Guide to
U.S. GOVERNMENT
PUBLICATIONS

New subordinate (level 2) classification numbers

New level 2 classes should be assigned as offices are established and issue publications. The next higher number should be assigned beginning with number 2 after the author symbol.

Usually the classes are not broken down more than one step from the parent agency, but some agencies are themselves broken down into other important issuing offices and it is advisable to establish classes further down the hierarchy as is the case with National Oceanic and Atmospheric Administration and Public Health Service.

(See previous examples.)

All of the subordinate offices in Public Health Service issue many publications, and the finer breakdown is necessary to keep the publications of each institute together.

If these institutes were not broken down as they are, there would not have been enough numbers to cover the many series they issue without using numbers assigned to another bureau, or attaching classes indiscriminately to other classes.

For examples of the problems encountered in not breaking a bureau down far enough, study the obsolete **FS 2.22:** classes assigned to the National Institutes of Health publications when Public Health Service was subordinate to the abolished Federal Security Agency.

New classes for third and fourth level organizations

When a new subordinate office is established, determine how the office fits into the agency organization, and the name of its parent organization. Determine how many levels are between the new organization and the departmental secretary or independent agency administrator. Use the letter of the agency, the number for the first level breakdown followed by a period, then a **100, 200,** or **300** class as appropriate, followed by a colon.

If not many publications are expected, consider assigning a series class rather than a subordinate agency class. (See previous Forest Service example-also, Chapter 2 Series Designations, Practical Application, New classes.)

If the agency is expected to issue many publications and has many smaller offices all of which will produce many publications, you may use **1000** numbers to differentiate between offices. There are very few cases where this will be necessary. If it does become necessary, the Public Health Service classes under **HE 20.** will serve as a guide.

Problems

Certain agencies in their infancy have been very inconsistent and changeable in the naming of their subordinate offices. This has presented many problems and certain classes which should have had a subordinate breakdown have been established under the parent agency. An example of this problem is the publications of the Environmental Protection Agency. The subordinate office names changed frequently during the first years of its existence.

Another problem is reorganization within an agency. Sometimes offices and functions are moved from one subordinate office to another. It is important in classifying to note the issuing office on each publication classified to ascertain that no reorganization has taken place that will affect the class. This is a particular problem in serials when the name of the serial remains the same, the publication looks the same, and the numbering follows along logically; but the issuing office has been transferred to another bureau or office.

Example:

> **ED 1.116/2:** *Institutions of higher education index, by state and congressional district.* The National Center for Education Statistics at one time was a subordinate office of the Department of Health, Education, and Welfare, and was moved in 1980 to the United States Department of Education.

It is important to change the classes with the first issue carrying the name of the new department or bureau. Always glance at the parent agency of any publication being classified to be sure that the subordinate office class is still correct. By checking constantly, the necessity for changing class numbers later can be avoided.

Chapter 2
Series Designations (after the period)

The number after the department, and subordinate bureau number is the series designation. This number is followed by a colon.

Series publications may carry volume numbers, volume numbers and issue numbers such as many periodicals or contins do; they may carry numbers only and have individual titles as the *Farmers Bulletins,* **A 1.9:(nos.)**, do; they may be issued by date and volume number as *Foreign Relations of the United States,* **S 1.1:(date)** is; or they may carry no numbers and have individual titles such as *Background Notes,* **S 1.123:(CT)**.

Category groups of publications without a common title printed on them have been assigned titles such as *Handbooks, Manuals, Guides,* and *General Publications.*

Standard reserved and category classes

At the present time the following numbers are reserved for the most common series issued by most Government offices:

.1	Annual report
.2	General publications
.3	Bulletins
.4	Circulars
.5	Laws
.6	Regulations, rules, and instructions
.7	Press releases
.8	Handbooks, manuals, guides
.9	Bibliographies and lists of publications
.10	Directories
.11	Maps and charts
.12	Posters
.13	Forms
.14	Addresses, lectures, etc.

Note: Numbers .1 through .4 were assigned when the classification system was established; numbers .5 through .8 were assigned in the 1950's as the scheme developed, .9 through .14 were assigned in 1985. Older classes will deviate from the current practice of using .5 through .8. When searching for laws, regulations, handbooks, etc., do not assume that the class has not been set up if you do not find it in .5 through .8 classes. Search further.

Under the pre-1985 100 breakdown, the standard classes are **.101:** for annual reports; **.102:** for general publications; **.103:** for bulletins, etc.

Examples:

C 55.300's:	National Marine Fisheries Service
C 55.301:	Annual report
C 55.302:	General publications
C 55.304:	Circulars
C 55.305:	Laws
C 55.306:	Regulations, rules, and instructions
C 55.308:	Handbooks, manuals, guides
C 55.308/2:	Handbooks (numbered)

Individual title series begin with **109, 209, 309,** etc., and with **115 , 215, 315,** etc., after the latter part of 1985, unless the series is related to the standard numbers just mentioned.

With the exception of annual reports, bulletins, and circulars, and certain numbered laws and regulations classes, these are "catch-all" or category classes which are determined by the type of material included in the publications themselves; to do this, the contents of the publication, as well as the titles, have to be studied.

Additional series issued by an office are given the next highest numbers in order of issuance, or attached to related series by use of slash-letters or numbers.

Subject related series are attached to established classes by use of a slash and numbers.

Examples:

I 28.37:	Minerals yearbook
I 28.37/a:	Preprints from Minerals yearbook
I 28.37/2:	Mineral perspective, MP (series)
I 28.37/3:	Mineral commodity profiles, MCP (series)

What to include in the category classes

Annual reports. This is for the annual report of the department, bureau, or office as a whole. Do not include annual reports on projects or on specific subjects; these should have separate classes elsewhere.

Annual reports may be issued by subordinate offices lower than the classification numbers have been broken down. In that case, a new class should be established and attached to the class for the annual report of the parent agency.

Examples:

C 13.1:	Annual report (National Bureau of Standards)
C 13.1/7:	Polymer Science and Standards Division annual report.

The determination as to whether a publication is the annual report of a department, bureau, or office can be made usually by looking at the title page, cover, or preface. However, a telephone call to the department, bureau or office will be the only way to get the necessary information occasionally.

General publications. Includes unnumbered publications of a miscellaneous nature. This is a "last resort" class. The publications are one-time publications which do not fit into any established series, or into any of the foregoing categories. There is no indication that the publications will be issued on a regular basis. This should be the last consideration for a publication, and should not be the starting point for determining a class number.

Bulletins and circulars. They are usually numbered by the offices issuing them.

Laws. The publications in this class contain the texts of Federal laws which are administered by the agencies issuing the publications. A publication which explains only parts of law or discusses the contents of laws should not be included in the Laws class. Possibly such publications may be classified as regulations under the law (Regulations, rules, and instructions class) or as guides to understanding a law (Handbooks, manuals, guides class). An overall description of a law may be classified under General publications. Follow the practice already established in individual Laws classes, since the above classification rules have been perceived in different ways over the years.

State laws on any subject should not be included in the Laws classes. State laws are not administered by agencies of the United States Government, and if they are published by the Federal Government, it is for information, not statutory purposes.

Regulations, rules, and instructions. These publications contain information on requirements of agencies. The information may pertain to the operation of an agency or to outside activities under an agency's jurisdiction.

Example: T 70.6:F 31/982-2 Regulations under Federal Alcohol Administration Act: Title 27, Code of Federal Regulations. (ATF P 5100.8 (12-82).)

A separate category class will not be established for Decisions and Orders. They should be assigned their own separate classes. Some decisions and orders were previously classed with Regulations, rules, and instructions, and Laws.

Press releases. This group includes agency news releases issued for the media. The publications may or may not have the word release or news on them. Press interviews, statements to the press, and news conferences with reporters should be included in the Press release classes, as well as the usual releases on various subjects.

Speeches, remarks, and addresses given before audiences are often issued as news releases. These should be classified individually in the Addresses class for the agencies releasing the information.

Handbooks, manuals, guides. These publications differ from regulations, rules, and instructions in that they do not have the force of law. They may include helpful information on any subject. In early years these publications were included in the Regulations, rules, and instruction classes. Beginning in the 1950's, new classes were established and handbooks, manuals, and guides were no longer included in the Regulations classes.

Example: T 70.8:N 47 News media guide to firearms (ATF P 1200.7 (178).)

To qualify in this class, the words "handbook", "guide", "manual", "how to", will have to be part of the title.

Example: Title page: How to become a depository library.

For a short time in 1984-1985, publications that were by nature handbooks, manuals, or guides got classed under this category class, even though the words "handbooks", "manual", or "guide" did not appear on the publications. This policy has been superseded by the instructions in the prior paragraph.

Bibliographies and lists of publications. This class includes any bibliographies, whether they are on specific subjects, or lists of all publications of an agency or bureau. An agency may issue annual or other periodic lists of publications with consistent titles which should be set up as separate classes, and not be included in a category class.

Directories. The publications will need to have the word directory as part of the title to qualify in this class.

Maps and charts. A chart can be defined in two ways: 1) a map designed primarily for navigation, either nautical or aeronautical; 2) a sheet exhibiting information in a tabular or graphic form.

Only charts failing under definition 1 should be classified as cartographic material. Tabular or graphic charts, often statistical in nature, should be classified as series documents, posters, or general publications.

Publications which consist of a mixture of cartographic, textual, and other illustrative content, and whose primary purpose is to acquaint visitors with parks, historical sites, etc., should not be classified as maps. These publications often have their own classes, such as the National Park Service Information Circulars. If individual class stems have not been established, these "tour guides" should be treated under the general rules for classification.

If a map's class must be modified by the addition of a date, use the date of publication. In many cases this will not be the date associated with the title. Examine the map closely for the presence of a GPO or other printing date and use that to qualify the class number.

In order to be consistent with past practices, maps issued in numbered series should continue to be classed in that series. Maps issued as U.S. Geological Survey open-file reports (I 19.78:) are an example of this type of material. However, new bureaus, offices, departments, etc., will have separate category classes for maps and charts.

Posters. A single sheet with material printed on one side only, including photographs and announcements.

Forms. Before this category class was established in the latter part of 1985, forms were treated in a special way. The department and bureau letters and numbers were assigned in the regular manner.

Example: T 22. for Internal Revenue Service

This designation was followed by the word form, a colon, then the identification numbers and/or letters printed on the form.
Example: T 22.Form: 1040 U.S. individual income tax return, Form 1040

Additional information, if needed, was added after the number by adding a slash and a word or abbreviation in the regular manner.

Example: T 22.Form:1040/sched. A,B Schedule A and B to Form 1040

Revisions and new editions were classified by use of a slash and a date.

Example: T 22.Form:1040/983

This category class should be reserved for publications that contain forms and/or instructions on how to fill them in. If the publications have textual material also, they should be classed somewhere else, most likely in General publications; follow this procedure even when the publication has a form number in the title page.

Addresses, lectures, etc. The titles of this category may vary from agency to agency, but the content of the classes is the same. This class includes addresses, lectures, speeches, remarks, statements, papers, etc., which were delivered before groups of people. The addresses may be issued as news releases. If so, they are taken from the press release classes and classified as addresses. Do not include statements to the press, or press conferences or interviews.

Practical Application

When a publication is received for classifying and the author symbol and subordinate office numbers have been determined, check the publication to determine the series class. The series designation number in the Superintendent of Documents classification scheme appears after the period and before the colon.

Ask yourself these questions when classifying a publication:

A. Is it a serial or otherwise recurring publication which has, or should have, a separate class? The preface may indicate that it is the first in a series of annual, quarterly, monthly, etc., publications for which a class has not yet been established. It may be the annual report of an office. If a series number is printed on the publication, use it as part of the classification number if it is not a serial publication.

B. If a series designation does not appear on the publication, and the title does not have its own class, is it-

1. a bibliography?
2. an address or lecture given before a group? (Press interviews do not fall into this category, but are treated as press releases.)
3. regulations, rules, or instructions? (Usually this can be determined from the title, introduction, etc.)
4. a Federal law, or an act, which belongs in a Laws class?
5. a map, chart, or poster?
6. a reprint or preprint from another publication?
7. a directory?
8. a form?

If the publication does not fit into any of these categories, it may be classed in the General publications class. The General publications class is a "last resort" class for any publication which is not the first of a series, and does not fit into any other established class.

New classes. (Serials, etc.)

Any publication which is issued on a regular basis should have its own class. The frequency may be anywhere from daily to every three or more years.

If no class has been set up for a Publication which is the first in a new series, a new class should be established. Do not skip immediately to the end of the class and use the next highest number.

Look at the new publication, and see if it is related either by content or smaller issuing office to a class already established.

Examples:

C 55.309/2:	Current Fisheries Statistics
C 55.309/2-2:	Fisheries of the United States (annual)
C 55.309/2-3:	Marine Recreational Fisheries Statistics Survey, Atlantic and Gulf Coasts (annual)
C 55.309/2-4:	Frozen Fishery Products, Annual Summary

Sometimes it is advisable to keep all publications of a smaller office together instead of scattering them by type of material throughout the classes
for the parent agency.

Examples:

HE 23.1210:	National Center on Child Abuse and Neglect: Publications
HE 23.1210/2:	Child abuse and neglect research projects and publications (semiannual)
HE 23.1210/3:	Annual review of child abuse and neglect research
HE 23.1210/4:	National Center on Child Abuse and Neglect: User manuals (series)

Occasionally classes will be so tightly grouped that there is no number available in the spot which is the best for the new Series to be placed. In that case, a dash-number can be used. The following example will serve as a guide in applying this rule.

Energy Information Administration of the Energy Department issues a series of publications entitled Energy data reports. In an effort to keep all publications in the series together, the class E 3.11: was assigned to them. There are many subtitles on many subjects in the series. To keep the subtitles on the same subjects together, the (nos.) are used with (nos.) following them.

E 3.11:	Energy data report: Natural gas monthly report
E 3.11/2:	Energy data report: Natural gas liquids, monthly
E 3.11/2-2:	Energy data report: Naturalgas, annual
E 3.11/2-3:	Energy data report: World natural gas (annual)
E 3.11/2-4:	Energy data report: Underground storage of natural gas by interstate pipeline companies (annual)
E 3.11/2-5:	Energy data report: Natural sas deliveries etc. (annual)

All of the **E 3.11/2:** classes cover series relating to natural gas.

E 3.11/5:	Energy data report: Monthly petroleum supply
E 3.11/5-2:	Energy data report: Petroleum
E 3.11/5-3:	Energy data report: International petroleum (annual)
E 3.11/5-4:	Energy data report: Petroleum refineries in the U.S. and U.S. territories

All of the E 3.11/5: classes relate to petroleum. In order not to interfile these various subjects the dash-numbers were added to the slash-numbers. This makes it possible to add new classes related by Subject to established classes rather than to use a totally unrelated slash-number at the end of the **E 3.11:** classes when new titles are received.

Note that the first class, **E 3.11:**, does not have a -number even though **E 3.11/2:** is related by sub-title to it. The -number should be used only after a slash number. This means that a new series is not always classified exactly where it would be best. In that case some other adjustment must be made such as giving the new title a new **/number.**

If the publication being classified is unrelated to the publications in classes already established, find the highest number at the end of the issuing agency's classes and assign the next highest number.

In the case of a publication with two series designations printed on it, see the **Joint publications** heading in Chapter 1, Section 1.

If separate classes are needed for a serial title that is issued for every state in the United States, then the item number breakdown should be Incorporated in the classification numbers. If the publication covers more than one state, use the first one named when setting up the class.

When using item number's 01-09 the class numbers, omit the 0's.

ITEM NUMBER BREAKDOWN

Alabama	01
Alaska	02
Arizona	03
Arkansas	04
California	05
Colorado	06
Connecticut	07
Delaware	08
Florida	09
Georgia	10
Hawaii	11
Idaho	12
Illinois	13
Indiana	14
Iowa	15
Kansas	16
Kentucky	17
Louisiana	18
Maine	19
Maryland	20
Massachusetts	21
Michigan	22
Minnesota	23
Mississippi	24
Missouri	25

Examples:

Area wage survey, Pittsburgh, Pennsylvania metropolitan area
January 1985 edition: Bulletin 3030-3
January 1984 edition: Bulletin 3025-4
New classification number: L 2.121/38: (date)

If the series number uniquely identifies each state, then it is used in the classification number rather than the item number breakdown.

Examples:

County business patterns. New York
1982 edition: CBP-82-34
1981 edition: CBP-81-34
New classification number: C 3.204/3-34: (date)
    Not C 3.204/3-32: (date)

Ways of determining the necessity for a new class

There is no problem in deciding on a new class if the information is in the publication and it is clearly indicated as number **1** or the first in a series. Sometimes the physical makeup of a publication indicates that more will be forthcoming. Perhaps the publication has a stylized heading which will appear on future publications. Usually a "one-time" publication will not have a large heading which includes the issuing office and date, with an individual title farther down on the publication.

It may be necessary to call the issuing agency on publications which look as if they could be part of a series. Unfortunately, the agencies themselves may not know what will be published in the future. Future plans may depend on the reception of the initial publication, or on available funds. Base decisions on the information that can be discerned from the publications, or can be obtained from the issuing offices, which in most cases comes down to intent.

The series number may have been omitted in error from the publication. This might cause the publication to be classified in a category class. If at some later date, the series number becomes known, the class should be changed.

If the agency issues an erratum adding the series number to the publication, then the publication, in most cases, should be reclassified as part of the series. Consider what benefits and problems may occur if the class is changed, before changing the class in this situation.

A publication may be issued as a one-time publication with no plans for a series. Later, the issuing agency may decide that this publication should be issued annually. In that case, establish a new class beginning with the second publication issued, with a reference to the earlier class.

Example:
Note.-See, for earlier class, (class number of original publication)

Individual classes for specific titles in a numbered series

Certain agencies publish numbered series which include annual or other serial titles with different numbers assigned to them. Thus, the titles are scattered throughout the series, and may be difficult for the user to find. In this case, separate classes should be established by title, with Congressional reports/documents and committee prints that use the Senate numbering scheme being the exception. If possible, attach the new class to the existing numbered series class by using a dash or a slash; otherwise use the next available number. The series number will not be used after the colon of the new class designation; dates will be used, instead.

The one exception to the above rule is when a serial belonging to a numbered series is uniquely identified by a number that remains constant within the series-look at examples 1-2. However, the constant number can't have a changing number between itself and the class stem-look at example 3.

Example 1:
    Directory of professional workers in state agricultural experiment stations and other cooperating state institutions. (Annual)
A 1.76. Agriculture handbook series
A 1.76:305/980-81
A 1.76:305/981-82
A 1.76:305/982-83
A 1.76:305/984-85

Example 2:
    Current housing reports: Market absorption of apartments. (Quarterly)
C 3.215: Current housing report series
C 3.215:H 130-84-Q 3
C 3.215:H 130-84-Q 4

But

Example 3:
    Annual housing survey: Housing characteristics for selected metropolitan areas, St. Louis, MO-IL standard metropolitan statistical area
C 3-215: Current Housing Reports

The 1983 issue has on its cover: current housing reports **H-170-83-59.** The last two digits remain constant for the St. Louis, MO-IL metropolitan area, but since it is preceded by a changing year designation, a new class has to be established. In this case, **C 3.215/17-59: (date)** was used.

Numbered series, particularly new series, may present problems in certain cases. It is difficult to determine at times whether a series is a bureau series or a departmental series until several publications have been received. The Agricultural and State Departments' publications offer good examples of departmental series. Each subordinate office may contribute to the series. For example, in Agriculture Department series, no. 1 may carry Forest Service; no. 2, Agricultural Marketing Service; and no. 3. Statistical Reporting Service. All belong to one consecutively numbered series which should be kept together under Agriculture Department as a whole (A 1.) and not scattered under several subordinate office classes. A departmental series is not always readily identifiable from the publication, and a call to the agency may be necessary when the first publication in a new Agriculture or State Department series is received.

Do not confuse a departmental series number with a departmental control or identification number. The publication offices of some agencies assign numbers to their publications for identification of each specific publication, but this should not be considered a numbered publication series for classification purposes.

Example:
S 1.123:L 97/982 Background notes, Luxembourg. (Department of State publication 7856.)

The class **S 1.123:** is for Background notes series. The **7856** is the identification number that the State Department has assigned to the publication.

Example:
HE 3.19/2:109 Economic forecasting (Actuarial note 109, (SSA pub. no. 11-11500).)

The class **HE 3.19/2:** is for Actuarial notes. The SSA number is the Social Security Administration's identification or control number.

Example:
HE 23.3008:N 95/v.1 Nutrition service provider's guide. (DHHS publication no. (OHDS) 81-70671.)

The class **HE 23.3008:** is the category class for Handbooks, manuals, guides of the Administration on Aging. The DHHS publication number is the number assigned by the Department of Health and Human Services to identify this particular publication.

Basic manuals and transmittals. A basic manual or other publication may be issued infrequently, but if it has continuing transmittals, revised pages or frequent changes, the manual should have a separate class. In practice, this has not been done consistently, but a separate class should be established when a new edition of such a publication is received for classifying.

(See Chapter 5, subheading, Basic manuals.)

When the issuing agency changes before a new basic is issued, do not reclass the changes.

Preprints and separates. These classes include reprints and preprints from Government publications only. Reprints or articles from non-Government publications are sometimes issued by Government agencies when the contents of the particular articles pertain to the work of the agencies. Often an article is written by an employee of the reprinting agency. Reprints from non-Government publications issued by Government agencies have been classified in the General publications or other appropriate classes, and have not been treated as separates.

Separates or preprints classes are attached to the classes for the publications from which the separates are reprinted by use of a slash and lower case letters.

Examples:

I 28.37/a: Preprints from Minerals yearbook
J 1.5/a: Opinions of Attorney General (separate opinions)

In each of the above examples, the publications are later included in bound editions.

Chapter 3

Book Numbers
(after the colon)

The result of combining the designations for Government authors, bureaus, and series followed by a colon is the class stem.

Individual publication or book designations follow the class stem. The series number printed on the publication should be used in the class whenever possible. The number following the colon may be a volume number alone, a volume number and number; a number alone or in conjunction with letters; a date; or a combinat!on.. of these designations. The publication may carry no number and require a Cutter number from the Cutter table to complete the class.

Section 1,
Numbered Series

Numbered series designations appearing on the publications, as a rule, take precedence over the use of any other method of classifying the publications in that series. There are exceptions.

For numbered series, when each publication has an individual title, the original edition is classified simply by using the number printed on the publication.

Example:

A 13.52:154 Forest insect and disease leaflet 154, Phomopsis blight of junipers.

Revisions of numbered publications were classified by using the slash and additional figures beginning with /2.

Example:

A 13.52:154/2 (same title). revised October 1982.

To do away with the problem encountered when a revised edition of a numbered series is classed /2, and an earlier edition is received later, in the future, / (date) will be used. Under the new system, the 1983 edition of the above publication would be classed: **A 13.52:154/983**

Problems, exceptions, derivations

When classifying a publication in a class which uses the agency-provided numbering printed on the document, transcribe the numbering as it appears on the publication. For the purposes of Superintendent of Documents classification, "numbering" includes letters, symbols (such as "&"), and punctuation, as well as numbers.

It may be necessary to adjust the spacing within numbering to conform to the standard GPO classification spacing conventions.

Classification policy will be to use the numbering in the form in which it is provided by the issuing agency, and not to adjust or modify the numbering simply for the sake of consistency of style. However, agency-provided numbering may be changed as necessary to eliminate conflicts or correct printing errors.

The numbers printed on the publications may include letters and numbers identifying the series as well as the individual publication numbers. In that case, consider using some of the letters and numbers as part of the series title, and using only the distinctive part of the number in the class. This results in a shorter class. The decision of how much of the number to use should be decided when a new class is established, and continued consistently throughout the class.

Examples:

C 61.9:   Country market surveys CMS (series)

C 61.9:IPC/721/82   Country market survey, Industrial process controls, Algeria, CMS/IPC/721/82

The **CMS** is not used in the class because it is part of the series title for this class.

Examples:

HE 20.3173/2: ICRDB cancergrams

There are several subseries in this class so the individual subseries must be identified by using the subseries designations such as **CB 01** and **CT 10** in the class to identify certain fields of study. The complete classes are

HE 20.3173/2:CB 01/83/05
HE 20.3173/2:CT 10/83/05

using all of the letters and numbers printed on the publications in the class. If separate classes had been established for the **CB 01** series and the **CT 10** series, only the last four digits would have been required in the class.

Examples:

C 3.223/20:   Census of population and housing, Congressional districts of the 98th Congress, PHC (series)

C 3.223/20:80-4-44   1980 Census of population and housing, Congressional district Tennessee. PHC-80-4-44

The **PHC** is not used in the individual class. When the 2000 census publications are received, the title of the series can be adjusted and the Congressional districts determined as a result of the 2000 census can be included in this class using the **PHC 90(nos.)** which presumably, will be printed on the 1990 census publications.

Examples:

C 3.215/3:   Construction reports, Value of new construction put in place, C 30 (series)

C 3.215/3:C 30-83-1   Construction reports, Value of new construction put in place, January 1983, C 30-83-1

In this case, the **C 30** was used as part of the class. The class would have been complete without it, but at the time the class was established, it was decided to use the complete number for this series. Since the designations should be consistent within a class, continue to use the complete number as printed on the publication, in this class.

Sometimes numbers and letters on a new series are complicated and undecipherable at first glance. Gather a few of the publications together and compare the numbers.

What is the same on each one, and what is different?

Do some of the letters represent the series title?

Is part of the number different on each publication so that it can be used as part of the class?

Is part of the number the same on several publications but not on others?

What do the publications have in common that the other publications do not have? Does the number, perhaps, stand for a State name, or a field of study?

If no logical numbering scheme can be discerned from a group of the publications, or if only one publication is available, call the agency for an explanation of their numbering system. It is better to take the time to decipher the number and use it as part of the class, than to use Cutter numbers which may create problems later.

Some numbered series are issued in volumes or parts. If the number printed on the publication does not reflect the part or volume number, the volume number should be added to the class.

Examples:

A 1.76:529-47   A catalog of the Coleoptera of America north of Mexico, Family: Heteroceridae, Agriculture handbook 529-47.

A 1.76:529-49   A catalog of the Coleoptera of America north of Mexico, Family: Dryopidae. Agriculture handbook 529-49.

Each part of the catalog covers a separate family of Coleoptera. The Agriculture Department has assigned a series number that connects these publications to the other parts of the handbook, so no further breakdown in the class is necessary.

Example:

E 1.35/2:0063/v.2   Cost guide, DOE/MA-0063. volume 2.

The Energy Department has not included the volume number in its numbering system, so it must be added to the class.

(See also, Chapter 3, Section 3, Dates, Use of date in numbered series with a continuing title.)

Section 2,
Volume Numbers and Numbers

Periodicals often are designated by volume and number, but the designation is not limited to periodicals. In the class, the volume number is listed after the colon, followed by a slash, then by the number of the particular issue being classified.

Example:

L 241/2:29/6   Employment and earnings, volume 29, number 6, June 1982.

Sometimes a larger publication, in addition to carrying volume and number designations, will also carry a part or section number. If this occurs, another slash is added, followed by the abbreviation, pt. or sec. and the number.

Example:
L 2.41/2:29/6/pt.1
L 2.41/2:29/6/pt.2

The **pt.** is used as part of the class but not v. and no. When the classification system was established superior numbers were used, written as **L 2.412:296**, and placed on two lines breaking at the colon. The slashes in **L 2.41/2:29/6** replace writing the numbers as superior numbers for ease in writing, printing, and automating, but the meaning is still there. If a part number were added without the slash and the abbreviation pt., the class as written would be **L 2.412.2961** You cannot have a superior upon a superior number, so the slash in this case means to use the next line. The number **1** cannot stand alone on the third line, so **pt.** is used before it.

Some earlier classes used the abbreviations for volume and number as part of the class number.

Example:
LC 3.6/5:v.31/pt.1/no.1/sec.1-2
      Catalog of copyright entries, Third series, volume 31, part 1, Non-dramatic literary works, number 1, Jan-June 1977, sections 1 and 2.

If **v.** and **no.** were used as part of the class when the class was established, discontinue this practice when new issues are received. See p. 32 for exception to this rule.

Roman numerals should be converted to Arabic numerals in the classification numbers.

Revisions of publications identified by volume and number

Prior to 1985, revised publications identified by volume and number were classed by adding to the original edition class a slash and **/rev.**

Example:

L 2.41/2:29/6/rev.

In the future, revised publications will be classed by adding to the original edition class "/(date)"/.

Example:

L 2.41/2:29/10/985

A revised publication issued with a volume and number printed on it is more often issued as a corrected copy. In that case, the class would end with **/corr.**

Example:

L 2.41/2:29/6/corr.

(See Chapter 5 for classification instructions for handling correction sheets, errata sheets, etc.)

Section 3,
Dates

The date is used in the class for publications which have a constant title. Annual reports, quarterly reports, monthly reports, and weekly reports are examples. These may be on any subject and each title should have its own class.

Annual and less frequent publications. Use the last three digits of the date after the colon.

Example:

C 1.1:980 Annual report of the Department of Commerce.

For reports of publications covering more than one year, a combination of dates is used.

Example:

D 208.107:954-55 Annual register of the United States Naval Academy, 1954-1955.

How many digits are used in the second number depends on how many are needed for clarity. Always use at least two digits in the second date. A publication covering a century or more would require 3 digits in the second number.

Example: 895-995

With the arrival of the year 2000, some adjustment to the method of using dates is required. Probably the best solution is to use four digits rather than three. For example **895-2000** would be used for **1895** to **2000**.

Semiannual publications are treated in much the same way. The first publication would carry the three-digit date. The publication for the second half of the year would carry a dash-number (**-no.**).

Example:

TD 4.810.981 Semiannual report to Congress on the effectiveness of the Civil Aviation Security Program, Jan. 1-June 30. 1981.

TD 4.810:981-2 Same title, July 1-Dec. 31. 1981

A **-1** is not used on the first issue of a semiannual publication.

Quarterly, monthy, weekly, etc., publications are classified with a 3 digit date, a slash, and a number.

Example:

EP 1.21/17: EPA publications bibliography, Quarterly abstract bulletin.
982/1 Jan.-Mar. 1982 issue
982/2 Apr.-June 1982 issue

Use of date in numbered series with a continuing title.

Sometimes an agency will issue a series of publications beginning with; number **1** each year. Rather than add the date after the number, the date is used first to keep the year's publications together.

Example:

D 5.315:982/16 Notice to mariners, no. 16 for April 17, 1982

If the date is not used before the number, number **16** for all years will be filed next to each other and not be in logical order.

Sometimes the agencies producing the publications will incorporate the date in the series number that is assigned to the publication. In that case, treat the publication as a numbered series and use the date as it is incorporated in the series numbering system and printed on the publication.

Example:

LC 33.10:82-1 LC science tracer bullet 82-1, Jan. 1982.

A problem arises when an agency assigns the number in reverse order. For instance, if the Library of Congress had designated the **LC science tracer bullet** as **1-82**, the best thing would be to ignore the agency designation and use **982/1** in the class. However, this has not been done in many cases in the past when it would have been advisable.

When a new series is initiated by an agency, there is no way to be sure that the series numbering system will not be changed as the series is developed. If a series starts out as dated, then changes to a numbered series, start using the number as part of the class. In most cases, it will not be necessary to establish a new class.

Government publications are so varied in makeup, that there can be no "hard and fast" rules to handle each problem as it arises. Study the publications, consider past practices and future possibilities, and establish new classes or adapt old classes to follow a logical progression of a single series.

Problems

A publication carrying both a release date and a date for the statistics covered may create problems in selecting the correct date for the class number.

On a monthly publication, the statistics may cover January 1983. but the most visible date is a February 1983 release date. Do not decide immediately that the class should be **983/2** for the February issue. Look closely at classes assigned to earlier issues to determine which date is being used for classification purposes.

This is necessary particularly at the beginning of a new year. In general, it is better to use the date of the statistics in such cases; however, if the date of the statistics is not readily discernible, use the release date. This decision should be made when the class is first established, then followed consistently throughout the class.

Another example is an annual report that carries a release date only on the cover, but further examination indicates that the publication is the annual report for the previous year. Study classes for earlier issues to determine which date should be used to keep the class consistent.

Section 4,
Cutter Numbers

Cutter Table and its use

C.A. Cutter's Two-Figure Author Table, familiarly known as a Cutter table, was developed by Charles A. Cutter in the 1800's as a library tool for organizing library materials alphabetically. There is also a three-figure table. Both the two- and three-figure tables are used in the Superintendent of Documents classification scheme, and are available from commercial library supply houses.

Cutter numbers are used when there are no series numbers to identify the publications and dates are not appropriate for identification. Cutter numbers are used to distinguish publications in the category classes, as well as in other unnumbered series classes.

The 2-figure Cutter table is used for most publications. Words beginning with letters in the table are given appropriate letters and numbers. When a word falls between two numbers, always choose the preceding number,

Example:
Cutter table:
Chem: 42
Chi: 43
Chim: 44
Chl: 45
Words being Cuttered:
Chemistry: C 42
Cherries: C 42
Children: C 43
Chimes: C 44
China: C 44

The **3-figure table** is used for separates and in some classes where a finer breakdown is necessary to keep publications on a particular subject together. Since the **2-** and **3-figure** tables are compatible, they may be used in the same class when necessary for better organization of the publications within the class. However, new use of the **3-figure** table should be limited as a last resort measure. If possible, use a different Cutter word.

For example, in some Agriculture Department classes there are Cuttered publications for **peaches** and **pears**. Using the 2-figure Cutter table, all publications on both subjects would be interfiled under **P 31**. By using a 3 figure table, peaches would be **P 313**; and pears, **P 316**, thus separating each subject.

Publications being Cuttered under the same beginning letters within a class are separated from one another by / (nos.). The first publication will bear only the Cutter number such as **C 42**. As other publications with other titles are received, they will be classed **C 42/2, C 42/3**, etc. If there are a large number of publications within a class Cuttered under the same term, try to find a more distinctive Cutter word. If the same Cutter number is being applied to different subjects, consider using the 3-figure table for a finer breakdown.

Revisions or later editions of a title which has been Cuttered, are distinguished from the earlier editions by /(date).

Example:
Soviet Union (map)
PrEx 3.10/4:So 8 (Original edition)
PrEx 3.10/4:So 8/981 (Revised edition, 1981)
PrEx 3.10/4:So 8/981-2 (2d revision for 1981)

Dates for publications revised the same year as the original issue

The date should be added to the revised issue by using a hyphen-number.

Examples:
D 21 (Issued in 1982)
D 21/982-2 (Second or revised edition, 1982)

The **982-2** indicates that **D 21** was also issued in **1982**. It is not necessary to go back and add the date to the first publication. When both publications are issued in the same year, do not use the date alone without a (no.).

Examples:
D 21 (Issued in 1982)

INCORRECT:
D 21/982 (Revised of new edition also issued in 1962. See above correct example.)

Revisions are classified and filed as followed:

C 42	(original edition of 1st title)
C 42/961	(revised 1961 edition of 1st titles)
C 42/2	(original edition of 2d title requiring this Cutter number)
C 42/2/980	(revised 1980 edition of 2d title)
C 42/2/980-2	(2d revised edition 1980 of 2d title)
C 42/2/981	(revised 1981 edition of 2d title)
C 42/3	(original edition of 3d title, issued in 1962)
C 42/3/962-2	(revised edition of original 1982 edition of 3d title)

Filing order for Cutter numbers. Cutter numbers are filed alphabetically by letter, then digit by digit, not necessarily in numerical order. This is true whether the 2- or 3-figure Cutter tables or both together are used. By filing digit by digit, the publications will remain in alphabetical order. If filed in strict numerical order, the publications will not be in alphabetical order.

Examples:
Chemistry: C 42
Cherries: C 424
Children: C 437
Chimes: C 44
China: C 441
Classification: C 56

Any slash numbers added to the Cutters are filed numerically.

Special Cutter Numbers

Geographic names beginning with common terms such as **Fort, Saint, Mount, San, etc.,** are Cuttered from the first word. The first letter of the second word is transcribed in lower case after the Cutter number.

Examples:
Fort Washington: F 77 w
San Diego: Sa 5 d
San Francisco: Sa 5 f

In the case of similar names, when the geographic name begins with common terms such as **Fort Saint, Mount. etc.,** more than one letter may be used after the Cutter number to keep the place names separate.

Examples:

> I 29.21:F 77 ma Fort Matansas National
> Monument, Fla.
> I 29.21:F 77 mc Fort McHenry National
> Monument, Md.
> I 29.21:F 77 mo Fort Moultrie, S.C.

If the words **Saint, Mount, etc.,** are abbreviated on the publications, Cutter the words as if they were spelled out, thus **St.** would be Saint for Cuttering purposes.

State Cutter numbers have been devised so that each State will have its own distinctive number. Following are the Cutter numbers that should be used in all classes when a State name is being Cuttered:

Alabama	Al 1 b
Alaska	Al 1 s
Arizona	Ar 4 i
Arkansas	Ar 4 k
California	C 12
Colorado	C 71
Connecticut	C 76
Delaware	D 37
D.C.	D 63
Florida	F 66
Georgia	G 29
Hawaii	H 31
Idaho	Id 1
Illinois	Il 6
Indiana	In 2
Iowa	Io 9
Kansas	K 13
Kentucky	K 41
Louisiana	L 93
Maine	M 28
Maryland	M 36
Massachusetts	M 38
Michigan	M 58
Minnesota	M 66
Mississippi	M 69 i
Missouri	M 69 o
Montana	M 76
Nebraska	N 27
Nevada	N 41
New Hampshire	N 42 h
New Jersey	N 42 j
New Mexico	N 42 m
New York	N 42 y
North Carolina	N 81 c
North Dakota	N 81 d
Ohio.	Oh 3
Oklahoma	Ok 4
Oregon	Or 3
Pennsylvania	P 38
Rhode Island	R 34
South Carolina	So 8 c
South Dakota	So 8 d
Tennessee	T 25
Texas	T 31
Utah	Ut 1
Vermont	V 59
Virginia	V 81
Washington	W 27
West Virginia	W 52 v
Wisconsin	W75
Wyoming	W 99

Acronyms and **initialisms** are Cuttered from the first word spelled out when the full form of the acronym is known or is stated in the book.

Examples:

> MCRL (Master Cross Reference List) M 39
> CETA (Comprehensive Employment Training Act)
> C 73

If the words the letters represent cannot easily be determined, Cutter from the initials as they appear on the publication or choose another term when possible.

Example: CENTAC program (meaning unknown) C 33

Selecting Cutter Words

This, perhaps, is the most difficult part of the class to keep consistent. There are as many different ideas on the best word to Cutter as there are classifiers assigning the numbers. In most cases, a Cutter word selection is neither right nor wrong, but a matter of deciding which word is best for that particular publication in that particular class.

If the publication being classified is a revised edition of an earlier publication, it should be Cuttered the same as the original with addition of **/(date).**

Check class under all possible Cutter words for similar publications first. If none is found, use the following guidelines in selecting Cutter words.

Basic rule

Cutter from the first significant word in the title which denotes the subject of the book. In cases of doubt between terms, choosethe term which comes first in the title.

Examples:

> Increasing the **nutritive** value of wood and forest procducts.
> Report and recommendations on **range** conditions.
> **Pine** reforestation task force report.
> How the rural community **fire** protection program can help you.
> Progress report on the **cartographic** activities of the U.S.
> Proceedings of a symposium on preliminary results from the Sept. 1979 **Researcher/Pierce**
> Present and recommended U.S. Government research in **seafloor** engineering.
> Behavior and neurology of **lizards**
> Victims of **rape**
> Owlie Skywarn on flash **floods**

Exceptions

1. Avoid Cuttering under words which are common to the agency, particularly words in the name of the agency.

Examples:

> forest-Forest Service
> health-Public Health Services
> labor-Bureau of Labor Statistics
> wood-Forest Service

2. Avoid Cuttering under terms such as National, Federal, United States, Government, etc., unless absolutely necessary. Also, avoid using terms such as symposium, workshop, report, etc.

Examples:

> National climate program
> National estuarine sanctuary program
> Present and recommended U.S. Government research in seafloor.
> 4th international symposium on free radical stabilization.

3. When a title begins with a meaningless or catch phrase, Cutter from the substantive part of the title which denotes the contents of the book.

Examples:

> Fishing for compliments? Try sea fare from NOAA
> Paradise regained? Surface mining control and reclamation.
> Of cats and rats: Studies of the neural basis of agression.

If there is only a catch phrase for the title, Cutter a word from the phrase.

4. Cutter under the name of an agency only when it is the sole subject of the publication.

5. Geographic names.

a. In classes where the subject matter is similar (i.e., draft environmental impact statements) Cutter from the first word of the geographic location.

Examples:

> Adam's Rib Ski area: draft environmental impact statement
> Draft environmental statement: Alsea Planning Unit

Oil and gas lease applications of the Los Padres National Forest: draft environmental assessment

b. In more general classes the geographic location should be weighed against the first subject term. Check the class for past practice. In case of doubt, prefer the geographic term, especially when the subject term is common to the class.

Examples:

> Gravity survey of Amargosa Desert area of Nevada
> Water-resources inventory. Antelope Valley
> The effects of decreased nutrient loading on the limnology of Diamond Lake, Oregon
> But Formation and transport of oxidants along Gulf Coast

c. Areas within national parks and forests should be Cuttered under the name of the park or forest.

Examples:

> Sleeping Bear Dunes National Lakeshore: Alligator Hill cross country ski trail (I 29.6/3:Sl 2 b/6)
> Sleeping Bear Dunes National Lakeahore: Empire Bluff cross country ski trail (I 29.6/3:Sl 2 b/7)

In cases of doubt concerning geographic terms, examine the class for past practice and try to follow the pattern if one has been established.

d. When Cuttering using a geographic term consisting of a proper personal name, base the Cutter on the first word in the name.

For example, a Forest Service map of the George Washington National Forest should be classified as: A 13.28:G 29

If, however, there is an established practice within a particular class Cuttering from the last name, continue that practice to keep related publications together. For example, a 1982 Forest Service information pamphlet on the George Washington National Forest is received, and in the master classification file there is:

> A 13.13:W 27 George Washingon National Forest, 1958
> A 13.13:W 27/969 George Washington National Forest, 1969.
> A 13.13:W 27/975 George Washington National Forest, 1975, assign the class A 13.13:W 27/982 to keep the material together.

e. Maps should be Cuttered using the name of the geographic area covered. i.e. country, national park, national forest, etc. Forest Service maps should be Cuttered under the first-named national forest depicted. If the map shows a particular trail, wilderness area, or feature within a forest, use the Cutter for the forest. This will collect all maps covering a single forest or park into a unified sequence in the shelf list and **Monthly calalog.**

6. Related publications. When a publication is bibliographically related to another publication, class using the same Cutter whenever possible.

a. Multiple volumes in a set with a collective title should all be Cuttered under the same term in the collective title.

b. Multiple volumes in a set lacking a collective title may be kept together only when all titles are known and all titles share a common word. If titles are unknown, do not try to keep the set together, instead, Cutter under the most appropriate word in each title.

c. Publications in different classes which are related, such as draft and final environmental impact statements, should be Cuttered under the same term.

d. Serials should be removed from general classes when it is discovered that the title is being issued annually or more frequently, and separate classes should be assigned. When this is done, Cutter numbers are not needed in the class, with a few exceptions made in the boards, commissions, committees, and congressional classes, which do have Cutters in the class stems.

Dates and other information after the Cutter number

Whenever a date is used after a Cutter number, and additional numbers are needed, use a slash and a word or abbreviation between the slash and the number to show exactly what the number means.

Example:
PrEx 3.10/4:So 8/981/sh.2 Soviet Union (map), sheet 2

Sometimes the date as written on the publication is not compatible with the Superintendent of Documents classification scheme and its punctuation. A good illustration of the problem is **1984/85 NEH Fellowship Programs.** The class for the basic title is **NF 3.2:F 33/11.** The first thought is to use the date as printed on the publication, but a slash in the date after a Cutter number is not permitted. The correct handling of the date in this case is:

NF: 3.2:F 33/11/984-85

Convert the slash printed on the publication to a hyphen in the class. Note that unlike previous years when the date was used in a Cuttered class because it was part of the title of a publication, the future trend is to limit the use of dates only to indicate new editions.

Problems

Sometimes a prolific series requiring Cutter numbers becomes so crowded that it is advisable to devise some scheme to avoid an overabundance of /(nos.) on a particular Cutter. This happens often in classes for maps and environmental impact statements that cover comparatively small areas. One way to avoid having long complicated classes is to set up separate classes by State, and Cutter the small areas under each State. This does create many separate smaller classes, but it keeps publications on one State together and makes Cuttering and the location of specific publications easier.

Another solution to the problem is to assign a number after the colon for each State in a single series class, then Cutter the small area after the number.

The State names should not be tacked on to a class with a slash after the Cutter for two reasons. One, it is meaningless by itself in the class; two, it makes the class too long.

Also, in such prolific classes the 3-figure Cutter table may be used for a finer breakdown of similar words.

Formatting class numbers

The format of the Supt. of Docs. classification number is critical for the proper construction of the number itself and for accurate sorting and searching of class numbers in automated systems. One important aspect of the construction of the class number is the use of spacing. Generally, a space must be inserted between letters and numbers in the class number unless there is intervening punctuation, The only exception is the use of parenthesis. One space must be inserted before and after a parenthesis whether it is preceded or followed by a letter or number, unless the parenthesis is followed by intervening punctuation.

Correct formatting:	Incorrect formatting:
A 1.10.B 68	A 1:10:B68
C 16.21/a:17	C 16.21/ a:17
D 5.317:616 (717-5) A	D 5.317:616(717-5) A
AE 2.106/3:26/pt.1	AE 2.106/3:26/pt. 1

Chapter 4

Congressional and Related Publications (X and Y classes)

Section 1, Boards, Commissions, and Committees (Y 3.)

Those agencies established by act of Congress or under authority of act of Congress, not specifically designated in the Executive Branch of the Government, are grouped under **Y 3.,** one of the agency symbols assigned to Congressional publications.

Agency designations. The classification numbers of the publications of these agencies are then literally pushed over to the right so that instead of the series designation following the period, the individual agency designation follows it. This agency designation is derived from the two-figure Cutter table, by Cuttering the first main word of the agency name. The Cutter number is followed by a colon.

Examples:
Y 3.Ad 6. Administrative Conference of the United States
Y 3.Se 4: Selective Service System

Series designations for publications of these agencies then follow the colon instead of preceding it as is done in other classes.

Examples:
Y 3.Ad 6:1 Annual report
Y 3.Ad 6:2 General publications

Individual book numbers are then added to the series designation by use of a slash, or by a blank space if the series designation is followed by Cutters.

Examples:
Y 3.Ad 6:1/983
Y 3.Ad 6:2 C 21

Breakdown of the components of the **Y 3.Ad 6:1/963** class:

Y 3.	Congressional publications
.Ad 6:	Issuing Agency
:1	Series
:1/983	Individual book number

Practical application

Author symbols. When publications from a new committee, commission, task force, or interagency organization are received, it is necessary to determine how the agency was set up, and how it fits into the total Government organization. Often this information is not included in the publication and must be obtained from the agency itself.

There are many informal interagency groups that fall into this category as well as those specifically set up by law. Congress may request a report on a certain subject. In order to comply with this request, several agencies may work together as a group because the subject of the report comes under their varied jurisdictions. These loosely formed committees will publish one report, and for classification purposes are assigned **Y 3.** author designations. In such cases, the committee may publish only the one report, then cease to exist.

When it has been determined that the new agency designation should be **Y 3.,** assign the Cutter number from the two-figure table, using the first main word from the agency name. This is followed by a colon.

Example:

Y 3.Am 3:	American Battle Monuments Commission
Y 3.L 61:	National Commission on Libraries and Information Science

Check all active and inactive files to be sure the number has not been used previously. A slash and numbers are used to distinguish between author designations having the same or similar first word in their names.

Examples:

Y 3.F 31/8:	Federal Deposit Insurance Corporation
Y 3.F 31/15:	Federal Council on Aging

In later years, because there are so many agencies beginning with Federal, a more descriptive word in the name of the agency is used for the Cutter number.

Examples:

Y 3.El 2/3:	Federal Election Commission
Y 3.P 19:	Federal Paperwork Commission

This applies to such words as **Advisory, National,** and **Interagency,** also.

(Subordinate offices.) The **Y 3.** classes make no provision for a breakdown for publications of smaller offices. Most of the organizations are small themselves, and have no subdivisions other than, perhaps, working groups.

A few of the larger organizations do have subdivisions. The Tennessee Valley Authority is an example. An effort was made to attach classes for publications of one office together by using -nos. with classes already established, as was done with the **HE 23.1210:** classes, the example given in Chapter 2. Office names changed and this attempt to organize by smaller issuing office was not totally satisfactory.

Subordinate offices are disregarded in assigning classes in the **Y 3.** classes except when the office name is part of the title of the series. Classes are related to each other by subject matter.

Series designation follows the colon. These series designations are assigned in the regular way, and the standard classes are used when necessary, or reserved for future use.

Examples:

Y 3.N 88:	Nuclear Regulatory Commission
Y 3.N 88:1	Annual report
Y 3.N 88:2	General publications

If a commission or committee is established to make a study, submits a report to Congress, then goes out of existence, only the 1 class (Y 3. :1) is set up. This class is entitled **Report** rather than **Annual report.** In preparing the report, the commission may issue background papers, task force reports, interim reports, or such. In that case, either the **General publications class** (Y 3. :2) or a class for the specific title of the series may be set up (Y 3. :9). Numbers 2 through 8 (prior to 1985) and 2 through 14 (after the latter part of 1985) are always reserved for the standard classes even though they may never be used.

Series of the same or related subjects are attached to each other by -(nos.)

Examples:

Y 3.Oc 1:10-2	Administrative Law Judge and Commission decisions
Y 3.Oc 1:10-3	Index to Decisions of Occupational Safety and Health Review Commission
Y 3.Oc 1:10-4	Citator to Decisions of Occupational Safety and Health Review Commission

Individual book numbers are added after the series designation. A slash is used after the series designation if the book number begins with a number. If the book number begins with a letter as in Cuttered classes, a space with no punctuation is used between the elements.

Examples:

Y 3.N 88:1/982	Nuclear Regulatory Commission, 1982 annual report
Y 3.T 25:2 B 84	Floods on Tuckasegee River and Deep Creek in vicinity of Bryson City, N.C.

Numbered series. Use a slash between the series designation and the individual book number.

Examples:

Y 3.N 88:10/0868   A collection of mathematical modes for dispersion in surface water and groundwater, NUREG-0868.

Prior to 1985, a revised edition of a numbered publication in a **Y 3.** class was designated by **/rev.** In the future, all revisions will be classed by adding **/(date)** to the original edition class.

Examples:
Y 3.N 88:10/0868/rev.
Y 3.N 88:10/0870/985

A numbered publication issued in volumes is classified by using a slash, the letter v. and the number.

Example: Y 3.N 88:10/0868/v.1

A numbered publication carrying both volume and number is classified by adding a comma after the volume number, then the letters no. before the actual numbers.

Example: Y 3.N 88:10/0868/v.1,no.2

In a numbered series, after the first book number, informative letters should precede any additional numbers, such as pt. for part numbers, **Chap.** for chapter numbers, **rp.** for report numbers, etc.

Example: Y 3.N 88:10/0868/rp.17 not 0868/17

(Dates.) Use a slash after the series designation and the 3-digit date or dates, as necessary.

Example:
Y 3.B 78:1/1982 Annual report of the Board for International Broadcasting. 1982.

When a publication is issued quarterly, monthly, weekly, etc., use a hyphen after the 3-digit date and the number assigned to that particular issue.

Example:
Y 3.Oc 1:10-2/982-8 Occupational Safety and Health Review Commission decisions, table of citations, August 1982 issue.

Do not use a slash between date and issue number in **Y 3.** classes as is done in other classes mentioned in earlier chapters.

Cutter numbers. When a Cutter is used, leave a space between the series designation and the Cutter number. Do not use any punctuation to separate these two elements.

Example:
Y 3.C 76/3:2 K 54/3/982 For Kids' Sake--Think Toy Safety Revised Sept. 1982.

Slash numbers are used to separate titles using the same Cutter numbers as in the regular classes. Dates for revisions, and any other information are added, separated by slashes in the regular way. See above example.
An additional number other than a date after a Cutter number should carry an abbreviation or word before it to explain the additional number. This is true of any Cuttered publication.

Example:
Y 3.T 22/2:2 F 95/2/no.1 Synthetic fuels for transportation background paper

The word number may or may not be printed on the publication, but such an abbreviation should still be used in the class. Avoid tacking on unexplained numbers.

Section 2, Congressional Record and House and Senate journals (X)

The class stem for the **Congressional record** (bound edition) is **X** followed by a period. The period is followed by the number of the Congress, a slash, and the session number, then a colon.

Examples:
X.95/2:
X.96/1:

The volume number, the abbreviation **pt.**, and the part number complete the class.

Example:
X.96/1:125/pt.19 Congressional record, 96th Congress. 1st session, volume 125, part 19, Sept 13-20, 1979.

The daily Congressional Record is treated as a preprint for classification purposes by using **/a** as part of the class stem. Then the class is formed by using the Congress and session numbers, the volume and issue numbers.

Example:
X/a.96/1:129/1 Congressional record, volume 129, no.1, Jan. 3, 1963.

The House and Senate journals have been assigned **XJH** and **XJS** respectively. The letters are followed by Congress and session number, then the part number.

Example:
XJH:96-2/pt.1 Journal of House of Representatives, 96th Congress, 2d session. part 1.

Section 3, Congress, House, and Senate (Y 1.)

All unnumbered publications of the Congress as a whole, the House of Representatives, and the Senate are grouped into three separate classes regardless of type of material. Following are the class designations:

Y 1.1: Congress as a whole, and conference committee publications without the names of specific established committees printed on them
Y 1.2: House of Representatives publications
Y 1.3: Senate publications

Classes in most of the above series are completed by adding a Cutter number after the colon. The publications may be manuals, bibliographies, compilations of laws, or any other type of material. Separate classes are not established for specific kinds of material. None of the publications classified in these series carries a Congressional committee name on it, and all are treated as miscellaneous unnumbered publications. Individual book numbers and revisions are handled the same as in other Cuttered classes.

Example:
Y 1.2:T 23/982 Telephone directory. Spring 1982 Issued by the House of Representatives.

The Senate has numbered all of its publications since the beginning of the oath Congress. The numbers printed on the publications are used now rather than Cutter numbers.

Example:
Y 1.3:S.pub.98-15 United States Senate telephone directory. May 1983

If, at a later date, the House of Representatives or Congress starts numbering its publications, the numbers printed on the publications should be used in the **Y 1.1:** or **Y 1.2:** class as appropriate.
A few exceptions have been made for specific titles of House and Senate publications by establishing separate classes for them. These are attached by **/(nos.)** to the appropriate classes.

Examples:
Y 1.2: House of Representatives publications
Y 1.2/2: House calendar
Y 1.3: Senate publications
Y 1.3/3: Senate calendar

Such additional classes are completed in the usual way using numbers, dates, or Cutter number as appropriate in each case after the colon.

Numbered House and Senate documents and reports have separate classes. Originally, the individual numbered documents and reports were not assigned specific classes, and were filed simply by number in individual groups.

Examples:

House and Senate documents and reports of the 86th Congress. 2d session. 86-2:H.doc.21
86-2:H.rp.100
86-2:S.doc.11
86-2:S.rp.35

During the 96th Congress, an X preceded the Congress and session numbers to aid in the computer production of the **Monthly Catalog of United States Government Publications.**

Examples:
House and Senate documents of the 96th Congress. 2d session.
X 96-2:H.doc.353
X 96-2:S.doc.62

These old numbering systems were in effect through the publications of the 96th Congress.
Beginning with the 97th Congress, the publications were assigned Y 1.1/(nos.): classes.

Examples:
Y 1.1/5: Senate reports
Y 1.1/8: House reports

The number as it is printed on the report follows the colon.

Examples:
Y 1.1/5:97-570 Senate Report 97-570
Y 1.1/8:97-914 House report 97-914

Since the House and Senate incorporated the Congress number in their numbering systems, no adjustment to the class is necessary to differentiate between the publications of various Congresses.
Subordinate offices. The classification scheme for the publications of Congress does not provide for an orderly incorporation of classes for publications of subordinate offices. In recent years, subordinate offices have been issuing their own publications, thus presenting problems in the best way to expand the classification system. Publications of two such offices have been handled in two different ways.
The class, **Y 3.T 22/2:**, was established in July 1974 for the publications of the Technology Assessment Office, United States Congress. The individual series classes are set up and used as in any **Y 3.** class. (See Section 1 of this Chapter.)
Y 10. was established in March 1975 for the publications of the Congressional Budget Office, United States Congress. The individual series classes are set up and used as in regular department and agency classes. (See Chapter 2.)
Future new classes for publications of subordinate offices of Congress would do well to follow the Y 10. example, rather than the **Y 3.** example. This will avoid mixing the letters rather than numbers, and some by letters and numbers.
Some committees do not number their publications, so the class is completed by using Cutter numbers.

Components of a class:

Y 4.   Congressional Committees
.J 89/1:   Committee designation
    :97/54   Individual
                          book number

Practical application

Serial numbers

The numbers and letters should be used as they are printed on the publication as far as possible.

Examples:

Y 4.B 22/3:S.Hrg. 98-12   Nomination of Edwin J. Gray, hearing . . . 98th Cong., 1st sess . . . S.Hrg. 98-12

Y 4.Ag 8/1:97-BBBB   Surplus Agricultural Commodities Act, hearing . . . 97th Cong., 2d sess . . . Serial no. 97-BBBB

Y 4.B 22/1:97-95   HUD field reorganization . . . Hearing. 97th Cong., 2d sess . . . Serial no. 9795

When a serial number does not incorporate the number of the Congress as has been done in the above examples, the Congress number must be added to the class after the colon, followed by a slash, then the serial number.

Example:

Y.J 89/1:97/54   Lanham Trademark Act amendment, hearing . . . 97th Cong., 2d sess . . . Serial 54.

The slash in the class indicates at a glance that the Congress number is not printed as part of the serial number of the publication.

Compare:

Y 4.J 89/1:97/54   Serial number 54 without the Congress number printed onthe publication.

Y 4.B 22/1:97-95   Serial 97-95 incorporating the Congress printed on the publication.

Part numbers.

The serial numbers are assigned in different ways to the Committee publications. Many hearings are issued in parts. A committee may assign the same serial number to all parts, so that it is necessary to use the part numbers in the classes.

Examples:

Y 4.J 89/2:J-97-7/pt. 3   Department of Justice confirmations hearing. . . part 3. . . Serial no. J-97-7. (Parts 1 and 2 are also designated Serial J-97-7.)

Y 4.In 8/14:97-9/pt. 10   Additions to the National Wilderness Preservation System, hearing . . . Serial 97-9, part 10. (Parts 1-9 are also designated Serial 97-9.)

Some committees assign separate serial numbers to each part of a hearing. The part number should be used in the class in such cases:

Examples:

Y 4.B 22/1:97-53   Housing and Urban-Rural Recovery Act, hearings, part 2. Serial no. 97-53

Congressional subordinate office classes with the boards, committees, and commissions classes.

Neither class is wrong, it is a question of which type of class for Congressional subordinate offices is more compatible with the basic principles of the classification system.

Star prints

Corrected editions of Congressional documents are issued as star prints. These documents have a star printed at the lower left-hand corner of the title page or cover. Sometimes the words "star print" also appear adjacent to the star. Star prints are new, revised editions. The class number for a star print should include "/corr." after the number assigned to the original edition.

Examples:
Y 1.1/5:97-77 **original edition**
Y 1.1/5:97-177/corr. **star print**

Section 4, Congressional Committee Publications (Y 4.)

The working committees of Congress such as Appropriations, Judiciary, etc., are grouped under **Y 4.**, one of the agency symbols assigned to Congress. As in the **Y 3.** classifications outlined in Section 1 of this Chapter, an author designation based on the name of the Committee and derived from the Cutter table follows the period and is followed by a colon.

Examples:
Y 4.J 89/1: House Committee on the Judiciary
Y 4.J 89/2: Senate Committee on the Judiciary

Unlike the **Y 3.** classes, the figure /1 is used in the Committee classes when it is known that there are both House and Senate Committees with the same name.

If other committees are appointed using the Cutter number, **J 89**, slash numbers beginning with the next highest number would be used as the author designation.

With this method of classifying Congressional committee publications, the classes for publications of House, Senate, and Joint committees are intermixed.

Examples:

Y 4.Ap 6/1:	House Appropriations
Y 4.Ap 6/2:	Senate Appropriations
Y 4.B 22/1:	House Banking, Finance and Urban Affairs
Y 4.B 22/3	Senate Banking, Housing and Urban Affairs
Y 4.Ec 7:	Joint Economic Committee
Y 4.Ed 8/1:	House Education and Labor
Y 4.F 29:	Senate Finance
Y 4.L 61/2:	Joint Committee on the Library

No provision is made for separate classes for subcommittees under the committees.

Separate series classes, with a few exceptions, are not assigned in the **Y 4.** classes. All publications including committee prints, hearings, manuals, bibliographies, etc., are included in a single class,

After the author designation and colon is the individual **book number.** The individual book numbers are assigned by using a Cutter number or serial number depending upon the designation, if any, which is printed on each publication.

Serial numbers appearing on publications should be used in the class. The numbers may or may not be identified by the word **serial** on the publications. These numbers usually begin with number one for each Congress. Some committees use the number of the Congress in conjunction with the serial numbers, and others do not. Some identify their publications by letters rather than numbers, and some by letters and numbers.

Some committees do not number their publications, so the class is completed by using Cutter numbers.

Components of a class:

Y 4.	Congressional Committees
.J 89/1:	Committee designation
:97/54	Individual book number

Practical application

Serial numbers

The numbers and letters should be used as they are printed on the publication as far as possible.
Examples:

Y 4.B 22/3:S.Hrg. 98-12   Nomination of Edwin J. Gray, hearing . . . 98th Cong., 1st sess . . . S.Hrg. 98-12

Y 4.Ag 8/1:97-BBBB   Surplus Agricultural Commodities Act, hearing . . . 97th Cong., 2d sess . . . Serial no. 97-BBBB

Y 4.B 22/1:97-95   HUD field reorganization . . . Hearing. 97th Cong., 2d sess . . . Serial no. 9795

When a serial number does not incorporate the number of the Congress as has been done in the above examples, the Congress number must be added to the class after the colon, followed by a slash, then the serial number.

Example:

Y 4.J 89/1:97/54   Lanham Trademark Act amendment, hearing . . . 97th Cong., 2d sess . . . Serial 54.

The slash in the class indicates at a glance that the Congress number is not printed as part of the serial number of the publication.

Compare:

Y 4.J 89/1:97/54   Serial number 54 without the Congress number printed on the publication.

Y 4.B 22/1:97-95   Serial 97-95 incorporating the Congress printed on the publication.

Part numbers. The serial numbers are assigned in different ways to the Committee publications. Many hearings are issued in parts. A committee may assign the same serial number to all parts, so that it is necessary to use the part numbers in the classes.

Examples:

Y 4.J 89/2:J-97-7/pt. 3   Department of Justice confirmations hearing. . . part 3. . . Serial no. J-97-7. (Parts 1 and 2 are also designated Serial J-97-7.)

Y 4.In 8/14:97-9/pt. 10   Additions to the National Wilderness Preservation System, hearing . . . Serial 97-9, part 10. (Parts 1-9 are also designated Serial 97-9.)

Some committees assign separate serial numbers to each part of a hearing. The part number should be used in the class in such cases:

Examples:

Y 4.B 22/1:97-53   Housing and Urban-Rural Recovery Act, hearings, part 2. Serial no. 97-53

Y 4.B 22/1:97-55   Housing and Urban-Rural Recovery Act, hearings, part 4. Serial no. 97-55.

When part 1 of a numbered serial is received, look at other publications in the class to determine whether the part number has been necessary in this particular class in similar cases. Presumably the committee is consistent in assigning serial numbers to publications issued in parts, and earlier examples can be followed. When part 2 or later numbers are received, it is easy to determine whether to use the part number in the class by locating the earlier parts.

Cutter numbers are used for publications not carrying serial numbers or letters. The rules for Cuttering hearings are the same as for other publications. (See Chapter 3, Section 4.)

There are a few problems that are, perhaps, unique to the hearings. One problem is how to handle such words as **Nominations, United States and Legislation.** Use these words for Cutter words only when absolutely necessary.

A hearing may be entitled **Nominations** only. The hearing may cover one or several names but they are not listed in the heading title. In this case, Cutter under **Nominations**.

Example:

Y 4.L 11/4:N 72/982-4   Nomination, hearing

The date is added after a slash with hyphen-numbers as necessary, as is done with any Cuttered publication.

If the heading title carries one or more names after the word **Nomination**, Cutter under the name of the first person listed.

Examples:

Y 4.F 76/2:K 38   Nomination of Richard T.
                         Kennedy, hearing.
Y 4.-   Nominations of Joe Lister, John
                         Doe, and Mary Brown,
                         hearing.
   :L 69

Avoid using **United States** and **Legislation** as Cutter words when possible. Congress is involved with legislation and the United States, and presumably most of their publications deal with these subjects. If Legislation or United States is the only word in the title, use it for the Cutter word; otherwise, choose another word. A hearing may be on United States relations with another country. Even though the United States may be used first in the title, Cutter under the name of the foreign country. **Legislation on energy** may be the title of a publication. Cutter under **energy** rather than Legislation. The name of the committee issuing the publication may affect your choice of Cutter, and an exception to the above rule may be necessary. The Committee on Energy may issue a publication entitled **Legislation on energy**. According to the rules, neither word is a good Cutter word, since the committee itself is involved totally with energy. In that case, it is permissible to Cutter under Legislation. Study the publications, the names of the issuing offices, the method of handling other publications in the class, and decide on the best Cutter word.

Classify like titles together even though they are not revisions or new editions of the same titles. For example, if Richard T. Kennedy is nominated for two separate positions, classify under the same Cutter and use the date after a slash at the end of the class for the second publication.

Examples:

   Y 4.F 76/2:K 38   Hearing held in 1981
   Y 4.F 76/2:K 38/983   Hearing held in 1983

If the dates for both hearings are **1983.** use **-(no.)** after the date for the second hearing. The classes would be:

Y 4.F 76/2.K 38   Hearing held in 1983, but no date
                         is used in the class.
Y 4.F 76/2:K 38/983-2   Hearing also held in 1983.

It is not necessary to go back and add the date to the first publication.

Hearings and committee prints under the same Cutter number are classified by using slash numbers. Even though the titles may be exactly the same, give the second publication received a different slash number. Do not use the same slash number for a hearing and a committee print.

Examples:
   K 38 Nomination of Kennedy (hearing)
   K 38/2 Nomination of Kennedy (committee print)

Bill numbers may be the only title of a publication. This presents a problem. One way to handle the situation is to Cutter a word from the title of the bill.

Example:
   Y 4.-:En 2
   S.1234 (This is the complete title of hearing)

The subject of the bill is energy so that is selected as the Cutter word.

The other way to handle the problem is to Cutter the S alone. Cuttering the letter alone is less informative than Cuttering a word and in years to come it is doubtful that a user will search for a bill number to find a publication on a certain subject.

While either method may be used, the way such publications are handled should be consistent within a class.

Before choosing a Cutter word, look in the master file under all possible Cutter words so that all like titles will be Cuttered under the same word and to be sure that the publication in question is not a duplicate.

Numbers may appear as part of titles, and be required in the classes.

Convert Roman numerals to Arabic numerals in the classes.

Example:
   Miscellaneous tax bills, XVII, hearing.

Though the word number, part, section, or volume does not appear in the title before the number, use an abbreviation of some such designation before the number when it is added at the end of the class. Numbers should not be tacked onto the end of a Cuttered class with no explanation.

   Correct: Y 4.-:T 19/981/no.17

   Incorrect: Y 4.-:T 19/981-82/17

Dates in the title of a hearing should be used in a Cuttered class even though there has been no earlier publication with a similar title.

Example:

Y 4.G 74/9:Ar 2/981   Arctic Research and Policy Act
                        of 1981, hearings

Problems and deviations.

A committee may issue its publications in a variety of ways. The hearings may have serial designations and the committee prints may not. That means that part of the class may be numbered, and part Cuttered. Use the same class stem for both types of material.

Examples:

Y 4.Ag 8/1:B 85/2/982   Report of the Committee on
                        Agriculture . . . to the
                        Committee on the Budget
                        . . . Committee print
Y 4.Ag 8/1:97-JJJ   Review of tobacco price
                        support program costs.
                        hearing. Serial no. 97-JJJ.

Another committee may use serial numbers for hearings, and letters for committee prints. These are classified under the same class stem.

Example:

Y 4.En 2/3:97-GG   Natural Gas regulation study
                        Committee print 97-GG.
Y 4.En 2/3:97-119   Telecommunications Act of
                        1982, hearings Serial no.
                        97-119.

Designation changes. In recent years more committees have been assigning serial numbers to their publications. As the committees add, drop, or change their serial designations, the class should be adapted to cover these changes. When the committee has indicated that it will be changing from Cutters to numbers or vice versa, the class should be changed at the beginning of a new Congress or a new session of Congress.

Series. No regular numbered series designations other than Serials are used as a general rule. Usually the committees issue only hearings and committee prints. When series do occur within the publications of a Committee, they have been treated in various ways. Some examples follow:

Y 4.P 93/1:1/97-1   Congressional directory.

The series designation **1** following the colon has been used. The individual booknumber indicating the Congress and session follow. Note the slash and hyphen separating the various components of the series and book number for the 97th Congress, 1st session.

Y 4.Ec 7:Ec 7/982-2   Economic indicators, Feb. 1982

This is a monthly periodical issued by the Joint Economic Committee. It has been assigned a place in the group of publications issued by this Committee by use of the Cutter designation following the colon (instead of the regular numerical series designation) based on the subject word economic. The book numbers for individual issues are designated by year of issue, and number corresponding to month of issue, as **982-2** for February 1982, **982-3** for March 1982, etc. These are added to the series designation Ec 7 following the colon and separated by a slash.

Reports also issued as committee prints. Committee names are often printed on House and Senate reports as well as the assigned House and Senate report numbers. Occasionally a committee will issue a report as a committee print. It may or may not have the words Committee Print on it, and it may have House or Senate report printed on it with no number assigned to it.

, If the publication has the number of the report printed on it, it is not a committee print and should be classified in the appropriate **Y 1.** class. (See Section 3 of this chapter.)

If the report number has not been printed on the publication, classify it as committee print in the appropriate Committee class.

Joint hearings. When two committees hold a hearing jointly and publish the results in one hearing, classify the publication under the first Committee listed.

Example:

Y 4.F 76/1:Ag 8/2   Agricultural development in the
                        Caribbean and Central
                        America, joint hearing
                        before . . .Committee on
                        Foreign Affairs and . . .
                        Committee on Agriculture,
                        House of Representatives .
                        . . Serial no. 97-ZZZ.

This is classified under Committee on Foreign Affairs. Serial no. **97-ZZZ** is the serial number assigned by the Committee on Agriculture so it is not used in this class.

Publications prepared by one committee for the use of another committee. These publications are usually issued as committee prints. This is most prevalent when the joint Committee on Taxation prepares summaries, descriptions, and analyses of bills for the Senate Committee on Finance and the House Committee on Ways and Means. It is necessary to determine which committee actually published the committee print.

If the heading on the publication reads joint committee print, classify it under the Joint Committee on Taxation.

If there is no heading, look at the next page to see. If names of members of the committee are listed as they often are on committee prints. Classify under the committee to which the members belong.

If there is no heading, and no members' names are listed, look in the classification files to determine what has been done in similar situations, and classify accordingly.

New classes for new and reorganized committees

As new committees are formed, set up new committee classes by Cuttering the first main word in the title of the committee, checking all active and inactive files to determine the correct slash number to be used.

If two or more existing committees are merged into one committee, set up a new number for the committee.

Examples:

   Y 4.Ag 8/2: Senate Committee on
                Agriculture and Forestry.
   Y 4.N 95:   Senate Select Committee on
                Nutrition and Human
                Needs
   Y 4.Ag 8/3: Senate Committee on
                Agriculture, Nutrition and
                Forestry.

When the first two committees were merged to form the third committee, a new author designation was assigned to it.

If a committee name changes to include other subjects, but completed committees were not merged, use the existing class and change the name of the class.

Examples:
   House Committee on Y 4.B 22/1: Banking and
         Currency.
   House Committee on Y 4.B 22/1: Banking,
         Housing, and Urban Affairs.
   House Committee on Y 4.B 22/1: Banking,
         Finance, and Urban Affairs.

This should be done only when the first important word of the name of the committee remains the same. If the name of the committee changes to Finance, Banking, and Urban Affairs, a new class should be set up with **Finance** as the Cutter word.

Chapter 5

Exceptions, Problems, and Miscellaneous Instructions

Section 1, Special Treatment of Publications of Certain Authors

While the foregoing principles and rules govern the classification of the publications and documents of most Government authors, special treatments are employed for those of certain Government agencies. These consist of classes assigned to:

1. Some series issued by the Interstate Commerce Commission.
2. Boards, Commissions, and Committees established by act of Congress or under authority of act of Congress, not specifically designated in the Executive Branch of the Government. (See Chapter 4, Section 1.)
3. Congress and its working committees. (See Chapter 4, Sections 2-4.)
4. Multilateral international organizations in which the United States participates.
5. President and the Executive Office of the President including Committees and Commissions established by executive order and reporting directly to the President.

Interstate Commerce Commission

The classes assigned to publications of this agency were revised in December 1914 to provide better groupings of material than could formerly be given due to the lack of bureau breakdowns within the Commission at that time. Accordingly, those publications of the Commission as a whole, such as annual reports, general publications, bulletins, circulars, etc., continued to follow the regular form of classification, while all others were grouped by subject.

This subject grouping took the place of bureau breakdowns and was designated by adding the first three or four letters of the subject word to the main agency designation of IC 1.

Examples:

IC 1 acci.	Publications relating to accidents.
IC 1 exp.	Publications relating to express companies.

The series designations and individual book numbers were then assigned under each subject grouping as though it were a regular bureau.

Example:
IC 1 acci. 3:3

Accident bulletin no. 3

A list of current subject breakdowns is contained in *List of Classes of United States Government Publications Available for Selection by Depository Libraries*.

Multilateral International Organizations in which the United States Participates

Many of the publications of these organizations are published simultaneously by the United States and other countries. The United States portions of these organizations may also publish separately, for example, the United States National Commission for UNESCO. Since participation by the United States is in the realm of foreign relations, such publications are classed under the State Department with two main class designations assigned as follows:

S 3. Arbitrations and Mixed Commissions to Settle International Disputes

S 5. International Congresses, Conferences, and Commissions

The individual organizations are then treated as subordinate bureaus or offices, a number being assigned to each as it begins to publish, but following the period rather than preceding it as in regular class construction. Individual book numbers are assigned after the colon, using the 2-figure Cutter table and based on the principal subject word of the title.

However, if the organization proves to be a prolific publisher, issuing several definite series of publications, each is distinguished by adding a slash and digits beginning with 2 to the number assigned to the organization as a bureau designation, as in the case of related series in regular class construction. For example, some of the series issued by the U.S. National Commission for UNESCO are classed as follows:

S 5.48/9:	Addresses
S 5.48/10:	Maps and posters
S 5.48/11:	Executive committee, summary of notice of meetings

Individual book numbers are then assigned in the regular way.

Only publications of the United States delegations or commissions are classified. Publications issued by the international organization as a whole (e.g. United Nations) are not considered United States Government publications and are not assigned Superintendent of Documents classification numbers.

President and Executive Office of the President, including Committees and Commissions Established by Executive Order and Reporting Directly to the President

The agency symbol assigned to the President of the United States is Pr followed by the number corresponding to the ordinal number of succession to the presidency, as **Pr 42**, William Clinton, 42nd President of the United States. Breakdowns under the agency symbol follow normal methods of classification expansion. However, in recent years, presidents have appointed many special committees and commissions to study particular problems and to report their findings directly to the Chief executives. These organizations usually cease to exist after making their reports. Since their publications are usually few in number, normal bureau treatment is not practical and special treatment is therefore indicated to prevent establishment of classes which will not be used, and in addition to keep together the publications of all such organizations appointed by one president.

Beginning with those appointed by President Eisenhower, one series class (**Pr—.8:**) has been assigned for all such committees and commissions. A Cutter designation using the 2-figure table is then assigned to each based on the principal subject word of its name, as **Pr 34.8:H 81**, President's Advisory Committee on Government Housing Policies and Programs. Publications of the committee are distinguished by addition of the slash and Cutter numbers based on the principal subject word of the title as normal classification. In ordinary usage a double Cutter number is not assigned to a publication. The **Pr—.8:** class is an exception.

Examples:

Pr 40.8:Et 3/L 62/2	Deciding to forego life-sustaining treatment, ethical, medical, and legal issues in treatment decisions.
Pr 40.8:Et 3/H 34/2/v.3	Securing access to health care, v.3.

Both of the examples are publications of the President's Commission for Study of Ethical Problems in Medicine and Biomedical and Behavioral Research established by Public Law 95622 in 1978.

When a class has been established for a Committee, the class continues under the establishing President, even though a new President may be elected. If the new President renews the establishment of the Committee, then the class is transferred to the .8 class for the renewing President.

Beginning with the administration of President Kennedy, the continuing offices assigned to the President which make up the Executive Office of the President, have been given permanent classes under the symbol PrEx. Thus, with a change in administration it is no longer necessary to change the classes for such offices as Management and Budget Office, Council of Economic Advisers, Council on Environmental Quality, etc. These have been given breakdowns as subordinate offices of the Executive Office of the President.

Example:
PrEx 2.   Management and Budget Office

Series and book numbers are then assigned in the usual manner.

Section 2, Miscellaneous

Contins

The following are procedures for assigning classification numbers to contins based on their designations.

A. Date.
1. If two issues are combined within the same year, use the **date/both** numbers separated by a comma.

e.g. 979/3,4

a. If two issues for two different years are combined, use dates and separated by a comma.

e.g. 979/4,980/1

2. If a publication is monthly. but is not issued in August, then make the September issue number 9, and make a note for the shipping list and on the contin card.
3. When a new title begins with an issue other than the January issue, give it the designation 1 and designate all future issues for that year accordingly.

e.g. If a monthly publication begins with the September issue, it will be given the number 1 and there will only be four numbers for that year. The January issue of the following year will begin again with number one.

B. Numbers; and letters and numbers.
1. If a publication has consecutive numbering which continues from year to year, then the numbering alone is sufficient.

e.g. January 1980. no. 27 would be designated :27

C. Special issues.
1. All special issues should be carefully scrutinized for content and publication pattern. If issued on a regular basis, they should be given a different class and cataloged separately.
2. Special issues published irregularly or on a one-time basis, will be assigned the same classification stem as the contin and cataloged separately.

D. Indexes.
1. An index should be given the same classification number as the publication it indexes.
2. In some cases indexes were in the past given separate classification numbers. These will remain as they are and will have to be cataloged and classed individually.

E. Date.
1. If there is only one index per year, use year/ind.

e.g. 979/ind.

2. If there is more than one index, then indicate which months are covered.

e.g. Semiannual index covering Jan.-June would be classed: 979/1-6/ind. The annual index. if cumulative, would be classed: 979/1-12/ind.

F. Numbers.
1. Use the numbers which are indexed/ind.

e.g. T 43.12:1-53/ind.

G. V. nos. & nos.
1. If the index covers complete volume, use volume number/ind.

e.g. E 3.27:4/ind.

2. If the index covers part of volumes, include numbers as follows:

e.g. E 3.27:4/1-6/ind.

E 3.27:4/7-12/ind. (semiannual, not cumulative)

E 3.27:4/1-12/ind. (2d, cumulative issue)

H. Supplements.

A. If issued three or more times a year with the same title, they will be given the same classification number and recorded on the contincard.

1. These will probably be issued as a supplement to a specific issue.

e.g. A 105.23:3/5/supp.

If not issued to a particular issue, use date or volume no./supp.-nos.

e.g. FR 26.15:979/supp.-2
GS 3.1812/supp.-6

B. If issued annually, semiannually or infrequently. If there is no special title, give it the same classification number as the contin stem and catalog separately.

C. With separate title. Supplement issued annually, etc. with a separate title (such as the *Periodicals Supplement*) should be classed on a green slip, and given a separate classification number. These will require a different cataloging record.

Summaries

1. If connected by numbering to a contin, such as no. 13 of a monthly, or no. 5 of a quarterly, etc., then give it the same classification number as the contin, and treat it as such.

e.g. C 3.158:M 28 (80)-13

2. Otherwise, all annual summaries should be classed on green slips and cataloged separately. If classed by date, then give the summary a separate classification number.

e.g. Medicaid management reports (quarterly) HE 22.410:
Medicaid management report.
Annual summary: HE 22.410/2:

Abbreviations and shortened words

In an effort to keep the classes short and compact, many abbreviations and otherwise shortened words are used when necessary to describe a particular publication. Always use lower case letters.

Use the following abbreviations for these terms which may or may not appear on the documents, but are needed in the class number:

Addenda, addendum	add.
Amendment	amdt.
amendments	Appendix,
app.	appendices
Book, books	bk.
Change, Changes	ch.
Chapter, chapters	chap.
Corrected copy	corr.
Correction sheet	corr.sh.
Index	ind.
Module	mod.
Number	no.
Page, pages	p. (when followed by page no.)
Part, parts	pt.
Preliminary	prelim.
Report, reports	rp. (not rp. no.)
Section, sections	sec.
Sheet, sheets	sh.
Subpart	subpt.
Summary, summaries	sum.
Supplement	supp.
Transmittal, transmittal sheet	trans.
Volume	v.

Note that both singular and plural are treated as singular in the class.

Occasionally other words may be necessary in a class to separate two publications on the same subject. There may be a report and a descriptive brochure or folder on a particular project. Rather than give the folder a separate **/(no.)**, thereby perhaps separating it from the project report, use the same class as the project report and add a slash and a word, shortened if necessary. The word may or may not be printed in the title. It could be **/desc.** (for description), **/folder**, or perhaps another word that has been used on the publication itself. The shortened version of words used may not be accepted abbreviations in general writing, but they will be descriptive for classification purposes. Be sure to shorten long words. No word should be longer than seven letters.

Sets of publications to be used together by instructors and students frequently require such descriptive words to keep the publications together as a set. Below are examples of shortened words that may be used when applicable. Some adjustment may be necessary depending on the wording of the publications themselves and what publications are included in the set.

Workbook	wkbk.
Instructor's guide	inst.
Guidelines	guide
Student guide	stud.
Manual	man.
Course outline	course

In most cases it is not necessary to use more than one word to identify the publication. The use of the words is flexible to fit the particular set of publications being classified.

For example: A set includes a study guide, an instructor's guide, a student workbook, and course outline.

Study guide	guide
Instructor's guide	inst.
Student workbook	wkbk.
Course outline	course

Since there are two guides, the word guide was used on the study guide. The sameset could also be done as follows:

Study guide	study
Instructor's guide	guide
Student workbook	stud.
Course outline	course

If later a student manual appeared, it could be classed **/man.**

If there are several sets of such publications in one class, be consistent in the designations used within that class. Since the sets of publications vary so much in format and wording, it is difficult to make a hard and fast rule that can be applied to the best advantage to each set.

Length of class number

A classification number can have as many characters as can be input in the **099** field of an OCLC record. The current limit is 47 characters, but this number might change. One solution for classification numbers having more than 47 characters is to use " . . . "

Basic manuals and changes

Basic manuals are publications issued in looseleaf format which are updated by transmittal or change sheets issued periodically. After a number of changes have been issued, a consolidated reprint may be issued incorporating the basic manual and all changes to date. In many cases a new edition will be issued later. The following are guidelines for classifying such manuals.

These are basic guidelines for standard cases. The nature of basic manuals is such that they frequently do not follow the standard pattern. Individual decisions will need to be made on a case-by-case basis.

Basic manuals. It is preferable that basic manuals with frequent changes be given separate classes, rather than be included in general **Handbooks, manuals, guides** classes. This should be applied only when new basics are received, so that the new class begins with a basic edition. A new basic may be a completely revised edition, or a reprint of an earlier edition incorporating all changes to date.

When classing the basic, always include the date of issuance in the class. This date will be used for all future publications until a new basic is issued.

Examples:
A 103.8/3.973
TD 4.308:Ae 8/981

Prior to 1985, if a basic was classed as part of a numbered series and the same number was retained for each edition, a number was used to indicate successive editions. In the future, add /**(date)** to the class.

Examples:
TD 4.6:124 1st edition
TD 4.6:124/2 2nd edition
TD 4.6:124/985 3rd edition

Occasionally a basic will be called **installment 1** or **transmittal 1.** Use the date in the class, but do not class as **transmital** or **installment 1.**

Changes, transmittal sheets, etc. Most change sheets will bear a numerical or chronological designation which is included in the class along with the date of the basic edition. In general, use the designation given, do not create numbers.

Unfortunately there is little consistency in the numbering of change sheets in accordance with the issuance of basic manuals. In theory, when a new edition is published the numbering should revert to number one. This is not always the case. Thus, the classifier must be aware of new editions so that the appropriate date can be added to the change sheets.

Reprints. Frequently a basic and its changes will be consolidated and reprinted through a particular change or date. This will constitute a new edition for classification purposes.

Dates and volume numbers, or Volume numbers and dates

The question of whether to use the date or the volume number first arises frequently. Which is used first in the class depends on the publication and the meaning of the date and volume numbers in the class.

If the publication being classified is one of a set of publications which reports on a year's activities, the date will come first, then the volume number. Each volume may cover a specific subject. A publication may be divided into volumes only because of the quantity of material, with no specific titles to the volumes.

Examples:

S 1.1:951/v.5   Foreign relations of the United States, 1951; volume 5. The Near East and Africa.

S 1.1:951/v.6   Foreign relations of the United States, 1951, volume 6, Asia and the Pacific.

Occasionally a situation may arise when the volume number should be listed first. In this case the volumes may be used alone and are revised individually and irregularly.

Examples:
    D 7.6/4:D 26/v.4/981
    D 7.6/4:D 26/v.9/982

These are volumes of the Defense integrated data system procedures manual.
Volume 4 is entitled Item identification, volume 9 is Document identifier code input/output formation.

Using the date first in this case would make it difficult for the user to discover the latest edition of the volume he wanted to use. The logical organization is to keep the set together by volume number with the latest edition being in the set. Filing by date would not keep the volumes in order unless they were all revised the same year.

Foreign language publications

A foreign language publication is classified the same as the English edition with a slash followed by the name of the language spelled out at the end of the class.

Examples:

HE 20.3038:R 11   The search for health: Rabies, a dreaded disease.

HE 20.3038:R 11/Spanish   En busca de buena salud: La rabia, enfermedad temible.

Capitalize the name of the language. This is one of the rare exceptions to the rule of using lower case letters when words are added at the end of the class.
The English word that is Cuttered and its equivalent in the foreign language may not be spelled alike, but the Cutter for the English word is used in both classes.
Changes within classes. The use of adequate references will eliminate many errors. Notes should be placed in appropriate places when classes are changed, or the method of classifying within the class is changed. This may involve changing from Cutters to numbers, from 2-figure to 3-figure Cutter table, changing the Cutter word of a particular title for one reason or another, etc.
Part numbers, chapter numbers, section numbers, etc. Part, chapter, title, section or other numbers may be needed at the end of classes for any type of publications. Usually the need will be apparent from the titles and format of the publications. These are added as nacessary after a slash at the end of the class. Occasionally you may need to use more than one of these designations on a single publication, but be careful not to use more than are necessary.
A good example is *Code of Federal regulations, Title 20, Employees' benefits, Parts 1-399, Revised April 1, 1985.* The class is:

AE 2.106/3:20/pt.1-399/985

Preliminary and final reports

When a preliminary or draft report is classified use /prelim. or /draft at the end of the class. When the final edition is received, use the same class without the / prelim. or /draft. In most cases it is not necessary to use /final in the class for the final report.

Examples:

I 1.98:C 63/7   Final Uinta-Southwestern Utah regional coal environmental impact statement.

I 1.98:C 63/7/draft   Draft Uinta-Southwestern Utah regional coal environmental impact statement.

Reprints

A reprint is a new printing of an item made from the original type image. The printing may reproduce the original exactly, or it may contain more or less slight variations, such as changes in names of officials, or in date of printing.
Reprints are not classified. However, if the basic is not received in the library but a reprint is, the latter will be classed using the regular methods of classification; never add /rep. Prior to 1985, reprints of looseleaf material incorporating changes were classified by adding /rep. at the end of the original class. This indicated that it was not an exact reprint; instead, it had additional material.

Revised pages, changes, errata, correction sheets, etc.

Amendments, changes, revised pages, corrections, errata, etc., are issued frequently to modify publications which have been printed. To classify these, use the class for the original publication followed by a slash (/) and descriptive letters to identify the amending publications.
Amendments. Use the class on the original publication and add /amdt. The publication may read **amendment, amendments,** or **amendment** sheet but the class should use the abbreviation for the singular form. No other letters are necessary.
If another amendment to the same publication is issued and does not carry a number, use a hyphen and the figure 2.

Examples:
    /amdt.-2

Continue adding numbers to each successive amendment so that each publication has a distinctive number.
If the amendment number is printed on the publication, use that number in the class.

Examples:
    /amdt. 1
    /amdt. 82-1

A hyphen between amdt. and the number indicates that the amendment itself did not have a number printed on it. If no hyphen, that indicates that the amendment number was printed on the publication.
Changes. Change sheets are handled in the same way as the amendments, using the abbreviation ch., and the hyphen if the change numbers are not printed on the publication.

Examples:
    /ch. Number not printed on the publication.
    /ch.-3 Number not printed on the publication.
    /ch.5 Number is printed on the publication.

Erratum, Errata.

Classification of errata sheets for publications may be handled in several ways depending on how they were issued by the agency or received by the Library Programs Service.

1) An errata sheet that is a bound page in a document requires no action.
2) Errata sheet that are inserted in a publication at the time of receipt should be classified the same as the parent document with addition of /errata. This class is for identification purposes only, in the event that the parts become separated during handling. No individual temporary card is needed, but the temporary card for the parent publication should be annotated to show that an errata was also issued.
3) A separately issued errata sheet should have its own SuDocs class number, which is based on the class of the parent document with the addition / errata.

Examples:

HE 20.3152:C 48   (parent document)
HE 20.3152:C 48/errata   (separately issued errata)

4) A separately issued errata whose parent publication has not been received should not be classified.

Corrections and correction sheets. To distinguish between corrected copies and corrections sheets, use /corr.sh. at the end of the class for a list of corrections. Very likely the only word in the title or heading will be Corrections. A corrected copy of the whole publication is classified /corr. and all correction lists are classified /corr.sh.
Revised pages and transmittals. Revised pages are classified /rev.pages. It is important to include the word pages in the class, to distinguish from a revised edition of the complete publication. Sometimes it is helpful to include the page numbers in the class, particularly if many revised pages are issued at different times.
Often revised pages are issued to looseleaf material, and the agency **numbers the transmittals.** Use the words and numbers that the agency assigns whenever possible. This may result in /rev.pages 2 or /trans.2 in the class. Study previous examples in the series and follow that practice.

Summaries, executive summaries, etc.

All summaries, executive or otherwise, are classified by using /sum. at the end of the class. Other words should not be used with /sum. unless it is necessary to avoid conflict with a class already used. Thus, an executive summary would be classified /sum. unless that designation has already been used in the class.

Two or more types or publications issued in a set

All publications in a set with a common title may or may not be the same type of material. There may be a report with an accompanying map, for example. Each will have a separate class number written on it. Classify the report in its appropriate class. Classify the map by using the same number as assigned to the report and add /map at the end of the class. Do not classify a map in a Maps and charts class if it is part of a set or is to be used with another publication.
Another set with a common title but no volume numbers may include a bibliography, a manual, a report, and a chart. Decide which publication is the main publication and classify in the appropriate class. Classify the other publications with the main publication by using the class for the main publication, a slash, then a word or shortened word for each of the other publications.
If the publications have similar titles but are not issued as a set, classify the publications separately, each in its appropriate class.

Locally assigned SuDocs Numbers

Government publications are classified once they are received at the Library Programs Service. GPO receives numerous requests from libraries wanting a SuDocs classification number for fugitive publications. To alleviate this problem, GPO suggests two methods for libraries to construct their own SuDocs classes. However, every library should work out a method that best serves its own needs and patrons, and should feel completely free in assigning these numbers.

1) For documents falling in existing classes, the class stem in the List of Classes can be used, a Cutter number, date, or series number is added after the colon, and an arbitrary designation such as "X" is placed at the end to indicate that it is a locally assigned number.
2) After General Publication classes, the numbers 2 through 9 or 2 through 14, after the latter part of 1985 when dealing with new offices, bureaus, departments, etc., are slashed, and 2 through infinity are dashed if needed.

Examples:
    A 1.2/2:
    A 112.2/14:

Agencies having all publications listed in a single class, like the **Y.4's** (Congressional committees), will use the above system with the only class available.

Examples:
    Y 4.Ag 8/3-4:

TABLE OF CONTENTS

DEPARTMENT OF AGRICULTURE
(1862–   )

CREATION AND AUTHORITY

The Department of Agriculture was created by an act of Congress approved May 15, 1862 (12 Stat. 387, 5 U.S.C. 511 , 514, 516), and until 1889 was administered by a Commissioner of Agriculture. By act of February 9, 1889 (25 Stat. 659; 5 U.S.C. 512), the powers and duties of the Department was enlarged. It was made the eighth executive department in the Federal Government, and the Commissioner became the Secretary of Agriculture.

INFORMATION

1400 Independence Avenue, SW
Washington, D.C. 20250
(202) 720-2791
http://www.usda.gov

A 1.1   • Item 6 (MF)
REPORT OF THE SECRETARY OF AGRICULTURE.
1862–   [Annual]

The annual report on agriculture began in 1837 with a 2-page statement in the Report of the Commissioner of Patents, and formed part of his report (making a separate volume after 1849) until 1862, when the Department of Agriculture was established. The annual report was issued from 1862– 1893 in one volume and from 1894– 1936 in two volumes: one the report proper (A 1.1), containing the Secretary's report and the purely executive reports of the several chiefs of bureaus, divisions, and offices; the other, the Yearbook of Agriculture (A 1.10), embracing the Secretary's report and a collection of special articles on agricultural science.
ISSN 0082-9803

A 1.1/2:date   • Item 6-B
INFORMATION AND TECHNICAL ASSISTANCE DELIVERED BY THE DEPARTMENT OF AGRICULTURE IN FISCAL YEAR. [Annual]
Discontinued.

A 1.1/3:date   • Item 6-G (MF)
SEMIANNUAL REPORT, OFFICE OF INSPECTOR GENERAL.

Earlier title: Office of Inspector General, Agricultural Research Service, Annual Report.

A 1.1/4:date
ANNUAL REPORT TO THE SECRETARY OF AGRICULTURE BY THE JOINT COUNCIL ON FOOD AND AGRICULTURAL SCIENCES. [Annual]

A 1.1/4-2:date   • Item 6-J (MF)
ANNUAL REPORT ON THE FOOD AND AGRICULTURAL SCIENCES.

A 1.1/4-3:date   • Item 6-N
APPRAISAL OF THE PROPOSED BUDGET FOR FOOD AND AGRICULTURAL SCIENCES REPORT TO THE PRESIDENT AND CONGRESS. [Annual]
An appraisal of the proposed budget for food and agricultural sciences by the National Agricultural Research and Extension Users Advisory Board.

A 1.1/5:date   • Item 6-J (MF)
REPORT ON USDA HUMAN NUTRITION RESEARCH AND EDUCATION ACTIVITIES, A REPORT TO CONGRESS. [Annual]

A 1.1/6:date   • Item 6-J (MF)
OFFICE OF INSPECTOR GENERAL FY, ANNUAL PLAN.

A 1.2:CT   • Item 10
GENERAL PUBLICATIONS.

A 1.2:B 83   • Item 10
NATIONAL BRUCELLOSIS COMMITTEE: PROCEEDINGS. [Annual]

A 1.2:P 43/3   • Item 10
PROGRESS REPORT OF PESTICIDES AND RELATED ACTIVITIES. [Annual]
Limited

A 1.2/10:date
PRIORITIES FOR RESEARCH, EXTENSION AND HIGHER EDUCATION. [Annual]

A 1.2/11:date   • Item 6-L
FIVE-YEAR PLAN FOR THE FOOD AND AGRICULTURAL SCIENCES. [Biennial]

Issued by the Joint Council on Food and Agricultural Sciences as required by PL 97-98.

A 1.2/12:date   • Item 6-K
ACCOMPLISHMENTS FOR RESEARCH, EXTENSION, AND HIGHER EDUCATION. [Annual]

Issued by the Joint Council on Food and Agricultural Sciences as required by Section 1407 of PL 95-113 as amended by PL 97-98. Summarizes ongoing research, extension, and teaching programs, their accomplishments and expectation.

A 1.2/13:date   • Item 6-S (MF)
FISCAL YEAR PRIORITIES AND FISCAL YEAR ACCOMPLISHMENTS FOR RESEARCH, EXTENSION, AND HIGHER EDUCATION, A REPORT TO THE SECRETARY OF AGRICULTURE.
Discontinued 1997.

A 1.3:nos.
DEPARTMENT BULLETINS. 1– 1500. 1913– 1929.

Superseded by Technical Bulletins A 1.36. Nos. 1-1125 have title Bulletin.
– INDEX. 1– 1500. 1936. 384p.

A 1.3/2:nos.
MANAGEMENT BULLETINS.

A 1.4/2:nos.   • Item 8
CIRCULARS. 1– 982. 1927– 1956.

A 1.5/1:nos.
MISCELLANEOUS CIRCULARS. 1st series, 1– 3. 1897.
Series discontinued with no. 3, 1897 (The Mississippi River Flood). [Report No. 2] and resumed in 1923 with no. 3 (The Relation of Agricultural Education to Farm Organizations).

A 1.5/2:nos.
MISCELLANEOUS. 2nd series, 3– 110. 1923– 1929.
See note above (A 1.5/1). Superseded by Miscellaneous Publications.

A 1.6:nos.
SPECIAL REPORTS. 1– 65. 1897– 1883.

A 1.7:nos.
MISCELLANEOUS SPECIAL REPORTS. 1– 11. 1883– 1886.

A 1.8:nos.
REPORTS. 1– 117. 1862– 1918.
Nos. 1– 58 were issued, 1862– 1898, without numbers.

A 1.9   • Item 9
FARMERS' BULLETINS. 1–   1889– [Irregular]
PURPOSE:– To give farmers, ranchers, and others useful information on agriculture presented in a concise, non-technical, and popular style.
Of all the publications of the Department of Agriculture, or for that matter the whole U.S. Government, the Farmers' Bulletins are the most well known. Designed to meet the needs of the individual farmer or rancher, the Bulletins give the particular application of agricultural information, stressing directions and recommendations. The Bulletins are well illustrated and are written in a popular style, making for easy and interesting reading.
Many of the titles are kept in print by revisions necessitated by the addition of new methods, current research, etc. Such publications present

problems in accessioning and binding. Many libraries need keep only the latest editions, while others will want to keep all editions to show the changes in agricultural research and the resulting recommendations. Quite a few of the Bulletins are superseded by later Bulletins with new numbers assigned.
The Farmers' Bulletins are published in editions ranging from 20,000 to 100,000 copies.
– INDEXES.
Indexes have been issued for the following series of numbers:

1– 250
1– 750
1– 1000
1001– 1500
1501– 1750

Title-pages and tables of contents were issued for each 25 Bulletins through Farmers' Bulletin 2000. This service was discontinued, along with other indexing services.

A 1.10   • Item 17
YEARBOOK OF AGRICULTURE. 1894–1993 [Annual]

PURPOSE:– To make available an authoritative and comprehensive treatment on an important agricultural subject.
The Yearbook of Agriculture is one of the more widely known Government publications. It grew out of the requirement of the Act of January 12, 1895, which required the Secretary of Agriculture to submit his annual report to Congress in two parts-part 1 being his summary report, and part 2 a review of developments. This was accomplished in one volume in the Yearbook of Agriculture. From its beginning until 1936, the Yearbook consisted of the summary report, a series of un-related articles on current agricultural research or study, and an appendix of statistical tables.
In 1936, a drastic change was made in this series. It was decided to devote each volume to one broad subject of interest, addressed to all Americans in general, and to the farmer in particular. The general annual report of the Secretary of Agriculture and the statistical section were dropped from the Yearbook and published separately. The annual report did appear in the 1936 and 1937 volumes, but not in any subsequent volumes. A brief digest of statistical tables also appeared in the 1936 volume, but disappeared after that. The statistical section was made a separate series and has been published since 1936 under the title, Agricultural Statistics.
The articles are both technical and popular in approach. While not intended as a definitive edition or an all-inclusive coverage of a single subject, the Yearbooks do cover a lot of ground and provide libraries within expensive reference tools to the various fields of agriculture.

A 1.10/a:CT   • Item 17
YEARBOOKS (separates). [Irregular]
Discontinued.

A 1.11:nos.
REGULATIONS. 1936–

A 1.11/2:nos.
IMPORT REGULATIONS.

A 1.11/3:CT   • Item 11-C
HANDBOOKS, MANUALS, GUIDES.

A 1.11/4:nos.   • Item 11-C
AUDIT GUIDE SERIES. [Irregular]
Non-depository.

A 1.12:nos.
GENERAL ORDERS.

A 1.13.:CT
SPECIAL ORDERS.

A 1.14/1:date&nos.
DEPARTMENT CIRCULARS. 1905. nos. 1– 5.

A 1.14/2:nos.
DEPARTMENT CIRCULARS. 1– 425. 1919– 1927.
Superseded by Circulars A 1.4/2

A 1.15:nos.
FOOD INSPECTION DECISIONS. 1– 212. 1905– 34.

A 1.16:nos.
NOTICES OF JUDGEMENT, FOOD AND DRUG ACT.

A 1.17:date
INSECTICIDE DECISIONS.

A 1.18:nos.
NOTICES OF INSECTICIDE ACT JUDGEMENT.

    Included in A 34.6

A 1.19:date
REGULATIONS OF DEPARTMENT OF AGRICULTURE.

A 1.20:v.nos.
DEPARTMENTAL CIRCULARS. v. 1, no. 1– 8. 1915.

A 1.21
FARM-MANAGEMENT OFFICE CIRCULARS.

    Changed to A 37.4

A 1.22:v.nos.
WEEKLY NEWS LETTER [To Crop Correspondents].
    v. 1– 9. 1913– 1921.

    Superseded by Official Record, A 1.33

A 1.23:v.nos.   • Item 14
JOURNAL OF AGRICULTURAL RESEARCH. v. 1-78.
    1913– 1949.

    The publication was superseded in 1921, with
    v. 22, no. 10 and resumed in 1923, with v. 23, no.
    1.

A 1.24:nos.
FOOD THRIFT SERIES. 1– 5. 1917.

A 1.25:CT
SPECIFICATIONS.

A 1.26:nos.
UNITED STATES FOOD LEAFLETS. 1– 20. 1917– 18.

A 1.27:nos.
JOINT ORDERS.

A 1.28:nos.
JOINT CIRCULARS. 1– 6. 1918– 1920.

    Issued jointly with the Treasury Department.

A 1.29:nos.
LIBRARY LEAFLETS. 1– 20. 1919.

A 1.30:CT
ATLAS OF AMERICAN AGRICULTURE ADVANCE
    SHEETS. 1– 8. 1917– 35.

A 1.31:date or nos.
PRESS NOTICES.

A 1.32   • Item 80-H
POSTERS AND MAPS. [Irregular]

A 1.32/2:CT
AUDIOVISUAL MATERIALS.

A 1.33:v.nos.
OFFICIAL RECORD, DEPARTMENT OF AGRICULTURE.
    1– 12. 1922– 1933.
    Supersedes A 1.22, Weekly Newsletter [to
    crop correspondents].

A 1.34:nos.   • Item 15 (MF)
STATISTICAL BULLETINS. 1–   1923–   [Irregular]

    PURPOSE:– To publish needed statistics on
    agriculture obtained and compiled as part of the
    work of the Department on such subjects as pro-
    duction, movement from the farm, receipts at
    principal markets, farm and market prices, ex-
    ports and imports, etc.
    Data appearing in these Bulletins are usually
    in their final form and cover a large period of time.

A 1.34/2:date   • Item 15 MF
FEDERAL MILK ORDER MARKET STATISTICS. [An-
nual]

    Discontinued.

A 1.34/3:date   • Item 15 MF
WORLD INDICES OF AGRICULTURAL AND FOOD
PRODUCTION. [Irregular]

A 1.34/4:date   • Item 15 MF
FOOD CONSUMPTION, PRICES, AND EXPENDI-
TURES. [Annual]

A 1.34/5:date
POULTRY PRODUCTION, DISPOSITION, AND IN-
COME, FINAL ESTIMATES. [Triennial]

A 1.35:nos.   • Item 12
LEAFLETS. 1–   1927–   [Irregular]

    PURPOSE:– To provide brief statements of
    information as contained in the Farmers' Bulletins
    or Home and Garden Bulletins, but in a briefer
    form, usually ranging from one to eight pages.

A 1.36:nos.   • Item 16 (MF)
TECHNICAL BULLETINS. 1–   1927–   [Irregular]

    PURPOSE:– To publish substantial original
    contributions to scientific or technical knowledge,
    usually the full, final report on a research project
    or of a major segment of a large research project.

    – INDEXES.

        The following indexes have been pub-
    lished:
                1– 500 1937. 249 p.
        501– 750
        This indexing service has been discon-
    tinued.

A 1.37:nos.
WITH THE CORN BORER. [Weekly]

A 1.38:nos.   • Item 13-A (MF)
MISCELLANEOUS PUBLICATIONS. 19–   1927–

    Both technical and nontechnical publications
    that do not conform to the size or type of material
    specified for the other series.

A 1.38/2:date   • Item 13-A-1 (P) (EL)
FACTS ABOUT U.S. AGRICULTURE. [Annual]

    PURPOSE:– To present facts about U.S. ag-
    riculture in such areas as farm production, in-
    come, and values, agricultural planning and pro-
    ductivity, and food marketingand distribution.
    Earlier A 1.38: (item 13-1).

A 1.39:nos.
NATIONAL LAND-USE PLANNING COMMITTEE PUB-
LICATIONS.

A 1.40
ADDRESSES. [Irregular]

A 1.41:nos.
MEMORANDUM.

A 1.42:CT
AGRICULTURE DEPARTMENT GRADUATE SCHOOL
PUBLICATIONS.

A 1.43:nos.
BUDGET AND FINANCE CIRCULARS.

A 1.44:nos.
PERSONNEL CIRCULARS.

A 1.45:nos.
OPERATION DIVISION CIRCULARS.
    Later A 60.4

A 1.46:nos.
DISCUSSION GROUP TOPICS.

A 1.47:date   • Item 1 (P) (EL)
AGRICULTURAL STATISTICS. 1936–   [Annual]

    PURPOSE:– To bring together each year the
    more important series of statistics concerning
    agriculture and closely related subjects.
    Prior to 1936, the data appeared in the Sta-
    tistical Section of the Yearbook of Agriculture.
    Historical series are usually limited to the last 10
    years. The issue for 1952 contains longer series
    of years for most of the tables.

A 1.47/2:date   • Item 1-A (E)
AGRICULTURAL STATISTICS. [Annual]

    Issued on CD-ROM

A 1.48:CT
WORLD'S POULTRY CONGRESS AND EXPOSITION,
    CLEVELAND , OHIO, JULY 28– AUGUST 7, 1939
    (7th).

A 1.49:nos.
INTERBUREAU FORAGE COMMITTEE PUBLICA-
TIONS I.F.C.

A 1.50:vol.nos.
COTTON LITERATURE, SELECTED REFERENCES.
    Earlier A 36.76
    Later A 17.13

A 1.51:date
EXTENT OF AERIAL PHOTOGRAPHY BY AGRICUL-
TURE DEPARTMENT, COMPLETED, IN
PROGRESS AND APPROVED. [Monthly]

A 1.52
CROPS AND MARKETS. v. 4–   1927–
    Prior to July 1939, A 36.11/3
    Supersedes another publication of the same
    title and its supplement, issued by the Depart-
    ment of Agriculture, and continues the volume
    numbering of the Supplement.

A 1.53
NOTES ON GRADUATE STUDIES AND RESEARCH
IN HOME ECONOMICS AND HOME ECONOMICS
EDUCATION.

    Slightly varying titles.

A 1.54:CT
FARM HANDBOOKS (by States).

A 1.55:nos.
HYDROLOGIC BULLETINS. 1–   1941–

A 1.56:vol
AGRICULTURAL LABOR SITUATION. [Monthly]

A 1.57:vol   • Item 15A (EL)
USDA NEWS v. 1–   1942–   [Biweekly]
    ISSN 0364-5290

A 1.58
[This class was not used]

A 1.58/a   • Item 2
AGRICULTURE DECISIONS. v. 1–   1942– [Semian-
nual]
    Sub-title:-Decisions of the Secretary of Agri-
    culture under the Regulatory Laws Administered
    in the United States Department of Agriculture
    (including Court Decisions).
    PURPOSE:– To make available to the public,
    in an orderly and accessible form, decisions is-
    sued under regulatory laws administered in the
    Department of Agriculture.
    The decisions may be described generally as
    those which are made in proceedings of a quasi-
    judicial (as contrasted with quasi-legislative) char-
    acter, and which, under applicable statutes, can
    be made by the Secretary of Agriculture, or an
    officer authorized by law to act in his stead, only
    after notice and hearing or opportunity for hear-
    ing have been given. These decisions do not
    include rules and regulations of general applica-
    tion which are required to be published in the
    Federal Register.
    The decisions published are numbered seri-
    ally in the order in which they appear in Agricul-
    ture Decisions. It is unnecessary to cite the docket
    or decision number. Prior to 1942, the Secretary's
    decisions were identified by docket and decision
    numbers (for example, D-578; S- 1150). Such
    citation of a case in these volumes generally
    indicates that the decision is not published in the
    Agriculture Decisions. Decisions prior to 1942 were
    not published and are available in the Department
    files only.
    The December issue contains a cumulative
    list of decisions reported for the year, by act;
    docket numbers arranged in consecutive order,
    and cumulative subject-index by act.
    Citation:A.D.

Principal statutes concerned are:
Agricultural Marketing Agreement Act of 1937.
Commodity Exchange Act.
Grain Standards Act.
Packers and Stockyards Act, 1921.
Perishable Agricultural Commodities Act, 1930.
United States Warehouse Act.
ISSN 0002-1741

A 1.59:nos.
[AGRICULTURE WAR INFORMATION SERIES] PUBS. DESIGN. AWI-No. 1– 116. 1942– 1945.
Superseded by Agriculture Information Series (A 1.64).

A 1.60:nos.   • Item 7
BIBLIOGRAPHICAL BULLETINS. 1–   1943–

Discontinued.

A 1.60/2:CT   • Item 32-B-1
BIBLIOGRAPHIES AND LISTS OF PUBLICATIONS. [Irregular]

A 1.60/3:nos.   • Item 32-B-1
BIBLIOGRAPHIES AND LITERATURE OF AGRICULTURE. Series.

Note:-Since this series has been issued by various Agricultural offices, and therefore, classified A 106.110/3, A 105.55, and A 13.11/3, it has been decided to reclassify it as A 1.60/3 and to leave it there regardless of which Agriculture Department office may issue it in the future.

A 1.61:nos.
ADMINISTRATIVE SERIES. 1–   1943–

A 1.62:nos.
GENERAL DEPARTMENTAL CIRCULARS. 1– 69. 1943– 1945.

A 1.63:CT
INTERBUREAU COMMITTEE ON POST-WAR PROGRAMS PUBLICATIONS.

A 1.64:nos.
AGRICULTURE INFORMATION SERIES.
Supersedes Agricultural War Information Series (A 1.59).

A 1.65:nos.
NUTRITION AND FOOD CONSERVATION SERIES.
Earlier A 80.123

A 1.66:nos.
DISCUSSION SERIES.
A 1–   1935–
B 1–
Earlier A 35.126

A 1.67:v.nos.
CONSUMERS' GUIDE. [Monthly]

Earlier A 80.808

A 1.68:nos.   • Item 14-A
PROGRAM AIDS. PA 1–   1946–

PURPOSE:– To publish information as needed on current programs of the Department, such as acreage allotments, marketing quotas, insect pest control, soil conservation, 4-H club work, etc.

A 1.69:nos.
WAR RECORDS, MONOGRAPHS. 1– 2. 1946.

A 1.70:CT
FAMINE EMERGENCY COMMITTEE PUBLICATIONS.

A 1.71:CT
FACT SHEETS.

A 1.72:CT
AGRICULTURAL RESEARCH AND MARKETING ACT PUBLICATIONS.
Changed to A 87.2 and A 87.7

A 1.73:nos.
COMMODITY STATISTICS. 1–   1943–
Earlier A 82.18

A 1.74:nos.   • Item 13
MANAGEMENT IMPROVEMENT. 1– 3.   – 1949.

Discontinued.

A 1.75:nos.`   • Item 4 (MF) (EL)
AGRICULTURE INFORMATION BULLETINS. 1– 1949–   [Irregular]

PURPOSE:– To publish information of a more specialized character than that included in the Farmers Bulletins, Home and Garden Bulletins, or Leaflets. Written in a popular and nontechnical style.

A 1.75:402   • Item 4
ONE HUNDRED YEARS OF FEDERAL FORESTRY. 1976.

A photographic album of the U.S. Forest Service and the men and women who have applied the science of developing, caring for, or cultivation forests in the century since 1876.

A 1.75/2:date   • Item 4
FINANCIAL CHARACTERISTICS OF U.S. FARMS.

A 1.76:nos.   • Item 3 (P) (EL)
AGRICULTURAL HANDBOOKS. 1–   1950–   [Irregular]

PURPOSE:– To publish manuals of information on agriculture and home economics. Designed for ready reference tools, such as manuals, guidebooks, specifications, glossaries and lists of plants.

A 1.76/2:date   • Item 3
AGRICULTURE CHARTBOOK. [Annual]

Economic charts on various agricultural subjects. Enlargements of these charts are also available and A 43.50.

Discontinued.

A 1.76/2-2:date   • Item 3
AGRICULTURAL CHARTBOOK ENLARGEMENTS. [Annual]Discontinued.

A 1.77:nos.   • Item 11 (P) (EL)
HOME AND GARDEN BULLETINS. 1–   1950– [Irregular]

PURPOSE:– To present in a popular style information on home and garden subjects, such as home building; growing flowers, vegetables, and fruit for home use; controlling insect pest, etc.

A 1.78:nos.   • Item 5
AGRICULTURE MONOGRAPHS. 1–   1950–

Discontinued.

A 1.79:
MEMORANDUM TO HEADS OF DEPARTMENT OF AGRICULTURE AGENCIES.

A 1.80
PRESS RELEASES. [Irregular]

The Press Service issues approximately 2,000 to 3,000 releases a year on the various programs and services of the department. Releases are numbered consecutively for each year. For those interested in knowing what releases have been issued, the following two recurring lists are very helpful:

– DAILY SUMMARY. [Monday-Friday]

Lists the title of each press release and for the more important ones, gives a paragraph summary of their contents. Also lists the more important periodic reports issued the same day.
– WEEKLY SUMMARY. [Weekly]
Issued at the beginning of each week for the listing (titles only) of the press releases issued during the preceeding week.

A 1.80/2   • Item 6-C
OUTLOOK FOR AGRICULTURAL EXPORTS. [Irregular]

Gives data on U.S. agricultural trade balance; agricultural exports, by commodity and by destination regions; and U.S. imports of selective competitive and noncompetitive commodities.
Later A 93.43

A 1.80/3:date
OIG NEWS. [Irregular] (Office of the Inspector General)

PURPOSE:– To serve as the official publication of the Office of the Inspector General. Discontinued in 1980 or 1981.

A 1.81:nos.
DEFENSE FOOD DELEGATIONS.

A 1.82   • Item 13-B (MF)
MARKETING RESEARCH REPORTS. 1–   1952– [Irregular]

PURPOSE:– To make available semitechnical or semipopular information resulting from marketing research, usually covering transportation, processing and marketing farm products.

Discontinued.

A 1.83:
AGRICULTURE IN NATIONAL DEFENSE. [Weekly]

A 1.84   • Item 13-C (MF)
PRODUCTION RESEARCH REPORTS. 1–   1956– [Irregular]

PURPOSE:– To make available popular or semitechnical reports on production research, including reports on less complete research projects than are reported in the Technical Bulletins, with emphasis on the application of the information in the production of farm products.

Discontinued.

A 1.85:date   • Item 13-D
PROGRESS IN RURAL DEVELOPMENT PROGRAM, ANNUAL REPORTS.

Discontinued.

A 1.85/2:date   • Item 6-D (MF)
RURAL DEVELOPMENT GOALS, ANNUAL REPORT OF THE SECRETARY OF AGRICULTURE TO THE CONGRESS. 1st– 1974–

Discontinued.

A 1.86   • Item 11-A
HOUSEHOLD FOOD CONSUMPTION SURVEY (year), REPORTS.

Prepared by Consumer and Food Economics Research Division, Agricultural Research Service.
1955 survey issued in 13 parts.
1954-66, Report 1–

Discontinued.

A 1.87:nos.   • Item 11-B (MF)
HOME ECONOMICS RESEARCH REPORTS. 1– 1957–   [Irregular]

PURPOSE:– To make available semitechnical or technical reports on home economics research.

A 1.87:41   • Item 11-B
AVERAGE WEIGHT OF MEASURED CUP OF VARIOUS FOODS. 1969. Reprinted 1977. 26.

Useful data for those engaged in the development, standardization, and testing of food preparation formulas for homes and institutions.

A 1.88:nos.　　　　　　　　**• Item 16-A (MF)**
UTILIZATION RESEARCH REPORTS. 1–　1957–
[Irregular]

　　PURPOSE:– To make available semitechnical or semipopular information resulting from utilization research.
　　Discontinued.

A 1.89:date　　　　　　　　**• Item 80-E (MF)**
TELEPHONE DIRECTORY. [Semiannual] (Office of Plant and Operations)

　　Covers Washington, D.C. area. Issued in March and October
　　Superseded by Telephone Directory, Alphabetical Listing (A 1.89/4).
　　ISSN 0161-4673

A 1.89/2:date
OFFICIALS OF DEPARTMENT OF AGRICULTURE.
　　Earlier A 1.2:Of 2/2

A 1.89/3:CT　　　　　　　　**• Item 80-E**
DIRECTORIES.
　　Formerly distributed to Depository Libraries under Item 6-A.

A 1.89/4:date　　　　　　　　**• Item 80-E (MF)**
TELEPHONE DIRECTORY, ALPHABETICAL LISTING. [Semiannual]
　　Supersedes Telephone Directory (A 1.89).

A 1.90:CT
PLANT DISEASE, DECAY, ETC., CONTROL ACTIVITIES OF DEPARTMENT OF AGRICULTURE, REPORTS.

A 1.91:CT
BREEDING RESEARCH AND IMPROVEMENT ACTIVITIES OF DEPARTMENT OF AGRICULTURE, REPORTS.

A 1.92:date　　　　　　　　**• Item 13-E**
NATIONAL FIRE PREVENTION WEEK. [Annual]Earlier

　　A 1.2:F 51 and A 1.2:F 51/2

　　Discontinued.

A 1.93:date　　　　　　　　**• Item 6-H (MF)**
BUDGET ESTIMATES FOR UNITED STATES DEPARTMENT OF AGRICULTURE.
　　Earlier A 1.2:B 85

A 1.94:CT　　　　　　　　**• Item 13-F**
REPORTS OF TECHNICAL STUDY GROUPS ON SOVIET AGRICULTURE. 1– 11.　– 1963.

　　Discontinued.

A 1.95:nos.　　　　　　　　**• Item 13-G**
MARKETING BULLETINS. 1–　1959–　[Irregular]

　　PURPOSE:– To give popular presentations of information on agricultural marketing.

　　Discontinued.

A 1.96　　　　　　　　**• Item 13-H**
NATIONAL FARM SAFETY WEEK. [Annual]

　　Four-page release issued to promote National Farm Safety Week, usually in July. Contains statistical tables on types of farm accidents and suggestions on how individuals and groups can cooperate to prevent such accidents.
　　Discontinued.

A 1.97
CHECKLIST OF REPORTS ISSUED BY ECONOMIC RESEARCH SERVICE AND STATISTICAL REPORTING SERVICE, AE-CL– (Series). 1–　1961–　[Monthly]
　　Discontinued. Information presently contained Agricultural Outlook (A 93.10/2).
　　ISSN 0364-1031

A 1.98:date　　　　　　　　**• Item 18-B**
AGRICULTURAL OUTLOOK CHARTBOOK. [Annual]

　　Issued by Economic Research Service, Foreign Agricultural Service, Agricultural Research Service.

A 1.99　　　　　　　　**• Item 13-I**
PERIODIC REPORTS OF AGRICULTURAL ECONOMICS, ECONOMIC RESEARCH SERVICE, STATISTICAL REPORTING SERVICE. 1962–　[Annual]

　　Lists and describes the various periodic reports issued by the Economic Research Service and Statistical Reporting Service. Includes calendars of release dates for the various Crop Reporting Board releases and the outlook and situation reports.
　　Supersedes Periodic Reports of the Agricultural Marketing Service.
　　Discontinued 1973.

A 1.99/2:v.nos.&nos.
DIGEST OF WORLD AGRICULTURE.

A 1.100　　　　　　　　**• Item 12-A**
PICTURE STORIES. 1–　1956–　[Irregular]

　　PURPOSE:– To offer photographs available from the USDA to the general public (free to newspapers and magazines, priced to others) on Department programs, and to illustrate Department programs, serving at times almost as an illustrated press release.
　　Consists of a brief story with ample illustrations of photographs which may be ordered from the USDA.
　　Discontinued.

A 1.100/2
PHOTO SERIES. 1–　[Irregular]

　　PURPOSE:– Similar to Picture Stories listed above, except that there is no story, merely a series of illustrations, with captions, on a particular Department program.

A 1.101
CCC MONTHLY SALES LIST. [Monthly]
　　Issued as a USDA Press release. Textual summary. Monthly sales list gives for each commodity: sales price or method of sale.

A 1.102
ORDERLY LIQUIDATION OF STOCK OF AGRICULTURAL COMMODITIES HELD BY THE COMMODITY CREDIT CORPORATION AND THE EXPANSION OF MARKETS FOR SURPLUS AGRICULTURAL COMMODITIES. [Annual]
　　Later A 99.9

A 1.103　　　　　　　　**• Item 569-C-3**
FARM RESOURCES AND FACILITIES RESEARCH ADVISORY COMMITTEE REPORT.

　　See AE 1.103

A 1.104:nos.　　　　　　　　**• Item 14-B**
SCIENCE STUDY AIDS. 1–　1970–　[Irregular] (Educational Service Branch, Agricultural Research Center)

　　PURPOSE:– To provide teaching aids in the field of agriculture and related subjects. They are developed by teachers working with the research staff of the Agricultural Research Service. They are not intended to be complete teaching units, but to serve as supplements to regular teaching programs, providing up-to-date, research-related activities.
　　Discontinued.

A 1.105:CT
WATER AND RELATED LAND RESOURCES [by area].

A 1.106:nos.
REFERENCE REPORTS WORKING MATERIALS FOR SOUTHEAST WISCONISN RIVERS BASIN.

A 1.107:nos.　　　　　　　　**• Item 42-C (MF)**
ECONOMIC RESEARCH SERVICE REPORT 234– 1972–　[Irregular]
　　PURPOSE:– To make available semitechnical and semipopular information resulting from agricultural economics research.
　　Earlier A 93.28
HIRED FARM WORKING FORCE OF (year). [Annual]
　　Gives data on the number, characteristics, and earnings of persons who did any farm work for wages at any time during the year. Surveys were make since 1945, with the exceptions for the years 1953 and 1955.
　　Formerly Agricultural Economic Reports

A 1.107/2:date　　　　　　　　**• Item 42-C MF**
FOOD COST REVIEW. [Annual]

A 1.107/3:date　　　　　　　　**• Item 42-C**
FOOD MARKETING REVIEW. [Biennial]

A 1.108:date
USDA/AID NEWS DIGEST.

A 1.109:date　　　　　　　　**• Item 11-D**
MEAT AND POULTRY INSPECTION, REPORT OF THE SECRETARY OF AGRICULTURE. 1972–　[Annual]

　　This report is submitted to Congress as required by section 301(c)(4) of the Federal Meat Inspection Act (21 U.S.C 661), section 17 of the Wholesome Meat Act (21 U.S.C. 691), and section 27 and 5(c)(4) of the Poultry products Inspection Act, as amended (21 U.S.C 470 and 21 U.S.C. 454).
　　Later A 110.11/2

A 1.109/2:date　　　　　　　　**• Item 11-D (MF)**
FOREIGN MEAT INSPECTION. 1st– 1968–　[Annual]
　　Report submitted by the Secretary of Agriculture to the Committee on Agriculture, House of Representatives, and the Committee on Agriculture and Forestry, Senate as required by the Federal Meat Inspection Act, as amended (Public Law 90-201, 81 Stat. 591).
　　Contains numerous tables and provides information on the leading countries exporting meat to the United States.
　　See A 110.11/2

A 1.110:nos.　　　　　　　　**• Item 11-F**
AGRICULTURAL SUPPLY AND DEMAND ESTIMATES. [Irregular] (Outlook and Situation Board)

　　PURPOSE:– To provide as rapidly as possible USDA's current assessments of developments on the commodity scene. The assessments are made by an interagency board of USDA experts. They are released in tabular form, with a brief commentary, after 3 p.m. on the day following the issuance of major crop production, grain stocks, or planting intentions reports by the Statistical Reporting Service.
　　Supply-demand reports present statistics, by crop, covering the balance of supply (production, stocks, imports) and demand (domestic use, exports, carry-over) for the current marketing season. Rough indications of the supply-demand balance for one season ahead also may be included. ERS Situation Reports for individual commodities contain fuller discussions of the estimates and their implications.
　　ISSN 0162-5586

A 1.111:date　　　　　　　　**• Item 6-E (MF)**
ANNUAL REPORT ON LOCATION OF NEW FEDERAL OFFICES AND OTHER FACILITIES. 1st–　1974– 1979　[Annual]

　　PURPOSE:– To report the efforts during the fiscal year of all Federal departments and agencies to locate their new offices and other facilities in rural areas as required by Section 901(b) of the Agricultural Act of 1970 (84 Stat. 1383) as amended by Section 601 of the Rural Development Act of 1972 (86 Stat. 674). Executive Order 11797 dated July 31, 1974, delegated to the Secretary of the Agriculture the responsibility for preparing and submitting the annual report to Congress.　The reports of the Departments and agencies have been summarized for quick reference. Part I consists of narratives, directives and policy statements reflecting efforts of all concerned in implementing the policies and procedures of this Act. Part II is a statistical outline by agency of all new facilities established or relocated during the fiscal year. For convenience of the reader, defini-

DIVISION OF AGROSTOLOGY

tions of rural and urban areas, location selection codes, and usage codes are included.
Discontinued 1979.

A 1.113:date • Item 11-E (MF)
FINANCIAL AND TECHNICAL ASSISTANCE PROVIDED BY THE DEPARTMENT OF AGRICULTURE AND THE DEPARTMENT OF HOUSING AND URBAN DEVELOPMENT FOR NON-METROPOLITAN PLANNING DISTRICT, ANNUAL REPORT TO CONGRESS.

Discontinued 1974.

A 1.114:nos. • Item 25-D (MF)
CONSERVATION RESEARCH REPORTS. 1– [Irregular]

Earlier A 77.23

A 1.115:v.nos.& nos. • Item 24-R
SUGAR AND SWEETENER OUTLOOK AND SITUATION. v. 1– 1976–

PURPOSE:– To provide market news and situation and outlook information on sugar, sugarcane, sugarbeets, corn sweeteners (corn syrup, dextrose, and high-fructose corn syrup), honey, saccharin, molasses, sugar-containing products, cocoa, and chocolate.
Supersedes Sugar and Sweetener Situation (A 93.31/2) and Sugar Market News (A 88.54).
Former title: Sugar and Sweetener Report.
ISSN 0362-9511

A 1.116:CT • Item 2 (MF)
RURAL TELEPHONE BANK PUBLICATIONS. [Irregular]

A 1.116:date • Item 2
RURAL TELEPHONE BANK ANNUAL REPORT

A 1.117:date
QUARTERLY REPORT OF THE GENERAL SALES MANAGER.

Later A 67.43

A 1.118 • Item 24-S
QUICK-QUIZ (series).

Discontinued 1978.

A 1.119:date • Item 24-T
FOOD FOR PEACE, ANNUAL REPORT ON PUBLIC LAW 480.

PURPOSE:– To report on agricultural export activities during the previous year, including both sales and foreign donations programs.
Later A 67.44

A 1.120:date • Item 24-V
HORSE PROTECTION ENFORCEMENT. [Annual]

Annual report submitted by the Secretary of Agriculture to the President of the United States and to Congress.
Later 101.22

A 1.121:nos. • Item 90-B
AGRICULTURE FACT SHEETS, AFS– (series). [Irregular]

Earlier A 107.14
Discontinued.

A 1.125:nos.
SMALL FARM FAMILY NEWSLETTER. [Irregular]

Discontinued with no. 8 (Summer 1981).

A 1.126
DIGEST OF CONGRESSIONAL PROCEEDINGS.

A 1.127:date • Item 6-F (MF)
AGRICULTURE AND THE ENVIRONMENT. 1– 1980– [Annual]

PURPOSE:– To summarize the activities of the Office of Environmental Quality for the past year, which include coordinating environmental issues such as use and conservation of land, water, and forest resources among agriculture agencies, and representing the Secretary on broad departmental issues.
Discontinued.

A 1.128:nos. • Item 13-C
LAND USE NOTES. (Committee on Land Use)
Presents news items on U.S. land use plans.

A 1.129:date
NEWSLETTER. [Bimonthly] (Office of Operations and Finance)

A 1.129/2:date
ALERT, ADMINISTRATIVE NEWS HIGHLIGHTS FOR SUPERVISORS. [Monthly]

A 1.130:CT • Item 13-H-1 (MF)
NATIONAL AGRICULTURAL LANDS STUDY: REPORTS AND PUBLICATIONS.

Discontinued.

A 1.130/2:nos. • Item 13-H-1 (MF)
NATIONAL AGRICULTURAL LANDS STUDY: INTERIM REPORTS. 1– 1980– [Irregular]

Reports on an interagency study of total U.S. agricultural lands initiated to determine whether they are being statisfactorily allocated among competing uses by the private market and, if not, whether there is a need for government initiatives to protect farm land.

Discontinued.

A 1.131:CT • Item 13-H-2
FACTS ABOUT (various subjects) (series). [Irregular]

Earlier editions classified in various offices within the Department of Agriculture.

Discontinued.

A 1.132:date • Item 13-J (MF)
AGRISTARS ANNUAL REPORT.

Discontinued.

A 1.133:nos. • Item 13-L
NEWS. [Irregular]

Press release material.
Later A 21.7/4
Non-depository

A 1.133/2:nos. • Item 13-M
NEWS, DAILY SUMMARY.

Later A 21.7/2
Non-depository

A 1.133/3:nos. • Item 13-N
NEWS, FEATURE. [Irregular]

Later A 21.7/3
Non-depository

A 1.134:date • Item 13-K
SELECTED SPEECHES AND NEWS RELEASES. [Weekly]
See A 21.24/2

A 1.135: • Item 6-R (MF)
AG IN THE CLASSROOM NOTES. [Bimonthly]

A newsletter for the Agriculture in the Classroom program, sponsored by the Agriculture Department to help students understand the important role of agriculture in the U.S. economy.

A 1.136:date • Item 6-M (MF)
ANNUAL REPORT, USDA GRAIN STORAGE, HANDLING AND PROCESSING SAFETY COORDINATING SUBCOMMITTEE. [Annual]

A 1.137/2: • Item 6-P
USDA PHOTO FEATURE (series).
Each issue contains black and white photographs whichillustrate a different topic.

Discontinued.

A 1.138:date • Item 6-H (MF)
U.S. DEPARTMENT OF AGRICULTURE BUDGET SUMMARY. [Annual]

Discontinued.

A 1.141:CT • Item 90-B
ISSUE BULLETIN.

Discontinued.

A 1.142 • Item 15-A
ELECTRONIC PRODUCTS. [Irregular]

A 1.143:date • Item 25-D (MF)
NEWS RELEASES AND OTHER NEWS MATERIAL.

Discontinued.

A 1.144:date • Item 10-A (MF)
AGRICULTURE OUTLOOK, CONFERENCE PROCEEDINGS. [Annual]

DIVISION OF ACCOUNTS AND DISBURSEMENTS
(1893– 1925)

A 2.1:date
ANNUAL REPORTS.

A 2.2:CT
GENERAL PUBLICATIONS.

A 2.3:nos.
BULLETINS.

A 2.4:CT
CIRCULARS.

A 2.5:date
EXPENDITURES OF DEPARTMENT OF AGRICULTURE.

DIVISION OF AGROSTOLOGY
(1895– 1901)

CREATION AND AUTHORITY

The Division of Agrostology was originally a part of the Division of Botany (A 6) in the Department of Agriculture. On July 1, 1895, it was established as an independent division of the Department of Agriculture. On July 1, 1901, it was consolidated with certain other divisions and offices to form the Bureau of Plant Industry (A 19).

A 3.1:date
ANNUAL REPORTS.

A 3.2:CT
GENERAL PUBLICATIONS.

A 3.3:nos.
BULLETINS.

A 3.4:nos.
CIRCULARS.

BUREAU OF ANIMAL INDUSTRY
(1884–1942)

CREATION AND AUTHORITY

The Bureau of Animal Industry was established within the Department of Agriculture by act of Congress, approved May 29, 1884 (23 Stat. 31), succeeding the Veterinary Division. By Executive Order 9069 of February 23, 1942, it became a part of the Agricultural Research Administration (A 77.200).

A 4.1:date
ANNUAL REPORTS.
Later A 77.201

A 4.2:CT
GENERAL PUBLICATIONS.
Later A 77.202

A 4.3:nos.
BULLETINS.

A 4.4:nos.
CIRCULARS.

A 4.5:nos.
B.A.I. ORDERS.
Later A 77.218

A 4.5/a:CT
– SEPARATES.

A 4.6:date
MAP OF DISTRICTS INFECTED WITH SPLENETIC FEVER.

A 4.7:nos.
RULES.

A 4.8:date
REGULATIONS.
Later A 77.206

A 4.9:nos.
PRESS BULLETINS.

A 4.10:date
MEAT INSPECTION DIRECTORY.

A 4.11:date
ADDRESS LIST OF (meat) INSPECTORS.

A 4.12:nos.
MEAT INSPECTION RULINGS.

A 4.13
SERVICE AND REGULATORY ANNOUNCEMENTS.
[Monthly]
Later A 77.208

A 4.14:date
DIRECTORY OF BUREAU OF ANIMAL INDUSTRY.
Later A 77.221

A 4.15:CT
ANIMALS IMPORTED FOR BREEDING PURPOSES, ETC.

A 4.16:CT
POSTERS.
Later A 77.220

A 4.16/2:CT
LIVESTOCK HEALTH SERIES (Posters).

A 4.17:nos.
MILK PLANT LETTERS. [Monthly]
Later A 44.17

A 4.18:pt.nos.
INDEX-CATALOGUE OF MEDICAL AND VETERINARY ZOOLOGY.
Later A 77.219

A 4.19:date
INTERNATIONAL VETERINARY CONGRESSES PROCEEDINGS.

A 4.19/a:CT
– SEPARATES.

A 4.20:nos.
DECLARATIONS.

A 4.21:date
SUMMARY OF BANG'S DISEASE WORK IN COOPERATION WITH VARIOUS STATES. [Monthly]
Later A 77.212

A 4.22:date
SUMMARY OF TUBERCULOSIS ERADICATION IN COOPERATION WITH VARIOUS STATES. [Monthly]
Later A 77.216

A 4.23:date
SUMMARY OF BANG'S DISEASE CONTROL PROGRAM CONDUCTED BY BUREAU OF ANIMAL INDUSTRY IN COOPERATION WITH VARIOUS STATES. [Monthly]
Later A 77.213

A 4.24:nos.
EXTENSION POULTRY HUSBANDMAN. [Annual]
Earlier A 53.5/12

A 4.25:nos.
EXTENSION ANIMAL HUSBANDMAN. [Quarterly]
Later A 77.214

A 4.26:nos.
ANIMAL HUSBANDRY DIVISION MIMEOGRAPHS, A.H.D.
Later A 77.209

A 4.27:nos.
ANIMAL NUTRITION DIVISION PUBLICATIONS, A.N.D.
Later A 77.210

A 4.28:vol.
MONTHLY RECORD, ADMINISTRATION OF PACKERS AND STOCKYARDS ACT.
Earlier A 39.5
Superseded by A 66.18

A 4.29:date
STATEMENT OF INDEMNITY CLAIMS AND AVERAGES IN COOPERATIVE BANG'S DISEASE WORK. [Monthly]
Later A 77.211

A 4.30:date
STATEMENT OF INDEMNITY CLAIMS AND AVERAGES IN COOPERATIVE TUBERCULOSIS ERADICATION. [Monthly]
Later A 77.215

A 4.31:nos.
NOTICES, ACTIVITIES OF LICENSED ESTABLISHMENTS SUPERVISED BY VIRUS-SERUM CONTROL DIVISION. [Monthly]

A 4.32:nos.
ADMINISTRATIVE NOTICES.

A 4.33:date
NAMES OF COUNTIES DECLARED TO BE MODIFIED ACCREDITED BANG'S DISEASE-FREE AREAS.

A 4.34:CT
ADDRESSES.

BUREAU OF BIOLOGICAL SURVEY
(1905–1939)

CREATION AND AUTHORITY

The Division of Ornithology and Mammalogy, also called the Division of Economic Ornithology and Mammalogy, was established within the Department of Agriculture on July 1, 1866. On July 1, 1896, it was renamed the Division of Biological Survey and on July 1, 1905, it became the Bureau of Biological Survey. Reorganization Plan No. 2 of 1939, effective July 1, 1939, transferred the Bureau to the Department of the Interior (I 47)

A 5.1:date
ANNUAL REPORTS.
Later I 47.1

A 5.2:CT
GENERAL PUBLICATIONS.
Later I 47.2

A 5.3:nos.
BULLETINS.

A 5.4:nos.
CIRCULARS.

A 5.5:nos.
NORTH AMERICAN FAUNA.
Later I 49.30

A 5.6:nos.
SERVICE AND REGULATORY ANNOUNCEMENTS.

A 5.6/a:
– SEPARATES.

A 5.7:date
ANNUAL REPORTS OF GOVERNOR OF ALASKA ON ALASKA GAME LAW.

A 5.8:date
DIRECTORY OF OFFICERS AND ORGANIZATIONS CONCERNED WITH PROTECTION OF BIRDS AND GAME.

This had been issued annually since 1900 as Circulars (A 5.4) no. 94 being the one for 1912.

A 5.9:nos.
OPEN SEASON FOR GAME.
Later I 47.8

A 5.9/2:CT
POSTERS.

Alaska Game Commission

A 5.10/1:date
ANNUAL REPORTS.

A 5.10/2:CT
GENERAL PUBLICATIONS.

A 5.10/3:
BULLETINS.

A 5.10/4:nos.
CIRCULARS.
Later I 49.12

A 5.10/5:nos.
SERVICE AND REGULATORY ANNOUNCEMENTS.

Bureau of Biological Survey (Continued)

A 5.11:nos.
WILDLIFE RESEARCH AND MANAGEMENT LEAFLETS.
Later I 47.7

A 5.12:nos.
WILDLIFE REVIEW.
Later I 47.9

A 5.13:CT
LISTS OF PUBLICATIONS.
Later I 47.12

A 5.14:CT
ADDRESSES.
Later I 47.13

A 5.15:vol.
BIRD BANDING NOTES.
Later I 47.10

A 5.16:nos.
BIRD MIGRATION MEMORANDUM.
Later I 49.31

DIVISION OF BOTANY
(1869– 1901)

CREATION AND AUTHORITY

The Division of Botany was established within the Department of Agriculture in March 1869. On July 2, 1901, it was consolidated with other divisions to form the Bureau of Plant Industry (A 19).

A 6.1:date
ANNUAL REPORTS.

A 6.2:CT
GENERAL PUBLICATIONS.

A 6.3:nos.
BULLETINS.

A 6.4:nos.
CIRCULARS.

A 6.5:v.nos.
CONTRIBUTIONS FROM U.S. NATIONAL HERBARIUM.

A 6.5/a:CT
– SEPARATES.

A 6.6:nos.
INVENTORIES.

BUREAU OF CHEMISTRY
(1901– 1927)

CREATION AND AUTHORITY

The Division of Chemistry was established within the Department of Agriculture by act of Congress, approved May 15, 1862. The Division became the Bureau of Chemnistry on July 1, 1901. The Bureau was abolished on July 1, 1927, and its functions transferred to the Food, Drug and Insecticide Administration (A 46) and the Bureau of Chemistry and Soils (A 47).

A 7.1:date
ANNUAL REPRTS.

A 7.2:CT
GENERAL PUBLICATIONS.

A 7.3:nos.
BULLETINS.

A 7.3/a:CT
– SEPARATES.

A 7.4:nos.
CIRCULARS.

A 7.5:nos.
FOOD INSPECTION DECISIONS.

A 7.6:nos.
SERVICE AND REGULATORY ANNOUNCEMENTS.

A 7.6/2:nos.
– SUPPLEMNTS.

A 7.6/2a
– SEPARATES.

A 7.63
INDEXES.

A 7.7:date
TEA INSPECTION SERVICE, ANNUAL REPORTS.

A 7.8:date
FOOD AND DRUG REVIEW. [Monthly]
Later A 46.5
Changed to A 47.7

A 7.9:date
REVIEW OF U.S. PATENTS RELATING TO INSECTICEDES AND FUNGICIDES. [Quarterly]
Later A 47.7

ENTOMOLOGICAL COMMISSION
(1880– 1882)

CREATION AND AUTHORITY

The Entomological Commission was established within the Department of the Interior by Act of Congress, approved March 3, 1877 (19 Stat. 357). The Commission was transferred to the Department of Agriculture by acts of Congress, approved June 16, 1880 (21 Stat. 276), and March 3, 1881 (21 Stat. 383). The Commission was discontinued June 30, 1882.

A 8.1:nos.
ANNUAL REPORTS.

A 8.2:CT
GENERAL PUBLICATIONS [none issued].

A 8.3:nos.
BULLETINS.

A 8.4:nos.
CIRCULARS [none issued under Agriculture Department].

BUREAU OF ENTOMOLOGY
(1904– 1934)

CREATION AND AUTHORITY

The Division of Entomology was established within the Department of Agriculture in 1878. The Division became the Bureau of Entomology on July 1, 1904. On July 1, 1934, the Bureau merged with the Bureau of Plant Quarantine (A 48) to form the Bureau of Entomology and Plant Quarantine (A 56) by the Agricultural Appropriation Act of 1935 (48 Stat. 467).

A 9.1:date
ANNUAL REPORTS.

A 9.2:CT
GENERAL PUBLICATIONS.

A 9.3:nos.
BULLETINS.

A 9.4:nos.
CIRCULARS (1st series).

A 9.5:nos.
CIRCULARS (2nd series).

A 9.6:nos.
BULLETINS (new series).

A 9.7:v.nos.
INSECT LIFE.

A 9.8:nos.
TECHNICAL SERIES.

A 9.9:CT
POSTERS

A 9.9:
EUROPEAN CORN BORER.

A 9.10:vol.
INSECT PEST SURVEY BULLETIN. [Monthly, March to November]
Earlier A 56.18

A 9.11:nos.
FOREST ENTOMOLOGY BRIEFS.

A 9.12:nos.
MONTHLY LETTERS.
Later A 56.12

A 9.13:date
PUBLICATIONS OF BUREAU OF ENTOMOLOGY AVAILABLE FOR FREE DISTRIBUTION.

A 9.14:vol.
ENTOMOLOGY CURRENT LITERATURE. [Bimonthly]
Later A 56.10

A 9.15:vol.
BLISTER RUST NEWS. [Monthly]
Earlier A 19.21

A 9.16:E-nos.
E SERIES.
Later A 56.19

OFFICE OF EXPERIMENT STATIONS
(1923– 1942)

CREATION AND AUTHORITY

The Office of Experiment Stations was established within the Department of Agriculture on October 1, 1888, pursuant to the Hatch Act, approved March 2, 1887. Pursuant to the Smith-Lever Act, approved May 8, 1914, and related acts, the Secretary of Agriculture established the States Relations Service on July 1, 1915 to supervise the work of the Office of Experiment Stations. When the States Relations Service was abolished in 1923, the Office of Experiment Stations was reestablished within the Office of the Secretary of Agriculture by the Agriculture Appropriation Act of 1924, approved February 26, 1923 (42 Stat. 1289) and Departmental Memorandum 436, effective July 1, 1923. By Executive Order 9069 of February 23, 1942, the Office was transferred along with other agencies to form the Agricultural Research Administration, (A 77.400). Departmental Memorandum 1320, Supplement 4, dated November 2, 1953, transferred the functions of the Office to the Agricultural Research Service.

A 10.1/1:date
ANNUAL REPORTS.
Later A 77.401

A 10.1/2:date
REPORT ON AGRICULTURAL EXPERIMENT STATIONS.
Later A 77.401/2

A 10.2:CT
GENERAL PUBLICATIONS.

A 10.3:nos.
BULLETINS.

A 10.4:nos.
CIRCULARS.

A 10.5:nos.
MISCELLANEOUS BULLETINS.

A 10.6:v.nos.
EXPERIMENT STATION RECORD.
    Later A 77.408

A 10.6/2:incl.n.
GENERAL INDEX TO EXPERIMENT STATION
    RECORD.

A 10.7:nos.
FOOD AND DIET CHARTS (discontinued).

A 10.8:nos.
IRRIGATION AND INVESTIGATION SCHEDULES.

Hawaii Agricultural
Experiment Station

A 10.9/1:date
ANNUAL REPORTS.

A 10.9/1a:CT
    – SEPARATES.

A 10.9/2:CT
GENERAL PUBLICATIONS.

A 10.9/3:nos.
BULLETINS.

A 10.9/4:nos.
CIRCULARS [none issued].

A 10.9/5:nos.
PRESS BULLETINS.

Alaska Agricultural
Experiment Station

A 10.10/1:date
ANNUAL REPORTS.
    Later A 77.441

A 10.10/1a:CT
    – SEPARATES.

A 10.10/2:CT
GENERAL PUBLICATIONS.
    Later A 77.442

A 10.10/3:nos.
BULLETINS.
    Later A 77.443

A 10.10/4:nos.
CIRCULARS.
    Later A 77.444

A 10.11:v.nos.
EXPERIMENT STATION WORK.

Porto Rico Agricultural
Experiment Station

A 10.12/1:date
ANNUAL REPORTS.
    Later A 77.461

A 10.12/1a:CT
    – SEPARATES.

A 10.12/2:CT
GENERAL PUBLICATIONS.
    Later A 77.462

A 10.12/3:nos.
BULLETINS.
    Later A 77.462

A 10.12/4:nos.
CIRCULARS.
    Later A 77.464

Office of
Experiment Stations (Continued)

A 10.13:nos.
FARMER'S INSTITUTE LECTURES.

A 10.14:date
LIST OF PUBLICATIONS OF OFFICE OF EXPERI-
    MENT STATIONS ON AGRICULTURAL EDUCA-
    TION.

A 10.15:date
LIST OF PUBLICATIONS OF OFFICE OF EXPERI-
    MENT STATIONS ON FOOD AND NUTRITION OF
    MAN.

A 10.16:date
LIST OF PUBLICATIONS OF OFFICE OF EXPERI-
    MENT STATIONS ON IRRIGATION AND DRAIN-
    AGE.

A 10.17:date
LIST OF STATION PUBLICATIONS RECEIVED BY
    OFFICE OF EXPERIMENT STATIONS.

A 10.18:date
INSTITUTIONS IN UNITED STATES GIVING INSTRUC-
    TION IN AGRICULTURE.

A 10.19:date
ADDRESS LIST OF AGRICULTURAL EXPERIMENT
    STATIONS.

A 10.20:date
ADDRESS LIST OF AGRICULTURAL AND MECHANI-
    CAL COLLEGES.

A 10.21:nos.
(FOOD) CHARTS, COMPOSITION OF FOOD MATE-
    RIALS.

A 10.21/2:nos.
FOOD SELECTION AND MEAL PLANNING CHARTS.

Guam Agricultural
Experiment Station

A 10.22/1:date
ANNUAL REPORTS.

A 10.22/2:CT
GENERAL PUBLICATIONS.

A 10.22/3:nos.
BULLETINS.

A 10.22/4:nos.
CIRCULARS.

A 10.22/5:nos.
EXTENSION CIRCULARS.

Office of
Experiment Stations (Continued)

A 10.23:date
STATES RELATIONS SERVICE.

    List of Workers in subjects pertaining to Ag-
riculture.

A 10.24:CT
COOPERATIVE EXTENSION WORK IN AGRICULTURE
AND HOME ECONOMICS.

A 10.25:date
ADDRESS LIST OF STATE INSTITUTIONS AND
    OFFICERS IN CHARGE OF AGRICULTURAL
    EXTENSION WORKS UNDER SMITH-LEVER ACT.

    To provide for cooperative agricultural exten-
sion work between agricultural college and Department of Agriculture.

Virgin Island Agricultural
Experiment Station

A 10.26/1:date
ANNUAL REPORTS.

A 10.26/2:CT
GENERAL PUBLICATIONS.

A 10.26/3:nos.
BULLETINS.

A 10.26/4:nos.
CIRCULARS.

Office of
Experiment Stations (Continued)

A 10.27:CT
ADDRESSES.
    Later A 77.407

OFFICE OF FIBER
INVESTIGATIONS
(1891– 1989)

CREATION AND AUTHORITY

    The Office of Fiber Investigations was estab-
lished within the Department of Agriculture on
January 1, 1891. On Jun 30, 1898, its work was
transferred to the Division of Botany (A 6).

A 11.1:date
ANNUAL REPORTS.

A 11.2:CT
GENERAL PUBLICATIONS [none issued].

A 11.3:nos.
BULLETINS.

A 11.4:nos.
CIRCULARS.

A 11.5:nos.
REPORTS.

DIVISION OF FOREIGN MARKETS
(1901– 1903)

CREATION AND AUTHORITY

    The Section of Foreign Markets was estab-
lished within the Department of Agriculture on
March 20, 1894. On July 1, 1902, it became the
Division of Foreign Markets. The Division was
placed under the Bureau of Statistics (A 27) on
July 1, 1903.

A 12.1:date
ANNUAL REPORTS.

A 12.2:CT
GENERAL PUBLICATIONS [none issued].

A 12.3:nos.
BULLETINS.

A 12.4:nos.
CIRCULARS.

FOREST SERVICE
(1905–   )

CREATION AND AUTHORITY

The Division of Forestry was established within the Department of Agriculture by order of the Secretary of the Department of Agriculture in 1880. The name was changed to the Bureau of Forestry on July 1, 1901 and to the Forest Service on July 1, 1905.

INFORMATION

Office of Communications
Forest Service
Department of Agriculture
P.O. Box 96090
Washington, D.C. 20090-6090
(202) 205-8333
http://www.fs.fed.us

A 13.1   • **Item 80**
REPORT OF THE CHIEF OF THE FOREST SERVICE. 1883–   [Annual]

Report is for the fiscal year. Of special interest is the section devoted to the various research projects currently being conducted by the Forest Service. Since 1938, contains a Statistical Tables section.

Discontinued.

A 13.1/2:date
CALIFORNIA REGION, PROGRESS REPORTS, PROGRESS IN (year). 1952–   [Annual]

PURPOSE:– To report progress in achieving land management objectives during the year by the California Region.

A 13.1/3:date   • **Item 80 (MF)**
REPORT OF THE FOREST SERVICE, FISCAL YEAR (date). [Annual]

A 13.1/4   • **Item 85-B (EL)**
ANNUAL PERFORMANCE PLAN. [Annual]

A 13.2:CT   • **Item 84**
GENERAL PUBLICATIONS.

A 13.3:nos.   • **Item 84-F**
BULLETINS. 1– 127. 1887– 1913; 1986–   [Irregular]

A 13.4
CIRCULARS. 1– 216. 1886– 1913.

A 13.5:v
REPORT ON FORESTRY. v. 1– 4. 1878– 84.

A 13.6:nos.
PRESS BULLETINS. 1– 197. 1900– 1907.

A 13.7:CT
NOTES ON FOREST TREES SUITABLE FOR PLANTING IN THE U.S. 1903–

A 13.8:date
FIELD PROGRAM (and Service Notes). 1904– 1920. [Monthly 1904– 1910; Quarterly 1910– 1920]

A 13.8/2:date
SERVICE DIRECTORY. 1920– 1949.

A 13.9:nos.
FOREST PLANTING LEAFLETS. 1– 24. 1905– 1906.

A 13.10   • **Item 84-A (MF)**
LAND AREAS OF THE NATIONAL FOREST SYSTEM. 1905–   [Annual]

Lists all areas administered by or through the Forest Service in the United States, Puerto Rico and the Virgin Islands, including National Forest, Purchase Units, Grasslands, Wild and Scenic Rivers, and other areas of interest.
Former title: National Forest System Areas.

Previously distributed to depository libraries under Item 86

A 13.11:date
LISTS OF PUBLICATIONS. 1905–

A 13.11/2:CT   • **Item 85-A**
LISTS OF PUBLICATIONS.

A 13.12:nos.
SILVICAL LEAFLETS. 1– 53. 1907– 1912.

A 13.13:CT   • **Item 85**
INFORMATION PAMPHLETS RELATING TO NATIONAL FORESTS

A 13.13/2:CT/date
NATIONAL FORESTS, REPORTS OF ACTIVITIES DURING YEAR.

A 13.13/3:date
NATIONAL FORESTS, LANDS OF MANY USES, REPORT FOR (Year). [Annual] (California Region)

A 13.14:nos.
AMENDMENTS TO 1911 EDITION OF USE BOOK AND NATIONAL FOREST MANUAL.

A 13.14/1:date
USE BOOK. 1905– 1918. [Irregular]
Changed from A 3.2
A manual of information about the National Forests.

A 13.14/2
USE BOOK SECTIONS.
Changed from A 3.2

A 13.14/3:date
NATIONAL FOREST MANUAL. 1911– 1913.

Regulations of the Secretary of Agriculture and instructions to forest officers relating to the general administration of the Forest Service, and the protection and use of the National forest.
Changed from A 3.2

A 13.14/4:CT
NATIONAL FOREST MANUAL, SECTIONS.
Changed from A 3.2

A 13.14/5:nos.
AMENDMENTS TO USE BOOK AND NATIONAL FOREST MANUAL.
Changed from A 13.14

A 13.15:date
WHOLESALE PRICES OF LUMBER, BASED ON ACTUAL SALES MADE F.O.B. MILL. 1910– 1912.

A 13.16:date
WHOLESALE PRICES OF LUMBER, BASED ON ACTUAL SALES MADE F.O.B. EACH MARKET.

A 13.17:nos.
FOREST ATLAS. 1913.

A 13.18:CT
FORESTRY LAWS.

A 13.19:date
FOREST WORKER. 1924– 1933. [Bimonthly]

A 13.20/1:CT
POSTERS.

A 13.20/2:nos.
STANDARD POSTERS.

A 13.20/3:CT   • **Item 80-G**
POSTERS (Miscellaneous).

A 13.20/4:dt.&nos.
COOPERATIVE FOREST FIRE PREVENTION PROGRAM.

A 13.21:nos.
PROGRESS REPORT OF FOREST TAXATION INQUIRY. 1– 18. 1928– 1933.

A 13.21/2:date
STATE FOREST TAX LAW DIGEST.

A 13.22:date
INFORMATION REGARDING EMPLOYMENT ON NATIONAL FORESTS.
Changed from A 13.2

A 13.23:date
INDEX OF STANDARD FORMS.

A 13.24:date
FIRE HANDBOOK. REGION 7.
Changed from A 13.2

A 13.25:date
FORESTRY CURRENT LITERATURE.
Superseded by A 17.18:E

A 13.26:vol.
NATIONAL PLAN FOR AMERICAN FORESTRY

Forest Products Laboratory

A 13.27/1
ANNUAL REPORT OF RESEARCH.

A 13.27/2:CT   • **Item 85-A**
GENERAL PUBLICATIONS.

A 13.27/3
BULLETINS.

A 13.27/4
CIRCULARS.

A 13.27/5
LAWS.

A 13.27/6:CT
REGULATIONS, RULES AND INSTRUCTIONS.

A 13.27/7   • **Item 85-A**
LIST OF PUBLICATIONS ON [subject].
Subject bibliographies of Forest Products Laboratory publications.

A 13.27/7-2:date   • **Item 85-A (MF)**
DIVIDENDS FROM WOOD RESEARCH. [Semiannual]

A 13.27/8
LISTS OF PUBLICATIONS. [Semiannual]

Annotated bibliography, arranged by broad subjects such as those used in the subject lists, of all publications issued during the six months period. Serves as a supplement to the regular subject lists, each of which shows all of the publications on a given subject which are still available for distribution. Entries appearing in the semiannual publication eventually become a part of the subject bibliographies as each is revised.

A 13.27/9:nos.   • **Item 83-B-3**
TECHNICAL NOTE SERIES, WSDG-TN– (nos). 1– 1980–   [Irregular]
WSDG = Watershed Systems Development Group

A 13.27/10:date
LOG OF THE LABORATORY, ITEMS OF CURRENT RESEARCH.

A 13.27/11:date
RESEARCH IN FOREST PRODUCTS.

A 13.27/12:CT
ADDRESSES.

A 13.27/13:nos.
REPORTS TO AID NATION'S DEFENSE EFFORT.

A 13.27/14:nos.
RESEARCH REPORTS.

A 13.27/15:date   • **Item 85-A-3 (MF)**
TECHNOLOGY TRANSFER OPPORTUNITIES. [Biennial]

Reports describe technology transfer opportunities. Describes results of studies and their potential for application.
Earlier A 1.38
Earlier published in A 13.27/2, A 13.27/7, A 13.27/12 and A 13.27/13.

FOREST SERVICE (Continued)

A 13.28:CT   • Item 80-G
MAPS AND CHARTS.

A 13.28/a   • Item 80-G
OTTAWA NATIONAL FOREST (SERIES).

A 13.28/2:CT
SHEETS OF NATIONAL ATLAS OF UNITED STATES.
1962–

A 13.28/3:CT   • Item 80-G
SHAWNEE SPORTSMAN'S MAPS (series). [Irregular]

A 13.29:nos.
WESTERN RANGE.

Northern Rocky Mountain Forest and Range Experiment Station

A 13.30/1:date
ANNUAL REPORTS.

A 13.30/2:CT
GENERAL PUBLICATIONS.

A 13.30/5:nos.
FOREST SURVEY RELEASE: PROGRESS REPORTS.

A 13.30/6:nos.
PROGRESS REPORTS.

A 13.30/7:nos.
RESEARCH NOTES. 1–   1940–

A 13.30/8:nos.
STATION PAPERS. 1– 35.   – 1953.

A 13.30/9:v.nos.
SELECTED BIBLIOGRAPHY OF RANGE MANAGE-
MENT LITERATURE. v. 1– v.2, no. 15. 1947– 1950.

A 13.30/10:v.nos. & nos.
RANGE RESEARCH HI-LITES. v. 1–   1949–

A 13.30/11:nos.
MISCELLANEOUS PUBLICATIONS.

FOREST SERVICE (Continued)

A 13.31:nos.   • Item 80-A
AN AMERICAN WOOD, (name) (series). [Irregular]
Former title: American Woods (series).

Discontinued.

A 13.31/2:CT
FOREIGN WOOD SERIES.

A 13.32:v.nos.   • Item 82-A-6 (EL)
FIRE MANAGEMENT TODAY. v. 1–   1936–
[Quarterly]

A quarterly review devoted to the technique
of forest fire control. Articles cover theory, relationships, prevention, equipment, detection, communication, transportation, cooperation, planning,
organization, training, fire fighting, methods of
reporting, and statistical systems.
Index for year appears in the October issue.
Former titles: Fire Control Notes, prior to v.
34, no. 2, Spring 1973 issue. Fire management.
Notes prior to v. 60, no. 1.
ISSN 0095-5450

A 13.32/2:date   • Item 82-D-2 (MF)
WILDFIRE STATISTICS. [Annual]

Tables include summary table, which gives
forest area number of fires, area burned, by group
and State; number of forest fires, by cause and
by size, for group and State; areas burned by
forest fires, by type classes.
Formerly titled: Forest Fire Statistics.

A 13.32/2-2:CT   • Item 82-D-11
WILDLIFE UNIT TECHNICAL SERIES. [Irregular]

Discontinued.

A 13.32/3   • Item 82-D-6 (MF)
ANNUAL FIRE REPORT FOR NATIONAL FORESTS,
CALENDAR YEAR (date). [Annual]

A compilation of forest fire statistics for fires
occurring on national forest land and other lands
protected by the Forest Service. Tables include
number of fires by general causes, area burned
by general causes, area burned and damage,
damage by major causes, and number of fires by
major causes and size classes.

A 13.32/4:nos.   • Item 82-D-9
FOREST FIRE NEWS. [Semiannual]
Prepared on behalf of the North American
Forestry Commission's Fire Management Study
Group.
Contains news of U.S. forest fires. Also in-
cludes news concerning important fires in other
countries.

Non-depository

A 13.33:vol
CONSTRUCTIVE HINTS. v. 1– v. 8. 1935– 1942.
[Biweekly]

A 13.34:CT
FARM WOODLANDS OF STATES (Charts) (by States).

A 13.35:CT
ADDRESSES.

A 13.36:CT   • Item 86-B
REGULATIONS, RULES AND INSTRUCTIONS (Mis-
cellaneous).
Includes handbooks and manuals.

A 13.36/2:CT   • Item 86-C
HANDBOOKS, MANUALS, GUIDES. Formerly in A
13.36

A 13.36/2-2:date   • Item 86-H
FOREST SERVICE ORGANIZATIONAL DIRECTORY.
[Annual]
Shows the organization of the forest Service
with the addresses and telephone numbers of the
main field office and units. Lists personnel chiefly
responsible for the various units.

A 13.36/2-3:date   • Item 86-H
INTERMOUNTAIN REGION ORGANIZATION DIREC-
TORY [Annual]

See item 79-B-9

A 13.36/2-6:nos.   • Item 86-C
RECREATION GUIDE (R8-RG series).

A 13.36/2-7:v.nos/nos.   • Item 86-C
RECREATION GUIDE TO GRAND MESA,
UNCOMPAHGRE AND GUNNISON NATIONAL
FORESTS.

A 13.36/3:nos.
MANAGING YOUR WOODLAND, HOW TO DO IT
GUIDES. 1–   1959–

A 13.36/4:nos.   • Item 81-B
TRAINING TEXT (series). 1–   [Irregular]

Non-depository

A 13.36/5:CT   • Item 86-C
AREA GUIDE PRELIMINARY SERIES. [Irregular]

Non-depository

A 13.36/12:CT   • Item 86-C
FEDERAL RESEARCH NATURAL AREAS IN [various
States].

A 13.37:nos.
GENERAL SURVEY OF FOREST SITUATION. 1–
1958–

A 13.38:nos.
CLUB SERIES. PUBS. DESIG. CS 1–   1938–

A 13.39:nos.
LEGISLATION RELATING TO TOWN AND COMMU-
NITY FORESTS. LG 1–

Southern Forest Experiment Station

A 13.40/1   • Item 80
ANNUAL REPORTS. [Annual]

A 13.40/1-2:date   • Item 82-D-4 (MF)
ANNUAL LETTER.

Discontinued.

A 13.40/2:CT   • Item 84-Y
GENERAL PUBLICATIONS.

A 13.40/5:nos.
FOREST SURVEY RELEASES. 1– 87. 1962

A 13.40/6:nos.   • Item 86-C
OCCASIONAL PAPERS. 1– 194.   – 1962.

A 13.40/7:nos.
SOUTHERN FORESTRY NOTES. 1– 142. – 1962.
[Bimonthly]

A 13.40/8:CT
BIBLIOGRAPHIES.

A 13.40/8-2:date
RECENT PUBLICATIONS OF SOUTHERN FOREST
EXPERIMENT STATION. January– June 1976.
[Irregular]

Titles varies.
Merged with Forest Research News for the
South (A 13.40/11) to form Research Accom-
plished (A 13.40/8-4).
Earlier A 13.40/8:P 96

A 13.40/8-3   • Item 82-D-4 (MF)
PUBLICATIONS OF THE SOUTHERN FOREST EX-
PERIMENT STATION. [Annual]

List of publications issued during the year.
ISSN 0149-9769
See A 13.63/13

A 13.40/8-4:date   • Item 82-D-5 (MF)
RESEARCH ACCOMPLISHED.

Formed by combining Recent Publications of
the Southern Forest Experiment Station (A 13.40/
8-2) and Forest Research News for the South (A
13.40/11).
ISSN 034-6769

Discontinued.

A 13.40/9:nos.
SOUTHERN FOREST INSECT REPORTER. 1–
1954–

A 13.40/10:v.nos. & nos.
SOUTHERN FOREST RESEARCH. v. 1–   1960–
[Irregular]

A 13.40/11:date
FOREST RESEARCH NEWS FOR THE SOUTH. 1967–
[Irregular]

PURPOSE:– To provide a newsletter to disseminate information about Southern Forest Experiment Station research in particular and Forest Service research in general to land managers, forestry students, newspaper, television, and
radio editors, and through them to the general
public.
Former title: Forest Research News for the
Midsouth.
Merged with Recent Publications of the Southern Forest Experiment Station (A 13.40/8-2) to
form Research Accomplished (A 13.40/8-4).

A 13.40/12:nos.   • Item 82-D-8 (MF)
TECHNICAL PUBLICATIONS, SA-TP (series). 1–
[Irregular]

FOREST SERVICE (Continued)

A 13.41:nos.
FOREST RESEARCH PROJECT REPORTS. 1. 1938.

Northeastern Forest Experiment Station

A 13.42/1   • Item 82-D
ANNUAL REPORT. [Annual]

Discontinued.

A 13.42/2:CT   • Item 79-A
GENERAL PUBLICATIONS.

A 13.42/6:CT
REGULATIONS, RULES AND INSTRUCTIONS.

A 13.42/6-2:CT   • Item 79-A-1
HANDBOOKS, MANUALS, GUIDES.

A 13.42/7:nos.
TECHNICAL NOTES. 1–   1930–

A 13.42/8:nos.
OCCASIONAL PAPERS. 1– 10. 1936– 1940.

A 13.42/8-2:nos.
OCCASIONAL PAPERS. 1– 5. 1938– 1942.

A 13.42/9:nos.
ANTHRACITE SURVEY PAPERS. 1–   1940–

A 13.42/10:nos.
FOREST SURVEY NOTES. 1–   1946–

A 13.42/11:nos.
FOREST MANAGEMENT NOTES. 1–   1946–

A 13.42/12:nos.
FOREST MANAGEMENT PAPERS. 1–   1964–

A 13.42/13:nos.
FOREST ECONOMIC NOTES. 1–   1946–

A 13.42/14:nos.
FOREST PRODUCTS PAPERS. 1–   1946–

A 13.42/15:nos.
STATION NOTES. 1–   1947–

A 13.42/16:nos.
STATION PAPERS. 1–   1949–
    Changed from A 13.67/8

A 13.42/17:nos.
FOREST SURVEY RELEASES. 1–   1948–
    Changed from A 13.67/7

A 13.42/18:nos.
FOREST PRODUCT NOTES. 1–   1945–

A 13.42/19
BEACH UTILIZATION SERIES. [Irregular] 1–   1951–

    Prepared by the Northeastern Technical Committee on Utilization of Beach in cooperation with the Northeastern Forest Experiment Station.

A 13.42/20:nos.
NORTHEASTERN RESEARCH NOTES.

A 13.42/21:CT
FOREST STATISTICS SERIES (by States).

A 13.42/22:date
NORTHEASTERN PEST REPORTER. 1957–
[Irregular]

A 13.42/23
NEW PUBLICATIONS AVAILABLE.

A 13.42/24   • Item 84
TREES FOR RECLAMATION (series). [Irregular]

    See item 84-D

A 13.42/25:nos.   • Item 84-D
NE-INF– (series). [Irregular]

A 13.42/26:nos.   • Item 79-A-3 (MF)
NORTHEASTERN RESOURCE BULLETINS, NE-RB–
(series). [Irregular]

    See item 83-B-5

A 13.42/27:nos.   • Item 79-A-5 (MF)
NORTHEASTERN RESEARCH NOTES, NE- RN–
(series).

    See item 83-B-4

A 13.42/28:nos.   • Item 79-A-2 (MF)
NORTHEASTERN GENERAL TECHNICAL REPORTS,
NE-GTR– (series). [Irregular]

    See item 83-B-6

A 13.42/29:nos.   • Item 79-A-4 (MF)
NORTHEASTERN RESEARCH PAPERS, NE-RP–
(series). [Irregular]

    "See item 83-B

Southwestern Forest and Range Experiment Station

A 13.43/1:date
ANNUAL REPORTS.

A 13.43/2:CT
GENERAL PUBLICATIONS.

A 13.43/7:nos.
RESEARCH NOTES.

A 13.43/8:nos.
RESEARCH REPORT.

FOREST SERVICE (Continued)

A 13.44:CT
CHARTS.

A 13.45:nos.
TABLES (Statistical). T 1–

A 13.46:nos.   • Item 86-A
USEFUL TREES OF UNITED STATES. 1–   1941–

    Discontinued.

A 13.47:date
WHY DID IT HAPPEN? 1944– 1946.

A 13.48:date
LIFE LINE. 1– 2. 1947.

A 13.49:nos.
[EQUIPMENT DEVELOPMENT] REPORTS. ED 1–
1944.

A 13.49/2:nos.
EQUIPMENT DEVELOPMENT REPORT R.M. (Series).
RM 1–   1956–

A 13.49/3
TECHNICAL EQUIPMENT REPORTS. F 1–   1958–
[Irregular]

    Illustrated series designed to present new ideas for equipment useful in forestry work. Each report varies from 6 to 10 pages in length.

A 13.49/4:nos.   • Item 82-D-3 (MF)
EQUIPMENT DEVELOPMENT AND TEST REPORTS,
EDT–   (Series). EDT 2400-1–   1967–

    Discontinued.

A 13.49/4-2:CT
EQUIP TIPS. [Irregular] (Equipment Development Center)

    PURPOSE:– To assist forest managers, equipment managers, and equipment engineers in maintaining a current awareness of equipment technology and development relevant to forest resource management.
    Covers new equipment, modification, or uses of equipment pertinent to forest operations that appear on the market; tips on techniques or changes in the applications of equipment already in use; sketches, drawings, photos, or schematics illustration changes to equipment or applications; and safety tips involving equipment.
    Loose-leaf, punched for ring binder.
    Earlier publications numbered in the ED&T series, A 14.49/4.

A 13.49/5:date   • Item 82-D-1
EQUIPMENT DEVELOPMENT AND TEST PROGRAM,
PROGRESS, PLANS, FISCAL YEAR. [Annual]

    The Forest Service Equipment Development and Test (ED&T) program is conducted to provide forest managers and engineers with useful and current information on equipment, vehicles, and materials. Technology developed through research in engineering, forestry, and other applicable fields is utilized in the program. These reports contain capsule versions of work done in the fiscal year, and plans for the following FY on various ED&T projects, in areas such as engineering, recreation, personal safety, pest control, timber management, range management, wildlife and fire control. Contains list of available publications, alphabetical subject index, and numerical index.

    Non-depository

A 13.50:nos.   • Item 83
FOREST RESOURCE REPORTS. 1–   1950–   [Irregular]

    PURPOSE:– To provide economic information on forest resources, mainly timber, including inventories, data on utilization, and requirements for forest products.
    Each report covers a State or group of States.

A 13.50:20/2   • Item 83
OUTLOOK FOR TIMBER IN THE UNITED STATES.
Rev. 1974. 394 p. il.

    PURPOSE:– To provide an analysis of the Nation's timber situation as of 1970. Statistics on the current area and condition of the Nation's forest land, inventories of standing timber, and timber growth and removals by individual States are also included.

A 13.51:v.nos.&nos.   • Item 86-D
TREE PLANTERS' NOTES. 1– 180, Nov. 1950– Dec.
1966; v. 18–   March 1967–   [Quarterly]

    Publication for nurserymen and planters of forests and shelterbelts. Presents brief articles on techniques of forestation and forest nursery practice and results of experiments.
    Once a year one issue is devoted to the release of two separate publications, listed below:

    1) (Year) Seed and Planting Stock Dealers. Directory of Commercial Dealers in Seeds and Planting Stock for Common Trees and Shrubs.
    2) (Year) Report, Forest and Windbarrier Planting and Seeding in the U.S.
    Prior to 1969, issued separately. Beginning in 1969 issued as A 13.51/2.
    Other title: Tree Planters' Notes for Planters of Forests and Shelterbelts and for Nursery-Men.
    Subtitle varies.
    Index by: Biological Abstracts.
    ISSN 0564-1829
    Indexes:
    Nos. 1– 49. 1961.
    57– 63. 1964.
    64– 69. 1965.

A 13.51/2:date   • Item 86-D (MF)
FOREST PLANTING, SEEDING, AND SILVICAL
TREATMENTS IN THE UNITED STATES. 1969–
[Annual]

    Formerly issued, prior to 1969, as part of Tree Planters' Notes, A 13.51.
    ISSN 0147-9075
    Earlier title: Forest and Windbarrier Planting and Seeding in the United States, Report.

    See A 13.110/14

A 13.52:nos • Item 82-A (P) (EL)
FOREST INSECT AND DISEASE LEAFLETS. 1–
1955–   [Irregular]

Briefly describes importance and facts bearing on detection and control of forest insects and diseases. Includes their distribution, hosts, evidences of pest activity, description of the organism, life history, habits and known control measures. Includes illustrations and a map showing the known distribution. Signed articles are by members of the various forestry experiment stations.

Former title: Forest Pest Leaflets.

A 13.52/2 • Item 82-B (MF) (EL)
FOREST INSECT AND DISEASE CONDITIONS IN THE UNITED STATES. 1954–   [Annual]

Prepared by the Division of Forest Insect Research.
PURPOSE:– To provide an annual summary of the status of the more important forest insects in a country wide forest insect conditions report. Reports for 1951– 53 were released as supplements to the Cooperative Economic Insect Report. Published by the Plant Pest Control Division of the Agricultural Research Service.
Arrangement is by forest regions. Contains an index to insects.
Earlier title: Forest Insect Conditions in the United States.

A 13.52/3:nos.
NORTHEASTERN FOREST PEST REPORTER. (Region 7)

A 13.52/4:nos.
SOUTHERN FOREST PEST REPORTER. (Southern Region)

A 13.52/5:nos.
BUG BUSINESS. (Division of Timber Management, Denver)

A 13.52/6 • Item 82-D-7 (MF)
FOREST INSECT AND DISEASES CONDITIONS IN THE PACIFIC NORTHWEST. [Annual]
Earlier title: Forest Insect Conditions in the Pacific Northwest.

A 13.52/7 • Item 82-D-7 (MF)
FOREST INSECT AND DISEASE CONDITIONS IN THE NORTHERN REGION. [Annual]

PURPOSE:– To report status of conditions caused by forest insects. Report is for the calendar year.
Earlier title: Forest Insect Conditions in the Northern Region.

A 13.52/8
NORTHEASTERN AREA STATE AND PRIVATE FORESTRY [Publications]. [Irregular]

Publications are designated by letter (field office), year, and number.
D–   Delaware, Ohio
S–   St. Paul, Minn.

A 13.52/9:date • Item 82-B (MF)
FOREST PEST CONDITIONS IN THE NORTH EAST [Annual]

A 13.52/10-2:nos. • Item 82-A-4
NEWSLETTER, FOREST PEST MANAGEMENT METHODS APPLICATION GROUP.

PURPOSE:– To present information on management of forest pests in relation to such forest resources as timber, wildlife, recreation and scenic values, and water. Newsletters are expected to contain drawings and black and white photographs, and to be issued as seldom as two per year.

Non-depository

A 13.52/10-3:date • Item 82-A-4
FOREST PEST MANAGEMENT METHODS APPLICATIONS GROUP: REPORTS (series). [Irregular]

Discontinued.

A 13.52/10-4:nos. • Item 82-A-4
PEST ALERT (NA-TP series).

A 13.52/11:date • Item 82-B-1 (MF)
FOREST INSECT AND DISEASE CONDITIONS IN THE SOUTHWEST. [Annual]

Includes a status of insects by name, status of diseases by type of disease, and insect and disease conditions on State and private lands in Arizona and New Mexico.

A 13.52/12:date • Item 80-J (MF) (EL)
FOREST INSECT AND DISEASE CONDITIONS, INTERMOUNTAIN REGION. [Annual]

PURPOSE:– To provide an annual report on causes of tree mortality and defoliation such as bark beetles, Western spruce budworm, etc.
Earlier A 13.65/2:In 7

A 13.52/13:date • Item 80-J-1 (MF)
FOREST INSECT AND DISEASE CONDITIONS IN THE ROCKY MOUNTAIN REGION. [Annual]

A 13.53:
INTERIM TECHNICAL REPORTS.

See A 13.153

A 13.54:date
BLISTER RUST CONTROL IN CALIFORNIA, COOPERATIVE PROJECT OF STATE AND FEDERAL AGENCIES AND PRIVATE OWNERS, ANNUAL REPORTS.

A 13.55 • Item 83-A
FOREST SERVICE FILMS AVAILABLE ON LOAN FOR EDUCATIONAL PURPOSES TO SCHOOLS, CIVIC GROUPS, CHURCHES, TELEVISION. [Irregular]

Discontinued 1975.

A 13.56:date
SOUTHERN REGION REPORT. [Annual]

A 13.57:date
INTERMOUNTAIN REGION YEARBOOKS.

A 13.58
NATIONAL FOREST TIMBER SALE ACCOMPLISHMENTS FOR FISCAL YEAR. 1962–   [Annual]

PURPOSE:– To summarize National Forest timber sale at the end of each fiscal year and make these accomplishments known to Forest Service Personnel and other interested persons.

A 13.58/2
STUMPAGE PRICES FOR SAWTIMBER SOLD FROM NATIONAL FORESTS, BY SELECTED SPECIES AND REGION. [Quarterly & Annual]

Annual issue for fiscal year.

A 13.59:date
WHITE PINE BLISTER CONTROL, ANNUAL REPORT.

A 13.60:nos.
STATE LAW FOR SOIL CONSERVATION. (Division of State Cooperation)

Lake States Forest Experiment Station

A 13.61/1:date
ANNUAL REPORTS.

A 13.61/2:CT
GENERAL PUBLICATIONS.

A 13.61/7:nos.
LAKE STATES ASPEN REPORTS. 1–   1947–

A 13.61/8:nos.
STATION PAPERS. 1–   1945–

A 13.61/9:nos.
MISCELLANEOUS REPORTS.

A 13.61/10:nos.
TECHNICAL NOTES.

A 13.61/11:nos.
ECONOMIC NOTES.

A 13.61/12:date
PUBLICATIONS BY LAKE STATES FOREST EXPERIMENT STATION [list]. [Annual]

Pacific Southwest Forest and Range Experiment Station

A 13.62/1
ANNUAL REPORT. [Annual]

A 13.62/2:CT
GENERAL PUBLICATIONS.

A 13.62/7:nos.
FOREST RESEARCH NOTES.

A 13.62/8:nos.
FOREST SURVEY RELEASES.

A 13.62/9:nos.
MISCELLANEOUS PAPERS.

A 13.62/10:nos.
TECHNICAL PAPERS. 1–   1953–

A 13.62/11:date • Item 82-G (MF)
STAFF PUBLICATIONS.
Earlier A 13.62/2:P 96

A 13.62/11-2:CT
BIBLIOGRAPHIES AND LISTS OF PUBLICATIONS.

A 13.62/11-3:date • Item 82-G
PUBLICATIONS NEWLY AVAILABLE. [Quarterly]

Prior to 1974, issued as List of Available Publications.

Discontinued.

A 13.62/12:CT
HANDBOOKS, MANUALS, GUIDES.

A 13.62/13
WHAT'S NEW IN RESEARCH. 1967. [Irregular]
PURPOSE:– To keep forest land managers, and others, interested in conservation of natural resources informed about the research program at the Pacific Southwest Forest and Range Experiment Station.
Includes notices of recent publications.

Southeastern Forest Experiment Station

A 13.63/1
ANNUAL REPORT. [Annual]

A 13.63/2:CT • Item 84
GENERAL PUBLICATIONS.
See A 13.150

A 13.63/3
RESEARCH AT SOUTHEASTERN FOREST EXPERIMENT STATION. [Annual]
Includes list of publications by members of staff including cooperators for the calendar year.

A 13.63/7:nos.
FOREST SURVEY RELEASES.

A 13.63/8:nos.
TECHNICAL NOTES.

A 13.63/9:nos.
STATION PAPERS. 1–   1949–

A 13.63/10:nos.
RESEARCH NEWS.

A 13.63/11:nos.
RESEARCH NOTES.

A 13.63/12
HICKORY TASK FORCE REPORTS. 1–   1955– [Irregular]

PURPOSE:– To to promote the utilization of hickory. Technical reports on various aspects of hickory wood, its properties, uses, etc.

A 13.63/13 • Item 82-D-4
RESEARCH INFORMATION DIGEST, RECENT PUB-
LICATIONS OF SOUTHEASTERN FOREST
EXPERIMENT STATION. [Semiannual]

List of publications issued during the year.
Title varies.

A 13.63/13-2:CT • Item 82-D-4
BIBLIOGRAPHIES AND LIST OF PUBLICATIONS.
[Irregular]

See A 13.150/2

A 13.63/14:nos.
SOUTHEASTERN FOREST INSECT AND DISEASE
NEWSLETTERS

A 13.63/15:CT • Item 84
HANDBOOKS, MANUALS, GUIDES.
See 13.150/3

Institute of Tropical Forestry

A 13.64/1
ANNUAL REPORT. [Annual]

A 13.64/2:CT
GENERAL PUBLICATIONS.

A 13.64/7:v.nos.
CARIBBEAN FORESTER. 1– 24. – 1963. [Quar-
terly]

A 13.64/8:nos.
TROPICAL FOREST NOTES. 1– 14. –1963.

A 13.64/9:date
LIST OF AVAILABLE PUBLICATIONS FOR DISTRI-
BUTION. [Annual]

A 13.64/10:nos.
OCCASIONAL PAPERS. 1–   [Irregular]

Intermountain Forest and Range Experiment Station

A 13.65/1
ANNUAL REPORT. [Annual]

A 13.65/2:CT • Item 79-B
GENERAL PUBLICATIONS.

See A 13.151

A 13.65/3:nos.
BULLETINS.

A 13.65/7:nos.
RESEARCH PAPERS. 1– 17. – 1962.

Superseded by Forest Service Research Papers (A 13.78).

A 13.65/8:nos.
RESEARCH NOTES. 1– 104. – 1962.

Superseded by Forest Service Research Notes
(A 13.79).

A 13.65/9:nos.
MISCELLANEOUS PUBLICATIONS (Series). 1– 16.
– 1962.

A 13.65/10:nos.
FOREST SURVEY RELEASES. 1– 5. – 1962.

A 13.65/11:nos. & nos
RANGE IMPROVEMENT NOTES. [Quarterly]

A 13.65/12:CT
HANDBOOKS, MANUALS, GUIDES.

A 13.65/12-2:nos. • Item 79-B (MF)
PERFORMANCE GUIDES (series). [Irregular]

Discontinued.

A 13.65/13:CT
ADDRESSES.

A 13.65/14
PUBLICATIONS BY STAFF AND COOPERATORS,
INTERMOUNTAIN FOREST AND RANGE
EXPERIMENT STATION. [Annual]

A 13.65/14-2:CT • Item 79-B-2 (MF)
BIBLIOGRAPHIES AND LISTS OF PUBLICATIONS.

See A 13.151/2

A 13.65/14-3:nos. • Item 79-B-2
RECENT REPORTS (series). 1–   1967– [Irregu-
lar]

PURPOSE:– To serve as an announcement
of Station publications.
ISSN 0364-8494

See item 79-D-8

A 13.65/15:date
INTERCOM.
ISSN 0146-3551

A 13.65/16:CT • Item 79-B-1
MAPS. [Irregular]

See A13.151/3

A 13.65/17 • Item 79-B-3 (MF)
CULTURAL RESOURCE REPORT (series). [Irregular]

Each report evaluates a different site for possible inclusion in the National Register of Historic
Places.

Pacific Northwest Research Station

A 13.66/1:date • Item 79-C-2 (MF)
ANNUAL REPORT. [Annual]

Discontinued 1966.

A 13.66/2:CT • Item 79-C
GENERAL PUBLICATIONS.

A 13.66/6:CT • Item 84
REGULATIONS, RULES AND INSTRUCTIONS.

A 13.66/7:nos.
FOREST RESEARCH NOTES.

A 13.66/8:nos.
FOREST SURVEY REPORTS.

A 13.66/9:nos.
RANGE RESEARCH REPORTS.

A 13.66/10:nos.
RESEARCH PAPERS.

A 13.66/11:nos.
SILVICAL SERIES. 1–   1957–

A 13.66/12:CT • Item 79-C-1
HANDBOOKS, MANUALS, GUIDES.

A 13.66/13:nos. • Item 86-E (MF)
PRODUCTION, PRICES EMPLOYMENT, AND TRADE
IN NORTHWEST FOREST INDUSTRIES. 1963–
[Quarterly]

PURPOSE:– To provide current information
on lumber and plywood production, prices, employment in the forest industries, international
trade in logs and lumber, volume and average
prices of stumpage sold by public agencies, and
other related items.
Former title: Production, Prices, Employment
and Trade in Pacific Northwest Forest Industries.
ISSN 0364-1252

A 13.66/14:date/nos. • Item 85-A-1 (EL)
RECENT PUBLICATIONS OF THE PACIFIC NORTH-
WEST RESEARCH STATION. [Quarterly]
Earlier title: Recent Publications of the Pa-
cific Northwest Forest and Range Experiment
Station.
Formerly: List of Available Publications.
ISSN 0364-8486

A 13.66/15 • Item 85-A-1
BIBLIOGRAPHIES AND LISTS OF PUBLICATIONS.
[Annual]

List of publications issued during the year.

A 13.66/15:P 96 • Item 85-A
ANNOTATED LIST OF PUBLICATIONS OF THE
PACIFIC NORTHWEST FOREST AND RANGE
EXPERIMENT STATION. 1966– [Annual]

Continues Publications of the Pacific
Northwest Forest and Range Experiment Sta-
tion.
ISSN 0565-9485

A 13.66/15-2:date • Item 85-A-1
PUBLICATIONS OF THE PACIFIC NORTHWEST FOR-
EST AND RANGE EXPERIMENT STATION. [An-
nual]

A 13.66/16:nos.
WOOD OUTDOOR STRUCTURES: GENERAL INFOR-
MATION.

A 13.66/17:nos.
ADMINISTRATIVE REPORT (series). [Irregular]
Administrative use only.

A 13.66/18:nos. • Item 85-A-1
ECOL TECH PAPER. [Irregular]

A 13.66/19 • Item 85-A-2 (EL)
SCIENCE FINDINGS. [Monthly]

Northeastern Forest Experiment Station

A 13.67/1:date
ANNUAL REPORTS.

A 13.67/2:CT • Item 84
GENERAL PUBLICATIONS.

A 13.67/7:nos.
FOREST SURVEY RELEASE.
Changed to A 13.42/17

A 13.67/8:nos.
STATION PAPERS.
Changed to A 13.42/16

A 13.67/9:nos.
TECHNICAL NOTES. 1–

A 13.67/10:nos.
FOREST PRODUCTS PAPERS. 1–   1946–

Central States Forest Experiment Station

A 13.68/1
ANNUAL REPORT. [Annual]

A 13.68/2:CT
GENERAL PUBLICATIONS.

A 13.68/7:nos.
TECHNICAL PAPERS. 1–   192. – 1962.

A 13.68/8:nos.
MISCELLANEOUS RELEASES. 1– 35. – 1962.

A 13.68/9:nos.
FOREST SURVEY RELEASES. 1– 22. – 1959.

A 13.68/10:nos.
STATION NOTES. 1– 157. – 1962.

A 13.68/11:v.nos.
FOREST PEST OBSERVER. v. 1–   1957– [Ir-
regular]

A 13.68/12:CT
BIBLIOGRAPHIES AND LISTS OF PUBLICATIONS.

A 13.68/12-2
PUBLICATIONS. [Annual]
List of publications issued during the year.

**Rocky Mountain Forest and
Range Experiment Station**

A 13.69/1
ANNUAL REPORT. [Annual]

A 13.69/2:CT   • Item 79-D
GENERAL PUBLICATIONS.

    See A 13.151

A 13.69/7:nos.
STATION PAPERS.

A 13.69/8:nos.
RESEARCH NOTES.

A 13.69/9:nos.
FOREST SURVEY RELEASES. 1–   1959–

A 13.69/10:date   • Item 79-D-2
NEW PUBLICATIONS. [Quarterly]

A 13.69/10-2:date   • Item 79-D-2
PUBLICATIONS FOR [year]. 1970–   [Annual]

    Discontinued.

A 13.69/10-3:CT
BIBLIOGRAPHIES AND LISTS OF PUBLICATIONS.

A 13.69/11:nos.
EISENHOWER CONSORTIUM BULLETINS.

A 13.69/12:CT   • Item 79-D-3
HANDBOOKS, MANUALS, GUIDES.

A 13.69/13:date   • Item 80-A-1 (MF)
PROCEEDINGS OF THE ANNUAL WESTERN INTER-
NATIONAL FOREST DISEASE WORK CONFER-
ENCE. 1–   1953–
    27th. Sept. 25-28, 1979 Salem, Oregon

    Discontinued.

A 13.69/14:nos.
RESOURCES EVALUATION NEWSLETTER. REN 1–
1980–
    Supersedes Resources Inventory Notes (I
53.24).

    Discontinued.

A 13.69/15:nos.   • Item 79-D-4
RM-TT– (series). [Irregular]
    Each report deals with a different topic.

    Discontinued.

FOREST SERVICE (Continued)

A 13.70:CT
RELEASES.

A 13.71:
REPORT OF FOREST SERVICE TRAINING ACTIVI-
TIES, CIVILIAN CONSERVATION CORPS.

A 13.72:CT   • Item 79-S
CONSERVATION TEACHING AIDS.

    Previously distributed to Depository Libraries
under Item 81-A.

A 13.72/2:nos.
CONSERVATION VISTAS, REGIONAL CONSERVA-
TION EDUCATION NEWSLETTER SERVING
OREGON AND WASHINGTON. 1–

**Northern Forest
Experiment Station**

A 13.73/1
ANNUAL REPORT. [Annual]

A 13.73/2:CT
GENERAL PUBLICATIONS.

A 13.73/8:nos.
STATION PAPERS. 1–   1953–

A 13.73/9:nos.
TECHNICAL NOTES.

A 13.73/10:nos.
MISCELLANEOUS PUBLICATIONS. 1–   1960–

FOREST SERVICE (Continued)

A 13.74
FOREST TREE NURSERIES IN THE UNITED STATES.
[Annual]

    A directory, giving location and ownership,
name of resident nurseryman, and production in
fiscal year for Federal, State, and private nurseries.
    Punched for ring binder.

A 13.75
REPORT OF FOREST AND WINDBARRIER PLANT-
ING IN THE UNITED STATES. [Annual]

    Provides a statistical summary of planting
activities for the calendar year, compiled from
information furnished by the State Foresters and
other appropriate public officials of each State
and Federal agency concerned.
    Also known as the Annual Planting Report,
which title appears on the cover sheet of the Tree
Planters' Notes.
    Punched for ring binder.

A 13.76:date
DEMAND AND PRICE SITUATION FOR FOREST PROD-
UCTS. [Annual]
    Earlier A 13.2:D 39

A 13.77:date
LUMBER MANUFACTURING, WOOD USING AND AL-
LIED ASSOCIATIONS.
    Earlier A 13.2:L 97/9 and A 13.2:L 97/15.

A 13.78:letters-nos.   • Item 83-B (MF) (EL)
RESEARCH PAPERS.

    PURPOSE:– To present results, analyses and
conclusions arising from formal studies or experiments in the fields of timber management, wood
utilization, forest economics and timber marketing, watershed management, range management,
forest recreation, strip-mine reclamation, forest
fire control, and forest insect and disease control, The papers give a fairly complete story and
many represent the final results of the various
studies and experiments conducted under the
guidance of the experiment stations.
    Abstract cards are inserted for those who
want to maintain an index to the individual papers.
    Also published in microfiche.

A 13.79:letters-nos.   • Item 83-B-4 (MF)
RESEARCH NOTES.

    PURPOSE:– To present observational infor-
mation and reports on new techniques or instruments. Included in this series are the how- to-do-
type of publication, reports of incidental discovery, and progress reports of research being conducted, but not completed.
    Also published in microfiche.

A 13.79/2:date   • Item 83-B-4 (MF)
PULPWOOD PRICES IN THE SOUTHEAST. [Annual]

    Earlier A 13.79

A 13.79/3:date   • Item 83-B-4 (MF)
BULLETIN OF HARDWOOD MARKET STATISTICS.
[Semiannual]

A 13.79/4:date   • Item 83-B-10 (EL)
U.S FOREST PRODUCTS ANNUAL MARKET REVIEW
AND PROSPECTS. [Annual]

A 13.80:letters-nos.   • Item 83-B-5 (MF)
RESOURCE BULLETINS.

    PURPOSE:– To present information on forest
resources and related information on production
and use of forest products.

A 13.80/2:letters & nos.
RESOURCE REPORTS. [Irregular]

A 13.80/3:date   • Item 83-B-5 (EL)
PULPWOOD PRODUCTION IN THE NORTHEAST. [An-
nual]

A 13.80/4:date   • Item 83-B-5 (EL)
SOUTHERN PULPWOOD PRODUCTION. [Annual]

A 13.80/5:date   • Item 83-B-5 (MF) (EL)
PULPWOOD PRODUCTION IN THE NORTH- CENTRAL
REGION BY COUNTY. [Annual]
    Earlier A 13.80

A 13.80/5-2   • Item 83-B-9 (MF)
PULPWOOD PRODUCTION IN THE LAKE STATES.
[Annual]

A 13.80/6:   • Item 83-B-5 (MF)
FOREST STATISTICS FOR NORTHWEST FLORIDA.
[Annual]

A 13.81:nos.
[FOREST SERVICE TRANSLATIONS]. FS–

**North Central Forest
Experiment Station**

A 13.82/1:date   • Item 84
ANNUAL REPORT.

A 13.82/2:CT   • Item 79-E
GENERAL PUBLICATIONS.

A 13.82/8:CT   • Item 79-E-1
HANDBOOKS, MANUALS, GUIDES. [Irregular]

A 13.82/9:date   • Item 79-E (MF)
NEW FROM NORTH CENTRAL. 1965–   [Semian-
nual]

    Earlier title: List of Publications, Annotated.
    Earlier issued annually
    Lists and annotates the publications of the
Station.

A 13.82/9-2:   • Item 79-E-4 (MF) (EL)
NC (NORTH CENTRAL) NEWS. [Monthly]

A 13.82/10   • Item 79-E-2
TECHNICAL BRIEF (series).

A 13.82/11:date   • Item 79-E-3 (MF)
RESEARCH ATTAINMENT REPORT, FISCAL YEAR.
[Annual]

FOREST SERVICE (Continued)

A 13.83:date   • Item 83-C-2 (MF) (EL)
ANNUAL GRAZING STATISTICAL REPORT.

    Also issued on CD-ROM.

A 13.84:nos.
ENGINEERING TECHNICAL INFORMATION SYSTEM:
TECHNICAL REPORTS. 1968–   [Irregular]
    PURPOSE:– To provide a method of dissemi-
nating technical information among Forest Service employees. The publication is an in-house
document containing material related to the activities of Forest Service engineers. The series
provides Forest Service Engineers an opportunity to publish their ideas or have the ideas of
authors outside the Forest Service reprinted for
the dissemination to and for use by all Forest
Service employees.

A 13.84/2:nos.   • Item 83-C (MF)
ENGINEERING TECHNICAL INFORMATION
SYSTEM:EM. (series). [Irregular]

A 13.84/3:v. nos & nos.   • Item 83-C-1
FIELD NOTES. v. 1–   1969–   [Monthly]
    Previous title: Engineering Technical Infor-
mation System, Field Notes.
    Other previous title: Engineering Field Notes.
    ISSN 0364-2631

    Discontinued.

A 13.85:nos.
TRAINING TEXTS. 1–

A 13.86 • Item 82-C
FOREST SERVICE COMMENTS ON RESOLUTIONS RELATING TO THE NATIONAL FOREST SYSTEM AS ADOPTED.

Discontinued 1970.

A 13.87:date
WATERSHED MANAGEMENT RESEARCH, SEMI-ANNUAL REPORT.

A 13.87/2:nos. • Item 83-B-1 (MF)
WSDG TECHNICAL PAPERS, WSDG-TP– (series). 1– 1980– [Irregular] (Watershed System Development Group)

Discontinued.

A 13.87/3:nos. • Item 83-B-2 (MF)
APPLICATION DOCUMENT SERIES, WSDG-AD– (nos.). [Irregular] (Watershed System Development Group)

Discontinued.

A 13.87/4:nos. • Item 83-B-3
TECHNICAL NOTES, WSDG-TN– (series). [Irregular] (Watershed Systems Development Group)

Discontinued.

A 13.88:letters-nos. • Item 83-B-6 (MF) (EL)
GENERAL TECHNICAL REPORTS. [Irregular]
Also Issued on CD-ROM.

A 13.88:PSW-13 • Item 83-B
WILDLAND PLANNING GLOSSARY. 252 p.

Contains more than 1400 terms useful in wildland and related resource planning which are defined.

A 13.89:date • Item 82-D-10
FOREST-GRAM SOUTH.

A dispatch of current technical information for direct use by practicing forest resource managers in the South, concerning subjects such as infestations of the Southern pine beetle.

Discontinued.

A 13.89/2:date • Item 79-E
NEW FROM NORTH CENTRAL PUBLICATIONS. [Annual]

A 13.90:date • Item 80-D
RESOURCE DECISIONS IN THE NATIONAL FORESTS OF THE EASTERN REGION. [Quarterly]

A 13.91:nos. • Item 80-D
CURRENT INFORMATION REPORTS. 1– [Irregular]

Discontinued.

A 13.92:CT • Item 80-F (MF)
FINAL ENVIRONMENTAL IMPACT STATEMENTS AND RELATED MATERIALS. [Irregular]
Earlier title: Final Environmental Impact Statements.

A 13.92/2:nos. • Item 80-F (MF)
DRAFT ENVIRONMENTAL IMPACT STATEMENTS AND RELATED MATERIALS. [Irregular]
Also Issued on CD-ROM.
Earlier title: Draft Environmental Statements.

A 13.93:CT • Item 82-B (MF)
FOREST INSECT AND DISEASE MANAGEMENT/ EVALUATION REPORTS.

Discontinued.

A 13.93/2:nos. • Item 82-B
FOREST INSECT AND DISEASE MANAGEMENT/SURVEY REPORTS.

Non-depository

A 13.93/3:CT • Item 82-B (MF)
FOREST INSECT AND DISEASE MANAGEMENT (series). [Irregular]
Covers miscellaneous reports.

Discontinued.

A 13.93/4 • Item 82-B-4 (MF)
FOREST INSECTS AND DISEASES GROUP TECHNICAL PUBLICATIONS.

A 13.94:nos.
ARCHEOLOGICAL REPORTS.

A 13.95:date/nos. • Item 79-F (MF)
FORESTRY RESEARCH WEST. [Quarterly]
Earlier title: Forestry Research, What's New in the West.

A 13.95/2:date
FORESTRY RESEARCH WEST. [Quarterly]

A 13.96:nos. • Item 83-B-7
FOREST PRODUCT UTILIZATION TECHNICAL REPORTS. 1– [Irregular]

Discontinued.

A 13.97:nos.
BIOLOGICAL EVALUATION (series). [Irregular]

A 13.98:nos.
FRIDAY NEWSLETTER. [Weekly]

A 13.98/2:nos.
QUADS, REPORT ON ENERGY ACTIVITIES. [Monthly]

Issued as a supplement to Friday Newsletter (A 13.98) Prior to December 1979.

A 13.98/3:date
FOREST SERVICE HISTORY LINE.

A 13.99:nos. • Item 82-B-2
NWGC HANDBOOKS. 1– 1979– [Irregular] (National Wildfire Coordinating Group)

PURPOSE:– To coordinate the programs of the Department of Agriculture, the Department of the Interior and State Programs in wildfire prevention and control.

Non-depository

A 13.99/8:CT • Item 83-B-8
NATIONAL WILDLIFE COORDINATING GROUP: HANDBOOKS, MANUALS, GUIDES. [Irregular]

A 13.100:nos. • Item 82-B-3
FIELD IDENTIFICATION CARDS. (Southeastern Area State and Private Forestry Office)

Flash cards, 13 x 8 cm., with colored photograph on one side and descriptive information, area map and plant symbols on the verso. Each card identifies a rare and sensitive botanical species found in the Southeast.

Discontinued.

A 13.101:CT • Item 84-B (MF)
CULTURAL RESOURCES OVERVIEW (series). [Irregular]
Series of cultural resource overviews for the State of New Mexico, prepared jointly by the Bureau of Land Management and the Forest Service, and used as baseline documents for planning efforts in New Mexico.

Discontinued.

A 13.101/2:nos. • Item 84-B-1
STUDIES IN CULTURAL RESOURCE MANAGEMENT. [Irregular] (Pacific Northwest Region)
PURPOSE:– To provide historical and architectural surveys of historical landmarks listed in the National Register of Historic Places.

A 13.102:nos. • Item 84
NORTHEASTERN AREA, NA-FR– (series). 1– [Irregular]
See A 13.110/9

A 13.102/2:nos. • Item 84
SA-FR (series).

A 13.102/3:nos. • Item 82-A-3
MISCELLANEOUS REPORTS, SA-MA– (series). [Irregular] (Southeastern Area).

Discontinued.

A 13.103 • Item 82-A-1
ALASKA REGION REPORTS. 1– [Irregular]

Series covers various subjects concerning the forests of Alaska, such as trees, timber, forest pests, etc.

Discontinued.

A 13.103/2 • Item 82-A
ALASKA REGION LEAFLETS. [Irregular]

Discontinued.

A 13.104:CT • Item 80-H-1
POSTERS. [Irregular]

A 13.104/2:CT • Item 80-H-2
AUDIOVISUAL MATERIALS.

Discontinued.

A 13.105:nos. • Item 82-A-2
GENERAL REPORTS, SA-GR– (series). 1– [Irregular]

SA = Southeastern Area.
Later A 13.110/12

A 13.105/2:nos. • Item 82-A-5
MANAGEMENT BULLETIN (series). [Irregular]

Each bulletin deals with a different management topic, such as managing the family forest in the South.

A 13.105/3:lts. nos. • Item 82-A-5
UTILIZATION REPORT (Series).

A 13.105/4:lts. nos. • Item 82-A-5
PROTECTION REPORT (Series).

A 13.106:nos. • Item 79-K
NA-FB/P (series). [Irregular]

Superseded by State and Private Forestry: Forestry Bulletins (A 13.110/10).

A 13.106/2:nos. • Item 79-L
FORESTRY BULLETINS, SB-FB/P– (series). 1– [Irregular]

Superseded by State and Private Forestry: Forestry Bulletins (A 13.110/10).

A 13.106/2-2:nos.
FORESTRY BULLETINS, SA-FB-U– (series). [Irregular] (Southeastern Area)

A 13.106/3:nos. • Item 84-C
NA-FB/M (series). [Irregular] (Northeastern Area)

Each folder is devoted to a single subject of popular interest.
Superseded by State and Private Forestry: Forestry Bulletins (A 13.110/10).

A 13.106/3-2:nos. • Item 84-C-1
NA-GR– (series). [Irregular] (Northeastern Area)
Later A 13.110/12

A 13.106/4:nos.
NORTHEASTERN INFORMATION SERIES. NE-INF– [Irregular]

A 13.107:CT • Item 80-G
SPECIES RANGE MAPS (series). [Irregular]

A 13.108:date
WESTFORNET MONTHLY ALERT.

A 13.109:date • Item 86-D
U.S. FOREST PLANTING REPORT. [Annual]
Discontinued.

A 13.110/2:CT • Item 86-F-1
STATE AND PRIVATE FORESTRY: GENERAL PUBLICATIONS.

A 13.110/8:CT • Item 86-F
STATE AND PRIVATE FORESTRY: HANDBOOKS, MANUALS, GUIDES. [Irregular]

A 13.110/9:letters-nos. • Item 79-M (MF)
STATE AND PRIVATE FORESTRY: FORESTRY REPORTS.

A 13.110/10:nos. • Item 79-M-1 (MF)
STATE AND PRIVATE FORESTRY: FORESTRY BULLETINS. [Irregular]

Consists of bulletins formerly classed A 13.106, A 13.106/2, and A 13.106/3.
Bulletins concern miscellaneous forestry subjects and may consist of a single sheet.

A 13.110/11:letters-nos. • Item 86-F-1
STATE AND PRIVATE FORESTRY: MISCELLANEOUS REPORTS.

A 13.110/12:letters-nos. • Item 84-C-2 (MF)
STATE AND PRIVATE FORESTRY: GENERAL REPORTS (Series). [Irregular]

Includes reports NA-GR and SA-GR formerly classified A 13.106/3-2 and A 13.105.

A 13.110/13 • Item 86-G (MF)
STATE AND PRIVATE FORESTRY: TECHNICAL PUBLICATIONS. [Irregular]

A 13.110/14 • Item 84-I (MF)
TREE PLANTING IN THE UNITED STATES . . .

A 13.110/14:letters-nos.
STATE AND PRIVATE FORESTRY: TECHNICAL REPORTS.

A 13.110/15 • Item 86-F-2
NE/NA-INF (series).

A 13.110/17 • Item 86-F-4 (EL)
UPDATE, FOREST HEALTH TECHNOLOGY, ENTERPRISE TEAM UPDATE.

A 13.111:date • Item 80-F-1
WOODSY OWL'S CAMPAIGN CATALOG. [Annual]

Catalog of materials such as posters, wallet cards, patches, and pens and pencils that promote the Woodsy Owl campaign for environmental improvement.
Discontinued.

A 13.111/2 • Item 80-F-2
SMOKEY'S CAMPAIGN CATALOG. [Biennial]
Discontinued.

A 13.112:date • Item 84-E
VOLUNTEER OPPORTUNITIES. [Annual] (Intermountain Region)

A 13.112/2:nos. • Item 84-E
VOLUNTEERS IN THE NATIONAL FORESTS (series).

A 13.113:date • Item 84-G (EL)
U.S. TIMBER PRODUCTION, TRADE, CONSUMPTION, AND PRICE STATISTICS. [Annual]

PURPOSE:– To present statistical information on theproduction, trade, consumption, and price of timber products in the U. S. Although most data are national, some applies to regions, states, and Canada.
Earlier A 1.38

A 13.113/2:date • Item 84-A-2 (MF)
THE NATIONAL TIMBER BRIDGE INITIATIVE FISCAL YEAR. [Annual]
Discontinued.

A 13.114: • Item 84-H (MF)
STOCKHOLDERS' REPORT. [Annual]

This publication's title reflects the concept of U.S.citizens as being stockholders in our national forests, such as the Huron-Manistee National Forests. Reports present information on the national forests' fish and wildlife, fire management, minerals management, roads/ trails, and receipts.

A 13.114/2:CT • Item 80 (EL)
NATIONAL FOREST ANNUAL REPORTS (Various Regions).

A 13.114/4 • Item 80 (MF)
NATIONAL FOREST ANNUAL REPORTS (Various Regions).
See A 13.114/2

A 13.115/2: • Item 79-M-2 (MF)
FOREST PEST CONDITIONS REPORT FOR THE NORTHEASTERN AREA. [Annual]

PURPOSE:– To provide information on insect and disease conditions of trees in the Northeastern area of the U.S., including declines and increases in pest infestations. Points out pest and disease conditions oftrees in some individual states.

A 13.116:date/nos. • Item 79-N
FOREST SERVICE REPORT TO CONGRESS: IMPLEMENTATION OF SECTION 318 OF THE INTERIOR AND RELATED AGENCIES APPROPRIATION ACT FOR FISCAL YEAR . . . [Monthly]
Discontinued.

A 13.117:date • Item 85-A-1 (MF)
IMPORTANT FACTS ABOUT THE PACIFIC NORTHWEST REGION. [Annual]

A 13.118:nos. • Item 85-A-4
GIS APPLICATION NOTE (Series).

A 13.119:v.nos./nos. • Item 79-F
EXPERIENCE THE WILLAMETTE NATIONAL FOREST. [Quarterly]

A 13.120:v.nos./nos. • Item 82-D-6
MOUNTAIN VIEWS. [Quarterly]
Discontinued.

A 13.121:date • Item 82-D-6
HEADWATER HERALD. [Three times a year]
Discontinued.

A 13.122:date • Item 79-F (MF)
THE NATIONAL FORESTS, AMERICA'S GREAT OUTDOORS. [Three times a year]

A 13.123:date/nos. • Item 79-N (MF)
MONTHLY ALERT. (Rocky Mountain Research Station)

A 13.124 • Item 79-B (MF)
FISHERIES, WILDLIFE, AND TES SPECIES CHALLENGE COST-SHARE PROGRAM REPORT FOR THE INTERMOUNTAIN REGION (FY).

A 13.124/2:date • Item 84-G (MF)
CHALLENGE COST-SHARE PROGRAM REPORT. [Annual]
Discontinued.

A 13.125 • Item 84-E
WORKING TOGETHER FOR RURAL AMERICA.
Discontinued.

A 13.128:nos. • Item 84
YOUR CHANGING FOREST, NEWS ON THE BLACK HILLS NATIONAL FOREST PLAN REVISION.
Non-depository

A 13.129:CT • Item 84-E
PACIFIC NORTHWEST RESEARCH STATION: MISCELLANEOUS PUBLICATIONS.

A 13.130:date • Item 84 (MF)
BUDGET EXPLANATORY NOTES FOR COMMITTEE ON APPROPRIATIONS.

A 13.131:nos. • Item 84-E
THE CATALYST. [Quarterly]

A 13.133:date • Item 84-E-1
WILDLIFE, FISH, RARE PLANT, PARTNERSHIP UPDATE. [Annual]

A 13.134 • Item 84-A-1 (MF)
FHM-NC (series). (National Center of Forest Health Management)

A 13.136 • Item 84-J (MF)
HEALTH HAZARDS OF SMOKE. [Semiannual]

A 13.137:nos. • Item 84-A-3 (MF)
TECHNOLOGY AND DEVELOPMENT PROGRAM (series).

A 13.138:nos. • Item 84-A-4 (EL)
THE SHAWNEE QUARTERLY, THE SHAWNEE NATIONAL FOREST SCHEDULE OF PROJECTS.

A 13.140 • Item 15-A-2 (E)
ELECTRONIC PRODUCTS. [Irregular]

A 13.141 • Item 15-A-2 (EL)
GYPSY MOTH NEWS.

A 13.150: • Item 84-K
SOUTHERN RESEARCH STATION: GENERAL PUBLICATIONS.

A 13.150/1: • Item 84-K-4
ANNUAL REPORT SOUTHERN RESEARCH STATION:

A 13.150/2: • Item 84-K-1 (MF)
SOUTHERN RESEARCH STATION: BIBLIOGRAPHIES AND LISTS OF PUBLICATIONS.

A 13.150/3: • Item 84-K-2
SOUTHERN RESEARCH STATION: HANDBOOKS, MANUALS, GUIDES.

A 13.150/4: • Item 84-K-3 (EL)
SOUTHERN RESEARCH STATION DIRECTORY OF RESEARCH SCIENTISTS.

A 13.150/5: • Item 82-K-4 (EL)
COMPASS:RECENT PUBLICATIONS OF THE SOUTHERN RESEARCH STATION. [Quarterly]

A 13.151:CT • Item 79-B-5
ROCKY MOUNTAIN RESEARCH STATION: GENERAL PUBLICATIONS.

A 13.151/2: • Item 79-B-6 (MF)
ROCKY MOUNTAIN RESEARCH STATION: BIBLIOGRAPHIES AND LISTS OF PUBLICATIONS.

A 13.151/2-2: • Item 79-D-9 (EL)
NEW PUBLICATIONS ROCKY MOUNTAIN RESEARCH STATION. [Quarterly]

A 13.151/2-3: • Item 79-D-8
RECENT REPORTS (Rocky Mountain Research Station).
Discontinued.

A 13.151/3: • Item 79-B-4
ROCKY MOUNTAIN RESEARCH STATION: MAPS.

A 13.151/4: • Item 79-B-7
ROCKY MOUNTAIN RESEARCH STATION: HANDBOOKS, MANUALS, GUIDES.

A 13.151/4-2: • Item 79-B-9 (MF)
ROCKY MOUNTAIN RESEARCH STATION DIRECTORY.

A 13.151/5:letters-nos. • Item 79-B-8
PROCEEDINGS RMRS-P. (Rocky Mountain Research Station (Series).

A 13.151/6 • Item 80-B-1 (EL)
RMRScience. [Quarterly]

A 13.151/7 • Item 79-B-11 (EL)
ANNUAL REPORT.

A 13.152: • Item 79-B-10 (MF)
FOREST MANAGEMENT PROGRAM ANNUAL REPORT (NATIONAL SUMMARY).

A 13.153 • Item 15-A-2 (EL)
INTERNATIONAL PROGRAMS NEWS. [Irregular]

A 13.154 • Item 15-A-2 (EL)
FOREST HEALTH HIGHLIGHTS.

A 13.155 • Item 84-L (EL)
THE NATURAL INQUIRER, A RESEARCH AND SCIENCE JOURNAL.

A 13.156:date • Item 84-M
BRIEFING BOOK, ALASKA REGION. [Annual]

A 13.157 • Item 84-L-1 (EL)
SOUTHERN REGION ANNUAL MONITORING AND EVALUATION REPORTS. [Annual]

DIVISION OF GARDENS AND GROUNDS (1862– 1901)

CREATION AND AUTHORITY

The Division of Gardens and Grounds was established within the Department of Agriculture in September 1862. On July 1, 1901, the Division was consolidated with certain other agencies to form the Bureau of Plant Industry (A 19).

A 14.1:date
ANNUAL REPORTS.

A 14.2:CT
GENERAL PUBLICATIONS [none issued].

A 14.3:nos.
BULLETINS [none issued].

A 14.4:nos.
CIRCULARS [none issued].

OFFICE IRRIGATION INQUIRY (1890– 1896)

A 15.1:date
ANNUAL REPORTS.

A 15.2:CT
GENERAL PUBLICATIONS.

A 15.3:nos.
BULLETINS.

A 15.4:nos.
CIRCULARS [none issued].

BOARD OF LABOR EMPLOYMENT (1902– 1904)

CREATION AND AUTHORITY

The Board of Labor Employment was established within the Department of Agriculture, pursuant to regulations issued by the President, dated July 2, 1902. Discontinued in 1904, when its work was taken over by the Civil Service Commission (CS).

A 16.1:date
ANNUAL REPORTS.

A 16.2:CT
GENERAL PUBLICATIONS.

A 16.3:nos.
BULLETINS [none issued].

A 16.4:nos.
CIRCULARS [none issued].

NATIONAL AGRICULTURAL LIBRARY (1962– 1978, 1981–   )

CREATION AND AUTHORITY

In commemoration of its 100th anniversary on May 15, 1962, the Library of the Department of Agriculture was renamed the National Agricultural Library. Secretary's Memorandum 1927, Supplement 1, dated December 19, 1977 transferred the National Agricultural Library to the Science and Education Administration effective January 24, 1978. The name was changed to Technical Information Systems (A 106.100). The Science and Education Administration (A 106) was abolished on June 17, 1981 and the Technical Information Systems was transferred to the reestablished National Agricultural Library.

INFORMATION

National Agricultural Library
10301 Baltimore Ave.
Beltsville, MD 20705
(301) 504-5755
Fax: (301) 504-6110
http://www.nal.usda.gov

A 17.1:date • Item 95-F
REPORT OF THE LIBRARIAN. 1893/94– 1952/53.
Later A 106.101

A 17.2:CT • Item 95-A-1
GENERAL PUBLICATIONS.
Later A 106.102
Discontinued.

A 17.2:D 62 • Item 95
DIRECTORY OF INFORMATION RESOURCES IN AGRICULTURE AND BIOLOGY. 1971. 523 p.
A directory of Federal organizations, units of land-grant colleges and universities, and their campus affiliated organizations arranged alphabetically, by State.

A 17.3:nos.
BULLETINS. 1– 76. 1894– 1912.

A 17.4:nos.
CIRCULARS.
(None issued)

A 17.5:nos.
LIST OF DUPLICATES OFFERED AS EXCHANGES.
1–   1901–

A 17.6:v.nos
MONTHLY BULLETINS. v. 1– 4. 1910– 1913.

Contains list of accessions to the library, formerly issued in Bulletin series (A 17.3).

A 17.7:nos.
LIBRARY LEAFLETS. 1– 8. 1918– 1919.
Prior to May 5, 1919, classified A 1.29.

A 17.8:nos. • Item 94
BIBLIOGRAPHICAL CONTRIBUTIONS. 1– 35. 1919– 1939.
Discontinued.

A 17.9:vol.
AGRICULTURAL LIBRARY NOTES. v. 1– v. 17, no. 6. 1926– 1942. [Monthly]

A 17.10:vol.
AGRICULTURAL ECONOMICS LITERATURE. v. 1– 16, no. 6   – 1942.
Earlier A 36.20
Later A 17.18:A

A 17.11:vol.
PLANT SCIENCE LITERATURE, SELECTED REFERENCES. v. 1– v. 15, no. 26.   – 1942. [Weekly]
Later A 17.18:D

A 17.12:date
LISTS OF AGRICULTURAL EXPERIMENT STATION PUBLICATIONS RECEIVED BY LIBRARY.   – 1942. [Monthly]
Earlier A 10.7
Later A 77.409

A 17.13:vol.
COTTON LITERATURE, SELECTED REFERENCES. [Monthly]
Earlier A 1.50

A 17.14:vol.
ENTOMOLOGY CURRENT LITERATURE, SELECTED REFERENCES. v. 1– v. 11, no. 3.   – 1942. [Bimonthly]
Earlier A 56.10
Later A 17.18:C

A 17.15:vol.
SOIL CONSERVATION LITERATURE, SELECTED CURRENT REFERENCES. v. 1– v. 6, no. 3.   – 1942. [Bimonthly]
Earlier A 57.20

A 17.16:vol.
AGRICULTURE IN DEFENSE. v. 1–   1941– [Weekly]

A 17.17 • Item 95-A
LIBRARY LISTS. 1–   1942–   [Irregular]
Bibliographies.
Later A 106.110/2

A 17.17:1
SELECTED LIST OF AMERICAN AGRICULTURAL BOOKS IN PRINT AND CURRENT AGRICULTURAL PERIODICALS.

A 17.17:25
AVAILABLE BIBLIOGRAPHIES AND LISTS. 1946– [Irregular]

A 17.17:41
COOPERATION IN AGRICULTURE. 1954– 1964.

A 17.17:75
SERIAL PUBLICATIONS INDEXED IN BIBLIOGRAPHY OF AGRICULTURE. 1st ed.–   1963–   [Irregular]

A 17.18:vol
BIBLIOGRAPHY OF AGRICULTURE (by sections). [Monthly]
Section A supersedes, July 1942, A 17.10, Section B supersedes, July 1942, A 70.7, Section C supersedes, July 1942, A 17.14, Section D supersedes July 1942, A 17.11, Section E supersedes A 13.25.
Effective 1970, published privately.

A 17.18/2:CT • Item 95-A-2
BIBLIOGRAPHIES AND LISTS OF PUBLICATIONS.
Later A 106.110

A 17.18/2:Se 6 • Item 95-D
SERIALS CURRENTLY RECEIVED BY THE NATIONAL AGRICULTURAL LIBRARY. [Irregular]

A list of approximately 15,000 serials held by the National Agricultural Library. The serials cover such topics as animal science, biochemistry, botany, consumer science, economics, entomology, food and nutrition, management science, natural resources, technical agriculture, and many others.

A 17.18/3:date • Item 95-A
FOOD AND NUTRITION INFORMATION AND EDUCA-
TIONAL MATERIALS CENTER. CATALOG.

A 17.18/4:nos. • Item 95-A-2
QUICK BIBLIOGRAPHIC SERIES. [Irregular]

Bibliographies are not in depth but are a substantial resource for recent investigations on a
given topic. They are derived from computerized
on-line searches of the AGRICOLA data base.

A 17.18/5:date • Item 95-A-2 (EL)
LIST OF JOURNALS INDEXED IN AGRICOLA. [Annual]

A 17.18/6:date-nos. • Item 95-A-2
AGRI-TOPICS (Series). [Irregular]

A 17.18/7:nos. • Item 95-A-2
BIBLIOGRAPHIC SERIES: CURRENT TITLES LIST-
ING. [Quarterly]

Discontinued.

A 17.19:v.nos.&nos.
DAILY DIGEST.
Administrative.

A 17.20:nos. • Item 95-B
PESTICIDES DOCUMENTATION BULLETIN. v. 1– v. 5.
1965– 1969. [Biweekly]

PURPOSE:– To provide an index to the literature on pest control, broadly defined. Covers diseases, pests, and parasites of plants and animals; pest, parasite, and disease control; entomology in general; biological states of plants and
animals as they are affected by chemicals and
biologicals; weeds; and residues of economic poisons wherever found.
Since December 1967, a computer-produced
categorized bibliography with subject biographical, author, and organizational indexes. Each item
appearing in the Bulletin is maintained in magnetic tape files which are fully searchable.
Semiannual Cumulative Index is sent separately.
Discontinued.

A 17.21:CT
PRESS RELEASES.

A 17.22:CT • Item 95-C-1
HANDBOOKS, MANUALS, GUIDES.

A 17.23:v.nos.&nos. • Item 95-F (P) (EL)
AGRICULTURAL LIBRARIES INFORMATION NOTES.
v. 1– 1975– [Monthly]
ISSN 0095-2699
Later A 106.109

A 17.24:nos. • Item 95-A-3
SPECIAL REFERENCE BRIEFS. [Irregular]
Each reference brief lists publications per-
taining to a different agricultural topic.

A 17.25: • Item 95-A-4
SEARCH TIPS SERIES.
Each issue provides tips on searching a par-
ticular topic.
Discontinued.

A 17.26 • Item 95-A-5
ANIMAL WELFARE LEGISLATION: BILLS SUBMIT-
TED TO THE CONGRESS.
Earlier titled: Animal Welfare Legislation: Bills
and Public Laws.
Discontinued.

A 17.27:nos. • Item 95-C-1 (MF)
AWIC (Animal Welfare Information Center) (Series).

A 17.27/2 • Item 95-C-1
ANIMAL WELFARE INFORMATION CENTER NEWS-
LETTER. [Quarterly]

A 17.27/3:nos. • Item 95-C-2
AWIC RESOURCE SERIES.

A 17.28:nos. • Item 95-A-2
AIC (Aquaculture Information Center) (Series).

A 17.29:nos. • Item 95-A-2
RURAL INFORMATION CENTER PUBLICATION
SERIES.

A 17.30 • Item 95-A-6 (E)
FOOD & NUTRITION RESEARCH BRIEFS.

A 17.31 • Item 95-A-6 (E)
ELECTRONIC PRODUCTS.

A 17.32 • Item 95-A-7 (EL)
EDUCATIONAL AND TRAINING OPPORTUNITIES IN
SUSTAINABLE AGRICULTURE. [Annual]

DIVISION OF MICROSCOPY
(1871– 1895)

CREATION AND AUTHORITY

The Division of Microscopy was established
within the Department of Agriculture in 1871 and
secured divisional status in 1885. The Division
was abolished in 1895.

A 18.1:date
ANNUAL REPORTS.

A 18.2:CT
GENERAL PUBLICATIONS.

A 18.3:nos.
BULLETINS.

A 18.4:nos.
CIRCULARS.

A 18.5:nos.
FOOD PRODUCTS.

BUREAU OF PLANT INDUSTRY
(1901– 1942)

CREATION AND AUTHORITY

The Bureau of Plant Industry was established
within the Department of Agriculture on July 1,
1901, pursuant to Act of Congress, approved
March 2, 1901, by the consolidation of the Division of Agrostology (A 3), the Division of Botany
(A 6), the Division of Gardens and Grounds (A
14), the Division of Pomology (A 20), the Division
of Seeds (A 24), the Seed and Plant Introduction
Section (A 23), the Division of Vegetable Physiology and Pathology (A 28), and the Arlington Experimental Farm. By Executive Order 9069 of
February 23 1942, the Bureau was made a part of
the Agricultural Research Administration (A
77.500)

A 19.1:date
ANNUAL REPORTS.
Later A 77.501

A 19.2:CT
GENERAL PUBLICATIONS.
Later A 77.502

A 19.3:nos.
BULLETINS.

A 19.4
CIRCULARS.

A 19.5:sec.nos.
FOOD PRODUCTS.

A 19.6:CT
SEED AND PLANT INTRODUCTION AND DISTRIBU-
TION.

A 19.7:CT
HORTICULTURAL INVESTIGATIONS.

A 19.8:date
(LIST OF) BULLETINS OF BUREAU OF PLANT IN-
DUSTRY.

A 19.9:CT
HINTS TO SETTLERS (on irrigation projects).

A 19.10:date
LIST OF PUBLICATIONS OF THE BUREAU OF PLANT
INDUSTRY.

A 19.11:CT
GRAIN STANDARDIZATION.

A 19.12:nos.
INVENTORIES OF SEEDS AND PLANTS IMPORTED
BY OFFICE OF FOREIGN SEED AND PLANT IN-
TRODUCTION.
Later A 77.515

A 19.13:nos.
SERVICE AND REGULATORY ANNOUNCEMENTS.

A 19.14:CT/date
WORK OF RECLAMATION PROJECT EXPERIMENT
FAR (by name of project).

A 19.15:date
NEW PLANT INTRODUCTIONS (annual lists).

A 19.16:nos.
PLANT IMMIGRANTS. [Monthly]

A 19.17:nos.
COTTON, TRUCK, AND FORAGE CROP DISEASE
CIRCULARS.

A 19.18:v.nos.
PLANT DISEASE BULLETINS.
Later Plant Disease Reporter, (A 77.511).

A 19.18/a:CT
– SEPARATES.

A 19.19:nos.
PLANT DISEASE BULLETINS, SUPPLEMENTS.

A 19.19/a:
– SEPARATES.

A 19.20:nos.
AGRICULTURAL TECHNOLOGY CIRCULARS.

A 19.21:vol
BLISTER RUST NEWS. [Monthly]

A 19.22:vol
BOTANY, CURRENT LITERATURE. [Fortnightly]
Later A 19.22/2

A 19.22/2:vol.
PLANT SCIENCE LITERATURE, SELECTED REFER-
ENCES. [Weekly]
Later A 17.11

A 19.23:vol
AGRONOMY, CURRENT LITERATURE. [Fortnightly]
Later A 19.22/2

A 19.24:date
WEEKLY STATION REPORTS OF OFFICE OF DRY
LAND AGRICULTURE INVESTIGATIONS.
Later A 77.508

A 19.25:vol.
WEEKLY REPORTS OF OFFICE OF WESTERN IRRI-
GATION AGRICULTURE.

A 19.26:nos.
PLANT DISEASE POSTERS.
Later A 77.517

A 19.27:vol.
HORTICULTURAL CROPS AND DISEASES DIVISION.
[Semimonthly]
Later A 77.510

A 19.28:CT
PAPERS IN RE.
Later 77.513

A 19.29:vol.
FORAGE CROP GAZETTE. [Monthly]

News letter for Staff Workers, Division of Forage Crops and Diseases.
Later A 77.509

A 19.30:date
ALFALFA IMPROVEMENT CONFERENCES, REPORTS.

A 19.31:CT
SOIL SURVEY REPORTS (lists of by States).
Earlier A 47.5/a

A 19.32:date/nos.
SOIL SURVEY [Reports].
Earlier A 47.5

A 19.33:CT
ADDRESSES.
Later A 77.507

A 19.34:nos.
[DRY-LAND] AGRICULTURE.

Publications designated D.L.A.-no.
Changed from A 19.2

A 19.35:nos.
CONTRIBUTIONS TOWARD A FLORA OF NEVADA.
Later A 77.527

A 19.36:nos.
H. T. & S. OFFICE REPORTS
Later A 77.523

DIVISION OF POMOLOGY
(1886– 1901)

CREATION AND AUTHORITY

The Division of Pomology was established within the Department of Agriculture on July 1, 1886. The Division was consolidated along with certain other agencies to form the Bureau of Plant Industry (A 19) on July 1, 1901, pursuant to act of Congress, approved March 2, 1901.

A 20.1:date
ANNUAL REPORTS.

A 20.2:CT
GENERAL PUBLICATIONS.

A 20.3:nos.
BULLETINS.

A 20.4:nos.
CIRCULARS

OFFICE OF COMMUNICATIONS
(1987–   )

CREATION AND AUTHORITY

The Office of Communication was combined with the Office of Congressional and Public Affairs and the Office of Intergovernmental Affairs in 1978 to form the Office of Governmental and Public Affairs (A 107).

INFORMATION

Office o f Communications
USDA
Whitten Bldg. Rm. 220-A
Washington, D.C. 20250-1301
(202) 720-4623
Fax: (202) 720-5043
http://www.usda.gov/agencies/ocpage.htm

A 21.1:date   • Item 89
ANNUAL REPORTS.

A 21.2:CT   • Item 90
GENERAL PUBLICATIONS.

A 21.3:nos.
BULLETINS. 1– 10. 1896– 1913.

A 21.4:nos.
CIRCULARS. 1– 19. 1901– 1912.

A 21.5:ed.nos.
LIST OF BULLETINS AND CIRCULARS ISSUED BY DEPARTMENT OF AGRICULTURE FOR DISTRIBUTION. 1st– 14th ed. 1897– 1906.

A 21.6/1:date
MONTHLY LIST OF PUBLICATIONS (of Department of Agriculture). 1892– 1924.

A 21.6/2:date
MONTHLY LIST OF PUBLICATIONS (of Department of Agriculture) FOR FOREIGN DISTRIBUTION. 1904– 1910.

A 21.6/3:nos.
NEW PUBLICATIONS. 1– 63. 1924– 1929.

A 21.6/4:date
PUBLICATIONS OF DEPARTMENT OF AGRICULTURE AVAILABLE FOR DISTRIBUTION.

A 21.6/5   • Item 92
BIMONTHLY LIST OF PUBLICATIONS AND VISUALS. 1896–   [Bimonthly]

A four-page listing of Department series publications. Includes recent motion pictures.
Formerly Bimonthly List of Publications and Motion Pictures prior to July-August 1973 issue.
ISSN 0092-5896
Later A 107.10

A 21.6/6:date
WEEKLY SUMMARY.
See also A 107.17

A 21.7:CT.
PRESS NOTICES.

A 21.7/2:nos.
NEWS, DAILY SUMMARY. [Daily]
Earlier A 1.133/2

A 21.7/3:nos.
NEWS, FEATURE. [Irregular]

Earlier A 1.133/3

A 21.7/4:nos.
NEWS. [Irregular]
Earlier A 1.133.

A 21.8:ed.no
PRICE LIST OF PUBLICATIONS OF DEPARTMENT OF AGRICULTURE FOR SALE BY SUPERINTENDENT OF DOCUMENTS. 1st– 13th ed. 1896– 1906.

A 21.9/1:date
FARMERS' BULLETINS (Available for Distribution). 1896– 1923.

A 21.9/2:date
FARMERS' BULLETINS OF INTEREST TO PERSONS RESIDING IN CITIES OR TOWNS. 1910– 1922.

A 21.9/3:date
FARMERS' BULLETINS (Complete List).

A 21.9/4:date
FARMERS' BULLETINS (Subject List).

A 21.9/5:v.nos.
FARMERS' BULLETINS (Indexes).

A 21.9/6:date
SUBJECT LIST OF FARMERS' BULLETINS (Front Space).

A 21.9/7:date
FARMERS' BULLETINS (Subject List) (Back Space).

A 21.9/8:nos.   • Item 91
LIST (series). 1–   [Irregular]

Later A 107.12
The following lists are revised from time-to-time:

A 21.9/8:1
LIST OF PUBLICATIONS AVAILABLE FOR DISTRIBUTION BY MEMBERS OF CONGRESS. [Semiannual]

Lists the Departmental series which are available for distribution by Members of Congress and in stock as of January 1 and July 1. Arranged by subject.

A 21.9/8:5   • Item 91
POPULAR PUBLICATIONS FOR FARMER, SUBURBANITE, HOMEMAKER, CONSUMER. 1944. [Irregular]
Later A 107.12:5

A 21.9/8:11   • Item 91
LIST OF AVAILABLE PUBLICATIONS OF THE UNITED STATES DEPARTMENT OF AGRICULTURE. 1929–   [Annual]
Later A 107.12:11

A 21.9/9:date
LIST OF AVAILABLE FARMERS BULLETINS AND LEAFLETS.

®eLIST OF PUBLICATIONS (general). 1913– 1921.

A 21.11:CT
MAPS.

A 21.12:date
INDEXES TO YEARBOOKS OF DEPARTMENT OF AGRICULTURE.
Earlier A 21.3:7, 9, 10

A 21.13:nos.
LIVESTOCK SHORT COURSE.

A 21.13/1:nos.
RADIO SERVICE, LIVESTOCK SHORT COURSE. 1– 8. 1926– 1927.

A 21.13/2:nos.
RADIO SERVICE, DAIRY SHORT COURSE. 1– 8. 1926– 1927.

A 21.13/3:nos.
RADIO SERVICE, POULTRY SHORT COURSE. 1– 8. 1926– 1927.

A 21.13/4:nos.
RADIO SERVICE, FARM ECONOMIC SERIES. 1– 3. 1927– 1928.

A 21.13/5:CT
RADIO RECORDS.

A 21.13/6:date
RADIO SERVICE, CONSUMER FACTS. [Weekly]

A 21.13/7:date
RADIO SERVICE, FARM FLASHES.

A 21.13/8:date
RADIO SERVICE, HOUSEKEEPERS' CHATS. [Daily]

A 21.13/9:nos.
RADIO SERVICE, AGRICULTURE IN DEFENSE. 1– 12. 1940.

A 21.14:vol.nos.
DAILY DIGEST. v. 1– v. 84, no. 24. 1927– 1942.

A 21.15:nos.
CLIP SHEETS. [Weekly]

A 21.16:CT
NATIONAL FARM DATA PROGRAM, 1932– 40 (by
States).

A 21.17:nos.
FOOD FOR FREEDOM PROGRAM, BACKGROUND
INFORMATION SERIES.

A 21.18:nos.
FOOD INFORMATION SERIES. 1– 102. 1943– 1945.

A 21.19:nos.
FOOD FIGHTS FOR FREEDOM ROUND-UP. 1– 18.
1944. [Weekly]

A 21.20:CT
POSTERS.

A 21.21:dt.&nos.
FARM MOBILIZATION FACT SHEETS. 1– 15. 1952.

A 21.22:
HOMEMAKER NEWS.

A 21.23
RELEASES.

A 21.24:CT
ADDRESSES.

A 21.24/2:date   • Item 13-K (MF)
SELECTED SPEECHES AND NEWS RELEASES.
[Weekly]
          Earlier A 1.134

A 21.25:nos.
RURAL DEVELOPMENT PROGRAM NEWS. [Irregu-
lar]
          Replaced by A 21.15/3

A 21.25/2:nos.
RURAL RESOURCE LEAFLETS.
          Cancelled by Y 3.R 88/2:8/nos.

A 21.25/3
RURAL AREAS DEVELOPMENT NEWSLETTER. 1–
119. [Monthly]

          PURPOSE:– To encourage rural development
by informing interested people and groups, such
as local civic leaders, about what is being done
to improve rural areas. It reports on conservation
and recreation projects, construction of rural community sewage and water systems, the efforts of
small communities to attract industry to their town
and other activities to develop rural areas. It also
reports on local vocational retraining programs,
adult education classes and attempts of rural
people to add to their income by such projects as
vacation farms or other recreational facilities.
          Supersedes Rural Development Program
News (A 21.15 and Y 3.R 88/2:9).

A 21.26:nos.
PICTURE STORY (series).
          Changed to A 1.100

A 21.27:nos.
CONSUMER INFORMATION TV PROGRAM PACK-
AGES, SUGGESTED SCRIPTS.

A 21.28:CT   • Item 90-A
HANDBOOKS, MANUALS, GUIDES.

A 21.29
SERVICE, USDA'S REPORT TO CONSUMERS. 1–
1963–   [Monthly]
          ISSN 0037-2544
          Later A 107.11

A 21.30:nos.
RESPONSE, REPORT ON ACTIONS FOR A BETTER
ENVIRONMENT. 1– 1971–   [Irregular]

          PURPOSE:– To present information on the
Department's many areas of action to remedy
environmental problems, showing how department
programs protect and improve the environment
through research, forestry, conservation, and a
wide range of rural and community services.

A 21.31:date
CATALYST FOR RURAL DEVELOPMENT. 1–   Feb.
1972– Jan. 1973. [Bimonthly]

A 21.32:nos.
FPL [Farm Paper Letter].1– 1942–   [Weekly]
(farm press only)
          ISSN 0364-0922
          Later A 107.13

A 21.33:date
FOOD AND HOME NOTES. 1943–   [Weekly] (Press
Division)
          PURPOSE:– To provide the mass media with
pertinent information on food, fiber, and housing
information. In addition to the mass media, this
publication is also directed to nutritionists, home
economists, and educators.
          ISSN 0090-9688

A 21.34:letters-nos.   • Item 90-E-1 (EL)
FARM BROADCASTERS LETTERS. [Weekly]

A 21.36:v.nos.&nos.   • Item 90-D-1
INSIDE INFORMATION.
          See also A 107.15
          Discontinued.

A 21.37   • Item 91
LISTS OF AVAILABLE PUBLICATIONS OF THE U.S.
DEPARTMENT OF AGRICULTURE.
          Discontinued.

BUREAU OF PUBLIC ROADS
(1918– 1939)

CREATION AND AUTHORITY

          The Bureau of Public Roads traces its history
to the Office of Road Inquiry, which was established within the Department of Agriculture on
October 3 1893, under authority of the Agricultural Appropriation Act for fiscal 1894. By Reorganization Plan No. 1 of 1939, effective July 1,
1939, the Bureau was transferred to the Federal
Works Agency as the Public Roads Administration (FW 2).

A 22.1:date
ANNUAL REPORTS.
          Later FW 2.1

A 22.2:CT
GENERAL PUBLICATIONS.
          Later FW 2.2

A 22.3:nos.
BULLETINS.

A 22.4:nos.
CIRCULARS.

A 22.5:date
PUBLICATIONS.

A 22.6:v.nos.
PUBLIC ROADS. [Monthly]
          Later FW 2.7

A 22.7:CT
SPECIFICATIONS.

A 22.7/a:CT
          – SEPARATES.

A 22.8:CT
HIGHWAY TRANSPORTATION SURVEYS (by States).

A 22.9:CT
MAPS AND ATLASES.
          Later FW 2.12

A 22.9/2:CT
TRANSPORTATION MAPS.
          Later FW 2.13

A 22.10:vol.
HIGHWAYS, CURRENT LITERATURE. [Weekly]
          Later FW 2.8

A 22.11:CT
ADDRESSES.

A 22.12:nos.
PLANNING SURVEY MEMORANDUM.
          Later FW 2.9

A 22.13:nos.
STATE-WIDE HIGHWAY PLANNING SURVEYS.
          New Bulletins for Bureau Managers.
          Later FW 2.10

A 22.14:nos.
INFORMATION SERIES.
          Later A 53.10

A 22.15:CT
ADDRESSES.

SEED AND PLANT
INTRODUCTION SECTION
(1898– 1901)

CREATION AND AUTHORITY

          The Seed and Plant Introduction Section was
established within the Department of Agriculture
in 1898. The Section was consolidated along with
certain other agencies to form the Bureau of Plant
Industry (A 19), effective July 1, 1901.

A 23.1:date
ANNUAL REPORTS.

A 23.2:CT
GENERAL PUBLICATIONS.

A 23.3:nos.
BULLETINS.

A 23.4:nos.
CIRCULARS.

DIVISION OF SEEDS
(1868– 1901)

CREATION AND AUTHORITY

          The Division of Seeds, later known as the
Division of Congressional Seed Distribution, was
established in 1868. The Division was consolidated along with certain other agencies to form
the Bureau of Plant Industry (A 19), effective
July 1, 1901.

A 24.1:date
ANNUAL REPORTS.

A 24.2:CT
GENERAL PUBLICATIONS [none issued].

A 24.3:nos.
BULLETINS [none issued].

A 24.4:nos.
CIRCULARS [none issued].

A 24.5:date
REPORTS OF SPECIAL AGENT FOR PURCHASE AND
DISTRIBUTION OF SEEDS.

SILK SECTION
(1889– 1891)

A 25.1:date
ANNUAL REPORTS.

A 25.2:CT
GENERAL PUBLICATIONS [none issued].

A 25.3:nos.
BULLETINS.

A 25.4:nos.
CIRCULARS [none issued].

BUREAU OF SOILS
(1901– 1927)

CREATION AND AUTHORITY

The Division of Agricultural Soils was established within the Department of Agriculture by
order of the Secretary of Agriculture, dated February 15, 1894. By an appropriation act, approved
March 2, 1895, the Division became independent
of the Weather Bureau, under which agency it
had been functioning. In 1897, it became the
Division of Soils and effective July 1, 1901, it
became the Bureau of Soils. The Agricultural Appropriations Act of 1928, effective July 1, 1927,
merged the Bureau with the Bureau of Chemistry
(A 7) to form the Bureau of Chemistry and Soils
(A 47)

A 26.1:date
ANNUAL REPORTS.

A 26.2:CT
GENERAL PUBLICATIONS.

A 26.3:nos.
BULLETINS.

A 26.4:nos.
CIRCULARS.

A 26.5:date
FIELD OPERATIONS OF BUREAU OF SOILS.
    Later A 47.5

A 26.5/a:CT
SOIL SURVEYS.
    Later A 47.5

A 26.6/1:date
LISTS OF PUBLICATIONS.

A 26.6/2:date
CLASSIFIED LIST OF PUBLICATIONS.

A 26.7:nos.
SERVICE AND REGULATORY ANNOUNCEMENTS.

BUREAU OF CROP ESTIMATES
(1914– 1922)

CREATION AND AUTHORITY

The Division of Statistics was established
within the Department of Agriculture in 1863. On
July 1, 1903, it became the Bureau of Statistics.

By act of Congress, approved June 30, 1914, the
Bureau was reorganized as the Bureau of Crop
Estimates, which in turn merged with the Bureau
of Markets to form the Bureau of Markets and
Crop Estimates (A 36) in 1921.

A 27.1:date
ANNUAL REPORTS.

A 27.2:CT
GENERAL PUBLICATIONS.

A 27.3:nos.
BULLETINS.

A 27.4:nos.
CIRCULARS.

A 27.5:date
CROP CIRCULARS.

A 27.6:vol.
CROP REPORTER. [Monthly]

A 27.6/2:vol.
MONTHLY CROP REPORTS.
    Later A 36.10

A 27.7:date
MONTHLY CROP SYNOPSIS.

A 27.8:nos.
MISCELLANEOUS SERIES, BULLETIN.

A 27.9:vol.
STATISTICAL REPORTS.

A 27.10:CT
MAPS OF STATES.

A 27.11:nos.
FOREIGN CROP AND LIVESTOCK REPORTS. [Semi-
monthly]
    Later A 36.19

DIVISION OF VEGETABLE
PHYSIOLOGY AND PATHOLOGY
(1895– 1901)

CREATION AND AUTHORITY

The Mycological Section was established
within the Division of Botany (A 6) of the Department of Agriculture in 1886. This Section was
known as the Section of Vegetable Pathology
from 1887 until 1890, when it became an independent Division of Vegetable Pathology within the
Department by act of Congress, approved July
14, 1890 (26 Stat. 283). On March 2, 1895, the
name was changed to Division of Vegetable Physiology and Pathology. The Division was consolidated along with certain other agencies to form
the Bureau of Plant Industry (A 19) on July 1,
1901.

A 28.1:date
ANNUAL REPORTS.

A 28.2:CT
GENERAL PUBLICATIONS.

A 28.3:nos.
BULLETINS.

A 28.4:nos.
CIRCULARS.

A 28.5:v.nos.
JOURNAL OF MYCOLOGY.

WEATHER BUREAU
(1890– 1940)

CREATION AND AUTHORITY

The Weather Bureau was established within
the Department of Agriculture under act of Congress, approved October 1, 1890 (26 Stat. 653).
Reorganization Plan No. 4 of 1940, effective June
30, 1940, transferred the Bureau to the Department of Commerce (C 30).

A 29.1:date
ANNUAL REPORTS.
    Later C 30.1

A 29.2:CT
GENERAL PUBLICATIONS.
    Later A 30.2

A 29.3:nos.
BULLETINS.

A 29.4:nos.
CIRCULARS.

A 29.5:letters
BULLETINS.

A 29.5/a:CT
– SEPARATES.
    Later C 30.3/2

A 29.6:vol.
MONTHLY WEATHER REVIEW.
    Later C 30.14

A 29.6/a 1:dist.no. date & no.
CLIMATOLOGICAL SERVICE OF BUREAU, DIST.
NO.

A 29.6/2:nos.
– SUPPLEMENTS.

A 29.7:dt. & nos.
NATIONAL WEATHER BULLETIN.

A 29.7/2:date
WEEKLY WEATHER AND CROP BULLETIN.
    Later C 30.11

A 29.8:vol.
CLIMATE AND HEALTH.

A 29.9:nos.
COLD WAVE BULLETIN.

A 29.10:pt.nos.
DAILY RIVERS STAGES.
    Begins with part 4. Pt. 1-3, see W 42.19.
    Later C 30.24

A 29.11:letter
INSTRUMENT ROOM [or division] CIRCULARS.
    Later C 30.4

A 29.12:CT
INSTRUCTIONS.
    Later C 30.6

A 29.13:date
METEOROLOGICAL CHART OF GREAT LAKES.

A 29.13/2:date
METEOROLOGICAL CHART OF GREAT LAKES [2nd
series 1911– 13].

A 29.14:date
MONTHLY REPORT OF RIVER AND FLOOD SERVICE.

A 29.15:nos.
SANITARY CLIMATOLOGY CIRCULARS.

A 29.16:date
SNOW AND ICE BULLETIN.

A 29.17:date
STORM BULLETIN.

A 29.18:date
DAILY WEATHER MAP.
      Later C 30.12

A 29.19:date
SPECIAL RIVER BULLETINS.

A 29.20:nos.
COTTON REGION WEATHER CROP BULLETIN.

A 29.21:v.nos.
BULLETIN OF MOUNTAIN WEATHER OBSERVATORY.

A 29.22:CT
SPECIFICATIONS.

A 29.23:date
METEOROLOGICAL CHART OF NORTH ATLANTIC
      OCEAN. [Monthly]

A 29.25:date
METEOROLOGICAL CHART OF SOUTH ATLANTIC
      OCEAN. [Monthly]

A 29.26:date
METEOROLOGICAL CHART OF SOUTH PACIFIC
      OCEAN. [Monthly]
      Later C 30.20

A 29.27:date
METEOROLOGICAL CHART OF INDIAN OCEAN.
      [Monthly]

A 29.28:date
ROSTER OF COMMISSIONED OFFICERS AND
      EMPLOYEES.

A 29.29:vol.
CLIMATOLOGICAL DATA (by section).
      Later C 30.18

A 29.29/2:vol.
CLIMATOLOGICAL DATA BY SECTIONS. [Monthly]

A 29.30:date
MONTHLY METEOROLOGICAL SUMMARY.

A 29.30/2:date
      –WASHINGTON, D.C.
      Later C 30.10

A 29.30/3:date
      –HONOLULU, HAWAII.
      Later C 30.17

A 29.30/4:date
      – ERIE, PA.
      Later C 30.17

A 29.30/5:date
      –FT. WORTH, TEXAS.
      Later C 30.17

A 29.30/6:date
      – MIAMI, FLORIDA.
      Later C 30.17

A 29.30/7:date
      – HATTERAS, NORTH CAROLINA.
      Later C 30.17

A 29.30/8:date
      –CHARLOTTE, NORTH CAROLINA.
      Later C 30.17

A 29.30/9:date
      – MILES CITY, MONTANA.
      Later C 30.17

A 29.30/10:date
      – OSWEGO, NEW YORK.
      Later C 30.17

A 29.30/11:date
      – WALLA WALLA, WASHINGTON.
      Later C 30.17

A 29.30/12:date
      –DUBUQUE, IOWA.
      Later C 30.17

A 29.30/13:date
      – LANDER, WYOMING.

A 29.30/14:date
      – PORT ARTHUR, TEXAS.

A 29.30/15:date
      – PUEBLO, COLORADO.

A 29.30/16:date
      – EL PASO, TEXAS.

A 39.30/17:date
      –ALBUQUERQUE, N. MEXICO.

A 29.30/18:date
      – ASHEVILLE, NORTH CAROLINA.

A 29.30/19:date
      – BAKER, OREGON.

A 29.30/20:date
      – ESCAMBIA, MICHIGAN.

A 29.30/21:date
      – ROSEBURG, OREGON.

A 29.30/22:date
      – MOBILE, ALABAMA.

A 29.30/23:date
      – CORPUS CHRISTI, TEXAS.

A 29.30/24:date
      – GREEN BAY, WISCONSIN.

A 29.30/25:date
      – RAPID CITY, SOUTH DAKOTA.

A 29.30/26:date
      –GREENSBORO, NORTH CAROLINA.

A 29.30/27:date
      – LYNCHBURG, VIRGINIA.

A 29.30/28:date
      – BROWNSVILLE, TEXAS.

A 29.30/29:date
      – PORTLAND, MAINE.

A 29.30/30:date
      – TATOOSH ISLAND, WASHINGTON.

A 29.30/31:date
      – SEATTLE, WASHINGTON.

A 29.30/32:date
      – PALESTINE, TEXAS.

A 29.30/33:date
      – KALISPELL, MONTANA.

A 29.30/34:date
      – EDFORD, OREGON.

A 29.30/35:date
      –YAKIMA, WASHINGTON.

A 29.30/36:date
      – CONCORD, NEW HAMPSHIRE.

A 29.30/37:date
      – CHATTANOOGA, TENNESSEE.

A 29.30/38:date
      – CAPE HENRY, VIRGINIA.

A 29.31:date
PUBLICATIONS OF WEATHER BUREAU AVAIL-
      ABLE FOR DISTRIBUTION.

A 29.31/2:CT
LIST OF PUBLICATIONS (miscellaneous).

A 29.31/3:date
      PRICE LIST OF PUBLICATIONS.
      Later C 30.17

A 29.32:date
      NEW ENGLAND HIGHWAY WEATHER BULLETIN.

A 29.33:date
CLIMATOLOGICAL DATA, ALASKA SECTION.
      Later C 30.21

A 29.34:date
CLIMATOLOGICAL DATA, HAWAII SECTION.
      Later C 30.19

A 29.35:date
CLIMATOLOGICAL DATA, PORTO RICO SECTION.

      Superseded by Climatological Data, West
Indies and Caribbean Service, (A 29.36).

A 29.36:date
CLIMATOLOGICAL DATA, WEST INDIES AND
      CARIBBEAN SERVICE.
      Later C 30.20

A 29.37:nos.
FORECAST DIVISION CIRCULARS.

      Also to include publications classified as A
29.32/2 which was cancelled.
      Later C 20.23.

A 29.38:date
WEATHER OUTLOOK. [Weekly]
      Later C 30.13

A 29.39:dt.&nos.
WEEKLY COTTON REGION BULLETINS. [Weekly
      during cotton season]
      Later C 30.13

A 29.40:v.nos.
MONTHLY BULLETINS OF HAWAIIAN VOLCANO
      OBSERVATORY.
      Later I 19.28

A 29.41:date
MARINE CALENDAR, ATLANTIC.

A 29.42:date
MARINE CALENDAR, PACIFIC.

A 29.43:date
WEEKLY CORN AND WHEAT REGION BULLETIN.
      Later C 30.7

A 29.43/2:date
WEEKLY CORN AND WHEAT REGION BULLETIN.
      [Daily except Sundays and Holidays during crop
      season]
      Later C 30.8

A 29.44:nos.
CLIMATIC CHARTS FOR U.S.

A 29.45:date
UNITED STATES METEOROLOGICAL YEARBOOK.

      Formerly issued as part of A 29.1
      Later C 30.25

A 29.46:CT
ADDRESSES.

APPOINTMENT CLERK
(1896–1916)

A 30.1:date
ANNUAL REPORTS.

A 30.2:CT
GENERAL PUBLICATIONS [none issued].

A 30.3:nos.
BULLETINS [none issued].

A 30.4:nos.
CIRCULARS [none issued]

CHIEF CLERK
(1898– 1925)

A 31.1:date
ANNUAL REPORTS.

A 31.2:CT
GENERAL PUBLICATIONS.

A 31.3:nos.
BULLETINS [none issued].

A 31.4:nos.
CIRCULARS [none issued].

BOARD OF FOOD AND DRUG
INSPECTION
(1907– 1914)

CREATION AND AUTHORITY

The Board of Food and Drug Inspection was established within the Department of Agriculture in May 1907, pursuant to order of Secretary of Agriculture dated April 25, 1907. The Board was terminated on February 1, 1914, and its functions transferred to the Bureau of Chemistry (A 7), and the Office of the Solicitor of the Department of Agriculture (A 33).

A 32.1:date
ANNUAL REPORTS.

A 32.2:CT
GENERAL PUBLICATIONS.

A 32.3:nos.
BULLETINS [none issued].

A 32.4:nos.
CIRCULARS [none issued].

A 32.5:nos.
FOOD INSPECTION DECISIONS.

A 32.6:nos.
NOTICES OF JUDGMENT, FOOD AND DRUG ACT.

GENERAL COUNSEL
(1955–   )

INFORMATION

General Counsel
Department of Agriculture
107 Jamie L. Whitten Federal Bldg.
1400 Independence Avenue, SW
Washington, D.C. 20250
(202) 720-3351
Fax: (202) 720-8666

A 33.1:date • Item 123
ANNUAL REPORTS.

Discontinued.

A 33.2:CT • Item 124
GENERAL PUBLICATIONS.

Discontinued.

A 33.3:nos.
BULLETINS.

A 33.4:nos.
CIRCULARS. 1–   908–

A 33.5:CT
PAPERS IN RE.

A 33.6:CT
REGULATIONS, RULES, AND INSTRUCTIONS.

A 33.7:date • Item 125
LAWS.
Changed from A 33.2:L 44

INSECTICIDE AND FUNGICIDE
BOARD
(1910– 1927)

CREATION AND AUTHORITY

The Insecticide and Fungicide Board was established within the Department of Agriculture by General Order 143, dated December 22, 1910. The Board was abolished and its functions transferred to the Food, Drug, and Insecticide Administration (A 46) on June 30, 1927.

A 34.1:date
ANNUAL REPORTS.

A 34.2:CT
GENERAL PUBLICATIONS.

A 34.3:nos.
BULLETINS.

A 34.4:nos.
CIRCULARS.

A 34.5:nos.
INSECTICIDE DECISIONS.

A 34.6:nos.
SERVICE AND REGULATORY ANNOUNCEMENTS.
Includes Notices of Judgment.
Earlier A 1.18
Later A 46.7

FEDERAL HORTICULTURE
BOARD
(1912– 1928)

CREATION AND AUTHORITY

The Federal Horticultural Board was established within the Department of Agriculture on August 21, 1912, pursuant to the Plant Quarantine Act, approved August 20, 1912. The Board was superseded in 1928 by the Plant Quarantine and Control Administration (A 48).

A 35.1:date
ANNUAL REPORTS.
Later A 56.1

A 35.2:CT
GENERAL PUBLICATIONS.
Later A 56.2

A 35.3:nos.
BULLETINS.

A 35.4:nos.
CIRCULARS.

A 35.5:nos.
NOTICES OF QUARANTINE.
Later A 48.5

A 35.6:nos.
PLANT QUARANTINE DECISIONS.

A 35.7:date
CIRCULAR OF INFORMATION
Later A 48.11

A 35.8:CT
REGULATIONS, PLANT.
Later A 56.6

A 35.9:nos.
SERVICE AND REGULATORY ANNOUNCEMENTS.
Later A 48.7

A 35.10:nos.
ANNUAL LETTER OF INFORMATION.
Later published as a supplement or addition to Service and Regulatory Announcements.

BUREAU OF AGRICULTURAL
ECONOMICS
(1922– 1953)

CREATION AND AUTHORITY

The Bureau of Agricultural Economics was established within the Department of Agriculture on July 1, 1922, pursuant to the Agricultural Appropriation Act of 1923, approved May 11, 1922, consolidating the Bureau of Markets and Crop Estimates and the Office of Farm Management and Farm Economics (A 37). The Bureau was abolished by Departmental Memorandum 1320, Supplement 4, dated November 2, 1953, transferring its functions to the Agricultural Marketing Service (A 88) and Agricultural Research Service (A 77).

A 36.1:date • Item 20
ANNUAL REPORTS.

Discontinued.

A 36.2:CT • Item 22
GENERAL PUBLICATIONS.

Discontinued.

A 36.3
BULLETINS.

A 36.4
CIRCULARS.

A 36.5:nos.
SERVICE AND REGULATORY ANNOUNCEMENTS.
Later A 66.27

A 36.6:vol.
SEED REPORTER.
Later Superseded by A 36.9

A 36.7:vol.
FOOD SURVEYS.
Superseded by A 36.9

A 36.8:nos.
REPORTS ON FOREIGN MARKETS FOR AGRICULTURAL PRODUCTS.

A 36.9:vol
MARKET REPORTER.

Supersedes the Seed Reporter (A 36.6) and Food Surveys (A 36.7).

A 36.10:vol.
MONTHLY CROP REPORTER.
Earlier A 27.6/2

A 36.11:vol.
WEATHER, CROPS, AND MARKETS. [Weekly]

A 36.11/2:vol.
CROPS AND MARKETS. [Monthly]
Later A 1.52, A 88.24/3

A 36.11/3:vol.
CROPS AND MARKETS. [Monthly]

A 36.12:v.nos.
AGRICULTURAL COOPERATION. [Fortnightly]
Later FF 1.12

A 36.13:nos.
AGRICULTURAL ECONOMICS BIBLIOGRAPHIES.

A 36.14:vol.
FOREIGN CROPS AND MARKETS. [Weekly]
Later A 64.8

A 36.15:vol.
AGRICULTURAL SITUATION. [Monthly]
Later A 88.8

A 36.15/2:v.nos.
– SPECIAL EDITION FOR CROP AND PRICE REPORTERS. [Monthly]
Earlier A 36.15/a

A 36.16:vol
B.A.E. NEWS. [Weekly]
A 36.17:nos.
– LIBRARY SUPPLEMENTS. [Monthly]
Superseded by A 36.20

A 36.18:CT
CHARTS.

A 36.19:nos.
FOREIGN CROP AND LIVESTOCK REPORTS. [Semi-monthly]
Earlier A 27.11
Later A 36.14

A 36.20:v.nos.
AGRICULTURAL ECONOMICS LITERATURE. [Monthly]
Supersedes BAE News, Library Supplements (A 36.17).
Later A 17.10

A 36.21:v.nos.
STATE AND FEDERAL MARKETING ACTIVITIES AND OTHER ECONOMIC WORK. [Weekly]
Later A 66.14

A 36.22:CT
POSTERS.
Later A 66.21

A 36.23:vol.
FARM POPULATION AND RURAL LIFE ACTIVITIES. [Quarterly]

A 36.24:nos.
EGG STANDARDIZATION LEAFLETS.

A 36.25:CT
HANDBOOKS, MANUALS, GUIDES.
Changed from A 36.2

A 36.25/2:CT
REGULATIONS, RULES, AND INSTRUCTIONS.
Includes Handbooks and Manuals.

A 36.26:date
CROP AND MARKET NEWS RADIO BROADCAST SCHEDULES.

A 36.27/1:date
COTTON GRADE AND STAPLE REPORTS. GEORGIA. [Monthly during the height of the growing season].

A 36.27/2:date
COTTON GRADE AND STAPLE REPORTS, TEXAS AND OKLAHOMA. [Monthly during the height of the ginning season]

A 36.28:date
PRICE SITUATION. [Monthly]
Later Demand and Price Situation.
Later A 88.9

A 36.29:date
MIMEOGRAPHED MATERIAL: CROP REPORTS.
See A 66.11
Later A 88.24

A 36.29/2:date
MILK PRODUCTION. [Monthly]

A 36.29/3:date
FRUIT. [Monthly]

A 36.29/4
SUGAR PRODUCTION CROP REPORT AS OF [date].

A 36.29/5
TOBACCO, CROP REPORT AS OF [date].

A 36.30:date
MIMEOGRAPHED MATERIAL: COTTON REPORTS.
Later A 66.9

A 36.31:date
MIMEOGRAPHED MATERIAL: ESTIMATES OF COTTON CROPS. REVISED.

A 36.32:date
FRUIT CROP PROSPECTS. (includes nut crops)
Later A 66.39

A 36.33:date
LIVESTOCK REPORTS.
Later A 66.42

A 36.34:date
POTATO AND SWEET POTATO CROP PROSPECTS.

A 36.35:CT
UNITED STATES STANDARDS FOR FRUITS AND VEGETABLES.
Later A 66.16

A 36.35/2:CT
UNITED STATES STANDARDS.
Later A 66.16
A 36.36:nos.
WORLD WOOL SITUATION.

A 36.37:CT
OUTLINE MAPS.

A 36.37/2:CT
MAPS (miscellaneous).

A 36.38:date
PLANTING INTENTIONS.
Later A 66.33, A 88.24/4

A 36.39:nos.
FOREIGN SERVICE REPORTS.
Later A 67.11

A 36.40:nos.
WORLD COTTON PROSPECTS. [Monthly]

A 36.40/2:nos.
COTTON SITUATION. [Monthly]
Later A 88.11/8

A 36.41:nos.
WORLD DAIRY PROSPECTS. [Monthly]

A 36.42:nos.
WORLD FLAXSEED PROSPECTS. [Monthly]

A 36.43:nos.
WORLD HOG AND PORK PROSPECTS. [Monthly]

A 36.44:nos.
WORLD WHEAT PROSPECTS. [Monthly]

A 36.45:nos.
FOREIGN NEWS ON TOBACCO.

A 36.46:nos.
FOREIGN NEWS ON VEGETABLES.
Later A 64.13

A 36.47:nos.
WORLD DRY BEAN PROSPECTS.

A 36.48:CT
MARKET NEWS SERVICE ON FRUITS AND VEGETABLES.

A 36.49:CT
PAPERS IN RE.

A 36.50:CT   • Item 18-B
OUTLINE CHARTS.

Discontinued.

A 36.51:CT
ADDRESSES.

A 36.52:CT
ESTIMATED NUMBERS OF APPLE TREES BY VARIETIES AND AGES IN COMMERCIAL AND FARM ORCHARDS (slightly varying title).

A 36.53:nos.
FOLDERS; GRAIN STANDARDS.

A 36.54:date
DAIRY AND POULTRY MARKET STATISTICS ANNUAL SUMMARIES.
Later A 66.35

A 36.55:date
STATE AGRICULTURAL AND MARKETING OFFICERS.
Later A 66.45

A 36.56:nos.
SMUTTY WHEAT REPORTS.
Later A 66.30

A 36.57:date
DIRECTORY OF TEACHERS GIVING COURSES IN RURAL SOCIOLOGY AND RURAL LIFE.

A 36.58:date
AGRICULTURAL ECONOMIC REPORTS AND SERVICES.

Later A 66.19

A 36.59:date
CHECK LIST OF STANDARDS FOR FARM PRODUCTS.
Later A 66.26

A 36.60:date
LIST OF MANUFACTURERS AND JOBBERS OF FRUIT AND VEGETABLE CONTAINERS.

A 36.61:date
PRODUCTION AND CARRY OVER OF FRUIT AND VEGETABLE CONTAINERS.

A 36.62:CT
BIBLIOGRAPHIES.

A 36.63:CT
FARM REAL ESTATE TAXES.
Later A 77.15, A 83.9/6

A 36.64:nos.
UTILIZATION OF AMERICAN COTTON STUDIES.

A 36.65:date
DAIRY SITUATION. [Monthly]
Later A 88.14/4

A 36.66:date
WEEKLY EUROPEAN CITRUS FRUIT MARKET CABLE.
Later A 64.12

A 36.67:date
WEEKLY EUROPEAN FRUIT MARKET CABLE.
Later A 64.13

A 36.68:date
CASH INCOME FROM FARM MARKETINGS. [Monthly]

A 36.69:date
EMPLOYMENT ON FARMS OF CROP REPORTERS.
[Monthly]
    Later A 66.10

A 36.70:CT   •Item 22-A
LIST OF PUBLICATIONS.
    Changed from A 36.Z/2

    Discontinued.

A 36.70/2:date
CHECK LIST OF PRINTED AND PROCESSED PUBLI-
    CATIONS. [Monthly]
    Superseded by A 88.33

A 36.71:date
DAIRY OUTLOOK. [Annual]

A 36.72:date
POULTRY AND EGG OUTLOOK. [Annual]

A 36.73:date
COTTON MARKET REVIEW. [Weekly]
    Later A 66.8

A 36.74:date
UNITED STATES WINTER WHEAT AND RYE REPORTS.
    [Annual]

    Later A 66.48, A 88.19/11

A 36.75:nos.
PRICES PAID BY FARMERS.

A 36.76:vol.
COTTON LITERATURE, SELECTED REFERENCES.
    [Monthly]
    Later A 1.50

A 36.77:date
FARM WAGE RATES AND RELATED DATA. [Quar-
    terly]
    Later A 66.10

A 36.78:CT
TAX DELINQUENCY OF RURAL REAL ESTATE.

A 36.79:nos.
FOREIGN NEWS ON APPLES.
    Issued by Foreign Agricultural Service.
    Later A 64.9

A 36.80:nos.
FOREIGN NEWS ON CITRUS FRUITS.

A 36.81/1:date
RECEIPTS FROM SALE OF PRINCIPAL FARM PROD-
    UCTS BY STATES. [Monthly]

A 36.81/2:date
MONTHLY RECEIPTS FROM SALE OF PRINCIPAL
    FARM PRODUCTS BY STATES. [Monthly]

A 36.82:date
CAPACITY OF ELEVATORS, REPORTING GRAIN
    STOCKS. [Weekly]

A 36.83:CT
AGRICULTURAL OUTLOOKS (individual).

A 36.84/1:nos.
WORLD FEED GRAIN PROSPECTS.

A 36.84/2:nos.
FEED PROSPECTS.
    Publications designated F-nos.

A 36.85:nos.
HOG SITUATION. [Monthly]

A 36.86:nos.
WHEAT SITUATION. [Monthly]
    Later A 88.18/8

A 36.87:nos.
FEED GRAIN SITUATION. [Monthly]
    Superseded by A 36.117

A 36.88:vol.
FOREIGN AGRICULTURE, REVIEW OF FOREIGN
    FARM POLICY, PRODUCTION, AND TRADE.
    [Monthly]
    Later A 64.7

A 36.89:nos.
WOOL SITUATION. [Monthly]

    After May 1942, Livestock and Wool Situa-
    tion, A 36.141

A 36.90:nos.
BEEF CATTLE SITUATION. [Monthly]

A 36.91:nos.
SHEEP AND LAMB SITUATION. [Monthly]

A 36.92:nos.
CROP REPORTING PROCEDURE.
    Publications designated C.R.P.
    Later A 66.22

A 36.93:nos.
GRAIN INVESTIGATIONS [publications].
    Publications designated U.S.G.S.A.-G.I.

A 36.94:nos.
TOBACCO SITUATION.
    Publications designated TS
    Later A 88.34/2

A 36.95
FRUIT AND VEGETABLE SITUATION.
    Publications designated FVS

A 36.96:nos.
POULTRY AND EGG SITUATION. [Monthly]
    Publications designated PES
    Later A 88.15/3

A 36.97:nos.
FATS AND OILS SITUATION. [Monthly]
    Later A 88.32

A 36.98:vol.
MARKET REVIEWS AND STATISTICAL SUMMARIES
    OF LIVESTOCK, MEATS AND WOOL. [Weekly]
    Later A 66.13

A 36.99:nos.
FRUIT SITUATION.
    Publications designated TFS
    Later A 88.12/7

A 36.100:nos.
VEGETABLE SITUATION. [Monthly]
    Publications designated TVS
    Later A 88.12/8

A 36.101:date
TRUCK CROP ESTIMATE REPORTS.
    Publications designated TC
    Later A 66.17, A 88.12/6

A 36.102:date
POULTRY AND EGG PRODUCTION REPORTS.
    [Monthly]
    Slightly varying titles.

A 36.103:date
LAND POLICY CIRCULARS. [Monthly]
    Supersedes A 61.9

A 36.104:nos.
LAND ECONOMICS REPORTS.
    Supersedes A 61.8

A 36.105:nos.
SEMI-MONTHLY HONEY REPORTS.
    Later A 66.12

A 36.106:nos.
WEEKLY PEANUT REPORTS.
    Later A 66.15

A 36.107:date
COLD STORAGE REPORTS. [Monthly]
    Later A 66.7

A 36.108:CT
LAND USE PROJECTS (by States).

A 36.109:CT
FARM-MORTGAGE RECORDINGS (by States).

A 36.110:date
RESEARCH-REFERENCE ACCESSIONS.
    Earlier A 61.15

A 36.111:vol
AGRICULTURAL FINANCE REVIEW. [Semiannual]
    Later A 77.14

A 36.112:nos.
LAND ECONOMICS DIVISION. BULLETINS.

A 36.113:nos.
ECONOMIC LIBRARY LISTS.

A 36.114:CT
COTTON ESTIMATED ACREAGE, YIELD, AND PRO-
    DUCTION (by States).

A 36.115:date
QUARTERLY FLAX MARKET REVIEW.
    Later A 66.25

A 36.116:nos.
LIVESTOCK SITUATION. [Monthly]

    A consolidation of Beef Cattle Situation (A
    36.90), Hog Situation (A 36.85) and Sheep and
    Lamb Situation (A 36.91). After May 1942 Live-
    stock and Wool Situation (A 36.141) also.

A 36.117:nos.
FEED SITUATION.
    Supersedes A 36.87
    Later A 88.18/12

A 36.118:nos.
FARM MANAGEMENT REPORTS.

A 36.119:CT
WORLD WAR [1914– 18] AND 1939 EUROPEAN WAR
    (by commodities).

A 36.120:nos.
COUNTY PLANNING SERIES.

A 36.121:nos.
LAND ECONOMICS DIVISION, BULLETINS.

A 36.122:nos.
FARM INCOME SITUATION. [Monthly]
    Publications designated FIS-nos.
    Later A 88.9/2

A 36.123:date
FARM POPULATION ESTIMATES. [Annual]
    Changed from A 36.2
    Later A 88.21

A 36.124:date
FARM RETURNS, SUMMARY OF REPORTS OF FARM
    OPERATORS. [Annual]
    Changed from A 36.2

A 36.125:CT
FARM VALUE, GROSS INCOME, AND CASH INCOME
    FROM FARM PRODUCTION.
    Changed from A 36.2

A 36.126:nos.
[DISCUSSION SERIES.]
    Publications designated DS-nos.
    Earlier A 43.13
    Later A 1.66

A 36.127:nos.
EDITORIAL REFERENCE SERIES.

A 36.128:nos.
FLIERS.
    Issued in cooperation with Extension Ser-
    vice.

A 36.129:vol.
AGRICULTURAL SITUATION IN RELATION TO BANK-
    ING. [Quarterly]

A 36.130:nos.
RICE SITUATION.
    Publications designated RS
    Later A 88.18/18

A 36.131:nos.
MIGRATION AND SETTLEMENT ON PACIFIC COAST, REPORTS.

A 36.132:CT
AGRICULTURAL LOANS BY STATES. [Semiannual]

A 36.133:nos.
AGRICULTURAL HISTORY SERIES.

A 36.134:nos.
STATISTICS AND AGRICULTURE.

A 36.135:CT
TRUCK CROP FARMS, ADJUSTMENTS ON (by States).

A 36.136:nos.
RURAL LIFE STUDIES.

A 36.137/1:CT
AGRICULTURAL CENSUS ANALYSES: CHANGES IN LAND IN FARMS BY SIZE OF FARM.

A 36.137/2:CT
AGRICULTURAL CENSUS ANALYSES: CHANGES IN NUMBER OF FARMS BY SIZE OF FARM.

A 36.138:date
FARM-RETAIL PRICE SPREADS. [Monthly]

A 36.139:nos.
DAIRY PRODUCTION. [Monthly]
    Later A 66.44, A 88.14/2

A 36.140:date
FARM LABOR REPORTS. [Monthly]
    Earlier A 66.10
    Later A 88.25

A 36.141:nos.
LIVESTOCK AND WOOL SITUATION.

    Prior to May 1942, see Wool Situation (A 36.89) and Livestock Situation (A 35.116).
    Later A 36.158, A 36.159

A 36.142:nos.
POST-WAR PLANS.

A 36.143:nos.
MARKETING AND TRANSPORTATION SITUATION. [Monthly]
    Publications designated MTS-no.
    Monthly A 88.26/2

A 36.144:CT
RADIO TALKS.

A 36.145:nos.
FARMER AND THE WAR.

A 36.146:nos.
DISCUSSION [leaflets].
    Publications designated D-nos.
    Earlier A 43.9

A 36.147:nos.
NATIONAL FOOD SITUATION.

    Publications designated NFS-nos.
    Earlier A 36.2:F 73/2
    Later A 88.37

A 36.148:CT
WATER FACILITIES AREA PLANS (by States).

A 36.149:CT
WATER UTILIZATION SECTION, LAND ECONOMICS DIVISION, PUBLICATIONS.
    See also A 36.148

A 36.150:nos.
WAR RECORDS PROJECT, REPORTS

A 36.151:nos.
STATISTICAL SUMMARY. [Monthly]
    Later A 88.28

A 36.152:date
FLUID MILK PRICES IN CITY MARKETS. [Monthly]
    Later A 88.14/3

A 36.153:date
EVAPORATED, CONDENSED, AND DRIED MILK REPORTS. [Monthly]
    Later A 88.14

A 36.154:date
HATCHERY PRODUCTION. [Monthly]
    Later A 88.15/5

A 36.155:date
LIQUID, FROZEN AND DRIED EGG PRODUCTION. [Monthly]
    Later A 88.15

A 36.156:nos.
SURVEYS OF WAGE AND WAGE RATES IN AGRICULTURE, REPORTS.

A 36.157:nos.
FARM COST SITUATION.
    Later A 77.14/2

A 36.158:nos.
LIVESTOCK AND MEAT SITUATION. [Monthly]
    Formerly included in A 36.141
    Later A 88.16/8

A 36.159:nos.
WOOL SITUATION. [Quarterly]
    Formerly included in A 36.141
    Later A 88.35

A 36.160:date
AGRICULTURAL OUTLOOK DIGEST. [Monthly]
    Later A 88.8/2

A 36.161:date
STOCKS OF EVAPORATED AND CONDENSED MILK HELD BY WHOLESALE GROCERS. [Quarterly]
    Later A 88.14/5

A 36.162:date
LIVESTOCK SLAUGHTER, BY STATES. [Monthly]
    Later A 88.16/2

A 36.163:date
AGRICULTURAL PRICES. [Monthly]
    Later A 88.9/3

A 36.164:date
PEANUTS, STOCKS AND PROCESSING. [Monthly]
    Later A 88.10/2

A 36.165:date
MILK SUGAR. [Monthly]

A 36.166:date
DRY CASE IN, ESTIMATED PRODUCTION AND STOCKS, UNITED STATES. [Monthly]

A 36.167:v.nos.
AGRICULTURAL ECONOMICS RESEARCH. [Quarterly]

A 36.168:nos.
CURRENT DEVELOPMENTS IN FARM REAL ESTATE MARKET.
    Earlier A 36.2:R 22/8
    Later A 77.13

A 36.169:nos.
HARVARD STUDIES IN MARKETING FARM PRODUCTS.

A 36.170:date
CANNED POULTRY. [Monthly]
    Later A 88.15/2

A 36.171:date
CONSUMER PURCHASES OF SELECTED FRESH FRUITS, CANNED AND FROZEN JUICES, AND DRIED FRUITS. [Monthly]
    Later A 88.12/4

A 36.171/2:date
CONSUMER PURCHASES OF FRUITS AND JUICES BY REGIONS AND RETAIL OUTLETS. [Quarterly]
    Formerly A 36.172
    Later A 88.12/4-2

A 36.172:date
REGIONAL DISTRIBUTION AND TYPES OF STORES WHERE CONSUMERS BUY SELECTED FRESH FRUITS, CANNED AND FROZEN JUICES, AND DRIED FRUITS. [Quarterly]

A 36.173:date
CONSUMER BUYING PRACTICES FOR SELECTED FRESH FRUITS, CANNED AND FROZEN JUICES, AND DRIED FRUITS, RELATED TO FAMILY CHARACTERISTICS, REGION AND CITY SIZE.

A 36.174:date
STOCKS OF FEED GRAINS. [Quarterly]

A 36.174/2:date
STOCKS OF WHEAT AND RYE. [Quarterly]

A 36.175:date
MARKETING MARGINS FOR FLORIDA ORANGES IN 10 MAJOR CITIES. [Monthly during the season]

A 36.176:date
SEED CROPS. [Irregular]
    Later A 88.30

A 36.177
NAVAL STORES REPORT. [Monthly]
    Changed from A 36.2:N 22
    Later A 88.29

A 37.177/2:date
NAVAL STORES REPORT. [Quarterly]
    Changed from A 36.2:N 22

A 36.178
SPECIAL NEWS LETTERS.

A 36.179
AVERAGE SEMI-MONTHLY RETAIL MEAT PRICES AT NEW YORK, CHICAGO AND KANSAS CITY.

A 36.180
DRY MILK REPORTS.

A 36.181:
CATTLE AND CALVES: WEEKLY AVERAGE PRICE PER 100 POUNDS (by localities).

A 36.182:
WAREHOUSES LICENSED UNDER UNITED STATES WAREHOUSE ACT.

A 36.183
SHEEP AND LAMBS: WEEKLY AVERAGE PRICE PER 100 POUNDS (by localities).

A 36.184
FARM PRODUCTS PRICES. [Monthly]

A 36.185
SOUTHERN RICE STOCKS AND MOVEMENT REPORTS.

A 36.186
CALIFORNIA RICE STOCKS AND MOVEMENT REPORTS.

A 36.187
UNLOADS OF TOMATOES IN 66 CITIES BY STATES OF ORIGIN.

A 36.188
SEASON TOBACCO MARKET NEWS REPORTS TYPE 12.

A 36.189
TOBACCO MARKET REVIEWS.

A 36.190
MEAT GRADED BY BUREAU OF AGRICULTURAL ECONOMICS.

A 36.191
SUMMARY OF COLD STORAGE STOCKS.

A 36.192
GRAIN INSPECTOR'S LETTERS.

A 36.193
FRUIT AND VEGETABLE INSPECTION SERVICE, INSPECTOR'S GUIDE.

A 36.194
REPORTS ON HATCHERY SALES IN CALIFORNIA.

A 36.195
EXPORT AND IMPORT REPORTS. [Monthly]

A 36.196
CREAMERY BUTTER AND AMERICAN CHEESE PRO-
DUCTION ESTIMATES.

A 36.197
COLD STORAGE HOLDINGS BY STATES.

A 36.198
ADDRESS LISTS.

A 36.199
ANIMALS SLAUGHTERED UNDER FEDERAL MEAT
INSPECTION IN DISTRICTS REPRESENTED BY
CITIES.

A 36.200
MOHAIR PRODUCTION AND INCOME.

A 36.201
SHIPPING POINT INSPECTION CIRCULARS.

A 36.202
LIVESTOCK MOVEMENT AT 12 MARKETS.

A 36.203
RECEIPTS AND DISPOSITION OF LIVESTOCK AT
PUBLIC STOCKYARDS.

A 36.204
HOGS WEEKLY AVERAGE PRICE PER 100 POUNDS.

A 36.205
HATCHERY REPORTS.

A 36.206
QUALITY OF GRAIN CROPS BASED ON INSPECTED
RECEIPTS AT REPRESENTATIVE MARKETS.

A 36.207
CATTLE, CALVES, AND VEALERS: TOP PRICES AND
BULK OF SALES, CHICAGO.

A 36.208
NEBRASKA WEEKLY WEATHER AND CROP REPORT.

A 36.209
CATTLE ON FEED.

A 36.209/2
CATTLE ON FEED, ILLINOIS, IOWA, NEBRASKA.

A 36.209/3
CATTLE ON FEED, ILLINOIS.

A 36.209/4
CATTLE ON FEED, IOWA. [Quarterly]

A 36.209/5
CATTLE ON FEED, NEBRASKA.

A 36.209/6
CATTLE ON FEED, IDAHO.

A 36.210:v.nos.&nos.
VIRGINIA CROPS AND LIVESTOCK. [Monthly]
Later A 88.31

OFFICE OF FARM MANAGEMENT AND FARM ECONOMICS (1915– 1922)

CREATION AND AUTHORITY

The Office of Farm Management was established within the Bureau of Plant Industry (A 19)
of the Department of Agriculture in 1905. On July
1, 1915, the Office was placed under the Office
of the Secretary of Agriculture. In 1919, the Office was redesignated the Office of Farm Management and Farm Economics. In 1920, it was
made an independent unit within the Department
and on July 1, 1922, the Office merged with the
Bureau of Markets and Crop Estimates (A 36) to
form the Bureau of Agricultural Economics (A
36).

A 37.1:date
ANNUAL REPORTS.

A 37.2:CT
GENERAL PUBLICATIONS.

A 37.3:nos.
BULLETINS.

A 37.4
CIRCULARS.
Changed from A 1.21

A 37.5:CT
MAPS.

A 37.6
DIRECTORY OF AMERICAN AGRICULTURAL ORGA-
NIZATIONS.

FIXED NITROGEN RESEARCH LABORATORY (1921– 1926)

A 38.1:date
ANNUAL REPORTS.

A 38.2:CT
GENERAL PUBLICATIONS.

A 38.3
BULLETINS.

A 38.4
CIRCULARS.

PACKERS AND STOCKYARDS ADMINISTRATION (1921– 1927)

CREATION AND AUTHORITY

The Packers and Stockyards Administration
was established within the Department of Agriculture in 1921, pursuant to provisions in the Packers and Stockyards Act of 1921. The Administration was abolished on July 1, 1927, and its functions transferred to the Bureau of Animal Industry (A 4).

A 39.1:date
ANNUAL REPORTS.

A 39.2:CT
GENERAL PUBLICATIONS.

A 39.3
BULLETINS.

A 39.4
CIRCULARS.

A 39.5:v.nos.
MONTHLY RECORD.
Later A 4.28

EXHIBITS OFFICE (1921– 1922)

A 40.1:date
ANNUAL REPORTS.

A 40.2:CT
GENERAL PUBLICATIONS.

A 40.3
BULLETINS.

A 40.4
CIRCULARS.

GRAIN FUTURES ADMINISTRATION (1922– 1936)

CREATION AND AUTHORITY

The Grain Futures Administration was established within the Department of Agriculture pursuant to the Grain Futures Act, approved September 21, 1922 (42 Stat. 998). The Administration
was abolished on July 1, 1936, and its functions
assumed by the Commodity Exchange Administration (A 59) by order of the Secretary of Agriculture pursuant to the Commodity Exchange Act,
approved Jun 15, 1936.

A 41.1:date
ANNUAL REPORTS.

A 41.2:CT
GENERAL PUBLICATIONS.

A 41.3:nos.
BULLETINS.

A 41.4:CT
CIRCULARS.

A 41.5:CT
LAWS.

A 41.6:CT
REGULATIONS.

A 41.7:vol.
TRADE IN GRAIN FUTURES. [Monthly]
Later A 59.7

BUREAU OF HOME ECONOMICS
(1923– 1942)

CREATION AND AUTHORITY

The Office of Home Economics was established within the States Relations Service of the Department of Agriculture on July 1, 1915, pursuant to the Smith-Lever Act, approved May 8, 1914. On July 1, 1923, the Office became the Bureau of Home Economics and given bureau status. Under Executive Order 9069 of February 23, 1942, the Bureau was placed along with certain other agencies under the newly created Agricultural Research Administration (A 77.700).

A 42.1:date
ANNUAL REPORTS.
Later A 77.701

A 42.2:CT
GENERAL PUBLICATIONS.
Later A 77.702

A 42.3:nos.
BULLETINS.

A 42.4:nos.
CIRCULARS.

A 42.5:nos.
HOME ECONOMICS PUBLICATIONS.

A 42.6:nos.
HOME ECONOMICS BIBLIOGRAPHIES.

A 42.7:nos.
NUTRITION CHARTS.

A 42.7/2:nos.
HOUSEHOLD REFRIGERATION CHARTS.

A 42.7/3:nos.
CHILD FEEDING CHARTS.

A 42.7/4:nos.
MEAT COOKING CHARTS.

A 42.7/5:nos.
CLOTHING SELECTION CHARTS.

A 42.7/6:nos.
POULTRY COOKING CHARTS.

A 42.8:CT
STUDY OF CONSUMER PURCHASES.

A 42.9:CT
ADDRESSES.

EXTENSION SERVICE
(1970– 1978; 1981–   )

CREATION AND AUTHORITY

The Extension Service was established within the Department of Agriculture on July 1, 1923, pursuant to the Agricultural Appropriations Act of 1924, approved February 26, 1923 (42 Stat. 1289). Under Executive Order 9322 of March 26, 1943, the Extension Service was consolidated with certain other agencies into the Administration of Food Production and Distribution, the name of which was changed to War Food Administration (A 80.300) by Executive Order 9334 of April 19, 1943. Upon termination of the War Food Administration, it was returned to the direct control of the Secretary of Agriculture by Executive Order 9577 of June 29, 1953, the Extension Service was

placed under the administrative supervision of the Assistant Secretary for Federal-States Relations (A 43) and the name changed to Federal Extension Service. In 1970, the Agency was redesignated Extension Service. The Extension Service was consolidated with certain other agencies to form the Science and Education Administration (A 106) by Secretary's Memorandum 1927, Supplement 1, dated December 19, 1977, effective January 24, 1978. The Science and Education Administration (A 106) was abolished on June 17, 1981 and certain functions returned to the reestablished Extension Service (A 43). Became part of Cooperative State, Research, Education, and Extension Service under Department of Agriculture's reorganization in 1995.

A 43.1:date   •Item 59
ANNUAL REPORTS.
See also A 80.301

Discontinued.

A 43.2:CT   • Item 61-D
GENERAL PUBLICATIONS.
See also A 80.302

A 43.3
BULLETINS.

A 43.4   • Item 59-A
EXTENSION SERVICE CIRCULARS. ESC 1–   1926–
[Irregular]

Discontinued 1977.

COOPERATIVE EXTENSION WORK OFFICE

A 43.5/1:date
ANNUAL REPORTS. 1923– 1929.

A 43.5/2:CT
GENERAL PUBLICATIONS.

A 43.5/3:nos.
BULLETINS.

A 43.5/4:
CIRCULARS.

A 43.5/5:v.nos.
BOYS AND GIRLS 4-H CLUB LEADER. v. 1– v. 4, no. 3. 1927– 1930. [Monthly]
Superseded by A 43.7

A 43.5/6:nos.
TIMELY EXTENSION INFORMATION. 1– 298. 1926– 1939.
Later A 43.4

A 43.5/7:vol.
EXTENSION PATHOLOGIST. v. 1– v. 7, no. 1. 1923– 1929. 1– 35. 1932– 1939.
Later A 43.20

A 43.5/8:nos.
LANTERN SLIDE SERIES. 1– 556.   – 1958.
Later A 43.19

A 43.5/9:date
LIST OF EXTENSION PUBLICATIONS OF STATE AGRICULTURAL COLLEGES RECEIVED BY OFFICE OF EXPERIMENT STATIONS LIBRARY. [Monthly]

A 43.5/10:CT
SERIES OF EDUCATIONAL ILLUSTRATIONS (Charts).
Later A 43.22

A 43.5/11:nos.
EXTENSION FORESTER.
Later A 43.17

A 43.5/12:date
EXTENSION POULTRY HUSBANDMAN.
Later A 4.24

A 43.5/13:nos.
HERE AND THERE WITH HOME DEMONSTRATION WORKERS. 1– 16. 1929.

A 43.5/14:vol.
HOME DEMONSTRATION REVIEW. v. 1, nos. 1– 4. 1930. [Monthly]
Superseded by A 43.7

A 43.5/15:nos.
SOUTHERN ECONOMIC EXTENSION. 1– 6. 1930– 1931.

A 43.5/16:date
WHEAT PRODUCTION ADJUSTMENT. 1930–   1931.

A 43.5/17:nos.
AGRICULTURE ECONOMICS EXTENSION. 1– 18. 1931– 1935.

A 43.5/18:nos.
MISCELLANEOUS EXTENSION PUBLICATIONS. 1– 62. 1932– 1941.

A 43.5/19:CT
ADDRESSES.

A 43.5/20:nos.
WILDLIFE CONSERVATION AND RESTORATION NOTES.

A 43.5/21:nos.
EXTENSION MARKETING NEWS. 1– 5. 1929– 1930. [Monthly]
Later A 43.18

Federal Extension Service
(Continued)

A 43.6:nos.
TIMELY EXTENSION INFORMATION.

A 43.7   • Item 60
EXTENSION SERVICE REVIEW. v. 1–   1930–
[Monthly]
PURPOSE:– To serve as a source of ideas and useful information on how extension workers might help people utilize their own resources, to farm more efficiently, and to make the home and community a better place in which to live.
Consists of short, signed articles, mostly by extension workers at the county level.
Issued Monthly prior to May-June 1973.
Indexed by: Index to U.S. Government Periodicals.
ISSN 0014-5408
See also A 106.10

Discontinued.

A 43.8:CT   • Item 61-F
POSTERS. [Irregular]
See also A 80.308

A 43.9:nos.
DISCUSSION [Leaflets].
Pubs. desig. D-no.
Later A 36.146

A 43.9/2:date
GARDEN FACTS FOR GARDEN LEADERS. [Monthly]
Formerly Garden and Home Food Perservation Facts.

A 43.10:nos.
DISCUSSION SERIES. DA 1– 4. 1935.

A 43.11:nos.
DISCUSSION SERIES. DB 1– 3. 1935.

A 43.12:nos.
DISCUSSION SERIES. DC 1– 2. 1935.

A 43.13:DS-nos.
DISCUSSION SERIES. DS 1– 18. 1936– 1939.

A 43.14:nos.
PARENT EDUCATION MESSENGER. 1– 6. 1935– 1936.

A 43.15:vol.
4-H FORAGE. v. 1– v. 11, no. 6   – 1937. [Daily except Sunday, during week of National 4-H Club camp held annually during June]

A 43.15/2:vol.
4-H RECORD, NATIONAL 4-H CLUB CAMP, WASHINGTON, D.C. v. 1– v. 4, no. 4. 1938– 1941.

A 43.16:CT • Item 61-A
REGULATIONS, RULES, AND INSTRUCTIONS.
Includes handbooks and manuals.

A 43.16/2:CT • Item 61-B
HANDBOOKS, MANUALS, GUIDES.

A 43.17:date
EXTENSION FORESTER. 1939– 1941.
Earlier A 43.5/11

A 43.18:nos.
EXTENSION MARKETING NEWS. 10– 46. 1939– 1942.
[Monthly]
Earlier A 43.5/21, prior to no. 10.

A 43.19:nos.
LECTURE NOTES FOR FILMSTRIP SERIES. 1– 684.
– 1948.
Earlier A 43.5/8
See also A 80.309

A 43.20:ser.nos.
PATHOLOGY; NEWS LETTER FOR EXTENSION
WORKERS INTERESTED IN PLANT DISEASE
CONTROL. 36– 48. 1939– 1942.
Earlier A 43.5/7 prior to no. 36

A 43.21:CT
ADDRESSES.
See also A 80.310

A 43.22:gr.nos.
SERIES OF EDUCATIONAL ILLUSTRATIONS (Charts).
Earlier A 43.5/10

A 43.23:date
FILM STRIPS OF U.S.D.A., PRICE LISTS.
Earlier A 43.5/2:F 48/2

A 43.24:date
MOTION PICTURES OF DEPARTMENT OF AGRICUL-
TURE.

A 43.25:program nos.
NATIONAL 4-H MUSIC HOUR. [Monthly, National 4-H
Club Radio Program; Descriptive Notes].

A 43.26:nos.
EXTENSION FARM LABOR CIRCULARS.
Earlier A 80.311

A 43.27:
WEEKLY NEWS SERIES.

A 43.28:
RANDOM FORESTRY NOTES FOR EXTENSION
FORESTERS.

A 43.29:nos.
GARDEN AND HOME FOOD PRESERVATION FACTS.
[Monthly]
Replaced by A 43.29/2

A 43.29/2
GARDEN FACTS FOR GARDEN LEADERS. 1954–
1957. [Bimonthly]

A 43.30:nos.
CLEAN GRAIN NOTES FOR COOPERATORS IN
CLEAN GRAIN PROGRAM. 1– [Irregular]

A 43.31:CT
FOLDER SUGGESTIONS.

A 43.32:date
LIST OF STATE EXTENSION ENTOMOLOGISTS AND
EXTENSION AGRICULTURISTS.

A 43.33 • Item 61-C
TRENDS IN FORAGE CROPS VARIETIES. 1956–
[Annual]

PURPOSE:– To disseminate information on
forage crops varieties being grown in the U.S. To
assist producers and merchants in balancing the
supply of and demand for seed of the various
forage varieties, especially where seed are grown
in one area of the country for use in another. This
publication summarizes acreages of forage crops
by States, regions, and the U.S. It also points out

likely trends for acreage changes for each variety.
Discontinued.

A 43.33/2
NEW CROP VARIETIES. 1– 1959– [Annual]

Compiled in cooperation with state extension
agronomists and the Agricultural Research Service.

A 43.34:date
ANNUAL INVENTORY OF AVAILABLE USDA POPU-
LAR PUBLICATIONS. FOR USE OF STATE AND
COUNTY EXTENSION OFFICES IN ORDERING
USDA PUBLICATIONS.

A 43.34/2:CT
BIBLIOGRAPHIES AND LISTS OF PUBLICATIONS.

A 43.35:nos.
YOU CAN SURVIVE, RURAL DEFENSE FACT SHEETS.
1– 1962–

A 43.35/2:nos.
KNOWLEDGE FOR SURVIVAL, YOU CAN SURVIVE!
NEWSLETTER TO STATE EXTENSION PROGRAM
LEAFLETS, RURAL DEFENSE. [Monthly]

A 43.36:nos.
IDEAS, 4-H AND YOUTH DEVELOPMENT (series). 1–

A 43.37:CT
[STATE PUBLICATIONS ISSUED IN COOPERATION
WITH FEDERAL EXTENSION SERVICE].

A 43.38
STATISTICAL SUMMARY, RURAL AREAS DEVELOP-
MENT AND AREA REDEVELOPMENT,
QUARTERLY PROGRESS REPORT. 1966–
[Quarterly]

A 43.39
NOTES TO AGENTS ON [subject] (series). [Irregular]

A 43.40
SANITATION SERIES. 1– 1965– [Irregular]
PURPOSE:– To provide home economics extension or village workers in the less developed
countries sound information on sanitation in easy
to read format with appropriate illustration.
Prepared for Agency for International Development, this series has also been translated into
French and Spanish.
Some issues are reprints of former ER&T
series.

A 43.49:date
CRD NEWSLETTER.

A 43.49/2:date
AGRICULTURAL PROGRAMS. [Monthly]

A 43.49/3 • Item 61-H
EXTENSION SERVICE UPDATE, COMMUNITY AND
RURAL DEVELOPMENT (CRD). [Bimonthly]

Contains short items on community and rural
development aswell as a calendar of events and
publications and educational aids on thattopic.

Discontinued.

A 43.50:date • Item 61-E
AGRICULTURAL CHARTBOOK ENLARGEMENTS. [An-
nual]

Consists of enlargements of charts from the
Agricultural Chartbook (A 1.76/2).

A 43.51 • Item 61-G
LIST OF AVAILABLE USDA PUBLICATIONS FOR SALE
FROM GPO. [Annual]

Lists USDA publications for sale by GPO showing date of issue or revision, GPO stock number,
and price.

Discontinued.

BUREAU OF DAIRY INDUSTRY
(1926– 1942)

CREATION AND AUTHORITY

The Dairy Division was established within the
Bureau of Animal Industry (A 4) of the Department of Agriculture on July 1, 1895. By act of
Congress, approved May 29, 1924, the Division
was given bureau status as the Bureau of Dairying. In 1926, the name was changed to Bureau of
Dairy Industry. Executive Order 9069 of February
23, 1942, transferred the Bureau along with certain other agencies to the Agricultural Research
Administration (A 77.600).

A 44.1:date
ANNUAL REPORTS.
Later A 77.601

A 44.2:CT
GENERAL PUBLICATIONS.
Later A 77.602

A 44.3
BULLETINS [none issued].

A 44.4
CIRCULARS [none issued].

A 44.5:nos.
SERVICE AND REGULATORY ANNOUNCEMENTS.

A 44.6:v.nos.
COW TESTING ASSOCIATION LETTER. [Monthly]
Later A 77.608

A 44.7:nos.
MILK PLANT LETTERS. [Monthly]
Earlier A 4.17

A 44.8:nos.
MILK INSPECTOR LETTERS. [Monthly]

A 44.9:nos.
DAIRY LIBRARY LIST.

A 44.10:nos.
ORDERS.

A 44.11:date
PUBLICATIONS RELATING TO DAIRY INDUSTRY.
[Twice a year]

A 44.12:CT
ADDRESSES.
Later A 77.607

OFFICE OF AGRICULTURAL
INSTRUCTION
(1926)

A 45.1:date
ANNUAL REPORTS.

A 45.2:CT
GENERAL PUBLICATIONS.

A 45.3
BULLETINS.

A 45.5:CT
SERIES OF EDUCATIONAL ILLUSTRATIONS FOR
SCHOOLS (poster).

FOOD AND DRUG ADMINISTRATION (1930–1940)

CREATION AND AUTHORITY

The Food, Drug, and Insecticide Administration was established within the Department of Agriculture by the Agricultural Appropriation Act of 1928, approved January 18, 1927 (44 Stat. 1002). The name was changed to the Food and Drug Administration by Agriculture Appropriation Act of 1931, approved May 27, 1930 (46 Stat. 422). Reorganization Plan No. 4 of 1940, effective June 30, 1940 transferred the Food and Drug Administration to the Federal Security Agency (FS 7).

A 46.1:date
ANNUAL REPORTS.
    Later FS 7.1

A 46.2:CT
GENERAL PUBLICATIONS.
    Later FS 7.2

A 46.3
BULLETINS.

A 46.4
CIRCULARS.

A 46.6:incl.nos.
NOTICE OF JUDGMENT UNDER FOOD AND DRUG ACT. [Irregular]
    Later FS 7.11

A 46.7:incl.nos.
NOTICE OF JUDGMENT UNDER INSECTICIDE ACT. [Irregular]
    Earlier A 34.6
    Later A 66.46

A 46.8:nos.
NOTICE OF JUDGMENT UNDER REGULATIONS OF NAVAL STORES. [Irregular]

A 46.9:nos.
NOTICE OF JUDGMENT UNDER CAUSTIC POISON ACT. [Irregular]
    Later FS 7.9

A 46.10
[Vacant].

A 46.11:nos.
SERVICE AND REGULATORY ANNOUNCEMENTS, IMPORT MILK. [Irregular]
    Changed from A 46.5/1
    Earlier A 7.8
    Later FS 13.4

A 46.12:nos.
SERVICE AND REGULATORY ANNOUNCEMENTS, FOOD AND DRUG. [Irregular]
    Changed from A 46.5/2

A 46.12/a:CT
– SEPARATES.

A 46.13:nos.
SERVICE AND REGULATORY ANNOUNCEMENTS, CAUSTIC POISON. [Irregular]
    Changed from A 46.5/3
    Later FS 13.110

A 46.14:nos.
SERVICE AND REGULATORY ANNOUNCEMENT, TEA. [Irregular]
    Later FS 7.14

A 46.15:nos.
SERVICE AND REGULATORY ANNOUNCEMENTS, INSECTICIDE AND FUNGICIDE. [Irregular]

A 46.16:CT
PAPERS IN RE.

A 46.17:nos.
MICROANALYTICAL DIVISION PUBLICATIONS.
    Later FS 7.16

A 46.18:nos.
SERVICE AND REGULATORY ANNOUNCEMENTS, NAVAL STORES.

A 46.19:nos.
SERVICE AND REGULATORY ANNOUNCEMENTS, FOOD, DRUG AND COSMETIC.
    Later FS 7.8

BUREAU OF CHEMISTRY AND SOILS (1927–1938)

CREATION AND AUTHORITY

The Bureau of Chemistry (A 7) and Bureau of Soils (A 26), created in 1901, were combined in 1927 into the Bureau of Chemistry and Soils. In 1938 the soils units transferred to other agencies of the Department and the remaining units of the Bureau of Chemistry and Soils and the Bureau of Agricultural Engineering (A 53) were consolidated to form the Bureau of Agricultural Chemistry and Engineering (A 70).

A 47.1:date
ANNUAL REPORTS.

A 47.2:CT
GENERAL PUBLICATIONS.

A 47.3:
BULLETINS.

A 47.4
CIRCULARS.

A 47.5:CT & nos.
SOIL SURVEY REPORTS.
    Earlier A 1.64/1,2 and A 26.5
    Later A 19.32

A 47.5/a:CT
– SEPARATES.

A 47.5/2:CT
SOIL SURVEY (of States).
    See for separates from Field Operations, 1899–1922, (A 26.5/2). Individual reports classified as A 26.5/a and A 47.5
    Later A 19.31

A 47.6:CT
PAPERS IN RE.

A 47.7:vol.
REVIEW OF U.S. PATENTS RELATING TO PEST CONTROL. [Monthly]
    Earlier A 7.9
    Later A 56.17

A 47.8:date
INSECTICIDE DIVISION PUBLICATIONS (lists).
    Later A 56.15

A 47.9:nos.
MIMEOGRAPHED CIRCULARS.
    Superseded by A 70.4

A 47.10:CT
ADDRESSES.

BUREAU OF PLANT QUARANTINE (1932–1934)

CREATION AND AUTHORITY

The Plant Quarantine and Control Administration was established within the Department of Agriculture in 1928, succeeding the Federal Horticultural Board (A 35). The name was changed in 1932 to Bureau of Plant Quarantine, pursuant to the Agricultural Appropriation Act of 1933 (47 Stat. 640). The Bureau of Plant Quarantine was combined with the Bureau of Entomology (A 9) to form the Bureau of Entomology and Plant Quarantine (A 56) by the Agricultural Appropriation Act of 1935 (48 Stat. 467), effective July 1, 1934.

A 48.1:date
ANNUAL REPORTS.

A 48.2:CT
GENERAL PUBLICATIONS.

A 48.3
BULLETINS.

A 48.4
CIRCULARS.

A 48.5:nos.
NOTICE OF QUARANTINE.
    Earlier A 35.5
    Later A 56.14

A 48.6:nos.
MEMORANDUM

A 48.7:nos.
SERVICE AND REGULATORY ANNOUNCEMENT.
    Earlier A 35.9
    Later A 56.14

A 48.7/a:CT
– SEPARATES.

A 48.7/2:CT
– SEPARATES. LIST OF INTERCEPTED PLANT PESTS.
    Later A 56.14/2

A 48.8:CT
REGULATIONS, RULES, AND INSTRUCTIONS.
    Supersedes A 36.8
    Later A 56.6

A 48.9:CT
POSTERS.

A 48.10:nos.
ADMINISTRATIVE MEMORANDUM.
    Later A 56.16

A 48.11:nos.
CIRCULAR OF INFORMATION.
    Earlier A 35.7
    Later A 56.9

PERSONNEL OFFICE (1925–   )

A 49.1:date   • Item 96
ANNUAL REPORTS.
    Discontinued.

A 49.2:CT   • Item 97
PUBLICATIONS.
    Discontinued.

A 49.3:nos.
BULLETINS. 1– 14. 1938– 1949.
　　Superseded by Personnel Bulletins (A 49.3/
　2).

A 49.3/2:vol.
PERSONNEL BULLETINS. v. 1– v. 2, no. 1. 1940–
　1942.
　　Supersedes Bulletins (A 49.3).

A 49.4:nos.
P.B.A. CIRCULARS. 1– 259. 1925– 1934.

A 49.4/2:nos.
PERSONNEL CIRCULARS. 1– 116. 1934– 1941.

A 49.5:CT　　　　　　　　　　　• Item 98
LAWS.
　　Discontinued.

A 49.7:
MEMORANDUM FOR CHIEFS OF BUREAUS AND
　OFFICES.

A 49.8:CT　　　　　　　　　　　• Item 97
HANDBOOKS, MANUALS, GUIDES. [Irregular]
　　Discontinued.

ALASKA COMMISSION FOR DEPARTMENT OF AGRICULTURE (1927– 1928)

A 50.1:date
ANNUAL REPORTS.

A 50.2:CT
GENERAL PUBLICATIONS.

A 50.3
BULLETINS.

A 50.4
CIRCULARS.

FARMERS' SEED LOAN OFFICE (1929– 1933)

CREATION AND AUTHORITY

　　The Farmers' Seed Loan Office was established within the Department of Agriculture pursuant to Public Resolution 92, 70th Congress, approved February 25, 1929, for the handling of
applications for seed loans from flood and storm
damaged areas. The Office was also referred to
as the Farmers' Seed and Fertilizer Loan Office.
The Office was transferred to the Farm Credit
Administration (FCA) by Executive Order 6084 of
March 27, 1933.

A 51.1:date
ANNUAL REPORTS.

A 51.2:CT
GENERAL PUBLICATIONS.

A 51.3
BULLETINS.

A 51.4
CIRCULARS.

A 51.5
LAWS.

A 51.6:CT
REGULATIONS.

NATIONAL ADVISORY LOAN COMMITTEE (1931)

A 52.1:date
ANNUAL REPORTS.

A 52.2:CT
GENERAL PUBLICATIONS.

A 52.3
BULLETINS.

A 52.4
CIRCULARS.

A 52.5
LAWS.

A 52.6
REGULATIONS.

BUREAU OF AGRICULTURAL ENGINEERING (1931– 1938)

CREATION AND AUTHORITY

　　The Bureau of Agricultural Engineering was
established within the Department of Agriculture
on July 1, 1931, pursuant to the Agricultural Appropriation Act of 1932 (46 Stat. 1266), continuing the work of the Division of Agricultural Engineering of the Bureau of Public Roads (A 22). The
Bureau merged with the Bureau of Chemistry and
Soils (A 47) to form the Bureau of Agricultural
Chemistry and Engineering (A 70) by order of the
Secretary of Agriculture, October 16, 1938.

A 53.1:date
ANNUAL REPORTS.

A 53.2:CT
GENERAL PUBLICATIONS.

A 53.3:nos.
BULLETINS.

A 53.4
CIRCULARS.

A 53.5
LAWS.

A 53.6
REGULATIONS.

A 53.7
MAPS.

A 53.8
POSTERS.

A 53.9:vol.
AGRICULTURAL ENGINEERING, CURRENT
　LITERATURE. [Monthly]
　　Later A 70.7

A 53.10:nos.
INFORMATION SERIES.
　　Earlier A 22.14
　　Later A 70.11

A 53.11:CT
LISTS OF PUBLICATIONS.

A 53.12:CT
ADDRESSES.

A 53.13:CT
BIBLIOGRAPHIES.
　　Changed from A 53.2

CROP PRODUCTION LOAN OFFICE (1918– 1933)

CREATION AND AUTHORITY

　　The Crop Production Loan Office was established within the Department of Agriculture pursuant to letter of the President, dated July 26,
1918. The Office was consolidated with certain
other agencies to form the Farm Credit Administration (FCA) by Executive Order 6084 of March
27, 1933, effective May 27, 1933.

A 54.1:date
ANNUAL REPORTS.

A 54.2:CT
GENERAL PUBLICATIONS.

A 54.3
BULLETINS.

A 54.4
CIRCULARS.

AGRICULTURAL ADJUSTMENT ADMINISTRATION (1933– 1942)

CREATION AND AUTHORITY

　　The Agricultural Adjustment Administration
was established within the Department of Agriculture pursuant to the Agricultural Adjustment Act,
approved May 12, 1933 (48 Stat. 31). By Executive Order 9069 of February 23, 1942, it was
consolidated along with certain other agencies to
form the Agricultural Conservation and Adjustment Administration (A 76.400).

A 55.1:date
ANNUAL REPORTS.
　　Later A 76.401

A 55.1/a:nos.
　– SEPARATES.

A 55.2:CT
GENERAL PUBLICATIONS.
　　Later A 76.402

A 55.3
BULLETINS.

A 55.5:CT
LAWS.

A 55.6:CT
REGULATIONS.
　　For Sugar Regulations see A 36.6 (Jan. 1940).
　　Later A 76.406

A 55.7:CT
POSTERS.

A 55.7/2:nos.
REGIONAL CONTACT CHARTS.
　　Pub. desig. RC

A 55.7/3:nos.
REGIONAL CONTACT CHARTS, 2d series.

A 55.7/4:nos.
REGIONAL CONTACT CHARTS, 3d SERIES.

A 55.8:nos.
LICENSE SERIES.

A 55.9:nos.
MARKETING AGREEMENT SERIES.
        Changed to A 65.9

A 55.10:T-nos.
CIGAR TOBACCO ADJUSTMENT PROGRAM.

        Includes cigar tobacco acreage adjustment
program.

A 55.11:vol.
NEWS DIGEST. [Weekly]

A 55.12:vol.
CONSUMERS' GUIDE. [Biweekly]
        Later A 75.108

A 55.13
CODE OF FAIR COMPETITION SERIES.

A 55.14:CH-3
CORN HOG CHARTS.

A 55.15:CT
ADDRESSES.
        Later A 80.609

A 55.16:nos.
ADMINISTRATIVE ORDERS.

A 55.17:nos.
CONTINENTAL U.S. BEET SUGAR ORDERS.

A 55.18:nos.
PUERTO RICO SUGAR ORDERS.
        Later A 63.8

A 55.18/2:nos.
PUERTO RICO TAX FUND ORDERS.

A 55.18/3:nos.
PUERTO RICO ADMINISTRATIVE RULINGS.

A 55.19:nos.
GENERAL SUGAR ORDERS.

A 55.20:nos.
RICE ADMINISTRATIVE ORDERS.

A 55.21:nos.
DOCKETS (usually mim.).
        Later A 65.8

A 55.22:nos.
TO FARM JOURNAL EDITORS. [Weekly]

A 55.23:nos.
COTTON PRODUCTION ADJUSTMENTS.

A 55.24:CT
PAPERS IN RE.

A 55.25:nos.
COMMODITY INFORMATION SERIES: COTTON
        LEAFLETS.

A 55.25/2:nos.
COMMODITY INFORMATION SERIES: TOBACCO.

A 55.25/3:nos.
COMMODITY INFORMATION SERIES: MILK
        LEAFLETS.

A 55.25/4:nos.
COMMODITY INFORMATION SERIES: WHEAT
        CIRCULARS.

A 55.25/5:nos.
COMMODITY INFORMATION SERIES: WHEAT LEAF-
        LETS.

A 55.25/6:nos.
COMMODITY INFORMATION SERIES: POTATO LEAF-
        LETS.

A 55.25/7:nos.
COMMODITY INFORMATION SERIES: CORN-HOG
        LEAFLETS.

A 55.25/8:nos.
COMMODITY INFORMATION SERIES: RYE
        LEAFLETS.

A 55.25/9:CT
COMMODITY INFORMATION SERIES (miscella-
        neous).

A 55.26:vol.
LAND POLICY REVIEW. [Monthly]

        Later Land Policy Circulars, Bureau of Agri-
        cultural Economics, (A 36.103).

A 55.27:vol
SUMMARY OF PRESS COMMENTS. [Weekly]

A 55.28:nos.
HAWAII TAX FUND ORDERS.

A 55.29:nos.
DISCUSSION STATEMENTS.

A 55.30:nos.
[CORN-HOG BOARD OF REVIEW PUBLICATIONS].

A 55.31:nos.
[TOBACCO LETTERS].
        Pubs. desig. TL before numbers.

A 55.32:CT
COMMITTEEMEN'S LETTERS (by commodity).

A 55.33:nos.
CURRENT INFORMATION STATEMENTS.

A 55.34:nos.
CIRCULAR LETTERS, CORN-HOG WORK.

        Earlier numbers issued by Director of Exten-
        sion Work, later ones usually by Agricultural Ad-
        justment Administration and Extension Service
        Cooperating. All are classified in A 55.34.

A 55.34/2:dt.&nos.
CIRCULAR LETTERS, CORN-HOG WORK.
        First issue Jan. 11, 1935.

A 55.34/3:CA-nos.
CORN-HOG CIRCULAR LETTERS.

A 55.35:nos.
CIRCULAR LETTERS: WHEAT WORK.

A 55.36:nos.
ORDER SERIES.
        Later A 65.7

A 55.37:nos.
SUGAR DETERMINATION.

        Pubs. desig. S.D. no.
        Later A 63.7, A 76.307, A 80.117

A 55.38:nos.
[PEANUT LETTERS.]
        Pubs. desig. Form PL-no.

A 55.39:nos.
COTTON EDUCATIONAL MEETINGS.

A 55.40:CT
STATE SUMMARY SERIES.

A 55.41:v.nos.
BETTER MARKETING. [Biweekly]

Agricultural Conservation Program
East Central Region

A 55.42:date
ANNUAL REPORT.

A 55.42/2:CT
GENERAL PUBLICATIONS.
        Later A 80.2142

A 55.42/3:nos.
BULLETINS.
        Later A 55.42/9

A 55.42/5:nos.
REGIONAL INFORMATION SERIES.

A 55.42/6:nos.
[JOINT LETTERS.]

A 55.42/7:nos.
COMMITTEEMEN'S LETTERS.

A 55.42/8:nos.
ADMINISTRATIVE LETTERS.

A 55.42/9:CT
PROGRAMS BY STATES.
        Preceeded by A 55.42/3
        Later A 80.613

A 55.42/10:CT
REGULATIONS, RULES, AND INSTRUCTIONS.
        Includes Handbooks and Manuals.

A 55.42/11:vol.
A.A.A. FLASHES, FACTS FOR COMMITTEEMEN.
        Later A 76.410

Agricultural Conservation Program
North Central Region

A 55.43
ANNUAL REPORT.

A 55.43/2:CT
GENERAL PUBLICATIONS.
        Later A 79.452

A 55.43/3:nos.
BULLETINS.

A 55.43/5
REGIONAL INFORMATION SERIES LEAFLETS.

A 55.43/6:CT
REGULATIONS, RULES, AND INSTRUCTIONS.

A 55.43/7:nos.
COMMITTEEMEN'S LETTERS.

A 55.43/8:nos.
[MISCELLANEOUS SERIES.]

A 55.43/9:nos.
STATE COMMITTEE [letters].

A 55.43/10:nos.
COTTON MARKETING QUOTAS LETTERS.

A 55.43/11:CT
A.A.A.N.C.R. AGRICULTURAL CONSERVATION PRO-
        GRAM BY STATES. NCR. 501–

Agricultural Conservation Program
Northeast Region

A 55.44:date
ANNUAL REPORT.

A 55.44/2:CT
GENERAL PUBLICATIONS.
        Later A 76.462

A 55.44/3:nos.
BULLETINS.

A 55.44/5:CT
REGIONAL INFORMATION SERIES.

A 55.44/6:nos.
JOINT LETTERS.

A 55.44/7:nos.
COMMITTEEMEN'S LETTERS.

A 55.44/8:nos.
ADMINISTRATIVE LETTERS.

A 55.44/9:nos.
NEWS LETTERS.

A 55.44/10:CT
SOIL-BUILDING PRACTICES APPLICABLE IN STATES.

A 55.44/11:CT
REGULATIONS, RULES, AND INSTRUCTIONS.

Includes Handbook and Manual.
Later A 76.466

A 55.44/12:CT
OUTLINE OF AGRICULTURAL CONSERVATION PROGRAM (By States).

A 55.14/13:v.
FACTS FOR NORTHEAST COMMITTEEMEN.

A 55.44/14:CT
AGRICULTURAL CONSERVATION PROGRAM (by States).

**Agricultural Conservation Program
Southern Region**

A 55.45
ANNUAL REPORT.

A 55.45/2:CT
GENERAL PUBLICATIONS.
Later A 76.472

A 55.45/3:nos.
BULLETINS.

A 55.45/5:nos.
REGIONAL INFORMATION SERIES LEAFLETS.

A 55.45/6:nos.
SOUTHERN REGION MISCELLANEOUS SERIES, ITEMS.

A 55.45/7:nos.
COMMITTEEMEN LETTERS.

A 55.45/8:nos.
SOUTHERN REGION AGRICULTURAL CONSERVATION.

A 55.45/9:nos.
ANNOUNCEMENTS.

A 55.45/10:nos.
[PROCEDURE RELATIVE TO CLAIMS.]

A 55.45/11:nos.
HANDBOOKS, AGRICULTURAL AND RANGE CONSERVATION PROGRAMS (by States) ACP, SOUTHERN REGION. COTTON MARKET QUOTA LETTERS.

A 55.45/12:CT
HANDBOOKS, AGRICULTURAL CONSERVATION PROGRAMS.
Later A 76.476

**Agricultural Conservation Program,
Western Region**

A 55.46
ANNUAL REPORT.

A 55.46/2:CT
GENERAL PUBLICATIONS.

Later A 76.482

A 55.46/3:nos.
BULLETINS.

A 55.46/5:nos.
REGIONAL INFORMATION SERIES LEAFLETS.

A 55.46/6:nos.
STATE COMMITTEE LETTERS.

A 55.46/7:nos.
COMMITTEEMEN'S LETTERS.

A 55.46/8:nos.
[ADMINISTRATIVE LETTERS.]

A 55.46/9:nos.
COUNTY COMMITTEE MEMORANDUM.

A 55.46/10:nos.
STATE OFFICE MEMORANDUM.

A 55.46/11:CT
HANDBOOKS, AGRICULTURAL AND RANGE CONSERVATION PROGRAM (by States).

A 55.46/12:CT
PROCEDURE (by States).

A 55.46/13:CT
COUNTY OFFICE PROCEDURE (by States).

A 55.46/14:
COMMITTEE PROCEDURE.

A 55.46/15
REGULATIONS, RULES, AND INSTRUCTIONS.
Later A 76.486

A 55.47:nos.
MARKETING INFORMATION SERIES.
Leaflets.

**Agricultural Conservation Program
Insular Region**

A 55.48
ANNUAL REPORT.

A 55.48/2:CT
GENERAL PUBLICATIONS.

A 55.48/3:CT
BULLETINS.

A 55.48/5:nos.
ANNOUNCEMENTS.

A 55.49:nos.
CONSUMERS' COUNSEL SERIES, PUBLICATIONS.
Later A 75.111

**Agricultural Adjustment Administration
(Continued)**

A 55.50:nos.
COMMUNITY DISCUSSION PAPERS.

A 55.51:nos.
[INFORMATION FILE, INSERTS.]

A 55.52:vol.
CONSUMERS MARKET SERVICE.
Later A 75.109

A 55.53:nos.
CONSUMER STUDY OUTLINE.

A 55.54:le no.
MARKETING INFORMATION SERIES.
Later A 65.12

A 55.55:CT
NUMBER OF FARMS PARTICIPATING IN 1934 AAA VOLUNTARY CONTROL PROGRAMS (by States).

A 55.56:date
CONSUMER NOTES.
Later A 75.110

A 55.57:CT
SCHEDULES OF PAYMENTS TO HOLDERS OF COTTON OPTIONS AND PARTICIPATION TRUST CERTIFICATES BY CONGRESSIONAL DISTRICT OF STATES.

A 55.58:nos.
BRIEFLY SPEAKING.

A 55.59:nos.
MARKETING AND MARKETING AGREEMENTS DIVISION, MARKETING SECTION PUBLICATIONS.

A 55.60:nos.
STATISTICAL PUBLICATIONS.

A 55.61:nos.
TECHNICAL CHARTS.
Pubs. desig. TC

A 55.62:date
STATEMENTS OF EXPENDITURES.
Later A 76.409

A 55.63:CT
CONSUMERS' COUNSEL DIVISION, GENERAL PUBLICATIONS.
Later A 75.102

A 55.64:vol.
WEEKLY SUMMARY: AAA PRESS RELEASES.

A 55.65:nos.
P.C. PRODUCER-CONSUMER SERIES.

A 55.66:nos.
SUGAR BEET SUGAR ORDERS.

A 55.67:nos.
MAINLAND CANE SUGAR ORDERS.

A 55.68:nos.
FLUE-CURED TOBACCO LETTERS.

A 55.69:CT
REGULATIONS, RULES, AND INSTRUCTIONS.
Later A 76.406

A 55.70:nos.
[INSTRUCTIONS RELATIVE TO SUGAR BEET PROGRAM.]
Pubs. desig. SB-no.
Changed from A 55.2
See also A 63.11

A 55.71:nos.
GENERAL INFORMATION SERIES.
Pubs. desig. G-no.
Changed from A 55.2; A 55.7; A 55.15
Later A 76.408

A 55.72:nos.
[CONSUMERS' SERVICE.]
Pubs. desig. CS-no.

A 55.73:nos.
[MISCELLANEOUS SERIES.]
Earlier A 63.10

BUREAU OF ENTOMOLOGY AND PLANT QUARANTINE
(1934– 1942)

CREATION AND AUTHORITY

The Bureau of Entomology and Plant Quarantine was established within the Department of Agriculture by Agricultural Appropriation Act of 1935 (48 Stat. 467), effective July 1, 1934, combining the Bureau of Entomology (A 9) and the Bureau of Plant Quarantine (A 48). Executive Order 9069 of February 23, 1942, transferred the Bureau along with certain other agencies to form the Agricultural Research Administration (A 77).

A 56.1:date
ANNUAL REPORTS.
Earlier A 35.1
Later A 77.301

A 56.2:CT
GENERAL PUBLICATIONS.
Earlier A 35.2
Later A 77.302

A 56.3
BULLETINS.

A 56.4
CIRCULARS.

A 56.5
LAWS.

A 56.6:CT
REGULATIONS, RULES, AND INSTRUCTIONS.
Earlier A 35.8; A 48.8

A 56.7:CT
MAPS.

A 56.8
POSTERS.

A 56.9:nos.
[CIRCULARS OF INFORMATION].

Earlier A 48.11

A 56.10:vol.
ENTOMOLOGY CURRENT LITERATURE. [Bimonthly]
Earlier A 9.14
Later A 17.14

A 56.11:nos.
[ENTOMOLOGY TECHNIC SERIES].
Pubs. desig. ET

A 56.12:vol.
NEWS LETTER. [Monthly]
Earlier A 9.12

A 56.13:nos.
NOTICES OF QUARANTINE.
Earlier A 48.5
Later A 77.317

A 56.14:nos.
SERVICE AND REGULATORY ANNOUNCEMENTS.
Earlier A 48.7

A 56.14/a:CT
 – SEPARATES.
Later A 77.308/a

A 56.14/2:date
LIST OF INTERCEPTED PLANT PESTS.
Earlier A 48.7/2
Later A 77.308/2

A 56.15:date
INSECTICIDE DIVISION PUBLICATIONS. [Quarterly]
Earlier A 47.8

A 56.16:nos.
ADMINISTRATIVE MEMORANDUM.
Pubs. desig. EQ-nos.
Earlier A 48.10

A 56.17:vol.
REVIEW OF UNITED STATES PATENTS RELATING
TO PEST CONTROL. [Monthly]
Issued by Insecticide Division.
Earlier A 47.7
Later A 77.311

A 56.18:vol.
INSECT PEST SURVEY BULLETIN. [Monthly]
Earlier A 9.10
Later A 77.310

A 56.19:E-nos.
E [series].
Earlier A 9.16
Later A 77.312

A 56.20:nos.
PICTURE SHEETS.
Later A 77.320

A 56.21:vol.
EXTENSION ENTOMOLOGIST.
Later A 77.309

A 56.22:CT
ADDRESSES.

A 56.23:CT
PAPERS IN RE.
Later A 77.315

A 56.24:nos.
INSECTS IN RELATION TO NATIONAL DEFENSE,
CIRCULARS.
Later A 77.316

A 56.25:nos.
FOREIGN PLANT QUARANTINES IN SERVICE TRAIN-
ING SERIES.

A 56.26
FOREIGN PLANT QUARANTINE MEMORANDUM.

NATURAL RESOURCES CONSERVATION SERVICE
(1935– 1942, 1945–   )

CREATION AND AUTHORITY

Natural Resources Conservation Service was
established as the Soil Conservation Service
within the Department of Agriculture under authority of the Soil Conservation Act of 1935 (49
Stat. 163), approved April 27, 1935, superseding
the Soil Erosion Service (I 30) which has been
transferred to the Department of Agriculture from
the Department of the Interior on March 25, 1935.
Executive Order 9060 of February 23, 1942, consolidated it with other agencies in the Department
of Agriculture to form the new Agricultural Conservation and Adjustment Administration (A
76.200). From December 5, 1942 until March 26,
1943, it was under the Food Production Administration (A 79.200); from 1943 until June 30, 1945,
under the War Food Administration (A 80.200 and
A 80.500). Executive Order 9577 of June 29,
1945 placed the Service under the direct control
of the Secretary of Agriculture (A 57). In 1994,
the Natural Resources Conservation Service assumed the functions of the Soil Conservation
Service.

INFORMATION

Natural Resources Conservation Service
Department of Agriculture
1400 Independence Ave. SW
Washington, D.C. 20250
Fax: (202) 720-7690
http://www.nres.usda.gov

A 57.1:date   • Item 119
ANNUAL REPORTS.
See also A 76.201
Discontinued.

A 57.1/2   • Item 119-B
CONSERVATION HIGHLIGHTS, DIGEST OF THE
PROGRESS REPORT OF THE SOIL CONSERVA-
TION SERVICE. 1–   [Annual]

Brief resume giving the highlights of the
Service's activities for the fiscal year. Similar in
format and nature to the Program Aids issued by
the Department of Agriculture, this is intended for
wide distribution.
See A57.9/2

A 57.1/3:CT
SOIL CONSERVATION SERVICE. [State Reports]

A 57.1/4:date   • Item 119-C
COLORADO STATE OFFICE: ANNUAL REPORT.

PURPOSE:– To summarize activities of the
Colorado StateOffice of the Service. Includes
Colorado's conservation goals and objectives,
its soil and water resources, and financing of
conservation practices.

A 57.2:CT   • Item 120
GENERAL PUBLICATIONS.
See also A 76.202

A 57.2:C 76   • Item 120
CONSERVATION DISTRICTS. [Annual]

Gives status of organizations, by States; approximate acreage; and farms in organized districts.

ISSN 0160-2969

A 57.3:nos.
BULLETINS. 1–   1936–

A 57.4
CIRCULARS.

A 57.5:CT
LAWS.

A 57.6:CT
REGULATIONS, RULES AND INSTRUCTIONS.

Includes handbooks and manuals.

A 57.6/2:CT   • Item 120-A
HANDBOOKS, MANUALS, GUIDES.

A 57.6/2:En 3   • Item 120
SCS NATIONAL ENGINEERING HANDBOOK. [Ir-
regular]

Issued in sections and chapters, punched
for ring binder.

A 57.6/3:CT   • Item 120-A
IRRIGATION GUIDES [for areas].
Earlier A 57.6/2

A 57.6/4:nos.
CONSERVATION GUIDE SHEETS. 1–   [Irregular]

A 57.7:CT
MAPS (by states).

A 57.7/2:CT
MAPS (by subjects).

A 57.8:CT
POSTERS.

A 57.8/2:CT
AMERICA THE BEAUTIFUL (posters). 1966.

Set of 52 posters 20 x 24 inches. Colored
pictures.

A 57.9   • Item 122
SOIL CONSERVATION. v. v. 1–   1935–   [Monthly]

PURPOSE:– To serve as the official organ of
the Soil Conservation Service.
Monthly illustrated periodicals concerned with
soil and water conservation. The articles, some
technical but mostly popular, cover soil and water conservation, watershed programs, activities
of local soil conservation districts and how the
U.S. Soil Conservation Service provides them with
technical help.
Index issued separately covering each volume.
DISTRIBUTION:– Free distribution is limited
to a very small number of workers and official
cooperators of the Department engaged in soil
conservation activities, to libraries, agricultural
colleges, experiment stations and similar institu-
tions.
Indexed by:–
Biological and Agricultural Index.
Index to U.S. Government Periodicals.
ISSN 0038-0725
Superseded by Soil and Water Conservation
News
(A 57.9/2).

A 57.9/2:v.nos.&nos.   • Item 122
SOIL AND WATER CONSERVATION NEWS. v. 1–
1980–   [Monthly]
Supersedes Soil Conservation (A 57.9)
Discontinued.

A 57.10:nos.
ADMINISTRATIVE PUBLICATIONS. 1–   1935–

A 57.11:nos.
ADMINISTRATIVE REPORTS. 1– 3. 1936– 1938.

A 57.12:nos.
ENGINEERING PUBLICATIONS. 1–   1935–

A 57.13:nos.
MISCELLANEOUS PUBLICATIONS. 1–   1938–

A 57.14:nos.
SEDIMENTATION STUDIES. 1–   1936–

A 57.15   • Item 121-D (MF)
TECHNICAL PUBLICATIONS. SCS-TP 1–   [Irregular]

A 57.16:nos.
REGIONAL BULLETINS. 1–   1936–

A 57.17:nos.
PROCEDURE FOR MAKING SOIL CONSERVATION SURVEYS, OUTLINES. 1–

A 57.18:nos.
UPPER MISSISSIPPI VALLEY REGION, PUBLICATIONS. R5-Ms-1–

A 57.19:nos.
EXPERIMENT STATION REPORTS. SCS-ESR 1–

A 57.20:vol
SOIL CONSERVATION LITERATURE, SELECTED CURRENT REFERENCES. v. 1–   [Bimonthly]
Later A 17.15

A 57.21:nos.
TECHNICAL TABLES. SCS-TT–

A 57.21/2:date
PRECIPITATION IN MUSKINGUM RIVER BASIN. [Monthly]

A 57.22:date   • Item 120-B
INVENTORY OF SOIL, WATER, AND RELATED RESOURCES. [Annual]

PURPOSE:– To summarize data collected for the the National Resources Inventory on land use, soil erosion, and cropland quality for a particular county.

A 57.23:nos.
CHARTS. 1–   1938–

A 57.23/2:CT
SHEETS ON NATIONAL ATLAS OF UNITED STATES.

A 57.24:CT   • Item 121
EROSION AND RELATED LAND USE CONDITIONS (by Projects).
Later A 76.212
Discontinued.

A 57.24/2:nos.
EROSION SURVEYS.

A 57.25
ADDRESSES. [Irregular]

A 57.26:CT
LAND USE AND SOIL CONSERVATION, INFORMATIONAL MATERIALS AVAILABLE TO PUBLIC, LEAFLETS (by Regions).

A 57.27:nos.
BIBLIOGRAPHIES. SCS-B-1–   1940–

A 57.27/2:nos.
SOIL CONSERVATION BIBLIOGRAPHIES. 1–4. 1940–1942.

A 57.28:nos.
ENGINEERING DIVISION PUBLICATIONS. SCS-ED-1–   1937–
Earlier A 36.55

A 57.29:nos.
ECONOMIC PUBLICATIONS. SCS-EC-1–   1940–

A 57.30:nos.
CONSERVATION FOLDERS. 1–   1940–
Later A 76.210

A 57.31:nos.
HOURLY PRECIPITATION ON UPPER OHIO AND SUSQUEHANNA DRAINAGE BASINS. SCS-PC 1–12. 1938. [Monthly]
Precipitation charts.

A 57.32
SOIL AND WATER CONSERVATION DISTRICTS, STATUS OF ORGANIZATION, BY STATES, APPROXIMATE ACREAGE, AND FARMS IN ORGANIZED DISTRICTS. 1938–   [Annual]

Gives in tabular form, as of July 1, by State and soil conservation districts approximate total acres and number of farms, and general location (county or counties).

A 57.33:nos.
CONSERVATION EDUCATION REPORTS. 1–5. 1946–1947.

A 57.34:v.nos.
SUMMARY OF RESEARCH PROJECTS MONTHLY REPORTS. v. 1– v. 5, no. 3. 1947– 1951.

A 57.35:nos.
TECHNICAL LETTER. SED-1–   1939.

A 57.36:date   • Item 118
ABSTRACTS OF RECENT PUBLISHED MATERIAL ON SOIL AND WATER CONSERVATION.
Discontinued.

A 57.37:
WOODLAND MANAGEMENT PLAN, AGREEMENTS AND FARM CODES.

A 57.38:CT   • Item 102-B-1– 102-B-53
SOIL SURVEYS. 1899–   [Irregular]

PURPOSE:– To publish findings of soil surveys including detailed soil maps and descriptions of soil types in a given area usually a county, for use of anyone needing scientific information regarding soil in a particular area.
Since 1957, soil boundaries have been plotted on aerial photographs by soil scientists examining soils in the field. Recognition is given to all soil characteristics that affect their use, including texture, structure, chemical composition, and other properties of the individual layers of the soil as well as total depth, slope, stoniness, degree of erosion, and any other features that influence how the soils respond to management.
Each survey consists of a report, accompanied by a series of soil maps, superimposed on aerial photos. The report includes a general description of the area, descriptions of the soils, formation and classification of soils, glossary, literature cited, and a guide to mapping units and capability. The maps consist of a general map of the entire area, a series of strip aerial photos upon which the soil information has been added, and an index to the map sheets. The usual map scale is 1:20,000 or 1:15,840, depending upon the needs of the area.
DISTRIBUTION:– Beginning in 1973, distribution has been by the Soil Conservation Service. Prior to that the surveys were sold by the Superintendent of Documents.
A soil survey published by the U.S. Department of Agriculture that is still in print can be obtained in one of the following ways:
Land users in the area surveyed and professional workers who have use for the survey can obtain a free copy from the State or local office of the Soil Conservation Service, from their county agent, or from their Congressman. Soil conservation district offices and county agricultural extension offices have copies of local soil surveys that can be used for reference.
See A 57.38/32

A 57.38:list/date   • Item 102-A
LISTS OF PUBLISHED SOIL SURVEYS. [Annual]

Lists by States and counties soils surveys which have been published, date of survey, and whether survey is out-of-print.

A 57.38/1-2   • Item 102-B-1
SOIL SURVEY REPORTS (Alabama).

A 57.38/2:CT   • Item 102-B-35 (MF)
SOIL AND WATER CONSERVATION DISTRICT RESOURCES INVENTORIES (series). [Irregular]
Discontinued.

A 57.38/2-2   • Item 102-B-2
SOIL SURVEY REPORTS (Alaska).

A 57.38/3   • Item 102-B-3
SOIL SURVEY REPORTS (Arizona).

A 57.38/4   • Item 102-B-4
SOIL SURVEY REPORTS (Arkansas).

A 57.38/5   • Item 102-B-5
SOIL SURVEY REPORTS (California).

A 57.38/6   • Item 102-B-6
SOIL SURVEY REPORTS (Colorado).

A 57.38/7   • Item 102-B-7
SOIL SURVEY REPORTS (Connecticut).

A 57.38/8   • Item 102-B-8
SOIL SURVEY REPORTS (Delaware).

A 57.38/9   • Item 102-B-9
SOIL SURVEY REPORTS (Florida).

A 57.38/10   • Item 102-B-10
SOIL SURVEY REPORTS (Georgia).

A 57.38/11   • Item 102-B-11
SOIL SURVEY REPORTS (Hawaii).

A 57.38/12   • Item 102-B-12
SOIL SURVEY REPORTS (Idaho).

A 57.38/13   • Item 102-B-13
SOIL SURVEY REPORTS (Illinois).

A 57.38/14   • Item 102-B-14
SOIL SURVEY REPORTS (Indiana).

A 57.38/15   • Item 102-B-15
SOIL SURVEY REPORTS (Iowa).

A 57.38/16   • Item 102-B-16
SOIL SURVEY REPORTS (Kansas).

A 57.38/17   • Item 102-B-17
SOIL SURVEY REPORTS (Kentucky).

A 57.38/18   • Item 102-B-18
SOIL SURVEY REPORTS (Louisiana).

A 57.38/19   • Item 102-B-19
SOIL SURVEY REPORTS (Maine).

A 57.38/20   • Item 102-B-20
SOIL SURVEY REPORTS (Maryland).

A 57.38/21   • Item 102-B-21
SOIL SURVEY REPORTS (Massachusetts).

A 57.38/22   • Item 102-B-22
SOIL SURVEY REPORTS (Michigan).

A 57.38/23   • Item 102-B-23
SOIL SURVEY REPORTS (Minnesota).

A 57.38/24   • Item 102-B-24
SOIL SURVEY REPORTS (Mississippi).

A 57.38/25   • Item 102-B-25
SOIL SURVEY REPORTS (Missouri).

A 57.38/26   • Item 102-B-26
SOIL SURVEY REPORTS (Montana).

A 57.38/27   • Item 102-B-27
SOIL SURVEY REPORTS (Nebraska).

A 57.38/28   • Item 102-B-28
SOIL SURVEY REPORTS (Nevada).

A 57.38/29   • Item 102-B-29
SOIL SURVEY REPORTS (New Hampshire).

A 57.38/30   • Item 102-B-30
SOIL SURVEY REPORTS (New Jersey).

A 57.38/31   • Item 102-B-31
SOIL SURVEY REPORTS (New Mexico).

A 57.38/32   • Item 102-B-32
SOIL SURVEY REPORTS (New York).

A 57.38/33   • Item 102-B-33
SOIL SURVEY REPORTS (North Carolina).

A 57.38/34   • Item 102-B-34
SOIL SURVEY REPORTS (North Dakota).

A 57.38/35   • Item 102-B-35
SOIL SURVEY REPORTS (Ohio).

A 57.38/36   • Item 102-B-36
SOIL SURVEY REPORTS (Oklahoma).

A 57.38/37   • Item 102-B-37
SOIL SURVEY REPORTS (Oregon).

A 57.38/38   • Item 102-B-38
SOIL SURVEY REPORTS (Pennsylvania).

A 57.38/39   • Item 102-B-39
SOIL SURVEY REPORTS (Rhode Island).

A 57.38/40   • Item 102-B-40
SOIL SURVEY REPORTS (South Carolina).

A 57.38/41   • Item 102-B-41
SOIL SURVEY REPORTS (South Dakota).

A 57.38/42   • Item 102-B-42
SOIL SURVEY REPORTS (Tennessee).

A 57.38/43   • Item 102-B-43
SOIL SURVEY REPORTS (Texas).

A 57.38/44   • Item 102-B-44
SOIL SURVEY REPORTS (Utah).

A 57.38/45   • Item 102-B-45
SOIL SURVEY REPORTS (Vermont).

A 57.38/46   • Item 102-B-46
SOIL SURVEY REPORTS (Virginia).

A 57.38/47   • Item 102-B-47
SOIL SURVEY REPORTS (Washington).

A 57.38/48   • Item 102-B-48
SOIL SURVEY REPORTS (West Virginia).

A 57.38/49   • Item 102-B-49
SOIL SURVEY REPORTS (Wisconsin).

A 57.38/50   • Item 102-B-50
SOIL SURVEY REPORTS (Wyoming).

A 57.38/51   • Item 102-B-53
SOIL SURVEY REPORTS (Outlying Areas).

A 57.39:
MECHANICAL ANALYSES OF DATA FOR SOIL TYPES [By County].

A 57.40:nos.
REGION 5, NORTHERN GREAT PLAINS: SCS AIDS. 1– 1952–

A 57.40/2:nos.
– JOB SHEETS.

A 57.40/3:nos.
– SCS FLOOD REPORTS.

A 57.41:
WORK AND MANAGEMENT IMPROVEMENT. [Irregular]

A 57.42:
SOIL SURVEY FIELD LETTER.

A 57.43:nos.   • Item 101-A
SOIL SURVEY LABORATORY MEMORANDUMS. 1– [Irregular]
    Earlier A 77.525

A 57.44   • Item 119-A (MF)
CONSERVATION INFORMATION. SCS- CI-1– 1955– [Irregular]

    Discontinued.Discontinued.

A 57.45
CONSERVATION AIDS. SCS-CA-1– 1955– [Irregular]

WATER SUPPLY OUTLOOK REPORTS.

The climate of the cultivated and populated areas of the West is characterized by relatively dry summer months. Such precipitation as occurs falls mostly in the winter and early spring months when it is of little immediate benefit to growing crops. Most of this precipitation falls as mountain snow which stays on the ground for month, melting later to sustain streamflow during the period of greatest demand during late spring and summer. Thus, nature provides in mountain snow an imposing water storage facility.

The amount of water stored in mountain snow varies from place to place as well as from year to year and accordingly, so does the runoff of the streams. The best seasonal management of variable western water supplies results from advance estimates of the streamflow.

A snow survey consists of a series of about ten samples taken with specially designed snow sampling equipment along a permanently marked line, up to 1000 feet in length, called a snow course. The use of snow sampling equipment provides snow depth and water equivalent values for each samplingpoint. The average of these values is reported as the snow survey measurement for a snow course.

Snow surveys are made monthly or semi-monthly beginning in January or February and continue through the snow season until April, May or June. Currently more than 1400 western snow courses are measured each year. These measurements furnish the key data for water supply forecasts.

The reports, which are secured through Federal, State, private cooperation, contain detailed information on snow survey measurements, streamflow forecasts, reservoir storage, soil moisture and other guide data to water management and conservation decisions.

Requests for sample copies or mailing lists may be made either directly with the individual offices or the Portland office, which acts as a coordinating ordering service for the individual reports.

A 57.46   • Item 102-B-3 (MF)
ARIZONA. [Semimonthly (January-April)]

    Prepared by the Soil Conservation Service, 807 W. Washington Street, Phoenix, Arizona in cooperation with the Salt River Water Users Association and the Arizona Agricultural Experiment Station.
    ISSN 0364-4987

A 57.46/2
MONTANA. [Monthly (January-June)]

    Prepared by the Soil Conservation Service, Box 855, Bozeman, Montana 59715, in cooperation with the Montana Agricultural Experiment Station
    Annual issue of special measurements published separately.

A 57.46/3:date   • Item 102-B-26 (MF)
MONTANA AND NORTHERN WYOMING. [Monthly (February-May)]
    ISSN 0566-0416

    Discontinued.

A 57.46/3-2:date
WATER SUPPLY OUTLOOK FOR MONTANA AND FEDERAL-STATE-PRIVATE COOPERATION SNOW SURVEYS: SNOW PILLOW RECORDS.

A 57.46/4   • Item 102-B-28 (MF)
NEVADA. [Monthly (January-May)]
    Prepared by the Soil Conservation Service, 1483 Wells Avenue, Reno, Nevada in cooperation with the Nevada Department of Conservation and Natural Resources.

A 57.46/4-2:date   • Item 102-B-28 (MF)
NEVADA ANNUAL DATA SUMMARY WATER YEAR.

A 57.46/5   • Item 102-B-37 (MF)
OREGON. [Monthly (January-May)]

    Prepared by the Soil Conservation Service, 511 N. W. Broadway, Portland, Oregon 97209, in cooperation with the Oregon State University and the State Engineer of Oregon. Annual summary issued separately.
    ISSN 0566-0394

    Discontinued.

A 57.46/5-2:date
WATER SUPPLY SUMMARY AND OUTLOOK FOR OREGON AND FEDERAL-STATE- PRIVATE COOPERATIVE SNOW SURVEYS.

A 57.46/5-3:date   • Item 102-B-37 (MF)
OREGON ANNUAL DATA SUMMARY, WATER YEAR. [Annual]

A 57.46/6   • Item 102-B-44 (MF)
UTAH WATER SUPPLY OUTLOOK. [Monthly (January – June)]

    Prepared by the Soil Conservation Service, Room 4012, Federal Building, Salt Lake City, Utah 84111, in cooperation with the State Engineer of Utah.
    ISSN 0364-4995

A 57.46/6-1:date
FALL WATER SUPPLY SUMMARY FOR UTAH AND FEDERAL-STATE-PRIVATE COOPERATIVE SNOW SURVEYS. [Annual]

A 57.46/6-3:date   • Item 102-B-44 (MF)
UTAH, ANNUAL DATA SUMMARY. [Annual]

A 57.46/7   • Item 102-B-47 (MF)
BASIN OUTLOOK REPORTS (WASHINGTON). [Monthly (February – June)]

    Prepared by the Soil Conservation Service, 301 Hutton Building, Spokane, Washington, 99204, in cooperation with the Washington State Department of Conservation.
    ISSN 0364-5357

A 57.46/7-2:date   • Item 102-B-47 (MF)
WASHINGTON ANNUAL DATA SUMMARY WATER YEAR.

A 57.46/8   • Item 102-B-5
RIVER BASINS, FALL WATER SUPPLY SUMMARY. [Annual]

    Issued October 1. Prepared by the Soil Conservation Service, 511 N.W. Broadway, Portland, Oregon 97209.

    Discontinued.

A 57.46/9   • Item 102-B-6
COLORADO AND NEW MEXICO. [Monthly (February-May)]

    Covers Colorado River, Platte River, Arkansas River, and Rio Grande River drainage basins. Prepared by the Soil Conservation Service, Colorado Experiment Station, Fort Collins, Colorado 80521, in cooperation with the Colorado State University, State Engineer of Colorado, and State Engineer of New Mexico.
    Annual issue of special measurements issued separately.

    See A 57.56/19

A 57.46/9-2:date
FEDERAL STATE COOPERATIVE SNOW SURVEYS AND WATER SUPPLY FORECASTS FOR COLORADO, RIO GRANDE, PLATTE, AND ARKANSAS DRAINAGE BASINS, LIST AND LOCATION OF SNOW COURSES AND SOIL MOISTURE STATIONS, SEASONS.

A 57.46/10   • Item 102-B-50 (MF)
WYOMING. [Monthly (February-June)]

    Prepared by the Soil Conservation Service, Casper, Wyoming 82601, in cooperation with the State Engineer of Wyoming.
    ISSN 0364-5263

A 57.46/11   • **Item 102-B-12 (MF)**
IDAHO. [Monthly (January–June)]

Prepared by the Soil Conservation Service, Box 2709, Boise, Idaho in cooperation with the Idaho State Reclamation Engineer. ISSN 0566-0408

A 57.46/12
WESTERN UNITED STATES. [Monthly (February–May)]

Includes the Columbia River drainage in Canada. Prepared by the Soil Conservation Service, 511 N.W. Broadway, Portland, Oregon 97209, in collaboration with the California Department of Water Resources and British Columbia Department of Lands, Forests, and Water Resources.
Later A 57.46/12-2
ISSN 0364-5355

A 57.46/12-2:date   • **Item 102-B-5 (EL)**
WATER SUPPLY OUTLOOK FOR THE WESTERN UNITED STATES. [Monthly, January–May]
Earlier   A 57.46/12 and C 55.113

A 57.46/13:date   • **Item 102-B-2**
ALASKA SNOW SURVEYS AND FEDERAL-STATE PRIVATE COOPERATIVE SURVEYS. [Monthly]

(Soil Conservation Service, 204 E. Fifth Avenue, Room 217, Anchorage, Alaska 95501)
Prepared by the Soil Conservation Service in cooperation with the Alaska Soil Conservation District, Corps of Engineers, Reclamation Bureau, Alaska Highway Commission, Alaska Agricultural Experiment Station.
Earlier title: Snow Surveys and Water Supply Outlook for Alaska.

A 57.46/13-2:date
SUMMARY OF SNOW MEASUREMENTS FOR ALASKA.

A 57.46/13-3:date   • **Item 102-B-2 (MF)**
ALASKA SNOW SURVEY, ANNUAL DATA SUMMARY. [Annual]

A 57.46/14:date
FALL WATER SUPPLY SUMMARY FOR NEVADA. [Annual]

Earlier A 57.2:N 41

A 57.46/15
FEDERAL-STATE-PRIVATE COOPERATIVE SNOW SURVEYS FOR COLORADO.

A 57.46/16:date
SNOW SURVEY PHASE OF PROJECT SKYWATER, COLORADO, ANNUAL REPORT. [Annual]
Report covers fiscal year.

A 57.46/17:date
SNOW SURVEY AND SOIL MOISTURE MEASUREMENT, BASIC DATA SUMMARY FOR WESTERN UNITED STATES, INCLUDING COLUMBIA RIVER DRAINAGE IN CANADA.

Earlier A 57.2:Sn 6/12

A 57.46/18:date/nos.   • **Item 102-B-31**
NEW MEXICO WATER SUPPLY OUTLOOK AND FEDERAL-STATE-PRIVATE COOPERATIVE SNOW SURVEYS. [Monthly]

A 57.46/18-2:date   • **Item 102-B-31 (MF)**
NEW MEXICO ANNUAL DATA SUMMARY, WATER YEAR. [Annual]

A 57.46/19:date   • **Item 102-B-6**
COLORADO WATER SUPPLY OUTLOOK AND FEDERAL-STATE-PRIVATE COOPERATIVE SNOW SURVEY. [Monthly]

A 57.46/19-2:date   • **Item 102-B-6 (MF)**
COLORADO ANNUAL DATA SUMMARY, WATER YEAR (date). [Annual]

A 57.46/20   • **Item 102-B-54 (EL)**
BASIN OUTLOOK REPORTS (Western States).

A 57.47:date
WIND EROSION CONDITIONS, GREAT PLAINS, SUMMARY OF LOCAL ESTIMATES. [Irregular]

A 57.48:nos.
SOILS MEMORANDUM.

A 57.49:date & CT
CONGRESS OF INTERNATIONAL SOCIETY OF SOIL SCIENCE PUBLICATIONS.

A 57.50:CT
TECHNICAL MEMORANDUM…TO UNITED STATES STUDY COMMISSION, SOUTHEAST RIVER BASINS.

A 57.51:nos.   • **Item 121-B (MF)**
TECHNICAL RELEASES. 1–   [Irregular]

Discontinued.

A 57.52:nos.   • **Item 121-A (MF)**
SOIL SURVEY INVESTIGATION REPORTS. 1– 1967–   [Irregular]

PURPOSE:– To make available technical information from cooperative laboratory and field investigations of soils in the United States, Puerto Rico, and the Virgin Islands.
Some volumes contain only soil descriptions and physical, chemical and mineralogical data from the soil survey laboratories, while others contain reports of completed studies on soil genesis.

A 57.53:letters-nos.
CONSERVATION PLANNING MEMORANDUM.

A 57.54:date   • **Item 121-B-1 (MF)**
NATIONAL PLANT MATERIALS CENTERS: ANNUAL TECHNICAL REPORTS.

PURPOSE:– To summarize the calendar year activities of the Center, which functions in various locations throughout the United States to introduce exchange, and observe grasses, legumes, trees, and shrubs with potential value in soil and water conservation. Contains some text but consists mainly of highly technical lists of plants received, tested, and evaluated for performance.

A 57.54/2   • **Item 121-B-1 (MF)**
ANNUAL TECHNICAL REPORT OF THE CAPE MAY PLANT MATERIALS CENTER.

A 57.54/3:date   • **Item 121-B-1 (MF)**
ANNUAL REPORT MANHATTAN PLANT MATERIALS CENTER. [Annual]

A 57.55:CT
PLANT MATERIALS ANNUAL PROGRESS REPORTS.

A 57.56   • **Item 121-H**
HABITAT MANAGEMENT FOR [Various Animals].

Discontinued.

A 57.56/2   • **Item 121-H-1 (EL)**
FISH & WILDLIFE HABITAT MANAGEMENT LEAFLETS . [Irregular]

A 57.57:CT
APPRAISAL OF POTENTIALS FOR OUTDOOR RECREATIONAL DEVELOPMENT [by Area].

A 57.58:nos.
SOIL SURVEY INTERPRETATIONS FOR WOODLANDS, PROGRESS REPORTS W–   (series).

A 57.59:CT
WATERSHED WORK PLAN [by Area].
Earlier A 57.2

A 57.60:date
OBSERVATIONAL STUDY OF AGRICULTURAL ASPECTS OF ARKANSAS RIVER MULTIPLE-PURPOSE PROJECT, ANNUAL REPORT. 1969–

A 57.61:CT
CLASSIFICATION AND CORRELATION OF SOILS [by areas]. (Western Regional Technical Service Center, Portland, Oregon)

A 57.62:CT
RESOURCE CONSERVATION AND DEVELOPMENT PLANS.

A 57.63:nos.
CONSERVATION AGRONOMY TECHNICAL NOTES (numbered). (Western Region, Portland, Oregon)

A 57.64:CT   • **Item 121-E (MF)**
FLOOD PLAIN REPORT [various locations].

A 57.64/2:CT   • **Item 121-E (MF)**
FLOOD HAZARD ANALYSES (series). [Irregular]

Discontinued 1979.

A 57.64/3:CT
FLOOD HAZARD STUDIES [various rivers, creeks, and areas]. [Irregular]

Discontinued 1979.

A 57.64/4   • **Item 102-B-6**
FLOOD PLAIN MANAGEMENT STUDY. [Irregular]

A 57.65:CT   • **Item 121-C (MF)**
RESOURCE CONSERVATION DEVELOPMENT PLAN. [Irregular]

Earlier title: Data Environmental Impact Statements.

A 57.65/2:CT   • **Item 121-C (MF)**
FINAL ENVIRONMENTAL IMPACT STATEMENTS. [Irregular]

A 57.66:date
ANNUAL PLAN. (Columbia Blue Mountain Resource Conservation and Development Project)

A 57.67:nos.
AGRONOMY TECHNICAL NOTES.

A 57.68:CT   • **Item 121-F**
MAPS AND POSTERS. [Irregular]

A 57.69:CT   • **Item 121-F**
IMPORTANT FARMLANDS. [Irregular]
Map series for various counties.
Non-Government Publication.

A 57.69/2:CT
SOIL INTERPRETIVE MAPS (for various subjects).

A 57.70:date
CURRENT DEVELOPMENTS. [Irregular]

A 57.71:CT   • **Item 121-F**
POSTERS. [Irregular]

A 57.72:CT   • **Item 121-G**
SPECIAL REPORTS (SERIES). [Irregular]
Miscellaneous topics pertaining to the work of the Soil Conservation Service.

A 57.73   • **Item 121-C (MF)**
SOIL AND WATER CONSERVATION RESEARCH NEEDS EXECUTIVE SUMMARY. [Biennial]

A 57.74   • **Item 121-G**
HISTORICAL NOTES (series).

A 57.75:date   • **Item 121-G-1**
CONSERVATION AND YOUR COMMUNITY.

A 57.76:   • **Item 121-G-2 (E)**
ELECTRONIC PRODUCTS (misc.).

A 57.77:   • **Item 121-G-2 (EL)**
SOIL QUALITY INFORMATION SHEETS.

A 57.78:   • **Item 121-G-3 (EL)**
NCSS (NATIONAL COOPERATIVE SOIL SURVEY) NEWSLETTER.

OFFICE OF BUDGET AND FINANCE

A 58.1:date • Item 33-A
ANNUAL REPORTS.

Discontinued.

A 58.2:CT
GENERAL PUBLICATIONS.

A 58.3
BULLETINS.

A 58.4:nos.
BUDGET AND FINANCE CIRCULARS.

A 58.7:nos.
BUDGET AND FINANCE MEMORANDUMS.

A 58.8
BULLETIN FOR INFORMATION OF BUDGET, FISCAL, PROCUREMENT AND ADMINISTRATIVE PERSONNEL.

COMMODITY EXCHANGE ADMINISTRATION
(1936– 1942)

CREATION AND AUTHORITY

The Commodity Exchange Administration was established within the Department of Agriculture by memorandum of the Secretary of Agriculture effective July 1, 1936, pursuant to provisions of Act of congress, approved June 15, 1936, succeeding the Grain Futures Administration (A 41). Executive Order 9069 of February 23, 1942, grouped the Administration together with certain other agencies to form the Agricultural Marketing Administration (A 75.200).

A 59.1:date
ANNUAL REPORTS.

Later A 75.201

A 59.2:CT
GENERAL PUBLICATIONS.
Later A 75.202

A 59.5:CT
LAWS.

A 59.6:CT
REGULATIONS, RULES, AND INSTRUCTIONS.
Earlier A 41.7

A 59.7:vol.
TRADE IN GRAIN FUTURES. [Monthly]
Later A 75.209

A 59.8:vol.
COMMODITY EXCHANGE ADMINISTRATION LITERATURE, SELECTED REFERENCES CATALOGUED IN THE LIBRARY. [Monthly]

A 59.9:CT
ADDRESSES.

A 59.10:date
BALES OF COTTON DELIVERED IN SETTLEMENT OF FUTURE ON NEW YORK AND NEW ORLEANS COTTON EXCHANGES.

A 59.11:vol.
TRADE IN COTTON FUTURES. [Monthly]
Later A 75.208

A 59.12:vol.
TRADE IN WOOL TOP FUTURES. [Monthly]
Later A 75.210

A 59.13
ALPHABETICAL LIST OF FUTURES COMMISSION MERCHANTS REGISTERED UNDER COMMODITY EXCHANGE ACT, ETC.

A 59.14
ALPHABETICAL LIST OF FLOOR BROKERS REGISTERED UNDER COMMODITY EXCHANGE ACT, WITH ADDRESSES OF EACH REGISTRANT.

A 59.15
DIRECTORY OF PRINCIPAL AND BRANCH OFFICES OF REGISTERED FUTURES COMMISSION MERCHANTS, ARRANGED GEOGRAPHICALLY.

A 59.16
DIRECTORY OF ITEM 10 CORRESPONDENTS AND SOLICITORS, ETC., SOLICITING OR ACCEPTING COMMODITY FUTURES ORDERS ON BEHALF OF FUTURE COMMISSION MERCHANTS.

PLANT AND OPERATIONS OFFICE
(1939–   )

A 60.1:date • Item 71-A
ANNUAL REPORTS.

A 60.2:CT • Item 71
GENERAL PUBLICATIONS.

A 60.4
CIRCULARS. (Oct. 1 1934– July 9, 1936).

Earlier A 1.45

A 60.4/2:nos.
CIRCULARS. (July 31, 1936–   ).

A 60.4/3:nos.
PLANT AND OPERATIONS CIRCULARS.

A 60.6:CT • Item 72
REGULATIONS, RULES AND INSTRUCTIONS. MISCELLANEOUS.

A 60.7:nos.
MEMORANDUM.

A 60.7/2:nos.
PLANT AND OPERATIONS MEMORANDUM.

FARM SECURITY ADMINISTRATION
(1937– 1942, 1945– 1946)

CREATION AND AUTHORITY

The Resettlement Administration (Y 3.R 31) was established as an independent agency by Executive Order 7020 of April 30, 1935. The Administration was transferred to the Department of Agriculture by Executive Order 7530 of December 31, 1936, effective January 1, 1937. The name was changed to Farm Security Administration by Secretary's Memorandum of September 1, 1937. Executive Order 9280 of December 5, 1942, transferred the Administration to the Food Production Administration (A 79)

A 61.1:date
ANNUAL REPORTS.
Later A 80.701

A 61.2:CT
GENERAL PUBLICATIONS.
Later A 80.702

A 61.7:CT
REGULATIONS, RULES, AND INSTRUCTIONS

Includes Handbooks and Manuals.
Later A 80.706

A 61.8:nos.
LAND USE PLANNING PUBLICATION.
Superseded by A 36.104
Earlier Y 3.R 31:23

A 61.9:nos.
LAND POLICY CIRCULARS. [Monthly]
Superseded by A 36.103
Earlier Y 3.R 31:9

A 61.10:nos.
SOCIAL RESEARCH REPORTS.

A 61.11:CT
SURVEYS OF AGRICULTURAL LABOR CONDITIONS.

A 61.12:CT
PROJECT SUMMARIES (by subject).

A 61.13:CT
MAPS (by subject).

A 61.14:nos.
RESEARCH REPORTS.

A 61.15:date
RESEARCH-REFERENCE ACCESSIONS. [Semimonthly]
Earlier Y 3.R 31:29
Later A 36.110

A 61.16:CT
ADDRESSES.
Later A 80.707

A 61.17:CT
POSTERS.

A 61.18:nos.
LEAFLETS-FOR-ACTION.
Later A 80.708

A 61.19:nos.
STATUS AND PROGRESS REPORTS, RELEASES.
Earlier A 80.709

FEDERAL CROP INSURANCE CORPORATION
(1938– 1942, 1947–   )

CREATION AND AUTHORITY

The Federal Crop Insurance Corporation was established within the Department of Agriculture by the Federal Crop Insurance Act, approved February 16, 1938 (52 Stat. 72). Executive Order 9060 of February 23, 1942, consolidated the Corporation with other agencies to form the Agricultural Conservation and Adjustment Administration (A 76.100), which in turn was consolidated into the Food Production Administration (A 79.300) by Executive Order 9280 of December 5, 1942. The Corporation was made a part of the War Food Administration (A 80.900) by Executive Order 9334 of April 19, 1943. The War Food Administration was abolished by Executive Order 9577 of June 29, 1945. Secretary's Memorandum 118, Supplement 1, dated October 8, 1945, placed the Corporation within the Production and Marketing Administration (A 82.200). In 1947, the Corporation again became independent within the Department of Agriculture. (A 62). Consolidated with the Agricultural Stabilization and Conservation and the Farmers' Home Administration in 1995 to form the Farm Service Agency. The Corporation now functions under the Risk Management Agency, Department of Agriculture.

INFORMATION

Risk Management Agency
Stop 0801
1400 Independence Avenue
South Bldg., Rm. 6624
Washington, DC 20250
(202) 720-2832
Fax: (202) 720-0756

A 62.1:date • Item 71-A (MF)
ANNUAL REPORTS. 1st– 1939–

Formerly distributed to Depository Libraries under Item 70.
ISSN 0160-2314

A 62.2:CT • Item 71
GENERAL PUBLICATIONS.

A 62.6:nos.
REGULATIONS (numbered). 1– 1938–

A 62.6/2:CT • Item 72
REGULATIONS, RULES, AND INSTRUCTIONS.

A 62.7:nos.
GENERAL INFORMATION SERIES. 1– 1938–

A 62.8:CT
ADDRESSES.

A 62.9:nos.
INFORMATION (series). 1– 22. 1939– 1942.

A 62.10:nos.
KANSAS LEAFLETS. 1– 1940–

A 62.11:nos.
GENERAL PROCEDURE. 1– 7. 1939– 1940.

A 62.12:nos.
NORTH DAKOTA LEAFLETS. 1– 1940.

A 62.13:date • Item 71-B
CROP INSURANCE UPDATE. [Monthly]

Title varies: All-Risk Update; FCIC Update. Short articles and tables provide information regarding FCIC insurance on various crops. Discontinued.

A 62.15:CT • Item 71-E
HANDBOOKS, MANUALS AND GUIDES.

A 62.16:date • Item 71-C
GUIDE TO CROP INSURANCE PROTECTION. [Annual]

A 62.17: • Item 71-C-1 (EL)
CROP INSURANCE RESEARCH AND DEVELOPMENT BULLETINS (R&D Bulletins).

A 62.18: • Item 71-C-1 (E)
ELECTRONIC PRODUCTS (misc.)

SUGAR DIVISION
(1938– 1942)

CREATION AND AUTHORITY

The Sugar Division, originally established within the Agricultural Adjustment Administration (A 55), was made an independent division in the Department of Agriculture on October 16, 1938, by Secretary's Memorandum 783. By Executive Order 9069 of February 23, 1942, it was placed under the Agricultural Conservation and Adjustment Administration, where it was redesignated the Sugar Agency (A 76.300).

A 63.1:date
ANNUAL REPORTS.

A 63.2:CT
GENERAL PUBLICATIONS.

A 63.3
BULLETINS [none issued].

A 63.4
CIRCULARS [none issued].

A 63.5
LAWS [none issued].

A 63.6:CT
REGULATIONS.
Earlier A 55.6

A 63.7:nos.
SUGAR DETERMINATION.

Pubs. desig. SD-nos.
Earlier A 55.37
Later A 76.307

A 63.8:nos.
PUERTO RICO ORDERS.
Earlier A 55.18

A 63.9:nos.
SUGAR INFORMATION SERIES, PUBLICATIONS.

A 63.10:nos.
MISCELLANEOUS SERIES.
Later A 55.73

A 63.11:nos.
INSTRUCTIONS RELATIVE TO SUGAR BEET PROGRAM.

Changed from A 63.2
See also A 55.70

FOREIGN AGRICULTURAL SERVICE
(1938– 1939)

CREATION AND AUTHORITY

The Foreign Agriculture Service was established by the Act of June 5, 1930. Its officers reported directly to the Foreign Agricultural Service Division in the Bureau of Agricultural Economics (A 36) during the period from 1930 until December 1, 1938 when the Service became a separate agency within the Department of Agriculture. By Reorganization Plan 2 of 1939, the Service was transferred to the Department of State. Other Division personnel and its economic research functions were transferred to the Office of Foreign Agricultural Relations (A 67).

A 64.1:date
ANNUAL REPORTS.

A 64.2:CT
GENERAL PUBLICATIONS.

A 64.7:vol.
FOREIGN AGRICULTURE, REVIEW OF FOREIGN FARM POLICY, PRODUCTION, AND TRADE. [Monthly]
Earlier A 36.88
Later A 67.7

A 64.8:vol.
FOREIGN CROPS AND MARKETS. [Weekly]
Earlier A 36.14
Later A 67.8

A 64.9:nos.
F.S.A. (series).
Earlier A 36.79
Later A 67.12

A 64.10:CT
ADDRESSES.

A 64.11:nos.
FRUIT FLASHES, FOREIGN NEWS ON FRUITS BY CABLE AND RADIO: CITRUS FRUITS. [Weekly]
Earlier A 36.66
Later A 67.9

A 64.12:nos.
FRUIT FLASHES, FOREIGN NEWS ON FRUITS BY CABLE AND RADIO: DECIDUOUS FRUITS. [Weekly]
Earlier A 36.67
Later A 67.10

A 64.13:nos.
FOREIGN SERVICE ON VEGETABLES.

Earlier A 36.46

DIVISION OF MARKETING AND MARKETING AGREEMENTS
(1937–1940)

CREATION AND AUTHORITY

The Division of Marketing and Marketing Agreements was established within the Department of Agriculture by Marketing Agreement Act of 1937. By Reorganization Plan No. 3, of 1939, the Division was merged with the Federal Surplus Commodities Corporation (A 69) to form the Surplus Marketing Administration (A 73), effective June 30, 1940.

A 65.1:date
ANNUAL REPORTS.

A 65.2:CT
GENERAL PUBLICATIONS.

A 65.5:CT
LAWS.

A 65.7:nos.
MARKETING ORDERS.
    Earlier A 55.36
    Later A 73.8

A 65.8:nos.
DOCKETS.
    Earlier A 55.21

A 65.9:nos.
MARKETING AGREEMENT SERIES.
    Earlier A 55.9
    Later A 73.9

A 65.10:nos.
MARKETING SECTION PUBLICATIONS.

A 65.11:CT
ADDRESSES.

A 65.12:letters-nos.&nos.
MARKETING INFORMATION SERIES.
    Earlier A 55.54

AGRICULTURAL MARKETING SERVICE
(1939–1942)

CREATION AND AUTHORITY

The Agricultural Marketing Service was established within the Department of Agriculture by Secretary's Memorandum 830, dated July 7, 1939, pursuant to the Agricultural Appropriations Act of 1940, approved June 30, 1939 (53 Stat. 939). The Service was consolidated with other agencies to form the Agricultural Marketing Administration (A 75) by Executive Order 9069 of February 23, 1942.

A 66.1:date
ANNUAL REPORTS.

A 66.2:CT
GENERAL PUBLICATIONS.

A 66.6:CT
REGULATIONS, RULES, AND INSTRUCTIONS.

A 66.7:date
COLD STORAGE REPORTS. [Monthly]
    Earlier A 36.107
    Later A 75.8

A 66.8:date
COTTON MARKET REVIEW. [Weekly]
    Earlier A 36.73
    Later A 75.9

A 66.9:date
COTTON REPORTS. [Monthly July-Dec.]
    Earlier A 36.30

A 66.10:date
FARM LABOR REPORTS. [Monthly]
    Varying title.
    Earlier A 36.69
    Later A 36.140

A 66.10:date
FARM WAGE RATES AND RELATED DATA. [Quarterly]
    Earlier A 36.77

A 66.11:date
GENERAL CROP REPORTS. [Monthly except Feb. and March]
    Earlier A 36.29

A 66.12:nos.
HONEY REPORTS. [Semiannual]

    Earlier A 36.105
    Later A 75.11

A 66.13:vol
LIVESTOCK, MEATS, AND WOOL; MARKET REVIEWS AND STATISTICS. [Weekly]
    Earlier A 36.98
    Later A 75.10

A 66.14:vol.
MARKETING ACTIVITIES. [Monthly]
    Earlier A 36.21
    Later A 75.13

A 66.15:nos.
PEANUT REPORTS. [Weekly]
    Earlier A 36.106
    Later A 75.12

A 66.16:CT
U.S. STANDARDS FOR FRUITS AND VEGETABLES.
    Earlier A 36.35
    Later A 75.19

A 66.17:dt.&nos.
TRUCK CROP ESTIMATE REPORTS.
    Pubs. Desig. TC-nos.
    Earlier A 36.101

A 66.18:vol.
P. AND S. DOCKET, MONTHLY REPORT OF ACTION TAKEN ON CASES ARISING UNDER PACKERS AND STOCKYARDS ACT.
    Supersedes A 4.28
    Later A 75.14

A 66.19:date
REPORTS ISSUED BY AGRICULTURAL MARKETING SERVICE.

    Earlier A 36.58

A 66.20:date
TRUCK RECEIPTS OF FRESH FRUITS AND VEGETABLES.
    Earlier A 36.48:F 94/2

A 66.21:CT
POSTERS.
    Earlier A 36.22

A 66.22:nos.
CROP REPORTING PROCEDURE.
    Earlier A 36.92

A 66.23:CT
ADDRESSES.

A 66.24:date
CAR-LOT SHIPMENTS OF FRUITS AND VEGETABLES, BY COMMODITIES, STATES, AND MONTHS.
    Earlier A 36.2:F 94/10

A 66.24/2:date
CARLOT SHIPMENTS OF . . . FROM STATIONS IN U.S.
    Earlier A 36.2:F 94/21

A 66.25:date
FLAX MARKET REVIEW. [Quarterly]
    Earlier A 36.115

A 66.26:date
CHECK LIST OF STANDARDS FOR FARM PRODUCTS.
    Earlier A 36.59

A 66.27:nos.
SERVICE AND REGULATORY ANNOUNCEMENTS.
    Earlier A 36.5
    Later A 75.16

A 66.28:date
DRIVEN-IN RECEIPTS OF LIVESTOCK.
    Earlier A 36.2:L 75/5

A 66.29:date
CROP REPORTS TO BE ISSUED BY CROP REPORTING BOARD.
    Earlier A 36.2:C 88/7

A 66.30:nos.
SMUTTY WHEAT REPORTS.
    Earlier A 36.56

A 66.31:vol.
A.M.S. NEWS. [Semimonthly]

A 66.32:CT
LIST OF PUBLICATIONS.

A 66.33:date
PROSPECTIVE PLANTINGS.
    Earlier A 36.38

A 66.34:date
FARM PRODUCTION AND INCOME FROM MEAT ANIMALS.
    Earlier A 36.2:M 46/5

A 66.35:date
DAIRY AND POULTRY MARKET STATISTICS, ANNUAL SUMMARIES.
    Earlier A 36.54

A 66.36:date
LIVESTOCK, MEATS, AND WOOL, MARKET STATISTICS AND RELATED DATA (annual compilation).
    For weekly issues, see A 66.13
    Earlier A 36.2:L 74/8

A 66.37:date
QUALITY AND PRICES OF COTTON LINTERS PRODUCED IN UNITED STATES.
    Earlier A 36.2:C 82/56

A 66.38:date
DIRECTORY [of] MARKET NEWS BROADCASTS.
    Earlier A 36.2:M 34/3

A 66.39:date
FRUIT AND NUT CROP PROSPECTS.
    Earlier A 36.32

A 66.40:date
CAR-LOT UNLOADS OF CERTAIN FRUITS AND VEGETABLES. [Annual]
    Earlier A 36.48:F 94

A 66.41:CT
COTTON, ESTIMATED ACREAGE, YIELD AND PRODUCTION.

A 66.42:date
LIVESTOCK REPORTS.
    Earlier A 36.33

A 66.43:date
POULTRY AND EGG PRODUCTION. [Monthly]

A 66.44:nos.
DAIRY PRODUCTION. [Monthly]
    Later A 36.139

A 66.45:date
STATE AGRICULTURAL DEPARTMENTS AND MARKETING AGENCIES, WITH NAMES OF OFFICIALS.
Earlier A 36.55

A 66.46:incl. nos.
NOTICES OF JUDGMENT UNDER INSECTICIDE ACT.
Earlier A 46.7
Later A 75.15

A 66.47:CT
CORN, ESTIMATED PLANTED ACREAGE, YIELD, AND PRODUCTION BY STATES.

A 66.48
WINTER WHEAT AND RYE REPORTS.
Earlier A 36.74

A 66.49:date
ANNUAL REPORTS ON TOBACCO STATISTICS.

FOREIGN AGRICULTURAL SERVICE
(1953–   )

CREATION AND AUTHORITY

The Foreign Agricultural Service was established within the Department of Agriculture by Secretary's Memorandum 1320, Supp. 1, dated March 10, 1953, which also abolished the Office of Foreign Agricultural Relations.

INFORMATION

Information Division
Foreign Agricultural Service
USDA
Stop 1004
1400 Independence Avenue, SW
Washington, DC 20250-1004
(202) 690-1980
Fax: (202) 690-2159
E-mail:info@fas.usda.gov
http://www.fas.usda.gov

A 67.1:date   • Item 75
ANNUAL REPORTS.
Discontinued.

A 67.1/2:date   • Item 77-A
FOREIGN AGRICULTURE. [Annual]
Discontinued.

A 67.2:CT   • Item 77
GENERAL PUBLICATIONS.

A 67.3:nos.   • Item 76-A
FOREIGN AGRICULTURAL BULLETINS.
Discontinued.

A 67.6:CT
REGULATIONS, RULES, AND INSTRUCTIONS.

A 67.7:v.nos.&nos.   • Item 76
FOREIGN AGRICULTURE, A REVIEW OF FOREIGN FARM POLICY, PRODUCTION, AND TRADE. v. 1– 256. 1927– 1962. [Monthly]

Combined with Foreign Crops and Markets (A 67.8) to from Foreign Agriculture (A 67.7/2).

A 67.7/2:v.nos.&nos.   • Item 76
FOREIGN AGRICULTURE, INCLUDING FOREIGN CROPS AND MARKETS. 1–   1963–   [Weekly]

PURPOSE:– To inform interested persons and organizations in the United States of important world developments affecting U.S. exports and imports of agricultural products.
Contains brief signed articles, written in popular style. Departments include: Market Developments & Export Programs; World Crops and Mar-

kets (which contains statistical tables).
Released on Friday of each week.
Combines Foreign Agriculture (A 67.7) and Foreign Crops and Markets (A 67.8) which prior to 1963 were published separately.
Annual index included in final issue.
Indexed by: Index to U.S. Government Periodicals.
ISSN 0015-7163
See A 67.7/3

A 67.7/3:v.nos./nos.   • Item 76
AGEXPORTER. [Monthly]

A 67.8:v.nos.&nos.   • Item 76-C (EL)
FOREIGN CROPS AND MARKETS. v. 1– 85. 1919– 1962. [Weekly]

PURPOSE:– To assist the foreign marketing of U.S. farm products by keeping the Nation's agricultural interests informed of current crops and livestock developments abroad, foreign trends in production, prices, supplies and consumption of farm products, and other factors affecting world agricultural trade. Statistical tables supplement new items.
Issues were numbered beginning with v. 4, no. 4 (March 1, 1922); those proceeding being unnumbered.
Combined in 1963 with Foreign Agriculture (A 67.7) to form a new weekly publication, Foreign Agriculture (A 67.7/2).

A 67.8/2:date
– MONTHLY SUPPLEMENT.
Superseded by A 67.19

A 67.8/3
WORLD AGRICULTURAL PRODUCTION AND TRADE, STATISTICAL REPORT. 1963–1975. [Monthly]

Contains a series of reports on world crop and livestock production and trade.
Supersedes World Summaries, Crops and Livestock, which were published prior to 1963 as a supplement to Foreign Crops and Markets.

RELEASE DATE OF (year) WORLD AGRICULTURAL REPORT. [Annual]

List by release date commodity, and contents, the appearing in World Agricultural Production and Trade, Statistical Report.
Issued early in January of each year.

A 67.9:nos.
FRUIT FLASHES, FOREIGN NEWS ON FRUITS BY CABLE AND RADIO: CITRUS [Fruits]. 1– 234. – 1940. [Weekly]
Earlier A 64.11

A 67.10:nos.
FRUIT FLASHES, FOREIGN NEWS ON FRUITS BY CABLE AND RADIO: DECIDUOUS [Fruits]. 1– 248. – 1941. [Weekly]
Earlier A 64.12

A 67.11:nos.
[FOREIGN SERVICE REPORTS].
Earlier A 36.39

A 67.12:nos.
[FOREIGN STATISTICS ON APPLES AND OTHER DECIDUOUS FRUITS].
Earlier A 64.9

A 67.13
ADDRESSES. [Irregular]

A 67.14:nos.
[FOREIGN SERVICE ON VEGETABLES]. FSV 1– 123. – 1941.
Earlier A 64.23

A 67.15:v.nos.
AGRICULTURE IN THE AMERICAS. v. 1– 7. 1941– 1947.

A 67.16   • Item 76-E
FOREIGN AGRICULTURE REPORTS. FAR 1–   1942– [Irregular]

PURPOSE:– To provide an orderly outlet for comprehensive treatment of various phases of agricultural policy programs, production, consumption, and trade of foreign countries.
The majority of the reports are devoted to a single commodity situation in a single country, such as the tobacco industry in Italy or the citrus industry in Southern Africa Some reports cover the world situation for a single commodity. Material presented is of a more permanent and technical nature.
PROSPECTS FOR FOREIGN TRADE IN [Commodity].

Provides a situation and outlook releases for various agricultural commodities. Each release covers the world situation, including stocks, production, trade, consumption, price movements; factors affecting export outlook; and developing markets abroad for U.S. products. Charts and statistical tables supplement the textual summaries. Some issues contain list of Foreign Agricultural Service publications on the commodity covered in reports.

A 67.17:CT
ECONOMIC PLANS OF INTEREST TO THE AMERICAS.

A 67.18:letters/nos.   • Item 76-J (MF) (EL)
FOREIGN AGRICULTURAL CIRCULARS. [Irregular]

Supplements information appearing in Foreign Crops and Markets and other Foreign Agricultural Service publications. While many of the reports are issued on a one-time basis and cover a specific subject or country, many of the reports are released on a periodic basis. The Circulars contain both textual summaries and statistical tables. Releases are issued for the following commodities with examples of the more important coverage within each sub-division of this series of releases.

A 67.18:ATH nos.   • Item 76-J
AGRICULTURAL TRADE HIGHLIGHTS.

A 67.18:ECG nos.   • Item 76-J
MONTHLY SUMMARY OF EXPORT CREDIT GUARANTEE PROGRAM ACTIVITY, COMMODITY CREDIT CORPORATION.

A 67.18:EMG nos.   • Item 76-J
EXPORT MARKETS OF U.S. GRAIN AND PRODUCTS.

A 67.18:FATP/nos.   • Item 76-J
FOREIGN AGRICULTURAL TRADE POLICY AND ANALYSIS. 1–

A 67.18:FC/nos.   • Item 76-J
COTTON. 1–

ISSN 0145-0875

A 67.18:FCAN/nos.   • Item 76-J
CANNED FRUIT. 1–
ISSN 0145-0905

A 67.18:FCB/nos.   • Item 76-J
COCOA BEANS. 1–
ISSN 0145-0883

A 67.18:FCF/nos.   • Item 76-J
CITRUS FRUITS. 1–
ISSN 0145-0891

A 67.18:FCOF/nos.   • Item 76-J
COFFEE. 1–
ISSN 0145-0913

A 67.18:FD/nos.   • Item 76-J
DAIRYING. 1–
ISSN 0145-093X

A 67.18:FDAP/nos.   • Item 76-J
DECIDUOUS FRUIT. 1–
ISSN 0145-0948

A 67.18:FDF/nos.   • Item 76-J
DRIED FRUITS. 1–

ISSN 0145-0956

A 67.18:FDLMT • **Item 76-J**
MEAT AND DAIRY MONTHLY IMPORTS.

A 67.18:FDLP nos. • **Item 76-J**
DAIRY, LIVESTOCK, AND POULTRY: U.S. TRADE AND PROSPECTS.

A 67.18:FDMI nos. • **Item 76-J**
DAIRY MONTHLY IMPORTS.

A 67.18:FDP/nos. • **Item 76-J**
DRY BEANS AND PEAS. 1–

A 67.18:FDR/nos. • **Item 76-J**
DRIED PULSES. 1–
ISSN 0145-0964

A 67.18:FFO/nos. • **Item 76-J**
FATS, OILS, AND OILSEEDS. 1–

A 67.18:FFV/nos. • **Item 76-J**
FRESH VEGETABLES.1–

A 67.18:FFVS • **Item 76-J**
U.S. SEED EXPORTS.
Earlier title: Seeds, Field and Vegetables.
ISSN 0145-1006

A 67.18:FG • **Item 76-J**
GRAIN: WORLD MARKETS AND TRADE.
Previously: World Grain Situation and Outlook.
ISSN 0145-0195

A 67.18:FH/nos. • **Item 76-J**
HOPS. 1–
ISSN 0145-028X

A 67.18:FHON/nos. • **Item 76-J**
HONEY. 1–
ISSN 0145-0972

A 67.18:FHORT nos. • **Item 76-J**
HORTICULTURAL PRODUCTS REVIEW.

A 67.18:FL&P:date • **Item 76-J**
LIVESTOCK AND POULTRY: WORLD MARKETS AND TRADE... CIRCULAR SERIES

A 67.18:FLM/nos. • **Item 76-J**
LIVESTOCK AND MEATS. 1–
ISSN 0145-0980

A 67.18:FN/nos. • **Item 76-J**
NUTS. 1–

A 67.18:FOL/nos. • **Item 76-J**
TABLE OLIVES. 1– 1976– [Irregular]

A 67.18:FOP/nos. • **Item 76-J**
OILSEEDS AND PRODUCTS. 1–
ISSN 0145-0921

A 67.18:FPE/nos. • **Item 76-J**
POULTRY AND EGGS. 1–
ISSN 0145-0182

A 67.18:FR/nos. • **Item 76-J**
RICE. 1–
ISSN 0145-0999

A 67.18:FS/nos. • **Item 76-J**
SUGAR, MOLASSES AND HONEY. 1–

Mergers Sugar (FS-nos.) and Honey (FHON-nos).
ISSN 0145-0859

A 67.18:FT/nos. • **Item 76-J**
TOBACCO. 1–
ISSN 0145-0867

A 67.18:FTEA/nos. • **Item 76-J**
TEA, SPICES, AND OTHER TROPICAL PRODUCTS. 1–
ISSN 0092-8011

A 67.18:FTROP/nos. • **Item 76-J**
TROPICAL PRODUCTS: WORLD MARKETS AND TRADE.

A 67.18:FVEG/nos. • **Item 76-J**
FRESH AND PROCESSED VEGETABLES. 1–

A 67.18:FVF/nos. • **Item 76-J**
VEGETABLE FIBERS. 1–
ISSN 0092-8046

A 67.18:FW/nos. • **Item 76-J**
WOOL. 1–
ISSN 0145-0840

A 67.18:SG • **Item 76-J**
USSR GRAIN SITUATION AND OUTLOOK.

A 67.18:WAP • **Item 76-J**
WORLD AGRICULTURAL PRODUCTION.

A 67.18:WCP • **Item 76-J**
WORLD CROP PRODUCTION.

A 67.18:WP nos. • **Item 76-J**
WOOD PRODUCTS: INTERNATIONAL TRADE AND FOREIGN MARKETS.

A 67.18/2:date • **Item 76-J (MF)**
WORLD COCOA SITUATION. [Semiannual]
Earlier A 67.18:FCB
Discontinued.

A 67.18/3 • **Item 77-B-1 (EL)**
U.S. PLANTING SEED TRADE. [Monthly]

A 67.19:date
FOREIGN AGRICULTURAL TRADE. [Monthly]

Supersedes Foreign Crops and Markets Monthly Supplement A 67.8/2
Later A 93.17

A 67.19/2:date
– STATISTICAL REPORT FOR CALENDAR YEAR.
Later A 93.17/3

A 67.19/3:date
– FISCAL YEAR WITH COMPARISONS.
Later A 93.17/6

A 67.19/4:date
– BY COMMODITY AND BY COUNTRY, ANNUAL FISCAL YEAR.

A 67.19/5:date
– VALUE BY COUNTRIES, CALENDAR YEAR WITH COMPARISONS.
Later A 93.17/4

A 67.19/6:CT&date
– UNITED STATES TRADE IN AGRICULTURAL PRODUCTS WITH INDIVIDUAL COUNTRIES BY CALENDAR YEAR.
Earlier A 67.19

A 67.19/7:date
– UNITED STATES IMPORTS OF FRUITS AND VEGETABLES UNDER QUARANTINE BY COUNTRIES OF ORIGIN AND PORTS OF ENTRY, ANNUAL FISCAL YEAR.
Earlier A 67.2:F 94
Later A 93.17/5

A 67.19/8:date
– DIGEST OF UNITED STATES. [Monthly]

Contains material formerly included in A 67.19 and A 67.8
Later A 93.17/2

A 67.19/9:nos.
SUMMARY OF CIRCULAR. [Irregular]

A 67.20:nos. • **Item 78**
INTERNATIONAL AGRICULTURAL COLLABORATION SERIES.
Discontinued.

A 67.21:date
FOREIGN TRADE IN FARM MACHINERY AND SUPPLIES. [Monthly]

A 67.22:
BRITISH-AMERICAN AGRICULTURAL NEWS SERVICE.

A 67.23:date
WORLD COTTON PRICES. [Weekly]

A 67.24:date • **Item 76-B**
FOREIGN AGRICULTURAL SITUATION, MAPS AND CHARTS. [Annual]
Earlier A 67.2:C 38 and A 67.2:C 38/2
Discontinued.

A 67.25:nos. • **Item 76-D**
WORLD TOBACCO ANALYSIS (Quarterly).
Designated Circular FT-nos.
Discontinued.

A 67.26 • **Item 76-G (MF)**
FOREIGN AGRICULTURAL SERVICE, MISCELLANEOUS. FAS-M-1– 1956–

PURPOSE:– To provide an outlet for specialized information, often of an ephemeral nature, on various phases of agriculture.

A 67.26:201 • **Item 76-G**
FOOD AND AGRICULTURAL EXPORT DIRECTORY. 1969– [Annual] (Export Trade Services Division)

PURPOSE:– To provide an updated listing of State and government agencies, companies, trade associations, and others willing to assist and provide services to U.S. firms interested in exporting U.S. foods and agricultural products.

A 67.27:date • **Item 78-A**
WORLD AGRICULTURAL SITUATION. [Annual]
Earlier A 67.2:Ag 8/9
Later A 93.29

A 67.28:date • **Item 76-F**
COMPETITIVE POSITION OF UNITED STATES FARM PRODUCTS ABROAD. [Annual]
Earlier A 67.2:F 22
Discontinued.

A 67.29:date • **Item 75-A**
DEVELOPING FOREIGN MARKETS FOR U.S. FARM PRODUCTS, SUMMARY OF PROMOTIONAL ACTIVITY. [Annual]
Discontinued.

A 67.30:CT
PROSPECTS FOR FOREIGN TRADE IN [various commodities].

A 67.30:C 82
– COTTON. [Annual]

A 67.30:D 14
– DAIRY CATTLE AND DAIRY AND POULTRY PRODUCTS. [Annual]

A 67.30:F 94
– FRUITS, VEGETABLES, TREE NUTS. [Annual]

A 67.30:L 75
– LIVESTOCK AND MEAT. [Annual]

A 67.30:Oi 5
– OILSEEDS AND OILSEED PRODUCTS. [Annual]

A 67.30:T 55
– TOBACCO. [Annual]

A 67.30:W 56
– WHEAT, RICE, FEED GRAINS, DRY PEAS, DRY BEANS, SEEDS, HOPS. [Annual]

A 67.31:nos.
FOREIGN TRAINING LETTER TO FOREIGN AGRICULTURAL CONTRACTS AT LAND-GRANT COLLEGE.

A 67.31/2:
FAS LETTER TO AGRICULTURAL ATTACHES AND OFFICERS.

A 67.31/3:
FOREIGN TRAINING LETTERS.

A 67.32:date
U.S. AGRICULTURAL EXPORTS. [Annual]
Earlier A 67.2:Ex 7/2
Later A 93.90

A 67.32/2:date
U.S. AGRICULTURAL IMPORTS, FACT SHEET. [Annual]
Later A 93.30/2

A 67.33:nos.
BIBLIOGRAPHIES AND LISTS OF PUBLICATIONS.

A 67.34:CT
INTERNATIONAL ANIMAL FEED SYMPOSIUM
REPORTS.

A 67.35   • **Item 76-H**
REPORT OF UNITED STATES GOVERNMENT TO THE
FOOD AND AGRICULTURAL ORGANIZATION OF
THE UNITED NATIONS. [Triennial]
Discontinued.

A 67.36:CT
INDICES OF AGRICULTURAL PRODUCTION IN [vari-
ous] COUNTRIES.
Later A 93.32

A 67.37
ANNUAL SUMMARY OF FOREIGN AGRICULTURAL
TRAINING AS OF [date]. [Annual]

Prepared by the International Agricultural Development Service.
Describes in brief textual summaries, pictures,
maps and statistical tables the work of training of
agricultural participants in the exchange-of-per-
sons programs sponsored both privately and by
the Government.

A 67.38:date
DOCUMENT RETRIEVAL SUBJECT INDEX. 1968–
[Monthly]

This subsystem is one part of the FAS Information Management System and is designed to
enable FAS to store and retrieve the information
for the benefit of end-users contained in foreign
agricultural reports and related material.
Each issue is cumulative for the year.
Each report is indexed by country, commodity or commodity group and/or certain selected
topics.

A 67.39:nos.
AGRICULTURAL TRADE POLICY, ATP– (series).
[Irregular]

A 67.40:date   • **Item 76-K (EL)**
U.S. EXPORT SALES. [Weekly]

Prior to October 31, 1974 issued by Statisti-
cal Reporting Service (A 92.38).
ISSN 0145-0352
Discontinued.

A 67.40/2:date   • **Item 76-K (EL)**
TRADE LEADS. [Weekly]
Earlier titled: Export Briefs.

A 67.40/3:date
CONTRACTS FOR U.S. FOOD PRODUCTS. [Monthly]

A 67.40/4:date   • **Item 76-K (MF)**
U.S. EXPORTS OF REPORTED AGRICULTURAL
COMMODITIES FOR (dates), MARKETING YEARS.
[Annual]

Data for the report is derived from weekly
reports submitted by exporters of U.S. agricultural commodities and summarized at the end of
each market year. Exports are shown by country
and region.

A 67.40/5:date   • **Item 76-K-1 (MF)**
TRADE POLICIES AND MARKET OPPORTUNITIES
FOR U.S. FARM EXPORTS, ANNUAL REPORT.
[Annual]

Presents information on trade policies of foreign countries and the effects of those policies
on market opportunities for U. S. farm exports, as
required by Section 1132 of the Food Security

Act of 1985. Tables present data on U. S. trade
partners and U. S. farm products for export.

A 67.41:date
EEO FACT SHEET FROM OFFICE OF THE ADMINIS-
TRATOR.

A 67.42:nos.   • **Item 76-L (MF)**
WEEKLY ROUNDUP OF WORLD PRODUCTION AND
TRADE, WR (series).

Contains short articles on agriculture and
trade as well as statistical tables showing different kinds of agricultural production in various
countries.
Discontinued.

A 67.42/2:nos.
FAS REPORT, STATUS OF U.S. SUGAR IMPORT
QUOTAS. [Weekly]

Alternate title: Sugar Import Notice.

A 67.43:date   • **Item 77-A-3**
QUARTERLY REPORT OF THE GENERAL SALES
MANAGER.

Consists largely of statistical tables showing
sales to foreign countries.
Earlier A 1.117
Discontinued.

A 67.44:date   • **Item 24-T (MF)**
FOOD FOR PEACE, ANNUAL REPORT ON PUBLIC
LAW 480.
Earlier A 1.119

A 67.45:nos.   • **Item 76-M**
AGRICULTURAL TRADE HIGHLIGHTS. [Monthly]

Discontinued.

A 67.46:date   • **Item 76-M (EL)**
AGRICULTURAL EXPORT ASSISTANCE UPDATE
QUARTERLY REPORT.

A 67.47:date   • **Item 76-J-1 (EL)**
MONTHLY SUMMARY OF EXPORT CREDIT GUAR-
ANTEE PROGRAM ACTIVITY.

A 67.48:date/nos.   • **Item 76-K**
U.S. EXPORT SALES, OUTSTANDING EXPORT SALES
(UNSHIPPED BALANCES) ON . . .

A 67.49   • **Item 77-B**
DIRECTORIES

A 67.50   • **Item 77-B-1 (E)**
ELECTRONIC PRODUCTS. (MISC.)

RURAL UTILITIES SERVICE
(1994–   )

CREATION AND AUTHORITY

The Rural Electrification Administration (Y 3.R
88) was established as an emergency agency by
Executive Order 7037 of May 11, 1935. It became a permanent agency in 1936 and was transferred to the Department of Agriculture by the
President's Reorganization Plan 2 of 1939.

Abolished by Secretary's Memorandum 1010-
13, October 20, 1994, functions assumed by Rural
Utilities Services.

INFORMATION

Natural Resources Conservation Service
4051 South Agricultural Bldg.
1400 Independence Ave., SW
Washington, DC 20250
(202) 720-9540
Fax: (202) 720-1725
http://www.usda.gov/rus/home/home.htm

A 68.1   • **Item 115 (MF)**
REPORT OF THE ADMINISTRATOR OF THE RURAL
ELECTRIFICATION ADMINISTRATION. 1936–
[Annual]

Annual report of the Administrator made to
the Secretary of Agriculture for the fiscal year.
Includes statistical tables of operations.
ISSN 0083-3193

A 68.1/2:date   • **Item 115-A-1 (MF)**
ANNUAL STATISTICAL REPORT, RURAL ELECTRIFI-
CATION BORROWERS. [Annual]
Contains financial and statistical information
about the operations of over 900 REA electric
borrowers individually and as a group. Data in the
report are on a calendar year basis, since most
borrowers close their books on December 31.
Data on borrowers which are not cooperatives
are also included in the Federal Power Commission annual reports on the electric utility industry.

A 68.1/3   • **Item 115-A-2 (MF)**
STATISTICAL REPORT, RURAL TELECOMMUNICA-
TIONS PHONE BORROWERS. [Annual]

Presents financial and statistical information
on the REA rural telephone program and is based
on REA loan records and statistical reports submitted by over 600 borrowers. Data are on a calendar year basis.
Former titles: Annual Statistical Report, Rural
Telephone program. Annual Statistical Report,
Rural Telephone Borrowers

A 68.1/4:date   • **Item 115-A-3 (MF)**
ANNUAL REPORT OF ENERGY PURCHASED BY REA
BORROWERS, CALENDAR YEAR. 1st–   1939–

A 68.2:CT   • **Item 116**
GENERAL PUBLICATIONS.

Earlier Y 3.R 88:2

A 68.3:nos.   • **Item 116 (MF)**
RUS BULLETINS. [Irregular]

A 68.3:ind.   • **Item 116**
CURRENT REA PUBLICATIONS.

Issued in looseleaf form.

A 68.5:CT   • **Item 116-B**
LAWS.

A 68.6:CT
REGULATIONS, RULES AND INSTRUCTIONS.

A 68.6/2   • **Item 116-A**
LIST OF MATERIAL ACCEPTABLE FOR USE ON SYS-
TEMS OF REA ELECTRIFICATION BORROWERS
AND LIST OF MATERIALS ACCEPTED ON A TRIAL
BASIS. [Annual] (REA Bulletin 43-5)

Gives listing of electrical materials acceptable for use on distribution transmission and plant
systems of REA borrowers
Subscription includes basic manual and three
quarterly supplements.

A 68.6/3:sec.nos.   • **Item 116-A-1 (MF)**
TELEPHONE OPERATORS' MANUAL.

A 68.6/4   • **Item 116-A-2**
TELECOMMUNICATIONS ENGINEERING AND CON-
STRUCTION MANUAL. [Irregular]

Earlier title: Telephone Engineering and Construction Manual.
Issued in sections, punched for ring-binder.

A 68.6/5   • **Item 116-A-3 (P) (EL)**
LIST OF MATERIALS ACCEPTABLE FOR USE ON
TELEPHONE SYSTEMS OF REA BORROWERS.
[Annual] (REA Bulletin 344-2)

Gives names of the manufacturers together
with the catalog numbers for items acceptable for
use on telephone systems of REA borrowers.
These items are referred to in the Telephone System Construction Contract and other telephone
documents.
Subscription price includes the basic volume,
issued in April, and bi-monthly supplements.

A 68.6/6:CT   • **Item 116-A-4**
HANDBOOKS, MANUALS, GUIDES. [Irregular]

A 68.7:nos.
CONSTRUCTION REPORTS.
Earlier Y 3.R 88:13

A 68.8:nos.
PROGRESS BULLETINS, GENERAL.

A 68.9:vol   • **Item 117**
RURAL ELECTRIFICATION NEWS. [Monthly]
Earlier Y 3.R 99:9

Discontinued

A 68.10:date
[LIBRARY LIST OF PAMPHLETS, BOOKS, ETC.]
[Weekly]

Earlier Y 3.R 88:17

A 68.11:nos.
ELECTRO-ECONOMY SUPPLEMENTS.

A 68.12:CT
POSTERS.

A 68.13:nos.
STATISTICAL BULLETINS. [Monthly]
Later see also A 68.13/2, A 68.13/3

A 68.13/2
QUARTERLY STATISTICAL BULLETIN, ELECTRIC
PROGRAM.

Gives authorization, loans approved, and
funds advanced to borrowers; loans approved by
purpose and loan estimate miles and consumers
(cumulative totals); loans approved by type of
borrowers and purpose as of last day of month;
loans approved by type and status of borrowers;
funds advanced, payments and balance outstanding as of last day of preceding month; loans
approved (cumulative totals) and loan estimate
miles and consumers (cumulative totals) by
States.

A 68.13/3:nos.
QUARTERLY STATISTICAL BULLETIN, TELEPHONE
PROGRAM.

Formerly included in Monthly Statistical Bulletin, Electric and Telephone Programs, (A 68.13).
Gives loan authorizations, allocations, and
funds advanced to borrowers; loan estimate miles
and subscribers, loan allocations by purpose;
loan allocations and advanced to borrowers (as
of last day of month); applications, loan allocations, and funds advanced to borrowers, by
States; loan estimate miles and subscribers, by
States.

A 68.14   • **Item 115-A**
ADDRESSES. [Irregular]
Discontinued

A 68.15:v.nos.&nos.
LINEMAN. [Monthly]

A 68.16:nos.
SUGGESTED CO-OP ELECTRIFICATION ADVISER
TRAINING OUTLINE

A 68.17:
ENGINEERING MEMORANDUM.

A 68.18:v.nos.&nos.   • **Item 117-A**
RURAL LINES. v. 1– 10. 1954– 1963. [Monthly]
PURPOSE:– To provide a monthly review of
the REA-financed rural electrification and rural
telephone activity in the United States.
Supersedes Rural Electrification News (A
68.9).
Discontinued

A 68.19:date
ELECTRIC FARMING NEWS EXCHANGE OF INTER-
INDUSTRY FARM ELECTRIC UTILIZATION COUN-
CIL. [Irregular]
Changed from A 68.2:El 2/9

A 68.20
NUMBER AND PERCENTAGE OF FARMS ELECTRI-
FIED WITH CENTRAL STATION SERVICE. 1948–
[Annual]

Prepared by Statistical Services Section, Accounting and Statistics Branch.
Single page release giving total number of
farms receiving central station electric service
as of Dec. 31 of year, with comparable data for
1935, 1940, and 1950, for U.S. and States.

A 68.21:nos.
STAFF INSTRUCTIONS.

A 68.22:nos.   • **Item 117-B (MF)**
ENVIRONMENTAL IMPACT STATEMENTS. [IRREGU-
LAR]

A 68.24:nos.   • **Item 115-A-4 (E)**
ELECTRONIC PRODUCTS
Issued on CD-ROM

FEDERAL SURPLUS COMMODITIES CORPORATION (1935– 1940)

CREATION AND AUTHORITY

The Federal Surplus Relief Corporation (Y 3.F
31/9) was established as an independent agency
on October 4, 1933, under authority of the National Industrial Recovery Act approved June 16,
1933 (48 Stat. 195). On November 18, 1935, the
name was changed to Federal Surplus Commodities Corporation and the agency was placed under the Secretary of Agriculture as its
Administrator. Act of Congress (50 Stat. 323) and
the Agricultural Adjustment Act of 1938 (52 Stat.
38) made the Corporation a formal part of the
Department of Agriculture. Reorganization Plan
No. 3 1940, effective June 30, 1940, merged the
Corporation with certain other agencies to form
the Surplus Marketing Administration (A 73)

A 69.1:date
ANNUAL REPORTS.

Earlier Y 3.F 31/9:1

A 69.2:CT
GENERAL PUBLICATIONS.

Earlier Y 3.F 31/9:2

A 69.7:CT
ADDRESSES.

A 69.8:CT
FACTS ON SURPLUS FOODS.

Issuing agency omitted from publications.

A 69.9:nos.
GENERAL INFORMATION SERIES.

Pubs. desig. GI-nos.

BUREAU OF AGRICULTURAL CHEMISTRY AND ENGINEERING (1939– 1942)

CREATION AND AUTHORITY

The Bureau of Agricultural Chemistry and Engineering was established within the Department
of Agriculture on July 1, 1939, pursuant to the
Agricultural Appropriation Act of 1940, approved
June 30, 1939, consolidating the Bureau of Chemistry and Soils (A 47) and the Bureau of Agricultural Engineering (A 53). Executive Order 9060 of
February 23, 1942, made the Bureau of part of
the Agricultural Research Administration (A
77.100).

A 70.1:date
ANNUAL REPORTS.
Later A 77.101

A 70.2:CT
GENERAL PUBLICATIONS.
Later A 77.102

A 70.4:nos.
CIRCULAR SERIES.
Supersedes A 47.9
Later A 77.104

A 70.7:vol.
CURRENT LITERATURE IN AGRICULTURAL ENGI-
NEERING. [Monthly]
Earlier A 53.9
Later A 17.18:B

A 70.8:CT
ADDRESSES.

A 70.9:CT
BIBLIOGRAPHIES.

A 70.10:CT
LISTS OF PUBLICATIONS.

A 70.11:nos.
INFORMATION SERIES.
Earlier A 53.10
Later A 77.518

COMMODITY CREDIT CORPORATION
(1939– 1943)

CREATION AND AUTHORITY

The Commodity Credit Corporation (Y 3.C 73) was established October 17, 1933, pursuant to Executive Order 6340 of October 15, 1933, under the laws of the State of Delaware, as an agency of the United States. Reorganization Plan No. 1 of 1939, effective July 1, 1939, transferred the corporation to the Department of Agriculture. Executive Order 9322 of March 26, 1943, placed it along with certain other agencies under the Food Production and Distribution Administration (A 80), the name of which changed to War Food Administration by Executive Order 9334 of April 19, 1943.

A 71.1:date
ANNUAL REPORT.
    Earlier Y 3.C 73:1
    Later A 80.401

A 71.2:CT
GENERAL PUBLICATIONS.
    Earlier Y 3.C 73:2
    Later A 80.402

A 71.6:CT
REGULATIONS, RULES, AND INSTRUCTIONS.
    Earlier Y 3.C 73:6
    Later A 80.406

A 71.7:date
STATEMENT OF LOANS AND COMMODITIES OWNED.
    [Semimonthly]
    Earlier Y 3.C 73:12
    Later A 80.407

A 71.8:CT
ADDRESSES.

A 71.9:nos.
FOOD TRADE LETTERS. [Weekly]
    Later A 80.410

A 71.10:CT
FACT SHEETS.

FARM CREDIT ADMINISTRATION
(1939– 1942, 1943)

CREATION AND AUTHORITY

The Farm Credit Administration (FCA) was established as an independent agency by Executive Order 6084 of March 27, 1933. Under Reorganization Plan No. 1 of 1939, made effective July 1, 1939, the Farm Credit Administration was transferred to the Department of Agriculture. Executive Order 9280 of December 5, 1942 placed it under the Food Production Administration (A 79.100). Executive Order 9322 of March 26, 1943 returned it to the Secretary of Agriculture (A 72). Public Law 83-202, approved August 6, 1953, made it an independent agency (FCA) effective December 4, 1953.

A 72.1:date   • Item 62
ANNUAL REPORT.
    Earlier FCA 1.1
    Discontinued.

A 72.2:CT   • Item 65
GENERAL PUBLICATIONS.
    Earlier FCA 1.2
    Discontinued.

A 72.3:nos.
BULLETINS.
    Earlier FCA 1.3

A 72.4:nos.
CIRCULARS (numbered).
    Earlier FCA 1.4
    Later A 89.4

A 72.4:le-nos.
CIRCULARS (lettered-numbered).
    Earlier FCA 1.4/2

A 72.6:CT
REGULATIONS, RULES, AND INSTRUCTIONS.

A 72.7:nos.
LEAFLETS.
    Pubs. desig. L-nos.

A 72.8:nos.
MISCELLANEOUS REPORTS.
    Earlier FCA 1.13

A 72.9:nos.
SPECIAL REPORTS.
    Earlier FCA 1.21

A 72.10:nos.
NEWS FOR FARMER COOPERATIVES. [Monthly]
    Earlier FCA 1.10
    Later A 89.8

A 72.11:CT
ADDRESSES.
    Earlier FCA 1.9

A 72.12:date
QUARTERLY REPORTS ON LOANS AND DISCOUNTS.
    Earlier FCA 1.12

A 72.13:vol.
COOPERATIVE SAVINGS WITH FEDERAL CREDIT UNIONS. [Bimonthly]
    Earlier FCA 1.14/2
    Later Y 3.F 31/8:12

A 72.14:date
MONTHLY REPORTS OF ORGANIZATION AND OPERATIONS OF FEDERAL CREDIT UNIONS.
    Earlier FCA 1.15
    Later Y 3.F 31/8:13

A 72.15:vol.
FARM CREDIT QUARTERLY. [Quarterly]
    Earlier FCA 1.7

A 72.16:date
JOINT STOCK LAND BANKS, PROGRESS IN LIQUIDATION INCLUDING STATEMENTS OF CONDITION. [Quarterly]
    Earlier FCA 1.7/2

A 72.17:CT
FARMER CO-OPS (by States).
    Earlier FCA 1.19

A 72.18:nos.
SUMMARY OF CASES RELATING TO FARMERS' COOPERATIVE ASSOCIATIONS.
    Earlier FCA 1.18
    Later A 89.9

A 72.19:date
ANNUAL REPORTS ON OPERATIONS OF FEDERAL CREDIT UNIONS.
    Earlier FCA 1.16
    Later Y 3.F 32/8:14

A 72.20:CT
COOPERATIVE-CREAMERY ROUTES (by States) [Preliminary Summaries].

A 72.21:CT
LISTS OF PUBLICATIONS.

A 72.22:date
COOPERATIVE RESEARCH AND SERVICE DIVISION; QUARTERLY REPORTS.

A 72.23:nos.
WAR CIRCULARS.

A 72.24:nos.
CONFIDENTIAL REPORTS.

A 72.25:date
SUMMARY OF OPERATIONS OF PRODUCTION CREDIT ASSOCIATIONS. [Annual]
    Later FCA 1.22

SURPLUS MARKETING ADMINISTRATION
(1940– 1942)

CREATION AND AUTHORITY

The Surplus Marketing Administration was established within the Department of Agriculture by Reorganization Plan No. 3 of 1940, effective June 30, 1940 consolidating the Federal Surplus Commodities Corporation (A 69) and the Division of Marketing and Marketing Agreements of the Agricultural Adjustment Administration (A 55). By Executive Order 9069 of February 23, 1942, the Administration was consolidated with the Agricultural Marketing Service (A 66) and the Commodity Exchange Administration (A 59) to form the Agricultural Marketing Administration (A 75).

A 73.1:date
ANNUAL REPORTS.

A 73.2:CT
GENERAL PUBLICATIONS.

A 73.7:nos.
MARKETING AGREEMENT SERIES.
    Earlier A 65.9

A 73.8:nos.
MARKETING ORDERS.
    Earlier A 65.7
    Later A 75.20

A 73.9
ADDRESSES.

A 73.10:CT
LISTS OF PUBLICATIONS.

A 73.11:nos.
[FOOD STAMP SERIES.]
    Pubs. desig. FS-no.

A 73.12:nos.
[SUPPLEMENTARY COTTON PROGRAM SERIES.]
    Pubs. desig. SC-nos.

A 73.13:nos.
[SCHOOL LUNCH SERIES.]
    Pubs. desig. SL-no.

A 73.14:CT
PAPERS IN RE.

OFFICE FOR AGRICULTURAL WAR RELATIONS (1941–1943)

CREATION AND AUTHORITY

The Office of Agricultural Defense Relations was established within the Department of Agriculture by Secretary's Memorandum 905, dated May 17, 1941, pursuant to request of the President by letter of May 5, 1941, which transferred to the Secretary of Agriculture functions previously assigned to the Agriculture Division of the Advisory Commission to the Council of National Defense. In December 1941, the name was changed to Office for Agricultural War Relations. Executive Order 9280 of December 5, 1942, transferred those functions pertaining to food production to the Food Production Administration (A 79) and those pertaining to food distribution to the Food Distribution Administration (A 78). Other functions were absorbed by other agencies of the Department of Agriculture. By June 14, 1943, the liquidation of the Office was completed.

A 74.1:date
ANNUAL REPORT.

A 74.2:CT
GENERAL PUBLICATIONS.

A 74.7:series nos.
FARM DEFENSE PROGRAM.

A 74.8:CT
ADDRESSES.

AGRICULTURAL MARKETING ADMINISTRATION (1942)

CREATION AND AUTHORITY

The Agricultural Marketing Administration was established within the Department of Agriculture by Executive Order 9069 of February 23, 1942, consolidating the Surplus Marketing Administration (A 73), the Agricultural Marketing Service (A 66), and the Commodity Exchange Administration (A 59). Executive Order 9280 of December 5, 1942, consolidated the Administration with other agencies to form the Food Distribution Administration (A 78).

A 75.1:date
ANNUAL REPORT.

A 75.2:CT
GENERAL PUBLICATIONS.

A 75.7:CT
ADDRESSES.

A 75.8:date
COLD STORAGE REPORTS. [Monthly]
    Earlier A 66.7
    Later A 78.7

A 75.9:date
COTTON MARKET REVIEW. [Weekly]
    Earlier A 66.8
    Later A 78.9

A 75.10:vol.
LIVESTOCK, MEAT AND WOOL; MARKET REVIEWS AND STATISTICS. [Weekly]
    Earlier A 66.13
    Later A 78.11

A 75.11:nos.
HONEY REPORTS. [Semimonthly]
    Earlier A 66.12
    Later A 78.10

A 75.12:nos.
PEANUT REPORTS. [Weekly]
    Earlier A 66.15
    Later A 78.12

A 75.13:vol.
MARKETING ACTIVITIES. [Monthly]
    Earlier A 66.14
    Later A 78.14

A 75.14:vol.
P. AND S. DOCKET, MONTHLY REPORT OF ACTION TAKEN ON CASES ARISING UNDER PACKERS AND STOCKYARDS ACT.
    Earlier A 66.18
    Later A 78.15

A 75.15:nos.
NOTICES OF JUDGMENT UNDER INSECTICIDE ACT.
    Earlier A 66.46
    Later A 78.13

A 75.16:nos.
SERVICE AND REGULATORY ANNOUNCEMENTS.
    Earlier A 66.27
    Later A 80.118

A 75.17:CT
POSTERS.

A 75.18:nos.
SCHOOL LUNCH SERIES.
    Pubs. desig. SL-nos.
    Earlier A 73.13

A 75.19:CT
UNITED STATES STANDARDS FOR FRUITS AND VEGETABLES.
    Earlier A 36.35/1, A 36.35/2, A 66.15
    Later 80.221

A 75.20:nos.
MARKETING ORDERS.
    Earlier A 65.7 and A 73.8
    Later A 80.116

CONSUMERS' COUNSEL DIVISION (1942–1943)

CREATION AND AUTHORITY

The Consumers' Counsel Office was established within the Agricultural Adjustment Administration (A 55.63) by the Agricultural Adjustment Act of 1933, approved May 12, 1933. In 1935, it became the Consumers' Counsel Division. Secretary's Memorandum 988, dated February 13, 1942, transferred the Division to the Agricultural Marketing Administration. The Division was terminated in 1943.

A 75.101:date
ANNUAL REPORTS.
    Earlier A 55.63:R 29

A 75.102:CT
GENERAL PUBLICATIONS.
    Earlier A 55.63

A 75.108:vol.
CONSUMERS' GUIDE. [Monthly from June through September, Semimonthly from October through May]
    Earlier A 55.12
    Later A 78.8

A 75.109:vol.
CONSUMERS' MARKET SERVICE. [Semimonthly]
    Earlier A 55.52

A 75.110:v.nos.&nos.
CONSUMER NOTES CLIPSHEET. [Weekly]
    Earlier A 55.56

A 75.111:nos.
CONSUMERS' COUNSEL SERIES PUBLICATIONS.
    Earlier A 55.49

COMMODITY EXCHANGE ADMINISTRATION (1942–1947)

CREATION AND AUTHORITY

The Commodity Exchange Administration (A 59) was established within the Department of Agriculture by memorandum of the Secretary of Agriculture, effective July 1, 1936, pursuant to provisions of Act of Congress, approved June 15, 1936, succeeding the Grain Futures Administration (A 41). Executive Order 9069 of February 23, 1942, grouped the Administration together with certain other agencies to form the Agricultural Marketing Administration. Executive Order 9577 of June 29, 1945, transferred the functions of the Administration to the Secretary of Agriculture. By Secretary's Memorandum 1185, dated January 21, 1947, the Commodity Exchange Administration was abolished and succeeded by the Commodity Exchange Authority (A 85).

A 75.201:date
ANNUAL REPORTS.
    Earlier A 59.1

A 75.202:CT
GENERAL PUBLICATIONS.
    Earlier A 59.2

A 75.208:vol.
TRADE IN COTTON FUTURES. [Monthly]
    Earlier A 59.11
    Later A 82.30

A 75.209:vol.
TRADE IN GRAIN FUTURES. [Monthly]
    Earlier A 59.7
    Later A 82.29

A 75.210:vol.
TRADE IN WOOL TOP FUTURES. [Monthly]
    Earlier A 59.12

AGRICULTURAL CONSERVATION AND ADJUSTMENT ADMINISTRATION (1942)

CREATION AND AUTHORITY

The Agricultural Conservation and Adjustment Administration was established within the Department of Agricultural by Executive Order 9069 of February 23, 1942, which transferred to it the Agricultural Adjustment Administration (A 55), the Soil Conservation Service (A 57), the Federal Crop Insurance Corporation (A 62), and the Sugar Division of Agricultural Adjustment Administration (A 55). Executive Order 9280 of December, 5 1942 consolidated the Administration along with certain other agencies into the Food Production Administration (A 79).

A 76.1:date
ANNUAL REPORTS.

A 76.2:CT
GENERAL PUBLICATIONS.

FEDERAL CROP INSURANCE CORPORATION (1942)

CREATION AND AUTHORITY

The Federal Crop Insurance Corporation (A 62) was consolidated with other agencies to form the Agricultural Conservation and Adjustment Administration by Executive Order 9060 of February 23, 1942. Executive Order 9280 of December 5, 1942 placed the Corporation in the Food Production Administration (A 79.300).

A 76.101:date
ANNUAL REPORTS.
Earlier A 62.1
Later A 79.301

A 76.102:CT
GENERAL PUBLICATIONS.
Earlier A 62.2
Later A 79.302

A 76.106:CT
REGULATIONS, RULES, AND INSTRUCTIONS.
Earlier A 62.6/2
Later A 79.306

A 76.107
ADDRESSES.

A 76.108:nos.
F.C.I. INFORMATION SERIES.
Earlier A 62.9
Later A 80.907

SOIL CONSERVATION SERVICE (1942)

CREATION AND AUTHORITY

The Soil Conservation Service (A 57) along with certain other agencies was consolidated to form the Agricultural Conservation and Adjustment Administration by Executive Order 9069 of February 23, 1942. Executive Order 9280 of December 5, 1942, transferred the Service to the Food Production Administration (A 79.200).

A 76.201:date
ANNUAL REPORTS.
Earlier A 57.1
Later A 79.201

A 76.202:CT
GENERAL PUBLICATIONS.
Earlier A 57.2
Later A 79.202

A 76.208:vol.
SOIL CONSERVATION; OFFICIAL ORGAN. [Monthly]
Earlier A 57.9
Later A 79.207

A 76.209:date
PRECIPITATION IN MUSKINGUM RIVER BASIN. [Monthly]
Earlier A 57.21

A 76.210:nos.
CONSERVATION FOLDERS.
Earlier A 57.30

A 76.211
TECHNICAL PUBLICATIONS.
Later A 80.2011

A 76.212:nos.
PHYSICAL LAND SURVEYS.
Earlier A 57.24
Later A 80.2012

A 76.213:nos.
MISCELLANEOUS PUBLICATIONS.
Earlier A 57.13

A 76.214:date
SOIL CONSERVATION DISTRICTS. [Monthly]
Earlier A 57.32
Later A 80.2009

A 76.215:nos.
SPECIAL REPORTS OF SEDIMENTATION SECTION, OFFICE OF RESEARCH.
Later A 80.2013

SUGAR AGENCY (1942)

CREATION AND AUTHORITY

The Sugar Division (A 63), originally established within the Agricultural Adjustment Administration (A 55), was made an independent division in the Department of Agriculture on October 16, 1938, by Departmental Memorandum 783. By Executive Order 9069 of February 23, 1942, it was placed under the Agricultural Conservation and Adjustment Administration, where it was redesignated the Sugar Agency. By Executive Order 9280 of December 5, 1942, the functions of the Sugar Agency was transferred to the Food Distribution Administration (A 80.100).

A 76.301:date
ANNUAL REPORTS.

A 76.302:CT
GENERAL PUBLICATIONS.

A 76.307:nos.
SUGAR DETERMINATION.
Pubs. desig. S.D. no.
Earlier A 55.37
Later A 80.117

AGRICULTURAL ADJUSTMENT AGENCY (April– December 1942)

CREATION AND AUTHORITY

The Agricultural Adjustment Administration (A 55) along with certain other agencies were consolidated to form the Agricultural Conservation and Adjustment Administration (A 76) by Executive Order 9069 of February 23, 1942. Office Memorandum 113, dated April 13, 1942, changed the name to Agricultural Adjustment Agency. Executive Order 9280 of December 5, 1942, grouped it with other agencies to form the Food Production Administration (A 79.400).

A 76.401:date
ANNUAL REPORTS.
Earlier A 55.1
Later A 79.401

A 76.402:CT
GENERAL PUBLICATIONS.
Earlier A 55.2
Later A 79.402

A 76.406:CT
REGULATIONS, RULES, AND INSTRUCTIONS.
Earlier A 55.6, A 55.69

A 76.408:nos.
GENERAL INFORMATION SERIES.
Pubs. desig. G-no.
Earlier A 55.71
Later A 80.614

A 76.409:date
STATEMENT OF EXPENDITURES. [Monthly]
Earlier A 55.62

A 76.410:vol.
AAA FLASHES, FACTS FOR COMMITTEEMEN.
[Monthly]
    Earlier A 55.42/11

East Central Region Publications
North Central Region Publications
Northeast Region Publications

A 76.462:CT
GENERAL PUBLICATIONS.
    Earlier A 55.44/2

A 76.466:CT
REGULATIONS, RULES, AND INSTRUCTIONS.
    Earlier A 55.44/11
    Later A 80.2166

Southern Region Publications

A 76.472:CT
GENERAL PUBLICATIONS.
    Earlier A 55.45/2
    Later A 80.2172

A 76.476:CT
REGULATIONS, RULES, AND INSTRUCTIONS.
    Earlier A 55.45/12
    Western Region Publications

A 76.482:CT
GENERAL PUBLICATIONS.
    Earlier A 55.46/2
    Later A 80.2182

A 76.486:CT
REGULATIONS, RULES, AND INSTRUCTIONS.
    Earlier A 55.46/15
    Later A 80.2186

AGRICULTURAL RESEARCH SERVICE
(1953– 1978, 1981–   )

CREATION AND AUTHORITY

The Agricultural Research Administration was established within the Department of Agriculture by Executive Order 9060 of February 23, 1942, to which were transferred the Bureau of Agricultural Chemistry and Engineering (A 70), the Bureau of Animal Industry (A 4), the Bureau of Dairy Engineering (A 44), the Bureau of Home Economics (A 42), and the Bureau of Plant Industry (A 19). The various bureaus were regrouped by Departmental Memorandum 1320, Supplement 4, dated November 2, 1953, to form the newly designated Agricultural Research Service. The Agricultural Research Service was consolidated with certain other agencies to form the Science and Education Administration (A 106) by Secretary's Memorandum 1927, Supplement 1, dated December 19, 1977, effective January 28, 1978. In 1981, the Science and Education Administration was abolished and the Agricultural Research Service was reestablished.

INFORMATION

Information Staff
Agricultural Research Service
Department of Agriculture
Room 1-2251
5601 Sunnyside Avenue
Beltsville, Maryland 20705-5128
(301) 504-1636
Fax: (301) 504-1648
http://www.ars.usda.gov

A 77.1:date   • Item 26-A-5
RESEARCH PROGRESS IN (year), A REPORT OF THE AGRICULTURAL RESEARCH SERVICE. [Annual]

    Former title: Annual Report.

A 77.2:CT   • Item 26-A-1
GENERAL PUBLICATIONS.

    Formerly distributed to Depository Libraries under Item 26.

A 77.2:Av   • Item 26
REPORT OF AGRICULTURAL AVIATION RESEARCH CONFERENCES. 1st–   1953–
[Irregular]
    Discontinued.

A 77.2:Ut 3
SUMMARY REPORT OF UTILIZATION RESEARCH AND DEVELOPMENT, FISCAL YEAR (date). [Annual]

A 77.6/2:nos.   • Item 111
SERVICE AND REGULATORY ANNOUNCEMENTS.
    Earlier A 82.23

A 77.6/3:CT   • Item 26-A-3
HANDBOOKS, MANUALS, GUIDES.
    Discontinued.

A 77.7
RESEARCH ACHIEVEMENT SHEET, R.A.S.– (series). 1–   [Irregular]

A 77.8:date   • Item 113
REPORT OF ACTIVITIES UNDER RESEARCH AND MARKETING ACT. [Annual]
    Earlier A 87.1
    Discontinued.

A 77.9:CT
RELEASES.

A 77.10   • Item 25-A-1
ADDRESSES. [Irregular]
    Discontinued.

A 77.11
ADMINISTRATOR'S MEMORANDUM.

A 77.12:v.nos.&nos.   • Item 25-A (EL)
AGRICULTURAL RESEARCH. v. 1–   1953–
[Monthly]

    PURPOSE:– To report late research findings to those who work directly with farmers, processors, marketing agencies, and the general public.
    Consists of technical articles.
    See also A 106.9
    Indexed by: Index to U.S. Government Periodicals.
    ISSN 002-161X

A 77.12/a:CT   • Item 25-A
AGRICULTURAL RESEARCH (Separates). [Monthly]

A 77.13:nos.
CURRENT DEVELOPMENTS IN FARM REAL ESTATE MARKET.
    Earlier A 36.168
    Later A 77.15 and A 93.9/4

A 77.14:nos.   • Item 18-A
AGRICULTURAL FINANCE REVIEW.
    Earlier A 36.111
    Later A 93.910

A 77.14/2:nos.
FARM COST SITUATION. [Irregular]
    Earlier A 36.157
    Later A 77.15 and A 92.9/3

A 77.14/3:date
DEPOSITS OF COUNTY BANKS: INDEX NUMBERS OF TOTAL, DEMAND AND TIME DEPOSITS SELECTED GROUPS OF STATES, SPECIFIED PERIODS.
    Later A 93.9/7

A 77.15:nos.   • Item 25-B (MF)
ARS (series). [Irregular]

    Publications in the ARS series are designated by a double numbering scheme. The first series of numbers designate the Division responsible for the publication, the second, the number of the publication within each sub-series.

The Agricultural Research Service does not maintain a central office from which all its publications may be obtained. Requests for specific titles or series must be requested from the individual Division.
    The following ARS numbered sub-series are currently in use:

20	Office of the Administrator
22	Information Division
25	Budget and Finance Division
26	Personnel Division
27	Administrative Services Division
28	Agricultural Research Center
33	Entomology Research Division
34	Crops Research Division
41	Soil and Water Conservation Research Division
42	Agricultural Engineering Research Division
44	Animal Science Research Division
45	Animal Disease and Parasite Research Division
51	Market Quality Research Division
52	Transportation and Facilities Research Division
61	Human Nutrition Research Division
62	Consumer and Food Economics Research Division
63	Clothing and Housing Research Division
71	Northern Utilization Research and Development Division (Peoria, Illinois)
72	Southern Utilization Research and Development Division (New Orleans, Louisiana)
73	Eastern Utilization Research and Development Division (Philadelphia, Pennsylvania)
74	Western Utilization Research and Development Division (Albany, California)
81	Plant Protection Division
82	Plant Quarantine Division
91	Animal Health Division
92	Animal Inspection and Quarantine Division
93	Meat Inspection Division

34 Crops Research Division

34-[nos.] CROPS RESEARCH: RESULTS OF REGIONAL COTTON VARIETY TESTS BY COOPERATING AGRICULTURAL EXPERIMENT STATIONS. [Annual]

41 Soil and Water Conservation Branch

41-75 [nos.] ABSTRACTS OF RECENT PUBLISHED MATERIAL ON SOIL AND WATER CONSERVATION. 1–   1949–   [Irregular]

    Prepared by the Soil and Water Conservation Research Division.
    PURPOSE:– To bring together a summary of current published information about soil and water conservation for ready reference of those engaged in soil and conservation work.
    Abstracts cover such subjects as watershed management, water management, basic soil problems, erosion control, soil management, plant management, economic and social problems, biology, soil surveys.
    Supersedes SCS Research Summaries.

INDEX

    Nos 9– 21. ARS 41– 59. February 1963. 299 p.
    The first 8 issues were indexed individually.
    44 Animal Husbandry Research Division

44-[nos.] DHIA COW PERFORMANCE INDEX LIST, REGISTERED PROGENY OF DHIA SIRES. [Quarterly]

    Contains sire summary information, by breeds, compiled from data received by the Dairy Cattle Research Branch.

44-[nos.] DHIA SIRE SUMMARY LIST. [Annual]

Contains sire summary information, by breeds, compiled from data received by the Dairy Cattle Research Branch.

Frequency varies.

44-2 BREED DISTRIBUTION OF NPIP PARTICIPATING FLOCKS BY STATES AND DIVISIONS. 1943– [Annual]

PURPOSE:– To show trends in the prevalence or popularity of varieties of chickens in breeding flocks in States and geographic regions of the United States.

44-3 TABLES ON HATCHERY AND FLOCK PARTICIPATION IN THE NATIONAL POULTRY IMPROVEMENT PLAN. [Annual]

Gives two-year comparisons of number of hatcheries and egg capacity, by States and Divisions; summary of hatchery and flock participation in the National Poultry Improvement Plan, for selected years.

44-4 TABLES ON HATCHERY AND FLOCK PARTICIPATION IN THE NATIONAL TURKEY IMPROVEMENT PLAN. [Annual]

Gives two-year comparisons of number of hatcheries and egg capacity, by States and Divisions; summary of hatchery and flock participation in the National Turkey Improvement Plan, for selected years.

44-6 HATCHERIES AND DEALERS PARTICIPATING IN THE NATIONAL POULTRY IMPROVEMENT PLAN. [Annual]

Directory of hatcheries and dealers participating in the National Poultry Improvement Plan. Revised editions are kept up-to-date by supplements issued irregularly throughout the year.

44-7 ANNUAL R.O.P AND PERFORMANCE TEST SUMMARY. 1940– [Annual]

PURPOSE:– To provide a summary of official egg production records of poultry breeding stock.

44-11 TURKEYS IN NTIP FLOCKS AND THEIR DISTRIBUTION BY STATES AND VARIETIES. 1954– [Annual]

PURPOSE:– To show trends in the prevalence of popularity of varieties of turkeys in breeding flocks in States and geographic regions of the United States.

44-13 TURKEY PERFORMANCE TESTS. [Annual]

Report of results of central turkey meat production test and statistical analysis of performance records.

The detailed provisions for the tests are contained in USDA Miscellaneous Publication 739.

44-79 REPORT OF EGG PRODUCTION TESTS, UNITED STATES AND CANADA. 1960– [Annual]

PURPOSE:– To provide a summary and analysis of the results of performance records compiled in sample egg production tests.

62 Consumer and Food Economics Research Division

62-5 FAMILY ECONOMICS REVIEW.

See A 77.708.

74 Western Regional Research Laboratory

74-[nos.] NATIONAL CONFERENCE ON WHEAT UTILIZATION RESEARCH PROCEEDINGS. 1st–

74-[nos.] NATIONAL POTATO UTILIZATION CONFERENCE REPORT. 1st–

74-[nos] REPORT ON DRY BEAN RESEARCH CONFERENCE. 1st–

74-[nos.] TECHNICAL ALFALFA CONFERENCE. PROCEEDINGS. 1–

82 Plant Quarantine Division

82-2 SUMMARY OF ACTIVITIES, PLANT QUARANTINE DIVISION. [Annual]

Textual summary and statistical tables on activities for the fiscal year. Tables give ship inspection activities, foreign mail inspections, transit inspection, cargo inspection, number of quarantine material interception, number of plant pest interceptions, comparative summary of activities.

82-6 LIST OF INTERCEPTED PLANT PESTS. [Annual]

Prepared by the Plant Quarantine Division. Covers the fiscal year.
Earlier A 77.308/2 prior to 1966.
Later A 101.10/2:82-5

91 Animal Disease Eradication Division

91-41 COOPERATIVE STATE-FEDERAL BRUCELLOSIS ERADICATION.

Gives over-all national summary and individual State reports. Includes charts and maps. Data are for the calendar year.

91-44 COOPERATIVE STATE-FEDERAL TUBERCULOSIS ERADICATION, PROGRESS REPORT, FISCAL YEAR (date). 1963– [Annual]

PURPOSE:– To provide information concerning progress in eradicating tuberculosis from the domestic livestock in individual States and in the Nation.

91-54 POULTRY DISEASES ACTIVITIES REPORT. [Annual]

91-56 COOPERATIVE STATE-FEDERAL HOG CHOLERA ERADICATION PROGRAM, PROGRESS REPORT (year). 1963– [Annual]

PURPOSE:– To provide a general outline of the progress made during the calendar year in the Cooperative State-Federal hog cholera eradication program, as well as to describe some of the problems facing the program during the year ahead. Compiled from a comprehensive year-end survey and from regular reports received during the year.

91-57 COOPERATIVE STATE-FEDERAL BRUCELLOSIS ERADICATION PROGRAM, PROGRESS REPORT. [Annual]

A 77.15/2:date　　　　　　• Item 25-B (MF)
ARS DIRECTORY. [Semiannual]

A 77.15/3:nos.　　　　　　• Item 25-B-1
SOIL ORGANIC MATTER LEVELS IN THE CENTRAL GREAT PLAINS.

A 77.16:nos.
PRODUCTION ECONOMICS RESEARCH BRANCH PUBLICATIONS. PERB 1– 4. 1954.

A 77.16/2:nos.
PUBLICATIONS ISSUED. 1– 1954– (Production Economics Research Branch)

Later A 93.18

A 77.17:CT.
LIST OF PUBLICATIONS AND BIBLIOGRAPHIES.

Congress in 1938 authorized the establishment of four regional laboratories to conduct basic and applied research designed to expand, improve and develop through science and technology the utilization of American farm crops. Each laboratory is responsible for research on those crops indigenous to that region of the country. They are:

EASTERN DIVISION:– Eastern deciduous fruits; Eastern vegetables; meat; dairy products; animal fats; hides, tanning materials, and leather; honey; maple products; tobacco; wood by-products; plant precursors of cortisone; biologically active plant compounds; and allergens of agricultural products.

NORTHERN DIVISION:– Cereal grains; corn, wheat, grain sorghum, and oats; oilseeds; soybean, flaxseed, safflower, and erucic acid-containing oilseeds; new crops screening.

SOUTHERN DIVISION:– Cotton and cottonseed; tung fruit, pine gum; Southern fruits and vegetables, including citrus, sweetpotatoes, and cucumbers; sugarcane; rice; peanuts; new crops.

WESTERN DIVISION:– Western fruits, nuts, vegetables, rice; poultry products; forage crops; wheat; barley; wool and mohair; sugar beets; drybeets; dry beans and peas; castor beans; new crops.

The majority of the publications, if not all, issued by the four regional laboratories consists of reprints of articles which have appeared in technical journals.

Each Division publishes a list semiannually, which includes all the articles published in technical journals and authored by the staff of the various laboratories and field stations within each Division. Each entry contains a sample abstract of the contents of the article. Included also is a list of patents developed under and assigned to the Department of Agriculture.

Publications are also issued in the ARS series (ARS 71-, 72-, 73-, and 74-sub-series).

A 77.17/2
LIST OF PUBLICATIONS AND PATENTS, WITH ABSTRACTS. List 1– [Semiannual] (Western Utilization Research and Development Division)
Earlier A 77.2:P 96/2

A 77.17/3　　　　　　• Item 26-C-1
PUBLICATIONS AND PATENTS. [Semiannual] (Southern Utilization Research and Development Division)
Earlier A 77.2:P 96/3
Discontinued.

A 77.17/4　　　　　　• Item 26-C-1 (MF)
PUBLICATIONS AND PATENTS. [Semiannual] (Eastern Utilization Research and Development Division)
Earlier A 77.15:73
Discontinued.

A 77.17/5　　　　　　• Item 26-C-1 (MF)
PUBLICATIONS AND PATENTS. [Annual] (Northern Utilization Research and Development Division)
Earlier A 77.15:71
Discontinued.

A 77.17/6:date　　　　　　• Item 26-C-1
RECENT PUBLICATIONS OF RANGE RESEARCH, ARID SOUTH AREA. [Annual]

Covers Arizona, New Mexico, Nevada, and Utah area.
Discontinued.

A 77.18　　　　　　• Item 22-A-1
CORRESPONDENCE AIDS, CA- (series). [Irregular]
Later A 106.23

A 77.19:CT
SHEETS OF NATIONAL ATLAS OF UNITED STATES.

A 77.20:fascile no.&pt.no.　　　　　　• Item 25-C
GENERAL CATALOGUE OF HOMOPTERA.
Discontinued.

A 77.21:date
MANUSCRIPTS APPROVED BY DIVISIONS FOR PUBLICATION.

A 77.22:nos.   • Item 26-B
USDA CONSUMER EXPENDITURE SURVEY RE-
PORTS. 1–   1961–
    Discontinued.

A 77.23   • Item 25-D
CONSERVATION RESEARCH REPORTS. 1–   1965–
    [Irregular]
    Later A 1.114

A 77.24:date
SOUTHWEST BRANCH ANNUAL REPORT. 1966–
    (Soil and Water Conservation Research Division)

A 77.25:v.nos.&nos.
NOTES FROM WASHINGTON, INTERNATIONAL PRO-
GRAMS DIVISION.

A 77.26:date
U.S. NATIONAL ARBORETUM: ANNUAL REPORT.

A 77.27:date
ADVISORY COMMITTEE FOR THE U.S. MEAT ANI-
MAL RESEARCH CENTER: REPORT OF MEET-
INGS. [Irregular]
    Title varies.

A 77.28:nos.
ARS NATIONAL RESEARCH PROGRAM, NRP- (series). [Irregular]

A 77.29:nos.
NE REGIONAL STAFF LETTER.

A 77.30:letters-nos.   • Item 22-A-5 (MF)
AGRICULTURAL REVIEWS AND MANUALS.
    Earlier A 106.12
    Discontinued.

A 77.31:letters-nos.   • Item 25-B (MF)
ADVANCES IN AGRICULTURAL TECHNOLOGY, AAT
(series).
    Published in microfiche.
    Earlier A 106.24
    Discontinued.

A 77.32:letters-nos.   • Item 22-A-8 (MF)
AGRICULTURAL RESEARCH RESULTS, ARR– (series). [Irregular]

    Miscellaneous highly technical reports of re-
    search carried out in the various field research
    centers of the Agricultural Research Service.
    See also A 106.13
    Discontinued.

A 77.32/2   • Item 26-A-7 (EL)
QUARTERLY REPORT OF SELECTED RESEARCH
PROJECTS.

A 77.33:date
CROP PRODUCTION RESEARCH. [Annual]

A 77.34:date   • Item 22-A-13 (MF)
POST HARVEST SCIENCE AND TECHNOLOGY RE-
SEARCH. [Annual]
    Discontinued.

A 77.35   • Item 26-A-2 (MF)
AGRICULTURAL INVENTIONS CATALOG. [Semian-
nual]

    Earlier title: Inventions Available for Licens-
    ing.

A 77.36:date   • Item 26-A-4
NATIONAL POTATO GERMPLASM EVALUATION AND
ENHANCEMENT REPORT. [Annual]

    Tables present tentative results of replicated
    yield trails of potato crops in various states.

A 77.37:date   • Item 101
U.S. DAIRY FORAGE RESEARCH CENTER.

A 77.38   • Item 101-A-1 (MF)
U.S. NATIONAL ARBORETUM CONTRIBUTION
(series).

A 77.38/2:CT   • Item 101-A-3
U.S. NATIONAL ARBORETUM ELITE PLANT.

A 77.39:date   • Item 26-A-6 (MF)
ANNUAL REPORT OF THE WESTERN WHEAT QUAL-
ITY LABORATORY CORP.

A 77.40:CT   • Item 15-A-1 (E)
ELECTRONIC PRODUCTS.

BUREAU OF AGRICULTURAL AND INDUSTRIAL CHEMISTRY (1943– 1953)

CREATION AND AUTHORITY

    The Bureau of Agricultural Chemistry and
Engineering (A 70) was transferred along with
other agencies to form the Agricultural Research
Administration. By Executive Order 9060 of February 23, 1942. In February 1943, the name was
changed to Bureau of Agricultural and Industrial
Chemistry while certain of its functions were transferred to the Bureau of Plant Industry, Soils, and
Agricultural Engineering (A 77.500). The Bureau
was abolished and its functions transferred to
the Agricultural Research Service (A 77) by
Secretary's Memorandum 1320, Supplement 4 of
November 2, 1953.

A 77.101:date   • Item 23
ANNUAL REPORTS. 1942– 1943.
    Earlier A 70.1
    Discontinued.

A 77.102:CT   • Item 24
GENERAL PUBLICATIONS.
    Earlier A 70.2
    Discontinued.

A 77.104:nos.
[CIRCULAR SERIES] ACE 1– 260.   – 1943.
    Earlier A 70.4

A 77.104/2:nos.
[CIRCULAR SERIES] AIC 1–   – 1943.
    Supersedes A 77.104

A 77.108:CT
ADDRESSES.

A 77.109:nos.
PROGRESS IN CANDY RESEARCH, REPORT. 1–

PUBLICATIONS RELATING TO THE CARE OF ANIMALS AND POULTRY (1953– 1978)

CREATION AND AUTHORITY

    The Bureau of Animal Industry (A 4) was
transferred along with other agencies to form the
Agricultural Research Administration by Executive Order 9060 of February 23, 1942. The Bureau
was abolished and its functions transferred to
the Agricultural Research Service (A 77) by
Secretary's Memorandum 1320, Supplement 4,
of November 2, 1953.

A 77.201:date   • Item 27
ANNUAL REPORTS. 1942– 1953.
    Earlier A 4.1
    Discontinued

A 77.201/2:date
MEAT INSPECTION BRANCH, SUMMARY OF ACTIVI-
TIES. 1954. [Annual]
    Earlier A 77.202:M 46
    Later A 77.15:93-2
    Discontinued.

A 77.202:CT   • Item 30
GENERAL PUBLICATIONS.
    Discontinued.

A 77.202:B 83/16   • Item 30
PROCEEDINGS OF THE NATIONAL BRUCELLOSIS
COMMITTEE AND PROGRESS REPORT OF THE
COOPERATIVE STATE- FEDERAL BRUCELLOSIS
ERADICATION PROGRAM. 1967–   [Annual]
(Animal Health Division)

    PURPOSE:– To furnish recommendations
    of the National Brucellosis Committee, Live-
    stock Conservation, Inc., and the U.S. De-
    partment of Agriculture on the progress or
    trends of program activities of the Coopera-
    tive State-Federal Brucellosis Eradication
    Program.
        Includes statistical data.
        Prior to 1967, reports issued separately.
    The Proceedings classified A 1.2:B 83 and A
    77.202:B 83/16 and the Progress Report is-
    sued as ARS 91-57, (A 77.15).
        Discontinued.

A 77.206:CT   • Item 32
REGULATIONS, RULES, AND INSTRUCTIONS
    Earlier A 4.8
    Discontinued.

A 77.206/2:CT   • Item 30-A
HANDBOOKS, MANUALS, GUIDES [Relating to Animal
Industry].
    Discontinued.

A 77.208:nos.   • Item 33
SERVICE AND REGULATORY ANNOUNCEMENTS. 1–
565.   – 1954. [Monthly]
    Earlier A 4.13
    Discontinued.

A 77.209:nos.
A.H.D. [Animal Husbandry Divisions] (series). 1– 153.
    – 1954.
    No. 153 designated A.P.H.
    Earlier A 4.26

A 77.210
A.N.D [Animal Nutrition Division] (series). 1– 7. – 1942.
    Earlier A 4.27

A 77.211:date
BANG'S DISEASE WORK; STATEMENT OF INDEM-
NITY CLAIMS AND AVERAGES IN COOPERA-
TIVE.
    Earlier A 4.29
    Later combined in A 77.216/2

A 77.212:date
SUMMARY OF BRUCELLOSIS (Bang's Disease) WORK
IN COOPERATION WITH VARIOUS STATES.
[Monthly]
    Earlier A 4.21
    Later combined in A 77.216/2

A 77.212/2
SUMMARY OF BOVINE BRUCELLOSIS ERADICA-
TION ACTIVITIES IN COOPERATION WITH
STATES. [Annual] (Animal Health Division)
    Data for fiscal year.

A 77.212/3:date
STATISTICAL TABLES SHOWING PROGRESS OF
ERADICATION OF BRUCELLOSIS AND TUBER-
CULOSIS IN LIVESTOCK IN UNITED STATES AND
TERRITORIES FOR FISCAL YEAR.
    Earlier A 77.202:B 83/9

A 77.212/4
COOPERATIVE STATE-FEDERAL BRUCELLOSIS
ERADICATION PROGRAM STATISTICAL TABLES,
FISCAL YEAR (date). [Annual] (Animal Health Division)

Tables give summary of bovine brucellosis
eradication in cooperation with the States for year
and 1935 to date; statement of cooperative brucellosis testing in the U.S., 1935 to date; calf
vaccinations, number and percent, 1942 to date;
goats and swine tested for brucellosis, by States;
market cattle testing, brucellosis eradication program.
Later A 101.18/2

A 77.212/5
COOPERATIVE STATE-FEDERAL TUBERCULOSIS
ERADICATION PROGRAM, STATISTICAL TABLES,
FISCAL YEAR (date). [Annual] (Animal Health Di-
vision)

Tables give summary of tuberculosis eradication work with cattle, swine, and poultry.

A 77.212/6
COOPERATIVE STATE-FEDERAL BRUCELLOSIS
ERADICATION PROGRAMS. [Quarterly]

A 77.212/6-2:date
COOPERATIVE STATE-FEDERAL BRUCELLOSIS
ERADICATION PROGRAM, CHARTS AND MAPS.
FISCAL YEAR.

A 77.212/7:date
SUMMARY OF BRUCELLOSIS ERADICATION ACTIVI-
TIES IN COOPERATION WITH VARIOUS STATES
UNDER CULL AND DRY COW TESTING PRO-
GRAM. [Monthly] (Animal Health Division)

A 77.212/8:date
SUMMARY OF BRUCELLOSIS ERADICATION ACTIVI-
TIES IN COOPERATION WITH THE VARIOUS
STATES UNDER THE MARKET CATTLE TESTING
PROGRAM. [Monthly] (Animal Disease Eradica-
tion Division)

A 77.212/9:date
DISEASE CONTROL SERVICES ACTIVITIES. [Quar-
terly]

A 77.213:date
SUMMARY OF BRUCELLOSIS (Bang's Disease) CON-
TROL PROGRAM CONDUCTED BY BUREAU OF
ANIMAL INDUSTRY IN COOPERATION WITH
VARIOUS STATES. [Monthly]
Earlier A 4.23

A 77.214:nos.
EXTENSION ANIMAL HUSBANDMAN. 1– 66. – 1942.
[Quarterly]
Earlier A 4.25

A 77.215:date
STATEMENT OF INDEMNITY CLAIMS AND AVER-
AGES IN COOPERATIVE TUBERCULOSIS ERADI-
CATION.   – 1942. [Monthly]
Earlier A 4.30

A 77.216:date
SUMMARY OF TUBERCULOSIS ERADICATION IN
COOPERATION WITH VARIOUS STATES.
[Monthly]
Earlier A 4.22
Later A 77.216/2

A 77.216/2:date
SUMMARY OF BOVINE TUBERCULOSIS ERADICA-
TION IN COOPERATION WITH VARIOUS STATES,
STATEMENT OF INDEMNITY AND AVERAGES IN
COOPERATIVE BOVINE BRUCELLOSIS WORK.
[Monthly]
Combines A 77.216, A 77.212, and A 77.211

A 77.217:nos.
NOTICES: ACTIVITIES OF LICENSED ESTABLISH-
MENTS SUPERVISED BY VIRUS-SERUM CON-
TROL DIVISION. [Monthly]
Earlier A 4.31
Replaced by A 77.226/2

A 77.218:nos.   • Item 38
ORDERS.
Earlier A 4.5

A 77.219:pt.nos.   • Item 31
INDEX-CATALOGUE OF MEDICAL AND VETERINARY
ZOOLOGY.
Earlier A 4.18
ISSN 0096-2570

A 77.219/2:nos.   • Item 31 (MF)
– SUPPLEMENTS.
Later A 106.15/2
Discontinued.

A 77.219/3:CT   • Item 31 (MF)
INDEX-CATALOGUE OF MEDICAL AND VETERI-
NARY ZOOLOGY [by Subject].

A 77.219/4:nos.   • Item 31
INDEX-CATALOGUE OF MEDICAL AND
VETERINARY ZOOLOGY, SPECIAL PUBLI-
CATIONS, (numbered). 1–
ISSN 0097-2769
Later A 106.15
Discontinued.

A 77.220:CT
POSTERS.
Earlier A 4.16/1

A 77.221:date   • Item 29
DIRECTORY OF BUREAU OF ANIMAL INDUSTRY.
Earlier A 4.14
Discontinued.

A 77.221/2:date   • Item 32-A
WORKING REFERENCE OF LIVESTOCK REGULA-
TORY ESTABLISHMENTS.
Replaces A 77.221

A 77.222:CT
VESTOCK HEALTH SERIES (Posters).

A 77.223:CT
ADDRESSES.

A 77.224:
REPORT OF DEVELOPMENTS ON ERADICATION OF
VESICULAR EXANTHEMA.

A 77.225:date
REPORT ON INCIDENCE OF ANTHRAX IN ANIMALS
IN UNITED STATES. [Monthly]

A 77.226:nos.
BIOLOGICAL PRODUCTS NOTICES.

A 77.226/2:nos.
BIOLOGICAL PRODUCTS MEMO. [Irregular]

Replaces VSC notices (A 77.217:) and VSC
letters.

A 77.226/3:nos.
VETERINARY BIOLOGICS DIVISION NOTICES. 1–
1965–   [Irregular]
Later A 101.14

A 77.227:date
NATIONAL STATUS ON CONTROL OF GARBAGE
FEEDING. [Monthly] (Animal Health Division)
PURPOSE:– To summarize information on gar-
bage fed swine.
ISSN 0364-8060
Later A 101.20

A 77.228:nos.
APH-CORRESPONDENCE AID (series).

A 77.228/2:nos.
[CORRESPONDENCE AIDS] CA (series). (Animal Disease Eradication Division)

A 77.229
ANIMAL MORBIDITY REPORT. [Monthly]
Later A 101.12

A 77.229/2
– [ANNUAL REPORTS.] [Twice a year] (Animal
Health Division)

Gives number of infected herds or flocks
reported, by States and diseases.
Separate reports issued for fiscal and
calendar years.

A 77.230
REPORTED INCIDENCE OF INFECTIOUS EQUINE
ENCEPHALOMYELITIS AND RELATED
ENCEPHALITIDES IN THE UNITED STATES, CAL-
ENDAR YEAR (Date). [Annual] (Animal Disease
Eradication Division)

Tables gives, by State, equine cases reported
and seasonal incidence-number equine cases
(estimated), for calendar year.

A 77.230/2
REPORTED ANTHROPOD-BORNE ENCEPHALIDITES
IN HORSES AND OTHER EQUIDAE. 1935–
[Annual] (Animal Health Division)

PURPOSE:– To summarize field reports from
the Animal Health Division field stations and to
serve as an aid to public health officials in their
assessment of viral activity of various agents.
Gives brief summary reports by States and
supplemented by statistical summaries for the
current year, by States, and for previous years
for the U.S.
Report is for the calendar year.

A 77.231
INCIDENCE OF BLUETONGUE REPORTED IN SHEEP
DURING CALENDAR YEAR (date). [Annual] (Ani-
mal Health Division)

Table gives incidence of bluetongue as reported in the United States during the calendar
year, by States affected. Maps.

A 77.232:date
REPORTED INCIDENCE OF RABIES IN UNITED
STATES. [Annual]
Earlier A 77.202:R 11/4

A 77.233
COOPERATIVE STATE-FEDERAL SHEEP AND
CATTLE SCABIES ERADICATION, PROGRESS
REPORT. [Annual] (Animal Health Division)

PURPOSE:– To report on the progress made
in scabies eradication for sheep and cattle including advances which may be adaptable for
wide scale application.
Report is for the fiscal year.
Earlier A 77.202:Sh 3/8
Later A 77.233/2 and A 77.233/3

A 77.233/2
ANNUAL REPORT OF COOPERATIVE STATE-
FEDERAL SHEEP SCABIES ERADICATION
ACTIVITIES, FISCAL YEAR (date). [Annual]
(Animal Health Division)

A 77.233/3
ANNUAL REPORT OF COOPERATIVE PSOROPTIC
CATTLE SCABIES ERADICATION ACTIVITIES,
FISCAL YEAR (date). [Annual] (Animal Health Di-
vision)

Textual summary report of work accomplished
during the fiscal year, supplemented by statistical tables and maps.

A 77.233/4
COOPERATIVE STATE-FEDERAL SHEEP AND
CATTLE SCABIES, EPIDEMIOLOGY AND RE-
LATED ACTIVITIES. 1954–   [Annual] (Animal
Health Division)

PURPOSE:– To report on the progress made
in scabies eradication for sheep and cattle including advances which may be adaptable for
widescale application.
Report covers the fiscal year.

A 77.234:date
NORTHEASTERN STATES REGIONAL POULTRY
BREEDING PROJECT. ANNUAL REPORT.

A 77.235:date
WESTERN STATES REGIONAL TURKEY BREEDING PROJECT. ANNUAL REPORT.

A 77.236:date
NORTH CENTRAL STATES REGIONAL POULTRY BREEDING PROJECT. ANNUAL REPORT.

A 77.237
REPORT OF COOPERATIVE CATTLE FEVER TICK ERADICATION ACTIVITIES. FISCAL YEAR (date). [Annual] (Animal Health Division)

　　　Textual summary of activities during the fiscal year. Maps.

A 77.237/2
NATIONAL TICK SURVEILLANCE PROGRAM. [Annual] (Animal Health Division)
　　　Covers the calendar year.
　　　Formerly National Tick Survey. (A 77.202:T 43/2)

A 77.238:CT
MAPS [Concerning Animal Industry].

A 77.239
FACILITIES AND EQUIPMENT FACT SHEET. MID-FE-1–   1963–   [Irregular] (Meat Inspection Division)

　　　Brief summaries of suggestions for improvement of facilities and equipment used in the meat packing industry.

A 77.239/2
CHEMICAL EVALUATION AND CONTROL FACT SHEETS. MID-SEC-1–   1964–   [Irregular] (Meat Inspection Division)

A 77.240
PSOROPTIC SHEEP SCABIES OUTBREAKS IN (State). [Annual] (Animal Health Division)

A 77.241:date
COOPERATIVE STATE-FEDERAL HOG CHOLERA ERADICATION PROGRAM PROGRESS REPORT. [Annual]

A 77.242
EQUINE PIROPLASMOSIS PROGRESS REPORT. 1966–   [Annual] (Animal Health Division)

　　　PURPOSE:– To provide a summary of the State-Federal cooperative program efforts against equine piroplasmosis and to summarize equidemiological findings relating to Babesia caballi and Babesia equi.
　　　Report is for the fiscal year.

A 77.243:CT
BIBLIOGRAPHIES AND LISTS OF PUBLICATIONS RELATING TO ANIMAL RESEARCH.

A 77.244
EQUINE INFECTIOUS ANEMIA, PROGRESS REPORT AND HISTORY IN THE UNITED STATES. 1968– [Annual] (Animal Health Division)

　　　PURPOSE:-To inform regulatory researh and other segments of the veterinary profession activities for the fiscal year.

A 77.245:v.nos./nos.   • **Item 88-B**
FAMILY ECONOMICS REVIEW. [Quarterly]
　　　See A 98.20

PUBLICATIONS RELATING TO ENTOMOLOGY AND PLANT QUARANTINE (1953–1978)

CREATION AND AUTHORITY

　　　The Bureau of Entomology and Plant Quarantine (A 56) was transferred along with other agencies to form the Agricultural Research Administration by Executive Order 9060 of February 23, 1942. The Bureau was abolished and its functions transferred to the Agricultural Research Service (A 77) by Secretary's Memorandum 1320, Supplement 4, dated November 2, 1953.

A 77.301:date   • **Item 43**
ANNUAL REPORTS.   – 1953.
　　　Earlier A 56.1
　　　Discontinued.

A 77.302:CT   • **Item 44**
GENERAL PUBLICATIONS.
　　　Earlier A 56.2
　　　Discontinued.

A 77.302:F 96   • **Item 44**
ANNOTATED INDEX OF REGISTERED FUNGICIDES AND NEMATICIDES, THEIR USES IN THE UNITED STATES. 1969. 1392 p.

A 77.302:P 43/4   • **Item 44**
U.S.D.A. SUMMARY OF REGISTERED AGRICULTURAL PESTICIDE CHEMICAL USES. [Irregular] (Pesticides Regulation Division)

A 77.306:CT   • **Item 47**
REGULATIONS, RULES, AND INSTRUCTIONS.
　　　Discontinued.

A 77.306/2:nos.
ADMINISTRATIVE INSTRUCTIONS [under sections of the Plant Quarantine Act].
　　　Reprint from Federal Register.

A 77.306/3:CT
HANDBOOKS MANUALS, GUIDES [Relating to Entomology and Plant Quarantine].

A 77.308:nos.   • **Item 48**
SERVICE AND REGULATORY ANNOUNCEMENTS. 1–
　　　1914–   [Quarterly]
　　　Earlier A 56.14. A 48.7, A 35.9
　　　Discontinued.

A 77.308/2:date   • **Item 48**
LIST OF INTERCEPTED PLANT PESTS. 1941– [Annual]
　　　Earlier A 56.14/2
　　　Later A 77.15:82-6

A 77.308/3:nos.
PQ [Plant Quarantine] (series). 1–
　　　Designated BEPQ prior to December 1953.
　　　Earlier A 56.9

A 77.308/4:nos.
P.P.C. [Plant Pest Control] (series). 1–

　　　Notices relating to insects reprinted from the Federal Register.
　　　Earlier in PQ series (A 77.308/3).

A 77.308/5:date   • **Item 48**
PLANT REGULATORY ANNOUNCEMENTS.
　　　Discontinued.

A 77.309:vol
EXTENSION ENTOMOLOGIST.
　　　Earlier A 56.21

A 77.310:vol
INSECT PEST SURVEY BULLETINS. [Monthly]
　　　Earlier A 56.18

A 77.310/2:date
THE MORE IMPORTANT INSECT RECORDS. [Monthly]

A 77.310/3:dt&nos.
INSECT PEST SURVEY, SPECIAL SUPPLEMENTS.
　　　Earlier A 77.310:22/sp.supp. 1– 13.

A 77.311:vol
REVIEW OF UNITED STATES PATENTS RELATED TO PEST CONTROL. v. 1– 29. 1956.
　　　Earlier A 56.17

A 77.312:nos.
E [Entomology] (Series). 1–
　　　Earlier A 56.19

A 77.313:nos.
ET [Entomological Technical] (series). 1–
　　　Earlier A 56.11

A 77.314:
ADMINISTRATIVE MEMORANDUM.
　　　Earlier A 56.16

A 77.314/2:nos.
PLANT QUARANTINE MEMORANDUM.

A 77.315:CT
PAPERS IN RE.
　　　Earlier A 56.23

A 77.316:nos.
INSECTS IN RELATION TO NATIONAL DEFENSE CIRCULARS.
　　　Earlier A 56.24

A 77.317:nos.   • **Item 45**
NOTICES OF QUARANTINE.
　　　Earlier A 56.13
　　　Discontinued.

A 77.317/2:nos.
PLANT QUARANTINE P.P.C. (Series).

　　　Formerly included in BEPQ-Q series, A 77.317.

A 77.318:date
LIST OF PUBLICATIONS AND PATENTS OF DIVISION OF INSECTICIDE INVESTIGATIONS.
　　　Earlier A 56.15

A 77.318/2:date
LIST OF U.S. PATENTS GRANTED MEMBERS OF DIVISION OF INSECTICIDE INVESTIGATIONS.
　　　Earlier A 77.318

A 77.319:CT
POSTERS.

A 77.320   • **Item 46**
PICTURE SHEETS. 1–   [Irregular] (Plant Pest Control Division)

　　　Contains colored illustrations. Poster
　　　Discontinued.

A 77.321:CT
ADDRESSES.

A 77.322:dt.&nos.
COTTON INSECT CONDITIONS.

A 77.323:nos.
EC [Entomological Control] (series). 1–   1948– (Bureau of Entomology and Plant Quarantine)

A 77.324:v.nos.&nos.
COOPERATIVE ECONOMIC INSECT REPORT. v. 1–   1951–   [Weekly] (Plant Pest Control Division)

　　　Condensation of reports from cooperating State, Federal, and industrial entomologists and other agricultural workers. Includes in addition to the reports, a 30-day week.
　　　Later A 101.9

A 77.324/2:v.nos.
– SPECIAL REPORTS.

A 77.324/3:CT
COOPERATIVE ECONOMIC INSECT REPORT [unnumbered miscellaneous reports].

A 77.325   • **Item 109**
NOTICES OF JUDGEMENT UNDER FEDERAL INSEC-
TICIDE, FUNGICIDE, AND RODENTICIDE ACT.
1–   1912–   [Irregular] (Pesticides Regulation
Division)

Brief notices of judgement relating to cases
arising in the U.S. District Counts.
Citation: I.F.R.
Discontinued.

A 77.326:date
JAPANESE BEETLE-EUROPEAN CHAFER CONTROL
PROGRAM, ANNUAL REPORT.

A 77.327:date
COOPERATIVE PEST CONTROL PROGRAMS. [Irregu-
lar]

A 77.327/2
PLANT PEST CONTROL COOPERATIVE PROGRAMS,
WESTERN REGION, FISCAL YEAR (date). [An-
nual]

Gives brief textual summary, statistical table,
map, and pictures, showing the work done on
pest eradication and control.

A 77.328:date   • **Item 43-A**
CONFERENCE REPORT ON COTTON INSECT RE-
SEARCH AND CONTROL: [Annual]
Earlier A 77.302:C 82
Discontinued.

A 77.329
PLANT QUARANTINE IMPORT REQUIREMENTS OF
(country). [Irregular] (Plant Quarantine Division)

Each release issued for a separate country.
Punched for three-ring binder.
Later A 101.11

A 77.330:CT
POSTERS.

OFFICE OF EXPERIMENT STATIONS (1942– 1953)

CREATION AND AUTHORITY

The Office of Experiment Stations (A 10) was
transferred along with other agencies to form the
Agricultural Research Administration by Executive Order 9060 of February 23, 1942. The Office
was abolished and its functions transferred to
the Agricultural Research Service (A 77) by
Secretary's Memorandum 1320, Supplement 4,
dated November 2, 1953.

A 77.401:date   • **Item 50**
ANNUAL REPORTS.
Earlier A 10.1/2
Discontinued.

A 77.401/2:date
REPORT ON AGRICULTURAL EXPERIMENT
STATIONS.
Earlier A 10.1/2
Discontinued.

A 77.402:CT   • **Item 51**
GENERAL PUBLICATIONS.
Earlier A 10.2
Discontinued.

A 77.406:CT   • **Item 51-A**
REGULATIONS, RULES, AND INSTRUCTIONS.
Discontinued.

A 77.407:CT
ADDRESSES.
Earlier A 10.27

A 77.408:vol.
EXPERIMENT STATION RECORD. [Monthly]
Earlier A 10.6

A 77.409:date
LISTS OF AGRICULTURAL EXPERIMENT STATION
PUBLICATIONS RECEIVED BY THE OFFICE.
[Monthly]
Earlier A 10.12

A 77.410:nos.
OES CIRCULAR LETTERS. [Weekly]

A 77.411:v.nos.
BIBLIOGRAPHY ON POULTRY INDUSTRY, CHICK-
ENS, TURKEYS, AQUATIC FOWL, GAMEBIRDS.
v. 1–   [Annual]

Alaska Agricultural Experiment Station

A 77.441:date
ANNUAL REPORTS.
Earlier A 10.10/1
Discontinued.

A 77.442:CT   • **Item 54**
GENERAL PUBLICATIONS.
Earlier A 10.10/2
Discontinued.

A 77.443:nos.   •**Item 52**
BULLETINS.
Earlier A 10.10/3
Discontinued.

A 77.444:nos.   • **Item 53**
CIRCULARS.
Earlier A 10.10/4
Discontinued.

Puerto Rico Agricultural Experiment Station

A 77.461:date   • **Item 55**
ANNUAL REPORT.
Earlier A 10.12/1
Discontinued.

A 77.462:CT   • **Item 58**
GENERAL PUBLICATIONS.
Earlier A 10.12/2
Discontinued.

A 77.463:nos.   •**Item 56**
BULLETINS.
Earlier A 10.12/3
Discontinued.

A 77.464:nos.   • **Item 57**
CIRCULARS.
Earlier A 10.12/4
Discontinued.

Hawaii Agricultural Experiment Station

A 77.481:date
ANNUAL REPORTS.

Earlier A 10.9/1

A 77.482:CT
GENERAL PUBLICATIONS.
Earlier A 10.9/2

A 77.483:nos.
BULLETINS.
Earlier A 10.9/3

A 77.484:nos.
CIRCULARS.
Earlier A 10.9/4

A 77.487:nos.
TECHNICAL BULLETINS. 1–   1943–

[Virgin Islands Agricultural Experiment Station]

A 77.491:date   • **Item 58-A**
REPORT OF VIRGIN ISLANDS AGRICULTURAL RE-
SEARCH AND EXTENSION PROGRAM.

A 77.492:CT
GENERAL PUBLICATIONS.

PUBLICATIONS RELATING TO HORTICULTURE (1953– 1978)

CREATION AND AUTHORITY

The Bureau of Plant Industry (A 19) was transferred along with other agencies to form the Agricultural Research Administration by Executive
Order 9060 of February 23, 1942. By
Administrator's Memorandum 5, dated February
12, 1943, the engineering research functions of
the Bureau of Agricultural Chemistry and Engineering were transferred to the newly designated
Bureau of Plant Industry, Soils, and Agricultural
Engineering. By Secretary's Memorandum 1320,
Supplement 4, dated November 2, 1953, the Bureau was abolished and its function transferred
to the Agricultural Research Service (A 77).

A 77.501:date   • **Item 99**
ANNUAL REPORTS.
Earlier A 19.1
Discontinued.

A 77.502:CT   • **Item 100**
GENERAL PUBLICATIONS.
Earlier A 19.2
Discontinued.

A 77.507:CT
ADDRESSES.
Earlier A 19.33

A 77.508:date
DRY LAND AGRICULTURE DIVISION, WEEKLY
STATION REPORTS.
Earlier A 19.24

A 77.509:vol
FORAGE CROP GAZETTE, NEWS LETTER FOR
STAFF WORKERS, DIVISION OF FORAGE
CROPS AND DISEASES. [Monthly]
Earlier A 19.29

A 77.509:vol
FRUIT AND VEGETABLE CROPS AND DISEASES
DIVISION, SEMI-MONTHLY NEWS LETTERS.
Earlier A 19.27

A 77.511   • **Item 100-B**
PLANT DISEASE REPORTER. v. 1–   1917–
[Monthly] (Crops Research Division)

Indexed by:–
Bibliography of Agriculture.
Biological Abstracts.
Biological and Agricultural Index.
Chemical Abstract.
Index to U.S. Government Periodicals.
Nuclear Science Abstracts.
Selected Water Resources Abstracts
ISSN 0032-0811
Earlier A 19.18
Later A 106.21

A 77.512:nos.
PLANT DISEASE REPORTER SUPPLEMENTS.
Earlier A 19.19

A 77.513:CT
PAPERS IN RE.
Earlier A 56.23

A 77.514:date • Item 102
SOIL SURVEY REPORTS.
Earlier A 19.32
Later A 57.38
Discontinued.

A 77.515 • Item 101
PLANT INVENTORY. 1– 1898– [Annual]

Prepared by New Crops Research Branch, Crops Research Division.
See also A 106.11

A 77.516:nos. • Item 101-A-2 (MF)
NFS REPORTS (series)

A 77.517:nos.
PLANT DISEASE POSTERS.
Earlier A 19.26

A 77.518:nos.
INFORMATION SERIES.
Earlier A 70.11

A 77.519:CT
COOPERATIVE INTER-AMERICAN PLANTATION RUBBER DEVELOPMENT.

A 77.520:nos.
PLANT DISEASE SURVEY SPECIAL PUBLICATIONS.
1– 1950–

A 77.521:date • Item 99-A
BIBLIOGRAPHY OF WEED INVESTIGATIONS. [Quarterly]
Discontinued.

A 77.522:nos.
RESEARCH REPORTS.

A 77.523:nos.
H. T. & S. OFFICE REPORTS.
Earlier A 19.36
Later A 88.39

A 77.524:date
SOIL SURVEY FIELD LETTERS. [Irregular]

A 77.525:nos. • Item 101-A
SOIL SURVEY LABORATORY MEMORANDUMS.
Later A 57.34
Discontinued.

A 77.526:nos. • Item 100-A-1
NATIONAL ARBORETUM CONTRIBUTIONS. 1– [Irregular]

Previously distributed to depository libraries under Item 100-A.
Discontinued.

A 77.526/2:nos. • Item 100-A
NATIONAL ARBORETUM LEAFLETS.
Discontinued.

A 77.527:nos.
CONTRIBUTIONS TOWARD A FLORA OF NEVADA.
Earlier A 19.35

A 77.528:nos.
PROGRESS IN SOIL AND WATER CONSERVATION RESEARCH, QUARTERLY REPORTS.

A 77.529:
RSIM– (series).

A 77.530:date
PROGRESS REPORT, ANNUAL VARIETAL AND ENVIRONMENTAL STUDY OF FIBER AND SPINNING PROPERTIES OF COTTONS. [Annual]
Earlier A 77.502 and A 77.2

A 77.531:date
REPORT OF ALFALFA IMPROVEMENT CONFERENCE. [Biennial]

A 77.532:date
ANNUAL REPORT OF VEGETABLE BREEDING IN SOUTHEASTERN UNITED STATES, HAWAII, AND PUERTO RICO.

A 77.533:nos.
SERIES 1, EVALUATION OF FOREIGN FRUITS AND NUTS.

A 77.534
CR [Crop Research] (series). [Irregular] (Crop Research Division)

PUBLICATIONS RELATING TO DAIRY RESEARCH (1953– 1978)

CREATION AND AUTHORITY

The Bureau of Dairy Industry (A 44) was transferred along with other agencies to form the Agricultural Research Administration (A 77.600) by Executive Order 9069 of February 23, 1942. The Bureau was abolished and its functions transferred to the Agricultural Research Service by Secretary's Memorandum 1320, Supplement 4, of November 2, 1953.

A 77.601:date • Item 41
ANNUAL REPORTS.

Earlier A 44.1

Discontinued.

A 77.602:CT • Item 42
GENERAL PUBLICATIONS RELATING TO DAIRY RESEARCH.
Earlier A 44.2
Discontinued.

A 77.607:CT
ADDRESSES.
Earlier A 44.12

A 77.608:v.nos.&nos. • Item 25-A-2
DAIRY-HERD-IMPROVEMENT LETTER. v. 1– 1925– [Irregular] (Northeastern Region)

Issued for the National Cooperative Dairy Herd Improvement Program.
ISSN 0085-7580
See also A 106.34
Discontinued 984/3

A 77.609:nos.
BDI-INF (Series).

Changed from A 77.602 and A 77.607

PUBLICATIONS RELATING TO HOME ECONOMICS AND HUMAN NUTRITION (1953– 1978)

CREATION AND AUTHORITY

The Bureau of Home Economics (A 42) was transferred along with other agencies to form the Agricultural Research Administration (A 77.700) by Executive Order 9069 of February 23, 1942. In 1943 the name was changed to Bureau of Human Nutrition and Home Economics. The Bureau was abolished and its functions transferred to Agricultural Research Service, (A 77) by Secretary's Memorandum 1320, Supplement 4, dated November 2, 1953.

A 77.701:date • Item 87
ANNUAL REPORTS.
Earlier A 42.1
Discontinued.

A 77.702:CT • Item 88
GENERAL PUBLICATIONS.
Earlier A 42.2
Discontinued.

A 77.706:CT • Item 88-A
REGULATIONS, RULES, AND INSTRUCTIONS.
Discontinued.

A 77.707:CT
POSTERS.

A 77.708:date • Item 88-B
FAMILY ECONOMICS REVIEW. 1943– [Quarterly]
(ARS-62-5)

Supersedes Wartime Family Living and Rural Family Living.
Indexed by: Index to U.S. Government Periodicals.
ISSN 0425-676X
Later A 106.17

See A 77.245

A 77.709:nos.
COMMODITY SUMMARY. 1– 10. 1949– 1950.

A 77.710 • Item 88-C
NUTRITION PROGRAM NEWS. [Bimonthly]

FOOD DISTRIBUTION ADMINISTRATION (1942– 1943)

CREATION AND AUTHORITY

The Food Distribution Administration was established within the Department of Agriculture by Executive Order 9280 of December 5, 1942, to which were transferred the Agricultural Marketing Administration (A 75), the Sugar Agency (A 63), and certain other offices concerned with food distribution. By Executive Order 9322 of March 26, 1943, the Administration was consolidated with certain other agencies to form the Administration of Food Production and Distribution (A 80.100).

A 78.1:date
ANNUAL REPORTS.
Later A 80.101

A 78.2:CT
GENERAL PUBLICATIONS.
    Later A 80.102

A 78.6:CT
REGULATIONS, RULES, AND INSTRUCTIONS.
    Later A 80.106

A 78.7:date
COLD STORAGE REPORTS. [Monthly]
    Earlier A 75.8
    Later A 80.107

A 78.8:vol.
CONSUMERS' GUIDE. [Monthly]
    Earlier A 75.8
    Later A 80.108

A 78.9:date
COTTON MARKET REVIEW. [Weekly]
    Earlier A 75.9
    Later A 80.109

A 78.10:nos.
HONEY REPORTS. [Semimonthly]
    Earlier A 75.11
    Later A 80.110

A 78.11:vol.
LIVESTOCK, MEATS AND WOOL; MARKET REVIEW
    AND STATISTICS. [Weekly]
    Earlier A 75.10
    Later A 80.111

A 78.12:nos.
PEANUT REPORTS. [Weekly]
    Earlier A 75.12
    Later A 80.112

A 78.13:incl.nos.
NOTICES OF JUDGEMENT UNDER INSECTICIDE ACT.
    Earlier A 75.15
    Later A 80.113

A 78.14:vol.
MARKETING ACTIVITIES. [Monthly]
    Earlier A 75.13
    Later A 80.114

A 78.15:v.nos.
P. AND S. DOCKET, MONTHLY REPORTS OF ACTION
    TAKEN ON CASES ARISING UNDER PACKERS
    AND STOCKYARDS ACT.
    Earlier A 75.14
    Later A 80.115

A 78.16:nos.
MEAT INSPECTION DIVISION MEMORANDUMS.

FOOD PRODUCTION ADMINISTRATION
(1942– 1943)

CREATION AND AUTHORITY

    The Food Production Administration was es-
tablished within the Department of Agriculture by
Executive Order 9280 of December 5, 1942, to
which were transferred the Agricultural Conservation and Adjustment Administration (A 76) (except the Sugar Agency), the Farm Credit Administration, (A 72), the Farm Security Administration (A 61), and certain other offices dealing with
food production. By Executive Order 9322 of
March 26, 1943, the Administration was consolidated with certain other agencies to form the
Administration of Food Production and Distribution (A 80.200).

A 79.1:date
ANNUAL REPORTS.
    Later A 80.201

A 79.2:CT
GENERAL PUBLICATIONS.
    Later A 80.202

A 79.7:nos.
FOOD PRODUCTION MEMORANDUM.
    Later A 80.208

FARM CREDIT ADMINISTRATION
(1942– 1943)

CREATION AND AUTHORITY

    The Farm Credit Administration was trans-
ferred to the Food Production Administration by
Executive Order 9280 of December 5, 1942. Executive Order 9322 of March 26, 1943 returned it
to the Secretary of Agriculture as an independent
bureau (A 72).

A 79.101:date
ANNUAL REPORT.
    Earlier A 72.1

A 79.102:CT
GENERAL PUBLICATIONS.
    Earlier A 72.2

A 79.107:v.nos.& nos.
NEWS FOR FARMER COOPERATIVES. [Monthly]
    Earlier A 72.10

A 79.108:date
SEMIANNUAL REPORT ON LOANS AND DISCOUNTS.
    Earlier A 72.12

SOIL CONSERVATION SERVICE
(1942– 1943)

CREATION AND AUTHORITY

    The Soil Conservation Service (A 76.200), as
a subordinate bureau within the Agricultural Conservation and Adjustment Administration, was
transferred to the Food Production Administration by Executive Order 9280 of December 5,
1942. By Executive Order 9322 of March 26,
1943, the Service was placed within the Administration of Food Production and Distribution (A
80.2000), which was renamed the War Food Administration by Executive Order 9334 of April 19,
1943.

A 79.201:date
ANNUAL REPORTS.
    Earlier A 76.201
    Later A 80.2001

A 79.202:CT
GENERAL PUBLICATIONS.
    Earlier A 76.202
    Later A 80.2002

A 79.207:v.nos.
SOIL CONSERVATION; OFFICIAL ORGAN. [Monthly]
    Earlier A 76.208
    Later A 80.2007

FEDERAL CROP INSURANCE CORPORATION
(1942– 1943)

CREATION AND AUTHORITY

    The Federal Crop Insurance Corporation (A
76.100) was transferred to the Food Production
Administration by Executive Order 9280 of December 5, 1942. Executive Order 9322 of March
26, 1943 transferred the Corporation to the Administration of Food Production and Distribution
(A 80.900).

A 79.301:date
ANNUAL REPORT.
    Earlier A 76.101
    Later A 80.901

A 79.302:CT
GENERAL PUBLICATIONS.
    Earlier A 76.102
    Later A 80.902

A 79.306:CT
REGULATIONS, RULES, AND INSTRUCTIONS.
    Earlier A 62.6/2 and A 76.106
    Later A 80.906

AGRICULTURAL ADJUSTMENT AGENCY
(1942– 1943)

CREATION AND AUTHORITY

    The Agricultural Adjustment Agency (A
76.400), a subordinate agency within the Agricultural Conservation and Adjustment Administration, was transferred to the Food Production Administration by Executive Order 9280 of December 5, 1942. Executive Order 9322 of March 26,
1943 transferred the agency to the Administration of Food Production and Distribution (A
80.2100).

A 79.401:date
ANNUAL REPORT.
    Earlier A 76.401
    Later A 80.2101

A 79.402:CT
GENERAL PUBLICATIONS.
    Earlier A 76.402
    Later A 80.2102

A 79.406:CT
REGULATIONS, RULES, AND INSTRUCTIONS.
    Earlier A 76.406
    Later A 80.2106

A 79.441
EAST CENTRAL REGION PUBLICATIONS.

A 79.451
NORTH CENTRAL REGION PUBLICATIONS.

A 79.452:CT
GENERAL PUBLICATIONS.
    Earlier A 55.43/2
    Later A 80.2152

A 79.458:CT
PRODUCTION PRACTICES, 1943 FARM PROGRAM.

A 79.461
NORTHEAST REGION PUBLICATIONS.

A 79.471
SOUTHERN REGION PUBLICATIONS.

A 79.481
WESTERN REGION PUBLICATIONS.

WAR FOOD ADMINISTRATION
(1943– 1945)

CREATION AND AUTHORITY

    The Administration of Food Production and Distribution was established within the Department of Agriculture by Executive Order 9322 of March 26, 1943, under which were placed the Food Production Administration (A 79) (except the Farm Credit Administration), the Food Distribution Administration (A 78), the Commodity Credit Corporation (A 71) and the Extension Service (A 43). Executive Order 9334 of April 19, 1943, changed the name to War Food Administration. The War Food Administration was terminated by Executive Order 9577 of June 29, 1945, effective June 30, 1945.

A 80.1:date
ANNUAL REPORTS.

A 80.2:CT
GENERAL PUBLICATIONS.

A 80.6:CT
REGULATIONS, RULES, AND INSTRUCTIONS.

A 80.7:CT
ADDRESSES.

A 80.8:CT
POSTERS.

OFFICE OF DISTRIBUTION
(1944– 1945)

CREATION AND AUTHORITY

    The Food Administration (A 78) was consolidated with certain other agencies to form the Administration of Food Production and Distribution by Executive Order 9322 of March 26, 1943. On January 21, 1944, the name of the Food Distribution Administration was changed to Office of Distribution. The Office was abolished by Executive Order 9577 of June 29, 1945, effective June 30, 1945.

A 80.101:date
ANNUAL REPORTS.
    Earlier A 78.1

A 80.102:CT
GENERAL PUBLICATIONS.
    Earlier A 78.2

A 80.106:CT
REGULATIONS, RULES, AND INSTRUCTIONS.
    Earlier A 78.6

A 80.107:date
COLD STORAGE REPORTS.
    Earlier A 78.7
    Later A 80.807

A 80.108:vol.
CONSUMERS' GUIDE. [Monthly]
    Earlier A 78.8
    Later A 80.808

A 80.109:date
COTTON MARKET REVIEW. [Weekly]
    Earlier A 78.9
    Later A 80.809

A 80.110:nos.
HONEY REPORTS. [Semimonthly]
    Earlier A 78.10
    Later A 80.810

A 80.111:v.nos.
LIVESTOCK, MEATS AND WOOL; MARKET REVIEWS
    AND STATISTICS. [Weekly]
    Earlier A 78.111
    Later A 80.811

A 80.112:nos.
PEANUT REPORTS. [Weekly]
    Earlier A 78.112
    Later A 80.812

A 80.113:incl.nos.
NOTICES OF JUDGMENT UNDER INSECTICIDE ACT.
    Earlier A 78.13 and A 80.823

A 80.114:v.nos.
MARKETING ACTIVITIES. [Monthly]
    Earlier A 78.14
    Later A 80.813

A 80.115:v.nos.
P. AND S. DOCKET, MONTHLY REPORTS OF ACTION
    TAKEN ON CASES ARISING UNDER PACKERS
    AND STOCKYARDS ACT.
    Earlier A 78.15
    Later 80.814

A 80.116:nos.
MARKETING ORDERS.
    Earlier A 75.20
    Later A 80.825

A 80.116:CT
MARKETING ORDERS (miscellaneous).

A 80.117:nos.
SUGAR DETERMINATION.
    Earlier A 55.37 and A 76.307
    Later A 80.817

A 80.118:nos.
SERVICE AND REGULATORY ANNOUNCEMENTS.
    Earlier A 75.16
    Later A 82.23

A 80.119:nos.
COMMODITY STATISTICS.
    Later A 80.826

A 80.120:CT
ADDRESSES.

A 80.121:CT
UNITED STATES STANDARDS FOR FUITS, ETC.
    Earlier A 75.19
    Later 80.822

A 80.122:CT
POSTERS.

A 80.123:nos.
NUTRITION AND FOOD CONSERVATION BRANCH
    PUBLICATIONS.
    Later A 1.65

A 80.124:date
STOCKS OF LEAF TOBACCO OWNED BY DEALERS
    AND MANUFACTURERS. [Quarterly]
    Earlier A 75.2:T 55/3
    Later A 80.821

A 80.125:nos.
FOOD TRADE LETTERS. [Weekly]
    Later A 80.410

A 80.126:nos.
CONTAINER NOTES.

A 80.127:date
INDUSTRIAL NUTRITION SERVICE. [Monthly]

A 80.128:v.nos.
COTTON PRICE STATISTICS, MONTHLY AVERAGES.
    Later A 80.815

A 80.129:date
QUARTERLY SOYBEAN MARKET REVIEW.
    Later A 80.818

A 80.130:date
MARGARINE PRODUCTION. [Monthly]
    Later A 80.820

A 80.131:CT
FACT SHEETS.

A 80.132:date
FOOD SUPPLY REPORTS. [Monthly]
    Later 80.816

A 80.133:vol.
COTTON LINTERS REVIEW. [Weekly]

    Later A 80.819
A 80.134:v.nos.
U.S. COTTON QUALITY REPORT FOR GINNINGS.
    Later A 80.824 and A 82.28

A 80.135:nos.
NUTRITION NEWS LETTER. [Monthly]
    Earlier Pr 32.4502:N 95/7 and A 80.830

A 80.136
FEDERAL FOOD REPORTER.

A 80.137
NUTRITION KIT.

A 80.138
SCHOOL LUNCH KIT.

OFFICE OF PRODUCTION
(1944– 1945)

CREATION AND AUTHORITY

    The Food Production Administration (A 79) was transferred by Executive Order 9322 of March 26, 1943 to the Administration of Food Production and Distribution (A 80.200). On January 21, 1944, the name of the Food Production Administration was changed to Office of Production. The Office was abolished by Executive Order 9577 of June 29, 1945, effective June 30, 1945.

A 80.201:date
ANNUAL REPORTS.
    Earlier A 79.1

A 80.202:CT
GENERAL PUBLICATIONS.

A 80.206:CT
REGULATIONS, RULES, AND INSTRUCTIONS.

A 80.207:CT
ADDRESSES.

A 80.208:nos.
FOOD PRODUCTION MEMORANDUMS.
    Earlier A 79.9

EXTENSION SERVICE
(1943–1945)

CREATION AND AUTHORITY

The Extension Service (A 43) was placed within the Administration of Food Production and Distribution (A 80.300) by Executive Order 9322 of March 26, 1943. Executive Order 9577 of June 29, 1945 returned the Service to the Secretary of Agriculture (A 43), effective June 30, 1945.

A 80.301:date
ANNUAL REPORTS.
See also A 43.1

A 80.302:CT
GENERAL PUBLICATIONS.
See also A 43.2

A 80.304:nos.
EXTENSION SERVICE CIRCULARS.
Earlier A 43.4

A 80.306:CT
REGULATIONS, RULES, AND INSTRUCTIONS.

A 80.307:v.nos.
EXTENSION SERVICE REVIEW. [Monthly]
See also A 43.7

A 80.308:CT
POSTERS.
Earlier A 43.8

A 80.309:nos.
LECTURES FOR SLIDEFILMS.
Earlier A 43.19

A 80.310:CT
ADDRESSES.
See also A 43.21

A 80.311:nos.
EXTENSION FARM LABOR CIRCULARS.
Later A 43.26

COMMODITY CREDIT ADMINISTRATION
(1943–1945)

CREATION AND AUTHORITY

The Commodity Credit Corporation (A 71) was placed along with other agencies under the Administration of Food Production and Distribution (A 80.400) by Executive Order 9322 of March 26, 1943. Executive Order 9577 of June 29, 1945 returned control of the Administration to the Secretary of Agriculture, effective June 30, 1945. By Secretary's Memorandum 1118, dated August 18, 1945, the Administration became a part of the Production and Marketing Administration (A 82.300), effective August 20, 1945.

A 80.401:date
ANNUAL REPORTS.
Earlier A 71.1
Later A 82.301

A 80.402:CT
GENERAL PUBLICATIONS.
Earlier A 71.2
Later A 82.302

A 80.406:CT
REGULATIONS, RULES, AND INSTRUCTIONS.
Earlier A 71.6
Later A 82.306

A 80.407:date
STATEMENTS OF LOANS AND COMMODITIES OWNED. [Monthly]
Earlier A 71.7
Later A 82.307

A 80.408:CT
ADDRESSES.

A 80.410:nos.
FOOD TRADE LETTERS. [Weekly]
Earlier A 71.9

SOIL CONSERVATION SERVICE
(1944–1945)

CREATION AND AUTHORITY

The Soil Conservation Service (A 80.2000), functioned as an independent agency within the War Food Administration during the period from January 21, 1944 until June 30, 1945 (A 80.500), at which time Executive Order 9577 returned the Soil Conservation Service to the direct control of the Secretary of Agriculture (A 57).

A 80.501:date
ANNUAL REPORTS.
Earlier A 80.2001
Later A 57.1

A 80.502:CT
GENERAL PUBLICATIONS.
Earlier A 80.2002
Later A 57.2

A 80.507:v.nos.
SOIL CONSERVATION. [Monthly]
Earlier A 80.2007
Later A 57.9

A 80.508:date
SOIL CONSERVATION DISTRICTS. [Monthly]
Earlier A 80.200
Later A 57.32

A 80.509:nos.
TECHNICAL PUBLICATIONS.
Earlier A 80.2011

A 80.510
PHYSICAL LAND SURVEYS.
Earlier A 80.2012

AGRICULTURAL ADJUSTMENT AGENCY
(1944–1945)

CREATION AND AUTHORITY

The Agricultural Adjustment Agency (A 80.2100), a subordinate agency within the War Food Administration became an independent agency within that Administration effective January 21, 1944, by an Administration Memorandum. When the War Food Administration was terminated by Executive Order 9577 of June 29, 1945, the functions of the Agricultural Adjustment Agency was transferred to the Secretary of Agriculture, such change being made permanent by Reorganization Plan No. 3 of 1946, effective July 16, 1946. The Agency was terminated and its functions transferred to the Production and Marketing Administration (A 82) by Secretary's Memorandum 1118, dated August 18, 1945.

A 80.601:date
ANNUAL REPORTS.
Earlier A 80.2101
Later A 83.1

A 80.602:CT
GENERAL PUBLICATIONS.
Earlier A 80.2101
Later A 83.2

A 80.606:CT
REGULATIONS, RULES, AND INSTRUCTIONS.
Includes Handbooks and Manuals.
Earlier A 80.2106
Later A 83.6

A 80.607:CT
POSTERS, CONSERVATION PRACTICES.

A 80.608:CT
AGRICULTURAL CONSERVATION PRACTICES (by states).
Later A 82.111

A 80.609:CT
ADDRESSES.
Earlier A 55.15
Later A 82.113

A 80.610
SPECIAL SERVICES MEMORANDUMS.
Later A 83.7

A 80.611:CT
COMMITTEEMAN'S PRACTICE HANDBOOKS (by states).
Later A 82.107

A 80.612:CT
INSTRUCTIONS FOR COMPLETING FARM PLANS (by states).

A 80.613:CT
AGRICULTURAL CONSERVATION PROGRAM (by states).

A 80.614:nos.
GENERAL INFORMATION SERIES.
Earlier A 76.408

FARM SECURITY
ADMINISTRATION
(1942– 1946)

CREATION AND AUTHORITY

The Farm Security Administration (A 61) became an agency within the War Food Administration (A 80.700) by Executive Order 9280 of December 5, 1942. On January 21, 1944, the Farm
Security Administration became a separate
agency directly responsible to the War Food Administrator. Executive Order 9577 of June 29,
1945, returned the Administration to the Jurisdiction of the Secretary of Agriculture. The Farm
Security Administration was abolished by Act of
Congress, approved August 15, 1946 (60 Stat.
1062), succeeded by the Farmers' Home Administration (A 84).

A 80.701:date
ANNUAL REPORTS.
   Earlier A 61.1

A 80.702:CT
GENERAL PUBLICATIONS.
   Earlier A 61.2

A 80.706:CT
REGULATIONS, RULES, AND INSTRUCTIONS.
   Earlier A 61.7

A 80.707:CT
ADDRESSES.
   Earlier A 61.16

A 80.708:nos.
LEAFLETS FOR ACTION.
   Earlier A 61.18

A 80.709:dt.nos.
FAMILY PROGRESS REPORT, RELEASES.
   Earlier A 61.19

OFFICE OF MARKETING SERVICE
(January– June 1945)

CREATION AND AUTHORITY

The Office of Marketing Services was established within the War Food Administration on January 1, 1945 by authority of the War Food
Administrator's Memorandum 27, dated December 13, 1944, to succeed the Office of Distribution (A 80.100). Executive Order 9577 of June
29, 1945, effective June 30, 1945, placed the
Office under the jurisdiction of the Secretary of
Agriculture (A 81).

A 80.801:date
ANNUAL REPORT.
   Later A 81.1

A 80.802:CT
GENERAL PUBLICATIONS.
   Later A 81.2

A 80.807:v.nos.
COLD STORAGE REPORTS. [Monthly]
   Earlier A 80.107
   Later A 81.7

A 80.808:v.nos.
CONSUMERS' GUIDE. [Monthly]
   Earlier A 80.108
   Later A 1.67

A 80.809:v.nos.
COTTON MARKET REVIEW. [Weekly]
   Earlier A 80.109
   Later A 81.9

A 80.810:v.nos.
HONEY REPORTS. [Semimonthly]
   Earlier A 80.110
   Later A 81.10

A 80.811:v.nos.
LIVESTOCK, MEATS AND WOOL, MARKET REVIEWS
   AND STATISTICS. [Weekly]
   Earlier A 80.111
   Later A 81.11

A 80.812:v.nos.
PEANUT REPORTS. [Weekly]
   Earlier A 80.112
   Later A 81.12

A 80.813:v.nos.
MARKETING ACTIVITIES. [Monthly]
   Earlier A 80.114
   Later A 81.13

A 80.814:v.nos.
P. AND S. DOCKET, MONTHLY REPORTS OF ACTION
   TAKEN ON CASES ARISING UNDER PACKERS
   AND STOCKYARDS ACT.
   Earlier A 80.115
   Later A 81.14

A 80.815:v.nos.
COTTON PRICE STATISTICS. [Monthly]
   Earlier A 80.128
   Later A 81.17

A 80.816:date
FOOD SUPPLY REPORTS. [Monthly]
   Earlier A 80.132
   Later A 82.16

A 80.817:nos.
SUGAR DETERMINATION.
   Earlier A 80.117
   Later A 81.16

A 80.818:date
SOYBEAN MARKET SUMMARY. [Quarterly]

   Earlier A 80.129
   Later A 81.18

A 80.819:vol.
COTTON LINTERS REVIEW. [Weekly]
   Earlier A 80.133
   Later A 81.8

A 80.819:vol.
COTTON LINTERS REVIEW. [Weekly]
   Earlier A 80.133
   Later A 81.8

A 80.820:date
MARGARINE PRODUCTION. [Monthly]
   Earlier A 80.130
   Later A 82.26

A 80.821:date
TOBACCO STOCKS REPORTS. [Quarterly]

   Earlier A 80.124
   Later A 82.11

A 80.822:CT
UNITED STATES STANDARDS FOR FRUITS, ETC.
   Earlier A 80.121
   Later A 81.15

A 80.823:nos.
NOTICES OF JUDGMENT UNDER INSECTICIDE ACT.
   Earlier A 80.133
   Later A 81.15

A 80.824:vol.
U.S. COTTON QUALITY REPORT FOR GINNINGS.
   Earlier A 80.134
   Later A 82.28

A 80.825:nos.
MARKETING ORDERS.
   Earlier A 80.116
   Later A 82.22

A 80.826:nos.
[COMMODITY STATISTICS.]
   Earlier A 80.119
   Later A 82.18

A 80.827:v.nos.
COMMERCIAL GRAIN STOCKS REPORTS. [Weekly]
   Later A 81.9

A 80.828:v.nos.
FEED MARKET REVIEW. [Weekly]

A 80.829:v.nos.
RICE MARKET REVIEW. [Weekly]
   Later A 81.21

A 80.830:nos.
NUTRITION NEWS LETTERS. [Monthly]
   Earlier A 80.135
   Later A 81.2

FEDERAL CROP INSURANCE
CORPORATION
(1943– 1945)

CREATION AND AUTHORITY

The Federal Crop Insurance Corporation (A
79.300), a subordinate unit within the Food Production Administration, was transferred to the
War Food Administration (A 80.900) by Executive
Order 9334 of April 19, 1943. The War Food Administration was abolished by Executive Order
9577 of June 29, 1945. Secretary's Memorandum
118, Supplement 1, dated October 8, 1945, placed
the Corporation within the Production and Marketing Administration (A 82.200).

A 80.901:date
ANNUAL REPORT.
   Earlier A 79.301
   Later A 82.201

A 80.902:CT
GENERAL PUBLICATIONS.
   Earlier A 79.302
   Later A 82.202

A 80.906:CT
REGULATIONS, RULES, AND INSTRUCTIONS.
   Earlier A 79.306

A 80.907:nos.
INFORMATION SERIES.
   Earlier A 76.108
   Later A 82.207

SOIL CONSERVATION SERVICE
(1943–1944)

CREATION AND AUTHORITY

The Soil Conservation Service, a subordinate bureau within the Food Production Administration (A 79.200) during the period December 5, 1942 until March 26, 1943, was transferred by Executive Order 9322 to the Administration of Food Production and Distribution (A 80.2000), which agency was renamed the War Food Administration by Executive Order 9334 of April 19, 1943. By an Administration Memorandum, the Service functioned from January 21, 1944 until June 30, 1945 as an independent agency (A 80.500) within the War Food Administration.

A 80.2001:date
ANNUAL REPORTS.
Earlier A 79.201
Later A 80.501

A 80.2002:CT
GENERAL PUBLICATIONS.

Earlier A 79.202
Later A 80.502

A 80.2007:v.nos.
SOIL CONSERVATION.
Earlier A 79.207

A 80.2008:CT
ADDRESSES.

A 80.2009:date
SOIL CONSERVATION DISTRICTS. [Monthly]
Earlier A 76.214

A 80.2010:date
DAILY TOTALS OF PRECIPITATION IN MUSKINGUM RIVER BASIN. [Monthly]

A 80.2011:nos.
[TECHNICAL PUBLICATIONS.]
Earlier A 76.211
Later A 80.509

A 80.2012:nos.
PHYSICAL LAND SURVEYS.
Earlier A 76.212
Later A 80.510

A 80.2013:nos.
SPECIAL REPORTS OF SEDIMENTATION SECTION, OFFICE OF RESEARCH.
Earlier A 76.215

AGRICULTURAL ADJUSTMENT AGENCY
(1943–1944)

CREATION AND AUTHORITY

The Agricultural Adjustment Agency (A 79.400), a subordinate agency within the Food Production Administration, as transferred to the Administration of Food Production and Distribution (A 80.2100) by Executive Order 9322 of March 26, 1943. By Administration Memorandum, the Agency functioned independently within the War Food Administration (A 80.600), effective January 21, 1944.

A 80.2101:date
ANNUAL REPORTS.
Earlier A 79.401
Later A 80.601

A 80.2102:CT
GENERAL PUBLICATIONS.
Earlier A 79.402
Later A 80.602

A 80.2106:CT
REGULATIONS, RULES, AND INSTRUCTIONS.
Earlier A 79.406
Later A 80.606

East Central Region

A 80.2142:CT
GENERAL PUBLICATIONS.
Earlier A 55.42/2

North Central Region

A 80.2152:CT
GENERAL PUBLICATIONS.
Earlier A 79.452

A 80.2158:CT
PRODUCTION-CONSERVATION PROGRAM, COMMITTEEMEN'S HANDBOOKS.

A 80.2161
NORTHEAST REGION.

A 80.2162:CT
GENERAL PUBLICATIONS.

A 80.2166:CT
REGULATIONS, RULES, AND INSTRUCTIONS.
Earlier A 76.466

A 80.2171
SOUTHERN REGION PUBLICATIONS.

A 80.2172:CT
GENERAL PUBLICATIONS.
Earlier A 76.472

Western Region

A 80.2182:CT
GENERAL PUBLICATIONS.
Earlier A 76.482

A 80.2186:CT
REGULATIONS, RULES, AND INSTRUCTIONS.
Earlier A 76.48

OFFICE OF MARKETING SERVICES
(July 1– August 20, 1945)

CREATION AND AUTHORITY

The Office of Marketing Services was established within the War Food Administration of the Department of Agriculture on January 1, 1945, by authority of the War Food Administrator's Memorandum 27, dated December 13, 1944, to succeed the Office of Distribution (A 80.100). Executive Order 9577 of June 29, 1945, placed the Office under the jurisdiction of the Secretary of Agriculture. Secretary's Memorandum 1118, dated August 18, 1945, effective August 20, 1945, consolidated the Office with certain other agencies to form the Production and Marketing Administration (A 82).

A 81.1:date
ANNUAL REPORTS.
Earlier A 80.801

A 81.2:CT
GENERAL PUBLICATIONS.
Earlier A 80.802

A 81.7:vol.
COLD STORAGE REPORTS. [Monthly]
Earlier A 80.807

A 81.8:vol.
COTTON LINTERS REVIEW. [Weekly]
Earlier A 80.819
Later A 82.8

A 81.9:vol.
COTTON MARKET REVIEW. [Weekly]
Earlier A 80.809
Later A 92.9

A 81.10:vol.
HONEY REPORTS. [Semimonthly]
Earlier A 80.810
Later A 82.12

A 81.11:vol.
LIVESTOCK, MEATS AND WOOL, MARKET REVIEWS AND STATISTICS. [Weekly]
Earlier A 80.811
Later A 82.7

A 81.12:vol.
PEANUT REPORTS. [Weekly]
Earlier A 80.812
Later A 82.10

A 81.13:vol.
MARKETING ACTIVITIES. [Monthly]
Earlier A 80.813
Later A 82.17

A 81.14:vol.
P. AND S. DOCKET, MONTHLY REPORT OF ACTION TAKEN ON CASES ARISING UNDER PACKERS AND STOCKYARDS ACT.

Earlier A 81.814
Later A 82.14

A 81.15:CT
UNITED STATES STANDARDS FOR GRADES OF [fruits, vegetables, etc.]
Earlier A 80.822
Later A 82.20

A 81.16:nos.
[SUGAR DETERMINATION].
Earlier A 80.817
Later A 82.19

A 81.17:vol.
COTTON PRICE STATISTICS. [Monthly]
   Earlier A 80.815
   Later A 82.13

A 81.18:date
SOYBEAN MARKET SUMMARY. [Quarterly]
   Earlier A 80.818
   Later A 82.21

A 81.19:v.nos.
COMMERCIAL GRAIN STOCKS REPORTS. [Weekly]
   Earlier A 80.827
   Later A 82.31

A 81.20:v.nos.
FEED MARKET REVIEW. [Weekly]
   Earlier A 80.828
   Later A 82.32

A 81.21:v.nos.
RICE MARKET REVIEW. [Weekly]
   Earlier A 80.829
   Later A 82.23

AGRICULTURAL STABILIZATION AND CONSERVATION SERVICE (1961– 1994)

CREATION AND AUTHORITY

The Production and Marketing Administration was established within the Department of Agriculture by Secretary's Memorandum 1118, dated August 18, 1945, effective August 20, 1945, consolidating the Agricultural Adjustment Agency (A 83), the Office of Marketing Services (A 81), and certain other offices of the Department of Agriculture. The Production and Marketing Administration was succeeded by the Commodity Stabilization Service, effective November 2, 1953 by Secretary's Memorandum 1320, Supplement 4. The name was changed to Agricultural Stabilization and Conservation Service by Secretary's Memorandum 1458 of June 14, 1961, effective June 5, 1961.

Abolished October 20, 1994, and functions assumed by the Farm Service Agency.

A 82.1:date   • Item 104
ANNUAL REPORTS.
   Discontinued.

A 82.1/2:CT/date   • Item 110-B-1– B-55
ANNUAL REPORTS [by States].
   Discontinued.

A 82.2:CT   • Item 106
GENERAL PUBLICATIONS.

A 82.3:nos.
BULLETINS.

A 82.3/2:date
EXPORT CORN MEAL BULLETIN.

A 82.3/3
CORN MEAL FOR DOMESTIC DISTRIBUTION. [Monthly]

   Formerly Domestic Corn Meal Bulletin.

A 82.3/4
CORN (Hominy) GRITS FOR DOMESTIC DISTRIBUTION. [Monthly]

   Formerly Domestic Corn (Hominy) Grits Bulletins.

A 82.3/5:date
EXPORT WHEAT FLOUR BULLETIN.

A 82.3/6
WHEAT FLOUR FOR DOMESTIC DISTRIBUTION. [Monthly]

   Formerly Domestic Wheat Flour Bulletin.

A 82.3/7
CORN MEAL FOR EXPORT DISTRIBUTION. [Monthly]

   Formerly Export Corn Meal Price Bulletin.

A 82.3/8
CORN MEAL. [Monthly]

   Formerly Export Corn Meal Port Bulletin.

A 82.3/9
WHEAT FLOUR FOR EXPORT DISTRIBUTION. [Monthly]

   Formerly Export Wheat Flour Price Bulletin.
INFORMATION RELEASES, PORT ALLOCATIONS.

   PURPOSE:– To furnish information concerning millers supplying commodities, amounts, type and pack, port of exit, destination country and distribution agency.
   Separate release issued for the following commodity:

A 82.3/10
WHEAT FLOUR. [Monthly]

   Formerly Export Wheat Flour Port Bulletin.

A 82.5:CT   • Item 107
LAWS.

A 82.6:CT   • Item 110
REGULATIONS, RULES, AND INSTRUCTIONS.

A 82.6/2
S.R. [Sugar Requirements and Quotas] (series). – December 31, 1974. [Irregular]

   Regulations reprinted from the Federal Register relating to sugar requirements and quotas allotted for import into the United States.

A 82.6/3:nos.
SOIL BANK HANDBOOKS.

A 82.6/4:CT   • Item 106-A
HANDBOOKS, MANUALS, GUIDES.

A 82.7:v.nos.
LIVESTOCK, MEATS AND WOOL, MARKET REVIEWS AND STATISTICS. [Weekly]
   Earlier A 81.11
   Later A 88.16/4

A 82.8:v.nos.
COTTON LINTERS REVIEW. [Weekly]
   Earlier A 81.8
   Later A 88.11/3

A 82.9:v.nos.
ARKET REVIEW. [Weekly]
   Earlier A 81.9
   Later A 88.11/2

A 82.10:v.nos.
PEANUT REPORTS. [Weekly]
   Earlier A 81.12
   Later A 88.10

A 82.11:date
TOBACCO STOCKS REPORTS. [Quarterly]
   Earlier A 80.821
   Later A 88.34

A 82.12:v.nos.
HONEY REPORTS. [Semimonthly]
   Earlier A 81.10
   Later A 88.19

A 82.13:v.nos.
COTTON PRICE STATISTICS. [Monthly]
   Earlier A 81.17
   Later A 88.11/9

A 82.14:nos.
P. AND S. DOCKET, MONTHLY REPORT OF ACTION TAKEN ON CASES ARISING UNDER PACKERS AND STOCKYARDS ACT
   Earlier A 81.14
   Later A 88.16/5

A 82.15:v.nos.
COLD STORAGE REPORTS. [Monthly]
   Earlier A 81.7
   Later A 88.20

A 82.16:v.nos.
FOOD SUPPLY REPORTS. [Monthly]
   Restricted.
   Earlier A 80.816

A 82.17:v.nos.   • Item 107-A
MARKETING ACTIVITIES. [Monthly]
   Earlier A 81.13
   Later A 88.26
   Discontinued.

A 82.17/a:CT
REPRINT FROM MARKETING ACTIVITIES.

A 82.18:nos.
[COMMODITY STATISTICS.]
   Earlier A 80.826
   Later A 1.73

A 82.19   • Item 112
S.D [Sugar Determination] (series). [Irregular]

   Regulations reprinted form the Federal Register relating to prices and wages for the sugarcane industry.

   Discontinued.

A 82.20:CT
UNITED STATES STANDARDS FOR GRADES OF [fruits, vegetables, etc.].
   Earlier A 81.15
   Later A 88.6/2

A 82.21:date
SOYBEAN MARKET SUMMARY. [Quarterly]
   Earlier A 81.18

A 82.22   • Item 108
MARKETING ORDERS.
   Earlier A 80.825
   Discontinued.

A 82.23:nos.
SERVICE AND REGULATORY ANNOUNCEMENTS.
   Earlier A 80.118
   Later A 88.6/3, A 77.6/2
   Discontinued.

A 82.24
ADDRESSES. [Irregular]

A 82.25
POSTERS.
   Later A 88.28

A 82.26:date
MARGARINE PRODUCTION. [Monthly]
   Earlier A 80.820

A 82.27:nos.
SERVING MANY. [Monthly]

A 82.28:v.nos.
UNITED STATES COTTON QUALITY REPORT FOR GINNINGS.
   Earlier A 80.824, A 80.134
   Later A 88.11

A 82.29:v.nos.
TRADE IN GRAIN FUTURES. [Monthly]
　　Earlier A 75.209
　　Later A 85.8

A 82.30:v.nos.
TRADE IN COTTON FUTURES. [Monthly]
　　Earlier A 75.209
　　Later A 85.7

A 82.31:v.nos.
COMMERCIAL GRAIN STOCKS REPORTS. [Weekly]
　　Earlier A 81.19
　　Later A 88.18/2

A 82.31/2:CT
COMMERCIAL GRAIN STOCKS REVISED FIGURES
　　FOR CALENDAR YEAR.
　　Later A 88.18:2-2

A 82.32:v.nos.
FEED MARKET REVIEW.
　　Earlier A 81.20
　　Later A 88.18/4

A 82.33:v.nos.
RICE MARKET REVIEW. [Weekly]
　　Earlier A 81.21
　　Later A 88.18/9

A 82.34:nos.
NOTICES OF JUDGEMENT UNDER INSECTICIDE ACT.
　　Earlier A 80.823

A 82.35:date
FEED MARKET SUMMARY. [Quarterly]
　　Later A 88.18/3

A 82.36:date
COLD STORAGE STOCKS OF FROZEN FRUITS AND
　　VEGETABLES BY CONTAINER SIZE. [Monthly]

AGRICULTURAL CONSERVATION PROGRAM

　　Through the Agricultural Conservation Program, administered by the Department of Agriculture, the Federal Government shares with the farmers and ranchers in the United States, Puerto Rico, and the Virgin Islands the cost of carrying out approved soil-building and soil and water conservation practices, including related wildlife and beautification conservation practices in accordance with provisions established by the Department of Agriculture.　The following publications are issued on a recurring basis in connection with the program.

A 82.37　　　　　　　　　　　　**• Item 103-A-1– 50**
HANDBOOKS. [Annual]

　　Separate handbook issued for each State. Contains the same text as the National Bulletin with additional illustrations and tables applicable to the particular State or territory.
　　Later A 82.89
　　Discontinued.

A 82.37:M 32　　　　　　　　　　　**• Item 103-B**
MAPS. 1944–　[Irregular]

　　Contains a series of U.S. State outline maps, showing, by dots, the extent and distribution of some of the conservation measures carried out under the Agricultural Conservation Program. For complete data, the statistical volumes listed above should be consulted.
　　List published in 1964.
　　Discontinued.

A 82.37:N 21　　　　　　　　　　**• Item 103-A-50**
NATIONAL BULLETIN.

　　Contains the provisions of the program, including distribution of funds, State and county agricultural conservation programs, practice completion requirements, Federal cost-shares, general provisions relating to Federal cost-sharing, definitions; authority, availability of funds, and applicability; conservation practices.
　　Bulletin kept up-to-date by annual supplements covering needed changes.

A 82.37:Su 6/4　　　　　　　　　　**• Item 103-B**
　　SUMMARY. 1965–　[Annual]

　　PURPOSE:– To serve as an administrative tool for the personnel of the Department and those in the States engaged in conservation work. Brings together comprehensive data collected by county and State Agricultural Stabilization and Conservation Committees relative to conservation measures performed on farms participating in the Agricultural Conservation Program.
　　Discontinued.

A 82.37/2:CT
PUBLICATIONS.

A 82.37/3:CT
STATISTICAL SUMMARIES [various commodity programs].

A 82.37/3:C 82/81　　　　　　　　**• Item 103-B**
UPLAND COTTON PROGRAM. 1964– [Annual]

A 82.37/3:F 32/2　　　　　　　　**• Item 103-B**
FEED GRAIN AND WHEAT STABILIZATION PROGRAM. 1965–　[Annual]

　　For year 1962-65, published separately as Feed Grain Program (A 82.37/3:F 32) and Wheat Stabilization Program (A 82.37/3:W 56).

A 82.38:date
DOMESTIC DAIRY MARKET REVIEW. [Monthly]
　　Later A 88.13

A 82.38/2:date
– STATISTICAL SUPPLEMENT. [Monthly]
　　Later A 88.13/2

A 82.39:date
EGG AND POULTRY MARKETS REVIEW. [Monthly]

　　Later A 88.13, A 88.13/3

A 82.39/2:date
– STATISTICAL SUPPLEMENT. [Monthly]
　　Later A 88.13/4

A 82.40:CT
FACT SHEETS.

A 82.41:date
RECEIPTS AND DISPOSITION OF LIVESTOCK AT
　　66 PUBLIC MARKETS. [Monthly]
　　Later A 88.16

A 82.42:date
ESTIMATED REFRIGERATOR CAR MOVEMENT OF
　　DOMESTIC FRESH FRUITS AND VEGETABLES
　　BY REGIONS.　– 1950. [Monthly]

A 82.43:date
USDA FOOD DELIVERIES.　– 1950. [Monthly]

A 82.44:date
PURCHASE REPORT.　– 1949. [Monthly]

A 82.45:date
SUMMARY OF CARLOT SHIPMENTS. [Weekly]
　　Later A 88.12

A 82.46:date
CARLOT UNLOADS OF FRUITS AND VEGETABLES
　　AT WASHINGTON, D.C. [Monthly]
　　Later A 88.12/5

A 82.47
SUGAR REPORTS. 1–　1948– 1975. [Monthly]

　　PURPOSE:– To provide statistics and data useful to the sugar trade, students of sugar marketing, ASCS field officials, and to Agricultural Stabilization and Conservation Committee offices.
　　Includes market review, administrative actions, and statistical series.
　　January issue contains index for previous year.
　　Information continued in Sugar Market News (A 88.54).

A 82.48:nos.
NUTRITION NEWS LETTERS. [Monthly]
　　Earlier A 81.2:N 95
　　Later A 77.710

A 82.49:date
RICE, STOCKS AND MOVEMENT, CALIFORNIA
　　MILLS. [Monthly]
　　Later A 88.18/11

A 82.50:date
RICE, STOCKS AND MOVEMENT, SOUTHERN MILLS.
　　[Monthly]

A 82.51:date
UNFINISHED COTTON CLOTH PRICES, COTTON
　　PRICES, AND MILL MARGINS. [Monthly]
　　Later A 88.116

A 82.52:date
WEEKLY SUMMARY OF WHOLESALE PRICES OF
　　FRUITS AND VEGETABLES AT NEW YORK AND
　　CHICAGO.
　　Later A 88.12/3

A 82.53:date
WEEKLY SUMMARY OF F.O.B. PRICES OF FRESH
　　FRUITS AND VEGETABLES IN REPRESENTATIVE
　　SHIPPING DISTRICTS.
　　Later A 88.12/2

A 82.54:date
USDA MEAT PRODUCTION REPORTS. [Weekly]
　　Later A 88.17

A 82.55:date　　　　　　　　　　　　**• Item 105**
DIGEST OF DECISIONS OF SECRETARY OF
　　AGRICULTURE UNDER PERISHABLE AGRICULTURAL COMMODITIES ACT.
　　Discontinued.

A 82.56:nos.
NOTICES OF JUDGEMENT UNDER FEDERAL INSECTICIDE, FUNGICIDE, AND RODENTICIDE ACT.

A 82.57:date
RELEASES.

A 82.58:v.nos.
SURVEY OF CAPACITY OF REFRIGERATED
　　STORAGE WAREHOUSES IN UNITED STATES.
　　[Biennial]

A 82.59:
PRODUCTION AND INSPECTION REPORTS.

A 82.59/2:date
ALFALFA MEAL PRODUCTION. [Monthly]
　　Later A 88.18/5

A 82.59/3:date
BREWERS' DRIED GRAIN PRODUCTION. [Monthly]
　　Later A 88.18/6

A 82.59/4:date
DISTILLERS' DRIED GRAIN PRODUCTION. [Monthly]
　　Later A 88.17/7

A 82.59/5:date
SOYBEAN INSPECTION REPORT. [Monthly]

A 82.60:date
PURCHASE REPORTS.　–1958

A 82.61:date
SALES REPORTS.　–1958

A 82.61/2:date
PURCHASE AND SALES REPORTS. [Irregular]

A 82.62:v.nos.&nos.
WEEKLY MOLASSES MARKET REPORTS.
　　Later A 88.23

A 82.63:
PMA PROCEDURE CHECK LIST. [Irregular]

A 82.64:nos.
DFO [DEFENSE FOOD ORDERS].

A 82.65:
COTTONSEED REVIEW, SOUTH CENTRAL AREA.

A 82.65/2:v.nos.&nos.
–SOUTHEASTERN AREA.

A 82.65/3:v.nos.&nos.
–SOUTHWESTERN AREA.

A 82.66
INDUSTRIAL NUTRITION SERVICE.

A 82.67:
FARMERS WEEKLY COTTON PRICE QUOTATIONS.

A 82.68:
COTTON QUALITY REPORT FOR GINNINGS, WESTERN UPLAND COTTON.

A 82.69:
ESTIMATED GRADE AND STAPLE LENGTH OF UPLAND COTTON GINNED (by States).

A 82.70:
COTTON QUALITY REPORTS FOR GINNINGS (by States).

A 82.71:v.nos.
GRAIN MARKET NEWS AND STATISTICAL REPORT. [Weekly]
Later A 88.18

A 82.72:date
PRIMARY SUGAR DISTRIBUTION FOR WEEK.

A 82.72/2:nos.
MONTHLY DELIVERIES OF SUGAR BY STATES.

A 82.72/3:date
SUGAR PRODUCTION AND MOVEMENT REPORT. [Monthly]
Later A 82.47

A 82.73:v.nos.&nos.
SPOT COTTON QUOTATIONS, DESIGNATED MARKETS. [Daily]
Later A 88.11/4

A 82.74:le.-nos.
ANNOUNCEMENTS (of Sales).

A 82.75:
DISSEMINATION OF RESEARCH RESULTS [on poultry and egg marketing subjects]. [Issued 5 or 6 times a year]
Later A 88.15/8

A 82.76
PESTICIDE REVIEW (year). [Annual]

Present statistical data, including estimates, on production and consumption of chemicals that are used to control pests.
Previous title: Pesticide Station for (year).

A 82.77   • Item 110-A-2 (MF)
FERTILIZER SUPPLY (year). 1966/67– [Annual]

Presented on a fiscal year basis, giving as complete a picture as possible of the fertilizer supplies that are expected to be available to farmers. Includes supporting statistical tables and a list of references to current fertilizer data sources.
Previous title: Fertilizer Situation for (year).
ISSN 0503-5198
Discontinued

A 82.78:date
ACQUISITION AND DISPOSAL OF CCC PRICE-SUPPORT INVENTORY. [Annual]
Earlier A 82.2:P 93/2

A 82.79:CT
SOIL BANK SUMMARIES.

A 82.79/2:date   • Item 104-A
CONSERVATION RESERVE PROGRAM OF SOIL BANK, STATISTICAL SUMMARIES.
Discontinued.

A 82.80:date
WHAT WE ARE DOING ABOUT AGRICULTURAL SURPLUSES. [Irregular]
Earlier A 82.2:Su 7

A 82.81:nos.
FEDERAL MILK ORDER MARKET STATISTICS, SUMMARY. [Monthly]
Earlier A 88.14/11

A 82.81/2:date
BULK COOLING TANKS ON FARMS SUPPLYING FEDERAL MILK ORDER MARKETS. [Annual]
Earlier A 88.40/26

A 82.82   • Item 110-A
ASCS BACKGROUND INFORMATION. BI-1–
[Irregular]

PURPOSE:– To provide brief information on the Agricultural Stabilization and Conservation Service and its various programs.
Formerly CSS Background Information.
Discontinued.

A 82.82/2:CT   • Item 110-A
ASCS COMMODITY FACT SHEETS. [Irregular]
Discontinued.

A 82.83:date
INFORMATION RELEASES.

A 82.83/2:date
SUMMARY OF LOAN ACTIVITY AND OPERATING RESULTS THROUGH (date) ISSUED BY CCC. [Monthly]

A 82.84:CT
MAPS, CHARTS, POSTERS. [Irregular]

A 82.84:Ae 8
ASCS AERIAL PHOTOGRAPHY STATUS MAPS. [Annual] (2505 Parley's Way, Salt Lake City, Utah 84109)

Gives for each county the portion of the county photographed, year of photography, number of photo-index sheets, plus other information.
ISSN 0503-5228
Earlier A 82.2:Ae 8

A 82.85:nos.
ENVIRONMENTAL STATEMENTS. [Irregular]

A 82.86:
PORT ALLOCATIONS OF [various commodities].

A 82.87:date
COMMODITY PURCHASES FOR DOMESTIC DISTRIBUTION.

A 82.87/2:date
COMMODITY PURCHASES FOR EXPORT DISTRIBUTION.

A 82.88:CT   • Item 106-B
BIBLIOGRAPHIES AND LISTS OF PUBLICATIONS. [Irregular]
Discontinued.

A 82.89:CT
AGRICULTURAL CONSERVATION PROGRAM (by States).
Earlier A 82.37

A 82.89/2:date   • Item 110-A-1 (MF)
AGRICULTURAL CONSERVATION PROGRAM, FISCAL YEAR STATISTICS SUMMARY. [Annual]

Gives statistical data on conservation practices.
Discontinued.

A 82.90:date   • Item 110-A-2 (MF)
STATE DATA PROFILES, CALENDAR YEAR (date), SELECTED ASCS PROGRAM ACTIVITY AND OTHER AGRICULTURAL DATA. [Annual]

Gives statistical data for the U.S. and by State, by program and/or commodity for ASCS payments to producers, cash receipts from farm marketings, commodity loans made, etc.
Discontinued.

A 82.91:CT
MAPS AND ATLASES. [Irregular]

A 82.92:date   • Item 110-A-3 (MF)
FORESTRY INCENTIVES PROGRAM, FROM INCEPTION OF PROGRAM THROUGH (date). [Annual]

Tables summarizes practices by states under the Forestry Incentives Program. The Program's purpose is to increase the U.S. supply of timber products from private nonindustrial forestlands.
Discontinued.

A 82.93:date   • Item 110-A-4 (MF)
EMERGENCY CONSERVATION PROGRAM, FISCAL YEAR SUMMARY. [Annual]

Tables summarizes conservation practices by states under the Emergency Conservation Program. The objective of this program is to rehabilitate farmlands damaged by wind, erosion, floods, hurricanes, drought, etc.

A 82.94:date   • Item 110-A-5 (MF)
WATER BANK PROGRAM, FROM INCEPTION OF PROGRAM THROUGH (DATE). [Annual]

A 82.98   • Item 24-G-3 (MF)
WAREHOUSES LICENSED UNDER U.S. WAREHOUSE ACT. [Annual]
Discontinued.

FIELD SERVICE BRANCH (1945–   )

CREATION AND AUTHORITY

The Field Service Branch was established as a bureau within the Production and Marketing Administration by authority of Memorandum 1118 of the Secretary of Agriculture, dated August 18, 1945, effective August 20, 1945.

A 82.101:date
ANNUAL REPORTS.
Earlier A 83.1

A 82.102:CT
GENERAL PUBLICATIONS.
Earlier A 83.2

A 82.106:CT
REGULATIONS, RULES, AND INSTRUCTIONS.

A 82.107:CT
COMMITTEEMAN'S PRACTICE HANDBOOKS (by States).
Earlier A 80.611

A 82.108:CT
POSTERS.

A 82.109:nos.
SPECIAL SERVICES MEMORANDUMS.
Earlier A 83.7

A 82.110:CT
AGRICULTURAL CONSERVATION PROGRAM (by States).
Earlier A 80.613

A 82.111:CT
HANDBOOK OF CONSERVATION PRACTICES (by States).
Earlier A 80.608

A 82.112:CT
AGRICULTURAL CONSERVATION PROGRAM (by States).
Earlier A 82.112

A 82.113:CT
ADDRESSES.
Earlier A 80.609

FEDERAL CROP INSURANCE CORPORATION (1945– 1947)

CREATION AND AUTHORITY

The Federal Crop Insurance Corporation (A 80.900), a subordinate unit of the War Food Administration, was transferred to the Production and Marketing Administration by Secretary's Memorandum 118, Supplement 1, dated October 8, 1945. Returned to the jurisdiction of the Secretary of Agriculture (A 62) by Secretary's Memorandum 1196, of June 26, 1947, effective July 1, 1947.

A 82.201:date
ANNUAL REPORTS.
    Earlier A 80.901

A 82.202:CT
GENERAL PUBLICATIONS.
    Earlier A 80.902

A 82.207:nos.
INFORMATION (series).
    Earlier A 80.907

COMMODITY CREDIT CORPORATION (1945–   )

CREATION AND AUTHORITY

The Commodity Credit Corporation (A 80.400), a subordinate unit within the War Food Administration, was transferred to the Production and Marketing Administration (A 82.300) by Secretary's Memorandum 1118, Supplement 1, dated June 29, 1945, effective July 1, 1945.

INFORMATION

Information Division
Commodity Credit Corporation, Foreign Agricultural Service
Department of Agriculture
Stop 1004
1400 Independence Ave., SW
Washington, D.C. 20250
(202) 720-3111
Fax: (202) 418-9125

A 82.301   • Item 34 (MF)
REPORT OF THE PRESIDENT OF THE COMMODITY CREDIT CORPORATION. 1940–   [Annual]

Gives summary of operations for the fiscal year, made by the President of the Corporation to the Secretary of Agriculture.

A 82.302:CT   • Item 35
GENERAL PUBLICATIONS.
    Earlier A 80.402

A 82.305:CT   • Item 36
LAWS.

A 82.306:CT   • Item 37
REGULATIONS, RULES, AND INSTRUCTIONS.
    Earlier A 80.406

A 82.307:date
STATEMENT OF LOANS AND COMMODITIES OWNED. [Quarterly]
    Earlier A 80.407

A 82.308   • Item 35-A (MF)
REPORT OF FINANCIAL CONDITIONS AND OPERATIONS, AS OF [date]. [Quarterly]

Contains financial statements, program results, loan operations, and inventory operations of the Commodity Credit Corporation.

REPORT OF PRICE SUPPORT COMMODITIES OWNED AS OF (date). [Weekly]

One-page statistical release which gives estimated total stocks for date and change from a year ago; estimated cost value, dollars per unit, total value, and change from a year ago for various commodities.
Discontinued.

A 82.309:date
CCC LOANS ON COTTON. [Weekly]

A 82.310:date
ACTIVE AND ANNOUNCED PRICE SUPPORT PROGRAMS APPROVED BY BOARD OF DIRECTORS. [Monthly]

A 82.310/2:date
PRICE SUPPORT PROGRAM, CHARTS AND TABLES, SELECTED ACTIVITIES. [Quarterly]

A 82.310/3
CCC PRICE SUPPORT PROGRAM DATA. 1968– [Irregular]

Supersedes Active and Announced Price Support Programs Approved by the Board of Directors through (date) (A 82.310).

A 82.311   • Item 34-A (MF)
COMMODITY CREDIT CORPORATION CHARTS. [Annual]

Provides a cumulative graphic summary, supplemented by statistical tables, of operations of the Commodity Credit Corporation from 1933 through the end of the current fiscal year. Only the latest edition need be retained.
    Earlier A 82.301:C 38
    Discontinued.

AGRICULTURAL ADJUSTMENT AGENCY (July– August 1945)

CREATION AND AUTHORITY

The Agricultural Adjustment Agency (A 80.600), an independent unit within the War Food Administration, was transferred to the jurisdiction and control of the Secretary of Agriculture by Executive Order 9577 of June 29, 1945. The Agency was abolished and its functions transferred to the Production and Marketing Administration by Secretary's Memorandum 1118, dated August 18, 1945, effective August 20, 1945.

A 83.1:date
ANNUAL REPORTS.
    Earlier A 80.601

A 83.2:CT
GENERAL PUBLICATIONS.
    Earlier A 80.602

A 83.6:CT
REGULATIONS, RULES, AND INSTRUCTIONS.
    Earlier A 80.606

A 83.7:nos.
SPECIAL SERVICES MEMORANDUMS.
    Earlier A 80.610

FARMERS' HOME ADMINISTRATION (1946– 1994)

CREATION AND AUTHORITY

The Farmers' Home Administration was established in the Department of Agriculture in accordance with Public Law 731, 79th Congress, approved August 14, 1946. The same law abolished the Farm Security Administration whose functions, etc., were merged into the Farmers' Home Administration on November 1, 1946.

Abolished December 27, 1994, and functions assumed by the Consolidated Farm Service Agency and the Rural Housing and Community Development Service.

A 84.1:date   • Item 67
ANNUAL REPORTS. 1947– 1953.
    Discontinued.

A 84.2 CT   • Item 68
GENERAL PUBLICATIONS.
    Discontinued.

A 84.6:CT   • Item 69
REGULATIONS, RULES, AND INSTRUCTIONS.
    Discontinued.

A 84.6/2:CT   • Item 68-A
HANDBOOKS, MANUALS, GUIDES.
    Discontinued.

A 84.7:date
MONTHLY REPORT OF FARMERS HOME ADMINISTRATION.

A 84.8:CT
ADDRESSES.

A 84.9:nos.
FARMERS HOME ADMINISTRATION FEATURES.

A 84.10:nos.
ENVIRONMENTAL STATEMENTS. [Irregular]

A 84.11   • Item 24-B-6
FYI/FMHA. [Weekly]

Contains short news items for the information of Farmers Home Administration.
    Discontinued.

A 84.12:date   • Item 65-B (MF)
ANNUAL REPORT ON THE HEW/USDA RURAL HEALTH FACILITIES AGREEMENT.
    Discontinued.

A 84.15:date   • Item 68-C
POSTERS. [Irregular]

A 84.16:date-nos.   • Item 69-A
FORMS.

A 84.17   • Item 68-A-1 (MF)
RURAL HOUSING (New Jersey). [Annual]

COMMODITY EXCHANGE AUTHORITY (1947–1974)

CREATION AND AUTHORITY

The Commodity Exchange Authority was established within the Department of Agriculture by Secretary's Memorandum 1185 of January 21, 1947, succeeding the Commodity Exchange Administration (A 75.200). By act of October 23, 1974 (88 Stat. 1414), the agency was abolished and functions transferred to the Commodity Futures Trading Commission (Y 3.C 73/5).

A 85.1:date • Item 38
ANNUAL REPORTS. 1947–1953.
  Discontinued.

A 85.2:CT • Item 39
GENERAL PUBLICATIONS.

A 85.6:CT • Item 40
REGULATIONS, RULES, AND INSTRUCTIONS.
  Discontinued.

A 85.6:C 73 • Item 40
COMMODITY EXCHANGE ACT, AS AMENDED, REGULATIONS OF THE SECRETARY OF AGRICULTURE THEREUNDER, ORDERS OF THE COMMODITY EXCHANGE COMMISSION PURSUANT TO SEC. 4a AND 5a (4).

A 85.7:v.nos.
TRADE IN COTTON FUTURES. v. 1–20. 1940–1963. [Monthly]
  Earlier A 82.30

A 85.8:v.nos.
TRADE IN GRAIN FUTURES. v. 1–30. 1951–1963. [Monthly]
  Earlier A 82.29

A 85.9:nos.
COMMITMENTS OF TRADERS IN COMMODITY FUTURES: COTTON, FROZEN CONCENTRATED ORANGE JUICE, POTATOES. 1– 1946– [Monthly]

Previous title: Commitments of Large Traders in Cotton Futures.
  Absorbed A 85.9/3 beginning December 1959.
  Later Y 3.C 73/5:9

A 85.9/2
COMMITMENTS OF TRADERS IN WHEAT, CORN, OATS, RYE SOYBEANS, SOYBEAN OIL, SOYBEAN MEAL, SHELL EGGS. [Monthly]
  Title varies.
  Later Y 3.C 73/5:9/2

A 85.9/3:nos.
COMMITMENTS OF TRADERS IN WOOD AND WOOL TOP FUTURES. –1959.

Combined with A 85.9 beginning Dec. 1959.

A 85.10:CT
ADDRESSES.

A 85.11
FUTURES TRADING AND OPEN CONTRACTS IN POTATOES. – January 2, 1974. [Daily]
  Title varies.

A 85.11/2
FUTURES TRADING IN COTTON, WOOL AND WOOL TOPS. – January 3, 1974. [Daily]

A 85.11/3:nos.
FUTURES TRADING AND OPEN CONTRACTS IN POTATOES. [Daily]

A 85.11/4:nos.
FUTURES TRADING AND OPEN CONTRACTS IN BUTTER, EGGS AND POTATOES, [Chicago Mercantile Exchange]. [Daily]

A 85.11/5:nos.
FUTURES TRADING AND OPEN CONTRACTS IN COTTON AND COTTONSEED OIL [New Orleans Cotton Exchange]. [Daily]

A 85.11/6:nos.
FUTURES TRADING AND OPEN CONTRACTS IN SOYBEAN MEAL AND COTTONSEED MEAL. [Memphis Board of Trade Clearing Association]. [Daily]

A 85.11/7
FUTURES TRADING AND OPEN CONTRACTS IN WHEAT, CORN, OATS, RYE, SOYBEANS AND PRODUCTS. – January 3, 1974. [Daily]

Gives daily volume of trading (sales), including exchanges of futures for cash, and open contracts (one side only) as reported by clearing members as of close of business for wheat, corn, oats, rye, soybeans, soybean oil, soybean meal, lard, and cotton.

A 85.11/8
FUTURES TRADING AND OPEN CONTRACTS IN FROZEN CONCENTRATED ORANGE JUICE [on Citrus Associates of New York Cotton Exchange] 1– 1969– [Daily]

A 85.12:nos.
WEEKLY REPORT [Cotton].

A 85.13:date
LIST OF PUBLICATIONS OF COMMODITY EXCHANGE AUTHORITY.
  Earlier A 85.2:P 96

A 85.14:date
STOCKS OF GRAIN IN DELIVERABLE POSITIONS FOR CHICAGO BOARD OF TRADE, FUTURES CONTRACTS IN EXCHANGE– APPROVED AND FEDERALLY LICENSED WAREHOUSES, AS REPORTED BY THOSE WAREHOUSES. [Weekly] (Commodity Exchange Authority, 141 West Jackson Blvd., Chicago, Illinois 60604)

Title varies.
Gives stocks represented by outstanding warehouse receipts as reported by licensed warehouse, by grain and grade, as of date (Friday), previous week, and previous years.
  Later Y 3.C 73/5:10

A 85.15
MONTHLY SUMMARY OF COMMODITY FUTURES STATISTICS. [Monthly]

Provides summary statistics on volume of trading and open contracts, by markets and for all markets combined, and month-end closing prices on principal markets for commodities under the Commodity Exchange Act.

A 85.15/2:v.nos.&nos.
MONTHLY COMMODITY FUTURES STATISTICS FOR FUTURES TRADING IN COMMODITIES REGULATED UNDER THE COMMODITY EXCHANGE ACT. v. 1– 7, no 6. 1967– Dec. 1973

A 85.16:nos. • Item 39-A
MARKET SURVEY REPORTS. 1– 1971– [Irregular]

A 85.17:nos.
WEEKLY REPORTS.
  Later Y 3.C 73/5:11

OFFICE OF FOOD AND FEED CONSERVATION (1948)

A 86.1:date
ANNUAL REPORTS.

A 86.2:CT • Item 73
GENERAL PUBLICATIONS.
  Discontinued.

A 86.7:nos. • Item 74
OFFICE FOR FOOD AND FEED CONSERVATION NUMBERED PUBLICATIONS.
  Discontinued.

A 86.8:nos.
POSTERS.

OFFICE OF THE ADMINISTRATOR OF THE MARKETING ACT (1947–1949)

A 87.1:date
ANNUAL REPORT.
  Later A 77.8

A 87.2:CT • Item 114
GENERAL PUBLICATIONS.
  Discontinued.

A 87.7:CT
ADDRESSES.

AGRICULTURAL MARKETING SERVICE (1972–   )

CREATION AND AUTHORITY

The Agricultural Marketing Service (A 66) was established within the Department of Agriculture by Secretary's Memorandum 830, dated July 7, 1939, pursuant to Agricultural Appropriations Act of 1940, approved June 30, 1939 (53 Stat. 939). The Service was consolidated with other agencies to form the Agricultural Marketing Administration (A 75) by Executive order 9060 of February 23, 1942. It was reestablished by Secretary's Memorandum 1320, Supplement 4, dated November 2, 1953, pursuant to Reorganization Plan No. 2 of 1953, and placed under the administrative supervision of the Assistant Secretary for Marketing and Foreign Agriculture. The name was changed to Consumer and Marketing Service, effective February 8, 1965. The name changed back to Agricultural Marketing Service effective April 2, 1972.

INFORMATION
  Information Staff
  Agricultural Marketing Svc.
  Department of Agriculture
  1400 Independence Ave., SW
  Washington, D.C. 20250
  (202) 720-8998
  Fax: (202) 720-8477
  http://www.ams.usda.gov

A 88.1:date
ANNUAL REPORTS.

A 88.2:CT • Item 24-B
GENERAL PUBLICATIONS.

A 88.2:G 76/6 • Item 24-B
LIST OF INSPECTION POINTS UNDER THE GRAIN STANDARDS ACT. 1961– [Irregular]

Grain Division. Directory D-3.
PURPOSE:– To show the places in the United States where grain inspection services are provided regularly under the authority of the U.S. Grain Standards Act and is for use by the grain trade in determining the best routing to obtain inspection services.
Issued in looseleaf form and punched for three-ring binder.

A 88.2:M 59/28 • Item 24-B
SUMMARIES OF FEDERAL MILK MARKETING ORDERS. [Irregular]

Milk Marketing Orders Division.
Issued in looseleaf form. Includes revised Federal Register citations for all markets, and summaries for Appalachian, Austin-Waco, Central West Texas, Corpus Christi, and Lubbock-Plainview orders.

A 88.3/2:nos.
RECRUITING BULLETINS.

A 88.5:CT • Item 24-O
LAWS.

A 88.6:CT • Item 107-B
REGULATIONS, RULES, AND INSTRUCTIONS.

A 88.6:C 42 • Item 107-B
LIST OF CHEMICAL COMPOUNDS AUTHORIZED FOR USE UNDER USDA POULTRY, MEAT, RABBIT AND EGG PRODUCTS INSPECTION PROGRAMS.

Prepared by the Technical Services Division. Previously published as AMS 419.
Latest edition: Rev. October 1971.

A 88.6:P 41 • Item 107-B
REGULATIONS (OTHER THAN RULES OF PRACTICE) UNDER THE PERISHABLE AGRICULTURAL COMMODITIES ACT, 1930, AND PERISHABLE AGRICULTURAL COMMODITIES ACT. 1930– [Irregular]

Latest edition: Regulations effective January 1, 1969 published as C&MS-25.
Contains the regulations (7 CFR Part 46) under the Perishable Agricultural Commodities Act, 1930 and the text of the Perishable Agricultural Commodities Act, 1930, as amended.

A 88.6/2:CT • Item 24-B-2 (MF) (EL)
UNITED STATES STANDARDS FOR GRADES OF [Commodity]. [Irregular]
Standards are used in marketing farm products in the United States. The use of these quality standards is, in most cases, voluntary. They are used in many instances by manufacturers or by packers in quality control work. They are also used as the basis of the Federal and Federal-State grading services.
The publication Checklist of U.S. Standards for Farm Products (AMS-210), lists all of the Federal standards which the U.S. Department of Agriculture has in effect. Some of them are listed as tentative or proposed standards. These are the ones that have not been officially promulgated but are offered by ISDA for use under commercial conditions to test their practicability or as a basis for discussion. They are subject to further study and investigation before being officially recommended. The Federal standards listed in the above Checklist are available from the individual commodity divisions within the Agricultural Marketing Service which developed and issued the standards. Those not officially promulgated are issued in offset or mimeographed form. Those which have been are issued in the Service and Regulatory Announcements series.
Later A 103.6/2

A 88.6/2:G 761 •
OFFICIAL GRAIN STANDARDS OF THE UNITED STATES. Rev. 1970. 66 p. il.

Presents the official United States standards for wheat, corn, barley, oats, rye, grain sorghums, flaxseed and mixed grain.

A 88.6/3 • Item 111
SERVICE AND REGULATORY ANNOUNCEMENTS, SRA-C&MS– (series). 1– [Irregular]

Formerly published as ARA-AMS– (series).
PURPOSE:– To publish information as needed in the enforcement and administration of regulatory acts and in the administration of acts providing for the furnishing of services by the Department of Agriculture.
The majority of this service covers standards officially promulgated through publication first in the Federal Register, then in the Code of Federal Regulations. Other material covered in this series includes regulations required by regulatory acts, notices of judgement, decisions.

A 88.6/3:188 • Item 111
REGULATIONS GOVERNING MEAT INSPECTION OF THE U.S. DEPARTMENT OF AGRICULTURE. [Irregular]

Subscription includes basic volume plus supplements for an indefinite period.
Contains regulations governing the meat inspection activities of the Department of Agriculture as governed by the Code of Federal Regulations, Title 9, Chapter III, Subchapters A and D.

A 88.6/4:CT • Item 24-P
HANDBOOKS, MANUALS, GUIDES.

A 88.6/4:G 76 • Item 24-P
GRAIN INSPECTION MANUAL. [Irregular]

Covers the sampling, inspection, grading, and certification of grain under the United States Grain Standards Act as amended.

A 88.6/4:M 46 • Item 24-P
MANUAL OF MEAT INSPECTION PROCEDURES OF THE DEPARTMENT OF AGRICULTURE. [Irregular]

Subscription includes basic manual plus supplementary material for indefinite period. Issued in looseleaf form.
Contains instructions on procedures to be used in carrying out the laws and regulations relating to Federal meat inspection.
Previously published by the Agricultural Research Service (A 77.206/2:M 46).
Later published as Manual of Meat Inspection Procedures by the Animal and Plant Health Inspection Service (A 101.6/2).

A 88.6/4:P 86 • Item 24-P
POULTRY INSPECTORS HANDBOOK. [Irregular]

Poultry Division, Inspection Branch.
Implements title 7, Code of Federal Regulations, part 81. Issued in looseleaf form.

A 88.6/4:P 86/2 • Item 24-P
GUIDELINES FOR IMPLEMENTATION OF SANITARY REQUIREMENTS IN POULTRY ESTABLISHMENTS. [Irregular]

PURPOSE:– Designed to help in understanding the public health reasons for some of the requirements concerning facilities, sanitation, and operating procedures in official establishments. It is further intended to aid in understanding what constitutes satisfactory compliance with the requirements.
Subscription includes basic manual plus supplementary material for an indefinite period.
Issued in looseleaf form and punched for 3-ring binder.

A 88.6/4:Sa 5 • Item 24-P
SANITATION HANDBOOK OF CONSUMER PROTECTION PROGRAMS. [Irregular]

PURPOSE:– To be used as a tool by those concerned with the sanitary processing of meat and meat products. It brings together the sanitation guidelines to be followed in all meat plants producing meat under Federal inspection.
Designed primarily for C&MS meat inspectors in plants operating under State or municipal meat inspection programs.
The Sanitation Handbook should be used in conjunction with Manual of Meat Inspection of the United States Department of Agriculture.
Issued in looseleaf form and punched for 3-ring binder. Subscription includes basic manual plus supplementary material for an indefinite period.

A 88.6/5 • Item 24-P
USDAW-C&MS VISUAL AIDS (series). 1– 1966– [Irregular]

A 88.6/6:CT • Item 116-A
HANDBOOKS, MANUALS, GUIDES. [Irregular]

A 88.7:
RELEASES.

A 88.8:v.nos. • Item 19
AGRICULTURAL SITUATION. [Monthly]
Earlier A 36.15
Later A 92.23

A 88.8/2:date
AGRICULTURAL OUTLOOK DIGEST. [Monthly]
Earlier A 26.160
Later A 93.10

A 88.8/3:date • Item 18-B
AGRICULTURAL OUTLOOK CHARTS. [Annual]
Earlier A 36.50:C 38/3
Later A 1.98

A 88.9:date • Item 21-A
DEMAND AND PRICE SITUATION. [Monthly]
Earlier A 36.28
Later A 93.9/2

A 88.9/2:nos. • Item 21-C
FARM INCOME SITUATION. [Bimonthly]
Earlier A 36.122
Later A 93.9

A 88.9/3:date • Item 18-C
AGRICULTURAL PRICES. [Monthly]
Earlier A 36.163

A 88.9/4:date
AGRICULTURAL PRICES, LOUISIANA CROP REPORTING SERVICE.

A 88.9/5:date • Item 18-C
AGRICULTURAL PRICES, ANNUAL SUMMARY.

Desig. Pr 1-3
Later A 92.16/2

A 88.10:v.nos.
PEANUT MARKET NEWS. [Weekly] (Fruit and Vegetable Division)
Former title: Weekly Peanut Report.
Later A 82.10

A 88.10/2:date
PEANUTS, STOCKS AND PROCESSING. [Monthly]
Earlier A 36.164
Later A 92.14

A 88.10/2-2:date
PEANUTS, STOCKS AND PROCESSING. [Annual]
Later A 92.14/2

A 88.10/3:date
LIST, PEANUT SHELLERS AND CRUSHERS. [Annual]

A 88.10/4:date
TREE NUTS BY STATES. [Annual]
Earlier A 88.1:N 95
Later A 92.27

A 88.10/5:date
PECAN REPORT, LOUISIANA CROP REPORTING SERVICE.

A 88.10/5-2:date
ANNUAL PECAN SUMMARY, LOUISIANA CROP REPORTING SERVICE.

A 88.10/6:date
LIST, PEANUT PROCESSORS (users of raw peanuts).
Later A 92.14/4

A 88.11:v.nos.&nos.
COTTON QUALITY CROP OF (year). v. 1–   [Annual] (Cotton Division)
Title varies
Earlier A 82.28
ISSN 0093-4429

A 88.11/2   • **Item 24-B-12 (EL)**
WEEKLY COTTON MARKET REVIEW.
Earlier A 82.9
ISSN 0145-0360

A 88.11/3:v.nos.&nos.
MONTHLY COTTON LINTERS REVIEW.
Formerly Weekly Cotton Linters Review.
Earlier A 82.8
ISSN 0027-0318

A 88.11/4   • **Item 24-B-12 (EL)**
DAILY SPOT COTTON QUOTATIONS.

Earlier title: Spot Cotton Quotations, Designated Markets.
Earlier A 82.73

A 88.11/5:date
COTTON PRODUCTION. [Monthly, June– December]
Earlier A 36.30
Later A 92.20

A 88.11/6:date
UNFINISHED COTTON CLOTH PRICES, COTTON PRICES AND MILL MARGINS. [Monthly]
Earlier A 82.51

A 88.11/7:v.nos.
ESTIMATED GRADE AND STAPLE LENGTH OF UPLAND COTTON GINNED IN UNITED STATES.

A 88.11/8:nos.   • **Item 212-M**
COTTON SITUATION. [Issued 6 times a year]
Earlier A 36.40/2
Later A 93.24

A 88.11/9:v.nos.
COTTON PRICE STATISTICS. [Monthly]
Earlier A 82.13
ISSN 0010-9827

A 88.11/10:date
PRICES OF COTTON CLOTH AND RAW COTTON, AND MILL MARGINS FOR CERTAIN CONSTRUCTIONS OF UNFINISHED CLOTH. [Monthly]

A 88.11/10-2:date
MILL MARGINS REPORT, COTTON CLOTH AND YARN VALUES, COTTON PRICES AND MILL MARGINS FOR UNFINISHED CARDED COTTON CLOTH AND YARN, REVISED ESTIMATES. [Annual] (Cotton Division)
Title varies.
Earlier A 88.2:C 82/6

A 88.11/10-3:date
MILL MARGINS REPORT [New Series]. v. 1– v. 49, no. 5. – December 1973. [Monthly]

A 88.11/11:date
COTTON VARIETIES PLANTED IN EARLY PRODUCING SECTION OF TEXAS, (year). [Annual] (Market News Section, Cotton Division)
Earlier A 88.2:C 82/3

A 88.11/12:date
CHANGES FOR GINNING COTTON, COSTS OF SELECTED SERVICES INCIDENT TO MARKETING, AND RELATED INFORMATION, SEASON.
Earlier A 88.2:C 82/10

A 88.11/13:date   • **Item 24-P-1**
COTTON VARIETIES PLANTED. [Annual]

PURPOSE:– To provide statistical data on varieties of cotton planted in the U.S.
Published in microfiche (24x).
Earlier A 88.2:C 82/11
Discontinued.

A 88.11/14:date
QUALITY OF COTTON IN CARRY-OVER. [Annual]
Earlier A 88.2:C 82/7

A 88.11/15:date   • **Item 24-P-1**
COTTONSEED QUALITY, CROP OF (year). [Annual] (Market News Section, Cotton Division, Box 17723, Memphis, Tennessee)
Earlier A 88.2:C 82
Discontinued.

A 88.11/16:date
COTTON PRODUCTION: COTTON AND COTTONSEED PRODUCTION. [Annual]
Earlier A 88.2:C 82/2

A 88.11/17:date
COTTON FIBER AND PROCESSING TEST RESULTS. [Semimonthly during harvesting season]
Earlier in AMS-nos. (A 88.40)
ISSN 0566-5469

A 88.11/17-2   • **Item 24-B-1 (MF)**
SUMMARY OF COTTON FIBER AND PROCESSING TEST RESULTS, CROP OF (year). [Annual] (Cotton Division)

A 88.11/18:nos.
FUTURES TRADING AND OPEN CONTRACTS [Wheat, Corn, Oats, etc.] ON CHICAGO BOARD OF TRADE. [Daily except Sat., Sun. & Legal Holidays]

A 88.11/19:date
COTTON GIN EQUIPMENT [Annual] (Market News Section, Cotton Division)

Earlier A 88.2:C 82/14

A 88.11/20:v.nos.&nos.
LONG STAPLE COTTON REVIEW. v. 1–   1962– [Monthly] (Cotton Division, Market News Section)

PURPOSE:– To consolidate and make available to interested parties current economic information and statistics bearing on long staple and extra long staple cotton. Included in this classification are domestic upland cotton, 1-1/8" and longer, produced principally in West Texas and New Mexico; American Pima cotton; and foreign growths, mainly Egyptian and Peruvian.
ISSN 0565-2022

A 88.11/21:date
AVERAGE PREMIUMS AND DISCOUNTS FOR CCC SETTLEMENT PURPOSES FOR OFFERS RECEIVED. [Irregular] (Cotton Division)

A 88.11/22:v.nos.&nos.
COTTON MARKET NEWS. [Weekly]

A 88.11/23:v.nos.&nos.   • **Item 24-B-17 (EL)**
QUALITY OF COTTON CLASSED UNDER SMITH-DOXEY ACT, UNITED STATES. v. 1–   [Weekly]

Formed by merger of Quality of Cotton Classed under Smith-Doxey Act, Western States, and for Southern States.

A 88.11/24:date
WEEKLY REPORT OF CERTIFICATED STOCK IN LICENSED WAREHOUSES.

A 88.12:date
WEEKLY SUMMARY OF FRUIT AND VEGETABLE CARLOT SHIPMENTS.
Earlier A 82.45
Replaced by A 88.12/22

A 88.12/2:date
WEEKLY SUMMARY OF F.O.B. PRICES OF FRESH FRUITS AND VEGETABLES IN REPRESENTATIVE SHIPPING DISTRICTS
Earlier A 82.53

A 88.12/3:date
WEEKLY SUMMARY OF WHOLESALE PRICES OF FRESH FRUITS AND VEGETABLES AT NEW YORK CITY AND CHICAGO.
Earlier A 82.52

A 88.12/4:date
CONSUMER PURCHASES OF FRUITS AND JUICES. [Monthly]
Earlier A 36.171

A 88.12/4-2:date   • **Item 20-A**
SWEETPOTATO REPORT, LOUISIANA CROP REPORTING SERVICE.
Discontinued.

A 88.12/5:date
CARLOT UNLOADS OF FRUITS AND VEGETABLES BY COMMODITIES. [Monthly]
Earlier A 82.46

A 88.12/6:dt.&nos.
COMMERCIAL VEGETABLES TC (series).
Earlier A 36.101
Later A 92.11

A 88.12/6-2:CT   • **Item 24-E**
[TRUCK CROPS] TC-SERIES. [Annual]
Earlier A 88.2:v. 52 & A 88.2:v. 52/2
Later A 92.11/10 & A 92.11/10-2

A 88.12/7   • **Item 21-K**
FRUIT SITUATION.
Earlier A 36.99
Later A 93.12/3

A 88.12/8:nos.   • **Item 21-L**
VEGETABLE SITUATION.
Earlier A 36.100
Later A 93.12/2

A 88.12/9:date
MERCHANTABLE POTATO STOCKS, WITH COMPARISONS.

A 88.12/10:date
STATE CARLOT SHIPMENTS OF FRUITS AND VEGETABLES, BY COMMODITIES, COUNTIES, AND BILLING STATIONS. [Annual]

A 88.12/11:date
SOUTH CHERRY REPORT. [Annual]
Earlier A 88.2
Later A 92.11/3

A 88.12/12:date
CRANBERRIES. [Annual]
Earlier A 88.2:C 85
Later A 92.11/6

A 88.12/13:date
HYBRID CORN. [Annual]
Earlier A 88.2:C 81/2

A 88.12/14:date
POPCORN PRODUCTION. [Annual]

Earlier A 88.2:P 81
Later A 92.11/7

A 88.12/15:date
APPLES, PRODUCTION BY VARIETIES, WITH COMPARISONS. [Annual]
Earlier A 88.2:Ap 5
Later A 92.11/9

A 88.12/16:date
PRODUCTION, FARM DISPOSITION, AND VALUE OF PRINCIPAL FRUITS AND TREE NUTS. [Annual]
Earlier A 88.2:F 94

A 88.12/17:date
WASHINGTON, D.C. UNLOADS OF FRESH FRUITS AND VEGETABLES. [Annual]
Earlier A 88.2:F 94/2

A 88.12/18:date
FRUIT AND VEGETABLE MARKET NEWS, WEEKLY ARRIVAL SUMMARY.
Replaced by A 88.12/22

A 88.12/19:date
POTATOES AND SWEETPOTATOES, ESTIMATES BY STATES AND SEASONAL GROUPS. [Annual]
    Earlier A 1.34:190
    Later A 92.11/4

A 88.12/20:date
FRUITS, NONCITRUS, BY STATE, PRODUCTION, USE, VALUE. [Annual]
    Earlier A 88.2:F 94/9
    Later A 92.11/2

A 88.12/21:date
CITRUS FRUITS BY STATES, PRODUCTION, USE, VALUE. [Annual]
    Earlier A 88.2:C 49
    Later A 92.11/8

A 88.12/22:nos.
FRESH FRUIT AND VEGETABLE MARKET NEWS, WEEKLY SUMMARY. WS– (series). [Weekly]
    Replaces A 88.12 and A 88.12/18
    ISSN 0094-4858

A 88.12/22-2:date
FRESH FRUIT AND VEGETABLE WHOLESALE MARKET PRICES. 1968–   [Annual] (Fruit and Vegetable Division, Market News Branch)

    Presents data on wholesale market price information, from the Washington, D.C. Market News field office, selected each Wednesday form the daily Fresh Fruit and Vegetable Market News Report.

A 88.12/22-3:date
FRESH FRUIT AND VEGETABLE PRICES. [Annual]

A 88.12/23:date
LOUISIANA ANNUAL VEGETABLE SUMMARY, LOUISIANA CROP REPORTING SERVICE.

A 88.12/24:date
ANNUAL SWEETPOTATO SUMMARY, LOUISIANA CROP REPORTING SERVICE.

A 88.12/24-2:date
SWEETPOTATO REPORT, LOUISIANA CROP REPORTING SERVICE.

A 88.12/25:date
ONION STOCKS. [Annual]
    Earlier A 88.2:On 4
    Later A 92.11/12

A 88.12/26:date
VEGETABLE REPORT, LOUISIANA CROP REPORTING SERVICE.

A 88.12/27:date
PROSPECTIVE STRAWBERRY ACREAGE, LOUISIANA CROP REPORTING SERVICE.

A 88.12/28:date
FRESH PRODUCTS STANDARDIZATION AND INSPECTION BRANCH, ANNUAL PROGRESS REPORT.

A 88.12/29:date
MARKETING OF SOUTH CAROLINA PEACHES, SUMMARY OF SEASON.

A 88.12/30:CT/date
MARKET NEWS SERVICE OF FRUITS AND VEGETABLES.
    Earlier A 36.48 & A 88.2:P 31

A 88.12/31   • **Item 19-A (MF)**
FRESH FRUIT AND VEGETABLE UNLOADS, FVUS (series). 1– 1972–   [Irregular] (Fruit and Vegetable Division, Market News Branch)

    Data for each of the cities covered include 3-year comparison by commodities and mode of transport; city totals by months and States of origin; by commodities, mode of transport, States of origin and months.
    Previously published in the C&MS series (A 88.40/2)
    Issued in the following sub-series:–

A 88.12/31:1   • **Item 19-A**
EASTERN CITIES. [Annual]

    Previously published as C&MS-3 (A 88.40/2:3).
    Covers:
    Albany, N.Y.
    Baltimore, Md.
    Boston, Mass.
    Buffalo, N.Y.
    New York, N.Y. (Includes Newark, N.J.)
    Philadelphia, Pa.
    Pittsburgh, Pa.
    Providence, R.I.
    Washington, D.C.

A 88.12/31:2   • **Item 19-A**
MIDWESTERN CITIES. [Annual]

    Previously published as C&MS-5 (A 88.40/2:5).
    Covers:
    Chicago, Ill.
    Cincinnati, Ohio
    Cleveland, Ohio
    Detroit, Mich.
    Indianapolis, Ind.
    Kansas City, Mo.
    Louisville, Ky.
    Milwaukee, Wisc.
    Minneapolis, Minn. (Includes St. Paul, Minn.)
    St. Louis, Mo.
    Wichita, Kans.

A 88.12/31:3   • **Item 19-A**
SOUTHERN CITIES. [Annual]

    Previously published as C&MS-6 (A 88.40/2:6).
    Covers:
    Atlanta, Ga.
    Birmingham, Ala.
    Columbia, S.C.
    Dallas, Tex.
    Ft. Worth, Tex.
    Houston, Tex.
    Memphis, Tenn.
    Miami, Fla.
    Nashville, Tenn.
    New Orleans, La.
    San Antonio, Tex.

A 88.12/31:4   • **Item 19-A**
WESTERN CITIES. [Annual]

    Previously published as C&MS-4 (A 88.40/2:4).
    Later A 88.12/31-2
    ISSN 0501-4611
    Covers:
    Denver, Colo.
    Los Angeles, Calif.
    Portland, Oreg.
    Salt Lake City, Utah
    San Francisco, Calif. (Includes Oakland Calif.)
    Seattle, Wash. (Includes Tacoma, Wash.)

A 88.12/31:5   • **Item 19-A**
TOTAL FOR 41 CITIES. 1955–   [Annual]

    Gives unloads for each city in two tables: 1) Outlines reported commodity totals by months with a three-year totals comparison, and 2) Outlines annual city total for each reported commodity by States of origin. Truck unloads, expressed in carlot equivalents, are reported for 41 U.S. and 5 Canadian cities.
    Title for 1959 and prior years: Carlot Unloads of Certain Fruits and Vegetables in 100 U.S. and 5 Canadian Cities.
    Previously published as C&MS 7 (A 88.40/2:7)
    ISSN 0090-3086

A 88.12/31:6   • **Item 19-A**
FRESH FRUIT AND VEGETABLE SHIPMENTS BY STATES, COMMODITIES, COUNTIES, STATIONS, CALENDAR YEAR (date). 1920– [Annual]

    Reports shipments of fresh fruits and vegetables by stations and months for each commodity. Arrangement is by State, counties, and stations.
    Issued 1920– 35 in the Statistical Bulletin series. Published prior to 1971 as C&MS-13 (A 88.40/2:13) and prior to 1964 as AMS-41 (A 88.40:41).
    ISSN 0565-2065

A 88.12/31:7   • **Item 19-A**
FRESH FRUIT AND VEGETABLE SHIPMENTS, BY COMMODITIES, STATES, MONTHS, CALENDAR YEAR (date). [Annual]

    Tables include summary by commodities and month, by origins and months, domestic shipments by commodities and shipments and imports by origin for 10-year period. Main tables give shipments by origins and months for each commodity.
    Released in April or May.
    Published prior to 1971 as C&MS-14 (A 88.40/2:14).
    ISSN 0160-2942

A 88.12/31-2:date   • **Item 19-A (MF)**
FRESH FRUIT AND VEGETABLE ARRIVALS IN WESTERN CITIES, BY COMMODITIES, STATES, AND MONTHS. [Annual]

    Earlier A 88.12/31:4

A 88.12/31-3:date   • **Item 19-A**
FRESH FRUIT AND VEGETABLE SHIPMENTS, BY COMMODITIES, STATES, AND MONTHS. [Annual]

A 88.12/31-4:date   • **Item 19-A (MF)**
FRESH FRUIT AND VEGETABLE ARRIVAL TOTALS. [Annual]

A 88.12/32:v.nos.&nos.
FRUIT AND VEGETABLE TRUCK RATE REPORT. [Weekly]

A 88.12/33:date
MARKETING ORDER ACTIONS, A SUMMARY OF ACTIONS UNDER MARKETING ORDERS FOR FRUIT, VEGETABLES, AND SPECIALTY CROPS. [Weekly]

A 88.13:date
MONTHLY DOMESTIC DAIRY MARKETS REVIEW.

A 88.13/2:date
STATISTICAL SUPPLEMENT OF MONTHLY DOMESTIC DAIRY MARKETS REVIEW.
    Earlier A 82.38/2

A 88.13/3:date
MONTHLY EGG AND POULTRY MARKETS REVIEW.
    Earlier A 82.39

A 88.13/4:date
STATISTICAL SUPPLEMENT TO MONTHLY EGG AND POULTRY MARKET REVIEW.
    Earlier A 82.39/2

A 88.14:date
EVAPORATED, CONDENSED, AND DRY MILK REPORT. [Monthly]
    Earlier A 36.153
    Later A 92.10/4

A 88.14/2:date
DAIRY PRODUCTION. [Monthly]
    Earlier A 36.139
    Later A 92.10

A 88.14/3:date
FLUID MILK AND CREAM REPORT. [Monthly]
    Earlier A 36.152
    Later A 92.10/3

A 88.14/4:nos. • Item 21-B
DAIRY SITUATION. [Bimonthly]
    Earlier A 36.65
    Later A 93.13

A 88.14/5:date
STOCKS OF EVAPORATED AND CONDENSED MILK
   HELD BY WHOLESALE GROCERS. [Quarterly]
    Earlier A 36.161

A 88.14/6:date
HOUSEHOLD PURCHASES OF BUTTER, CHEESE,
   NONFAT DRY MILK SOLIDS AND MARGARINE.
   [Monthly]

A 88.14/7:date • Item 24-F
MILK PRODUCTION ON FARMS AND STATISTICS OF
   DAIRY PLANT PRODUCTS. [Annual]
    Earlier A 88.2:M 59
    Later A 92.10/6

A 88.14/8:date • Item 24-F
MILK, FARM PRODUCTION, DISPOSITION, AND
   INCOME.
    Earlier A 88.2:M 59/2
    Later A 92.10/2

A 88.14/9:nos.
MILK DISTRIBUTORS, SALES AND COSTS MDSC
   (series). [Quarterly]
    Later A 93.13/2

A 88.14/10:date • Item 24-F
PRODUCTION OF MANUFACTURED DAIRY PROD-
   UCTS. [Annual]
    Earlier A 88.2:D 14/2
    Later A 92.10/5

A 88.14/11:nos. • Item 24-B-3 (MF) (EL)
FEDERAL MILK ORDER MARKET STATISTICS, FMOS–
   (series). 1–   [Bimonthly]

    Tables give number of producers, average
daily deliveries of milk per producer, average
percentage of butterfat in such milk. Federal order markets; Federal milk order minimum Class 1
and market average blend prices for milk at 3.5
percent butterfat content, f.o.b. market or other
indicated point, receipt of milk from producers,
and producer milk in Class 1: minimum prices
established by Federal milk orders, f.o.b. market
or other indicated point, for milk at basic test with
butterfat differentials; Federal milk order Class 1
formula price information and gross Class 1 usage; whole milk, skim milk items, milk and cream
mixtures, and cream sold in marketing areas defined by Federal milk orders, for markets where
such information is available; prices and economic indexes in Federal milk order formulas to
determine (current month) prices. Textual summary.
    ISSN 0501-4670

A 88.14/11-2:date • Item 24-B-3 (MF)
FEDERAL MILK ORDER MARKET STATISTICS. [An-
   nual]

A 88.14/11-3 • Item 24-B-11 (MF)
SOURCES OF MILK FOR FEDERAL ORDER MARKETS
   BY STATE & COUNTY. [Irregular]

A 88.14/12 • Item 21-Q (EL)
DAIRY PLANTS SURVEYED AND APPROVED FOR
   USDA GRADING SERVICE. [Quarterly]
    Previously published as AMS 509.
    See also A 103.12
    ISSN 0565-2049

A 88.14/13 • Item 24-B-9 (MF)
DAIRY MARKET STATISTICS, ANNUAL SUMMARY.

A 88.15:date
LIQUID, FROZEN, AND DRIED EGG PRODUCTION.
   [Monthly]
    Earlier A 36.155
    Later A 92.9/4

A 88.15/2:date
CANNED POULTRY. [Monthly]
    Earlier A 36.170

A 88.15/3:nos. • Item 21-F
POULTRY AND EGG SITUATION.
    Earlier A 36.196
    Later A 93.20

A 88.15/4:date
TURKEYS TESTED BY OFFICIAL STATE AGENCIES.
   [Monthly]
    Later A 92.9/2

A 88.15/5:date
HATCHERY PRODUCTION. [Monthly]
    Earlier A 36.154
    Later A 92.9/6

A 88.15/6:date
COMMERCIAL HATCHERY REPORT.

A 88.15/7:date
WEEKLY POULTRY SLAUGHTER REPORT.

A 88.15/8:
DISSEMINATION OF RESEARCH RESULTS [on Poultry & Egg Marketing Subjects]. [Issued 5 or 6
   times a year]
    Earlier A 82.75

A 88.15/9:date
POULTRY USED IN CANNING AND OTHER PRO-
   CESSED FOODS. [Monthly]
    Later A 92.9/5

A 88.15/9-2:date
POULTRY SLAUGHTERED UNDER FEDERAL INSPEC-
   TION AND POULTRY USED IN CANNING AND
   PROCESSED FOODS. [Annual]

A 88.15/10:date
CHICKENS RAISED ON FARMS. [Annual]
    Earlier A 88.2:C 43/4
    Later A 92.9/7

A 88.15/10-2:date
CHICKENS RAISED, LOUISIANA CROP REPORTING
   SERVICE.

A 88.15/11:date
TURKEYS RAISED ON FARMS. [Annual]
    Earlier A 88.2:T 84/2
    Later A 92.9/8

A 88.15/11-2:date
TURKEYS RAISED, LOUISIANA CROP REPORTING
   SERVICE.

A 88.15/12:date
TURKEY BREEDER HENS ON FARMS. [Annual]
    Earlier A 88.2:T 84
    Later A 92.9/11

A 88.15/13:date
COMMERCIAL BROILER PRODUCTION. [Annual]
    Earlier A 88.2:B 78
    Later A 92.9/10

A 88.15/14:date
CHICKEN AND EGGS, LAYERS AND EGG PRODUC-
   TION, MONTHLY. [Annual]
    Earlier A 88.2:Eg 3
    Later A 92.9/13

A 88.15/15:date
BROILER CHICKS PLACED. [Annual]
    Earlier A 88.2:C 43
    Later A 92.9/14

A 88.15/16:date
FARM PRODUCTION, DISPOSITION, CASH
   RECEIPTS AND GROSS INCOME, TURKEYS.
   [Annual]
    Earlier A 88.2:T 84/3
    Later A 92.9/15

A 88.15/17:date
CHICKENS AND EGGS, LAYERS AND RATE OF LAY,
   FIRST OF EACH MONTH. [Annual]
    Earlier A 88.2:C 43/2
    Later A 92.9/12

A 88.15/18:date • Item 21-F
CHICKENS AND EGGS, FARM PRODUCTION, DIS-
   POSITION, CASH RECEIPTS, GROSS INCOME,
   CHICKENS ON FARMS, COMMERCIAL BROIL-
   ERS, BY STATES. [Annual]
    Earlier A 88.2:C 43/3
    Later A 92.9/3

A 88.15/19:date
PULLET CHICK REPLACEMENTS FOR BROILER
   HATCHERY SUPPLY FLOCKS. [Annual]
    Later A 92.9

A 88.15/20:date
COMMERCIAL EGG MOVEMENT REPORT. [Weekly]

A 88.15/21:date
BROILER CHICK REPORT, LOUISIANA CROP RE-
   PORTING SERVICE.

A 88.15/22:date
HATCHERY PRODUCTION, LOUISIANA CROP RE-
   PORTING SERVICE.

A 88.15/23 • Item 40-B-1 (MF)
LIST OF PLANTS OPERATING UNDER USDA POUL-
   TRY AND EGG INSPECTION AND GRADING
   PROGRAMS. [Semiannual]

    Numerical List of Plants Operating under Poul-
try Inspection Service was published separately
for 1957 as AMS 45.
    Revised in the Spring and Fall of each year.
    Previously published as AMS 15.
    See also A 103.10

A 88.15/24:date • Item 21-U
BROILER MARKETING FACTS.   – 1976 [Quarterly]

    ISSN 0360-2911
    Discontinued.

A 88.15/25:date • Item 21-V
TURKEY MARKETING FACTS.
    Discontinued.

A 88.16:date
RECEIPTS AND DISPOSITION OF LIVESTOCK AT
   PUBLIC MARKETS. [Monthly]
    Earlier A 82.41

A 88.16/2:date
LIVESTOCK SLAUGHTER BY STATES. [Monthly]
    Earlier A 36.162

A 88.16/2-2:date
LIVESTOCK SLAUGHTER, LOUISIANA CROP RE-
   PORTING SERVICE.

A 88.16/3:date
PIG CROP REPORT. [Semiannual]
    Earlier A 36.2:P 62
    Later A 92.18/7

A 88.16/3-2:date
PIG CROP REPORT, LOUISIANA CROP REPORT-
   ING SERVICE.

A 88.16/4:v.nos.&nos. • Item 24-C-2 (MF)
LIVESTOCK, MEAT, WOOL, MARKET NEWS,
   WEEKLY SUMMARY AND STATISTICS. (Livestock
   Division)

    Former title: Market News, Livestock Divi-
sion, Market Reviews and Statistics.
    Earlier A 82.7

A 88.16/5:date
P. AND S. DOCKET, MONTHLY REPORT OF ACTION
   STOCKYARDS ACT.

A 88.16/5-2:v.nos.&nos.
PACKERS AND STOCKYARDS RESUME. [Monthly]
    Replaces A 88.16/5

A 88.16/6:date
CATTLE ON FEED.
    Later A 92.18/6

A 88.16/7:date
CATTLE ON FEED, ILLINOIS, IOWA, NEBRASKA,
   IDAHO, AND CALIFORNIA.

A 88.16/8:nos. • **Item 24-C**
LIVESTOCK AND MEAT SITUATION.
　　Earlier A 36.158
　　Later A 93.15

A 88.16/9:date
LIVESTOCK SLAUGHTER AND MEAT PRODUCTION.
　[Monthly]
　　Later A 92.18/3

A 88.16/10:date
CALF CROP REPORT.
　　Earlier A 88.2:C 12
　　Later A 92.18/5

A 88.16/10-2:date
CALF CROP, LOUISIANA CROP REPORTING
　SERVICE.

A 88.16/11:date
LAMB CROP REPORT.

　　Earlier A 88.2:C 12
　　Later A 92.18/4

A 88.16/12:date
LAMB FEEDING SITUATION. [Annual]
　　Earlier A 88.2:L 16/2

A 88.16/13:date
SHEEP AND LAMB ON FEED. [Annual]
　　Earlier A 88.2:Sh 3
　　Later A 92.18.9

A 88.16/14:date • **Item 21-N**
LIVESTOCK AND POULTRY INVENTORY. [Annual]
　　Earlier A 88.2:L 75/8
　　Later A 92.18/8

A 88.16/15:date
SALABLE [and total] RECEIPTS OF LIVESTOCK AT
　PUBLIC MARKETS, IN ORDER OF VOLUME.
　[Annual]

　　Earlier A 88.2:L 75

A 88.16/16:date
TOTAL LIVESTOCK SLAUGHTER, MEAT AND LARD
　PRODUCTION. [Annual]
　　Earlier A 88.2:L 75/3

A 88.16/17:date • **Item 24-J**
COMMERCIAL LIVESTOCK SLAUGHTER, NUMBER
　AND LIVE WEIGHT, BY STATES, MEAT AND LARD
　PRODUCTION, UNITED STATES, BY MONTHS.
　[Annual]
　　Later A 92.18

A 88.16/18:date
SHIPMENTS OF STOCKER AND FEEDER CATTLE
　AND SHEEP. [Monthly]
　　Later A 92.18/2

A 88.16/18-2:date
CATTLE AND SHEEP, SHIPMENTS OF STOCKER AND
　FEEDER CATTLE AND SHEEP INTO SELECTED
　NORTH CENTRAL STATES. [Annual]
　　Earlier A 88.2:C 29/5

A 88.16/19:date
LAMB CROP AND WOOL PRODUCTION, LOUISIANA
　CROP REPORTING SERVICE.

A 88.16/20:date • **Item 32-A**
DIRECTORY OF MEAT AND POULTRY INSPECTION
　PROGRAM ESTABLISHMENTS, CIRCUITS AND
　OFFICIALS. 1954–　[Bimonthly]

　　Includes list of establishments operating un-
　der Federal Meat Inspection, public stockyards
　under Animal Disease Eradication inspection, li-
　censed manufactures of biological products,
　pathological laboratories, trained diagnosticians,
　and State officials in charge of animal disease
　control.
　　Published in loose-leaf form and punched for
　3-ring binder.
　　Formerly Working Reference of Livestock
　Regulatory Establishments, Circuits and Officials.

A 88.17:date
USDA MEAT PRODUCTION REPORTS. [Weekly]
　　Earlier A 82.54

A 88.17/2:date
MEAT SCRAPS AND TANKAGE PRODUCTION. [Semi-
　annual]
　　Earlier A 88.2:M 46
　　Later A 92.17/2

A 88.17/3:date • **Item 24-H**
MEAT ANIMALS, FARM PRODUCTION, DISPOSITION,
　AND INCOME BY STATES. [Annual]
　　Later A 92.17

A 88.17/4:CT • **Item 24-N**
INSTITUTIONAL MEAT PURCHASE SPECIFICATIONS.
　[Irregular]

　　Later A 103.15
　　Issued in the following series:
　　　100 Fresh Beef (A 88.17/4:B 29)
　　　200 Fresh Lamb and Mutton (A 88.17/4:L
　16)
　　　300 Fresh Veal and Calf (A 88.17/4:V 48)
　　　400 Fresh Pork (A 88.17/4:P 82)
　　　400-F Frozen Pork (A 88.17/4:P 82/2)
　　　500 Cured, Smoked, or Fully-Cooked Pork
　　　　Products (A 88.17/4:P 82/3)
　　　600 Cured, Dried, and Smoked Beef Prod-
　ucts
　　　　　(A 88.17/4:B 39/2)
　　　700 Edible By-Products (A 88.17/4:Sa 8)
　　　1000 Portion-Cut Meat Products (A 88.17/4:M 46)

A 88.17/5:v.nos.&nos.
MEAT HYGIENE ABSTRACTS.

A 88.17/6
MIP [Meat Inspection Program] GUIDELINES. 1–
　[Irregular]

A 88.17/6:6
TECHNICAL TERMS OF THE MEAT INDUSTRY. 1968.
　76 p.

A 88.17/7:date • **Item 21-S**
FEDERAL MEAT AND POULTRY INSPECTION,
　STATISTICAL SUMMARY FOR (year). 1969–
　[Annual] (C&MS-80)

　　Supersedes Federal Meat Inspection, Statis-
　tical Summary for (year) (C&MS-54) (A 88.40/2).
　　Later A 101.6/3

A 88.17/8 • **Item 21-T**
MEAT AND POULTRY INSPECTION PROGRAM, PRO-
　GRAM ISSUANCES.

A 88.18:v.nos.
GRAIN MARKET NEWS AND STATISTICAL REPORT.
　[Weekly]
　　Earlier A 82.71
　　Merged with Feed Market News (A 88.18/4) to
　form Grain and Feed Market News (A 88.18/4-2).
　　ISSN 0364-099X

A 88.18/2:v.nos.
COMMERCIAL GRAIN STOCKS REPORTS. [Weekly]
　　Earlier A 82.31

A 88.18/2-2:CT
COMMERCIAL GRAIN STOCKS [Revised Figures for
　Calendar Year].
　　Earlier A 82.31/2

A 88.18/3:date
FEED MARKET SUMMARY. [Quarterly]
　　Earlier A 82.35

A 88.18/4:v.nos.&nos.
FEED MARKET NEWS, WEEKLY SUMMARY AND
　STATISTICS. (Grain Division)

　　Formerly Weekly Feed Review.
　　Earlier A 82.32
　　Merged with Grain Market News (A 88.18) to
　form Grain and Feed Market News (A 88.18/4-2).
　　ISSN 0364-2046

EGRAIN AND FEED MARKET NEWS. [Weekly]

　　Formed by the merger of Grain Market News
　(A 88.18) and Feed Market News (A 88.18/4).

A 88.18/5:date
ALFALFA MEAL PRODUCTION. [Monthly]
　　Earlier A 82.59/2

A 88.18/6:date
BREWERS' DRIED GRAINS PRODUCTION. [Monthly]
　　Earlier A 82.59/3

A 88.18/6-2:date
BREWERS' DRIED GRAINS, UNITED STATES,
　PRODUCTION AND STOCKS IN HANDS OF PRO-
　DUCERS. [Annual]
　　Earlier A 88.2:B 75

A 88.18/7:date
DISTILLERS' DRIED GRAINS PRODUCTION. [Monthly]
　　Earlier A 82.59/3

A 88.18/7-2:date
DISTILLERS' DRIED GRAINS, UNITED STATES, PRO-
　DUCTION BY KINDS BY MONTHS. [Annual]
　　Earlier A 88.2:D 63

A 88.18/8:nos. • **Item 21-I**
WHEAT SITUATION.
　　Earlier A 36.86
　　Later A 93.11

A 88.18/9:v.nos.&nos.
RICE MARKET NEWS. [Weekly] (Grain Division)

　　Former title: Weekly Rice Market Review.
　　Earlier A 82.33
　　ISSN 0364-8087

A 88.18/10:date
RICE, STOCKS AND MOVEMENTS: CALIFORNIA
　MILLS. [Monthly]
　　Earlier A 82.49

A 88.18/11:date
CROP PRODUCTION, WINTER WHEAT AND RYE.
　[Annual]
　　Earlier A 36.74
　　Later A 92.15/4

A 88.18/12:nos. • **Item 21-E**
FEED SITUATION.
　　Earlier A 36.117
　　Later A 93.11/2

A 88.18/13:date
STOCKS OF FLAXSEED, STOCKS OF SOYBEANS.

A 88.18/13-2:date
SOYBEANS AND FLAXSEED SUMMARY, CROP YEAR.

A 88.18/14:date
STOCKS OF GRAIN IN ALL POSITIONS. [Quarterly]
　　Earlier A 88.2:G 76
　　Later A 92.15

A 88.18/15:date
STORAGE CAPACITY OF ELEVATORS REPORTING
　COMMERCIAL GRAIN STOCKS. [Annual]
　　Earlier A 88.2:C 76/2

A 88.18/16:date
WHEAT AND RYE SUMMARY, CROP YEAR.

A 88.18/17:date
ROUGH AND MILLED RICE STOCKS.
　　Later A 91.15/2

A 88.18/18 • **Item 21-P**
RICE SITUATION.
　　Earlier A 36.130
　　Later A 92.11/3

A 88.18/19:date
SOYBEANS HARVESTED FOR BEANS BY COUN-
　TRIES, ACREAGE, YIELD, PRODUCTION.
　[Annual]
　　Earlier A 88.2:So 9/2
　　Later A 92.15/3

A 88.18/20:v.nos.&nos.
RICE MARKET NEWS SUPPLEMENT, ROUGH RICE
RECEIPTS. [Weekly]

A 88.18/21:v.nos.&nos.
GRAIN MARKET NEWS, QUARTERLY SUMMARY AND
STATISTICS.

Consolidation of separate quarterly reports
for wheat, oats, barley, rye, flaxseed, corn, grain
sorghums, and soybeans, which were classed A
88.42.

A 88.18/22:date
CROP PRODUCTION: QUARTERLY GRAIN STOCKS
IN FARMS, REVISED ESTIMATES.

A 88.18/23:date
ANNUAL RICE SUMMARY, LOUISIANA CROP RE-
PORTING SERVICE.

A 88.18/24:date
WINTER WHEAT REPORT, LOUISIANA CROP RE-
PORTING SERVICE.

A 88.18/25:date
LOUISIANA SOYBEANS FOR BEANS, ACREAGE,
YIELD AND PRODUCTION.

A 88.18/26:date
RICE PRODUCTION, LOUISIANA CROP REPORTING
SERVICE.

A 88.18/27:v.nos.&nos.
GRAIN DIVISION NEWS. ADMINISTRATIVE.

A 88.18/28:v.nos.&nos.
SOUTHERN RICE INSPECTED FOR EXPORT.

A 88.19   • Item 24-B-8
NATIONAL HONEY MARKET NEWS. [Monthly]

Presents such honey market news as prices
paid to beekeepers in major producing states by
packers, handlers, and other large users.
Former title: Semimonthly Honey Report
Earlier A 82.12
ISSN 0364-2054

Co-Op Publication

A 88.19/2:date
HONEY REPORT. [Annual]
Earlier A 88.2:H 75/3
Later A 92.28
A 88.19/2-2:date
HONEY REPORT, LOUISIANA CROP REPORTING
SERVICE.

A 88.19/2-3:date
HONEY PRODUCTION.

A 88.19/3:date
HONEY, ANNUAL SUMMARY.
Earlier A 88.2:H 75
Later A 92.28/2

A 88.20:v.nos.
COLD STORAGE REPORT. [Monthly]
Earlier A 82.15
Later A 92.21

A 88.20/2:date   • Item 24-G
SUMMARY OF REGIONAL COLD STORAGE HOLD-
INGS. [Annual]
Earlier A 88.2:C 67
Later A 92.21/2

A 88.20/3:date   • Item 24-G
CAPACITY OF REFRIGERATED WAREHOUSES IN
UNITED STATES.
Earlier A 1.34
Later A 92.21/3

A 88.21:date
FARM POPULATION, ANNUAL ESTIMATES BY
STATES, MAJOR GEOGRAPHICAL DIVISION,
AND REGIONS.
Earlier A 36.123

A 88.21/2:date
NUMBER OF FARMS BY STATES.
Earlier A 88.2:F 22/2

A 88.22
[ADDRESSES]. [Irregular]

A 88.23:v.nos&nos.   • Item 24-B-12 (EL)
MOLASSES MARKET NEWS. [Weekly] (Grain Divi-
sion)
Former Title: Weekly Molasses Market Re-
port
Earlier A 82.62
ISSN 0145-0662

A 88.23/2:date
MOLASSES MARKET NEWS. MARKET SUMMARY.
[Annual]

A 88.24:date   • Item 20-B
CROP PRODUCTION. [Monthly]
Earlier A 36.39
Later 92.24

A 88.24/2:CT
CROP REPORT AS OF . . . VARIOUS CROPS.

NOTE:– Information appears in Crop Production (A 88.24).

A 88.24/3:v.nos.   • Item 21
CROPS AND MARKETS. [Annual]
Earlier A 36.22/2
Discontinued.

A 88.24/4:date   • Item 20-B
CROP PRODUCTION, PROSPECTIVE PLANTINGS.
[Annual]

This class replaces and cancels A 88.30/2
Earlier A 36.38
Later A 92.24/2

A 88.24/5:date
CROP VALUES.
Earlier A 88.2:C 88/5
Later A 92.24/3

A 88.24/6:date
LOUISIANA ANNUAL CROP SUMMARY, LOUISIANA
CROP REPORTING SERVICE.

A 88.24/7:date
GENERAL CROP REPORT, LOUISIANA CROP RE-
PORTING SERVICE.

A 88.25:date
FARM LABOR. [Monthly]
Earlier A 36.140
Later A 92.12

A 88.26:date
MARKETING ACTIVITIES. [Monthly]
Earlier A 82.17

A 88.26/2:nos.   • Item 21-G
MARKETING AND TRANSPORTATION SITUATION.
[Quarterly]
Desig. MTS-nos.
Earlier A 26.143
Later A 93.14

A 88.26/3   • Item 24-K
AGRICULTURAL MARKETING. v. 1–16. 1956–1971.

PURPOSE:– To keep publications, organizations, officials and individuals who are concerned
with the marketing of farm products informed about
current agricultural marketing.
Brings together up-to-date information on programs carried on by Federal, State, municipal,
and commercial marketing agencies; reports on
preliminary findings under authorized marketing
research projects; summaries of reports issued
on completed projects; and reports on activities
in agricultural marketing; such as the formulation
of standards, inspection and grading, market news,
administration of regulatory legislation, and the
various food distribution programs.
Supersedes Marketing Activities.
Discontinued.

A 88.26/4   • Item 18-D
ACREAGE-MARKETING GUIDES. AMG 1–   1958–
[Annual]

PURPOSE:– To provide the best estimates of
the acreage of particular vegetables required,
with average yields, to supply the quantity of
these vegetables deemed necessary to meet the
market need anticipated for the coming season.
The information is presented to the grower in
sufficient time for him to consider the facts as he
develops his plans for the forthcoming season.
The fundamental concept behind the guides program is that, given the best information possible,
the grower will be in a better position to make
intelligent decisions for his and the industry's
best interest. Compliance with the guides on the
part of growers is voluntary.
Guides issued prior to the 1958 season appear in the AMS series.
Issued in the following parts:

SPRING AND EARLY-SUMMER POTATOES. 1963–
[Annual]
Issued in November of preceeding year.
Prior to 1963, published in Spring Vegetables,
Spring Melons, Spring Potatoes.

SPRING VEGETABLES AND MELONS. 1956–
[Annual]
Issued in November of preceeding year.
Former title: Spring Vegetables, Spring
Melons, Spring Potatoes. Beginning with crop
year 1963. Spring Potatoes, published sepa-
rately.

SUMMER AND FALL POTATOES. 1956–   [Annual]
Issued in February of current year.
Former title: Summer Potatoes, Fall Pota-
toes.

SUMMER AND FALL VEGETABLES, MELONS,
SWEETPOTATOES. 1956–   [Annual]
Issued in February of current year.
Former title: Summer and Fall Vegetables
for Fresh Market, Summer Melons, Sweet
potatoes.

VEGETABLES FOR COMMERCIAL PROCESSING.
1956–   [Annual]
Issued in February of Current year.

WINTER VEGETABLES AND POTATOES. 1956–
[Annual]
Issued in August of preceeding year.
Former title: Winter Vegetables, Winter
Potatoes.
Discontinued.

A 88.26/5   • Item 18-D
PMG [Poultry Marketing Guides] (series). 1–   1966–

PURPOSE:– To help producers and market-
ers of poultry tailor their plans to the prospective
market situation.

BROILER MARKETING GUIDE. [Quarterly]

EGG MARKETING GUIDE. [Semiannual]

TURKEY MARKETING GUIDE. [Annual]

A 88.27:v.nos.   • Item 18
AGRICULTURAL ECONOMICS RESEARCH. [Quarterly]
Earlier A 36.167
Later A 93.26

A 88.28:nos.
STATISTICAL SUMMARY. [Monthly]
Earlier A 36.151
Later A 92.13

A 88.29:date
NAVAL STORES REPORT. [Monthly]
Earlier A 36.177
Later A 92.25

A 88.29/2:date
NAVAL STORES REPORT. [Annual]
Later A 95.25/2

A 88.30:date
SEED CROPS.
Earlier A 36.176
Later A 92.16/a, A 92.19/2, A 92.19/3

A 88.30/2:
CROP PRODUCTION, PROSPECTIVE PLANTINGS. [Annual]

A 88.30/3:date
SEED CROPS ANNUAL SUMMARY.
Earlier A 88.2:Se 3/3
Later A 92.19/4

A 88.30/4:date • **Item 24-I**
FIELD AND SEED CROPS, FARM PRODUCTION, FARM DISPOSITION, VALUE, BY STATES. [Annual]
Later A 92.19

A 88.30/5:date
VEGETABLE-SEED STOCKS.

A 88.30/6:date
SEED CROPS, CERTIFIED SEED POTATO REPORT.
Designated Pot. 3
Later A 92.19/6

A 88.30/7:date
PROSECUTIONS AND SEIZURES UNDER THE FEDERAL SEED ACT. 1951– [Annual]

Summarizes facts of individual court actions taken under Federal Seed Act during the preceding fiscal year.

A 88.31:v.nos.
VIRGINIA CROPS AND LIVESTOCK. [Monthly]
Earlier A 36.97
Later A 92.22

A 88.32:nos. • **Item 21-D**
FATS AND OILS SITUATION. [Monthly]
Earlier A 36.97
Later A 93.23

A 88.33:date
CHECKLIST OF REPORTS AND CHARTS ISSUED BY AGRICULTURAL MARKETING SERVICE.

A 88.33/2:CT
BIBLIOGRAPHIES AND LISTS OF PUBLICATIONS.

A 88.33/3:CT
[CHECKLIST OF REPORTS ISSUED BY AGRICULTURAL MARKETING SERVICE] SUPPLEMENTS.

Formerly classified as supplements to individual numbers in A 88.33.
Designated CL-(letters) supplement.

A 88.34:date • **Item 24-D (MF)**
TOBACCO STOCKS REPORT. [Quarterly]
Earlier A 82.11
ISSN 0360-439X

A 88.34/2:nos. • **Item 24-D**
TOBACCO SITUATION. [Issued 4 times a year]
Earlier A 36.94
Later A 93.25

A 88.34/3:date
DARK AIR-CURED TOBACCO MARKET REVIEW. [Annual]
Earlier A 88.2:T 55/3
Later A 88.34/8

A 88.34/4:date
FIRE-CURED TOBACCO MARKET REVIEW. [Annual]
Earlier A 88.2:T 55/5
Later A 88.34/8

TOBACCO MARKET REVIEW. [Annual]

(Tobacco Division)
Consists mainly of statistical tables covering sales, receipts, prices, composition of crops, percentage distribution, and warehouse charges. Textual summaries, give review of tobacco markets.
Issued in the following sections:

A 88.34/5 • **Item 24-D (MF)**
LIGHT AIR-CURED. [Annual]

Issued in two parts:
Part 1. Type 32, Maryland. (Issued in June)
Part 2. Type 31, Burley. (Issued in February of following year)

A 88.34/6 • **Item 24-D (MF)**
FLUE-CURED. [Annual]

Issued in March. Covers types 11, 12, 13, and 14.

A 88.34/7:nos. • **Item 24-D (MF)**
WEEKLY TOBACCO MARKET NEWS SUMMARY.

A 88.34/8:date • **Item 24-D**
FIRE-CURED AND DARK AIR-CURED TOBACCO MARKET REVIEW. [Annual]

Issued in May. covers types 21, 22, 23, 35, 36, and 37.
Earlier A 88.34/3 and a 88.34/4
Discontinued.

A 88.34/9 • **Item 24-D**
TOBACCO CROP SUMMARY.

A 88.34/10 • **Item 24-D**
TOBACCO MARKET NEWS SUMMARY. [Annual]

A 88.34/11:date
QUARTERLY REPORT OF MANUFACTURE AND SALES OF SNUFF, SMOKING, AND CHEWING TOBACCO. (Tobacco Division)

A 88.34/12:date • **Item 24-D (MF)**
ANNUAL REPORT ON TOBACCO STATISTICS.

A 88.35:nos. • **Item 21-O**
WOOL SITUATION. [Quarterly]
Earlier A 36.159
Later A 93.19

A 88.35/2:date
SHORN WOOL PRODUCTION. [Annual]
Earlier A 88.2:W 88/2
Later A 92.29

A 88.35/3:date
WOOL PRODUCTION AND VALUE OF SALES. [Annual]
Earlier A 88.2:W 88/4
Later A 92.29/3

A 88.35/4:date
MOHAIR PRODUCTION AND VALUE OF SALES. [Annual]
Earlier A 88.2:M 72
Later A 92.29/4

A 88.35/5:date
WOOL AND MOHAIR PRICES, MARKETING YEAR.
Later A 92.29/2

A 88.36:date • **Item 21-J**
SUGAR SITUATION. [Annual]

Formerly World Sugar Situation (A 36.2:Su 3).
Later A 93.31

A 88.37:nos. • **Item 21-H**
NATIONAL FOOD SITUATION. [Quarterly]
Earlier A 36.174
Later A 93.16

A 88.37/2:nos.
PLENTIFUL FOODS, PF- (series). – July 1973. [Monthly]

Superseded by Food Marketing Alert (A 88.37/3).

A 88.37/3:nos.
FOOD MARKETING ALERT. [Monthly]

Supersedes Plentiful Food (A 88.37/2).

A 88.38:CT • **Item 24-B-5**
POSTERS.
Earlier A 85.25

A 88.39:nos.
H.T. & S. OFFICE REPORTS.
Earlier A 77.523

A 88.40:nos. • **Item 19-A (MF)**
AMS (series).

Superseded by C&MS (series) (A 88.40/2), 1965– 1972.

SOURCES OF MILK FOR FEDERAL ORDER MARKETS, BY STATE AND COUNTY. 1957– [Irregular]
PURPOSE:– To present information relating to milk supply areas for handlers regulated under Federal milk marketing orders, which are authorized by the Agricultural Marketing Agreement Act of 1937.
Presents a breakdown of producer deliveries of milk to Federal order markets according to the State and counties from which these deliveries originated.
Discontinued.

A 88.40/2 • **Item 19-A**
C&MS (series). 1– 1965– 1972. [Irregular]

A complete listing of all C&MS (series) may be found in the Checklist of Major U.S. Government Series, Volume 1, Department of Agriculture.
Superseded AMS (series) (A 88.40), 1965– 1975.

A 88.40/2:2 • **Item 19-A**
MOLASSES MARKET NEWS ANNUAL SUMMARY. 1954– [Annual]

A 88.40/2:3 • **Item 19-A**
FRESH FRUIT AND VEGETABLE UNLOADS IN EASTERN CITIES. [Annual]

Previously published as A 88.40:427
Later published as FVUS-1 (A 88.12/31:1)

A 88.40/2:4 • **Item 19-A**
FRESH FRUIT AND VEGETABLE UNLOADS IN WESTERN CITIES. [Annual]

Previously published as A 88.40:428
Later published as FVUS-4 (A 88.12/31:4).

A 88.40/2:5 • **Item 19-A**
FRESH FRUIT AND VEGETABLE UNLOADS IN MIDWESTERN CITIES. 1962– [Annual]

Previously published as A 88.40:492
Later published as FVUS-2 (A 88.12/31:2).

A 88.40/2:6 • **Item 19-A**
FRESH FRUIT AND VEGETABLES UNLOADS IN SOUTHERN CITIES. 1962– [Annual]

Previously published as A 88.40:493
Later published as FVUS-3 (A 88.12/31:3).

A 88.40/2:7 • **Item 19-A**
FRESH FRUIT AND VEGETABLE UNLOAD TOTALS FOR 41 CITIES, CALENDAR YEAR (date). 1955– [Annual] (Market News Branch, Fruit and Vegetable Division)

Previously published as A 88.40:25
Later published as FVUS-5 (A 88.12/31:5).

A 88.40/2:12 • **Item 19-A**
FRESH FRUIT AND VEGETABLE SHIPMENTS BY STATES, COMMODITIES, COUNTIES, STATIONS, CALENDAR YEAR (date). 1920– [Annual] (Market News Branch, Fruit and Vegetable Division)

Issued 1920– 35 in the Statistical Bulletin series. Previously published prior to 1964 as A 88.40:41
Later published as FVUS-6 (A 88.12/31:6).

A 88.40/2:14 • Item 19-A
FRESH FRUIT AND VEGETABLE SHIPMENTS, BY COMMODITIES, STATES, MONTHS, CALENDAR YEAR (date). [Annual] (Market News Branch, Fruit and Vegetable Division)

Previously published as A 88.40:36
Later published as FVUS-7 (A 88.12/31:7).

A 88.40/2:17 • Item 19-A
DIRECTORY OF STATE DEPARTMENTS OF AGRICULTURE. [Annual] (Administrative Services Divisions)

Gives State marketing service agencies and the names of key officials of the State departments of agriculture. Arranged by State. Includes the Virgin Islands and Puerto Rico. Also gives the National Association of State Departments of Agriculture, Agricultural Marketing Act Advisory Committee, National Association of Marketing Officials, National Plant Board, United States Livestock Sanitary Association, and key officials of the U.S. Department of Agriculture.
Previously published as A 88.40:27

A 88.40/2:18 • Item 19-A
RICE ANNUAL MARKET SUMMARY. [Annual]

Prepared by the Grain Division. Formerly published as A 88.40:277.
Gives statistical data on prices, production, distribution, shipments, receipts, CCC and foreign activities.

A 88.40/2:20 • Item 19-A
SUMMARY OF ACTIVITIES, MEAT INSPECTION DIVISION. [Annual]

Covers fiscal year. Gives textual summary of activities of the division with supporting statistical tables.

A 88.40/2:21 • Item 19-A
FEDERAL-STATE MARKET NEWS REPORTS, DIRECTORY OF SERVICES AVAILABLE.

A 88.40/2:44 • Item 19-A
GRAIN CROP QUALITY, (year) CROPS. [Annual]

A 88.40/2:53 • Item 19-A
AVAILABLE PUBLICATIONS OF USDA'S CONSUMER AND MARKETING SERVICE (except Market News Reports). [Annual]

A 88.40/2:54 • Item 19-A
FEDERAL MEAT INSPECTION, STATISTICAL SUMMARY FOR (year). [Annual]

A 88.40/3:nos. • Item 19-A
AMS HEADLINES. [Quarterly]

Non-depository

A 88.41:
SPECIAL NEWS LETTER. [Monthly]

A 88.42:
FIELD RELEASES OF AGRICULTURAL MARKETING SERVICE.

A 88.42/2:CT
[STATE PUBLICATIONS ISSUED IN COOPERATION WITH AGRICULTURAL MARKETING SERVICE].

A 88.43:date
OFFICES OF PROCESSED PRODUCTS STANDARDIZATION AND INSPECTION BRANCH. [Annual]
Earlier A 88.2:P 94/3

A 88.43/2 • Item 21-R
PLANTS UNDER USDA CONTINUOUS INSPECTION, PROCESSED FRUITS AND VEGETABLES AND RELATED PRODUCTS. [Annual] (Processed Products Standardization and Inspection Branch, Fruit and Vegetable Division)

List firms, headquarters and plant locations with list of foods covered. Under this type of service, an inspector is on duty continuously while the plant is in operation. To qualify for this service, plants must meet highstandards of sanitation in accordance with Department regulations.
Previously published as AMS 100 and C&MS-SRA 186.

Discontinued.

A 88.42/3:v.nos.&nos.
COTTONSEED REVIEW. [Weekly]

Earlier A 88.42:C 82/2

A 88.44:date
STOCK OF HOPS. [Semiannual]

Earlier A 88.2:H 77
Later A 92.30

A 88.45:date
FARM TELEPHONES. [Annual]

Earlier A 88.2:P 56
Later A 88.2:T 23

A 88.45/2:date
FARM TELEPHONE AND ELECTRICITY COMBINED REPORT.

See for separate reports A 88.45 and A 88.46

A 88.46:date
FARM ELECTRICITY REPORT. [Annual]

Earlier A 88.2:El 2/3

A 88.47:date • Item 34-L
CUT FLOWERS, PRODUCTION AND SALES.

Later A 92.32
A 88.48:date • Item 24-M
NURSERY PRODUCTS, PRODUCTION AND SALES.

Later A 92.31

A 88.49:nos.
MISSISSIPPI WEEKLY WEATHER-CROPS BULLETINS.

A 88.49/2:date
LOUISIANA WEEKLY WEATHER AND CROP BULLETIN.

A 88.50
TYPE A TOPICS, NATIONAL SCHOOL LUNCH PROGRAM. 1966– [Monthly (September– May)]

Issued by the Food and Nutrition Service.
PURPOSE:– A four-page monthly newsletter issued during the school year and intended as a helpful and educational tool to provide guidance for school lunch managers. A different theme is used each school year.

A 88.51:date
MOLASSES MARKET NEWS, MARKET SUMMARY (year). 1954– [Annual] (Grain Division)

Formerly issued in the C&MS series (A 88.40/2:2)

A 88.52:v.nos.&nos. • Item 24-B-7 (MF)
OFFICIAL JOURNAL OF THE PLANT VARIETY PROTECTION OFFICE. 1973– [Quarterly] (Plant Variety Protection Office, 10301 Baltimore Ave., Beltsville, MD 20705-2351)
PURPOSE:– To provide the public with pertinent information relating to the operations of the Plant Variety Protection Office; to disseminate technological and other information available to the Office that would encourage innovation and promote progress in plant breeding; and provide instructions issued by the Office and related information.

A 88.53/2 • Item 24-B-12 (EL)
VARIETY PROTECTION DATABASE.

A 88.53:date • Item 21-W
EGG MARKETING FACTS.

Discontinued.

A 88.54:v.nos.&nos.
SUGAR MARKET NEWS. [8 times a year] (Fruit and Vegetable Division)

Quarterly issues combined with Sugar and Sweetener Report (A 1.115).

A 88.55:date
PROGRAM NOTES. [Weekly]

A 88.56:date • Item 24-G-3 (MF)
WAREHOUSES LICENSED UNDER U.S. WAREHOUSE ACT. [Annual]

Lists warehouses licensed under the U.S. Warehouse Act, by city and State and by type of warehouse.

A 88.57:nos. • Item 24-B-4 (MF)
AMS FOOD PURCHASES. [Weekly]

Lists the week's purchases of food for domestic feeding programs such as the school lunch program, bid information, and awards.
Published earlier as FSQS Food Purchases (A 103.11).

A 88.57/2 • Item 24-B-4
AMS FOOD PURCHASES, QUARTERLY SUMMARY.

Lists commodities purchased for the quarter.
Discontinued 983/3

A 88.58:date
AMS IN ACTION. [Monthly]

A 88.59:date • Item 24-B-1
DIRECTORY OF STATE DEPARTMENTS OF AGRICULTURE. [Biennial]
Discontinued

A 88.60:date/nos. • Item 24-B-1 (EL)
PESTICIDE DATA PROGRAM. [Annual]

A 88.61 • Item 24-B-1
LIVESTOCK & SEED DIVISION (series).

A 88.63 • Item 24-B-10 (EL)
ITEMS OF INTEREST IN SEED CONTROL. [Quarterly]

A 88.64 • Item 24-B-12 (E)
ELECTRONIC PRODUCTS.

A 88.65:date • Item 24-B-13
BEAN MARKET NEWS.

A 88.66 • Item 24-B-12 (EL)
MARKET NEWS REPORTS.

A 88.67 • Item 24-B-12 (EL)
FOOD PURCHASE REPORTS & INVITATIONS TO BID.

A 88.68:date • Item 24-B-14 (EL)
GRAIN TRANSPORTATION REPORT. [Weekly]

A 88.68/2 • Item 24-B-12 (EL)
GRAIN TRANSPORTATION PROSPECT. [Irregular]

A 88.69: • Item 24-B-15
DIRECTORIES.

A 88.69/2: • Item 24-B-16
NATIONAL DIRECTORY OF FARMERS MARKETS. [Biennial]

A 88.70 • Item 24-B-18 (EL)
OCEAN FREIGHT RATE BULLETIN. [Quarterly]

FARMER COOPERATIVE SERVICE
(1953– 1978)

CREATION AND AUTHORITY

The Farmer Cooperative Service was established within the Department of Agriculture by Departmental Memorandum 1320, Supplement 4, dated November 2, 1953. The Service was consolidated along with certain other agencies to form the Economics, Statistics, and Cooperatives Service (A 105) by Secretary's Memorandum 1927, Supplement 1, of December 19, 1977, effective January 2, 1978.

A 89.1:date
ANNUAL REPORTS.

A 89.2:CT   • Item 65-C
GENERAL PUBLICATIONS.
   Discontinued.

A 89.3   • Item 63
FCS BULLETINS. 1–   1934–   [Irregular]

PURPOSE:– To present findings of research studies and material of a more technical nature on farmer cooperatives.
   Discontinued.

A 89.3/a
BULLETIN REPRINTS. 1–   1954–   [Irregular]

PURPOSE:– To present findings of general interest and long-term value for members of farmer cooperatives and students of cooperation.

A 89.4/2   • Item 64
FCS EDUCATIONAL CIRCULARS. 1–   1954–   [Irregular]

PURPOSE:– To present educational information of widespread interest and long-term value for members of farmer cooperatives and students and teachers in vocational agriculture.
   Discontinued.

A 89.8:v.nos.&nos.   • Item 66
FARMER COOPERATIVES. v. 1–   1934–   [Monthly]

Index issued separately.
Prior to v. 42, no. 11 (February 1976) titled News for Farmer Cooperatives.
Indexed by: Index to U.S. Government Periodicals.
ISSN 0364-0736
Later A 105.19

A 89.8/a:nos.
– REPRINTS.

Reprints of the more popular articles appearing in the monthly periodical.
Earlier A 72.10/a 2

A 89.9:nos.
SUMMARY OF COOPERATIVE CASES.
   Earlier A 72.18

A 89.9/2
SUMMARY OF COOPERATIVE CASES, LEGAL SERIES. 1–   1957–   [Quarterly]

PURPOSE:– To keep lawyers, accountants, managements and employees of farmer cooperatives, and others interested up-to-date on the latest court rulings and administrative agency rulings affecting cooperatives.
Supersedes Summary of Cooperative Cases (A 89.9), Summary Nos. 1– 69, published from March 1939 through November 1956. All cases of lasting interest reported in the series have been included in FCS Bulletin 10, Legal Phases of Farmer Cooperatives.

A 89.10
ADDRESSES. [Irregular]

A 89.11   • Item 65-A
GENERAL REPORTS. 1–   1954–   [Irregular]

PURPOSE:– To present findings of short-term value to managements of farmer cooperatives and students of cooperation. Series is used to publish reports quickly and to report on preliminary findings. Includes handbooks, statistical reports, etc.
   Discontinued.

A 89.12:nos.
SERVICE REPORTS.

A 89.13:CT   • Item 62-A
BIBLIOGRAPHIES AND LISTS OF PUBLICATIONS.
   Discontinued.

A 89.14
EDUCATIONAL AIDS. 1–   1954–   [Irregular]

PURPOSE:– Designed specifically for training and demonstration use by Federal Extension Service personnel and other educators working with 4-H Clubs, vocational agriculture students and adult education groups.

A 89.15   • Item 65-B
FCS INFORMATION (series). 1–   1955–   [Irregular]

PURPOSE:– Brief publications, often in leaflet form, using text, pictures or drawings to present highlights of a bulletin, circular, speech or article, or to make available other information of general interest.
   Later A 105.38/2

A 89.15:2   • Item 65-B
FARMER COOPERATIVE FILMS.

A 89.15:4   • Item 65-B
LIST OF PUBLICATIONS. [Biennial]

Annotated list by broad subjects. Also contains a numerical list of the series. Supplements issued in odd years and main volumes in even years.

A 89.16:date
HIGHLIGHTS OF ANNUAL WORKSHOP OF FARMER COOPERATIVE SERVICE.
   Earlier A 89.2:F 22/date

A 89.17:date
MIDWEST REGIONAL MEMBER RELATIONS CONFERENCE SPONSORED BY AMERICAN INSTITUTE OF COOPERATION AND FARMER COOPERATIVE SERVICE.

A 89.17/2:date
NORTH CENTRAL REGIONAL MEMBERSHIP RELATIONS CONFERENCE.

A 89.18:date
NATIONAL RESEARCH AND TEACHING CONFERENCE IN AGRICULTURAL COOPERATION.

A 89.19   • Item 64-A
FCS RESEARCH REPORTS. 1–   1968–   [Irregular]

Publications in this series range from technical reports based on research projects to less technically written reports directed primarily toward cooperative management and students of cooperatives as well as agricultural leaders. They include findings of both short and long time studies.
   Later A 105.38

STATISTICS OF FARMER COOPERATIVES. [Annual]

Gives number of associations and membership, business volume, farm produce marketed for patrons, farm supplies purchased for patrons, and services.
   Covers fiscal year.
Prior to 1966, published in the General Reports series (A 89.11).
   Later A 105.31

A 89.20:nos.   • Item 64-B (MF)
SPECIAL REPORT SERIES.

AGRICULTURAL CONSERVATION PROGRAM SERVICE
(1953– 1961)

CREATION AND AUTHORITY

The Agricultural Conservation Program Service was established within the Department of Agriculture by Secretary's Memorandum 1320, Supplement 4, dated November 2, 1953. Except for a change in name, the Service carries on the duties and functions of the Agricultural Conservation Programs Branch (A 82.37) of the Production and Marketing Administration (A 82), which was abolished. Merged with Commodity Stabilization Service (A 82) by Secretary's Memorandum 1446, Supplement 2, dated April 19, 1961, effective April 24, 1961.

A 90.1:date
ANNUAL REPORTS.

A 90.2:CT
GENERAL PUBLICATIONS.

A 90.8:CT
AGRICULTURAL CONSERVATION PROGRAM (by States) HANDBOOKS.
   Earlier A 82.37

A 90.9:CT
ADDRESSES.

A 90.10:date
AGRICULTURAL CONSERVATION PROGRAM, STATISTICAL SUMMARY. [Annual]
   Earlier A 90.2:St 2

A 90.10/2:date
AGRICULTURAL CONSERVATION PROGRAM, SUMMARY. [Annual]
   Earlier A 90.2:Su 6

OFFICE OF ADMINISTRATIVE MANAGEMENT
(1960–   )

A 91.1:date
ANNUAL REPORTS.

A 91.2:CT
GENERAL PUBLICATIONS.

A 91.8:nos.
OAM PUBLICATIONS.

NATIONAL AGRICULTURAL STATISTICS SERVICE
(1986–   )

CREATION AND AUTHORITY

The Statistical Reporting Service was established as a program agency within the Department of Agriculture by Memorandum 1446, Supplement 1, of the Secretary of Agriculture, dated April 3, 1961. The Service was consolidated along with certain other agencies to form the Economics, Statistics, and Cooperatives Service (A 105) by Secretary's Memorandum 1927, Supplement 1, of December 19, 1977, effective January 2, 1978. The Economics and Statistics Service (A 105) was abolished on June 17, 1981 and certain functions were returned to the reestablished Statistical Reporting Service (A 92). In 1986 the name was changed to National Agricultural Statistics Service

INFORMATION

Executive Assistant to the Administrator
NASS
Department of Agriculture
4117 South Agriculture Building
1400 Independence Avenue, SW
Washington, D.C. 20250-2000
(202) 720-5141
Fax: (202) 690-2090
Toll Free: (800) 727-9540
http://www.usda.gov/nass

A 92.1:date
ANNUAL REPORTS.

A 92.2:CT   • Item 122-A-7
GENERAL PUBLICATIONS.

Formerly distributed to Depository Libraries under Item 122-A-1.

A 92.8:CT   • Item 122-A-9
HANDBOOKS, MANUALS, GUIDES.

A 92.9:date
PULLET CHICKS FOR BROILER SUPPLY FLOCKS. [Monthly] (Crop Reporting Board) (Pou 2-7)

Title varies.
Discontinued with November 1969 issue. Data now included in Eggs, Chickens, and Turkeys (A 92.9/16).
Earlier A 88.15/19

A 92.9/2:date
TURKEYS AND CHICKEN TESTED. [Monthly] (Crop Reporting Board) (Pou 1-2)

Discontinued with December 1969 issue. Data now published on a quarterly basis in Eggs, Chickens, and Turkeys (A 92.9/16)
Earlier A 88.15/4.

A 92.9/3:date   • Item 21-F (EL)
CHICKENS AND EGGS, INCLUDING BROILER PRODUCTION, DISPOSITION, CASH RECEIPTS, AND GROSS INCOME. [Annual] (Crop Reporting Board) (Pou 2-3)
Earlier A 88.15/18

A 92.9/4   • Item 21-F-2 (MF)
EGG PRODUCTS, LIQUID, FROZEN, DRIED PRODUCTION UNDER FEDERAL INSPECTION. [Monthly] (Crop Reporting Board) (Pou 2-5)

Title varies.
See also A 105.12/2
Earlier A 88.15
ISSN 0145-3904

A 92.9/5:date   • Item 21-F (EL)
POULTRY SLAUGHTERED FEDERAL INSPECTION AND POULTRY USED IN FURTHER PROCESSING. [Monthly] (Crop Reporting Board) (Pou 2-1)

Title varies.
Earlier A 88.15/9
Later A 105.12/5
ISSN 0364-2682

A 92.9/6:date   • Item 21-F (EL)
HATCHERY PRODUCTION. [Annual] (Crop Reporting Board) (Pou 1-1)

Discontinued with November 1969 issue. Data now contained in Eggs, Chickens, and Turkeys (A 92.9/16).
Earlier A 88.15/5

A 92.9/7:date
CHICKENS, NUMBER RAISED, PRELIMINARY ESTIMATES. [Annual] (Crop Reporting Board) (Pou 2-2)

Earlier A 88.15/10

A 92.9/8:date
TURKEYS RAISED. [Annual]

(Crop Reporting Board) (Pou 3-2)
Earlier A 88.15/11

A 92.9/9:date
TURKEY BREEDER HENS HATCHING SEASON INTENTIONS. (Crop Reporting Board) (Pou 3-4)

A 92.9/10:date
COMMERCIAL BROILERS PRODUCTION IN 22 STATES. [Annual] (Crop Reporting Board) (Pou 2-7)

Earlier A 88.15/13

A 92.9/11:date
TURKEY BREEDER HENS [on farms]. [Annual]

(Crop Reporting Board) (Pou 3-3)
Earlier A 88.15/12

A 92.9/12:date
LAYERS, POTENTIAL LAYERS AND RATE OF LAY FIRST OF MONTH. [Monthly]

(Crop Reporting Board) (Pou 2-8)
Earlier A 88.15/17

A 92.9/13:date   • Item 21-F-2 (MF)
CHICKENS AND EGGS, LAYERS AND EGG PRODUCTION. [Annual] (Crop Reporting Board) (Pou 2-4)

See also A 105.12/7
Earlier A 88.15/14

A 92.9/14:date
BROILER CHICKS PLACED IN 22 STATES. [Annual] (Crop Reporting Board) (Pou 2-7)
Earlier A 88.15/15

A 92.9/15:date   • Item 21-F (MF)
POULTRY PRODUCTION AND VALUE. [Annual]
Earlier A 88.15/16

A 92.9/16:date   • Item 21-F-1 (EL)
CHICKENS AND EGGS. [Monthly] (Crop Reporting Board) (Pou 1-1)

Replaces Hatchery Production (A 92.9/6), Turkeys and Chickens Tested (A 92.9/2), Pullet Chicks for Broiler Hatchery Supply Flocks (A 92.9), and Egg Production (formerly a part of Crop Production).
Earlier title: Eggs, Chickens and Turkeys.
See also A 105.12/3

A 92.9/17:date   • Item 21-F-1 (EL)
TURKEYS. [Biennial] (Crop Reporting Board) (Pou 3)

A 92.9/17-2:date   • Item 21-F-1 (EL)
TURKEY HATCHERY. [Monthly] (Crop Reporting Board) (Pou 3)

A 92.10:date   • Item 24-F (EL)
MILK PRODUCTION. [Monthly] (Crop Reporting Board) (Da 1-1)
Earlier A 88.14/2
Later A 105.17

A 92.10/2:date   • Item 24-F (EL)
MILK PRODUCTION, DISPOSITION, AND INCOME. [Annual] (Crop Reporting Board) (Da 1-2)
See also A 105.17/5
Earlier A 88.14/8

A 92.10/3:date   • Item 24-F
FLUID MILK AND CREAM REPORT.   – June 1973. [Monthly] (Crop Reporting Board) (Da 1-3)
Earlier A 88.14/3

A 92.10/4:date
EVAPORATED, CONDENSED, AND DRY MILK REPORT. [Monthly] (Crop Reporting Board) (Da 2-6)

Earlier A 88.14

A 92.10/5:date   • Item 24-F (EL)
PRODUCTION OF MANUFACTURED DAIRY PRODUCTS. [Annual] (Crop Reporting Board) (Da 2-1)
Earlier A 88.14/10
See also A 105.17/4

A 92.10/6:date   • Item 24-F
MILK PRODUCTION AND DAIRY PRODUCTS, ANNUAL STATISTICAL SUMMARY. (Crop Reporting Board) (Da 3)
Earlier A 88.14/7

A 92.10/7:date   • Item 24-F (EL)
DAIRY PRODUCTS. [Monthly] (Crop Reporting Board) (Da 2-6)
Later A 105.17/3

A 92.10/8   • Item 15-A-3 ((EL)
CHEDDAR CHEESE PRICES. [Weekly]

A 92.11:date • **Item 24-E (EL)**
VEGETABLES.

Issued in two sections:

– FRESH MARKET. [Monthly] (Crop Reporting Board) (Vg 2-1)

Annual summary issued separately in December (A 92.11/10-2)

– PROCESSING. [15 times a year] (Crop Reporting Board) (Vg 3-1)

Annual summary issued in December (A 92.11/10)
Earlier A 88.12/5

A 92.11/2:date • **Item 122-A-4 (EL)**
FRUITS, NONCITRUS, BY STATES, PRODUCTION, USE, VALUE. [Annual] (Crop Reporting Board) (FrNt 2-1)

Issued in two parts.
Earlier A 88.12/20

A 92.11/2-2:date • **Item 122-A-4 (MF)**
NONCITRUS FRUITS AND NUTS. [Annual] (Crop Reporting Board) (FrNt 1-3)

Two reports issued: 1) Annual summary of production, use, price, and value, issued in January; and 2) Midyear supplement of production, use, price, and value, issued in July.
See also A 105.11

A 92.11/2-3:date • **Item 122-A-4 (MF)**
NONCITRUS FRUITS AND NUTS. MIDYEAR SUPPLEMENT. [Annual] (FrNt 1-3)
Earlier A 92.11/2-2
Discontinued.

A 92.11/2-4:date • **Item 122-A-12**
WALNUT PRODUCTION.

A 92.11/2-5 • **Item 122-A-15 (EL)**
ALMOND PRODUCTION. [Annual]

A 92.11/3:date • **Item 122-A-13 (EL)**
CHERRY PRODUCTION. [Annual] (Crop Reporting Board) (FrNt 2-4)
Earlier title: Sour Cherry Report.
Earlier A 88.12/11

A 92.11/3-2:date
CHERRY UTILIZATION. [Annual] (Crop Reporting Board) (FrNt 2-4)
Former title: Sour Cherry Report.
See also A 105.11/3

A 92.11/4:date • **Item 20-B-1 (EL)**
POTATOES AND SWEETPOTATOES, ESTIMATES BY STATES AND SEASONAL GROUPS. [Annual] (Crop Reporting Board) (Pot 1-6)

Earlier A 88.12/19

A 92.11/5:date
IRISH POTATOES, UTILIZATION OF CROP WITH COMPARISONS. [Annual] (Crop Reporting Board) (Pot 1-3)
Earlier A 88.2P 84/6

A 92.11/6:date • **Item 122-A-4 (EL)**
CRANBERRIES, INDICATED PRODUCTION. [Annual] (Crop Reporting Board) (SpCr 1)
Earlier A 88.12/21

A 92.11/7:date
POPCORN ACREAGE FOR HARVEST. [Annual]
Earlier A 88.12/14

A 92.11/8:date • **Item 24-E-1 (EL)**
CITRUS FRUITS BY STATES, PRODUCTION, USE, VALUE. [Annual] (Crop Reporting Board) (FrNt 3-1)
Earlier A 88.12/21

A 92.11/9:date • **Item 122-A-4**
COMMERCIAL APPLES, PRODUCTION BY VARIETIES, WITH COMPARISONS. [Annual] (Crop Reporting Board) (FrNt 2-2-2)
Earlier A 88.12/15
Discontinued.

A 92.11/10:date • **Item 24-E**
VEGETABLES, PROCESSING, ANNUAL SUMMARY. [Annual] (Crop Reporting Board) (Vg 3-2)
Earlier A 88.12/6-2:V 52/2
See 92.11/10-2

A 92.11/10-2:date • **Item 24-E (EL)**
VEGETABLES, FRESH MARKET, ANNUAL SUMMARY. (Crop Reporting Board) (Vg 2-2)
Earlier A 88.12/6-2:V 52/2
See also A 105.24/2

A 92.11/10-3:date
TOTAL COMMERCIAL PRODUCTION OF ALL VEGETABLES AND MELONS FOR FRESH MARKET AND PROCESSING. [Annual] (Crop Reporting Board) (Vg 1)
Earlier A 92.2:V 52

A 92.11/10-4:date • **Item 24-E (MF)**
CELERY. [Monthly] (Crop Reporting Board) (Vg 2-1-1)

ISSN 0364-2690
See also A 105.45
Discontinued.

A 92.11/10-5:date • **Item 24-E (EL)**
MUSHROOMS. [Annual] (Crop Reporting Board) (Vg 2-1-2)

A 92.11/10-6:date
VEGETABLES, PRELIMINARY ACREAGE, YIELD, PRODUCTION AND VALUE. [Annual]

A 92.11/11:date • **Item 20-B-1 (EL)**
POTATO STOCKS. [6 times a year] (Crop Reporting Board)

Former titles: Potatoes and Sweetpotatoes; Total Potato Stocks.
Earlier A 88.12/9
See also A 105.24/5
ISSN 0364-2259

A 92.11/12:date
ONION STOCKS. [Annual] (Crop Reporting Board) (Vg 4)

Earlier A 88.12/15

A 92.11/13:date
BUSH BERRIES, INDICATED YIELD AND PRODUCTION. (Crop Reporting Board) (FrNt 5)

A 92.11/14:date
VEGETABLES, PROCESSING. [Irregular]
Earlier A 92.11

A 92.12:date • **Item 21-F-5 (EL)**
FARM LABOR. [Quarterly] (Crop Reporting Board) (La 1)

Earlier A 88.25
Discontinued with May 22, 1983 issue.
Later A 105.44
ISSN 0363-8545

A 92.13:nos.
STATISTICAL SUMMARY. 1– 337. – 1970. [Monthly]

Designed for ready-reference desk use, each four-page issue covers such items as figures on average prices received by farmers; livestock and livestock products; farm employment; index figures for production and prices; current estimates of cash receipts for farm marketings, by States; cash receipts from farming. Textual summaries.
Earlier A 88.28

A 92.14:date • **Item 122-A-3 (EL)**
PEANUT STOCKS AND PROCESSING. [Monthly] (Crop Reporting Board) (GrLg 11-2)

Issued in March and October.
Earlier A 88.10/2
See also A 105.29
ISSN 0499-0579

A 92.14/2:date • **Item 122-A-3 (MF)**
PEANUT STOCKS AND PROCESSING, SEASONAL REPORT. [Annual] (Crop Reporting Board) (GrLg 22-2-1)

Earlier A 88.10/2-2
Discontinued.

A 92.14/3:date • **Item 122-A-11**
LIST, PEANUT MILLERS (Shellers and Crushers).

Discontinued.

A 92.14/4:date
LIST, PEANUT PROCESSORS.

A 92.15:date • **Item 122-A-3 (EL)**
GRAIN STOCKS. [Quarterly] (Crop Reporting Board) (GrLg 11-1)

Prior to October 24, 1975, entitled Stocks of Grain in All Positions.
Earlier A 88.18/4
Later A 105.20

A 92.15/2:date
RICE STOCKS, ROUGH AND MILLED. [Quarterly] (Crop Reporting Board) (GrLg 11-3)

Earlier A 88.18/17
Later A 105.42

A 92.15/3:date
SOYBEANS HARVESTED FOR BEANS BY COUNTIES. [Annual] (Crop Reporting Board) (GrLg 9-1)

Earlier A 88.18/19

A 92.15/4:date
CROP PRODUCTION, WINTER WHEAT AND RYE. [Annual] (Crop Reporting Board) (CrPr 2-3)

Earlier A 88.18/11

A 92.15/5:date • **Item 122-A-3 (MF)**
STOCKS OF SOYBEANS IN ALL POSITIONS. [Annual] (Crop Reporting Board) (GrLg 11-1)

Later A 105.20/5
Discontinued.

A 92.16:date • **Item 18-C (EL)**
AGRICULTURAL PRICES. [Monthly] (Crop Reporting Board) (Pr-1)

Earlier A 88.9/3
Later A 105.26
ISSN 0002-1601

A 92.16/2:date • **Item 18-C (EL)**
AGRICULTURAL PRICES, ANNUAL SUMMARIES. (Crop Reporting Board) (Pr 1-3)

Earlier issued annually.
Discontinued.
Earlier A 88.9/5
See also A 105.26/2

A 92.16/3:date • **Item 18-C (MF)**
PRICES RECEIVED, MINNESOTA-WISCONSIN MANUFACTURING GRADE MILK. [Annual] (Pr 1-4)

Earlier title: Prices Received by Farmers for Manufacturing Grade Milk in Minnesota and Wisconsin.

A 92.17:date   • Item 24-H (EL)
MEAT ANIMALS, FARM PRODUCTION, DISPOSITION,
AND INCOME, BY STATES. [Annual] (Crop Re-
porting Board) (MtAn 1-1)

    Earlier A 88.17/3

A 92.17/2
MEAT MEAL AND TANKAGE PRODUCTION, SEMI-
ANNUAL REPORT.   – 1965. (Crop Reporting
Board) (MtAn 3)

    Earlier A 88.17/2
    Later 105.23/6

A 92.18:date   • Item 24-J (EL)
LIVESTOCK SLAUGHTER. [Annual] (Crop Reporting
Board) (MtAn 1-2-1)

    Earlier A 88.16/17
    See also A 105.23/4-2

A 92.18/2:date
SHIPMENTS OF STOCKER AND FEEDER CATTLE
AND SHEEP.   – 1962. [Monthly] (Crop Reporting
Board) (MtAn 5-3-3)

    Earlier A 88.16/18

A 92.18/3:date   • Item 24-J (EL)
LIVESTOCK SLAUGHTER. [Monthly]

    Earlier title: Livestock Slaughter and Meat
Production.
    Prior to July 1982 issue, issued monthly.
    ISSN 0499-0544
    Earlier A 88.16/9
    See also A 105.23/4

A 92.18/4:date
LAMB CROP. [2 times a year] (Crop Reporting Board)
(MtAn 5-1)

    Earlier A 88.16/11

A 92.18/5:date
CALF CROP. [2 times a year] (Crop Reporting Board)
(MtAn 2-2)

    Earlier A 88.16/10

A 92.18/6:date   • Item 21-N-1 (EL)
CATTLE ON FEED, CATTLE SOLD FOR SLAUGHTER,
SELECTED MARKETS. [Monthly] (Crop Reporting
Board) (MtAn 2-1)

    ISSN 0364-202X
    Earlier A 88.16/6
    Later A 105.16

A 92.18/6-2:date   • Item 21-N (EL)
CATTLE INVENTORY, SPECIAL REPORT ON NUM-
BER OF CATTLE AND CALVES ON FARMS BY
SEX AND WEIGHT, UNITED STATES, (date).
[Irregular] (Crop Reporting Board) (LvGn)

    See also A 105.23

A 92.18/6-3   • Item 21-N-11 (EL)
UNITED STATES AND CANADA CATTLE.

A 92.18/7:date   • Item 24-H (EL)
HOGS AND PIGS. [Quarterly] (Crop Reporting Board)
(MtAn 4)

    Entitled Pig Crop Report, prior to June 1968.
    Earlier A 88.16/3
    See also A 105.23
    ISSN 0565-2189

A 92.18/8:date   • Item 21-N (EL)
SHEEP AND GOAT INVENTORY. [Annual] (Crop Reporting Board) (LvGn 1)

    Supersedes Livestock and Poultry Inventory.
Title varies.
    See also A 105.23/8
    Earlier A 88.16/14

A 92.18/9:date   • Item 21-N-10 (EL)
SHEEP. (Crop Reporting Board) (MtAn 5-2)

    Earlier title: Sheep and Lambs on Feed. This
title was discontinued with March 17, 1982 issue.
    Earlier: A 88.16/3
    See also: A 105.47

A 92.18/10:date
WESTERN RANGE AND LIVESTOCK REPORT.
[Monthly] (Crop Reporting Board) (MtAn 2-3)

A 92.18/11:date   • Item 24-J (EL)
MINK PRODUCTION, PELTS PRODUCED IN (year).
[Annual] (Crop Reporting Board) (MtAn 6)

    Later A 105.48

A 92.19:date   • Item 24-I
FIELD AND SEED CROPS, PRODUCTION, FARM USE,
SALES, VALUE BY STATES. [Annual] (Crop Re-
porting Board) (CrPr 1)

    Earlier A 88.30/4

A 92.19/2:CT
SEED CROPS FORECASTS. [Irregular] (Crop Reporting Board) (SeHy 1-1)

    Earlier A 88.30

A 92.19/3:CT
SEED CROPS STOCK REPORTS. [Irregular] (Crop
Reporting Board) (SeHy 1-4)

    Earlier A 88.30

A 92.19/4:date
SEED CROPS, ANNUAL SUMMARY. (Crop Reporting
Board) (SeHy 1-3)

    Earlier A 88.30/3
    Later A 105.18

A 92.19/5:date
FIELD SEEDS, SUPPLY AND DISAPPEARANCE.
[Annual] (Crop Reporting Board) (SeHy 1-2)

    Earlier A 88.2:Se 3/6

A 92.19/6:date
SEED CROPS, CERTIFIED SEED POTATO REPORT.
– 1964. [Annual] (Crop Reporting Board) (Pot 3)

    Earlier A 88.30/6

A 92.19/7:date
SEED CROPS: VEGETABLE SEED REPORT. [Annual]

A 92.19/9:date
CRIMSON CLOVER. [Annual] (Crop Reporting Board)

A 92.19/10:date
RED CLOVER. [Annual] (Crop Reporting Board)

A 92.19/11:date
TIMOTHY. [Annual] (Crop Reporting Board)

A 92.19/12:date
TALL FESCUE, SOUTHERN STATES. [Annual] (Crop
Reporting Board)

A 92.19/13:date
TALL FESCUE, OREGON. [Annual] (Crop Reporting
Board)

A 92.19/14:date
ALFALFA. [Annual] (Crop Reporting Board)

A 92.19/15:date
FIELD SEED STOCKS. (Crop Reporting Board) (SeHy
1-3)

A 92.19/16:date
VEGETABLE SEED STOCKS. [Annual] (Crop Reporting Board) (SeHy 1-1)

A 92.19/17:date
VEGETABLE SEEDS. [Annual] (Crop Reporting Board)
(SeHy 1-1)

A 92.20:date
COTTON PRODUCTION. [7 times a year] (Crop Reporting Board) (Cn 1)

    Earlier A 88.11/5

A 92.21:v.nos.&nos.   • Item 24-G-1 (EL)
COLD STORAGE REPORT. [Monthly] (Crop Reporting
Board) (CoSt 1)

    Earlier A 88.20
    Later A 105.33
    ISSN 0091-1297

A 92.21/2:date   • Item 24-G-4 (EL)
SUMMARY OF REGIONAL COLD STORAGE HOLD-
INGS. [Annual] (Crop Reporting Board) (CoSt 3)

    Formerly distributed to Depository Libraries
under Item 24-G.
    Earlier A 88.20/2
    See also A 105.33/2

A 92.21/3:date   • Item 24-G (EL)
CAPACITY OF REFRIGERATED WAREHOUSES IN
UNITED STATES. [Biennial] (Crop Reporting Board)
(CoSt 2)

    Earlier A 88.20/3
    See also A 105.33/3

A 92.22:v.nos.&nos.
VIRGINIA CROPS AND LIVESTOCK. [Monthly]

    Earlier A 88.31

A 92.23   • Item 19
AGRICULTURAL SITUATION. v. 1– 1921–   [11
times a year]

    Contains brief reviews of current marketing
and economic developments affecting farmers.

A 92.23/2:date
DIGEST FOR REPORTERS.   – August 1975. [Monthly]
(Crop Reporting Board)

    ISSN 0364-2658

A 92.24:date   • Item 20-B (EL)
CROP PRODUCTION. [Monthly] (Crop Reporting
Board) (CrPr 2-2)

    Earlier A 88.24
    Later A 105.9
    ISSN 0363-8561

A 92.24/2:date   • Item 20-B-3 (EL)
CROP PRODUCTION, PROSPECTIVE PLANTINGS.
[Annual] (Crop Reporting Board) (CrPr 2-4)
    Earlier A 88.24/4

A 92.24/3:date   • Item 20-B-5 (EL)
CROP VALUES, SEASON AVERAGE PRICES
RECEIVED BY FARMERS AND VALUE OF PRO-
DUCTION. [Annual] (Crop Reporting Board) (CrPr
2-1-1)
    Earlier A 88.24/5

A 92.24/4:date   • Item 20-B-2 (EL)
CROP PRODUCTION, ANNUAL SUMMARY.

    Gives acreage, yield and production.

A 92.24/4-2:date   • Item 20-B-2 (MF)
CROP PRODUCTION, ACREAGE. [2 issues per year]
(Crop Reporting Board) (CrPr 2-2)

A 92.24/5:date   • Item 18-A (EL)
FARM NUMBERS LAND IN FARMS. [Annual]

    Earlier title: Farm Numbers.
    Briefly absorbed by Crop Production, Annual
Summary (A 92.24/4).

A 92.25:date
NAVAL STORES. [Monthly]

    Earlier A 88.29

A 92.25/2:date
NAVAL STORES. [Annual] (Crop Reporting Board)
(SpCr 3)

    Earlier A 88.29/2
    Later A 105.49

A 92.26:CT
ADDRESSES.

A 92.27:date
TREE NUTS BY STATES. [Annual] (Crop Reporting
Board) (FrNt 4-1)

    Earlier A 88.10/4

A 92.28:date
HONEY REPORT. [Annual] (Crop Reporting Board)
(Hny)

    Earlier A 88.19/2

A 92.28/2:date   • Item 18-E (EL)
HONEY. [Annual] (Crop Reporting Board) (Hny)

    Earlier title: Honey Production, Annual Sum-
mary.
    Earlier A 88.19/3

A 92.29:date
SHORN WOOL PRODUCTION. [Annual] (Crop Reporting Board) (MtAn 5-3)

    Earlier A 88.35/2

A 92.29/2:date
WOOL AND MOHAIR PRICES. [Annual] (Crop Reporting Board) (Pr 1-2)

    Earlier A 88.35/5

A 92.29/2-19:nos.   • Item 78-A (MF)
PACIFIC RIM AGRICULTURE AND TRADE REPORTS:
SITUATION AND OUTLOOK SERIES (Series).

A 92.29/3:date
WOOL PRODUCTION AND VALUE. [Annual] (Crop
Reporting Board) (MtAn 5-3)

    Earlier A 88.35/3

A 92.29/4:date
MOHAIR PRODUCTION AND VALUE. [Annual] (Crop
Reporting Board) (MtAn 5-3)

    Earlier A 88.35/4
    Later 92.29/5

A 92.29/5:date   • Item 21-N-9 ((EL)
WOOL AND MOHAIR. [Annual] (Crop Reporting Board)
(MtAn 5-3)

    Earlier title: Wool and Mohair Production, Price
and Value.
    Earlier A 92.29/2, A 92.29/3, A 92.29/4

A 92.30:date   • Item 122-A-3 (EL)
HOP STOCKS. (Crop Reporting Board) (SpCr 2)
    Earlier title: Socks of Hops.
    Earlier A 88.44
    See also A 105.36

A 92.31:date   • Item 24-M
NURSERY PRODUCTS, PRODUCTION AND SALES.
– 1962. [Annual] (Crop Reporting Board) (SpCr
6-2)

    Earlier A 88.48
    Discontinued.

A 92.32:date   • Item 24-L (EL)
FLORICULTURE CROPS, PRODUCTION AREA AND
SALES. [Annual] (Crop Reporting Board) (SpCr 6-
1)

    Earlier title: Flowers and Foliage Plants, Pro-
duction and Sales.
    Entitled Cut Flowers, prior to 1965
    Earlier A 88.47

A 92.33:date
WHEAT PASTURE REPORT. [Monthly, October–
December] (Crop Reporting Board) (MtAn 2-5)

A 92.34:   • Item 18-C-1
SRS (series). 1– 1962– [Irregular]

    A 92.34:1   • Item 24-Q
    DIRECTORY OF REFRIGERATED WAREHOUSES
    IN THE UNITED STATES. 1947– [Irregular]

        A directory of those refrigerated warehouses
    participating in the Department's biennial survey
    of the capacity of refrigerated warehouses in the
    United States.

        Discontinued.

    A 92.34:5   • Item 24-Q
    PLANTS MANUFACTURING DAIRY PRODUCTS.

    A 92.34:8   • Item 24-Q
    NUMBER OF LIVESTOCK SLAUGHTER PLANTS.

A 92.35:CT   • Item 122-A-8
BIBLIOGRAPHIES AND LISTS OF PUBLICATIONS.
[Irregular]

    A 92.35:C 88
    CROP REPORTING BOARD, (year) ISSUANCE
    DATES AND CONTENTS. [Annual] (Crop
    Reporting Board)

A 92.35/2   • Item 122-A-8
AGRICULTURAL STATISTICS BOARD CATALOG.

    Earlier title: Crop Reporting Board Catalog.
    Earlier A 92.35:C 88
    Discontinued.

A 92.36:CT
[STATE REPORTS ISSUED IN COOPERATION WITH
STATISTICAL REPORTING SERVICE].

    Note:– Use State CT, subject CT, and date.

A 92.37:date   • Item 122-A-2 (MF)
CONSUMPTION OF COMMERCIAL FERTILIZERS AND
PRIMARY PLANT NUTRIENTS IN UNITED STATES.
[Annual] (Crop Reporting Board) (SpCr 7)

    Later A 105.41/2
    Discontinued.

A 92.37/2:date   • Item 122-A-2 (MF)
COMMERCIAL FERTILIZERS. [Annual] (Crop Reporting Board) (SpCr 7-1-1)

    ISSN 0364-2593
    Later A 105.41
    Discontinued.

A 92.37/3:date   • Item 122-A-2
COMMERCIAL FERTILIZERS, CONSUMPTION BY
CLASS FOR YEAR ENDED (date). [Annual]

    Discontinued.

A 92.38:date
EXPORTS. [Weekly] (Crop Reporting Board) (Exp 1-
1)

    Later A 67.40

A 92.39:date   • Item 20-B-4 (MF)
ACREAGE. [Annual] (Crop Reporting Board) (CrPr 2-
2)

    See also A 105.36

A 92.40:date   • Item 18-A (EL)
FARM PRODUCTION EXPENDITURES FOR (year).
[Annual]

    Earlier A 105.35/2

A 92.41:date   • Item 18-C-2 (MF)
SUGAR MARKET STATISTICS. [Quarterly] (SpCr 4)

    Earlier A 105.53
    Discontinued.

A 92.42:date   • Item 122-A-6 (EL)
SMALL GRAINS, ANNUAL SUMMARY AND CROP
WINTER WHEAT AND RYE SEEDINGS.

A 92.43:date   • Item 122-A-3 (EL)
RICE STOCKS.

A 92.44:date   • Item 21-F-4 (EL)
CATFISH. [Monthly]

    PURPOSE:– To present narrative and tabular
    data on production, sale, and average prices of
    farm-raised catfish. Also includes data on catfish
    imports.
    Earlier A 105.52

A 92.44/2:date
TROUT.

    Discontinued in 1983.

A 92.44/2-2:date   • Item 21-F-4 (EL)
CATFISH PRODUCTION. [Quarterly]

A 92.44/3:date   • Item 21-F-7 (MF)
TROUT PRODUCTION. [Annual]

A 92.45   • Item 21-F-6 (EL)
ALASKA FARM REPORTER. [Monthly]

    PURPOSE– To present information on milk
    production, potato stocks, egg production, hog
    and pig numbers, and U. S. prices received index.

    Co-Op Publication

A 92.46:date/nos.   • Item 21-F-1 (EL)
BROILER HATCHERY. [Weekly]

A 92.47:date   • Item 141 (EL)
COTTON GINNINGS. [Annual]

    Replaces C 3.20 and C 3.20/3.

A 92.48   • Item 122-A-8 (EL)
ALASKA AGRICULTURE STATISTICS. [Annual]

A 92.49   • Item 18-C-3 (MF)
SRB RESEARCH REPORT (series).

    Discontinued.

A 92.50:date   • Item 122-A-10 (MF)
AGRICULTURAL CHEMICAL USAGE, VEGETABLES,
SUMMARY. [Annual]

A 92.51   • Item 15-A-3 (E)
ELECTRONIC PRODUCTS.

A 92.52:nos.   • Item 15-A-4
FORMS.

A 92.53:nos.   • Item 15-B-10 to 55-(P)(EL)
CENSUS OF AGRICULTURE.

A 92.53/56   • Item 15-B-56
CENSUS OF AGRICULTURE. Vol. 1, Geographic Area
Series.

    Issued on CD-ROM

A 92.53/57:date/vol./nos. • Item 15-B-58 (P)(EL)
CENSUS OF AGRICULTURE, FINAL VOLUMES.
(Misc.)

A 92.54   • Item 15-B-57 (P)(EL)
CENSUS OF AGRICULTURE, VOL 2, SUBJECT SE-
RIES.

ECONOMIC RESEARCH SERVICE
(1961– 1978; 1981–   )

CREATION AND AUTHORITY

    The Economic Research Service was estab-
lished within the Department of Agriculture by
Memorandum 1446, Supplement 1, of the Secretary of Agriculture, dated April 3, 1961. The Service was consolidated along with certain other
agencies to form the Economics, Statistics, and
Cooperatives Service (A 105) by Secretary's
Memorandum 1927, Supplement 1, of December
19, 1977, effective January 2, 1978. The Economics and Statistics Service (A 105) was abolished on June 17, 1981 and certain functions
were returned to the reestablished Economic
Research Service (A 93).

INFORMATION

    Economic Research Service
    Department of Agriculture
    4145 N. 1800 M Street, NW
    Washington, D.C. 20236-5831
    (202) 694-5000
    Fax: (202) 694-5757
    http://www.ers.usda.gov

A 93.1:date
ANNUAL REPORTS.

A 93.2:CT   • Item 42-T
GENERAL PUBLICATIONS.

    Formerly distributed to Depository Libraries
under Item 42-H.

A 93.8:CT
HANDBOOKS, MANUALS, GUIDES.

A 93.9   • Item 21-C
FARM INCOME SITUATION. FIS 1–   1940–   [4
times a year]

    Analysis of situation and outlook for farm
income. Charts. Tables on estimates of cash receipts from farm marketing, by commodity groups;
Government payments; index numbers of cash
receipts and of physical volumes of farm
marketings; State estimates of cash receipts from
sales of crops and livestock quarterly estimates
of gross and net farm income, seasonally adjusted at annual rates; income of farm and nonfarm population compared. Annual supplement
shows Government payments to farmers, value
of home consumption for crops and livestock,
gross and net farm income by States; cash receipts and home consumption by commodities;
and cash receipts from farm marketings by States,
by major individual commodities.
    Issued in February, April, July, and November
    Earlier A 88.9/2
    Merged with other publications to form Agri-
cultural Outlook (A 93.10/2).

    Discontinued.

A 93.9/2`   • Item 21-A
DEMAND AND PRICE SITUATION. DPS 1–   1937–
[Quarterly]

    Analysis of agricultural and general economic
situation and outlook. Special articles. Tables on
economic factors affecting agriculture (production, employment, income, prices); retail sales of
food; manufacturing and retail inventories and
stock-sales ratios; indexes of industrial production of major industrial groups, supply and utilization of farm products; and prices received and
paid by farmers.
    Issued in February, May, August, and Novem-
ber.
    Earlier A 88.9
    Merged with other publications to form Agri-
cultural Outlook (A 93.10/2).
    ISSN 0501-9133

    Discontinued.

A 93.9/3   • Item 42-A
FARM COST SITUATION. 1–   1946–   [Annual]

    Analysis of situation and outlook for availabil-
ity and costs of farm labor, farm power, and machinery, feeds, livestock on feed or to be fed,
seeds, fertilizer, building materials, and pesticides;
land values and rentals, interest, taxes, and insurance, and costs on farm of different types.
    Issued in November
    Earlier A 77.14/2 and A 77.15

A 93.9/4   • Item 42-A (MF)
FARM REAL ESTATE MARKET DEVELOPMENTS. CD
1–   1942–   [Semiannual]

    Former title: Current Developments in Farm
Real Estate Market.
    Earlier A 77.13 and A 77.15
    See also A 105.19/2

    Discontinued.

A 93.9/5   • Item 42-A
FARM-MORTGAGE LENDING EXPERIENCE OF 19
LIFE INSURANCE COMPANIES, FEDERAL LAND
BANKS, AND FARMERS HOME ADMINISTRATION,
FML- (series). 1–   1961–   [Semiannual]

    PURPOSE:– To provide current information on
farm mortgage loans made by three farm mortgage made lenders. Compares mortgages owned
at beginning of the period, the mortgages acquired and repaid during the period, and those
owned at the end of the period. Other items are
also included, such as mortgages loan commitments and mortgages in process of foreclosure.
    For the period 1956-1960, published in the
ARS-43 series.

A 93.9/6   • Item 42-A (MF)
FARM REAL ESTATE TAXES, RECENT TRENDS AND
DEVELOPMENTS. RET 1–   1961–   [Annual]

    Gives the amount per acre and the amount
per $100 of full value levied on farm real estate,
by years and by States and geographic division.
Also includes total tables levied by years.
    Earlier A 77.15 and A 36.63

    Discontinued.

A 93.9/7
DEPOSITS OF COUNTY BANKS: INDEX NUMBERS
OF TOTAL, DEMAND, AND TIMES DEPOSITS,
SELECTED GROUPS OF STATES, SPECIFIED
PERIODS. [Irregular]

    Earlier A 77.14/3

A 93.9/8   • Item 42-D (EL)
AGRICULTURAL INCOME AND FINANCE, SITUATION
AND OUTLOOK REPORT. [Quarterly]

    Earlier title: Agricultural Finance Outlook.
    Earlier A 77.15
    See also A 105.19/3

A 93.9/9:date
FARM REAL ESTATE DEBT, RED (series).

A 93.9/10   • Item 18-A (MF)
AGRICULTURE FINANCIAL REVIEW. v. 1–   1938–
[Annual]

    PURPOSE:– To present research in agricul-
tural credit, taxation, farm insurance, and in other
fields relating to general financial conditions in
agriculture. Contains signed articles as well as
brief reports on current developments in the field
of agricultural finance, reviews of recent publications and summaries of research projects underway. Also included are a statistical appendix, list
of available publications and reports related to
agricultural finance, and a list of signed articles
for previous volumes.
    Main volume is issued in the Fall.
    Prior to May 1978 (v. 38) issue, published by
Economic Research Service (A 93.9/10).
    Earlier A 77.14
    Later A 105.35
–SUPPLEMENT

    Issued in mid-year to make available at
an earlier date certain statistical date which
would ordinarily be included in the annual
volumes.
    Later A 93.9/10-2

A 93.9/10-2:nos.   • Item 18-A (MF)
AGRICULTURAL FINANCE STATISTICS, AFS- (series).
1–   1973–   [Annual] (Agricultural Finance
Branch, Farm Production Economics Division)

    PURPOSE:– To provide reliable data pertain-
ing to, or related to, the financing of agriculture in
the United States.
    Formerly issued as an annual supplement of
the Agricultural Finance Review (A 93.9/10).

A 93.9/11
COST AND RETURNS. FCR 1–   1961–   [Annual]

    Each publication in this series covers a par-
ticular type of commercial farm (dairy farms, egg-
producing farms, wheat farms, etc.) for a particular State or area. Statistics cover size of farm,
land use, numbers of livestock, crop and livestock production, investment, cash receipts, cash
expenditures, net cash farm income, value of
perquisites, changes in inventories of livestock
and machinery and buildings, net farm income,
charge for capital, and return to operator and
family labor. Indexed numbers are included for 11
important summary Items. A map shows the location, which tables show the amount of land, labor,
and capital for each type of farm studied.
    Summary statistics are contained in Farm
Costs and Returns, Commercial Farms, by Type,
Size, and Location (Agriculture Information Bulletin 230, revised annually).

    The following reports are issued on a recur-
ring basis:

COMMERCIAL BROILER FARMS, GEORGIA.

COMMERCIAL CORN BELT FARMS. [Annual]

COMMERCIAL COTTON FARMS. [Annual]

COMMERCIAL DAIRY FARMS, NORTHEAST AND
    MIDWEST. [Annual]

COMMERCIAL EGG-PRODUCING FARMS, NEW
    JERSEY. [Annual]

COMMERCIAL TOBACCO FARMS, COASTAL PLAIN, NORTH CAROLINA. [Annual]

COMMERCIAL TOBACCO-LIVESTOCK FARMS, BLUEGRASS AREA, KENTUCKY AND PENNY-ROYAL GRASS AREA, KENTUCKY AND PENNY-ROYAL AREA, KENTUCKY-TENNESSEE. [Annual]

COMMERCIAL WHEAT FARMS, PLAINS AND PACIFIC NORTHWEST. [Annual]

MIGRATORY SHEEP RANCHES, UTAH-NEVADA. [Annual]

NORTHWEST CATTLE RANCHES. [Annual]

SOUTHWEST CATTLE RANCHES. [Annual]

WESTERN LIVESTOCK RANCHES. [Annual]

A 93.9/12 • Item 42-A
FARM MORTGAGE DEBT. FMD 1– 1963– [Annual]

PURPOSE:– To show the total amount of farm-mortgage debt outstanding and the amounts held by principal lender groups, nationally for a number of years and by States for the most recent year.
From 1956– 60, published as ARS-43 by the Agriculture Research Service.

Discontinued.

A 93.10 • Item 42-K
AGRICULTURAL OUTLOOK DIGEST. AOD 1– 1947– 1975. [Monthly]

A 2- to 4-page digest of current situation highlights and shortrun outlook for agricultural production, supplies, domestic and export demand, prices and income. Includes background on general economic situation and outlook.
Issued monthly, except December.
Merged with other publications to form Agricultural Outlook (A 93.10/2).

Discontinued.

A 93.10/2:nos • Item 42-M (EL)
AGRICULTURAL OUTLOOK. [11 times/yr.]

The Farm Income Situation (A 92.9), Demand and Price Situation (A 92.9/2), Marketing and Transportation Situation (A 92.14), and the Agricultural Outlook Digest (A 93.10) have been merged into the Agricultural Outlook Report.
ISSN 0099-1066
Later A 105.27

A 93.11 • Item 21-I (EL)
WHEAT OUTLOOK AND SITUATION REPORT. WS 1– 1936– [4 times a year]

Title varies.
ISSN 0364-2305
Earlier A 88.18/8
See also A 105.20/3

A 93.11/2 • Item 21-E (EL)
FEED OUTLOOK AND SITUATION REPORT. FDS 1– 1939– [Quarterly]

Former title: Feed Outlook and Situation.
First published under title: Feed Situation.
Earlier A 88.18/2
See also A 105.20/2
ISSN 0014-9578

A 93.11/2-2:date • Item 21-E (MF)
FEED, OUTLOOK AND SITUATION YEARBOOK. [Annual]

See A 93.11/2

A 93.11/2-3:date • Item 21-I (MF)
WHEAT SITUATION AND OUTLOOK YEARBOOK. [Annual]

See A 93.11

A 93.11/3:date • Item 21-P (EL)
RICE, SITUATION AND OUTLOOK REPORT. [Quarterly]

Earlier A 88.18/18
See also A 105.20/24

A 93.12:nos.
CONSUMER PURCHASES OF CITRUS AND OTHER JUICES, CPFJ (series).

Earlier A 88.12/4

A 93.12/2:date • Item 21-L
VEGETABLE TABLES AND SPECIALTIES SITUATION AND OUTLOOK REPORT [Semiannual]

Earlier title: Vegetable Situation and Outlook
ISSN 0042-3084
Earlier A 88.12/8
See also A 105.24

A 93.12/2-3:date • Item 21-L (MF)
VEGETABLE TABLES AND SPECIALTIES SITUATION AND OUTLOOK YEARBOOK. [Annual]

See A 93.12/3

A 93.12/3:date • Item 21-K (EL)
FRUIT AND TREE NUTS.

Title varies.
Earlier A 88.12/7
See also A 105.11/2
ISSN 0364-8648

A 93.12/3-2:date • Item 21-K
FRUIT, SITUATION AND OUTLOOK YEARBOOK. [Annual]

A 93.11/4 • Item 21-P (EL)
RICE YEARBOOK. (RCS-nos.) [Annual]

A 93.13:nos. • Item 21-B (MF)
DAIRY OUTLOOK AND SITUATION REPORT. DS 1– 1931– [5 times a year]

Analysis of dairy situation and outlook. Special articles. Charts. Tables on dairy situation at a glance, number of milk cows and heifers, milk production, and factors affecting milk production; output of dairy products, stocks, imports, and exports; commercial and total disappearance of fluid and manufactured dairy products; Federal milk marketing order program; USDA dairy support program; prices farmers receive for milk and cream; wholesale and retail prices of dairy products; world dairy information.
ISSN 0011-5703
Formerly issued 5 times a year.
Former title: Dairy Situation.
Earlier A 88.14/9
See also A 105.17/2
See 93.46/3

A 93.13/2:nos.
MILK DISTRIBUTORS, SALES AND COSTS. [Quarterly]

Earlier A 88.14/9

A 93.13/2-2:date • Item 21-B (MF)
DAIRY, SITUATION AND OUTLOOK YEARBOOK. [Annual]

See 93.13

A 93.14 • Item 21-G
MARKETING AND TRANSPORTATION SITUATION. MTS 1– 198. 1942– 1975. [Quarterly]

Analysis of situation and outlook for marketing and transportation of farm foods. Special articles on agricultural marketing. Charts. Tables on statistical summary of market information; market basket of farm foods: retail cost, farm value, marketing spread, and farmer's share of retail cost of 46 farm food products; marketing bill for farm foods by commodity groups, components of marketing bill: labor cost, transportation, corporate profits and other selected costs; labor cost per hour and per unit of product unit of product, profit ratios for marketing firms, prices of nonfarm inputs purchased by food marketing firms, percentage of income spent for food.
Issued in February, May, August, and November.
Earlier A 88.26/2
Merged with other publications to form Agricultural Outlook (A 93.10/2).

Discontinued

A 93.15 • Item 24-C
LIVESTOCK AND MEAT SITUATION. LMS 1– 1947– [6 times a year]

Combined with Poultry and Egg Outlook and Situation (A 93.20) to form Livestock and Poultry (A 93.46).
Earlier A 88.16/8
See also A 105.23/2
ISSN 0024-516X

Discontinued.

A 93.16 • Item 21-H
NATIONAL FOOD REVIEW. NFS 1– 1939– 1977. [Quarterly]

Earlier A 88.37
Later A 105.15
See also A 105.15

A 93.16/2:nos. • Item 42-P (MF)
AGRICULTURAL-FOOD POLICY REVIEW. AFPR 1–

Later A 105.50
Discontinued.

A 93.16/3:nos. • Item 21-H (EL)
NATIONAL FOOD REVIEW. NFR 1– 1978– [Quarterly]

Earlier A 105.15

A 93.17:date • Item 42-E
FOREIGN AGRICULTURAL TRADE OF UNITED STATES, STATISTICAL REPORT. [Monthly]

Earlier A 67.19

A 93.17/2:date • Item 42-E
FOREIGN AGRICULTURAL TRADE OF UNITED STATES, DIGEST. [Monthly]

Earlier A 67.19/8

A 93.17/3:date • Item 42-E
U.S. FOREIGN AGRICULTURAL TRADE STATISTICAL REPORT. [Annual]

(Foreign Demand and Competition Division, Statistics Program Area)
Supplement to the Monthly Foreign Agricultural Trade of the United States (A 93.17).
Report covers fiscal year.
Continues Foreign Agricultural Trade of the United States Statistical Report.
Earlier A 67.19/2
See also A 105.14/2

Discontinued.

A 93.17/4 • **Item 42-E**
FOREIGN AGRICULTURAL TRADE OF UNITED STATES, TRADE BY COUNTRIES. [2 times a year]

Report for fiscal year issued in April, for calendar year in September.
Tables give for export and imports: value of agricultural products, by country of destination (or origin); quantity and value of principal agricultural products, by countries.
Earlier A 67.19/5

A 93.17/5:date
FOREIGN AGRICULTURAL TRADE OF UNITED STATES, IMPORTS OF FRUITS AND VEGETABLES UNDER QUARANTINE BY COUNTRIES OF ORIGIN AND PORTS OF ENTRY, FISCAL YEAR.

Earlier A 67.19/7

A 93.17/6:date
FOREIGN AGRICULTURAL TRADE OF UNITED STATES, FISCAL YEAR.

Earlier A 67.19/3

A 93.17/7:date/nos. • **Item 42-E**
FATUS (Foreign Agricultural Trade of the United States).

Incorporates Foreign Agricultural Trade Digest of the United States (A 93.17/2), Foreign Agricultural Trade of the United States Statistical Reports (A 93.17) and Government Program Export Series.
Annual calendar and fiscal year export and import statistics are released in yearly supplements and classed separately: Trade by Countries (A 93.17/4); and Trade by Commodities (A 93.17/8).
ISSN 0046-4546
See also A 105.14

Discontinued.

A 93.17/7-2:date • **Item 42-E (MF)**
FOREIGN AGRICULTURAL TRADE OF THE UNITED STATES, FISCAL YEAR SUPPLEMENT. [Annual]

Discontinued.

A 93.17/7-3:date • **Item 42-E (MF)**
FOREIGN AGRICULTURE TRADE OF THE UNITED STATES, CALENDAR YEAR SUPPLEMENT. [Annual]

A 93.17/7-4:date • **Item 42-E (MF)**
FOREIGN AGRICULTURAL TRADE OF THE UNITED STATES, CALENDAR YEAR: SUPPLEMENTARY TABLES. [Annual]

Discontinued.

A 93.17/7-5:date • **Item 42-E (MF)**
U.S. AGRICULTURAL TRADE UPDATE. [Monthly]

A 93.17/8 • **Item 42-E**
FOREIGN AGRICULTURAL TRADE OF UNITED STATES, TRADE BY COMMODITIES. [2 times a year]

Report for fiscal year issued in January, for calendar year in June.
Tables give total exports and imports by commodities, with no breakdown by countries as is given in report listed below. Tables give quantity and value, by commodity, with two year comparisons.

A 93.18:nos.
PUBLICATIONS RECEIVED.

Earlier A 77.16/2

A 93.18/2:CT
BIBLIOGRAPHIES AND LISTS OF PUBLICATIONS.

A 93.18/3:date • **Item 42-T-1**
REPORTS FROM USDS's ECONOMIC RESEARCH SERVICE. [Quarterly]

Lists and annotates ERS reports in various categories and contains ordering forms.

Discontinued.

A 93.18/3-2:date
NEW REPORTS. [Weekly]

A 93.19 • **Item 21-O**
WOOL SITUATION. TWS 1– 1947– 1975. [4 times a year]

Analysis of situation and outlook for wool. Special articles. Charts. Tables on statistical summary; prices, number of stock sheep and lambs on farms and ranches; production of wool in specified countries, exports and imports; production of manmade fiber; estimated world production and consumption of wool; weekly rate of consumption of apparel and carpet wool on woolen and worsted systems; percentage distribution of apparel wool consumption; percentage distribution of fibers consumed for spinning of carpet and rug yarns; woolen and worsted systems; percentage distribution of fibers consumed for spinning of carpet and rug yarns; woolen and worsted fabric production; cuttings and percentage distribution of cuttings of clothing.
Issued in February, May, August, and October.
Earlier A 88.35
Combined with Cotton Situation (A 93.24) to form Cotton and Wool Situation (A 93.24/2).

A 93.20 • **Item 21-F**
POULTRY AND EGG SITUATION. PES 1– 1937– [5 times a year]

Combined with Livestock and Meat Outlook and Situation (A 93.15) to form Livestock and Poultry (A 93.46).
Earlier A 88.15/3
See also A 105.12/4
ISSN 0032-5708

A 93.21 • **Item 42-W (MF)**
ERS- (Series). 1– 1961– [Irregular]

Includes nonperiodic publications of the Economic Research Service not included in the Department-wide series. May include preliminary reports of agriculture research, less complete research projects than are reported in the Agricultural Economic Reports and the Marketing Research Reports; non-administrative agency guides and handbooks not of sufficient general interest to be included in the Agricultural Handbook series; reference lists; and reprints of major articles from periodicals.
Later A 105.13
Discontinued.

A 93.21/2 • **Item 76-G**
ERS- FOREIGN (series). 1– 1961– [Irregular]

Majority of the reports is devoted to a single country, usually covering the agricultural situation of agricultural trade of that particular country. Similar type of reports published by the Foreign Agricultural Service prior to the establishment of the Economic Research Service and the transfer of certain functions of the Foreign Agricultural Service to the new agency at the time of its establishment. The following four regional reports are issued as supplements to the World Agricultural Situation, which since 1964 has been published in the Foreign Agricultural Economic Report series.
Regional reports give a review of the past year and an outlook for the coming year. Released early in the calendar year. In July and August, short mid-year reviews of the situation in each of the regions are issued.

AFRICA AND WEST ASIA AGRICULTURAL SITUATION. [Annual]

MIDYEAR REVIEW.

REVIEW OF [year].

FAR EAST AND OCEANIA AGRICULTURAL SITUATION. [Annual]

MIDYEAR REVIEW.

REVIEW OF [year].

WESTERN HEMISPHERE AGRICULTURAL SITUATION. [Annual]

MIDYEAR REVIEW.

REVIEW OF [year].

EXPORT FACT SHEET AND IMPORT FACT SHEET. [Annual]

Summaries reprinted from monthly issues of Foreign Agricultural Trade of the United States.
Previously issued as two separate publications (A 93.17/7a:Ex 75 and A 93.17/7a:Im 7).

A 93.21/3:nos. • **Item 42-N (MF)**
AGERS (series). 1– [Irregular]

A 93.21/4:nos. • **Item 21-N-2 (MF)**
ESS- (series).

Earlier A 105.56
Discontinued.

A 93.22
[ADDRESSES]. [Irregular]

A 93.23 • **Item 21-D**
FATS AND OILS SITUATION. FOS 1– 310. 1937– 1983. [5 times a year]

Earlier A 88.32
See also A 105.28
Superseded by Oil Crops Outlook and Situation Report (A 93.23/2).
ISSN 0014-8865

See 93.23/2

A 93.23/2:nos. • **Item 21-D (EL)**
OIL CROPS OUTLOOK AND SITUATION REPORT. OCS 1– 1983– [Quarterly]

Continues Fats and Oils Situation (A 93.23).

A 93.23/2-2:date • **Item 21-D**
OIL CROPS, SITUATION AND OUTLOOK YEARBOOK. [Annual]

See 93.23/2

A 93.24 • **Item 21-M**
COTTON SITUATION, CS 1– 270. 1937– 1975. [5 times a year]
Analysis of cotton situation and outlook. Special articles. Charts. Tables on acreage, yield, production, and stocks; USDA price support programs; spot prices of specified growths of cotton; domestic use (including cotton used in textile items delivered to military forces); foreign trade; and prices and consumption of cotton linters.
Issued in January, March, May, August, and November.

Earlier A 88.11/8
Combined with Wool Situation (A 93.19) to form Cotton and Wool Situation (A 93.24/2).

A 93.24/2 • Item 21-M (EL)
COTTON AND WOOL SITUATION. CWS 1– 1975–
[Quarterly]

Supersedes Wool Situation (A 93.19) and Cotton Situation (A 93.24).

See also A 105.16
ISSN 0360-2184

A 93.24/2-2: • Item 21-M (MF)
COTTON AND WOOL, SITUATION AND OUTLOOK YEARBOOK. [Annual]

See 93.24/2

A 93.24/3 • Item 21-M (MF)
COTTON AND WOOL UPDATE.

Discontinued.

A 93.25:nos. • Item 24-D-1 (EL)
TOBACCO, SITUATION AND OUTLOOK REPORT. [2 times/yr.]
Earlier title: Tobacco Situation.
Earlier A 88.34/2
See also A 105.32
ISSN 0040-8344

A 93.25/2:date • Item 24-D-1 (MF)
TOBACCO, SITUATION AND OUTLOOK YEARBOOK, TS-1. [Annual]

See A 93.25

A 93.26:v.nos./nos. • Item 18
THE JOURNAL OF AGRICULTURAL ECONOMIC RESEARCH. [Quarterly]

Earlier title: Agricultural Economics Research.
Earlier A 88.27
Later A 105.21
ISSN 0002-1423
Discontinued.

A 93.27 • Item 42-B (MF)
FOREIGN AGRICULTURAL ECONOMIC REPORTS. 1–
1961– [Irregular]

See also A 105.22

WORLD AGRICULTURE SITUATION. [Annual]

PURPOSE:– To appraise the state of world agriculture for the year just ended and the outlook for the year to come. Covers the demand-supply situation by region and commodity and discusses important changes in prices and other factors affecting agriculture. Included are indices of total and per capita agricultural production by region and for the world, and trends for recent years.
Regional situation reports are also issued annually, and since 1964 have been published in the ERS-Foreign series.

Earlier A 93.29
Later A 93.29/2

A 93.28 • Item 42-C
AGRICULTURAL ECONOMIC REPORTS. 1–233. 1961–1972. [Irregular]

Later A 1.107

A 93.29:date
WORLD AGRICULTURAL SITUATION. 1962–1963. [Annual]

Earlier A 67.27
Later A 93.27

A 93.29/2:nos. • Item 78-A (MF)
WORLD AGRICULTURAL OUTLOOK AND SITUATION. WAS 1– 1971– [Quarterly]

Earlier part of the Foreign Agricultural Economic Reports (A 93.27)
ISSN 0084-1358

See also A 105.10/3
Discontinued.

A 93.29/2-2:date • Item 78-A (MF)
AGRICULTURAL SITUATION SUPPLEMENTS (various areas). [Irregular]

Superseded by Outlook and Situation Reports (A 93.29/2-3).

See also A 105.23/4

See A 93.29/2-3

A 93.29/2-3:nos. • Item 78-A (MF)
OUTLOOK AND SITUATION REPORTS (various areas). [Irregular]

Continues World Agricultural Situation Supplements (A 93.29/2-2).

A 93.29/2-4:date • Item 78-B (MF)
AGRICULTURAL LAND VALUES AND MARKETS, OUTLOOK AND SITUATION REPORT. [Annual]

PURPOSE:– To present farmland values in historical perspective, including farm sales and cropland rents. Compares current and past farmland values and discusses the outlook for the future.

Discontinued. Information included in Agricultural Resources and Environmental Indicators, Agricultural Handbooks and updated by by AREI Updates A 93.47/3.

A 93.29/2-5:date • Item 78-A (MF)
OUTLOOK AND SITUATION REPORTS, EAST ASIA. [Annual]

Earlier A 93.29/2-19

A 93.29/2-6:date • Item 78-A (MF)
MIDDLE EAST AND NORTH AFRICA, SITUATION AND OUTLOOK REPORT. [Annual]

Earlier title: Outlook and Situation Reports, Middle East and North Africa.
Earlier A 93.29/2-3

Ceased in 1994.

A 93.29/2-7:date • Item 78-A (MF) (EL)
NEWLY INDEPENDENT STATES AND THE BALTICS, SITUATION AND OUTLOOK SERIES. [Annual]

Earlier A 93.29/2-3
Formerly: Outlook and Situation Reports, USSR; Former USSR Outlook and Situation Reports.

A 93.29/2-8:date • Item 78-A (MF)
USSR, SITUATION AND OUTLOOK REPORT. [Annual]

Earlier title: Outlook and Situation Reports, USSR.
Earlier A 93.29/2-3
See A 93.29/2-19

A 93.29/2-9:date • Item 78-A (EL)
WESTERN EUROPE, SITUATION AND OUTLOOK REPORT. [Annual]

Earlier title: Outlook and Situation Report, Western Europe.

Earlier A 93.29/2-3

A 93.29/2-10:date • Item 78-A (MF)
EASTERN EUROPE, SITUATION AND OUTLOOK REPORT. [Annual]

Earlier title: Outlook and Situation Reports, Eastern Europe.

Earlier A 93.29/2-3
See A 93.29/2-9

A 93.29/2-11:date • Item 78-A (MF) (EL)
OUTLOOK AND SITUATION REPORTS, CHINA. [Annual]

Earlier A 93.29/2-3

A 93.29/2-12:date • Item 78-A (MF)
OUTLOOK AND SITUATION REPORTS, LATIN AMERICA. [Annual]

Earlier A 93.29/2-3
See A 93.29/2-18

A 93.29/2-13:date • Item 78-A (MF)
SUB-SAHARAN AFRICA, SITUATION AND OUTLOOK REPORT. [Annual]

Earlier title: Outlook and Situation Reports, Sub-Saharan Africa.
Earlier A 93.29/2-3

See A 1993.29/2-6

A 93.29/2-14:date • Item 78-A (MF)
CROPLAND USE AND SUPPLY, OUTLOOK AND SITUATION REPORT. [Annual]
Discontinued. Merged into Agricultural Resources, Input, Outlook and Situation A 93.47

A 93.29/2-15:date • Item 78-A (MF)
SOUTH ASIA OUTLOOK AND SITUATION REPORT. [Annual]

See A 93.29/2-19

A 93.29/2-16:date • Item 78-A
NORTH AMERICA AND OCEANIA OUTLOOK AND SITUATION REPORT. [Annual]

See A 93.29/2-18

A 93.29/2-17:nos.
OUTLOOK AND SITUATION, SUMMARY.

A 93.29/2-18: • Item 78-A (MF)
WESTERN HEMISPHERE, OUTLOOK AND SITUATION REPORT. [Annual]

Discontinued.

A 93.29/2-19:ltrs/nos. • Item 78-A (MF) (EL)
ASIA AND PACIFIC RIM, SITUATION AND OUTLOOK SERIES. [Annual]

A 93.29/2-20 • Item 78-A-2 (EL)
NAFTA, SITUATION AND OUTLOOK SERIES. [Annual]
Formerly: Western Hemisphere Situation and Outlook Series

A 93.29/2-21 • Item 78-A-3 (MF)
EUROPE UPDATE, AGRICULTURE AND TRADE REPORT. [Quarterly]

Discontinued.

A 93.29/3 • Item 11-F (EL)
WORLD AGRICULTURAL SUPPLY AND DEMAND ESTIMATES. 1– [Irregular]

PURPOSE:– To provide as rapidly as possible USDA's current assessments of developments on the commodity scene. The assessments are made by an interagency board of USDA experts. They are released in tabular form, with a brief commentary, after 3 p.m. on the day following the issuance of major crop production, grain stocks, or planting intentions reports by the Statistical Reporting Service.
Supply-demand reports present statistics, by crop, covering the balance of supply (production, stocks, imports) and demand (domestic use, exports, carryover) for the current balance for one season. Rough indications of the supply-demand balance for one season ahead also may be included. ERS Situation Reports for individual commodities contain fuller discussions of these estimates and their implications.
Earlier A 1.110
ISSN 0162-5586

A 93.30:date
U.S. AGRICULTURAL EXPORTS, FACT SHEET. [Annual]

Earlier A 67.32

A 93.30/2:date
U.S. AGRICULTURAL IMPORTS, FACT SHEETS.

   Earlier A 67.32/2

A 93.31:nos.   • **Item 21-J**
SUGAR SITUATION. SUS 1–   [Annual]

   Tables include world production of centrifugal cane and beet sugar; number of farms growing sugar beets and sugar-cane; centrifugal sugar; production in specified countries; acreage; production; wholesale prices; distribution, edible syrups, corn sweeteners, corn syrup, maple sugar and syrup, honey, molasses, industrial molasses. Textual summary.

   Earlier A 88.36
   Discontinued.

A 93.31/2   • **Item 24-R**
SUGAR AND SWEETENER SITUATION. SSS-1–
1975. [Quarterly]

   Superseded by Sugar and Sweetener Report (A 1.115).

A 93.31/3:v.nos.&nos.   • **Item 24-R (EL)**
SUGAR AND SWEETENER, OUTLOOK AND SITUATION. [3 times a year]

   See also A 105.53/2

A 93.31/3-2:date   • **Item 24-R (MF)**
SUGAR AND SWEETENER, SITUATION AND OUTLOOK YEARBOOK. [Annual]

   Earlier A 93.31/3
   See A 93.31/3

A 93.32:CT
INDICES OF AGRICULTURAL PRODUCTION IN [various] COUNTIES.

   Earlier A 67.36

A 93.33   • **Item 42-F**
FARM INDEX. v. 1–   1962–   [Monthly]

   Later A 105.27/2
   ISSN 0014-7982

A 93.33/2:v.nos.&nos.   • **Item 19**
FARMLINE. v. 1–   1980–   [Monthly]

   Earlier A 105.10/4
   Discontinued.

A 93.34:nos.   • **Item 42-J**
FOREIGN GOLD AND EXCHANGE RESERVES. 1962–
1970. [Semiannual]

   Presents an analysis of current international financial trends and the impact of such developments on gold and exchange holdings of foreign countries and international institutions for the most recent period. The U.S. balance of payments as it reflects recent trade and financial developments having a bearing on the overall payments position is discussed in general. New balance of payments developments which influence the level of gold and dollar holdings abroad are analyzed in connection with the report. Periodically special reports are written on a timely international trade for financial topic.
   Superseded by World Monetary Conditions in Relation to Agricultural Trade (A 93.34/2).

A 93.34/2:nos.   • **Item 42-J**
WORLD ECONOMIC CONDITIONS IN RELATION TO AGRICULTURAL TRADE. 1–   1971–   [Semiannual]

   The name has been changed from World Monetary Conditions in Relation to Agricultural Trade. Supersedes Foreign Gold and Exchange Reserves (A 93.34).

   Later A 105.22/2

A 93.35:v.nos.
NET MIGRATION OF THE POPULATION, BY AGE, SEX AND COLOR.

A 93.36:nos.   • **Item 42-R (MF)**
FERTILIZER SITUATION. FS-1–   [Annual]

   Gives outlook, inventories, use, import-export review, work situation, and supply and demand projections.

   Discontinued.

A 93.37:date   • **Item 42-C**
FDD [Foreign Development Division] REPORTS. 1– [Irregular]

A 93.37/2:nos.
ERS FIELD REPORTS.

A 93.38:nos.   • **Item 77-A-1**
FOREIGN ECONOMIC DEVELOPMENT REPORT. 1–

   [Irregular]

   Prepared in cooperation with the Agency for International Development. Each report includes an abstract and key words for that report.
   Earlier A 100.9

   Discontinued.

A 93.39:date   • **Item 21-N-2**
AGRICULTURE ECONOMICS REPORTS. [Annual]

   Earlier title: Research Abstracts.
   Earlier A 105.25/2

A 93.40:letters-nos.   • **Item 21-N-4**
FARMERS' NEWSLETTER. [Irregular]

   Earlier A 105.10/2
   Discontinued.

A 93.41:nos.   • **Item 24-G-2 (MF)**
RURAL DEVELOPMENT RESEARCH REPORTS. 1– [Irregular]

   See also A 105.40

A 93.41/2:nos.   • **Item 21-N-6 (EL)**
RURAL DEVELOPMENT PERSPECTIVES. RDP 1–
1978–   [Irregular]

   Earlier A 105.40/2

A 93.41/3   • **Item 21-N-8 (EL)**
RURAL CONDITIONS AND TRENDS. [3 times/yr.]

A 93.42:nos.   • **Item 24-C-1**
AQUACULTURE OUTLOOK AND SITUATION. AS 1–
1981–   [Semiannual]

   See also A 105.23/2-2
   Discontinued 1982.

A 93.43:date/nos.   • **Item 6-C (EL)**
OUTLOOK FOR U.S. AGRICULTURAL EXPORTS.

   Earlier title: Agricultural Exports.
   Published jointly with Foreign Agricultural Service.

   Title varies.
   Earlier A 1.80/2

A 93.44:nos.   • **Item 42-W-1 (MF) (EL)**
ERS STAFF REPORTS. 1–   [Irregular]

A 93.44/2:date   • **Item 42-W-1**
ABSTRACTS OF STAFF REPORTS. [3 times a year]

   Discontinued.

A 93.44/3:date   • **Item 42-10-1**
U.S. IMPORTS OF FRUITS AND VEGETABLES UNDER PLANT QUARANTINE REGULATIONS. [Annual]

   Earlier A 93.44
   Discontinued.

A 93.44/4:date   • **Item 42-W-1 (MF)**
COTTON GINNING CHARGES, HARVESTING PRACTICES, AND SELECTED MARKETING COSTS. [Annual]

   Earlier A 93.44

A 93.44/5   • **Item 42-W-2 (MF)**
ERS STAFF PAPER (numbered). [Irregular]

A 93.45:date   • **Item 42-F-1**
ECONOMIC INDICATORS OF THE FARM SECTOR. [5 times a year]

   Issued in the following reports:–

   Jan.   Production and Efficiency Statistics.
   June   Costs of Production.
   Aug.   Income and Balance Sheet Statistics.
   Oct.   State Income and Balance Sheet Statistics.
   Nov.   Farm Sector Review.

   Formerly published in Statistical Bulletins (series), (A 1.34).

   Discontinued.

A 93.45/2:date   • **Item 42-F-1**
ECONOMIC INDICATORS OF THE FARM SECTOR, COSTS OF PRODUCTION. [Annual]

   Earlier A 93.45

   Discontinued.

A 93.45/2-2:date   • **Item 42-F-1**
ECONOMIC INDICATORS OF THE FARM SECTOR, COST OF PRODUCTION: LIVESTOCK AND DAIRY. [Annual]

   Discontinued.

A 93.45/3:date   • **Item 42-F-1**
ECONOMIC INDICATORS OF THE FARM SECTOR, NATIONAL FINANCIAL SUMMARY. [Annual]

   Discontinued.

A 93.45/4:date   • **Item 42-F-1**
ECONOMIC INDICATORS OF THE FARM SECTOR, FARM SECTOR REVIEW. [Annual]

A 93.45/5:date   • **Item 42-F-1 (MF)**
ECONOMIC INDICATORS OF THE FARM SECTOR, PRODUCTION AND EFFICIENCY STATISTICS. [Annual]

   Discontinued.

A 93.45/6   • **Item 42-F-1**
ECONOMIC INDICATORS OF THE FARM SECTOR, STATE FINANCIAL SUMMARY. [Annual]

A 93.45/7:date   • **Item 42-F-2 (MF)**
FARM BUSINESS ECONOMICS REPORT. [Annual]

A 93.46:date   • **Item 24-C (MF)**
LIVESTOCK AND POULTRY. [Quarterly]

   Supersedes Livestock and Meat Outlook and Situation (A 93.15) and Poultry and Egg Outlook and Situation (A 93.20).

   See A 93.46/3

A 93.46/2:date   • **Item 24-C (MF)**
LIVESTOCK AND POULTRY UPDATE. [Monthly]

   See A 93.46/3

A 93.46/3   • **Item 24-C (EL)**
LIVESTOCK, DAIRY AND POULTRY SITUATION AND OUTLOOK.

A 93.46/3-2   • **Item 24-C (MF)**
POULTRY OUTLOOK, SUPPLEMENT TO LIVESTOCK, DAIRY, AND POULTRY SITUATION AND OUTLOOK.

   See A 93.46/3

A 93.46/3-3   • **Item 24-C (MF)**
DAIRY OUTLOOK, SUPPLEMENT TO LIVESTOCK, DAIRY, AND POULTRY SITUATION AND OUTLOOK.

   See A 93.46/3

A 93.46/3-4   • Item 24-C (MF)
HOG OUTLOOK, SUPPLEMENT TO LIVESTOCK, DAIRY, AND POULTRY SITUATION AND OUTLOOK.

See A 93.46/3

A 93.46/3-5   • Item 24-C-5
CATTLE AND SHEEP OUTLOOK, SUPPLEMENT TO LIVESTOCK, DAIRY, AND POULTRY SITUATION AND OUTLOOK.

A 93.46/3-6   • Item 24-C-7 (EL)
AQUACULTURE OUTLOOK, SUPPLEMENT TO LIVESTOCK, DAIRY, AND POULTRY SITUATION AND OUTLOOK. [Semiannual]

A 93.47:date/nos.   • Item 24-C-3 (MF)
AGRICULTURAL RESOURCES, INPUTS, SITUATION AND OUTLOOK REPORT.

Earlier title: Inputs Outlook and Situation Report.
Issues assess supply, demand, and price prospects for pesticides, farm energy, farm machinery, and fertilizer.

Discontinued.

A 93.47/2:date   • Item 24-C-4 (MF)
AGRICULTURAL RESOURCES: CROPLAND, WATER CONSERVATION SITUATION AND OUTLOOK REPORT. [Annual]

Earlier title: Agricultural Resources, Cropland, Water, and Conservation.

See A 93.47

A 93.47/3   • Item 24-C (EL)
AREI UPDATES.

A 93.48:date   • Item 78-A-1
WORLD FOOD NEEDS AND AVAILABILITIES. [Annual]

Prepared by an Interagency Food Aid Analysis Working Group established by the President in 1984 to assess the food needs of the developing world.

Discontinued.

A 93.49:date   • Item 42-T-2 (MF)
ARED NEWSLETTER. [Quarterly]

ARED = Agricultural Rural Economics Division
PURPOSE:– To summarize activities of the various branches and sections of the Agricultural and Rural Economics Division.

A 93.50:nos.
SUMMARY OF REPORT.

A 93.51:date   • Item 42-T-3 (MF)
U.S. RICE DISTRIBUTION PATTERNS. [Annual]

The sole source of detailed information on U.S. domestic rice distribution patterns for the marketing year and assesses proportional market shares and trends. Provides information on rice distribution by states through narrative and tables.

Earlier A 1.34

Discontinued.

A 93.52:   • Item 42-T-5 (MF)
FOOD SPENDING IN AMERICAN HOUSEHOLDS. [Annual]

Narrative and tables provides such information as average weekly total food expenditures per person for food consumed at home and for food consumed away from home. Tabulates 133 food categories by 10 householdsocioeconomic characteristics.

Earlier A 1.34

Discontinued.

A 93.53:   • Item 42-T-4 (MF)
COSTS OF PRODUCING MILK. [Annual]

Contains data in the form of narrative, tables, and graphson costs of producing milk in various regions of the U.S.

Earlier A 1.107
Discontinued.

A 93.54   • Item 42-B
LIST OF PUBLICATIONS (miscellaneous).

A 93.55   • Item 42-D-1 (EL)
AQUACULTURE SITUATION AND OUTLOOK REPORT.

A 93.56   • Item 24-C-6 (MF)
INDUSTRIAL USES OF AGRICULTURAL MATERIALS, SITUATION AND OUTLOOK REPORT.

Discontinued July 1977.

A 93.58   • Item 42-T-6 (MF)
POTATO FACTS. [Semiannual]

Discontinued.

A 93.59   • Item 42-T-7 (MF)
ERS-NASS INFORMATION DIRECTORY. [Semiannual]

A 93.60:nos.   • Item 42-T-8 (EL)
FOOD ASSISTANCE AND NUTRITION RESEARCH REPORT. [Series]

A 93.61:date   • Item 42-T-9 (MF) (EL)
FOOD ASSISTANCE AND NUTRITION RESEARCH PROGRAM.

COOPERATIVE STATE RESEARCH, EDUCATION AND EXTENSION SERVICE (1961– 1978; 1981–   )

CREATION AND AUTHORITY

The Cooperative State Experiment Station Service was established within the Department of Agriculture by Secretary's Memorandum no. 1462, Supplement 1, dated August 30, 1961. The Name was subsequently changed to Cooperative State Research Service. The Service was consolidated along with certain other agencies to form the Science and Education Administration (A 106) by Secretary's Memorandum 1927, Supplement 1, dated December 19, 1977, effective January 28, 1978. In 1981, the Science and Education Administration was abolished and functions returned to the reestablished Cooperative State Research Service; changed to present name in 1995.

INFORMATION

Office of the Administrator
Cooperative State Research, Education and Extension Service
Department of Agriculture
305 Administration Bldg.
1400 Independence Ave., SW
Washington, D.C. 20250
(202) 720-4423
Fax: (202) 720-8987
http://www.reeusda.gov

A 94.1:date
ANNUAL REPORTS.

A 94.2:CT   • Item 40-A-2
GENERAL PUBLICATIONS.

A 94.2:F 76/date   • Item 40-A-2
FORESTRY RESEARCH PROGRESS IN (year) McINTIRE-STENNIS COOPERATIVE FORESTRY RESEARCH PROGRAM. 1965– [Annual]

PURPOSE:– To provide information essential in identifying future research directions. The years's projects are subdivided by subject matter, and include lists of publication arising from each project.

A 94.6:CT   • Item 40-A-10
RULES, REGULATIONS, INSTRUCTIONS.

A 94.8:CT   • Item 40-A-3
HANDBOOKS, MANUALS, GUIDES. [Irregular]

A 94.9:CT
ADDRESSES.

A 94.10   • Item 40-A-4
CSRS (series). [Irregular]

Supersedes CSESS (series).
FUNDS FOR RESEARCH AT STATE AGRICULTURE EXPERIMENT STATIONS. [Annual]

Contains statistical tables on organization and personnel of the experiment stations, publications issued, federal funds available to experiment stations, obligations and appropriations under the Hatch Act., Regional Research Fund, McIntire-Stennis Act, Experiment Station Facilities Act, grants and contracts. Also contains a list of Agricultural Experiment Stations in the United States.
Releases for data prior to 1961 were contained in the ARS 23 (series) of the Agriculture Research Service.

Discontinued.

A 94.11   • Item 40-A-1
AGRICULTURAL SCIENCE REVIEW. v.1– 1 1, no. 2. 1963– 1973. [Quarterly]
PURPOSE:– To facilitate planning and coordination of information of agricultural research by publishing critical, comprehensive reviews of published research, research in progress, and trends in research. Primary research reports are not included.

– INDEXES.

Vols. 1– 5, 1963– 1967 in v. 5, no. 4.

Discontinued.

A 94.12:nos.
EXPERIMENT STATION LETTERS. 1949–   [Weekly]

PURPOSE:– To provide informal communication from the CSRS Administrator to Directors of State Research in Agriculture and Forestry: Deans of agricultural colleges, Directors of State Agricultural Experiment Stations and of forestry schools, and other research scientists upon request. Contents include administrative Items, status of current legislation, research highlights, and other announcements of interest.

A 94.13:nos.
CSRS RESEARCH INFORMATION LETTER. [Monthly]

A 94.14:date   • Item 40-A-5 (MF)
INVENTORY OF AGRICULTURAL RESEARCH. [Annual]

Consists of statistical tables on research conducted by USDA, State Experiment Stations, Forestry Schools, etc.

A 94.15:date
GENETIC BASES FOR RESISTANCE TO AVIAN DIS-
EASES, NORTHEASTERN STATES REGIONAL
PROJECT. [Annual]

A 94.16:   • **Item 40-A-6 (MF)**
PROGRAM SOLICITATION, SMALL BUSINESS IN-
NOVATION RESEARCH PROGRAM. [Annual]

A solicitation from the Agriculture Department
of science-based small business firms to submit
research proposals under the Small Business Innovation Research Program.

A 94.17:date   • **Item 40-A-6**
THE DIRECTORY OF SMALL-SCALE AGRICULTURE.
[Annual]

Discontinued.

A 94.18:date/nos.   • **Item 40-A-6 (P) (EL)**
NRI RESEARCH HIGHLIGHTS.

A 94.18/2   • **Item 40-A-6 (EL)**
NRI ANNUAL REPORT.

A 94.19:date   • **Item 40-A-7 (MF)**
NATIONAL SARE/ACE REPORT TO CONGRESS.
[Annual]

A 94.20   • **Item 40-A-8 (EL)**
CSREES - UPDATE.

A 94.21   • **Item 40-A-8 (EL)**
CONNEX NEWSLETTER.

A 94.22   • **Item 40-A-8 (E)**
ELECTRONIC PRODUCTS.

A 94.23:v.nos/nos.   • **Item 40-A-9 (EL)**
SMALL FARM DIGEST.

A 94.24   • **Item 40-A-11 (EL)**
NATIONAL RESEARCH INITIATIVE COMPETITIVE
GRANTS PROGRAM. [Annual]

INTERNATIONAL AGRICULTURAL
DEVELOPMENT SERVICE
(1961–1969)

CREATION AND AUTHORITY

The International Agricultural Development
Service was established by Secretary's Memorandum of July 12, 1963. Secretary's Memorandum of March 28, 1969 transferred its functions
and delegations of authority to the Foreign Agricultural Service (A 67).

A 95.1   • **Item 92-A**
YEAR OF PROGRESS, ANNUAL SUMMARY. 1965–
[Annual]

Discontinued.

A 95.2:CT
GENERAL PUBLICATIONS.

A 95.9:nos.
INTERNATIONAL AGRICULTURAL DEVELOPMENT,
MONTHLY NEWSLETTER TO COOPERATORS IN
AGRICULTURAL TECHNICAL ASSISTANCE AND
TRAINING PROGRAMS AROUND THE WORLD.

A 95.10
IADS-S- [Survey] (series). 1–   [Irregular]

Reports of surveys made on agriculture in
foreign countries, each report being for a separate country.

A 95.10/2
IADS-C– [Consultants] (series) [Irregular]

Reports of short term investigations made on
agricultural development in foreign countries.

A 95.10/3:nos.
IADS-T- (series).

A 95.11
ADDRESSES. [Irregular]

AGRICULTURAL DEVELOPMENT, IADS NEWS
DIGEST. 1968–   [Monthly]

Four-page news summary of Items on the
activities of the International Agricultural Development Service and general news of international
agricultural development.

PACKERS AND STOCKYARDS
ADMINISTRATION
(1967–1978)

CREATION AND AUTHORITY

The Packers and Stockyards Administration
was established within the Department of Agriculture by Secretary's Memorandum 1613, supplement 1, effect May 8, 1967. The Agency administers the Packers and Stockyards Act of 1921 (42
Stat. 159; 7 U.S.C. 181 et seq.), as amended. The
Administration was consolidated into the Agricultural Marketing Service (A 88) by Secretary's
Memorandum 1927 of January 15, 1978.

A 96.1:date   • **Item 96-A-2**
ANNUAL REPORT.

A 96.2:CT   • **Item 96-A-3**
GENERAL PUBLICATIONS.

A 96.5:CT   • **Item 96-A-1**
LAWS.

Discontinued.

A 96.9
PACKERS AND STOCKYARDS RESUME. v. 1–
1963–   [Monthly]

Summary of administrative and judicial proceedings on formal complaints and other activities under the Packers and Stockyards Act, 1921,
as amended. In addition to the summaries of proceedings in progress, those initiated and completed, and those pending, also contains amendments to the regulations and policy statements
as issued.
The Packers & Stockyards Act is a Federal
statute which safeguards free and competitive
marketing of livestock, poultry and meat by regulating business practices of those engaged in
interstate livestock and poultry marketing, meat
packing and the merchandising of these commodities.
Supersedes P & S Docket.
Prior to v. 4, no. 25, May 19, 1967, published
by the Packers and Stockyards Division, Consumer and Marketing Service (A 88.16/5-2).

A 96.10:nos.   • **Item 96-A-2**
RESEARCH REPORTS (nos.) [Irregular]

Earlier title: P&SA (series).

Discontinued.

A 96.11:nos.   • **Item 96-A-2**
SCALES AND WEIGHING MEMORANDUMS.

RURAL COMMUNITY
DEVELOPMENT SERVICE
(1968–1970)

CREATION AND AUTHORITY

The Rural Community Development Service
was established within the Department of Agriculture in 1968. The Service was abolished February
2, 1970 by Secretary's Memorandum 1679.

A 97.1:date
ANNUAL REPORT.

A 97.2:CT   • **Item 114-A**
GENERAL PUBLICATIONS.

Discontinued.

FOOD AND NUTRITION SERVICE
(1969–   )

CREATION AND AUTHORITY

The Food and Nutrition Service was established within the Department of Agriculture by the Secretary's Memorandum 1659, Supplement 1, dated August 8, 1969.

INFORMATION

Food and Nutrition Service
Department of Agriculture
Park Office Center
3101 Park Center Drive
Alexandria, Virginia 22302
(703) 305-2062
Fax: (703)305-2908
http://www.fns.usda.gov/fns

A 98.1
ANNUAL REPORT.

A 98.2:CT • Item 74-A-1
GENERAL PUBLICATIONS.

A 98.8:CT • Item 74-A-4
HANDBOOKS, MANUALS, GUIDES. [Irregular]

A 98.8/2:nos. • Item 74-A-4
FNS (FS) HANDBOOKS. 1–   [Irregular]

A 98.9:nos. • Item 74-A-2 (MF)
FNS- (series). 1–   1969–   [Irregular]

PURPOSE:– To provide educational and informational materials for participants in USDA's family feeding programs (Food Stamps and Commodity Distribution) and child nutrition programs (School Lunch, breakfast and non-school food service activities), information and guidelines for State and local public and private agencies through which Food and Nutrition Service programs are administered.
Some publications previously published in the C&MS series (A 88.40/2).

ANNUAL STATISTICAL REVIEW, FOOD AND NUTRITION PROGRAMS, FISCAL YEAR (date).

A 98.10:date
TYPE A TOPICS, NATIONAL SCHOOL LUNCH PROGRAM. 1966– 1977. [Monthly, September-May]

PURPOSE:– A four-page monthly newsletter issued during the school year and intended as a helpful and educational tool to provide guidance for school lunch managers. A different theme is used each school year.
Subtitles varies.
Earlier A 88.50, A 77.202:Sh 3/13.

A 98.11:v.nos.&nos. • Item 74-A-3
FOOD AND NUTRITION. v. 1, no.1–   June 1971– [Quarterly]

PURPOSE:– To report on the Federal assistance programs administered by the U.S. Department of Agriculture's Food and Nutrition Service. It shows their impact on people, the activities of public and private agencies in helping those in need of food assistance, and outstanding work of individuals or groups of volunteers in furthering the drive to eliminate malnutrition in the United States. Programs include the food stamp and direct food assistance for needy families, and the school lunch, school breakfast, non-school food service and related child nutrition programs.

Free distribution is limited to cooperating State and local agencies, professional groups working with school programs of low-income families, persons who can further disseminate food and nutrition information, including the general press, and libraries.
ISSN 0046-4384

Discontinued.

A 98.11/3:nos.
FOOD AND NUTRITION, NEWSLETTER OF THE FOOD AND NUTRITION SERVICE. [Irregular]

A 98.12:date
REACHING PEOPLE. 1972–   [Bimonthly]

PURPOSE:– To aid State agencies in developing their outreach program as provided in the Food Stamp Act of 1964 as amended in 1971. Reports on activities in the various States.

A 98.14:date
WICommunique, ISSUES OF THE SPECIAL SUPPLEMENTAL FOOD PROGRAM FOR WOMEN, INFANTS, AND CHILDREN. [Quarterly]

A 98.14/2:date • Item 74-A-5 (MF)
NATIONAL ADVISORY COUNCIL ON MATERNAL, INFANT AND FETAL NUTRITION: BIENNIAL REPORT.

Summarizes activities of the Council in its ongoing study of the Special Supplemental Food Program for Women, Infants, and Children related programs to determine what areas of such programs need improvement.

A 98.15:date • Item 74-A-1
DIRECTORY OF COOPERATING AGENCIES. [Annual]

Discontinued.

A 98.16:CT • Item 74-A-6
POSTERS. [Irregular]

A 98.17:date • Item 74-A-5 (MF)
STUDY OF WIC PARTICIPANT AND PROGRAM CHARACTERISTICS. [Biennial]

A 98.18:CT • Item 74-A-1
REGULATIONS, RULES, AND INSTRUCTIONS.

A 98.19:v.nos./nos. • Item 74-A-7
COMMODITY FOODS. [Irregular]

A 98.19/2 • Item 74-A-8 (E)
COST OF FOOD AT HOME ESTIMATED FOR FOOD PLANS AT FOUR COST LEVELS. [Monthly]

A 98.20 • Item 74-A-9 (EL)
FAMILY ECONOMICS AND NUTRITION REVIEW. [Quarterly]

A 98.21 • Item 74-A-10 (EL)
CHARACTERISTICS OF FOOD STAMP HOUSEHOLDS. [Annual]

A 98.21/2 • Item 74-A-11 (EL)
CHARACTERISTICS OF FOOD STAMP HOUSEHOLDS ADVANCE REPORT. [Annual]

EXPORT MARKETING SERVICE
(1969– 1974)

CREATION AND AUTHORITY

The Export Marketing Service was established within the Department of Agriculture on March 28, 1969, by the Secretary of Agriculture under authority of revised, statutes (5 U.S.C. 301), and Reorganization Plan 2 of 1953. Merged with Foreign Agricultural Service (A 67) by the Secretary's Memorandum of December 7, 1973, effective February 3, 1974.

A 99.1:date
ANNUAL REPORT.

A 99.2:CT
GENERAL PUBLICATIONS.

A 99.6:CT
REGULATIONS, RULES, AND INSTRUCTIONS.

A 99.9:date
ORDERLY LIQUIDATION OF STOCKS OF AGRICULTURAL COMMODITIES HELD BY THE COMMODITY CREDIT CORPORATION AND EXPANSION OF MARKETS FOR SURPLUS AGRICULTURAL COMMODITIES. [Annual]

Annual report submitted by the Secretary of Agriculture in response to section 201 (b) of Public Law 540, 84th Congress.
Part 1 gives quantities of surplus commodities on hand, sales and disposition methods used, and quantities of CCC commodities moved into consumption channels. Part 1 gives the methods of disposition to be utilized and the estimated quantities that can be sold or disposed of during the succeeding twelve months.
Earlier A 1.102

FOREIGN ECONOMIC DEVELOPMENT SERVICE (1969–1972)

CREATION AND AUTHORITY

The Foreign Economic Development Service was established within the Department of Agriculture by the Secretary of Agriculture, effective December 1, 1969. It was abolished by order of the Secretary on February 6, 1972 and functions and authorities transferred to the Economic Research Service (A 93).

A 100.1:date
ANNUAL REPORT.

A 100.1/2:date
FOREIGN ECONOMIC DEVELOPMENT SERVICE ANNUAL SUMMARY. 1969–   [Annual]

PURPOSE:– To summarize the USDA's international assistance efforts in the areas of development strategy and policy, technical assistance and research, nutrition improvement, and foreign training.
Prepared in cooperation with Agency for International Development.

A 100.2:CT
GENERAL PUBLICATIONS.

A 100.9:nos.   • Item 77-A-1
FOREIGN ECONOMIC DEVELOPMENT REPORTS (numbered). 1–   [Irregular]

Later A 93.38
A 100.10:nos.   • Item 77-A-2
FEDS STAFF PAPERS. 1–   [Irregular]

Discontinued.

ANIMAL AND PLANT HEALTH INSPECTION SERVICE (1972–   )

CREATION AND AUTHORITY

The Animal and Plant Health Service was established within the Department of Agriculture by Secretary Memorandum 1744, Supplement 1, October 29, 1971. Functions of the Animal Health Division (A 77.200) and the Plant Protection Division (A 77.300) of the Agricultural Research Service were transferred to the newly established agency. The name was changed to Animal and Plant Health Inspection Service in April 1972.

INFORMATION

Legislative and Public Affairs
Animal and Plant Health Inspection Service
Department of Agriculture
1147 South Agriculture Bldg.
1400 Independence Ave. SW
Washington, D.C. 20250
(202) 720-2511
Fax: (202) 720-3982
http://www.aphis.usda.gov

A 101.1:date
ANNUAL REPORT.

A 101.2:CT   • Item 30-A-5
GENERAL PUBLICATIONS.

Earlier A 77.202 and A 77.302

A 101.2:D 63/2   • Item 30-A-5
DIRECTORY OF ANIMAL DISEASE DIAGNOSTIC LABORATORIES, 1975. 1976

(Diagnostic Services, National Animal Disease Laboratory, Ames, Iowa)
The information is provided as a guide to where various types of laboratory diagnostic tests are available and as an overview of what types of procedures are being performed at any given laboratory. Included in this Directory is information on laboratories performing diagnostic tests for diseases of domestic and wild animals as well as diseases of animals that also affect man.

A 101.2/10:date   • Item 30-A-13 (MF)
VETERINARY BIOLOGICAL PRODUCTS, LICENSEES AND PERMITTEES. [Semiannual]

Lists all licensed establishments, licensees, and permittees with their subsidiaries and divisions, as well as the biological products they are authorized to produce or import.
Earlier A 101.2

A 101.6:CT   • Item 107-B
REGULATIONS, RULES, AND INSTRUCTIONS.

A 101.6:C 42   • Item 107-B
LIST OF CHEMICAL COMPOUNDS AUTHORIZED FOR USE UNDER USDA POULTRY, MEAT, RABBIT AND EGG PRODUCTS INSPECTION PROGRAMS. [Irregular]

Later A 103.13

A 101.6/2:date   • Item 30-A-4
MEAT AND POULTRY INSPECTION REGULATIONS. [Irregular]

(Includes basic manual plus supplementary material for an indefinite period)
Formerly published by Agricultural Marketing Service (A 88.6/4:M 46).
Later published by Food Safety and Quality Service (A 103.6/4).

Discontinued.

A 101.6/2-2:date   • Item 32-A-1
ISSUANCES OF MEAT AND POULTRY INSPECTION PROGRAM. [Monthly] (Meat and Poultry Program [Issuance Coordination Staff, Technical Services])

Prior to January 1975 issued as APHIS Meat and Poultry Inspection Program, Program Issuances for the Period (date).
Formerly issued biweekly.
Formerly distributed to depository libraries under Item No. 30-A-4.
Later A 103.9/2
ISSN 0364-1368

Discontinued.

A 101.6/3:date   • Item 21-S (MF)
FEDERAL MEAT AND POULTRY INSPECTION, STATISTICAL SUMMARY FOR (year). [Annual]

PURPOSE:– To present a statistical summary of the activities conducted by the Meat and Poultry Inspection Program of the Animal and Plant Health Inspection Service.
Formerly published by the Agricultural Marketing Service, (A 88.17/7).

Discontinued.

A 101.6/4:date   • Item 32-A-2
ACCEPTED MEAT AND POULTRY EQUIPMENT. (MPI-2)

Earlier A 101.2:Eq 5
Later A 103.6/3

A 101.8:CT   • Item 30-A-3
HANDBOOKS, MANUALS, GUIDES.

A 101.8:M 46/2   • Item 30-A-3
MEAT AND POULTRY INSPECTION MANUAL AND COMPILATION OF MEAT AND POULTRY INSPECTION ISSUANCES. [Irregular] (Includes basic manual plus monthly changes for an indefinite period) (Meat and Poultry Inspection Program)

An official publication of procedural guidelines and instructions to aid all MPI employees in enforcing laws and regulations related to Federal meat and poultry inspection.
Absorbed Compilation of Meat and Poultry Inspection Issuances (A 110.9).
Later A 103.8/3

A 101.9:v.nos.&nos.
COOPERATIVE ECONOMIC INSECT REPORT. v. 1–1951–   [Weekly]

(Economic Insect Survey and Detection Staff, Plant Protection and Quarantine Programs)
Condensation of reports received from cooperating State, Federal and industrial entomologists and other agricultural workers. Includes in addition to the report, a 30-day Weather Bureau outlook and review of the weather for the week.
Volume index issued separately.
Earlier A 77.324

A 101.9/2:v.nos&nos.
COOPERATIVE PLANT PEST REPORT. [Weekly]

Continues Cooperative Economic Insect Report (A 101.9).
ISSN 0363-0889

A 101.10:nos.   • Item 30-A-1
APHS (series). [Irregular]

A 101.10/2:nos.   • Item 30-A-1 (MF)
APHIS- (series). [Irregular]

Supersedes APHS- (series) (A 101.10).

A 101.10/2:82-5   • Item 30-A-1
LIST OF INTERCEPTED PLANT PESTS. [Annual] (Plant Protection and Quarantine Programs)

PURPOSE:– To summarize the records of plant pests found in, on, or with plants, plant products, baggage, and means of conveyance (1) imported into or entering the United States and its possessions, (2) offered for entry but refused, (3) held in quarters or stores of planes or ships, (4) offered for entry for immediate transportation and exportation in bond, (5) in domestic shipments to the mainland from the States of Alaska and Hawaii, and the offshore possessions, including the American Virgin Islands, Guam, and Puerto Rico, or (6) in preclearance inspection at Nassau in the Bahamas.
The pests listed include insects, snails, fungi, bacteria, nematodes, and viruses of known or potential plant quarantine significance to the United States. Some common organisms are included if such limited distribution in the United States is worthy of mention.
Presented in tabular form, gives pest and host; country of origin; number of interceptions in consumption, nonentry, propagation; State in which pests were collected.
ISSN 0092-6825
Earlier A 77.15:82-6

A 101.10/3:CT
APHIS FACTS.

A 101.11:CT   • Item 30-A-6
PLANT QUARANTINE IMPORT REQUIREMENTS OF [various countries]. [Irregular]

Each report is prepared as a guide to plant quarantine import requirements for nurserymen, plant quarantine officials, and others concerned with plant exports to a particular country from the U.S., its possessions, or Puerto Rico.

Official Use Only.

A 101.12:date
ANIMAL MORBIDITY REPORT. [Monthly] (Animal Health Diagnostic Laboratories, Veterinary Services)

Issued by the Agricultural Research Service (A 77.229) prior to July 1971 issue.
ISSN 0091-0872

A 101.12/2:date
ANIMAL MORBIDITY REPORT. [Annual Summaries] (Veterinary Services Diagnostic Laboratory, Veterinary Services)

Gives number of infected herds or flocks reported, by States and diseases.
Separate reports issued for calendar and fiscal years.
Issued by the Agricultural Research Service (A 77.299/2) prior to 1972.

A 101.13:date • **Item 30-A-9**
DIRECTORY OF ANIMAL DISEASE DIAGNOSTIC LABORATORIES. [Annual]

Discontinued.

A 101.14:date
VETERINARY BIOLOGICS NOTICES. 1– 1965– [Irregular]

Earlier A 77.226/3

A 101.15:date • **Item 32-A**
MEAT AND POULTRY INSPECTION DIRECTORY. 1954– [Bimonthly]

Title varies: Working Reference of Livestock Regulatory Establishments, Circuits and Officials; – 1976, Directory of Meat and Poultry Inspection Establishments; 1977, APHIS Program Service Directory; July 1977– Meat and Poultry Inspection Directory.
Earlier A 88.16/20
Later A 103.9

A 101.17:date • **Item 30-A-10 (MF)**
FOREIGN ANIMAL DISEASES REPORT. 1972– [Quarterly] (Emergency Programs, Veterinary Services)

PURPOSE:– To provide information pertaining to animal disease situations on a national and international basis; to keep livestock producers and dealers in livestock abreast of import and export restrictions, quarantines and changes in regulations; and provide a forum for the exchange of scientific information in entomology, veterinary medicine, and other disciplines interested in animal and plant health.
ISSN 0091-8199

Ceased in 1995.

A 101.18:date • **Item 30-A-12 (MF)**
COOPERATIVE STATE-FEDERAL BOVINE TUBERCULOSIS ERADICATION PROGRAM, STATISTICAL TABLES. [Annual]

Report covers fiscal year.

Discontinued.

A 101.18/2:date • **Item 30-A-12 (MF)**
COOPERATIVE STATE-FEDERAL BRUCELLOSIS ERADICATION PROGRAM, STATISTICAL TABLES. [Annual]

Earlier A 77.212/4

Discontinued.

A 101.18/3:date
COOPERATIVE STATE-FEDERAL BRUCELLOSIS ERADICATION PROGRAM: BRUCELLOSIS BULLETIN. [Irregular] (Veterinary Services)

A 101.19:CT • **Item 32-A-4**
BIBLIOGRAPHIES AND LISTS OF PUBLICATIONS. [Irregular]

A 101.20:date
NATIONAL STATUS ON CONTROL OF GARBAGE-FEEDING. [Monthly]

Earlier A 77.277

A 101.21:date • **Item 30-A-8**
APHIS ORGANIZATIONAL DIRECTORY.

Discontinued.

A 101.22:date • **Item 24-V (MF) (EL)**
HORSE PROTECTION ENFORCEMENT. [Annual]

Earlier A 1.120

A 101.22/2:date • **Item 24-V (MF)**
ANIMAL WELFARE ENFORCEMENT FISCAL YEAR.

A 101.23:v.nos.&nos.
PLANT PEST NEWS. [Irregular]

A 101.24:nos. • **Item 30-A-11**
ANIMAL CARE MATTERS. v. 1, nos. 1–6. 1981. [Quarterly]

Contains news items concerned with the humane treatment of animals as required by the Animal Welfare Act.

Discontinued.

A 101.25:CT • **Item 30-A-14**
POSTERS. [Irregular]

A 101.26: • **Item 30-A-15 (MF)**
ANIMAL WELFARE: LIST OF LICENSED DEALERS. [Annual]
Lists animal welfare licensed dealers by state, showing licensee's name, firm name, and address.
Earlier A 101.2:An 5/5

A 101.27: • **Item 30-A-16 (MF)**
SUMMARY OF ACTIVITIES. [Annual]

Summarizes activities of the various National Veterinary Services Laboratories, which comprise the only Federal facilities in the U.S. which evaluate veterinary biologics and diagnose animal diseases, both domestic and foreign.

A 101.28 • **Item 30-A-8 (MF) (EL)**
ANIMAL DAMAGE CONTROL PROGRAM.

A 101.29:date/nos. • **Item 30-A-17**
NWRC RESEARCH UPDATE. [Annual]

Formerly DWRC Research Update

A 101.29/2:nos. • **Item 30-A-17 (MF)**
DWRC RESEARCH REPORT (series).

A 101.30 • **Item 30-A-18 (EL)**
TECHNICAL REPORTS.

A 101.31 • **Item 30-A-18 (EL)**
FACT SHEETS.

A 101.32 • **Item 30-A-18 (EL)**
ELECTRONIC PRODUCTS.

A 101.33:date • **Item 30-A-19**
NATIONAL PSEUDORABIES REPORTS. [Quarterly]

A 101.34 • **Item 30-A-20 (EL)**
LIST OF LABORATORIES APPROVED TO RECEIVE SOIL. [Quarterly]

RURAL DEVELOPMENT POLICY OFFICE
(1981– 1986)

CREATION AND AUTHORITY

The Rural Development Service was established by Secretarial order in 1973. Its functions were transferred to Office of Rural Development Coordination and Planning in the Farmers' Home Administration (A 84) by Secretarial order in 1978. The Rural Development Policy Office was established by Secretary's Memorandum 1020-3 of October 26, 1981. It was abolished in 1986 through lack of funding.

A 102.1:date
ANNUAL REPORT.

A 102.2:CT • **Item 31-A-2**
GENERAL PUBLICATIONS.

Discontinued.

A 102.8:CT • **Item 31-A-1**
HANDBOOKS, MANUALS, GUIDES. [Irregular]

Discontinued.

FOOD SAFETY AND QUALITY SERVICE
(1977– 1981)

CREATION AND AUTHORITY

The Food Safety and Quality Service was established within the Department of Agriculture on March 14, 1977. The Service was abolished and its functions transferred to the Food Safety and Inspection Service (A 110) on June 17, 1981.

A 103.1:date
ANNUAL REPORTS.

A 103.2:CT • **Item 31-C**
GENERAL PUBLICATIONS. [Irregular]

Later A 110.2

A 103.6/2:CT • **Item 21-T-5**
UNITED STATES STANDARDS FOR [various foods].

Earlier A 88.6/2

Discontinued.

A 103.6/3:date • **Item 32-A-2**
ACCEPTED MEAT AND POULTRY EQUIPMENT. (MPI-2)

Earlier A 101.6/4
Later A 110.12

A 103.6/4:nos. • **Item 30-A-4**
MEAT AND POULTRY INSPECTION REGULATIONS. (Subscription includes basic volume plus monthly changes for an indefinite period)

Covers meat inspection, poultry inspection, rabbit inspection, voluntary inspection and certification service of meat and poultry, humane slaughter of livestock.
Formerly published by Animal and Plant Health Inspection Service (A 101.6/2).
Later A 110.6/2

Discontinued.

A 103.8:CT • Item 32-A-3
HANDBOOKS, MANUALS GUIDES. [Irregular]

Later A 110.8

A 103.8/2:nos. • Item 21-T-3
MPI [Meat and Poultry Inspection] GUIDELINES (Series). 1– [Irregular] (Meat and Poultry Inspection Program Training Staff)

PURPOSE:– To assure uniform examination of animals, sets forth minimum requirements for veterinarians to follow in examining animals.

Discontinued.

A 103.8/3:date • Item 30-A-3
MEAT AND POULTRY INSPECTION MANUAL. [Irregular] (Subscription includes basic manual plus supplementary material for an indefinite period)

PURPOSE:-To serve as an official publication of procedural guidelines and instructions to aid all MPI employees in enforcing laws and regulations related to Federal meat and poultry inspection.
Earlier A 101.8/2

A 103.9:date • Item 32-A
MEAT AND POULTRY INSPECTION DIRECTORY. [Semiannual]
Includes list of establishments operating under Federal Meat Inspection, public stockyards under Animal Disease Eradication Inspection, licensed manufacturers of biological products, pathological laboratories, trained diagnosticians, and State officials in charge of animal disease control.
Published in loose-leaf form and punched for 3-ring binder.
Earlier A 101.15
Later A 110.11

A 103.9/2:date • Item 21-T
ISSUANCES OF MEAT AND POULTRY INSPECTION PROGRAM. [Monthly]

Includes CFR amendments, MPI-VS Bulletins, MPI Directives, and changes to Meat and Poultry Inspection Manual.
ISSN 0364-1368
Earlier A 101.6/2-2

A 103.10:date • Item 40-B-1
LIST OF PLANTS OPERATING UNDER USDA AND EGG GRADING AND EGG PRODUCTS INSPECTION PROGRAMS. [Semiannual]
PURPOSE:– To provide a list of plants officially approved by the Agricultural Marketing Service to receive inspection or grading services for poultry or eggs.
Part 1 is a list, arranged by States, of officially approved plants which are operating under the Poultry Products Inspection Act, giving by code the type of service each plant receives. Part 2 is a list, arranged by States, of officially approved plants receiving voluntary grading and inspection services on shell eggs and egg products, with code for type of service each plant receives. Part 3 is a cross-index which lists official plant numbers in numerical sequence, together with the page number on which the plant name and location are to be found. Part 4 is the Organization Directory of the Poultry Division for Washington D.C. and its field offices.
Revised in the Spring and Fall of each year.
See also A 88.15/23

A 103.11:v.nos.&nos.
FSQS FOOD PURCHASES, WEEKLY SUMMARY.

Later published as AMS Food Purchases (A 88.57).

A 103.11/2:date
FSQS FOOD PURCHASE, ANNUAL SUMMARY. 1977–

Continues AMS Food Purchases, Annual Summary.

A 103.11/3:nos.
FSQS FACTS. [Irregular]

A 103.11/4:date
FSQS FOOD PURCHASES. [Quarterly]

A 103.12:date • Item 21-Q
DAIRY PLANTS SURVEYED AND APPROVED FOR USDA GRADING SERVICE. (Poultry and Dairy Quality Division)

List of dairy plants surveyed and approved by the U.S. Department of Agriculture under regulations governing inspection and grading of manufactured or processed dairy products. Gives, by States, name of firm, location, and products manufactured, processed, or packaged.
See also A 88.14/12
ISSN 0565-2049

A 103.13:date • Item 21-T-1 (MF)
LIST OF CHEMICAL COMPOUNDS AUTHORIZED FOR USE UNDER USDA MEAT, POULTRY, RABBIT AND EGG INSPECTION PROGRAMS. [Annual] (Meat and Poultry Inspection Program)
Supersedes List of Chemical Compounds Authorized for Use Under USDA Poultry, Meat, Rabbit, and Egg Products Inspection Programs (A 101.6:C 42).

Discontinued.

A 103.14:nos. • Item 21-T-2
FSQS- (Series). 1– [Irregular]

Superseded by FSIS- (series) (A 110.13).

A 103.15:CT • Item 24-N
INSTITUTIONAL MEAT PURCHASE SPECIFICATIONS. [Irregular]

The U.S Department of Agriculture, through its Meat Grading Service, makes available to large-scale purchasers of meat an Acceptance Service designed to assure such agencies that meats they purchase comply with detailed specifications approved by USDA. These publications contain descriptions of the various meat products customarily purchased for institutional users of meats.
Earlier A 88.17/4

Discontinued.

A 103.16:date • Item 21-T-4
FOOD FOR CONSUMERS. [Irregular]

PURPOSE:– To provide a newsletter containing short releases on a variety of food subjects of interest to consumers.

A 103.17:date
CHIT CHAT, AN ADMINISTRATIVE LETTER FOR DIVISION EMPLOYEES. (Poultry and Dairy Quality Division)

A 103.18:CT • Item 21-T-6
POSTERS. [Irregular]

Discontinued.

FEDERAL GRAIN INSPECTION SERVICE
(1976–   )

CREATION AND AUTHORITY

The Federal Grain Inspection Service was established within the Department of Agriculture on November 20, 1976.

INFORMATION
Public Affairs/Public Information Staff
Federal Grain Inspection Service
Department of Agriculture
1099 South Agriculture Building
1400 Independence Avenue, SW
Washington, D.C. 20250
(202) 720-5091
Fax: (202) 205-9237

A 104.1:date • Item 31-B-4 (MF)
ANNUAL REPORT.

A 104.2:CT • Item 31-B-3
GENERAL PUBLICATIONS.

A 104.6:CT • Item 31-B-1
REGULATIONS, RULES, INSTRUCTIONS. [Irregular]

A 104.6/2:date • Item 24-P-2
OFFICIAL UNITED STATES STANDARDS FOR GRAIN.

Earlier A 88.6/2:G 761

A 104.6/3:CT • Item 24-P-2
STANDARDS FOR FRUITS AND VEGETABLES. [Irregular]

Earlier A 1.120
Discontinued.

A 104.8:CT • Item 31-B-2
HANDBOOKS, MANUALS, AND GUIDES. [Irregular]

A 104.10:date
CONVEYER.

PURPOSE:– To provide an administrative letter to FGIS employees.

A 104.11:date
INSPECTION AND WEIGHING UPDATE. [Irregular]

A 104.12:date • Item 24-P-3
U.S. EXPORT CORN QUALITY. [Annual]

See A 104.12/2-3

A 104.12/2:date • Item 24-P-3
U.S. EXPORT SOYBEAN QUALITY. [Annual]

See A 104.12/2-3

A 104.12/2-2:date • Item 24-P-3
U.S. EXPORT WHEAT QUALITY. [Annual]

See A 104.12/2-3

A 104.12/2-3:date • Item 24-P-3 (MF)
U.S. GRAIN EXPORT QUALITY REPORT, WHEAT, CORN, SOYBEANS. [Annual]

A 104.12/2-4:date • Item 24-P-3 (MF)
U.S. . . . . CROP QUALITY. [Annual]

A 104.12/2-5:CT • Item 24-P-3
U.S. WHEAT QUALITY. [Annual]

A 104.12/3:date • Item 31-B-5 (MF)
FGIS UPDATE. [Quarterly]

FGIS = Federal Grain Inspection Service
PURPOSE:– To present short items on activities of the Federal GrainInspection Service.
Discontinued.

A 104.13   • Item 31-B-1 (MF)
DIRECTORIES.

ECONOMICS AND STATISTICS
SERVICE
(1980–1981)

CREATION AND AUTHORITY

The Economics, Statistics, and Cooperatives Service was established within the Department of Agriculture by Secretary's Memorandum 1927, Supplement 1, dated December 19, 1977, effective January 2, 1978, to which were transferred the functions of the former Economic Research Service (A 93), the Statistical Research Service (A 92), Farmer Cooperative Service (A 89), and the Economic Management Support Center. Redesignated the Economics and Statistics Service by Secretary's Memorandum 2025 of September 17, 1980 when certain functions were transferred to the newly established Agricultural Cooperative Service (A 109). The Service was abolished on June 17, 1981 and its functions returned to the reestablished Statistical Reporting Service (A 92) and the Economic Research Service (A 93).

A 105.1:date
ANNUAL REPORT.

A 105.2:CT   • Item 21-N-5
GENERAL PUBLICATIONS. [Irregular]

Discontinued.

A 105.8:CT   • Item 21-N-3
HANDBOOKS, MANUALS, GUIDES. [Irregular]

Discontinued.

A 105.9:date   • Item 20-B
CROP PRODUCTION. [Monthly] (Crop Reporting Board) (CrPr 2-2)

See also (A 92.24).
ISSN 0363-8561

A 105.9/2:date   • Item 20-B (MF)
CROP PRODUCTION, ANNUAL SUMMARY. (Crop Reporting Board) (CrPr 2-1)

Earlier A 92.24
See 92.24/4

A 105.9/3:date   • Item 20-B (MF)
PROSPECTIVE PLANTINGS. [Annual] (Crop Reporting Board) (CrPr 2-4)

Prior to January 20, 1978 issue, published by the Statistical Reporting Service (A 92.24/2).

A 105.9/4:date   • Item 24-I (MF)
FIELD CROPS, PRODUCTION, DISPOSITION, VALUE. [Annual] (Crop Reporting Board) (CrPr 1)

Earlier A 92.19

A 105.10:v.nos.&nos.   • Item 19
AGRICULTURAL SITUATION. v. 1–   1921– 1980. [Monthly]

Prior to v. 61, no. 10 (November 1977) issued by the Statistical Reporting Service.
Merged with Farm Index (A 105.27/2) to form Farmline (A 105.10/4).

A 105.10/2:letter & nos.   • Item 21-N-4
FARMERS' NEWSLETTER. [Irregular]

PURPOSE:– To help readers make production and marketing decisions. Separate subseries for wheat, feed, livestock, oilseeds, cotton, and general.
Former title: Commodity Outlook for Farmers.
Later A 93.40

A 105.10/3   • Item 78-A
WORLD AGRICULTURE OUTLOOK AND SITUATION. WAS 1–   1971–   [Annual]

PURPOSE:– To appraise world agriculture for the past year and present the outlook for the coming year.
Former title: World Agricultural Situation.
See also A 93.29/2

A 105.10/3-2:date   • Item 78-A
WORLD AGRICULTURAL SITUATION SUPPLEMENTS. [Irregular]

A 105.10/4:v.nos.&nos.   • Item 19
FARMLINE. v. 1–   1980–   [Monthly]

Replaces Agricultural Situation (A 105.10) and Farm Index (A 105.27/2).
Later A 93.33/2

A 105.11:date   • Item 122-A-4
NONCITRUS FRUITS AND NUTS, ANNUAL SUMMARY. (Crop Reporting Board)

Earlier A 92.11/2-2

A 105.11/2:nos.   • Item 21-K
FRUIT SITUATION. FS-1–   1937–   [4 times a year]

Analysis of situation and outlook for fruit and tree nuts. Special articles. Charts. Tables on season average price per unit received by growers; production of fruits and nuts; canned fruit and fruit juices; pack and cold-storage holdings; citrus fruit production; oranges, total weekly fresh shipments from producing points; apples, production; apples, pears, and miscellaneous fruits and nuts, cold-storage holdings; strawberries, acreage, yield and production; fruits and tree nuts, per capita utilization; selected fruits, monthly retail prices.
Issued in January, June, August, and October.
Prior to March 1978 (TFS-206) issue published by the Economic Research Service (A 93.12/3).
ISSN 0364-8648

A 105.11/3:date
CHERRY UTILIZATION. [Annual] (Crop Reporting Board) (FrNt 2-4)

See also A 92.11/3-2

A 105.11/4:date
CHERRIES. [Annual] (Crop Reporting Board) (FrNt 2-4)

A 105.12/2:date
EGG PRODUCTS. [Monthly] (Crop Reporting Board) (Pou 2-5)

ISSN 0256-3904
Earlier A 92.9/4

A 105.12/3:date   • Item 21-F-1
EGGS, CHICKENS, AND TURKEYS. [Monthly] (Crop Reporting Board) (Pou 1-1)
Statistical tables showing egg production, number of layers, egg-type, chicks hatched, turkeys hatched, by State, month, and year.
ISSN 0093-013X
See also A 92.9/16

A 105.12/3-2:date   • Item 21-F
HATCHERY PRODUCTION. [Annual] (Crop Reporting Board) (Pou 2-3)

Formerly issued with Eggs, Chickens, and Turkeys (A 92.9/16).

A 105.12/4:nos.   • Item 21-F
POULTRY AND EGG SITUATION. PES-1–   1937– [5 times a year]

Analysis of situation an outlook for poultry and eggs. Special articles. Charts. Tables on hatchery operations; production; federal inspection; processing; storage stocks; consumption; government purchases; farm, wholesale, and retail prices; feed prices and poultry product-feed price ratios for eggs, broilers, and turkeys.
Issued in February, April, June, September, and October.
See also A 93.20
ISSN 0032-5708

A 105.12/5   • Item 21-F
POULTRY SLAUGHTER. [Monthly] (Crop Reporting Board) (Pou 2-1)

Earlier A 92.9/5

A 105.12/6:date   • Item 21-F
POULTRY, PRODUCTION, DISPOSITION AND INCOME. [Annual] (Crop Reporting Board)

See also A 92.9/3

A 105.12/7:date   • Item 21-F-2 (MF)
LAYERS AND EGG PRODUCTION. [Annual] (Crop Reporting Board) (Pou 2-4)

Earlier A 92.9/13

A 105.13:nos.   • Item 42-I
ERS- (series). [Irregular]

Earlier A 93.21

A 105.14:date   • Item 42-E
FOREIGN AGRICULTURAL TRADE OF THE UNITED STATES. [Monthly]

Analytical review of the foreign agricultural trade of the United States, emphasizing current status and outlook for U.S. agricultural trade, including Food-for-peace shipments. Exports are estimated for one month later than that reported by the Bureau of the Census. Summarized cumulative data on quantity and value from July 1 of the current year with comparisons for the corresponding period of the current year. Government program information consists of quantity and value totals for individual commodities and countries. Detail is provided on sales for dollars, P.L. 480 by title, CCC and Export-Import Bank credit, and total exports. Also included are fiscal year estimates of the value of exports assisted by payments-in-kind and by sales below domestic market prices as well as estimates of the amount of export assistance paid.
See also A 93.17/7

A 105.14/2:date   • Item 42-E
FOREIGN AGRICULTURAL TRADE STATISTICAL REPORT. [Annual]

Earlier A 93.17/3

A 105.15:nos.   • Item 21-H
NATIONAL FOOD REVIEW. NFR 1–   1978–

Supersedes National Food Situation (A 93.16).
Later A 93.16/3
ISSN 0161-4274

A 105.16:date   • Item 21-M
COTTON AND WOOL SITUATION. CWS 1–   1975– [Quarterly]

PURPOSE:– To analyze supply and demand, price, and outlook for cotton and wool. Includes tables and charts presenting current data on production, market movement, stocks, consumption, prices, and foreign trade. Relevant special studies are frequently included.
See also A 93.24/2
ISSN 0360-2184

A 105.17:date
MILK PRODUCTION. [Monthly] (Crop Reporting Board) (Da 1-1)

ISSN 0026-4202
Earlier A 92.10

A 105.17/2:nos. • **Item 21-B**
DAIRY SITUATION. DS 1– 1931– [5 times a year]

Analysis of dairy situation and outlook. Special articles. Charts. Tables on dairy situation at a glance, number of milk cows and heifers, milk production, and factors affecting milk production; output of dairy products, stocks, imports, and exports; commercial and total disappearance of fluid and manufactured dairy products; Federal milk marketing order program; USDA dairy support program; prices farmers receive for milk and cream; wholesale and retail prices of dairy products; world dairy information.
Issued in March, May, July, September, and November.

See also A 93.13
ISSN 0011-5703

A 105.17/3:date
DAIRY PRODUCTS. [Monthly] (Crop Reporting Board) (Da 2-6)

Earlier A 92.10/7

A 105.17/4:date • **Item 24-F**
DAIRY PRODUCTS, ANNUAL SUMMARY (year). (Crop Reporting Board) (Da 2-1)

See also A 92.10/5

A 105.17/5:date • **Item 24-F**
MILK PRODUCTION, DISPOSITION, INCOME. [Annual] (Crop Reporting Board) (Da 1-2)

Earlier A 92.10/2

A 105.18:date • **Item 24-W (MF)**
SEED CROPS, ANNUAL SUMMARY.

Gives data on area harvested, yield, production, price and value of alfalfa, Kentucky Bluegrass, and red clover.

A 105.18/3:date
RED CLOVER SEED. [Annual] (Crop Reporting Board) (SeHy 1-3)

A 105.18/4:date
TIMOTHY SEED. [Annual] (Crop Reporting Board) (SeHy 1-3)

A 105.18/5:date
ALFALFA SEED. [Annual] (Crop Reporting Board) (SeHy 1-3)

A 105.19:v.nos.&nos. • **Item 66**
FARMER COOPERATIVES. v. 1– 1934– [Monthly]
PURPOSE:– To present articles concerned with the operations and management of farmers' cooperatives, and with recent developments in outstanding cooperatives in various parts of the country.
Prior to v. 42, no. 11 (February 1976) entitled News for Farmer Cooperatives.
ISSN 0364-0736
Earlier A 89.8

A 105.19/2:nos. • **Item 42-A**
FARM REAL ESTATE MARKET DEVELOPMENTS. CD 1– 1942– [Semiannual]

PURPOSE:– To summarize trends in farmland values, volume of sales, financing farm purchases, and factors affecting the land market. Includes index numbers of estimated average value per acre by States and graphic material.

See also A 93.9/4

A 105.19/3:nos. • **Item 42-D (MF)**
AGRICULTURAL FINANCE OUTLOOK. AFO 1– 1961– [Annual]

Analysis of situation and outlook for financial developments, including farm income and expenditures, balance sheet of agriculture, farm real estate values, farm debts, and regional situation and outlook.

Issued in November
Earlier A 93.9/8

A 105.20:date • **Item 122-A-3**
GRAIN STOCKS. [Quarterly] (Crop Reporting Board) (GrLg 11-1)

See also A 92.15

A 105.20/2:nos. • **Item 21-E**
FEED OUTLOOK AND SITUATION. FS-1– 1939– [5 times a year]

Analysis of situation and outlook for feed grains and other feeds. Special articles. Charts. Tables on feed prices and livestock-feed price ratios; feed concentrate supplies and consumption (total and per animal unit); feed grain (corn, sorghum grain, oats and barley) acreage, yield, production, supplies and utilization, market receipts, and prices; government programs and price support activity; exports and imports of feed grains and other feeds; high-protein feed supplies and utilization; hay acreage, yield, production, supply, utilization, and prices.
Issued in February, April, May, August, and November.

See also A 93.11/2
Former title: Feed Situation.
ISSN 0014-9578

A 105.20/3:nos. • **Item 21-I**
WHEAT SITUATION. WS 1– 1936– [4 times a year]

Analysis of situation and outlook for wheat and rye. Special articles. Charts. Tables on acreage, yield, production; free and CCC Stocks; loans and purchase agreements; average prices per bushel received by farmers and weighted average cash price; domestic use and exports; and world trade for both wheat and rye.
Issued in February, May, July, and November.

See also A 93.11
ISSN 0364-2305

A 105.20/4:nos. • **Item 21-P**
RICE OUTLOOK AND SITUATION. RS-1– 1956– [Annual]

Analysis of situation and outlook for rice. Special articles. Charts. Tables on acreage, yield, and production, acreage allotments, by States; CCC price support operations; consumption, U.S.; average wholesale price at leading markets; supply and distribution, U.S.; world production and trade.

Issued in January.
See also A 93.11/3
Former title: Rice Situation.

A 105.20/5:date
SOYBEAN STOCKS. [Annual] (Crop Reporting Board) (GrLg 11-1)

Earlier A 92.15/5

A 105.20/6:date • **Item 122-A-6**
SMALL GRAINS, ANNUAL SUMMARY AND CROP WINTER WHEAT AND RYE SEEDINGS. [Annual] (Crop Reporting Board) (CrPr 2-2)

A 105.21:v.nos.&nos. • **Item 18**
AGRICULTURAL ECONOMICS RESEARCH. v. 1– 1949– [Quarterly]

PURPOSE:– To present technical articles which deal with methods, results, and findings of research in agricultural economics, statistics, and marketing.
Gives data on the number, characteristics, and earnings of persons who did any farm work for wages at any time during the year. Surveys were made since 1945, with the exceptions for the years 1953 and 1955.
Issued in January, April, July and October.
Prior to January 1978, issued by the Economic Research Service (A 93.26).
ISSN 0002-1423

A 105.22:nos. • **Item 42-B**
FOREIGN AGRICULTURAL ECONOMIC REPORTS. 1– 1961– [Irregular]

PURPOSE:– To make available semitechnical or semipopular information resulting from economic studies and analyses of foreign agricultural situation.
See also A 93.27

A 105.22/2:nos. • **Item 42-J (MF)**
WORLD ECONOMIC CONDITIONS IN RELATION TO AGRICULTURAL TRADE. WEC-1– 1971– [Semiannual]

Former title: World Monetary conditions in Relation to Agricultural Trade.
Earlier A 93.34/2

Discontinued 1978.

A 105.23:date • **Item 21-N**
CATTLE INVENTORY. [Annual] (Crop Reporting Board) (LvGn)

See also A 92.18/6-2

A 105.23/2:nos. • **Item 24-C**
LIVESTOCK AND MEAT OUTLOOK AND SITUATION. LMS 1– 1947– [6 times a year]

Analysis of situation and outlook for livestock and meat. Special articles. Charts. Tables on production and consumption per person of red meat; retail prices and marketing margins for meat; foreign trade in meat, by countries; number of cattle and calves on farms; number of cattle slaughtered under Federal inspection; number of cattle calves on feed and fed cattle marketings; market price per 100 pounds of selected class of meat animals; estimated net returns in cattle feeding program; imports of cattle from Canada and Mexico; pig crop and pig slaughter; hog-corn ratio during fall breeding season; sheep and lambs on farms and ranches, lamb crop, number slaughtered, and wool production; selected price statistics for meat animals; selected marketing, slaughter and stocks statistics for animals and meat.
Issued in February, March, May, August, October, and November,
See also A 93.15
Former title: Livestock and Meat Situation.

A 105.23/2-2:nos. • **Item 24-C-1**
AQUACULTURE OUTLOOK AND SITUATION, AS- (series). 1– 1981– [Semiannual]

Presents the current outlook and situation of the controlled cultivation of such aquatic animals as trout, catfish, crayfish, and freshwater prawns.
Later A 93.42

A 105.23/3:date • **Item 21-N-1**
CATTLE ON FEED. [Monthly] (Crop Report Board) (MtAn 2-1)

ISSN 0364-202X
Earlier A 92.18/6

A 105.23/4:date • **Item 24-J**
LIVESTOCK SLAUGHTER. [Monthly] (Crop Reporting Board) (MtAn 1-2)

ISSN 0499-0544
See also A 92.18/3

A 105.23/4-2:date • **Item 24-J (MF)**
LIVESTOCK SLAUGHTER, ANNUAL SUMMARY. [Annual] (Crop Reporting Board) (MtAn 1-2-1)

Earlier A 92.18

A 105.23/5:date • **Item 24-H**
HOGS AND PIGS. [Quarterly] (Crop Reporting Board) (MtAn 4)

See also A 92.18/7
ISSN 0565-2189

A 105.23/6:date • **Item 24-H**
MEAT ANIMALS, PRODUCTION, DISPOSITION, AND INCOME. [Annual] (Crop Reporting Board) (MtAn 1-1)

Earlier A 92.17

A 105.23/7-2:date
LAMB CROP AND WOOL. [Annual] (Crop Reporting Board) (MtAn 5-1)

See also A 92.18/4

A 105.23/8:date • **Item 21-N**
SHEEP AND GOATS. [Annual] (Crop Reporting Board) (LvGn 1)

Title varies.
Earlier A 92.18/8

A 105.24:nos. • **Item 21-L**
VEGETABLE SITUATION. TVS 1– 1937– [4 times a year]

Analysis of situation and outlook for vegetables. Special articles. Charts. Tables on civilian per capita consumption of commercially produced fresh vegetables, canned and frozen vegetables, and potatoes; commercial acreage and production; representative prices; index numbers of prices received by farmers; packs and current stocks.
Issued in January, April, July, and October.
See also A 93.12/2
ISSN 0042-3084

A 105.24/2:date • **Item 24-E**
VEGETABLES, (year) ANNUAL SUMMARY. (Crop Reporting Board) (Vg 2-2)

Earlier A 92.11/10-2

A 105.24/2-2:date
VEGETABLES. [Monthly] (Crop Reporting Board) (Vg 2-1)

Earlier A 92.11

A 105.24/5:date
POTATO STOCKS. [Monthly, Dec.-May]

Title varies.
See also A 92.11/11
A 105.24/6:date
MUSHROOMS. [Annual] (Crop Reporting Board) (Vg 2-1-2)

See also A 92.11/10-5

A 105.25:nos. • **Item 21-N-2**
ESCS- (series). 1– 1978– [Irregular]

PURPOSE:– To provide a series of miscellaneous reports covering a wide variety of subjects relating to agricultural economics, statistics, and cooperatives.
Supersedes ERS (series) (A 93.21) and SRS (series) (A 92.34).

Previously distributed to Depository Libraries under Item 21-T-1.
ESCS Economics, Statistics, and Cooperatives Service.
Superseded by ESS (series) (A 105.56).

A 105.25/2:date • **Item 21-N-2**
ESCS RESEARCH ABSTRACTS.

Later A 93.39

A 105.26:date • **Item 18-C**
AGRICULTURAL PRICES. [Monthly] (Crop Reporting Board) (Pr 1)

See also A 92.16
ISSN 0002-1601

A 105.26/2:date • **Item 18-C (MF)**
AGRICULTURAL PRICES, ANNUAL SUMMARY. (Crop Reporting Board) (Pr 1-3)

See also A 92.16/2

A 105.27:nos. • **Item 42-M**
AGRICULTURE OUTLOOK. AO-1– 1975– [Monthly]

PURPOSE:– To bring together on an aggregate basis the outlook for food and agriculture, including sections related to commodities, food marketing, world agriculture and trade, farm income, transportation, inputs, and the general economy.
Statistical material on farm income, marketing spreads, prices, production, foreign trade and general economic indicators are featured.
Prior to April 1978, published by the Economic Research Service (A 93.10/2).
ISSN 0099-1066

A 105.27/2:v.nos.&nos. • **Item 42-F**
FARM INDEX. v. 1– 1962– [Monthly]

PURPOSE:– To provide in a nontechnical language the results of ESCS's broad research program. Articles are grouped according to the special interests of farming, rural life, marketing, the foreign market, and the consumer. Regular features are a digest of the agricultural outlook, a table with the latest figures for 45 leading indicators of economic development in agriculture, marketing, and the general economy, and brief reviews of current government publications.
Prior to v. 17 no. 2 (February 1978) issue published by the Economic Research Service (A 93.33).
Merged with Agricultural Situation (A 105.10) to form Farmline (A 105.10/4).
ISSN 0014-7982

A 105.28:nos. • **Item 21-D**
FATS AND OILS OUTLOOK SITUATION. FOS 1– 1937– [5 times a year]

Analysis of situation and outlook. Special articles. Charts. Tables on wholesale prices, supply and disposition, exports and imports, production of fats and oils (both edible and nonedible); index numbers of wholesale prices of fats and oils; prices received by farmers and prices at terminal markets for specified oil-bearing materials and oil-meals; special tables for soybeans, flaxseed and linseed oil, castor beans, castor oil, inedible tallow and grease, soap and synthetic detergents, tung oil, tung nuts, and tall oil.
Issued in January, April, June, September and November.
See also A 93.23
Former title: Fats and Oils Situation.
ISSN 0014-8865

A 105.29:date • **Item 24-L**
PEANUT STOCKS AND PROCESSING. [Monthly] (Crop Reporting Board) (GrLg 11-2)

ISSN 0499-0579
Earlier A 92.14

A 105.30:date • **Item 24-L**
FLORICULTURE CROPS. [Annual] (SpCr 6-1)

Prior to 1978 issue published by the Statistical Reporting Service under the title Flowers and Foliage Plants (A 92.32).

Later A 109.10
See also A 92.32

A 105.31:nos. • **Item 64-A**
RESEARCH REPORTS. 1– 1968– [Irregular]

Earlier A 89.19

A 105.32:nos. • **Item 24-D**
TOBACCO SITUATION. TS-1– 1937– [Quarterly]

Analysis of tobacco situation and outlook. Special articles. Charts. Tables on statistical summary: cigarettes; total output, domestic consumption and exports: tobacco products; consumption per capita, 18 years and older: cigars; output and domestic consumption, consumption of cigars per males 18 years and over: output of manufactured tobacco; exports of unmanufactured tobacco; domestic supplies; season average price and price support operations; acreage; yield per acre; cash receipts from Federal taxes; tobacco manufacture; net sales, net income, and profit ratios.
Issued in March, June, September and December.
See also A 93.25
ISSN 0040-8344

A 105.33:date • **Item 24-G-1**
COLD STORAGE. [Monthly] (Crop Reporting Board) (CoSt 1)

Earlier A 92.21

A 105.33/2:date • **Item 24-G (MF)**
REGIONAL COLD STORAGE HOLDINGS. [Annual] (Crop Reporting Board) (CoSt 3)

See also Summary of Regional Cold Storage Holdings (A 92.21/2).
ISSN 0145-4846

A 105.33/3:date • **Item 24-G (MF)**
CAPACITY OF REFRIGERATED WAREHOUSES. [Annual] (Crop Reporting Board) (CoSt 2)

See also A 92.21/3

A 105.35:nos. • **Item 18-A (MF)**
AGRICULTURAL FINANCE REVIEW. v. 1– 1938– [Annual]

PURPOSE:– To present research in agricultural credit, taxation, farm insurance, and in other fields relating to the general financial conditions in agriculture.
Contains signed articles as well as brief reports on current developments in the field of agricultural finance, reviews of recent publications and summaries of research projects underway. Also included are a statistical appendix, list of available publications and reports related to agricultural finance, and a list of signed articles from previous volumes.
Vol. 38-42 (1978-1982) issued under this class number.
See also A 93.9/10.
Prior to May 1978 (v. 38) issue, published by Economic Research Service (A 93.9/10).

A 105.35/2:date • **Item 18-A**
FARM PRODUCTION EXPENDITURES FOR (year).
[Annual]

> Later A 92.40

A 105.36:date
HOP STOCKS. [2 times a year] (Crop Reporting Board)
(SpCr 2)

> See also A 92.30

A 105.38:nos. • **Item 64-A**
COOPERATIVE RESEARCH REPORTS. [Irregular]
Supersedes FCS Research Reports (A 89.19),
formerly issued by the Farmer Cooperative Service.

A 105.38/2:nos. • **Item 65-B**
COOPERATIVE INFORMATION REPORTS. 1–
1978– [Irregular]

> Supersedes Information Series (A 89.15), formerly issued by the Farmer Cooperative Service.

A 105.39:date • **Item 20-B (MF)**
ACREAGE. (Crop Reporting Board) (CrPr 2-2)

> See also A 92.39

A 105.40:nos. • **Item 21-N-7**
RURAL DEVELOPMENT RESEARCH REPORTS. 1–
[Irregular]

> PURPOSE:– To provide a series of studies that pertain to various issues of rural concern, such as farm population, federal outlays in non-metropolitan areas, etc.

> Later A 93.41

> Discontinued.

A 105.40/2:date • **Item 21-N-6**
RURAL DEVELOPMENT PERSPECTIVES. RDP 1–
1978– [Irregular]
PURPOSE:– To translate results of varied
social science research into information useful in
the formation of public policy for rural people and
communities.

> Later A 93.41/2

A 105.41:date
COMMERCIAL FERTILIZERS. [Monthly] (Crop Reporting Board) (SpCr 7-1-1)

> See also A 92.37/2

A 105.41/2:date • **Item 122-A-2**
COMMERCIAL FERTILIZERS. [Annual] (Crop Reporting Board) (SpCr 7)

> Earlier A 92.37/3

A 105.42:date
RICE STOCKS, ROUGH AND MILLED. [Quarterly] (Crop Reporting Board) (GrLg 11-3)

> Earlier A 92.15/2

A 105.43:date
POTATO STOCKS.

A 105.44:date
FARM LABOR. [Monthly] (Crop Reporting Board) (La 1)

> Earlier A 92.12

A 105.45:date
CELERY. [Monthly] (Crop Reporting Board) (Vg 2-1-1)

> ISSN 0364-2690
> See also A 92.11/10-4

A 105.47:date
SHEEP AND LAMBS ON FEED. [3 times a year] (Crop Reporting Board) (MtAn 5-2)

> Earlier A 92.18/9

A 105.48:date
MINK. [Annual] (Crop Reporting Board) (MtAn 6)

> Earlier A 92.18/11

A 105.49:date
NAVAL STORES. [Monthly] (Crop Reporting Board) (SpCr 3)

> Earlier A 92.25
> Discontinued in 1982.

A 105.50 • **Item 42-P**
AGRICULTURAL-FOOD POLICY REVIEW. AFPR 1–

> [Irregular]

> See also A 93.16/2

A 105.51:v.nos.&nos.
EEO NEWSLETTER.

A 105.52:date
CATFISH. [Monthly] (Crop Reporting Board) (SpCr 8)

> Previously published by the National Marine Fisheries Service as Farm Raised Catfish Processor's Report.

> Later A 92.44

A 105.53:v.nos.&nos. • **Item 122-A-2**
SUGAR MARKET STATISTICS. (SpCr 4)

> Superseded by Sugar and Sweetener, Outlook and Situation (A 105.53/2).

> Later A 92.41

A 105.53/2:v.nos.&nos. • **Item 24-R**
SUGAR AND SWEETENER, OUTLOOK AND SITUATION.

> Supersedes Sugar Market Statistics.
> See also A 93.31/3.

A 105.54:date
WOOL AND MOHAIR. [Annual] (Crop Reporting Board) (MtAn 5-3)

> Earlier A 92.29/5

A 105.55:nos. • **Item 32-B-1**
BIBLIOGRAPHIES AND LITERATURE OF AGRICULTURE. BLA 1– 1978– [Irregular]

> Prepared by the Institute of Home Economics, in cooperation with the Interagency Committee on Nutrition Education and School Lunch.
> Four-page newsletter of activities on nutrition education and the school lunch program.
> Earlier A 106.110/3

A 105.56 • **Item 21-N-2**
ESS- (series). 1– [Irregular]

> ESS Economics and Statistics Service.
> Supersedes ESCS (series) (A 105.25)
> Later A 93.21/4

A 105.57:date
ABSTRACTS OF ESS STAFF REPORTS [Irregular]

SCIENCE AND EDUCATION ADMINISTRATION (1978– 1981)

CREATION AND AUTHORITY

The Science and Education Administration was established within the Department of Agriculture by Secretary's Memorandum, Supplement 1, dated December 19, 1977, consolidating the Agricultural Research Service (A 77), Cooperative State Research Service (A 94), Extension Service (A 43) and the National Agricultural Library (A 17). The Administration was abolished on June 17, 1981 and its functions returned to the reestablished Extension Service (A 43), the Agricultural Research Service (A 77), and the Cooperative State Research Service (A 94).

A 106.1:date
ANNUAL REPORT.

A 106.2:CT • **Item 22-A-3**
GENERAL PUBLICATIONS. [Irregular]

A 106.8:CT • **Item 22-A-1**
HANDBOOKS, MANUALS, GUIDES. [Irregular]

A 106.9:v.nos.&nos. • **Item 25-A**
AGRICULTURAL RESEARCH. v. 1– 1953–
[Monthly]

> PURPOSE:– To present results of U.S. Department of Agriculture research projects in livestock management, crops, soils, fruits and vegetables, poultry, and related agricultural fields.
> See also A 77.12
> ISSN 0002-161X

A 106.10 • **Item 60**
EXTENSION REVIEW. v. 1– 1930– [Quarterly]

> Includes pertinent information on agriculture extension programs of the United States, 4-H Club work, conservation, home demonstration, community cooperation, etc.
> Continues: Extension Service Review (A 43.7) (ISSN 0014-5408)
> Indexed by: Index to U.S. Government Periodicals.
> See also A 43.7

A 106.11:nos. • **Item 101**
PLANT INVENTORY. 1– 1898– [Annual]

> See also A 77.515

A 106.12:letters-nos. • **Item 22-A-5**
AGRICULTURAL REVIEW AND MANUALS. ARM- (series). [Irregular]

> Includes technical publications covering miscellaneous topics that are of interest to the mission of the Agriculture Department.

> See also A 77.30

A 106.13:letters-nos. • **Item 22-A-8**
AGRICULTURAL RESEARCH RESULTS, ARR- (series). [Irregular]

> Miscellaneous highly technical reports of research carried out in the various field research centers of the Science and Education Administration.
> Published in microfiche (24x).
> See also A 77.32

A 106.14:date • Item 22-A-2 (MF)
SOIL, WATER, AIR SCIENCES RESEARCH ANNUAL REPORT.

PURPOSE:– To provide a brief overview on research aimed toward development of cultural practices and cropping systems that assure efficient use of soil, water, and air while providing adequate protection for sustained use.

A 106.14/2 • Item 22-A-6
DIRECTORY, NATURAL RESOURCES LOCATIONS.

Earlier title: Soil, Water, Air Science Directory.

INDEX-CATALOGUE OF MEDICAL AND VETERINARY ZOOLOGY.

Issuing agency varies: 1952– 54, Zoological Division of the Bureau of Animal Industry; 1955– 57, Animal Disease and Parasite Research Branch; 1958– 66, Animal Disease and Parasite Research Division; 1966– 70, Beltsville Parasitological Laboratory; 1971– 72, National Animal Parasite Laboratory; 1972– 77, Animal Parsitology Institute; 1978– , Science and Education Administration.

A 106.15:nos. • Item 31 (MF)
– SPECIAL PUBLICATION. 1–   [Irregular]

Earlier A 77.219/4

A 106.15/2:nos. • Item 31 (MF)
– SUPPLEMENT. 1–   1953–   [Irregular]

Supplements 1– 14 have Authors section only; supplements 15–   include Parasite-Subject Catalogue section.
Earlier A 77.219/2

A 106.16:CT • Item 22-A-4 (MF)
BIBLIOGRAPHIES AND LISTS OF PUBLICATIONS.

A 106.16/2:date • Item 22-A-4 (MF)
ANNUAL INVENTORY OF AVAILABLE USDA PUBLICATIONS FOR STATE AND COUNTY EXTENSION OFFICES IN ORDERING USDA PUBLICATIONS.
Earlier A 43.34

A 106.17:date • Item 88-B
FAMILY ECONOMICS REVIEW. 1943–   [Quarterly]

PURPOSE:– To report current developments in family and food economics, and economic aspects of home management. Summarizes other Government reports in the home economics field.
Includes index of articles for previous year and annual outlook issue.
See also A 77.708

A 106.18:nos. • Item 22-A-7
AGRICULTURE INFORMATION POSTERS. 1–   [Irregular]

A 106.19:CT • Item 22-A-9 (MF)
CATALOG OF SEED AND VEGETABLE STOCK AVAILABLE FROM THE SOUTHERN REGIONAL PLANT INTRODUCTION STATION [for various plants]. [Irregular]

PURPOSE:– To provide a cumulative tabular inventory of plant materials grown at the Station or by State Experiments under the S-9 "New Plants" project.
Published in microfiche (24x).
Discontinued.

A 106.20: • Item 88-C
NUTRITION PROGRAM NEWS. [Bimonthly]
Discontinued.

A 106.21:v.nos.&nos. • Item 100-B
PLANT DISEASE REPORTER. v. 1–   1917– [Monthly]
PURPOSE:– To provide reports, summaries, observations, and comments submitted voluntarily by qualified observers, as a service to plant pathologists throughout the country.
Earlier A 77.511

Discontinued.

A 106.22 • Item 22-A-10 (MF)
NATIONAL POULTRY IMPROVEMENT PLAN REPORTS. 1–   1979–   [Irregular]

Reports contain statistical data in tabular form and other information about activities, participants, etc. under the plan for improvement of poultry, poultry products, and hatcheries
Published in microfiche (24x).

A 106.23:letters-nos. • Item 22-A-1 (MF)
CORRESPONDENCE AIDS, CA- (series). [Irregular]

Earlier A 77.18

Discontinued.

A 106.24:letters-nos. • Item 25-B (MF)
ADVANCES IN AGRICULTURAL TECHNOLOGY, ATT (series). [Irregular]

See A 77.31

A 106.25:date • Item 22-A-11 (MF)
ANNUAL REPORT OF THE NATIONAL RESEARCH PROGRAMS, CROP PRODUCTION.

PURPOSE:– To provide a summary of activities and examples of recent findings in the Administration's research concerning crop production and protection technology.
Companion report, covering crop protection issued separately (A 106.25/2).

A 106.25/2:date • Item 22-A-11 (MF)
ANNUAL REPORT OF THE NATIONAL RESEARCH PROGRAMS, CROP PROTECTION.

Issued as a companion report to entry above (A 106.25).

A 106.26:nos.
VEGETABLES FOR THE HOT, HUMID TROPICS (series). [Irregular]

Earlier A 106.2:V 52

A 106.26/2:nos.
CULTIVATION OF NEGLECTED TROPICAL FRUITS WITH PROMISE (series). [Irregular]

Earlier A 106.2:C 89

A 106.27:date
SUGARCANE VARIETY TESTS IN FLORIDA, HARVEST SEASON. [Irregular]

Earlier published in the ARS (series) (A 77.15).

A 106.27/2
PROCEEDINGS OF THE TECHNICAL SESSION ON CANE SUGAR REFINING RESEARCH. [Annual]

A 106.28:date • Item 22-A-12 (MF)
REGIONAL COTTON VARIETY TESTS. [Annual]

Earlier published in the ARS (series) (A 77.15).

A 106.28/2:date
ANNUAL CONFERENCE REPORT ON COTTON-INSECT RESEARCH AND CONTROL.

Earlier A 77.328

A 106.29:date
PROCEEDINGS OF THE SOUTHERN PASTURE AND FORAGE CROP IMPROVEMENT CONFERENCE. [Annual]

A 106.33:date • Item 25-A-3 (MF)
LIVESTOCK AND VETERINARY SCIENCES, ANNUAL REPORT OF THE NATIONAL RESEARCH PROGRAMS. (Veterinary Sciences Staff)

PURPOSE:– To improve the effectiveness of research, extension, and teaching in the food and agricultural sciences. Contains brief descriptions of research accomplishments concerning livestock, insects, diseases, equipment and housing.

Discontinued.

A 106.34:v.nos.&nos. • Item 25-A-2
DAIRY HERD IMPROVEMENT LETTER. v. 1–   1925– [Irregular]

See also A 77.608

A 106.35:date
CRD NEWSLETTER. [Monthly, except August]

Earlier A 43.49

A 106.36:date
AGRONOMY, WEED SCIENCE, SOIL CONSERVATION, AGRICULTURAL PROGRAMS. [Quarterly] (SEA-Extension)

Issued for State extension specialists.

A 106.37:nos.
RESEARCH INFORMATION LETTER. [Monthly] (Cooperative Research)

Discontinued with the November 1982 issue.

A 106.37/2:nos.
RESEARCH INFORMATION ABSTRACTS. [Monthly] (Cooperative Research)

Discontinued with the November 1982 issue.

A 106.38:date
NE REGIONAL STAFF LETTER. [Bimonthly]

Earlier A 77.29
COST OF FOOD AT HOME ESTIMATED FOR FOOD PLANS AT FOUR COST LEVELS. (Consumer and Food Economics Institute)

Issued for the following regions:–

A 106.39:date
U.S. AVERAGE. [Quarterly] (CFE [Adm]- 329)

A 106.39/2:date
NORTHEAST REGION. [Annual] (CFE [Adm]-330)

A 106.39/3:date
NORTH CENTRAL REGION. [Annual] (CFE [Adm]-331]

A 106.39/4:date
WESTERN REGION. [Annual] (CFE [Adm]- 332)

A 106.39/5:date
COST OF FOOD AT HOME ESTIMATED FOR FOOD PLANS AT THREE COST LEVELS, SOUTHERN REGION. [Annual] (Consumer and Food Economics Institute) (CFE [Adm]-333)

A 106.40:date
ANIMAL HEALTH SCIENCE RESEARCH ADVISORY BOARD. [Annual]

A 106.41:nos.
SEA NEWSMAKERS.

A 106.42:date • Item 22-A-14 (MF)
FOOD AND AGRICULTURE COMPETITIVELY
AWARDED RESEARCH AND EDUCATION
GRANTS. [Annual]

Includes such information as organization,
principal investigator, amount, and agreement
period.

A 106.42/2:date • Item 22-A-14 (MF)
ACTIVE FOREIGN AGRICULTURAL RESEARCH.

TECHNICAL INFORMATION SYSTEMS
(1978–1981)

CREATION AND AUTHORITY

The Technical Information Systems was established within the Science and Education Administration on January 2, 1978, superseding the
National Agricultural Library (A 17). The Science
and Education Administration (A 106) was abolished on June 17, 1981 and the Technical Information Systems was transferred to the reestablished National Agricultural Library (A 17).

A 106.101:date • Item 95-E
ANNUAL REPORT.
Earlier A 17.1

A 106.102:CT • Item 95-G
GENERAL PUBLICATIONS. [Irregular]
Earlier A 17.2
Discontinued.

A 106.109:v.nos.&nos. • Item 95-F
AGRICULTURAL LIBRARIES INFORMATION NOTES.
v. 1–   1975–   [Monthly]

PURPOSE:– To provide descriptions of information activities and resources in the field of
agriculture; a forum for all components of the
Department of Agriculture concerned with provision of information services; solutions of information problems developed in one location that
can be shared with others; information about what
is going on at the National Agricultural Library
and in the agri-research world.   Prior to February 1978 (v. 4, no.2) issue, published by the
National Agricultural Library (A 17.23).
ISSN 0095-2699

A 106.110:CT • Item 95-D
BIBLIOGRAPHIES AND LISTS OF PUBLICATIONS.
[Irregular]
Earlier A 17.18/2
Discontinued.

A 106.110/2:nos. • Item 95-A (MF)
LIBRARY LISTS. 1–   1942–   [Irregular]
Bibliographies.
Earlier A 17.17
Discontinued 1978.

A 106.110/3:nos. • Item 32-B-1
BIBLIOGRAPHIES AND LITERATURE OF AGRICUL-
TURE. BLA 1–   1978–   [Irregular]

PURPOSE:– To provide miscellaneous bibliographies covering topics connected with the work
of the Department of Agriculture.
Later A 105.55

A 106.111:date • Item 88-C
NUTRITION PROGRAM NEWS. [Bimonthly]

Prepared by the Institute of Home Economics, in cooperation with the Interagency Committee on Nutrition Education and School Lunch.
Four-page newsletter of activities on nutrition
education and the school lunch program.
Earlier A 77.710

OFFICE OF CONGRESSIONAL
RELATIONS
(1978–   )

CREATION AND AUTHORITY

The Office of Governmental and Public Affairs was established within the Department of
Agriculture in 1978, combining the former Office
of Communication (A 21), the Office of Congressional and Public Affairs, and the Office of Intergovernmental Affairs.
Name changed.

INFORMATION
Office of Congressional Relations
Department of Agriculture
1400 Independence Ave. SW, Rm. 213-A
Washington, D.C. 20250
(202) 720-7095
Fax: (202) 720-8077

A 107.1:date
ANNUAL REPORT.

A 107.2:CT • Item 90
GENERAL PUBLICATIONS. [Irregular]

A 107.8:CT • Item 90-C
HANDBOOKS, MANUALS, GUIDES. [Irregular]

A 107.9:date
FOOD AND HOME NOTES. [Weekly]
ISSN 0090-9688

A 107.10:date • Item 92
PUBLICATIONS AND VISUALS, QUARTERLY LIST.

Previously published bimonthly.
Former title: Bimonthly List of Publications
and Visuals.
Earlier A 21.6/5

A 107.11:nos.
SERVICE, USDA'S REPORT TO CONSUMERS. 1–
1963–   [Monthly]
PURPOSE:– To inform the public about consumer services of the Department. It tells of new
research developments in food, clothing, and
housing; offers information about gardening, recreation, nutrition, shopping tips, etc. The newsletter features brief items which editors may en-
large upon, or clubs may use or further develop in
their programs.
Earlier A 21.29

A 107.12:nos. • Item 91
LIST (series). 1–   [Irregular]
Earlier A 21.9/8
Discontinued.

A 107.12:5 • Item 91
POPULAR PUBLICATIONS FOR THE FARMER,
SUBURBANITE, HOMEMAKER, CONSUMER.
[Irregular]
Earlier A 21.9/8:5

A 107.12:11 • Item 91
LIST OF AVAILABLE PUBLICATIONS. [Annual]

Lists available publications (Departmental series only) from the Department of Agriculture or by purchase from the Superintendent of Documents. Arranged by broad subjects and sub-topics. Included is information
on the various periodicals and Department
series issued by the USDA.
Earlier A 21.9/8:11

A 107.13:nos. • Item 90-E
FARM PAPER LETTER. FPL 1–   1942–   [Weekly]
[farm press only]
Earlier A 21.32
Superseded by A 107.13/3

A 107.13/2:nos.
FARM BROADCASTERS LETTERS. [Weekly]
ISSN 0364-5444
See also A 21.34

A 107.13/3:nos. • Item 90-E
FARM PAPER LETTER. FPL 1000–   1985–
[Weekly]

PURPOSE:– To provide a service for agricultural writers throughout the United States, both
farm editors of daily newspapers and editorial
staffers of farm magazines. Essentially, it is designed to keep the farm press abreast with news
highlights of the week at the Department of Agriculture.
Supersedes A 107.13/3 due to redesignation
of issues starting with 1000 for 1985 issues.
Discontinued.

A 107.14:nos. • Item 90-B
AGRICULTURE FACT SHEETS, AFS- (series).
[Irregular]
Earlier A 21.35
Later A 1.121

A 107.15:nos.&nos. • Item 90-D-1
INSIDE INFORMATION. [Weekly]
See A 21.36

A 107.16:nos.
ISSUE BRIEFING PAPERS (series). [Irregular]

A 107.17:date
WEEKLY SUMMARY (Press Division)
See also A 21.6/6

A 107.18:date • Item 90-D
MAJOR NEWS RELEASES AND SPEECHES. [Weekly]

PURPOSE:– To present the week's news releases and speeches related to Agriculture Department activities.
Title varies.
See A1.143

OFFICE OF TRANSPORTATION
(1980–1990)

A 108.1:date
ANNUAL REPORT.

A 108.2:CT • Item 91-B
GENERAL PUBLICATIONS.

A 108.9:date
TRANSPORTATION UPDATE. [Monthly]

A 108.10:v.nos.&nos.
FRUIT AND VEGETABLE TRUCK COST REPORT.
[Monthly]

A 108.11:nos. • Item 91-A (MF)
OT- (series). 1–   [Irregular]

Includes studies on all phases of transportation of agricultural produce such as meat, fruit,
and vegetables.
Discontinued.

A 108.12:date • Item 91-C (MF)
GRAIN TRANSPORTATION SITUATION. [Weekly]

A 108.12/2:date • Item 91-C (MF)
BIMONTHLY GRAIN UPDATE.

Supplements Grain Transportation Situation
(A 108.12).
Discontinued.

RURAL BUSINESS-
COOPERATIVE SERVICE

IINFORMATION

Rural Business-Cooperative Service
South Agriculture Building
1400 Independence Ave., SW
Washington, DC 20250
(202) 690-4730
Fax:(202) 690-4737
http://www.rurdev.usda.gov/RBS

Formerly: Agricultural Cooperative Service

A 109.1:date   • **Item 65-C-1**
ANNUAL REPORT.

A 109.2:CT   • **Item 65-B**
GENERAL PUBLICATIONS. [Irregular]

A 109.9:nos.   • **Item 64-C (MF)**
SERVICE REPORT. 1–   1980–   [Irregular]

Each report concerns a different subject of
interest to the Service such as attitudes toward
cooperatives by bank trust and professional farm
managers.
ACS Agricultural Cooperative Service.

A 109.10:nos.   • **Item 64-A (MF)**
RBS RESEARCH REPORT (series). [Irregular]
Earlier A 105.31
Previously: ACS Research Reports

A 109.10/2:nos.   • **Item 65-B (MF)**
COOPERATIVE INFORMATION REPORTS. 1–
1981–   [Irregular]

A 109.11:v.nos.&nos.   • **Item 66**
FARMER COOPERATIVES. v. 1–   1934–   [Monthly]

Composed of articles concerned with the operations and management of farmers' cooperatives, and with recent developments in outstanding cooperatives in various parts of the country.
Former title: News for Farmer Cooperatives.
ISSN 0364-0736
Earlier A 105.19

A 109.11/2:date   • **Item 64-C (EL)**
FARMER COOPERATIVE STATISTICS. [Annual]
Earlier A 109.

FOOD SAFETY AND INSPECTION
SERVICE
(1981–   )

CREATION AND AUTHORITY

The Food and Safety and Inspection Service
was established on June 17, 1981 to supersede
the Food Safety and Quality Service (A 103) which
was abolished.

INFORMATION

Administrator
Food Safety and Inspection Service
Department of Agriculture
1400 Independence Ave. SW, 331-E
Washington, D.C. 20250
(202) 720-7025
Fax: (202) 205-0158
http://www.fsis.usda.gov

A 110.1:date
ANNUAL REPORTS.

A 110.2:CT   • **Item 31-C**
GENERAL PUBLICATIONS. [Irregular]
Earlier A 103.2

A 110.6/2:yr.-nos.   • **Item 21-T**
MEAT AND POULTRY INSPECTION REGULATIONS.

(Includes basic manual plus supplementary
material for an indefinite period)
Contains regulations for slaughter and processing of livestock, poultry, as well as for certain voluntary services and humane slaughter.
Earlier A 103.6/4

A 110.6/2-2:date   • **Item 21-T**
MEAT AND POULTRY INSPECTION REGULATIONS
(reprint). [Irregular]
Earlier A 103.6/4

A 110.8:CT   • **Item 32-A-3**
HANDBOOKS, MANUALS, GUIDES.
Earlier A 103.8

A 110.8/2:date   • **Item 31-C-1**
MEAT AND POULTRY INSPECTION MANUAL. (Includes basic manual plus monthly supplements
for an indefinite period)

PURPOSE:– To provide an official publication
of procedural guidelines and instructions to aid
all MPI employees in enforcing the laws and regulations related to Federal meat and poultry inspection.
Earlier A 103.8/3
Discontinued.

A 110.8/3   • **Item 32-A-6**
CHEMISTRY LABORATORY GUIDEBOOK.

PURPOSE:– To provide a reference book of
methods available for the analysis of the natural
constituents, additives, and biological and environmental residues, and biological residues that
may occur in meat and poultry products.

A 110.9:date   • **Item 31-C-1 (MF)**
COMPILATION OF MEAT AND POULTRY INSPEC-
TION ISSUANCES. [Monthly]

Former title: Issuance of the Meat and Poul-
try Inspection Program.
Discontinued as a separate subscription.
Earlier A 103.9/2
Later A 110.15:10
Combined with Meat and Poultry Inspection
Manual (A 101.8:M 46/2).

A 110.9/2:date   • **Item 31-C-1**
COMBINED COMPILATION OF MEAT AND POULTRY
INSPECTION ISSUANCES. [Annual]

Earlier title: Combined Meat and Poultry Inspection Issuances.

A 110.10   • **Item 21-T-4**
FOOD NEWS FOR CONSUMERS. v. 1–   1984–
[Irregular]

Published prior to 1984 Summer Issue without volume and issue numbers.
Non-depository.

A 110.11:date   • **Item 32-A (MF)**
MEAT AND POULTRY INSPECTION DIRECTORY.
[Semiannual]

Includes list of establishments operating under Federal Meat Inspection, public stockyards
under Animal Disease Eradication Inspection, licensed manufactures of biological products,
pathological laboratories, trained diagnosticians,
and State officials in charge of animal disease
control.
Issued in microfiche.
Earlier A 103.9

A 110.11/2:date   • **Item 11-D (MF)**
MEAT AND POULTRY AND EGG PRODUCTS INSPEC-
TION, REPORT OF THE SECRETARY OF AGRI-
CULTURE. 1972–   [Annual]

Includes CFR amendments, MPI-VS Bulletins,
MPI Directives, and changes to Meat and Poultry
Inspection Manual.
Earlier A 1.109/2

A 110.12:date   • **Item 32-A-2**
ACCEPTED MEAT AND POULTRY EQUIPMENT.
Earlier A 103.6/3

Ceased in Nov. 1995.

A 110.13:nos.   • **Item 21-T-2**
FSIS- (series). 1–   [Irregular]
Supersedes FSQS- (series) (A 103.14).

A 110.13/2   • **Item 21-T-2 (MF)**
FSIS BACKGROUND (Various Titles).

A 110.14:date   • **Item 31-C-2 (MF)**
FOREIGN PLANTS CERTIFIED TO EXPORT MEAT
TO THE UNITED STATES. [Annual]

Report submitted to Congress pursuant to
Section 20 of the Federal Meat Inspection Act.
Lists by foreign country the plants certified
as eligible to export meat to the Uninted States.
Lists plant number, addresses, and dates of re-
view.

See A 110.14/2

A 110.14/2   • **Item 31-C-2 (MF)**
FOREIGN COUNTRIES AND PLANTS CERTIFIED TO
EXPORT MEAT AND POULTRY TO THE UNITED
STATES.

A 110.15:date   • **Item 32-A-7 (MF)**
LIST OF PROPRIETARY SUBSTANCES AND NON-
FOOD COMPOUNDS AUTHORIZED FOR USE
UNDER USDA INSPECTION AND GRADING PRO-
GRAMS. [Annual]

PURPOSE:– To list proprietary substances
used in thepreparation of products and nonfood
compounds, for use in slaughtering and processing plants operating under the US Agriculture Department poultry, meat,rabbit, shell egg grading,
and egg products inspection programs.

Earlier in A 1.38

Discontinued.

A 110.15:10   • **Item 32-A-7 (MF)**
COMBINED COMPILATION OF MEAT AND POULTRY
INSPECTION ISSUANCES. [Annual]

Earlier A 110.9/2

A 110.16:CT   • **Item 31-C**
DIRECTORIES.

A 110.17   • **Item 21-T-2 (MF)**
FSIS FOOD SAFETY REVIEW. [Quarterly]

A 110.18:date   • **Item 31-C-1**
STANDARDS AND LABELING POLICY BOOK.

A 110.19   • **Item 31-C-1 (EL)**
THE FOOD SAFETY EDUCATOR. [Quarterly]

A 110.20   • **Item 31-C-3 (E)**
ELECTRONIC PRODUCTS.

A 110.21   • **Item 32-C-4**
POSTERS.

HUMAN NUTRITION INFORMATION SERVICE
(1981–   )

A 111.1:date   • **Item 125-B-1**
ANNUAL REPORTS.

A 111.2:CT   • **Item 125-B-1**
GENERAL PUBLICATIONS. [Irregular]
    Discontinued.

A 111.8:CT   • **Item 125-B-2**
HANDBOOKS, MANUALS, GUIDES. [Irregular]
    Discontinued.

A 111.9:letters-nos.   • **Item 125-B (MF)**
NATIONWIDE FOOD CONSUMPTION SURVEY (year),
REPORTS. [Irregular]

    Series of national and regional reports taken
    from Surveys made in 1965-66 and 1977-78.
    Discontinued.

A 111.9/2:nos.   • **Item 125-B (MF)**
NATIONWIDE FOOD CONSUMPTION SURVEY (year),
PRELIMINARY REPORTS.
    Discontinued.

A 111.9/3:date/nos.   • **Item 125-B (MF)**
CONTINUING SURVEY OF FOOD INTAKE BY INDI-
VIDUALS.
    Discontinued.

FARM SERVICE AGENCY

Previously: Consolidated Farm Service Agency

INFORMATION

    Public Affairs Staff
    Farm Service Agency
    Dept. of Agriculture
    3624 South Agriculture Bldg.
    Washington, DC 20250
    (202) 720-7809
    Fax: (202) 720-9105
    http://www.fsa.usda.gov

A 112.1:date
ANNUAL REPORT.

A 112.1/2   • **Item 31-H-1 (MF)**
EMERGENCY CONSERVATION PROGRAM, FISCAL
YEAR STATISTICAL SUMMARY.

A 112.2:CT   • **Item 68-E**
GENERAL PUBLICATIONS.

A 112.5   • **Item 68-6-1**
LAWS.

A 112.6   • **Item 68-6**
REGULATIONS, RULES, INSTRUCTIONS.

A 112.8:CT   • **Item 68-F**
HANDBOOKS, MANUALS AND GUIDES.

A 112.9   • **Item 68-F-1**
BIBLIOGRAPHIES AND LISTS OF PUBLICATIONS.

A 112.15:CT   • **Item 68-E-1 (P) (EL)**
CFSA COMMODITY FACT SHEET.

A 112.17   • **Item 68-E-2 (E)**
CROP INSURANCE RESEARCH AND DEVELOPMENT
BULLETINS.
    See A 62.17

A 112.18   • **Item 68-E-3**
POSTERS.

A 112.19   • **Item 68-E-4**
FORMS.

A 112.20:   • **Item 68-E-5 (EL)**
CROP INSURANCE MANAGER'S BULLETINS (series).

A 112.21:   • **Item 68-E-5 (E)**
ELECTRONIC PRODUCTS (misc.)

A 112.22:   • **Item 68-E-6 (EL)**
U.S. WAREHOUSE ACT LICENSED WAREHOUSES.

THE GRAIN INSPECTION, PACKERS AND STOCKYARDS ADMINISTRATION

INFORMATION

    Chief Information Officer
    Grain Inspection, Packers
        and Stockyards Administration
    Department of Agriculture
    1093 South Agriculture Bldg.
    Washington, DC 20250
    (202) 690-3204
    Fax: (202) 205-9237
    Toll Free: (800) 998-3447

A 113.1:date   • **Item 31-H (EL)**
ANNUAL REPORTS.

A 113.1/2   • **Item 31-H-1 (MF)**
EMERGENCY CONSERVATION PROGRAM, FISCAL
YEAR STATISTICAL SUMMARY.

A 113.2:CT   • **Item 31-F**
GENERAL PUBLICATIONS.

A 113.8:CT   • **Item 31-G**
HANDBOOKS, MANUALS, AND GUIDES.

A 113.10:   • **Item 31-J (MF) (EL)**
OFFICIAL UNITED STATES STANDARDS FOR GRAIN.

A 113.10/2   • **Item 31-J (EL)**
OFFICIAL UNITED STATES STANDARDS FOR RICE.

A 113.10/3   • **Item 31-J (EL)**
OFFICIAL UNITED STATES STANDARDS FOR
BEANS.

A 113.10/4   • **Item 31-J (EL)**
OFFICIAL UNITED STATES STANDARDS FOR PEAS
AND LENTILS.

A 113.11:   • **Item 31-J-1**
DIRECTORIES.

A 113.12:   • **Item 31-J-2**
REGULATIONS, RULES, INSTRUCTIONS.

A 113.14:   • **Item 31-J-3 (E)**
ELECTRONIC PRODUCTS. (Misc.)

A 113.15:   • **Item 31-J-4 (EL)**
PACKERS AND STOCKYARDS STATISTICAL REPORT.
    [Annual]

RURAL DEVELOPMENT

A 114.2:   • **Item 34-A-1**
GENERAL PUBLICATIONS.

A 114.10:   • **Item 34-A-2**
DIRECTORIES.

INFORMATION
    Rural Development
    Legislative and Public Affairs Staff
    Stop 0705
    Dept. of Agriculture
    1400 Independence Ave., SW
    Washington, DC 20250-0320
    (202) 720-6903

RURAL HOUSING SERVICE

INFORMATION

    Rural Development
    Legislative and Public Affairs Staff
    Stop 0705
    Dept. of Agriculture
    1400 Independence Ave., SW
    Washington, DC 20250-0320
    (202) 720-6903

A 115.2:   • **Item 35-A-1**
GENERAL PUBLICATIONS

ACTION
(1971–1994)

CREATION AND AUTHORITY

    ACTION was created as an independent
agency within the executive branch of the government under provisions of Reorganization Plan
1 of 1971, effect July 1, 1971, and Executive
Order 11603 of June 30, 1971. It was reorganized by act of October 1, 1973 (87 Stat. 405),
and functions relating to SCORE and ACT programs were transferred to the Small Business
Administration by EO 11871 of July 18, 1975 (40
ER 30915). Functions exercised by the director
of ACTION prior to March 31, 1995, were transferred to the Corporation for National and community Service (Y 3.N 21/29) (107 Stat. 888 and
Proclamation 6662 of April 4, 1994 (57 FR 16507)).

AA 1.1:date   • **Item 74-C-4 (MF)**
ANNUAL REPORT. 1st–   1972–
    See Y3.N21/29

AA 1.1/2   • **Item 74-C-4 (MF)**
ACTION, OFFICE OF THE INSPECTOR GENERAL,
SEMIANNUAL REPORT.
    See Y3.N21/29

AA 1.2:CT   • **Item 74-C-3**
GENERAL PUBLICATIONS.
    See Y3.N21/29

AA 1.8:CT   • **Item 74-C-11**
HANDBOOKS, MANUALS, GUIDES.
    See Y3.N21/29

AA 1.8/2:nos. • **Item 74-C-5**
HANDBOOKS (numbered).
    See Y3.N21/29

AA 1.9:date • **Item 857-H-13**
VISTA FACT BOOK. – 1972. [Monthly]

    Includes list of active projects, with directory
of names of project contracts and local sponsors.
    Earlier PrEx 10.21

AA 1.9/2:date • **Item 857-H-13**
DOMESTIC PROGRAMS FACT BOOK. [Quarterly]
    ISSN 0363-6860
    Discontinued.

AA 1.9/3:v.nos.&nos. • **Item 74-C-7**
VISTA CURRENTS. [Irregular]

    PURPOSE:– To provide technical assistance
for VISTA (Volunteers in Service to America), Volunteers and their sponsoring organizations. Contains short articles and lists of sources for further information on VISTA projects and planned
activities.
    Discontinued.

AA 1.9/4
ACTION PROGRAM HIGHLIGHTS.

    See Y3.N21/29

AA 1.9/5:nos. • **Item 30-A-2**
UPDATE ON ACTION. [Quarterly]

    See Y3.N21/29

AA 1.9/6 • **Item 30-A-2**
NATIONAL VISTA NEWS. [Quarterly]

    Later Y.3.N 21/29:17-15

AA 1.9/11-2 • **Item 30-A-2**
RSVP EXCHANGE.

AA 1.10:v.nos.&nos. • **Item 74-C-1**
TRANSITION, A MAGAZINE FOR FORMER ACTION
    VOLUNTEERS. v. 1– v. 2, no. 8. – August 1973.
    [Monthly]

AA 1.11:nos. • **Item 30-A-2**
ACTION PAMPHLETS. [Irregular]

AA 1.11/2:nos. • **Item 74-C-6**
ACTION FLYERS. [Irregular]
    Discontinued in 1979.

AA 1.12:date
BI-ANNUAL STATISTICAL SUMMARY. 1971–

AA 1.13:v.nos.&nos. • **Item 74-C-2**
INTERACTION. v. 1–   [Monthly]

    ISSN 0094-7105

    Discontinued.

AA 1.14:date & nos.
ACTION NEWS DIGEST. 1973–

    PURPOSE:– To portray current media cover-
age of ACTION and its international and domestic
volunteer programs. Drawn from thousands of clippings from newspapers, magazines and specialized publications, the clippings reproduced in the
News Digest attempt to reflect the range and
tone of news and editorial comment about AC-
TION. 400 copies of the News Digest are issued
each month; circulation is to ACTION staff members and interested outside parties who request
it. Contains 10 sections: general news, colum-
nists, editorials, letters to the editor, photo features, volunteers, School Partnership Program,
recruiting and training, and staff.

AA 1.15:date
ACTION UPDATE.

AA 1.16:v.nos.&nos. • **Item 74-C-8**
RECONNECTION. v. 1– 3.   – 1981.

    PURPOSE:– To serve as a newsletter for
former Peace Corps personnel and Vista volunteers. Consists of brief articles, book reviews,
photographs, notices about reunions, activities,
employment opportunities, etc.
    Discontinued 1981.

AA 1.17:nos. • **Item 74-C-9**
PEACE CORPS IN [various countries]. [Irregular]

    PURPOSE:– To provide informational folders
for Peace Corps volunteers, each devoted to a
separate country and containing black and white
photographs, a map of the country, and narrative
on the history, economy, government, and Peace
Corps activities in that country.
    Discontinued.

AA 1.18:CT • **Item 74-C-10**
POSTERS. [Irregular]
    See Y3.N21/29

AA 1.19:ltrs.nos. • **Item 74-C-12**
FORMS. [Irregular]
    See Y3.N21/29

AA 1.20:CT • **Item 74-C-13**
DIRECTORIES. [Irregular]

AA 1.21 • **Item 30-A-2**
FGP EXCHANGE. [Quarterly]
    See Y3N21/29

AA 1.22:CT • **Item 74-C-3**
FACT SHEETS.
    See Y3N21/29

OLDER AMERICANS VOLUNTEER PROGRAMS
(1971–   )

CREATION AND AUTHORITY

    The Older Americans Volunteer Programs was
established by the President and placed within
ACTION on July 1, 1971.

AA 2.1:date
ANNUAL REPORT. • **Item 74-B-1**
GENERAL PUBLICATIONS.
    See Y3N21/29

AA 2.9:nos.
OLDER AMERICANS IN ACTION. 1– 16. – October
    1973. [Monthly]

AA 2.10:date • **Item 74-B-2**
PRIME TIMES. v. 1–   1978– [Bimonthly]

    PURPOSE:– To provide a newsletter for and
about older volunteers in the Retired Senior Volunteer Program, the Foster Grandparent, and the
Senior Companion Programs– a forum where issues that affect older Americans, as individuals
and volunteers, can be fruitfully discussed.

    Discontinued.

NATIONAL CENTER FOR SERVICE LEARNING
(1980–   )

AA 3.1:date
ANNUAL REPORT.

AA 3.2:CT
GENERAL PUBLICATIONS.

AA 3.8:CT • **Item 74-D-2**
HANDBOOKS, MANUALS, GUIDES.
    See Y3N21/29

AA 3.9:v.nos.&nos. • **Item 74-D-1**
SYNERGIST. v. 1– 11.   – 1982. [3 times a year]

    PURPOSE:– To provide a journal for the Na-
tional Student Volunteer Program.
    Issued in Spring, Fall, and Winter.
    ISSN 0049-2752
    Discontinued.

PEACE CORPS
(1971– 1981)

CREATION AND AUTHORITY

    The Peace Corps was established within the
Department of State (S 19) by Executive Order
10924, effective March 1, 1961 and the Peace
Corps Act of September 22, 1961, as amended
(75 Stat. 612; 22 U.S.C. 2501 et seq.). The functions, powers, and responsibilities were transferred to ACTION by Reorganization Plan 1 of
1971, effective July 1, 1971. The Peace Corps
was transferred from ACTION to become an independent agency (PE 1) within the executive department by the International Security and Development Act of 1981 (95 Stat. 612), approved
February 21, 1982.

AA 4.1:date • **Item 900-D**
ANNUAL REPORT.
    Earlier S 19.1

AA 4.2:CT • **Item 900-D**
GENERAL PUBLICATIONS.
    Earlier S 19.2
    See PC 1.2

AA 4.8:CT
HANDBOOKS, MANUALS, GUIDES.

AA 4.8/2:nos. • **Item 74-E**
PROGRAM AND TRAINING JOURNAL MANUAL
    SERIES. 1–   [Irregular]
    Later PE 1.10

AA 4.8/3:nos.
INFORMATION COLLECTION AND EXCHANGE,
    MANUAL SERIES, 1–   [Irregular]

AA 4.9:date
BIBLIOGRAPHIES AND LISTS OF PUBLICATIONS.

AA 4.10:nos.
PROGRAM AND TRAINING JOURNAL REPRINT
    SERIES.

AA 4.10/2:v.nos.&nos. • **Item 74-E-1**
PEACE CORPS TIMES. v. 1–   1978– [Monthly]
    Later PE 1.9

AA 4.12:nos.
INFORMATION COLLECTION AND EXCHANGE, RE-
    PRINT SERIES, R 1–   [Irregular]

ARMS CONTROL AND DISARMAMENT AGENCY (1961– 1998)

CREATION AND AUTHORITY

The United States Arms Control and Disarmament Agency was established by the act approved September 26, 1961 (75 Stat. 631; 22 U.S.C. 2551).

Abolished by an Act of October 21, 1998 (112 Stat. 2681-767) and functions transferred to the Secretary of State.

AC 1.1:date • Item 125-A-12 (MF)
ACDA ANNUAL REPORT TO CONGRESS. 1st– 1961–   [Annual]

Submitted by the Director to the President and Congress Pursuant to the Arms Control and Disarmament Act. Covers the Calendar year.
Also issued in the House Document series.
Formerly distributed to Depository Libraries under item number 124-A-4 and 125-A-9.
Discontinued.

AC 1.2:CT • Item 125-A-3
GENERAL PUBLICATIONS.

AC 1.9 • Item 125-A-1
GENERAL SERIES. 1–   1961–   [Irregular]
Discontinued.

AC 1.10 • Item 125-A-2
ECONOMIC SERIES. 1–   1962–   [Irregular]
Discontinued.

AC 1.11
DISARMAMENT DOCUMENT SERIES. 1–   [Irregular]

Continues series published by former agency, U.S. Disarmament Administration, Department of State (S 1.117/3).
Consists primarily of statements of U.S. Representatives to the United Nations on matters dealing with disarmament or nuclear test bans, texts of notes exchanged by U.S. and U.S.S.R., resolutions, etc.

AC 1.11/2 • Item 865-B
DOCUMENTS ON DISARMAMENT. 1945/59– [Annual]

Presents basic official documents regarding international developments on disarmament, arms control, and related matters, including texts of speeches, statements and papers in various forums such as the United Nations General Assembly. The international negotiations and the activities of the U.S. Arms Control and Disarmament Agency during the year are included in this publication. Bibliography, topical list of documents, and other bibliographical aids are also included.
Prior to 1961, issued by the Department of State (S 1.117).
Discontinued 1991.

AC 1.12 • Item 125-A-5 (MF)
ADDRESSES. [Irregular]
Discontinued.

AC 1.13:CT • Item 125-A-6 (MF)
BIBLIOGRAPHIES AND LISTS OF PUBLICATIONS.
Discontinued.

AC 1.13/2-2 • Item 125-A-11 (MF)
CURRENT ARTICLES OF INTEREST CUMULATIVE INDEX.
Discontinued.

AC 1.14
REPORT ON U.S. GOVERNMENT RESEARCH AND STUDIES IN THE FIELD OF ARMS CONTROL AND DISARMAMENT MATTERS. [Semiannual]
AC 1.15 • Item 125-A-7
RESEARCH REPORTS. [Irregular]
Discontinued.

AC 1.16:[nos.] • Item 125-A-8
WORLD MILITARY EXPENDITURES AND RELATED DATA. 1965–   [Annual]

PURPOSE:– To assess the size and impact of the world's military expenditures. The survey covers 120 countries, all those for which factual data exist or for which there is some reasonable basis for estimation.

AC 1.17: • Item 125-A-10
ARMS CONTROL UPDATE. [Monthly]

PURPOSE:– To inform the public on administration activities in the area of arms control through features and articles on such topics as negotiating with the Soviets.
Discontinued.

NATIONAL ARCHIVES (1934– 1949)

CREATION AND AUTHORITY

The National Archives was established by the National Archives Act, approved June 19, 1934 (48 Stat. 1122). The National Archives was transferred to the General Services Administration by the Federal Property and Administrative Services Act of 1949 (63 Stat. 378), effective July 1, 1949. The National Archives was succeeded by the National Archives and Records Service (GS 4), which was established on December 11, 1949.

AE 1.1:date
ANNUAL REPORTS.
Later GS 4.1

AE 1.2:CT
GENERAL PUBLICATIONS.
Later GS 4.2

AE 1.3:nos.
BULLETINS.
Later GS 4.3

AE 1.4:nos.
CIRCULARS.

AE 1.6:CT
REGULATIONS, RULES, AND INSTRUCTIONS.
Later GS 4.6

AE 1.7:nos.
NATIONAL ARCHIVES ACCESSIONS. [Quarterly]
Later GS 4.8

AE 1.8:date
ANNUAL REPORTS OF ARCHIVIST OF FRANKLIN D. ROOSEVELT LIBRARY.
Later GS 4.9

AE 1.9:nos.
STAFF INFORMATION CIRCULARS.
Later GS 4.12

AE 1.10:nos.
PRELIMINARY INVENTORIES.
Later GS 4.10

AE 1.11:nos.
SPECIAL LISTS.
Later GS 4.7

AE 1.12:nos.
REFERENCE INFORMATION CIRCULARS.
Later GS 4.15

AE 1.13:nos.
MISCELLANEOUS PROCESSED DOCUMENTS.

AE 1.14:nos.
RECORDS ADMINISTRATION STUDIES.
AE 1.15:nos.
PRELIMINARY CHECKLISTS.

AE 1.16:CT
ADDRESSES.

AE 1.17:nos.
INDEXES.

AE 1.18:nos.
SPECIAL REPORTS.

AE 1.19:nos.
INVENTORIES OF WORLD WAR II.

AE 1.20:dt&nos.
CIRCULAR LETTERS.

AE 1.21:nos.
NATIONAL ARCHIVES FACSIMILES.

NATIONAL ARCHIVES AND RECORDS ADMINISTRATION
(1985–   )

CREATION AND AUTHORITY

The National Archives and Records Administration was established by an act of October 19, 1984 (98 Stat. 2280; 44 U.S.C. 2101 et. seq.), effective April 1, 1985 to succeed the National Archives and Records Service in the General Services Administration (GS 4).

INFORMATION
National Archives and
Records Administration
8601 Adelphi Road
College Park, MD 20740-6001
(301) 713-6800
Fax: (301) 837-0483
Toll-Free: (866) 272-6272
http://www.nara.gov

AE 1.101:date   • **Item 569-G (MF)**
ANNUAL REPORT.
Summarize activities of the National Archives and Records Administration.

AE 1.101/2   • **Item 569-G-1 (MF)**
OFFICE OF INSPECTOR GENERAL, SEMIANNUAL REPORT TO THE CONGRESS.

AE 1.101/3   • **Item 569-G-2 (EL)**
(INFORMATION SECURITY OVERSIGHT OFFICE) ANNUAL REPORT.

AE 1.102:CT   • **Item 569-B-2**
GENERAL PUBLICATIONS. [Irregular]
Official Use Only

AE 1.103:date• **Item 569-C-3**
NARA BULLETIN.
Bulletins from the National Archives and Records Administration to heads of federal agencies on miscellaneous topics.
Earlier GS 4.18/2

AE 1.103:date   • **Item 569-C-3**
NARA BULLETIN.

AE 1.108   • **Item 569-B**
HANDBOOKS, MANUALS AND GUIDES.

AE 1.108   • **Item 569-B**
GUIDES TO THE MICROFILMED RECORDS OF THE GERMAN NAVY. [Irregular]
Earlier GS 4.18/2

AE 1.109   • **Item 569-C-2**
QUARTERLY UPDATE.
This publication was suspended from April 1988 to January 1991.
Earlier GS 4.17/5-3

AE 1.110:CT   • **Item 569-C-3**
BIBLIOGRAPHIES AND LISTS OF PUBLICATIONS. [Irregular]
Earlier GS 4.17/3

AE 1.110/2:CT   • **Item 569-C-2**
LIST OF AUDIOVISUAL MATERIALS PRODUCED BY THE UNITED STATES GOVERNMENT. [Irregular]
Earlier GS 4.17/5-2
Discontinued.

AE 1.110/3:CT   • **Item 569-E**
POSTERS. [Irregular]
Earlier GS 4.26

AE 1.110/4:date   • **Item 569-C-2**
MEDIA RESOURCE CATALOG FROM THE NATIONAL AUDIOVISUAL CENTER. [Irregular]
Earlier AE 1.110:M 46
Discontinued.

AE 1.110/5:   • **Item 569-C-5 (MF)**
FEDERAL AUDIOVISUAL ACTIVITY, FISCAL YEAR.

This report on expenditure of audiovisual funds by federal agencies complies with Office of Management and Budget (OMB) Circular A-114.

AE 1.111:v.nos.&nos.
PROLOGUE. [Quarterly]
Earlier GS 4.23

AE 1.112:nos.   • **Item 570-C-1 (MF)**
GUIDES TO GERMAN RECORDS MICROFILMED AT ALEXANDRIA, VIRGINIA. [Irregular]
Earlier GS 4.18

AE 1.112/2:nos.   • **Item 570-C (MF)**
GUIDES TO THE MICROFILMED RECORDS OF THE GERMAN NAVY, 1850-1945.

AE 1.113:nos.   • **Item 569**
GENERAL INFORMATION LEAFLETS (series). 1– [Irregular]

PURPOSE:– To acquaint the general public with the facilities and services of the National Archives and Records Service. Includes such items as a leaflet about the National Archives in general, the regulations for the public use of records, list of publications, slides, and photographs, and sources for genealogical research.
Earlier GS 4.22

AE 1.114:date   • **Item 569-A-1 (MF)**
NATIONAL HISTORICAL PUBLICATIONS AND RECORDS COMMISSION: ANNUAL REPORT.
Earlier GS 4.14/3

AE 1.114/2:   • **Item 569-A-2 (MF) (EL)**
ANNOTATION, THE NEWSLETTER OF THE NATIONAL HISTORICAL PUBLICATIONS AND RECORDS COMMISSION. [3 times a year]

Newsletter on activities of the National Historical Publications and Records Commission. Contains articles on such matters as regional records projects funded by the Commission and recent records products.

AE 1.114/3:letter+nos./date   • **Item 569-A-3**
NATIONAL HISTORICAL PUBLICATIONS AND RECORDS COMMISSION: GENERAL PUBLICATIONS.

AE 1.115:nos.   • **Item 570-A (MF)**
SPECIAL LIST (series). 1–   1942–   [Irregular]

Lists of material in the National Archives covering subjects rather than agencies as the Preliminary Inventories do. Covers all types of documents, films, maps, population schedules, etc., under the jurisdiction of the National Archives.

AE 1.115:nos.   • **Item 570-A (MF)**
FEDERAL POPULATION AND MORTALITY SCHEDULES (years), IN THE NATIONAL ARCHIVES AND THE STATES. [Irregular]
Earlier GS 4.7

AE 1.116:date
ON THE RECORD. [Annual]

AE 1.117:   • **Item 569-B-4 (MF)**
NEWS FROM THE ARCHIVES. [Quarterly]

A quarterly compilation by the National Archives and Records Administration.
Discontinued.

AE 1.117/2:v.nos./nos.   • **Item 569-H**
THE RECORD, NEWS FROM THE NATIONAL ARCHIVES AND RECORDS ADMINISTRATION.
Temp. Suspended

AE 1.118:   • **Item 569-B-3**
NATIONAL ARCHIVES UPDATE. [Quarterly]

The National Archives Education Branch publishes Update aspart of its community, technical, and junior college program. Intended to helppublicize the holdings, resources, and educational services of the National Archives that can supplement and enrich college instruction. May reproduce federal records considered permanently valuable.

AE 1.119:   • **Item 569-C-4**
NATIONAL ARCHIVES MICROFILM PUBLICATIONS PAMPHLET DESCRIBING ...
Earlier GS 4.20

AE 1.121:   • **Item 569-B-6 (MF)**
RECORD FACTS UPDATE. [Quarterly]

Published by the Records Administration Information Center to share news about records administration throughout the Federal records community. Contains news items on records management and a calendar of comingevents of interest to managers of recorded information.

AE 1.122:date   • **Item 569-B-2 (MF)**
NATIONAL ARCHIVES AND RECORDS ADMINISTRATION TELEPHONE DIRECTORY.

Discontinued.

AE 1.123:nos.   • **Item 569-B-4**
ARCHIVES II RESEARCHER BULLETIN.
Discontinued.

AE 1.124:nos.   • **Item 569**
REFERENCE INFORMATION PAPER (series).

AE 1.125   • **Item 569-B-7 (MF)**
NATIONAL ARCHIVES AND RECORDS ADMINISTRATION STRATEGIC PLAN FOR A CHALLENGING FEDERAL ENVIRONMENT. [Annual]

AE 1.126   • **Item 569-I (E)**
QUARTERLY COMPILATION OF PERIODICAL LITERATURE REFLECTING THE USE OF RECORDS IN THE NATIONAL ARCHIVES. [Quarterly]
Discontinued.

AE 1.127   • **Item 569-I (E)**
ELECTRONIC PRODUCTS.

AE 1.128:   • **Item 569-I (EL)**
QUARTERLY COMPILATION OF PERIODICAL LITERATURE REFLECTING THE USE OF RECORDS IN THE NATIONAL ARCHIVES. [Quarterly]

AE 1.129   • **Item 569-I-01 (P) (EL)**
NATIONAL ARCHIVES, CALENDAR OF EVENTS. [Bi-monthly]

FEDERAL REGISTER DIVISION
(1935–1949)

CREATION AND AUTHORITY

The Federal Register Division was established within the National Archives by Act of Congress, approved July 26, 1935. The Federal Register Division was succeeded by the Office of the Federal Register (GS 4.100).

AE 2.1:date
ANNUAL REPORTS.

Later GS 4.101

AE 2.2:CT
GENERAL PUBLICATIONS.

Later GS 4.102

AE 2.5:CT
LAWS.

AE 2.6:CT
REGULATIONS, RULES, AND INSTRUCTIONS.

AE 2.7:vol.
FEDERAL REGISTER.

Later GS 4.107

AE 2.8:vol.
CODE OF REGULATIONS OF U.S. OF AMERICA.

AE 2.9:date
CODE OF FEDERAL REGULATIONS OF UNITED STATES CUMULATIVE SUPPLEMENTS.

AE 2.10:incl.dts.
– CUMULATIVE SUPPLEMENTS.

AE 2.11:date
UNITED STATES GOVERNMENT MANUAL.

Earlier Pr 33.407
Later GS 4.109

AE 2.12:title nos.
CODE OF FEDERAL REGULATIONS.

Earlier AE 2.8
Later GS 4.108

FEDERAL REGISTER OFFICE
(1985–   )

CREATION AND AUTHORITY

The Federal Register Office (GS 4.100) was transferred from the General Services effective April 1, 1985.

INFORMATION

Office of the Federal Register
National Archives and Records Administration
700 Pennsylvania Avenue, N.W.
Washington, D.C. 20408
(202) 523-4534
Fax: (202) 523-6866
E-mail: info@fedreg.nara.gov
http://www.nara.gov/fedreg

Street Address:
800 North Capitol Street, NW
Washington, DC 20002

AE 2.102:CT   **• Item 574**
GENERAL PUBLICATIONS. [Irregular]

• Item 573-D (MF)

AE 2.106:v. nos./nos.   **• Item 573-C (P)**
FEDERAL REGISTER. [Daily]   **• Item 573-D (MF)**

Published daily except Sunday, Monday, and day following official Federal holiday. Includes full text of Presidential Proclamations and Executive Orders, and any order, regulation, notice, or similar document promulgated by Federal administrative agencies which has general applicability and legal effect.

The material first presented in the daily issues of the Federal Register is later codified and published in the Code of Federal Regulations.
Citation: F.R.
Indexed by:–
Chemical Abstracts
Selected Water Resources Abstracts
Earlier GS 4.107

Non-depository

AE 2.106   **• Item 573-F (EL)**
FEDERAL REGISTER: INCLUDES PRESIDENTIAL PROCLAMATIONS, EXECUTIVE ORDERS, RULES, REGULATIONS, AND NOTICES. [Daily]
Online service available on Internet or via asynchronous connection. Issued when the Federal Register is published.

AE 2.106/a   **• Item 573**
FEDERAL REGISTER REPRINT SERIES (and unnumbered separates). [Irregular]

• Item 573-C (P) (EL)
AE 2.106/2:date/nos.   **• Item 573-D (MF)**
CODE OF FEDERAL REGULATIONS, LSA, LIST OF CFR SECTIONS AFFECTED. [Monthly]

AE 2.106/2-2:date   **• Item 573-C (P) (EL)**
LIST OF CFR SECTIONS AFFECTED (Cumulative).

• Item 572-C (MF) (EL)
AE 2.106/3   **• Item 572-B (P) (EL)**
CODE OF FEDERAL REGULATIONS (Hardcopy).
PURPOSE:– To provide, in a single series of volumes, the codification of all executive and administrative rules and regulations, originally published in the Federal Register, having a general applicability and the effects of law.
Arranged into broad subject groups, or titles, similar to scheme used in the United States Code. Each volume of the Code of Federal Regulations is revised annually except three volumes (Title 32-National Defense [Parts 590-699]; Title 35-Panama Canal; and Title 37-Patents, Trademarks, and Copyrights). These volumes are supplemented annually with cumulative pocket supplements which when used with the basic volumes give a complete text of the rules and regulations as of January 1 of the current year.
For those maintaining complete sets of the Code, the Superintendent of Documents provides a yearly subscription service which includes all pocket supplements and completely revised-volumes issued during the year.
Citation: C.F.R
Earlier GS 4.108
Following is a list of the basic titles:

Title 1- General Provisions.
Title 2- Congress.
Title 3- The President.
Title 3A- The President, Appendix.
Title 4- Accounts.
Title 5- Administrative personnel.
Title 6- Agricultural Credit (Vacated).
Title 7- Agriculture.
Title 8- Aliens and Nationality.
Title 9- Animals and Animal Products.
Title 10- Energy.
Title 11- Federal Elections.
Title 12- Banks and Banking.
Title 13- Business Credit and Assistance.
Title 14- Aeronautics and Space.
Title 15- Commerce and Foreign Trade.
Title 16- Commercial Practices.
Title 17- Commodity and Securities Exchanges.
Title 18- Conservation of Power and Water Resources.
Title 19- Customs Duties.
Title 20- Employees' Benefits.
Title 21- Food and Drugs.
Title 22- Foreign Relations.
Title 23- Highways.
Title 24- Housing and Urban Development.
Title 25- Indians.
Title 26- Internal Revenues.
Title 27- Alcohol, Tobacco Products and Firearms.
Title 28- Judicial Administration.
Title 29- Labor.
Title 30- Mineral Resources
Title 31- Money and Finance, Treasury.
Title 32- National Defense.
Title 32A- National Defense, Appendix.
Title 33- Navigation and Navigable Waters.
Title 34- Education.
Title 35- Panama Canal.
Title 36- Parks, Forests, and Pubic Property.
Title 37- Patents, Trade-marks, and Copyrights.
Title 38- Pensions, Bonuses and Veteran's Relief.
Title 39- Postal Service.
Title 40- Protection of the Environment.
Title 41- Public Contracts and Property Management.
Title 42- Public Health.
Title 43- Public Lands, Interior.
Title 44- Emergency Management and Assistance.
Title 45- Public Welfare.
Title 46- Shipping.
Title 47- Telecommunication.
Title 48- Federal Acquisition Regulations System.
Title 49- Transportation.
Title 50- Wildlife and Fisheries.
GENERAL INDEX.

AE 2.106/3-2:date • Item 572
CFR INDEX AND FINDING AIDS. [Annual]

AE 2.106/4:date/v. • Item 573
PRIVACY ACT ISSUANCES COMPILATION. [Annual]
Discontinued.

AE 2.106/4-2 • Item 574-C-1 (EL)
PRIVACY ACT ISSUANCES COMPILATION.
Issued on CD-ROM.

AE 2.108:CT • Item 574-B
HANDBOOKS, MANUALS, GUIDES. [Irregular]

AE 2.108/2:date • Item 577 (P) (EL)
UNITED STATES GOVERNMENT MANUAL. [Annual]

Official handbook about the Federal Government containing sections describing the creation and authority, organization, and functions of the agencies in the legislative, judicial, and executive branches. Supplemental information following these sections include brief descriptions of quasi-official agencies and selected international organizations; selected boards, committees and commissions; commonly used abbreviations of the names of agencies and departments; organizational charts of the Departments and selected agencies; list of executive agencies and functions of the Federal Government abolished, transferred, or terminated subsequent to March 4, 1933; list of representative publications of the Government agencies.
Prior to 1973 entitled United States Government Organization Manual.

Earlier GS 4.109

AE 2.109: • Item 577-A (EL)
WEEKLY COMPILATION OF PRESIDENTIAL DOCUMENTS.

Published every Monday, contains statements, messages and other Presidential materials released by the White House up to Friday (5:00 p.m.) each week. Includes such items as addresses and remarks, appointments and nominations, bill signings, executive orders, letters, memorandums, etc. of special interest, new conferences, proclamations, swearing-in ceremonies, etc. Included also is a checklist of White House news releases not included in the Compilation, a list of acts approved by the President.
Earlier GS 4.114

AE 2.110:Cong.-nos. • Item 575 (P) (EL)
SLIP LAWS (Public). [Irregular]

Slip Laws are published immediately after enactment in two series: Public Laws and Private Laws. The individual copies of the public laws are offered in subscription form from the Superintendent of Documents; those for private laws are available upon request for a specific law from the House Document Room as long as the supply lasts.
The texts of the laws first appearing as slip laws are collected into the bound volumes of the Statutes at Large. Notation is made on the slip laws of the pagination to be used in the forthcoming bound volume, thereby permitting early citation of volume and page for reference purposes.
Earlier GS 4.110

AE 2.110/2 • Item 575-A
PRIVATE LAWS AND PUBLIC LAWS.

Earlier GS 4.110/3

AE 2.111:v.nos. • Item 576
UNITED STATES STATUTES AT LARGE. [Annual]

Annual bound volumes containing texts of all the laws and concurrent resolutions enacted for each session of Congress, as well as the texts of the reorganization plans, amendments to the Constitution, and proclamations.
Citation: Stat.
Earlier GS 4.111
Earlier S 7.9

AE 2.112:date • Item 574-B-1
RECORDS ADMINISTRATION TRAINING. [Annual]

Brochure on records administration training classes.

Discontinued.

AE 2.113:date • Item 574-A-1
CODIFICATION OF PRESIDENTIAL PROCLAMATIONS AND EXECUTIVE ORDERS. [Irregular]

PURPOSE:– To provide in one convenient reference source proclamations and Executive orders which have general applicability and continuing effect. The publication is an editorial codification and is not intended to be used as a definitive legal authority.

Earlier GS 4.113/3

Discontinued.

AE 2.114:date • Item 574-A
PUBLIC PAPERS OF THE PRESIDENT OF THE UNITED STATES. [Annual]

Earlier GS 4.113

AE 2.115 • Item 574-C (E)
ELECTRONIC PRODUCTS. [Irregular]

BROADCASTING BOARD OF GOVERNORS

CREATION AND AUTHORITY

Board originally functioned under the U.S. Information Agency. It became an independent agency in October 1999, as mandated by the Foreign Affairs Reform and Restructuring Act (P.L. 105-277) of 1998.

INFORMATION

Broadcasting Board of Governors
330 Independence Ave. SW
Washington, D.C. 20237
(202) 619-2538
Fax: (202) 619-1241
http://www.bbg.gov

B 1.1 • Item 1100-B (EL)
ANNUAL REPORT.

B 1.2 • Item 1100-B-1
GENERAL PUBLICATIONS

B 1.15 • Item 1100-B-2 (E)
ELECTRONIC PRODUCTS

INTERNATIONAL BROADCASTING BUREAU (1994–   )

CREATION AND AUTHORITY

Established by the International Broadcasting Act of 1994 (P.L. 103-236) under the U.S. Information Agency. Became an independent agency in October 1999, as mandated by the Foreign Affairs Reform and Restructuring Act (P.L. 105-277) of 1998.

INFORMATION

Office of External Affairs
International Broadcasting Bureau
330 Independence Ave. SW
Washington, D.C. 20237
(202) 619-2538
Fax: (202) 619-1241
E-mail: pubaff@voa.gov
http://www.ibb.gov

B 2.1   **• Item 1100-C**
GENERAL PUBLICATIONS.

DEPARTMENT OF COMMERCE (1913–   )

CREATION AND AUTHORITY

The Department of Commerce and Labor was established as an executive department by act of Congress, approved February 14, 1903 (32 Stat. 825) to which certain agencies of the Treasury Department, the Department of State, and the Department of the Interior were transferred. It became the Department of Commerce by act of Congress, approved March 4, 1913 (37 Stat. 736), which transferred all labor functions to the newly created Department of Labor (L 1).

INFORMATION

Office of Public Affairs
Department of Commerce
Fourteenth Street and Constitution Ave. NW
Washington, D. C. 20230
(202) 482-2000
http://www.doc.gov

C 1.1:date   **• Item 126 (MF)**
ANNUAL REPORT OF SECRETARY, DEPARTMENT OF COMMERCE AND LABOR. 1st– 10th. 1903– 1912.

Also issued in House Documents series, 1912.

C 1.1:date   **• Item 126**
COMMERCE IN [year], ANNUAL REPORT OF THE SECRETARY OF COMMERCE. 1st–   1913– [Annual]
Also issued in House Documents series, 1913– 20.
Printed editions for 1943– 45 not issued.
Prior to 1960, issued as Annual report.
Report covers the fiscal year.
Covers the services and information provided to industry and business by the Department of Commerce.

C 1.1/2:date • Item 126-D-11 (EL)SEMIANNUAL REPORT OF THE INSPECTOR GENERAL TO CONGRESS. (Office of the Inspector General)

C 1.1/2-2:date   **• Item 126-H (MF)**
OFFICE OF INSPECTOR GENERAL, AUDIT AND INSPECTION PLAN (FY). [Biennial]

C 1.1/3:   **• Item 126-C-5 (MF)**
ANNUAL PERFORMANCE REPORT, MINORITY BUSINESS DEVELOPMENT AGENCY. [Annual]

Summarizes the performance of the Minority Business Development Agency in terms of minority clients assisted, businesses started and assisted, dollars generated, and accomplishments through networking.

C 1.1/4:date   **• Item 126-F (MF)**
ANNUAL REPORT ON U.S. EXPORT COMPETITIVENESS AS REQUIRED BY SECTION 206 OF THE 1992 EXPORT ENHANCEMENT ACT.

C 1.1/5:date   **• Item 126-G (MF)**
COMMERCE WORKS! A SUMMARY OF THE ECONOMIC ACCOMPLISHMENTS OF THE DEPARTMENT.

Discontinued.

C 1.1/6:date   **• Item 126-A-1(E)**
NATIONAL EXPORT STRATEGY. [Annual]
Previously C 1.2:EX

C 1.1/7   **• Item 126-A-2 (EL)**
U.S. GOVERNMENT WORKING GROUP ON ELECTRONIC COMMERCE. [Annual]

C 1.2:CT   **• Item 128**
GENERAL PUBLICATIONS.

[C 1.3]
BULLETINS.

None issued.

C 1.4:
CIRCULARS.

C 1.4/2:letters-nos.
DEPARTMENT CIRCULARS.

C 1.5:date
ESTIMATES OF APPROPRIATIONS FOR DEPARTMENT OF COMMERCE. 1905.

C 1.6:nos.
DECISIONS. 1– 120. July 9, 1903– February 8, 1912.

C 1.6/3   **• Item 306-A**
ARMED FORCES REPORT, ARMED FORCES DAY. [Annual]

Continues: Speakers' Guide for Service Spokesmen, Power for Peace, Armed Forces Day.

C 1.7:CT
REPORTS OF TRADE CONDITIONS. 1906– 1909.

Also published in Special Agents series (C 10.13).

C 1.8:CT
RULES AND REGULATIONS.

C 1.8/2:nos.
DEFENSE AIR TRANSPORTATION ADMINISTRATIVE ORDERS. 1– [10]. [1960].

Reprinted from the Federal register.

C 1.8/3:CT   **• Item 128-A**
HANDBOOKS, MANUALS, GUIDES.

C 1.8/4   **• Item 128-A-1 (MF)**
FEDERAL METEOROLOGICAL HANDBOOKS. 1– 1968–   [Irregular]

C 1.8/4:3   **• Item 128-A**
RADIOSONDE OBSERVATIONS. 1969–   [Irregular]

Supersedes publication Manual of Radiosonde Observations (WBAN), Circular P, issued by the Weather Bureau (C 30.4:P).
Issued in looseleaf form. Prepared in cooperation with the Department of Defense.

C 1.9/1:date
NATIONAL COUNCIL OF COMMERCE, PROCEEDINGS OF ANNUAL MEETINGS. 1st– 3d. 1907– 1909.

C 1.9/2:date
NATIONAL COUNCIL OF COMMERCE, PROCEEDINGS OF QUARTERLY MEETINGS OF EXECUTIVE COMMITTEE. 1st. Apr. 7, 1909.

C 1.10:CT
INTERNATIONAL CONFERENCE ON SAFETY AT SEA, REPORTS. 1913– 1914.

See also S 5.29

C 1.10/2:CT
INTERNATIONAL CONFERENCE ON SAFETY OF LIFE AT SEA, LONDON, 1929, REPORTS. 1929.

See also S 5.29.

C 1.11:CT
TABLES TO CONVERT [FOREIGN MONEYS, WEIGHTS AND MEASURES INTO U.S. STANDARDS]. 1911.

Originally published by the Bureau of Statistics, Department of the Treasury.

C 1.12:CT
POSTERS. 1918.

C 1.13:CT
ELIMINATION OF WASTE SERIES. 1923– 1932.

C 1.14:CT
NATIONAL COMMITTEE ON WOOD UTILIZATION. PUBLICATIONS.

The National Committee on Wood Utilization was established in 1925 by direction of the President. The Committee was abolished by Executive Order 6179-B of June 16, 1933.

C 1.15:CT
PRESIDENT'S ORGANIZATION OF UNEMPLOYMENT RELIEF. PUBLICATIONS.

The President's Emergency Committee for Employment was established in Oct. 1930. On Aug. 19, 1931, the Committee was reorganized as the President's Organization on Unemployment Relief. The Organization ceased to exist on June 30, 1932.

Publications printed for the Organization by the Department of Commerce are included in this class. Those printed by the Organization itself are classified Y 3.P 92.

C 1.16:date
CATALOGUE OF BOOK AND BLANKS FURNISHED BY DEPARTMENT OF COMMERCE TO CUSTOMS OFFICERS. 1906– 1933.

C 1.17:CT
ACCIDENT PREVENTION CONFERENCE. PUBLICATIONS. 1936– 1938.

Group called together in Dec. 1935 by the Secretary of Commerce at the request of the President to consider ways and means of making life safer on land, sea, and air.

Includes posters and reports on accident prevention.

C 1.18
ADDRESSES. [Irregular]

C 1.18/2:CT
[ADDRESSES ISSUED AS PRESS RELEASES]. [Irregular]

C 1.19:date
WEEKLY BUSINESS SURVEY OF KEY CITIES. 1935– 1939.

C 1.20:nos.
STORIES OF AMERICAN INDUSTRY. 1– 24. 1937– 1938.

C 1.21:CT
NATIONAL CONFERENCES ON STREET AND HIGHWAY SAFETY. 1st– 4th. 1924– 1934.

C 1.22:pt.nos.
ST. LAWRENCE SURVEY [Reports]. 1– 7. 1941.

C 1.23:nos.
BANKING INSTITUTIONS OWNED AND OPERATED BY NEGROES, ANNUAL REPORTS. 1st– 4th. 1941– 1944.

C 1.24:v.nos.&nos.   • Item 127
BUSINESS SERVICE CHECKLIST. v. 1– 33. July 5, 1946– 1978. [Weekly]

Lists publications, releases, etc., issued by the Department of Commerce and its various subordinate agencies. All series except press releases and similar material are cumulated in the annual supplements to Department of Commerce Publications, A Catalog and Index.
ISSN 0007-7062

C 1.24/2:date   • Item 127
COMMERCE NEWS, RECENT COMMERCE PUBLICATIONS. 1979–   [Biweekly]
Supersedes Business Service Checklist (C 1.24).

C 1.24/3:v.nos.&nos.   • Item 127
COMMERCE PUBLICATIONS UPDATE. v. 1–   1980– [Biweekly]

PURPOSE:– To provide a listing of all publications and press releases issued by the Department of Commerce during the preceeding two week period. Also highlights publications of special interest as well as the latest figures in 19 key areas of business and economic activity, such as personal income, consumer prices, employment, and housing.

Discontinued.

C 1.25:v.nos.
DOMESTIC COMMERCE. v. 34, no. 7– v. 35, no. 9.

July 1946– Sept. 1947. [Monthly]
Sub-titles vary.
Issued 3 times a month (10th, 20th, 30th), 1927– Aug. 30, 1940; weekly, Sept. 30, 1940– Apr. 29, 1943; monthly, May 1943– June 1946.
Issued 1927– 1946 by the Bureau of Foreign and Domestic Commerce (C 18.32).

C 1.26   • Item 130
EXPORT CONTROL, QUARTERLY REPORTS. 1st– July/Sept. 1947–   [Quarterly]
Title varies: July/Sept.– Oct./Dec. 1947, Report under the Second Decontrol Act of 1947; Jan./March 1948– Jan./March 1950, Export Control and Allocation Powers.
Report submitted by the Secretary of Commerce to Congress pursuant to the Export Control Act of 1949.
Later C 57.411

C 1.27:nos.
WORLD WAR II HISTORY OF DEPARTMENT OF COMMERCE.

C 1.28:date   • Item 129
RUBBER, ANNUAL REPORT. 1st– 7th. 1949– 1955.

Report covers fiscal year.

Discontinued.

C 1.29:nos.
MERITORIOUS SUGGESTIONS DIGEST. v. 1, no. 1– 2. 1949– 1950.

C 1.30:
QUARTERLY REPORT OF BUDGETARY OPERATIONS.

C 1.31:
LIBRARY REFERENCE LIST, SELECTED LIST OF CURRENT ACQUISITIONS. [Monthly]

C 1.32
PRESS RELEASES. [Irregular]
Distribution of the press releases of the Department of Commerce and its constituent bureaus on a mailing list basis restricted to the press and other informational media. The releases are listed in the weekly Business Service Checklist. Requests for individual releases listed in the Checklist are filled as long as the supply lasts.

C 1.32/2:nos.
SCIENCE AND TECHNOLOGY NEWS FEATURES. 1959– No longer published.

C 1.32/3:nos.
CENTURY 21 U.S. SCIENCE EXHIBIT RELEASES. 1960.
No longer published.

C 1.32/4
DEPARTMENT OF COMMERCE TRADE TIPS ON THE WORLD MARKET. 1966–   [Weekly]
News release of highlights from World Trade Opportunities section of International Commerce (C 42.8).

C 1.32/5:date
COMMERCIAL NEWSLETTER MATERIAL.

C 1.32/6:date
DOMESTIC AND INTERNATIONAL BUSINESS NEWS TO USE FOR TRADE ASSOCIATION PERIODICALS. 1970–   [Irregular]

C 1.32/7:date
TELECOMMUNICATIONS OFFICE: PRESS RELEASES. 1971–

C 1.32/8:let&nos.   • Item 128-E
UNITED STATES DEPARTMENT OF COMMERCE NEWS. [Irregular]

C 1.33:nos.
PATENT ABSTRACT SERIES. 1–   1954–

C 1.34:nos.
EMPLOYEE SURVIVAL BULLETIN.

C 1.35:nos.
SUPERVISION SERIES.
DEPARTMENT ORDERS. 1–

C 1.37   • Item 126-D (MF)
TELEPHONE DIRECTORY. [Annual]
Early issues classified C 1.2:T 23

C 1.37/2:date   • Item 126-C-4
MEGA-MARKETPLACE EAST, DIRECTORY OF WOMEN BUSINESS OWNERS. [Annual]

Directory for use by private industry and government officials in contracting for– and by women business owners in marketing their products and services. Lists representation at the Megamarketplace East conference including women-owned businesses and regional procurement offices.

Discontinued.

C 1.37/3:   • Item 126-C-4
DIRECTORY OF WOMEN BUSINESS OWNERS, MEGAMARKETPLACE EAST/WEST. [Annual]

Discontinued.

C 1.38:nos.
COMMERCE LOG.

C 1.39:date   • Item 126 (MF)
COMMERCE BUDGET IN BRIEF, FISCAL YEAR.

C 1.40:nos.
COMMERCE NEWS DIGEST.

C 1.41
OUTLOOK AND YEAR-END ECONOMIC REVIEW. [Annual]

Issued as a press release, gives brief review of the past year and a summary of the outlook for the coming year.
Issues prior to 1961 classified C 1.2:Ec 7/2.

C 1.42:v.nos.&nos.
EXPORT EXPANSION TIDINGS.
Issued by National Export Expansion Council.

C 1.42/2:v.nos.&nos.
EXPORT EXPANSION COUNCIL NEWS.

C 1.42/3:CT   • Item 128-B
AL EXPORT EXPANSION COUNCIL. PUBLICATIONS.

Discontinued.

C 1.43:v.nos.&nos.
FIELD SERVICE NEWSLETTER.

C 1.44:date
LIST OF EXPORT LICENSES APPROVED.

C 1.45:nos.
STATISTICAL PROFILE, REDEVELOPMENT AREA SERIES. SP 1– [143]. 1962– [1963].
Prepared for the Area Redevelopment Administration by the Bureau of the Census.
Replaces class C 3.228.

C 1.45/2:nos.
STATISTICAL PROFILES, RURAL REDEVELOPMENT AREAS, SP (Series). SPB 1– [49]. 1962– [1963].
Prepared for the Area Redevelopment Administration by the Bureau of the Census.

C 1.46:CT
EXPORT ORIGIN STUDIES [by State]. 1962.

C 1.47:CT
GREAT LAKES PILOTAGE ADMINISTRATION. PUBLICATIONS.

The Great Lakes Pilotage Administration was established within the Department of Commerce to administer the Great Lakes Pilotage Act of 1960, as amended (74 Stat. 259). Administration of the act was transferred to the Department of Transportation pursuant to act of Congress Oct. 15, 1966 (80 Stat. 931).

C 1.47:R 26
GREAT LAKES PILOTAGE REGULATIONS AND
RULES AND ORDERS. [Irregular]
Reprint of title 46, Code of Federal Regu-
lations, part 401 and 402.

C 1.47:St 2
STATISTICAL REPORT, GREAT LAKES PILOT-
AGE. 1964– 1966. [Annual]

C 1.48:yr.nos.   • Item 129-A
STAFF REPORTS. 63-1. 1963.
Issued by the office of Assistant Secretary
of Commerce for Science and Technology.
Discontinued.

C 1.49:nos.
TDC EMPLOYEE NEWS BULLETIN. 1–
Published for employees of the Technical
Documentation Center.

C 1.50:yr.-nos.   • Item 231-B
OVERSEAS BUSINESS REPORTS, OBR-(series). 64-
85– 1964– [Irregular]

Issued 1962– 1964, by Bureau of International Commerce (C 42.20); 1964– 73, by the
Department of Commerce (C 1.50); 1973– by
Domestic and International Business Administration (C 57.11).

C 1.51:date
TRADE CENTER ANNOUNCEMENTS. [Irregular]

C 1.52:nos.
NORTHEAST CORRIDOR TRANSPORTATION
PROJECT. TECHNICAL PAPERS. 1– 1965–

Office of State
Technical Service

The Office of State Technical Services was
established within the Department of Commerce
by Department Order 7A of November 19, 1965,
pursuant to the act of September 14, 1965 (79
Stat. 679), to administer and coordinate the State
Technical Services program.

C 1.53:nos.
STATE TECHNICAL SERVICES NEWSLETTERS. 1–
1966– [Bimonthly]

PURPOSE:– To serve as an interchange of
information among the States about their respective programs and activities conducted under the
State Technical Services Act and to provide information, pertaining to the objectives and goals
of the program, that is not ordinarily available
within the States.

C 1.53/2   • Item 128-C
ANNUAL REPORT. 1st– 1966–
Discontinued.

C 1.53/3:date
LIST OF STATE DESIGNATED AGENCIES, OFFICIALS
AND WORKING CONTRACTS.   – 1969. [Irregu-
lar]
Earlier issued classified C 1.2:St 2/6.

C 1.53/4:nos.
PRESS RELEASES. [Irregular]

DEPARTMENT OF COMMERCE
(Continued)
C 1.54:CT   • Item 126-A
BIBLIOGRAPHIES AND LISTS OF PUBLICATIONS.

C 1.54:P 41   • Item 126-A
U.S. DEPARTMENT OF COMMERCE PERIODI-
CALS TO AID BUSINESS MEN. [Irregular]

C 1.54/2:date   • Item 126-A
CATALOG AND INDEX, U.S. DEPARTMENT OF COM-
MERCE PUBLICATIONS. 1972– [Annual]

Continues the annual supplements to United
States Department of Commerce Publications (C
1.2:P 96/supp).
Superseded by Publications Catalog of the
U.S. Department of Commerce (C 1.54/2-2).

C 1.54/2-2:date   • Item 126-A
PUBLICATIONS CATALOG OF THE U.S. DEPARTMENT
OF COMMERCE.

Supersedes United States Department of Commerce Publications Catalog and Index, Supplements
(C1.54/2).

C 1.55:nos.
DIB [DOMESTIC AND INTERNATIONAL BUSINESS]
COMPUTER NEWS. 1– 1967– [Irregular]

Minority Business
Development Agency

The Office of Minority Business Enterprise
was established within the Department of Commerce pursuant to Executive Order 11458 of March
5, 1969. The Office was superesed by the Minority Business Develpment Agency November 1,
1979 by Executive Order 11625 of October 13,
1971.

C 1.56:date   • Item 126-B
DIRECTORY OF PRIVATE PROGRAMS FOR MINORITY
BUSINESS ENTERPRISE. 1969– [Annual]
Issued by Office of Minority Business Enterprise.
Discontinued.

C 1.57:nos.
PRESS RELEASES. [Irregular]

C 1.57/2:date   • Item 126-C
OMBE OUTLOOK, NEWS FROM THE OFFICE OF
MINORITY BUSINESS ENTERPRISE. 1970– 1972.
[Monthly]

PURPOSE:– To provide information of successful minority enterprises; notices of technical
assistance available to entrepreneurs; information on new minority enterprise programs; listings
of appropriate new publications; summaries of
legislative action affecting minority enterprise;
and descriptions of Federal and local minority
enterprise programs.
Superseded by Access (C 1.57/4).

C 1.57/3:date   • Item 128-D
NATIONAL ROSTER OF MINORITY PROFESSIONAL
CONSULTING SERVICES. 1971– [Irregular]
(Government Programs Coordination Division, Of-
fice of Minority Business Enterprise)
Discontinued.

C 1.57/4:date-nos.   • Item 126-C (MF)
ACCESS. 1973– [Monthly]

PURPOSE:– To inform the publication of the
latest developments in minority business enterprise to include legislation, success stories, opportunities available in both technical and financial assistance.
Supersedes OMBE Outlook (C 1.57/2).
ISSN 0091-5688
Discontinued.

C 1.57/5:date
MARKETING AND PROCUREMENT BRIEFS. [Irregu-
lar] (Office of Minority Business Enterprise)
Published in cooperation with the National
Minority Purchasing Council.

DEPARTMENT OF COMMERCE
(Continued)
C 1.58:v.nos.&nos.   • Item 127-A
COMMERCE TODAY. v. 1– 6. 1970– 1975. [Biweekly]
Incorporates International Commerce (C 42.8).
Superseded by Commerce America (C 1.58/
2).

C 1.58/2   • Item 127-A
COMMERCE AMERICA. v. 1– 1976– [Biweekly]
Supersedes Commerce Today (C 1.58).
Superseded by Business America (C 1.58/4).
ISSN 0361-0438

C 1.58/3:CT/date
COMMERCE AMERICA [by State]. [Monthly]

C 1.58/4:v.nos.&nos.   • Item 127-A
BUSINESS AMERICA. 1978– [Biweekly]

PURPOSE:– To provide a news review of the
Department of Commerce's activities affecting
private enterprise. Includes reports on domestic
business, economic affairs, overseas trade (including foreign sales leads), scientific research,
applied technology and authoritative comment on
current national and international business problems.
Supersedes Commerce America (C 1.58/2).
Later C 61.18

Office of Telecommunication

The Office of Telecommunication was established within the Department of Commerce by
Department Order 30-5A, effective September 20,
1970.

C 1.59:nos.   • Item 240
IONOSPHERIC PREDICTIONS. 95– 103. Nov. 1970–
July 1971. [Monthly]

Issued 1963– 1966, by Central Radio Propagation Laboratory, National Bureau of Standards;
1966– 1970, by Central Radio Propagation Laboratory, Environmental Science Services Administration; 1970– 1971, by Institute for Telecommunication Sciences, Office of Telecommunications.
PURPOSE:– To provide an aid in determining
the best sky-wave frequencies over any transmission path, at any time of day, for average
conditions for the month. Issued three months in
advance, each issue provides tables of numerical coefficients that define the functions describing the predicted worldwide distribution of foF2
and M(3000)F2 and maps for each even hour of
universal time of MUF(Zero)F2 and MUF(4000)F2.
Discontinued.

C 1.60:nos.   • Item 126-D-1
TELECOMMUNICATIONS RESEARCH AND ENGI-
NEERING REPORTS. OT/ITSRR 1–
Discontinued.

C 1.60/2:nos.   • Item 126-D-3
OT SPECIAL PUBLICATION (series). [Irregular]
Later C 60.9

C 1.60/3:nos.
REPORTS, OTR- (series). [Irregular]

PURPOSE:– To provide important contributions to existing knowledge but of less breadth
than a monograph, such as results of completed
projects and major activities; specific major accomplishments; or OT coordinated activities.
Later C 60.10

C 1.60/4:nos.   • Item 126-D-3
BULLETINS, OTB- (series). [Irregular]

C 1.60/5:date
IRAC [Interdepartment Radio Advisory Committee]
GAZETTEER. 1973– [Irregular] (Frequency Man-
agement Support Division)
Contains two sections, part 1 gives place
into code, and part 2, code into place.

C 1.60/6:nos.
TELE-IRAC (series). [Irregular]

C 1.60/7:nos.   • Item 126-D-5
OT CONTRACTOR REPORTS. [Irregular]
Later C 60.12

C 1.60/8:nos.
OT TECHNICAL MEMORANDUMS. [Irregular]
Later C 60.11

DEPARTMENT OF COMMERCE
(Continued)

C 1.61:date   • Item 126-D-2 (MF)
INTERAGENCY AUDITOR TRAINING CENTER BUL-
LETIN. [Annual]
Covers fiscal year.

Discontinued.

C 1.62:CT   • Item 126-D-4
OFFICE OF TECHNOLOGY ASSESSMENT AND
FORECAST: PUBLICATIONS.
Discontinued.

C 1.63:CT   • **Item 126-C-2**
POSTERS. [Irregular]

C 1.64:CT
COUNTRY COMMERCIAL PROGRAM FOR [various
      countries].
            Prepared in cooperation with the various Em-
bassies of the Department of State.

C 1.64/2:CT
COMMERCIAL RESOURCE ALLOCATION GUIDES [for
various countries]. [Irregular]

C 1.65:date
NEVADA TODAY, DEVELOPMENTS IN BUSINESS,
      TECHNOLOGY AND INTERNATIONAL TRADE.
      [Monthly]

C 1.66:nos.   • **Item 126-D-6 (MF)**
INTERAGENCY TASK FORCE ON PRODUCT LIABIL-
      ITY, ITFPL- (series). [Irregular]
            Discontinued.

C 1.66/2:CT
INTERAGENCY TASK FORCE ON PRODUCT LIABIL-
      ITY: PUBLICATIONS. [Irregular]

C 1.67:date
COMMERCE LIBRARY BULLETIN. [Bimonthly]

C 1.68:CT
ENVIRONMENTAL IMPACT STATEMENTS. [Irregular]

C 1.69:date   • **Item 855-C**
STATISTICAL REPORTER. [Monthly] (Office of Federal Statistical Policy and Standards)

            PURPOSE:– To provide an interchange of in-
formation among Government employees engaged
in statistical and research activities. Contains
articles as well as news notes of new statistical
publications and personnel notes.
            See also PrEx 2.11
            ISSN 0039-050X

C 1.70:nos.   • **Item 126-D-7 (MF)**
STATISTICAL POLICY WORKING PAPERS. 1–
      [Irregular] (Office of Federal Statistical Policy and
      Standards)

            PURPOSE:– To encourage further discussion
of the technical issues and to stimulate policy
actions which flow from technical findings.
            Later PrEx 2.28

C 1.71:date   • **Item 126-D-8 (MF)**
NATIONAL VOLUNTARY LABORATORY ACCREDITA-
      TION: ANNUAL REPORT. 1st–   1977–

            PURPOSE:– To summarize the activities of
the National Voluntary Laboratory Accreditation
Program, which provides for the establishment
and implementation of programs to accredit laboratories capable of satisfactory testing products,
calibrating standards and instruments, and evaluating design and specification of products.
            Earlier C 57.2:F 84
            Discontinued.

C 1.72:date   • **Item 126-D-9 (MF)**
FOOTWEAR INDUSTRY REVITALIZATION PROGRAM,
      ANNUAL PROGRESS REPORT. 1st–   1978–

            PURPOSE:– To present the record of progress
of the Administration's unique effort to assist a
basic American industry to modernize and adjust
to import competition.
            Discontinued.

C 1.73:nos.   • **Item 126-D-12 (MF)**
TECHNICAL PAPERS. 1–   1979–   [Irregular] (Office
      of Federal Statistics Policy and Standards)

            PURPOSE:– To provide a series of working
documents on technical aspects of statistical
activities.
            Discontinued.

C 1.74:date   • **Item 126-D-13**
FRANCHISING IN THE ECONOMY. 1st–
      [Annual]

            PURPOSE:– To present information regard-
ing the growth of franchising and its effects on
the U.S. marketing system. Information is based
on individual returns from firms representing the
vast majority of business format franchising sales
and establishments and from other sources.
            Earlier C 57.2:F 84
            Later C 62.16.

C 1.75:date   • **Item 853-A**
FEDERAL STATISTICAL DIRECTORY. 1st ed.–
      1955–   [Irregular]

            PURPOSE:– Designated to serve as a guide
to facilitate communication with offices concerned
with particular statistical functions.
            Lists, by organizational units within each
agency, the names, office addresses, and telephone numbers of professional, technical, and
administrative personnel associated with statistical and related activities of the agencies of the
executive branch of the Federal Government.
            Earlier PrEx 2.10
            Discontinued 1979.

C 1.76:   • **Item 231-G-3**
COMMERCE BUSINESS DAILY. [Daily, Monday-Fri-
day]

            Subtitle: Synopsis of U.S. Government Pro-
posed Procurement, Sales, and Contract Awards.
            The Synopsis is of particular value to firms
interested in bidding on U.S. Government purchases, surplus property offered for sale, or in
seeking subcontract opportunities from the prime
contractors. It lists current information received
daily from military and civilian procurement offices.
            ISSN 0095-3423
            Earlier C 57.20

C 1.77:CT   • **Item 126-D-14 (MF)**
INTEGRATED RESOURCES AND SERVICES FOR [vari-
ous subjects]. [Irregular]

            Each issue briefly describes the activities of
the Department's various operating units in a different area of service such as waterfronts, energy, etc.
            Published in microfiche (24x).
            Discontinued.

C 1.78:v.nos.&nos.   • **Item 126-C-1**
COMMERCE, JOURNAL OF MINORITY BUSINESS. v.
      1–   1981–   [Quarterly]

            PURPOSE:-To present short articles and news
items on minority business enterprises and government programs and legislation intended to aid
them.
            Discontinued.

C 1.79:v.nos.&nos.   • **Item 126-C-3**
MINORITY BUSINESS TODAY. [Bimonthly] (Minority
Business Development Agency)

            Contains short articles and news items on
minority business enterprises and government
programs intended to aid them.
            Discontinued.

C 1.80:CT   • **Item 128-F**
NEXT GENERAL WEATHER RADAR (series). [Irregu-
lar]
            Discontinued.

C 1.81   • **Item 128-G**
STUDIES IN THE ECONOMICS OF PRODUCTION.

            PURPOSE:– To provide a comprehensive col-
lection of analyses of the economics of production in such U.S. industries as plastics, iron and
steel, and motor vehicles.
            Discontinued.

C 1.82:date   • **Item 128-H (EL)**
SMALL BUSINESS INNOVATION RESEARCH FOR
      FISCAL YEAR. [Annual]

            Solicitations by the Commerce Department
for small business firms to submit research proposals under the Small Business Innovation Research Program.

C 1.83:   • **Item 126 (MF)**
APPENDIX, BUDGET OF THE UNITED STATES GOV-
ERNMENT, DEPARTMENT OF COMMERCE CHAP-
TER.
            Discontinued.

C 1.84:date   • **Item 128-J (MF)**
U.S. AUTOMOBILE INDUSTRY. [Annual]

            PURPOSE:– To summarize the performance
and competitive condition of the U.S. automobile
industry and its outlook for the future.
            Earlier C 1.2:Au 8/4/date
            Discontinued.

C 1.85:date
NATIONAL ASSOCIATION OF WOMEN BUSINESS
OWNERS, MEMBERSHIP ROSTER. [Annual]
            Earlier C 1.2:M 51

C 1.86   • **Item 126 (MF)**
APPENDIX, BUDGET OF THE UNITED STATES GOV-
ERNMENT, DEPARTMENT OF COMMERCE CHAP-
TER.

C 1.86:date   • **Item 128-K (MF)**
SCIENCE AND TECHNOLOGY FELLOWSHIP PRO-
GRAM. [Annual]
            PURPOSE:– To describe the fellowship pro-
gram, which encourages the personal growth and
professional development of selected individuals
in Commerce Department scientific programs.
            Earlier C 1.2:Sci 2/4
            Discontinued.

C 1.87:   • **Item 128-K-1 (MF)**
STATE STATISTICAL AND ECONOMIC ABSTRACT
SERIES (series).

            The Department expects this to become a
state-by-state series that provides information
on a particular state's contribution to U.S. exports, its population and households, its labor
markets, its economy, etc.
            Discontinued.

C 1.88:date   • **Item 128-L (CD)**
NATIONAL TRADE DATA BANK. [Monthly]
            Issued on CD-ROM.
            Discontinued.

C 1.88/2:date   • **Item 128-N (E)**
NATIONAL ECONOMIC SOCIAL & ENVIRONMENTAL
DATA BANK (NESEDB).
            Issued on CD-ROM.
            Discontinued.

C 1.89   • **Item 128-M (E)**
ELECTRONIC PRODUCTS. [Irregular]

C 1.90   • **Item 128-K (MF)**
JAPANESE TECHNICAL LITERATURE BULLETIN.
[Quarterly]
            Discontinued.

C 1.91   • **Item 128-P (EL)**
STAT-USA.
            Online Service available on the Internet.

C 1.91/2   • **Item 128-P (EL)**
STAT-USA: THE NEWSLETTER.

C 1.93:   • **Item 128-R (MF)**
RESEARCH SERIES (OIMA).

C 1.94   • **Item 128-M (EL)**
PACESETTER (newsletter).

MINORITY BUSINESS DEVELOPMENT AGENCY (1979–   )

NFORMATION

Office of the Director
Minority Business Development Agency
Department of Commerce
5055 Herbert Clark Hoover Building
14th Street and Constitution Ave. NW
Washington, DC 20230
(202) 482-5061
http://www.mbda.gov

C 1.102:CT   • Item 231-B-4
GENERAL PUBLICATIONS.

C 1.108:CT   • Item 231-B-4
HANDBOOKS, MANUALS, GUIDES.

C 1.108/2   • Item 231-B-4
FRANCHISE OPPORTUNITIES HANDBOOK.

Earlier published by the International Trade
Administration, C 61.31

C 1.112:CT
POSTERS.

C 1.115   • Item 231-B-25 (MF)
ANNUAL BUSINESS ASSISTANCE REPORT, FISCAL
YEAR.

TECHNOLOGY ADMINISTRATION

INFORMATION

Department of Commerce
14th St. & Constitution Ave. NW
Washington, DC 20230
Fax: (202) 501-2492
http://www.ta.doc.gov

C 1.202   • Item 129-B
GENERAL PUBLICATIONS.

DIVISION OF ALASKAN FISHERIES (1903–1908)

C 2.1:date
ANNUAL REPORTS ON SALMON FISHERIES.
Earlier T 35.6

C 2.2:CT
GENERAL PUBLICATIONS.

C 2.3
BULLETINS [none issued].

C 2.4
CIRCULARS [none issued].

BUREAU OF THE CENSUS (1903–1972, 1975–   )

CREATION AND AUTHORITY

The United States Census Office was established within the Department of the Interior (I 14) on July 1, 1902, pursuant to act of Congress, approved, March 6, 1902 (32 Stat. 51). On July 1, 1903, it was transferred to the Department of Commerce and Labor under the name of the Bureau of the Census. Upon the creation of the Department of Labor, the Bureau remained with the Department of Commerce. On January 1, 1972, the Bureau was placed under the newly created Social and Economic Statistics Administration (C 56.200) by the Secretary of Commerce. The Social and Economic Statistics Administration was discontinued in 1975.
Bureau of Census publications issued during the period 1972–1975 were designated in the C 56.200 class.

INFORMATION

Bureau of the Census
Department of Commerce
Federal Office Building 3
Silver Hill and Suitland Roads
Suitland, MD 20746
(301) 457-4608
http://www.census.gov

C 3.1:date
ANNUAL REPORTS. 1904–[1948].
See also C 56.201

C 3.2:CT   • Item 146
GENERAL PUBLICATIONS.
See also C 56.202

C 3.3:nos.   • Item 131
BULLETINS. 5–[202]. 1903–[1965].
Bulletins 1–4 classified I 14.3

– CENSUS OF MANUFACTURES [by States]. 1904–

– COTTON PRODUCTION AND DISTRIBUTION, YEAR ENDING JULY 31. 1905–[1965] [Annual]

Title varies: 1905, American Cotton Supply and Its Distribution; 1906–1914, Supply and Distribution of Cotton; 1915–[1965] Cotton Production and Distribution.
Continuation of series, Commercial Cotton Crops, 1899–1904, issued by Bureau of Statistics, Department of Agriculture, as Bulletins 17, 19, 28, and 34.

– COTTON PRODUCTION IN THE UNITED STATES.

1914– issued as a separate publication (C 3.32).

– MORTALITY STATISTICS. 1908–1922.

– NEGROES IN THE UNITED STATES. 1904–

– STOCKS OF LEAF TOBACCO. 1917–1928.

Discontinued.

C 3.3/2:v.nos.
CENSUS BULLETINS, OFFICIAL INFORMATION FOR CENSUS EMPLOYEES.

C 3.3/3
CENSUS BULLETIN, OFFICIAL INFORMATION FOR CENSUS EMPLOYEES.

C 3.4:nos.
CIRCULARS.

C 3.4/2:nos.
CIRCULAR LETTERS.

C 3.5:CT
SPECIAL REPORTS. 1900–1913.

C 3.6:CT   • Item 147
REGULATIONS, RULES AND INSTRUCTIONS.

C 3.6/2:CT   • Item 146-A
HANDBOOKS, MANUALS, GUIDES.

C 3.6/2:C 33
CENSUS TRACT MANUAL.

1934–1947, classified C 3.6:C 33.
Defines census tracts and discusses the need for tracts, what areas are eligible for them, and how to establish them. Also discusses the appointment of census tract key persons, ways to make tract statistics useful, census tract revisions, tract related areas, and other selected statistical areas.
Following supplements issued separately:

A. Membership of Advisory Committees on Census Tracts and Small Areas.
B. List of Areas with Approved Census Tracts in 1960.
C. List of Census Tract Key Persons.
D. List of Census Bureau Regional Directors.

C 3.6/2:C 33/2   • Item 146-A
CENSUS USER'S GUIDE. 1969– [Irregular] (Includes basic manual plus supplementary material for an indefinite period) (User Communication Staff, Data and Access Use Laboratory)

Issued in two parts:
Pt. 1. Includes text covering such subjects as the collection and processing of 1970 data, data delivery media (computer tapes, microfilm, and printed materials), maps and information on how to obtain census materials; and 3 appendixes containing the census user's dictionary, comparison of printed reports and summary tapes, and glossary.
Pt. 2. Contains appendixes specifically related to the use of census summary tapes and the Address Coding Guide. Particularly for those who plan to obtain tapes or who want complete information on the data content of the summary tapes.

C 3.6/2-2:nos.   • Item 146-A-1
CPS INTERVIEWER MEMORANDUM (series). [Irregular]

CPS = Current Population Survey
PURPOSE:– To provide information on the Current Population Survey, whose primary purpose is to collect up-to-date facts about the number of persons in the U.S. who are employed, unemployed, or not in the market for jobs. One example is a memorandum that transmits revisions to the CPS Interviewer's Manual.
Discontinued.

C 3.7:nos.
MANUFACTURES DIVISION. SPECIAL BULLETINS. 3–10. 1903–1905.
Nos. 1–2 not printed.

C 3.8/1:vol
PHILIPPINE ISLANDS CENSUS, 1903. REPORTS

C 3.8/2:nos.
PHILIPPINE ISLANDS CENSUS, 1903. BULLETINS.

C 3.9:date
COTTON GINNING REPORTS. 1905–1911.
Later classified C 3.20

C 3.10:date
OFFICIAL REGISTER OF THE UNITED STATES. 1907–1932. [Annual]

Biennial, 1907–1925, Annual 1926–
Published in two volumes, 1907–1912, one volume 1913–
Issued 1816–1860, by Department of State (S 1.11); 1861–1905, by Department of the Interior (I 1.25); 1933–1959, by Civil Service Commission (CS 1.31).

C 3.11:CT
HEADS OF FAMILIES AT 1st CENSUS. 1790. 1907–1908.

C 3.12
FOREST PRODUCTS. 1906– 1912.

The following sub-series appeared each year:

1. Pulp-Wood Construction.
2. Lumber, Lath, and Shingles.
3. Slack Cooperage Stock.
4. Tanbark and Tanning Extract.
5. Veneers.
6. Tight Cooperage Stock.
7. Wood Distillation.
8. Cross-ties Purchased.
9. Poles Purchased
10. Forest Products of the States.

C 3.12/1:nos.
FOREST PRODUCTS, 1907. 1– 10. 1907– 1909.

C 3.12/2:nos.
FOREST PRODUCTS, 1908. 1– 10. 1909– 1911.

C 3.12/3:nos.
FOREST PRODUCTS, SERIES 1909. 1– 10. 1911.

C 3.12/4:nos.
FOREST PRODUCTS, 1910 SERIES. 1– 9. 1912.
No. 10 not issued.

C 3.12/5:nos.
FOREST PRODUCTS, 1911 SERIES. 1– 9. 1913

C 3.12/6:nos.
FOREST PRODUCTS, 1912.

C 3.12/7:CT
FOREST PRODUCTS. 1923– [1943]. [Biennial]

Continues the above series.

C 3.13:CT
LIST OF PUBLICATIONS (by subject). 1930– 1940.

C 3.13:date
LIST OF SUBJECTS (by date). 1905– 1910

C 3.14
13th CENSUS, 1910.

C 3.14/1:CT
BULLETINS, POPULATION (by States). 1911– 1912.

C 3.14/2:CT
BULLETINS, AGRICULTURE (by States). 1911– 1913.

C 3.14/3:CT
BULLETINS, MANUFACTURED (by States). 1912.

C 3.14/4:CT
BULLETINS, MINES (by States).

C 3.14/5:CT
BULLETINS [Miscellaneous] (by States).

C 3.14/6:CT
GENERAL BULLETINS. 1912.

C 3.14/7:CT
SPECIAL BULLETINS. 1912– 1913.

C 3.14/8:CT
BULLETINS, IRRIGATION (by States). 1912.

C 3.15:CT
ABSTRACTS, 13th CENSUS, 1910, WITH SUPPLEMENTS ONLY FOR INDIVIDUAL STATES. (by States). 1913

Statistics of population, agriculture, manufactures, and mining for United States, States, and principal cities, with supplements for individual States.

Supplements for individual States also issued separately (C 3.15/a).

C 3.16:vol
CENSUS REPORTS (FINAL VOLUMES) 13th CENSUS, 1910. 11 v. 1913.

C 3.17:CT
PRESS SUMMARIES, 13th CENSUS, 1910. 1910– 1911.

C 3.18/1:nos.
TOBACCO REPORTS. SEMI-ANNUAL. [Semiannual]

C 3.18/2:latest date covered
TOBACCO REPORTS [ADVANCE INFORMATION].

C 3.19:nos.
CIRCULARS OF INFORMATION.

C 3.20 • **Item 141**
REPORT ON COTTON GINNINGS BY STATES (Preliminary). [11 times a season (August– January)]

Each report shows ginnings prior to specified date during each cotton-ginning season (August through January). An end-of-season report is issued as Report on Cotton Ginned, Crop of (year). Issued in A-10 series.
See also C 56.239/2
Later: A 92.47

C 3.20/2:CT&date
COTTON GINNED (by States).

C 3.20/3 • **Item 141**
REPORT ON COTTON GINNINGS BY COUNTIES. [6 times during season (Sept.– Dec.)]

Reports issued as of the first of the month, September through December and following March (end-of-season report). Gives preliminary figures by counties on cotton ginned from the season's growth prior to specified date, with two-year comparisons. Quantities are in running bales, not including linters. Issued A-20 series.
See also C 56.239
Later: A 92.47

C 3.20/4
CONSOLIDATED COTTON REPORT. [Monthly (August– December)]

One page press release, issued jointly with the Agricultural Marketing Service, as of the first of each month, August through December. Gives ginnings (running bales); indicated total production and abandonment, acres left for harvest, yield per acre of lint cotton, condition (percent of normal). Issued in the A-10 series.

C 3.21:date
REPORT OF COTTON CONSUMED, ON HAND, IMPORTED, AND EXPORTED, AND ACTIVE SPINDLES (preliminary report).

C 3.22:date
COTTON SEED CRUSHED AND LINTERS OBTAINED.

C 3.23:CT
SPECIAL CENSUS, 1923, HIGH POINT, N.C.; VIRGIN ISLANDS 1917.

C 3.24: • **Item 134**
BIENNIAL CENSUS OF MANUFACTURES. 1923–
Discontinued 1977.

C 3.24/1:date
BIENNIAL CENSUS OF MANUFACTURES (FINAL VOLUMES).
See also C 56.244

C 3.24/2:CT • **Item 135**
CENSUS OF MANUFACTURES: GENERAL PUBLICATIONS.

C 3.24/3:date&CT • **Item 137-A-1– 51**
GEOGRAPHIC AREA (by States).

C 3.24/3 • **Item 137-A-1**
ALABAMA.

C 3.24/3 • **Item 137-A-2**
ALASKA.

C 3.24/3 • **Item 137-A-3**
ARIZONA.

C 3.24/3 • **Item 137-A-4**
ARKANSAS.

C 3.24/3 • **Item 137-A-5**
CALIFORNIA.

C 3.24/3 • **Item 137-A-6**
COLORADO.

C 3.24/3 • **Item 137-A-7**
CONNECTICUT.

C 3.24/3 • **Item 137-A-8**
DEAWARE.

C 3.24/3 • **Item 137-A-9**
FLORIDA.

C 3.24/3 • **Item 137-A-10**
GEORGIA.

C 3.24/3 • **Item 137-A-11**
HAWAII.

C 3.24/3 • **Item 137-A-12**
IDAHO.

C 3.24/3 • **Item 137-A-13**
ILLINOIS.

C 3.24/3 • **Item 137-A-14**
INDIANA.

C 3.24/3 • **Item 137-A-15**
IOWA.

C 3.24/3 • **Item 137-A-16**
KANSAS.

C 3.24/3 • **Item 137-A-17**
KENTUCKY.

C 3.24/3 • **Item 137-A-18**
LOUISIANA.

C 3.24/3 • **Item 137-A-19**
MAINE.

C 3.24/3 • **Item 137-A-20**
MARYLAND.

C 3.24/3 • **Item 137-A-21**
MASSACHUSETTS.

C 3.24/3 • **Item 137-A-22**
MICHIGAN.

C 3.24/3 • **Item 137-A-23**
MINNESOTA.

C 3.24/3 • **Item 137-A-24**
MISSISSIPPI.

C 3.24/3 • **Item 137-A-25**
MISSOURI.

C 3.24/3 • **Item 137-A-26**
MONTANA.

C 3.24/3 • **Item 137-A-27**
NEBRASKA.

C 3.24/3 • **Item 137-A-28**
NEVADA.

C 3.24/3 • **Item 137-A-29**
NEW HAMPSHIRE.

C 3.24/3 • **Item 137-A-30**
NEW JERSEY.

C 3.24/3 • **Item 137-A-31**
NEW MEXICO.

C 3.24/3 • **Item 137-A-32**
NEW YORK.

C 3.24/3 • **Item 137-A-33**
NORTH CAROLINA.

C 3.24/3 • **Item 137-A-34**
NORTH DAKOTA.

C 3.24/3 • **Item 137-A-35**
OHIO.

C 3.24/3 • **Item 137-A-36**
OKLAHOMA.

C 3.24/3 • **Item 137-A-37**
OREGON.

C 3.24/3 • Item 137-A-38
PENNSYLVANIA.

C 3.24/3 • Item 137-A-39
RHODE ISLAND.

C 3.24/3 • Item 137-A-40
SOUTH CAROLINA.

C 3.24/3 • Item 137-A-41
SOUTH DAKOTA.

C 3.24/3 • Item 137-A-42
TENNESSEE.

C 3.24/3 • Item 137-A-43
TEXAS.

C 3.24/3 • Item 137-A-44
UTAH.

C 3.24/3 • Item 137-A-45
VERMONT.

C 3.24/3 • Item 137-A-46
VIRGINIA.
C 3.24/3 • Item 137-A-47
WASHINGTON.

C 3.24/3 • Item 137-A-48
WEST VIRGINIA.

C 3.24/3 • Item 137-A-49
WISCONSIN.

C 3.24/3 • Item 137-A-50
WYOMING.

C 3.24/3 • Item 137-A-51
DISTRICT OF COLUMBIA.

C 3.24/3-nos. • Item 137-A-1– 51
CENSUS OF MANUFACTURES: GEOGRAPHIC AREA
SERIES, [State].

C 3.24/4: • Item 136
CENSUS OF MANUFACTURES: INDUSTRY SERIES.
See also C 56.244/6

C 3.24/5: • Item 135
PRESS SUMMARIES.

C 3.24/6:CT
RULES, REGULATIONS AND INSTRUCTIONS.

C 3.24/7:CT
CENSUS OF MANUFACTURES, MAPS

C 3.24/8:ser.nos. • Item 135
CENSUS OF MANUFACTURES, PRELIMINARY RE-
PORTS.
See also C 56.244/5

C 3.24/8-2:dt./le&nos.
INDUSTRY AND PRODUCT REPORTS.

C 3.24/8-3:dt/nos.
PRELIMINARY GENERAL STATISTICS.

C 3.24/8-4:dt/letters-nos.
AREA REPORT MC(P)-S SERIES. [Irregular]

C 3.24/8-5:ltrs.-nos. • Item 135
CENSUS OF MANUFACTURERS, PRELIMINARY
REPORT, SUMMARY SERIES.

C 3.24/9:le-nos. • Item 134-A (MF)
ANNUAL SURVEY OF MANUFACTURES SERIES, (M)
(date) (AS– nos.)
See also C 56.221

C 3.24/9-2 • Item 134-A
ANNUAL SURVEY OF MANUFACTURES. 1949/50–
[Annual]

The Annual Survey of Manufactures was initiated in 1949 and has been conducted since that
time for years not covered by the Census of
Manufactures (1954 and 1958). Covers approximately 50,000 plants out of a total of about
300,000. Included are all large plants, accounting
for approximately two-thirds of the total manufac-

turing employment in the United States, and a
sample of the much more numerous small plants.
The Annual Survey Program is designed to
provide estimates of general statistics (employment, payrolls, manhours, value added by manufacture, etc.) for industry groups and selected
industries; general statistics for geographic division, States, and large standard metropolitan statistical areas, cross-classified by major industry
groups; value of shipments for classes of products; expenditures for new plant and equipment,
for select industries; industry groups, and for
States and large standard metropolitan statistical areas; and value of manufacturers' inventories, for industry groups and selected industries.
Time lag for the bound volume is approximately two years. Individual chapters are released
in advance of publication in the MAS- (series).
Current data is published in preliminary form in
the various Current Industrial Reports.
See also C 56.221/2

C 3.24/9-3:CT
– REPORTS.

C 3.24/9-4:CT • Item 134-A
– MISCELLANEOUS PUBLICATIONS.

C 3.24/9-5:date
PUBLICATION ANNOUNCEMENT AND ORDER
FORM.
Earlier C 3.24/9-2

C 3.24/9-6:date • Item 134-A
VALUE OF PRODUCT SHIPMENTS.

C 3.24/9-7:date • Item 134-A
STATISTICS FOR INDUSTRY GROUPS AND IN-
DUSTRIES. [Annual]

C 3.24/9-8:date • Item 134-A
EXPENDITURES FOR PLANT AND EQUIPMENT,
BOOK VALUE OF FIXED ASSETS, RENTAL
PAYMENTS FOR BUILDINGS AND EQUIP-
MENT, DEPRECIATION AND RETIREMENTS.
[Annual]
Discontinued 1985.

C 3.24/9-9:date • Item 134-A
GEOGRAPHIC AREA STATISTICS. [Annual]

C 3.24/9-10:date • Item 134-A
ANNUAL SURVEY OF MANUFACTURES, ORIGIN
OF MANUFACTURED PRODUCTS. [Annual]

Earlier title: Annual Survey of Manufactured
Products.
Earlier C 3.24/9-2
Discontinued 1985.

C 3.24/9-11 • Item 134-A
ANNUAL SURVEY OF MANUFACTURES, VALUE
OF MANUFACTURERS' INVENTORIES.
[Annual]
Earlier C 3.24/9
Discontinued 1985.

C 3.24/9-12:nos. • Item 135
MANUFACTURING: ANALYTICAL REPORT SE-
RIES.

C 3.24/10:date
ANNOUNCEMENTS, CENSUS OF MANUFACTURES.

C 3.24/11– /15 • Item 135
CENSUS OF MANUFACTURES. 1810– [Quinquen-
nial]

The Census of Manufactures, first taken in
1810, provides detailed data on manufacturing
activity for small geographic areas, individual industries, products shipped, and materials consumed. This census was taken decennially 1810–
1900, except for the year 1830 when no canvass
was made; quinquennially 1900– 1919; and biennially thereafter through 1939. Interrupted by World
War II, the manufactures census was again conducted for the years 1947, 1954, and 1958. Now
authorized to be conducted quinquennially, the
next manufactures census will cover the year
1963.

C 3.24/12:date/MC-nos. • Item 135
– SUBJECT BULLETIN MC (Series).
See also C 56.244/8

C 3.24/13:dt.&nos.
– [SPECIAL REPORTS] BULLETIN MC– (series).

C 3.24/13-2:dt./&nos.
SPECIAL REPORT MC 58 (1)– D (11) (Series).

C 3.24/14:pt.nos.
LOCATION OF MANUFACTURING PLANTS BY
INDUSTRY, COUNTY, AND EMPLOYMENT
SIZE.
Later C 3.24/15

C 3.24/15:dt./nos. • Item 135
CENSUS OF MANUFACTURES: SUPPLEMEN-
TARY REPORTS.
See also C 56.244/3

C 3.25:date
COTTONSEED RECEIVED, CRUSHED, AND ON HAND,
ETC. PRELIMINARY REPORT.

C 3.26:date
BIRTH, STILL-BIRTH AND INFANT MORTALITY
STATISTICS, ANNUAL REPORT.

C 3.27:CT
CENSUS OF WAR COMMODITIES.

C 3.28
14TH CENSUS 1920.

C 3.28/1:date • Item 154-B-3
ANNUAL REPORTS.
See C3.281/2

C 3.28/2:CT
GENERAL PUBLICATIONS.

C 3.28/3:
BULLETINS.

C 3.28/4:
CIRCULARS.

C 3.28/5:vol.
FINAL REPORTS

C 3.28/6:CT
RULES, REGULATIONS AND INSTRUCTIONS.

C 3.28/7:date
ABSTRACTS AND COMPENDIUM.

C 3.28/8:CT
BULLETINS, POPULATION (by States).

C 3.28/9:CT
BULLETINS, POPULATION (Misc.) [Including
Occupations].

C 3.28/10:CT
BULLETINS, AGRICULTURE (by States).

C 3.28/11:CT
BULLETINS, AGRICULTURE (Misc.).

C 3.28/12:CT
BULLETINS, IRRIGATION (by States). [1921–
1922].

C 3.28/13:CT
BULLETINS, DRAINAGE.

C 3.28/14:CT
BULLETINS, MANUFACTURES (by States).

C 3.28/15:CT
BULLETINS, MANUFACTURES (by Industries).

C 3.28/16:CT
BULLETINS, FOREST PRODUCTS.

C 3.28/17:CT
BULLETINS, MINES AND QUARRIES (by States).

C 3.28/18:CT
BULLETINS, MINES AND QUARRIES (by Industries).

C 3.28/19:CT
STATE COMPENDIUMS.

C 3.29:CT
FINANCIAL STATISTICS OF STATE GOVERNMENTS.

C 3.30:nos.   • Item 154-A
CENSUS MONOGRAPHS.

C 3.31
CENSUS OF AGRICULTURE.

C 3.31/1:date
FINAL COLUMNS.

C 3.31/2:CT
STATE BULLETINS.

C 3.31/3:CT
STATE BULLETINS, 2d Series (Statistics by Counties).

C 3.31/4   • Item 152-A-1– A-40
CENSUS OF AGRICULTURE. 1840–   [Quinquennial]
    The first United States Census of Agriculture was taken in 1840 in conjunction with the Sixth Decennial Census. Each Decennial Census thereafter through 1950 included a census of agriculture, A mid-decennial agricultural census was initiated January 1, 1925. Under legislation enacted in 1952 and revised in 1957, the census of agriculture is now conducted as of October for the years ending in "4" and in "9". Census of irrigation and drainage augment the census of agriculture every 10 years (for years ending in "9").

C 3.31/5:CT   • Item 152
SPECIAL REPORTS.
    See also C 56.227/2

C 3.31/6:CT   • Item 153
1953 SAMPLE CENSUS OF AGRICULTURE.
    Discontinued.

C 3.31/7:nos.   • Item 152-B-1– B-53
– PRELIMINARY REPORTS, SERIES AC.

C 3.31/7-52   • Item 152-B-52
– PRELIMINARY AND/OR ADVANCE REPORTS (U.S. Summary).

C 3.31/7-53   • Item 152-B-53
– PRELIMINARY AND/OR ADVANCE REPORTS (Outlying Areas).

C 3.31/8:dt.&nos.
– ANNOUNCEMENTS.

C 3.31/9:date   • Item 152
– GENERAL REPORTS.

C 3.31/10:dt/CT
SHEETS OF NATIONAL ATLAS OF UNITED STATES.

C 3.31/11:dt.nos.
– STATISTICS BY SUBJECTS, SERIES AS 54-3. [Irregular]

C 3.31/12:date/v.   • Item 152
– FINAL VOLUMES [other than area reports, general reports, and special reports].
    See also C 56.227/3

C 3.31/13:CT
CENSUS OF AGRICULTURE, COUNTY DATA.

C 3.32:date   • Item 141
REPORT ON COTTON GINNINGS. 1922–   [Annual]

    Earlier title: Cotton Production in the United States.
    Comparative summary of U.S. production of cotton and linters, crops of 1899 to date. Main tables give State and county data.
    Discontinued.

C 3.33/1:CT
SURVEY OF CURRENT BUSINESS. [Monthly]
    Later C 18.35

C 3.33/2:CT
RECORD BOOK OF BUSINESS STATISTICS.

C 3.34:date
SURVEY OF CURRENT BUSINESS, WEEKLY SUPPLEMENTS.
    Later C 18.36

C 3.35:date
CENSUS OF RELIGIOUS BODIES.
    Changed from C 3.2

C 3.36:date
SUPPLY AND DISTRIBUTION OF COTTON IN UNITED STATES.

C 3.37:
15TH CENSUS, 1930.

C 3.37/1:date
ANNUAL REPORTS.

C 3.37/2:CT
GENERAL PUBLICATIONS.

C 3.37/3:
BULLETINS.

C 3.37/4:
CIRCULARS.

C 3.37/5:CT
FINAL VOLUMES.

C 3.37/6:CT
RULES, REGULATIONS AND INSTRUCTIONS.

C 3.37/7:date
ABSTRACT.

C 3.37/8:CT
POPULATION BULLETINS, 1st SERIES (by States).

C 3.37/9:CT
POPULATION BULLETINS, 2d SERIES (by States).

C 3.37/10:CT
POPULATION BULLETINS. FAMILIES.

C 3.37/11:CT
AGRICULTURE (by States).

C 3.37/12:CT
AGRICULTURE, 1st SERIES (by States).

C 3.37/13:CT
AGRICULTURE, 2d SERIES (by States)

C 3.37/14:CT
AGRICULTURE, 3d, SERIES (by States)

C 3.37/15:CT
AGRICULTURE (MISCELLANEOUS REPORTS).

C 3.37/16:CT
UNEMPLOYMENT BULLETINS (by States).

C 3.37/17:CT
CENSUS OF DISTRIBUTION (BY PLACE NAMES) PRELIMINARY.

C 3.37/18:CT
CENSUS OF DISTRIBUTION, MERCHANDISING SERIES.

C 3.37/19:CT
CENSUS OF DISTRIBUTION. PRELIMINARY REPORTS, STATES SUMMARY SERIES (by States).

C 3.37/20:CT
CENSUS OF DISTRIBUTION. COUNTY SERIES, PRELIMINARY (by States).

C 3.37/21:CT
CENSUS OF DISTRIBUTION. CONSTRUCTION INDUSTRY, STATE SERIES.

C 3.37/22:CT
CENSUS OF DISTRIBUTION. RETAIL DISTRIBUTION (by States).

C 3.37/23:CT
CENSUS OF DISTRIBUTION. WHOLESALE TRADE BULLETINS, STATE SERIES.

C 3.37/24:CT
IRRIGATION, AGRICULTURAL LANDS (by States).

C 3.37/25:CT
DRAINAGE OF AGRICULTURAL LANDS (by States).

C 3.37/26:CT
MANUFACTURES. INDUSTRY SERIES.

C 3.37/27:CT
MANUFACTURES (Miscellaneous).

C 3.37/28:CT
MANUFACTURES. STATE SERIES.

C 3.37/29:
[RESERVED FOR OTHER MANUFACTURES SERIES].

C 3.37/30:CT
FINAL BULLETINS (U.S. Territorial Possessions).

C 3.37/31:CT
OCCUPATIONAL STATISTICS.

C 3.37/32:CT
CENSUS OF MINES AND QUARRIES.

C 3.37/33:CT
CENSUS OF MINES AND QUARRIES (by States).

C 3.37/34:CT
CENSUS OF DISTRIBUTION. DISTRIBUTION OF AGRICULTURAL COMMODITIES.

C 3.37/35:CT
CENSUS OF DISTRIBUTION. WHOLESALE DISTRIBUTION. TRADE SERIES.

C 3.37/36:CT
CENSUS OF DISTRIBUTION. HOTELS. PRELIMINARY REPORT.

C 3.37/37:CT
CENSUS OF DISTRIBUTION. WHOLESALE DISTRIBUTION. SPECIAL SERIES.

C 3.37/38:CT
CENSUS OF DISTRIBUTION. SMALL CITY AND RURAL TRADE SERIES.

C 3.37/39:CT
CENSUS OF DISTRIBUTION, RETAIL DISTRIBUTION TRADE SERIES.

C 3.37/40:CT
CENSUS OF DISTRIBUTION. RETAIL DISTRIBUTION. SPECIAL SERIES.

C 3.38:dt.&CT
CENSUS OF ELECTRICAL INDUSTRIES.

C 3.38/2:CT
– INSTRUCTIONS FOR PREPARING REPORTS.

C 3.38/2:dt.&nos.
– ELECTRIC LIGHT AND POWER PLANTS.

C 3.39:dt.(later v.)
SUMMARY OF MORTALITY FROM AUTOMOBILE ACCIDENTS. [Monthly]

C 3.40:date
MORTALITY STATISTICS.

C 3.41:vol
WEEKLY HEALTH INDEX.
    Later FS 2.107

C 3.41/2:date
– ANNUAL MORTALITY SUMMARIES.

C 3.42:date
LEATHER GLOVES AND MITTENS. [Monthly]
    Multigraphed.

C 3.43:date
PRODUCTION OF BOOTS AND SHOES. [Monthly]

C 3.44:date
PRELIMINARY REPORT ON HARNESS LEATHER AND SKIVERS. [Monthly]

C 3.45:date
REPORT ON HIDES, SKINS AND LEATHER. [Monthly]

C 3.46:date
MARRIAGE AND DIVORCE. ANNUAL REPORTS.

C 3.47:date
FINANCIAL STATISTICS OF CITIES HAVING A POPULATION OF OVER 30,000.

C 3.47/2:date
FINANCIAL STATISTICS OF CITIES HAVING A POPULATION OF OVER 100,000.
Later C 3.142

C 3.48:date
FINANCIAL STATISTICS OF STATES.
Later C 3.141

C 3.49:CT
FINANCIAL STATISTICS OF STATE AND LOCAL GOVERNMENT (COMPILATION).
Earlier C 3.2:W 37/2– 2

C 3.49/2:date
FINANCIAL STATISTICS OF STATE AND LOCAL GOVERNMENT.

C 3.50:CT
DIGEST OF STATE LAWS RELATING TO TAXATION AND REVENUE.

C 3.51:date
ACTIVITY OF MACHINERY IN WOOL MANUFACTURES. [Monthly]

C 3.52:date
WOOL CONSUMPTION REPORTS. [Monthly]
Mimeographed.

C 3.52/2:date
WOOL STOCK REPORTS. [Quarterly]
Superseded by C 3.52/3

C 3.52/3
COMMERCIAL STOCKS OF WOOL AND RELATED FIBERS, TOPS, MOILS, WASTE CLIPS AND RAGS IN U.S. [Quarterly]
Supersedes C 3.52/2

C 3.52/4:date
WOOL MANUFACTURES. [Monthly]

C 3.53:date
ACTIVITY IN COTTON SPINNING INDUSTRY. [Monthly]

C 3.54:date
PHYSICIAN'S POCKET REFERENCE TO INTERNATIONAL LIST OF CAUSES OF DEATH.
Changed from C 3.2

C 3.55:date
MANUFACTURE AND SALE OF FARM EQUIPMENT.
Changed from C.2

C 3.56:date
ANIMAL AND VEGETABLE FATS AND OILS.
Changed from C 3.2

C 3.57:nos.
DISTRIBUTION OF SALES (ROTOPRINT).

C 3.58:date
CURRENT INDUSTRIAL REPORTS (Multigraphed).
Changed from C 3.2

C 3.59:date
MENTAL PATIENTS IN STATE HOSPITALS.

Changed from C 3.2
Later FS 2.59

C 3.59/2:date
PATIENTS IN HOSPITALS FOR MENTAL DISEASE.

C 3.60:date
MENTAL DEFECTIVES AND EPILEPTICS IN STATE INSTITUTIONS.
Changed for C 3.2

C 3.61:CT
MAPS (Minor Civil Divisions).

C 3.62:CT
MAPS (outline).

C 3.62/2:CT • **Item 146-K-1**
MAPS (miscellaneous) INCLUDES U.S. OUTLINE MAPS.

C 3.62/3:CT
SHEETS OF NATIONAL ATLAS OF UNITED STATES.
See also C 3.31/10

C 3.62/4 • **Item 146-K**
GE-50 UNITED STATES MAPS. 1–   1963–   [Irregular]
See also C 56.242

C 3.62/5 • **Item 140-B**
CONGRESSIONAL DISTRICT ATLAS. [Biennial]
Shows boundaries of the congressional districts.
See also C 56.213/2

C 3.62/6 • **Item 140-B-2**
COUNTY SUBDIVISION MAPS. 1930–   [Decennial]

State base maps showing counties and minor civil subdivisions. Prepared for each decennial population census. Separate map for each State, except Delaware and Maryland; Connecticut, Massachusetts, and Rhode Island; and New Hampshire and Vermont. Map also available for Puerto Rico.

C 3.62/7 • **Item 146-K**
URBAN ATLAS, TRACT DATA FOR STANDARD METROPOLITAN STATISTICAL AREAS, GE 80– (series).
The atlases in this series provide a graphic presentation of selected census tract statistics as reported in the 1970 Census of Population and Housing. Using the same boundaries in defining the standard metropolitan statistical areas (SMSA's), these maps will depict data from 65 of the largest SMSA's that were in existence at the time of 1970 census.
Each atlas reports data for a single SMSA and contains 12 detailed maps in a large (15 x 19 inches) format, presenting color-coded data for each tract of the metropolitan area concerned. Data are presented on the following subjects: Population density; percentage of the total population under 18 years of age and 65 years of age and older; black population as percentage of the total population; percentage of all persons 25 years old and over who are high school graduates; median family income; percentages of the total labor force employed in blue collar occupations; median housing value; mediancontract rent; percentage of all housing units which are owner occupied; percentage of all occupied units constructed from 1960 to March 1970; and interrelationship of family income and educational attainment.
Each atlas also contains a table of comparative statistics for the purpose of relating the general characteristics of the metropolitan area to the Nation as a whole, to the State in which the metropolitan area is located, and to the counties and larger places located within the metropolitan area.
See also C 56.242/4
Discontinued 1980.

C 3.62/8:nos. • **Item 146-K**
GE-70 MAP SERIES. 1–   1973–   [Irregular]

C 3.62/9 • **Item 146-S (CD)**
COUNTY BLOCK MAPS. [Irregular]
Issued on CD-ROM.

C 3.62/10:nos. • **Item 146-K**
UNITED STATES MAPS (GE-90 series).

C 3.63:date
KNIT WOOL GLOVES AND MITTENS.

C 3.64:date
WORK CLOTHING (Garments Cut).

C 3.65:CT
CENSUS OF AMERICAN BUSINESS, 1933.

C 3.66:date
WEEKLY BUSINESS SURVEY OF 33 CITIES.
Varying titles. Number of cities varies.

C 3.67:vol.
VITAL STATISTICS, SPECIAL REPORTS.
Later FS 2.109

C 3.67/2:CT
VITAL STATISTICS, SPECIAL REPORTS (abstracts).

C 3.68:date
AIR CONDITIONING SYSTEMS AND EQUIPMENT. [Monthly]
Title varies slightly.

C 3.69:date
AUTOMOBILE FINANCING. [Monthly]

C 3.70:date
AUTOMOBILES. [Monthly]

C 3.71:date
BABBITT METAL. [Monthly]
Beginning January 1936, title reads Whitebase Antifriction Bearing Metals.

C 3.72:date
BATHROOM ACCESSORIES (Recessed and Attachable, All Clay). [Monthly]

C 3.73
CELLULOSE PLASTIC PRODUCTS (Nitrocellulose and Cellulose Acetate Sheets, Rods and Tubes). [Monthly]

C 3.74:date
COMMERCIAL STEEL CASTINGS. [Monthly]

C 3.75:date
CONVECTION-TYPE RADIATORS. [Monthly]

C 3.76:date
DISTILLATE OIL BURNERS. [Monthly]

C 3.77:date
SHIPMENTS OF DOMESTIC PUMPS, WATER SYSTEMS, AND WINDMILLS. [Monthly]

C 3.78:date
SHIPMENTS OF DOMESTIC WATER SOFTENING APPARATUS. [Monthly]

C 3.79:date
EDIBLE GELATION. [Quarterly]

C 3.80:date
ELECTRICAL INDUSTRIAL TRUCKS AND TRACTORS. [Monthly]

C 3.81:date
ELECTRIC LOCOMOTIVES (mining and industrial). [Quarterly]

C 3.82:date
ELECTRICAL GOODS. [Quarterly]

C 3.83:date
FABRICATED STEEL PLATE. [Monthly]

C 3.84:date
FIRE EXTINGUISHING EQUIPMENT, REPORT OF SHIPMENTS. [Monthly]

C 3.85:date
FLOOR AND WALL TILE (except quarry tile).

C 3.86:date
GALVANIZED RANGE BROILERS AND TANKS FOR HOT WATER HEATERS. [Monthly]
Prior to January 1936 title reads: Range Boilers.

C 3.87:date
HOSIERY. [Monthly]

C 3.88:date
SALES OF LACQUERS. [Quarterly]

C 3.89:date
MALLEABLE IRON CASTINGS. [Monthly]

C 3.90:date
SHIPMENTS OF MEASURING AND DISPENSING
    PUMPS, GASOLINE, OIL, ETC. [Monthly]
    Title varies slightly.

C 3.91:date
MECHANICAL STOKERS. [Monthly]

C 3.92:date
MEN'S YOUTH'S AND BOY'S CLOTHING CUT. [Monthly]
    Title varies slightly.

C 3.93:date
OIL BURNERS. [Monthly]

C 3.94:date
PAINT, VARNISH, LACQUER, AND FILLERS. [Monthly]
    Title varies.

C 3.95:date
PAPERBOARD. [Monthly]

C 3.96:date
PLASTIC PAINTS, COLD WATER PAINTS, AND
    CALCIMINES. [Monthly]

C 3.97:date
PLUMBING BRASS. [Monthly]

C 3.98:date
PORCELAIN ENAMELED FLATWARE. [Monthly]

C 3.99:date
LAIN PLUMBING FIXTURES (ALL CLAY). [Monthly]

C 3.100:date
PREPARED ROOFING. [Monthly]

C 3.101:date
PRODUCTION OF METHANOL. [Monthly]

C 3.102:date
PUBLIC MERCHANDISE WAREHOUSING. [Monthly]

C 3.103:date
NEW ORDERS FOR PULVERIZERS, FOR PULVER-
    IZED FUEL INSTALLATIONS. [Monthly]

C 3.104:date
PYROXYLIN-COATED TEXTILES. [Monthly]

C 3.105:date
RAILROAD LOCOMOTIVES. [Monthly]

C 3.106:date
STEEL BARRELS AND DRUMS. [Monthly]
    Title varies slightly.

C 3.107:date
STEEL BOILERS. [Monthly]

C 3.108:date
STEEL OFFICE FURNITURE, SHELVING, AND LOCK-
    ERS, AND FIREPROOF SAFES. [Monthly]

C 3.109:date
STRUCTURAL CLAY PRODUCTS (Common Brick, Face
    Brick, Vitrified Paving Brick, Hollow Building Tile).
    [Monthly]

C 3.110:date
SULPHURIC ACID, PRODUCTION, STOCKS, ETC.
    REPORTED BY FERTILIZER MANUFACTURES.
    [Monthly]

C 3.111:date
SUPERPHOSPHATES, PRODUCTION, ETC., RE-
    PORTED BY FERTILIZER MANUFACTURES.
    [Monthly]

C 3.112:date
TERRA COTTA. [Monthly]

C 3.113:date
UNDERWARE AND ALLIED PRODUCTS. [Monthly]

C 3.114:date
VITREOUS-CHINA PLUMBING FIXTURES. [Monthly]

C 3.115:date
WHEAT AND WHEAT-FLOUR STOCKS HELD BY
    MILLS. [Quarterly]

C 3.116:date
WHEAT GROUND AND WHEAT-MILLING PRODUCTS.
    [Monthly]

C 3.117:date
WHEAT GROUND AND WHEAT-MILLING PRODUCTS,
    BY STATES. [Monthly]

C 3.118:date
WHEAT GROUND AND WHEAT-MILLING PRODUCTS,
    MERCHANT AND OTHER MILLS. [Quarterly]

C 3.119:date
RED CEDAR SHINGLES. [Quarterly]

C 3.120
CENSUS OF BUSINESS.

C 3.120/1:CT
CENSUS OF BUSINESS, 1935. FINAL REPORTS.

C 3.120/2:CT
CENSUS SURVEY OF BUSINESS, 1937– 38. [Re-
    ports].

C 3.121:date
SOYBEAN CRUSH PRODUCTS. PRELIMINARY RE-
    PORT. [Quarterly]

C 3.122:date
PRODUCTION OF LINSEED OIL. PRELIMINARY RE-
    PORT. [Quarterly]

C 3.123:date
PRODUCTION, CONSUMPTION, AND STOCKS OF
    FATS AND OILS. PRELIMINARY REPORT.
    [Quarterly]

C 3.124:date
FATS AND OILS SUBJECTED TO SUPPHONATION.
    [Quarterly]

C 3.125:date
COTTONSEED PRODUCTS MANUFACTURED AND ON
    HAND AT OIL MILLS BY STATES.

C 3.126:date
THE REGISTAR. [Monthly]
    Later FS 2.11

C 3.127:date
MONTHLY VITAL STATISTICS BULLETINS.
    Later FS 2.110

C 3.128:vol.
WEEKLY ACCIDENT BULLETINS.

C 3.128/2:date
ANNUAL SUMMARIES.

C 3.128/3:date
SUMMARY OF MOTOR VEHICLE ACCIDENT
    FATALITIES. [Quarterly]

C 3.129:date
KNIT FABRIC GLOVES. [Monthly]

C 3.130:date
IMPORTED DATES PACKED AND SHIPPED. [Monthly]

C 3.131:nos.
NEGRO STATISTICS BULLETIN.
    Transferred from C 18.19

C 3.132:CT
ADDRESSES.
    See also C 56.257

C 3.133   • **Item 147-C**
CURRENT BUSINESS REPORTS: MONTHLY WHOLE-
    SALE TRADE. [Monthly]

    Earlier title: Monthly Wholesale Trade Report:
    Sales and Inventories.
    Gives sales and inventory trends and stocks-
    sales ratios of merchant wholesalers, by kind of
    business and geographic divisions. Charts.
    See also C 56.219
    ISSN 0363-8553

C 3.133/2   • **Item 147-C**
MONTHLY WHOLESALE TRADE, SALES AND INVEN-
    TORIES. [Monthly]
    See C1.133/4

C 3.133/3:date   • **Item 147-C**
WHOLESALE TRADE, ANNUAL SALES AND YEAR-
    END INVENTORIES OF MERCHANT WHOLESAL-
    ERS. [Annual] (Current Business Reports)
    See C3.133/4

C 3.133/4:date   • **Item 147-C (P) (EL)**
COMBINED ANNUAL AND REVISED MONTHLY
    WHOLESALE TRADE. [Annual]

C 3.133/5:date   • **Item 147-C-1 (P) (EL)**
ANNUAL BENCHMARK REPORT FOR WHOLESALE
    TRADE.

C 3.134   • **Item 150 (P) (EL)**
STATISTICAL ABSTRACT OF THE UNITED STATES.
    1st– 1879–   [Annual]
        PURPOSE:– To provide a one-volume basic
    reference guide to the statistical tables issued
    by the U.S. Government agencies as well as pri-
    vate firms and research organizations.
        The volume is divided into subject sections,
    each of which is preceded by a brief summary
    giving an explanation of terms used, major source,
    and origin of data used. Most of the tables are on
    an annual basis with data for preceding years
    included for historical comparisons. Supplement-
    ing the tables are charts which illustrate the more
    important economic and social trends. New tables
    are included in each volume as needed, thus
    keeping abreast of the time by providing data on
    new developments and interests. Cross-refer-
    ences are given to series in Historical Statistics
    of the United States. Detailed subject index.
        Also issued in the House Document Series.
    See also C 56.243
        Also issued on CD-ROM.
        The following titles have been issued as
    supplement to the Abstract:

C 3.134/2:CT   • **Item 151**
SUPPLEMENTS TO STATISTICAL ABSTRACT OF
    UNITED STATES.
    See also C 56.243/2

C 3.134/2:C 76   • **Item 151**
CONGRESSIONAL DISTRICT DATA BOOK. 87th
    Cong.–   1961–   [Irregular]

        PURPOSE:– To provide a handy refer-
    ence volume for Congressmen and their con-
    stituents to have within arm's reach a statis-
    tical picture of each Congressional district.
    Presents statistical information from recent
    Censuses of Population, Housing, Agricul-
    ture, Business, Manufactures, Mineral Indus-
    tries, and from other governmental and pri-
    vate sources for Congressional districts.
        Supplements are issued for individual
    States in the event that the States are redis-
    tricted. Latest edition in 1964 covers the dis-
    tricts of the 88th Congress with individual
    State supplements issued for the districts of
    the 90th Congress.
    See also C 56.243/2:C 76

C 3.134/2:C 83/2   • **Item 151**
COUNTY AND CITY DATA BOOK. [Irregular]

        Latest edition: 1972.
        Statistics include agriculture; bank de-
    posits; births, deaths, and marriages; busi-
    ness units; city finances and employments;
    city school systems; climate; dwelling units;
    electric bills; hospitals; manufactures; new
    dwelling units; population characteristics; re-
    tail and wholesale trade; services; telephones.
        Presents a large and varied selection of
    items taken from the most recent Censuses
    of Agriculture, Business, and Manufactures.
    Covers areas such as cities; Congressional
    districts; regions, divisions, and States;
    smaller urban places; standard metropolitan
    areas.
        Special appendix on Congressional dis-
    tricts. Includes explanatory notes and source
    citations.
    See also C 56.243/2:C 83

C 3.134/2:C 83/2 • Item 151-D (CD)
COUNTY AND CITY DATA BOOK. [Irregular]
Issued on CD-ROM.

C 3.134/2:H 62 • Item 151
HISTORICAL STATISTICS OF THE UNITED STATES,
COLONIAL TIMES TO 1970. 1975. 2 v.

A two-part compendium updating and expanding the second edition, Historical Statistics of the United States, Colonial Times to 1957.

This bicentennial edition includes more than 12,500 time series, mostly annual, providing a statistical history of U.S. social, economic, political, and geographic development during periods from 1610 to 1970. The series are organized in 24 chapters and 50 subchapters on such subjects as population, vital statistics, health, labor, prices, income, welfare, climate, agriculture, forestry, fisheries, minerals, construction, housing, manufactures, transportation, communications, energy, commerce, banking, and government, among others, plus a separate chapter devoted to colonial and pre-Federal statistics. Accompanying text cites sources, defines technical term, and includes discussion of methodology, qualifications, and reliability of data. Also included are a time-period index indication which time series begin within specified 10-or 20-year time segments and a detailed alphabetical subject index.

Data later than 1970 are presented for many of the series in annual issues of the Statistical Abstract of the United States. A special historical appendix in each Abstract, beginning with the 1975 edition, links the historical series to specific Abstract tables.

Supersedes previous edition covering periods 1789– 1945 and 1610– 1957.

Also issued as house Document.

C 3.134/2:St 2 • Item 151
USA STATISTICS IN BRIEF. 1st. ed.– 1972–
[Annual]

C 3.134/2-1:date • Item 151-D-1 (E)
COUNTY AND CITY DATA BOOK (Statistical Abstract of the U.S. Supplement). [Irregular]
Issued on CD-ROM.

C 3.134/2-2:date • Item 151
USA STATISTICS IN BRIEF. [Annual]

C 3.134/3 • Item 150-A
POCKET DATA BOOK, USA (year). 1967– [Biennial]

Presents, in two parts, a compact selection of statistics covering the current social, economic, and political life of the Nation. The first part consists of charts and graphs in color and concise factual commentary; the second provides condensed statistical tables and additional charts in 30 subject-matter section. Many of the tables in part 2 have totals, the most recent data, or the most significant percentages printed in color for immediate recognition. The source agencies are identified for each table, and footnotes and tables titles have been simplified for easy use of the book.
Also issued in the House Document series.
See also C 56.243/3
Discontinued.

C 3.134/4:nos. • Item 140-B-1
CONGRESSIONAL DISTRICT DATA, CDD- (series). 1971– [One series of separate State reports issued for each Congress]

A series of separate State reports presenting population and housing data and recent election statistics for districts of each Congress. The five single district States– Alaska, Delaware, Nevada, Vermont and Wyoming– are covered in one report. The population figures show the number of persons in the State and each Congressional district by race, sex, residence, and broad age groups; population per square mile; and percent change in population. The housing data show total number of housing units, units lacking complete plumbing, number and value or monthly rent of owner- and renter-occupied units, and units

with more than one person per room. The elections data show vote cast on Congressional and Presidential elections, by major party. Also included are explanatory text and one or more maps showing Congressional district boundaries, counties, and selected cities.
See also C 56.213
Later C 3.223/20

C 3.134/5:date • Item 150
STATE AND METROPOLITAN AREA DATA BOOK.
Subtitle: A Statistical Abstract Supplement.

C 3.134/5-2 • Item 150 (P) (EL)
STATE AND METROPOLITAN AREA DATA BOOK, A STATISTICAL SUPPLEMENT.
Issued on CD-ROM.

C 3.134/6:CT • Item 150-B-1 (E)
USA COUNTIES, A STATISTICAL ABSTRACT SUPPLEMENT.
Issued on CD-ROM.

C 3.134/7:date • Item 150-B (E)
STATISTICAL ABSTRACT OF THE UNITED STATES.
[Annual]
Issued on CD-ROM.

C 3.135:date
MONTHLY COMPARATIVE SALES OF CONFECTIONERY AND COMPETITIVE CHOCOLATE PRODUCTS.
Earlier C 18.72/11

C 3.136:date
QUARTERLY CANNED FOODS STOCKS REPORTS.
Earlier C 18.72/12

C 3.137:date
LIST OF REPORTS AND PUBLICATIONS RELATING TO VITAL STATISTICS.

C 3.138:date
RETAIL SALES, INDEPENDENT STORES, SUMMARY FOR STATES. [Monthly]

CURRENT RETAIL TRADE REPORTS.

Issued on the 10th of the month following month of report. Gives advance monthly estimates of retail dollar sales volume for major kind-of- business groups and for all kinds of business combined, collected, collected from a subsample of the Census Bureau's retail trade reporting panel. Formerly titled: Advance Retail Sales Report and Advance Report on Retail Trade.

All series of the Current Retail Trade Reports are sold as a single subscription which includes the following subseries:–

C 3.138/2:date
RETAIL TRADE REPORT, UNITED STATES SUMMARY. [Monthly]

C 3.138/3 • Item 147-B (EL)
MONTHLY RETAIL TRADE REPORT. [Monthly]

Gives estimated dollar sales of all retail stores and Group II stores, by kind of business for current month with comparisons for previous months; estimated monthly sales of Group I retail stores, by Census region and by kind of business; estimated weekly sales during current month of Group II retail grocery stores; percentage changes in sales, all kinds of business combined, for stores or firms operating 1 to 10 stores, for selected standard metropolitan areas. Charts.
See also C 56.219/4
ISSN 0363-8448

C 3.138/3-2 • Item 147-B
ANNUAL RETAIL TRADE REPORT. [Annual]

Gives estimates of sale of all retail stores and those of organizations operating 11 or more retail stores, United States and Census regions, by kind of business. Year-end merchandise inventories, sales-inventory ratios, and accounts receivable balances held by retailers, by kind of business, United States.
See also C 56.291/4-2
See C3.138/3-3

C 3.138/3-3 • Item 147-B
REVISED MONTHLY RETAIL SALES IN INVENTORIES.
Earlier title: Month Retail Sales.
Supersedes Monthly Retail Trade, Sales and Accounts Receivable (C 3.138/3).
See C.138/3-7

C 3.138/3-4:date • Item 147-B (P) (EL)
CURRENT BUSINESS REPORTS, SERVICE ANNUAL SURVEY. [Annual]

C 3.138/3-5:date • Item 147-B-1
MOTOR FREIGHT TRANSPORTATION AND WAREHOUSING SURVEY. [Annual]

PURPOSE:– To present survey results through narrative, tables, and graphs. Statistics are summarized by kind-of-business classification. Estimates are derived from a sample of employer firms only.

C 3.138/3-6:date • Item 147-B (P) (EL)
CURRENT BUSINESS REPORTS: ANNUAL SURVEY OF COMMUNICATION SERVICES.

C 3.138/3-7 • Item 147-B
COMBINED ANNUAL AND REVISED MONTHLY RETAIL TRADE.

C 3.138/3-8 • Item 147-B-2 (P) (EL)
ANNUAL BENCHMARK REPORT FOR RETAIL TRADE.

C 3.138/4 • Item 147-B
ADVANCE MONTHLY RETAIL SALES REPORT.
[Monthly]
See also C 56.219/6
Discontinued 1980.

C 3.138/5:yr.-week no. • Item 147-B
WEEKLY RETAIL SALES REPORT. [Weekly]

Issued Thursday following week covered, presents estimated weekly sales of retail stores in the United States, based on a subsample of the sample used for the Monthly Retail Trade Report. Formerly entitled: Weekly Sales of Retail Stores.
See also C 56.219/7
ISSN 0363-8510

C 3.139:date
VITAL STATISTICS OF THE UNITED STATES.
Prior to 1937, vital statistics data compiled by Census Bureau were published annually in two volumes, Mortality Statistics (C 3.40) and Birth, Stillbirth and Infant Mortality Statistics (C 3.26).
Later FS 2.112

C 3.140:vol
STATE AND LOCAL GOVERNMENT QUARTERLY EMPLOYMENT SURVEY.

C 3.140/2 • Item 148-A
GOVERNMENT EMPLOYMENT GE (series). [Annual]
Earlier title: Public Employment in (year).

Gives number of public employees and amount of monthly payrolls as of October, by level and type of Government; employment and payrolls of State and local government and by function. Charts.
Previously published as State Distribution of Public Employment in (year).

C 3.140/2-3:date • Item 148-A
CITY EMPLOYMENT IN (year). [Annual]
Earlier C 3.140/2

C 3.140/2-4:date • Item 148-A
PUBLIC EMPLOYMENT IN (year). [Annual]
Earlier C 3.140/2

C 3.140/2-5:date • Item 148-A
COUNTY GOVERNMENT EMPLOYMENT. [Annual]
Earlier C 3.140/2

C 3.140/2-6:date • Item 148-A
LOCAL GOVERNMENT EMPLOYMENT IN MAJOR COUNTY AREAS. [Annual]
Discontinued.
Ceased in 1985.

C 3.141:vol • Item 149
FINANCIAL STATISTICS OF STATES, 1938–
Earlier C 3.48
Later C 3.191/2
Discontinued.

C 3.142:vol
FINANCIAL STATISTICS OF CITIES. 1938–
Earlier C 3.47
Later C 3.191/2
Discontinued.

C 3.143:date
BLOWERS, FANS, UNIT HEATERS, AND ACCESSORY EQUIPMENT. [Quarterly]
Prior to January 1940 data included in C 3.68.

C 3.144:date
WARM-AIR FURNACES, WINTER AIR-CONDITIONING SYSTEMS, AND ACCESSORY EQUIPMENT. 1940-1944. [Quarterly]
Prior to January 1940, included in C 3.68. After 1944, reports are in Facts for Industry, C 3.158:21-3.

C 3.145:nos. • Item 148-A
STATE AND LOCAL GOVERNMENT SPECIAL STUDIES. 1– 1936–
See also C 56.231
Discontinued.

C 3.145/2:dt.&nos.
CENSUS OF GOVERNMENTS ADVANCE RELEASE CGA (series).

C 3.145/3:date
CENSUS OF GOVERNMENTS, ANNOUNCEMENTS.

C 3.145/4 • Item 148-A
CENSUS OF GOVERNMENTS. [Quinquennial]

During the past century, and up to 1942, the Census of Governments was taken at 10-year intervals, providing more complete and detailed information on State and local governments than is reported on a current basis. The law now provides that such a census be taken at 5-year (rather than 10-year) intervals. The Census of Governments for the year 1957 was the first taken since 1942.
See also C 56.247/2

C 3.145/5:date/nos. • Item 148-A
CENSUS OF GOVERNMENTS; PRELIMINARY REPORTS.
See also C 56.247

C 3.145/6 • Item 146-E
QUARTERLY SUMMARY OF FEDERAL, STATE, AND LOCAL TAX REVENUE. 1963– [Quarterly]

Gives national totals of State and local tax revenue by level of government and by type of tax; property tax collections in 123 selected major county areas; and collections of selected State taxes, by States.
Former title: Quarterly Summary of State and Local Tax Revenue.
See also C 56.231/2
ISSN 0501-7718

C 3.146:date
ILLUMINATING GLASSWARE MANUFACTURES, SALES AND CREDITS. [Monthly]

C 3.147 • Item 147-A
QUARTERLY SUMMARY OF FOREIGN COMMERCE OF THE UNITED STATES. 1866– [Quarterly]

Gives data on imports and exports by commodities, countries, customs districts, and economic classes on a cumulative basis through each quarter, with some data for the preceding year. In addition, contains separate detail on shipping weight and value of waterborne exports and imports, and shipping weight of total outbound and inbound vessel shipments of merchandise by customs districts and selected ports.
Discontinued.

C 3.148:date
COTTON LINTERS PRODUCED AND ON HAND AT OIL MILLS BY TYPE OF CUT, BY STATES. PRELIMINARY.
Superseded by C 3.149

C 3.149:date
COTTONSEED RECEIVED, CRUSHED AND ON HAND; COTTON LINTERS PRODUCED; AND LINTERS ON HAND AT OIL MILLS. PRELIMINARY REPORTS. [Monthly]
Supersedes C 3.25 and C 3.148

C 3.150:letters-date&v. nos. • Item 148
SCHEDULES.
See also C 56.210/3

C 3.150:A
SCHEDULE A. STATISTICAL CLASSIFICATION ON COMMODITIES IMPORTED INTO THE UNITED STATES WITH RATES OF DUTY AND TARIFF PARAGRAPHS.

This schedule exhibits the statistical commodity classifications used in compiling the official United States import statistics. It shows the complete commodity description and commodity code number for each statistical classification used in the published report and machine tabulations of United States imports. In addition, it shows the county, custom district, commodity vessel classifications, as well as the units of quantities used in the compilation of the data.

C 3.150:B
SCHEDULE B. STATISTICAL CLASSIFICATION OF DOMESTIC AND FOREIGN COMMODITIES EXPORTED FROM THE UNITED STATES. [Irregular]

(Includes basic volume plus supplementary changes for an indefinite period)
Latest edition: March 1971.
This schedule shows commodity classification numbers required to be used on Shipper's Export Declarations. Arrangement is by Schedule B number, with a commodity description and items included, unit of quantity, and date established, also given.
Also includes Code Classification of Countries (Schedule C) and Code Classification of U.S. Customs Districts and Ports (Schedule D).

C 3.150:C
SCHEDULE C. CODE CLASSIFICATION OF COUNTRIES.

C 3.150:D
SCHEDULE D. CODE CLASSIFICATION OF U.S. CUSTOMS DISTRICTS AND PORTS.

C 3.150:G
SCHEDULE G. CONSOLIDATION OF SCHEDULE B COMMODITY CLASSIFICATIONS FOR USE IN PRESENTATION OF U.S. EXPORT STATISTICS.

C 3.150:H
SCHEDULE H. STATISTICAL CLASSIFICATION AND CODE NUMBERS OF SHIPMENTS OF MERCHANDISE TO ALASKA FROM UNITED STATES. [Irregular]

C 3.150:J
SCHEDULE J. CODE CLASSIFICATION OF FLAG OF VESSEL.

C 3.150:K
SCHEDULE K. CODE CLASSIFICATION OF FOREIGN PORTS BY GEOGRAPHIC TRADE AREA AND COUNTRY.

C 3.150:L
SCHEDULE L. STATISTICAL CLASSIFICATION OF FOREIGN MERCHANDISE REPORTS IN IN-TRANSIT TRADE OF UNITED STATES.

C 3.150:N
SCHEDULE N. METHOD OF TRANSPORTATION CODE, EXPORTS.

C 3.150:P
SCHEDULE P. COMMODITY CLASSIFICATION FOR REPORTING SHIPMENTS FROM PUERTO RICO TO U.S.

C 3.150:Q
SCHEDULE Q. COMMODITY CLASSIFICATION FOR COMPILING STATISTICS ON SHIPMENTS FROM U.S.

C 3.150:R
SCHEDULE R. CODE CLASSIFICATION AND DEFINITIONS OF FOREIGN TRADE AREAS.

C 3.150:S
SCHEDULE S. STATISTICAL CLASSIFICATION OF DOMESTIC AND FOREIGN MERCHANDISE EXPORTED FROM U.S.

C 3.150:T
SCHEDULE T. STATISTICAL CLASSIFICATION OF IMPORTS INTO U.S. ARRANGED IN SHIPPING COMMODITY GROUPS.

C 3.150:W
SCHEDULE W. STATISTICAL CLASSIFICATION OF U.S. WATERBORNE EXPORTS AND IMPORTS.

C 3.150:X
SCHEDULE X. STATISTICAL CLASSIFICATION OF DOMESTIC AND FOREIGN MERCHANDISE EXPORTED FROM UNITED STATES BY AIR ARRANGED IN SHIPPING COMMODITY GROUPS.

C 3.150:Y
SCHEDULE Y. STATISTICAL CLASSIFICATION OF IMPORTS INTO UNITED STATES ARRANGED IN SHIPPING COMMODITY GROUPS.

C 3.150/2:nos.
SCHEDULE, CHANGES. 16-A– 1942– (P.B. nos.) (Public Bulletin)

C 3.150/3:nos.
[COLLECTORS' BULLETIN.]

C 3.150/4
UNITED STATES IMPORT DUTIES ANNOTATED. [Irregular]

Prepared with the cooperation and assistance of the U.S. Tariff Commission and the Department of the Treasury.
Provides a statistical classification schedule which contains statistical reporting numbers and commodity descriptions to be used by importers in preparing import entry and withdrawal forms from which the official United States statistics are compiled. Presented in tabular form, includes tariff paragraph number, reporting number, description unit of quantity, rate of duty (full rate and reduced rate and effective date). Index.
Includes text of Schedule C and Schedule D.

C 3.150/5:nos. • Item 148
UNITED STATES IMPORT DUTIES ANNOTATED, PUBLIC BULLETINS.

C 3.150/6 • Item 148
U.S. IMPORTS FOR CONSUMPTION & GENERAL IMPORTS. TARIFF SCHEDULES ANNOTATED BY COUNTRY. 1965– [Annual]

Gives the quantity and value of imports for consumption and general imports for commodities as classified by the Tariff Schedules of the United States Annotated (TSUSA), by country of origin.
Effective September 1963, the TSUSA classifications are used by importers in furnishing data on import documents, and the import statistics are reported by the Bureau of the Census are initially compiled in terms of TSUSA classification.

C 3.151:date
SALES FINANCE COMPANIES. [Monthly]
Replaces C 3.69

C 3.152:vol
CURRENT MORTALITY ANALYSIS. [Monthly]
Later FS 2.108

C 3.153:date
ELECTIONS.

C 3.154:date
FACTORY CONSUMPTION OF ANIMAL AND VEGETABLE FATS AND OILS BY CLASSES OF PRODUCTS. [Quarterly]

C 3.155:nos.
MONTHLY REPORTS ON LABOR FORCE.

C 3.156:nos.
LABOR FORCE BULLETIN.

C 3.157:date
UNITED STATES EXPORTS OF DOMESTIC MERCHANDISE TO LATIN AMERICAN REPUBLICS.

C 3.157/2:date
UNITED STATES EXPORTS OF FOREIGN MERCHANDISE TO LATIN AMERICAN REPUBLICS.

C 3.157/3:date
UNITED STATES GENERAL IMPORTS FROM LATIN AMERICAN REPUBLICS.

C 3.157/4:date
UNITED STATES EXPORTS OF DOMESTIC AND FOREIGN MERCHANDISE TO CANADA (Including Lend-lease Exports).

C 3.157/5:date
UNITED STATES GENERAL IMPORTS FORM CANADA, EXCLUDING STRATEGIC AND CRITICAL MATERIALS AND MILITARY EQUIPMENT.

C 3.158   • **Item 142-A (EL)**
CURRENT INDUSTRIAL REPORTS. [Monthly]

Gives current statistics on commodity production and shipments for approximately 5,000 products accounting for more than one-third of all U.S. manufacturing.

The series include monthly, quarterly, semiannual, and annual reports. Publication schedules vary for individual industries. All monthly and quarterly series include annual summaries. Data collected in this current and continuing program are later used in the inter-censal publication Annual Survey of Manufactures.

The system of numbering commodity surveys in the Current Industrial Reports series is designed to relate them closely to the Standard Industrial Classification followed in the 1954 and 1958 Census of Manufactures. In 1957, the system was revised and many reports were renumbered to adhere more closely to the SIC. The numbering system used on the published reports consists of 1) the letter "M" which has been used to designate Manufactures, and since 1966, the designation MA for annual releases. 2) two digits which identify the principal Standard Industrial Classification major group to which the commodities included in the Current Industrial Reports series are generally related, and 3) and alphabetic (or numeral-alphabetic) designation to identify uniquely such survey within the 2-digit group.
Supersedes Facts for Industry.
See also C 56.216

C 3.158/2:nos.   • **Item 142-A**
ADVANCE REPORT ON DURABLE GOODS MANUFACTURES, SHIPMENTS AND ORDERS.

C 3.158/3:date   • **Item 142-A**
CURRENT INDUSTRIAL REPORTS: MANUFACTURING TECHNOLOGY. [Annual]
Discontinued.

C 3.158/4:date   • **Item 142-A-1 (P) (EL)**
CURRENT INDUSTRIAL REPORTS, MANUFACTURING PROFILES. [Annual]

C 3.159:date   • **Item 143**
FOREIGN COMMERCE AND NAVIGATION OF UNITED STATES.
Earlier C 18.19
Discontinued.

C 3.160:CA-nos.&nos.
POPULATION [Congested Areas].

C 3.161:dt.&nos.
POPULATION, SPECIAL REPORTS.

C 3.162:nos.
STATE DOCUMENTS.

C 3.163:v.nos.
CENSUS PUBLICATIONS
See for other lists of census publications C 3.2:P 96/3, C 3.2:P 96/4, C 3.13 and C 3.19.
See also C 56.222

C 3.163/2:date   • **Item 138**
CENSUS PUBLICATIONS, LIST OF PUBLICATIONS ISSUED. [Monthly]
Formerly C 3.163:2
See also C 56.222/2

C 3.163/3   • **Item 138 (EL)**
CENSUS CATALOG AND GUIDE. 1946–   [Quarterly]

Quarterly issues are cumulative-to-annual volume, with monthly supplements. Beginning with 1964, includes unpublished materials. Arrangement is by Administrative Divisions. Detailed annotation.
Monthly supplements (C 3.163/2) include new and discontinued items, special reports and regular publications issued less frequently than quarterly, but do not contain annotation.
Previous titles: Bureau of the Census Catalog of Publications; Catalog of United States Census Publications; and Bureau of the Census Catalog.
See also C 56.222

C 3.163/4   • **Item 138-A-1 (MF)**
BIBLIOGRAPHIES AND LISTS OF PUBICATIONS.
Earlier title Miscellaneous Lists.
See also C 56.222/3

C 3.163/4-2:CT   • **Item 138-A**
NUMERIC LIST OF PRODUCT CLASS CODES, COMMODITY TRANSPORTATION SURVEY.

Reference list for coding the major products shown on each invoice transcribed on the Invoice Transcription Records of Form TC-9408(x).
Discontinued 1977.

C 3.163/5   • **Item 143-A**
FOREIGN SOCIAL SCIENCE BIBLIOGRAPHIES. 1–1961–   [Irregular]

Issued as P-92 series.
A series of bibliographies of social science periodicals and monographs published in the Communist Bloc and other countries using so- called "difficult" languages. Twenty-two such documents are planned in the series, prepared by the Foreign Manpower Research Office, Bureau of the Census under a grant from the Office of Science Information Service, National Science Foundation. Each issue covers a separate country.
Bibliographic entries are included for the following subjects: General social sciences, cultural anthropology, economics, education, history, human geography, law, linguistics, political science, public health, social philosophy, social psychology, sociology, statistics, and bibliography.

C 3.163/6:CT   • **Item 131-G**
DATA FINDERS. [Irregular]

Series of eight publications designed to familiarize the reader with the content and use of various Census Bureau publications and services. Covers the following subjects:– Government, Business Statistics, Industrial, Energy, Economic Surveys, Construction, Foreign Trade, and Agriculture.
Discontinued.

C 3.163/7   • **Item 138-A-2**
MONTHLY PRODUCT ANNOUNCEMENT. [Monthly]
See C3.163/7-2

C 3.163/7-2   • **Item 138-A-5 (EL)**
CENSUS PRODUCT UPDATE. [Biweekly]

C 3.163/8:nos.   • **Item 138-A-3**
PRODUCT PRIMERS (numbered). 1–   [Irregular]
Discontinued.

C 3.163/9:nos.   • **Item 138-A-4 (MF)**
COLLEGE CURRICULUM SUPPORT PROJECT UPDATES (numbered). 1–   [Irregular]
Discontinued.

C 3.164:nos.&dt.   • **Item 144**
[FOREIGN TRADE] REPORTS.
See also C 56.210
Discontinued.

CURRENT IMPORTS

C 3.164:110-date   • **Item 144 (MF)**
UNITED STATES IMPORTS OF MERCHANDISE FOR CONSUMPTION: COMMODITY BY COUNTRY OF ORIGIN. – 1964. [Monthly, with calendar year summaries]
Earlier titles: United States General Imports of Merchandise; Commodity by Country of Origin, prior to Dec. 1947. United States Imports for Consumption of Merchandise; Commodity of Country by Origin, 1947-June 1949.
No monthly report issued for July-Dec. 1944.
Replaced by FT 125, beginning 1964.

C 3.164:120-date   • **Item 144 (MF)**
UNITED STATES IMPORTS OF MERCHANDISE FOR CONSUMPTION: COUNTRY OF ORIGIN BY SUBGROUP. 1943– 1964. [Monthly, with calendar year summaries]

Superseded by FT 125, beginning Feb. 1964.

C 3.164:121-date   • **Item 144 (MF)**
UNITED STATES GENERAL IMPORTS AND IMPORTS FOR CONSUMPTION FROM CANADA AND MEXICO, EXCLUDING STRATEGIC, MILITARY AND CRITICAL MATERIALS, COUNTRY BY COMMODITY TOTALS. 1943– 1944.
Earlier C 3.157/5:942

C 3.164:125-date   • **Item 144 (MF)**
U.S. IMPORTS OF MERCHANDISE FOR CONSUMPTION. 1943– 1966. [Monthly, cumulative]
Supersedes FT 120 and FT 110, beginning Feb. 1964.

C 3.164:130-date   • **Item 144-A-1 (MF)**
UNITED STATES GENERAL IMPORTS OF COTTON MANUFACTURES: COUNTRY OF ORIGIN BY GENEVA AGREEMENT CATEGORY. [Monthly]

Each issue cumulative to annual.
Gives net quantity (current month and cumulative-to-date) of United States general imports of cotton manufactures, country of origin by Geneva agreement category.
ISSN 0095-7530

C 3.164:135-date   • **Item 144-A-6 (MF)**
U.S. GENERAL IMPORTS AND IMPORTS FOR CONSUMPTION, SCHEDULE A COMMODITY AND COUNTRY. 1967–   [Monthly]

Title varies.
Contains information on United States general imports and imports for consumption for the current month and cumulative for the current year by all methods of transportation combined. Data are presented for total dollar value for Schedule A groupings of commodities (i.e., section, division, group, and subgroup) and all net quantity and value for Schedule A 7-digit commodity by country of origin arrangement.
ISSN 0095-5493

C 3.164:150-date • Item 144-A-3 (MF)
U.S. GENERAL IMPORTS– SCHEDULE A COMMODITY GROUPINGS, GEOGRAPHIC AREA, COUNTRY, AND METHOD OF TRANSPORTATION. 1967– [Annual]

Issued monthly, January– July 1967.
Gives total dollar value of general imports by all methods of transportation combined and separate data showing the value and shipping weight of trade handled by vessel and by air. Data are shown for Schedule A groupings of commodities (i.e., section, division, group, and subgroup) by method of transportation; and data in terms of the approximately 600 subgroups classifications of Schedule A are shown in commodity subgroups by country of origin arrangement. Information of the number of items included in the 5-percent random sample of import entries used for estimating shipments valued under $251 is shown.

C 3.164:155/date • Item 144-A-4 (MF)
U.S. GENERAL IMPORTS, WORLD AREA AND COUNTRY OF ORIGIN BY SCHEDULE A COMMODITY GROUPINGS. [Annual]

Earlier title: U.S. General Imports- Geographic Area, Country, Schedule A Commodity Groupings, and Method of Transportation. Issued monthly, January– July 1967.
Gives dollar value of general imports by all methods of transportation combined and separate data showing the value and shipping weight of trade handled by vessel and by air. Data are shown for Schedule A groupings of commodities (i.e., section, division, group, and subgroup) by method of transportation; world area of origin by Schedule A subgroup and method of transportation; and continent and country of origin by Schedule A commodity groupings and method of transportation. Information on the number of items included in the 5-percent random sample of import entries used for estimating shipments valued under $251 is also included.

Discontinued.

C 3.164:210-date • Item 144-A-5
U.S. IMPORTS FOR CONSUMPTION AND GENERAL IMPORTS, SIC-BASED PRODUCTS AND AREA. 1964– [Annual]

Import data originally compiled under the approximately 10,000 classes of the Tariff Schedules of the United States Annotated are rearranged and summarized into approximately 2,000 classes based on the Standard Industrial Classification.
Discontinued.

C 3.164:231-date • Item 144 (MF)
GENERAL IMPORTS OF MERCHANDISE INTO UNITED STATES BY AIR, COMMODITY BY COUNTRY OF ORIGIN. 1945– 1947. [Monthly]

C 3.164:232-date • Item 144 (MF)
GENERAL IMPORTS OF MERCHANDISE INTO UNITED STATES BY AIR, COUNTRY OF ORIGIN BY COMMODITY. 1945– 1947. [Monthly]

C 3.164:246-date • Item 144-A-6 (MF)
U.S. IMPORTS FOR CONSUMPTION AND GENERAL IMPORTS– TSUSA COMMODITY BY COUNTRY: (year). [Annual]

Gives net quantity and value of U.S. imports for consumption, by commodity, unit of quantity, and country of origin.
Discontinued.

C 3.164:247/date • Item 144-A-6 (MF)
U.S. IMPORTS FOR CONSUMPTION, HARMONIZED TSUSA COMMODITY BY COUNTRY OF ORIGIN, FT 247. [Annual]

C 3.164:350-date • Item 144 (MF)
U.S. GENERAL IMPORTS, COMMODITY, COUNTRY AND METHOD OF TRANSPORTATION. Jan.-Dec. 1966. [Monthly, with issue for calendar year]

C 3.164:380-date • Item 144 (MF)
UNITED STATES, AIRBORNE GENERAL IMPORTS OF MERCHANDISE, COMMODITY BY COUNTRY OF ORIGIN. 1962– 1964. [Monthly, with calendar year issue]

Superseded by FT 785, beginning Jan. 1965.

C 3.164:390-date • Item 144 (MF)
UNITED STATES AIRBORNE GENERAL IMPORTS OF MERCHANDISE, COUNTRY OF ORIGIN BY COMMODITY. (Schedule Y). 1962– 1964. [Monthly, with annual issue]

Superseded by FT 785, beginning Jan. 1965.

CURRENT EXPORTS

C 3.164:400-date • Item 144 (MF)
UNITED STATES EXPORTS OF DOMESTIC AND FOREIGN MERCHANDISE (including lend-lease exports). 1942– 1946. [Monthly]

C 3.164:405-date • Item 144 (MF)
UNITED STATES EXPORTS OF DOMESTIC AND FOREIGN MERCHANDISE UNDER LEND-LEASE PROGRAM, CALENDAR YEAR, 1944. [Only one issued]

C 3.164:410-date • Item 144-A-7 (MF)
U.S. EXPORTS– COMMODITY BY COUNTRY. [Monthly & Annual]
Monthly cumulative to annual.
Gives quantity and value of individual commodities exported, by country of destination. Commodity detail shown is that of Schedule B. The value of export shipments individually valued $100– 1,999 to Canada and $100– 499 to countries other than Canada (about 8 percent of total export value is estimated by sampling.
Previous title prior to 1964 date United States Exports of Domestic and Foreign Merchandise. Commodity by Country of Destination, issued in two parts.
ISSN 0098-0242

C 3.164:415-date • Item 144 (MF)
UNITED STATES EXPORTS OF DOMESTIC AND FOREIGN MERCHANDISE UNDER LEND-LEASE PROGRAM, COMMODITY BY COUNTRY OF DESTINATION. 1945– 1946. [Monthly]

C 3.164:416-date • Item 144 (MF)
UNITED STATES EXPORTS OF DOMESTIC AND FOREIGN MERCHANDISE UNDER UNITED NATIONS RELIEF AND REHABILITATION PROGRAM, COMMODITY BY COUNTRY OF DESTINATION. 1945– 1946. [Monthly]

C 3.164:420-date • Item 144 (MF)
U.S. EXPORTS, COUNTRY BY COMMODITY GROUPINGS. 1943– 1966. [Monthly]

Earlier titles; United States Exports of Domestic and Foreign Merchandise (Including Lend-lease Exports), 1943– 1946. United States Exports of Domestic and Foreign Merchandise, Country of Destination by Subgroup, 1948– 1964.
Earlier C 3.157:942 pt. 2, sec. 1-4, prior to 1943.

C 3.164:421-date • Item 144 (MF)
UNITED STATE EXPORTS OF DOMESTIC AND FOREIGN MERCHANDISE UNDER LEND-LEASE PROGRAM, COUNTRY OF DESTINATION BY COMMODITY. 1943– 1944. [Monthly]

C 3.164:425-date • Item 144 (MF)
UNITED STATES EXPORTS OF DOMESTIC AND FOREIGN MERCHANDISE UNDER LEND-LEASE PROGRAM, COUNTRY OF DESTINATION BY COMMODITY. 1945– 1946. [Monthly]

C 3.164:426-date • Item 144 (MF)
UNITED STATES EXPORTS OF DOMESTIC AND FOREIGN MERCHANDISE UNDER UNITED NATIONS RELIEF AND REHABILITATION PROGRAM, COUNTRY OF DESTINATION BY COMMODITY. 1944– [1946]. [Monthly]

C 3.164:446-nos. • Item 144-A-18 (MF)
U.S. EXPORT, SCHEDULE B, COMMODITY BY COUNTRY. [Annual]

Consists mainly of tables showing the physical movement of domestic and foreign merchandise out of the United States and Puerto Rico to foreign countries.
Discontinued.

C 3.164:447/date • Item 144-A-18 (MF)
U.S. EXPORTS, HARMONIZED SCHEDULE B COMMODITY BY COUNTRY, FT-447. [Annual]
Discontinued.

C 3.164:450-date • Item 144-A-8 (MF)
U.S. EXPORTS, SCHEDULE B COMMODITY GROUPINGS, GEOGRAPHIC AREA, COUNTRY, AND METHOD OF TRANSPORTATION. 1967– [Annual]
Issued monthly, January– July 1967.
Gives for calendar year, total dollar value of United States exports of domestic and foreign merchandise by all methods of transportation combined and separate data showing the value and shipping weight of exports handled by vessel and air. The data are shown by Schedule B groupings of commodities (i.e., section, division, group, and subgroup) by method of transportation; and data in terms of the approximately 600 subgroup classifications of Schedule B are shown by method of transportation, and country and world area destinations. Information is also presented on the number of items included in the 10 percent random sample of export declarations used for estimating shipments valued $100– 1,999 to Canada and on U.S. exports of foreign merchandise in terms of Schedule B subgroups, by method of transportation. Discontinued.

C 3.164:455/date • Item 144-A-9 (MF)
U.S. EXPORTS, WORLD AREA BY SCHEDULE B COMMODITY GROUPINGS. [Annual]

Earlier title: U.S. Exports, Geographic Area, County, Schedule B, Commodity Groups and Method of Transportation.
Gives, for calendar year, total dollar value of United States exports of domestic and foreign merchandise by all methods of transportation combined and separate handled by vessel and air. The data are shown by Schedule B groupings of commodities (i.e., section, division, group, and subgroup) by method of transportation; world area of destination by Schedule B commodity subgroup classification; and continent and country of destination by Schedule B commodity section, division group, and subgroup arrangement. Information is also presented on the number of items included in the 10-percent random sample of export declarations used for estimating shipments valued $100– 1,999 to Canada and on U.S. exports of foreign merchandise in continent by country of destination agreement.
Issued monthly, January– July 1967.
Discontinued.

C 3.164:526-date • Item 144 (MF)
UNITED STATES EXPORTS OF PETROLEUM AND PETROLEUM PRODUCTS OF DOMESTIC ORIGIN, COMMODITY BY COUNTRY OF DESTINATION.

C 3.164:527-date • Item 144 (MF)
U.S. EXPORTS OF PETROLEUM AND PETROLEUM PRODUCTS OF DOMESTIC ORIGIN, COMMODITY BY CUSTOMS DISTRICT.

C 3.164:576-date   • Item 144 (MF)
UNITED STATES IMPORTS FOR IMMEDIATE
CONSUMPTION, ENTRIES INTO BONDED
MANUFACTURING WAREHOUSE FOR MANU-
FACTURE AND EXPORTS, ENTRIES INTO
BONDED STORAGE WAREHOUSE AND WITH-
DRAWALS FROM BONDED STORAGE WARE-
HOUSE FOR CONSUMPTION OF
PETROLEUM AND ITS PRODUCTS. Aug.-Dec.
1947. [Monthly]

C 3.164:600-date   • Item 144 (MF)
U.S. WATERBORNE FOREIGN TRADE, TRADE
AREA BY U.S. COASTAL DISTRICT. 1964–
1966. [Monthly, with annual issue]

C 3.164:610-date   • Item 144-A-10 (MF)
U.S. EXPORTS OF DOMESTIC MERCHANDISE,
SIC-BASED PRODUCTS AND AREA. 1965–
[Annual]

Gives data on net quantity and value of
shipment of U.S. exports of domestic merchandise. Data are shown by the Standard
Industrial Classification (SIC) based export
product code, arranged by commodity and
world area of destination. Additional tables
show the conversion of Schedule B to a classification system based on the SIC by: (1)
SIC-based export product, showing the assigned Schedule B numbers, and (2) Schedule B number, showing the SIC-based export
product code to which assigned. Also included
are tables showing the principal differences
between the SIC-based output and export
product codes by: (1) SIC-based export product arrangement, and (2) SIC-based output
product code arrangement.
Discontinued.

C 3.164:731-date   • Item 144 (MF)
UNITED STATES EXPORTS BY AIR OF DOMES-
TIC AND FOREIGN MERCHANDISE
COMMODITY BY COUNTRY OF DESTINA-
TION. 1946–1947. [Monthly]

C 3.164:732-date   • Item 144 (MF)
UNITED STATES EXPORTS BY AIR OF DOMES-
TIC AND FOREIGN MERCHANDISE
COUNTRY OF DESTINATION BY COMMOD-
ITY. 1946–[1947]. [Monthly]

C 3.164:750-date   • Item 144 (MF)
U.S. EXPORTS, COMMODITY, COUNTRY, AND
METHOD OF TRANSPORTATION. Jan.-Dec.
1966. [Monthly, with issue for calendar year]

C 3.164:780-date   • Item 144 (MF)
UNITED STATES AIRBORNE EXPORTS OF
DOMESTIC AND FOREIGN MERCHANDISE,
COMMODITY (Schedule X) BY COUNTRY OF
DESTINATION. 1962–1964. [Monthly, with cal-
endar year issue]

Beginning January 1965, superseded by
U.S. Exports and Imports by Air (C 3.164:785).

C 3.164:785-date   • Item 144 (MF)
U.S. EXPORTS AND IMPORTS BY AIR. 1965–
[Monthly, with calendar year issue]

Supersedes U.S. Imports by Air, General
Imports of Merchandise, Commodity by Coun-
try (C 3.164:380); U.S. Imports by Air, Gen-
eral Imports of Merchandise, Country by Com-
modity, (C 3.164:390) U.S. Exports by Air,
Commodity by Country, (C 3.164:780); and
U.S. Exports by Air, Country by Commodity,
(C 3.164:790).

C 3.164:790-date   • Item 144 (MF)
U.S. EXPORTS BY AIR, COUNTRY BY COMMOD-
ITY. 1962–1965. [Monthly, with calendar year
issue]

Earlier title: United States Airborne Ex-
ports of Domestic and Foreign Merchandise,
Country of Destination by Commodity, prior to
April 1964.
Beginning January 1965, superseded by
U.S. Exports and Imports by Air, (C 3.164:785).

**CURRENT TRADE WITH PUERTO RICO
AND WITH U.S. POSSESSIONS**

C 3.164:800-date   • Item 144-A-11 (MF)
UNITED STATES TRADE WITH PUERTO RICO
AND WITH UNITED STATES POSSESSIONS.
[Monthly & Annual]

Gives net quantity, value, and shipping
weight of individual commodities, shipped between continental United States and individual
territories and possessions; commodities
shipped to the United States from Puerto Rico
and Virgin Islands, and commodity totals every quarter for the smaller possessions. Annual summary issued separately.
ISSN 0565-1204

CURRENT SUMMARY REPORTS

C 3.164:810-date   • Item 144-A-17 (MF)
UNITED STATES FOREIGN TRADE– BUNKER
OIL AND COAL LADEN IN THE UNITED
STATES ON VESSELS. [Monthly & Annual]

Gives quantity laden on American vessels and on foreign vessels engaged in foreign trade, by customs district of lading, and
total value. Annual summary issued separately.
ISSN 0363-6798

C 3.164:859-date   • Item 144 (MF)
UNITED STATES EXPORTS AND IMPORTS OF
GOLD AND SILVER, TOTAL UNITED STATES
TRADE IN GOLD AND SILVER AND UNITED
STATES TRADE IN GOLD AND SILVER WITH
LATIN AMERICAN REPUBLICS AND CANADA.
1942–1945. [Annual]

C 3.164:895   • Item 144-A-11 (EL)
U.S. TRADE WITH PUERTO RICO AND U.S. POS-
SESSIONS, FT-895. [Monthly, with annual is-
sue]

C 3.164:900   • Item 144-A-6 (EL)
U.S. MERCHANDISE TRADE: SEASONALLY AD-
JUSTED EXPORTS, IMPORTS, AND TRADE
BALANCE, FT-900. [Monthly]
Value, for each month of the current and
preceding calendar years, is shown for: U.S.
export, general imports and merchandise trade
balance, adjusted for seasonal and working-
day variation; U.S. exports excluding Department of Defense (DoD) Military Assistance
Program grant-aid shipments (domestic and
foreign exports– seasonally adjusted and
unadjusted; domestic exports– unadjusted);
exports including DoD grant-aid shipments,
unadjusted; U.S. imports of merchandise (general imports– seasonally adjusted and unadjusted; imports for consumption– unadjusted);
U.S. exports of domestic merchandise– Schedule B sections and selected divisions, including DoD Military Assistance Program grant-
aid shipments, seasonally adjusted and unadjusted; and U.S. general imports of merchandise by Schedule A sections, seasonally adjusted and unadjusted.
This report replaces reports C 3.164:900-
E and C 3.164:900-I which were discontinued
with the release of the March 1968 issue.
Subscription also includes subscriptions
to C 3.164:975, C 3.164:985, and C 3.164:986.
ISSN 0361-0047

C 3.164:900-A   • Item 144-A-21 (EL)
IMPORTS OF STEEL PRODUCTS. [Monthly]

C 3.164:920   • Item 144-A-6 (MF)
U.S. MERCHANDISE TRADE; SELECTED HIGH-
LIGHTS, FT-920. [Monthly]
See C3.164:920

C 3.164:925/date   • Item 144-A-6 (MF)
U.S. MERCHANDISE TRADE: EXPORTS,
GENERAL IMPORTS, AND IMPORTS FOR
CONSUMPTION. [Monthly]
Discontinued.

C 3.164:927   • Item 144-A-6 (MF)
U.S. MERCHANDISE TRADE: EXPORTS AND
GENERAL IMPORTS BY COUNTY.

C 3.164:930-date   • Item 144 (MF)
UNITED STATES FOREIGN TRADE. 1941–1966.
[Monthly]

C 3.164:947   • Item 144-B (MF)
U.S. EXPORTS AND IMPORTS BY HARMONIZED
COMMODITY.

C 3.164:950-date   • Item 144 (MF)
UNITED STATES FOREIGN TRADE. 1939–1966.
[Monthly]

C 3.164:951-date   • Item 144 (MF)
UNITED STATES FOREIGN TRADE, TRADE WITH
E.C.A. COUNTRIES. 1948–1951. [Monthly]

C 3.164:954-date   • Item 144 (MF)
UNITED STATES FOREIGN TRADE, TRADE WITH
U.S.S.R. AND OTHER EASTERN EUROPE.
1948–1951. [Monthly]

C 3.164:960-date   • Item 144 (MF)
UNITED STATES EXPORTS UNDER UNITED NA-
TIONS RELIEF AND REHABILITATION PRO-
GRAM DURING . . . 1945–1946.

C 3.164:970-date   • Item 144 (MF)
UNITED STATES FOREIGN TRADE, TRADE BY
CUSTOMS DISTRICT. 1943–1966. [Monthly]

C 3.164:971-date   • Item 144 (MF)
UNITED STATES FOREIGN TRADE, TRADE BY
AIR. 1946–1947. [Monthly]

C 3.164:972-date   • Item 144 (MF)
UNITED STATES FOREIGN TRADE, WATER-
BORNE TRADE BY UNITED STATES PORTS.
1946–[1952]. [Monthly]

C 3.164:973-date   • Item 144 (MF)
UNITED STATES FOREIGN TRADE, WATER-
BORNE TRADE BY TRADE AREA. 1964–
[1952]. [Monthly]

C 3.164:975-date   • Item 144-A-13 (MF)
VESSEL ENTRANCES AND CLEARANCES: CAL-
ENDAR YEAR (date). 1945–   [Annual]

Gives number and net registered tonnage
of American and foreign flag vessels entered
and cleared, with cargo and in foreign trade
of the U.S. by customs district and port of
entry.

C 3.164:976-date   • Item 144 (MF)
SHIPMENT UNDER THE UNITED STATES
FOREIGN AID PROGRAMS MADE ON ARMY-
OR NAVY-OPERATED VESSELS (AMERICAN
FLAG) BY PORT OF LADING BY COUNTRY
OF DESTINATION. 1948–[1952]. [Monthly]

Earlier title: Participation of American and
Foreign-Flag Vessels in shipments under
United States Foreign Relief programs, prior
to Jan. 1949.

C 3.164:980-date   • Item 144 (MF)
UNITED STATES TRADE WITH THE TERRITO-
RIES AND POSSESSIONS. 1942–1946.

C 3.164:981-date   • Item 144 (MF)
SHIPPING WEIGHT AND DOLLAR VALUE OF
MERCHANDISE LADEN ON AND UNLADEN
FROM VESSELS AT UNITED STATES PORTS
DURING THE IN-TRANSIT MOVEMENT OF
THE MERCHANDISE FROM ONE FOREIGN
COUNTRY TO ANOTHER. 1948–[1952].
[Monthly]

C 3.164:985-date-nos. • **Item 144-A-6 (MF)**
U.S. WATERBORNE EXPORTS AND GENERAL IMPORTS. [Monthly]

Earlier title: U.S. Waterborne Foreign Trade Summary Report.

Gives shipping weight and value of U.S. waterborne exports of domestic and foreign merchandise, outbound in-transit merchandise and shipments of Department of Defense controlled cargo and "special category" non-Department of Defense controlled cargo, on dry cargo and tanker vessel, by customs district and port of lading. Shipping weight and value of U.S. waterborne general imports and inbound in-transit merchandise, on dry cargo and tanker vessels, by customs district and port of unlading. Shipping weight of U.S. exports of domestic and foreign merchandise and of general imports of merchandise by trade area, type of vessel service, and amount carried on U.S. flag vessels, Department of Defense controlled cargo exported by vessel under the U.S. foreign aid programs, and "special category" non-Department of Defense controlled cargo exported by vessel-coastal district of lading by type of service and amounts carried on U.S. flag and foreign flag vessels, and on U.S. flag vessels. Detailed figures are for current month; summary figures are given for previous months for comparative purposes.

Effective with statistics from January 1967, C 3.164:985 was expanded to include data formerly shown in report U.S. Waterborne Foreign Trade. Trade Area by U.S. Coastal District, (C 3.164:600).

Subscription included with subscription to C 3.164:900.

C 3.164:986-date • **Item 144-A-15 (MF)**
U.S. AIRBORNE EXPORTS AND GENERAL IMPORTS, SHIPPING WEIGHT AND VALUE. [Annual]

Earlier title: United States Airborne Foreign Trade and Customs District by Continent.

Gives shipping weight and value of U.S. airborne exports of domestic and foreign merchandise by selected customs district of lading, and shipping weight and value of U.S. airborne general import of merchandise by selected customs district of unlading, both by continent.

Subscription included with subscription to C 3.164:900.
ISSN 0095-7771

C 3.164:990-date • **Item 144-A-16 (MF)**
HIGHLIGHTS OF U.S. EXPORTS AND IMPORT TRADE. 1967– [Monthly]

Gives data on quantity and value of United States exports (domestic and foreign merchandise), and imports (general and for consumption). Statistics for exports are shown by selected Schedule A commodity groupings and principal commodities. Data for exports and imports are presented by world area, country of destination (exports), country of origin (imports), U.S. customs districts and regions, and method of transportation. Figures are given for the current month, the previous month, cumulative year-to-date, and comparisons with a year ago.
ISSN 0565-0941

C 3.164:2402-date • Item 144 (MF)
UNITED STATES GOLD AND SILVER MOVEMENTS IN (Month). [Monthly & Annual]

Gives gold and silver export and import data for ore and base bullion, refined bullion, and for U.S. coin, foreign coin, and total (dollar, formonth, preceding month, and month a year ago). Annual summary issued separately.

C 3.164/2:CT
SPECIAL FOREIGN TRADE REPORTS. 1962–

C 3.164/2-2:date
UNITED STATES GENERAL IMPORTS OF COTTON MANUFACTURES, TQ-2003, COUNTRY OF ORIGIN BY AGREEMENT CATEGORY ARRANGEMENT. [1963]– [Semimonthly]

C 3.164/2-3:date
UNITED STATES GENERAL IMPORTS OF COTTON MANUFACTURES; TQ-2004, COMBINED COUNTRY TOTALS . . .; TQ-2005, AGREEMENT CATEGORY TOTALS . . .; TQ-2002, SELECTION AGREEMENT CATEGORY. . . [1963]– [Semimonthly]

C 3.164/2-4:
UNITED STATES GENERAL IMPORTS OF WOOL MANUFACTURES EXCEPT FLOOR COVERINGS, WOOL GROUPINGS BY COUNTRY OF ORIGIN AND SCHEDULE A COMMODITY BY COUNTRY OF ORIGIN, TQ-2201. [1963]– [Monthly]

C 3.164/2-5:date
UNITED STATES GENERAL IMPORTS OF WOOL MANUFACTURE EXCEPT FOR FLOOR COVERINGS, COUNTRY OF ORIGIN BY WOOL GROUPING, TQ-2202. [1963]–

C 3.164/2-6:date
UNITED STATES GENERAL IMPORTS OF WOOL MANUFACTURE EXCEPT FLOOR COVERINGS, QUANTITY TOTALS IN TERMS OF EQUIVALENT SQUARE YARDS IN COUNTRY OF ORIGIN BY COMMODITY GROUPING ARRANGEMENT, TQ-2203. [1963]–

C 3.164/2-7:date
UNITED STATES GENERAL IMPORTS OF TEXTILE MANUFACTURES, EXCEPT COTTON AND WOOL, GROUPING BY COUNTRY OF ORIGIN AND SCHEDULE A COMMODITY BY COUNTRY OF ORIGIN TQ-2501.

C 3.164/2-8:date
UNITED STATES GENERAL IMPORTS OF COTTON MANUFACTURES; TQ-2190, SCHEDULE BY A COUNTRY OF ORIGIN TOTALS . . . WHICH BECAME EFFECTIVE IN JAN. 1962; TQ-2191, SCHEDULE A BY COUNTRY OF ORIGIN TOTALS . . . WHICH BECAME EFFECTIVE IN OCT. 1962. [1963]– [Monthly]

C 3.165:CT
SUMMARY OF BIOSTATISTICS.

C 3.166:date
UNITED STATES FOREIGN TRADE STATISTICS PUBLICATIONS. [Monthly]

C 3.167:date • **Item 145**
FOREIGN TRADE STATISTICS NOTES. [Monthly]
Discontinued.

C 3.168:date
CANNED FRUITS AND VEGETABLES, PRODUCTION AND WHOLESALE DISTRIBUTION. [Monthly]
Superseded by C 3.189

C 3.169:date
COFFEE INVENTORIES AND ROASTINGS. [Monthly]

C 3.170:nos.
CITY DOCUMENTS.

C 3.171:nos.
GOVERNMENT ORGANIZATIONS.

C 3.172:date
TRENDS IN ELECTRICAL GOODS TRADE. [Monthly]

C 3.173:date
RETAIL TRADE REPORT, NEW ENGLAND. [Monthly]
Superseded by C 3.138/3

C 3.174:date
RETAIL TRADE REPORT, MIDDLE ATLANTIC REGION. [Monthly]
Superseded by C 3.138/3

C 3.175:date
RETAIL TRADE REPORT, SOUTH ATLANTIC REGION. [Monthly]
Superseded by C 3.138/3

C 3.176:date
RETAIL TRADE REPORT, EAST NORTH CENTRAL. [Monthly]
Superseded by C 3.138/3

C 3.177:date
RETAIL TRADE REPORT, EAST SOUTH CENTRAL. [Monthly]
Superseded by C 3.138/3

C 3.178:date
RETAIL TRADE REPORT, WEST NORTH CENTRAL. [Monthly]
Superseded by C 3.138/3

C 3.179:date
RETAIL TRADE REPORT, WEST SOUTH CENTRAL. [Monthly]
Superseded by C 3.138/3

C 3.180:date
RETAIL TRADE REPORT, MOUNTAIN REGION. [Monthly]
Superseded by C 3.138/3

C 3.181:date
RETAIL TRADE REPORT, PACIFIC REGION. [Monthly]
Superseded by C 3.138/3

C 3.182:date
TRENDS IN DRUG TRADE. [Monthly]

C 3.183:date
TRENDS IN GROCERY TRADE. [Monthly]

C 3.184:date
TRENDS IN TOBACCO TRADE. [Monthly]

C 3.185:date
SERVICE TRADE REPORTS. [Monthly]

C 3.186 • **Item 142-C-2**
CURRENT POPULATION REPORTS. 1– 1947– [varies]

Subscription includes reports issued in series P-20, P-23, P-25, P-27, and P-60.
See also C 56.218
One-time studies and irregular sub-series may appear in the various series in addition to the following recurring publications.

C 3.186:P-20 • **Item 142-C-1 (EL)**
POPULATION CHARACTERISTICS. 1– 1947–
ISSN 0363-6836

EDUCATIONAL ATTAINMENT. [Annual]

Gives years of school completed for persons 14 years old and over by age groups, race, sex, type and region of residence, employment status, mobility status, major occupation group, and income of employed males.

FERTILITY OF POPULATION. [Irregular]

Tables show fertility of women by: Age, marital status, married and husband present; age of woman for the noninstitutional and the total population of the United States.

GEOGRAPHIC MOBILITY. [Annual]

HOUSEHOLDS AND FAMILIES, BY TYPE: (year). [Annual]

Gives number of family units by type, percent of these units by type. Additional tables give figures for United States on number and percent of households, by type, by color of head and farm-nonfarm residence; average population per household and family; households by type and age of head.

HOUSEHOLD AND FAMILY CHARACTERISTICS. [Annual]

Includes data on households, families, subfamilies, and quasi households, and population in these units by age, for the U.S., urban and rural, civilian population; households, families, married couples, parent-child groups, and unrelated individuals, by total and urban and rural nonfarm characteristics of households, families, and unrelated individuals, each by type, and of all subfamilies and husband-wife subfamilies.

MARITAL STATUS AND FAMILY STATUS: (date). [Annual]

Gives for the civilian population, U.S.: marital status by age and sex for the total, for rural-farm persons, for nonwhite persons; and also family status by age and sex.

MOBILITY OF THE POPULATION OF THE UNITED STATES. 1948–   [Annual]

Gives for the civilian population 1 year old and over, for the United States: mobility status and type of mobility; place of residence and color, percent distribution by metropolitan- nonmetropolitan and urban-rural residence, age and sex, and percent distribution by color and sex for regions, each by region of residence of previous year of migration. Also includes employment status of the male civilian population 14 years old and over, and labor force status, marital status, and age of the civilian female population 18 years old and over, each by mobility status and type of mobility.
Covers year March to March.

NEGRO POPULATION: March (year). [Annual]

Gives social and economic characteristics of the Negro population as of March.

SCHOOL ENROLLMENT: OCTOBER (year). [Annual]

Gives for the civilian noninstitutional population 5 to 34 years old, U.S.: fall school enrollment by age and sex, October (selected years), with additional information on current October data for urban and rural residence, color, and type of school, marital status for the population 14 to 34 years old enrolled in school, and living arrangements for college students.

C 3.186:P-23   • Item 142-C-2 (EL)
SPECIAL STUDIES. [21]–   [1954]–
        ISSN 0498-8485

C 3.186:P-25   • Item 142-C-3
POPULATION ESTIMATES AND PROJECTION. 1– 1947–

ESTIMATES OF THE POPULATION OF THE UNITED STATES JANUARY 1, 1950 TO (date). [Monthly]

Gives estimated population including and excluding Armed Forces overseas, and of the civilian population, by months.

ESTIMATES OF THE POPULATION OF THE UNITED STATES AND COMPONENTS OF POPULATION CHANGE. [Annual]

Gives estimates of the population of the United States including Armed Forces overseas, 1950 to date, with components of population change (births, deaths, net civilian immigration, and net change in number and percent), and increase in population since 1950.

ESTIMATES OF THE POPULATION OF THE UNITED STATES, BY AGE, COLOR, AND SEX. [Annual]

Gives estimates of the total population of the United States including the Armed Forces overseas, the total population residing in continental United States and the civilian population of continental United States by age, color, and sex.

C 3.186:P-26   • Item 142-C-4
FEDERAL-STATE COOPERATIVE PROGRAM FOR POPULATION ESTIMATES. 1–   1969–

This series of reports presents population estimates for countries for selected States in which the figures are prepared by State agency as part of the Federal-State Cooperative Program for Local Population Estimates. The objective of this cooperative program is the development and publication of State-prepared county population figures using the methods which have been standardized and which have been mutually agreed upon by the States and the Bureau of the Census. The results are also designed to be consistent with the results of any special censuses (Series P-28) conducted in the specified State.
        ISSN 0565-0917

C 3.186:P-27   • Item 142-C-5
FARM POPULATION OF THE UNITED STATES: (year). [Annual]

Gives population of the United States, including Armed Forces overseas, and farm population, April 1950 to date; estimated civilian population living on farms, by age and sex, and employment status and industry of civilian population 14 years old and living on farms.

C 3.186:P-28   • Item 142-C-6
SPECIAL CENSUS OF (city or area). [Irregular]

Gives population by sex and color for city or other area as of the date special census was taken. Reports show increase in population between April 1, 1960 and date of special census. For places of 50,000 population or more, age by race and sex is reported. Special censuses are taken at the request of and expense of the area involved.

C 3.186:P-29   • Item 142-C
SPECIAL CENSUSES, SUMMARIES. 230–   1947–

C 3.186:P-50
LABOR FORCE. 1– 91. 1947–1959. [Irregular]

C 3.186:P-51
LABOR FORCE, MONTHLY REPORT ON THE LABOR FORCE. 1–204. 1947–1959.

C 3.186:P-59
LABOR FORCE, GROSS CHANGES IN THE LABOR FORCE. 1–   1949–1951. [Monthly]

C 3.186:P-60   • Item 142-C-7(EL)
CONSUMER INCOME. 1–   1948–

INCOME IN (year) OF FAMILIES IN THE UNITED STATES. 1967–   [Annual]

Published prior to 1967 in Income of Families and Persons in the United States.

INCOME IN (year) OF PERSONS IN THE UNITED STATES. [Annual]

Published prior to 1967 in Income of Families and Persons in the United States.

C 3.186:P-65   • Item 142-C
CONSUMER BUYING INDICATORS. 1–   1963–

RECENT PURCHASES OF CARS, HOUSES AND OTHER DURABLES AND EXPECTATIONS TO BUY DURING THE MONTH AHEAD: SURVEY DATA THROUGH (current quarter). 1–   1963– [Quarterly]
        Data on household expectations to purchase automobiles, houses, and household durables within specified periods of time. Also data on recent purchases and recent and expected changes in family income.

C 3.186:P-70   • Item 142-C-8
HOUSEHOLD ECONOMIC STUDIES, ECONOMIC CHARACTERISTICS OF HOUSEHOLDS IN THE UNITED STATES. [Quarterly]

PURPOSE:– To present data on the distribution of income and wealth and participation in government programs by various segments of the U.S. population, by race, spanish origin, and region, based on the continuing Survey of Income and Program Participation.
        See C3.186:P-70/2

C 3.186:P-70/2-nos.   • Item 142-C-8 (EL)
HOUSEHOLD ECONOMIC STUDIES, Series P-70. [Quarterly]
        Earlier title: Economic Characteristics of Households in the United States.

C 3.186:P-95   • Item 142-C-8
INTERNATIONAL POPULATION REPORTS. 50– 1957–
        (Nos. 1– 49 are classified and not available)

C 3.186:2:date   • Item 142-C-7
MONEY INCOME OF HOUSEHOLDS, FAMILIES, AND PERSONS IN THE UNITED STATES. [Annual]
        See C3.186:22

C 3.186:3:date   • Item 142-C-1
VOTING AND REGISTRATION IN THE ELECTION OF NOVEMBER (date). [Biennial]
        Earlier C 3.186:P 20

C 3.186:3-2:date   • Item 142-C-1
VOTING AND REGISTRATION IN THE ELECTION OF (name). [Biennial]
        Earlier C 3.186:P-20/405

C 3.186:4:date   • Item 142-C-2
CHILD SUPPORT AND ALIMONY, CURRENT POPULATION REPORTS. [Annual]
        Discontinued.

C 3.186:5:date   • Item 142-C-2
AFTER-TAX MONEY INCOME ESTIMATES OF HOUSEHOLDS, CURRENT POPULATION REPORTS. [Annual]
        Earlier C 3.186:P 23
        Discontinued.

C 3.186:6:date   • Item 142-C-1
MARITAL STATUS AND LIVING ARRANGEMENTS. [Annual]
        Earlier C 3.186:P-20

C 3.186:7:date   • Item 142-C-3
ESTIMATES OF THE POPULATION OF THE UNITED STATES TO (date).
        Earlier C 3.186:P 25

C 3.186:7-2:date   • Item 142-C-3
ESTIMATES OF THE POPULATION OF THE UNITED STATES, BY AGE, SEX, AND RACE. [Irregular]
        Earlier C 3.186

C 3.186:7-3:date   • Item 142-C-3
ESTIMATES OF THE POPULATION OF THE UNITED STATES AND COMPONENTS OF CHANGE. [Annual]
        Earlier C 3.186:P 25

C 3.186:8:date   • Item 142-C-2
POPULATION PROFILE OF THE UNITED STATES, CURRENT POPULATION REPORTS. [Annual]
        Earlier C 3.186:P-23

C 3.186:9:date   • Item 142-C-1
HOUSEHOLDS, FAMILIES, MARITAL STATUS, AND LIVING ARRANGEMENTS, ADVANCE REPORT. [Annual]
        Earlier C 3.186:P-20

C 3.186:10:date   • Item 142-C-1
FERTILITY OF AMERICAN WOMEN: CURRENT POPULATION REPORTS. [Annual]
        Earlier C 3.186:P-20

C 3.186:11:date   • Item 142-C-7
MONEY INCOME AND POVERTY STATUS OF FAMILIES AND PERSONS IN THE UNITED STATES. [Annual]
        Earlier C 3.186:P-20

C 3.186:12:date   • Item 142-C-1 (P) (EL)
SCHOOL ENROLLMENT-SOCIAL AND ECONOMIC CHARACTERISTICS OF STUDENTS. [Annual]

C 3.186/12-2:date • **Item 142-C-1**
SCHOOL ENROLLMENT, SOCIAL AND ECONOMIC
CHARACTERISTICS OF STUDENTS (Advance
Report). [Annual]
Earlier C 3.186:P-20
See C3.186/12

C 3.186/13:date • **Item 142-C-7**
CHARACTERISTICS OF HOUSEHOLDS AND
PERSONS RECEIVING SELECTED NONCASH
BENEFITS. [Annual]
Earlier C 3.186:P-60
Discontinued.

C 3.186/14:date • **Item 142-C-1**
HISPANIC POPULATION IN THE UNITED STATES,
ADVANCE REPORT. [Annual]
Earlier title: Persons of Spanish Origin in the
United States, . . .
Earlier C 3.186:P-20

C 3.186/14-2:date • **Item 142-C-1**
THE HISPANIC POPULATION IN THE UNITED STATES.
[Annual]

C 3.186/15:date • **Item 142-C-3**
PROJECTIONS OF THE NUMBER OF HOUSEHOLDS
AND FAMILIES. [Quinquennial]
Earlier C 34.186:P-25

C 3.186/16:date • **Item 142-C-7**
CHARACTERISTICS OF THE POPULATION BELOW
THE POVERTY LEVEL. [Annual]
Earlier C 3.186:P-60
Discontinued.

C 3.186/17:date • **Item 142-C-1**
HOUSEHOLD AND FAMILY CHARACTERISTICS. [Annual]
Earlier C 3.186:P-20

C 3.186/17-2 • **Item 142-C-16 (EL)**
AMERICA'S FAMILIES AND LIVING ARRANGE-
MENTS. [Annual]

C 3.186/18:date • **Item 142-C-1**
GEOGRAPHICAL MOBILITY. [Annual]

C 3.186/19:date • **Item 142-C-9**
ESTIMATES OF THE POPULATION OF PUERTO RICO
AND THE OUTLYING AREAS. [Irregular]

PURPOSE:– To present estimates of the popu-
lation of the Commonwealth of Puerto Rico, the
Virgin Islands of the U.S., American Samoa,
Guam, and the Commonwealth of Northern
Mariana Islands.
Designated Series P-25 (nos.).

C 3.186/20: • **Item 142-C-4**
PROVISIONAL ESTIMATES OF THE POPULATION
OF COUNTIES. [Annual]
Discontinued.

C 3.186/20-2:date • **Item 142-C-4**
CURRENT POPULATION REPORTS, LOCAL POPU-
LATION ESTIMATES, COUNTY POPULATION
ESTIMATES. [Biennial]
Earlier C 3.186:P-26

C 3.186/21: • **Item 142-C-3**
STATE POPULATION AND HOUSEHOLD ESTIMATES
WITH AGE, SEX, AND COMPONENTS OF
CHANGE. [Annual]
Discontinued.

C 3.186/22: • **Item 142-C-7**
POVERTY IN THE UNITED STATES. [Annual]

C 3.186/23: • **Item 142-C-10**
EDUCATIONAL ATTAINMENT IN THE UNITED STATES.
[Annual]
Contains data on trends in educational at-
tainment and includes gender, racial, and regional
differences.
Designated Series P-20 (nos.).

C 3.186/25:date • **Item 142-C-5**
RESIDENTS OF FARMS & RURAL AREAS. [Annual]
Earlier titled: Farm Population of the United
States.

C 3.186/26: • **Item 142-C-3**
PROJECTIONS OF THE POPULATION OF VOTING
AGE, FOR STATES. [Biennial]

C 3.186/27: • **Item 142-C-11**
NORTHEAST, POPULATION AND PER CAPITA IN-
COME ESTIMATES FOR COUNTIES AND INCOR-
PORATED PLACES. [Biennial]

Local Population Estimates from Series P- 26
(C 3.186:P-26/(Item 142-C-4).
Tables present population and calendar year
per capita income estimates for counties and
subcounty areas of CT, MA, ME, NH, NJ, NY, PA,
RI, and VT.

C 3.186/27-2: • **Item 142-C-12**
WEST, POPULATION AND PER CAPITA INCOME
ESTIMATES FOR COUNTIES AND INCORPO-
RATED PLACES. [Biennial]

Local Population Estimates from Series P- 26
(C 3.186:P-26/(Item 142-C-4).
Tables present population and calendar year
per capita income estimates for counties and
subcounty areas of AK, AZ, CA, CO, HI, MT, NV,
OR, UT, WA, and WY.
Discontinued.

C 3.186/27-3: • **Item 142-C-13**
WEST NORTH CENTRAL, POPULATION AND PER
CAPITA INCOME ESTIMATES FOR COUNTIES
AND INCORPORATED PLACES. [Biennial]

Local Population Estimates from Series P- 26
(C 3.186:P-26/(Item 142-C-4).
Tables present population and calendar year
per capita income estimates for counties and
subcounty areas of IA, KS, MN, MO, NE, ND, and
SD.
Discontinued.

C 3.186/27-4: • **Item 142-C-14**
EAST NORTH CENTRAL, POPULATION AND PER
CAPITA INCOME ESTIMATES FOR COUNTIES
AND INCORPORATED PLACES. [Biennial]

Local Population Estimates from Series P- 26
(C 3.186:P-26/(Item 142-C-4).
Tables present population and calendar year
per capita income estimates for counties and
subcounty areas of IL, IN, MI, OH, and WI.
Discontinued.

C 3.186/27-5: • **Item 142-C-15**
SOUTH, POPULATION AND PER CAPITA INCOME
ESTIMATES FOR COUNTIES AND INCOR-
PORATED PLACES. [Biennial]

Local Population Estimates from Series P- 26
(C 3.186:P-26/(Item 142-C-4).
Tables present population and calendar year
per capita income estimates for counties and
subcounty areas of AL, AR, DE, DC, FL, GA, KY,
LA, MD, MS,NC, OK, SC, TN, TX, VA, and WV.
Discontinued.

C 3.187:nos.
LABOR FORCE MEMORANDUMS.

C 3.188:CT
COMMITTEE ON 1950 CENSUS OF THE AMERICAS.

C 3.189 • **Item 131-B**
CANNED FOOD REPORT. [5 times a year]

Reports issued as of the 1st of January, April,
June, July, and November. Gives total stocks of
wholesale distributors and warehouses of retail
multi-unit organizations, of specified canned foods.
November, April, and June reports cover 17 items,
January and July issues cover 31 items. January
report gives breakdown by two can size groups.
Discontinued with the July 1, 1981 issue.
See also C 56.219/8
ISSN 0145-5664
Discontinued.

C 3.190:date
TRENDS IN JEWELRY TRADE. [Monthly]

C 3.191:dt.&nos • **Item 146-C.**
GOVERNMENTAL FINANCES IN UNITED STATES.
Later C 3.191/2
Discontinued.

C 3.191/2 • **Item 146-E**
GOVERNMENTAL FINANCES, GF- (series). 1–
1965–   [Annual]

Combines the three series previously published separately– City Finances, CF-(series) (C
3.142), State Finances, SF- (series) (C 3.141),
and Governmental Finances, GS-(series) (C
3.191).
See also C 56.209
Discontinued.

CHART BOOK ON GOVERNMENTAL FINANCES
AND EMPLOYMENT: (year). 1966–
[Annual]

PURPOSE:– To provide, in graphic form,
a summary of key facts on Federal, State
and local governmental finances and employment drawn from previous Bureau of Census
Reports.

CITY GOVERNMENT FINANCES IN (year). [Annual]

Earlier published in City Finances series
(C 3.142). Previous title: Summary of City
Government Finances in (year).

COMPENDIUM OF STATE GOVERNMENT
FINANCES IN (year). [Annual]

Gives detailed State financial data for
fiscal year. Includes a national summary of
State finances for year and previous years
and summarizes financial aggregates, by
States.
Previously published in State Finances
series. (C 3.141).

FINANCES OF EMPLOYEE-RETIREMENT SYS-
TEMS OF STATE AND LOCAL GOVERNMENTS
IN (year). 1963/64–   [Annual]

Previously published in Government Finances in the United States series (C 3.191).

GOVERNMENTAL FINANCES IN (year). [Annual]

Previously published in Governmental Finances series (C 3.191).

LOCAL GOVERNMENT FINANCES IN SELECTED
METROPOLITAN AREAS IN (year). [Annual]

Covers the 38 standard metropolitan statistical areas recorded as the most populous
in the Nation by the Census of Population of
1960, when each of them had at least 700,000
inhabitants.
Gives revenue, by source; direct general
expenditure by type (current and capital) and
by function; revenue and expenditure of public utilities; indebtedness by type; total expenditure for personal services; and cash
and security holdings.

STATE TAX COLLECTION IN (year). [Annual]

Earlier published in State Finances series (C 3.141).

SUMMARY OF GOVERNMENTAL FINANCES IN
(year). 1953–   [Annual]

Gives revenues by type and source; expenditure by type, function, character, and
object, amount spent for personal services
and construction, and an exhibit of inter-governmental expenditure for selected functions;
debt outstanding, issues, and retired; and
State and local Government cash and security
holdings. Charts.

SUMMARY OF STATE GOVERNMENT FINANCES IN (year). [Annual]

Gives summary financial aggregates; per capita general revenue, general expenditures, and debt; general revenue by source; summary of expenditure by character and object, and by function; capital outlay and intergovernmental expenditure in total and for selected functions; insurance trust revenue and expenditure; debt outstanding by term and character and long-term debt issued and redeemed.
Previously published in State Finances series (C 3.141).

C 3.191/2-2:date   • **Item 146-E**
FINANCES OF EMPLOYEE-RETIREMENT SYSTEMS OF STATE AND LOCAL GOVERNMENTS. [Annual]

Gives receipts, payments, and cash and security holdings of employee-retirement systems administered by State and local governments.
Earlier C 3.191/2
Discontinued.

C 3.191/2-3:date   • **Item 146-E**
STATE GOVERNMENT FINANCES. [Annual]
Earlier C 3.191/2
Ceased with 1991/92.

C 3.191/2-4:date   • **Item 146-E**
GOVERNMENTAL FINANCES IN (year). [Annual]

Gives data on Governmental revenues and expenditures of State and local governments.
Earlier C 3.191/2
Ceased with 1991/92.

C 3.191/2-5:date   • **Item 146-E**
CITY GOVERNMENT FINANCES IN (year). [Annual]

Gives for each of the six population groups of cities with population of 25,000 and over: general, utility, and employee-retirement revenue and expenditures aggregates; general revenue, by source; expenditure data by character, object, and function; utility finance, by type; city employee-retirement system finances; and debt outstanding, issued and retired. Two year comparisons. Charts.
Earlier C 3.191/2
Ceased with 1991/92.

C 3.191/2-6:date   • **Item 146-E**
FINANCES OF PUBLIC SCHOOL SYSTEMS IN (year). [Annual]
See C3.191/2-10

C 3.191/2-7:date   • **Item 146-E**
COUNTY GOVERNMENT FINANCES. [Annual]
Earlier C 3.191/2:GF- (series).
Ceased with 1991/92.

C 3.191/2-8:date   • **Item 146-E (EL)**
STATE GOVERNMENT TAX COLLECTIONS. [Annual]

Gives State tax revenue, by type of tax; sales and gross receipts tax revenue; and license tax revenue.

C 3.191/2-9:date   • **Item 146-E**
LOCAL GOVERNMENT FINANCES IN MAJOR COUNTY AREAS. [Annual]
Earlier C 3.191/2
Ceased with 1985-86.

C 3.191/2-10:date   • **Item 146-E (P) (EL)**
GOVERNMENT FINANCES: PUBLIC EDUCATION FINANCES. [Annual]

C 3.191/3:date   • **Item 146-L**
GOVERNMENT FINANCES AND EMPLOYMENT AT A GLANCE.
Discontinued.

C 3.192:dt.&nos.
COUNTY FINANCES.

C 3.193:nos.
FARMS OF NONWHITE FARM OPERATORS, NUMBER OF FARMS, LAND IN FARM, CROPLAND HARVESTED, AND VALUE OF LAND AND BUILD-INGS, BY TENURE, CENSUSES OF 1945 AND 1940 (BY STATES).

C 3.194:nos.
SURVEY OF WORLD WAR II VETERANS AND DWELLING UNIT VACANCY AND OCCUPANCY (IN SPECIFIED AREAS).

C 3.195:date
WEEKLY STATEMENT OF GOLD AND SILVER EXPORTS AND IMPORTS, UNITED STATES.

C 3.196:date   • **Item 144**
GOLD AND SILVER MOVEMENTS: UNITED STATES. [Monthly]

C 3.196/2:date
SUMMARY OF U.S. EXPORTS AND IMPORTS OF GOLD AND SILVER, FISCAL YEAR.

C 3.196/3:date   • **Item 144**
SUMMARY OF U.S. EXPORTS AND IMPORTS OF GOLD AND SILVER, CALENDAR YEAR.

C 3.197:date
TRENDS IN DAY GOODS TRADE. [Monthly]

C 3.198:v.nos.
LIST OF ACQUISITIONS OF MUNICIPAL REFERENCE SERVICE. [Semimonthly]

C 3.199:date
PUBLICATIONS OF FOREIGN COUNTRIES, ANNOTATED ACCESSION LIST. [Quarterly]
See also C 56.238

C 3.200:date
TRENDS IN WHOLESALE WINERS AND SPIRITS TRADE. [Monthly]

C 3.201:nos.
FARM POPULATION.

C 3.202   • **Item 132 & 133**
CENSUS OF BUSINESS. 1929–   [Quinquennial]

A complete Census of Business was taken for each of the years 1929, 19331935, 1939, 1948, 1954, and 1958. Those for 1929 and 1939 were taken as part of the 1930 and 1940 Decennial Censuses; those for 1933 and 1935 were special projects. The Business Census is now authorized to be taken quinquennially, the next one being scheduled for 1963.
See also C 56.251

C 3.202/2:CT
– RETAIL TRADE BULLETINS (by States).
See also C 56.251/2

C 3.202/3:CT
– WHOLESALE TRADE BULLETINS (by States).

C 3.202/4:CT
– SERVICE TRADES BULLETINS (by States).

C 3.202/5:nos.   • **Item 132**
– FINAL VOLUMES.

C 3.202/6:CT   • **Item 133**
– SUBJECT BULLETINS, RETAIL TRADE.

C 3.202/7:CT   • **Item 133**
– SUBJECT BULLETINS, SERVICE TRADES.

C 3.202/8:CT   • **Item 133**
– SUBJECT BULLETINS, WHOLESALE TRADES.

C 3.202/9:CT
– RETAIL, WHOLESALE, SERVICE TRADES, SUBJECT BULLETIN RWS (series).

C 3.202/10:CT
– TRADE SERIES, BULLETINS.

C 3.202/11:CT
– CENSUS MONOGRAPHS.

C 3.202/12:le-nos.
PRELIMINARY REPORTS.

C 3.202/12-2:le&nos.   • **Item 132-A**
– PRELIMINARY AREA REPORTS.
See also C 56.252/2

C 3.202/13:dt.&nos.   • **Item 132-A**
– CENTRAL BUSINESS DISTRICT STATISTICS BULLETIN CBD (series).

C 3.202/14:date
–ANNOUNCEMENTS.

C 3.202/15:date   • **Item 133**
– PUERTO RICO.

C 3.202/16:date/EC-nos.
–MANUFACTURES, MINERALS INDUSTRIES, EC (series).

C 3.202/17:nos.
– ADVANCE REPORTS.

C 3.202/18:letters-nos.   • **Item 133**
– SPECIAL REPORTS.

C 3.202/19:date   • **Item 132-A**
– MERCHANDISE LINE SALES, BC-MLS (series).
1–   1970–   [Irregular]

PURPOSE:– To present data on retailers' sales by merchandise lines, reflecting a continuing demand for information regarding the degree with such different lines of merchandise are sold in different kinds of business. The tables in these reports provide data 1) on the number and total sales of establishments in a specified kind of business; 2) on the number and total sale of those establishments reporting their sales by the 25 broad merchandise lines; 3) on the percentage of total sales accounted for by each of the 25 broad lines; and 4) for establishments handling a specific line, what percent their total sales is represented by sales of that line. Additional detailed merchandise line breakdowns within the broad lines are shown for selected kinds of business.

C 3.203:nos.
SPECIAL STATISTICAL REPORTS ON UNITED STATES WATER-BORNE COMMERCE. [Monthly]
Changed from C 3.2:W 29/2

C 3.204   • **Item 133-A-1– A-55**
COUNTY BUSINESS PATTERNS, (year). 1st ed– 1943–   [Annual]

Gives statistics for States, counties, and standard metropolitan statistical areas for all private nonfarm activities and nonprofit membership organizations reported under the Federal Insurance Contributions Act, for the following subjects; employees, mid-March pay period; taxable payrolls, January– March; total number of reporting units; and reporting units by employment size class.
The State reports present the principal data items by detailed industry level (4-digit Standard Industrial Classification) for States and counties; for Standard Metropolitan Statistical Areas, the data are shown by major industry group (2-digit Standard Industrial Classification). Data are given for detailed kinds of business within the broad industry groups of agricultural services; forestry and fisheries; mining; contract construction; manufacturing; transportation and public utilities; wholesale trade; retail trade; finance, insurance, and real estate; and services.
Separate volumes issued for U.S. Summary and for each State as well as for Puerto Rico and Outlying Areas.
The first ten editions from 1943– 1962 were issued irregularly.
The reports are subsequently assembled and reissued in final form in a buckram-bound set of five volumes.
See also C 56.233

C 3.204/2
COUNTY BUSINESS PATTERNS, (year) (Final Reports). 1964–   [Annual]

The individual 53 volumes of the preliminary edition (listed above) are later assembled and reissued in a buckram-bound set of five volumes with corrections which occurred after the publication of the individual State reports inserted in the appropriate part of the reports.

C 3.204/3-1– 53:date   • **Item 133-A-1– 53**
COUNTY BUSINESS PATTERNS, UNITED STATES. [Annual]

C 3.204/4:date   • **Item 133-E (CD) (EL)**
COUNTY BUSINESS PATTERNS. [Annual]
Issued on CD-ROM.

C 3.204/5   • **Item 133-A-54 (EL)**
COUNTY BUSINESS PATTERNS (various states).

C 3.205   • **Item 139**
P-90 INTERNATIONAL POPULATION STATISTICS REPORTS. 1–   [Irregular]

C 3.205/2:nos.
STATISTICAL BRIEFS FROM AROUND THE WORLD. [Irregular]

C 3.205/3   • **Item 146-F**
ISPO [International Statistical Program Office] (series). 1–   [Irregular]

See also C 56.266
WORLD POPULATION: RECENT DEMOGRAPHIC ESTIMATES FOR THE COUNTRIES AND REGIONS OF THE WORLD. ISP-WP–   1973– [Annual]

C 3.205/4   • **Item 146-F**
ISP [INTERNATIONAL STATISTICAL PROGRAM] SUPPLEMENTAL COURSE SERIES. 1–   1968– [Irregular]

The courses cover lectures in basic applied sampling, principles of demography, agricultural economics, computer language, and similar topics to supplement the materials presented in case studies and censuses.
Discontinued.

C 3.205/5:nos.   • **Item 139**
DEMOGRAPHIC REPORTS FOR FOREIGN COUNTRIES, P 96- (series). 1–   1969–   [Irregular]

PURPOSE:– To investigate current and prospective demographic conditions in various countries and to provide long-range socioeconomic planners and other interested individuals with quantitative information regarding the projected changes in the size and structure of the population of a particular country, with; the ultimate aim of helping to establish a schedule of priorities for future demands, such as food, employment, schools, hospitals, and housing.

C 3.205/6   • **Item 146-F-1**
INTERNATIONAL RESEARCH DOCUMENTS, ISP-RD- (series).

PURPOSE:– To provide a series of demographic and socio-economic reports and studies prepared for project sponsors or presented at conferences which may be of interest to professionals other than those for whom originally prepared.
See also C 56.226/2
Discontinued.

C 3.205/8:date   • **Item 146-F-2 (P) (EL)**
STATISTICAL BRIEF FROM THE BUREAU OF THE CENSUS (series). [Irregular]

PURPOSE:– To provide statistical data on a different topic, such as age structure of the U. S. population in the 21st century.

C 3.205/9:date   • **Item 145-F-3 (P) (EL)**
BUREAU OF THE CENSUS, INTERNATIONAL BRIEF.

C 3.206:
CENSUS SUPERVISOR. [Monthly]

C 3.207:
LIBRARY NOTES. [Monthly]

C 3.207/2   • **Item 146-R**
INFORMATION EXCHANGE. [Monthly]
Non-Government Publication.

C 3.208   • **Item 146-B**
GE-10 GEOGRAPHIC REPORTS. 1– 1963– [Irregular]

C 3.208/2   • **Item 146-B**
GE-20 AREA MEASUREMENT REPORTS. 1– [Irregular]

Series consists of one report for each State and a U.S. summary. A bound volume combining all of these reports is planned at the completion of the series.
Provides surface area measurements for selected geographic units. The land area, water area, and total area are given in square miles for each country and component minor civil division or census county division, and each place with 1,000 or more inhabitants in 1960. The 1960 population and population per square mile are shown for each area.
Discontinued.

C 3.209:CT
RELEASES CGS (series).

See also C 56.207

C 3.209/2:nos.
INDUSTRY [RELEASES].

C 3.210:
TIPS.

C 3.211:nos.
CENSUS OF THE AMERICAS, POPULATION CENSUS, URBAN AREA DATA.

C 3.211/2   • **Item 144-A**
UNITED STATES WATERBORNE FOREIGN COMMERCE, GREAT LAKES AREA [year]. 1955– [Annual]

PURPOSE:– To provide annual statistical information on the foreign commerce handled through U.S. ports in the Great Lakes region.
1955, 1956, and 1957 reports were issued as Business Reports of the Department of Commerce. Beginning with the 1958 report, issued by the Bureau of the Census.
This series of reports is published in view of the current wide spread interest in the impact of the Saint Lawrence Seaway Project on the foreign trade of both the Great Lakes and sea board regions of the United States.
Additional information on the commerce of the Great Lakes waterways and harbors is published by the Corps of Engineers in its publication, Waterborne Commerce of the United States, Part 3.
Discontinued.

C 3.211/2
UNITED STATES WATERBORNE FOREIGN COMMERCE, A REVIEW OF [year]. [Annual]

PURPOSE:– To provide an analysis of United States foreign waterborne commerce for the calendar year, giving comparative data for previous year.   Deals primarily with the regular commercial import and export cargo segment of the foreign waterborne commerce of the United States. Supplemental data on the relatively less important aspect of the waterborne commerce such as in-transit cargo, Department of Defense controlled foreign aid cargo; and shipments of "special category" commodities are included. Excluded from all the figures are shipment to the United States Armed forces abroad of supplies and equipment for their own use.

C 3.211/3:CT
BUSINESS INFORMATION SERVICE: GENERAL PUBLICATIONS.

C 3.211/4:les-nos.   • **Item 141-B**
BUSINESS REPORTS.
Discontinued.

C 3.211/5   • **Item 148-B**
MONTHLY DEPARTMENT STORE SALES IN SELECTED AREAS. 1966– Jan. 1981. [Monthly]

Series measure total sales of department stores in selected areas.
See also C 56.219/3
Discontinued with the Jan. 1981 issue.
ISSN 0360-4179
Discontinued Jan. 1981.

C 3.212:nos.   • **Item 151-A (MF)**
TECHNICAL PAPERS. 1–   [Irregular]
See also C 56.215/2

C 3.212/2   • **Item 151-C (MF)**
TECHNICAL NOTES. 1–   1968–   [Irregular]

Presents fragments from research investigations undertaken by the Bureau of the Census staff members, bringing together some reports and memorandums in areas of methodological research related primarily to the design, analysis, or evaluation of various Bureau sample surveys and censuses.
See also C 56.215
Discontinued.

C 3.213:date
PETROLEUM PRODUCTS, SECONDARY INVENTORIES AND STORAGE CAPACITY.

C 3.214   • **Item 151-B (MF)**
WORKING PAPERS. 1–   1954–   [Irregular]
PURPOSE:– To make available to the public certain working documents of general interest.
See also C 56.229

C 3.215:letters-nos.&nos.   • **Item 141-A (EL)**
HOUSING AND CONSTRUCTION REPORTS (series).
See also C 56.214

HOUSEHOLDS WITH TELEVISION SETS IN THE UNITED STATES. 1–   [Irregular]

Surveys made at various times, usually one during each year. Gives percentages of households with television sets for U.S., regions, inside and outside standard metropolitan statistical areas, by residence (urban, by size of place; rural nonfarm; rural farm), and by size of household.

C 3.215:H-111
VACANT HOUSING UNITS IN THE UNITED STATES. 1–   [Quarterly]

Gives rental vacancy rates and homeowner vacancy rates for the United States, regional, and inside and outside standard metropolitan statistical areas, current quarter compared with same quarter a year ago.
Former title: Vacant Dwelling Units in the United States.
See also C 56.214
ISSN 0498-8469

C 3.215:H-130/data
CURRENT HOUSING REPORTS.   [Quarterly, with annual summary]

C 3.215:H-170   • **Item 141-A**
ANNUAL HOUSING SURVEY: HOUSING CHARACTERISTICS FOR SELECTED METROPOLITAN AREAS. H-170– 1974–   [Triennial]

Housing surveys conducted in 60 SMSAs divided in 3 groups, approximately 20 each, with one group interviewed every three years on a rotating basis. First group was interviewed April 1974– March 1975.

C 3.215/2 • **Item 140-A-1**
HOUSING STARTS IN (Month). [Monthly]

Gives estimates of housing starts, nonfarm and total, including figures for the following: New housing units started, by ownership, with seasonally adjusted annual rate of private starts; by type of structure; by metropolitan– non- metropolitan location and region.
Previous title: Nonfarm Housing Starts in (Month).
See also C 56.211/3
ISSN 0498-8442

C 3.215/3:C 30-nos. • **Item 140-A-2 (EL)**
CONSTRUCTION REPORTS: VALUE OF NEW CONSTRUCTION PUT IN PLACE, C30-(series).

Gives estimates of the value of new construction put in place, by type of construction, for month, two preceding months, and month a year ago.
See also C 56.211/5
ISSN 0363-8294

C 3.215/4:C 40-nos. • **Item 140-A-3**
CURRENT CONSTRUCTION REPORTS, HOUSING UNITS AUTHORIZED BY BUILDING PERMITS.

Annual summary, issued separately, provides similar data for 12,000 permit-issuing places including breakdown or housing units authorized by number of units in residential structures.
Previous titles: New Housing Units Authorized by Local Building Permits and New Dwelling Units Authorized in Local Building Permits.
See also C 56.211/4
ISSN 0363-8790
Discontinued.

C 3.215/5 • **Item 140-A-4**
AUTHORIZED CONSTRUCTION– WASHINGTON, D.C. AREA. C 41- (series). [Monthly]

Gives number of new dwelling units and permit valuation of building construction authorized in the standard metropolitan area of Washington, D.C.
See also C 56.211/6
ISSN 0498-8418
Discontinued.

C 3.215/6:nos. • **Item 140-A-4**
CONSTRUCTION REPORTS: BUILDING PERMITS: C 42- (series).

New residential construction authorized in permit issuing places, C 42- series.

C 3.215/7:le-nos.
CONSTRUCTION REPORTS: BUILDING PERMITS, C 40- (series).

C 3.215/8 • **Item 140-A-5 (EL)**
PART 1– EXPENDITURES ON RESIDENTIAL ADDITIONS, ALTERATIONS, MAINTENANCE AND REPAIRS, AND REPLACEMENTS. 1–   1961– [Annual]
Issued quarterly during 1961, annually since 1962. Beginning with data for 1963, issued in two parts.
For part 1, expenditures are shown according to general categories (number of housing units in property, size of property, nonfarm- farm status, etc.) and some specific types of construction work (plumbing, roofing, painting, heat, central air conditioning, remodeling, etc.). In addition to information provided for expenditures on all residential properties, this report also shows selected statistics for one to four housing unit properties with one unit owner occupied.

PART 2– EXPENDITURES FOR ADDITIONS, ALTERATIONS, MAINTENANCE AND REPAIRS, AND REPLACEMENTS ON 1-HOUSING-UNIT OWNER-OCCUPIED PROPERTIES. 1963– [Annual]

Part 2 is concerned only with the expenditures by owners on 1-housing-unit owner-occupied properties and shows expenditures in relationship to property, household, and geographic characteristics, which include value and age of the residential structure, household income, household composition, age and education of the household head, and location of property.
See also C 56.211/7
ISSN 0501-7645

C 3.215/8-2:date • **Item 1140-A-5**
CURRENT CONSTRUCTION REPORTS, SPECIAL STUDIES, EXPENDITURES FOR NONRESIDENTIAL IMPROVEMENTS AND REPAIRS. [Triennial]
Discontinued.

C 3.215/9 • **Item 140-A-6 (EL)**
CURRENT CONSTRUCTION REPORTS, NEW ONE-FAMILY HOUSES SOLD AND FOR SALE.

Monthly reports are supplemented by quarterly and annual summaries.
Monthly reports provide estimates of sales of new private, nonfarm, one-family homes, current month with revised figures for specified prior months. Gives numbers of new homes sold each month and for sale at end of each month, by stage of construction; median number of months from start to date and from completion to sale, by month of sale; and median number of months since start and since completion of homes for sale.
Quarterly reports supplement and expand the information in the monthly reports and also provide additional cross tabulations of data by sales price categories, by type of financing, and by geographic regions.
The annual report (the first report covered the year 1963) supplements and expands the information presented in the quarterly reports.
Earlier title: Sales of New One-Family Homes.
See also C 56.211/2
ISSN 0363-8537

C 3.215/9-2:nos. • **Item 140-A-7**
CONSTRUCTION REPORTS: PRICE INDEX OF NEW ONE-FAMILY HOUSES SOLD, C 27 (series).
See also C 56.211/2-2
ISSN 0093-4011
Now included in C 3.215/9

C 3.215/9-3:ltrs.nos. • **Item 140-A-6**
CHARACTERISTICS OF NEW HOUSING. [Annual]
Earlier C 3.215/9

C 3.215/10 • **Item 148-A**
CONSTRUCTION EXPENDITURE OF STATE AND LOCAL TAX REVENUE. 1965–   [Quarterly]

Gives nationwide figures on construction expenditure of State and local governments, by level of government and by function, for current quarter and specified prior periods.
See also C 56.223
ISSN 0363-8316

C 3.215/11:nos.
CONSTRUCTION REPORTS C 40/21 HOUSING AUTHORIZED BY BUILDING PERMITS AND PUBLIC CONTRACTS. 1–   1969–

Consolidation of C 3.215/4 and C 3.215/6.

C 3.215/12:date • **Item 140-A-10**
CONSTRUCTION REPORTS: PERMITS ISSUED FOR DEMOLITION OF RESIDENTIAL STRUCTURES IN SELECTED CITIES, C 45 (series)
See also C 56.211/8
Discontinued [List of Classes, 1980/4].
Discontinued.

C 3.215/13:letters-nos. • **Item 140-A-8 (EL)**
CONSTRUCTION REPORTS: HOUSING COMPLETIONS, C 22- (series). C 22-69–   1970– [Monthly]

Supplements data in Construction Reports, C 20, Housing Starts (C 3.215/2). Gives information on the number of housing units completed, irrespective of when construction started. Includes data on completions by ownership (private, public), by type of structure (units in 1, 2-4, and 5 or more family buildings), by location inside and outside of standard metropolitan statistical ar-

eas, and by 4 broad census regions.
See also C 56.211
ISSN 0363-8804

C 3.215/14:nos.
CURRENT HOUSING REPORTS, H-105-(series).
See also C 56.214/2

C 3.215/15 • **Item 140-A-9**
CURRENT CONSTRUCTION REPORTS: NEW RESIDENTIAL CONSTRUCTION IN SELECTED METROPOLITAN AREAS, C21- (series).

Earlier title: Construction Reports: New Residential Construction in Selected Standard Metropolitan Statistical Areas (ISSN 0145-0212).
Ceased 4th Quarter, 1998.

C 3.215/16:date • **Item 141-A**
ANNUAL HOUSING SURVEY, SUPPLEMENTARY REPORT, NO. 1, SUMMARY OF HOUSING CHARACTERISTICS FOR SELECTED METROPOLITAN AREAS. [Annual]
Earlier C 3.215
Ceased 1994.

C 3.215/17-nos.date • **Item 156-B-nos.**
ANNUAL HOUSING SURVEY: HOUSING CHARACTERISTICS FOR SELECTED STANDARD METROPOLITAN STATISTICAL AREA. [Biennial]
Earlier C 3.215

C 3.215/17-21:date • **Item 156-B-9**
MIAMI, FLORIDA, STANDARD METROPOLITAN STATISTICAL AREA. [Biennial]

C 3.215/17-29:date • **Item 156-B-49**
MILWAUKEE, WISCONSIN, PRIMARY METROPOLITAN STATISTICAL AREA. [Irregular]
Earlier C 3.215

C 3.215/17-31:date • **Item 156-B-46**
NORFOLK-VIRGINIA BEACH-NEWPORT NEWS, VIRGINIA, METROPOLITAN STATISTICAL AREA. [Biennial]
Earlier C 3.215

C 3.215/17-34:date • **Item 156-B-37**
PORTLAND, OREGON-WASHINGTON, STANDARD METROPOLITAN STATISTICAL AREAS. [Biennial]
See C 3.215

C 3.215/17-44:date • **Item 156-B-32**
BUFFALO, NEW YORK, CONSOLIDATED METROPOLITAN STATISTICAL AREA. [Irregular]
See C 3.215

C 3.215/17-45:date • **Item 156-B-35**
CLEVELAND, OHIO PRIMARY METROPOLITAN STATISTICAL AREA. [Biennial]
Earlier C 3.215

C 3.215/17-49:date • **Item 156-B-43**
HOUSTON, TEXAS STANDARD METROPOLITAN AREAS. [Biennial]
See C 3.215

C 3.215/17-50:date • **Item 156-B-14**
INDIANAPOLIS, INDIANA, METROPOLITAN STATISTICAL AREA. [Biennial]
Earlier C 3.215

C 3.215/17-52:date • **Item 156-B-17**
LOUISVILLE, KENTUCKY-INDIANA, STANDARD STATISTICAL AREAS. [Biennial]
See C 3.215

C 3.215/17-58:date • **Item 156-B-5**
SACRAMENTO, CALIFORNIA, STANDARD METROPOLITAN STATISTICAL AREA. [Biennial]
See C 3.215

C 3.215/17-60:date • **Item 156-B-47**
SEATTLE-EVERETT, WASHINGTON STANDARD METROPOLITAN STATISTICAL AREAS. [Biennial]
See C 3.215

C 3.215/17-61:date • Item 156-B-5
SAN JOSE, CALIFORNIA, PRIMARY METRO-
POLITAN STATISTICAL AREA. [Biennial]
See C 3.215

C 3.215/17-84:date • Item 156-B-44
SALT LAKE CITY, UTAH. [Biennial]

C 3.215/18:date • Item 156-B-52
ANNUAL HOUSING SURVEY: HOUSING CHARAC-
TERISTICS OF RECENT MOVERS.
Now included in 141-A.

C 3.215/18-2:date • Item 156-B-52
ANNUAL HOUSING SURVEY: URBAN AND RURAL
HOUSING CHARACTERISTICS.
Earlier C 3.215

C 3.215/18-3:date • Item 156-B-nos.
ANNUAL HOUSING SURVEY: ENERGY-RELATED
HOUSING CHARACTERISTICS. [Annual]
Earlier C 3.215
Discontinued.

C 3.215/19 • Item 156-P (CD)
AMERICAN HOUSING SURVEY. [Biennial]
Issued on CD-ROM.

C 3.215/20:date&nos. • Item 156-B-52 (P) (EL)
AMERICAN HOUSING BRIEF (AHB) FROM THE
AMERICAN HOUSING SURVEY.

C 3.216:dt.nos • Item 158
CENSUS OF MINERAL INDUSTRIES: [Industry] BUL-
LETINS MI- (series).
See also C 56.236/3

C 3.216/2:date-no. • Item 158
– [STATE] BULLETIN MI- (series).

See also C 56.236/4
C 3.216/3:date/letters&nos. • Item 158
– PRELIMINARY REPORTS.

C 3.216/3-2:date/letters&nos.
– INDUSTRY AND PRODUCT REPORTS.

C 3.216/4:date/letters • Item 158
– [SUBJECT] BULLETIN MI- (series).
See also C 56.236/5

C 3.216/5:date • Item 157
– FINAL VOLUMES.
Discontinued 1977.

C 3.216/6:date
– ANNOUNCEMENTS.

C 3.216/7 • Item 158
– SUMMARY SERIES.

C 3.217:date/nos.
INTERNATIONAL NEWS LETTER. [Admin.].

C 3.218:date
RECONDITIONED STEEL BARRELS AND DRUMS
REPORT. [Quarterly]

C 3.218/2:CD 90-AOA • Item 154-B-3
1990 CENSUS OF POPULATION AND HOUSING,
SPECIAL TABULATION ON AGING, FEDERAL RE-
GION 1, CONNECTICUT-MAINE-MASSACHU-
SETTS-NEW HAMPSHIRE-RHODE ISLAND-
VERMONT, CD 90-AOA1.
Issued on CD-ROM.

C 3.219:date
PUERTO RICO CENSUSES, ANNOUNCEMENTS.

C 3.220:date
CENSUS TELEPHONE LISTING OF BUREAU
ACTIVITIES. ADMIN.

C 3.221:dt/v.no.pt.no.
NATIONAL HOUSING INVENTORY.

C 3.222:date&nos.
COMPANY STATISTICS BULLETINS, CENSUS OF
BUSINESS, MANUFACTURES AND MINERAL IN-
DUSTRIES.

C 3.223:CT • Item 154
CENSUS OF POPULATION: GENERAL PUBLICA-
TIONS.
Earlier C 3.950-2:

C 3.223/2:date/letters-nos. • Item 159-A-1– A-54
CENSUS OF POPULATION: PRELIMINARY RE-
PORTS.

C 3.223/3:date/nos.
CENSUS OF POPULATION AND HOUSING:
ANNOUNCEMENTS.

C 3.223/4:date/ltrs.-nos. • Item 159-A-1– A-54

(CENSUS OF POPULATION: ADVANCE REPORTS.)

NOTE:– Includes PC (A 1)-nos. Final Popula-
tion Counts.
PC (A 2)-nos. General Population Character-
istics.
PC (A 3)-nos. General Social and Economic
Characteristics.
Later C 3.223/19

C 3.223/5:date/nos. • Item 159-C-1– C-53
U.S. CENSUS OF POPULATION: NUMBER OF
INHABITANTS.

C 3.223/6:date/nos. • Item 159-C-1– C-53
CENSUS OF POPULATION: GENERAL POPULATION
CHARACTERISTICS, PC 80-1-B Series.

C 3.223/6-2 • Item 154-A-1
CENSUS OF POPULATION: GENERAL
POPULATION CHARACTERISTICS FOR
AMERICAN INDIAN AND ALASKA NATIVE AR-
EAS (Series 90-CP-1-1A).

C 3.223/6-3 • Item 154-A-2
CENSUS OF POPULATION: GENERAL
POPULATION CHARACTERISTICS FOR MET-
ROPOLITAN STATISTICAL AREAS (Series 90-
CP-1-1B).

C 3.223/6-4 • Item 154-A-3
CENSUS OF POPULATION: GENERAL
POPULATION CHARACTERISTICS FOR UR-
BANIZED AREAS (Series 90-CP-1-1C).

C 3.223/7:date/nos. • Item 159-C-1– C-53
CENSUS OF POPULATION: GENERAL SOCIAL AND
ECONOMIC CHARACTERISTICS, PC (1)-C Se-
ries.

C 3.223/7-2 • Item 154-A-1
CENSUS OF POPULATION: SOCIAL AND ECO-
NOMIC CHARACTERISTICS FOR AMERICAN
INDIAN AND ALASKA NATIVE AREAS (Se-
ries 90-CP-2-1A).

C 3.223/7-3 • Item 154-A-2
CENSUS OF POPULATION: SOCIAL AND ECO-
NOMIC CHARACTERISTICS FOR METRO-
POLITAN STATISTICAL AREAS (Series 90-
CP-2-1B).

C 3.223/7-4 • Item 154-A-3
CENSUS OF POPULATION: SOCIAL AND
ECONOMIC CHARACTERISTICS FOR
URBANIZED AREAS (Series 90-CP-2-1C).

C 3.223/7-5:nos. • Item 154
1990 CENSUS PROFILE (numbered).

C 3.223/8:date/nos • Item 159-C-1– C-53
CENSUS OF POPULATION. DETAILED CHARACTER-
ISTICS. PC 80-(1)-D Series.

C 3.223/9:date/pt.nos. • Item 159-A-1– A-54
CENSUS OF POPULATION. CHARACTERISTICS OF
THE POPULATION. BOUND VOLUMES.

C 3.223/10 • Item 159-G
CENSUS OF POPULATION: SUBJECT REPORTS, PC
80-2 (series).

C 3.223/11:date/nos. • Item 156-K-1– K-53
CENSUS OF POPULATION AND HOUSING, CENSUS
TRACT REPORTS, PHC 80-2 (Series) (State).

C 3.223/11-2:CT • Item 156-K-52
CENSUS OF POPULATION AND HOUSING: FIND-
ERS GUIDE TO CENSUS TRACT REPORTS (Se-
ries 90-CPH-3)

C 3.223/12 • Item 154 (MF)
CENSUS OF POPULATION. PC 80-S1 1970–
[Decennial]

C 3.223/13:date/nos. • Item 159-A-1– A-54
UNITED STATES CENSUSES OF POPULATION AND
HOUSING: GEOGRAPHIC IDENTIFICATION
CODE SCHEME, PHC (2) (series).

C 3.223/13-2:Reg. • Item 154
GEOGRAPHIC IDENTIFICATION CODE SCHEME [by
regions].

C 3.223/14:nos. • Item 154
GRAPHIC PAMPHLETS GP (series).

C 3.223/15:date/nos. • Item 154
CENSUSES OF POPULATION AND HOUSING:
CENSUS COUNTY DIVISION BOUNDARY DE-
SCRIPTION, PHC 80-E series.

C 3.223/16:nos. • Item 154
EVALUATION AND RESEARCH REPORTS ER PHC
80-E (series).

C 3.223/17:date-nos. • Item 159-A-1– A-54
EMPLOYMENT PROFILES FOR SELECTED LOW-
INCOME AREAS, PHC (3) (series).

C 3.223/18 • Item 159-B-1– B-54
CENSUS OF POPULATION AND HOUSING: PRELIMI-
NARY REPORTS PHC 80-P (series) (State).

C 3.223/19 • Item 159-B-1– 53
CENSUS OF POPULATION AND HOUSING: ADVANCE
REPORTS PHC 80-V (series) (State).
Earlier C 3.223/4 and C 3.224

C 3.223/20 • Item 159-C-1– C-53
CENSUS OF POPULATION AND HOUSING: CON-
GRESSIONAL DISTRICTS OF THE 103RD
CONGRESS PHC 90-4 (series) (State).
Earlier C 3.134/4

C 3.223/21:nos. • Item 154
CENSUS OF POPULATION AND HOUSING: PROVI-
SIONAL ESTIMATES OF SOCIAL ECONOMIC
AND HOUSING CHARACTERISTICS, PHC 80-S
1-1 (series). [Irregular]

C 3.223/21-2:nos. • Item 156-M-1– 53
CENSUS OF POPULATION AND HOUSING: ADVANCE
ESTIMATES OF SOCIAL ECONOMIC, AND HOUS-
ING CHARACTERISTICS, SUPPLEMENTARY
REPORTS, PHC-A2- (series). [Irregular]

C 3.223/22: • Item 154-B
CENSUS OF POPULATION AND HOUSING: USERS
GUIDE (Series PHC 80-R1).

Earlier title: Census of Population and Housing, Reference Reports.

C 3.223/22:80-R1 • Item 154-B
CENSUS OF POPULATION AND HOUSING: USERS
GUIDE PHC 80-R1 (series).

C 3.223/22:80-R2 • Item 154
CENSUS OF POPULATION AND HOUSING: HISTORY,
PHC 80-R2 (series).

C 3.223/22:80-R3 • Item 154
CENSUS OF POPULATION AND HOUSING: ALPHA-
BETICAL INDEX OF INDUSTRIES AND OCCUPA-
TIONS PHC 80-R3 (series).

C 3.223/22:80-R4 • Item 154
CENSUS OF POPULATION AND HOUSING: CLASSI-
FIED INDEX OF INDUSTRIES AND OCCUPATIONS
PHC 80-R4 (series).

C 3.223/22:80-R5 • Item 154
CENSUS OF POPULATION AND HOUSING: GEO-
GRAPHIC IDENTIFICATION CODE SCHEME, PHC
80-R5 (series).

C 3.223/22:90-R   • **Item 154-A-4**
CENSUS OF POPULATION AND HOUSING: REFER-
ENCE REPORTS, SERIES CPH-90-R.
     Later: C 3.223/22-2

C 3.223/22:90-R1   • **Item 154-A-5**
1990 CENSUS OF POPULATION AND HOUSING,
GUIDE PART B. GLOSSARY, CPH-R-1B.

C 3.223/22:90-R2   • **Item 154-A-6**
CENSUS OF POPULATION AND HOUSING: HISTORY,
CPH-90-R2.

C 3.223/22:90-R3   • **Item 154-A-7**
CENSUS OF POPULATION AND HOUSING: ALPHA-
BETICAL INDEX OF INDUSTRIES AND
OCCUPATIONS, SERIES CPH-90-R3.

C 3.223/22:90-R4   • **Item 154-A-8**
CENSUS OF POPULATION AND HOUSING:
CLASSIFIED INDEX OF INDUSTRIES AND OC-
CUPATIONS, SERIES CPH-90-R4.

C 3.223/22:90-R5   • **Item 154-A-9**
CENSUS OF POPULATION AND HOUSING: GEO-
GRAPHIC IDENTIFICATION CODE SCHEME,
SERIES CPH-90-R5.

C 3.223/22-2   • **Item 154-B**
CENSUS OF POPULATION AND HOUSING: USERS
GUIDE (SERIES PHC 90-R).
     Earlier: C 3.223/22:90-R

C 3.223/23   • **Item 154-M-1– M-53**
CENSUS OF POPULATION AND HOUSING:
SUMMARY CHARACTERISTICS FOR GOVERN-
MENTAL UNITS AND STANDARD METROPOLI-
TAN STATISTICAL AREAS, PHC 90-3 (series)
(State).

C 3.223/24   • **Item 159-B-53**
CENSUS OF POPULATION AND HOUSING TABULA-
TION AND PUBLICATION PROGRAM FOR
PUERTO RICO (Series 90-CPH-1).

C 3.223/25   • **Item 154-B-54 (MF)**
POPULATION PAPER LISTINGS (PPL series).

C 3.223/26   • **Item 146-L-1**
POPULATION DIVISION WORKING PAPER SERIES.

C 3.223/27:nos.   • **Item 154-B-55 (MF)**
POPULATION DIVISION... WORKING PAPER
SERIES... TECHNICAL WORKING PAPERS.

C 3.224:date/letters-nos.   • **Item 156-A**
CENSUS OF HOUSING: ADVANCE REPORTS. IN-
CLUDES HOUSING CHARACTERISTICS, STATES,
HC (A 1) (series).

C 3.224/2:date/letters-nos.
CENSUS OF HOUSING: PRELIMINARY REPORTS.

C 3.224/3:80-1-A   • **Item 156-B-1– B-53**
CENSUS OF HOUSING: GENERAL HOUSING CHAR-
ACTERISTICS HC 80-1-A (series) (State).

C 3.224/3:90-CH-1   • **Item 156-B-1-51**
CENSUS OF HOUSING: GENERAL HOUSING CHAR-
ACTERISTICS (Series 90-CH-1) (State).

C 3.224/3:90-CH-1   • **Item 156-B-52**
CENSUS OF HOUSING: GENERAL HOUSING CHAR-
ACTERISTICS (Series 90-CH-1) (U.S. Summary).

C 3.224/3:90-CH-1   • **Item 156-B-53**
CENSUS OF HOUSING: GENERAL HOUSING CHAR-
ACTERISTICS (Series 90-CH-1) (Outlying Areas).

C 3.224/3:90-CH-2   • **Item 156-B-1—51**
CENSUS OF HOUSING: DETAILED HOUSING CHAR-
ACTERISTICS (Series 90-CH- 2) (State).

C 3.224/3:90-CH-2   • **Item 156-B-52**
CENSUS OF HOUSING: DETAILED HOUSING CHAR-
ACTERISTICS (Series 90-CH- 2) (U.S. Summary).

C 3.224/3:90-CH-2   • **Item 156-B-53**
CENSUS OF HOUSING: DETAILED HOUSING CHAR-
ACTERISTICS (Series 90-CH- 2) (Outlying Areas).

C 3.224/3-2   • **Item 155-A-1**
CENSUS OF HOUSING: GENERAL HOUSING CHAR-

ACTERISTICS FOR AMERICAN INDIAN AND
ALASKA NATIVE AREAS (Series 90-CH-1-1A).

C 3.224/3-3   • **Item 155-A-2**
CENSUS OF HOUSING: GENERAL HOUSING CHAR-
ACTERISTICS FOR METROPOLITAN STATISTI-
CAL AREAS (Series 90-CH-1-1B).

C 3.224/3-4   • **Item 155-A-3**
CENSUS OF HOUSING: GENERAL HOUSING CHAR-
ACTERISTICS FOR URBANIZED AREAS (Series
90-CH-1-1C).

C 3.224/3-5   • **Item 155-A-1**
CENSUS OF HOUSING: DETAILED HOUSING CHAR-
ACTERISTICS FOR AMERICAN INDIAN AND
ALASKA NATIVE AREAS (Series 90-CH-2-1A)

C 3.224/3-6   • **Item 155-A-2**
CENSUS OF HOUSING: DETAILED HOUSING CHAR-
ACTERISTICS FOR METROPOLITAN STATISTI-
CAL AREAS (Series 90-CH-2-1B).

C 3.224/3-7   • **Item 155-A-3**
CENSUS OF HOUSING: DETAILED HOUSING CHAR-
ACTERISTICS FOR URBANIZED AREAS (Series
90-CH-2-1C).

C 3.224/3-8:nos.   • **Item 140-A-6**
1990 HOUSING HIGHLIGHTS (Series CH-S)

C 3.224/4   • **Item 156-B-1– B-53**
CENSUS OF HOUSING: METROPOLITAN HOUSING
HC 80-2 (series) (State).

     A Census of Housing was taken as part of
the Decennial Censuses of 1940 and 1950 and
again conducted in 1960.

C 3.224/4-2:date   • **Item 146-T**
CENSUS OF HOUSING: METROPOLITAN HOUSING
CHARACTERISTICS, CH-3-1.

C 3.224/5   • **Item 156-J-1– J-53**
CENSUS OF POPULATION AND HOUSING: BLOCK
STATISTICS PHC 80-1 (series) (State).

C 3.224/6   • **Item 155-A**
CENSUS OF HOUSING: COMPONENTS OF INVEN-
TORY CHANGE HC 80-4 (series).

C 3.224/7:date/pt.nos.   • **Item 155-A**
CENSUS OF HOUSING. RESIDENTIAL FINANCE. HC
80-5 series.

C 3.224/8   • **Item 155-A**
CENSUS OF HOUSING: SUPPLEMENTARY REPORT
HC 80-SI-1 (series).

C 3.224/9:date/v.nos.   • **Item 155**
CENSUS OF HOUSING: FINAL VOLUMES.

C 3.224/10:date/nos.   • **Item 155-A**
CENSUS OF HOUSING, SUBJECT REPORTS HC 90-
3 (7)- (series). 1–   [Irregular]

C 3.224/11:ltrs-nos.   • **Item 155-A**
1990 CENSUS OF POPULATION AND HOUSING CON-
TENT DETERMINATION REPORTS: (Series).

C 3.224/12:date   • **Item 155-C (CD)**
CURRENT POPULATION SURVEY. [Annual]
     Issued on CD-ROM.

C 3.224/12-2:date   • **Item 155-C-1 (E)**
INCOME AND POVERTY, CURRENT POPULATION
SURVEY. [Annual]
     Issued on CD-ROM.

C 3.224/13:1990 CH-4-1   • **Item 155-A-4**
1990 CENSUS OF HOUSING, RESIDENTIAL
FINANCE, CH-4-1.

C 3.224/13-2   • **Item 155-A-5 (EL)**
HOUSING VACANCY SURVEY. [Quarterly]

C 3.225:
PROCEDURAL STUDIES OF CENSUSES.
     Earlier C 3.950-19

C 3.225/3-3:letters-nos.   • **Item 133**
CENSUS OF RETAIL TRADE: INDUSTRY SERIES.

C 3.226   • **Item 131-A**
ENTERPRISE STATISTICS.

     ES 1 BUSINESS CONDITIONS DIGEST. 1961–
[Monthly]

     Brings together many of the economic
times series found most useful by business
analysts and forecasters. Almost 500 economic indicators are presented in a form that
is convenient for analysts with different approaches to the study of current business
conditions and prospects (e.g., the national
income model, the leading indicators, and anticipations and intentions) as well as for analysts who use combinations of these approaches. Various other types of data (such
as the diffusion indexes) are provided to facilitate complete analysis.
     The report is organized into six major sec-
tions, as follows: (a) National income and
product; (b) cyclical indicators: (c) anticipations and intentions; (d) other key indicators;
(e) analytical measures; and (f) international
comparisons. Several appendixes present
historical data, series descriptions, seasonal
adjustment factors, and measures of variability.
     Formerly Business Cycle Developments.
Subscription service includes a separate
summary table Advanced BCD, which is mailed
in advance of the monthly reports.
     See also C 56.111

C 3.226/2:nos.   • **Item 151-A**
BCD TECHNICAL PAPERS.

C 3.226/3
ADVANCE BCD [Business Condition Digest]. [Monthly]
     Subscription included with Business Condi-
tions Digest.
     See also C 56.111/2

C 3.227   • **Item 131-C**
CENSUS TRACT MEMOS. 1–   1961–   [Irregular]

     PURPOSE:– To make information more uni-
formly available to Census Tract Committees and
other national and local users of tract data and to
reduce the necessity for individual letters on subjects of general interest to members of the approximately 230 local Census Tract Committees
in about 200 standard metropolitan statistical areas. Series serves to solicit the aid of Committees, to inform them as new plans affecting census tracts and other Bureau activities evolve,
and to bring the ideas and activities of the various Committees to the attention of all those who
are interested and would profit from such knowledge.
     See also C 56.235/2

C 3.227/2   • **Item 131-C**
GE-40 CENSUS TRACT PAPERS. 1–   1966–
[Irregular]

     Text of papers presented in Census Tract
Conferences. Census Tract papers were previously published in Census Working Papers, 7,
10– 13, 17, and 11.
     See also C 56.235

C 3.228:nos.
STATISTICAL PROFILE SERIES SP.

     Prepared from Area Redevelopment Adminis-
tration.
     Replaced by C 1.45:

C 3.229 • Item 160-B
ES 2 U.S. COMMODITY EXPORTS AND IMPORTS RELATED TO OUTPUT. 1– 1968&57– [Annual]

PURPOSE:– To help meet the need for a systematic body of statistical information on the relation between U.S. domestic output and U.S. commodity exports and imports.
Basic detailed tables show value data for agricultural, forestry, fisheries, mineral, and manufactured commodity groups and also quantity data where appropriate and available. Also includes historical series on value of exports and imports and their relationships to output, for 5-digit and 4-digit Standard Industrial Classification commodity groups.
See also C 56.232

C 3.230 • Item 142-B
ES 3 ENTERPRISE STATISTICS: (year). 1 (58)– 1963– [Irregular]

Studies based on the Censuses of Business, Manufactures, and Mineral Industries. Series have been published for the 1958 and 1963 Census.
See also C 56.228

C 3.230/2:letters-nos. • Item 142-B
ENTERPRISE STATISTICS, PRELIMINARY REPORTS.

C 3.231:nos. • Item 227-B (MF)
MANUFACTURES, SHIPMENTS, INVENTORIES, AND ORDERS, SERIES M 3-1.

Formerly Industry Survey.
See also C 56.245

C 3.232:nos.
RESEARCH DOCUMENTATION LIST. [Official Use].

C 3.233:CT • Item 160-D
CENSUS OF TRANSPORTATION, PUBLICATIONS.

See also C 56.246

C 3.233/2:nos. • Item 160-D
– ADVANCE AND/OR PRELIMINARY REPORTS.
See also C 56.246/2

C 3.233/3 • Item 160-D
CENSUS OF TRANSPORTATION. 1963– [Quinquennial]

The 1963 Census of Transportation was the first census of this type and was conducted as four major projects– Commodity Transport Survey, Passenger Transportation Survey, Truck Inventory and Use Survey, and Bus and Truck Carrier Survey.
Plans call for such a census every five years hereafter, coincident with other economic censuses of business, manufactures, and mineral industries. Under legislation enacted in 1963, these census will be taken in the future for the years ending in 2 and 7.
See also C 56.246/3

C 3.233/4:date
– ANNOUNCEMENT AND ORDER FORMS.

C 3.233/4-2:date/nos.
PUBLICATION PROGRAM.

C 3.233/5:letters-nos. • Item 160-D
FINAL REPORTS.
See also C 56.246/2

C 3.233/6:date • Item 154-C-1 (E)
TRUCK INVENTORY AND USE SURVEY (TIUS).
Issued on CD-ROM

C 3.234:date • Item 133-C
CENSUS OF COMMERCIAL FISHERIES: FINAL VOLUMES.
Later C 3.223/19

C 3.234/2:date
CENSUS OF COMMERCIAL FISHERIES, PRELIMINARY REPORTS.

C 3.235 • Item 160-B-1
U.S. EXPORTS AND IMPORTS, WORKING-DAY AND SEASONAL ADJUSTMENT FACTORS AND MONTHS FOR CYCLICAL DOMINANCE (MCD). 1965– [Annual]

Gives for exports and imports the unadjusted series, the series adjusted for working days and seasonality, the estimate trend-cycle component provided by the MCD moving average, and the historical estimates of the trend-cycle provided by the weighted 15-month moving average.

C 3.236 • Item 146-D
GREEN COFFEE INVENTORIES AND ROASTINGS. [Quarterly]

Gives estimates of green coffee inventories held by roasters, importers, and dealers as of the period covered and selected prior years; and roastings of green coffee by quarters during current and previous years.
See also C 56.219/2
Discontinued with 2nd quarter 1981.

C 3.237:v.nos.&nos.
CENSUS BUREAU STATISTICAL DAILY.

C 3.238:v.nos./nos. • Item 148-C
CENSUS AND YOU.

Earlier title: Data User News.
PURPOSE:– To keep both the users and the producers of small-area informed as to the needs, new programs, publications, and other relevant items which may be of interest to readers.
Previous titles: Small-Area Data Activities and Small Area Data Notes.
Vols 7– 10 were classified C 56.217.
ISSN 0096-9877

C 3.238/a • Item 148-C (MF)
DATA USER NEWS (Separates).

C 3.238/2:nos. • Item 142-B-1 (MF)
SMALL-AREA STATISTICS PAPERS, SERIES. GE 41-1– [Irregular]

C 3.238/3:nos.
CENSUS UPDATE, SUPPLEMENT TO DATA USER NEWS.

C 3.238/4:date • Item 148-C (MF)
NATIONAL CLEARINGHOUSE FOR CENSUS DATA SERVICES ADDRESS LIST. [Annual]
Former title: Summary Tape Processing Centers and State Data Centers Address List.
Earlier C 3.2:T 16

C 3.238/5 • Item 148-C (EL)
TELEPHONE CONTACTS FOR DATA USERS. [Irregular]

C 3.238/6:nos. • Item 148-C
PRODUCT/ACTIVITY STATUS BULLETIN. [Monthly]

C 3.238/7:nos.
DATA DEVELOPMENTS. [Irregular]

C 3.238/8:date
STATE DATA CENTER EXCHANGE. [Quarterly]

C 3.239 • Item 141-C
MONTHLY SELECTED SERVICES RECEIPTS. 1966– [Monthly]

PURPOSE:– To provide summary statistics for selected services by major kind of business group. Gives estimated monthly receipts of establishments for selected services, by kind of business group, for current month and 12 preceeding months, and trends (percent change) in receipts, by kind of business group, current month, previous month, and month a year ago. Data are shown for the United States, both unadjusted and adjusted for seasonal variations, and trading day differences.
Kinds of business groups included are hotels, motels, camps, and other lodging places (except rooming and boarding houses, organization hotels and lodging houses operating on a membership basis); personal service, including laundries and dry cleaning, beauty and barber

shops, funeral service, photographic studios, etc.; business services, including advertising agencies, consumer credit and collection agencies, news syndicates, private employment agencies, miscellaneous repair services (electrical, watch, furniture, etc.); motion pictures, including production and distribution, related services and heaters; amusement and recreation services.
See also C 56.219/5
ISSN 0092-038X

C 3.239/2:date • Item 141-C
MONTHLY SELECTED SERVICES RECEIPTS, REVISED [Compilations]. [Irregular]

C 3.240 • Item 142-D
DATA ACCESS DESCRIPTIONS, MATCHING STUDIES SERIES, MS-(nos.). 1– 1967– [Irregular]

PURPOSE:– To provide introductions to means of access to unpublished data of the Bureau of Census, for persons with data requirements not fully met by published reports.
See also C 56.212

C 3.240/2 • Item 142-D
DATA ACCESS DESCRIPTIONS: AUTOMATED ADDRESS CODING GUIDE AND DATA RETRIEVAL SERIES, ACC-(nos.). 1– 1967– [Irregular]

C 3.240/3 • Item 142-D
DATA ACCESS DESCRIPTIONS: CENSUS TABULATIONS AVAILABLE ON COMPUTER TAPE SERIES CT-(nos).
See also C 56.212/3

C 3.240/4 • Item 142-D
DATA ACCESS DESCRIPTIONS, POLICY AND ADMINISTRATION SERIES, PA-(nos). 1– 1968– [Irregular]
PURPOSE:– To provide a means of access to unpublished data of the Bureau of the Census for persons with data requirements not fully met by published reports.

C 3.240/5 • Item 142-D
DATA ACCESS DESCRIPTIONS: COLLECTION, EVALUATION AND PROCESSING SERIES, CEP-(nos). 1– 1968– [Irregular]
See also C 56.212

C 3.240/6:nos. • Item 142-D
DATA ACCESS DESCRIPTIONS: CENSUS GEOGRAPHY SERIES, CG-(nos). 1– 1969–
Intended as introductions to means of access to Census Bureau data for persons with data requirements not fully met by printed reports.
See also C 56.212/5

C 3.240/7:nos. • Item 142-D
DATA ACCESS DESCRIPTION [Miscellaneous].
Earlier C 56.212/6

C 3.241 • Item 142-E
DEFENSE INDICATORS. 1968– [Monthly]

This report brings together the principal time series on defense activity which influence short-term changes in the national economy. These include series on obligations, contracts, orders, shipments, inventories, expenditures, employment and earnings. The approximate 30 times series included are grouped in accordance with the time at which the activities they measure occurred in the defense order-production- delivery process. Most are monthly though a few are quarterly. This publication provides original and seasonally adjusted basic data in monthly, quarterly, and annual form. Charts and analytical tables are included to facilitate interpretation.
Supersedes Selected Economic Indicators(D 1.43) published by the Department of Defense.
See also C 56.110

C 3.242 • Item 148-E (EL)
FINANCES OF SELECTED PUBLIC EMPLOYEE
RETIREMENT SYSTEMS, GR- (series). 1968–
[Quarterly]

Gives for current quarter and specified prior
periods summary data on cash and security holdings of 100 major employee-retirement systems
of State and local governments. Data are shown
for cash and deposits, Federal, State and local
government securities, corporate bonds and
stocks, mortgages, and other securities.
Former title: Holdings of Selected Public Employee Retirement Systems.
See also C 56.224

C 3.243
FINANCIAL MANAGEMENT SYSTEMS SERIES.
FMSS-1– [Irregular]

C 3.244:nos. • Item 131-D (MF)
CENSUS USE STUDY REPORTS.
See also C 56.220

C 3.245:letters-nos. • Item 133-D-1
CENSUS OF CONSTRUCTION INDUSTRIES:
ADVANCE INDUSTRY REPORTS.
See also C 56.254/2

C 3.245/2:date
CENSUS OF CONSTRUCTION INDUSTRIES:
ANNOUNCEMENTS AND ORDER FORMS.
See also C 56.254

C 3.245/3:date/nos. • Item 133-D-2
CENSUS OF CONSTRUCTION INDUSTRIES: FINAL
REPORTS. 1– 1967– [Irregular]
By States.
See also C 56.254/3

C 3.245/4:date/v.nos. • Item 133-D-2
CENSUS OF CONSTRUCTION INDUSTRIES: FINAL
VOLUMES.

C 3.245/5: • Item 133-D-2
CENSUS OF CONSTRUCTION INDUSTRIES:
SPECIAL REPORTS.
See also C 56.254/5

C 3.245/6 • Item 133-D-2
CENSUS OF CONSTRUCTION INDUSTRIES: PRE-
LIMINARY INDUSTRY STATISTICS CC (series).

C 3.245/7:letters-nos. • Item 133-D-2
CENSUS OF CONSTRUCTION INDUSTRIES: GEO-
GRAPHIC AREA STUDIES. [Irregular]

C 3.245/8 • Item 133-D-3
CENSUS OF CONSTRUCTION INDUSTRIES, SUB-
JECT SERIES.

C 3.246:nos. • Item 142-F (MF)
COMPUTERIZED GEOGRAPHIC CODING SERIES.
GE 60-1– 1971– [Irregular]

C 3.247:nos.
DUAList (series). 1– 1971– [Irregular]
See also C 56.241

C 3.248:nos.
SCRIS REPORTS.

C 3.249:letters&nos. • Item 131-E (MF)
GBF/DIME SYSTEMS, (GEO nos.).

C 3.249/2:letters-nos • Item 131-E (MF)
GEOGRAPHIC BASE (DIME) FILE, CUE, [Correction-
update-extension]. (Geographic Division)
See also C 56.255

C 3.250 • Item 132
WOMAN OWNED BUSINESSES, WB- (series).
[Irregular]

C 3.251:nos.
STATUS, A MONTHLY CHARTBOOK OF SOCIAL AND
ECONOMIC TRENDS.

C 3.252:nos. • Item 131-F
FACTFINDER FOR THE NATION, CFF-(series).
[Irregular]

C 3.253:letters-nos. • Item 131-H
ECONOMIC CENSUSES: REFERENCE SERIES.
[Irregular]

Includes various reference tools relating to
the Censuses of Retail Trade, Wholesale Trade,
Service, Construction, Mineral Industries, Manufactures, and Transportation.

C 3.253/2 • Item 147-A-1
ECONOMIC CENSUSES OF OUTLYING AREAS, OAC
(Series).
See also C 56.259

C 3.253/3:date • Item 146-P
HISTORY OF THE ECONOMIC CENSUSES.
[Quinquennial]

Economic censuses cover such areas as retail
and wholesale trades, service, construction and
manufactures, and mineral industries.
Earlier C 3.2:Ec 7/4

C 3.254:nos. • Item 131-J (MF)
[FOREIGN-OWNED U.S. FIRMS] FOF (series). 1–
1979– [Irregular]

PURPOSE:– To provide selected characteristics of U.S. firms with 10% or more of voting
stock or other equity rights owned by a foreign
entity.

C 3.255:CT • Item 133
CENSUS OF RETAIL TRADE: GENERAL PUBLICA-
TIONS. [Irregular]
See also C 56.251

C 3.255/2:letters-nos. • Item 132-A-1– 132-A-54
CENSUS OF RETAIL TRADE: GEOGRAPHIC AREA
STATISTICS. [Irregular]
See also C 56.251/2

C 3.255/2-2:letters-nos. • Item 132-A-1– 132-A-
53
CENSUS OF RETAIL TRADE: GEOGRAPHIC AREA
STATISTICS, ADVANCE REPORTS. [Irregular]

C 3.255/3:letters-nos. • Item 133
CENSUS OF RETAIL TRADE: SUBJECT REPORTS.
[Irregular]
See also C 56.251/3

C 3.255/3-2:letters-nos. • Item 133
CENSUS OF RETAIL TRADE: PRELIMINARY REPORT
INDUSTRY SERIES.

C 3.255/3-3 • Item 133
CENSUS OF RETAIL TRADE: INDUSTRY SERIES.

C 3.255/4:letters-nos • Item 133 (MF)
CENSUS OF RETAIL TRADE: RETAIL MERCHANDISE
LINES SERVICE. [Irregular]
See also C 56.251/4

C 3.255/5:letters-nos. • Item 132-A-1– 132-A-53
CENSUS OF RETAIL TRADE: MAJOR RETAIL
CENTERS STATISTICS. [Irregular]

Separate reports are to issued for each State
having one or more standard metropolitan statistical areas (SMSA's) and for the District of Columbia (49 reports). Statistics are presented on
number of establishments, sales, payroll, and
employment for each SMSA, for each city of
100,000 inhabitants or more and its central business district (CBD), and for other major retail
center (MCR's) in the SMSA that have 100 or
more retail establishments. In addition, number of
stores is shown by kind of retail business, and
sales are shown for three major kind-of-business
categories for smaller delineated MCR's within
the SMSA.
See also C 56.251/5

C 3.255/6:date/v.nos. • Item 132
CENSUS OF RETAIL TRADE: FINAL VOLUMES.
[Quinquennial]
See also C 56.251/6

C 3.255/7:nos. • Item 133
CENSUS OF RETAIL TRADE: NONEMPLOYER
STATISTICS SERIES.

C 3.255/8 • Item 132-A-54
CENSUS OF RETAIL TRADE: GEOGRAPHIC AREA -
SUMMARY.

C 3.255/8-2 • Item 132-A-56 (EL)
CENSUS OF RETAIL TRADE: GEOGRAPHIC AREA
SERIES (various states).

C 3.256:CT • Item 133-B-1
CENSUS OF WHOLESALE TRADE: GENERAL PUB-
LICATIONS. [Irregular]
See also C 56.252

C 3.256/2:letters-nos. • Item 132-B-1– 132-B-53
CENSUS OF WHOLESALE TRADE: GEOGRAPHIC
AREA SERIES. [Irregular]
See also C 56.252/3

C 3.256/2-2:letters-nos. • Item 132-B-1– 32-B-54
CENSUS OF WHOLESALE TRADE: GEOGRAPHIC
AREA SERIES, ADVANCE REPORTS. [Irregular]
Discontinued.

C 3.256/3:letters-nos. • Item 133-B-1
CENSUS OF WHOLESALE TRADE: SUBJECT SE-
RIES. [Irregular]
See also C 56.252/4

C 3.256/3-2:letters-nos. • Item 133-B-1
CENSUS OF WHOLESALE TRADE: PRELIMINARY
REPORT INDUSTRY SERIES. [Irregular]
Earlier title: U.S. Census of Wholesale Trade
Industry Series.

C 3.256/4:date • Item 132
CENSUS OF WHOLESALE TRADE: FINAL REPORTS.
[Quinquennial]
See also C 56.252/5

C 3.256/5:letters-nos. • Item 133-B-1 (MF)
CENSUS OF WHOLESALE TRADE: WHOLESALE
COMMODITY LINE SALES. [Irregular]

C 3.256/6:letters-nos. • Item 133-B-1
CENSUS OF WHOLESALE TRADE: INDUSTRY SE-
RIES WC (series).

C 3.256/7 • Item 132-B-54
CENSUS OF WHOLESALE TRADE: GEOGRAPHIC
AREA-SUMMARY.

C 3.256/7-2 • Item 132-B-55 (EL)
CENSUS OF WHOLESALE TRADE: GEOGRAPHIC
AREA SERIES (various states).

C 3.257:CT • Item 133-C-1
CENSUS OF SERVICE INDUSTRIES: GENERAL PUB-
LICATIONS. [Irregular]
See also C 56.253

C 3.257/2:letters-nos • Item 132-C-1– 132-C-53
CENSUS OF SERVICE INDUSTRIES: GEOGRAPHIC
AREA SERIES. [Irregular]
See also C 56.253/3

C 3.257/2-2:letters-nos. • Item 132-C-1-132-C-53
CENSUS OF SERVICE INDUSTRIES: GEOGRAPHIC
AREA SERIES, ADVANCE REPORTS. [Irregular]
Discontinued.

C 3.257/3:letters-nos. • Item 133-C-1
CENSUS OF SERVICE INDUSTRIES: SUBJECT SE-
RIES [Irregular]
See also C 56.253/4

C 3.257/3-2:letters-nos. • Item 133-C-1
CENSUS OF SERVICE INDUSTRIES: ADVANCE SUB-
JECT REPORTS. [Irregular]

C 3.257/3-3:letters-nos. • Item 133-C-1
CENSUS OF SERVICE INDUSTRIES: PRELIMINARY
REPORT INDUSTRY SERIES.

C 3.257/3-4:letters-nos. • Item 133-C-1
CENSUS OF SERVICE INDUSTRIES, INDUSTRY SE-
RIES. [Irregular]

C 3.257/4:date • Item 132
CENSUS OF SERVICE INDUSTRIES: FINAL RE-
PORTS. [Quinquennial]
See also C 56.253/5
Discontinued 1977.

C 3.257/5:ltrs.-nos. • Item 133-C-1
CENSUS OF SERVICE INDUSTRIES: NONEMPLOYER STATISTICS SERIES.

C 3.256/6 • Item 132-C-54
CENSUS OF SERVICE INDUSTRIES: GEOGRAPHIC AREA-SUMMARY.

C 3.256/6-2 • Item 132-C-55 (EL)
CENSUS OF SERVICE INDUSTRY: GEOGRAPHIC AREA SERIES (various states).

C 3.258:nos. • Item 160-E-2
SURVEY OF MINORITY-OWNED BUSINESS ENTER-PRISES, MB (series). [Irregular]
See also C 56.250
Discontinued.

C 3.259:nos. • Item 142-D (MF)
ECONOMIC RESEARCH REPORTS. 1– [Irregular]

C 3.260:nos. • Item 148-D (MF)
BOUNDARY AND ANNEXATION SURVEY, GE-30 (series). [Annual]

PURPOSE:– To report on surveys designed to obtain boundary change and corporate status information from incorporated places of 2,500 or more inhabitants. Includes tables by States and places.
Discontinued.

C 3.261: • Item 145-A (MF)
SPECIAL DEMOGRAPHIC ANALYSES, CDS- (series). [Irregular]

PURPOSE:– To provide insight, perspective, and analyses of important demographic trends and patterns. Mainly tables and statistical information.

C 3.262:date • Item 148-F
DIRECTORY OF DATA FILES. [Quarterly] (Data Users Service Division)

PURPOSE:– To provide a directory of the data files maintained by the Bureau of the Census, including subjects such as agriculture, economics, geographic, governments, population, housing, and general data.
Discontinued.

C 3.263:nos. • Item 148-G
RETAIL SALES AND INVENTORIES OF FUEL OIL, SBR- (series). [Monthly]

Contains information on stocks and sales of fuel oil in the U.S. by retail oil dealers. Report is derived from sample surveys of fuel oil dealers and information is showned by fuel oil type, monthly totals, and geographic areas.
Published jointly with Energy Information Administration and also designated DOE/EIA- 0195.
Also published in microfiche.
Discontinued with March 1981 issue.
Discontinued.

C 3.263/2:nos. • Item 148-G
WHOLESALE FUEL OIL DISTRIBUTORS STOCK AND SALES, SBR-W- (series). [Monthly]

Published jointly with Energy Information Administration and also designated DOE/EIA- 0197.
Contains information on stocks and sales of fuel oil in the U.S. by selected kinds of wholesale businesses in the U.S.
Also published in microfiche.
Discontinued with March 1981 issue.

C 3.263/3:nos. • Item 148-G
INVENTORIES AND SALES OF FUEL OIL AND MOTOR GASOLINE, WHOLESALE DISTRIBUTIONS. [Monthly]
Also published in microfiche.
Discontinued with March 1981 issue.

C 3.264:nos. • Item 142-D-1 (MF)
FOREIGN ECONOMIC REPORTS. 1– [Irregular]

Consists of highly technical and specialized studies of Communist countries.
Earlier C 59.12
Discontinued.

C 3.265:nos.
OCCASIONAL PAPERS. [Irregular]

C 3.266:date • Item 137-B
FEDERAL EXPENDITURES BY STATE FOR FISCAL YEAR. [Annual]

Prepared pursuant to the Consolidated Federal Funds Report Act of 1982 (P.L. 97-326). Consists chiefly of tables showing the geographic distribution of Federal funds by State and territory.

C 3.266/2:date • Item 137-B
CONSOLIDATED FEDERAL FUNDS REPORT FISCAL YEAR. [Annual]

C 3.266/3 • Item 154-B-2 (CD) (EL)
CONSOLIDATED FEDERAL FUNDS REPORT.
Issued on CD-ROM.

C 3.267:date • Item 536-A (MF) (EL)
QUARTERLY FINANCIAL REPORT FOR MANUFAC-TURING, MINING, AND TRADE CORPORATIONS. 1947– [Quarterly]

PURPOSE:– To produce, each calendar quarter, an income statement and balance sheet for all manufacturing corporations, classified by both industry and size.
Covers more than 40 income statement and balance sheet items for industry and size groups of all enterprises classified as manufacturers, except newspapers, which are required to file Federal corporate income tax form 1120.
Published jointly with the Securities and Exchange Commission.
Earlier FT 1.18

C 3.268:nos. • Item 144-K (MF)
SPECIAL PUBLICATION, P10/PoP (series).
Discontinued.

C 3.269:date • Item 144-A-19
TRADE AND EMPLOYMENT. [Quarterly]

PURPOSE:– To present tabular data that measures changes in U.S. imports and related domestic employment. The initial report covers first quarter 1982 through second quarter 1984 and contains 112 pages. Succeeding reports will be quarterly, and pagination will vary.
Discontinued.

C 3.270:CT • Item 144-A-20
POSTERS. [Irregular]

C 3.271:nos. • Item 146-N (MF)
1990 PLANNING CONFERENCE SERIES. [Irregular]
This series reports on conferences being held to plan the 1990 Decennial Census.
Discontinued.

C 3.272:nos. • Item 146-M
FORMS. [Irregular]

C 3.273:date
TRAINING BRANCH NEWSLETTER. [Semiannual]

C 3.275 • Item 154-B (E)
ELECTRONIC PRODUCTS.

C 3.276:v.nos/nos. • Item 148-F
CONSUMER SPENDING UPDATE. [Quarterly]
Discontinued.

C 3.277:CT • Item 154-C (CD) (EL)
ECONOMIC AND AGRICULTURE CENSUSES. [Irregular]
Issued on CD-ROM.

C 3.277/2 • Item 154-C-2 (EL)
1977 ECONOMIC S CENSUSES.

C 3.277/3 • Item 160-E-2 (P) (EL)
COMPANY STATISTICS SERIES (ECONOMIC CENSUS).

C 3.278:date • Item 154-D (CD)
FOREIGN TRADE DATA. [Monthly]
Issued on CD-ROM.
Discontinued.

C 3.278/2:date • Item 154-D (CD)
U.S. IMPORTS OF MERCHANDISE. [Monthly]
Issued on CD-ROM.

C 3.278/3:date • Item 154-D (CD)
U.S. EXPORTS OF MERCHANDISE. [Monthly]
Issued on CD-ROM.

C 3.279 • Item 154-E (CD)
TIGER/LINE FILES - 1990 CENSUS VERSION.
Issued on CD-ROM.

C 3.279/2:CD-CTSI-v.nos. • Item 154-E-1 (CD)(DVD)
TIGER/CENSUS TRACT STREET INDEX, VERSION 2.

Volume 1 contains data for CT, MA, ME, NH, RI, VT, NJ, NY, PA: vol 2; IL, IN, MI, OH, WI: vol 3; CO, IA, KS, MN, MO, MT, NE, ND, SD, WY: vol 4; DE, DC, FL, GA, MD, NC, SC, VA, WV.
Issued on CD-ROM AND DVD.

C 3.279/3 • Item 154-E-3 (DVD) (EL)
TIGER/LINE REDISTRICTING-CENSUS.

C 3.281:CT • Item 154-B-1 (CD)
CENSUS OF POPULATION AND HOUSING, PUBLIC LAW 94-171 DATA (CD-ROM).

C 3.281/2 • Item 154-B-3 (CD)
1990 CENSUS OF POPULATION AND HOUSING SPECIAL TABULATION ON AGING.
Issued on CD-ROM.

C 3.282:date • Item 154-F (CD)
SUMMARY TAPE FILES: STF 1. [Irregular]
Issued on CD-ROM.

C 3.282/2 • Item 154-F-1 (CD)
SUMMARY TAPE FILES: STF 3. [Irregular]
Issued on CD-ROM.

C 3.282/2-2 • Item 154-F-1 (CD)
SUMMARY TAPE FILES-STF4. [Irregular]

C 3.282/3 • Item 154-F (CD)
CENSUS OF POPULATION AND HOUSING BLOCK STATISTICS. [Irregular]
Issued on CD-ROM.

C 3.282/4:CD-nos. • Item 154-F-5 (CD)
CONGRESSIONAL DISTRICTS OF THE UNITED STATES, SUMMARY TAPE FILES.
Issued on CD ROM.

C 3.282/5:CD-nos. • Item 154-F-6 (CD)
CONGRESSIONAL DISTRICT ATLAS. [Biennial]
Issued on CD ROM.

C 3.283:CT • Item 154-F-2 (CD)
CENSUS/EQUAL EMPLOYMENT OPPORTUNITY (EEO) SPECIAL FILE.
Issued on CD-ROM.

C 3.284 • Item 154-F-3 (CD)
COUNTY-TO-COUNTY MIGRATION FILE.
Issued on CD-ROM.

C 3.285 • Item 154-F-4 (CD)
PUBLIC USE MICRODATA FILES (PUMS).
Issued on CD-ROM.

C 3.286 • Item 154-G (CD)
SUBJECT REPORTS.
Issued on CD-ROM.

C 3.287:nos. • Item 148-F (P) EL)
PRODUCT PROFILE (Series).

C 3.288:nos. • Item 142-C-9
POPULATION TRENDS. [Irregular]

C 3.289 • Item 146-A-2 (EL)
ANNUAL CAPITAL EXPENDITURES.

C 3.291:nos. • Item 135-A
CENSUS OF FINANCIAL, INSURANCE, AND REAL ESTATE INDUSTRIES.

C 3.292:nos. • Item 160-D-1
CENSUS OF TRANSPORTATION, COMMUNICATIONS, AND UTILITIES.

C 3.293 • Item 146-A-3
ASA/NSF/CENSUS BUREAU RESEARCH FELLOW PROGRAM.

C 3.294:date • Item 154-B-1 (EL)
HOUSING VACANCIES AND HOMEOWNERSHIP SURVEY.
Issued on CD-ROM.

C 3.295 • Item 154-B-1 (EL)
CENSUS BUREAU NEWS RELEASES.

C 3.296:v.nos./nos • Item 146-A-4 (P) (EL)
ROAD TO THE UNITED STATES CENSUS 2000 (series).
Issued in paper and electronic formats.

C 3.297:date • Item 154-B-14 (CD)
AMERICAN COMMUNITY SURVEY.
Issued on CD-ROM.

C 3.298:date • Item 154-B-13 (CD)
ZIP CODE BUSINESS PATTERNS.
Issued on CD-ROM.

C 3.299:nos. • Item 154-B-15 (MF)
INTERNATIONAL PROGRAMS CENTER STAFF PAPER.

C 3.300 • Item 154-B-15 (EL)
AMERICAN FACTFINDER.

C 3.301 • Item 154-B-17 (CD) (DVD)
LANDVIEW IV/THE FEDERAL GEOGRAPHIC DATA.
Issued on CD-ROM and DVD.

C 3.940
16th CENSUS, 1940.

C 3.940-1:CT
GENERAL PUBLICATIONS.

C 3.940-5:CT
FINAL VOLUMES

C 3.940-6:CT
REGULATIONS, RULES, AND INSTRUCTIONS.

C 3.940-7:CT
POSTERS.

C 3.940-8:CT
NARRATIVES.

C 3.940-9:CT
IRRIGATION OF AGRICULTURAL LANDS (by States).

C 3.940-10:CT
RETAIL TRADE (by States).

C 3.940-11:CT
SERVICE ESTABLISHMENTS (by States).

C 3.940-12:CT
MINERAL INDUSTRIES, 1939.

C 3.940-13:CT
POPULATIONS, 1st Series (by States)

C 3.940-13/2:CT
POPULATION, 2d Series.

C 3.940-14:CT
AGRICULTURE, 1st Series (by States).

C 3.940-15:CT
AGRICULTURE, 2d Series (by States).

C 3.940-16:CT
AGRICULTURE, 3d Series (by States).

C 3.940-17:CT
TERRITORIES AND POSSESSIONS REPORTS (Individual Reports).

C 3.940-18:CT
MANUFACTURES (by Industries).

C 3.940-19:CT
MANUFACTURES, 1939: STATE SERIES.

C 3.940-21:CT
CENSUS OF BUSINESS, 1939.

> See for earlier censuses; C 3.65, C 3.120/1, and C 3.120/2

C 3.940-22:CT
CENSUS OF BUSINESS, 1939: RETAIL TRADE (Miscellaneous).

C 3.940-23:CT
CENSUS OF BUSINESS, 1939: RETAIL TRADE (by States).

C 3.940-24:CT
CENSUS OF BUSINESS, 1939, RETAIL TRADE, COMMODITY SALES (by Commodities).

C 3.940-25:CT
CENSUS OF BUSINESS, 1939: WHOLESALE TRADE (by States).

C 3.940-26:CT
CENSUS OF BUSINESS, 1939: WHOLESALE TRADE (Miscellaneous).

C 3.940-28:CT
CENSUS OF BUSINESS, 1939: CONSTRUCTION (by States).

C 3.940-30:CT
HOUSING, 1st SERIES (by States).

C 3.940-31:CT
HOUSING SUPPLEMENT TO 1st SERIES: HOUSING BULLETINS (by States).

C 3.940-32:CT
HOUSING, 2d Series (by States).

C 3.940-33:CT
HOUSING, 3d Series (by States).

C 3.940-34:CT
HOUSING, 4th series (by States).

C 3.940-37:CT
POPULATION, 3d SERIES (by States).

C 3.940-37/2:CT
POPULATION, 4th SERIES (by States).

C 3.940-38:CT
POPULATION AND HOUSING (by States).

C 3.940-39:CT
POPULATION, OUTLYING POSSESSIONS.

C 3.950
17th CENSUS, 1950.

C 3.950-3:CT
GENERAL PUBLICATIONS.

C 3.950-4:PC-nos.&nos.
SERIES PC REPORTS.

C 3.950-4/2:HC-nos.&nos.
SERIES HC REPORTS.

C 3.950-4/3:nos. or letters
1950 CENSUS OF POPULATION AND HOUSING ANNOUNCEMENTS.

C 3.950-6:CT
REGULATIONS, RULES, AND INSTRUCTIONS.

C 3.950-7:CT
UNITED STATES CENSUS OF POPULATION, 1950: NUMBER OF INHABITANTS (by States).

C 3.950-7/2:CT
– CENSUS TRACTS.

C 3.950-7/3:CT
GENERAL CHARACTERISTICS (by States).

C 3.950-7/4:CT
– DETAIL CHARACTERISTICS (by States), 1950 POPULATION CENSUS REPORT P-C (series).

C 3.950-7/5:v.nos.
– (FINAL VOLUMES).

C 3.950-7/6:nos.-les.
– SPECIAL REPORTS, P-E (series).

C 3.950-8:CT
UNITED STATES CENSUS OF POPULATION, 1950: BLOCK STATISTICS REPORTS.

C 3.950-8/2:CT
– GENERAL CHARACTERISTICS (by States), REPORT H-A (series).

C 3.950-8/3:nos.
– NONFARM HOUSING CHARACTERISTICS [of Standard Metropolitan Areas], 1950 HOUSING CENSUS REPORT H-B (series).

C 3.950-8/4:
HOUSING CENSUS SEPARATE REPORTS AND BULLETINS.

C 3.950-8/5:v.nos.
CENSUS OF HOUSING, 1950; (Final Volumes).

C 3.950-9:v.nos.
UNITED STATES CENSUS OF AGRICULTURE, 1950 (Final Volumes).

C 3.950-9/2:CT
– V.1, COUNTIES AND STATE ECONOMIC AREAS SEPARATES.

C 3.950-9/3:CT
– IRRIGATION OF AGRICULTURAL LANDS (by States).

C 3.950-9/4:CT
LOCATION OF IRRIGATED LAND, MAPS (by States).

C 3.950-9/5:chap. nos
UNITED STATES CENSUS OF AGRICULTURE, 1950: V. 2 GENERAL REPORT (separates).

C 3.950-9/6:nos.
UNITED STATES CENSUS OF AGRICULTURE, 1950: ANNOUNCEMENTS.

C 3.950-10:nos.
PROCEDURAL STUDIES OF 1950 CENSUSES
Later see C 3.225

COAST AND GEODETIC SURVEY (1903–1965)

CREATION AND AUTHORITY

The Coast and Geodetic Survey (T 11) was transferred from the Department of the Treasury to the newly formed Department of Commerce and Labor effective July 1, 1903. It remained with the Department of Commerce in 1913 when the separation of the Commerce and Labor Departments took place. It was transferred to the Environmental Science Services Administration (C 52) by Reorganization Plan No. 2 of 1965, effective July 13, 1965.

C 4.1:date
ANNUAL REPORT OF THE DIRECTOR.
Earlier T 11.1
Discontinued.

C 4.2:CT
GENERAL PUBLICATIONS.

C 4.3:nos.
BULLETINS.

C 4.4:nos.
CIRCULARS.
Earlier T 11.4

C 4.4/2:nos.
CIRCULARS, 2d SERIES, 1913–1917.

C 4.4/3:nos.
CIRCULARS, 3d SERIES, 1919–

C 4.4/4
P. & A. CIRCULARS.

C 4.5:date
CATALOGS OF CHARTS, COAST PILOTS AND TIDE
TABLES.

C 4.5/a:CT
– SEPARATES.

C 4.5/2:nos.
NAUTICAL CHARTS AND OTHER PUBLICATIONS
RECENTLY ISSUED.
Some read Nautical Charts Recently Issued.

C 4.6/1
COAST PILOTS. 1869–

PURPOSE:– To furnish information required
by the navigator that cannot be shown conveniently on nautical charts. Each coast pilot covers a certain section of the coast.
Introductory sections in each volume give
indexes of nautical charts available, general information of services by the Coast and Geodetic
Survey, the Coast Guard, Corps of Engineers,
Weather Bureau, Naval Oceanographic Office,
Immigration and Naturalization Service, and the
Public Health Service. Also included is information on radio broadcasts and time signals. The
navigation regulations are given for the area
involved as taken from the sections of the Code
of Federal Regulations, Title 33, Navigation and
Navigable Waters.
Individual chapters are devoted to particular
sections of the coast and under each is included
general information relative to the coast and harbors, port information relative to the coast and
harbors, port information, and sailing directions
for coasting and entering harbors.
The appendix in each volume includes lists of
publications of interest to the navigator, directory of Government district or field offices, storm
warning stations, etc., climatological tables of
representative ports, conversion tables, distances
between ports, and distance of visibility of objects at sea at various heights.
Supplements to each pilot, containing changes
from various sources, are issued early each year.
Each supplement is complete in itself and cancels all previous issues. The latest supplement,
together with "Notices to Mariners" subsequent
to it, correct the book to date.
Prior to 1869, Coast Pilot matters appeared
in appendixes to the Survey's Annual Reports.
Now published in cloth editions with paper
supplements in the following volumes:

C 4.6/1:1   • **Item 203**
ATLANTIC COAST, EASTPORT TO CAPE COD.
7th edition (1965).

C 4.6/1:2   • **Item 203**
ATLANTIC COAST, CAPE COD TO SANDY HOOK.
7th edition (1966).

C 4.6/1:3   • **Item 203**
ATLANTIC COAST, SANDY HOOK TO CAPE
HENRY.

8th edition (1966).

C 4.6/1:4   • **Item 203**
ATLANTIC COAST, CAPE HENRY TO KEY WEST.
7th edition (1964).

C 4.6/2:CT   • **Item 207**
U.S. COAST PILOT, WEST INDIES.
Discontinued.

C 4.6/3:CT
INSIDE ROUTE PILOT (ATLANTIC AND GULF
COASTS).

C 4.6/4   • **Item 204**
GULF COAST, PUERTO RICO, AND VIRGIN ISLANDS.
1st–   1926–
6th edition (1965).

C 4.7/1   • **Item 206**
PACIFIC COAST, CALIFORNIA, OREGON, WASHING-
TON, AND HAWAII.
10th edition (1968).

C 4.7/2   • **Item 201**
ALASKA, DIXON ENTRANCE TO CAPE SPENCER.
11th edition (1962).

C 4.7/3   • **Item 202**
ALASKA, CAPE SPENCER TO BEAUFORT SEA. 1st–
1916–
7th edition (1964).

[HAWAIIAN ISLANDS].
Now included in Coast Pilot 7 (C 4.7/1) above.

C 4.7/4:CT
COAST PILOT NOTES, HAWAIIAN ISLANDS.

C 4.7/5:date
U.S. COAST PILOT, HAWAIIAN ISLANDS.

C 4.7/6:date
WARTIME INFORMATION TO MARINERS SUPPLE-
MENTING U.S. COAST PILOTS.

C 4.7/7:date
U.S. COAST PILOT, ALASKA, ALEUTIAN ISLANDS.
Discontinued.

C 4.8:date
LAWS RELATING TO COAST AND GEODETIC SUR-
VEY.

C 4.9:nos.
MAPS AND CHARTS.
Earlier T 11.9

C 4.9/2:CT
MAPS AND CHARTS (unnumbered).

C 4.9/3:R-nos.
RADIO CHARTS.

C 4.9/4:CT
AERONAUTICAL CHARTS.
Formerly C 23.10/3

C 4.9/5:nos.
REGIONAL AERONAUTICAL CHARTS.
Formerly C 23.10/4

C 4.9/6:date
AERONAUTICAL CHARTS; LISTS OF PUBLISHED
CHARTS, ETC.
Changed from C 4.2:Ae 8.

C 4.9/7:nos.
CHART CORRECTION NOTICES.

C 4.9/8:nos.
WORLD AERONAUTICAL CHARTS. [Restricted]

C 4.9/9:nos.
ROUTE CHARTS.

C 4.9/10:nos.
INSTRUMENT APPROACH AND LANDING CHARTS.

C 4.9/11:nos.
AIRPORT OBSTRUCTION PLANS.

C 4.9/11-2
AIRPORT OBSTRUCTION PLANS, MONTHLY
BULLETIN.

C 4.9/11-3
AIRPORT OBSTRUCTION PLANS, BIMONTHLY
BULLETIN.

C 4.9/12:nos.
RADIO FACILITY CHARTS.

C 4.9/13:date
AERONAUTICAL CHARTS, DATES OF LATEST
PRINTS.
Earlier C 3.2:C 38/5

C 4.9/13-2:date
LATEST EDITIONS OF U.S. AIR FORCE AERO-
NAUTICAL CHARTS. [Quarterly]

C 4.9/14:nos.
INSTRUMENT APPROACH CHARTS, I.L.S.

C 4.9/15:area
DANGER AREA CHARTS.

C 4.9/16:nos.
INSTRUMENT APPROACH CHART, RADIO BEACON.

C 4.9/17:nos.
ROUTE CHARTS.

C 4.9/18:date
DATES OF LATEST PRINTS, INSTRUMENT FLIGHT
CHARTS. [Monthly]
Title varies.
Earlier C 4.9/10

C 4.9/18-2:date
INSTRUMENT APPROACH PROCEDURE CHARTS,
[ALASKA, HAWAII, U.S. PACIFIC ISLANDS].

C 4.9/19:date
EASTERN UNITED STATES, DATES OF LATEST
PRINTS, INSTRUMENT APPROACH PROCEDURE
CHARTS AND AIRPORT OBSTRUCTION PLANS
(OP). [Monthly]
Earlier C 4.9/18

C 4.9/20:date
WESTERN UNITED STATES, DATES OF LATEST
PRINTS, INSTRUMENT APPROACH PROCEDURE
CHARTS AND AIRPORT OBSTRUCTION PLANT
(OP). [Monthly]
Earlier C 4.9/18

C 4.9/21:CT
SHEETS OF NATIONAL ATLAS OF UNITED STATES.

C 4.9/22:date
MILITARY FIELDS UNITED STATES, DATES OF
LATEST EDITIONS, INSTRUMENT APPROACH
PROCEDURE CHARTS. [Quarterly]

C 4.10:nos.
LEAFLETS FOR DISTRIBUTION FROM SURVEY'S
EXHIBITION AT LOUISIANA PURCHASE EXPO-
SITION, ST. LOUIS, MISSOURI, 1904.

C 4.11:nos.
NOTICE TO MARINERS.
Earlier T 11.11

C 4.12:CT
REGULATIONS, RULES, AND INSTRUCTIONS.
Earlier T 11.12

C 4.12/2:
BUREAU PERSONNEL MANUAL. [Administrative]

C 4.12/3:
BUREAU OF FINANCE MANUAL. [Administrative]

C 4.12/4:CT
HANDBOOKS, MANUALS, GUIDES.

C 4.12/5:nos.   • **Item 192-B**
C & GS TECHNICAL MANUALS. 1–   1969–

C 4.13:date
TIDE TABLES, ATLANTIC COAST FOR (CALENDAR
YEAR).
Earlier T 11.13

C 4.14:date
TIDE TABLES, PACIFIC COAST FOR (CALENDAR
YEAR).
Earlier T 11.14
Replaced by C 4.15/2

,,

C 4.15 • Item 196– 199
TIDE TABLES. 1853– [Annual]

PURPOSE:– To provide mariners with advance information relative to the rise and fall of the tide. These tide tables, published a year in advance, give the predicted times and heights of high and low waters for every day in the year for a number of reference stations and the differences for obtaining similar predictions for numerous other places.

Tide tables for the use of mariners have been published by the Coast and Geodetic Survey since 1853. For a number of years these tables appeared as appendixes to the annual reports of the Superintendent of the Survey, and consisted of more or less elaborate means for enabling the mariner to make his own prediction of tides as the occasion arose. The first tables to give predictions for each day were those for the year 1867, which contained daily predictions for 19 stations and tidal differences for 124 stations. The tide tables are now issued in four volumes, containing daily predictions for 195 reference ports and differences and ranges for about 5,000 stations.

In addition to the full daily predictions and the differences and ranges for auxiliary stations, the publications include table for obtaining the approximate height of the tide at any time, a table of local mean time of sunrise and sunset for every fifth day of the year for different latitudes, a table for the reduction of local mean time to standard time, and a table of the Greenwich mean time of the moon's phases, apogeem perigee, greatest north and south and zero declination, and the time of the solar equinoxes and solstices.

Issued in the following four parts:

C 4.15/2:date
TIDE TABLES, PACIFIC OCEAN AND INDIAN OCEAN.

C 4.15/3:date
TIDE TABLES, ATLANTIC OCEAN.

C 4.15/3a:date
– SEPARATES.

C 4.15/4 • Item 197
EAST COAST OF NORTH AND SOUTH AMERICA (INCLUDING GREENLAND). [Annual]

C 4.15/5 • Item 199
WEST COAST OF NORTH AND SOUTH AMERICA (INCLUDING THE HAWAIIAN ISLANDS). [Annual]

C 4.15/6 • Item 196
CENTRAL AND WESTERN PACIFIC OCEAN AND INDIAN OCEAN. 1867– [Annual]

C 4.15/7 • Item 198
EUROPE AND WEST COAST OF AFRICA (INCLUDING MEDITERRANEAN SEA). [Annual]

C 4.15/8:CT
SPECIAL TIDE TABLES.

C 4.16:nos.
RESULTS OF OBSERVATIONS MADE AT C. & G. SURVEY MAGNETIC OBSERVATORIES.
Publications designated MO-nos.

C 4.17:CT
SPECIFICATIONS.

C 4.18/1:date
COAST AND GEODETIC SURVEY SUBOFFICE, MANILA. CATALOG OF CHARTS, SAILING DIRECTIONS AND TIDE TABLES.
Earlier T 11.19/1

C 4.18/2:date
NOTICE TO MARINERS.
Earlier T 11.19/2

C 4.18/3:sec.nos.
SAILING DIRECTIONS.
Earlier T 11.19/3

C 4.18/4:date
GENERAL INSTRUCTIONS FOR SURVEYS IN PHILIPPINE ISLANDS.

C 4.18/5:pt.nos.
COAST AND GEODETIC SURVEY SUBOFFICE, MANILA, U.S. COAST PILOT, PHILIPPINE ISLANDS.

C 4.19 • Item 193
SPECIAL PUBLICATIONS. 1– [Irregular]

C 4.19/a:CT
– SEPARATES.

C 4.19/2 • Item 193
PUBLICATIONS. 1957– [Irregular]

PURPOSE:– To provide a medium for publication of monographs in the fields of mathematics, geodetic astronomy, nautical and aeronautical cartography, geodetic and hydrographic surveying, photogrammetry, and the following divisions of geophysics: geodesy, geomagnetism, gravity, seismology, physical oceanography and tidal phenomena.

The Publications series carried a hyphenated number. The first element of the number indicates the subject category, the second element indicates the number of the publication within that subject category. This series supersedes the "Special Publications" series. Existing Special Publications will not be renumbered in the Publications series.

Classification of subject numbers:

10 General
20 Hydrography
30 Tides and Currents
31 Oceanography
40 Geomagnetism
41 Seismology
60 Geodesy (General)
61 Leveling
62 Triangulation
63 Gravity
64 Geodetic Astronomy
65 State Plane Coordinate Systems
70 Topography and Photogrammetry
80 Cartography and Reproduction

C 4.19/2a:CT
– SEPARATES.

C 4.20:date
BULLETIN, COAST SURVEY BULLETIN. [Monthly]

C 4.21:CT
DIGEST OF GEODETIC PUBLICATIONS. TIDAL CURRENT TABLES. [Annual]
PURPOSE:– To provide mariners with advance information relative to the tidal current, a periodic horizontal flow of water accompanying the rise and fall of the tide.

Current tables for the use of mariners have been published by the Coast and Geodetic Survey since 1890 for the Atlantic coast and 1898 for the Pacific coast.

Tables include daily predictions of the times of slack water and the times and velocities of strength of flood and ebb currents for a number of waterways together with differences for obtaining predictions for numerous other places. Supplementary tables include velocity of current at any time, duration of slack, rotary tidal currents.

Published a year in advance. Issued in the following two parts:

C 4.22 • Item 190
ATLANTIC COAST OF NORTH AMERICA. 1890– [Annual]

Includes a description of the Gulf Stream.

C 4.22/a:date
– SEPARATES.

C 4.23 • Item 191
PACIFIC COAST OF NORTH AMERICA AND ASIA. 1898– [Annual]

C 4.24:CT
MAGNETIC DECLINATIONS (by States).

C 4.24:nos.
MAGNETIC DECLINATIONS (by nos.).
Publications designated MD-nos.

C 4.25:date
SEISMOLOGICAL REPORTS. [Quarterly]

C 4.25/2 • Item 208
UNITED STATES EARTHQUAKES. 1928– [Annual]

PURPOSE:– To provide a summary of earthquake activity in the United States and regions outside the U.S. under its jurisdiction for the calendar year. Technical in nature, this annual report contains narrative and tabular summaries pertaining to geodetic work of seismological interest, tidal disturbances of seismic origin, fluctuations in well-water levels, and narrative summaries of the characteristics and effects of the principal earthquakes experienced during the year.

A history of the more important shocks of the country appears in "Earthquake History of the United States" (Pub. 41-1), issued in two parts. Part 1 covers the continental United States and Alaska (exclusive of California and western Nevada).

A summary of the earthquake program as carried out in the United States is outlined briefly in "Earthquake Investigation in the United States" (S.P. 282).

Current data may be found in the "Quarterly Engineering Seismology Bulletin."

Time lag of publication is about 2 years (information for calendar year 1959 was published in 1961).

C 4.25/3
PROGRESS DURING . . . STRONG-MOTION EARTHQUAKE IN CALIFORNIA AND ELSEWHERE. [Official Use]

For information on the subject see C 4.25/2.

C 4.25/4:nos.
QUARTERLY SEISMOLOGY BULLETIN MSP (series).

C 4.26:date
MAGNETIC OBSERVATIONS.

C 4.27:CT • Item 195
TIDE TABLES (Individual Harbors).
Discontinued.

C 4.28:nos.
CURRENT DIAGRAMS.

C 4.29:CT • Item 194
TIDAL CURRENT CHARTS.
Discontinued.

C 4.30:vol.
GEODETIC LETTERS. [Quarterly]

C 4.31:nos.
FIELD ENGINEERS BULLETINS. [Annual]

C 4.32:CT
TIDAL BENCH MARKS (by States).

C 4.32/2:CT
INDEX MAPS, TIDAL BENCH MARKS.

C 4.32/3
TIDAL BENCH MARKS. [Loose leaf, by individual stations]

C 4.33:nos.
DENSITY OF SEA WATER (D.W.)

C 4.34:nos.
WATER TEMPERATURES, COAST AND GEODETIC SURVEY TIDE STATIONS.
Publications designated TW-nos.

C 4.35:nos.
TIDAL HARMONIC CONSTANTS.
Publications designated TW-no.

C 4.36
ANTARCTIC SEISMOLOGICAL BULLETIN. [Quarterly]

Published in cooperation with the Scientific Committee on Antarctic Research of International Council of Scientific Unions.

C 4.36/2:nos.
PRELIMINARY DETERMINATION OF EPICENTERS.

C 4.36/2-2:date
PRELIMINARY DETERMINATION OF EPICENTERS, MONTHLY LISTING.
   Later C 44.412

C 4.37:CT
GEOGRAPHIC NAMES IN COASTAL AREAS (by States).

C 4.38:nos.
MAGNETOGRAMS.
   See for old series C 4.16

C 4.39
SECOND-ORDER LEVELING, LIST OF STANDARD ELEVATIONS.

C 4.40:letters-nos.
MAGNETIC HOURLY VALUES HV (series).

C 4.40/2
MAGNETOGRAMS AND HOURLY VALUES. 1950–
   [Annual]

   PURPOSE:– To provide information on mean hourly values of magnetic declination, horizontal intensity and vertical intensity of the earth's field recorded at each Coast and Geodetic Survey magnetic observatory.
   Separate publications are issued for each station. Time-lag of publication varies from two to four years.
   DISTRIBUTION:– Issued in small editions for official distribution to specialists engaged in geophysical research.

C 4.41:nos.
JOURNAL. [Irregular, about once a year].
   Superseded by C 4.41/2

C 4.41/2   • Item 192-A
TECHNICAL BULLETINS. 1–   1958–   [Irregular]

   PURPOSE:– To report on new developments in instrumentation and survey procedures and on the results of other research and development in the various fields of the Bureau's activities.
   Issued in two series; a numbered series for those publications for sale by the Superintendent of Documents and a lettered series for those available from the Coast and Geodetic Survey.
   Supersedes the "Journal, Coast and Geodetic Survey."
   Discontinued.

C 4.41/3:letters
TECHNICAL BULLETINS, SPECIAL.

C 4.42:nos.
MSA-nos.

C 4.43:nos.
MSS-nos.

C 4.44:nos.
INFORMATION LEAFLET, MM-nos.

C 4.45
BUZZARD.

C 4.46
PERSONAL PANORAMA.

C 4.47:nos.
RELEASES CGS (series).

C 4.48:nos.
PHOTOGRAMMETRIC INSTRUCTIONS.

C 4.49:nos.
PUBLICATIONS NOTICE PN SERIES. [Irregular]

C 4.50:CT
BIBLIOGRAPHIES AND LISTS OF PUBLICATIONS.

C 4.51:v.nos.&nos.
SURVEY WITH SAFETY. [Administrative]

C 4.52:CT
POSTERS.

C 4.53:CT
ADDRESSES.

C 4.54:v.nos.&nos.
EARTHQUAKE INFORMATION BULLETIN.

C 4.55:nos.
DIGEST OF SCIENCE AND ENGINEERING PRESENTATIONS.

C 4.56
ANTARCTIC TRAVERSE (series). 1–   1960-61–
   [Annual]

   PURPOSE:– To present results of magnetic observations made by scientists on annual overland geophysical traverses of the Antarctic Continent. Each one in the series gives a season's results in the form of tabular data.

BUREAU OF CORPORATIONS
(1903– 1944)

CREATION AND AUTHORITY

   The Bureau of Corporations was established within the Department of Commerce and Labor by act of Congress, approved February 14, 1903. Upon the establishment of the Federal Trade Commission (FT) by the act of Congress, approved September 26, 1944, the Bureau was abolished and its functions transferred to the Commission.

C 5.1:date
ANNUAL REPORTS.

C 5.2:CT
GENERAL PUBLICATIONS.

   C 5.2/a:CT
   – SEPARATES.

C 5.3
BULLETINS [none issued].

C 5.4
CIRCULARS [none issued].

BUREAU OF FISHERIES
(1903– 1939)

CREATION AND AUTHORITY

   The United States Fish Commission (FC 1) was established by Joint Resolution of Congress, approved February 9, 1871. By 1880, the Commission was known as the United States Fish and Fisheries Commission. Upon the creation of the Department of Commerce and Labor on February 14, 1903, the Commission became a part of the Department and its name was changed to Bureau of Fisheries. By Reorganization Plan No. 2 of 1939, effective July 1, 1939, the Bureau of Fisheries was transferred from the Department of Commerce to the Department of the Interior (I 45).

C 6.1:date
ANNUAL REPORTS.
   Later I 45.1

C 6.2:CT
GENERAL PUBLICATIONS.
   Later I 45.2

C 6.3:v.nos.
BULLETINS.
   Earlier FC 1.3

C 6.3/2:nos.
BULLETINS (numbered).

C 6.4:nos.
CIRCULARS.

C 6.5:nos.
STATISTICAL BULLETINS.
   Earlier FC 1.5
   Later I 45.8

C 6.6:date
LIST OF PUBLICATIONS OF THE BUREAU OF FISHERIES AVAILABLE FOR DISTRIBUTION.

C 6.7:nos.
ECONOMIC CIRCULARS.

Alaska Fisheries Service

C 6.8/1:date
ANNUAL REPORTS.
C 6.8/2:CT
GENERAL PUBLICATIONS.

C 6.8/4:nos.
CIRCULARS.

Bureau of Fisheries (Continued)

C 6.9:date
FISHERIES SERVICE BULLETIN. [Monthly]
   Later I 45.7

C 6.10:CT
POSTERS.

C 6.11:date
PACIFIC COAST SALMON PACK.
   Later I 45.15

C 6.12:nos.
INVESTIGATIONAL REPORTS.
   Later I 45.19

C 6.13:nos.
FISHERY CIRCULARS.
   Superseded by I 49.4

C 6.14:nos.
INQUIRY MEMORANDA.
   Later I 45.12

C 6.15:nos.
SCIENTIFIC INQUIRY MEMORANDA.
   Later I 45.13

C 6.16:nos.
LIBRARY BULLETINS, RECENT ACCESSIONS. [Monthly]
   Later I 45.10

C 6.17:nos.
BLACK BASS AND ANGLERS DIVISION PUBLICATIONS.
   Later I 45.17

C 6.18:vol.
FISHERY MARKET NEWS. [Monthly]
   Later I 45.9

BUREAU OF IMMIGRATION AND NATURALIZATION
(1906–1913)

CREATION AND AUTHORITY

The Bureau of Immigration (T 21) was transferred from the Treasury department to the newly created Department of Commerce and Labor on July 1, 1903. On July 14, 1906, the Bureau was changed to the Bureau of Immigration and Naturalization under an act of Congress, approved June 29, 1906, when functions pertaining to naturalization were added and a Division of Naturalization (C 7.10) was created within the Bureau. By act of Congress, approved March 4, 1913 (37 Stat. 736), the Bureau of Immigration and Naturalization was transferred to the Department of Labor and separated into two separate Bureaus (L 3 and L 6).

C 7.1:date
ANNUAL REPORTS.
    Earlier T 21.1
    Later L 3.1

C 7.2:CT
GENERAL PUBLICATIONS.
    Earlier T 21.2
    Later L 3.2

C 7.3:nos.
BULLETINS [none issued].

C 7.4:nos.
CIRCULARS.
    Earlier T 21.4
    Later L 3.4

C 7.5:date
CHINESE EXCLUSION TREATIES, LAWS AND REGULATIONS.
    Earlier T 21.5
    Later L 3.7

C 7.6:date
IMMIGRATION LAWS AND REGULATIONS.
    Earlier T 21.5
    Later L 3.5

C 7.7:CT
DECISIONS.

C 7.8:date
IMMIGRATION BULLETIN. [Monthly]

C 7.9:CT
TERMS, CONDITIONS AND LIMITATIONS, WITH FORM PROPOSAL.

Naturalization Division

C 7.10/1:date
ANNUAL REPORTS.
    Later 6.1

C 7.10/2:CT
GENERAL PUBLICATIONS.
    Later L 6.2

C 7.10/3:nos.
BULLETINS.
    Later L 6.3

C 7.10/4:nos.
CIRCULARS [none issued].

C 7.10/5:date
NATURALIZATION LAWS AND REGULATIONS.
    Later L 6.5

Information Division

C 7.11/1:date
ANNUAL REPORTS.

C 7.11/2:CT
GENERAL PUBLICATIONS.

C 7.11/3:nos.
BULLETINS [none issued].

C 7.11/4:nos.
CIRCULARS [none issued].

C 7.11/5:nos.
AGRICULTURAL OPPORTUNITIES.

BUREAU OF LABOR
(1903–1913)

CREATION AND AUTHORITY

The Bureau of Labor was established within the Department of Commerce and Labor by act of Congress, approved February 14, 1903 (32 Stat. 827), which also abolished the Department of Labor (La), an independent agency without executive rank. This bureau was superseded by the Bureau of Labor Statistics (L 2) on March 4, 1913.

C 8.1:date
ANNUAL REPORTS.
    Earlier La 1.1
    Later L 2.1

C 8.2:CT
GENERAL PUBLICATIONS.
    Earlier La 1.2
    Later L 2.2

C 8.3:v.nos
BULLETINS. [Bimonthly]
    Earlier La 1.3

C 8.3/2:whole nos.
BULLETINS. [Irregular]

C 8.4:nos.
CIRCULARS [none issued].

C 8.5:nos.
SPECIAL REPORTS.
    Earlier La 1.5

C 8.6:date
REPORT ON HAWAII.
    Earlier La 1.7

BUREAU OF LIGHTHOUSES
(1910–1939)

CREATION AND AUTHORITY

The Lighthouse Board (T 25) was transferred from the Treasury Department to the Department of Commerce and Labor on July 1, 1903. By act of Congress, approved June 17, 1910 (36 Stat. 537), the Lighthouse Board was succeeded by the Bureau of Lighthouses. The Bureau was abolished by Reorganization Plan No. 2 of 1939, effective July 1, 1939, and its functions transferred to the Coast Guard (T 47) in the Treasury Department.

C 9.1:date
ANNUAL REPORTS.
    Earlier T 25.1

C 9.2:CT
GENERAL PUBLICATIONS.
    Earlier T 25.2

C 9.3:nos.
BULLETINS.
    Earlier T 25.3
    Superseded by C 9.26

C 9.4:nos.
CIRCULARS.
    Earlier T 25.4

C 9.5:date
LIGHTS, BUOYS, AND DAY MARKS, 1st DISTRICT.
    Earlier T 25.5

C 9.6:date
LIGHTS, BUOYS, AND DAY MARKS, 2d DISTRICT.
    Earlier T 25.6

C 9.7:date
LIGHTS, BUOYS, AND DAY MARKS, 3rd DISTRICT.
    Earlier T 25.7

C 9.8:date
LIGHTS, BUOYS, AND DAY MARKS, 4th DISTRICT.
    Earlier T 25.8

C 9.9:date
LIGHTS, BUOYS, AND DAY MARKS, 5th DISTRICT.
    Earlier T 25.9

C 9.10:date
LIGHTS, BUOYS, AND DAY MARKS, 6th DISTRICT.
    Earlier T 25.10

C 9.11:date
LIGHTS, BUOYS, AND DAY MARKS, 7th DISTRICT.
    Earlier T 25.11

C 9.12:date
LIGHTS, BUOYS, AND DAY MARKS, 8th DISTRICT.
    Earlier T 25.12

C 9.13:date
LIGHTS, BUOYS, AND DAY MARKS, 9th DISTRICT.
    Earlier T 25.13

C 9.14:date
LIGHTS, BUOYS, AND DAY MARKS, 10th DISTRICT.
    Earlier T 25.14

C 9.14/2:date
LIST OF BUOYS, 19th DISTRICT, HAWAIIAN AND SAMOAN ISLANDS.

C 9.15:date
LAWS RELATIVE TO LIGHT HOUSE ESTABLISHMENT PASSED AT [ ] SESSION [ ] CONGRESS.
    Earlier T 25.15

C 9.16:date
LAWS AND REGULATIONS RELATING TO LIGHTHOUSE ESTABLISHMENT.
    Earlier T 25.15

C 9.17:date
LIGHTS, BUOYS AND DAY MARKS, 1st– 9th DISTRICTS.
    Earlier T 25.16

C 9.18:date
LIGHTS AND FOG SIGNALS, NORTHERN LAKES AND RIVERS AND CANADA 3rd AND 9th– 11th DISTRICTS.
    Earlier T 25.17

C 9.19:date
LIGHTS, BUOYS AND DAYMARKS, 16th– 19th DISTRICT.

C 9.20:date
NOTICE TO MARINERS. [Irregular]
    Earlier T 25.19
    Superseded by C 9.26

C 9.21:date
LIGHTS ON WESTERN RIVERS.
    Earlier T 25.20

C 9.22:CT
SPECIFICATIONS.
    Earlier T 25.21

C 9.23:date
INSTRUCTIONS TO LIGHTKEEPERS.
Earlier T 25.22

C 9.24:date
LIGHTS, BUOYS AND DAYMARKS, 3rd DIVISION.
Earlier T 25.23

C 9.25:CT
REGULATIONS, MISCELLANEOUS.
Earlier T 25.24

C 9.26:date
NOTICE TO MARINERS. [Weekly]
Supersedes Notice to Mariners, issued irregularly (C 9.20) and Bulletins (C 9.3).
Later T 47.19

C 9.27:date
LIGHTS, BUOYS AND DAYMARKS, 13th DISTRICT.

C 9.28:date
LIGHTS, BUOYS AND DAYMARKS, 14th DISTRICT.

C 9.29:date
AIDS TO NAVIGATION, 15th DISTRICT.

C 9.29/2:v.nos.
LIGHT LIST, LIGHTS, BUOYS, AND DAY MARKS, MISSISSIPPI AND OHIO RIVERS, 15th LIGHTHOUSE DISTRICT.
Combines publications which have been classed as C 9.27; C 9.28; and C 9.29.

C 9.30:date
LIGHT AND FOG SIGNALS OF UNITED STATES AND CANADA ON NORTHERN LAKES AND RIVERS (3rd and 10th– 12th districts).

C 9.31:nos.
LIGHTHOUSE SERVICE BULLETIN. [Monthly]
Changed to Coast Guard Bulletin (T 47.21).

C 9.32:date
BUOY LIST, 10th LIGHTHOUSE DISTRICT.

C 9.33:date
BUOY LIST, 11th LIGHTHOUSE DISTRICT.

C 9.34:date
BUOY LIST, 12th LIGHTHOUSE DISTRICT.

C 9.35:date
BUOY LIST, 16th LIGHTHOUSE DISTRICT.

C 9.36:date
BUOY LIST, 17th LIGHTHOUSE DISTRICT.

C 9.37:date
BUOY LIST, 18th LIGHTHOUSE DISTRICT.

C 9.38:CT
NOTICE TO MARINERS.

C 9.38/1:nos.
POSTER NOTICE TO MARINERS, ATLANTIC COAST.

C 9.38/2:nos.
POSTER NOTICE TO MARINERS, PACIFIC COAST.

C 9.38/3:nos.
POSTER NOTICE TO MARINERS, GREAT LAKES.

C 9.39:date
BUOY LIST, 10th TO 12th LIGHTHOUSE DISTRICTS.

C 9.40:nos.
CIRCULAR LETTER.

C 9.41:dt.&nos.
NOTICE TO MARINERS, GREAT LAKES. [Weekly]
Later T 47.20

C 9.42:date
LOCAL LIGHT LIST, 1st AND 2nd DISTRICTS.

C 9.43:date
LOCAL LIGHT LIST, 3rd DISTRICT.

C 9.44:date
LOCAL LIGHT LIST, 4th AND 5th DISTRICTS.

C 9.45:date
LOCAL LIGHT LIST, 7th AND 8th DISTRICTS.

C 9.46:date
LOCAL LIGHT LIST, 16th AND 17th DISTRICTS.

C 9.47:date
LOCAL LIGHT LIST, 17th AND 18th DISTRICTS.

C 9.48:date
LOCAL LIGHT LIST, 6th DISTRICT

C 9.49:date
LOCAL LIGHT LIST, 6th AND 7th DISTRICTS.
Later T 47.23

C 9.50:date
LIGHT LIST, 1st– 5th DISTRICTS. (North Atlantic Coast of U.S.) [Annual]
Replaces C 9.42; C 9.43; and parts of C 9.44
Later T 47.24

C 9.51:date
LIGHT LIST, 5th– 9th DISTRICTS (South Atlantic and Gulf Coasts of U.S.). [Annual]
Replaces parts of C 9.17; C 9.44; and C 9.45.

C 9.52:date
LIGHT LIST, 5th– 8th DISTRICTS (Atlantic Coast of U.S. Intra-Coastal Waterway, Hampton Roads to Rio Grande including inside waters). [Annual]

C 9.53:CT
MAPS.
The radio beacon system maps transferred to T 47.22; in the Classification they were C 9.53:R 11, R 11/2, R 11/3

BUREAU OF MANUFACTURERS
(1903– 1912)

CREATION AND AUTHORITY

The Bureau of Manufacturers was established within the Department of Commerce and Labor on July 1, 1903, pursuant to act of Congress, approved February 14, 1903. By act of Congress, approved August 23, 1912, the Bureau of Manufacturers merged with the Bureau of Statistics (C 14) to form the Bureau of Foreign and Domestic Commerce (C 18).

C 10.1:date
ANNUAL REPORTS.

C 10.2:CT
GENERAL PUBLICATIONS.

C 10.3:nos.
BULLETINS [none issued].

C 10.4:nos.
CIRCULARS [none issued].

C 10.5/1:nos.
DAILY CONSULAR AND TRADE REPORTS (old series). [Monthly]
Earlier C 14.6

C 10.5/2:dt.&nos.
DAILY CONSULAR AND TRADE REPORTS, SERIES JULY 5, 1910– JUNE 29, 1912.

C 10.6:nos.
DAILY CONSULAR AND TRADE REPORTS.
Earlier C 14.8
Later C 18.5

C 10.7:v.nos.
SPECIAL CONSULAR REPORTS.
Earlier C 14.10
Later C 18.9

C 10.8:date
COMMERCIAL RELATIONS.
Earlier C 14.15
Later C 18.16

C 10.9:date
REVIEW OF WORLD'S COMMERCE.
Earlier C 14.15

C 10.10:nos.
TARIFF SERIES.
Later C 18.12

C 10.11
REPORT ON TRADE CONDITIONS.
Changed to C 10.13

C 10.12:nos.
CONSULAR REPORTS. ANNUAL SERIES.
Later C 18.11

C 10.13:nos.
SPECIAL AGENTS SERIES.

C 10.14:v.nos.
WEEKLY CONSULAR AND TRADE REPORTS.
Later C 18.5/1

C 10.15:nos.
CONFIDENTIAL BULLETINS.

C 10.16:nos.
FOREIGN TARIFF NOTE.
Later C 18.13

C 10.17:nos.
MISCELLANEOUS SERIES.
Later C 18.15

BUREAU OF NAVIGATION
(1903– 1932)

CREATION AND AUTHORITY

The Bureau of Navigation (T 30) was transferred from the Treasury Department to the newly created Department of Commerce and Labor on July 1, 1903. The Bureau was consolidated with the Steamboat Inspection Service (C 15) to form the Bureau of Navigation and Steamboat Inspection (C 25) by act of Congress, approved June 30, 1932 (47 Stat. 415).

C 11.1:date
ANNUAL REPORTS.
Earlier T 30.1

C 11.2:CT
GENERAL PUBLICATIONS.
Earlier T 30.2

C 11.3:nos.
BULLETINS [none issued].

C 11.4:nos.
CIRCULARS [none issued].

C 11.5:date
ANNUAL LIST OF MERCHANT VESSELS.
Earlier T 30.5
Later C 25.11

C 11.6:date
NAVIGATION LAWS.
Earlier T 30.6
Later C 25.5/2

Radio Service

Later Radio Division (C 24).

C 11.7/1:date
ANNUAL REPORTS.

Issued as part of Annual Report of Commissioner of Navigation.

C 11.7/2:CT
GENERAL PUBLICATIONS.

C 11.7/3:nos.
BULLETINS-RADIO SERVICE BULLETINS.

C 11.7/4
CIRCULARS.

C 11.7/5:date
RADIO COMMUNICATION LAWS AND REGULATIONS.

C 11.7/6:date
LIST OF RADIO STATIONS OF THE UNITED STATES.
Later C 24.5

Bureau of Navigation (Continued)

C 11.8:date
AMERICAN DOCUMENTED SEAGOING MERCHANT
VESSELS OF 500 GROSS TONS AND OVER, 4
DEGREE. [Monthly]

C 11.9:nos.
GENERAL LETTER.

C 11.10:date
MERCHANT MARINE STATISTICS.
Later C 25.10

SHIPPING COMMISSIONERS
(1903– 1938)

CREATION AND AUTHORITY

The control of the Shipping Commissioners
was transferred from the Navigation Bureau (T
30) to the newly created Department of Commerce and Labor on July 1, 1903.

C 12.1:date
ANNUAL REPORTS.

C 12.2:CT
GENERAL PUBLICATIONS [none issued].

C 12.3:nos.
BULLETINS [none issued].

C 12.4:nos.
CIRCULARS [none issued].

NATIONAL INSTITUTE OF
STANDARDS AND TECHNOLOGY
(1934–   )

CREATION AND AUTHORITY

The Bureau of Standards was established
within the Department of the Treasury by act of
Congress, March 3, 1901 (31 Stat. 1449, as
amended; 15 U.S.C. 171-286), to succeed the
Office of Standard Weights and Measures, established in 1830 as a section of the Coast Survey. The Bureau was transferred to the Department of Commerce and Labor by act of February
14, 1903. Upon separation of the two Departments in 1913, the Bureau remained under the
Department of Commerce. In 1934, the name was
changed to National Bureau of Standards. The
name was changed in 1989 to National Institute
of Standards and Technology.

INFORMATION

National Institute of Standards
and Technology
Department of Commerce
100 Bureau Dr.
Stop 3460
Gaithersburg, MD 20899-3460
(301) 975-6478
Fax: (301) 926-1630
http://www.nist.gov

C 13.1:date   • **Item 238 (MC)**
ANNUAL REPORT.
Earlier title: Technical Highlights of the National Bureau of Standards.
PURPOSE:– To provide an illustrated summarized report of the research and development
activities of the National Bureau of Standards in
the fields of physics, chemistry, engineering, and
mathematics during the fiscal year.
Brief accounts are included relating to projects
completed or in progress in the Bureau's scientific and technical divisions, including electricity
and electronics, optics and meteorology, heat,
atomic and radiation physics, chemistry, mechanics, organic and fibrous materials, metallurgy,
mineral projects, building technology, applied
mathematics, data processing systems, cryogenic
engineering, radio propagation, radio standards,
and basic instrumentation. A statement of the
Bureau's testing, calibration, and Standard
Samples activities by Divisions is also included,
as well as a review of its technical services and
cooperation, both national and international. For
bibliographical reference, a complete list of NBS
publications and patents is provided for the fiscal
year period.
Published 1958– 63 as Research Highlights
of the National Bureau of Standards.
Published in the Special Publications series.

C 13.1/2:date
CENTER FOR RADIATION RESEARCH, TECHNICAL
HIGHLIGHTS, FISCAL YEAR.

C 13.1/3:date
INSTITUTE FOR APPLIED TECHNOLOGY, TECHNI-
CAL HIGHLIGHTS, FISCAL YEAR.

C 13.1/4:date
INSTITUTE FOR BASIC STANDARDS, TECHNICAL
HIGHLIGHTS, FISCAL YEAR.

C 13.1/5:date
INSTITUTE FOR MATERIALS RESEARCH, TECHNI-
CAL HIGHLIGHTS, FISCAL YEAR.

C 13.1/5-2:date
INSTITUTE FOR MATERIAL RESEARCH, METAL-
LURGY DIVISION, TECHNICAL HIGHLIGHTS,
FISCAL YEAR. [Annual]

C 13.1/6:date
CENTER FOR COMPUTER SCIENCES AND TECH-
NOLOGY TECHNICAL HIGHLIGHTS, FISCAL
YEAR.

C 13.1/7:date   • **Item 238-A (MF)**
POLYMER SCIENCE AND STANDARDS DIVISION,
ANNUAL REPORT.

C 13.1/8:date
NATIONAL MEASUREMENT LABORATORY, CENTER
FOR ANALYTICAL CHEMISTRY: ANNUAL RE-
PORT.

C 13.1/9:date   • **Item 247-D (MF)**
CENTER FOR MATERIALS SCIENCE: ANNUAL
REPORT.

C 13.1/10:date
NATIONAL MEASUREMENT LABORATORY, CENTER
FOR BASIC STANDARDS: ANNUAL REPORT.

C 13.2:CT   • **Item 244**
GENERAL PUBLICATIONS.

C 13.2:R 31/4   • **Item 244**
RESEARCH AND DEVELOPMENT PROJECTS.
[Annual]

Prepared by the Management Analysis

Section.
Project listing, key word index, project
leaders. Covers fiscal year.

C 13.2:St 2/2   • **Item 244**
DIRECTORY OF STANDARDS LABORATORIES
IN THE UNITED STATES. [Irregular]

C 13.3:vol.
BULLETINS.

C 13.3/2:vol.
DECENNIAL INDEX TO BULLETINS.

C 13.3/3:nos.
ADMINISTRATIVE BULLETINS.

C 13.3/4:nos.   • **Item 244-G (MF)**
TIME AND FREQUENCY BULLETIN. [Monthly]

Contains information on the time and frequency activities of the National Bureau of Standards. Includes tables showing time scale information, International Timing Center comparisons,
etc.

C 13.4:nos.   • **Item 242**
CIRCULARS.
Superseded by C 13.44
Discontinued.

C 13.5:nos.
CIRCULARS OF INFORMATION.
Earlier T 41.5

C 13.6:CT
REGULATIONS, RULES, AND INSTRUCTIONS.

C 13.6/2:CT   • **Item 245-A**
HANDBOOKS, MANUALS, GUIDES (unnumbered).

C 13.6/3:nos.
CRYOGENIC MATERIALS DATA HANDBOOK.
Earlier C 31.6/2:C 88

C 13.7:date
CONFERENCE ON WEIGHTS AND MEASURES.

C 13.8:nos.
TECHNOLOGIC PAPERS.

C 13.8/2:vol.
TECHNOLOGIC PAPERS. BOUND VOLUMES.

C 13.9:serial nos.
SPECIFICATIONS, INTERNATIONAL AIRCRAFT STAN-
DARDS.

C 13.10   • **Item 247 (MF) (EL)**
SPECIAL PUBLICATIONS. 1–   [Irregular]

PURPOSE:– To provide material of a particular nature and quantity, which includes proceedings of high-level national and international conferences sponsored by National Bureau of Standards, precision measurement and calibration
volumes, NBS Research Highlights, and other
special publications appropriate to this grouping.
Effective April 1968 the name of the series
was changed from Miscellaneous Publications
with a continuation of the numbering system established under the former title.

DIRECTORY OF UNITED STATES STANDARDIZA-
TION ACTIVITIES. [Irregular]

PURPOSE:– To provide a descriptive inventory of the work of American organizations involved in standardization activities.

HYDRAULIC RESEARCH IN THE UNITED STATES. 1951– [Annual]

Describes research and development projects conducted during the year in hydraulic and hydrologic laboratories of universities and Federal agencies in the United States and Canada. The status of continuing projects covered by previous issues of the publication is reported upon, as well as on new projects in progress, and results of completed work is given. A list of the contributing laboratories is also included.

For each project the following information is given: a) number and title of project; b) project conducted for; c) correspondent; d) nature of project; e) description; f) present status; g) results; h) publications.

PROCEEDINGS OF THE STANDARDS LABORATORY CONFERENCES. 1962– [Irregular]

Presents the proceedings of the national meetings of the National Conference of Standards Laboratories. Includes the papers presented, plus the transcriptions of discussion panels. Also included is a report of the business and information session.
Aug. 8-10,1962 Boulder, Colo. MP 248
May 9-12, 1966 Washington, D.C. MP 291

REPORT OF THE NATIONAL CONFERENCE ON WEIGHTS AND MEASURES. 1st– 1905– [Annual]

Report records the full proceedings of the Conference, including the texts of the opening addresses. Papers delivered by delegates, committee reports, and a complete list of the persons attending the Conference are also included.

INDEX TO REPORTS OF THE NATIONAL CONFERENCE ON WEIGHTS AND MEASURES, 1st– 56th, 1905– 71. (SP 377)

STANDARDS YEARBOOKS. 1927– 1933. [Annual]

TECHNICAL HIGHLIGHTS OF THE NATIONAL BUREAU OF STANDARDS.
For entry, see C 13.1

C 13.10:250-1– • Item 247
CALIBRATION AND TEST SERVICES OF THE NATIONAL BUREAU OF STANDARDS. (Miscellaneous Publications 250)

PURPOSE:– To provide a descriptive listing of most of the test and calibration work done at the National Bureau of Standards with the respective fees. Includes list of publications referred to in the text.

MEASUREMENT USERS BULLETIN. 1– 1968– [Irregular]

Issued as supplements to Miscellaneous Publication 250.

C 13.10:258 • Item 247
FOREIGN-LANGUAGE AND ENGLISH DICTIONARIES IN THE PHYSICAL SCIENCES AND ENGINEERING, SELECTED BIBLIOGRAPHY, 1952– 1963. 1964. 190 p.

(Miscellaneous Publication 258)

C 13.10:260 • Item 247
STANDARD REFERENCE MATERIALS. 1951– [Irregular] (Office of Standard Reference Materials) (Special Publication 260)

An entire current listing of standard reference materials arranged in logical sequence giving normal values of certified properties plus information for ordering.

Editions are supplemented by Price and Availability Listing of Standard Reference Materials.

C 13.10:260-1–
STANDARD REFERENCE MATERIALS: [Specific Subjects]. 1– 1964– [Irregular]

C 13.10:288 • Item 247
DIRECTORY OF UNITED STATES STANDARDIZATION ACTIVITIES. 1967. 276 p. (Miscellaneous Publication 288)

C 13.10:305 • Item 247
PUBLICATIONS OF THE NATIONAL BUREAU OF STANDARDS. [Irregular]

PURPOSE:– To provide a complete list, with brief abstracts, of the Bureau publications as well as papers appearing in outside journals.

C 13.10:329 • Item 247
INDEX OF U.S. VOLUNTARY ENGINEERING STANDARDS. 1971. 984 p. (Special Publication 329)
A computer-produced index containing the permuted titles of more than 19,000 voluntary engineering and related standards, specifications, test methods, and recommended practices, in effect as of December 31, 1969, published by some 360 United States technical societies, professional organizations, and trade associations.

C 13.10:352 • Item 247
WORLD INDEX OF PLASTIC STANDARDS. 1971. 445 p. (Special Publications 352)
Contains the titles of more than 9,000 national and international standards on plastics and related materials which were in effect as of December 31, 1970. Serves a reference for design engineers, purchasing agents and others who want to know if there are standards covering a particular plastics material, product or test method.

C 13.10:375 • Item 247
INDEX OF STATE SPECIFICATIONS AND STANDARDS. 1973. 377 p.

This computer-produced Index contains the permuted titles of more than 6,000 State purchasing specifications and standards, issued by State purchasing offices through 1971, and related information.

C 13.10:390 • Item 247
INDEX OF INTERNATIONAL STANDARDS. [Irregular]

Provides a computer produced index of international standards, recommendations, test methods, analyses, and specifications, containing over 2,700 standards titles of five international organizations. The index is based on the Key-Word-In-Context System.

C 13.10:417 • Item 247
DIRECTORY OF UNITED STATES STANDARDIZATION ACTIVITIES. 1975. 223 p.
This directory serves as a guide to standardization activities in the U.S. Included in the Directory are summaries of the standardization activities of trade associations, technical and other professional societies representing industry and commerce, and State and Federal governments. Contains current descriptive summaries of more than 580 organizations, including nonengineering and nonindustry groups.

C 13.10:440 • Item 247
COLOR UNIVERSAL LANGUAGE AND DICTIONARY OF NAMES. Rev. 1976. 184 p. il.

This book combines the Universal Color Language (UCL), which has been revised, and the seventh printing of the Color Names Dictionary. The UCL provides readers with all the well known color-order systems and methods of designating color. It interrelates them in six correlated levels of fineness of color designation, each higher level indicating a finer division of the color solid. The designations are intended to be accurate enough to satisfy a scientist, usable enough to satisfy a manufacturer, and uncomplicated enough to be understood by the average person. Instructions are included for the application of the UCL at each level.

The Dictionary of Color Names contains the names of more than 7,500 individual colors, and gives their ISCC-NBS numbers.

C 13.10:480-20 • Item 247
DIRECTORY OF LAW ENFORCEMENT AND CRIMINAL JUSTICE ASSOCIATIONS AND RESEARCH CENTERS. 1978. 46 p.

Lists national, nonprofit professional and volunteer social action associations, and research centers which are active in the fields of law enforcement and criminal justice.
Prepared for the Law Enforcement Assistance Administration, Department of Justice.

C 13.10:483 • Item 247
INDEX OF U.S. NUCLEAR STANDARDS. 1977. 78 p.

Contains the titles of more than 1,200 nuclear and nuclear-related standards, specifications, test methods, codes, and recommended practices published by technical societies, professional organizations, trade associations, and U.S. Government agencies.

C 13.10:500-42 • Item 247
GUIDE TO COMPUTER PROGRAM DIRECTORIES. 1977. 167 p. (Special Publication 500-22)

C 13.10:739 • Item 247
DIRECTORY OF FEDERAL GOVERNMENT CERTIFICATION AND RELATED PROGRAMS. 1998 [Special Publication 739]

C 13.10:800-nos. • Item 247
COMPUTER SECURITY - GUIDE. [Special Publication 800-18]

C 13.10:950-1 • Item 247
ADVANCED TECHNOLOGY PROGRAM. PERFORMANCE OF COMPLETED PROJECTS. [Special Publication 950-1]

C 13.10/2: • Item 247
MEASUREMENT USERS BULLETIN.

C 13.10/3:date • Item 247 (MF)
REPORT OF THE NATIONAL CONFERENCE ON WEIGHTS AND MEASURES. [Annual]
Earlier C 13.10

C 13.10/3-2 • Item 247-L (EL)
NIST CONFERENCE CALENDAR. [Monthly]

C 13.10/3-3 • Item 247-J (MF)
NCWM PUBLICATIONS (series).

C 13.10/4:date • Item 247 (MF)
LASER INDUCED DAMAGE IN OPTICAL MATERIALS. [Annual]
Earlier C 13.10
Discontinued.

C 13.11 • Item 245 (P) (EL)
HANDBOOKS. H 1– 1918– [Irregular]

Recommended codes of engineering and industrial practice, including safety codes, developed in cooperation with the national organizations and others concerned. In many cases the recommended requirements are given official status through their incorporation in local ordinances by State and municipal regulatory bodies.

C 13.11/2:date • Item 245
NIST HANDBOOK, SPECIFICATIONS, TOLERANCES, AND OTHER TECHNICAL REQUIREMENTS FOR WEIGHING AND MEASURING DEVICES. [Annual]

Earlier title: NBS Handbook, Specifications, Tolerances, and Other Technical Requirements for Weighing and Measuring Devices.

C 13.12 • **Item 249**
SIMPLIFIED PRACTICE RECOMMENDATIONS. R 1–
1923–   [Irregular]

PURPOSE:– To provide recommendations developed by voluntary cooperation among manufacturers, distributors, consumers, and other interests upon the initiative of any of these groups, through a regular procedure of the Commodity Standards Division.

The Recommendations give the sizes, kinds, and types of specific manufactured articles that are produced and stocked for the trade in greatest quantity, or methods applicable to them, which may be used effectively to keep variety to a minimum.

Recommendations in printed form are designated R-(nos.)-(year) and are for sale by the Superintendent of Documents. Certain recommendations which are not available in printed form, but due to a continued limited trade interest are maintained by the Commodity Standards Division in mimeographed or other form of copy. They are so designated in the Classified List and are available upon request from the Commodity Standards Division free of charge. A List of Commercial Standards and Simplified Practice Recommendations is available upon request.
Discontinued.

C 13.12/2:nos.
LIMITATION OF VARIETY RECOMMENDATIONS.

C 13.13 • **Item 250**
DIMENSIONS, NBS. v. 1–   1925– 1981. [10 times a year]

PURPOSE:– To summarize the current research developments and testing activities of the Bureau.

The issues are about 16 pages in length. The articles are brief, with emphasis on the results of research and their significance, chosen for their importance to other scientists, engineers, and to industry. Resumes of longer research reports, important national and international conferences on fundamental science in which the Bureau has represented the Nation, and a bibliography of all publications by members of the staff as published are included. Also included, when applicable, is a brief description of new standard materials available from the bureau. This keeps its catalog Standard Materials (Circular 552 [3rd ed.]) up-to-date.

Index contained in the December issues.
Titled Technical News Bulletin prior to the August 1973 issue.
ISSN 0093-0458
Discontinued.

C 13.14:date
WHOLESALE PRICES OF BUILDING MATERIALS. [Monthly]

C 13.15:nos.
NEWS PUBLICATIONS. [Monthly List]

C 13.16:nos. • **Item 247-A-1**
LETTER CIRCULARS.
Discontinued.

C 13.17:nos.
CERTIFICATE OF ANALYSES OF STANDARD SAMPLES.

C 13.18:CT
PRESS NOTICES.

C 13.19:nos.
AMERICAN MARINE STANDARDS COMMITTEE.

C 13.20 • **Item 243**
COMMERCIAL STANDARDS. CS 1–   [Irregular]

PURPOSE:– To provide a recorded voluntary standard of the trade on specific items.

Commercial Standards are specifications that establish quality levels for manufactured products in accordance with the principal demands of the trade. They give technical requirements for materials, construction, dimensions, tolerances, testing, grading, marking, labeling, or other details, so as to promote sound commercial prac-

tices in the manufacture, marketing and application of the products. The standards are developed by voluntary cooperation among manufacturers, distributors, consumers, and other interests, upon the initiative of any of these groups, through regular procedures of the Commodity Standards Division.

A List of Commercial Standards are Simplified Practice Recommendations is available upon request.

The standards are designated CS-(nos.)-(year).
Earlier C 18.276 and C 41.25

C 13.20/2 • **Item 243**
PRODUCT STANDARDS, PS-(series). 1966–   [Irregular] (Engineering Standards Service)

Product Standards are developed by manufacturers, distributors, and users in cooperation with the Office of Engineering Standards Services of the National Bureau of Standards. The purpose of a Product Standard may be either (1) to establish standards of practice for sizes, dimensions, varieties, or other characteristics of specific products; or (2) to establish quality criteria, standard methods of test, rating, certification, and labeling of manufactured products.
Discontinued.

C 13.21:vol
COMMERCIAL STANDARDS. [Monthly]

C 13.22 • **Item 246-E**
JOURNAL OF RESEARCH. v. 1–   1928–
[Bimonthly]

PURPOSE:– To report National Bureau of Standards research and development in physics, mathematics, chemistry, and engineering.

Contains comprehensive scientific papers, giving complete details of the work, including laboratory data, experimental procedures, and theoretical and mathematical analyses. Illustrated with photographs, drawings, and charts.

Each issue contains an annotated bibliography of publications issued by the National Bureau of Standards, including papers published in outside journals.

Supersedes Bulletin of the Bureau of Standards.

Beginning in July 1959, the Journal was issued in four separate sections and from 1966 to 1977 in three sections. Starting in 1977 Sections A and B were consolidated to form one section.

C 13.22/sec.A • **Item 246-A**
A. PHYSICS AND CHEMISTRY. v. 63– 81. 1959– 1977. [Bimonthly]

Covers the broad range of physical and chemical research, with major emphasis on standards of physical measurement, fundamental constants, and properties of matter.

Index contained in the November– December issues. Title page and table of contents were issued separately.
Indexed by:
Chemical Abstracts.
Engineering Index Annual.
Engineering Index Monthly.
Nuclear Science Abstracts.
International Aerospace Abstracts.
ISSN 0022-4332
Discontinued.

C 13.22/sec.B • **Item 246-B**
B. MATHEMATICAL SCIENCES. v. 63– 81. 1959– 1977. [Quarterly]

Includes studies and compilations designed mainly for mathematicians and theoretical physicists. Topics in mathematical statistics, theory of experiment design, numerical analysis, theoretical physics and chemistry, logical design and programming of computers and computer systems. Short numerical tables.

Index contained in the October– December issues. Title page and table of contents issued separately.

Title prior to January 1968: Mathematics and Mathematical Physics.
ISSN 0098-8979
Discontinued.

C 13.22/sec.C • **Item 246-C**
C. ENGINEERING AND INSTRUMENTATION. v. 63– 76, no. 2. 1959– June 1972. [Quarterly]

Presents results of interest chiefly to the engineer and the applied scientist. Covers many of the new developments in instrumentation resulting from the Bureau's work in physical measurement, data processing, and development of test methods. Also covers such fields as acoustics, applied mechanics, building research, and cryogenic engineering.

Index contained in the October– December issues. Title page table of contents issued separately.
Discontinued.

C 13.22/sec.D:v.nos.&nos.
D. RADIO SCIENCE. [Bimonthly]

Effective with the January 1966 issue, published by the Environmental Science Services Administration (C 52.9).
Earlier entitled Radio Propagation.
Discontinued.

C 13.22/a:CT
RESEARCH PAPERS, SEPARATES FROM THE JOURNAL OF RESEARCH.

C 13.22/2:vol.
JOURNAL OF RESEARCH. BOUND VOLUMES.

The Journal is also issued in bound form at a later date. Prior to July 1959, two volumes were issued each year. Beginning with July 1959, the bound volumes are issued for each section and on an annual basis, except for the six-month period, July– December 1959.

C 13.23:nos.
NATIONAL SCREW THREAD COMMISSION.

C 13.24:nos.
FEDERAL SPECIFICATIONS BOARD, UNITED STATES GOVERNMENT MASTER SPECIFICATIONS.

C 13.25:nos.
BUILDING AND HOUSING PUBLICATIONS.

C 13.26:vol.
REPORT ON CURRENT HYDRAULIC LABORATORY RESEARCH IN U.S.

C 13.26/2:date
HYDRAULIC LABORATORY BULLETIN, SERIES B.

C 13.27:nos.
TECHNICAL INFORMATION ON BUILDING MATERIALS FOR USE IN DESIGN OF LOW-COST HOUSING.

C 13.28:date
NEWS BULLETIN OF PAPER SECTION. [Monthly]

C 13.29:nos. • **Item 241**
BUILDING MATERIALS AND STRUCTURES REPORT.
Superseded by C 13.44
Discontinued.

C 13.29/2 • **Item 241-A (MF)**
BUILDING SCIENCE SERIES. 1–   1965–
[Irregular]

PURPOSE:– To disseminate technical information developed at the National Bureau of Standards on building materials, components, systems, and whole structures.

The series presents research results, test methods, and performance criteria related to the structural and environmental functions and the durability and safety characteristics of building elements and systems. Similar in style and content to the NBS Building Materials and Structures Reports, published from 1938 to 1959.

C 13.30:nos.
[MATHEMATICAL TABLES.]

C 13.31:nos.
BASIC RADIO PROPAGATION PREDICTIONS. [Monthly]

C 13.31/2:
RADIO PROPAGATION FORECASTS.

C 13.31/3:nos.
CENTRAL RADIO PROPAGATION LABORATORY IONOSPHERIC PREDICTIONS. [Monthly]
    Continuation of C 13.31
    Later C 52.10

C 13.32   • Item 239
APPLIED MATHEMATICS SERIES. AMS 1–   1948–   [Irregular]

    Contains mathematical tables, manuals and studies of special interest to physicists, engineers, chemists, biologists, mathematicians, computer programs and others engaged in scientific and technical work.
    Some volumes are reissues, to meet a continuing demand, of the Mathematical Tables prepared by the Project for the Computation of Mathematical Tables conducted by the Federal Works Agency, Works Project Administration, for the City of New York, under the scientific sponsorship of and made available through the National Bureau of Standards. Publications of the Mathematical Tables are now out of print. When the Applied Mathematics Division was established at the National Bureau of Standards in July 1947, the Mathematical Tables Project became identified with the unit known as the Computation Laboratory.
    Discontinued.

C 13.32:55   • Item 239
HANDBOOK OF MATHEMATICAL FUNCTIONS. 1972. 1046 p. il.

    Includes every special function normally needed by anyone who uses tables in his work. Now all reference needs– even bibliographies– are supplied in one convenient volume. This important compendium expands the work of past authors: It increases the number of functions covered, presents more extensive numerical tables, and gives larger collections of mathematical properties of the tabulated functions. Rational approximation formulas, tailored to the modern electronic computers, are included for all functions. To the scientist who must do his own calculations, these formulas are valuable. Everyone who needs to refer to tables of mathematical functions may want to have this definitive Handbook.

C 13.33:nos.
CENTRAL RADIO PROPAGATION LABORATORY REPORTS.

C 13.33/2
QUARTERLY REPORT OF CENTRAL PROPAGATION LABORATORY.

C 13.33/3:nos.
LIST OF REPORTS RECEIVED IN LIBRARY. (Central Radio Propagation Laboratory)

C 13.33/4:nos.
LIST OF UNCLASSIFIED REPORTS RECEIVED FROM DEPT. OF ARMY, SIGNAL CORPS. (Central Radio Propagation Laboratory)

    An internal administrative document and report of the Division to the Director of the National Bureau of Standards.

C 13.34:nos.   • Item 248
THERMAL PROPERTIES OF GASES [Tables].
    Discontinued.

C 13.35:CT
ADDRESSES.

C 13.36:nos.
[RELEASES OF GENERAL INFORMATION] TRG (Series).

C 13.36/2:CT
NEW PUBLICATIONS FORM NBS. [Irregular]
    Prior to January 1974 issued as NBS Publications Announcements.
        ISSN 0364-8605

C 13.36/3:nos.
[RELEASES PERTAINING TO PERSONNEL] TRP (Series).

C 13.36/4:date
RELEASES [Miscellaneous].

C 13.36/5
NBS PUBLICATIONS NEWSLETTER. 1–   1963–   [Quarterly]

    PURPOSE:– To assist science librarians, documentalists and science information specialists to make better utilization of the publications output of the National Bureau of standards and to cope more effectively with the information explosion.
    Written in a friendly chatter style, tells of new publications and services both of the National Bureau of Standards and the Clearinghouse for Federal Scientific and Technical Information.
    Prior to 1966, issued irregular.
        ISSN 0364-1775.

C 13.36/6:date
TECHNICAL NEWS FROM DEPARTMENT OF COMMERCE, NATIONAL BUREAU OF STANDARDS.

                                          • Item 238-B (P)
C 13.36/7   • Item 247-L (EL)
NIST UPDATE.

    Intended as a guide for editors on recent activities at the Bureau, which is the nation's physical sciences and engineering measurement laboratory. Each issue contains short items on various subjects such as automation, chemistry, and industrial standards.
    Earlier title: NBS Update.
    Official Use Only.

C 13.37:nos.   • Item 240-A-1
LIST OF PUBLICATIONS, LP (Series).

C 13.37/2:date/nos.
BIBLIOGRAPHY ON THE HIGH TEMPERATURE CHEMISTRY AND PHYSICS OF MATERIALS IN THE CONDENSED STATE.

C 13.37/3:nos.
BIBLIOGRAPHY ON THE HIGH TEMPERATURE CHEMISTRY AND PHYSICS OF GASES AND GAS-CONDENSED PHASE REACTIONS.

C 13.37/4:CT   • Item 240-A
BIBLIOGRAPHIES AND LISTS OF PUBLICATIONS.

C 13.37/5:nos.
SUPERCONDUCTING DEVICES AND MATERIALS. [Quarterly]

    PURPOSE:– To provide a literature survey of publications and reports pertaining to superconducting devices and to theory and experiment related to superconducting devices.
    Discontinued in 1980.
        ISSN 0039-5714

C 13.37/6:nos.
LIQUEFIED NATURAL GAS, LITERATURE SURVEY. 70-1–   1970–   [Quarterly] (Cryogenic Data Center, Cryogenics Division, Institute for Basic Standards, Boulder, Colorado 80302)

    Contains bibliography arranged by subject headings, with author index, or current literature in the field of liquefied natural gas. Also provides news of interest and a list of bibliographies which have been prepared by the Cryogenic Data Center and are available to the public. The literature surveys and bibliographies are the results of literature searches conducted by the Data Center's information storage and retrieval system.

Discontinued in 1980.
    ISSN 0024-4228.

C 13.37/7:date
LIBRARY. [Monthly]

C 13.38:nos. or CT
REPORTS [on Projects].

C 13.39:nos.
TECHNICAL MEMORANDUM (Applied Mathematics Division).

C 13.40:nos.
BUILDING RESEARCH, SUMMARY REPORTS. OFFICIAL USE ONLY.

C 13.41:date
GRADUATE SCHOOL ANNOUNCEMENT OF COURSES. [Annual]
    Administrative.
    Earlier C 13.2:G 75

C 13.42:v.nos.&nos.
NBS STANDARD. OFFICIAL USE.

C 13.43:date
NATIONAL APPLIED MATHEMATICS LABORATORIES. PROJECTS AND PUBLICATIONS, QUARTERLY REPORT.

C 13.44   • Item 247-A (MF)
MONOGRAPHS. Mono 1–   1959–   [Irregular]

    Monographs are usually contributions to the technical literature which are too lengthy for publication in the Journal of Research. They often provide extensive compilations of information on subjects related to the Bureau's technical program.
    Supersedes Circulars.

C 13.45:nos.
NATIONAL BUREAU OF STANDARDS CERTIFICATE OF CALIBRATION.

C 13.46:nos.   • Item 249-A (MF)
TECHNICAL NOTES. TN 1–   1959–   [Irregular]

    PURPOSE:– To supplement the Bureau's regular publications program. Provides a means for making available scientific information of a transient of limited interest. They are available by purchase from the Office of Technical Services.

FLAMMABLE FABRICS PROGRAM. 1970–   [Annual]

    PURPOSE:– To report to the Congress on standards developed during the calendar year for wearing apparel as required under the Flammable Fabrics Act.

INSTITUTE FOR MATERIALS RESEARCH, ANALYTICAL CHEMISTRY DIVISION. ANNUAL REPORTS OF SECTIONS.

    Each of the nine sections of the Analytical Chemistry Division of the National Bureau of Standards prepares an informal summary describing the progress of its work for the past year. These reports are the medium by which that information is presented which is of help to others but which will not be treated fully in regular publications. Areas of work which are not to be published are considered in detail while those which are being written up for publication in the journal literature are covered in a much more abbreviated form. Information obtained and techniques developed which usually do not find their way into the regular literature, including the unspectacular "negative results" are included. In addition, there are included experimental techniques and procedures, the designs and modifications of equipment, etc., which often require months to perfect but which often are covered in only a line or two of a journal article.
    The Analytical Chemistry Division was established as a separate division at the National Bureau of Standards on September 1, 1963, and became part of the Institute for

Materials Research in the February 1, 1964 reorganization. Annual reports of the nine sections are as follows:
All reports are for the fiscal year:

ACTIVATION ANALYSIS SECTION

ACTIVATION ANALYSIS: COCKCROFT-WALTON GENERATOR NUCLEAR REACTOR, LINAC. 1966– [Annual]

ANALYTICAL COORDINATION CHEMISTRY SECTION

ANALYTICAL COORDINATION CHEMISTRY: TITRIMETRY, GRAVIMETRY, FLAME PHOTOMETRY, SPECTROPHOTOMETRY, AND GAS EVOLUTION. 1965– [Annual]

ANALYTICAL MASS SPECTROMETRY SECTION

SUMMARY OF ACTIVITIES. 1966 [Annual]

Covers studies in the field of developing instrumentation and devising analytical techniques which will improve the precision of isotope radio measurements.

ELECTROCHEMICAL ANALYSIS SECTION

SUMMARY OF ACTIVITIES. 1965– [Annual]

Covers studies in ionic processes occurring in solutions, with areas of analytical measurement where ionic equilibria play a part, and with the explanation of solution behavior in terms of the interactions of ionic solutes with solvent molecules.

MICROCHEMICAL ANALYSIS SECTION

SUMMARY OF ACTIVITIES. 1965– [Annual]
Covers studies in the following fields of analytical competence; gas analysis by mass spectrometry and other techniques, polarography, a.c. polarography, coulometry, electroanalytical measurements, microscopy, wet chemistry, conventional elemental microchemical analysis.

ORGANIC CHEMISTRY SECTION

ORGANIC CHEMISTRY: AIR POLLUTION STUDIES CHARACTERIZATION OF CHEMICAL STRUCTURES; SYNTHESIS OF RESEARCH MATERIALS: NOVEL RESEARCH MATERIALS: ISOTOPIC METHODS FOR ANALYSIS OF CARBOHYDRATES; OCCURRENCE, PREPARATION, AND PROPERTIES OF NATURALLY OCCURRING MONOSACCHARIDES (including 6-deoxy sugars); STANDARD REFERENCE MATERIALS (organic). 1965– [Annual]

RADIOCHEMICAL ANALYSIS SECTION

RADIO CHEMICAL ANALYSIS, NUCLEAR INSTRUMENTATION, RADIATION TECHNIQUES, NUCLEAR CHEMISTRY, RADIOISOTOPE TECHNIQUES. 1964– [Annual]

SEPARATION AND PURIFICATION SECTION

SUMMARY OF ACTIVITIES. 1967– [Annual]

SPECTROCHEMICAL ANALYSIS SECTION

ACTIVITIES OF THE NBS SPECTROCHEMICAL ANALYSIS SECTION. 1965– [Annual]

Covers instrumental elementary analysis, especially for those spectroscopic techniques that are capable of multielement determinations, including optical, X-ray, and mass spectroscopy.

C 13.46:814   • Item 249-A
MECHANIZED INFORMATION SERVICES CATALOG. 1974. 47 p. il.

Describes currently available data bases containing information sources and services.

C 13.46/2:date   • Item 249-A (MF)
NBS REACTOR: SUMMARY OF ACTIVITIES. [Annual]
Earlier C 13.46

C 13.47:date   • Item 248-A
PRESIDENT RESEARCH ASSOCIATESHIPS, POST-DOCTORAL, TENABLE AT NATIONAL BUREAU OF STANDARDS. [Annual]
Earlier C 13.2:R 31/3
Discontinued.

C 13.48:nos.   • Item 248-B (MF)
NATIONAL STANDARD REFERENCE DATA SERIES, NSRDS-NBS– (series). 1– 1964– [Irregular]

The National Standard Reference Data System is a government-wide effort to give to the technical community of the United States the optimum access to the quantitative data of physical science, critically evaluated and compiled for convenience. This program was established in 1963 by the President's Office of Science and Technology, acting upon the recommendation of the Federal Council for Science and Technology. The National Bureau of Standards has been assigned the responsibility for administering the effort. The general objective of the System is to coordinate and integrate existing data evaluation and compilation activities into a systematic, comprehensive program, supplementing and expanding technical coverage when necessary, establishing and maintaining standards for the output of the participating groups, and providing mechanisms for the dissemination of the output as required.

For operational purposes, NSRDS compilation activities are organized into seven categories as listed below. The data publications of the NSRDA, which may consist of monographs, loose-leaf sheets, computer tapes, or any other useful product, will be classified as belonging to one or another of these categories. An additional General category will include reports on detailed classification schemes, lists of compilations considered to be Standard Reference Data, status reports, and similar material.
Categories covered by NSRDA Data Series:
General
Nuclear Properties
Atomic and Molecular Properties
Solid State Properties
Thermodynamic and Transport Properties
Chemical Kinetics
Colloid and Surface Properties
Mechanical Properties of Materials

C 13.48/2:CT
NBS STANDARD REFERENCE MATERIALS [Announcements]. [Irregular] (Office of Standard Reference Materials)

C 13.48/3:v.nos.&nos.
REFERENCE DATA REPORT. [Bimonthly]

Sub-title: An Informal Communication of the National Standard Reference Data System.

C 13.48/4:CT   • Item 248-B (MF)
STANDARD REFERENCE MATERIALS (series). [Irregular]
Earlier C 13.2:St 2/5

C 13.48/4-2:nos.   • Item 248-B (EL)
NIST STANDARD REFERENCE MATERIALS PRICE LIST. [Annual]
Also published in microfiche.

C 13.48/4-3   • Item 24-B (P) (EL)
STANDARD REFERENCE MATERIALS PRICE LIST. [Quarterly]

C 13.49   • Item 248-C
REVIEW OF SELECTED U.S. GOVERNMENT RESEARCH AND DEVELOPMENT REPORTS, OTR– (Series). 1– [Irregular] (Office of Technical Resources, Institute of Applied Technology)
Discontinued.

C 13.50
NEWS FOR USERS OF NBS STANDARD REFERENCE MATERIALS. 1– 1967– [Quarterly] (Office of Standard Reference Materials, Institute of Materials Research)

PURPOSE:– To communicate on a regular basis with persons in science and industry who need and use Standard Reference Materials, giving the status of NBS programs and encouraging comments and suggestions which will lead to improvements on new programs.

C 13.51:nos.   • Item 247-E
BIWEEKLY CRYOGENICS AWARENESS SERVICE. 1–
Compiled by the Cryogenic Data Center, Cryogenics Division, Institute for Basic Standards, Boulder, Colorado.
Prior to list no. 565, issued as Cryogenic Data Center, Current Awareness Service, Publications and Reports of Interest in Cryogenic Noted.
Discontinued in 1980.
ISSN 0364-0868

C 13.52:nos.   • Item 248-D
FEDERAL INFORMATION PROCESSING STANDARDS PUBLICATIONS. 1– 1968– [Irregular] (Includes all new FIPS publications and supplements for an indefinite period)

PURPOSE:– To announce and maintain Federal information processing standards, to provide information of general interest and a complete index of relevant standards publications and specifications. The publications which announce the adoption of standards provide necessary policy, administrative, and guidance information for their effective implementation and utilization.

C 13.53:nos.   • Item 247-B (MF)
NBS CONSUMER INFORMATION SERIES. 1971– [Irregular]

PURPOSE:– To help the consumer make informed decisions in the marketplace.
Discontinued.

C 13.54:date   • Item 247-F
ELECTROMAGNETIC METEOROLOGY, CURRENT AWARENESS SERVICE. Sept. 1970– [Monthly] (Electromagnetic Meteorology Information Center, Boulder, Colorado 80302)

Abstracts of selected articles on measurement techniques and standards of electromagnetic quantities from D-C to millimeter-wave frequencies.
ISSN 0046-1709
Discontinued.

C 13.55:date   • Item 247-C (MF)
MODEL WEIGHTS AND MEASURES ORDINANCE (year), PROVISIONS AS ADOPTED BY THE NATIONAL CONFERENCE ON WEIGHTS AND MEASURES.

The Model Weights and Measures Ordinance is a compilation of the requirements in the Model State Weights and Measures Law and the Model Regulations designed to be adopted thereunder. Its purpose is to provide for a comprehensive weights and measures program at the city or county level. It is designed to complement State activity in this area.

C 13.55/2:date
NATIONAL WEIGHTS AND MEASURES LAW, (year). [Annual]

PURPOSE:– To provide a model weights and measures law, adopted by the National Conference on Weights and Measures.

C 13.55/3:date   • Item 247-C (MF)
MODEL STATE REGULATIONS [on various subjects] AS ADOPTED BY THE NATIONAL CONFERENCE ON WEIGHTS AND MEASURES. [Irregular] (Office of Weights and Measures)

PURPOSE:– To provide the States with suggested model laws on such subjects as weights and measures, unit pricing method of sale of commodities, registration of servicemen and service agencies, as adopted by the National Conference on Weights and Measures.

C 13.56:nos.
OVERLAP, MEASUREMENT AGREEMENT THROUGH PROCESS EVALUATION. 1–   [Irregular]

C 13.57:CT
EXPERIMENTAL TECHNOLOGY INCENTIVES PROGRAM, PROGRAM AREA DESCRIPTION.

C 13.57/2:nos.   • **Item 247-H (MF)**
NIST-GCR GRANTEE/CONTRACTOR REPORT (Series).

Earlier title NBS-GCR Grantee/Contractor Report (Series).
GCR = Grants Contractor Report.

C 13.58:nos.   • **Item 247-D (MF)**
NISTIR-(Series). 1973–   [Irregular]

A special series of interim or final reports on work performed by NBS for outside sponsors (both government and non-government).
Earlier title: National Bureau of Standards Interagency Reports.

C 13.58/2:date   • **Item 247-D (MF)**
TECHNICAL ACTIVITIES, CENTER FOR ANALYTICAL CHEMISTRY. [Annual]
Earlier C 13.58
Discontinued.

C 13.58/3:date   • **Item 247-D (MF)**
TECHNICAL ACTIVITIES, OFFICE OF STANDARD REFERENCE DATA. [Annual]
Earlier C 13.58

C 13.58/4:   • **Item 247-D (MF)**
FIRE RESEARCH PUBLICATIONS. [Annual]
Discontinued.

C 13.58/5:   • **Item 247-D (MF)**
NIST SERIAL HOLDINGS.

Earlier title: NBS (National Bureau of Standards) Serial Holdings.

C 13.58/6:   • **Item 247-D (MF)**
DOUBLE-LEVEL METALLIZATION: ANNUAL REPORT.
Discontinued.

C 13.58/7:date   • **Item 247-D (MF)**
DIRECTORY OF NVLAP ACCREDITED LABORATORIES. [Annual]

C 13.58/9:   • **Item 247-D (MF)**
TECHNICAL ACTIVITIES, CENTER FOR CHEMICAL PHYSICS. [Annual]
Discontinued

C 13.58/10:   • **Item 247-D (MF)**
TECHNICAL PUBLICATION ANNOUNCEMENTS. [Quarterly]

C 13.58/11   • **Item 247-D (MF)**
TECHNICAL PROGRESS BULLETIN. [Quarterly]

C 13.59:date
PROJECT SUMMARIES FY (year), CENTER FOR BUILDING TECHNOLOGY. [Annual] (Institute for Applied Technology)

C 13.60:date   • **Item 247-G**
NBS TIME AND FREQUENCY BROADCAST SERVICES.
See C13.10

C 13.61:v.nos.&nos.
FIREVIEW. (Center for Fire Research)

C 13.62:date
CONFERENCE BRIEFS. [Quarterly]

C 13.63:v.nos.&nos.
VOICE OF Z39, NEWS ABOUT LIBRARY, INFORMATION SCIENCE, AND PUBLISHING STANDARDS.

[Quarterly] (American National Standards Committee Z39)

C 13.64:CT   • **Item 224-A**
MAPS, CHARTS, POSTERS.

C 13.64/2:CT
AUDIOVISUAL MATERIAL. [Irregular]

C 13.65:date   • **Item 246-F**
POSTDOCTORAL RESEARCH ASSOCIATESHIPS. [Annual]
Earlier C 13.2:R 31/6
Discontinued.

C 13.65/2:date   • **Item 246-F (MF)**
ENGINEERING POSTDOCTORAL RESEARCH ASSOCIATESHIP PROGRAM. [Annual]
Discontinued.

C 13.66:date   • **Item 244-B (MF)**
WEIGHTS AND MEASURES DIRECTORY. [Annual]

C 13.66/2:v.nos.&nos.
WEIGHTS AND MEASURES TODAY. [Irregular]

C 13.66/3:date   • **Item 244-B**
DIRECTORY OF ASSOCIATE MEMBERS, NATIONAL CONFERENCE ON WEIGHTS AND MEASURES. [Annual]

C 13.67:date
YELLOW BOOK. [Annual]

C 13.68:date   • **Item 244-E (MF)**
ANNUAL ACCOMPLISHMENTS REPORT, AFFIRMATIVE ACTION PROGRAM FOR MINORITIES AND WOMEN. [Annual]

Describes the goals, activities, and accomplishments of the affirmative action program for minorities and women of the National Bureau of Standards.
Discontinued.

C 13.69:CT   • **Item 244-C-1**
DIRECTORIES (NBS). [Irregular]

C 13.69/2:date
DIRECTORY OF VOTING MEMBERS (NATIONAL INFORMATION STANDARDS ORGANIZATION). [Annual]

C 13.69/3:date   • **Item 244-C**
DIRECTORY OF DoC STAFF MEMBERSHIPS ON OUTSIDE STANDARDS COMMITTEES. [Annual]

C 13.70:date   • **Item 244-F**
TBT NEWS. [Bimonthly] [Irregular]

TBT=Technical Barriers to Trade
Contains brief items on technical barriers to trade.
Non-depository

C 13.70/2:   • **Item 244-F-1 (MF)**
NATIONAL MEASUREMENT LABORATORY, NEWS FEATURES. [Annual]

Contains selected National Measurement Laboratory news releases, articles from the technical press, and information on NML conferences and workshops.
Discontinued.

C 13.71:date   • **Item 238-A (MF)**
TECHNICAL ACTIVITIES, SURFACE SCIENCE DIVISION. [Annual]
Discontinued.

C 13.72:date   • **Item 244-D (MF)**
STATUS REPORT OF THE ENERGY-RELATED INVENTIONS PROGRAM. [Annual]

This program is jointly operated by NBS and the DoE under Section 14 of the Federal Nonnuclear Energy Research and Development Act. NBS evaluates inventions and forwards them to DoE with its recommendations as to possible support.
Discontinued.

C 13.73:date   • **Item 238-A-1 (MF)**
INSTITUTE FOR COMPUTER SCIENCES AND TECHNOLOGY: ANNUAL REPORT.
Discontinued.

C 13.74:v.nos.&nos.
SCI-TECH INFORMATION.

C 13.75:date   • **Item 244-F (P) (EL)**
TECHNOLOGY AT A GLANCE. [Quarterly]

C 13.75/5
SUPERCONDUCTING DEVICES. 1965–   [Quarterly]

Issued by the Cryogenic Data Center, Institute for Basic Standards.
Publications and reports pertaining to superconducting devices and to theory and experiment related to superconducting devices.

C 13.76   • **Item 244-G (EL)**
CSL BULLETIN. [Monthly]

C 13.77:date   • **Item 238-B-1**
COMPUTER SYSTEMS LABORATORY, ANNUAL REPORT.
Discontinued.

C 13.78:v.nos./nos.   • **Item 244-G-1**
RESEARCH UPDATE. [Quarterly]

C 13.79   • **Item 247-L (E)**
ELECTRONIC PRODUCTS.

BUREAU OF STATISTICS
(1903– 1912)

CREATION AND AUTHORITY

The Bureau of Statistics was established within the Department of Commerce and Labor on July 1, 1903, consolidating the Bureau of Statistics (T 37) of the Treasury Department with the Bureau of Foreign Commerce (S 4) of the Department of State. The Bureau was consolidated with the Bureau of Manufacturers (C 10) to form the Bureau of Foreign and Domestic Commerce (C 18) by act of Congress, approved August 23, 1912.

C 14.1:date
ANNUAL REPORTS.
Earlier T 37.1

C 14.2:CT
GENERAL PUBLICATIONS.

C 14.3:date
BULLETINS, EXPORTS OF DOMESTIC BREAD STUFFS.
Earlier T 37.3/1 & T 37.3/4
Later C 18.3

C 14.4:nos.
CIRCULARS [none issued].

C 14.5:date
COMMERCIAL RELATIONS.
Earlier S 4.1
Later C 10.8

C 14.6:nos.
DAILY CONSULAR REPORTS.
Earlier S 4.5
Later C 10.5/1

C 14.7:date
INDEX TO DAILY CONSULAR REPORTS.
Earlier S 4.6

C 14.8:v.nos.
MONTHLY CONSULAR REPORTS.
Earlier S 4.7
Later C 10.6

C 14.9:date
INDEX TO MONTHLY CONSULAR REPORTS.
Earlier S 4.8

C 14.10:v.nos.
SPECIAL CONSULAR REPORTS.
Earlier S 4.9
Later C 10.7

C 14.11:date
LIST OF PUBLICATIONS.

C 14.12:date
TOTAL VALUES OF IMPORTS AND EXPORTS.
[Monthly]
Earlier T 37.7
Later C 18.6

C 14.13:date
ADVANCE SHEETS FROM MONTHLY SUMMARY OF
COMMERCE AND FINANCE.
Earlier T 37.9

C 14.14:date
MONTHLY SUMMARY OF COMMERCE AND FINANCE.
Earlier T 37.8

C 14.15:date
REVIEW OF THE WORLD'S COMMERCE.
Earlier S 4.12
Later C 10.9

C 14.16:date
STATISTICAL ABSTRACTS OF THE UNITED STATES.
Earlier T 37.10
Later C 18.14

C 14.17:letters-nos.
CLASSIFICATION SCHEDULES.
Later C 18.18

C 14.18:date
IMPORTED MERCHANDISE ENTERED FOR CON-
SUMPTION IN UNITED STATES, ETC.
Later C 18.17

C 14.19:date
SAILING DATES OF STEAMSHIPS FROM THE PRIN-
CIPAL PORTS OF THE UNITED STATES TO
PORTS IN FOREIGN COUNTRIES. [Monthly]

STEAMBOAT-INSPECTION
SERVICE
(1903– 1932)

CREATION AND AUTHORITY

The Steamboat-Inspection Service (T 38) was
transferred from the Treasury Department to the
newly created Department of Commerce and Labor on July 1, 1903. By act of Congress, approved June 30, 1932, the Service was consolidated with the Bureau of Navigation (C 11) to
form the Bureau of Navigation and Steamboat
Inspection (C 25).

C 15.1:date
ANNUAL REPORTS.
Earlier T 38.1

C 15.2:CT
GENERAL PUBLICATIONS.

C 15.3:nos.
BULLETINS [none issued].

C 15.4:nos.
CIRCULARS.
Earlier T 38.4

C 15.5:date
LAWS GOVERNING STEAMBOAT INSPECTION SER-
VICE.
Earlier T 38.5/1
Later C 25.5

C 15.6:ed.nos.
STEAMBOAT INSPECTORS' MANUAL.
Earlier T 38.6

C 15.7:date
LIST OF OFFICERS OF MERCHANT STEAM, MOTOR
AND SAIL VESSELS LICENSED DURING (calen-
dar year).
Earlier T 38.7

C 15.8:date
PILOT RULES.
Earlier T 38.8
Later C 25.8; C 25.9

C 15.9:date
GENERAL RULES AND REGULATIONS.
Earlier T 38.9

C 15.9/2:date
SUPPLEMENT TO GENERAL RULES AND REGULA-
TIONS.

C 15.9/3:dt.& rule no.
REVISION OF RULES (all classes).

C 15.10:nos.
STEAMBOAT-INSPECTION SERVICE BULLETIN.
Later C 25.3

DIVISION OF PRINTING AND
PUBLICATIONS

C 16.1:date
ANNUAL REPORTS.

C 16.2:CT
GENERAL PUBLICATIONS.

C 16.3:nos.
BULLETINS [none issued].

C 16.4:nos.
CIRCULARS [none issued].

C 16.5:date
LIST OF PUBLICATIONS OF THE DEPARTMENT OF
COMMERCE AND LABOR AVAILABLE FOR DIS-
TRIBUTION.

C 16.6:date
MONTHLY LIST OF PUBLICATIONS.

C 16.7:CT
LIST OF PUBLICATIONS (Miscellaneous).

APPOINTMENTS DIVISION
(1910– 1925)

C 17.1:date
ANNUAL REPORTS.

C 17.2:CT
GENERAL PUBLICATIONS.

C 17.3:nos.
BULLETINS.

C 17.4:nos.
CIRCULARS.

BUREAU OF FOREIGN AND
DOMESTIC COMMERCE
(1912– 1953)

CREATION AND AUTHORITY

The Bureau of Foreign and Domestic Commerce was established within the Department of

Commerce and Labor by act of Congress, approved August 23, 1912, consolidating the Bureau of Statistics (C 14) and the Bureau of Manufacturers (C 10). The Bureau remained within the
Department of Commerce upon the establishment
of the Department of Labor. In the departmental
reorganization of 1953, the Bureau was abolished
and its functions transferred to other offices in
the Department, among them the Business and
Defense Services Administration (C 41) and the
Bureau of Foreign Commerce (C 42).

C 18.1:date
ANNUAL REPORTS.

C 18.2:CT
GENERAL PUBLICATIONS.

C 18.3:dt.& nos.
BULLETINS, EXPORTS OF DOMESTIC BREAD-
STUFFS, ETC. [Monthly]
Earlier C 14.3

C 18.3/2:nos.
NATIONAL INDUSTRIAL RECOVERY ACT.

C 18.3/3
INTERNATIONAL BULLETINS [Administrative].

C 18.4:nos.
CIRCULARS.

C 18.5:dt.&nos.
DAILY CONSULAR AND TRADE REPORTS.
Earlier C 10.6

C 18.5/1:vol.
FOREIGN COMMERCE WEEKLY. 1940–
Entitled Commerce Reports 1927-1940.
Earlier C 10.14
Later C 42.8

C 18.5/2:CT
SUPPLEMENTS TO COMMERCE REPORTS, ANNUAL
SERIES.

C 18.5/3:date
MONTHLY SUPPLEMENTS TO COMMERCE
REPORTS.

C 18.6:date
TOTAL VALUES OF IMPORTS AND EXPORTS.
[Monthly]
Earlier C 14.12

C 18.6/2:date
VALUE OF EXPORTS, INCLUDING REEXPORTS . . .
BY GRAND DIVISIONS AND PRINCIPAL COUN-
TRIES. [Monthly]

C 18.6/3:date
ANALYSIS OF ECONOMIC GROUPS OF DOMESTIC
EXPORTS FROM AND IMPORTS INTO U.S.
[Monthly]
Early numbers read "Analysis of Domestic."

C 18.7:date
MONTHLY SUMMARY OF FOREIGN COMMERCE OF
UNITED STATES.

C 18.8:date
ADVANCE SHEETS FROM MONTHLY SUMMARY OF
THE FOREIGN COMMERCE OF THE UNITED
STATES. [Monthly]

C 18.9:nos.
SPECIAL CONSULAR REPORTS.
Earlier C 10.7

C 18.10:date
SAILING DATES OF STEAMSHIPS FROM THE PRIN-
CIPAL PORTS OF THE UNITED STATES TO
PORTS IN FOREIGN COUNTRIES. [Monthly]

C 18.11:nos.
SPECIAL AGENTS SERIES.
Earlier C 10.13

C 18.12:nos.
[FOREIGN] TARIFF SERIES.
Earlier C 10.10

C 18.13:nos.
FOREIGN TARIFF NOTES.
  Earlier C 10.16

C 18.14:date
STATISTICAL ABSTRACT OF THE UNITED STATES.
  Earlier C 14.16
  Later C 3.134

C 18.15:nos.
MISCELLANEOUS SERIES.

C 18.16:date
COMMERCIAL RELATIONS.
  Earlier C 10.8

C 18.17:date
IMPORTED MERCHANDISE ENTERED FOR CON-
  SUMPTION IN UNITED STATES, AND DUTIES
  COLLECTED THEREON DURING THE QUARTER
  ENDING.
  Earlier C 14.18 and C 14.17

C 18.18:letters
CLASSIFICATION SCHEDULES.
  Later C 3.150

C 18.18/2:CT
CLASSIFICATION OF IMPORTS AND EXPORTS.

C 18.19:date
FOREIGN COMMERCE AND NAVIGATION.
  Later C 3.159

C 18.20:nos.
COMMERCIAL STANDARDS.

C 18.21:nos.
MONTHLY LETTER.

C 18.22/1:date
LIST OF PUBLICATIONS FOR SALE BY THE SUPER-
  INTENDENT OF DOCUMENTS; ETC.

C 18.22/2:date
CATALOGUE OF BUREAU PUBLICATIONS.
  Issued about once a year.

C 18.22/3:CT
LISTS OF PUBLICATIONS.

C 18.23:nos.
CONFIDENTIAL CIRCULARS.

C 18.24:nos.
INDUSTRIAL STANDARDS.

C 18.25:nos.
TRADE INFORMATION BULLETINS.

C 18.26:date
COMMERCE YEARBOOKS.

C 18.26/2:date
FOREIGN COMMERCE YEARBOOKS.
  Earlier C 18.26:1926 and C 18.26:1932

C 18.27:nos.
TRADE PROMOTION SERIES.
  Displaces C 18.9; C 18.11; C 18.15

C 18.28:nos.
DOMESTIC COMMERCE SERIES.

C 18.29:CT
CONVERSION TABLES.

C 18.30:nos.
ELECTRICAL STANDARDS.

C 18.31:CT
PRESS NOTICES.

C 18.32:nos.
DOMESTIC COMMERCE. [Irregular]
  Later C 1.25

C 18.32/2:nos.
DOMESTIC COMMERCE NEWS LETTER. [Monthly]

C 18.33:nos.
DISTRIBUTION COST STUDIES.

C 18.34:nos.
FOREIGN PORT SERIES.

C 18.35:vol.
SURVEY OF CURRENT BUSINESS. [Monthly]

  Changed from C 3.33
  Later C 43.8

C 18.35/2:CT
– SPECIAL SUPPLEMENTS.
    Earlier C 18.2:In 2/2
    Later C 43.8/3

C 18.36:date
SURVEY OF CURRENT BUSINESS, WEEKLY
  SUPPLEMENT.
    Earlier C 3.34
    Later C 43.8/2

C 18.37:date
SURVEY OF CURRENT BUSINESS, ANNUAL
  SUPPLEMENT.
    Later C 43.8/4

C 18.38:CT
AID FOR ANALYZING MARKETS (by States).
  Changed from C 18.2

C 18.39:CT
BIBLIOGRAPHIES (including reading lists).
  Changed from C 18.Z/1

C 18.40:CT
RADIO TALKS.
  Changed from C 18.Z/2

C 18.41:nos.
MARKET RESEARCH SERIES.

C 18.42:nos.&CT
REAL PROPERTY INVENTORY.

C 18.43:nos.
ADVERTISING ABROAD. [Monthly]

C 18.44:CT
ADVERTISING MEDIA IN CERTAIN FOREIGN COUN-
  TRIES.

C 18.45:nos.
AERONAUTICAL WORLD NEWS.

C 18.46:vol.
AERONAUTICS EXPORT NEWS. [Weekly]

C 18.47:nos.
AGRICULTURAL IMPLEMENTS & FARM EQUIPMENT,
  MONTHLY EXPORT AND IMPORT BULLETIN.

C 18.49:nos.
AUTOMOTIVE WORLD NEWS.

C 18.50:vol.
BIMONTHLY REVIEW OF MEDICINAL PREPARATION
  EXPORTS.

C 18.51:vol.
BIMONTHLY REVIEW OF TOILET PREPARATIONS
  EXPORTS.

C 18.52:nos.-lets.
BOX SERIES.

C 18.52/2:nos.-lets.
CIGAR BOX SERIES.

C 18.53:date
BRITISH EXPORTS OF ELECTRICAL APPARATUS.
  [Monthly]

C 18.54:nos.
BUILDING ABROAD. [Fortnightly]

C 18.54/2:date
BUSINESS SITUATION AT HOME AND ABROAD.
  [Weekly]

C 18.55:date
CHEMICALS AND ALLIED PRODUCTS ENTERED FOR
  CONSUMPTION.

C 18.57:date
COMMERCIAL NOTES ON CANADA. [Weekly]

C 18.59/1:nos.-lets.
COMPARISONS OF INTERNATIONAL GRAY CLOTH
  PRICES. [Quarterly]

C 18.59/2:nos.
CONSTRUCTION ABROAD, CONSTRUCTION CIRCU-
  LAR NO.

C 18.60:nos.
COOPERAGE SERIES.

C 18.61:letters
COST OF CURRENT SERIES. (Electrical Equipment
  Division)

C 18.62:nos.-let.
COTTON GOODS IN WORLD MARKETS. [Weekly]

C 18.63:letters-nos.
CURRENT RELEASES OF NON-THEATRICAL FILM.

C 18.64:nos.
DISTRICT OFFICE RELEASES [Confidential]. [Weekly]

C 18.65:nos.
DOOR SERIES.

C 18.66:nos.-letters
DRY GOODS MERCHANTS' WORLD NEWS LETTER.
  [Monthly]

C 18.67:nos.
ELECTRICAL AND RADIO WORLD TRADE NEWS.

C 18.68:nos.
END-MATCHED SOFTWOOD LUMBER SERIES.

C 18.69:nos.
ESSENTIAL OIL PRODUCTION AND TRADE.

C 18.70:nos.
EUROPEAN FINANCIAL NOTES.

C 18.71:nos.
FAR EASTERN FINANCIAL NOTES.

C 18.72:date
FOOD STUFFS AROUND THE WORLD.

C 18.72/1:v.nos.
CANNED AND DRIED FOODS.

C 18.72/2:date
FISHERY NEWS. [Biweekly]

C 18.72/3:v.nos.
FRESH FRUITS AND VEGETABLES.

C 18.72/4:v.nos.
GRAIN AND GRAIN PRODUCTS. [Biweekly]

C 18.72/5:v.nos.
MEATS, LIVESTOCK, FATS AND OILS.

C 18.72/6:v.nos.
SUGAR, CONFECTIONERY, NUTS.

C 18.72/7:v.nos.
TROPICAL PRODUCTS.

C 18.72/8:v.nos.
WORLD DAIRY AND POULTRY NEWS SECTION.

C 18.72/9:v.nos.
WORLD NEWS ON RICE.

C 18.72/10:date
FOREIGN BEAN MARKET INFORMATION.

C 18.72/11:date
MONTHLY COMPARATIVE SALES OF CONFECTION-
  ERY.

  Later C 3.135

C 18.72/12:nos.
QUARTERLY CANNED FOODS STOCK REPORT.

  Later C 3.136

C 18.72/13:date
WEEKLY FRUIT EXPORTS.

C 18.73:v.nos.
FOREIGN COMMUNICATION NEWS.

C 18.74:date
FOREIGN CONSTRUCTION NEWS. [Weekly]

C 18.75:date
FOREIGN EXCHANGE RATES. [Monthly]

C 18.76:H-nos.
HARDWARE TRADE BULLETIN.

C 18.77:nos.
FOREIGN HIGHWAY NEWS. [Weekly]

C 18.78:nos.-letters
FOREIGN KNIT GOODS LETTER: SPECIAL BULLE-
TINS.

C 18.79:v.nos.
COMPARATIVE LAW SERIES, MONTHLY WORLD
REVIEW.

C 18.80:letters
FOREIGN LUMBER TARIFF SERIES.

C 18.81:nos.
FOREIGN MARKET BULLETIN.

C 18.82:nos.
FOREIGN MARKETS FOR BUILDERS' HARDWARE
[Confidential].

C 18.83:nos.
FOREIGN MARKETS FOR HAND TOOLS [Confiden-
tial].

C 18.84:nos.
FOREIGN MARKETS FOR HEATING AND COOKING
APPLIANCES [Confidential].

C 18.85:nos.
FOREIGN MARKETS FOR SCALES AND OTHER
WEIGHING DEVICES.

C 18.85/2:nos.
FOREIGN MARKETS FOR METALS & MINERALS
CIRCULARS.
Earlier C 18.91/2

C 18.86:nos.-letters
FOREIGN PETROLEUM STATISTICS.

C 18.86/2:nos.
FOREIGN PETROLEUM STATISTICS. [Monthly]

C 18.87:CT
FOREIGN RADIO BROADCASTING SERVICES.

C 18.88:v.nos.
FOREIGN RAILWAY NEWS.
C 18.88/2:nos.-letters
FOREIGN RAILWAY NEWS, WEEKLY [Confidential].
[Weekly]

C 18.88/3:nos.
– SUPPLEMENTS [Confidential].

C 18.88/4:nos.
– SPECIAL CIRCULARS.

C 18.89:v.nos.
FOREIGN SHIPPING NEWS.

C 18.90:nos.
FOREIGN TRADE MARK APPLICATION SERVICE.
Publications designated FTA-nos.

C 18.91:nos.
FOREIGN TRADE NOTES, MINERALS AND METALS
AND PETROLEUM. [Biweekly]

C 18.91/2:v.nos.
FOREIGN TRADE NOTES, MINERALS AND METALS.
[Monthly]
Later C 18.85/2

C 18.91/3:v.nos.
FOREIGN TRADE NOTES, PETROLEUM. [Biweekly]

C 18.92:nos.-letters
FOREIGN YEAR TRADE NOTES.

C 18.92/2:nos.
FOREST PRODUCTS DIVISION CIRCULARS.

C 18.92/3:nos.-letters
FOREST PRODUCTS DIVISION PAPER CIRCULARS
[Confidential].

C 18.93:nos.
FUR BEARING ANIMALS ABROAD, NEWS JOTTINGS
FROM FIELD FOR AMERICAN BREEDERS, BUL-
LETINS.

C 18.94:nos.-letters
FUR TRADE DEVELOPMENTS. [Monthly]

C 18.95:nos.
GENERAL LEGAL BULLETIN, FOREIGN LAWS
AFFECTING AMERICAN BUSINESS.

C 18.96/1:nos.
GEOGRAPHIC SECTION, STATISTICAL RESEARCH
DIVISION, SPECIAL CIRCULARS.

C 18.96/2:v.nos.
GEOGRAPHIC NEWS.

C 18.97:nos.
IMPLEMENTS & TRACTOR NOTES.

C 18.98:nos.
INDUSTRIAL MACHINERY LETTERS. [Semimonthly]

C 18.99:nos.
INDUSTRIAL PROPERTY BULLETIN.

C 18.99/2:nos.
INSURANCE AND LABOR LAW SERIES.

C 18.100:date
INTERNATIONAL COAL TRADE. [Monthly]

C 18.101:nos.-letters
INTERNATIONAL KNIT GOODS NEWS. [Monthly]
Earlier C 18.78

C 18.102:v.nos.
INTERNATIONAL PETROLEUM TRADE. [Monthly]

C 18.103:nos.
IRISH FREE STATE TRACTOR EXPORTS.

C 18.104:nos.
IRON AND STEEL FORTNIGHTLY.

C 18.104/2:v.nos.& supp.nos.
– SUPPLEMENTS.

C 18.106:nos.
LATIN AMERICAN CIRCULARS.

C 18.107:nos.
LATIN AMERICAN FINANCIAL NOTES.

C 18.108:nos.
LEATHER ADVERTISING CIRCULARS. [Monthly]

C 18.109:nos.
LEATHER FOREIGN MARKETS BULLETINS.

C 18.109/2:nos.
FOREIGN MARKETS BULLETINS FOR RAW MATERI-
ALS.

C 18.110:nos.
LEATHER FORTNIGHTLY.

C 18.111:nos.
LEATHER MANUFACTURERS ADVERTISING
CIRCULARS. [Monthly]

C 18.112:nos.
LEATHER MANUFACTURERS REST IN FOREIGN
MARKETS.

C 18.113:nos.-letters
LINENS AND LACES. [Monthly]

C 18.114:nos.-letters
LUMBER TARIFF MANUALS.

C 18.114/2:nos.
MANUAL OF FOREIGN LUMBER TARIFFS.

C 18.115:nos.-letters
MOTION PICTURES ABROAD.

C 18.116:nos.-let & let-nos.
MOTION PICTURES EDUCATIONAL [AND] INDUS-
TRIAL.

C 18.116/2:date
MOTION PICTURE THEATERS THROUGHOUT THE
WORLD. [Annual]

C 18.117:nos. & nos.lets
NEW USES OF COTTON SERIES.

C 18.118:nos.
PLUMBING SUPPLIES REPORTS.

C 18.119:nos.-letters
POLE SERIES [Confidential].

C 18.120:CT
WORLD RADIO MARKETS.

C 18.120/2:CT
WORLD RADIO MARKETS SERIES.

C 18.120/3:date
RADIO MARKETS CHECKLIST OF CIRCULARS.

C 18.120/4:date
WORLD RADIO MARKETS, INDEX.

C 18.121:date
RAYON AND OTHER SYNTHETIC TEXTILE FIBER
IMPORTS. [Monthly]

C 18.122::nos.
RUG AND FLOOR COVERING MATERIAL NOTES.
[Quarterly]

C 18.123:nos.
RUSSIAN ECONOMIC NOTES.

C 18.124:v.nos.
SIDE RUNS OF PAPER TRADE.

C 18.125:nos.-letters
SILK AND RAYON AND OTHER SYNTHETIC TEXTILE
FIBERS. [Monthly]

C 18.126:nos.-letters
SISAL, HEMP, JUTE AND MISCELLANEOUS FIBERS.
[Monthly]

C 18.127:nos.
SPECIAL BULLETINS, TEXTILE DIVISION.

C 18.128:v.nos.
SPECIAL CEMENT BULLETINS.

C 18.130/1:nos.
SPECIAL CIRCULARS, AGRICULTURAL IMPLEMENTS
DIVISION.

C 18.130/2:nos.
SPECIAL CIRCULARS: EXPORTS OF HARVESTERS
& BINDERS & COMBINES FROM THE UNITED
STATES. [Monthly]

C 18.131:nos.
SPECIAL CIRCULARS, AUTOMOTIVE DIVISION [Con-
fidential].

C 18.131/2:nos.
SPECIAL CIRCULARS, AUTOMOTIVE-AERONAUTICS
TRADE DIVISION. [Irregular]

C 18.132:nos.
SPECIAL CIRCULARS, CHEMICAL DIVISION.

C 18.133:nos.
SPECIAL CIRCULARS, COMMERCIAL LACES DIVI-
SION.

C 18.134:nos.
SPECIAL CIRCULARS, ELECTRICAL EQUIPMENT
DIVISION.

C 18.135:nos.
SPECIAL CIRCULARS, FINANCE DIVISION.

C 18.136:nos.
SPECIAL CIRCULARS, FOODSTUFFS DIVISION.

C 18.137:nos.
SPECIAL CIRCULARS, FOREIGN CONSTRUCTION
DIVISION.

C 18.138:nos.
SPECIAL CIRCULARS, INDUSTRIAL MACHINERY
DIVISION.

C 18.139:nos.
SPECIAL CIRCULARS, IRON & STEEL DIVISION.
Later C 18.141/2

C 18.140/1:nos.
SPECIAL CIRCULARS, LEATHER & RUBBER DIVI-
SION.

C 18.140/2:nos.
RUBBER NEWS LETTER. [Semimonthly]
Earlier C 18.143

C 18.141:nos.
SPECIAL CIRCULARS, LUMBER DIVISION.

C 18.141/2:nos.
IRON AND STEEL FORTNIGHTLY, INTERMEDIATE
ISSUE.
Earlier C 18.139

C 18.142:nos.
SPECIAL CIRCULAR.

C 18.143:nos.
SPECIAL CIRCULARS, RUBBER DIVISION.
Later C 18.140/2

C 18.145:nos.
SPECIAL CIRCULARS, TRANSPORTATION DIVISION
[Confidential].

C 18.146:nos.
SPECIAL SERIES, PAPER DIVISION.

C 18.147:nos.
TARIFF CORRECTION CIRCULAR.

C 18.148:nos.-letters
TEXTILE MAINTENANCE NOTES. [Monthly]

C 18.149:nos.
TEXTILE RAW MATERIALS.

C 18.150:nos.
TEXTILE AND ALLIED PRODUCTS.

C 18.151:nos.& nos.let.
TIE SERIES.

C 18.152:nos.
TOBACCO MARKETS AND CONDITIONS ABROAD.

C 18.152/2:date
U.S. EXPORT & IMPORT TRADE IN LEAF AND MANU-
FACTURED TOBACCO.

C 18.153:CT
TRADE LIST.
Later C 42.10

C 18.154:date
MONTHLY TRADE REPORT, CHINA.

C 18.155:date
MONTHLY TRADE REPORT, JAPAN.

C 18.156:date
QUARTERLY TRADE REPORT, SOUTHEASTERN
ASIA.

C 18.157:vol.
TRADE REVIEW OF CANADA.

C 18.158:date
VALUES OF GERMAN EXPORTS OF ELECTRICAL
APPARATUS & EQUIPMENT. [Monthly]

C 18.159:nos.-let nos.
VENEER AND PLYWOOD SERIES.

C 18.160:nos.
VITAL STATISTICS OF LATIN AMERICA.

C 18.161:nos.-letters
WEARING APPAREL IN WORLD MARKETS. [Monthly]

C 18.162:nos.-letters
WEEKLY COTTON SERVICE BULLETINS.

C 18.163:nos.
WORLD LUMBER DIGEST.

C 18.164:nos.
WORLD ELECTRICAL MARKETS.
Later C 18.220/3

C 18.165:vol.
WORLD RETAIL PRICES AND TAXES ON GASOLINE,
KEROSENE AND MOTOR LUBRICATING OILS.
[Quarterly]

C 18.166:date
WORLD SURVEY OF FOREIGN RAILWAYS.

C 18.167:nos.-letters
WORLD TRADE IN COAL TAR TIES.

C 18.168:nos.
WORLD TRADE IN DENTAL PREPARATIONS (WTDP-
nos).

C 18.169:nos.
WORLD TRADE IN EXPLOSIVES.

C 18.170:nos.
WORLD TRADE IN INSECTICIDES.

C 18.171:nos.
WORLD TRADE PAINTS AND VARNISHES.

C 18.172:nos.
WORLD TRADE IN PLASTIC PAINTS.

C 18.173:nos.
WORLD TRADE IN PLASTICS.

C 18.174:nos.
WORLD TRADE IN PREPARED MEDICINES.

C 18.175:nos.
WORLD TRADE IN SYNTHETIC AROMATICS.

C 18.176:nos.
WORLD TRADE IN TOILET PREPARATIONS.

C 18.177:nos.
WORLD TRADE IN VETERINARY PREPARATIONS.

C 18.178:nos.
WORLD TRADE IN WOOD, FURNITURE, FLOOR,
METAL AND AUTOMOBILE POLISHES.

C 18.179:v.nos.
WORLD TRADE NOTES ON CHEMICALS AND AL-
LIED PRODUCTS.

C 18.180:date
WORLD WIDE MOTION PICTURE DEVELOPMENTS.

C 18.181:nos.-letters
WORLD'S WOOL DIGEST. [Weekly]

C 18.182
BUSINESS INFORMATION SERVICE.
Superseded by C 18.228

C 18.183
BUSINESS INFORMATION SERVICE.

C 18.184:CT
BASIC DATA ON IMPORT TRADE AND TRADE
BARRIERS.

C 18.185:nos.
UNITED STATES FOREIGN TRADE STATISTICS.

C 18.186:nos.
LEATHER RAW MATERIALS BULLETIN.

C 18.186/2:nos.
INTERNATIONAL TRADE IN GOAT SKINS.

C 18.186/3:nos.
INTERNATIONAL TRADE IN SHEEP SKINS.

C 18.187:v.nos.
WORLD MACHINERY NEWS.

C 18.188:CT
FINANCIAL DATA ON HOUSING, PRELIMINARY.

C 18.189:date
MONTHLY TRADE REVIEW OF FRANCE.

C 18.190:date
TREND OF U.S. FOREIGN TRADE. [Monthly]

C 18.191::vol.
HOME AND ABROAD WITH BUREAU OF FOREIGN
AND DOMESTIC COMMERCE. [Fortnightly]

C 18.192:nos.
[FOREIGN TARIFFS.]

C 18.193:nos.
NEGRO AFFAIRS DIVISION, BULLETINS.

Division transferred to Census Bureau July
1, 1937.
Later C 3.131

C 18.194:vol.
DIGEST OF TRADE HINTS FOR PAINT AND VARNISH
MERCHANTS.

C 18.195:date
MANUFACTURERS SALES AND COLLECTIONS ON
ACCOUNTS RECEIVABLE.

C 18.196:date
WHOLESALE TRADE. [Monthly]

C 18.197:date
MANCHURIAN SOY BEAN TRADE.

C 18.198:date
U.S. FOREIGN TRADE IN PULP AND PAPER. [Monthly]

C 18.199:date
PHILIPPINE COPRA MARKET.

C 18.199/2:date nos.
PHILIPPINE COPRA MARKET. [Weekly]
Earlier C 18.185:3043

C 18.200:CT
LIST OF STATE AND LOCAL TRADE ASSOCIATIONS
(by states).

C 18.200/2:CT
STATE-LOCAL BUSINESSMEN'S ORGANIZATIONS.

C 18.201:vol.
RUBBER PRODUCTS TRADE NEWS.

C 18.202:nos.
EXPORT MARKET SERIES.

C 18.203:vol.
FOODSTUFFS AROUND THE WORLD.

C 18.204:CT
TRADE OF THE UNITED STATES WITH.

C 18.205:v.nos.
TARIFF ITEM.

C 18.206:nos.
ECONOMIC SERIES.

C 18.207:date
TRADE OF U.S. WITH JAPAN, CHINA, HONG KONG,
AND KWANTUNG. [Monthly]

C 18.208:v.nos.
FOREIGN INLAND WATERWAY NEWS, INTER-
COASTAL WATERWAYS, RIVERS, LAKES,
CANALS, EQUIPMENT. [Monthly]

C 18.209:date
TUNG OIL MONTHLY, PRODUCTION IN AMERICA,
FOREIGN TRADE, ETC.

Prior to December 1983, see C 18.185:2890.

C 18.210:CT
ADDRESSES.

C 18.211:CT
U.S. FOREIGN TRADE (by commodities).
    Title varies.
    Changed from C 18.2

C 18.212:date
CURRENT DEVELOPMENTS IN DRUG DISTRIBU-
    TION. [Monthly]

C 18.213:date
CURRENT DEVELOPMENTS IN ELECTRICAL TRADE.
    [Monthly]

C 18.214:date
CURRENT DEVELOPMENTS IN FOOD DISTRIBU-
    TION. [Monthly]

C 18.215:date
CURRENT DISTRIBUTION DEVELOPMENTS IN HARD-
    WARE AND ALLIED TRADES. [Monthly]

C 18.216:vol.
AUTOMOTIVE FOREIGN TRADE MANUAL.

C 18.217:CT
REGULATIONS, RULES, AND INSTRUCTIONS.
    Includes Handbooks and Manuals.

C 18.218:date
FOOD EXPORTS AND IMPORTS. [Monthly]

C 18.219:date
INDUSTRIAL BANKING, COMPANIES, INSTALLMENT
    LOANS TO CONSUMERS. [Monthly]

C 18.220:pt.nos.   • Item 231
INDUSTRIAL REFERENCE SERVICE.
    Later C 34.10
    Discontinued.

C 18.220/2:CT
RADIO, TELEPHONE, TELEGRAPH.
    Earlier C 18.20

C 18.220/3:nos.
WORLD ELECTRICAL MARKETS.
    Earlier C 18.164

C 18.221:nos.
INDUSTRIAL REFERENCE SERVICE, BUSINESS
    SERVICE.

C 18.222:date
PERSONAL FINANCE COMPANIES, INSTALLMENT
    LOANS TO CONSUMERS. [Monthly]

C 18.223:vol.   • Item 226
INTERNATIONAL REFERENCE SERVICE.
    Later C 34.11
    Discontinued.

C 18.223/2:nos.
REPORTS ON GENEVA TARIFF CONCESSIONS.

C 18.224:date
INDUSTRY SURVEY: MANUFACTURERS' INVENTO-
    RIES, SHIPMENTS, INCOMING BUSINESS [AND]
    UNFILLED ORDERS. [Monthly]
    Later C 43.9

C 18.225:nos.
INDUSTRIAL SERIES.

C 18.226:date
CREDIT UNIONS, INSTALLMENT LOANS TO CON-
    SUMERS. [Monthly]

C 18.227:CT
MARKETING LAWS SURVEY PUBLICATIONS.

C 18.228:CT
INQUIRY REFERENCE SERVICE.
    Supersedes C 18.182
    Later C 41.8/3; C 42.9

C 18.228/2:CT
INQUIRY REFERENCE SERVICE: COUNTY BASIC
    DATA SHEETS, SELECTED COUNTIES BY
    STATES.

C 18.229:date
PULP AND PAPER INDUSTRY REPORTS. [Monthly]
    Later C 40.11

C 18.230:date   • Item 222
INDUSTRY REPORTS: LUMBER. [Monthly]
    Discontinued.

C 18.231:date   • Item 225
INDUSTRY REPORTS: SUGAR, MOLASSES AND
    CONFECTIONARY. [Monthly]
    Discontinued.

C 18.232:date
INDUSTRY REPORTS: DOMESTIC TRANSPORTA-
    TION. [Monthly]

C 18.233:date
INDUSTRY REPORT: CONSTRUCTION AND CON-
    STRUCTION MATERIALS. [Monthly]
    Later C 40.10

C 18.234:date   • Item 216
INDUSTRY REPORT: CANNED FRUITS AND VEG-
    ETABLES, PRODUCTION AND WHOLESALE DIS-
    TRIBUTION.
    Discontinued.

C 18.235:date   • Item 217
INDUSTRY REPORT: CHEMICALS AND ALLIED PROD-
    UCTS. [Monthly]
    Discontinued.

C 18.236:date
INDUSTRY REPORT: CRUDE DRUGS, GUMS,
    BALSAMS, AND ESSENTIAL OILS. [Monthly]

C 18.237:date
INDUSTRY REPORT: DRUGS AND PHARMACEUTI-
    CALS. [Monthly]

C 18.238:date   • Item 221
INDUSTRY REPORT: FATS AND OILS. [Monthly]
    Discontinued.

C 18.239:date
INDUSTRY REPORT: LEATHER. [Monthly]

C 18.240:date   • Item 218
INDUSTRY REPORT: COFFEE, TEA, AND SPICES.
    [Quarterly]
    Discontinued.

C 18.241:date   • Item 224
INDUSTRY REPORT: RUBBER. [Bimonthly]
    Discontinued.

C 18.242:date
CONTAINERS AND PACKAGING. [Quarterly]
    Later C 40.13

C 18.266:nos.
CURRENT EXPORT BULLETINS.
    Earlier Pr 32.5807
    Later C 42.11/2

C 18.267:nos.
COMPREHENSIVE EXPORT SCHEDULES.
    Earlier Pr 32.5808
    Later C 42.1

C 18.268:nos.
SMALL BUSINESS AIDS.
    Later C 40.7/2

C 18.269:v.nos.&nos.
BULLETIN OF COMMERCE.
    Later C 41.10

C 18.270:date   • Item 210
BUSINESS ESTABLISHMENT, EMPLOYMENT AND
    TAXABLE PAY ROLLS UNDER OLD-AGE AND
    SURVIVORS INSURANCE PROGRAM.
    Later C 3.204
    Discontinued.

C 18.271:nos.   • Item 213
[DOMESTIC COMMERCE SERIES.]
    Discontinued.

C 18.272:date
AMERICAN CONVENTIONS. [Quarterly]

C 18.273:nos.   • Item 227
[INTERNATIONAL TRADE SERIES.]
    Discontinued.

C 18.274:nos.   • Item 230
TRANSPORTATION SERIES.
    Discontinued.

C 18.275:nos.   • Item 209
[BUSINESS ECONOMICS SERIES.]
    Discontinued.

C 18.276:nos.
COMMERCIAL STANDARDS.
    Earlier C 13.20
    Later C 41.25

C 18.277:nos.
SIMPLIFIED PRACTICE RECOMMENDATIONS.
    Earlier C 13.12/1
    Later C 41.20

C 18.278
FOREIGN TRANSACTIONS OF U.S. GOVERNMENT.
    [Quarterly]

C 18.279
FOREIGN AID BY THE U.S. GOVERNMENT.
    [Quarterly]
    Later C 43.11

C 18.280
WORLD TRADE DIRECTORY REPORTS.

C 18.281:nos.
BUSINESS NEWS REPORTS OBE [releases].
    Later C 43.7

C 18.281/2:nos.
OFFICE OF INDUSTRY AND COMMERCE RELEASES
    OIC (series).

C 18.281/3:nos.
OFFICE OF INTERNATIONAL TRADE RELEASES OIT
    (series).

C 18.282
WORLD ECONOMIC NOTES.

C 18.283
DOMESTIC TRADE DIGEST.

C 18.284:nos.
SYNOPSIS OF U.S. GOVERNMENT PROPOSED
    PROCUREMENT AND CONTRACT AWARDS.
    [Daily, Monday through Friday except Federal le-
    gal holidays]
    Later C 41.9

C 18.285:date
DOMESTIC ECONOMIC DEVELOPMENTS, WEEKLY
    BUSINESS INDICATORS.

C 18.285/2:date
DOMESTIC ECONOMIC DEVELOPMENTS, MONTHLY
    BUSINESS INDICATORS. [Weekly]

CHILDREN'S BUREAU
(1912– 1913)

CREATION AND AUTHORITY

    The Children's Bureau was created by act of
Congress of April 9, 1912 (37 Stat. 79, as
amended; 42 U.S.C. 191 et seq.). The Bureau
was transferred to the newly created Department
of Labor (L 5) by act of March 4, 1913 (37 Stat.
737; 5 U.S.C. 616).

C 19.1:date
ANNUAL REPORTS.
    Later L 5.1

C 19.2:CT
GENERAL PUBLICATIONS.
    Later L 5.2

C 19.3:nos.
BULLETINS.

C 19.4:nos.
CIRCULARS.

C 19.5:nos.
MONOGRAPHS.
Later L 5.8

WASTE RECLAMATION SERVICE
(1919)

CREATION AND AUTHORITY

The Waste Reclamation Service was established within the Department of Commerce on January 1, 1919. The Service ceased to function on June 30, 1919.

C 20.1:date
ANNUAL REPORTS.

C 20.2:CT
GENERAL PUBLICATIONS.

C 20.3
BULLETINS.

C 20.4
CIRCULARS.

PATENT AND TRADEMARK OFFICE
(1975–   )

CREATION AND AUTHORITY

The Patent Office (I 23) was transferred from the Department of the Interior to the Department of Commerce by Executive Order 4175 of March 17, 1925. The name was changed to Patent and Trademark Office by act of January 2, 1975 (88 Stat. 1949; 35 U.S.C. 1 note).

INFORMATION

General Information Services Division
Patent and Trademark Office
Crystal Plaza 3, Rm. 2002
Washington, DC 20231
(703) 308-4455
http://www.uspto.gov

C 21.1:date
ANNUAL REPORTS TO CONGRESS (calendar years). 1925–1927.

Prior to April 1, 1925, see I 23.1/1

C 21.1/2　　　　　　　• Item 251 (MF)
ANNUAL REPORT OF THE COMMISSIONER OF PATENTS. 1837–　[Annual]

C 21.1/3　　　　　　　• Item 251-A (EL)
TRADEMARK PUBLIC ADVISORY COMMITTEE ANNUAL REPORT.

C 21.1/4　　　　　　　• Item 251-A-1 (EL)
PATENT PUBLIC ADVISORY COMMITTEE ANNUAL REPORT.

C 21.2:CT　　　　　　　• Item 254
GENERAL PUBLICATIONS.

C 21.2:T 67　　　　　　　• Item 254
GENERAL INFORMATION CONCERNING TRADEMARKS. [Irregular]

C 21.3　　　　　　　• Item 252
CLASSIFICATION BULLETINS. 1–　[Irregular]

Contain changes in classification of patents as well as definitions of new and revised classes and subclasses.

C 21.3/2:nos./date　　　　　• 252-A (MF)
PATENT CLASSIFICATION DEFINITIONS. [Irregular]

PURPOSE:– To describe new and revised classes and subclasses and changes in the classification of patents as necessary. Under the Patent Office classification system, U.S. patents are classified on a subject basis under approximately 310 classes and 65,000 sub-classes.
AUDIENCE:– Patent searchers, librarians, patent attorneys, researchers, or any person using the Patent Office Search Center or other collections of U.S. patents.
Also published in microfiche (24x).

Discontinued.

C 21.3/3:　　　　　　　• Item 252-A (MF)
RECLASSIFICATION ORDERS (series).

Reclassification orders are related to List of Patent Classification Definitions, C 21.3/2, but each is a one time issuance in the nature of a newspaper.

C 21.4:
CIRCULARS [none issued].

C 21.5:v.nos.&nos.　　• Item 260-A (P)
　　　　　　　　　• Item 260-B (MF)
OFFICIAL GAZETTE OF UNITED STATES PATENT OFFICE: PATENTS. v. 1–　[Weekly]

This publication is the official journal relating to patents and trademarks. It is issued each Tuesday simultaneously with the weekly issue of patents. It contains a select figure of the drawings and one claim of each patent granted on that day, an illustration of each trademark published for opposition, a list of trademarks registered, and other trademark information; decisions in patent and trademark cases rendered by the courts and the Patent Office; notices of patent and trademark suits; index of patentees; disclaimers filed; list of patents available for license or sale; and much general information such as orders, notices, changes in rules, changes in classification, etc.
Each calendar month covers one volume, consisting of four or five issues. A title page, list of contents, etc. is issued for each volume and included in the subscription.
Citation: O. G. Pat. Off.
ISSN 0098-1133

C 21.5/a 1:v.nos.
– SEPARATES. CLASSIFICATION OF PATENTS. [Weekly]

Changed from I 12.8/a 3

C 21.5/a 2
DECISION LEAFLETS. [Weekly]

Decisions of the Commissioner of Patents and U.S. Courts; register of patents available for license or sale; tabulation of condition of work in each examining division.

C 21.5/a 3
TRADEMARK SUPPLEMENT. [Weekly]

Contains trademark notices, trademark applications published for opposition, list of trademark applicants, classified list of registered trademarks.

C 21.5/a 4:v.nos.
– INDEX. [Weekly]

C 21.5/a 5:CT　　　　　• Item 260
– SEPARATES, MISCELLANEOUS.
Changed from I 23.8/a 6
See C 21.5/5

C 21.5/a 6:date
– SEPARATES. CHANGED IN CLASSIFICATION OF INVENTIONS. [Irregular]
Changed from I 23.8/a 2

C 21.5/a 7:v.nos.
– SEPARATES. APPLICATIONS VESTED IN ALIEN PROPERTY CUSTODIAN.

C 21.5/a 8
PATENT ABSTRACT SECTION. 1968–　[Weekly]

Extract from the Official Gazette of the Patent Office containing the descriptive matter relating to patents only.

　　　　　　　　　• Item 255-A (P)
C 21.5/2:date　　　　　• Item 255-B (MF)
INDEX OF PATENTS ISSUED FROM THE PATENT OFFICE. 1920–　[Annual]

Beginning with the 1966 edition, issued in two volumes:
Part 1. List of Patentees.
Part 2. Index to Subjects of Inventions.
Contains cross reference index, which presents an index according to the original patent classification and an index according to the cross-reference classification.

　　　　　　　　　• Item 256-C (P)
C 21.5/3　　　　　　　• Item 256-D (MF)
INDEX OF TRADEMARKS ISSUED FROM THE PATENT OFFICE. [Annual]

Contains an alphabetical index of trademark registrants, registration numbers, dates published, classification of goods for which registered, and decisions published. Index for the calendar year.
ISSN 0099-0809

　　　　　　　　　• Item 260-C (P)
C 21.5/4:v.nos.&nos.　　• Item 260-D (MF)
OFFICIAL GAZETTE OF U.S. PATENT OFFICE, TRADEMARKS. v. 883–　1971–　[Weekly]

Earlier: Part of Official Gazette, C 21.5, prior to v. 883.
ISSN 0360-5132

C 21.5/4/a:date　　　　　• Item 260
PATENT AND TRADEMARK OFFICE NOTICES. [Weekly]
Reprinted from the Official Gazette.

C 21.5/4-2:date　　　　　• Item 260
PATENT AND TRADEMARK OFFICE NOTICES. [Annual]

C 21.5/5:date　　　　　• Item 260-C
CONSOLIDATED LISTING OF OFFICIAL GAZETTE NOTICES RE PATENT AND TRADEMARK OFFICE PRACTICES AND PROCEDURES, PATENT NOTICES. [Annual]
Earlier C 21.5/a 5

C 21.6　　　　　　　• Item 253
DECISIONS OF THE COMMISSIONER OF PATENTS AND OF UNITED STATES COURTS IN PATENT AND TRADEMARK CASES. 1869–　[Annual]

Cumulation of the decisions printed in the weekly Official Gazette.
Also published in the House Documents series.
Discontinued.

C 21.7　　　　　　　• Item 261
PATENT LAWS. [Irregular]

A compilation of the patent laws in force. Latest edition: January 3, 1961.

C 21.7/2:date
U.S. STATUTES CONCERNING THE REGISTRATION OF TRADEMARKS.
Earlier I 23.11/2

C 21.7/3:date
U.S. STATUTES CONCERNING THE REGISTRATION OF PRINTS AND LABELS.
Earlier I 23.11/3

C 21.7/4 • **Item 261**
TRADEMARK LAWS. [Irregular]

Compilation of trademark laws in force. Latest edition: January 1, 1959.

C 21.8:date • **Item 263**
RULES OF PRACTICE.
Earlier I 23.13
Discontinued.

C 21.9 • **Item 262-A (MF)**
ROSTER OF ATTORNEYS AND AGENTS REGISTERED TO PRACTICE BEFORE THE U.S. PATENT OFFICE. [Irregular]
See C 21.9/2

C 21.9/2 • **Item 262-A (MF) (EL)**
PATENT ATTORNEYS AND AGENTS AVAILABLE TO REPRESENT INVENTORS BEFORE THE UNITED STATES PATENT OFFICE.

A list of those registered patent attorneys and agents who are available to accept employment by inventors. It includes the names of those who are full-time employees of corporations who have stated that they are, nevertheless, free to represent clients other than their employers.

C 21.10:CT
BRIEFS.
Earlier I 23.15

C 21.11:date
SPECIFICATIONS AND DRAWINGS OF PATENTS.
Earlier I 23.14

C 21.12 • **Item 258**
MANUAL OF CLASSIFICATION. [Irregular]

Contains a list of all the classes and subclasses of inventions in the Patent Office classification of patents, subject matter index and other information relating to classification.
Subscription includes basic volume, issued in loose-leaf form and punched for 3-ring binder, plus revised pages for approximately two years.
ISSN 0145-0654

C 21.12/2:date • **Item 257**
INDEX TO U.S. PATENT CLASSIFICATION SYSTEM.

Included in subscription to Manual of Classification.

C 21.12/3:date/nos.
INDEX TO THE U.S. PATENT CLASSIFICATION. [Semiannual]

C 21.13:date
PATENT OFFICE NEWS LETTER. [Monthly]

C 21.14:CT • **Item 262**
REGULATIONS, RULES, AND INSTRUCTIONS.

C 21.14:P 27 • **Item 262**
RULES OF PRACTICE IN PATENT CASES. [Irregular] (Includes basic manual plus supplementary material for an indefinite period)

C 21.14:T 67/2 • **Item 254-A**
TRADEMARK RULES OF PRACTICE OF THE PATENT OFFICE, WITH FORMS AND STATUTES. [Irregular] (Includes basic volume plus supplementary material for an indefinite period)

C 21.14/2:CT • **Item 254-A**
HANDBOOKS, MANUALS, GUIDES.

C 21.14/3:nos. • **Item 254-A**
SUPERVISOR AND PERSONNEL ADMINISTRATION (numbered). 1–

C 21.15 • **Item 259 (EL)**
MANUAL OF PATENT EXAMINING PROCEDURES. [Irregular]

PURPOSE:– To serve primarily as a detailed reference work on patent examining practice and procedure for use by the Examining Corps of the Patent Office.

Subscription includes basic manual plus supplementary service for an indefinite period. Issued in loose-leaf form and punched for 3-ring binder.
ISSN 0364-2453

C 21.15/2:nos. • **Item 256-A**
TRADEMARK EXAMINING PROCEDURE DIRECTIVES. 1– 1971– [Irregular] (Includes basic volume plus supplementary material for an indefinite period)
Discontinued.

C 21.16
[PRESS RELEASES] [Irregular]

C 21.17:CT
BIBLIOGRAPHIES AND LISTS OF PUBLICATIONS. [Irregular]

C 21.17/2:nos.
LIST OF RECENT ACCESSIONS AND FOREIGN PATENT TRANSLATIONS OF THE SCIENTIFIC LIBRARY. [Monthly]

C 21.18:nos.
RESEARCH AND DEVELOPMENT REPORTS. 1– [Irregular]

C 21.19:nos.
NOTES ON PATENT MATTERS. 1– [Irregular]

C 21.20:CT
ADDRESSES. [Irregular]

C 21.21:nos.
EMPLOYEE BULLETIN. 1–

C 21.22:CT
TRANSLATIONS OF [Foreign] PATENTS. [Irregular]

C 21.23:CT
PATENTS.

Class assigned for libraries wanting to assign SuDocs numbers to their patents.

C 21.24:CT • **Item 256-B (MF)**
OFFICE OF TECHNOLOGY AND FORECAST: PUBLICATIONS. [Irregular]
Discontinued.

C 21.24:T 22 • **Item 254**
TECHNOLOGY ASSESSMENT AND FORECAST, REPORT. 1st– 1973– [Semiannual] (Office of Technology Assessment and Forecast)

PURPOSE:– To review patent activity in selected portions of the patent file of over 11,000,000 patent documents and to disseminate such information to U.S. business, industry and the scientific and engineering communities.

C 21.25:CT • **Item 256-B (MF)**
PATENT PROFILES. [Irregular]
Discontinued.

C 21.26:date • **Item 256-A-1**
GENERAL INFORMATION CONCERNING TRADEMARKS. [Irregular]

PURPOSE:– To present a brief introduction to trademark matters, including definition and functions of trademarks and actions that must be taken by applicants. Revised and updated periodically.

C 21.26/2 • **Item 256-A-2 (P) (EL)**
GENERAL INFORMATION CONCERNING PATENTS. [Irregular]

PURPOSE:– To present general information on patents and the operation of the Patents and Trademark Office. Contains information on preparing an application, forms needed and fees.

C 21.27:date • **Item 255 (MF)**
PATENTEE/ASSIGNEE INDEX. [Quarterly]
Discontinued.

C 21.28:CT • **Item 254-B (MF)**
DIRECTORIES. [Irregular]

C 21.28/2 • **Item 254-B-2 (MF)**
INFORMATION DIRECTORY. [Quarterly]

C 21.30 • **Item 254-B-1 (EL)**
PRODUCTS AND SERVICES CATALOG. [Annual]

C 21.31:date • **Item 260-E**
USAPAT SUBSCRIBER NOTICE.

C 21.31:nos. • **Item 260-E (DVD)**
USAPAT, FACSIMILE IMAGES OF UNITED STATES PATENTS.
Issued on DVD.

C 21.31/2:date • **Item 154-B-4 (DVD)**
PATENTS BIB.
Issued on DVD.

C 21.31/3:date • **Item 154-B-5 (DVD)**
PATENTS CLASS, CURRENT CLASSIFICATIONS OF US PATENTS, ISSUED 1790 TO PRESENT.
Issued on DVD.

C 21.31/4:date • **Item 154-B-6 (E)**
PATENTS ASSIGN, U.S. PATENTS ASSIGNMENTS RECORDED AT THE USPTO 1980 AUGUST TO PRESENT.
Issued on CD-ROM.

C 21.31/5:date • **Item 154-B-7 (E)**
PATENTS ASSIST, FULL TEXT OF PATENT SEARCH TOOLS.
Issued on CD-ROM.

C 21.31/6:date • **Item 154-B-8**
PATENTS SNAP, CONCORDANCE OF U.S. PATENT APPLICATION SERIAL NUMBERS TO U.S. PATENT NUMBERS.
Issued on CD-ROM.
Ceased with 1998.

C 21.31/7:date • **Item 154-B-9 (E)**
TRADEMARKS REGISTERED, BIBLIOGRAPHIC INFORMATION FROM REGISTERED US TRADEMARKS.
Issued on CD-ROM.

Merged with C 21.31/14. See C21.31/18.

C 21.31/8:date • **Item 154-B-10 (E)**
TRADEMARKS PENDING, BIBLIOGRAPHIC INFORMATION FROM PENDING US TRADEMARKS.
Issued on CD-ROM.
Merged with C 21.31/14. See C21.31/18.

C 21.31/9:date • **Item 154-B-11**
TRADEMARKS ASSIGN, U.S. TRADEMARKS ASSIGNMENTS RECORDED AT THE USPTO.
Issued on CD-ROM.

C 21.31/10:date/nos. • **Item 154-B-12 (DVD)**
TRADEMARKS ASSIST.
Issued on DVD.

C 21.31/11:nos. • **Item 260-E-1 (CD)**
USAMARK: FASCIMILE IMAGES OF REGISTERED UNITED STATES TRADEMARKS.
Issued on CD-ROM.

C 21.31/12: • **Item 260-E-2 (EL)**
CASSIS CURRENTS NEWSLETTER.

C 21.31/13:date/nos. • **Item 154-H-2 (DVD)**
PATENTS AND TRADEMARKS, ASSIGN.
Issued on DVD-ROM.

C 21.31/14:date • **Item 154-H-3**
TRADEMARKS REGISTERED.
Issued on DVD-ROM.
Merged with C 21.31/8. See C 21.31/18.

C 21.31/16: • **Item 154-H-1 (DVD)**
PATENTS BIB AND PATENTS SNAP.
Issued on DVD-ROM.

C 21.31/17: • **Item 260-E-4 (EL)**
U.S. PATENT APPLICATIONS (database)

C 21.31/18: • **Item 154-H-7**
TRADEMARKS BIB.
Issued on DVD-ROM.
Previously C 21.31/8 and C 21.31/14

C 21.32: • Item 260-E-2 (E)
ELECTRONIC PRODUCTS (misc.)

C 21.33: • Item 260-E-2 (EL)
PTO PULSE. [Weekly]
Editions cumulate to monthly.

C 21.33/2 • Item 260-E-3 (EL)
USPTO TODAY. [Monthly]

C 21.33/2-2 • Item 260-E-3 (EL)
USPTO TODAY. [Quarterly]

BUREAU OF MINES
(1925– 1934)

CREATION AND AUTHORITY

The Bureau of Mines (I 28) was transferred from the Department of the Interior to the Department of Commerce by Executive Order 4239 of June 4, 1925, effective July 1, 1925 and returned to the Department of the Interior by Executive Order 6611 of February 22, 1934, effective April 23, 1934.

C 22.1:date
ANNUAL REPORTS.

C 22.2:CT
GENERAL PUBLICATIONS.

C 22.3:nos.
BULLETINS.

C 22.4
CIRCULARS.

C 22.5:nos.
TECHNICAL PAPERS.
Later I 28.7

C 22.6:nos.
MINERS' CIRCULARS.
Changed from I 28.6
Later I 28.6

C 22.7/1:date
PUBLICATIONS OF BUREAU OF MINES.

C 22.7/2:date
INDEX TO BUREAU OF MINES PUBLICATIONS.

C 22.7/3:nos.
NEW PUBLICATIONS.
Changed from I 28.5/2

C 22.8:date
MINERAL RESOURCES OF UNITED STATES (calendar years).
Changed from I 19.8
Later I 28.37

C 22.8/2:date
MINERALS YEARBOOK.
Later I 28.37

C 22.9:date
PETROLEUM STATISTICS. [Monthly]
Changed from I 28.8
Later I 28.18/2

C 22.9/2:date
PETROLEUM STATISTICS. [Annual]

C 22.10:nos.
SCHEDULES.
Changed from I 28.8

C 22.11:nos.
INFORMATION CIRCULARS.
Later I 28.27

C 22.12:nos.
REPORTS OF INVESTIGATIONS.
Later I 28.23

C 22.13:nos.
ECONOMIC PAPERS.
Later I 28.38

C 22.14:nos.
WEEKLY COAL REPORT.
Earlier I 19.30
Later I 28.33

C 22.15:nos.
MONTHLY COKE REPORT.
Later I 28.30

C 22.16:date
COMMERCIAL STOCKS OF COAL. [Quarterly]
First published intermittently.

C 22.17:date
PRELIMINARY ESTIMATES OF PRODUCTION OF COAL AND BEEHIVE COKE.
Later I 28.31

C 22.18:CT
RULES, REGULATIONS, AND INSTRUCTIONS HANDBOOKS.
Later I 28.16

C 22.19:nos.
COAL MINE FATALITIES. [Monthly]

C 22.19/2:date
COAL MINE FATALITIES. [Monthly]
Supersedes C 22.19
Later I 28.10/2

C 22.20:CT
MAPS.

C 22.21:nos.
GENERAL SURVEY OF CONDITIONS IN COAL INDUSTRY. [Monthly]

C 22.22:dt.&nos.
MONTHLY COAL MARKET SUMMARY.

C 22.23:nos.
MONTHLY COAL DISTRIBUTION REPORT.

C 22.24:nos.
MONOGRAPHS.
Later I 28.40

C 22.25:date
RECENT ARTICLES ON PETROLEUM AND ALLIED SUBSTANCES. [Monthly]

C 22.26/1:CT
MOTION-PICTURE FILMS, (Miscellaneous List).

C 22.26/2:date
MOTION-PICTURE FILMS. [Semiannual]
Later I 28.35

C 22.27:nos. • Item 255
BIBLIOGRAPHY OF FIRE HAZARDS AND PREVENTION AND SAFETY, IN PETROLEUM INDUSTRY.

C 22.28:nos.
MINERAL MARKET REPORTS.
Later I 28.28

C 22.29:nos.
MONTHLY CEMENT STATEMENT.
Later I 28.29

C 22.30:nos.
CONSUMPTION OF EXPLOSIVES. [Monthly]

C 22.31:nos.
HEALTH AND SAFETY STATISTICS.
Later I 28.26

C 22.32:nos.
GEOPHYSICAL ABSTRACTS. [Monthly]
Later I 28.25

C 22.33:nos.
QUARTERLY GYPSUM REPORTS.
Later I 28.32

C 22.34:date
STATISTICS OF BITUMINOUS COAL LOADED FOR SHIPMENT ON RAILROADS AND WATERWAYS AS REPORTED BY OPERATORS. [Annual]

C 22.35:nos.
QUESTION AND ANSWER HANDBOOKS.
Later I 28.48

BUREAU OF AIR COMMERCE
(1934– 1938)

CREATION AND AUTHORITY

The Aeronautics Branch was established within the Department of Commerce pursuant to provisions of the the Air Commerce Act of 1926, approved May 20, 1926 (44 Stat. 568). The name was changed to Bureau of Air Commerce by administrative order of Secretary of Commerce, July 1, 1934. Executive Order 7959 of August 22, 1938, transferred the functions of the Bureau of Air Commerce to the Civil Aeronautics Authority (CA 1).

C 23.1:date
ANNUAL REPORTS.

C 23.2:CT
GENERAL PUBLICATIONS.

C 23.3
BULLETINS.

C 23.4
CIRCULARS.

C 23.5:nos.
AERONAUTICAL BULLETINS, STATE SERIES.

For nos. 1-526 see Air Service (W 87.27/1).

C 23.6:date
REGULATIONS (general).

C 23.6/a:CT
HANDBOOKS, REGULATIONS AND MANUALS (miscellaneous).

C 23.6/2:CT
CIVIL AIR REGULATIONS-HANDBOOKS, REGULATIONS AND MANUALS.
Miscellaneous, Individual.

C 23.6/3:nos.
REGULATIONS.
Later CA 1.6 (Sept. 1939) and CA 1.9 (April 1940).

C 23.6/3:date
CIVIL AIR REGULATIONS (compilations).

C 23.6/5:chap.&pt.nos.
MANUAL OF OPERATIONS.
Later CA 1.15

C 23.7:nos.
AIRWAY BULLETIN (looseleaf). [Irregular]

This series will take the place of Aeronautical Bulletins, State series, Route information series and state summaries series (W 87.21/1-3).

C 23.7/2:nos.
AIRWAY BULLETINS.

C 23.7/3:nos.
AIRPORT BULLETINS.

C 23.8:nos.
INFORMATION BULLETINS.
Superseded by C 23.11

C 23.9:v.nos.
DOMESTIC AIR NEWS.

C 23.10/1:nos.
AIRWAY MAPS.

C 23.10/2:CT
AIRWAY MAPS (miscellaneous).

C 23.10/3:letters
AIRWAY MAPS.
    Later C 4.9/4

C 23.10/4:nos.
REGIONAL AERONAUTICAL CHARTS.
    Later C 4.9/5

C 23.11:nos.
AERONAUTICS BULLETIN.
    Supersedes Information Bulletin (C 23.8).

C 23.12:vol.
AIR COMMERCE BULLETIN. [Monthly]
    Later CA 1.8

C 23.13
LIAISON COMMITTEE ON AERONAUTICS RADIO
    RESEARCH.

C 23.14:nos.
INSPECTION SERVICE MEMORANDUM.

C 23.15:date
WEEKLY NOTICES TO AIRMEN.
    Later CA 1.7

C 23.16:letters-nos.
INSTRUCTION BULLETINS.
    Superseded by Manuals (CA 1.10).

C 23.17:nos.
ARMY NAVY COMMERCE COMMITTEE ON AIRCRAFT-
    REQUIREMENTS.
    Later C 31.113

C 23.18:date
TABULATION OF AIR NAVIGATION RADIO AIDS.
    [Monthly]
    Earlier issued Quarterly.
    Later CA 1.9

C 23.19:nos.
REPORTS.
    Later CA 1.11

C 23.20:date
DOMESTIC SCHEDULED AIR LINE OPERATION STA-
    TISTICS. [Monthly]
    Earlier CA 1.22 and C 32.112

C 23.21
720 HOUR CHECK. [Monthly]

RADIO DIVISION
(1927– 1932)

CREATION AND AUTHORITY

    The Radio Service was established within the
Bureau of Navigation (C 11) of the Department of
Commerce in 1910. On March 31, 1927, it was
made a separate agency within the Department
and redesignated as the Radio Division. On July
20, 1932, the Division was abolished and its functions transferred to the Federal Radio Commission (RC 1) pursuant to act of Congress, approved June 30, 1932 (47 Stat. 417).

C 24.1:date
ANNUAL REPORTS.

C 24.2:CT
GENERAL PUBLICATIONS.

C 24.3:nos.
RADIO SERVICE BULLETINS. [Monthly]

C 24.4
CIRCULARS.

C 24.5:date
RADIO STATIONS OF THE U.S.

    Issued annually in two separate pamphlets
as follows: Commercial and Government Radio
Stations; Amateur Radio Stations.
    Earlier C 11.7/6

BUREAU OF MARINE
INSPECTION AND NAVIGATION
(1936– 1942)

CREATION AND AUTHORITY

    The Bureau of Navigation and Steamboat In-
spection was established within the Department
of Commerce by act of Congress approved June
30, 1932 (47 Sat. 415), consolidating the Steamboat Inspection Service (C 15) and the Bureau of
Navigation (C 11). By act of Congress, approved
May 27, 1936 (49 Stat. 1380), the name was
changed to Bureau of Marine Inspection and Navigation. Executive Order 9083 of February 28,
1942, transferred functions of the Bureau of Marine Inspection and Navigation to the Bureau of
Customs (T 17) of the Treasury Department and
the Coast Guard of the Navy Department. This
transfer was made permanent by Reorganization
Plan No. 3 of 1946, effective July 16, 1946 and
the Bureau was abolished.

C 25.1:date
ANNUAL REPORTS.

C 25.2:CT
GENERAL PUBLICATIONS.

C 25.3:nos.
BULLETINS. [Monthly]
    Earlier C 15.10

C 25.4
CIRCULARS.

C 25.5:date
LAWS GOVERNING STEAMBOAT INSPECTION.
    See for earlier edition C 15.5.

C 25.5/2:date
NAVIGATION LAWS OF U.S. [Issued every 4 years]
    Earlier C 11.6

C 25.6/1:date
GENERAL RULES AND REGULATIONS.

    C 25.6/2:nos.
    – SUPPLEMENTS.

C 25.6/3:CT
REGULATIONS, MISCELLANEOUS.

C 25.7:vol.
CURRENT SHIPPING DATA. [Monthly]

C 25.8:date
PILOT RULES FOR RIVERS WHOSE WATERS FLOW
    INTO GULF OF MEXICO AND THEIR TRIBU-
    TARIES AND RED RIVER OF THE NORTH.
    Earlier C 15.8

C 25.9:date
PILOT RULES FOR CERTAIN INLAND WATERS OF
    ATLANTIC AND PACIFIC COASTS OF GULF OF
    MEXICO.
    Earlier C 15.8

C 25.10:date
MERCHANT MARINE STATISTICS.
    Earlier C 11.20

C 25.11:date
MERCHANT VESSELS OF U.S.
    Earlier T 37.11, T 30.5, C 11.5
    Later C 25.15

C 25.12:vol.
MERCHANT MARINE BULLETIN. [Monthly]
    Later N 24.24

C 25.13:nos.
CIRCULAR LETTERS.
    Superseded by N 24.27

C 25.14:nos.
RULES AND REGULATIONS SERIES.

C 25.15:nos.
REPORT SERIES.

C 25.16:nos.
EDUCATIONAL SERIES.

C 25.17:CT
POSTERS.

FEDERAL EMPLOYMENT
STABILIZATION OFFICE
(1934– 1939)

CREATION AND AUTHORITY

    The Federal Employment Stabilization Board
was established by the Employment Stabilization
Act of February 10, 1931. In 1934, the Board was
abolished and its functions transferred to the
Federal Employment Stabilization Office as its
successor. The functions of the Office, which
was inactive after June 1935, were transferred to
the National Resources Planning Board (Pr
32.300).

C 26.1:date
ANNUAL REPORTS.

C 26.2:CT
GENERAL PUBLICATIONS.

C 26.3
BULLETINS.

C 26.4
CIRCULARS.

SHIPPING BOARD BUREAU
(1933– 1936)

CREATION AND AUTHORITY

    The United States Shipping Board Bureau was
established within the Department of Commerce
by Executive Order 6166 of June 10, 1933 which
abolished the United States Shipping Board (SB
1) and transferred its functions to the Department of Commerce. The Bureau was abolished
when its functions were transferred by act of
Congress, approved June 29, 1936 (49 Stat.
1985) to the United States Maritime Commission (MC 1).

C 27.1:date
ANNUAL REPORTS.

C 27.2:CT
GENERAL PUBLICATIONS.

    Earlier SB 1.2

C 27.3
BULLETINS.

C 27.4
CIRCULARS.

C 27.5
LAWS.

C 27.6:date
REGULATIONS.
　　Includes rules.

C 27.7:
MAPS.

C 27.8:
POSTERS.

C 27.9:
RESEARCH DIVISION REPORTS.

C 27.9/1:date
AMERICAN FLAG SERVICES IN FOREIGN TRADE
WITH U.S.
　　Later MC 1.12

C 27.9/2:CT
COMPARATIVE STATEMENT OF FOREIGN COM-
MERCE OF U.S. PORTS BY STATES.
　　Later MC 1.10

C 27.9/3:date
COMPARATIVE SUMMARY OF WATER BORNE
FOREIGN COMMERCE (Calendar and fiscal
years).
　　Earlier SB 7.5/399
　　Later MC 1.19

C 27.9/4:q-date and a-date
IMPORTS AND EXPORTS OF COMMODITIES BY U.S.
COASTAL DISTRICTS AND FOREIGN TRADE
REGIONS. [Quarterly, Fiscal and Calendar Years]
　　Report D.R. 275
　　Earlier SB 7.5/275
　　Later MC 1.11

C 27.9/5:date
MERCHANT FLEET IN SERVICE ON GREAT LAKES.
[Semiannual]
　　Report D.R. 1111

C 27.9/6:date
OCEAN GOING MERCHANT FLEETS OF PRINCIPAL
MARITIME NATIONS, VESSELS OF 2,000 GROSS
TONS AND OVER. [Semiannual]
　　Report D.R. 100
　　Earlier SB 7.5/100
　　Later MC 1.16

C 27.9/7:date
QUARTERLY REPORT ON EMPLOYMENT OF AMERI-
CAN MERCHANT VESSELS.
　　Report D.R. 300
　　Earlier SB 7.5/300
　　Later MC 1.16

C 27.9/8:date
STATUS OF VESSEL CONSTRUCTION AND RECON-
DITIONING UNDER MERCHANT MARINE ACTS
OF 1920 AND 1928. [Monthly]
　　Report D.R. 1105
　　Earlier SB 7.5/1105

C 27.9/9:date
U.S. WATER BORNE INTERCOASTAL TRAFFIC BY
PORTS OF ORIGIN AND DESTINATION AND PRIN-
CIPAL COMMODITIES, (fiscal and calendar years).
　　Report D.R. 317
　　Earlier SB 7.5/317
　　Later MC 1.9

C 27.9/10:date
REPORT ON VOLUME OF WATER BORNE FOREIGN
COMMERCE OF U.S. BY PORTS OF ORIGIN AND
DESTINATION (fiscal years).
　　Earlier SB 7.2:C 73
　　Later MC 1.17

C 27.9/11:date
WATER BORNE FOREIGN AND DOMESTIC COM-
MERCE OF U.S. (calendar years).
　　Report D.R. 295
　　Earlier SB 7.5/295
　　Later MC 1.20

C 27.9/12:date
WATER BORNE PASSENGER TRAFFIC OF U.S. (fis-
cal and calendar years).
　　Report D.R. 157
　　Earlier SB 7.5/157
　　Later MC 1.15

C 27.9/13:CT
RESEARCH DIVISION MAPS.
　　Earlier SB 7.6
　　Later MC 1.14

C 27.10:CT
PAPERS IN RE.
　　Earlier SB 1.13

C 27.11:date
ANNUAL REPORT AND GENERAL FINANCIAL STATE-
MENT.
　　Earlier SB 10.7

BUSINESS ADVISORY COUNCIL
(1935– 1953)

CREATION AND AUTHORITY

　　The Business Advisory and Planning Council
was established within the Department of Commerce on June 26, 1933. On April 11, 1935, the
name was changed to Business Advisory Council.

C 28.1:date
ANNUAL REPORTS.

C 28.2:CT
GENERAL PUBLICATIONS.

INLAND WATERWAYS
CORPORATION
(1939– 1953)

CREATION AND AUTHORITY

　　The Inland Waterways Corporation (W 103)
was transferred from the War Department to the
Department of Commerce by Reorganization Plan
No. 2 of 1939, effective July 1, 1939. The Corporation was sold to the Federal Waterways Corporation under a contract of July 24, 1953, and
renamed the Federal Barge Lines, Inc. An act of
July 19, 1963, provided for the liquidation of the
Corporation.

C 29.1:date
ANNUAL REPORTS.

　　Earlier W 103.1

C 29.2:CT
GENERAL PUBLICATIONS.

　　Earlier W 103.2

WEATHER BUREAU
(1940– 1965)

CREATION AND AUTHORITY

　　The Weather Bureau (A 29) was transferred
from the Department of Agriculture to the Department of Commerce by Reorganization Plan No. 4
of 1940, effective June 30, 1940. The Bureau
was placed under the Environmental Science
Services Administration (C 52) by Reorganization
Plan No. 2 of 1965, effective July 13, 1965.

C 30.1:date
ANNUAL REPORTS.

C 30.2:CT
GENERAL PUBLICATIONS.

C 30.3:nos.
BULLETINS.

C 30.3/2　　　　　　　　　　　**• Item 273-B**
CLIMATIC SUMMARY OF THE UNITED STATES,
SUPPLEMENT.

　　Carries on the data in Bulletin W for the
period 1931-1952. Separate publication issued
for each State.

C 30.4　　　　　　　　　　　　　**• Item 273**
CIRCULARS. [Irregular]
Discontinued.

C 30.4:B　　　　　　　　　　　　**• Item 273**
INSTRUCTIONS FOR CLIMATOLOGICAL
OBSERVERS. [Irregular]

C 30.4:M　　　　　　　　　　　　**• Item 273**
MANUAL OF MARINE METEOROLOGICAL
OBSERVATIONS. [Irregular]

　　Issued in loose leaf form with marginal
index tabs.

C 30.4:N　　　　　　　　　　　　**• Item 273**
MANUAL OF SURFACE OBSERVATION (WBAN).
1928–　[Irregular]

　　Issued in loose leaf form. Kept up-to-date
by "Changes."
　　Published in cooperation with the Air Force
and Navy.

C 30.4:O　　　　　　　　　　　　**• Item 273**
MANUAL OF WINDS-ALOFT OBSERVATIONS. [Ir-
regular]

C 30.6:CT
REGULATIONS, RULES, AND INSTRUCTIONS.

C 30.6/2:CT
HANDBOOKS, MANUALS, GUIDES.
　　Earlier C 30.6

C 30.6/2:B 26　　　　　　　　　**• Item 275-E**
MANUAL OF BAROMETRY. [Irregular]

　　v. 1, 1st ed., 1963.

C 30.6/2:R 11　　　　　　　　　**• Item 275-E**
MANUAL FOR RADIOSONDE CODE (WBAN). [Ir-
regular]

　　3rd ed. January 1, 1968.
　　Standards and procedures for coding
radiosonde reports.

C 30.6/2:Sy 7/2　　　　　　　　**• Item 275-E**
MANUAL FOR SYNOPTIC CODE (WBAN).
[Irregular]

　　2nd ed. January 1, 1966.
　　Issued in looseleaf form.
　　Standards and procedures for coding of
synoptic reports.

C 30.6/2:W 72   • **Item 275-E**
MANUAL FOR UPPER WIND CODE (WBAN). 1st
ed–   [Irregular]

Prepared in cooperation with Air Weather
Service, Air Force, and Naval Weather Service, Navy.
Issued in looseleaf form.
3rd ed., January 1, 1968.

C 30.6/3:nos.
FORECASTING GUIDE.

C 30.6/4   • **Item 275-E**
WEATHER BUREAU FORECASTERS HANDBOOKS.
1–   1968–   [Irregular] Office of Meteorological Operations.

PURPOSE:– To provide information and instruction in the derivation of weather forecasts.

C 30.6/5   • **Item 275-E**
WEATHER BUREAU ENGINEERING HANDBOOKS,
EHB- (series). 1–   [Irregular]

C 30.6/6:nos.
WEATHER BUREAU OBSERVING HANDBOOKS.

C 30.7:dt.&nos.
CORN AND WHEAT REGION BULLETINS. [Weekly
during season, April-September]
Issued at Chicago.
Earlier A 29.43

C 30.8:date
CORN AND WHEAT REGION BULLETINS. [Daily except
Sundays & Holidays during season, April-
September]

Issued at Region Center of Weather Bureau,
Chicago, Illinois.
Earlier A 29.43/2

C 30.9:dt.&nos.
COTTON REGION BULLETIN. [Weekly durning season
April-October]
Issued at New Orleans.
Earlier A 29.39

C 30.9/2
CROP BULLETIN.

C 30.10:date
METEOROLOGICAL SUMMARY, WASHINGTON, D.C.
[Monthly]
Earlier A 29.30/2
Later C 30.10:1

C 30.10:1/date
STATION METEOROLOGICAL SUMMARY, WASHING-
TON.
Earlier C 30.10
Later 30.56/1

C 30.10:2/date
STATION METEOROLOGICAL SUMMARY, SAN JUAN,
P.R. [Monthly]
Earlier C 30.45
Later 30.56/2

C 30.10:3/date
STATION METEOROLOGICAL SUMMARY, LOS
ANGELES, CALIFORNIA. [Monthly]

C 30.10/2:1/date
SPECIAL METEOROLOGICAL SUMMARIES, WASH-
INGTON NATIONAL AIRPORT, WASHINGTON,
D.C. [Monthly]

C 30.10/2:2/date
SPECIAL METEOROLOGICAL SUMMARIES, SAN
JUAN, P.R. [Monthly]

C 30.10/2:3/date
SPECIAL METEOROLOGICAL SUMMARIES, LOS
ANGELES WB AIRPORT, CALIFORNIA [Monthly]

C 30.10/2:4/date
SPECIAL METEOROLOGICAL SUMMARIES,
BURBANK WB AIRPORT, CALIFORNIA. [Monthly]

C 30.10/2:5/date
SPECIAL METEOROLOGICAL SUMMARIES,
DETROIT, MICHIGAN WB AIRPORT. [Monthly]

C 30.10/3:CT
LOCAL CLIMATOLOGICAL SUMMARY WITH COM-
PARATIVE DATA.

C 30.11
WEEKLY WEATHER AND CROP BULLETIN,
NATIONAL SUMMARY. v. 1–   1924–   [Weekly]
Issued on Tuesday of each week, the Bulletin
contains an account of weather conditions and
their effect on crops throughout the United States,
for the week ending at 7:30 a.m., e.s.t., each
Tuesday. In particular, it covers the effects of
weather on crop development and farm operations, especially as featured in "Weather of the
Week" and special mention of weather conditions
affecting the more important crops. Tables of temperature and precipitation are included with departures from normal; also charts showing the
same data and their distribution throughout the
country. During the winter season snow and ice
conditions are published in lieu of most of the
"Special Telegraphic Summaries" which normally
appear in the Bulletin. These summaries are reported by the Weather Bureau State Climatologists in cooperation with the State and Federal
agricultural agencies concerning crop-weather
conditions in their respective States.
Most issues of the Bulletin feature special
articles on various aspects of weather, crops,
and agricultural activities, as space permits. Also
"Special Weather Summary" editions are infrequently issued to cover very unusual conditions.
An index of the special articles is contained
in the final issue of each year.
Bulletins issued for local areas are listed in
Volume 3 of this Guide.

C 30.11/2:date
UTAH WEATHER, CROPS AND LIVESTOCK.

C 30.12:date
WEATHER MAPS. [Daily]
Earlier A 29.18

C 30.13:date
WEATHER OUTLOOK. [Weekly]
Earlier A 29.38

C 30.14   • **Item 277**
MONTHLY WEATHER REVIEW. v. 1–   1872–
[Monthly]
PURPOSE:– To serve as a medium for tech-
nical contributions in the field of meteorology,
principally in the branches of synoptic and ap-
plied meteorology.
In addition to the scientific articles, each is-
sue contains an article descriptive of the atmo-
spheric circulation during the month over the
Northern Hemisphere with particular references
to the effect on weather in the United States.
Index and table of contents contained in the
December issues.

C 30.14/a:CT
– SEPARATES, MISCELLANEOUS.

C 30.14/a 2:date
– SEPARATES: WEATHER OF OCEANS. [Monthly]

C 30.15:nos.   • **Item 278**
– SUPPLEMENTS.
Discontinued.

C 30.16:CT/dt.   • **Item 272**
METEOROLOGICAL SUMMARIES (CT by States).
[Annual]

Earlier A 29.30/2 to A 29.30/38
Discontinued.

C 30.17:date
PRICE LIST OF PUBLICATIONS.
Earlier A 29.31/3

C 30.17/2:pt.nos.
WEATHER BUREAU PUBLICATIONS.

C 30.17/3:CT   • **Item 272-B**
BIBLIOGRAPHIES AND LISTS OF PUBLICATIONS.
Discontinued.

C 30.18:vol.
CLIMATOLOGICAL DATA FOR UNITED STATES BY
SECTIONS. [Monthly]
Earlier A 29.29

C 30.18/2
– BOUND EDITION.

C 30.18/3:v.nos.
– ALABAMA.

C 30.18/4:v.nos.
– ARIZONA.

C 30.18/5:v.nos.
– ARKANSAS.

C 30.18/6:v.nos.
– CALIFORNIA.

C 30.18/7:v.nos.
– COLORADO.

C 30.18/8:v.nos.
– FLORIDA.

C 30.18/9:v.nos.
– GEORGIA.

C 30.18/10:v.nos.
– IDAHO.

C 30.18/11:v.nos.
– ILLINOIS.

C 30.18/12:v.nos.
– INDIANA.

C 30.18/13:v.nos.
– IOWA. [Monthly]

C 30.18/14:v.nos.
– KANSAS.

C 30.18/15:v.nos.
– KENTUCKY.

C 30.18/16:v.nos.
– LOUISIANA.

C 30.18/17:v.nos.
– MARYLAND AND DELAWARE.

C 30.18/18:v.nos.
– MICHIGAN.

C 30.18/19:v.nos.
– MINNESOTA.

C 30.18/20:v.nos.
– MISSISSIPPI.

C 30.18/21:v.nos.
– MISSOURI.

C 30.18/22:v.nos.
– MONTANA.

C 30.18/23:v.nos.
– NEBRASKA.

C 30.18/24:v.nos.
– NEVADA.

C 30.18/25:v.nos.
– NEW ENGLAND.

C 30.18/26:v.nos.
– NEW JERSEY.

C 30.18/27:v.nos.
– NEW MEXICO.

C 30.18/28:v.nos.
– NEW YORK.

C 30.18/29:v.nos.
– NORTH CAROLINA.

C 30.18/30:v.nos.
– NORTH DAKOTA.

C 30.18/31:v.nos.
– OHIO.

C 30.18/32:v.nos.
– OKLAHOMA.

C 30.18/33:v.nos.
– OREGON.

C 30.18/34:v.nos.
– PENNSYLVANIA.

C 30.18/35:v.nos.
– SOUTH CAROLINA.

C 30.18/36:v.nos.
– SOUTH DAKOTA.

C 30.18/37:v.nos.
– TENNESSEE.

C 30.18/38:v.nos.
– TEXAS.

C 30.18/39:v.nos.
– UTAH. [Monthly]

C 30.18/40:v.nos.
– VIRGINIA.

C 30.18/41:v.nos.
– WASHINGTON.

C 30.18/42:v.nos.
– WEST VIRGINIA.

C 30.18/43:v.nos.
– WISCONSIN.

C 30.18/44:v.nos.
– WYOMING.

C 30.18/45:date
[CLIMATOLOGICAL DATA MAP]. [Monthly]

C 30.19:vol.
CLIMATOLOGICAL DATA, HAWAII SECTION. [Monthly]

Earlier A 29.34

C 30.19/2:v.nos.
CLIMATOLOGICAL DATA, PACIFIC. [Monthly]

C 30.20:vol.
CLIMATOLOGICAL DATA, WEST INDIES AND CARIBBEAN SERVICE. [Monthly]

Earlier A 29.26

C 30.20/2:v.nos.
CLIMATOLOGICAL DATA: PUERTO RICO AND VIRGIN ISLANDS.

Later C 55.214/37

C 30.21:vol.
CLIMATOLOGICAL DATA, ALASKA SECTION.

Earlier A 29.33

C 30.21/2 • Item 273-D
CLIMATOLOGICAL DATA FOR ARCTIC STATIONS. [Annual]
Prepared in cooperation with the National Science Foundation.

C 30.21/3 • Item 273-D
CLIMATOLOGICAL DATA FOR ANTARCTIC STATIONS. 1– 1962– [Annual]

Prepared in cooperation with the National Science Foundation.

C 30.22:CT
MAPS AND CHARTS.

C 30.22/2:CT
MAPS AND CHARTS (sets).

C 30.22/3
COASTAL WARNING FACILITIES CHARTS. [Irregular]

C 30.22/4:CT
SHEETS OF NATIONAL ATLAS OF UNITED STATES.

C 30.22/5:date/pt.nos.
INTERNATIONAL GEOPHYSICAL YEAR WORLD WEATHER MAPS. July 1953– December 1958. [Monthly]

C 30.22/6:CT
WEATHER BUREAU MARINE SERVICES CHARTS.

C 30.23:nos.
RADIO CIRCULARS.

Earlier A 29.37

C 30.24 • Item 274
DAILY RIVER STAGES. v. 1– 1903– [Annual]

Contains daily river stage data for approximately 625 stations located on the principal rivers of the United States.

C 30.25:date • Item 276
UNITED STATES METEOROLOGICAL YEARBOOK.

Earlier A 29.45
Discontinued.

C 30.26:
CORRESPONDENCE COURSE, ELEMENTS OF SURFACE WEATHER OBSERVATIONS, LESSONS.

C 30.27:date
DAILY SYNOPTIC SERIES, HISTORICAL WEATHER MAPS, NORTHERN HEMISPHERE SEA LEVEL. (For Official Use Only) [Monthly]

C 30.28 • Item 281
TECHNICAL PAPERS. 1– 1943– [Irregular]

These papers present technical data, meteorological charts and tables, and other technical information compiled for the use of research meteorologists, weather forecasters, climatologists, weather observers, other workers in the atmospheric sciences.

Discontinued.

C 30.29 • Item 279
RESEARCH PAPERS. 1– 1943– [Irregular]

Reports on original research in which at least part of the answer to a specific meteorological problem has been worked out and is presented as a contribution to knowledge of the weather.
Papers published in this series usually are too long or detailed for publication in a technical journal.

Discontinued.

C 30.30:date
HYDROLOGIC BULLETIN, HOURLY AND DAILY PRECIPITATION, NORTH ATLANTIC DISTRICT. [Monthly]

C 30.31:date
HYDROLOGIC BULLETIN, HOURLY AND DAILY PRECIPITATION, SOUTHEAST DISTRICT. [Monthly]

C 30.32:date
HYDROLOGIC BULLETIN, HOURLY AND DAILY PRECIPITATION, OHIO RIVER DISTRICT. [Monthly]

C 30.33:date
HYDROLOGIC BULLETIN, HOURLY AND DAILY PRECIPITATION, UPPER MISSISSIPPI DISTRICT. [Monthly]

C 30.34:date
HYDROLOGIC BULLETIN, HOURLY AND DAILY PRECIPITATION, MISSOURI RIVER DISTRICT. [Monthly]

C 30.35:date
HYDROLOGIC BULLETIN, HOURLY AND DAILY PRECIPITATION, LOWER MISSISSIPPI-WEST GULF DISTRICT. [Monthly]

C 30.36:date
HYDROLOGIC BULLETIN, HOURLY AND DAILY PRECIPITATION, PACIFIC DISTRICT. [Monthly]

C 30.37:date
HYDROLOGIC BULLETIN, HOURLY AND DAILY PRECIPITATION, SOUTH PACIFIC DISTRICT. [Monthly]

C 30.37/2:date
DAILY AND HOURLY PRECIPITATION DATA, HYDROLOGIC NETWORK REGION 7, SOUTHWESTERN DISTRICT, WEATHER BUREAU OFFICE, ALBURQUERQUE, NEW MEXICO.

C 30.38:date
DAILY SYNOPTIC SERIES, HISTORICAL WEATHER MAPS, NORTHERN HEMISPHERE 3,000 DYNAMIC METERS. [Monthly]

C 30.39:date
DAILY SYNOPTIC SERIES, HISTORICAL WEATHER MAPS, SOUTHWEST PACIFIC, SEA LEVEL. [Monthly]

C 30.40:date
DAILY SYNOPTIC SERIES, HISTORICAL WEATHER MAPS, NORTH AMERICA, 10 KILOMETERS. [Monthly]

C 30.41:date
DAILY SYNOPTIC SERIES, HISTORICAL WEATHER MAPS, NORTH AMERICA, 13 KILOMETERS. [Monthly]

C 30.42:date
DAILY SYNOPTIC SERIES, HISTORICAL WEATHER MAPS, NORTH AMERICA, 16 KILOMETERS. [Monthly]

C 30.43:date
DAILY WEATHER BULLETIN.

C 30.43/2
– NORFOLK, VA.

C 30.43/3
– NEW YORK CITY.

C 30.43/4
– BISMARK, N. DAK.

C 30.43/5
– HOUSTON, TEX.

C 30.43/6
– DALLAS, TEX.

C 30.44 • Item 275-A
HYDROMETEOROLOGICAL REPORTS. 1– 1938– [Irregular]

This series of reports has special application in engineering, mostly in the design of hydraulic structures. Reports dwell generally on discussions of area rainfall, thunderstorms, hurricanes, and dewpoints, and studies of particular river basins with estimates of maximum possible precipitation and the associated meteorological conditions.

C 30.44/2:nos.
HYDROMETEOROLOGICAL SECTION TECHNICAL PAPERS.

C 30.45:date
CLIMATOLOGICAL SUMMARY: SAN JUAN, P.R. [Monthly]

Later C 30.10:2

C 30.46
AVERAGE MONTHLY WEATHER OUTLOOK. v. 1–
1946–   [Semimonthly]

Shows in graphic form (for broad geographic areas) the atmospheric circulation, temperature departures, and precipitation amounts as observed for the preceeding month and also as anticipated for the coming 30-day period, based on the best indications available. The Outlook is not a specific forecast in the usual meteorological sense, but instead is an estimate of the rainfall and temperature for the next 30 days.

C 30.47
HEATING DEGREE DAY BULLETIN.

C 30.48:nos.   • Item 282
WEATHER BUREAU TRAINING PAPERS.

Discontinued.

C 30.49
DAILY SERIES, SYNOPTIC WEATHER MAPS.

PART 1. NORTHERN HEMISPHERE SEA LEVEL AND 500 MILLIBAR CHARTS. [Monthly]
Consists of a sea-level and an upper-air constant pressure surface (500-millibar) map for each day of the month.
PART 2. NORTHERN HEMISPHERE DATA TABULATIONS, DAILY BULLETIN.

Discontinued with the December 31, 1964 issue.

C 30.49/2:date
DAILY SERIES, SYNOPTIC WEATHER MAPS, PART 2, NORTHERN HEMISPHERE DATA TABULATIONS, DAILY BULLETIN.

Formerly monthly and classed C 30.49

C 30.49/3:date
DAILY SERIES, SYNOPTIC WEATHER MAPS, NORTHERN HEMISPHERE, 100 MILLIBAR AND 50 MILLIBAR CHARTS.

C 30.50
MONTHLY CLIMATIC DATA FOR THE WORLD. [Monthly]

Surface data table gives pressure, temperature, relative humidity, precipitation by country and selected cities; upper aid data table gives dynamic height, temperature, and dew point at specific pressure levels, by country and selected cities.

C 30.50/2:date
MONTHLY CLIMATIC DATA FOR WORLD, SUPPLEMENTS. [Annual]

C 30.51
CLIMATOLOGICAL DATA, NATIONAL SUMMARY. v. 1– 1950–   [Monthly & Annual]
Contains general summary of weather conditions, condensed climatological summary for the States, climatological data by stations for the States, Pacific Area, and West Indies, degree days and severe storm data, river stages and flood data, and upper air data.

CLIMATOLOGICAL DATA [State Sections]. v. 1– 1914–   [Monthly & Annual]

Issued in 47 sections, one for each State with the following exceptions: Maryland and Delaware issued together, one section issued for the New England States (Connecticut, Maine, Massachusetts, New Hampshire, Rhode Island, and Vermont), plus sections for Pacific Area, West Indies and Caribbean section, Puerto Rico and Virgin Islands.
Contains climatological data for stations within each section, consisting of a narrative concerning the month's weather for the section, and tables listing information such as daily and monthly precipitation, temperature, wind movements, etc.
Annual summary issued separately, presenting data on an annual basis, similar to the material published in the monthly issues.

C 30.52:CT
TERMINAL FORECASTING REFERENCE MANUAL (by Terminals).

C 30.53:v.nos.
LIBRARY CIRCULAR. [Monthly]

C 30.54
DAILY MISSOURI-MISSISSIPPI RIVER BULLETIN. [Daily]

Prepared by the River Forecast Center, St. Louis, Missouri.
Formerly: Daily Mississippi River Stage and Forecast Bulletin.

C 30.54/2
– COLUMBIA, SOUTH CAROLINA.

C 30.54/3
– HOUSTON, TEXAS.

C 30.54/4
DAILY WEATHER AND RIVER BULLETIN, ALBUQUERQUE, NEW MEXICO. [Daily (April 1-June 30)]

C 30.54/5
– JACKSON, MISSISSIPPI.

C 30.54/6
– LITTLE ROCK, ARKANSAS.

C 30.54/7
DAILY RIVER BULLETIN, MEMPHIS, TENNESSEE AREA. [Daily]

Formerly Daily Weather and River Bulletin.
Beginning with data for July 1965, includes Vicksburg, Miss., area (C 30.54/13).

C 30.54/8
– MOBILE, ALABAMA.

C 30.54/9
– MONTGOMERY, ALABAMA.

C 30.54/10
– NEW ORLEANS, LOUISIANA. [Daily]

C 30.54/11
– SACRAMENTO, CALIFORNIA.

C 30.54/12
DAILY RIVER AND RAINFALL BULLETINS, SHREVEPORT, LOUISIANA AREA. [Daily]

C 30.54/13
– VICKSBURG, MISSISSIPPI.

C 30.54/14
DAILY WEATHER AND RIVER BULLETIN: LA CROSSE, WISCONSIN.

C 30.54/15
– CAIRO, ILLINOIS.

C 30.54/16
– CHARLESTON, SOUTH CAROLINA.

C 30.54/17
DAILY OHIO RIVER BULLETIN. [Daily]

C 30.54/18
DAILY WEATHER AND RIVER BULLETIN: PORTLAND, OREGON.

C 30.55
DAILY RIVER BULLETIN: DAVENPORT, IOWA.

C 30.55/2
– ATLANTA, GEORGIA.

C 30.55/3
– EVANSVILLE, INDIANA.

C 30.55/4
– PITTSBURGH, PENNSYLVANIA.

C 30.56
LOCAL CLIMATOLOGICAL DATA. [Monthly and Annual]

Issued for approximately 290 stations. Tables give local climatological data, including temperature, precipitation, wind, sunshine, sky cover, thunderstorms or distant lightning, weather restricting visibility, hourly precipitation.

MONTHLY SUPPLEMENTS.

Issued for approximately 200 stations where 24-hourly observations are taken. Tables give occurrences for temperature and wind speed, relative humidity; wind direction and speed, hourly and daily precipitation amounts; ceiling-visibility; sky cover, wind, and relative humidity; temperatures; 6-hourly observations on sky cover, pressure, psychometic data, and wind. Monthly figures. Two-year comparisons.

ANNUAL SUMMARY.

Issued for approximately 220 stations. Contains narrative climatological summary, meteorological data for current year, normals, means, and extremes, comparative temperature, precipitation, degree days, and snowfall data for earlier years.

C 30.56/1:date
LOCAL CLIMATOLOGICAL DATA, WASHINGTON, D.C. [Monthly]

Formerly Station Meteorological Summary (C 30.10:1).

C 30.56/2:date
– SAN JUAN, PUERTO RICO. [Monthly]

Formerly Station Meteorological Summary (C 30.10:2).

C 30.56/3:date
– CHICAGO, ILLINOIS.

C 30.56/4:date
– ROANOKE, VIRGINIA.

C 30.56/5
– RALEIGH, NORTH CAROLINA.

C 30.56/6:date
– INNEAPOLIS, MINNESOTA.

C 30.57
DAILY UPPER AIR BULLETIN.

C 30.58
WATER SUPPLY FORECASTS.

C 30.59– C 30.59/43
HOURLY PRECIPITATION DATA. [Monthly & Annual]

Issued in 42 sections, one for each State, except that data for Maryland and Delaware are issued in one release, the New England States (Connecticut, Maine, Massachusetts, New Hampshire, Rhode Island, and Vermont) are issued in one release, and no releases are issued for Alaska and Hawaii.
Gives daily totals and hourly precipitation data by stations. The annual issue recapitulates the monthly tables, and carries a station index and location map.

C 30.59/2:v.nos.&nos.
– ALASKA.

C 30.59/3:v.nos.&nos.
– ARIZONA.

C 30.59/4:v.nos.&nos.
– ARKANSAS.

C 30.59/5:v.nos.&nos.
– CALIFORNIA.

C 30.59/5-2:date
– CALIFORNIA, MONTHLY AND SEASONAL PRECIPITATION (fiscal year).

C 30.59/6:v.nos.&nos.
– COLORADO.

C 30.59/7:v.nos.&nos.
– FLORIDA.

C 30.59/8:v.nos.&nos.
– GEORGIA.

C 30.59/9:v.nos.&nos.
– IDAHO.

C 30.59/10:v.nos.&nos.
– ILLINOIS.

C 30.59/11:v.nos.&nos.
– INDIANA.

C 30.59/12:v.nos.&nos.
– IOWA.

C 30.59/13:v.nos.&nos.
– KANSAS.

C 30.59/14:v.nos.&nos.
– KENTUCKY.

C 30.59/15:v.nos.&nos.
– LOUSIANA.

C 30.59/16:v.nos.&nos.
– MARYLAND AND DELAWARE.
C 30.59/17:v.nos.&nos.
– MICHIGAN.

C 30.59/18:v.nos.&nos.
– MINNESOTA.

C 30.59/19:v.nos.&nos.
– MISSISSIPPI.

C 30.59/20:v.nos.&nos.
– MISSOURI.

C 30.59/21:v.nos.&nos.
– MONTANA.

C 30.59/22:v.nos.&nos.
– NEBRASKA.

C 30.59/23:v.nos.&nos.
– NEVADA.

C 30.59/24:v.nos.&nos.
– NEW ENGLAND.

C 30.59/25:v.nos.&nos.
– NEW JERSEY.

C 30.59/26:v.nos.&nos.
– NEW MEXICO.

C 30.59/27:v.nos.&nos.
– NEW YORK.

C 30.59/28:v.nos.&nos.
– NORTH CAROLINA.

C 30.59/29:v.nos.&nos.
– NORTH DAKOTA.

C 30.59/30:v.nos.&nos.
– OHIO.

C 30.59/31:v.nos.&nos.
– OKLAHOMA.

C 30.59/32:v.nos.&nos.
– OREGON.

C 30.59/33:v.nos.&nos.
– PENNSYLVANIA.

C 30.59/34:v.nos.&nos.
– SOUTH CAROLINA.

C 30.59/35:v.nos.&nos.
– SOUTH DAKOTA.

C 30.59/36:v.nos.&nos.
– TENNESSEE.

C 30.59/37:v.nos.&nos.
– TEXAS.

C 30.59/38:v.nos.&nos.
– UTAH.

C 30.59/39:v.nos.&nos.
– VIRGINIA.

C 30.59/40:v.nos.&nos.
– WASHINGTON.

C 30.59/41:v.nos.&nos.
– WEST VIRGINIA.

C 30.59/42:v.nos.&nos.
– WISCONSIN.

C 30.59/43:v.nos.&nos.
– WYOMING.

C 30.59/44   • **Item 273-B**
PRECIPITATION DATA FROM STORAGE-GAGE
STATIONS.

C 30.59/45
STORAGE-GAGE PRECIPITATION DATA FOR WEST-
ERN UNITED STATES. v. 1–   [Annual]

v. 8 July 1962– June 1963.

C 30.59/46:v.nos.&nos.
HOURLY PRECIPITATION DATA: HAWAII.

C 30.60
[PRESS RELEASES]. [Irregular]

C 30.61:nos.   • **Item 273-A**
COOPERATIVE STUDIES REPORTS.

Discontinued.

C 30.61/2:nos.
COOPERATIVE STUDIES TECHNICAL PAPERS.
[Irregular]

C 30.62
DAILY TEMPERATURE, DEGREE DAY AND PRECIPI-
TATION NORMALS.

C 30.62/2
MONTHLY NORMAL TEMPERATURES, PRECIPITA-
TION AND DEGREE DAYS.

See C 30.2:T 24/3

C 30.62/3
PACIFIC NORTHWEST MONTHLY PRECIPITATION
AND TEMPERATURE. [Monthly]

C 30.63
TRAINING PAPERS.

C 30.64:sec.nos.   • **Item 275-B**
INVENTORY OF UNPUBLISHED CLIMATOLOGICAL
TABULATIONS.

Discontinued.

C 30.65:nos.   • **Item 272-A**
AVIATION SERIES.

Discontinued.

C 30.66:CT
KEY TO METEOROLOGICAL RECORDS DOCUMEN-
TATION.

C 30.66/2   • **Item 275-C**
KEY TO METEOROLOGICAL RECORDS DOCUMEN-
TATION. [Irregular]

PURPOSE:– To provide guidance information
to research personnel and others making use of
observed data.

C 30.66/3:CT
– 6.11, DECADAL CENSUS OF WEATHER
STATIONS BY STATES.

C 30.67:nos.
CLIMATIC GUIDES (CLIMATOGRAPHY OF THE
UNITED STATES NO. 40-nos.).

C 30.68:nos/CT
SUMMARY OF HOURLY OBSERVATIONS (CLIMA-

TOGRAPHY OF THE UNITED STATES NO. 30-
nos.).

C 30.69:nos.
[LETTER SUPPLEMENTS] L.S. SERIES.

C 30.70:nos.
NATIONAL HURRICANE RESEARCH PROJECT
REPORTS.

C 30.70/2
REPORTS. 1–   1961–   [Irregular]

C 30.71
CLIMATOLOGICAL SUBSTATION SUMMARIES.

CLIMATOGRAPHY OF THE UNITED STATES.

PURPOSE:– To include summaries of data
covering periods in excess of one year.
Publications in this series are designated by
a double set of numbers. The first number designating the publication, the second being the State
number.
The following sub-series are in this series

C 30.71/2:nos.
CLIMATOGRAPHY OF UNITED STATES 10-NOS.
CLIMATIC SUMMARY [by regions].

Earlier A 29.5/a

C 30.71/2:10   • **Item 273-B**
CLIMATIC SUMMARY OF THE UNITED STATES,
1930 edition (Bulletin W).

Separate publication issued for each
State. Contains historical data from establishment of each station through 1930.

C 30.71/3:nos.
CLIMATOGRAPHY OF UNITED STATES, 60-NOS.
CLIMATES OF THE STATES.

C 30.71/3:60   • **Item 273-B**
CLIMATES OF THE STATES.

Separate publications issued for each
State. Contains narrative climatic information,
climatic summary tables, normals, means and
extremes of weather, temperature, precipitation and storm charts, location of weather
stations and types of observations taken.

C 30.71/4:nos.
DECENNIAL CENSUS OF UNITED STATES CLIMATE;
MONTHLY NORMALS OF TEMPERATURE, PRE-
CIPITATION, AND HEATING DEGREE DAYS,
CLIMATOGRAPHY OF UNITED STATES NO. 81-
(series).

C 30.71/5:nos.
DECENNIAL CENSUS OF UNITED STATES CLIMATE,
SUMMARY OF HOURLY OBSERVATIONS, 75th
MERIDIAN TIME ZONE, CLIMATOGRAPHY OF
UNITED STATES 82 (series).
C 30.71/5:82   • **Item 279-A**
DECENNIAL CENSUS OF UNITED STATES
CLIMATE, SUMMARY OF HOURLY OBSER-
VATIONS.

This series is being prepared under the
Decennial Census of United States Climate,
1960 program, covering most of the Weather
Bureau stations. All data are based on monthly
data published in Local Climatological Data
Supplements for all or part of the period 1951–
1960. Where the full 10-year period is not
covered by the monthly data, summaries are
based on the period 1956– 1960.
This series supersedes Summary of Hourly
Observations, 30- (series) (Listed above).

C 30.71/6:nos.   • **Item 273-B**
CLIMATOGRAPHY OF UNITED STATES 21 (series).
Discontinued.

C 30.71/6:21 • Item 273-B
CLIMATIC SUMMARIES OF RESORT AREAS.
[Irregular]
50. CLIMATIC CHARTS FOR THE UNITED STATES.

Nothing has been issued in this sub-series.

C 30.71/7:nos.
DECENNIAL CENSUS OF UNITED STATES CLIMATE:
CLIMATOGRAPHY OF UNITED STATES (Miscellaneous Series).

C 30.71/7:83 • Item 273-B
DECENNIAL CENSUS OF UNITED STATES CLIMATE, HEATING DEGREE DAY NORMALS.

C 30.71/7:84 • Item 273-B
DECENNIAL CENSUS OF UNITED STATES CLIMATE, DAILY NORMALS OF TEMPERATURE AND HEATING DEGREE DAYS.

C 30.71/7:85 • Item 273-B
DECENNIAL CENSUS OF UNITED STATES CLIMATE, MONTHLY AVERAGES FOR STATE CLIMATIC DIVISIONS.

Data for 1931– 1960.

C 30.71/8:nos.
DECENNIAL CENSUS OF UNITED STATES CLIMATE, CLIMATIC SUMMARY OF UNITED STATES, SUPPLEMENT 1951– 60, CLIMATOGRAPHY OF UNITED STATES, NO. 86- (series).

C 30.71/8:86 • Item 273-B
DECENNIAL CENSUS OF UNITED STATES: CLIMATIC SUMMARY OF UNITED STATES, SUPPLEMENT FOR 1951– 1960.

C 30.72 • Item 275-D
MARINERS WEATHER LOG. [Bimonthly]

PURPOSE:– To provide information on weather over the oceans and Great Lakes. Gale table gives selected weather observations from vessels in the North Atlantic Ocean.
Index in November issue.

C 30.73:date
DIRECTORY OF WEATHER BROADCASTS. [Annual]
Earlier C 30.2:B 78

C 30.74:v.nos.
STORM DATA. v. 1–   1959–   [Monthly]

Contains reports and statistical data on severe storms, by States, with a description of the storm damage reported in the month.
Information of this nature prior to 1959 appeared in Climatological Data-National Summary and prior to 1950 in Monthly Weather Review.

C 30.75:date • Item 273-B
RESEARCH PROGRESS AND PLANS OF THE WEATHER BUREAU, FISCAL YEAR (date). 1960–
[Annual]
Discontinued.

C 30.75/2:date • Item 273-E
CURRENT FEDERAL METEOROLOGICAL RESEARCH AND DEVELOPMENT ACTIVITIES. 1962/63–
[Annual]
Discontinued.

C 30.76:date • Item 273-C
DAILY AEROLOGICAL CROSS-SECTION POLE TO POLE ALONG MERIDIAN 75 DEGREE W FOR THE IGY PERIOD, JULY 1957– DEC. 1958.
[Monthly]

Note 18 in series.
Discontinued.

C 30.77:date • Item 279-C
SUMMER STUDENT TRAINEE REPORT. [Annual]

Earlier C 30.2:T 68
Student papers.
Discontinued.

C 30.78:CT
STUDY KITS.

C 30.79 • Item 282-A
WEATHER SERVICE FOR MERCHANT SHIPPING.
1st–   [Irregular]

PURPOSE:– To provide a directory service containing details of all U.S. and principal foreign radio stations making scheduled broadcasts of marine weather bulletins to merchant ships. Broadcast bulletins described in this publication contain warnings and forecasts applicable to major ocean areas of the world where service is available.
Information includes time of transmission, call signs, frequency K.C., contents of transmission, and remarks. Includes maps showing areas covered.
Latest edition: 15th, February 1967.

C 30.80:nos.
NATIONAL METEOROLOGICAL CENTER TECHNICAL MEMORANDUMS.

C 30.81:CT
ADDRESSES.

C 30.82:nos.
TECHNICAL NOTES.

C 30.83
OPERATIONS OF THE WEATHER BUREAU. [Semiannual]

C 30.84:nos
EASTERN REGION RADAR PROGRESS REPORT.

C 30.85
WATER SUPPLY OUTLOOK FOR WESTERN UNITED STATES. v. 1–   [Monthly]

Prior to 1969, entitled Water Supply Forecasts for Western United States.

C 30.86:date
OBSERVERS QUARTERLY.
Discontinued.

C 30.87:nos.
SYSTEMS DEVELOPMENT OFFICE REPORTS (numbered).

C 30.88:date
COOPERATIVE OBSERVER, REGIONAL NEWS LETTER, WESTERN REGION, SALT LAKE CITY, UTAH.

CIVIL AERONAUTICS AUTHORITY (1940– 1959)

CREATION AND AUTHORITY

The Civil Aeronautics Authority (CA 1) was established as an independent agency under the Civil Aeronautics Act of 1938 (52 Stat. 973), composed of the Authority, an Administrator, and the Air Safety Board. By Reorganization Plan Nos. 3 and 4 of 1940, effective June 30, 1940, the five-member Board was changed to the Civil Aeronautics Board, the Air Safety Board abolished, and the functions of the Administrator placed under the Secretary of Commerce. While the Civil Aeronautics Authority was a part of the Department of Commerce, it performed no administrative functions.

C 31.1:date
ANNUAL REPORTS.

Earlier CA 1.1

C 31.2:CT
GENERAL PUBLICATIONS.

Earlier 1.2

C 31.5:CT
LAWS.

C 31.6:CT
REGULATIONS, RULES, AND INSTRUCTIONS. INCLUDES HANDBOOKS AND MANUALS.

C 31.7:vol.
CIVIL AERONAUTICS JOURNAL. [Bimonthly]

Earlier CA 1.17
Later C 31.118

C 31.8:date
TABULATION OF AIR NAVIGATION RADIO AIDS.
[Monthly]

Earlier CA 1.9
Later C 31.108

C 31.9:vol.
WEEKLY NOTICES TO AIRMEN.

Earlier CA 1.7
Later C 31.109

C 31.10:dt.&nos.
SPECIAL NOTICES TO AIRMEN.

Earlier CA 1.7/2
Later C 31.110

C 31.11:nos.
TECHNICAL DEVELOPMENT REPORTS.

Earlier C 23.19
Later C 31.119

C 31.12:nos.
TECHNICAL DEVELOPMENT NOTES.

Later C 31.125

CIVIL AERONAUTICS ADMINISTRATION (1940– 1959)

CREATION AND AUTHORITY

The Civil Aeronautics Administration was established within the Department of Commerce by Departmental Order 52, dated August 29, 1940, pursuant to Reorganization Plan Nos. 3 and 4 of 1940, effective June 30, 1940, which placed those functions which had previously been administered by the Administrator of Civil Aeronautics under the direction and supervision of the Secretary of Commerce. The functions, funds, and personnel of the Civil Aeronautics Administration, were integrated into the newly established Federal Aviation Agency (FAA 1) on January 1, 1959, pursuant to the Federal Aviation Act of 1958 (Public Law 726, 85th Congress, second session, approved August 23, 1958).

C 31.101:date • Item 165
ANNUAL REPORTS.

Discontinued.

C 31.102:CT • Item 168
GENERAL PUBLICATIONS.

Discontinued.

C 31.103:nos.
CIVIL AERONAUTICS BULLETINS.

Earlier CA 1.3

C 31.103/2:nos.
AIRPORT ENGINEERING BULLETINS, PROC.
[Administrative]

C 31.103/4:nos.
MAINTENANCE ENGINEERING BRANCH TRAINING
BULLETIN, OJT NOS. [Administrative]

C 31.104/2
AIR TRAFFIC CONTROL PERFORMANCE STAN-
DARDS CIRCULARS, PROC. [Administrative]

C 31.104/3
AIR TRAFFIC CONTROL TRAINING CIRCULAR, PROC.
[Administrative]

C 31.105:CT   • Item 169
LAWS.

    Discontinued.

C 31.106:CT   • Item 172
REGULATIONS, RULES, AND INSTRUCTIONS.

    Discontinued.

C 31.106/2:date
ANC PROCEDURES FOR CONTROL OF AIR TRAF-
FIC.
    Earlier 31.106:T 67/3
    Later FAA 3.9

C 31.106/3:nos./CT
ATC MANUAL. [Official Use]

C 31.106/4:nos.
MAINTENANCE OPERATIONS DIVISION INSTRUC-
TIONS. [Administrative]

    Later FAA 1.6/3

C 31.106/5:CT
HANDBOOKS, MANUALS, GUIDES (unnumbered).

    Earlier C 31.106

C 31.107:nos.   • Item 170
MANUALS (numbered).

    Earlier CA 1.10

    Discontinued.

C 31.107/2:v.nos.
CIVIL AERONAUTICS MANUALS [by volume num-
ber].

    Earlier C 31.107
    Later FAA 1.34

C 31.108:date
TABULATION OF AIR NAVIGATION RADIO AIDS.
[Monthly]

    Earlier CA 1.10

C 31.109:vol.
WEEKLY NOTICES TO AIRMEN.

    Earlier C 31.9
    Superseded by C 31.127

C 31.110:date
SPECIAL NOTICES TO AIRMEN.

    Earlier C 31.10

C 31.111:nos.
CERTIFICATES AND INSPECTIONS DIVISION RE-
LEASES.

    Earlier CA 1.21
    Later FAA 5.7

C 31.112:date
DOMESTIC AIR CARRIER OPERATION STATISTICS.
[Monthly]

    Earlier CA 1.22

C 31.113:nos.
ARMY NAVY CIVIL COMMITTEE ON AIRCRAFT RE-
QUIREMENTS PUBLICATIONS.

    Earlier C 23.17
    Transferred to Y 3.Ar 5/3:7

C 31.114:nos.
FLIGHT ENGINEERING REPORTS.

C 31.115:CT
CIVIL AERONAUTICS ADMINISTRATION, MAPS.

    Earlier CA 1.13
    Later FAA 3.12

C 31.116:chap.&pt.nos.
MANUAL OF OPERATIONS.

    Earlier CA 1.15
    Superseded by C 31.116/2

C 31.116/2:v.Chap & pt. nos.
FEDERAL AIRWAYS MANUAL OF OPERATIONS.
    Supersedes C 31.116

C 31.116/3:nos.-letters
MODIFICATION WORK ORDERS.
    Earlier W 1.56
    Later FAA 4.9

C 31.117:chap. nos.
INSPECTION HANDBOOK.

C 31.118:vol.   • Item 166
CIVIL AERONAUTICS JOURNAL. [Bimonthly]
    Discontinued.

C 31.119:nos.   • Item 175
TECHNICAL DEVELOPMENT REPORTS.

    Earlier C 31.11
    Later FAA 2.8

    Discontinued.

C 31.120:nos.
SPECIFICATIONS.

    Pubs. designated CAA-nos.
    Later FAA 1.13

C 31.120/2
AIRCRAFT SPECIFICATIONS (subscription).

    Consists of specifications, alphabetical in-
    dex, aircraft listing and monthly supplementary
    service, aircraft listing.
    Formerly C 31.102:Ai 7/37
    Later FAA 1.29

C 31.120/3
ENGINE AND PROPELLER SPECIFICATIONS (subscription).

    Consists of specifications, alphabetical in-
    dexes, engine listing, propeller listing and monthly
    supplements.
    Earlier title: Aircraft Engine Listing Propeller
    Listing.
    Formerly C 31.102:Ai 7/39 and C 31.102:R 94
    Later FAA 1.29/2

C 31.121:nos.
FLIGHT INFORMATION BULLETINS.

    Aircraft listing formerly C 31.102:Ai 7/3

C 31.122:CT
POSTERS.

C 31.123:nos.
STUDY OF AIR TRAFFIC CONTROL, REPORTS.

C 31.124:CT
ADDRESSES.

C 31.125:nos.
TECHNICAL DEVELOPMENT NOTES.
    Earlier C 31.13

C 31.126:date
DIRECTORY OF AIRFIELDS, U.S. ARMY & NAVY [Re-
stricted]. [Bimonthly]

C 31.127:vol.   • Item 162
AIRMAN'S GUIDE. [Biweekly]

    Supersedes C 31.109 and C 31.121:3
    Later FAA 1.23
    Discontinued.

C 31.128:v.nos.   • Item 167
FLIGHT INFORMATION MANUAL. [Semiannual]

    Companion publication to Airman's Guide
    (C 31.127).
    Later FAA 1.20
    Discontinued.

C 31.129:CT
[TECHNICAL PAPERS].

C 31.130:date   • Item 173
MILITARY AND CIVIL AIRCRAFT AND AIRCRAFT
ENGINE PRODUCTION, MONTHLY PRODUCTION
REPORT. [Restricted]
    Discontinued.

C 31.131:nos.
REPORTS OF DIVISION OF RESEARCH.

C 31.131/2:nos.
SPECIAL SERIES REPORTS OF DIVISION OF RE-
SEARCH.

C 31.132:date
CIVIL AIRCRAFT BY STATES AND BY COUNTIES
WITHIN STATES. [Monthly]

C 31.132/2:date
UNITED STATES ACTIVE CIVIL AIRCRAFT BY STATE
AND COUNTY.
    Earlier C 31.102:Ai 7/50
    Later FAA 1.35

C 31.133:v.nos.
INTERNATIONAL NOTAMS. [Daily]

    Later FAA 1.26

C 31.134:v.nos.• Item 164-A
ALASKA FLIGHT INFORMATION MANUAL.

    Later FAA 1.21

    Discontinued.

C 31.135:v.nos.
ALASKA AIRMAN'S GUIDE.

    Later FAA 1.24

C 31.136:v.nos.
AIRMAN'S GUIDE, 9TH REGION SUPPLEMENT
[PACIFIC OCEAN AREA]. [Monthly]

    Supplements C 31.127
    Later FAA 1.25

C 31.137:CT   • Item 163
AIRPORT MANAGEMENT SERIES

    Discontinued.

C 31.138:nos.   • Item 176
TECHNICAL MANUALS.

    Later FAA 5.8

    Discontinued.

C 31.139:v.nos.   • Item 168-A
INTERNATIONAL FLIGHT INFORMATION MANUAL.
[Quarterly]

    Later FAA 1.22

    Discontinued.

C 31.140:pt.nos.   • **Item 171**
REGULATIONS OF ADMINISTRATOR.

Later FAA 1.6/4

Discontinued.

C 31.141:nos.   • **Item 164**
AIRWAYS OPERATING AND TRAINING SERIES BULLETINS.

Discontinued.

C 31.142:date   • **Item 161**
ANNUAL REPORTS OF AIR NAVIGATION DEVELOPMENT BOARD.

Discontinued.

C 31.142/2
AIR NAVIGATION DEVELOPMENT BOARD RELEASES.

C 31.142/3:nos.
AIR NAVIGATION DEVELOPMENT BOARD REPORTS, PROC.

C 31.142/4:nos.
AIR NAVIGATION DEVELOPMENT BOARD TECHNICAL SPECIFICATIONS.

C 31.143:letters-nos.
TECHNICAL STANDARDS ORDERS.

Later FAA 1.38

C 31.143/2:date
TECHNICAL STANDARDS REGISTER. [Annual]

C 31.144:date   • **Item 174**
STATISTICAL HANDBOOK OF CIVIL AVIATION.

Later FAA 1.32

Discontinued.

C 31.145:CT   • **Item 163-A**
AIRPORT PLANNING.

Discontinued.

C 31.145/2:date   • **Item 170-B**
NATIONAL AIRPORT PLAN.

Earlier C 31.102:Ai 7/16
Later FAA 4.8

Discontinued.

C 31.145/3:date
ANNUAL REPORT OF OPERATIONS UNDER FEDERAL AIRPORT ACT.

Earlier C 31.105:M 31
Later FAA 1.30

C 31.146:nos.
RELEASES.

C 31.146/2:nos.
[PROFILES] P SERIES.

C 31.147:date   • **Item 163-B**
AIRWORTHINESS DIRECTIVE SUMMARY.

Earlier C 31.102:Ai 7/34

Discontinued.

C 31.147/2:nos.
CAA AIRWORTHINESS DIRECTIVE. [Biweekly]

Later FAA 1.28

C 31.148
SUMMARY OF FEDERAL-AIR AIRPORT PROGRAM. [Monthly]

C 31.149
OFFICE OF FEDERAL AIRWAYS MAINTENANCE ENGINEERING DIVISION NEWSLETTER. [Bimonthly]

C 31.150
AIRCRAFT EMERGENCY EVACUATION REPORTS.

C 31.151:date   • **Item 174-A**
STATUS OF CAA RELEASES, MANUALS, AND REGULATIONS. [Quarterly]

Later FAA 1.18

Discontinued.

C 31.152
MONTHLY COMMENT ON AVIATION TRENDS.

C 31.153:date   • **Item 161-A**
AIR COMMERCE TRAFFIC PATTERNS.

Later FAA 4.11

Discontinued.

C 31.153/2:date
INTERNATIONAL AIR COMMERCE TRAFFIC PATTERN, U.S. FLAG CARRIERS, CALENDAR YEAR.

Earlier C 31.102:T 67/4

C 31.154
CAA MEMO.

C 31.155
BASIC SUPERVISION.

C 31.156:nos.
AIRFRAME AND EQUIPMENT ENGINEERING REPORTS.

C 31.157:date   • **Item 169-A**
LOCATION IDENTIFIERS.

Earlier C 31.102:L 78
Later FAA 3.10

Discontinued.

C 31.158
FEDERAL AIRWAYS AIR TRAFFIC ACTIVITY. [Semiannual]

Later FAA 1.27

C 31.159
CAA NEWS DIGEST.

C 31.160:date   • **Item 174-B**
STATISTICAL STUDY OF U.S. CIVIL AIRCRAFT. [Annual]

Earlier C 31.102:Ac 2/2
Later FAA 1.15

Discontinued.

C 31.160/2:date
GENERAL AVIATION ACCIDENTS (NON-AIR CARRIER), STATISTICAL ANALYSIS. [Annual]

Earlier C 31.102:St 2
Later FAA 1.32/2

C 31.161
ELECTRONIC EQUIPMENT MODIFICATION.

C 31.161/2:nos.
AIRBORNE ELECTRONICS MODIFICATION. [Administrative]

C 31.162:date
LIST OF PUBLICATIONS.

Earlier C 31.102:P 96/2
Later FAA 1.10

C 31.162:date
GENERAL MAINTENANCE INSPECTION AIDS. [Annual with Monthly Supplements]
Later FAA 1.31

C 31.163:date   • **Item 168-B**
GENERAL MAINTENANCE INSPECTION AIDS. [Annual with Monthly supplements]
Later FAA 1.31
Discontinued.

C 31.163/2:nos.
GENERAL MAINTENANCE ALERT BULLETINS.
Later FAA 1.31/2

C 31.163/3:date
UNITED STATES STANDARD FLIGHT INSPECTION MANUAL.
Later FAA 5.9

C 31.164
POWER PLANT ENGINEERING REPORTS.

C 31.165:date
ENROUTE IFR AIR TRAFFIC SURVEY. [Annual]
Later FAA 3.11

C 31.166:nos.   • **Item 170-A**
QUALITY CONTROL DIGESTS.
Later FAA 5.11
Discontinued.

C 31.167:date   • **Item 166-A**
FEDERAL AIRWAY PLAN.
Earlier C 31.102:Ai 7/52
Later FAA 1.37
Discontinued.

C 31.168:nos.   • **Item 168-C**
JET AGE PLANNING, PROGRESS REPORTS.
Later FAA 1.36
Discontinued.

C 31.169:nos.
ADMINISTRATOR'S NOTICE. [Administrative]

CIVIL AERONAUTICS BOARD
(1940– 1978)

CREATION AND AUTHORITY

The Civil Aeronautics Board was established within the Department of Commerce under Reorganization Plans 3 and 4 of 1940, effective June 30, 1940. The Board was made an independent agency by the Federal Aviation Act of 1958 (72 Stat. 731), effective January 1, 1959.
Note:– For the period from January 1959 until June 1978, the C 31.200 SuDocs classes continued to be used for CAB publications. In June 1978, a new class, CAB 1, was assigned for all publications issued after that date.

C 31.201   • **Item 178**
ANNUAL REPORT. 1941–   [Annual]

Reports activities of the Board for the fiscal year.

C 31.202:CT   • **Item 183**
GENERAL PUBLICATIONS.

C 31.203/2
ACCIDENT PREVENTION BULLETIN, U.S. GENERAL AVIATION.

C 31.205:CT   • **Item 184**
LAWS.

Later CAB 1.5

C 31.205:Ae 8   • **Item 184**
AERONAUTICAL STATUTES AND RELATED MATERIAL, FEDERAL AVIATION ACT OF 1958 AND OTHER PROVISIONS RELATING TO CIVIL AERONAUTICS. 1940–   [Irregular]

Compiled by the Office of General Counsel.

C 31.206:serial nos.
REGULATIONS.
Earlier CA 1.6

C 31.206/2:CT   • **Item 186**
REGULATIONS, RULES, AND INSTRUCTIONS.

C 31.206/2:L 52/date • Item 186
CIVIL AERONAUTICS BOARD LEGISLATIVE HISTORY OF REGULATIONS. [Irregular] (Includes basic volume plus supplementary material for an indefinite period)

C 31.206/3:nos.
SPECIAL CIVIL AIR REGULATIONS.

C 31.206/4:nos.
SAFETY INVESTIGATION REGULATIONS, SIR (series).

C 31.206/5 • Item 186
UNIFORM SYSTEM OF ACCOUNTS AND REPORTS FOR CERTIFICATED ROUTE AIR CARRIERS IN ACCORDANCE WITH SEC. 407 OF THE FEDERAL AVIATION ACT. [Irregular]

> This publication is not included in the subscription to Regulations listed above.
> This system of accounts and reports is applicable to all certificate route air carriers holding Certificates of Public Convenience and Necessity subject to the provisions of the Federal Aviation Act of 1958, as amended.
> Issued in looseleaf form and punched for 3-ring binder.
> Subscription price includes basic volume and supplementary material for an indefinite period.

C 31.206/6
ORGANIZATION REGULATIONS. OR 1– [Irregular]

> Issued under authority of Reorganization Plan No. 3 of 1961.

C 31.206/7 • Item 186
REGULATIONS OF THE CIVIL AERONAUTICS BOARD. [Irregular]

> Later CAB 1.16

C 31.206/8
PARTS 375–377. SPECIAL REGULATIONS. SPR 1– [Irregular]

> Regulations established under authority from the Federal Aviation Act of 1953.
> ISSN 0364-7706

C 31.206/9:CT • Item 186
HANDBOOKS, MANUALS, GUIDES. [Irregular]

> Formerly included in Regulations, Rules, and Instructions (C 31.206/2).
> Later CAB 1.8

C 31.207:serial nos.
ORDERS.

> Earlier CA 1.12

C 31.208
WEEKLY SUMMARY OF ORDERS AND REGULATIONS. [Weekly]

> Gives in tabular form order number, docket number, summary, and data adopted or orders and regulations.
> ISSN 0364-7099

C 31.209:pt.nos. • Item 180
CIVIL AIR REGULATIONS.

> Earlier CA 1.19

> Discontinued.

C 31.209/2:nos.
CIVIL AIR REGULATIONS DRAFT RELEASE.

> Later FAA 1.6/5

C 31.210:nos.
SPECIAL TARIFF PERMISSION UNDER SECTION 224.1 OF ECONOMIC REGULATIONS.

> Earlier CA 1.16

C 31.211 • Item 179
CIVIL AERONAUTICS BOARD REPORTS. v. 1– 1938/40– [Irregular]

> Later CAB 1.21

C 31.211/a:v.nos.
ECONOMIC DECISIONS.

C 31.211/2
DOCKETS. PRELIMINARY.

C 31.211/3 • Item 179 (MF)
CUMULATIVE INDEX-DIGEST. [Irregular]

> Economic Cases
> Aug. 1938– May 1955. 1963.
> June 1955– April 1960. 1966.

> Discontinued.

C 31.212:CT
PAPERS IN RE.

C 31.213:CT
REPORTS OF INVESTIGATIONS OF ACCIDENTS INVOLVING CIVIL AIRCRAFT.

C 31.214:CT • Item 187
SAFETY BULLETINS.

> Discontinued.

C 31.215
ADDRESSES. [Irregular]

> Later CAB 1.25

C 31.216:v.nos.
FOREIGN AIR NEWS DIGEST. [Fortnightly]

C 31.217:CT
MAPS.

C 31.218:date
AIR TRAFFIC SURVEY [Maps].

C 31.219:date
REPORT OF FORMAL ECONOMIC PROCEEDINGS. [Monthly]

C 31.220 • Item 186
PARTS 200-299. ECONOMIC REGULATIONS. ER 1– [Irregular]

> Incorporated are all the substantive rules adopted as authorized by Titles I and IV of the Federal Aviation Act of 1958 and statements of general policy or interpretations thereof for the guidance of the public, in connection with economic regulatory functions of the Board.

C 31.220/2:date • Item 182
ECONOMIC REGULATIONS (compilation).

> Discontinued.

C 31.221:date
APPLICATIONS AND/OR AMENDMENTS THERETO FILED WITH CIVIL AERONAUTICS BOARD. [Weekly]

> ISSN 0364-1295
> Later CAB 1.23

C 31.222:CT
[CARRIER AIRLINES].

> See for Directory of Scheduled Common Carrier Airlines of the World, C 31.202:Ai 7/2.

C 31.223:nos. • Item 188
SAFETY STUDIES.

> Discontinued.

C 31.224 • Item 185
PARTS 300-211. PROCEDURAL REGULATIONS. PR 1– [Irregular]

> Established July 1, 1919, as amended, comprising rules and principles adopted by the Board under authority of section 204(a) of the Act, describing the administrative procedure by which the board operates with respect to the public.

> Discontinued.

C 31.224/2:nos.
REGULATIONS AND POLICY STATEMENTS.

C 31.225:dt.&nos. • Item 177
AIRLINE TRAFFIC SURVEY. [Semiannual]

> Changed from C 31.202:Ai 7/5

> Discontinued.

C 31.226
PRESS RELEASES. [Irregular]

C 31.227
CALENDAR OF PREHEARING CONFERENCES HEARINGS, AND ARGUMENTS CONFERENCES.

C 31.228
AGREEMENTS FILED WITH CAB UNDER 412(a) DURING WEEK ENDING. . .

C 31.229:date
RECURRENT REPORT OF MILEAGE AND TRAFFIC DATA: DOMESTIC LOCAL SERVICE CARRIERS. [Monthly]

> **C 31.229/2:date**
> – QUARTERS [comparisons].

> **C 31.229/3:date**
> – 12 MONTHS ENDING [comparisons].

C 31.229/4:date
RECURRENT REPORT OF MILEAGE AND TRAFFIC DATA: DOMESTIC HELICOPTER SERVICE, CERTIFICATED AIRMAIL CARRIERS. [Monthly]

> **C 31.229/5:date**
> – [Comparisons].

C 31.230:date
RECURRENT REPORT OF MILEAGE AND TRAFFIC DATA: DOMESTIC AIR MAIL TRUNK CARRIERS. [Monthly]

> **C 31.230/2:date**
> – QUARTERS [comparisons].

> **C 31.230/3:date**
> – 12 MONTHS ENDING [comparisons].

C 31.231:date
RECURRENT REPORT OF MILEAGE AND TRAFFIC DATA: FOREIGN, OVERSEAS & TERRITORIAL AIR MAIL CARRIERS. [Monthly]

> **C 31.231/2:date**
> – QUARTERS [comparisons].

> **C 31.231/3:date**
> – 12 MONTHS ENDING [comparisons].

C 31.232:date
RECURRENT REPORT OF MILEAGE AND TRAFFIC DATA: ALL CERTIFICATED AIR CARGO CARRIERS. [Monthly]

> **C 31.232/2:date**
> – QUARTERS [comparisons].

> **C 31.232/3:date**
> – 12 MONTHS ENDING [comparisons].

C 31.233:date
RECAPITULATION BY CARRIER GROUPS, CERTIFICATED AIR CARRIERS. [Monthly]

> **C 31.233/2:date**
> – QUARTERS [comparisons].

> **C 31.233/3:date**
> – 12 MONTHS ENDING [comparisons].

C 31.234:date
RECURRENT REPORT OF FINANCIAL DATA: DOMESTIC AIR MAIL TRUNK CARRIERS, QUARTERS [comparisons].

C 31.234/2:date
– 12 MONTHS ENDING [comparisons].

C 31.235:date
CERTIFICATED AIR CARRIER FINANCIAL DATA: DOMESTIC LOCAL SERVICE [quarterly comparisons].

Some of the following class numbers were formerly assigned to Recurrent Report of Financial Data series. The title has been changed from Recurrent Report of Financial Data to Certificated Air Carrier Financial Data.

C 31.235/2:date
CERTIFICATED AIR CARRIER FINANCIAL DATA: DOMESTIC LOCAL SERVICE 12-MONTH COMPARISONS. [Quarterly]

C 31.236:date
CERTIFICATED AIR CARRIER FINANCIAL DATA: FOREIGN OR OVERSEAS [quarterly comparisons].

C 31.236/2:date
CERTIFICATED AIR CARRIER FINANCIAL DATA: FOREIGN OR OVERSEAS [12-month comparisons].

C 31.237:date
RECURRENT REPORT OF FINANCIAL DATA: ALL CERTIFICATED AIR CARGO CARRIERS, QUARTERS [comparisons].

C 31.237/2:date
– 12 MONTHS ENDING [comparisons].

C 31.238:date
CERTIFICATED AIR CARRIER FINANCIAL DATA: RECAPITULATION BY CARRIER GROUPS [quarterly comparisons].

C 31.238/2:date
CERTIFICATED AIR CARRIER FINANCIAL DATA: RECAPITULATION BY CARRIER GROUPS [12-month comparisons]. [Quarterly]

C 31.239:date
DOMESTIC AIR CARRIERS (trunk lines), COMPARATIVE STATEMENT OF BALANCE SHEET DATA. [Semiannual]

C 31.240:v.nos.&nos.   • Item 177-A-3
AIR CARRIER FINANCIAL STATISTICS. v. 1– [Quarterly]

ISSN 0565-1352
Later CAB 1.17

C 31.240/2
SUMMARY OF AIR CARRIER STATISTICS.

C 31.240/3:date   • Item 177-A-3
QUARTERLY INTERIM FINANCIAL REPORT, CERTIFIED ROUTE AIR CARRIERS AND SUPPLEMENTAL AIR CARRIERS.
Later CAB 1.14

C 31.241   • Item 177-A-2
AIR CARRIER TRAFFIC STATISTICS. [Monthly]

ISSN 0098-0404
Later CAB 1.13

C 31.241/2:v.nos.&nos.
AIR CARRIER ANALYTICAL CHARTS AND SUMMARIES, INCLUDING SUPPLEMENTAL AIR CARRIER STATISTICS. v. 1– 12, no. 1. 1963– March 1970. [Quarterly]

This publication supplements the Monthly Air Carrier Traffic Statistics and the quarterly Air Carrier Financial Statistics. Data are presented in chart form, supplemented by statistical tables. This is the only publication carrying data on supplemental air carriers.
Supersedes Supplement to Air Carrier Traffic Statistics. Previous titles: Monthly Report of Air Carrier Traffic Statistics; Certificated Air Carrier Traffic Statistics; and Recurrent Reports of Airline Mileage and Traffic Financial Data. The December 31, 1962 issue had title Supplement to Reports of Air Carrier Financial and Traffic Statistics.

C 31.241/3:date   • Item 177-A-17
COMMUTER AIR CARRIER TRAFFIC STATISTICS. [Quarterly]

Later CAB 1.11

C 31.242:date
CERTIFICATED AIR CARRIER FINANCIAL DATA: DOMESTIC HELICOPTER SERVICE [quarterly comparisons].

C 31.242/2:date
CERTIFICATED AIR CARRIER FINANCIAL DATA: DOMESTIC HELICOPTER SERVICE [12-month comparisons]. [Quarterly]

C 31.243:date
CERTIFICATED AIR CARRIER FINANCIAL DATA: TERRITORIAL INTRA-ALASKA AND OTHER ALASKA [quarterly comparisons].

C 31.243/2:date
CERTIFICATED AIR CARRIER FINANCIAL DATA: TERRITORIAL INTRA-ALASKA AND OTHER THAN ALASKA [12-month comparisons]. [Quarterly]

C 31.244:date
RESUME OF U.S. CIVIL AIR CARRIER AND GENERAL AVIATION AIRCRAFT ACCIDENTS, CALENDAR YEAR.

Earlier C 31.202:Ac 8

C 31.244/2:date
AERIAL CROP CONTROL ACCIDENTS. [Annual]

Earlier C 31.202:Ac 2/12

C 31.244/3:date
ACCIDENTS IN U.S. CIVIL AIR CARRIER AND GENERAL AVIATION OPERATIONS. [Annual]

Earlier C 31.202:Ac 2/13

C 31.244/4:date
SUMMARY REPORTS OF ACCIDENTS, U.S. CIVIL AVIATION. [Semimonthly]

C 31.244/5:date
BRIEFS OF ACCIDENTS, U.S. GENERAL AVIATION. [Semimonthly]

C 31.244/6:date
BRIEFS OF ACCIDENTS, U.S. CIVIL AVIATION. [Monthly]

C 31.245:date
ANNUAL REVIEW: AIRWORTHINESS CIVIL AIR REGULATIONS MEETING. ADMIN.

C 31.246:date
ALL-CARGO CARRIERS [quarterly comparisons].

C 31.246/2:date
ALL-CARGO CARRIERS [12-month comparisons].

C 31.247:date
OTHER CARRIERS [quarterly comparisons].

C 31.247/2:date
OTHER CARRIERS [12-month comparisons].

C 31.248:date
TELEPHONE DIRECTORY.

Earlier C 31.202:T 23

C 31.249   • Item 183-A (MF)
HANDBOOK OF AIRLINE STATISTICS. 1944– [Annual]

PURPOSE:– Designated to serve as a ready-reference source on the history and current status of commercial air transport in the United States.
For each airline, statistics are given showing trends in passenger, freight, express, and mail revenues and traffic; flying operation expense; aircraft maintenance expense; aircraft depreciation; promotion and sales expenses; administrative expenses, as well as data on capital gains, interest expense, income taxes, subsidy, dividends, investment, long-term debt, and rates of return on stockholder equity and investment.
The basic data can be updated by use of the monthly Air Carrier Traffic Statistics and the quarterly Air Carrier Financial Statistics.

C 31.250
AIR TRANSPORT ECONOMICS IN JET AGE, STAFF RESEARCH REPORTS.

C 31.251:date
AIRPORT ACTIVITY STATISTICS ON CERTIFICATED ROUTE AIR CARRIERS. [Semiannual]

Issued jointly by CAB and Federal Aviation Agency. Combination of former Air Commerce Traffic Pattern (FAA 8.9) of FAA and Airport Activity Statistics of Certificated Route Air Carriers of CAB.

C 31.252:nos.
BUREAU OF SAFETY PAMPHLET, BOSP (series).

C 31.252/2:nos.
BUREAU OF SAFETY REPORTS, BOSR (series).

C 31.253:date   • Item 177-A-4
LOCAL SERVICE AIR CARRIERS' UNIT COSTS. 1963– [Semiannual]
Issued pursuant to rule 1109 of the Rule of Practices in Economic Proceedings.
Former title: Certificated Air Carrier Financial Data: Domestic Local Service.
Later CAB 1.12

C 31.253/2
LOCAL SERVICE AIR CARRIER, SELECTED FLIGHT LOAD DATA BY CITY PAIR, BY FREQUENCY GROUPING, BY AIRCRAFT TYPE. 1963– [Annual]

PURPOSE:– To present arrangements of local service carriers' average flight passenger load data, initially required to furnish a basis for Use It or Lose It segment load analyses in formal proceedings, and additionally, to provide such data in summary form readily adaptable to flight load analyses for other uses.

C 31.254   • Item 177-A-15
LIST OF U.S. CARRIERS. [Semiannual]

Later CAB 1.26

C 31.255   • Item 177-A-20
LIST OF PUBLICATIONS. [Annual]

Non-Government Publication

C 31.256:date
TO MAYOR OF EACH CITY WITH LOCAL AIRLINE SERVICE.

C 31.257
SUBSIDY FOR UNITED STATES CERTIFICATED AIR
CARRIERS. 1st–   1952–   [Annual]

> Prepared by the Bureau of Economics, Local
> Service Division.

C 31.258:nos.
REGIONAL AIR CARGO WORKSHOP.

C 31.259   • **Item 177-A-1**
AIRCRAFT OPERATING COST AND PERFORMANCE
REPORT. v. 1–   1965–   [Annual]

> Later CAB 1.22

C 31.259/2:date   • **Item 177-A-1**
AIRCRAFT OPERATING COST AND PERFORMANCE
REPORT, FISCAL YEAR. [Annual]

C 31.260:v.nos.&nos.   • **Item 177-A-5**
AIRLINE INDUSTRY ECONOMIC REPORT. v. 1–
[Quarterly]

> Later CAB 1.18

C 31.261:date   • **Item 177-A-6**
SCHEDULE ARRIVAL PERFORMANCE IN THE TOP
200 MARKETS BY CARRIER. [Monthly]

> ISSN 0145-9295
> Later CAB 1.19

C 31.262:date   • **Item 177-A-7**
SEASONALLY ADJUSTED CAPACITY AND TRAFFIC:
SCHEDULED INTERNATIONAL OPERATIONS,
INTERNATIONAL TRUNKS. [Monthly]
> Later in C 31.262/5

C 31.262/2:date   • **Item 177-A-7**
SEASONALLY ADJUSTED CAPACITY AND TRAFFIC:
SCHEDULED OPERATIONS, SYSTEM TRUNKS.
[Monthly]
> Later in C 31.262/5

C 31.262/3
SEASONALLY ADJUSTED CAPACITY AND TRAFFIC:
SCHEDULED DOMESTIC OPERATIONS, DOMES-
TIC TRUNKS. [Monthly]
> Later in C 31.262/5

C 31.262/4:date   • **Item 177-A-7**
SEASONALLY ADJUSTED CAPACITY AND TRAFFIC
SCHEDULED OPERATIONS, LOCAL SERVICE
CARRIERS.
> Later in C 31.262/5

C 31.262/5:date   • **Item 177-A-7**
SEASONALLY ADJUSTED CAPACITY AND TRAFFIC
SCHEDULED OPERATIONS: SYSTEM TRUNKS
AND REGIONAL CARRIERS. [Monthly]

> Formerly carried in four separate publica-
> tions:– System Trunks (C 31.262/2), Domestic
> Trunks (C 31.262/3), International Trunks (C
> 31.262), and Local Service Carriers (C 31.262/4).
> Later CAB 1.20

C 31.263:date   • **Item 177-A-8 (MF)**
PRODUCTIVITY AND COST OF EMPLOYMENT:
LOCAL SERVICE CARRIERS, CALENDAR YEAR.
[Annual]

> Cancelled.

C 31.263/2:date   • **Item 177-A-8 (MF)**
PRODUCTIVITY AND COST OF EMPLOYMENT: SYS-
TEM TRUNKS, CALENDAR YEAR. [Annual]

> Cancelled.

C 31.264:date   • **Item 177-A-9**
QUARTERLY CARGO REVIEW.

> Cancelled.

C 31.264/2:date   • **Item 177-A-19**
TRENDS IN SCHEDULED ALL-CARGO SERVICE. 1st
ed.–   [Biennial]

> Cancelled.

C 31.265:nos.   • **Item 177-A-11**
AIR FREIGHT LOSS AND DAMAGE CLAIMS. 1– 19.
1972– 1976. [Quarterly]

> Superseded by C 31.265/2

C 31.265/2:v.nos.   • **Item 177-A-11 (MF)**
AIR FREIGHT LOSS AND DAMAGE CLAIMS FOR
THE SIX MONTHS ENDED (date). 1–   1977–
[Semiannual]

> Supersedes C 31.265

> Discontinued.

C 31.265/3:v.nos.   • **Item 177-A-11 (MF)**
AIR FREIGHT LOSS AND DAMAGE CLAIMS, ANNUAL
SUMMARIES. 1–

> Discontinued.

C 31.265/4:date   • **Item 177-A-22 (MF)**
U.S. INTERNATIONAL AIR FREIGHT TRAFFIC. [Annual]

> PURPOSE:– To present a series of statistical
> reports on traffic and financial statistical data on
> U.S. international air freight activity. Focuses gen-
> eral attention on the U.S. two-way foreign trade
> and more particular attention on the movement of
> goods by air.

> Discontinued.

C 31.266:date   • **Item 177-A-10 (MF)**
LOCAL SERVICE CARRIER PASSENGER
ENPLANEMENTS. [Annual]

> Discontinued.

C 31.266/2:date   • **Item 177-A-12 (MF)**
TRUNKLINE CARRIER DOMESTIC PASSENGER
ENPLANEMENTS. [Annual]

> Separate report issued for calendar and fis-
> cal years.

> Discontinued.

C 31.267:date   • **Item 177-A-13**
FUEL CONSUMPTION AND COST, CERTIFICATED
ROUTE AND SUPPLEMENTAL AIR CARRIERS,
DOMESTIC AND INTERNATIONAL OPERATIONS.
1977–   [Monthly]

C 31.267/2:date   • **Item 177-A-13**
FUEL COST AND CONSUMPTION, CERTIFIED ROUTE
AND SUPPLEMENTAL AIR CARRIERS, DOMES-
TIC AND INTERNATIONAL OPERATIONS,
TWELVE MONTHS ENDED (date). [Annual]

> Later CAB 1.15/2

C 31.268:date   • **Item 177-A-14**
PASSENGERS DENIED CONFIRMED SPACE. [Annual]

> Separate reports issued for calendar and fis-
> cal years.
> Later CAB 1.9

C 31.268/2:date   • **Item 177-A-14 (MF)**
UNACCOMMODATED PASSENGERS, BY CARRIER
AND MARKET. [Annual]

C 31.269:date   • **Item 177-A-16**
COACH TRAFFIC, REVENUE, YIELD AND AVERAGE
ON-FLIGHT TRIP LENGTH BY FARE CATEGORY
FOR THE 48-STATE OPERATIONS OF THE
DOMESTIC TRUNKS. [Quarterly]

> Later CAB 1.24

> Discontinued.

C 31.270:date   • **Item 177-A-18**
ANNUAL ECONOMIC REPORT OF AIR FREIGHT
FORWARDERS.

> Discontinued.

C 31.271:date   • **Item 177-A-21**
DOMESTIC JET TRENDS. 1st ed.–   1974–
[Biennial]

> Later CAB 1.29

C 31.272:date
SUMMARY OF PRESCRIBED UNIT COSTS AND
HOURLY RATE FOR RETURN ON INVESTMENT
AND TAX ALLOWANCE. [Annual]

NATIONAL INVENTORS COUNCIL
(1940– 1963)

CREATION AND AUTHORITY

> The National Inventors Council was estab-
> lished by the Secretary of Commerce in August
> 1940 with the full concurrence of the President.
> The C 34 classes were cancelled October 1947
> and publications changed to C 18 classes.

C 32.1:date
ANNUAL REPORTS.

C 32.2:CT
GENERAL PUBLICATIONS.

C 32.7:nos.
INFORMATION BULLETINS.

C 32.8:dt.&nos.   • **Item 250-D-1**
TECHNICAL PROBLEMS AFFECTING NATIONAL
DEFENSE.

> Discontinued.

RECONSTRUCTION FINANCE
CORPORATION
(1942– 1945)

CREATION AND AUTHORITY

> The Reconstruction Finance Corporation (FL
> 5) was transferred from the Federal Loan Agency
> to the Department of Commerce by Executive
> Order 9071 of February 24, 1942. The Corpora-
> tion was returned to the Federal Loan Agency
> pursuant to act of Congress, approved February
> 24, 1945 (59 Stat. 5).

C 33.1:date
ANNUAL REPORTS.

> Earlier FL 5.1

C 33.2:CT
GENERAL PUBLICATIONS.

> Earlier FL 5.2

C 33.4:nos.
CIRCULARS.

> Earlier FL 5.4

C 33.5:CT
LAWS.
    Earlier FL 5.5

C 33.7:date
QUARTERLY REPORTS.
    Earlier FL 5.7

C 33.8:CT
PAPERS IN RE.

    Earlier FL 5.10

C 33.9:letters
REGULATIONS-WAR DAMAGE CORPORATION.

C 33.10:CT
ADDRESSES.

    Earlier FL 5.9

C 33.11:date
SUMMARY OF SURPLUS PROPERTY. [Semimonthly]

    Later FL 5.11

OFFICE OF INTERNATIONAL TRADE OPERATIONS (1945)

CREATION AND AUTHORITY

The Office of International Trade Operations was established within the Department of Commerce by Departmental Order 6, dated October 21, 1945. By Departmental Order 10, effective December 18, 1945, the Office merged with the Division of International Economy to form the Office of International Trade in the Bureau of Foreign and Domestic Commerce.

C 34.:date
ANNUAL REPORTS.

C 34.2:CT
GENERAL PUBLICATIONS.

C 34.7:nos.
CURRENT EXPORT BULLETINS.

    Earlier Pr 32.5807

C 34.8:nos.
COMPREHENSIVE EXPORT SCHEDULES.

    Earlier Pr 32.5808

C 34.9:date
TRADE RELATIONS BULLETIN.

C 34.10:v.nos.
INDUSTRIAL REFERENCE SERVICE.

    Earlier C 18.220

C 34.11:v.nos.
INTERNATIONAL REFERENCE SERVICE.

    Earlier C 18.223

OFFICE OF TECHNICAL SERVICES (1946– 1953)

CREATION AND AUTHORITY

The Office of the Publication Board was created in the Department of Commerce to succeed the Publication Board (Y 3.P 96/6). The Office was later known as the Office of Declassification and Technical Service. On July 1, 1945 the Office was renamed Office of Technical Services. On October 1, 1953, the Office was placed under the newly created Business and Defense Services Administration (C 41) in the Department of Commerce.

C 35.1:date
ANNUAL REPORT.

C 35.2:CT
GENERAL PUBLICATIONS.

C 35.7:v.nos.
BIBLIOGRAPHY OF SCIENTIFIC AND INDUSTRIAL REPORTS. [Weekly]

    Earlier Y 3.P 96/6:9
    Later C 41.21

C 35.7/2:nos.
NEWSLETTER. [Monthly]
    Earlier C 41.21/2

C 35.7/3:nos.
NUMERICAL INDEX SUPPLEMENT TO BIBLIOGRAPHY OF TECHNICAL REPORTS.

C 35.8:nos.
TECHNICAL SERVICES.

C 35.9:v.nos.
FEDERAL SCIENCE PROGRESS. [Monthly]

C 35.10:nos.
OFFICE OF TECHNICAL SERVICES REPORTS SUITABLE FOR COMMERCIAL PUBLICATIONS, BULLETINS.

C 35.11:CT
BIBLIOGRAPHY OF REPORTS.

    Later C 41.23/2 and C 41.23/3

C 35.11/2:nos.
BIBLIOGRAPHY OF MOTION PICTURES AND FILM STRIPS, FB (series).

    Later C 41.23

C 35.11/3:nos.
BIBLIOGRAPHY OF REPORTS SB (series).

C 35.12:nos.
OTS TECHNOLOGY GUIDE CIRCULARS.

C 35.13:nos.
TECHNICAL DIVISION REPORTS.

C 35.13/2:nos.
TECHNICAL DIVISION REPORTS IR (series)

    Later C 41.26/2

C 35.14
QUESTIONS & ANSWER SERVICE.

C 35.15:nos.
RELEASES OTS (series).

OFFICE OF DOMESTIC COMMERCE (1945– 1947)

CREATION AND AUTHORITY

The Office of Domestic Commerce was established within the Department of Commerce by Departmental Order 10, of December 18, 1945. The C 36 classes were cancelled October 1947 and publications changed to C 18 classes.

C 36.1:date
ANNUAL REPORTS.

C 36.2:CT
GENERAL PUBLICATIONS.

C 36.7:nos.
INDUSTRIAL SERIES.

    Earlier C 18.225

C 36.8:CT
INQUIRY REFERENCE SERVICE.

    Earlier C 18.228

BUREAU OF PUBLIC ROADS (1949– 1966)

CREATION AND AUTHORITY

The Bureau of Public Roads (GS 3) was transferred from the General Services Administration to the Department of Commerce by Reorganization Plan No. 7 of 1949, effective August 20, 1949. Pursuant to Public Law 89-670, approved October 15, 1966, the Bureau was made a component of the newly established Department of Transportation (TD 2.100).

C 37.1:date   • Item 264
HIGHWAY PROGRESS (Year) ANNUAL REPORT OF THE BUREAU OF PUBLIC ROADS. [Annual]

    Earlier GS 3.1

C 37.2:CT
GENERAL PUBLICATIONS.

    Earlier GS 3.2

C 37.4/2:nos.
HYDRAULIC ENGINEERING CIRCULARS.

C 37.5:CT
LAWS.

    Earlier FW 2.5

C 37.6:CT
REGULATIONS, RULES, AND INSTRUCTIONS.

C 37.6/2:CT
HANDBOOKS, MANUALS, GUIDES (unnumbered).

    Earlier C 37.6

C 37.7:CT   • Item 267
PRESIDENT'S HIGHWAY SAFETY CONFERENCE.

    Earlier FW 2.18

    Discontinued.

C 37.8:v.nos.
PUBLIC ROADS, JOURNAL OF HIGHWAY RESEARCH.
[Bimonthly]

    Earlier GS 3.8

C 37.9:date
TRAFFIC VOLUME TRENDS. [Monthly]

    Earlier GS 3.7

C 37.9/2:date
TRAFFIC SPEED TRENDS.

    Later TD 2.115

C 37.10:v.nos.&nos.
HIGHWAYS CURRENT LITERATURE. [Weekly]

 Earlier FW 2.8

C 37.11:CT
TRANSPORTATION MAPS.

    Earlier FW 2.13

C 37.12:v.nos.
PLANNING, CURRENT LITERATURE. [Weekly]

    Earlier FW 1.15

C 37.12/2:v.nos.&nos.
URBAN TRANSPORTATION RESEARCH AND PLAN-
NING, CURRENT LITERATURE.

    Later TD 2.112/2

C 37.13:CT
MAPS (miscellaneous).

    Earlier FW 2.12

C 37.14
RELEASES.

C 37.14/2:nos.
NINTH PAN AMERICAN HIGHWAY CONGRESS,
INAUGURAL TOURS INTERAMERICAN HIGHWAY
NEWS.

C 37.15
ADMINISTRATION AND MANAGEMENT, CURRENT
LITERATURE. [Biweekly]

C 37.16
NEWS IN PUBLIC ROADS. [Monthly]

C 37.17:date
HIGHWAY STATISTICS. [Annual]

    Earlier C 37.2:H 53

C 37.17/2:date
HIGHWAY STATISTICS, SUMMARIES.

    Earlier FW 2.2:H 53/8
C 37.18   • Item 265-B
HIGHWAY FINANCE. [Annual]

C 37.19:date
RECEIPTS FOR STATE ADMINISTERED HIGHWAYS
(Official Distribution). [Annual]

C 37.19/2:date
DISBURSEMENTS FOR STATE ADMINISTERED HIGH-
WAYS. [Annual]

C 37.19/3:date
RECEIPTS FOR TOLL ROAD AND CROSSING FA-
CILITIES. [Annual]

C 37.19/4:date
DISBURSEMENTS FOR TOLL ROAD AND CROSS-
ING FACILITIES. [Annual]

C 37.20:nos.
ELECTRONIC COMPUTER PROGRAM LIBRARY
MEMORANDUM.

C 37.21:CT
ADDRESSES.

C 37.22:date
PRICE TRENDS FOR FEDERAL-AID HIGHWAY CON-
STRUCTION (Official Use). [Quarterly]

    Earlier C 37.2:H 53/5

C 37.23   • Item 263-C
HYDRAULIC DESIGN SERIES. 1–   1960–
[Irregular]

C 37.24:nos.
HIGHWAY RESEARCH NEWSLETTER (Official Use).

C 37.25:nos.
HIGHWAY CONSTRUCTION CONTRACTS AWARDED
BY STATE HIGHWAY DEPARTMENTS (For Offi-
cial Distribution).

C 37.26:nos.
HIGHWAY PLANNING NOTES. [Irregular]

C 37.27:nos.   • Item 265-D
HIGHWAY PLANNING TECHNICAL REPORTS.

    Discontinued.

C 37.28:CT
BIBLIOGRAPHIES AND LISTS OF PUBLICATIONS.

C 37.29:nos.
PUBLIC ROADS ROUND-UP. [Weekly]

    Official distribution.

C 37.30:date
HIGHWAY RESEARCH AND DEVELOPMENT
STUDIES.

C 37.31:v.nos.&nos.
BPR EMERGENCY READINESS NEWSLETTER.

    Official distribution.

C 37.32:nos.
BPR PROGRAM (series).

C 37.33:CT
POSTERS.

OFFICE OF INDUSTRY COOPERATION
(1947– 1948)

CREATION AND AUTHORITY

    The Office of Industry Cooperation was es-
tablished within the Department of Commerce in
January 1948 pursuant to act of Congress, ap-
proved December 30, 1947 (61 Stat. 945) and
Executive Order 9919 of January 3, 1948. The
Office was terminated during 1948.

C 38.1:date   • Item 232
ANNUAL REPORTS.

    Discontinued.

C 38.2:CT   • Item 232
GENERAL PUBLICATIONS.

    Discontinued.

FEDERAL MARITIME BOARD
(1950– 1961)

CREATION AND AUTHORITY

    The Federal Maritime Board was established
within the Department of Commerce by Reorganization Plan No. 21 of 1950, effective May 24,
1950. Reorganization Plan No. 7 of 1961, effective August 12, 1961, abolished the Board and
transferred its regulatory functions to the Federal
Maritime Commission (C 39.200), and functions
relating to subsidization of merchant marine to
the Secretary of Commerce.

C 39.101:date
ANNUAL REPORTS.

C 39.102:CT
GENERAL PUBLICATIONS.

C 39.106:CT
REGULATIONS, RULES, AND INSTRUCTIONS.

C 39.106/2:date
INDEX OF CURRENT REGULATIONS OF FEDERAL
MARITIME BOARD, MARITIME ADMINISTRATION,
NATIONAL SHIPPING AUTHORITY.

    Later C 39.206/4

C 39.108:v.nos.
FEDERAL MARITIME BOARD REPORTS, DECISIONS
(bound volumes).

    Earlier MC 1.22
    Later FMC 1.10

  C 39.108/a:nos.
  – SEPARATES.

    Earlier MC 1.22/a
    Later FMC 1.10/a

C 39.109:dt.&nos.
FEDERAL MARITIME BOARD AND MARITIME AD-
MINISTRATION RELEASES NR (series).

C 39.109/2:nos.
FEDERAL MARITIME BOARD, MARITIME ADMINIS-
TRATION RELEASES SP [Speeches].

    Later C 39.210/2

MARITIME ADMINISTRATION
(1950– 1981)

CREATION AND AUTHORITY

    The Maritime Administration was established
by Reorganization Plan 21 of 1950, effective May
24, 1950. The Administration was transferred to
the Department of Transportation (TD 11) by Public Law 97-31 of August 6, 1981 (95 Stat. 151).

C 39.201   • Item 233
ANNUAL REPORT. 1950–   [Annual]
    Report submitted by the Maritime Administra-
tion to Congress through the Secretary of Commerce for the fiscal year.
    Also published in the House Document se-
ries.
    Later TD 11.1

C 39.202:CT • Item 235
GENERAL PUBLICATIONS.

> Earlier MC 1.2
> Later TD 11.2

C 39.202:B 87/date • Item 235
BULK CARRIERS IN THE WORLD FLEET.

> Gives list of bulk carriers in the world fleet by country of registry, showing name, year built, gross, deadweight, speed and draft. Additional tables gives frequency distribution by age, speed and draft for selected years. Covers oceangoing merchant type ships of 1,000 gross tons and over and excludes vessels on the Great Lakes.
> Supersedes Ore Carriers and Ore/Oil Carriers in the World Fleet (C 39.202:Or 3).
> Later TD 11.20

C 39.202:F 76/date • Item 235
ESSENTIAL UNITED STATES FOREIGN TRADE ROUTES. [1953]– [Irregular]

> Gives description and map for the essential trade routes, with listings of U.S. steamship lines and commodities moving over them.

C 39.202:M 53/2/date
UNITED STATES MERCHANT MARINE, BRIEF HISTORY. [1957]– [Irregular]

C 39.202:Oc 2/date
REVIEW OF UNITED STATES OCEANBORNE FOREIGN TRADE. [Annual]

C 39.202:R 31/date • Item 235
RESEARCH AND DEVELOPMENT PROGRESS. 1st– 1968– [Annual]

> PURPOSE:– To keep the Maritime Industry current on the research and development programs of the Maritime Administration's Office of Research and Development.
> Includes list of current contracts, contract status, summaries of technical reports completed, In-House Studies and Technical Papers.
> Covers fiscal year.

C 39.202:Se 1/2/date
MARITIME MANPOWER REPORT: SEA FARING, LONGSHORE, AND SHIPYARD EMPLOYMENT AS OF (date). [Semiannual]

C 39.202:Su 1/2/date • Item 235
MARITIME SUBSIDIES. [Irregular]

> PURPOSE:– To provide a comparison of the subsidies and aids that are offered by different countries which influence the competitive sphere in which their vessels must operate. The subsidies and aids of each nation are detailed in the text, and are preceded by a brief run-down of each nation's economic background and events in their maritime industries.
> Later TD 11.27

C 39.202:W 12/date • Item 235
SEAFARING WAGE RATES, ATLANTIC, GULF AND PACIFIC DISTRICTS. [1964]– [Irregular]

C 39.205:CT
LAWS.

> Earlier MC 1.5

C 39.206:CT • Item 237
REGULATIONS, RULES, AND INSTRUCTIONS.

> Earlier MC 1.6

C 39.206/2:nos.
NSA (National Shipping Authority) ORDERS.

C 39.206/3:CT • Item 235-B
HANDBOOKS, MANUALS, GUIDES.

> Later TD 11.8

C 39.206/3:Se 1 • Item 235-B
SEAFARING GUIDE, AND DIRECTORY OF LABOR-MANAGEMENT AFFILIATIONS. 1969. 85 p.

> Lists U.S. flag shipowners, operators and/or agents who are parties to collective bargaining agreements with maritime unions and Government agencies involved with maritime labor, seafaring unions, longshore unions, shipyard unions and shipowner associations.

C 39.206/4 • Item 237
INDEX OF CURRENT REGULATIONS OF THE MARITIME ADMINISTRATION, MARITIME SUBSIDY BOARD, NATIONAL SHIPPING AUTHORITY. [Annual]

> PURPOSE:– To provide a convenient reference index for those persons required to use or comply with the regulations of the Federal Maritime Board, the Maritime Administration, or the National Shipping Authority.
> Contains numerical index of general orders, outline of codified general orders, subject index of general orders; numerical, subject, and symbol indexes of NSA orders.
> Later TD 11.22

C 39.207
[PRESS RELEASES]. [Irregular]

C 39.208:date
EMPLOYMENT REPORT OF UNITED STATES FLAG MERCHANT FLEET, OCEANGOING VESSELS 1,000 GROSS TONS AND OVER. [Quarterly] (Office of Subsidy Administration, Division of Statistics) (MAR-560-13)

> Summarizes the employment activity of the United States Flag Merchant Fleet. Presents the ownership, status, and area of employment of United States flag ships, by type, and in greater detail, the area of employment and ownership of combination passenger and cargo ships, freighters, and tankers.

C 39.209
NATIONAL SHIPPING AUTHORITY: SAFETY BULLETIN. [Quarterly]

C 39.210:CT
ADDRESSES.

C 39.210/2:nos.
ADDRESSES, MA-SP- (series). [Irregular]

> Earlier C 39.109/2

C 39.211:date • Item 236-C (MF)
MERCHANT SHIPS BUILT IN UNITED STATES AND OTHER COUNTRIES IN EMPLOYMENT REPORT OF UNITED STATES FLAG MERCHANT SEAGOING VESSELS 1,000 TONS AND OVER.
Discontinued.

C 39.212 • Item 236-B
MERCHANT FLEETS OF THE WORLD. 1956– [Annual]

> Gives seagoing steam and motor ships of 1,000 gross tons and over, by type of vessel and country of registration. Country summaries give number of ships, gross tons and deadweight tons as of last day of period covered; distribution by type of ship; new construction; transfers in and/or out; losses and/or scrappings.

> See TD 11.14

C 39.212/2:date
NEW SHIP DELIVERIES, CALENDAR YEAR.

> Discontinued.

C 39.212/3:date • Item 233-H
NEW SHIP CONSTRUCTION, OCEANGOING SHIPS OF 1,000 GROSS TONS AND OVER IN UNITED STATES AND FOREIGN SHIPYARDS. 1946– [Annual]

> PURPOSE:– To show the number and tonnage, by type (freighters, tankers, etc.), of new merchant ships being built and/or on order throughout the world.

> Arranged by country of construction and country of intended registration (flag).
> Later TD 11.15

C 39.213:date
DRY CARGO SERVICE AND AREA REPORT, UNITED STATES DRY CARGO SHIPPING COMPANIES BY SHIPS OWNED AND/OR CHARTERED TYPE OF SERVICE AND AREA OPERATED.

> Earlier C 39.202:D 84

C 39.214:date
UNITED STATES AND CANADIAN GREAT LAKES FLEETS. [Annual]

> Main table presents in tabular form, by owner, parent company, and name of ship: type, year built, gross tons, deadweight tons, speed (knots) and draft. Supplementary summary tables include U.S. Flag Great Lakes ships by owners, U.S. Flag Great Lakes fleet and Canadian owner Great Lakes fleet frequency distribution of gross tons, deadweight tons, and age.

C 39.215:date
CHARTER REPORT, GOVERNMENT-OWNED DRY-CARGO VESSELS, OPERATED BY BAREBOAT CHARTERS AND/OR AGENTS OF MARITIME ADMINISTRATION. [Monthly]

> Official use.

C 39.216:nos.
SHIPBUILDING PROGRESS REPORT FOR MONTH ENDING.
Official Distribution.

C 39.216/2:date • Item 236-E (MF)
RELATIVE COST OF SHIPBUILDING IN VARIOUS COASTAL DISTRICTS OF THE UNITED STATES, REPORT TO CONGRESS. 1st– 1963– [Annual]

> Report made annually by the Secretary of Commerce to Congress pursuant to Section 213(c) of the Merchant Marine Act of 1936, as amended.
> PURPOSE:– To report on studies made on the relative cost of construction or reconditioning of comparable ocean vessels in shipyards in the various coastal districts of the United States. The report also makes recommendations as to how such shipyards may compete for work on an equalized basis.
> See TD 11.15/2

C 39.217:date • Item 236-F
VESSEL INVENTORY REPORT, UNITED STATES FLAG DRY CARGO AND TANKER FLEETS, 1,000 GROSS TONS AND OVER. [Semiannual] (Division of Statistics) (MAR-560-19)

> Later TD 11.11

C 39.218:date • Item 235-A
HANDBOOK OF MERCHANT SHIPPING STATISTICS. [Annual]

> Discontinued.

C 39.219:nos.
MarAd SAFETY REVIEW. [Monthly]

> Prior to August 1970 issued as Reserve Fleet Safety Review.

C 39.220:nos.
VALUE ENGINEERING INFORMATION LETTERS. OFFICIAL USE.

C 39.221:date • Item 236-D
PARTICIPATION OF PRINCIPAL NATIONAL FLAGS IN UNITED STATES OCEANBORNE FOREIGN TRADE. [Annual]

> Discontinued.

C 39.222:date • **Item 233-B (MF)**
DOMESTIC WATERBORNE TRADE OF THE UNITED STATES. [Annual]

Gives for dry cargo ships and tank ships: shipping areas to receiving areas and receiving areas from shipping areas, by commodity; shipping port to receiving port and receiving port from shipping port, total tonnage. Summary charts give historical data.
Former title: Domestic Oceanborne and Great Lakes Commerce of the United States.
Later TD 11.19

C 39.223:CT • **Item 340**
PORT SERIES.

NEW SHIP CONSTRUCTION. [Semiannual]

Part 1 gives deliveries and Part 2 merchant ships under construction and on order during calendar or fiscal year, number and deadweight tonnage of oceangoing steam and motor ships of 1,000 gross tons and over by country in which built and for whom built for tankers and freighters, combination passenger and cargo ships, freighters, tankers.

C 39.223/2:date/nos.
HIGHLIGHTS OF MarAd PORT ACTIVITIES. 1–
1973– [Irregular] (Office of Ports and Intermodal Systems)

PURPOSE:– To inform the principal elements of the U.S. port industry (public and private port operators) about the various technical and promotional port programs carried out by the Maritime Administration.

C 39.224:date • **Item 237-A (MF)**
STATISTICAL ANALYSIS OF WORLD'S MERCHANT FLEETS SHOWING AGE, SIZE, SPEED, AND DRAFT BY FREQUENCY GROUPINGS, AS OF (date). 1956– [Biennial]

Later TD 11.12

C 39.225:date
COURSE OF INSTRUCTION AT MERCHANT MARINE ACADEMY.

C 39.226:v.nos. • **Item 233-A-2**
DECISIONS OF THE MARITIME SUBSIDY BOARD. v. 1– 1961/64– [Irregular]

v. 1 Aug. 1961– Sept. 1964

Discontinued.

C 39.227:CT • **Item 233-C**
BIBLIOGRAPHIES AND LISTS OF PUBLICATIONS.

Later TD 11.9

C 39.227:P 96 • **Item 233-C**
PUBLICATIONS OF THE MARITIME ADMINISTRATION. [Irregular] (Office of Public Affairs)

C 39.227:T 22 • **Item 233-C**
TECHNICAL REPORT INDEX, MARITIME ADMINISTRATION RESEARCH AND DEVELOPMENT. 1967– [Annual]

PURPOSE:– To make readily available to the public, and in particular to the Maritime Industry, knowledge of the accessibility of the research performed under the Maritime Administration's Office of Research and Development.
Each issue is cumulative and contains a subject index, a corporate source of reports index, and a technical report index (arranged numerically by report number).

C 39.227/2:v.nos.&nos.
MARATEC R & D TECHNOLOGY TRANSFER JOURNAL. [Bimonthly]

Later TD 11.26

C 39.228:date
SHIPS REGISTERED UNDER LIBERIAN, PANAMA-
NIAN, AND HONDURAN FLAGS DEEMED BY THE NAVY DEPARTMENT TO BE UNDER EFFECTIVE U.S. CONTROL. 1963– [Quarterly]

PURPOSE:– To reflect the owners and stock control of a list of foreign flag (Liberia, Panama, and Honduras) ships deemed by the Navy Dept. to be under the effective control of the U.S. Also includes a summary table showing the number and tonnage of the fleet by type of ship.

C 39.229:date
OCEANGOING MERCHANT SHIPS OF 1,000 GROSS TONS AND OVER SCRAPPED AND LOST DURING THE CALENDAR YEAR (date). 1946– [Annual] (Report MAR-560-23)

PURPOSE:– To record the number and tonnage of merchant ships scrapped or lost during the calendar year. Arranged by country and type of ship, giving the name, year built, gross and deadweight tonnage of each vessel scrapped or lost.

C 39.230:date • **Item 233-E**
OCEANGOING FOREIGN FLAG MERCHANT TYPE SHIPS OF 1,000 GROSS TONS AND OVER OWNED BY THE UNITED STATES PARENT COMPANIES [Annual] (Office of Subsidy Administration, Division of Statistics)

Part I gives a summary, by flag, showing type, number of ships and tonnage; a listing showing the United States parent companies and their foreign affiliates; and a name listing of ships by owner showing where built, flag and other characteristics. Part II gives a summary, by flag, showing type, number of ships and tonnage; and a listing by owner showing name or hull number, if available, and other characteristics of ships under construction.
Later TD 11.16

C 39.231:date
CONTAINERSHIPS UNDER CONSTRUCTION AND ON ORDER (including conversions) IN UNITED STATES AND FOREIGN SHIPYARDS OCEANGOING SHIPS OF 1,000 GROSS TONS AND OVER. [Semiannual] (Office of Subsidy Administration, Division of Statistics)

Gives containerships under construction and/or on order; ships with partial capacities for containers and/or vehicles under construction and/or on order; and merchant vessels converted to containerships in United States shipyards, by country of construction shipyard, giving deadweight, number of standard 20' containers, speed, scheduled delivery date, and owner.

C 39.232:date
UNITED STATES FLAG CONTAINERSHIPS AND UNITED STATES FLAG SHIPS WITH PARTIAL CAPACITIES FOR CONTAINERS AND/OR VEHICLES. 1966– [Semiannual]

PURPOSE:– To show the number of containerships operating under U.S. flag. Arranged by owner showing vessel name, year built, speed, container capacity, etc.

C 39.233:date • **Item 233-D (MF)**
CONTAINERIZED CARGO STATISTICS. 1968– [Quarterly] (Office of Government Aid, Division of Trade Studies)

One of a statistical series of containerized cargo reports released for the information of industry and interested government agencies.
The report is designed to cover the trade areas which have the greatest concentration of container shipping– U.S. North Atlantic/United Kingdom and European Continent (Trade Route 5-7-8-9) and U.S. Pacific/Far East (Trade Route 29).
Formerly Foreign Oceanborne Trade of the United States Container Cargo, Selected Trade Routes.
Later TD 11.21

C 39.234/2:date
MarAd PRESS CLIPS.

C 39.235:date
MARITIME MANPOWER REPORT: SEAFARING, LONGSHORE, AND SHIPYARD EMPLOYMENT AS OF (date). – 1974. [Monthly] (Office of Maritime Manpower) (MAR 750-10)

Gives totals for seafaring jobs abroad, longshore employment and shipyard employment. For shipboard jobs, table gives, breakdown by types for cargo ships, tanks, passenger/combination, and total for month, previous month, and month a year ago.
Earlier C 39.202:Se 1/2

C 39.236:date
SEAWORD, DEVELOPMENTS IN AMERICAN FLAG SHIPPING. 1971– [Quarterly] (Office of Market Development)

PURPOSE:– To provide exporters and importers with a digest of the latest developments in American flag shipping. Conveys a modern image of the U.S. flag fleet and supports the Maritime Administration's efforts to urge shippers to use U.S. flag vessels.
ISSN 0364-8397

C 39.237:date • **Item 233-F (MF)**
INVENTORY OF AMERICAN INTERMODAL EQUIPMENT, (year). 1972– [Annual] (Division of Intermodal Transport, Office of Ports and Intermodal Systems)

PURPOSE:– To present an inventory of intermodal equipment owned by U.S. steamship or leasing companies. The types of intermodal equipment tested are containers, chassis, shipborne barges, and vessels. Each type of equipment is classified as to either its dimensions, capacities or ratings.

C 39.238:date
MERCHANT MARINE DATA SHEET. [Monthly]

ISSN 0364-8427
Later TD 11.10

C 39.239:CT • **Item 333-G (MF)**
FINAL ENVIRONMENTAL IMPACT STATEMENTS. [Irregular]
Discontinued.

C 39.240:date • **Item 333-H**
UNITED STATES OCEANBORNE FOREIGN TRADE ROUTES. [Annual]

PURPOSE:– To provide detailed information on cargoes moving on United States foreign waterborne trade routes both in U.S.-flag and foreign-flag vessels. Includes narrative and tables showing commodity flow information by type of service and trade route.
Supersedes Essential United States Foreign Trade Routes (C 39.202:F 76).
Later TD 11.13

C 39.241:date • **Item 333-J (MF)**
INTERNATIONAL SHIPBORNE BARGE REGISTER. [Annual]
Earlier C 39.202:B 23
Later TD 11.24

C 39.243:nos. • **Item 233-K**
CAORF (series). [Irregular] (Computer Aided Operations Research Facility)

Highly technical reports.
Also published in microfiche (24x).
Later TD 11.18

C 39.244:nos.
NMRC (series). (National Maritime Research Center)

Later TD 11.17

C 39.245:date • **Item 233-I**
NATIONAL SHIPBUILDING RESEARCH PROGRAM (various subjects) (series). [Irregular]

Highly technical reports on various shipbuilding research subjects.

Discontinued.

C 39.246:letters-nos.   • Item 233-J
TECHNICAL REPORTS, MA-RD- (series). [Irregular]

    Later TD 11.23

NATIONAL PRODUCTION AUTHORITY (1950–1953)

CREATION AND AUTHORITY

    The National Production Authority was established within the Department of Commerce on September 11, 1950, by Executive Order 10161 of September 9, 1950, pursuant to the Defense Production Act of 1950 (64 Stat. 798). The Authority was abolished by Departmental Order, dated October 1, 1953, and its functions transferred to the Business and Defense Services Administration (C 41) of the Department of Commerce.

C 40.1:date
ANNUAL REPORTS.

C 40.2:CT   • Item 250-A
GENERAL PUBLICATIONS.

    Discontinued.

C 40.6:CT   • Item 250-B
REGULATIONS, RULES, AND INSTRUCTIONS.

    Discontinued.

C 40.6/2:nos.
NPA REGULATIONS.

    Later C 41.6/2

C 40.6/3:nos.
NPA DELEGATIONS.

    Later C 41.6/3

C 40.6/4:letters-nos.
NPA ORDERS.

    Later C 41.6/4

C 40.6/5:nos.
CMP REGULATIONS.

C 40.6/6:nos.
DESIGNATION OF SCARCE MATERIALS.

C 40.6/7:nos.
NPA ORGANIZATION STATEMENTS.

C 40.6/8:date
NPA REGULATORY MATERIAL AND FORMS DIGEST. [Monthly with weekly supplements in intervening weeks]

C 40.6/9:nos.
DMS [Defense Materials System] REGULATIONS.
    Later C 41.6/6

C 40.7:nos.
BUSINESS INFORMATION SERVICE: DEFENSE PRODUCTION AIDS.

C 40.7/2:nos.
SMALL BUSINESS AIDS (series).

    Earlier C 18.268

C 40.8:nos.
RELEASES.

C 40.9:nos.
NPA NOTICES.

    Later C 41.6/5

C 40.10:v.nos.
CONSTRUCTION AND BUILDING MATERIALS, MONTHLY INDUSTRY REPORT.

    Earlier C 18.233
    Later C 41.30

C 40.11:v.nos.&nos.
PULP, PAPER AND BOARD INDUSTRY REPORT. [Quarterly]

    Earlier C 18.229
    Later C 41.32

C 40.12:v.nos.
CONTAINERS AND PACKAGING INDUSTRY REPORTS. [Quarterly]

    Earlier C 18.242
    Later C 41.33

C 40.13:nos.   • Item 250-C
QUESTIONS AND ANSWERS ON CONTROLLED MATERIALS PLAN, Q & A (series).

    Discontinued.

C 40.14:date
UNITED STATES CONSUMPTION OF RUBBER. [Monthly]

    Later C 41.31

C 40.15:date
NPA PRODUCTION SERIES, QUARTERLY INDEXES OF SHIPMENTS FOR PRODUCTS OF METAL-WORKING INDUSTRIES.

C 40.16
MINUTES OF [Meetings of Committees of Various Industries].

C 40.17:CT
MATERIALS SURVEY REPORTS.

C 40.18:nos.
HISTORICAL REPORTS ON DEFENSE PRODUCTION. (Official use only)

BUREAU OF DOMESTIC COMMERCE (1970–1972)

CREATION AND AUTHORITY

    The Business and Defense Services Administration was established within the Department of Commerce by Departmental Order 152, dated October 1, 1953. The Administration was abolished and its functions transferred to the Bureau of Domestic Commerce (C 41) by Departmental Order 40-1A, effective September 15, 1970. By a Departmental Order of November 17, 1972, the Bureau was placed within the newly established Domestic and International Business Administration (C 57.500).

C 41.1:date
ANNUAL REPORTS.

C 41.2:CT   • Item 215
GENERAL PUBLICATIONS.

    C 41.2:M 34/3   • Item 215
    FACTS FOR MARKETERS: STANDARD METROPOLITAN STATISTICAL AREAS IN [ ] REGION GEOGRAPHICAL DIVISION. 1966–   [Irregular]
    Published for the following regions

        New England
        Middle Atlantic
        South Atlantic
        East North Central
        East South Central
        West North Central
        West South Central

        Mountain
        Pacific

C 41.3:nos.
BUSINESS SERVICE BULLETIN BSB (series). [Irregular]

C 41.3/2:v.nos.&nos.
BDSA BULLETINS, INFORMATION OF INTEREST OF EMPLOYEES.

C 41.3/3:nos.
BULLETIN, NATIONAL EXECUTIVE RESERVE. 1–

C 41.5:CT
LAWS.

C 41.6:CT
REGULATIONS, RULES, AND INSTRUCTIONS.

C 41.6/2:nos.
BDSA REGULATIONS.

    Earlier NPA Regulations, C 40.6/2
    Replaced by C 41.BDSAOT, September 1960 and DPS Regulations, C 41.6/2-2, in 1971.

C 41.6/2-2:nos.
DPS REGULATIONS (numbered). 1–   1953– (Defense Priorities System)

    These are the basic rules of the priorities system administered by BDC.
    Earlier BDSA Regulations, C 41.6/2.

C 41.6/3:nos.
BDSA DELEGATIONS.

    These are delegations other than emergency delegations that provide for the delegation of authority to other agencies or officials of the government by the Director of the Bureau of Domestic Commerce.
    Earlier NPA Delegations, C 40.6/3
    Later C 41.BDSAOT, September 1960.

C 41.6/3-2:nos.
BDSA REPORTING DELEGATIONS. [2]–   [1966]–

C 41.6/4:letters-nos.
BDSA ORDERS. [Irregular]
    Earlier NPA Notices (C 40.9).
    Later C 41.6/4:BDSAOT, September 1960, and BDC Notices, (C 41.6/5-2).

C 41.6/5:nos.
BDSA NOTICES.
    Earlier NPA Notices. C 40.9
    Later C 41.6/4-2:BDSAOT

C 41.6/5-2:nos.
BDC NOTICES. 1–   1970–   [Irregular]

    Published actions issued by the director, BDC, which are nonregulatory in nature, but pertain to the administration of BDC functions under the Defense Production Act of 1950, as amended.

C 41.6/6:nos.
DMS REGULATIONS. 1–
    Earlier C 40.6/9
    Later C 41.BDSAOT, September 1960.

C 41.6/7:date
BACKGROUND TO INDUSTRIAL MOBILIZATION, MANUAL FOR EXECUTIVE RESERVISTS.

C 41.6/8:nos.
BDSA EMERGENCY DELEGATIONS. 1–   1968–

    These are actions that provide for the emergency delegation of priorities and allocations of authority to individuals occupying named positions, in a line of succession, in the event of attack upon the United States.
    Earlier BDSA Emergency Delegations.
    Superseded by C 41.BDSAOT, September 1960.

C 41.6/9:CT   • Item 215-G
HANDBOOKS, MANUALS, GUIDES.

C 41.6/10:CT • Item 215-K
INDUSTRIAL MARKETING GUIDES.
Discontinued.

C 41.6/11:nos.
RULES OF PRACTICE. 1–   (Part of subscription to
C 4.BDSAOT)

C 41.6/12 • Item 215-G & 310-B-3
INDUSTRIAL CIVIL DEFENSE HANDBOOKS.
[Irregular]

C 41.7
PRESS RELEASES. [Irregular] (Press only)

C 41.8:CT
BUSINESS INFORMATION SERVICE.

C 41.8/2:nos.
– AREA AND INDUSTRIAL DEVELOPMENT AIDS.

C 41.8/3:CT/date
– ANNUAL SURVEYS.
        Earlier C 18.228

C 41.9
COMMERCE BUSINESS DAILY.
        Later C 57.20

C 41.9/2:nos.
BULLETIN CBD-S (series).

C 41.10:v.nos.&nos.
BULLETIN OF COMMERCE. [Weekly]
        Earlier C 18.269

C 41.11 • Item 215-A
MARKETING INFORMATION GUIDE. v. 1– 18. 1954–
1971. [Monthly]

        PURPOSE:– Published in the interest of bet-
ter marketing and selling.
        Contains annotations of selected current ma-
terials of value to those marketing and distributing our Nation's goods and services. Includes
Government reports, international organization
materials, and business, professional, and institutional materials. Important articles appearing in
periodicals are also included.
        Includes quarterly cumulative year-to-date in-
dexes.
        Previously titled: Distribution Data Guide.
        Discontinued.

C 41.12CT • Item 215-E
BIBLIOGRAPHIES AND LISTS OF PUBLICATIONS.
Discontinued.

C 41.12:P 96/2 • Item 215-E
BDSA PUBLICATIONS. [Semiannual]
        List of BDSA publications in print.

C 41.13
BIWEEKLY REVIEW, NEWS AND INFORMATION OF
INTEREST TO FIELD OFFICES.

C 41.14:CT • Item 215-C
ESTABLISHING AND OPERATING [Business].
        Formerly in C 18.225 and C 18.271
        Discontinued.

C 41.15
ADDRESSES. [Irregular]

C 41.16:CT • Item 215-J
MOTION PICTURES ABROAD.
        Discontinued.

C 41.17 • Item 215-Q
WORLD MOTOR VEHICLE PRODUCTION AND REG-
ISTRATION. 1960–   [Annual]

        Gives data on production of motor vehicles,
by country; summary of world motor vehicle registration, as of January 1, by world areas; detailed presentation of registration information, by
area and country. Two year comparisons.
        Later C 57.21

C 41.18 • Item 215-H
PRINTING AND PUBLISHING. [Quarterly]
        Later C 57.311

C 41.19 • Item 215-D
CONFECTIONERY SALES AND DISTRIBUTION.
[Annual]

        Former title: Confectionery Manufacturers'
Sales and Distribution.
        Later C 57.13

C 41.20:nos.
SIMPLIFIED PRACTICE RECOMMENDATIONS.
        Earlier C 18.277
        Later C 13.12

C 41.21 • Item 270
U.S. GOVERNMENT RESEARCH. v. 1–   1946–
[Semimonthly]

        PURPOSE:– To announce new reports of re-
search and development released by the Army,
Navy, Air Force, Atomic Energy Commission, and
other agencies of the Federal Government, the
majority of which is available for sale by the OTS.
        The first section is compiled by the Armed Ser-
vices Technical Information Agency (known as
ASTIA) and is called Department of Defense
agency which services DOD agencies and their
contractors with military research information. The
section is called Non-Military and Older Military
Research Reports. This section contains the reports which are collected by OTS and include
new reports of the Atomic Energy Commission
and other civilian agencies publishing research
and development reports. It also includes military
research reports not to be found in TAB. The joint
announcement program of ASTIA and OTS began
with the July 5, 1961 issue.
        Indexes are issued separately for January-
March, January-June, July-September, and July-
December.
        Supersedes 1946-49, Bibliography of Scien-
tific and Industrial Reports, 1949-54, Bibliography of Technical Reports.
        Earlier C 35.7
        Later C 51.9/3

C 41.21/2:nos.
TECHNICAL REPORTS NEWS LETTERS. [Monthly]
        Earlier C 35.7/2
        Discontinued.

[C 41.21/3]
PRICE LIST, SELECTIVE BIBLIOGRAPHY OF
GOVERNMENT RESEARCH REPORTS AND
TRANSLATIONS. SB 1–   [Irregular]

C 41.21/3:nos.
CATALOG OF TECHNICAL REPORTS CTR (series).
        Earlier C 35.11/3

C 41.21/4:date
NEW RESEARCH AND DEVELOPMENT REPORTS
AVAILABLE TO INDUSTRY. [Official Use]

C 41.21/5:v.nos.&nos.
KEYWORDS INDEX TO U.S. GOVERNMENT TECH-
NICAL REPORTS (Permuted Title Index).
[Semimonthly]

C 41.22:CT
TECHNICAL SERVICES OFFICE GENERAL PUBLI-
CATIONS.
        Earlier C 35.2

C 41.23:nos.
BIBLIOGRAPHY OF MOTION PICTURES AND FILM
STRIPS, FB (series).
        Earlier C 35.11/2

C 41.23/2:nos.
BIBLIOGRAPHY OF REPORTS IB (series).
        Earlier C 35.11

C 41.23/3:nos.
SELECTED INDUSTRIAL FILMS SIF (series).

C 41.23/4:CT
BIBLIOGRAPHIES AND LISTS OF PUBLICATIONS,
TECHNICAL SERVICES OFFICE.

C 41.24
TECHNICAL DIGEST SERVICE. [Monthly]

C 41.25:nos.
COMMERCIAL STANDARD CS (series).
        Earlier C 18.276
        Later C 13.20

C 41.26:nos.
TECHNICAL DIVISION REPORT, TAS (series).
        Earlier C 35.13

C 41.26/2:nos.
– IR (series).
        Earlier C 35.13/2

C 41.27:v.nos.&nos.
ARNA DEVELOPMENT BULLETIN. [Bimonthly]
        Later C 45.9 and C 46.9

C 41.27/2:nos.
FEDERAL REFERENCE MATERIAL FOR STATE,
ECONOMIC DEVELOPMENT AGENCIES.

C 41.28:nos.
TECHNICAL SERVICES OFFICE RELEASES.

C 41.28/2:date
SPECIAL ANNOUNCEMENT CONCERNING
RESEARCH REPORTS FROM DEPARTMENT OF
COMMERCE OTS.

C 41.29:nos. • Item 215-R
ATOMIC ENERGY COMMISSION RESEARCH RE-
PORTS FOR SALE BY OFFICE OF TECHNICAL
SERVICES.
        Earlier Y 3.At 7:15
        Discontinued.

C 41.30:v.nos.
INDUSTRY REPORT: CONSTRUCTION AND BUILD-
ING MATERIALS. [Monthly]
        Earlier C 40.10

C 41.30/2:CT
CONSTRUCTION AND BUILDING MATERIALS,
STATISTICAL SUPPLEMENTS.

C 41.30/3 • Item 219
CONSTRUCTION REVIEW. v. 1–   1955–   [Monthly]
        Later C 57.310

C 41.30/4 • Item 219
STATISTICAL SUPPLEMENTS. [Irregular]

C 41.30/5:date • Item 219-A
QUARTERLY SUMMARY FOR FUTURE CONSTRUC-
TION ABROAD.

C 41.31:date
UNITED STATES CONSUMPTION OF RUBBER.
[Monthly]
        Earlier C 40.14

INDUSTRY REPORTS

        The following reports contain mainly statisti-
cal data on production, consumption, inventories, exports and imports, etc. with brief textual
summaries of conditions, outlook, changes, etc.

C 41.32 • Item 223
PULP, PAPER, AND BOARD. v. 1–   1944–
[Quarterly]
        Later C 57.313

C 41.33 • Item 220
CONTAINERS AND PACKAGING. v. 1–   1948–
[Quarterly]
        Later C 57.314

C 41.34 • Item 220-A
COPPER. v. 1–   1954–   [Quarterly]
        Later C 57.312

C 41.34/2 • Item 220-A
ANNUAL STATISTICAL SUPPLEMENT. 1st–   1957–
[Annual]
        Later C 57.312/2

C 41.35 • Item 216-A
CHEMICALS. v. 1– 19. 1954– December 1971/May
1972. [Quarterly]
        Former title: Chemical and Rubber.
        Discontinued.

C 41.36:v.nos.   • Item 220-B
INDUSTRY REPORT: INTERNATIONAL IRON AND
STEEL. [Quarterly]
        Discontinued.

C 41.37
MONTH-END SUMMARY OF DOMESTIC TRADE SER-
VICES RENDERED BY FIELD OFFICES.

C 41.38:CT   • Item 638-A
MATERIALS SURVEYS.
        Earlier C 40.17
        Discontinued.

C 41.39:date
MONTHLY MOTOR TRUCK PRODUCTION REPORTS.

C 41.40:nos.
SOVIET BLOC INTERNATIONAL GEOPHYSICAL
YEAR INFORMATION. [Weekly]

        Published from February 14, 1958 to January
1, 1959.
        Later Y 3.J 66:14

C 41.41:v.nos.
TECHNICAL TRANSLATIONS. [Semimonthly]

C 41.42
ECONOMIC REPORT, ER- (series). 1960–   [An-
nual]

        Issued as a press release, each report cov-
ers a single industry, containing a review of the
preceeding year, the prospects for the coming
year, with supplemental statistical data. The material covered in the individual releases are consolidated and reprinted in a single volume, U.S.
Industrial Outlook (C 41.42/3).

C 41.42/2:nos.
[MIDYEAR REVIEW] MR- (series).

C 41.42/3   • Item 215-L
U.S. INDUSTRIAL OUTLOOK. 1960–   [Annual]

        PURPOSE:– To present in a single volume
the various individual Outlook Studies on selected
U.S. industries which were previously issued as
press releases.
        Each release is on an individual industry and
contains a review of the preceeding year, the
prospects for the coming year, with supplemental
background data and statistics.

C 41.42/4:date   • Item 215-L
INDUSTRIAL OUTLOOK AND ECONOMY AT MIDYEAR.
[Semiannual]
        Supersedes U.S. Industrial Outlook, (C 41.42/
3).
        Earlier C 41.2:Ec 7

C 41.43:nos.
AUTOMATICS.
        Designated PB 141095T

C 41.43/2:nos.
AUTOMATICS AND TELEMECHANICS ABSTRACTS.
[Monthly]
        Designated PB 141096T

C 41.44:nos.
AUTOMOBILE INDUSTRY [abstracts]. [Monthly]
        Designated PB 14110T

C 41.45:nos.
EXPLORATION AND CONSERVATION OF NATURAL
RESOURCES [abstracts]. [Monthly]
        Designated PB 141135T

C 41.46:nos.
GEOCHEMISTRY [abstracts]. [Monthly]
        Designated PB 14110T

C 41.46/2:nos.
BULLETIN OF MOSCOW SOCIETY OF NATURALISTS,
GEOLOGICAL DIVISION [abstracts]. [Bimonthly]
        Designated PB 14100T

C 41.46/3:nos.
GEODESY AND CARTOGRAPHY [abstracts].
[Monthly]

        Designated PB 14100T

C 41.46/4:nos.
NEWS OF ACADEMY OF SCIENCES OF USSR,
GEOGRAPHY SERIES [abstracts]. [Bimonthly]
        Designated PB 14110T

C 41.46/5:nos.
NEWS OF ACADEMY OF SCIENCES OF USSR,
GEOLOGY SERIES [abstracts]. [Monthly]
        Designated PB 141106T

C 41.46/6:nos.
NEWS OF ALL-UNION GEOGRAPHICAL SOCIETY.
1– 5. [   ]– 1959. [Bimonthly]

C 41.47:nos.
HYDRAULIC AND ENGINEERING CONSTRUCTION
[abstracts]. [Monthly]
        Designated PB 14109T

C 41.47/2:nos.
MECHANIZATION OF CONSTRUCTION [abstracts].
[Monthly]
        Designated PB 141093T

C 41.47/3:nos.
HYDRAULIC ENGINEERING AND SOIL IMPROVE-
MENT [abstracts]. [Monthly]
        Designated PB 141092T

C 41.48:nos.
JOURNAL OF ACOUSTICS [abstracts]. [Quarterly]
        Designated PB 141039T

C 41.49:nos.
RADIO ENGINEERING [abstracts]. [Monthly]
        Designated PB 141105T

C 41.49/2:nos.
RADIO ENGINEERING AND ELECTRONICS
[abstracts]. [Monthly]

        Designated PB 141106T

C 41.49/3:nos.
RADIO [abstracts]. 1–   1959–
        Discontinued.

C 41.50:nos.
REPORTS OF ACADEMY OF SCIENCES USSR
[abstracts]. [3 times a month]
        Designated PB 14106T

C 41.50/2:nos.
REPORTS OF ACADEMY OF SCIENCES USSR
[abstracts]. [Monthly]
        Designated PB 14106T

C 41.50/3:nos.
NEWS OF ACADEMY OF SCIENCES OF USSR, DE-
PARTMENT OF TECHNICAL SERVICES [ab-
stracts]. [Monthly]

        Designated PB 14109T

C 41.50/4:nos.
HERALD OF ACADEMY OF SCIENCES OF USSR
[abstracts]. [Monthly]
        Designated PB 141025T
C 41.50/5:nos.
NEWS OF ACADEMY OF SCIENCES OF ESTONIA
SSR, TECHNICAL AND PHYSIOMATHEMATICAL
SCIENCES [abstracts]. [Quarterly]
        Designated PB 14108T

C 41.50/6:nos.
HERALD OF MOSCOW UNIVERSITY, PHYSIO-
MATHEMATICAL AND NATURAL SCIENCES SE-
RIES [abstracts]. [Monthly]
        Designated PB 141051T

C 41.50/7:nos.
NEWS OF ACADEMY OF SCIENCES OF ARMENIAN
SSR, PHYSIOMATHEMATICAL, NATURAL AND
TECHNICAL SCIENCES SERIES [abstracts].
[Monthly]

C 41.50/8:nos.
HERALD OF LENINGRAD UNIVERSITY, MATHEMAT-
ICS, MECHANICS, AND ASTRONOMY SERIES
[abstracts]. [Quarterly]
        Designated PB 141037T

C 41.50/9:nos.
HERALD OF ACADEMY OF SCIENCES OF KAZAKH
SSR [abstracts]. [Monthly]
        Designated PB 141026T

C 41.51:nos.
STEEL [abstracts]. [Monthly]
        Designated PB 141136T

C 41.52:nos.
PROGRESS OF PHYSICAL SCIENCES [abstracts].
[Monthly]
        Designated PB 141049T

C 41.52/2:nos.
JOURNAL OF EXPERIMENTAL AND THEORETICAL
PHYSICS [abstracts]. [Monthly]
        Designated PB 141052T

C 41.52/3:nos.
NEWS OF ACADEMY OF SCIENCES OF USSR,
PHYSICS SERIES [abstracts]. [Monthly]
        Designated PB 14104T

C 41.52/4:nos.
NEWS OF INSTITUTES OF HIGHER LEARNING OF
MINISTRY OF HIGHER EDUCATION, PHYSICS,
[abstracts]. [Bimonthly]
        Designated PB 141043T

C 41.52/5:nos.
HERALD OF LENINGRAD UNIVERSITY, PHYSICS
AND CHEMISTRY SERIES [abstracts]. [Quarterly]
        Designated PB 141050T

C 41.56/6:nos.
JOURNAL OF TECHNICAL PHYSICS [abstracts].
[Monthly]
        Designated PB 141053T

C 41.52/7:nos.
NEWS OF ACADEMY OF SCIENCES OF USSR, GEO-
PHYSICS SERIES [abstracts]. [Monthly]

        Designated PB 141042T

C 41.52/8:nos.
PHYSICS IN SCHOOL [abstracts]. 1–
Discontinued.

C 41.53:nos.
JOURNAL OF GENERAL CHEMISTRY [abstracts].
[Monthly]
        Designated PB 141075T

C 41.53/2:nos.
NEWS OF ACADEMY OF SCIENCES, USSR, DEPART-
MENT OF CHEMICAL SCIENCE [abstracts].
[Monthly]
        Designated PB 141055T

C 41.53/3:nos.
PROGRESS OF CHEMISTRY [abstracts]. [Monthly]
        Designated PB 141070T

C 41.53/4:nos.
JOURNAL OF INORGANIC CHEMISTRY [abstracts].
[Monthly]
        Designated PB 140074T

C 41.53/5:nos.
JOURNAL OF PHYSICAL CHEMISTRY [abstracts].
[Monthly]
        Designated PB 141072T

C 41.53/6:nos.
JOURNAL OF ANALYTICAL CHEMISTRY [abstracts].
[Bimonthly]
        Designated PB 141071T

C 41.53/7:nos.
CHEMICAL INDUSTRY [abstracts]. [Issued 8 times a
year]
        Designated PB 141059T

C 41.53/8:nos.
NEWS OF INSTITUTES OF HIGHER LEARNING, CHEMISTRY, AND CHEMICAL TECHNOLOGY [abstracts]. [Bimonthly]
Designated PB 141056T

C 41.53/9:nos.
SCIENTIFIC REPORTS OF HIGHER SCHOOLS, CHEMISTRY AND CHEMICAL TECHNOLOGY [abstracts]. [Quarterly]
Designated PB 141066T

C 41.53/10:nos.
CHEMICAL SCIENCE AND INDUSTRY [abstracts]. [Monthly]
Designated PB 141058T

C 41.53/11:nos.
JOURNAL OF APPLIED CHEMISTRY [abstracts]. [Monthly]
Designated PB 141076T

C 41.54:nos.
NONFERROUS METALS [abstracts]. [Monthly]
Designated PB 41139T

C 41.54/2:nos.
PHYSICS OF METAL AND METALLOGRAPHY [abstracts]. [Bimonthly]

C 41.54/3:nos.
METALLURGIST [abstracts]. [Monthly]
Designated PB 141132T

C 41.54/4:nos.
SCIENTIFIC REPORTS OF HIGHER SCHOOLS, METALLURGY [abstracts]. [Quarterly]
Designated PB 141133T

C 41.54/5:nos.
MINING JOURNAL [abstracts]. [Monthly]
Designated PB 141127T

C 41.54/6:nos.
AUTOMATIC WELDING [abstracts]. [Monthly]
Designated PB 141125T

C 41.54/7:nos.
METALLOGRAPHY AND HEAT TREATMENT OF METALS [abstracts]. [Monthly]
Designated PB 141131T

C 41.54/8:nos.
WELDING PRACTICE [abstracts]. [Monthly]
Designated PB 141138T

C 41.54/9:nos.
JOURNAL OF ABSTRACTS, METALLURGY [abstracts]. [Monthly]
Designated PB 141140T

C 41.54/10:nos.
FOUNDRY PRACTICE [abstracts]. [Monthly]
Designated PB 141130T

C 41.55:nos.
CHEMISTRY AND TECHNOLOGY OF FUELS AND OILS [abstracts].
Designated PB 141060T

C 41.55/2:nos.
PETROLEUM WORKER [abstracts]. [Monthly]
Designated PB 141085T

C 41.55/3:nos.
PETROLEUM ECONOMY [abstracts]. [Monthly]
Designated PB 141086T

C 41.55/4:nos.
NEWS OF INSTITUTES OF HIGHER LEARNING, PETROLEUM AND GAS [abstracts]. 1– 1959– Discontinued.

C 41.56:nos.
CIVIL AVIATION [abstracts]. [Monthly]
Designated PB 141078T

C 41.56/2:nos.
NEWS OF INSTITUTES OF HIGHER LEARNING, AERONAUTICAL ENGINEERING [abstracts]. [Quarterly]
Designated PB 141401T

C 41.57:nos.
ENGINEERING FOR YOUTH [abstracts]. [Monthly]
Designated PB 141024T

C 41.58:nos.
PLANT LABORATORY [abstracts]. [Monthly]
Designated PB 141207T

C 41.59:nos.
HERALD OF COMMUNICATIONS [abstracts]. [Monthly]
Designated PB 141108T

C 41.60:nos.
HEAT POWER ENGINEERING [abstracts]. [Monthly]
Designated PB 141089T

C 41.60/2:nos.
POWER ENGINEERING [abstracts]. [Monthly]
Designated PB 141048T

C 41.60/3:nos.
POWER ENGINEERING BULLETIN [abstracts]. [Monthly]
Designated PB 141083T

C 41.60/4:nos.
INDUSTRIAL POWER ENGINEERING [abstracts]. [Monthly]
Designated PB 141078T

C 41.61:nos.
APPLIED MATHEMATICS AND MECHANICS [abstracts]. [Bimonthly]
Designated PB 141034T

C 41.61/2:nos.
NEWS OF INSTITUTES OF HIGHER LEARNING OF MINISTRY OF HIGHER EDUCATION, USSR, MATHEMATICS [abstracts]. [Bimonthly]
Designated PB 141032T

C 41.61/3:nos.
JOURNAL OF ABSTRACTS, MATHEMATICS [abstracts]. [Monthly]
Designated PB 141038T

C 41.61/4:nos.
PROGRESS OF MATHEMATICAL SCIENCES [abstracts]. [Bimonthly]
Designated PB 141036T

C 41.61/5:nos.
NEWS OF ACADEMY OF SCIENCES OF USSR, MATHEMATICS SERIES [abstracts]. [Bimonthly]
Designated PB 141031T

C 41.61/6:nos.
MATHEMATICS SYMPOSIUM [abstracts]. [Monthly]
Designated PB 141033T

C 41.61/7:nos.
UKRANIAN MATHEMATICS JOURNAL [abstracts]. [Quarterly]
Designated PB 141035T

C 41.61/8:nos.
THEORY OF PROBABILITY AND ITS APPLICATIONS [abstracts]. [Quarterly]

C 41.62:nos.
VOCATIONAL AND TECHNICAL EDUCATION ABSTRACTS. [Monthly]
Designated PB 141022T

C 41.63:nos.
OPTICS AND SPECTROSCOPY [abstracts]. [Monthly]
Designated PB 141047T

C 41.64:nos.
COKE AND CHEMISTRY [abstracts]. [Monthly]
Designated PB 141063T

C 41.65:nos.
MACHINE BUILDER [abstracts]. [Monthly]
Designated PB 14116T

C 41.65/2:nos.
MACHINE TOOLS AND TOOLS [abstracts]. [Monthly]
Designated PB 14116T

C 41.65/3:nos.
JOURNAL OF ABSTRACTS, MECHANICS [abstracts]. [Monthly]
Designated PB 141124T

C 41.65/4:nos.
HERALD OF MACHINE BUILDING [abstracts]. [Monthly]
Designated PB 141122T

C 41.65/5:nos.
MECHANIZATION OF LABOR AND HEAVY WORK [abstracts].
Designated PB 14117T

C 41.65/6:nos.
NEWS OF INSTITUTES OF HIGHER LEARNING, ELECTROMECHANICS [ABSTRACTS]. [Monthly]

C 41.65/7:nos.
SCIENTIFIC REPORTS OF HIGHER SCHOOLS, ELECTROMECHANICS AND AUTOMATION [abstracts]. [Quarterly]
Designated PB 141102T

C 41.65/8:nos.
SCIENTIFIC REPORTS OF HIGHER SCHOOLS, MACHINE CONSTRUCTION AND INSTRUMENTS MANUFACTURE. 1–
Discontinued

C 41.66:nos.
ELECTRICITY [abstracts]. [Monthly]
Designated PB 141098T

C 41.66/2:nos.
HERALD OF ELECTRICAL INDUSTRY [abstracts]. [Monthly]
Designated PB 141107T

C 41.66/3:nos.
JOURNAL OF ABSTRACTS, ELECTRICAL ENGINEERING [abstracts]. [Monthly]

Designated PB 141109T

C 41.66/4:nos.
ELECTRICAL COMMUNICATIONS [abstracts]. [Monthly]
Designated PB 141102T

C 41.67:nos.
SCIENCE AND LIFE [abstracts]. [Monthly]
Designated PB 141020T

C 41.68:nos.
GLASS AND CERAMICS [abstracts]. [Monthly]
Designated PB 141068T

C 41.69:nos.
JOURNAL OF SCIENTIFIC AND APPLIED PHOTOGRAPHY AND CINEMATOGRAPHY [abstracts]. [Bimonthly]
Designated PB 141073T

C 41.69/2:nos.
NEWS OF INSTITUTES OF HIGHER LEARNING OF MINISTRY OF HIGHER EDUCATION USSR, GEODESY AND AERIAL PHOTOGRAPHY [abstracts]. [Bimonthly]
Designated PB 141007T

C 41.70:nos.
RAW AND VULCANIZED RUBBER [abstracts]. [Monthly]
Designated PB 141057T

C 41.71:nos.
CEMENT [abstracts]. [Bimonthly]
Designated PB 141094T

C 41.71/2:nos.
CONCRETE AND REINFORCED CONCRETE [abstracts]. [Monthly]
Designated PB 141090T

C 41.72:nos.
STANDARDIZATION [abstracts]. [Bimonthly]

C 41.73:nos.
ASTRONOMICAL JOURNAL [abstracts]. [Bimonthly]
Designated PB 141028T

C 41.74:nos.
ATOMIC ENERGY [abstracts]. [Monthly]
    Designated PB 141082T

C 41.75:nos.
MEASUREMENT TECHNIQUES [abstracts].
    [Bimonthly]
    Designated PB 14112T

C 41.76:nos.
REFRACTORIES [abstracts]. [Monthly]

    Designated PB 141134T

C 41.77:nos.
INSTRUMENTS AND EXPERIMENTAL TECHNIQUES
    [abstracts]. [Bimonthly]
    Designated PB 141120T

C 41.77/2:nos.
INSTRUMENT MANUFACTURE [abstracts]. [Monthly]
    Designated PB 14119T

C 41.78:nos.
METEOROLOGY AND HYDROLOGY [abstracts].
    [Monthly]
    Designated PB 141045T

C 41.79:nos.
CRYSTALLOGRAPHY [abstracts]. [Bimonthly]
    Designated PB 141065T

C 41.80:nos.
OXYGEN [abstracts]. [Bimonthly]

    Designated PB 141062T

C 41.81:nos.
COLLOID JOURNAL [abstracts]. [Bimonthly]
    Designated PB 141064T

C 41.82:nos.
BULLETIN OF INVENTIONS [abstracts]. [Monthly]
    Designated PB 141014T

C 41.83:nos.
REFRIGERATION ENGINEERING [abstracts].
    [Quarterly]
    Designated PB 141061T

C 41.84:nos.
ENGLISH ABSTRACTS OF SELECTED ARTICLES
    FROM SOVIET BLOC AND MAINLAND CHINA
    TECHNICAL JOURNALS: SERIES 1, PHYSICS,
    GEOPHYSICS, ASTROPHYSICS, ASTRONOMY,
    ASTRONAUTICS, AND APPLIED MATHEMATICS.
    [Monthly]
    Designated 61-11, 140.

C 41.84/2:nos.
– SERIES 2, CHEMISTRY, CHEMICALS, AND
    CHEMICAL PRODUCTS. [Monthly]
    Designated 61-11, 141.

C 41.84/3:nos.
– SERIES 3, METALLURGY, METALS, METAL
    PRODUCTS, AND NONMETALLIC MINERALS.
    [Monthly]
    Designated 61-11, 142.

C 41.84/4:nos.
– SERIES 4, ENGINEERING (MECHANICAL,
    ELECTRICAL, AERONAUTICAL, NUCLEAR,
    PETROLEUM, STRUCTURAL, AND CIVIL),
    MACHINERY AND EQUIPMENT (GENERAL
    AND SPECIAL PURPOSE). [Monthly]
    Designated 61-11, 144.
  C 41.84/5:nos.
– SERIES 5, COMMUNICATIONS, TRANSPOR-
    TATION, NAVIGATION, ELECTRICAL AND
    ELECTRONIC EQUIPMENT, SYSTEMS AND
    DEVICES, INCLUDING AIRCRAFT AND
    MISSILE EQUIPMENT. 1–[34]. 1961–[1963].
    [Monthly]
    Designated 61-11, 145.

C 41.84/6:nos.
– SERIES 6, GENERAL SCIENCE AND MISCEL-
    LANEOUS, INCLUDING METEOROLOGY,
    OCEANOGRAPHY, BIOLOGY, ASTRO-
    BIOLOGY, BOTANY, ZOOLOGY, MEDICAL
    SCIENCE, AEROMEDICINE, EDUCATION,
    FUEL, FUEL PRODUCTS, AND POWER.
    [Monthly]
    Designated 61-11, 146.

C 41.84/7:nos.
– SERIES 7, GEOPHYSICS AND ASTRONOMY.
    Designated 62-11703.

C 41.85:date
TRANSLATED SWISS PATENTS (first claim only).
    Earlier C 41.22:Sw 6

C 41.85/2:date
TRANSLATED POLISH PATENTS (first claim only).
    Earlier C 41.22:P 75

C 41.88   • Item 215-F
SALAD DRESSING, MAYONNAISE AND RELATED
    PRODUCTS. [Annual]
    Later C 57.316

C 41.89:nos.
AREA DEVELOPMENT AID: AREA TREND SERIES.
    Earlier C 45.13

C 41.90   • Item 130-B
INDUSTRY TREND SERIES. 1–   1968– [Irregu-
    lar]
    Discontinued.

C 41.90/2:nos.
INDUSTRIAL LOCATION SERIES.
    Earlier 45.8/3

C 41.90/3:CT
INDUSTRIAL FACT SHEETS.
    Earlier 45.8

C 41.90/4:CT   • Item 215-T
BDSA INDUSTRY GROWTH STUDIES.
    Discontinued.

C 41.90/5:CT
PATTERNS OF INDUSTRIAL GROWTH (series).

C 41.91:CT   • Item 215-I
WORLD SURVEY OF AGRICULTURAL MACHINERY
    AND EQUIPMENT.
    Discontinued.

C 41.92:CT   • Item 215-N
FOREIGN TRADE INFORMATION ON INSTRUMEN-
    TATION [by country].
    Earlier C 41.3
    Discontinued.

C 41.93:CT   • Item 215-M
SELECTED UNITED STATES MARKETING TERMS
    AND DEFINITIONS ENGLISH– [Foreign Lan-
    guage].
    Discontinued.

C 41.94:nos.
CURRENT REVIEW OF SOVIET TECHNICAL PRESS.

C 41.95:date
BUREAU OF SHIPS, SHOP PRACTICE SUGGES-
    TIONS. [Semiannual]

C 41.96   • Item 215-O
WORLD SURVEY OF CIVIL AVIATION. 1960–
    [Irregular]

    Series of foreign market surveys of civil air-
craft and aeronautical products throughout the
world. Discusses aircraft fleet composition and
commercial and general flight operations, with
special emphasis given to market potential, trade
and investment opportunities, and competitive
factors affecting sales of U.S. aircraft and
aeronautical products.
    Separate reports issued for countries or ar-
eas.
    Discontinued.

C 41.97:nos.   • Item 215-P
COMMUNITY DEVELOPMENT SERIES.
    Discontinued.

C 41.98:CT
MARKET FOR U.S. LEATHER AND SHOES IN [vari-
    ous foreign countries].

C 41.99:date
VALUE OF PRIME CONTRACTS AWARDED BY FED-
    ERAL AGENCIES IN AREAS OF SUBSTANTIAL
    LABOR SURPLUS. [Quarterly]
    Later C 46.10

C 41.100:CT
HOUSEHOLD AND COMMERCIAL POTTERY
    INDUSTRY IN [various countries].

C 41.101   • Item 215-U
UNITED STATES LUMBER EXPORTS. [Annual]
    Later C 57.24

C 41.101/2   • Item 215-U
UNITED STATES LUMBER IMPORTS. [Annual]

    Statistical tables give U.S. lumber imports,
softwood lumber imports, and hardwood lumber
imports, by species and area and country of destination.
    Data compiled from Bureau of the Census
Report FT 125, United States Imports of Merchandise for Consumption.

C 41.102:v.nos.&nos.
OTS BRIEFS.

C 41.103:CT
MARKET FOR SELECTED U.S. ELECTRIC HOUSE-
    WARES IN [various countries].

C 41.104:CT
MARKET FOR U.S. TELECOMMUNICATIONS EQUIP-
    MENT IN [various countries]. [1961]–

C 41.105:CT
MARKET FOR U.S. MICROWAVE, FORWARD SCAT-
    TER, AND OTHER RADIO COMMUNICATIONS
    EQUIPMENT AND RADAR IN [various countries].

C 41.106:CT
MARKET FOR SELECTED U.S. HOUSEHOLD AND
    COMMERCIAL GAS APPLIANCES IN [various
    countries].

C 41.107:CT   • Item 215-S
BDSA EXPORT POTENTIAL STUDIES.
    Discontinued.

C 41.108   • Item 215-V
UNITED STATES FOREIGN TRADE IN PHOTO-
    GRAPHIC GOODS. [Annual]

    Statistical tables give exports and imports of
photographic equipment and supplies.
    Discontinued.

C 41.109
FOREIGN MARKET SURVEYS. [Irregular]

    PURPOSE:– To make available to U.S. indus-
try the foreign market surveys contracted for by
the Department of Commerce in planning for Trade
Centers and Trade Fairs to help U.S. firms develop or expand export trade.
    Each survey covers a particular commodity
in a country. Covers such topics as market indicators, market analysis, and competitive factors.

C 41.110:nos.   • Item 215-W
INDUSTRIAL CIVIL DEFENSE NEWSLETTER.
    Discontinued.

C 41.111   • Item 215-X
FACTS ABOUT WHOLESALING (series). [Irregular]
    Discontinued.

C 41.112
ALUMINUM IMPORTS AND EXPORTS.

C 41.112/2:date
UNITED STATES EXPORTS OF ALUMINUM. [Annual]
(Aluminum and Magnesium Industries Operations)

Gives statistics, by country, in thousands of
pounds for exports of ingot, scrap, and
semifabricated products.
Later C 57.10

C 41.112/3:date
UNITED STATES IMPORTS OF ALUMINUM. [Annual]
(Aluminum and Magnesium Industries Operations)
Later C 57.10/2

C 41.112/4:date
ALUMINUM METAL SUPPLY AND SHIPMENTS OF
PRODUCTS TO CONSUMERS. [Quarterly]
Earlier C 41.2:Al 8/4
Later C 57.14

C 41.113:nos.
EXECUTIVE RESERVIST, BULLETIN FROM INDUS-
TRIAL MOBILIZATION, FOR MEMBERS OF
NATIONAL DEFENSE EXECUTIVE RESERVE. 1–

C 41.114:date
STEEL IMPORT DATA. September 1969–   [Monthly]
Limited distribution
Later C 57.209

C 41.BDSAOT
BDSA OFFICIAL TEXTS. [Irregular]

Supersedes: BDSA Regulations (C 41.6/2),
BDSA Delegations (C 41.6/3), BDSA Orders
(C 41.6/4), BDSA Notices (C 41.6/5), DMS Regu-
lations (C 41.6/6), and BDSA Emergency Delega-
tions (C 41.6/8).
Earlier NPA Official Text.
Later BDC Official Texts (C 41.BDCOT).

C 41.BDCOT
BDC OFFICIAL TEXTS. [Irregular]

Earlier BDSA Official Texts (C 41.BDSAOT).

BUREAU OF INTERNATIONAL
COMMERCE
(1963– 1972)

CREATION AND AUTHORITY

The Bureau of International Commerce was
established by the Secretary on February 1, 1963,
by Department Order 182, under authority provided by Reorganization Plan 5 of 1950. Functions were transferred to the Domestic and International Business Administration (C 57.400), effective November 17, 1972.

C 42.1:date
ANNUAL REPORTS.

C 42.2:CT   • **Item 231-A**
GENERAL PUBLICATIONS.

C 42.2:Am 3   • **Item 231-A**
SOURCES FOR INFORMATION ON AMERICAN
FIRMS FOR INTERNATIONAL BUYERS. Rev.
1971. 37 p.

Lists sources from which names, addresses, and commercial information on business firms in the United States and in its
noncontiguous areas are available. The business directories are limited to those which
are revised periodically or kept up to date
with supplements.

C 42.3/2:nos.
INVESTMENT OPPORTUNITIES ABROAD, BULLE-
TINS. [Semimonthly]

C 42.6:CT   • **Item 213-F**
REGULATIONS, RULES, AND INSTRUCTIONS.
Discontinued.

C 42.6:Ex 7/2   • **Item 213-F**
SUMMARY OF U.S. EXPORT CONTROL REGU-
LATIONS. [Irregular]

Describes the Department of Commerce
responsibility in the administration of the Export Control Act. Lists country designations.
Cites categories of commodities and products requiring license; instructions for submitting application; types of license and features of each, how to handle mail shipments,
and helpful hints in applying for a license.
Includes specimens of forms, such as application for export license, export license document, request for amendment of license, and
shipper's export declaration.

C 42.6/2:CT   • **Item 213-E**
HANDBOOKS, MANUALS, GUIDES.

C 42.6/3:CT
EXPORT MARKET GUIDES.

C 42.7
PRESS RELEASES. [Irregular] (Press only)

C 42.8   • **Item 214**
INTERNATIONAL COMMERCE. v. 1– 26 no. 33. 1940–
October 5, 1972. [Weekly]

PURPOSE:– To present foreign economic and
commercial information of a current nature in a
form convenient for use by U.S. businessmen
engaged in international trade.
Departments:– Briefs on World Commerce,
Commodity News, Economic Conditions Abroad,
Foreign Government Actions, Investment Activities, U.S. Government Actions, World Trade Leads.
Brief articles and news items. Includes notices of new publications of the Department of
Commerce as well as foreign publications of interest to businessmen.

Special issues:– World Trade in Review (review of six-month period with outlook for international trade, travel, and investment) appears in
the April and October issues.
Previous title: Foreign Commerce Weekly.
Superseded by Commerce Today (C 1.58).
Discontinued.

C 42.8/a:H 717/2
WORLD HOLIDAYS LISTED, A GUIDE FOR BUSI-
NESS TRAVEL. 1970. 27 p.

Lists business holidays for 120 nations.

C 42.8/2:CT
INTERNATIONAL COMMERCE, SUPPLEMENTS.

C 42.8/3   • **Item 214**
AUTOMATED CUMULATIVE INDEX.   – 1970. [Quar-
terly]

Country and subject indexes.

C 42.9:CT
BUSINESS INFORMATION SERVICE.
Earlier C 18.228

C 42.9/2:nos.
– WORLD TRADE SERIES.
Earlier C 18.228:W 89

C 42.9/3:CT
– INTERNATIONAL TRADE STATISTICS SERIES.
Earlier C 18.228:T 67

C 42.10:CT
TRADE LISTS.
Earlier C 18.153
Later C 57.22

C 42.10/2:date   • **Item 231-G-2**
TRADE LIST CATALOG, [Annual]
Discontinued.

C 42.11:date   • **Item 211**
EXPORT CONTROL REGULATIONS. 1941–   [Annual]

Subscription service includes a set of divid-
ers and supplementary material issued as Export
Control Bulletins, (C 42.11/3). Issued in loose
leaf form, punched for 3-ring binder.
Entitled Comprehensive Export Schedule,
prior to 1969.
Earlier C 18.267 and C 49.208
Later C 57.409

C 42.11/2   • **Item 212**
CURRENT EXPORT BULLETIN. 1–   [Irregular]

Issued as a supplement to the Comprehensive Export Schedule and include the subscription to that publication.
Pages are perforated and punched for 3-ring
binder so that they may be inter-filed with the
pages of the basic volume.
Formerly Current Control Bulletin.

DOING BUSINESS IN [Country].

See Reports of Trade Missions listed below.

C 42.11/3:nos.   • **Item 212**
EXPORT CONTROL BULLETIN. 1–   1969–
[Irregular] (Included in subscription to Export Con-
trol Regulations, C 42.11)

Beginning June 1969, supersedes Current Export Bulletin, (C 42.11/2).
Later C 57.409/2

C 42.12:date   • **Item 214-A**
FOREIGN COMMERCE YEARBOOK [none issued].
Discontinued.

C 42.13:date
INDEX TO WORLD TRADE INFORMATION SERVICE
REPORTS.
Replaces C 42.9, C 42.9/2, C 42.9/3

C 42.13/1:nos.
WORLD TRADE INFORMATION SERVICE: PT. 1, ECO-
NOMIC REPORTS.
Later C 49.8/1

C 42.13/2:nos.
WORLD TRADE INFORMATION SERVICE: PT. 2,
OPERATIONS REPORTS.
Later C 49.8/2

C 42.13/3:nos.
WORLD TRADE INFORMATION SERIVCE: PT. 3,
STATISTICAL REPORTS.
Later C 49.8/3

C 42.13/4:nos.
WORLD TRADE INFORMATION SERVICE: PT. 4,
UTILITIES ABROAD.

C 42.13/5:nos.
WORLD TRADE INFORMATION SERVICE: PT. 5,
FAIRS & EXHIBITIONS.

C 42.14:CT
COUNTRY-BY-COMMODITY SERIES.

C 42.14/2:CT
VALUE SERIES.

C 42.15:CT   • **Item 231-D**
BIBLIOGRAPHIES AND LISTS OF PUBLICATIONS.

C 42.15:C 41   • **Item 231-D**
SEMIANNUAL CHECKLIST, BUREAU OF INTER-
NATIONAL COMMERCE INTERNATIONAL
BUSINESS PUBLICATIONS. [Semiannual]

   Lists publications in print. Also includes
some publications of other agencies devoted
to international commerce.
   Checklist appears in the January and July
issues of International Commerce and later is
published as a separate.
   Previous title: International Business Publications Checklist.
   Continues the lists of predecessor agencies, Checklist of BFC Publications and International Trade Checklist.
   Later C 57.115

C 42.15/2
FOREIGN MARKET REPORTS SERVICE, LISTING.
1– 12. 1967–   [Monthly]

   Lists unclassified airgrams recently received
in the Commerce Department containing information helpful to business in foreign market research.
   Superseded by Foreign Market Reports, Accession Listing (C 42.15/3).

EXPORT MARKET GUIDES. 1964–   [Irregular]

   Background data to sales throughout the
world, by country and by product. Prepared in
advance of trade center shows, trade fairs,
and exhibitions to assist U.S. businessmen
planning to participate. Provide description of
markets, sales opportunities, demand for
items on sale international competition, sales
approach, expected attendance and sales
and technical requirements.

C 42.15/3   • **Item 231-G**
FOREIGN PRODUCTION AND COMMERCIAL RE-
   PORTS. 1–   1968–

   This series consists of reports received by
the Department of Commerce from specialists in
U.S. Foreign Service posts abroad. They include
commodity oriented reports on production and
other developments in agriculture, manufacturing, mining, fisheries, power and fuels, transportation, distribution and trade, construction and
communication field.
   Includes monthly and cumulative annual indices.
   Earlier title: Foreign Market Reports, Accession Listings, prior to no. 3, 1969.   Earlier: Foreign Reports Service, Listing, (C 42.15/2).

C 42.15/3-2:date   • **Item 231-G**
CUMULATIVE INDEX TO FOREIGN PRODUCTION
AND COMMERCIAL REPORTS. 1968/69–

   Earlier Foreign Market Reports.

C 42.15/3-3:CT   • **Item 231-G**
INDEX TO FOREIGN PRODUCTION AND COMMER-
   CIAL REPORTS, CUMULATIVE INDEXES [by sub-
   jects]. [Irregular]

C 42.16:CT   • **Item 231-C**
DOING BUSINESS WITH [various countries].
   Discontinued.

C 42.17:nos.
INFORMATION SOURCES ON INTERNATIONAL
TRAVEL.

C 42.18
ADDRESSES. [Irregular]

C 42.19:CT
REPORTS OF UNITED STATES TRADE MISSIONS.
   Later C 48.9

C 42.20:nos.
OVERSEAS BUSINESS REPORTS.
   Replaces C 49.8/1 to C 49.8/3
   Later C 1.50

C 42.20/2:CT
MARKET FOR U.S. PRODUCTS [by country].

C 42.21
EXPORT LICENSES APPROVED AND REEXPORTA-
TIONS AUTHORIZED. [Daily]
   Later C 57.40

C 42.22:nos.
LISTINGS OF REPORTS PREPARED FOR FOREIGN
SERVICE OF UNITED STATES.

C 42.23:date
EXPORT SUCCESS STORY.

C 42.23/2:CT
EXPORT SALES PROMOTIONS ANNOUNCEMENTS.

C 42.24:date
INTERNATIONAL CONFERENCE CALENDAR.
   [Administrative]

C 42.25:CT
INVESTMENT OPPORTUNITY INFORMATION.

TRADE LISTS. [Irregular]

   Most of these lists furnish, for a particular
country, names and addresses of foreign firms
(of importers and dealers or of manufacturers
and exporters, as the case may be), classified
by commodity; others are listings of professional
groups, institutions, and service organizations
by country. The lists include names and addresses
of the principal firms engaged in a specified
commodity trade or names and addresses of service or professional groups, etc., with information on the relative size, type of operation, products handled, and sales territory. They also provide a summary of general conditions governing
trade in specified products. For some of the smaller
countries simple listings of businessmen often
with indication of the commodities handled, are
furnished.
   The number of commodity classifications
made available for any particular country is based
on the established channels of trade and actual
or potential commerce in the merchandise covered.

C 42.26
TRENDS IN U.S. FOREIGN TRADE. 1966–
   [Irregular]

C 42.27:nos.
PARIS AIR SHOW NEWSLETTER.

C 42.27/2:nos.
PARIS AIR SHOW NEWS FILLERS.

SHARE OF MARKET REPORTS. [Annual]

   Statistical reports on leading world import markets for manufactured products available for sale
to U.S. exporters.
   Issued in two sub-series.

Commodity Series.

   Tables show the values of shipments for
each of 1,127 manufactured commodities, as
supplied to the 69 major importing countries
by the world's 14 principal exporting nations.

Country Series.

   Gives shipments of 1,127 commodities
from these 14 major suppliers into each of 33
importing countries, mainly those in Europe,
the tables present total imports and imports
from the United States and the European
Economic Community.

   A complete list of this series is available
from the Washington Office or any of the
Department of Commerce Field Offices. Also
listed in the Semiannual Checklist.

C 42.28   • **Item 213-H**
STATE EXPORT-ORIGIN SERIES: EXPORTS FROM
[State]. 1966–   [Irregular]

   Data covering 1966 was published in 1968.
Separate release for each State.
   Discontinued.

C 42.29
KENNEDY ROUND, SPECIAL REPORTS. [Irregular]

C 42.30   • **Item 231-I**
FOREIGN ECONOMIC TRENDS AND THEIR IMPLI-
CATIONS FOR UNITED STATES, ET (series).
[Irregular]
   Later C 57.111

C 42.31:nos.
INTERNATIONAL MARKETING INFORMATION SER-
VICE, IMIS (series). 69-1–   1969–   [Irregular]
   Later C 57.116

C 42.31/2:CT   • **Item 231-J**
INTERNATIONAL MARKETING INFORMATION SER-
VICE: COUNTRY MARKET SURVEY. [1969]–
[Irregular]
   Discontinued.

C 42.31/3:date
MARKET SHARE REPORT CATALOG.

C 42.31/4:nos.
EXPORT MARKET DIGEST, EMD- (series).

C 42.32:date   • **Item 231-K**
RESEARCH ON U.S. INTERNATIONAL TRADE. [1970]–

   Discontinued.

C 42.33:CT   • **Item 231-G-1**
GLOBAL MARKET SURVEY.

C 42.34:date
INTERNATIONAL ECONOMIC INDICATORS.
[Quarterly] (International Trade Analysis Division)
   Later C 57.19

OFFICE OF BUSINESS ECONOMICS
(1953– 1972)

CREATION AND AUTHORITY

   The Office of Business Economics was established within the Department of Commerce by
a Departmental Order dated December 1, 1953.
The Office was transferred to the Social and Economic Statistics Administration and renamed the
Office of Economic Analysis (C 56.100), effective January 1, 1972.

C 43.1:date
ANNUAL REPORTS.

C 43.2:CT   • **Item 227-H**
GENERAL PUBLICATIONS.
   Discontinued.

C 43.7
[PRESS RELEASES]. [Irregular]

   The following release is issued on a recurring
basis

   C 43.7
   BUSINESS NEWS REPORTS, OBE- (series).
   [Monthly & Quarterly]

C 43.8 • Item 288
SURVEY OF CURRENT BUSINESS. v. 1– 1921–
[Monthly]

PURPOSE:– To disseminate significant economic indicators for business use, including analytical findings of the Office of Business Economics as well as over 2,500 statistical series originating from both public and private sources.

The first section is devoted to the business situation, special analyses, and articles, supported by charts and tables, on various aspects of the Nation's economy, information on trends in industry, outlook and other points pertinent to the business world. An overall summary is given in The Business Situation, the introduction to each issue.

The second section, Current Business Statistics, contains over 2,500 statistical series giving the latest monthly or quarterly data. Data which appear in these series are compiled for historical reference in the various supplements listed below. The monthly data are supplemented by the weekly release, Business Statistics.
Later C 56.109

C 43.8/2:date • Item 229
–WEEKLY SUPPLEMENT.
Earlier C 18.36
Later C 57.109/2

C 43.8/3:CT
SUPPLEMENTS (Special) TO SURVEY OF CURRENT BUSINESS.
Earlier C 18.35/2

C 43.8/4 • Item 228
BUSINESS STATISTICS. [Biennial]

PURPOSE:– To provide businessmen and others interested in the progress of the American economy a handy and comprehensive reference book supplementing the up-to-date indicators published in the current monthly issues.

Gives monthly figures for the last four years and yearly (monthly average) for year 1929 to date. General tables cover general business indicators; commodity prices; construction and real estate; domestic trade; employment and population; finance; and international transactions of the United States. Individual commodity data cover production, trade, employment, imports and exports, stocks, and prices. Includes explanatory notes on sources and methods of the data presented. Index.

C 43.9:date
INDUSTRY SURVEY, MANUFACTURERS' SALES, INVENTORIES, NEW AND UNFILLED ORDERS.
[Monthly]
Earlier C 18.224

C 43.10:nos.
ECONOMIC REPORT TO THE SECRETARY OF COMMERCE. [Official Use]

C 43.11:date
FOREIGN GRANTS AND CREDITS BY THE UNITED STATES GOVERNMENT.
Official use.
Earlier C 18.279

C 43.11/2:date
FOREIGN CREDITS BY UNITED STATES GOVERNMENT. [Annual]
Later T 1.45

C 43.12:date
GUIDE TO CURRENT BUSINESS DATA. [Weekly]

C 43.13:CT
ADDRESSES.

C 43.14:nos.
STAFF PAPERS.

Renamed Office of Economic Analysis and on January 1, 1972 became a part of the Social and Economic Statistics Administration.

OFFICE OF INTERNATIONAL TRADE FAIRS
(1955– 1961)

CREATION AND AUTHORITY

The Office of International Trade Fairs was established within the Department of Commerce by Departmental Order 159, effective January 27, 1955. The Office was transferred to the Bureau of International Business Operations (C 48.100) in 1961.

C 44.1:date
ANNUAL REPORTS.

C 44.2:CT • Item 232-A
GENERAL PUBLICATIONS.
Discontinued.

C 44.7:nos.
RELEASES.
Later C 48.107

C 44.8:v.nos.&nos. • Item 232-B
FAIR FACTS, INFORMATION FOR AMERICAN INDUSTRY. [Quarterly]
Discontinued.

C 44.9:CT
ADDRESSES.
Later C 48.109

OFFICE OF AREA DEVELOPMENT
(1956– 1958)

CREATION AND AUTHORITY

The Office of Area Development was established as a primary organization unit of the Department of Commerce by Departmental Order 164, effective August 10, 1956. The functions of the Office were transferred to the Business and Defense Services Administration (C 41) in 1958.

C 45.1:date
ANNUAL REPORTS.

C 45.2:CT • Item 130-A
GENERAL PUBLICATIONS.
Discontinued.

C 45.7:nos.
RELEASES.

C 45.8:CT
INDUSTRIAL FACT SHEETS.
Later C 41.90/3

C 45.8/2:nos.
AREA DEVELOPMENT AID, INDUSTRY TREND SERIES.
Later C 41.90

C 45.8/3:nos.
AREA DEVELOPMENT AID: INDUSTRIAL LOCATION SERIES.
Later C 41.90/2

C 45.9:v.nos.
AREA DEVELOPMENT BULLETIN. [Bimonthly]
Earlier C 41.27
Later C 46.9

C 45.10
STAFF PAPERS.

C 45.11:date
CONFERENCE OF STATE PLANNING AND DEVELOPMENT OFFICERS WITH FEDERAL OFFICIALS, SUMMARIES. [Annual]

C 45.12:CT
ADDRESSES.

C 45.13:nos.
AREA TREND SERIES.
Later C 41.80

C 45.14:date
AREA DEVELOPMENT MEMORANDUM FOR STATE PLANNING AND DEVELOPMENT OFFICES.

C 45.15:CT
BIBLIOGRAPHIES AND LISTS OF PUBLICATIONS

ECONOMIC DEVELOPMENT ADMINISTRATION
(1965–)

CREATION AND AUTHORITY

The Area Redevelopment Administration was established within the Department of Commerce on May 8, 1961, pursuant to the Area Development Act (75 Stat. 47). The Administration was terminated August 31, 1965 and its functions transferred to the Economic Development Administration (C 46).

INFORMATION

Economic Development Administration
Department of Commerce
Herbert Clark Hoover Bulding
14th Street And Constitution Avenue, NW
Washington, D.C. 20230
(202) 482-2309
Fax: (202) 482-0995
http://www.doc.gov/eda

C 46.1 • Item 130-F (MF)
ANNUAL REPORT. 1st– 1966– [Annual]

Report submitted by the Secretary of Commerce to Congress pursuant to the Public Works and Economic Development Act of 1965. Report covers fiscal year.

C 46.2:CT • Item 130-D
GENERAL PUBLICATIONS.

C 46.5:CT • Item 130-T
LAWS. [Irregular]

C 46.6:CT • Item 130-C-1
REGULATIONS, RULES, AND INSTRUCTIONS.

C 46.7
[PRESS RELEASES]. [Irregular]

C 46.7/2:date
INDUSTRIAL NEWS. [Irregular]

C 46.8:CT • Item 130-C
HANDBOOKS, MANUALS, GUIDES.

C 46.8:C 73 • Item 130-C
HANDBOOK OF FEDERAL AID TO COMMUNITIES. 1966– [Irregular]

C 46.8/2:CT
AREA REDEVELOPMENT BOOKSHELF OF COMMUNITY AIDS.

C 46.9:v.nos.&nos.
AREA DEVELOPMENT BULLETIN. [Bimonthly]
Earlier C 41.27

C 46.9/2   • Item 215-B
ECONOMIC DEVELOPMENT. v. 1– 10, no. 6. 1965–
June 1973. [Monthly]

PURPOSE:– To provide information of EDA
policies and procedures, to report on experiences
of community and regional development groups.
Includes annotated list of publications, both
government and nongovernment of interest to
those participating in the EDA programs. Also
includes list of technical assistance studies, prepared under contract to the Department of Commerce, and available through the Department of
Commerce, and available through the
Department's Library.

Prior to v. 2, no. 8, October 1965 issue, entitled Redevelopment and issued by the predecessor agency, Area Redevelopment Administration.

Discontinued.

C 46.9/3:date   • Item 130-N
ECONOMIC DEVELOPMENT U.S.A.
Discontinued.

C 46.9/4:date
DEVELOPMENT LETTER.

C 46.9/5:date
DEVELOPMENT U.S.A. [Bimonthly]

PURPOSE:– To serve as a newsletter for the
Economic Development Administration.

C 46.10:date
VALUE OF PRIME CONTRACTS AWARDED BY FED-
ERAL AGENCIES IN AREAS OF SUBSTANTIAL
LABOR SURPLUS. [Quarterly]
Earlier C 41.99

C 46.11
ADDRESSES. [Irregular]

C 46.12:CT
STATE OFFICERS ANALYZER SHEETS. OFFICIAL
USE.

C 46.13:nos.
INFORMATION NEWS SERVICE. ADMINISTRATIVE.

C 46.14:nos.
AREA DESIGNATION STATUS REPORTS.

C 46.15:date
ARA INFORMATION MEMO.

C 46.16:CT   • Item 130-E
Q & A (series).
Discontinued.

C 46.17:CT   • Item 130-J
MAPS AND CHARTS, QUALIFIED AREAS

C 46.18:CT   • Item 130-K
BIBLIOGRAPHIES AND LISTS OF PUBLICATIONS.

C 46.19:date   • Item 130-G
ACCELERATED PUBLIC WORKS PROGRAM, DIREC-
TORY OF APPROVED PROJECTS. [Monthly]
Discontinued.

C 46.19/2   • Item 130-J (MF)
EDA DIRECTORY OF APPROVED PROJECTS. [Semi-
annual]

Lists projects approved for assistance under
Public Law 89-136, passed Aug. 26, 1965.
Discontinued.

C 46.20:nos.   • Item 130-H
ARA CASE BOOK.
Discontinued.

C 46.21:nos.
MONTHLY OEDP STATUS REPORT.

C 46.22:CT
EDA FIELD REPORTS. [Irregular] (Office of Public
Affairs)
Formerly ARA Field Reports.

C 46.22/2:CT
ARA STAFF STUDIES.

C 46.23:date
QUARTERLY CUMULATIVE REPORT OF TECHNICAL
ASSISTANCE.

C 46.24:CT   • Item 130-I
ECONOMIC REDEVELOPMENT RESEARCH.
Discontinued.

C 46.25   • Item 130-J (MF)
QUALIFIED AREAS UNDER PUBLIC WORKS AND
ECONOMIC DEVELOPMENT ACT OF 1965,
PUBLIC LAW 89-136, REPORTS. 1–   1965–
[Annual]
Discontinued.

C 46.25/2   • Item 130-J (MF)
AREAS ELIGIBLE FOR FINANCIAL ASSISTANCE
DESIGNATED UNDER THE PUBLIC WORKS AND
ECONOMIC DEVELOPMENT ACT OF 1965, RE-
PORTS. 1–   1966–   [Irregular]

C 46.25/3:date   • Item 130-J (MF)
DESIGNATED REDEVELOPMENT AREAS UNDER THE
PUBLIC WORKS AND ECONOMIC DEVELOP-
MENT ACT OF 1965.
Discontinued.

C 46.26   • Item 130-M
RESEARCH REVIEW. 1967–   [Annual]

Published by the Office of Economic Research for the employees of the Economic Development Administration.
Discontinued.

C 46.27:CT   • Item 130-L
URBAN BUSINESS PROFILE (series).

PURPOSE:– To serve as a meaningful vehicle to introduce the prospective small urban
entrepreneur to selected urban-oriented businesses; to provide a better understanding of the
opportunities, requirements, and problems associated with particular businesses; to provide guidelines on types of information required for location-
specific feasibility studies; and to assist urban
development groups in their business creation
activities.
Discontinued.

C 46.28:date
EDA NEWS CLIPS. [Irregular]

C 46.29:CT   • Item 130-P
ECONOMIC DEVELOPMENT RESEARCH REPORTS.
[Irregular]
Discontinued.

C 46.30:CT   • Item 130-R (MF)
ENVIRONMENTAL IMPACT STATEMENTS. [Irregular]

UNITED STATES TRAVEL AND TOURISM ADMINISTRATION (1961– 1996)

CREATION AND AUTHORITY

The United States Travel Service was estab-
lished by the Secretary of Commerce, effective
July 1, 1961, pursuant to the International Travel
Act of 1961 (75 Stat. 129; 22 U.S.C. 2121 note).
The name was changed to United States Travel
and Tourism Administration by Public Law 97-63,
October 16, 1981. Abolished by P.L. 104-288,
October 11, 1996

C 47.1:date   • Item 271-A
ANNUAL REPORT. 1st–   1962–

Earlier title: Program Report of the United
States Travel Service
Report submitted by the Secretary of Com-
merce to the President and Congress pursuant to
Section 5 of the International Travel Act of 1961.

Summarizes activities of the U.S. Travel Ser-
vice, established to encourage more tourists to
visit the United States.
First report covered period July 1961– March
1962. Subsequent reports cover period April–
September and October– March.
Frequency varies: Semiannual 1962– 1964;
annual 1965–
Former title: Semiannual Report of the Secre-
tary of Commerce on the United States Travel
Service.
ISSN 0502-5397

C 47.2:CT   • Item 271-A-1
GENERAL PUBLICATIONS.

C 47.2:P 69   • Item 271-A-1
PLANT TOURS FOR INTERNATIONAL VISITORS
TO THE UNITED STATES. 1969/70–
[Irregular]
PURPOSE:– To provide a listing of plant
tours given as part of the program to welcome international visitors to the United States.
The list arranged by State and city, is also
classified by industry for those who are interested in locating plants of a particular industry.

C 47.2:T 64/3   • Item 271-A-1
INVENTORY OF FEDERAL TOURISM PRO-
GRAMS, FEDERAL AGENCIES COMMIS-
SIONS, PROGRAMS REVIEWED FOR THEIR
PARTICIPATION IN THE DEVELOPMENT OF
RECREATION, TRAVEL, AND TOURISM IN
THE UNITED STATES. 1970. 84 p.

PURPOSE:– To provide information on the
extent to which the Federal Government is a
participant in travel, recreation and tourism
development. The programs reviewed in this
report have been categorized into the following eight major areas: Natural resources; recreation; cities; historic areas; transportation;
data; travelers and cultural attractions.

C 47.7
PRESS RELEASES. [Irregular]

C 47.8
INFORMATION SOURCES ON INTERNATIONAL
TRAVEL. 1–   [Irregular]

C 47.9
ADDRESSES. [Irregular]

C 47.10:CT
POSTERS.

C 47.10/2
U.S.T.S. [poster series]. [Irregular]

C 47.11:CT
MAPS.

C 47.12:CT   • Item 271-A-2
HANDBOOKS, MANUALS, GUIDES.

C 47.12/2:nos.
TRAVELER'S GUIDES TO SPECIAL ATTRACTIONS.
1–   1976–   [Irregular]

C 47.13:CT   • Item 271-B-6
BIBLIOGRAPHIES AND LISTS OF PUBLICATIONS.

C 47.14:v.nos.&nos.
NEWSLETTER. v. 1–

C 47.15:date   • Item 271-A-4 (MF)
SUMMARY AND ANALYSIS OF INTERNATIONAL
TRAVEL TO THE U.S. [Monthly] (Office of Re-
search and Analysis)

Gives statistics on visitor arrivals to the U.S.
and market analysis of international travel by
residents of foreign countries.
Former title: Statistical Summary and Analy-
sis of Foreign Visitor Arrivals, U.S. Citizen and
Non-U.S. Citizen Departures.
Earlier issue entitled Travel and Travel Dollar
Flow into and out of the United States.
ISSN 0095-3482
Discontinued.

C 47.15/2
PLEASURE AND BUSINESS VISITORS TO U.S. BY PORT OF ENTRY AND MODE OF TRAVEL. [Semiannual]

Published biannually 1963– 1968; annually 1969– 1972; semiannually 1973–
Earlier C 47.2:V 83

C 47.15/3 • Item 271-B (MF)
MAJOR METROPOLITAN MARKET AREAS. 1970–
[Quarterly]
Discontinued.

C 47.15/4:date • Item 271-A-3 (MF)
ARRIVALS AND DEPARTURES BY SELECTED PORTS, STATISTICS OF FOREIGN VISITOR ARRIVALS AND U.S. CITIZEN DEPARTURES ANALYZED BY U.S. PORTS OF ENTRY AND DEPARTURE. 1963– [Semiannual]

PURPOSE:– To provide comparative statistics on an annual basis with respect to arrivals and departures by country of residence and debarkation and mode of travel.
Issued bi-annually 1963– 1968.
Discontinued.

C 47.15/5 • Item 271-A-4
INTERNATIONAL TRAVELERS TO THE U.S., ANNUAL SUMMARY.
Discontinued.

C 47.15/6:date • Item 271-A-5 (MF)
FOREIGN VISITOR ARRIVALS BY SELECTED PORTS, CALENDAR YEAR.
Discontinued.

C 47.15/7:date • Item 271-A-4 (MF)
IN-FLIGHT SURVEY. [Quarterly]
Discontinued.

C 47.16:nos. • Item 271-B-8
[TRAVEL FOLDERS] USTS (series).
Earlier C 47.2
Discontinued.

C 47.17:date • Item 271-B-4
FESTIVAL USA. [Annual]

PURPOSE:– To provide a listing of events to be held throughout the country during the year, including major sporting events in auto racing, horse racing, tennis, golf, skiing, surfing, and boating. Events are listed in chronological order with exact date and location, and are designated as major or local events.
Earlier C 47.2:F 42
Discontinued 1976.

C 47.18:CT • Item 271-B-5 (MF)
PATTERNS OF FOREIGN TRAVEL IN THE U.S. [Annual]

Separate reports for various regions in the U.S. as well as a summary report.
Discontinued.

C 47.19:CT • Item 271-B-7 (MF)
STUDY OF THE INTERNATIONAL TRAVEL MARKET [various countries]. [Irregular]
Discontinued.

C 47.20:date • Item 271-B-9 (MF)
MARKETING U.S. TOURISM ABROAD.

Former title:Review of USTTA International Markets, and Summary of Cooperative Advertising Opportunities.
PURPOSE:– To describe the broad outlook for inbound tourism to the United States from various foreign countries.

BUREAU OF INTERNATIONAL BUSINESS OPERATIONS (1961– 1963)

CREATION AND AUTHORITY

The Bureau of International Business Operations was established by the Secretary of Commerce on August 8, 1961, by authority of Departmental Orders 173 and 174, to plan and operate the international action programs of the Department. The Bureau was abolished by Departmental Order 182 of February 1, 1963.

C 48.1:date
ANNUAL REPORTS.

C 48.2:CT • Item 232-D-1
GENERAL PUBLICATIONS.
Discontinued.

C 48.8:CT
ADDRESSES.

C 48.9:CT
REPORTS OF UNITED STATES TRADE MISSION.
Earlier C 42.19

C 48.10:CT • Item 232-D-2
HANDBOOKS, MANUALS, GUIDES.
Discontinued.

OFFICE OF INTERNATIONAL TRADE FAIRS (1961– 1963)

CREATION AND AUTHORITY

The Office of International Trade Fairs (C 44) was placed within the Bureau of International Business Operations in 1961. The Office was abolished in 1963.

C 48.101:date
ANNUAL REPORTS.
Earlier C 44.1

C 48.102:CT
GENERAL PUBLICATIONS.
Earlier C 44.2

C 48.107:nos.
PRESS RELEASES.
Earlier C 44.1

C 48.108:nos.
OITF POLICY STATEMENTS.

C 48.109:CT
ADDRESSES.
Earlier C 44.9

BUREAU OF INTERNATIONAL PROGRAMS (1961– 1963)

CREATION AND AUTHORITY

The Bureau of International Programs was established within the Department of Commerce on August 8, 1961, by Departmental Orders 173 and 174. The Bureau was abolished by Departmental Order 182 of February 1, 1963.

C 49.1:date
ANNUAL REPORTS.

C 49.2:CT
GENERAL PUBLICATIONS.

C 49.8/1:nos.
WORLD TRADE INFORMATION SERVICE, PART 1, ECONOMIC REPORTS.
Earlier C 42.13/1
Later C 42.20

C 49.8/2:nos.
WORLD TRADE INFORMATION SERVICE, PART 2, OPERATIONS REPORT.
Earlier C 42.13/2
Later C 42.20

C 49.8/3:nos.
WORLD TRADE INFORMATION SERVICE, PART 3, STATISTICAL REPORTS.
Earlier C 42.13/3
Later 42.20

C 49.9:CT
SENDING GIFT PACKAGES TO VARIOUS COUNTRIES.
Earlier C 42.2

C 49.10:CT
BIBLIOGRAPHIES AND LISTS OF PUBLICATIONS.

C 49.11:CT • Item 232-C-1
INFORMATION FOR UNITED STATES BUSINESSMEN [by country].
Discontinued.

C 49.12:CT
COUNTRY-BY-COMMODITY SERIES.

C 49.13:CT
ADDRESSES.

OFFICE OF REGIONAL ECONOMICS (1961– 1963)

CREATION AND AUTHORITY

The Office of Regional Economics was established within the Bureau of International Programs by Departmental Order 173 of August 8, 1961. The Office was abolished in 1963.

C 49.101:date
ANNUAL REPORT [none issued].

C 49.102:CT
GENERAL PUBLICATIONS [none issued].

OFFICE OF EXPORT CONTROL
(1961– 1963)

CREATION AND AUTHORITY

The Office of Export Control was established within the Bureau of International Programs by Departmental Order 173 of August 8, 1961. The Office was abolished in 1963.

C 49.201:date
ANNUAL REPORT.

C 49.202:CT
GENERAL PUBLICATIONS.

C 49.206:CT
REGULATIONS, RULES, AND INSTRUCTIONS.

C 49.208:date
COMPREHENSIVE EXPORT SCHEDULE.
    Earlier C 42.11
    Later C 42.11

C 49.208/a:CT
COMPREHENSIVE EXPORT SCHEDULE (separates).
    Earlier C 42.11/a

C 49.208/2:nos.
CURRENT EXPORT BULLETINS.
    Earlier C 42.1162
    Later C 42.11/2

C 49.209:date
EXPORT LICENSES APPROVED AND REEXPORTATIONS AUTHORIZED. [Daily, Monday-Friday, except Federal Legal Holidays]
    Later C 42.21

OFFICE OF INTERNATIONAL ECONOMIC PROGRAMS
(1961– 1963)

CREATION AND AUTHORITY

The Office of International Economics Programs was established within the Bureau of International Programs, by Departmental Order 173 of August 8, 1961. The Office was abolished in 1963.

C 49.301:date
ANNUAL REPORTS.

C 49.302:CT
GENERAL PUBLICATIONS.

C 49.309:CT
ADDRESSES.

COMMUNITY RELATIONS SERVICE
(1962– 1966)

CREATION AND AUTHORITY

The Community Relations Service was established within the Department of Commerce by title X of the Civil Rights Act of 1962 (78 Stat. 241; 42 U.S.C. 2000a). The Service was transferred to the Department of Justice (J 23) by Reorganization Plan 1 of 1966, effective April 11, 1966.

C 50.1:date
ANNUAL REPORT.
    Later J 23.1

C 50.2:CT
GENERAL PUBLICATIONS.
    Later J 23.2

C 50.3/2:nos.
NATIONAL CITIZENS COMMITTEE BULLETIN.

C 50.7:date
PRESS RELEASES.

C 50.7/2:date
CRS MEDIA RELATIONS, NEWSPAPERS, MAGAZINES, RADIO, TELEVISION.

C 50.8:CT
HANDBOOKS, MANUALS, GUIDES.
    Later J 23.8

C 50.9:CT
ADDRESSES.

NATIONAL TECHNICAL INFORMATION SERVICE
(1970–   )

CREATION AND AUTHORITY

The Clearinghouse for Federal Scientific and Technical Information was established within the Department of Commerce in 1965, succeeding the Office of Technical Services in the Business and Defense Services Administration (C 41). The Clearinghouse was superseded by the National Technical Information Service on September 2, 1970.

INFORMATION

National Technical Information Service
Department of Commerce
Sills Building
5285 Port Royal Road
Springfield, Virginia 22161
(703) 605-6400
Toll free: (800) 553-NTIS
http://www.ntis.gov

C 51.1:date   • Item 188-A-7 (MF)
ANNUAL REPORTS.

C 51.2:CT   • Item 271
GENERAL PUBLICATIONS.

C 51.7/2
FAST ANNOUNCEMENTS. [Irregular]

Announcements of reports of U.S. and foreign research.

C 51.7/3:nos.
SPECIAL ANNOUNCEMENTS.
    Earlier C 41.28/2

C 51.7/4
CFSTI NEWS. 1968–   [Irregular]

A newsletter highlighting new Clearinghouse products and services.

C 51.7/5:CT
GOVERNMENT REPORTS TOPICAL ANNOUNCEMENTS. [Semimonthly]

Previous title: Clearinghouse Announcements in Science and Technology.
Superseded by the Weekly Government Abstracts (C 51.9/5– C 51.9/31))
Issued in the following categories:–

Aeronautics and aerodynamics.
Agriculture and food.
Area planning and development.
Astronomy and astrophysics.
Atmospheric sciences.
Behavioral and social sciences.
Biological and medical sciences.
Chemistry.
Civil, structural and marine engineering.
Communication systems.
Detection and countermeasures.
Earth sciences.
Economics, business and commerce.
Electrotechnology.
Energy conversion (non-propulsive).
Industrial and mechanical engineering.
Library and information sciences.
Mathematical sciences.
Methods, instrumentation and equipment.
Military sciences.
Missile technology.
Navigation, guidance and control.
Nuclear science and technology.
Oceanscience and engineering.
Ordance.
Physics.
Propulsion and fuels.
Peprography and recording devices.
Safety engineering and protection.
Space technology.

C 51.7/6:date
NTIS MONTHLY MARKETING.
    No longer published.

C 51.8:CT   • Item 188-A-2
HANDBOOKS, MANUALS, GUIDES.

C 51.9:v.nos.&nos.   • Item 270
GOVERNMENT REPORTS INDEX. 1965– 1975. [Semimonthly]
Published concurrently with the Government Reports Announcements. Indexes each issue by subject, personal and corporate author, contract number, and accession/report number.
From 1965– 1967 issued as Government-Wide Index to Federal Research and Development Reports with separate volume numbering; 1968– 1971, U.S. Government Research and Development Reports Index; 1971– 1975 Government Reports Index.
Discontinued with no. 6, March 21, 1975 issue. Merged with Government Reports Announcements (C 51.9/3) effective no. 7, April 4, 1975.

C 51.9/2:v.nos.&nos.   • Item 270
GOVERNMENT REPORTS INDEX, QUARTERLY CUMULATIVE. 1968– 1971.

Published in two sections

Section 1. Subject Index.
Section 2. Personal and Corporate Author, Contract and Accession Number Indexes.
Superseded by Government Reports Annual Index (C 51.9/4)

C 51.9/3:v.nos.&nos. • Item 270
GOVERNMENT REPORTS ANNOUNCEMENTS AND INDEX. v. 1– 1946– [Semimonthly]

PURPOSE:– To provide abstracts from all newly released Government-funded research and development reports and foreign translations. Features quick-scan format; cross references (including title, price and corporate author); edge index to subject fields; and a report number locator list. Covers over 50,000 reports from some 225 Government units annually.

Title varies: January 1946– June 1959, Bibliography of Scientific and Industrial Reports; July 1949– September 1954, Bibliography of Technical Reports; October 1954– December 1964, U.S. Government Research Reports; January 1965– March 1971, U.S. Government Research and Development Reports; March 1971– 1975, Announcements and Index.

Absorbed Government Reports Index (C 51.9) effective with no. 7, April 4 1977 issue.
Earlier C 41.21
ISSN 0097-9007

Discontinued.

C 51.9/4:v.nos.&nos. • Item 270
GOVERNMENT REPORTS ANNUAL INDEX. v. 71– 1971–

Supersedes Government Reports Index, Quarterly Cumulative (C 51.9/2)
Published in six sections

Section 1. Subject Index, A– L
Section 2. Subject, – Z
Section 3. Personal Author Index.
Section 4. Corporate Author Index.
Section 5. Contract Number, Accession/Report Number Index.
Section 6. Accession/Report Number Index [continued].

WEEKLY GOVERNMENT ABSTRACTS, WGA- (series).

The Weekly Government Abstracts newsletters have been designed as a more frequent and improved eventual replacement for the semimonthly Government Reports Topical Announcements (C 51.7/5).

Each newsletter reports on such technical advances as the testing of new materials and processes now in use, development of new techniques and methods toward solutions of business and social problems, ways to improve existing products and methods, and modifications of materials and analytical and physical processes.

Issued as subscriptions for the following subseries
Discontinued.

C 51.9/5:nos.
ENVIRONMENTAL POLLUTION AND CONTROL.
ISSN 0364-4936

C 51.9/6:nos.
ADMINISTRATION.

Formerly Management Practice and Research.
ISSN 0364-7986

C 51.9/7:nos.
MATERIALS SCIENCES. [Weekly]
ISSN 0364-4928

C 51.9/8:nos.
COMPUTERS, CONTROL, AND INFORMATION THEORY. [Weekly]

C 51.9/9:nos.
TRANSPORTATION. [Weekly]

C 51.9/10:nos.
BUILDING TECHNOLOGY. [Weekly]

C 51.9/11:nos.
NASA EARTH RESOURCES SURVEY PROGRAM.
ISSN 0364-6440

C 51.9/12:nos.
BEHAVIOR AND SOCIETY.
ISSN 0145-0034

C 51.9/13:nos.
BIOMEDICAL TECHNOLOGY AND ENGINEERING.
ISSN 0364-4952

C 51.9/14:nos.
URBAN TECHNOLOGY.
ISSN 0363-7417

C 51.9/15:nos.
LIBRARY AND INFORMATION SCIENCES.
ISSN 0364-6467

C 51.9/16:nos.
INDUSTRIAL AND MECHANICAL ENGINEERING.
ISSN 0364-6483

C 51.9/17:nos.
BUSINESS AND ECONOMICS.
ISSN 9364-7978

C 51.9/18:nos.
ENERGY.

ISSN 0148-446X

C 51.9/19:nos.
AGRICULTURE AND FOOD.
ISSN 0364-7994

C 51.9/20:nos.
CHEMISTRY.

C 51.9/21:nos.
CIVIL AND STRUCTURAL ENGINEERING.
ISSN 0145-0344

C 51.9/22:nos.
ELECTROTECHNOLOGY.

C 51.9/23:nos.
GOVERNMENT INVENTIONS FOR LICENSING.
ISSN 0364-6491

C 51.9/24:nos.
MEDICINE AND BIOLOGY.
ISSN 0364-6432

C 51.9/25:nos.
NATURAL RESOURCES.
ISSN 0364-4979

C 51.9/26:nos.
OCEAN TECHNOLOGY AND ENGINEERING.
ISSN 0364-6424

C 51.9/27:nos.
PHYSICS.

C 51.9/28:nos.
COMMUNICATION.
ISSN 0364-4944

C 51.9/29:nos.
HEALTH PLANNING.

C 51.9/30:nos.
PROBLEM-SOLVING TECHNOLOGY FOR STATE AND LOCAL GOVERNMENTS.
ISSN 0364-6459

C 51.9/31:nos.
INFORMATION FOR INNOVATORS, AND INTERDISCIPLINARY INFORMATION SERVICE. [Bimonthly]

C 51.9/32:date
FOREIGN TECHNOLOGY. [Weekly]

C 51.9/33:date
MANUFACTURING TECHNOLOGY. [Weekly]

C 51.10:date
MONTHLY PROGRESS REPORT. OFFICIAL USE.

C 51.11:CT • Item 188-A-1
BIBLIOGRAPHIES AND LISTS OF PUBLICATIONS.
Earlier C 41.23/4

C 51.11/2:date • Item 188-A-3
DIRECTORY OF COMPUTERIZED SOFTWARE. 1976– [Annual]

Former title: Directory of Computerized Data Files and Related Software from Federal Agencies.

C 51.11/2-2:date • Item 188-A-3
DIRECTORY OF COMPUTERIZED DATA FILES. [Annual]

Continues: Directory of Computerized Data Files and Related Software (C 51.11/2)
Former title: Directory of Computerized Data Files and Related Technical Reports.

C 51.11/3:date • Item 188-A-1
[SELECTED REPORTS] (series). [Monthly]

Title varies.
Includes best new research titles available from NTIS.

C 51.11/4:nos. • Item 188-A-5
NTIS INFORMATION SERVICES, GENERAL CATALOGS. 1– [Irregular]

Earlier C 51.2:N 21t
NOTE:– Item 188-A-5 was cancelled November 22, 1977.
Discontinued.

C 51.11/5:CT • Item 188-A-5
DIRECTORY OF COMPUTER SOFTWARE APPLICATIONS. [Irregular]
Discontinued.

C 51.11/6:date • Item 188-A-6
JACS [Journal Article Copy Service] DIRECTORY.

The Journal Article Copy Service is a service which NTIS provides its deposit account customers with rapid delivery of journal article copies under copyright license from the journal publishers.
Discontinued.

C 51.11/7:date • Item 188-A-4
NTIS DIGEST. [Quarterly]
Discontinued.

C 51.11/8:date • Item 188-A-1
NTIS PRODUCTS AND SERVICES CATALOG.
Earlier C 51.11

C 51.12 • Item 188-A-8
SPECIAL FOREIGN CURRENCY SCIENCE INFORMATION PROGRAM. LIST OF TRANSLATIONS IN PROCESS FOR FISCAL YEAR, COORDINATED AND ADMINISTERED BY THE NATIONAL SCIENCE FOUNDATION. [Annual]

Lists English translation of highly technical foreign publications in scientific disciplines such as the physical and life sciences. Designed primarily to supplement the information needs of U.S. government research scientists.
Discontinued.

C 51.13:date • Item 188-A-4 (MF)
NTIS SEARCHERS. [Monthly]

C 51.13/2:CT/date • Item 188-A-4
PUBLISHED SEARCH BIBLIOGRAPHIES. [Irregular]

Items taken from the NTIS Bibliographic data base.

C 51.13/2-2:date • Item 188-A-4
NTIS PUBLISHED SEARCH MINI CATALOG. [Annual]
Discontinued.

C 51.13/3:CT • Item 188-A-1
FOREIGN TECHNOLOGY ALERT-BIBLIOGRAPHY (series). [Irregular]
Discontinued.

C 51.14:date/nos. • Item 188-A-12
NEWS LINE. [Quarterly] (Available on the NTIS subscribers)

C 51.15:date • Item 188-A-9
DIRECTORY OF FEDERAL STATISTICAL DATA FILES.

PURPOSE:– To list and describe machine-readable data files by various Federal agencies, giving availability information.
Also published in microfiche.
Discontinued.

C 51.16:date • Item 188-A-10
CATALOG OF GOVERNMENT PATENTS. [Irregular]

C 51.16/2 • Item 188-A-10
CATALOG OF GOVERNMENT INVENTIONS AVAILABLE FOR LICENSING. [Annual]
Discontinued.

C 51.17 • Item 188-A-11
TECH NOTES.
See 51.17/12

C 51.17:date • Item 188-A-11
COMPUTERS. [Monthly]

C 51.17/2:date • Item 188-A-11
ELECTROTECHNOLOGY. [Monthly]
See C 51.17/12

C 51.17/3:date • Item 188-A-11
ENERGY. [Monthly]
See C 51.17/12

C 51.17/4:date • Item 188-A-11
ENGINEERING. [Monthly]
See C 51.17/12

C 51.17/5:date • Item 188-A-11
LIFE SCIENCES. [Monthly]
See C 51.17/12

C 51.17/6:date • Item 188-A-11
MACHINERY AND TOOLS. [Monthly]
See C 51.17/12

C 51.17/7:date • Item 188-A-11
MANUFACTURING. [Monthly]
See C 51.17/12

C 51.17/8:date • Item 188-A-11
MATERIALS. [Monthly]
See C 51.17/12

C 51.17/9:date • Item 188-A-11
PHYSICAL SCIENCES. [Monthly]
See C 51.17/12

C 51.17/10:date • Item 188-A-11
TESTING AND INSTRUMENTATION. [Monthly]
See C 51.17/12

C 51.17/11:date • Item 188-A-11
FEDERAL TECHNOLOGY CATALOG, SUMMARIES OF PRACTICAL TECHNOLOGY, NTIS TECH NOTES ANNUAL INDEX.
Discontinued.

C 51.17/12:date • Item 188-A-11
TECH NOTES. [Monthly]
Replaces C 51.17 through C 51.17/10
Discontinued.

C 51.18:date • Item 188-A-13
CORPORATE AUTHOR AUTHORITY LIST. [Annual]
Discontinued.

C 51.19:CT • Item 188-A-14 (MF)
DIRECTORIES. [Irregular]

C 51.19/2:date • Item 188-A-15 (MF)
DIRECTORY OF FEDERAL AND STATE BUSINESS ASSISTANCE. [Annual]

A reference linking technology-oriented U.S. companies with federal and state business assistance resources.
Discontinued.

C 51.19/2-2:date
DIRECTORY OF FEDERAL LABORATORY AND TECHNOLOGY RESOURCES, A GUIDE TO SERVICES, FACILITIES, AND EXPERTISE. [Annual]

C 51.19/3 • Item 188-A-14 (MF)
DIRECTORY OF JAPANESE TECHNICAL REPORTS. [Annual]

Discontinued.

C 51.19/4:date • Item 188-A-14 (MF)
DIRECTORY OF U.S. GOVERNMENT DATAFILES FOR MAINFRAMES & MICROCOMPUTERS.
Discontinued.

C 51.19/5:date • Item 188-A-16 (MF)
DIRECTORY OF U.S. GOVERNMENT SOFTWARE FOR MAINFRAMES & MICROCOMPUTERS. [Annual]
Ceased in 1995.

C 51.20:date • Item 188-A-4
U.S. GOVERNMENT ENVIRONMENTAL DATAFILES & SOFTWARE.
Discontinued.

C 51.21:nos. • Item 271-C
NTIS TECH EXPRESS. [Quarterly]

ENVIRONMENTAL SCIENCE SERVICES ADMINISTRATION (1965– 1970)

CREATION AND AUTHORITY

The Environmental Science Services Administration was established within the Department of Commerce by Reorganization Plan No. 2, effective July 13, 1965, to which were transferred the Coast and Geodetic Survey (C 4) and the Weather Bureau (C 30). The Administration was abolished by Reorganization Plan No. 4 of 1970, effective October 3, 1970, and its functions transferred to the National Oceanic and Atmospheric Administration (C 55).

C 52.1:date
ANNUAL REPORTS.

C 52.2:CT • Item 208-B-1
GENERAL PUBLICATIONS.
Discontinued.

C 52.3/2:date
ENVIRONMENTAL DATA BULLETIN.
Later C 55.203

C 52.6:CT• Item 208-B-5
REGULATIONS, RULES, AND INSTRUCTIONS.
Discontinued.

C 52.7
PRESS RELEASES. [Irregular] (Press only)

C 52.7/2:date
RADIO-TELEVISION NEWS.

C 52.7/3:nos.
PUBLICATION ANNOUNCEMENTS.

C 52.7/4 • Item 208-B-8
ESSA NEWS. v. 1– [Weekly]
Discontinued.

C 52.8:CT • Item 208-B-2
HANDBOOKS, MANUALS, GUIDES.
Discontinued.

C 52.8/2
ESSA RESEARCH LABORATORIES TECHNICAL MANUALS. 1– 1968– [Irregular]

C 52.9:v.nos.&nos.
RADIO SCIENCE. [Monthly]

Replaces Section D of Journal of Research (C 13.22/Sec. D).

C 52.10 • Item 240
IONOSPHERIC PREDICTIONS. [Monthly]
Discontinued.

C 52.11:CT
CLIMATIC MAPS OF UNITED STATES.

C 52.11/2
DAILY WEATHER MAPS, WEEKLY SERIES. 1968– [Weekly]

Features for each day of the weekly period, Monday through Sunday, a surface weather map of the United States showing weather conditions observed daily at 7 a.m. EST throughout the country. Three other smaller maps on each page show the pattern of winds and temperatures near the 18,000-foot level at 7 a.m. EST; the highest and lowest temperatures for the previous day at selected stations in the United States; and the areas over which precipitation was reported in the preceding 24 hours. Forecasts for the District of Columbia and vicinity are also given. A complete explanation of the maps and the weather symbols used are included.
Supersedes Daily Weather Map, published by the Weather Bureau (C 30.12), which was discontinued with the April 14, 1968 issue.

C 52.12
ADDRESSES. [Irregular]

C 52.13 • Item 208-B-3
ESSA MONOGRAPHS. 1– 1966– [Irregular]

PURPOSE:– To provide authoritative treatises covering in both breadth and depth a selected field, area, or specialized topic of scientific inquiry, engineering achievement, or optional technical application.
Discontinued.

C 52.14 • Item 208-B-9
ESSA WORLD. v. 1– 1966– [Quarterly]

Official employee publication.
Discontinued.

C 52.15:letters-nos.
ESSA TECHNICAL REPORTS. 1966– [Irregular]

PURPOSE:– To report the results of a single research project or completed phase of research, or to present the results of scientific or engineering analysis in a single field of specialization.
The Technical Reports are designated by letters for the major agency components and individual research installations.

C 52.15/2:letters-nos.
ESSA TECHNICAL MEMORANDUMS. 1965– [Irregular]

PURPOSE:– To report on work in progress, to describe technical procedures and practices, to report to a limited distribution list (as, for example, in the case of reports to outside sponsors), and for various other types of reporting at the discretion of the agency directors.
The Technical Memorandums are designated by letters for the major agency components (Coast and Geodetic Survey, Environmental Data Service, Weather Bureau, Institutes for Environmental Research, National Environmental Satellite Center, and ESSA Research Laboratories), letter designations for the individual research centers within the major components, and numerical for individual reports within each sub-series. Whenever the name of a component or research center is changed, the letter designation is also changed, but the numerical designations are given on a continuous basis and not reassigned to "1." In some instances, a sub-series is a continuation of previously published series and as such, the numerical designations are also on a continuous basis.

C 52.16
DATA REPORT, METEOROLOGICAL ROCKET NET-WORK FIRINGS. v. 1– 1964– [Monthly]

Contains tabulations and plotted soundings of meteorological rocket-sounding data (wind and temperature) for very high altitudes and computed pressure, density, and speed of sound data.
A brief monthly summary has been initiated beginning with the 1965 data reports. This summary, found immediately before the addendum, is designed to compare the mean profile for the current month with long-term means for the same month.

C 52.16/2
UPPER ATMOSPHERE GEOPHYSICS, REPORTS UAG-(series). 1– 1968– [Irregular] (Environmental Data Service, World Data Center A)

C 52.17   • Item 208-B-4
FEDERAL PLAN FOR METEOROLOGICAL SERVICES AND SUPPORTING RESEARCH. 1968– [Annual]

Covers fiscal year.
Prepared by Office of Federal Coordinator for Meteorological Services and Supporting Research.
PURPOSE:– To provide Congress and the Executive Branch with a coordinated, overall plan for Government meteorological services and for those research and development programs whose immediate objective is to improve meteorological services.

C 52.18:nos.
SOLAR-GEOPHYSICAL DATA, IER-FB-(series). [Monthly]

C 52.19:nos.
ATMOSPHERIC SCIENCES LIBRARY: ACCESSION LIST.

C 52.20   • Item 208-B-6
ESSA PROFESSIONAL PAPERS. 1– 1967– [Irregular]

PURPOSE:– To provide the results of extensive individual research, an analytical treatise of somewhat narrower scope than a monograph, or a scientifically useful compilation of voluminous tables of authoritative data or information yielded by research or experiment in a given specialty.

C 52.21
BIBLIOGRAPHY ON THE CLIMATE OF [Country] WB/BC- (series). 1– 1955– [Irregular]

Bibliographies on the climate of foreign countries. Some bibliographies were not published, but available on microfilm from the manuscript copies.
Prepared by the Environmental Data Service.

C 52.21/2:nos.
WB/TA (series).
Earlier C 30.17/3:So 8

C 52.21/3:CT   • Item 208-B-11
BIBLIOGRAPHIES AND LISTS OF PUBLICATIONS. Discontinued.

C 52.21/4:date
SCIENTIFIC AND TECHNICAL PUBLICATIONS OF ESSA RESEARCH LABORATORIES.

Formerly entitled: Scientific and Technical Publications of Institutes for Environmental Research.

C 52.21/4-2:date
SCIENTIFIC AND TECHNICAL PUBLICATIONS OF ESSA RESEARCH LABORATORIES: EARTH SCIENCES LABORATORIES. [Semiannual]

Scientific Documentation Division, Boulder, Colorado.

C 52.21/5:date
MANAGEMENT INFORMATION ON ERL'S SCIENTIFIC AND TECHNICAL PUBLICATIONS. [Annual] Discontinued.

C 52.22:letters-nos.
ESSA OPERATIONAL DATA REPORTS.

C 52.23:date
COLLECT REPRINTS, ESSA INSTITUTE FOR OCEANOGRAPHY. [Annual]

C 52.24:nos.
BOMEX BULLETIN.
Later C 55.18

C 52.25:date   • Item 208-B-12
ESSA SCIENCE AND ENGINEERING. [Biennial]
Earlier C 52.2:Sci 2
Discontinued.

REGIONAL ECONOMIC DEVELOPMENT OFFICE
(Jan. 6– Dec. 22, 1966)

CREATION AND AUTHORITY

The Regional Economic Development Office was established by the Secretary of Commerce on January 6, 1966, pursuant to the Public Works, and Economic Development Act of 1965 (79 Stat. 552; 42 U.S.C. 3131). The Office was abolished by Departmental Order 5A, December 22, 1966, and functions vested in the Economic Development Administration (C 46).

C 53.1:date
ANNUAL REPORT.

C 53.2:CT
GENERAL PUBLICATIONS.

C 53.7:date
PRESS RELEASES.

C 53.9:CT   • Item 269-A-1
BIBLIOGRAPHIES AND LISTS OF PUBLICATIONS. Discontinued.

OFFICE OF FOREIGN DIRECT INVESTMENTS
(1968– 1974)

CREATION AND AUTHORITY

The Office of Foreign Direct Investments was established within the Department of Commerce by the Secretary of Commerce on January 2, 1968, to carry out provisions of Executive Order 11387 of January 1, 1968. Functions were terminated on January 29, 1974.

C 54.1:date
ANNUAL REPORT.

C 54.2:CT   • Item 232-E-1
GENERAL PUBLICATIONS.

C 54.6:CT   • Item 232-E
REGULATIONS, RULES, AND INSTRUCTIONS.

C 54.7:nos.
PRESS RELEASES. (Foreign Direct Investments Office)

C 54.9:CT
ADDRESSES.

NATIONAL OCEANIC AND ATMOSPHERIC ADMINISTRATION
(1970–)

CREATION AND AUTHORITY

The National Oceanic and Atmospheric Administration was established within the Department of Commerce on October 3, 1970 by Reorganization Plan 4 of 1970.

INFORMATION

Office of Public Affairs
National Oceanic and
Atmospheric Administration
14th St. and Constitution Ave. NW
Department of Commerce
Washington, D.C. 20230
(202) 482-6090
Fax: (202) 482-3154
http://www.noaa.gov

C 55.1
ANNUAL REPORT.

C 55.1/2:date   • Item 250-E-26 (MF)
ANNUAL REPORT ON THE STATUS OF U.S. LIVING MARINE RESOURCES.

C 55.1/3:date   • Item 250-G (MF)
NOAA ANNUAL OPERATING PLAN.

C 55.2:CT   • Item 250-E-2
GENERAL PUBLICATIONS.

C 55.4:nos.
NOAA CIRCULAR (series).

C 55.6:CT   • Item 250-E-6
REGULATIONS, RULES AND INSTRUCTIONS.

C 55.7:nos.
PRESS RELEASES. [Irregular]

Includes science and engineering news from NOAA and radio-TV news.

C 55.8:CT   • Item 250-E-15
HANDBOOKS, MANUALS, GUIDES. [Irregular]

C 55.8/2:nos.   • Item 250-E-15
NOAA HANDBOOKS. [Irregular]

C 55.8/3:letters-nos.   • Item 250-E-15
NOAA MANUALS (numbered).

C 55.9:v.nos.
NOAA WEEK.

C 55.9/2:date
THIS WEEK IN NOAA. [Weekly]

C 55.9/3:date
RESOURCE MANAGEMENT QUARTERLY INFORMATION SUMMARY.

C 55.11:v.nos.&nos. • Item 277
MONTHLY WEATHER REVIEW. v. 1– 101. 1872– 1973.
[Monthly]

PURPOSE:– To serve as a medium for technical contributions in the field of meteorology, principally in the branches of synoptic and applied meteorology.

In addition to the scientific articles, each issue contains an article descriptive of the atmospheric circulation during the month over the Northern Hemisphere with particular references to the effect on weather in the United States.

Index and table of contents contained in the December issues.

Earlier C 30.14 prior to v. 98, no. 11.

Commencing with volume 102 (1974), published by the American Meteorological Society, 45 Beacon Street, Boston, Massachusetts 02108.

C 55.12:nos. • Item 250-E (MF) (EL)
FEDERAL COORDINATOR FOR METEOROLOGICAL SERVICES AND SUPPORTING RESEARCH, FCM (series).

C 55.13:letters-nos. • Item 208-C-1 (MF)
NOAA TECHNICAL REPORTS. 1966–   [Irregular]

PURPOSE:– To report the results of a single research project or completed phase of research, or to present the results of scientific or engineering analysis in a single field of specialization.

The Technical Reports are designated by letters for the major agency components and individual research installations.

Earlier title: ESSA Technical Reports, (C 52.15).

C 55.13:CZ/SP-nos. • Item 208-C-11
CZ/SP (series).

C 55.13:EDIS-nos. • Item 208-C-1
EDIS (series).

C 55.13:ERL-nos. • Item 208-C-2
ERL (series).

C 55.13:NESDIS-nos. • Item 208-C-12
NESDIS (series).

C 55.13:NESS-nos. • Item 208-C-3
NESS (series).

C 55.13:NMFS-nos. • Item 208-C-4
NMFS (series).

C 55.13:NOS-nos. • Item 208-C-5
NOS (series).

C 55.13:NWS-nos. • Item 208-C-6
NWS (series).

C 55.13:OOE-nos. • Item 208-C-8
OOE (series).

C 55.13:OTES-nos. • Item 280-C-10
OTES (series).

C 55.13/2:letters-nos. • Item 208-C-9 (MF)
NOAA TECHNICAL MEMORANDUMS. 1965–
[Irregular]

PURPOSE:– To report on work in progress, to describe technical procedures and practices, to report to a limited distribution list (as, for example, in the case of reports to outside sponsors), and for various other types of reporting at the discretion of the agency directors.

The Technical Memorandums are designated by letters for the major agency components (Coast and Geodetic Survey, Environmental Data Service, Weather Bureau, Institutes for Environmental Research, National Environmental Satellite Center, and ESSA Research Laboratories), letter designations for the individual research centers within the major components, and numerical for individual reports within each sub-series. Whenever the name of a component or research center is changed, the letter designation is also changed, but the numerical designations are given on a continuous basis and not reassigned to "1". In some instances, a sub-series is a continuation of a previously published series and as such, the numerical designations are also on a continuous basis.

Previously distributed to Depository Libraries under item 208-B-7

Earlier title: ESSA Technical Memorandums (C 52.15/2).

C 55.13/2:EDS-nos. • Item 208-C-1
EDIS (series).

C 55.13/2:ERL-nos. • Item 208-C-2
ERL (series).

C 55.13/2:NESDIS-nos. • Item 208-C-12 (MF)
NESDIS (series).

C 55.13/2:NESS-nos. • Item 208-C-3
NESS (series).

C 55.13/2:NMFS-nos. • Item 208-C-4
NMFS (series).

C 55.13/2:NOS-nos. • Item 208-C-5
NOS (series).

C 55.13/2:NWS-nos. • Item 208-C-6
NWS (series).

C 55.13/2:OAO-nos. • Item 208-C-13 (MF)
OAO (series).

C 55.13/2:OAR-nos. • Item 208-C-14
OAR (series).

C 55.13/2-2 • Item 208-C-12
PUBLICATIONS AND FINAL REPORTS ON CONTRACTS AND GRANTS. [Annual]
Discontinued.

C 55.13/3:letters-nos. • Item 208-C-6 (MF)
NOAA COMPUTER PROGRAMS AND PROBLEMS (by region). [Irregular]

Previous title: NOAA Western Region Computer Programs and Problems.
Discontinued.

C 55.13/4:nos. • Item 208-C-6 (MF)
NWS-TDL-CP- (series). [Irregular]
Discontinued.

C 55.13/5:nos. • Item 208-C-6 (MF)
TDL-CP- (series).
Discontinued.

C 55.13/6 • Item 208-C-15 (MF)
NOAA SPECIAL REPORTS, NOS OMA-(series). [Irregular]
Discontinued.

C 55.14:v.nos.&nos. • Item 250-E-1 (MF)
NOAA. v. 1–   1971–   [Quarterly]

PURPOSE:– To acquaint readers with the policies and programs of the agency.
Supersedes ESSA (C 52.14)
Indexed by: Index to U.S. Government Periodicals.
ISSN 0014-0821
Discontinued.

C 55.14/a:date • Item 250-E-1
– SEPARATES. [Semiannual]
Discontinued.

C 55.15:nos. • Item 250-E-3
NOAA PROGRAM PLANS. (Office of Plans and Programs)
Discontinued.

C 55.16:date • Item 250-E-4
FEDERAL PLAN FOR MARINE ENVIRONMENTAL PREDICTION, FISCAL YEAR.

C 55.16/2:date • Item 208-B-4 (MF)
FEDERAL PLAN FOR METEOROLOGICAL SERVICES AND SUPPORTING RESEARCH, FISCAL YEAR (date). 1968–   [Annual] (Federal Coordinator for Meteorological Services and Supporting Research)

PURPOSE:– To provide Congress and the Executive Branch with a coordinated, overall plan for Government meteorological services and for those research and development programs whose immediate objective is to improve meteorological services.
Earlier C 52.17

C 55.17:nos. • Item 250-E-5
NOAA PUBLICATIONS ANNOUNCEMENTS.
Later C 55.228/2
Discontinued.

C 55.18:nos. • Item 250-E-2
BOMEX [Barbados Oceanographic and Meteorological Experiment] BULLETIN. 1– 12. 1968– 1975.
[Irregular]

PURPOSE:– To document planning and execution of the Barbados Oceanographic and Meteorological Experiment (BOMEX), conducted in the summer of 1969. Post-experiment Bulletins have dealt with the progress of the 100 individual investigations, and with the processing of the bulk of the data (done at the Center for Experiment Design and Data Analysis, Environmental Data Service, NOAA).

C 55.19:nos. • Item 250-E-7
NOAA PHOTOESSAYS. 1–   1971–   [Irregular]
Discontinued.

C 55.20:date-nos. • Item 250-E-8
NATURAL DISASTER SURVEY REPORTS. NDSR.
[Irregular]

C 55.21:nos. • Item 250-E-10
INTERNATIONAL FIELD YEAR FOR GREAT LAKES: IFYGL BULLETINS. 1–   1972–   [Irregular]
Discontinued.

C 55.21/2:date
INTERNATIONAL FIELD YEAR FOR GREAT LAKES: NEWS RELEASES. [Irregular]

Joint Canadian and United States program on environmental and water resources research.

C 55.21/3:date • Item 250-E-16
INTERNATIONAL FIELD YEAR FOR THE GREAT LAKES: PROCEEDINGS, IFYGL SYMPOSIUM, ANNUAL MEETINGS OF THE AMERICAN GEOPHYSICAL UNION.
Discontinued.

C 55.21/4:nos. • Item 250-E-17
INTERNATIONAL FIELD YEAR FOR THE GREAT LAKES: TECHNICAL MANUAL SERIES. 1–
[Irregular]
Discontinued.

C 55.21/5:CT • Item 250-G
IFYGL ATLASES.

C 55.22:nos. • Item 250-E-9
NOAA ATLASES. 1–   1971–   [Irregular] (Environmental Data Service)

C 55.22/a:CT • Item 250-F
MAPS.

C 55.22/2:CT • Item 250-F
MAPS. [Irregular]

C 55.22/3:CT • Item 250-F
POSTERS.

C 55.23
ATMOSPHERIC SCIENCES AND MARINE AND EARTH SCIENCES: LIBRARY ACCESSION LIST.

C 55.24:CT
ADDRESSES. [Irregular]

C 55.25:nos. • Item 208-B-6 (MF)
NOAA PROFESSIONAL PAPERS. 1–   [Irregular]

C 55.26:CT • Item 250-E-11
BIBLIOGRAPHIES AND LISTS OF PUBLICATIONS.
[Irregular]

C 55.27:date • Item 834-R (MF)
WEATHER MODIFICATION, SUMMARY REPORT. [Annual]

Report submitted by the Foundation to the President pursuant to section 3(a) of the National Science Foundation Act of 1950, as amended by Public Law 510, 85th Congress for the fiscal year.
The Weather Modification Program is administered by the National Science Foundation through grants and contracts with universities and other research groups. It is managed as an integral part of the Foundation's much broader program for atmospheric sciences.
In addition to reporting the Foundation's activities during the fiscal year, the report summarized the work being carried on by other Government agencies in the field of weather modification.
Earlier NS 1.21
See also C 55.27/2

C 55.27/2:date • Item 834-R (MF)
WEATHER MODIFICATION ACTIVITY REPORTS. 1973– [Annual]

Issued pursuant to Public Law 92-205, December 18, 1971, and amended February 15, 1974, which requires the reporting of all nonfederally sponsored weather modification activities in the United States and its territories.

C 55.27/3:date • Item 834-R (MF)
WEATHER MODIFICATION REPORTING PROGRAM. [Annual]

C 55.28:nos. • Item 275-A
HYDROMETEOROLOGICAL REPORTS. 1– 1938– [Irregular]

This series of reports has special application in engineering, mostly in the design of hydraulic structures. Reports dwell generally on discussions of area rainfall, thunderstorms, hurricanes, and dewpoints, and studies of particular river basins with estimates of maximum possible precipitation and the associated meteorological conditions.
Earlier C 30.44

C 55.29:date • Item 250-E-12
NOAA UNDERSEA RESEARCH PROGRAM, FISCAL YEAR REPORTS.

Former title: Manned Undersea Science and Technology Program, Fiscal Year Reports.
Discontinued.

C 55.29/2:date • Item 250-E-31
SYMPOSIA SERIES FOR UNDERSEA RESEARCH, NOAA'S UNDERSEA RESEARCH PROGRAM. [Annual]

C 55.29/3:date • Item 250-E-31
NATIONAL UNDERSEA RESEARCH PROGRAM TECHNICAL REPORT (Series).
Discontinued.

C 55.30:v.nos.&nos.
DATA BUOY TECHNICAL BULLETIN. v. 1– 1973– [Quarterly] (NOAA Data Buoy Office, Bay St. Louis, Mississippi 39520)

PURPOSE:– To disseminate technical information concerning the Data Buoy Program and keep the national and international data buoy communities informed on the status of environmental data buoy technology.
Formerly Data Buoy Newsletter.
ISSN 0364-4898

C 55.31:date • Item 250-E-13 (MF)
REPORT TO CONGRESS ON OCEAN DUMPING AND OTHER MAN-INDUCED CHANGES TO OCEAN ECOSYSTEMS. 1st– 1973– 1974. [Annual]

Report submitted for the calendar year in compliance with Section 201, Title II of the Marine Protection, Research, and Sanctuaries Act of 1972 (Public Law 92-532). The report describes significant Federal research programs and activities carried out during the year.
Superseded by Report to Congress on Ocean

Pollution, Overfishing and Offshore Development (C 55.31/2).

C 55.31/2:date • Item 250-E-13 (MF)
REPORT TO CONGRESS ON OCEAN POLLUTION, OVERFISHING AND OFFSHORE DEVELOPMENT. 1975– 1983. [Annual]

Submitted in compliance with Section 202(c), Title II of the Marine Protection, Research, and Sanctuaries Act of 1972 (Public Law 92-532).
Supersedes C 55.31
Superseded by C 55.31/3
Discontinued.

C 55.31/3:date • Item 250-E-13 (MF)
REPORT TO CONGRESS ON OCEAN POLLUTION, MONITORING AND RESEARCH. [Annual]
Supersedes C 55.31/2

C 55.32:date • Item 250-E-14 (MF)
REPORT TO THE CONGRESS ON COASTAL ZONE MANAGEMENT. 1st– 1973– [Annual]

Report submitted by the Secretary of Commerce to the President and Congress pursuant to Section 313 (a) and (b) of the Coastal Zone Management Act of 1972 (Public Law 92-583).
The report is to include a list of all approved State coastal zone management programs; a list of participating States and their accomplishments; an itemization of the funds allocated to the States; identification of any State programs which have been disapproved; identification of any Federal activities found to be inconsistent with approved State programs; a summary of regulations issued or in effect during the year; a summary of the national strategy for the coastal zone and discussion of the roles of the Federal, State, regional and local governments in the program; a summary of major problems encountered in administering the Act and a list of any proposed legislation felt necessary for improved operation of the Act.

C 55.32/2:CT • Item 250-E-20
COASTAL ZONE MANAGEMENT TECHNICAL ASSISTANCE DOCUMENTS.
Discontinued.

C 55.32/3:date • Item 250-E-14
STATE COASTAL ZONE MANAGEMENT ACTIVITIES. [Annual]

C 55.32/4:nos.
OCZM GUIDELINE PAPERS. (Office of Coastal Zone Management)

C 55.32/5:date
PUBLIC SUPPORT FOR COASTAL ZONE MANAGEMENT PROGRAMS IMPLEMENTATION OF THE COASTAL ZONE MANAGEMENT ACT OF 1972. [Annual] (Coastal Zone Management Advisory Committee)

C 55.32/6:CT • Item 250-E-22
MANAGEMENT PLANS (series). [Irregular] (Office of Coastal Zone Management)

Each plan explains the purpose of a specific marine sanctuary; describes the ecosystem under protection, and threats to the natural resources; and summarizes the Office's plan to manage and conserve the marine sanctuary.

C 55.32/7 • Item 128-M-3 (CD) (EL)
COASTAL ZONE CONFERENCE PROCEEDINGS. [Biennial]

C 55.33:nos.
TECHNICAL SERIES REPORTS. [Irregular]

C 55.34:CT • Item 250-E-18 (MF)
DRAFT ENVIRONMENTAL IMPACT STATEMENTS.

C 55.34/2:CT • Item 250-E-18 (MF)
FINAL ENVIRONMENTAL IMPACT STATEMENTS. [Irregular]

C 55.35:nos. • Item 250-E-19 (MF)
NOAA DUMPSITE EVALUATION REPORTS. [Irregular]
Discontinued.

C 55.36:nos. • Item 250-E-25
NOAA DATA REPORTS. - (series). 1– 1980– [Irregular] (Office of Marine Pollution Assessment)

C 55.37:nos.
SATELLITE APPLICATIONS INFORMATION NOTES.

C 55.38:date • Item 250-E-21
SEA GRANT BIENNIAL REPORT.
Published annually prior to 1977-79 report.

C 55.38/2:date • Item 250-E-21 (MF)
NATIONAL SEA GRANT PROGRAM ANNUAL RETREAT REPORT.
Earlier C 55.2:Se 1/8

C 55.39:nos. • Item 250-E-23
AQUATIC SCIENCES AND FISHERIES INFORMATION SYSTEM: ASFIS REFERENCE SERIES. [Irregular]

The Aquatic Sciences and Fisheries Information System is an international United Nations information system for the science and technology of freshwater environments. Separate titles deal with rules, geographic authority lists, formats, codes, etc., on which the system is based and will be revised as necessary.

C 55.40:date • Item 250-E-24 (MF)
UNIVERSITIES AND THEIR RELATIONSHIPS WITH THE NATIONAL OCEANIC AND ATMOSPHERIC ADMINISTRATION. [Annual]

Reports on the Administration's relations with universities in terms of both direct contacts involving use of NOAA personnel, monies, plant and equipment, and indirect contacts not involving funds transfers. Contains many tables on awards, grants, contracts, and other agreements with universities.

C 55.40/2 • Item 250-E-33
SUB MARINUS. [Quarterly]

A quarterly review of NOAA's Office of Undersea Research Activities at various universities and other locations.
Discontinued.

C 55.41:CT
AUDIOVISUAL MATERIALS.

C 55.42:date • Item 250-E-27 (MF)
OCEAN THERMAL ENERGY CONVERSION, REPORT TO CONGRESS, FISCAL YEAR. [Annual]

Report submitted to Congress, pursuant to Section 405 of the Ocean Thermal Energy Conservation Act of 1980, which concerns generation of electricity from the temperature differences between warm and cold water.

C 55.43:date • Item 250-E-26 (MF)
OFFICE OF MARINE POLLUTION ASSESSMENT: ANNUAL REPORT.
Summarizes activities and accomplishments of the Office in its primary goal of providing scientific information that will guide policy decisions on marine pollution issues. Sets forth OMPA emphasis and objectives for the coming five years.
Discontinued.

C 55.43/2:date • Item 250-F-26 (MF)
OFFICE OF MARINE POLLUTION ASSESSMENT, TECHNICAL PLAN FOR FISCAL YEAR. [Annual]

C 55.44:date • Item 250-E-28 (MF)
NATIONAL CLIMATE PROGRAM: ANNUAL REPORT.

Report submitted to Congress pursuant to Section 7 of the National Climate Program Act. Summarizes significant achievements of the program, which is participated in by several Federal agencies.

C 55.45:nos. • Item 619-F-1
LANDSAT DATA USERS NOTES. 1–   [Bimonthly]

PURPOSE:– To inform the user community, in newsletter format, regarding Landsat products, systems, and related remote sensing developments.
Formerly published by Geological Survey (I 19.78).
Non-government.

C 55.46:date
THIS WEEK IN NOAA. [Weekly]

C 55.47:nos. • Item 250-E-29
TRANSMITTALS (NOAA Washington Area Personnel Locator). [Semiannual]

Directory of NOAA personnel and organizations in the Washington metropolitan area. Each transmittal comprises the latest directory and is complete within itself.
Discontinued.

C 55.48:CT • Item 250-E-30 (MF)
DIRECTORIES. [Irregular]

C 55.48/2:date • Item 250-E-29 (MF)
NOAA ORGANIZATION DIRECTORY (series).

C 55.49:nos. • Item 250-E-32 (MF)
NOAA ESTUARY-OF-THE-MONTH, SEMINAR SERIES.

Each report contains proceedings of a seminar on the issues, resources, status, and management of a different estuary, such as the Delaware Bay.
Replaced by C 55.49/2

C 55.49/2 • Item 250-E-32 (MF)
NOAA COASTAL OCEAN PROGRAM, REGIONAL SYNTHESIS SERIES.
Replaces C 55.49
Discontinued.

C 55.49/3:nos. • Item 250-E-34 (EL)
NOAA COASTAL OCEAN PROGRAM, DECISIONS ANALYSIS SERIES.

C 55.49/4:date • Item 250-E-35 (EL)
NOAA COASTAL OCEAN PROGRAM, PROJECT NEWS UPDATE. [Quarterly]

C 55.49/5 • Item 250-E-37 (EL)
COASTAL SERVICES. [Bimonthly]

C 55.50 • Item 250-E-3 (MF)
THE SPOKEFISH MONTHLY.
Discontinued.

C 55.51:v.nos.&nos. • Item 250-E-33
COAST AND GEODETIC SURVEY C & GS UPDATE. [Quarterly]
Discontinued.

C 55.52:v.nos.&nos. • Item 250-E-3
EARTH SYSTEM MONITOR. [Quarterly]

C 55.53 • Item 128-M-2 (EL)
NOAA REPORT.

C 55.54 • Item 128-M-2 (E)
ELECTRONIC PRODUCTS.

C 55.55: • Item 128-M-2 (EL)
ACCP (Atlantic Climate Change Program) NEWSLETTER.

C 55.56:date • Item 250-E-36
GLOBE OFFLINE. [Quarterly]

**National Oceanographic
Instrumentation Center**

C 55.70:date
TESTS IN PROGRESS SHEET. [Quarterly]
Earlier D 203.32

C 55.71:nos. • Item 275-G
INSTRUMENT FACT SHEET, IFS- (series). 1–   May 1964–   [Irregular]

PURPOSE:– To report the results of technical evaluation of oceanographic research instrumentation (generally developed and manufactured commercially) conducted by the National Oceanographic Instrumentation Center.
Earlier D 203.32/2

C 55.72:CT
NATIONAL OCEANOGRAPHIC INSTRUMENTATION CENTER PUBLICATIONS.

C 55.73:letter-nos.
TECHNICAL BULLETINS. [Irregular]

NATIONAL WEATHER SERVICE
(1970–   )

CREATION AND AUTHORITY

The National Weather Service was established within the National Oceanic and Atmospheric Administration of the Department of Commerce by Department Organization Order 25-5A, effective October 9, 1970 superseding the Weather Bureau (C 30).

INFORMATION

Chief Information Office
National Weather Service
Department of Commerce
Washington DC 20230
(301) 713-1360
Fax: (301) 713-0610
http://www.nws.noaa.gov

C 55.101:date
ANNUAL REPORT.

C 55.102:CT • Item 275
GENERAL PUBLICATIONS.

C 55.106:CT • Item 278-A
RULES, REGULATIONS, AND INSTRUCTIONS.
Earlier C 30.6

C 55.108:CT • Item 275-E
HANDBOOKS, MANUALS, GUIDES.
Earlier C 30.6/2

C 55.108/2:nos. • Item 275-E
WEATHER SERVICE OBSERVING HANDBOOKS. 1–   1969–   [Irregular]

PURPOSE:– To prescribe uniform instructions for standard weather observing and reporting techniques. They are intended to provide a framework within which the observer can find a system for identifying meteorological phenomena and reporting their occurrence in an understandable format. Agreements with the World Meteorological Organization, international and domestic aviation interests, and civil and military weather services provide the basis for which standards are developed.
Supersedes Manual of Marine Meteorological Observations, Circular M, 12th ed., March 1964.
Earlier C 30.6/6

C 55.108/3:nos. • Item 275-E
FORECASTERS HANDBOOKS. 1–   1967–   [Irregular] (Office of Meteorological Operations)

PURPOSE:– To provide forecasters in the National Weather Service and other meteorologists with technical information to aid them in their forecasting duties.

C 55.108/4:nos. • Item 275-G
COMMUNICATIONS HANDBOOKS. 1–   [Irregular]

(Communications Division, Office of Meteorological Operations)

C 55.108/5:nos. • Item 275-G
ENGINEERING HANDBOOKS, EHS- (series). [Irregular]

C 55.108/6 • Item 275-E (MF)
AFOS HANDBOOK (series).

C 55.109:v.nos.&nos. • Item 275-F
MONTHLY AND SEASONAL WEATHER OUTLOOK. v. 1–   1946–   [Semimonthly]

Shows in graphic form (for broad geographic areas) the atmospheric circulation, temperature departures, and precipitation amounts as observed for the preceeding month and also as anticipated for the coming 30-day period, based on the best indications available. The Outlook is not a specific forecast in the usual meteorological sense, but instead is an estimate of the rainfall and temperature for the next 30 days.
Former title: Average Monthly Weather Outlook.
Earlier C 30.46, prior to v. 24, no. 20.
ISSN 0090-0613
Discontinued.

C 55.110:date
OHIO RIVER SUMMARY AND FORECASTS. [Daily, except Sat., Sun., and Holidays]

Previous title Daily Ohio River Bulletin.
Earlier C 30.54/17, prior to the Oct. 12, 1970 issue.
ISSN 0145-031X

C 55.110/2:date
RIVER SUMMARY AND FORECASTS [Memphis, Tenn. area]. [Daily, except Sat., Sun., and Holidays]

Beginning with data for July 1965, includes Vicksburg, Miss. area (C 30.54/13).
Previous titles: Daily Weather and River Bulletin, Daily River Bulletin [Memphis, Tenn. area].
Earlier C 30.54/7, prior to the Oct. 16, 1970 issue.
Effective March 1, 1973 combined with River Summary and Forecast, New Orleans (C 55.110/2-2) and published as River Summary and Forecast (C 55.110/7).

C 55.110/2-2:date
RIVER SUMMARY AND FORECAST, NEW ORLEANS, LOUISIANA. [Daily]

Earlier C 30.54/10
Effective March 1, 1973 combined with River Summary and Forecast, Memphis (C 55.110/2) and published as River Summary and Forecast (C 55.110/7).

C 55.110/3:date
MISSOURI-MISSISSIPPI RIVER SUMMARY AND FORECASTS. [Daily, except Sat. and Sun.]

Previous titles: Daily Mississippi River Stage and Forecast Bulletin, daily Missouri-Mississippi River Bulletin.
Earlier C 30.54, prior to November 24, 1970.
ISSN 0364-7552

C 55.110/4:date
DAILY WEATHER AND RIVER BULLETIN [Albuquerque, New Mexico area]. [Daily, April 1– June 30 only]
Earlier C 30.54/4
ISSN 0364-5819

C 55.110/5:date
DAILY WEATHER AND RIVER BULLETIN [New Orleans, La. area].
Earlier C 30.54/10

C 55.110/6:date
DAILY WEATHER AND RIVER BULLETIN [Shreveport, La. area].
Earlier C 30.54/12

C 55.110/7:date
RIVER SUMMARY AND FORECAST, [Lower Mississippi Region]. March 1, 1973–   [Daily, except Sun. and Holidays] (National Weather Service, Lower Mississippi River Forecast Center, 1010 Gause Road, Slidell Louisiana 70458)

Replaces and combines former River Summary and Forecasts for Memphis, Tennessee (C 55.110/2) and New Orleans, Louisiana (C 55.110/2-2).
ISSN 0145-0298

C 55.111:date   • Item 278-B (MF)
OPERATIONS OF NATIONAL WEATHER SERVICE. 1st ed.–   1970–   [Semiannual]

Previous title Operations of the Weather Bureau (C 30.83).
Discontinued.

C 55.112:CT
MARINE WEATHER SERVICES CHARTS. [Irregular]

Radio broadcast schedules of stations, Weather Bureau office telephone numbers, and locations of warning display stations are shown for weather forecasts for boating areas in the United States and Puerto Rico.
Previous title Weather Bureau Marine Services Charts (C 30.22/6).

C 55.113:v.nos.&nos.
WATER SUPPLY OUTLOOK FOR WESTERN UNITED STATES, WATER YEAR. v. 23, no. 1–   Jan. 1, 1971–   [Monthly, Jan.-May]

Prior to 1969, entitled Water Supply Forecasts for Western United States.
Earlier C 30.85
ISSN 0364-3433

C 55.113/2:date   • Item 275-R (MF)
WATER SUPPLY OUTLOOK FOR NORTHEASTERN UNITED STATES. [Monthly]

C 55.114:date
PACIFIC NORTHWEST MONTHLY PRECIPITATION AND TEMPERATURE. – September 1974.

Earlier C 30.62/3
Beginning with October 1974 issue, information incorporated into the Pacific Northwest Water Resources Summary (I 19.46).

C 55.115:date
NUMERICAL WEATHER PREDICTION ACTIVITIES, NATIONAL METEOROLOGICAL CENTER. 1968– [Semiannual]

PURPOSE:– To inform users of products, and university groups and foreign weather services about changes made in operations. Includes information on operational product development, communications, automation, changes to numerical models and research development on new forecast models and procedures.
Earlier C 30.2:N 91

C 55.116:nos.
ENGINEERING BITS AND FAX. [Engineering Division]

PURPOSE:– To provide an engineering newsletter for National Weather Service engineering staff.

C 55.117:v.nos.   • Item 274
DAILY RIVER STAGES. v. 1–   1903–   [Annual]

PURPOSE:– To provide daily river stage data for over 600 stations located on the principal rivers of the United States.
Prior to 1949, entitled Daily River Stages at River Gage Stations on Principal Rivers of the United States.
Earlier C 30.24

C 55.117/2:v.nos.   • Item 274
RIVER FORECASTS PROVIDED BY THE NATIONAL WEATHER SERVICE. v. 1–   1972–   [Annual]
Later C 55.285

C 55.118
COOPERATIVE OBSERVER.

PURPOSE:– To improve cooperative observer's morale and to instruct the observer in observational techniques, thus increasing the quality of weather observations taken by them. In addition, it serves as a communications link between the cooperative observer and the National Weather Service offices utilizing their reports.

The regional newsletters are published by the National Climatic Center, Asheville, North Carolina 28801, and issued in the following editions:–

C 55.118:v.nos.&nos.
WESTERN REGION. v. 1–   1963–   [Quarterly]

C 55.118/2:v.nos.&nos.
SOUTHERN REGION. v. 1–   1963–   [Quarterly]

C 55.118/3:v.nos.&nos.
CENTRAL REGION. v. 1–   1963–   [Quarterly]

C 55.118/4:v.nos.&nos.
EASTERN REGION. v. 1–   1963–   [Quarterly]

C 55.118/5:v.nos.&nos.
PACIFIC REGION. v. 1–   1963–   [Quarterly]

C 55.118/6:v.nos.&nos.
NATIONAL COOPERATIVE OBSERVER NEWSLETTER. v. 1–   [Quarterly]

C 55.119:date   • Item 282-A
SELECTED WORLDWIDE WEATHER BROADCASTS. [Irregular]

Covers radiotelegraph and radiotelephone broadcasts, VHF-FM continuous weather broadcasts, and radiofacsimile broadcasts.
Prepared in cooperation with Naval Weather Service Command, Department of the Navy.
Continues Weather Service from Merchant Shipping (C 30.79).
Former title: Worldwide Marine Weather Broadcasts.

C 55.121:nos.
TRAINING PAPERS. 1–   [Irregular]

C 55.122:CT   • Item 275-P
MAPS AND CHARTS. [Irregular]
Earlier C 30.22

C 55.123:v.nos.&nos.   • Item 275-H
GULFSTREAM. v. 1–   1975–   [Monthly]

Provides positions of the Gulf Stream plus eddys for the beginning and end of each month; selected bathythermographs; mean sea surface temperature (SST), SST anomaly (the difference between the monthly mean SST and historical mean); monthly SST change; surface temperature observations; and a special article each month concerning research done in the Gulf Stream area.
Continues publication issued by the Naval Oceanographic Office from 1966-1974 (D 203.29).
Consolidated with Fishing Information (C 55.319) to form Oceanographic Monthly Summary (C 55.123/2).
ISSN 0565-8543

C 55.123/2:v.nos.&nos.   • Item 275-H
OCEANOGRAPHIC MONTHLY SUMMARY. v. 1, no. 1– Jan. 1981–
Consolidates Gulfstream (C 55.123) and Fishing Information (C 55.319).
Discontinued.

C 55.124:CT   • Item 275-I
BIBLIOGRAPHIES AND LISTS OF PUBLICATIONS. [Irregular]

C 55.125:CT   • Item 275-M
AUDIOVISUAL MATERIALS. [Irregular]

C 55.126:CT   • Item 275-J (MF)
FORECAST TRACKS AND PROBABILITIES FOR HURRICANES (by name). [Irregular]

Each report is a compilation of the forecast tracks and probabilities of a different well known historical hurricane. Intended for use by local officials and other disaster preparedness officials. Reports contain an introduction, forecast tracks, and tables.
Discontinued.

C 55.127:date   • Item 275-K (P) (EL)
AWARE. [Quarterly]

PURPOSE:– To provide information on activities of the National Weather Service and other government agencies directed toward coping with natural disasters and weather.
Earlier titled: Disaster Preparedness Report.

C 55.128:nos.   • Item 275-L (MF)
TECHNICAL PROCEDURES BULLETINS.
Discontinued.

C 55.129:date   • Item 275-N
CLIMATE REVIEW, METROPOLITAN WASHINGTON. [Monthly]

Weather maps, tables, and narratives highlight metropolitan Washington climate in a historical perspective in terms of temperatures, precipitation, sunshine, wind gusts, etc.

C 55.129/2:nos.   • Item 275-S
THE CLIMATE BULLETIN. [Monthly]

Earlier title Weekly Climate Bulletin. Earlier issued weekly, now issued monthly.
Discontinued.

C 55.130:CT   • Item 275-T
POSTERS. [Irregular]

C 55.131:v.nos./nos.   • Item 275-J
DIAGNOSTICS REPORT OF THE NATIONAL HURRICANE CENTER. [3 times a year]
Discontinued.

C 55.132   • Item 275 (MF)
CRITICAL PATH. [Quarterly]
Discontinued.

C 55.133   • Item 275-F-1 (MF)
NATIONAL IMPLEMENTATION PLAN FOR MODERNIZATION OF THE NATIONAL WEATHER SERVICE. [Annual]
Discontinued.

C 55.134   • Item 275-K-1
A SUMMARY OF NATURAL HAZARD DEATHS IN THE UNITED STATES. [Annual]

C 55.135   • Item 275-D (EL)
MARINERS WEATHER LOG. [3 times/yr.]

PURPOSE:–To provide information on weather over the oceans and Great Lakes. Gale table gives selected weather observations from vessels in the North Atlantic Ocean.
Index in November issue.
Earlier C 55.299/2

C 55.136   • Item 275-W
CLIMATE PREDICTION CENTER ATLAS.

National Centers for Environmental Prediction
Formerly: National Meteorological Center

C 55.190:CT   • Item 250-E-2
NATIONAL METEOROLOGICAL CENTER PUBLICATIONS.

C 55.191/2:date   • Item 276-B-1 (MF)
CLIMATE ANALYSIS CENTER, ANNUAL ACHIEVEMENTS.

C 55.193:date
SEMIMONTHLY MEANS OF SEA SURFACE TEMPERATURE. [Semimonthly]

C 55.194:date   • Item 276-A
CLIMATE DIAGNOSTIC BULLETIN. [Monthly]

PURPOSE:– To provide the scientific community with an overview of the state of the global climate system. Contains maps of mean, and when appropriate, anomaly fields which will include sea surface temperature, outgoing longwave radiations, etc.

C 55.195:date   • Item 273-D-4
DAILY WEATHER MAPS. [Weekly]
    Earlier C 55.213

C 55.196:date   • Item 276-B (MF)
NMC MONTHLY PERFORMANCE SUMMARY. [Monthly]

PURPOSE:– To summarize performance of the National Meteorological Center in forecasting weather.
    Due to budget restraints this publication was suspended between 1986 and 1988.
    Discontinued.

C 55.197   • Item 276-B (MF)
RESEARCH HIGHLIGHTS OF THE NMC DEVELOPMENT DIVISION.
    Discontinued.

NATIONAL ENVIRONMENTAL SATELLITE, DATA, AND INFORMATION SERVICE (1970–   )

CREATION AND AUTHORITY

The Environmental Data Service was established within the National Oceanic and Atmospheric Administration of the Department of Commerce by Department Organization Order 25-5A, effective October 9, 1970.

INFORMATION

NESDIS
NOAA
Department of Commerce
Herbert Clark Hoover Bldg.
14th Street and Constitution Ave. NW
Washington, DC 20230
(301) 713-3578
Fax: (301) 713-1249
http://www.nesdis.noaa.gov

C 55.201:date
ANNUAL REPORT.

C 55.201/2:date   • Item 273-D-25 (MF)
NATIONAL GEOPHYSICAL DATA CENTER: ANNUAL REPORT.

C 55.202:CT   • Item 273-D-1
GENERAL PUBLICATIONS.

C 55.202:C 99/871-977   • Item 273-D-1
TROPICAL CYCLONES OF THE NORTH ATLANTIC OCEAN, 1871– 1977. 1978. 170 p.

Over the 107-year period 1871– 1977, a total of 850 tropical cyclones have been reported over the North Atlantic. This publication discusses the classification of tropical cyclones and the sources and accuracy of cyclone data; summarizes a great deal of statistical information pertaining to the cyclones; and presents a cyclone tracking chart showing the origin, course, and meteorological changes of the cyclones of each of the 107 years.

C 55.202:Ea 7   • Item 273-D-1
EARTHQUAKE HISTORY OF THE UNITED STATES. 1973. 208 p. il.

This well written history of prominent earth-quakes in the United States from historical times through 1970, is documented with earthquake data. Explanations of terms and tabular data have been included to assist the reader in understanding this study of earth quakes, many of which have been devastatingly destructive to life and property. Earthquakes are listed and described by region and State, and maps and photographs accompany the text.

C 55.203:date
ENVIRONMENTAL DATA BULLETIN. – June 1971. [Bimonthly]

Earlier C 52.3/2, prior to the October 1970 issue.
    Superseded by Environmental Data Service, (C 55.222).

C 55.208:CT   • Item 273-D-6
HANDBOOKS, MANUALS, GUIDES.

C 55.209:v.nos.&nos.   • Item 273-D-12 (EL)
WEEKLY WEATHER AND CROP BULLETIN. v. 1– 1924–   [Weekly]

Issued on Tuesday of each week, the Bulletin contains an account of weather conditions and their effect on crops throughout the United States for the week ending at 7:30 a.m., e.s.t., each Tuesday. In particular, it covers the effects of weather on crop development and farm operations, especially as featured in Weather of the Week and special mention of weather conditions affecting the more important crops. Tables of temperature and precipitation are included with departures from normal; also charts showing the same data and their distribution throughout the country. During the winter season snow and ice conditions are published in lieu of most of the .Special Telegraphic Summaries which normally appear in the Bulletin. These summaries are reported by the Weather Bureau State Climatologist in cooperation with the State and Federal Agricultural Agencies concerning crop-weather condition in their respective States.
    Most issues of the Bulletin feature special articles on various aspects of weather, crops, and agricultural activities, as space permits. Also Special Weather Summary editions are infrequently issued to cover very unusual conditions.
    An index of the special articles is contained in the final issue of each year.
    ISSN 0043-1974
    Earlier C 30.11, prior to v. 57, no. 40.

C 55.210:v.nos.&nos.   • Item 275-D
MARINERS WEATHER LOG. [Bimonthly]
    ISSN 0025-3367
    Earlier C 30.72, prior to v. 14, no. 6.
    Later C 55.299/2.

C 55.211:v.nos.&nos.   • Item 273-D-22 (EL)
MONTHLY CLIMATIC DATA FOR THE WORLD. [Monthly]

Surface data table gives pressure, temperature, relative humidity, precipitation, by country and selected cities; upper aid data table gives dynamic height, temperature, and dew point at specific pressure levels, by country and selected cities.
    ISSN 0027-0296
    Earlier C 30.50, prior to v. 23, no. 5.

C 55.212:v.nos.&nos.   • Item 274-B (EL)
STORM DATA. v. 1–   1959–   [Monthly]

Contains reports and statistical data on severe storms, by States, with a description of the storm damage reported in month.
    Information of this nature prior to 1959 appears in Climatological Data– National Summary and prior to 1950 in Monthly Weather Review.
    ISSN 0039-1972
    Earlier C 30.74 prior to v. 12, no. 9.

C 55.213:date/nos.   • Item 273-D-4
DAILY WEATHER MAPS, WEEKLY SERIES. 1968– [Weekly]

Features for each day of the weekly period, Monday through Sunday, a surface weather map of the United States showing weather condition observed daily at 7 a.m. EST throughout the country. Three other smaller maps on each page show the pattern of winds and temperatures near the 18,000-foot level at 7 a.m. EST; the highest and lowest temperatures for the previous day at selected stations in the United States; and the areas over which precipitation was reported in the preceding 24 hours. Forecasts for the district of Columbia and vicinity are also given. A complete explanation of the maps and the weather symbols used are included.
    Supersedes Daily Weather Map, published by the Weather Bureau (C 30.12), which was discontinued with the April 14, 1968 issue.
    Earlier C 52.11/2 prior to the Oct. 26– Nov. 1, 1970 issue.
    See C 55.195

C 55.213/2
DAILY SERIES, SYNOPTIC WEATHER MAPS.
    PART 1. NORTHERN HEMISPHERE SEA LEVEL AND 500 MILLIBAR CHARTS. [Monthly]

Consists of a sea-level and upper-air constant pressure surface (500-millibar) map for each day of the month.
    ISSN 0566-5566
    Earlier C 30.49 prior to the July 1962 issue.

C 55.214:v.nos.&nos.   • Item 277-A-52
CLIMATOLOGICAL DATA, NATIONAL SUMMARY. v. 1–   1950– 1980. [Monthly & Annual]

Contains general summary of weather conditions, condensed climatological summary for the States, climatological data by stations for the States, Pacific Area, and West Indies, degree days and severe storm data, river stages and flood data and upper air data.
    ISSN 0095-4365
    Earlier C 30.51, prior to v. 21, no. 6.

Discontinued Dec. 1980.

C 55.214/2-C 55.214/47   • Item 277-A-1
CLIMATOLOGICAL DATA [State sections]. v. 1– 1914–   [Monthly & Annual]

Contains climatological data for stations within each section, consisting of a narrative concerning the month's weather for the section, and tables listing information such as daily and monthly precipitation, temperature, wind movements, etc.
    Annual summary issued separately, presenting data on an annual basis, similar to the material published in the monthly issues.
    Issued for the following

C 55.214/2   • Item 277-A-1 (MF)
ALABAMA.

    ISSN 0145-0050
    Earlier C 30.18/2

C 55.214/3   • Item 277-A-2 (MF)
ALASKA.

    ISSN 0364-5762
    Earlier C 30.21

C 55.214/4   • Item 277-A-3 (MF)
ARIZONA.

    ISSN 0145-0387
    Earlier C 30.18/4

C 55.214/5   • Item 277-A-4 (MF)
ARKANSAS.

    ISSN 0364-605X
    Earlier C 30.18/5

C 55.214/6   • Item 277-A-5 (MF)
CALIFORNIA.

    ISSN 0145-0069
    Earlier C 30.18/6

C 55.214/7   • Item 277-A-6 (MF)
COLORADO.

  ISSN 0145-0506
  Earlier C 30.18/7

C 55.214/8   • Item 277-A-9 (MF)
FLORIDA.

  ISSN 0145-0484
  Earlier C 30.18/8

C 55.214/9   • Item 277-A-10 (MF)
GEORGIA.

  ISSN 0145-0492
  Earlier C 30.18/9

C 55.214/10   • Item 277-A-54 (MF)
HAWAII.

  ISSN 0095-4373
  Earlier C 30.18/10

C 55.214/11   • Item 277-A-12 (MF)
IDAHO.

  ISSN 0145-0514
  Earlier C 30.19

C 55.214/12   • Item 277-A-13 (MF)
ILLINOIS.

  ISSN 0145-0522
  Earlier C 30.18/11

C 55.214/13   • Item 277-A-14 (MF)
INDIANA.

  ISSN 0145-0530
  Earlier C 30.18/12

C 55.214/14   • Item 277-A-15 (MF)
IOWA.

  ISSN 0145-0468
  Earlier C 30.18/13

C 55.214/15   • Item 277-A-16 (MF)
KANSAS.

  ISSN 0145-0417
  Earlier C 30.18/14

C 55.214/16   • Item 277-A-17 (MF)
KENTUCKY.

  ISSN 0145-0433
  Earlier C 30.18/15

C 55.214/17   • Item 277-A-18 (MF)
LOUISIANA.
  ISSN 0145-0409
  Earlier C 30.18/16

C 55.214/18   • Item 277-A-55 (MF)
MARYLAND AND DELAWARE.

  ISSN 0145-0549
  Earlier C 30.18/17

C 55.214/19   • Item 277-A-22 (MF)
MICHIGAN.

  ISSN 0145-045X
  Earlier C 30.18/18

C 55.214/20   • Item 277-A-23 (MF)
MINNESOTA.

  ISSN 0145-0476
  Earlier C 30.18/19

C 55.214/21   • Item 277-A-24 (MF)
MISSISSIPPI.

  ISSN 0145-0424
  Earlier C 30.18/20

C 55.214/22   • Item 277-A-25 (MF)
MISSOURI.
  ISSN 0364-6068
  Earlier C 30.18/21

C 55.214/23   • Item 277-A-26 (MF)
MONTANA.

  ISSN 0145-0395
  Earlier C 30.18/22

C 55.214/24   • Item 277-A-27 (MF)
NEBRASKA.

  ISSN 0145-0441
  Earlier C 30.18/23

C 55.214/25   • Item 277-A-28 (MF)
NEVADA.

  ISSN 0364-5312
  Earlier C 30.18/24

C 55.214/26   • Item 277-A-56 (MF)
NEW ENGLAND.

  ISSN 0364-5339
  Earlier C 30.18/25

C 55.214/27   • Item 277-A-30 (MF)
NEW JERSEY.

  ISSN 0364-5614
  Earlier C 30.18/26

C 55.214/28   • Item 277-A-31 (MF)
NEW MEXICO.

  ISSN 0364-5622
  Earlier C 30.18/27

C 55.214/29   • Item 277-A-32 (MF)
NEW YORK.

  ISSN 0364-5606
  Earlier C 30.18/28

C 55.214/30   • Item 277-A-33 (MF)
NORTH CAROLINA.

  ISSN 0145-0794
  Earlier C 30.18/29

C 55.214/31   • Item 277-A-34 (MF)
NORTH DAKOTA.

  ISSN 0364-5029
  Earlier C 30.18/30

C 55.214/32   • Item 277-A-35 (MF)
OHIO.

  ISSN 0364-5584
  Earlier C 30.18/31

C 55.214/33   • Item 277-A-36 (MF)
OKLAHOMA.

  ISSN 0364-4960
  Earlier C 30.18/32

C 55.214/34   • Item 277-A-37 (MF)
OREGON.

  ISSN 0364-5851
  Earlier C 30.18/33

C 55.214/35
PACIFIC.

  Earlier C 20.19/2

C 55.214/36   • Item 277-A-38 (MF)
PENNSYLVANIA.

  ISSN 0364-5843
  Earlier C 30.18/34

C 55.214/37   • Item 277-A-53 (MF)
PUERTO RICO AND VIRGIN ISLANDS.

  ISSN 0500-4780
  Earlier C 30.20/2

C 55.214/38   • Item 277-A-40 (MF)
SOUTH CAROLINA.

  ISSN 0364-5037
  Earlier C 30.18/35

C 55.214/39   • Item 277-A-41 (MF)
SOUTH DAKOTA.

  ISSN 0364-5045
  Earlier C 30.18/36

C 55.214/40   • Item 277-A-42 (MF)
TENNESSEE.

  ISSN 0364-5010
  Earlier C 30.18/37

C 55.214/41   • Item 277-A-43 (MF)
TEXAS.

  ISSN 0364-6041
  Earlier C 30.18/38

C 55.214/42   • Item 277-A-44 (MF)
UTAH.

  ISSN 0364-5592
  Earlier C 30.18/39

C 55.214/43   • Item 277-A-46 (MF)
VIRGINIA.

  ISSN 0364-5630
  Earlier C 30.18/40

C 55.214/44   • Item 277-A-47 (MF)
WASHINGTON.

  ISSN 0364-5320
  Earlier C 30.18/41

C 55.214/45   • Item 277-A-48 (MF)
WEST VIRGINIA.

  ISSN 0364-5371
  Earlier C 30.18/42

C 55.214/46   • Item 277-A-49 (MF)
WISCONSIN.

  ISSN 0364-5304
  Earlier C 30.18/43

C 55.214/47   • Item 277-A-50 (MF)
WYOMING.

  ISSN 0364-5002
  Earlier C 30.18/44

C 55.214/48
WEST INDIES AND THE CARIBBEAN.

C 55.214/49   • Item 273-D
ARCTIC REGIONS.

  Earlier C 30.21/2
  Discontinued.

C 55.214/50   • Item 273-D
ANTARCTIC REGIONS.

  Earlier C 30.21/3
  Item 273-D-113 (MF)
  Discontinued.

C 55.214/51   • Item 277-B (EL)
CLIMATOLOGIC DATA.

  (Various states).

C 55.215:nos./pt.nos.   • Item 273-D-13 (MF)
SOLAR-GEOPHYSICAL DATA [reports]. [Monthly]

  Separate annual descriptive text issued.
  Pt. 1, Prompt Reports; pt. 1, Comprehensive
  Reports.
  ISSN 0038-0911
  Earlier C 52.18 prior to no. 314.

C 55.216– C 55.216/44 • Item 274-A-51– A-56 (MF)
HOURLY PRECIPITATION DATA [State Sections].
[Monthly & Annual]

　　Gives daily totals and hourly precipitation data by stations. The annual issue recapitulates the monthly tables, and carries a station index and location map.

　　Issued for the following

C 55.216　　　　　• Item 274-A-1 (MF)
ALABAMA.

　　ISSN 0364-6076
　　Earlier C 30.59

C 55.216/2　　　　• Item 274-A-3 (MF)
ARIZONA.

　　ISSN 0364-6084
　　Earlier C 30.59/3

C 55.216/3　　　　• Item 274-A-4 (MF)
ARKANSAS.

　　ISSN 0090-2683
　　Earlier C 30.59/4

C 55.216/4　　　　• Item 274-A-5 (MF)
CALIFORNIA.

　　ISSN 0364-6092
　　Earlier C 30.59/5

C 55.216/5　　　　• Item 274-A-6 (MF)
COLORADO.

　　ISSN 0364-6106
　　Earlier C 30.59/6

C 55.216/6　　　　• Item 274-A-9 (MF)
FLORIDA.

　　ISSN 0364-6114
　　Earlier C 30.59/7

C 55.216/7　　　　• Item 274-A-10 (MF)
GEORGIA.

　　ISSN 0364-6122
　　Earlier C 30.59/8

C 55.216/8　　　　• Item 274-A-54 (MF)
HAWAII AND PACIFIC.

　　ISSN 0364-6130
　　Earlier C 30.59/46

C 55.216/9　　　　• Item 274-A-12 (MF)
IDAHO.

　　ISSN 0364-6149
　　Earlier C 30.59/9

C 55.216/10　　　• Item 274-A-13 (MF)
ILLINOIS.

　　ISSN 0364-6157
　　Earlier C 30.59/10

C 55.216/11　　　• Item 274-A-14 (MF)
INDIANA.

　　ISSN 0364-6165
　　Earlier C 30.59/11

C 55.216/12　　　• Item 274-A-15 (MF)
IOWA.

　　ISSN 0364-6173
　　Earlier C 30.59/12

C 55.216/13　　　• Item 274-A-16 (MF)
KANSAS.

　　ISSN 0364-6181
　　Earlier C 30.59/13

C 55.216/14　　　• Item 274-A-17 (MF)
KENTUCKY.

　　ISSN 0364-5401
　　Earlier C 30.59/14

C 55.216/15　　　• Item 274-A-18 (MF)
LOUISIANA.

　　ISSN 0364-5398
　　Earlier C 30.59/15

C 55.216/16　　　• Item 274-A-55 (MF)
MARYLAND AND DELAWARE.

　　ISSN 0364-538X
　　Earlier C 30.59/16

C 55.216/17　　　• Item 274-A-22 (MF)
MICHIGAN.

　　ISSN 0364-6205
　　Earlier C 30.59/17

C 55.216/18　　　• Item 274-A-23 (MF)
MINNESOTA.

　　ISSN 0364-6211
　　Earlier C 30.59/18

C 55.216/19　　　• Item 274-A-24 (MF)
MISSISSIPPI.

　　ISSN 0364-622X
　　Earlier C 30.59/19

C 55.216/20　　　• Item 274-A-25 (MF)
MISSOURI.

　　ISSN 0364-6238
　　Earlier C 30.59/20

C 55.216/21　　　• Item 274-A-26 (MF)
MONTANA.

　　ISSN 0364-6246
　　Earlier C 30.59/21

C 55.216/22　　　• Item 274-A-27 (MF)
NEBRASKA.

　　ISSN 0364-6254
　　Earlier C 30.59/22

C 55.216/23　　　• Item 274-A-28 (MF)
NEVADA.

　　ISSN 0364-6262
　　Earlier C 30.59/23

C 55.216/24　　　• Item 274-A-56 (MF)
NEW ENGLAND.

　　ISSN 0364-6270
　　Earlier C 30.59/24

C 55.216/25　　　• Item 274-A-30 (MF)
NEW JERSEY.

　　ISSN 0364-6289
　　Earlier C 30.59/25

C 55.216/26　　　• Item 274-A-31 (MF)
NEW MEXICO.

　　ISSN 0364-6297
　　Earlier C 30.59/26

C 55.216/27　　　• Item 274-A-32 (MF)
NEW YORK.

　　ISSN 0364-6300
　　Earlier C 30.59/27

C 55.216/28　　　• Item 274-A-33 (MF)
NORTH CAROLINA.

　　ISSN 0364-6219
　　Earlier C 30.59/28

C 55.216/29　　　• Item 274-A-34 (MF)
NORTH DAKOTA.

　　ISSN 0364-6327
　　Earlier C 30.59/29

C 55.216/30　　　• Item 274-A-35 (MF)
OHIO.

　　ISSN 0364-6335
　　Earlier C 30.59/30

C 55.216/31　　　• Item 274-A-36 (MF)
OKLAHOMA.

　　ISSN 0364-6343
　　Earlier C 30.59/31

C 55.216/32　　　• Item 274-A-37 (MF)
OREGON.

　　ISSN 0364-6351
　　Earlier C 30.59/32

C 55.216/33　　　• Item 274-A-38 (MF)
PENNSYLVANIA.

　　ISSN 0364-619X
　　Earlier C 30.59/33

C 55.216/34　　　• Item 274-A-40 (MF)
SOUTH CAROLINA.

　　ISSN 0364-636X
　　Earlier C 30.59/34

C 55.216/35　　　• Item 274-A-41 (MF)
SOUTH DAKOTA.

　　ISSN 0364-6378
　　Earlier C 30.59/35

C 55.216/36　　　• Item 274-A-42 (MF)
TENNESSEE.

　　ISSN 0364-6386
　　Earlier C 30.59/36

C 55.216/37　　　• Item 274-A-43 (MF)
TEXAS.

　　ISSN 0364-6882
　　Earlier C 30.59/37

C 55.216/38　　　• Item 274-A-44 (MF)
UTAH.

　　ISSN 0364-6920
　　Earlier C 30.59/38

C 55.216/39　　　• Item 274-A-46 (MF)
VIRGINIA.

　　ISSN 0364-6874
　　Earlier C 30.59/39

C 55.216/40　　　• Item 274-A-47 (MF)
WASHINGTON.

　　ISSN 0364-6912
　　Earlier C 30.59/40

C 55.216/41　　　• Item 274-A-48 (MF)
WEST VIRGINIA.

　　ISSN 0364-6904
　　Earlier C 30.59/41

C 55.216/42　　　• Item 274-A-49 (MF)
WISCONSIN.

　　ISSN 0364-6939
　　Earlier C 30.59/42

C 55.216/43　　　• Item 274-A-50 (MF)
WYOMING.

　　ISSN 0364-6890
　　Earlier C 30.59/43

C 55.216/44 • Item 274-A-53 (MF)
PUERTO RICO.

ISSN 0090-2691

C 55.216/45 • Item 274-A-57 (EL)
HOURLY PRECIPITATION DATA, & COUNTIES.

(Various states).

C 55.217:date
LOCAL CLIMATOLOGICAL DATA. [Monthly & Annual]
(National Climatic Center, Asheville, N.C. 28801)

Issued for approximately 290 stations. Tables
give local climatological data, including temperature, precipitation, wind, sunshine, sky cover,
thunderstorms or distant-lightning, weather restricting visibility, hourly precipitation.

MONTHLY SUPPLEMENTS.

Issued for approximately 200 stations
where 24-hourly observations are taken.
Tables give occurrences for temperature and
wind speed, hourly and daily precipitation
amounts; ceiling- visibility; sky cover, wind,
and relative humidity; temperatures; 6-hourly
observation on sky cover, pressure,
psychmetric data, and wind. Monthly figures.
Two-year comparisons.

ANNUAL SUMMARY.
Earlier C 30.56
Later C 55.287

C 55.217/2:date
LOCAL CLIMATOLOGICAL DATA. WASHINGTON, D.C.,
DULLES NATIONAL AIRPORT. [Monthly]

Later C 55.287/3

C 55.218:date/nos.
IONOSPHERIC DATA. – Sept. 1974. [Monthly] (National Climatic Center, Asheville, N.C.)

Data compiled by Aeronomy and Space Center, Boulder, Colorado.

C 55.219:nos. • Item 275-C
KEY TO METEOROLOGICAL RECORDS DOCUMEN-
TATION [miscellaneous reports]. [Irregular]

PURPOSE:– To provide guidance information
to research personnel and others making use of
observed data.
Earlier C 30.66/2

C 55.219:5.3 • Item 275-C
CATALOG OF METEOROLOGICAL SATELLITE
DATA: ESSA 9 AND NOAA 1 TELEVISION
CLOUD PHOTOGRAPHY. [Quarterly]

C 55.219/2:nos. • Item 275-C
KEY TO GEOPHYSICAL RECORDS DOCUMENTA-
TION. 1– 1972– [Irregular]

C 55.219/3:nos. • Item 275-C
KEY TO OCEANOGRAPHIC RECORDS DOCUMEN-
TATION. 1– 1973– [Irregular]

Includes such publications as bibliographies,
data listing, user's guides, data reports, atlases,
data inventories, data submission guides, and
data processing manuals.

C 55.219/4:date-nos. • Item 275-C
KEY TO METEOROLOGICAL RECORDS, 5.4. ENVI-
RONMENTAL SATELLITE IMAGERY (series).
[Monthly]

ISSN 0091-5262

Discontinued.

C 55.219/5:nos. • Item 273-D-5
KEY TO OCEANIC AND ATMOSPHERIC INFORMA-
TION SOURCES. 1– 1974– [Irregular]

World Data Center A

C 55.220:nos. • Item 273-D-17 (MF)
UPPER ATMOSPHERE GEOPHYSICS, REPORT UAG-
(series). 1– 1968– [Irregular]

Earlier C 52.16

C 55.220/2:date • Item 834-N-2
OCEANOGRAPHY CATALOGUE OF ACCESSIONED
SOVIET PUBLICATIONS. [Irregular]

Published as a supplement to Catalogue of
Accessioned Publications.

C 55.220/2-2:date • Item 834-N-2
WORLD DATA CENTER A, OCEANOGRAPHY, CATA-
LOG OF ACCESSIONED PUBLICATIONS.
[Annual]

C 55.220/2-3:date • Item 834-N-2
WORLD DATA CENTER A OCEANOGRAPHY, CATA-
LOGUE OF DATA, WDCA-OC-(series).

C 55.220/3:date • Item 834-N-2
WORLD DATA CENTER A, OCEANOGRAPHY, CATA-
LOGUE OF DATA. [Annual]

Earlier title: Oceanography Semiannual Report of the Oceanographic Data Exchange.

C 55.220/4 • Item 834-N-2
PUBLICATIONS (unnumbered).

C 55.220/5:nos. • Item 273-D-15 (MF)
WORLD DATA CENTER A FOR SOLID EARTH
GEOPHYSICS REPORT, SE SERIES (numbered).
[Irregular]

Earlier title: Report, SE- (series).

C 55.220/5:25
DIRECTORY OF WORLD SEISMOGRAPH
STATIONS.

Vol. 1. THE AMERICAS. 1980. 465 p.
charts, maps.

C 55.220/5-2:CT • Item 273-D-21
WORLD DATA CENTER A: PUBLICATIONS (unnumbered). [Irregular]

Consists of all publications which do not fit
into any other established series of the Center.
Discontinued.

C 55.220/6 • Item 273-D-18 (MF)
GLACIOLOGICAL DATA REPORT, GD-(nos). [Irregular]

Also published in microfiche.
Supersedes Glaciological Notes (I 19.60).

C 55.220/7:CT • Item 273-D-19 (MF)
WORLD DATA CENTER A, METEOROLOGY:
PUBLICATIONS (unnumbered). [Irregular]

C 55.220/8:nos. • Item 273-D-18
WORLD DATA CENTER A FOR GLACIOLOGY (Snow
and Ice): NEW ACCESSIONS LIST. [Quarterly]

Discontinued.

C 55.220/9:nos. • Item 273-D-17 (MF)
STP NEWSLETTER (Series).
Non-depository.

C 55.220/10:nos. • Item 273-D-21
WORLD DATA CENTER-A FOR MARINE GEOLOGY
AND GEOPHYSICS REPORT.

**Environmental Data
Service (Continued)**

C 55.221:nos. • Item 273-B
CLIMATOGRAPHY OF THE UNITED STATES; CLIMATE
OF THE UNITED STATES. 60-1– 1959–

Separate publications issued for each State.
Contains narrative climatic information, climatic
summary tables, normals, means and extremes
of weather, temperature, precipitation and storm
charts, location of weather station and types of
observations taken.
Earlier C 30.71/3
Discontinued.

C 55.221/2:nos. • Item 279-A
DECENNIAL CENSUS OF U.S. CLIMATE.
Earlier C 30.71/5
Discontinued.

C 55.222:date • Item 273-D-7
ENVIRONMENTAL DATA AND INFORMATION SER-
VICE. v. 1– 12. 1971– 1981. [Bimonthly] (Environ-
mental Data Service)

PURPOSE:– To inform EDS cooperators,
colleagues, and contributors of recent develop-
ments in its services and programs and in the
general field of scientific data and information
management.
Supersedes National Oceanographic Data
Center Newsletter (C 55.290) and Environmental
Data Bulletin (C 55.203).
ISSN 0364-0116
Discontinued 1981.

C 55.223:nos.
ABSTRACTS OF EARTHQUAKE REPORTS FOR THE
UNITED STATES, MSA- (series).
Earlier C 55.417
Later I 19.69

C 55.224:date • Item 273-D-2
INTERIM LISTS OF PERIODICALS IN COLLECTION
OF ATMOSPHERIC SCIENCES LIBRARY AND
MARINE AND EARTH SCIENCES LIBRARY. [Ir-
regular] (Libraries Division, Environmental Sci-
ence Information Center)
Discontinued.

C 55.225:v.nos.
STORAGE-GAGE PRECIPITATION DATA FOR WEST-
ERN UNITED STATES.

C 55.226:date • Item 208
UNITED STATES EARTHQUAKES. 1928– [Annual]
(National Geophysical Data Center)
Earlier C 55.417/2
Beginning with 1981 issue published by Geo-
logical Survey (I 19.65/2).

C 55.227:date • Item 273-D-3
INTERNATIONAL DECADE OF OCEAN EXPLORA-
TION, PROGRESS REPORTS. 1973– [Annual]

PURPOSE:– To provide the scientific community and other interested persons with information, data inventories, and lists of scientific
reports derived from U.S. IDOE projects.

C 55.228:nos. • Item 193
PUBLICATIONS (numbered). 1957– [Irregular]

PURPOSE:– To provide a medium for publication of monographs in the fields of mathematics,
geodetic astronomy, nautical and aeronautical cartography, geodetic and hydrographic surveying,
photogrammetry, and the following divisions of
geophysics: geodesy, geomagnetism, gravity,
seismology, physical oceanography and tidal phenomena.
The Publications series carried a hyphenated
number. The first element of the number indicates
the subject category, the second element, the
number of the publication within that subject category. This series supersedes the Special Publications series. Existing Special Publications will
not be renumbered in the Publications series.
Classification of subject numbers
10 General
20 Hydrography
30 Tides and Currents
31 Oceanography
40 Geomagnetism
41 Seismology
60 Geodesy
61 Leveling
62 Triangulation
63 Gravity
64 Geodetic Astronomy
65 States Plane Coordinate Systems
70 Topography and Photogrammetry
80 Cartography and Reproduction
Earlier C 55.419
Discontinued.

C 55.228/2:nos. • Item 193
NOAA SCIENTIFIC AND TECHNICAL PUBLICATIONS ANNOUNCEMENTS.
Earlier C 55.17
Discontinued 984/6,7.

C 55.229:CT • Item 273-D-8
BIBLIOGRAPHIES AND LISTS OF PUBLICATIONS. [Irregular]

C 55.229/2:nos.
ACCESSIONS LIST. [Monthly]

C 55.229/3:yr.-nos. • Item 273-D-8
PACKAGED LITERATURE SEARCHES (series). [Irregular]
Also published in microfiche.
Discontinued.

C 55.230:CT • Item 273-D-9
POSTERS. [Irregular]

C 55.231:CT • Item 273-D-10
MAPS AND ATLASES. [Irregular]

C 55.232:date • Item 273-D-11
ENVIRONMENTAL INVENTORIES. [Irregular]

PURPOSE:– To show in an easily understandable from the various types of environmental data available from the Environmental Data Service. The inventory illustrates in graphic form the types and amounts of data available for specific geographical regions.
Discontinued.

C 55.233:date • Item 273-D-14 (MF)
CLIMATE IMPACT ASSESSMENT, FOREIGN COUNTRIES. [Weekly]

Highly technical summaries of precipitation, temperature, and miscellaneous data for the United States, Canada, U.S.S.R., China, Asia, India, and South America. Snow and ice boundaries for the Northern Hemisphere and any major abnormal weather occurrences are also included. Contains maps and tables.
Published in microfiche (24x).
Former title: Environmental/Resource Assessment and Information.
Discontinued Dec. 1986.

C 55.233/2:date • Item 273-D-14 (MF)
CLIMATE IMPACT ASSESSMENT, U.S. [Weekly]

Formerly included in Environmental/ Resource Assessment and Information (C 55.233).
Discontinued Mar. 1987.

C 55.233/3:date • Item 273-D-14 (MF)
CLIMATE IMPACT ASSESSMENT, FOREIGN COUNTRIES ANNUAL SUMMARY.
Discontinued.

C 55.233/4:date • Item 273-D-14 (MF)
CLIMATE IMPACT ASSESSMENT, UNITED STATES, ANNUAL SUMMARY.
Discontinued.

C 55.234:date • Item 273-D-16
CEAS ACTIVITIES. [Annual] (Center for Environmental Assessment Services)

Summarizes the Center's activities which include responsibility for producing quantitative impact assessments of the effects of weather, climate, energy, water and other key sectors of the U.S. economy.
Discontinued.

C 55.235:nos. • Item 273-D-20
CURRENT ISSUE OUTLINE (series). [Irregular]

Each issue provides an objective background review on a current topic of high general interest, such as acid rain. Contains bibliographies of selected material so that the reader can pursue the subject in great depth.
Discontinued.

C 55.236:nos.
ARSLOE INFORMAL REPORT (series). 1– [Irregular]

ARSLOE Atlantic Remote Sensing Land Ocean Experiment.

C 55.237:date • Item 273-D-14
MARINE ENVIRONMENTAL ASSESSMENT, GULF OF MEXICO, ANNUAL SUMMARY.
Discontinued.

C 55.237/2:date • Item 273-D-14
MARINE ENVIRONMENTAL ASSESSMENT: CHESAPEAKE BAY. [Quarterly]
Discontinued.

C 55.237/3:date • Item 273-D-14 (MF)
MARINE ENVIRONMENTAL ASSESSMENT: CHESAPEAKE BAY; ANNUAL SUMMARY. [Annual]
Discontinued.

C 55.238:nos. • Item 273-D-23
NATIONAL ENVIRONMENTAL DATA REFERRAL SERVICE PUBLICATION, NEDRES– (series).
Discontinued.

C 55.239:nos.ltrs.&nos. • Item 273-D-24
DATA ANNOUNCEMENTS (series). [Irregular]
Each issue announces data on a different subject.
Discontinued.

C 55.240:v.nos./nos. • Item 273-D-24
THE PALEOCLIMATE DATA RECORD. [Irregular]
Discontinued.

C 55.241 • Item 193 (MF)
NOAA PALEOCLIMATE PUBLICATIONS SERIES REPORT (Series).

C 55.242 • Item 273-D-26 (MF)
NOAA ATLAS NESDIS (series).

National Climate Center

C 55.280:v.nos.&nos.
DATA REPORT: HIGH ALTITUDE METEOROLOGICAL DATA. v. 1– 1964– [Monthly]

Contains tabulations and plotted soundings of meteorological rocket-sounding data (wind and temperature) for very high altitudes and computed pressure, density, and speed of sound data.
A brief monthly summary has been initiated beginning with the 1965 data reports. This summary, found immediately before the addendum, is designed to compare the mean profile for the current month with long-term means for the same month.
Previous title Data Report, Meteorological Rocket Network Firings, prior to v. 6, no. 1, Jan. 1969.
ISSN 0364-7579
Earlier C 52.16 prior to v. 6, no. 3.

C 55.280/2:v.nos.
DATA REPORT, HIGH ALTITUDE METEORLGICAL DATA, INTERNATIONAL DELAYED DATA ISSUE.

C 55.281:CT • Item 274-A
NATIONAL CLIMATIC CENTER PUBLICATIONS.

C 55.281/2:v.nos.&nos.
FIVE DAY FINAL.

C 55.281/2:date • Item 128-M-1 (CD)
GLOBAL DAILY SUMMARY, TEMPERATURE AND PRECIPITATION, [date].
Issued on CD-ROM.

C 55.281/2-2:CT • Item 274-F (E)
ELECTRONIC PRODUCTS.

C 55.281/2-3:v.nos. • Item 274-F-1 (CD)
U.S. DIVISIONAL AND STATION CLIMATIC DATA AND NORMALS.
Issued on CD-ROM.

C 55.281/2-4:date • Item 274-F-2 ((CD))
COOPERATIVE SUMMARY OF THE DAY. [Annual]
Issued on CD-ROM

C 55.281/2-5:v.nos./nos. • Item 274-F-3 (CD)
CHART SERIES A, SURFACE AND UPPER AIR WEATHER CHARTS. [Monthly]
Issued on CD-ROM.

C 55.281/2-6:v.nos./nos. • Item 274-F-4 (E)
CHART SERIES B, INITIAL ANALYSIS AND FORECAST CHARTS. [Monthly]
See C 55.281/2-5
Issued on CD-ROM.

C 55.281/2-7:v.nos./nos. • Item 274-F-5 (E)
CHART SERIES C, TROPICAL STRIP/PRECIPITATION AND OBSERVED WEATHER CHARTS. [Monthly]
See C 55.281/2-5
Issued on CD-ROM.

C 55.281/3:v.nos.&nos.
STATE CLIMATOLOGIST. [Quarterly]

C 55.282:v.nos.
MARINE CLIMATOLOGICAL SUMMARIES. [Annual]

C 55.283:letters-nos.
ATMOSPHERIC TURBIDITY AND PRECIPITATION CHEMISTRY DATA FOR THE WORLD.

C 55.284:date • Item 274-D
GLOBAL ATMOSPHERIC BACKGROUND MONITORING FOR SELECTED ENVIRONMENTAL PARAMETERS, BAPMoN (series). [Annual]

BAPMoN = Background Air Pollution Monitoring Network
Sponsored by the World Meteorological Organization in cooperation with NOAA and EPA.
Tables present worldwide data on atmospheric turbidity, precipitation, atmospheric carbon dioxide, and suspended particulate matter.
Discontinued.

C 55.285:v.nos. • Item 274
RIVER FORECASTS PROVIDED BY THE NATIONAL WEATHER SERVICE. v. 1– 1972– [Annual]
ISSN 0093-7177
Earlier C 55.117/3

C 55.286:CT/date
CLIMATOGRAPHY OF THE UNITED STATES, NO. 81 (series). MONTHLY NORMALS OF TEMPERATURE, PRECIPITATION, AND HEATING AND COOLING DEGREE DAYS. (National Climatic Center, Federal Building, Asheville, North Carolina 28801)

Separate report issued for each State. Latest series covers period 1941-1970.
Earlier C 30.71/4

C 55.286/2:CT/date
CLIMATOGRAPHY OF THE UNITED STATES, NO. 85 (series). MONTHLY AVERAGES OF TEMPERATURE AND PRECIPITATION FOR STATE CLIMATIC DIVISION. (National Climatic Center, Federal Building, Asheville, North Carolina 28801)

Separate report issued for each State. Latest series covers period 1941– 1970
Earlier C 30.71/7

C 55.286/3:CT
CLIMATOGRAPHY OF THE UNITED STATES, NO. 90. (1965-1974): AIRPORT CLIMATOLOGICAL SUMMARY.

C 55.286/5:CT
CLIMATOGRAPHY OF THE UNITED STATES NO. 60 (by State).

Previously published as Climates of the States (C 30.71/3).

C 55.286/6– C 55.286/6-53 • Item 274-E-9– E-53
LOCAL CLIMATOLOGICAL DATA. [Monthly]

C 55.286/6:date • Item 274-E-1
ALABAMA.

C 55.286/6-2:date • Item 274-E-2
ALASKA.

C 55.286/6-3:date • Item 274-E-3
ARIZONA.

C 55.286/6-4:date   • Item 274-E-4
ARKANSAS.

C 55.286/6-5:date   • Item 274-E-5
CALIFORNIA.

C 55.286/6-6:date   • Item 274-E-6
COLORADO.

C 55.286/6-7:date   • Item 274-E-7
CONNECTICUT.

C 55.286/6-8:date   • Item 274-E-8
DELAWARE.

C 55.286/6-9:date   • Item 274-E-51
DISTRICT OF COLUMBIA.

C 55.286/6-10:date   • Item 274-E-9
FLORIDA.

C 55.286/6-11:date   • Item 274-E-10
GEORGIA.

C 55.286/6-12:date   • Item 274-E-11
HAWAII.

C 55.286/6-13:date   • Item 274-E-12
IDAHO.

C 55.286/6-14:date   • Item 274-E-13
ILLINOIS.

C 55.286/6-15:date   • Item 274-E-14
INDIANA.

C 55.286/6-16:date   • Item 274-E-15
IOWA.

C 55.286/6-17:date   • Item 274-E-16
KANSAS.

C 55.286/6-18:date   • Item 274-E-17
KENTUCKY.

C 55.286/6-19:date   • Item 274-E-18
LOUISIANA.

C 55.286/6-20:date   • Item 274-E-19
MAINE.

C 55.286/6-21:date   • Item 274-E-20
MARYLAND.

C 55.286/6-22:date   • Item 274-E-21
MASSACHUSETTS.

C 55.286/6-23:date   • Item 274-E-22
MICHIGAN.

C 55.286/6-24:date   • Item 274-E-23
MINNESOTA.

C 55.286/6-25:date   • Item 274-E-24
MISSISSIPPI

C 55.286/6-26:date   • Item 274-E-25
MISSOURI.

C 55.286/6-27:date   • Item 274-E-26
MONTANA.

C 55.286/6-28:date   • Item 274-E-27
NEBRASKA.

C 55.286/6-29:date   • Item 274-E-28
NEVADA.

C 55.286/6-30:date   • Item 274-E-29
NEW HAMPSHIRE.

C 55.286/6-31:date   • Item 274-E-30
NEW JERSEY.

C 55.286/6-32:date   • Item 274-E-31
NEW MEXICO.

C 55.286/6-33:date   • Item 274-E-32
NEW YORK.

C 55.286/6-34:date   • Item 274-E-33
NORTH CAROLINA.

C 55.286/6-35:date   • Item 274-E-34
NORTH DAKOTA.

C 55.286/6-36:date   • Item 274-E-35
OHIO.

C 55.286/6-37:date   • Item 274-E-37
OKLAHOMA.

C 55.286/6-38:date   • Item 274-E-37
OREGON.

C 55.286/6-39:date   • Item 274-E-53
PACIFIC.

C 55.286/6-40:date   • Item 274-E-38
PENNSYLVANIA.

C 55.286/6-41:date   • Item 274-E-39
RHODE ISLAND.

C 55.286/6-42:date   • Item 274-E-40
SOUTH CAROLINA.

C 55.286/6-43:date   • Item 274-E-41
SOUTH DAKOTA.

C 55.286/6-44:date   • Item 274-E-42
TENNESSEE.

C 55.286/6-45:date   • Item 274-E-43
TEXAS.
C 55.286/6-46:date   • Item 274-E-44
UTAH.

C 55.286/6-47:date   • Item 274-E-45
VERMONT.

C 55.286/6-48:date   • Item 274-E-46
VIRGINIA.

C 55.286/6-49:date   • Item 274-E-47
WASHINGTON.

C 55.286/6-50:date   • Item 274-E-53
WEST INDIES.

C 55.286/6-51:date   • Item 274-E-48
WEST VIRGINIA.

C 55.286/6-52:date   • Item 274-E-49
WISCONSIN.

C 55.286/6-53:date   • Item 274-E-50
WYOMING.

C 55.286/6-54   • Item 274-G (EL)
LOCAL CLIMATOLOGICAL DATA. (Various states).

C 55.286/8:CT/date
CLIMATOGRAPHY OF THE UNITED STATES NO. 84.

    PURPOSE:– To give daily temperature, heating and cooling degree days and precipitation.

C 55.287
LOCAL CLIMATOLOGICAL DATA, ANNUAL SUMMARIES.

    Contains narrative climatological summary, meteorological data for current year, normals, means, and extremes, comparative temperature, precipitation, degree days, and snowfall data for earlier years.
    Earlier C 55.217
    In 1980, the following SuDocs Class Numbers were assigned from C 55.287 through C 55.287/55 the Local Climatological Data, monthly and annual summaries for approximately 288 weather stations.

C 55.287/2:date
LOCAL CLIMATOLOGICAL DATA (National Airport).
    Earlier C 55.217
    See C 55.286/6

C 55.287/3:date
LOCAL CLIMATOLOGICAL DATA (Dulles International Airport).
    Earlier C 55.217/2
    See C 55.286/6-2

C 55.287/3-2:date
LOCAL CLIMATOLOGICAL DATA, WASHINGTON, D.C. DULLES INTERNATIONAL AIRPORT ANNUAL SUMMARY WITH COMPARATIVE DATA. [Annual]

C 55.287/4– C 55.287/55
LOCAL CLIMATOLOGICAL DATA. (Monthly and annual summaries)

    Issued for the following stations:–

Alabama

    C 55.287/4:date   • Item 274-E-4
    BIRMINGHAM.
      See C 55.286/6-3

    C 55.287/4-2:date
    BIRMINGHAM, MUNICIPAL AIRPORT.

    C 55.287/4-3:date
    HUNTSVILLE.

    C 55.287/4-4:date
    MONTGOMERY.

    C 55.287/4-5:date
    MOBILE.

Alaska

    C 55.287/5:date   • Item 274-E-4
    ANCHORAGE.
      See C 55.286/6-4

    C 55.287/5-2:date
    ANNETTE.

    C 55.287/5-3:date
    BARROW.

    C 55.287/5-4:date
    BARTER ISLAND.

    C 55.287/5-5:date
    BETHEL.

    C 55.287/5-6:date
    BETTLES.

    C 55.287/5-7:date
    BIG DELTA.

    C 55.287/5-8:date
    COLD BAY.

    C 55.287/5-9:date
    FAIRBANKS.

    C 55.287/5-10:date
    GULKANA.

    C 55.287/5-11:date
    HOMER.

    C 55.287/5-12:date
    JUNEAU.

    C 55.287/5-13:date
    KING SALMON.

    C 55.287/5-14:date
    KODIAK.

    C 55.287/5-15:date
    KOTZEBUE.

    C 55.287/5-16:date
    McGRATH.

    C 55.287/5-17:date
    NOME.

    C 55.287/5-18:date
    SAINT PAUL ISLAND.

    C 55.287/5-19:date
    TALKEETNA.

    C 55.287/5-20:date
    UNALAKLEET.

C 55.287/5-21:date
VALDEZ.

C 55.287/5-22:date
YAKUTAT.

Arizona

C 55.287/6:date   • Item 274-E-5
FLAGSTAFF.
    See C 55.286/6-5

C 55.287/6-2:date
PHOENIX.

C 55.287/6-3:date
TUCSON.

C 55.287/6-4:date
WINSLOW.

C 55.287/6-5:date
YUMA.

Arkansas

C 55.287/7:date   • Item 274-E-6
FORT SMITH.
    See C 55.286/6-6

C 55.287/7-2:date
LITTLE ROCK.

C 55.287/7-3:date
NORTH LITTLE ROCK.

California

C 55.287/8:date   • Item 274-E-7
BAKERSFIELD.
    See C 55.286/6-7

C 55.287/8-2:date
BISHOP

C 55.287/8-3:date
BLUE CANYON.

C 55.287/8-4:date
EUREKA.

C 55.287/8-5:date
FRESNO.

C 55.287/8-6:date
LONG BEACH.

C 55.287/8-7:date
LOS ANGELES, CIVIC CENTER.

C 55.287/8-8:date
LOS ANGELES, INTERNATIONAL AIRPORT.

C 55.287/8-9:date
MOUNT SHASTA.

C 55.287/8-10:date
OAKLAND.

C 55.287/8-11:date
RED BLUFF.

C 55.287/8-12:date
SACRAMENTO.

C 55.287/8-13:date
SAN DIEGO.

C 55.287/8-14:date
SAN FRANCISCO, FEDERAL OFFICE BUILDING.

C 55.287/8-15:date
SAN FRANCISCO, INTERNATIONAL AIRPORT.

C 55.287/8-16:date
SANTA MARIA.

C 55.287/8-17:date
STOCKTON.

Colorado

C 55.287/9:date   • Item 274-E-8
ALAMOSA.
    See C 55.286/6-8

C 55.287/9-2:date
COLORADO SPRINGS.

C 55.287/9-3:date
DENVER.

C 55.287/9-4:date
GRAND JUNCTION.

C 55.287/9-5:date
PUEBLO.

Connecticut

C 55.287/10:date   • Item 274-E-51
BRIDGEPORT.
    See C 55.286/6-9

C 55.287/10-2:date
HARTFORD.

Delaware

C 55.287/11:date   • Item 274-E-9
WILMINGTON.
    See C 55.286/6-10

Florida

C 55.287/12:date   • Item 274-E-10
APALACHICOLA.
    See C 55.286/6-11

C 55.287/12-2:date
DAYTONA BEACH.

C 55.287/12-3:date
FORT MYERS.

C 55.287/12-4:date
JACKSONVILLE.

C 55.287/12-5:date
KEY WEST.

C 55.287/12-6:date
MIAMI.

C 55.287/12-7:date
ORLANDO.

C 55.287/12-8:date
PENSACOLA.

C 55.287/12-9:date
TALLAHASSEE.

C 55.287/12-10:date
TAMPA.

C 55.287/12-11:date
WEST PALM BEACH.

Georgia

C 55.287/13:date   • Item 274-E-11
ATHENS.
    See C 55.286/6-12

C 55.287/13-2:date
ATLANTA.

C 55.287/13-3:date
AUGUSTA.

C 55.287/13-4:date
COLUMBUS.

C 55.287/13-5:date
MACON.

C 55.287/13-6:date
ROME.

C 55.287/13-7:date
SAVANNAH.

Hawaii

C 55.287/14:date   • Item 274-E-12
HILO.
    See C 55.286/6-13

C 55.287/14-2:date
HONOLULU.

C 55.287/14-3:date
LIHUE.

C 55.287/14-4:date
KAHULUI.

Idaho

C 55.287/15:date   • Item 274-E-13
BOISE.
    See C 55.286/6-14

C 55.287/15-2:date
LEWISTON.

C 55.287/15-3:date
POCATELLO.

Illinois

C 55.287/16:date   • Item 274-E-14
CAIRO.
    See C 55.286/6-15
C 55.287/16-2:date
CHICAGO.

C 55.287/16-3:date
MOLINE.

C 55.287/16-4:date
PEORIA.

C 55.287/16-5:date
ROCKFORD.

C 55.287/16-6:date
SPRINGFIELD.

C 55.287/16-7:date
CHICAGO, MIDWAY AIRPORT.

Indiana

C 55.287/17:date   • Item 274-E-15
EVANSVILLE.
    See C 55.286/6-16

C 55.287/17-2:date
FORT WAYNE.

C 55.287/17-3:date
INDIANAPOLIS.

C 55.287/17-4:date
SOUTH BEND.

Iowa

C 55.287/18:date   • Item 274-E-16
DES MOINES.
    See C 55.286/6-17

C 55.287/18-2:date
DUBUQUE.
C 55.287/18-3:date
SIOUX CITY.

C 55.287/18-4:date
WATERLOO.

C 55.287/18-5:date
BURLINGTON.

Kansas

C 55.287/19:date   • Item 274-E-17
CONCORDIA.
    See C 55.286/6-18

C 55.287/19-2:date
DODGE CITY.

C 55.287/19-3:date
GOODLAND.

C 55.287/19-4:date
TOPEKA.

C 55.287/19-5:date
WICHITA.

Kentucky

C 55.287/20:date • **Item 274-E-18**
GREATER CINCINNATI AIRPORT, BOONE
COUNTY.
See C 55.286/6-19

C 55.287/20-2:date
LEXINGTON.

C 55.287/20-3:date
LOUISVILLE.

C 55.287/20-4:date
JACKSON.

Louisiana

C 55.287/21:date • **Item 274-E-19**
BATON ROUGE.
See C 55.286/6-20

C 55.287/21-2:date
LAKE CHARLES.

C 55.287/21-3:date
NEW ORELEANS.

C 55.287/21-4:date
SHREVEPORT.

Maine

C 55.287/22:date • **Item 274-E-20**
CARIBOU.
See C 55.286/6-21

C 55.287/22-2:date
PORTLAND.

C 55.287/22-3:date
BALTIMORE, MARYLAND.

Massachusetts

C 55.287/23:date • **Item 274-E-21**
BLUE HILL OBSERVATORY, MILTON.
See C 55.286/6-22

C 55.287/23-2:date
BOSTON.

C 55.287/23-2:date
WORCESTER.

Michigan

C 55.287/24:date • **Item 274-E-22**
ALPENA.
See C 55.286/6-23

C 55.287/24-2:date
DETROIT, CITY AIRPORT.

C 55.287/24-3:date
DETROIT, METROPOLITAN AIRPORT.

C 55.287/24-4:date
FLINT.

C 55.287/24-5:date
GRAND RAPIDS.

C 55.287/24-6:date
HOUGHTON LAKE.

C 55.287/24-7:date
LANSING.

C 55.287/24-8:date
MARQUETTE.

C 55.287/24-9:date
MUSKEGON.

C 55.287/24-10:date
SAULT SAINTE MARIE.

Minnesota

C 55.287/25:date • **Item 274-E-23**
DULUTH.
See C 55.286/6-24

C 55.287/25-2:date
INTERNATIONAL FALLS.

C 55.287/25-3:date
ROCHESTER.

C 55.287/25-4:date
SAINT CLOUD.

C 55.287/25-5:date
MINNEAPOLIS-SAINT PAUL.

Mississippi

C 55.287/26:date • **Item 274-E-24**
MERIDIAN.
See C 55.286/6-25

C 55.287/26-2:date
JACKSON.

Missouri

C 55.287/27:date • **Item 274-E-25**
COLUMBIA.
See C 55.286/6-26
C 55.287/27-2:date
KANSAS CITY, DOWNTOWN AIRPORT.

C 55.287/27-3:date
KANSAS CITY, INTERNATIONAL AIRPORT.

C 55.287/27-4:date
SAINT JOSEPH.

C 55.287/27-5:date
SAINT LOUIS.

C 55.287/27-6:date
SPRINGFIELD.

Montana

C 55.287/28:date • **Item 274-E-26**
BILLINGS.
See C 55.286/6-27

C 55.287/28-2:date
GLASCOW.

C 55.287/28-3:date
GREAT FALLS.

C 55.287/28-4:date
HAVRE.

C 55.287/28-5:date
HELENA.

C 55.287/28-6:date
KALISPELL.

C 55.287/28-7:date
MILES CITY.

C 55.287/28-8:date
MISSOULA.

Nebraska

C 55.287/29:date • **Item 274-E-27**
GRAND ISLAND.
See C 55.286/6-28

C 55.287/29-2:date
LINCOLN.

C 55.287/29-3:date
NORFOLK.

C 55.287/29-4:date
NORTH PLATTE.

C 55.287/29-5:date
SCOTTSBLUFF.

C 55.287/29-6:date
VALENTINE.

C 55.287/29-7:date
OMAHA, EPPLEY AIRFIELD.

C 55.287/29-8:date
OMAHA, NATIONAL WEATHER SERVICE FORE-
CAST OFFICE.

Nevada

C 55.287/30:date • **Item 274-E-28**
ELKO.
See C 55.286/6-29

C 55.287/30-2:date
ELY.
C 55.287/30-3:date
RENO.

C 55.287/30-4:date
WINNEMUCCA.

C 55.287/30-5:date
LAS VEGAS.

New Hampshire

C 55.287/31:date • **Item 274-E-29**

CONCORD.
See C 55.286/6-30
C 55.287/31-2:date
MOUNT WASHINGTON OBSERVATORY, GORHAM.

New Jersey

C 55.287/32:date • **Item 274-E-30**
ATLANTIC CITY, ATLANTIC CITY STATE MARINA.
See C 55.286/6-31

C 55.287/32-2:date
ATLANTIC CITY, AVIATION FACILITIES EXPERI-
MENT CENTER.

C 55.287/32-3:date
NEWARK.

C 55.287/32-4:date
TRENTON.

New Mexico

C 55.287/33:date • **Item 274-E-31**
ALBUQUERQUE.
See C 55.286/6-32

C 55.287/33-2:date
CLAYTON.

C 55.287/33-3:date
ROSWELL.

New York

C 55.287/34:date • **Item 274-E-32**
ALBANY.
See C 55.286/6-33

C 55.287/34-2:date
BINGHAMTON.

C 55.287/34-3:date
BUFFALO.

C 55.287/34-4:date
NEW YORK, CENTRAL PARK OBSERVATORY.

C 55.287/34-5:date
NEW YORK, JOHN F. KENNEDY INTERNATIONAL
AIRPORT.

C 55.287/34-6:date
NEW YORK, LA GUARDIA AIRPORT.

C 55.287/34-7:date
ROCHESTER.

C 55.287/34-8:date
SYRACUSE.

North Carolina

C 55.287/35:date   • Item 274-E-33
ASHEVILLE.
    See C 55.286/6-34

C 55.287/35-2:date
CAPE HATTERAS.

C 55.287/35-3:date
CHARLOTTE.

C 55.287/35-4:date
GREENSBORO, HIGH POINT, WINSTON-SALEM
AIRPORT.

C 55.287/35-5:date
RALEIGH.

C 55.287/35-6:date
WILMINGTON.

North Dakota

C 55.287/36:date   • Item 274-E-34
BISMARCK.
    See C 55.286/6-35

C 55.287/36-2:date
FARGO.

C 55.287/36-3:date
WILLISTON.

Ohio

C 55.287/37:date   • Item 274-E-35
AKRON.
    See C 55.286/6-36

C 55.287/37-2:date
CINCINNATI.

C 55.287/37-3:date
CLEVELAND.

C 55.287/37-4:date
COLUMBUS.

C 55.287/37-5:date
DAYTON.

C 55.287/37-6:date
MANSFIELD.

C 55.287/37-7:date
TOLEDO.

C 55.287/37-8:date
YOUNGSTOWN.

Oklahoma

C 55.287/38:date   • Item 274-E-36
OKLAHOMA CITY.
    See C 55.286/6-37

C 55.287/38-2:date
TULSA.

Oregon

C 55.287/39:date   • Item 274-E-37
BURNS.
    See C 55.286/6-38

C 55.287/39-2:date
EUGENE.

C 55.287/39-3:date
PENDLETON.

C 55.287/39-4:date
PORTLAND.

C 55.287/39-5:date
SALEM.

C 55.287/39-6:date
SEXTON SUMMIT.

C 55.287/39-7:date
ASTORIA.

C 55.287/39-8:date
MEDFORD.

Pennsylvania

C 55.287/40:date
ALLENTOWN.
    See C 55.286/6-39

C 55.287/40-2:date
AVOCA.

C 55.287/40-3:date
ERIE.

C 55.287/40-4:date
HARRISBURG.

C 55.287/40-5:date
PHILADELPHIA.

C 55.287/40-6:date
PITTSBURGH.

C 55.287/40-7:date
WILLIAMSPORT.

Puerto Rico

C 55.287/41:date
SAN JUAN.
    See C 55.286/6-40
Rhode Island

C 55.287/42:date
BLOCK ISLAND.
    See C 55.286/6-41

C 55.287/42-2:date
PROVIDENCE.

South Carolina

C 55.287/43:date
CHARLESTON, MUNICIPAL AIRPORT.
    See C 55.286/6-42

C 55.287/43-2:date
CHARLESTON, U.S. CUSTOM HOUSE.

C 55.287/43-3:date
COLUMBIA.

C 55.287/43-4:date
GREENVILLE-SPARTANBURG AIRPORT, GREER.

South Dakota

C 55.287/44:date
HURON.
    See C 55.286/6-43

C 55.287/44-2:date
SIOUX FALLS.

C 55.287/44-3:date
RAPID CITY.

C 55.287/44-4:date
ABERDEEN.

Tennessee

C 55.287/45:date
BRISTOL-JOHNSON CITY-KINGSPORT.
    See C 55.286/6-44

C 55.287/45-2:date
CHATTANOOGA.

C 55.287/45-3:date
MEMPHIS.

C 55.287/45-4:date
KNOXVILLE.

C 55.287/45-5:date
NASHVILLE.

C 55.287/45-6:date
OAK RIDGE.

Texas

C 55.287/46:date
ABILENE.
    See C 55.286/6-45

C 55.287/46-2:date
AMARILLO.

C 55.287/46-3:date
AUSTIN.

C 55.287/46-4:date
BROWNSVILLE.

C 55.287/46-5:date
CORPUS CHRISTI.

C 55.287/46-6:date
DALLAS-FORT WORTH.

C 55.287/46-7:date
DEL RIO.

C 55.287/46-8:date
EL PASO.

C 55.287/46-9:date
GALVESTON.

C 55.287/46-10:date
HOUSTON.

C 55.287/46-11:date
LUBBOCK.

C 55.287/46-12:date
MIDLAND-ODESSA.

C 55.287/46-13:date
PORT ARTHUR.

C 55.287/46-14:date
SAN ANGELO.

C 55.287/46-15:date
SAN ANTONIO.

C 55.287/46-16:date
VICTORIA.

C 55.287/46-17:date
WACO.

C 55.287/46-18:date
WICHITA FALLS.

Utah

C 55.287/47:date
MILFORD.
    See C 55.286/6-46

C 55.287/47-2:date
SALT LAKE CITY.

Vermont

C 55.287/48:date
BURLINGTON.
    See C 55.286/6-47

Virginia

C 55.287/49:date
LYNCHBURG.
    See C 55.286/6-48

C 55.287/49-2:date
NORFOLK.

C 55.287/49-3:date
RICHMOND.

C 55.287/49-4:date
ROANOKE.

C 55.287/49-5:date
WALLOPS ISLAND.

Washington

C 55.287/50:date
OLYMPIA.
   See C 55.286/6-49

C 55.287/50-2:date
QUILLAYUTE.

C 55.287/50-3:date
SEATTLE. (National Weather Service Urban Site, 2725 Montlake Blvd., East)

C 55.287/50-4:date
SEATTLE, SEATTLE-TACOMA AIRPORT.

C 55.287/50-5:date
SPOKANE.

C 55.287/50-6:date
STAMPEDE PASS.

C 55.287/50-7:date
WALLA WALLA.

C 55.287/50-8:date
YAKIMA.

West Virginia

C 55.287/51:date
BECKELEY.
   See C 55.286/6-51

C 55.287/51-2:date
CHARLESTON.

C 55.287/51-3:date
ELKINS.

C 55.287/51-4:date
HUNTINGTON.

C 55.287/51-5:date
PARKERSBURG.

Wisconsin

C 55.287/52:date
GREEN BAY.
   See C 55.286/6-52

C 55.287/52-2:date
LA CROSSE.

C 55.287/52-3:date
MADISON.

C 55.287/52-4:date
MILWAUKEE.

Wyoming

C 55.287/53:date
CASPER.
   See C 55.286/6-53

C 55.287/53-2:date
CHEYENNE.

C 55.287/53-3:date
LANDER.

C 55.287/53-4:date
SHERIDAN.

Pacific

C 55.287/54:date
GUAM.

C 55.287/54-2:date
JOHNSTON ISLAND.

C 55.287/54-3:date
KHAJALEIN ISLAND.

C 55.287/54-4:date
KOROR ISLAND.

C 55.287/54-5:date
MAJURO, MARSHALL ISLANDS.

C 55.287/54-6:date
PONAPE ISLAND.

C 55.287/54-7:date
TRUK, CAROLINE ISLANDS.

C 55.287/54-8:date
WAKE ISLAND.

C 55.287/54-9:date
YAP ISLAND.

American Samoa

C 55.287/55:date
PAGO PAGO.

C 55.287/2– 54   • **Item 274-E-1– 53 (MF)**
LOCAL CLIMATOLOGICAL DATA: [State], MONTHLY AND ANNUAL SUMMARIES.

   In 1984, the following SuDocs Class Numbers were also assigned to the State Summaries from C 55.287/2 through C 55.287/54, causing a duplication of these numbers.
   Once this problem of duplication is resolved, the correct class numbers will be included in the next edition of this Guide.

C 55.287/2   • **Item 274-E-1**
– ALABAMA.

C 55.287/3   • **Item 274-E-2**
– ALASKA.

C 55.287/4   • **Item 274-E-3**
– ARIZONA.

C 55.287/5   • **Item 274-E-4**
– ARKANSAS.

C 55.287/6   • **Item 274-E-5**
– CALIFORNIA.

C 55.287/7   • **Item 274-E-6**
– COLORADO.

C 55.287/8   • **Item 274-E-7**
– CONNECTICUT.

C 55.287/9   • **Item 274-E-8**
– DELAWARE.

C 55.287/10   • **Item 274-E-51**
– DISTRICT OF COLUMBIA.

C 55.287/11   • **Item 274-E-9**
– FLORIDA.

C 55.287/12   • **Item 274-E-10**
– GEORGIA.

C 55.287/13   • **Item 274-E-11**
– HAWAII.

C 55.287/14   • **Item 274-E-12**
– IDAHO.

C 55.287/15   • **Item 274-E-13**
– ILLINOIS.

C 55.287/16   • **Item 274-E-14**
– INDIANA.

C 55.287/17   • **Item 274-E-15**
– IOWA.

C 55.287/18   • **Item 274-E-16**
– KANSAS.

C 55.287/19   • **Item 274-E-17**
– KENTUCKY.

C 55.287/20   • **Item 274-E-18**
– LOUISIANA.

C 55.287/21   • **Item 274-E-19**
– MAINE.

C 55.287/22   • **Item 274-E-20**
– MARYLAND.

C 55.287/23   • **Item 274-E-21**
– MASSACHUSETTS.

C 55.287/24   • **Item 274-E-22**
– MICHIGAN.

C 55.287/25   • **Item 274-E-23**
– MINNESOTA.

C 55.287/26   • **Item 274-E-24**
– MISSISSIPPI.

C 55.287/27   • **Item 274-E-25**
– MISSOURI.

C 55.287/28   • **Item 274-E-26**
– MONTANA.

C 55.287/29   • **Item 274-E-27**
– NEBRASKA.

C 55.287/30   • **Item 274-E-28**
– NEVADA.

C 55.287/31   • **Item 274-E-29**
– NEW HAMPSHIRE.

C 55.287/32   • **Item 274-E-30**
– NEW JERSEY.

C 55.287/33   • **Item 274-E-31**
– NEW MEXICO.

C 55.287/34   • **Item 274-E-32**
– NEW YORK.

C 55.287/35   • **Item 274-E-33**
– NORTH CAROLINA.

C 55.287/36   • **Item 274-E-34**
– NORTH DAKOTA.

C 55.287/37   • **Item 274-E-35**
– OHIO.

C 55.287/38   • **Item 274-E-36**
– OKLAHOMA.

C 55.287/39   • **Item 274-E-37**
– OREGON.

C 55.287/40   • **Item 274-E-52**
– PACIFIC.

C 55.287/41   • **Item 274-E-38**
– PENNSYLVANIA.

C 55.287/42   • **Item 274-E-39**
– RHODE ISLAND.

C 55.287/43   • **Item 274-E-40**
– SOUTH CAROLINA.

C 55.287/44   • **Item 274-E-41**
– SOUTH DAKOTA.

C 55.287/45   • **Item 274-E-42**
– TENNESSEE.

C 55.287/46   • **Item 274-E-43**
– TEXAS.

C 55.287/47   • **Item 274-E-44**
– UTAH.

C 55.287/48   • **Item 274-E-45**
– VERMONT.

C 55.287/49   • **Item 274-E-46**
– VIRGINIA.

C 55.287/50   • **Item 274-E-47**
– WASHINGTON.

C 55.287/51   • **Item 274-E-53**
– WEST INDIES.

C 55.287/52   • **Item 274-E-48**
– WEST VIRGINIA.

C 55.287/53   • **Item 274-E-49**
– WISCONSIN.

C 55.287/54   • **Item 274-E-50**
– WYOMING.

C 55.287/56:CT
LOG RECORD OF WEATHER OBSERVATIONS.

C 55.287/57:nos.
HISTORICAL INDEX.

C 55.287/58:nos.   • **Item 274-D-3 (MF)**
HISTORICAL CLIMATOLOGY SERIES, ATLASES.
[Irregular]

Issues contain U.S. maps of Palmer Moisture Anomaly Indices or temperature departures from the mean on a monthly or seasonal basis over a period of many years. The maps illustrate spatial or temporal variablity of drought or temperature in the U.S.

C 55.287/59:nos.
AREALLY-WEIGHTED DATA.

C 55.287/60:nos.   • **Item 274-D-1 (MF)**
POPULATION-WEIGHTED DATA.
Tabulation designed to provide heating fuel demand information on a state-by-state basis. This allows comparison of fuel demand for the current year to normal and also to conditions of the pervious year.

C 55.287/60-2:date   • **Item 274-D-1 (MF)**
MONTHLY STATE, REGIONAL AND NATIONAL HEATING DEGREE DAYS WEIGHTED BY POPULATION.

C 55.287/60-3:date   • **Item 274-D-2 (MF)**
MONTHLY STATE, REGIONAL AND NATIONAL COOLING DEGREE DAYS WEIGHTED BY POPULATION.

Tabulation designed to provide cooling energy demand information on a state-by-state basis. Data allows comparison of the energy demand for the current year to normal and also to conditions in the previous year.

C 55.287/61   • **Item 274-F-6 (EL)**
CLIMATE VARIATIONS BULLETIN.

C 55.287/62:   • **Item 274-F-7 (EL)**
TECHNICAL REPORT SERIES (Research Customer Service Group).

C 55.287/63:   • **Item 274-G-1 (CD)**
NATIONAL CLIMATIC DATA CENTER PERIODICAL PUBLICATIONS. [Quarterly]
Issued on CD-ROM.

C 55.288:CT/date
INDEX OF ORIGINAL SURFACE WEATHER RECORDS FOR STATIONS IN [various States].

C 55.289:v.nos.&nos.
MONTHLY SUMMARY SOLAR RADIATION DATA.A
Discontinued with the Dec. 1980 issue, No 12.

National Oceanographic Data Center

C 55.290:nos.
NEWSLETTER. – June 1971. [Monthly]
Earlier D 203.24/2
Superseded by Environmental Data Service, (C 55.222)

C 55.291:date   • **Item 273-D-1**
HIGHLIGHTS NATIONAL OCEANOGRAPHIC DATA CENTER. – [1970].

PURPOSE:– To set forth progress made in the Center's efforts to provide prompt and economical services to meet the requirements of their data users.
Earlier D 203.24/2:N 21

C 55.291/2:date   • **Item 192-B-2 (MF)**
NATIONAL OCEANOGRAPHY DATA CENTER: ANNUAL REPORT.

Summarizes Center activities in carrying out its mission as U.S. national facility established to acquire, process, archive, and disseminate global oceanographic data.

C 55.292:CT   • **Item 192-B-1**
PUBLICATIONS. [Irregular]
Earlier D 203.24/3

C 55.297:   • **Item 192-B-5**
WORLD OCEAN ATLAS.
Issued on CD-Rom

C 55.297:T:nos.   • **Item 192-B-05**
NOAA ENVIRONMENTAL BUOY DATA
Issued on CD-Rom

C 55.298:CT   • **Item 192-B-3**
HANDBOOKS, MANUALS, GUIDES. [Irregular]

C 55.299:nos.   • **Item 192-B-4**
NODC ENVIRONMENTAL INFORMATION SUMMARIES. [Irregular]

C 55.299/2:v.nos.&nos.   • **Item 279-D**
MARINERS WEATHER LOG. [Bimonthly] (National Oceanographic Data Center)
Discontinued.

PURPOSE:– To provide information on weather over the oceans and Great Lakes. Gale table gives selected weather observations from vessels in the North Atlantic Ocean.
Index in November issue.
Earlier C 55.210
Later C 55.135

NATIONAL MARINE FISHERIES SERVICE
(1970–   )

CREATION AND AUTHORITY
The National Marine Fisheries Service was established within the National Oceanic and Atmospheric Administration of the Department of Commerce by Department Organization Order 25-5A, effective October 9, 1970.

INFORMATION

Public Affairs Office
National Marine Fisheries Service
NOAA
Department of Commerce
1315 East-West Hwy.
Silver Spring, Md. 20910
(301) 713-2239
http://www.nmfs.noaa.gov

C 55.301:date   • **Item 609-C-2 (MF)**
ANNUAL REPORT.

C 55.301/2:date
NMFS NORTHWEST REGION, ORGANIZATION AND ACTIVITIES, FISCAL YEAR.

C 55.302:CT   • **Item 609-C-1**
GENERAL PUBLICATIONS.

C 55.303/2:nos.
BULLETINS. (Southwest Fisheries Center)

C 55.303/2-2:date
FISHING INFORMATION, SUPPLEMENTS. [Semimonthly, October– May](Southwest Fisheries Center)

For period June– September, information contained in Bulletins series (C 55.303/2).

C 55.304:nos.   • **Item 609**
CIRCULARS. 1– 1964– [Irregular]

Popular and semitechnical publications of general and regional interest intended to aid in conservation and management.
Earlier titles: Fishery Circulars and Wildlife Circulars.
Earlier I 49.4

C 55.305:CT   • **Item 609-C-4**
LAWS. [Irregular]

C 55.306:CT   • **Item 609-C-5**
REGULATIONS, RULES, AND INSTRUCTIONS. [Irregular]

C 55.308:CT   • **Item 609-C-3**
HANDBOOKS, MANUALS, GUIDES. [Irregular]
C 55.308:An 4   • **Item 609-C-3**
ANGLERS' GUIDE TO THE UNITED STATES ATLANTIC COAST.

Large, (14" X 16 1/2") and well illustrated these fascinating guides are excellent geographical studies of marine recreational fishing. Each guide includes: a summary description of each fishing area with facts on tides, composition and configuration of shore areas, climate variances, and general fishing information; a section entitled "Most Commonly Caught Fish" including pictures and descriptions of fish indigenous to each region; a glossary of fishing and general marine terms; and colorful fishing map atlases.

Section I, Passamaquoddy Bay, Maine to
        Cape Cod. 1974. 15 p. il.
Section II, Nantucket Shoals to Long
        Island Sound. 1974. 15 p. il.
Section III, Block Island to Cape May,
        New Jersey. 1974. 19 p. il.
Section IV, Delaware Bay to False Cape,
        Virginia. 1974. 15 p. il.
Section V, Chesapeake Bay.
Section VI, False Cape, Virginia to
        Altamaha Sound, Georgia
Section VII, Altamaha Sound, Georgia to
        Fort Pierce Inlet, Florida.
Section VIII, St. Lucie Inlet, Florida to
        Dry Tortugas.

C 55.308:An 4/2   • **Item 609-C-3**
ANGLERS' GUIDE TO THE UNITED STATES PACIFIC COAST. 1977. 139 p. il.

Similar in format to the Guides to the Atlantic Coast (C 55.308:An 4).

C 55.308/2:nos.   • **Item 609-C-3**
HANDBOOKS (numbered). 1– [Irregular]

C 55.309:date   • **Item 610-A**
FROZEN FISH REPORT (preliminary). [Monthly]

Issued about the 15th of each month. Gives summaries of freezings of fish and shellfish for the previous month and holdings at end of month, Canadian holdings. More detailed information contained in Frozen Fish Report.
ISSN 0364-0604
Earlier I 49.8 prior to the September 1970 issue.

C 55.309/2:nos. • Item 610-A
CURRENT FISHERIES STATISTICS CFS (series). CFS
1–   1941–   [Monthly]
Earlier I 49.8/2 prior to the July 1970 issue.

C 55.309/2-2:date • Item 610-A
FISHERIES OF THE UNITED STATES. [Annual]

This title has been taken out of Current Fisheries Statistics (C 55.309/2) and given its own class.

C 55.309/2-3:date • Item 610-A (MF)
MARINE RECREATIONAL FISHERY STATISTICS SURVEY, ATLANTIC AND GULF COASTS. [Annual]
Earlier C 55.309/2
Discontinued.

C 55.309/2-4:date • Item 610-A
CURRENT FISHERY PRODUCTS, ANNUAL SUMMARY.
Previous issued under C 55.309/2 class.

C 55.309/2-5:date • Item 610-A
MARINE RECREATIONAL FISHERY STATISTICS SURVEY, PACIFIC COAST. [Annual]
Discontinued

C 55.309/2-6:date
U.S. PRODUCTION OF FISH FILLETS AND STEAKS, ANNUAL SUMMARY. [Annual]

C 55.309/2-7:date • Item 610-A (EL)
FISH MEAL AND OIL. [Quarterly]
Earlier C 55.309/2

C 55.309/2-8:date • Item 610-A
FROZEN FISHERY PRODUCTS (preliminary). [Monthly]

C 55.309/2-8:995/4 • Item 610-A
FROZEN FISHERY PRODUCTS, COMMERCE NEWS, APRIL SUPPLY OF FROZEN SEAFOOD DOWN FROM MARCH.
This issue is the last printed copy. Future issues are available through National Marine Fisheries Service Fax-on-Demand 1-301-713-1415.

C 55.309/2-9:date • Item 610-A (MF)
PROCESSED FISHERY STATISTICS, ANNUAL SUMMARY. [Annual]
Earlier C 55.309/2
Discontinued

C 55.309/2-10:date • Item 610-A-1 (P) (EL)
IMPORTS AND EXPORTS OF FISHERY PRODUCTS, ANNUAL SUMMARY. [Annual]

Tables compare quantity and valve of fishery imports and exports (including shrimp and tuna) with that of the previous year.
Earlier C 55.309/2

Sectional Bulletins

ALASKA FISHERIES.

CHESAPEAKE FISHERIES. (Maryland and Virginia)

ISSN 0162-6132

GREAT LAKES FISHERIES. (Great Lakes, Michigan, Ohio, Wisconsin, and Minnesota)

GULF FISHERIES. (West Coast of Florida, Alabama, Mississippi, Louisiana, and Texas)

ISSN 0162-6078

MIDDLE ATLANTIC FISHERIES. (New York, New Jersey, and Delaware)
MISSISSIPPI RIVER FISHERIES. (Alabama, Arizona, Arkansas, Idaho, Illinois, Indiana, Iowa, Kansas, Kentucky, Louisiana, Minnesota, Mississippi, Montana, Nebraska, North Dakota, Oklahoma, South Dakota, Tennessee, Texas, West Virginia, and Wisconsin)

ISSN 0148-5261

NEW ENGLAND FISHERIES. (Maine, New Hampshire, Massachusetts, Rhode Island, and Connecticut)

ISSN 0094-3215

PACIFIC COAST STATES FISHERIES. (Washington, Oregon, and California)

SOUTH ATLANTIC FISHERIES. (North Carolina, South Carolina, Georgia, and East Coast of Florida)

STATE LANDING BULLETINS

Current information on the commercial yield of fishery products is provided in this series of monthly and annual landings bulletins published cooperatively by the Branch of Statistics, Bureau of Commercial Fisheries, and the State Fishery Departments.

Data on over 97 percent of the total domestic catch of fish and shellfish are now collected on a current basis. The statistical information in the reports varies considerably depending upon the information available, but each contains information on the volume of landings by species in the individual States and some indicate the value of the landings. the bulletins for some States also include the catch, by gear, county or district of landing, and the area.

Issued for the following States:–

ALABAMA. 1950– 1979.
ISSN 0364-0108

CALIFORNIA. 1955– 1979.

FLORIDA. 1950– 1979.
ISSN 0364-0590

GEORGIA. 1956– 1979.
ISSN 0364-0515

HAWAII. 1960– 1979. [Annual only]

LOUISIANA. 1954– 1979.
ISSN 0364-0493

MAINE. 1946– 1979.
ISSN 0364-0523

MARYLAND. 1960– 1979.

MASSACHUSETTS. 1947– 1979.
ISSN 0364-0485

MICHIGAN. – 1971.

MISSISSIPPI. 1950– 1979.
ISSN 0364-0469

NEW JERSEY. 1952– 1979.
ISSN 0364-0450

NEW YORK. 1954– 1979.

NORTH CAROLINA. 1955– 1979.
ISSN 0364-0477

OHIO. – 1971.

OREGON. 1960– 1979. [Annual only]

RHODE ISLAND. 1954– 1979.
ISSN 0364-0442

SOUTH CAROLINA. 1957– 1979.
ISSN 0364-0183

TEXAS. 1949– 1979.
ISSN 0162-6159

VIRGINIA. 1960– 1979.
ISSN 0364-0167

WASHINGTON. 1960– 1979 [Annual only]

WISCONSIN. – 1971.

CANNED FISHERY PRODUCTS, (year) ANNUAL SUMMARY (CFS series).

FISH MEAL AND OIL (CFS series). [Monthly]

Gives production of fish meal, scrap, and condensed solubles, and fish oil for month and calendar year to date. Two year comparisons.
ISSN 0364-0140
Earlier I 49.8/2 prior to the August 1970 issue.

FISH STICKS, FISH PORTIONS, AND BREADED SHRIMP (CFS series). [Annual]

Gives production of fish sticks, cooked and uncooked, by month for quarter. Two year comparisons. Also monthly tables on production of fish sticks with three year comparisons.
Previous title: Fish Stick Report.
ISSN 0364-0612
Earlier I 49.8/2 prior to the July-September 1970 issue.

FISHERIES OF THE UNITED STATES (CFS series). [Annual]

(Division of Statistics and Market News)

FROZEN FISHERY PRODUCTS (CFS series). [Monthly]

Discontinued with June 1974 issue.
ISSN 0364-0604
Earlier I 49.8/2 prior to the June 1970 issue.

GULF COAST SHRIMP DATA (CFS series). [Monthly]

Prepared in cooperation with Fishery Agencies of Florida, Alabama, Mississippi, Louisiana, and Texas.
ISSN 0364-0507
Earlier I 49.8/2 prior to the June 1970 issue.
IMPORTS AND EXPORTS OF FISHERY PRODUCTS, (year) ANNUAL SUMMARY (CFS series).
INDUSTRIAL FISHERY PRODUCTS, (year) ANNUAL SUMMARY (CFS series).
PACKAGED FISHERY PRODUCTS, (year) ANNUAL SUMMARY (CFS series).

SHRIMP LANDINGS (CFS series). 1956–   [Monthly]

Gives landings for shrimp by species, size, and State.
ISSN 0364-0434
Earlier I 49.8/2 prior to no. 5385, June 1970.

C 55.309/3 • Item 610-A
FISH MEAL AND OIL MARKET REVIEW, CURRENT ECONOMIC ANALYSIS I (series).
PURPOSE:– To provide current economic information on supply and demand of fish meal, fish oil, and fish solubles so that the prices and quantity of these commodities are more stable on an annual and seasonal basis than they have been in the past. This includes information on production, stocks, and rates of consumption for various levels of prices.
Indexed by: Index to U.S. Government Periodicals.
ISSN 0093-8327
Earlier title: Industrial Fishery Products, Situation and Outlook.
Earlier I 49.8/9 prior to no. 11, dated Oct. 1970.
Discontinued.

C 55.309/4 • Item 610-A
SHELLFISH MARKET REVIEW, CURRENT ECONOMIC ANALYSIS S (series). [Irregular]
PURPOSE:– To provide a current description of the demand and supply conditions of major food finfish products including shrimp, northern lobsters, spiny lobsters, scallops, crabs, oysters, and clams.
Earlier title: Shellfish Situation and Outlook.
Indexed by: Index to U.S. Government Periodicals.
ISSN 0098-8014
Earlier I 49.8/8 prior to no. 19 dated Oct. 1970.
Discontinued.

C 55.309/5:nos. • Item 610-A (MF)
FOOD FISH MARKET REVIEW AND OUTLOOK, CEA-
F- (series). 1–   [3 times a year] (Market Re-
search and Services Division) (Current Economic
Analysis)

PURPOSE:– To provide a current description
of the demand and supply conditions of major
food finfish products including fish blocks, fish
sticks and portions, canned salmon, fish fillets
and steaks, canned tuna. The information is presented in textual summaries, tabular and graphic
forms for each and quick readability. This information is used by the industry to make pricing
and operating decisions so that prices of these
products will be more stable on an annual and
seasonal basis and that quantities will be available to consumers on a more uniform basis
throughout the year.
Indexed by: Index to U.S. Government Periodicals.
ISSN 0091-8105
Earlier I 49.8/6 prior to Dec. 1970 issue.
Discontinued.

C 55.309/6:nos.
FOOD FISH FACTS.

C 55.310:v.nos.&nos. • Item 609-A (EL)
MARINE FISHERIES REVIEW. v. 1–   1939–   [Quar-
terly]

A review of developments and news items of
the fishery industry. Contains articles, trends,
and developments.
Departments: Research in Service Laborato-
ries; Trends and Developments; Foreign Activi-
ties; Fishery Indicators; Federal Actions, Recent
Fishery Publications.
Title varies: 1939– 1945, Fishery Market News;
1946– 1972, Commercial Fisheries Review; 1973–
Marine Fisheries Review.
Volume index issued separately.
Indexed by:–
Biological Abstracts,
Index to U.S. Government Periodicals.
ISSN 0090-1830
Earlier I 49.10 prior to v. 32, no. 10.

C 55.310/2:v.nos.&nos. • Item 609-B
MARINE FISHERIES ABSTRACTS. v. 1– 27. 1948–
1974. [Monthly]

PURPOSE:– Designed to serve the needs of
fishery scientists, engineers, and managers in
industry, academic institutions, and government
by supplying timely information of current progress
in fishery research and technology.
Contains summaries of selected articles from
trade, engineering, and scientific journals dealing
with the entire spectrum of fishery science.
Formerly Commercial Fisheries Abstracts prior
to March 1973 (v. 26, no. 3).
Earlier I 49.10 prior to v. 32, no. 10.
Discontinued.

C 55.311:v.nos.&nos. • Item 611-B
FISHERY INDUSTRIAL RESEARCH. v. 1–   1962–
[Irregular]

PURPOSE:– To report on scientific investigations of fishery technology, economics, exploratory fishing, and gear research.
Earlier I 49.26/2 prior to v. 6, no. 4.
Discontinued.

C 55.312:nos. • Item 614-B
SPECIAL SCIENTIFIC REPORT: FISHERIES. 1–
1949–
Earlier I 49.15/2
Discontinued.

C 55.313:v.nos.&nos. • Item 611 (EL)
FISHERY BULLETIN. 1–   1931–   [Quarterly]
Technical reports of scientific investigation
of fishery biology, consisting of separates from
the Fishery Bulletin of the Fish and Wildlife Service. The Bulletins are numbered consecutively
and are assigned to volumes. There is no fixed
number of Bulletins which constitute a volume,
each varying from one to sixteen or more Bulle-

tins. Paging is continuous with each volume, with
title pages and lists of contents issued sepa-
rately.
Prior to vol. 47, separates were issued as
Documents.
Indexed by:–
Bibliography of Agriculture.
Biological Abstracts.
Chemical Abstracts.
Index to U.S. Government Periodicals.
Selected Water Resources Abstracts.
ISSN 0090-0656

C 55.313/2 • Item 616-K-7 (EL)
MMPA BULLETIN   [Quarterly]

C 55.314:nos. • Item 611-D
FISHERY LEAFLETS.
Replaced by Fishery Facts (C 55.322).

C 55.314/2:nos.
FOREIGN FISHERIES LEAFLETS.

C 55.315:CT • Item 609-C-7
POSTERS.

C 55.316:nos. • Item 615
STATISTICAL DIGESTS. 1–   1942–
Supersedes Administrative Reports. Consists
of the following sub-series:
FISHERY STATISTICS OF THE UNITED STATES.
1939–   [Annual] (Statistics and Market News
Division)

Contains detailed statistics, analytic textual reviews, and graphic presentations on
the commercial fisheries of the United States.
Includes historical tables.
Published in the Statistical Digest series
since 1939. Data for 1958 were published in
the Administrative Report series of the De-
partment of the Interior. Data prior to 1938
were published in the Administrative Report
series of the former Bureau of Fisheries.
Issuing body varies: 1939– 55, Fish and
Wildlife Service; 1956– 67, Bureau of Com-
mercial Fisheries; 1968–   National Marine
Fisheries Service.
Continues: Fishery Industries of the
United States.
ISSN 0095-7682
Earlier I 49.32

C 55.317:nos.
RESOURCE REPORTS (series). 1–   1972–   [Ir-
regular]

C 55.318:letters-nos. • Item 616-K (EL)
FISHERY MARKET NEWS. [3 times a week]

Gives data on landings, market receipts, imports, wholesale prices, for fresh and frozen fish,
shellfish, and by-products.

C 55.319:date
FISHING INFORMATION. [Monthly] (Southwest Fisheries Center, National Marine Fisheries Service,
8604 La Jolla Shores Drive, La Jolla, California
92037)

C 55.320:nos. • Item 611-F
FISHERY MARKET DEVELOPMENT SERIES. 1–
1966–   [Irregular]
Earlier I 49.49/2
Discontinued.

C 55.321:nos. • Item 616
TEST KITCHEN SERIES. 1–   1950–   [Irregular]
Pamphlets on buying and cooking fish and
shellfish.
Earlier I 49.39
Discontinued.

C 55.322:nos. • Item 611-D
FISHERY FACTS, FSHFA- (series). 1–   1972–
[Irregular]

PURPOSE:– To provide a publication series
for disseminating practical information regarding
scientific and technical research findings that
can be applied by one or more specialized fisher-

ies related user groups.
Replaces Fishery Leaflets (C 55.314).

C 55.323:date • Item 616-D (MF)
GRANT-IN-AID FOR FISHERIES PROGRAM ACTIVI-
TIES. [Annual]

PURPOSE:– To give a listing of completed
and ongoing projects financed under Public Law
88-309, Public Law 89-304 which are administered by the Office of State-Federal Relationships, National Marine Fisheries Service, to keep
the public informed of the efforts and accomplishments of the Federal Government, in cooperation with the States, in the area of fisheries of
the United States.
Discontinued.

C 55.324:nos. • Item 616-G
DATA REPORTS. 1–   1964–   [Irregular]

PURPOSE:– To provide compilations of
unanalyzed or partially analyzed data collected
during biological, limnological, or oceanographic
investigations.
Reports also available in microfiche.
Earlier I 49.59
Discontinued.

C 55.325:nos. • Item 616-L-1
TRANSLATED TABLES OF CONTENTS OF CURRENT
FOREIGN FISHERIES, OCEANOGRAPHIC, AND
ATMOSPHERIC PUBLICATIONS. 1–   [Irregular]

Lists translated tables of contents of current
foreign fisheries, oceanographic, and atmospheric
publications believed to be of interest to scientists, researchers, administrators, business
people, and the industry in general.

C 55.325/2:nos. • Item 616-L-2
RECEIVED OR PLANNED CURRENT FISHERIES,
OCEANOGRAPHIC, AND ATMOSPHERIC TRANS-
LATIONS, A- (series). [Irregular]

Lists fisheries, oceanographic, atmospheric,
and related articles, periodicals, and publications
translated or considered for translation and believed to be of interest to scientists, researchers, administrators, business people, and the industry in general.

C 55.325/3:nos. • Item 616-L-3
SURVEY OF FOREIGN FISHERIES, OCEANO-
GRAPHIC, AND ATMOSPHERIC LITERATURE, C-
(series). [Irregular]

Contains full translations, detailed summaries, or abstracts of foreign articles. All salient
points of the material are covered.

C 55.325/4:nos. • Item 616-L-3 (MF)
SURVEY OF FOREIGN FISHERIES, TRANSLATED
TABLES OF CONTENTS, AND NEW TRANSLA-
TIONS. [Bimonthly]

C 55.326:CT
NORTHWEST FISHERIES CENTER: PUBLICATIONS.
[Irregular]

C 55.327:date • Item 616-H (MF)
ADMINISTRATION OF THE MARINE MAMMAL PRO-
TECTION ACT OF 1972. 1st–   [Annual]

C 55.328:CT • Item 616-I (MF)
ENVIRONMENTAL IMPACT STATEMENTS. [Irregular]

C 55.329:date
CENTRAL, WESTERN, AND SOUTH PACIFIC FISH-
ERIES DEVELOPMENT PROGRAM REPORT FOR
CALENDAR YEAR. [Annual]

C 55.330:date • **Item 616-J (MF)**
ANNUAL REPORT, FISHERY CONSERVATION AND
MANAGEMENT ACT. 1st–   1977–

PURPOSE:– To report on the activities of the
Regional Fishery Management Councils and the
Department of Commerce with respect to fishery
management plans, regulations to implement such
plans, and other activities relating to the conservation and management of fishery resources that
were undertaken during the year. Report submitted to Congress pursuant to the Fishery Conservation and Management Act of 1976.
Discontinued.

C 55.331:nos. • **Item 616-K-3 (MF)**
SOUTHWEST FISHERIES CENTER: REPORT OF
ACTIVITIES [Quarterly].

Highlights fisheries research conducted by
Honolulu, La Jolla, and Tiburon Laboratories, and
the Pacific Environmental Group.
Discontinued.

C 55.331/2:date/nos. • **Item 616-K-1 (EL)**
NORTHWEST AND ALASKA FISHERIES CENTER,
QUARTERLY REPORT.

Earlier title: Monthly Report (Northwest and
Alaska Fisheries Centers).

C 55.331/3: • **Item 616-K-5 (MF)**
NORTHWEST FISHERIES SCIENCE CENTER, QUAR-
TERLY REPORT.
Discontinued.

C 55.332:CT • **Item 616-L**
BIBLIOGRAPHIES AND LISTS OF PUBLICATIONS.
[Irregular]

C 55.332:So 1 • **Item 616-L**
UNITED STATES FISHERIES SYSTEMS AND
SOCIAL SCIENCES: A BIBLIOGRAPHY OF
WORK AND DIRECTORY OF RESEARCHERS.
1979. 162 p. map.

C 55.334:date • **Item 616-K-3 (MF)**
COLLECTED REPRINTS.

C 55.335: • **Item 609-C-6 (MF)**
COASTAL ZONE AND ESTUARINE STUDIES (series).
[Irregular]

Studies deal with miscellaneous estuarine
subjects such as migration, characteristics of
various species of fish.
Discontinued.

C 55.336: • **Item 616-K-2**
COUNCIL MEMORANDUM. [Monthly]

PURPOSE:– To present fishery news and
individual reports on the various regional fishery
management councils.
Discontinued.

C 55.337:letters-nos. • **Item 609-C-8**
ADMINISTRATIVE REPORTS (series). [Irregular]
Discontinued.

C 55.337/2:date • **Item 609-C-8 (MF)**
SEAFOOD DEALERS OF THE SOUTHWEST REGION.
Discontinued.

C 55.338:date • **Item 609-C-9 (EL)**
APPROVED LIST, SANITARY INSPECTED FISH
ESTABLISHMENTS. [Semiannual]

C 55.338/2:date • **Item 616-C-9 (MF)**
LIST OF FISHERY COOPERATIVES IN THE UNITED
STATES. [Annual]
Discontinued.

C 55.339:date • **Item 609-A-1**
MARINE RECREATIONAL FISHERIES. [Annual]

Proceedings of the annual Marine Recreational
Fisheries Symposium. Published for such organizations as the National Coalition for Marine Fisheries Service. Proceedings are expected to contain maps, photographs, tables, and graphs, and
to be about 220 pages in length.
Discontinued.

C 55.340:date • **Item 609-C-10 (MF)**
ANNUAL REPORT HABITAT CONSERVATION
PROGRAM. [Annual]

PURPOSE– To provide information on the Na-
tional Habitat Program, Management Programs of
the Southeast, Northeast, Alaska, Northwest, and
Southwest Regions as well as Marine Pollution
Research Programs for the regional centers.
Discontinued.

C 55.341:date • **Item 616-K-4 (MF)**
NATIONAL SYSTEMATICS LABORATORY REPORT
FOR CALENDAR YEAR (date). [Annual]

C 55.343:date
ANNUAL REPORT DALL PORPOISE-SALMON RE-
SEARCH.

C 55.344:date • **Item 616-K-6 (P) (EL)**
SFA UPDATE. [Irregular]

C 55.345:date • **Item 616-K-7 (E)**
ELECTRONIC PRODUCTS (MISC.)
uP/10W (Misc.)

C 55.346 • **Item 616-K-8 (EL)**
BILLFISH NEWSLETTER. (Southwest Fisheries Science Center) [Annual]

NATIONAL OCEAN SERVICE
(1970–   )

CREATION AND AUTHORITY

The National Ocean Service was established
within the National Oceanic and Atmospheric Administration of the Department of Commerce by
Departmental Organization Order 25-5A, effective October 9, 1970.

INFORMATION

National Ocean Service
NOAA
SSMC4, 13th Fl.
1305 East West Hwy.
Silver Spring, MD 20910
(301) 713-3070
Fax: (301) 713-4269
http://www.nos.noaa.gov

C 55.401:date • **Item 189-A (MF)**
ANNUAL REPORT.

C 55.401/2:date
MONTHLY REPORT OF ACTIVITIES.

C 55.402:CT • **Item 192**
GENERAL PUBLICATIONS.

C 55.408:CT • **Item 192-B**
HANDBOOKS, MANUALS, GUIDES. [Irregular]

C 55.408/2:nos. • **Item 192-B (MF)**
NOS TECHNICAL MANUALS. [Irregular]
Continues C&GS Technical Manuals (C 4.12/
5).

C 55.409:date
DATES OF LATEST EDITIONS, AERONAUTICAL
CHARTS. [Every 4 weeks]
ISSN 0364-5800
Earlier C 4.9/13 prior to the November 2, 1970
issue.

C 55.409/2:date • **Item 191-B-7**
DATES OF LATEST EDITIONS, NAUTICAL CHARTS
AND MISCELLANEOUS, MAPS. [Quarterly]

C 55.410:v.nos.&nos. • **Item 191-A**
EARTHQUAKE INFORMATION BULLETIN. [Bimonthly]
Earlier C 4.54
Later C 55.611

C 55.411:date • **Item 192-A-1**
U.S. TERMINAL PROCEDURES.

(IAP) charts present aeronautical data required to execute instrument approaches. Covers U.S., Puerto Rico, and Virgin Islands. Revised every 56 days. Change Notices issued every 28 days.
Includes Airport Obstruction Charts (OC) and
Turbine Data Sheets (T).
Earlier C 4.9/18 prior to the November 1, 1970
issue.
Earlier titled: Instrument Approach Procedure
Charts.
Now issued by the Federal Aviation Administration under TD 4.80.

C 55.411/2:date
INSTRUMENT APPROACH PROCEDURE CHARTS
[Alaska, Hawaii, U.S. Pacific Islands]. [Bimonthly]

Includes Airport Obstruction Charts (OC) and
Turbine Data Sheets (T).
Earlier C 4.9/18-2 prior to the November 2,
1970 issue.

C 55.411/3:date • **Item 192-A-2**
AIRPORT OBSTRUCTION CHARTS. [Bimonthly]
Non-depository.

C 55.411/3-2 • **Item 192-A-2**
LATEST EDITIONS, AIRPORT OBSTRUCTION
CHARTS. [Quarterly]

OC are 1:12,000-scale graphics showing airport obstructions establishing instrument approach
and departure procedures, etc. Revised as required by the FAA. ODS tabulates the OC, lists all
objects with and elevation on the OC. This ODS is
issued with the OC. The Dates of Latest Editions
is a pamphlet listing airports alphabetically by
state then associated city, then airport by name.
Non-depository.

C 55.411/4:CT • **Item 192 (MF)**
DATA ATLAS.

C 55.412:date • **Item 192-C**
PRELIMINARY DETERMINATION OF EPICENTERS.
[Monthly]
Earlier C 4.36/2-2 prior to the July 1970 is-
sue.
Later C 55.690

C 55.413:CT • **Item 207-A-1**
BIBLIOGRAPHIES AND LISTS OF PUBLICATIONS.

C 55.413/2:nos. • **Item 207-A-1 (MF)**
NATIONAL OCEAN SURVEY ABSTRACTS. [Annual]

C 55.413/3:date • **Item 207-A-1 (MF)**
PUBLICATIONS OF THE NATIONAL GEODETIC
SURVEY. [Irregular]
Earlier C 55.413:G 29/2

C 55.414:CT
ANTARCTIC SEISMOLOGICAL BULLETIN. [Quarterly]

Published in cooperation with the Scientific
Committee on Antarctic Research of the International Council of Scientific Unions.
Earlier C 4.36 prior to the April-June 1970
issue.

C 55.415:nos.
PRESS RELEASES, NOS (series). [Irregular]

C 55.416:date • **Item 192-A-3**
FLIGHT INFORMATION PUBLICATION: SUPPLEMENT,
ALASKA.

A joint civil/military flight information publication containing an airport/facility directory, special notices, procedures, etc. A single volume
designed for use with the Enroute, Alaska Terminal Area, World Aeronautical, and Sectional Aeronautical Charts. Issued every 56 days.

C 55.416/2:letters/date • Item 192-A-4
FLIGHT INFORMATION PUBLICATIONS, AIRPORT/
FACILITY DIRECTORY.

Pilot's manual provides data on airports, seaplane bases, heliports, navigation aids, operational procedures, etc. Covers conterminous U.S.,
Puerto Rico, and the Virgin Islands. These volumes are revised every 56 days.

C 55.416/3: • Item 192-A-5
STANDARD TERMINAL ARRIVAL (STAR) CHARTS.

PURPOSE– To expedite air traffic control arrival route procedures, to facilitate transition between enroute and instrument approach operations through graphics and text. One bound volume, arranged by city name, for U.S., Puerto
Rico, and Virgin Islands, except Alaska. Five Profile Descent Charts are included.
Issued every 56 days.

C 55.416/4: • Item 192-A-6
ALASKA TERMINAL CHARTS.

Contains all terminal flight procedures, e.g.
instrument approach charts, standard terminal
arrival charts, airport diagrams, etc., for civil and
military aviation in Alaska.
Published in one volume every 56 days.

C 55.416/5: • Item 192-A-7
STANDARD INSTRUMENT DEPARTURE (SID)
CHARTS, EASTERN U.S.
Expedites clearance delivery and facilitates
transition between takeoff and enroute operations. These two bound books arranged alphabetically by city names, furnish pilots departure
routing clearance through graphics and text.
Also includes Puerto Rico and the Virgin Islands
Revised every 56 days.

C 55.416/6:date/nos. • Item 192-A-7
STANDARD INSTRUMENT DEPARTURE (SID)
CHARTS, WESTERN UNITED STATES.

C 55.416/7: • Item 192-A-8
VFR/IFR PLANNING CHART.

Used for pre-flight planning of long flights.
C 55.416/7: is in two pieces that assemble to
form a composite VFR (Visual Flight Rules) plan-
ning chart on one side and an IFR (Instrument
Flight Rules) planning charton the other.
Revised every 56 days.

C 55.416/7-1:date/nos. • Item 192-A-8
IFR WALL PLANNING CHART: WEST, LOW ALTITUDE,
U.S. [Bimonthly]

C 55.416/7-2 • Item 192-A-8
FLIGHT CASE PLANNING CHART. [Semiannual]

This publication is similar to VFR/IFR Planning Chart (C 55.416/7) with added information
such as Flight Service Stations, etc.
Revised every 24 weeks.

C 55.416/8:date/nos. • Item 192-A-9
NORTH ATLANTIC ROUTE CHART.

Designed for Air Traffic Controllers in
monitoringtransatlantic flights. Depicts major
coastal airports, oceanic control areas. May be
used for pre- and in-flight planning.

C 55.416/9: • Item 192-A-10
NORTH PACIFIC OCEANIC ROUTE CHART (1 sheet
full size).

1:12,000,000
Designed for FAA air traffic controller's use in
monitoring transoceanic air traffic. Contains
established intercontinental air routes.
Revised every 24 weeks.

C 55.416/9-2 • Item 192-A-10
NORTH PACIFIC OCEANIC ROUTE CHART (4 area
charts).

1:7,000,000
Designed for FAA air traffic controller's use in
monitoring transoceanic air traffic. Contains
established intercontinental air routes. Charts
cover Northwest, Northeast, Southwest, Southeast areas.
Revised every 8 weeks.

C 55.416/10: • Item 192-A-11
SECTIONAL AERONAUTICAL CHARTS.

Designed for visual navigation of slow to medium speed aircraft. Charts cover the conterminous U.S. Topographic information includes the
relief and a judicious selection of visual check-
points used for flight under visual flight rules.
Most revised semiannually.

C 55.416/11: • Item 192-A-12
TERMINAL AREA CHARTS (VFR).

Charts depict airspace designated as Terminal Control Areas (TCA), for use by pilots operating from airfields within or near TCAs. Contain
information similar to that on Sectional Charts but
in much greater detail.
Revised semiannually.

C 55.416/12: • Item 192-A-13
U.S. GULF COAST VFR AERONAUTICAL CHART.
Designed primarily for helicopter operations
in the Gulf of Mexico area. Includes information
on offshore mineral leasing areas and high density helicopter activity areas.
Revised annually.

C 55.416/12-2: • Item 192-A-14
VFR HELICOPTER CHART OF LOS ANGELES.
Each single sheet chart shows principal heli-
copter routes for its respective area.
All charts are revised as required.

C 55.416/12-3 • Item 192-A-14
NEW YORK HELICOPTER ROUTE CHART.

Each single sheet chart shows principal helicopter routes for its respective area.
All charts are revised as required.

C 55.416/12-4: • Item 192-A-14
WASHINGTON HELICOPTER ROUTE CHART.

Each single sheet chart shows principal helicopter routes for its respective area.
All charts are revised as required.

C 55.416/12-5 • Item 192-A-14
CHICAGO HELICOPTER ROUTE CHART.

Each single sheet chart shows principal helicopter routes for its respective area.
All charts are revised as required.

C 55.416/12-6 • Item 192-A-13
GRAND CANYON VFR AERONAUTICAL CHART, (GEN-
ERAL AVIATION).

C 55.416/12-7 • Item 192-A-23
BOSTON HELICOPTER ROUTE CHART.

C 55.416/12-8:date • Item 192-A-25
ATLANTA HELICOPTER ROUTE CHART.

C 55.416/12-9:date • Item 192-A-26
HOUSTON HELICOPTER ROUTE CHART.

C 55.416/13: • Item 192-A-15
WORLD AERONAUTICAL CHARTS.

Charts cover land areas for navigation by
moderate speed aircraft and aircraft operating at
high altitudes. Includes Alaska, the U.S., Northern Mexico, and the Caribbean Islands.
Most charts are revised and updated annually.

C 55.416/14 • Item 192-A-16
IFR ENROUTE LOW ALTITUDE (U.S.).

Charts provide aeronautical information for
navigation under instrument flight rules in the low
altitude stratum (below 18,000 feet) for conterminous U.S.
Revised every 56 days.
Earlier titled: Enroute Area Charts (U.S.) Low
Altitude.

C 55.416/15: • Item 192-A-17
ENROUTE LOW ALTITUDE CHARTS (ALASKA).

Charts provide aeronautical information for
navigation under flight rules in the low altitude
stratum (below 18,000 feet) for Alaska.
Charts are issued every 56 days.

C 55.416/15-2 • Item 192-A-18
IFR AREA CHARTS (U.S.).

Charts provide aeronautical information for
navigation under instrument flight rules in the low
altitude stratum (below 18,000 feet) for Eastern
and Western U.S.
Revised every 56 days.
Earlier title: Enroute Area Charts (U.S.) Low
Altitude.

C 55.416/15-3 • Item 192-A-24
IFR/VFR LOW ALTITUDE PLANNING CHART.

C 55.416/16: • Item 192-A-19
ENROUTE HIGH ALTITUDE CHARTS, U.S.
Charts are designed for navigation at or above
18,000 feet for the conterminous U.S.
These charts are revised and issued every
56 days.

C 55.416/16-2: • Item 192-A-20
ENROUTE HIGH ALTITUDE CHARTS (ALASKA).

Charts are designed for navigation at or
above 18,000 feet.
Revised and issued every 56 days.

C 55.416/17: • Item 192-A-21
ENROUTE HIGH ALTITUDE PLANNING CHARTS (U.S.).
Designed specifically for IFR enroute
planning at or above 18,000 feet. May be
used for pre- and in-flight planning. Contains
published jet routes, restricted areas.
Revised every 56 days.
Discontinued.

C 55.416/18:date-nos. • Item 192-A-5
SPECIAL NOTICE (series). [Irregular]

C 55.417:nos.
ABSTRACTS OF EARTHQUAKE REPORTS FOR THE
UNITED STATES, MSA- (series).
Earlier C 4.42
Later C 55.223

C 55.417/2:date • Item 208
UNITED STATE EARTHQUAKES. [Annual]
Earlier C 4.25/2
Later C 55.226

C 55.418:nos./date
NAUTICAL CHART CATALOGS.

Lists nautical charts and related publications
of the National Ocean Survey, ordering information, and information on the classification of smallcraft and conventional charts.
Earlier C 4.5

C 55.418:1/date • Item 191-B-1
1. ATLANTIC AND GULF COASTS, INCLUDING
PUERTO RICO AND THE VIRGIN ISLANDS.
[Annual]

C 55.418:2/date • Item 191-B-2
2. PACIFIC COAST, INCLUDING HAWAII, GUAM,
AND SAMOA ISLANDS. [Annual]

C 55.418:3/date • Item 191-B-3
3. ALASKA, INCLUDING THE ALEUTIAN ISLANDS.
[Annual]

C 55.418:4/date • **Item 191-B-4**
4. GREAT LAKES AND ADJACENT WATERWAYS. [Annual]

C 55.418:5 • **Item 191-B-18**
BATHYMETRIC MAPPING PRODUCTS (CATALOG) 5, UNITED STATES BATHYMETRIC AND FISHING MAPS. [Annual]

Catalog includes topographic/bathymetric maps, bathymetric fishing maps, and IHB GEBCO plotting sheets.
See C 55.418/7

C 55.418:6 • **Item 191-B-19**
6. GUIDE TO NOAA NAUTICAL PRODUCTS & SERVICES. [Irregular]

C 55.418/2:date • **Item 191-B-6**
NATIONAL OCEAN SURVEY CATALOG OF AERONAUTICAL CHARTS AND RELATED PUBLICATIONS. [Quarterly]

PURPOSE:– To show index coverage of aeronautical charts published and distributed by the National Ocean Survey. Included in the information is chart purpose and description, with ordering instructions.

C 55.418/3:date • **Item 191-D**
DEFENSE MAPPING AGENCY AERONAUTICAL CHARTS AND PUBLICATIONS AVAILABLE FROM NOAA'S NATIONAL OCEAN SERVICE. [Annual]
Published quarterly prior to August 1, 1971 by the cost and Geodetic Survey (C 4.9/13-2). Earlier issued monthly.
Earlier titled: Latest Editions of U.S. Air Force Aeronautical Charts. (ISSN 0364-6793).

C 55.418/4:date
MILITARY FIELDS, UNITED STATES, INSTRUMENT APPROACH PROCEDURE CHARTS. –January 1973. [Quarterly]

Published by the Coast and Geodetic Survey prior to April 1, 1971 (C 4.9/22).

C 55.418/5: • **Item 191-B-12**
RECREATIONAL CHARTS (series).

Each recreational chart deals with a different waterway.

C 55.418/6: • **Item 191-B-11**
MAPS AND CHARTS.

Includes miscellaneous maps and charts on various topics pertaining to the work of the Service.

C 55.418/6-2:CT • **Item 191-B-11**
POSTERS. [Irregular]

C 55.418/7:(numbers) • **Item 191-B-13**
CHARTS (LISTED IN) CHARTS AND PUBLICATIONS CATALOG 1, UNITED STATES ATLANTIC AND GULF COASTS.

Includes charts from Cape Hatteras to Rio Grande; Puerto Rico; and Virgin Islands. Includes different kinds of charts such as harbor, coast, intra coastal waterway, and sailing charts. The type of chart is color-coded in the catalog itself. Revised as required.

C 55.418/7:(numbers) • **Item 191-B-14**
CHARTS (LISTED IN) CHARTS AND PUBLICATIONS CATALOG 2, UNITED STATES PACIFIC COAST.

Includes various charts from San Diego to Vancouver Island; Hawaii; Guam; and the Samoan Islands. Includes different kinds of charts such as harbor, coast, general, sailing, and international charts. The type of chart is color-coded in the catalog itself. Revised as required.

C 55.418/7:(numbers) • **Item 191-B-15**
CHARTS (LISTED IN) CHARTS AND PUBLICATIONS CATALOG 3, UNITED STATES ALASKA.

Includes Alaska Coast and Aleutian Islands. Includes different kinds of charts such as harbor, coast, general, sailing, and international charts. The type of chart is color-coded in the

catalog itself. Revised as required.

C 55.418/7:(numbers) • **Item 191-B-16**
CHARTS (LISTED IN) CHARTS AND PUBLICATIONS CATALOG 4, UNITED STATES GREAT LAKES.

Includes waterways adjacent to the Great Lakes. Includes different kinds of charts such as harbor, coast, general, canoe, and sailing charts. The type of chart is color-coded in the catalog itself. Revised as required.

C 55.418/7: • **Item 191-B-17**
MAPS (LISTED IN) BATHYMETRIC MAPPING PRODUCTS CATALOG 5, UNITED STATES BATHYMETRIC AND FISHING MAPS.

Includes topographic/bathymetric maps, bathymetric fishing maps, geophysical maps, and IHB GEBCO plotting sheets. Revised as required.

C 55.419:nos. • **Item 193**
NOS PUBLICATIONS (numbered). 1957– [Irregular]
Earlier C 4.19, C 4.19/2
Later C 55.228

C 55.420:date • **Item 338 (MF)**
GREAT LAKES PILOT. [Annual]
PURPOSE:– To supply full descriptions of physical conditions and the particulars of constantly changing conditions not adapted to adequate or prompt representation of the charts.
Bearings are true and distances are expressed in statute miles. Supplements information given upon charts published by Lake Survey Center. Supersedes all previous pilots for above mentioned waters.
Price includes six monthly supplements, issued during the navigation season, May to October.

C 55.420/2:date • **Item 199-A**
GREAT LAKES WATER LEVELS. [Annual]

TIDE TABLES. 1853–   [Annual]

PURPOSE:– To provide mariners with advance information relative to the rise and fall of the tide. These tables, published a year in advance, give the predicted times and heights of high and low waters for every day in the year for a number of reference stations and the differences for obtaining similar predictions for numerous other places.
Tide tables for the use of mariners have been published by the Coast and Geodetic Survey since 1853. For a number of years these tables appeared as appendixes to the annual reports of the Superintendent of the Survey, and consisted of more or less elaborate means for enabling the mariner to make his own prediction of tides as the occasion arose. The first tables to give predictions for each day were those for the year 1867, which contained daily predictions for 19 stations and tidal differences for 124 stations. The tide tables are now issued in four volumes, containing daily predictions for 195 reference ports and differences and ranges for about 5,000 stations.
In addition to the full daily predictions and the differences and ranges for auxiliary stations, the publications include tables for obtaining the approximate height of the tide at any time, a table of local mean time of sunrise and sunset for every fifth day of the year for different latitudes, a table for the reduction of local mean time to standard time, and a table of the Greenwich mean time of the moon's phases, apogee, perigee, greatest north and south and zero declination, and the time of the solar equinoxes and solstices.
Issued in the following four parts:

C 55.421:date • **Item 199**
TIDE TABLES, HIGH AND LOW WATER PREDICTION, WEST COAST OF NORTH AND SOUTH AMERICA INCLUDING HAWAIIAN ISLANDS. [Annual]

These tide tables and those following include predictions of the times and heights of high and low waters for every day in the year for many of the more important harbors, and

differences for obtaining predictions for numerous other places.
Earlier C 4.15/5

C 55.421/2:date • **Item 197**
TIDE TABLES, HIGH AND LOW WATER PREDICTIONS, EAST COAST OF NORTH AND SOUTH AMERICA INCLUDING GREENLAND. 1949– [Annual]
Earlier C 4.15/4

C 55.421/3:date • **Item 198**
TIDE TABLES, HIGH AND LOW WATER PREDICTIONS, EUROPE AND WEST COAST OF AFRICA, INCLUDING THE MEDITERRANEAN SEA. 1950– [Annual]

Includes index map of tide table coverage and list of publications relating to tides and tidal currents.
Earlier C 4.15/7

C 55.421/4:date • **Item 196**
TIDE TABLES, HIGH AND LOW WATER PREDICTIONS, CENTRAL AND WESTERN PACIFIC OCEAN AND INDIAN OCEAN. [Annual]
Earlier C 4.15/6

C 55.421/5:date • **Item 199-A-1 (CD)**
TIDE & TIDAL CURRENT TABLES.
Issued on CD-ROM.

C 55.422:v.nos.
UNITED STATES COAST PILOTS. [Irregular]
Earlier C 4.6/1

C 55.422:1/date • **Item 203**
ATLANTIC COAST, EASTPORT TO CAPE COD.

C 55.422:2/date • **Item 203**
ATLANTIC COAST, CAPE COD TO SANDY HOOK.

C 55.422:3/date • **Item 203**
ATLANTIC COAST, SANDY HOOK TO CAPE HENRY.

C 55.422:4/date • **Item 203**
ATLANTIC COAST, CAPE HENRY TO KEY WEST.

C 55.422:5/date • **Item 204**
ATLANTIC COAST, GULF OF MEXICO, PUERTO RICO, AND VIRGIN ISLANDS.

C 55.422:6/date • **Item 207-A-3**
GREAT LAKES.

C 55.422:7/date • **Item 206**
PACIFIC COAST, CALIFORNIA, OREGON, WASHINGTON, AND HAWAII.

C 55.422:8/date • **Item 201**
PACIFIC COAST, ALASKA, DIXON ENTRANCE TO CAPE SPENCER.

C 55.422:9/date • **Item 202**
PACIFIC AND ARCTIC COASTS, ALASKA, CAPE SPENCER TO BEAUFORT SEA.

C 55.423:date • **Item 207-A-2 (MF)**
SHIP OPERATIONS REPORT, NATIONAL OCEAN SURVEY. 1969– [Annual]

This report summarizes the work programs of NOAA ships carried on during the field season. Its purpose is to present, in summary form advance information on the seasonal programs conducted by the ships. It is prepared for in-house dissemination in the National Ocean Survey, for collaborating and interested agencies with which the Survey operates, and for use by members of the scientific and oceanographic communities.
The report is arranged by projects with a brief history of each project, a summary description of the project, and the work accomplished. Progress sketches are included for some of the projects.
Discontinued.

C 55.424:CT
TIDAL CURRENT CHARTS.

These publications each consist of a set of 12 charts which depict, by means of arrows and figures, the direction and velocity of the tidal current for each hour of the tidal cycle. The charts, which may be used for any year, present a comprehensive view of the tidal current movement in the respective waterways as a whole and also supply a means for readily determining for any time the direction and velocity of the current at various localities throughout the water areas covered.
Earlier C 4.29

TIDAL CURRENT TABLES. [Annual]

PURPOSE:– To provide mariners with advance information relative to the tidal current, a periodic horizontal flow of water accompanying the rise and fall of the tide.
Current tables for the use of mariners have been published by the Coast and Geodetic Survey since 1890 for the Atlantic Coast and 1898 for the Pacific coast.
Tables include daily predictions of the times of slack water and the times and velocities of strength of flood and ebb currents for a number of waterways together with differences for obtaining predictions for numerous other places. Supplementary tables include velocity of current at any time, duration of slack, rotary tidal currents.
Published a year in advance. Issued in the following two parts:

C 55.425:date   • **Item 190**
– ATLANTIC COAST OF NORTH AMERICA. [Annual]

Includes list of publications relating to tides and tidal currents.
Earlier C 4.22

C 55.425/2:date   • **Item 191**
– PACIFIC COAST OF NORTH AMERICA AND ASIA.
Earlier C 4.23

C 55.425/3   • **Item 190**
REGIONAL TIDE AND TIDAL CURRENT TABLES. [Biennial]

C 55.426:nos.
EARTHQUAKE DATA REPORTS, EDR-(series).

C 55.427:date   • **Item 192-A-22**
UNITED STATES GOVERNMENT FLIGHT INFORMATION PUBLICATION: PACIFIC CHART SUPPLEMENT. [Issued every 8 weeks, with amendment notices issued every 28 days]

Designed for use with Enroute Charts and the Sectional Aeronautical Charts covering Hawaii and the area of the Pacific served by U.S. facilities.
The supplement is published every 56 days and an Amendment Notice is published 4 weeks after issue.
Chart Supplement (TD 4.16).

C 55.428:date   • **Item 191-B**
COLLECTED REPRINTS. 1976– [Annual]

PURPOSE:–To present those papers of greatest significance which have been presented or published in the calendar year. Included are papers published in-house and those professional journals which aid in the research and development function in science and engineering.
Discontinued.

C 55.429:nos.   • **Item 191-C**
NOS OCEANOGRAPHIC CIRCULATORY SURVEY REPORTS. 1– 1978– [Irregular]

PURPOSE:– To provide reports which contain information from circulatorysurveys by the National Ocean Survey, covering currents, tides, temperatures and salinity for the Nation's navigational waterways.
Discontinued.

C 55.430:
HORIZONTAL CONTROL DATA.

C 55.430/2:date
ALPHABETICAL INDEX TO HORIZONTAL CONTROL DATA.

C 55.431:nos.   • **Item 191-B-5**
EDUCATIONAL PAMPHLETS (series). 1– [Irregular] (Physical Science Services Branch, Office of Program Development and Management)

Series publicizes the program services of the National Ocean Survey.

C 55.432:date   • **Item 199**
SUPPLEMENTAL TIDAL PREDICTIONS, ANCHORAGE, NIKISHKA, SELDOVIA, AND VALDEZ, ALASKA. [Annual]
Earlier C 55.402:An 21
Supplements C 55.421

C 55.433:nos.   • **Item 191-C-1 (MF)**
OUTER CONTINENTAL SHELF ENVIRONMENTAL ASSESSMENT PROGRAM FINAL REPORTS OF PRINCIPAL INVESTIGATORS. 1– [Irregular]

Former Title: Environmental Assessment of the Alaskan Continental Shelf Principal Investigators Reports (C 55.622).
Discontinued.

C 55.434   • **Item 191-B-8 (MF)**
NOAA NATIONAL STATUS AND TRENDS PROGRAM AND QUALITY ASSURANCE PROGRAM FOR MARINE ENVIRONMENTAL MEASUREMENTS. [Quarterly]

PURPOSE:– To disseminate information to those involved in the Quality Assurance and National Status and Trends Programs.
Discontinued.

C 55.435:v.nos.&nos.
COASTAL WAVES PROGRAM FIELD WAVE DATA. [Quarterly]

C 55.436   • **Item 191-B-9 (MF)**
NATIONAL STATUS AND TRENDS PROGRAM, WATER QUALITY CRUISE DATA REPORTS (series). [Irregular]

C 55.436/2   • **Item 191-B-10 (MF)**
NATIONAL STATUS AND TRENDS PROGRAM FOR MARINE ENVIRONMENTAL QUALITY.

Each issue deals with a different topic.

C 55.436/3:date   • **Item 191-B-10 (MF)**
NATIONAL STATUS AND TRENDS PROGRAM FOR MARINE ENVIRONMENTAL QUALITY, FY PROGRAM DESCRIPTION. [Biennial]
Discontinued.

C 55.436/4:date   • **Item 191-B-9 (MF)**
NATIONAL STATUS AND TRENDS PROGRAM, WATER QUALITY ANNUAL REPORT.

C 55.437:date
IRIS, EARTH ORIENTATION BULLETIN. [Monthly]

C 55.438:date   • **Item 207-A-1 (MF)**
STATES' ACTIVITIES REPORT, [Biennial]

C 55.439:date   • **Item 191-B-9 (MF)**
REPORT TO THE CONGRESS ON OCEAN POLLUTION, MONITORING, AND RESEARCH. [Annual]

C 55.440:nos./date   • **Item 378-E-22**
DEFENSE MAPPING AGENCY PUBLIC SALE NAUTICAL CHARTS AND PUBLICATIONS. [Annual]

Earlier D 5.351/2

C 55.440:1   • **Item 378-E-11**
NAUTICAL CHARTS AND PUBLICATIONS, REGION 1, UNITED STATES AND CANADA.

C 55.440:2   • **Item 378-E-11**
NAUTICAL CHARTS AND PUBLICATIONS, REGION 2, CENTRAL AND SOUTH AMERICA AND ANTARCTICA.

C 55.440:3   • **Item 378-E-11**
NAUTICAL CHARTS AND PUBLICATIONS, REGION 3, WESTERN EUROPE, ICELAND, GREENLAND, AND THE ARCTIC.

C 55.440:4   • **Item 378-E-11**
NAUTICAL CHARTS AND PUBLICATIONS, REGION 4, SCANDINAVIA, BALTIC, AND THE FORMER SOVIET UNION.

C 55.440:5   • **Item 378-E-11**
NAUTICAL CHARTS AND PUBLICATIONS, REGION 5, WESTERN AFRICA AND THE MEDITERRANEAN.

C 55.440:6   • **Item 378-E-11**
NAUTICAL CHARTS AND PUBLICATIONS, REGION 6, INDIAN OCEAN.

C 55.440:7   • **Item 378-E-11**
NAUTICAL CHARTS AND PUBLICATIONS, REGION 7, AUSTRALIA, INDONESIA, AND NEW ZEALAND.

C 55.440:8   • **Item 378-E-11**
NAUTICAL CHARTS AND PUBLICATIONS, REGION 8, OCEANIA.

C 55.440:9   • **Item 378-E-11**
NAUTICAL CHARTS AND PUBLICATIONS, REGION 9, EAST ASIA.

C 55.441:date   • **Item 192-D**
NATIONAL SHELLFISH REGISTER OF CLASSIFIED GROWING WATERS. [Quinquennially]

C 55.442:   • **Item 192-D-1 (MF)**
ENVIRONMENTAL IMPACT STATEMENT.

NATIONAL EARTH SATELLITE SERVICE
(1971–   )

C 55.501:date
ANNUAL REPORT.

C 55.502:CT   • **Item 207-B-1**
GENERAL PUBLICATIONS.
Discontinued.

C 55.508:CT   • **Item 207-B-2**
HANDBOOKS, MANUALS, GUIDES. [Irregular]
Discontinued.

C 55.509:date
BIBLIOGRAPHY OF NATIONAL ENVIRONMENTAL SATELLITE SERVICE.

C 55.510:date   • **Item 207-B-3**
SATELLITE ACTIVITIES OF NOAA. [Annual]

PURPOSE:– To present information on satellite activities of various components of NASA, including the National Earth Satellite Service.
Discontinued.

ENVIRONMENTAL RESEARCH LABORATORIES
(1971–   )

C 55.601:date
ANNUAL REPORT.

C 55.601/2:date   • Item 207-C-3 (MF)
PACIFIC MARINE ENVIRONMENTAL LABORATORY: ANNUAL REPORT.

C 55.601/3:date   • Item 208-E-1 (MF)
NATIONAL HURRICANE RESEARCH LABORATORY, FISCAL YEAR PROGRAMS, FISCAL YEAR PROJECTIONS. [Annual]

Summarizes laboratory activities in hurricane research.

C 55.601/4:date   • Item 208-E-3 (MF)
RESEARCH FACILITIES CENTER: ANNUAL REPORT. [Annual]

Summarizes Center activities in carrying out its mission of providing instrumental aircraft to support various atmospheric/oceanic research programs of National Oceanic and Atmospheric Administration elements and other government agencies.
Discontinued.

C 55.601/5:date   • Item 208-E-4 (EL)
GEOPHYSICAL FLUID DYNAMICS LABORATORY: ACTIVITIES, PLANS. [Annual]

C 55.602:CT   • Item 207-C-1
GENERAL PUBLICATIONS.

C 55.608:CT   • Item 207-C-4
HANDBOOKS, MANUALS, GUIDES. [Irregular]

C 55.609:nos.
HURRICANE RESEARCH PROGRESS REPORTS. 1– [Irregular]

C 55.610:nos.
ANTARCTIC SEISMOLOGICAL BULLETIN. [Quarterly]

PURPOSE:– To publish phase readings received by radio from Antarctic stations.
Issued by the National Ocean Survey and classified C 55.414 prior to the January-March 1971 issue.

C 55.611:v.nos.&nos.   • Item 191-A
EARTHQUAKE INFORMATION BULLETIN. 1967– [Bimonthly]

PURPOSE:– To provide current information on earthquake and seismological activities of interest to both general and specialized readers.
Earlier C 55.410, prior to v. 3, no. 5, September-October 1971.
Beginning with v. 5, no. 4, July-August 1973, issued by the Geological Survey (I 19.65).

C 55.612:date   • Item 208-B-10
COLLECTED REPRINTS, (year): ATLANTIC OCEANOGRAPHIC AND METEOROLOGICAL LABORATORIES. 1970– [Annual]

C 55.612/2:date   • Item 208-B-10
COLLECTED REPRINTS, (year) WAVE PROPAGATION LABORATORY. 1971– [Biennial] (Environmental Research Laboratories, Boulder, Colorado 80302)

C 55.612/3:date   • Item 208-B-10
COLLECTED REPRINTS, (year): ATMOSPHERIC PHYSICS AND CHEMISTRY LABORATORY. [Annual]
Discontinued.

C 55.613/2:date
ADMINISTRATIVE BULLETIN.

C 55.614:CT
ADDRESSES.

C 55.615:nos.
ERL PROGRAM PLAN (series). [Irregular]

C 55.615/2:date   • Item 207-C-3 (MF)
PROGRAMS AND PLANS, ENVIRONMENTAL RESEARCH LABORATORIES. [Annual]
Also published in microfiche.

C 55.616:CT   • Item 207-C-6
BIBLIOGRAPHIES AND LISTS OF PUBLICATIONS. [Irregular]

C 55.617:nos.   • Item 207-C-2
MESA [Marine Ecosystems Analysis Programs] REPORTS. 1– 1974– [Irregular] (Marine Ecosystems Analysis Program Office)
Discontinued.

C 55.618:nos.   • Item 207-C-5 (MF)
GEOPHYSICAL MONITORING FOR CLIMATIC CHANGE, SUMMARY REPORTS (numbered). [Irregular]

C 55.620:date   • Item 208-E-2 (MF)
GREAT LAKES ENVIRONMENTAL RESEARCH LABORATORY: ANNUAL REPORT 1st– 1977– (2300 Washtenaw Avenue, Ann Arbor, Michigan 48104)

C 55.620/2:date   • Item 208-E-2 (MF)
TECHNICAL PLAN FOR THE GREAT LAKES ENVIRONMENTAL RESEARCH LABORATORY. [Annual]
Discontinued.

C 55.621:yr.-nos.
AIR RESOURCES ATMOSPHERIC TURBULENCE AND DIFFUSION LABORATORY: ANNUAL REPORT.

C 55.622:date   • Item 208-C-7
ENVIRONMENTAL ASSESSMENT OF THE ALASKAN CONTINENTAL SHELF, PRINCIPAL INVESTIGATOR'S REPORTS. [Irregular]
Later C 55.433.

C 55.622/2:date   • Item 208-C-7 (MF)
ENVIRONMENTAL ASSESSMENT OF THE ALASKAN CONTINENTAL SHELF. [Annual]

PURPOSE:– To provide annual reports of the principal investigations conducted on the Alaskan Continental Shelf.
Also published in microfiche.
Discontinued.

C 55.622/3:CT   • Item 208-C-7 (MF)
ENVIRONMENTAL ASSESSMENT OF THE ALASKAN CONTINENTAL SHELF [various publications]. [Irregular]
Discontinued.

C 55.623:nos.   • Item 208-D
BAO REPORTS. 1– 1979– [Irregular] (Boulder Atmospheric Observatory)

Highly technical reports on such subjects as boundary- layer dynamics, air pollution chemistry, and relationships between these areas of science and larger-scale meteorology.
Discontinued.

C 55.624:CT   • Item 273-D-10
MAPS AND CHARTS. [Irregular]

C 55.625:date   • Item 208-E (MF)
NATIONAL SEVERE STORMS LABORATORY, ANNUAL REPORT, FISCAL YEAR (date).

Summarizes Laboratory activities in its function of studying severe storm circulations and dynamics and investigating techniques for improved storm detection and prediction.

C 55.626:date   • Item 207-C-7 (MF)
WEATHER RESEARCH PROGRAM, ANNUAL REPORT.

C 55.626/2:date   • Item 207-C-7 (MF)
PROGRAM FOR REGIONAL OBSERVING AND FORECASTING SERVICES. [Annual]

PURPOSE:– To summarize the activities of the program, whose mission is to improve short-range operational weather services through the development, testing and transfer of scientific and technological advances.

C 55.627:nos   • Item 207-C-5 (EL)
PRELIMINARY REPORT AND FORECAST OF SOLAR GEOPHYSICAL DATA.

C 55.628   • Item 207-C-8 (EL)
FSL FORUM. [Irregular]

NATIONAL EARTHQUAKE INFORMATION CENTER

C 55.690:date   • Item 192-C
PRELIMINARY DETERMINATION OF EPICENTERS, MONTHLY LISTING. (Information Center)

PURPOSE:– To provide a chronological listing of all earthquakes located by the National Ocean Survey to scientific and general users. Contains date and time of each shock, its geographic location, the region in which it centered and damage comments, its depth and magnitude, and the number of seismic stations used in computing these data.
Later I 19.66.

C 55.691:CT   • Item 192-C-1
NATIONAL EARTHQUAKE INFORMATION CENTER [Publications]. [Irregular]

OCEANIC AND ATMOSPHERIC RESEARCH OFFICE

INFORMATION

Oceanic and Atmospheric
  Research Office
National Oceanic and
  Atmospheric Administration
14th & Constitution Ave NW
Washington, DC 20230
(301) 713-2458
Fax: (301) 713-0163
http://www.oar.noaa.gov

C 55.702:   • Item 207-D
GENERAL PUBLICATIONS.

C 55.703:   • Item 207-D-1 (MF)
NATIONAL ACID PRECIPITATION ASSESSMENT PROGRAM, REPORT TO CONGRESS. [Biennial]

SOCIAL AND ECONOMIC STATISTICS ADMINISTRATION (1972–1975)

CREATION AND AUTHORITY

The Social and Economic Statistics Administration was established within the Department of Commerce on January 1, 1972 to which was transferred the Bureau of the Census (C 3) and the Office of Business Economics (C 43), which was renamed The Bureau of Economic Analysis. The Administration was abolished by Department of Commerce Organization Orders 35-1A and 2A, effective August 4, 1975. The Bureau of the Census (C 3) and the Bureau of Economic Analysis (C 59) were restored to independent status within the Department of Commerce.

C 56.1:date
ANNUAL REPORT.

C 56.2:CT   • Item 147-D-1
GENERAL PUBLICATIONS.

C 56.9:v.nos.
LIBRARY NOTES.
        Earlier C 3.207

BUREAU OF ECONOMIC ANALYSIS (1972–1975)

CREATION AND AUTHORITY

The Bureau of Economic Analysis was established within the Social and Economic Statistics Administration of the Department of Commerce on January 1, 1971 by the Secretary of Commerce to supersede the former Office of Business Economics (C 43). The Bureau regained independent status within the Department of Commerce (C 59) when the Social and Economic Statistics Administration was abolished by Department Organization Orders 35-1A and 2A, effective August 4, 1975.

C 56.101:date
ANNUAL REPORT.
        Earlier C 43.1
        Later C 59.1

C 56.102:CT   • Item 130-D-1
GENERAL PUBLICATIONS.
        Earlier C 43.2
        Later C 59.2

C 56.107:nos.
PRESS RELEASES. [Irregular]
        Earlier C 43.7

C 56.109:v.nos.&nos.   • Item 228
SURVEY OF CURRENT BUSINESS. v. 1–   1921–
[Monthly]

        Index by: Index to U.S. Government Periodicals.
        Earlier C 43.8
        Later C 59.11

C 56.109/2:date   • Item 229
BUSINESS STATISTICS, WEEKLY SUPPLEMENT TO SURVEY OF CURRENT BUSINESS.
        (Included in subscription to Survey of Current Business)
        Earlier C 43.8/2
        Later C 59.11/2

C 56.109/3:date   • Item 228
BUSINESS STATISTICS, BIENNIAL SUPPLEMENT TO SURVEY OF CURRENT BUSINESS.
        Earlier C 43.8/4
        Later C 59.11/3

C 56.109/4:CT   • Item 228
SPECIAL SUPPLEMENTS TO SURVEY OF CURRENT BUSINESS.
        Earlier C 43.8/3
        Later C 59.11/4

C 56.110:date   • Item 142-E
DEFENSE INDICATORS. 1968–   [Monthly] (ES 2)

        Supersedes Selected Economic Indicator (D 143) published by the Department of Defense.
        Earlier C 3.241
        Later C 59.10

C 56.111:date   • Item 131-A
BUSINESS CONDITIONS DIGEST. 1961–   [Monthly] (ES 1)

        Formerly Business Cycle Developments. Subscription service includes a separate summary table Advanced BCD (C 56.111/2), which is mailed in advance of the monthly reports.
        Indexed by: Index to U.S. Government Periodicals.
        Earlier C 3.226
        Later C 59.9

C 56.111/2   • Item 131-A
ADVANCE BCD, [Business Conditions Digest]. [Monthly] (Included in subscription to Business Conditions Digest)
        Later C 59.9/3

C 56.112:P-nos./nos.   • Item 139
INTERNATIONAL POPULATION STATISTICS REPORTS. P- (series) [Irregular]
        Earlier C 3.205

C 56.112/2:P-(nos./nos.)   • Item 142-C
INTERNATIONAL POPULATION REPORTS SERIES.
        (Foreign Demographic Analysis Division)
        Earlier C 3.186:P

C 56.113:nos.   • Item 142-G
BUREAU OF ECONOMIC ANALYSIS STAFF PAPERS, BEA-SP- (series). 1–   1963–   [Irregular]
        Later C 59.14

C 56.114:v.nos.&nos.
SESA INQUIRIES. Admin.

BUREAU OF THE CENSUS (1972–1975)

CREATION AND AUTHORITY

The Bureau of Census (C 3) was established within the Social and Economic Statistics Administration on January 1, 1972. The Bureau regained independent status within the Department of Commerce (C 3) when the Administration was abolished by Organization Orders 35-1A and 2A, effective August 4, 1975.

C 56.201:date
ANNUAL REPORT.
        See also C 3.1

C 56.202:CT   • Item 146
GENERAL PUBLICATIONS.
        See also C 3.2

C 56.206:CT   • Item 147
REGULATIONS, RULES AND INSTRUCTIONS.

C 56.207:date-nos.   • Item 146
PRESS RELEASES.
        See also C 3.209

C 56.208:CT   • Item 146-A
HANDBOOKS, MANUALS, GUIDES.

C 56.209   • Item 146-E
GOVERNMENTAL FINANCES, GF- (series). 1–
        1965–   [Annual]
        See also C 3.191/2

C 56.209/2   • Item 148-A
GOVERNMENT EMPLOYMENT, GE (series). [Irregular]

C 56.210:nos.&date   • Item 144
U.S. FOREIGN TRADE [Reports].
        See also C 3.164

CURRENT IMPORTS

FT 146 U.S. IMPORT FOR CONSUMPTION, TSUSA COMMODITY BY COUNTRY OF ORIGIN. – May 1974. [Monthly]

        Presents data on the net quantity and dollar value in terms of Customs appraisal, transaction value at port of exportation (free alongside ship– f.a.s.), value at port of entry (cost, insurance, freight– c.i.f.), and import charges of U.S. imports classified according to the Tariff Schedules of the United States Annotated (TSUSA). The data are presented for the current month and cumulative to date for the current year. Figures for each TSUSA commodity are given by country of origin under the following TSUSA schedules: Animal and vegetable products; wood and paper, and printed matter; textiles fibers and textile products; nonmetallic minerals and products; metals and metal products; specified products and miscellaneous and nonenumerated products; and special classification provisions. Similar figures are given in an appendix to the tariff schedules.
        A technical explanation of the new import data, including the definition for each valuation used in this report, is presented in the introduction.

C 56.210/2:date   • Item 146-G
GUIDE TO FOREIGN TRADE STATISTICS, (year). [Annual] (Foreign Trade Division)
        See also C 3.6/2:F 76
        Discontinued.

C 56.210/3:letters-date • Item 148
U.S. FOREIGN TRADE: SCHEDULES.
See also C 3.150

C 56.210/4:nos.
U.S. GENERAL IMPORTS [various commodities].
See also C 3.164/2-2 through 2-8

C 56.211:nos. • Item 140-A
CONSTRUCTION REPORTS: HOUSING COMPLE-
TIONS, C 22- (series). C 22-69– 1970–
[Monthly]
See also C 3.215/13

C 56.211/2:nos. • Item 140-A
CONSTRUCTION REPORTS: NEW ONE- FAMILY
HOMES SOLD AND FOR SALE, C 25- (series).
[Monthly]
See also C 3.21/9

C 56.211/2-2:nos. • Item 140-A
CONSTRUCTION REPORT: PRICE INDEX OF NEW
ONE-FAMILY HOUSES SOLD, C 27-(series).
[Quarterly]
See C 3.215/9-2

C 56.211/3:nos. • Item 140-A
CONSTRUCTION REPORTS: HOUSING STARTS, C
20- (Series). [Monthly]

Previous title: Nonfarm Housing Starts in
(month).
See also C 3.215/2

C 56.211/4:nos. • Item 140-A
CONSTRUCTION REPORTS: HOUSING AUTHORIZED
BY BUILDING PERMITS AND PUBLIC CON-
TRACTS, C 40 (series).
See also C 3.215/4

C 56.211/5:nos. • Item 140-A
CONSTRUCTION REPORTS: VALUE OF NEW CON-
STRUCTION PUT IN PLACE, C 30-(Series).
[Monthly]
See also C 3.215/3

C 56.211/6:nos. • Item 140-A
CONSTRUCTION REPORTS: AUTHORIZED
CONSTRUCTION, WASHINGTON, D.C. AREA,
C 41-(Series). [Monthly]

See also C 3.21/5

C 56.211/7:nos. • Item 140-A
CONSTRUCTION REPORTS: RESIDENTIAL ALTER-
ATIONS AND REPAIRS, EXPENDITURES ON
RESIDENTIAL ADDITIONS, ALTERATIONS, MAIN-
TENANCE AND REPAIRS, AND REPLACEMENTS,
C 50-(Series). 1– 1961– [Annual]

Issued quarterly during 1961, annually since
1962. Beginning with data for 1963, issued in two
parts.

Part 1– EXPENDITURES IN RESIDENTIAL ADDI-
TIONS, ALTERATIONS, MAINTENANCE AND
REPAIRS, AND REPLACEMENTS.

Part 2– EXPENDITURES FOR ADDITIONS, AL-
TERATIONS, MAINTENANCE AND REPAIRS,
AND REPLACEMENTS ON 1-HOUSING-UNIT
OWNER-OCCUPIED PROPERTIES.

See also C 3.215/8

C 56.211/8:date • Item 140-A
CONSTRUCTION REPORTS: HOUSING UNITS
AUTHORIZED FOR DEMOLITION IN PERMIT-
ISSUING PLACES, (year), C 45-(Series). 1968–
[Annual]
See also C 3.215/12

C 56.212:nos. • Item 142-D
DATA ACCESS DESCRIPTION: COLLECTION, EVALU-
ATION, AND PROCESSING SERIES. CEP 1–
1968– [Irregular]
See also C 3.240/5

C 56.212/2:nos.
CENSUS USERS BULLETINS. 1– 1972–
[Irregular] (Office of the Director)

C 56.212/3:nos. • Item 142-D
DATA ACCESS DESCRIPTIONS: CENSUS TABULA-
TIONS AVAILABLE ON COMPUTER TAPE SE-
RIES, CT- (Series).
See also C 3.240/3

C 56.212/4:nos. • Item 142-D
DATA ACCESS DESCRIPTIONS: ECONOMIC
CENSUSES PRINTED REPORTS SERIES, ECPR
(series). 1– 1972– [Irregular]

PURPOSE:– To provide a means of introduction to means of access to Bureau of the Census
data.

C 56.212/5:nos. • Item 142-D
DATA ACCESS DESCRIPTION: CENSUS GEOGRAPHY
SERIES, CG-(nos.). 1– 1969– [Irregular]
See also C 3.240/6

C 56.212/6:CT • Item 146
DATA ACCESS DESCRIPTIONS: MISCELLANEOUS
SERIES.
Later C 3.240/7

C 56.213:nos. • Item 140-B-1
CONGRESSIONAL DISTRICT DATA, CDD- (Series).
See also C 3.134/4

C 56.213/2:date • Item 140-B
CONGRESSIONAL DISTRICT ATLAS. (Geography
Division)
See also C 3.62/5

C 56.213/3:nos.
CONGRESSIONAL DISTRICT DATA, COMPUTER PRO-
FILE.

C 56.214:nos. • Item 141-A
CURRENT HOUSING REPORTS.
See also C 3.215
Includes the following sub-series:

H-111. HOUSING VACANCIES. [Quarterly] (Subscription includes H-111 and H-121 series)
H-121. HOUSING CHARACTERISTICS. [Irregular]

C 56.214/2:nos. • Item 141-A
CURRENT HOUSING REPORTS, H-150-(series).
[Irregular]

C 56.215:nos. • Item 151-C
TECHNICAL NOTES. 1– 1968– [Irregular]
See also C 3.212/2

C 56.215/2 • Item 151-A
TECHNICAL PAPERS. 1– [Irregular]
See also C 3.212

C 56.26:letters-nos. • Item 142-A
CURRENT INDUSTRIAL REPORTS. [Varies]
See also C 3.158

C 56.217:v.nos.&nos. • Item 148-C
DATA USER NEWS. [Monthly]

Former title: Small-Area Data Notes, prior to
v. 10, no. 2, Feb. 1975.
See also C 3.238

C 56.217/2:nos.
SMALL-AREA STATISTICS, GE-41- (Series). [Irregu-
lar]

C 56.218:P-nos.&nos. • Item 142-C
CURRENT POPULATION REPORTS. 1947–
[Varies]

(Subscription includes Series P-20, P-23,
P-25, P-26, P-27, P-28 summaries, P-60, and
P-65 for one year)
See also C 3.186

C 56.218/2:nos. • Item 139
COUNTRY DEMOGRAPHIC PROFILES FOR FOREIGN
COUNTRY SERIES, ISP 30-(Series). 1– 1973–
[Irregular]

C 56.219:nos. • Item 147-C
CURRENT BUSINESS REPORTS: MONTHLY WHOLE-
SALE TRADE, SALES AND INVENTORIES, BW-
(Series).
See also C 3.133

C 56.219/2:nos. • Item 146-D
CURRENT BUSINESS REPORTS: GREEN COFFEE,
INVENTORIES, IMPORTS, ROASTINGS, BG-(Se-
ries). [Quarterly]
See also C 3.236

C 56.219/3:nos. • Item 148-B
SPECIAL CURRENT BUSINESS REPORTS: MONTHLY
DEPARTMENT STORE SALES IN SELECTED
AREAS, BD- (Series).
See also C 3.211/5

C 56.219/4:nos. • Item 147-B
CURRENT BUSINESS REPORTS: MONTHLY RETAIL
TRADE, SALES AND ACCOUNTS RECEIVABLE,
BR- (series).

(Includes Weekly Retail Sales [C 56.219/7]
and Annual Retail Sales Report [C 56.219/4-2])
See also C 3.138/3

C 56.219/4-2:date • Item 147-B
CURRENT BUSINESS REPORTS: RETAIL TRADE.
[Annual]
(Included with Monthly Retail Trade [C 56.219/
4])
See also C 3.138/3-2

C 56.219/5:nos. • Item 141-C
CURRENT BUSINESS REPORTS: MONTHLY
SELECTED SERVICE RECEIPTS, BS-(Series).
See also C 3.239

C 56.219/6:nos. • Item 141-C
CURRENT BUSINESS REPORTS: ADVANCE
MONTHLY RETAIL SALES, CB- (Series).

(Included in subscription to Monthly Retail
Trade)
See also C 3.138/4

C 56.219/7:nos.
CURRENT BUSINESS REPORTS: WEEKLY RETAIL
SALES, CB- (Series).
(Included with Monthly Retail Trade [C 56.219/
4])
See also C 3.138/5

C 56.219/8:nos. • Item 131-B
CURRENT BUSINESS REPORTS: CANNED FOOD,
STOCK, PACK, SHIPMENTS, B-1-(Series). [5
times a year]
see also

C 56.220:CT • Item 131-D
CENSUS USE STUDIES.
See also C 3.244

C 56.221:letters-nos. • Item 134-A
ANNUAL SURVEY OF MANUFACTURES, M (date)
(AS) (series).
See also C 3.24/9

C 56.221/2:date • Item 134-A
ANNUAL SURVEY OF MANUFACTURES: ANNUAL
VOLUMES. 1949/50–
See also C 3.24/9-2

C 56.222:date • Item 138
BUREAU OF CENSUS CATALOG. 1946– [Quar-
terly to Annual]
See also C 3.163/3

C 56.222/2:date • Item 138
– MONTHLY SUPPLEMENT.

(Included with subscription to the Catalog)
See also C 3.163/2

C 56.222/2-2: • Item 138
– [HISTORICAL COMPILATIONS].

C 56.222/3:CT • Item 138
BIBLIOGRAPHIES AND LISTS OF PUBLICATIONS.

C 56.222/3:M 56/date • Item 138
CENSUS BUREAU METHODOLOGICAL
RESEARCH, (year), ANNOTATED LIST OF
PAPERS AND REPORTS. [Annual]
See also C 3.163/4

C 56.223:nos. • Item 148-A
CONSTRUCTION EXPENDITURE OF STATE AND LOCAL GOVERNMENTS, GC-(Series). [Quarterly]
See also C 3.215/10

C 56.223/10:date/v.&pt. nos. • Item 159
CENSUS OF POPULATION: SUBJECT REPORTS, PC(2) series. [Irregular]

C 56.223/12:date-nos. • Item 154
CENSUS OF POPULATION, (year), SUPPLEMENTARY REPORTS PC (S1)- (Series). [Irregular]
A series of reports on individual subjects from the Census of Population.

C 56.223/16:date/nos • Item 154
CENSUS OF POPULATION AND HOUSING: EVALUATION AND RESEARCH PROGRAM, PHC(E) series. [Irregular]

PURPOSE:– Designed to produce data on the accuracy of selected subject matter or on the effectiveness of specific methodological features of the census-taking process. Data are from the Census of Population and Housing.

C 56.224:nos. • Item 148-A
HOLDINGS OF SELECTED PUBLIC EMPLOYEE RETIREMENTS SYSTEMS, GR- (Series). [Quarterly]
See also C 3.242

C 56.226:nos./nos. • Item 146-F
SERIES ISP, CENTS [Census Tabulation System]. [Irregular] (International Statistical Programs Division)
See also C 3.205/3

C 56.226/2:nos.
INTERNATIONAL RESEARCH DOCUMENTS, ISP-RD- (Series). 1– 1975– [Irregular]

PURPOSE:– To provide a series of demographic and socio-economic reports and studies prepared for project sponsors or presented at conferences which may be of interest to professionals other than those for whom originally prepared.

C 56.227:date • Item 152-A-1 to 39
CENSUS OF AGRICULTURE: AREA REPORTS. [Irregular]

C 56.227/2:date • Item 152
CENSUS OF AGRICULTURE: SPECIAL REPORTS. [Irregular] (Agriculture Division)
See also C 3.31/5

C 56.227/3:date • Item 152
CENSUS OF AGRICULTURE: FINAL VOLUMES [other than Area Reports and Special Reports]. [Irregular]
See also C 3.31/12

C 56.227/4: • Item 152-B-1– B-52
CENSUS OF AGRICULTURE: PRELIMINARY AND/OR ADVANCE REPORTS.

C 56.227/5:CT
CENSUS OF AGRICULTURE: GENERAL PUBLICATIONS.
Discontinued.v

C 56.228:nos • Item 142-B
ENTERPRISE STATISTICS, ES- (Series). [Irregular]
See also C 3.230

C 56.229:nos. • Item 151-B
WORKING PAPERS. 1– 1954– [Irregular]
See also C 3.214

C 56.229/2:nos. • Item 151-B
WORKING PAPERS, PUBLICATION ORDER FORMS. 1– [Irregular]

C 56.230:nos. • Item 141-A
CURRENT HOUSING REPORTS: MARKET ABSORPTION OF APARTMENTS, H-130- (Series). [Quarterly]

Issued jointly with the Department of Housing and Urban Development.

C 56.231 • Item 148-A
STATE AND LOCAL GOVERNMENT SPECIAL STUDIES. 1– 1936– [Irregular]
See also C 3.145

C 56.231/2:date • Item 146-E
QUARTERLY SUMMARY OF STATE AND LOCAL TAX REVENUE, GT- (Series).
See also C 3.145/6

C 56.232:nos. • Item 160-B
U.S. COMMODITY EXPORTS AND IMPORTS AS RELATED TO OUTPUT. ES 2, No. 1– 1958/59– [Annual]
See also C 3.229

C 56.233:nos. • Item 133-A
COUNTY BUSINESS PATTERNS, (year), CBP (series). 1st. ed.– 1943– [Annual] (Economic Statistics and Surveys Division)
See also C 3.204

C 56.234:nos. • Item 146-H
WE THE AMERICANS (series). 1– 1972– [Irregular]
Reports from the 1970 census.
Discontinued.

C 56.235:nos. • Item 131-C
CENSUS TRACT PAPERS, GE-40- (Series). 1– 1966– [Irregular]

C 56.235/2 • Item 131-C
CENSUS TRACT MEMOS. 1– 1961– [Irregular]
See also C 3.227

C 56.236:CT
CENSUS OF MINERAL INDUSTRIES [Publications]. [Irregular]

C 56.236/2:letters-nos.
CENSUS OF MINERAL INDUSTRIES: PRELIMINARY REPORTS. [Irregular]

C 56.236/3:date/nos. • Item 158
CENSUS OF MINERAL INDUSTRIES: [Industry] BULLETINS MI- (Series). [Irregular]
See also C 3.216

C 56.236/4:date/nos. • Item 158
CENSUS OF MINERAL INDUSTRIES: AREA SERIES. [Irregular]
See also C 3.216/2

C 56.236/5:date/nos. • Item 158
CENSUS OF MINERAL INDUSTRIES: SUBJECT SERIES. [Irregular]
See also C 3.216/4

C 56.236/6:date • Item 157
CENSUS OF MINERAL INDUSTRIES: SUBJECT, INDUSTRY, AND AREA STATISTICS. [Irregular]

C 56.237:nos. • Item 142-F
COMPUTERIZED GEOGRAPHIC CODING, GE 60- (Series). 1– 1971– [Irregular]
Discontinued.

C 56.238:date
FOREIGN STATISTICAL PUBLICATIONS, ACCESSIONS LIST. [Quarterly]

(Limited Distribution) (International Statistical Programs Division)
See also C 3.199

C 56.239:nos. • Item 141
COTTON GINNINGS, REPORT ON COTTON GINNINGS BY COUNTIES, A 20- (Series). [6 times a year]
See also C 3.20/3

C 56.239/2:nos. • Item 141
COTTON GINNINGS, REPORT ON COTTON GINNINGS BY STATES, A 10- (Series). [Irregular]
See also C 3.20

C 56.239/3:date
COTTON GINNINGS, REPORT ON COTTON GINNINGS. (by States) A10– (series)
Earlier C 3.20
Later C 3.20/3

C 56.240 • Item 146-J
EMPLOYMENT AND POPULATION CHANGES, SPECIAL ECONOMIC REPORTS, ES 20- (Series).
Discontinued.

C 56.241:nos.
DAUList (series). 1–

C 56.242:nos. • Item 146-K
UNITED STATES MAPS, GE 50- (Series). [Irregular]
See also C 3.62/4

C 56.242/2:nos. • Item 146-K
U.S. MAPS, GE 70- (Series). 1– 1973– [Irregular]

C 56.242/3:CT
MAPS. (miscellaneous)
Earlier C 3.62/2

C 56.242/4:nos.
URBAN ATLAS, TRACT DATA FOR STANDARD METROPOLITAN STATISTICAL AREAS, GE 80- (Series). [Irregular]
See also C 3.62/7

C 56.243:date • Item 150
STATISTICAL ABSTRACT OF THE UNITED STATES. 1st ed– 1879– [Annual]
See also C 3.134
The following titles have been issued as supplements to the Abstract:

C 56.243/2:CT • Item 151
SUPPLEMENTS TO THE STATISTICAL ABSTRACT OF THE UNITED STATES.
See also C 3.134/2

C 56.243/2:C 76 • **Item 151**
CONGRESSIONAL DISTRICT DATA BOOK. 87th
Cong. 1961–   [Irregular]
See also C 3.134/2:C 76

C 56.243/2:C 83 • **Item 151**
COUNTY AND CITY DATA BOOK. [Irregular]
See also C 3.134/2:C 83/2

C 56.243/3:date • **Item 151**
POCKET DATA BOOK. 1967–   [Biennial]
See also C 3.134/3

C 56.244 • **Item 134**
CENSUS OF MANUFACTURES: FINAL VOLUMES.
See also C 3.24/1

C 56.244/2:CT • **Item 135**
CENSUS OF MANUFACTURES: GENERAL PUBLICA-
TIONS.

C 56.244/3:date/nos. • **Item 135**
CENSUS OF MANUFACTURES: SUPPLEMENTARY
REPORTS.

See also C 3.24/15

C 56.244/4:date
CENSUS OF MANUFACTURES: ANNOUNCEMENTS
AND ORDER FORMS.
Earlier C 3.24/10

C 56.244/5:date-nos.
CENSUS OF MANUFACTURES: PRELIMINARY RE-
PORTS. [Irregular]
See also C 3.24/8

C 56.244/6:date/nos. • **Item 136**
CENSUS OF MANUFACTURES: INDUSTRY SERIES
MC- (nos.) [Irregular] (Industry Division)

For each of the 450 manufacturing industries
(or groups of industries), the reports provide preliminary industry totals for quantity and value of
products shipped, value added by manufacture,
cost of materials, expenditures for new plant and
equipment, and employment. Tables present U.S.
industry totals for general statistics; geographic
division and State industry totals for general statistics; quantity and value of individual products
shipped; and quantity and cost of materials consumed by establishments in the industry. The
data are presented with comparable historical data.
See also C 3.24/4

C 56.244/7:date/nos. • **Item 137**
CENSUS OF MANUFACTURES: AREA SERIES.
[Irregular]

Each State report presents general manufacturing statistics for the State, Standard Metropolitan Statistical Areas, and counties.

C 56.244/8:date/nos. • **Item 135**
CENSUS OF MANUFACTURES: MANUFACTURERS'
INVENTORIES. [Irregular]
See also C 3.24/12

C 56.245:nos. • **Item 227-B**
MANUFACTURERS' SHIPMENTS, INVENTORIES AND
ORDERS, M3- (Series).
See also C 3.231

C 56.246:CT • **Item 160-D**
CENSUS OF TRANSPORTATION: GENERAL PUBLI-
CATIONS. [Irregular]
See also C 3.233

C 56.246/2:date/nos. • **Item 160-D**
CENSUS OF TRANSPORTATION: FINAL REPORTS.
See also C 3.233/2 and C 3.233/5

C 56.246/3:v.nos. • **Item 160-D**
CENSUS OF TRANSPORTATION: [Volumes]. [Irregu-
lar]

C 56.247:date/nos. • **Item 148-A**
CENSUS OF GOVERNMENTS: PRELIMINARY RE-
PORTS.
See also C 3.145/5

C 56.247/2:date/v.nos.&nos. • **Item 148-A**
CENSUS OF GOVERNMENTS. [Irregular]
See also C 3.145/4

C 56.248:nos.
RESEARCH DOCUMENTS. 1–   [Irregular] (International Demographic Statistics Center)

C 56.249:date
BOUNDARY AND ANNEXATION SURVEY, ANNUAL
REPORTS.
See also C 3.260

C 56.250:nos. • **Item 160-E**
SURVEY OF MINORITY-OWNED BUSINESS ENTER-
PRISES, MB (series). [Irregular]

See also C 3.258

C 56.251:CT • **Item 133**
CENSUS OF RETAIL TRADE: GENERAL PUBLICA-
TIONS. [Irregular]

See also C 3.255

C 56.251/2:date/nos. • **Item 132-A-10**
CENSUS OF RETAIL TRADE: AREA STATISTICS (series). [Irregular] (Business Division)

This series of reports presents data by kind
of business for States, standard metropolitan
statistical areas (SMSA's), areas outside SMSA's,
counties and cities with 500 establishments or
more, cities of 2,500 inhabitants or more, and all
counties (but in less kind-of- business detail).
Data are provided on number of establishments,
sales, payroll, and employees; and on number of
proprietorship and partnership establishments.
Data are also given for States and SMSA's based
on 1967 Standard Industrial Classifications. The
appendixes provide and explanation of terms and
other pertinent information.
See also C 3.255/2

C 56.251/3:date/nos. • **Item 133**
CENSUS OF RETAIL TRADE: SUBJECT REPORTS.
[Irregular]

See also C 3.255/3

C 56.251/4:date/letters • **Item 133**
CENSUS OF RETAIL TRADE: RETAIL MERCHANDISE
LINES SERVICE. [Irregular]

See also C 3.255/4

C 56.251/5:date/nos. • **Item 132-A-1–A-54**
CENSUS OF RETAIL TRADE: MAJOR RETAIL
CENTERS IN STANDARD METROPOLITAN STA-
TISTICAL AREAS, RC-(Series). [Irregular] (Busi-
ness Division)

See also C 3.255/5

C 56.251/6:date • **Item 132**
CENSUS OF RETAIL TRADE: FINAL VOLUMES.
[Quinquennial]

Supersedes Census of Business, Retail Trade.

C 56.251/7: • **Item 132-A-1–A-54**
CENSUS OF RETAIL TRADE: PRELIMINARY AREA
REPORTS.

C 56.252:CT • **Item 133**
CENSUS OF WHOLESALE TRADE: GENERAL
PUBLICATIONS. [Irregular]
See also C 3.256

C 56.252/2:letters-nos. • **Item 132-A-1– A-54**
CENSUS OF WHOLESALE TRADE: PRELIMINARY
AREA SERIES. [Irregular]

See also C 3.202/12-2

C 56.252/3:date-nos. • **Item 132-A-1–A-54**
CENSUS OF WHOLESALE TRADE: AREA STATIS-
TICS (series). [Irregular] (Business Division)

This series of reports presents data by kind
of business for States, standard metropolitan
statistical areas (SMSA's), counties and cities
with 300 establishments or more and cities of
2,500 inhabitants or more and all counties (but in
less kind-of-business detail). Data are provided
on number of establishments, receipts, payrolls,
and employees, and on number of proprietorship
and partnership establishments. Data are also
given for States and SMSA's based on 1967 Standard Industrial Classifications. The appendixes
provide an explanation of terms and other pertinent information.
See also C 3.256/2

C 56.252/4:letters-nos. • **Item 133**
CENSUS OF WHOLESALE TRADE: SUBJECT SE-
RIES. [Irregular]
See also C 3.256/3

C 56.252/5 • **Item 132**
CENSUS OF WHOLESALE TRADE: FINAL VOLUMES.
[Irregular]

See also C 3.256/4

C 56.253:CT • **Item 133**
CENSUS OF SELECTED SERVICE INDUSTRIES:
GENERAL PUBLICATIONS. [Irregular]

See also C 3.257

C 56.253/2:letters-nos. • **Item 132-A-1– A-54**
CENSUS OF SELECTED SERVICE INDUSTRIES:
PRELIMINARY AREA SERIES. [Irregular]

See also C 3.202/12-2

C 56.253/3:date-nos. • **Item 132-A-1– A-54**
CENSUS OF SELECTED SERVICE INDUSTRIES:
AREA STATISTICS SERIES. [Irregular]
See also C 3.257/2

C 56.253/4 • **Item 133**
CENSUS OF SELECTED SERVICE INDUSTRIES:
SUBJECT REPORTS. [Irregular]
See also C 3.257/3

C 56.253/5:date • **Item 132**
CENSUS OF SELECTED SERVICE INDUSTRIES:
FINAL VOLUMES. [Quinquennial]

Supersedes Census of Business: Selected
Service Industries.

C 56.254:CT
CENSUS OF CONSTRUCTION INDUSTRIES: GEN-
ERAL PUBLICATIONS. [Irregular]
See also C 3.245/2

C 56.254/2:date
CENSUS OF CONSTRUCTION INDUSTRIES: PRE-
LIMINARY REPORTS. [Monthly]
See also C 3.245

C 56.254/3:date/nos. • **Item 133-D-2**
CENSUS OF CONSTRUCTION INDUSTRIES: FINAL
REPORTS. 1–   1967–   [Irregular]
See also C 3.245/3

C 56.254/4:nos. • **Item 133-D-2**
CENSUS OF CONSTRUCTION INDUSTRIES: AREA
STATISTICS. [Irregular]

C 56.254/5:nos. • **Item 133-D-2**
CENSUS OF CONSTRUCTION INDUSTRIES:
SPECIAL REPORTS.
See also C 3.245/5

C 56.254/6:date • **Item 133-D-2**
CENSUS OF CONSTRUCTION INDUSTRIES: BOUND
VOLUMES. [Quinquennial]

See also C 3.245.6

C 56.255:CT or nos. • **Item 131-E**
GEOGRAPHIC BASE (DIME) FILE, CUE, [Correction-
update-extension]. (Geography Division)

See also C 56.202:G 29

C 56.256:nos.
METHODOLICAL RESEARCH DOCUMENTATION,
QUARTERLY LIST.

C 56.257:CT
ADDRESSES. [Irregular]

See also C 3.132

C 56.258:yr.-nos.
CENSUS PORTRAITS. CP 73-1–   1974–

Each report in the CP-73 series is a concise summary of basic information from the 1960 and 1970 Censuses of Population and Housing and the 1969 and 1964 Censuses of Agriculture. Separate report issued for each State, the District of Columbia, and Puerto Rico.

C 56.259:nos.   • Item 147-A-1
ECONOMIC CENSUSES OF OUTLYING AREAS. [Irregular]

See also C 3.253/2

C 56.260:nos.   • Item 160-E
SURVEY OF MINORITY-OWNED BUSINESS ENTERPRISES, MB- (Series). [Irregular]

INDUSTRY AND TRADE ADMINISTRATION
(1977– 1980)

CREATION AND AUTHORITY

The Domestic and International Business Administration was established within the Department of Commerce by Department Organization Order 40-1, effective November 17, 1972. The name was changed to Industry and Trade Administration in 1977. The Administration was abolished and its functions transferred to the International Trade Administration (C 61) on January 2, 1980.

C 57.1:date
ANNUAL REPORTS.

C 57.2:CT   • Item 231-B-1
GENERAL PUBLICATIONS.

C 57.7:nos.
PRESS RELEASES. [Irregular]

C 57.8:CT   • Item 231-B-5
HANDBOOKS, MANUALS, GUIDES. [Irregular]

C 57.9:CT
ADDRESSES.

C 57.10:date
UNITED STATES EXPORTS OF ALUMINUM. [Annual]

Separate reports issued for preliminary and final data.
Earlier C 41.112/2

C 57.10/2:date
UNITED STATES IMPORTS OF ALUMINUM. [Annual]

Separate reports issued for preliminary and final data.
Earlier C 41.112/3

C 57.11:nos.   • Item 231-B
OVERSEAS BUSINESS REPORTS. [Irregular]

Combines the three parts of the former World Trade Information Service (C 49.8). Prior to September 1964, published by the Bureau of International Commerce, and later is released as a separate.
Later C 61.12

C 57.12:date   • Item 231-B-2
OVERSEAS TRADE PROMOTION CALENDAR.

Later C 57.117

C 57.13:date   • Item 215-D
CONFECTIONARY MANUFACTURERS' SALES AND DISTRIBUTION. 1st–   1929–   [Annual]

This annual survey is conducted at the request and with the financial support of the National Confectioners Association, assisted by the National Candy Wholesalers Association and the Chocolate Manufacturers Association.
Statistical tables give production sales, consumption, and foreign trade.
Earlier C 41.19.

Discontinued.

C 57.14:date
ALUMINUM IMPORTS AND EXPORTS. [Monthly]

Statistical tables gives for sources of supply: domestic primary production, unwrought imports, domestic secondary recovery, recovery from imported scrap, imports of mill products, and total sources of supply; for shipments of products to consumers: total, reported for defense, and other.
ISSN 0364-8524
Published by the Bureau of Domestic Commerce prior to the November 1972 issue (C 41.112).

C 57.15:CT   • Item 231-B-3
BIBLIOGRAPHIES AND LISTS OF PUBLICATIONS.

Later C 61.15

C 57.16:date   • Item 231-B-4
FRANCHISE OPPORTUNITIES HANDBOOK. [Annual]

Earlier C 41.6/9:F 84
Later C 62.14

C 57.17:CT
TRADE DATA (series).

C 57.18:date   • Item 215-L
U.S. INDUSTRIAL OUTLOOK. 1960–   [Annual]

Earlier C 57.309
Later C 62.17

C 57.19:date
INTERNATIONAL ECONOMIC INDICATORS AND COMPETITIVE TRENDS. [Monthly] (International Trade Analysis Staff)

PURPOSE:– To present a wide variety of comparative economic statistics for the United States and seven major competitor nations (France, Federal Republic of Germany, Italy, Netherlands, United Kingdom, Japan, and Canada) for recent periods.
Statements on the economic outlook and recent past trends comprise Section 1. Tables and charts of Section 2 compare quarterly changes in key competitive indicators. Section 3 includes monthly, quarterly, and annual indicators in 108 tabulations. Technical notes, definitions, and sources are provided in Section 4.
Earlier C 42.34

C 57.19/2:date   • Item 231-B-6
INTERNATIONAL ECONOMIC INDICATORS AND COMPETITIVE TRENDS. [Quarterly] (International Trade Analysis Staff)

Indexed by: Index to U.S. Government Periodicals.
ISSN 0149-1873
Later C 61.14

C 57.20:   • Item 231-G-3
COMMERCE BUSINESS DAILY. [Daily, Monday– Friday]

Subtitle: Synopsis of U.S. Government Proposed Procurement, Sales, and Contract Awards.
The Synopsis is of particular value to firms interested in bidding on U.S. Government purchases, surplus property offered for sale, or in seeking subcontract opportunities from prime contractors. It lists current information received daily from military and civilian procurement offices.
ISSN 0095-3423
Earlier C 41.9

C 57.21:date   • Item 215-Q
WORLD MOTOR VEHICLE AND TRAILER PRODUCTION AND REGISTRATION. [Annual]

Earlier C 41.17
Discontinued.

C 57.22:CT
TRADE LISTS.

Earlier C 42.10

C 57.23:date
TRENDS IN U.S. FOREIGN TRADE. [Monthly]

C 57.24:date   • Item 215-U
U.S. LUMBER EXPORTS. [Annual]

Statistical tables give U.S. lumber imports, softwood lumber imports, and hardwood lumber imports, by species and area and country of destination.
Data compiled from Bureau of the Census Report FT 125, United States Imports of Merchandise for Consumption.
Earlier C 41.101

Discontinued.

C 57.24/2:date   • Item 215-U
U.S. LUMBER IMPORTS. [Annual]

C 57.25:date   • Item 231-B-8
VOLUNTARY INDUSTRIAL ENERGY CONSERVATION. [Quarterly]

Later E 1.22

C 57.26:CT
BUREAU OF INTERNATIONAL ECONOMIC POLICY AND RESEARCH: REPORTS, STUDIES, DATA.

C 57.27:date   • Item 231-B-9
TRADE OPPORTUNITY PROGRAM, TOP BULLETIN. [Weekly]

Later C 61.13

C 57.28:date
U.S. TRADE STATUS WITH COMMUNIST COUNTRIES. [Monthly]

Earlier C 57.413

C 57.29:CT   • Item 231-M-1– -50
STATE EXPORT SERIES. [Irregular]

Series of 50 reports, one for each State, consisting of data in tabular and graphic form on various kinds of exports.
Later C 61.30

C 57.30:date   • Item 130
REPORT ON U.S. EXPORT CONTROLS TO THE PRESIDENT AND THE CONGRESS. 1st–   1947– [Semiannual]

Report submitted by the Secretary of Commerce to Congress pursuant to the Export Control Act of 1949.
Earlier C 57.411
Later C 61.24

C 57.31:CT
AUDIOVISUAL MATERIALS. [Irregular]

BUREAU OF EXPORT DEVELOPMENT (1977–   )

CREATION AND AUTHORITY

The Bureau of International Commerce (C 42) was placed within the Domestic and International Business Administration of the Department of Commerce by Organization Order 40-1, effective November 17, 1972. In 1977, the name was changed to Bureau of Export Development.

INFORMATION

Bureau of Export Development
Department of Commerce
Washington, D. C. 20230

C 57.101:date
ANNUAL REPORTS.

Earlier C 42.1

C 57.102:CT • Item 231-A
GENERAL PUBLICATIONS.

C 57.108:CT • Item 231-E
HANDBOOKS, MANUALS, GUIDES.

Earlier C 42.6/2

C 57.109:CT • Item 231-G-1
GLOBAL MARKET SURVEYS.

Earlier C 42.33

C 57.110:date/nos. • Item 231-G
INDEX TO FOREIGN MARKET REPORTS. [Irregular]

Formerly Index to Foreign Production and Commercial Reports.
ISSN 0094-2634
Earlier C 42.15/3
Later C 61.16

C 57.111:nos. • Item 231-I
FOREIGN ECONOMIC TRENDS AND THEIR IMPLICATIONS FOR THE UNITED STATES, FET-(series). [Semiannual or Annual]

Separate reports issued for individual countries. Reports on larger countries issued semiannually.
Indexed by: Index to U.S. Government Periodicals.
ISSN 0090-9467
Earlier C 42.30

C 57.112:nos. • Item 231-G-1
COUNTRY MARKET SURVEYS, CMS-(series). [Irregular]

Prior to December 1973 entitled Export Market Digest.
These reports are bound together by industries and distributed as Global Market Surveys (C 57.109).
Later C 61.9

C 57.113:date
QUARTERLY SUMMARY OF FUTURE CONSTRUCTION ABROAD. (Trade Opportunities Section, Office of Export Development)

Earlier C 41.30/5
Discontinued.

C 57.114:nos. • Item 219-C
COMMERCIAL NEWS USA. [Bimonthly]

Former title: Commercial News for the Foreign Service.
ISSN 0161-9772

C 57.115:CT • Item 231-D
BIBLIOGRAPHIES AND LIST OF PUBLICATIONS.

C 57.115:In 2 • Item 231-D
INDEX TO INTERNATIONAL BUSINESS PUBLICATIONS. [Semiannual]

Earlier C 43.15:C 41

C 57.116:CT • Item 219-B
INTERNATIONAL MARKETING INFORMATION SERVICE, IMIS (series). 69-1– 1969–   [Irregular]

PURPOSE:– To serve in the Commerce Department's effort to increase U.S. exports. Includes Country Market Digest, Exhibitor's Export Market Guide, World Markets for U.S. Exports, Market Share Reports, and Country Market Surveys.
Earlier C 42.31

C 57.117:date • Item 231-B-2
OVERSEAS EXPORT PROMOTION CALENDAR. [Quarterly]
PURPOSE:– To help U.S. business firms take advantage of the extensive sales opportunities in overseas markets.
ISSN 0364-8362
Prior to July 1974 issued by the Domestic and International Business Administration and entitled Overseas Trade Promotions Calendar (C 57.12).

C 57.117/2:CT
INTERNATIONAL MARKETING EVENTS INFORMATION SERIES. [Irregular]

PURPOSE:– To provide a market research summary for individual industries in specific foreign countries.

C 57.117/3:CT • Item 231-B-10
INTERNATIONAL MARKETING EVENTS: EXPORT MARKETING GUIDES. [Irregular]

PURPOSE:– To provide summary information in support of trade promotion events, exhibitions, etc. for American exporters, and others. Includes data on trade potential, categories of trade, marketing information, trade groups, Commerce Department exhibition services, etc.

C 57.118:CT • Item 219-B
CONSUMER GOODS RESEARCH.

C 57.119:CT • Item 231-L
COUNTRY MARKET SECTORAL SURVEYS.

C 57.120:nos. • Item 231-P
FORMS.

C 57.121:CT • Item 231-A
DIRECTORIES.

BUREAU OF RESOURCES AND TRADE ASSISTANCE (1972–   )

CREATION AND AUTHORITY

The Bureau of Resources and Trade Assistance was established within the Domestic and International Business Administration of the Department of Commerce on November 17, 1972 by Department Organization Orders 10-3 and 40-1.

INFORMATION

Bureau of Resources and
Trade Assistance Bureau
Department of Commerce
Washington, D. C. 20230

C 57.201:date
ANNUAL REPORTS.

C 57.202:CT • Item 231-C-2
GENERAL PUBLICATIONS.

Discontinued.

C 57.208:CT
HANDBOOKS, MANUALS, GUIDES.

C 57.209:date
STEEL IMPORT DATA, SHIPMENTS FROM EXPORTING COUNTRIES IN CALENDAR YEAR.   – May 1975. [Annual] (Office of Import Programs)

Gives data by TSUSA number, country of origin, customs region, and grade.
Earlier C 41.114

C 57.210:CT • Item 231-C-1
BIBLIOGRAPHIES AND LISTS OF PUBLICATIONS. [Irregular]

Discontinued.

BUREAU OF COMPETITIVE ASSESSMENT AND BUSINESS POLICY (1972– 1974)

CREATION AND AUTHORITY

The Bureau of Competitive Assessment and Business Policy was established within the Domestic and International Business Administration of the Department of Commerce by Department Organization Order 40-1, effective November 17, 1972.

C 57.301:date
ANNUAL REPORTS.

Earlier C 41.1

C 57.302:CT • Item 215
GENERAL PUBLICATIONS. [Irregular]

C 57.309:date • Item 215-L
U.S. INDUSTRIAL OUTLOOK, (year), WITH PROJECTIONS TO (year). [Annual]

Earlier C 41.42/4
Later C 57.18

C 57.310:v.nos.&nos. • Item 219
CONSTRUCTION REVIEW. v. 1–   1955–   [Monthly] (Construction and Forest Products Division) (Industry Reports)

Indexed by: Index to U.S. Government Periodicals.
Prior to v. 19, no. 3 (March 1973) issued by the Bureau of Domestic Commerce (C 41.30/3).
Later C 57.509

C 57.311:v.nos.&nos. • Item 215-H
PRINTING AND PUBLISHING. [Quarterly] (Construction and Forest Products Division) (Industry Report)

Issued by the Bureau of Domestic Commerce (C 41.18) prior to v. 14, no. 1, January 1973.
Later C 57.510

C 57.312:v.nos.&nos. • **Item 220-A**
COPPER. v. 1– 1954– [Quarterly] (Including annual issue) (Materials Division) (Industry Report)

Annual statistical supplement issued separately (C 57.312/2)
Issued by the Bureau of Domestic Commerce (C 41.34) prior to v. 19, no. 2, January 1973.
Later C 57.512

C 57.312/2:nos. • **Item 220-A**
– (Year) ANNUAL STATISTICAL SUPPLEMENT. (Included in subscription of Copper) (Materials Division) (Industry Report)

Earlier C 41.341/2
Later C 57.512/2

C 57.313:v.nos.&nos. • **Item 223**
PULP, PAPER AND BOARD. v. 1– 1944– [Quarterly] (Includes annual review) (Construction and Forest Products Division) (Industry Report)

Issued by the Bureau of Domestic Commerce (C 41.32) prior to v. 28, no. 1, January 1973.
Later C 57.511

C 57.314:v.nos&nos. • **Item 220**
CONTAINERS AND PACKAGING. v. 1– 1948– [Quarterly] (Industry Report)

Earlier C 41.33
Later C 57.513

C 57.315:date
NOTICE TO TRADE [various commodities].

C 57.316:date • **Item 215-F**
SALAD DRESSING, MAYONNAISE AND RELATED PRODUCTS. [Annual]

Earlier C 41.88
Later C 57.514

EAST–WEST TRADE BUREAU
(1972–   )

CREATION AND AUTHORITY

The East-West Trade Bureau was established within the Domestic and International Business Administration of the Department of Commerce by Organization Order 40-1, effective November 17, 1972.

INFORMATION

East-West Trade Bureau
Department of Commerce
Washington, D.C. 20230

C 57.401:date
ANNUAL REPORTS.

C 57.402:CT • **Item 212-A-1**
GENERAL PUBLICATIONS. [Irregular]
Discontinued.

C 57.408:CT • **Item 212-A-3**
HANDBOOKS, MANUALS, GUIDES. [Irregular]
Discontinued.

C 57.409:date • **Item 211**
EXPORT ADMINISTRATION REGULATIONS. (Includes basic volume plus a set of dividers and supplementary material issued as Export Control Bulletins (C 57.409/2))

Entitled Comprehensive Export Schedule, prior to 1969.
ISSN 0094-8411
Earlier C 18.267. C 42.11, and C 42.208
Later C 61.23

C 57.409/2 • **Item 212**
EXPORT ADMINISTRATION BULLETIN. 1– 1969– [Irregular] (Included in subscription to Export Control Regulations)

Prior to no. 77, issued by the Bureau of International Commerce (C 42.11/3).
Prior to no. 104, November 19, 1973, entitled Export Control Bulletin.
ISSN 0363-8308

C 57.410:date
EXPORT LICENSES APPROVED AND REEXPORTS AUTHORIZED. [Daily]

ISSN 0364-5452
Earlier C 41.21
Later C 61.20

C 57.411:date • **Item 130**
EXPORT ADMINISTRATION REPORTS. 1st– [Semiannual]

Title varies: July/Sept.– Oct./Dec. 1947, Report under the Second Decontrol Act of 1947; Jan./Mar. 1948– Jan./Mar. 1950, Export Control and Allocation Powers; – Jan./Mar. 1973, Export Control, Quarterly Reports.
Report submitted by the Secretary of Commerce to Congress pursuant to the Export Control Act of 1949.
Earlier C 1.26

C 57.412:CT • **Item 212-A-2**
MARKET ASSESSMENTS FOR [various countries] [Irregular]

Discontinued.

C 57.413:date
U.S. TRADE STATUS WITH COMMUNIST COUNTRIES. [Monthly]

Earlier C 57.412:So 1
Later C 57.28

BUREAU OF DOMESTIC
COMMERCE
(1974– 1980)

CREATION AND AUTHORITY

The Bureau was abolished and its functions transferred to the Bureau of Industrial Economics (C 62) on January 2, 1980 pursuant to the Reorganization Plan of 1979 (44 Fr 69273).

C 57.501:date
ANNUAL REPORT.

C 57.502:CT • **Item 215**
GENERAL PUBLICATIONS. [Irregular]

Earlier C 57.302

C 57.508:CT • **Item 215-G**
HANDBOOKS, MANUALS, GUIDES. [Irregular]

Earlier C 41.6/9

C 57.509:v.nos.&nos. • **Item 219**
CONSTRUCTION REVIEW. v. 1– 1955– [Monthly] (Construction and Forest Products Division)

Indexed by:–
Business Periodicals Index.
Index to U.S. Government Periodicals.
Public Affairs Information Service.
ISSN 0010-6917
March-October 1973, issued by the Bureau of Competitive Assessment and Business Policy (C 57.310).
Later 62.10

C 57.510 • **Item 215**
PRINTING AND PUBLISHING. [Quarterly] (Construction and Forest Products Division) (Industry Report)

Indexed by: Index to U.S. Government Periodicals.
ISSN 0032-8588
Earlier C 57.311
Later C 62.9

C 57.511:v.nos.&nos. • **Item 223**
PULP, PAPER AND BOARD. v. 1– 1944– [Quarterly] (Includes annual review) (Construction and Forest Products Division) (Industry Report)

Indexed by: Index to U.S. Government Periodicals.
ISSN 0033-412X
Earlier C 57.313
Later C 62.11

C 57.512:v.nos.&nos. • **Item 220-A**
COPPER. v. 1– 1954– [Quarterly]

Annual statistical supplement issued separately (C 57.512/2).
ISSN 0097-7829
Earlier C 57.312

C 57.512/2:nos. • **Item 220-A**
COPPER, (year) ANNUAL STATISTICAL SUPPLEMENT. (included in subscription of Copper)

Earlier C 57.312/3
Later C 62.12/2

C 57.513:v.nos.&nos. • **Item 220**
CONTAINERS AND PACKAGING. v.1– 31. 1948– 1978. [Quarterly]

Indexed by: Index to U.S. Government Periodicals.
ISSN 0090-578X
Earlier C 57.314
Discontinued.

C 57.514:date • **Item 215-F**
SALAD DRESSING, MAYONNAISE, AND RELATED PRODUCTS. [Annual]

This annual survey is conducted at the request and with the financial support of several leading manufacturers, the Mayonnaise and Salad Dressing Institute, and the Glass Containers Manufacturers Association.
The Bureau of Census cooperates with BDSA in developing the statistics contained in the report and publishes the data in summary form in Current Industrial Report Series M-20 F, Salad Dressing, Mayonnaise and Related Products.
Statistics over production, consumption, sales and exports.
Earlier C 57.316

Discontinued.

C 57.515:CT
BIBLIOGRAPHIES AND LISTS OF PUBLICATIONS.

UNITED STATES FIRE ADMINISTRATION
(1978– 1979)

CREATION AND AUTHORITY

The National Fire Prevention and Control Administration was established by the Federal Fire Prevention and Control Act of 1974, approved October 29, 1974 (88 Stat. 1535; 15 U.S.C. 2201). In 1978, the name was changed to United States Fire Administration by act of October 5, 1978 (92 Stat. 932). The Administration was transferred to the Federal Emergency Management Agency (FEM 1.100) by Reorganization Plan No. 3 of 1978, effective April 1, 1979, pursuant to Executive Order 12127 of March 31, 1979.

C 58.1:date • **Item 216-A-2**
ANNUAL REPORT. 1st– 1974–

Later FEM 1.101

C 58.2:CT • **Item 216-A-1**
GENERAL PUBLICATIONS.

C 58.7:nos.
PRESS RELEASES.

Later FEM 1.102

C 58.8 • **Item 216-A-3**
HANDBOOKS, MANUALS, GUIDES.

C 58.9:CT
ADDRESSES.

C 58.10:date • **Item 215-L-1**
FIREWORD, A BULLETIN FROM THE NATIONAL FIRE PREVENTION AND CONTROL ADMINISTRATION. [Irregular]

ISSN 0145-1227
Discontinued.

C 58.11:v.nos.&nos • **Item 215-L-2**
FIRE TECHNOLOGY ABSTRACTS. v. 1– 1976– [Bimonthly]

ISSN 0148-6675
Later FEM 1.109

C 58.12:date • **Item 215-L-3**
CATALOG OF GRANTS, CONTRACTS, AND INTER-AGENCY TRANSFERS. [Annual]

PURPOSE:– To provide a status report on programs and projects of the National Fire Prevention and Research Office.
Discontinued.

C 58.13:date • **Item 216-A-2**
FIRE IN THE UNITED STATES. 1978– [Annual]

PURPOSE:– To provide data on deaths, injuries, dollar loss, and incidents at the National, State, and local levels.

BUREAU OF ECONOMIC ANALYSIS
(1975–)

CREATION AND AUTHORITY

The Bureau of Economic Analysis (C 56.100) regained independent status within the Department of Commerce when the Social and Economic Statistics Administration was abolished by Department Organization Orders 35-1A and 2A, effective August 4, 1975.

INFORMATION

Bureau of Economic Analysis
Department of Commerce
1441 L Street N.W.
Washington, D.C. 20230
(202) 606-9900
http://www.bea.doc.gov

Publications Website:
http://www.bea.doc.gov/bea/
uguide.htm#_1_33/

C 59.1:date
ANNUAL REPORT.
Earlier C 56.101

C 59.2:CT • **Item 130-D-1**
GENERAL PUBLICATIONS.
Earlier C 56.102

C 59.8:CT • **Item 130-D-2**
HANDBOOKS, MANUALS, GUIDES. [Irregular]

C 59.9:date • **Item 131-A**
BUSINESS CONDITIONS DIGEST. [Monthly]

PURPOSE:– To bring together many of the economic times series found most useful by business analysts and forecasters. Almost 500 economic indicators are presented in a form that is convenient for analysts with different approaches to the study of current business conditions and prospects (e.g., the national income model, the leading indicators, and anticipations and intentions) as well as for analysts who use combinations of these approaches. Various other types of data (such as the balance of payments) and analytical measures (such as the diffusion indexes) are also provided to facilitate complete analysis.

The report is organized into six major sections, as follows: (A) National income and product; (B) cyclical indicators; (C) anticipations and intentions; (D) other key indicators; (E) analytical measures; and (F) international comparisons. Several appendixes present historical data, series descriptions, seasonal adjustment factors, and measures of variability.

Indexed by: Index to U.S. Government Periodicals.
Earlier C 56.111
Discontinued v. 30/3.

C 59.9/2:date • **Item 131-A**
ADVANCE BCD, [Business Conditions Digest]. – 1977. [Monthly] (Included in subscription to Business Conditions Digest)

PURPOSE:– To provide summary data on important data prior to its publication in the Business Conditions Digest.

C 59.9/3:CT • **Item 131-A**
BUSINESS CONDITIONS DIGEST, SUPPLEMENTS.
Discontinued.

C 59.10:date • **Item 142-E**
DEFENSE INDICATORS. [Monthly]
This report brings together the principal time series on defense activity which influence short-term changes in the national economy. These include series on obligations, contracts, orders, shipments, inventories, expenditures, employment

and earnings. The approximate 30 time series included are grouped in accordance with the time at which the activities they measure occur in the defense order-productiondelivery process. Most are monthly though a few are quarterly. This publication provides original and seasonally adjusted basic data in monthly, quarterly, and annual form. Charts and analytical tables are included to facilitate interpretation.

Supersedes Selected Economic Indicators (D 1.43) published by the Department of Defense.
ISSN 0418-5013
Earlier C 56.110
Discontinued.

C 59.11:v.nos.&nos. • **Item 228 (P) (EL)**
SURVEY OF CURRENT BUSINESS. v. 1– 1921– [Monthly]

PURPOSE:– To disseminate significant economic indicators for business use, including analytical findings of the Office of Business Economics as well as over 2,500 statistical series originating from both public and private sources.

The first section is devoted to the business situation, special analyses, and articles, supported by charts and tables, on various aspects of the Nation's economy, information on trends in industry, outlook and other pointspertinent to the business world. An overall summary is given in The Business Situation, the introduction to each issue.

The second section, Current Business Statistics, contains over 2,500 statistical series giving the latest monthly or quarterly data. Data which appear in these series are compiled for historical reference in the various supplements listed below. The monthly data are supplemented by the weekly release, Business Statistics.
Indexed by:–
Business Periodicals Index.
Index to U.S. Government Periodicals.
Industrial Arts Index.
Public Affairs Information Service.
ISSN 0039-6222
Earlier C 56.109

C 59.11/a:CT • **Item 228**
REPRINTS (separates). [Irregular]
Discontinued.

C 59.11/1:date • **Item 228-A (CD) (E)**
SURVEY OF CURRENT BUSINESS. [Annual]
Issued on CD-ROM.

C 59.11/2:date • **Item 229**
BUSINESS STATISTICS, WEEKLY SUPPLEMENT. (Included in subscription to the Survey of Current Business)

ISSN 0090-7669
Earlier C 56.109/2
Discontinued.

C 59.11/3:date • **Item 228-A-1**
BUSINESS STATISTICS, BIENNIAL SUPPLEMENT TO SURVEY OF CURRENT BUSINESS. 1st ed.– 1932– [Biennial]

PURPOSE:– To provide businessmen and others interested in the progress of the American economy a handy and comprehensive reference book supplementing the up-to-date indicators published in the current monthly issues.

Gives monthly figures for the last four years and yearly (monthly average) for years 1929 to date. General titles cover general business indicators; commodity prices; construction and real estate; domestic trade; employment and population; finance; and international transactions of the United States. Individual commodity data cover stocks and prices. Includes explanatory notes and sources and methods of the data presented. Index.
Earlier title: Business Statistics.
Earlier C 56.109/3

C 59.11/4:CT • **Item 228-A-2**
SUPPLEMENT (Special) TO SURVEY OF CURRENT BUSINESS. [Irregular]

Earlier title: Special Supplements to the Survey of Current Business.

C 59.11/4:In 2/929-74 • **Item 228**
NATIONAL INCOME AND PRODUCT ACCOUNTS OF THE UNITED STATES, 1929– 74. 1976. 360 p.

C 59.11/5 • **Item 228-A-3**
NATIONAL INCOME AND PRODUCT ACCOUNTS OF THE UNITED STATES.

C 59.11/5-2 • **Item 228-A-4 (CD)**
NATIONAL INCOME AND PRODUCTS ACCOUNTS OF THE UNITED STATES. [Annual]

C 59.11/5-3 • **Item 228-A-5 (EL)**
NATIONAL INCOME AND PRODUCTS ACCOUNTS OF THE UNITED STATES. [Monthly]

C 59.12:nos.
FOREIGN ECONOMIC REPORTS.

C 59.13:nos. • **Item 139**
INTERNATIONAL POPULATION REPORTS, P-91- (series). 1– [Irregular]

C 59.13/2:90/nos. • **Item 139**
INTERNATIONAL POPULATION STATISTICS REPORTS, P 90- (series). 1– [Irregular]

C 59.14:nos. • **Item 142-G (MF)**
BUREAU OF ECONOMIC ANALYSIS STAFF PAPERS. 1– 1963– [Irregular]

PURPOSE:– To present reports on BEA research that is more specialized or less well established than BEA research generally made available to the public.
Earlier C 56.113

C 59.15:CT • **Item 142-H**
MAPS. [Irregular]

C 59.16/1– C 59.16/51:date • **Item142-J-1–142-J-52**
STATE QUARTERLY ECONOMIC DEVELOPMENTS.

Separate report issued for each State and the District of Columbia on current economic development data.
Superseded by one-volume report covering all 50 States and D.C. (C 59.16/52).

C 59.16/52:date • **Item 142-J**
STATE QUARTERLY ECONOMIC DEVELOPMENTS.

Combines in one volume the individual state reports formerly published separately (C 59.16/1– C 59.16/51).
Gives statistical data on market prices, employment, construction, etc. for each State and D.C.

C 59.17:date • **Item 130-D-3 (MF)**
OBERS, BEA REGIONAL PROJECTIONS. [Quinquennial]

Projects national, State, and area economic activity, mainly through tables.
OBERS Acronym for cooperative effort of Office of Business Economics (now BEA) and the Department of Agriculture's Economic Research Service.
1980 report published in 11 volumes.
Issued in microfiche.

C 59.18:date • **Item 130-D-4**
LOCAL AREA PERSONAL INCOME. [Annual]

Tables present local area personal income statistics over a six-year period in one national summary volume and in one volume for each of eight regions, by counties and Standard Metropolitan Statistical Areas.
Also published in microfiche.

C 59.19:letters-nos. • **Item 130-D-5**
METHODOLOGY PAPERS. U.S. NATIONAL INCOME AND PRODUCT ACCOUNTS, BEA-MP(series). [Irregular]

PURPOSE:– To describe methods used to estimate U.S. national income and product accounts. Each report deals with a different component of national income.

C 59.20:date • **Item 130-D-7**
FOREIGN DIRECT INVESTMENT IN THE U.S., OPERATIONS OF U.S. AFFILIATES OF FOREIGN COMPANIES. [Annual]

Presents estimates covering the financial structure and operations of nonbank U.S. affiliates of foreign direct investors.
Earlier C 61.25/2

C 59.20/2:date • **Item 130-D-6**
U.S. DIRECT INVESTMENT ABROAD, OPERATIONS OF U.S. PARENT COMPANIES AND THEIR FOREIGN AFFILIATES, PRELIMINARY ESTIMATES. [Annual]

PURPOSE:– To present preliminary results of a survey of U.S. direct investments abroad. Tables present data on the financial structure and operations of a sample of nonbank U.S. companies and their nonbank foreign affiliates.

C 59.20/3 • **Item 130-D-11**
FOREIGN DIRECT INVESTMENT IN THE UNITED STATES, ESTABLISHMENT DATA FOR MANUFACTURING.

C 59.21:date • **Item 130-D-8**
NATIONAL ECONOMIC ACCOUNTING TRAINING PROGRAM. [Annual]

These brochures present information on curriculum, candidate requirements, application procedures, and program costs.
Cancelled.

C 59.22: • **Item 130-D-9**
BIBLIOGRAPHIES AND LISTS OF PUBLICATIONS.

Includes miscellaneous bibliographies covering topics concerning the work of the Bureau.

C 59.23:CT • **Item 130-D-10**
FORMS. [Irregular]

C 59.24:date • **Item 130-U (CD)**
REGIONAL ECONOMIC INFORMATION SYSTEM (REIS). [Annual]
Issued on CD-ROM.

C 59.25 • **Item 130-U (CD)**
SPI STATE PERSONAL INCOME. 1969-[date].
Issued on CD-ROM.

C 59.26: • **Item 130-U-3 (E)**
ELECTRONIC PRODUCTS (misc.).

C 59.27: • **Item 130-U-4 (CD)**
FIXED REPRODUCIBLE TANGIBLE WEALTH OF THE UNITED STATES.
Issued on CD-ROM.

NATIONAL TELECOMMUNICATIONS AND INFORMATION ADMINISTRATION (1978–   )

CREATION AND AUTHORITY

The National Telecommunication and Information Administration was established within the Department of Commerce by Executive Order 12046 of March 27, 1978.

INFORMATION

National Telecommunications and Information Administration
Department of Commerce
Herbert Clark Hoover Building
1401 Constitution Ave, NW
Washington, D.C. 20230
(202) 482-7002
Http://www.ntia.doc.gov

C 60.1:date
ANNUAL REPORT.

C 60.2:CT • **Item 126-E-4**
GENERAL PUBLICATIONS. [Irregular]

C 60.8:CT • **Item 126-E-2**
HANDBOOKS, MANUALS, GUIDES.

C 60.9:nos. • **Item 126-D-3 (MF)**
SPECIAL PUBLICATIONS, NTIA-SP-(series). [Irregular]

Supersedes OT Special Publications (C 1.60/2).

C 60.10:nos. • **Item 126-D-3 (MF)**
NTIA REPORTS. [Irregular]

Supersedes OT Reports (C 1.60/3).
Also issued in microfiche

C 60.11:nos. • **Item 126-D-10 (MF)**
TECHNICAL MEMORANDUM SERIES, NTIA-TM-(nos.). [Irregular]

PURPOSE:– To provide, in a highly technical format, outlines, preliminary results, summaries, notes, etc. of scientific and technical research. Includes topics such as electromagnetic compatibility, technical standards for cable TV, radio propagation, etc.
Supersedes OT Technical Memorandums (C 1.60/8).

C 60.12:nos. • **Item 126-D-5 (MF)**
CONTRACTOR REPORTS, NTIA-CR-(series). [Irregular]
Earlier C 1.60/7

C 60.13:CT • **Item 126-E-1**
BIBLIOGRAPHIES AND LISTS OF PUBLICATIONS. [Irregular]

C 60.14:date • **Item 126-E-3 (MF) (EL)**
INSTITUTE FOR TELECOMMUNICATION SCIENCES: ANNUAL TECHNICAL PROGRESS REPORT.

PURPOSE:– To summarize the progress made in the technical work of the various divisions of the Institute, in its mission to manage the telecommunications program of the Administration.

C 60.15:date • **Item 126-E-5 (MF)**
REPORT OF THE INTERDEPARTMENT RADIO ADVISORY COMMITTEE. [Semiannual]

Summarizes the activities of the Committee, which serves inan advisory capacity to the NTIA Administrator in discharging his responsibilities pertaining to use of the electro magnetic spectrum.
Discontinued.

C 60.16 • **Item 126-E-6**
POSTERS.

INTERNATIONAL TRADE ADMINISTRATION (1980–   )

CREATION AND AUTHORITY

The International Trade Administration was established by the Secretary of Commerce on January 2, 1980 to succeed the Industry and Trade Administration (C 57).

INFORMATION

Office of Public Affairs
International Trade Administration
Herbert Clark Hoover Building
14th St. and Constitution Ave. NW
Washington, DC 20230
(202) 482-5819
Toll Free: (800) 872-8723
Fax: (202) 482-4821
http://www.ita.doc.gov

C 61.1:date
ANNUAL REPORT.

C 61.2:CT • **Item 231-B-1**
GENERAL PUBLICATIONS. [Irregular]

C 61.8:CT • **Item 231-B-5**
HANDBOOKS, MANUALS, GUIDES. [Irregular]

Earlier C 57.8

C 61.8/2:date • **Item 231-B-5 (MF)**
GUIDEBOOK, CARIBBEAN BASIN INITIATIVE. [Annual]

Earlier C 61.8:C 19

C 61.9:nos. • **Item 231-G-1**
COUNTRY MARKET SURVEY, CMS- (series). [Irregular]

Earlier C 57.112
Discontinued.

C 61.9/2:CT • **Item 231-G-1**
GLOBAL MARKET SURVEY, EUROPEAN MARKET.

Earlier C 57.109
Discontinued.

C 61.10:v.nos.&nos. • **Item 219-C**
COMMERCIAL NEWS USA. v. 1–   [Monthly]

Earlier C 57.114

Cooperative.

C 61.10/2 • **Item 219-C**
COMMERCIAL NEWS USA, NEW PRODUCTS ANNUAL DIRECTORY.

Cooperative.

C 61.11:CT • **Item 231-I**
FOREIGN ECONOMIC TRENDS AND THEIR IMPLICATIONS FOR THE UNITED STATES, FET-(series). [Semiannual or Annual]

Separate reports issued for individual countries. Reports on larger countries issued semiannually.
Earlier C 57.111
Discontinued.

C 61.11/2: • **Item 231-N (MF)**
ANNUAL FOREIGN POLICY REPORT TO CONGRESS.
Report to Congress on foreign policy related to trade in accordance with Section 6 of the Export Administration Act of 1979, as amended (the act) and EO 12214.

C 61.12:nos. • **Item 231-B**
OVERSEAS BUSINESS REPORTS. [Irregular]

PURPOSE:– To provide information of interest to exporters, importers, investors, manufacturers, researchers, and all who are interested in international trade and economic conditions throughout the world.
Issued 1962– 1964 by the Bureau of International Commerce (C 42.20); 1964– 1973 by the Department of Commerce (C 1.50).
Indexed by: Index to U.S. Government Periodicals.
Earlier C 57.11
The following sub-series are issued on an irregular basis:

BASIC DATA ON THE ECONOMY OF (country).

PURPOSE:– To provide basic information on the economic structure of specified countries, emphasizing those aspects which are of most interest to U.S. foreign traders and investors, enabling them to make preliminary judgments as to the advisability of initiating, continuing, or expanding operations in a given country.
Includes general information of geography, population, and standard of living; government; structure of the economy; industrial sectors; labor force; finance; foreign trade; government role in the economy; and outlook for the economy. Also includes a map of the country and a brief bibliography.

ESTABLISHING A BUSINESS IN (country).

PURPOSE:– To provide a "How to" report on going into business in selected countries.
Covers government policy on investment, entry and repatriation of capital, trade factors affecting investment, business organizations, registration, regulations affecting employment, and taxation.

FOREIGN TRADE REGULATIONS OF (country).

PURPOSE:– To cover trade policy, tariff structure, basis of duty assessment, customs surcharges, sales and other internal taxes, documentation and fees, labeling and marking requirements, special customs provisions, nontariff import trade controls, local country's controls and United States controls. Also gives addresses of foreign government offices in the U.S. and U.S. offices in the foreign country covered in the report.
Combines the former Import Tariff System, Licensing and Exchange Controls, portions of Marking and Labeling Requirements, plus a summary of information from Preparing Shipments subseries formerly published in the World Trade Information Service.

MARKET FACTORS IN (country).

PURPOSE:– To assess the climate for exporting to individual countries with discussion by commodity groups

MARKET FOR (product) IN (country).

PURPOSE:– To present the scope and nature of the market, distribution facilities and services, trade regulations and practices, and market analysis for selected commodities. Contains statistical tables, maps and illustrations.

SELLING IN (country).

PURPOSE:– To provide a guide on selling in the foreign market, with emphasis on the marketing system in each country, and on government procurement as appropriate.

See C 1.88

C 61.13:date • **Item 231-B-9**
TOP [Trade Opportunities Program] BULLETIN. [Weekly]

Indexes trade opportunities according to product, giving codes and showing country of origin, type of opportunity-sale lead, representation inquiry, or foreign government tender, and notice number.
Earlier C 57.27
Discontinued Aug. 1987.

C 61.13/2:nos. • **Item 231-B-9 (MF)**
INDEX OF TRADE OPPORTUNITIES. [Semiannual]

Also published in microfiche.
Discontinued March 1985.

C 61.14:v.nos.&nos. • **Item 231-B-6**
INTERNATIONAL ECONOMIC INDICATORS. v. 1– 1975–   [Quarterly]

Earlier C 57.19/2

C 61.15 • **Item 231-B-3**
BIBLIOGRAPHIES AND LISTS OF PUBLICATIONS. [Irregular]

C 61.16:date
INDEX TO FOREIGN MARKET REPORTS. [Irregular]

Earlier C 57.110

C 61.17:CT • **Item 231-B-11 (MF)**
EAST-WEST TRADE POLICY STAFF PAPERS. [Semiannual]

Each paper deals with trends of U.S. trade with a different country. Issued in microfiche (24x).

C 61.18:v.nos.&nos. • **Item 127-A**
BUSINESS AMERICA. v. 1–   1978–   [Biweekly]

PURPOSE:– To provide a news review of the Department of Commerce's activities affecting private enterprise. Includes reports on domestic business, economic affairs, overseas trade (including foreign sales leads), national and international business problems.
Supersedes Commerce America (C 1.58/2).
Earlier C 1.58/4
Discontinued; see C 61.18/2
Previously Business America.
Discontinued.

C 61.18/2: • **Item 127-A (EL)**
EXPORT AMERICA. [Monthly]

C 61.18/3:date
BUSINESS AMERICA, MICHIGAN.

C 61.19:date • **Item 231-B-2**
EXPORT PROMOTION CALENDAR. [Quarterly]

PURPOSE:– To serve in the Commerce Department's effort to increase U.S. exports. Includes Country Market Digest, Exhibitor's Export Market Guide, World Markets for U.S. Exports, Market Share Reports, and Country Market Surveys.
Former title: Overseas Export Promotion Calendar.
Earlier C 42.31
Discontinued.

C 61.19/2: • **Item 231-B-22 (MF)**
FOREIGN BUYER PROGRAM EXPORT INTEREST DIRECTORY (series).

Consists of directories intended for prospective foreign buyers which list U.S. companies interested in international business. Each directory is issued in connection with a different international trade conference.

C 61.20:date
EXPORT LICENSES APPROVED AND REEXPORTS AUTHORIZED. [Daily] (Office of Export Administration)

Earlier C 57.410

C 61.21:CT • **Item 231-B-10**
INTERNATIONAL MARKETING EVENTS, MARKET RESEARCH SUMMARY.

Non-government publication.

C 61.21/3:CT
INTERNATIONAL MARKETING EVENTS: COUNTRY MARKET SURVEY.

C 61.22:date
U.S. TRADE STATUS WITH COMMUNIST COUNTRIES. [Monthly] (Office of East-West Policy and Planning)
    Earlier C 57.28

C 61.23:date   **• Item 211**
EXPORT ADMINISTRATION REGULATIONS. (Includes basic volume plus a set of dividers and supplementary material issued as Export Administration Bulletins (C 61.23/2))

    PURPOSE:– To provide a compilation of official regulations and policies governing the export licensing of the commodities and technical data. It also contains a new Commodity Control List, which replaces the Positive List, the General Licenses GHK Commodity List, and others.
    Previous title: Export Control Bulletin. Entitled Comprehensive Export Schedule, prior to 1969.
    Earlier C 57.409, C 18.267, C 42.111, and C 42.208

    See C 63.23

C 61.23/a   **• Item 211**
– SEPARATES.

    See C 63.23/A

C 61.23/2:nos.   **• Item 212**
EXPORT ADMINISTRATION BULLETIN. 1–   1969–

    Published as a supplement to Export Administration Regulations (C 61.23).
    Previous title: Export Control Bulletin.
    Earlier C 57.409/2

C 61.24:date   **• Item 130 (MF)**
EXPORT ADMINISTRATION ANNUAL REPORT. 1– 1947–   [Semiannual]

    Report submitted to Congress pursuant to the Export Control Act of 1949.
    Earlier C 57.30
    Discontinued.

C 61.25:date   **• Item 231-B-12**
OPEC DIRECT INVESTMENT IN THE UNITED STATES. [Annual]

    Consists mainly of tables on direct investment in the United States by Organization of Petroleum Exporting Countries. Lists such information as name of U.S. company, state where located, and foreign owner.
    Discontinued.

C 61.25/2:date   **• Item 231-B-12**
FOREIGN DIRECT INVESTMENT IN THE UNITED STATES. [Annual]

    Earlier C 61.2:In 8/2
    Later C 59.20
    Discontinued.

C 61.25/3:nos.
MONTHLY REPORT ON FOREIGN DIRECT INVESTMENT ACTIVITY IN THE UNITED STATES.

    Former title: Foreign Direct Investment Activity in the United States.
    Discontinued.

C 61.26:date   **• Item 231-B-13 (MF)**
U.S. PRODUCTION, IMPORTS AND IMPORT/ PRODUCTION RATIOS FOR COTTON, WOOL AND MAN-MADE TEXTILES AND APPAREL. [Annual]

    Tables provide data on the import penetration of cotton, wool, and man-made fiber textile and apparel products in the U.S. for the current and preceding nine years. Tables show the ratio of such imports to domestic U.S. production.
    Earlier C 61.2:C 82
    Discontinued.

C 61.27:date
TRADEWINDS.

C 61.28:date   **• Item 231-B-14**
U.S. TRADE PERFORMANCE IN (year) AND OUTLOOK. [Annual]
    Discontinued.

C 61.28/2:date   **• Item 231-B-14 (EL)**
U.S. FOREIGN TRADE HIGHLIGHTS. [Annual]

C 61.29:date   **• Item 231-B-15**
INTERNATIONAL DIRECT INVESTMENT, GLOBAL TRENDS AND THE U.S. ROLE. [Annual]

    Provides policymakers and the public with an overview of the growth and global distribution of international direct investment, including directinvestment abroad by the U.S., foreign direct investment in the U.S., and the concerns and policy issues raised by the international direct investment.
    Discontinued.

C 61.30:CT   **• Item 231-M-1– 50**
STATE EXPORT SERIES, (State) EXPORTS. [Irregular]

    Separate report issued for each State.
    Earlier C 57.29
    See 61.30/1-C 61.30/50

C 61.30/nos.   **• Item 231-M-1– 50 (MF)**
STATE EXPORT SERIES [State].
    Discontinued.

C 61.31:date   **• Item 231-B-4**
FRANCHISE OPPORTUNITIES HANDBOOK. [Annual]
    PURPOSE:– To assist in the establishment of minority group businesses. Included is general information on franchising, suggestions and checklists to assist and protect the potential investor, guides to other sources of information.
    Earlier C 62.14
    Later C 1.108/2

C 61.31/2:date   **• Item 126-D-13**
FRANCHISING IN THE ECONOMY.
    Earlier C 62.16

C 61.32:date   **• Item 231-B-16**
DIRECTORY OF EMPLOYEES FOR THE INTERNATIONAL TRADE ADMINISTRATION. [Quarterly]

C 61.33:CT   **• Item 231-B-17**
POSTERS. [Irregular]

C 61.34:date   **• Item 215-L**
U.S. INDUSTRIAL OUTLOOK. [Annual]
    Earlier C 62.17
    Discontinued.

C 61.34/2:date   **• Item 215-L-6**
U.S. GLOBAL TRADE OUTLOOK. [Annual]
    Discontinued.

C 61.34/3:date   **• Item 215-L-7**
U.S. GLOBAL TRADE OUTLOOK 1995-2000 TOWARD THE 21ST CENTURY.
    Issued on CD-ROM.

C 61.35:v.nos./nos.   **• Item 231-B-20**
CARIBBEAN BASIN INITIATIVE BUSINESS BULLETINS. [Monthly]

    Bulletins provide information on business and investment opportunities in Caribbean countries.
    Replaced by LA/C Business Bulletin (C 61.35/ 2).

C 61.35/2   **• Item 231-B-20 (MF)**
LA/C BUSINESS BULLETIN. [Monthly]

    Replaces Caribbean Basin Initiative Business Bulletins (C 61.35).
    Discontinued.

C 61.36:date
TRADEWINDS. [Bimonthly]

C 61.37:v.nos.&nos.   **• Item 219**
CONSTRUCTION REVIEW. v. 1–   [Quarterly]

Contains articles, statistical tables, construction legislation news (when Congress is in session), and construction regulations.
    Earlier C 62.10
    Ceased in 1997.

C 61.38:date   **• Item 231-B-21**
LATIN AMERICAN TRADE REVIEW. [Annual]

    Analyzes major trends in Latin America's trade from the perspective of the U.S. Summarizes trade impact and its implications for U.S. exports. Contains brief country studies on Latin American countries from Argentina to Venezuela.
    Discontinued.

C 61.39   **• Item 231-B-19**
TRADE WORLD MICHIGAN. [Monthly]

    News from the U.S. Department of Commerce for the business community in Michigan.
    Discontinued.

C 61.39/2:date
USA TRADE WORLD NEVADA. [Bimonthly]

C 61.39/3:date/nos.   **• Item 231-B-19**
TRADE WORLD ILLINOIS. [Bimonthly]

C 61.39/4:date/nos.   **• Item 231-B-19**
USA TRADE WORLD, PENNSYLVANIA & DELAWARE.

C 61.39/5:date/nos.   **• Item 231-B-19**
TRADE WORLD NEW YORK. [Quarterly]

C 61.39/6:date   **• Item 231-B-24**
TRADE WORLD, OHIO.
    Formerly: USA Trade World, Ohio

C 61.40:   **• Item 231-B-23**
U.S. MERCHANDISE TRADE POSITION AT MIDYEAR. [Annual]

    PURPOSE– To present the U.S. trade position at midyear inrelation to the developed countries, the developing countries, and the centrally planned economies. Also presents bilateral total trade data.
    Ceased in 1991.

C 61.41:date   **• Item 231-B-20 (MF)**
EUROPE NOW. [Quarterly]
    Discontinued.

C 61.42:date   **• Item 231-B-20 (EL)**
BISNIS BULLETIN. [Monthly]

C 61.42/2   **• Item 231-B-20 (EL)**
BISNIS SEARCH OF PARTNERS.

C 61.43   **• Item 231-B-20 (EL)**
EASTERN EUROPE BUSINESS BULLETIN. [Monthly]

C 61.44   **• Item 231-B-22 (MF)**
DIRECTORIES.

C 61.45:date   **• Item 231-B-26**
THE BIG EMERGING MARKETS, OUTLOOK AND SOURCEBOOK. [Annual]

C 61.46   **• Item 231-B-27 (EL)**
MONTHLY TRADE UPDATE.

C 61.47   **• Item 231-B-27 (E)**
ELECTRONIC PRODUCTS.

C 61.48:date   **• Item 215-L-8**
U.S. INDUSTRY AND TRADE OUTLOOK. [Annual]

C 61.49:   **• Item 231-B-28 (MF)**
MARKETING U.S. TOURISM ABROAD. [Annual]

C 61.50:   **• Item 231-B-27 (EL)**
U.S. EXPORTS OF TEXTILES AND APPAREL PRODUCTS.

C 61.51:   **• Item 231-B-27 (EL)**
TEXTILE AND APPAREL TRADE BALANCE REPORT.

C 61.52:   **• Item 231-B-27 (EL)**
U.S. IMPORTS OF TEXTILE AND APPAREL PRODUCTS.

C 61.53: • Item 231-B-27 (EL)
THE MAJOR SHIPPERS REPORT.

C 61.54: • Item 231-B-27 (EL)
U.S. TEXTILE AND APPAREL CATEGORY SYSTEM.

C 61.56 • Item 231-B-29 (MF) (EL)
RESULTS OF SERVICES CONFERENCE. [Biennial]

BUREAU OF INDUSTRIAL ECONOMICS (1980–1984)

CREATION AND AUTHORITY

The Bureau of Industrial Economics was established in the Department of Commerce on January 2, 1980 pursuant to Reorganization Plan No. 3 of 1979 (44 FR 69273) superseding the Bureau of Domestic Commerce (C 57.500). Effective January 22, 1984, the Bureau was abolished by Secretarial Order (49 FR 4538) and its functions transferred to other units of the Department.

C 62.1:date
ANNUAL REPORT.

C 62.2:CT • Item 215
GENERAL PUBLICATIONS. [Irregular]
Discontinued.

C 62.9:v.nos.&nos. • Item 215-H
PRINTING AND PUBLISHING. v. 1– 23. – 1982.
[Quarterly] (Industry Report)
Earlier C 57.510
Discontinued v. 23/n.1.

C 62.10:v.nos.&nos. • Item 219
CONSTRUCTION REVIEW. v. 1– 1955– [Monthly]
Earlier C 57.509
Later C 61.37

C 62.11:v.nos.&nos. • Item 223
FOREST PRODUCTS REVIEW. v. 1–37. 1944–1982.
[Quarterly] (Industry Report)
Former title: Pulp, Paper, and Board.
Earlier C 57.511
Discontinued v. 37/4.

C 62.12:v.nos.&nos. • Item 220-A
COPPER. v. 1– 1954– [Quarterly] (Industry Report)
Earlier C 57.512
Discontinued.

C 62.12/2:date • Item 220-A
COPPER, ANNUAL STATISTICAL SUPPLEMENT.
Earlier C 57.512/2
Discontinued.

C 62.13:date
ALUMINUM IMPORTS AND EXPORTS. [Monthly]
(Office of Basic Industries)
Earlier C 57.14

C 62.14:date • Item 231-B-4
FRANCHISE OPPORTUNITIES HANDBOOK.
Earlier C 57.16
Later C 61.31

C 62.15:nos. • Item 218-C (MF)
STAFF PAPERS, BIE-SP- (series). [Irregular]
Discontinued.

C 62.16:date • Item 126-D-13
FRANCHISING IN THE ECONOMY. [Annual]

PURPOSE:– To present information regarding the growth of franchising and its effects on the U.S. marketing system. Information is based on individual returns from firms representing the vast majority of business format franchising sales and establishments and from other sources.
Earlier C 1.74
Later C 61.31/2
Discontinued.

C 62.17:date • Item 215-L
U.S. INDUSTRIAL OUTLOOK FOR 200 INDUSTRIES WITH PROJECTIONS FOR (year). [Annual]

PURPOSE:– To present in a single volume the various individual Outlook Studies on selected U.S. industries which were previously issued as press releases.
Each release is on an individual industry and contains a review of the preceding year, the prospects for the coming year, with supplemental background data and statistics.
Earlier C 57.18
Later C 61.34

C 62.18:CT • Item 218-A (MF)
SEMINAR ON INDUSTRIAL ISSUES (series). [Irregular]

Each issue presents a condensed transcript of a seminar on a different industrial issue.
Discontinued.

C 62.19:date • Item 218-B
INDUSTRIAL ECONOMICS REVIEW. [Irregular]

Consists of articles on industrial developments and issues of current concern, such as technological growth and high technology in U.S. industries. Contains tables and graphs.
Discontinued.

BUREAU OF INDUSTRY AND SECURITY

CREATION AND AUTHORITY

Name changed April 18, 2002, to better reflect the breadth of the Bureau's activities. Formerly Bureau of Export Administration.

INFORMATION

Bureau of Industry and Security
Herbert Clark Hoover Building
14th Street and Constitution Ave., NW
Washington DC 20230
(202)482-2000
Fax: (202)482-2387
http://www.bxa.doc.gov

C 63.1:date • Item 231-S (MF) (EL)
ANNUAL REPORTS.

C 63.2:CT • Item 231-S-1
GENERAL PUBLICATIONS.

C 63.8:CT • Item 231-S-4
HANDBOOKS, MANUALS, GUIDES.

C 63.10: • Item 231-S-6
DIRECTORIES.

C 63.13: • Item 231-S-5
FORMS.

C 63.23:date/nos. • Item 231-S-2
REGULATIONS.

C 63.24: • Item 231-S-7 (EL)
BUREAU OF EXPORT ADMINISTRATION FACT SHEETS.

C 63.25: • Item 231-S-7 (E)
ELECTRONIC PRODUCTS (misc.).

C 63.28:date • Item 231-S-2
EXPORT ADMINISTRATION REGULATIONS.

CIVIL AERONAUTICS AUTHORITY (1938– 1940)

CREATION AND AUTHORITY

The Civil Aeronautics Authority was established as an independent agency under the Civil Aeronautics Act of 1938 (52 Stat. 973), composed of the Authority, an Administrator, and the Air Safety Board. By Reorganization Plan Nos. 3 and 4 of 1940, effective June 30, 1940, the five-member Board was changed to the Civil Aeronautics Board, the Air Safety Board abolished, and the functions of Administrator placed under the Secretary of Commerce (C 31). While the Civil Aeronautics Authority was a part of the Department of Commerce, it performed no administrative functions.

CA 1.1:date
ANNUAL REPORTS.
Later C 31.1

CA 1.2:CT
GENERAL PUBLICATIONS.
Later C 31.2

CA 1.3:nos.
CIVIL AERONAUTICS BULLETINS.
Later C 31.103

CA 1.6:serial nos.
REGULATIONS.
Earlier C 23.6/3
Later C 31.206

CA 1.7:vol.
WEEKLY NOTICES TO AIRMEN.
Later C 31.9

CA 1.7/2:date.&nos.
SPECIAL NOTICE TO AIRMEN.
Later C 31.10

CA 1.8:vol.
AIR COMMERCE BULLETINS. [Monthly]
Earlier C 23.12
Superseded by CA 1.17

CA 1.9:date
TABULATION OF AIR NAVIGATION RADIO AIDS.
[Monthly]
Earlier C 23.18
Later C 31.8

CA 1.10:nos.
MANUALS (numbered).
Supersedes C 23.16
Later C 31.107

CA 1.11:nos.
PLANNING AND DEVELOPMENT REPORTS.
Earlier C 23.19

CA 1.12:serial nos.
ORDERS.
Earlier CA 1.14
Later C 31.207

CA 1.13:CT
MAPS.
Later C 31.115

CA 1.14:date
RULES OF PRACTICE UNDER TITLE 4, REGULATIONS AND ORDERS.

Later Regulations (CA 1.16) and Orders (CA 1.12)..

CA 1.15:chap.&pt. nos.
MANUAL OF OPERATIONS.
Earlier C 23.6/5
Later C 31.116

CA 1.16:nos.
SPECIAL TARIFF PERMISSION.
Later C 31.210

CA 1.17:vol.
CIVIL AERONAUTICS JOURNAL. [Semimonthly]
Supersedes CA 1.8
Later C 31.7

CA 1.18:date
WEEKLY SUMMARY OF ORDERS AND REGULATIONS ISSUED BY THE AUTHORITY.
Later C 31.208

CA 1.19:pt.nos.
CIVIL AIR REGULATIONS.
Earlier C 23.6/3
Later C 31.209

CA 1.20:nos.
TECHNICAL DEVELOPMENT REPORTS.

CA 1.21:nos.
CERTIFICATE AND INSPECTION DIVISION RELEASES.
Later C 31.111

CA 1.22:date
DOMESTIC AIR CARRIER OPERATIONS STATISTICS. [Monthly]
Earlier C 23.20
Later C 31.12

CA 1.23:vol.
CIVIL AERONAUTICS AUTHORITY REPORTS.

CA 1.24
MAINTENANCE INSTRUCTION BULLETINS. [Admin.]

CIVIL AERONAUTICS BOARD (1978– 1985)

CREATION AND AUTHORITY

The Civil Aeronautics Board (C 31.200) was established within the Department of Commerce by Reorganization Plans 3 and 4 of 1940, effective June 30, 1940. The Board was made an independent agency by the Federal Aviation Act of 1958 (72 Stat. 731), effective January 1, 1959. The Board was abolished and and its functions transferred to the Department of Transportation (TD 1) and the United States Postal Service (P 1) effective in part on December 31, 1981; in part on January 1, 1983; and in part on January 1, 1985; under title XIV of the Federal Aviation Act of 1958 (92 Stat. 1744; 49 U.S.C. app. 1551), as amended and by the Civil Aeronautics Bord Sunset Act of 1984, approved October 4, 1984 (98 Stat. 1703; 49 U.S.C. app. 1301 note).

Note:– For the period from January 1959 until June 1978, the C 31.200 SuDocs classes continued to be used for CAB publications. In June 1978, this new class was assigned for publications issued after that date.

CAB 1.1:date   • Item 178
ANNUAL REPORT.
Earlier C 31.201
Discontinued.

CAB 1.2:CT   • Item 183
GENERAL PUBLICATIONS. [Irregular]
Discontinued.

CAB 1.5:CT   • Item 184
LAWS. [Irregular]
Earlier C 31.205
Discontinued.

CAB 1.6:CT   • Item 186
REGULATIONS, RULES, AND INSTRUCTIONS.
Earlier C 31.206/2
Discontinued.

CAB 1.8:CT   • Item 186
HANDBOOKS, MANUALS, GUIDES. [Irregular]
Earlier C 31.206/9
Discontinued.

CAB 1.9:date   • Item 177-A-14 (MF)
PASSENGERS DENIED CONFIRMED SPACE. [2 times a year]

Separate reports issued for calendar and fiscal years.
Earlier C 31.268
Discontinued in 1977.

CAB 1.10:date   • Item 177-A-23 (MF)
SUMMARY OF PRESCRIBED UNIT COSTS AND HOURLY RATE FOR RETURN ON INVESTMENT AND TAX ALLOWANCES. [Annual]
Discontinued in 1977.

CAB 1.11:date   • Item 177-A-17 (MF)
COMMUTER AIR CARRIER TRAFFIC STATISTICS. [Semiannual]
Earlier C 31.241/3
See TD 10.9/2

CAB 1.12:date   • Item 177-A-4
LOCAL SERVICE AIR CARRIERS' UNIT COSTS. 1963–1981. [Semiannual]
PURPOSE:– To implement the requirements of Subpart K of CAB Rules of Practice (part 302, Procedural Regulations) that each part in a CAB route proceeding submit cost estimates– for local service air carriers' service modification– in accordance with the standardized method for costing such changes in operations.
Earlier C 31.253
Discontinued Dec. 1981.

CAB 1.13:date   • Item 172-A-2
AIR CARRIER TRAFFIC STATISTICS. v.1–   [Monthly]

Tables show changes in revenue load factors and capacity operated, changes in revenue ton-miles, revenue ton-miles, revenue passenger and passenger-miles revenue load factor, average revenue load and passenger load, average seats available; available ton-mile and seat-mile capacity, schedule performance factor and revenue aircraft miles. Two year comparisons for month and 12 months with percent change. Charts.
Beginning with 1st issue of 1980, volume and issue numbers dropped from publication.
ISSN 0098-0404
Earlier C 31.241
Discontinued 984/8.

CAB 1.14:date   • Item 177-A-3
QUARTERLY INTERIM FINANCIAL REPORT, CERTIFICATED ROUTE AIR CARRIERS AND CHARTER AIR CARRIERS.
Earlier C 31.240/3
Discontinued.

CAB 1.15:date   • Item 177-A-3
FUEL COST AND CONSUMPTION. 1977– 1981. [Monthly]
Sub-title varies.
Earlier C 31.267
Discontinued.

CAB 1.15/2:date   • Item 177-A-13 (MF)
FUEL COST AND CONSUMPTION, TWELVE MONTHS ENDED DECEMBER 31, (year). [Annual]
Earlier C 31.267/2
Discontinued.Discontinued.v

CAB 1.16:date   • Item 186
REGULATIONS OF THE CIVIL AERONAUTICS BOARD. [Irregular]

Regulations of the Board consists of five types. They are published in the Federal Register and codified in the Code of Federal Regulations under Title 14. Release information is included in the Weekly Summary of Orders and Regulations. Notices of proposed rulings are also circu-

lated to interested persons.
Earlier C 31.206/7
Discontinued.

CAB 1.17:v.nos.&nos.   • Item 177-A-3
AIR CARRIER FINANCIAL STATISTICS. [Quarterly]

Table 1, Income Statement Data, gives tables and for individual airlines data on operating revenues, expenses and profits, nonoperating income and expenses, unappropriated retained earnings, and adjusted U.S. mail and subsidy revenue for quarter and 12 months ending quarter, with two year comparisons.
Table 2, Earning Position and Average Investment.
Table 3, Balance Sheet Data.
Earlier C 31.240
Discontinued June 1984.

CAB 1.18:v.nos.&nos.   • Item 177-A-5
AIRLINE INDUSTRY ECONOMIC REPORT. [Quarterly]
Earlier C 31.260
Discontinued.

CAB 1.19:date   • Item 177-A-6
SCHEDULE ARRIVAL PERFORMANCE IN THE TOP 200 MARKETS BY CARRIER. [Monthly]

Beginning with the November 1979 issue, volume and issue number have been discontinued.
ISSN 0145-9295
Discontinued 981/7.

CAB 1.20:date   • Item 177-A-7
SEASONALLY ADJUSTED TRAFFIC AND CAPACITY, MAJOR SCHEDULED SERVICE, SYSTEM, DOMESTIC AND INTERNATIONAL OPERATIONS. [Monthly]

Former title: Seasonally Adjusted Capacity and Traffic, Scheduled Operations, System, Domestic and International Trunks Plus Local Service Carriers.
Earlier C 31.262/5
Cancelled.

CAB 1.21:nos.   • Item 179 (MF)
CIVIL AERONAUTICS BOARD REPORTS. v.1–1938/40–   [Irregular]

Opinions of the Board are first issued as separates and are available upon request from the Board. The Opinions are later published in bound volumes as reports.
The opinions set forth matters considered, findings, conclusions, and decisions, and usually include an order in such cases as route awards to domestic or foreign carriers, mergers, mail routes, enforcement, and policy.
Beginning with volume 17, Economic and Safety Enforcement Cases are bound together. Prior to volume 17, they were issued in separate volumes.
Earlier C 31.211
Discontinued.

CAB 1.22:v.nos.   • Item 177-A-1 (MF)
AIRCRAFT OPERATING COST AND PERFORMANCE REPORT, FISCAL YEAR. [Annual] (Cost and Statistics Division, Bureau of Accounts and Statistics)

PURPOSE:– To present direct aircraft operating cost per block hour and on several other unit bases together with a variety of measures of aircraft performance relating to utilization, capacity, speed, productivity, fuel consumption and traffic carried. Breakdowns are given by aircraft equipment groups and aircraft equipment type both on a carrier group and individual carrier basis.
Earlier C 31.259
See TD1.53

CAB 1.22/2:   • Item 177-A-1
AIRCRAFT OPERATING COST AND PERFORMANCE REPORT. [Annual]
Discontinued with FY 1978/79 report.

CAB 1.23:nos.
APPLICATIONS AND/OR AMENDMENTS THERETO FILED WITH THE CIVIL AERONAUTICS BOARD. [Weekly]

Gives brief summary of applications with date, docket number, type of service, terminals, and intermediate points.
Earlier C 31.221

CAB 1.24:date
TRUNK CARRIERS– COACH CLASS, TRAFFIC, REVENUE, YIELD, ENPLANEMENTS AND AVERAGE ON-FLIGHT TRIP LENGTH BY FARE CATEGORY. [Monthly]

Earlier C 31.269

CAB 1.25:CT
ADDRESSES. [Irregular]
Earlier C 31.215

CAB 1.26:date   • Item 177-A-15 (MF)
LIST OF U.S. AIR CARRIERS. [Semiannual]

PURPOSE:– To inform the public of current addresses and presidents of certificated air carriers and air freight forwarders.
Issued as of August 1 and February 1.
Earlier C 31.254
Discontinued.

CAB 1.27:date   • Item 177-A-24
REPORTS ON AIRLINE SERVICE, FARES TRAFFIC, LOAD FACTORS AND MARKET SHARES. [Irregular]

Contains statistical data on such subjects as Average Yields by Fare Flexibility Category; Changes in Domestic Scheduled Market Shares; Summary of Aircraft Departures, by City; etc.
Discontinued 984/3.

CAB 1.28:date   • Item 177-A-25 (MF)
TELEPHONE DIRECTORY. [Quarterly]
Discontinued 980/2.

CAB 1.29:date   • Item 177-A-21
DOMESTIC JET TRENDS. 1st ed.–   1974– [Biennial]
PURPOSE:– To present tables and charts showing unit cost and performance data for turbofan/turbojet aircraft operated by the domestic trunk and local carriers in domestic operations.
Earlier C 31.271
Discontinued in 1979.

CAB 1.29/2:date   • Item 177-A-21
INTERNATIONAL JET TRENDS. 1st ed–   1979–
Discontinued.

CAB 1.31:date/trans.nos.
C.A.B ECONOMIC ORDERS AND OPINIONS. [Daily]

CAB 1.32:date/trans.nos.
C.A.B. WEEKLY LIST OF AGREEMENTS FILED UNDER SEC. 412(a) OF THE FEDERAL AVIATION ACT.

CAB 1.33:date/trans.nos.
C.A.B. WEEKLY CALENDAR OF PREHEARING CONFERENCES, HEARINGS AND ARGUMENTS.

CAB 1.34:date/trans.nos.
C.A.B. ADVANCE DIGEST SERVICE. [Monthly]

CAB 1.35:date/trans.nos.
C.A.B. PREHEARING CONFERENCE REPORTS. [Irregular]

CAB 1.36:date/trans.nos.
C.A.B. NOTICES OF PREHEARING CONFERENCE HEARINGS AND ORAL ARGUMENTS. [Irregular]

CAB 1.37:date/trans.nos.
C.A.B. NOTICES OF PROPOSED RULEMAKING AND AMENDMENTS TO ALL REGULATIONS. [Irregular]

CAB 1.38:date/trans.nos.
C.A.B. INITIAL AND RECOMMENDED DECISIONS OF ADMINISTRATIVE LAW JUDGES. [Irregular]

CAB 1.39:date   • Item 177-A-26
AIR CARRIER INDUSTRY SCHEDULED SERVICE TRAFFIC STATISTICS. [Quarterly]

Tables present statistics on the scheduled service activities of air carriers in the medium regional group, by airline companies, for the current quarter and the current and previous 12 months.
Discontinued 986/1.

FEDERAL COMMUNICATIONS COMMISSION
(1934–   )

CREATION AND AUTHORITY

The Federal Communications Commission was created by the Communications Act of 1934 (48 Stat. 1064; 15 U.S.C. 21; 47 U.S.C. 35, 151-609), and administers that act, as amended. it also has additional regulatory jurisdiction under the provisions of the Communications Satellite Act of 1962 (76 Stat. 419; 47 U.S.C. 701-744).

INFORMATION

Information Division
Federal Communications Commission
445 12th Street S.W.
Washington, D.C. 20554
(202) 418-0200
Fax: (202) 418-0232
Toll Free: (888) 225-5322
http://www.fcc.gov

CC 1.1   • Item 283 (MF) (EL)
ANNUAL REPORT. 1st–   1935–   [Annual]

CC 1.1/2:date   • Item 287-A
SUMMARY OF ACTIVITIES, IN FISCAL [year].
Inactive.

CC 1.2:CT   • Item 285
GENERAL PUBLICATIONS.
Earlier RC 1.2

CC 1.2:M 43   • Item 285
MAJOR MATTERS BEFORE THE COMMISSION. [Annual]

CC 1.2/2   • Item 285-C
DIRECTORY OF FIELD CONTACTS FOR THE COORDINATION OF THE USE OF RADIO FREQUENCIES. [Annual]
See CC 1.2/10

CC 1.2/10:date   • Item 285-C
DIRECTORY OF FIELD CONTACTS FOR THE COORDINATION OF THE USE OF RADIO FREQUENCIES. [Annual]

CC 1.3:
BULLETINS.

CC 1.3/2:nos.
RADIO SERVICE BULLETINS. [Semimonthly]
Earlier RC 1.3

CC 1.3/2:nos.
ADM BULLETINS.

CC 1.3/3
INF BULLETINS. [Irregular]
Desig. PB 141106T

CC 1.4:
CIRCULARS.

CC 1.5:CT   • Item 286
FEDERAL LAWS.

CC 1.6:CT   • Item 287
RULES AND REGULATIONS.

CC 1.6/1– CC 1.6/11   • Item 287
FEDERAL COMMUNICATIONS COMMISSION RULES AND REGULATIONS. [Irregular]

The Federal Communications Commission grouped the various rules and regulations into 11 volumes, arrange by FCC part numbers.
Discontinued in 1983.

CC 1.7:nos.   • Item 287
FEDERAL RULES AND REGULATIONS (in parts).
Discontinued.

CC 1.7/2:nos.
–AMENDMENTS.

CC 1.7/3:nos.
–CORRECTION SHEETS.

CC 1.7/4:CT   • Item 285-A
HANDBOOKS, MANUALS, GUIDES.

CC 1.8:CT
POSTERS, FEDERAL, MAPS.

CC 1.9:CT
PAPERS IN RE.
Earlier RC 1.7

CC 1.10:date
LIST OF RADIO BROADCAST STATIONS. [Weekly]

Call letters assigned expecting amateurs.
Earlier RC 19, CC 2.7

CC 1.11:CT
EXAMINER'S REPORTS, BROADCAST DIVISION.

CC 1.11/2:CT
EXAMINER'S REPORTS, TELEGRAPH DIVISION.

CC 1.11/3:CT
EXAMINER'S REPORTS, TELEPHONE DIVISION.

CC 1.12:vol   • Item 284
FEDERAL COMMUNICATIONS REPORTS.
Contains decisions, reports and orders.

CC 1.12/a 1:CT
FEDERAL COMMUNICATIONS COMMISSION REPORTS. SEPARATES. DECISIONS, BROADCAST DIVISION.

CC 1.12/a 2:CT
– SEPARATES. DECISIONS, TELEGRAPH DIVISION.

CC 1.12/a 3:CT
– SEPARATES. DECISIONS, TELEPHONE DIVISION.

CC 1.12/a 4:CT
– SEPARATES. COMMISSION ORDERS.

CC 1.12/a 5:CT
– SEPARATES. BROADCAST DIVISION ORDERS.

CC 1.12/a 6:CT
– SEPARATES. TELEGRAPH DIVISION ORDERS.

CC 1.12/a 7:CT
– SEPARATES. TELEPHONE DIVISION ORDERS.

CC 1.12/a 8:date
MEMORANDUM, OPINIONS, AND ORDERS, INITIAL DECISIONS, ETC. [Irregular]

ISSN 0364-8052

CC 1.12/a 9:v.nos.
– SEPARATES. SELECTED DECISIONS AND REPORTS. [Weekly]

CC 1.12/2   • Item 284
FEDERAL COMMUNICATIONS COMMISSION REPORTS: SECOND SERIES.
Discontinued.

CC 1.12/2a • Item 284-A
FEDERAL COMMUNICATIONS COMMISSION
REPORTS. DECISIONS, REPORTS, PUBLIC
NOTICES, AND OTHER DOCUMENTS OF THE
FEDERAL COMMUNICATIONS COMMISSION (2d
series). v. 1– 1965– [Weekly]

Supersedes Federal Communications Commissions Reports, Selected Decisions and Reports of the Federal Communications Commission, of which the final issue was v. 38, no. 20, July 9, 1965.
Contains all decisions, reports, memorandum, opinions, orders, statements of policy, public notices, and all other official utterances and acts which are or may be of precedential value of public interest.
Later appears in bound volumes (CC 1.12/2). See CC 1.12/3

CC 1.12/3:v.nos.&nos. • Item 284
FCC RECORD. [Biweekly]
Earlier CC 1.12/2

CC 1.13
QUARTERLY OPERATING DATA OF TELEGRAPH CARRIERS.
(FCC Form 82)

Tables gives revenues, expenses, and other items for month and year-to-month by carrier. Two year comparisons. Included are companies having annual operating revenues in excess of $150,000.
Former title: Operating Data from Monthly Reports of Large Telegraph Carriers Filing Annual and Monthly Reports.

CC 1.14
QUARTERLY OPERATING DATA OF 70 TELEPHONE CARRIERS. (FCC Form 81)

Consists of two tables. Gives selected operating revenues, operating expenses and taxes, and other income items, and deductions for month and previous twelve-month period for all FCC respondents, principal telephone subsidiaries of ATT companies and affiliates, long lines department of ATT, and other FCC respondents. Two year comparisons.
Former title: Operating Data from Monthly Reports of Telephone Carries Filing Annual and Monthly Reports.

CC 1.14/2
STATISTICS OF CLASS A TELEPHONE CARRIERS REPORTING ANNUALLY TO THE COMMISSION, AS OF DECEMBER 31 (year) AND FOR YEAR THEN ENDED. [Annual]

Gives balance sheet data (assets and liabilities), income and earned surplus statement, dividends, operating statistics, employment and pensions, for all companies, Bell companies, and non-Bell companies.

CC 1.15
ADDRESSES. [Irregular]

CC 1.16:nos.
TARIFF CIRCULARS.

CC 1.17:nos.
TELEGRAPH ACCOUNTING CIRCULARS.

CC 1.18:nos.
TELEPHONE ACCOUNTING CIRCULARS.

CC 1.19:nos.
APPLICATIONS PENDING IN COMMISSION FOR EXEMPTION FROM RADIO PROVISIONS OF INTERNATIONAL CONVENTION FOR SAFETY OF LIFE AT SEA CONVENTION, LONDON, 1929, TITLE 3, Pt. 2 OF COMMUNICATIONS ACT OF 1934, ETC., REPORTS.

CC 1.20:nos.
DECISIONS; REPORTS [of action taken].

CC 1.20/2:nos.
ACTIONS OF COMMISSION, REPORTS [broadcast].
Earlier CC 1.20

CC 1.20/3:nos.
ACTIONS OF COMMISSION, REPORTS (Telephone and Telegraph).
Earlier CC 1.20

CC 1.21:date
LIST OF RADIO BROADCAST STATIONS, ALPHABETICALLY BY CALL LETTERS. [Annual]

CC 1.22:date
LIST OF RADIO BROADCAST STATIONS BY FREQUENCY. [Annual]

Prior to 1938 see CC 2.11

CC 1.23:date
LIST OF RADIO BROADCAST STATIONS BY STATE AND CITY. [Annual]
Prior to 1938 see CC 2.12

CC 1.24:date
RADIO BROADCAST STATIONS IN UNITED STATES, CONTAINING ALTERATIONS AND CORRECTIONS. [Monthly]
Prior to 1938 see CC 2.13

CC 1.25
RADIO SERVICE BULLETINS. [Semimonthly]
Earlier CC 2.3

CC 1.26:nos.
REPORTS OF APPLICATIONS RECEIVED IN RADIO BROADCAST STATIONS.
Earlier CC 2.8

CC 1.26/2:nos.
STANDARD BROADCAST APPLICATIONS READY AND AVAILABLE FOR PROCESSING PURSUANT TO SEC. 1.354 (c) OF COMMISSION'S RULES, LISTS. [Irregular]

CC 1.26/3:nos.
FM BROADCAST APPLICATIONS ACCEPTED FOR FILING AND NOTIFICATION OF CUT-OFF DATE. [Irregular]

CC 1.26/4:nos.
AM BROADCAST APPLICATIONS ACCEPTED FOR FILING AND NOTIFICATION OF CUT-OFF DATE. [Irregular]

CC 1.26/5:nos.
TV BROADCAST APPLICATIONS ACCEPTED FOR FILING AND NOTIFICATION OF CUT-OFF DATE. [Irregular]

CC 1.26/6:date
FM AND TV TRANSLATOR APPLICATIONS READY AND AVAILABLE FOR PROCESSING AND NOTIFICATION OF CUT-OFF DATE. [Irregular]

CC 1.27:nos.
REPORTS OF APPLICATIONS RECEIVED IN TELEGRAPH SECTION.

CC 1.28:nos.
REPORTS OF APPLICATIONS RECEIVED IN TELEPHONE SECTION.

CC 1.29:nos.
REPORTS OF CONSTRUCTION PERMITS RETIRED TO CLOSED FILES, ETC. [Monthly]

Earlier CC 3.9

CC 1.30:sec.nos.
SELECTED FINANCIAL AND OPERATING DATA FROM ANNUAL REPORTS.

CC 1.31:date
RELAY BROADCAST STATIONS.

CC 1.32:nos.
ACTIONS ON MOTIONS, REPORTS.

CC 1.33:nos.
ACTION IN DOCKET CASES, REPORTS.

CC 1.33/2:nos.
COMMISSION INSTRUCTIONS IN DOCKET CASES.

CC 1.34:dt.&nos.
APPLICATIONS [for permits], ETC.

CC 1.35:date • Item 288 (EL)
STATISTICS OF COMMUNICATIONS COMMON CARRIERS, YEAR ENDED (date). [Annual]

Compilation of financial and operating information secured under the Communications Act of 1934 and from all common carriers engaged in interstate or foreign communication service.
Covers telephone carriers, domestic and international telegraph carriers, and includes the intercorporate relations of all the carriers and controlling companies reporting to the Commission.

CC 1.36:nos.
NEW DOMESTIC PUBLIC LAND MOBILE RADIO SERVICE APPLICATIONS ACCEPTED FOR FILING DURING PAST WEEK.

CC 1.36/2:nos.
COMMON CARRIER ACTIONS, REPORTS, PUBLIC NOTICES.

CC 1.36/3:nos.
COMMON CARRIER TARIFF FILINGS, REPORTS, PUBLIC NOTICES.

CC 1.36/4:nos.
OVERSEAS COMMON CARRIER SECTION 214 APPLICATIONS FOR FILING. [Irregular]

CC 1.36/5:nos.
DOMESTIC PUBLIC LAND MOBILE RADIO SERVICE [action], PUBLIC NOTICES.

CC 1.36/6:nos.
COMMON CARRIER PUBLIC MOBILE SERVICES INFORMATION. [Weekly]

CC 1.36/8
POINT TO POINT MICROWAVE RADIO SERVICE. [Weekly]

CC 1.36/9:nos.
APPLICATIONS ACCEPTED FOR FILING BY PRIVATE RADIO BUREAU. [Irregular]

CC 1.36/10:nos.
PRIVATE RADIO BUREAU. [Weekly]

CC 1.37:nos.
PUBLIC NOTICES. [Press releases]

CC 1.37/2:nos.
GENERAL INFORMATION [releases].

CC 1.37/3:nos.
EXPERIMENTAL ACTIONS, REPORTS, PUBLIC NOTICES.

CC 1.38:
PUBLIC NOTICES: PETITIONS FOR RULE MAKING FIELD.

CC 1.38/2:nos.
OFFICE OF THE SECRETARY PETITIONS FOR RECONSIDERATION OF ACTIONS IN RULE MAKING PROCEEDINGS FILED, PUBLIC NOTICES.

CC 1.39:nos.
PUBLIC NOTICES: SAFETY AND SPECIAL RADIO SERVICES, REPORT. [Weekly]

CC 1.39/2:nos.
SAFETY AND SPECIAL ACTIONS, REPORTS, PUBLIC NOTICES.

CC 1.39/3:nos. • Item 287-B
SAFETY AND SPECIAL RADIO SERVICES BULLETINS. (numbered)
Inactive.

CC 1.39/4:nos.
APPLICATIONS ACCEPTED FOR FILING BY SAFETY AND SPECIAL RADIO SERVICES BUREAU. [Irregular]

CC 1.40:nos.
FIXED PUBLIC SERVICE APPLICATIONS RECEIVED FOR FILING DURING PAST WEEK, PUBLIC NOTICES. [Weekly]

CC 1.41
STATISTICS OF PRINCIPAL DOMESTIC AND INTER-NATIONAL TELEGRAPH CARRIERS REPORTING TO THE COMMISSION AS OF DECEMBER 31 (year) AND FOR YEAR THEN ENDED. [Annual]

Gives condensed balance sheet, income and earned surplus statement, dividends operating revenues and expenses plant and operating statistics, employees and compensation, by carrier. Figures are for calendar year.

CC 1.42:date
HEARING CALENDARS. [Irregular]

CC 1.42/2:date
FCC CALENDAR OF EVENTS FOR THE WEEK OF (date).

CC 1.42/3:date
EXPARTE PRESENTATIONS IN INFORMAL RULEMAKINGS. [Weekly]

CC 1.42/4:date
ORAL ARGUMENT [before a panel of the Review Board].

CC 1.43:date
FINAL TV BROADCAST FINANCIAL DATA. [Annual]

CC 1.43/2   • Item 287-C
AM-FM BROADCAST FINANCIAL DATA. [Annual]

Gives statistical data on revenue for all AM, AM/FM, and FM stations.
Discontinued.

CC 1.44:nos.
REQUEST FOR NEW OR MODIFIED BROADCAST CALL SIGNS.

CC 1.45:nos.
CATV REQUESTS FILED PURSUANT TO SEC. 74.1107(a) OF THE RULES, PUBLIC NOTICE.

CC 1.45/2:nos.
CATV ACTIONS REPORTS.

CC 1.45/3:nos.
CABLE TELEVISION AUTHORIZATION ACTIONS. PUBLIC NOTICES.

CC 1.46:nos.
REPORT R- (series). OFFICE OF CHIEF ENGINEER.

CC 1.47:nos.
CABLE TELEVISION SERVICE APPLICATIONS, REPORTS, PUBLIC NOTICES. [Irregular]

CC 1.47/2:nos.
CABLE TELEVISION RELAY SERVICE, APPLICATIONS, REPORTS, PUBLIC NOTICES. [Irregular]

CC 1.47/3:nos.
CABLE TELEVISION CERTIFICATE OF COMPLIANCE ACTIONS. [Irregular]

CC 1.47/4:nos.
DOMESTIC FIXED SATELLITE SERVICES. [Irregular]

CC 1.47/5:date
POLE ATTACHMENT FILINGS. [Irregular]

CC 1.48:nos.
TYPE APPROVAL ACTIONS, REPORTS, PUBLIC NOTICES. [Irregular]

CC 1.48/2:nos.
EQUIPMENT CERTIFICATION AND TYPE ACCEPTANCE ACTIONS, REPORTS, PUBLIC NOTICES. [Irregular]

CC 1.49:v.nos.&nos.
FCC ACTIONS ALERT. v. 1–   1975–   [Weekly]

A weekly summary of commission actions.
ISSN 0145-1170

CC 1.50:date   • Item 285-B
MAJOR MATTERS BEFORE THE FEDERAL COMMUNICATIONS COMMISSION. [Annual]

PURPOSE:– To serve as a means of informing Congress and the public of the status of significant proceedings in progress before the Commission. A detailed discussion of each proceeding is included.
Earlier CC 1.2:M 43
Discontinued.

CC 1.51:date
FCC FILINGS. [Irregular]

CC 1.52:date
COMMISSION MEETING AGENDA. [Irregular]

CC 1.53:date   • Item 283-A (MF)
TELEPHONE DIRECTORY. [Biennial]

CC 1.54:v.nos.&nos.
DAILY DIGEST.

CC 1.55/2   • Item 283-B
FORMS. [Irregular]

CC 1.56   • Item 285-D (EL)
FEDERAL COMMUNICATION COMMISSION DAILY.

CC 1.57:   • Item 285-D (E)
ELECTRONIC PRODUCTS (misc.).

CC 1.58:date   • Item 285-D (EL)
CCB (Common Carrier Bureau) REPORTS.

CC 1.59:CT   • Item 285-E
CONSUMER NEWS.

CC 1.60/1-1   • Item 283-A-1 (EL)
CIB (Consumer Information Bureau) ANNUAL REPORT.

CC 1.60/1-2   • Item 283-A-2 (EL)
CIB (Consumer Information Bureau) GENERAL PUBLICATIONS.

FEDERAL COMMUNICATIONS COMMISSION

NOTE:– Classes CC 2 through CC 4 became inactive in 1937.

Broadcast Division

CC 2.1:date
ANNUAL REPORTS.

CC 2.2:CT
GENERAL PUBLICATIONS.

CC 2.3:nos.
RADIO SERVICE BULLETINS. [Semimonthly]
Earlier RC 1.3
Later CC 1.25

CC 2.7:date
CALL LETTERS ASSIGNED. [Weekly, July–September]
1935 titled: Call Signals Assigned.

CC 2.8:nos.
REPORTS OF APPLICATIONS RECEIVED.
Slightly varying title.

CC 2.9:nos.
REPORTS (of action taken). [Weekly]

CC 2.10:date
LIST OF RADIO BROADCAST STATIONS, ALPHABETICALLY BY CALL LETTERS.
For alterations and corrections see CC 2.13
Earlier RC 1.9

CC 2.11:date
LIST OF RADIO BROADCAST STATIONS, BY FREQUENCY.
For alterations and corrections see CC 2.13
Earlier RC 1.9

CC 2.12:date
LIST OF RADIO BROADCAST STATIONS, BY ZONE AND STATE.
For alterations and corrections see CC 2.13
Earlier RC 1.9

CC 2.13:date
RADIO BROADCAST STATIONS IN U.S., CONTAINING ALTERATIONS AND CORRECTIONS.

Telegraph Division

CC 3.1:date
ANNUAL REPORTS.

CC 3.2:CT
GENERAL PUBLICATIONS.

CC 3.7:nos.
REPORTS OF APPLICATIONS RECEIVED.
Title varies slightly.

CC 3.8:nos.
REPORTS OF ACTION TAKEN. [Weekly]

CC 3.9:nos.
REPORTS OF CONSTRUCTION PERMITS RETIRED TO CLOSED FILES.
Later CC 1.29

Telephone Division

CC 4.1:date
ANNUAL REPORTS.

CC 4.2:CT
GENERAL PUBLICATIONS.

CC 4.7:nos.
REPORTS OF APPLICATIONS RECEIVED.
Slightly varying titles.

CC 4.8:nos.
RELEASE (of action taken) PRIOR TO JANUARY 22, 1936, REPORTS.

CC 4.9:nos.
REPORTS OF CONSTRUCTION PERMITS RETIRED TO CLOSED FILES.

UNITED STATES COMMISSION ON CIVIL RIGHTS (1957–   )

CREATION AND AUTHORITY

The Commission on Civil Rights was established by Public Law 85-315, approved September 9, 1957 (71 Stat. 634; 42 U.S.C. 1975), as amended by act of December 14, 1967 (81 Stat. 582). The Commission was reestablished by the United States Commission on Civil Rights Act of 1983 (97 Stat. 1301). Renamed November 2, 1994 by Stat. 4683.

INFORMATION

Commission on Civil Rights
624 9th St. NW
Washington, D. C. 20425
(202) 376-8177
Fax: (202) 376-7672
http://www.usccr.gov

CR 1.1   • Item 288-A (MF)
ANNUAL REPORTS. 1st–   1959–   [Annual]

CR 1.2:CT • Item 288-A
GENERAL PUBLICATIONS.

CR 1.6:CT
REGULATIONS, RULES, AND INSTRUCTIONS.

CR 1.6/2:CT • Item 288-A-2
HANDBOOKS, MANUALS, GUIDES.

CR 1.6/3:CT • Item 288-A
WORKING WITH YOUR SCHOOLS. [Irregular]
Handbooks of State Advisory Committees.
Discontinued in 1971.

CR 1.7:date
PRESS RELEASES.

CR 1.8:CT • Item 288-A-1
HEARINGS AND CONFERENCES BEFORE COMMIS-
SION ON CIVIL RIGHTS. [Irregular]

Transcripts of hearings and conferences held
in various cities covering civil rights issues.
Formerly distributed to depository libraries
under item 288-A-4.

CR 1.9 • Item 288-A-4
BIBLIOGRAPHIES, LISTS OF PUBLICATIONS.
[Irregular]

CR 1.10:nos. • Item 288-A-5
CLEARINGHOUSE PUBLICATIONS. 1– 1965–
[Irregular]

PURPOSE:– To carry out responsibilities delegated to the Commission by the Civil Rights Act
of 1964 to serve as a clearinghouse for civil
rights information.
Subjects include equal opportunity in agriculture, education, employment in both public and
private sectors, health and welfare services, and
voting rights.
Former title: CCR Special Publications.

CR 1.10:15 • Item 288-A (EL)
CIVIL RIGHTS DIRECTORY. Rev. 1970. 181 p.

Lists officials of 38 Federal agencies who
are responsible for monitoring, administering,
coordinating, and enforcing various aspects
of equal opportunity laws and policies; Federal officials with liaison responsibility for programs of special interest to Spanish- speaking groups; national private organizations with
civil rights programs; official State agencies
with civil rights responsibilities; and county
and municipal commissions with civil rights
responsibilities.

CR 1.11:CT
URBAN STUDIES.

CR 1.11/2:nos. • Item 288-A
CLEARINGHOUSE PUBLICATIONS: URBAN SERIES.
1– 1970–

CR 1.12 • Item 288-A
NEW PERSPECTIVES. v. 1– 1968– [Quarterly]

PURPOSE:– To provide authoritative information on civil rights matters by presenting articles on current events, report of government
and non- government activities, book reviews,
and analyses on civil rights developments in all
sections of the nation.
Former titles: Civil Rights Digest and Perspectives, Civil Rights.
Indexed by: Index to U.S. Government Periodicals.
ISSN 0009-7969

CR 1.13:CT
MAPS AND CHARTS. [Irregular]

CR 1.14:CT • Item 288-A
SCHOOL DESEGREGATION IN [Various Localities].
[Irregular]
Discontinued in 1979.

CR 1.15 • Item 288-A-5
CIVIL RIGHTS UPDATE. [Irregular]

Newsletter concerning civil rights activities
of the Commission.

CR 1.16:date • Item 288-A-9 (MF)
TELEPHONE DIRECTORY.

CR 1.17:v.nos./nos. • Item 288-A-10
CIVIL RIGHTS JOURNAL.

CIVIL SERVICE COMMISSION
(1883– 1979)

CREATION AND AUTHORITY

The United States Civil Service Commission
was created by act of Congress on January 16,
1883 (5 U.S.C. 1101). Over the years its authority
has been broadened by additional legislation and
Executive orders. The Commission was abolished
by Executive Order 12107, effective January 1,
1979, and its functions transferred to the newly
established Office of Personnel Management (PM
1) and the Merit Systems Protection Board (MS
1).

CS 1.1 • Item 290
ANNUAL REPORT. 1st– 1884– [Annual]

Report submitted by the Commission to the
President for the fiscal year.
Information included in the Appendix are statistical tables, report on agency training activities, political activity case, Federal personnel legislation. Executive Orders relating to personnel
management and significant judicial decisions are
also included.
Also published in the House Document series.

CS 1.2:CT • Item 295
GENERAL PUBLICATIONS.

CS 1.3:nos.
BULLETINS.

CS 1.3/2:nos.
MANAGEMENT SCIENCES INSTITUTE, PHILADEL-
PHIA REGION: BULLETINS.

CS 1.4:nos.
CIRCULARS.

CS 1.5:
SERVICE AND REGULATORY ANNOUNCEMENTS.

CS 1.6:CT
INSTRUCTION AND INFORMATION FOR APPLICANTS
AND FOR BOARDS OF EXAMINERS.

CS 1.7:date
LAWS, RULES AND REGULATIONS.

CS 1.7/2:date • Item 297
LAWS, RULES AND REGULATIONS (special).

CS 1.7/3:nos.
ORGANIZATION AND POLICY MANUAL LETTERS
(Admin).

CS 1.7/4:CT • Item 296-B
HANDBOOKS, MANUALS, GUIDES.
Earlier CS 1.7/2
Later PM 1.8

CS 1.7/4:C 18 • Item 296-B
FEDERAL CAREER DIRECTORY, GUIDE FOR
COLLEGE STUDENTS. [Irregular]

This directory presents specific information about Federal careers and the agencies
offering career positions. The book is intended
as a reference and guide for graduating college students, but will also be valuable to
persons with work experience and no degree.
A look at the major Federal career occupations is provided, describing the nature of the
work, the qualifications required, and career
possibilities, Each of the major Federal agencies is also described, along with where to
write for information.

CS 1.7/5 • Item 296-B
MANUAL ON FUND-RAISING WITHIN THE FEDERAL
SERVICES FOR VOLUNTARY HEALTH AND WEL-
FARE AGENCIES. [Irregular]

Subscription includes basic manual plus
supplemental material for an indefinite period. Issued in looseleaf form punched for ring binder.
PURPOSE:– Official medium of the Chairman
of the United States Civil Services Commission
for advertising policies, procedural and informational material of a reference nature about the
fund-raising program of the Federal Services. It is
for the guidance of Federal officials and representatives of recognized voluntary health and
welfare agencies.

CS 1.8:date
MANUAL OF EXAMINATIONS.

CS 1.9:
INSTRUCTIONS TO APPLICANTS, 1st DISTRICT,
BOSTON, MASSACHUSETTS.

CS 1.10:
– 2d DISTRICT, NEW YORK CITY.

CS 1.11:
– 3d DISTRICT, PHILADELPHIA, PA.

CS 1.12:
– 4th DISTRICT, WASHINGTON, D.C.

CS 1.13:
– 5th DISTRICT, ATLANTA, GEORGIA.

CS 1.14:
– 6th DISTRICT, CINCINNATI, OHIO.

CS 1.15:
– 7th DISTRICT, CHICAGO, ILLINOIS.

CS 1.16:
– 8th DISTRICT, SAINT PAUL, MINNESOTA.

CS 1.17:
– 9th DISTRICT, SAINT LOUIS, MISSOURI.

CS 1.18:
– 10th DISTRICT, NEW ORLEANS, LOUISIANA.

CS 1.19:
– 11th DISTRICT, SEATTLE, WASHINGTON.

CS 1.20:
– 12th DISTRICT, SAN FRANCISCO, CALIFORNIA.
CS 1.21:
– 13th DISTRICT, DENVER, COLORADO.

CS 1.22:date
INFORMATION CONCERNING TRANSFERS.

CS 1.23:date
ON CONCERNING REINSTATEMENTS.

CS 1.24:date
INFORMATION CONCERNING REMOVALS, REDUC-
TIONS, SUSPENSIONS AND FURLOUGHS.

CS 1.25:date
INFORMATION CONCERNING TEMPORARY
APPOINTMENTS.

CS 1.26 & CS 1.27 • Item 292
[ANNOUNCEMENTS OF EXAMINATIONS]. [Irregular]

Intended as poster announcements for forthcoming examinations to be held by the Civil Service Commission.
Later PM 1.21/2

CS 1.26/2:CT
POSTERS.

CS 1.26/3:nos. • Item 292
ANNOUNCEMENTS OF EXAMINATIONS, 4th DIS-
TRICT.

CS 1.26/4:nos. • Item 292
ANNOUNCEMENTS OF EXAMINATIONS, FIELD AND
LOCAL.

CS 1.27:CT
SCHEDULE OF EXAMINATIONS FOR 4th- CLASS POSTMASTERS (by States).

CS 1.28:form nos. • Item 292
ANNOUNCEMENTS OF EXAMINATIONS (General Series).
Later PM 1.21

CS 1.28:2279/nos. • Item 292
AN 2279, CURRENT FEDERAL EXAMINATION ANNOUNCEMENTS. 1– 1923– [Bimonthly]

Prior to issue 214 entitled Current Federal Civil Service Announcements.
ISSN 0364-2704

CS 1.28:2280/issue nos. • Item 292
AN 2280. BEST OPPORTUNITIES FOR FEDERAL EMPLOYMENT. 1– 173. 1951– 1975. [Bimonthly]

Earlier: Local and Regional Civil Service Examinations Offering Best Job Opportunities, AN 2280, prior to 1970.

ISSN 0364-2712

CS 1.28:2300/nos. • Item 292
AN 2300. PLACES WHERE CIVIL SERVICE EXAMINATIONS ARE HELD. 1– 1953– [Irregular]

CS 1.28:2301/nos. • Item 292
AN 2301. CIVIL SERVICE COMMISSION OFFICES. 1– 1954– [Irregular]

CS 1.28:2602-WA/nos. • Item 292
AN 2602-WA. CURRENT LOCAL ANNOUNCEMENTS COVERING WASHINGTON, D.C. METROPOLITAN AREA. 1– 1969– [Bimonthly]

ISSN 0364-5797

CS 1.29:nos.
RETIREMENT CIRCULARS.

CS 1.29/2:date
RETIREMENT REPORTS, FISCAL YEAR, C.S. RETIREMENT ACT, PANAMA CANAL ANNUITY ACT.
Earlier CS 1.2:R 31

CS 1.29/3 • Item 301-A
REPORT, CIVIL SERVICE REQUIREMENT, FEDERAL EMPLOYEES' GROUP LIFE INSURANCE, FEDERAL EMPLOYEES HEALTH BENEFITS, RETIRED FEDERAL EMPLOYEES HEALTH BENEFITS, FISCAL YEAR (date). [Annual]

CS 1.29/4:date
DIGEST OF SELECTED FEDERAL RETIREMENT SYSTEMS. [Annual]

CS 1.30:date
VETERAN PREFERENCE (in Appointment to Civil Offices under U.S. Government-Form 1481).

CS 1.31:date
OFFICIAL REGISTER OF THE UNITED STATES. 1816– 1959. [Annual]

Sub-title: Persons Occupying Administrative and Supervisory Positions in Legislative, Executive and Judicial Branches of Federal Government and in the District of Columbia.
Issued by the Department of State, 1816– 1861 (S 1.11); Department of the Interior, 1861– 1905 (I 1.25); and the Bureau of the Census, 1907– 1932 (C 3.10).
Issued biennially 1816– 1921.
Discontinued.

CS 1.32:date
CIVIL EMPLOYMENT AND PAYROLLS IN EXECUTIVE BRANCH OF U.S. GOVERNMENT. [Monthly]

CS 1.32/2:date
MONTHLY REPORT OF FEDERAL EMPLOYMENT.
Replaces CS 1.32

CS 1.33:date
PERSONNEL STATISTICS REPORTS. [Semiannual]

Varying titles.

CS 1.34:date
POLITICAL ACTIVITY AND POLITICAL ASSESSMENTS OF FEDERAL OFFICE- HOLDERS AND EMPLOYEES.
Changed from CS 1.2:P 75/1-15

CS 1.35:nos.
RECRUITING CIRCULARS, 4th CIVIL SERVICE DISTRICT.

CS 1.35/2:nos.
RECRUITING CIRCULARS, 4th CIVIL SERVICE REGION (1944–).

CS 1.36:CT
CLASS SPECIFICATIONS. PRELIMINARY DRAFTS.

CS 1.37:nos.
TRANSFER CIRCULARS.

CS 1.38:nos.
DEPARTMENTAL CIRCULARS, OCCUPATIONAL DEFERMENT SERIES.

CS 1.39 • Item 291
POSITION CLASSIFICATION STANDARDS FOR POSITIONS SUBJECT TO THE CLASSIFICATION ACT OF 1949. [Bimonthly] (Includes basic volume plus changes for an indefinite period).
Contains new position classification standards of the Civil Service Commission as issued. Also contains changes in position classification standards as they occur.
Later PM 1.30

CS 1.39/2:GS-nos.
[POSITION CLASSIFICATION STANDARDS CONCERNING POSITIONS IN ONE AGENCY].

CS 1.39/3:CT
POSITION CLASSIFICATION PLANS FOR [various cities or districts].

CS 1.40:letter-nos. • Item 300
P.D.C. MANUALS.

Discontinued.

CS 1.41:nos. • Item 294
FEDERAL PERSONNEL MANUAL, TRANSMITTAL SHEETS.
Later PM 1.14

CS 1.41/2:trans.sh.nos.
– SPECIAL REPRINT.

CS 1.41/3:nos. • Item 294
FEDERAL PERSONNEL MANUAL BULLETIN, INSTALLMENTS AND LETTERS. [Irregular]

Official medium of the U.S. Civil Service Commission for issuing its personnel regulations, instructions, and suggestions to other agencies.
Subscription can be placed for the entire series of basic volumes plus supplementary material for an indefinite period or for the individual supplements as listed below.
Later PM 1.14/2

CS 1.41/4:nos. • Item 294
– SUPPLEMENTS.

271- 1. DEVELOPMENT OF QUALIFICATION STANDARDS.
271- 2. TESTS AND OTHER APPLICANT APPRAISAL PROCEDURES.
292- 1. PERSONNEL DATA STANDARDS.
293-31. PERSONNEL RECORDS AND FILES.
296-31. PROCESSING PERSONNEL ACTIONS.
305- 1. EMPLOYMENT UNDER THE EXECUTIVE ASSIGNMENT SYSTEM.
330- 1. EXAMINING PRACTICES.
335- 1. EVALUATION OF EMPLOYEES FOR PROMOTION AND INTERNAL PLACEMENT.

339-31. REVIEWING AND ACTING ON MEDICAL CERTIFICATES.
512- 1. JOB GRADING SYSTEM FOR TRADES AND LABOR OCCUPATIONS.

Part 1, contains basic information; Part 2, description of the Standards and Individual Job Standards (issued bimonthly); and Part 3, occupational definitions.
532- 1. COORDINATED FEDERAL WAGE SYSTEM.
532- 2. NON-APPROPRIATED EMPLOYEES.
711- 1. LABOR MANAGEMENT RELATIONS.
711- 2. LABOR MANAGEMENT CASE FINDER.
731- 1. DETERMINING SUITABILITY FOR FEDERAL EMPLOYMENT.
752- 1. ADVERSE ACTION, LAW AND REGULATIONS, ANNOTATED Discontinued
792- 1. OCCUPATIONAL HEALTH SERVICES FOR CIVILIAN EMPLOYEES.
792- 2. ALCOHOLISM AND DRUG ABUSE PROGRAM.
831- 1. RETIREMENT.
870- 1. LIFE INSURANCE.
890- 1. FEDERAL EMPLOYEES HEALTH BENEFITS.
910- 1. NATIONAL EMERGENCY READINESS OF FEDERAL PERSONNEL MANAGEMENT.
990- 1. LAWS, EXECUTIVE ORDERS, RULES AND REGULATIONS.
990- 2. HOURS OF DUTY, PAY, AND LEAVE, ANNOTATED.
990- 3. NATIONAL EMERGENCY STANDBY REGULATIONS AND INSTRUCTIONS, PERSONNEL AND MANPOWER.

CS 1.42:nos.
EQUIPMENT MAINTENANCE SERIES, BULLETINS.

CS 1.42/2 • Item 294
JOB GRADING SYSTEM FOR TRADES AND LABOR OCCUPATIONS, TRANSMITTALS. [Irregular]

Federal Personnel Manual, Supplement 512- 1.

CS 1.43:date
BEST FEDERAL JOB OPPORTUNITIES. [Bimonthly]

CS 1.43/2:date
BEST BETS FOR RETURNING VETERANS IN WASHINGTON, D.C. AREA. [Bimonthly]
Earlier CS 1.2:V 64/8

CS 1.44 • Item 296
HANDBOOK OF OCCUPATIONAL GROUPS AND SERIES OF CLASSES. [Irregular]

Covers occupational groups and series of classes established under the Federal- Classification Plan.
Subscription includes basic volume plus supplementary material for an indefinite period.
Later PM 1.8/2

CS 1.45 • Item 290-A
HANDBOOKS.
Later PM 1.8/3

CS 1.45:X 118 • Item 290-A
QUALIFICATION STANDARDS FOR WHITE COLLAR POSITIONS UNDER THE GENERAL SCHEDULE. [Irregular] (Includes basic manual plus monthly revised pages for an indefinite period)
Later PM 1.8/3:X-118

CS 1.46:nos. • Item 293
EXAMINING CIRCULARS.
Discontinued.

CS 1.46/2:nos.
EXAMINING CIRCULARS, 4th CIVIL SERVICE RE-
GION.

CS 1.47:nos.
SPECIAL BULLETINS.

CS 1.48   • **Item 299**
PAMPHLETS. 1–   1947–   [Irregular]

PURPOSE:– To inform the public about em-
ployment opportunities and other aspects of the
Federal merit system
Later PM 1.10
The following titles are issued on a periodic
basis:

ANNUAL REPORT OF FEDERAL CIVILIAN
EMPLOYMENT BY GEOGRAPHIC AREA. 1st–
1967–   [Annual] (Manpower Statistics Division, Bureau of Manpower Information Systems) (SM 68)

PURPOSE:– To show the number of civilian employees of the Federal Government by
State and county of duty station (generally,
place where employees works), as well as by
Standard Metropolitan Statistical Area. Data
presented are derived from the Annual Geographic Distribution of Federal Civilian Employment Survey.

PAY STRUCTURE ON THE FEDERAL CIVIL SER-
VICE. 1946–   [Annual]

Pamphlet 33.
Figures are as of June 30. Statistical summaries of employment and compensation of
the Federal Government.
1967 issued as a monograph.

CS 1.48:T-7   • **Item 299**
EMPLOYEE TRAINING IN THE FEDERAL SER-
VICE, FISCAL YEAR (date). [Annual] (Bureau
of Training)

Supplements the general summary included in the Annual Report.

CS 1.48/2   • **Item 295**
BEM [Bureau of Executive Management] PAMPHLETS.
1–   1967–   [Irregular]

PURPOSE:– To inform about the Executive
Assignment System.

CS 1.49:nos.
GENERAL DISPLACEMENT NOTICES.

CS 1.50:nos.
CIRCULAR LETTERS, 4th CIVIL SERVICE REGION.

CS 1.51:nos.
RECRUITING BULLETINS.

CS 1.52:nos.   • **Item 301**
RECRUITING BULLETINS.
Discontinued.

CS 1.53:
RECRUITING AUTHORITY CIRCULARS.

CS 1.54   • **Item 300-A**
PERSONNEL MANAGEMENT SERIES. 1–   1951–
[Irregular]

PURPOSE:– To provide general guides for
the strengthening of personnel management and
programs.
Later PM 1.28

CS 1.55:date
FEDERAL EMPLOYMENT STATISTICS BULLETIN.
[Monthly]

CS 1.55/2   • **Item 293-E**
FEDERAL CIVILIAN WORKFORCE STATISTICS.
[Monthly]

Supersedes Federal Employment Statistics
Bulletin (CS 1.55) and Monthly Report of Federal
Employment (CS 1.32/2).
Prior to 1977 entitled Federal Civilian Man-

power Statistics.
Later PM 1.15

CS 1.56:nos.
HOW FEDERAL AGENCIES DEVELOP MANAGE-
MENT TALENT, MANAGEMENT STAFF
DEVELOPMENT SERIES REPORTS.

CS 1.57
PRESS RELEASES. [Irregular] (press only)

CS 1.58   • **Item 300-B**
PERSONNEL METHODS SERIES. 1–   1955–
[Irregular]

PURPOSE:– To provide general guides for
improving techniques in personnel management.
Discontinued.

CS 1.58/2:nos.   • **Item 290-M**
EVALUATION METHODS SERIES. 1–   1975–
Discontinued.

CS 1.59   • **Item 293-A**
FEDERAL FACTS. 1–   1956–   [Irregular]

CS 1.60   • **Item 290-B**
ADDRESSES. [Irregular]
Discontinued.

CS 1.61:CT   • **Item 290-E**
BIBLIOGRAPHIES AND LISTS OF PUBLICATIONS.
Later PM 1.22

CS 1.61/2
DISSERTATIONS AND THESES RELATING TO
PERSONNEL ADMINISTRATION. [Annual]

Compiled by the Library.

CS 1.61/3:nos.   • **Item 300-A-1**
PERSONNEL BIBLIOGRAPHY SERIES. 1–   1960–
[Irregular updated biennially]
Later PM 1.22/2

CS 1.61/4:date-nos.   • **Item 300-A-2**
INDEX TO CIVIL SERVICE COMMISSION INFORMA-
TION. 1–   1975–   [Quarterly] (Library)

PURPOSE:– To include, but not limited to,
information required to be available under section
552(a)(2) of the Freedom of Information Act.
ISSN 0145-1251
Inactive.

CS 1.62:v.nos.&nos.   • **Item 300-D**
PERSONNEL LITERATURE. v. 1–   1941–   [Monthly]
ISSN 0031-5753
Later PM 1.16

CS 1.63:date
ORGANIZATIONS DESIGNATED UNDER E.O. 10450;
CONSOLIDATED LIST (SCS FORM 385).

CS 1.64:date   • **Item 300-C**
PRESIDENT'S AWARDS FOR DISTINGUISHED FED-
ERAL CIVILIAN SERVICE. [Annual]

CS 1.65   • **Item 296-A**
INTERAGENCY TRAINING PROGRAMS. 1962–
[Annual & Monthly]

PURPOSE:– To provide information about
training programs offered in the Washington, D.C.
area on an interagency basis.

ANNUAL BULLETIN.

Published before the beginning of each
fiscal year, gives complete course descriptions and nomination information listed by
content indices for subject and agency. This
basic volume is updated by new course descriptions by monthly publications which are
so designated that they may be clipped and
the contents inserted into looseleaf copy of
annual IATPB maintained by the agency training office.
Includes Annual Calendar, previously published separately, gives titles, dates, and
course numbers of all IATPB listings arranged
chronologically.

MONTHLY CALENDAR.

Includes titles, dates, course numbers,
and nomination deadlines for two months,
arranged chronologically. Updates new
courses, new dates, cancellations, and nomination deadlines.

CS 1.65/2   • **Item 296-A**
DIRECTORY OF ADP TRAINING. 1966–

Continuation of the service inaugurated in
1960 by the Bureau of the Budget in its publication Orientation and Training Courses in Automatic Data Processing.

CS 1.65/3:date   • **Item 296-A**
EXECUTIVE SEMINAR CENTERS [programs].
Earlier CS 1.2:Ex 3/6

CS 1.65/4:date   • **Item 291-D**
INTERAGENCY TRAINING COURSES, CALENDAR.
[Quarterly]
ISSN 0145-1049
Later PM 1.19/2

CS 1.65/5:date   • **Item 296-A**
GENERAL MANAGEMENT TRAINING CENTER, CAL-
ENDAR OF TRAINING COURSES, FISCAL YEAR.
[Annual]
Earlier CS 1.2:M 31/4

CS 1.65/6:date   • **Item 296-A**
NATIONAL INTERAGENCY TRAINING CURRICULUM.

CS 1.65/7:CT   • **Item 290-H-5**
MANAGEMENT ANALYSIS SERIES. [Irregular]

PURPOSE:– To provide a series of training
courses covering such subjects as productivity,
flow charting, paperwork management, from the
management analysis point of view.
Later PM 1.49

CS 1.65/8:CT
PROGRAM MANAGEMENT SERIES. [Irregular]

CS 1.65/9:CT   • **Item 291-G**
CATALOGS OF TRAINING COURSES [on various sub-
jects].

CS 1.65/10:date   • **Item 291-F**
PERSONNEL MANAGEMENT TRAINING CENTER
COURSE CATALOG. [Annual]
Discontinued.

CS 1.66   • **Item 290-C**
CIVIL SERVICE JOURNAL. v. 1–   1960–
[Quarterly]
ISSN 0009-7985
Later PM 1.11

CS 1.67:nos.
COMMISSION LETTERS.

CS 1.68   • **Item 290-D**
CIVIL SERVICE RECRUITER. [Irregular]

Published periodically between September and
June.
Discontinued.

CS 1.69   • **Item 293-B**
FEDERAL NEWS CLIP SHEET. [Monthly]
Later PM 1.12

CS 1.70:date
UNIVERSITY-FEDERAL AGENCY CONFERENCE ON
CAREER DEVELOPMENT, CONFERENCE RE-
PORTS.

PERSONNEL RESEARCH AND DEVELOPMENT CENTER

CS 1.71:nos.
TECHNICAL SERIES.
Administrative.

CS 1.71/2:nos.   • **Item 290-J**
PROFESSIONAL SERIES.
Inactive.

CS 1.71/3:nos. • Item 290-P
TECHNICAL STUDIES. [Irregular] (Bureau of Policies
and Standards)
Discontinued.

CS 1.71/4:nos. • Item 291-E
TECHNICAL MEMORANDUM.
Discontinued.

CS 1.71/5:date • Item 290-R (MF)
FISCAL YEAR [report]. [Annual]
Discontinued.

CS 1.71/6:nos.
TECHNICAL NOTES. [Irregular]

CS 1.71/7:nos. • Item 290-P-1
PERSONNEL RESEARCH REPORTS. [Irregular]
Later PM 1.43

CS 1.71/8:CT
OPERATION PAPERS.

CIVIL SERVICE COMMISSION
(Continued)

CS 1.72 • Item 291-A
CURRENT FEDERAL WORKFORCE DATA. 1964–
[Semiannual]

PURPOSE:– To provide statistical tabulations
of Federal employment, turnover and hiring data.
Companion volumes to Federal Workforce Outlook, which projects trends to a four-year period.
Discontinued.

CS 1.72/2 • Item 291-A
FEDERAL WORKFORCE OUTLOOK. 1965/68–
[Annual]

Gives four-year projections of employment,
based on current and expected trends in agency
programs and in the occupational composition of
the Federal workforce.
Companion volume to Current Federal
Workforce Data, which gives current data.
Discontinued.

CS 1.72/3:date
FEDERAL EMPLOYMENT OUTLOOK. [Quarterly]

CS 1.73:nos. • Item 290-F
SALARY TABLES, EXECUTIVE BRANCH OF THE
GOVERNMENT. 1– [Irregular]
Earlier GA 1.10
Later PM 1.9

CS 1.74 • Item 293-C
FEDERAL EMPLOYMENT OF WOMEN. [Quarterly]

Prepared by the Bureau of Management Services for the Interdepartmental Committee on the
Status of Women.
Contains statistical breakdown of women
employed by Federal agencies by agencies, grade,
occupational group, and geographical area.
Discontinued.

CS 1.74/2:v.nos.&nos. • Item 290-H-2
WOMEN IN ACTION, AN INFORMATION SUMMARY
FOR THE FEDERAL WOMEN'S PROGRAM. v. 1–
1971– [Bimonthly]

Newsletter containing short articles on various subjects relating to the working woman.
Later PM 1.20

CS 1.75 • Item 291-B
COORDINATOR'S SCOREBOARD, REVIEW OF
WHAT'S NEW IN PLACEMENT OF THE HANDI-
CAPPED. 1962– [Annual]

Employment Programs for the Handicapped.
PURPOSE:– To inform about placements of
the handicapped in Federal agencies as well as
about program highlights and changes.
Discontinued.

CS 1.76:v.nos.&nos. • Item 291-C
EEO SPOTLIGHT. v. 1– [Bimonthly] (Office of Assistant Executive Director)

Prior to v. 6, no. 3, entitled Equal Opportunity
in Federal Employment, Newsletter.
Later PM 1.18

CS 1.76/2:nos. • Item 290-L
EEO FOR STATE AND LOCAL GOVERNMENTS
(series). 1–
Later PM 1.18/2

CS 1.77:v.nos.&nos.
CONGRESSIONAL RECORD DIGEST.

CS 1.78:nos.
MERIT SYSTEM METHODS.
Earlier FS 1.25

CS 1.79:v.nos.&nos. • Item 290-I
ADMINISTRATOR'S ALERT. [Monthly]
Discontinued.
ISSN 0364-541X

CS 1.80:nos. • Item 293-D
FEDERAL LABOR-MANAGEMENT CONSULTANT. 71-
1– 1971– [Biweekly] (Office of Labor-
Management Relations)
ISSN 0046-3418
Later PM 1.13

CS 1.80/2:nos • Item 290-Q
LABOR MANAGEMENT RELATIONS ISSUES IN
STATE AND LOCAL GOVERNMENTS. [Irregular]
Inactive.

CS 1.81:date
STATE SALARY RANGES OF SELECTED CLASSES
OF POSITIONS IN EMPLOYMENT SECURITY–
PUBLIC WELFARE– PUBLIC HEALTH, MENTAL
HEALTH– CIVIL DEFENSE, VOCATIONAL
REHABILITATION. 1971– [Annual] (Bureau of
Intergovernmental Personnel Programs)

CS 1.82:nos. • Item 295
PERSONNEL ADVISORY SERIES. 1– 1970–
[Irregular]
ISSN 0364-1325

CS 1.83:nos.
INCENTIVE AWARDS NOTES. 1– 1955–
[Bimonthly] (Office of Incentive Systems)

PURPOSE:– To help incentive awards administrators nationwide to do their job by providing a
media for exchanging current ideas and innovations in improving incentive awards activities, highlights on effective practice among Government
agencies and industry incentive awards efforts,
and extracts from studies of interest, speeches,
and articles.
Later PM 1.27/2

CS 1.84:nos. • Item 290-G
FEDERAL TRAINER, INFORMATION EXCHANGE FOR
THE FEDERAL TRAINING COMMUNITY. 1– [Ir-
regular] (Bureau of Training)

ISSN 0364-1325

CS 1.85:nos. • Item 290-H
EXECUTIVE PERSONNEL MANAGEMENT TECHNI-
CAL ASSISTANCE PAPERS, EMMTAP. 1– 1973–
[Irregular]

PURPOSE:– To assist agency personnel in
the implementation of effective programs in all
areas of executive manpower management. The
guidelines reflect and reinforce the broad requirements for an executive development program as
established in the Guidelines for Executive Development in the Federal Service issued by the
Civil Service Commission in October 1971.
Discontinued Nov. 1978.

CS 1.86:date
INTERGOVERNMENTAL PERSONNEL NOTES. 1971–
[Bimonthly]

PURPOSE:– To present current information
about program activity under the intergovernmental
Personnel Act of 1970 (IPA); to present other
information of interest to managers in State and
local governments (i.e., upcoming conferences,
new publications, new developments such as legal decisions affecting personnel management in
State and local governments); and to recognize

outstanding management achievements in State
and local governments.
The Act authorizes such mechanisms for
strengthening management capabilities of State
and local governments as direct grants-in-aid,
technical assistance, intergovernmental mobility
assignments, State and local participation in federal training programs, and administration of the
Standards for a Merit System of Personnel Administration in connection with a number of other
Federal assistance programs.
ISSN 0146-3012
Later PM 1.27

CS 1.87:date • Item 290-K
INTERAGENCY ADVISORY GROUP: ANNUAL RE-
PORT. 1st– 1965–

PURPOSE:– To serve as a major framework
for action by the Interagency Advisory Group
and its committees during the coming fiscal year
as well as listing the accomplishments and
achievements in meeting its goals and objectives
established for the preceeding year.
Also includes the report of the Personnel Directors Conference.
Discontinued.

CS 1.88:date • Item 290-N
TELEPHONE DIRECTORY.
Earlier CS 1.2:T 23
Later PM 1.31

CS 1.89:CT
POSTERS. [Irregular]
Earlier PM 1.35

CS 1.90:v.nos.&nos.
OCCUPATIONAL HEALTH REPORTER.
ISSN 0145-1219

CS 1.91:v.nos.&nos. • Item 290-H-1
FIRST LINE, NEWSLETTER FOR FEDERAL SUPER-
VISORS AND MIDMANAGERS. v. 1– 1976–
[Bimonthly]
ISSN 0145-1243
Later PM 1.17

CS 1.92:CT
NATIONAL INDEPENDENT STUDY CENTER:
. CORRESPONDENCE COURSES.

CS 1.93:date
EMPLOYMENT OF DISABLED AND VIETNAM ERA
VETERANS IN FEDERAL GOVERNMENT. [Semi-
annual]

CS 1.94:date • Item 290-H-6
CURRENT IPA PROJECTS FOR IMPROVED STATE
AND LOCAL MANAGEMENT. [Irregular]

PURPOSE:– To provide current information
of Intergovernmental Personnel Act (IPA) grant
programs to improve personnel management and
training in the public sector.
Former title: Report of IPA Grant Activity.
Discontinued 1978-1.

CS 1.95:date • Item 290-H-4
STATE AND LOCAL PERSONNEL SYSTEMS, ANNUAL
STATISTICAL REPORT. (Bureau of Intergovern-
mental Personnel Programs)

PURPOSE:– To provide base line indicators
for evaluation of the effectiveness of State and
local personnel administration. Data developed
by individual jurisdictions can be compared with
the national averages present in this report as a
starting point in self-evaluation.
ISSN 0148-950X
Discontinued 1977.

CS 1.96:v.nos.&nos. • Item 290-H-3
DIGEST OF SIGNIFICANT DECISIONS. [Bimonthly]

PURPOSE:– To provide a selection of significant cases in terms of an application of policy,
regulations of law thereto, or a clear, concise
statement of application of policy, regulations or
law in the cases involved. Selected decisions of
the Federal Employee Appeals Authority, the Appeals Review Board, and the Commissioners are
included.
Inactive.

COMMUNITY SERVICES ADMINISTRATION (1974– 1981)

CREATION AND AUTHORITY

The Community Services Administration was established by the Headstart, Economic Opportunity, and Community Partnership Act of 1974 (88 Stat. 2291; 42 U.S.C. 2701 note) as the successor to the Office of Economic Opportunity. The Administration was abolished and its functions transferred to the Office of Community Services in the Department of Health and Human Services by Public Law 97-35 of August 13, 1981 (95 Stat. 519; 42 U.S.C. 2941).

CSA 1.1:date • **Item 361-C**
ANNUAL REPORT.
    Discontinued.

CSA 1.1/2:date • **Item 361-D**
OFFICE OF THE INSPECTOR GENERAL: SEMI-ANNUAL REPORT TO THE CONGRESS.
    Discontinued.

CSA 1.2:CT • **Item 361-A**
GENERAL PUBLICATIONS.
    Discontinued.

CSA 1.2:Ac 2 • **Item 361-A**
ACCESSIBILITY ASSISTANCE, A DIRECTORY OF CONSULTANTS ON ENVIRONMENTS FOR HANDICAPPED PEOPLE. 1978. 202 p.

CSA 1.8:CT
HANDBOOKS, MANUALS, GUIDES.

CSA 1.8/2:nos. • **Item 857-H-2**
HANDBOOKS, MANUALS, GUIDES (numbered).
    Earlier PrEx 10.8/5
    Discontinued.

CSA 1.8/3:nos. • **Item 857-H-2**
CSA GUIDANCE (series).
    Discontinued.

CSA 1.9:nos. • **Item 857-H-17**
PAMPHLETS. [Irregular]
    Earlier PrEx 10.23
    Discontinued.

CSA 1.10:CT • **Item 361-A-1– 53 (MF)**
GEOGRAPHIC DISTRIBUTION OF FEDERAL FUNDS IN (States). 1975– [Annual] (Office of Operations, Division of State and Local Government)

    PURPOSE:– To present the dollar outlays of the Executive Branch of the Federal government by agency, program, and influence activities for every county of the United States and for each city of 25,000 population or more.
    Supersedes series, Federal Outlays in [State] published by the Office of Economic Opportunity (PrEx 10.24).
    Separate report issued for each State, covering the fiscal year.
    Summary report issued as Federal Outlays in Summary.
    Former title: Federal Outlays, Reports of Federal Governments Impact by State, County and Large City.
    Discontinued 1980.

CSA 1.11:v.nos.&nos. • **Item 361-B**
OPPORTUNITY II. v. 1– 2. 1978– 1980. [Quarterly]

    PURPOSE:– To provide information on the anti-poverty program of the Community Services Administration. Includes articles with illustration that amplify various aspects of the program.
    Discontinued 1980

CANAL ZONE GOVERNMENT (1951– 1979)

CREATION AND AUTHORITY

The Canal Zone Government was established by act of Congress approved September 26, 1950 (64 Stat. 1041), which limited its functions to maintaining civil government of the Canal Zone. The Canal Zone Government was superseded by the Panama Canal Commission (Y 3.P 19/2) pursuant to the Panama Canal Act of 1979 (93 Stat. 452), approved September 27, 1979.

CZ 1.1 • **Item 360**
PANAMA CANAL COMPANY, ANNUAL REPORT. 1st– [Annual]

    Continues Annual Report of the Governor of the Panama Canal.
    ISSN 0475-6126
    See Y3.P19/2

CZ 1.2:CT
GENERAL PUBLICATIONS.
    Earlier PaC 1.2

CZ 1.6:CT
REGULATIONS, RULES, AND INSTRUCTIONS.

CZ 1.7:
RELEASES.

CZ 1.8:v.nos. • **Item 360-A**
PANAMA CANAL REVIEW. [Semiannual]
    ISSN 0031-0646
    Earlier PaC 1.11
    Later Y 3.P 19/2:10

CZ 1.9:date
ANNUAL REPORT OF INSURANCE BUSINESS TRANSACTED IN CANAL ZONE.

CZ 1.10
SCHEDULE OF RATES FOR SUPPLIES AND SERVICES FURNISHED AT THE PANAMA CANAL AND SUPPLEMENTS. Admin.

CZ 1.11:v.nos.&nos.
PANAMA CANAL SPILLWAY. [Weekly]
    ISSN 0364-8044
    Later Y 3.P 19/2:9

DEPARTMENT OF DEFENSE (1949–   )

CREATION AND AUTHORITY

The Department of Defense was established as an executive department of the Government by the National Security Act Amendments of 1949 (61 Stat. 499 as amended), succeeding the National Military Establishment (M 1).

INFORMATION

    Office of the Assistant Secretary
      of Defense (Public Affairs)
    2E800
    The Pentagon
    Washington, D.C. 20301-1400
    (703) 697-9312
    Http://www.defenselink.mil

    Publications
    http://www.defenselink.mil/
    pubs/almanac/osd.html

D 1.1:date • **Item 306-A-2 (EL)**
DEPARTMENT OF DEFENSE ANNUAL REPORT.

    Continues: Report of Secretary of Defense to the Congress on the Budget, Authorization Request, and Defense Programs.
    Report submitted by the Secretary of Defense pursuant to section 202(d) of the National Security Act, as amended, for the fiscal year.
    The report includes the annual reports of the Secretary of the Army, Secretary of the Navy, and Secretary of the Air Force. Also includes annual report of the Reserve Forces Policy Board.
    Generalized and in summary form, the reports deal with current operations, new equipment, research and development, manpower, logistics, training, etc. Well illustrated with pictures and charts. A brief appendix contains statistical tables giving annual operational data.
    Published semiannual, July/Dec. 1949– Jan./June 1958; annual FY 1959–
    Formerly distributed to depository libraries under item No. 310.
    Continues: Annual Report, Department of Defense (ISSN 0082-8954)
    ISSN 0191-6513

D 1.1/2:CT
ANNUAL REPORTS OF ASSISTANTS TO SECRETARY OF DEFENSE.

D 1.1/3:date • **Item 306-A-1 (MF)**
ANNUAL REPORT OF THE SECRETARY OF DEFENSE ON RESERVE FORCES.

D 1.1/3-2 • **Item 306-A-1 (MF)**
RESERVE COMPONENT PROGRAMS.

    Earlier title: Annual Report of the Reserve Forces Policy Board.

D 1.1/4:date • **Item 306-A-2 (MF)**
YOUR DEFENSE BUDGET. [Annual]

D 1.1/5:date • **Item 306-A-14 (MF)**
ANNUAL REPORT OF THE DEPUTY ASSISTANT SECRETARY OF DEFENSE (INSTALLATIONS).

D 1.1/6:date • **Item 306-A-17 (MF) (EL)**
REPORT TO THE CONGRESS ON THE BALLISTIC MISSILE DEFENSE ORGANIZATION. [Annual]

    Formerly: Report to the Congress on the Strategic Defense Initiative.

    Describes the DoD's research and technology program efforts needed to meet the goals of the President's Strategic Defense Initiative. It responds to Section 1102 of the DoD Defense Authorization Act, FY 1985.

D 1.1/7:date • **Item 306-A-18 (MF)**
ANNUAL REPORT TO THE CONGRESS, FISCAL YEAR EXECUTIVE SUMMARY. [Annual]

    PURPOSE– To summarize the Defense Secretary's annual report to the Congress. Deals with such matters as provision for the common defense; threats, military balances, and net assessments; U.S. interests, national security objectives, and strategy, and the defense budget.

D 1.1/7-2:date • **Item 306-A-14**
ANNUAL REPORT TO THE CONGRESS FISCAL YEAR . . . INSTALLATIONS. [Annual]

D 1.1/8:date • **Item 306-A-18 (MF)**
DIS (Defense Investigative Service) ACHIEVEMENTS.

D 1.1/9:date • **Item 306-A-2 (MF)**
DOD INSPECTOR GENERAL SEMIANNUAL REPORT TO CONGRESS.

D 1.1/10 • **Item 306-H (MF)**
ANNUAL TEST REPORT, DEPARTMENT OF DEFENSE DEPENDENTS SCHOOLS.

D 1.1/11:date • **Item 306-J (MF)**
PLANNERS AND PROJECT MANAGERS ANNUAL REPORT.
    See D 103.132

D 1.2:CT • **Item 306**
GENERAL PUBLICATIONS.

D 1.2:P 94/8
REAL AND PERSONAL PROPERTY OF THE DEPARTMENT OF DEFENSE, AS OF JUNE 30. [Annual] (Office of the Comptroller)

Report submitted to the President and to Congress in compliance with Section 410 of Title IV of the National Security Act of 1947, as amended, and as codified in Section 2701 of title 10, United States Code.
Later D 1.58/2

D 1.3/2:v.nos.&nos. • Item 304-C
DEFENSE INDUSTRY BULLETIN. v. 1– 8. 1965– 1972. [Monthly]

PURPOSE:– To serve as a means of communication from the Department of Defense and its components to actual and potential defense contractors, labor, and other interests. It provides information and guidance on official policies, programs, procedures, activities and developments concerning the management of research, development and acquisition of equipment, supplies and services needed in the national defense effort.
Merged with Defense Management Journal (D 1.38/2) effective Spring 1972 issue.

Discontinued.

D 1.3/3: • Item 306-B-2
SECURITY AWARENESS BULLETIN.
Discontinued.

D 1.5:CT
LAWS.
D 1.6:CT • Item 309
REGULATIONS, RULES, AND INSTRUCTIONS.
Earlier M 1.6

D 1.6/2:CT • Item 306-A
HANDBOOKS, MANUALS, GUIDES.

D 1.6/2-2:nos. • Item 306-A (MF)
DEPENDENTS SCHOOLS MANUALS. [Irregular]

D 1.6/2-3:date • Item 306-A (MF)
GUIDE TO THE EVALUATION OF EDUCATIONAL EXPERIENCES IN THE ARMED SERVICES. [Biennial]
Earlier D 1.6/2:Ed 8

D 1.6/3 • Item 306-A (MF)
SPEAKERS' GUIDE FOR SERVICE SPOKESMEN, POWER FOR PEACE, ARMED FORCES DAY. [Annual]
Earlier D 6.8
Discontinued.

D 1.6/4 • Item 306-B-1
JOINT FEDERAL TRAVEL REGULATIONS: VOLUME 1, MEMBERS OF UNIFORMED SERVICES. [Irregular]
Earlier title: Joint Travel Regulations.

Vol 1. MEMBERS OF THE UNIFORMED SERVICES. [Annual & Monthly] (Includes basic volume plus 11 monthly supplements. Issued in looseleaf form).

Gives basic statutory regulations concerning travel and transportation allowances of members of the uniformed services, including the Army, Navy, Marine Corps, Air Force, Coast Guard, Coast and Geodetic Survey, and the Public Health Service.
See D 1.6/4-5

D 1.6/4-2:date
JOINT FEDERAL TRAVEL REGULATIONS, VOL. 1. [Irregular]
Earlier D 1.6/4:date

D 1.6/4-5:date • Item 306-C-1 (EL)
JOINT FEDERAL TRAVEL REGULATIONS.
Issued on floppy diskettes.

D 1.6/5:date • Item 306-C
JOINT TRAVEL REGULATIONS: VOL. 2. CIVILIAN PERSONNEL. [Annual & Monthly] (Includes basic volume plus 11 monthly supplements. Issued in looseleaf form)

Provides uniform per diem, travel, and transportation allowance regulations for civilian personnel of the Department of Defense.

D 1.6/6 • Item 306-D
LCC [Life Cycle Costing].
Discontinued.

D 1.6/7:CT • Item 310-N (MF)
ENGINEERED PERFORMANCE STANDARDS FOR REAL PROPERTY MAINTENANCE ACTIVITIES. [Irregular]

Formerly published by the Naval Facilities Engineering Command and classed D 209.14.

D 1.6/8:date • Item 306-E (MF)
DoD DIRECTIVES SYSTEM QUARTERLY INDEX.

Part 1 indexes DoD directives and instructions by number, Part 2, by subject. Part 3 contains the DoD Distribution List, and Part 4 lists the final opinions, statements of policy and administrative staff manuals and instructions that affect the public.
Published in microfiche.
Discontinued.

D 1.6/8-2:nos. • Item 306-E
DEPARTMENT OF DEFENSE DIRECTIVES (series). [Irregular]

D 1.6/9:nos. • Item 310-E-3
MEPCOM REGULATIONS. [Irregular]

D 1.6/10:nos. • Item 310-E (MF)
DCAA REGULATIONS (series). [Irregular] (Defense Contract Audit Agency)
Discontinued.

D 1.6/11:date • Item 303
FEDERAL ACQUISITION REGULATIONS. [Irregular]

Subscription service consists of a basic manual and supplementary material issued for an indeterminate period.
Together with agency supplemental regulations, the Federal Acquisition Regulation (FAR), the primary regulation for use by all Federal Executive Agencies in their acquisition of supplies and services with appropriate funds, replaces the current Federal Procurement Regulations System (GS 1.6/5), the Defense Acquisition Regulation (D 1.13), and the NASA Procurement Regulation (NAS 1.6/2).
It precludes agency acquisition regulations that unnecessarily repeat, paraphrase, or otherwise restate the FAR and limits agency acquisition relations to those necessary to implement FAR policies and procedures within an agency. It also provides for coordination, simplicity, and uniformity in the Federal acquisition process.
The DoD FAR Supplement must be read in conjunction with the FAR for DoD acquisitions, and the NASA FAR Supplement must be read in conjunction with the FAR for NASA acquisitions.

D 1.6/11-2: • Item 303
FEDERAL ACQUISITION CIRCULAR.

D 1.6/11-3 • Item 307-A (P) (EL)
AR TODAY (ACQUISITION REFORM TODAY). [Bi-monthly]

D 1.6/12:date • Item 310-E-19 (MF)
DoD DIRECTORY OF CONTRACT ADMINISTRATION SERVICES COMPONENTS. [Semiannual]

PURPOSE:– To list the components assigned to providing contract administration services (CAS) within designated geographic areas and at specified contractor plants.

D 1.6/13:nos. • Item 309
DEPARTMENT OF DEFENSE INSTRUCTION (series). [Irregular]

D 1.6/14:date • Item 306-A
MILITARY CAREER GUIDE, EMPLOYMENT AND TRAINING OPPORTUNITIES IN THE MILITARY. [Biennial]
Replaced by D 1.6/15

D 1.6/15:date • Item 306-A
MILITARY CAREERS: A GUIDE TO MILITARY OCCUPATIONS AND SELECTED MILITARY CAREER PATHS.
Replaces D 1.6/14

D 1.6/16 • Item 306-A--23 (EL)
SUBCONTRACTING DIRECTORY. [Annual]

D 1.6/17 • Item 306-A--23 (EL)
SMALL BUSINESS SPECIALISTS. [Annual]

D 1.6/18 • Item 306-A--25
DEPARTMENT OF DEFENSE MILITARY COMMISSION ORDER.

D 1.7 • Item 304-H (CD)
DEPARTMENT OF DEFENSE TELEPHONE DIRECTORY. [3 times/yr.]

ISSN 0363-6844

D 1.7/1:date • Item 304-H-2 (E)
DEPARTMENT OF DEFENSE TELEPHONE DIRECTORY. [Triennial]

D 1.7/2:date/nos. • Item 304-H-1
MAPAD SYSTEM.

MAPAD = Military Assistance Program Address Directory
Contains the addresses of country representatives, freight forwarders and customers- within-country required for releasing Foreign Military Sales and Military Assistance Program Grant Aid shipments.
Earlier D 7.6/4:M 59/6

D 1.8:date
MILITARY NEGOTIATION REGULATIONS.
Later RnB 1.6/4

D 1.9:date • Item 302
ARMED SERVICES CATALOG OF MEDICAL MATERIAL.

D 1.9/2:date
– STANDARD PRICE SUPPLEMENT.

D 1.9/3:nos.
– CHANGE BULLETINS.

D 1.9/4:date
– ALPHABETICAL INDEX.

D 1.9/5:date
ARMED SERVICES CATALOG OF MEDICAL MATERIEL. COMPONENT PARTS SUPPLEMENT.

D 1.9/6:date
– COMPONENT PARTS SUPPLEMENT.

D 1.10 • Item 305
ARMED FORCES INSTITUTE MANUALS. [Irregular]
Discontinued.

D 1.10/2:date
USAFI INFORMATION LETTER.

D 1.10/3:date
USAFI SUPPLY NOTICE.

D 1.10/4:date
USAFI CATALOG.

D 1.10/5:v.nos.&nos. • Item 310-C
DIALOG FOR THE SERVICE EDUCATION OFFICER. v. 1, nos 1– 4. Feb.– June 1971. (Armed Forces Institute)
Discontinued.

D 1.10/6:date
CORRESPONDENCE COURSES OFFERED BY PARTICIPATING COLLEGES AND UNIVERSITIES THROUGH THE UNITED STATES ARMED FORCES INSTITUTE. [Annual]

D 1.11:v.nos.
UNITED STATES ARMED FORCES MEDICAL JOURNAL. [Monthly]
Discontinued.

D 1.11/2:v.nos.
MEDICAL TECHNICIANS BULLETIN, SUPPLEMENT TO U.S. ARMED FORCES MEDICAL JOURNAL. [Bimonthly]
> Replaces Hospital Corps Quarterly M 203/2
> Discontinued.

D 1.12
MILITARY SPECIFICATIONS. [Irregular]

D 1.12/2:le-nos.
MILITARY SPECIFICATIONS. TEMPORARY.

D 1.12/3:le-nos.
INTERIM MILITARY SPECIFICATIONS.

D 1.13   **• Item 303**
ARMED SERVICES PROCUREMENT REGULATION.

> Latest basic volume: 1973 edition.
> This regulation for the Department of Defense uniform policies and procedures relating to the procurement of supplies and services under the authority of chapter 137, title 10, United States Code, or under other statutory authorization. The regulation applies to all purchases and contracts made by the Department of Defense, within or without the continental United States for the procurement of supplies and services with obligated appropriated funds.
> Beginning with the 1960 edition, extensive changes in the format have been made, including a uniform system of type size, numbering, indentation, and paragraphing. In addition, some of the material has been relocated and realined to afford a more orderly presentation and to provide a logical basis for future expansion. Other minor changes have also been made in this edition which will serve to increase its usefulness and conciseness.
> Subscription price includes basic volume, issued in looseleaf form and punched for 3-ring binder, plus supplementary material for period of approximately 2 years.
> Subscription also includes Defense Procurement Circulars.

D 1.13/2   **• Item 304**
DEFENSE ACQUISITION REGULATIONS, SUPPLEMENTS. 1–   1982–

> Former title: Armed Services Procurement Regulations.
> Earlier M 1.8/2

D 1.13/2-2   **• Item 304**
ARMED SERVICES PROCUREMENT REGULATION SUPPLEMENT, ASPA- (series). 1–   1966– [Irregular]

D 1.13/2-3:date   **• Item 304**
ARMED SERVICES PROCUREMENT REGULATIONS SUPPLEMENT, HQ USAF. [Monthly] (Includes basic volume plus monthly supplemental pages for an indefinite period)

> Implements the Armed Services Procurement Regulation and establishes for the Air Force uniform policies, procedures, and instructions relating to the procurement of supplies and services.
> Supersedes Air Force Procurement Instructions (D 301.6/4).

D 1.13/3:nos.   **• Item 304**
DEFENSE ACQUISITION CIRCULARS. [Irregular] see above

> Included in subscription to Armed Services Procurement Regulation.
> Former title: Defense Procurement Circulars.
> ISSN 0364-6734

D 1.13/4   **• Item 303**
ARMED SERVICES PROCUREMENT MANUAL, ASPM- (series). 1–   1965–   [Irregular]

D 1.14:date
ARMED FORCES SONG FOLIO. [Monthly]
> Earlier D 202.10

D 1.15:date   **• Item 349**
MANUAL FOR COURTS-MARTIAL, UNITED STATES. [Irregular]

> This is the legal manual authorized by the Department of the Army for all courts-martial proceedings. It contains all relevant rules, procedures, and preparations, required for the operation of the courts-martial. Also included are appendices containing pertinent forms for the legal counsels and basic legal documents such as the Constitution and the Uniform Code of Military Justice.
> See for earlier issues of Manual for Courts-martial, Air Force M 301.6:C 83 and Army M 107.7

D 1.15/2:date   **• Item 349**
MANUAL FOR COURTS-MARTIAL, ARMY SUPPLEMENT.
> Formerly classified in D 1.15

D 1.15/3:date   **• Item 349**
MANUAL FOR COURTS-MARTIAL, AIR FORCE SUPPLEMENT.
> Formerly classified D 1.15

D 1.15/4   **• Item 349**
MANUAL FOR COURTS-MARTIAL, NAVY SUPPLEMENT.

D 1.16:sec.nos.&fasc.nos.
ATLAS OF TUMOR PATHOLOGY.

D 1.16/2:CT   **• Item 306-B**
MEDICAL MUSEUM OF ARMED FORCES INSTITUTE OF PATHOLOGY PUBLICATIONS.
> Discontinued.

D 1.16/3:fascicle nos.   **• Item 310-D**
ATLAS OF TUMOR PATHOLOGY, 2d SERIES.
> Later D 101.117/3

D 1.16/4:CT   **• Item 310-G**
ARMED FORCES INSTITUTE OF PATHOLOGY: PUBLICATIONS. [Irregular]

D 1.17:
QUALIFIED PRODUCTS LISTS.

D 1.18:v.nos.
DIGEST OF OPINIONS, JUDGE ADVOCATE GENERAL OF ARMED FORCES. [Quarterly]

D 1.18/2
DIGEST OF OPINIONS: JUDGE ADVOCATES GENERAL OF ARMED FORCES.

D 1.19:dates   **• Item 311-A (EL)**
UNITED STATES COURT OF MILITARY APPEALS AND THE JUDGE ADVOCATES GENERAL OF THE ARMED FORCES AND THE GENERAL COUNSEL OF THE DEPARTMENT OF THE TREASURY. ANNUAL REPORT. 1951/52–   [Annual]

> Report issued for the calendar year pursuant to article 67(g) of the Uniform Code of Military Justice, 10 U.S.C. 867(g).
> Report for year 1951/52 ends May 31; for 1952/53–   Dec. 31.

D 1.19/2:CT
UNITED STATES COURT OF MILITARY APPEALS, PUBS. (other than annual reports).

D 1.19/3   **• Item 311-B**
DIGEST ANNOTATED AND DIGESTED OPINIONS, U.S. COURT OF MILITARY APPEALS.
> Discontinued.

D 1.20:v.nos.
CURRENT LIST OF MEDICAL LITERATURE. [Monthly]
> Earlier D 104.7
> Later D 8.8

D 1.21:date   **• Item 348**
DIGEST OF DECISIONS OF ARMED SERVICES BOARD OF CONTRACT APPEALS.
> Earlier 108.2:C 76/942-50

D 1.22   **• Item 302-A**
ARCTIC BIBLIOGRAPHY. v. 1–   1953–   [Annual]
> Prepared for and in cooperation with the Department of Defense, under the direction of the Arctic Institute of North America.
> Discontinued.

D 1.23:
HEADQUARTERS EUROPEAN COMMAND, PUBLICATIONS.

D 1.23/2:v.nos.&nos.
HISTORICAL DIVISION, SPECIAL STUDIES SERIES.

D 1.24:CT
GENERAL HEADQUARTERS, FAR EAST COMMAND, GENERAL PUBLICATIONS.

D 1.24/2:nos.
MILITARY HISTORY SECTION: JAPANESE OPERATIONAL MONOGRAPH SERIES.

D 1.25:CT
NATIONAL SECURITY AGENCY PUBLICATIONS.

D 1.25/2:nos.
– [TRAINING PROGRAM] TP (series).

D 1.25/8:CT   **• Item 306-A-6**
HANDBOOKS, MANUALS, GUIDES. [Irregular]
> Discontinued.

D 1.26:date
FEATURE SECTIONS OF JOURNALS IN NWC LIBRARY. [Annual]

> Issued by Periodicals and Documents Section, National War College Library.

D 1.26/2:date
LIST OF PERIODICALS IN NWC LIBRARY. [Annual]

D 1.26/3:v.nos.&nos.
PERIODICAL LITERATURE BULLETINS. National War College Library

D 1.26/4:v.nos.&nos.
BOOK NEWS. National War College Library

D 1.27:
EMERGENCY MANAGEMENT OF NATIONAL ECONOMY.

D 1.27/2:CT
ECONOMIC MOBILIZATION STUDIES.

D 1.28:date
ANNUAL REPORT OF ARMY-AIR FORCE WAGE BOARD.
> Earlier D 101.2:W 12

D 1.29
COURTS-MARTIAL REPORTS, HOLDINGS AND DECISIONS OF JUDGE ADVOCATES GENERAL, BOARDS OF REVIEW, AND UNITED STATES COURT OF MILITARY APPEALS. v. 1–   1951/52–   [Annual]

> Sold by Lawyer Co-operative Publishing Company, Rochester, N.Y.
> Supersedes Board of Review and Judicial Council, of the Army; Courts-Martial Orders of the Navy, and Courts-Martial reports of the Judge Advocate General of the Air Force.

D 1.30:nos.
ARMED SERVICES MEDICAL PROCUREMENT AGENCY; MEMORANDUM REPORTS.

D 1.31:date   **• Item 304-A**
COBOL [common business oriented language].
> Discontinued.

D 1.32:CT
U.S. ANTARCTIC PROJECTS OFFICER. PUBLICATIONS.
> Later D 201.15/2

D 1.32/2:v.nos.&nos.
U.S. ANTARCTICS PROJECTS OFFICER. BULLETIN.
> See D 301.89/14

D 1.33:CT   **• Item 304-D**
BIBLIOGRAPHIES AND LIST OF PUBLICATIONS.

D 1.33/2:nos.   **• Item 304-D-1 (MF)**
FRIDAY REVIEW OF DEFENSE LITERATURE. [Weekly]
> Later D 2.19/8

D 1.33/3:date
DEPARTMENT OF DEFENSE BIBLIOGRAPHY OF LOGISTICS STUDIES AND RELATED DOCUMENTS.
　　Updated by supplements.

D 1.33/3-2:date
ANNUAL DEPARTMENT OF DEFENSE BIBLIOGRAPHY OF LOGISTICS STUDIES AND RELATED DOCUMENTS.

D 1.33/4:date　　　　　　　• Item 304-D (EL)
CATALOG OF DIOR REPORTS. [Annual] (Directorate for Information Operations and Reports)
　　Also published in microfiche.

D 1.33/5:date　　　　　　　• Item 304-D (MF)
INDEX OF DCAA NUMBERED PUBLICATIONS AND MEMORANDUMS. [Quarterly]
　　See D 1.33/5-2

D 1.33/5-2　　　　　　　• Item 304-D (MF)
INDEX OF DCAA MEMORANDUMS FOR REGIONAL DIRECTORS (MRDs). [Quarterly]

D 1.33/6:date
CATALOG OF LOGISTICS MODELS. [Annual]

D 1.33/7:date　　　　　　• Item 304-D-2 (MF)
DANTES EXTERNAL DEGREE CATALOG. [Annual]

D 1.33/7-2:date　　　　　　• Item 304-D-3 (MF)
DANTES INDEPENDENT STUDY CATALOG. [Annual]

D 1.34:v.nos.&nos.
CD NEWS FEATURE PAGE.
　　Earlier PrEx 4.7/4

D 1.34/2:v.nos.&nos.
CD NEWSPICTURES.
　　Earlier Pr 34.760

D 1.35:nos.
JOINT MILITARY PACKAGING TRAINING CENTER COURSE OUTLINES.

D 1.36:date
BRIEF OF THE ORGANIZATION AND FUNCTIONS, SECRETARY OF DEFENSE, DEPUTY SECRETARY OF DEFENSE, DEPUTY SECRETARY OF DEFENSE, ETC.

D 1.37:nos.
FTG TIF (series).
　　Later D 301.45/31-4

D 1.38:date　　　　　　　• Item 304-B
DEPARTMENT OF DEFENSE COST REDUCTION PROGRAM, ANNUAL PROGRESS REPORT. 1st– 1962/63–　[Annual]
　　Title varies.
　　ISSN 0011-7595

D 1.38/2:v.nos.&nos.　　　　• Item 304-B
DEFENSE MANAGEMENT JOURNAL. v. 1–　1965– [Bimonthly]

　　Includes cost reduction goals and accomplishments; policies and procedures of the cost reduction systems; cost reduction techniques and processes in all functional areas from which savings are derived; new developments in concepts and philosophy that affect cost reduction objectives; and specific cost reduction examples, with attribution where appropriate.
　　Title varies: Dec. 1963– Feb. 1966, Cost Reduction Report: Spring 1966– Summer 1967, Cost Reduction Journal; Fall 1967– Defense Management Journal.
　　Effective Spring 1972, absorbed Defense Industry Bulletin (D 1.3/2).
　　Issued quarterly prior to v. 14(1978)
　　Indexed by: Index to U.S. Government Periodicals.
　　ISSN 0011-7595
　　Discontinued.

D 1.39:nos.
NATIONAL COMMUNICATIONS SYSTEM MEMORANDA. Offical Use.

D 1.39/2:nos.
NATIONAL COMMUNICATIONS SYSTEM INSTRUCTIONS. Offical Use.

D 1.39/3:nos.
NATIONAL COMMUNICATIONS SYSTEM CIRCULARS. Offical Use.

D 1.40　　　　　　　　• Item 304-E
COUNTRY LAW STUDIES. [Irregular]

　　Prepared by Judge Advocate General's Corps, Army.
　　Discontinued.

D 1.41:v.nos.&nos.　　　• Item 304-G (P) (EL)
PROFILE: LIFE IN THE ARMED FORCES. v. 1– 1957–　[Monthly during school year]

　　Titled High School News Service Report prior to November 1976.
　　Indexed by: Index to U.S. Government Periodicals.

D 1.41/2:date　　　　　　• Item 304-G-1
FUTURES FOR THE CLASS OF . . .

　　Earlier title: High School News Service Report, Basic Fact Edition, School Year.

D 1.42:nos.　　　　　　　• Item 310-A
SHOCK AND VIBRATION MONOGRAPHS. 1– [Irregular]
　　Later D 210.27/3
　　Discontinued.

D 1.43:nos.
SELECTED ECONOMIC INDICATORS. [Monthly]

D 1.44:CT　　　　　　　• Item 304-F
RESOURCE MANAGEMENT MONOGRAPHS.
　　Discontinued.

D 1.45:nos.　　　　　　　• Item 310-B (MF)
DEFENSE MANAGEMENT EDUCATION AND TRAINING CATALOG.

D 1.45/2:date　　　　　　• Item 310-B (MF)
ADP TRAINING CATALOG. [Biennial] (DoD 5160.49-C)
　　Discontinued.

D 1.45/3:date　　　　　　• Item 310-B (MF)
DISAM CATALOG. [Annual]

D 1.46:nos.　　　　　　　• Item 310-E
DEFENSE CONTRACT AUDIT AGENCY PAMPHLETS, DCAAP- (series). [Irregular]

D 1.46/2:nos.　　　　　　• Item 310-E-2
DEFENSE CONTRACT AUDIT AGENCY MANUAL, DCAAM- (series).

D 1.46/3:date
DCAA BULLETIN. (Defense Contract Audit Agency)

D 1.46/4:date　　　　　　• Item 310-E-1 (MF)
DIRECTORY OF DCAA OFFICES. [2 times a year] (Defense Contract Audit Agency)

　　Consists of separate sections listing DCAA Headquarters offices and its six regional offices. Contains a section on geographical responsibility of various offices, alphabetical and organizational indexes, etc.

D 1.46/5:date　　　　　　• Item 310-E (MF)
REPORT ON ACTIVITIES DEFENSE CONTRACT AUDIT AGENCY. [Annual]
　　Continues: Report on Operations.

D 1.46/5-2　　　　　　　• Item 310-P (MF)
DEFENSE CONTRACT AUDIT AGENCY AND STRATEGIC PLAN.

D 1.46/6:v.nos.&nos.　　　• Item 310-E-20 (MF)
DEFENSE CONTRACT AUDIT AGENCY BULLETIN. [Monthly]

　　The official newsletter of the Defense Contract Audit Agency. Contains articles on DCAA employees and the audit/management operations of the agency.

D 1.47:nos.
ELECTROMAGNETIC COMPATIBILITY ANALYSIS CENTER, ECAP-PR–　(series).

D 1.48:date　　　　　　　• Item 310-E-10
PROCUREMENT FROM SMALL AND OTHER BUSINESS FIRMS. [11 times a year] (OASD (Comptroller) Directorate for Information Operations)

　　ISSN 0145-0255
　　Discontinued D 1984.

D 1.48/2:date　　　　　• Item 310-E-10 (MF)
SMALL BUSINESS PERFORMANCE, BY CLAIMANT PROGRAM. [Annual]
　　Discontinued.

D 1.48/3:date　　　　　• Item 310-E-10 (MF) (EL)
SMALL BUSINESS INNOVATION RESEARCH (SBIR) PROGRAM. [Annual]

D 1.49:letters-nos.
OPERATIONAL NAVIGATION CHARTS, ONC (series).

D 1.50:nos.
MANPOWER DEVELOPMENT RESEARCH PROGRAM, REPORT MR- (series).

D 1.50/2:nos.
MANPOWER RESEARCH REPORT, MA-(series).

D 1.51:date　　　　　　　• Item 310-F
MILITARY-CIVILIAN OCCUPATIONAL SOURCE BOOK. 1975–
　　Discontinued.

D 1.52:date
MANPOWER REQUIREMENTS REPORT. [Annual]

D 1.53:v.nos.&nos.　　　　• Item 310-H
CONCEPTS. v. 1– 5. 1976– 1982. [Quarterly]

　　PURPOSE:– To disseminate information concerning new developments and effective actions taken relative to the management of defense systems programs and defense systems acquisitions.
　　Indexed by: Index to U.S. Government Periodicals.
　　Prior to 1982, entitled Defense Systems Management Review.
　　ISSN 0363-7727
　　Discontinued v.5/4.

D 1.54:CT　　　　　　　• Item 310-I (MF)
MILITARY COMPENSATION BACKGROUND PAPERS. [Irregular]

D 1.55:v.nos.&nos.　　　　• Item 310-J
SOLDIER, SAILOR, AIRMAN, MARINE (SSAM). v. 1– 63. 1978– 1983. [Monthly]

　　Newspaper-type publication providing information and entertainment to improve the morale and welfare of U.S. military personnel, their dependents and Defense Department civilian employees.
　　Discontinued No. 63.

D 1.56:nos.　　　　　　　• Item 310-K
POSTERS. [Irregular]

D 1.56/2:CT
AUDIOVISUAL MATERIAL.

D 1.57:date　　　　　　• Item 310-E-16 (MF)
100 COMPANIES RECEIVING THE LARGEST DOLLAR VOLUME OF PRIME CONTRACT AWARDS. [Annual]

D 1.57/2　　　　　　　• Item 310-E-16 (MF)
FIVE-HUNDRED CONTRACTORS RECEIVING THE LARGEST DOLLAR VOLUME OF PRIME CONTRACTS FOR RDT&E. FISCAL YEAR. [Annual]

　　Report covers fiscal year.

D 1.57/2-2:date　　　　　• Item 310-E-13 (MF)
TOP FIVE CONTRACTORS RECEIVING THE LARGEST DOLLAR VOLUME OF PRIME CONTRACT AWARDS IN EACH STATE. [Annual]

D 1.57/3:date • **Item 310-E-13 (EL)**
PRIME CONTRACT AWARDS. [Annual]

D 1.57/3-2:date • **Item 310-E-13 (MF)**
PRIME CONTRACT AWARDS BY STATUTORY AUTHORITY, NUMBER OF ACTIONS, AND NET VALUE BY DEPARTMENT. [Annual]

Discontinued.

D 1.57/3-3:date • **Item 310-E-13 (MF)**
ALPHABETICAL LIST OF DoD PRIME CONTRACTORS. [Semiannual]

Discontinued.

D 1.57/3-4:date • **Item 310-E-13 (MF)**
ALPHABETICAL SUMMARY OF PRIME CONTRACT AWARDS OVER $25,000. [Semiannual]

Discontinued.

D 1.57/3-5:date • **Item 310-E-13 (EL)**
PRIME CONTRACT AWARDS, SIZE DISTRIBUTION. [Annual]

D 1.57/4:date • **Item 310-E-13 (MF)**
PRIME CONTRACT AWARDS BY SERVICE CATEGORY AND FEDERAL SUPPLY CLASSIFICATION. [Annual]

Report covers fiscal year.

D 1.57/5:date • **Item 310-E-13 (EL)**
PRIME CONTRACT AWARDS BY REGION AND STATE. [Annual]

Report covers fiscal year.

D 1.57/6:date • **Item 310-E-13 (MF)**
PRIME CONTRACT AWARDS BY STATE. [Annual]

Discontinued.

D 1.57/6-2:date • **Item 310-E-13**
MILITARY PRIME CONTRACT AWARDS BY STATE. [Annual]

Discontinued.

D 1.57/7:date • **Item 310-E-13 (MF)**
PRIME CONTRACT AWARDS IN LABOR SURPLUS AREAS. [Semiannual]

Provides detailed information on Department of Defense prime contract awards over $10,000 for performance in labor surplus areas, chiefly through tables. Supporting data are presented by state, county, and city, according to the purchasing department making the awards.

Discontinued.

D 1.57/8:date • **Item 310-E-21 (EL)**
EDUCATIONAL AND NONPROFIT INSTITUTIONS RECEIVING PRIME CONTRACT AWARDS FOR RESEARCH, DEVELOPMENT, TEST AND EVALUATION. [Annual]

PURPOSE:– To present data on DoD prime contract awards over $10,000 made to educational and nonprofit institutions.

D 1.57/9:date • **Item 310-E-18 (EL)**
COMPANIES PARTICIPATING IN THE DEPARTMENT OF DEFENSE SUBCONTRACTING PROGRAM. [Semiannual]

PURPOSE:– To present subcontract data collected from large firms that have received at least $500,000 or $1,000,000 for construction.

D 1.57/10:date • **Item 306-A (MF)**
DEFENSE ACQUISITION MANAGEMENT DATA SYSTEM CODE TRANSLATIONS. [Annual]

D 1.57/11:date • **Item 310-E-13 (MF)**
ESTIMATED EXPENDITURES FOR STATES AND SELECTED AREAS. [Annual]

D 1.57/11-2:date • **Item 310-E-13 (MF)**
ESTIMATED DEFENSE EXPENDITURES FOR STATES. [Annual]

D 1.58:date
MAP BOOK OF MAJOR MILITARY INSTALLATIONS. [Biennial]

D 1.58/2:date • **Item 310-E-12 (MF)**
REAL AND PERSONAL PROPERTY. [Annual]

Provides a variety of data on the types and amounts of real and personal property owned by the Department of Defense for reports on the status, cost, capacity, condition, use, maintenance, and management of real property of the military departments.
Earlier D 1.2:P 94/8
Discontinued.

D 1.58/3:date • **Item 310-E-16 (MF)**
WORKING CAPITAL FUNDS. [Annual]

Discontinued.

D 1.58/4:date • **Item 310-E-22 (MF) (EL)**
ATLAS/STATE DATA ABSTRACT FOR THE UNITED STATES. [Annual]

PURPOSE:– To provide information on DoD personnel, payroll outlays, and prime contracts over $25,000. Contains maps and statistical summaries for each state, Guam, and Puerto Rico plus an index of major military installations and industrial facilities.

D 1.59:date • **Item 310-L (MF)**
DEFENSE INFORMATION SCHOOL: CATALOG. [Annual]

Contains catalog of courses offered by the Defense Information School in carrying out its mission of providing public affairs training for officers, enlisted personnel, and civilian employees selected for such assignment at all levels of command in the Department of Defense.

D 1.59/2:date • **Item 310-M (MF)**
CATALOG. [Annual] (Defense Systems Management College)

Provides a catalog of courses offered by the College in its threefold mission of education, research, and information dissemination.

D 1.59/2-2 • **Item 310-M-2 (MF) (EL)**
DSMC TECHNICAL REPORT.

D 1.59/2-3:date • **Item 310-M-3 (MF)**
DSMC IN REVIEW: A QUALITY JOURNEY. [Annual]

D 1.59/3:date • **Item 310-M (MF)**
DEFENSE ACQUISITION UNIVERSITY CATALOG. [Annual]

D 1.60 • **Item 304-B-1 (EL)**
PROGRAM MANAGER. [Bimonthly]

PURPOSE:– To serve as a newsletter for the Defense Systems Management College.

D 1.61:date • **Item 310-E-8 (MF)**
MILITARY MANPOWER STATISTICS. [Monthly]

Ceased with Dec. 1997.

D 1.61/2:date • **Item 310-E-6 (MF)**
CIVILIAN MANPOWER STATISTICS. [Monthly]

D 1.61/3:date • **Item 310-E-7 (MF)**
WORLDWIDE MANPOWER DISTRIBUTION BY GEOGRAPHICAL AREA. [Quarterly]

D 1.61/4:date • **Item 310-E-9 (MF)**
SELECTED MANPOWER STATISTICS. FISCAL YEAR. [Annual]

Also published in microfiche.

D 1.61/5:date • **Item 310-E-14 (EL)**
DISTRIBUTION OF PERSONNEL BY STATE AND BY SELECTED LOCATIONS. [Annual]

Tables show distribution of DoD duty military and direct hire civilian personnel by state, according to component.

D 1.61/6:date • **Item 310-E-15 (EL)**
WORLDWIDE U.S. ACTIVE DUTY MILITARY PERSONNEL CASUALTIES. [Quarterly]

D 1.61/7:date • **Item 310-G-8 (MF)**
RESERVE MANPOWER STATISTICS. [Annual]

D 1.61/8:date • **Item 310-E-24 (MF)**
GENERAL/FLAG OFFICER WORLDWIDE ROSTER. [Quarterly]

Rosters show duty title, name, rank, service, date assigned, and date of rank of each officer.

D 1.61/9 • **Item 310-E-6 (MF)**
SUPPLY SYSTEM INVENTORY REPORT (DIOR).

D 1.62:date • **Item 310-E-5 (MF)**
SELECTED MEDICAL CARE STATISTICS. [Quarterly]

D 1.62/2:date • **Item 310-E-5 (MF)**
HEALTH MANPOWER STATISTICS. [Annual]

D 1.63:nos. • **Item 306-A-3**
MILITARY CHILD CARE PROJECT (series). [Irregular] (Dod 6060.1-M)

Consists of three sub-series:

STAFF DEVELOPMENT SERIES.

CHILD ENVIRONMENT SERIES.

ADMINISTRATIVE GUIDEBOOK SERIES.

Discontinued.

D 1.63/2:v.no.
MILITARY FAMILY. [Bimonthly]

D 1.64:date • **Item 310-E-4 (MF)**
COMMERCIAL ACTIVITIES INVENTORY REPORT AND FIVE YEAR REVIEW SCHEDULE. [Annual] (DoD 4100.33-INV)

Tabular presentation of DoD inventory of commercial activities and DoD contract support services, by DoD component, State, installation, and function.

Discontinued.

D 1.65:nos. • **Item 310-E-3**
MEPCOM- (series). [Irregular] (Military Enlistment Processing Command)

Discontinued.v

D 1.65/2:nos.
MEMCPM REGULATIONS. [Irregular] (Military Enlistment Processing Command)

D 1.66:date • **Item 310-E-11 (MF)**
FOREIGN MILITARY SALES, FOREIGN MILITARY CONSTRUCTION SALES, AND MILITARY ASSISTANCE FACTS. [Annual] (Defense Security Assistance Agency)

Earlier D 1.2:F 76

D 1.67:date • **Item 310-M-1 (MF)**
BULLETIN OF THE SCHOOL OF MEDICINE, UNIFORMED SERVICES UNIVERSITY OF THE HEALTH SCIENCES. [Annual]

Presents information on the School, including curriculum, graduate medical education, admissions and student status, faculty and administration, and sudent body.

D 1.67/2:date • **Item 310-M-1 (MF)**
GRADUATE EDUCATION BULLETIN, UNIFORMED SERVICES UNIVERSITY OF THE HEALTH SCIENCES. [Annual]

D 1.67/3 • **Item 310-M-1 (MF)**
STUDENT HANDBOOK. [Annual]

D 1.67/4 • Item 310-M-1 (MF)
DEPARTMENT OF OBSTETRICS AND GYNECOLOGY.
[Annual]

D 1.68:date • Item 306-F
OVERSEAS EMPLOYMENT OPPORTUNITIES FOR
EDUCATORS. [Annual]

Provides information on overseas employment
opportunities in DoD Dependent Schools. Includes
eligibility standards, position categories, application procedures, salary and benefits, housing,
and shipment of household goods.
Earlier D 1.2:Ed 8

D 1.69:date • Item 306-A-12 (MF)
U.S. GOVERNMENT'S PREFERRED PRODUCTS LIST.
[Quarterly]

Identifies telecommunications and informa-
tion-processing equipment and systems which
conform to approved national security performance
standards.

See D 1.69/2

D 1.69/2:date • Item 306-A-12 (MF)
INFORMATION SYSTEMS SECURITY PRODUCTS AND
SERVICES CATALOGUE. [Quarterly]

D 1.70:date • Item 304-D
AUDIOVISUAL RELEASE ANNOUNCEMENTS.

Discontinued.

D 1.71:letters-nos. • Item 306-A (MF)
HEADSTART (series). [Irregular]

D 1.72:date • Item 306-A (MF)
DoD DOCUMENT IDENTIFIERS. [Irregular] (DoD
4000.25-13-S2)

D 1.73:date • Item 306-A-4 (MF)
DEFENSE SMALL BUSINESS INNOVATION RE-
SEARCH PROGRAM. [Annual]

Invites small business firms with strong research and development capabilities in science
or engineering in the topic areas described, to
submit proposals under this program solicitation.
Objectives include stimulating technological innovation in the private sector and increasing commercial application of DoD- supported research.

See D 1.48/3

D 1.74:date • Item 306-A-5
MILITARY FORCES IN TRANSITION.

Earlier title: Soviet Military Power.
Formerly classed in D 1.2

Discontinued.

D 1.75:nos.-letters-nos. • Item 310-E-17
DoDDS PAMPHLETS (series). [Irregular]

DoDDS = Department of Defense Dependents
Schools.

D 1.76:date • Item 314-G
INDEX OF SPECIFICATIONS AND STANDARDS.
[Annual]

D 1.76/2:date • Item 314-G
FEDERAL SUPPLY CLASSIFICATION LISTING OF DoD
STANDARDIZATION DOCUMENTS. [Bimonthly]

PURPOSE:– Designed as an administrative
tool of the Defense Standardization Program (DSP)
for Review/user data used in specification coordination, for determination of the scope of documents covered by federal Supply Classification
area assignments under the DSP, and for other
DSP purposes requiring such a list of standardization documents.
Earlier D 7.14/2

See D 1.76

D 1.77:date
LIST OF DEPARTMENT OF DEFENSE PURCHASING
OFFICES. [Annual]

D 1.78 • Item 303-A
CONSOLIDATED FEDERAL SUPPLY CATALOG.

D 1.79 • Item 306-A-9 (MF)
COMPUTER SECURITY CENTER, CSC- EPL-(series).
[Irregular]

Discontinued.

D 1.79/2 • Item 306-A-8 (MF)
NATIONAL COMPUTER SECURITY CENTER, NCSC-
WA- (series). [Irregular]

D 1.79/3:nos. • Item 306-A-11 (MF)
CSC-STD (series). [Irregular]

Each issue of the series relates to a different
computer security topic.

D 1.79/4: • Item 306-A-19
NCSC-TG (series).

Issued by the National Computer Security
Center. Each issue is expected to discuss a different topic, such as guidelines for auditing in
automatic data procession systems that process
classified and other sensitive information.

D 1.80:date • Item 306-A-7 (MF)
FEDERAL VOTING ASSISTANCE PROGRAM. [Annual]

PURPOSE:– To summarize program activities required by the Federal Voting Assistance
Act of 1955 and the Overseas Citizens Voting
Rights Act of 1975. These Acts cover all members of the Armed Forces and Merchant Marines
and their dependents, and all other U.S. citizens
overseas.

D 1.81:date • Item 306-A-10
DEPARTMENT OF DEFENSE PROGRAM FOR RE-
SEARCH AND DEVELOPMENT. [Annual]

PURPOSE:– To present the DoD program for
research and development. Discusses the U.S.-
USSR R & D development balance, strategic and
non-strategic nuclear programs, and tactical warfare programs.

D 1.82:date • Item 306-A-13
CHAMPUS CHARTBOOK OF STATISTICS. [Semian-
nual]

PURPOSE:– To provide an overview of information on the total CHAMPUS program. Additional
statistics enable the user to compare CHAMPUS
with other health care systems.
CHAMPUS = Civilian Health and Medical Program of the Uniformed Services.
Earlier D 1.2:C 49/2

D 1.83 • Item 306-A-15
TECHNICAL INFORMATION MEMORANDUM (series).

D 1.84 • Item 306-A-16 (MF)
FEDERAL RADIONAVIGATION PLAN. [Biennial]

PURPOSE:– To provide information on the
management of those radionavigation systems
which are used by both the military and civil sectors. It is the official source of navigation policy
for the Departments of Transportation and Defense.

D 1.85 • Item 310-E-23
CONGRESSIONAL PRESENTATION FOR SECURITY
ASSISTANCE PROGRAMS, FISCAL YEAR (date).
[Annual]

Submitted to the Congress in explanation and
support of the budget request for the security
assistance programs. Designed to demonstrate
how security assistance programs serve our foreign policy goals and help to achieve national
security objectives. Describes these programs
by country.

See 0876

D 1.86: • Item 306-A-20 (EL)
THE DISAM JOURNAL OF INTERNATIONAL SECU-
RITY ASSISTANCE MANAGEMENT. [Quarterly]

DISAM = Defense Institute of Security Assistance Management
Issues are expected to contain articles on
such topics as the security assistance and related bilateral affairs of the Joint United States
Military Group, Assistance Military/Advisory
Group– Spain.

D 1.87: • Item 306-A-21
MILSTRIP. [Irregular]
MILSTRIP = Military Standards Requisitioning and Issue Procedures.
Provides uniform procedures, data elements,
codes, formats, etc., for usein data processing
used in requisitioning, issuing, and returning DoD
materiel.
Earlier D 7.6/17

D 1.87/2: • Item 306-A-21 (EL)
MILSTRIP ROUTING AND IDENTIFIER AND DISTRI-
BUTION CODES.

MILSTRIP = Military Standards Requisitioning and Issue Procedures.
Provides uniform procedures, data elements,
codes, formats, etc., for usein data processing
used in requisitioning, issuing, and returning DoD
materiel.
Earlier D 7.6/16

D 1.87/3:date • Item 306-A-1
MISTRIP, DEFENSE PROGRAM FOR REDISTRIBU-
TION OF ASSETS (DEPRA) PROCEDURES.

MILSTRIP = Military Standards Requisitioning and Issue Procedures.

D 1.88:nos. • Item 306-A-20
STANDARDIZATION AND DATA MANAGEMENT NEWS-
LETTER. [Quarterly]

Non-depository.

D 1.89 • Item 306-A-1 (MF)
SIXTH QUADRENNIAL REVIEW OF MILITARY
COMPENSATION.

D 1.90:date • Item 306-A
MILITARY WOMEN IN THE DEPARTMENT OF
DEFENSE.

Discontinued.

D 1.91:date • Item 310-D-23
THE DEPARTMENT OF DEFENSE CRITICAL TECH-
NOLOGIES PLAN FOR THE COMMITTEES ON
ARMED SERVICE, UNITED STATES CONGRESS.
[Annual]

D 1.91/2:date • Item 310-E-23 (MF)
TECHNOLOGY APPLICATIONS REPORT. [Annual]

D 1.92:nos. • Item 306-G
IACC (Series).

D 1.93 • Item 306-A-11 (MF)
IDA (Institute for Defense Analyses) REPORT (series).

D 1.94:date • Item 434-B-1 (MF)
STRATEGIC AND CRITICAL MATERIALS REPORT TO
THE CONGRESS. [Semiannual]
Earlier FEM 1.12

Discontinued.v

D 1.95:CT • Item 307-A (E)
ELECTRONIC PRODUCTS. [Irregular]

D 1.95/2:date • Item 307-A-11 (CD)
DEFENSE ACQUISITION DESKBOOK. [Quarterly]

Issued on CD-ROM.

D 1.95/3:date • Item 307-A-14 (E)
UNCLASSIFIED DOD ISSUANCES ON CD-ROM.
[Semiannual]
Issued on CD-ROM.

D 1.95/4 • Item 307-A-15 (EL)
DOD ISSUANCES AND DIRECTIVES.
   Online Database.

D 1.95/5 • Item 307-A-16 (EL)
GULF NEWS. [Bimonthly]

D 1.96: • Item 307-A (EL)
VOTING INFORMATION NEWS.

D 1.97:date • Item 434-B-1 (EL)
DEFENSE ENVIRONMENTAL RESTORATION PRO-
GRAM: ANNUAL REPORT TO CONGRESS.

D 1.97/2:date • Item 434-B-2
ANNUAL REPORT AND STRATEGIC INVESTMENT
PLAN. [Annual]

D 1.98:date • Item 306-F
UNITED STATES SPECIAL OPERATIONS FORCES,
POSTURE STATEMENT.

D 1.100:v.nos./nos. • Item 306-H-1
WORLD WAR II, DISPATCH. [Quarterly]

   Discontinued.

D 1.101:date • Item 306-A-22 (MF)
ANNUAL STATEMENT OF ASSURANCE.

D 1.103:v.nos./nos. • Item 306-F-1 (MF)
ACQUISITION REVIEW QUARTERLY: JOURNAL OF
THE DEFENSE ACQUISITION UNIVERSITY.

D 1.104: • Item 307-A (E)
DFAS: THE DOD ACCOUNTING FIRM. [Monthly]

   Discontinued.

D 1.104/3: • Item 307-A (EL)
MILITARY PERSONNEL UPDATE.

D 1.105:v.nos./nos. • Item 306-F-2 (EL)
APPLIED LANGUAGE AND LEARNING. [Semiannual]

D 106 • Item 307-A (EL)
HPC (HIGH PERFORMANCE COMPUTING) MODERN-
IZATION PLAN. [Annual]

D 107 • Item 307-B (EL)
DEFENSE SCIENCE BOARD (DSB) GENERAL PUB-
LICATIONS.

D 1.107/2 • Item 307-B-1 (EL)
DBS NEWSLETTER. [Quarterly]

AMERICAN FORCES
INFORMATION SERVICE
(1977–   )

CREATION AND AUTHORITY

   The Armed Forces Information and Education
Division was established within the National Military Establishment on May 1, 1949, succeeding
the Army-Air Force Troop Information and Education Division (M 104). The Division was made a
part of the Department of Defense by the National Security Act Amendments of 1949 (61 Stat.
499 as amended). The name was changed to
Office of Armed Forces Information and Education on April 9, 1952, by direction of the Assistant
Secretary of Defense (Manpower and Personnel).
The name was changed in 1968 to Armed Forces
Information Service and again in 1971 to Office
of Information for the Armed Forces. In 1977 the
name was changed back to Armed Forces Information Service. Name changed to American Forces
Information Service.

INFORMATION

   American Forces Information Service
   Department of Defense
   601 North Fairfax Street
   Suite 311
   Alexandria, VA 22314
   (703) 428-0711
   http://www.defenselink.mil/AFIS

D 2.1:date
ANNUAL REPORTS.

D 2.2:CT • Item 313
GENERAL PUBLICATIONS.

D 2.3/2 • Item 312-A (MF)
VOTING INFORMATION BULLETINS. 1–   1965–
[Irregular]

   Internal use only.

D 2.6:CT
REGULATIONS, RULES, AND INSTRUCTIONS.

D 2.7:nos.
ARMED FORCES TALK.

   Earlier M 104.7

   Discontinued.

D 2.7/2:nos.
ARMED FORCES INFORMATION PAMPHLETS.

D 2.8 • Item 312-E
HANDBOOKS, MANUALS, GUIDES. [Irregular]

   Discontinued.

   D 2.8 • Item 314 & 312-A
   POCKET GUIDES TO [country]. PG 1–
   [Irregular]

      Brief guides for troops stationed in for-
   eign country, covering all phases of information on the land, climate, customs, etc.

D 2.9 • Item 312-F
POSTERS, DoD P- (series). 1–   [Irregular]

D 2.9/2:date • Item 312-F
DEFENSE BILLBOARD. [Monthly]

   See D 2.9

D 2.10:nos.
FACT SHEETS, DoD FACT SHEETS.

   Superseded by Information Guidance Series
   (D 2.17).

D 2.11:nos. • Item 313-A
YOU AND YOUR USA SERIES.

   Discontinued.

D 2.11/2:nos.
YOU AND YOUR U.S.A. SERIES.

D 2.12:nos.
RESEARCH REPORTS.

D 2.12/2:nos.
ATTITUDE RESEARCH BRANCH: REPORTS.

D 2.13:nos. • Item 313-B
KNOW YOUR COMMUNIST ENEMY SERIES.

   Discontinued.

D 2.14 • Item 312-A
DoD PAMPHLETS. [Irregular]

   Superseded by Information Guidance Series
   (D 2.17).

D 2.15:v.nos.&nos.
FOR COMMANDERS, THIS CHANGING WORLD.
[Semimonthly]

   ISSN 0010-2482

D 2.15/2:v.nos.&nos. • Item 312-B
COMMANDERS DIGEST. v. 1–21. 1965–1978. [Weekly]

   Contains official information, news and policy.
   Indexed by: Index to U.S. Government Peri-
   odicals.
   Supersedes For Commanders, This Changing
   World (D 2.15).
   Superseded by Command (D 2.15/3).
   ISSN 0010-2482

D 2.15/2-2:nos. • Item 312-B
COMMANDERS DIGEST INDEXES.

D 2.15/3:vol.nos.&nos. • Item 312-B (EL)
DEFENSE. v. 1–   1978–   [Irregular] (Armed Forces
Press Service)

   Former titles: Command; Command Policy
   Supersedes Commanders Digest (D 2.15/2).

D 2.15/4:vol.nos. • Item 312-B-1 (EL)
DEFENSE ISSUES. [Irregular]

   Each issue concerns a different defense issue.

D 2.16 • Item 312-C
ALERT (series). 1–   [Irregular]

   Discontinued.

D 2.17:nos. • Item 312-E
INFORMATION GUIDANCE SERIES. 1971–
[Monthly]

   PURPOSE:– To disseminate quickly to the
   Armed Forces commanders and personnel current information and policy from the Department
   of Defense and other Federal agencies that will
   contribute to a better understanding of national
   defense programs and aid them in accomplishing
   their missions through increased professional
   knowledge.
   Supersedes Fact Sheet (D 2.10) and DoD
   Pamphlet (D 2.14) series.

   Discontinued 1978.

D 2.18:nos. • Item 312-D
CIVILIAN HEALTH AND MEDICAL PROGRAM OF UNI-
FORMED SERVICE [FACT SHEETS], CHAMPUS.
FS-1–   [Irregular]

   Contains information on miscellaneous subjects dealing with health care of the Armed Forces
   under the CHAMPUS program.

D 2.19 • Item 424-B-1 (MF)
CURRENT NEWS, EARLY BIRD EDITION. [5 times a
week]

   Discontinued.

D 2.19/2 • Item 424-B-2 (MF)
RADIO-TV DEFENSE DIALOG. [5 times a week]

Discontinued.

D 2.19/3 • Item 424-B-4 (MF)
CURRENT NEWS, SUPPLEMENTAL CLIPS. [5 times a week]

Discontinued.

D 2.19/4 • Item 424-B-5 (MF)
CURRENT NEWS, SPECIAL EDITION. [3 times a week]

Discontinued.

D 2.19/5 • Item 424-B-8 (MF)
CURRENT NEWS, DEFENSE MANAGEMENT EDITION. [Biweekly]

Discontinued with No. 89-5.

D 2.19/7 • Item 424-B-5 (MF)
CURRENT NEWS, SPECIAL EDITION, SELECTED STATEMENTS. [Bimonthly]

Discontinued.

D 2.19/8 • Item 304-D-1 (MF)
CURRENT NEWS, THE FRIDAY REVIEW. [Weekly]

PURPOSE:– To bring to the attention of key DoD personnel current literature of interest to them in their official capacities. Four or five such publications are reviewed in each six-page issue.
Also issued to depository libraries under item number 424-B-2.
Earlier D 1.33/2

D 2.20: • Item 312-B-2 (E)
ELECTRONIC PRODUCTS (misc.).

D 2.21: • Item 312-B-2 (EL)
AFPS NEWS.

PUBLICATIONS RELATING TO INDUSTRIAL MOBILIZATION AND SECURITY
(1953–   )

CREATION AND AUTHORITY

The Munitions Board (M 5) was established within the National Military Establishment by the National Security Act of 1947 (61 Stat. 499). The Board continued under the Department of Defense upon its establishment in 1949. The Board was abolished by Reorganization Plan No. 6 of 1953, effective June 30, 1953, and its functions transferred to the Secretary of Defense.

D 3.1:date
ANNUAL REPORTS.

Earlier M 5.1

D 3.2:CT • Item 317
GENERAL PUBLICATIONS.
Earlier M 5.2

Discontinued.

D 3.5:CT • Item 317-B
LAWS.

Discontinued.

D 3.6:CT • Item 319
REGULATIONS, RULES, AND INSTRUCTIONS.
Discontinued.

D 3.6/2:
MANUAL OF POLICIES AND PROCEDURE FOR MILITARY SPECIFICATIONS.

D 3.6/3:CT • Item 319
HANDBOOKS, MANUALS, GUIDES RELATING TO INDUSTRIAL MOBILIZATION AND SECURITY.

Discontinued.

D 3.7:nos.
MILITARY STANDARDS.

Earlier M 5.8
Later D 7.10

D 3.8:nos. • Item 318
MUNITIONS BOARD MANUALS.

Discontinued.

D 3.9:nos. • Item 316
ANC BULLETINS AND DOCUMENTS.

Earlier M 6.9

Discontinued.

D 3.10:date • Item 317-A
INDEX OF MILITARY SPECIFICATIONS AND STANDARDS, MILITARY INDEX. v. 1. [Semiannual]

Superseded by 7.14

Discontinued.

D 3.11:letters
INDUSTRIAL SECURITY POSTER PIN (series).

D 3.11/2:
[INDUSTRIAL SECURITY STATEMENTS.]

D 3.11/3:
[INDUSTRIAL SECURITY CARTOONS.]

D 3.11/4:nos.
INDUSTRIAL SECURITY LETTER.

D 3.11/5:nos.
POSTERS.

D 3.12:nos. • Item 317-C
INDUSTRIAL PERSONNEL SECURITY REVIEW PROGRAM, ANNUAL REPORTS.

Discontinued.

D 3.13:nos.
MANPOWER AWARENESS SERIES.

PUBLICATIONS RELATING TO RESEARCH AND DEVELOPMENT
(1953–   )

CREATION AND AUTHORITY

The Research and Development Board (M 6) was established within the National Military Establishment by the National Security Act of 1947 (61 Stat. 499). The Board continued under the Department of Defense upon its establishment in 1949. the Board was abolished by Reorganization Plan No. 6 of 1953, effective June 30, 1953, and its functions transferred to the Secretary of Defense.

D 4.1:date
ANNUAL REPORTS.

Earlier M 6.1

D 4.2:CT • Item 320
GENERAL PUBLICATIONS.

Abolished and functions vested in the Secretary of Defense by Reorganization Plan 6 of 1953.
Earlier M 6.2

Discontinued.

D 4.8:CT
BIBLIOGRAPHIES AND LISTS OF PUBLICATIONS.

Issued by Office of Director of Defense Research and Development.

D 4.9:nos.
PARTS SPECIFICATION MANAGEMENT FOR RELIABILITY. PSMR-nos.

D 4.10:CT • Item 320-A
HANDBOOKS, MANUALS, GUIDES RELATING TO RESEARCH AND DEVELOPMENT.

Discontinued.

D 4.11:nos.
PLASTICS TECHNICAL EVALUATION CENTER: PLASTIC REPORTS.

D 4.11/2:nos. • Item 315-E-1 (MF)
PLASTICS TECHNICAL EVALUATION CENTER: (PLASTIC) NOTES. 1–   [Irregular]

PURPOSE:– To present technical information on current developments, engineering, and application work in the field of plastics and adhesives.
Published in microfiche (24x)

Discontinued.

D 4.12:nos. • Item 310-A
SHOCK AND VIBRATION BULLETINS. 1–   [Irregular] (Shock and Vibration Information Center, Naval Research Laboratory)

D 4.12/2:v.nos.&nos. • Item 320-A-1
SHOCK AND VIBRATION DIGEST. v. 1–   1969– [Monthly] (Director, Navy Publications and Printing Service Office, Bldg. 157-2, Washington Navy Yard, Washington, D.C. 20390) (Office of Director of Defense Research and Engineering, Department of Defense)

Contains short articles on sound, shock, and vibration technology with references, news briefs, reviews of meetings, and abstracts from the current shock and vibration literature.
Later D 210.27
ISSN 0583-1024

JOINT CHIEFS OF STAFF
(1949–   )

CREATION AND AUTHORITY

The Joint Chiefs of Staff was established within the Department of Defense by Public Law 216, 81st Congress, approved August 10, 1949.

INFORMATION

Public Affairs
Joint Chiefs of Staff
Department of Defense
200 Joint Chiefs of Staff
The Pentagon, Room 2D844
Washington, DC 20318-0200
(703) 697-4272
http://www.defenselink.mil/pubs/almanac/joint_staff.html

D 5.1:date
ANNUAL REPORT.

D 5.2:CT • Item 315
GENERAL PUBLICATIONS.

D 5.8:nos.
JANP (series).

D 5.8/2:nos. • **Item 315-A-1**
CJCS GUIDE TO THE CHAIRMAN'S READINESS SYSTEM.

D 5.9:date • **Item 315-A**
NATIONAL SECURITY SEMINAR: PRESENTATION. [Annual]
> Continues: National Resources Conference Conducted by Industrial College of Armed Forces. Earlier D 5.2:R 31

> Discontinued.

D 5.9/2 • **Item 315-A (MF)**
NATIONAL SECURITY SEMINAR PRESENTATION OUTLINES AND READING LIST. 1948– [Twice a year]

> PURPOSE:– To present facts regarding the status of our national security, some of the national and international problems involved, and the importance of the civilian-military team in national security.
> It is designed to increase general understanding of the need for cooperation and preparations for times of national danger, and is designed primarily as a training program for Reserve officers, as well as a source of information for the local citizenry who affect and influence community action.
> Title varies.

> Discontinued.

D 5.9/3:CT
NATIONAL SECURITY MANAGEMENT (series). [Irregular]

D 5.9/4:CT • **Item 315-B**
MONOGRAPH SERIES.

D 5.10:nos.
[MONOGRAPH] M-nos. INDUSTRIAL COLLEGE OF THE ARMED FORCES.

D 5.10/2:nos.
[LECTURES] L-(series) INDUSTRIAL COLLEGE OF THE ARMED FORCES.

D 5.10/3 • **Item 315-B**
MONOGRAPHS. R 1– 1944– [Irregular]

> ICAF monograph publications are employed as instructional matter within the School of Resident Studies, and supplement the lectures, seminars, and textual information studies there. They are primarily designed to reiterate economic-oriented areas of instruction with application to the Government and military establishments.
> The catalog of Publication is now published every two years, and is the only R-series publication which is available for distribution outside the College.

D 5.10/4:nos.
STUDENT COMMITTEE REPORT SR– (series). (Industrial College of Armed Forces)

D 5.10/5:nos.
[Correspondence Course Textbooks]. vol. 1– (series) (Industrial College of Armed Forces)

D 5.11 • **Item 315-B**
INDUSTRIAL COLLEGE OF THE ARMED FORCES CATALOG. 1946/47– [Annual]

> PURPOSE:– To promulgate the mission, organization, history, and academic program of the school, and to provide general information concerning extracurriculum programs such as sports, social activities, and facilities available to the students of the College.

> Inactive.

D 5.12 • **Item 315-C**
JOINT PUBLICATIONS (series). 1– 1959– [Irregular]
> Earlier title: JCS Pubications (Series).

> See D 5.21

D 5.12:1 • **Item 315-C**
DICTIONARY OF MILITARY AND ASSOCIATED TERMS. 1979. 377 p.

D 5.12/2:nos. • **Item 315-C-1 (MF)**
JOINT CHIEFS OF STAFF (Series).

> See D 5.12

D 5.12/3 • **Item 315-C-4 (EL)**
DEPARTMENT OF DEFENSE DICTIONARY OF MILITARY AND ASSOCIATED TERMS.
> Issued on CD-ROM.

D 5.13:CT • **Item 315-A**
INDUSTRIAL COLLEGE OF THE ARMED FORCES: PUBLICATIONS.

D 5.13/2:nos.
INDUSTRIAL COLLEGE OF ARMED FORCES. INFORMATIONAL CIRCULARS.

D 5.14:nos.
DEFENSE ATOMIC SUPPORT AGENCY: TECHNICAL ANALYSIS REPORT DASA (series).

D 5.14/2:nos.
DASIAC SPECIAL REPORTS. (Defense Atomic Support Agency, Information and Analysis Center)

D 5.15:CT
BIBLIOGRAPHIES AND LISTS OF PUBLICATIONS.

D 5.16:date • **Item 315-E**
INDUSTRIAL COLLEGE OF THE ARMED FORCES: PERSPECTIVES IN DEFENSE MANAGEMENT. [Irregular]
> Discontinued 1975-76.

D 5.17:CT
NATIONAL WAR COLLEGE: PUBLICATIONS. [Irregular]

D 5.18:CT • **Item 315-C-1 (MF)**
ADDRESSES.

D 5.19:date • **Item 315-C-2**
UNITED STATES MILITARY POSTURE FOR FY (date). [Annual]

> Augments and amplifies Joint Chiefs of Staff reports and statements at Congressional hearings in support of the U.S. Defense Budget. Discontinued.

D 5.20 • **Item 315-A (EL)**
JOINT FORCE QUARTERLY.

D 5.21:date/nos. • **Item 315-C-3 (CD) (EL)**
JOINT ELECTRONIC LIBRARY.
> Issued on CD-ROM.

DEFENSE INFORMATION SYSTEMS AGENCY
(1960–   )

CREATION AND AUTHORITY

> The Defense Communications Agency was established on May 12, 1960, as an agency of the Defense Department under the direction, authority, and control of the Secretary of defense. Renamed. Defense Information Systems Agency by Department of Defense Directive 5105.19 dated June 25, 1991. The Director is responsible to the Secretary of Defense through the Joint Chiefs of Staff.

INFORMATION

> Chief Information Officer
> Defense Information Systems Agency
> Washington, DC 20305
> (703) 681-2062
> Fax: (703) 607-4081
> http://www.disa.mil

D 5.102:CT • **Item 315-D-4**
GENERAL PUBLICATIONS.

D 5.104:nos. • **Item 315-D (MF)**
DCA CIRCULARS.

D 5.109:CT • **Item 315-D-1 (MF)**
NATIONAL MILITARY COMMAND SYSTEM INFORMATION PROCESSING SYSTEM 360 FORMATTED FILE SYSTEM (NIPS 360 FFS). [Irregular] (National Military Command System Support Center)

> Discontinued.

D 5.110:nos. • **Item 315-D (MF)**
TECHNICAL MEMORANDUMS. [Irregular] (Joint Technical Support Activity)

D 5.111:date • **Item 315-D-2 (MF)**
DEFENSE COMMUNICATIONS SYSTEM GLOBAL, AUTOMATIC VOICE NETWORK TELEPHONE DIRECTORY. [Semiannual]

> Contains both alphabetical listing within geographical areas and departmental listings of Automatic Voice Network (AUTOVON) telephone numbers. This network is provided for the transmission of official, essential information only and is subject to communications management monitoring at all times.
> Earlier title: Global Autovon Telephone Directory.

> Discontinued.

D 5.112 • **Item 315-D-3**
DISA. (Defense Information Systems Agency)

DEFENSE INTELLIGENCE AGENCY
(1961–   )

CREATION AND AUTHORITY

> The Defense Intelligence Agency was established as an agency of the Department of Defense by DoD Directive 5105.21, dated August 1, 1961, under provisions of National Security Act of 1947, as amended, to operate under direction, authority, and control of the Secretary of Defense. The chain of command runs from the Secretary of Defense, through the Joint Chiefs to Staff to the Director.

INFORMATION

> Defense Intelligence Agency
> 7400 Defense Pentagon
> Washington, D.C. 20301-7400
> (202) 695-1757
> http://www.dia.mil

D 5.201:date
ANNUAL REPORT.

D 5.202:CT • **Item 315-F-1**
GENERAL PUBLICATIONS.

D 5.203:date
DoD AERONAUTICAL CHART BULLETINS.

> Earlier D 301.59

D 5.206/2 • **Item 315-F-6**
DEFENSE INTELLIGENCE AGENCY REGULATIONS (series). [Irregular]

D 5.208:date
DoD AERONAUTICAL CHART UPDATING MANUAL (CHUM). [Monthly]

> Earlier D 302.59/4

D 5.208/2:CT • **Item 315-F-6**
HANDBOOKS, MANUALS, GUIDES. [Irregular]

D 5.208/3:nos.
MANUALS, DIAM- (series). [Irregular]

D 5.209:nos.   • Item 315-F-2
REVIEW OF SOVIET GROUND FORCES. RSGF 1-77– Aug. 1977–   [Monthly] (Defense Intelligence Report)

PURPOSE:– To provide up-to-date information on a wide variety of topics of general interest throughout the Department of Defense. Consists of translations of selected articles from the Soviet press and background articles written by DIA analysts on Soviet tactics, training, equipment, and organization.

Non-depository.

D 5.210:date   • Item 315-F-3 (MF)
DEFENSE INTELLIGENCE SCHOOL: ACADEMIC CATALOG. [Annual] Catalog of courses offered by the Defense Intelligence School to military and civilian personnel of the Army, Navy, and Air Force.

D 5.210/2:   • Item 315-F-3 (MF)
QUARTERLY GRADUATE BULLETIN.

D 5.211:date   • Item 315-F-5 (MF)
BIBLIOGRAPHY OF SOVIET LASER DEVELOPMENTS. [Bimonthly]

Compiled under an interagency agreement to document current Soviet-bloc developments in the quantum electronics field. Most entries come from about 30 periodicals known to publish the most significant findings in Soviet laser technology.

D 5.211/2:   • Item 315-F-7
BIBLIOGRAPHIES AND LISTS OF PUBLICATIONS.

D 5.212:date   • Item 315-F-3
QUARTERLY BULLETIN, INTELLIGENCE CONTINUING EDUCATION PROGRAM.

Discontinued.

D 5.213:CT   • Item 315-F-4
POSTERS. [Irregular]

NATIONAL IMAGERY AND MAPPING AGENCY
(1972–   )

CREATION AND AUTHORITY

The National Imagery and Mapping Agency was established as the Defense Mapping Agency under the Department of Defense on January 1, 1972, under the provisions of the National Security Act of 1947, as amended, to operate under the direction, authority, and control of the Secretary of Defense. Functions transferred to the National Imagery and Mapping Agency by P.L. 104-201, Sept. 23, 1996 (110 Stat. 2677).

INFORMATION

Public Affairs Office
National Imagery and Mapping Agency
4600 Sangamore Rd.
Bethesda, MD 20816-5003
(301) 227-7397 or (301) 227-2057
Toll Free: (800) 826-0342
http://www.nima.mil

D 5.301:date   • Item 379-A-11 (MF)
ANNUAL REPORT.

Summarizes activities of DMA and gives its accomplishments in terms of products produced.

D 5.302:CT   • Item 379-A-10
GENERAL PUBLICATIONS.

D 5.308   • Item 379-A-13
HANDBOOKS, MANUALS, GUIDES.

D 5.315:date/nos.   • Item 379-A (P) (EL)
NOTICE TO MARINERS. [Weekly]

ISSN 0092-1262
Earlier D 203.8

D 5.315/2:date/v.nos   • Item 379-A
SUMMARY OF CHART CORRECTIONS.

D 5.316:date-nos.
MEMORANDUM FOR AVIATORS.   – June 1973. [Irregular]
Earlier D 203.11

D 5.317:nos./date   • Item 378-D
HYDROGRAPHIC/TOPOGRAPHIC CENTER: PUBLICATIONS (numbered).
Earlier: H. O. Publications.
Earlier D 203.22

D 5.317:9   • Item 378
AMERICAN PRACTICAL NAVIGATOR. 1975 ed. 2 v.

The first edition of this famous compendium on navigation appeared in 1802, authored by the brilliant mathematician, astronomer, and seaman, Nathaniel Bowditch, a name virtually synonymous with navigation. This great work has endured because "it has combined the best thoughts of each generation of navigators, who have looked to it as their final authority." The U.S. Navy Hydrographic Office has included timely information in this reprint of the revised 1962 edition, consistent with modern navigational practices and techniques. Major sections of this volume include: Fundamentals; Piloting and Dead Reckoning; Electronic Navigation; Celestial Navigation; Oceanography; Weather; and Hydrography.
Earlier D 203.22:9

DoD FLIGHT INFORMATION PUBLICATIONS.

D 5.317:nos.   • Item 378-F
LORAN TABLES.
See D 5.317/4

D 5.317:nos.   • Item 378-G
OMEGA TABLES.
See D 5.317/5

D 5.317:nos.   • Item 378-E
SAILING DIRECTIONS. [Irregular]
See D 5.317/3

D 5.317/2:nos./date   • Item 378-D
HYDROGRAPHIC/TOPOGRAPHIC CENTER PUBLICATIONS (numbered).

D 5.317/3   • Item 378-E
HYDROGRAPHIC/TOPOGRAPHIC CENTER PUBLICATIONS: SAILING DIRECTIONS.

D 5.317/4   • Item 378-F
HYDROGRAPHIC/TOPOGRAPHIC CENTER PUBLICATIONS: LORAN TABLES.

D 5.317/5   • Item 378-G
HYDROGRAPHIC/TOPOGRAPHIC CENTER PUBLICATIONS: OMEGA TABLES.

D 5.318:v.nos.&nos.
LOW ALTITUDE INSTRUMENT APPROACH PROCEDURES.

D 5.318/2:CT/date
HIGH ALTITUDE INSTRUMENT APPROACH PROCEDURES.

D 5.318/3:date
LOW ALTITUDE APPROACH PROCEDURES, UNITED STATES MILITARY AVIATION NOTICE.

D 5.318/4:letters & nos./date
ENROUTE HIGH AND LOW ALTITUDE, U.S.

D 5.318/5:date
GENERAL PLANNING, GP- (series). [Issued every 24 weeks]

D 5.318/5-2:date
AREA PLANNING, NORTH AND SOUTH AMERICA, AP/1- (series). [Issued every 12 weeks]

D 5.318/5-3:date
AREA PLANNING, SPECIAL USE AIRSPACE, NORTH AND SOUTH AMERICA, AP/1A-(series). [Issued every 16 weeks]

D 5.318/6:date
AREA CHARTS, U.S.

D 5.318/7:date
ENROUTE IFR-SUPPLEMENT, UNITED STATES.

D 5.318/8:date
VFR-SUPPLEMENT, UNITED STATES.

D 5.318/8-2:date
ENROUTE CHANGE NOTICE, DoD FLIP ENROUTE VFR SUPPLEMENT UNITED STATES. [Irregular]

Supersedes Military Aviation Notice, DoD Flip Enroute VFR Supplement United States.

D 5.319:CT   • Item 617 (MF)
GAZETTEERS. [Irregular]

Each volume covers a single country or group of countries and is generally the most comprehensive yet produced. The gazetteers constitute the authoritative source of geographic names in the areas covered, and their spelling and application, that are official for use by our Federal Government. Also included are the more important unapproved names or spellings cross-referenced to the approved ones. They include new and changed names resulting from changes in administrative divisions or other governmental actions, and new forms or spelling resulting from orthographic changes officially adopted and implemented by those countries.
Previously published by the Board on Geographic Names (I 33.8).

D 5.319/2   • Item 617-B (EL)
GEONET NAME SERVER.
Database.

D 5.319/3   • Item 378-E-6
PUBLIC SALE CATALOG-TOPOGRAPHICAL MAPS AND PUBLICATIONS. [Annual]

D 5.320:v.nos.&nos.
SURF 'N' TURF. (Hydrographic/Topographic Center)

Newsletter for the personnel of the Center.

D 5.321:CT
TERRAIN ANALYSIS (series). (Hydrographic/Topographic Center)

Defense Mapping Agency Maps

D 5.322   • Item 379-A-1– 9
ONC– OPERATIONAL NAVIGATION CHARTS.

Maps in this series are issued for the following geographic areas: (1) Africa, (2) Antarctica, (3) Arctic Regions, (4) Asia and Eastern Europe, (5) Europe, (6) Central and South America, (7) North America, (8) Pacific, and (9) the World. The scale used for maps in this series is 1:1,000,000.

D 5.323   • Item 379-B-1– 9
JNC– JET NAVIGATION CHARTS.

Maps in this series are issued for the following geographic areas: (1) Africa, (2) Antarctica, (3) Arctic Regions, (4) Asia and Eastern Europe, (5) Europe, (6) Central and South America, (7) North America, (8) Pacific, and (9) the World. The scale used for maps in this series is 1:2,000,000.

D 5.324 • Item 379-C-1– 9
GNC– GLOBAL NAVIGATION CHARTS.

Maps in this series are issued for the following geographic areas: (1) Africa, (2) Antarctica, (3) Arctic Regions, (4) Asia and Eastern Europe, (5) Europe, (6) Central and South America, (7) North America, (8) Pacific, and (9) the World. The scale used for maps in this series is 1:5,000,000.

D 5.325 • Item 379-D-1– 9
SERIES 1105– AREA OUTLINE MAPS.

Maps in this series are issued for the following geographic areas: (1) Africa, (2) Antarctica, (3) Arctic Regions, (4) Asia and Eastern Europe, (5) Europe, (6) Central and South America, (7) North America, (8) Pacific, and (9) the World. The scale used for maps in this series are 1:5,000,000, 1:10,000,000 and 1:20,000,000.

D 5.325/2 • Item 379-G-1– 9
SERIES 1146– AREA OUTLINE MAPS.

Maps in this series are issued for the following geographic areas: (1) Africa, (2) Antarctica, (3) Arctic Regions, (4) Asia and Eastern Europe, (5) Europe, (6) Central and South America, (7) North America, (8) Pacific, and (9) the World. The scale used for maps in this series is 1:7,000,000.
Discontinued.

D 5.326 • Item 379-E-1– 9
SERIES 1106– THE WORLD.

Maps in this series are issued for the following geographic areas: (1) Africa, (2) Antarctica, (3) Arctic Regions, (4) Asia and Eastern Europe, (5) Europe, (6) Central and South America, (7) North America, (8) Pacific, and (9) the World. The scale used for maps in this series is 1:5,000,000.
Discontinued.

D 5.326/2 • Item 379-F
SERIES 1107– THE WORLD.

The scale used for maps in this series are 1:6,000,000 and 1:135,000,000.

Discontinued.

D 5.326/4 • Item 379-F-1
SERIES 1144– THE WORLD.

The scale used for maps in this series is 1:22,000,000.

D 5.326/5 • Item 379-F-2
SERIES 1145– THE WORLD.

The scale used for maps in this series is 1:35,000,000.

D 5.326/6 • Item 379-F-3
SERIES 1148– THE WORLD.

The scale used for maps in this series is 1:35,000,000.
Discontinued.

D 5.326/7 • Item 379-J-1– 9
SERIES 1301– THE WORLD.

Maps in this series are issued for the following geographic areas: (1) Africa, (2) Antarctica, (3) Arctic Regions, (4) Asia and Eastern Europe, (5) Europe, (6) Central and South America, (7) North America, (8) Pacific, and (9) the World. The scale used for maps in this series is 1:1,000,000.
Discontinued.

D 5.326/8 • Item 379-F-15
SERIES 1150– THE WORLD.

The scale used for maps in this series is 1:14,000,000.

D 5.327 • Item 379-H-1– 9
SERIES 1147– WORLD PLOTTING SERIES.

Maps in this series are issued for the following geographic areas: (1) Africa, (2) Antarctica, (3) Arctic Regions, (4) Asia and Eastern Europe,

(5) Europe, (6) Central and South America, (7) North America, (8) Pacific, and (9) the World. The scale used for maps in this series are 1:9,000,000 and 1:18,000,000.
Discontinued.

D 5.328 • Item 378-K-E-7
SERIES 1209– EUROPE.

Maps in this series are issued for the following geographic areas: (1) Asia and Eastern Europe, (2) Europe, and (3) the World. The scale used for maps in this series is 1:2,000,000.

D 5.329 • Item 379-L-1– 3
SERIES 1211S– MID-EAST BRIEFING GRAPHIC.

Maps in this series are issued for the following geographic areas: (1) Africa, (2) Asia and Eastern Europe, and (3) Europe. The scale used for maps in this series is 1:3,500,000.
Discontinued.

D 5.330 • Item 379-M-1– 3
SERIES 1308– MID-EAST BRIEFING MAPS.

Maps in this series are issued for the following geographic areas: (1) Africa, (2) Asia and Eastern Europe, and (3) the World. The scale used for maps in this series is 1:1,500,000.

D 5.331 • Item 379-F-4
SERIES 2201– AFRICA.

The scale used for maps in this series is 1:2,000,000.
See D 5.355

D 5.332 • Item 379-F-5
SERIES 5103– USSR-ADMINISTRATIVE AREAS.

The scale used for maps in this series is 1:8,000,000.
See D 5.355

D 5.333 • Item 379-F-6
SERIES 5104– USSR AND ADJACENT AREAS.

The scale used for maps in this series is 1:8,000,000.
See D 5.355

D 5.334 • Item 379-N-1– 3
SERIES 5211– ARABIAN PENINSULA.

Maps in this series are issued for the following geographic areas: (1) Africa, (2) Asia and Eastern Europe, and (3) Europe. The scale used for maps in this series is 1:2,000,000.

D 5.335 • Item 379-F-7
SERIES 5213– SE ASIA BRIEFING MAP.

The scale used for maps in this series is 1:2,000,000.
See D 5.355

D 5.336 • Item 379-F-8
SERIES 5305– EASTERN ASIA.

The scale used for maps in this series is 1:1,500,000.
Discontinued.

D 5.337 • Item 379-F-9
SERIES 8205 AND 8206– UNITED STATES.

The scale used for maps in this series is 1:3,500,000.
Discontinued.

D 5.338 • Item 379-F-10
SERIES 9201– NEW ZEALAND.

The scale used for maps in this series is 1:2,000,000.
Discontinued.

D 5.339 • Item 379-F-11
SERIES 9203– U.S. TRUST TERRITORY OF THE PACIFIC.

The scale used for maps in this series is 1:4,000,000.
Discontinued.

D 5.340 • Item 379-F-12
SERIES L302– JAPAN ROAD MAPS.

The scale used for maps in this series is 1:1,000,000.
Discontinued.

D 5.341 • Item 379-F-13
SERIES L351– KOREA ROAD MAPS.

The scale used for maps in this series is 1:7,000,000.
Discontinued.

D 5.342 • Item 379-F-14
SERIES M305– OFFICIAL ROAD MAPS FOR ALLIED FORCES– EUROPE.

The scale used for maps in this series is 1:1,000,000.
Discontinued v. 5/11.

D 5.343 • Item 379-P-1– 9
GENERAL (38) NAUTICAL CHARTS.

Charts in this series are issued for the following regions: Region 1– U.S. and Canada; Region 2– Central and South America; Region 3– Western Europe, Iceland, and Greenland; Region 4– Scandinavia, Baltic, and USSR; Region 5– Western Africa and the Mediterranean; Region 6– Indian Ocean; Region 7– Australia, Indonesia and New Zealand; Region 8– Oceania; Region 9– East Asia.

D 5.344 • Item 379-Q-1– 9
INTERNATIONAL (45) CHART SERIES.

Charts in this series are issued for the following regions: Region 1– U.S. and Canada; Region 2– Central and South America; Region 3– Western Europe, Iceland, and Greenland; Region 4– Scandinavia, Baltic, and USSR; Region 5– Western Africa and the Mediterranean; Region 6– Indian Ocean; Region 7– Australia, Indonesia and New Zealand; Region 8– Oceania; Region 9– East Asia.

D 5.345 • Item 379-R-1– 9
GREAT CIRCLE (8) SAILING AND POLAR CHARTS.

Charts in this series are issued for the following regions: Region 1– U.S. and Canada; Region 2– Central and South America; Region 3– Western Europe, Iceland, and Greenland; Region 4– Scandinavia, Baltic, and USSR; Region 5– Western Africa and the Mediterranean; Region 6– Indian Ocean; Region 7– Australia, Indonesia and New Zealand; Region 8– Oceania; Region 9– East Asia.

D 5.346 • Item 379-R-1– 9
GREAT CIRCLE (58) TRACKING CHARTS.

Charts in this series are issued for the following regions: Region 1– U.S. and Canada; Region 2– Central and South America; Region 3– Western Europe, Iceland, and Greenland; Region 4– Scandinavia, Baltic, and USSR; Region 5– Western Africa and the Mediterranean; Region 6– Indian Ocean; Region 7– Australia, Indonesia and New Zealand; Region 8– Oceania; Region 9– East Asia.

D 5.347 • Item 379-S-1– 9
OMEGA PLOTTING (31) CHARTS SERIES 7500.

Charts in this series are issued for the following regions: Region 1– U.S. and Canada; Region 2– Central and South America; Region 3– Western Europe, Iceland, and Greenland; Region 4– Scandinavia, Baltic, and USSR; Region 5– Western Africa and the Mediterranean; Region 6– Indian Ocean; Region 7– Australia, Indonesia and New Zealand; Region 8– Oceania; Region 9– East Asia.
Discontinued.

D 5.347/2 • Item 379-S-1– 9
OMEGA PLOTTING (112) CHARTS SERIES 7600.

Charts in this series are issued for the following regions: Region 1– U.S. and Canada; Region 2– Central and South America; Region 3– Western Europe, Iceland, and Greenland; Region 4– Scandinavia, Baltic, and USSR; Region 5– Western Africa and the Mediterranean; Region 6– Indian Ocean; Region 7– Australia, Indonesia and New Zealand; Region 8– Oceania; Region 9– East Asia.

D 5.348 • Item 379-T-1– 9
LORAN A (19) PLOTTING CHARTS SERIES 7300.

Charts in this series are issued for the following regions: Region 1– U.S. and Canada; Region 2– Central and South America; Region 3– Western Europe, Iceland, and Greenland; Region 4– Scandinavia, Baltic, and USSR; Region 5– Western Africa and the Mediterranean; Region 6– Indian Ocean; Region 7– Australia, Indonesia and New Zealand; Region 8– Oceania; Region 9– East Asia.
Discontinued.

D 5.348/2 • Item 379-T-1– 9
LORAN C (44) PLOTTING CHARTS SERIES 7800.

Charts in this series are issued for the following regions: Region 1– U.S. and Canada; Region 2– Central and South America; Region 3– Western Europe, Iceland, and Greenland; Region 4– Scandinavia, Baltic, and USSR; Region 5– Western Africa and the Mediterranean; Region 6– Indian Ocean; Region 7– Australia, Indonesia and New Zealand; Region 8– Oceania; Region 9– East Asia.

D 5.349 • Item 379-W-1– 9
DISPLAY PLOTTING CHARTS 1°36' (12).

Charts in this series are issued for the following regions: Region 1– U.S. and Canada; Region 2– Central and South America; Region 3– Western Europe, Iceland, and Greenland; Region 4– Scandinavia, Baltic, and USSR; Region 5– Western Africa and the Mediterranean; Region 6– Indian Ocean; Region 7– Australia, Indonesia and New Zealand; Region 8– Oceania; Region 9– East Asia.

D 5.349/2 • Item 379-W-1– 9
DISPLAY PLOTTING CHARTS 1°– 1'(87).

Charts in this series are issued for the following regions: Region 1– U.S. and Canada; Region 2– Central and South America; Region 3– Western Europe, Iceland, and Greenland; Region 4– Scandinavia, Baltic, and USSR; Region 5– Western Africa and the Mediterranean; Region 6– Indian Ocean; Region 7– Australia, Indonesia and New Zealand; Region 8– Oceania; Region 9– East Asia.

D 5.349/3 • Item 379-W-1– 9
DISPLAY PLOTTING CHARTS 1°– 2' (200).

Charts in this series are issued for the following regions: Region 1– U.S. and Canada; Region 2– Central and South America; Region 3– Western Europe, Iceland, and Greenland; Region 4– Scandinavia, Baltic, and USSR; Region 5– Western Africa and the Mediterranean; Region 6– Indian Ocean; Region 7– Australia, Indonesia and New Zealand; Region 8– Oceania; Region 9– East Asia.

D 5.349/4 • Item 379-W-1– 9
DISPLAY PLOTTING CHARTS 1°– 3' (85).

Charts in this series are issued for the following regions: Region 1– U.S. and Canada; Region 2– Central and South America; Region 3– Western Europe, Iceland, and Greenland; Region 4– Scandinavia, Baltic, and USSR; Region 5– Western Africa and the Mediterranean; Region 6– Indian Ocean; Region 7– Australia, Indonesia and New Zealand; Region 8– Oceania; Region 9– East Asia.

D 5.350 • Item 379-Y-1– 9
COASTAL CHARTS (4000).

Charts in this series are issued for the following regions: Region 1– U.S. and Canada; Region 2– Central and South America; Region 3– Western Europe, Iceland, and Greenland; Region 4– Scandinavia, Baltic, and USSR; Region 5– Western Africa and the Mediterranean; Region 6– Indian Ocean; Region 7– Australia, Indonesia and New Zealand; Region 8– Oceania; Region 9– East Asia.

NATIONAL IMAGERY AND MAPPING AGENCY (Continued)

D 5.351:v.no./date
Part 1. AEROSPACE PRODUCTS.

D 5.351/2 • Item 378-E-22
DEFENSE MAPPING AGENCY PUBLIC SALE NAUTICAL CHARTS AND PUBLICATIONS.

A series of comprehensive reference of coastal, harbor, and approach charts for Regions 1-9. Contains information concerning the availability, prices, and ordering instructions for public sale charts.
Later C 55.440

D 5.351/2:1/date • Item 378-E-11
– VOLUME 1, UNITED STATES AND CANADA. [Annual]

D 5.351/2:2/date • Item 378-E-12
– VOLUME 2, CENTRAL AND SOUTH AMERICA AND ANTARCTICA. [Annual]

D 5.351/2:3/date • Item 378-E-13
– VOLUME 3, WESTERN EUROPE, ICELAND, GREENLAND, AND THE ARCTIC. [Annual]

D 5.351/2:4/date • Item 378-E-14
– VOLUME 4, SCANDINAVIA, BALTIC, AND USSR. [Annual]

D 5.351/2:5/date • Item 378-E-15
– VOLUME 5, WESTERN AFRICA AND THE MEDITERRANEAN. [Annual]

D 5.351/2:6/date • Item 378-E-16
– VOLUME 6, INDIAN OCEAN. [Annual]

D 5.351/2:7/date • Item 378-E-17
– VOLUME 7, AUSTRALIA, INDONESIA, AND NEW ZEALAND. [Annual]

D 5.351/2:8/date • Item 378-E-18
– VOLUME 8, OCEANIA. [Annual]

D 5.351/2:9/date • Item 378-E-19
– VOLUME 9, EAST ASIA. [Annual]

D 5.351/2:10/date • Item 378-E-20
– VOLUME 10, MISCELLANEOUS CHARTS AND PUBLICATIONS. [Annual]

Describes DMA hydrographic products, including the Hydrographic Products Bulletin System, chart numbering and stock numbers, portfolio designations, chart terms, and chart and publication procedures. Contains information concerning the availability, prices, and ordering instructions for public sale charts.

D 5.351/2-2:nos. • Item 38-E-11
QUARTERLY BULLETIN FOR PART 2, HYDROGRAPHIC PRODUCTS. [Quarterly]

Earlier: Monthly Bulletin for Part 2, Hydrographic Products.

D 5.351/2-3:date
DEFENSE MAPPING AGENCY CATALOG OF MAPS, CHARTS, AND RELATED PRODUCTS, SEMI-ANNUAL BULLETIN DIGEST, PART 2, HYDROGRAPHIC PRODUCTS. [Semiannual]

D 5.351/3:date • Item 378-E-6
PUBLIC SALE CATALOG: TOPOGRAPHIC MAPS AND PUBLICATIONS. [Annual]

Contains information concerning the availability, purchase prices, and ordering instructions for DMA-produced products for public sale.

D 5.351/3-2:date • Item 378-E-8
PUBLIC SALE CATALOG: AERONAUTICAL CHARTS AND PUBLICATIONS. [Annual]

Contains information concerning the availability, purchase prices, and ordering instructions for DMA-produced products for public sale.

D 5.352:date • Item 378-D-1 (MF)
CATALOG AND COURSE DESCRIPTIONS OF THE DEFENSE MAPPING SCHOOL. [Annual]
Describes course offerings for two years. Non-depository.

D 5.352/2:nos. • Item 378-D-2 (MF)
STUDENT TEXTS, ST- (series). [Irregular]
Discontinued.

D 5.353:CT • Item 378-E-37
MAPS, CHARTS, AND ATLASES.

D 5.354
NAVIGATION CHARTS.

D 5.354 • Item 378-E-3
GNC: GLOBAL NAVIGATION AND PLANNING CHARTS.

Charts suitable for aeronautical planning, operations over long distances, and enroute navigation in long range, high altitude, high speed aircraft. Charts show principal cities, towns and drainage, primary roads and railroads, prominent cultural features and shaded relief. Standard Index Chart is included. Scale: 1:5,000,000. Revised as required.

D 5.354 • Item 378-E-2
JNC: JET NAVIGATION CHARTS.

Charts suitable for long range, high altitude, high speed navigation. Topographic features include large cities, roads, railroads, drainage and relief. All aeronautical information necessary is shown. Standard Index Chart is supplied. Scale: 1:2,000,000. Revised as required.

D 5.354 • Item 378-E-1
ONC: OPERATIONAL NAVIGATION CHARTS.

Charts support high-speed radar navigation requirements of aircraft at medium altitudes. Uses include visual, celestial, and radio navigation. Standard Index Chart is supplied. Scale: 1:1,000,000. Revised as required.

D 5.354 • Item 378-E-5
TPC: TACTICAL PILOTAGE CHARTS.

Charts support high speed, low altitude, radar and visual navigation of high performance tactical and reconnaissance aircraft at very low through medium altitudes. Stand Index Chart is supplied. Scale: 1:500,00. Revised as required.

D 5.355:1105 • Item 378-E-4
SERIES 1105: AREA OUTLINE MAPS.

Characteristics: International and major subdivision boundaries delineated; national capital cities of major importance shown; drainage patterns. Scale: 1:20,000,000. Revised as required.

D 5.355:1144 • Item 378-E-35
SERIES 1144: THE WORLD.

Topographic map of the world. Scale 1:22,000,000. Revised as required.
Distributed by the U.S. Geological Survey on behalf of the Defense Mapping Agency.

D 5.355:1145 • Item 378-E-35
SERIES 1145: THE WORLD

Topographic map of the world. Scale
1:30,000,000. Revised as required.
Distributed by the U.S. Geological Survey on
behalf of the Defense Mapping Agency.

D 5.355:1150 • Item 378-E-35
SERIES 1150: THE WORLD.

Topographic map of the world. Scale
1:14,000,000. Revised as required.
Distributed by the U.S. Geological Survey on
behalf of the Defense Mapping Agency.

D 5.355:1209 • Item 378-E-7
SERIES 1209: EUROPE.

Characteristics: International boundaries,
major civil subdivisions and administrative boundaries; towns, and roads classified by administrative importance; railways in operation; airports,
etc. Scale: 1:2,000,000. Revised as required.

D 5.355:1308 • Item 378-E-9
SERIES 1308: MIDDLE EAST BRIEFING MAP.

Characteristics: Armistice and international
boundaries and populated places shown; roads
classified; railroads, oil pipelines and drainage
shown; airfields symbolized. Depicts Cyprus,
Egypt, Iraq, Israel, Jordan, Lebanon, Saudi Arabia,
Syria, and Turkey. Scale: 1:1,500,000. Revised
as required.

D 5.355:2201 • Item 379-F-4
SERIES 2201: AFRICA.

Characteristics: International major administrative boundaries delineated; cities, towns, and
roads classified by importance, vegetation, drainage features relating to arid areas shown. Scale
1:2,000,000. Revised as required.

D 5.355:5103 • Item 379-F-5
SERIES 5103: ADMINISTRATIVE AREAS OF THE
USSR.

Characteristics: Boundaries delineated for
USSR internally for republics; foreign countries;
Chinese provinces. Series comprises of one planimetric map showing hydrographic features, pipelines etc. Scale 1:8,000,000. Revised as require.

D 5.355:5104 • Item 379-F-6
SERIES 5104: USSR AND ADJACENT AREAS.

Characteristics: Boundaries delineated as international, interstate, and provincial; roads classified by surface, towns symbolized by population, etc. Series comprises of one topographic
map showing drainage patterns, water and land
features. Scale 1:8,000,000. Revised as required.

D 5.355:5211 • Item 378-E-10
SERIES 5211: ARABIAN PENINSULA.

Characteristics: Relief indicated by hachur-
ing; types of sand areas differentiated; roads
and population places classified; railroads and
petroleum facilities shown, etc. Scale:
1:2,250,000. Revised as required.

D 5.355:5213 • Item 379-F-7
SERIES 5213: SOUTHEAST ASIA BRIEFING MAP.

Characteristics: International boundaries
delineated, populated places classified by importance, principal roads and airfields shown. Series
comprises of one topographic sheet depicting
Burma, China, Kampuchea, Laos, Thailand, and
Vietnam. Scale 1:2,000,000.

D 5.356
CHARTS.

D 5.356
CHARTS (listed in) CATALOG OF MAPS, CHARTS,
AND RELATED PRODUCTS, PART 2, HYDRO-
GRAPHIC PRODUCTS.

D 5.356:nos./date • Item 378-E-21
– VOLUME 1, UNITED STATES AND CANADA.

Includes coastal, harbor, and approach
charts for Hawaii, Gulf of Mexico, Atlantic
and Pacific coasts of the U.S. and Canada,
Great Lakes, and Arctic Canada produced by
DMA. Those charts offered by the NOS/GPO
map program are not included here. Revised
as required.

D 5.356:nos./date • Item 378-E-22
– VOLUME 2, CENTRAL AND SOUTH AMERICA,
AND ANTARCTICA.

Includes coastal, harbor, and approach
charts for Mexico, Central America, Isthmus
of Panama, Brazil. . ., and Antarctica. Revised as required.

D 5.356:nos./date • Item 378-E-23
– VOLUME 3, WESTERN EUROPE, ICELAND,
GREENLAND, AND THE ARCTIC.

Includes coastal, harbor, and approach
charts, for Ireland, Great Britain and France,
Scotland, Netherlands, Ireland and Irish Sea,
English Channel area, and Spain. Revised as
required.

D 5.356:nos./date • Item 378-E-24
– VOLUME 4, SCANDINAVIA, BALTIC, AND USSR.

Includes coastal, harbor, and approach
charts for the Barents Sea area, the Coast of
Norway, Southern coast of Norway, Sweden
and approach to the Baltic. Revised as required.

D 5.356:nos./date • Item 378-E-25
– VOLUME 5, WESTERN AFRICA, AND THE MEDI-
TERRANEAN.

Includes coastal, harbor, and approach
charts for the West Cost of Africa, Mediterranean and the Black Seas, Aegean Sea. . .,
the Cape of Good Hope and various islands.
Revised as required.

D 5.356:nos./date • Item 378-E-26
– VOLUME 6, INDIAN OCEAN.

Includes coastal, harbor, and approach
charts for the Republic of South Africa, and
Mozambique Channel area, the Red Sea, Gulf
of Aden to the Persian Gulf, Arabian Sea,
Bay of Bengal area. . . Revised as required.

D 5.356:nos./date • Item 378-E-27
– VOLUME 7, AUSTRALIA, INDONESIA, AND NEW
ZEALAND.

Includes coastal, harbor, and approach
charts for Sumatra, Borneo, Java to Timor,
New Guinea, Australia, and New Zealand and
vicinity. Revised as required.

D 5.356:nos./date • Item 378-E-28
– VOLUME 8, OCEANIA.

Includes harbor, coastal, and approach
charts for the Islands Mariana, Bismarck Ar-
chipelago, Caroline, Marchall, Wake, Solomon,
Gilbert, etc. Revised as required.

D 5.356:nos./date • Item 378-E-29
– VOLUME 9, EAST ASIA.

Includes coastal, harbor, and approach
charts for China, Philippine Islands, Vietnam,
Eastern Malay Peninsula, Gulf of Tonkin, North
and South Korea, etc. Revised as required.

D 5.356 • Item 378-E-34
DISPLAY PLOTTING CHARTS.

Charts in degrees, minutes, and seconds
used to plot departure and destination points
for Regions 1-9. Revised as required.

D 5.356 • Item 378-E-30
GENERAL NAUTICAL AND INTERNATIONAL NAU-
TICAL CHARTS.

Charts cover Regions 1-9 and show nature and shape of the coasts, depths of water, prominent landmarks, nautical symbols.
etc. Scales vary widely for the General Nautical Charts. Scales are generally 1:10,000,000
or 1:3,500,000 for the International Nautical
Charts. Revised as required.

D 5.356 • Item 378-E-31
GREAT CIRCLE SAILING, POLAR AND TRACK-
ING CHARTS.

Charts primarily cover the Atlantic, Pacific, and Indian Oceans. Include geophysical and reference charts. Revised as required.

D 5.356 • Item 378-E-33
LORAN C PLOTTING CHARTS.

LOng RAnge Navigation (LORAN) charts
used primarily by aircraft flying over ocean
routes, generally for distances of 1000 to
1500 nautical miles. Charts include a series
of hyperbolas that represent time differences
for LORAN radio frequencies for Regions 1-9.
Revised as required.

D 5.356 • Item 378-E-32
OMEGA PLOTTING CHARTS.

Very long-distance navigation system
where position is determined by measuring
differences in travel time of continuous wave
signals separated by 5000 to 6000 nautical
miles. Charts cover Regions 1-9. Revised as
required.

D 5.358:letters/date • Item 378-E-36 (CD)
DIGITAL CHART OF THE WORLD (DCW).
Issued on CD-ROM.

D 5.359:v.nos./nos. • Item 379-A-12
NAVIGATOR. [Quarterly]
Ceased Spring 1996.

D 5.360: • Item 378-E-38 (E)
ELECTRONIC PRODUCTS (misc.).

D 5.361: • Item 378-E-38 (EL)
FACT SHEETS.

NATIONAL DEFENSE UNIVERSITY
(1977–)

CREATION AND AUTHORITY

The National Defense University was established by the Department of Defense on January
16, 1976, merging the Industrial College of the
Armed Forces and the National War College.

INFORMATION

Chief Information Officer
Ft. McNair
National Defense University
300 5th Ave. SW Building 62
Washington DC 20319-5066
(202) 685-4246

D 5.401:date • Item 378-H-8 (MF)
ANNUAL REPORT.

D 5.402:CT • Item 378-H-1
GENERAL PUBLICATIONS.

D 5.406:CT • Item 378-H-10
REGULATIONS, RULES, INSTRUCTIONS. [Irregular]

D 5.408:CT • Item 378-H-7
HANDBOOKS, MANUALS, GUIDES. [Irregular]

D 5.408/2:date • Item 378-H-7
JOINT STAFF OFFICER'S GUIDE. [Annual]

D 5.409:yr.nos. • **Item 378-H-7 (MF)**
NATIONAL SECURITY AFFAIRS MONOGRAPHS.
[Irregular]

PURPOSE:– To disseminate the results of innovative research studies in selected areas of national strategy formulation and management of national security resources.

D 5.409/2:yr.nos. • **Item 378-H (MF)**
NATIONAL SECURITY AFFAIRS ISSUE PAPERS.
Published in microfiche

D 5.410:CT • **Item 378-H-4 (MF)**
NATIONAL SECURITY MANAGEMENT (series).
[Irregular] (Industrial College of the Armed Forces)

D 5.410/2
NATIONAL SECURITY MANAGEMENT PROGRAMS
INSTRUCTOR'S GUIDE (series).

D 5.411:CT • **Item 378-H-2**
BIBLIOGRAPHIES AND LISTS OF PUBLICATIONS.
[Irregular]

D 5.411/2:nos. • **Item 378-H-2 (MF)**
NDU RESEARCH ABSTRACTS. 1– 1984–
[Annual]
Discontinued.

D 5.411/3:date • **Item 378-H-2 (MF)**
FOR YOUR INFORMATION, NEW ACQUISITIONS.
[Monthly]
Earlier title: New Books.

D 5.411/4:date • **Item 378-H-2**
CATALOGED SERIAL HOLDINGS. [Quarterly]
Discontinued.

D 5.412:date • **Item 378-H-3**
PROCEEDINGS OF THE NATIONAL SECURITY
AFFAIRS CONFERENCE. [Annual]
Discontinued.

D 5.413 • **Item 378-H-5**
NATIONAL SECURITY ESSAY SERIES.
Discontinued.

D 5.413/2:CT • **Item 378-H-5**
ARMED FORCES STAFF COLLEGE ESSAYS ON COM-
MAND ISSUES. [Irregular]

D 5.414:date • **Item 378-H-6 (MF)**
NATIONAL DEFENSE UNIVERSITY CATALOGUE. [An-
nual]
PURPOSE:– To describe the curriculum and courses offered by the University, including the Industrial College of the Armed Forces, the Na-
tional War College, and the Armed Forces Staff
College.

D 5.414/2:date • **Item 378-H-6 (MF)**
DoD COMPUTER INSTITUTE: NDU-DODCI COURSE
CATALOG. [Annual]

D 5.414/3:date • **Item 378-H-6 (MF)**
DoD COMPUTER INSTITUTE: COURSE INFORMA-
TION. [Annual]

D 5.415: • **Item 378-H-9 (MF)**
NATIONAL WAR COLLEGE STRATEGIC STUDIES
(series). [Irregular]

D 5.415/9 • **Item 378-H-11 (MF)**
ELECTIVE COURSE READINGS (series). [Irregular]

Elective miscellaneous course readings reproduced from various sources for use in the
courses of the National Defense University.

D 5.416:nos. • **Item 378-H-5(MF) (EL)**
MC NAIR PAPERS (series).

D 5.417:nos. • **Item 378-H-12 (EL)**
STRATEGIC FORUM. (Institute for National Strategic
Studies)

D 5.417/2 • **Item 378-H-14 (EL)**
INSTITUTE FOR NATIONAL STRATIGIC STUDIES:
GENERAL PUBLICATIONS.

D 5.418 • **Item 378-H-13 (MF)**
WORKSHOP (Series). (Institute for National Strategic Studies)

OFFICE OF PUBLIC AFFAIRS
(1962–   )

INFORMATION

Office of Public Affairs
1400 Defense Pentagon
Washington DC 20301-1400
(703) 697-9312
Fax: (703) 695-4299

D 6.1:date
ANNUAL REPORTS.

D 6.2:CT
GENERAL PUBLICATIONS.

D 6.6:CT
REGULATIONS, RULES, AND INSTRUCTIONS.

D 6.7:dt.&nos.
RELEASES.

D 6.7/2:dt./nos.
ADDRESSES S (series).

D 6.8:v.nos.
HANDBOOKS, MANUALS, GUIDES.

DEFENSE LOGISTICS AGENCY
(1977–   )

CREATION AND AUTHORITY

The Defense Supply Management Agency
was established within the Department of Defense by the Defense Cataloging and Standardization Act approved July 1, 1952 (66 Stat. 318).
The Agency was abolished by Reorganization Plan
No. 6 of 1953, effective June 30, 1953, and its
functions transferred to the Office of the Secretary of Defense. The Defense Supply Agency
was established by the Secretary of Defense to
succeed the Defense Supply Management Agency.
The name changed to Defense Logistics Agency
by DoD Directive 5105.22 of January 22, 1977.

INFORMATION

Defense Logistics Agency
8725 John J. Kingman Road
Suite 1421
Fort Belvoir, VA 22060-6221
(202)767-5200
http://www.dla.mil

D 7.1:date • **Item 314-M**
REPORTS. [Annual]

D 7.1/2:date
ANNUAL HISTORICAL SUMMARY: DEFENSE LO-
GISTICS SERVICE CENTER, BATTLE CREEK,
MICH.

D 7.1/3:date
ANNUAL HISTORICAL SUMMARY: DEFENSE IN-
DUSTRIAL PLANT EQUIPMENT CENTER.

D 7.1/4:CT
ANNUAL HISTORICAL SUMMARY: DEFENSE
CONTRACT ADMINISTRATION SERVICES [by
region].

D 7.1/5:date
ANNUAL HISTORICAL SUMMARY: DEFENSE
ELECTRONICS SUPPLY CENTER.

D 7.1/6:date
ANNUAL HISTORICAL SUMMARY: DEFENSE
FUEL SUPPLY CENTER.

D 7.1/6-2:date • **Item 314-M (MF)**
FACT BOOK, DEFENSE FUEL SUPPLY CENTER.
[Annual]

D 7.1/7:CT/date
ANNUAL HISTORICAL SUMMARY: DEFENSE DE-
POTS.

D 7.1/8:date
ANNUAL HISTORICAL SUMMARY: DEFENSE
GENERAL SUPPLY CENTER.

D 7.1/9:date
ANNUAL HISTORICAL SUMMARY: DEFENSE
CONSTRUCTION SUPPLY CENTER.

D 7.1/10:date
ANNUAL HISTORICAL SUMMARY: DEFENSE
DOCUMENTATION CENTER.

D 7.1/11:date
ANNUAL HISTORICAL SUMMARY: DEFENSE IN-
DUSTRIAL SUPPLY CENTER.

D 7.1/12:date
ANNUAL HISTORICAL SUMMARY: DEFENSE
PRODUCTION SUPPORT OFFICE.

D 7.1/13:date
ANNUAL MANAGEMENT REPORT OF THE DE-
FENSE SUPPLY AGENCY.
Discontinued.

D 7.2:CT • **Item 314-A**
GENERAL PUBLICATIONS.

D 7.6:CT • **Item 314-A**
REGULATIONS, RULES, AND INSTRUCTIONS.

D 7.6/2:nos. • **Item 314-A**
CATALOGING HANDBOOKS.
Issued in the following parts and sections:
Discontinued.

D 7.6/2:2-1 • **Item 314-A**
H 2-1 FEDERAL SUPPLY CLASSIFICATION, PART
1, GROUPS AND CLASSES. [Annual]

Contains the classification structure of
the Federal Supply Classification, showing all
groups and classes presented in the arrangement of the 4-digit FSC code numbering system.
Revised at least annually, usually in January.

D 7.6/2:2-2 • **Item 314-A**
H 2-2 FEDERAL SUPPLY CLASSIFICATION, PART
2, NUMERIC INDEX OF CLASSES. [Monthly
& Quarterly]

Contains the names of items within each
class listed alphabetically under the class
number and title. The classes are shown, group
by group, in the numeric order of the code-
numbering system.
Basic volume kept up-to-date by quarterly addenda and monthly supplements. Subscription price includes basic volumes, supplements, and addenda for indefinite period.
When new addenda are received, all preceding cumulative supplements may be discarded, but the addenda must be retained
until a new basic volume is issued.
ISSN 0145-0573

D 7.6/2:2-3 • Item 314-A
H 2-3 FEDERAL SUPPLY CLASSIFICATION, PART 3, ALPHABETICAL INDEX. [Monthly]

Contains an index of all names of items, which appear in Part 2, arranged in alphabetical order. Opposite each name is shown the applicable FSC class code number.

Issued in loose-leaf form and punched for 3-ring binder. Kept up-to-date by monthly supplements. Subscription price includes the basic volume plus the monthly supplements for an indefinite period.
ISSN 0145-059X

D 7.6/2:4-1 • Item 314-A
H 4-1 FEDERAL SUPPLY CODE FOR MANUFACTURERS, PART 1, NAME TO CODE. [Monthly]

List in alphabetical sequence the names of manufacturers which have or are currently producing items used by the Federal Government, followed by the five-digit numerical code assigned to each. Also provides the address of each manufacturer and related historical and affiliation date where pertinent.

Kept up-to-date by monthly supplements. Subscription price includes the basic volume plus monthly supplements for an indefinite period. Issued in loose-leaf form and punched for 3-ring binder.
ISSN 0145-0557

D 7.6/2:4-2 • Item 314-A
H 4-2 FEDERAL SUPPLY CODE FOR MANUFACTURERS, PART 2, CODE TO NAME. [Monthly]

Lists in numerical sequence the five digit codes followed by the manufacturer's name and address to which the code has been assigned.

Issued in loose-leaf form and punched for 3-ring binder. Kept up-to-date by monthly supplements. Subscription price includes basic volume plus monthly supplements for and indefinite period.
ISSN 0145-0565

D 7.6/2:4-3 • Item 314-A
H 4-3 FEDERAL SUPPLY CODE FOR MANUFACTURERS (Excluding United States and Canada). [Quarterly]

Contains only assigned codes to manufacturers outside the United States and Canada by items procured by the NATO Member Nations.

Subscription service includes cumulative quarterly supplements for an indefinite period.

D 7.6/2:6 • Item 314-A
FEDERAL ITEM NAME DIRECTORY FOR SUPPLY CATALOGING, HANDBOOK H 6.

Section A. ALPHABETIC INDEX OF NAMES. July 1972. 596 p. (includes basic volume plus cumulative bimonthly supplements for an indefinite period)

Section B. Subsection 1, NUMERIC INDEX OF ITEM NAME CODES TO FEDERAL ITEM IDENTIFICATION NAMES AND FEDERAL ITEM IDENTIFICATION GUIDES: Subsection 2, ALPHANUMERIC INDEX GUIDES TO ITEM NAME CODES. July 1972. 280 p.(includes basic volume plus cumulative bimonthly supplements for an indefinite period)

D 7.6/2:6-1 • Item 314-A
H 6-1 FEDERAL ITEM IDENTIFICATION GUIDES FOR SUPPLY CATALOGING, PART 1, INDEXES, SUPPLEMENTS. [Bimonthly]

An Index of all names, description patterns, reference drawings, and abbreviations and symbols approved by the Cataloging Division, Defense Logistics Service Center, Defense Supply Agency, Department of Defense, for use by ITEM identification writers.

Issued in the following sections:

A. ALPHABETIC INDEX OF NAMES.
B. NUMERIC INDEX OF DESCRIPTION PATTERNS AND ITEM NAME CODES.
C. ABBREVIATIONS AND SYMBOLS.

Subscription service includes basic volumes plus cumulative supplements for an indefinite period. Issued in loose-leaf form, punched for 3-ring binder.

Classified D 7.8:1, but placed in this sequence with the other Handbook sections.

D 7.6/2:6-2 • Item 314-A
H 6-2 FEDERAL ITEM IDENTIFICATIONS GUIDES FOR SUPPLY CATALOGING, PART 2, DESCRIPTION PATTERNS.

The Defense Logistics Supply Center of the Defense Supply Agency, Department of Defense, has issued the 1964 edition of the Federal Item Identification Guides for Supply Cataloging Handbook, Part 2, H 6-2, Description Patterns and Part 3, H 6-3, Reference Drawings, Sections A through J, on a subscription basis, including supplements, issued irregularly, for an indefinite period.

The material in the current Cataloging Handbook H 6-2 is divided substantially into two areas, one, descriptive patterns and the other reference drawings. In this re-publication, the description patterns appear in Cataloging Handbook H 6-2, while the reference drawings are published in the Cataloging Handbook H 6-3, both conveniently grouped into appropriate Sections as referred to below.

Section A of the Cataloging Handbook H 6-2 contains those description patterns covering items which may be classified in two or more Federal Supply Classification groups, when those groups are represented in two or more Cataloging Handbook H 6-2, Sections B through J. Consequently, it is recommended that a purchaser interested in a particular Federal Supply Classification group purchase the Sections covering that group and also purchase Section A to insure that he will receive, in both the basic and supplemental form all description patterns and reference drawings pertinent to the Federal Supply Cataloging group involved.

The Federal Supply Classification (FSC) groups covered by each of these subscription service sections are listed below together with the pertinent subscription rate. Each subscription service section consists of Cataloging Handbooks H 6-2, Description Patterns, H 6-3, Reference Drawings and supplements, issued irregularly, for an indefinite period. In loose- leaf form, punched for 3-ring binder.

D 7.6/2:6-3 • Item 314-A
H 6-3 FEDERAL ITEM IDENTIFICATION GUIDES FOR SUPPLY CATALOGING, PART 3, REFERENCE DRAWINGS.

Sections A– J were discontinued in October 1971.

D 7.6/2:6-2&3/sec. A • Item 314-A
– SECTION A. [Irregular]

Section A contains those descriptive pattern covering items which may be classified in two or more Federal Supply Classification Groups, when those groups are represented in two or more Cataloging Handbook H 6-2 Sections (B– J).

D 7.6/2:6-2&3/sec. B • Item 314-A
– SECTION B. [Irregular]

Contains FSC groups.

22. Railway equipment.
23. Motor vehicles, trailers, and cycles.
24. Tractors.
25. Vehicular equipment components.
26. Tires and tubes.
28. Engines, turbines, and components.
29. Engine accessories.
30. Mechanical power transmission equipment.
31. Bearing.

38. Construction, mining, excavating, and highway maintenance equipment.
39. Materials handling equipment.

D 7.6/2:6-2&3/sec. C • Item 314-A
– SECTION C. [Irregular]

Contains FSC groups:

32. Woodworking machinery and equipment.
34. Metalworking machinery.
37. Agricultural machinery and equipment.
51. Hand tools.
52. Measuring tools.

D 7.6/2:6-2&3/sec. D • Item 314
– SECTION D. [Irregular]

Contains FSC groups:

35. Service and trade equipment.
40. Rope, cable, chain, and fittings.
42. Fire fighting, rescue, and safety equipment.
49. Maintenance and repair shop equipment.
81. Containers, packaging, and packing supplies.

D 7.6/2:6-2&3/sec. E • Item 314-A
– SECTION E. [Irregular]

Contains FSC groups:

41. Refrigerators and air conditioning equipment.
43. Pumps and compressors.
44. Furnace, steam plant, and drying equipment, and nuclear reactors.
45. Plumbing, heating, and sanitation equipment.
46. Water purification and sewage treatment equipment.
47. Pipe, tubing, hose and fittings.
48. Valves.
54. Prefabricated structures and scaffolding.
55. Lumber, millwork, plywood, and veneer.
56. Construction and building materials.
95. Metal bars, sheets, and shapes.

D 7.6/2:6-2&3/sec. F • Item 314-A
– SECTION F. [Irregular]

Contains FSC groups:

58. Communication equipment.
59. Electrical and electronic equipment components.
61. Electric wire, and power distribution equipment.
62. Lighting fixtures and lamps.
63. Alarm and signal systems.
66. Instruments and laboratory equipment.

D 7.6/2: 6-2&3/sec. G • Item 314-A
– SECTION G. [Irregular]

Contains FSC groups:

65. Medical, dental, and veterinary equipment and supplies.
67. Photographic equipment.
68. Chemical and chemical products.
79. Cleaning equipment and supplies.
80. Brushes, paints, sealers, and adhesives.
87. Agricultural supplies.
89. Subsistence.
91. Fuels, lubricants, oils, and waxes.

D 7.6/2:6-2&3/sec. H • Item 314-A
– SECTION H. [Irregular]

Contains FSC groups:

53. Hardware and abrasives.
93. Nonmetallic fabricated materials.
94. Nonmetallic crude materials.

96.   Ores, minerals, and their primary
       products.

D 7.6/2:6-2&3/sec. I   • **Item 314-A**
– SECTION I. [Irregular]

   Contains FSC groups.

36.   Special industry machinery.
71.   Furniture.
72.   Household and commercial furnishings
       and appliances.
73.   Food preparation and serving
       equipment.
74.   Office machines and data processing
       equipment.
75.   Office supplies and devices.
76.   Books, maps, and other publications.
77.   Musical instruments, phonographs,
       and home-type radios.
78.   Recreational and athletic equipment.
83.   Textiles, leathers, and furs.
85.   Toiletries.
88.   Live animals.
99.   Miscellaneous.

D 7.6/2:6-2&3/sec. J   • **Item 314-A**
– SECTION J. [Irregular]
   Contains FSC groups.

10.   Weapons.
11.   Atomic ordance.
12.   Fire control equipment.
13.   Ammunition and explosives.
14.   Guided missiles.
15.   Aircraft; and airframe structural
       components.
16.   Aircraft components and accessories.
17.   Aircraft launching, landing, and ground
       handling equipment.
18.   Space vehicles.
19.   Ships, smallcraft, pontoons, and
       floating docks.
20.   Ship and marine equipment.
69.   Training aids and devices.

D 7.6/2:7   • **Item 314-A**
H 7 MANUFACTURERS PART AND DRAWING NUM-
BERING SYSTEMS. [Irregular]

D 7.6/2:8-1/2   • **Item 314-A**
H 8-1 NONGOVERNMENT ORGANIZATION CODES
FOR MILITARY STANDARD CONTRACT ADMIN-
ISTRATION PROCEDURES: NAME TO CODE.
[Irregular] (Includes basic volumes plus quarterly
supplements) (Defense Logistics Services Cen-
ter, Battle Creek, Michigan 49016)

   An alphabetical listing of the names of
business establishments referenced to their
assigned five-digit code. Related historical
data are shown.

D 7.6/2:8-2/2   • **Item 314-A**
H 8-2 NONGOVERNMENT ORGANIZATION CODES
FOR MILITARY STANDARD CONTRACT ADMIN-
ISTRATION PROCEDURES: CODE TO NAME.
[Irregular] (Included with H 8-1) (Defense Logis-
tics Services Center, Battle Creek, Michigan
49016)

   An alphanumeric listing of the assigned five-
digit codes referenced to the applicable names of
business establishments.
ISSN 0364-8478

D 7.6/2-2:nos.   • **Item 314-A-1 (MF)**
CATALOGING HANDBOOKS (numbered). [Microfiche
edition 48x] [Annual]

D 7.6/2-2:4-3/date   • **Item 314-A-1**
NATO SUPPLY CODE FOR MANUFACTURERS.
     Former title: Federal Supply Code for Manu-
facturers (Excluding United States and
Canada).
D 7.6/2-2:5/date
CORPORATE COMPLEX. [Bimonthly]

D 7.6/3:nos.   • **Item 314-A (MF)**
MANUALS, M- (series). [Irregular]

D 7.6/3:4120.3-M   • **Item 314-A**
DEFENSE STANDARDIZATION AND SPECIFICA-
TION PROGRAM POLICIES, PROCEDURES
AND INSTRUCTIONS.
     (Subscription includes supplements is-
sued irregularly for an indefinite period)

D 7.6/4:CT   • **Item 314-A**
HANDBOOKS, MANUALS, GUIDES. [Irregular]

D 7.6/4:M 59   • **Item 314-A**
MILITARY STANDARD REQUISITIONING AND
ISSUE PROCEDURE, MILSTRIP-(series).
[Irregular]

D 7.6/4:M 59/6   • **Item 314-A**
MILITARY ASSISTANCE PROGRAM ADDRESS
DIRECTORY. 1977. 792 p.
     Contains the addresses of the country
representatives, freight forwarders, and customers within-country required for releasing
Foreign Military Sales and Military Assistance
Program Grant Aid shipments, and addresses
required for forwarding of related documentation. Also contains information and detailed
instructions for users of the directory and
automated file.

D 7.6/4-2   • **Item 314-A-3**
STANDARDIZATION OF WORK MEASUREMENT.

D 7.6/4-3:nos.   • **Item 314-A (MF)**
DGSCM (series). [Irregular] (DGSCM 4155.1)

D 7.6/5   • **Item 314-A-6**
DEFENSE LOGISTICS PROCUREMENT REGULA-
TIONS. [Irregular]

     PURPOSE:– To establish policies, procedures
and delegations of authority governing the procurement of supplies and services by the Defense Supply Agency under Chapter 137, Title
10, of the U.S. Code.
     Subscription includes basic manual plus
supplementary material for an indefinite period.

D 7.6/6:nos.   • **Item 314-A**
DEFENSE LOGISTICS AGENCY REGULATIONS,
DLAR- (series). [Irregular]

D 7.6/7:nos.   • **Item 314-A (MF)**
DEFENSE LOGISTICS AGENCY HANDBOOKS, DLAH-
(series). [Irregular]

D 7.6/7:5025.1:pt. 2/date   • **Item 314-A**
QUARTERLY LISTING OF INTERIM ISSUANCES.
(Defense Supply Agency, Cameron Station,
Alexandria, Virginia 22314)

     Issued as part 2 of Handbook DSAH
5025.1, DSA Index of Publications.

D 7.6/7-2:nos.   • **Item 314-A**
GOVERNMENT VEHICLE OPERATORS GUIDE TO
SERVICE STATIONS FOR GASOLINE, OIL AND
LUBRICATION. [Irregular] (Defense Fuel Supply
Center)

D 7.6/8:nos.   • **Item 314-A**
DEFENSE LOGISTICS AGENCY MANUALS, DLAM-
(series). [Irregular]

D 7.6/9:nos.   • **Item 314-A**
HEADQUARTERS MANUAL, HQM-(series). [Irregular]

D 7.6/10:nos.   • **Item 314-A**
DSA-DLSC MANUALS. [Irregular] (Defense Logistics
Service Center)

D 7.6/11:nos.
QUALITY AND RELIABILITY ASSURANCE HAND-
BOOKS. [Irregular]

D 7.6/12:date   • **Item 314-A-2 (MF)**
DoD ACTIVITY ADDRESS DIRECTORY (microfiche
edition).

D 7.6/13:nos.   • **Item 314-A-4**
DEFENSE REUTILIZATION AND MARKETING
SERVICE, DRMS-H (series). [Irregular]

     Continues: Defense Property Disposal Ser-
vice, DPDS-H (series).

D 7.6/14:nos.   • **Item 314-A-5 (MF)**
DEFENSE ADMINISTRATIVE SUPPORT CENTER
HANDBOOKS, DASCH-(series). [Irregular]

D 7.6/15:date   • **Item 314-A**
FOREIGN MILITARY SALES CUSTOMER PROCE-
DURES (series).

D 7.6/16:date   • **Item 314-A**
MILSTRIP ROUTING IDENTIFIER AND DISTRIBUTION
CODES.
     Later D 1.87/2

D 7.6/17:date   • **Item 314-A**
MILSTRIP MILITARY STANDARD REQUISITIONING
AND ISSUE PROCEDURES. [Annual]
     Later D 1.87

D 7.6/18:nos.   • **Item 314-A (MF)**
TM-DPSC- (series).

D 7.6/19:nos./date   • **Item 314-A**
DEFENSE LOGISTICS INFORMATION SYSTEM
(DLIS) PROCEDURES MANUAL.

     DIDS = Defense Integrated Data System
     Earlier titled: DIDS (Defense Integrated Data
System) Procedures Manual.
     Earlier D 7.6/4:D 26

D 7.6/20:date   • **Item 314-A-13**
CUSTOMER ASSISTANCE HANDBOOK. [Biennial]

     PURPOSE:– To provide DLA's worldwide
customers with a practical, ready reference for
codes used in the Defense Logistics Standard
systems. Contains information on other logistics
management systems used in supply operations.
     Earlier D 7.6/4:C 96

D 7.6/21:   • **Item 314-A-16**
DRMS WORLD. [Monthly]
     DRMS = Defense Reutilization and Marketing
Service

D 7.8/1   • **Item 314-A**
FEDERAL ITEM IDENTIFICATION GUIDES FOR SUP-
PLY CATALOGING, PART 1.
     See entry under D 7.6/2:6-1

D 7.9:group nos.   • **Item 314-B**
FEDERAL SUPPLY CATALOG, DEPARTMENT OF
DEFENSE SECTION.
     Discontinued.

D 7.9/2:date   • **Item 314-A-8 (MF)**
FEDERAL SUPPLY CATALOG FOR CIVIL AGENCIES,
DESCRIPTIVE AND MANAGEMENT DATA LIST.

D 7.10:nos.   • **Item 314-J**
MILITARY STANDARDS, MIL-STD- (series). [Irregu-
lar]

     A military specification, formerly known as
Joint Army-Navy Specification and designated
with the prefix JAN, is a departmental specification covering materials, products, or services used
only or predominantly by military activities. Covers a military-type item or service required in their
operatings.

D 7.10:726C   • **Item 314-J**
726 PACKAGING REQUIREMENTS CODE.
[Irregular]

     PURPOSE:– To establish and define a
system for coding essential preservation and
packaging data.
     Subscription includes basic manual plus
supplementary material for an indefinite period. Issued in loose-leaf form, punched for
ring binder.
     Latest edition 1968.

D 7.10/2:nos.
MILITARY STANDARDS (preliminary).

D 7.11:date
ALPHABETICAL LISTING, REGISTER OR PLANNED
MOBILIZATION PRODUCERS, MANUFACTURERS
OF WAR MATERIAL REGISTERED UNDER
PRODUCTION ALLOCATION PROGRAM. [Annual]

D 7.11/2:date/vols. • **Item 314-A (MF)**
REGISTER PLANNED EMERGENCY PRODUCERS.
[Annual] (Office of Assistant Secretary of Defense, Installations and Logistics) (DoD 4005.3-H)

　　Issued in the following volumes:

　　　　Vol. 1. ALPHABETICAL LISTING.
　　　　Vol. 2. GEOGRAPHICAL LISTING.
　　　　Vol. 3. ASPPO LISTING.

D 7.12:date
ACTIVE STANDARDIZATION PROJECTS, STANDARDS, SPECIFICATIONS, STUDIES AND HANDBOOKS. [Quarterly]

D 7.13:nos. • **Item 314-C**
STANDARDIZATION DIRECTORIES. SD 1–　[Irregular]
　　Discontinued.

D 7.13:1 • **Item 314-C**
1. DIRECTORY AND PLANNING SCHEDULE OF FSC CLASS AND AREA ASSIGNMENTS. [Quarterly]

D 7.13/2:date
DEFENSE STANDARDIZATION PROGRAM, DIRECTORY OF POINTS OF INTEREST. [Quarterly]
　　Discontinued.

D 7.13/3:nos.
PRODUCTION EQUIPMENT DIRECTORY D (series).

D 7.14:date • **Item 314-G**
DEPARTMENT OF DEFENSE INDEX OF SPECIFICATIONS AND STANDARDS. [Bimonthly]

　　Subscription service consists of two parts with cumulative supplements.
　　Consolidated edition of the Indexes of Military Specifications formerly published by the Department of the Air Force (D 301.28), the Department of the Army (D 101.34), and the Department of the Navy (D 212.10).
　　Issued in two parts: Part 1, Alphabetical Listing, and Part 2, Numerical Listing.
　　ISSN 0363-8464
　　See D 1.76

D 7.14/2:date • **Item 314-G**
FEDERAL SUPPLY CLASSIFICATION LISTING OF DoD STANDARDIZATION DOCUMENTS. [Bimonthly]

　　Supersedes Part 3 of Department of Defense Index of Specifications (D 7.14).
　　ISSN 0565-2669
　　See D 1.76/2

D 7.15: • **Item 314-H**
QUALITY CONTROL AND RELIABILITY TECHNICAL REPORTS. TR 1–　[Irregular]
　　Earlier D 7.2:M 42 and D 7.6/4:T 28

D 7.15/2:nos. • **Item 314-A-9 (MF)**
TECHNICAL REPORTS, DTIC/TR- (series). [Irregular]

　　DTIC = Defense Technical Information Center

D 7.16:CT • **Item 314-A-7**
BIBLIOGRAPHIES AND LISTS OF PUBLICATIONS.
　　Discontinued.

D 7.16/2:date
REGION INDEX OF PUBLICATIONS, FORMS AND FORM LETTERS. (DCASR LA H 5025.1)

D 7.17:date • **Item 314-K**
DCSC FISCAL YEAR PROCUREMENT ESTIMATES CATALOG. [Annual]

　　Issued by Defense Construction Supply Center.
　　Discontinued.

D 7.18:date
SMALL BUSINESS REPORT.

D 7.19:nos.
DSA POSTER SERIES. [Irregular]

D 7.19/2:CT • **Item 314-A-10**
POSTERS. [Irregular]

D 7.20:date • **Item 314-L**
CONSOLIDATED MASTER CROSS REFERENCE LIST, C-RL-1.
　　Discontinued.

D 7.20/2 • **Item 314-L-1 (MF)**
– [MICROFICHE EDITION].
　　Discontinued.

D 7.20/3:nos. • **Item 314-L-4 (MF)**
MASTER CROSS REFERENCE LIST, MARINE CORPS, MCRL 1–

　　Lists items of supply that pertain to the Marine Corps by National Stock Numbers, reference numbers, and manufacturers' codes cross-referenced to each other. Contains all non-security reference numbers of active NSN's except such items as Production Equipment Codes, ammunition codes, etc.
　　Each issue supersedes the previous quarter. Published in microfiche (48x).
　　Discontinued.

D 7.21:date
ANNUAL REPORT TO CONGRESS ON NATIONAL INDUSTRIAL RESERVE UNDER PUBLIC LAW 883, 80th CONGRESS.

D 7.22:date • **Item 314-O**
DCAS MANUFACTURING COST CONTROL DIGEST.
v. 1–　1975–　[Annual] (Defense Contract Administration Services)
　　Inactive.

D 7.23:nos.
QUALITY ASSURANCE, QA REPORTER. [Quarterly]

D 7.24:date • **Item 314-P (EL)**
DFSC [Defense Fuel Supply Center] FUEL LINE. [Quarterly]

　　PURPOSE:– To provide timely, factual information on policies, plans, operations and technical developments of the Defense Fuel Supply Center.

D 7.24/2 • **Item 314-P (MF)**
AVFUEL & AVOIL INTO PLANE CONTRACT LISTING. [Irregular]

D 7.25:date • **Item 314-A (MF)**
IDENTIFICATION LISTS. IL- (Series). [Irregular]

　　Published in microfiche.

D 7.26:nos.
FEDERAL ITEM LOGISTICS DATA RECORDS.

　　Published in microfiche.

D 7.27:date
DPDS DEMIL REFERENCE FICHE.

　　Published in microfiche.

D 7.28:date • **Item 314-L-7 (MF)**
FREIGHT CLASSIFICATION DATA FILE. [Quarterly]
　　Published for use by activities involved in traffic management to determine transportation rates, etc. Contains shipping data for National Stock Numbers in the Defense Logistics Services Center Total Item Record.
　　Each issue supersedes previous issues.
　　Discontinued.

D 7.29:date
CATALOG MANAGEMENT DATA.
　　Issued in microfiche.

MANAGEMENT DATA LIST

　　Provides requisitioners with supply management data necessary to acquire and account for an item of supply. Items not included are certain subsistence, ammunition, forms and publications, crytographic, and other highly selective items. The index is in numeric sequence according to the National Item Identification numbers.
　　Published in microfiche (48x).

D 7.29/2:date
AIR FORCE. [Monthly]

D 7.29/3:date • **Item 314-L-5 (MF)**
ARMY. [Monthly]
　　See 7.29/6

D 7.29/4:date • **Item 314-L-2 (MF)**
NAVY. [Monthly]
　　Discontinued.

D 7.29/5:date • **Item 314-L-6 (MF)**
MARINE CORPS. [Quarterly]
　　Discontinued.

D 7.29/6:date • **Item 314-L-3 (MF)**
CONSOLIDATED MANAGEMENT DATA LIST, ML-C basic. [Monthly]

　　Lists supply management data on all National Stock Numbers recorded in the Catalog Management Data segment of the Total Item Record. Contains supply management data for all items submitted to the Defense Logistics Services Center by the Military Services, Defense Supply Services, and the General Services Administration.
　　Published in microfiche.
　　Discontinued.

D 7.30:nos. • **Item 314-R (MF)**
NOT FOR WOMEN ONLY. 1–　[Quarterly] (Federal Women's Program Committee)

D 7.31:date • **Item 314-P-1 (MF)**
DFSC CHRONICLE. [Monthly] (Defense Fuel Supply Center)

　　PURPOSE:– To provide a newsletter for DFSC employees, covering activities and personnel notes of interest, as well as general interest articles on various subjects usually fuel related.
　　Discontinued.

D 7.32:date • **Item 314-T (MF)**
HAZARDOUS ITEM LISTING. [Annual] (subscription consists of basic volume plus quarterly cumulative supplements)
　　PURPOSE:– To provide data elements for items included in the DoD Hazardous Materials Information System. This is basic reference data for use by DoD to comply with the more stringent regulatory controls established for hazardous materials.
　　Published in microfiche (48x) only.
　　Discontinued.

D 7.32:date • **Item 314-V (CD)**
HAZARDOUS MATERIALS INFORMATION SYSTEM. [Quarterly]

　　Issued on CD-ROM.
　　See D 212.16

D 7.32/2-2 • **Item 314-T**
HMTC ABSTRACT BULLETIN. [Quarterly]
　　Discontinued.

D 7.32/3: • **Item 314-A-20 (EL)**
HTIS BULLETIN.

D 7.33:v.nos. • **Item 314-A-8**
INTRODUCTION TO FEDERAL SUPPLY CATALOGS AND RELATED PUBLICATIONS.
　　Discontinued.

D 7.33/2 • **Item 314-A-14**
FEDERAL CATALOG SYSTEM, TRAINING COURSE CATALOG. [Annual]

　　PURPOSE– To provide information concerning the courses offered by the Defense Logistics Services Center. Describes each class, giving cost, training materials available, and registration information.
　　Discontinued.

D 7.33/3:nos. • **Item 314-A-14**
DLSC LINE. [Quarterly]

　　DLSC LINE = Defense Logistics Services Center Logistics Information Notice Express.
　　Discontinued.

D 7.34 • Item 314-A-20 (EL)
SEALED BID/INVITATION FOR BIDS.

Earlier title: Sealed Bids (series).

D 7.34/2:yr. and no. • Item 314-A-12 (MF)
DECLARED EXCESS PERSONAL PROPERTY LIST-
ING. [Weekly]
Lists excess personal property available for
distribution to all elements of the Defense Department, U.S. Coast Guard, approved DoD contractors, and authorized foreign governments (subject to provisions of DoD 5105.38-M, Military Assistance and Sale Manual).
Discontinued.

D 7.35:CT • Item 314-A-11
ENVIRONMENTAL IMPACT STATEMENTS. [Irregular]
PURPOSE:– To describe the effects on the
environment of different construction or other alteration, such as a fuel pier relocation project of
the Defense Logistics Agency.
Earlier D 7.2

D 7.36:date • Item 314-L-1 (MF)
DOD INTERCHANGEABILITY AND SUBSTITUTABIL-
ITY (I&S), PARTS I & II. [Monthly]
Discontinued.

D 7.37:date • Item 314-L-1
DOD MEDICAL CATALOG. [Monthly]
See D 7.37/2

D 7.38: • Item 314-A-15 (MF)
FOOD SERVICE EQUIPMENT CATALOG. [Annual]

A catalog of the most widely used National
Stock Numbers for Food Service Equipment. Includes end items and accessories for overseas,
field, and aircraft use. Provided by DLA for use
by federal civil agencies and DoD activities.

D 7.39:date • Item 314-X
HAZARDOUS MATERIALS INFORMATION SYSTEM.
[Monthly]

D 7.40:v.nos.&nos. • Item 314-R (MF)
TQM QUARTERLY. [Quarterly]
Discontinued.

D 7.41:date/nos. • Item 314-V (EL)
DLAPS PUBLICATIONS [Quarterly]

DLAPS = Defense Logistics Agency Publishing System.
Issued on CD-ROM.

D 7.41/2:nos. • Item 314-V-1 (EL)
FORM FLOW. [Quarterly]
Issued on CD-ROM.

D 7.42:nos. • Item 314-A-17 (EL)
MMSLD LETTER (series).
Discontinued.

D 7.43:v.nos/nos. • Item 314-A-18 (EL)
LOG LINES, DLA NEWS CUSTOMERS CAN USE.
[Quarterly]

D 7.43/2 • Item 314-A-19
DCSC COMMUNICATOR. [Quarterly]
Discontinued.

D 7.45 • Item 314-A-20 (E)
ELECTRONIC PRODUCTS.

D 7.46: • Item 314-A-20 (EL)
POLICY LETTERS (series).

ARMED FORCES MEDICAL LIBRARY
(1952– 1956)

CREATION AND AUTHORITY

In 1836, the Library of the Surgeon General's
Office was established. It later became known as
the Army Medical Library. The Army Medical Library was redesignated as the Armed Forces
Medical Library, a joint agency of the Army, Navy,
and Air Force, by Section 1, General Order 49 of
the Department of the Army, dated May 9, 1952,
pursuant to authority vested in the Secretary of
Defense by the National Security Act of 1947, as
amended. By act of Congress, approved August
3, 1956 (70 Stat. 960), the National Library of
Medicine (FS 2.200) was established within the
Public Health Service and the Armed Forces Medical Library was abolished and transferred to the
newly created library.

D 8.1:date
ANNUAL REPORT.

D 8.2:CT
GENERAL PUBLICATIONS.

D 8.8:v.nos.&nos.
CURRENT LIST OF MEDICAL LITERATURE. [Monthly]
D 1.20 has been cancelled.
Earlier D 104.7
Later FS 2.208

D 8.9:nos.
INDEX CATALOGUE OF ARMED FORCES MEDICAL
LIBRARY.
The new class D 104.8 not used.
Earlier M 102.8
Discontinued.

D 8.10:CT
[BIBLIOGRAPHIES.]
Later FS 2.209

NORTH ATLANTIC TREATY ORGANIZATION

NOTE:– Class D 9 was established in the
SuDocs Classification Scheme for the convenience of users for publications of the multilateral
organizations in which the United States participates.

D 9.1
REPORTS.

D 9.8:CT
SUPREME ALLIED COMMANDER IN EUROPE PUB-
LICATIONS.

DEFENSE TECHNICAL INFORMATION CENTER
(1969–   )

D 10.1:date
ANNUAL REPORTS.

D 10.2:CT • Item 314-E
GENERAL PUBLICATIONS.

D 10.3/2:nos.
TECHNICAL ABSTRACTS BULLETINS.

D 10.3/3:nos.
TECHNICAL ABSTRACTS BULLETINS, INDEX.

D 10.3/4:nos.
TECHNICAL ABSTRACTS BULLETINS, QUARTERLY
INDEXS.

D 10.6:CT
REGULATIONS, RULES, AND INSTRUCTIONS.

D 10.7/2 • Item 314-E-1 (MF)
DTICH (series).

D 10.8:nos.
TITLE ANNOUNCEMENT BULLETIN. [Irregular]

D 10.8/2:nos.
– AD NUMERICAL INDEX.

D 10.9
BIBLIOGRAPHIES AND LISTS OF PUBLICATIONS.

D 10.10:nos.
KEYWORDS IN CONTEXT TITLE INDEX.

D 10.11:v.nos./nos. • Item 314-E-1 (EL)
DTIC DIGEST. [Quarterly]

D 10.11/2 • Item 314-E-3 (MF)
THE DTIC REVIEW.

D 10.12:CT • Item 314-E-2
BIBLIOGRAPHIES AND LISTS OF PUBLICATIONS.

D 10.13 • Item 314-E-4 (EL)
MILITARY CRITICAL TECHNOLOGIES.

Online database.

ARMED SERVICES PETROLEUM PURCHASING AGENCY
(1949– 1959)

D 11.1:date
ANNUAL REPORT.

D 11.2:CT
GENERAL PUBLICATIONS.

D 11.3:nos.
OIL CONTRACT BULLETIN, IFB- (series).
Discontinued.

NATIONAL GUARD BUREAU
(1958–)

CREATION AND AUTHORITY

Established in the Department of Defense as a joint bureau of the Department of the Army and the Department of the Air Force by the Department of Defense reorganization act of 1958 (Public Law 599), 85th Congress, 2d session, approved August 6, 1958.

INFORMATION

Public Affairs Chief
National Guard Bureau
Jefferson Plaza 1
1411 Jefferson Davis Hwy.
Arlington, VA 22202-3259
(703) 607-2540
http://www.ngb.dtic.mil

D 12.1:date • Item 355 (MF)
ANNUAL REPORTS.
Earlier D 112.1

D 12.1/2:date • Item 355 (MF)
DISTRICT OF COLUMBIA NATIONAL GUARD: ANNUAL REPORT.

D 12.1/3:date • Item 355-A (MF)
UTAH NATIONAL GUARD, ANNUAL REPORT.

D 12.2:CT • Item 356
GENERAL PUBLICATIONS.
Earlier D 112.2, D 301.2

D 12.3:v.nos.&nos.
NATIONAL GUARD BUREAU BULLETINS. Admin.

D 12.3/2:nos.
NGB PUBLICATIONS BULLETIN. [Irregular]

D 12.6:nos. • Item 358
REGULATIONS.
Earlier D 112.6

D 12.8:nos. • Item 358 (MF)
PAMPHLETS.

D 12.8/2:nos. • Item 358
TECHNICAL PERSONNEL PAMPHLETS. 1–
[Irregular]
Discontinued.

D 12.9:date • Item 358-A
OFFICIAL ARMY NATIONAL GUARD REGISTER. [Annual]

An alphabetical listing of all officers and warrant officers of the Army National Guard currently serving in an active status or assigned to the Inactive National Guard.
Earlier D 112.8

Non-depository.

D 12.9/2:date • Item 358-A (MF)
AIR NATIONAL GUARD REGISTER.

Earlier D 112.8/2

D 12.10:CT • Item 358
HANDBOOKS, MANUALS, GUIDES (unnumbered).

D 12.10/2:nos. • Item 358 (MF)
NGB MANUALS (numbered).

D 12.11:nos. • Item 358-B
ANG- (series). [Irregular] (Air National Guard)

Consists of recruitment folders, each devoted to a particular job in the Air National Guard.

D 12.12:nos. • Item 358-B-1
ARNG- (series). [Irregular]
Consists mainly of recruitment folders for the Army National Guard, Army Reserve, and Army ROTC programs.

D 12.12/2 • Item 358-B-1
OKARNG- (series). [Irregular]

D 12.13:nos. • Item 358-B-1
INSTRUCTOR SET (series). [Irregular]

D 12.14:CT • Item 358-C
POSTERS.

D 12.14/2:v.nos.&nos. • Item 358-C
NATIONAL GUARD ON GUARD. [Monthly]

Internal use only.

D 12.15:CT • Item 358-D
FACT SHEETS (series). [Irregular]

Fact sheets are provided for individuals who desire information on joining the Air National Guard. Each describes opportunities in a particular occupational area, such as physician, optometrist, or nurse, etc.

D 12.16: • Item 356-A
EDUCATION SERVICE PLAN, WISCONSIN NATIONAL GUARD. [Annual]

Informs members of the Wisconsin Army National Guard about various educational programs that are available to them.

Discontinued.

D 12.17:date • Item 358-B
THE NATIONAL GUARD UPDATE (AIR). [Semiannual]

D 12.17/2:date • Item 358-B-1
THE NATIONAL GUARD UPDATE (ARMY). [Semi-annual]

D 12.20 • Item 356-A-1
ARMY NATIONAL GUARD LINEAGE SERIES.

OFFICE OF CIVIL DEFENSE
(1961– 1964)

CREATION AND AUTHORITY

The civil defense functions of the Office of Civil and Defense Mobilization (PrEx 4) were transferred to the Department of Defense by Executive Order 10952 of July 20, 1961 establishing the Office of Civil Defense. In 1964, the Office was transferred to the Department of the Army (D 119).

D 13.1:date
ANNUAL REPORT.

Later D 119.1

D 13.1/2:date
ANNUAL STATISTICAL REPORT.

Earlier PrEx 4.1/2
Later D 119.1/2

D 13.2:CT
GENERAL PUBLICATIONS.

Later D 119.2

D 13.3/2
INFORMATION BULLETINS.

Later D 119.3/2

D 13.3/3
SURPLUS PROPERTY BULLETIN.

Earlier PrEx 4.3/5

D 13.8:CT
HANDBOOKS, MANUALS, GUIDES.

Earlier PrEx 4.12
Later D 119.8

D 13.8/2:nos.
POCKET MANUALS PM (series).

Earlier PrEx 4.12/6

D 13.8/3
[HANDBOOK] H (series).
Earlier Pr 34.761/2, PrEx 4.12/3
Later D 119.8/2

D 13.8/4:nos.
[NATIONAL PLAN FOR CIVIL DEFENSE] NP-nos.

D 13.8/5:nos.
STUDENT MANUALS SM (series).
Earlier Pr 34.761/7
Later D 119.8/8

D 13.8/6:nos.
PROFESSIONAL GUIDE PSD-PG (series).

Issued by Protective Structures Division.

D 13.8/7:nos.
INSTRUCTOR'S GUIDE IG (series).
Earlier PrEx 4.12/5
Later D 119.8/7

D 13.8/8:le-nos.
FEDERAL GUIDANCE FOR STATE AND LOCAL CIVIL DEFENSE, FS (series).
Later D 119.8/3

D 13.8/9:pt. (les)
FEDERAL CIVIL DEFENSE GUIDE.
Later D 119.8/4

D 13.8/10:nos.
TECHNICAL MANUALS.
Earlier PrEx 4.12/4
Later D 14.8/7

D 13.9:nos.
MISCELLANEOUS PUBLICATIONS MP (series).

Earlier Pr 34.759, PrEx 4.14
Later D 119.11

D 13.10:nos.
LEAFLET L (series).

Earlier PrEx 4.13
Later D 119.13

D 13.11:nos.
PUBLIC BOOKLET PB (series).

D 13.12:nos.
TECHNICAL REPORT TR (series).
Earlier Pr 34.763
Later D 119.9

D 13.13:nos.
PROTECTIVE STRUCTURES DIVISION, TECHNICAL MEMORANDUMS. [Administrative]

D 13.14:CT
ADDRESSES.
Later D 119.12

D 13.15:les-nos.
PROTECTIVE STRUCTURES, SHELTER DESIGN SERIES.

D 13.16:date
WESTERN TRAINING CENTER, CATALOGS AND
SCHEDULE OF COURSES.

D 13.17:v.nos.&nos.
CD NEWS FEATURE PAGE.
    Earlier D 1.34

D 13.17/2:v.nos.&nos.
CD NEWSPICTURES.
    Earlier D 1.34/2
    Later D 119.10

D 13.18:nos.
REGION EIGHT NEWS.

DEFENSE CIVIL PREPAREDNESS AGENCY
(1972– 1979)

CREATION AND AUTHORITY

    The Defense Civil Preparedness Agency was
established as a separate agency of the Department of Defense by direction of the Secretary of
Defense, effective May 5, 1972, succeeding the
Office of Civil Defense. The Agency was abolished and its functions transferred to the Federal
Emergency Management Agency (FEM 1) by Executive Order 12148 of July 20, 1979 effective
July 15, 1979.

D 14.1:date   • Item 320-B-4
ANNUAL REPORT. 1st–   1972–

    Earlier D 119.1

D 14.1/2:date   • Item 857-D-17
ANNUAL STATISTICAL REPORT, FISCAL YEAR (date).

    (Statistics and Reports Division, Office of
the Comptroller)
    Earlier D 119.1/2

D 14.2:CT   • Item 857-D-2
GENERAL PUBLICATIONS. [Irregular]

    Earlier D 119.2
D 14.8:CT   • Item 857-D-8
HANDBOOKS, MANUALS, GUIDES. [Irregular]
    Earlier D 119.8

D 14.8/2:nos.   • Item 320-B-1 (MF)
STUDENT MANUAL, SM- (series). [Irregular]
    Earlier D 119.8/8

D 14.8/3:nos.   • Item 857-D-10
HANDBOOKS, H- (series). [Irregular]
    Earlier D 119.8/2

D 14.8/4:nos.   • Item 857-D-12 (MF)
INSTRUCTOR'S GUIDES, IG- (series). [Irregular]

    Earlier D 119.8/7

D 14.8/5:nos.   • Item 320-B-3
FEDERAL GUIDANCE FOR STATE AND LOCAL CIVIL
    DEFENSE, FG- (series). [Irregular]

    Earlier D 119.8/3
D 14.8/6:nos.   • Item 857-D-8
CPG (series). [Irregular]
    Later D 14.17

D 14.8/7:nos.
TM (series).
    Earlier D 13.8/10

D 14.9:nos.   • Item 320-B-2 (MF)
TECHNICAL REPORTS. TR 1–   [Irregular]
    Earlier D 119.9

D 14.10:nos.   • Item 857-D-11 (MF)
MISCELLANEOUS PUBLICATIONS. MP-1–
[Irregular]

    Earlier D 119.11

D 14.11:nos.   • Item 320-B-9
HS [Home Study] (series). 1–   1971–   [Irregular]
    Earlier D 119.15

D 14.12:nos.   • Item 857-D-5
LEAFLETS, L- (series). 1–   [Irregular]
    Earlier D 119.13
    Later FEM 1.11

D 14.13:v.nos.&nos.
SURVIVAL.   – January 1974. [Irregular]
    (Region 2)

D 14.13/2:nos.
INFORMATION BULLETIN. [Irregular]

D 14.14:v.nos.&nos.   • Item 320-B-10
FORESIGHT, CIVIL PREPAREDNESS TODAY. v. 1–
1974–   [Bimonthly]

    PURPOSE:– To serve as a forum to exchange
information and ideas on civil preparedness
throughout the United States. Contains brief articles and news items. Includes notes on new
publications and audiovisual materials.
    ISSN 0093-6049

D 14.15
K–   (series)
    Earlier D 14.2

D 14.16:nos.   • Item 320-B-8
BUILDING WITH ENVIRONMENTAL PROTECTION,
    DESIGN CASE STUDIES. [Irregular]
    Earlier D 119.14

D 14.17:nos.   • Item 320-B-11 (MF)
RESEARCH STUDIES, RS- (series). [Irregular]

    PURPOSE:– To provide basic planning, guid-
ance and data to the Defense Civil Preparedness
Agency and State personnel in developing plans
for nuclear civil protection.
    Earlier D 14.8/6

D 14.18:CT
AUDIOVISUAL MATERIAL.

DEFENSE THREAT REDUCTION AGENCY
(1959–   )

CREATION AND AUTHORITY

    The Defense Atomic Support Agency was es-
tablished in 1959. The Agency was redesignated
as the Defense Nuclear Agency in 1971, pursuant to DoD Directive 5105.31.
    Renamed June 14, 1995; functions transfered
to the Defense Threat Reduction Agency September 30, 1998.

D 15.1:date
ANNUAL REPORT.

D 15.1/2:   • Item 379-B-10 (MF)
ARMED FORCES RADIOBIOLOGY RESEARCH IN-
    STITUTE: ANNUAL RESEARCH REPORT, AFRRL
    ARR-(series).

D 15.2:CT   • Item 379-B-11
GENERAL PUBLICATIONS. [Irregular]

D 15.9:CT   • Item 379-B (MF)
FACT SHEETS.

D 15.10:nos.   • Item 306
U.S. ATMOSPHERIC NUCLEAR WEAPONS TESTS,
    NUCLEAR TEST PERSONNEL REVIEW. [Irregular]

D 15.11:CT
AUDIOVISUAL MATERIALS. [Irregular]

D 15.12:   • Item 379-B-10 (MF)
ARMED FORCES RADIOBIOLOGY RESEARCH
    INSTITUTE: SCIENTIFIC REPORTS, AFRRI SR–
    (series). [Irregular]

D 15.12/2:   • Item 379-B-10 (MF)
ARMED FORCES RADIOBIOLOGY RESEARCH IN-
    STITUTE: TECHNICAL REPORTS, AFRRI TR–
    (series). [Irregular]

D 15.12/3:date   • Item 379-B-10 (MF)
ARMED FORCES RADIOBIOLOGY RESEARCH IN-
    STITUTE: REPORTS, AFRRI-R- (series). [Quar-
    terly]

D 15.12/4:nos.   • Item 379-B-10 (MF)
AFRRI-CR- (series). [Irregular]

D 15.13:nos.   • Item 379-B-12 (MF)
TECHNICAL REPORTS, DNA-TR- (series). [Irregular]

DEPARTMENT OF THE ARMY
(1949–   )

CREATION AND AUTHORITY

    The Department of the Army was made a
military department within the Department of Defense in lieu of its prior status as an executive
department (M 101) by Public law 216, 81st Congress, approved August 10, 1949.

INFORMATION

    Office of the Chief of Public Affairs
    Department of the Army
    1500 Army Pentagon
    Washington, D.C. 20310-1500
    (703) 695-5135
    Fax: (703) 614-3354
    http://www.army.mil

D 101.1:date
ANNUAL REPORTS.

    Earlier M 101.1

D 101.1/2:date   • Item 325
REPORT OF THE CHIEF OF STAFF OF THE UNITED
    STATES ARMY.

D 101.1/3:date   • Item 325-B-9 (MF)
ANNUAL HISTORICAL REVIEW, UNITED STATES
    ARMY SOLDIER SUPPORT CENTER.

    PURPOSE:– To review the history and sum-
marize the activities of the Center, which is the
Army's focal point for promotion of troop morale.

D 101.1/4:date   • Item 325-B-10 (MF)
AMC LABORATORIES AND RESEARCH, DEVELOP-
    MENT AND ENGINEERING CENTERS, TECHNI-
    CAL ACCOMPLISHMENTS. [Annual]

D 101.1/4-2:   • Item 325-B-20 (EL)
U.S. ARMY MATERIEL COMMAND, ANNUAL
    HISTORICAL REVIEW.

    Covers AMC headquarters' activities in ac-
complishing its mission of providing materiel to
U.S. land forces.

D 101.1/5:date   • Item 325-B-12 (MF)
ANNUAL HISTORICAL REVIEW, ARMAMENT, MUNITIONS AND CHEMICAL COMMAND, (AMCCOM) (series).

Discontinued.

D 101.1/6:date
HISTORY ANNUAL SUPPLEMENT.

Earlier D 101.2:F 77 J

D 101.1/7:date   • Item 330-E (MF)
ANNUAL REPORT (U.S. ARMY RESEARCH INSTITUTE FOR THE BEHAVIORAL AND SOCIAL SCIENCES). [Annual]

D 101.1/7-2:date   • Item 330-E (MF)
BASIC RESEARCH IN BEHAVIORAL AND SOCIAL SCIENCES: U.S. ARMY RESEARCH INSTITUTE ANNUAL REPORT. [Annual]

D 101.1/8:date   • Item 322-S (MF)
75th USA MANEUVER AREA COMMAND, ANNUAL REPORT AND HISTORICAL SUPPLEMENT.

PURPOSE:– To summarize Command activities in accomplishing its mission of writing and conducting training exercises and tests for Army Reserves and National Guard units throughout the western two-thirds of the United States.

D 101.1/9:date   • Item 325-B-17 (MF)
HEADQUARTERS, FIRST UNITED STATES ARMY, DEPUTY CHIEF OF STAFF, INFORMATION MANAGEMENT, ORGANIZATION, MISSION, AND FUNCTIONS. [Biennial]

PURPOSE:– To set forth the organization, mission, and functions of the Deputy Chief of Staff for Information Management, First U.S. Army. Summarizes activities of the various divisions and other organizational units of DCSIM.

D 101.1/10:date   • Item 325-A-1 (MF)
FACILITIES ENGINEERING AND HOUSING ANNUAL SUMMARY OF OPERATIONS.

See D 101.1/15

D 101.1/11:date   • Item 325-B-21 (MF)
ARMY RESEARCH LABORATORY, ANNUAL REVIEW.

D 101.1/11-2   • Item 325-B-27 (MF)
ARMY RESEARCH LABORATORY STRATEGIC PLAN FOR FISCAL YEAR. [Biennial]

D 101.1/12:date   • Item 325-B-23 (MF)
ARMY RESERVE FORCES POLICY COMMITTEE, ANNUAL REPORT.

D 101.1/13:date   • Item 325-B-24 (MF)
ANNUAL REPORT OF THE SECRETARY OF THE ARMY ON CIVIL WORKS ACTIVITIES.

D 101.1/14:date   • Item 325-B-25 (MF)
ARMY FOCUS. [Annual]

D 101.1/15:date   • Item 325-B-22 (MF)
PROGRESS REPORT USAISC. [Annual]

D 101.1/16:date   • Item 325-B-28 (MF)
ARMY TECHNOLOGY.

D 101.1/17   • Item 307-A-8 (EL)
DEPARTMENT OF THE ARMY ANNUAL FINANCIAL REPORT.

D 101.2:CT   • Item 325
GENERAL PUBLICATIONS.

Earlier M 101.2

D 101.2:F 96   • Item 325
LAST SALUTE, CIVIL AND MILITARY FUNERALS, 1921– 1969. 1972. 482 p. il.

"Our national tradition of honoring prominent officials is never more in evidence than following the death of an American dignitary. The ceremonies of the public funeral salute his accomplishments in life and demonstrate the Nation's recognition of a debt owed for his services." This volume covers the ceremonies conducted between 1921 and 1969 for 26 eminent American officials, four foreign diplomats on assignment in the United States, and the unknown American servicemen killed in World War I, World War II, and the Korean War. These officials include Pershing, Marshall, MacArthur, Hoover, John Kennedy, Robert Kennedy, and Eisenhower.

D 101.3:dt.&nos.
JOINT ARMY AND AIR FORCE BULLETINS.

Earlier M 101.3

D 101.3/2:nos.
MILITARY TRAFFIC MANAGEMENT BULLETINS. ADMINISTRATIVE.

D 101.3/3   • Item 329-A
U.S. ARMY AUDIT AGENCY BULLETINS. [Irregular]

Discontinued.

D 101.3/3-2:nos.   • Item 329-A
U.S. ARMY AUDIT AGENCY PAMPHLETS. [Irregular]

Discontinued.

D 101.3/4:nos.
ADVANCE PLANNING PROCUREMENT INFORMATION BULLETIN, APPI (series).

D 101.3/5   • Item 322-B
EMPLOYMENT BULLETIN, CURRENT OPENINGS, G-11 AND ABOVE, AT ARMY MATERIAL COMMAND ACTIVITIES THROUGHOUT THE UNITED STATES. [Irregular]

Discontinued.

D 101.3/6:v.nos./nos.   • Item 323-A
MANPRINT BULLETIN. [Bimonthly]

See D 101.3/6-2

D 101.3/6-2:v.nos./nos.   • Item 323-A (EL)
MANPRINT. [Quarterly]

Coordinated Recruitment Branch

D 101.4:dt.&nos.   • Item 324-B-1 (MF)
CIRCULARS.

Earlier M 101.4

D 101.4/2:nos.   • Item 322-K-2 (MF)
USASSC FIELD CIRCULARS, FC- (series). [Irregular]

USASSC = U.S. Army Soldier Support Center.

D 101.4/3:nos.   • Item 324-B (MF)
SECOND ARMY, 2A CIRCULARS (series). [Irregular]

D 101.4/4:nos.   • Item 324-B-1 (MF)
1A CIRCULAR (series).

1A = First Army.

D 101.4/5:date   • Item 325-B-19
AMC CIRCULARS (series). [Irregular]

AMC = Army Materiel Command

D 101.6:CT   • Item 323
REGULATIONS, RULES, AND INSTRUCTIONS.

D 101.6/2:
CIVILIAN PERSONNEL REGULATIONS.

D 101.6/3:
CIVILIAN PERSONNEL PROCEDURES MANUAL.

D 101.6/4   • Item 327-A (MF)
ARMY PROCUREMENT PROCEDURES. [Irregular]

Issued in looseleaf form.

D 101.6/5:CT   • Item 325-B
HANDBOOKS, MANUALS, GUIDES. [Irregular]

D 101.6/6:CT
AREA HANDBOOKS.

D 101.6/7:nos.   • Item 325-B-7 (MF)
TEC LESSONS (series). [Irregular]

Includes miscellaneous lessons on various subjects pertaining to the work of different components of the Army.

D 101.6/8:letters-nos.   • Item 325-B (MF)
AMCCOM HANDBOOKS. [Irregular] (Munitions and Chemical Command)

D 101.6/9:nos.   • Item 325-B-14 (MF)
QMS- (series). [Irregular]

D 101.6/10:   • Item 322-K-4
BELVIOR RESEARCH, DEVELOPMENT, AND ENGINEERING CENTER: HANDBOOKS, (series). [Irregular]

D 101.6/11:date   • Item 325-B
U.S. ARMY POCKET RECRUITING GUIDE. [Annual]

D 101.7:dt.&nos.
GENERAL ORDERS.

Earlier M 101.7

D 101.8:dt.&nos.
SPECIAL ORDERS.

Earlier M 101.18

D 101.9   • Item 323
ARMY REGULATIONS, AR- (series). [Irregular]

D 101.9/2:nos.   • Item 323
ARMY MATERIAL COMMAND REGULATIONS, AMCR (series).

D 101.9/2-2:nos.   • Item 323
AMC SUPPLEMENT 1 TO AR (series). [Irregular]

D 101.9/3   • Item 323
SUPPLY AND MAINTENANCE COMMAND REGULATIONS.

D 101.9/4:nos.   • Item 323
HEADQUARTERS FORT McCOY REGULATIONS. [Irregular]

D 101.9/5:nos.   • Item 323
USAREC REGULATIONS. [Irregular] (United States Army Recruiting Command)

D 101.9/6:nos.   • Item 323
FIRST ARMY, 1A REGULATIONS. [Irregular]

1A = First Army

D 101.9/7   • Item 323
ARL REGULATIONS.

D 101.10:nos.   • Item 328
SPECIAL REGULATIONS.

Earlier M 101.32

Discontinued.

D 101.11:nos.   • Item 329
TECHNICAL MANUALS, TM- (series). [Irregular]

Earlier M 101.18

D 101.11:30-nos. • **Item 329**
GUIDES TO SPOKEN LANGUAGE INTRODUC-
TORY SERIES. [Irregular]

Issued for the following languages:–
French. 30-302
German. 30-306
Greek. 30-350
Italian. 30-303
Japanese. 30-341
Malay. 30-330
Norwegian. 30-310
Portuguese. 30-301
Russian. 30-344
Spanish. 30-300
Tagalog. 30-340
Turkish. 30-318

D 101.11/2 • **Item 329**
TECHNICAL MANUALS. [Irregular]

Discontinued.

D 101.12 • **Item 322 (EL)**
SOLDIERS. v. 1– 1946– [Monthly]

PURPOSE:– To keep personnel of the Army
aware of trends and developments of professional
concern. The digest is published under supervision of the Army Chief of Information, providing
timely and authoritative information on policies,
plans, and operations, and the technical developments of the Department of the Army to the Active Army, Army National Guard, and Army Reserve. It also serves as a vehicle for timely expression of the views of the Secretary of the
Army and the Chief of Staff and assists in the
achievement of information objectives of the
Army.
Contains brief illustrated articles of timely interest. Some issues are devoted to one subject,
such as a Special Air Force Issue, etc.
Index contained in the December issues.
Supersedes I & E Digest.
Prior to June 1966, entitled Army Information
Digest, 1966– 1971, Army Digest.
Indexed by: Index to U.S. Government Peri-
odicals.
ISSN 0093-8440

D 101.12/2:v.nos.&nos. • **Item 322-K (MF)**
SOLDIER SUPPORT JOURNAL. v. 1– 1980–
[Bimonthly] (Army Soldier Support Center)

Covers personnel management functions for
which the Center has training and combat development responsibility. Primarily for the military
personnel managers.

D 101.13:dt.&nos.
CIVILIAN PERSONNEL AND PAYROLL LETTERS.

D 101.14:dt.&nos.
GENERAL COURT-MARTIAL ORDERS.
Earlier M 101.14

D 101.15:nos. • **Item 322-A (MF) (CD)**
SUPPLY BULLETINS.

Earlier M 101.27

D 101.16:sec.nos.&le. nos. • **Item 322-A (MF)**
SUPPLY CATALOGS.

Earlier 101.12

D 101.16/2:nos.
DEPARTMENT OF ARMY SUPPLY MANUAL SM
(series).

D 101.16/3:date • **Item 322-A-15 (CD)**
CONSOLIDATED PUBLICATION OF COMPONENT
LISTS. [Semiannual]

Issued on CD-ROM.
D 101.17:v.nos. • **Item 326**
OFFICERS' CALL. [Monthly]
Earlier M 101.33
Discontinued.

D 101.18:nos.
REDUCTION TABLES.
Earlier M 101.31

D 101.19:nos.
TABLES OF ORGANIZATION AND EQUIPMENT.
Earlier M 101.2

D 101.19:nos. • **Item 327-E (MF)**
ARMY AUTOMATION REVIEW. [Bimonthly] (Computer
Systems Command, Fort Belvoir, Virginia)
Continues: Army ADP Review.
Discontinued [MC June 1980].

D 101.20:nos. • **Item 324**
FIELD MANUALS, FM- (series). [Irregular]
Discontinued.

D 101.20/2:nos. • **Item 324-A (MF)**
ARMY TRAINING AND EVALUATION PROGRAM,
ARTEP- (series). [Irregular]

D 101.20/3: • **Item 324-C (MF)**
ARMY TRAINER. [Quarterly] (Training and Doctrine
Command)

Provides timely information on training plans,
policies, and developments, and promotes an exchange of firsthand knowledge and experiences
among Active and Reserve components, as well
as Department of the Army civilians who are responsible for training.
Discontinued.

D 101.20/4:nos.
SOLDIER TRAINING PUBLICATIONS, STP- (series).

D 101.21:nos.
GRAPHIC TRAINING AIDS.
Earlier W 1.53

• **Item 327-P (E)**
D 101.22:nos. • **Item 327-E (MF)**
PAMPHLETS. [Irregular]

Indexed by: Index to U.S. Government Peri-
odicals.
The following are issued on a recurring basis:
See D 101.114

• **Item 327-P (E)**
• **Item 327-E (MF)**
CONSOLIDATED INDEX OF ARMY PUBLICA-
D 101.22:25-30/date TIONS AND BLANK FORMS. [Semiannual]

This Item will no longer be distributed in microfiche. Some Information is on CD-ROM.

D 101.22:27 • **Item 327**
JUDGE ADVOCATE LEGAL SERVICE. [Irregular]

Index issued semiannually.
ISSN 0364-247X

D 101.22:27-50 • **Item 327-F**
ARMY LAWYER. v. 1– 1971– [Monthly] (Judge
Advocate General's School, Charlottesville,
Va.)

PURPOSE:– To disseminate legal infor-
mation on military justice,
claims,administrative law, legal logistics, and
legal assistance to Department of the Army
military and civilian attorneys.
Issued by the Judge Advocate General's
Office (D 108.11) prior to April 1973.
Indexed by: Index to U.S. Government
Periodicals.
ISSN 0364-1287

D 101.22:27-100 • **Item 327-G**
MILITARY LAW REVIEW. [Quarterly]

PURPOSE:– To provide a medium for the
military lawyer, active and reserve, to share
the product of his experience and research
with fellow lawyers in the Department of the
Army.
Indexed by: Index to U.S. Government
Periodicals.
ISSN 0026-4040

D 101.22:165 • **Item 327-H**
MILITARY CHAPLAINS' REVIEW. [Quarterly]
ISSN 0360-9693
Earlier D 101.73
Later D 101.114

D 101.22:210-1 • **Item 327-H**
UNITED STATES ARMY INSTALLATIONS AND
MAJOR ACTIVITIES IN CONTINENTAL U.S.
[Annual]

D 101.22:360 • **Item 327**
COMMANDERS CALL. [Bimonthly]
Prior to July-August 1975 issued quar-
terly.
ISSN 0160-3744

D 101.22:360-400 • **Item 327**
POCKET GUIDE TO [Country]. [Irregular]

PURPOSE:– To provide American military
personnel stationed in or visiting foreign countries a brief background of the countries and
their peoples.
Issued for the following countries:–

Caribbean. 360-412
France. 360-402
Germany. 360-404
Great Britain. 360-400
Greece. 360-408
Italy. 360-401
Korea. 360-414
Low Countries [Netherlands, Belgium and
Luxembourg]. 360-416
Middle East [Iran, Iraq, Israel, Jordan, Leba-
non, Libya, Saudi Arabia, Syrian Arab Re-
public, and the United Arab Republic.]
360-417
Okinawa. 360-413
Philippines. 360-415
Spain. 360-409
Taiwan. 360-406
Thailand. 360-403
Turkey. 360-407
Vietnam. 360-411

D 101.22:550 • **Item 327**
[AREA AND COUNTRY BIBLIOGRAPHIC SUR-
VEYS.]

PURPOSE:– To provide an annotated
bibliography of publications available in the
open holdings of the Army Library in the Pentagon. The bibliographies include a wide range
of source material, backed by supplementary
material such as charts, maps, etc.
The following compilations have been published:–

Africa. 550-5
Communist China. 550-9

PURPOSE:– To present a bibliography
of a wide range source material, received
during the period 1971– 1976, on a number of
subjects which are important keys to a knowledge of this region and its people. Some of
the subject areas are; military posture, economic aspects, science and technology, life
in communist China today, and more.

Communist Eastern Europe. 550-8
Communist North Korea. 550-11
Japan, Okinawa, Republic of China (Tai-
wan), Korea.
Latin America and the Caribbean. 550-7
Middle East. 550-2
Middle East, strategic hub and North Africa. 550-16
Pacific Islands and Trust Territories. 550-
10
Peninsular Southeast Asia. 550-14

PURPOSE:– To present a bibliography
with annotations supported by 36 appendixes
comprised of charts, tables, maps, and texts
of military, political, economic, and sociological nature. The maps, 17 of which are in color,
provide the regional geographic picture of
peninsular Southeast Asia, as well as the
political and economic aspects of Burma,
Cambodia, Laos, and Thailand.
Ryukyu Islands. 550-4
Southeast Asia, Australia, Indonesia, Malaysia, New Zealand, Philippines,
Singapore. 550-12
Sudan. 550-27
USSR. 550-6
Discontinued.

D 101.22:550   • **Item 327-J**
U.S. AREA HANDBOOK FOR (Country). [Irregular]

    Each handbook covers the sociological, political, economic, and military background of the individual country, including extensive bibliographies to enable the reader to locate other sources for more detailed information in the areas of special interest. Handbooks are revised and updated from time to time.
    Issued for the following countries:–

Afghanistan. 550-65
Albania. 550-98
Algeria. 550-44
Angola. 550-59
Argentina. 550-73
Australia. 550-169
Austria. 550-176
Bangladesh. 550-175
Belgium. 550-170
Bolivia. 550-66
Brazil. 550-20
Bulgaria. 550-168
Burma. 550-61
Burundi. 550-73
Cambodia. 550-50
Ceylon. 550-96
Chad. 550-159
Chile. 550-77
Colombia. 550-26
China. 550-60
Costa Rica. 50-90
Cuba. 550-152
Cyprus. 550-22
Czechoslovakia. 550-158
Democratic Republic of Sudan. 550-27
Democratic Republic of the Congo (Congo Kinshasa). 550-67
Dominican Republic. 550-54
East Germany. 550-155
Ecuador. 550-52
El Salvador. 550-150
Ethiopia. 550-28
Federal Republic of Germany. 550-173
Finland. 550-167
Germany. 550-29
Ghana. 550-153
Greece. 550-87
Guatemala. 550-78
Guinea. 550-174
Guyana. 550-82
Haiti. 550-164
Hashemite Kingdom of Jordan. 550-34
Honduras. 550-151
Hungary. 550-165
India. 550-21
Indian Ocean Territories. 550-154
Indonesia. 550-39
Iran. 550-68
Iraq. 550-31
Israel. 550-25
Italy. 550-182
Ivory Coast. 550-69
Jamaica. 550-177
Japan. 550-30
Kenya. 550-56
Korea. 550-41
Laos. 550-58
Lebanon. 550-24
Liberia. 550-38
Libya. 550-85
Malawi. 550-172
Malaysia and Singapore. 550-45
Mauritania. 550-161
Mexico. 550-79
Mongolia. 550-76
Morocco. 550-49
Mozambique. 550-64
Nepal, Bhutan, and Sikkim. 550-35
Nicaragua. 550-88
Nigeria. 550-157
North Korea. 550-81
Oceania. 550-94
Pakistan. 550-48
Panama. 550-46
Paraguay. 550-156
People's Republic of China. 550-60
People's Republic of the Congo (Congo Brazzaville). 550-91
Peripheral States of the Arabian Peninsula. 550-92
Persian Gulf States. 550-185
Peru. 550-42
Philippines. 550-72
Poland. 550-162
Portugal. 550-181
Republic of China. 550-63
Republic of Korea. 550-41
Republic of South Africa. 550-93

Republic of Tunisia. 550-89
Republic of Turkey. 550-80
Romania. 550-160
Rwanda. 550-84
Saudi Arabia. 550-51
Senegal. 550-70
Sierra Leone. 550-180
Somalia. 550-86
Southern Rhodesia. 550-171
Soviet Union. 550-95
Spain. 550-179
Syria. 550-47
Tanzania. 550-62
Thailand. 550-53
Trinidad and Tobego. 550-178
Turkey. 550-80.
Uganda. 550-74
United Arab Republic (Egypt). 550-43
United Republic of Cameroon. 550-166
Uruguay. 550-97
Venezuela. 550-71
Vietnam. 550-40
Vietnam, North. 550-57
Vietnam, South. 550-55
Yemens. 550-183
Yugoslavia. 550-99
Zambia. 550-75

D 101.22:715-4   • **Item 327**
DEPARTMENT OF THE ARMY PRIME CONTRACTS ($1 million and over) PLACED WITH INDUSTRY, NON- PROFIT ORGANIZATIONS, COLLEGES, AND UNIVERSITIES. [Monthly]

D 101.22:600   • **Item 327-J (MF)**
THE ARMY HEALTH PROMOTION PROGRAM, FIT TO WIN.

D 101.22:750-10/date   • **Item 327-E**
U.S. ARMY EQUIPMENT INDEX OF MODIFICATION WORK ORDERS. [Quarterly]

D 101.22:   • **Item 327-P (E)**
PAMPHLETS: ELECTRONIC PRODUCTS.

D 101.22/2:nos.
IG PAMPHLETS. ADMINISTRATIVE.

D 101.22/3   • **Item 322-A (MF)**
DARCOM PAMPHLETS (numbered). [Irregular]
    Earlier title: Army Material Command, Amc Pamphlets. [Irregular]

D 101.22/3:310.1   • **Item 322-A**
MILITARY PUBLICATIONS: INDEX OF AMC PUBLICATIONS AND BLANK FORMS.

D 101.22/3:335-1   • **Item 322-A**
REPORTS, REGISTER OF APPROVED RECURRING REPORTS. [Quarterly]

D 101.22/3:385   • **Item 322-A**
SAFETY DIGEST. [Bimonthly]
    Prepared by Safety Division.

D 101.22/4:nos.
UNITED STATES ARMY, ALASKA, PAMPHLETS.

D 101.22/5   • **Item 322-A (MF)**
SUPPLY AND MAINTENANCE COMMAND, SMC PAMPHLETS. [Irregular]

D 101.22/6:nos.   • **Item 327-K (MF)**
MTMC PAMPHLETS. [Irregular] (Military Traffic Management Command)

    Covers various areas of traffic management, highway transportation, etc.

D 101.22/7:nos.   • **Item 322-A-1 (MF)**
U.S. ARMY RECRUITING COMMAND PAMPHLETS, USAREC PAM- (series). [Irregular]

D 101.22/8:nos.   • **Item 322-A-1 (MF)**
ERADCOM PAMPHLET (series). [Irregular] (Electronic Research and Development Command)

D 101.22/9:nos.   • **Item 322-A (MF)**
2A PAMPHLETS (series). [Irregular]
    2A Second Army

D 101.22/9-2:nos.   • **Item 322-A (MF)**
1A PAMPHLETS (series). [Irregular]
    1A First Army.

D 101.22/10:nos.   • **Item 322-A (MF)**
HEADQUARTERS FORT GEORGE G. MEADE PAMPHLETS (series). [Irregular]

D 101.22/11:nos.   • **Item 322-A (MF)**
USAAVNC PAM- (series). [Irregular]

D 101.22/12:nos.   • **Item 325-B**
AMCCOMP- (series). [Irregular]
    AMCCOMP = Army Armament, Munitions and Chemical Command (pamphlet).

D 101.22/13:nos.   • **Item 322-A (MF)**
FH PAM (series). [Irregular]
    FH = Fort Hood

D 101.22/14:nos.   • **Item 327-E (MF)**
USAADASCH PAM (series). [Irregular]

    USAADASCH = United States Army Air Defense Artillery School

D 101.22/15:nos.   • **Item 322-A-2 (MF)**
FORT LEE PAMPHLETS (series). [Irregular]

D 101.22/16:nos.   • **Item 322-A-1 (MF)**
U.S. ARMY MILITARY PERSONNEL CENTER: PAMPHLETS (series). [Irregular]

D 101.22/17:nos.   • **Item 327-M (MF)**
CID PAMPHLET (series). [Irregular]
    Contains short articles on the U.S. Army Criminal Investigation Command, its laboratories, and regions.

D 101.22/18:nos.   • **Item 327-E (MF)**
FORT JACKSON PAMPHLETS (series). [Irregular]

D 101.22/19   • **Item 322-A-3**
AHS PAMPHLETS. [Irregular]
    AHS = Academy of Health Sciences.

D 101.22/20:nos.   • **Item 322-A-4**
USAARMC PAMPHLETS (series). [Irregular]
    USAARMC = U.S. Army Armor Center

D 101.22/21:nos.   • **Item 322-A-5**
USAFAC PAMPHLET (series). [Irregular]
    USAFAC = U.S. Army Finance and Accounting Center

D 101.22/22:nos.   • **Item 322-A-6 (MF)**
TRADOC PAMPHLET (series). [Irregular]
    TRADOC = Training and Doctrine Command

D 101.22/23   • **Item 322-A-7**
10TH MOUNTAIN DIVISION (LI) AND FORT DRUM: PAMPHLETS (series). [Irregular]

D 101.22/24:nos.   • **Item 322-B-2**
LABORATORY COMMAND: PAMPHLETS, LABCOM-P- (series). [Irregular]
    Pamphlets on miscellaneous topics pertaining to the mission of the Army Laboratory Command. One example is a pamphlet on technology to win.

D 101.22/25:nos.   • **Item 322-A-8 (P) (EL)**
CENTER FOR ARMY LESSONS LEARNED (Series).

D 101.22/25-2:   • **Item 307-A-8 (EL)**
NEWS FROM THE FRONT!

D 101.22/26:date/v.nos.   • **Item 322-A-9**
CTC TRENDS, COMBAT MANEUVER TRAINING CENTER (CMTC)

D 101.22/27:date   • **Item 322-A-10 (EL)**
CTC TRENDS, NTC. [Quarterly]

D 101.22/28   • **Item 322-A-11 (EL)**
CTC TRENDS, JOINT READINESS TRAINING CENTER (JRTC).

D 101.22/29:date   • **Item 322-A-12**
CTC TRENDS, BATTLE COMMAND TRAINING PROGRAM (BCTP).

D 101.22/29-2:date   • **Item 322-A-14**
BCBST, PERCEPTIONS II, FY . . . [Annual]
    BCBST = Brigade Command and Battle Staff Training Team.

D 101.22/30   • Item 322-A-13 (EL)
CTC QUARTERLY BULLETIN.

D 101.22/31:CT   • Item 325-B-30
ARMY ROTC (pamphlets).

D 101.23:nos.
TABLE OF ALLOWANCES.
    Earlier M 101.29

D 101.24:dt.&nos.   • Item 324-B (MF)
TRAINING CIRCULARS.
    Earlier M 101.22

D 101.25:nos.   • Item 329
TECHNICAL BULLETINS.
    Earlier M 101.13

D 101.26:dt.&nos.
CIVILIAN PERSONNEL CIRCULARS.
    Earlier M 101.20

D 101.27:date   • Item 330
UNITED STATES ARMY INDEX OF SPECIFICATIONS,
    INCLUDING MILITARY (MIL and JAN) STAN-
    DARDS. [Annual with Monthly sup.]
    Earlier M 101.23
    Discontinued.

D 101.28:nos.
U.S. ARMY SPECIFICATIONS.
    Earlier M 101.26

D 101.29:sec.&le-nos.
MODIFICATION WORK ORDERS.
    Earlier W 1.56

D 101.30:
ARMY-NAVY-AIR FORCE, LIST OF PRODUCTS QUALI-
    FIED UNDER MILITARY SPECIFICATIONS.

D 101.31:dt.&nos.
SPECIAL COURT-MARTIAL ORDERS.
    Earlier M 101.2:Sp 3

D 101.32:nos.
MEMORANDUMS.
    Earlier M 101.24

D 101.32/2:nos.
MEMO AG (series). [Irregular]

D 101.33:nos.
JOINT ARMY AND AIR FORCE PROCUREMENT
    CIRCULARS.

D 101.33/2:dt.&nos.
ARMY PROCUREMENT CIRCULARS.

D 101.33/3:dt.&nos.
PROCUREMENT LEGAL SERVICE CIRCULARS.

D 101.34:date
INDEX OF SPECIFICATIONS AND STANDARDS USED
    BY DEPARTMENT OF ARMY, MILITARY INDEX. v.
    2. [Semiannual]
    Later D 7.14

D 101.35:nos.   • Item 322-H
POSTERS.
    Earlier M 101.34

D 101.35/2:CT
AUDIOVISUAL MATERIALS.

D 101.35/3   • Item 322-H
AMD POSTERS (series).

D 101.36:date
DEPARTMENT OF ARMY CHIEFS AND EXECUTIVES
    [Organization chart]. [Bimonthly]
    Later D 102.23

D 101.37:nos.   • Item 323-D
CIVILIAN PERSONNEL PAMPHLETS.
    Earlier M 101.35
    Discontinued No. 80.

D 101.38:
ARMED SERVICES ELECTRO STANDARDS AGENCY,
    LISTS.

D 101.39:dt.&nos.
CIVILIAN PERSONNEL NEWS LETTER. [Monthly]

D 101.39/2:nos.
ARMY PERSONNEL NEWSLETTER.
    Supersedes D 101.39

D 101.39/3:nos.   • Item 325-B-8
ARMY PERSONNEL LETTER. [Monthly]
    See D 101.39/4

D 101.39/4:date   • Item 325-B-8 (MF)
ARMY PERSONNEL BULLETIN. [Monthly]
    Former title: Army Personnel Letter (D 101.39/
    3).
    Discontinued.

D 101.40:date   • Item 325-A
UNITED STATES ARMY OCCUPATIONAL HANDBOOK.
    Discontinued.

D 101.41:
INSPECTION GUIDES.

D 101.41/2
IG NOTES. ADMIN.

D 101.42:CT
HEADQUARTERS, U.S. ARMY, EUROPE, PUBLICA-
    TIONS.

D 101.42/2:CT
HISTORICAL DIVISION PUBLICATIONS.

D 101.42/3:date   • Item 325-B-4 (EL)
MEDICAL BULLETIN. [Bimonthly] (Headquarters, 7th
    Medical Command)

      PURPOSE:– To provide the professional mili-
tary medical community in Europe with a medium
for timely exchange of important health care information.

D 101.42/4:date   • Item 323-A-1 (MF)
EURARMY. [Monthly]
      Published by Headquarters, U.S. Army Eu-
rope, and Seventh Army. Its purpose is to assist
in fulfilling Command information objectives by
keeping assigned personnel informed of their mission, responsibilities, and opportunities.
    Discontinued.

D 101.43:v. nos.&nos.   • Item 323-A (P) (EL)
ARMY RESERVE MAGAZINE. v. 1–   1955–
    [Bimonthly]

      PURPOSE:– To increase the effectiveness
of the Army Reserve as an instrument of National
Defense by encouraging interest and participation in the Army Reserve training, insuring a source
of timely information for Army Reserve membership and stimulating activities that enhance Army
Reserve prestige and morale.
      Brief articles on various phases of the Re-
serve Program. Also includes news articles. Each
issue is 16 pages. Published by the Chief, U.S.
Army Reserve and ROTC Affairs.
      Formerly Army Reservist.
      Indexed by: Index to U.S. Government Peri-
odicals.

D 101.43/2:nos.   • Item 323-A
RPI- (series).

D 101.43/2-2:nos.   • Item 323-A-2
APA (no. series).

D 101.44
PSYCHOLOGICAL WARFARE SCHOOL SPECIAL
    TEXTS.

D 101.45:CT
ADDRESSES.

D 101.46/2:CT
HUMAN RESEARCH UNIT NO. 2, OFFICE, CHIEF OF
    ARMY FIELD FORCES, FORT ORD, CALIF., PUB-
    LICATIONS.

D 101.46/3:CT
HUMAN RESEARCH UNIT NO. 3, OFFICE, CHIEF OF
    ARMY FIELD FORCES, FORT BENNING, GA.,
    PUBLICATIONS.

D 101.47   • Item 321-A
ARMY AVIATION DIGEST. [Monthly]

      PURPOSE:– To provide information of an op-
erational or functional nature concerning safety
and aircraft accident prevention, training, maintenance, operations, research and development,
aviation medicine and other related data.
      Indexed by: Index to U.S. Government Peri-
odicals.
    Discontinued.

D 101.47/2:nos.
ARMY AVIATION SCHOOL, FORT RUCKER, ALA.,
    SPECIAL BIBLIOGRAPHY.

D 101.47/3   • Item 325-C-1 (MF)
STUDENT HANDOUT (series). [Irregular]
    Discontinued.

D 101.47/4:CT   • Item 325-C-1 (MF)
STUDENT HANDBOOK (series). [Irregular]
    Discontinued.

D 101.47/5:nos.   • Item 325-C-2 (MF)
PROGRAMMED TEXT, USAAVNA PT-(series). [Irregu-
    lar] (U.S. Army Aviation Center)
    Discontinued.

D 101.47/6:nos.   • Item 325-C-1 (MF)
STUDENT REFERENCE BOOK (series). [Irregular]
    Discontinued.

D 101.47/7:CT   • Item 325-C-2 (MF)
PROGRAMMED LESSON (series). [Irregular]
    Discontinued.

D 101.47/8:CT   • Item 325-B-13
STUDENT PACKAGE (series). [Irregular]

      Lessons on miscellaneous subjects for stu-
dents of U.S. Army schools.
    Discontinued.

D 101.48:nos.   • Item 327-D
ROTC MANUALS. [Irregular]

D 101.49:
SPECIAL BIBLIOGRAPHY, ARTILLERY & GUIDED
    MISSILE SCHOOL LIBRARY.

D 101.50   • Item 327-B
PROGRESS, U.S. ARMY. [Annual]
      A well-illustrated, attractive booklet showing
the activities of the various branches of the Army
performed during the past year.
    Discontinued.

D 101.51:date
JOINT MILITARY-INDUSTRY PACKAGING AND MA-
    TERIALS HANDLING SYMPOSIUM.

D 101.52   • Item 330-B
UNITED STATES ARMY RESEARCH AND DEVELOP-
    MENT SERIES. 1–   [Irregular]
    Discontinued.

D 101.52/2:date   • Item 323-C
ARMY RESEARCH TASK SUMMARIES. [Annual]
    Discontinued.

D 101.52/3:date/nos.   • **Item 323-B (EL)**
ARMY AL & T BULLETIN. [Bimonthly]

　　　　PURPOSE:– To improve informal communication among all segments of the Army scientific
community and other Government R & D agencies; to further understanding of Army R & D
progress, problem areas, and program planning;
to stimulate more closely integrated and coordinated effort among the widely dispersed and dif-
fused Army R & D activities; to maintain a closer
link from top management through all levels to
scientists, engineers, and technicians at the
bench level; to express views of leaders, as pertinent to their responsibilities, and to keep personnel informed on matters germane to their welfare and pride of service.
　　　　Prepared by Office of Chief, Research and
Development.
　　　　Prior to the March-April 1978 (v. 19, no. 2)
issue entitled Army Research and Development.
Name was Army RD & A Bulletin until the March -
April 2000 volume.
　　　　Indexed by: Index to U.S. Government Periodicals.
　　　　ISSN 0162-7082

D 101.52/4:date/v.nos.
U.S. ARMY RESEARCH AND DEVELOPMENT PRO-
GRAM GUIDE.
　　　　Earlier D 101.6:R 31

D 101.52/5
RESEARCH IN PROGRESS, CALENDAR YEAR.
　　[Annual]

D 101.52/5-2:nos.
ARMY RESEARCH OFFICE (Durham) HISTORICAL
　　SUMMARY.

D 101.52/5-3:date
U.S. ARMY RESEARCH OFFICE (Durham) ENGINEER-
ING SCIENCES DIVISION ENGINEERING
PROJECTS ACCOMPLISHMENTS.

D 101.52/5-4:date   • **Item 330-G (MF)**
RESEARCH IN PROGRESS: PHYSICS, ELEC-
TRONICS, MATHEMATICS, GEOSCIENCES.
[Annual] (Army Research Office)
　　　　Formerly included in Research in Progress
(D 101.52/5).

D 101.52/5-5:date   • **Item 330-G (MF)**
RESEARCH IN PROGRESS: METALLURGY AND
MATERIALS SCIENCES, MECHANICS AND
AERONAUTICS, CHEMISTRY AND BIOLOGICAL
SCIENCES. [Annual] (Army Research Office)
　　　　Formerly included in Research in Progress
(D 101.52/5).
　　　　Discontinued.

D 101.52/6   • **Item 323-C**
UNITED STATES ARMY HUMAN FACTORS RESEARCH
AND DEVELOPMENT, ANNUAL CONFERENCE.
　　1st–　[Annual]
　　　　Chief of Research and Development.

D 101.52/7
ARO-D- (series). [Irregular]

D 101.52/8:v.nos.&nos.
BIOLOGICAL EFFECTS OF ELECTROMAGNETIC
RADIATION. [Quarterly]
　　　　Sub-title: A digest of current literature and a
forum of communication.

D 101.53:v.nos.&nos.
INFANTRY SCHOOL QUARTERLY.

D 101.54   • **Item 323-C**
ARMY RESEARCH OFFICE, ARO REPORTS. 1–
　　[Irregular]
　　　　Prepared by Office of Chief, Research and
Development.

D 101.55:nos.   • **Item 330-A**
UNITED STATES ARMY SERVICE CENTER FOR THE
ARMED FORCES; PAMPHLETS.
　　　　Desig. USASCAF pamphlet (nos.).
　　　　Discontinued.

D 101.56:CT   • **Item 327-L**
BIBLIOGRAPHIES AND LISTS OF PUBLICATIONS.

D 101.57:CT
DICTIONARIES, GLOSSARIES, ETC.

D 101.58:nos.
FIRING TABLES.

D 101.59:nos.
ARMY SUBJECT SCHEDULES.

D 101.60:nos.   • **Item 330-E (MF)**
RESEARCH INSTITUTE FOR THE BEHAVIORAL AND
SOCIAL SCIENCES: TECHNICAL PAPERS.

D 101.60/2:nos.   • **Item 330-E-1 (MF)**
ARMY RESEARCH INSTITUTE FOR BEHAVIORAL
AND SOCIAL SCIENCES: RESEARCH REPORTS.
　　　　Published in microfiche (24x).

D 101.60/3:nos.
ARMY RESEARCH INSTITUTE FOR THE BEHAVIORAL
AND SOCIAL SCIENCES: R & D UTILIZATION
REPORTS. [Irregular]

D 101.60/4:nos.   • **Item 330-E (MF)**
ARMY RESEARCH INSTITUTE FOR THE BEHAVIORAL
AND SOCIAL SCIENCES: TECHNICAL REPORTS.
[Irregular]

D 101.60/5:nos.   • **Item 330-E-1 (MF)**
RESEARCH PRODUCT (series). [Irregular] (Army Re-
search Institute for the Behavioral and Social
Sciences)

D 101.60/6:nos.   • **Item 330-E**
ARMY RESEARCH INSTITUTE FOR THE BEHAVIORAL
AND SOCIAL SCIENCES: SPECIAL REPORTS
(series). [Irregular]

D 101.60/7:date   • **Item 329-B (MF)**
ARI NEWSLETTER. [Quarterly]

D 101.60/8   • **Item 330-E-2 (MF)**
ARMY RESEARCH INSTITUTE FOR THE BEHAVIORAL
SCIENCES, STUDY REPORT. (Series)

D 101.61   • **Item 325-C**
OFFICIAL BULLETINS, NATIONAL TROPHY
MATCHES. [Annual]
　　　　National Board for Promotion of Rifle Prac-
tice.
　　　　Discontinued.

D 101.62:CT   • **Item 327-A**
ARMY AUDIT AGENCY PUBLICATIONS.
　　　　See D 101.3/3 for Army Audit Agency Bulle-
tins.

D 101.63:date   • **Item 325-D**
MANAGEMENT IMPROVEMENT PROGRAM,
PLOWBACK, IMPROVEMENTS REPORTS. [Semi-
annual]
　　　　Discontinued.

D 101.64:CT
ARMY LANGUAGE SCHOOL, PRESIDIO OF
MONTEREY, CALIF., PUBLICATIONS.

D 101.65:nos.• Item 325-E
AMC HISTORICAL STUDIES.
　　　　Discontinued.

D 101.66   • **Item 329-B**
TRANSPORTATION PROCEEDINGS. v. 1–　1967–
[Monthly]
　　　　Official magazine of the Military Traffic Management and Terminal Service.
　　　　PURPOSE:– To provide timely and authoritative information on policies, plans, operations,
and technical developments in the defense transportation field.

D 101.66/2:v.nos.&nos.   • **Item 329-B**
TRANSLOG. v. 1–　1970–　[Monthly]

　　　　PURPOSE:– To provide timely and authoritative information on policies, plans, operations,
and technical developments in the defense transportation field.
　　　　Indexed by: Index to U.S. Government Periodicals.
　　　　ISSN 0041-1639
　　　　See D 101.66/2-2

D 101.66/2-2:v.nos./nos.   • **Item 329-B (P) (EL)**
TRANSLOG, DEFENSE TRANSPORTATION SYSTEM
BULLETIN. [Monthly]

D 101.66/3:v.nos.&nos.   • **Item 330-F**
MTMC EXPEDITER. v. 1–　1978–　(Military Traffic
Management Command)

　　　　PURPOSE:– To provide an authorized unofficial publication of Headquarters, Military Traffic
Management Command, issued to spread the word
on important developments and obtain feedback
on policies and procedures.
　　　　Discontinued.

D 101.66/4:date/nos.   • **Item 329-B**
TRANSPORTATION CORPS. [Quarterly]
　　　　Ceased in 1994.

D 101.67   • **Item 323-C-1**
TECHNICAL REPORTS. [Irregular]
　　　　Discontinued.

D 101.67/2:date   • **Item 323-C-2**
BESRL [Behavior and Systems Research Labora-
tory] WORK PROGRAM, FISCAL YEAR (date).
[Annual] (Office of the Chief of Research and
Development)

　　　　Gives background information on research
projects being conducted during the fiscal year.

D 101.68   • **Item 329-C**
HALLMARK. v. 1–　1968–　[Monthly]
　　　　ISSN 0040-1352
　　　　Discontinued.

D 101.69:v.nos.&nos.   • **Item 322-C (EL)**
ARMY LOGISTICIAN. v. 1–　1968–　[Bimonthly]

　　　　Prepared by the Army Logistics Management
Center.
　　　　PURPOSE:– To provide timely and authorita-
tive information on U.S. Army logistics plans,
policies, doctrine, procedures, operations and
developments to the Active Army, Army National
Guard, and U.S. Army Reserve.
　　　　Indexed by: Index to U.S. Government Peri-
odicals.
　　　　ISSN 0004-2528

D 101.70:date
ARMY MATERIAL COMMAND COORDINATED
RECRUITING PROGRAM ANNUAL PROGRESS
REPORT. 1st–　[Annual]
　　　　Report covers fiscal year.

D 101.71:date   • **Item 322-D**
ARROWHEAD. 1– 49.　– March 1973. [Monthly] (Army
Combat Developments Command, Ft. Belvoir, Va.)
　　　　Discontinued.

D 101.72:v. nos./nos.   • **Item 325-K (EL)**
PARAMETERS, JOURNAL OF THE U.S. ARMY WAR
COLLEGE. [Quarterly]

　　　　Contains articles that provide a forum for military officers and civilians concerned with military
affairs to exchange thoughts on such subjects
as land warfare, national and international security, military history strategy, and leadership.

D 101.73:v.nos.&nos.   • **Item 322-E**
MILITARY CHAPLAINS' REVIEW. v. 1–　1972–
[Quarterly]
　　　　Later D 101.22:165

D 101.74:CT   • **Item 322-F**
VIETNAM STUDIES (series). [Irregular]
　　　　Discontinued.

D 101.75   • **Item 322-G**
GENERAL INFORMATION LEAFLETS. 1–　[Irregular]
　　　　Discontinued.

D 101.76:CT
SPECIAL BIBLIOGRAPHIES. (Library, General Staff
College, Fort Leavenworth, Kansas)

D 101.77:date • Item 330-C-1 (EL)
AIR DEFENSE ARTILLERY. 1976– [Quarterly] (Army Air Defense School, Ft. Bliss, Tex.)

PURPOSE:– To keep school and field unit personnel informed of, and dialoging on, air defense developments worldwide.
ISSN 0091-9225
Continues Air Defense Trends.
Depository Item 330-C cancelled.
Prior to 1983, Air Defense Magazine.
Discontinued.

D 101.77/2:v.nos.&nos. • Item 330-C-2 (EL)
FIELD ARTILLERY JOURNAL. [Bimonthly]

Contains articles that disseminate professional knowledge, report on field artillery's progress, and promote understanding and cooperation among different arms of the military.

D 101.78: • Item 325
USA ARMOR SCHOOL SUBCOURSES. [Irregular]

D 101.78/2:v.nos.&nos. • Item 322-M (EL)
ARMOR, THE MAGAZINE OF MOBILE WARFARE. v. 1– [Bimonthly] (Army Armor School)

PURPOSE:– To disseminate knowledge of the military arts and sciences, with special attention to mobility in ground warfare. Contains articles, letters, news notes, and other features.
ISSN 0004-2420

D 101.79:CT • Item 322-A
ARMY FOREIGN SCIENCE AND TECHNOLOGY CENTER: PUBLICATIONS. [Irregular]

D 101.80:nos.
AMMRC TR- (series). [Irregular] (Army Materials and Mechanics Research Center)

D 101.81:CT
ARMY SCIENTIFIC ADVISORY PANEL: PUBLICATIONS. [Irregular]

D 101.82:CT • Item 325-F-7 (MF)
ENVIRONMENTAL IMPACT STATEMENT.

D 101.83:date • Item 332-F (MF)
ARMY COMMUNICATIONS COMMAND: ANNUAL REPORT.
Discontinued.

D 101.84:v.nos.&nos. • Item 325-F-1 (P) (EL)
MILITARY INTELLIGENCE. v. 1– [Quarterly] (U.S. Army Intelligence Center and School, Ft. Huachuca, Arizona)

PURPOSE:– To provide a professional development resource for military and civilian intelligence personnel. Contains articles and short news items.
Indexed by Index to U.S. Government Periodicals.
ISSN 0026-4024
Continues: MI Magazine.

D 101.84/2:v.nos.&nos. • Item 325-F-4 (MF)
MILITARY POLICE JOURNAL. [Quarterly]

Contains information about military police functions in combat, battlefield support, etc. Objectives are to inform and motivate, increase knowledge, improve performance, and provide a forum for exchange of ideas.

D 101.85:v. nos./nos. • Item 325-F
JOURNAL OF THE U.S. ARMY INTELLIGENCE AND SECURITY COMMAND. v. 1– 1977–

PURPOSE:– To serve as an educational and informational media for members of the Army Intelligence and Security Command and the intelligence community.
For the period 1977– April 1980, issued as numbered volumes and issues.

D 101.86:v.nos.&nos.
ARMY ADMINISTRATOR. [Quarterly]

D 101.87:nos. • Item 325-F (EL)
PS, THE PREVENTIVE MAINTENANCE MONTHLY. Issue 1–

PURPOSE:– To provide soldiers assigned to combat, combat support, maintenance, and supply with an informative magazine containing articles on preventive maintenance information for specific military equipment. Presented in a colored comic book format.
Note:– Discontinued in the depository system with issue no. 342.
ISSN 0475-2953
Discontinued.

D 101.88:nos. • Item 325-I (MF)
OFFICER SPECIALTY (series). 1– [Irregular] (Army Tactical (Combat Support)/Strategic Intelligence)

Career opportunity brochures for the cadets in the United States Military Academy, Reserve Officer Training Corps, and Officer Cadet Schools for specialized fields such as public affairs, subsistence management, etc.
Discontinued.

D 101.89:date/nos. • Item 323-E (EL)
RESOURCE MANAGEMENT. [Quarterly]

PURPOSE:– To provide a forum for free expression of mature, professional thought on the art and science of Army resource management.
Previous title: Resource Management Journal.

D 101.90:nos. • Item 325-B-1
DESIGN GUIDES. [Irregular]

PURPOSE:– To aid architects in designing realistic, cost-effective facilities.
Prepared by the Army's Chief of Engineers.
Discontinued.

D 101.91:date • Item 322-C-1
ARMY ORGANIZATIONAL EFFECTIVENESS JOURNAL. [Quarterly]

PURPOSE:– To inform and act as a forum for commanders and military and civilian leaders on applying the Organizational Effectiveness process in unitsand organizations throughout the Army. Seeks to foster research and methods for evaluating the contributions of OE to combat readiness.
Former title: OE (Organizational Effectiveness) Communique.
Discontinued.

D 101.92:v.nos.&nos. • Item 322-J
MILITARY MEDIA REVIEW. v. 1– 1974– [Quarterly] (Defense Information School)

PURPOSE:– To provide Public Affairs personnel of all services with military media- related articles, black and white photographs, and drawings.
Discontinued.

D 101.93 • Item 322-L (MF)
EDUCATIONAL SERVICES BROCHURE AND SCHEDULE OF COURSES. (Pentagon Education Center)

Gives schedule of Degree Programs offered through the Center in cooperation with various colleges and universities.
Previous title: Schedule of Education Courses and Special Programs.
Discontinued.

D 101.93/2:date • Item 322-L (MF)
TOWER UNIVERSITY. EDUCATION SERVICE PLAN. [Annual]
Discontinued.

D 101.93/3:date • Item 322-L (MF)
EDUCATIONAL PROGRAMS AT FORT BENJAMIN HARRISON. [Annual]
Discontinued.

D 101.94: • Item 325-B-2 (MF)
ARMY MANAGEMENT COURSE (series). [Irregular] (Army Management Engineering Training Activity)
Consists of texts developed for use in resident courses at the Activity in such subjects as technical data package development and management.
Discontinued.

D 101.94/2: • Item 325-B-3 (MF)
DEFENSE MANAGEMENT JOINT COURSE (series). [Irregular] (Army Management Engineering Training Activity)
Consists of texts developed for use in resident courses at the Activity in such subjects as defense work methods and standards. Includes both course books and work books.

D 101.94/3:date • Item 325-B-3 (MF)
ARMY MANAGEMENT ENGINEERING TRAINING ACTIVITY: COURSE CATALOG. [Annual]
Discontinued.

D 101.95:date • Item 322-N
WEAPON SYSTEMS. [Annual]
Describes and pictures Close Combat, Air Defense, Fire Support, Combat Support, Mission Areas, Combat Service Support, Combat Control and Communications, and Strategic Conflict Weapon Systems.

D 101.96:v.nos.&nos. • Item 325-B-18 (MF)
ALL POINTS BULLETIN, THE ARMY FINANCIAL MANAGEMENT NEWSLETTER. [Monthly]
Contains items of general and technical interest to comptroller, finance, and accounting personnel.
Non-depository.

D 101.96/2:date
ALL POINTS BULLETIN, JTELS SITE IDENTIFICATION DIRECTORY. [Bimonthly]

D 101.96/3:date • Item 325-B-18 (MF)
ALL POINTS BULLETIN AUTOVON DIRECTORY. [Annual]

D 101.97:CT
TELEPHONE DIRECTORY (by area).

D 101.98:date • Item 323-F
HISTORICAL REVIEW, U.S. ARMY BELVOIR RESEARCH AND DEVELOPMENT CENTER. [Annual]

PURPOSE:– To summarize Command activities in fulfilling its mission of fielding combat support and construction engineer equipment.
Former title: Historical Review, U.S. Army Mobility Equipment Research and Development Command.

D 101.99:date • Item 322-P (MF)
CONUS ARMY INSTALLATIONS/ACTIVITIES BY CONGRESSIONAL DISTRICT. [Annual]
CONUS = Continental United States
Consists of a Continental United States headquarters map, a Civil Works District/Division map, and state maps showing Army Installations.
Discontinued.

D 101.100:nos. • Item 322-R (MF)
CHEMICAL RESEARCH AND DEVELOPMENT CENTER, CRDC-SP- (series). [Irregular]

D 101.101:nos. • Item 325-B
DIAGRAM BOOKLETS (series). [Irregular]

D 101.102:nos.
ADVANCE SHEETS (series). [Irregular]

D 101.103: • Item 325-B-5 (MF)
ARMY INSTITUTE FOR PROFESSIONAL DEVELOPMENT: SUBCOURSE ISO-(series). [Irregular]
Discontinued.

D 101.104: • Item 323-A (MF)
RSC- (series).
Discontinued.

D 101.105:nos.   • **Item 325-B (MF)**
WORKBOOK (series). [Irregular]
Discontinued.

D 101.106:nos.   • **Item 322-A-1 (MF)**
USAREC RESEARCH NOTES (series). [Irregular]
USAREC = U.S. Army Recruiting Command.
Discontinued.

D 101.106/2:nos.   • **Item 322-A-1 (MF)**
USAREC RESEARCH MEMORANDUMS (numbered).
[Irregular]
Discontinued.

D 101.106/3:v.nos.&nos.   • **Item 321-B-1**
RECRUITER JOURNAL. [Monthly]

PURPOSE:– To serve as the house organ of
the U.S. Army Recruiting Service and to be the
medium of exchange of ideas on recruiting and
reenlistment. Presents successful means developed by recruiters and reenlistment personnel so
that others on the same duty may use the same
media. It elaborates and clarifies contents of official directives, etc.
Earlier D 118.9

D 101.106/3 a: • **Item 321-B-2**
RECRUITER JOURNAL (separates).
Consists of materials extracted from
D 101.106/3
Internal use only.

D 101.107:nos.   • **Item 325-D-1 (MF)**
PRACTICAL EXERCISES (series). [Irregular]

Practical exercises, performance guides, self-
instructional texts, information sheets, equipment
manuals, and special texts, pertaining to training
at the U.S. Army Signal Center and Fort Gordon
(Georgia).
Discontinued.

D 101.107/2:nos.
LESSON PERFORMANCE TEST GRADING SHEETS
(series). [Irregular]

D 101.107/3:   • **Item 325-D-1 (MF)**
STUDENT PERFORMANCE GUIDES (series).
[Irregular]
Discontinued.

D 101.107/3-2   • **Item 325-D-1 (MF)**
PERFORMANCE GUIDES (series). [Irregular]
Discontinued.

D 101.107/4:CT   • **Item 325-D-2 (MF)**
COURSE MANAGEMENT PLAN AND PROGRAM OF
INSTRUCTION (series). [Irregular]
Discontinued.

D 101.107/5:nos.   • **Item 325-D-2 (MF)**
READING BOOKS (series). [Irregular]
Discontinued.

D 101.107/6:nos.   • **Item 325-D-1 (MF)**
SELF-INSTRUCTIONAL TEXTS (series). [Irregular]
Discontinued.

D 101.107/7:nos.
PROGRAMMER'S MANUAL (series). [Irregular]

D 101.107/8:nos.   • **Item 325-D-1 (MF)**
INFORMATION SHEETS (series). [Irregular]
Discontinued.

D 101.107/9:nos.
MANUALS (series). [Irregular]

D 101.107/10:nos.   • **Item 325-D-2 (MF)**
PROGRAMMED INSTRUCTION (series). [Irregular]
Discontinued.

D 101.107/11:CT   • **Item 325-D-1 (MF)**
BASIC ELECTRONICS TRAINING (series). [Irregular]
Discontinued.

D 101.107/12:nos.   • **Item 325-D-1 (MF)**
INFORMATION BOOKLETS (series). [Irregular]
Discontinued.

D 101.107/13:letters-nos.   • **Item 325-D-1 (MF)**
EQUIPMENT MANUALS (series). [Irregular]
Discontinued.

D 101.107/14:nos.   • **Item 325-D-1 (MF)**
SPECIAL TEXT (series). [Irregular]
Discontinued.

D 101.107/15:CT   • **Item 325-D-2 (MF)**
PROGRESS CHECK BOOK (series). [Irregular]
Discontinued.

D 101.108:CT   • **Item 325-B-6 (MF)**
TRADOC HISTORICAL MONOGRAPH SERIES.
[Irregular]
TRADOC = Training and Doctrine Command

D 101.108/2   • **Item 325-B-6**
TRADOC HISTORICAL STUDY SERIES.

D 101.109   • **Item 323-G**
ANNUAL HISTORICAL REVIEW, ROCK ISLAND
ARSENAL.
Discontinued.

D 101.110:   • **Item 323-H (MF)**
REPORTS CONTROL SYMBOL DARCOM MANUFAC-
TURING TECHNOLOGY, RCS DRCMT- (series).
[Irregular]

Includes various reports on manufacturing
methods and technology, such as project summary reports, each of which may be updated
annually or semiannually.
Discontinued.

D 101.111   • **Item 322-K-1 (MF)**
REFERENCE BOOK (series). [Irregular]
Discontinued.

D 101.111/2   • **Item 322-K-1 (MF)**
SPECIAL TEXT (series). [Irregular]
Discontinued.

D 101.112   • **Item 325-F-2 (MF)**
ARMY INTELLIGENCE CENTER AND SCHOOL: SupR
(series).
Discontinued.

D 101.112/2:letters-nos.
STUDENT INFORMATION SHEETS (series). [Irregu-
lar]

D 101.113:nos.   • **Item 325-B-11**
LUBRICATION ORDERS, LO- (series). [Irregular]
Lubrication orders for systems such as field
artillery missile systems. The orders are actually
manuals with drawings and instructions for lubricating such systems.
Non-depository.

D 101.114:date&nos.   • **Item 327-H (EL)**
ARMY CHAMPLAINCY [Quarterly]
Earlier D 101.22:165
Continues Military Chaplains' Review

D 101.115:date   • **Item 322-K-3 (MF)**
BELVOIR RESEARCH AND DEVELOPMENT CENTER:
CONTAINER SYSTEM HARDWARE STATUS RE-
PORT. [Annual]
This report deals with the necessity for the
U.S. Army to rely on the use of containers in
shipping all commodities as a result of a shift by
the Merchant Marine industry from the breakbulk
fleet to containerships.
Discontinued.

D 101.116:date   • **Item 325-F-3**
DETECTIVE. [Semiannual]

Contains articles providing information on
criminal investigative techniques to U.S. Army
Criminal Investigation Command special agents
and staff members as well as to other members
of the military and civilian law enforcement communities.
Formerly issued Quarterly.
Discontinued.

D 101.117:v.nos.&nos.   • **Item 325-B-15 (EL)**
AFIP LETTER. [Bimonthly]
AFIP = Armed Forces Institute of Pathology.
Contains short news items on activities of
the Armed Forces Institute of Pathology.

D 101.117/3:nos.   • **Item 310-D**
TUMORS OF THE ADRENAL, SECOND SERIES.
[Irregular]
Earlier D 1.16/3
Non-government publication.

D 101.117/4:nos.   • **Item 310-D**
ATLAS OF TUMOR PATHOLOGY, THIRD SERIES.

D 101.117/5   • **Item 310-D-1 (MF)**
AFIP (Armed Forces Institute of Pathology) ANNUAL
REPORT.

D 101.117/6   • **Item 310-D-2 (MF)**
ARMED FORCES INSTITUTE OF PATHOLOGY
ANNUAL RESEARCH PROGRAMS REPORT.

D 101.117/7:date   • **Item 325-B-26 (EL)**
LEGAL MEDICINE OPEN FILE. [Annual]

D 101.118:date   • **Item 327-E**
OFFICERS' CALL. [Bimonthly]
Former title: Commanders' Call (D 101.22:360).
Discontinued.

D 101.118/2:date   • **Item 327-E**
COMMANDERS' NOTES. [Bimonthly]
Discontinued.

D 101.118/3:date   • **Item 327-E**
NCO CALL.
Previous title: Sargents Business
Discontinued.

D 101.118/4:date   • **Item 327-E**
SOLDIERS' SCENE. [Bimonthly]
Discontinued.

D 101.118/5:nos.   • **Item 327-E-1**
COMMAND INFORMATION PACKAGE.
See D 101.2:C73/13/

D 101.119:date   • **Item 325-B**
LOGISTICS SYSTEMS. [Annual]
Earlier D 101.6/5
Discontinued.

D 101.120:CT   • **Item 325-M**
DIRECTORIES. [Irregular]

D 101.120/2:date   • **Item 325-M-1**
WORLDWIDE PUBLIC AFFAIRS OFFICES DIREC-
TORY. [Annual]

PURPOSE:– To list key personnel of public
affairs offices and activities associated with the
U.S. Army, listed by state and by countries.
Discontinued.

D 101.120/4:date   • **Item 325-M-2**
GARRISON COMMANDERS DIRECTORY. [Annual]

D 101.121:date   • **Item 325-B-16 (MF)**
ARMY BUDGET, FISCAL YEAR.

D 101.121/2:date   • **Item 325-B-29**
FISCAL YEAR BUDGET ESTIMATES.

D 101.122:   • **Item 325-R (MF)**
SAGAMORE ARMY MATERIALS RESEARCH CON-
FERENCE PROCEEDINGS (series).

The proceedings of each research conference are expected to relate to a different topic.
Discontinued.

D 101.123   • **Item 307-A-8 (EL)**
ARMY FAMILIES. [Quarterly]

D 101.124:v.nos./nos.   • **Item 325-F-3**
SPECIAL WARFARE (The Professional Bulletin of the
John F. Kennedy Special Warfare Center &
School).

D 101.125:v.nos./nos.   • **Item 307-A-8 (EL)**
COUNTERMEASURE.

D 101.127:v.nos./nos.   • Item 327-E (EL)
THE NCO JOURNAL. [Quarterly]

D 101.128   • Item 307-A-8 (EL)
MERCURY. [Monthly]

D 101.129/3:date   • Item 307-A-4 (E)
MILITARY TRAFFIC MANAGEMENT COMMAND PUB-
    LICATIONS. [Quarterly]
    Issued on CD-ROM
    Discontinued.

D 101.129/4:date   • Item 327-P-1 (EL)
ELECTRONIC FORMS. [Annual]
    Issued on CD-ROM.

D 101.129/5:date   • Item 307-A-6 (CD)
AMC CD-ROM. PUBLICATIONS. [Annual]
    Official use only.

D 101.129/6:CT   • Item 307-A-8 (E)
ELECTRONIC PRODUCTS.

D 101.130:date   • Item 325-B
ENVIRONMENTAL COMPLIANCE ASSESSMENT SYS-
    TEM (ECAS) ANNUAL REPORT.
    Discontinued.

D 101.131   • Item 325-F-5 (MF)
USAAVSCOM TM (series).

D 101.132   • Item 325-F-6 (MF)
USAAVSCOM TR (series).
    See D 101.134

D 101.133   • Item 324-A-1 (MF)
ARL-TR (series).

D 101.136:   • Item 307-A-8 (EL)
EMPLOYEE RELATIONS BULLETIN.

D 101.137:   • Item 307-A-8 (EL)
TAPES NEWSLETTER.

D 101.138:   • Item 307-A-8 (EL)
CIVILIAN PERSONNEL BULLETINS (CPBs).

D 101.139:   • Item 307-A-8 (EL)
PUBLICATIONS BULLETIN.

D 101.140:   • Item 307-A-8 (EL)
SES BULLETINS.

D 101.141:   • Item 307-A-8 (EL)
ARMY ECHOES.

D 101.142:   • Item 307-A-8 (EL)
INSTALLATIONS: NEWS FOR AND ABOUT BASOPS.

D 101.143:   • Item 307-A-8 (EL)
ECONOMIC BULLETINS. [Monthly].

D 101.144:   • Item 307-A-8 (EL)
TALON.

D 101.145:   • Item 307-A-8 (E)
CATALYST.
    Suspended.

D 101.146:   • Item 307-A-8 (EL)
STRATEGIC STUDIES INSTITUTE, GENERAL PUB-
    LICATIONS.

D 101.146/2   • Item 307-A-17
STRATEGIC STUDIES INSTITUTE, CONFERENCE
    REPORT.

D 101.146/3   • Item 307-A-18
LETORT PAPERS. (Series)

D 101.146/4   • Item 307-A-19
ARMY ISSUE PAPER. (Series)

D 101.146/5   • Item 307-A-22
IMPLEMENTING PLAN COLOMBIA. (Special Series)

D 101.146/6   • Item 307-A-23 (EL)
STRATEGY CONFERENCE SERIES.

D 101.146/7   • Item 307-A-24
STRATEGIC STUDIES INSTITUTE, SPECIAL REPORT.

D 101.146/8   • Item 307-A-25 (EL)
STUDIES IN ASYMMETRY. (Series)

D 101.147   • Item 307-A-8 (EL)
RED THRUST STAR.

ADJUTANT GENERAL'S OFFICE
(1949–   )

CREATION AND AUTHORITY

The Adjutant General's Department is subordinate to the Department of the Army; which was
made a military department within the Department
of Defense in lieu of its prior status as an executive department within the National Military Establishment, by Public Law 216, 81st Congress,
approved August 10, 1949.

INFORMATION
    The Adjutant General's Office
    Department of the Army
    The Pentagon
    Room 2E532
    Washington, D.C. 20310

D 102.1:date   • Item 368
ANNUAL REPORTS.
    Discontinued.

D 102.2:CT   • Item 331
GENERAL PUBLICATIONS.
    Earlier M 108.2

D 102.6:CT
REGULATIONS, RULES, AND INSTRUCTIONS.

D 102.6/2:CT   • Item 331-A
HANDBOOKS, MANUALS, GUIDES.

D 102.7:nos.
CONSOLIDATED REPORT OF ACCESSIONS.
    [Monthly]
    Earlier M 108.9

D 102.8:v.nos.
TRIALS OF WAR CRIMINALS BEFORE NUREMBERG
    MILITARY TRIBUNALS.
    Discontinued.

D 102.9
ARMY REGISTER. 1813–   [Annual]

    Issued in the following three volumes:

        Vol. 1. United States Army Active and Re-
            tired List.
        Vol. 2. Army of the United States and Other
            Retired Lists.
        Vol. 3. Officers' Honorary Retired List.

    Also published in the House Documents se-
ries.
    Discontinued.

D 102.10:date
ARMY HIT KIT OF POPULAR SONGS. [Monthly]
    Earlier M 117.7
    Later D 1.14

D 102.11:CT   • Item 332-A
SUPREME COMMANDER FOR ALLIED POWERS,
    PUBLICATIONS.
    Earlier W 1.84
    Discontinued.

D 102.11/2:date
EXPORTS AND IMPORTS. [Monthly]

D 102.11/3:date
REPORT OF JAPAN'S EXPORT SHIPMENTS AND
    IMPORT RECEIPTS STATED BY AREAS AND
    COUNTRIES OF DESTINATION AND ORIGIN,
    WITH VALUE EXPRESSED IN UNITED STATES
    DOLLARS. [Monthly]

D 102.11/4:date
MONTHLY JAPANESE FOREIGN TRADE STATISTICS.

D 102.12:nos.
NATURAL RESOURCES SECTION WEEKLY SUM-
    MARY.

D 102.13:nos.
WEEKLY REPORT ON JAPAN.
    Earlier M 105.22

D 102.14:nos.
MEMORANDUM FOR JAPANESE GOVERNMENT.
    Earlier M 105.23

D 102.15:nos.
SCIENCE AND TECHNOLOGY IN JAPAN, REPORTS.
    Earlier M 105.24

D 102.16:nos.
OFFICIAL GAZETTE [Japanese] ENGLISH EDITION.

D 102.17:nos.
[MEMORANDUM OF INFORMATION.]

D 102.18:nos.&se.nos.
SUPREME COMMANDER FOR ALLIED POWERS:
    JAPANESE ECONOMIC STATISTICS BULLETIN.
    [Monthly]

D 102.19:nos.
MILITARY GOVERNMENT OF RYUKYU ISLANDS:
    RYUKYU STATISTICAL BULLETIN. [Monthly]

D 102.19/2:nos.
UNITED STATES CIVIL ADMINISTRATION OF RYUKYU
    ISLANDS; SPECIAL BULLETINS.

D 102.19/3:nos.
CIVIL AFFAIRS ACTIVITIES IN RYUKYU ISLANDS.
    [Semiannual]

D 102.19/4:date
RYUKYU ISLANDS, ANNUAL REPORT TO FOOD AND
    AGRICULTURE ORGANIZATION OF THE UNITED
    NATIONS.

D 102.20:nos.
SUPREME COMMANDER FOR ALLIED POWERS:
    NATURAL RESOURCES SECTION REPORTS.
    Earlier W 1.80
    Later M 105.25

D 102.20/2:nos.
NATURAL RESOURCES SECTION, PRELIMINARY
    STUDY.
    Earlier W 1.80/2

D 102.21:nos.
TECHNICAL PAPERS.

D 102.22:nos.
GAZETTE OF THE ALLIED COMMISSION FOR AUS-
    TRIA. [Monthly]
    Earlier W 1.82

D 102.23:date
DEPARTMENT OF ARMY CHIEFS AND EXECUTIVES
    (organization chart). [Quarterly]
    Earlier D 101.36

D 102.24:nos.
ARMY FORCES FAR EAST, AFFE PAMPHLETS.

D 102.25:CT
ADJUTANT GENERAL'S SCHOOL, FORT BENJAMIN
    HARRISON, INDIANA, REPORTS AND PUBLICA-
    TIONS.

D 102.26:CT
POSTERS.

D 102.27:nos.
PRB TECHNICAL RESEARCH NOTES.
    Earlier D 101.60

D 102.27/2:nos.
PRB TECHNICAL RESEARCH REPORTS.
    Earlier D 101.60/2

D 102.27/3:nos.
PRB REPORTS.

D 102.28   • Item 332-B
SPECIAL BIBLIOGRAPHIES. 1–   [Irregular]
Discontinued.

D 102.28/2:CT
BIBLIOGRAPHIES AND LISTS OF PUBLICATIONS.

D 102.28/3:nos.
SELECTED CURRENT ACQUISITIONS, LISTS.

D 102.28/4:nos.
SPECIAL LISTS.
Issued by Army Library.

D 102.28/5:nos.
SELECTED PERIODICAL LITERATURE, LISTS.

D 102.29:nos.
SPECIAL STUDIES.

D 102.75:CT
RECRUITING PUBLICITY BUREAU PUBLICATIONS.
Earlier M 108.75

D 102.76:v.nos.   • Item 332-C
RECRUITING JOURNAL. [Monthly]
Earlier M 108.80
Later D 118.9
Discontinued.

D 102.77:v.nos.
LIFE OF SOLDIER AND AIRMAN. [Monthly]
Earlier M 108.77

D 102.78:nos.
RECRUITING PUBLICITY BUREAU POSTERS.
Earlier M 108.78

D 102.79:nos.
PRS NOS. (Personnel Research Section)

D 102.80:date   • Item 332-D
TIPS, ARMY PERSONNEL MAGAZINE. [Quarterly]
(U.S. Army Personnel Information Activity, Army
Adjutant General School)

PURPOSE:– To provide information and guidance on all phases of military personnel operations.
Discontinued.

D 102.81:v.nos.&nos.   • Item 332-E
ACCESS.
Earlier title: Community and Family Sentinel.
Discontinued.

D 102.82:date   • Item 332-G (MF)
ARMY CLUB SYSTEM, ANNUAL REPORT.

PURPOSE:– To summarize the financial activities of Army Clubs in the United States and
abroad, including achievements in training, personnel, entertainment, procurement, and other
programs.

D 102.82/2:date   • Item 332-G (MF)
ARMY MORALE, WELFARE, AND RECREATION,
FISCAL YEAR ANNUAL REPORT.

Former title: Army Morale Support Fund, Annual Report.

D 102.83:v.nos.&nos.   • Item 332-H (EL)
INFANTRY. v. 1–   [Quarterly] (Army Infantry School)

PURPOSE:– To provide current information
on infantry organization, weapons, equipment,
tactics, and techniques; and to serve as a forum
for professional ideas.
Sub-title: A Professional Journal for the Combined Arms Team.

D 102.84:v.nos.&nos.   • Item 332-J (MF)
WOLVERINE GUARD. [Monthly]

Publication of the Adjutant General's Office
in Lansing, Michigan. Contains articles pertaining
to the Army National Guard.

CORPS OF ENGINEERS
(1949–   )

CREATION AND AUTHORITY

The Engineer Department (M 110), Army Department, was made subordinate to the Department of Defense under Provisions of Public law
216, 81st Congress, approved Aug. 10, 1949.

INFORMATION

Public Affairs Office
Chief of Engineers
Washington, D.C. 20314
(202) 761-0001
http://www.hqda.army.mil/daen

PUBLICATIONS

Publications Office
Chief of Engineers
U.S. Army
Washington, D.C. 20310

D 103.1   • Item 334 (MF)
ANNUAL REPORT OF THE CHIEF OF ENGINEERS,
ARMY, ON CIVIL WORKS ACTIVITIES. [Annual]

Report covers fiscal year and is issued in two
volumes. Volume 1 covers civil work activities in
the field of rivers and harbors, flood control, beach
erosion control, and related purposes. Volume 2
contains specific project data.
Also issued in House Document Series.

D 103.1/a:date   • Item 334
– SEPARATES.

D 103.1/2   • Item 334 (MF)
WATERBORNE COMMERCE OF THE UNITED STATES.
[Annual]

Beginning with the Calendar Year 1953, the
Statistics of Waterborne Commerce has been
published in five parts by the regional offices of
the Corps of Engineers. Prior to 1953, the statis-
tics were published annually as Part 2 of the
Annual Report of the Chief of Engineers.
Tables give tonnage of freight traffic by com-
modities; comparative statement of traffic, trips
and drafts of vessels.
Parts include:
Part 2. Gulf Coast, Mississippi River
System and Antilles (Puerto
Rico and Virgin Islands).
Part 3. Great Lakes Area.
Part 4. Pacific coast, Alaska, and Pacific
Islands Area.
Part 5. National Summaries.
Supplement 1. Domestic Inland Traffic
Areas of Origin and
Destination of Principal
Commodities.
Supplement 2. Water Carriage Ton-Miles.

D 103.1/3:date   • Item 334-A-5
GREAT LAKES–ST. LAWRENCE SEAWAY WINTER
NAVIGATION BOARD: ANNUAL REPORT.
Discontinued.

D 103.1/4:date   • Item 334 (MF)
ANNUAL REPORT OF THE CHIEF OF ENGINEERS
ON CIVIL WORKS ACTIVITIES, EXTRACT
REPORTS OF THE LOWER MISSISSIPPI VAL-
LEY DIVISION AND MISSISSIPPI RIVER COM-
MISSION. [Annual]

D 103.2:CT   • Item 337
GENERAL PUBLICATIONS.

D 103.2:B 76   • Item 337
BRIDGES OVER NAVIGABLE WATERS OF THE
UNITED STATES.

Contains a list of the locations and owner
of each bridge over navigable waters of the

United States, and gives such pertinent information as the distance from the mouth of
the body of water it spans, type of bridge,
clearance (horizontal and vertical), date plans
were approved, and type of traffic traveling
over the bridge.

Issued in the following parts:
Part 1. Atlantic Coast.
Part 2. Gulf and Mississippi River
System.
Part 3. Great Lakes.
Part 4. Pacific Coast.
Since 1961 issued by Coast Guard (TD
5.2:B 76).

D 103.4   • Item 337-B-2 (MF)
CIRCULARS, EC- (series). [Irregular]

D 103.6:CT   • Item 341
REGULATIONS, RULES, AND INSTRUCTIONS.
Earlier M 110.6

D 103.6/2:cap.nos.   • Item 341
ORDERS AND REGULATIONS.
Earlier W 7.8/2

D 103.6/3   • Item 338-A
MANUALS, EM- (series). [Irregular]

D 103.6/4   • Item 341 (MF)
REGULATIONS, ER- (series). [Irregular]

D 103.6/5:CT   • Item 337-B
HANDBOOKS, MANUALS, GUIDES.

D 103.6/6   • Item 337-B
DG (series).
DG = Design Guide.

D 103.6/7:CT   • Item 337-B-15
LESSONS (series). [Irregular]
Earlier D 103.6/5

D 103.6/8:nos.   • Item 337-B-15
INSTRUCTIONAL MATERIALS . . . FOR U.S. ARMY
RESERVE SCHOOLS. [Irregular]

D 103.7:dt.&nos.
GENERAL ORDERS.
Earlier M 110.14

D 103.8:no./date   • Item 340
PORT SERIES. 1–   1921–   [Irregular]

Gives pertinent data on port facilities, such
as harbor conditions, port customs, regulations,
services, fuel and supplies, loading and shipping
facilities, regulations, commerce of the port.

D 103.9:pt.nos.&chap.nos.   • Item 336
ENGINEERING MANUAL FOR MILITARY CONSTRUC-
TION.
Earlier M 110.13
Discontinued.

D 103.9/2:nos.
GUIDE SPECIFICATIONS FOR MILITARY CONSTRUC-
TION.

D 103.9/3:nos.
GUIDE SPECIFICATION FOR CIVIL WORKS CON-
STRUCTION.

D 103.10   • Item 343
TRANSPORTATION SERIES. 1–   1926–
Covers transportation lines and cargo ves-
sels.
Issued for the following parts:

3. Great Lakes System.
4. Mississippi River System and the Gulf
Intercoastal Waterway. ISSN 0361-8986
5. Atlantic, Gulf, and Pacific Coasts. ISSN
0361-0125
Discontinued.

D 103.11:nos.   • Item 339
MISCELLANEOUS SERIES.
Earlier M 110.12
Discontinued.

D 103.12:date
INDEX OF SPECIFICATIONS USED BY CORPS OF ENGINEERS.
    Earlier M 110.9

D 103.13:date
STATISTICAL REPORT OF MARINE COMMERCE OF DULUTH-SUPERIOR HARBOR, MINN. AND WIS.

D 103.14:pt.nos.chap.nos. • Item 335
ENGINEERING MANUAL, CIVIL WORKS CONSTRUCTION.
    Earlier M 110.7
    Discontinued.

BEACH EROSION BOARD

D 103.15:nos. • Item 342
TECHNICAL REPORTS.
    Earlier M 110.307
    Discontinued.

D 103.15/2:nos.
MISCELLANEOUS PAPERS.

D 103.16:v.nos.&nos.
BULLETIN OF BEACH EROSION BOARD. [Quarterly]
    Earlier M 110.303

Corps of Engineers (Continued)

D 103.17:date • Item 341-A
ST. MAYS FALLS CANAL, MICH., STATISTICAL REPORT OF LAKE COMMERCE PASSING THROUGH CANALS AT SAULT STE. MARIE, MICH., AND ONTARIO.
    Earlier M 110.16
    Discontinued.

D 103.17/2
STATISTICAL REPORT OF COMMERCE PASSING THROUGH CANALS AT SAULTE STE. MARIE, MICH. AND ONTARIO, SALT WATER SHIP MOVEMENTS FOR SEASON OF (year). [Annual]

D 103.18 • Item 337-A
LAKE SERIES. 1–   1931–

    Gives pertinent data on port facilities, such as harbor conditions, port customs, regulations, services, fuel and supplies, loading and shipping facilities, regulations, commerce of the port, for the ports located in the Great Lakes region.
    Discontinued.

D 103.19:nos.
TECHNICAL MEMORANDUM OF BEACH EROSION BOARD.
    Earlier M 110.308

ARMY MAP SERVICE

D 103.20:CT
PUBLICATIONS.
    Earlier W 7.33

D 103.20/2:nos.
AMS TECHNICAL MANUALS.

D 103.20/3:nos.
BULLETINS.
    Earlier M 110.20

D 103.20/4:nos.
TECHNICAL REPORTS.

D 103.20/6:nos. • Item 334-A-28 (MF)
ETL- (series). [Irregular] (Engineer Topographic Laboratories)
    Discontinued.

D 103.20/7:date • Item 334-A-1
ARMY BATTLEFIELD ENVIRONMENT.
    Bulletins consist of unclassified information on such topics as battlefield environments, space activities, field exercises and work related to military applications of environmental sciences and technology.
    Earlier title: Army Environmental Sciences.
    Discontinued.

D 103.20/8:v.nos./nos. • Item 334-A-31 (MF)
DIGITAL DATA DIGEST. [Quarterly]

Corps of Engineers (Continued)

D 103.21:chap.nos. • Item 336
ENGINEERING MANUAL FOR EMERGENCY CONSTRUCTION.
    Discontinued.

D 103.21/2:nos.
GUIDE SPECIFICATIONS FOR EMERGENCY-TYPE MILITARY CONSTRUCTION. Desig CE-E-nos.

D 103.22 • Item 334-A
[ENGINEER REPORTS.] [Irregular]
    Reports to Congress on individual engineering projects performed by the Corps of Engineers. Also published in the House Documents series.

D 103.22/2:date • Item 334-A (MF)
PROJECTS RECOMMENDED FOR DEAUTHORIZATION, ANNUAL REPORT. 1st–   1975–
    Also issued in House Document Series.
    Discontinued.

D 103.22/3 • Item 337-B-18
DEH DIGEST. [Bimonthly]

D 103.23:CT
BOARD OF ENGINEERS FOR RIVERS AND HARBORS, REPORT OF HEARINGS.

WATERWAYS EXPERIMENT STATION
Vicksburg, Mississippi

D 103.24:nos.
BULLETINS.

D 103.24/2:letters-nos. • Item 334-A-16 (MF)
TECHNICAL REPORTS. [Irregular]

    Covers preliminary or final results of assigned engineering investigations.
    Supersedes Technical Memorandum series.

D 103.24/3:nos.
TRANSLATIONS.

D 103.24/4 • Item 334-A-7 (MF)
MISCELLANEOUS PAPERS. [Irregular]
    Includes reports, professional papers, interoffice or intra-office memoranda, published principally for record purposes and which have no prescribed distribution.

D 103.24/5 • Item 334-A-19 (MF)
RESEARCH REPORTS. [Irregular]
    Reports of basic research studies.

D 103.24/6 • Item 334-A-12 (MF)
LIST OF PUBLICATIONS OF THE ARMY ENGINEER WATERWAYS EXPERIMENT STATION AVAILABLE FOR PURCHASE. [Annual]

D 103.24/7 • Item 334-A-7 (MF)
INSTRUCTION REPORTS. [Irregular]
    Publications containing instructions or guidance for making tests, operating equipment, or similar purposes.

D 103.24/8:nos.
ANNUAL SUMMARY OF INVESTIGATIONS IN SUPPORT OF CIVIL WORKS PROGRAM FOR CALENDAR YEAR.

D 103.24/9:letters-nos. • Item 334-A-7 (MF)
CONTRACT REPORTS. [Irregular]

D 103.24/10
WATERWAYS EXPERIMENT STATION CAPABILITIES. [Irregular]

D 103.24/11:nos.
WATERWAYS EXPERIMENT STATION, EERO TECHNICAL REPORT. (Explosives Excavation Research Office)

D 103.24/12:nos.
PAVEMENTS AND SOIL TRAFFICABILITY INFORMATION ANALYSIS CENTER, PSTIAC REPORTS. [Irregular]

D 103.24/13:nos.
AQUATIC PLANT CONTROL PROGRAM, TECHNICAL REPORTS [Irregular]

D 103.24/14:nos. • Item 334-A-16 (EL)
WIS REPORTS (series). [Irregular]

    WIS = Wave Information Study.

D 103.24/15:nos. • Item 334-A-27 (MF)
WATER OPERATIONS TECHNICAL SUPPORT: WOTS. [Irregular]

    Earlier title: Environmental and Water Quality Operations Studies.

D 103.24/16:ltrs.&nos.
ENVIRONMENTAL EFFECTS OF DREDGING. [Irregular]

D 103.24/19 • Item 334-A-28 (MF)
EIRS BULLETIN. [Irregular]

Corps of Engineers (Continued)

D 103.25:nos.
ENGINEER RESEARCH AND DEVELOPMENT LABORATORIES REPORTS.

D 103.25/2
TECHNICAL REPORTS, TR- (series). 1–   [Irregular]

D 103.26:nos.
SIPRE REPORTS.

D 103.27 • Item 335-C (MF)
ANNUAL FISH PASSAGE REPORT, NORTH PACIFIC DIVISIONS. [Annual]

    Includes Bonneville, The Dalles, McNary and Ice Harbor Dams, Columbia and Snake Rivers, Oregon and Washington.
    Prepared by Army Engineer Districts, Portland and Walla Walla.
    Discontinued.

D 103.27/2:nos.
BONNEVILLE HYDRAULIC LABORATORY, REPORTS.

D 103.28:nos.
REPORTS OF COMMITTEE ON TIDAL HYDRAULICS.

D 103.28/2:nos.
TECHNICAL BULLETIN OF COMMITTEE ON TIDAL HYDRAULICS.

D 103.29:nos.
ENGINEER INTELLIGENCE NOTES.

D 103.30
PRESS RELEASES. [Irregular]

D 103.30/2:date
ARKANSAS RIVER WATER BASIN NEWS.

D 103.30/3:date
PRESS RELEASE: ARKANSAS WATER BASIN NEWS.

ARCTIC CONSTRUCTION AND FROST EFFECTS LABORATORY

D 103.31:nos.
TECHNICAL REPORTS.

D 103.31/2:nos.
MISCELLANEOUS PAPERS.

D 103.31/3:nos.
TRANSLATIONS.

Corps of Engineers (Continued)

D 103.32:nos.
MILITARY HYDROLOGY BULLETINS.

ARMY COLD REGIONS RESEARCH AND ENGINEERING LABORATORY
Hanover, New Hampshire 03755

D 103.33
TECHNICAL REPORTS. [Irregular]

D 103.33/2:nos.   • Item 335-B (MF)
SPECIAL REPORTS.

D 103.33/3/letters-nos.
RESEARCH REPORTS. 1–   [Irregular]

D 103.33/4
TRANSLATIONS (series). 1–   [Irregular]

D 103.33/5:CT
GENERAL PUBLICATIONS.

D 103.33/6:date
LIST OF PUBLICATIONS.

D 103.33/7:nos.   • Item 335-B (MF)
CRREL MONOGRAPHS. [Irregular]
    CRREL = Cold Regions Rsearch and Engineering Laboratory.

D 103.33/8:date
CRREL IN ALASKA, ANNUAL REPORT (year).
    Gives account of the work performed in Alaska during the year by the Cold Regions Research and Engineering Laboratory.
    Contains bibliographies.

D 103.33/9:date
RESEARCH DIVISION, QUARTERLY PROGRESS REPORT. – Jan.-Mar. 1974.

D 103.33/10:date
QUARTERLY PROGRESS REPORT. – July-Sept. 1973.

D 103.33/11:date
R & D NOTES. [Irregular]

D 103.33/12:nos.   • Item 335-B (MF)
CRREL REPORTS. [Irregular]

D 103.33/13   • Item 335-B-1 (MF)
COLD REGIONS TECHNICAL DIGEST.

D 103.33/14:nos.
COLD REGIONS TECHNICAL DIGEST (series). [Irregular]

Corps of Engineers (Continued)

D 103.34:nos.
RECRUITMENT ANNOUNCEMENTS. ADMIN.

D 103.35:CT   • Item 334-A-6
WATER RESOURCES DEVELOPMENT BY ARMY CORPS OF ENGINEERS IN [State]. [Irregular]
    Earlier D 103.2:W 29

D 103.35/1:date   • Item 335-A-1
WATER RESOURCES DEVELOPMENT IN ALABAMA. [Biennial]

D 103.35/2:date   • Item 335-A-2
WATER RESOURCES DEVELOPMENT IN ALASKA. [Biennial]

D 103.35/3:date   • Item 335-A-3
WATER RESOURCES DEVELOPMENT IN ARIZONA. [Biennial]

D 103.35/4:date   • Item 335-A-4
WATER RESOURCES DEVELOPMENT IN ARKANSAS. [Biennial]

D 103.35/5:date   • Item 335-A-5
WATER RESOURCES DEVELOPMENT IN CALIFORNIA. [Biennial]

D 103.35/6:date   • Item 335-A-6
WATER RESOURCES DEVELOPMENT IN COLORADO. [Biennial]

D 103.35/7:date   • Item 335-A-7
WATER RESOURCES DEVELOPMENT IN CONNECTICUT. [Biennial]

D 103.35/8:date   • Item 335-A-8
WATER RESOURCES DEVELOPMENT IN DELAWARE IN (year). [Biennial]
    Earlier D 103.35:D 37

D 103.35/9:date   • Item 335-A-9
WATER RESOURCES DEVELOPMENT IN FLORIDA. [Biennial]

D 103.35/10:date   • Item 335-A-10
WATER RESOURCES DEVELOPMENT IN GEORGIA. [Biennial]

D 103.35/11:date   • Item 335-A-11
WATER RESOURCES DEVELOPMENT IN HAWAII. [Biennial]

D 103.35/12:date   • Item 335-A-12
WATER RESOURCES DEVELOPMENT IN IDAHO. [Biennial]
    Earlier D 103.35:Id 1

D 103.35/13:   • Item 335-A-13
WATER RESOURCES DEVELOPMENT IN ILLINOIS. [Biennial]

D 103.35/14:date   • Item 335-A-14
WATER RESOURCES DEVELOPMENT IN INDIANA. [Annual]

D 103.35/15:   • Item 335-A-15
WATER RESOURCES DEVELOPMENT IN IOWA. [Biennial]

D 103.35/16:date   • Item 335-A-16
WATER RESOURCES DEVELOPMENT IN KANSAS. [Biennial]

D 103.35/17:date   • Item 335-A-17
WATER RESOURCES DEVELOPMENT IN KENTUCKY. [Annual].

D 103.35/18:date   • Item 335-A-18
WATER RESOURCES DEVELOPMENT IN LOUISIANA. [Biennial]

D 103.35/19:date   • Item 335-A-19
WATER RESOURCES DEVELOPMENT IN MAINE. [Biennial]

D 103.35/20:date   • Item 335-A-20
WATER RESOURCES DEVELOPMENT IN MARYLAND. [Quadrennial]
    Earlier D 103.35:M 36

103.35/21:date   • Item 335-A-21
WATER RESOURCES DEVELOPMENT IN MASSACHUSETTS. [Biennial]

D 103.35/22:date   • Item 335-A-22
WATER RESOURCES DEVELOPMENT IN MICHIGAN. [Biennial]

D 103.35/23:date   • Item 335-A-23
WATER RESOURCES DEVELOPMENT IN MINNESOTA. [Annual]

D 103.35/24:date   • Item 335-A-24
WATER RESOURCES DEVELOPMENT IN MISSISSIPPI. [Biennial]

D 103.35/25:date   • Item 335-A-25
WATER RESOURCES DEVELOPMENT IN MISSOURI. [Irregular]
    Earlier D 103.35:M 69 o

D 103.35/26:date   • Item 335-A-26
WATER RESOURCES DEVELOPMENT IN MONTANA. [Biennial]

D 103.35/27:date   • Item 335-A-27
WATER RESOURCES DEVELOPMENT IN NEBRASKA. [Biennial]

D 103.35/28:date   • Item 335-A-28
WATER RESOURCES DEVELOPMENT IN NEVADA. [Biennial]

D 103.35/29:date   • Item 335-A-29
WATER RESOURCES DEVELOPMENT IN NEW HAMPSHIRE. [Biennial]

D 103.35/30:date   • Item 335-A-30
WATER RESOURCES DEVELOPMENT IN NEW JERSEY (year). [Biennial]
    Earlier D 103.25

D 103.35/31:   • Item 335-A-31
WATER RESOURCES DEVELOPMENT IN NEW MEXICO. [Biennial]

D 103.35/32:date   • Item 335-A-32
WATER RESOURCES DEVELOPMENT IN NEW YORK. [Quadrennial]
    Earlier D 103.35:N 42 y

D 103.35/33:date   • Item 335-A-33
WATER RESOURCES DEVELOPMENT IN NORTH CAROLINA. [Irregular]

D 103.35/34:date   • Item 335-A-34
WATER RESOURCES DEVELOPMENT IN NORTH DAKOTA. [Biannual]
    Earlier D 103.35:N 81 d

D 103.35/35:date   • Item 335-A-35
WATER RESOURCES DEVELOPMENT IN OHIO. [Biennnial]

D 103.35/36:date   • Item 335-A-36
WATER RESOURCES DEVELOPMENT IN OKLAHOMA. [Biennial]

D 103.35/37;date   • Item 335-A-37
WATER RESOURCES DEVELOPMENT IN OREGON. [Biennial]

D 103.35/38:date   • Item 335-A-38
WATER RESOURCES DEVELOPMENT IN PENNSYLVANIA. [Biennial]

D 103.35/39:date   • Item 335-A-39
WATER RESOURCES DEVELOPMENT IN RHODE ISLAND. [Biennial]

D 103.35/41:date   • Item 335-A-41
WATER RESOURCES DEVELOPMENT IN SOUTH DAKOTA. [Biennial]

D 103.35/42:date   • Item 335-A-42
WATER RESOURCES DEVELOPMENT IN TENNESSEE. [Biennial]

D 103.35/43:date   • Item 335-A-43
WATER RESOURCES DEVELOPMENT IN TEXAS. [Biennial]

D 103.35/44:date   • Item 335-A-44
WATER RESOURCES DEVELOPMENT IN UTAH. [Biennial]

D 103.35/45:date   • Item 335-A-45
WATER RESOURCES DEVELOPMENT IN VERMONT. [Biennial]

D 103.35/46:date   • Item 335-A-46
WATER RESOURCES DEVELOPMENT IN VIRGINIA. [Quadrennial]

D 103.35/47:date   • Item 335-A-47
WATER RESOURCES DEVELOPMENT IN WASHINGTON. [Biennial]

D 103.35/48:date   • Item 335-A-48
WATER RESOURCES DEVELOPMENT IN WEST VIRGINIA. [Biennial]

D 103.35/49:   • Item 335-A-49
WATER RESOURCES DEVELOPMENT IN WISCONSIN. [Annual]

D 103.35/50:date   • Item 335-A-50
WATER RESOURCES DEVELOPMENT IN WYOMING. [Biennial]

D 103.35/51:date   • Item 335-A-49
WATER RESOURCES DEVELOPMENT IN DISTRICT OF COLUMBIA. [Irregular]
    Earlier D 103.35:D 63

D 103.35/52:date   • Item 335-A-52
WATER RESOURCES DEVELOPMENT, U.S. SUMMARY.

D 103.35/53:date • Item 335-A-53
WATER RESOURCES DEVELOPMENT IN (OUTLYING AREAS).

D 103.36 • Item 334-B
DIGEST OF DECISIONS OF CORPS OF ENGINEERS BOARD OF CONTRACT APPEALS. v. 1– 1954/59– [Annual]
Discontinued.

ARMY POLAR RESEARCH AND DEVELOPMENT CENTER FORT BELVOIR

D 103.37:CT
GENERAL PUBLICATIONS.

D 103.37/2:nos.
REPORTS.

OHIO RIVER DIVISION LABORATORIES

D 103.38:nos.
TECHNICAL REPORTS. [Irregular]

D 103.38/2:nos.
MISCELLANEOUS PAPERS. [Irregular]

D 103.38/3
TECHNICAL MEMORANDUMS. [Irregular]

Corps of Engineers (Continued)

D 103.39:CT • Item 334-A-22
BIBLIOGRAPHIES AND LISTS OF PUBLICATIONS.

D 103.39:P 96/date
PUBLICATIONS AVAILABLE FOR PURCHASE, U.S. ARMY ENGINEER WATERWAYS EXPERIMENT STATION AND OTHER CORPS OF ENGINEERS AGENCIES. [Annual] (Army Engineer Waterways Experiment Station, Box 60, Vicksburg, Mississippi 39180)

D 103.40:CT/dt.
MILITARY GEOLOGY (series).

MISSOURI RIVER DIVISION

D 103.41:nos.
M.R.D. SEDIMENT SERIES.

D 103.41/2:date
MISSOURI RIVER MAIN STEM RESERVIORS, ANNUAL OPERATING PLAN AND SUMMARY OF ACTUAL OPERATION.

D 103.41/3:nos.
MISSOURI RIVER MAIN STREAM RESERVOIR REGULATION STUDIES.

COASTAL ENGINEERING RESEARCH CENTER 5201 Little Falls Road, N.W. Washington, D.C. 20016

D 103.42
TECHNICAL MEMORANDUMS. 1– 1964– [Irregular]

D 103.42/2
MISCELLANEOUS PAPERS. 1– 1954– [Irregular]

D 103.42/3
CERC BULLETIN AND SUMMARY REPORT OF RESEARCH, FISCAL YEAR (date). v. 1964– [Annual]

D 103.42/4
REPRINTS, R- (series). [Irregular]

D 103.42/5 • Item 334-A-23 (MF)
TECHNICAL REPORTS. 1– [Irregular]
Distribution to depository libraries previously made under item 342.

D 103.42/6:nos. • Item 334-A-9 (MF)
SPECIAL REPORTS. [Irregular]

D 103.42/7:nos. • Item 334-A-15 (MF)
GITI [General Investigation of Tidal Inlets] REPORTS. 1– [Irregular]
Series of general investigations prepared jointly by the U.S. Army Coastal Engineering Research Center, Fort Belvoir, Virginia and the U.S. Army Engineer Waterways Experiment Station, Vicksburg, Mississippi.
PURPOSE:– To provide highly technical reports, containing quantitative data for use in the design of inlets and inlet improvements.

D 103.42/8:nos. • Item 334-A-20 (MF)
MISCELLANEOUS REPORTS. 1– [Irregular]

D 103.42/10:yr.-nos. • Item 334-A-24 (MF)
TECHNICAL PAPERS. [Irregular]

D 103.42/11:v.nos.&nos. • Item 337-B-20 (EL)
THE CERCULAR.
Earlier title: Quarterly Circular Information Bulletin.

D 103.42/12:nos. • Item 334-A-18 (MF)
COASTAL ENGINEERING TECHNICAL AIDS (numbered).
Discontinued.

D 103.42/13:date • Item 334-A-20 (MF)
PRELIMINARY DATA SUMMARY. [Monthly]

Corps of Engineers (Continued)

D 103.43:nos. • Item 338-B
PAMPHLET EP (series).

D 103.43:1105-2-3 • Item 338-B
DIRECTORY OF ENVIRONMENTAL LIFE SCIENTISTS, 1974. 1974. 9 v.

PURPOSE:– To provide a list of environmental life scientists in the United States. Each entry consists of name, address, scientist's skills, principal field, and research being conducted.
See the following volumes:–

Vol. 1. North Pacific Region.
2. South Pacific Region.
3. Missouri River Region.
4. Southwest Region.
5. North Central Region.
6. Lower Mississippi Region.
7. North Atlantic Region.
8. Ohio River Valley Region.
9. South Atlantic Region.

D 103.43/2:nos. • Item 338-B-1 (MF)
ENGINEER HISTORICAL STUDIES. 1– 1981– [Irregular]
This sub-series published as EP 870 in the Pamphlet series (D 103.43).

D 103.43/2-2:CT • Item 338-B-1 (MF)
ENVIRONMENTAL HISTORY SERIES. [Irregular]

D 103.43/3:nos. • Item 338-B
DISTRICT PAMPHLETS, DP- (series). [Irregular]

D 103.43/4 • Item 338-B-2 (MF)
STUDIES IN MILITARY ENGINEERING (series). [Irregular]
Discusses significant actions undertaken by engineer troops in the 20th century. Its aim is to teach Engineer Officers lessons in military history that relate directly to their professional responsibilities.
Discontinued.

D 103.44 • Item 334-A-29 (MF)
HYDRAULIC LABORATORY: TECHNICAL REPORTS. [Irregular] (Army Engineer Division, North Pacific)
Discontinued.

D 103.45 • Item 334-A-26 (MF)
STAGES AND DISCHARGES OF MISSISSIPPI RIVER AND TRIBUTARIES IN THE VICKSBURG DISTRICT. 1965– [Annual]
Data formerly contained in Stages and Discharges of Mississippi River and Its Outlets and Tributaries (D 103.309).

D 103.45/2 • Item 334-A-26 (MF)
STAGES AND DISCHARGES OF MISSISSIPPI RIVER AND TRIBUTARIES IN THE MEMPHIS DISTRICT. 1965– [Annual]
Data formerly contained in Stages and Discharges of Mississippi River and Its Outlets and Tributaries (D 103.309).

D 103.45/3 • Item 334-A-26 (MF)
STAGES AND DISCHARGES OF MISSISSIPPI RIVER AND TRIBUTARIES IN THE ST. LOUIS DISTRICT. 1965– [Annual]

D 103.45/4 • Item 334-A-26 (MF)
STAGES AND DISCHARGES OF THE MISSISSIPPI RIVER AND TRIBUTARIES AND OTHER WATERSHEDS IN THE NEW ORLEANS DISTRICT. 1965– [Annual]

D 103.46:nos.
POTAMOLOGY INVESTIGATIONS.

D 103.47 • Item 334-A-10 (MF)
FLOOD PLAIN INFORMATION (series). [Irregular]

D 103.47/2 • Item 334-A-11
FLOODS IN [location]; HOW TO AVOID DAMAGE. [Irregular]
Prepared from data in Flood Plain Information.

D 103.48:v.nos.&nos. • Item 342-B
WATER SPECTRUM. v. 1– 14. 1949– 1983. [Quarterly]

PURPOSE:– To serve as a forum for the open discussion of issues and choices in resolving water resources problems.
Indexed by: Index to U.S. Government Periodicals.
ISSN 0043-1435
Discontinued 1983.

D 103.49:nos.
RESOURCES ATLAS PROJECT: THAILAND, ATLAS. 1– 1969– [Irregular] (Engineering Agency for Resources Inventories)

D 103.49/2:CT • Item 334-C
BOATERS MAPS (series). [Irregular]

PURPOSE:– To provide a series of maps for various Corps of Engineer projects where recreational opportunities are available. Maps show landmarks and boating hazards, with boating and fishing rules, and other information about the project on the verso.
No longer a depository item.
Discontinued.

D 103.49/3:CT • Item 334-C-1
MAPS AND POSTERS. [Irregular]

D 103.49/3-2:CT • Item 334-C-1
ATLASES. [Irregular]

D 103.49/4:CT
AUDIOVISUAL MATERIALS. [Irregular]

ENGINEER AGENCY FOR RESOURCES INVENTORIES 4701 North Sagamore Road Washington, D.C. 20016

D 103.50:nos.
EARI DEVELOPMENT RESEARCH SERIES REPORTS. 1– 1969– [Irregular]

PURPOSE:– To make available to others the results of the Agency's project oriented but supportive research findings not included within project publications. Publications deal mainly with resources of foreign countries.

D 103.50:3
3. NATURAL RESOURCES, A SELECTION OF BIBLIOGRAPHIES. 1970.

Lists bibliographies on natural resources of foreign countries.

Corps of Engineers (Continued)

D 103.51:nos.
HONOLULU DISTRICT: TECHNICAL REPORTS.

D 103.52:nos.   • Item 334-A-1
CONTRACT REPORTS. 1–   [Irregular]
Discontinued.

CONSTRUCTION ENGINEERING RESEARCH LABORATORY
Champaign, Illinois

D 103.53:nos.   • Item 335-A (MF) (EL)
TECHNICAL REPORTS. [Irregular]

D 103.53/2:letters-nos.   • Item 335-A (MF)
TECHNICAL MANUSCRIPTS. [Irregular]

D 103.53/3:letters-nos.
PRELIMINARY REPORTS. [Irregular]

D 103.53/4:letters-nos.
SPECIAL REPORTS. [Irregular]

D 103.53/5:nos.   • Item 335-A (MF)
INTERIM REPORTS. M-1–   [Irregular]

D 103.53/6:letters-nos.
TECHNICAL INFORMATION PAMPHLETS.

D 103.53/7:letters-nos.   • Item 335-A (MF)
SPECIAL REPORTS. [Irregular]

D 103.53/8   • Item 335-D (MF)
ADP REPORTS.

D 103.53/11   • Item 335-D-1 (MF)
THE CUTTING EDGE, RESEARCH & DEVELOPMENT FOR SUSTAINABLE ARMY INSTALLATIONS. [Quarterly]

Corps of Engineers (Continued)

D 103.54:nos.
NCG [Nuclear Catering Group] TECHNICAL REPORTS. 1–   [Irregular]

HYDROLOGIC ENGINEERING CENTER
Davis, California

D 103.55:nos.
TECHNICAL PAPERS.

D 103.55/2:CT
GENERAL PUBLICATIONS.

D 103.55/3:date
ANNUAL REPORT.

D 103.55/4:nos.
RESEARCH NOTES.

D 103.56:CT
PRESS RELEASES.

INSTITUTE OF WATER RESOURCES

D 103.57:nos.   • Item 337-B-3 (MF)
IWR CONTRACT REPORTS (numbered). [Irregular]
Reports of research conducted under contract to the Institute of Water Resources on various topics in the water resources field, such as, water planning, and water supplies.

D 103.57/2:nos.
CENTER FOR ECONOMIC STUDIES.

D 103.57/3:date   • Item 337-B-4 (MF)
ANNUAL REPORT.
Summarizes the activities, programs, and accomplishments of the Institute in its mission to assist the Corps of Engineers in water resources planning.
Discontinued.

D 103.57/4:nos.
IWR PAMPHLETS.

D 103.57/5:nos.   • Item 337-B-3 (MF)
INSTITUTE FOR WATER RESOURCES: RESEARCH REPORTS. 1–   [Irregular]

D 103.57/6:date-letters-nos. • Item 337-B-3 (MF)
MISCELLANEOUS PAPERS (series). [Irregular]

D 103.57/8:date-letters-nos. • Item 337-B-3 (MF)
POLICY STUDIES (series). [Irregular]

D 103.57/9:date-nos.   • Item 337-B-3 (MF)
WORKING PAPERS (series). [Irregular]

D 103.57/10   • Item 337-B-3 (MF)
IWR PROCEEDINGS (series).
Earlier: Economic and Social Analysis Workshop: Proceedings.

D 103.57/11   • Item 337-B-9 (MF)
IWR USER'S MANUAL. [Irregular]

D 103.57/12:date   • Item 337-B-3 (MF)
PERFORMANCE MONITORING SYSTEM: SUMMARY OF LOCK STATISTICS. [Semiannual]
Earlier issued Quarterly.
Discontinued.

D 103.57/13   • Item 337-B-3 (MF)
ALTERNATIVE DISPUTE RESOLUTION SERIES.

Corps of Engineers (Continued)

D 103.58:date
LIST OF ILLINOIS RIVER TERMINALS, DOCKS, MOORING LOCATIONS, AND WAREHOUSES. (St. Louis District, Corps of Engineers, 210 North 12th Street, St. Louis, Missouri 63101)

D 103.58/2:date
LIST OF MISSISSIPPI RIVER TERMINALS, DOCKS, MOORING LOCATIONS, AND WAREHOUSES.

D 103.59:nos.
U.S. ARMY ENGINEER DISTRICT, LOS ANGELES: REPORTS (numbered). [Irregular]

D 103.60:nos.   • Item 344-A-3
WASTEWATER MANAGEMENT REPORTS. [Irregular]
Discontinued.

D 103.61:date
COLUMBIA RIVER WATER MANAGEMENT REPORT FOR WATER YEAR.

D 103.62:CT   • Item 334-A-13 (MF)
ENVIRONMENTAL IMPACT STATEMENT [by area].

D 103.63:date/nos.
LAKE ERIE WATER QUALITY NEWSLETTER. [Quarterly] (Army Engineer District, 17776 Niagara Street, Buffalo, New York 14207)
Superseded by D 103.63/2

D 103.63/2:nos.
LAKE ERIE WASTEWATER MANAGEMENT STUDY PUBLIC INFORMATION FACT SHEET.
Supersedes D 103.63

D 103.64:nos.
COMMITTEE ON CHANNEL STABILIZATION: TECHNICAL REPORTS. 1– 1965–   [Irregular]

D 103.66   • Item 337-B-5
NAVIGATION CHARTS (Various Rivers).
Each publication consists of navigation charts representing channel lines and conditions for a particular river and its tributaries. Includes bridge profiles, colored illustrations of aids to navigation, etc.
Revised annually.
Discontinued.

D 103.66:CT   • Item 337-B-5
MISSOURI RIVER.

D 103.66/2:CT   • Item 337-B-5
OHIO RIVER.

D 103.66/3:CT   • Item 337-B-5
CUMBERLAND RIVER NAVIGATION CHARTS.
Discontinued.

D 103.66/4:CT   • Item 337-B-5
ALLEGHANEY AND MONONGAHELA RIVERS.

D 103.66/5:CT   • Item 337-B-5
TENNESSEE RIVER.
Discontinued.

D 103.66/6:CT   • Item 377-B-5
MISSISSIPPI RIVER.
Discontinued.

D 103.66/7:date   • Item 337-B-14 (MF)
NAVIGATION CONDITIONS FOR (name). [Annual]
PURPOSE– To present information on the navigability of various rivers at different points, for example, the Mississippi River from the Ohio River to the Gulf of Mexico.
Issued by the Office of the Division Engineer, North Central Division, Chicago, Illinois, and designated Division Bulletin (nos.).

D 103.67:date   • Item 337-B-1 (MF)
DISTINGUISHED DESIGN AWARDS. [Annual]
Program was initiated to recognize excellence in the design of structures and in area developments by the Corps of Engineers Designing Division and District Offices and their consulting firms of the environmental design professions. Awards are given to the designing offices and consulting firms for winning architectural, engineering, and landscape architectural entries.
ISSN 0360-070X

D 103.68:date   • Item 334-A-14 (MF)
REPORT TO CONGRESS ON ADMINISTRATION OF OCEAN DUMPING ACTIVITIES. 1st– 1976– [Annual]
Issued pursuant to the Marine Protection, Research and Sanctuaries Act of 1972 (P.L. 92-953).
Discontinued.

D 103.68/2:date   • Item 334-A-14 (MF)
OCEAN DUMPING REPORT FOR CALENDAR YEAR (date) DREDGED MATERIAL. [Annual]
Discontinued.

D 103.69:v.nos.&nos.   • Item 334-A-21 (EL)
ENGINEERS UPDATE. v. 1– 1977– [Monthly]
PURPOSE:– To provide engineering personnel with newsletters giving information on Corps of Engineers activities and personnel news.

D 103.70   • Item 334-A-25
ENVIRONMENTAL HARMONY AT (various places).

D 103.71:date   • Item 334-D (MF)
OFFICER DIRECTORY. [Annual]
Lists officers and warrant officers in certain specialties, by name and grade.

D 103.72:v.nos.&nos.
THE REMR BULLETIN: NEWS FROM THE REPAIR, EVALUATION, MAINTENANCE AND REHABILITATION RESEARCH PROGRAM. [Irregular]

D 103.73:v.nos.&nos.
CERL ABSTRACTS, INFORMATION EXCHANGE BULLETIN. [Irregular]

D 103.74:v.nos.&nos.
CERL REPORTS, INFORMATION EXCHANGE BULLETIN. [Irregular]

ENGINEER SCHOOL
Fort Belvoir, Virginia

D 103.101:date
ANNUAL REPORTS.
Earlier M 110.402

D 103.102:CT   • Item 337-B-10
GENERAL PUBLICATIONS. [Irregular]
Earlier M 110.402

D 103.105   • Item 421-E-7 (MF)
ECONOMIC RESOURCES IMPACT STATEMENTS. [Annual]

D 103.107:nos.
ENGINEER SCHOOL LIBRARY BULLETIN.
Earlier M 110.407

D 103.108:nos.
WEEKLY PERIODICAL INDEX.

D 103.108/2:CT   • Item 337-B-12
HANDBOOKS, MANUALS, GUIDES. [Irregular]
Earlier M 110.408

D 103.109:nos.   • Item 337-B-6 (MF)
ENGINEER SCHOOL SPECIAL TEXT, ST (series).

D 103.109/2:CT   • Item 337-B-7 (MF)
PROGRAMMED TEXTS. [Irregular]

D 103.109/3   • Item 337-B-7 (MF)
FB PAMPHLET (series). [Irregular]
FB = Fort Belvoir.

D 103.110:CT
MASTER LESSON PLANS PREPARED FOR USE AT
ENGINEER SCHOOL ONLY.

D 103.111:nos.
COURSES, ENGINEER SCHOOL, FT. BELVOIR, VA.
ADMIN.

D 103.111/2:nos.   • Item 334-A-4
CORRESPONDENCE COURSE PROGRAM, SUB-
COURSES. (Army Engineer School)
Discontinued.

D 103.112:nos.
CONFERENCE NOTES.
Official use.

D 103.112/2:nos.
STUDENT MATERIAL FOR USE WITH CONFERENCE
NOTES. Proc.

D 103.112/4:nos.   • Item 337-B-11
ENGINEER CENTER TEAM MINUTES. [Bimonthly]
PURPOSE:– To summarize presentations and
discussions of the Engineer Center Team at Fort
Belvoir, Virginia on miscellaneous topics pertain-
ing to the mission of the center.
Discontinued.

D 103.113:nos.
USAR TRAINING BULLETIN. [Monthly]

D 103.114:CT
BIBLIOGRAPHIES AND LISTS OF PUBLICATIONS,
ENGINEER SCHOOL.
Formerly in D 103.102

D 103.115:v.nos.&nos.   • Item 334-A-2 (EL)
ENGINEER. v. 1 [Quarterly]

PURPOSE:– To provide factual and in-depth
information of interest to all engineer units.
Index by: Index to U.S. Government Periodicals.
ISSN 0046-1989

D 103.116:date   • Item 334-B-1 (P) (EL)
MONTHLY BULLETIN OF LAKE LEVELS FOR THE
GREAT LAKES.

Folder consisting of graphs and tables that
compare current levels of each of the Great Lakes
with 1900-1979 average and extreme levels and
also project probable levels for the next six
months. Mean lake levels are also compared with
those of the same month of the previous year
and with maximum and minimum years of the
past.

D 103.116/2:nos.   • Item 334-B-1
GREAT LAKES LEVELS UPDATE. [Monthly]

D 103.117:letters-nos.
PUBLIC NOTICE, LMNOD-SP- (series). [Irregular]

D 103.118:nos.   • Item 337
EXPLORE (series). 1–   [Irregular]

D 103.119:date   • Item 334-E (MF)
ARMY FACILITIES ENERGY PLAN. [Annual]

D 103.120:CT   • Item 337-B-6 (MF)
U.S. ARMY ENGINEER SCHOOL: STUDENT WORK-
BOOK (series).

D 103.120/2:CT   • Item 337-B-6 (MF)
U.S. ARMY ENGINEER SCHOOL: STUDENT HAND-
OUT (series).

D 103.120/3:CT   • Item 337-B-6
STUDENT PAMPHLET (series).

D 103.121:date   • Item 337-B-8 (MF)
LESSONS LEARNED IN CONTRACTING RPMA.
[Annual] (S-12)
Intended as a management tool for teaching
lessons learned in the contracting of Real Prop-
erty Maintenance Activities and housing.
RPMA = Real Property Maintenance Activi-
ties.

D 103.122   • Item 337-B-13
FESA(series). [Irregular]
FESA = Facilities Engineering Support Agency.
Discontinued.

D 103.122/2:   • Item 337-B-16
FESA BRIEFS. [Quarterly]
FESA=Facilities Engineering Support Agency
Discontinued.

D 103.122/3:v. & no.   • Item 337-B-18 (EL)
PUBLIC WORKS DIGEST. [Monthly]

PURPOSE:– To provide extended coverage
of major DEH stores.
Earlier title: DEH (Directorate of Engineering
and Housing) Digest.
Earlier issued bimonthly.

D 103.122/4:date-nos.   • Item 338-B (MF)
CEHSC-P PAM (series).
Discontinued.

D 103.123:   • Item 337-B-17
EDUCATION SERVICES BROCHURE. [Annual]
Describes education programs and courses
offered through the U.S. Army Engineering Center and Fort Belvoir.

D 103.124:   • Item 334-A-30
WATER SAFETY PROGRAM CATALOG. [Annual]
Contains colored illustrations of posters, video
public service announcements, T-shirts, baseball
caps, and billboards that may be used to promote
the Corps of Engineers water safety program.
Discontinued.

D 103.125:v.nos./nos.   • Item 334-A-31 (MF)
TECH-TRAN. [Quarterly]
Discontinued.

D 103.126:v.nos./nos.   • Item 334-A-31 (EL)
THE ENVIRONMENTAL UPDATE. [Quarterly]

D 103.128   • Item 337-B-19 (CD)
NEPA/BRAC. [Annual]
Issued on CD-ROM.

D 103.130   • Item 337-A-1 (MF)
NDC REPORT (series).

D 103.132   • Item 306-J (MF)
PLANNERS AND PROJECT MANAGERS PROGRAM.
[Annual]

D 103.135   • Item 337-B-20 (E)
ELECTRONIC PRODUCTS.

LAKE SURVEY OFFICE

D 103.201:date
ANNUAL REPORTS.
Earlier M 110.101

D 103.202:CT
GENERAL PUBLICATIONS.
Earlier M 110.102

D 103.203   • Item 338
GREAT LAKES PILOT. [Annual]
Subscription includes basic volume plus
supplements issued during the year.

D 103.203/2
BULLETINS, B- (series). [Semiannual]
Contains articles and short reports of projects
being conducted.

D 103.208:date
CATALOG OF CHARTS OF THE GREAT LAKES AND
CONNECTING WATERS, ALSO LAKE CHAM-
PLAIN, NEW YORK CANALS, MINNESOTA
ONTARIO BORDER LAKES. [Annual]
Earlier D 103.2:C 38/3

D 103.209
RESEARCH REPORTS, PR- (series). [Irregular]

D 103.210
MISCELLANEOUS PAPERS, MP- (series). [Irregular]

D 103.211
BASIC DATA REPORTS, BD- (series). [Irregular]

MISSISSIPPI RIVER COMMISSION

D 103.301:date
ANNUAL REPORTS.
Earlier M 110.201

D 103.302:CT
GENERAL PUBLICATIONS.
Earlier M 110.202

D 103.307:CT
MAPS.Earlier M 110.208

D 103.308:CT
TOPOGRAPHIC QUADRANGLE MAPS OF ALLUVIAL
VALLEY OF LOWER MISSISSIPPI RIVER.

Earlier W 31.9

D 103.308/2:date
INDEX OF TOPOGRAPHIC QUADRANGLE MAPS OF
ALLUVIAL VALLEY OF LOWER MISSISSIPPI
RIVER.
Earlier W 31.9/2

D 103.309:date
STAGES AND DISCHARGES, MISSISSIPPI RIVER
AND ITS OUTLETS AND TRIBUTARIES. [Annual]
Earlier M 110.207

D 103.309/2:date
ANNUAL MAXIMUM, MINIMUM, AND MEAN
DISCHARGES OF MISSISSIPPI RIVER AND ITS
OUTLETS AND TRIBUTARIES.

D 103.310:nos.
PERIODIC INSPECTION REPORTS.

ARMY MEDICAL DEPARTMENT
(1950–   )

D 104.1   • Item 349-C
ANNUAL REPORT, SURGEON GENERAL, UNITED
STATES ARMY. 1818–   [Annual]

PURPOSE:– To provide a factual and objective resume of the professional and administrative worldwide activities and accomplishments of
the Army Medical Service.
Discontinued with the 1975 issue.
Discontinued.

D 104.2:CT   • Item 351-A
GENERAL PUBLICATIONS.
Earlier M 102.2
Discontinued.

D 104.3:v.nos.
BULLETIN OF ARMY MEDICAL DEPARTMENT.
[Monthly]
Earlier M 102.3

D 104.6/2 • Item 351-C
HANDBOOKS, MANUALS, GUIDES. [Irregular]

D 104.7:v.nos.
CURRENT LIST OF MEDICAL LITERATURE. [Weekly]
Earlier M 102.7
Later D 8.8
Discontinued.

D 104.8:
INDEX-CATALOGUE OF LIBRARY OF SURGEON GENERAL'S OFFICE, 4th SERIES.

D 104.9:nos. • Item 349-A
MEDICAL DEPARTMENT EQUIPMENT LIST.
Earlier M 102.9
Discontinued.

D 104.10:CT
ARMY MEDICAL LIBRARY BIBLIOGRAPHIES.
Discontinued.

D 104.10/2:CT • Item 351-B
BIBLIOGRAPHIES AND LISTS OF PUBLICATIONS.

D 104.11:CT • Item 352-A
MEDICAL DEPARTMENT OF THE ARMY IN WORLD WAR II.
Discontinued.

D 104.11/2:CT • Item 352-A-1 (MF)
MEDICAL DEPARTMENT, UNITED STATES ARMY IN VIETNAM. [Irregular]

D 104.12:date
MEDICAL RESEARCH AND DEVELOPMENT BOARD, RESEARCH PROGRESS REPORT. [Annual]
Discontinued.

D 104.12/2:nos.
MEDICAL RESEARCH AND DEVELOPMENT BOARD, RESEARCH PROGRESS REPORT. [Quarterly]
Discontinued.

D 104.13 • Item 352-C
MEDICAL SCIENCE PUBLICATIONS. 1– [Irregular]
Prepared by the Walter Reed Army Institute of Research, Walter Reed Army Medical Center.
Discontinued.

D 104.14:nos.
ARMY MEDICAL RESEARCH LABORATORY REPORTS.

WALTER REED ARMY MEDICAL CENTER

D 104.15:nos.
WALTER REED ARMY INSTITUTE OF RESEARCH, RESEARCH REPORTS WRAIR (series).
Internal use only.

D 104.15/2:nos.
ARMY PROSTHETICS RESEARCH LABORATORY. TECHNICAL REPORTS.

D 104.15/3:date • Item 352-E (MF)
ANNUAL PROGRESS REPORT.

D 104.15/4:nos.
WALTER REED ARMY INSTITUTE FOR RESEARCH, WALTER REED ARMY MEDICAL CENTER: HEALTH DATA PUBLICATIONS.

D 104.15/5:v.nos.&nos. • Item 330-D
PROGRESS NOTES. v. 1– 1968– [Monthly] (Department of Medicine)

PURPOSE:– To provide interested physicians with information pertaining to the practice of medicine at Walter Reed Army Medical Center. Articles are written by Department of Medicine staff and residents and cover subjects of interest in clinical internal medicine.
ISSN 0145-0204
Discontinued.

ARMY MEDICAL DEPARTMENT
(Continued)

D 104.16 • Item 349-D
ANNUAL REPORT, DEPENDENTS' MEDICAL CARE PROGRAM. [Annual]
Discontinued.

D 104.17
REPORTS. 1– [Irregular]

D 104.17/list
BIBLIOGRAPHY OF U.S. ARMY MEDICAL RESEARCH AND NUTRITION LABORATORY REPORTS AND REPRINTS FOR (year). [Annual]

D 104.18:nos.
ARMED SERVICES RESEARCH AND DEVELOPMENT REPORT ON INSECT AND RODENT CONTROL. [Quarterly]
Admin. only.

D 104.18/2:date
ARMED FORCES PEST CONTROL BOARD. ANNUAL REPORTS.

D 104.19
REPORT OF ACTIVITIES. [Annual]

D 104.20:v.nos.
HEALTH OF THE ARMY.

D 104.21:nos.
AEROMEDICAL RESEARCH UNIT, FORT RUCKER, ALA.; USAARU REPORTS.

D 104.22:date
SURGICAL RESEARCH UNIT, BROOKE ARMY MEDICAL CENTER, FORT SAM HOUSTON, TEXAS: ANNUAL RESEARCH PROGRESS REPORT.

D 104.23:date • Item 349-A-1
ABSTRACTS FROM ANNUAL AND TECHNICAL REPORTS SUBMITTED BY USAMRDC CONTRACTORS/GRANTEES. [Quarterly]
Discontinued.

D 104.23/2:date • Item 349-A-2
ADVANCED ABSTRACTS OF SCIENTIFIC AND TECHNICAL PAPERS SUBMITTED FOR PUBLICATION AND PRESENTATION. [Quarterly]
Discontinued.

D 104.24:v.nos.&nos. • Item 352-D
NEWSLETTER OF THE U.S. ARMY MEDICAL DEPARTMENT. v. 1– v. 4. no 3. 1970-1973. [Quarterly] (Office of Surgeon General)

PURPOSE:– To develop a greater unity and understanding among Army Medical Department personnel and to serve as a medium for dissemination of timely information not normally and readily available in other media published by the U.S. Army.
Superseded by AMEDD Spectrum (D 104.26).
Discontinued.

D 104.25:nos.
BIOMEDICAL REPORTS OF THE 406 MEDICAL LABORATORY.

D 104.26:v.nos.&nos.
AMEDD SPECTRUM. v. 1, no. 1– 3. 1974. [Quarterly]
Supersedes Newsletter of the U.S. Army Medical Department (D 104.24).

D 104.27:date • Item 352-F (MF)
UNITED STATES ARMY MEDICAL RESEARCH INSTITUTE OF INFECTIOUS DISEASE: ANNUAL PROGRESS REPORT.

D 104.28:v.nos.&nos. • Item 352-G
PERSPECTIVES. v. 1– 1975– [Monthly]
Discontinued.

D 104.29:nos.
LETTERMAN ARMY INSTITUTE OF RESEARCH: INSTITUTE REPORTS. [Irregular]

D 104.30:date • Item 352-H (MF)
ANNUAL HISTORICAL REPORT, AMEDD ACTIVITIES FOR THE CALENDAR YEAR. (Army Medical Bioengineering Research and Development Laboratory)
Discontinued.

D 104.31:nos. • Item 352-J (MF)
FAMC PAMPHLETS (series). [Irregular] (Fitzsimons Army Medical Center)
Discontinued.

D 104.31/2: • Item 352-J (MF)
TEXT PAMPHLETS (series). [Irregular]

D 104.31/3 • Item 352-J-2 (MF)
ARMY MEDICAL EQUIPMENT AND OPTICAL SCHOOL: STUDENT HANDOUTS (series). [Irregular]
Discontinued.

D 104.32:nos. • Item 352-J-1 (MF)
WRAMC PAM (series).

D 104.33:CT
AUDIOVISUAL MATERIALS. [Irregular]

D 104.34: • Item 351-D
POSTERS.

D 104.35:pt.nos./v.nos. • Item 352-F (MF)
TEXTBOOK OF MILITARY MEDICINE (series).

D 104.36:CT • Item 352-J-3 (E)
ELECTRONIC PRODUCTS (misc.).

PUBLICATIONS RELATING TO ORDNANCE
(1968–)

D 105.1:date
ANNUAL REPORTS.
Earlier M 111.1

D 105.2:CT • Item 359
GENERAL PUBLICATIONS.
Earlier M 111.2

D 105.3:nos.
ORDANCE CORPS BULLETIN. Admin.
Earlier W 34.3

D 105.6:CT
REGULATIONS, RULES AND INSTRUCTIONS.
Earlier W 34.12/1, W 34.12/2

D 105.6/2 • Item 359-B
ORDNANCE CORPS MANUALS, ORDM-(series). [Irregular]
Discontinued.

D 105.6/3:CT • Item 325-L
HANDBOOKS, MANUALS, GUIDES. [Irregular]

D 105.6/4:nos. • Item 325-G (MF)
JOB AIDS (numbered). [Irregular] (Army Ordnance and Chemical Center and School)

PURPOSE:– To provide a series of self- teaching instructions for accomplishing various job-related tasks in the U.S. Army, such as trouble-shooting clutches on wheeled vehicles.
Discontinued.

D 105.7:v.nos.
ORDNANCE DEPARTMENT SAFETY BULLETIN.
Indexed by: Index to U.S. Government Periodicals.
Earlier M 111.7

D 105.8:dt.&nos.
ORDNANCE DEPARTMENT ORDERS.
Earlier M 111.8

D 105.9 • **Item 359-A**
ORDNANCE CORPS PAMPHLETS, ORDP-(series).
[Irregular]
   Discontinued.

D 105.9/2:nos. • **Item 325-G**
OCO PAMPHLETS (series). [Irregular]
   OCO = Office Chief of Ordnance.
   Discontinued.

D 105.9/3:nos. • **Item 325-G**
USAAPGISA PAMPHLETS (series). [Irregular]
   USAAPGISA = U.S. Army Aberdeen Proving
   Ground Installation Support Activity
   Discontinued.

D 105.10:nos. • **Item 325-G (MF)**
MEMORANDUM REPORT BRL-MR (Series).
   Discontinued.

   D 105.10/2:
   – REPORTS.

   D 105.10/3:nos.
   – TECHNICAL NOTES.

D 105.10/3-2:nos. • **Item 325-G (MF)**
TECHNICAL REPORT, BRL TR (series).
   Discontinued.

D 105.10/4:nos.
ORDANCE COMPUTER RESEARCH REPORTS.

D 105.11
TECHNICAL REPORTS. [Irregular]

D 105.11/2
REPORTS. [Irregular]

D 105.12:nos.
PICATINNY ARSENAL, DOVER, N.J., TECHNICAL
REPORTS.

   D 105.12/2:nos.
   – TECHNICAL NOTES.

D 105.12/3
TECHNICAL REPORTS, FRL-TR- (series). [Irregular]

D 105.12/4
TECHNICAL NOTES, FRL-TN- (series). [Irregular]

D 105.12/5
TECHNICAL MEMORANDUMS. 1– [Irregular]

D 105.13:nos.
RODMAN PROCESS LABORATORY, WATERTOWN
ARSENAL, REPORTS.

D 105.13/2:nos.
WATERTOWN ARSENAL LABORATORY, REPORT
WAL (series).

D 105.13/2-2:nos.
WATERTOWN ARSENAL LABORATORY: TECHNICAL
REPORT (series).

D 105.13/2-3:nos.
WATERTOWN ARSENAL: TECHNICAL REPORT
WARD-TR (series).

D 105.13/2-4:nos.
METALLURGICAL ADVISORY COMMITTEE ON
TITANIUM INFORMATION BULLETINS.

D 105.13/3:nos.
ORDNANCE MATERIALS RESEARCH OFFICES,
WATERTOWN ARSENAL, OMRO PUBLICATIONS.

D 105.14 • **Item 325-J (MF)**
TECHNICAL REPORTS, RT- (series). 1– [Irregular]

D 105.14/2
TECHNICAL REVIEW. v. 1– [Irregular]

D 105.14/3:nos.
HARRY DIAMOND LABORATORIES, WASHINGTON,
D.C. TM–

D 105.14/4:nos.
HDL [Harry Diamond Laboratories] TECHNICAL DIS-
CLOSURE BULLETIN.

D 105.14/5:nos. • **Item 325-J (MF)**
HARRY DIAMOND LABORATORIES: SPECIAL
REPORTS. [Irregular]

D 105.15:nos.
ARMY BALLISTIC MISSILE AGENCY, DC-TR- (series).

D 105.16
REPORTS. CCL- (series). [Irregular]

D 105.17
REPORTS. [Irregular]

D 105.17/2
MEMORANDUM REPORTS. [Irregular]

D 105.17/3:nos.
FRANKFORD ARSENAL: TECHNICAL MEMORAN-
DUMS.

D 105.17/4:nos.
FRANKFORD ARSENAL: TECHNICAL REPORTS.
[Irregular]

D 105.18
REPORTS. [Irregular]

D 105.18/2
LAND LOCOMOTION LABORATORY REPORTS.
[Irregular]

D 105.19
TECHNICAL REPORTS. SA-TR- (series). [Irregular]

D 105.20
TECHNICAL REPORTS. WVT- (series). [Irregular]

D 105.21:nos.
MISSILE PURCHASE DESCRIPTION, MPD (series).
ADMINISTRATIVE.

D 105.22
REPORTS, RE-TR- (series). [Irregular]

D 105.22/2
REPORTS, RT-TR- (series). [Irregular]

D 105.22/2-2
REPORTS, RG-TR- (series). [Irregular]

D 105.22/3:nos.
ARMY MISSILE COMMAND. REDSTONE SCIENTIFIC
INFORMATION CENTER, REDSTONE ARSENAL,
ALABAMA, RSIC- (series).

D 105.23
IRIG DOCUMENTS. [Irregular]

D 105.24
TECHNICAL MEMORANDUMS. [Irregular]

D 105.25:nos. • **Item 325-G**
ARMY ORDNANCE CENTER AND SCHOOL,
ABERDEEN PROVING GROUND, MARYLAND:
SPECIAL TEXTS, ST- (series). [Irregular]
   Discontinued.

D 105.26
TECHNICAL REPORTS, AMRA CR- (series). [Irregu-
lar]

D 105.27 • **Item 325-G**
OSPAM- (series). 1– [Irregular]
   Discontinued.

D 105.28:CT
SUPPLEMENTAL TRAINING MATERIAL (series).
[Irregular]

D 105.29:v.nos.&nos. • **Item 325-P**
ORDNANCE MAGAZINE. [Quarterly]

   PURPOSE:– To provide timely information in
such areas as ordnance specialities, readiness,
and material maintenance. Contains articles intended to promote the professional development
of members of the worldwide ordnance community.
   Discontinued.

D 105.30:v.nos.&nos. • **Item 325-J**
HARRY DIAMOND LABORATORIES: DIMENSIONS.
[Monthly]
   Discontinued.

D 105.31: • **Item 325-L-1**
SCHOOL OF MILITARY PACKAGING TECHNOLOGY
BOOKLETS, SMPT- BKLT-(series). [Irregular]
   Discontinued.

D 105.32: • **Item 325-S**
POSTERS.

D 105.33:CT • **Item 325-P**
USAEHA PAMPHLET (series).
   USAEHA = U.S. Army Environmental Hygiene
Agency.
   Discontinued.

QUARTERMASTER CORPS
(1949–   )

D 106.1:date
ANNUAL REPORTS.
   Earlier M 112.1

D 106.2:CT • **Item 363**
GENERAL PUBLICATIONS.
   Earlier M 112.2

D 106.3/2:nos.
QUARTERMASTER FOOD AND CONTAINER
INSTITUTE FOR ARMED FORCES: LIBRARY BUL-
LETIN.

   D 106.3/3:nos.
   – SUPPLEMENTS.

D 106.3/4:date/no. • **Item 363-D (EL)**
QUARTERMASTER PROFESSIONAL BULLETIN.
[Quarterly]

D 106.4
QMC CIRCULARS. ADMIN.

D 106.6:CT • **Item 364**
REGULATIONS, RULES, AND INSTRUCTIONS.
   Earlier M 112.6
   Discontinued.

D 106.6/2:nos. • **Item 364**
QUARTERMASTER CORPS MANUAL QMC (series).
   Discontinued.

D 106.7:v.nos.
DEPOT AND MARKET CENTER OPERATIONS.
[Bimonthly]
   Restricted.
   Earlier M 221.7

D 106.8:nos.
QMC HISTORICAL STUDIES.

D 106.8/2 • **Item 363-A**
QMC HISTORICAL STUDIES, SERIES II. 1–   1956–
[Irregular]
   Covers post-World War II period.
   Discontinued.

D 106.8/3:CT • **Item 363-A**
HISTORICAL PUBLICATIONS (unnumbered).
   Discontinued.

D 106.9
FOOTWEAR AND LEATHER SERIES REPORTS. 1–
[Irregular]

D 106.9/2
TEXTILE SERIES REPORTS. 1– [Irregular]

D 106.9/2-2:nos.
TEXTILE ENGINEERING LABORATORY REPORTS.

D 106.9/3:nos.
ENVIRONMENTAL PROTECTION DIVISION
REPORTS.

D 106.9/4:nos.
ENVIRONMENTAL PROTECTION DIVISION, TECHNICAL REPORT EP (series).

D 106.9/5:nos.
CHEMICAL AND PLASTICS DIVISION, TECHNICAL REPORT CP (series).

D 106.10:nos.
TECHNICAL LIBRARY BIBLIOGRAPHIC SERIES.
    Earlier M 112.10

D 106.10/2:CT
BIBLIOGRAPHIES AND LISTS OF PUBLICATIONS (unnumbered).

D 106.10/3
BIBLIOGRAPHIC SERIES.

D 106.11:date
INDEX QUARTERMASTER CORPS SPECIFICATIONS.
    [Quarterly]

D 106.12   • **Item 364-A**
STATISTICAL YEARBOOK OF THE QUARTERMASTER CORPS. [Annual]
    Beginning with Fiscal Year 1955, the Yearbooks have been presented on a program basis, including the following programs: installations; command and management; manpower; training; procurement; industrial mobilization; supply; distribution and maintenance; services; construction; research and development, and foreign aid activity. Index. Map. Charts.
    Discontinued.

D 106.13   • **Item 363-B**
QMC PAMPHLETS. [Irregular]
    Discontinued.

D 106.14:date
INDEX, COORDINATED PURCHASE DESCRIPTIONS.

D 106.15:CT
ADDRESSES.

D 106.16:nos.
QMFCIAF REPORTS.
    Issued by Quartermaster Food and Container Institute for Armed Forces.

D 106.17:nos.
EARTH SCIENCES DIVISION: TECHNICAL REPORT ES (series).

D 106.17/2:nos.
EARTH SCIENCES DIVISION: SPECIAL REPORT S (series).

D 106.18:v.nos.Qtr.nos.
ACTIVITIES REPORT.

D 106.19:nos.
OPERATION STUDIES.

D 106.20:nos.
U.S. ARMY NATICK LABORATORIES. FOOD DIVISION, NATICK, MASS. TECHNICAL REPORT FD- (series).

D 106.21:nos.   • **Item 363 (MF)**
NATICK LABORATORIES, NATICK, MASS.: TECHNICAL REPORTS.
    This series consists of reports numbered in one series, which were formerly numbered in separate series.
    Earlier D 106.9 & D 106.17

D 106.22:nos.   • **Item 363-C (MF)**
ARMY QUARTERMASTER SCHOOL CORRESPONDENCE SUBCOURSE, QM-(series).
    Discontinued.

TROOP INFORMATION AND EDUCATION DIVISION (1949– 1954)

D 107.1:date
ANNUAL REPORTS.
    Earlier M 104.1

D 107.2:CT   • **Item 367**
GENERAL PUBLICATIONS.
    Earlier M 104.2
    Discontinued.

D 107.7:v.nos.
REPORT TO ARMY. [Semimonthly]
    Earlier M 104.8
    Later D 101.43

OFFICE OF JUDGE ADVOCATE GENERAL (1949–   )

INFORMATION

    The Judge Advocate General
    Department of the Army
    1777 N. Kent St.
    Rosslyn, VA 22209-2194
    (703) 697-5151
    Fax: (703) 588-0133
    http://www.jagcnet.army.mil

D 108.1:date
ANNUAL REPORTS.
    Earlier M 107.1

D 108.2:CT   • **Item 348**
GENERAL PUBLICATIONS.
    Earlier M 107.2

D 108.3:v.nos.   • **Item 347**
BULLETIN OF JUDGE ADVOCATE GENERAL OF ARMY. [Quarterly]
    Earlier M 107.3
    Discontinued.

D 108.5:CT
LAWS.

D 108.5/2:date   • **Item 348-A**
MILITARY LAWS OF UNITED STATES (Army).
    Earlier W 1.8/1
    Discontinued.

D 108.7:date
MANUAL FOR COURTS MARTIAL, ARMY.

D 108.8:date   • **Item 348-B**
MEMORANDUM OPINIONS OF JUDGE ADVOCATE GENERAL OF THE ARMY.
    Discontinued.

D 108.9:nos.
SPECIAL TEXT OF JUDGE ADVOCATE GENERAL'S SCHOOL.

D 108.9/2:date
JUDGE ADVOCATE GENERAL'S SCHOOL: COMMANDANT'S ANNUAL REPORT.

D 108.10:CT   • **Item 348-C**
HANDBOOKS, MANUALS, GUIDES.

D 108.11:date   • **Item 348-D**
ARMY LAWYER. v. 1–   1971–   [Monthly]

    (Judge Advocate General's School, Charlottesville, VA.)
    Later D 101.22:27-50

D 108.12:CT   • **Item 348-F**
POSTERS. [Irregular]

LEGAL SERVICES AGENCY (1978–   )

D 108.101:date
ANNUAL REPORT.

D 108.102:CT
GENERAL PUBLICATIONS.

D 108.109:v.nos.&nos.   • **Item 348-E**
ADVOCATE. v. 1– 16. 1969– 1984. [Bimonthly]
    Absorbed January 1985 by the Army Lawyer (D 101.22:27-50).
    Discontinued v.16/2.

MILITARY ACADEMY (1949–   )

INFORMATION

    United States Military Academy
    West Point, New York 10996
    (845) 938-4011
    html://www.usma.army.mil

D 109.1:date
ANNUAL REPORT.
    Earlier M 109.1

D 109.2:CT   • **Item 354**
GENERAL PUBLICATIONS.
    Earlier M 109.2

D 109.6:CT
REGULATIONS, RULES, AND INSTRUCTIONS.
    Earlier M 109.6

D 109.6/2:date
REGULATIONS FOR UNITED STATES CORPS OF CADETS PRESCRIBED BY COMMANDANT OF CADETS.
    Earlier M 109.6/2

D 109.7
OFFICIAL REGISTER OF OFFICERS AND CADETS.
    1818–   [Annual]

D 109.8   • **Item 353**
CATALOGUE. [Annual]
    Gives description of the courses offered at the Military Academy and general information for those interested in admission to the Academy.
    Discontinued.

D 109.9:date   • **Item 359-C**
STUDENT CONFERENCE ON UNITED STATES AFFAIRS. [Annual]

D 109.10:nos.
USMA LIBRARY BULLETIN.

D 109.11:CT   • **Item 354-A**
MAPS AND ATLASES. [Irregular]

D 109.12:CT   • **Item 354-B**
HANDBOOKS, MANUALS, GUIDES. [Irregular]

D 109.15   • **Item 354-C (MF)**
USCC PAMPHLET.

COMMAND AND GENERAL STAFF COLLEGE
(1949–   )

Fort Leavenworth, Kansas 66027

D 110.1:date • Item 359-C
ANNUAL REPORTS.
Earlier M 119.1

D 110.2:CT • Item 359-C
GENERAL PUBLICATIONS.
Earlier M 119.2

D 110.7 • Item 359-C (EL)
MILITARY REVIEW. v. 1–   1922–   [Monthly]
Available in English, Spanish, or Portuguese editions.
Annual index issued separately.
ISSN 0026-4148

D 110.7/2:v.nos.&nos. • Item 359-C-1 (EL)
SPANISH EDITION. [Monthly]

D 110.7/3:v.nos.&nos. • Item 359-C-2 (EL)
PORTUGUESE EDITION. [Bimonthly]

D 110.8:nos.
SPECIAL ORDERS.
Earlier W 28.6

D 110.9:nos. • Item 359-C (MF)
LEAVENWORTH PAPERS (series). [Irregular]

D 110.10:nos.
REFERENCE BOOKS, RB- (series).

D 110.11:nos. • Item 359-C (MF)
RESEARCH SURVEYS. [Irregular] (Combat Studies Institute)

D 110.12 • Item 359-C (MF)
HISTORICAL BIBLIOGRAPHY (Series).

D 110.13:letter&no. • Item 359-C-3 (E)
ELECTRONIC PRODUCTS. (Misc.)

ARMY ELECTRONICS RESEARCH AND DEVELOPMENT COMMAND
(1968–   )

INFORMATION

Army Electronics Research
and Development Command
Department of Defense
2800 Powder Mill Road
Adelphi, Maryland 20783
(202) 394-1076

D 111.1:date
ANNUAL REPORTS.
Earlier W 42.2

D 111.2:CT • Item 365
GENERAL PUBLICATIONS.
Discontinued.

D 111.6:CT • Item 365-A
REGULATIONS, RULES AND INSTRUCTIONS.
Discontinued

D 111.7:v.nos. • Item 366
MARS BULLETIN.
Discontinued.

D 111.8:date
INDEX OF SIGNAL CORPS SPECIFICATIONS AND STANDARDS.

D 111.9
TECHNICAL MEMORANDUMS. [Irregular]

D 111.9/2
ENGINEERING REPORTS. [Irregular]

D 111.9/3
TECHNICAL REPORTS. [Irregular]

D 111.9/4:nos.
ARMY ELECTRONICS COMMAND, FORT MONMOUTH, N.J.: RESEARCH AND DEVELOPMENT TECHNICAL REPORTS, ECOM (series). [Irregular]

Formerly: Army Electronics Research and Development Laboratories, Fort Monmouth, N.J.: Technical Reports, AELRDL-TR (series).

D 111.9/5
ATMOSPHERIC SCIENCES LABORATORY: TECHNICAL REPORTS, ASL-TR (series). [Irregular]

D 111.9/6:nos. • Item 343-C (MF)
ATMOSPHERIC SCIENCES LABORATORY: CONTRACTOR REPORTS, ASL-CR (series). [Irregular]
Highly technical reports of research on topics pertaining to meteorology and atmospheric sciences, such as cloud/fog analysis system and application routines, electrical conductivity measurement in the stratosphere.
Discontinued.

D 111.10:nos.
[PUBLICATIONS] SIG (nos.)

D 111.11:CT • Item 343-C-1
HANDBOOKS, MANUALS, GUIDES. [Irregular]

D 111.12:nos.
U.S. ARMY ELECTRONIC PROVING GROUND, USAEPG-SIG (series).

D 111.13:CT • Item 365-B
BIBLIOGRAPHIES AND LISTS OF PUBLICATIONS.
Discontinued.

D 111.14:v.nos.&nos. • Item 343-C-2 (EL)
ARMY COMMUNICATOR, VOICE OF THE SIGNAL CORPS. [Quarterly]

PURPOSE:– To promote professional development of Army Communication through presenting information and new ideas and concepts relating to communications and electronics.
ISSN 0362-5745

NATIONAL GUARD BUREAU
(1949–1958)

CREATION AND AUTHORITY

The National Guard Bureau (M 114) was made subordinate to the Department of the Army within the Department of Defense by Public Law 216, 81st Congress, approved August 10, 1949. The Bureau was established in the Department of Defense (D 12) as a joint bureau of the Department of the Army and the Department of the Air Force by Department of Defense Reorganization act of 1958 (Public law 85-599), approved August 6, 1958.

D 112.1:date
ANNUAL REPORTS.
Earlier M 114.1
Later D 12.1

D 112.2:CT
GENERAL PUBLICATIONS.
Earlier M 114.2
Later D 12.2

D 112.4:dt.&nos.
NGB CIRCULARS.
Earlier M 114.4

D 112.6:nos.
NATIONAL GUARD REGULATIONS.
Earlier M 114.6
Later D 12.6

D 112.6/2:CT
REGULATIONS, RULES, AND INSTRUCTIONS.

D 112.7:nos. • Item 357
NATIONAL GUARD BUREAU MANUAL.
Earlier W 70.8
Discontinued.

D 112.8:date
OFFICIAL NATIONAL GUARD REGISTER.
Earlier W 70.5
Later D 12.9

D 112.8/2:date
AIR NATIONAL GUARD REGISTER.
Later D 12.9/2

PANAMA CANAL
(1949–1950)

D 113.1:date
ANNUAL REPORTS.
Earlier M 115.1
Later PAC 1.1

D 113.2:CT • Item 361
GENERAL PUBLICATIONS.
Earlier M 115.2
Later PAC 1.2
Discontinued.

D 113.7:date
TIDE TABLES, BALBOA AND CRISTOBAL, CANAL ZONE.
Earlier M 115.7
Later PAC 1.7

D 113.8:nos.
CANAL ZONE JUNIOR COLLEGE CATALOGUES.
Earlier M 115.9
Later PAC 1.8

D 113.9:CT
PANAMA RAILROAD COMPANY PUBLICATIONS.
Later PAC 1.9

D 113.10:date
ANNUAL REPORT OF INSURANCE BUSINESS TRANSACTED IN CANAL ZONE.
Earlier M 115.10
Later PAC 1.10

CENTER OF MILITARY HISTORY
(1974–   )

CREATION AND AUTHORITY

The Historical Division (M 103) was established within the Department of the Army in 1949. In 1950, the Division was redesignated the Office of the Chief of Military History. In 1974, it became the Center of Military History.

INFORMATION
U.S. Army Center of Military History
Ft. McNair, Bldg. 35
103 Third Ave. SW
Washington, DC 20319-5058
(202) 685-2194
http://www.army.mil/cmh-pg

D 114.1:date
ANNUAL REPORTS.

D 114.2:CT   • Item 344
GENERAL PUBLICATIONS.
Earlier M 103.2

  D 114.2:Am 3   • Item 344
WAR OF THE AMERICAN REVOLUTION. 1976. 257 p. il.

    PURPOSE:– To provide a brief narrative history of the war, a chronology of military events, and a bibliography of over a thousand titles of books, articles, and published source materials on the American Revolution.

  D 114.2:M 59   • Item 344
AMERICAN MILITARY HISTORY. 1973. 720 p. il.
    Traces the development of the American Army and its impact on American history in times of peace as well as war.

D 114.7:CT   • Item 345
UNITED STATES ARMY IN WORLD WAR II.
Earlier M 103.7

D 114.7/2:nos.   • Item 345
UNITED STATES ARMY IN WORLD WAR II: MASTER INDEX, READER'S GUIDE.

D 114.7/3:CT   • Item 345
UNITED STATES ARMY IN VIETNAM (series). [Irregular]

D 114.7/4:CT   • Item 344-G
U.S. ARMY IN ACTION SERIES.

D 114.7/5:CT   • Item 344-G
THE U.S. ARMY CAMPAIGNS OF WORLD WAR II.

D 114.8:   • Item 345
WORLD WAR I (1917–19) PUBLICATIONS.

D 114.9:   • Item 344-G
ARMED FORCES IN ACTION (series).
Earlier M 103.8
Discontinued.

D 114.10:date   • Item 344-B (MF)
PUBLICATIONS OF OFFICE, CHIEF OF MILITARY HISTORY.

D 114.10/2:date   • Item 344-B
ARMY HISTORICAL PROGRAM, FISCAL YEAR.

D 114.11:v.nos.   • Item 343-G
ARMY LINEAGE BOOK.
Discontinued.

  D 114.11:2
v. 2. INFANTRY. 1953. 859 p. il.

  D 114.11:Ar 5
ARMOR-CAVALRY, Part 1. REGULAR ARMY AND ARMY RESERVE. 1969. 477 p. il.

Presents the story of the armored cavalry division of the regular and reserve army, complete with photographs and charts. The authors describe the origins and development of the U.S. Cavalry, from its revolutionary beginnings, through its frontier heyday, up through the time horse soldiers were discarded for tank operators and helicopter pilots. Even as the vehicles changed, the function of the unit, reconnaissance and security, remained basically the same for the Vietnam soldier as it was in the age of George Washington and the famous "Light Horse" troops. The book also includes histories of the armored regiments and tank battalions of World War II, whose modern descendants make up the bulk of the armored cavalry division. Also featured are pictures of insignias and coats of arms of various units, as well as the stories behind those symbols and units.

D 114.12:CT   • Item 344-F
HANDBOOKS, MANUALS, GUIDES. [Irregular]

D 114.13:CT   • Item 344-B-1
POSTERS, ETC.

D 114.14:nos.   • Item 344-D (MF)
SPECIAL BIBLIOGRAPHICAL SERIES. 1– [Irregular] (U.S. Army Military Research Collection, Carlisle Barracks, Pa.)

D 114.14/2:v.nos.&nos.
U.S. ARMY MILITARY RESEARCH COLLECTION, CARLISLE BARRACKS, PA, PERSPECTIVES IN MILITARY HISTORY.

D 114.15:date   • Item 344-C
DEPARTMENT OF THE ARMY HISTORICAL SUMMARY.
1971/72–   [Annual]
ISSN 0092-7880

D 114.16:date&nos.   • Item 344-H (MF)
ARMY MUSEUM NEWSLETTER. 1–   1969– [Irregular] (Army Center of Military History)

    PURPOSE:– To provide information and guidance of all persons in the Army Museum System, and all others responsible for the use and safekeeping of historical items in the U.S. Army. Aim is to provide Army museum personnel with otherwise unobtainable information concerning activities, plans, and projects of Army museums in order that they may profit professionally thereby. Newsletter also explains official policy, interprets Army regulations, provides reminders on administrative matters and sets up a medium for exchange of historical properties between museums.
ISSN 0004-2536
Discontinued.

D 114.17:CT   • Item 344-E
SPECIAL STUDIES SERIES. [Irregular]

D 114.18:CT   • Item 345-A (MF)
INDOCHINA MONOGRAPHS (series). [Irregular]
Published in microfiche (24x) only.
    Monographs by officers of the Cambodian, Laotian, and South Vietnamese armed forces during the Vietnam War.

D 114.19:CT   • Item 344-G
ARMY HISTORICAL SERIES. [Irregular]

D 114.19/2:CT   • Item 344-G (MF)
HISTORICAL ANALYSIS SERIES.

D 114.19/3:CT   • Item 344-G
HISTORICAL STUDIES (series). [Irregular]

D 114.20:nos.   • Item 345-B (MF)
ARMY HISTORY [Quarterly]
Formerly: Army Historian

D 114.21:   • Item 344-J (E)
ELECTRONIC PRODUCTS (misc.).

PUBLIC INFORMATION DIVISION

This class (D 115) was assigned for the 1950 revision of the Depository Classification List, by apparently never was used.
Prior to August 1949 classed M 118.

CHEMICAL CORPS
(1949–   )

D 116.1:date
ANNUAL REPORTS.

D 116.2:CT   • Item 346-A-1
GENERAL PUBLICATIONS.

D 116.8:date
INDEX OF CHEMICAL CORPS SPECIFICATIONS.

D 116.9:date
ALPHABETICAL LIST OF CMIC DIRECTIVES.

D 116.9/2:date
INDEX TO CMLC DIRECTIVES. Admin.

D 116.10:nos.
CHEMICAL CORPS PURCHASE DESCRIPTION.

D 116.11:date
INDEX OF CHEMICAL CORPS DRAWINGS.

D 116.12:date
PROCEEDINGS OF ANNUAL STATISTICAL ENGINEERING SYMPOSIUM.

D 116.13:nos.
CHEMICAL WARFARE LABORATORIES: CWL SPECIAL PUBLICATIONS.

D 116.14:nos.
ENGINEERING COMMAND REPORT, ENCR (series).

D 116.15
CRDL SPECIAL PUBLICATIONS. [Irregular]

D 116.15/2:nos.
CHEMICAL RESEARCH AND DEVELOPMENT LABORATORIES: TECHNICAL REPORT SRDLR (series).

D 116.16:date
INDEX OF INSTRUCTION MANUALS OR INSPECTION AIDS. [Annual]

D 116.17:date/no.   • Item 346-A (MF)
ARMY CHEMICAL REVIEW. [Semiannual]
    Professional journal of the Chemical Corps. Contains articles about Chemical Corps functions related to nuclear, biological, chemical, smoke and flame field expedients, and also reconnaissance combat support.

U. S. ARMY AIR MOBILITY RESEARCH AND DEVELOPMENT COMMAND
(1968–   )

D 117.1:date
ANNUAL REPORTS.
Earlier W 109.301

D 117.2:CT
GENERAL PUBLICATIONS.

D 117.8:nos.
TRANSPORTATION RESEARCH AND DEVELOPMENT COMMAND: RESEARCH TECHNICAL MEMORANDUMS.

D 117.8/2:nos. • Item 322-B-1 (MF)
APPLIED TECHNOLOGY LABORATORY, U.S. ARMY RESEARCH AND TECHNOLOGY LABORATORIES (AVRADCOM). [Irregular]
Earlier title: Army Air Mobility Research and Development Laboratory, Fort Eutis, Virginia: USAAMRDL Technical Reports.

D 117.8/2-2:date
TECHNICAL REPORTS PUBLISHED IN (year). [Annual]

D 117.8/3:nos.
ARMY TRANSPORTATION RESEARCH COMMAND: INTERIM REPORTS.

D 117.8/4:nos. • Item 322-B-1 (MF)
USARTL-TN, TECHNICAL NOTES.
Earlier: Army Air Mobility Research and Development Laboratory, Fort Eustis, Virginia: USAAMRDL Technical Reports.

D 117.8/6:nos.
U.S. AIR MOBILITY R & D LABORATORY: USAAMRDL CR- (series).

D 117.9:nos.
TC IN THE CURRENT NATIONAL EMERGENCY, HISTORICAL REPORT NO.

D 117.9/2:CT
TC IN THE CURRENT NATIONAL EMERGENCY: THE POST KOREAN EXPERIENCE.

D 117.10:nos.
TREC REPORTS.

D 117.11:nos.
ARMY TRANSPORTATION ENGINEERING AGENCY: USATEA REPORTS.

OFFICE OF PERSONNEL OPERATIONS
(1949–   )

D 118.1:date
ANNUAL REPORTS.

D 118.2:CT
GENERAL PUBLICATIONS.

D 118.9:v.nos.&nos. • Item 321-B-1
RECRUITER JOURNAL. v. 1–   1948–   [Monthly]
Published under the supervision of the Publicity Office, Enlisted Personnel Directorate, for the Army Recruiting Service.
Prior to August 1962, issued by the Adjutant General's Office (D 102.76).
Title varies: 1948– 1962, Recruiting Journal of the Army; 1963– 1978, Recruiting and Career Counseling Journal; 1978– 1979, U.S. Army Recruiting and Reenlisting Journal; 1979– 1984, All Volunteer.
ISSN 0049-545X
Later D 101.106/3
See D 101.106/3

OFFICE OF CIVIL DEFENSE
(1964–1972)

CREATION AND AUTHORITY

The Office of Civil Defense (D 13) was placed within the Department of the Army in 1964. In 1972, the Office was succeeded by the Defense Civil Preparedness Agency (D 14), an agency within the Department of Defense.

D 119.1 • Item 320-B-4
ANNUAL REPORT. 1961/62–   [Annual]
Later D 14.1

D 119.1/2 • Item 857-D-17
ANNUAL STATISTICAL REPORT, FISCAL YEAR (date). 1st–   1961/62–   [Annual]
Prepared by the Statistics and Reports Division, Office of Comptroller.

D 119.2:CT • Item 857-D-2
GENERAL PUBLICATIONS.
Earlier D 13.2
Later D 14.2

D 119.3/2
INFORMATION BULLETIN. [Irregular]

D 119.3/3:CT
FG (series).

D 119.8:CT • Item 857-D-8
HANDBOOKS, MANUALS, GUIDES.
Earlier D 13.8

D 119.8/2 • Item 857-D-10
HANDBOOKS. H 1–   [Irregular]

D 119.8/3 • Item 320-B-3
FEDERAL GUIDANCE FOR STATE AND LOCAL CIVIL DEFENSE, FG- (series). [Irregular]

D 119.8/3:E 5.11 • Item 320-B-3
FEDERAL RADIOLOGICAL FALLOUT MONITORING STATION DIRECTORY. [Irregular]

D 119.8/4 • Item 320-B-3
FEDERAL CIVIL DEFENSE GUIDE. [Irregular]
Issued in parts and chapters. Punched for ring binder, loose-leaf.

D 119.8/5 • Item 320-B-7
TECHNICAL MEMORANDUMS (numbered). [Irregular]
Discontinued.

D 119.8/6 • Item 320-B-3
PROFESSIONAL MANUALS, PM- (series). [Irregular]

D 119.8/7 • Item 857-D-12
INSTRUCTOR'S GUIDES, IG- (series). [Irregular]

D 119.8/8 • Item 320-B-1
STUDENT MANUALS, SM- (series). [Irregular]
Later D 14.8/2

D 119.9 • Item 320-B-2
TECHNICAL REPORTS. TR 1–   [Irregular]
Later D 14.9

D 119.10
CD NEWSPICTURES. [Irregular]

D 119.11 • Item 857-D-11
MISCELLANEOUS PUBLICATIONS, MP-(series). 1–   [Irregular]
Later D 14.10

D 119.12
ADDRESSES. [Irregular]

D 119.13 • Item 857-D-5
LEAFLETS, L- (series). [Irregular]

D 119.14:nos • Item 320-B-8
BUILDINGS WITH FALLOUT PROTECTION, DESIGN CASE STUDIES. DCS-1–   1968–   [Irregular]

PURPOSE:– To illustrate to architects and engineers how fallout shelters can be incorporated into buildings through application of radiation protection design techniques at little or no cost.

D 119.15:nos. • Item 320-B-9
HS [Home Study] (series). 1–   1971–   [Irregular]
Later D 14.11

OFFICE OF PROVOST MARSHAL GENERAL
(1969–   )

D 120.1:date
ANNUAL REPORT.

D 120.2:CT
GENERAL PUBLICATIONS.

D 120.8:CT • Item 362-A
HANDBOOKS, MANUALS, GUIDES.

DEPARTMENT OF THE NAVY
(1949–   )

CREATION AND AUTHORITY

The Department of the Navy, together with the office of the Secretary of the Navy, was established by act of Congress, approved April 30, 1798 (1 Stat. 553). For 9 years prior to that date, by provision of act of Congress, approved August 7, 1789 (1 Stat. 49), the conduct of naval affairs was under the Secretary for the Department of War. The Department of the Navy was incorporated in the National Military Establishment by the National Security Act of 1947 (61 Stat. 499). The National Security Act Amendments of 1949, approved August 10, 1949 (63 Stat. 578) redesignated the National Military Establishment as the Department of Defense.

INFORMATION

Office of Information
Department of the Navy
The Pentagon
Washington, D.C. 20350
(202) 697-5342
Fax: (202) 697-8921
http://www.navy.mil

D 201.1:date • Item 399-E (MF)
REPORT TO THE CONGRESS. [Annual]
Earlier title: SECNAV/CNO Report.
Effective with FY 1983, Annual Report of the Department of the Navy (D 201.1) and Annual Report of Office of Naval Operations (D 207.1) combined to form SECNAV/CNO Report.

D 201.1/1-2 • Item 307-A-21 (EL)
HIGHLIGHTS OF THE DEPARTMENT OF THE NAVY FY...BUDGET. [Annual]

D 201.1/2:date • Item 370
FINANCIAL REPORT, FISCAL YEAR, OFFICE OF COMPTROLLER.
Replaces D 212.8

D 201.1/3:date • Item 399-E
NAVY PERSONNEL RESEARCH AND DEVELOPMENT CENTER: ANNUAL REPORT.
Discontinued.

D 201.2:CT • Item 370
GENERAL PUBLICATIONS.
Earlier M 201.2

D 201.2:Se 4/2 • Item 370
SELLING TO NAVY PRIME CONTRACTORS. 1952–   [Irregular]

D 201.3/2:nos.
ELECTRONICS INFORMATION BULLETIN.

D 201.5:CT • Item 371
LAWS.
Earlier M 201.10
Discontinued.

D 201.6:CT • Item 373
REGULATIONS, RULES, AND INSTRUCTIONS.
Earlier N 1.19

D 201.6/2:v.nos. • Item 370-A
NAVY COMPTROLLER MANUAL.
Supersedes D 212.6:Su 7/949 and N 20.13:Su 7/2/946

D 201.6/3:
NAVY COMPTROLLER MANUAL, ADVANCE CHANGES.

D 201.6/4:
NAVCOMPT INSTRUCTION NOS.

D 201.6/5:
NAVCOMP NOTICE.

D 201.6/6:date
OFFICE EQUIPMENT HANDBOOK.

D 201.6/7:index nos.
OFFICE EQUIPMENT GUIDE.

D 201.6/8:index nos.
OFFICE EQUIPMENT NEWS.

D 201.6/9:
NAVY PROPERTY REDISTRIBUTION AND DISPOSAL REGULATIONS.

D 201.6/10 • Item 373 (MF)
NAVY PROCUREMENT DIRECTIVES. [Irregular]

PURPOSE:– To implement the Armed Services Procurement Regulation (ASPR) and establish for the Department of the Navy uniform policies and procedures relating to the procurement of supplies and services.
Subscription includes basic manual plus supplementary material for an indefinite period. Issued in loose-leaf form, punched for 3-ring binder.
ISSN 0147-7102

D 201.6/10-2 • Item 373 (MF)
– SUPPLEMENTS.

D 201.6/11:date • Item 373
INDEX TO NAVY PROCUREMENT INFORMATION.
Earlier D 201.2:P 94/3

D 201.6/12:CT • Item 370-A
HANDBOOKS, MANUALS, GUIDES.
Formerly in D 201.6

D 201.6/13:dt.&nos.
NAVY CURRENT PROCUREMENT DIRECTIVES, NCPD (series).

D 201.6/14:date
SURVEY OF PROCUREMENT STATISTICS. [Quarterly] (Naval Material Command) (NAVMAT P-4200)
Annual issue published separately.
ISSN 0565-8497

D 201.7:date
TELEPHONE DIRECTORY.
Earlier M 201.8

D 201.7/2:date
NAVAL MATERIAL COMMAND TELEPHONE DIRECTORY.

D 201.8:dt.&nos. • Item 369
COURT-MARTIAL ORDERS.
Earlier M 201.9
Discontinued.

D 201.9:series nos. • Item 373-B
YOUR NAVY, FROM THE VIEWPOINT OF THE NATION'S FINEST ARTISTS [lithographic prints, announcement and order form].
Discontinued.

D 201.11: • Item 372
U.S. NAVY REGULATIONS.

D 201.12:CT
POTOMAC RIVER NAVAL COMMAND PUBLICATIONS.

D 201.13:
MILITARY STANDARD MIL-STD (Navy) SERIES.

D 201.14 • Item 371-A
NAVY MANAGEMENT REVIEW. v. 1– 1956–
[Monthly]

PURPOSE:– To publicise better management practices as they exist within the Navy and Marine Corps; to disseminate information about "management improvement" techniques, their applications and probable benefits. Covers industrial methods, improved office methods, electronic data processing, management science, and organization review and analysis.
Discontinued.

D 201.15:date • Item 373-A
UNITED STATES ANTARCTIC PROGRAMS, ANNUAL REPORT.

D 201.15/2:CT • Item 373-A (MF)
NAVAL SUPPORT FORCE, ANTARCTICA, PUBLICATIONS.
Earlier D 1.32
Discontinued.

D 201.15/3 • Item 373-A (MF)
NAVAL SUPPORT FORCE ANTARCTICA: MONOGRAPH (series).

D 201.16:CT
ADDRESSES.

D 201.16/3:nos.
SCIENTIFIC MONOGRAPHS. [Irregular] (Naval Research Office, Tokyo)

D 201.17 • Item 369-B
DIRECTION, THE NAVY PUBLIC AFFAIRS MAGAZINE. [Monthly]
Guidelines in public information for commanders and public information offices.
Indexed by: Index to U.S. Government Periodicals.
ISSN 0419-1854

D 201.18:v.nos.&nos.
CIVILIAN MANPOWER MANAGEMENT, JOURNAL OF NAVY AND CIVILIAN PERSONNEL MANAGEMENT. [Quarterly]

D 201.19:CT • Item 370-G
POSTERS. [Irregular]

D 201.19/2:CT • Item 370-A
AUDIOVISUAL MATERIALS.

D 201.20:nos. • Item 370-B
MC REPORTS. [Irregular] (Maury Center for Ocean Science)
Discontinued.

NAVAL WEAPONS LABORATORY
Dahlgren, Virginia 22448

D 201.21:nos.
NWL TECHNICAL REPORTS. TR 1– [Irregular]

Combined with D 201.21/3 to form class D 201.21/5.

D 201.21/2:nos.
NWL ADMINISTRATIVE REPORTS. AR 1– [Irregular]

D 201.21/3:nos.
WHITE OAK LABORATORY: TECHNICAL REPORTS, NSWC/WOL/TR- (series).
Combined with D 201.21 to form class D 201.21/5.

D 201.21/4:nos.
DAHLGREN LABORATORY: CONTRACT REPORTS, CR- (series).

D 201.21/5:yr.-nos. • Item 370-D (MF)
NAVAL SURFACE WEAPONS CENTER, TECHNICAL REPORTS, NSWC-TR-(series). [Irregular]

Highly technical reports concerning the laboratory testing and evaluation of various systems prior to their use, covering such subjects as sur-face weapons, satellites, environmental protection, etc.
This class combines D 201/21 and D 21.3
Discontinued.

D 201.21/6:yr.-nos. • Item 307-D (MF)
NAVAL SURFACE WEAPONS CENTER, NSWC-AP-(series). [Irregular]
Discontinued.

D 201.21/6-2 • Item 370-D
NWC ADMINISTRATIVE PUBLICATION (series).
Discontinued.

D 201.21/7:nos. • Item 370-D
NSWC MP (series).
Discontinued.

D 201.21/8:date • Item 370-D-1 (MF)
NAVAL SURFACE WARFARE CENTER DAHLGREN DIVISION, TECHNICAL DIGEST. [Annual]

Naval Air Development Center
Warminster, Pennsylvania

D 201.22:nos.
REPORTS, NADC-CS- (series). [Irregular]

Naval Weapons Center
China Lake, California

D 201.23:nos.
NWC TECHNICAL PUBLICATIONS, TP-(series). [Irregular]

DEPARTMENT OF THE NAVY
(Continued)

D 201.24:date
NavNews, A NAVY NEWS SERVICE. – Sept. 1975. [Irregular] (Office of Chief of Information, Naval Internal Relations Activity)

D 201.25:v.nos./nos. • Item 370-C
NAVY FAMILY LIFELINE.
Earlier titled: Wifeline. [Annual]

D 201.26:date
NAVY EDITOR SERVICE. [Biweekly]

D 201.27:v.nos.&nos. • Item 373-C
NCEL TECHDATA.

D 201.28:CT
ENVIRONMENTAL IMPACT STATEMENTS.

D 201.29:nos. • Item 370-E (MF)
TECHNICAL REPORTS. [Irregular] (Naval Training Equipment Center)
Published in microfiche.

D 201.30:date • Item 370-F (MF)
U.S. NAVAL CONTROL OF SHIPPING REPORT. [Annual]

Functions as a communication medium between activities involved with the Naval Control of Shipping Organization to keep members informed of developments.
Discontinued.

D 201.31: • Item 370-A-1 (MF)
CNTT- (series). [Irregular]

CNTT = Chief Naval Technical Training

D 201.31/2:letters-nos. • Item 307-A-1 (MF)
CNATT- (series). [Irregular]

D 201.31/3:letters-nos.-date • Item 370-A-1 (MF)
CHIEF OF NAVAL AIR TRAINING, CNAT-(series). [Irregular]

D 201.32:v.nos.&nos. • **Item 374-A-1 (EL)**
FATHOM, SURFACE SHIP AND SUBMARINE SAFETY
REVIEW. [Quarterly]
PURPOSE:– To present the most accurate
information currently available on the subject of
nautical accident prevention.
Indexed by: Index to U.S. Government Peri-
odicals.
Earlier D 202.20

D 201.33 • **Item 370-H (MF)**
HISTORY OF THE CHAPLAIN CORPS, U.S. NAVY.
[Irregular]
Earlier D 208.2:C 36

D 201.34:nos. • **Item 370-J**
NPRDC-TR- (series). [Irregular]
NPRDC = Navy Personnel Research and De-
velopment Center.
Discontinued.

D 201.35: • **Item 370-K**
LONG RANGE ACQUISITION ESTIMATES. [Annual]

PURPOSE– To present long range acquisition estimates intended principally to increase
the number of qualified suppliers for Navy program requirements but also to provide industry
with business planning information relating to prospective competitive opportunities.

D 201.36:date • **Item 370-C**
UPDATE (Electronics Manufacturing Productivity
Facility). [Quarterly]
Discontinued.

D 201.37:date • **Item 370-K (MF)**
Consolidated Subject Index. [Annual]
Discontinued.

D 201.38 • **Item 370-H**
BIBLIOGRAPHY.

D 201.39:CT • **Item 373-C**
WWII FACT SHEET (series).
Discontinued.

D 201.40:CT • **Item 307-A-2 (E)**
ELECTRONIC PRODUCTS.

D 201.42:v.nos./nos. • **Item 370-A-2**
TECHNOLOGY TRANSFER TODAY, GAINING THE
COMPETITIVE EDGE.
Discontinued.

D 201.43:date/nos. • **Item 370-A-3**
SPACE TRACKS.

D 201.44: • **Item 307-A-2 (EL)**
ABM (Acquisition & Business Management) ONLINE.
[Weekly]

NAVAL AIR SYSTEMS COMMAND
(1966–   )

CREATION AND AUTHORITY

The Bureau of Aeronautics (M 208) was transferred along with the Department of the Navy to
the Department of Defense upon its establishment in 1949. In September 1959, the Bureau
merged with the Bureau of Ordnance to form the
Bureau of Naval Weapons (D 217).
The Naval Air Systems Command was established in 1966 and its publications assigned to
the D 202 class.

INFORMATION

Naval Air Systems Command
Bldg. 2272, Ste. 540
47123 Buse Road Unit #IPT
Patuxent River, MD. 20670-1547
(301) 757-7825
Fax: (301) 757-7756
http://www.navair.navy.mil

D 202.1:date
ANNUAL REPORTS.
Earlier M 208.2

D 202.2:CT • **Item 374**
GENERAL PUBLICATIONS.
Earlier M 208.2

D 202.2:An 8
ANTARCTIC BIBLIOGRAPHY. 1951. 147 p.

Covers biological, geo-physical, and geographical sciences.

D 202.2:At 6
U.S. NAVY MARINE CLIMATIC ATLAS OF THE
WORLD. 1955– 69. 8. v.

PURPOSE:– To provide a source for those
requiring an up-to-date qualitative knowledge
of the climates of the oceans. Volumes 1– 7
cover the individual oceans, while volume 8
covers meteorological information on surface
and upper levels of the atmosphere over
oceans and adjacent land masses.

D 202.2:Av 5/2/910-70 • **Item 374**
UNITED STATES NAVAL AVIATION, 1910– 1970.
[2nd edition] Rev. 1971. 440 p. il.

Gives a chronological record of significant events in Naval Aviation's growth and
development from its beginning in 1910
through December 1970.

D 202.6:CT • **Item 376**
REGULATIONS, RULES, AND INSTRUCTIONS.
Earlier M 208.6

D 202.6/2:date
BUREAU OF AERONAUTICS MANUAL.
Earlier N 28.7

D 202.6/3:
BUAER INSTRUCTIONS.
Administrative.

D 202.6/4:
BUAER INSTRUCTION NAVAER.
Administrative.

D 202.6/5:
BUAER NOTICE.
Administrative.

D 202.6/6:
BUAER NOTICE NAVAER.
Administrative.

D 202.6/7:CT • **Item 374-E**
HANDBOOKS, MANUALS, GUIDES.
Earlier D 202.6
Formerly distributed to Depository Libraries
under item 374-B.

D 202.6/8:nos. • **Item 374-C**
[LANGUAGE GUIDES] PT- (series).
Discontinued.

D 202.7:dt.&nos.
TECHNICAL NOTES.
Earlier M 208.10

D 202.8:dt.&nos.
TECHNICAL ORDERS.
Earlier M 208.7

D 202.9:v.nos./nos. • **Item 375 (EL)**
NAVAL AVIATION NEWS. 1919–   [Monthly]

PURPOSE:– To disseminate information on
safety, training, maintenance, and technical data
concerning the various phases of Navy and Marine air activities.
Index contained in the December issues.
Indexed by: Index to U.S. Government Periodicals.
ISSN 0028-1417

D 202.9/2:nos.
NAVAL AVIATION NEWS. [Monthly]
Restricted. Changed from D 207.7/2

D 202.10:dt.&nos.
FLIGHT SAFETY BULLETINS.
Earlier M 207.8

D 202.11:
MILITARY STANDARD (designs).

D 202.12:
AVIATION CIRCULAR LETTER.

D 202.13:v.nos./nos. • **Item 374-A-2 (EL)**
APPROACH v. 1–   1955–   [Monthly]
Contains articles, editorials, and the most
accurate information currently available on the
subject of aviation accident prevention.
Earlier titles: Approach, Naval Aviation Safety
Review; Approach/MECH. See D 202.19 for MECH.

D 202.14:nos.
NAVAL AIR DEVELOPMENT CENTER, JOHNSVILLE,
PA. AERONAUTICAL ELECTRONIC AND ELEC-
TRICAL LABORATORY, REPORT NADC-EL
(series).
Later D 217.19

D 202.15:CT
CHARTS AND POSTERS.

D 202.16:nos.
BUAER REPORT.

D 202.17:date
EMPLOYMENT OPPORTUNITIES.
Earlier D 217.9

D 202.18:nos.
WHAT'S HAPPENING IN THE PERSONNEL FIELD.
Earlier D 217.9

D 202.19:date/nos. • **Item 374-A-3 (EL)**
MECH. [Quarterly]

PURPOSE:– To provide current information
on maintenance, caused mishap prevention and
general aviation ground safety.
Earlier issued bimonthly.
Merged with Approach to form Approach/
MECH (see D 202.13). Reactivated in 1997.
Indexed by: Index to U.S. Government Peri-
odicals.
ISSN 0025-6471

D 202.20:v.nos.&nos. • **Item 374-A-1**
FATHOM, SURFACE SHIP AND SUBMARINE SAFETY
REVIEW. v. 1–   [Quarterly] (Naval Safety Cen-
ter)
Later D 201.32
ISSN 0014-8822

D 202.21:CT
BIBLIOGRAPHIES AND LISTS OF PUBLICATIONS.

D 202.22:v.nos.&nos.
T.I.S.C.A [Technical Information System for Carrier
Aviation] TECHNICAL INFORMATION INDEXES:
NAVAL CARRIER AVIATION ABSTRACT BULLE-
TIN WITH CROSS REFERENCE INDEX.

D 202.23:nos.
NAVAL AIR DEVELOPMENT CENTER REPORTS
NADA (series).

NAVAL OCEANOGRAPHIC OFFICE
(1962–   )

CREATION AND AUTHORITY

The Hydrographic Office (M 202) was transferred along with the Department of the Navy to
the Department of Defense upon its establishment in 1949. The name was changed to Naval
Oceanographic Office by Public Law 87-533 approved July 10, 1962.

INFORMATION
Naval Oceanographic Office
Department of the Navy
Stennis Space Center, Mississippi 39522

D 203.1   • Item 377-A
ANNUAL REPORT. [Annual]

D 203.2:CT   • Item 377
GENERAL PUBLICATIONS.
Earlier M 202.

D 203.3:nos.
HYDROGRAPHIC BULLETINS. [Weekly]
Earlier M 202.3

D 203.3/2:nos.
BIWEEKLY INFORMATION BULLETIN.

D 203.3/3:nos.
THE BULLETIN. Admin.

D 203.4:nos.   • Item 377-B
CIRCULARS.
Earlier M 202.4

D 203.7:dt.&nos.
NOTICE TO AVIATORS. [Biweekly]
Earlier M 202.7

D 203.8
NOTICE TO MARINERS. [Weekly]
Part 1, Atlantic and Mediterranean. Part 2,
Pacific and Indian Oceans.
Prepared in cooperation with the Coast Guard.
Notice to Mariners Relating to Great Lakes and
Tributary Waters West of Montreal is published
by the Coast Guard (TD 5.10).
Semiannual index.

D 203.8/2:dt.&nos.
NOTICE TO MARINERS. [Semimonthly]
Restricted.
Earlier M 202.8/2

D 203.8/3
SPECIAL NOTICE TO MARINERS. [Annual]
Prepared jointly with the Coast and Geodetic
Survey.

D 203.9:dt.&nos.
NOTICE TO MARINERS RELATING TO GREAT LAKES
AND TRIBUTARY WATERS WEST OF MONTREAL.
[Weekly]
Earlier M 202.9

D 203.9/2:nos.
LOCAL HYDROGRAPHIC MEMORANDUM FOR AVIA-
TORS.

D 203.10:dt.&nos.
NOTICE TO MARINERS, NORTH AMERICAN-
CARIBBEAN EDITION. [Weekly]
Earlier M 202.10

D 203.11:dt.&nos.
MEMORANDUM FOR AVIATORS.
Earlier M 202.11

D 203.12:date
TIDE, MOON AND SUN CALENDAR, BALTIMORE,
MD. [Monthly]

D 203.13:date
TIDE CALENDAR FOR HAMPTON ROADS (Sewalls
Pt.) VA. [Monthly]

D 203.14:date
TIDE CALENDAR, SAVANNAH, GA. [Monthly]
Earlier M 202.14

D 203.14/2:date
SUN AND MOON TABLES FOR CLEVELAND, OHIO.
[Monthly]

D 203.15:date
PILOT CHARTS OF CENTRAL AMERICAN WATERS;
NO. 3500. [Monthly]
Earlier M 202.15

D 203.16:date
PILOT CHART OF INDIAN OCEAN; NO. 2603. [Monthly]
Earlier M 202.15

D 203.17:date
PILOT CHART OF NORTH ATLANTIC OCEAN; NO.
1400. [Monthly]
Earlier M 202.17

D 203.18:date
PILOT CHART OF SOUTH ATLANTIC OCEAN; NO.
2600. [Quarterly]
Earlier M 202.18

D 203.19:date
PILOT CHART OF NORTH PACIFIC OCEAN; NO. 1401.
[Monthly]
Earlier M 202.19

D 203.20:date
PILOT CHART OF SOUTH PACIFIC OCEAN; NO. 2601.
[Quarterly]
Earlier M 202.20

D 203.21:nos.
MAPS AND CHARTS.
Earlier M 202.21

D 203.21/2
U.S. NAVAL OCEANOGRAPHIC OFFICE CHART
CORRECTION LIST. [Semiannual]

D 203.21/3:date
HYDROGRAPHIC OFFICE CHART, CORRECTION
LIST, ARRANGED ACCORDING TO CONSECU-
TIVE NUMBERS.

D 203.22   • Item 378
PUBLICATIONS. 1–   [Irregular]

Publications of the Naval Oceanographic Office are published in this numbered series and
include sailing directions, light lists, radio aids,
manuals, tables, atlases for nautical and aerial
navigation, weather summaries.
Material covered by the Naval Oceanographic
Office is exclusive of the continental United
States. For similar publications covering the United
States, consult the publications of the Coast and
Geodetic Survey and the Coast Guard. Super-
sedes H. O. Publications, for title designation,
but the numbering system has remained the same.
Effective August 15, 1960, certain Hydrographic
Office publications were assigned new numbers.

LIST OF LIGHTS AND FOG SIGNALS. [Irregular]

Basic volumes kept up-to-date by
Changes which are sold for 50¢ each.
Each volume is revised every few years
with annual supplements issued between editions to provide an up-to-date service for
mariners. Except for the volume on Antarctica, all Sailing Directions are published in
loose- leaf form with a standard price of $4.50
per volume, which includes the ring binder, or
$3.00 per volume without the binder. When a
volume is sold, all Changes in effect at the
time of sale are furnished without additional
cost. Later Changes are available at 35¢ each.

SAILING DIRECTIONS.

PURPOSE:– To furnish information required by the navigator that cannot be shown
conveniently on nautical charts.
Discontinued.

D 203.22:1-P/date   • Item 378
CATALOG OF PUBLICATIONS. (N.O. Pub. 1-P)
[Annual]

D 203.22:9   • Item 378
AMERICAN PRACTICAL NAVIGATOR. Revised
1962, Reprinted 1972. 1524 p. il.

D 203.22:9/tab.   • Item 378
TABLES FROM AMERICAN PRACTICAL NAVIGA-
TOR (BOWDITCH). 1969. 1058. p.

For the convenience of the navigator, 34
navigational tables from the American Practical Navigator (Bowditch) have been extracted
and published separately in this bound volume. These tables have been specifically
selected, prepared, and designed for shipboard use. They consist of various conversion, piloting, traverse, meteorological, math-

ematical, specialized celestial sight reduction, and other tables useful to the mariner.
D 203.22:102   • Item 378
INTERNATIONAL CODE OF SIGNALS, UNITED
STATES EDITION. 1968. 156 p. il. (H. O. Pub.
102)
Gives signals for visual, sound, and radio communications as adopted by the 4th
assembly of the Inter-Governmental Maritime
Consultative Organization in 1965.
A valuable addition to the library of all
boat owners, whether the boat is a small pleasure craft or a large cruising yacht. There are
more than 2000 signals listed for distress
and emergency, maneuvers, navigation and
hydrography, meteorology and weather, medical assistance and advice, and other situations likely to confront a boatsman. The book
answers many questions regarding the meaning of various flag hoists, radio/telephone procedures, signalling for assistance, and more.

D 203.22:150   • Item 378
WORLD PORT INDEX. 4th ed. 1971. 360 p. il.
Gives location, characteristics, facilities,
and available services of ports and shipping
facilities throughout the world. The application chart and Sailing Direction is given for
each place listed. Information compiled through
November 30, 1970.

D 203.22:151   • Item 378
DISTANCES BETWEEN PORTS. 1965. 220 p. (H.
O. Pub. 151)
Former title: Table of Distances between
Ports. Supersedes H.O. 117.

D 203.22:220   • Item 378
NAVIGATION DICTIONARY. 2d ed. 1969. 292 p.
(H. O. Pub. 220)

PURPOSE:– To supply the need for a
comprehensive, authoritative dictionary of
navigational terms by furnishing the navigator of any type craft definitions that represent present usage. Terms and expressions
are listed alphabetically according to standard dictionary practice, followed by the plural (or singular) form if unusual.

D 203.22/2:date&serial nos.
MONTHLY CORRECTIONS AFFECTING PORTFOLIO
CHART LIST AND INDEX- CATALOG OF NAUTI-
CAL CHARTS AND PUBLICATIONS.
Restricted.

D 203.22/3   • Item 377-C
SPECIAL PUBLICATIONS, SP- (series). 1–
[Irregular]
Discontinued.

National Oceanographic
Data Center

D 203.23:nos.
HYDRO NOTICE.

D 203.24:nos.   • Item 377-D
NATIONAL OCEANOGRAPHIC DATA CENTER PUB-
LICATIONS (numbered).
Discontinued.

D 203.24:C   • Item 377-D
CATALOG SERIES. C 1–   1965–   [Irregular]

D 203.24:G   • Item 377-D
GENERAL SERIES. G 1–   [Irregular]

D 203.24:G-13   • Item 377-D
QUESTIONS ABOUT THE OCEANS. 1969. 121 p.

Presents factual material on the marine
sciences for use by young people at all grade
levels and supplies teachers with a suitable
introduction to selected marine subjects with
specific references for additional information
on each topic. All answers were thoroughly
researched and guides to further reading on
each question are supplied.

D 203.24:M   • Item 377-D
MANUAL SERIES. M 1–   [Irregular]

D 203.24/2:nos.
NATIONAL OCEANOGRAPHIC DATA CENTER NEWS-
LETTER.
Later C 55.290

D 203.24/3:CT
NATIONAL OCEANOGRAPHIC DATA CENTER
PUBLICATIONS (unnumbered).

D 203.24/4
ANNOUNCEMENTS. [Irregular]

D 203.24/5
NATIONAL OCEANOGRAPHIC DATA CENTER, LIST
OF FULLY PROCESSED OCEANOGRAPHIC
CRUISE. [Irregular]

D 203.24/6
NODC QUARTERLY ACCESSIONS, COMPUTER
PRODUCED INDEXES, AMERICAN METEORO-
LOGICAL SOCIETY METEOROLOGICAL AND
GEOASTROPHYSICAL ABSTRACTS. v. 1–
1966–   [Quarterly]

D 203.25:nos.
TRANSLATIONS.

D 203.26:nos.
TECHNICAL REPORTS. 1–   [Irregular]

D 203.26/2:nos.
INFORMAL REPORTS.

D 203.27
POSTERS. [Irregular]

D 203.28:v.nos.&nos.
NAVAL OCEANOGRAPHIC NEWSLETTER.
Discontinued.

D 203.29:v.nos.&nos.
MONTHLY SUMMARY, THE GULF STREAM. v. 1–
1966– 1974. [Monthly]
Gives position of northern edge of the Gulf
Stream, associated temperatures, and tempera-
ture anomalies for western North Atlantic.
Continued by the National Weather Service
(C 55.123).

D 203.29/2:nos.
– SUPPLEMENTS.

D 203.30:nos.
NEWS RELEASES.

D 203.31:nos.   • Item 377-E
GLOBAL OCEAN FLOOR ANALYSIS AND RESEARCH
DATA SERIES. 1–   1969–   [Irregular]

PURPOSE:– To make oceanographic data
obtained on successive cruises of the Ocean
Floor Analysis Division available to the oceanographic community and to the general public as
soon as possible after the raw data are collected
and to keep all the data from a cruise together
under one cover.
Issued in large, heavy volumes, the data
contain computer-drawn Mercator charts and profiles of navigation, bathymetry, magnetics and
other underway data; computer-drawn plots of
salinity, temperature, and sound velocity as a
function of depth; and reproductions of the precision echograms, seismic reflection profiles
records, and selected ocean-bottom photographs.

NATIONAL OCEANOGRAPHIC INSTRUMENTATION CENTER

D 203.32:date
TESTS IN PROGRESS SHEET. 1966–   [Quarterly]

PURPOSE:– To inform subscribers regarding
testing programs currently underway at the Center, the status of the Instrument Fact Sheet in
which the results will be reported, and the testing
programs planned in the near future.

D 203.32/2:nos.
INSTRUMENT FACT SHEET, IFS- (series). [Irregular]

D 203.32/3:letters-nos.
TECHNICAL BULLETIN.

D 203.33:date   • Item 377-H (MF)
NATIONAL OCEANOGRAPHIC FLEET OPERATING
SCHEDULES. [Annual] (RP- 34)
Earlier D 218.11

D 203.34:CT   • Item 307-A-3 (E)
ELECTRONIC PRODUCTS.

OFFICE OF CIVILIAN MANPOWER MANAGEMENT (1966–   )

CREATION AND AUTHORITY

The Office of Industrial Relations (M 204)
was transferred along with the Department of the
Navy to the Department of Defense upon its establishment in 1949. The name was changed to
the Office of Civilian Manpower Management in
1966.

D 204.1:date
ANNUAL REPORTS.
Earlier M 204.1

D 204.2:CT   • Item 378-C
GENERAL PUBLICATIONS.
Earlier M 204.2
Discontinued.

D 204.6:CT   • Item 378-A
REGULATIONS, RULES, AND INSTRUCTIONS.

D 204.6/2:CT   • Item 378-B
HANDBOOKS, MANUALS, GUIDES.

D 204.7   • Item 379
SAFETY REVIEW. v. 1– 29. 1944– 1972. [Monthly]
(NAVSO P-52)
PURPOSE:– To provide all levels of manage-
ment with information encouraging greater effort
in accident prevention in the Naval Service.
Discontinued.

D 204.8:v.nos.
PERSONNEL OF NAVAL SHORES ESTABLISHMENT.
[Quarterly]
Restricted
Earlier D 204.8

D 204.9:v.nos.&nos.   • Item 369-C (MF)
ADVISOR, NAVY CIVILIAN MANPOWER MANAGE-
MENT. v. 1–   [Quarterly]
(NAVSO P-3016)
Prior to Winter 1975 issued as Journal of
Navy Civilian Manpower Management.
ISSN 0364-0426
Discontinued.

OFFICE OF JUDGE ADVOCATE GENERAL (1949–   )

CREATION AND AUTHORITY

The Office of the Judge Advocate General
was authorized by act of Congress, approved
June 8, 1880 (21 Stat. 164).

INFORMATION

Office of Judge Advocate General
Department of the Navy
200 Stovall Street
Alexandria, Virginia 22332
(703) 614-7420
Fax: (202) 685-5461
http://www.jag.navy.mil

D 205.1:date
ANNUAL REPORTS.
Earlier M 214.1

D 205.2:CT   • Item 380
GENERAL PUBLICATIONS.
Earlier M 214.2

D 205.6:CT   • Item 382-A
REGULATIONS, RULES, AND INSTRUCTIONS.

D 205.6/2:CT   • Item 380-A
HANDBOOKS, MANUALS, GUIDES.

D 205.7:v.   • Item 381 (MF)
NAVAL LAW REVIEW. v. 1–   1947–   [Semiannual]

PURPOSE:– To promote legal forehandedness
among naval personnel charged with the administration of naval law.
Former title: JAG Journal.

D 205.8:CT   • Item 382
LAWS.
Discontinued.

D 205.9:date   • Item 380-B (MF)
FEDERAL TAX INFORMATION FOR ARMED FORCES
PERSONNEL. [Annual]
Discontinued.

BUREAU OF MEDICINE AND SURGERY (1949–   )

CREATION AND AUTHORITY

The Bureau of Medicine and Surgery (M 203)
was transferred along with the Department of the
Navy to the Department of Defense upon its establishment in 1949.

INFORMATION

Public Affairs Specialist
Bureau of Medicine and Surgery
Department of the Navy
2300 E Street NW
1306 Potomac Annex, Bldg. One
Washington, DC 20372-5300
(202) 762-3218
Fax: (202) 762-3750
http://navymedicine.med.navy.mil/

D 206.1:date
ANNUAL REPORTS.
Earlier M 203.1

D 206.1/2:date   • Item 388 (MF)
SUMMARIES OF RESEARCH, NAVAL DENTAL RE-
SEARCH INSTITUTE.

D 206.1/3:date   • Item 388 (MF)
COMMAND HISTORICAL REPORT. [Annual]

D 206.2:CT   • Item 385
GENERAL PUBLICATIONS.
Earlier M 203.2

D 206.3:v.nos.
NAVAL MEDICAL BULLETIN. [Bimonthly]
Earlier M 203.3

D 206.3/2   • Item 385-A-1 (EL)
NAVY MEDICAL AND DENTAL MATERIEL BULLETIN.

D 206.6:CT   • Item 387
REGULATIONS, RULES, AND INSTRUCTIONS.
Earlier M 203.6

D 206.6/2:
BUMED INSTRUCTIONS. ADMIN.

D 206.6/3:CT   • Item 385-B
HANDBOOKS, MANUALS, GUIDES.
Formerly in D 206.6

D 206.6/3:H 79 • Item 385-B
HANDBOOK OF THE HOSPITAL CORPS, UNITED STATES NAVY. 1914– [Irregular]

Following a brief chapter sketching the history of the Hospital Corps, the remaining chapters of the book cover such subjects as anatomy and physiology; first aid; nursing procedures, dietary principles; preventive medicine; pharmacology, and toxicology; pharmacal chemistry; laboratory procedures; embalming; nuclear, chemical, and biological war defense; and administration of the Medical Department.

Subscription covers the basic volume, which consists of a loose-leaf binder and approximately 17 chapters with separators. The various chapters are issued separately as they are revised.

D 206.6/3:Sn 1 • Item 385-B
POISONOUS SNAKES OF THE WORLD. 1972. 220 p. il.

Classified by areas of the world, each dangerous snake is described, many with photographs. If an antidote to the snake's venom is available, the place to obtain it is included. Suggestions for preventing snakebite and instructions in practical first aid are also included.

D 206.7:v.nos.&nos. • Item 385-D (EL)
U.S. NAVY MEDICINE. [Bimonthly]

PURPOSE:– To provide Navy medical personnel official and professional information on medicine, dentistry, and allied health sciences.
Index issued separately.
Former title: Medical News Letter.
ISSN 0364-6807

D 206.7/a • Item 385-D
– SEPARATES.
Discontinued.

D 206.8:chap.nos. • Item 386
MANUAL OF MEDICAL DEPARTMENT, NAVY.
Earlier M 203.12
Discontinued.

D 206.8/2:date • Item 385-B (MF)
MANUAL OF MEDICAL DEPARTMENT, NAVY. [Irregular] (NAVMED P-117)

D 206.9:project nos.&rp.nos.
NAVAL MEDICAL RESEARCH INSTITUTE REPORTS.
Earlier M 203.8

NAVAL SUBMARINE MEDICAL CENTER
Submarine Base
Groton, Connecticut 06340

D 206.10 • Item 385-C (MF)
REPORTS. 1– [Irregular]

D 206.10/2:nos.
MEMORANDUM REPORTS. 1– [Irregular]

D 206.10/3:nos.
SPECIAL REPORTS. [Irregular]

BUREAU OF MEDICINE AND SURGERY
(Continued)
D 206.11:date • Item 388 (MF)
MEDICAL STATISTICS, NAVY, STATISTICAL REPORT OF THE SURGEON GENERAL, NAVY, OCCURRENCE OF DISEASES AND INJURIES IN THE NAVY FOR FISCAL YEAR (date). [Annual]
(NAVMED P-5027)
Discontinued.

D 206.12:nos. • Item 385-A
HISTORY OF MEDICAL DEPARTMENT OF NAVY IN WORLD WAR II.
Discontinued.

D 206.12/2:date
HISTORY OF MEDICAL DEPARTMENT OF UNITED STATES NAVY.
Discontinued.

D 206.13:
BUMED CIRCULAR LETTER.

D 206.14:nos.
NAVAL MEDICAL RESEARCH INSTITUTE: LECTURE AND REVIEW SERIES.

D 206.15 • Item 388-A
STATISTICS OF NAVY MEDICINE. v. 1– 1945– [Quarterly]

Sub-title: Quarterly Highlights of Trends and Facts.
Covers admission rates, daily number of patients occupying beds, patients admitted, outpatient service, incident rates, and industrial health.
Discontinued.

NAVAL SCHOOL OF
AVIATION MEDICINE
Pensacola, Florida

D 206.16:
RESEARCH REPORTS. [Irregular]

D 206.17
SUMMARIES OF RESEARCH REPORTED ON DURING CALENDAR YEAR (date). [Annual]

NAVAL AEROSPACE MEDICINE CENTER
Pensacola, Florida 32512

D 206.18:nos.
NAVAL AEROSPACE MEDICAL INSTITUTE, NAMI-(series). 1– [Irregular]

NAVAL MEDICAL FIELD RESEARCH
LABORATORY
Camp Lejeune, North Carolina 28542

D 206.19:v.nos.&nos.
REPORTS. v. 1– [Irregular]

BUREAU OF MEDICINE AND SURGERY
(Continued)

D 206.20:CT
BIBLIOGRAPHIES AND LISTS OF PUBLICATIONS.

NAVAL MEDICAL NEUROPSYCHIATRIC
RESEARCH UNIT
San Diego, California 92152

D 206.21:nos.
REPORTS. [Irregular]

D 206.21/2:date
ABSTRACTS OF COMPLETED RESEARCH.

NAVAL HEALTH RESEARCH CENTER

D 206.22:CT • Item 388-B
PUBLICATIONS. [Irregular]

D 206.23:CT • Item 385-E
POSTERS. [Irregular]

D 206.24 • Item 385-A-1 (E)
ELECTRONIC PRODUCTS.

OFFICE OF NAVAL OPERATIONS
(1949–   )

CREATION AND AUTHORITY

The Office of Naval Operations (M 207) was transferred along with the Department of the Navy to the Department of Defense upon its establishment in 1949.

INFORMATION
Public Affairs
Chief of Naval Operations
Department of the Navy
4A-686 Pentagon
Washington, DC 20350-2000
(703) 697-6154
Fax: (703) 693-9408
http://www.n4.hq.navy.mil

D 207.1:date • Item 399-E
ANNUAL REPORTS.

Effective with FY 1983, combined with Annual Report of the Department of the Navy (D 201.1) to form the SECNAV/CNO Report (D 201.1).
Earlier M 207.1
See D 201.1

D 207.2:CT • Item 399
GENERAL PUBLICATIONS.
Earlier M 207.2

D 207.6:CT • Item 400
REGULATIONS, RULES, AND INSTRUCTIONS.
Earlier M 207.6

D 207.6/2:CT • Item 399-C
HANDBOOKS, MANUALS, GUIDES.

D 207.7:nos.
NAVAL AVIATION NEWS. [Monthly]
Changed to D 202.9
Earlier M 207.7

D 207.7/2:nos.
NAVAL AVIATION NEWS. [Monthly]
Restricted.
Changed to D 202.9/2
Earlier M 207.7/2

D 207.8:
O & NAV INSTRUCTIONS. ADMIN.

D 207.9:nos.
NAVAL WARFARE PUBLICATIONS.
Desig. NWP-nos.

D 207.10:v.nos. • Item 399-A
DICTIONARY OF AMERICAN NAVAL FIGHTING SHIPS.

D 207.10/2:CT • Item 399-A-2
HISTORICAL PUBLICATIONS.

D 207.10/3:nos. • Item 399-A-1
UNITED STATES NAVY AND THE VIETNAM CONFLICT (series). 1– 1977– [Irregular]

D 207.10/4:nos. • Item 399-A-2
CONTRIBUTIONS TO NAVAL HISTORY (Series).
Later D 221.19

D 207.11:CT • Item 399-B
BIBLIOGRAPHIES AND LISTS OF PUBLICATIONS.

D 207.12:v.nos. • Item 399-D
NAVAL DOCUMENTS OF THE AMERICAN REVOLUTION. v. 1–

D 207.13 • Item 400-A
SHIPBUILDING AND CONVERSION PROGRAM. [Annual]
Discontinued.

D 207.14:CT • Item 400-B (MF)
EXCERPTS FROM SLIDE PRESENTATIONS BY THE OFFICE OF CHIEF OF NAVAL OPERATIONS.

D 207.15:v.nos.&nos. • Item 400-C
NAVY LIFELINE, NAVAL SAFETY JOURNAL. v. 1– 1972– [Bimonthly] (Naval Safety Center, Norfolk, Virginia 23511)
Indexed by: Index to U.S. Government Periodicals.

D 207.15/2:date • Item 403-D
ASHORE, A NAVAL SAFETY CENTER PUBLICATION. [Bimonthly]
Previously Titled Safety Line

D 207.16:CT
POSTERS.

D 207.17:nos. • Item 401 (EL)
ALL HANDS, BUREAU OF NAVAL PERSONNEL
INFORMATION BULLETIN. 303– 1942–
[Monthly]

Contains articles of general interest about
the Navy and its operations. Intended as a popular magazine for sailors, but of interest also to
the general public.
Supersedes Bureau of Navigation Bulletin.
Indexed by: Index to U.S. Government Periodicals.
ISSN 0002-5577
Earlier D 208.3

D 207.18:v.nos.&nos. • Item 400-D (EL)
SURFACE WARFARE. v. 1– 1975– [Bimonthly]

PURPOSE:– To further the objectives of the
Chief of Naval Operations by disseminating information to the surface warfare community which
will increase professionalism, improve readiness,
and enhance a sense of common identity and
esprit.
ISSN 0145-1073

D 207.18/2 • Item 400-D-1 (EL)
UNDERSEA WARFARE. [Quarterly]

D 207.19:v.nos.&nos. • Item 403-D
NAVY CHAPLAINS BULLETIN. v. 1– 1983–

PURPOSE:– To provide a source of information and inspiration for all Navy Chaplains, active
duty, retired, reserve, as well as serve as a medium of communication between the Navy Chaplain Corps and civilian religious groups.
Articles cover such items as human relations,
ministry in stress situations, career planning in
the chaplaincy, pastoral counseling, etc.
Supersedes publication published by Naval
Training Support Command (D 208.3/2).

D 207.19/2:v.nos.&nos. • Item 403-D (MF)
NAVY CHAPLAIN. [Quarterly]
Earlier D 207.19

D 207.20 • Item 399-A-3
COMBAT NARRATIVES (series).

NAVAL TECHNICAL TRAINING COMMAND
(1971–)

CREATION AND AUTHORITY

The Naval Technical Training Command was
established August 1, 1971, and operates under
the direction of the Chief of Naval Operations.

INFORMATION

Naval Technical Training Command
Naval Air Station
Millington, Tennessee 38054

D 207.101
ANNUAL REPORT.

D 207.102:CT
GENERAL PUBLICATIONS.

D 207.108:CT • Item 403-A
HANDBOOKS, MANUALS, GUIDES.

D 207.109:nos. • Item 404
MODULAR INDIVIDUALIZED LEARNING FOR ELEC-
TRONICS TRAINING, MIL-(series). [Irregular]

NAVAL EDUCATION AND TRAINING COMMAND
(1972–)

CREATION AND AUTHORITY

The Naval Training Command was established
on July 1, 1972, and operates under the direction
of the Chief of Naval Operations.

INFORMATION

Naval Education and Training Command
Naval Air Station
Pensacola, Florida 32508
(904) 452-3613

D 207.201:date
ANNUAL REPORT.

D 207.202:CT • Item 404-A-3
GENERAL PUBLICATIONS.

D 207.208:CT • Item 404-A-2
HANDBOOKS, MANUALS, GUIDES.

D 207.208/2:CT • Item 404
RATE TRAINING MANUALS. 1972– [Irregular]

D 207.208/3:nos. • Item 404 (MF)
PERSONNEL QUALIFICATION STANDARDS (series).
[Irregular]

D 207.208/4:CT • Item 404 (MF)
[NAVY TRAINING TEXT MATERIALS]. [Irregular]
Earlier D 208.11/2

D 207.208/5:nos. • Item 404 (MF)
OFFICER CORRESPONDENCE COURSES (series).
[Irregular]

D 207.208/6:nos. • Item 404 (MF)
OFFICER TEXT (series).

D 207.208/7:date • Item 404
LIST OF TRAINING MANUALS AND CORRESPON-
DENCE COURSES. [Annual]

D 207.209 • Item 404-A-1 (MF)
CAMPUS, NAVY EDUCATION AND TRAINING.
[Monthly] (Chief of Naval Education and Training)
ISSN 0096-1361
Earlier D 208.11/2

D 207.215: • Item 404-A-4 (MF)
USEFUL INFORMATION FOR NEWLY COMMIS-
SIONED OFFICERS. [Annual]
Contains information on such matters as the
Naval officer' scareer in the Navy, orders to duty,
first duty advice, personal affairs, etc.

D 207.216: • Item 404-A-5
BIBLIOGRAPHY FOR ADVANCED STUDY. [Annual]

PURPOSE– To provide a list of training manu-
als and other publications in support of the Naval
Standards and Occupational Standards pre-
scribed in Section 1; Manual of Navy Enlisted
Manpower and Personnel Classifications and
Occupational Standards (D 208.6/3:C 56/4).

D 207.217: • Item 404-A-6 (E)
ELECTRONIC PRODUCTS (misc.).

CHIEF OF NAVAL RESERVE
(1978–)

INFORMATION

Naval Reserve Center
Department of the Navy
Department of Defense
Anacostia, S.E., Room 351
Washington, D.C. 20374
(202) 433-2623

D 207.301:date
ANNUAL REPORT.

D 207.302:CT
GENERAL PUBLICATIONS. [Irregular]

D 207.309 • Item 404-P-1 (EL)
NAVAL RESERVIST NEWS.
Supersedes Naval Reservist (D 208.10).

D 207.310: • Item 404-P-1 (E)
ELECTRONIC PRODUCTS (misc.).

NAVAL DOCTRINE COMMAND

D 207.402: • Item 404-R
GENERAL PUBLICATIONS.

D 207.415: • Item 404-R-1 (E)
ELECTRONIC PRODUCTS.

D 207.416: • Item 404-R-1 (EL)
DOCTRINE NOTES.

NAVAL MILITARY PERSONNEL COMMAND
(1972–)

CREATION AND AUTHORITY

The Bureau of Naval Personnel (M 206) was
transferred along with the Department of the Navy
to the Department of Defense upon its establishment in 1949. The name was changed to Naval
Training Support Command in 1972.

INFORMATION

Naval Military Personnel Command
Department of the Navy
Washington, D.C. 20390

D 208.1:date
ANNUAL REPORTS.
Earlier M 206.1

D 208.2:CT • Item 403
GENERAL PUBLICATIONS.
Earlier M 206.2

D 208.3:nos. • Item 401
ALL HANDS, BUREAU OF NAVAL PERSONNEL
CAREER PUBLICATIONS. 303– 1942–
[Monthly]
Supersedes Bureau of Navigation Bulletin.
Former title: All Hands, Bureau of Naval Per-
sonnel Information Bulletin.
Indexed by: Index to U.S. Government Peri-
odicals.
Later D 207.17

D 208.3/2 • Item 403-D
NAVY CHAPLAINS BULLETIN. 1943– 1983. [Irregular]
Former title: Navy Chaplains Newsletter.
Superseded by publication of the same name issued by the Office of Naval Operations (D 207.19).
ISSN 0028-1654
See D 207.19

D 208.3/3:v.nos.&nos.
ITEMS OF INTEREST. [Monthly] (Office of the Chief of Chaplains)

D 208.6:CT • Item 406
REGULATIONS, RULES, AND INSTRUCTIONS.
Earlier M 206.6

D 208.6/2:date • Item 403-A (MF)
NAVAL MILITARY PERSONNEL MANUAL. (includes basic manual plus supplements for an indefinite period)
Former title: Bureau of Naval Personnel Manual.

D 208.6/3:CT • Item 403-A
HANDBOOKS, MANUALS, GUIDES.
Earlier D 208.6

D 208.6/3-2:date • Item 403-A (MF)
DIVISION OFFICER'S PLANNING GUIDE. [Annual]

D 208.6/3-4:date • Item 403-A (MF) (EL)
MANUAL OF NAVY ENLISTED MANPOWER AND PERSONNEL CLASSIFICATIONS AND OCCUPATIONAL STANDARDS, SECTION 2, NAVY ENLISTED CLASSIFICATIONS. [Quarterly]

D 208.6/4:CT • Item 403-A-1
PORT GUIDES. [Irregular]
Discontinued.

D 208.6/5:CT • Item 403-A-2
FOREIGN LANGUAGE PHRASE CARDS. [Irregular]
PURPOSE:– To provide in convenient format the commonly used phrases of a specific language, to be used as a guide to the spoken language. Separate language to each card.
Discontinued.

D 208.7 • Item 402
NAVAL TRAINING BULLETIN. 1945– 1972. [Quarterly]
Features contributed articles on such current programs as Regular and Reserve shipboard training and exercises, People-to-People, leadership, physical fitness, enlisted training of personnel in all ratings, officer education, and applicable civil and military graduate education. Also includes sections providing recent information of specific training publications, seamanship and navigation safety (Davy Jones' Locker), schools and courses, book reviews, security training, and training aids.
Discontinued.

D 208.8:nos.
SEA CLIPPER. [Weekly]
Earlier M 206.8

D 208.9:CT
INSTRUCTOR'S TRAINING AIDS GUIDE.

D 208.10 • Item 405-A
NAVAL RESERVIST, NEWS OF INTEREST TO THE NAVAL RESERVIST. 1946– [Quarterly]
Indexed by: Index to U.S. Government Periodicals.
Later D 207.309
Discontinued.

D 208.11 • Item 404
[NAVY TRAINING COURSES]. [Irregular]
Textbooks for courses given to enlisted personnel in the various occupations of the Navy.

D 208.11/2 • Item 404
[NAVY TRAINING TEXT MATERIALS]. [Irregular]
Later D 207.208/4

D 208.11/3 • Item 405
NAVY LIFE, READING AND WRITING FOR SUCCESS IN THE NAVY.

D 208.12 • Item 405 (MF)
REGISTER OF COMMISSIONED AND WARRANT OFFICERS OF THE NAVY AND MARINE CORPS AND RESERVE OFFICERS ON ACTIVE DUTY. [Annual]
List is as of January 1.

D 208.12/2 • Item 405 (MF)
REGISTER OF COMMISSIONED AND WARRANT OFFICERS OF THE UNITED STATES NAVAL RESERVE. 1921– [Annual]
List is as of July 1.

D 208.12/3 • Item 405 (MF)
REGISTER OF RETIRED COMMISSIONED AND WARRANT OFFICERS, REGULAR AND RESERVE, OF THE UNITED STATES NAVY AND MARINE CORPS. [Annual]

D 208.12/3-2:v./no. • Item 405-C-1 (EL)
SHIFT COLORS, THE NEWSLETTER FOR NAVY RETIREES. [Quarterly]
Contains miscellaneous short items of interest primarily to Navy retirees.

D 208.13:pt.nos. • Item 402-A
CASE INSTRUCTION, CASES.
Earlier N 17.31
Discontinued.

D 208.14:nos.
U.S. NAVAL POSTGRADUATE SCHOOL. TECHNICAL REPORTS.

D 208.14/2:nos.
– RESEARCH PAPERS.

D 208.14/3:nos.
– REPRINTS.

D 208.14/4:date
– CATALOGUE.

D 208.14/5:CT
– THESES.

D 208.14/6:CT
– PUBLICATIONS.

D 208.15:CT • Item 401-A
BIBLIOGRAPHIES AND LISTS OF PUBLICATIONS.

D 208.16:.v.nos.&nos. • Item 403-B
NAVY RECRUITER.
Discontinued.

D 208.17:v.nos.&nos.
NAVAL HISTORY, SUPPLEMENTS. Admin.

D 208.18:nos.
TECHNICAL BULLETINS.

D 208.19:date • Item 403-C (EL)
LINK, ENLISTED PERSONNEL DISTRIBUTION BULLETIN. [Quarterly]

D 208.20:CT • Item 401-B (MF)
FINAL ENVIRONMENTAL IMPACT STATEMENTS.

D 208.21:v.nos.&nos.
OFFICER PERSONNEL NEWSLETTER.

D 208.22:date • Item 405-C (EL)
PERSPECTIVE. [Bimonthly]
Sub-title: A Newsletter for Navy Officers
Newsletter furnishing Navy officers with information on such matters as educational and advancement opportunities, assignments, and billeting.

D 208.23: • Item 403-A-3
MONOGRAPH SERIES. [Irregular]
Consists of monographs on the history of the Chaplain Corps of the U.S. Navy.

D 208.24:date • Item 405-B (MF)
BIENNIAL OFFICER BILLET SUMMARY (Junior Officer Edition).
PURPOSE:– To provide a comprehensive display of many types and broad ranges of billets within the Navy for the grades Warrant Officer through Lieutenant. Tables list billets in various categories such as subspecialties and shore duty.

D 208.24/2 • Item 405-B-1 (MF)
BIENNIAL OFFICER BILLET SUMMARY (Senior Officer Edition).

D 208.25:date • Item 405
NAVY MILITARY PERSONNEL STATISTICS. [Quarterly]
No longer a depository item. For internal/administrative use only under 44 U.S.C. section 1902.
Official use only.

D 208.26:date • Item 403-A (MF)
NAVY GUIDE FOR RETIRED PERSONNEL AND THEIR FAMILIES. [Quinquennial]

D 208.28 • Item 405-B-2 (E)
ELECTRONIC PRODUCTS. (Misc.)

NAVAL ACADEMY
(1949–)

INFORMATION

United States Naval Academy
121 Blake Road
Annapolis, Maryland 21402-5100
(410) 293-1000
http://www.usna.edu

D 208.101:date
REPORT OF BOARD OF VISITORS TO NAVAL ACADEMY. [Annual]
Earlier M 206.101

D 208.102:CT • Item 391
GENERAL PUBLICATIONS.
Earlier M 206.102

D 208.107 • Item 389 (MF)
ANNUAL REGISTER OF THE UNITED STATES NAVAL ACADEMY. [Annual]

D 208.108:date • Item 392
REGULATIONS GOVERNING ADMISSION OF CANDIDATES INTO NAVAL ACADEMY AS MIDSHIPMEN AND SAMPLE EXAMINATION QUESTIONS. [Annual]
Earlier M 206.108

D 208.109:date • Item 390-A
ANNAPOLIS, THE UNITED STATES NAVAL ACADEMY CATALOG. [Annual]
Title varies: – 1964 called United States Naval Academy Catalogue of Information; 1965–73, United States Naval Academy Catalog; 1974– Annapolis, United States Naval Academy Catalog.

D 208.110:date
UNITED STATES NAVAL ACADEMY, SUPERINTENDENT'S STATEMENT TO BOARD OF VISITORS. [Annual]

D 208.111:date • Item 390-B (MF)
TRIDENT SCHOLARS. [Annual]

PURPOSE:– To provide a brief biographical sketch of Scholars each year, a resume of their projects, information about their faculty advisors, and a listing of the members of the Trident Scholars Committee.
Discontinued.

D 208.112:v.nos.&nos. • Item 390-C (MF)
ARNOLDIAN. v. 1– [Semiannual]
Former title: Arnold Newsletter.
ISSN 0160-4848
Discontinued.

D 208.115: • Item 390-D
HANDBOOKS, MANUALS, GUIDES.

NAVAL WAR COLLEGE
(1949–   )

D 208.201:date
ANNUAL REPORTS.
Earlier M 206.201

D 208.202:CT • **Item 408-A-1**
GENERAL PUBLICATIONS.
Earlier M 206.202

D 208.207:v.nos. • **Item 408-A**
INTERNATIONAL LAW STUDIES. v. 1–   [Irregular]

D 208.207/2 • **Item 408-A**
– INDEXES.

D 208.209:v.nos.&nos. • **Item 408-A-3 (EL)**
NAVAL WAR COLLEGE REVIEW. v. 1–   1948–
[Quarterly]
Consists of general interest, professional, and educational articles, and literature reviews on topics such as politics, law, history, etc., of interest to military officers and other readers.

D 208.210:v.nos.&nos. • **Item 408-A-2**
HISTORICAL MONOGRAPH SERIES. 1–   1975–
[Irregular]

D 208.211: • **Item 408-A-4**
LOGISTICS LEADERSHIP SERIES.

D 208.212 • **Item 408-A-5 (EL)**
NEWPORT PAPERS.

NAVAL FACILITIES
ENGINEERING COMMAND
(1966–   )

CREATION AND AUTHORITY

The Bureau of Yards and Docks (M 205) was transferred along with the Department of the Navy to the Department of Defense upon its establishment in 1949. The Bureau was abolished and its functions transferred to the Naval Facilities Engineering Command by reorganization of May 1, 1966.

INFORMATION

Naval Facilities Engineering Command
Department of the Navy
Washington Navy Yard
1322 Patterson Ave. SE
Washington, DC 20374-5065
(202) 685-1833
http://www.navfac.navy.mil

D 209.1:date • **Item 418-C (MF)**
ANNUAL REPORTS.
Earlier M 205.1

D 209.1/2
PROGRESS REPORT, FISCAL YEAR (date). [Annual]

D 209.2:CT • **Item 418**
GENERAL PUBLICATIONS.
Earlier M 205.2

D 209.7:v.nos. • **Item 420**
U.S. NAVY CIVIL ENGINEER CORPS BULLETIN.
[Monthly]
Earlier M 205.7
Discontinued.

D 209.8:nos. • **Item 419**
TECHNICAL DIGEST. [Monthly]
Earlier M 205.8
Discontinued.

D 209.9:date
REGISTER OF CIVIL ENGINEER CORPS COMMISSIONED AND WARRANT OFFICERS OF UNITED STATES NAVY AND NAVAL RESERVE ON ACTIVE DUTY. [Quarterly]

D 209.10:nos. • **Item 419-A**
TECHNICAL PUBLICATIONS NAVDOCKS TP (series).
Discontinued.

D 209.11:nos.&le.
SPECIFICATIONS.
Earlier N 21.10

D 209.12
TECHNICAL MEMORANDUMS. [Irregular]

D 209.12/2
TECHNICAL REPORTS. 1–   [Irregular]

D 209.12/3:nos.
TECHNIAL NOTES.

D 209.12/4 • **Item 418-D (MF)**
NCEL CONTRACT REPORT (series).

D 209.13:v.nos./nos. • **Item 419-B (P) (EL)**
NAVY CIVIL ENGINEER. v. 1–   1960–   [3 times/yr.]
Features articles on the Navy's worldwide shore establishments, including technical articles on planning and designing, construction, maintenance, public works, utilities, transportation. Navy housing and real estate, and the Naval Civil Engineering Laboratory. Also includes research and development, disaster control, and features articles on Civil Engineer Corps officers and Seabees.
Supersedes U.S. Naval Civil Engineer Corps Bulletin (D 209.7) and BuDocks Technical Digest (D 209.8).
Frequency varies: 1960– July 1967, bimonthly; August 1967–   monthly.
Title varies: some issues carry title Navy Civil Engineer News.
Indexed by: Index to U.S. Government Periodicals.
ISSN 0096-9419

D 209.14:CT • **Item 418-A**
HANDBOOKS, MANUALS, GUIDES.

D 209.14/2 • **Item 418-A**
DESIGN MANUALS, DM (series). [Irregular]

D 209.15:CT • **Item 418-B**
INDEX OF BUREAU OF YARDS AND DOCKS PUBLICATIONS.
Discontinued.

D 209.16:nos.
NAVFAC TECHNICAL TRAINING CENTER: NTTC COURSES.

D 209.17:date • **Item 418-D (MF)**
DIRECTORY, NAVY CIVIL ENGINEER CORPS. [Semiannual] (NAVFAC P-1)
Discontinued.

D 209.17/2: • **Item 418-A-1**
NAVFAC-P- (series). [Irregular]
Consists of publications on miscellaneous topics, such as amanual that provides editorial criteria for approval of all documents. Prepared for publication by the Command.

D 209.17/2-2: • **Item 418-A-2**
NAVFACENGCOM DOCUMENTATION INDEX. [Annual]
A consolidated subject index called "Keywords out of Context" (KWOC). Selected keywords taken from the contents of official instructions, publications, specifications, etc., and related documents with the same keywords are grouped together.
Discontinued.

D 209.18: • **Item 418-E (MF)**
ENERGY AND ENVIRONMENTAL NEWS. [Quarterly]
Contains short news items on conservation and efficient use of energy and protection of the environment.
Discontinued.

OFFICE OF NAVAL RESEARCH
(1949–   )

CREATION AND AUTHORITY

The Office of Naval Research (M 216) was transferred along with the Department of the Navy to the Department of Defense upon its establishment in 1949.

INFORMATION

Office of Naval Research
Ballston Towers No. 1
800 North Quincy Street
Arlington, Virginia 22217-5660
(202) 692-4767
http://www.onr.navy.mil

D 210.1:date • **Item 407-A**
ANNUAL REPORTS.
Earlier M 216.1
Discontinued.

D 210.2:CT • **Item 407**
GENERAL PUBLICATIONS.
Earlier M 216.2

D 210.2:Sh 2 • **Item 407**
SENSORY BIOLOGY OF SHARKS, SKATES, AND RAYS. 1978. 666 p. il.
PURPOSE:– To review the research of the sensory organs of sharks, skates, and rays, including vision, hearing, chemical sense, electrical and magnetic senses, as well as the behavior of the animals in the wild.

D 210.3/2:v.nos. • **Item 407-C-3 (MF)**
TECHNICAL DISCLOSURE BULLETIN. [Quarterly] (Assistant Chief for Patents)
PURPOSE:– To disseminate scientific and technical data which may be of interest to the private sector. Bulletins concisely describe and illustrate inventions developed by Naval facilities and contractors.
ISSN 0364-3646
Discontinued.

D 210.3/3:v.nos. • **Item 407-C-1**
SCIENTIFIC BULLETIN. (Office of Naval Research/Tokyo) [Quarterly]
Presents highly technical articles covering recent developments in Far East (particularly Japan) scientific research in areas such as plasma physics, gaseous electronics, radioisotopes, tropical cyclones, etc. Also contains agenda of international conferences.
Discontinued.

D 210.5:letters-nos.
ONR SYMPOSIUM REPORTS.

D 210.6:CT • **Item 408**
REGULATION, RULES, AND INSTRUCTIONS.
Discontinued.

D 210.6/2:CT • **Item 407-F**
HANDBOOKS, MANUALS, GUIDES.

D 210.7:date
SCIENTIFIC PERSONNEL BULLETIN. [Monthly]

D 210.8 • **Item 407-H (MF)**
NRL REPORTS. 1–   [Irregular] (National Research Laboratory)
PURPOSE:– To publish research findings conducted by or under contract to the Office of Naval Research. The majority of the reports issued are the final reports issued after completion of each task or project.
The unclassified or declassified reports only are listed in the Monthly Catalog. These are for sale by the Office of Technical Services. Each report contains an abstract and an detachable catalog card of the report covered. The series now numbers more than 5,000 reports.
Published in microfiche.

D 210.8:7070 • Item 407-H
TABLE OF ALL PRIMITIVE ROOTS FOR PRIMES LESS THAN 5000. 1970. 590 p.

D 210.8/2:nos. • Item 407-H-1 (MF)
NRL MEMORANDUM REPORT (series).

D 210.8/3:nos.
TECHNICAL REPORTS.

D 210.8/3-2:nos.
ONR TECHNICAL REPORT RLT (series).

D 210.9:dt.&nos.
NRL REPRINTS.

D 210.10:
DAILY UPPER AIR BULLETIN.

D 210.11:v./nos. • Item 407-C (EL)
NAVAL RESEARCH REVIEWS. v. 1–31. 1948–1978. [Quarterly]
    PURPOSE:– To report in a brief and concise manner on the various research projects conducted by the Naval Research organizations as well as the contractors outside the Government performing research for the Navy.
    Former title: Research Reviews.
    Indexed by:–
        Chemical Abstracts
        Biological Abstracts
        Index to U.S. Government Periodicals
        International Aerospace Abstracts
        Nuclear Science Abstracts
    ISSN 0028-145X

D 210.12 • Item 407-B
NAVAL RESEARCH LOGISTICS QUARTERLY. v. 1– 1954– [Quarterly]
    PURPOSE:– Devoted to the dissemination of scientific information in logistics and economics, presenting research and expository papers, including those in certain areas of mathematics, statistics, and economics, relevant to the overall effort to improve the efficiency and effectiveness of logistics operations.
    Published in the months of March, June, September, and December.
    Indexed by: Index to U.S. Government Periodicals.
    Note:– Discontinued as a government publication with the December 1982 issue. Beginning in 1983 published by John Wiley & Sons with the cooperation of the Office of Naval Research.
    ISSN 0028-1441
    Discontinued.

D 210.13
NRL [Naval Research Laboratory] BIBLIOGRAPHIES. 1– [Irregular]

D 210.13:13
LITERATURE OF SPACE SCIENCE AND EXPLORATION. 1958. 264 p.

D 210.13/2:CT
BIBLIOGRAPHIES AND LISTS OF PUBLICATIONS.

D 210.14
TECHNICAL REPORTS, NAVTRADEVCEN– (series). [Irregular]

D 210.14/2
INDEX OF PUBLICATIONS. [Annual]

D 210.14/3:nos.
HUMAN ENGINEERING REPORT.

D 210.14/4:nos.
TRAINING SUPPORT DEVELOPMENTS. 1– [6 times a year] (Naval Training Equipment Center, Orlando, Florida)
    Entitled Training Device Developments prior to no. 59, January 1973.

D 210.14/5:nos.
SURVIVAL PLANT RECOGNITION CARDS. [Irregular] (Naval Training Device Center)

D 210.15:nos. • Item 407-D (MF)
ONR REPORT ARC (series). [Irregular]
    Earlier title: ONR Reports DR (series).
    Those scientific or technical reports not appropriate for either the Survey of Naval Sciences or Symposium Reports and falling in the special reports class are assigned DR numbers.
    Former title: ACR [Assistance Chief for Research] Research Reports. ACR– (series).
    Discontinued.

D 210.16:nos.
TECHNICAL REPORTS. NAVAL RESEARCH OFFICE LONDON.
    Issued by U.S. Embassy, London.

D 210.16/2:date • Item 407-C-4 (MF)
ESN INFORMATION BULLETIN. [Monthly]
    Earlier title: European Scientific Notes.
    Issued by U.S. Embassy, London.
    Contains brief articles intended to call attention to current developments in European science and technology activities.
    Discontinued.

D 210.16/3:nos. • Item 407-C-1 (MF)
SCIENTIFIC MONOGRAPHS. 1– [Irregular]
    Also published in microfiche.

D 210.17
REPORT OF NRL PROGRESS. –1979 [Monthly]
    Published by the Naval Research Laboratory.
    Contains general articles of scientific interest, reports on progress of work by the various divisions of the Laboratory, and lists of NRL technical reports, patents, published papers, and papers, presented by NRL staff members at professional meetings.
    Indexed by:–
        Chemical Abstracts
        Engineering Index
    ISSN 0500-0505

D 210.17/2:date • Item 407-C-2 (MF)
NAVAL RESEARCH LABORATORY, REVIEW. [Annual]
    Reviews NRL accomplishments resulting from its multidisciplinary program of scientific research and advanced technologic development directed toward and improved materials, equipment, techniques, and systems for the Navy.
    Discontinued.

D 210.17/2 a:CT • Item 407-C-2 (MF)
NAVAL RESEARCH LABORATORY REVIEW (Separates). [Annua]

D 210.17/3:date • Item 407-C-2 (MF)
NAVAL RESEARCH LABORATORY, FACT BOOK. [Annual]

D 210.17/4:date • Item 407-C-2 (MF)
MATERIALS SCIENCE & ENGINEERING RESEARCH, RESEARCH PROGRAMS AND PUBLICATIONS. [Annual]

D 210.18
SCIENCE EDUCATION PROGRAM. v. 1– [Semiannual] Naval Research Laboratory.

D 210.19:date
SYMPOSIUM ON NAVAL HYDRODYNAMICS.

D 210.20:date • Item 407-E
NAVAL RESEARCH TASK SUMMARY. [Annual]
    Discontinued.

D 210.21:date
NAVAL RESEARCH LABORATORY QUARTERLY ON NUCLEAR SCIENCE AND TECHNOLOGY. PROGRESS REPORTS. LIMITED DISTRIBUTION.

D 210.22
USRL RESEARCH REPORTS. 1– [Irregular]

D 210.23:date
DIRECT ENERGY CONVERSION LITERATURE ABSTRACTS.
    Earlier title: Thermoelectricity Abstracts.

D 210.24:v.nos.&nos.
DIGITAL COMPUTER NEWSLETTER.

D 210.25:nos.
TEST AND EVALUATION REPORTS.

D 210.26:date&nos.
NAVY SCIENTIFIC AND TECHNICAL INFORMATION PROGRAM, NEWSLETTER.

D 210.27:v.nos.&nos. • Item 320-A-1
SHOCK AND VIBRATION DIGEST. [Monthly]
    Earlier D 4.12/2
    Discontinued.

D 210.27/2:nos. • Item 320-A-1
SHOCK AND VIBRATION BULLETIN. [Annual]

D 210.27/3 • Item 320-A-2
SHOCK AND VIBRATION MONOGRAPH, SVM-(series). [Irregular]
    Earlier D 1.42
    Discontinued.

D 210.28:date • Item 407-C-5 (MF)
OCEANIC BIOLOGY PROGRAM ABSTRACT BOOK, FY. [Annual]
    Discontinued.

NAVAL OCEAN RESEARCH AND DEVELOPMENT ACTIVITY

D 210.101:date
ANNUAL REPORT.

D 210.102:CT
GENERAL PUBLICATIONS.

D 210.109:nos. • Item 407-G (MF)
NORDA REPORTS. 1– [Irregular]
    Discontinued.

NAVAL SEA SYSTEMS COMMAND (1966–   )

CREATION AND AUTHORITY

    The Bureau of Ships (M 210) was transferred along with the Department of the Navy to the Department of Defense upon its establishment in 1949. The Bureau was abolished and its functions transferred to the Naval Ship Systems Command effective May 1, 1966.

INFORMATION

    Naval Sea Systems Command
    1333 Isaac Hull Ave. SE
    Washington, Navy Yard, D.C. 20376
    (202) 781-0000
    http://www.navsea.navy.mil

D 211.1:date • Item 412-F (MF)
ANNUAL REPORTS.
    Earlier M 210.1

D 211.2:CT • Item 412
GENERAL PUBLICATIONS.
    Earlier M 210.2

D 211.3:nos.
BULLETIN OF INFORMATION. [Quarterly]
    Earlier M 210.3

D 211.3/2:v.nos.&nos.
BULLETIN. Admin.

D 211.6:CT • Item 414
REGULATIONS, RULES, AND INSTRUCTIONS.

D 211.6/2:CT • Item 412-B
HANDBOOKS, MANUALS, GUIDES.
    Formerly in D 211.6

D 211.7:chap.nos.   • **Item 413**
BUREAU OF SHIPS MANUAL.
    Earlier M 210.8
    Discontinued.

D 211.7/2:nos.
–CHANGES.
    Earlier M 210.8/2

D 211.7/3:chap.nos.
BUREAU OF SHIPS TECHNICAL MANUAL.
    Formerly D 211.7

D 211.8   • **Item 412-A**
NAVAL SHIP SYSTEMS COMMAND TECHNICAL
NEWS. v. 1– 17. 1952– 1968. [Monthly]
    Contains articles of interest to naval archi-
tects, ship builders, naval officers, ship repair
personnel, and others concerned with building or
maintaining vessels and their components.
    Prior to May 1966, entitled Bureau of Ships
Journal.
    Discontinued.

D 211.9:nos.   • **Item 412-C (MF)**
NAVAL SHIP RESEARCH AND DEVELOPMENT CEN-
TER REPORTS. [Irregular]
    Discontinued.

D 211.9/2:nos.
DAVID W. TAYLOR MODEL BASIN REPORT R- (series).

D 211.9/3
AERO REPORTS. [Irregular]

D 211.9/4:nos.
DAVID TAYLOR MODEL BASIN: TRANSLATIONS.

D 211.9/5:date   • **Item 412-C (MF)**
INTERNATIONAL CONFERENCE ON NUMERICAL
SHIP HYDRODYNAMICS: PROCEEDINGS. 1st–
1975–
    1st. October 20– 22, 1975.

D 211.10
INDUSTRIAL NOTES.

D 211.11:nos.
NAVY ELECTRONICS LABORATORY REPORTS.

D 211.11/2:CT
NAVY ELECTRONICS LAB., SAN DIEGO, CALIF.,
PUBLICATIONS (Misc.).

D 211.12:nos.
PAMPHLET NBS (series).

D 211.13:nos.
U.S. NAVAL RADIOLOGICAL DEFENSE LABORATORY,
RESEARCH AND DEVELOPMENT REPORT
USNRDL (series).

D 211.13/2
RESEARCH AND DEVELOPMENT TECHNICAL RE-
PORTS, USNRDL-TR- (series). [Irregular]

D 211.13/3
REVIEWS AND LECTURES, R & L- (series). [Irregu-
lar]

D 211.14:nos.
BUREAU OF SHIPS TRANSLATIONS.

D 211.15:nos.
NAVAL ENGINEERING EXPERIMENT STATION,
ANNAPOLIS. MD., REPORT E.E.S. (series).

D 211.16:nos.
RUBBER LABORATORY, MARE ISLAND NAVAL SHIP-
YARD, VALLEJO, CALIFORNIA, REPORTS.

D 211.17:nos.
BOSTON NAVAL SHIPYARD: MATERIALS LABORA-
TORY, EVALUATION REPORT.

D 211.18:CT
NEW YORK NAVAL SHIPYARD, BROOKLYN, N.Y.,

D 211.19:nos.
MATERIALS LABORATORIES, PUGET SOUND NAVAL
SHIPYARD: EVALUATION REPORTS.

D 211.20:date
DIRECTORY.

D 211.21
USL REPORTS. 1–   [Irregular] (Navy Underwater
Sound Laboratory, New London, Connecticut
06321)
D 211.22:v.nos.&nos.   • **Item 412-D**
FACEPLATE. [Quarterly]
    Official magazine for divers of the U.S. Navy.
Indexed by: Index to U.S. Government Peri-
odicals.
    D v.16/1

D 211.22/2:   • **Item 412-E-2 (EL)**
FACEPLATE.

D 211.23:CT
NAVAL TORPEDO STATION, KEYPORT, WASHING-
TON: PUBLICATIONS.

D 211.24:v.nos.&nos.
NAVSEA JOURNAL.

D 211.25:v.nos.&nos.   • **Item 412-E (MF)**
COMMODORE. [Biweekly]
    Contains standard features, such as the Com-
manding Officer's Comments, Navy News Briefs,
and short articles.

D 211.26:v.nos/nos.   • **Item 412-E**
EXPLOSIVES SAFETY. [Quarterly]

D 211.28:date   • **Item 412-E-1**
YEAR IN REVIEW CARDEROCK DIVISION.

D 211.29:   • **Item 412-E-2 (E)**
ELECTRONIC PRODUCTS (misc.).

D 211.30:   • **Item 412-E-2 (EL)**
FINANCIAL POLICY AND PROCEDURES UPDATE.
    [Quarterly].

NAVAL SUPPLY SYSTEMS COMMAND
(1966–   )

CREATION AND AUTHORITY

    The Bureau of Supplies and Accounts (M 213)
was transferred along with the Department of the
Navy to the Department of Defense upon its establishment in 1949. The Bureau was abolished
and its functions transferred to the Naval Supply
Systems Command effective May 1, 1966.

INFORMATION

Naval Supply Systems Command
Department of the Navy
5450 Carlisle Pike
PO Box 2050
Mechanicsburg PA 17055-0791
(717) 605-2287
Fax: (717) 605-5938
http://www.navsup.navy.mil

D 212.1:date   • **Item 415-A-1 (MF)**
ANNUAL REPORT.
    See D 212.1/2

D 212.1/2:date   • **Item 415-A-1 (MF)**
ANNUAL REPORT, NAVAL PUBLICATIONS AND FORM
CENTER.

D 212.2:CT   • **Item 415**
GENERAL PUBLICATIONS.
    Earlier M 213.2

D 212.6:CT   • **Item 417**
REGULATIONS, RULES, AND INSTRUCTIONS.
    Earlier M 213.6

D 212.6/2:nos.
INSTRUCTION MEMORANDUM.

D 212.6/3:CT   • **Item 415-B**
HANDBOOKS, MANUALS, GUIDES.
    Earlier D 212.6

D 212.7:dt.&pt.nos.
INDEX OF SPECIFICATIONS USED BY NAVY DE-
PARTMENT.
    Earlier M 213.9
D 212.8:date   • **Item 416**
NAVAL EXPENDITURES.
    Earlier M 213.10
    Discontinued.

D 212.9:nos.
NAVY DEPARTMENT SPECIFICATIONS.
    Earlier M 213.7

D 212.10:date   • **Item 415-A**
INDEX OF SPECIFICATIONS AND STANDARDS USED
BY DEPARTMENT OF THE NAVY, MILITARY IN-
DEX. v. 3 [Semiannual]
    Later D 7.14
    Discontinued.

D 212.10/2:date
INDEX OF SPECIFICATIONS AND STANDARDS USED
BY DEPARTMENT OF THE NAVY, MILITARY IN-
DEX, v. 3, SPECIFICATIONS CANCELLED OR
SUPERSEDED. [Annual]

D 212.11
INSTRUCTION MEMORANDUM.

D 212.11/2:nos.
AFLOAT ACCOUNTING INSTRUCTION MEMORAN-
DUM.

D 212.11/3:nos.
BUSANDAINST [Bureau of Supplies and Accounts
Instructions]. Official Use

D 212.12:nos.
RESEARCH AND DEVELOPMENT DIVISION
REPORTS.

D 212.13:nos.
BUSANDA NOTICE. ADMIN.

D 212.14:v.nos.&nos.   • **Item 417-A (MF) (EL)**
NAVY SUPPLY CORPS NEWSLETTER. [Bimonthly]
ISSN 0360-716X

D 212.15:CT   • **Item 415-C**
BIBLIOGRAPHIES AND LISTS OF PUBLICATIONS.
    Discontinued.

D 212.16:date   • **Item 307-A-1 (CD)**
HAZARDOUS MATERIAL CONTROL AND MANAGE-
MENT/HAZARDOUS MATERIALS INFORMATION
SYSTEM. [Quarterly]
    Issued on CD-ROM.

D 212.16/2   • **Item 307-A-1 (CD)**
ERAF (Environmental Reporting Assist File). [Quar-
terly]

NAVAL OBSERVATORY
(1949–   )

CREATION AND AUTHORITY

    The Naval Observatory (M 212) was trans-
ferred along with the Department of the Navy to
the Department of Defense upon its establishment in 1949.

INFORMATION

Naval Observatory
Department of the Navy
34th and Massachusetts Avenue, N.W.
Washington, D.C. 20392-5100
(202) 653-1541

D 213.1:date
ANNUAL REPORTS.
Earlier M 212.1

D 213.2:CT • Item 397
GENERAL PUBLICATIONS.
Earlier M 212.2

D 213.4:nos. • Item 393-A-1
CIRCULARS.

D 213.7:date • Item 393
AIR ALMANAC. [Semiannual]
    PURPOSE:– To provide in a convenient form
the astronomical data required for air navigation.
    Published approximately one year in advance
of data presented.
    Formed by the union of the American Air Almanac and British Air Almanac.

D 213.8 • Item 394
ASTRONOMICAL ALMANAC. 1855– [Annual]
    Contains information relating to the sun,
moon, planets, stars, eclipses, ephemerides, and
satellites for the year covered.
    Published from one to two years in advance
of data presented.
    Former title, prior to 1981, American Ephemeris and Nautical Almanac.

D 213.8/2:date
IMPROVED LUNAR EPHEMERIS.

D 213.8/3:date • Item 396-A
ASTRONOMICAL PHENOMENA FOR THE YEAR [date].
1951– [Annual]
    Reprint of selected pages from the American
Ephemeris and Nautical Almanac covering data
on eclipses, rising and setting phenomena of the
sun and of the moon, and other astronomical
phenomena for the year covered.
    Published one to two years in advance of
data presented.

D 213.9 • Item 396 (MF)
ASTRONOMICAL PAPERS PREPARED FOR USE OF
    AMERICAN EPHEMERIS AND NAUTICAL
    ALMANAC. v. 1– 1822– [Irregular]

D 213.10 • Item 398
PUBLICATIONS OF NAVAL OBSERVATORY, 2d
    SERIES. v. 1– [Irregular]

D 213.11:date • Item 395
NAUTICAL ALMANAC FOR THE YEAR [date]. 1855–
    [Annual]
    Information contained in this volume has been
extracted from the American Ephemeris and Nautical Almanac and is greatly expanded to provide
ready access to the astronomical data required
for ocean navigation. The Almanac includes the
ephemerides of the sun, moon, Aries, Venus,
Mars, Jupiter, and Saturn; daily charts of sunrise, sunset, twilights, moonrise, and moonset;
star charts, tables of the sidereal hour angles
and declination of 173 stars; Polaris tables; tables
of standard times; tables for conversion of arc to
time; tables of increments and corrections for the
sun, moon, planets, and Aries; altitude correction tables for the sun, moon, stars, and planets;
and more.
    In addition to its obvious importance to professional navigators, many others will find the
Nautical Almanac invaluable. Student navigator
will discover that the section on chart explanations is helpful in interpreting and utilizing the
data. Astronomers, astrologers, and others who
know their own location but wish to find the positions of the stars will find that the Almanac can
also be used in reverse.
    Published from one to two years in advance
of data presented.
    ISSN 0077-619X

D 213.12:nos.
EPHEMERIS OF SUN, POLARIS, AND OTHER
    SELECTED STARS.
    Earlier I 53.8

D 213.14:date • Item 393-A
ALMANAC FOR COMPUTERS. [Annual]

    PURPOSE:– To present and explain navigational, astronomical, and stellar tables as well as
applications of Day of the Year, Julian Date, Sidereal Time, and other astronomical data.

D 213.15 • Item 397-A
NEWS FROM THE NAVAL OBSERVATORY, STARGAZING NOTES FOR . . . [Monthly]
    A popular newsletter on Naval observations of the planets, the moon, meteors, and
other events in the sky.

D 213.16:CT • Item 397
HANDBOOKS, MANUALS, GUIDES. [Irregular]

MARINE CORPS
(1949–   )

CREATION AND AUTHORITY

    The Marine Corps (M 209) was transferred
along with the Department of the Navy to the
Department of Defense upon its establishment in
1949.

INFORMATION

    U.S. Marine Corps
    Department of the Navy
    Washington, D.C. 20380-1775
    (202) 614-2500
    Fax: (703) 697-7246
    http://www.usmc.mil

    Physical Address:
    U.S. Marine Corps
    Columbia Pike and Southgate Road
    Arlington Annex
    Arlington, VA 22204

D 214.1:date • Item 384-A-7
COMMANDANT OF THE MARINE CORPS FY POSTURE
    STATEMENT. [Annual]
    Summarizes the posture, plans, and programs
of the Marine Corps.
    Earlier M 201.9

D 214.2:CT • Item 383
GENERAL PUBLICATIONS.
    Earlier M 209.2

D 214.6:CT • Item 384-C
REGULATIONS, RULES, AND INSTRUCTIONS.

D 214.7: • Item 384
RELEASES.

D 214.9:date • Item 384 (MF)
MARINE CORPS MANUAL.
    Earlier M 209.9

D 214.9/2:CT • Item 384
HANDBOOKS, MANUALS, GUIDES.

D 214.9/2:F 59 • Item 384
FLAG MANUAL. 1970. 94 p. il.
    Gives a brief history of the American flag
and lists the proper times and manner in which
the flag is to be displayed and folded.

D 214.9/3:nos. • Item 384 (MF)
TECHNICAL MANUALS, TM- (series). [Irregular]

D 214.9/4 • Item 384
FLEET MARINE FORCE MANUALS, FMFM- (series).
    1– [Irregular]

D 214.9/6:nos. • Item 384-A-8
FLEET MARINE FORCE REFERENCE PUBLICATIONS,
    FMFRP (series).

D 214.9/7:nos. • Item 384-A-10
MARINE AIR TRAFFIC CONTROL DETACHMENT HANDBOOK, PCN NOS.

D 214.9/8:nos. • Item 384-A-12 (MF)
MCRP (Marine Corp Reference Publication) SERIES.

D 214.9/9 • Item 384-A-13 (EL)
MARINE CORP DOCTRINE MANUALS. (Series)

D 214.10 • Item 384-A
RESERVE MARINE. [Monthly]
    ISSN 0034-5547
    Discontinued.

D 214.11 • Item 383-D (MF)
OFFICERS ON ACTIVE DUTY IN THE MARINE CORPS.
    [Annual]
    PURPOSE– To present lineal precedence information for officers in the Marine Corps Reserve on active duty for use in determining promotion eligibility and relative seniority.
    Designated NAVMC P-1005.
    Earlier title: Combined Lineal List of Officers
on Active Duty in the Marine Corps.

D 214.11/2 • Item 383-A
LINEAL LIST OF COMMISSIONED AND WARRANT
    OFFICERS OF THE MARINE CORPS RESERVES.
    [Annual]
    Discontinued.

D 214.11/3 • Item 383-D (MF)
OFFICERS IN THE MARINE CORPS RESERVE.
    [Annual]

D 214.12:CT • Item 384-B
[REGIMENTAL AND SQUADRON HISTORIES.]
    Discontinued.

D 214.13:CT • Item 383-B
HISTORICAL PUBLICATIONS.
    Includes Marine Corps Monographs.

    D 214.13:R 32/775-83 • Item 383-B
    MARINES IN THE REVOLUTION: A HISTORY OF
    CONTINENTAL MARINES IN THE AMERICAN
    REVOLUTION, 1775– 1783. 1975. 516 p. il.
    PURPOSE:– To describe the Marines'
contributions to the struggle for American independence. It contains dozens of illustrations, including maps, portraits and depictions of battles.

D 214.14
MARINE CORPS HISTORICAL REFERENCE SERIES.
    1– [Irregular]
    Prepared by Historical Branch, G-3 Division.

D 214.14/2
MARINE CORPS HISTORICAL REFERENCE PAMPHLETS. [Irregular]
    Prepared by Historical Branch, G-3 Division.

D 214.14/3 • Item 383-C
OCCASIONAL PAPERS. [Irregular]

D 214.14/4:CT • Item 383-C
MARINES IN WORLD WAR II COMMERORATIVE
SERIES.

D 214.15
MARINE CORPS HISTORICAL BIBLIOGRAPHIES.
    [Irregular]
    Prepared by Historical Branch, G-3 Division.

D 214.16:CT • Item 384-E
LITHOGRAPHS.
    Discontinued.

D 214.16/2:letters
MARINE CORPS PHOTOGRAPHS SET.

D 214.16/3:CT
AUDIOVISUAL MATERIAL. [Irregular]

D 214.16/4:CT • Item 384-F
POSTERS. [Irregular]

D 214.17:nos.
MUSEUM MANUSCRIPT REGISTER SERIES.

D 214.18:v.nos.&nos.
COLLEGE MARINE. [Monthly during school year]

D 214.19:nos.
MARINE CORPS PAPERS SERIES.

D 214.20:v.nos.&nos. • Item 383-B-1
FORTITUDINE, NEWSLETTER OF MARINE CORPS HISTORICAL PROGRAM. [Quarterly]
Published for the Marine Corps and for friends of Marine Corps history. Contains articles on Corps history plus other features on recent books of historical interest, etc.

D 214.21:v.nos.&nos.
MARINE CORPS GAZETTE.

D 214.22:date • Item 384-D (MF)
FOOD SERVICE INFORMATION BULLETIN. [Irregular]
Administrative use only.

D 214.23:v.nos.&nos. • Item 384-A-6 (P) (EL)
CONTINENTAL MARINE AND DIGEST. [10 times a year]
Published by the 4th Marine Division (Rein)/ 4th Marine Aircraft Wing, New Orleans, LA. This magazine is for information purposes only and in no way shall be considered directive in nature.

D 214.23/2:v.nos.&nos. • Item 384-A-4
DIXIE DIGEST. [Monthly]
Published for regular and reserve personnel and units in the Sixth Marine Corps District in Atlanta, Georgia. Contains articles on Marine Corps activities.

D 214.24:v.nos.&nos. • Item 384-A-1 (EL)
MARINES, OFFICIAL MAGAZINE OF THE U.S. MARINE CORPS. [Quarterly]

Published to keep U.S. Marines informed about current Marine plans, policies, programs, and activities.

D 214.25:nos. • Item 384-G (MF)
MCI- (series). [Irregular]
MCI = Marine Corps Institute
Consists of courses offered by the Marine Corps Institute, each of which concerns a different subject.

D 214.26 • Item 384-A-5
CRESCENT CITY MARINE. [Quarterly]
Published by the 4th Marine Division (Rein) 4th Marine Aircraft Wing, New Orleans, Louisiana. Issues contain articles on Marine activities.

D 214.26/2:v.nos.&nos. • Item 384-A-5
FOUR THE CORPS. [Irregular]

D 214.27:date • Item 384-A-2 (EL)
CONCEPTS AND ISSUES. [Annual]
This publication is a ready reference that presents the framework and substance of the Marine Corps' program, such as its contribution to national security through ground combat and aviation combat elements.

D 214.28 • Item 384-A-3
PUBLICATIONS STOCKED BY THE MARINE CORPS. [Quarterly]

D 214.29 • Item 384
MARINE CORPS TRAVEL INSTRUCTIONS MANUAL. [Irregular]

D 214.29/2 • Item 384-H
MARINE CORPS INSTITUTE ORDERS (series). [Monthly]
Each Order deals with a different topic. Discontinued.

D 214.30:date • Item 384-A-6
NOTES. [Bimonthly]

D 214.31:v.nos./nos. • Item 384-A-9
OUTREACH. [Quarterly]

D 214.32:v.nos./nos. • Item 307-A-10 (CD)
MARINE CORPS DIRECTIVES ELECTRONIC LIBRARY.
Issued on CD-ROM.

D 214.34:CT • Item 384-A-11 (E)
ELECTRONIC PRODUCTS (misc.).

D 214.35: • Item 384-A-11 (EL)
SEMPER FIDELIS.

D 214.36: • Item 384-A-14 (EL)
MARINE FORCES RESERVE NEWS. [Monthly]

NAVAL ORDNANCE SYSTEMS COMMAND
(1966–   )

CREATION AND AUTHORITY

The Bureau of Ordnance (M 211) was transferred along with the Department of the Navy to the Department of Defense upon its establishment in 1949. The Bureau was abolished and its functions transferred to the Naval Ordnance Systems Command effective May 1, 1966.

INFORMATION

Naval Ordnance Systems Command
Department of the Navy
Washington, D.C. 20360

D 215.1:date
ANNUAL REPORTS.
Earlier M 211.1

D 215.2:CT • Item 410-A
GENERAL PUBLICATIONS.
Earlier M 211.2
Discontinued.

D 215.6:CT • Item 411
REGULATIONS, RULES, AND INSTRUCTIONS.
Earlier M 211.6
Discontinued.

D 215.6/2:CT • Item 409-A
HANDBOOKS, MANUALS, GUIDES.

D 215.7 • Item 410
NAVORD REPORTS. 1–   [Irregular]
Discontinued.

LITHOGRAPHS.

D 215.8:date
EMPLOYMENT OPPORTUNITIES. [Bimonthly]
Later D 217.9

D 215.9 • Item 410-A
ORDNANCE PAMPHLETS, OP- (series). 1– [Irregular]

D 215.10:nos.
TECHNICAL REPORT NGF (series). (Engineering Research and Evaluation Division, Engineering Department, Naval Gun Factory).

D 215.11:nos.
U.S. NAVAL ORDNANCE TEST STATION, INYOKERN, TECHNICAL MEMORANDUMS.

D 215.12:CT
U.S. NAVAL PROPELLANT PLANT PUBLICATIONS.
Later D 217.15

D 215.13:nos.
NAVAL ORDNANCE LABORATORY, CORONA, CALIFORNIA: REPORTS.
Later D 217.20

D 215.14:nos.
NWL TECHNICAL REPORT TR- (series). (Naval Weapons Laboratory)

Earlier D 217.7

D 215.15:v.nos.&nos. • Item 410-B (MF)
FOCUS (Joint Center for Integrated Product Data Environment). [Quarterly]

MILITARY SEALIFT COMMAND
(1970–   )

CREATION AND AUTHORITY

The Military Sea Transportation Service was established by directive of the Secretary of Defense, dated August 2, 1949, consolidating the troop transportation functions of the Naval Transportation Service and the Army Transportation Corps. The name was changed to Military Sealift Command in 1970.

INFORMATION

Public Affairs
Military Sealift Command
Washington Navy Yard
914 Charles Morris Ct. SE
Washington, DC 20398-5540
(202) 685-5055
Fax: (202) 685-5067
Toll Free: 1-888-SEALIFT
http://www.msc.navy.mil

D 216.1:date • Item 388-B-3
ANNUAL REPORTS.

D 216.2:CT • Item 388-B-2
GENERAL PUBLICATIONS.

D 216.6:CT
REGULATIONS, RULES, AND INSTRUCTIONS.

D 216.6/2:CT • Item 388-B-4
HANDBOOKS, MANUALS, GUIDES. [Irregular]

D 216.8 • Item 388-B-1
SEALIFT, MAGAZINE OF THE MILITARY SEALIFT COMMAND. v. 1– 29. 1951– 1979. [Monthly]
PURPOSE:– To disseminate items of technical and professional interest concerning the Military Sea Transportation Service operations, including such subjects as safety at sea, training, ship construction, rescues, Arctic and Antarctic operations, oceanography and hydrography, missile tracking, and ocean logistic support to the Armed Forces.
Previous titles: Military Sea Transportation Service Magazine, Sealift Magazine, and Military Sealift Command.
Indexed by: Index to U.S. Government Periodicals.

D 216.9:date/pt.nos.&nos.
FINANCIAL AID STATISTICAL REPORT.

D 216.10:CT
POSTERS. [Irregular]

D 216.11:CT • Item 307-A-12 (E)
ELECTRONIC PRODUCTS.

BUREAU OF NAVAL WEAPONS
(1959– 1966)

CREATION AND AUTHORITY

The Bureau of Naval Weapons was established by act of August 18, 1959 (73 Stat. 395; 10 U.S.C. 5131, 5153), to replace the Bureau of Ordnance (D 215) and the Bureau of Aeronautics (D 202). The Bureau was abolished by Department of Defense Reorganization Order of March 9, 1966, effective May 1, 1966, and functions were transferred to Secretary of the Navy (31 F.R. 7188).

D 217.1:date
ANNUAL REPORTS.

D 217.2:CT   • Item 408-B-1
GENERAL PUBLICATIONS.
  Discontinued.

D 217.4/2:nos.
ENGINEERING CIRCULARS.

D 217.6/2
[INSTRUCTIONS] BUWEPSINST (series).

D 217.7:v.nos.&nos.
TECHNICAL PROGRESS REPORTS, RESEARCH
  AND DEVELOPMENT.
    Earlier M 120.7

D 217.8:date
NAVAL AVIATION NEWS. [Monthly]
    Earlier D 202.9

D 217.9:date
EMPLOYMENT OPPORTUNITIES. [Bimonthly]

    Earlier D 215.8

D 217.10:v.nos.&nos.
APPROACH, NAVAL AVIATION SAFETY REVIEW.
  [Monthly]
    Earlier D 202.13

Naval Avionic Facility
Indianapolis, Indiana

  Conducts research, design, development,
engineering production, overhaul, repair, and modernization of avionics equipment.

D 217.11
AFI-TP- (series). 1–   [Irregular]

D 217.12   • Item 410-A
ORDANCE PAMPHLETS, OP- (series). [Irregular]

D 217.13:nos.
WHAT'S HAPPENING IN THE PERSONNEL FIELD.

D 217.14:CT   • Item 408-13-B-2
HANDBOOKS, MANUALS, GUIDES.
  Discontinued.

D 217.15:CT
U.S. NAVAL PROPELLANT PLANT, PUBLICATIONS.
    Earlier D 215.12

D 217.16:le-nos.
STANDARDS LABORATORY CROSS-CHECK PROCE-
  DURE, DEPARTMENT OF NAVY, BUWEPS-
  BUSHIPS CALIBRATION PROGRAM.

D 217.16/2:le-nos.
STANDARDS LABORATORY INSTRUMENT CALIBRA-
  TION PROCEDURE, DEPARTMENT OF NAVY,
  BUWEPS-BUSHIPS CALIBRATION PROGRAM.

D 217.16/2-2:date
CALIBRATION PROCEDURE CHANGE NOTICE
  BOOK.

D 217.16/3:le-nos.
STANDARDS LABORATORY MEASUREMENTS SYS-
  TEM OPERATION PROCEDURE, DEPARTMENT
  OF NAVY, BUWEPS-BUSHIPS CALIBRATION
  PROGRAM.

D 217.16/4:le-nos.
TECHNICAL MANUAL, DEPARTMENT OF NAVY,
  BUWEPS-BUSHIPS CALIBRATION PROGRAM.

D 217.16/4-2:le-nos.
TECHNICAL MANUAL, NAVY CALIBRATION PRO-
  GRAM, MEASUREMENT SYSTEMS OPERATION
  PROCEDURE.

D 217.16/5:le-nos.
FABRICATION INSTRUCTIONS, DEPARTMENT OF
  NAVY, BUWEPS-BUSHPS CALIBRATION PRO-
  GRAM.

D 217.16/6:nos.
MODIFICATION INSTRUCTIONS.

D 217.16/7:le-nos.
STANDARDS LABORATORY INSTRUMENT CALIBRA-
  TION TECHNIQUE.

D 217.16/8:nos.
TECHNICAL MANUAL: CROSS-CHECK PROCEDURE.

Naval Weapons Laboratory
Dahlgren, Virginia

  Conducts research and development, design
and technical evaluation programs dealing with
weapons, ballistics, ordnance, and astronautics.

D 217.17
NWL REPORTS. 1–   [Irregular]

D 217.17/2   • Item 408-B-3
TECHNICAL MEMORANDUMS. [Irregular]
  Discontinued.

D 217.18   • Item 410
NAVWEPS REPORTS. [Irregular]
  Supersedes NavOrd Reports (D 215.7)

FIELD AGENCY PUBLICATIONS
Aeronautical Electronic and Electrical
Laboratory
Johnsville, Pennsylvania

  The Naval Air Development Center conducts
research, design, development, tests, and evaluation of optimum naval air systems and components with major emphasis on broad categories
of combat air, air defense, and antisubmarine
warfare.

D 217.19
REPORTS, NADC-EL- (series). [Irregular]

D 217.20:nos.
NAVAL ORDANCE LABORATORY, CORONA, CALI-
  FORNIA, NOLC REPORTS.
    Earlier D 215.13

Aeronautical Engine Laboratory
Naval Air Material Center
Philadelphia, Pennsylvania

  Conducts research, design, development,
tests, and evaluation of launching and recovery
devices and related equipment for aircraft and
guided missiles; aircraft powerplants and the components and accessories, fuels, and lubricating
oils; all materials and processes which enter into
the construction, overhaul, maintenance, and
operation of naval aircraft.

D 217.21
NAMC-AEL- (series). [Irregular]

Naval Ordnance Laboratory
White Oak, Maryland

  Conducts research, design, development,
tests, and technical evaluation of complete ordnance systems, assemblies, components, and
materials pertaining to existing, advance and proposed weapons, principally in the fields of missiles and underwater ordnance.

D 217.22
TECHNICAL REPORTS, NOLTR- (series). [Irregular]

D 217.22/2:nos.
NEWS FOR RELEASE.

Naval Ordnance Test Station
China Lake, California

D 217.23
TECHNICAL PUBLICATIONS, NOTS-TP (series).
  [Irregular]

D 217.24
DAYLIGHTER. (U.S. Navy Weather Research Facility,
Naval Air Station, Norfolk, Va.)

D 217.25:date
BUREAU OF NAVAL WEAPONS DIRECTORY,
  ORGANIZATIONAL LISTING AND CORRESPON-
  DENCE DESIGNATIONS.

D 217.26:nos.
NAVAL MISSILE CENTER: NMC-MP (series).

Naval Air Test Center
Pautuxent River, Maryland

  Conducts tests and evaluation of aircraft,
weapons systems and their components.

D 217.27
TECHNICAL REPORTS: [Irregular]

OFFICE OF THE
OCEANOGRAPHER OF THE NAVY
(1967–   )

INFORMATION

  Office of the Oceanographer of the Navy
  U.S. Naval Observatory
  Washington, D.C. 20390-5100
  (202) 762-1020
  Fax:(202) 762-1025
  http://oceangrapher.navy.mil

D 218.1:date
ANNUAL REPORT.

D 218.2:CT   • Item 377
GENERAL PUBLICATIONS.

D 218.9:nos.   • Item 377-G (MF)
PAMPHLETS. 1–   [Irregular]
    Earlier PrEx 12.9

D 218.10:nos.
REFERENCE PUBLICATIONS (series).

D 218.11:date   • Item 377-H
NATIONAL OCEANOGRAPHIC FLEET OPERATING
  SCHEDULES.
    Later D 203.33

D 218.15   • Item 377-G-1 (E)
ELECTRONIC PRODUCTS. (Misc.)

SPACE AND NAVAL WARFARE
SYSTEMS COMMAND
(1968–   )

CREATION AND AUTHORITY

  The Electronic Systems Command was es-
tablished within the Department of the Navy on
May 1, 1966. Name changed to Space and Naval
Warfare Systems Command.

INFORMATION

  Public Affairs
  Space and Naval War Systems Command
  4301 Pacific Hwy.
  San Diego, CA 92110-3127
  (619) 524-3428
  Fx: (619) 524-3469
  http://www.enterprise.spawar.navy.mil/
  spawarpublicsite

D 219.1:date
ANNUAL REPORT.

D 219.2:CT • Item 414-A-1
GENERAL PUBLICATIONS.

D 219.8:CT • Item 414-A
HANDBOOKS, MANUALS AND GUIDES.

NAVAL WEATHER SERVICE COMMAND

INFORMATION

Naval Weather Service Headquarters
Washington Navy Yard
Washington, D.C. 20390

D 220.1:date
ANNUAL REPORTS.

D 220.2:CT • Item 415-D-2
GENERAL PUBLICATIONS.

D 220.8:CT • Item 374-B
HANDBOOKS, MANUALS, GUIDES.

D 220.8:St 7 • Item 374-B
MARINERS WORLDWIDE CLIMATIC GUIDE TO
TROPICAL STORMS AT SEA. 1974. 426 p. il.
This guide provides general climatic knowledge about tropical cyclones in all parts of the world. It is designed to aid in understanding the information received from weather forecast centers. Several hundred charts of the world's ocean areas are included, as well as information on winds and waves, an explanation of tropical warning systems, storm photographs, and tips to the mariner.

D 220.9:date
PROJECT STORMFURY, ANNUAL REPORT.

D 220.10:CT • Item 415-D-1 (MF)
SUMMARY OF SYNOPTIC METEOROLOGICAL OBSERVATIONS.
Consists of tables of summary data on marine surface observations recorded aboard vessels of varying registry. Issued in a number of volumes for each marine area of the world. Each volume issued as a separate microfiche.
Issued in microfiche (24x).
Discontinued.

D 220.11:date
ANNUAL TYPHOON REPORT. (Fleet Weather Center/
Joint Typhoon Warning Center)

NAVAL DATA AUTOMATION COMMAND (1980– 1992)

D 221.1:date
ANNUAL REPORT.

D 221.2:CT • Item 415-D-4
GENERAL PUBLICATIONS. [Irregular]

D 221.8:CT • Item 415-D-7
HANDBOOKS, MANUALS, GUIDES.

D 221.9:v.nos.&nos.
ACCESS, THE NAVY DATA AUTOMATION REVIEW.
[Bimonthly]

NAVAL HISTORICAL CENTER

D 221.2:CT • Item 415-D-4
GENERAL PUBLICATIONS.

D 221.16 • Item 415-D-3
THE U.S. NAVY IN THE MODERN WORLD SERIES.

D 221.17:nos. • Item 415-D-4 (MF)
NAVAL HISTORY BIBLIOGRAPHIES (series).

D 221.18:CT • Item 415-D-6 (E)
ELECTRONIC PRODUCTS (Misc).

D 221.19:nos. • Item 399-A-4
CONTRIBUTIONS TO NAVAL HISTORY (series).
Earlier D 207.10/4

DEPARTMENT OF THE AIR FORCE (1949–   )

CREATION AND AUTHORITY

The Department of the Air Force (M 301) was made a military department within the Department of Defense upon its establishment by the National Security Amendments of 1949 (63 Stat. 578).

INFORMATION

Department of the Air Force
Pentagon
Washington, D.C. 20330-1000
(202) 696-6720
Fax: (703) 696-7273
http://www.af.mil

D 301.1:date • Item 421-G (MF)
ANNUAL REPORTS.
Discontinued.
Earlier M 301.1

D 301.1/2:date • Item 421-G (MF)
UNITED STATES AIR FORCE HISTORY PROGRAM,
SUMMARY OF ACTIVITIES. [Annual]
Discontinued.

D 301.1/3:date • Item 421-G-1
AIR FORCE ISSUES BOOK. [Annual]

D 301.2:CT • Item 424
GENERAL PUBLICATIONS.
Earlier M 301.2

D 301.3:dt.&nos.
AIR FORCE BULLETINS.

D 301.3/2:v.nos./nos. • Item 424-K
SPACE TACTICS BULLETIN.
Official use only.

D 301.6:nos. • Item 425
AFR REGULATIONS.
Earlier M 301.6

D 301.6:0-2/date • Item 425
NUMERICAL INDEX OF STANDARD AND RECURRING AIR FORCE PUBLICATIONS.

D 301.6:0-8/date • Item 425
NUMERICAL INDEX OF SPECIALTY TRAINING STANDARDS. [Quarterly]

D 301.6:0-9/date • Item 425
NUMERICAL INDEX OF DEPARTMENTAL FORMS.

D 301.6:0-12/date • Item 425
FUNCTIONAL INDEX OF DEPARTMENTAL FORMS.
[Quarterly]
Internal use only.

D 301.6:0-20/date • Item 425
NUMERICAL INDEX OF STANDARD AND RECURRING AIR FORCE PUBLICATIONS AVAILABLE TO SECURITY ASSISTANCE CUSTOMERS. [Quarterly] (AF Regulation 0-20)
Internal use only.

D 301.6:0-22/date • Item 425
NUMERICAL INDEX OF STANDARD AND RECURRING AIR FORCE PUBLICATIONS AVAILABLE TO NATO SECURITY ASSISTANCE CUSTOMERS. [Quarterly] (AF Regulation 0-22)
Internal use only.

D 301.6:50-5
USAF FORMAL SCHOOLS. [Quarterly]

D 301.6/2:CT • Item 425
REGULATIONS, RULES AND INSTRUCTIONS.
Earlier M 301.6

D 301.6/2-2:date • Item 425 (MF)
AIR FORCE ACTIVITY ADDRESS CODE NAME/
ORGANIZATION TO CODE. [Quarterly]
Internal use only.

D 301.6/2-3 • Item 425-C
AFAC (series).

D 301.6/3:nos.
MATS REGULATIONS.

D 301.6/4:date • Item 425
AIR FORCE PROCUREMENT INSTRUCTION.
Superseded by Headquarters U.S.A.F. Armed Services Procurement Regulation Supplement (D 1.13/2-3).

D 301.6/4-2:date&nos.
PROCUREMENT NEWSLETTER. (AFRP 70-1)

D 301.6/5:CT • Item 424-F
HANDBOOKS, MANUALS (unnumbered), GUIDES.

D 301.6/5:H 62 • Item 424-F
UNITED STATES AIR FORCE HISTORY, A GUIDE TO DOCUMENTARY SOURCES. 1973. 245 p. il. PURPOSE:– To provide amateur historians and researchers with the locations of collections of primary and secondary documents on the Air Force, as far back as the Civil War when Union soldiers were sent aloft in balloons. There are more than 700 entries, with a description of the contents of each collection, and more than 50 photographs.

D 301.6/5-2:date • Item 424-F-1 (MF)
HANDBOOK FOR SERVICE ATTACHES ACCREDITED TO THE DEPARTMENT OF THE AIR FORCE. [Semiannual]
Contains official titles, addresses and photographs of attaches accredited to the Air Force. Also includes AF International Affairs Division personnel.
Non-depository.

D 301.6/6:nos.
CIVIL AIR PATROL REGULATIONS. Admin.

D 301.6/7 • Item 425-B (MF)
WESTERN SPACE AND MISSILE CENTER: REGULATIONS, WSMCR- (series). [Irregular]
Discontinued.

D 301.6/8:nos./v. • Item 474-F-6
AIR FORCE HANDBOOK (series).

D 301.7 • Item 421
MANUALS, AFM- (series). [Irregular]

D 301.7:51-37 • Item 421
INSTRUMENT FLYING. (Subscription includes basic manual plus changes for an indefinite period)

D 301.7/2:
AFTRC MANUALS.

D 301.7/3:
CONAC MANUALS.

D 301.7/4   • **Item 421**
CIVIL AIR PATROL MANUALS, CAPM-(series).
[Irregular]

D 301.7/5   • **Item 421**
AACS MANUALS. [Irregular]

D 301.7/6   • **Item 421**
MATS MANUALS, MM- (series). [Irregular]

D 301.7/7:nos.
ATRC MANUAL.

D 301.8:v.nos.&nos.   • **Item 422 (EL)**
CITIZEN AIRMAN. v. 1–   [Bimonthly]
    Published for the Air Force Reserve, Air Na-
    tional Guard, and Civil Air Patrol.
    Indexed by: Index to U.S. Government Peri-
    odicals.
    Frequency varies.
    Former title: Air Reservist.
    ISSN 0002-2535

D 301.9:date
UNITED STATES AIR FORCE RADIO FACILITY
    CHARTS, EUROPE, AFRICA, MIDDLE EAST.
    Earlier M 301.7

D 301.9/2:v.nos.&nos.
MILITARY AVIATION NOTICES. [Weekly]
    Earlier M 301.17/2

D 301.9/3:date
SPECIAL NOTICES, SUPPLEMENT TO RADIO FA-
    CILITY CHARTS AND INFLIGHT DATA, EUROPE.
    [Monthly]

D 301.9/4:date
FLIGHT INFORMATION PUBLICATIONS: ENROUTE
    HIGH ALTITUDE, EUROPE, AFRICA, MIDDLE
    EAST. [Monthly]
    Earlier M 301.7

D 301.9/5:v.nos.&nos.
MILITARY AVIATION NOTEICES, CORRECTIONS TO
    FLIP ENROUTE EUROPE AND NORTH AFRICA.

D 301.10:date
UNITED STATES AIR FORCE RADIO FACILITY
    CHARTS, CARIBBEAN AND SOUTH AMERICAN
    AREA. [Bimonthly]

D 301.10/2:nos.
MILITARY AVIATION NOTICES, CORRECTIONS TO
    FLIP PUBLICATIONS, CARIBBEAN AND SOUTH
    AMERICA.
    Earlier M 301.19

D 301.11:date
UNITED STATES AIR FORCE, UNITED STATES NAVY
    RADIO FACILITY CHARTS, NORTH ATLANTIC
    AREA.
    Replaced by D 301.13/3
    Earlier M 301.15

D 301.11/2:v.nos.
MILITARY AVIATION NOTICES, NORTH ATLANTIC AND
    EAST CANADA.

D 301.12:date
UNITED STATES AIR FORCE AND UNITED STATES
    NAVY RADIO FACILITY CHARTS, CENTRAL- PA-
    CIFIC-FAR EAST. [Monthly]
    Earlier M 301.16

D 301.12/2:dt.&nos.
MILITARY AVIATION NOTICES, PACIFIC.

D 301.12/3:date
FLIGHT INFORMATION PUBLICATION: TERMINAL,
    LOW ALTITUDE, PACIFIC AND SOUTHEAST ASIA.
    [Monthly]

D 301.12/4:date
–**TERMINAL, HIGH ALTITUDE, PACIFIC AND**
SOUTHEAST ASIA. [Monthly]

D 301.13:date
UNITED STATES AIR FORCE, UNITED STATES NAVY
    AND ROYAL CANADIAN AIR FORCE RADIO
    FACILITY CHARTS, WEST CANADA AND ALASKA.
    [Bimonthly]
    Replaced by D 301.13/3

D 301.13/2:dt.&nos.
MILITARY AVIATION NOTICES, WEST CANADA AND
    ALASKA.

D 301.13/3:date
UNITED STATES AIR FORCE, NAVY, ROYAL CANA-
    DIAN AIR FORCE AND ROYAL CANADIAN NAVY
    RADIO FACILITY CHARTS AND IN-FLIGHT DATA,
    ALASKA, CANADA AND NORTH ATLANTIC.
    [Monthly]
    Replaces D 301.11 and D 301.13

D 301.13/4:v.nos.&nos.
MILITARY AVIATION NOTICES, CORRECTIONS TO
    ENROUTE-LOW ALTITUDE- ALASKA.

D 301.13/5:date/M-nos.
FORMATION PUBLICATION: ENROUTE INTER-
    MEDIATE ALTITUDE, UNITED STATES. [Issued
    every 4 weeks]
    Issued in 4 sections, M-1, and M-2, M-3, M-
    4, M-5, M-6, M-7, and M-8.

D 301.13/6:date
–TERMINAL, LOW ALTITUDE, AFRICA AND SOUTH-
    WEST ASIA. [Monthly]

D 301.14:v.nos.&nos.
CADO TECHNICAL DATA DIGEST.
    Earlier M 301.9

D 301.15:date
ALPHABETICAL LIST, U.S. AIR FORCE AND AIR
    FORCE-NAVY AERONAUTICAL STANDARD
    DRAWINGS. [Semiannual]
    Replaced by D 301.16/2
    Earlier M 301.12

D 301.16:date
NUMERICAL LIST OF U.S. AIR FORCE AND AIR
    FORCE-NAVY AERONAUTICAL STANDARD
    DRAWINGS. [Monthly]
    Earlier M 301.12
    Later D 301.16/2

D 301.16/2:date
INDEX OF U.S. AIR FORCE, AIR FORCE- NAVY AERO-
    NAUTICAL AND MILITARY (MS) STANDARDS
    (sheet form). [Semiannual]
    Replaces D 301.15 and D 301.16

D 301.17:dt.&nos.
NUMERICAL INDEX OF TECHNICAL PUBLICATIONS.
    Restricted.
    Earlier M 301.13

D 301.17/2:nos.
TECHNICAL ORDERS.
    Degignated TO-nos.

D 301.18:date
INDEX OF SPECIFICATIONS AND BULLETINS AP-
    PROVED FOR U.S. AIR FORCE PROCUREMENT.

D 301.19:nos.
SPECIFICATIONS BULLETINS.

D 301.20:nos.
TECHNICAL PUBLICATIONS FOR AIR FORCE TECH-
    NICAL LIBRARIES, BOOK LISTS.
    Earlier M 301.8

D 301.22:
QUALIFIED PRODUCTS LIST.

D 301.22/2:nos.
PERFERRED PARTS LISTS. Desig. ANG-nos.3

D 301.23:nos.
AIR NATIONAL GUARD MANUALS.

D 301.24:nos.
AIR FORCE LETTERS.

D 301.24/2:nos.
AIR FORCE POLICY LETTER FOR COMMANDERS

FROM OFFICE OF SECRETARY OF AIR FORCE.
    Admin.

D 301.24/3:nos.
–SUPPLEMENTS.

D 301.25
AIR STAFF. [Irregular]
    Organizational chart.

D 301.26   • **Item 422-A**
AIR UNIVERSITY REVIEW. v. 1–   1947–
    [Bimonthly]

    PURPOSE:– Published, as a professional jour-
    nal of the U.S. Air Force, to stimulate profes-
    sional thought concerning the developments and
    employment of aerospace forces.
    Contains non-technical and semi-technical
    articles. Well illustrated.
    Subscriptions available from Air University
    Book Department.
    Indexed by: Index to U.S. Government Peri-
    odicals.
    ISSN 0002-2594
    See D 301.26/24

D 301.26:947-87/ind.   • **Item 422-A**
AIR UNIVERSITY REVIEW INDEX.

D 301.26/2   • **Item 424-I (EL)**
AIR UNIVERSITY LIBRARY INDEX TO MILITARY
    PERIODICALS. v. 1–   1949–   [Quarterly]
    Quarterly issues are superseded by annual
    and triennial volumes.
    Provides a subject index to significant ar-
    ticles, news items and editorials appearing in over
    60 English language military and aeronautical pe-
    riodicals not indexed in readily available commer-
    cial indexing services.
    Previous title: Air University Periodical In-
    dex.
    Available to libraries, on an exchange basis,
    from the Air University Library.
    ISSN 0002-2586

D 301.26/2-2:date
AIR UNIVERSITY LIBRARY MASTER LIST OF PERI-
    ODICALS. [Annual]

D 301.26/3:CT   • **Item 422-R (MF)**
AIR UNIVERSITY DOCUMENTARY RESEARCH STUD-
    IES.
    Discontinued.

D 301.26/3-2:date/nos.   • **Item 422-R (MF)**
AIR UNIVERSITY COMPENDIUM OF RESEARCH
    TOPICS. [Annual]
    Discontinued.

D 301.26/4:date
USAF EXTENSION COURSE CATALOG.

D 301.26/5:
ECI LETTER.

D 301.26/6:CT   • **Item 422-K**
AIR UNIVERSITY PUBLICATIONS.

D 301.26/6-8:CT   • **Item 424-F-2**
AIR UNIVERSITY: HANDBOOKS, MANUALS, GUIDES.
    [Irregular]

D 301.26/6-9:CT   • **Item 422-K-2 (MF)**
SCHOOL OF ADVANCED AIRPOWER STUDIES
    (series).

D 301.26/7:CT
AIR UNIVERSITY, HUMAN RESOURCES RESEARCH
    INSTITUTE, RESEARCH MEMORANDUM.

D 301.26/7-2:ltrs.nos.   • **Item 422-R-3**
RESEARCH REPORTS (series). [Irregular]
    Each Report is concerned with a different
    topic. One example is an analysis of Soviet pres-
    ence in Vietnam issued by the Air University Press
    at Maxwell Air Force Base, Alabama.
    Discontinued.

D 301.26/7-3:   • **Item 424-F-3 (MF)**
STUDENT REPORT (series).
    Discontinued.

D 301.26/7-4:nos.
MODULE (series). [Irregular]

D 301.26/8:nos.
ADTIC PUBLICATIONS.

D 301.26/9:
ECI CLIP SHEET. [Monthly]

D 301.26/10:nos.
TECHNICAL RESEARCH REPORTS PUB. BY AIR FORCE PERSONNEL AND TRAINING CENTER AIR RESEARCH AND DEVELOPMENT COMMAND.

D 301.26/11:nos.
SPECIAL BIBLIOGRAPHIES.
    Issued by Air University.

D 301.26/12:CT   • Item 421-E-4 (MF)
AIR UNIVERSITY, AFROTC [text books].
    Text books covering a wide spectrum of subjects that are relevant to the curriculum of the Air University.
    Discontinued.

D 301.26/13:
RESEARCH REPORTS.
    Cancelled see D 301.26/23-2

D 301.26/13-2:nos.
AIR UNIVERSITY, SCHOOL OF AVIATION MEDICINE: [Publications].

D 301.26/13-3:date
PUBLICATIONS OF SCHOOL OF AVIATION MEDICINE, INDEX, FISCAL YEAR.

D 301.26/13-4
AEROMEDICAL REVIEW. [Irregular]

D 301.26/13-5:CT
SCHOOL OF AVIATION MEDICINE: GENERAL PUBLICATIONS.

D 301.26/13-6:nos.   • Item 422-C-1 (MF)
SCHOOL OF AEROSPACE MEDICINE: TECHNICAL DOCUMENTARY REPORT SAM-TDR (series).
    Technical reports on miscellaneous topics pertaining to the mission of the USAF School of Aerospace Medicine, Brooks AFB, Texas.
    Discontinued.

D 301.26/13-6:1056
    TECHNICAL DOCUMENTARY REPORTS, SAM-TDR- (series). [Irregular]

D 301.26/13-6:1057
    TECHNICAL REPORTS, SAM-TR- (series). [Irregular]

D 301.26/14:v.nos.&nos.
CONTACT. ADMIN.

D 301.26/15:date
RESEARCH AND SPECIAL STUDIES PROGRESS REPORT. [Annual]

D 301.26/16:date   • Item 422-R-1 (MF)
AIR UNIVERSITY CATALOG. [Annual]
    Describes schools and professional organizations that make up the Air University and the educational opportunities available in each school.
    Discontinued.

D 301.26/16-2:date
GUIDE TO AIR UNIVERSITY.

D 301.26/17:nos.
ECI COURSES.

D 301.26/17-2:nos.   • Item 421-E-4 (MF)
EXTENSION COURSE INSTITUTE, AIR UNIVERSITY: CAREER DEVELOPMENT COURSE, CDC– (series). [Irregular]
    Discontinued.

D 301.26/17-3:nos.   • Item 421-E-4 (MF)
COURSE (series). [Irregular]
    Discontinued.

D 301.26/17-4   • Item 421-E-4 (MF)
MODULE.
    Discontinued.

D 301.26/17-5:nos.   • Item 421-E-4 (MF)
VOLUME REVIEW EXERCISE (series). [Irregular]
    Discontinued.

D 301.26/18:v.nos.
AIR FORCE INSTITUTE OF TECHNOLOGY, AIR UNIVERSITY, U.S. AIR FORCE CATALOGUE.

D 301.26/19:nos.
USAF HISTORICAL STUDIES.

D 301.26/20:v.nos.   • Item 424-I (MF)
AIR UNIVERSITY ABSTRACTS OF RESEARCH REPORTS. [Annual]
    Discontinued.

D 301.26/21:v.nos.&nos.
AIR UNIVERSITY LIBRARY SELECTED DOCUMENTS ACCESSION LIST. [Weekly]

D 301.26/22:v.nos.&nos.
AIR UNIVERSITY LIBRARY SELECTED ACQUISITIONS. [Monthly]

D 301.26/23:   • Item 422-R-2 (MF)
UNITED STATES AIR FORCE, COMMANDS AND AGENCIES BASIC INFORMATION. [Annual] (Air University)
    Designed for use in military instructional programs and provides current general information regarding USAF organizations and their activities.
    Discontinued.

D 301.26/24:v.nos./nos.   • Item 422-A (EL)
AEROSPACE POWER JOURNAL. [Quarterly]
    Formerly: Airpower Journal

D 301.26/24-2   • Item 422-A-1 (EL)
AEROSPACE POWER JOURNAL (Portuguese). [Quarterly] Formerly: Airpower Journal

D 201.26/24-3   • Item 422-A-2 (EL)
AEROSPACE POWER JOURNAL (Hispanoamericana). [Quarterly] Formerly: Airpower Journal

D 301.26/25:nos.   • Item 422-K-1 (MF)
AIR WAR COLLEGE STUDIES IN NATIONAL SECURITY (series).

D 301.27:nos.   • Item 421
AIR WEATHER SERVICE MANUAL.
    Earlier M 301.2
    Discontinued.

D 301.27/2:letters-nos.
AIR WEATHER SERVICE PAMPHLET, AWSP (series).

D 301.28:date   • Item 424-A
INDEX OF SPECIFICATIONS AND RELATED PUBLICATIONS USED BY AIR FORCE, MILITARY INDEX. v. 4. [Semiannual]
    Later D 7.14
    Discontinued.

D 301.29:
AIR FORCE-NAVY AERONAUTICAL DESIGN STANDARDS.

D 301.30:
AIR FORCE-NAVY AERONAUTICAL STANDARDS.

D 301.31:
U.S. AIR FORCE STANDARDS.

D 301.32:
NOTICE.

D 301.33:
ANA NOTICE. [Weekly]

D 301.34:
ANA BULLETIN.

D 301.35   • Item 421-A (MF)
AIR FORCE PAMPHLETS, AFP- (series). [Irregular]
    Discontinued.

D 301.35/2:nos.
CIVIL AIR PATROL PAMPHLET CAPP (series).

D 301.35/3   • Item 421-A (MF)
PAMPHLETS, AFSCP- (series). [Irregular]

D 301.35/5:nos.   • Item 421-A (MF)
AIR FORCE RESERVE PAMPHLETS, AFRESP- (series). [Irregular]

D 301.35/6:nos.   • Item 421-A (MF)
F.E. WARREN AFB, FEWP- (series). [Irregular]

D 301.35/7:nos.   • Item 421-A (MF)
MALMSTROM AIR FORCE BASE PAMPHLET (series). [Irregular]

D 301.35/8:   • Item 421-A-1
AFCC PAMPHLETS (series).
    AFCC = Air Force Communications Command
    Discontinued.

D 301.35/9:   • Item 424-F-4 (MF)
ARPC PAMPHLET (series).
    ARPC = Air Reserve Personnel Center

D 301.36:nos.
AIR TRAINING COMMAND, HUMAN RESOURCES RESEARCH CENTER: LIST OF PUBLICATIONS.

D 301.36/2:nos.
    – TECHNICAL REPORTS.

D 301.36/3:nos.
    – RESEARCH BULLETINS.

D 301.36/4:nos.
    – RESEARCH REVIEWS.

D 301.36/5:CT
    – INFORMATION BULLETINS.

D 301.36/6:nos.
RESEARCH REPORT AFPTRC-TN (series).

D 301.36/7:nos.
DEVELOPMENT REPORT AFPTRC-TN (series).

D 301.36/8:nos.
[CREW RESEARCH LABORATORY] TECHNICAL MEMORANDUMS CRL- TM-Nos.
    Official use only.

D 301.36/9:nos.
– LABORATORY NOTES. CRL-IN-NOS. [unpublished draft].

D 301.36/10:CT
BIBLIOGRAPHIES AND LISTS OF PUBLICATIONS. OPERATIONAL APPLICATIONS OFFICE.

D 301.37:nos.
CADO RECLASSIFICATION BULLETIN.

D 301.38:v.nos.&nos.
AIR TRAINING. [Monthly]

D 301.38/2:v.nos.&nos.
TRAINING ANALYSIS AND DEVELOPMENT, INFORMATION BULLETIN.

D 301.38/3:CT
AIR TRAINING COMMAND, MISCELLANEOUS PUBLICATIONS.

D 301.38/4   • Item 424-C
NAVIGATOR. [Quarterly]
    PURPOSE:– To disseminate useful, timely, and interesting technical information relative to the navigator's duties.
    Previous title: Aircraft Observer.
    Indexed by: Index to U.S. Government Periodicals.
    ISSN 0028-1557
    Discontinued v.33/3.

D 301.38/5:date
ON THE JOB TRAINING PROGRAM, JP SERIES.

D 301.38/6:nos.
ATC PAMPHLET. (Air Training Command)

D 301.38/7 • Item 424-G
INSTRUCTORS' JOURNAL. v. 1– 9, no. 4. – Spring 1972. [Quarterly] (Air Training Command)
PURPOSE:– To serve as a medium in which the instructor might gain expression in spotlighting his accomplishments through the exchange of ideas. Also disseminates news of professional developments in the fields of education and training with emphasis on new methods and technology.
Discontinued.

D 301.38/8:nos. • Item 424-C-1 (MF)
INFORMATION BULLETINS. 1– [Irregular] (Air Training Command, Environmental Information Division)
PURPOSE:– To provide useful environmental information for individuals and teachers, which will enable the user to overcome many difficulties met in survival situations and in normal operations.
Discontinued.

D 301.38/9 • Item 424-C-1
AIR TRAINING COMMAND HISTORICAL MONOGRAPH (series).
Discontinued.

D 301.39:nos.
AIR WEATHER SERVICE: TRAINING GUIDES.

D 301.40:nos.
AIR WEATHER SERVICE. TECHNICAL REPORTS.
Earlier M 301.22

D 301.40/2:nos.
ENVIRONMENTAL TECHNICAL APPLICATIONS CENTER. TECHNACAL NOTES.

D 301.41:
[This Class Changed to D 301.26/3]

D 301.42:nos.
AIR WEATHER SERVICE: BIBLIOGRAPHY.

D 301.42/2:nos.
AEROSPACE SCIENCES REVIEW.
AWS recurrring publication 105-2.

D 301.43:
RADIO FACILITY CHARTS AND SUPPLEMENTARY INFORMATION, UNITED STATES, LF/MF EDITION.

D 301.43/2:date
RADIO FACILITY CHARTS UNITED STATES, VOR EDITION.
Official use only.

D 301.43/3:date
FLIGHT INFORMATION PUBLICATION: ENROUTE-HIGH ALTITUDE, UNITED STATES, NORTHEAST [and Southeast]. [Issued every 4 weeks]
Later D 5.318/4

D 301.43/3-2:date
FLIGHT INFORMATION PUBLICATION: ENROUTE-HIGH ALTITUDE, UNITED STATES, NORTHWEST [and Southwest]. [Issued every 4 weeks]

D 301.44:/v.nos./nos. • Item 423-A (EL)
FLYING SAFETY. v. 1– 1945– [Monthly]

Contains articles on fields of flight, aircraft engineering, training, and safety measures in the air and on the ground, published in the interest of safer flying.
Earlier title: Aerospace Safety.
Indexed by: Index to U.S. Government Periodicals.
ISSN 0001-9429

D 301.44/2:v.nos.nos. • Item 422-T (EL)
THE COMBAT EDGE. [Monthly]

D 301.44/3 • Item 422-T-1 (EL)
TORCH, SAFETY MAGAZINE OF AETC. [Monthly]

D 301.45:CT • Item 422-B (MF)
AIR FORCE SYSTEMS COMMAND: PUBLICATIONS. [Irregular]
Issued as WADC-TR-53-373 and supplements.
Contains abstracts of technical reports published by the Air Force Materials Laboratory during the fiscal year. Reports on research con-

ducted by the Air Force Materials Laboratory personnel as well as that conducted on contract are included.
Each entry gives subject, investigator, contract, abstract and whether available from the Clearinghouse for Federal Scientific and Technical Information.
Earlier: Review of the Air Force Materials Research and Development Program.

D 301.45/2:nos.
GEOPHYSICAL RESEARCH PAPERS.

D 301.45/3:nos.
RELEASES. AIR RESEARCH AND DEVELOPMENT COMMAND.

D 301.45/4 • Item 421-E-6 (MF)
AIR FORCE GEOPHYSICS LABORATORY: TECHNICAL REPORTS, AFGL-TR (series).
Earlier: Air Force Cambridge Research Center: AFCRC Technical Reports.

D 301.45/4-2:nos.
AFCRC TECHNICAL NOTES TN (series).

**Field Agency Publications
Air Force
Cambridge Research Laboratories
Hanscom Field
Bedford, Massachusetts 0l730**

Conduct and sponsor basic and applied research in electronics and geophysics, the program combines a substantial intramural research effort with a large contractual program.

D 301.45/4-3
AFCRL- (series). [Irregular]

D 301.45/4-4: • Item 421-E-6 (MF)
DAILY MAGNETOGRAMS FOR ... FROM THE AFGL NETWORK. [Annual]
Discontinued.

D 301.45/5
TECHNICAL DOCUMENTARY REPORTS, WADC-TDR- (series). [Irregular]

D 301.45/6:nos.
AF TECHNICAL REPORTS, WRIGHT AIR DEVELOPMENT CENTER.

D 301.45/7:nos.
HFORL MEMORANDUM TN (series).
Issued by Human Factors Operations Research Laboratories, Air Research & Development Command, Bolling Air Force Base, Washington, D.C.

D 301.45/8:nos.
HFORL REPORT TR (series).

D 301.45/9
AIR FORCE SURVEYS IN GEOPHYSICS. 1– [Irregular]

D 301.45/10
INSTRUMENTATION PAPERS. 1– [Irregular]

D 301.45/11:date
NEW SHIP TECHNIQUES AND DEVELOPMENT OF RESEARCH SERVICES DIVISION, ANNUAL REPORT.

ELECTRONIC RESEARCH DIRECTORATE

D 301.45/12:date
[TECHNICAL MEMORANDUM] ERD-CRRK-TM (series).

D 301.45/12-2:nos.
TECHNICAL NOTE ERD-TN (series).

D 301.45/13:nos.
WADC TECHNICAL NOTES.

AIR FORCE SYSTEMS COMMAND

D 301.45/14 • Item 421
MANUALS, AFSCM- (series). [Irregular]

D 301.45/14-2 • Item 421 (MF)
REGULATIONS, AFSCR (series).

D 301.45/14-2:0-2/date • Item 421
NUMERICAL INDEX OF AFSC PUBLICATIONS. [Quarterly]
Discontinued.

D 301.45/14-2:0-9/date • Item 421
NUMERICAL AND FUNCTIONAL INDEX OF COMMAND FORMS. [Quarterly]

D 301.45/15:date
QUARTERLY INDEX OF TECHNICAL DOCUMENTARY REPORTS.

**GEOPHYSICS RESEARCH DIRECTORATE
Air Force Cambridge Research Center**

D 301.45/16:nos.
GRD RESEARCH NOTES.

D 301.45/16-2:nos.
TECHNICAL NOTES, GRD-TN (series).

D 301.45/16-3:nos
GRD TECHNICAL REPORT, TR (series).

D 301.45/16-4:date
ANNUAL REPORT.

D 301.45/17
TECHNICAL REPORTS, AFMDC-TR- (series). [Irregular]

D 301.45/17-2
TECHNICAL NOTES, AFMDC-TN- (series). [Irregular]

AIR FORCE OFFICE OF SCIENTIFIC RESEARCH

D 301.45/18:nos.
TECHNICAL NOTES, AFOSR-TN- (series).

D 301.45/19:nos. • Item 422-B (MF)
TECHNICAL REPORTS, AFOSR-TR- (series).

D 301.45/19-2 • Item 422-B
AFOSR- (series). [Irregular]

D 301.45/19-2:700
AIR FORCE SCIENTIFIC RESEARCH BIBLIOGRAPHY. 1950/56– [Irregular]
PURPOSE:– To provide ready access to both the published (professional journal) literature and Air Force Technical reports resulting from the extramural support of basic research by the Air Force.
Abstracts are arranged by contractor, with indexes for contracts, OSR control numbers, authors, and subjects. A mathematical subject classification index is also included.

Vol. 1 1950-56
Vol. 2 1957-58
Vol. 3 1959

D 301.45/19-3:nos.
– AFOSR TECHNICAL DOCUMENTS.

D 301.45/19-4:nos.
– DIRECTORATE OF RESEARCH ANALYSIS, AFOSR/DRA (series).

D 301.45/19-5:date • Item 424-B-10 (MF)
U.S. AIR FORCE PLAN FOR DEFENSE RESEARCH SCIENCES. [Annual]
PURPOSE:– To describe research planned for the coming fiscal year in seven different technical areas: Life Sciences, Materials, Geophysics, Aerospace Vehicles, Propulsion and Power, Weaponry, and Electronics.

D 301.45/19-6:date • Item 422-B (MF)
TECHNICAL REPORT SUMMARIES. [Quarterly]

D 301.45/19-7:date   • **Item 422-B-2 (MF)**
RECENT RESEARCH ACCOMPLISHMENTS OF THE
AIR FORCE OFFICE OF SCIENTIFIC RESEARCH.
[Annual]
    PURPOSE:– To summarize research accom-
plishments of the Office in such areas as aero-
space structures, chemistry, and mathematics.

D 301.45/19-8:date   • **Item 422-B (MF)**
CHEMICAL AND ATMOSPHERIC SCIENCES PRO-
GRAM REVIEW. [Annual]

D 301.45/19-9:date   • **Item 422-B**
DIRECTORATE OF ELECTRONIC AND MATERIAL
SCIENCES FY PROGRAM. [Annual]
    Discontinued.

D 301.45/19-10:   • **Item 422-B (MF)**
DIRECTORATE OF MATHEMATICAL AND INFORMA-
TION SCIENCES, AIR FORCE OFFICE OF
SCIENTIFIC RESEARCH, RESEARCH SUMMA-
RIES.
    Discontinued.

D 301.45/19-11   • **Item 422-B**
SURFACE REACTIONS IN THE SPACE ENVIRON-
MENT. [Annual]

D 301.45/19-12   • **Item 421-A-2 (MF)**
AFOSR PAMPHLET.

AIR FORCE SPECIAL
WEAPONS CENTER

D 301.45/20:nos.
TECHNICAL REPORTS, AFSWC-TR.

D 301.45/20-2:nos.
TECHNICAL NOTES, AFSWC-TN.

D 301.45/20-3
TECHNICAL DOCUMENTARY REPORTS, AFSWC-
TDR- (series). [Irregular]

D 301.45/21:nos.   • **Item 421-A (MF)**
AIR FORCE SYSTEMS COMMAND: TECHNICAL RE-
PORTS, AFSC-TR- (series)
    Formerly: Air Research and Development
Command: Technical Reports, ARDC-TR-(series).
    Discontinued.

D 301.45/21-2:nos.   • **Item 421-A (MF)**
SD-TR (series).

D 301.45/22:le-nos.
WRIGHT AERONAUTICAL SERIAL REPORTS.

D 301.45/23:nos.
AIR FORCE MISSILE TEST CENTER: TECHNICAL
REPORTS, AFMTC-TR-(series).

D 301.45/23-1:nos.
AFMTCP-AIR FORCE MISSILE TEST CENTER.

D 301.45/23-2:nos.
AFMTCP-AIR FORCE MISSILE TEST CENTER.

D 301.45/24:nos.
AIR FORCE COMMAND AND CONTROL DEVELOP-
MENT DIVISION: TECHNICAL NOTES AFCCDD-
TN (nos.).

D 301.45/25:nos.
ARL TECHNICAL REPORTS.

AERONAUTICAL SYSTEMS DIVISION

D 301.45/26:nos.   • **Item 424-E**
ASD TECHNICAL NOTE TN (series).
    Discontinued.

D 301.45/26-2   • **Item 424-E**
TECHNICAL REPORTS, ASD-TR- (series). [Irregular]

D 301.45/26-3
TECHNICAL DOCUMENTARY REPORTS, ASD-TDR-
(series). [Irregular]

AIR FORCE
HUMAN RESOURCES LABORATORY

D 301.45/27   • **Item 421-E-3 (MF)**
ARMSTRONG LABORATORY TECHNICAL REPORT.
    PURPOSE:– To document research findings
of laboratory staff in support of Air Force personnel planning; methods of selecting, classifying,
and evaluating personnel; method of improving
retention and utilization of personnel; methods
for structuring and evaluating Air Force jobs.
    Libraries participating in the Documents Ex-
pediting Project receive automatic distribution of
all issues given general release.
    Formerly Technical Documentary Report, PRL-
TDR- (series).
    Earlier title: AL-TR (series).

ABSTRACTS OF PERSONNEL RESEARCH
    REPORTS. [Annual]
        Issued as the final report of each yearly
series.
        1954-65 PRL-TDR-65-23

TECHNICAL REPORTS, ESD-TR- (series).
    [Irregular]

D 301.45/27-2:nos.
TECHNICAL REPORT MEMORANDUM AFHRL
    (TT)-TRM (series). 1–   [Irregular]

D 301.45/27-3:nos.
TECHNICAL REPORT ANALYSIS CONDENSA-
TION EVALUATION (TRACE).

D 301.45/27-4:nos.   • **Item 421-E-3 (MF)**
ARMSTRONG LABORATORY TECHNICAL PAPER.
    Earlier title: AL-TP (series).

D 301.45/27-5:date   • **Item 421-E-3 (MF)**
AIR FORCE HUMAN RESOURCES LABORATORY:
    ANNUAL REPORT.

D 301.45/27-6:date   • **Item 421-E-3**
QUARTERLY R&D SUMMARY.
    Discontinued.

D 301.45/27-7:date   • **Item 421-E-3 (MF)**
AFHRL-SR (series).

D 301.45/27-8:date   • **Item 421-E-3**
AFHRL NEWSLETTER. [Quarterly]

D 301.45/27-10:date   • **Item 421-E-3**
FISCAL YEAR ... AIR FORCE TECHNICAL OB-
JECTIVE DOCUMENT. [Annual]
    Discontinued.

D 301.45/27-11   • **Item 421-E-13 (MF)**
ARMSTRONG LABORATORY, AL/HR-CR (series).

D 301.45/28
TECHNICAL REPORTS, ESD-TR- (series). [Irregular]

D 301.45/28-2
TECHNICAL DOCUMENTARY REPORTS, ESD-TDR-
(series). [Irregular]

AIR FORCE SYSTEMS COMMAND
Andrews Air Force Base

D 301.45/29:nos.
PRESS RELEASES.

D 301.45/29-2:CT
ADDRESSES.

D 301.45/30
TECHNICAL REPORTS, AAL-TR- (series). [Irregular]

D 301.45/30-2
TECHNICAL DOCUMENTARY REPORTS, AAL-TDR-
(series). [Irregular]

D 301.45/30-3
TECHNICAL NOTES, TN- (series). [Irregular]

D 301.45/31
TECHNICAL REPORTS. FTC-TR- (series). [Irregular]

D 301.45/31-2
TECHNICAL DOCUMENTARY REPORTS, FTC-TDR-
(series). [Irregular]

D 301.45/31-3:nos.
–TECHNICAL INFORMATION MEMORANDUM
FTC-TM (series).

D 301.45/31-4
TECHNICAL INFORMATION HANDBOOKS, FTC-TIH-
(series). [Irregular]

AEROSPACE MEDICAL
RESEARCH LABORATORY

D 301.45/32
TECHNICAL DOCUMENTARY REPORTS, AMRL-TDR-
(series). [Irregular]

D 301.45/32-2
AMRL MEMORANDUMS. [Irregular]

D 301.45/32-3   • **Item 422-B-1 (MF)**
TECHNICAL REPORTS, AMRL-TR (series). [Irregular]

ARNOLD ENGINEERING
DEVELOPMENT CENTER

D 301.45/33:nos.
TECHNICAL REPORTS, AEDC-TR.

D 301.45/33-2
TECHNICAL DOCUMENTARY REPORTS, AEDC-TDR-
(series). [Irregular]

D 301.45/33-3:nos.
TECHNICAL NOTES, AEDC-TN.

D 301.45/33-4:date   • **Item 421-E-3**
TEST HIGHLIGHTS. [Quarterly]

RESEARCH AND TECHNOLOGY
DIVISION

D 301.45/34:v.nos.&nos.
RTD TECHNOLOGY BRIEFS.

D 301.45/34-2
TECHNICAL DOCUMENTARY REPORTS, RTD-TDR-
(series). [Irregular]

D 301.45/34-3
AIR FORCE WEAPONS LABORATORY: TECHNICAL
REPORT AFWL-TR (series).

D 301.45/35:nos.
AIR FORCE WEAPONS LABORATORY. RESEARCH
AND TECHNOLOGY DIVISION. AFWL-TDR.

D 301.45/36:nos.
BALLISTIC SYSTEMS DIVISION. TECHNICAL DOCU-
MENTARY REPORT BSD-TDR.

D 301.45/37:nos.
OPERATIONAL APPLICATIONS LABORATORY. AIR
FORCE CAMBRIDGE RESEARCH CENTER, OAL-
TM.

D 301.45/38:date   • **Item 421-E (MF)**
AIR FORCE SYSTEMS COMMAND ANNUAL REPORT.
    Discontinued.

D 301.45/38-2:   • **Item 421-E-10 (MF)**
HUMAN SYSTEMS DIVISION, ANNUAL REPORT.
    PURPOSE– To summarize activities of the
division in its role as the systems independent,
human-centered advocate for the Air Force in
weapons system development, deployment and
operations.
    Discontinued.

D 301.45/39
ENVIRONMENTAL RESEARCH PAPERS. 1–
    [Irregular]

D 301.45/40
PHYSICAL SCIENCES RESEARCH PAPERS. 1–
    1964–   [Irregular]

D 301.45/41:date
CRYOGENIC MATERIALS DATA HANDBOOK, YEARLY
    SUMMARY REPORTS. [Contractor Report by Non-
    Govt. Organization].

D 301.45/42
SPECIAL REPORTS. [Irregular]

D 301.45/43
GEOPHYSICS AND SPACE DATA BULLETIN.
[Quarterly]

D 301.45/44:nos.
AIR FORCE INSTITUTE OF TECHNOLOGY: NEW
BOOKS IN LIBRARY.

D 301.45/45
TECHNICAL DOCUMENTARY REPORTS, AL-TDR-
(series). [Irregular]

D 301.45/45-2:nos.
AIR FORCE AVIONICS LABORATORY TECHNICAL
REPORTS, AFAL-TR- (series). [Irregular]

RESEARCH AND TECHNOLOGY
DIVISION
Air Force Systems Command
Wright-Patterson
Air Force Base, Ohio

AF FLIGHT DYNAMICS LABORATORY

D 301.45/46:nos.
TECHNICAL DOCUMENTARY REPORT FDL-TDR.

D 301.45/46-2:nos.   • Item 422-B (MF)
TECHNICAL REPORTS, AFFDL-TR.

AF MATERIALS LABORATORY

D 301.45/47:nos.
TECHNICAL DOCUMENTARY REPORT ML-TDR.

D 301.45/47-2:nos.
TECHNICAL REPORT AFML-TR.

SYSTEMS ENGINEERING GROUP

D 301.45/48:nos.
TECHNICAL DOCUMENTARY REPORT, SEG-TDR.

D 301.45/48-2:nos.
SYSTEMS ENGINEERING GROUP: TECHNICAL RE-
PORTS SEG-TM (series).

D 301.45/49:nos.
ARDC TECHNICAL PROGRAM PLANNING DOCUMENT
AF ARPD.
    Formerly AF TPPD.

AIR PROVING GROUND CENTER
Elgin Air Force Base, Florida

D 301.45/50:nos.
TECHNICAL NOTE, APGC-TN.

D 301.45/50-2:nos.
TECHNICAL REPORT, APGC-TR.

AIR FORCE AERO PROPULSION
LABORATORY

D 301.45/51:nos.
TECHNICAL DOCUMENTARY REPORT, APL-TDR.

D 301.45/51-2:nos.
TECHNICAL REPORT, AFAPL-TR.

D 301.45/52
TECHNICAL REPORTS, AMD-TR- (series). [Irregular]

D 301.45/52-2:nos.
AEROMEDICAL RESEARCH LABORATROY: TECH-
NICIAL DOCUMENTARY REPORT ARL-TDL
(series).

D 301.45/53:nos.
MAINTENANCE LABORATORY. AIR FORCE PERSON-
NEL TRIANING RESEARCH CENTER ML-TM (se-
ries).

D 301.45/54:date
RESEARCH AND TECHNOLOGY BRIEFS.

D 301.45/55:nos.
SAMSO-TR (series).

D 301.45/56:v.nos.&nos.   • Item 442-P
FEEDBACK. v. 1– 3 1979– 1981. [Quarterly] (Deputy
for Avionics Control)
    PURPOSE:– To provide a newsletter giving
information on Air Force activities, conferences,
etc., in the area of development, production, procurement, etc. of electrical and electronic devices and systems for aviation.
    Discontinued Dec. 1981.

D 301.45/57:nos.   • Item 422-B (MF)
TECHNICAL REPORTS, AFWAL-TR- (series).
[Irregular] (Air Force Wright Aeronautics Labora-
tory)

D 301.45/58:   • Item 422-B-3
AIR FORCE SYSTEMS COMMAND: HANDBOOKS,
MANUALS, GUIDES.
    Discontinued.

DEPARTMENT OF THE
AIR FORCE (Continued)

D 301.46:
AIR FORCE PUBLIC INFORMATION LETTER.

D 301.46/2:nos.
–SUPPLEMENTS.

D 301.47:v.nos.&nos.   • Item 422-C
AIRCRAFT FLASH. [Monthly]
    Discontinued.

D 301.48:date
UNITED STATES AIR FORCE, NAVY, ROYAL CANA-
DIAN AIR FORCE, AND ROYAL CANADIAN NAVY
SUPPLEMENTARY FLIGHT INFORMATION,
NORTH AMERICAN AREA (excluding Mexico and
Caribbean area).

D 301.48/2:dt./nos.
MILITARY AVIATION NOTICES, CORRECTIONS.
[Monthly]

D 301.49:date
UNITED STATES AIR FORCE AND NAVY SUPPLE-
MENTARY FLIGHT INFORMATION, EUROPE,
AFRICA, AND MIDDLE EAST.

D 301.49/2:dt.&nos.
MILITARY AVIATION NOTICES, CORRECTIONS TO
SUPPLEMENTARY FLIGHT INFORMATION,
EUROPE, AFRICA AND MIDDLE EAST. [Monthly]

D 301.49/3:v.nos.
AERONAUTICAL CHART & INFORMATION BULLE-
TIN, EUROPE, AFRICA AND MIDDLE EAST, NEW
EDITIONS OF AERONAUTICAL CHARTS PUB-
LISHED. [Monthly]

D 301.49/4:letters-nos.
LUNAR CHARTS AND MOSAICS SERIES.

D 301.50:date
UNITED STATES AIR FORCE AND NAVY SUPPLE-
MENTARY FLIGHT INFORMATION DOCUMENT,
PACIFIC AND FAR EAST.

D 301.50/2:dt.&nos.
MILITARY AVIATION NOTICES, CORRECTIONS TO
SUPPLEMENTARY FLIGHT INFORMATION DOCU-
MENT, PACIFIC AND FAR EAST.

D 301.51:date
SUPPLEMENTARY FLIGHT INFORMATION DOCU-
MENT, CARIBBEAN AND SOUTH AMERICAN.
Proc.
    Later D 301.52

D 301.51/2:dt.&nos.
USAF MILITARY AVIATION NOTICES, AMENDING
SFID, CARIBBEAN AND SOUTH AMERICA.

D 301.52:date
U.S. AIR FORCE AND U.S. NAVY FLIGHT PLANNING
DOCUMENT.
    Replaces D 301.48 through D 301.51/2

D 301.52/2:date
QUARTERLY CHECK LIST, USAF/USN FLIGHT IN-
FORMATION PUBLICATIONS, PLANNING.

D 301.52/3:nos.
MILITARY AVIATION NOTICES: CORRECTIONS TO
FLIGHT INFORMATION PUBLICATIONS.

D 301.53:nos.
GROUND ACCIDENT ABSTRACTS.

D 301.53/2:date
GROUND ACCIDENT ABSTRACTS. [Monthly] Proc.
Offical Use.

D 301.54:nos.   • Item 424-D
INFORMATION SERVICES FACT SHEETS.

D 301.55:nos.   • Item 421-E-5
AIR FORCE VISUAL AID SERIES.

D 301.56   • Item 424-B
MAC FLYER. v. 1–   1954–   [Monthly] (Military
Airlift Command)
    Contains interesting articles designed to gain
greater safety and efficiency in MAC air opera-
tions.
    Merged with Airlift (D 301.56/5) into The MAC
Forum (D 301.56/7).
    Formerly: MATS (Military Air Transportation
Service) Flyer.
    Indexed by: Index to U.S. Government Peri-
odicals.
    ISSN 0024-788X
        See D 301.56/7.

D 301.56/2:date
MATS QUARTERLY SCHEDULE.

D 301.56/3:date
MILITARY AIRLIFT COMMAND: AIRLIFT SERVICE
MANAGEMENT REPORT. [Annual]

D 301.56/5:date   • Item 424-B-13
AIRLIFT, THE JOURNAL OF THE AIRLIFT OPERA-
TIONS SCHOOL. [Quarterly]
    Merged with The MAC Flyer (D 301.56) into
The MAC Forum (D 301.56/7).

D 301.56/7:v.nos./nos.   • Item 424-B
THE MOBILITY FORUM. [Bimonthly]
    Product of the merger of MAC Flyer (D 301.56)
and Airlift (D 301.56/5).
    Earlier title: The MAC Forum.

D 301.57
TECHNICAL REPORTS, RADC-TR- (series). [Irregu-
lar]

D 301.57/2:nos.
– RADC-TN (series).

D 301.57/3
TECHNICAL DOCUMENTARY REPORTS, RADC-TDR-
(series). [Irregular]

D 301.58:
AIRCRAFT ACCIDENT AND MAINTENANCE REVIEW.
    Later D 306.8

AERONAUTICAL CHART AND
INFORMATION CENTER
Second and Arsenal Streets
St. Louis, Missouri 63ll8

D 301.59
BULLETIN. [Monthly]

D 301.59/2:nos.
ACIC TECHNICAL REPORTS.

D 301.59/3:v.nos.&nos.
SQUADRON BULLETIN.
    Official use.

D 301.59/4
CHART UPDATING MANUAL. [Monthly]

D 301.59/5
BULLETIN DIGEST, NEW AND REVISED EDITIONS
OF AERONAUTICAL CHARTS ON ISSUE AS OF
(date). [Semiannual]

DEPARTMENT OF THE
AIR FORCE (Continued)

D 301.60:v.nos./nos. • Item 422-D (EL)
AIRMAN, OFFICIAL JOURNAL OF THE AIR FORCE.
v. 1–   1957–   [Monthly]
PURPOSE:– To present to Air Force personnel in a readable and attractive style, Air Force
policy, doctrine, personnel programs, achievements and historical data.
Indexed by: Index to U.S. Government Periodicals.
ISSN 0002-2756

D 301.61:nos.
PLANNING DIVISION PROCESS AND PROCEDURES.
ADMIN.

D 301.62:nos.
PACAF [Pacific Air Forces] BASIC BIBLIOGRAPHIES.

D 301.62/2:CT • Item 424-I
BIBLIOGRAPHIES AND LISTS OF PUBLICATIONS.

D 301.63:CT
AIR FORCE RESERVE OFFICER TRAINING CORPS
[textbooks].

D 301.64
TRANSLATIONS. [Irregular]

D 301.65:v.nos.&nos. • Item 421-B
AIR FORCE ENGINEERING AND SERVICES QUAR-
TERLY. v. 1–
Edited and published by the Civil Engineering
Center, Institute of Technology, Air University.
Provides a medium of exchange of profes-
sional ideas and information which will result in a
more effective civil engineering function in the Air
Force.
Prior to v. 16, no. 3, August 1975, published
as Air Force Civil Engineer.
Indexed by: Index to U.S. Government Peri-
odicals.
ISSN 0364-188X
Discontinued v 27/1

D 301.65/2: • Item 421-B (MF)
ESL-TR (series).
ESL-TR = Engineering and Services Labora-
tory Technical Reports
Discontinued.

D 301.66:nos.
ALASKAN AIR COMMAND, ARCTIC AEROMEDICAL
LABORATORY: TECHNICAL NOTES.

D 301.67:nos.
AIR MATERIAL COMMAND: TECHNICAL REPORTS.
Desig. AMC technical reports.

D 301.68:CT
AIR FORCE BALLISTIC MISSILE DIVISION, PUBLI-
CATIONS.

OFFICE OF AEROSPACE RESEARCH

D 301.69:nos.
OAR NEWS.

D 301.69/2:nos.
AERONAUTICAL RESEARCH LABORATORY, ARL
(series).

D 301.69/3: • Item 422-B
OAR (series) (numbered). [Irregular]

AIR FORCE RESEARCH RESUMES. 1959–
[Annual]
PURPOSE:– To provide those individuals
concerned with the administration, conduct
and application of research with an index of
current intra- and extra-mural Air Force research efforts. Includes descriptions of individual research efforts, a performing- organization index, principal- investigator index,
contract-grant-number index, and subject index.

OAR PROGRESS (year). 1965–   [Annual]

PURPOSE:– To portray for higher-echelon managers, members of Congress, and the general public, the progress that OAR has made
during the fiscal year. This progress is re-
flected in what Hq OAD and its subordinate
units are doing, how they are managing their
resources, and the type of research being
conducted.

OAR QUARTERLY INDEX OF CURRENT RE-
SEARCH RESULTS. [Quarterly]
PURPOSE:– To provide research- infor-
mation/ document searchers with a list of
technical reports generated by OAR for both
in-house and sponsored efforts during the
period covered.
Includes bibliography, corporate-author
index, author index, contract/grant index,
project-number index, and KWIC (Key-Word-
In-Context) index of report titles.
Cumulative indexes have been issued for
the period 1959-62, and annually beginning
with 1963.

RESEARCH OBJECTIVES (year). [Annual]
PURPOSE:– To acquaint the members of
the scientific community with those areas of
sciences which are of paramount to the Air
Force by presenting a clear statement of OAR
goals and the scope of the OAR program.

D 301.69/4:date
IN-HOUSE LIST OF PUBLICATIONS, AERONAUTI-
CAL RESEARCH LABORATORY.

D 301.69/5:CT • Item 422-B
PUBLICATIONS.

D 301.69/6 • Item 424-H
RESEARCH REVIEW. 1962– 1970. [Monthly]
Annual index issued separately.
Superseded by Air Force Research Review
(D 301.69/6-2).

D 301.69/6-2:date/nos. • Item 424-H
AIR FORCE RESEARCH REVIEW. 1970–1971.
[Bimonthly] (Technical Information Division, Air
Force Systems Command)
PURPOSE:– To contribute to the exchange
of information concerning Air Force conducted
and sponsored research activities.
Supersedes OAR Research Review (D 301.69/
6).   Discontinued.

D 301.69/7:date
LIST OF OAR RESEARCH EFFORTS. [Quarterly]

D 301.69/8:date
OAR QUARTERLY INDEX OF CURRENT RESEARCH
RESULTS.
Earlier D 301.69/3:64-5

D 301.69/9 • Item 422-E
ANNUAL REPORT. [Annual]
Discontinued.

D 301.69/10
MONOGRAPHS. 1964–   [Irregular]
PURPOSE:– To make available to the U.S.
scientific community significant nontechnical reports related to Air Force research.

DEPARTMENT OF THE AIR FORCE
(Continued)

D 301.70:v.nos.&nos.
INTERCEPTOR.

D 301.71:nos.
SPACE SYSTEMS DIVISION: TECHNICAL DOCUMEN-
TARY REPORT TDR (series).

D 301.72:v.nos.&nos. • Item 423-B
AIR FORCE DRIVER, THE AUTOMOTIVE MAGAZINE
OF THE U.S. AIR FORCE. v. 1–   1957–
[Monthly]
Presents information on cars, bikes, trucks,
drivers and driving, including tips on what's new
in cars, motorcycles, accessories, protective
clothing, equipment, and maintenance.
Previous title: Driver, Automotive Magazine
of the Air Force.

Indexed by: Index to U.S. Government Peri-
odicals.
ISSN 0002-2373
Discontinued Dec. 1986.

D 301.72/2:v.nos./nos. • Item 421-C-3 (EL)
ROAD & REC. [Quarterly]

D 301.73:v.nos./nos. • Item 421-C (EL)
AIR FORCE COMPTROLLER. v. 1–   1967–   [Quar-
terly]
PURPOSE:– To provide timely information to
Air Force Comptroller personnel relating to mission accomplishment; to assist them in solving
problems and improving efficiency of operation;
to communicate new developments and techniques; and to stimulate professional thought and
development.
Indexed by: Index to U.S. Government Periodicals.
ISSN 0002-2365

D 301.74:v.nos.&nos.
ACCOUNTING AND FINANCE TECH. DIGEST.
[Biweekly] Offical Use.

D 301.75:nos.
AEROSPACE SPAEECH SERIES. Offical Use.

D 301.75/2:nos.
AIR FORCE FACT SHEETS. Offical Use.
Superseded by D 301.75/2-2

D 301.75/3:CT
AIR FORCE INFORMATION SERIES.

D 301.76:nos. • Item 421-E-1
LITHOGRAPH SERIES.
Series of color lithographs, 17 x 22 inches,
depicting the United States Air Force through
photographs and paintings, suitable for framing.
Issued in sets of 12 illustrations.

D 301.76/2:date • Item 421-E-2
USAF HISTORICAL AIRCRAFT PHOTOPAKS.

D 301.76/3 • Item 421-E
LITHOGRAPH SERIES CATALOG.

D 301.76/4:nos. • Item 421-E-1
U.S. AIR FORCE FINE ARTS SERIES. 1978–
[Irregular]

D 301.76/5:CT • Item 421-E-5
POSTERS. [Irregular]

D 301.76/7:CT • Item 421-E-9
MAPS. [Irregular]

D 301.77:nos.
AIR FORCE MACHINABILITY DATA CENTER-AFMDC–
(series).

D 301.78:date • Item 421-D (MF)
PROCEEDINGS OF MILITARY HISTORY SYMPO-
SIUM. 1st–   [Biennial] (Office of Air Force His-
tory)

D 301.79:nos. • Item 421-F
SOVIET MILITARY THOUGHT SERIES. 1–   1973–
[Irregular]
PURPOSE:– To make available significant and
representative Soviet military writings translated
and published under the auspices of the Air Force.
Discontinued.

D 301.79:9 • Item 421-F
DICTIONARY OF BASIC MILITARY TERMS: A
SOVIET VIEW. 1976. 256 p.
Contains more than 1600 military terms
used by officers of the Soviet armed forces.
Written by the U.S.S.R. General Staff Academy and translated by the U.S. Air Force, this
volume is actually a small military encyclopedia. It defines Soviet operational and tactical
terms, discusses arms terminology, and includes many terms found in writings on military strategy.

D 301.80:nos. • Item 424 (EL)
COMMUNITY COLLEGE OF THE AIR FORCE
GENERAL CATALOG. 1–   1973–   [Annual]
(Community College of the Air Force, Randolph
AFB, Texas)

D 301.80/2:date • **Item 424-B-18**
GENERAL CATALOG: MAC NCO ACADEMY WEST.
[Annual]
    MAC NCO = Military Airlift Command, Non-
commissioned Officer Academy
    PURPOSE:– To list and describe courses of-
fered and to provide other information on such
matters as student life, graduation activities, etc.

D 301.81:v.nos.&nos. • **Item 422-F**
COMBAT CREW. v. 1–   1951–   [Monthly]
    ISSN 0010-213X

D 301.82:CT • **Item 422-M**
ARMY AIR FORCES IN WORLD WAR II (series).
[Irregular]
    Formerly distributed to Depository Libraries
under Item 345.

D 301.82/2:v.nos. • **Item 422-M**
U.S. AIR SERVICE IN WORLD WAR I. v. 1–   1978–
[Irregular] (Office of Air Force History)
    Series of hardcover illustrated volumes of
World War I documentation.

D 301.82/3:CT • **Item 422-M**
UNITED STATES AIR FORCE GENERAL HISTORIES
(series).

D 301.82/4:CT • **Item 422-M-1**
UNITED STATES AIR FORCE SPECIAL STUDIES.
[Irregular]

D 301.82/5:CT • **Item 422-M-1**
UNITED STATES AIR FORCE REFERENCE SERIES.
[Irregular]

D 301.82/6:CT • **Item 422-M-2**
AIR STAFF HISTORICAL STUDY (series). [Irregular]
    Studies will concern miscellaneous topics
pertaining to the history of the Air Force.

D 301.82/7:CT • **Item 422-M-1**
CENTER FOR AIR FORCE HISTORY PUBLICATIONS.

D 301.83:date • **Item 422-G (MF)**
AIR FORCE BUDGET. [Annual]

D 301.83/2:date • **Item 422-G-1**
BUDGET ESTIMATES AIRCRAFT AND MISSILE PRO-
CUREMENT. [Annual]
    See D 301.83/3

D 301.83/3:date • **Item 422-G-1 (EL)**
THE USAF STATISTICAL DIGEST.

D 301.84:v.nos.&nos. • **Item 422-H**
MAINTENANCE. v. 1–   1976–   [Quarterly]
    Designed for aircraft maintenance technicians
and munitions maintenance personnel. Includes
informative articles, accident prevention information, experience sharing and other topics emphasizing aircraft and munitions safety.
    ISSN 0364-7145
    Discontinued v. 11/3.

D 301.85:v.nos. • **Item 422-I**
STUDIES IN COMMUNIST AFFAIRS. (series).
    See D 301.83/3

D 301.86:v.nos.&nos. • **Item 422-J**
USAF SOUTHEAST ASIA MONOGRAPH SERIES. v.
1–   1976–   [Irregular]

D 301.86/2:CT • **Item 422-J**
UNITED STATES AIR FORCE IN SOUTHEAST ASIA
(series).

D 301.87:nos.
AIR FORCE CIVIL ENGINEERING CENTER: AFCEC-
TR (series).

D 301.88:nos.
AIR FORCE OFFICE OF SPECIAL INVESTIGATIONS,
AFOSIP- (series). [Irregular]

D 301.89: • **Item 424-B-1 (MF)**
CURRENT NEWS. [5 times a week]
    Reproduces news items from various sources
that are of interest to key DoD personnel in their
official capacities.
    Issued as Part 1, Early Bird Edition; Part 2,

Main Edition.
    Also published in the following supplemental
series:
    See D 2.19

D 301.89/2: • **Item 424-B-2 (MF)**
RADIO-TV DEFENSE DIALOG. [5 times a week]
    Briefly summarizes news items from radio and
TV broadcasts and then treats them individually,
giving excerpts.
    See D 2.19/2

D 301.89/3:date • **Item 424-B-3**
WEEKEND EDITION. [Weekly]
    Discontinued Dec. 1985.

D 301.89/4:date • **Item 424-B-4 (MF)**
SUPPLEMENTAL CLIPS. [5 times a week]
    Reprints articles from newspapers, radio and
television news broadcasts, and periodicals.
    See D 2.19/3

D 301.89/5:nos. • **Item 424-B-5 (MF)**
SPECIAL EDITION. [3 times a week]
    Consists of reprints from newspapers and
periodicals, sometimes devoting some issues to
a single subject.
    See D 2.19/4

D 301.89/5-2:date • **Item 424-B-5 (MF)**
CURRENT NEWS SPECIAL EDITION, SELECTED
STATEMENTS. [Bimonthly]
    See D 2.19/7

D 301.89/6:nos. • **Item 424-B-6 (MF)**
ENERGY EDITION. [Weekly]
    Highlights and reprints of news items that
deal with energy problems worldwide.
    Non-depository.

D 301.89/6-2:date • **Item 424-B-17 (MF)**
AIR FORCE ENERGY CONSERVATION PLAN.
[Annual]
    PURPOSE:– To provide policy guidance to
Air Force activities which prepare and implement
energy conservation programs and to set forth
results of such programs.
    Discontinued.

D 301.89/7:nos. • **Item 424-B-7 (MF)**
FOREIGN MEDIA EDITION. [Biweekly]
    Highlights and reprints news items from for-
eign media worldwide. Translations are extracted
and compiled from various Foreign Broadcast Information Service reports and other sources.
    Discontinued Dec. 1986.

D 301.89/8 • **Item 424-B-8**
CURRENT NEWS, DEFENSE MANAGEMENT EDITION.
[Biweekly]
    Earlier: Fraud and Waste Edition.
    Highlights and reprints news items related to
fraud and waste.
    See D 2.19/5

D 301.89/9:date • **Item 424-B-9 (MF)**
EQUAL OPPORTUNITY EDITION. [Bimonthly]
    Highlights and reprints news items related to
equal opportunity.
    Discontinued.

D 301.89/10:date
NEWS SUMMARY. [Biweekly]

D 301.89/11:nos.
CURRENT NEWS DEFENSE MANAGEMENT EDITION.
[Biweekly]

D 301.89/13: • **Item 424-B-4 (MF)**
CURRENT NEWS, SUPPLEMENTAL SPECIAL
EDITION. [Irregular]

D 301.89/14: • **Item 304-D-1 (MF)**
THE FRIDAY REVIEW OF DEFENSE LITERATURE.
[Weekly]
    Later D 1.33/2
    See D 2.19/8

D 301.90:v.nos. • **Item 422-L**
ENCYCLOPEDIA OF U.S. AIR FORCE AIRCRAFT AND
MISSILE SYSTEMS. [Irregular]

Series includes a variety of titles dealing with
development, deployment, and operations of
fighter aircraft, Air Force bombers, transports,
trainers, and other military aircraft and missile
systems.
    Vol. 1. Post-World War II Fighters, 1945– 1973.

D 301.91:v.nos.&nos. • **Item 422-N (EL)**
AIR FORCE JOURNAL OF LOGISTICS. v. 1–
[Quarterly] (Air Force Logistics Management
Center) (AFRP-400-1)

    PURPOSE:– To provide the Air Force logis-
tics personnel with brief reports on in-progress or
recently completed logistics research and studies.
    Former title: Pipeline.

D 301.92:CT • **Item 424-C-2 (MF)**
ENVIRONMENTAL IMPACT STATEMENTS. [Irregular]

D 301.93:v.nos.&nos
AIR WAR IN INDOCHINA (series). [Irregular] (Airpower
Research Institute, Air University)

D 301.94:v.nos.&nos. • **Item 422-T**
TAC ATTACK. [Monthly] (Tactical Air Command)
    Safety magazine of the Tactical Air Command.
Includes articles on safety in flight and on the
ground. Intended for aviators, maintenance mechanics, munitions handlers, and support workers. Some material is technical, but the writing is
normally simple and straightforward.
    ISSN 0494-3880
    Discontinued.

D 301.95:date • **Item 424 (MF)**
AIR FORCE ROTC FOUR YEAR COLLEGE SCHOL-
ARSHIP PROGRAM APPLICATION BOOKLET
FOR HIGH SCHOOL STUDENTS ENTERING COL-
LEGE IN THE (year) FALL TERM. [Annual]

D 301.96:CT • **Item 422-M-1**
USAF WARRIOR STUDIES. [Irregular] (Office of Air
Force History)
    Issued in support of Project Warrior, which
seek to create and maintain within the Air Force
an environment where Air Force people at all levels can learn from the past and apply the
warfighting experiences of past generations.

D 301.97:nos.
FOUR BY SIX. [7 times a year]

D 301.98:date • **Item 424-B-11**
THUNDERBIRD PUBLICITY BOOK. [Annual]

    PURPOSE:– To provide data to help publicity
directors publicize Thunderbird aerial demonstrations. Contains selected news items, pilot
biographies, and enlisted roster, with drawings of
aircraft and maneuvers.

D 301.99 • **Item 424-B-12 (MF)**
SAFETY, FIRE PREVENTION, AND OCCUPATIONAL
HEALTH MANAGEMENT, BY OBJECTIVES RE-
VIEW. [Annual]

    PURPOSE:– To present USAF implementing
actions and results obtained in the areas of safety,
fire prevention, and occupational health. Compares current year with three prior years.
    Discontinued.

D 301.100:date • **Item 421-C-2 (MF)**
UNPUBLISHED COMPTROLLER GENERAL DECI-
SIONS, WITH INDEX. [Semiannual]
    Consists of a basic set of 207 microfiche
which contain virtually all unpublished decisions
issued since June 1955 as well as miscellaneous
older decisions. Supplemental fiche are added to
the set every six months.

 • **Item 424-B-14 (P)**
D 301.101 • **Item 307-A-5 (EL)**
INTERCOM.
    Issued in newspaper format, contains news
items.
    Internal Use Only.

D 301.102:v.nos.&nos. • Item 424-B-15 (MF)
USAF FIGHTER WEAPONS REVIEW. [Quarterly]
Published by U.S. Fighter Weapons School at
Nellis AFB, Nevada. Contains articles on fighter
weapons.
Discontinued.

D 301.103:v.nos.&nos.
FLITE NEWSLETTER. v. 1–   [Quarterly]

FLITE = Federal Legal Information Through
Electronics.
Earlier D 302.10

D 301.104:CT • Item 424-B-16
DIRECTORIES. [Irregular]

D 301.104/2: • Item 424-B-20 (MF)
AIR FORCE LOGISTICS COMMAND, HILL AIR FORCE
BASE, TELEPHONE DIRECTORY. [Annual]
Contains organizational and classified list-
ings of Air Force installations as well as a general
information section.

D 301.104/3: • Item 424-B-19 (MF)
LOS ANGELES AIR FORCE STATION, TELEPHONE
DIRECTORY. [Annual]
Contains organizational and alphabetical per-
sonnel listings plus AUTOVON listings for Air Force
installations.

D 301.104/4: • Item 424-B-21
U.S. AIR FORCE PUBLIC AFFAIRS STAFF DIREC-
TORY. [Annual]
Identifies public affairs staff personnel in key
positions at Air Force installations Worldwide and
those assigned to unified commands and special
organizations. Listings are in alphabetical order
by installation and also by individuals' names.
Discontinued.

D 301.104/5:date • Item 424-B-16
STRATEGIC AIR COMMAND, WURTSMITH AIR
FORCE BASE, TELEPHONE DIRECTORY.
[Annual]
Discontinued.

D 301.104/6: • Item 424-B-23 (MF)
STRATEGIC AIR COMMAND, GRISSOM AIR FORCE
BASE TELEPHONE DIRECTORY. [Annual]

PURPOSE– To list principal organizations
served by the Grissom AFB Telephone System.
Contains General Information, Organizational and
classified listing sections, and base maps.
Discontinued.

D 301.104/7: • Item 424-B-22 (MF)
STRATEGIC AIR COMMAND, VANDENBERG AIR
FORCE BASE TELEPHONE DIRECTORY. [Annual]
Lists principal organizations served by the
Vandenberg Telephone System. Contains organi-
zational, classified, and personnel listings, and a
map of Vandenberg AFB.
Discontinued.

D 301.104/9:nos. • Item 424-B-36
AIR FORCE ADDRESS DIRECTORY.

D 301.105 • Item 421-E-7 (MF)
ECONOMIC RESOURCE IMPACT STATEMENT, FIS-
CAL YEAR, K. I. SAWYER AFB. [Annual]
Discontinued.

D 301.105/2:date • Item 421-E-7
ECONOMIC RESOURCE IMPACT STATEMENT, FY,
GRAND FORKS AIR FORCE BASE. [Annual]
Discontinued.

D 301.105/3:date • Item 421-E-7 (MF)
ECONOMIC RESOURCE IMPACT STATEMENT, FY
(date), KELLY AIR FORCE BASE. [Annual]
Discontinued.

D 301.105/4:date • Item 421-E-7 (MF)
ECONOMIC RESOURCE IMPACT STATEMENT, FY
(date), GEORGE AIR FORCE BASE, CALIFOR-
NIA. [Annual]
Discontinued.

D 301.105/5:date • Item 421-E-7 (MF)
ECONOMIC RESOURCE IMPACT STATEMENT, FY
(date), LUKE AIR FORCE BASE, NEW MEXICO.
[Annual]
Discontinued.

D 301.105/6: • Item 421-E-7 (MF)
ECONOMIC RESOURCE IMPACT STATEMENT,
HOLLOMAN AFB, NEW MEXICO. [Annual]
Discontinued.

D 301.105/7: • Item 421-E-7
ECONOMIC RESOURCE IMPACT STATEMENT,
ANDREWS AIR FORCE BASE. [Annual]

D 301.105/8:date • Item 421-E-7
ECONOMIC RESOURCE IMPACT STATEMENT FY,
305TH AIR REFUELING WING, GRISSOM AIR
FORCE BASE, INDIANA. [Annual]
Discontinued.

D 301.105/9:date • Item 421-E-7 (MF)
CHANUTE TECHNICAL TRAINING CENTER ECO-
NOMIC RESOURCE IMPACT STATEMENT, FY
(date). [Annual]

D 301.105/10:date • Item 421-E-11 (MF)
ECONOMIC RESOURCE IMPACT STATEMENT.
Discontinued.

D 301.105/11:date • Item 421-E-12 (MF)
ECONOMIC IMPACT TINKER AIR FORCE BASE, FY
[date]. [Annual]
Discontinued.

D 301.106 • Item 421-E-8
ESC IN REVIEW. [Biennial]
ESC = Electronic Security Command.
PURPOSE:– To summarize activities of the
various centers, wings, groups, and squadrons
of the Command.
Discontinued.

D 301.107: • Item 424-J (MF)
LCCEP ANNUAL REPORT.
LCCEP = Logistics Civilian Career Enhance-
ment Program
Summarizes the Logistics Civilian Career
Enhancement Program's history, operational ac-
tivities, and future plans.

D 301.108: • Item 424-F-5
BAND NEWS FROM THE UNITED STATES AIR FORCE
BAND, WASHINGTON, D. C. [Quarterly]
The Band News will list upcoming concerts,
highlight new groups or programs and in form on
who's coming and going in the Band. The USAF
Band provides free indoor and outdoor concerts
throughout Washington, D. C.and the surrounding
area in various locations.
Discontinued.

D 301.109:nos. • Item 424
INFORMATION BROCHURE FOR HANDLING AIR
FORCE CONSTITUENT INQUIRIES.
Discontinued.

D 301.111:v.nos./nos. • Item 422-N (MF)
HOTLINE, THE AIR FORCE C4 JOURNAL. [Quarterly]
Discontinued.

D 301.112:date • Item 421-H
UNITED STATES AIR FORCE STATISTICAL DIGEST.
Discontinued.

D 301.116:date/nos./v.nos. • Item 307-A-7 (CD)
AIR FORCE ELECTRONIC PUBLISHING LIBRARY OF
DEPARTMENTAL PUBLICATIONS AND FORMS.
[Monthly]
Issued on CD-ROM.

D 301.116/3:date • Item 307-A-13 (EL)
AIR EDUCATION AND TRAINING COMMAND ELEC-
TRONIC PUBLISHING LIBRARY, AETCEPL.
Issued on CD-ROM.

D 301.117:date/nos. • Item 422-N-1
ENVIRO-VISION 2020. [Quarterly]
Discontinued.

D 301.118:CT • Item 307-A-5 (E)
ELECTRONIC PRODUCTS.

D 301.118/2:CT • Item 307-A-9 (CD)
INTERACTIVE COURSEWARE.
Issued on CD-ROM.

D 301.119 • Item 307-A-5 (EL)
TIG BRIEF.

D 301.120 • Item 307-A-5 (EL)
U.S. AIR FORCE POLICY LETTER DIGEST.

D 301.121:date • Item 424-J-1 (EL)
ASC MSRC, [Seminnual] JOURNAL.

D 301.122: • Item 307-A-5 (EL)
AIR FORCE NEWS.

D 301.123: • Item 307-A-5 (EL)
AVIANO VIGILEER.

D 301.124: • Item 307-A-5 (EL)
CYBERSPOKESMAN.

D 301.125: • Item 307-A-5 (EL)
LEADING EDGE. [Monthly].

D 301.126: • Item 307-A-5 (EL)
ECOTONE. [Monthly].

D 301.127: • Item 307-A-5 (EL)
IMA UPDATE ISSUES. [Bimonthly]

D 301.128: • Item 307-A-5 (EL)
UNITED STATES AIR FORCE FACT SHEETS.

OFFICE OF JUDGE ADVOCATE GENERAL
(1949–   )

INFORMATION

Office of the Judge Advocate General
Department of the Air Force
1420 Air Force Pentagon
Washington, DC 20330-1420
(202) 614-5732
http://hqja.jag.af.mil

D 302.1:date
ANNUAL REPORTS.

D 302.2:CT • Item 428
GENERAL PUBLICATIONS.

D 302.6:CT • Item 427-A
REGULATIONS, RULES, AND INSTRUCTIONS.

D 302.7:v.nos.&nos.
DIGEST OF THE JUDGE ADVOCATE GENERAL OF
THE AIR FORCE. v. 1– 3. 1949– 1961. [Quarterly]

D 302.8:CT • Item 427-D
HANDBOOKS, MANUALS, GUIDES. [Irregular]
Earlier D 302.6

D 302.9:v.nos.&nos. • Item 427-B
AIR FORCE LAW REVIEW. v. 1–   1959–
[Semiannual] (AFRP 110-1)
Contains surveys of important legislative, ad-
ministrative, and judicial developments in military
and related law fields. Many of the issues are
devoted to a related topic, such as Special Mili-
tary Criminal Law Issue, Special Air Force Logis-
tics Command Issue, Special Litigation Issue,
etc.
Bimonthly prior to 1969.
Prior to v. 16, issued as Air Force JAG Law
Review.
Citation: AF L. Rev.
Indexed by: Index to U.S. Government Peri-
odicals.
ISSN 0094-8381

D 302.10:v.nos.&nos.
FLITE NEWSLETTER. v. 1–   [Quarterly] (Flight Division, Executive Services, 3800 York Street, Denver, Colorado 80205)
 FLITE = Federal Legal Information Through Electronics.
 Prior to v. 3, no. 3 October/December 1974 issued as LITE Newsletter.
 Later D 301.103
 ISSN 0364-6785

D 302.11:v.nos.&nos.   • **Item 427-C (MF)**
REPORTER. v. 1–   1977–   [Quarterly]
 PURPOSE:– To provide a forum for the exchange of information pertinent to the practice of law in the military as well as the civilian community.
 Frequency varies: 1977– Dec. 1978, Quarterly; Feb. 1979–   Bimonthly.
 ISSN 0193-1834

D 302.12:date   • **Item 427-A-1 (MF)**
CIVIL LAW OPINIONS OF THE JUDGE ADVOCATE GENERAL, AIR FORCE. [Irregular]
 A compilation of opinions originally published in annual paperback editions. They are reproduced verbatim and no attempt has been made to ascertain the current validity of any opinion.

ADMINISTRATIVE SERVICES DIRECTORATE
(1958–   )

INFORMATION

 Administrative Services Directorate
 Department of the Air Force
 Washington, D.C. 20330

D 303.1:date
ANNUAL REPORTS.
 Earlier M 302.1

D 303.2:CT   • **Item 427**
GENERAL PUBLICATIONS.
 Earlier M 302.2
 Discontinued.

D 303.7:date   • **Item 421-C-1 (MF)**
AIR FORCE REGISTER. [Annual]

 Formerly distributed to Depository Libraries under item no. 426.
 Vol. 1. Active Lists.
 Vol. 2. Retired Lists.
 Discontinued.

D 303.8:date
ACTIVITIES SERVICED BY HEADQUARTERS USAF MAIL CENTER. [Monthly]
 Discontinued.

D 303.9:date
AIR FORCE WRITING. AIR FORCE RECURRING PUBLICATION 10-1. [Quarterly]
 Discontinued.

SURGEON GENERAL OF THE AIR FORCE
(1949–   )

CREATION AND AUTHORITY

 Established by Department of Air Force General Order 35, dated June 8, 1949, effective July 1, 1949. Name changed from Air Force Medical Service to Surgeon General of the Air Force.

INFORMATION

 Surgeon General of the Air Force
 Bolling Air Force Base
 Bldg. 5681
 110 Luke Ave.
 Washington, DC 20332-7050
 (202) 767-4797
 Fax: (202) 404-7084
 http://www.satx.olisa.mil/af/sa/index.htm

D 304.1   • **Item 428-A (MF)**
ANNUAL REPORT. [Annual]
 Prepared by the Office of the Special Assistant for Historical Affairs and Technical Information, Office of the Surgeon General, based on reports prepared by the staff officers and commands.
 Discontinued.

D 304.2:CT   • **Item 428-B**
GENERAL PUBLICATIONS.

D 304.7:date
RELEASES.

D 304.8:v.nos./nos.   • **Item 428-D**
MEDICAL SERVICE DIGEST. [Bimonthly]
 Index issued separately.
 Discontinued.

D 304.9:nos.   • **Item 428-B-1 (EL)**
AIR FORCE MEDICAL LOGISTICS LETTER. [Biweekly]

D 304.9/2:date   • **Item 428-E (MF)**
USAF MEDICAL LOGISTICS DIRECTORY. [Annual]
 Earlier D 304.2:L 82
 Discontinued.

D 304.10   • **Item 428-F**
MCP- (series). [Irregular]

D 304.11   • **Item 428-E (MF)**
ADVANCED EDUCATION PROGRAM IN GENERAL DENTISTRY.

D 304.12   • **Item 428-B-1**
ELECTRONIC PRODUCTS. (Misc.)

AIR FORCE ACADEMY
(1954–   )

INFORMATION

 Air Force Academy
 Department of the Air Force
 Air Force Academy, Colorado 80840
 (303) 472-4040-5001

D 305.1:date
ANNUAL REPORTS.

D 305.2:CT   • **Item 425-A-1**
GENERAL PUBLICATIONS.

D 305.6/2:CT   • **Item 425-A-1**
HANDBOOKS, MANUALS, GUIDES. [Irregular]

 D 305.6/2:Ad 6   • **Item 425-A-1**
 ADMISSIONS GUIDE. [Annual]

D 305.6/3:date   • **Item 425-A-1**
CURRICULUM HANDBOOK.

D 305.6/4:date   • **Item 425-A-1**
ACADEMIC MAJORS HANDBOOK. [Annual]

D 305.8   • **Item 425-A (MF)**
CATALOG. 1–   1955–   [Annual]
 Title varies.

D 305.8/2   • **Item 425-A**
U.S. AIR FORCE ACADEMY BULLETIN. [Annual]
 Discontinued.

D 305.8/3   • **Item 425-A-11**
INSTRUCTIONS TO APPLICANTS, CLASS OF . . . [Annual]
 This booklet provides information on how to apply for admission to the Air Force Academy and also serves as a guidance tool to inform the applicant of his potential to qualify for admission.

D 305.8/4   • **Item 425-A-11**
INSTRUCTION TO CANDIDATES, CLASS OF . . . [Annual]

D 305.9:date
REPORT OF BOARD OF VISITORS.

D 305.10:nos.   • **Item 425-A-4 (MF)**
HARMON MEMORIAL LECTURES IN MILITARY HISTORY. 1–   [Annual]

D 305.10/2:   • **Item 425-A-4 (MF)**
IRA C. EAKER DISTINGUISHED LECTURE ON NATIONAL DEFENSE POLICY. [Annual]
 This lecture series commemorates the many and significant contributions to national defense policy and security made by General Eaker, the air power pioneer, columnist, and commentator.

D 305.11   • **Item 425-A-7 (MF)**
UNITED STATES AIR FORCE ACADEMY ASSEMBLY, PROCEEDINGS. 1st–   [Annual]
 Prepared by Department of Political Science.

D 305.12   • **Item 425-A-3**
SPECIAL BIBLIOGRAPHY SERIES. 1–   [Irregular]

D 305.12/2:CT   • **Item 425-A-3**
BIBLIOGRAPHIES AND LISTS OF PUBLICATIONS. [Annual]

 D 305.12/2:D 36/v.nos.   • **Item 425-A-3**
 SELECTED READINGS AND DOCUMENTS ON POSTWAR AMERICAN DEFENSE POLICY. v. 1–   [Quarterly]

D 305.13
PROCEEDINGS OF MILITARY HISTORY SYMPOSIUM.
 See also D 301.78

D 305.14:nos.
RESEARCH REPORTS.

D 305.15:nos.   • **Item 425-A-1 (MF)**
USAFA-TR- (series).

D 305.16.:date   • **Item 425-A-2**
CONTRAILS, AIR FORCE CADET HANDBOOK. [Annual]

 PURPOSE:– To provide cadets with an introduction to basic military concepts, the Air Force and its heritage, the Academy, etc.

D 305.16/2:   • **Item 425-A-10**
DASH ONE, A GUIDE TO CADET TRAINING AND DEVELOPMENT. [Annual]

 PURPOSE– To describe the philosophy and objectives of the Air Force Academy Cadet Training Program and general guidelines for its administration.

D 305.17:date   • **Item 425-A-5 (MF)**
FORMULARY, USAF ACADEMY HOSPITAL. [Annual]

 PURPOSE:– To list and describe pharmaceuticals for the benefit of prescribers, pointing out any significant interactions. Intended to serve as initial reference only. More in-depth information should be obtained from other sources.

D 305.18:date   • **Item 425-A-3 (MF)**
DISCOVERY: FACULTY PUBLICATIONS AND PRESENTATIONS, FISCAL YEAR (date). [Annual]

D 305.19:letters-nos.   • **Item 425-A-6 (MF)**
TEXTBOOK/COURSEBOOK (series). [Irregular]

D 305.20:CT   • **Item 425-A-9**
DIRECTORIES. [Irregular]

D 305.21:v.nos.&nos.   • **Item 425-A-8**
UNITED STATES AIR FORCE ACADEMY JOURNAL OF PROFESSIONAL MILITARY ETHICS. [Annual]
 Discontinued.

D 305.21/2:nos. • Item 425-A-8 (MF)
JOURNAL OF LEGAL STUDIES.

D 305.22:date • Item 425-A-8 (MF)
ICARUS: THE CADET CREATIVE WRITING MAGA-
ZINE. [Annual]

D 305.22/2:date • Item 425-A-8 (MF)
MINDFLIGHTS.

D 305.22/3 • Item 425-A-12 (MF)
WAR, LITERATURE, AND THE ARTS. [Semiannual]

D 305.23 • Item 425-A-13 (EL)
SOLDIER-SCHOLAR, A JOURNAL OF CONTEM-
PORARY MILITARY THOUGHT. [Irregular]

D 305.24: • Item 425-A-14 (EL)
INSS OCCASIONAL PAPER, REGIONAL SERIES.

INSPECTOR GENERAL OF AIR FORCE
(1956–   )

INFORMATION

> Inspector General of the Air Force
> 1140 Air Force Pentagon
> Washington, DC 20330-1140
> (703) 588-1531
> Fax: (703) 697-4293
> http://www.ig.hq.af.mil

D 306.1:date
ANNUAL REPORTS.

D 306.2:CT
GENERAL PUBLICATIONS.

D 306.8 • Item 428-C
AEROSPACE MAINTENANCE SAFETY. v. 1–   1946–
[Monthly]
> Presents articles designed to encourage
safety in the operation of aircraft by preventive
maintenance.
> Previous titles: Aircraft Accident and Main-
tenance Review and Aerospace Accident and
Maintenance Review.
> Discontinued.

DEFENSE MATERIALS PROCUREMENT AGENCY
(1951–1953)

CREATION AND AUTHORITY

> The Defense Materials Procurement Agency
was established by Executive Order 10281 of
August 28, 1951. The Agency was abolished by
Executive Order 10480 of August 14, 1953, and
its functions transferred to the Materials Division
of the Emergency Procurement Service.

DM 1.1:date
ANNUAL REPORT.

DM 1.2:CT
GENERAL PUBLICATIONS.

DM 1.6:CT
REGULATIONS, RULES, AND INSTRUCTIONS.

DM 1.6/2:nos.
DELEGATIONS. [Irregular]

DM 1.6/3:nos.
MINERAL ORDERS MO (series).

DM 1.6/4:nos.
OPERATING PROCEDURES. [Proc. Admin.]

DM 1.6/5:nos.
COMPLIANCE AND SECURITY MEMORANDUMS.
[Admin.]

DM 1.7:nos.
RELEASES.

DEFENSE PRODUCTION ADMINISTRATION
(1951–1953)

CREATION AND AUTHORITY

> The Defense Production Administration was
established by Executive Order 10200 of January 3, 1951, pursuant to the Defense Production
Act of 1950 (64 Stat. 798). Executive Order 10433
of February 4, 1953, abolished the Defense Production Administration and transferred its functions to the Office of Defense Mobilization (Pr
33.1000).

DP 1.1:date
ANNUAL REPORTS.
> Earlier Pr 33.1101

DP 1.2:CT • Item 430-B-2
GENERAL PUBLICATIONS.
> Earlier Pr 33.1102
> Discontinued.

DP 1.6:CT
REGULATIONS, RULES, AND INSTRUCTIONS.

DP 1.6/2:nos.
DELEGATIONS.

DP 1.6/3:nos.
REGULATIONS DPA (series).

DP 1.7:nos.
RELEASES.

DP 1.8:v.nos • Item 430-B-1
DEFENSE PRODUCTION RECORD. [Weekly]

DP 1.9:nos.
LIST OF BASIC MATERIALS AND ALTERNATES.
> Discontinued.

DP 1.10:nos.
DEFENSE PRODUCTION NOTES. [Irregular]

DP 1.11
DEFENSE PRODUCTION BRIEFS. PROC.

DP 1.12
SUMMARY OF DPA-NPA OPERATIONS.

DEPARTMENT OF ENERGY
(1977–   )

CREATION AND AUTHORITY

> The Department of Energy was established
by the Department of Energy Organization Act,
approved August 4, 1977 (91 Stat. 569) and effective October 1, 1977, pursuant to Executive
Order 1200, of September 13, 1977. The act consolidated the major Federal energy functions into
one Cabinet-level Department, transferring to the
Department of Energy all the responsibilities of
the Energy Research and Development Administration (ER 1); the Federal Energy Administration
(FE 1); the Federal Power Administration (FP 1);
the Alaska Power Administration, (I 68), the
Bonneville Power Administration (I 44), the Southeastern Power Administration (I 65), and the Southwestern Power Administration (I 59), all from the
Department of Interior; as well as certain functions relating to energy from various agencies.

INFORMATION

> Public Inquiries
> Department of Energy
> Forrestal Building
> 1000 Independence Avenue, S.W.
> Washington, D.C. 20585
> (202) 586-5575
> http://www.energy.gov

E 1.1:date • Item 429-J-1 (MF)
ANNUAL REPORT.

E 1.1/2:date • Item 429-T-36 (MF)
OFFICE OF THE INSPECTOR GENERAL: ANNUAL
REPORT.

E 1.1/3:date • Item 429-A-11 (MF)
LARAMIE ENERGY TECHNOLOGY CENTER: ANNUAL
REPORT.

E 1.1/4:date • Item 429-A-13 (MF)
BROOKHAVEN HIGHLIGHTS. [Annual]
> Summarizes activities of Brookhaven Labo-
ratory at Upton, New York, in conducting a broad
range of basic and applied research programs in
the physical and life sciences.

E 1.1/5:date • Item 429-A-8 (MF)
ARGONNE NATIONAL LABORATORY: ANNUAL RE-
PORT.

E 1.1/6:date • Item 429-A-25 (MF)
INHALATION TOXICOLOGY RESEARCH INSTITUTE,
ANNUAL REPORT.
> PURPOSE– To summarize activities of the
Institute, which investigates effects on human
health of inhalation of airborne materials.
> Earlier E 1.28
> Non-Govt. in 1996.

E 1.2:CT • Item 429-A
GENERAL PUBLICATIONS. [Irregular]

E 1.6:CT • Item 429-A-9 (P) (EL)
REGULATIONS, RULES, AND INSTRUCTIONS.
[Irregular]

E 1.7:nos.
PRESS RELEASES. [Irregular]

E 1.7/2:v.nos.&nos.
DEPARTMENT OF ENERGY INFORMATION: WEEKLY
ANNOUNCEMENTS.
> Earlier ER 1.12

E 1.7/3:date
DOE PETROLEUM DEMAND WATCH. [Weekly] (DOE/
EIA-0161)

E 1.8:CT • Item 429-B
HANDBOOKS, MANUALS, GUIDES. [Irregular]

E 1.8/2:nos.
FEDERAL ENERGY GUIDELINES. [Weekly]
> Earlier FE 1.8/5

E 1.8/3 • Item 429-D
STUDY GUIDES. [Irregular]

> PURPOSE:– To provide brief guides to be
used in connection with Department of Energy
films.

E 1.8/4:date • Item 429-D-1
GUIDE TO THE U.S. DEPARTMENT OF ENERGY,
BOARD OF CONTRACT APPEALS AND CON-
TRACT ADJUSTMENT BOARD. [Annual]
> PURPOSE:– To be used as a reference tool
in presenting appeals to the Board in an orderly
and consistent manner.
> Discontinued.

E 1.8/5 • Item 429-A-42 (EL)
FUEL ECONOMY GUIDE. [Annual]

E 1.9:nos.   • **Item 429-C**
INTERDISCIPLINARY STUDENT/TEACHER MATERIALS IN ENERGY, THE ENVIRONMENT, AND THE ECONOMY. 1–   1977–   [Irregular]
Discontinued.

E 1.10:nos.   • **Item 429-E (MF)**
CONFERENCE (series). [Irregular]
Published in microfiche.

E 1.11:v.nos.&nos.   • **Item 474-A-2**
ENERGY ABSTRACTS FOR POLICY ANALYSIS. v. 1– 1975–   [Monthly]
ISSN 0098-5104
Earlier ER 1.9
Discontinued v.15.

E 1.12:date   • **Item 429-F (MF)**
TELEPHONE DIRECTORY. [Semiannual]

E 1.12/2:date   • **Item 419-F-1 (MF)**
BROOKHAVEN NATIONAL LABORATORY: TELEPHONE DIRECTORY. [Annual]

E 1.12/3:date   • **Item 429-F (EL)**
NATIONAL TELEPHONE DIRECTORY. (DOE/AD-0022)

E 1.12/4:date   • **Item 429-F (MF)**
TELEPHONE DIRECTORY, ROCKWELL INTERNATIONAL, ROCKY FLATS PLANT. [Semiannual]

E 1.13:CT   • **Item 429-G**
BIBLIOGRAPHIES AND LISTS OF PUBLICATIONS. [Irregular]

E 1.13/2:   • **Item 429-M**
ENERGY LIBRARY, JOURNALS AVAILABLE. (DOE/OAS-0008)
Discontinued.

E 1.13/3:nos.
DOE TRANSLATION LIST.

E 1.13/4:nos.   • **Item 429-G**
SELECTED DOE HEADQUARTERS PUBLICATIONS. 1– 1978–   [Irregular]

     Previously published as DOE-AD (series) (E 1.32).
Discontinued.

E 1.13/5   • **Item 429-G (MF)**
NEW AT THE ENERGY LIBRARY. [Monthly]

E 1.14:date   • **Item 434-A-8**
ENERGY REPORTER.
Earlier FE 1.19
Discontinued.

E 1.15:nos.   • **Item 429-T-23 (MF)**
DEFENSE PROGRAMS, DOE/DP- (series). [Irregular]
Discontinued.

E 1.15/2:date   • **Item 429-T-23 (MF)**
SEMIANNUAL REPORT ON STRATEGIC SPECIAL NUCLEAR MATERIAL INVENTORY DIFFERENCES. [Semiannual]
Earlier E 1.15
Discontinued.

E 1.16:nos.   • **Item 429-H (MF)**
ENVIRONMENT, DOE/EV (series).

E 1.16/2:nos.   • **Item 429-H (MF)**
ENVIRONMENTAL READINESS DOCUMENTS, DOE/ERD (series). 1–   [Irregular]

     PURPOSE:– To review and evaluate the environmental status of an energy technology during the several phases of development of that technology.
Discontinued.

E 1.17:v.nos.&nos.   • **Item 474-A-6**
ENERGY RESEARCH ABSTRACTS. [Semimonthly]

     PURPOSE:– To provide abstracting and indexing coverage of all scientific and technical reports, journal articles, conference papers and proceedings, books, patents, theses, and monographs originated by the Department of Energy, its laboratories, energy centers, and contractors.
     Cumulative semiannual index issued separately.

     Previously published by the Energy Research and Development Administration (ER 1.15) prior to the October 31, 1977 issue.   Indexed by: Chemical Abstracts.
ISSN 0160-3604
Discontinued.

E 1.17/2   • **Item 429-X (EL)**
DOE REPORTS BIBLIOGRAPHIC DATABASE.

E 1.18:nos.   • **Item 429-P (MF)**
ENERGY TECHNOLOGY, DOE/ET (series).

E 1.19:nos.   • **Item 429-N (MF) (EL)**
ENERGY RESEARCH, DOE/ER (series).

E 1.19/2   • **Item 429-N (MF)**
ENERGY RELATED LABORATORY EQUIPMENT CATALOG. [Monthly]
Earlier E 1.19

E 1.19/3:date   • **Item 429-N (MF)**
SUMMARIES OF FY (date) RESEARCH IN NUCLEAR PHYSICS. [Annual]
Earlier E 1.19
Discontinued.

E 1.19/4:v.nos./nos.   • **Item 429-N (EL)**
ER NEWS. [Quarterly]

E 1.20:letters-nos.   • **Item 429-R (EL)**
ENVIRONMENTAL IMPACT STATEMENTS, DOE/EIS-(series). [Irregular]

E 1.20/2:nos.   • **Item 429-R (MF)**
ENVIRONMENTAL ASSESSMENT, DOE/EA (series).
Earlier E 4.9

E 1.20/3:nos.   • **Item 429-R (MF)**
DOE/EH (series).

E 1.20/4   • **Item 429-R-1 (MF)**
ENVIRONMENTAL RADON PROGRAM, SUMMARIES OF RESEARCH. [Annual]

E 1.20/5   • **Item 429-X-26 (EL)**
SANDIA TECHNOLOGY. [Quarterly]

E 1.21:date   • **Item 429-S**
ENERGY-RELATED DOCTORAL SCIENTISTS AND ENGINEERS IN THE UNITED STATES.

     PURPOSE:– To provide information about the number and characteristics of doctoral level engineers and scientists in primarily energy- related activities.
Discontinued.

E 1.22:nos.   • **Item 231-B-8**
VOLUNTARY INDUSTRIAL ENERGY CONSERVATION. [Quarterly]
Earlier C 57.25

E 1.23:nos.   • **Item 474-A-4 (EL)**
MATERIALS AND COMPONENTS IN FOSSIL ENERGY APPLICATIONS. [Bimonthly]
ISSN 0145-9244
Earlier ER 1.13

E 1.24:date   • **Item 429-T (MF)**
NATIONAL SURVEY OF COMPENSATION PAID SCIENTISTS AND ENGINEERS ENGAGED IN RESEARCH AND DEVELOPMENT ACTIVITIES. [Annual]
ISSN 0486-8816

E 1.25:nos.   • **Item 429-T-1 (MF)**
[INFORMATION PUBLICATIONS] DOE/OPA (series). [Irregular] (Office of Public Affairs)

E 1.26:nos.   • **Item 429-T-2 (MF)**
CONSERVATION AND SOLAR APPLICATIONS, DOE/CS (series).
Discontinued.

E 1.26/2:nos.   • **Item 429-E-2**
Wx, WEATHERIZATION BULLETIN. 1–   1980– [Irregular] (Office of Weatherization Assistance Programs) (DOE/CS-6047)
     Bulletin from the Department of Energy for use of local weatherization program operators, who weatherize private homes through insulating, weatherstripping, caulking, making furnaces

more efficient, etc.
Publication discontinued 1980-81
ANNUAL REPORT TO CONGRESS ON THE AUTOMOTIVE TECHNOLOGY DEVELOPMENT PROGRAM. 1st–   1979–

E 1.27:date   • **Item 429-T-3 (MF)**
ANNUAL REPORT TO THE PRESIDENT AND CONGRESS ON THE STATE OF ENERGY CONSERVATION PROGRAM. 1st–   1976–
ISSN 0161-1674

E 1.28:nos.   • **Item 429-T-4 (MF)**
CONTRACTOR RESEARCH AND DEVELOPMENT REPORTS. [Irregular]

E 1.28/2:date   • **Item 429-T-4**
QUARTERLY PROGRESS REPORT ON FISSION PRODUCT BEHAVIOR IN LWRs.

E 1.28/7:date   • **Item 429-T-4**
HIGH-TEMPERATURE GAS-COOLED REACTOR SAFETY STUDIES FOR THE DIVISION OF REACTOR SAFETY RESEARCH QUARTERLY PROGRESS REPORT.

E 1.28/10:date   • **Item 429-T-4**
NOISE DIAGNOSTICS FOR SAFETY ASSESSMENT, STANDARDS, AND REGULATION. [Quarterly]

E 1.28/15:   • **Item 474-B-8**
ANNUAL WATER QUALITY DATA REPORT.

     Water quality data report for the Waste Isolation Pilot Plant. The WIPP project is operated by the Energy Department to conduct research and development on safe disposal of radioactive wastes.

E 1.28/16:date   • **Item 474-B-8**
ECOLOGICAL MONITORING PROGRAM AT THE WASTE ISOLATION PILOT PLANT, ANNUAL REPORT.
Discontinued.

E 1.28/17:v.nos.&nos.   • **Item 474-B-8 (EL)**
OAK RIDGE NATIONAL LABORATORY REVIEW. [Quarterly]

E 1.28/18   • **Item 474-B-8 (MF)**
SCIENCE & TECHNOLOGY IN REVIEW. [Quarterly]
Discontinued.

E 1.29:date   • **Item 429-T-5**
CONSUMER BRIEFING SUMMARY. 1978– 1979. [Irregular]

     PURPOSE:– To provide highlights of briefings and Department of Energy activities of greatest interest to energy consumers. Major technique for informing the public about DOE programs and policies.
     Superseded by Energy Consumer (E 1.29/2).

E 1.29/2:date   • **Item 429-T-5**
ENERGY CONSUMER. v. 1–   1979– 1981–D 1980.

     Supersedes Consumer Briefing Summary (E 1.29).
     Prior to 1980 issues, issued with volume and number designations.

E 1.30:nos.   • **Item 429-T-7 (MF)**
RESOURCE APPLICATIONS, RA- (series). [Irregular]

     PURPOSE:– To provide information on various energy related resource applications, such as inventory of power plants, and strategic petroleum reserves.

     GEOTHERMAL ENERGY, RESEARCH, DEVELOPMENT, AND DEMONSTRATION PROGRAM. 1st–   1977–   [Annual]

     STRATEGIC PETROLEUM RESERVE. 1st– 1977–   [Annual]

E 1.31:date • Item 474-A-13
COAL, QUARTERLY REPORTS: GASIFICATION.

Prior to 1977 published by the Energy Research and Development Administration (ER 1.28/4).
Discontinued [List of Classes, 1980/4]
ISSN 0362-5184

E 1.31/2:date • Item 474-A-13
COAL, QUARTERLY REPORTS: POWER AND COMBUSTION.
Prior to 1977 published by the Energy Research and Development Administration (ER 1.28).
ISSN 0362-8361
Discontinued,

E 1.31/3:date • Item 474-A-13
COAL, QUARTERLY REPORTS: LIQUEFACTION.
Prior to 1977 published by the Energy Research and Development Administration (ER 1.28/2).
Discontinued [List of Classes, 1980/4]
ISSN 0362-7934

E 1.31/4:date • Item 474-A-13
COAL, QUARTERLY REPORTS: DEMONSTRATION PLANTS.
Prior to 1977 published by the Energy Research and Development Administration (ER 1.28/3).
Discontinued [List of Classes, 1980/4]
ISSN 0362-5176
Discontinued.

E 1.32:nos. • Item 429-T-8
ADMINISTRATION, DOE/AD (series). [Irregular]
Series of publications on various subjects related to administration of the Department of Energy.

E 1.33:nos. • Item 429-T-6 (MF)
INTERGOVERNMENT AND INSTITUTIONAL RELATIONS, IR- (series). 1– [Irregular]
Discontinued.

E 1.33:0049 • Item 429-T-6
EMPLOYMENT IN NUCLEAR ENERGY ACTIVITIES, A HIGHLIGHTS REPORT. [Biennial] (Division of Labor Affairs and Manpower Assessment) (DOE/IR-0049)
Previously published by Energy Research and Development Administration.
ISSN 0148-4575
Discontinued.

E 1.33/2 • Item 429-H-1
DOE/CA- (series).

E 1.33/2:10879-01 • Item 429-H-1
CONSUMER ENERGY ATLAS. 1980. 251 p. il.

PURPOSE:– To help consumers find answers to energy-related questions. Included are lists of executives, Federal offices, Congressional offices, State Government agencies, national energy organizations, and energy publications.
Discontinued.

E 1.33/3:nos. • Item 429-H-2 (MF)
DOE/PA- (series). (Office of Public Affairs)

PURPOSE:– To provide miscellaneous publications on energy subjects, such as news photo catalogs and tips on energy savers.

E 1.34:date • Item 429-T-46 (MF)
CONGRESSIONAL BUDGET REQUEST. [Annual]

PURPOSE:– To present detailed information on Congressional budget requests for the Department of Energy during the fiscal year covered. Includes narrative, tables, and charts which provide data.

E 1.34/2:date • Item 429-T-46 (MF)
CONGRESSIONAL BUDGET REQUEST, U.S. DEPARTMENT OF THE INTERIOR. [Annual] (DOE/MA-0058)
See E 1.34

E 1.34/3:date • Item 429-T-46 (MF)
CONGRESSIONAL BUDGET REQUEST, U.S. DEPARTMENT OF JUSTICE. (DOE/MA- 0059)
See E 1.34

E 1.34/4:date
CONGRESSIONAL BUDGET REQUEST, FEDERAL ENERGY REGULATORY COMMISSION. (DOE/MA-0060)

E 1.35:nos. • Item 429-T-14 (MF) (EL)
CONTROLLER, CR- (series). [Irregular]

E 1.35/2:nos. • Item 429-T-14 (MF)
DOE/MA- (series).
MA = Management Assessment.

E 1.35/2-2:date • Item 429-T-14 (MF)
BUDGET HIGHLIGHTS. [Annual]
Earlier E 1.35/2

E 1.35/2-3:date • Item 429-T-14 (MF)
LISTING OF AWARDEE NAMES, ACTIVE AWARDS. [Quarterly]

E 1.35/2-5 • Item 429-T-67 (MF)
LISTING OF AWARDEE NAMES, INACTIVE AWARDS.

E 1.35/2-6 • Item 429-N-3 (MF)
LISTING OF AWARDEE NAMES, RETIRED AWARDS. [Annual]

E 1.35/2-7:date • Item 429-N-2 (MF)
DIRECTORY OF AWARDEE NAMES. [Annual]

E 1.35/3:date
QUARTERLY STATUS OF DEPARTMENT OF ENERGY PROJECTS. [Quarterly] (DOE/ MA-0006)

E 1.35/4:date • Item 429-A-26 (MF)
ANNUAL PROCUREMENT AND FINANCIAL ASSISTANCE REPORT. [Annual]
Summarizes the Energy Department's procurement and financial assistance activities.

E 1.36:nos. • Item 429-T-9 (MF)
ENVIRONMENTAL DEVELOPMENT PLAN, DOE/EDP- (series). 1– [Irregular]

PURPOSE:– To provide basic documents for planning and managing environmental requirements of energy technology development.
Earlier ER 1.33
Discontinued.

E 1.36:0046 • Item 429-T-9
FOSSIL FUEL UTILIZATION. 1979– [Annual] (Office of Energy Technology) (DOE/EDP-0046)
Continues Direct Combustion Program; Advanced Powers Systems; and Conservation Research and Technology.

E 1.36/2:date • Item 429-T-9
URANIUM ENRICHMENT ANNUAL REPORT.

E 1.37:date
ENVIRONMENTAL QUARTERLY. (Environmental Measurements Laboratory)
Indexed by: Chemical Abstracts.
ISSN 0161-5742
Earlier ER 1.27

E 1.38:nos. • Item 429-T-18
SOLAR ENERGY RESEARCH AND DEVELOPMENT REPORT. 1– [Irregular] (DOE/ET-0044)

PURPOSE:– To provide a newsletter highlighting activities in solar energy research. Includes a Solar Energy Calendar of events and meetings.
Discontinued with Oct. 1979 issue.
Earlier ER 1.32

E 1.38/2:date • Item 429-P-3 (MF)
SOLAR THERMAL POWER SYSTEMS, ANNUAL TECHNICAL PROGRESS REPORT.

E 1.38/2-2:date • Item 429-P-4 (MF)
SOLAR THERMAL POWER SYSTEMS: PROGRAM SUMMARY.
Earlier E 1.18:0018/1

E 1.38/3:CT • Item 429-P-5
SCIENCE ACTIVITIES IN ENERGY (series). [Irregular]
Consists of folders of materials for teaching fourth through tenth grade students about energy principles and problems. Each folder concerns a different subject.

E 1.38/4:v.nos.&nos. • Item 429-T-51
SOLAR LAW REPORTER. v. 1– 3. 1979– 1982. [Bimonthly]

PURPOSE:– To serve as an information exchange and as a forum for the presentation and discussion of important issues related to the legal institutions affecting the development of solar energy. Intended for lawyers and other professionals.
Discontinued.

E 1.38/4:date • Item 429-P-6 (MF)
WIND ENERGY PROGRAM OVERVIEW. [Annual]

E 1.38/5:date • Item 429-P-6 (MF)
WIND POWER TODAY. [Annual]
Earlier: E 1.38/4
Formerly: Wind Energy Program Overview

E 1.39:nos. • Item 429-T-13 (MF)
VOLUNTARY BUSINESS ENERGY CONSERVATION PROGRAM, PROGRESS REPORTS. 1– [Semiannual]
PURPOSE:– To provide a summary of progress in energy conservation made by the U.S. business community participating in the Department's Voluntary Business Energy Conservation Program. Provides tangible evidence of business and industry's commitments to the vital national objective of improved energy efficiency.
Discontinued.

E 1.39/2:date • Item 429-A-37 (MF)
SMALL BUSINESS REPORT TO CONGRESS FOR FISCAL YEAR.

E 1.40:date • Item 429-T-10 (MF)
ANNUAL PROCUREMENT OPERATIONS REPORT. 1st– 1977–
PURPOSE:– To present energy related procurement activities concerning development of energy resources, and the search for alternate sources of energy. Includes statistics and charts showing solar, geothermal, fossil energy comments and obligations for the fiscal year.

E 1.41:date • Item 429-T-17
U.S. CENTRAL STATION NUCLEAR ELECTRIC GENERATING UNITS, SIGNIFICANT MILESTONES. [Quarterly] (DOE/ET-0030)

PURPOSE:– To provide a status report listing operating and pending nuclear power units showing owner, capacity, type of reactor, dates contract awarded, etc.
Discontinued.

E 1.42:date • Item 429-T-16 (MF)
ANNUAL REPORT OF RADIATION EXPOSURES FOR DOE AND DOE CONTRACTOR EMPLOYEES. 1st– 1968– (DOE/EV-0011)

E 1.43:nos. • Item 429-P-1 (MF)
TRANSLATION SERIES, DOE-TR– (nos.). [Irregular]
Translations of publications originally published in a foreign language. Consists of highly technical reports on various phases of energy.
Published in microfiche (24x).
Discontinued.

E 1.44:nos.
RADIOBIOLOGY. [Bimonthly] (DOE-TR-4)
Earlier ER 1.26

E 1.45:v.nos.&nos. • Item 429-T-19
ELECTRIC AND HYBRID VEHICLE PROGRAM, EHV/ QUARTERLY REPORT. 1– 15.– 1981.
Contains articles reporting on electric vehicle research progress. Also includes departments, such as Program Update, Abstracts, Literature Available, and Calendar, to keep readers informed on quarterly developments.
Discontinued.

E 1.45/2:date   • Item 429-T-19
ELECTRIC AND HYBRID VEHICLES PROGRAM, AN-
NUAL REPORT TO CONGRESS.

E 1.46:nos.   • Item 429-T-26
ADMINISTRATIVE SERVICES, DOE/OAS-(series).
[Irregular]

E 1.47:date   • Item 429-T-35 (MF)
INDUSTRIAL ENERGY EFFICIENCY IMPROVEMENT
PROGRAM, ANNUAL REPORT. (DOE/CS-0033)

    PURPOSE:– To provide a report on the
progress toward the achievement of the industrial energy efficiency improvement targets by
the Energy Policy and Conservation Act Title III,
Part D.
    Discontinued.

E 1.48:nos.   • Item 429-T-36 (MF) (EL)
OFFICE OF INSPECTOR GENERAL, DOE/IG- (series). [Irregular]

E 1.49:nos.   • Item 429-T-27
PROCUREMENT AND CONTRACTS MANAGEMENT,
DOE/PR- (series). [Irregular]

    PURPOSE:– To provide a series of reports
dealing with procurement systems which involve
information on contracts, grants, agreements, and
small purchase transactions.

E 1.50:date   • Item 429-T-28
ENERGY MANAGEMENT IN THE FEDERAL GOVERN-
MENT. 1st–   1977–   [Annual]

    PURPOSE:– To describe, in an annual report
submitted to the President, Federal departmental
and agency accomplishments in energy conservation and to provide details of current activities
and future plans to achieve improved efficiency
in the use of energy.
    Discontinued.

E 1.50/2:date   • Item 429-T-28 (MF)
ANNUAL REPORT ON IN-HOUSE ENERGY MANAGE-
MENT.
    Also published in microfiche.

E 1.51:date   • Item 429-T-29 (MF)
NATIONAL URANIUM RESOURCE EVALUATION: AN-
NUAL ACTIVITY REPORT.

    PURPOSE:– To summarize technical activi-
ties of the Grand Junction Office undertaken during
the calendar year to support the National Uranium Resource Evaluation Program.

E 1.52:date   • Item 429-T-30 (MF)
ENERGY MATERIALS COORDINATING COMMITTEE:
ANNUAL TECHNICAL REPORT. 1st–   1978–

    PURPOSE:– To provide and exchange point
for the coordination of interdepartmental materials projects. Describes energy related programs
and projects of various divisions.
    Discontinued.

E 1.53:date   • Item 429-T-41 (EL)
SCIENCE AND TECHNOLOGY REVIEW. [Monthly]
(Lawrence Livermore Laboratory)

    PURPOSE:– To provide highly technical ar-
ticles on accomplishments in magnetic fusion
energy, biomedical and environmental research.
    Earlier title: Energy and Technology Review.

E 1.53/2:v.nos.&nos.   • Item 429-E-1 (EL)
LBL RESEARCH REVIEW. v. 1–   1976–   [Quar-
terly] (Lawrence Berkeley Laboratory)

    PURPOSE:– To present news of activities of
the Lawrence Berkeley Laboratory which is operated by the University of California under contract to the Department of Energy. The
Laboratory's aim is to contribute to human knowledge about the natural world and to use this
knowledge to solve society's problems.
    Former title: LBL News Magazine.

E 1.53/3:v.nos.&nos.   • Item 429-A-3
NEWSLINE. v. 1–   1970–   [Bimonthly] (Lawrence

Livermore National Laboratory)

    PURPOSE:– To provide a newsletter to report
on various laboratory research projects and activities.
    Discontinued.

E 1.53/4:v.nos.&nos.
ENERGINFO. [Bimonthly]

E 1.53/5   • Item 429-E-4 (EL)
BREAKTHROUGHS. (3 times/yr.)

E 1.54:v.nos.&nos.   • Item 429-T-37 (EL)
DoE THIS MONTH. v. 1–   1978–   [Monthly]

    PURPOSE:– To provide a newspaper for De-
partment of Energy employees and others interested in the energy field. Includes coverage of
events, programs, and activities that are of interest and relevance to the Department of Energy.
    Former title: Energy Insider prior to February
1984.

E 1.55:date   • Item 429-T-31
ENERGY INFORMATION DATA BASE: SUBJECT THE-
SAURUS. [Irregular] (Technical Information Center)

    PURPOSE:– To provide structural vocabu-
lary that allows for machine storage and retrieval
of energy information developed by the staff during its subject indexing activities.
    Earlier ER 1.11:TID-7000

E 1.55/2:date
ENERGY INFORMATION DATA BASE: SUBJECT
CATEGORIES.

E 1.55/3:date
ENERGY INFORMATION DATA BASE ENERGY
CATEGORIES.

E 1.56:date   • Item 429-T-34
COAL CONVERSION SYSTEMS TECHNICAL DATA
BOOK. [Irregular] (includes basic looseleaf manual
and supplements for an indefinite period)
    Highly technical publication designed to pro-
vide a single source of information on coal conversion facilities.
    Discontinued.

E 1.57:nos.   • Item 429-T-33
FACTSHEETS. [Irregular] (EDM-1043)
    Series of leaflets, produced by the National
Science Teachers Association under contract with
the Department of Energy, covering such subjects as fuels from plants, solar heating and cooling, and energy conservation.

E 1.58:date   • Item 429-T-38
SOLAR BULLETIN. [Irregular]

    PURPOSE:– To provide a list of documents
which contain the latest findings of the National
Solar Heating and Cooling Demonstration Program.
    Discontinued 1980.

E 1.59:date   • Item 434-A-3
REPORT TO CONGRESS ON THE ECONOMIC IM-
PACT OF ENERGY ACTIONS AS REQUIRED BY
PUBLIC LAW 93-275, SECTION 18 (d). [Annual]

E 1.60:nos.   • Item 429-T-39 (MF)
OFFICE OF THE SECRETARY, DOE/S-(series).
[Irregular]

    E 1.60:0010   • Item 429-T-39
    SECRETARY'S ANNUAL REPORT TO CON-
    GRESS, POSTURE STATEMENT, OUTLOOK
    AND PROGRAM REVIEW. (DOE/S-0010)

E 1.61:date   • Item 429-T-50
ENERGY HISTORY REPORT. [Monthly]

    PURPOSE:– To provide a newsletter type pub-
lication designed to serve as a forum for all those
interested in the history of energy and to provide
a report of research activities in a systematic
study of energy history, including brief articles,
book review, research and news notes.
    Discontinued Jan. 1981.

E 1.62:date   • Item 429-T-57
NATIONAL ENERGY PLAN. [Biennial]

    PURPOSE:– To report to Congress, as re-
quire by Title VIII of Public Law 95-91, describing
the Administration's plan to fulfill energy production, utilization, and conservation objectives necessary to satisfy projected U.S. energy needs.
Includes statistical data and graphs.

E 1.63:date   • Item 429-T-58
WEEKLY PETROLEUM STATUS REPORT. (Energy
Emergency Policy Committee) (DOE/EPC-12)

    PURPOSE:– To provide statistical data on
petroleum, gasoline, and heating oil, derived from
company reports and other data systems.

E 1.64:date   • Item 429-P
ALLOY DEVELOPMENT FOR IRRADIATION PERFOR-
MANCE. [Quarterly] (DOE/ET-0058)

E 1.65:date   • Item 429-N-1 (MF)
DAMAGE ANALYSIS AND FUNDAMENTAL STUDIES.
[Quarterly] (DOE/ET-0065)
    Provides a working technical record for use
of the DAFS program participants, the fusion en-
ergy program in general, and the Department of
Energy.
    Sub-title: Quarterly Progress Report.

E 1.66:date
GEOTHERMAL ENERGY UPDATE. [Monthly]

E 1.67:date   • Item 429-T-63
ENERGY BRIEFS FOR EDITORS/NEWS DIRECTORS.
[Irregular]

    Printed on glossy paper with camera ready
copy and reproducible photographs, to be used
as hand-outs to editors and news directors. Contains brief interviews and news items on all phases
of energy.
    Publication discontinued.

E 1.67/2:nos.   • Item 435-E-7
DoE FEATURE, NF- (series). [Irregular]

    Series of short features concerning energy
conservation, new technologies, and the nature
of the energy problem. Prepared for editors and
printed on glossy paper in newspaper format.

E 1.68:nos.   • Item 474-B (MF)
NUCLEAR ENERGY, DOE/NE (series). [Irregular] (DOE/
EIA-0194)

    PURPOSE:– To describe the Department of
Energy nuclear programs and positions in such
areas as fission energy and nuclear waste management. Intended for Congress, the research
community, and interested public. Includes annual reports on nuclear programs as well as legal
reports.

E 1.68/2   • Item 474-B-7 (MF)
DOE/RW- (series). [Irregular]
    Each issue is concerned with a different ra-
dioactive waste topic.
    RW Radioactive Waste.

E 1.68/2-2:date   • Item 474-B-7 (EL)
OCRWM BULLETIN. [Monthly]
    OCRWM = Office of Civilian Radioactive Waste
Management.

E 1.68/2-3:date   • Item 474-B-7
OCRWM BACKGROUNDER. [Monthly]
    OCRWM = Office of Civilian Radioactive Waste
Management.
    See E 1.68/2

E 1.68/2-4   • Item 474-B-9 (MF)
OCRWM PUBLICATIONS CATALOG. [Annual]
    OCRWM = Office of Civilian Radioactive Waste
Management.
    Provides citations of selected technical and
public information on the subject of high-level
radioactive waste management. Suitable for libraries and those individuals needing either a
broad base of information or a particular source.
    This annual is related to DOE/RW- (series),
E 1.68/2.

E 1.68/2-5:   • **Item 474-B-7**
IMPLEMENTATION PLAN FOR DEVELOPMENT OF
FEDERAL INTERIM STORAGE FACILITIES FOR
COMMERCIAL SPENT NUCLEAR FUEL. [Annual]
Discontinued.

E 1.68/2-6:date   • **Item 474-B-7 (MF)**
QUARTERLY REPORT ON PROGRAM COST AND
SCHEDULE. [Quarterly]

E 1.68/2-7   • **Item 474-B-10 (EL)**
OFFICE OF CIVILIAN RADIOACTIVE WASTE MAN-
AGEMENT ANNUAL REPORT TO CONGRESS.

E 1.68/3   • **Item 474-B (MF)**
DOE/NS (Series).

E 1.68/4:nos.   • **Item 474-B-11 (MF)**
DOE/NP (Office of New Production Reactors) (series).

E 1.68/5:nos.   • **Item 474-B-12 (MF)**
DOE-NE-STD (Nuclear Safety Policy Standards) (series).

E 1.69:date   • **Item 429-A-2**
ENERGY FORUM. [Bimonthly]
      Newsletter containing information of interest
to State, county, regional and city levels of government. Contains short articles in the news style
format on activities of the Department including
Congressional and State legislation dealing with
energy.
      Discontinued with September 1980 issue.

E 1.70:CT   • **Item 474-B-2**
POSTERS. [Irregular]

E 1.70/2:CT
AUDIOVISUAL MATERIALS. [Irregular]

E 1.71:nos.   • **Item 474-B-1 (MF)**
DOE/GC- (series). [Irregular] (Office of General Counsel)

E 1.72:nos.
TECHNOLOGY APPLICATIONS (series).

E 1.73:date
QUARTERLY REPORT ON PRIVATE GRIEVANCES
AND REDRESSES.
      Earlier FE 1.26

E 1.74:nos.
MORGANTOWN ENERGY TECHNOLOGY CENTER:
      METC/EGSP- (series). [Irregular] (Eastern Gas
      Shales Project)

E 1.76:CT   • **Item 429-T-65 (MF)**
SMALL-SCALE APPROPRIATE ENERGY TECHNOL-
OGY GRANTS PROGRAM. [Irregular] (Pacific
Southwest Region)
      Highly technical reports on energy technol-
ogy projects.
      Discontinued.

E 1.77:nos.   • **Item 474-B-3 (MF)**
DOE/SR- (series). [Irregular]

E 1.78:v.nos.&nos.   • **Item 474-B-4**
ENERGY HISTORY SERIES. v. 1–   1980–   [Ir-
regular]

      PURPOSE:– To present a history of the en-
ergy function in the federal government in terms
of the organizational antecedents of the major
programs and offices which now comprise the
Department of Energy and which came from a
dozen different Federal departments and agencies. Each issue concerns a different office.
      Discontinued.

E 1.79:date   • **Item 429-E-3**
FUEL ECONOMY NEWS. 1980–   [Quarterly]
      Later TD 8.33

E 1.80:nos.   • **Item 474-C-2**
DOE/AF- (Alcohol Fuels Programs) (series). 1–
1980–   [Irregular]
      Discontinued.

E 1.80/2   • **Item 474-C-2**
ALCOHOL FUELS PROGRAMS TECHNICAL REVIEW.
[Irregular] (Solar Energy Research Institute)

      PURPOSE:– To provide technical information
in SERI programs in such areas as methanol
production research, alcohol utilization research,
and membrane research.

E 1.81:nos.   • **Item 474-C-1 (MF)**
DOE/PE (Policy and Evaluation) (series). [Irregular]

E 1.82:nos.   • **Item 429-A-4 (MF)**
DOE/IA (series). [Irregular]
      Consists of publications issued by the Assis-
tant Secretary for International Affairs.
      Discontinued.

E 1.83:v.nos.&nos.   • **Item 429-P-2**
SOLAR THERMAL REPORT. [Quarterly] (Solar Energy Research Institute)
      Newsletter on studies and experiments cur-
rently being conducted by the Institute.

E 1.84:nos.   • **Item 429-H-3 (MF)**
DOE/FE (series).

E 1.84/2:date   • **Item 474-B-5 (MF)**
NAVAL PETROLEUM AND OIL SHALE RESERVES,
ANNUAL REPORT OF OPERATIONS. [Annual]

E 1.84/3   • **Item 429-H-3**
FOSSIL ENERGY REVIEW. [Quarterly]
      Discontinued.

E 1.84/4:nos.   • **Item 429-H-3 (EL)**
CLEAN COAL TODAY. [Quarterly]

E 1.84/5   • **Item 429-H-12 (EL)**
CLEAN COAL TECHNOLOGY COMPENDIUM (TROPI-
CAL REPORTS).

E 1.84/6   • **Item 429-H-13 (EL)**
CLEAN COAL TECHNOLOGY DEMONSTRATION PRO-
GRAM, PROGRAM UPDATE. [Annual]

E 1.84/7   • **Item 429-H-14 (EL)**
CLEAN COAL TECHNOLOGY DEMONSTRATION PRO-
GRAM, PROJECT FACT SHEETS.

E 1.85:CT
SOLAR EDUCATIONAL PROGRAMS AND COURSES.
      [Irregular]

E 1.86:date
ARGONNE NATIONAL LABORATORY, DIVISION OF
EDUCATIONAL PROGRAMS: ANNUAL REPORT.

E 1.86/2:v.nos.&nos.   • **Item 429-A-8 (EL)**
ARGONNE NEWS. v. 1–   [Irregular] (Argonne National Laboratory)
      Provides short articles on Laboratory accom-
plishments, technological research, nuclear waste
management, etc.
      Non-depository.

E 1.86/3:v.nos.&nos.   • **Item 429-A-20 (EL)**
LOGOS. [3 times a year]
      Contains articles which focus primarily on
nuclear power, basic science, environmental biomedical studies, and alternate energy technology.

E 1.86/4   • **Item 429-A-22 (EL)**
ARGONNE NATIONAL LABORATORY: RESEARCH
AND HIGHLIGHTS. [Annual]

      PURPOSE:– To present significant develop-
ments at the Laboratory, which is a multidisciplinary
research center.

E 1.86/5:   • **Item 429-A-29**
ARGONNE COMPUTING NEWSLETTER. [Monthly]
      Contains news of activities of Argonne Na-
tional Laboratory Computing Services, which publishes it as an account of work sponsored by an
agency of the U.S. government. Contains computer center statistics, telephone numbers and
service schedule, and a subject index for the
newsletters.
      Discontinued.

E 1.86/6:date   • **Item 429-A-22 (MF)**
FACULTY AND STUDENT PROGRAMS. [Annual]

E 1.86/8   • **Item 429-X (EL)**
FUTURE DRIVE. [Quarterly]

E 1.86/10   • **Item 429-A-41 (EL)**
TECH TRANSFER HIGHLIGHTS.

E 1.87:date   • **Item 429-G-1**
SEIDB PUBLICATIONS BULLETIN: TECHNICAL IN-
FORMATION. [Quarterly] (Solar Energy Research
Institute)
      Lists technical publications by subject area.
      SEIDB Solar Energy Information Data Bank.
      Discontinued 1981.

E 1.88:nos.   • **Item 429-A-5 (MF)**
WSUN (series). [Irregular]
      Western Solar Utilization Network is a joint
program of the Department of Energy and Western States to further public awareness and commercialization of solar energy.
      Discontinued.

E 1.89:nos.   • **Item 429-H-4 (MF)**
DOE/CE- (series). [Irregular] (Conservation and Renewable Energy Office)

E 1.89/2:date   • **Item 429-H-4 (MF)**
FEDERAL ENERGY MANAGEMENT ACTIVITIES.
[Quarterly]
      Discontinued.

E 1.89/3:date   • **Item 429-H-5**
FIVE YEAR RESEARCH PLAN, NATIONAL PHOTO-
VOLTAICS PROGRAM. [Annual]

      PURPOSE– To project the research activities
needed during the next five years to continue the
rapid progress toward using photovoltaic technology for the large scale generation of economi-
cally competitive electric power.
      Discontinued.

E 1.89/4   • **Item 429-H-4 (EL)**
FEMP FOCUS. [Bimonthly]

E 1.90:nos.   • **Item 474-B-5 (MF)**
DOE/EP- (series). 1–   [Irregular]

      Consists of publications on emergency pre-
paredness subjects.
      EP = Emergency Preparedness

E 1.90/2:date   • **Item 474-B-6 (EL)**
STRATEGIC PETROLEUM RESERVE QUARTERLY
REPORT. [EP-0046]
      Information on the U.S. Strategic Petroleum
Reserve is presented in accordance with the
Energy Policy and Conservation Act of 1975, as
amended. Tables show SPR oil inventory and de-
livery statistics and current and projected stor-
age capacity.

E 1.90/3:nos.   • **Item 474-B-6 (MF)**
DOE/EM (series).

E 1.90/4   • **Item 429-X (EL)**
FULL CIRCLE.

E 1.90/5   • **Item 429-X (EL)**
SUBSISTENCE AND ENVIRONMENTAL HEALTH.

E 1.90/6   • **Item 429-X (EL)**
EM PROGRESS.

E 1.90/7   • **Item 429-X (EL)**
EM STATE FACT SHEETS.

E 1.90/8:   • **Item 474-B-13 (EL)**
PROJECT FACTS SHEETS.

E 1.90/9   • **Item 474-B-13 (EL)**
FACT SHEET OF FOSSIL ENERGY PROJECT.

E 1.90/10   • **Item 474-B-15 (EL)**
TECHNOLOGY FACT SHEET. (series)

E 1.91:date
SOLAR EVENTS CALENDAR AND CALL FOR PAPERS.
      [Quarterly]

E 1.92:date   • Item 429-A-6 (MF)
FERMILAB RESEARCH PROGRAM WORKBOOK.
[Annual]

E 1.92/2:date   • Item 429-A-7
FERMILAB REPORTS. [Monthly]
Reports issued by the Fermi National Accelerator Laboratory of Universities Research Association, Inc., under a Department of Energy contract.
No longer a depository item. For internal/administrative use only, under 44 U.S.C. section 1902.
Discontinued.

E 1.93:v.nos.&nos.   • Item 1051-H
NUCLEAR SAFETY. v. 1–   1959–   [Bimonthly]

PURPOSE:– To keep reactor designers, reactor builders, reactor fuel specialists, regulatory and public safety officials informed on the current developments in nuclear safety. Activities of the Commission's Advisory Committee on Reactor Safeguards and the Hazards Evaluation Branch are also summarized and recent safeguards reports are reviewed.
Indexed by:–
Biological Abstracts
Chemical Abstracts
Engineering Index Annual
Index to U.S. Government Periodicals
Nuclear Science Abstracts
Selected Water Resources Abstracts.
ISSN 0029-5604
Previously published by the Nuclear Regulatory Commission (Y 3.N 88:9) prior to the July-August 1981 issue.

E 1.94:nos.   • Item 429-A-15 (MF)
DOE/US- (series).

E 1.95:date   • Item 429-A-14 (MF)
SOUTHEASTERN POWER ADMINISTRATION: ANNUAL REPORT.
See E 8.1

E 1.95/2:date   • Item 492-A-19
SOUTHWESTERN POWER ADMINISTRATION: ANNUAL REPORT.
See E 8.1

E 1.96:v.nos.&nos.   • Item 429-A-12 (EL)
LOS ALAMOS SCIENCE. [Irregular]

E 1.96/2   • Item 429-A-23
LOS ALAMOS LABORATORY: RESEARCH HIGHLIGHTS. [Annual]

E 1.97:date   • Item 429-A-16 (MF)
LIQUID FOSSIL FUEL TECHNOLOGY, DOE/ BETC/ QPR- (series). [Quarterly] (Bartlesville Energy Technology Center)

PURPOSE:– To report progress in liquid fossil fuel technology in terms of extraction, processing, and utilization.
Discontinued.

E 1.98:   • Item 429-A-10
NBL CERTIFIED REFERENCE MATERIALS CATALOG. [Triennial] (New Brunswick Laboratory)

PURPOSE:– To provide lists of certified reference materials for use in nuclear and nuclear related analytical measurement activities.
Discontinued.

E 1.99:letters-nos. • Item 430-M-1- 40- 46 (MF)
CONTRACT REPORTS AND PUBLICATIONS.
With an abundance of reports being issued by the Department of Energy, reports are being issued under the following 40 item numbers:–

E 1.99   • Item 403-M-1
COAL AND COAL PRODUCTS.

E 1.99   • Item 430-M-2
PETROLEUM.

E 1.99   • Item 430-M-3
NATURAL GAS.

E 1.99   • Item 430-M-4
OIL SHALES AND TAR SANDS.

E 1.99   • Item 430-M-5
NUCLEAR FUELS.

E 1.99   • Item 430-M-6
FUSION FUELS.

E 1.99   • Item 430-M-7
ISOTOPE AND RADIATION SOURCE TECHNOLOGY.

E 1.99   • Item 430-M-8
HYDROGEN.

E 1.99   • Item 430-M-9
OTHER SYNTHETIC AND NATURAL FUELS.

E 1.99   • Item 430-M-10
HYDRO ENERGY.

E 1.99   • Item 430-M-11
SOLAR ENERGY.

E 1.99   • Item 430-M-12
GEOTHERMAL ENERGY.

E 1.99   • Item 430-M-13
TIDAL POWER.

E 1.99   • Item 430-M-14
WIND ENERGY.

E 1.99   • Item 430-M-15
ELECTRIC POWER ENGINEERING.

E 1.99   • Item 430-M-16
NUCLEAR POWER PLANTS.

E 1.99   • Item 430-M-17
NUCLEAR REACTOR TECHNOLOGY.

E 1.99   • Item 430-M-18
ENERGY STORAGE.

E 1.99   • Item 430-M-19
ENERGY PLANNING AND POLICY.

E 1.99   • Item 430-M-20
DIRECT ENERGY CONVERSION.

E 1.99   • Item 430-M-21
ENERGY CONSERVATION, CONSUMPTION AND UTILIZATION.

E 1.99   • Item 430-M-22
ADVANCE AUTOMOTIVE PROPULSION SYSTEMS.

E 1.99   • Item 430-M-23
MATERIALS.

E 1.99   • Item 430-M-24
CHEMISTRY.

E 1.99   • Item 430-M-25
ENGINEERING.

E 1.99   • Item 430-M-26
PARTICLE ACCELERATORS.

E 1.99   • Item 430-M-27
INSTRUMENTATION.

E 1.99   • Item 430-M-28
EXPLOSIONS AND EXPLOSIVES.

E 1.99   • Item 430-M-29
ENVIRONMENTAL SCIENCES, ATMOSPHERIC.

E 1.99   • Item 430-M-30
ENVIRONMENTAL SCIENCES, TERRESTRIAL.

E 1.99   • Item 430-M-31
ENVIRONMENTAL SCIENCES, AQUATIC.

E 1.99   • Item 430-M-32
ENVIRONMENTAL-SOCIAL ASPECTS OF ENERGY TECHNOLOGIES.

E 1.99   • Item 430-M-33
BIOMEDICAL SCIENCES, BASIC STUDIES.

E 1.99   • Item 430-M-34
BIOMEDICAL SCIENCES, APPLIED STUDIES.

E 1.99   • Item 430-M-35
HEALTH AND SAFETY.

E 1.99   • Item 430-M-36
GEOSCIENCES.

E 1.99   • Item 430-M-37
PHYSICS RESEARCH.

E 1.99   • Item 430-M-38
PHYSICS RESEARCH (Continued).

E 1.99   • Item 430-M-39
FUSION ENERGY.

E 1.99   • Item 430-M-40
GENERAL AND MISCELLANEOUS.

E 1.99   • Item 430-M-40 (MF)
ARMS CONTROL

E 1.99   • Item 430-M-41 (MF)
BIOMASS FUELS.

E 1.99   • Item 430-M-42 (MF)
SYNTHETIC FUELS

E 1.99   • Item 430-M-43 (MF)
FOSSIL-FUELED POWER PLANTS.

E 1.99   • Item 430-M-44 (MF)
POWER TRANSMISSION & DISTRIBUTION.

E 1.99   • Item 430-M-45 (MF)
ENVIRONMENTAL SCIENCES.

E 1.99   • Item 430-M-46 (MF)
PHYSICS.

E 1.99/2:date/nos.   • Item 429-T-68 (MF)
CONTRACTS FOR FIELD PROJECTS & SUPPORTING RESEARCH ON ...

E 1.99/3:v.nos./nos. • Item 429-G-2 (MF) (EL)
HUMAN GENOME NEWS. [Bimonthly]

E 1.99/5   • Item 429-H-7 (MF)
BIOFUELS UPDATE. [Quarterly]

E 1.99/5-2   • Item 429-H-10 (MF)
THE SOLAR DETOX UPDATE. [Semiannual]
Discontinued.

E 1.99/7   • Item 429-H-8 (MF)
INERTIAL CONFINEMENT FUSION QUARTERLY REPORT.

E 1.99/7-2:date   • Item 429-H-11 (MF)
INERTIAL CONFINEMENT FUSION, ICF ANNUAL REPORT.

E 1.99/8   • Item 429-P-7 (MF)
ENERGY EFFICIENCY AND RENEWABLE ENERGY CLEARING HOUSE. . . [Monthly]

E 1.99/11   • Item 429-P-8
See 1.53/2

E 1.99/13:nos.   • Item 429-P-7 (EL)
ENERGY EFFICIENCY AND RENEWABLE ENERGY, CLEARINGHOUSE. (Factsheets)

E 1.100:nos.
INFORMATION BULLETIN, NT (series).

E 1.101:nos.   • Item 429-A-17 (MF)
DOE/CP (series). [Irregular]
Consists of miscellaneous publications issued under the direction of the Assistant Secretary of Congressional, Intergovernmental, and Public Affairs.

E 1.102:nos.   • Item 429-T-39 (MF)
DOE/ES (series). [Irregular] (Office of the Executive Secretary)

E 1.103:CT   • Item 429-A-18
PPL DIGEST. [Irregular]
Published by the Princeton Plasma Physics Laboratory, which is engaged in the development of magnetic fusion energy under contract with the Department. Consists of one folded sheet with short news items regarding Laboratory development of magnetic fusion energy.

E 1.104   • Item 429-A-21 (MF)
DOE/OR- (series). [Irregular] (Office of Conservation and Renewable Energy)

E 1.105:date   • **Item 429-A-24 (MF)**
REACTOR PLANT FISCAL YEAR END REVIEW.
[Annual]

PURPOSE:– To summarize activities in such areas as plant and reactor production and safety, radiological improvement plan, and fuel processing.
Discontinued.

E 1.106:   • **Item 429-A-27**
RESEARCH AREAS. [Annual]
Describes research programs administered by Oak Ridge Associated Universities sponsored by the Energy Department. Describes research facilities participating and research areas available for study by potential applicants.

E 1.107   • **Item 429-A-28 (MF)**
RESEARCH SUMMARY. [Annual] (Materials Components Technology Division, Argonne National Laboratory)
Prepared by the Argonne National Laboratory's Materials and Components Technology Division, whose financial support comes primarily from the Energy Department.
Presents information on the Division's activities in connection with the design, fabrication, and testing of high-reliability materials.
Discontinued.

E 1.108:   • **Item 430-N-1**
NATIONAL PHOTOVOLTAICS PROGRAM REVIEW.
[Annual]
Prepared by the Solar Energy Research Institute for the Energy Department. Summarizes the Institute's progress in photovoltaic technology.

E 1.109:   • **Item 430-N**
R & D TECHNOLOGY TRANSFER, AN OVERVIEW.
[Annual]
Prepared by the Solar Energy Research Institute for the Energy Department. Summarizes SERI's accomplishments in the area of transferof its technological developments to the private sector.
Discontinued.

E 1.110:v.nos/nos.   • **Item 474-B-7**
PACIFIC BASIN CONSORTIUM FOR HAZARDOUS WASTE RESEARCH NEWSLETTER.

E 1.111   • **Item 429-X (E)**
ELECTRONIC PRODUCTS. [Irregular]

E 1.112   • **Item 429-H-3 (MF)**
PETC REVIEW. [Three times a year]
Discontinued. v

E 1.113:v.nos./nos.   • **Item 429-A-18 (EL)**
BEAM LINE. [Quarterly]

E 1.114   • **Item 429-A-18**
AFDC UPDATE, NEWS OF THE ALTERNATIVE FUELS DATA CENTER. [Quarterly]
See E 1.114/4

E 1.114/2:date   • **Item 429-A-18 (MF)**
FEDERAL ALTERNATIVE AND FUEL PROGRAM, ANNUAL REPORT TO CONGRESS.

E 1.114/3   • **Item 429-D-2 (MF)**
ALTERNATIVE FUELS IN TRUCKING. [Quarterly]
Discontinued.

E 1.114/4   • **Item 429-X (EL)**
ALTERNATIVE FUEL NEWS. [Bimonthly]

E 1.115   • **Item 429-H-9 (EL)**
INQUIRY. [Annual]

E 1.116:nos   • **Item 429-A**
DOE/OC. [Irregular]
Discontinued.

E 1.117   • **Item 429-H-6 (MF)**
DOE/SA (series).

E 1.118   • **Item 429-A-34 (MF)**
DOE/PO (series).

E 1.119   • **Item 429-A-35 (MF)**
CURRENT AWARENESS BUILDINGS ENERGY TECHNOLOGY, DOE/BET (series).

E 1.120:nos.   • **Item 429-A-33 (MF)**
DOE/EE (series).

E 1.120/2   • **Item 429-A-43 (EL)**
PARTNER UPDATE. [Bimonthly]

E 1.121   • **Item 429-A-32 (MF)**
DOE/HR (series).

E 1.122   • **Item 429-A-30 (MF)**
DOE/BU (series).

E 1.122/2   • **Item 429-A-39 (MF)**
FORECAST CONTRACTING AND SUBCONTRACTING OPPORTUNITIES. [Annual]

E 1.123   • **Item 429-A-31 (MF)**
DOE/RL (series).
Discontinued.

E 1.125:nos.   • **Item 429-A-36 (MF)**
DOE/FM (series).

E 1.126:nos.   • **Item 429-A-38 (MF)**
STAFF REPORT ELECTRIC POWER SUPPLY AND DEMAND FOR THE CONTIGUOUS UNITED STATES.
Discontinued.

E 1.128:   • **Item 429-X (E)**
OTT TIMES. [Quarterly]
Discontinued.

E 1.133:nos.   • **Item 429-A-40 (MF)**
REPORT OF INVESTIGATIONS.

E 1.134:   • **Item 429-X (EL)**
INFORUM.

E 1.135:   • **Item 429-X (EL)**
TRANSPORTATION SAFETY REGULATORY BULLETIN.

E 1.136:   • **Item 429-X (EL)**
OFFICE OF INSPECTOR GENERAL PUBLIC REPORTS (various series).

E 1.137:   • **Item 429-X-19 (EL)**
DOE INFORMATION BRIDGE.

E 1.137/2   • **Item 429-X (EL)**
PUBSCIENCE.

E 1.137/3   • **Item 429-X-23 (EL)**
GRAYLIT NETWORK.

E 1.138   • **Item 429-X-20 (CD)**
OFFICE OF INDUSTRIAL TECHNOLOGIES, REPORTS.
Issued in CD-Rom.

E 1.139   • **Item 429-X (EL)**
CMC (COOPERATIVEMONITORING CENTER) MONITOR NEWSLETTER.

E 1.140   • **Item 429-X-20 (CD)**
OIT TECHNICAL REPORTS. [Annual]
Issued in CD-Rom.

E 1.140/2   • **Item 429-X (EL)**
THE OIT (OFFICE OF INDUSTRIAL TECHNOLOGIES) TIMES. [Quarterly]

E 1.140/3   • **Item 429-X-25 (EL)**
ENERGY MATTERS (OIT NEWSLETTER)

E 1.141   • **Item 429-W-2 (EL)**
STATE RENEWABLE ENERGY NEWS. (3x/year)

E 1.142   • **Item 429-X-24 (EL)**
FEDERAL R & D PROJECT SUMMARIES.

E 1.143   • **Item 429-X-27 (EL)**
REPORT ON INADVERTENT RELEASES OF RESTRICTED DATA...THAT OCCURED BEFORE OCTOBER 17, 1998. [Quarterly]

E 1.144   • **Item 429-A-44 (EL)**
PROTECTING HUMAN SUBJECTS. [Quarterly]

FEDERAL ENERGY REGULATORY COMMISSION
(1977–   )

CREATION AND AUTHORITY

The Federal Energy Regulatory Commission was established within the Department of Energy by the Department of Energy Organization Act, approved August 4, 1977 (91 Stat. 569) effective October 1, 1977, pursuant to Executive Order 12009 of September 13, 1977.

INFORMATION

Federal Energy Regulatory Commission
Department of Energy
888 First Street, NE
Washington, D.C. 20426
(202) 208-0200
Fax: (202) 208-0147
http://www.ferc.gov

E 2.1:date   • **Item 429-V-10 (MF)**
ANNUAL REPORT.

E 2.2:CT   • **Item 429-V-4**
GENERAL PUBLICATIONS.

E 2.6:CT   • **Item 429-V-7**
RULES, REGULATIONS, AND INSTRUCTIONS.
[Irregular]

E 2.8:CT   • **Item 429-L-4**
HANDBOOKS, MANUALS, GUIDES. [Irregular]

E 2.9:v.nos.&nos.   • **Item 436-A**
FERC NEWS. v. 1–   1977–   [Weekly]
Supersedes FPC News (FP 1.25/3).
Discontinued.

E 2.10:nos.   • **Item 429-V-4**
ORDERS. [Irregular]

This material also appears in the Federal Register.

E 2.11:nos.   • **Item 429-V-3 (MF)**
ENVIRONMENTAL IMPACT STATEMENTS, FERC/EIS (series). [Irregular]

E 2.11/2:nos.   • **Item 429-V-3 (MF)**
DRAFT ENVIRONMENTAL IMPACT STATEMENTS, FERC/DEIS- (series).

E 2.11/3:CT   • **Item 429-V-3 (MF)**
ENVIRONMENTAL IMPACT STATEMENTS.

E 2.12:nos.   • **Item 429-V-1 (MF)**
DOE/FERC- (series). 1–   1978–   [Irregular]
Miscellaneous non-recurring publications related to energy regulatory matters.

E 2.12:0030   • **Item 429-V-1**
FEDERAL ENERGY REGULATORY COMMISSION PRODUCER MANUAL.
Subscription includes basic manual with quarterly changes for an indefinite period.
Prepared by the FERC staff for producer compliance with the provisions of the Natural Gas Policy Act of 1978.
Earlier E 2.8:P 94

E 2.12/2:date   • **Item 429-L-5 (MF)**
TELEPHONE DIRECTORY. [Quarterly]

E 2.12/3:   • **Item 429-W (MF)**
THE QUALIFYING FACILITIES REPORT. [Annual]
A cumulative list of filings made for small power production and cogeneration facilities as required by CR Title 18, Pt. 292. Lists facilities that qualify for certain benefits under the Public Utility Regulatory Policies Act of 1978.
Earlier E 2.12

E 2.13:date • Item 429-V-2
STAFF REPORT OF MONTHLY REPORT COST AND QUALITY OF FUELS FOR ELECTRIC UTILITY PLANTS. [Monthly]
Consists of tables compiled from statistics supplied by utility companies and plants.
ISSN 0163-2981
Discontinued.

E 2.14:date • Item 429-V-6
CRITICAL PROJECT STATUS REPORT. v.1– 4 . 1978– 1981. [Monthly]

PURPOSE:– To provide information using flow charts, necessary to monitor and control the progress of projects, that are likely to have a significant impact on the nation's energy supply or energy policy.
Discontinued June 1981.

E 2.14/2:v.nos.&nos. • Item 429-V-9
HEARING PROCESS STATUS REPORT (White Book). v. 1– 3. 1979– 1981. [Monthly]

PURPOSE:– To graphically display and track the progress of active or recently completed cases within the Federal Energy Regulatory Commission hearing process. Intended for FERC management to identify backlog, evaluate processes, etc.
Discontinued July 1981.

E 2.15:CT • Item 429-V-5
MAPS AND CHARTS. [Irregular]
Earlier FP 1.13

E 2.16:date • Item 429-V-11
REGULATORY CALENDAR. [Quarterly]

PURPOSE:– To provide a calendar of proposed rulemakings under acts such as the Natural Gas Act and the Natural Gas Policy Act. Rulemakings also concern such regulations as electric and hydroelectric regulations as well as Administration Rules and Practices. Each issue contains many proposed rulemakings consisting of one page each and containing a docket number, description, legal basis, and major states of completion.
Discontinued.

E 2.17:nos. • Item 438-C
FEDERAL ENERGY GUIDELINES: FERC REPORTS. [Weekly]
Includes precedential opinions, findings, orders, declarations, notices and decisions.
Consists of multi-looseleaf volumes, each of which is updated weekly to monthly with 100– 300 page supplements.
Companion volume to Federal Energy Guidelines: Statutes and Regulations (E 2.18).

E 2.18:nos. • Item 438-C-1
FEDERAL ENERGY GUIDELINES: STATUTES AND REGULATIONS. [Bimonthly]
Consists of multi-looseleaf volumes, each of which is updated weekly to monthly with 100– 300 page supplements.
Companion volume to Federal Energy Guidelines: FERC Reports (E 2.17).

E 2.18/2:date
FERC STATUTES AND REGULATIONS, REGULATIONS PREAMBLES.

E 2.18/3:date
FERC STATUTES AND REGULATIONS, PROPOSED REGULATIONS.

E 2.19:v.nos.&nos. • Item 429-V-2
MONITOR. v. 1– 1981– [Bimonthly]

PURPOSE:– To provide a newsletter on the Commission's activities.
Discontinued.

E 2.20:v.nos.&nos.
ALTERNATE FUELS.

E 2.22:date • Item 438-C-2 (MF)
NOTICES OF DETERMINATIONS BY JURISDICTIONAL AGENCIES UNDER THE NATURAL GAS POLICY ACT OF 1978. [Irregular]

PURPOSE:– To list notices of determination received by the Commission pursuant to the Natural Gas Policy Act of 1978 and 18 CFR 274.104. Contains special technical information intended primarily for those concerned with natural gas wells.

E 2.23: • Item 429-L-6 (MF)
STAFF DISCUSSION PAPER (series).

E 2.23/2 • Item 429-L-7 (MF)
PAPER NO. DPR (series).

E 2.24:CT • Item 429-W-1
FORMS. [Irregular]

E 2.25:date • Item 429-Y (MF)
THE CHRONICLE. [Monthly]
Discontinued.

E 2.26:date • Item 429-W (MF)
ALPHABETICAL LIST OF PROJECTS AND ALPHABETICAL LIST OF OWNERS PROJECTS LICENSED, EXEMPTED, AND APPLICATIONS PENDING. [Annual]
Discontinued.

ENERGY INFORMATION ADMINISTRATION
(1977–   )

CREATION AND AUTHORITY

The Energy Information Administration was established within the Department of Energy by the Department of Energy Organization Act, approved August 4, 1977 (91 Stat. 569) and effective October 1, 1977, pursuant to Executive Order 12009 of September 13, 1977.

INFORMATION

Energy Information Administration
Department of Energy
1000 Independence Ave. SW, E130
Washington, D.C. 20585-0601
(202) 586-8800
Fax: (202) 586-0329
http://www.eia.doe.gov

E 3.1:date • Item 429-J-1 (MF)
ANNUAL REPORT. 1st– 1977–
Presents historical account of work during the year, forecasts energy supply and demand, and imparts diverse energy statistics relating to past and present.

E 3.1/a:date • Item 429-J-1
ANNUAL ENERGY BALANCE.
Extract from Annual Report to Congress.

E 3.1/a-2:date • Item 429-J-1
ANNUAL ENERGY SUMMARY.
Material is extracted from the Annual Report.
Discontinued.

E 3.1/2:date 429-J-1 (MF)
ANNUAL ENERGY REVIEW. (DOE/EIA- 0384)
Replaces v. 2 of the Annual Report (E 1.1).
Discontinued.

E 3.1/2:date • Item 429-X-4
ANNUAL ENERGY REVIEW (Diskettes).

E 3.1/3:date • Item 429-J-1
SYNOPSIS OF THE ANNUAL ENERGY REVIEW AND OUTLOOK. [Annual] (DOE/EIA-0385)
Combines information from Annual Energy Review and Annual Energy Outlook, which were v. 2 and v. 3 of Annual Report (E 3.1).
Discontinued.

E 3.1/4:date • Item 429-J-1 (MF)
ANNUAL ENERGY OUTLOOK, WITH PROJECTIONS TO (year). (DOE/EIA 0383)
Replaces v. 3 of the Annual Report (E 1.1).

E 3.1/4-2:date • Item 429-J-1
COMPARISON OF ANNUAL ENERGY OUTLOOK, FORECASTS WITH OTHER FORECASTS, SUPPLEMENT TO THE ANNUAL ENERGY OUTLOOK. [Annual]
Discontinued. v

E 3.1/4-3:date • Item 429-J-1
ASSUMPTIONS FOR THE ANNUAL ENERGY OUTLOOK. [Annual]
Discontinued.

E 3.1/5:date • Item 429-J-3
PERSONAL COMPUTER-ANNUAL ENERGY OUTLOOK.
Issued on diskettes.
Discontinued.

E 3.1/5-2 • Item 429-X-8 (E)
MARKET PENETRATION MODELS. [Annual]
Issued on computer diskettes.
Discontinued.

E 3.2:CT • Item 429-T-11
GENERAL PUBLICATIONS. [Irregular]

E 3.8:CT • Item 429-T-24
HANDBOOKS, MANUALS, GUIDES. [Irregular]

E 3.9:date • Item 434-A-2 (EL)
MONTHLY ENERGY REVIEW.

PURPOSE:– To present current and historical statistics on production and disposition of major sources of energy in the United States.
ISSN 0095-356
Earlier FE 1.17

E 3.9/2:date • Item 434-C
MONTHLY ENERGY REVIEW DATABASE. [Monthly]
Issued on diskettes.
Discontinued.

E 3.10:letters-nos. • Item 429-J
ENERGY INFORMATION ADMINISTRATION REPORTS, DOE/EIA- (series). 1– [Irregular]
Discontinued.

ENERGY DATA REPORTS.

E 3.11:date • Item 435-E-10 (EL)
NATURAL GAS. (DOE/EIA-0130) [Monthly]
Gives current monthly and quarterly production of natural and synthetic gas, and net gas imports; marketed natural gas, by producing States.
Continues: Natural and Synthetic Gas.
Earlier I 28.98/4

E 3.11/2:date
NATURAL GAS LIQUIDS. May 1977– Dec. 1978. [Monthly]
Absorbed by Petroleum Statement (E 3.11/5) with Jan. 1979 issue.
Earlier I 28.47

E 3.11/2-2:date • Item 429-K-3 (EL)
NATURAL GAS ANNUAL. (Annual).

PURPOSE:– To present statistical data on production, interstate movement, consumption, etc. of natural gas, by State.
Note:– Reports for 1979, 1980, and 1981 were mistakenly classed in E 3.38. In 1983, these publications were reclassified in the present class. [Adm. Notes, Vol. 4, No. 1, January 1983.]
Earlier I 28.98/6

E 3.11/2-2 • Item 429-X-5 (E)
NATURAL GAS ANNUAL (Diskettes).

E 3.11/2-3:nos. • Item 435-E-11
WORLD NATURAL GAS. [Annual] (DOE/ EIA-0133)

Gives statistical data on world marketed natural gas production and international gas flow; natural gas either wasted or used for repressuring; and world natural gas trade, by continent.
Discontinued.

E 3.11/2-4:date • **Item 427-T-47**
UNDERGROUND STORAGE OF NATURAL GAS BY INTERSTATE PIPELINE COMPANIES. [Annual] (DOE/EIA-0151)

PURPOSE:– To present brief summary and statistical data in tabular and graphic form, including number of fields, quantity of gas, injections and withdrawals, cost, gas balances, etc.
Discontinued.

E 3.11/2-5:date • **Item 429-T-45**
NATURAL GAS DELIVERIES AND CURTAILMENTS TO END-USE CUSTOMERS AND POTENTIAL NEEDS FOR ADDITIONAL ALTERNATE FUELS. [Annual]

PURPOSE:– To present information and data in tabular form derived from Administration surveys for the heating season. Information deals exclusively with markets for end-use customers.
Discontinued.

E 3.11/2-6:date
SALES, REVENUE, AND INCOME FOR ELECTRIC UTILITIES. [Monthly]

Combined with Interstate Gas Prices and Financial Data (E 3.11/2-7) to form Financial Statistics of Electric Utilities and Interstate Natural Gas Pipeline Companies (E 3.11/2-8).

E 3.11/2-7:date
INTERSTATE GAS PRICES AND FINANCIAL DATA. [Monthly]

Combined with Sales, Revenue, and Income for Electric Utilities (E 3.11/2-6) to form Financial Statistics of Electric Utilities and Interstate Natural Gas Pipeline Companies (E 3.11/2-8).

E 3.11/2-8:date • **Item 429-T-61**
SALES, REVENUE, AND INCOME OF ELECTRIC UTILITIES. [Monthly]
Contains statistical data on sales, revenue, income, etc., for privately owned electric utilities, and major natural gas pipeline companies.
Formed by the combination of Sales, Revenue, and Income for Electric Utilities (E 3.11/2-6) and Interstate Gas Prices and Financial Data (E 3.11/7).
Former title: Financial Statistics of Electric Utilities and Interstate Natural Gas Pipeline Companies.
Absorbed by Electric Power Monthly (E 3.11/17-8) with October 1981 issue.
Discontinued.

E 3.11/2-9:date • **Item 435-E-19**
UNDERGROUND NATURAL GAS STORAGE IN THE UNITED STATES, (date) HEATING YEAR. [Annual] (DOE/EIA- 0239)
Gives statistical data on total U.S. underground natural gas storage for the current and previous heating year (April-March).
See E 3.11

E 3.11/2-10 • **Item 429-X-5 (E)**
NATURAL GAS ANNUAL.
Issued on diskettes.
Discontinued.

E 3.11/2-11:date • **Item 429-K-5 (MF)**
NATURAL GAS…ISSUES AND TRENDS. [Annual]

E 3.11/2-12 • **Item 434-A-20 (EL)**
NATURAL GAS WEEKLY MARKET UPDATE.

E 3.11/3:nos.
PENNSYLVANIA ANTHRACITE WEEKLY. 1– 136. – May 9, 1980.

Absorbed by Weekly Coal Report (E 3.11/4)
Earlier I 28.49/2

E 3.11/3-2:date • **Item 435-E-17**
COAL, PENNSYLVANIA ANTHRACITE. [Annual]

Gives statistical data on production, distribution, consumption, and exports of Pennsylvania anthracite.
Earlier I 28.50/4

E 3.11/3-3:date
PENNSYLVANIA ANTHRACITE DISTRIBUTION. [Annual]
Earlier I 28.50/3

E 3.11/4:nos. • **Item 435-E-12**
WEEKLY COAL PRODUCTION. (DOE/EIA 218)
Absorbed Pennsylvania Anthracite Weekly (E 3.11/3), effective May 9, 1980 issue.
Former title: Weekly Coal Report.
Earlier I 28.33
Discontinued.

E 3.11/5:nos. • **Item 435-J-1 (EL)**
PETROLEUM SUPPLY MONTHLY. [Monthly] (DOE/EIA 109)
Contains brief narrative and statistical tables on the production, importation, and disposition of crude petroleum, petroleum products, and natural gas liquids in the United States.
Prior to 1982, entitled Monthly Petroleum Statement.
Effective 1982, absorbed Availability of Heavy Fuel Oils by Sulfur Levels (E 3.11/8), Monthly Petroleum Statistics Report (E 3.12).
See E 3.11/5-5

E 3.11/5-2:date • **Item 434-A-23**
PETROLEUM STATEMENT. [Annual]
Consists mainly of tables showing supply, distribution, and stocks of crude petroleum, petroleum products, and natural gas liquids in the United States for the calendar year.
Combined with other reports to form Petroleum Supply Annual (E 3.11/5-5)
Earlier I 28.18/4
Discontinued.

E 3.11/5-3:date • **Item 642-A**
INTERNATIONAL PETROLEUM ANNUAL (date).

PURPOSE:– To present data on supply and demand for crude petroleum and refined products, output, imports, exports and reexports, domestic demand for refined products, by countries. Two-year comparisons.
Earlier I 28.43/3

E 3.11/5-4:date • **Item 435-J-1**
PETROLEUM REFINERIES IN THE UNITED STATES AND U.S. TERRITORIES. [Annual]
Consists of a brief narrative and tables on the number and capacity of U.S. petroleum refineries. Also projects crude oil inputs and outputs for the next two years.
Combined with other reports to form Petroleum Supply Annual (E 3.11/5-5)
Earlier I 28.17/2

E 3.11/5-5:date • **Item 435-J-1 (MF) (EL)**
PETROLEUM SUPPLY ANNUAL.
Formed by the union of Petroleum Statement (E 3.11/5-2); Petroleum Refineries in the United States and U.S. Territories (E 3.11/5-4); Sales of Liquid Petroleum Gases and Ethane (E 3.11/13); and Deliveries of Fuel Oil and Kerosene (E 3.40)

E 3.11/5-6 • **Item 435-J-1 (EL)**
INTERNATIONAL PETROLEUM STATISTICS REPORT. [Monthly]

E 3.11/6:date
DISTRICT V PETROLEUM STATEMENT. [Monthly]
Earlier I 28.45/3

E 3.11/6-2:date
P.A.D. DISTRICTS SUPPLY/DEMAND. [Annual]

E 3.11/6-3:date • **Item 435-G-1**
P.A.D. DISTRICTS SUPPLY/DEMAND. [Quarterly]
Earlier I 28.18/7
Discontinued.

E 3.11/6-4:nos. • **Item 435-E-13**
SUPPLY, DISPOSITION, AND STOCKS OF ALL OILS AND BY P.A.D. DISTRICTS AND IMPORTS INTO THE U.S., BY COUNTRY. [Monthly] (subscription consists of 17 reports) (DOE/EIA-0134)
Statistical data give supply, disposition, and stocks of all oils, by Petroleum Administration for Defense (PAD) Districts, and imports of petroleum products and crude oil into the United States.
Discontinued.

E 3.11/7:date • **Item 435-E-2 (MF)**
COAL DISTRIBUTION.

PURPOSE:– To present data on distribution of bituminous coal and lignite as provided by mandatory company reports.
Earlier title: Bituminous Coal and Lignite Distribution.
Earlier I 28.33/2

E 3.11/7-2:date
COAL, BITUMINOUS AND LIGNITE. [Annual]
Earlier I 28.42/3

E 3.11/7-3:date • **Item 435-E-2 (EL)**
COAL INDUSTRY ANNUAL. (DOE/EIA-0118)
Former title: Bituminous Coal and Lignite Production and Mine Operation.
Former title: Coal Production (year).

E 3.11/7-4:date • **Item 435-E-22**
COAL DISTRIBUTION COMPANIES IN THE UNITED STATES. [Annual]
Lists companies that submit coal distribution data to the Administration, including coal mining companies, wholesale coal dealers, (including brokers), and retail coal dealers.
Discontinued.

E 3.11/7-5:date • **Item 435-E-22 (MF)**
DIRECTORY OF COAL PRODUCTION OWNERSHIP. [Annual]
Also published in microfiche.
Discontinued.

E 3.11/7-6:date • **Item 435-E-26**
DEMONSTRATED RESERVE BASE OF COAL IN THE UNITED STATES. [Annual] (DOE/EIA-0280)
Discontinued.

E 3.11/7-7:date • **Item 435-E-27 (MF)**
COAL DATA, A REFERENCE. [Annual] (DOE/EIA-0064)
Written for a wide audience, for the purpose of broadening the reader's knowledge of coal deposits, mining, production, consumption, and exports of coal.
Earlier E 3.2:C 63

E 3.11/7-8:date • **Item 435-E-32 (MF)**
ANNUAL OUTLOOK FOR U.S. COAL. (DOE/ EIA-0333)
Discusses the historical as well as the future trends of coal production and consumption. Also discusses issues that could effect the coal industry, such as leasing.
Earlier E 3.2:C 63/5
Discontinued.

E 3.11/7-9: • **Item 435-E-34 (MF)**
ANNUAL PROSPECTS FOR WORLD COAL TRADE. (DOE/EIA-0363)
Discusses past and projects future U.S. world coal trade and examines factors affecting the growth of world demand for metallurgical and steam coal.

E 3.11/7-10 • **Item 429-K-4 (MF)**
ANNUAL OUTLOOK FOR OIL AND GAS.
Discontinued.

E 3.11/7-11 • **Item 429-X-9 (E)**
EIA PERSONAL COMPUTER PRODUCTS, INTERNATIONAL COAL STATISTICS DATA- BASE.
Issued on computer diskettes.
Discontinued.

E 3.11/8:date • Item 435-F
AVAILABILITY OF HEAVY FUEL OILS BY SUL-
FUR LEVEL. [Monthly] (DOE/EIA-0105)
    Consists of a brief narrative and statisti-
cal tables showing imports and waterborne
movements of heavy fuel oils.
    Previous title: Fuel Oils by Sulfur Con-
tent.
    Superseded by Petroleum Supply Monthly
(E 3.11/5).
    Earlier I 28.45/4

E 3.11/8-2:date • Item 435-F
AVAILABILITY OF HEAVY FUEL OILS BY SULFUR
LEVEL. [Monthly]

E 3.11/9:date • Item 435-G (EL)
QUARTERLY COAL REPORT. [Quarterly]. (DOE/
EIA 121)
    Consists of narrative and statistical tables
showing coke production, imports and exports, and distribution.
    Former title: Coke and Coal Chemicals.
    Formerly issued monthly
    Also published in microfiche.
    Title varies.
    ISSN 0162-6175
    Earlier I 28.30

E 3.11/9-2:date • Item 435-G
COKE AND COAL CHEMICALS. [Annual]
    Earlier I 28.30/4
    Discontinued with 1980 issue.
    Data continued in Coke and Coal Chemi-
cals (E 3.11/9).
    Discontinued.

E 3.11/10:date
CARBON BLACK. [Quarterly]
    Earlier I 28.88

E 3.11/10-2:date
CARBON BLACK. [Annual]
    Earlier I 28.88/2

E 3.11/11:date
FUEL OIL SALES. [Annual]
    Earlier I 28.45/5

E 3.11/11-2:date • Item 435-E-6
PRICES AND MARGINS OF NO. 2 DISTILLATE
FUEL OIL. – 1983. [Monthly] (DOE/EIA-
0013)
    Consists of a brief narrative with statisti-
cal tables showing the average prices of heating oil and margins across the country.
    Former title: Heating Oil and Price Mar-
gins.
    Merged with Monthly Petroleum Product
Price Report (E 3.24) to form Petroleum Marketing Monthly (E 3.13/4).
    Discontinued.

E 3.11/11-3:date • Item 434-A-20 (EL)
FUEL OIL AND KEROSENE SALES. [Annual]

E 3.11/11-4 • Item 429-X-12
FUEL OIL AND KEROSENE SALES. [Annual]
    Issued on floppy diskettes.
    Discontinued.

E 3.11/12:date
CRUDE-OIL AND PRODUCT PIPELINES.
[Triennial]

E 3.11/13:date • Item 435-E-21
SALES OF LIQUEFIED PETROLEUM GASES AND
ETHANE. [Annual]
    Gives sales of liquefied petroleum gases
and ethane for various uses.
    Former title: Liquefied Petroleum Gas
Sales.
    Combined with other reports to form Pe-
troleum Supply Annual (E 3.11/5-5)
    Discontinued.

E 3.11/14:date • Item 429-T-53
MAIN LINE NATURAL GAS SALES TO INDUS-
TRIAL USERS. [Annual] (DOE/ EIA-0219)

    PURPOSE:– To present data on main line
natural gas sales, by State, by natural gas
companies, and by customers within each
State.
    See E 3.11

E 3.11/15:date • Item 429-T-40
COST AND QUALITY OF FUELS. [Monthly]

    PURPOSE:– To summarize cost and qual-
ity of fossil fuels delivered to electric utility
plants each month.
    Discontinued Dec. 1982

E 3.11/15-2:date • Item 429-T-40
COST AND QUALITY OF FUELS FOR ELECTRIC
UTILITY PLANTS. [Annual] (DOE/EIA-0101)
    Summarizes data contained in the Monthly
Report of Cost and Quality of Fuels for Elec-
tric Plants (E 3.11/15).
    Discontinued.

E 3.11/16:date • Item 429-T-48
COKE DISTRIBUTION. [Annual]
    PURPOSE:– To present data on distribu-
tion of oven and beehive coke and breeze
(small sizes of coke) produced in the United
States. Includes total consumption, state
consumption, production, exports, etc.

E 3.11/16-2
COKE PRODUCERS. [Annual]
    Earlier I 28.30/2

E 3.11/17:date • Item 435-E
NATIONAL TRENDS IN ELECTRIC ENERGY
RESOURCE USE. [Quarterly]

    Discontinued with 1st quarter 1980 is-
sue.
    Combined with other reports to form Elec-
tric Power Monthly (E 3.11/17-8).

E 3.11/17-2:date • Item 435-E-4
RESIDENTIAL ELECTRIC BILLS IN MAJOR
CITIES. [Monthly] (DOE/EIA- 0004)
    Discontinued with 3rd quarter 1980 is-
sue.
    Combined with other reports to form Elec-
tric Power Monthly (E 3.11/17-8)

E 3.11/17-3:date • Item 435-E-4
ENERGY AND PEAK LOAD DATA. [Monthly] (DOE/
EIA-0050)
    PURPOSE:– To present statistical data
on net generation and peak loads of major
electrical utilities in the States.
    Discontinued with June 1980 issue.
    Combined with other reports to form Elec-
tric Power Monthly (E 3.11/17-8)

E 3.11/17-4:date • Item 429-T-52
PRELIMINARY POWER PRODUCTION, FUEL
CONSUMPTION, AND INSTALLED CAPACITY
DATA FOR (year). [Annual] (DOE/EIA-0049)
    PURPOSE:– To present statistical data
on electric utility and industrial installed capacity, power production, consumption and
stocks of fossil fuels for electric utilities.
    Discontinued.

E 3.11/17-5:date • Item 429-T-55
MONTHLY COMPARISONS OF PEAK DEMANDS
AND ENERGY LOAD. [Annual]
    Consists of brief narrative introduction
and tables summarizing monthly energy and
peak load data of the nation's major electric
utility systems for a five year period.
    Discontinued.

E 3.11/17-6:date • Item 429-T-52
PRELIMINARY POWER PRODUCTION, FUEL
CONSUMPTION AND INSTALLED CAPACITY
DATA. [Monthly]
    Discontinued with July 1980 issue.
    Combined with other reports to form Elec-
tric Power Monthly (E 3.11/17-8)
    Former title: Power Production, Consump-
tion and Capacity.

E 3.11/17-7:date • Item 429-T-52
POWER PRODUCTION, GENERATING CAPAC-
ITY. [Annual] (DOE-EIS-0052/1)
    Discontinued.

E 3.11/17-8:date • Item 435-E-18 (EL)
ELECTRIC POWER MONTHLY. (DOE/EIA-0226)
    Supersedes and contains the information
formerly found in the following reports:– Pre-
liminary Power Production, Fuel Consumption,
and Installed Capacity Data (E 3.11/17-6);
Energy and Peak Load Data (E 3.11/17-3);
National Trends in Electric Energy Resources
(E 3.11/17); Residential Electric Bills in Major
Cities (E 3.11/17-2).

E 3.11/17-9:date
ELECTRIC ENERGY AND PEAK LOAD DATA. [An-
nual]

E 3.11/17-10:date • Item 435-E-18 (EL)
ELECTRIC POWER ANNUAL. (DOE/EIA- 0348)
    Earlier E 3.11/17-4 and E 3.11/17-9

E 3.11/17-11:date • Item 435-E-18 (MF)
ELECTRIC POWER QUARTERLY. (DOE/EIA- 0397)
    Discontinued.

E 3.11/17-12 • Item 435-E-18 (MF)
ELECTRIC TRADE IN THE UNITED STATES.
[Biennial]

E 3.11/17-13:date • Item 429-X-13 (E)
MONTHLY POWER PLANT REPORT.
    Issued on floppy diskettes.

E 3.11/17-14:date/nos. • Item 429-X-14 (E)
MONTHLY ELECTRIC UTILITY SALES AND REV-
ENUE REPORT WITH STATE DISTRIBUTIONS.
[Monthly]
    Issued on floppy diskettes.
    Discontinued.

E 3.11/18:date • Item 435-E-20
ASPHALT SALES. [Annual] (DOE/EIA-0112)
    Contains mainly tables and graphs show-
ing sales of asphalt petroleum for various
uses such as cement, roofing road oils, etc.
    Earlier I 28.11/02
    Discontinued.

E 3.11/19:date • Item 435-E-5
GASOLINE PRICES (Preliminary Release).
[Monthly] (DOE/EIA-0043)
    Consists of a brief narrative with statisti-
cal tables showing the average retail selling
prices of gasoline across the country.
    Discontinued with the May 1980 issue.

E 3.11/20:date • Item 435-H
INTERNATIONAL ENERGY. [Annual] (DOE/EIA-
0219)

E 3.11/20-2:date • Item 435-H (EL)
INTERNATIONAL ENERGY PRICES. [Annual]
(DOE/EIA-0424)
    Discontinued.

E 3.11/20-3:date • Item 435-H (EL)
INTERNATIONAL ENERGY OUTLOOK (year) WITH
PROJECTIONS TO (year). [Annual]

E 3.11/20-4:date • Item 435-H
INTERNATIONAL OIL AND GAS EXPLORATION
AND DEVELOPMENT ACTIVITIES. [Quarterly]
    Discontinued.

E 3.11/20-5:date • Item 429-X-6 (E)
WEPS (World Energy Projection System). [An-
nual]
    Issued on computer diskettes.
    Discontinued.

E 3.11/20-6 • Item 435-H-1 (MF)
INTERNATIONAL OIL AND GAS EXPLORATION
AND DEVELOPMENT. [Annual]
    Discontinued.

E 3.12:date • Item 434-A-17
MONTHLY PETROLEUM STATISTICS REPORT. 1975–

PURPOSE:– To provide the public with up-to-date data on all relevant petroleum statistics. It contains graphs and statistical tables on refinery operations; refinery production of petroleum products; primary stocks of crude and petroleum products; and imports of crude oil, unfinished oils and petroleum products.
Prior to the August 1977 issue published by the Federal Energy Administration (FE 1.9/4).
Superseded by Petroleum Supply Monthly (E 3.11/5).
ISSN 0364-0205
See E 3.11/5-5

E 3.13:date • Item 434-A-19
PETROLEUM MARKET SHARES, REPORT ON SALES OF REFINED PETROLEUM PRODUCTS. 1974–Sept. 1981. [Monthly]

PURPOSE:– To provide current statistics on market shares of motor gasoline retailers.
Prior to the July 1977 issue published by the Federal Energy Administration (FE 1.12).
ISSN 0161-1941
Discontinued. v

E 3.13/2:date • Item 434-A-16
PETROLEUM MARKET SHARES, REPORT ON SALES OF RETAIL GASOLINE. [Monthly]
Prior to the July 1977 issue published by the Federal Energy Administration (FE 1.12/2).
Discontinued with September 1981 issue.

E 3.13/3:CT • Item 434-A-19
PETROLEUM MARKET SHARES: [REPORTS ON VARIOUS SUBJECTS].
Earlier FE 1.12/2

E 3.13/4:date • Item 434-A-20 (EL)
PETROLEUM MARKETING MONTHLY. 1983– [Monthly] (DOE/EIA-308)
Formed by the union of Prices and Margins of No. 2 Distillate Fuel Oil (E 3.11/11-2) and Monthly Petroleum Product Price Report (E 3.24).

E 3.13/4-2:date • Item 434-A-20 (EL)
PETROLEUM MARKETING. [Annual] (DOE/EIA-487)

E 3.13/5 • Item 434-A-20 (EL)
DISTILLATE WATCH. [Weekly]

E 3.13/6 • Item 434-A-20 (EL)
MOTOR GASOLINE WATCH. [Weekly]

E 3.13/7 • Item 434-A-20 (EL)
PROPANE WATCH. [Weekly]

E 3.13/8 • Item 434-A-20 (EL)
ON-HIGHWAY DIESEL PRICES. [Weekly]

E 3.13/9 • Item 434-A-20 (EL)
RETAIL GASOLINE PRICES. [Weekly]

E 3.14:CT/date • Item 437-A-1– A-53
NATIONAL ELECTRIC RATE BOOK. [Annual]

PURPOSE:– To present rate schedules for electric service in communities of 2,500 population or more, for residential, commercial, and industrial service.
Separate section issued for each State.
ISSN 0364-87095
Earlier FP 1.18
Discontinued.

E 3.15:date • Item 434-A-3
ENERGY INFORMATION, REPORT TO CONGRESS. – 1982. [Quarterly]
Report submitted to Congress pursuant to Public Law 93-319 (88 Stat. 262) giving summaries and statistical information on energy resource development of coal, natural gas, crude oil, and refined petroleum products. A section dealing with the development and operation of nuclear energy and nuclear power plants is also included.
Discontinued with 3rd quarter 1982 issue.
Information contained in March, June, September, and December issues of Monthly Energy Review (E 3.9).

ISSN 0148-494X
Earlier FE 1.15
Discontinued 1982.

E 3.16:date • Item 438-A
ALL ELECTRIC HOMES, ANNUAL BILLS. [Annual]
Prior to 1977 data published by the Federal Power Commission (FP 1.10).
Discontinued.

E 3.17:date • Item 429-T-25
STEAM-ELECTRIC PLANT CONSTRUCTION COST AND ANNUAL PRODUCTION EXPENSES. [Annual] (DOE/EIA-0033)

PURPOSE:– To present tables and plant data sheets issued as annual supplements to the Statistics Series (FP 1.21) issued by the former Federal Power Commission.
Merged with Gas Turbine Plant Construction (Eÿ203.17/2) to form Thermal-Electric Plant Construction (E 3.17/4).
ISSN 0161-7206

E 3.17/2:date • Item 425-T-25
GAS TURBINE ELECTRIC PLANT CONSTRUCTION COST AND ANNUAL PRODUCTION EXPENSES. [Annual] (DOE/EIA-0048)

PURPOSE:– To present tables and plant data sheets issued as annual supplements to the Statistics Series (FP 1.21) issued by the former Federal Power Commission.
Merged with Steam-Electric Plant Construction (Eÿ203.17) to form Thermal-Electric Plant Construction (Eÿ203.17/4).

E 3.17/3:date • Item 425-T-25
HYDRO ELECTRIC PLANT CONSTRUCTION COST AND ANNUAL PRODUCTION EXPENSES. [Annual]

PURPOSE:– To present tables and plant data sheets issued as annual supplements to the Statistics Series (FP 1.21) issued by the former Federal Power Commission.
Combined with Thermal-Electric Plant Construction Cost and Annual Production Expenses (E 3.17/4) to form Historical Plant Cost and Annual Production Expenses for Selected Electric Plants (E 3.17/4-2).
ISSN 0083-0798

E 3.17/4:date • Item 429-T-25
THERMAL-ELECTRIC PLANT CONSTRUCTION COST AND ANNUAL PRODUCTION EXPENSES. [Annual] (DOE/EIA-0323)
Formed by the merger of Steam-Electric Plant Construction (E 3.17) and Gas Turbine Electric Plant Construction (E 3.17/2).
Combined with Hydro-Electric Plant Construction Cost and Annual Production Expenses (E 3.17/3) to form Historical Plant Cost and Annual Production Expenses for Selected Electric Plants (E 3.17/4-2).

E 3.17/4-2:date • Item 429-T-25
HISTORICAL PLANT COST AND ANNUAL PRODUCTION EXPENSES FOR SELECTED ELECTRIC PLANTS. [Annual] (DOE/EIA-0455)

Supersedes Hydro-Electric Plant Construction Cost and Annual Production Expenses (E 3.17/3) and Thermal-Electric Plant Construction Cost and Annual Production Expenses (E 3.17/4).
Discontinued.

E 3.17/4-2:date • Item 429-T-25
ELECTRIC PLANT COST AND POWER PRODUCTION EXPENSES. [Annual].
Previous title: Historical Plant Cost and Annual Production Expenses for Selected Electric Plants.

E 3.17/5:date • Item 429-T-25
SURVEY OF NUCLEAR POWER PLANT CONSTRUCTION COSTS. [Annual] (DOE/EIA-0439)
Discontinued.

E 3.17/6:date • Item 429-T-25
NUCLEAR POWER PLANT CONSTRUCTION ACTIVITY. [Annual]
Discontinued.

E 3.18:date • Item 435-E
ELECTRIC POWER STATISTICS. – 1978 [Monthly]

PURPOSE:– To present monthly summaries of statistical data taken from reports filed by electric utilities with the Federal Power Commission. Covers production of energy and capacity of plants, fuel consumption of electric power plants, electric utility system loads, sales of electric energy, financial statistics of private utilities.
ISSN 0013-4139
Earlier FP 1.27
Discontinued.

E 3.18/2:date • Item 429-T-12
STATISTICS OF PRIVATELY OWNED ELECTRIC UTILITIES IN THE UNITED STATES. [Annual] (DOE/EIA-0044)

PURPOSE:– To present, for individual companies, detailed financial and operating information in the form of schedules consisting of balance sheets, income and earned surplus statements, capital stock and long-term debt, electric operating revenues, customers and sales by classes of service, electric operating expenses, utility plant, physical quantities.
Data prior to 1976 published by the Federal Power Commission (FP 1.21). Formerly distributed to depository libraries under item No. 440.
Merged with Statistics of Publicly Owned Electric Utilities (E 3.18/3) to form Financial Statistics of Selected Electric Utilities (E 3.18/4).
ISSN 0161-9004

E 3.18/3:date • Item 435-E-1
STATISTICS OF PUBLICLY OWNED ELECTRIC UTILITIES IN THE UNITED STATES. [Annual] (DOE/EIA-0146)

PURPOSE:– To present financial and operating information about publicly owned electric utilities operating in the United States.
Prior to the 1976 data report published by the Federal Power Commission in its FPC-S-(series) (FP 1.21).
Merged with Statistics of Privately Owned Electric Utilities in the United States (E 3.18/2) to form Financial Statistics of Selected Electric Utilities (E 3.18/4).

E 3.18/4:date • Item 435-E-1
FINANCIAL STATISTICS OF SELECTED ELECTRIC UTILITIES. [Annual]
Formed by the union of Statistics of Privately Owned Electric Utilities in the United States (E 3.18/2) and Statistics of Publicly Owned Electric Utilities (E 3.18/3) with report for 1982.
Later E 3.18/4-3

E 3.18/4-2:date • Item 435-E-1
FINANCIAL STATISTICS OF MAJOR U.S. INVESTOR-OWNED ELECTRIC UTILITIES.
Earlier title: Financial Statistics of Selected Investor-Owned Electric Utilities.

E 3.18/4-3:date • Item 435-E-1 (EL)
FINANCIAL STATISTICS OF MAJOR U.S. PUBLICLY OWNED ELECTRIC UTILITIES. [Annual]
Earlier title: Financial Statistics of Selected Publicly Owned Electric Utilities.
Earlier E 3.18/4

E 3.19:date • Item 429-T-20
SOLAR COLLECTOR MANUFACTURING ACTIVITY AND APPLICATIONS IN THE RESIDENTIAL SECTOR. [Semiannual] (DOE/EIA-0039)
PURPOSE:– To report on survey of private firms that manufacture and sell solar collectors. Includes descriptive statistics on economic activity in the solar heating and cooling area, and identifies production growth in the industry. Includes lists of manufacturers.
Discontinued [List of Classes, 1980/4].

E 3.19/2:date • Item 429-T-20 (EL)
SOLAR COLLECTOR MANUFACTURING ACTIVITY. [Annual] (DOE/EIA-1074)
Report is for fiscal year.

E 3.19/2-2 • Item 429-T-20 (EL)
RENEWABLE ENERGY: ISSUES AND TRENDS. [Annual]

E 3.19/3:date • **Item 435-E-28**
ACTIVE SOLAR INSTALLATIONS SURVEY. [Annual]
(DOE/EIA-3060)
Survey results are presented in narrative and tables on use of solar energy for space cooling and space and water heating in residential and commercial buildings.
Discontinued.

E 3.21:CT • **Item 438-B**
MAPS AND CHARTS. [Irregular]

E 3.22:date • **Item 429-J-1 (MF)**
ELECTRIC SALES AND REVENUE, DOE/EIA-540 [Annual]
PURPOSE:– To provide data on costs to consumers for representative amounts of electricity used per month for residential, commercial and industrial service.
Prior to the 1978 issue, published by the Federal Power Commission in its Rate Series (FP 1.10).
Earlier title: Typical Electric Bills.
Earlier issued under item number 429-T-32.
Discontinued.

E 3.23:date • **Item 429-T-42 (MF)**
QUARTERLY TRACKING SYSTEM, ENERGY USING AND CONSERVATION EQUIPMENT IN HOMES. [Irregular] (DOE/EIA-0067)
PURPOSE:– To provide reports on tracking system that monitors energy using and conservation installations in new and existing homes.
Discontinued.

E 3.24:date • **Item 434-A-20**
MONTHLY PETROLEUM PRODUCT PRICE REPORT. – 1983. [Monthly] (DOE/EIA- 0032)
Earlier FE 1.9/5
Merged with Prices and Margins of No. 2 Distillate Fuel Oil (E 3.11/11-2) to form Petroleum Marketing Monthly (E 3.13/4).

E 3.25:date • **Item 438-B-1**
STATISTICS OF INTERSTATE NATURAL GAS PIPELINE COMPANIES. [Annual]
PURPOSE:– To present financial and operating statistics compiled from Classes A and B companies annual reports to the Energy Information Administration.
Formerly published by the Federal Power Commission in its Statistical Series (FP 1.21).
Discontinued.

E 3.25/2:date • **Item 438-B-1**
GAS SUPPLIES OF INTERSTATE NATURAL GAS PIPELINE COMPANIES. [Annual]
Discontinued.

E 3.25/2-2 • **Item 431-J-2**
DOMESTIC NATURAL GAS RESERVES AND PRODUCTION DEDICATED TO INTERSTATE PIPELINE COMPANIES. [Annual] (Energy Data Report)
Contains narrative and tables on dedicated domestic natural gas reserves, which are those for which both the seller and pipeline have received certification authorization from the Federal Energy Regulatory Commission.
Previous title: Preliminary Report of Domestic Natural Gas Reserves and Production Dedicated to Interstate Pipeline Companies.
Discontinued.

E 3.25/3:date • **Item 435-E-15**
U.S. IMPORTS AND EXPORTS OF NATURAL GAS. [Annual] (Energy Data Report) (DOE/EIA-0188)
Consists largely of tables showing U.S. imports and exports of pipeline and liquefied natural gas for the current, previous, and certain past years.
Discontinued.

E 3.25/4:date • **Item 429-X-16 (E)**
ANNUAL REPORT OF MAJOR NATURAL GAS COMPANIES.
Issued on floppy diskettes.
Discontinued.

E 3.26:nos. • **Item 429-T-43 (MF)**
TECHNICAL MEMORANDUMS, TM- (series). [Irregular] (DOE/EIA-0103)

PURPOSE:– To provide a series of highly technical memoranda with information on sources and problems of providing energy for the United States.
Discontinued.

E 3.26/2:nos. • **Item 429-T-44 (MF)**
ANALYSIS MEMORANDUM, AM- (series). [Irregular] (DOE/EIA-0102)
PURPOSE:– To provide information and data on energy related topics, such as sources, production, utilization, and costs of energy.
Superseded by Technical Report (series) (E 3.26/3).
Discontinued.

E 3.26/3:nos. • **Item 429-T-43 (MF)**
TECHNICAL REPORT (series). [Irregular]
Supersedes Analysis Memorandum (series) (E 3.26/2).
Discontinued.

E 3.26/4:nos. • **Item 429-T-44 (MF)**
ANALYSIS REPORT, (series). 1– [Irregular]
Discontinued.

E 3.26/5:nos. • **Item 429-T-54**
SERVICE REPORTS. 1– 1979– [Irregular]

PURPOSE:– To present such topics as distributional aspects of gasoline rationing, alternate energy pricing, etc.
Discontinued.

E 3.26/6:nos. • **Item 435-E-9 (MF)**
MODEL DOCUMENTATION REPORTS. [Irregular]
Series of highly technical reports and manuals documenting and describing supply models.

E 3.26/7:nos. • **Item 429-T-44 (MF)**
DOE/EIA/CR- (series). [Irregular]
Discontinued.

E 3.27:date • **Item 429-T-49 (EL)**
EIA PUBLICATIONS DIRECTORY. [Annual]

PURPOSE:– To provide a listing of publications issued by the Energy Information Administration.

E 3.27/2:date • **Item 429-T-56**
ENERGY INFORMATION ADMINISTRATION ISSUANCES. [Semiannual]
Includes text of all publications issued during the six-month period covered. Accompanied by an index with access by DOE-EIA report number, title, and subject.
Published in microfiche (24x).
Discontinued.

E 3.27/3:nos. • **Item 429-T-62**
RECENT PRODUCTS OF APPLIED ANALYSIS. 1– 1979– [Quarterly] (DOE/EIA- 0203)

Contains abstracts of publications issued by the Office of Applied Analysis.
Discontinued.

E 3.27/4:nos. • **Item 429-T-49 (EL)**
EIA PUBLICATIONS, NEW RELEASES. [Bimonthly] (DOE/EIA-204)
Supplement to EIA Publications Directory (E 3.27).
Prior to 1982, issued biweekly.

E 3.27/5:date • **Item 429-T-49**
EIA DATA INDEX, AN ABSTRACT JOURNAL. [Semiannual]
Discontinued.

E 3.27/6:date • **Item 429-T-49 (EL)**
ENERGY EDUCATION RESOURCES, KINDERGARTEN THROUGH 12TH GRADE. [Annual]

E 3.27/7 • **Item 429-X-18**
EIA DIRECTORY OF ELECTRONIC PRODUCTS.

E 3.28:date
WINTER ENERGY DATA BULLETIN. [Monthly, October– February]

E 3.29:date • **Item 429-T-59 (MF)**
INVENTORY OF POWER PLANTS IN THE UNITED STATES. [Annual]

PURPOSE:– To list existing, standby, cut of service, retired and projected electric power plants by State. Includes data on type, capacity, fuel, county location, etc.

E 3.29/2 • **Item 429-T-69 (EL)**
INVENTORY OF NONUTILITY ELECTRIC POWER PLANTS IN THE UNITED STATES. [Annual]

E 3.30:CT • **Item 429-T-64 (MF)**
FOREIGN ENERGY SUPPLY ASSESSMENT PROGRAM SERIES. 1979– [Irregular]

PURPOSE:– To provide reports of studies on oil and natural gas resources of o-ther world entities, with estimates of future availability of oil and natural gas from these areas. Each report covers a separate country.
Discontinued.

E 3.31:date/nos. • **Item 429-K-1 (EL)**
SHORT-TERM ENERGY OUTLOOK. [Quarterly] (DOE/EIA-0202)

PURPOSE:– To provide quarterly projections for all energy products and monthly projections for motor gasoline and distillate fuel oil supply and disposition. Projections take into account recent and anticipated developments affecting the domestic energy situation. Contains tables and charts.

E 3.32:date • **Item 429-T-58 (EL)**
WEEKLY PETROLEUM STATUS REPORT. (DOE-EIA-0208)
Earlier E 1.63

E 3.32/2:nos. • **Item 429-T-58**
WEEKLY OIL UPDATE. – 1983. (DOE/EIA- 0231)
Discontinued with 83/18 (May 6, 1983) issue.

E 3.32/3 • **Item 429-T-58 (MF) (EL)**
WINTER FUELS REPORT. [Weekly]

E 3.33:date • **Item 435-E-8 (MF)**
ENERGY INFORMATION DIRECTORY. [Annual] (DOE/EIA-0205)

PURPOSE:– To provide energy information and referral assistance to Federal, State, and local governments, the academic community, business and industrial organizations, and to the general public. Contains organization charts.
Former title: Energy Information Referral Directory.

E 3.34:date • **Item 429-K-2 (EL)**
U.S. CRUDE OIL AND NATURAL GAS RESERVES, (year) ANNUAL REPORT. [Annual] (DOE/EIA-0216)
Presents estimates of the Nation's proved oil and natural gas reserves prepared from data submitted by selected oil and gas operators and verified by the Department.
Also issued on diskettes.

E 3.34 • **Item 429-X-1 (MF) (EL)**
U.S. CRUDE OIL, NATURAL GAS, AND NATURAL GAS LIQUIDS RESERVES (Diskettes).

E 3.34/2:date • **Item 429-K-4 (EL)**
OIL AND GAS FIELD CODE MASTER LIST. [Annual] (DOE/EIA-0370)
Lists unique codes by States for all U.S. oil and gas fields for use in EIA and Federal Energy Regulatory Commission forms and reports. Contains a Field Code Index.

E 3.34/3 • **Item 434-A-20 (EL)**
CRUDE OIL WATCH. [Weekly]

E 3.35:date • **Item 429-J-2**
BUYER/SELLER CODES AUTHORIZED FOR REPORTING TO THE FEDERAL ENERGY REGULATORY COMMISSION. [Annual] (DOE/EIA-0176)
Consists of a tabular listing of code numbers used to identify buyers and sellers of natural gas in the reporting of data to the Commission.
Earlier E 3.2:B 98
Discontinued.

E 3.37:date   • Item 435-K (EL)
PERFORMANCE PROFILES OF MAJOR ENERGY
PRODUCERS. [Annual] (DOE/EIA-0206)

PURPOSE:– To provide profiles of the performances of the major energy companies in such
areas as petroleum production and marketing.
Includes tables and graphs.

E 3.37/2:date   • Item 429-X-15
PERFORMANCE PROFILES OF MAJOR ENERGY
PRODUCERS.
Issued on floppy diskettes with paper docu-
mentation.
Discontinued.

E 3.37/3:date   • Item 429-X-17
FINANCIAL REPORTING SYSTEM, SELECTED
TABLES. [Annual]
Issued on diskettes.

E 3.38
Note:– This class was established and used
for the 1979, 1980, and 1981 reports of the Natu-
ral Gas Annual. These reports were returned to
the original class (E 3.11/2-2) in 1983. [Adm. Notes.
Vol. 4, No. 1, January 1983.]
E 3.39:date
ENERGY DATA CONTRACTS FINDER. [Quarterly]
(DOE/EIA-0259)
Discontinued.

E 3.40:date
DELIVERIES OF FUEL OIL AND KEROSENE IN (date).
(Energy Data Report)
Combined with other reports to form Petro-
leum Supply Annual (E 3.11/5-5).

E 3.41:nos.   • Item 435-L
ENERGY FACT SHEETS. 1–   [Irregular]
Correspondence aids, printed on a single
sheet, each on a particular subject, such as energy in transportation, solar collectors, and coal
as the primary source for electric utilities.
Discontinued.

E 3.42:date   • Item 435-E-24 (EL)
STATE ENERGY DATA REPORTS. [Annual]
Tables present estimates of annual energy
consumption at State and national levels by major economic sector and by principal energy type
for the last ten years. Includes documentation
describing how estimates were made for each
energy source. A separate supplement summarizes the findings.

E 3.42/2:date   • Item 435-E-24
STATE ENERGY OVERVIEW. [Annual] (DOE/EIA-
0354)
Earlier E 3.2:St 2/3
Distributed.

E 3.42/3:date   • Item 435-E-24 (MF)
STATE ENERGY PRICE AND EXPENDITURE REPORT.
[Annual]
Formerly classified E 3.2:P 93/4 and distrib-
uted to Depository Libraries under 429-T-11

E 3.42/4:date   • Item 435-P
STATE ENERGY PRICE AND EXPENDITURE DATA
SYSTEM.
Issued on diskettes.
Discontinued.

E 3.42/5   • Item 435-R
STATE ENERGY DATA SYSTEM.
Issued on diskettes.
Discontinued.

E 3.43:   • Item 435-M (MF)
RESIDENTIAL ENERGY CONSUMPTION SURVEY.
Each publication concerns a survey in a different area, such as housing characteristics, and
may be updated periodically. Survey results are
presented largely through tables and graphs.
Discontinued.

E 3.43/2:date   • Item 435-M
COMMERCIAL BUILDINGS CHARACTERISTICS. [Tri-
ennial]
Earlier titled: Nonresidential Buildings Energy
Consumption Survey.
Earlier issued annually.
Discontinued.

E 3.43/2-2:date   • Item 435-M
ENERGY CONSUMPTION SURVEY: COMMERCIAL
BUILDINGS CONSUMPTION AND EXPENDI-
TURES.
Earlier title: Nonresidential Buildings.

E 3.43/2-3:date   • Item 429-X-3
NONRESIDENTIAL BUILDINGS ENERGY CONSUMP-
TION SURVEY (NBECS) (Diskettes).
Discontinued.

E 3.43/2-4   • Item 429-X-11 (E)
COMMERCIAL BUILDINGS ENERGY CONSUMPTION
SURVEY (CBECS).
Issued on floppy diskettes with paper docu-
mentation.
Discontinued.

E 3.43/3:date   • Item 435-M
RESIDENTIAL ENERGY CONSUMPTION SURVEY:
HOUSING CHARACTERISTICS. [Annual] (DOE/
EIA-0314)
Earlier E 3.43:H 81

E 3.43/4:date   • Item 435-M (MF)
RESIDENTIAL ENERGY CONSUMPTION SURVEY:
CONSUMPTION AND EXPENDITURES. [Annual]
Earlier E 3.43:C 76
Discontinued.

E 3.43/5:date   • Item 429-X-2
RESIDENTIAL BUILDINGS ENERGY CONSUMPTION
SURVEY (Diskettes)
Discontinued.

E 3.43/6   • Item 435-M-1 (MF)
ENERGY CONSUMPTION SERIES.

E 3.44:date   • Item 435-E-25
INDEXES AND ESTIMATES OF DOMESTIC WELL
DRILLING COSTS. [Annual] (DOE/EIA-0347)
Discontinued.

E 3.44/2:date   • Item 435-E-29 (MF) (EL)
COSTS AND INDEXES FOR DOMESTIC OIL AND
GAS FIELD EQUIPMENT AND PRODUCTION OP-
ERATIONS. [Annual] (DOE/EIA-0185)
Presents estimated costs and indexes for
domestic oil and gas field equipment and produc-
tion operations.

E 3.45:date   • Item 435-E-30 (MF)
DIRECTORY OF ENERGY DATA COLLECTION
FORMS. [Annual] (DOE/EIA-0249)
Lists and describes statistical forms used by
the Department of Energy to gather basic energy
information. Provides an overview of the
Department's statistical data collection programs
for decision makers in government about industry.

E 3.46:date   • Item 435-E-31
SURVEY OF U.S. URANIUM EXPLORATION ACTIV-
ITY. [Annual] (DOE/EIA-0402)
Discontinued.

E 3.46/2:date   • Item 435-E-31
SURVEY OF UNITED STATES URANIUM MARKET-
ING ACTIVITY. [Annual]
Discontinued.

E 3.46/3:date   • Item 435-E-31 (MF)
DOMESTIC URANIUM MINING AND MILLING
INDUSTRY, (year) VIABILITY ASSESSMENT.
[Annual]
Discontinued.

E 3.46/3-2:date   • Item 429-X-10 (E)
OAK RIDGE URANIUM MARKET MODEL. [Annual]
Issued on computer diskettes.
Discontinued.

E 3.46/4:date   • Item 435-E-37
WORLD NUCLEAR FUEL CYCLE REQUIREMENTS.
[Annual]

PURPOSE:– To project domestic and foreign
requirements for natural uranium and enrichment
services as well as discharges of spent nuclear
fuel.
Earlier E 3.2:F 95/3

E 3.46/5:date   • Item 435-E-31 (EL)
URANIUM INDUSTRY. [Annual]

E 3.46/5-2:date   • Item 435-E-31 (MF)
URANIUM PURCHASES REPORT. [Annual]

E 3.47:date   • Item 435-E-33 (MF)
ENERGY CONSERVATION INDICATORS, ANNUAL
REPORT. (DOE/EIA-0441)

PURPOSE:– To present conservation indicators for the aggregate economy and for the five
major consuming sectors: residential, commercial, industrial, transportation, and electric utilities.
Former title: Annual Report of Energy Conservation Indicators.
Discontinued.

E 3.48:date   • Item 429-T-44 (MF)
DIRECTORY OF ENERGY INFORMATION ADMINIS-
TRATION MODEL ABSTRACTS. [Annual]

E 3.49   • Item 435-L-1
ENERGY FACTS. [Annual]

PURPOSE:– To provide a quick reference to
a broad range of domestic and international energy data, organized by energy source.
Discontinued.

E 3.50:date   • Item 435-E-35
ANNUAL OUTLOOK FOR U.S. ELECTRIC POWER.
[Annual]

PURPOSE:– To provide a history of and projections for U.S. electric utility markets. Includes
information on production, distribution, and costs
of electricity.
Discontinued.

E 3.51:date   • Item 435-E-36
COMMERCIAL NUCLEAR POWER, PROSPECTS FOR
THE UNITED STATES AND THE WORLD. [Annual]

PURPOSE:– To present prospects for commercial nuclear power for the United States and
the World.

E 3.51/2:date   • Item 429-X-7 (E)
WORLD INTEGRATED NUCLEAR EVALUATION SYS-
TEM. [Annual]
Issued on computer diskettes.
Discontinued.

E 3.52:date   • Item 435-E-38
PROFILES OF FOREIGN DIRECT INVESTMENT IN
U.S. ENERGY. [Annual]

PURPOSE:– To summarize activities in the
U.S. by foreign-owned or controlled companies
which also own or control U.S., energy sources
and supplies. Profiles and compares foreign-af-
filiated energy operations in the U.S. and U.S.
companies' energy operations abroad.
See E 3.37

E 3.53:date   • Item 429-J-1 (MF)
ENERGY FORECASTS FOR (year). [Annual]

E 3.54   • Item 429-J-1 (MF)
MANUFACTURING ENERGY CONSUMPTION SUR-
VEY: CONSUMPTION OF ENERGY. [Triennial]

E 3.54/2:date   • Item 429-J-1 (MF)
MANUFACTURING ENERGY CONSUMPTION
SURVEY: CHANGES IN ENERGY EFFICIENCY.
[Triennial]

E 3.54/3   • Item 429-J-1 (MF)
MANUFACTURING ENERGY CONSUMPTION SUR-
VEY: FUEL SWITCHING. [Triennial]
See E 3.54
E 3.55   • Item 435-N
OIL MARKET SIMULATION MODEL.
Issued on diskettes.
Discontinued.

E 3.56   • Item 429-K-1 (MF)
U.S. ENERGY INDUSTRY FINANCIAL DEVELOP-
MENTS. [Quarterly]
See E 3.58

E 3.57 • Item 429-K-6 (MF)
TECHNICAL REPORT TR (series).

E 3.58:date • Item 429-T-66 (MF)
ESTIMATES OF U.S. BIOMASS ENERGY CONSUMP-
TION. [Annual]
   Discontinued.

E 3.59:date • Item 429-K-7 (MF) (EL)
EMISSIONS OF GREENHOUSE GASES IN THE
UNITED STATES. [Annual]

E 3.59/2 • Item 429-K-10 (EL)
VOLUNTARY REPORTING OF GREENHOUSE GASES
ANNUAL REPORT.

E 3.59/3 • Item 429-K-11 (EL)
GREENHOUSE GAS VOLUNTEER (NEWSLETTER)

E 3.60:v.nos./nos. • Item 429-K-8 (E)
ENERGY INFODISC. [Quarterly]
   Issued on CD-ROM.

E 3.61 • Item 429-K--9 (E)
ELECTRONIC PRODUCTS. [Misc.]
   Issued on CD-ROM.

ECONOMIC REGULATORY
ADMINISTRATION
(1977–   )

CREATION AND AUTHORITY

The Economic Regulatory Administration was
established within the Department of Energy by
the Department of Energy Organization Act, approved August 4, 1977 (91 Stat. 569) and effective October 1, 1977, pursuant to Executive Order 12009 of September 13, 1977.

INFORMATION
   Economic Regulatory Administration
   Department of Energy
   Washington, D.C. 20585

E 4.1:date
ANNUAL REPORT.

E 4.2:CT • Item 429-L-1
GENERAL PUBLICATIONS. [Irregular]

E 4.8:CT • Item 429-L
HANDBOOKS, MANUALS, GUIDES. [Irregular]

E 4.9:nos. • Item 429-R
ENVIRONMENTAL ASSESSMENT, DOE/EA-(series).
   [Irregular]
   Later E 1.20/2

E 4.10:nos. • Item 429-T-21 (MF)
DOE/ERA- (series). [Irregular]

E 4.11:nos. • Item 429-L-3 (MF)
DOE/RG (series). [Irregular]
   Reports on the supply, demand for, and regu-
   lation of public utilities.

BONNEVILLE POWER
ADMINISTRATION
(1977–   )

CREATION AND AUTHORITY

The Bonneville Power Administration (I 44)
was transferred from the Department of Interior
to the Department of Energy by Act of August 4,
1977 (91 Stat. 565), effective October 1, 1977.

INFORMATION
   Bonneville Power Administration
   905 NE 11th Ave.
   Portland, Oregon 97232-4169
   (503) 230-5101
   http://www.bpa.gov

E 5.1:date • Item 606-A-3 (MF)
ANNUAL REPORT.
   Earlier I 44.1

E 5.1/2:date • Item 606-A-3 (MF)
QUARTERLY FINANCIAL REPORT.

E 5.2:CT • Item 606-A-1
GENERAL PUBLICATIONS. [Irregular]
   Earlier I 44.2

E 5.8:CT • Item 606-A-2
HANDBOOKS, MANUALS, GUIDES. [Irregular]

E 5.9:CT
AUDIOVISUAL MATERIALS. [Irregular]

E 5.10:date • Item 606-A-3 (MF)
RESEARCH AND DEVELOPMENT YEARBOOK.
   [Biennial]
   Discontinued.

E 5.10/2:date • Item 606-A-3 (MF)
RESEARCH AND DEVELOPMENT REPORT. [Biennial]
   See 5.10/2

E 5.11:date • Item 606-A-4 (MF)
FISH AND WILDLIFE ANNUAL PROJECT SUMMARY.
   [Annual]

   PURPOSE:– To summarize reports on projects
intended to protect, mitigate, and enhance fish
and wildlife resources affected by operation of
hydroelectric facilities on rivers.

E 5.12:date • Item 606-A-5
PACIFIC NORTHWEST AND ALASKA BIOENERGY
PROGRAM YEARBOOK. [Annual]

   PURPOSE:– To summarize activities of this
federal interagency program designed to promote
efficient and environmentally sound use of wood
for energy and other purposes.
   Discontinued.

E 5.13 • Item 606-A-6
IRRIGATION ENERGY EFFICIENCY (series). [Irregular]
   Each issue covers a separate subject.
   Discontinued.

E 5.14:date • Item 606-A-7 (MF)
GENERATION AND SALES STATISTICS. [Annual]
   Tables present statistics on the generation
and sales of electricity and compare them with
those of the previous year.

E 5.15: • Item 606-A-8
BACKGROUNDER. [Irregular]

E 5.16:date • Item 606-A-3 (MF)
OFFICE OF ENERGY RESOURCES YEARBOOK.
   [Annual]
   Discontinued.

E 5.23 • Item 606-A-9 (EL)
JOURNAL.

E 5.24 • Item 606-A-9 (E)
ELECTRONIC PRODUCTS.

WESTERN AREA POWER
ADMINISTRATION
(1977–   )

CREATION AND AUTHORITY

The Western Area Power Administration was
established by Department of Energy Organization Act (91 Stat. 578; 42 U.S.C. 7152) on December 21, 1977.

INFORMATION
   Western Area Power Administration
   12155 West Alameda Parkway
   Lakewood, CO 80228-2802
   (720) 962-7000
   http://www.wapa.gov

E 6.1:date • Item 430-K-4 (MF) (EL)
ANNUAL REPORT.

E 6.1/2 • Item 430-K
CUSTOMER CARE TECHNICAL BRIEF.

E 6.2:CT • Item 430-K-1
GENERAL PUBLICATIONS. [Irregular]

E 6.3/2 • Item 430-K
BIOMASS BULLETIN. [Quarterly]

E 6.3/2-2 • Item 430-K (P) (EL)
BIOMASS DIGEST.

E 6.8:CT • Item 430-K-2
HANDBOOKS, MANUALS, GUIDES. [Irregular]

E 6.9:CT • Item 430-K
BIBLIOGRAPHIES AND LISTS OF PUBLICATIONS.
   [Irregular]

E 6.10:CT • Item 430-K-3
MAPS AND CHARTS. [Irregular]

E 6.11 • Item 430-K
BIO TECH BRIEF.

E 6.11/2 • Item 430-K
CUSTOMER CARE TECHNICAL BRIEF.

ALASKA POWER
ADMINISTRATION

E 7.2:CT • Item 604-C-1
GENERAL PUBLICATIONS.

SOUTHEASTERN POWER
ADMINISTRATION

INFORMATION
   Southeastern Power Administration
   Samuel Elbert Building
   2 Public Square
   Elberton, GA 30635-1850
   (706) 213-3805

E 8.1:date • Item 430-K-7 (EL)
SOUTHEASTERN POWER ADMINISTRATION,
   ANNUAL REPORT.

E 8.2:CT • Item 430-K-5
GENERAL PUBLICATIONS. [Irregular]

E 8.8:CT   • Item 430-K-6
HANDBOOKS, MANUALS, GUIDES.

NATIONAL RENEWABLE ENERGY LABORTORY

E 9.2   • Item 430-P
GENERAL PUBLICATIONS.

E 9.8   • Item 430-P-1
HANDBOOKS, MANUAL, GUIDES.

BUREAU OF EFFICIENCY (1916–1933)

CREATION AND AUTHORITY

The Bureau of Efficiency was established by act of Congress, approved February 28, 1916 (39 Stat. 15). The Bureau was abolished by act of Congress, approved March 3, 1933 (47 Stat. 1519). effective June 3, 1933, and its functions transferred to the Bureau of the Budget.

EB 1.1:date
ANNUAL REPORT.

EB 1.2:CT
GENERAL PUBLICATIONS.

EB 1.3
BULLETINS.

EB 1.4
CIRCULARS.

EB 1.5:nos.
GENERAL CIRCULARS.

EMPLOYEES' COMPENSATION COMMISSION (1916–1946)

CREATION AND AUTHORITY

The Employees' Corporation was established by act of Congress, approved September 7, 1916 (39 Stat. 742). The Commission was abolished by Reorganization Plan No. 2 of 1946, effective July 16, 1946, and its functions transferred to the Federal Security Administrator.

EC 1.1:date
ANNUAL REPORTS.

Later FS 13.301
EC 1.2:CT
GENERAL PUBLICATIONS.

EC 1.3
BULLETINS.

EC 1.3/2:nos.
SPECIAL BULLETINS.

EC 1.4
CIRCULARS.

EC 1.5:date
REGULATIONS (general).

EC 1.5/2:nos.
REGULATIONS.

EC 1.5/3:nos.
RULES AND REGULATIONS.

EC 1.6:CT
REGULATIONS, RULES, AND INSTRUCTIONS.

EC 1.7
OPINIONS.

EC 1.8:nos.
ACCIDENT PREVENTION SERIES; BULLETINS.

EC 1.9:vol.
SAFETY BULLETINS. [Monthly]

DEPARTMENT OF EDUCATION (1979–   )

CREATION AND AUTHORITY

The Department of Education was established by the Department of Education Organization Act (93 Stat. 668), approved on October 17, 1979. The Education Division of the Department of Health, Education, and Welfare (HE 19), including the Office of Education (HE 19.100) were abolished and their functions transferred to the newly established Department.

INFORMATION

Information Resource Center
Department of Education
400 Maryland Avenue, SW
Washington, D.C. 20202
(202) 401-2000
Fax: (202) 401-0689
Toll Free: (800) 872-5327
http://www.ed.gov/index.isp

ED 1.1:date   • Item 455 (MF)
ANNUAL REPORT.

ED 1.1/2:date   • Item 455 (MF)
ADMINISTRATION OF PUBLIC LAWS 81-874 AND 81-815, ANNUAL REPORT OF THE COMMISSIONER OF EDUCATION. 1st–
Earlier HE 19.101/2
Discontinued.

ED 1.1/3:date   • Item 455-B-2
THE NATIONAL EDUCATION GOALS REPORT. [Annual]

ED 1.1/3-2:date   • Item 455-N-9 (E)
THE NATIONAL EDUCATION GOALS REPORT. Issued on CD-ROM.

ED 1.1/4   • Item 455-B-24 (MF)
SEMIANNUAL REPORTS TO CONGRESS ON AUDIT FOLLOW-UP.
Discontinued.

ED 1.1/5:date   • Item 455-B-25 (MF) (EL)
FINANCIAL MANAGEMENT STATUS REPORT AND 5-YEAR PLAN. [Annual]

ED 1.1/6   • Item 455-N (EL)
ANNUAL ACCOUNTABILITY REPORT.

ED 1.1/7   • Item 455-B-29 (P) (EL)
ANNUAL REPORT ON SCHOOL SAFETY.

ED 1.2:CT   • Item 455-B-2
GENERAL PUBLICATIONS.

ED 1.2/15:CT   • Item 766-C-25
BRAILLE PUBLICATIONS.

ED 1.2/16:v.nos./nos.   • Item 455-B-27
THE LAW, HIGHER EDUCATION, AND SUBSTANCE ABUSE PREVENTION, A BIANNUAL NEWSLETTER.

ED 1.2/17   • Item 455-P (EL)
CATALYST. [Quarterly]

ED 1.3/2:date   • Item 455-A-12
BULLETIN. 1980–   [Quarterly]
Continues BFSA Bulletin (HE 19.138).
Discontinued.

ED 1.3/3   • Item 455-B-26 (MF)
FEDERAL STUDENT LOAN PROGRAM BULLETIN.

ED 1.8:CT   • Item 461-B-1
HANDBOOKS, MANUALS, GUIDES. [Irregular]

ED 1.8/2:date   • Item 461-B-1 (MF)
STUDENT GUIDE, FIVE FEDERAL FINANCIAL AID PROGRAMS. [Annual]
Earlier ED 1.8:St 9/3

ED 1.8/3:   • Item 461-B-1
APPLICATION DEVELOPMENT GUIDE, TALENT SEARCH PROGRAM. [Triennial]

ED 1.8/4:nos.   • Item 461-B-9
NCBE, PROGRAM INFORMATION GUIDE SERIES.
These guides deal with current innovative teaching practices in bilingual education and in the education of limited English-proficient students. Each guide is concerned with a different topic.
Earlier title: Teacher Resource Guide.

ED 1.9:v.nos.&nos.   • Item 455-B-1
ED FACTS. v. 1–   1980–   [Monthly]

PURPOSE:– To provide a newsletter containing activities of the Department of Education in its goal of achieving equality and excellence in education.
Discontinued Oct. 1980.

ED 1.9/2:   • Item 455-B-19
WHAT'S NOTEWORTHY ON . . . (series).

ED 1.10:v.nos.&nos.   • Item 455-B
AMERICAN EDUCATION. [10 times a year]
Covers preschool to adult education, new research and demonstration projects, major education legislation, school and college bond data, grants, loans, contracts, and fellowships.
Indexed by:–
Current Index to Journals in Education
Education Index
Index to U.S. Government Periodicals
Language and Language Behavior Abstracts
Public Affairs Information Service
Reader's Guide to Periodical Literature
Earlier HE 19.115
Discontinued v. 21/3

ED 1.10/2:   • Item 455-B-18 (MF)
GUIDE TO DEPARTMENT OF EDUCATION PROGRAMS. [Annual]

PURPOSE:– To provide information needed to begin the process of applying for funding under individual federal education programs. Describes programs, gives authorizing legislation, who may apply, and contact.

ED 1.11:v.nos.&nos.   • Item 466-A
RESOURCES IN EDUCATION. [Monthly]
Earlier HE 19.210
NOTE:– Class cancelled. See ED 1.310.

ED 1.12:date   • Item 455-A-2 (MF)
RIGHT TO READ. [Annual]
Subtitle varies.
Earlier HE 19.125

ED 1.13:date   • Item 455-A-5 (MF)
ADVISORY COMMITTEE ON ACCREDITATION AND INSTITUTIONAL ELIGIBILITY: ANNUAL REPORT. 1st–
Earlier HE 19.130

ED 1.14:nos. • Item 460-C (MF)
CAMPUS BOARD PROGRAMS REPORT (series).
Notification to Congress in tabular form of approval of awards to institutions participating in the College Work-Study, the Supplemental Education Opportunity Grants, and the National Direct Student Loan Programs, showing authorized expenditures, and the estimated number of students involved.

ED 1.15:CT • Item 461-A-7 (MF)
MONOGRAPHS ON CAREER EDUCATION (series).
[Irregular]
Earlier HE 19.111
Discontinued.

ED 1.16:date • Item 455-B-3
ADVISORY COUNCIL ON DEVELOPING INSTITUTIONS: ANNUAL REPORT.
Summarizes activities of the Council in its administration of the Title III Program, which provides Federal support to develop qualifying institutions to strengthen their academic programs for the benefit of such educationally disadvantaged as Black, Hispanics, American Indians, etc.
Discontinued.

ED 1.17:CT • Item 455-D
BIBLIOGRAPHIES AND LISTS OF PUBLICATIONS.
[Irregular]
Earlier HE 19.128

ED 1.17/2:v.nos.&nos. • Item 455-D
RESOURCES IN WOMEN'S EDUCATIONAL EQUALITY. v. 1– 1977– [Irregular] (Far West Laboratory for Educational Research and Development)
Earlier HE 19.128:W 84/2
Discontinued.

ED 1.17/3:CT • Item 455-D
VOCATIONAL INSTRUCTIONAL MATERIALS AVAILABLE FROM FEDERAL AGENCIES.
Earlier: Vocational Instructional Materials for Marketing and Distributive Education.
Discontinued.

ED 1.18:date • Item 460-C-2
LIBRARY PROGRAMS, HEA TITLE II-C, STRENGTHENING RESEARCH LIBRARY RESOURCES PROGRAM. [Annual]
Lists information on Higher Education Act, Title II-C, grants to research libraries, including a description of projects being funded.
Discontinued.

ED 1.18/2: • Item 460-C-3
LIBRARY PROGRAMS, LIBRARY LITERACY PROGRAMS, ABSTRACTS OF FUNDED PROJECTS. [Annual]
Contains abstracts of projects funded under the Library Literacy Program, Title 6 of the Library Services and Construction Act, under which grants are awarded to state and local libraries in support of literacy projects nationwide.
Discontinued.

ED 1.18/3: • Item 460-C-4 (MF)
LIBRARY PROGRAMS, LIBRARY SERVICES FOR INDIAN TRIBES AND HAWAIIAN NATIVES PROGRAM. [Annual]

PURPOSE– To provide information on the funding of the Library Services and Construction Act Title 5 grants to Indian tribes and to organizations primarily serving Hawaiian natives.
Discontinued.

ED 1.18/3-2:date • Item 460-C-4 (MF)
LIBRARY PROGRAMS, LIBRARY SERVICES FOR INDIAN TRIBES AND HAWAIIAN NATIVES PROGRAM, REVIEW OF PROGRAM ACTIVITIES.
See ED 1.18/13

ED 1.18/4:date • Item 460-C-2
LIBRARY PROGRAMS, HEA TITLE II-B. [Annual]
See ED 1.338

ED 1.18/5:date • Item 460-C-2
LIBRARY PROGRAMS, INTERLIBRARY COOPERATION AND RESOURCE SHARING. [Annual]
Discontinued.

ED 1.18/6:date • Item 460-C-2
LIBRARY PROGRAMS, LIBRARY PROGRAMS FOR THE HANDICAPPED.
Discontinued.

ED 1.18/7:date • Item 460-C-2
LIBRARY PROGRAMS, PUBLIC LIBRARY CONSTRUCTION: AN OVERVIEW AND ANALYSIS. [Annual]
Discontinued.

ED 1.18/8:date • Item 460-C-2
LIBRARY PROGRAMS, LIBRARY SERVICES FOR INDIVIDUALS WITH LIMITED ENGLISH PROFICIENCY. [Annual]
Discontinued.

ED 1.19: • Item 460-A-14
OPPORTUNITIES ABROAD FOR EDUCATORS. [Annual]
Former title: Opportunities Abroad for Teachers.
Later IA 1.29
Discontinued.

ED 1.20:date • Item 455-A-13
DIRECTORY OF COMMUNITY EDUCATION PROJECTS. [Annual]
Earlier HE 19.132/3
Discontinued.

ED 1.21:date • Item 455-A-15
NATIONAL ADVISORY COMMITTEE ON BLACK HIGHER EDUCATION AND BLACK COLLEGES AND UNIVERSITIES: ANNUAL REPORT. 1st– 1977–
Earlier HE 19.140
Discontinued.

ED 1.22:v.nos.&nos. • Item 461-C-1
INFORMATION FROM HEALTH RESOURCE CENTER. v. 1– 1981–
Former title: Information from Health/Closer Look.
Earlier HE 19.119
Discontinued.

ED 1.23:CT • Item 461
FUND FOR THE IMPROVEMENT OF POST-SECONDARY EDUCATION: PUBLICATIONS. (Office of Educational Research and Improvement)
Earlier HE 19.9

ED 1.23:R 31/date • Item 461
RESOURCES FOR CHANGE, A GUIDE TO PROJECTS. [Annual]
Report covers fiscal year.
Earlier HE 19.9:R31

ED 1.23/2 • Item 461
FIPSE, APPLICATION FOR GRANTS UNDER THE COMPREHENSIVE PROGRAM, (Fiscal Year). [Annual]
FIPSE = Fund for the Improvement of Post-Secondary Education.
Earlier titled: FIPSE, Comprehensive Program Information and Application Procedures.

ED 1.23/3: • Item 461
THE FUND FOR THE IMPROVEMENT POSTSECONDARY EDUCATION, INNOVATIVE PROJECTS FOR STUDENT COMMUNITY SERVICE. [Annual]
Discontinued.

ED 1.23/4: • Item 461
THE FUND FOR THE IMPROVEMENT OF SECONDARY EDUCATION, LECTURES PROGRAM INFORMATION AND APPLICATION MATERIALS. [Annual]
Discontinued.

ED 1.23/5: • Item 461
THE FUND FOR THE IMPROVEMENT OF POSTSECONDARY EDUCATION (FIPSE), DRUG PREVENTION PROGRAMS IN HIGHER EDUCATION, INFORMATION AND APPLICATION PROCEDURES. [Annual]
Discontinued.

ED 1.23/6:date • Item 461-B-12
IPEDS INTEGRATED POSTSECONDARY EDUCATION DATA SYSTEM, INSTITUTIONAL CHARACTERISTICS. [Annual]
A form to be used in an Educational Department survey to determine the institutional characteristics of postsecondary institutions in the U.S. and its outlying areas, complete with instructions.
Discontinued.

ED 1.23/7:date • Item 461
FIPSE, DRUG PREVENTION PROGRAMS IN HIGHER EDUCATION, INFORMATION AND APPLICATION PROCEDURES FOR: THE INSTITUTION WIDE PROGRAM COMPETITION. [Annual]
Discontinued.

ED 1.23/8:date • Item 461
FIPSE, DRUG PREVENTION PROGRAMS IN HIGHER EDUCATION, INFORMATION AND APPLICATION PROCEDURES FOR: THE SPECIFIC APPROACHES TO PREVENTION COMPETITION, INVITATIONAL PRIORITY; HIGHER EDUCATION CONSORTIA FOR DRUG PREVENTION. [Annual]
Discontinued.

ED 1.23/9 • Item 461
THE FUND FOR THE IMPROVEMENT OF POSTSECONDARY EDUCATION (FIPSE), SPECIAL FOCUS COMPETITION: COLLEGE-SCHOOL PARTNERSHIPS TO IMPROVE LEARNING OF ESSENTIAL ACADEMIC SUBJECTS, KINDERGARTEN THROUGH COLLEGE. [Annual]
Discontinued.

ED 1.23/10:date • Item 461
FIPSE EUROPEAN COMMUNITY/UNITED STATES OF AMERICA JOINT CONSORTIA FOR COOPERATION IN HIGHER EDUCATION AND VOCATIONAL EDUCATION. [Annual]

ED 1.23/11:date • Item 461-A-25
FIPSE, DISSEMINATING PROVEN REFORMS.

ED 1.24:date • Item 455-K (MF)
TELEPHONE DIRECTORY.

ED 1.24/2:date • Item 455-D-1 (MF)
OERI DIRECTORY OF COMPUTER TAPES. [Annual]
OERI = Office of Educational Research and Improvement
Contains brief, non-technical synopses of the major computer tapes available for public sales distribution for the Office of Educational Research and Development.

ED 1.25:CT
PRESS RELEASES. [Irregular]

ED 1.26:date • Item 455-L (MF)
OFFICE OF INSPECTOR GENERAL: SEMI-ANNUAL REPORT TO CONGRESS.

ED 1.26/2 • Item 455-L-1 (MF)
SEMIANNUAL REPORTS TO CONGRESS ON AUDIT FOLLOW-UP.

ED 1.27:CT • Item 455-A-18
TERACY: MEETING THE CHALLENGE (series). [Irregular]
Discontinued.

ED 1.29:date • Item 455-A-3 (MF)
CATALOG OF FEDERAL EDUCATION ASSISTANCE PROGRAM. [Biennial]

PURPOSE:– To provide an indexed guide to the Federal Government's programs offering education benefits to the American people.
ISSN 0097-7802
Earlier HE 19.127

ED 1.29/2:date • Item 455-A-3
OSEA PROGRAM BOOK. [Annual]
Discontinued.

ED 1.30:date • Item 460
DIRECTORY OF EDUCATION ASSOCIATIONS.
The first section covers in a single alphabet, the following types of association:

1. Associations of educators and other persons directly concerned with schools and colleges.
2. Community health, service, or social welfare groups that relate certain of their activities to school and college programs.
3. Historical, learned, professional, research and scientific organizations growing out of or related to school and college activities.
4. Library and museum associations.
5. Organizations sponsoring youth activities in schools and colleges or suppplementing school or college programs.

The other section lists:
6. College professional fraternities, honor societies, and recognized societies (national).
7. State education associations.
8. Foundations.
9. Religious education associations.
10. International education associations.

Subject Index
ISSN 0160-0508
Earlier HE 19.113
Discontinued 1981

ED 1.30/2: • **Item 461-B-10**
DIRECTORIES.

ED 1.30/3: • **Item 461-B-11 (MF)**
THE CHALLENGE NETWORK MEMBERSHIP DIRECTORY. [Irregular]
Membership listings are arranged alphabetically by state, then by city, and then by the name of the school or district within each city. Includes names, titles, and phone numbers of contact persons active in substance abuse education and prevention in U.S. schools.

ED 1.30/4:date • **Item 461-B-10 (MF)**
DIRECTORY OF SERVICES.

ED 1.30/5 • **Item 461-B-10 (MF)**
NIDRR PROGRAM DIRECTORY.

ED 1.31:date • **Item 441-I**
PROGRAMS FOR THE HANDICAPPED. 1965– [Bimonthly]

PURPOSE:– To present information on Department of Education programs for the handicapped. Incidental information relating to the handicapped is also included. Certain issues are devoted to abstracts of mental retardation research projects sponsored by the Federal Government.
Previous title: Mental Retardation Reports.
ISSN 0565-2804
Earlier HE 1.23/4

ED 1.32:date • **Item 461-B (MF)**
ANNUAL REPORT TO CONGRESS ON THE IMPLEMENTATION OF THE EDUCATION OF THE HANDICAPPED ACT.
Report made by the Office of Education to Congress pursuant to the Education for All Handicapped Children Act of 1975 (P.L. 94-142; 89 Stat. 795). Report covers activities of the established centers on educational media and materials for the handicapped at various institutions of higher education. State and local educational agencies, and other appropriate non-profit agencies. These centers are contracted to design, develop, and adapt instructional materials to allow handicapped persons to use new education technology.
Former title: Report to Congress on the Implementation of Public Law 94-142.
Earlier HE 19.117/2

ED 1.32/2:date • **Item 461-B**
HIGHER EDUCATION AND THE HANDICAPPED, RESOURCE DIRECTORY. [Annual]
Discontinued.

ED 1.32/3:date
HANDICAPPED CHILDREN'S EDUCATION PROGRAM, GRANT ANNOUNCEMENTS.

ED 1.32/4:date • **Item 461-B**
HANDICAPPED CHILDREN'S EARLY EDUCATION PROGRAM. [Annual]

ED 1.33:CT • **Item 461-D-6 (MF)**
NATIONAL CENTER FOR RESEARCH IN VOCATIONAL EDUCATION: PUBLICATIONS. [Irregular]

ED 1.33/2:date • **Item 461-D-6 (MF)**
BIANNUAL PROFESSIONAL DEVELOPMENT PROGRAM. [Semiannual]
Discontinued.

ED 1.33/2-2:date • **Item 461-D-6**
PROJECTS IN PROGRESS. [Annual]
Earlier ED 1.310/2
Discontinued.

ED 1.33/3: • **Item 461-D-8**
VOCATIONAL EDUCATOR. [Quarterly]
Issued by the National Center for Research in Vocational Education at the Ohio State University. Issues are expected to deal with such topics as the Dropout Network, basic skills vocational education, and adult literacy.
Discontinued.

ED 1.33/5:v.nos./nos. • **Item 461-D-8 (EL)**
A.L.L. POINTS BULLETIN. [Bimonthly]

ED 1.34:date • **Item 461-B-3**
FEDERAL ASSISTANCE FOR PROGRAMS SERVING THE HANDICAPPED.

PURPOSE:– To provide a directory of Federal programs serving the handicapped grouped by formula grants to states, project grants, direct payments, and nonfinancial assistance.

ED 1.35:date • **Item 444-N**
FINANCIAL ASSISTANCE BY GEOGRAPHIC AREA. [Annual]

PURPOSE:– To provide data on all of the Department's domestic assistance programs, with separate sections for each of the ten regions. Shows amounts obligated for specific recipients and identifies recipients and their locations.

ED 1.36:CT • **Item 460-A-14**
EDUCATION AROUND THE WORLD (series). [Irregular]
Earlier HE 19.109

ED 1.37:CT • **Item 455-M**
POSTERS AND CHARTS. [Irregular]

ED 1.37/2:CT
AUDIOVISUAL MATERIALS.

ED 1.38:date • **Item 455-F**
ACCREDITED POSTSECONDARY INSTITUTIONS AND PROGRAMS. [Annual]
Earlier HE 19.145

ED 1.39:date • **Item 461-C-3 (MF) (EL)**
ANNUAL EVALUATION REPORT.
Earlier HE 19.101/3

ED 1.40:date • **Item 455-B-4**
NATIONAL DIRECT STUDENT LOAN STATUS OF DEFAULT AS OF (date). [Annual]
Data, by institution, with totals by State and aggregate United States.

ED 1.40/2:date • **Item 455-B-5 (EL)**
NATIONAL DEFENSE AND DIRECT STUDENT LOAN PROGRAM, DIRECTORY OF DESIGNATED LOW-INCOME SCHOOLS FOR TEACHER CANCELLATION BENEFITS. [Annual]
Directory of schools, by States, that have a high concentration of students from low-income families for National Defense Student Loan and National Direct Student Loan cancellation benefits for the school year.

ED 1.40/3 • **Item 455-B-4 (MF)**
COL- (series). [Irregular]
Discontinued.

ED 1.40/4:date • **Item 455-B-4 (MF)**
STATUS OF PERKINS LOAN DEFAULT AS OF . . .

ED 1.40/5 • **Item 455-D-3 (EL)**
DIRECT LOANS NEWSLETTER.

ED 1.40/6: • **Item 455-N (EL)**
DIRECT LOANS BULLETIN.

ED 1.41:date • **Item 455-J**
PROGRESS OF EDUCATION IN THE UNITED STATES OF AMERICA.
Earlier HE 19.133
Discontinued.

ED 1.41/2:date/nos. • **Item 455-J-1**
EDUCATION UPDATE: STUDENT LIAISON OFFICER'S MONTHLY MEMO TO STUDENTS. [Monthly]
Memo from the student who serves as the official link for the Education Department with the student leaders of the nation's post- secondary learning institutions. Issues will deal with topics of interest to students.
Discontinued.

ED 1.42:date • **Item 455-D (MF)**
HIGHER EDUCATION OPPORTUNITIES FOR MINORITIES AND WOMEN. [Annual]
Former title: Selected List of Postsecondary Education Opportunities for Minorities and Women.
Earlier ED 1.2:P 84

ED 1.42/2:CT
PROJECT ON THE STATUS AND EDUCATION OF WOMEN, FIELD EVALUATION DRAFT. [Irregular]

ED 1.43:nos.
ENGLISH LANGUAGE PROFICIENCY STUDY (series).

ED 1.44:date • **Item 455-A-10**
WOMEN'S EDUCATIONAL EQUITY ACT PROGRAM, ANNUAL REPORT. 1st– 1976–
Earlier HE 19.136

ED 1.45:date • **Item 461-B-1**
COUNSELOR'S HANDBOOK, A FEDERAL STUDENT AID REFERENCE.
Earlier HE 19.108:St 9/4

ED 1.45/2:date • **Item 455-B-6**
PELL GRANT FORMULA, (year). [Annual]
Intended to help applicants understand how the Department determines which students receive a Pell Grant. Includes calculation of Student Aid Index for both dependent and independent students, case studies, and a tax table.
Discontinued.

ED 1.45/3:nos. • **Item 455-B-6**
P- (series). [Irregular]

P = Pell

ED 1.45/3-2:date • **Item 455-B-6**
PELL GRANT PAYMENT SCHEDULE. [Annual]
Discontinued.

ED 1.45/4:date • **Item 461-B-4 (EL)**
FEDERAL STUDENT FINANCIAL AID HANDBOOK. [Irregular]
Intended to help post secondary institutions administer the major Federal student financial aid programs authorized under Title IV of the Higher Education Act of 1965 and its amendments.
Earlier ED 1.8:F 49/2

ED 1.45/5:date • **Item 461-B-14**
THE EFC FORMULA BOOK, THE EXPECTED FAMILY CONTRIBUTION FOR FEDERAL STUDENT AID. [Annual]

ED 1.46:date
JUSTIFICATIONS OF APPROPRIATION ESTIMATES FOR COMMITTEES ON APPROPRIATIONS, FISCAL YEAR. [Annual]

ED 1.46/2:date
JUSTIFICATIONS OF APPROPRIATION ESTIMATES FOR COMMITTEES ON APPROPRIATIONS, SUPPLEMENTS AND RESCISSIONS. [Annual]
Internal, not sent to depository libraries.

ED 1.47: • **Item 455-B-8**
REGULATIONS, RULES, INSTRUCTIONS. [Irregular]

ED 1.48:v.nos.&nos.   • Item 455-B-9
REHAB BRIEF. v. 1–   [irregular]

ED 1.49:nos.   • Item 455-B-10
FOCUS. 1–   [Irregular]
    Issued by the National Clearinghouse for Bi-
lingual Education. Each issue is devoted to a
single topic.
    Later ED 1.49/2-2

ED 1.49/2:date/nos.   • Item 455-B-10
NEW FOCUS.
    Earlier ED 1.49/2-2

ED 1.49/2-2   • Item 455-B-10
FOCUS OCCASIONAL PAPERS IN BILINGUAL EDU-
CATION.

ED 1.49/3:v.nos.-nos.   • Item 455-B-10
WORKPLACE NETWORK NEWS. [Quarterly]
    Discontinued.

ED 1.50:date   • Item 455-B-7
NEW APPLICATION FOR GRANTS UNDER
RESEARCH IN EDUCATION OF THE HANDI-
CAPPED. [Annual]
    See ED 1.2

ED 1.50/2:date
APPLICATION FOR GRANTS UNDER POST SECOND-
ARY EDUCATION PROGRAMS FOR HANDI-
CAPPED PERSONS. [Annual]

ED 1.50/3:date
APPLICATION FOR GRANTS UNDER HANDICAPPED
CHILDREN'S EARLY EDUCATION PROGRAM
DEMONSTRATION AND AUXILIARY ACTIVITIES.
[Annual]

ED 1.51:date
APPLICATION FOR GRANTS UNDER INDIAN EDU-
CATION PROGRAM. [Annual]
    See ED 1.2

ED 1.52:date   • Item 455-B-7
APPLICATION FOR GRANTS UNDER ADULT INDIAN
EDUCATION PROGRAMS. [Annual]
    See ED 1.2

ED 1.53:date   • Item 455-B-7
APPLICATION FOR GRANTS UNDER STRENGTHEN-
ING RESEARCH LIBRARY RESOURCES
PROGRAM. [Annual]
    See ED 1.2

ED 1.53/2:date
APPLICATION FOR BASIC GRANTS UNDER LIBRARY
SERVICES FOR INDIAN TRIBES AND HAWAIIAN
PROGRAM. [Annual]

ED 1.54:date   • Item 455-B-7
APPLICATION FOR FULBRIGHT-HAYS TRAINING
GRANTS. [Annual]
    See ED 1.2

ED 1.55:date   • Item 455-B-7
CONTINUATION APPLICATION FOR GRANTS UNDER
TALENT SEARCH PROGRAM. [Annual]
    See ED 1.2

ED 1.56:date   • Item 455-B-7
APPLICATION FOR GRANTS UNDER TITLE VI OF
THE HIGHER EDUCATION ACT OF 1965, AS
AMENDED. [Annual]
    See ED 1.2

ED 1.57:date   • Item 455-B-7
APPLICATION FOR GRANTS UNDER TITLE VI OF
THE HIGHER EDUCATION ACT OF 1965, AS
AMENDED. [Annual]
    See ED 1.2

ED 1.59:date   • Item 455-B-7
APPLICATION FOR GRANTS UNDER FULBRIGHT-
HAYS FOREIGN CURRICULUM CONSULTANTS.
[Annual]
    See ED 1.2

ED 1.59/2:date
APPLICATION FOR SEMINARS ABROAD PROGRAM.
[Annual]

ED 1.60:date   • Item 455-B-7
CONTINUATION APPLICATION FOR GRANTS UNDER
SPECIAL SERVICES FOR DISADVANTAGE STU-

DENTS PROGRAM. [Annual]
    See ED 1.2

ED 1.61:date
INSTRUCTIONS AND APPLICATION FOR GRANTS
UNDER THE SPECIAL NEEDS PROGRAM. [An-
nual]

ED 1.61/2:date   • Item 455-B-7
INSTRUCTIONS AND APPLICATION FOR GRANTS
UNDER THE STRENGTHENING PROGRAM.
[Annual]
    See ED 1.2

ED 1.62:date   • Item 455-B-7
APPLICATION FOR GRANTS UNDER FULBRIGHT-
HAYS GROUP PROJECTS ABROAD. [Annual]

ED 1.63:date
APPLICATION FOR GRANTS UNDER THE
SECRETARY'S DISCRETIONARY PROGRAM. [An-
nual]

ED 1.64:date   • Item 455-B-7
APPLICATION FOR GRANTS UNDER THE
SECRETARY'S DISCRETIONARY PROGRAM FOR
MATHEMATICS, SCIENCE, COMPUTER LEARN-
ING AND CRITICAL FOREIGN LANGUAGES.
[Annual]
    See ED 1.2

ED 1.65:date   • Item 455-B-12
NUMERIC LIST OF EDUCATIONAL INSTITUTIONS.
[Annual]

ED 1.66:date   • Item 455-B-11
ALPHABETIC LIST OF LENDERS. [Annual]

ED 1.67:date   • Item 455-B-11
NUMERIC LIST OF LENDERS. [Annual]
    Discontinued.

ED 1.68:date   • Item 455-B-12
ALPHABETICAL LIST OF EDUCATIONAL INSTITU-
TIONS.
    Discontinued.

ED 1.69:date   • Item 455-B-7
APPLICATION FOR GRANTS UNDER UPWARD
BOUND PROGRAM. [Annual]

ED 1.69/2:date   • Item 455-B-7
APPLICATION DEVELOPMENT GUIDE UPWARD
BOUND PROGRAM FOR PROGRAM YEAR (date).
[Annual]

ED 1.70:date   • Item 455-B-13 (MF)
VERIFICATION CASE STUDIES. [Annual]
    Discontinued.

ED 1.70/2:date
APPLICATION FOR GRANTS UNDER THE ENDOW-
MENT GRANT PROGRAM. [Annual]

ED 1.70/3:date
APPLICATION FOR GRANTS UNDER THE COOPERA-
TIVE EDUCATION PROGRAM. [Annual]

ED 1.70/4:date
APPLICATION FOR GRANTS UNDER REHABILITA-
TION RESEARCH, FIELD INITIATED RESEARCH.
[Annual]

ED 1.71:date   • Item 461-B-5
NEWS DIGEST. [Quarterly]
    Non-depository.

ED 1.71/2   • Item 461-B-7
EAST CENTRAL COMMUNIQUE. [Quarterly]
    PURPOSE:– To present information on the
activities of the East Central Network for Curriculum Coordination in Vocational and Technical Education.

ED 1.71/3   • Item 461-B-8
NCBE FORUM. [Bimonthly]
    NCBE = National Clearinghouse for Bilingual
Education
    PURPOSE:– To provide information on cur-
rent affairs concerning the education of limited
English proficient persons.
    Discontinued.

ED 1.72   • Item 455-B-14
REQUEST FOR PROPOSAL (series). [Irregular]
    Request for proposals in connection with the
awarding of contracts by the Education Department on various education topics.

ED 1.73   • Item 455-B-7
FORMS. [Irregular]

ED 1.74   • Item 455-A-4 (MF)
WORK-STUDY REPORTS (series). [Irregular]
    Earlier HE 19.129

ED 1.74/2:nos.   • Item 455-B-4 (MF)
CB (series). [Irregular]

ED 1.75:CT   • Item 461-B-6
OERI ANNOUNCEMENTS (series). [Irregular]
    Each publication announces a particular event
related to Office activities, such as the awarding
of Library Resources grants.

ED 1.76   • Item 455-B-16 (EL)
GEN- (series). [Irregular]
    Contains general information on Student Fi-
nancial Assistance programs. One example is an
issue on the Higher Education Amendments of
1986, which make major changes in all student
aid programs authorized under the Higher Education Act of 1965.

ED 1.76/2   • Item 455-B-16 (EL)
ANN. (series)

ED 1.76/2-2   • Item 455-B-16 (EL)
P. (series)

ED 1.76/3   • Item 455-B-16 (MF)
SSIG AND SG. (series)

ED 1.76/2-4   • Item 455-B-16 (EL)
L. (series)

ED 1.77:v.nos./nos.   • Item 455-B-20 (EL)
THE CHALLENGE. [Bimonthly]
    Each issue deals with a different educational
challenge.

ED 1.79:   • Item 455-B-17
NARIC, DISABILITY RESEARCH RESOURCES. [Semi-
annual]
    NARIC = National Rehabilitation Information
Center
    A publication of the National Rehabilitation
Information Center, which isfunded by the Na-
tional Institute on Disability and Rehabilitation
Research ofthe Education Department. Presents
information on disability research resources.
    Discontinued.

ED 1.79/2:v.nos./nos.   • Item 455-B-17
NARIC QUARTERLY.
    NARIC = National Rehabilitation Information
Center.
    Discontinued.

ED 1.79/3:nos.   • Item 455-B-17
A.T. QUARTERLY.
    Discontinued.

ED 1.80:   • Item 455-B-21
WORKING PAPER (series).

ED 1.81:   • Item 455-B-23
THE CONGRESSIONAL METHODOLOGY. [Annual]
    PURPOSE– To present Congressionally man-
dated formulas fordetermining a student's family
contribution under Perkins Loans, Supplemental
Educational Opportunity Grants, and College
Work-Study as well as the Guaranteed Student
Loan Program.
    Earlier: The Family Contribution Formula (ED
1.2:F 21).
    Discontinued.

ED 1.82:   • Item 455-B-22
FISAP WORKSHOP. [Annual]
    FISAP = Fiscal Operations Report/Applica-
tion to Participate
    PURPOSE– To present information and mate-
rials for the FISAP workshop,including overheads
and handouts for trainees: FISAP Update or Session and Campus- Based Highlights Session.

ED 1.83 • Item 455-N (E)
ELECTRONIC PRODUCTS. [Irregular]

ED 1.84:nos. • Item 455-B-17 (MF)
DISABILITY STATISTICS REPORT (Series).

ED 1.84/2 • Item 455-B-28
DISABILITY STATISTICS ABSTRACT.

ED 1.85 • Item 455-J-1
AMERICA 2000. [Weekly]
Discontinued.

ED 1.85/2:v.nos.&nos. • Item 455-J-1 (EL)
GOALS 2000, COMMUNITY UPDATE.

ED 1.85/3:v.nos./nos. • Item 455-J-1
OSERS, NEWS IN PRINT.

ED 1.85/4:date • Item 455-J-2
GOALS 2000 A PROGRESS REPORT.
Discontinued.

ED 1.86:v.nos.&nos. • Item 455-B-21
NIDRR CONSENSUS STATEMENT.

ED 1.87:CT • Item 455-B-23
A PROGRESS TO THE SECRETARY OF EDUCATION
FROM THE PRESIDENT'S ADVISORY COMMIS-
SION ON EDUCATIONAL EXCELLENCE FOR HIS-
PANIC AMERICANS.
See Pr 42.8

ED 1.87/4:v.nos./nos. • Item 461-B-6
INSIDE EDITION.

ED 1.89:date/nos. • Item 455-D-2
WHITE HOUSE INITIATIVE ON HISTORICALLY BLACK
COLLEGES AND UNIVERSITIES, NEWSLETTER.

ED 1.89/2:date • Item 455-D-2 (MF)
ANNUAL REPORT, PRESIDENTS BOARD OF ADVI-
SORS ON HISTORICALLY BLACK COLLEGES
AND UNIVERSITIES.

ED 1.90: • Item 455-N (E)
ED INITIATIVES.

ED 1.92 • Item 455-D-4
FEDERAL SCHOOL CODE LIST. [Annual]

ED 1.92/2 • Item 455-D-5 (EL)
FEDERAL SCHOOL CODE . (Database)

NATIONAL CENTER FOR
EDUCATION STATISTICS
(1979–   )

CREATION AND AUTHORITY

The National Center for Education (HE 19.300)
was transferred to the Department of Education
pursuant to the Department of Education Organization Act (93 Stat. 668), approved on October
17, 1979.

INFORMATION

National Center For Education Statistics
Department of Education
1990 K St. NW
Washington, D.C. 20006
(202) 502-7300
Fax: (202) 502-7466
http://nces.ed.gov

ED 1.101:date
ANNUAL REPORT.

ED 1.102:CT • Item 461-A-1
GENERAL PUBLICATIONS. [Irregular]

ED 1.108:CT • Item 461-A-3
HANDBOOKS, MANUALS, GUIDES. [Irregular]
Earlier HE 19.308

ED 1.108/2:nos. • Item 460-A-23
COMMUNITY INFORMATION IN EDUCATION, HAND-
BOOKS. 1–   [Irregular]
Earlier HE 19.308/2
Discontinued.

ED 1.108/3:date • Item 460-A-88 (MF)
STATE EDUCATION AGENCY OPERATIONS, REV-
ENUES, EXPENDITURES, AND EMPLOYEES.
[Biennial]
Provides a baseline statistical description of
education agency functions and a limited set of
data to aid in the management and support of
State Education Agency functions.

ED 1.109:date • Item 461-A-12 (P) (EL)
CONDITION OF EDUCATION.
Earlier HE 19.314

ED 1.109/a • Item 461-A-12 (P) (EL)
CONDITION OF EDUCATION (separates).

ED 1.109/2:date • Item 461-A-12
EDUCATION INDICTORS. [Annual]
Discontinued.

ED 1.109/2-2:nos. • Item 461-A-24 (P) (EL)
FINDINGS FROM THE CONDITION OF EDUCATION.
(National Center for Education Statistics).

ED 1.110:date • Item 455-F
ENROLLMENTS AND PROGRAMS IN NON-
COLLEGIATE POSTSECONDARY SCHOOLS. [An-
nual]
Earlier HE 19.337/2
Discontinued 1978

ED 1.111:date • Item 461-A-16 (MF)
EDUCATION DIRECTORY, COLLEGES AND
UNIVERSITIES. [Annual]
Earlier HE 19.324

ED 1.111/2:date • Item 460-B-1
DIRECTORY OF PUBLIC ELEMENTARY AND
SECONDARY EDUCATION AGENCIES. [Annual]
Earlier: Education Directory, Local Education
Agencies.
Discontinued.

ED 1.111/3:date • Item 461-A-16
EDUCATION DIRECTORY, STATE EDUCATION
AGENCY OFFICES. [Annual]
Earlier HE 19.324/3
Discontinued.

ED 1.111/4:date • Item 461-A-21 (P) (EL)
DIRECTORY OF POSTSECONDARY INSTITUTIONS.
[Annual]

ED 1.112:date • Item 460-B-1
STATISTICS OF PUBLIC ELEMENTARY AND
SECONDARY DAY SCHOOLS. 1954–   [Annual]

PURPOSE:– To disseminate timely and useful data by State and organization level on enrollment, classroom teachers, and schoolhousing in
full-time public elementary and secondary day
schools.
Earlier HE 19.326
Discontinued.

ED 1.112/2:date • Item 460-B-1
PUBLIC ELEMENTARY AND SECONDARY EDUCA-
TION IN THE UNITED STATES.
Discontinued.

ED 1.112/3:date • Item 460-B-1
ESTIMATES OF LOCAL PUBLIC SCHOOL SYSTEM
FINANCES. [Annual]
Discontinued.

ED 1.112/4:date
STATISTICS OF PUBLIC SCHOOL SYSTEMS IN
TWENTY LARGEST U.S. CITIES. [Annual]

ED 1.112/5:date • Item 460-B-1 (MF)
PREPRIMARY ENROLLMENT. [Annual]
Earlier HE 19.327
Discontinued.

ED 1.113:date • Item 460-A-10
DIGEST OF EDUCATION STATISTICS. [Annual]
Later ED 1.326
Earlier HE 19.315

ED 1.114: • Item 461-A-17
BIBLIOGRAPHIES AND LISTS OF PUBLICATIONS.
Earlier HE 19.317

ED 1.115:CT • Item 455-F-1 (MF)
CONTRACTOR REPORTS (series). [Irregular]

ED 1.116:date • Item 460-A-52
FINANCIAL STATISTICS OF INSTITUTIONS OF
HIGHER EDUCATION. [Annual]
Provides State and national totals of various
financial data acquired from institutions of higher
education in the questionnaire, Financial Statis-
tics of Institutions of Higher Education.
At head of title: Higher Education
Report covers fiscal year.
ISSN 0148-9305
Earlier HE 19.316/2
Discontinued.

ED 1.116/2:date • Item 460-A-52
INSTITUTIONS OF HIGHER EDUCATION, INDEX BY
STATE AND CONGRESSIONAL DISTRICT.
[Annual]
Earlier HE 19.322
Discontinued.

ED 1.116/3: • Item 460-A-52
STATE HIGHER EDUCATION PROFILES. [Annual]
Discontinued.

ED 1.117:date • Item 460-A-54
EARNED DEGREES CONFERRED. [Annual]

PURPOSE:– To provide data on baccalaureate and higher degrees. Data on awards below
the bachelor's level are contained in companion
volume, Associate Degrees and Other Formal
Awards Below the Baccalaureate (HE 19.333).
Earlier HE 19.329

ED 1.118:nos. • Item 461-A-8
NATIONAL ASSESSMENT OF EDUCATION
PROGRESS: REPORTS. [Irregular]
Earlier HE 19.312
Discontinued.

ED 1.118/2:nos. • Item 461-A-8
NATIONAL ASSESSMENT OF EDUCATIONAL
PROGRESS PUBLICATIONS (numbered).
Discontinued.

ED 1.119:date • Item 460-A-22
REVENUES AND EXPENDITURES FOR PUBLIC AND
ELEMENTARY AND SECONDARY EDUCATION.
[Annual]
Information in this report is designed to meet
the general information need of educational re-
searchers and the more specialized needs of
personnel administering programs under P.L. 81-
874, School Assistance in Federally Affected
Areas, and P.L. 89-10, the Elementary and Sec-
ondary Education Act of 1965 (ESEA).
At head of tile: ELementary and Secondary
Education. Report covers fiscal year.
More detailed expenditure and revenue data
published in Statistics of State School Systems
(HE 19.318).
Title varies.
Earlier HE 19.313
Discontinued.

ED 1.120:date • Item 460-A-10 (EL)
PROJECTIONS OF EDUCATION STATISTICS. [Annual]
Earlier HE 19.320

ED 1.120/2 • Item 460-D (MF)
STATISTICAL ANALYSIS REPORT (series).
Discontinued.

ED 1.121:date • Item 461-A-15
COLLEGE COSTS, BASIC STUDENT CHARGES, 4-
YEAR INSTITUTIONS. [Annual]
Contains tables that present college costs
by State at nearly 2,000 public and private four-
year colleges.
Combined with ED 1.121/2 to form ED 1.121/
3

ED 1.121/2:date   • **Item 461-A-15**
COLLEGE COSTS, BASIC STUDENT CHARGES, 2-YEAR INSTITUTIONS. [Annual]
    Companion volume to ED 1.121 (above).
    Combined with ED 1.121 to form ED 1.121/3

ED 1.121/3:date   • **Item 461-A-15**
COLLEGE COSTS, BASIC STUDENT CHARGES, 2-YEAR AND 4-YEAR INSTITUTIONS. [Annual]
    Combines ED 1.121 and ED 1.121/2

ED 1.122:date   • **Item 460-A-15**
LIBRARY STATISTICS OF COLLEGES AND UNIVERSITIES.

    PURPOSE:– To present data covering basic statistics on the library collections, staffing, hours of assistance, salaries, wages for hourly staff, library loan transactions, and operational expenditures by function.
    Issued in two parts: Part A, Summary Data; Part B, Institutional Data.
    Also published in microfiche.
    Earlier HE 19.338
    Discontinued.

ED 1.122/2:date   • **Item 460-B-2**
STATISTICS OF PUBLIC LIBRARIES. [Quadrennial]
    Presents statistical data on public libraries by State and city, largely through tables. Includes library collections, staffing, expenditures, receipts, loan transactions, and physical facilities.
    Discontinued.v

ED 1.122/3:date   • **Item 460-A-15**
LIBRARY STATISTICS OF COLLEGES AND UNIVERSITIES. [Triennial]

ED 1.123:date   • **Item 461-A-18**
PARTICIPATION IN ADULT EDUCATION. [Triennial]

    PURPOSE:– To present data on characteristics of adults who participate in educational or learning activities.
    Earlier HE 19.302
    Discontinued.

ED 1.124:date   • **Item 460-A-54**
FALL ENROLLMENT COLLEGES AND UNIVERSITIES. [Annual]
    Beginning with the survey for 1958, the publication has been issued in two separate volumes. The first, Institutional Data, is issued in the Fall to provide an early publication of opening (Fall) enrollment data for individual institutions. A companion publication, Analytic Report, is issued several months later, providing more detailed analysis of the data collected.
    A preliminary analytic report is presented annually in the January issue of Higher Education. Data from this and other surveys on enrollment later appeared in Chapter 4 of the Biennial Survey of Education, Statistics on Higher Education: Faculty, Students and Degrees.
    The purpose of the early fall survey is to provide a count of resident and extension enrollments as soon as possible after the beginning of the fall semester or quarter. Only students enrolled in courses creditable toward a bachelor's or higher degrees are included. A more comprehensive survey of resident and extension enrollment; both degree-credit and nondegree credit, in the fall semester or quarter, is also conducted in odd-numbered years. Data are published in a separate publication, Resident, Extension, and other Enrollments in Institutions of Higher Education, also issued in the Circular Series.
    Former title: Fall Enrollment in Higher Education.
    Earlier HE 19.325
    Discontinued.

ED 1.125:nos.   • **Item 460-B-3**
FRSS REPORTS (numbered). [Irregular]
    FRSS = Fast Response Survey System
    Each Survey concerns a different subject.
    Discontinued.

ED 1.126:nos.   • **Item 461-A-22 (MF)**
NCES BULLETINS. [Irregular]
    Bulletins on miscellaneous topics pertaining to the work of the Center. One example is a bulletin on public school district policies and practices with regard to arts and humanities instruction.

ED 1.127:date   • **Item 460-B-4**
SURVEY OF COLLEGE GRADUATES. [Annual]
    Questionnaire to be completed by individual college graduates providing general information as well as information on fellowships and scholarships, loans, jobs. preparation to teach, and field of teaching.
    Discontinued.

ED 1.128:nos.
NCES ANNOUNCEMENTS.

ED 1.129:date   • **Item 461-A-19**
DIRECTORY OF LIBRARY NETWORKS AND COOPERATIVE LIBRARY ORGANIZATIONS. [Quinquennial]
    Discontinued.

ED 1.130   • **Item 461-A-20**
DIRECTORIES. [Irregular]

ED 1.131:date
INSTRUCTIONAL FACULTY SALARIES FOR ACADEMIC YEAR. [Annual]

ED 1.132   • **Item 455-F-3**
TRENDS IN EDUCATION. [Annual]
    Tables project trends in U. S. education for a 20 year period. Projections are for kindergarten through higher education and include enrollments, graduations, and earned degrees.
    Discontinued.

ED 1.132/2:   • **Item 455-F-4 (MF)**
TRENDS IN BACHELORS AND HIGHER DEGREES. [Annual]
    PURPOSE– To present data on bachelors, masters, doctors, and first-professional degrees by sex of recipient and field of study for aten year period. This is considered the definitive national source of data ondegree awards and is part of the Higher Education General Information Survey.

ED 1.133:v.nos./nos.   • **Item 461-A-23**
SPEEDE/EXPRESS NEWSLETTER. [Quarterly]

ED 1.134   • **Item 461-A-27 (E)**
ELECTRONIC PRODUCTS. (Misc)

ED 1.135   • **Item 461-A-29 (EL)**
PUBLIC LIBRARIES IN THE UNITED STATES. [Annual]

REHABILITATION SERVICES ADMINISTRATION (1979–   )

CREATION AND AUTHORITY

    The Rehabilitation Services Administration (HE 23.4100) was transferred to the Department of Education pursuant to the Department of Education Organization Act (93 Stat. 668), approved on October 17, 1979.

INFORMATION

Rehabilitation Services Administration
Department of Education
Rm. 3329-MES
400 Maryland Ave., SW
Washington, DC 20202-2551
(202) 205-5482
http://www.ed.gov/offices/osers/rsa/

ED 1.201:date
ANNUAL REPORT.
    Earlier HE 23.4101

ED 1.202:CT   • **Item 529**
GENERAL PUBLICATIONS. [Irregular]
    Earlier HE 23.4102

ED 1.208:CT   • **Item 529-B**
HANDBOOKS, MANUALS, GUIDES.
    Earlier HE 23.4108

ED 1.209:CT   • **Item 506-C-5**
BIBLIOGRAPHIES AND LISTS OF PUBLICATIONS. [Irregular]

ED 1.209/2:date   • **Item 506-C-5 (MF)**
CATALOG OF CAPTIONED FILMS FOR THE DEAF. [Annual]

ED 1.209/2-2:date   • **Item 506-C-5 (MF)**
CATALOG OF EDUCATIONAL CAPTIONED FILMS/VIDEOS FOR THE DEAF. [Annual]
    Earlier ED 1.2:D 34
    See ED 1.209/2

ED 1.209/2-3:date   • **Item 506-C-5**
CATALOG OF CAPTIONED FEATURE AND SPECIAL INTEREST FILMS AND VIDEOS FOR THE HEARING IMPAIRED. [Annual]

ED 1.210   • **Item 529-D (MF)**
ANNUAL REPORT TO THE PRESIDENT AND CONGRESS.
    Earlier HE 1.609

ED 1.211:v.nos.&nos.   • **Item 506-C-4 (P) (EL)**
AMERICAN REHABILITATION. [Quarterly]
    Indexed by: Index to U.S. Government Periodicals
    ISSN 0362-4048
    Earlier HE 1.612

ED 1.212:nos.
FOCUS ON SPECIAL EDUCATION LEGAL PRACTICES. [Quarterly]

ED 1.213:   • **Item 506-C-7**
OSERS NEWS IN PRINT. [Quarterly]
    OSERS = Office of Special Education and Rehabilitative Services
    PURPOSE– To present news in the area of special education andrehabilitative services, such as placement of handicapped students in public schools.
    Discontinued.

ED 1.214:date   • **Item 529-D-1 (MF)**
APPLICATION FOR NEW GRANTS UNDER CERTAIN DIRECT GRANT PROGRAMS. [Annual]

ED 1.215:date   • **Item 529-D-2 (MF) (EL)**
NIDRR PROGRAM DIRECTORY. [Annual]

ED 1.215/2   • **Item 529-D-3**
DISABILITY STATISTICS REPORT (series).

ED 1.215/3:nos.   • **Item 529-D-4**
DISABILITY FORUM REPORT (series).

ED 1.215/4:   • **Item 529-D-3 (EL)**
DISABILITY STATISTICS ABSTRACT.

EDUCATIONAL RESEARCH AND IMPROVEMENT CENTER
(1986–)

CREATION AND AUTHORITY

The National Institute of Education (HE 19.200) was transferred to the Department of Education pursuant to the Department of Education Organization Act ((3 Stat. 668), approved October 17, 1979. The Institute was renamed Center of Educational Research and Improvement by act of October 17, 1986 (100 Stat. 1597).

INFORMATION

Office of Educational Research
    and Improvement
U.S. Dept. of Education
555 New Jersey Ave. NW
Washington, DC 20208-5500
(202) 219-1385
Fax: (202) 219-1402
http://www.ed.gov/offices/oeri

ED 1.301:date
ANNUAL REPORT.
    Earlier HE 19.201

ED 1.301/2:nos.   • **Item 461-D-21**
ERIC (Educational Resources Information Center) ANNUAL REPORT.

ED 1.302:CT   • **Item 461-D-5**
GENERAL PUBLICATIONS. [Irregular]
    Earlier HE 19.202

ED 1.303/2:date   • **Item 455-G-11**
OERI BULLETIN. [Quarterly]
    Formerly: Education Research Bulletin
    Discontinued.

ED 1.303/3:nos.   • **Item 455-G-11**
NEW INFORMATION FROM THE OFFICE OF EDUCATIONAL RESEARCH AND IMPROVEMENT. [Bimonthly]
    Discontinued.

ED 1.303/4:v.nos./nos. • **Item 455-G-11 (P) (EL)**
THE LINK.

ED 1.308:CT   • **Item 455-G-4**
HANDBOOKS, MANUALS, GUIDES.
    Earlier HE 19.208

ED 1.308/2:nos.   • **Item 455-G-4**
EDUCATION RESEARCH CONSUMER GUIDE (series). [Irregular]

ED 1.309:CT   • **Item 461-A-8**
NATIONAL ASSESSMENT OF EDUCATIONAL PROGRESS [reports]. [Irregular]
    Earlier HE 19.312/2

ED 1.310:v.nos.&nos.   • **Item 466-A**
RESOURCES IN EDUCATION. v. 1–　1966–
[Monthly]
    The Educational Resources Information Center (ERIC) of the Office of Education publishes a monthly abstract journal, Research in Education, which announces newly funded Bureau of Research projects and recently completed research or research related reports of interest to the educational community. Reports and projects are abstracted and indexed by subject, author, or investigator, and responsible institution.

The monthly issues are cumulated annually and published in two volumes on a Project Resume Index and the other a Report Resume Index.

The ERIC is a nationwide information network consisting of central staff at the Office of Education and 19 clearinghouses, each of which focuses on a specific field of education.

Reports cited in Research in Education may be secured in microfiche or hard copy from ERIC Document Reproduction Service, National Cash Register Company, 4936 Fairmont Avenue, Bethesda, Maryland 20014.

Reports of research for the period 1956– 1965 may be found in the two-volume Office of Education Reports, 1956– 65, Resumes (OE-12029) and Indexes (OE-12028).

Cumulative index issued semiannual.
Continues: Research in Education (ISSN 0034-5229).
Earlier HE 19.210

ED 1.310/2:nos.   • **Item 466-A-3 (MF)**
EDUCATION DOCUMENTS ANNOUNCED IN RIE. [Irregular]

Consists of the actual documents, classified by ED accession numbers, that are announced in Resources in Education (ED 1.310).
Also published in microfiche.

ED 1.310/3:date   • **Item 466-A-1 (MF)**
THESAURUS OF ERIC DESCRIPTORS. 1st ed.–
[Irregular] (Educational Research Information Center)

Presents the definitive vocabulary for education. Contains alphabetical and rotated descriptor, a two-way hierarchical term display, descriptor groups, and descriptor group display.
Formerly sent under item 466-A
Also published in microfiche.
Non-depository.

ED 1.310/3-2:date
THESAURUS OF ERIC DESCRIPTORS, ALPHABETICAL DISPLAY.

ED 1.310/3-3:date
THESAURUS OF ERIC DESCRIPTORS, HIERARCHICAL DISPLAY.

ED 1.310/3-4:date
THESAURUS OF ERIC DESCRIPTORS, ROTATED DISPLAY.

ED 1.310/4:v.nos.&nos. • **Item 466-A-2 (MF)**
CURRENT INDEX OF JOURNALS IN EDUCATION. [Monthly] (Educational Research Information Center)
Indexes by Journal, Subject, and Author, current periodical literature in about 780 major education journals. Contains annotations with descriptors. A separate section title New Thesaurus Terms lists new descriptors that supplement those in Thesaurus of ERIC Descriptors (ED 1.310/3).
Formerly sent under item 466-A.
Also published in microfiche.

ED 1.310/5:date   • **Item 466-A-5**
SELECTED PAPERS IN SCHOOL FINANCE. [Annual]

ED 1.310/6   • **Item 466-A-7 (EL)**
ERIC DATABASE. (Online database)

ED 1.311:CT   • **Item 465-B-1 (MF)**
PROGRAM ON TEACHING AND LEARNING. [Irregular]
Includes reports on conferences dealing with the educational and occupational needs of groups such as American Indian, Hispanic, and white ethnic women.
Discontinued.

ED 1.312:CT   • **Item 461-D-5**
WOMEN'S STUDIES, MONOGRAPH SERIES. [Irregular]
    Earlier HE 19.220
    Discontinued.

ED 1.313:date   • **Item 465-B-2**
GRANTS FOR RESEARCH ON DESEGREGATION, FISCAL YEAR. [Annual]

PURPOSE:– To provide annual announcements of the current year's competition for grants for research on desegregation in elementary and secondary schools and in higher education educational institutions.
Discontinued.

ED 1.314:nos.   • **Item 455-G-10 (MF)**
VOCATIONAL EDUCATION STUDY PUBLICATIONS. [Annual] (numbered).
    Earlier HE 19.219
    Discontinued.

ED 1.315:date   • **Item 455-G-7 (MF)**
NATIONAL COUNCIL ON EDUCATIONAL RESEARCH: ANNUAL REPORT. 1–　1975–
    Earlier HE 19.214
    Discontinued.

ED 1.316:v.nos.&nos.   • **Item 465-B-3**
NAEP NEWSLETTER. [Quarterly]
    NAEP = National Assessment of Education Progress.
    Earlier HE 19.209/2
    Discontinued.

ED 1.317:CT   • **Item 455-G-6**
BIBLIOGRAPHIES AND LISTS OF PUBLICATIONS.
    Earlier HE 19.213

ED 1.317/2   • **Item 455-G-6**
RECENT PUBLICATIONS OF THE DEPARTMENT OF EDUCATION. [Quarterly]
    Discontinued.

ED 1.317/3   • **Item 455-G-6**
PERSPECTIVES IN READING RESEARCH.
    Discontinued.

ED 1.317/4   • **Item 455-G-6**
ADVANCES IN EDUCATION RESEARCH. [Semiannual]
    Discontinued.

ED 1.318:date
NIE INFORMATION. [Quarterly]
    Earlier HE 19.209

ED 1.319:level nos/book nos.   • **Item 461-D-7**
INDIAN READING SERIES. 1981–　[Irregular]
    Consists of Indian elementary school reading textbooks on such subjects as Indian schools, festivals, tales and legends.
    Published on various reading levels.
    Discontinued.

ED 1.320:CT
AUDIOVISUAL MATERIAL.

ED 1.321:date   • **Item 455-G-9**
FUNDING OPPORTUNITIES AT NIE, FY (year). [Annual]
    Earlier HE 19.216/2
    Discontinued.

ED 1.322:CT   • **Item 455-G-11**
RESEARCH IN BRIEF (series). [Irregular]
    Each single sheet issue may describe a different NIE educational resource, such as Resources in Computer Education, or may give findings on a particular educational subject.

ED 1.322/2:nos.   • **Item 455-G-11**
ISSUE BRIEF (series). [Irregular]

ED 1.322/3:CT   • **Item 455-G-11**
EDUCATION RESEARCH REPORT (series).
    Discontinued.

ED 1.323:   • **Item 466-A-4**
BEST OF ERIC.
    ERIC = Educational Resources Information Center.
    Discontinued.

ED 1.324:nos.   • **Item 461-D-5**
REQUEST FOR PROPOSAL, NIE-R- (series). [Irregular]

ED 1.325:date
COMPUTER EDUCATION, A CATALOG OF PROJECTS SPONSORED BY THE U.S. DEPARTMENT OF EDUCATION.

ED 1.326:date • Item 461-D-9
DIGEST OF EDUCATION STATISTICS. [Annual]
    PURPOSE:– To provide a compilation of significant material pertaining to American education, on topics such as schools, enrollments, teachers, graduates, educational attainment, finances, and Federal programs in the field of education in the United States.
    Earlier ED 1.113

ED 1.327:date • Item 461-D-5
YOUTH INDICATORS, TRENDS IN THE WELL-BEING OF AMERICAN YOUTH. [Annual]

ED 1.328:CT • Item 455-G-9 (MF)
SURVEY REPORT (series). [Irregular]

ED 1.328/2 • Item 455-G-9 (MF) (EL)
ANALYSIS REPORT (Series).

ED 1.328/3:CT • Item 455-G-9 (MF) (EL)
E.D. TABS (Series).

ED 1.328/4:CT • Item 455-G-11
STATISTICS IN BRIEF (Series).

ED 1.328/5:CT • Item 455-G-9 (MF) (EL)
STATISTICAL ANALYSIS REPORT (Series).

ED 1.328/6:CT • Item 455-G-9 (MF)
RESEARCH AND DEVELOPMENT REPORT (Series).

ED 1.328/7:CT • Item 455-G-11
TECHNICAL REPORT (Series).

ED 1.328/8:date • Item 455-G-11 (EL)
FEDERAL SUPPORT FOR EDUCATION (Fiscal Year).

ED 1.328/9 • Item 455-G-14 (MF)
METHODOLOGY REPORT (series).

ED 1.328/10:CT • Item 455-G-17
NATIONAL CENTER FOR EDUCATION STATISTICS, TECHNICAL/METHODOLOGY REPORT.

ED 1.328/11 • Item 455-G-18 (MF)
DESCRIPTIVE REPORT.

ED 1.328/12:date • Item 455-G-19 (P) (EL)
PUBLIC ELEMENTARY AND SECONDARY EDUCATION STATISTICS: SCHOOL YEAR. [Annual]

ED 1.328/13:nos • Item 455-G-20 (EL)
EDUCATION STATISTICS. [Quarterly]

ED 1.329:date • Item 461-D-5 (MF)
DROPOUT RATES IN THE UNITED STATES. [Annual]

ED 1.330:CT • Item 461-G
DIRECTORIES.

ED 1.330/2:date • Item 461-G-1
DIRECTORY OF ERIC RESOURCE COLLECTION. [Annual]

ED 1.331:v.nos./nos. • Item 455-G-11
THE ERIC REVIEW. [Quarterly]

ED 1.331/2:nos. • Item 455-G-11
ERIC DIGEST. [Irregular]

ED 1.332:CT • Item 455-N-1 (CD)
SCHOOLS AND SAFETY STAFFING SURVEY.
    Issued on CD-ROM

ED 1.333:date • Item 455-N-2 (E)
NATIONAL POSTSECONDARY STUDENT AID STUDY (NPSAS).
    Issued on CD-ROM.

ED 1.334:date • Item 455-N-3 (E)
HIGH SCHOOL AND BEYOND.
    Issued on CD-ROM.

ED 1.334/2:CT • Item 455-N-4 (E)
ELECTRONIC PRODUCTS. [Irregular]

ED 1.334/3:date • Item 455-N-5 (E)
PUBLIC LIBRARY DATA, [date].
    (Diskettes)

ED 1.334/4:date • Item 455-N-6 (CD)
INTEGRATED POSTSECONDARY EDUCATION DATA SYSTEM IPEDS. [Annual]
    Issued on CD-ROM.

ED 1.334/5 • Item 455-N-7 (CD)
NATIONAL HOUSEHOLD EDUCATION SURVEY. [Biennial]

ED 1.334/6 • Item 455-N-8 (CD)
SCHOOL DISTRICT DATA BOOK.

ED 1.335:v.nos./nos. • Item 455-G-11 (P) (EL)
NAEPFACTS. [Irregular]

ED 1.335/2 • Item 455-G-11
FOCUS ON NAEP.

ED 1.335/3 • Item 455-G-13
NAEP . . . TECHNICAL REPORT. [Biennial]

ED 1.335/4 • Item 461-G-2 (EL)
NAEP TRENDS IN ACADEMIC PROGRESS.

ED 1.336:CT • Item 455-G-12
NATIONAL CENTER FOR EDUCATION STATISTICS, EDUCATION POLICY ISSUES: STATISTICAL PERSPECTIVES (series).
    Discontinued.

ED 1.336/2: • Item 461-D-22
PERSPECTIVES ON EDUCATION POLICY RESEARCH.

ED 1.337:date • Item 455-G-15 (EL)
FIELD INITIATED STUDIES PROGRAM, ABSTRACTS OF FUNDED PROJECTS. [Annual]

ED 1.338 • Item 455-G-16 (MF)
LIBRARY CAREER TRAINING PROGRAM, ABSTRACTS OF FUNDED PROJECTS TITLE 2-B. [Annual]

ED 1.340:v.nos/nos. • Item 461-D-1
ENC UPDATE. (Eisenhower National Clearinghouse) [Triennial]

ED 1.340/2:v.nos/nos. • Item 461-D-11
ENC FOCUS. [Irregular]

ED 1.340/3:v.nos./nos. • Item 461-D-16 (CD)
ENC, EISENHOWER NATIONAL CLEARINGHOUSE, A COLLECTION OF CURRICULUM STANDARDS AND FRAMEWORK.

ED 1.341:CT • Item 461-D-12 (P) (EL)
INDICATOR OF THE MONTH (series).

ED 1.342:date • Item 461-D-13
LEARNING CONNECTIONS NEWSLETTER.

ED 1.343:date • Item 461-D-14
EARLY CHILDHOOD UPDATE.
    Discontinued 1999.

ED 1.343/2:date • Item 461-D-20
EARLY CHILDHOOD DIGEST. [Quarterly]

ED 1.344 • Item 461-D-15
POSTERS.

ED 1.345:v.nos./nos. • Item 416-D-17
OPEN WINDOW, THE NEWSLETTER OF THE NATIONAL LIBRARY OF EDUCATION.

ED 1.346:v.nos./nos. • Item 461-D-18
BRIEFS (National Center for Early Development & Learning. [Quarterly].

ED 1.346/2:v.nos./nos. • Item 461-D-19
FACT SHEET (National Center for Early Development & Learning).

ED 1.347 • Item 461-A-26 (EL)
INDICATORS OF SCHOOL CRIME AND SAFETY. [Annual]

ED 1.348 • Item 461-D-23 (EL)
THE VISION (THE NEWSLETTER OF SERVE). [Irregular]

ED 1.348/2 • Item 461-D-24
A SERVE SPECIAL REPORT. (Various topics)

ED 1.348/3 • Item 461-D-25
SERVE-GENERAL PUBLICATIONS.

OFFICE OF ELEMENTARY AND SECONDARY EDUCATION

INFORMATION

Office of Elementary and
    Secondary Education
400 Maryland Ave., SW
Washington, DC 20202
(202) 401-0113
Fax: (202) 205-0310
http://www.ed.gov/offices/OESE

ED 1.401:date
ANNUAL REPORT.

ED 1.402:CT • Item 461-H
GENERAL PUBLICATIONS.

ED 1.408:CT • Item 461-B-2
HANDBOOKS, MANUALS, GUIDES.

ED 1.409:v.nos./nos. • Item 461-B-13
THE OUTLOOK. [Quarterly]
    Discontinued.

ED 1.410 • Item 461-H-1 (MF)
APPLICATION FOR GRANTS, FORMULA GRANTS TO LOCAL EDUCATIONAL AGENCIES. [Annual]

ED 1.411:date • Item 461-H-2 (P) (EL)
WEEA EQUITY RESOURCE CENTER AT EDC CATALOG. [Annual]

PRESIDENTIAL SCHOLARS COMMISSION

INFORMATION

Presidential Scholars Commission
Room 5E223, Federal Office Building 6
400 Maryland Avenue, SW
Washington, D.C. 20202-3521
(202) 205-0676
http://www.ed.gov/offices/OIIA/Recognition/
    PSP/commission

ED 1.500 • Item 466-B
REPORTS AND PUBLICATIONS.

ED 1.501:date • Item 466-B
ANNUAL REPORT.

ED 1.502:CT • Item 466-B
GENERAL PUBLICATIONS.

ENVIRONMENTAL PROTECTION AGENCY
(1970–   )

CREATION AND AUTHORITY

The Environmental Protection Agency was established as an independent agency pursuant to Reorganization Plan 3 of 1970, effective December 2, 1970.

INFORMATION

Environmental Protection Agency
Ariel Rios Federal Building
1200 Pennsylvania Ave. NW
Washington, DC 20004
(202) 260-1000
Toll Free: (888) 372-8255
http://www.epa.gov

EP 1.1:date • Item 431-I-4 (MF)
ANNUAL REPORT. 1st–   1971–

EP 1.1/2:date • Item 431-I-44
ANNUAL REPORT OF THE ACTIVITIES OF THE EFFLUENT STANDARDS AND WATER QUALITY INFORMATION ADVISORY COMMITTEE.
Discontinued.v

EP 1.1/3:date
OFFICE OF RESEARCH AND DEVELOPMENT, REGION 1: ANNUAL REPORT.

EP 1.1/4:date • Item 431-J-3 (EL)
SUMMARY OF THE BUDGET. [Annual]

Summarizes the President's budget for the Agency in such areas as air and water quality, research and development, state and local grants, and construction grants.

EP 1.1/5:date • Item 431-K-13
OFFICE OF THE INSPECTOR GENERAL: SEMIANNUAL REPORT.

EP 1.1/5-2 • Item 431-K-17 (EL)
QUARTERLY REPORT.

EP 1.1/6:date • Item 431-I-70 (MF)
ORD ANNUAL REPORT. [Annual]

EP 1.1/7:date • Item 431-I-82 (MF)
ROD ANNUAL REPORT FY (Record of Division).

EP 1.1/8 • Item 431-K-14 (MF)
CLEAN LAKES PROGRAM, ANNUAL REPORT.

EP 1.1/9 • Item 431-K-16 (EL)
REPORT OF THE GOOD NEIGHBOR ENVIRONMENTAL BOARD TO THE PRESIDENT AND CONGRESS OF THE UNITED STATES. [Annual]

EP 1.2:CT • Item 431-I-1
GENERAL PUBLICATIONS.

EP 1.2:Ai 7/5/date • Item 431-I-1
DIRECTORY OF AIR QUALITY MONITORING SITES ACTIVE IN (year). 1972–   [Annual]
ISSN 0093-5476

EP 1.2:St 2/972 • Item 431-I-1
COMPENDIUM OF STATE AIR POLLUTION CONTROL AGENCIES, 1972. 1972. 368 p. il. (Office of Legislation, Division of Intergovernmental Relations)

EP 1.2/7:date • Item 431-I-39
EPA PUBLICATIONS BIBLIOGRAPHY. [Quarterly]

EP 1.3:v.nos.&nos. • Item 431-I-8
EPA BULLETIN. v. 1–   1971–   [Monthly]

EP 1.3/2 • Item 431-I-8
EPA CITIZENS' BULLETIN. v. 1–   1971–   [Irregular]

PURPOSE:– To provide a compilation of previously issued news releases reissued occasionally for interested citizens.

Issues for September 1971 and November 1971 were unnumbered.
Discontinued.

EP 1.3/3:CT • Item 431-I-11 (MF)
ENGINEERING BULLETIN (Series).

EP 1.3/4:CT • Item 431-I-81
EMERGING TECHNOLOGY BULLETIN (Series).

EP 1.3/5:v.nos./nos. • Item 431-I-11 (MF)
EPA INTERMITTENT BULLETIN. [Irregular]

EP 1.5:CT • Item 431-I-2
LAWS.
Discontinued.

EP 1.5:L 44 • Item 431-I-2
CURRENT LAWS, STATUTES AND EXECUTIVE ORDERS. January 1972. 997 p.

PURPOSE:– To provide current legal authority under which the Agency operates. It is designed for quick reference through the tabbed index system, and amended laws or additional statutes and executive orders can be readily inserted within the system.
Issued in looseleaf form.
Binders must be purchased separately.

EP 1.5/2:CT • Item 431-I-2
ENVIRONMENTAL LAW SERIES. [Irregular]

PURPOSE:– To provide background information on the various environmental laws.
Discontinued.

EP 1.5/3:CT • Item 431-I-25
LEGAL COMPILATION, STATUTES AND LEGISLATIVE HISTORY, EXECUTIVE ORDERS, REGULATIONS, GUIDELINES AND REPORTS. 1973–   [Irregular]

PURPOSE:– To provide in a single ready-reference work the legal authority by which EPA performs the statutory and regulatory functions which were transferred to the Agency from other Federal departments by Reorganization Plan No. 3 of 1970.

It is composed of seven chapters: General, Air, Water, Solid Waste, Pesticides, Radiation, and Noise. All of the chapters, except Solid Waste and Noise, are to be published in several volumes for ease in handling. The General chapter contains materials concerning EPA's creation, organization and structure, as well as general legislation which overlaps several of the other categories.
Discontinued.

EP 1.5/3-2:nos. • Item 431-I-25
SUPPLEMENT. v. 1–   1973–   [Irregular]
Discontinued.

EP 1.5/3-3:date • Item 431-I-25
INDEX. 1974–   [Annual]
Discontinued.

EP 1.5/4:date • Item 431-I-25
INDEX OF EPA LEGAL AUTHORITY STATUTES AND LEGISLATIVE HISTORY, EXECUTIVE ORDERS, REGULATIONS.
Discontinued.

EP 1.6:CT • Item 431-I-56
REGULATIONS, RULES, AND INSTRUCTIONS.

EP 1.6/2:CT • Item 431-I-53 (MF)
BACKGROUND DOCUMENT FOR [various products], NOISE EMISSIONS REGULATIONS. [Irregular]

EP 1.6/3:CT • Item 431-I-53 (MF)
NOISE EMISSION STANDARDS FOR CONSTRUCTION EQUIPMENT, BACKGROUND DOCUMENT FOR [various items]. [Irregular]
Discontinued.

EP 1.7:date
PRESS RELEASES.

EP 1.7/2:date
ENVIRONMENTAL NEWS. Dec. 1970–   [Irregular]

PURPOSE:– To provide the press and other communications media with a steady and official source of information and data about program activities, projects, and other actions which EPA has initiated or is contemplating.

EP 1.7/3:date
SAFETY MANAGEMENT INFORMATION. – Jan. 1974. [Irregular] (EPA Safety Management Staff)

EP 1.7/4:nos.
ENVIRONMENT NEWS. [Monthly] (New England Regional Office, Boston, Massachusetts)
ISSN 0364-1317

EP 1.7/5:date
EPA TECHNICAL NOTES. [Irregular] (Public Affairs Office)

EP 1.7/6:date
EPAlert, TO ALERT YOU TO IMPORTANT EVENTS. [Biweekly] (Region 3, Public Affairs Division, 6th and Walnut Streets, Philadelphia, Pennsylvania 19106)
ISSN 0364-1309

EP 1.7/7:date
ENVIRONMENTAL NEWS SUMMARY.

EP 1.7/8:date
REGION 2 REPORT.

EP 1.7/9:date
ENVIRONMENTAL NEWS. (Corvallis Environmental Research Laboratory)

EP 1.8:CT • Item 431-K
HANDBOOKS, MANUALS, GUIDES.
Formerly distributed to depository libraries under item 431-I-5.
Discontinued.

EP 1.8/2:trans.nos. • Item 431-J-7
ASSISTANCE ADMINISTRATION MANUAL. [Irregular] (Includes basic manual plus supplemental material for an indefinite period)
Discontinued.

EP 1.8/3:CT • Item 431-K-1 (MF)
DEVELOPMENT DOCUMENT FOR EFFLUENT LIMITATIONS GUIDELINES AND NEW SOURCE PERFORMANCE STANDARDS FOR [various industries]. [Irregular] (Effluent Guidelines Division, Office of Water and Hazardous Materials)

PURPOSE:– To present the findings of extensive study for the purpose of developing effluent limitations guidelines for individual industries. Effluent limitations guidelines recommended set forth the degree of effluent reduction attainable through the applications of the best practicable control technology currently available.
Formerly distributed to depository libraries under item 431-I-5.
Discontinued.

EP 1.8/4:CT • Item 431-K-2 (MF)
ECONOMIC ANALYSIS OF PROPOSED EFFLUENT GUIDELINES. (series). [Irregular]
Formerly distributed to depository libraries under item 431-I-5
Discontinued.

EP 1.8/4-2:CT • Item 431-K-3 (MF)
ECONOMIC ANALYSIS OF PRETREATMENT STANDARDS SERIES.
Discontinued.

EP 1.8/4-3:CT • Item 431-K-3 (MF)
PROPOSED EFFLUENT GUIDELINES. [Irregular]
Discontinued.

EP 1.8/4-4:CT • Item 431-K-8 (MF)
INDUSTRIAL EFFLUENT STANDARDS. [Irregular]
Describes industrial effluent standards, such as new sources performance standards.
Discontinued.

EP 1.8/5:CT
BACKGROUND INFORMATION FOR STANDARDS OF PERFORMANCE. [Irregular]

EP 1.8/6:nos.   • **Item 431-I-50 (MF)**
OAQPS GUIDELINE SERIES. [Irregular] (Office of Air Quality Planning and Standards)

EP 1.8/7:nos.   • **Item 431-I-41 (MF)**
STATIONARY SOURCE ENFORCEMENT SERIES.

EP 1.8/8:CT   • **Item 431-I-52 (MF)**
WATER QUALITY MANAGEMENT GUIDANCE.
[Irregular]
    Discontinued.

EP 1.8/9:date   • **Item 431-I-70**
EXTRAMURAL PROGRAM GUIDE. [Annual] (Office of Research and Development)
    Former title: Program Guide.
    ISSN 0362-8876

EP 1.8/10:CT   • **Item 431-K-3**
ECONOMIC IMPACT ANALYSIS OF ALTERNATIVE POLLUTION CONTROL TECHNOLOGIES (series).
[Irregular]
    Discontinued.

EP 1.8/11:date   • **Item 431-K**
OPERATING YEAR GUIDANCE. [Annual]
    Discontinued.

EP 1.8/12:CT   • **Item 431-K (MF)**
WORKING FOR CLEAN WATER (series). [Irregular]

    PURPOSE:– To provide an information program for advisory groups.
    Discontinued.

EP 1.8/13   • **Item 431-K**
ACCESS EPA. [Annual]

EP 1.9:date
PROJECT REGISTER, PROJECTS APPROVED, MONTHLY SUMMARY.

    Earlier I 67.16/2

EP 1.9/2:date   • **Item 607-E**
PROJECT REGISTER, WASTE WATER TREATMENT CONSTRUCTION GRANTS. [Annual]
    List Projects approved under sec. 8 of the Federal Water Pollution Control Act (Public Law 84-660), as amended, and sec. 3 of the Public Works Acceleration Act (Public Law 87-658).
    Discontinued.

EP 1.10:CT   • **Item 431-I-6 (MF)**
ADDRESSES.

EP 1.11:date   • **Item 431-I-3**
COMPREHENSIVE STUDIES OF SOLID WASTE MANAGEMENT, ANNUAL REPORT. 1969–
    Earlier HE 20.1402:C 73.
    Discontinued.

EP 1.12:date   • **Item 431-I-22 (MF)**
TELEPHONE DIRECTORY. [Quarterly]

EP 1.12/2:date
OFFICE OF ADMINISTRATION AND RESOURCES MANAGEMENT, RESEARCH TRIANGLE PARK, N.C.: TELEPHONE DIRECTORY.

EP 1.12/3   • **Item 431-I-22 (MF)**
INFORMATION RESOURCES DIRECTORY.

EP 1.13:date
SOUTHWESTERN RADIOLOGICAL HEALTH LABORATORY: MONTHLY ACTIVITIES REPORT.

EP 1.14:date
WESTERN ENVIRONMENTAL RESEARCH LABORATORY: MONTHLY ACTIVITIES REPORT.

EP 1.14/2:date
WESTERN ENVIRONMENTAL RESEARCH LABORATORY: ANNUAL REPORT.

EP 1.15:date
NO NONSENSE.

EP 1.16:nos.   • **Item 473-A-1**
WATER POLLUTION CONTROL RESEARCH SERIES.
[Irregular]

    PURPOSE:– To describe the results and progress in the control and abatement of pollution in our Nation's waters. They provide a central source of information on the research, development, and demonstration activities in the water research program of the Environmental Protection Agency, through inhouse research and grants and contracts with Federal, State, and local agencies, research institutions, and industrial organizations.

EP 1.16/2:CT   • **Item 473-A-1**
CONFERENCE IN MATTERS OF POLLUTION OF NAVIGABLE WATERS, PROCEEDINGS. [Irregular]
    Title varies.

EP 1.17:nos.   • **Item 431-I-7 (MF)**
SOLID WASTE MANAGEMENT SERIES, SW.
    Consolidates HE 20.1408, HE 20.1409, EP 3.2, EP 3.5, EP 3.6, and EP 3.10.

    EP 1.17:58.25   • **Item 431-I-7**
    AVAILABLE INFORMATION MATERIALS. 1971–
    (Technical Information Staff)
    ISSN 0362-6601

EP 1.17/2:CT   • **Item 473-D-1**
REDUCING WASTE AT ITS SOURCE (series).
[Irregular]
    Discontinued

EP 1.17/3:v.nos.&nos.   • **Item 473-D-2**
SOLID WASTE MANAGEMENT MONTHLY ABSTRACTS BULLETIN. v. 1–   1973–

    Bibliography is arranged in categories corresponding to the various administrative, engineering, and operations phases of solid waste management.
    Annual subject and author index issued separately.
    Supersedes Accession Bulletin, Solid Waste Information Retrieval System.
    ISSN 0145-1235.
    Discontinued.

EP 1.17/4:date   • **Item 431-I-7**
SOLID WASTE NEWS BRIEF. (Municipal Environmental Research Laboratory)
    Discontinued.

EP 1.17/5:date   • **Item 431-I-7 (EL)**
REUSABLE NEWS. [Quarterly]

EP 1.17/6:date   • **Item 431-I-83 (MF)**
INNOVATIVE TREATMENT TECHNOLOGIES. [Annual]

EP 1.17/7   • **Item 431-J-17**
RECYCLING UPDATE. [Quarterly]

EP 1.17/8:nos   • **Item 431-J-20**
BUY-RECYCLED SERIES.

EP 1.18:v.nos.&nos.   • **Item 487-A-7**
ACCESSION BULLETIN, SOLID WASTE INFORMATION RETRIEVAL SYSTEM. v. 1–   1970–
[Monthly]
    Discontinued.

    PURPOSE:– To show both what is being published in the world literature pertaining to solid waste management and being abstracted for input into the Solid waste Information Retrieval System, covering the period 1964 to present.
    Earlier EP 3.3/2

EP 1.19:date
PACIFIC NORTHWEST ENVIRONMENTAL RESEARCH LABORATORY: QUARTERLY PROGRESS REPORT.
    – 1973. (National Environmental Research Center, Corvallis, Oregon)

    Published by the Water Quality Office (EP 2.22) prior to the July-September 1971 issue.
    Former title: Pacific Northwest Water Laboratory: Quarterly Progress Report.
    ISSN 0145-1103

EP 1.20
ENVIRONMENTAL INPUT. [Biweekly] Region VII, Kansas City, Missouri. Admin.

EP 1.21:CT   • **Item 431-I-9**
BIBLIOGRAPHIES AND LISTS OF PUBLICATIONS.

EP 1.21/2:date
MONTHLY TRANSLATIONS LIST AND CURRENT CONTENTS. (Translation Services Division)

    No longer published.

EP 1.21/3:date
CURRENT AWARENESS OF TRANSLATIONS.
[Monthly]

EP 1.21/4:nos.   • **Item 431-I-34**
SUMMARIES OF FOREIGN GOVERNMENT ENVIRONMENTAL REPORTS. 1–   [Monthly]
    Discontinued.

    ISSN 0094-3142

EP 1.21/5:nos.   • **Item 431-I-42 (MF)**
AIR POLLUTION ASPECTS OF EMISSION SOURCES: [various subjects], A BIBLIOGRAPHY WITH ABSTRACTS. [Irregular] (Air Pollution Technical Information Center)

    PURPOSE:– To report information of general interest in the field of air pollution. Abstracts arranged by subjects, with author and subject indexes.
    Earlier publications classified in AP- (series) (EP 4.9).
    Discontinued.

EP 1.21/6:date
ORD PUBLICATIONS SUMMARY. 1975– 1976. [Quarterly] (Technical Information Division, Office of Monitoring and Technical Support, Office of Research and Development)

    PURPOSE:– To notify the public of reports available from the Office of Research and Development. The ORD Publications Summary contains abstracts of new reports, bibliographical citations in report number order, alphabetical title listing, alphabetical performing organization index (the firm or laboratory or office who actually performed the work), personal author index. All indexes are referenced to the report number. The source of where the report can be purchased, either GPO or NTIS, is cited in the bibliographical citation.
    ORD reports are classified EP 1.23

EP 1.21/6-2:date   • **Item 431-I-39**
ORD PUBLICATIONS ANNOUNCEMENT. [Quarterly] (Office of Research and Development)

EP 1.21/7:date   • **Item 431-I-39**
EPA REPORTS BIBLIOGRAPHY QUARTERLY. (Library Systems Branch)

    ISSN 0360-2265

EP 1.21/7-2:date　　　• Item 431-I-39
EPA CUMULATIVE BIBLIOGRAPHY.

EP 1.21/7-3:date　　　• Item 431-I-39
PUBLICATIONS, A QUARTERLY GUIDE.

EP 1.21/8:nos.
AIR POLLUTION TECHNICAL PUBLICATIONS OF THE U.S. ENVIRONMENTAL PROTECTION AGENCY, QUARTERLY BULLETIN. 1–　1975–

　　Earlier EP 1.21:Ai 7

EP 1.21/9:date　　　• Item 431-I-68 (MF)
RESEARCH REPORTS, NATIONAL ENVIRONMENTAL RESEARCH CENTER, LAS VEGAS [list].

EP 1.21/10:date　　　• Item 431-I-9
ONLINE LITERATURE SEARCHING AND DATABASES. [Annual]

EP 1.22:nos.
ALASKA WATER LABORATORY, COLLEGE, ALASKA: REPORTS.

EP 1.22/2:date
ALASKA WATER LABORATORY QUARTERLY RESEARCH REPORTS.

　　Beginning July 1972, the Office of Research & Monitoring, now Office of Research & Development (ORD), research reports were grouped into series. These series were established to facilitate further development and application of environmental technology and previous groupings were eliminated to improve technology transfer and provide for maximum interface with related fields. Following establishment of these ORD-wide series all existing series designations, such as the Water Pollution Control Research Series, were discontinued.
　　In conjunction with the new ORD series designations, a report numbering system for all ORD research reports was also established. This numbering system is keyed to the report series assigned to the report and the following is a description of the system, including identifying report cover colors, which are also series related. This series identification pertains to all reports issued after July 1972.
　　Beginning July 1973, an Agency-wide numbering system (EPA-6nn/n-73-xxx) superseded the former ORD numbering system (EPA-Rn-73-xxx). This Agency-wide system is a direct extension of the former ORD system. All ORD reports are still classified into one of the various series.
　　For a listing of the series, see Indexed Bibliography of Office of Research and Development Reports (EP 1.21:In 2) and also ORD Publications Summary (EP 1.21/6).

EP 1.23:nos.　　　• Item 431-I-11 (MF)
ECOLOGICAL RESEARCH, 600/3- (series). [Irregular] (Office of Research and Development)

　　PURPOSE:– To describe research on the effects of pollution on humans, plant and animal species, and materials. Problems are assessed for their long and short-term influences. Investigations include formation, transport, and pathway studies to determine the fate of pollutants and their effects. This work provides the technical basis for setting standards to minimize undesirable changes in living organisms in the aquatic, terrestrial and atmospheric environments.
　　Formerly designated EPA-R3- (series).

EP 1.23/2:nos.　　　• Item 431-I-12 (MF)
ENVIRONMENTAL PROTECTION TECHNOLOGY, 600/2- (series). [Irregular] (Office of Research and Development)

　　PURPOSE:– To describe research performed to develop and demonstrate instrumentation, equipment and methodology to repair or prevent environmental degradation from point and non-point sources of pollution. This work provides the new or improved technology required for the control and treatment of pollution sources to meet environmental quality standards.
　　Formerly designated EPA-R2- (series).

EP 1.23/3:nos.　　　• Item 431-I-19 (MF)
SOCIOECONOMIC ENVIRONMENTAL STUDIES, 600/4- (series). [Irregular] (Office of Research and Development)

　　PURPOSE:– To describe research on the socioeconomic impact of environmental problems. This covers recycling and other recovery operations with emphasis on monetary incentives. The non-scientific realms of legal systems, cultural values, and business systems are involved. Because of their interdisciplinary scope, system evaluations and environmental management reports are included in this series.
　　Formerly designated EPA-R5- (series).

EP 1.23/4:nos.　　　• Item 431-I-23
ENVIRONMENTAL HEALTH EFFECTS RESEARCH, 600/1- (series). [Irregular] (Office of Research and Development)

　　PURPOSE:– To describe projects and studies relating to the tolerances of man for unhealthful substances or conditions. This work is generally assessed from a medical viewpoint, including physiological or psychological studies. In addition to toxicology and other medical specialties, study areas include biomedical instrumentation and health research techniques utilizing animals, but always with intended application to human health measures.
　　Formerly designated EPA-R1- (series).

EP 1.23/5:nos.　　　• Item 431-I-24 (MF)
ENVIRONMENTAL MONITORING, 600/4– (series). [Irregular] (Office of Research and Development)

　　PURPOSE:– To describe research conducted to develop new or improved methods and instrumentation for the identification and quantification of environmental pollutants at the lowest conceivable significant concentrations. It also includes studies to determine the ambient concentrations of pollutants in the environment and/or the variance of pollutants as a function of time or meteorological factors.
　　Formerly designated EPA-R4- (series).

EP 1.23/5:600/4-75-001　　　• Item 431-I-24
DIRECTORY OF EPA, STATE, AND LOCAL ENVIRONMENTAL ACTIVITIES. 1974. 384 p. il.

　　PURPOSE:– To present descriptions of Federal environmental quality monitoring programs and related State and local programs. Serves as a reference source for statistics on and descriptions of monitoring efforts on a State-by-State basis. The directory covers air and water quality, interstate water carrier supplies, pesticides, radiation, noise, and solid waste.

EP 1.23/5-2:date　　　• Item 431-I-24 (MF)
NATIONAL PERFORMANCE AUDIT PROGRAM, AMBIENT AIR AUDITS OF ANALYTICAL PROFICIENCY. [Annual]

EP 1.23/5-3:date　　　• Item 431-I-24 (MF)
PRECISION AND ACCURACY ASSESSMENTS FOR STATE AND LOCAL AIR MONITORING NETWORKS. [Annual]

EP 1.23/5-4:date　　　• Item 431-I-24
ACID PRECIPITATION IN NORTH AMERICA: ANNUAL DATA SUMMARY FROM ACID DEPOSITION SYSTEM DATA BASE. [Annual]

EP 1.23/6:nos.　　　• Item 431-J (MF)
MISCELLANEOUS SERIES, 600/9- (series). [Irregular] (Office of Research and Development)

　　Publications in this series are those not applicable to any of the other series published by ORD.

EP 1.23/6-2:date　　　• Item 431-J (MF)
EPA RESEARCH PROGRAM, ANNUAL REPORT.

EP 1.23/7:nos.　　　• Item 431-J-11
SCIENTIFIC AND TECHNICAL ASSESSMENTS REPORTS, 600/6- (series). [Irregular] (Office of Research and Development)

　　PURPOSE:– To described available scientific and technical knowledge on major pollutants that would be helpful in regulatory decision making or assessments of a major area of completed study. The series is used to present objective evaluations of existing knowledge– evaluations that point out the extent to which it is definitive, the validity of the data on which it is based, and the uncertainties and gaps that may exist. (Most of the reports are multimedia in scope and focus on single media only to the extent warranted.)

EP 1.23/8:nos.　　　• Item 431-I-62 (MF)
INTERAGENCY ENERGY-ENVIRONMENT RESEARCH AND DEVELOPMENT PROGRAM REPORTS. 600/7-(series) [Irregular]

EP 1.23/9:nos.　　　• Item 431-K-12 (MF)
EPA SPECIAL REPORTS. 1–　[Irregular] (EPA 600/8-[nos.])

EP 1.23/10:nos.　　　• Item 431-J-15
ENVIRONMENTAL TECHNOLOGY PARTNERSHIPS (series).

EP 1.24:v.nos.&nos.
EPA LOG, WEEKLY LOG OF SIGNIFICANT EVENTS.

EP 1.25:date
OIL POLLUTION RESEARCH NEWSLETTER. – March 1972. [Irregular] (Edison Water Quality Research Laboratory, National Environmental Research Center, Edison, New Jersey 08817)

EP 1.25/2:v.nos.&nos.　　　• Item 431-I-62
OIL POLLUTION ABSTRACTS. 1– 7.　– 1980. [Quarterly]

　　Formerly entitled Oil Pollution Report, and issued as part of EP 1.23/8.

EP 1.26:CT
POLICIES AND TRENDS IN MUNICIPAL WASTE TREATMENT (series). 1972–　[Irregular]

EP 1.27:v.nos.&nos.
YOUTH ADVISORY BOARD NEWSLETTER. [Irregular]

EP 1.28/5:date
REGION V PUBLIC REPORT. [Monthly] (Office of Public Affairs, Region V, Environmental Protection Agency, Chicago, Illinois)

　　Superseded by Environment Midwest (EP 1.28/7).

EP 1.28/6:date　　　• Item 431-I-36
ENVIRONMENT MIDWEST, TOGETHER. [Annual]

EP 1.28/7:date　　　• Item 431-I-43
ENVIRONMENTAL MIDWEST. [Monthly] (EPA, Public Affairs Office– Region V, 230 S. Dearborn, Chicago, Illinois 60604)

　　Supersedes Region V Public Report (EP 1.28/5).
　　Discontinued with Dec. 14, 1981 issue.
　　ISSN 0364-2151

EP 1.29:CT
WATER QUALITY STANDARDS SUMMARY [for various States] (series). 1972–　[Irregular]

EP 1.29/2:CT　　　• Item 431-I-14 (MF)
WATER QUALITY STANDARDS CRITERIA DIGEST, COMPILATION OF FEDERAL/STATE CRITERIA ON [various subjects]. 1972–　[Irregular]

　　PURPOSE:– To provide the general public as well as Federal, State, and local officials with a digest of Federal/State criteria or standards on various subjects connected with water quality.

EP 1.29/3:CT　　　• Item 431-I-14
AMBIENT WATER QUALITY CRITERIA FOR [various chemicals]. [Irregular]

　　Series is planned for the publication of 65 reports on various chemicals, each report on an individual chemical. at completion of the publication of the 65 reports, series is to be discontinued.

EP 1.30:date • Item 431-I-15
NOISE FACTS DIGEST. (Office of Noise Abatement and Control)

EP 1.31:date • Item 431-I-37
JOURNAL HOLDINGS REPORT. 1st–   1971– [Annual] (Library Systems Branch)

PURPOSE:– To provide a list of journal holdings of all Environmental Protection Agency libraries and the Library, Illinois Institute for Environmental Quality.

EP 1.32:date • Item 431-I-17 (MF)
EXPRO, LISTING OF EXTRAMURAL PROJECTS TO BE FUNDED IN FISCAL YEAR. [Annual] (Office of Research and Monitoring)

EP 1.33:date • Item 431-I-16
STATE AIR PROGRAMS, DIGEST, FISCAL YEAR (date). [Annual] (Division of Intergovernmental Relations, Office of Legislation)

EP 1.34:date • Item 431-I-20
LIFE– PASS IT ON, PRESIDENT'S ENVIRONMENTAL MERIT AWARDS PROGRAM.

Earlier EP 1.2:L 62

EP 1.34/2:nos.
LIFE– PASS IT ON, PAO- (series). 1–   (Environmental Protection Agency, Rocky Mountain Prairie Region, Box 2999, Denver, Colorado 80201)

EP 1.35:date • Item 431-I-32 (MF)
QUARTERLY AWARDS LISTING GRANTS ASSISTANCE PROGRAMS. (Grants Administration Division, Office of Administration)

Arranged by State, gives municipality, type of program, title, project director or community representative, grant number, type of grant, date of award, and amount of grant.

EP 1.35/2:nos. • Item 431-I-32
STATE AND LOCAL GRANT AWARDS. (Grants Administration Division) (EPA-GAD- 2)

EP 1.36:date
INSIDE EPA, PUBLICATION FOR EMPLOYEES.

EP 1.37:date
COASTAL POLLUTION RESEARCH HIGHLIGHTS. [Irregular] (Pacific Northwest Environmental Research Laboratory, Corvallis, Oregon 97330)

EP 1.37/2:nos.
PNERL WORKING PAPERS. [Irregular] (Pacific Northwest Environmental Research Laboratory)

EP 1.37/3:date
POLLUTANT IDENTIFICATION RESEARCH HIGHLIGHTS. [Irregular] (Southeast Environmental Research Laboratory)

EP 1.38:nos.
EPA ORDERS.

EP 1.39:date
QUARTERLY CALENDAR OF ENVIRONMENTAL MEETINGS. 1973–

EP 1.40:date
MONTHLY STATUS REPORT.

EP 1.41:date
INVENTORY OF INTERSTATE CARRIER WATER SUPPLY SYSTEMS. [Annual] (Water Supply Division)

PURPOSE:– To provide a listing of those water supply systems certified annually by the Regional Administrators of the Environmental Protection Agency which supply water to interstate carriers.

EP 1.42:date • Item 431-I-26
ENVIRONMENTAL FACTS. [Irregular]

Individual two-page facts sheets contain information on one phase of environment, such as energy, transportation controls, land use, and water.

EP 1.42/2 • Item 431-J-14 (MF) (EL)
ENVIRONMENTAL FACT SHEET.

EP 1.43:date • Item 431-I-33 (MF)
CLEAN WATER, REPORT TO CONGRESS (year). 1st– 1972–   [Annual]

Report submitted to Congress pursuant to Section 516(a) of the Federal Water Pollution Control Act. Reports for 1973 and subsequent years also contain information on water quality and sewage flow reduction as required by Sections 104(a)(5) and 104(o)(2) of the Federal Water Pollution Control Act.

EP 1.43/2:CT • Item 431-I-33 (MF)
GROUND WATER ISSUE.

Earlier EP 1.2:G 91

EP 1.44:date • Item 431-I-27
ENVIRONMENTAL STUDIES DIVISION, FY (year) PROGRAM. (Washington Environmental Research Center, Office of Research and Development).

EP 1.45:nos. • Item 431-I-28 (MF)
COMPREHENSIVE PLANNING SERIES. 1–   1973– [Irregular]

EP 1.46:date
NATIONAL ENVIRONMENTAL RESEARCH CENTER, RESEARCH TRIANGLE PARK, NORTH CAROLINA: ANNUAL REPORT.

EP 1.46/2:date
ENVIRONMENTAL RESEARCH IN (year). 1st– 1972–   [Annual] (National Environmental Research Center, Cincinnati, Ohio 45268)

The research program of the National Environmental Research Center in Cincinnati, Ohio, is directed toward solving major environmental problems of wastewater management and treatment, drinking water, solid wastes, toxicants from automobile exhaust and other sources, industrial and hazardous waste management and control, radioactivity emissions from nuclear power plants, and methods development and quality assurance.

EP 1.46/3:date
NATIONAL ENVIRONMENTAL RESEARCH CENTER, LAS VEGAS: QUARTERLY ACTIVITIES REPORT. (Office of Research and Development)

EP 1.46/4:date
GROSSE ILE LABORATORY: QUARTERLY REPORT.

EP 1.46/5:date • Item 431-I-57
INDUSTRIAL ENVIRONMENTAL RESEARCH LABORATORY: ANNUAL REPORT. (Research Triangle Park)

Formerly Control Systems Laboratory.

EP 1.46/5-2:date • Item 431-I-57
INDUSTRIAL ENVIRONMENTAL RESEARCH LABORATORY: (year) RESEARCH REVIEW. [Annual]

EP 1.46/6:date
ENVIRONMENTAL RESEARCH LABORATORY, DULUTH: QUARTERLY REPORT.

EP 1.46/7:date • Item 431-L-1
MUNICIPAL ENVIRONMENTAL RESEARCH LABORATORY: QUARTERLY REPORT.

EP 1.46/7-2:date • Item 431-L-1
MUNICIPAL ENVIRONMENTAL RESEARCH LABORATORY: REPORT OF PROGRESS. 1979– [Annual]

EP 1.46/8:v.nos.&nos. • Item 431-I-57
FGD [Flue Gas Desulfurization] QUARTERLY REPORT. v. 1–   [Quarterly]

EP 1.47:date • Item 431-I-29
NATIONAL AIR MONITORING PROGRAM: AIR QUALITY AND EMISSION TRENDS, ANNUAL REPORT.

EP 1.48:CT • Item 431-J-12
POSTERS. [Irregular]

EP 1.48/2:CT
AUDIOVISUAL MATERIALS.

EP 1.49:CT
NEWS OF ENVIRONMENTAL RESEARCH IN CINCINNATI.

EP 1.50:nos. • Item 431-I-30
UNITED STATES LPPSD TECHNICAL INFORMATION EXCHANGE DOCUMENTS. 1–   1973– [Irregular]
    Later ER 1.16

EP 1.51:nos.
SURVEILLANCE AND ANALYSIS DIVISION, REGION 9, SAN FRANCISCO, CALIFORNIA: TECHNICAL REPORTS.

EP 1.51/2:nos.
ANNAPOLIS FIELD OFFICE, MIDDLE ATLANTIC REGION 3, PHILADELPHIA, PA.: TECHNICAL REPORTS. 1–   [Irregular]

EP 1.51/3:nos.
SURVEILLANCE AND ANALYSIS DIVISION, REGION 8, DENVER COLORADO, TECHNICAL SUPPORT BRANCH: SA/TSB-1-(series). [Irregular]

EP 1.51/4:nos.
SURVEILLANCE AND ANALYSIS DIVISION, REGION 8: TECHNICAL INVESTIGATIONS BRANCH, SA/TIB- (series).

EP 1.51/5:nos.
DATA REPORT (series). 1–   [Irregular]

EP 1.51/6:nos.
SURVEILLANCE AND ANALYSIS DIVISION, REGION 10: WORKING PAPERS. [Irregular]

EP 1.52:date • Item 431-I-59
STATE AIR POLLUTION IMPLEMENTATION PLAN PROGRESS REPORT. 1973–   [Semiannual] (Office of Air and Waste Management, Office of Air Quality Planning and Standards)

EP 1.53:date • Item 431-J-4 (MF)
AIR QUALITY DATA, (date) QUARTER STATISTICS. 1974– 1978. [Quarterly & Annual] (Monitoring and Data Analysis Division)

PURPOSE:– To serve its users as a statistical summary report on ambient air quality which is submitted to EPA from air monitoring operations of State, local and Federal networks. It is organized with a separate section for each one of the six criteria pollutants. The format employed provides both parametric and non-parametric indices of air quality. The number of observations, the minimum and maximum value measured for the period of record, and the odd deciles plus the 95th and 99th percentiles are presented to describe the distribution of observed values at each site reported. Arithmetic and geometric means and standard deviations are also provided to give the reader some measure of central tendency and dispersion. Each summary line is preceded by the Air Quality Control Region within which the sampling site is located, the name of the city or county and the three digit site number. Codes are used to indicate the type of agency responsible for the laboratory analysis and the type of surveillance being conducted. The reports are confined to statistical summaries of reported data available at the time of publication. They do not present any type of trends analysis or interpretation of the data and its relationship to the National Ambient Air Quality Standards.

EP 1.53/2:CT • Item 431-I-76 (MF)
AIR QUALITY CRITERIA (series). [Irregular]

PURPOSE:– To present highly technical reports on specific air pollutants, covering physical and chemical properties, monitoring and measurement, environmental sources, effects on ecosystems and on human health.

EP 1.54:date
LIFECYCLE. [Monthly]

EP 1.55:CT
NATIONAL EMISSIONS INVENTORY OF SOURCES OF EMISSIONS.

EP 1.56:nos. • Item 431-I-73
MONTHLY LISTING OF AWARDS FOR CONSTRUCTION GRANTS FOR WASTEWATER TREATMENT WORKS. [Monthly] (Grants Administration Division)

PURPOSE:– To list all wastewater treatment facilities awards issued under Public Law 92-500. The awards are listed by State and information includes applicant identification, grant number, grant tile, award date, aware amount, grant step such as one-planning, two- design, three-construction, description of facility to be constructed and other data.
The March 1974 issue (PB 23130) provides a base listing of all grants awarded under Public Law 92-500. Beginning with the April 1974 issue (PB 231300-01) the listings contain awards for one month only and are numbered in sequence.
Also available in microfiche (24x).

EP 1.56/2:date
PROJECT REGISTER, WASTEWATER TREATMENT CONSTRUCTION GRANTS. – June 1973. [Monthly]

Superseded by Wastewater Treatment Construction Grants Data Base (EP 1.56).

EP 1.56/3:nos.
STATE MUNICIPAL PROJECT PRIORITY LISTS, GRANTS ASSISTANCE PROGRAMS.

EP 1.56/4:date • Item 431-L-5 (MF)
STATE PRIORITY LISTS FOR CONSTRUCTION GRANTS FOR WASTEWATER TREATMENT WORKS, FISCAL YEAR (date). [Annual]

PURPOSE:– To provide grant information for municipal wastewater treatment works projects assigned priority by the States and planned for funding by the Environmental Protection Agency.

EP 1.57:CT
FINAL ENVIRONMENTAL IMPACT STATEMENT FOR PROPOSED WASTE TREATMENT FACILITIES [Various Locations].

EP 1.57/2 • Item 431-I-55 (MF)
FINAL ENVIRONMENTAL IMPACT STATEMENT FOR WASTE TREATMENT FACIILITIES [Various Locations].

EP 1.57/3:CT • Item 431-I-55 (MF)
FINAL ENVIRONMENTAL IMPACT STATEMENTS.

EP 1.57/4:CT • Item 431-I-55 (MF)
DRAFT ENVIRONMENTAL IMPACT STATEMENTS.

EP 1.57/5:CT • Item 431-I-55
STANDARDS SUPPORT AND ENVIRONMENTAL IMPACT STATEMENTS. [Irregular]

EP 1.57/6:CT • Item 431-I-55 (MF)
DRAFT ENVIRONMENTAL STATUS REPORT.

EP 1.58:nos.
IMPLEMENTATION PLAN REVIEW FOR [various States] AS REQUIRED BY THE ENERGY SUPPLY AND ENVIRONMENTAL COORDINATION ACT.

EP 1.59:date • Item 431-I-40 (MF)
MONITORING AND AIR QUALITY TRENDS REPORT. 1971– [Annual] (Monitoring and Data Analysis Division)

PURPOSE:– To present an annual summary of nationwide status with respect to the National Ambient Air Quality Standards. Measurements for the following criteria pollutants are summarized: suspended particulate matter, sulfur dioxide, carbon monoxide, total oxidants and ozone and nitrogen dioxide. Appendices include the following statistics for individual monitoring stations: annual means and their ratios to annual standards, where applicable plus maximum short term concentrations and the number of violations, where a short term standard is exceeded.
Where representative data permit, nationwide

trends over the preceeding five years are analyzed. Special topics may also be included discussing studies of non-criteria pollutants, summaries of pollutant emissions, and the role of meteorological factors in transporting and dispersing pollutants.

EP 1.60:date
SOUTHEAST ENVIRONMENTAL RESEARCH LABORATORY: QUARTERLY SUMMARY.

EP 1.61:CT
EVALUATION OF [various States] WATER SUPPLY PROGRAM.

EP 1.62:date • Item 431-I-51 (MF)
COST OF CLEAN AIR. [Annual]

Report submitted by the Administrator to the Congress in compliance with Public Law 91-604. Earlier FS 1.35

EP 1.63:v.nos.
COLLECTION OF LEGAL OPINIONS.

EP 1.64:date • Item 431-I-49 (MF)
NATIONAL EMISSIONS REPORT. [Annual] (Office of Air and Waste Management, Office of Air Quality Planning and Standards, Research Triangle Park, North Carolina 27711)

EP 1.65:date • Item 431-I-54
SEMI-ANNUAL LIST OF REPORTS PREPARED FOR OR BY THE OFFICE OF TOXIC SUBSTANCES.

EP 1.66:v.nos. • Item 431-I-58
DECISIONS OF THE ADMINISTRATOR AND DECISIONS OF THE GENERAL COUNSEL. v. 1– 1974– [Irregular]

v. 1. September 1974– December 1975.

EP 1.67:v.nos.&nos. • Item 431-I-66
EPA JOURNAL. v. 1– 1975– [Quarterly]

Indexed by: Index to U.S. Government Periodicals.
ISSN 0145-1189

EP 1.67/a:CT • Item 431-I-66
EPA JOURNAL REPRINT. [Irregular]

EP 1.67/2:date • Item 431-J-5
EPA UPDATE. [Biweekly]

Provides factual, current information about Agency actions, programs, and policies. Published in newsletter format.

EP 1.68:nos. • Item 431-I-63
INTERAGENCY WORKING GROUP ON MEDICAL RADIATION: FEDERAL GUIDANCE REPORTS. 1– [Irregular]

EP 1.69:date • Item 431-I-64
ANNUAL REPORT TO CONGRESS ON ADMINISTRATION OF THE MARINE PROTECTION RESEARCH AND SANCTUARIES ACT OF 1972.

Earlier: Ocean Dumping in the United States.

EP 1.70:nos. • Item 431-I-65 (MF)
NOTICES OF JUDGMENT UNDER THE FEDERAL INSECTICIDE, FUNGICIDE, AND RODENTICIDE ACT. [Irregular]

EP 1.71:date • Item 431-I-67
WATER QUALITY MANAGEMENT BULLETIN. [Monthly]
Former title: 208 Bulletin.
Discontinued with the March 1980 issue.
ISSN 0146-3039

EP 1.72:nos.
LAKE MICHIGAN COOLING WATER STUDIES PANEL: REPORTS.

EP 1.73:nos. • Item 431-I-69 (MF)
FEDERAL NOISE PROGRAM REPORTS. 1– [Irregular]

EP 1.73/2:CT • Item 431-I-74
FOREIGN NOISE RESEARCH (series). [Irregular]

PURPOSE:– To report on results of noise research in foreign countries, covering such subjects as aviation, surface transportation, machinery and construction equipment.

EP 1.73/3:CT • Item 431-I-75
FEDERAL NOISE RESEARCH IN (various subjects). [Irregular]

PURPOSE:– To present reports of results of Federally sponsored noise control research on noise effects, surface transportation, machinery, construction and aircraft noise.

EP 1.74:CT • Item 431-I-71
DECISION SERIES. [Irregular]

PURPOSE:– To present the key issues and findings of the Interagency Energy/Environmental Research and Development program in a format conducive to efficient information transfer.

EP 1.75:CT • Item 431-I-72
WATER QUALITY MANAGEMENT ACCOMPLISHMENTS, COMPENDIUMS. 1– 1977–

PURPOSE:– To provide samples of solutions that Water Quality Management agencies have developed to deal with water quality problems.

EP 1.76:v.nos.&nos. • Item 856-E-2
102 MONITOR, ENVIRONMENTAL IMPACT STATEMENTS. v. 1– 11. 1970– 1981. [Monthly]

PURPOSE:– To provide abstracts of environmental impact statements and legislation of federal agencies concerning proposed projects of interest. Also includes articles on such subjects as international treaties, State environmental legislation, and NEPA Court decisions, along with a listing of EPA comments on impact statements.
Prior to v. 7, no. 11 (January 1978) issued by the Council on Environmental Quality (PrEx 14.10).

EP 1.77:date • Item 431-L
ENVIRONMENTAL PROGRAM ADMINISTRATORS. 1st– 1977– [Annual]

PURPOSE:– To facilitate and improve interstate cooperation and intergovernmental communications by providing a list of State officials and their areas of responsibility.
ISSN 0099-2275
Earlier EP 1.2:Ad 6

EP 1.78:nos. • Item 431-L-3 (MF)
TECHNICAL REPORTS. [Irregular] (Office of Water Supply)

EP 1.79:date • Item 431-L-2 (MF)
TOXIC SUBSTANCES CONTROL ACT, REPORT TO CONGRESS FOR FISCAL YEAR (date). 1st– 1977– [Annual]

Annual report submitted to Congress pursuant to the Toxic Substances Control Act. Includes summary of major problems encountered, and recommendations for additional legislation. Also contains list of substances with testing recommendations.
Former title: Administration of the Toxic Substances Control Act.
ISSN 0161-9780.

EP 1.79/2:nos. • Item 431-L-8
TOXICS INTEGRATION INFORMATION SERIES. 1st ed.– 1979– [Irregular]

Includes publications on various topics related to the coordination and integration of toxic substances programs policies, activities, and information on the various Federal agencies, public interest groups, industries and States.

DIRECTORY OF FEDERAL COORDINATIVE GROUPS FOR TOXIC SUBSTANCES.

1st ed. June 1979. 79-004
2nd ed. March 1980. 80-008

EP 1.79/3:CT • Item 431-L-8 (MF)
TOXICS INTEGRATION POLICY SERIES. [Irregular]

EP 1.79/4:date   • Item 431-L-15
REPORT OF INTERAGENCY SUBSTANCES DATA
COMMISSION. [Annual]

EP 1.80:date   • Item 431-I-77
ANNUAL CONFERENCE ON ADVANCED POLLUTION
CONTROL FOR THE METAL FINISHING INDUS-
TRY. 1st–   1978–

PURPOSE:– To present proceedings of the
Conference containing regulatory presentations,
as well as research and development presentations, by parties actively conducting research
and development programs. Covers air, water,
and solid waste problems associated with the
metal finishing industry.

EP 1.81:date   • Item 431-K-5
RESEARCH HIGHLIGHTS. 1977–   [Annual] (Office
of Research and Development)

Contains short articles on EPA's research to
educate the public and improve the environment
on such topics as Three Mile Island, Acid Rain,
Coastal Environment, and the Chesapeake Bay.

EP 1.81/2:date   • Item 431-K-4
RESEARCH OUTLOOK. [Annual]

PURPOSE:– To project research plans over a
five-year period for satisfying short-term regulatory requirements and anticipating future environmental problems in such areas as toxic substances, air and water quality, wastewaters and
spills, drinking water, etc.

EP 1.82:date   • Item 431-L-4 (MF)
TASK FORCE ON ENVIRONMENTAL CANCER AND
HEART AND LUNG DISEASES: ANNUAL REPORT
TO CONGRESS. 1st–   1978–

PURPOSE:– To outline the problems and
progress made by the Task Force in studying the
relationship between environmental pollution, and
human cancer and heart and lung diseases.

EP 1.83:date   • Item 431-I-80 (MF)
ANNUAL RESEARCH SYMPOSIUM. (Solid and
Hazardous Waste Research Division)

EP 1.84:date   • Item 431-L-6
WOMEN/CONSUMER CALENDAR OF EVENTS.
[Irregular]

PURPOSE:– To provide information on the
location, date, and theme of conferences and
meetings to be held by women/consumer associations and organizations.

EP 1.85:date   • Item 431-L-7
EPA ANNUAL REPORT TO POLLUTION ENGINEERS.

PURPOSE:– To provide pollution engineers
with an annual summary of Agency activities and
future plans for the control, reduction, and elimination of environmental pollution.

EP 1.86:date   • Item 431-I-79
STATE-EPA AGREEMENTS, ANNUAL REPORT.

PURPOSE:– To address the current status of
agreements which will help the Agency and the
States to integrate related environmental programs and manage personnel and grant resources
more effectively.

EP 1.87:CT   • Item 431-L-9
ENVIRONMENTAL QUALITY PROFILES (various
States). [Annual]

Individual reports of Alaska, Idaho, Oregon,
and Washington. Each report discusses progress
in environmental preservation, addresses some
of the problems and issues faced by the people
of those States, and identifies some solutions to
the problems and issues.

EP 1.87/2:date   • Item 431-L-14
ENVIRONMENTAL QUALITY PROFILE, PACIFIC
NORTHWEST REGION. [Annual]
Reports on environmental quality of the Pa-

cific Northwest Region in terms of air and water
quality, solid waste and hazardous substances
disposal, etc.

EP 1.88:letters-nos.   • Item 431-L-10 (MF)
CHESAPEAKE BAY PROGRAM (series). [Annual]

Series of highly-technical reports that identifies and resolves some of the Chesapeake Bay's
water quality problems, including such topics as
toxics, submerged aquatic vegetation,
euthrophication, environmental management, etc.

EP 1.89:CT   • Item 431-L-11 (MF)
RESEARCH SUMMARY (series). [Irregular]

Each issue describes a major area of the
Agency's research and development program such
as industrial wastewater, controlling hazardous
wastes, and its Chesapeake Bay program.

EP 1.89/2:nos.   • Item 431-L-12 (MF)
PROJECT SUMMARY (series).

EP 1.89/3   • Item 431-L-16
TEST METHOD (series). [Irregular]

EP 1.89/4:nos.   • Item 431-L-16 (MF)
SITE (Superfund Innovative Technology Evaluation)
(Series)

EP 1.89/4-2:nos.   • Item 431-L-16 (MF)
SITE (Superfund Innovative Technology Evaluation)
DEMONSTRATION BULLETIN.

EP 1.89/4-3   • Item 431-L-16 (MF)
SITE (Superfund Innovative Technology Evaluation)
TECHNOLOGY DEMONSTRATION SUMMARY.

EP 1.89/4-4   • Item 431-L-17 (MF)
THE SUPERFUND INNOVATIVE TECHNOLOGY
EVALUATION PROGRAM, ANNUAL REPORT TO
CONGRESS.

EP 1.89/5   • Item 431-L-16 (MF)
SUPERFUND EMERGENCY RESPONSE ACTIONS,
A SUMMARY OF FEDERALLY-FUNDED REMOV-
ALS, ANNUAL REPORT.

EP 1.90:date   • Item 431-K-6
RESEARCH AND DEVELOPMENT: PUBLIC AWARE-
NESS/PARTICIPATION SUPPORT PLAN, FISCAL
YEAR (date). [Annual]

EP 1.91:date
WATER QUALITY MANAGEMENT FIVE YEAR STRAT-
EGY FY-BASELINE. [Irregular]
Earlier EP 1.2:W 29/53

EP 1.92:date   • Item 431-K-7
QUARTERLY PROGRESS REPORT, NATIONWIDE
URBAN RUNOFF PROGRAM. [Quarterly]

PURPOSE:– To summarize the progress and
status of the Program, which functions to assess
urban runoff and to support regional, State, and
local program participants.

EP 1.93:date   • Item 431-J-1
ENVIRONMENTAL OUTLOOK. [Annual]

PURPOSE:– To project the environmental outlook in terms of scenarios for both high and low
economic and population growth and energy supply. Defines environmental problems and trends
associated with air and water quality, disposal of
solid and hazardous wastes, toxic substances,
radiation, etc.

EP 1.94:CT   • Item 431-K-9 (MF)
BIOLOGY AND CONTROL OF INSECT AND RELATED
PESTS OF [various animals]. [Irregular]

Each issue tells how to control pests of a
specific animal, such as how to control lice, ticks,
and other pests in horses.

EP 1.95:date   • Item 431-K-10 (MF)
ENVIRONMENTAL HOTLINE. 1– 1980–   [Annual]

Directory of private groups and public agencies (including EPA and other Federal agencies)
concerned with the environment.

EP 1.96   • Item 431-I-81
ENVIRONMENTAL RESEARCH BRIEF (series). [Irregu-
lar]

EP 1.97:date   • Item 431-J-8 (MF)
PUGET SOUND NOTES. [6 times a year]

Single sheet release giving short news items
on EPA efforts to reduce polluting of Puget Sound.

EP 1.98   • Item 431-J-9 (MF)
EPA NEWSLETTER, QUALITY ASSURANCE. [Semi-
annual]

Newsletter on activities of the Quality Assurance Branch of EPA's Environmental Monitoring
and Support Laboratory, Cincinnati, Ohio.

EP 1.99:CT   • Item 431-J-10
MAPS AND ATLASES. [Irregular]

EP 1.100:date
ENVIRONMENTAL PROTECTION AGENCY ADVISORY
COMMITTEES. [Annual]
Earlier EP 1.2:C 73/8

EP 1.101   • Item 431-J-6
FORMS.

EP 1.102:   • Item 431-J-13
DIRECTORIES. [Irregular]

EP 1.103:date   • Item 431-I-9
OSWER TRAINING COURSE CATALOG. [Annual]

EP 1.104   • Item 431-R (E)
ELECTRONIC PRODUCTS. [Irregular]

EP 1.104/2:date   • Item 431-R-1 (E)
EPA DOC. [Semiannual].
Issued on CD-ROM.

EP 1.104/3:date   • Item 431-R-2 (EL)
NATIONAL BIENNIAL RCRA HAZARDOUS WASTE
REPORT. [Biennial]
Issued on Floppy disk.

EP 1.104/4:nos.   • Item 431-R-3 (CD)
LANDVIEW II, MAPPING OF SELECTED EPA-
REGULATED SITES, TIGER/LINE AND CENSUS
OF POPULATION AND HOUSING.
Issued on CD-ROM

EP 1.104/5:date   • Item 431-R-5 (CD)
CERCLIS (Comprehensive Environmental Response
Compensation, and Liability Information System.
[Quarterly]

EP 1.105:nos.   • Item 431-I-7
BIOREMEDIATION. [Irregular]

EP 1.106:nos.   • Item 431-I-7 (EL)
TECH TRENDS. [Bimonthly]

EP 1.107:CT   • Item 431-L-5 (MF)
NATIONAL PRIORITIES LIST SITES.

EP 1.108:date   • Item 431-I-7
EARTH NOTES. [Quarterly]

EP 1.109   • Item 431-T (CD)
AIR CHIEF (Clearinghouse for Inventory and Emission Factors).

EP 1.110:date/nos.   • Item 431-I-70
ORD ENGINEERING HIGHLIGHTS.

EP 1.110/2:   • Item 431-I-84
ORD SCIENCE HIGHLIGHTS (series).

EP 1.111   • Item 431-R (EL)
MONTHLY HOTLINE REPORT.

EP 1.112   • Item 431-J-16 (MF)
SUPERFUND ACCOMPLISHMENTS IN . . .

EP 1.113:nos.   • Item 431-I-85 (P) (EL)
SECTOR NOTEBOOK PROJECT (series) (various industries).

RESEARCH HIGHLIGHTS NEWSLETTERS.

The following is a list of the newsletters published by the National Environmental Research Center and its associated laboratories. The newsletters are designed to keep Federal, State, and local officials, as well as representatives of colleges and industry, abreast of current research developments that may be of use in their own programs.

Organizations and individuals may be added to mailing lists by writing the Director, Office of Public Affairs, National Environmental Research Center, 200 S.W. 35th Street Corvallis, Oregon 97330.

Arctic Environmental Research Laboratory
College, Alaska

COLD CLIMATE RESEARCH HIGHLIGHTS.

Grosse Ile Laboratory
Grosse Ile, Michigan

GREAT LAKES RESEARCH HIGHLIGHTS.

Gulf Breeze Environmental Research Laboratory
Gulf Breeze, Florida

TOXIC ORGANICS – PESTICIDES RESEARCH HIGHLIGHTS.

Robert S. Kerr Environmental Research Laboratory
Ada, Oklahoma

AGRICULTURAL WASTE RESEARCH HIGHLIGHTS.
GROUNDWATER POLLUTION RESEARCH HIGHLIGHTS.
PETROLEUM AND ORGANIC CHEMICALS RESEARCH HIGHLIGHTS.
WATER QUALITY CONTROL RESEARCH HIGHLIGHTS.

National Ecological Research Laboratory
Corvallis, Oregon

TERRESTRIAL ECOLOGY RESEARCH HIGHLIGHTS.

National Marine Water Quality Laboratory
Narragansett, Rhode Island

MARINE ECOLOGY RESEARCH HIGHLIGHTS.

National Water Quality Laboratory
Duluth, Minnesota

FRESHWATER AQUATIC LIFE RESEARCH HIGHLIGHTS.

Pacific Northwest Environmental Research Laboratory
Corvallis, Oregon

COASTAL POLLUTION RESEARCH HIGHLIGHTS. (EP 1.37)
EUTROPHICATION RESEARCH HIGHLIGHTS.
LABORATORY SERVICES BRANCH.
NATIONAL LAKE SURVEY PROGRAM.
THERMAL POLLUTION RESEARCH HIGHLIGHTS.
WASTE TREATMENT RESEARCH HIGHLIGHTS.

Southeast Environmental Research Laboratory
Athens, Georgia
AGRICULTURAL AND INDUSTRIAL POLLUTION RESEARCH.
FRESHWATER ECOSYSTEM POLLUTION RESEARCH.
POLLUTANT IDENTIFICATION RESEARCH HIGHLIGHTS. (EP 1.37/3)

EP 1.114   • **Item 431-R (EL)**
INSIDE THE GREENHOUSE. [Quarterly]

EP 1.115   • **Item 431-I-87 (EL)**
IINVENTORY OF U.S. GREENHOUSE GAS EMMISIONS AND SINKS. [Annual]

EP 1.116   • **Item 431-I-88 (EL)**
THE STATE OF FEDERAL FACILITIES. [Biennual]

EP 1.117   • **Item 431-I-38 (EL)**
SMALL BUSINESS OMBUDSMAN UPDATE. [Semiannual]

OFFICE OF WATER
(1970–   )

CREATION AND AUTHORITY

The Office of Water Programs was established within the Environmental Protection Agency by Reorganization Plan 3 of 1970, effective December 2, 1970, superseding the Federal Water Quality Administration (I 67) of the Department of the Interior. Name changed to Office of Water.

INFORMATION

Office of Water
Environmental Protection Agency
1200 Pennsylvania Ave., NW
Washington, D. C. 20460
(202) 564-5700
Fax: (202) 564-0488
http://www.epa.gov/ow

EP 2.1:date
ANNUAL REPORT.

EP 2.2:CT   • **Item 473-A-1**
GENERAL PUBLICATIONS.

EP 2.3/2:letters-nos.   • **Item 473-A-7 (MF)**
TECHNICAL BULLETINS.

EP 2.3/3:date   • **Item 473-A-11**
EPA-IRC BULLETIN. [Irregular] (Instructional Resources Center)

PURPOSE:– To provide a newsletter on the projects of the National Training and Operational Technology Center aimed at providing wastewater treatment facility operators with training assistance in the form of printed, audio, and visual materials.
IRC = Instructional Resources Center

EP 2.3/4:date-nos.   • **Item 473-A-11 (EL)**
LABCERT BULLETIN. [Irregular]

EP 2.5:CT   • **Item 607-D**
LAWS.

EP 2.6:CT   • **Item 473-A-13**
REGULATIONS, RULES, AND INSTRUCTIONS. [Irregular]

EP 2.8:CT   • **Item 607-C**
HANDBOOKS, MANUALS, GUIDES.

Earlier I 67.8

EP 2.9:nos.
SELECTED SUMMARIES OF WATER RESEARCH.
Earlier I 67.12

EP 2.10:nos.   • **Item 473-A-1**
WATER POLLUTION CONTROL RESEARCH SERIES.

Earlier I 67.13/4
Later EP 1.16

EP 2.10:11024 EJC(nos.)   • **Item 473-A-1**
SELECTED URBAN STORM WATER RUNOFF ABSTRACTS. No. 11024EJC 10/70–   Oct. 1970–   [Quarterly]

Earlier I 67.13/4

EP 2.11:letters-nos.   • **Item 473-A-4 (MF)**
OIL AND HAZARDOUS MATERIAL PROGRAM SERIES.

EP 2.12:date
RESEARCH, DEVELOPMENT, AND DEMONSTRATION PROJECTS, GRANTS AND CONTRACT AWARDS.

EP 2.13:date   • **Item 607-E**
PROJECT REGISTER, PROJECTS APPROVED UNDER SEC. 8 OF FEDERAL WATER POLLUTION CONTROL ACT (Pub. Law 660, 84th Cong.), AS AMENDED AND SEC. 3, OF PUBLIC WORKS ACCELERATION ACT (Pub. Law 658, 87th Cong.).

Earlier I 67.16

EP 2.14:date/v.nos.   • **Item 473-A-2**
COST OF CLEAN WATER [Annual Report to Congress].

Earlier I 67.1/2

EP 2.15:date   • **Item 473-A-5**
NORTHWEST SHELLFISH SANITATION RESEARCH PLANNING CONFERENCE, PROCEEDINGS. [Annual] (Water Hygiene Division)

Earlier FS 2.2:Sh 4/6

EP 2.16:nos.   • **Item 483-F**
ANALYTICAL REFERENCE SERVICE REPORTS (numbered). 1–   1958–   [Irregular]

Earlier FS 2.300/5, HE 20.1113

EP 2.17:date   • **Item 473-A-1**
INVENTORY MUNICIPAL WASTE FACILITIES. [Annual] (Office of Media Programs)

Earlier I 67.22

EP 2.17/2:date   • **Item 473-A-9 (P) (EL)**
NATIONAL WATER QUALITY INVENTORY, REPORT TO CONGRESS. (Office of Water Planning and Standards)

EP 2.18:nos.
TR- (series). 1–   1971–

EP 2.19:nos.   • **Item 607-C-2**
ESTUARINE POLLUTION STUDY SERIES. 1– 1970–

Earlier I 67.21

EP 2.20:date   • **Item 498-A**
SEWAGE FACILITIES CONSTRUCTION, (year). [Annual]

PURPOSE:– To provide statistical data on sewage treatment works, collection sewer, waterworks, and combination construction.
Earlier I 67.11

EP 2.21:date   • **Item 473-A-6**
DIGEST OF STATE PROGRAM PLANS. 1969– [Annual]

PURPOSE:– To present information extracted from the State Program Plans submitted by the States to the Environmental Protection Agency for grants allocated under Section 7 of the Federal Water Pollution Control Act, as amended.

EP 2.22:date
PACIFIC NORTHWEST WATER LABORATORY: QUARTERLY PROGRESS REPORT. (National Environmental Research Center, Corvallis, Oregon)

EP 2.23:nos.
WORKING PAPERS. [Irregular]

Earlier I 67.23

EP 2.24:date   • **Item 496-C (MF)**
FISH KILLS CAUSED BY POLLUTION IN (year). 1st– 1960–   [Annual] (Data Reporting Branch, Monitoring and Data Support Division)

Summary report supported by statistical data.
Earlier I 67.9

EP 2.25:nos. • **Item 498-A-1 (MF)**
PESTICIDES STUDY SERIES. 1– 1972–
[Irregular]

PURPOSE:– To provide reports of technical research in the field of pesticides and their effect and relation to the environment.

EP 2.26:nos. • **Item 473-A-8 (MF)**
TECHNICAL STUDIES REPORTS, TS- (series).

EP 2.27:CT
RAPHIES AND LISTS OF PUBLICATIONS.

Earlier I 67.14

EP 2.28:nos. • **Item 473-A-10 (MF)**
MCD SERIES. 1– [Irregular] (Municipal Construction Division)

EP 2.28/2:nos. • **Item 474-A-19 (MF)**
FRD SERIES. 1– [Irregular] (Facility Requirements Division)

PURPOSE:– To emphasize environmental, economic, and political, as well as technological aspects of facility requirements for water facilities.

EP 2.29:date • **Item 473-A-12 (MF)**
OFFICE OF WATER OPERATING GUIDANCE AND ACCOUNTABILITY SYSTEM. [Annual]

Provides national direction to the Environmental Protection Agency, States, and the regulated community in carrying out water quality programs emanating from Federal statutes.

EP 2.29/2 • **Item 473-A-15 (MF)**
OFFICE OF WATER ENVIRONMENTAL AND PROGRAM INFORMATION SYSTEMS COMPENDIUM.

EP 2.30:date • **Item 473-A-14 (MF)**
INNOVATIVE AND ALTERNATIVE TECHNOLOGY PROJECTS, A PROGRESS REPORT. [Annual]

PURPOSE:– To provide an overview of progress in the implementation of innovative and alternative technologies under provisions of the Clean Water Act.

EP 2.32:nos. • **Item 431-I-11**
ECOLOGICAL RESEARCH SERIES. [Irregular]

EP 2.33 • **Item 473-A-16 (EL)**
CLEAN WATER SRF PROGRAM INFORMATION FOR THE STATE OF... (database) [Annual]

OFFICE OF SOLID WASTE
(1970–   )

CREATION AND AUTHORITY

The Office of Solid Waste Management (HE 20.1400) was transferred from the Department of Health, Education, and Welfare and placed within the Environmental Protection Agency by Reorganization Plan 3 of 1970, effective December 2, 1970.

INFORMATION

Office of Solid Waste
Environmental Protection Agency
1200 Pennsylvania Ave. NW
Washington, DC 20460
(202) 260-4610
Fax: (202) 260-3527

EP 3.1:date
ANNUAL REPORT.

EP 3.2:CT • **Item 487-A-1**
GENERAL PUBLICATIONS.

Cancelled and consolidated into Solid Waste Management Series (EP 1.17).

EP 3.3/2:v.nos.&nos. • **Item 487-A-7**
ACCESSION BULLETIN, SOLID WASTE INFORMATION RETRIEVAL SYSTEM.

Later EP 1.18

EP 3.5:CT • **Item 487-A-5**
LAWS.

Cancelled and consolidated into Solid Waste Management Series (EP 1.17).

EP 3.8:CT
HANDBOOKS, MANUALS, GUIDES.

Earlier HE 20.1408

EP 3.9:CT • **Item 487-A-3**
BIBLIOGRAPHIES AND LISTS OF PUBLICATIONS.

Cancelled and consolidated into Solid Waste Management Series (EP 1.17).

EP 3.10:date • **Item 487-A-4**
STATE SOLID WASTE PLANNING GRANTS, AGENCIES, AND PROGRESS, REPORT OF ACTIVITIES. [Annual]

PURPOSE:– To report on each State's progress and activities in making surveys of solid waste practices and development of solid waste management plans; in developing and passing legislation and regulations; and carrying on public relations and information activities.
Arranged by State and Interstate, and by regions.
Earlier similar publications: FS 2.2:So 4/12 and FS 2.2:So 4/13
Cancelled and consolidated into Solid Waste Management Series (EP 1.17).

EP 3.11:CT
POSTERS.

EP 3.12:date • **Item 487-A-6**
SOLID WASTE MANAGEMENT TRAINING BULLETIN OF COURSES.

AIR QUALITY PLANNING AND
STANDARDS OFFICE
(1971–   )

CREATION AND AUTHORITY

The Office of Air Pollution Control was established within the Environmental Protection Agency by Reorganization Plan 3 of 1970, effective December 2, 1970, superseding the National Air Pollution Control Administration (HE 20.1800) of the Department of Health, Education, and Welfare. The name was changed to Office of Air Programs in 1971.

INFORMATION

Office of Air Quality Planning and Standards
Policy Analysis & Communications Staff
Environmental Protection Agency
Research Triangle Park
NC 27771
(202) 541-5557
Fax: (202) 565-2055
http://www.epa.gov/oar/OAQPS

EP 4.1:date • **Item 483-E-25(EL)**
ANNUAL REPORT.
Earlier HE 20.1301

EP 4.2:CT • **Item 483-E-1**
GENERAL PUBLICATIONS.
Earlier HE 20.1302

EP 4.8:CT • **Item 483-E-2**
HANDBOOKS, MANUALS, GUIDES.

EP 4.9:nos. • **Item 483-E (MF)**
AIR POLLUTION CONTROL OFFICE PUBLICATIONS, AP- (series). 1– June 1963– [Irregular]

PURPOSE:– To report the results of scientific and engineering studies, and information of general interest in the field of air pollution. Includes coverage of Air Pollution Control Office intramural activities and of cooperative studies conducted in conjunction with state and local agencies, research institutes, and industrial organizations.
Earlier HE 20.1309

EP 4.9/2:nos. • **Item 483-E (MF)**
AIR POLLUTION CONTROL OFFICE PUBLICATION APTD- (series). 1– January 1968– [Irregular]

PURPOSE:– To report information on research and technical advances derived from internal activities and from contract.
Earlier HE 20.1309/2

EP 4.10:CT • **Item 483-E**
AIR POLLUTION REPORT, FEDERAL FACILITIES, AIR QUALITY CONTROL REGIONS. 1968– [Irregular]

PURPOSE:– To provide a detailed inventory of Federal facilities and a summary of the air pollution environs contributed by the facilities within the designated air quality control region. They cover the 34 largest metropolitan areas, with plans for an expanded scope to include similar documents for the entire State.
Earlier HE 20.1310/2

EP 4.11:v.nos.&nos. • **Item 483-E-3**
AIR POLLUTION ABSTRACTS. v. 1– 7. 1971– 1976. [Monthly]

PURPOSE:– To provide informative abstracts of approximately 1000 technical articles covering 1100 domestic and foreign serial publications patents, government reports, preprints, technical society papers, and proceedings.
Prepared by the Air Pollution Technical Information Center (APTIC), Office of Technical Information and Publications, Research Triangle Park, N.C. 27709.
Includes subject and personal author index.
Previous title: NAPCA Abstracts Bulletin.
ISSN 0027-5956
Earlier HE 20.1303

EP 4.12:CT • **Item 483-E-4**
ADDRESSES.
Earlier HE 20.1312

EP 4.13:date • **Item 483-E-6**
AIR POLLUTION TRAINING COURSES, (year) AND UNIVERSITY TRAINING PROGRAMS, EXTRA MURAL PROGRAMS, INSTITUTE FOR AIR POLLUTION TRAINING PLANNING AND SPECIAL PROJECTS.
Earlier HE 20.1303/4

EP 4.14:CT
DESCRIPTIONS OF [various] COURSES. [Irregular] (Manpower Development Staff)

EP 4.14/2:date • **Item 483-E-8**
CHRONOLOGICAL SCHEDULE, INSTITUTE OF AIR POLLUTION TRAINING COURSES. [Annual]

EP 4.15:CT
REAL PROPERTY OWNED BY THE FEDERAL GOVERNMENT IN [various States]. 1971– [Irregular] (Federal Sources Branch, Division of Compliance)

PURPOSE:– To provide an inventory report in the form of a summary compilation of the major facilities of real property owned by the Federal Government in the individual States.
The installations presented are listed alphabetically by the city in which they are located and includes a brief description of the installation, the agency which operates the facility, the GSA inventory number, the GSA location code, the total floor area of all the buildings and a size classification code.

EP 4.16:date • **Item 483-E-7 (MF)**
PROGRESS IN THE PREVENTION AND CONTROL OF AIR POLLUTION IN (year), REPORT TO CONGRESS. 1st– [Annual]

Report made to Congress pursuant to Section 313 of the Clean Air Act, which authorized a national program of air pollution research, regulation, and enforcement activities.

EP 4.17:CT • **Item 483-E-14 (MF)**
SOURCE CATEGORY SURVEY (series). [Irregular] (Emission Standards and Engineering Division)
Also published in microfiche.

EP 4.18:CT • **Item 483-E-11 (MF)**
DRAFT ENVIRONMENTAL IMPACT STATEMENTS. [Irregular]
Published in microfiche.

EP 4.18/2:CT • **Item 483-E-11 (MF)**
FINAL ENVIRONMENTAL IMPACT STATEMENTS. [Irregular]
Published in microfiche.

EP 4.19:CT • **Item 483-E-9 (MF)**
REVIEW OF STANDARDS OF PERFORMANCE FOR NEW STATIONARY SOURCES (various industries). [Irregular]

Title varies.
Each highly technical report reviews New Source Performance Standards for a different industry.

EP 4.20:CT • **Item 483-E-10 (MF)**
MANUFACTURING INDUSTRIES (various kinds) TECHNICAL DOCUMENTS. [Irregular] (Air Quality Planning and Standards Office)

Each Document covers an individual industry. Highly technical reports.
Also published in microfiche (24x).

EP 4.21: • **Item 483-E-12 (MF)**
APTI COURSES. [Irregular] (Air Pollution Training Institute)

Textbooks for students and instructors engaged in developing and improving air pollution control programs for EPA, State and local governments, industry, and academic institutions.

EP 4.22:date • **Item 483-E-13 (MF)**
NATIONAL EMISSIONS DATA SYSTEM (NEDS) FUEL USE REPORTS. [Annual]
Also published in microfiche.

EP 4.22/2:date • **Item 483-E-15**
NATIONAL AIR QUALITY AND EMISSIONS TRENDS REPORT. [Annual]
Earlier EP 1.47

EP 4.23:v.nos.&nos. • **Item 483-E-17**
NATIONAL AIR TOXICS INFORMATION CLEARINGHOUSE: NEWSLETTER. [Bimonthly]

Published to assist state and local air agencies making decisions on noncritical air pollutant emissions. Contains news items on EPA air quality activities in various parts of the country.

EP 4.24:date • **Item 483-E-16 (MF)**
NATIONAL AIR POLLUTANT EMISSION ESTIMATES. [Annual]

PURPOSE– To present estimates of trends in nationwide air pollutant emissions for the particulates sulfur oxides, nitrogen oxides, volatile organic compounds, carbon monoxide, and lead. Estimates are presented for each year from 1940 through the reported year.

EP 4.25:CT • **Item 483-E**
BIBLIOGRAPHIES AND LISTS OF PUBLICATIONS.

EP 4.26 • **Item 483-E-18 (MF)**
DIRECTORIES.

EP 4.27:letter & nos • **Item 483-E-24 (MF)**
FACT SHEETS (Environmental Protection Agency).

EP 4.28 • **Item 483-E-19 (E)**
ELECTRONIC PRODUCTS. (misc.)

EP 4.29 • **Item 483-E-19 (EL)**
ENERGY STAR HOMES UPDATE. [Irregular]

EP 4.30 • **Item 483-E-20 (CD)**
AIRSEXECUTIVE PLUS. (CD-ROM)

EP 4.31 • **Item 483-E-23 (EL)**
THE BENEFITS AND COSTS OF THE CLEAN AIR ACT. [Biennial]

EP 4.52 • **Item 483-E-22**
GENERAL PUBLICATIONS.

EP 4.58 • **Item 483-E-21**
HANDBOOKS, MANUALS, GUIDES.

OFFICE OF PREVENTION, PESTICIDES AND TOXIC SUBSTANCES
(1980–   )

CREATION AND AUTHORITY

The Office of Pesticides Programs was established within the Environmental Protection Agency by Reorganization Plan 3 of 1970, effective December 2, 1970. Name changed to Office of Pesticides and Toxic Substances in 1980.

INFORMATION

Communications Director
Office of Prevention, Pesticides and Toxic Substances
Environmental Protection Agency
1200 Pennsylvania Ave. NW
Washington, D.C. 20460
(202) 564-0341
Fax: (202) 564-0512
http://www.epa.gov/OPPTS

EP 5.1 • **Item 431-R-4 (EL)**
OFFICE OF PESTICIDE PROGRAMS ANNUAL REPORT.

EP 5.2:CT • **Item 473-B-1**
GENERAL PUBLICATIONS.

EP 5.6
REGULATIONS, RULES, AND INSTRUCTIONS.

EP 5.8:CT • **Item 473-B-2**
HANDBOOKS, MANUALS, GUIDES.

EP 5.8:P 43 • **Item 473-B-2**
DIGEST OF STATE PESTICIDE USE AND APPLICATION LAWS, GUIDE FOR ANALYZING PESTICIDE LEGISLATION. 1976. 303 p.

EP 5.8:P 75 • **Item 473-B-2**
CLINICAL HANDBOOK ON ECONOMIC POISONS, EMERGENCY INFORMATION FOR TREATING POISONING. 1971. 144 p. il.

This handbook was prepared primarily for the guidance of physicians in the diagnosis and treatment of persons who may have had

extensive or intensive exposure to economic poisons; however, it contains general information that may be of interest to others also.

EP 5.8/2:CT • **Item 473-B-2**
APPLY PESTICIDES CORRECTLY, A GUIDE FOR COMMERCIAL APPLICATORS (series). [Irregular]

EP 5.9:v.nos.&nos. • **Item 475-M**
PESTICIDES ABSTRACTS. v. 1– 1968– [Monthly]

PURPOSE:– To foster current awareness of the major worldwide literature pertaining to the effects of pesticides on humans. It represents a monthly review of more than 500 domestic and foreign journals.
Annual index issued separately.
Prior to the February 1974 issue, entitled Health Aspects of Pesticides, Abstract Bulletin.
ISSN 0093-3295.
Earlier HE 20.4011 prior to v. 4, no. 1.

EPA COMPENDIUM OF REGISTERED PESTICIDES.

PURPOSE:– To provide a compilation of all uses found on the labeling of pesticides registered by the Environmental Protection Agency. Each volume is sold separately and subscriptions include basic volumes plus supplemental material for an indefinite period.

EP 5.10
ADDRESSES.

EP 5.11:v.nos. • **Item 473-B-3**
EPA COMPENDIUM OF REGISTERED PESTICIDES.

EP 5.11/1 • **Item 473-B-3**
v. 1. HERBICIDES AND PLANT REGULATORS. [In preparation]

EP 5.11/2:date • **Item 473-B-3**
v. 2. FUNGICIDES AND NEMATICIDES. (Includes basic volume plus supplementary material for an indefinite period)

EP 5.11/3:date • **Item 473-B-3**
v. 3. INSECTICIDES, ACARICIDES, MOLLUSCICIDES, AND ANTIFOULING COMPOUNDS. [Irregular] (Includes basic manual plus supplementary material for an indefinite period) (Technical Services Division)

EP 5.11/4:date • **Item 473-B-3**
v. 4. RODENTICIDES AND MAMMAL, BIRD AND FISH TOXICANTS. 1973– [Irregular] (Includes basic manual plus supplementary material for an indefinite period) (Publications Branch, Pesticides Regulation Division)

EP 5.11/5:date • **Item 473-B-3**
v. 5. DISINFECTANTS. [In preparation]

EP 5.12:CT • **Item 473-B-11**
BIBLIOGRAPHIES AND LISTS OF PUBLICATIONS. [Irregular]

EP 5.13:nos.   • **Item 473-B-4 (MF)**
SUBSTITUTE CHEMICAL PROGRAM, INITIAL SCIENTIFIC AND MINIECONOMIC REVIEW OF [various chemicals]. [Irregular] (Criteria and Evaluation Division)

The Alternative (Substitute) Chemicals Program was initiated under Public Law 93-135 of October 24, 1973, to "provide research and testing of substitute chemicals." The legislative intent is to prevent using substitutes, which in essence are more deleterious to man and his environment, than a problem pesticide (one that has been suspended, cancelled, deregistered or in an "internal review" for suspected "unreasonable adverse effects to man or his environment"). The major objective of the program is to determine the suitability of substitute chemicals which now or in the future may act as replacements for those uses (major and minor) of pesticides that have been cancelled, or suspended, or are in litigation or under internal review for potential unreasonable adverse effects on man and his environment.

EP 5.14:CT   • **Item 473-B-5 (MF)**
ENVIRONMENTAL IMPACT STATEMENTS. [Irregular]

EP 5.15:v.nos.&nos.   • **Item 473-B-6 (EL)**
CHEMICALS-IN-PROGRESS BULLETIN.

PURPOSE:– To inform all persons concerned with the Toxic Substance Control Act about recent developments and near-term plans.
Previous title: TSCA Chemicals-in-Progress Bulletin.

EP 5.15/2:CT   • **Item 473-B-7 (MF)**
TSCA CHEMICAL ASSESSMENT SERIES. [Irregular]

Consists of chemical substances evaluation prepared by the Office of Testing and Evaluation scientists to implement provisions of the Toxic Substances Control Act.
TSCA = Toxic Substances Control Act

EP 5.15/3:CT   • **Item 473-B-9 (MF)**
TSCA ECONOMIC ANALYSIS SERIES. [Irregular]

Highly technical reports analyzing the potential economic impact on manufacturers of complying with testing rules for specified chemicals set by the Office to implement provisions of Toxic Substances Control Act.
TSCA = Toxic Substances Control Act.

EP 5.15/4:v.nos.&nos.   • **Item 473-B-10**
TSCA STATUS REPORT FOR EXISTING CHEMICALS. [Bimonthly]
PURPOSE:– To present in tabular form the status of chemicals of interest to the Office, in terms of what stages of evaluation they have been put through, such as the Chemical Hazard Information Profile, etc.
TSCA = Toxic Substances Control Act.

EP 5.16:v.nos.&nos.   • **Item 473-B-8**
PESTICIDES AND TOXIC SUBSTANCES MONITORING REPORT. v. 1– 1980– [Irregular] (Survey and Analysis Division)

The Survey and Analysis Division functions to detect and assess evidences of human and environmental exposure to pesticides and other toxic chemicals. Report provides potential users of monitoring information with a brief update on data programs and highlighted activities of the Field Studies Branch.

EP 5.17:CT   • **Item 473-B-12 (MF)**
PESTICIDE REGISTRATION STANDARDS. (series) [Irregular]

Each issue provides highly technical standards for registering a different pesticide active ingredient. All available information and the comprehensive Agency position on registration requirements for all products containing the ingredient are given.

EP 5.18:nos.   • **Item 431-E-14**
TOXIC INTEGRATION INFORMATION SERIES. [Irregular]

Includes publications on various topics related to the coordination and integration of toxic substances programs policies, activities, and information on the various Federal agencies, public interest groups, industries and States.
Earlier EP 1.79/2

EP 5.18/2:date   • **Item 473-B-14**
THE TOXICS-RELEASE INVENTORY: A NATIONAL PROSPECTIVE. [Annual]

EP 5.18/2-2:date   • **Item 473-B-14**
THE TOXICS-RELEASE INVENTORY: EXECUTIVE SUMMARY. [Annual]

EP 5.19:date   • **Item 473-B-13**
ADMINISTRATION OF THE PESTICIDE PROGRAMS. [Annual]

PURPOSE:– To summarize activities of the Office in its functions of regulating pesticides under the Federal Insecticide, Fungicide, and Rodenticide Act and the Federal Food, Drug, and Cosmetic Act.

EP 5.20:nos.   • **Item 473-B-15**
CHEMICAL INFORMATION FACT SHEETS. 1– [Irregular]

Each fact sheet describes and gives use patterns and other information on a different chemical.

EP 5.21:CT   • **Item 473-B-16**
POSTERS

EP 5.22:date   • **Item 473-G**
TOXIC CHEMICAL RELEASE INVENTORY (TRI). [Annual]

Issued on CD-ROM.

EP 5.22:CT   • **Item 473-G-1—G-50 (MF)**
TOXIC CHEMICAL RELEASE INVENTORY (State). [Annual] (MF)

EP 5.22:   • **Item 473-G-51**
TOXIC CHEMICAL RELEASE INVENTORY (District of Columbia). [Annual]

EP 5.22:   • **Item 473-G-52 (MF)**
TOXIC CHEMICAL RELEASE INVENTORY (U.S. Summary). [Annual]

EP 5.22:CT   • **Item 473-G-53 (MF)**
TOXIC CHEMICAL RELEASE INVENTORY (Outlying Areas). [Annual]

EP 5.22/2:date   • **Item 473-H (CD) (EL)**
TOXIC RELEASE INVENTORY. [Annual]

EP 5.22/3:date   • **Item 473-H-1**
TOXIC CHEMICAL RELEASE INVENTORY REPORTING FORM R AND INSTRUCTIONS. [Annual]

EP 5.23   • **Item 473-B-17 (MF)**
PROCEEDINGS DOCUMENT (series).

EP 5.24:CT   • **Item 473-B-18**
DIRECTORIES

EP 5.25   • **Item 473-B-19 (E)**
ELECTRONIC PRODUCTS. (misc.)

EP 5.26   • **Item 473-B-19 (EL)**
POLLUTION PREVENTION NEWS.

EP 5.27   • **Item 473-B-19 (EL)**
PESTICIDE REGISTRATION ELIGIBILITY DECISIONS (REDS).

EP 5.28   • **Item 473-B-19 (EL)**
EPP (ENVIRONMENTALLY PREFERABLE PURCHASING) UPDATE. [Irregular]

OFFICE OF RADIATION AND INDOOR AIR (1970–)

CREATION AND AUTHORITY

The Office of Radiation Programs was established within the Environmental Protection Agency by Reorganization Plan 3 of 1970, effective December 2, 1970, superseding the Bureau of Radiological Health (HE 20.4100) in the Public Health Service of the Department of Health, Education, and Welfare.
INFORMATION

Office of Radiation and Indoor Air
Environmental Protection Agency
1200 Pennsylvania Ave., NW
Washington, DC 20460
(202) 564-9320
Fax (202) 564-9651
http://www.epa.gov/air/oria.html

EP 6.1:date
ANNUAL REPORT.
Earlier HE 20.1501

EP 6.1/2:date   • **Item 431-I-47**
EPA REVIEW OF RADIATION PROTECTION ACTIVITIES. [Annual]

EP 6.2:CT   • **Item 431-I-18**
GENERAL PUBLICATIONS.
Earlier HE 20.1502

EP 6.8:CT   • **Item 498-C-3**
HANDBOOKS, MANUALS, GUIDES.

EP 6.9:v.nos.&nos.   • **Item 498-B**
RADIATION DATA AND REPORTS. [Monthly]

PURPOSE:– To bring together in one concise volume, the more pertinent month by month statistical information and reports on radiation in the environment.
Previous title: Radiological Data and Reports.
Indexed by: Index to U.S. Government Periodicals.
Earlier HE 20.1509

EP 6.10:nos.   • **Item 498-B-3**
RO/EERL SERIES. (Eastern Environmental Radiation Laboratory)

EP 6.10/2:nos.   • **Item 483-M**
ORP/SID (series). [Irregular] (Surveillance and Inspection Division)

Continuation of BRH/DER (series) (FS 2.314/3) formerly published by the Public Health Service.

EP 6.10/3:nos.   • **Item 431-I-13 (MF)**
TECHNICAL NOTE, ORP/CSD- (series). [Irregular] (Division of Criteria and Standards)

EP 6.10/4:nos.   • **Item 431-I-21 (MF)**
EPA/ORP- (series).

EP 6.10/6:date-nos.   • **Item 431-I-61 (MF)**
TECHNICAL NOTE ORP/LV- (series). [Irregular]

EP 6.10/7:nos.   • **Item 431-I-61 (MF)**
TECHNICAL NOTE ORP/TAD- (series).

EP 6.10/8:nos.   • **Item 431-I-61 (MF)**
TECHNICAL NOTE ORP/EAD (series).

EP 6.10/9:yr.-nos.   • **Item 431-L-13 (MF)**
ORP CONTRACT REPORTS. [Irregular]

Highly technical reports dealing, in general, with public exposure to radiation and, in particular, with such areas as analyzing the costeffectiveness of protective actions taken following a low-level disposition of radionulides.

EP 6.11:date   • Item 431-I-60 (MF)
RADIOLOGICAL QUALITY OF THE ENVIRONMENT.
[Annual]

EP 6.12:nos.
ENVIRONMENTAL RADIATION DATA REPORTS.
[Irregular]

EP 6.13:nos.   • Item 431-I-78 (MF)
TECHNICAL REPORTS. [Irregular]

EP 6.14:CT   • Item 431-K-11 (MF)
ENVIRONMENTAL IMPACT STATEMENTS. [Irregular]

    Series includes both draft and final statements.

EP 6.14/2:CT   • Item 431-K-11
REGULATORY IMPACT ANALYSIS (series). [Irregular]

EP 6.15   • Item 431-K-15 (EL)
NATURAL GAS STAR PARTNER UPDATE.

TECHNOLOGY TRANSFER
(1971–   )

CREATION AND AUTHORITY

    The Technology Transfer was established within the Environmental Protection Agency in September 1971.

INFORMATION

    Technology Transfer
    Environment Protection Agency
    Washington, D.C. 20460

EP 7.1:date
ANNUAL REPORT.

EP 7.2:CT   • Item 473-C-1
GENERAL PUBLICATIONS.

EP 7.8:CT   • Item 473-C-3
HANDBOOKS, MANUALS, GUIDES.

EP 7.8/2:CT   • Item 473-C-3 (MF)
PROCESS DESIGN MANUAL FOR [various subjects] (series). [Irregular]

EP 7.9:date   • Item 473-C-2
TECHNOLOGY TRANSFER.

    Previous title: Technology Transfer, The Bridge Between Research and Use.

EP 7.10:nos.   • Item 473-C-1 (MF)
TECHNOLOGY TRANSFER SEMINAR PUBLICATIONS (series).

EP 7.11:nos.   • Item 473-C-4 (MF)
EPA TECHNOLOGY TRANSFER CAPSULE REPORTS. 1–   [Irregular]

EP 7.12:nos.   • Item 473-C-5 (MF)
SULFUR OXIDES CONTROL TECHNOLOGY SERIES. [Irregular]

    PURPOSE:– To present highly technical series of summary reports on various engineering alternatives for controlling sulfur dioxide emissions. Intended for engineers, managers and decision makers.

OFFICE OF WETLANDS, OCEANS AND WATERSHEDS

INFORMATION

    Office of Wetlands, Oceans
    and Watersheds
    EPA
    1200 Pennsylvania Ave., NW
    Washington, DC 20460
    (202) 566-1146
    Fax: (202) 566-1147
    http://www.epa.gov/owow

EP 8.1:date
ANNUAL REPORT.

EP 8.2:CT   • Item 473-E
GENERAL PUBLICATIONS. [Irregular]

EP 8.8:CT   • Item 473-F
HANDBOOKS, MANUALS, GUIDES. [Irregular]

EP 8.15   • Item 473-E-1 (E)
ELECTRONIC PRODUCTS. (misc.)

EP 8.16   • Item 473-E-2 (EL)
COASTLINES.

CHEMICAL EMERGENCY PREPAREDNESS AND PREVENTION OFFICE

INFORMATION

    Officeof Emergency Preparedness
    and Prevention Office
    EPA
    Rm. 1448
    1200 Pennsylvania Ave., NW
    Washington, DC 20460
    (202) 564-8600
    Fax: (202) 564-8220
    http://www.epa.gov/ceppo

EP 9.2   • Item 431-W
GENERAL PUBLICATIONS.

EP 9.15   • Item 473-W-1 (E)
ELECTRONIC PRODUCTS. (Mics.)

EP 9.16   • Item 473-W-1 (EL)
CEPPO Alerts.

EP 9.17   • Item 473-W-1 (EL)
FACT SHEETS AND TECHNICAL ASSISTANCE BULLETINS.

ENERGY RESEARCH AND DEVELOPMENT ADMINISTRATION
(1975–1977)

CREATION AND AUTHORITY

    The Energy Research and Development Administration was established by the Energy Reorganization Act of 1974 (88 Stat. 1233; 3 U.S.C. 301), and activated on January 19, 1975 by Executive Order 11834 of January 15, 1975. Terminated and functions transferred to the Department of Energy by act of August 4, 1977 (91 Stat. 565), effective October 1, 1977.

ER 1.1:date
ANNUAL REPORT.

ER 1.2:CT   • Item 474-A-1
GENERAL PUBLICATIONS.

ER 1.5:CT   • Item 474-A-12
FINAL ENVIRONMENTAL IMPACT STATEMENTS. [Irregular]

ER 1.7:nos.
NEWS RELEASES.

ER 1.8:CT   • Item 474-A-9
HANDBOOKS, MANUALS, GUIDES.

ER 1.9:v.nos.&nos.   • Item 474-A-2
ENERGY ABSTRACTS FOR POLICY ANALYSIS. v. 1– 1975–   [Monthly]

    ISSN 0098-5104
    Earlier Y 3.At 7:59
    Later E 1.11

ER 1.10:v.nos.&nos.   • Item 1051-A
NUCLEAR SCIENCE ABSTRACTS. v. 1–33. 1948–1976. [Semimonthly]

    PURPOSE:– To serve scientists and engineers working in the field of atomic energy by abstracting as completely as possible the literature of nuclear science and engineering.

    Each issue contains abstracts, arranged under broad subject categories, together with author, report, and subject indexes.

    The literature that is abstracted and indexed is drawn from the following sources: 1) articles from scientific, engineering, and trade journals; 2) technical reports of the AEC and its contractors; 3) technical reports of other U.S. Government agencies and their contractors; 4) technical reports of foreign governments; 5) technical reports of industrial and institutional laboratories; 6) books; 7) monographs; 8) theses; 9) patents (domestic and foreign); and 10) serial publications of universities and learned societies.

    The number of items abstracted annually has increased from 4000 in the first year to approximately 42,000 in 1963, and continued growth at an increasing rate is in prospect. Coverage, especially of foreign literature and patents, has continued to be expanded.
    Indexed by: Chemical Abstracts
    ISSN 0029-5612
    Earlier Y 3.At 7:16
    Publications issued subsequent to June 30, 1967, are contained in Atomindex, published by UNIPUB, Box 433, Murray Hill Station, New York, New York 10016.

ER 1.10/2:v.nos.&nos.   • Item 1051-A
INDEXES. v. 1–   1948–   [Semiannual] (Technical Information Center, Office of Public Affairs)

    Prior to v. 31 issued by the Atomic Energy Commission (Y 3.At 7:16-5).
    The following cumulation has been published: v. 1–33. 1948–1976.

ER 1.11:letters-nos.   • Item 1051-C
RESEARCH AND DEVELOPMENT REPORTS. [Irregular]

    Declassified or unclassified technical reports. Majority of the reports is available by purchase from the Office of Technical Services. More popular titles are handled by the Superintendent of Documents.

    This series is subdivided by the issuing organizations of the reports, each sub-series designated by letter symbols to indicate the organization responsible for the report. For a listing of the symbols, see report Number Series used by the Technical Information Service in Cataloging Reports.
    Earlier Y 3.At 7:22

ER 1.12:v.nos.&nos.
INFORMATION FROM ERDA, WEEKLY ANNOUNCE-
MENTS.

Prior to v. 6, no. 8, entitled Information from
ERDA, Weekly Summary.
Contains research related information formerly covered by AEC News Releases (Y 3.At
7:32-2).
Superseded by Department of Energy Information: Weekly Announcements (E 1.7/2).

ER 1.12/2:date
INFORMATION FROM ERDA.

ER 1.12/3:date • Item 474-A-17
INFORMATION FROM ERDA: REFERENCE INFOR-
MATION. [Annual]

ER 1.13:nos. • Item 474-A-4
MATERIALS AND COMPONENTS IN FOSSIL ENERGY
APPLICATIONS, AND ERDA NEWSLETTER. 1–

ISSN 0145-9244
Later E 1.23

ER 1.14:CT
ERDA CRITICAL REVIEW SERIES.

ER 1.15:v.nos.&nos.
ERDA ENERGY RESEARCH ABSTRACTS. v. 1–
1976–   [Monthly and Annual]

Annual cumulative volume issued separately.
ISSN 0361-9869
Later E 1.17

ER 1.16:nos. • Item 431-I-30
UNITED STATES LPPSD [Low Pollution Power Systems
Development] TECHNICAL INFORMATION EX-
CHANGE DOCUMENTS. 1– 1973– [Irregu-
lar]

Under the auspices of the NATO Committee
on the Challenges of Modern Society, a Memorandum of Understanding concerning Low Pollution Power Systems Development (LPPSD) was
concluded between the appropriated agencies of
the following nations: the Federal Republic of
Germany, France, Italy, the Netherlands, the
United Kingdom, and the United States. This Memorandum included provisions for technical symposia, technical information exchange and collaborative projects.
These documents are published by the Energy Research and Development Agency as a
means of exchanging technical information on
research, development, and testing of low polluting power systems among all of the participants
in the Memorandum, so that each participant might
keep abreast of parallel LPPSD developments in
other countries part to the Memorandum.
Formerly issued by the Environmental Protection Agency (EP 1.50).

ER 1.17:date • Item 474-A-5
ERDA TELEPHONE DIRECTORY.

ER 1.18:nos.
ERDA TRANSLATION LISTS. 1– [Irregular]

PURPOSE:– To announce all unclassified
translations received or published by the ERDA's
Technical Information Center or brought to its
attention by other organizations in this country or
abroad. Both completed translations and those in
process are cited to help avoid duplication of
translating effort. It consists of three parts: Part
I –   Translations in Process; Part II Translations Completed; and Part III –   Miscellaneous
(includes translations completed by available on
loan only with the address of source of each
translation; also includes translations formerly
reported in process and subsequently cancelled).
Author, Report Number, and Source Indexes are
in each issue; a list of Newly Received Foreign
Books is also included.
AEC Translation List Index (TID-4028), published in May 1970, covers all translations cited
in issues of the AEC Translation List numbered
98-136 that were published from 1965 through
1969. Its supplement (TID-4028- S1-R1), published

in April 1974, covers all translations cited in issues of the AEC Translation List numbered 137-
154 (1970– 1973). The Translation Title List and
Cross Reference Guide (TID-4025 (Rev. 1) (Pt. 1))
and its supplements provide indexes, citations,
and availability information for translations announced prior to 1965.
Earlier Y 3.At 7:44-2

ER 1.19:date • Item 474-A-7
JOURNALS AVAILABLE IN THE ERDA LIBRARY. [Semi-
annual]

ER 1.20:CT
ADDRESSES.

ER 1.21:CT • Item 474-A-10
MAPS, CHARTS AND POSTERS.

ER 1.22:CT • Item 474-A-8
PROGRAM APPROVAL DOCUMENTS, EXECUTIVE
SUMMARIES. [Irregular]

ER 1.23:date • Item 474-A-11
LARAMIE ENERGY CENTER: ANNUAL REPORT.

ER 1.24:CT
BIBLIOGRAPHIES AND LISTS OF PUBLICATIONS.

ER 1.25:CT • Item 474-A-12
ENVIRONMENTAL IMPACT STATEMENT. [Irregular]

ER 1.26:v.nos.&nos.
RADIOBIOLOGY. [Bimonthly]

ISSN 0486-8816
Earlier ER 1.11:ERDA
Later E 1.44

ER 1.27:date
HEALTH AND SAFETY LABORATORY: ENVIRONMEN-
TAL QUARTERLY.

ISSN 0361-2341
Later E 1.37

ER 1.28:date • Item 474-A-13
COAL, QUARTERLY REPORTS: POWER AND COM-
BUSTION.

Beginning in 1977 published by the Department of Energy (E 1.31/2).
ISSN 0362-8361

ER 1.28/2 • Item 474-A-13
COAL, QUARTERLY REPORTS: LIQUEFACTION.

Beginning in 1977 published by the Department of Energy (E 1.31/3).
ISSN 0362-7934

ER 1.28/3 • Item 474-A-13
COAL, QUARTERLY REPORTS: DEMONSTRATION
PLANTS.

Beginning in 1977 published by the Department of Energy (E 1.31/4).

ER 1.28/4:date • Item 474-A-13
COAL, QUARTERLY REPORTS: GASIFICATION.

Beginning in 1977 published by the Department of Energy (E 1.31).
ISSN 0362-5184

ER 1.28/5:CT • Item 474-A-13
COAL TECHNICAL REPORTS.

ER 1.29:date • Item 474-A-14
ENERGY EFFICIENCY RESEARCH.

ER 1.30:letters-nos. • Item 474-A-15
PROGRAM RESEARCH AND DEVELOPMENT
ANNOUNCEMENTS, PRDA- (series). [Irregular]

ER 1.31:date • Item 474-A-16
GEOTHERMAL ENERGY RESEARCH, DEVELOPMENT
AND DEMONSTRATION PROGRAM, ANNUAL
REPORT. 1st–   1977–

ER 1.32:date
SOLAR ENERGY RESEARCH AND DEVELOPMENT
REPORT. [Monthly]

ER 1.33:date • Item 474-A-18
ENVIRONMENTAL DEVELOPMENT PLAN, OIL
SHALE. [Annual]

Report covers fiscal year.
Later E 1.36

ECONOMIC STABILIZATION
AGENCY
(1950– 1953)

CREATION AND AUTHORITY

The Economic Stabilization Agency was established by Executive Order 10161 of September 9, 1950, pursuant to Defense Production Act
of 1950 (64 Stat. 798). The Agency was terminated April 30, 1953, by Executive Order 10434
of February 6, 1953.

ES 1.1:date
ANNUAL REPORTS.

ES 1.2:CT
GENERAL PUBLICATIONS.

ES 1.6:CT
REGULATIONS, RULES, AND INSTRUCTIONS.

ES 1.6/2
REGULATIONS.

Includes: Ceiling Price Regulations, General
Regulations, Wage Procedure Regulations.

ES 1.6/3:nos.
GENERAL ORDERS. [Proc. Admin.]

ES 1.7/1:nos.
RELEASES.

ES 1.7/2:nos.
SPEECHES.

WAGE STABILIZATION BOARD
(1950– 1953)

CREATION AND AUTHORITY

The Wage Stabilization Board was established
within the Economic Stabilization Agency by Executive Order 10161 of September 9, 1950. The
Board was terminated on April 30, 1953, pursuant
to Executive Order 10434 of February 6, 1953
and provisions of Defense Production Act Amendments of 1952 (66 Stat. 296) and 1953 (67 Stat.
131).

ES 2.1:date
ANNUAL REPORTS.

ES 2.2:CT
GENERAL PUBLICATIONS.

ES 2.6:CT
REGULATIONS, RULES, AND INSTRUCTIONS.

ES 2.6/2:nos.
GENERAL REGULATIONS.

ES 2.6/3:nos.
GENERAL WAGE REGULATIONS.

ES 2.6/4:nos.
CONSTRUCTION INDUSTRY STABILIZATION COM-
MISSION REGULATIONS.

ES 2.6/5:nos.
RESOLUTIONS.

ES 2.7/1:le-nos.
RELEASES.

ES 2.7/2:nos.
WAGE STABILIZATION COMMITTEE RELEASES, WSC (series).

ES 2.8:nos.
INTERPRETATION BULLETINS.

OFFICE OF PRICE STABILIZATION (1950– 1953)

CREATION AND AUTHORITY

The Office of Price Stabilization was established within the Economic Stabilization Agency on January 24, 1951, by General Order 2 of the Administrator. The Office was terminated April 30, 1953, pursuant to Executive Order 10434 of February 6, 1953.

ES 3.1:date
ANNUAL REPORTS.

ES 3.2:CT
GENERAL PUBLICATIONS.

ES 3.5:CT
LAWS.

ES 3.6:CT
REGULATIONS, RULES, AND INSTRUCTIONS.

ES 3.6/2:nos.
ADMINISTRATIVE ORDERS.

ES 3.6/3:nos.
DISTRIBUTION ORDERS.

ES 3.6/4:nos.
GENERAL CEILING PRICE REGULATIONS.

ES 3.6/5:nos.
CEILING PRICE REGULATIONS.

ES 3.6/6:nos.
ENFORCEMENT AND PROCEDURE REGULATIONS.

ES 3.6/7:nos.
OPS GUIDES.

ES 3.6/8:nos.
DISTRIBUTION REGULATIONS.

ES 3.6/9:nos.
GENERAL OVERRIDING REGULATIONS.

ES 3.6/10:nos.
SUMMARY OF ORDERS.

ES 3.6/10-2:nos.
COMBINED SUMMARY OF ORDERS.

ES 3.6/11:nos.
DELEGATIONS OF AUTHORITY.

ES 3.6/12:nos.
PI-M (series).

ES 3.6/13:nos.
OPS TRADE GUIDE TP (series).

ES 3.6/14:nos.
GENERAL INTERPRETATIONS.

ES 3.6/15:nos.
OPS TRADE AIDE TA (series).

ES 3.6/16:date
ABSTRACTS OF PRICE REGULATIONS.

ES 3.6/17
GENERAL DISALLOWANCE ORDERS

ES 3.6/18
PRICE PROCEDURAL REGULATIONS.

ES 3.7/1:date
GENERAL PRESS RELEASES.

ES 3.7/2:nos.
SPEECHES.

ES 3.7/3:nos.
RELEASES RELATING TO ORDERS.

ES 3.7/4:nos.
[RELEASES RELATING TO QUESTIONS ON PRICE REGULATIONS AND ORDERS] TP (series).

ES 3.8:nos.
ADDRESSES.

ES 3.9:CT
OPS TRADE BULLETINS.

ES 3.10:date
DIRECTORY OF COMMODITIES AND SERVICES.

ES 3.10/2:date
DIRECTORY OF COMMODITIES AND SERVICES EXEMPTED OR SUSPENDED FROM PRICE CONTROL.

ES 3.11:nos.
PI-H (series)

SALARY STABILIZATION BOARD (1950– 1953)

CREATION AND AUTHORITY

The Salary Stabilization Board was established within the Economic Stabilization Agency on May 10, 1951, by General Order 8 of the Administrator, pursuant to the Defense Production Act of 1950 (63 Stat. 803). The Board was terminated April 30, 1953, pursuant to Executive Order 10434 of February 6, 1953, and the Defense Production Act Amendments of 1952 (66 Stat. 296) and 1953 (67 Stat 131).

ES 4.1:date
ANNUAL REPORTS.

ES 4.2:CT
GENERAL PUBLICATIONS.

ES 4.6:CT
REGULATIONS, RULES, AND INSTRUCTIONS.

ES 4.6/2:nos.
GENERAL SALARY STABILIZATION REGULATIONS GSSR (series).

ES 4.6/3:nos.
GENERAL SALARY ORDERS.

ES 4.6/4:nos.
INTERPRETATIONS.

ES 4.6/5:nos.
SALARY PROCEDURAL REGULATIONS.

ES 4.7
RELEASES.

OFFICE OF RENT STABILIZATION (1951– 1953)

CREATION AND AUTHORITY

The Office of Rent Stabilization was established within the Economic Stabilization Agency by General Order 9, dated July 31, 1951, of the Administrator, pursuant to the Housing and Rent Act of 1947 (61 Stat. 1932). The Office was abolished by Executive Order 10475 of July 31, 1953, pursuant to act of Congress, approved April 30, 1953 (67 Stat. 23), and its functions transferred to the Office of Defense Mobilization.

ES 5.1:date
ANNUAL REPORTS.

ES 5.2:CT
GENERAL PUBLICATIONS.

ES 5.5:CT
LAWS.

ES 5.6:CT
REGULATIONS, RULES, AND INSTRUCTIONS.

ES 5.7:nos.
RELEASES.

ES 5.7/2:CT
QUESTIONS AND ANSWERS ON RENT CONTROL.

NATIONAL ENFORCEMENT COMMISSION (1952– 1953)

CREATION AND AUTHORITY

The National Enforcement Commission was established within the Economic Stabilization Administration by General Order 18 of the Administrator, effective July 30, 1952. Upon the termination of the Economic Stabilization Administration, the functions of the Commission were transferred to the Attorney General by Executive Order 10494 of October 14, 1953.

ES 6.1:date
ANNUAL REPORTS.

ES 6.2:CT
GENERAL PUBLICATIONS.

ES 6.7:nos.
RELEASES.

COMMISSION OF FINE ARTS
(1910–   )

CREATION AND AUTHORITY

The Commission of Fine Arts was established by the act of May 17, 1910 (36 Stat. 371).

INFORMATION

Commission of Fine Arts
National Building Museum
441 F Street, N.W.
Washington, D. C. 20001
(202) 504-2200
Fax: (202) 504-2195
E-mail: fine_arts@os.doi.gov

FA 1.1   • Item 432
REPORT. 1st–   1911–   [Irregular]

FA 1.2:CT   • Item 432
GENERAL PUBLICATIONS.

FA 1.3:
BULLETINS.

FA 1.4:
CIRCULARS.

FEDERAL AVIATION AGENCY
(1958– 1967)

CREATION AND AUTHORITY

The Federal Aviation Agency was established by the Federal Aviation Act of 1958 (Public Law 726, 85th Congress, 2d session, approved August 23, 1958). Functions were transferred to the Federal Aviation Administration (TD 4) in the Department of Transportation by the Department of Transportation Act of October 15, 1966 (80 Stat. 931) effective April 1967.

FAA 1.1:date
SEMIANNUAL REPORTS.

FAA 1.2:CT
GENERAL PUBLICATIONS.

FAA 1.6:CT
REGULATIONS, RULES, AND INSTRUCTIONS.

FAA 1.5:CT
LAWS.

FAA 1.6/2:nos.
SPECIAL CIVIL AIR REGULATIONS.
Earlier C 31.206/3

FAA 1.6/3:nos.
MAINTENANCE OPERATIONS DIVISION INSTRUCTIONS. [Admin.]
Earlier C 31.106/4

FAA 1.6/4:nos.
REGULATIONS OF ADMINISTRATOR.
Earlier C 31.140
Later FAA 1.6/8

FAA 1.6/5:nos.
CIVIL AIR REGULATIONS DRAFT RELEASES.
Preliminary published in Federal Register.
Earlier C 31.209/2

FAA 1.6/6:pt.nos.
CIVIL AIR REGULATIONS.

Earlier C 31.209
Later FAA 1.6/8

FAA 1.6/7:nos.
SYSTEMS MAINTENANCE DIVISION INSTRUCTIONS.

Administrative.

FAA 1.6/8:pt.nos.
FEDERAL AVIATION REGULATIONS

Earlier FAA 1.6/6, FAA 1.6/4

FAA 1.6/9:date
RULES OF FLIGHT. [Annual]

FAA 1.7:nos.
RELEASES.

FAA 1.7/2:nos.
PRESS RELEASES T (series).

FAA 1.7/3:nos.
FAA NEWS [Dulles International Airport] DIA- (series).

FAA 1.7/4:date
NEWS FEATURES FROM FEDERAL AVIATION AGENCY.

FAA 1.8:CT
HANDBOOKS, MANUALS, GUIDES.

FAA 1.8/2:letters-nos.
FAA HANDBOOKS (numbered).

FAA 1.9:CT
DICTIONARIES, GLOSSARIES, ETC.

FAA 1.10:date
LIST OF FAA PUBLICATIONS.

Earlier C 31.162

FAA 1.10/2:nos.
BIBLIOGRAPHIES OF TECHNICAL REPORTS, INFORMATION RETRIEVAL LISTS.

FAA 1.10/3:nos.
BIBLIOGRAPHIC LIST.

FAA 1.11:v.nos.&nos.
FLY-BY, OFFICIAL EMPLOYEE PUBLICATION OF FEDERAL AVIATION AGENCY.

FAA 1.12
ADDRESSES.

FAA 1.13:nos.
FEDERAL AVIATION AGENCY SPECIFICATION. [Admin.]

Earlier C 31.120

FAA 1.14
SUMMARY OF SUPPLEMENTAL TYPE CERTIFICATES AND APPROVED REPLACEMENT PARTS.

Later FAA 5.12

FAA 1.15:date
GENERAL AVIATION ACCIDENTS (non-air carrier), STATISTICAL ANALYSIS, CALENDAR YEAR.

Earlier C 31.160/2

FAA 1.16:CT
MAPS AND CHARTS.

FAA 1.17:cl.nos.
FAA NATIONAL SUPPLY CATALOG. [Admin.]

FAA 1.18:date
STATUS OF CIVIL AIR REGULATIONS AND CIVIL AERONAUTICS MANUALS.

Earlier C 31.151

FAA 1.19:v.nos.&nos.
MANAGEMENT SERVICE NOTICES. [Monthly]

FAA 1.20:v.nos.
FLIGHT INFORMATION MANUAL.

Earlier C 31.128
Later FAA 3.13/2

FAA 1.21:v.nos.
ALASKA FLIGHT INFORMATION MANUAL.

Earlier C 31.134

FAA 1.22:v.nos.
INTERNATIONAL FLIGHT INFORMATIONAL MANUAL.

Earlier C 31.139
Later FAA 3.13

FAA 1.23:v.nos.&nos.
AIRMAN'S GUIDE. [Biweekly]

Earlier C 31.127

FAA 1.23/2:date
DIRECTORY OF AIRPORTS AND SEAPLANE BASES, AIRMAN'S GUIDE SUPPLEMENT.

FAA 1.24:v.nos.&nos.
ALASKA AIRMAN'S GUIDE, NOTICES TO AIRMEN. [Biweekly]

Earlier C 31.135

FAA 1.25:v.nos.&nos.
AIRMAN'S GUIDE AND FLIGHT INFORMATION MANUAL, PACIFIC SUPPLEMENT. [Semiannual]

Earlier C 31.136

FAA 1.25/2:date
AIRMAN'S GUIDE AND FLIGHT INFORMATION MANUAL.

FAA 1.25/3:v.nos.&nos.
AIRMAN'S GUIDE, PACIFIC SUPPLEMENT. [Semimonthly]

Earlier FAA 1.25
Later FAA 1.25/5

FAA 1.25/4:v.nos.
FLIGHT INFORMATION MANUAL, PACIFIC SUPPLEMENT.

Earlier FAA 1.25

FAA 1.25/5:v.nos.&nos.
PACIFIC AIRMAN'S GUIDE AND CHART SUPPLEMENT. [Monthly]

Earlier FAA 1.25/3

FAA 1.26:v.nos.&nos.
INTERNATIONAL NOTAMS. [Weekly]

Earlier C 31.133

FAA 1.27:date
FAA AIR TRAFFIC ACTIVITY.
Earlier C 31.158

FAA 1.27/2:date
ACTIVITIES AT AIR TRAFFIC CONTROL FACILITIES, FISCAL YEAR.

FAA 1.27/3:date
AIR TRAFFIC PATTERNS FOR VFR GENERAL AVIATION, FISCAL YEAR.

FAA 1.27/4:date
AIR TRAFFIC PATTERNS FOR IFR AND VFR AVIATION, CALENDAR YEAR.

FAA 1.28:nos.
FAA AIRWORTHINESS DIRECTIVES. [Biweekly]

Earlier C 31.147/2

FAA 1.28/2:date
SUMMARY OF AIRWORTHINESS DIRECTIVES FOR SMALL AIRCRAFT.

FAA 1.28/3:date
SUMMARY OF AIRWORTHINESS DIRECTIVES FOR LARGE AIRCRAFT.

FAA 1.29:date
AIRCRAFT SPECIFICATIONS.

Earlier C 31.120/2

FAA 1.29/2:date
ENGINE AND PROPELLER SPECIFICATIONS.

      Earlier C 31.120/3

FAA 1.30:date
ANNUAL REPORT OF OPERATIONS UNDER FEDERAL AIRPORT ACT.

      Earlier C 31.145/3

FAA 1.31:date
GENERAL MAINTENANCE INSPECTION AIDS SUMMARY AND SUPPLEMENTS.

      Earlier C 31.163

FAA 1.31/2:nos.
GENERAL MAINTENANCE ALERT BULLETINS.

      Earlier C 31.163/2

FAA 1.32:date
FAA STATISTICAL HANDBOOK OF AVIATION.

      Earlier C 31.144

FAA 1.32/2:date
STATISTICAL STUDY OF U.S. CIVIL AIRCRAFT. [Annual]

      Earlier C 31.160
      Later FAA 1.35/2

FAA 1.33:date
AIRCRAFT IN AGRICULTURE. [Annual]

      Earlier FAA 1.2:Ag 8

FAA 1.34:nos.
CIVIL AERONAUTICS MANUALS (numbered).

      Earlier C 31.107/2

FAA 1.34/1-8:nos.
CIVIL AERONAUTICS MANUALS. (1-8)

      Earlier C 31.132/2

FAA 1.35:date
UNITED STATES ACTIVE CIVIL AIRCRAFT BY STATE AND COUNTY.
      Earlier C 31.132/2

FAA 1.35/2:date
CENSUS OF U.S. CIVIL AIRCRAFT.

      Earlier FAA 1.32/2, FAA 1.35

FAA 1.35/3:date
UNITED STATES CIVIL AIRCRAFT REGISTER. [Semi-annual]

      Earlier FAA 5.14

FAA 1.36:nos.
JET AGE PLANNING PROGRESS REPORTS.

      Earlier C 31.168

FAA 1.37:date
FAA PLAN FOR AIR NAVIGATION AND AIR TRAFFIC CONTROL SYSTEMS.

      Earlier C 31.167

FAA 1.38:nos.
TECHNICAL STANDARDS ORDERS.

      Earlier C 31.143

FAA 1.39:date
GENERAL AVIATION AIRCRAFT USE.

FAA 1.40:date
AIRCRAFT INSTRUMENT APPROACHES, FISCAL YEAR.

FAA 1.41:v.nos.&nos.
AVIATION NEWS. [Monthly]

FAA 1.41/2:v.nos.&nos.
FAA AVIATION NEWS. [Monthly]

      Continuation of Aviation News, (FAA 1.41).

FAA 1.42:date
AVIATION FORECASTS, FISCAL YEARS.

FAA 1.43:date
FIELD FACILITY DIRECTORY. [Quarterly]

FAA 1.44:nos.
SECURITY REMINDER. (Official use)

FAA 1.45:nos.
TECHNICAL REPORTS.

      Earlier FAA 3.13/2

Bureau of Research and Development

FAA 2.1:date
PROGRAM AND PROGRESS REPORT.

FAA 2.2:CT
GENERAL PUBLICATIONS.

FAA 2.7:date
RELEASES.

FAA 2.8:nos.
TECHNICAL DEVELOPMENT REPORTS.

      Earlier C 31.119

FAA 2.8/2:nos.
REPORTS.

FAA 2.9:date
ANNUAL INTERNATIONAL AVIATION RESEARCH AND DEVELOPMENT SYMPOSIUM, REPORT OF PROCEEDINGS.

FAA 2.10:date
DESIGN FOR NATIONAL AIRSPACE UTILIZATIONAL SYSTEM.

FAA 2.11:v.nos.
CONSOLIDATED ABSTRACTS OF TECHNICAL REPORTS.

FAA 2.11/2:v.nos.
CONSOLIDATED ABSTRACTS OF TECHNICAL REPORTS: GENERAL DISTRIBUTION.

Bureau of Air Traffic Management

FAA 3.1:date
ANNUAL REPORTS.

FAA 3.2
GENERAL PUBLICATIONS.

FAA 3.6:CT
ATS MANUALS.

FAA 3.6/2:nos.
ATM DIRECTIVES.

FAA 3.8:CT
ATM MANUALS.

FAA 3.8/2:CT
HANDBOOKS, MANUALS, GUIDES.

FAA 3.9:date
AIR TRAFFIC CONTROL PROCEDURES.

      Formerly entitled ANC Procedures for Control of Air Traffic (C 31.106/2).

FAA 3.9/2:date
COMMUNICATIONS PROCEDURES, ATM-2-B.

FAA 3.10:date
LOCATION IDENTIFIERS.
      Earlier C 31.157

FAA 3.11:date
ENROUTE IFR AIR TRAFFIC SURVEY.

      Earlier C 31.165

FAA 3.11/2:date
IFR ALTITUDE USAGE PEAK DAY.

FAA 3.11/3:date
ENROUTE IFR PEAK DAY CHARTS, FISCAL YEAR.

FAA 3.12:CT
MAPS.

      Earlier C 31.115

FAA 3.13:v.nos.
INTERNATIONAL FLIGHT INFORMATION MANUAL.

      Earlier FAA 1.22

FAA 3.13/2:v.nos.
FLIGHT INFORMATION MANUAL.

      Earlier FAA 1.20

FAA 3.13/3:sec.nos./date
AIRMAN'S INFORMATION MANUAL.

FAA 3.14:date
ATS FACT BOOK. [Quarterly]

Bureau of Facilities

FAA 4.1:date
ANNUAL REPORTS.

FAA 4.2:CT
GENERAL PUBLICATIONS.

FAA 4.8:date
NATIONAL AIRPORT PLAN.

      Earlier C 31.145/2
      Later FAA 8.11

FAA 4.9:nos.
BUREAU OF FACILITIES MANUAL OF OPERATIONS.

      Earlier C 31.116/3

FAA 4.9/2:CT
HANDBOOKS, MANUALS, GUIDES.

FAA 4.9/3:date
AIRPORT DESIGN MANUAL.

FAA 4.10:date
STANDARD SPECIFICATIONS FOR CONSTRUCTION OF AIRPORTS.

      Earlier C 31.120

FAA 4.11:date
AIR COMMERCE TRAFFIC PATTERN, CALENDAR YEAR.

      Earlier C 31.153

FAA 4.12:nos.
PLANNING SERIES.

Bureau of Flight Standards

      The Bureau of Flight Standards was established in the Federal Aviation Agency pursuant to the Federal Aviation Act of 1958 (Public Law 726, 85th Congress, 2d session, approved Aug. 23, 1958).

FAA 5.1:date
ANNUAL REPORTS.

FAA 5.2:CT
GENERAL PUBLICATIONS.

FAA 5.7:nos.
BUREAU OF FLIGHT STANDARDS RELEASES.

      Earlier C 31.111

FAA 5.8:nos.
TECHNICAL MANUALS.

      Earlier C 31.138

FAA 5.8/2:CT
HANDBOOKS, MANUALS, GUIDES.

FAA 5.9:date
UNITED STATES STANDARD FACILITIES FLIGHT
CHECK MANUAL.

Earlier C 31.163/3

FAA 5.10:nos.
BUREAU PRACTICE. [Admin.]

FAA 5.11:nos.
QUALITY CONTROL DIGEST.

Earlier C 31.166

FAA 5.12:date
SUMMARY OF SUPPLEMENTAL TYPE CERTIFICATES
AND APPROVED REPLACEMENT PARTS.

Earlier FAA 1.14

FAA 5.13
STANDARD INSTRUMENT APPROACH PROCEDURE
[by type].

Official use.

FAA 5.14:date
UNITED STATES CIVIL AIRCRAFT REGISTER. [Semi-
annual]

Later FAA 1.35/3

FAA 5.15:date
ACCEPTABLE METHODS, TECHNIQUES, AND PRAC-
TICES: AIRCRAFT INSPECTION AND REPAIR.

FAA 5.16:date
ACCEPTABLE METHODS, TECHNIQUES, AND PRAC-
TICES: AIRCRAFT ALTERATIONS.

Bureau of National Capital Airports

FAA 6.1:date
ANNUAL REPORTS.

FAA 6.2:CT
GENERAL PUBLICATIONS.

Bureau of Aviation Medicine

FAA 7.1:date
ANNUAL REPORTS.

FAA 7.2:CT
GENERAL PUBLICATIONS.

FAA 7.8:date
LIST OF AVIATION MEDICAL EXAMINERS. [Semi-
annual]

FAA 7.9:CT
HANDBOOKS, MANUALS, GUIDES.

FAA 7.10
FAA AVIATION MEDICAL RESEARCH REPORTS.

FAA 7.10/2:nos.
CIVIL AEROMEDICAL RESEARCH INSTITUTE: TECH-
NICAL PUBLICATIONS.

FAA 7.11:v.nos.&nos.
MEDICAL NEWSLETTER. [Monthly]

FAA 7.12:nos.
[AVIATION MEDICAL REPORTS] AM (series).

FAA 7.13:nos.
AVIATION MEDICAL EDUCATION SERIES.

Airports Service

FAA 8.1:date
ANNUAL REPORTS.

FAA 8.2:CT
GENERAL PUBLICATIONS.

FAA 8.8:CT
HANDBOOKS, MANUALS, GUIDES.

FAA 8.9:date
AIR COMMERCE TRAFFIC PATTERN (scheduled
carrier), FISCAL YEAR.

Earlier FAA 4.11
Later combined in C 31.251

FAA 8.10:CT
FEDERAL-AID AIRPORT PROGRAM PUBLICATIONS.

FAA 8.11:date
NATIONAL AIRPORT PLAN, FISCAL YEARS.

Earlier FAA 4.8

FISH AND FISHERIES COMMISSION (1880–1903)

CREATION AND AUTHORITY

The United States Fish Commission was established by Joint Resolution of Congress, approved February 9, 1871. By 1880, the Commission was known as the United States Fish and
Fisheries Commission. Upon the creation of the
Department of Commerce and Labor on February
14, 1903, the Commission became a part of that
Department and its name was changed to Bureau
of Fisheries (C 6).

FC 1.1:pt.nos
ANNUAL REPORTS.

FC 1.2:CT
GENERAL PUBLICATIONS.

FC 1.3:v.nos.
BULLETINS.

Later C 6.3
FC 1.4:nos.
CIRCULARS.

FC 1.5:nos.
STATISTICAL BULLETINS.

Later C 6.5

FC 1.6:sec.nos.
FISHERIES AND FISHING INDUSTRIES.

FC 1.6/a:CT
– SEPARATES.

FC 1.7:CT
SPECIAL BULLETINS.

FARM CREDIT ADMINISTRATION (1933–1939, 1953–   )

CREATION AND AUTHORITY

The Farm Credit Administration was established as an independent agency by Executive
Order 6084 of March 27, 1933, by consolidation
of the Federal Farm Board (FF 1), the Federal
Farm Loan Bureau (T 40), certain functions of the
Reconstruction Finance Corporation dealing with
agricultural credit, the Crop Production Loan Office (A 54), and the Seed Loan Office. Under
Reorganization Plan No. 1 of 1939, made effective July 1, 1939, by Public Resolution 20, 76th
Congress, the Farm Credit Administration was
transferred to the Department of Agriculture (A
72). Executive Order 9280 of December 5, 1942
placed it under the Food Production Administration. Executive Order 9322 of March 26, 1943
returned it to the Secretary of Agriculture. Public

Law 202, 83d Congress, approved August 6, 1953,
made it an independent agency (FCA 1) effective
December 4, 1953. The agency currently operates under authorities in the Farm Credit Act of
1971, as amended.

INFORMATION

Office of Congressional and Public Affairs
Farm Credit Administration
1501 Farm Credit Drive
McLean, Virginia 22102-5090
(703) 883-4056
Fax: (703) 734-4785
Email: info-line@fca.gov
http://www.fca.gov

FCA 1.1   • Item 430-J-1 (MF)
ANNUAL REPORT OF THE FARM CREDIT
ADMINISTRATION ON THE WORK OF THE
COOPERATIVE FARM CREDIT SYSTEM. 1st–
1933–   [Annual]

Report submitted by the Administration to
Congress pursuant to section 3 of the Federal
Farm Loan Act; paragraph 3, section 4, of the
Agricultural Marketing Act, as amended; the Executive Order of March 27, 1933, creating the
Farm Credit Administration; and section 6 of the
1953 for the fiscal year.
Gives review of operations for the fiscal year,
including long term farm mortgage credit, short
and intermediate term credit, banks for cooperatives, and banks for cooperatives investment fund
(Agricultural Marketing Act revolving fund). Appendix tables give statistical data on operations.

FCA 1.1/2:date   • Item 430-J-1 (MF)
REPORT ON THE FINANCIAL CONDITION AND PER-
FORMANCE OF THE FARM CREDIT SYSTEM.

FCA 1.1/3   • Item 430-J-1 (EL)
FCA ANNUAL PERFORMANCE PLAN.

FCA 1.1/4   • Item 430-J-1 (EL)
FCA ACCOUNTABILITY REPORT.

FCA 1.1/5   • Item 430-J-1 (EL)
FCA STRATEGIC PLAN FY... [Irregular]

FCA 1.2:CT   • Item 430-J-2
GENERAL PUBLICATIONS.

Later A 72.2, FCA 1.1

FCA 1.3   • Item 430-J-9
FCA BULLETINS. 1–   1936–   [Monthly]

Bulletins include FCA Board actions and decisions, policy statement, directives and interpretations, proposed and final regulations, and
formal enforcement actions.
Earlier Bulletins were sent to depository libraries under item number 430-J-3.

FCA 1.3/2:nos.   • Item 430-J-6 (MF)
STATISTICAL BULLETINS. 1–   [Irregular]

FCA 1.4 & FCA 1.4/2   • Item 430-J-4
CIRCULARS. 1–   1933–   [Irregular]

Correspondence aids.
Circulars are issued in a numbered series
and also in three letter-number series. Each is
numbered individually and consecutively.
Letter-number series are:
A-Announcements of publications.
CR-Circulars on farm Credit.
E-Circulars of particular interest to
extension workers.

FCA 1.4/2:le
CIRCULARS (lettered).

Later A 72.4

FCA 1.4/3:le-nos.
CIRCULARS ON COOPERATIVE MARKETING.

FCA 1.5:
LAWS.

FCA 1.6:CT
REGULATIONS, RULES AND INSTRUCTIONS, ETC.

FCA 1.7:date
STATEMENT OF CONDITION OF FEDERAL LAND
BANKS, JOINT STOCK LAND BANKS, ETC.

Earlier T 48.6

FCA 1.7/2:date
STATEMENTS OF CONDITION OF JOINT STOCK LAND
BANKS.
Earlier FCA 1.7
Later A 72.16

FCA 1.8:nos.
POSTERS.

FCA 1.8/2:nos.
CHARTS.

FCA 1.9
ADDRESSES. [Irregular]

FCA 1.10:vol.
NEWS FOR FARMER COOPERATIVES. [Monthly]
Later A 72.10

FCA 1.11:vol.
FARM CREDIT NOTES. [Monthly]

FCA 1.12:date
MONTHLY REPORT ON LOANS AND DISCOUNTS.
Later A 72.12

FCA 1.12/2
LOANS AND DISCOUNTS OF FARM CREDIT BANKS
AND ASSOCIATIONS, ANNUAL REPORT. [Annual]

Statistical tables showing loans and discounts
made and loans and discounts outstanding, by
districts and States.
Previous title: Loans and Discounts of Lending Institutions Supervised by Farm Credit Administration.

FCA 1.13:nos.
MISCELLANEOUS REPORTS.

Later A 72.8

FCA 1.14:vol.
COOPERATIVE SAVINGS WITH FEDERAL CREDIT
UNIONS. [Monthly]

FCA 1.14/2:vol.
COOPERATIVE SAVINGS WITH FEDERAL CREDIT
UNIONS. [Bimonthly]

Later A 72.13

FCA 1.15:date
FEDERAL CREDIT UNIONS. [Monthly]

Later A 72.14

FCA 1.16:date
FEDERAL CREDIT UNIONS. QUARTERLY REPORT
ON OPERATIONS.

Later A 72.19

FCA 1.17:nos.
LECTURE NOTES FOR FILM STRIPS.

FCA 1.18:nos.
SUMMARIES.

Later A 72.18

FCA 1.19:CT
FARM COOPERATIVES (by States).

Later A 72.17

FCA 1.20:CT
LISTS OF PUBLICATIONS.

FCA 1.21:nos.
SPECIAL REPORTS.

Later A 72.9

FCA 1.22 • **Item 430-J-5**
PRODUCTION CREDIT ASSOCIATIONS, ANNUAL
SUMMARY OF OPERATIONS. [Annual]

Production credit associations are local cooperative lending organizations providing farmers and stockmen with a dependable source of
credit to finance their farming operations.
Report presents in tabular form the name and
locations of associations, number of members,
net worth as of December 31, and a summary of
lending operations.

FCA 1.23
REPORT TO THE FEDERAL LAND BANK ASSOCIA-
TIONS FOR YEAR ENDED JUNE 30 (date).
[Annual]

Title varies.
Report is for the fiscal year. Gives combined
statements of condition as of June 30 and of
income and expenses ended June 30 for the
Federal Land Bank Associations and Federal Land
Banks.
Previous title: Report to the National Farm
Loan Associations.

FCA 1.23/2 • **Item 430-J-9 (MF)**
ANALYSIS AND SUMMARY OF CONDITIONS AND
PERFORMANCES OF THE FARM CREDIT BANKS
AND ASSOCIATIONS. [Quarterly]

FCA 1.23/2-2:date • **Item 430-J-10 (EL)**
RISK ANALYSIS OF FARM CREDIT SYSTEM OPERA-
TIONS AND ECONOMIC OUTLOOK. [Quarterly]

FCA 1.24:date • **Item 430-J-8 (MF)**
AGRICULTURAL AND CREDIT OUTLOOK. [Annual]

PURPOSE:– To present information on the
general economic outlook, agricultural economic
outlook, policy issues, agricultural finance outlook, and the outlook for various commodities
such as meat, eggs, and feed grains.

FCA 1.24:date
FARM AND CREDIT OUTLOOK FOR [year].

FCA 1.25:nos. • **Item 430-J-7 (MF)**
FCA RESEARCH JOURNAL.

Consists of articles on such subjects as the
financial condition of young farmers after entry
and implications of deregulation and monetary
control for agricultural finance.
Also published in microfiche.

FCA 1.26 • **Item 430-J-11 (EL)**
FCA NEWSLINE. [Monthly]

FCA 1.28 • **Item 430-J-14 (EL)**
FINANCIAL PERFORMANCE INDICATORS. [Quarterly]

FEDERAL CIVIL DEFENSE
ADMINISTRATION
(1951– 1958)

CREATION AND AUTHORITY

The Federal Civil Defense Administration
(Pr 33.800) was established within the Office of
Emergency Management by Executive Order
10186 of December 1, 1950, and later established as an independent agency by the Federal
Civil Defense Act of 1950 (62 Stat. 1245), approved January 12, 1951. Under Reorganization
Plan 1 of 1958, effective July 1, 1958, the Office
of Defense Mobilization (Pr 34.200) and the Federal Civil Defense Administration were combined
to form the Office of Defense and Civilian Mobilization (Pr 34.700).

FCD 1.1:date
ANNUAL REPORTS.

Earlier Pr 33.801
Later Pr 34.701

FCD 1.1/2:date
ANNUAL STATISTICAL REPORT.

Later Pr 34.751/2

FCD 1.1/2:dt.&nos.
PROGRESS REPORTS.

Later Pr 34.751

FCD 1.2:CT
GENERAL PUBLICATIONS.

Earlier Pr 33.802
Later Pr 34.702

FCD 1.3:nos.
TECHNICAL BULLETINS.

Later Pr 34.753

FCD 1.3/2:nos.
ADVISORY BULLETINS.

FCD 1.6:CT
REGULATIONS, RULES, AND INSTRUCTIONS.

FCD 1.6/2:nos.
ADMINISTRATIVE GUIDES, AG (series).

FCD 1.6/3:nos.
TECHNICAL MANUAL TM (series).

Later Pr 34.761/3

FCD 1.6/4:nos.
HANDBOOK H (series).

Later Pr 34.761/2

FCD 1.6/5:nos.
INSTRUCTOR'S GUIDE IG (series).

FCD 1.6/5-2:CT
INTERIM INSTRUCTOR'S GUIDE.

Later PrEx 4.12/5-2

FCD 1.6/6
MANUALS.

FCD 1.6/7:nos.
PROGRAM GUIDE PG (series).

FCD 1.6/8:nos.
POCKET MANUAL PM (series).

Later Pr 34.761/5

FCD 1.7
RELEASES.

FCD 1.7/2:nos.
SPECIAL PROMOTION [releases] SP (series).

Later Pr 34.757/3

FCD 1.7/3:nos.
LEADER'S GUIDE, SPECIAL BULLETIN SERIES IN
SUPPORT OF ANNUAL NATIONAL CIVIL
DEFENSE WEEK.

Earlier FCD 1.6:L 45

FCD 1.8:v.nos.
CIVIL DEFENSE ALERT. [Monthly]

FCD 1.9:nos.
TRAINING AND EDUCATION BULLETIN TEB (series).

FCD 1.9/2:nos.
TRAINING BULLETIN, TRAINING OFFICER SERIES.

FCD 1.9/3:nos.
TRAINING BULLETIN, SCHOOL SERIES.

FCD 1.10:nos.
VOLUNTEER MANPOWER BOOKLET VM (series).

FCD 1.11:nos.
POSTER SERIES.

FCD 1.11/2:13-nos.
[PHOTOGRAPHS OF A-BOMB TEST, OPERATION DOORSTEP, YUCCA FLAT, NEVADA, MARCH 17, 1953].

FCD 1.12:v.nos.
IMPACT OF AIR ATTACK IN WORLD WAR II, SELECTED DATA FOR CIVIL DEFENSE PLANNING (Standard Research Institute Report).

  – DIVISION 1, PHYSICAL DAMAGE TO STRUCTURE, FACILITIES, AND PERSONS.

  FCS 1.12/2:v.nos.
  –DIVISION 2, EFFECTS ON GENERAL ECONOMY.

  FCD 1.12/3:v.nos.
  – DIVISION 3, SOCIAL ORGANIZATION, BEHAVIOR, AND MORALE UNDER STRESS.

FCD 1.12/4:CT
STRANFORD RESEARCH INSTITUTE, FINAL REPORTS.

FCD 1.13:nos.
PUBLIC AFFAIRS PA (series).

FCD 1.13/2:nos.
TECHNICAL ADVISORY SERVICES, HEALTH OFFICE, FOR YOUR INFORMATION, TAS (series).

FCD 1.13/3:nos.
OFFICE OF ADMINISTRATOR, FOR YOUR INFORMATION, AD (series).

FCD 1.13/4:nos.
OPERATIONS CONTROL SERVICES, FOR YOUR INFORMATION, OC (series). [Irregular]

FCD 1.13/5:nos.
EDUCATION SERVICES, FOR YOUR INFORMATION. [Irregular]

FCD 1.13/6:nos.
OFFICE OF EXECUTIVE ASSISTANT ADMINISTRATOR, FOR YOUR INFORMATION. [Irregular]

FCD 1.13/7:nos.
OFFICE OF GENERAL COUNSEL, FOR YOUR INFORMATION. [Irregular]

FCD 1.13/8:nos.
PLANNING STAFF, FOR YOUR INFORMATION [Releases].

FCD 1.13/9:nos.
INDUSTRIAL SURVIVAL, FOR YOUR INFORMATION. [Releases].

FCD 1.13/10:nos.
SURVIVAL SERIES, FOR YOUR INFORMATION. [Releases].

FCD 1.13/11:nos.
INFORMATION BULLETINS.
    Earlier FCD 1.13 to FCD 1.13/10
    Later Pr 34.753/2

FCD 1.14:nos.
TECHNICAL REPORT TR (series).
    Later Pr 34.763

FCD 1.15:v.nos.
FCDA PUBLIC AFFAIRS NEWSLETTER. [Monthly]

FCD 1.16:v.nos.&nos.
NEWS FEATURES. [Monthly]

FCD 1.16/2:v.nos.&nos.
NEWSPICTURES.
    Earlier Pr 34.757/4
    Later Pr 34.760

FCD 1.17:nos.
[PUBLIC AFFAIRS FLYER] PA-F (series).

FCD 1.17/2:nos.
[PUBLIC AFFAIRS] BOOKLET PA-B (series).
    Later Pr 34.764

FCD 1.18:date
REPORT ON WASHINGTON CONFERENCE OF MAYORS AND OTHER LOCAL GOVERNMENT EXECUTIVES ON NATIONAL SECURITY. [Annual]
    Earlier FCD 1.2:C 74/2

FCD 1.18/2:date
REPORT ON WASHINGTON CONFERENCE ON NATIONAL WOMEN'S ADVISORY COMMITTEE ON FCDA. [Annual]
    Earlier FCD 1.2:C 74/4

FCD 1.19:date
FEDERAL CIVIL DEFENSE ADMINISTRATION DIRECTORY.
    Earlier FCD 1.2:D 62

FCD 1.20:nos.
[LEAFLETS] L- (series).
    Earlier Pr 34.758

FCD 1.21:date
CIVIL DEFENSE PUBLICATIONS AVAILABLE FROM SUPERINTENDENT OF DOCUMENTS.
    Earlier FCD 1.2:P 96

FCD 1.21/2:date
INDEX FOR FEDERAL CIVIL DEFENSE ADMINISTRATION PUBLICATIONS. [Annual]
    Earlier FCD 1.2:In 2

FCD 1.22:nos.
MISCELLANEOUS PUBLICATIONS, MP (series).
    Later Pr 34.759

FCD 1.23:date
NATIONAL CIVIL DEFENSE WEEK PUBLICATIONS.
    Earlier FCD 1.2
    Later Pr 34.762

FCD 1.24:nos.
NEWSLETTER, BY, FOR, AND ABOUT WOMEN IN CIVIL DEFENSE. [Irregular]

FEDERAL ENERGY ADMINISTRATION
(1974– 1977)

CREATION AND AUTHORITY

    The Federal Energy Administration was established by the Federal Energy Administration Act of 1974 (88 Stat. 96), effective June 28, 1974, superseding the Federal Energy Office. The Administration was abolished and its functions transferred to the Energy Information Administration (E 3) of the Department of Energy by Act of August 4, 1977 (91 Stat. 565), effective October 1, 1977.

FE 1.1:date   • **Item 434-A-18**
ANNUAL REPORT.

FE 1.2:CT   • **Item 434-A-1**
GENERAL PUBLICATIONS.

FE 1.7:date
PRESS RELEASES.
    Earlier PrEx 21.7

FE 1.8:date   • **Item 434-A-14**
HANDBOOKS, MANUALS, GUIDES.

FE 1.8/2:CT   • **Item 434-A-11**
ENERGY HANDBOOKS FOR SMALL BUSINESSES. [Irregular]

FE 1.8/3:v./date
FEDERAL ENERGY GUIDELINES (basic volumes).

FE 1.8/4:v./date
FEDERAL ENERGY GUIDELINES, EXCEPTIONS AND APPEALS (basic volumes).

FE 1.8/5:nos.
FEDERAL ENERGY GUIDELINES, TRANSMITTALS.
    Later E 1.8/2

FE 1.8/6:CT
TIPS FOR TRUCKERS.

FE 1.9:date
PETROLEUM SITUATION REPORT. – April 4, 1975. [Weekly] (National Energy Information Center)

    Superseded by Monthly Petroleum Statistics Report (FE 1.9/4).

FE 1.9/2:date
PETROLEUM IMPORTS REPORTING SYSTEM, WEEKLY SITUATION REPORT. – September 6, 1974. (National Energy Information Center)

FE 1.9/3:date
WEEKLY PETROLEUM STATISTICS REPORTS. – April 4, 1975.

    Superseded by Monthly Petroleum Statistics Report (FE 1.9/4).

FE 1.9/4:date   • **Item 434-A-17**
MONTHLY PETROLEUM STATISTICS REPORT. 1975– (National Energy Information Center)

    ISSN 0364-0205
    Replaces Petroleum Situation Report (FE 1.9) and Weekly Petroleum Statistics Reports (FE 1.9/3).
    Later E 3.12

FE 1.9/5:date   • **Item 434-A-20**
MONTHLY PETROLEUM PRODUCT PRICE REPORT.

    Later E 3.24

FE 1.10:CT
ADDRESSES. [Irregular]

FE 1.11:nos.
DECISION LIST. [Weekly] (Office of Exceptions and Appeals)

    ISSN 0364-5835

FE 1.12:date   • **Item 434-A-16**
PETROLEUM MARKET SHARES. 1974– [Monthly] (National Energy Information Center)

    ISSN 0145-1278
    Later E 3.13

FE 1.12/2:CT   • **Item 434-A-16**
PETROLEUM MARKET SHARES, [REPORTS ON VARIOUS SUBJECTS]. [Irregular]

    Later E 3.13/2

FE 1.13:date   • **Item 434-A-6**
TELEPHONE DIRECTORY.

FE 1.14:date-nos.   • **Item 434-A-2**
MONTHLY ENERGY INDICATORS. – Aug. 1974. (National Energy Information Center)

FE 1.15:date   • **Item 434-A-3**
ENERGY INFORMATION REPORTED TO CONGRESS AS REQUIRED BY PUBLIC LAW 93-319. [Quarterly] (National Energy Information Center)

FE 1.15/2:date   • **Item 434-A-3**
REPORT TO CONGRESS ON THE ECONOMIC IMPACT OF ENERGY ACTIONS AS REQUIRED BY PUBLIC LAW 93-275, SECTION 18 (D). [Annual]

    ISSN 0360-330X

FE 1.16:date   • **Item 434-A-7**
FEDERAL ENERGY MANAGEMENT PROGRAM ANNUAL REPORTS.

FE 1.17:date
MONTHLY ENERGY REVIEW. 1974–   [Monthly]
(National Energy Information Center)

Indexed by: Index to U.S. Government Periodicals.
ISSN 0095-7356
Later E 3.9

FE 1.18:CT   • Item 434-A-5
PROJECT INDEPENDENCE [Publications]. [Irregular]

FE 1.19:date   • Item 434-A-8
ENERGY REPORTER, FEDERAL ENERGY ADMINISTRATION CITIZEN NEWSLETTER. 1975–
[Monthly] (Office of Communications and Public Affairs)

PURPOSE:– To present current and popular short news and feature articles on energy use, prices, conservation, etc., of interest to key communicators in government, industry, other private sectors,. and educational institutions.
ISSN 0363-8820
Later E 1.14

FE 1.20:nos.   • Item 434-A-13
TECHNICAL REPORTS. [Irregular] (Office of Policy and Analysis)

FE 1.21:nos.   • Item 434-A-9
FINAL ENVIRONMENTAL IMPACT STATEMENTS. [Irregular]

FE 1.22:nos.   • Item 434-A-10
CONSERVATION PAPERS. 1–   [Irregular]

FE 1.23:CT   • Item 434-A-12
BIBLIOGRAPHIES AND LISTS OF PUBLICATIONS. [Irregular]

FE 1.24:date   • Item 434-A-15
ENERGY INFORMATION IN THE FEDERAL GOVERNMENT, A DIRECTORY OF ENERGY SOURCES IDENTIFIED BY THE INTERAGENCY TASK FORCE ON ENERGY INFORMATION. [Annual]

FE 1.25:nos.   • Item 434-A-21
CONTINGENCY PLANS. 1–   [Irregular]

PURPOSE:– To present plans developed pursuant to the Energy Policy and Conservation Act (PL 94-163) to meet energy emergencies.

FE 1.26:date   • Item 434-A-22
QUARTERLY REPORT ON PRIVATE GRIEVANCES AND REDRESS.

FE 1.27:CT
INDUSTRIAL ENERGY CONSERVATION, FACT SHEETS. [Irregular]

FEDERAL EMERGENCY MANAGEMENT AGENCY
(1979–   )

CREATION AND AUTHORITY

The Federal Emergency Management Agency was established as an independent agency by Reorganization Plan No. 3 of 1978, effective April 1, 1979, pursuant to Executive Order 12127 of March 31, 1979, as amended by Executive Order 12148 of July 20, 1979.

INFORMATION

Office of Public Affairs
Federal Emergency Management Agency
Federal Center Plaza
500 C Street, S.W.
Washington, D.C. 20472
(202) 566-1600
Fax: (202) 646-2531
http://www.fema.gov

FEM 1.1:date   • Item 216-A-8 (MF)
REPORT TO THE PRESIDENT ON COMPREHENSIVE EMERGENCY MANAGEMENT. [Annual]

Purpose:– To summarize Agency activities as the focal point for comprehensive emergency management in nuclear attack, natural disasters such as floods and earthquakes, and man-made disasters such as arson, crime, terrorism, and radiological accidents.

FEM 1.1/2:region, date   • Item 216-A-8 (MF)
ANNUAL REPORT, FEDERAL EMERGENCY MANAGEMENT AGENCY (by Region).

FEM 1.2:CT   • Item 216-A-5
GENERAL PUBLICATIONS.

FEM 1.6:CT   • Item 216-A-13
REGULATIONS, RULES, AND INSTRUCTIONS. [Irregular]

FEM 1.8:CT   • Item 216-A-7
HANDBOOKS, MANUALS, GUIDES. [Irregular]

FEM 1.8/2:nos.   • Item 216-A-11 (MF)
CPG- (series). [Irregular]
Earlier D 14.8/6

FEM 1.8/3:nos.   • Item 857-D-10
HANDBOOKS, H- (series).
Earlier D 14.8/3

FEM 1.9:nos.   • Item 216-A-4
DISASTER INFORMATION. 1–   [Irregular]

PURPOSE:– To improve communication between the agency and people in private organizations, local, State, and the Federal Government who are involved in disaster litigation, preparedness, and response. Issued in newsletter format, contains information on specific disasters, State and Federal assistance provided, news items on legislation, and planning suggestions.
Earlier HH 12.9
[NOTE:– Fire Technology Abstracts was briefly assigned to this class number, which was cancelled and reassigned to FEM 1.109.]

FEM 1.10:date   • Item 434-B (MF)
NATIONAL DEFENSE EXECUTIVE RESERVE, ANNUAL REPORT TO THE PRESIDENT. 1st– 1979–

Summarizes the activities, status, and operations of the Reserve, which recruits and trains senior executives from the private sector to enter Government service in the event of a national emergency.

FEM 1.11:nos.   • Item 857-D-5
LEAFLET, L- (series). 1–   [Irregular]
Earlier D 14.12

FEM 1.12:date   • Item 434-B-1 (MF)
STOCKPILE REPORT TO THE CONGRESS. [Semiannual]
Earlier GS 1.22
Later D 1.94

FEM 1.13:nos.   • Item 320-B-9
HS [Home Study] (series). 1–   1971–   [Irregular]
Earlier D 14.11

FEM 1.14:date   • Item 216-A-6 (MF)
TELEPHONE DIRECTORY.

FEM 1.14/2:CT   • Item 216-A-20
DIRECTORIES. [Irregular]

FEM 1.15:CT   • Item 216-A-9 (MF)
ADDRESSES. [Irregular]

FEM 1.16:v.nos.&nos.   • Item 216-A-10
EMERGENCY MANAGEMENT. v. 1, no. 1–4. 1980– 1981. [Quarterly]

Presents articles on emergency planning and management in such situations as floods, volcanic eruptions, etc.

FEM 1.17:date
RESIDENTIAL PROGRAM HIGHLIGHTS. [Annual]

FEM 1.17/2:date   • Item 216-A-12 (EL)
EMERGENCY MANAGEMENT INSTITUTE, SCHEDULE OF COURSES. [Annual]

Former title: Emergency Management Institute, Resident Training Programs.

FEM 1.17/2-2   • Item 216-A-24 (EL)
CATALOG OF ACTIVITIES. [Annual]

FEM 1.17/3:date   • Item 216-A-12 (MF)
NATIONAL FIRE ACADEMY, CATALOG OF RESIDENT COURSES. [Annual]

FEM 1.18:nos.
DESIGN CASE STUDY (series). [Irregular]

FEM 1.19:date   • Item 216-A-14 (MF)
NATIONAL EARTHQUAKE HAZARD REDUCTION PROGRAM, A REPORT TO CONGRESS. [Annual]

Report submitted pursuant to Section 6 of the Earthquake Reduction Act of 1977 (PL 95-124), as amended. Highlights activities conducted during the fiscal year by all agency participants in the program.

FEM 1.20:date   • Item 216-A-16
FEMA NEWSLETTER. [Bimonthly]

Contains short articles on miscellaneous emergency management programs and activities.

FEM 1.21:CT   • Item 216-A-15
POSTERS. [Irregular]

FEM 1.22:   • Item 216-A-17 (MF)
RESEARCH PROJECTS. [Irregular]

FEM 1.23:date
WATERMARK. [Quarterly]

FEM 1.24:CT   • Item 216-A-18
BIBLIOGRAPHIES AND LISTS OF PUBLICATIONS. [Irregular]

FEM 1.25   • Item 216-A-19
EARTHQUAKE HAZARDS REDUCTION SERIES. [Irregular]

FEM 1.25   • Item 216-A-19
EARTHQUAKE HAZARDS REDUCTION SERIES. [Irregular]

FEM 1.26   • Item 216-A-21 (EL)
RECOVERY TIMES.

FEM 1.27   • Item 216-A-21 (E)
ELECTRONIC PRODUCTS. (Misc.)

FEM 1.28   • Item 216-A-25 (EL)
FEMA NEWS RELEASES.

UNITED STATES FIRE ADMINISTRATION
(1979–   )

CREATION AND AUTHORITY

The United States Fire Administration (C 58) was transferred from the Department of Commerce to the Federal Emergency Management Agency by Reorganization Plan No. 3 of 1978, effective April 1, 1979, pursuant to Executive Order 12127 of March 31, 1979.

INFORMATION

United States Fire Administration
Federal Emergency Management Agency
16825 South Seton Ave.
Emmitsburg, MD 21727
(301) 447-1018
Fax: (301) 447-1270
http://www.usfa.fema.gov

FEM 1.101:date • Item 216-A-2 (MF)
ANNUAL REPORT.
Earlier C 58.1

FEM 1.102:CT • Item 216-A-1
GENERAL PUBLICATIONS. [Irregular]

Earlier C 58.2

FEM 1.108:CT • Item 216-A-3
HANDBOOKS, MANUALS, GUIDES. [Irregular]
Earlier C 58.8

FEM 1.109:v.nos.&nos. • Item 215-L-2
FIRE TECHNOLOGY ABSTRACTS. v. 1– 5. 1977– 1982. [Bimonthly]

PURPOSE:– To provide comprehensive reference to the applied fire literature in a broad range of topics.
Earlier C 58.11

FEM 1.110:date • Item 215-L-4
RESOURCE EXCHANGE BULLETIN. [Irregular]

PURPOSE:– To provide a newsletter with information on Federal and other fire prevention and safety education programs, source materials, activities, etc. Intended for States, communities, fire educators, schools, etc.

FEM 1.110/2:date • Item 215-L-4
ARSON RESOURCE RESOURCE BULLETIN. [Irregular]
Former title: Arson Resource Bulletin.

FEM 1.110/3:date • Item 215-L-4
EMS [Emergency Medical Services] RESOURCE EXCHANGE BULLETIN. [Semiannual]

FEM 1.111:date • Item 215-L-5
FULLY INVOLVED. [Biweekly]

PURPOSE:– To provide news of the current firefighting conferences, tests of fire prevention equipment, job opportunities, and other matters of firefighting concern.

FEM 1.111/2:CT • Item 215-L-5
FULLY INVOLVED [special issues]. [Irregular]

FEM 1.115:nos. • Item 216-A-22 (EL)
TECHNICAL REPORT SERIES. [Irregular]

FEM 1.116 • Item 216-A-23 (EL)
FIREFIGHTER FATALITIES. [Annual]

FEM 1.117 • Item 216-A-26 (EL)
FIRE IN THE UNITED STATES. [Annual]

FEM 1.117/2 • Item 216-A-27
PROFILE ON FIRE IN THE UNITED STATES. [Annual]

FEDERAL INSURANCE ADMINISTRATION
(1979–   )

CREATION AND AUTHORITY

The Federal Insurance Administration (HH 10) was transferred from the Department of Housing and Urban Development to the Federal Emergency Management Agency by Reorganization Plan No. 3 of 1978, effective April 1, 1979, pursuant to Executive Order 12127 of March 31, 1979.

INFORMATION

Federal Insurance Administration
Federal Emergency Management Agency
Federal Center Plaza
500 C Street, SW
Washington, D.C. 20472
(202) 646-2781
http://www.fema.gov/fima

FEM 1.201:date • Item 439-A-2 (MF)
ANNUAL REPORT.

FEM 1.202:CT • Item 439-A-1
GENERAL PUBLICATIONS. [Irregular]

FEM 1.208:CT • Item 594-E
HANDBOOKS, MANUALS, GUIDES. [Irregular]

Earlier HH 10.8

FEM 1.209:nos. • Item 594-C-1– C-55 (MF)
FLOOD INSURANCE STUDIES (various areas). [Irregular]

Title varies: Some issues entitled Flood Insurance Reports.
Earlier HH 10.9

FEM 1.209/nos. • Item 594-C-1– 53 (MF)
FLOOD INSURANCE STUDIES (various areas) [State].

FEM 1.210:date • Item 594-D (MF)
NATIONAL FLOOD INSURANCE PROGRAM COMMUNITY STATUS BOOK, NATIONWIDE INFORMATION. [Bimonthly]

Lists both communities that participate in the National Flood Insurance Program with their entry dates and map effective dates; and also those that do not participate but who have had special flood hazards on which sanctions apply. Intended for lenders, property owners, Federal, State, and local agencies, and the general public.

FEM 1.210/1– /52 • Item 594-C-1– 53 (MF)
COMMUNITY STATUS BOOK (State). [Bimonthly]

Separate report issued for each State.

FEM 1.211:letters&nos. • Item 594-E
DISASTER RESPONSE AND RECOVERY.

FEDERAL FARM BOARD
(1929– 1933)

CREATION AND AUTHORITY

The Federal Farm Board was established as an independent agency by the Agricultural Marketing Act, approved June 15, 1929 (46 Stat. 11). By Executive Order 6084 of March 27, 1933, effective May 17, 1933, the Board was consolidated with certain other agencies to form the Farm Credit Administration.

FF 1.1:date
ANNUAL REPORTS.

FF 1.2:CT
GENERAL PUBLICATIONS.

FF 1.3
BULLETINS.

FF 1.4
CIRCULARS.

FF 1.5
LAWS.

FF 1.6
REGULATIONS

FF 1.7:v.nos.
AGRICULTURAL COOPERATION. [Fortnightly]

Earlier A 36.12

FF 1.8:date
REPORT OF ACTIVITIES.

FEDERAL HOUSING FINANCE BOARD
(1989 -   )

INFORMATION

Federal Housing Finance Board
1777 F Street, NW
Washington, DC 20006-5210
(202) 408-2500
Fax: (202) 408-1435
http://www.fhfb.gov

FHF 1.15 • Item 595-B (EL)
RATES & TERMS ON CONVENTIONAL HOME MORTGAGES ANNUAL SUMMARY.

FEDERAL HOME LOAN BANK BOARD
(1955–1989)

CREATION AND AUTHORITY

The Home Loan Bank Board (HH 4), a constituent agency of the Housing and Home Finance Agency was made an independent agency by the Housing Amendments of 1955 (69 Stat. 640) and redesignated the Federal Home Loan Bank Board. Abolished by an act of August 9, 1989 (103 Stat. 354, 415)

FHL 1.1 • Item 595
REPORT OF THE FEDERAL HOME LOAN BANK BOARD FOR THE YEAR ENDING DECEMBER 31. 1947– [Annual]

Report submitted by the Board to Congress pursuant to section 17(b) of the Federal Home Loan Bank Act for the calendar year.
Covers the operations of the Federal Home Loan Bank System, Federal Savings and Loan Insurance Corporation, and the Federal Savings and Loan System.

FHL 1.1/2:date • Item 595-A (MF)
ANNUAL REPORT, WORKFORCE PROFILE.

Designed to provide Bank Board managers with an overview of the agency's personnel management program.

FHL 1.2:CT • Item 596
GENERAL PUBLICATIONS.
Earlier HH 4.2
Later T 71.2

FHL 1.2:F 31/2 • Item 596
FEDERAL SAVINGS AND LOAN INSURANCE CORPORATION, FINANCIAL STATEMENTS. [Quarterly]

Issued as of March 31, June 30, September 30, and December 31.

FHL 1.6:CT • Item 597
REGULATIONS, RULES, AND INSTRUCTIONS.
Earlier HH 4.6
Later T 71.6

FHL 1.6:Sa 9 • Item 597
RULES AND REGULATIONS FOR FEDERAL SAVINGS AND LOAN SYSTEM, WITH AMENDMENTS TO [date]. 1933– [Irregular]

Kept up-to-date by insert sheets.

FHL 1.6/2:CT • Item 597
HANDBOOKS, MANUALS, GUIDES.
Later T 71.8

FHL 1.6/2:St 2 • Item 597
ANNOTATED MANUAL OF STATUTES AND REGU-
LATIONS OF THE FEDERAL HOME LOAN
BANK BOARD. Oct. 1973. 652 p. (includes
basic volume plus supplementary materials
for an indefinite period)

FHL 1.7 • Item 596-A-1
PRESS RELEASES. [Irregular]

FHL 1.7/2:date
FLOW OF SAVINGS IN SAVINGS AND LOAN ASSO-
CIATIONS. [Monthly]

Earlier HH 4.8/2

FHL 1.7/3:date
MORTGAGE LENDING ACTIVITY OF SAVINGS AND
LOAN ASSOCIATIONS. [Monthly]

Earlier HH 4.8/3

FHL 1.8
NONFARM REAL ESTATE FORECLOSURE REPORT.
[Quarterly & Annual]

Gives estimated nonfarm real estate foreclosures by month for five recent years, and annual
data prior to that period. Annual release issued in
March. Figures also appear in the Source Book.

FHL 1.8/2:date
REAL ESTATE FORECLOSURE REPORT. [Quarterly]
– 1970.

Replaces Nonfarm Real Estate Foreclosure
Report, (FHL 1.8).
Statistics now included in Journal of the Fed-
eral Home Loan Bank Board (FHL 1.27).

FHL 1.9:date
MORTGAGE RECORDING LETTER. [Monthly]

Earlier HH 4.9

FHL 1.10:date
SAVINGS, MORTGAGE FINANCING AND HOUSING
DATA. [Monthly]

Replaced by FHL 1.20
Earlier HH 4.10

FHL 1.11 • Item 597-A-1
SAVINGS AND HOME FINANCING. SOURCE BOOK.
1952– [Annual]

Statistical tables on various aspects of savings and home financing, with emphasis placed
on the institutions affiliated with the Federal Home
Loan Bank System and the Federal Savings and
Loan Insurance Corporation. Can be kept up-to-
date by use of the various periodic releases issued by the Board.
Later T 71.17

FHL 1.11/2:nos.
SAVINGS AND HOME FINANCING CHART BOOK.

FHL 1.12 • Item 597-A-2 (MF)
COMBINED FINANCIAL STATEMENTS OF MEMBERS
OF THE FEDERAL HOME LOAN BANK SYSTEM.
1947– [Annual]

Detailed data for member savings and loan
associations, insurance savings and loan associations, insured and uninsured state-chartered
member savings and loans associations, by savings capital size groups.
ISSN 0145-7845

FHL 1.12/2:date
FHLB SYSTEM S & LA's COMBINED FINANCIAL
STATEMENTS: SAVINGS AND HOME FINANCING
SOURCE BOOK. 1970– [Annual]

Combines two publications previously published as Savings and Home Financing Source
Book (FHL 1.11) and Combined financial statements of Members of the Federal Home Loan
Bank System (FHL 1.12).
Part 1 gives statistical data on various aspects of savings and home financing, with emphasis placed on the institutions affiliated with

the Federal Home Loan Bank System and the
Federal Savings and Loan Insurance Corporation. Can be kept up-to-date by use of the various
periodic releases issued by the Board.
Part 2 gives detailed data for member savings and loan associations, insured savings and
loan associations, Federal savings and loan associations, insured and uninsured state- chartered member savings and loans associations,
by savings capital size groups.

FHL 1.13:date
INVESTMENT OF INDIVIDUALS IN SAVINGS
ACCOUNTS, U.S. SAVINGS BONDS AND LIFE
INSURANCE RESERVES. [Annual]

Earlier HH 4.2:In 9

FHL 1.14
FEDERAL HOME LOAN BANK BOARD DIGEST. v. 1–
1958– [Monthly]

News organ for the activities of the Board
and the Federal Home Loan Bank System.
Index issued separately.

FHL 1.15
TRENDS IN THE SAVINGS AND LOAN FIELD. [Annual]

Presented in summary form, gives historical
figures of all operating savings and loan associations (including cooperative banks and homestead
associations). Supplemental tables give assets
and liabilities for current year by FHLB districts
and States.

FHL 1.15/2:date
SAVINGS AND LOAN ACTIVITY IN (Month). [Monthly]

FHL 1.16
ESTIMATED HOME MORTGAGE DEBT AND
FINANCING ACTIVITY. [Quarterly and Annual]

Gives estimated home mortgage loans outstanding, one- to four-family nonfarm homes;
estimated nonfarm mortgages of $20,000 or less
recorded. Historical tables. Figures also appear in
the Source Book.

FHL 1.17:date
PARTICIPATION LOAN TRANSACTIONS.

Earlier FHL 1.2:L 78

FHL 1.18
NONFARM MORTGAGE INVESTMENTS OF LIFE
INSURANCE COMPANIES. [Annual]

Gives nonfarm mortgage investments, by type
of property and mortgage loan; historical tables
on nonfarm mortgage loans held, nonfarm mortgages loans acquired, ratio of nonfarm holdings
to admitted assets, nonfarm real estate sold under contract and nonfarm real estate owned.
Charts.

FHL 1.19:date
CONVENTIONAL LOANS MADE IN EXCESS OF 80
PERCENT OF PROPERTY APPRAISAL BY FED-
ERAL SAVINGS AND LOAN ASSOCIATIONS.
[Quarterly]

FHL 1.20
ALL OPERATING SAVINGS AND LOAN ASSOCIA-
TIONS, SELECTED BALANCE SHEET DATA.
[Monthly]

Table 1 gives selected balance sheet data,
table 2 gives flow of savings and mortgage lending activity, by months for current and previous
year.
ISSN 0364-7536

FHL 1.20/2
FSLIC INSURED SAVINGS AND LOAN ASSOCIA-
TIONS, SAVINGS AND MORTGAGE ACTIVITY,
SELECTED BALANCE SHEET ITEMS. [Monthly]

Tables giving savings account and mortgage
lending activities, as well as various summarized
data of savings and loan associations. Textual
summary.

FHL 1.21:date
INSURED SAVINGS AND LOAN ASSOCIATIONS,
AVERAGE ANNUAL DIVIDEND RATES PAID. [An-
nual]

Earlier FHL 1.2:In 7/2

FHL 1.22:date
CONVENTIONAL LOANS MADE TO FINANCE AC-
QUISITION AND DEVELOPMENT OF LAND, FED-
ERAL SAVINGS AND LOAN ASSOCIATIONS.
[Quarterly]

FHL 1.23
ADDRESSES. [Irregular]

FHL 1.24:date
MORTGAGE INTEREST RATES ON CONVENTIONAL
LOANS, LARGEST INSURED SAVINGS AND LOAN
ASSOCIATIONS. [Monthly]

FHL 1.25
HOME MORTGAGE INTEREST RATES AND TERMS.
[Monthly]

Gives the average interest rate and other
characteristics of conventional first mortgage
loans originated by five major types of lenders for
the purchase of new and existing single-family
homes. Objective is to keep the Board informed
of trends and spread of rates. Textual interpretation points up main developments noted during
current and over recent periods, and variations
among FHLB districts.

FHL 1.25/2:date
HOME MORTGAGE INTEREST RATES CONTINUE TO
DECLINE IN EARLY (Month). [Monthly]

FHL 1.25/3:date • Item 596-A
CONVENTIONAL HOME MORTGAGE RATES IN
EARLY (month). [Monthly]

The news release presents narrative and tabular information on terms of conventional home
mortgages, including averages for selected metropolitan areas.
Later T 71.7

FHL 1.26:date
NUMBER OF FORECLOSURES [and rate of foreclo-
sure] BY FSLIC INSURED SAVINGS AND LOAN
ASSOCIATIONS. [Quarterly]

FHL 1.27 • Item 597-A-2
JOURNAL OF THE FEDERAL HOME LOAN BANK
BOARD. v. 1– 1968– [Monthly]

PURPOSE:– To expand information services
of the Federal Home Loan Bank Board activities
for the savings and loan industry, the news media, and the general public.
Contains statements by Board members,
changes in regulations, Board rulings and legal
opinions, and other articles of current interest in
the savings and mortgage lending fields.
Later T 71.15
Indexed by: Index to U.S. Government Periodicals
ISSN 0041-7645

FHL 1.28:date
ECONOMIC BRIEFS. [Monthly] (Office of Economic
Research)

PURPOSE:– To provide a capsule summary
of current economic conditions in the financial
and housing markets.
ISSN 0364-1279

FHL 1.29:date • Item 597-A-4 (MF)
SUMMARY OF SAVINGS ACCOUNTS BY GEO-
GRAPHIC AREA, FSLIC-INSURED SAVINGS AND
LOAN ASSOCIATIONS. [Annual]
Earlier FHL 1.2:Sa 9/4

FHL 1.30:date • Item 597-A-5 (MF)
ASSET AND LIABILITY TRENDS, ALL OPERATING
SAVINGS AND LOAN ASSOCIATIONS. [Annual]

Tables present selected financial and balance
sheet items for savings and loan associations by
States and by Federal Home Loan Bank Districts.
Earlier FHL 1.2:As 7

FHL 1.31:date • Item 596
MEMBERS OF THE FEDERAL HOME LOAN BANK
SYSTEM. [Annual]

Discontinued.

FHL 1.32:v.nos.&nos. • Item 597-A-3
HOUSING FINANCE REVIEW. v. 1– 1982–
[Quarterly]

Presents articles on such subjects as deposit costs and mortgage rates. Provides a forum for a continuing dialogue by providing articles on both sides of an issue. Articles include an abstract and references.

FHL 1.33:date • Item 597-A-6
THRIFT INSTITUTION ACTIVITY IN (month). [Monthly]
News release on thrift institution activity in such areas as assets and liabilities, mortgage lending, and deposit withdrawals.

FHL 1.34:date
ARM INDEX RATES. [Monthly]

FHL 1.35:nos. • Item 595-A-2 (MF)
RESEARCH WORKING PAPERS (series). [Irregular]

FEDERAL INTERDEPARTMENTAL SAFETY COUNCIL
(1939– 1950)

CREATION AND AUTHORITY

The Federal Interdepartmental Safety Council was established by Executive Order 8071 of March 21, 1939. The Council was succeeded by the Federal Safety Council (L 30), established by Executive Order 10194 of December 19, 1950.

FIS 1.1:date
ANNUAL REPORTS.

Later L 30.1

FIS 1.2:CT
GENERAL PUBLICATIONS.

Later L 30.2

FIS 1.7:CT
ADDRESSES.

FIS 1.8:v.nos.
FEDERAL SAFETY NEWS. [Bimonthly]

Replaced by Safety Standards (L 16.34).

FEDERAL LOAN AGENCY
(1939– 1947)

CREATION AND AUTHORITY

The Federal Loan Agency was established as an independent agency by Reorganization Plan No. 1 of 1939, effective July 1, 1939, which transferred to the Corporation those agencies established for the purpose of stimulating and stabilizing the financial, industrial, and commercial enterprises of the Nation. Executive Order 9070 of February 24, 1942, transferred those agencies performing housing functions from the Agency to the National Housing Agency. Executive Order 9071 of February 24, 1942, transferred the remaining agencies to the Office of the Secretary of Commerce. The later group was returned to the Federal Loan Agency by act of Congress, approved February 24, 1945 (59 Stat. 5). By act of Congress, approved June 30, 1947 (61 Stat 202),

the Agency was abolished and its functions transferred to the Reconstruction Finance Corporation (Y 3.R 24).

FL 1.1:date
ANNUAL REPORTS.

FL 1.2:CT
GENERAL PUBLICATIONS.

FL 1.7:CT
ADDRESSES.

FL 1.8:v.nos.
FEDERAL LOAN AGENCY NEWS. [Biweekly]

FEDERAL HOUSING ADMINISTRATION
(1939– 1942)

CREATION AND AUTHORITY

The Federal Housing Administration (Y 3.F 31/11) was transferred to the Federal Loan Agency by Reorganization Plan No. 1, effective July 1, 1939. Executive Order 9070 of February 24, 1942 transferred the Agency to the newly created National Housing Agency (NHA 2).

FL 2.1:date
ANNUAL REPORT.

Earlier Y 3.F 31/11:1
Later NHA 2.1

FL 2.2:CT
GENERAL PUBLICATIONS.

Earlier Y 3.F 31/11:2
Later NHA 2.2

FL 2.3
BULLETINS.

FL 2.4
CIRCULARS.

Earlier Y 3.F 31/11:4

FL 2.5:CT
LAWS.

Earlier Y 3.F 31/11:5

FL 2.6:CT
REGULATIONS, RULES, AND INSTRUCTIONS.

Earlier Y 3.F 31/11:7
Later NHA 2.6

FL 2.7:vol
CLIP SHEETS. [Weekly]

Earlier Y 3.F 31/11:14
Later NHA 2.10

FL 2.8:nos.
MAGAZINE DIGEST. [Weekly]

Earlier Y 3.F 31.11:21

FL 2.9:nos.
PRESS DIGEST. [Daily except Sat. and Sun.]

Earlier Y 3.F 31/11:38
Later NHA 2.9

FL 2.10:nos.
ADVERTISING DIGEST. [Weekly]

Earlier Y 3.F 31/11:39

FL 2.11:CT
MINIMUM CONSTRUCTION REQUIREMENTS FOR
NEW DWELLINGS.
Earlier Y 3.F 31/11:2 D 96/2-60

FL 2.12:vol
INSURED MORTGAGE PORTFOLIO. [Monthly]
Earlier Y 3.F 31/11:32
Later NHA 2.8

FL 2.13:date
AMORTIZATION SCHEDULES.
Earlier Y 3.F 31/11:36

FL 2.14:nos.
GENERAL ORDERS.
Earlier Y 3.F 31/11:16

FL 2.15:nos.
TECHNICAL BULLETINS.
Earlier Y 3.F 31/11:19

FL 2.16:nos.
LAND PLANNING BULLETINS.

FL 2.17:nos.
TECHNICAL CIRCULARS.
Earlier Y 3.F 31/11:40
Later NHA 2.12

FL 2.18:CT
ADDRESSES.
Earlier Y 3.F 31/11:10

FL 2.19:nos.
COMPTROLLER [circular letters].
Earlier Y 3.F 31/11:37
Later NHA 2.11

FL 2.20:nos.
ARCHITECTURAL BULLETINS.

FL 2.21:nos.
TECHNICAL LETTERS.

FEDERAL HOME LOAN BANK BOARD
(1939– 1942)

CREATION AND AUTHORITY

The Federal Home Loan Bank Board (Y 3.F 31/3) was transferred to the Federal Loan Agency by Reorganization Plan No. 1 of 1939, effective July 1, 1939. Under Executive Order 9070 of February 24, 1942, the Board was transferred to the National Housing Agency (NHA 3) and redesignated as the Federal Home Loan Bank Administration.

FL 3.1:date
ANNUAL REPORTS.
Earlier Y 3.F 31/3:1
Later NHA 3.1

FL 3.2:CT
GENERAL PUBLICATIONS.
Earlier Y 3.F 31/3:2
Later NHA 3.2

FL 3.5:CT
LAWS.
Later NHA 3.5

FL 3.6:CT
REGULATIONS, RULES, AND INSTRUCTIONS.
Later NHA 3.6

FL 3.7:v.nos.
FEDERAL HOME LOAN BANK REVIEW. [Monthly]

Earlier Y 3.F 31/3:9
Later NHA 3.8

FL 3.8:date
NON-FARM REAL ESTATE FORECLOSURES.
[Monthly]

> Earlier Y 3.F 31/3:10
> Later NHA 3.9

FL 3.9:CT
HOME OWNERS' LOAN CORPORATION PUBLICA-
TIONS.

> Earlier Y 3.F 31/3:8

ELECTRIC HOME AND FARM
AUTHORITY
(1939– 1942)

CREATION AND AUTHORITY

The Electric Home and Farm Authority (Y 3.EI
2/2) was transferred to the Federal Loan Agency
by Reorganization Plan No. 1 of 1939, effective
July 1, 1939. The Authority along with the Federal
Loan Agency was transferred to the Department
of Commerce by Executive Order 9071 of February 24, 1942 and terminated by Executive Order
9256 of October 13, 1942.

FL 4.1:date
ANNUAL REPORTS.

> Earlier Y 3.EI 2/2:1

FL 4.2:CT
GENERAL PUBLICATIONS.

> Earlier Y 3.EI 2/2:2

FL 4.4:nos.
CIRCULARS.

> Earlier Y 3.EI 2/2:4

RECONSTRUCTION FINANCE
CORPORATION
(1939– 1942)

CREATION AND AUTHORITY

The Reconstruction Finance Corporation (Y
3.R 24) was transferred to the Federal Loan
Agency by Reorganization Plan No. 1 of 1939,
effective July 1, 1939. The Corporation was transferred to the Department of Commerce (C 33) by
Executive Order 9071 of February 24, 1942.

FL 5.1:date
ANNUAL REPORTS.
> Earlier Y 3.R 24:1
> Later C 33.1

FL 5.2:CT
GENERAL PUBLICATIONS.
> Earlier Y 3.R 24:2
> Later C 33.2

FL 5.4:nos.
CIRCULARS.
> Earlier Y 3.R 24:4
> Later C 33.4

FL 5.5:CT
LAWS.
> Earlier Y 3.R 24.5
> Later C 33.5, Y 3.R 24:5

FL 5.6:CT
REGULATIONS, RULES, AND INSTRUCTIONS.

FL 5.7:date
QUARTERLY REPORTS.

> Earlier Y 3.R 24:7
> Later C 33.7

FL 5.8:date
REPORTS. [Monthly]

> When Congress is in session these reports
> are issued as House Documents.
> Earlier Y 3.R 24:11

FL 5.9:CT
ADDRESSES.

> Earlier Y 3.R 24:12
> Later C 33.10

FL 5.10:CT
PAPERS IN RE.

> Earlier Y 3.R 24:10
> Later C 33.8

FL 5.11:date
SUMMARY OF SURPLUS PROPERTY. [Semimonthly]

> Earlier C 33.11
> Later Pr 33.210

FL 5.12:date
RFC SURPLUS PROPERTY NEWS.

> Later Pr 33.207

FL 5.13:nos.
SURPLUS GOVERNMENT PROPERTY SPECIAL LIST-
INGS.

> Later Pr 33.209

FL 5.14:nos.
SURPLUS REPORTER.

FL 5.15:date
RFC SMALL BUSINESS ACTIVITIES. [Bimonthly]

FL 5.16:CT
FEDERAL NATIONAL MORTGAGE ASSOCIATION
INFORMATION CIRCULARS.

FL 5.17:date
FEDERAL NATIONAL MORTGAGE ASSOCIATION.
[Semiannual]

FEDERAL MEDIATION AND
CONCILIATION SERVICE
(1947–   )

CREATION AND AUTHORITY

The Federal Mediation and Conciliation Service was established by the Labor Management
Relations Act, 1947 (61 Stat. 153).

INFORMATION

Office of Information
Federal Mediation and Conciliation Service
2100 K Street, N.W.
Washington, D. C. 20427
(202) 606-8080
Fax: (202) 606-4251
http://www.fmcs.gov

FM 1.1   • Item 433 (MF)
ANNUAL REPORT. 1st–   1948–   [Annual]

> Report submitted by the Service to Congress
> pursuant to section 202(c) of the Labor Manage-
> ment Relations Act of 1947 for the fiscal year.

Included in a section devoted to significant
disputes in the various industries such as metals, missile and airframe, shipbuilding, atomic
energy, maritime, and food.

FM 1.2:CT   • Item 434
GENERAL PUBLICATIONS.

> Earlier L 19.2

FM 1.7:date
PRESS RELEASES.

FM 1.8:CT   • Item 434
ADDRESSES.

FM 1.9:nos.   • Item 433-A
GUIDELINES: INNOVATIVE COLLECTIVE BARGAIN-
ING CONTRACT PROVISIONS.

FEDERAL MARITIME
COMMISSION
(1961–   )

CREATION AND AUTHORITY

The Federal Maritime Commission was established by Reorganization Plan 7, effective August 12, 1961, as an independent agency to administer the functions and discharge the regulatory authorities under the Shipping Act, 1916;
Merchant Marine Act, 1920; Intercoastal Shipping Act, 1933; and Merchant Marine Act, 1936.

INFORMATION

Federal Maritime Commission
800 N. Capitol Street, NW
Washington, D.C. 20573
(202) 523-5725
Fax: (202) 523-3782
http://www.fmc.gov

FMC 1.1   • Item 233-A-1 (MF)
ANNUAL REPORT. 1st–   1962–   [Annual]

> Report submitted by the Chairman to Con-
> gress pursuant to section 103(e) of Reorganiza-
> tion Plan No. 7 of 1961, and section 208 of the
> Merchant Marine Act of 1936, for the fiscal year.

FMC 1.1/2   • Item 233-A-4 (EL)
FREEDON OF INFORMATION ACT ANNUAL REPORT.

FMC 1.2:CT   • Item 432-L-1
GENERAL PUBLICATIONS.

FMC 1.6:CT   • Item 237
REGULATIONS, RULES, AND INSTRUCTIONS.

FMC 1.6/2   • Item 233-A-10
HANDBOOKS, MANUALS, GUIDES.

FMC 1.7:nos.   • Item 233-A-9 (EL)
NEWS RELEASES, NR (series).

FMC 1.9
FEDERAL MARITIME COMMISSION SPEECHES, FMC
SP- (series). [Irregular]

FMC 1.9/2:CT
ADDRESSES.

FMC 1.9/3   • Item 233-A-5 (EL)
SPEECHES AND REMARKS.

FMC 1.10:v.nos.   • Item 233-A
DECISIONS OF THE MARITIME COMMISSION,
FEDERAL MARITIME BOARD, AND MARITIME
ADMINISTRATION. v. 1–   [Irregular]

> Published under the direction of the Federal
> Maritime Commission and the Maritime Adminis-
> tration.

FMC 1.10/a
FEDERAL MARITIME COMMISSION, DECISIONS, SEPARATES. [Irregular]

FMC 1.10/a2:date
[ORDERS, NOTICES, RULINGS AND DECISIONS (initial and final) ISSUED BY HEARING EXAMINERS AND BY THE COMMISSION IN FORMAL DOCKETED PROCEEDINGS BEFORE THE FEDERAL MARITIME COMMISSION] [Irregular]

FMC 1.10/2   • Item 233-A-6 (EL)
FORMAL DOCKET DECISIONS.

FMC 1.10/3   • Item 233-A-7 (EL)
SMALL CLAIMS DECISIONS (Informal Dockets).

FMC 1.11   • Item 432-L (MF)
APPROVED CONFERENCE, RATE AND INTERCONFERENCE AGREEMENTS OF STEAMSHIP LINES IN THE FOREIGN COMMERCE OF THE UNITED STATES. 1976–   [Annual]

   Issued in looseleaf form, punched for ring binder. Subscription includes basic manual plus supplementary material for an indefinite period.
   A compilation listing approved agreements of common carriers by water in the foreign commerce of the United States. It lists conference, rate and interconference agreements, showing agreement numbers, current membership, trade areas, representatives with addresses and other information pertaining to the agreements listed.

FMC 1.12:date   • Item 432-L-2 (MF)
AUTOMOBILE MANUFACTURERS MEASUREMENTS. [Annual]

   Tabular presentation of measurement data showing model, make, cubic feet, and weight of automobiles sold in the U.

FMC 1.13   • Item 233-A-8 (EL)
FORMS.

FMC 1.15   • Item 233-A-3 (EL)
TELEPHONE DIRECTORY.

IGN OPERATIONS ADMINISTRATION
(1953–1955)

CREATION AND AUTHORITY

   The Foreign Operations Administration was established by Reorganization Plan No. 7 of 1953, effective August 1, 1953, to administer the Mutual Security and Technical Cooperation (Point 4) programs. The Mutual Security Agency was abolished, while the Technical Cooperation Administration and the Institute of Inter-American Affairs (S 1.64) were transferred from the Department of State to the Foreign Operations Administration under Reorganization Plan No. 7. Under Executive Order 10610 of May 9, 1955, the Administration was abolished and its functions transferred to the newly established International Cooperation Administration (S 17) in the Department of State, effective July 1, 1955.

FO 1.1:date
ANNUAL REPORTS.
   Later S 17.1
FO 1.1/2:nos.
SEMIANNUAL REPORT ON OPERATIONS UNDER MUTUAL DEFENSE ASSISTANCE CONTROL ACT OF 1951.
   Earlier Pr 33.901/2
   Later S 17.1/2

FO 1.2:CT
GENERAL PUBLICATIONS.
   Later S 17.2

FO 1.3:nos.
PROCUREMENT INFORMATION BULLETINS.
   Later S 17.3

FO 1.3/2:nos.
TECHNICAL BULLETINS.

FO 1.5:CT
LAWS.

FO 1.6
REGULATIONS, RULES, AND INSTRUCTIONS.
   Later S 17.6

FO 1.6/2:nos.
REGULATIONS (Numbered).

FO 1.7
RELEASES.

FO 1.8:date
PROCUREMENT AUTHORIZATIONS AND ALLOTMENTS, EUROPEAN AND FAR EAST PROGRAMS. [Monthly]
   Earlier Pr 33.908

FO 1.9:date
PAID SHIPMENTS, EUROPEAN AND FAR EAST PROGRAM. [Monthly]
   Earlier Pr 33.909

FO 1.9/2:date
ALLOTMENTS, AUTHORIZATIONS, & PAID SHIPMENTS, DATA. [Monthly]
   Consolidation of FO 1.8 and FO 1.9

FO 1.10:date
MONTHLY REPORT ON EUROPEAN AND FAR EAST PROGRAMS.
   Earlier Pr 33.910
   Later S 17.10

FO 1.11:date
EUROPEAN PROGRAM, LOCAL CURRENCY COUNTERPART FUNDS. [Monthly]
   Earlier Pr 33.911

FO 1.11/2:date
FAR EAST PROGRAM, LOCAL CURRENCY COUNTERPART FUNDS. [Monthly]
   Earlier Pr 33.911/2

FO 1.11/3:date
COUNTERPART FUNDS AND FOA FOREIGN CURRENCY ACCOUNTS.
   Earlier FO 1.11 and FO 1.11/2
   Later S 17.11/3

FO 1.12
EUROPEAN AND FAR EAST PROGRAM, LOCAL CURRENCY COUNTERPART FUNDS. [Monthly]

   A Consolidation of FO 1.11 and FO 1.11/2.
   Earlier S 17.11/3

FO 1.13
SMALL BUSINESS CIRCULAR FOA/SBC (series).
   Later S 17.13

FO 1.13/2
SMALL BUSINESS CIRCULAR TCA/SBC (series).
   Earlier Pr 33.913/2

FO 1.14
SMALL BUSINESS MEMO FOA/SBM (series).
   Later S 17.14

FO 1.16:nos.
CONTACT CLEARING HOUSE SERVICE CCHS SUMMARY.
   Earlier Pr 33.916

FO 1.17:nos.
SMALL BUSINESS WEEKLY SUMMARY, TRADE OPPORTUNITIES AND INFORMATION FOR AMERICAN SUPPLIERS.
   Earlier Pr 33.917

FO 1.18:date
INDUSTRIAL PROJECTS BULLETIN. [Monthly]
   Later S 17.18

FO 1.22:date
REPORT OF COMMODITIES AND FUNDS FOR RELIEF AND REHABILITATION BY AMERICAN AGENCIES REGISTERED WITH ADVISORY COMMITTEE ON VOLUNTARY FOREIGN AID AS SHOWN ON THEIR MONTHLY SCHEDULE C 200 REPORTS OF EXPERTS [and Summary Statement of Income and Expenditures of Voluntary Relief Agencies Registered with Advisory Committee on Voluntary Foreign Aid as Shown in their Schedule C 100 Reports]. [Quarterly]

   Earlier S 1.99/3

FO 1.23
SRE SPECIAL PUBLICATIONS.

FO 1.23/2:CT
SPECIAL REPRESENTATIVE IN EUROPE PUBLICATIONS.

FO 1.24:nos.
FOA FACT SHEETS. [Irregular]

FO 1.25:CT
FOA COUNTRY SERIES.

   Earlier MSA Country Series (Pr 33.919).
   Later S 17.25

FO 1.26:nos.
FOA FINANCED AWARDS.

   Later S 17.26

FO 1.27:CT
MUTUAL SECURITY MISSION TO CHINA, PUBLICATIONS.

   Earlier Pr 33.921

FO 1.28
PLANT REQUIREMENTS REPORTS (series).

   Later S 17.28

FO 1.29:CT
TRAINING FILMS.

   Later S 17.29/1

FO 1.30
ECONOMIC FORCES IN UNITED STATES IN FACTS AND FIGURES.

   Earlier S 17.8

FO 1.31
NEWSLETTER ON COMMUNITY DEVELOPMENT IN TECHNICAL COOPERATION.

   Later S 17.31

FO 1.32:CT
BIBLIOGRAPHIES AND LISTS OF PUBLICATIONS.

FEDERAL POWER COMMISSION
(1920–1977)

CREATION AND AUTHORITY

   The Federal Power Commission was established on an interdepartmental basis by the Federal Water Power Act, approved June 10, 1920 (41 Stat. 1063) and organized as an independent regulatory agency by an amending act approved June 23, 1930 (46 Stat. 797). The Commission was abolished and its functions transferred to the Federal Energy Regulatory Commission (E 2) of the Department of Energy by Act of August 4, 1977 (91 Stat. 565), effective October 1, 1977.

FP 1.1   • Item 435
ANNUAL REPORT. 1st–   1921–   [Annual]

FP 1.2:CT • Item 436
GENERAL PUBLICATIONS.

FP 1.2:F 95 • Item 436
ANNUAL SUMMARY OF COST AND QUALITY OF STEAM-ELECTRIC PLANT FUELS. 1975–

    Mainly statistical tables.
    Covers fiscal year.

FP 1.2:W 89 • Item 436
WORLD POWER DATA. [Annual]

    Gives statistics on electric and generating capacity and electric energy production for almost all countries of the world and a number of their dependencies.
    Data includes electric energy production; per-capita electric energy production; installed generating capacity production, population and related data; electric energy production and average annual rate of growth; installed electric generating capacity, production, population, and related data, by major geographic divisions, and by geographic region and countries.

FP 1.3:
BULLETINS.

FP 1.4:
CIRCULARS.

FP 1.5:CT • Item 437
LAWS.

FP 1.6 • Item 437
RULES OF PRACTICE AND PROCEDURE. [Irregular]

    Includes general policy and interpretations, organization, and Administrative Procedure Act. Looseleaf. Subscription includes basic manual plus supplementary material for an indefinite period.

FP 1.6/2:CT
RATE SERIES, 1938.

FP 1.7:CT • Item 439
RULES AND REGULATIONS (miscellaneous).

FP 1.7:G 21/3 • Item 439
REGULATIONS UNDER THE NATURAL GAS ACT, AUGUST 1, 1967. [Irregular]

    Subscription includes basic manual plus supplementary material for an indefinite period.

FP 1.7:P 87/2 • Item 439
REGULATIONS UNDER FEDERAL POWER ACT. [Irregular]

    Subscription includes basic volume plus supplemental material for an indefinite period.

FP 1.7/2 • Item 439
UNIFORM SYSTEM OF ACCOUNTS PRESCRIBED FOR NATURAL GAS COMPANIES. [Irregular]

    Subscription includes basic manual plus supplemental material for an indefinite period.
    Contains Parts 201 (Class A and B), 104 (Class C) and 205 (Class D) of the Federal Power Commission's Rules and Regulations in Subchapter Fcomprising the Uniform Systems of Accounts for Natural Gas Companies in effect as of Sept. 1, 1968.

FP 1.7/3:date • Item 439
UNIFORM SYSTEM OF ACCOUNTS PRESCRIBED FOR PUBLIC UTILITIES AND LICENSES. [Irregular] (Includes basic manual plus supplementary material for an indefinite period) (A 106)

    ISSN 0364-9636

FP 1.7/4:nos.
STAFF REPORT, FPC/OCE (series). 1–   1974– [Irregular] (Office of Chief Engineer)

FP 1.8:date
RULES OF PRACTICE.

FP 1.8/2:CT
RULES OF PRACTICE.

FP 1.9:nos.
QUESTIONNAIRES.

FP 1.10 • Item 438-A
RATE SERIES. R 1–   1935–

    The following sub-series are issued on a recurring basis:

ALL-ELECTRIC HOMES IN THE UNITED STATES, ANNUAL BILLS, January 1 (year). 1963– [Annual]

TYPICAL ELECTRIC BILLS, TYPICAL NET MONTHLY BILLS AS OF JANUARY 1 (year), FOR RESIDENTIAL, COMMERCIAL, AND INDUSTRIAL SERVICES. 1936–   [Annual]

    Gives data for cities of 50,000 population and more. Basic tables give residential, service, commercial light service, commercial power service, and industrial service, by State and city, typical bills as of January 1. Includes historical tables from 1935.

FP 1.10/2:nos.
RATE SERIES 2, STATE REPORTS.

FP 1.11:date
PRODUCTION OF ELECTRICITY FOR PUBLIC USE IN U.S. [Monthly]
    Earlier I 19.33:

FP 1.11/2:date&nos.
PRODUCTION AND UTILIZATION OF ELECTRIC ENERGY IN UNITED STATES. [Monthly]
    Later FP 1.27

FP 1.11/3:date&nos.
CONSUMPTION OF FUEL FOR PRODUCTION OF ELECTRIC ENERGY. [Monthly]
    Later FP 1.27

FP 1.11/4:date
STOCKS OF COAL AND DAYS' SUPPLY. [Monthly]

FP 1.11/5:date&nos.
REVENUES AND INCOME OF PRIVATELY OWNED CLASS A & B ELECTRIC UTILITIES IN THE U.S. [Monthly]
    Later FP 1.27

FP 1.11/6:dt.&nos.
SALES OF ELECTRIC ENERGY TO ULTIMATE CONSUMERS. [Monthly]
    Later FP 1.27

FP 1.11/7:date
WEEKLY ELECTRIC OUTPUT, UNITED STATES.

FP 1.12 • Item 435-D
POWER SERIES. P 1–   1935–   [Irregular]

    Consists mainly of studies of estimated power requirements projected to a future date.

HYDROELECTRIC POWER RESOURCES OF THE UNITED STATES, DEVELOPED AND UNDEVELOPED. [Irregular]

    Gives developed potential hydroelectric power capacity available for possible development in U.S. as of January 1, with data arranged by major drainages and river basins, and by geographic divisions and States. Also includes maps showing locations of both federal and EPC-licensed plants.

WORLD POWER DATA. 1962–   [Annual]

    Gives statistics on electric generating capacity and electric energy production for almost all countries of the world and a number of their dependencies.
    Data includes electric energy production; per-capita electric energy production installed generating capacity production, population and

related data; electric energy production and average annual rate of growth; installed electric generating capacity, production, population, and related data, by major geographic divisions, and by geographic region and countries.

FP 1.13:CT • Item 438-B
MAPS.

FP 1.14:CT
ADDRESSES.

FP 1.15:letter
RATE SERIES A.

FP 1.16:CT
RATE SERIES B (by States).

FP 1.16/2:CT
TYPICAL ELECTRIC BILLS (by States).

FP 1.16/3:CT date
TYPICAL RESIDENTIAL ELECTRIC BILLS.
    Prior to 1942 FP 1.16/2

FP 1.16/4:CT date
TYPICAL COMMERCIAL AND INDUSTRIAL ELECTRIC BILLS.

FP 1.17:CT
PAPERS IN RE.

FP 1.18 • Item 437-A-1– 50
NATIONAL ELECTRIC RATE BOOK. [Annual]
    Issued as R-16.
    ISSN 0364-8095
    Later E 3.14

FP 1.18/2:date
NATIONAL ELECTRIC RATE BOOK BULLETIN SERVICE, IMPORTANT RATE CHANGES. [Monthly]

FP 1.19:nos.
ORDERS.

FP 1.20 • Item 438
FEDERAL POWER COMMISSION REPORTS, OPINIONS, AND ORDERS. v. 1–   1931– [Semiannual]

    Contains texts of opinions, intermediate decisions which have become final, general orders, list of independent producer orders. Index-digest to opinions and intermediate decisions. Subject Index.
    Current material is issued in the Preliminary Prints (listed below).
    Volumes 4-14 (1931-1955) issued on an annual basis. Beginning with volume 15 (Jan.- June 1956) issued on a semiannual basis.
    Citation: F.P.C.

CUMULATIVE INDEX-DIGEST. v. A. January 1973– December 1957. 1967.

FP 1.20/a
– PRELIMINARY PRINT. [Monthly]

FP 1.21 • Item 440
STATISTICAL SERIES. S 1– 1935–

The following sub-series are issued on a recurring basis:

FEDERAL AND STATE COMMISSION JURISDIC-
TION AND REGULATION, ELECTRIC, GAS,
AND TELEPHONE UTILITIES. 1st– 1941–
[Irregular]

Prepared by the Office of Accounting and
Finance in cooperation with the National Association of Regulatory Utility Commissioners and the Federal Communications Commission.
PURPOSE:– To present the results of a
survey of commission jurisdiction and regulation of electric, gas and telephone utilities in
each of the States, the District of Columbia,
Puerto Rico, and the Virgin Islands.

GAS SUPPLIES OF INTERSTATE NATURAL GAS
PIPELINE COMPANIES. 1969– [Annual]

HYDROELECTRIC PLANT CONSTRUCTION COST
AND ANNUAL PRODUCTION EXPENSES,
1953-1956.

Issued as S-130.
Similar to Steam-Electric Power Construction Cost and Annual Production Expenses
(listed below).

– SUPPLEMENTS. [Annual]

PRODUCTION OF ELECTRIC ENERGY AND
CAPACITY OF GENERATING PLANTS. 1940-
1954. [Annual]

SALES BY PRODUCERS OF NATURAL GAS TO
INTERSTATE PIPELINE COMPANIES. [Annual]

Gives sales by size groups, by States,
and by pricing areas, sales to individual purchasers; and pipeline companies' purchases
from producers and their own production.

SALES OF FIRM ELECTRIC POWER FOR
RESALE, BY PRIVATE ELECTRIC UTILITIES,
BY FEDERAL PROJECTS, BY MUNICIPALS.
[Annual]

STATISTICS OF INTERSTATE NATURAL GAS PIPE-
LINE COMPANIES. [Annual]

Gives for individual companies detailed
financial and operating information in the form
of statements of the balance sheet, income
and earned surplus statements, gas operating revenues, customers and sales, capital
stock and long-term debt, gas operating revenues, gas utility plant, gas accounts, data
on physical property, number of employees.
Statistics of Natural Gas Companies prior
to 1963.
Issued by the Energy Information Administration (E 3.25) starting in 1976.
STATISTICS OF PRIVATELY OWNED ELECTRIC
UTILITIES IN THE UNITED STATES. [Annual]

Prior to 1966, entitled Statistics of Electric Utilities in the United States, Classes A
and B Privately Owned Companies.
Beginning in 1976 issued by the Energy
Information Administration (E 3.18/2).

STATISTICS OF PUBLICLY OWNED ELECTRIC
UTILITIES IN THE UNITED STATES. [Annual]

Prior to 1966, entitled Statistics of Electric Utilities in the United States, Classes A
and B Publicly Owned Companies.
Beginning in 1976 issued by the Energy
Information Administration (E 3.18/3).

STEAM-ELECTRIC PLANT CONSTRUCTION COST
AND ANNUAL PRODUCTION EXPENSES,
1938-1947.

Basic volume issued as S-72.
Gives for each plant information on installed generating capacity, net generation,

peak demand, net continuous plant capability, cost of plant, production expenses, types,
quality and cost of fuels used, average BTU
per kilowatt-hour net generation, average
number of employees, type of construction.
Later E 3.17

– SUPPLEMENTS. [Annual]

FP 1.22:date
STATEMENT OF TAXES, DIVIDENDS, SALARIES AND
WAGES, CLASS A AND CLASS B PRIVATELY
OWNED ELECTRIC UTILITIES IN U.S. [Quarterly]

FP 1.23:date
EFFECT OF INCOME TAX LAW REVISION ON ELEC-
TRIC TAXES AND INCOME. [Quarterly]

FP 1.24:date
ELECTRIC UTILITY SYSTEM LOADS. [Monthly]

Later FP 1.27

FP 1.25
NEWS DIGEST. [Daily]

Issued for the information of the members
and staff of the Commission. Digests of news
items appearing in newspapers and periodicals.
Subscriptions are mailed on a weekly basis.

FP 1.25/2:nos.
RELEASE FOR PUBLICATION (series).

FP 1.25/3:v.nos. • Item 436-A
NEWS DIGEST. v. 1– 1968– 1977. [Weekly]

PURPOSE:– To provide a compilation of Federal Power Commission press releases; rate
change proposed by independent gas producers
and interstate pipeline companies; quality statements filed by independent producers; and listings of formal documents issued by the Federal
Power Commission.
Supersedes the following mailing lists of releases: all FPC press releases (ARR, G and PUB
mailing lists); Daily List of Formal Documents Issued (FDI); Notices of Pipeline Rate Revisions
(PIR); the Independent Producer Rate Change
Filings (IPRF); and the Independent Producer Rate
Schedule Quality Statements (FSQS).
Individual releases are still issued to the
press in the original form, but since January 1,
1968, issued in a new format so that they can be
reproduced for the weekly FPC News.
ISSN 0014-6080
Superseded by FERC News (E 2.9).

FP 1.25/4:nos.
PRESS RELEASES.

FP 1.26:date
FORMS AND PUBLICATIONS, LIST AND ORDER
BLANK. [Irregular]

Earlier FP 1.2:P 96/2

FP 1.27 • Item 435-E
ELECTRIC POWER STATISTICS. [Monthly]

Effective with data for January 1961, replaced
the five-part publication of the same title sold by
the Federal Power Commission.
Punched for 3-ring binder.
ISSN 0013-4139
Later E 3.18

FP 1.28:date
LIST OF ELECTRIC POWER SUPPLIERS WITH
ANNUAL OPERATING REVENUES OF $2,500,000
OR MORE CLASSIFIED AS PUBLIC UTILITIES
UNDER FEDERAL POWER ACT.

FP 1.29:CT
PLANNING STATUS REPORTS.

FP 1.30:date
COST OF PIPELINE AND COMPRESSOR STATION
CONSTRUCTION UNDER NON-BUDGET TYPE OF
CERTIFICATE AUTHORIZATIONS AS REPORTED
BY PIPELINE COMPANIES. [Annual]

FP 1.31:CT
EVALUATION REPORT, WATER RESOURCES
APPRAISAL FOR HYDROELECTRIC LICENSING.

FP 1.32:date
STAFF REPORT ON MONTHLY REPORT OF COST
AND QUALITY OF FUELS FOR STEAM-ELECTRIC
PLANT. [Quarterly] (Bureau of Power)

PURPOSE:– To provide a statistical summary
of data reported on FPC Form 423 by 744 steam-
electric plants with a capacity of 25 megawatts or
greater.

FP 1.33:CT
ENVIRONMENTAL IMPACT STATEMENTS.

FEDERAL PRISON INDUSTRIES, INC. (1934–1939)

CREATION AND AUTHORITY

The Federal Prison Industries, Inc. was created by Executive Order 6917 of December 11,
1934, to provide employment for all physically fit
inmates of Federal penal institutions. It was transferred to the Department of Justice (J 16.50), by
Reorganization Plan II, to be administered under
direction of the Attorney General, effective July
1, 1939.

FPI 1.1:date
ANNUAL REPORTS.

Later J 16.51

FPI 1.2:CT
GENERAL PUBLICATIONS.

Later J 16.52

FPI 1.7:CT
PRICE LISTS.

FEDERAL RESERVE SYSTEM BOARD OF GOVERNORS (1935–)

CREATION AND AUTHORITY

The Federal Reserve Board was established
by the Federal Reserve Act of December 23,
1913 (38 Stat 251). The name was changed to
Board of Governors of the Federal Reserve System by the Banking Act of 1935, approved August 23, 1935 (49 Stat 704).

INFORMATION

Office of Public Affairs
Board of Governors
Federal Reserve System
20th Street and Constitution Avenue, NW
Washington, D.C. 20551
(202) 452-3204
Fax: (202) 452-3819
http://www.federalreserve.gov

FR 1.1 • Item 441-A (MF)
ANNUAL REPORT. 1st– 1941– [Annual]

Published for the calendar year and includes
statistical tables.

FR 1.2:CT • Item 442
GENERAL PUBLICATIONS.

FR 1.3 • Item 443-C (MF)
FEDERAL RESERVE BULLETIN. v. 1– 1915–
[Monthly]

Presents articles of general and special interest, policy and other official statements issued by the Board, and statistical information relating to domestic financial and business developments and to international financial developments.

Departments: Law Department, Current Events and Announcements, National Summary of Business Conditions, Financial and Business Statistics (United States), Financial Statistics (International), Federal Reserve System Directory, Federal Reserve Board Publications.

Indexed by:–
Business Periodicals Index
Index to U.S. Government Periodicals
Public Affairs Information Service
ISSN 0014-9209

FR 1.3/a
REPRINTS.

The important articles of the Bulletin are reprinted for distribution to fill specific requests for information on the activities, etc. of the Board.

FR 1.3/2:vol
FEDERAL RESERVE BULLETIN.

FR 1.3/3:v.nos.
INDEX-DIGEST, FEDERAL RESERVE BULLETIN.

FR 1.4
CIRCULARS.

FR 1.5:nos.
REGULATIONS.

FR 1.6 • Item 443
REGULATIONS. [Irregular]

Separate pamphlets, designated by letters, revised as needed and kept up-to-date by one- or two-page amendments.

A. ADVANCES AND DISCOUNTS.
D. RESERVES OF MEMBER BANKS.
E. PURCHASE OF WARRANTS.
F. SECURITIES OF MEMBER STATE BANKS.
G. SECURITIES CREDIT BY PERSONS OTHER THAN BANKS, BROKERS, OR DEALERS.
H. MEMBERSHIP OF STATE BANKING INSTITUTIONS IN FEDERAL RESERVE SYSTEM.
I. ISSUE AND CANCELLATION OF CAPITAL STOCK OF FEDERAL RESERVE BANKS.
J. COLLECTION OF CHECKS AND OTHER ITEMS BY FEDERAL RESERVE BANKS.
K. CORPORATIONS ENGAGED IN FOREIGN BANKING AND FINANCING UNDER FEDERAL RESERVE ACT.
L. INTERLOCKING BANK RELATIONSHIPS UNDER THE CLAYTON ACT.
M. FOREIGN ACTIVITIES OF NATIONAL BANKS.
O. LOANS TO EXECUTIVE OFFICERS OF MEMBER BANKS.
P. MINIMUM SECURITY DEVICES AND PROCEDURES FOR FEDERAL RESERVE BANKS AND STATE MEMBER BANKS.
Q. INTEREST ON DEPOSITS.
R. RELATIONSHIPS WITH DEALERS IN SECURITIES UNDER SEC. 32 OF THE BANKING ACT OF 1933.
S. BANK SERVICE ARRANGEMENTS.
T. CREDIT BY BROKERS AND DEALERS.
U. CREDIT BY BANKS FOR PURPOSE OF PURCHASING OR CARRYING MARGIN STOCKS.
V. LOAN GUARANTEES FOR DEFENSE PRODUCTION.
X. REAL ESTATE CREDIT.
Y. BANK HOLDING COMPANIES.
Z. TRUTH IN LENDING.

FR 1.7:CT
PAPERS IN RE.

FR 1.8:dt.&nos.
INSTRUCTION, SPECIAL.

FR 1.8/2:CT
RULES, REGULATIONS AND INSTRUCTIONS, MISCELLANEOUS.

FR 1.8/3:CT • Item 443
HANDBOOKS, MANUALS, GUIDES.

FR 1.9
FEDERAL RESERVE PAR LIST, OCTOBER (year). – September 1975. [Annual]

Superseded by Memorandum on Exchange Charges (FR 1.9/2).

FR 1.9/2:date
MEMORANDUM ON EXCHANGE CHARGES. 1974– [Monthly]

PURPOSE:– To provide a list of banks upon which checks will be received by the Federal Reserve Banks and Branches for collection and credit. Includes an explanation and list of check routing symbols.
Supersedes Federal Reserve Par List (FR 1.9).

FR 1.10:date
DIGEST AND INDEX OF OPINIONS OF COUNSEL, INFORMAL RULINGS OF FEDERAL RESERVE BOARD AND MATTER RELATING THERETO, FROM FEDERAL RESERVE BULLETIN.

FR 1.11
SUMMARY REPORT, ASSETS AND LIABILITIES OF MEMBER BANKS. [3 times a year or more]

These statistics are tabulated from condition reports submitted by member banks following each official call, a minimum of three of which are required by law each year. The Comptroller of the Currency tabulates the national bank reports and published the results in the Abstract of Reports of Condition of National Banks. The combined statistics of national and State member banks appear in this publication.

Tables give assets and liabilities of all member banks, by class of bank, by Federal Reserve districts; classification of loans and United States Government district obligations of all member banks, by class of bank, by Federal Reserve districts, of reserve city and country member banks, by Federal Reserve districts; all members banks, by States; deposits and reserves by class of bank and Federal Reserve districts; assets and liabilities of State member banks, by Federal Reserve district.
Previous title: Member Bank Call Report.

FR 1.11/2
MEMBER BANK LOANS. [Issued on call dates] (Statistical Release E 3.4)
Preliminary figures of principal loan items of member banks on call dates, also includes changes from previous call dates. Final figures, given in more detail, appear in the Bulletin and also the Summary Report, Assets and Liabilities of Member Banks.

FR 1.11/3
MEMBER BANK INCOME. [Annual] (Statistical Release C 4)

Gives, by class of bank, preliminary figures on earnings, expenses, net current earnings before income taxes, recoveries, losses, profits before income taxes, taxes on net income, net profits, cash dividends declared, selected ratios.

Six months' figures are published in August and the calendar year figures in February. Final figures are given in more detail in the Bulletin.
Supersedes Member Bank Earnings (semiannual).

FR 1.11/4
DEPOSITS, RESERVES, AND BORROWINGS OF MEMBER BANKS. [Weekly] (Statistical Release J.1)

Cover-table gives for all member banks, central reserve city banks, reserve city banks, and country banks: gross demand deposits, net demand deposits, time deposits, demand balance due from domestic banks, reserves with Federal Reserve banks, and borrowing at Federal Reserve banks, taken from averages of daily figures.

Table (a) gives figures of demand deposits except interbank, time deposits for country banks in places with population of 15,000 or more, and country banks with population of less than 15,000 by Federal districts.

Table (b) continues the figures for places with population of less than 15,000 with breakdown by section and States.
ISSN 0364-2127

FR 1.11/5
STATE MEMBER BANKS OF THE FEDERAL RESERVE SYSTEM. [Monthly & Annual] (G4)

Includes nonmember banks that maintain clearing accounts with Federal Reserve Banks and corporations doing foreign banking or financing that maintain reserve accounts with the Federal Reserve Banks.

Annual volume lists banks by Federal Reserve District, State and city, as of December 31.
ISSN 0364-9601

– MONTHLY SUPPLEMENTS.

Lists changes, additions or deletions occurring during the month.
For weekly information, see Changes in State Bank Membership (listed above).

FR 1.11/6:date
DISTRIBUTION OF BANK DEPOSITS BY COUNTRIES AND STANDARD METROPOLITAN AREAS. [Biennial]

Earlier FR 1.2:D 44

FR 1.12:inc. dates
DIGEST OF RULINGS.

FR 1.13:date
FEDERAL RESERVE ACT, AS AMENDED (compilations).

FR 1.13/2:CT
LAWS.

FR 1.14:date
BANK DEBITS. [Weekly]

FR 1.15
FACTORS AFFECTING BANK RESERVES AND CONDITION STATEMENT OF F.R. BANKS. [Weekly] (Statistical Release H 4.1)

Cover-page gives weekly averages of daily figures and changes from preceding week and year. Additional tables give consolidated statement of condition of the twelve Federal Reserve Banks combined, and maturity distribution of loans and securities; statement of condition of each Federal Reserve Bank (assets and liabilities), and Federal Agent's accounts.

Figures later appear in the Bulletin.
Previous title: Weekly Averages of Member Bank Reserves, Reserve Bank Credit and Related Items and Statement of Condition of the Federal Reserve Bank.
ISSN 0364-961X

FR 1.15/2:date
RESERVE POSITIONS OF MAJOR RESERVE CITY BANKS [Weekly] (Statistical Release H.5)

Table on reserve positions of major reserve city banks gives reserve excess or deficiency, borrowings from Reserve Banks, net interbank Federal funds purchases or sales, and net basic reserve surplus or deficit. Table on Federal Funds transactions of major reserve city banks gives interbank Federal funds transactions and related transactions with U.S. Government securities dealers. Release issued on Friday covering week ended Wednesday of previous week. 2-page release.

FR 1.15/3:date
AGGREGATE RESERVES AND MEMBER BANK DEPOSITS. [Weekly] (Statistical Release H.3)

Table on Aggregate Reserves and Member Bank Deposits gives averages of daily figures, in billions of dollar, seasonally adjusted for member bank reserves and deposits subject to reserve requirements by weeks for current month and by months for previous year. Second Table gives Member Bank Deposits data not seasonally adjusted.
ISSN 0364-0582

FR 1.16
CONDITION OF WEEKLY REPORTING MEMBER BANKS IN LEADING CITIES. [Weekly] (Statistical Release H 4.2)

Cover-table gives summary of assets and liabilities of reporting member banks in leading cities for week with change from previous week and year. Second table, Condition of Weekly Reporting Member Banks in New York and Chicago, gives data for these two cities. This table is also released separately (listed below).
Table (a) gives assests and liabilities for all districts, Boston, New York, Philadelphia, Cleveland, Richmond, Atlanta, Chicago, St. Louis, Minneapolis, Kansas City, Dallas, and San Francisco.
Summary tables later appear in the Bulletin.
ISSN 0364-7331
Discontinued.

FR 1.16/2
CONDITION OF WEEKLY REPORTING MEMBER BANKS IN NEW YORK AND CHICAGO. [Weekly] (Statistical Release H 4.3)
Gives assets and liabilities for New York and Chicago, change since previous week and previous year. Figures later appear in the Bulletin and the entire release is included with the statement of Condition of Reporting Member Banks in Leading Cities (listed above). Textual summary.
Previous title: Condition of Weekly Reporting Member Banks in Central Reserve Cities.

FR 1.16/3:date
MONTHLY REPORT OF CONDITION FOR U.S. AGENCIES, BRANCHES AND DOMESTIC BANKING SUBSIDIARIES OF FOREIGN BANKS. (G 11 [412])

FR 1.17:date
BANK DEBITS, DEPOSITS, AND DEPOSIT TURNOVER. [Monthly] (Statistical Release G.6)

Gives debits to demand deposits, demand deposits, and annual rate of turnover, by Federal Reserve district and city. Figures appear in annual Bank Debits to Demand Deposit Accounts (listed above).
Previous title: Bank Debits and Deposit Turnover, and Bank Debits to Demand Deposit Accounts.
Discontinued.

FR 1.17/2
BANK DEBITS TO DEMAND DEPOSIT ACCOUNTS (except Interbank and U.S. Government Accounts). [Annual] (Statistical Release C.5)

Gives monthly and annual totals for Federal Reserve districts and 344 centers and annual rates of turnover of some groupings. Summaries appear in the Bulletin with seasonally adjusted turnover.

FR 1.17/3
DEBITS, DEMAND DEPOSITS, AND TURNOVER AT 233 INDIVIDUAL CENTERS. 1967– [Monthly] (Statistical Release G.11)
Arranged by FR district, State, and city.

FR 1.18:date
REPORT OF FINISHERS OF COTTON FABRICS. [Monthly]

FR 1.19
BUSINESS INDEXES. – Aug. 1973. [Monthly] (Statistical Release G.12.3)

Summary tables include industrial production, consumer durable goods, utility output, contracts (value), employment and payrolls, freight carloadings, department store sales. Additional tables for industrial production, output of consumer durable goods, and output of major household goods. Figures shown are for current month, two preceding months, and a month a year ago.

FR 1.19/2
NATIONAL SUMMARY OF BUSINESS CONDITIONS. [Monthly] (Statistical Release G.12.2)

Issued on or about the 15th of each month giving brief summary of industrial production, construction, employment, distribution, commodity prices, bank credit and reserves, security markets. Material later appears in the Bulletin.

FR 1.19/3:date
INDUSTRIAL PRODUCTION. [Monthly] (Statistical Release G.12.3)

Gives seasonally adjusted index, by industry, for month and twelve preceding months.
ISSN 0364-135X
Replaces National Summary of Business Conditions (FR 1.19/2) with June 15, 1973 issue.
Discontinued.

FR 1.20:date
DEPARTMENT STORE SALES, PRELIMINARY REPORTS. [Monthly]

Early issues read Retail Trade in U.S.

FR 1.21:date
WHOLESALE TRADE IN U.S. [Monthly]

FR 1.22:date
WEEKLY REVIEW OF PERIODICALS.
Includes quarterly supplement.

FR 1.22/2:date
SELECTED LIST OF ADDITIONS TO RESEARCH LIBRARY. (K.11)

FR 1.23
ADDRESSES. [Irregular]

FR 1.24:nos.
DEPARTMENT STORE SALES. [Weekly]

FR 1.24/2:date
DEPARTMENT STORE SALES, BY CITIES. v. 1–1971–1974. [Weekly] (Statistical Release H.11)

FR 1.24/3:date
DEPARTMENT STORE STOCKS. [Monthly] (Statistical Release G.7.4)

FR 1.24/4:date
DEPARTMENT STORE SALES AND STOCKS, BY MAJOR DEPARTMENTS. [Monthly] (Statistical Release G.7.3)

FR 1.24/5:date
DEPARTMENT STORE MERCHANDISING DATA. [Monthly] (Statistical Release G.7.4.1)

FR 1.24/6:date
DEPARTMENT STORE MERCHANDISING DATA. [Monthly] (Statistical Release G.7.4.1)

FR 1.24/7:date
DEPARTMENT STORE TRADE, UNITED STATES DISTRIBUTION OF SALES BY MONTHS. [Annual] (Statistical Release C.7.3.1)
Earlier FR 1.2:D 44/3

FR 1.24/8:date
DEPARTMENT STORE TRADE, UNITED STATES DISTRIBUTION OF SALES BY MONTHS. [Annual] (Statistical Release C.7.3.1)

Earlier FR 1.2:D 44/3

FR 1.24/9:date
DEPARTMENT STORE TRADE, UNITED STATES DEPARTMENTAL SALES INDEXES, WITHOUT SEASONAL ADJUSTMENT. [Annual] Proc.

Earlier FR 1.2: 44/3

FR 1.24/10:date
DEPARTMENT STORE TRADE, UNITED STATES DEPARTMENTAL STOCK INDEXES, WITHOUT SEASONAL ADJUSTMENT. [Annual] (Statistical Release C.7.3.4)

Earlier FR 1.2:D 44/3

FR 1.24/11:date
DEPARTMENT STORE TRADE, UNITED STATES DEPARTMENTAL STOCK-SALES RATIOS. [Annual] (Statistical Release C.7.3.5)

Earlier FR 1.2:D 44/3

FR 1.25:nos.
FEDERAL RESERVE CHART BOOKS.

FR 1.26
FINANCE COMPANIES. [Monthly] (Statistical Release G.20)

Gives amount at end of month and changes for outstanding credit held, credit extended, and number of motor vehicles financed by sales finance companies. A separate table gives data on total credit sales of new passenger cars as a percent of total number sold at retail.
Figures on amounts outstanding, extensions, and repayments later appear in the Bulletin.
Former title: Sales Finance Companies.
ISSN 0364-0132

FR 1.27:nos.
POSTWAR ECONOMIC STUDIES.

FR 1.28
ASSETS AND LIABILITIES OF ALL BANKS IN THE UNITED STATES. [Semiannual]

Mailing key: j.4 [formerly g.7]
Gives assets and liabilities of all banks in the United States for specified date, changes (percent) from month ago and year ago, for all banks, all commercial banks, all member banks, Reserve City banks (New York, Chicago, other), and country banks. Supplemental tables, Consolidated Condition statement for Banks and the Monetary System gives assets and liabilities for specified date, month ago and year ago, percent change from month ago and year ago.

STATISTICAL RELEASES.

The releases listed below are issued on a periodic basis to provide data on preliminary or current basis. Data on most of the tables are republished in the monthly Federal Reserve Bulletin with annual data summarized in the Chart Book.

FR 1.28/2
ALL BANKS IN THE UNITED STATES AND OTHER AREAS, PRINCIPAL ASSETS AND LIABILITIES BY STATES. [Semiannual] (Statistical Release E.4)

Tables give assets and liabilities for all banks, all commercial banks, and all mutual savings banks in the United States and other areas by States as of June 30 and December 31. Releases issued in April and October.

FR 1.28/3
ASSETS AND LIABILITIES OF ALL MEMBER BANKS, BY DISTRICTS. [Monthly] (Statistical Release G.7.1)

Gives loans and investments; reserves, cash, and bank balances, other assets, total assets; for liabilities and capital; gross demand deposits, time deposits, borrowing, other liabilities, and total capital accounts, by Federal Reserve districts.
ISSN 0364-0574

FR 1.28/4:date
ASSETS AND LIABILITIES OF ALL COMMERCIAL BANKS IN UNITED STATES. [Weekly] (Statistical Release H.8)

FR 1.29
RESEARCH LIBRARY, RECENT ACQUISITIONS. [Semimonthly]

Acquisition list of books, pamphlets, annuals, and U.S. Government publications.
Previous title: Selected List of Additions to the Research Library.
ISSN 0145-0301

FR 1.29/2:nos
RESEARCH LIBRARY, RECENT ACQUISITIONS. [Monthly] (G.15 [417])

Continues FR 1.29, with similar title.

FR 1.30   • Item 443-D (MF)
FEDERAL RESERVE CHART BOOK ON FINANCIAL AND BUSINESS STATISTICS. 1947– [Monthly]

Graphic presentation of the economic and financial data collected by the Division of Research and Statistics. The charts are brought up-to-date monthly.

FR 1.30/2   • Item 443-D (MF)
HISTORICAL CHART BOOKS. 1949– [Annual]

Included in subscription to the monthly series. Issued in September.
Covers the various series in the monthly charts plus additional data (mostly annual) not covered in the monthly issues.

FR 1.31:date
RELEASES.

FR 1.31/2
SUMMARY OF EQUITY SECURITY TRANSACTIONS AND OWNERSHIP OF DIRECTORS, OFFICERS, AND PRINCIPAL STOCKHOLDERS OF MEMBER STATE BANKS AS REPORTED PURSUANT TO SECTION 16(a) OF THE SECURITIES EXCHANGE ACT OF 1934. 1967– [Monthly] (Statistical Release G.16)

Gives in tabular form the name of the bank, reporting person, indirect account; relationship; date of transaction; transaction and ownership symbol; aggregate transactions; and month-end ownership.

FR 1.32
FOREIGN EXCHANGE RATES FOR WEEK. [Weekly] (Statistical Release H.10)

Gives daily rates in cents per unit of foreign currency, by country.
ISSN 0364-1333

FR 1.32/2
FOREIGN EXCHANGE RATES. [Monthly]

Gives average rates in cents per unit of foreign currency for month, two preceding months, and month a year ago, by county. Figures later appear in the Bulletin.
ISSN 0364-1341

FR 1.32/3:date/nos.
SELECTED INTEREST AND EXCHANGE RATES FOR MAJOR COUNTRIES AND THE U.S. [Weekly] (Statistical and Data Management Unit, Division of International Finance) (H.13)
ISSN 0364-8370

FR 1.32/4:date
INTEREST RATES CHARGED ON SELECTED TYPES OF BANK LOANS. [Monthly] (Statistical Release G.10)

Gives interest rates for month, previous month, and month a year ago for small short-term noninstallment loans to businesses, farm production loans, and consumer installment, and business loans (prime rate).
ISSN 0364-8508

FR 1.32/5:date
BANK RATES ON SHORT-TERM BUSINESS LOANS [Quarterly] (Statistical Release E.2)

Gives percentage distribution of dollar amount by size of loans for various interest rates for short-term, revolving credit, and long-term business loans.
ISSN 0364-2852

FR 1.32/6:date
SELECTED INTEREST RATES AND BOND PRICES. [Monthly]

FR 1.32/7:date
SELECTED INTEREST RATES AND BOND PRICES. [Weekly] (H.15)

Earlier FR 1.46/2

FR 1.33:dt.&nos.
CHANGES IN STATE MEMBER BANKS. [Weekly] (K.3)

List name and address of banks admitted, voluntary withdrawals, etc. Material later appears in the monthly supplements and annual, State Member Banks of the Federal Reserve System (listed below).
Previous title: Changes in State Bank Membership.
ISSN 0364-5436

FR 1.33/2:date
CHANGES IN STATUS OF BANKS AND BRANCHES DURING MONTH, NAME AND LOCATION OF BANKS AND BRANCHES.

FR 1.34:date
CONSUMER INSTALLMENT LOANS OF PRINCIPAL TYPES OF FINANCIAL INSTITUTIONS. [Bimonthly] (Statistical Release G.17.1)

FR 1.34/2:date
RETAIL INSTALLMENT CREDIT AND FURNITURE AND HOUSEHOLD APPLIANCE STORES. [Monthly] (Statistical Release G.17.2)

FR 1.34/3
DEPARTMENT STORE CREDIT. [Monthly] (Statistical Release G.17.3)

FR 1.34/4
AUTOMOBILE INSTALLMENT CREDIT DEVELOPMENTS. 1967– [Monthly] (Statistical Release G.26)

Gives extensions, average note, and cars financed, both seasonally adjusted and non-adjusted, for all lenders, bank direct loans, bank purchased papers, sales finance companies, and other lenders, for new cars and used cars, data for month, preceding month, and month a year ago.
January 1976 absorbed Automobile Loans by Major Finance Companies (FR 1.34/6) and Finance Rate and Other Terms on New and Used Car Installment Credit Contracts Purchased from Dealers of Major Auto Finance Companies (FR 1.34/5)
ISSN 0364-0566

– SUPPLEMENTS

1. Seasonally Adjusted Data. [Annual]
2. Seasonally Unadjusted Data. [Annual]

FR 1.34/5:date
FINANCE RATE AND OTHER TERMS ON NEW AND USED CAR INSTALLMENT CREDIT CONTRACTS PURCHASED FROM DEALERS OF MAJOR AUTO FINANCE COMPANIES. – 1975. [Monthly]

(Statistical Release G.11)

ISSN 0364-2747
Superseded by Automobile Installment Credit Developments (FR 1.43/4).

FR 1.34/6:date
AUTOMOBILE LOANS BY MAJOR FINANCE COMPANIES. – 1975. [Monthly] (Statistical Release G.25)

Superseded by Automobile Installment Credit Developments (FR 1.34/4).

FR 1.34/7:date
FINANCE RATE AND OTHER TERMS ON SELECTED CATEGORIES OF CONSUMER INSTALLMENT CREDIT EXTENDED BY FINANCE COMPANIES. [Monthly] (Statistical Release J.e)

Gives customer finance rate, average maturity, and average amount financed for mobile homes, other consumer goods, and personal loans for month and selected previous months.
ISSN 0364-2119

FR 1.34/8:date
AUTOMOBILE CREDIT.

ISSN 0364-0566

FR 1.34/9:date
FINANCE RATES AND OTHER TERMS ON SELECTED TYPES OF CONSUMER INSTALLMENT CREDIT EXTENDED BY MAJOR FINANCE COMPANIES (not seasonally adjusted). [Quarterly]

FR 1.35:date
STATEMENT OF VOLUNTARY CREDIT RESTRAINT COMMITTEE.

FR 1.35/2:nos.
BULLETIN OF VOLUNTARY CREDIT RESTRAINT COMMITTEE. Proc.

Later FR 1.3/1

FR 1.36
CONSUMER CREDIT. [Monthly] (Statistical Release G.19)

Gives consumer installment credit, by type of credit and type of holder, as of specified date, with change during month, month a year ago, and year ending at specified date; consumer installment credit extended and repaid, by type of credit, seasonally adjusted and unadjusted, for month, previous month and month a year ago; changes in consumer installment credit outstanding for automobile paper, other consumer goods paper, repair and modernization, and personal loans.
Figures later appear in the Bulletin.
ISSN 0364-2844

FR 1.36/2
CONSUMER INSTALLMENT CREDIT AT COMMERCIAL BANKS. – Dec. 1975. [Monthly] (Statistical Release G.18)

Gives amount outstanding and volume extended for automobile paper, other consumer goods paper, repair and modernization loans, and personal loans, for total and by Federal Reserve districts.
Figures on amounts outstanding and credit extended later appear in the Bulletin.

FR 1.36/3
CONSUMER LOANS MADE UNDER EFFECTIVE STATE SMALL LOANS LAWS. [Monthly] (Statistical Release G.21)

Gives amount and change from month ago and year ago for amounts of loans outstanding, end of month, and volume of loans made during month, for the current month, month a year ago, and month two years ago.

FR 1.36/4:date
CONSUMER INSTALLMENT CREDITS OF INDUSTRIAL LOAN COMPANIES. [Monthly] (Statistical Release G.18.3)

FR 1.36/5:date
CONSUMER INSTALLMENT CREDIT EXTENDED AND REPAID. [Monthly] (Statistical Release G.22)

FR 1.36/6:date
CONSUMER FINANCE COMPANIES, LOANS OUTSTANDING AND VOLUME OF LOANS MADE. [Monthly] (Statistical Release G.21)

FR 1.36/7:date
CONSUMER CREDIT AT CONSUMER FINANCE COMPANIES. [Monthly] (Statistical Release G.22)

FR 1.37:date
CROP REPORT, BY FEDERAL RESERVE DISTRICT. [Monthly during crop harvesting months, usually from July through November] (Statistical Release G.10)

FR 1.38
INDEX NUMBERS OF WHOLESALE PRICES. [Irregular] (G.8)

Gives index numbers for all commodities, farm products, processed foods, and other commodities, as well as subgroups under these major headings. Also included are index numbers for prices received by farmers and prices paid by farmers. Figures shown are for latest month, two preceding months, and month a year ago.
Figures later appear in the Bulletin, as well as in the Wholesale Price Index, published by the Department of Labor, and the Demand and Price Situation, issued by the Department of Agriculture.
ISSN 0364-8001
Discontinued.

FR 1.39
CHANGES IN COMMERCIAL AND INDUSTRIAL LOANS BY INDUSTRY. [Weekly] (Statistical Release H.12)

Cover-sheet gives changes in loans during the week as well as cumulative changes since mid-year and comparative period of previous year. Table (a) gives changes in commercial and industrial loans of a sample of weekly reporting member banks by industry and Federal Reserve district.
Figures later appear in the Bulletin.
ISSN 0564-9145

FR 1.39/2
COMMERCIAL AND INDUSTRIAL LOANS OUTSTANDING BY INDUSTRY. [Weekly] (Statistical Release H.12)

FR 1.39/3:date
LOAN COMMITMENTS AT SELECTED LARGE COMMERCIAL BANKS. [Monthly] (G.11 [432])

FR 1.39/4:date
MAJOR NONDEPOSIT FUNDS OF COMMERCIAL BANKS. [Monthly] (G.10[411])

FR 1.40
SALES, PROFITS, AND DIVIDENDS OF LARGE CORPORATIONS. [Quarterly] (Statistical Release E.6)

Gives quarterly figures on operating revenue, profits before and after taxes, and dividends for public utility corporations (railroad, electric power, and telephone) and for manufacturing corporation, by selected industries. Figures later appear in the Bulletin.

FR 1.41:date
RETAIL FURNITURE REPORT. [Monthly] (Statistical Release G.16)

FR 1.42:date
EMPLOYMENT IN NONAGRICULTURAL ESTABLISHMENTS. [Monthly] (Statistical Release G.12.4)

FR 1.43
INTERDISTRICT SETTLEMENT FUND. [Monthly] (Statistical Release G.15)

Table (a) gives summary of transactions for each Federal Reserve Bank showing the balance in fund at close of business at end of preceding month, clearings, withdrawals, deposits, transfers, net loss or gain through clearings and through combined clearings and transfers, and balance in fund at close of business at end of month.
Table (b) Federal Reserve Agents' Fund, gives the summary of transactions for the month showing the balance in fund at end of preceding month, withdrawals (transfers to bank), deposits (transfers from bank), and balance in fund at close of business at end of month.

FR 1.44
OPEN-MARKET MONEY RATES AND BOND PRICES. [Monthly] (Statistical Release G.13)

Gives average of daily figures for five current weeks, and two current months for rates on commercial paper, finance paper placed directly, bankers' acceptances, stock exchange call loans, yields on U.S. Government securities; corporate bond yields (Moody's) yields on State and local government AAA bonds, and prices on long-term Treasury Bonds.
All data, except rate on stock exchange call loans, later appear in the Bulletin.
ISSN 0364-8443

FR 1.45:date
FEDERAL RESERVE BOARD PUBLICATIONS.

Earlier FR 1.2:P 96

FR 1.45/2:nos.
CURRENT PERIODICAL ARTICLES. [Monthly]

FR 1.45/3:nos.
SELECTED CURRENT ARTICLES AND NEW PUBLICATIONS OF FEDERAL RESERVE SYSTEM.

FR 1.45/4:CT
BIBLIOGRAPHIES AND LISTS OF PUBLICATIONS.

FR 1.46
LIST OF STOCKS REGISTERED ON NATIONAL SECURITIES EXCHANGE AND OF REDEEMABLE SECURITIES OF CERTAIN INVESTMENT COMPANIES, AS OF JUNE 30. [Annual]

FR 1.46/2
U.S. GOVERNMENT SECURITIES YIELDS AND PRICES. [Weekly] (Statistical Release H.15)

Gives yields in percent per annum for specified securities; prices of bonds, due or callable in 10 years or more. Figures are daily with weekly averages of week, preceding week, and week a year ago.
Figures also appear in monthly release (listed below).
ISSN 0364-7080
Later FR 1.32/7

FR 1.46/3:date
U.S. GOVERNMENT SECURITY YIELDS AND PRICES (Yields in percent per annum). [Monthly] (Statistical Release G.14)

FR 1.46/4:date
OTC MARGIN STOCKS.

FR 1.47
MONEY STOCK MEASURES AND COMPONENTS OF MONEY STOCK MEASURES AND RELATED ITEMS. [Weekly] (Statistical Release H.6)

Gives monthly supply (total, currency component, and demand deposits component) and time deposits adjusted (all commercial banks) as averages of daily figures, in billions of dollars, seasonally adjusted. Supplemental table gives demand deposits, currency, and related items, as averages of daily figures, in billions of dollars, not seasonally adjusted.
Figures later appear in the Bulletin.
Former title: Demand Deposits, Currency, and Related Items.

FR 1.48
APPLICATIONS RECEIVED, OR ACTED ON, BY THE BOARD. [Weekly] (H.2)

Includes announcements of receipt of, and actions on, applications for 1) Branchs, foreign and domestic; 2) Edge Act and Agreement corporations and new branches thereof; 3) Admission to and withdrawal from membership of the System, and 4) Permission to carry reduced reserves.
ISSN 0364-5428

FR 1.49:nos.
REVIEW OF FOREIGN DEVELOPMENTS. PREPARED FOR INTERNAL CIRCULATION.

FR 1.50:date
OFFICIAL HOURS AND HOLIDAYS TO BE OBSERVED BY FEDERAL RESERVE OFFICES DURING YEAR (date). [Annual] (Division of Federal Reserve Bank Operation) (K.8)

Monthly prior to Nov. 29, 1973 release.

FR 1.51:nos.   • Item 443-A (MF)
STAFF ECONOMIC STUDIES. 1–   [Irregular]

Consists of studies prepared by the staff of the Federal Reserve Board of Governors and also the Federal Reserve Banks in the field of economic and financial subjects.

FR 1.52:date
WEEKLY SUMMARY OF BANKING AND CREDIT MEASURES. (Statistical Release H.9)

ISSN 0364-7102

FR 1.53:date
VOLUME AND COMPOSITION OF INDIVIDUALS' SAVING. [Quarterly] (Statistical Release E.8)

First table gives data for unadjusted quarterly flows, the second for seasonally adjusted annual rates.
ISSN 0364-9628

FR 1.54:date
MATURITY DISTRIBUTION OF EURO-DOLLAR DEPOSITS IN FOREIGN BRANCHES OF U.S. BANKS. [Monthly] (Statistical Release G.17)

FR 1.54/2:date
MATURITY DISTRIBUTION OF OUTSTANDING NEGOTIABLE TIME CERTIFICATES OF DEPOSIT. – Nov. 1973. [Monthly] (Statistical Release G.9)

Tables include Outstanding Negotiable Time Certificates of Deposit, Large Commercial Banks; and Maturity Distribution of Outstanding Negotiable Time Certificates of Deposit, Large Commercial Banks.
ISSN 0364-8036

FR 1.55:date
CAPACITY UTILIZATION IN MANUFACTURING, QUARTERLY AVERAGES, SEASONALLY ADJUSTED. (Statistical Release E.5)

Gives capacity utilization (per cent) for total manufacturing, primary processing, and advanced processing; and manufacturing output and capacity indexes.
ISSN 0364-2860

FR 1.55/2:date
CAPACITY UTILIZATION: MANUFACTURING AND MATERIALS. [Monthly]

Formerly Capacity Utilization in Manufacturing, Quarterly Averages, Seasonally Adjusted (FR 1.55).

FR 1.56:date
FLOW OF FUNDS, SEASONALLY ADJUSTED AND UNADJUSTED. [Quarterly] (Flow of Funds Section, Division of Research and Statistics)

Titled Flow of Funds, Seasonally Adjusted until 3rd quarter, 1975, when it merged with Flow of Funds, Unadjusted (FR 1.56/2).
Earlier FR 1.2:F 96/3

FR 1.56/2:date
FLOW OF FUNDS, UNADJUSTED. – 1975. [Quarterly] (Flow of Funds and Savings Section)

Effective 3rd quarter, 1975, merged with Flow of Funds, Adjusted (FR 1.56).

FR 1.57:date
ANNUAL REPORT TO CONGRESS ON THE FEDERAL TRADE COMMISSION IMPROVEMENT ACT FOR THE CALENDAR YEAR.

FR 1.58:nos.
SPECIAL STUDIES PAPERS. 1– [Irregular] (Division of Research and Statistics)

FR 1.59:date
ANNUAL STATISTICAL DIGEST.

FR 1.60:date
ANNUAL REPORT TO CONGRESS ON EQUAL CREDIT OPPORTUNITY ACT.

FR 1.61:CT
ADDRESSES. [Irregular]

FR 1.62:nos.
INTERNATIONAL FINANCE DISCUSSION PAPERS.

FR 1.63:nos.:   • Item 443-E-1– E-53
HOME MORTGAGE DISCLOSURE ACT DATA (State). [Annual]

Issued for each state, District of Columbia, U.S. Summary, and Outlying Areas.
FR 1.63/54   • Item 443-E-54 (EL)
HMDA AGGREGATE REPORTS.

FR 1.63/55   • Item 443-E-55 (EL)
HMDA DISCLOSURE REPORTS.

DEPARTMENT OF HEALTH, EDUCATION AND WELFARE (1953– 1969)

CREATION AND AUTHORITY

The Federal Security Agency was established by Reorganization Plan No. 1 of 1939, effective July 1, 1939, which transferred to the Agency the Office of Education (I 16), the Public Health Service (T 27), the Social Security Board (SS 1), the United States Employment Service (L 7), the Civilian Conservation Corps (Y 3.C 49), and the National Youth Administration (Y 3.N 21/14). The Agency was abolished and its units transferred to the Department of Health, Education, and Welfare (HE 1) by Reorganization Plan No. 1 of 1953, effective April 11, 1953.

NOTE:– During the period 1953-1969, the FS classes continued to be issued by the Department and its component agencies.

FS 1.1   • Item 444
ANNUAL REPORTS. [Annual]

Later HE 1.1

FS 1.2:CT
GENERAL PUBLICATIONS.

Later HE 1.2

FS 1.2:Ed 8/3   • Item 445
HEW OBLIGATIONS TO INSTITUTIONS OF HIGHER EDUCATION FISCAL YEAR, REFERENCE TABLES. [Annual] Office of Assistant Secretary for Health and Scientific Affairs.

FS 1.2:M 54   • Item 445
DIRECTORY OF STATE MERIT SYSTEMS. [Irregular]

FS 1.2:Su 7/2   • Item 445
DIRECTORY, DIRECTORS OF STATE AGENCIES FOR SURPLUS PROPERTY AND REGIONAL REPRESENTATIVES, DIVISION OF SURPLUS PROPERTY UTILIZATION. [Irregular]

FS 1.3
BULLETINS.

FS 1.3/2
PERSONNEL BULLETIN.

FS 1.4:nos.
AGENCY CIRCULARS.

FS 1.6:CT
REGULATIONS, RULES, AND INSTRUCTIONS.

FS 1.6/2:pt.nos.
AGENCY MANUALS. [Admin.]

FS 1.6/3:CT
HANDBOOKS, MANUALS, GUIDES.

Later HE 1.6/3

FS 1.6/4:nos.
EMERGENCY MANUAL GUIDES.

FS 1.6/5   • Item 445-A
HANDBOOK ON PROGRAMS OF THE DEPARTMENT OF HEALTH, EDUCATION, AND WELFARE. [Annual]

Later HE 1.6/5

FS 1.6/6   • Item 445-A
GRANTS-IN-AID AND OTHER FINANCIAL ASSISTANCE PROGRAMS ADMINISTERED BY THE DEPARTMENT OF HEALTH, EDUCATION, AND WELFARE. [Annual]
Later HE 1.6/6

FS 1.6/6-2
GRANTS ADMINISTRATION MANUAL CIRCULARS.

FS 1.6/7   • Item 445-A
GRANTS ADMINISTRATION MANUAL. [Irregular]

Later HE 1.6/7

FS 1.6/7-2:nos.
GRANTS ADMINISTRATION MANUAL CIRCULARS.

Later HE 1.6/7-2

FS 1.6/8   • Item 483-J
GUIDELINES FOR (Various Health Professionals and Sub-professionals) IN HOME HEALTH SERVICES. 1968– [Irregular]

FS 1.7:CT
ADDRESSES. [Irregular]

Later HE 1.7

FS 1.8:nos.
HERE'S YOUR ANSWER, PROGRAMS.

FS 1.9:nos.
I HEAR AMERICA SINGING (radio scripts). [Weekly]

FS 1.10:nos.
TRAINING MANUAL.

Later HE 1.10

FS 1.11:v.nos.&nos.
ACCESSION LIST, LIBRARY. [Biweekly]

FS 1.12:nos.
SUPERVISION AND MANAGEMENT SERIES.

FS 1.13:date
AGING. [Issued about 3 times a year]

Later FS 14.9

FS 1.13/2:nos.
REPORTS AND GUIDELINES FROM WHITE HOUSE CONFERENCE ON AGING (series).

FS 1.13/3:nos.
PATTERNS FOR PROGRESS IN AGING CASE STUDIES.

Later FS 14.9/5

FS 1.13/4:date
HIGHLIGHTS OF LEGISLATION ON AGING.

Later 14.9/2

FS 1.13/5:nos.
FACTS ON AGING.

Later FS 14.9/3

FS 1.14
AGENCY ORDERS.

FS 1.15
[PRESS RELEASES]. [Irregular]

Later HE 1.15

FS 1.15
[SURPLUS PROPERTY DISPOSED OF TO PUBLIC HEALTH AND EDUCATIONAL INSTITUTIONS]. [Quarterly]

FS 1.16
REGIONAL AND FIELD LETTER.

FS 1.17:date   • Item 444-D
FIELD DIRECTORY. [Annual]

Later HE 1.17

FS 1.17/2:date
REGIONAL OFFICE DIRECTORY, PROFESSIONAL AND ADMINISTRATIVE PERSONNEL. [Semiannual]

Earlier FS 1.2

FS 1.18:CT
BIBLIOGRAPHIES AND LISTS OF PUBLICATIONS.

Earlier FS 1.2
Later HE 1.18

FS 1.18/2:nos.
SELECTED REFERENCES ON AGING (numbered).

Later FS 14.9/4

FS 1.19   • Item 445-B
HEALTH, EDUCATION, AND WELFARE TRENDS. 1959– [Annual]

Later HE 1.19

FS 1.20:date
HEALTH, EDUCATION AND WELFARE INDICATORS. [Monthly]

FS 1.21:date
HEW FACTS AND FIGURES.

Earlier FS 1.2:H 77
Later HE 1.21

FS 1.22:date
STATE SALARY RANGES, SELECTED CLASSES [of position] IN EMPLOYMENT SECURITY, PUBLIC WELFARE, PUBLIC HEALTH, MENTAL HEALTH, VOCATIONAL REHABILITATION, CIVIL DEFENSE, EMERGENCY PLANNING. [Irregular]

FS 1.23:date   • Item 445-G
PROPOSED MENTAL RETARDATION PROGRAMS, FISCAL YEAR (date). 1966– [Annual]

Later HE 1.23

Secretary's Committee on Mental Retardation

FS 1.23/2
FISCAL YEAR APPROPRIATIONS FOR MENTAL RETARDATION PROGRAMS OF THE DEPARTMENT OF HEALTH, EDUCATION, AND WELFARE. [Annual]

FS 1.23/3   • Item 445-G
MENTAL RETARDATION GRANTS, FISCAL YEAR.
1964–   [Annual]

FS 1.23/4:nos.
PROGRAMS FOR THE HANDICAPPED. 1965–
[Irregular]

> Earlier title: Mental Retardation Report.
> Later HE 1.23/4

FS 1.23/5:date   • Item 445-G
MENTAL RETARDATION ACTIVITIES OF THE
DEPARTMENT OF HEALTH, EDUCATION, AND
WELFARE. [Annual]

> Later HE 1.23/5

FS 1.24
EDUCATIONAL TELEVISION FACILITIES PROGRAM:
PROGRAM BULLETINS. 1– 1963– [Irregular]

FS 1.24/2
EDUCATIONAL TELEVISION FACILITIES PROGRAM:
PUBLIC NOTICES. 1– 1963– [Irregular]

FS 1.25:nos.
MERIT SYSTEM METHODS.

FS 1.26   • Item 333-C & 460-A-87
EDUCATION AND TRAINING, ANNUAL REPORT OF
THE DEPARTMENT OF HEALTH, EDUCATION,
AND WELFARE TO THE CONGRESS ON TRAIN-
ING ACTIVITIES UNDER THE MANPOWER
DEVELOPMENT AND TRAINING ACT. 1– 1962–
[Annual]

> Earlier FS 1.2:Ed 8, FS 1.26

FS 1.27:nos.
HEW FIELD LETTER.

FS 1.28
TELEPHONE DIRECTORY.

FS 1.29
PROGRAM ANALYSIS (series). 1966–   [Irregular]

> Later FS 1.29

FS 1.30   • Item 445
SECRETARY'S LETTER. v. 1–

FS 1.31:date
GRANTS ADMINISTRATION REPORT. [Irregular]

> Later HE 1.31

FS 1.32:CT
TASK FORCE ON PRESCRIPTION DRUGS, PUBLI-
CATIONS.

> Later HE 1.32

FS 1.33:date   • Item 445-K
CAREER SERVICE BOARD FOR SCIENCE REPORTS.
1– 1968–

> Later HE 1.33

FS 1.34:date
HEW CONSUMER NEWSLETTERS.

FS 1.35   • Item 445
ANNUAL REPORT OF SECRETARY OF HEALTH,
EDUCATION, AND WELFARE TO CONGRESS IN
COMPLIANCE WITH PUBLIC LAW 90-148, AIR
QUALITY ACT OF 1967. 1– 1969– [Annual]

FS 1.36:nos.
PROJECT HEAD START (series).

> Earlier PrEx 10.12

FS 1.36/2:date
CHILD DEVELOPMENT OFFICE: MANUALS (numbered)

> Later HE 21.8/2

PUBLIC HEALTH SERVICE
(1939– 1969)

CREATION AND AUTHORITY

    The Public Health Service (T 27) was trans-
ferred from the Department of the Treasury to the
Federal Security Agency by Reorganization Plan
No. 1 of 1939, effective July 1, 1939. On April 11,
1953, it became a part of the newly created Department of Health, Education, and Welfare (HE
20) by Reorganization Plan No. 1 of 1953.

FS 2.1:date
ANNUAL REPORTS.
> Earlier T 27.1
> Later HE 20.1

FS 2.2:CT
GENERAL PUBLICATIONS.
> Earlier T 27.2
> Later HE 20.2

FS 2.2:Ad 9/2   • Item 485
PHS PUBLIC ADVISORY GROUPS, AUTHORITY,
STRUCTURE, FUNCTIONS. [Irregular]
> Later HE 20.2:Ad 9/2

FS 2.2:Ad 9/3   • Item 485
ROSTER OF MEMBERS OF PHS PUBLIC ADVI-
SORY GROUPS, COUNCILS, COMMITTEES,
BOARDS, PANELS, STUDY SECTIONS.
[Irregular]
> Later HE 20.2:Ad 9/3

FS 2.2:C 16/5   • Item 485
CANCER SERVICES, FACILITIES AND PRO-
GRAMS IN UNITED STATES. 1950–
[Irregular]
> Later HE 20.2:C 16/5

FS 2.2:D 54/7   • Item 485
DIGEST OF PREPAID DENTAL CARE PLANS.
1957– [Irregular]
> Later HE 20.2:D 54/7

FS 2.2:F 67/8   • Item 485
ANNUAL FLUORIDATION CENSUS REPORT.
[Annual]
> Later HE 20.2:F 67/8

FS 2.2:In 25/9
INDIAN HEALTH HIGHLIGHTS.
> Later HE 20.2:In 25/9

FS 2.2:M 31   • Item 485
HEALTH MANPOWER SOURCE BOOK. 1–
1952– [Irregular]
> Later HE 20.2:M 31

FS 2.2:P 75/2   • Item 485
DIRECTORY, POISON CONTROL CENTERS.
[Irregular]
> Later HE 20.2:P 75/2

FS 2.2:Sm 7/5   • Item 485
DIRECTORY OF ON-GOING RESEARCH IN
SMOKING AND HEALTH. 1– 1967–
[Annual]
> Later HE 20.2612

FS 2.2:T 68/6   • Item 485
NATIONAL CONFERENCE ON PUBLIC HEALTH
TRAINING, REPORT TO THE SURGEON
GENERAL. 1–
> Later HE 20.2:T 68/8

FS 2.2:T 69   • Item 485
HEALTH INFORMATION FOR TRAVEL IN [area].
[Irregular]
> Later HE 20.2:T 69

FS 2.3:nos.
PUBLIC HEALTH BULLETINS.
> Earlier T 27.12

FS 2.3/2:nos.
INFORMATION BULLETIN. [Admin.]

FS 2.3/3   • Item 486-H
TECHNICAL INFORMATION BULLETINS. 1– 1967–
[Irregular]

FS 2.4
CIRCULARS.

FS 2.4/2:nos.
CIRCULAR MEMOS [Conference on State Sanitary
Engineers].

FS 2.5:CT
LAWS.

FS 2.6:CT
REGULATIONS, RULES, AND INSTRUCTIONS.

FS 2.6/2:CT
HANDBOOKS, MANUALS, GUIDES.

> Earlier FS 2.6
> Later HE 20.1108

FS 2.6/2:nos.
PHS REHABILITATION GUIDE SERIES

> Later HE 20.1308, HE 20.2608

FS 2.6/3:CT
FILM GUIDES.

> Earlier FS 2.211/2
> Later 20.2558

FS 2.6/4:letters-nos.
HEALTH MOBILIZATION COURSE MANUAL [sections].
[Admin.]

FS 2.6/5:CT
AIR QUALITY CRITERIA.

FS 2.6/6   • Item 494-E
PHS REHABILITATION GUIDES SERIES. 1– 1967–
[Irregular]

FS 2.6/7   • Item 496-A
BHS [Bureau of Health Services] PROGRAMMED
INSTRUCTION (series). 1– 1968– [Irregular]

FS 2.6/8:CT
GUIDELINES FOR [Various Health Professionals and
Sub-professionals] IN HOME HEALTH SERVICES.

FS 2.7
PUBLIC HEALTH REPORTS. [Weekly]

> Earlier T 27.6/1

FS 2.7/a:nos.
REPRINTS. 1– 1913–

FS 2.7/a 2:nos.
– TUBERCULOSIS CONTROL ISSUES. [Monthly]

FS 2.7/2:v.nos.
– BOUND VOLUMES.
> Earlier T 27.6

FS 2.7/3:v.nos.
– TUBERCULOSIS CONTROL ISSUES, INDEX.

FS 2.8:nos.
SUPPLEMENTS TO PUBLIC HEALTH REPORTS.
> Earlier T 27.6/2

FS 2.9:vol.
VENEREAL DISEASE INFORMATION. [Monthly]
> Earlier T 27.26

FS 2.9/a:nos.
– REPRINTS.
> Earlier T 27.26/a

FS 2.10:nos.
SUPPLEMENTS TO VENEREAL DISEASE INFORMA-
TION BULLETIN.
> Earlier T 27.26/2

FS 2.11:nos.
VENEREAL DISEASE BULLETINS.

Earlier T 27.20

FS 2.11/2:date
CURRENT LITERATURE ON VENEREAL DISEASE.
[Irregular]

Later HE 20.2311

FS 2.11/2
ABSTRACTS OF CURRENT LITERATURE ON VENE-
REAL DISEASE. 1952–   [3 or 4 times a year]

FS 2.11/2
CURRENT LITERATURE ON VENEREAL DISEASE,
ABSTRACTS AND BIBLIOGRAPHY. [3 or 4 times
a year and Annual]

FS 2.11/3
STATISTICAL LETTER.

FS 2.11/4   • Item 500-B
VD FACT SHEET (year). 1–

Basic statistics on Venereal Disease problems in the United States.

FS 2.12:vol.
HOSPITAL NEWS. [Semimonthly]

Earlier T 27.33

FS 2.12/2:CT
HOSPITAL ELEMENTS, PLANNING AND EQUIPMENT
FOR 50-, AND 200-, BED GENERAL HOSPITALS.

FS 2.13   • Item 496
PUBLIC HEALTH ENGINEERING ABSTRACTS. v. 1–
1921–   [Monthly]

FS 2.14:nos.
GENERAL CIRCULARS.

Earlier T 27.15/3

FS 2.15:vol.
HEALTH OFFICER. [Monthly]

Earlier T 27.34

FS 2.16
CERTIFIED SHIPPERS OF FRESH AND FROZEN
OYSTERS, CLAMS, AND MUSSELS. [Monthly]

FS 2.16/2   • Item 494-B
PROCEEDINGS, NATIONAL SHELLFISH SANITATION
WORKSHOP. 1–   [Biennial]

FS 2.17:nos.
HOSPITAL DIVISION CIRCULARS.

Earlier T 27.24

FS 2.17/2:nos.
HOSPITAL DIVISION CIRCULARS, NEW SERIES. OCT.
1, 1943–

FS 2.18:nos.
HOSPITAL DIVISION SIMILAR LETTERS.

Earlier T 27.27

FS 2.18/2   • Item 494-C
ANNUAL STATISTICAL SUMMARY. [Annual]

Later HE 20.2709

FS 2.19:vol.
NATIONAL NEGRO HEALTH NEWS. [Quarterly]

Earlier T 27.30

FS 2.20:nos.
EDUCATIONAL PUBLICATIONS.

FS 2.21   • Item 481-A
PUBLIC HEALTH BIBLIOGRAPHY SERIES. 1–
[Irregular]

Later HE 20.11

FS 2.21:nos.   • Item 481-A
NATIONAL INSTITUTES OF HEALTH SCIENTIFIC DI-
RECTORY, (year), AND ANNUAL BIBLIOGRAPHY.
[Annual]

National Institutes of Health

FS 2.22:CT
GENERAL PUBLICATIONS.

Later HE 20.2402

FS 2.22:AI 6   • Item 507
NATIONAL INSTITUTES OF HEALTH ALMANAC.
[Irregular]

Later HE 20.3016

FS 2.22:M 52/40   • Item 507
DIRECTORY OF STATE MENTAL HEALTH
PERSONNEL AND REGIONAL OFFICES OF
DEPARTMENT OF HEALTH, EDUCATION, AND
WELFARE. [Irregular]

FS 2.22:M 52/44   • Item 507
MENTAL HEALTH RESEARCH FINDINGS (year).
[Annual]

FS 2.22:T 68/2
NIH LIBRARY TRANSLATIONS INDEX.

FS 2.22/2
N.I.H. RECORD.

FS 2.22/3:nos.
CANCER CONTROL LETTER.

FS 2.22/4   • Item 507-I
REFERENCE GUIDES. 1–   [Irregular]

FS 2.22/5:nos.
HEART HEALTH NEWS FOR HEALTH DEPARTMENTS.

FS 2.22/6:date
NATIONAL INSTITUTES OF HEALTH, ANNUAL
LECTURES.

Earlier FS 2.22:L 49

FS 2.22/7   • Item 507-D
PUBLIC HEALTH SERVICE GRANTS AND AWARDS.
1955–   [Annual]

FS 2.22/7-2   • Item 508-D
RESEARCH GRANTS INDEX, FISCAL YEAR. 1961–
[Annual]

Later HE 20.3013/2

FS 2.22/7-3   • Item 507-D
NATIONAL INSTITUTES OF HEALTH RESEARCH
GRANTS, FISCAL YEAR (date) FUNDS. [Annual]

FS 2.22/7-4   • Item 507-D
MENTAL HEALTH TRAINING GRANT AWARDS.
[Annual]

FS 2.22/7-5:date
NATIONAL INSTITUTES OF HEALTH TRAINING PRO-
GRAMS, FISCAL YEAR.

FS 2.22/8:date
RESEARCH AND TRAINING GRANTS AND AWARDS
OF PUBLIC HEALTH SERVICE. [Annual]

Earlier FS 2.2:R 31/3

FS 2.22/9:date
PAPERS APPROVED FOR PUBLICATION OR PRE-
SENTATION.

FS 2.22/10:nos.
PROGRESS REPORTS.

FS 2.22/11:date
HIGHLIGHTS OF HEART PROGRESS. [Annual]

Earlier FS 2.22:H 35/4

FS 2.22/11-2:date
PUBLIC HEALTH SERVICE SUPPORT OF CARDIO-
VASCULAR RESEARCH, TRAINING AND
COMMUNITY PROGRAMS. [Annual]

Earlier FS 2.22:C 17/4

FS 2.22/12:date
HIGHLIGHTS OF PROGRESS IN RESEARCH ON
NEUROLOGIC DISORDERS. [Annual]

FS 2.22/13:CT
BIBLIOGRAPHIES AND LISTS OF PUBLICATIONS.

Later HE 20.3012

FS 2.22/13-2
RECENT TRANSLATIONS. [Monthly]

Selected list.
Issued by NIH Library.

FS 2.22/13-3
PERIODICALS CURRENTLY RECEIVED IN NIH
LIBRARY. [Annual]

FS 2.22/13-4   • Item 506-B
CRIME AND DELINQUENCY ABSTRACTS.

Earlier title: International Bibliography on Crime
and Delinquency.
Later HE 20.2420

FS 2.22/13-5   • Item 506-A-2
ARTIFICIAL KIDNEY BIBLIOGRAPHY. v. 1–   1967–
[Quarterly]

Later HE 20.311

FS 2.22/13-6   • Item 506-A-3
FIBRINOLYSIS, THROMBOLYSIS, AND BLOOD CLOT-
TING, BIBLIOGRAPHY, ANNUAL COMPILATION.
1966–   [Annual]

Later HE 20.3209

FS 2.22/13-7:nos.
REPORTS ON REPRODUCTION AND POPULATION
RESEARCH (series).

FS 2.22/13-8:date
SCIENTIFIC DIRECTORY AND ANNUAL BIBLIO-
GRAPHY.

Earlier FS 2.21:75
Later HE 20.3017

FS 2.22/13-9
NIH QUARTERLY PUBLICATIONS LIST. 1969–
[Quarterly]

Later HE 20.3009

FS 2.22/14:date
HIGHLIGHTS OF PROGRESS IN RESEARCH ON CAN-
CER. [Annual]

FS 2.22/14-2   • Item 507-G
PROGRESS AGAINST CANCER. 1958–   [Annual]

Earlier FS 2.22:C 16/1
Later HE 20.3014

FS 2.22/15:CT
HANDBOOKS, MANUALS, GUIDES.

Earlier FS 2.22
Later HE 20.3208

FS 2.22/16:date
HIGHLIGHTS OF PROGRESS IN MENTAL HEALTH
RESEARCH.

FS 2.22/16-2   • Item 507-J
RESEARCH PROJECT SUMMARIES, NATIONAL
INSTITUTE OF MENTAL HEALTH. 1–   1963–
[Annual]

FS 2.22/17:date
HIGHLIGHTS OF RESEARCH PROGRESS IN AL-
LERGY AND INFECTIOUS DISEASES. [Annual]

FS 2.22/18 • **Item 507-L**
NATIONAL CANCER INSTITUTE MONOGRAPHS. 1–
[Irregular]

FS 2.22/19:CT
RUSSIAN SCIENTIFIC TRANSLATION PROGRAM
PUBLICATIONS.

FS 2.22/19-2:nos.
BULLETIN OF TRANSLATIONS FROM RUSSIAN MEDI-
CAL SCIENCES.

> Issued by Russian Scientific Translation Pro-
> gram.
> Internal use only.

FS 2.22/19-3:CT
TRANSLATIONS FOR NATIONAL INSTITUTES OF
HEALTH.

FS 2.22/20:date
HIGHLIGHTS OF RESEARCH PROGRESS IN GEN-
ERAL MEDICAL SCIENCES. [Annual]

FS 2.22/21:date
HIGHLIGHTS OF RESEARCH PROGRESS IN ARTHRI-
TIS AND METABOLIC DISEASES. [Annual]

FS 2.22/22:date
MEMBERS OF ADVISORY COUNCILS, STUDY
SECTIONS, AND COMMITTEES OF NATIONAL
INSTITUTES OF HEALTH. [Annual]

> Earlier FS 2.22:Ad 9

FS 2.22/22-2 • **Item 507-N**
NIH PUBLIC ADVISORY GROUPS: AUTHORITY,
STRUCTURE, FUNCTIONS.

> Later HE 20.3018

FS 2.22/23:date
HIGHLIGHTS OF PROGRESS IN RESEARCH ON
ORAL DISEASES. [Annual]

FS 2.22/24:date
PLANT SAFETY BRANCH HANDBOOKS.

FS 2.22/25:date
RESEARCH HIGHLIGHTS IN AGING. [Annual]

FS 2.22/25-2:date
RESEARCH PROGRAMS IN AGING.

> Earlier FS 2.22:Ag 4/2

FS 2.22/25-3:nos.
ADULT DEVELOPMENT AND AGING ABSTRACTS.

> Later FS 2.22:Ag 4/2

FS 2.22/26:date
ACTIVITIES OF THE NATIONAL INSTITUTES OF
HEALTH IN FIELD OF GERONTOLOGY. [Annual]

> Earlier FS 2.22:G 31

FS 2.22/27:nos.
NIMH ANALYSES SERIES.

FS 2.22/28 • **Item 507-M-1**
RESEARCH HIGHLIGHTS, NATIONAL INSTITUTES
OF HEALTH. [Annual]

> Earlier FS 2.22:R 31/5

FS 2.22/29 • **Item 507-Z-1**
PSYCHOPHARMACOLOGY BULLETIN. v. 1–
[Irregular]

> Earlier title: Psychopharmacology Service
> Center Bulletins.
> Later HE 20.2409

FS 2.22/29-2 • **Item 507-Z**
PSYCHOPHARMACOLOGY ABSTRACTS. v. 1–
1961–   [Irregular]

> Later HE 20.2409/2

FS 2.22/30 • **Item 507-A-9**
CANCER CHEMOTHERAPY REPORTS. 1–   1959–
[Irregular]

> Later HE 20.3160

FS 2.22/30-2
CANCER CHEMOTHERAPY ABSTRACTS. [Bimonthly]

> Later HE 20.3160/4

FS 2.22/30-3:v.nos.&nos.
CANCER CHEMOTHERAPY REPORTS PART 2.

> Later HE 20.3160/2

FS 2.22/30-4:v.nos.&nos.
CANCER CHEMOTHERAPY REPORTS PART 3, PRO-
GRAM INFORMATION.

> Later HE 20.3160/3

FS 2.22/31 • **Item 507-T**
MENTAL HEALTH MONOGRAPHS. 1–   1962–
[Irregular]

FS 2.22/32 • **Item 507-V**
NATIONAL CANCER INSTITUTE RESEARCH RE-
PORTS. 1–   1962–   [Irregular]

FS 2.22/32-2 • **Item 507-V**
RESEARCH REPORTS (unnumbered). [Irregular]

> Later HE 20.3166

FS 2.22/33 • **Item 507-U**
RESOURCES FOR MEDICAL RESEARCH, REPORTS.
1–   1962–   [Irregular]

> Later HE 20.3014

FS 2.22/34 • **Item 507-A-4**
HEART RESEARCH NEWS. [Irregular]

FS 2.22/35 • **Item 507-W**
RESOURCES ANALYSIS MEMOS. 1–   1959–
[Irregular]

FS 2.22/36:date
NATIONAL INSTITUTES OF HEALTH ORGANIZATION
HANDBOOK. [Annual]

FS 2.22/37 • **Item 507-V**
ANNUAL CONFERENCE OF MODEL REPORTING
AREA FOR BLINDNESS STATISTICS, PROCEED-
INGS. 1–   1962–   [Annual]

> Later HE 20.3759/2

FS 2.22/37-2 • **Item 507-Y**
STATISTICAL REPORT, ANNUAL TABULATIONS OF
MODEL REPORTING AREA FOR BLINDNESS
STATISTICS. 1962–   [Annual]

> Later HE 20.3759

FS 2.22/38 • **Item 507-A-5**
DATA ON PATIENTS OF OUTPATIENT PSYCHIATRIC
CLINICS IN THE UNITED STATES. 1959–
[Annual]

FS 2.22/38-2
DATA ON STAFF AND MAN-HOURS, OUTPATIENT
PSYCHIATRIC CLINICS IN THE UNITED STATES.
1959–   [Annual]

FS 2.22/38-3 • **Item 507-A-5**
OUTPATIENT PSYCHIATRIC CLINICS, COMMUNITY
SERVICE ACTIVITIES. [Irregular]

FS 2.22/38-4 • **Item 507-A-5**
DIRECTORY OF OUTPATIENT PSYCHIATRIC
CLINICS, PSYCHIATRIC DAYNIGHT SERVICES
AND OTHER MENTAL HEALTH RESOURCES IN
THE UNITED STATES AND TERRITORIES.
[Irregular]
> Earlier FS 2.22:P 95/5

FS 2.22/39 • **Item 507-A-1**
CARCINOGENESIS ABSTRACTS. v. 1–   1963–
[Monthly]
> Later HE 20.3159

FS 2.22/40 • **Item 507-A-5**
OUTPATIENT PSYCHIATRIC CLINICS, SPECIAL
STATISTICAL REPORTS [and Tables]. [Irregular]

FS 2.22/41 • **Item 507-A-3**
RESEARCH UTILIZATION SERIES. [Irregular]

FS 2.22/42 • **Item 507-D**
NATIONAL INSTITUTE OF MENTAL HEALTH TRAIN-
ING GRANT PROGRAM.

FS 2.22/43
RESEARCH PROFILES.

FS 2.22/44 • **Item 507-A-8**
PROCEEDINGS, PANEL PRESENTATIONS, ANNUAL
CONFERENCE ON MODEL REPORTING AREA
FOR MENTAL HOSPITAL STATISTICS. 1–
[Annual].

FS 2.22/45 • **Item 507-A-7**
PROCEEDINGS OF ANNUAL CONFERENCE, MENTAL
HEALTH CAREER DEVELOPMENT PROGRAM.
2nd–   1963–   [Annual]

FS 2.22/46
PATIENT MOVEMENT DATA, STATE AND MENTAL
HOSPITALS. [Annual]

> Earlier FS 2.22:M 52/39

FS 2.22/47 • **Item 507-A-13**
ARTHRITIS AND RHEUMATIC DISEASES AB-
STRACTS. [Monthly]

> Later HE 20.3312

FS 2.22/48 • **Item 507-A-12**
ANDROGENIC AND MYOGENIC ENDOCRINE BIO-
ASSAY DATA. [Irregular]

FS 2.22/48-2 • **Item 507-A-20**
ENDOCRINOLOGY INDEX. [Bimonthly]

> Later HE 20.3309

FS 2.22/49 • **Item 506-C**
MENTAL HEALTH DIRECTORY OF STATE AND
NATIONAL AGENCIES ADMINISTERING PUBLIC
MENTAL HEALTH AND RELATED PROGRAMS.
[Irregular]

> Later HE 20.2418

FS 2.22/50 • **Item 507-B-1**
CONFERENCE REPORT SERIES. [Irregular] National
Clearinghouse for Mental Health Information.

FS 2.22/50-2:date
DRUG DEPENDENCE AND ABUSE NOTES.

FS 2.22/50-3 • **Item 507-B-3**
OCCUPATIONAL MENTAL HEALTH NOTES. 1967–
[Irregular]

> Later HE 20.2411

FS 2.22/50-3
OCCUPATIONAL HEALTH NOTES. [Irregular]

FS 2.22/50-4
MENTAL HEALTH PROGRAM REPORTS. 1–   1967–
[Irregular]

> Later HE 20.2419

FS 2.22/50-5
MENTAL HEALTH DIGEST. v. 1–   1969–   [Monthly]

> Later 20.2410

FS 2.22/50-6:nos.
BULLETIN OF SUICIDOLOGY.

> Earlier FS 2.22:Su 3
> Later HE 20.2413

FS 2.22/50-7:date
DRUG DEPENDENCE.

FS 2.22/51   • Item 506-A-1
CURRENT PROJECTS IN PREVENTION, CONTROL,
AND TREATMENT OF CRIME AND DELINQUENCY.
v. 1–   [Semiannual]

FS 2.22/52   • Item 506-C-1
MENTAL RETARDATION ABSTRACTS. v. 1–   1964–
[Quarterly]

Later HE 17.113

FS 2.22/53   • Item 507-A-15
DIABETES LITERATURE INDEX. v. 1–   1966–
[Monthly & Annual]

Later HE 20.3310

FS 2.22/53-2   • Item 507-A-15
ANNUAL COMPILATION. [Annual]

Later HE 20.3310/2

FS 2.22/54   • Item 507-A-14
GASTROENTEROLOGY ABSTRACTS AND CITA-
TIONS. v. 1–   1966–   [Monthly]

Later HE 20.3313

FS 2.22/55   • Item 507-L-1
NINBD [National Institute of Neurological Diseases
and Blindness] MONOGRAPHS. 1–   1965–
[Irregular]

Earlier title: NINIM Monographs.
Later title: NINDS Monographs. [National
Institute of Neurological Diseases and Stroke.]
Later HE 20.3510

FS 2.22/56:v.nos.
READING GUIDE TO CANCER-VIROLOGY LITERA-
TURE.

FS 2.22/57:CT
NUTRITION SURVEYS [by country].

Earlier Y 3.In 8/13:2

FS 2.22/58
ADDRESSES. [Irregular]

FS 2.22/59   • Item 507-A-18
EPILEPSY ABSTRACTS. v. 1–   1967–   [Monthly]

Later HE 20.3509

FS 2.22/59-2:date
EPILEPSY ABSTRACTS (compilations).

Later HE 20.3509/2

FS 2.22/60:CT
NURSING CLINICAL CONFERENCES PRESENTED
BY NURSING DEPARTMENT OF CLINICAL
CENTER.

FS 2.22/61:nos.
CURRENT POPULATION RESEARCH REPORTS.

Later HE 20.3362

FS 2.22/62:date
NATIONAL INSTITUTES OF GENERAL MEDICAL
SCIENCES, ANNUAL REPORTS.

Later 20.3451

FS 2.22/63:CT
CHEMOTHERAPY FACT SHEETS.

Later HE 20.3164

FS 2.22/64   • Item 483-U
COMPUTER RESEARCH AND TECHNOLOGY
DIVISION: TECHNICAL REPORTS. 1–   1968–
[Irregular]

Later HE 20.3011

Public Health Service (Continued)

FS 2.23:nos.
NATIONAL INSTITUTE OF HEALTH, BULLETINS.
Earlier T 27.3

FS 2.24:CT
BIBLIOGRAPHIES.
Earlier T 27.40

FS 2.24:In 3   • Item 481-A
LIST OF HEALTH INFORMATION LEAFLETS AND
PAMPHLETS OF THE PUBLIC HEALTH SER-
VICE. [Annual]

FS 2.24/2   • Item 481-A
LIST OF PUBLICATIONS ISSUED BY THE PUBLIC
HEALTH SERVICE. [Semiannual]

Later HE 20.2012

FS 2.24/3:nos.
SELECTIVE LISTING OF RADIOLOGICAL HEALTH
DOCUMENTS, LISTS.

FS 2.24/4:date
SMOKING AND HEALTH BIBLIOGRAPHICAL BULLE-
TIN. [Monthly]

Later HE 20.2609

FS 2.25:nos.
FOLDERS.

Earlier T 27.43

FS 2.25:nos.
FOLDERS.

Earlier T 27.43

FS 2.26:CT
POSTERS.

Earlier T 27.19
Later FS 2.26/2

FS 2.26/2:nos.
PUBLIC HEALTH SERVICE POSTERS.

Earlier FS 2.26

FS 2.27:nos.
POSTERS, VD.

Earlier T 27.19:Sy 7

FS 2.28:date
CHRONOLOGICAL LIST OF OFFICIAL ORDERS TO
COMMISSIONED AND OTHER OFFICERS.

Earlier T 27.13

FS 2.29:nos.
MISCELLANEOUS PUBLICATIONS.

Earlier T 27.17

FS 2.30
ADDRESSES. [Irregular]

Earlier T 27.31
Later HE 20.1312

FS 2.31   • Item 488
JOURNAL OF THE NATIONAL CANCER INSTITUTE.
v. 1–   1940–   [Bimonthly]

Later HE 20.3161

FS 2.32:nos.
VD FOLDERS.

Earlier T 27.43

FS 2.33:nos.
WORKERS' HEALTH SERIES.

FS 2.34:date
CONFERENCE OF STATE AND TERRITORIAL HEALTH
OFFICERS WITH UNITED STATES PUBLIC
HEALTH SERVICE, TRANSACTIONS.
Earlier T 27.32

FS 2.35:nos.
COMMUNITY HEALTH SERIES.

FS 2.35/2   • Item 494-D
PORTRAITS IN COMMUNITY HEALTH. 1965–
[Irregular]

FS 2.36:nos.
[FILM ADVERTISEMENTS].

FS 2.36/2   • Item 497-A
PUBLIC HEALTH SERVICE FILM CATALOG. [Annual]

Later title: National Medical Audiovisual Center
Catalog.
Earlier FS 2.2:F 48/2
Later HE 20.3608/4

FS 2.37:CT
HEALTH LEAFLETS.

Earlier T 27.35/2

FS 2.38:nos.
SPECIAL VD EDUCATION CIRCULARS.

FS 2.39:nos.
VD EDUCATION CIRCULARS.

FS 2.40:nos.
LETTERS RELATIVE TO CURRENT DEVELOPMENTS
IN MEDICAL SCIENCE AND MEDICAL MILITARY
INFORMATION. [Semimonthly]

FS 2.41:nos.
MALARIA FOLDERS.

FS 2.42:nos.
T.B. FOLDERS.

FS 2.42/2:date
NEWLY REPORTED TUBERCULOSIS CASES AND
TUBERCULOSIS DEATHS, UNITED STATES AND
TERRITORIES. [Annual]

FS 2.42/3   • Item 500-D
REPORTED TUBERCULOSIS DATA. [Irregular]

Earlier FS 2.2:T 79/9
Later HE 20.2313

FS 2.43:nos.
NATIONAL INSTITUTE OF HEALTH, SPECIAL STUDY
SERIES.

FS 2.44
V.D. WAR LETTERS.

FS 2.45:vol.
INDUSTRIAL HYGIENE NEWS LETTER. [Monthly]

FS 2.45/2:nos.
OH-ACTIVITIES. (Division of Occupational Health)

FS 2.46:nos.
[NURSING EDUCATION] LEAFLETS.

FS 2.47
TRADE NAMES INDEX.

FS 2.48:vol.
CADET NURSE CORPS NEWS.

FS 2.49:nos.
EMPLOYEES' HEALTH SERVICE FOLDERS.

FS 2.50   • Item 486
HEALTH INFORMATION SERIES. 1–   1945–
[Irregular]
Later HE 20.10

FS 2.50/2   • Item 486
DON'T GAMBLE WITH YOUR HEALTH (series). 1968–
[Irregular]

FS 2.50/3   • Item 486
FEDERAL EMPLOYEE HEALTH SERIES. 1–   1968–
[Irregular]

FS 2.51:CT
RECRUITMENT IDEAS.

FS 2.52:date
COMPILATION OF PUBLIC HEALTH SERVICE REGU-
LATIONS.

FS 2.53:nos.
MENTAL HEALTH SERIES.

FS 2.53/2　　　　　　　　　　• Item 491-A
MENTAL HEALTH STATISTICS, CURRENT REPORT
SERIES, MHB. [Irregular]
　　Changed from FS 2.11:5
　　Later HE 20.2415/2, HE 17.117

FS 2.53/2-2:letters-nos.
MENTAL HEALTH STATISTICS.
　　Later HE 20.2415

FS 2.53/3　　　　　　　　　　• Item 491-A
MENTAL HEALTH MANPOWER, CURRENT STATISTI-
CAL AND ACTIVITIES REPORTS. 1–　　[Irregular]

FS 2.54:date
FREEDMEN'S HOSPITAL, ANNUAL REPORTS.
　　Earlier I 1.12/1

FS 2.54/2:CT
– GENERAL PUBLICATIONS.
　　Earlier I 1.12/2
FS 2.54/3:date
–BULLETINS, SCHOOL OF NURSING, AN-
NOUNCEMENTS.
　　Earlier FS 2.54/2:N 93/2

FS 2.55:v.nos.
FOR A HEALTHIER WORLD. [Monthly]

FS 2.56:nos.
STUDIES ON HOUSEHOLD SEWAGE DISPOSAL
SYSTEM.

FS 2.56/2:date
PUBLIC SEWAGE TREATMENT PLANT CONSTRUC-
TION.
　　Earlier FS 2.2:Se 8
　　Later I 67.11

FS 2.56/3:date
SEWAGE TREATMENT WORKS CONTRACT
AWARDS.

FS 2.56/4:date
WATER AND SEWER BOND SALES IN UNITED
STATES.
　　Later I 67.10

FS 2.57:nos.
CANCER SERIES.

FS 2.58:v.nos.&nos.
CDC BULLETINS. [Monthly]

FS 2.59　　　　　　　　　　• Item 494
PATIENTS IN MENTAL INSTITUTIONS. 1938–
[Annual]
　　Earlier C 3.59/2

FS 2.60:date
COMMUNICABLE DISEASE CENTER, ACTIVITIES.

FS 2.60/2:CT
COMMUNICABLE DISEASE CENTER PUBLICATIONS.
　　Later HE 20.2302

FS 2.60/3
COMMUNICABLE DISEASE CENTER, TECHNICAL
DEVELOPMENT SERVICES, SUMMARY OF
ACTIVITIES. [Quarterly]

FS 2.60/4:date
QUARTERLY REPORT, TRAINING BRANCH.

FS 2.60/5:nos.
CDC TECHNOLOGY BRANCH, SUMMARY OF INVES-
TIGATIONS. [Semiannual]

FS 2.60/6:date
COMMUNICABLE DISEASE CENTER RELEASES.

FS 2.60/7　　　　　　　　　　• Item 505-A
TRAINING GUIDE, INSECT CONTROL SERIES. Pt.
1–　[Irregular]
　　Later HE 20.2308

FS 2.60/7:CT
COMMUNICABLE DISEASE CENTER: HANDBOOKS,
MANUALS, GUIDES.
　　Earlier FS 2.60/2
　　TRAINING GUIDE, INSECT CONTROL SERIES.
　　[Irregular]
　　Later HE 20.2308
　　FS 2.60/7:Sy 7/2　　　　　• Item 505-A
　　SEROLOGIC TESTS FOR SYPHILIS. [Irregular]
　　Later HE 20.2308:Sy 7/2

FS 2.60/8:date
CDC TRAINING PROGRAM BULLETIN. [Annual]

FS 2.60/9　　　　　　　　　　• Item 508-A
MORBIDITY AND MORTALITY WEEKLY REPORT. v.
1–　1952–　[Weekly]
　　Earlier FS 2.107/2
　　Later HE 20.2310

FS 2.60/10　　　　　　　　　　• Item 508-H
FILM REFERENCE GUIDE FOR MEDICINE AND ALLIED
SCIENCES. 1956–　[Annual]
　　Earlier FS 2.21

FS 2.60/11:nos.
LIBRARY HORIZONS.

FS 2.60/12
NATIONAL COMMUNICABLE DISEASE CENTER SAL-
MONELLA SURVEILLANCE, REPORTS. 1–
　　Earlier FS 2.60/2:Sa 3/3
　　Later HE 20.2309

FS 2.60/12-2
NATIONAL COMMUNICABLE DISEASE CENTER SAL-
MONELLA SURVEILLANCE, ANNUAL SUMMARY.
[Annual]
　　Later HE 20.2309/2

FS 2.60/13
NATIONAL COMMUNICABLE DISEASE CENTER
HEPATITIS SURVEILLANCE, REPORTS. 1–
[Irregular]
　　Later HE 20.2309/5

FS 2.60/14:CT
NATIONAL COMMUNICABLE DISEASE CENTER NEU-
ROTROPIC VIRAL DISEASES SURVEILLANCE
[Reports].
　　Later HE 20.2309/8

FS 2.60/14:En 1
NATIONAL COMMUNICABLE DISEASE CENTER,
NEUROTROPIC VIRAL DISEASES
SURVIELLANCE: ANNUAL ENCEPHALITIS
SUMMARY. [Annual]
　　Later HE 20.2309/8:En 1

FS 2.60/14:P 75
NATIONAL COMMUNICABLE DISEASE CENTER
NEUROTROPIC VIRAL DISEASES SURVEIL-
LANCE, ANNUAL POLIOMYELITIS
SUMMARY. [Annual]

FS 2.60/15:CT
NATIONAL COMMUNICABLE DISEASE CENTER
ZOONOSES SURVEILLANCE [Reports].

FS 2.60/15:P 95
NATIONAL COMMUNICABLE DISEASE CENTER
ZOONOSES SURVEILLANCE, ANNUAL SUM-
MARY PSITTACOSIS. [Annual]

FS 2.60/16:nos.
NATIONAL COMMUNICABLE DISEASE CENTER SHI-
GELLA SURVEILLANCE REPORTS, ATLANTA,
GEORGIA. 1–　[Quarterly]
　　Later HE 20.2309/3

FS 2.60/17
NATIONAL COMMUNICABLE DISEASE CENTER RU-
BELLA SURVEILLANCE [Reports]. 1–
　　Later HE 20.2309/7

FS 2.60/18
NATIONAL COMMUNICABLE DISEASE CENTER
FOODBORNE OUTBREAKS, ANNUAL SUMMARY.
[Annual]
　　Later HE 20.2309/6

FS 2.60/19:date
CDC VETERINARY PUBLIC HEALTH NOTES.
　　Later HE 20.2312

FS 2.61:nos.
CANCER MORBIDITY SERIES.

FS 2.62　　　　　　　　　　• Item 500-A
PUBLIC HEALTH TECHNICAL MONOGRAPHS. 1–
1950–　[Irregular]

FS 2.63:date
UNITED STATES NATIONAL COMMITTEE ON VITAL
AND HEALTH STATISTICS, ANNUAL REPORTS.
　　Later FS 2.120

FS 2.63/2:CT
UNITED STATES NATIONAL COMMITTEE ON VITAL
AND HEALTH STATISTICS, GENERAL PUBLICA-
TIONS.

FS 2.64:nos.
WATER POLLUTION PUBLICATIONS.

FS 2.64/2　　　　　　　　　　• Item 502-A
WATER SUPPLY AND POLLUTION CONTROL. 1958–

FS 2.64/3:CT
NATIONAL CONFERENCE ON WATER POLLUTION,
PUBLICATIONS.

FS 2.64/4:CT
NATIONAL CONFERENCE ON WATER POLLUTION,
ADDRESSES, PAPERS, ETC.

FS 2.64/5:nos.
CLEAN WATER, ANNOUNCEMENTS [for radio and
television].

FS 2.64/6:date
BUILDING FOR CLEAN WATER, PROGRESS REPORT
ON FEDERAL INCENTIVE GRANTS FOR
MUNICIPAL WASTE TREATMENT, FISCAL YEAR.
　　Earlier FS 2.2:W 29/29
　　Later FS 16.9

FS 2.64/7:date
WATER POLLUTION CONTROL RESEARCH AND
TRAINING GRANTS, LIST OF AWARDS, RE-
SEARCH GRANTS, RESEARCH FELLOWSHIPS,
TRAINING GRANTS, DEMONSTRATION GRANTS.
　　Earlier FS 2.2:W 29/49

FS 2.64/8:date
SELECTED SUMMARIES OF WATER RESEARCH.
　　Later I 67.12

FS 2.65:date
NATIONAL MENTAL HEALTH PROGRAM PROGRESS
REPORTS. [Irregular]

FS 2.66
COMMISSIONED OFFICERS TRAVEL COMMITTEE,
MEMORANDA.

FS 2.66/2:nos.
DCO CIRCULARS.

FS 2.67
ADMINISTRATIVE BULLETINS.

FS 2.68:nos.
NATIONAL HEART INSTITUTE CIRCULARS.

FS 2.69 • **Item 468-A**
TUBERCULOSIS BEDS IN HOSPITALS AND SANA-
TORIA, INDEX OF BEDS AVAILABLE. 1946–
[Annual]

FS 2.70
FIELD MEMORANDUM, DIVISION OF FOREIGN QUAR-
ANTINE.

FS 2.71:nos.
INDUSTRIAL WASTE GUIDE SERIES.

FS 2.71/2 • **Item 487-B**
INVENTORY, MUNICIPAL AND INDUSTRIAL WASTE
FACILITIES. 1962– [Annual]

FS 2.72:dt.&nos.
MAP AND CHART SERIES.

FS 2.72/2 • **Item 500-C**
TUBERCULOSIS CHART SERIES. 1955– [Irregu-
lar]

FS 2.73:nos.
SPECIAL INFORMATION BULLETINS.

FS 2.73/2:date
NEW HEALTH AND HOSPITAL PROJECTS AUTHO-
RIZED FOR CONSTRUCTION UNDER CON-
TROLLED MATERIALS PLAN. [Monthly]

FS 2.74
HILL-BURTON PROJECT REGISTER. [Monthly]

> Earlier title: Hospital Facilities Division.
> Later HE 20.2509

FS 2.74/2:date
HOSPITAL AND MENTAL FACILITIES CONSTRUCTION
PROGRAM UNDER TITLE 6 OF PUBLIC HEALTH
SERVICE ACT, SEMIANNUAL ANALYSIS OF
PROJECTS APPROVED FOR FEDERAL AID.

> Earlier FS 2.2:H 79/19

FS 2.74/3 • **Item 486-D**
HOSPITAL AND MEDICAL FACILITIES SERIES UNDER
HILL-BURTON PROGRAM. [Irregular]

> Desig. PHS Publ 930-letter-nos.
> Later HE 20.2511
> Later title: Health Facilities Series.

FS 2.74/3:G-3
G-3. HILL-BURTON PUBLICATIONS. 1963–
[Irregular]

FS 2.74/4:nos.
HOSPITAL AND MEDICAL FACILITIES SERIES,
HEALTH PROFESSIONS EDUCATION.

FS 2.74/5 • **Item 486-D**
HOSPITAL AND MEDICAL FACILITIES SERIES,
FACILITIES FOR THE MENTALLY RETARDED.
1965– [Irregular]

FS 2.74/6:date
REPRESENTATIVE CONSTRUCTION COST OF HILL-
BURTON HOSPITALS AND RELATED HEALTH
FACILITIES. [Biannual]

> Later HE 20.2510, HE 1.109

FS 2.75
OFFICIAL CLASSIFICATION OF . . . WATERING
POINTS.

FS 2.76:nos.
SOURCES OF MORBIDITY DATA.

FS 2.76/2 • **Item 499-D**
HEALTH ECONOMIC STUDIES INFORMATION EX-
CHANGE. 1st– 1967– [Irregular]

FS 2.77 • **Item 483-C**
DIRECTORY OF LOCAL HEALTH UNITS. 1942–
[Irregular]

> Earlier FS 2.2:L 78
> Later HE 20.2015

FS 2.77/2 • **Item 483-B**
DIRECTORY OF STATE AND TERRITORIAL HEALTH
AUTHORITIES. [Irregular]

> Earlier FS 2.2:H 34/5
> Later HE 20.2015/2

FS 2.78:date
LIST OF ACCEPTABLE INTERSTATE CARRIER EQUIP-
MENT HAVING SANITATION SIGNIFICANCES.
[Semiannual]

FS 2.79
MEDICAL SUPPLY CATALOG. [Irregular]

FS 2.80 • **Item 493-A**
PUBLIC HEALTH PERSONNEL IN LOCAL HEALTH
UNITS. 1946– [Biennial]

> Earlier title: Organization and Staffing for Full
> Time Local Health Services.

FS 2.81:date
CENSUS OF NURSES EMPLOYED FOR PUBLIC
HEALTH WORK IN UNITED STATES, IN TERRI-
TORIES OF ALASKA AND HAWAII, AND IN
PUERTO RICO AND VIRGIN ISLANDS. [Biennial]

> Later HE 20.3110

FS 2.82:date
SALARIES OF STATE PUBLIC HEALTH WORKERS.

> Earlier FS 2.2:Sa 3/2

FS 2.83 • **Item 494-A**
PROCEEDINGS, ANNUAL CONFERENCE OF THE
SURGEON GENERAL, PUBLIC HEALTH SER-
VICE, AND CHIEF, CHILDREN'S BUREAU, WITH
STATE AND TERRITORIAL HEALTH OFFICERS.
1903– [Annual]

FS 2.83/2 • **Item 494-4**
PROCEEDINGS, BIENNIAL CONFERENCE OF STATE
AND TERRITORIAL DENTAL DIRECTORS WITH
PUBLIC HEALTH SERVICE AND CHILDREN'S
BUREAU. [Biennial]

FS 2.83/3 • **Item 494-A**
PROCEEDINGS, ANNUAL CONFERENCE, SURGEON
GENERAL, PUBLIC HEALTH SERVICE, WITH
STATE AND TERRITORIAL MENTAL HEALTH AU-
THORITIES. 1959– [Annual]

FS 2.83/4 • **Item 494-A**
PROCEEDINGS, CONFERENCE OF STATE SANITARY
ENGINEERS. 1st– 1920–

> Later HE 20.1010

FS 2.84
STATISTICAL SUMMARY OF MUNICIPAL WATER FA-
CILITIES. 1954– [Annual]

FS 2.84/2 • **Item 493-B**
PUBLIC HEALTH SERVICE WATER POLLUTION SUR-
VEILLANCE SYSTEM. 1957/58– [Annual]

> Earlier title: National Water Quality Network.

FS 2.84/3 • **Item 492-C**
MUNICIPAL WATER FACILITIES. INVENTORY. 1939–
[Quinquennial]

FS 2.84/4:CT
DIGEST OF WATER POLLUTION CONTROL LEGIS-
LATION (by States).

FS 2.84/5:nos.
PHS WATER POLLUTION SURVEILLANCE SYSTEM
APPLICATIONS AND DEVELOPMENT REPORTS.

> Formerly titled: National Water Quality Net-
> work Applications and Development Reports.

FS 2.85 • **Item 500-E**
HEALTH STATISTICS FROM THE U.S. NATIONAL
HEALTH SURVEY. 1958– [Irregular]

FS 2.85/2 • **Item 500-E**
VITAL AND HEALTH STATISTICS. 1963– [Irregular]

FS 2.85/3 • **Item 500-E**
LIFE TABLES. [Decennial]

FS 2.85/4:v.nos.&nos.
LIFE TABLES (bound volumes).

FS 2.86:CT
INDIANS ON FEDERAL RESERVATIONS IN UNITED
STATES [by area].

FS 2.86/2:date
REPORT ON INDIAN HEALTH. [Quarterly]

FS 2.86/3:date
DENTAL SERVICES FOR INDIANS, ANNUAL REPORT,
FISCAL YEAR.

> Later HE 20.2659

FS 2.86/4 • **Item 486**
TO THE 1ST AMERICANS, ANNUAL REPORT ON
THE INDIAN HEALTH PROGRAM. 1st– 1967–
[Annual]

> Earlier FS 2.2:Am 3
> Later HE 20.2014/2

FS 2.86/5:CT/date
INDIAN VITAL STATISTICS.

> Later HE 20.2660

FS 2.86/6
ANNUAL STATISTICAL REVIEW, HOSPITAL AND
MEDICAL SERVICES. [Annual]

FS 2.86/7:date
DIVISION OF INDIAN HEALTH, ANNUAL DISCHARGE
SUMMARY.

FS 2.87:nos.
DP PAMPHLETS.

FS 2.88:CT
DICTIONARIES, GLOSSARIES, ETC.

FS 2.89 • **Item 496-B**
MEDICAL INTERNSHIP IN U.S. PUBLIC HEALTH SER-
VICE HOSPITALS. [Annual]

> Earlier FS 22:In 85/2

FS 2.89/2 • **Item 496-B**
DENTAL INTERNSHIP IN U.S. PUBLIC HEALTH SER-
VICE HOSPITAL. [Irregular]

> Earlier FS 22:D 43/4

FS 2.89/3 • **Item 496-B**
PHARMACY RESIDENCES IN PUBLIC HEALTH
SERVICE HOSPITALS. [Irregular]

FS 2.89/4:date
DIETETIC INTERNSHIP, PUBLIC HEALTH SERVICE
HOSPITAL, STATEN ISLAND, N.Y.

FS 2.90 • **Item 498-B**
RADIOLOGICAL HEALTH DATA, MONTHLY REPORT.
1– 1960– [Monthly]

> Later HE 20.1100, HE 20.1509

FS 2.91:CT
ANNOUNCEMENT [of Examinations for Appointment
of Officers in Public Health Service].

FS 2.92
ROBERT A. TAFT SANITARY ENGINEERING CEN-
TER: TECHNICAL REPORTS. [Irregular]

FS 2.92/2:date
ENVIRONMENTAL SCIENCES AND ENGINEERING
TRAINING PROGRAM BULLETIN.

FS 2.92/3
BULLETINS OF COURSES, TRAINING PROGRAM
[Annual]

FS 2.92/4
TRAINING INSTITUTE OF ENVIRONMENTAL CON-
TROL ADMINISTRATION, BULLETIN OF
COURSES. [Annual]

FS 2.93 • Item 483-E
DIGEST OF STATE AIR POLLUTION LAWS. [Annual]

Earlier FS 2.2:Ai 7/11

FS 2.93/2:nos.
AIR POLLUTION ANNOUNCEMENTS.

FS 2.93/3
NATIONAL AIR POLLUTION CONTROL ADMINISTRA-
TION PUBLICATION, AP (series).

Later HE 20.1309

FS 2.93/3-2:nos.
NATIONAL AIR POLLUTION CONTROL ADMINISTRA-
TION PUBLICATIONS APTD (series).

Later HE 20.1309/2

FS 2.93/4 • Item 483-K
AIR POLLUTION, SULFUR OXIDES POLLUTION CON-
TROL, FEDERAL RESEARCH AND DEVELOP-
MENT, PLANNING AND PROGRAMMING. [Annual]

FS 2.93/5:CT
REPORTS FOR CONSULTATION ON AIR QUALITY
CONTROL REGIONS.

Later HE 20.1310

FS 2.93/6:CT • Item 483-S
APTIC [Air Pollution Technical Information Center]
BULLETIN. v. 1– [Irregular]

Later HE 20.1303/2

FS 2.94:date
POLLUTION-CAUSED FISH KILLS. [Annual]

Later I 67.9

FS 2.95 • Item 486-D
F-3. HILL-BURTON PROGRAM, PROGRESS REPORT.
[Annual]

Later HE 20.2509/2

FS 2.96
NATIONAL CLEARINGHOUSE FOR POISON
CONTROL CENTERS, BULLETINS. 1957–
[Monthly]

Later HE.1203/2, HE 20.4003/2

FS 2.97 • Item 500-F
TODAY'S HEALTH PROBLEMS, SERIES FOR TEACH-
ERS. 1– 1962– [Irregular]

FS 2.98:CT
NATIONAL CONFERENCE ON AIR POLLUTION, PUB-
LICATIONS, ADDRESSES, ETC.

FS 2.98/2:nos.
NATIONAL CONFERENCE ON AIR POLLUTION,
PAPERS (numbered).

FS 2.98/3:date
NATIONAL CONFERENCE ON AIR POLLUTION: COM-
MUNICATOR. [Irregular]

FS 2.99 • Item 496-D
HEALTH ECONOMICS SERIES. 1– 1962–
[Irregular]

National Office of Vital Statistics
(1946– 1969)

Under Reorganization plan no. 2, effective
July 16, 1946, the functions of the Bureau of the
Census with respect to vital statistics were transferred to the Federal Security Agency for administration by the Public Health Service.

FS 2.101:date
ANNUAL REPORTS.
Later HE 20.2201

FS 2.102:CT
GENERAL PUBLICATIONS.
Later HE 20.2202

FS 2.102:B 53/3 • Item 508
WHERE TO WRITE FOR BIRTH AND DEATH
RECORDS. [Irregular]

FS 2.102:B 53/7 • Item 508
WHERE TO WRITE FOR BIRTH AND DEATH
RECORDS OF U.S. CITIZENS WHO WERE
BORN OR DIED OUTSIDE OF THE UNITED
STATES AND BIRTH CERTIFICATIONS FOR
ALIEN CHILDREN ADOPTED BY U.S. CITI-
ZENS. [Irregular]

FS 2.102:D 64 • Item 508
WHERE TO WRITE FOR DIVORCE RECORDS.
1958– [Irregular]

FS 2.102:H 34 • Item 508
FACTS OF LIFE AND DEATH, SELECTED STATIS-
TICS ON NATION'S HEALTH AND PEOPLE.
[Irregular]

FS 2.102:M 34 • Item 508
WHERE TO WRITE FOR MARRIAGE RECORDS.
[Irregular]

FS 2.106:CT
REGULATIONS, RULES, AND INSTRUCTIONS.

FS 2.106/2:CT
HANDBOOKS, MANUALS, GUIDES RELATING TO
VITAL STATISTICS.

FS 2.107:v.nos.
MORTALITY INDEX. [Weekly]

Earlier C 3.41

FS 2.107/2:v.nos.
MORBIDITY AND MORTALITY WEEKLY REPORTS.

Later FS 2.60/9

FS 2.108:v.nos.
CURRENT MORTALITY ANALYSIS. [Monthly]

Earlier C 3.152
Later FS 2.116

FS 2.109:v.nos.
VITAL STATISTICS, SPECIAL REPORTS.

Earlier C 3.67

FS 2.110:v.nos.
VITAL STATISTICS BULLETIN. [Monthly]
Earlier C 3.127
Later FS 2.116

FS 2.111:v.nos.
THE REGISTAR. [Monthly]

Earlier C 3.126

FS 2.112 • Item 510
VITAL STATISTICS OF THE UNITED STATES. 1937–
[Annual]

Earlier C 3.139
Later HE 20.2212

FS 2.113:v.nos.
MARRIAGE REPORT. [Quarterly]

FS 2.114:v.nos.
MARRIAGE REPORT. [Monthly]

Later FS 2.116

FS 2.115:le-nos.
MENTAL HEALTH STATISTICS: CURRENT REPORTS.
Later FS 2.53/2

FS 2.116 • Item 508-B
MONTHLY VITAL STATISTICS REPORT. [Monthly]

Replaces Current Mortality Analysis (FS
2.108); Monthly Marriage Report (FS 2.114); and
Monthly Vital Statistics Bulletin (FS 2.110).
Later HE 20.2209

FS 2.117:date
COMMUNICABLE DISEASE SUMMARY. [Weekly]

FS 2.118:CT
ADDRESSES.

FS 2.119:nos.
COMPARISON DECK NOS.

FS 2.120
NATIONAL COMMITTEE ON VITAL AND HEALTH STA-
TISTICS; ANNUAL REPORT. [Annual]
Earlier FS 2.63
Later HE 20.2211

FS 2.121:CT
BIBLIOGRAPHIES AND LISTS OF PUBLICATIONS.

FS 2.122 • Item 509-A
PUBLIC HEALTH CONFERENCE ON RECORDS AND
STATISTICS; PROCEEDINGS. [Biennial]

Later HE 20.2214

FS 2.123 • Item 509-B
HEALTH RESOURCES STATISTICS. 1965–

Later HE 20.2215

National Library of Medicine
(1956– 1969)

The National Library of Medicine was established in the Public Health Service by Public Law
941, 84th Congress, approved August 3, 1956
(70 Stat. 960).

FS 2.201 • Item 508-L
ANNUAL REPORT. 1– [Annual]

Later HE 20.3601

FS 2.202:CT
GENERAL PUBLICATIONS.

Later HE 20.3602

FS 2.208:v.nos.
CURRENT LIST OF MEDICAL LITERATURE. [Monthly]

Earlier D 8.8
Later FS 2.208/2

FS 2.208/2 • Item 508-E
INDEX MEDICUS. v. 1– 1960– [Monthly]

Earlier FS 2.208
Later HE 20.3612

FS 2.208/3:date
LIST OF JOURNALS INDEXED IN INDEX MEDICUS.

Later HE 20.3612/4

FS 2.208/4 • Item 508-E
CUMULATED INDEX MEDICUS. v. 1– 1960–
[Annual]

Later HE 20.3612/3

FS 2.209:CT
BIBLIOGRAPHIES.
Earlier D 8.10

FS 2.209/2:v.nos.
BIBLIOGRAPHY OF MEDICAL REVIEWS.

FS 2.209/2-2 • Item 508-F
MONTHLY BIBLIOGRAPHY OF MEDICAL REVIEW. v.
1– 1968– [Monthly]
Later HE 20.3610

FS 2.209/3:v.nos.&nos.
BIBLIOGRAPHY OF MEDICAL TRANSLATIONS. [Semi-
monthly]

Earlier FS 2.209:T 26, which is considered v.
1 of this series.

FS 2.209/4:nos.
BIBLIOGRAPHY OF THE HISTORY OF MEDICINE.
[Annual, cumulated every five years]
Later HE 20.3651

FS 2.210:v.nos.
INDEX-CATALOGUE OF LIBRARY OF SURGEON GENERAL'S OFFICE.

FS 2.211:date
FILM REFERENCE GUIDE FOR MEDICINE AND ALLIED SCIENCES. [Annual]

> Earlier FS 2.202:F 48
> Later FS 2.60/10

FS 2.211/2:CT
MOTION PICTURE GUIDES (miscellaneous).

> Later FS 2.6/3

FS 2.211/3:CT
SELECTED LIST OF AUDIOVISUALS.

FS 2.212:date
MEDICAL SUBJECT HEADINGS.

FS 2.213:v.nos.&nos.
NATIONAL LIBRARY OF MEDICINE NEWS. [Monthly]

FS 2.214:CT
SCIENTIFIC TRANSLATION PROGRAM PUBLICATIONS.

FS 2.215
NOTES FOR MEDICAL CATALOGERS. v. 1–   1965– [Irregular]

> Later HE 20.3611

FS 2.215
CHILD WELFARE REPORTS. 1–   1946–   [Irregular]

FS 2.216   • Item 508-J
NATIONAL LIBRARY OF MEDICINE CURRENT CATALOG. 1966–

> Supersedes LC 30.13
> Later HE 20.3609

FS 2.216/2   • Item 508-J
CUMULATIVE LISTING. [Quarterly & Annual]

> Prior to January-March 1967 issue classified and sold as part of the subscription to the bi-weekly cumulation (FS 2.216).
> Later HE 20.3609/2

FS 2.216/3:date
– ANNUAL CUMULATION.

> Later HE 20.3609/3

FS 2.217:CT
HANDBOOKS, MANUALS, GUIDES.

> Later HE 20.3608

FS 2.218   • Item 508-M
TOXICITY BIBLIOGRAPHY. v. 1–   1968– [Quarterly]

> Later HE 20.3613

Public Health Service (Continued)

FS 2.300:let-nos.
ENVIRONMENTAL HEALTH SERIES.

> Later HE 20.1011

FS 2.300:AH   • Item 483-F
AH. ARCTIC HEALTH. 1–   1965–   [Irregular]

> Later HE 20.1011:AH

FS 2.300:AP
AP. AIR POLLUTION. 1–   [Irregular]

> Later HE 20.1011:AP

FS 2.300:RH   • Item 483-F
RH. RADIOLOGICAL HEALTH. 1–   1962– [Irregular]

> Later HE 20.1011:RH

FS 2.300/2:v.nos.
ENVIRONMENTAL HEALTH FACTORS, NURSING HOMES.

FS 2.300/3   • Item 486-G
RESEARCH GRANTS, ENVIRONMENTAL ENGINEERING AND FOOD PROTECTION, FISCAL YEAR (date). [Annual]

FS 2.300/4:nos.
URBAN ENVIRONMENTAL HEALTH PLANNING ADVISORY (series).

FS 2.300/5   • Item 483-F
ANALYTICAL REFERENCE SERVICE STUDIES. 1– [Irregular]

> Earlier FS 2.300:UIH-8, UIH-10, UIH-11, and WP-26
> Later HE 20.1113

FS 2.301:CT
TECHNICAL MEMORANDA FOR MUNICIPAL, INDUSTRIAL AND DOMESTIC WATER SUPPLIES, POLLUTION ABATEMENT, PUBLIC HEALTH [Southeast River Basins].

FS 2.302   • Item 486-E
HEALTH MOBILIZATION SERIES. 1963–   [Irregular]

> Later HE 20.2013
> Later title: Emergency Health Series.

FS 2.303   • Item 481-C
ACTIVITIES REPORT. 1964–   [Annual]

FS 2.304   • Item 483-G
FLUORIDATION CENSUS. [Annual]

> Earlier FS 2.2:D 67/9
> Later HE 20.3112

FS 2.305
OFFICE OF SOLID WASTES INFORMATION SERIES, SW- (series). 1–   1966–   [Irregular]

FS 2.306:yr.nos.
FOREIGN EPIDEMIOLOGICAL SUMMARY.

FS 2.307
AIR QUALITY DATA FROM NATIONAL AIR SAMPLING NETWORKS AND CONTRIBUTING STATE AND LOCAL NETWORKS. [Annual]

FS 2.307   • Item 483-N
AIR QUALITY DATA FROM NATIONAL AIR SURVEILLANCE NETWORKS AND CONTRIBUTING STATE AND LOCAL NETWORKS. 1966–

FS 2.308   • Item 485
CCPM [Commissioned Corps Personnel Manual] PAMPHLETS. 1–   [Irregular]

FS 2.309   • Item 485-A
HEALTH CONSEQUENCES OF SMOKING, A PUBLIC HEALTH SERVICE REVIEW: (year). 1967– [Annual]

FS 2.310   • Item 507
WORKSHOP SERIES OF PHARMACOLOGY SECTION, N.I.M.H. 1–   [Irregular]

FS 2.311   • Item 499-C
STUDIES IN MEDICAL CARE ADMINISTRATION. 1– 1967–   [Irregular]

FS 2.312   • Item 483-H
RHEUMATIC FEVER MEMO. 1–   1967–   [Irregular]

FS 2.313   • Item 483-L
PROGRESS REPORT, REGIONAL MEDICAL PROGRAMS FOR HEART DISEASE, CANCER, STROKE, AND RELATED DISEASES. [Annual]

> Earlier FS 2.22:H/35/13

FS 2.314
MORP [Medical and Occupational Radiation Program] (series). 1967–   [Irregular]

> Later HE 20.1516

FS 2.314/2
DMRE [Division of Medical Radiation Exposure] (series). [Irregular]

FS 2.314/3   • Item 483-M
DER [Division of Environmental Radiation] (series). [Irregular]

FS 2.315:date
CALENDAR OF NATIONAL MEETINGS. [Quarterly]

> Later HE 20.2009

FS 2.316   • Item 483-O
INJURY CONTROL RESEARCH LABORATORY: RESEARCH REPORTS, ICRL-RR- (series).

> Later HE 20.1116, HE 20.1809

FS 2.317
GRANTS-IN-AID AND OTHER FINANCIAL ASSISTANCE PROGRAMS, HEALTH SERVICES AND MENTAL HEALTH ADMINISTRATION. [Annual]

> Later HE 20.2016

FS 2.318:nos.
NATIONAL CENTER FOR HEALTH SERVICES RESEARCH AND DEVELOPMENT DIGEST.

> Later Focus, HE 20.2109

FS 2.319:date
PARTNERSHIP FOR HEALTH NEWS. [Irregular]

> Health Services and Mental Health Administration, Community Health Service, Arlington, Virginia.
> Later HE 20.2559

FS 2.320   • Item 483-R
EMERGENCY HEALTH SERVICES DIGEST. 1– 1969–   [Irregular]

> Later HE 20.13/2

FS 2.321:date
HEALTH SERVICES AND MENTAL HEALTH ADMINISTRATION PUBLIC ADVISORY COMMITTEES: AUTHORITY, STRUCTURE, FUNCTIONS.

> Later HE 20.2011

FS 2.321/2:v.nos.
HEALTH SERVICES AND MENTAL HEALTH ADMINISTRATION PUBLIC ADVISORY COMMITTEE: ROSTER OF MEMBERS.

> Later HE 20.2011/2

SOCIAL SECURITY ADMINISTRATION
(1946– 1969)

CREATION AND AUTHORITY

The Social Security Board (SS 1) was established as an independent agency by the Social Security Act, approved August 14, 1935 (49 Stat. 620). By Reorganization Plan No. 1 of 1939, effective July, 1939, the Board became a part of the Federal Security Agency. Reorganization Plan No. 2 of 1946, effective July 16, 1946, abolished the Board and transferred its functions to the newly created Social Security Administration. On April 11, 1953, the Social Security Administration became a part of the newly created Department of Health, Education, and Welfare (HE 3)

FS 3.1:date
ANNUAL REPORTS.
> Earlier SS 1.1
> Later HE 3.1

FS 3.2:CT
GENERAL PUBLICATIONS.

Earlier SS 1.2
Later HE 3.2

FS 3.3:vol. • Item 523
SOCIAL SECURITY BULLETIN. v. 1–   1938–
[Monthly]

Earlier SS 1.25
Later HE 3.3

FS 3.3/a2:date
PUBLIC ASSISTANCE. [Monthly]

Reprinted from Social Security Bulletin.
Earlier SS 1.25/a 1

FS 3.3/a3:date
OPERATIONS OF EMPLOYMENT SECURITY PRO-
    GRAM. [Monthly]

FS 3.3/2:date
SOCIAL SECURITY YEARBOOK.

FS 3.3/2a:nos.
PUBLIC ASSISTANCE REPORT.

Reprints from Social Security Yearbook.

FS 3.3/3:date • Item 523
SOCIAL SECURITY BULLETIN, ANNUAL STATISTI-
    CAL SUPPLEMENT. [Annual]

Issued as part of Bulletin for September from
1950 to 1955.
Later HE 3.3/3

FS 3.4 • Item 517
INFORMATION SERVICE CIRCULARS. ISC 1–   1957–
    [Irregular]

Earlier SS 1.4
Later HE 3.4

FS 3.5:CT
LAWS.

Earlier SS 1.5
Later HE 3.5

FS 3.6:CT
REGULATIONS, RULES, AND INSTRUCTIONS (mis-
    cellaneous).

Earlier SS 1.6
Later HE 3.6

FS 3.6/2:issue nos.
REGULATIONS NO. 4, OLD-AGE AND SURVIVORS
    INSURANCE (loose-leaf edition).

FS 3.6/3:CT
HANDBOOKS, MANUALS, GUIDES.
    Later HE 3.6/3

FS 3.6/4:nos. • Item 516-C
HEALTH INSURANCE FOR THE AGED, HIM- (series).
    1–   1966–   [Irregular]
    Later HE 3.6/4

FS 3.7:vol.
LAW ACCESSION LIST (of) LIBRARY.
    Earlier SS 1.22

FS 3.8:vol.
WEEKLY ACCESSION LIST (of) LIBRARY.
    Earlier SS 1.17

FS 3.9:nos.
BUREAU REPORTS. (Research and Statistics Bu-
    reau)
    Earlier SS 1.30

FS 3.10
ADDRESSES. [Irregular]
    Earlier SS 1.8

FS 3.11:nos.
BUREAU MEMORANDUM.
    Earlier SS 1.27

FS 3.12:nos.
RESEARCH MEMORANDUM.

FS 3.13:nos.
PUBLIC ASSISTANCE REPORTS.

NOTE:– Sent through as FS 3.2a:9 in D.I. no.
1705, December 1941.
    Later FS 14.213

FS 3.13/2:nos.
[PUBLIC ASSISTANCE INFORMATION] PAI- (series).

Later FS 14.213/2

FS 3.13/3:date
PUBLIC ASSISTANCE. [Annual]

FS 3.14:nos.
BUREAU OF CIRCULARS. (Public Assistance Bureau)

FS 3.14/2:date
ADVANCE RELEASE OF STATISTICS ON PUBLIC
    ASSISTANCE.

Later FS 14.209

FS 3.14/3:date
FINANCIAL STATISTICS FOR PUBLIC ASSISTANCE,
    CALENDAR YEAR.

FS 3.14/4:date
MONEY PAYMENTS TO RECIPIENTS UNDER STATE-
    FEDERAL ASSISTANCE PROGRAM, ANNUAL
    RELEASE.

FS 3.15:vol.
REVIEW OF OPERATIONS. [Monthly]

Earlier SS 1.33

FS 3.16:date
COMPARATIVE STATISTICS OF GENERAL ASSIS-
    TANCE OPERATIONS OF PUBLIC AGENCIES IN
    SELECTED LARGE CITIES. [Monthly]

FS 3.17:date
PUBLIC ASSISTANCE BUREAU APPLICATIONS: OLD-
    AGE ASSISTANCE, AID TO DEPENDENT CHIL-
    DREN, AID TO THE BLIND [and] GENERAL AS-
    SISTANCE.

FS 3.18:nos.
PLEASANTDALE FOLKS, 2d SERIES.

FS 3.19
ACTUARIAL STUDIES. 1–   [Irregular]

Earlier SS 1.34

FS 3.19/2
ACTUARIAL NOTES. 1–   1962–   [Irregular]

FS 3.20:nos.
ILLUSTRATIONS FROM STATE PUBLIC ASSISTANCE
    AGENCIES, CURRENT PRACTICES IN STAFF
    TRAINING.

FS 3.21:nos.
FACT SHEETS.

FS 3.22:CT
POSTERS.

FS 3.23:v.nos.
CASE RECORDS IN PUBLIC ASSISTANCE.

FS 3.24:date
DIGEST OF RULINGS (Old-age and Survivors Insur-
    ance).

FS 3.24/2:nos.
DIGEST OF RULINGS (OASI) TRANSMITTAL SHEETS.

FS 3.25:nos.
YOUR NEW SOCIAL SECURITY, FACT SHEETS.

FS 3.25/2:dt.&nos.
AMENDMENTS TO SOCIAL SECURITY LAW [fact
    sheets].

Designated OASI
Later HE 3.25/2

FS 3.26
DAILY PRESS DIGEST.

FS 3.27
FISCAL LETTERS.

FS 3.28
RESEARCH AND STATISTICS LETTERS.

FS 3.28/2
RESEARCH AND STATISTICS NOTES. [Irregular]

FS 3.28/3
RESEARCH AND STATISTICS LEGISLATIVE NOTES.
    1–   [Irregular]

FS 3.28/4:nos.
HEALTH INSURANCE STATISTICS, CMS (series).

FS 3.28/5
HEALTH INSURANCE STATISTICS, HI-(series). 1–
    1967–   [Irregular]

FS 3.28/6:date&nos.
MONTHLY BENEFIT STATISTICS: OLD-AGE
    SURVIVORS, DISABILITY, AND HEALTH INSUR-
    ANCE, SUMMARY BENEFIT DATA. [Monthly]

Later HE 3.28/6

FS 3.28/6-2:date
MONTHLY BENEFIT STATISTICS: CALENDAR YEAR
    BENEFIT DATA.

FS 3.28/6-3:date
MONTHLY BENEFIT STATISTICS: FISCAL YEAR BEN-
    EFIT DATA.

FS 3.29
UNEMPLOYMENT COMPENSATION PROGRAM LET-
    TERS.

FS 3.30
ADMINISTRATIVE ORDERS.

FS 3.31
STATE LETTERS.

FS 3.32
ADJUDICATION INSTRUCTIONS.

FS 3.33:nos.
INTERNATIONAL TECHNICAL COOPERATION
    SERIES.

Later HE 3.33

FS 3.34
INFORMATIONAL LETTERS.

FS 3.35 • Item 518-A
OASI- (series). 1–   1953–   [Irregular]

FS 3.36
OASIS. [Monthly]

FS 3.37:CT
HOW THEY DO IT, ILLUSTRATIONS OF PRACTICE
    IN ADMINISTRATION OF PUBLIC ASSISTANCE
    PROGRAMS.

FS 3.38:CT
BIBLIOGRAPHIES AND LISTS OF PUBLICATIONS.

Later HE 3.38

FS 3.39
CHARACTERISTICS OF FAMILIES RECEIVING AID
    TO DEPENDENT CHILDREN. [Biennial]

FS 3.39/2:date
AID TO DEPENDENT CHILDREN OF UNEMPLOYED
    PARENTS. [Monthly]

Earlier FS 3.2:C 43/4
Later FS 14.209

FS 3.39/3:date
STATISTICAL SUMMARY OF AID TO DEPENDENT
    CHILDREN OF UNEMPLOYED PARENTS.

FS 3.40:date • Item 516-A
HANDBOOK OF OLD-AGE AND SURVIVORS INSUR-
ANCE STATISTICS. 1937– [Annual]

Earlier FS 3.2:Ol 1/3
Later HE 3.40

FS 3.41:date • Item 520
ADVISORY COUNCIL ON SOCIAL SECURITY, RE-
PORT. [Quinquennial]

Later HE 3.41

FS 3.42:nos.
EMPLOYEE PUBLICATIONS.

Official use.

FS 3.43:date
CURRENT SOCIAL SECURITY PROGRAM OPERA-
TIONS. [Monthly]

Administrative.

FS 3.44:date/nos.
SOCIAL SECURITY RULINGS ON FEDERAL OLD-
AGE, SURVIVORS, AND DISABILITY INSURANCE.
[Monthly]

Later HE 3.44

FS 3.44/2:date • Item 523-A
SOCIAL SECURITY RULINGS, CUMULATIVE BULLE-
TINS. [Annual]

Later HE 3.44/2

FS 3.45:date
REASONS FOR OPENING AND CLOSING PUBLIC
ASSISTANCE CASES.

Later FS 14.214

FS 3.46:nos.
BENEFICIARY STUDIES NOTES.

FS 3.47:nos.
ANALYTICAL NOTES.

FS 3.48:nos.
NATIONAL SURVEY OF OLD-AGE AND SURVIVORS
INSURANCE BENEFICIARIES: HIGHLIGHT RE-
PORTS.

FS 3.49:nos. • Item 522-A
RESEARCH REPORTS. [Irregular]

Later HE 3.49

FS 3.49/2:date
INDEX TO RESEARCH REPORTS AND RESEARCH
AND STATISTICS NOTES.

FS 3.50:nos.
PUBLIC INFORMATION NOTES FIS (series).

FS 3.51:date • Item 515-A
HOME HEALTH AGENCIES. 1966– [Irregular]

Later HE 3.51

FS 3.51/2:date • Item 515-A
HOSPITALS. 1966– [Irregular]

Later HE 3.51/2

FS 3.51/3:date • Item 515-A
EXTENDED CARE FACILITIES. 1967– [Irregular]

Later HE 3.51/3

FS 3.51/4:date
DIRECTORY OF SUPPLIERS OF SERVICES: INDE-
PENDENT LABORATORIES.

Later HE 3.51/4

FS 3.51/5:date
DIRECTORY [of] MEDICARE PROVIDERS AND SUP-
PLIERS OF SERVICES.

FS 3.52 • Item 523-B
SOCIAL SECURITY INFORMATION, SSI-(series). 1–
1967– [Irregular]

Later HE 3.52

FS 3.52/2:nos. • Item 523-C
TECHNICAL INFORMATION BULLETINS, TIB- (series).
1– 1965– [Irregular]

Later HE 3.52/2

FS 3.53:
MEDICARE NEWSLETTER. [Irregular]

FS 3.54:series/nos.
DISABILITY STUDIES NOTES.

FS 3.54/2
FROM THE SOCIAL SECURITY SURVEY OF THE
DISABLED, REPORTS. [Irregular]

FS 3.55
HIR [Health Insurance Rulings] (series).

BUREAU OF EMPLOYMENT SECURITY (1939–1949)

CREATION AND AUTHORITY

The Bureau of Employment Security was established August 19, 1939, within the Social Security Board by the consolidation of the functions
of the Employment Service (L 7) of the Department of Labor and the Bureau of Unemployment
Compensation of the Social Security Board. Reorganization Plan No. 2 of 1946, effective July
16, 1946, made the Bureau a part of the Social
Security Administration. The Bureau, including the
United States Employment Service and the Unemployment Insurance Service, was transferred
to the Department of Labor (L 7) by Reorganization Plan No. 2 of 1949, effective August 20,
1949.

FS 3.101:date
ANNUAL REPORTS.

FS 3.102:CT
GENERAL PUBLICATIONS.

FS 3.105:CT
LAWS.

FS 3.106:CT
REGULATIONS, RULES, AND INSTRUCTIONS.

FS 3.107:vol.
EMPLOYMENT SERVICE NEWS. [Monthly]

Earlier L 7.14
Later Pr 32.5209

FS 3.108:vol.
UNEMPLOYMENT COMPENSATION INTERPRETA-
TION SERVICE, BENEFIT SERIES. [Monthly]

Later L 7.37

FS 3.109:vol.
UNEMPLOYMENT COMPENSATION INTERPRETA-
TION SERVICE, STATE SERIES. [Quarterly]

FS 3.110:nos.
EMPLOYMENT SECURITY MEMORANDUM.

FS 3.111:nos.
ADMINISTRATIVE STANDARDS BULLETINS.

FS 3.112:nos., vol. nos.&pt. nos.
INDUSTRIAL CLASSIFICATION CODE, STATE
OPERATIONS BULLETINS.

FS 3.112/2:vol.
INDUSTRIAL CLASSIFICATION CODE. 3d ed.

FS 3.113:date
LABOR MARKET DEVELOPMENTS. [Monthly]

FS 3.113/2:date
LABOR MARKET. [Monthly]

Later Pr 32.5211

FS 3.114:date
SUMMARY OF EMPLOYMENT SECURITY ACTIVITIES.
[Monthly]

Later L 7.40

FS 3.115:date
PRELIMINARY REPORTS OF EMPLOYMENT SECU-
RITY OPERATIONS. [Monthly]

FS 3.116:date
LABOR SUPPLY AND DEMAND IN SELECTED DE-
FENSE OCCUPATIONS, AS REPORTED BY
PUBLIC EMPLOYMENT OFFICES. [Bimonthly]

FS 3.117:date
LABOR SUPPLY AVAILABLE AT PUBLIC EMPLOY-
MENT OFFICES IN SELECTED DEFENSE
OCCUPATIONS. [Monthly]

FS 3.118:date&nos.
DURATION OF BENEFIT PAYMENTS.

FS 3.119:date&nos.
VOCATIONAL TRAINING ACTIVITIES OF PUBLIC
EMPLOYMENT OFFICES. [Monthly]

FS 3.120:date
FARM LABOR MARKET CONDITIONS.

FS 3.121:date
EMPLOYERS' ESTIMATES OF LABOR NEEDS IN
SELECTED DEFENSE INDUSTRIES. [Bimonthly]

FS 3.122:date
EMPLOYMENT AND WAGES OF WORKERS
COVERED BY STATE UNEMPLOYMENT COMPEN-
SATION LAWS: ESTIMATED. [Quarterly]

FS 3.123:date
NATIONAL CONFERENCE VETERANS' EMPLOYMENT
REPRESENTATIVES.

Earlier L 7.2:V 64

FS 3.124:letter-nos.
JOB FAMILY SERIES.

Later Pr 32.4212

FS 3.125:nos.
LEGISLATIVE REPORTS. [Monthly]

FS 3.126:nos.
SUMMARY OF AGRICULTURAL REPORTS. [Weekly]

Later Pr 32.5210

FS 3.127:CT
ADDRESSES.

FS 3.128:v.nos.
INSURED UNEMPLOYMENT. [Weekly]

Later L 7.38, L 7.37

FS 3.129:v.nos.
UNEMPLOYMENT INSURANCE CLAIMS. [Weekly]

Later L 7.39

FS 3.130:v.nos.
EMPLOYMENT SERVICE REVIEW. [Monthly]

Earlier L 7.18

FS 3.131:date
LABOR MARKET INFORMATION INDUSTRY SERIES:
CURRENT SUPPLEMENT. [Monthly]

Earlier L 7.23/2

FS 3.131/2:nos.
– BASIC STATEMENTS.

> Later L 7.23

FS 3.132:date
LABOR MARKET INFORMATION AREA SERIES, CUR-
RENT SUPPLEMENTS. [Monthly]

> Earlier L 7.22/2

FS 3.133:CT
OCCUPATIONAL GUIDE SERIES: JOB DESCRIP-
TIONS.

> Earlier L 7.32

FS 3.133/2:CT
OCCUPATIONAL GUIDE SERIES: LABOR MARKET
INFORMATION.

> Earlier L 7.32/2

FS 3.134:CT
LABOR MARKET SURVEY (by States).

FS 1.135
VETERANS EMPLOYMENT SERVICE NEWSLETTER.

CHILDREN'S BUREAU
(1946–1963)

CREATION AND AUTHORITY

The Children's Bureau (L 5) was transferred
to the Federal Security Agency pursuant to Reorganization Plan 2 of 1946. The Bureau was reassigned to the Welfare Administration (FS 14.100)
on January 28, 1963.

FS 3.201:date
ANNUAL REPORTS.

> Earlier L 5.1
> Later FS 14.101

FS 3.202:CT
GENERAL PUBLICATIONS.

> Earlier L 5.2
> Later FS 14.102

FS 3.205:CT
LAWS.

FS 3.206/2:CT
HANDBOOKS, MANUALS, GUIDES.

> Later FS 14.108

FS 3.207:v.nos.
THE CHILD. [Monthly]

> Superseded by FS 3.207/2
> Later L 5.35

FS 3.207/2:v.nos.
CHILDREN. [Bimonthly]

> Supersedes FS 3.207
> Later FS 14.109

FS 3.208:date
PRELIMINARY MONTHLY STATISTICAL REPORT ON
EMIC PROGRAM.

> Earlier L 5.50

FS 3.209:nos.
PUBLICATIONS.

> Earlier L 5.20
> Later FS 14.111

FS 3.210:nos.
FOLDERS.

> Earlier L 5.22
> Later FS 14.118

FS 3.212:nos.
CHILD GUIDANCE LEAFLETS, SERIES ON EATING,
FOR PARENTS.

> Earlier L 5.51

FS 3.212:nos.
OUR NATION'S CHILDREN.

> Earlier L 5.49

FS 3.213:date
PUBLICATIONS OF CHILDREN'S BUREAU.

> Earlier L 5.24

FS 3.213/2:CT
BIBLIOGRAPHIES AND LISTS OF PUBLICATIONS.

> Later FS 14.112

FS 3.214:nos.
STATISTICAL SERIES.

> Later FS 14.113

FS 3.215:nos.
CHILD WELFARE REPORTS.

> Earlier L 5.52

FS 3.216:nos.
MCH INFORMATION CIRCULARS.

FS 3.217:nos.
MIDCENTURY WHITE HOUSE CONFERENCE ON
CHILDREN AND YOUTH, PROGRESS BULLETINS.

FS 3.218
CC INFORMATION CIRCULARS.

FS 3.219:date
NEWS NOTES ON JUVENILE DELINQUENCY.
[Irregular]

FS 3.220:nos.
RESEARCH RELATING TO CHILDREN, INVENTORY
OF STUDIES IN PROGRESS.

> Changed from FS 3.202:R 31
> Later FS 14.114

FS 3.220/2:nos.
RESEARCH RELATING TO SPECIAL GROUPS OF
CHILDREN.
> Later FS 14.114/2

FS 3.221:CT
POSTERS.
> Earlier L 5.14

FS 3.222:date/nos.
JUVENILE DELINQUENCY, FACTS, FACETS.
> Later FS 14.115

FS 3.223   • Item 454-A
WORK WITH CHILDREN COMING BEFORE THE
COURTS. 1–   1961–   [Irregular]

FS 3.224:nos.
HEADLINER SERIES.
> Later FS 14.117

FS 3.225:CT
ADDRESSES.
> Later FS 14.110

BUREAU OF FEDERAL CREDIT
UNIONS
(1948– 1969)

CREATION AND AUTHORITY

The Bureau of Federal Credit Unions was established within the Federal Security Agency by
act of Congress, approved June 29, 1948, and
effective July 29, 1948. By agency order, it was
made a part of the Social Security Administration.
On April 11, 1953, the Social Security Administration became a part of the newly created Department of Health, Education, and Welfare (HE
3.300) by Reorganization Plan No. 1 of 1953.

FS 3.301   • Item 525
REPORT OF OPERATIONS. [Annual]

FS 3.302:CT
GENERAL PUBLICATIONS.

FS 3.303:v.nos.&nos.
BFCU BULLETIN.

> Later HE 3.303

FS 3.305:CT
LAWS.

FS 3.306:CT
REGULATIONS, RULES, AND INSTRUCTIONS.

FS 3.306/2:CT
HANDBOOKS, MANUALS, GUIDES.

FS 3.307:date
NEW FEDERAL CREDIT UNION CHARTERS, QUAR-
TERLY REPORT OF ORGANIZATION.

> Earlier Y 3.F 31/8:13

FS 3.308:CT
MAPS AND CHARTS.

FS 3.309   • Item 527-B
RESEARCH REPORTS. 1–   1969–   [Irregular]

FS 3.310:v.nos.&nos.
CREDIT UNION STATISTICS. [Monthly]

CIVILIAN CONSERVATION CORPS
(1939– 1943)

CREATION AND AUTHORITY

The Civilian Conservation Corps (Y 3.C 49)
was made a part of the Federal Security Agency
by Reorganization Plan 1, effective July 1, 1939.
The Labor-Federal Security Appropriation Act,
1943 (56 Stat. 569), provided for the liquidation of
the CCC no later than June 30, 1943.

FS 4.1:date
ANNUAL REPORTS.

FS 4.2:CT
GENERAL PUBLICATIONS.

FS 4.5
LAWS.

FS 4.7:nos.
FORESTRY PUBLICATIONS.
> Earlier Y 3.Em 3:7, Y 3.C 49:9

FS 4.8:date
SAFETY BULLETINS.

Earlier Y 3.C 49:7

FS 4.9:nos.
[PROJECT TRAINING SERIES].

Pubs. Desig. PT series no.
Earlier I 1.71

FS 4.10:nos.
CAMP LIFE ARITHMETIC WORKBOOKS.

OFFICE OF EDUCATION
(1939– 1969)

CREATION AND AUTHORITY

The Office of Education (I 16) was transferred to the Federal Security Agency by Reorganization Plan 1 of 1939, effective July 1, 1939.
On April 11, 1953, it became a part of the newly
created Department of Health, Education, and
Welfare (HE 5) by Reorganization Plan 1 of 1953.

FS 5.1:date
ANNUAL REPORTS.

Earlier I 16.1
Later HE 5.1

FS 5.1/2:nos.
ANNUAL REPORT OF COMMISSIONER . . .
CONCERNING ADMINISTRATION OF PUBLIC
LAWS 874 AND 851 (81st Congress).

FS 5.2:CT
GENERAL PUBLICATIONS.

Earlier I 16.2
Later HE 5.2

FS 5.2:T 68/2
STATE SUPERVISORS OF PUPIL TRANSPORTA-
TION, DIRECTORY. [Irregular]

FS 5.3:dt.&nos.
BULLETINS.

Earlier I 16.3

FS 5.3/2:nos.
SCHOOL ASSIGNMENTS IN FEDERALLY AFFECTED
AREAS, BULLETINS. [Admin.]

FS 5.3/3:nos.
COMMISSIONER'S BULLETINS. [Admin.]

FS 5.3/4:series nos.&nos.
FINANCIAL MANAGEMENT BULLETIN.

FS 5.4:nos.
CIRCULARS.

FS 5.4/2:nos.
LOOSE LEAF CIRCULARS.

FS 5.5:CT
LAWS.

FS 5.6:CT
REGULATIONS, RULES, AND INSTRUCTIONS.
Later HE 5.6

FS 5.6/2:CT
HANDBOOKS, MANUALS, GUIDES.

Earlier FS 5.6
Later HE 5.6/2

FS 5.7:vol.
SCHOOL LIFE. [Monthly except August and Septem-
ber]
Earlier I 16.26

FS 5.7/a 2:nos.
– PAN-AMERICAN CLUB NEWS.
Earlier FS 5.26/a2

FS 5.8
ADDRESSES. [Irregular]

Later HE 5.8

FS 5.9:date
PUBLICATIONS (General Lists).

FS 5.10:CT
PUBLICATIONS (Miscellaneous Lists).

Earlier I 16.14/2

FS 5.10/2:CT
SCHOOL FACILITIES SERVICES (Lists & References).

FS 5.10/3:date
GENERAL CATALOGS OF EDUCATIONAL FILMS. [An-
nual]

Earlier FS 5.2:F 48/5

FS 5.10/4:CT
REFERENCES ON LOCAL SCHOOL ADMINISTRA-
TION.

FS 5.10/5:date
CLEARINGHOUSE EXCHANGE OF PUBLICATIONS
OF STATE DEPARTMENTS OF EDUCATION
[Elementary Education Personnel].

FS 5.10/6:date
CLEARINGHOUSE EXCHANGE OF PUBLICATIONS
OF STATE DEPARTMENTS OF EDUCATION
[Secondary Education Personnel].

FS 5.11:nos.
[MISCELLANEOUS SERIES].

Pubs. desig. Misc. No.
Earlier I 16.54/5

FS 5.12:nos.
LANGUAGE USAGE SERIES.

Earlier I 16.75

FS 5.13/1:nos.
DEMOCRACY IN ACTION (radio scripts). [Weekly]

Earlier I 16.74

FS 5.13/2:nos.
DEMOCRACY IN ACTION: PUBLIC HEALTH SERIES
(radio scripts). [Weekly]

FS 5.13/3:nos.
DEMOCRACY IN ACTION: [Social Security] (radio
scripts). [Weekly]

FS 5.13/4:nos.
DEMOCRACY IN ACTION: [For Labor's Welfare] (radio
scripts). [Weekly]

FS 5.13/5:nos.
DEMOCRACY IN ACTION: CENSUS (radio scripts).
[Weekly]

FS 5.13/6:nos.
DEMOCRACY IN ACTION: ROOF OVER AMERICA
(Radio Script).

FS 5.14/1:nos.
THE WORLD IS YOURS (radio scripts). [Weekly]

Earlier I 16.56/2

FS 5.14/2:vol.
THE WORLD IS YOURS (radio scripts) SUPPLE-
MENTS.

Published weekly for 26 consecutive weeks
beginning in October 1939 by Columbia University Press, N.Y.

FS 5.15:nos.
GALLANT AMERICAN WOMEN (radio scripts).
[Weekly]

FS 5.16:nos.
BIBLIOGRAPHIES (numbered).

Prior to July 1, 1939 see I 16.46

FS 5.16/2:nos.
BIBLIOGRAPHIES, GUIDANCE AND STUDENT
PERSONNEL SECTION.

FS 5.17:nos.
PAMPHLETS.

Earlier I 16.43

FS 5.18:nos.
LEAFLETS.

Includes Guidance Leaflets.
Earlier I 16.44

FS 5.18/2:CT
GUIDANCE LEAFLETS.

Issued by Guidance and Student Personnel
Section.

FS 5.19:nos.
MARCH OF EDUCATION.

Earlier I 16.26/3

FS 5.20:CT
POSTERS.

Earlier I 16.27

FS 5.21:nos.
VOCATIONAL REHABILITATION DIVISION, LEAF-
LETS.

Earlier I 16.54/8

FS 5.22:nos.
EDUCATIONAL AND NATIONAL DEFENSE SERIES
PAMPHLETS.

FS 5.23:dt.&vol.nos.&chap.nos
BIENNIAL SURVEY OF EDUCATION IN UNITED
STATES.

Formerly issued in Bulletin Series, I 16.3 and
FS 5.3

FS 5.24:nos.
SERVICE BULLETINS ON DEFENSE TRAINING IN
VOCATIONAL SCHOOLS.

FS 5.25   • Item 460-A-20
EDUCATIONAL DIRECTORY. [Annual]

Earlier FS 5.3
Later HE 5.25

FS 5.26:v.nos.
EDUCATION FOR VICTORY. [Biweekly]

Replaces School Life, (FS 5.7) for duration of
the war.

FS 5.26/a 2:nos.
PAN-AMERICAN CLUB NEWS.

Earlier FS 5.35
Later FS 5.7/a2

FS 5.27:date
FREEDOM'S PEOPLE (radio scripts).

At intervals of about a month.

FS 5.28:nos.
VOCATIONAL REHABILITATION SERIES, BULLETINS.

Earlier issues included in I 16.54/3
Later FS 10.7

FS 5.29:nos.
VICTORY CORPS SERIES PAMPHLETS.

FS 5.30:nos.
[BULLETINS] MISC.

Earlier I 16.71

FS 5.31:nos.
INTER-AMERICAN EDUCATION DEMONSTRATION CENTERS.

FS 5.31/2:CT
INTER-AMERICAN EDUCATION DEMONSTRATION CENTERS (misc.)

FS 5.32:nos.
SCHOOL CHILDREN AND THE WAR SERIES, LEAFLETS.

FS 5.33:nos.
ADJUSTMENT OF COLLEGE CURRICULUM TO WARTIME CONDITIONS AND NEEDS, REPORTS.

FS 5.34:nos.
NUTRITION EDUCATION SERIES PAMPHLETS.

FS 5.35:nos.
PAN AMERICAN CLUB NEWS.

Later FS 5.26/a2

FS 5.36:nos.later dt.
NEWS EXCHANGE, EXTENDED SCHOOL SERVICES FOR CHILDREN OF WORKING MOTHERS, LETTERS.

FS 5.37:nos.
HIGHER EDUCATION.

FS 5.38:nos.
FAMILY CONTRIBUTIONS TO WAR AND POST-WAR MORALE.

FS 5.39:CT
STATISTICAL CIRCULARS.

FS 5.40:CT
PUBLICATIONS OF HOWARD UNIVERSITY.

Earlier I 1.18

FS 5.41:nos.
SPECIAL SERIES.

FS 5.42:nos.
ADULT EDUCATION IDEAS.

FS 5.43:nos.
SELECTED REFERENCES.

FS 5.44:nos.
EDUCATION BRIEFS.

FS 5.45:dt.&nos.
DEFENSE INFORMATION BULLETINS.

FS 5.45/2:nos.
CIVIL DEFENSE EDUCATION PROJECT, INFORMATION SHEETS. [Irregular]

FS 5.45/3:nos.
CIVIL DEFENSE EDUCATION PROJECT, CLASSROOM PRACTICES.

FS 5.46:nos.
PROGRESS REPORT OF SCHOOL FACILITIES SURVEY.

FS 5.47:nos.
SCIENTIFIC MANPOWER SERIES.

FS 5.47/2:nos.
INFORMATION BULLETINS (National Scientific Register).

FS 5.48
CIRCULAR LETTERS.

FS 5.49:nos.
ADULT EDUCATION REFERENCES.

FS 5.49/2:date
ADULT EDUCATION IN AMERICAN EDUCATION WEEK.

Title varies.
Earlier FS 5.2:Ad 9

FS 5.50:nos.
SPOTLIGHT ON ORGANIZATION AND SUPERVISION IN LARGE HIGH SCHOOLS.

FS 5.51:nos.
SPECIAL PUBLICATIONS.

FS 5.52:CT
TEACHING AIDS FOR DEVELOPING INTERNATIONAL UNDERSTANDING.

FS 5.53
SECONDARY EDUCATION. [Irregular]

FS 5.54:nos.
GUIDE LINES, GUIDANCE & PUPIL PERSONNEL SERVICE.

FS 5.55:CT
AVIATION EDUCATION SERIES. [Irregular]

FS 5.56
EDUCATION FACT SHEET. [Irregular]

FS 5.56/2:date
EDUCATION FACT SHEET. [Monthly]

FS 5.57:date
NEWSNOTES ON EDUCATION AROUND THE WORLD.

FS 5.57/2:nos.
INFORMATION ON EDUCATION AROUND THE WORLD.

FS 5.58:date
CONFERENCE ON ELEMENTARY EDUCATION REPORTS. [Annual]

Earlier FS 5.2:El 2/4

FS 5.58/2:date
CONFERENCE FOR SUPERVISORS OF ELEMENTARY EDUCATION IN LARGE CITIES. [Annual]

Earlier FS 5.2:El 2/4

FS 5.59:CT
STUDIES IN COMPARATIVE EDUCATION.

FS 5.60:date
AUDIOVISUAL EDUCATION DIRECTORS IN STATE DEPARTMENTS OF EDUCATION AND IN LARGE CITY SCHOOL SYSTEMS. [Annual]

FS 5.60/2:date
KEY AUDIOVISUAL PERSONNEL IN PUBLIC SCHOOLS AND LIBRARY SYSTEMS IN STATES AND LARGE CITIES AND IN LARGE PUBLIC COLLEGES AND UNIVERSITIES.
Earlier FS 5.2:Au 2/3, FS 5.60

FS 5.61:date
UNDERGRADUATE ENGINEERING CURRICULA ACCREDITED BY ENGINEER'S COUNCIL FOR PROFESSIONAL DEVELOPMENT. [Annual]
Earlier FS 5.2:En 3/7

FS 5.62:date
PROGRESS OF PUBLIC EDUCATION IN UNITED STATES OF AMERICA. [Annual]
Earlier FS 5.2:Ed 8/2

FS 5.63:nos.
SCHOLARSHIPS AND FELLOWSHIP INFORMATION.

FS 5.64:date
TEACHER EXCHANGE OPPORTUNITIES UNDER INTERNATIONAL EDUCATIONAL EXCHANGE PROGRAM. [Annual]
Earlier FS 5.2:El 2/4

FS 5.64/2:date
TEACHER EXCHANGE OPPORTUNITIES ABROAD, TEACHING, SUMMER SEMINARS UNDER INTERNATIONAL EDUCATIONAL EXCHANGE PROGRAM OF DEPARTMENT OF STATES [Announcements].
Earlier FS 5.2:Ex 2/6

FS 5.64/3:date
OPPORTUNITIES FOR TEACHERS OF FRENCH LANGUAGE AND LITERATURE. [Annual]
Earlier FS 5.2:T 22/12

FS 5.64/4:date
OPPORTUNITIES FOR TEACHERS OF SPANISH AND PORTUGUESE.

FS 5.65:v.nos.&nos.
CASE BOOK, EDUCATION BEYOND HIGH SCHOOL PRACTICES UNDERWAY TO MEET THE PROBLEM OF THE DAY.

FS 5.66:date
REPORT ON PRINCIPAL BILLS INTRODUCED INTO CONGRESS AFFECTING EDUCATION EITHER DIRECTLY OR INDIRECTLY. [Annual]
Earlier FS 5.2:Ed 8/3

FS 5.67:nos.
CITIZEN LEAFLETS.

FS 5.68:CT
LOCAL SCHOOL ADMINISTRATION BRIEFS.

FS 5.69:date
COOPERATIVE RESEARCH PROGRAM: PROJECTS UNDER CONTRACT.

FS 5.70:nos.
BULLETIN ON NATIONAL DEFENSE EDUCATION ACT, PUBLIC LAW 85-864. [Administrative]

FS 5.71:nos.
PROGRAM ACTIVITY REPORTS, PUBLIC LAW 85-864.

FS 5.72:date
BUSINESS AND PUBLIC ADMINISTRATION NOTES.

FS 5.73
PUBLIC SCHOOL FINANCE PROGRAM. 1947/48– [Biennial]

FS 5.73/2
STATE COMPILATIONS. 1953– [Biennial]

FS 5.74:v.nos.&nos.
HE INSTRUCTION IN AGRICULTURE, PROGRAMS, ACTIVITIES, DEVELOPMENTS.

FS 5.75:v.nos.&nos. • Item 455-B
AMERICAN EDUCATION. v. 1– 1965– [10 times a year]

Later HE 5.75

FS 5.76
MANPOWER DEVELOPMENT AND TRAINING, PROJECTS APPROVED. [Annual]

FS 5.77:nos. • Item 466-A
RESEARCH IN EDUCATION. v. 1– 1966– [Monthly & Annual]

Later HE 5.77

FS 5.78
COMMUNITY SERVICE AND CONTINUING EDUCATION, TITLE 1, HIGHER EDUCATION ACT OF 1965. 1967– [Irregular]

FS 5.79:date
ANNUAL REPORT OF COMPENSATORY EDUCATION PROGRAMS UNDER TITLE 1, ELEMENTARY AND SECONDARY EDUCATION ACT OF 1965. 1st– 1966– [Annual]

Earlier Title: Title 1, Elementary and Secondary Education Act of 1965, States Report.
Later HE 5.79

FS 5.80:nos. • Item 467-C
STATUS OF COMPLIANCE, PUBLIC SCHOOL DISTRICTS, 17 SOUTHERN AND BORDER STATES, REPORTS. 1– 1965– [3 times a year]
Later HE 5.80

FS 5.81:date
HIGHER EDUCATION REPORTS.
Later HE 5.81

FS 5.82 • Item 467-E
REPORT ON COOPERATIVE RESEARCH TO IMPROVE THE NATION'S SCHOOLS. 1957– [Annual]
Later HE 5.82

FS 5.83:date   • **Item 459-A**
COMPOSITE LIST OF ELIGIBLE INSTITUTIONS FOR GUARANTEED LOANS FOR COLLEGE STUDENTS, HIGHER EDUCATION ACT OF 1965. [Irregular]

Later HE 5.83

FS 5.83/2:date   • **Item 459-A**
COMPOSITE LIST OF ELIGIBLE INSTITUTIONS, NATIONAL VOCATION STUDENT LOAN INSURANCE ACT OF 1965. [Irregular]

Later HE 5.83/2

FS 5.84:CT
INSTITUTE PROGRAMS FOR ADVANCED STUDIES.

Later HE 5.84

FS 5.84:El 2   • **Item 460-A-58**
ELEMENTARY SCHOOL PERSONNEL. 1968/69– [Annual]

Later HE 5.84:El 2

FS 5.84:Se 2   • **Item 460-A-58**
SECONDARY SCHOOL PERSONNEL. 1968/69– [Annual]

Later HE 5.84:Se 2

FS 5.84:T 22   • **Item 460-A-58**
TRAINERS OF TEACHERS, OTHER EDUCATION PERSONNEL AND UNDERGRADUATES. 1968/69– [Annual]

Later FS 5.84:T 22

FS 5.85   • **Item 462-B**
NATIONAL ADVISORY COUNCIL IN VOCATIONS EDUCATION, ANNUAL REPORT. 1– 1969–

Later HE 5.85

FS 5.86:date
BETTER EDUCATION FOR HANDICAPPED CHILDREN, ANNUAL REPORT.

Later HE 5.86

Federal Radio Education Committee

Appointed by the Federal Communication Commission.

FS 5.101:date
ANNUAL REPORTS.

FS 5.103:nos.
BULLETINS OF FEDERAL RADIO EDUCATION COMMITTEE.

FS 5.106:CT
REGULATIONS, RULES, AND INSTRUCTIONS.

FS 5.107:v.nos.
SERVICE BULLETINS. [Monthly]

Vocational Division

FS 5.121:date
ANNUAL REPORTS.

FS 5.122:CT
GENERAL PUBLICATIONS.

Earlier I 16.54/2

FS 5.123:nos.
BULLETINS.

Earlier I 16.54/3

FS 5.126:CT
REGULATIONS, RULES, AND INSTRUCTIONS.

FS 5.127:nos.
[Miscellaneous] CIRCULARS.

Pubs. desig. Misc. Circular No.
Earlier I 16.54/7

FS 5.128:nos.
MONOGRAPHS.

Earlier I 16.54/9

FS 5.129:nos.
LEAFLETS.

Earlier I 16.54/8

FS 5.130:nos.
DEFENSE TRAINING LEAFLETS.

FS 5.130/2
VOCATIONAL TRAINING FOR DEFENSE (War Production) WORKERS, (Preemployment and Refresher Courses).

FS 5.131:date
DIGEST OF ANNUAL REPORTS OF STATE BOARDS FOR VOCATIONAL EDUCATION TO OFFICE OF EDUCATION, VOCATIONAL DIVISION.

Earlier issued in Misc. Series, (FS 5.11).

FS 5.132:CT
ADDRESSES.

FS 5.133:date
BASIC PREPARATORY PROGRAMS FOR PRACTICAL NURSES BY STATES AND CHANGES IN NUMBER OF PROGRAMS.

Earlier FS 5.122:N 93

Office of Education (Continued)

FS 5.210:nos.
MISCELLANEOUS PUBLICATIONS: GENERAL, OE 10,000-10,999.

Later HE 5.210

FS 5.210:10004   • **Item 460-A-10**
REPORT ON THE NATIONAL DEFENSE EDUCATION ACT. 1959– [Annual]

Later HE 5.210:10004

FS 5.210:10005   • **Item 460-A-10**
PROGRESS OF PUBLIC EDUCATION IN THE UNITED STATES OF AMERICA. [Annual]

Later HE 5.210:10005

FS 5.210:10024   • **Item 460-A-10**
DIGEST OF EDUCATIONAL STATISTICS. 1962– [Annual]

Later HE 5.210:10024

FS 5.210:10030   • **Item 460-A-10**
PROJECTIONS OF EDUCATIONAL STATISTICS TO (year). [Annual]

Later HE 5.210:10030

FS 5.211:nos.
MISCELLANEOUS PUBLICATIONS: PUBLICATIONS ABOUT OE AND HEW, OE 11,00-11,999.

Later HE 5.211

FS 5.211:11000   • **Item 460-A-11**
PUBLICATIONS OF THE OFFICE OF EDUCATION. [Irregular]

Later HE 5.211:11000

FS 5.211:11002   • **Item 460-A-11**
HANDBOOK, OFFICE OF EDUCATION. [Irregular]

Later FS 5.211:11002

FS 5.212
MISCELLANEOUS PUBLICATIONS: RESEARCH, OE 12,000-12,999.

FS 5.212   • **Item 460-A-14**
STUDIES IN COMPARATIVE EDUCATION, EDUCATION IN [country]. [Irregular]
Later HE 5.212

FS 5.212:12014   • **Item 460-A-12**
NATIONAL DEFENSE LANGUAGE DEVELOPMENT RESEARCH AND STUDIES. 1– 1958/59– [Irregular]

Later HE 5.212:12014

FS 5.212:12016   • **Item 460-A-12**
NATIONAL DEFENSE LANGUAGE DEVELOPMENT PROGRAM: COMPLETED RESEARCH, STUDIES, AND INSTRUCTIONAL MATERIALS. LISTS. 1– [Irregular]

Later FS 5.212:12016

FS 5.213:nos.
MISCELLANEOUS PUBLICATIONS: ADULT EDUCATION, OE 13,000-13,999.

Later HE 5.213

FS 5.214
MISCELLANEOUS PUBLICATIONS: INTERNATIONAL EDUCATION OE 14,000-14,999.

FS 5.214:[nos.]   • **Item 460-A-14**
STUDIES IN COMPARATIVE EDUCATION, BIBLIOGRAPHY: [year] PUBLICATIONS. 1958– [Annual]

FS 5.214:14003   • **Item 460-A-14**
INTERNATIONAL TEACHER DEVELOPMENT PROGRAM, ANNUAL REPORT TO BUREAU OF EDUCATIONAL AND CULTURAL AFFAIRS, DEPARTMENT OF STATE. 1956/57– [Annual]

Later HE 5.214:14003

FS 5.214:14031
EDUCATIONAL MATERIALS LABORATORY REPORTS. v. 1– [Irregular]

Later HE 5.214:14031

FS 5.214:14031   • **Item 460-A-14**
PROGRAM AND SERVICES, REPORT OF EDUCATIONAL MATERIALS LABORATORY, DIVISION OF INTERNATIONAL STUDIES AND SERVICES. [Irregular]

Later HE 5.214:14031

FS 5.214:14034
INFORMATION ON EDUCATION AROUND THE WORLD. 1– 1958– [Irregular]

Later HE 5.214:14034

FS 5.214:14035
NEWSNOTES ON EDUCATION AROUND THE WORLD. 1956– [Irregular]

Later HE 5.14:14035

FS 5.214:14046   • **Item 460-A-14**
ANNUAL REPORT ON THE TECHNICAL ASSISTANCE TRAINING PROGRAM IN EDUCATION. 1955– [Annual]

Later HE 5.214:14046

FS 5.214:14047   • **Item 460-A-14**
TEACHER EXCHANGE OPPORTUNITIES UNDER THE INTERNATIONAL EDUCATIONAL EXCHANGE PROGRAM. [Annual]

Later HE 5.214:14047

FS 5.215:nos.
MISCELLANEOUS PUBLICATIONS: LIBRARY SERVICES, OE 15,000-15,999.

Later HE 5.215

FS 5.215:15023   • **Item 460-A-15**
LIBRARY STATISTICS OF COLLEGES AND UNIVERSITIES, INSTITUTIONAL DATA. 1959/1960– [Annual]

Later HE 5.215:15023

FS 5.215:15031 • Item 460-A-15
LIBRARY STATISTICS OF COLLEGES AND UNIVERSITIES, ANALYTIC REPORT. [Annual]

Later HE 5.215:15031

FS 5.215:15033
STATISTICS OF PUBLIC LIBRARY SYSTEMS SERVING POPULATIONS OF 100,000 OR MORE. [Irregular]

Later HE 5.215:15033

FS 5.215:15034
STATISTICS OF PUBLIC LIBRARY SYSTEMS SERVING POPULATIONS OF 50,000-99,999. 1950– [Irregular]

Later HE 5.215:15034

FS 5.215:15035
STATISTICS OF PUBLIC LIBRARY SYSTEMS SERVING POPULATIONS OF 35,000-49,999. 1956/57– [Irregular]

Later HE 5.215:15035

FS 5.215:15046 • Item 460-A-15
LIBRARY EDUCATION DIRECTORY. [Biennial]

Later HE 5.215:15046

FS 5.215:15049 • Item 460-A-15
STATISTICS OF PUBLIC SCHOOL LIBRARIES. [Irregular]

Later 5.215:15049

FS 5.216:nos.
MISCELLANEOUS PUBLICATIONS: NURSERY SCHOOLS AND KINDERGARTENS, OE 16,000-16,999.

Later HE 5.216

FS 5.220:nos.
ELEMENTARY & SECONDARY EDUCATION: MISC., GENERAL STATISTICS, OE 20,000- 20,999.

Later HE 5.220

FS 5.220:20002A
SELECTED REFERENCES. 1– 1947– [Irregular]
Later HE 5.220:20002A

FS 5.220:20006
PRELIMINARY STATISTICS OF STATE SCHOOL SYSTEMS. [Biennial]
Later HE 5.220:20006

FS 5.220:20007 • Item 460-A-20
FALL [year] ENROLLMENT, TEACHERS, AND SCHOOL-HOUSING IN FULL-TIME PUBLIC ELEMENTARY AND SECONDARY DAY SCHOOLS. 1954– [Annual]
Later HE 5.220:20007

FS 5.220:20020 • Item 460-A-20
STATISTICS OF STATE SCHOOL SYSTEMS. 1959/60– [Biennial]
Later HE 5.220:20020

FS 5.220:20022
STATISTICS ON PUPIL TRANSPORTATION. 1947/48– [Irregular]
Later HE 5.220:20022

FS 5.220:20032 • Item 460-A-20
STATISTICS OF EDUCATION IN THE UNITED STATES. 1958/59– [Annual]
Later HE 5.220:20032

FS 5.220:20050 • Item 460-A-20
STATISTICS OF NONPUBLIC SECONDARY SCHOOLS. 1960/61– [Irregular]
Later HE 5.220:20052

FS 5.220:20064 • Item 460-A-20
STATISTICS OF NONPUBLIC ELEMENTARY SCHOOLS. [Irregular]
Later HE 5.220:20064

FS 5.220:20103 • Item 460-A-20
PACESETTERS IN INNOVATION. v. 1– 1966– [Annual]

Later HE 5.220:20103

FS 5.220:20108 • Item 460-A-20
ANNUAL REPORT, TITLE 2, ELEMENTARY AND SECONDARY EDUCATION ACT OF 1965, SCHOOL LIBRARY RESOURCES, TEXTBOOKS, AND OTHER INSTRUCTIONAL MATERIALS. 1– 1966– [Annual]

Later HE 5.220:20108

FS 5.221:nos.
MISCELLANEOUS PUBLICATIONS: BUILDINGS, EQUIPMENT, OE 21,000-21,999.

Later HE 5.221

FS 5.221:21033 • Item 460-A-21
CONDITION OF PUBLIC SCHOOL PLANTS. [Irregular]

Later HE 5.221:21033

FS 5.222:nos.
MISCELLANEOUS PUBLICATIONS: FINANCES, RECEIPTS, EXPENDITURES, OE 22,000-22,999.

Later HE 5.222

FS 5.222:22000 • Item 460-A-22
CURRENT EXPENDITURES PER PUPIL IN PUBLIC SCHOOL SYSTEMS. 1921/22– [Annual]

Later HE 5.22:22000

FS 5.222:22003 • Item 460-A-22
ADMINISTRATION OF PUBLIC LAWS 874 AND 815, ANNUAL REPORT. 1– 1951– [Annual]

Later HE 5.222:22003

FS 5.222:22009 • Item 460-A-22
BOND SALES FOR PUBLIC SCHOOL PURPOSES. 1959/60– [Annual]

Later HE 5.222:22009

FS 5.222:22013 • Item 460-A-22
REVENUE PROGRAMS FOR THE PUBLIC SCHOOLS IN THE UNITED STATES. 1949/50– [Irregular]

Later HE 5.222:22013

FS 5.222:22022 • Item 460-A-22
PROFILES IN SCHOOL SUPPORT, DECENNIAL OVERVIEW.

Later HE 5.222:22022

FS 5.222:22023 • Item 460-A-22
STATE PROGRAMS FOR PUBLIC SCHOOL SUPPORT.

Later HE 5.222:22023

FS 5.223:nos.
MISCELLANEOUS PUBLICATIONS: ADMINISTRATION, FACULTIES, SALARIES, OE 23,000-23,999.

Later HE 5.223

FS 5.223:23050 • Item 460-A-23
ADVISORY COUNCIL ON STATE DEPARTMENTS OF EDUCATION, ANNUAL REPORTS. 1– [Annual]

Later HE 5.223:23050

FS 5.224
MISCELLANEOUS PUBLICATIONS: ENROLLMENT, RETENTION, GRADUATES, OE 24,000- 24,999.

HEADLINER SERIES. 1– 1962– [Irregular]
Later HE 5.224

FS 5.224:24012 • Item 460-A-24
SUBJECT OFFERINGS AND ENROLLMENTS, GRADES 9-12, NONPUBLIC SECONDARY SCHOOLS.

Later HE 5.224:24012

FS 5.225:nos.
MISCELLANEOUS PUBLICATIONS: GUIDANCE, TESTING, COUNSELING, OE 25,000-25999.

Later HE 5.225

FS 5.225:25015 • Item 460-A-25
NDEA COUNSELING AND GUIDANCE INSTITUTES. [Irregular]

Later HE 5.225:25015

FS 5.225:25036 • Item 460-A-25
DIRECTORY OF COUNSELOR EDUCATORS. 1962– [Irregular]

FS 5.225:25037A • Item 460-A-25
DIRECTORY, STATE DEPARTMENT OF EDUCATION PERSONNEL FOR GUIDANCE, COUNSELING, AND TESTING. [Irregular]

Later HE 5.225:25037A

FS 5.226:nos.
MISCELLANEOUS PUBLICATIONS: CAREERS, OE 26,000-26,999.

Later HE 5.226

FS 5.226:26000 • Item 460-A-26
TEACHING OPPORTUNITIES, DIRECTORY OF PLACEMENT INFORMATION. 1955– [Irregular]

Later HE 5.226:26000

FS 5.227:nos.
MISCELLANEOUS PUBLICATIONS: FOREIGN LANGUAGES, OE 27,000-27,999.

Later HE 5.227

FS 5.228:nos.
MISCELLANEOUS PUBLICATIONS: HEALTH, PHYSICAL EDUCATION, RECREATION, OE 28,000-28,999.

Later HE 5.228

FS 5.229:nos.
MISCELLANEOUS PUBLICATIONS: MATHEMATICS, SCIENCE, OE 29,000-29,999.

Later HE 5.229

FS 5.229:29000 • Item 460-A-29
RESEARCH IN THE TEACHING OF SCIENCE. 1957/59– [Biennial]

Earlier title, 1950– 1957: Analysis of Research in the Teaching of Science
Later HE 5.229:29000

FS 5.229:29007 • Item 460-A-29
ANALYSIS OF RESEARCH IN THE TEACHING OF MATHEMATICS. 1952– [Biennial]
Later HE 5.229:29007

FS 5.230:nos.
MISCELLANEOUS PUBLICATIONS: LANGUAGE ARTS, READING, WRITING, SPEAKING, OE 30,000-30,999.
Later HE 5.230

FS 5.231:nos.
MISCELLANEOUS PUBLICATIONS: SOCIAL STUDIES, OE 31,000-31,999.
Later HE 5.231

FS 5.232:nos.
MISCELLANEOUS PUBLICATIONS: CURRICULUMS, SUBJECTS, ACTIVITIES (elementary only), OE 32,000-32,999.
Later HE 5.232

FS 5.233:nos.
MISCELLANEOUS PUBLICATIONS: CURRICULUMS, SUBJECTS, ACTIVITIES (Secondary & Elementary-Sec.) OE 33,000-33,999.

Later HE 5.233

FS 5.234:nos.
MISCELLANEOUS PUBLICATIONS: AUDIOVISUAL, OE 34,000-34,999.

Later HE 5.234

FS 5.234:34002   • **Item 460-A-34**
TITLE VII– NEW EDUCATIONAL MEDIA NEWS AND REPORTS. 1959–   [Irregular]

Later HE 5.234:34002

FS 5.234:34006   • **Item 460-A-34**
U.S. GOVERNMENT FILMS FOR PUBLIC EDUCATIONAL USE. 1955–   [Irregular]

Later HE 5.234:34006

FS 5.234:34013   • **Item 460-A-34**
PROJECTS INITIATED UNDER TITLE VII, NATIONAL DEFENSE EDUCATION ACT. Part A. 1962–   [Annual]

Later HE 5.234:34013

FS 5.234:34015   • **Item 460-A-34**
PROGRAMS, (year), GUIDE TO PROGRAMMED INSTRUCTIONAL MATERIALS AVAILABLE TO EDUCATORS BY (date). 1962–

Later HE 5.234:34015

FS 5.234:34016   • **Item 460-A-34**
EDUCATIONAL AM AND FM RADIO AND EDUCATION TELEVISION STATIONS, BY STATE AND CITY. [Irregular]

Later HE 5.234:34016

FS 5.234:34021   • **Item 460-A-34**
PROJECTS INITIATED UNDER TITLE VII, NATIONAL DEFENSE ACT (continued). Part B. [Annual]

Later HE 5.234:34021

FS 5.234:34039   • **Item 460-A-34**
CATALOG OF CAPTIONED FILMS FOR THE DEAF. [Irregular]

Earlier HE 5.234:34039

FS 5.235
MISCELLANEOUS PUBLICATIONS: ELEMENTARY AND SECONDARY EDUCATION: SPECIAL EDUCATION, EXCEPTIONAL CHILDREN, OE 35,000-35,999.

Later HE 5.235

FS 5.235:35003   • **Item 460-A-35**
EDUCATION OF EXCEPTIONAL CHILDREN AND YOUTH: SPECIAL EDUCATION PERSONNEL IN STATE EDUCATION DEPARTMENTS. 1955– [Irregular]

Later HE 5.235:35003

FS 5.235:35051
SPECIAL EDUCATION PERSONNEL IN STATE EDUCATION DEPARTMENTS. 1955– [Irregular]

Later HE 5.235:35051

FS 5.236:nos.
MISCELLANEOUS PUBLICATIONS: RURAL SCHOOLS, RURAL EDUCATION, OE 36,000–36,999.

Later HE 5.236

FS 5.237:nos.
MISCELLANEOUS PUBLICATIONS: EDUCATION OF THE DISADVANTAGED, OE 37,000– 37,999.

Later HE 5.237

FS 5.237:37013
TITLE 1 OF ELEMENTARY AND SECONDARY EDUCATION ACT OF 1965: ANNUAL REPORT. 1–   1956–   [Annual]

Later HE 5.237:37013

FS 5.238:nos.
MISCELLANEOUS PUBLICATIONS: EQUAL EDUCATIONAL OPPORTUNITIES, OE 38,000– 38,999.

Later HE 5.238

FS 5.250
HIGHER EDUCATION: MISCELLANEOUS, GENERAL STATISTICS, OE 50,000– 50,999.

FS 5.250   • **Item 460-A-50**
NEW DIMENSIONS IN HIGHER EDUCATION. 1– 1960–   [Irregular]

Later HE 5.250

FS 5.250:50002   • **Item 460-A-50**
STATISTICS OF LAND-GRANT COLLEGES AND UNIVERSITIES. 1895/96–   [Annual]

Later HE 5.250:500002

FS 5.250:50004   • **Item 460-A-50**
CLEARINGHOUSE OF STUDIES ON HIGHER EDUCATION, REPORTER. 1959–   [Irregular]

Later HE 5.250:50004

FS 5.250:50008   • **Item 460-A-50**
SURVEY OF STATE LEGISLATION RELATING TO HIGHER EDUCATION. 1956/57–   [Annual]

Later HE 5.250:50008

FS 5.250:50012   • **Item 460-A-50**
ACCREDITED HIGHER INSTITUTIONS. 1917– [Quadrennial]

Later HE 5.250:50012

FS 5.250:50023   • **Item 460-A-50**
FINANCIAL STATISTICS OF INSTITUTIONS OF HIGHER EDUCATION.

Later HE 5.250:50023

FS 5.250:50025
LAND-GRANT COLLEGES AND UNIVERSITIES, PRELIMINARY REPORT FOR YEAR ENDED JUNE 30, (year). [Annual]

Later HE 5.250:50025

FS 5.250:50052   • **Item 460-A-50**
DIRECTORY OF U.S. INSTITUTIONS OF HIGHER EDUCATION, FALL (year). 1967–

Later HE 5.250:50052

FS 5.251:nos.
MISCELLANEOUS PUBLICATIONS: BUILDINGS, EQUIPMENT, OE 51,000-51,999.

Later HE 5.251

FS 5.251:51016   • **Item 460-A-51**
HIGHER EDUCATION FACILITIES CLASSIFICATION AND PROCEDURES MANUAL. 1968– [Irregular]

Later HE 5.251:51016

FS 5.252:nos.
MISCELLANEOUS PUBLICATIONS: FINANCES, RECEIPTS, EXPENDITURES, OE 52,00052,999.

Later HE 5.252

FS 5.252:52004   • **Item 460-A-52**
BOND SALES FOR HIGHER EDUCATION. [Annual]

Later HE 5.252:52004

FS 5.252:52005   • **Item 460-A-52**
HIGHER EDUCATION, BASIC STUDENT CHARGES. 1962–   [Annual]

Later HE 5.252:52005

FS 5.253:nos.
MISCELLANEOUS PUBLICATIONS: ADMINISTRATION, FACULTIES, SALARIES, OE 53,000-53,999.

Later HE 5.253

FS 5.253:53000   • **Item 460-A-53**
FACULTY AND OTHER PROFESSIONAL STAFF IN INSTITUTIONS OF HIGHER EDUCATION. 1955–   [Biennial]

Later HE 5.253:53000

FS 5.253:53004   • **Item 460-A-53**
HIGHER EDUCATION PLANNING AND MANAGEMENT DATA. 1958–   [Annual]

Later HE 5.253:53004

FS 5.253:53014
SUMMARY REPORT, FACULTY AND OTHER PROFESSIONAL STAFF IN INSTITUTIONS OF HIGHER EDUCATION. 1955–   [Biennial]

Later HE 5.253:53014

FS 5.253:53015   • **Item 460-A-53**
HIGHER EDUCATION SALARIES. 1962– [Annual]

Later HE 5.253:53015

FS 5.253:53023   • **Item 460-A-53**
FACULTY SALARIES IN LAND-GRANT COLLEGES AND STATE UNIVERSITIES. 1935–   [Annual]

Later HE 5.253:53023

FS 5.254:nos.
MISCELLANEOUS PUBLICATIONS: ADMISSION, ENROLLMENT, RETENTION, DEGREES, GRADUATES, OE 54,000-54,999.

Later HE 5.254

FS 5.254:54000   • **Item 460-A-54**
RESIDENT, EXTENSION, AND OTHER ENROLLMENTS IN INSTITUTIONS OF HIGHER EDUCATION. 1953–   [Irregular]

Later HE 5.254:54000

FS 5.254:54001   • **Item 460-A-54**
JUNIOR-YEAR SCIENCE, MATHEMATICS, AND FOREIGN LANGUAGE STUDENTS, FIRST-TERM. 1957–

Later HE 5.254:54001

FS 5.254:54003   • **Item 460-A-54**
INSTITUTIONAL DATA. 1958–   [Annual]

Later HE 5.254:54003

FS 5.254:54004
ADVANCE REPORT ON ENGINEERING ENROLLMENT AND DEGREES, (year). 1949– [Annual]

Later HE 5.254:54004

FS 5.254:54006   • **Item 460-A-54**
ENGINEERING ENROLLMENTS AND DEGREES. 1949–   [Annual]

Later HE 5.254:54006

FS 5.254:54007   • **Item 460-A-54**
ANALYTIC REPORTS. 1958–   [Annual]

    Later HE 5.254:54007

FS 5.254:54009
SUMMARY REPORT ON SURVEY OF STUDENTS ENROLLED FOR ADVANCED DEGREES: FALL (year). 1959–   [Annual]

    Later HE 5.254:54009

FS 5.254:54010
SUMMARY REPORT OF BACHELOR'S AND HIGHER DEGREES CONFERRED DURING (school year). [Annual]

    Later HE 5.254:54010

FS 5.254:54012   • **Item 460-A-54**
GUIDE TO ORGANIZED OCCUPATIONAL CURRICULUMS IN HIGHER EDUCATION.

    Later HE 5.254:54012

FS 5.254:54013   • **Item 460-A-54**
EARNED DEGREES CONFERRED. 1948–   [Annual]

    Later HE 5.254:54013

FS 5.254:54019   • **Item 460-A-54**
ENROLLMENT FOR MASTERS AND HIGHER DEGREES, FALL (year), FINAL REPORT. 1959–   [Annual]

    Later HE 5.254:54019

OPENING FALL ENROLLMENT IN HIGHER EDUCATION. [Annual]

    Later HE 5.254:54023

FS 5.255:nos.
MISCELLANEOUS PUBLICATIONS: STUDENT FINANCIAL ASSISTANCE, OE 55,000-55,999.

    Later HE 5.255

FS 5.255:55001   • **Item 460-A-55**
NATIONAL DEFENSE STUDENT LOAN PROGRAM, INCLUDING PARTICIPATING INSTITUTIONS. 1958/59–   [Irregular]

    Later HE 5.255:55001

FS 5.255:55017   • **Item 460-A-55**
NATIONAL DEFENSE GRADUATE FELLOWSHIPS, GRADUATE PROGRAMS.

    Later HE 5.255:55027

FS 5.255:55027   • **Item 460-A-55**
FINANCIAL ASSISTANCE FOR COLLEGE STUDENTS, UNDERGRADUATE AND 1ST-PROFESSIONAL.

    Later HE 5.255:55027

FS 5.255:55034   • **Item 460-A-55**
MODERN FOREIGN LANGUAGE FELLOWSHIP PROGRAM, NATIONAL DEFENSE EDUCATION ACT, TITLE 6 AND NDEA RELATED AWARDS UNDER FULLBRIGHT-HAYS ACT. [Annual]

    Later HE 5.255:55034

FS 5.256:nos.
MISCELLANEOUS PUBLICATIONS: COURSES OF STUDY, SUBJECTS, OE 56,000– 56,999.

    Later HE 5.256

FS 5.257:nos.
MISCELLANEOUS PUBLICATIONS: JUNIOR COLLEGES, COMMUNITY COLLEGES, POST HIGH SCHOOL COURSES, OE 57,000– 57,999.

    Later HE 5.257

FS 5.258:nos.
MISCELLANEOUS PUBLICATIONS: TEACHER EDUCATION, OE 58,000– 58,999.

    Later HE 5.258

FS 5.280
VOCATIONAL EDUCATION. MISCELLANEOUS, OE 80,000– 80,999.

FS 5.280:[nos.]   • **Item 460-A-80**
AREA VOCATIONAL EDUCATION PROGRAM SERIES. 1–   1960–   [Irregular]

    Later HE 5.280

FS 5.280:80008   • **Item 460-A-80**
DIGEST OF ANNUAL REPORTS OF STATE BOARDS FOR VOCATIONAL EDUCATION TO THE OFFICE OF EDUCATION, DIVISION OF VOCATIONAL EDUCATION. 1933–   [Annual]

    Later 5.280:80008

FS 5.281:nos.
MISCELLANEOUS PUBLICATIONS: AGRICULTURAL EDUCATION, OE 81,000– 81,999.

    Later HE 5.281

FS 5.281:81002   • **Item 460-A-81**
SUMMARIES OF STUDIES IN AGRICULTURAL EDUCATION, SUPPLEMENTS. 1–   1943–   [Annual]

    Later HE 5.281:81002

FS 5.282:nos.
MISCELLANEOUS PUBLICATIONS: DISTRIBUTIVE EDUCATION, OE 82,000– 82999.

    Later HE 5.282

FS 5.283:nos.
MISCELLANEOUS PUBLICATIONS: HOME ECONOMICS EDUCATION, OE 83,000– 83,999.

    Later HE 5.283

FS 5.283:83008   • **Item 460-A-83**
HOME ECONOMICS IN INSTITUTIONS GRANTING BACHELOR'S OR HIGHER DEGREES. [Biennial]

    Later HE 5.283:83008

FS 5.284:nos.
MISCELLANEOUS PUBLICATIONS: TRADE & INDUSTRIAL EDUCATION, OE 84,000– 84,999.

    Later HE 5.284

FS 5.285:nos.
MISCELLANEOUS PUBLICATIONS: PRACTICAL NURSE EDUCATION, OE 85,000– 85,999.

    Later HE 5.285

FS 5.286:nos.
MISCELLANEOUS PUBLICATIONS: BUSINESS EDUCATION, OE 86,000-86,999.

    Later HE 5.286

FS 5.287:nos.
MISCELLANEOUS PUBLICATIONS: MANPOWER DEVELOPMENT AND TRAINING, OE 87,000– 87,999.

    Later HE 5.287

NATIONAL YOUTH ADMINISTRATION (1939– 1942)

CREATION AND AUTHORITY

    The National Youth Administration (Y 3.N 21/4) was transferred to the Federal Security Agency by Reorganization Plan No. 1 of 1939, effective July 1, 1939. It was transferred to the War Manpower Commission (Pr 32.5250) by Executive Order 9247 of September 17, 1942, where it functioned within the Bureau of Training.

FS 6.1:date
ANNUAL REPORTS.

    Earlier Y 3.N 21/14:1
    Later Pr 32.5251

FS 6.2:CT
GENERAL PUBLICATIONS.

    Earlier Y 3.N 21/14:2
    Later Pr 32.5252

FS 6.4:nos.
CIRCULARS.

FS 6.6:CT
REGULATIONS, RULES, AND INSTRUCTIONS.

FS 6.7:nos.
LETTERS (to State Youth Administrators).

    Earlier Y 3.N 21/14:7

FS 6.8:nos.
INFORMATION EXCHANGE BULLETINS.

FS 6.9:nos.
RELATED TRAINING LETTERS.

FS 6.10:CT
TOMORROW'S WORK (by industries).

FS 6.11:nos.
MODERN WORLD AT WORK.

FS 6.12:nos.
HANDBOOK OF PROCEDURES MEMORANDUM.

    Later Pr 32.5257

FS 6.13:nos.
WEEKLY SUMMARIES OF EDITORIAL COMMENT ON NATIONAL YOUTH ADMINISTRATION.

    Proc. Pubs. design. EC-no.

FS 6.14:nos.
TECHNICAL INFORMATION CIRCULARS

    Earlier Y 3.N 21/14:11

FS 6.15:CT
ADDRESSES.

FS 6.16:nos.
SAFETY BULLETINS.

FS 6.17:nos.
MANUAL OF FINANCE AND STATISTICS MEMORANDUM.

    Later Pr 32.5258

FOOD AND DRUG ADMINISTRATION
(1940–1946)

CREATION AND AUTHORITY

The Food and Drug Administration (A 46) was transferred to the Federal Security Agency by Reorganization Plan No. 4 of 1940, effective June 30, 1940, Reorganization Plan No. 2 of 1946, effective July 16, 1946, placed the Administration under the newly established Office of Special Services (FS 13.100)

FS 7.1:date
ANNUAL REPORTS.

Earlier A 46.1
Later FS 13.101

FS 7.2:CT
GENERAL PUBLICATIONS.

Earlier A 46.2
Later FS 13.102

FS 7.4:nos.
FOOD AND DRUG CIRCULARS.

FS 7.6:CT
REGULATIONS, RULES, AND INSTRUCTIONS.

Later FS 13.106

FS 7.7:vol.
FOOD AND DRUG REVIEW. [Confidential]

Earlier A 46.5
Later FS 13.107

FS 7.8:nos.
SERVICE AND REGULATORY ANNOUNCEMENTS, FOOD, DRUG, AND COSMETIC.

Earlier A 46.19
Later FS 13.115

FS 7.9:nos.
NOTICE OF JUDGMENT UNDER CAUSTIC POISON ACT.

Earlier A 46.9
Later FS 13.112

FS 7.10:nos.
NOTICES OF JUDGMENT UNDER FEDERAL FOOD, DRUG AND COSMETIC ACT, FOODS.

Earlier A 46.20
Later FS 13.109

FS 7.11:nos.
NOTICES OF JUDGMENT UNDER FOOD AND DRUGS ACT.
Earlier A 46.6

FS 7.12:nos.
NOTICES OF JUDGMENT UNDER FEDERAL FOOD, DRUG, AND COSMETIC ACT: DRUGS AND DEVICES.
Earlier A 46.22

FS 7.13:nos.
NOTICES OF JUDGMENT UNDER FEDERAL FOOD, DRUG, AND COSMETIC ACT: COSMETICS.
Earlier A 46.21
Later FS 13.113

FS 7.14:nos.
SERVICE AND REGULATORY ANNOUNCEMENTS, TEA.
Earlier A 46.14

FS 7.15:nos.
MISCELLANEOUS PUBLICATIONS.

Later FS 13.111

FS 7.16:nos.
MICROANALYTICAL DIVISION PUBLICATIONS.

Earlier A 46.17

FS 7.17:nos.
NOTICES OF JUDGMENT SUMARIZING JUDICIAL REVIEW OF ORDERS UNDER SEC. 701 (F) OF FEDERAL FOOD, DRUG AND COSMETIC ACT.

Later FS 13.116

COORDINATOR OF HEALTH, WELFARE, AND RELATED DEFENSE ACTIVITIES OFFICE
(1941)

FS 8.1:date
ANNUAL REPORTS.

FS 8.2:CT
GENERAL PUBLICATIONS.

FS 8.7:CT
ADDRESSES.

FS 8.8:nos.
RECREATION BULLETINS.

Later Pr 32.4509

FS 8.9:nos.
FAMILY SECURITY CONFIDENTIAL BULLETINS.

Later Pr 32.451

FS 8.10
NEWS LETTER. [Admin.]

OFFICE OF COMMUNITY WAR SERVICES
(1943–1946)

CREATION AND AUTHORITY

The Office of Community War Services was established as an integral part of the Office of the Administrator under Executive Order 9338 of April 29, 1943, and a Federal Security Agency order implementing it, to enable the Administrator to carry out recreation activities under provisions of Executive Order 8890 of September 3, 1941. The Office was terminated December 31, 1946, pursuant to act of Congress, approved July 26, 1946 (60 Stat. 695).

FS 9.1:date
ANNUAL REPORTS.

Earlier Pr 32.4501

FS 9.2:CT
GENERAL PUBLICATIONS.

Earlier Pr 32.4502

FS 9.6:CT
REGULATIONS, RULES, AND INSTRUCTIONS

Includes Handbooks and Manuals.
Earlier Pr 32.4506

FS 9.7:CT
RECREATION BULLETINS.

Earlier Pr 32.4509

FS 9.8:CT
ADDRESSES.

FS 9.9:nos.
[CONTACT REPORTS].

OFFICE OF VOCATIONAL REHABILITATION
(1943–1946)

CREATION AND AUTHORITY

The Office of Vocational Rehabilitation was established within the Federal Security Agency by Agency Order 3, Supplement 1, dated September 4, 1943. Reorganization Plan No. 2 of 1946, effective July 16, 1946, placed the Office under the newly established Office of Special Services (FS 13.200).

FS 10.1:date
ANNUAL REPORTS.

Later FS 13.201

FS 10.2:CT
GENERAL PUBLICATIONS.

Later FS 13.202

FS 10.6:CT
REGULATIONS, RULES, AND INSTRUCTIONS.

Later FS 13.206

FS 10.7:nos.
VOCATIONAL REHABILITATION SERIES, BULLETINS.

Earlier FS 5.28

FS 10.8:CT
ADDRESSES.

Later FS 13.208

ST. ELIZABETH'S HOSPITAL
(1940–1969)

FS 11.1:date
ANNUAL REPORTS.

Earlier I 1.14/1

FS 11.2:CT
GENERAL PUBLICATIONS.

Earlier I 1.14/2

COMMITTEE ON PHYSICAL FITNESS (1943–1945)

CREATION AND AUTHORITY

The Committee on Physical Fitness was established within the Federal Security Agency by Executive Order 9338 of April 19, 1943, to succeed the Office of Defense Health and Welfare Services. The Committee was terminated on June 30, 1945.

FS 12.1:date
ANNUAL REPORTS.

FS 12.2:CT
GENERAL PUBLICATIONS.

FS 12.6:CT
REGULATIONS, RULES, AND INSTRUCTIONS.

OFFICE OF SPECIAL SERVICES (1946–1950)

CREATION AND AUTHORITY

The Office of Special Services was established within the Federal Security Agency pursuant to Reorganization Plan No. 2 of 1946, effective July 16, 1946, to supervise the Food and Drug Administration and the Office of Vocation Rehabilitation. The Office was abolished in 1950.

FS 13.1:date
ANNUAL REPORTS.

FS 13.2:CT
GENERAL PUBLICATIONS.

FOOD AND DRUG ADMINISTRATION (1946–1969)

CREATION AND AUTHORITY

The Food and Drug Administration (FS 7) was placed under the Office of Special Services by Reorganization Plan No. 2 of 1946, effective July 16, 1946. On April 11, 1953, it was placed under the Public Health Service (HE 20.1200) in the newly created Department of Health, Education and Welfare.

FS 13.101
ANNUAL REPORTS. 1928–   [Annual]

Later HE 20.1201

FS 13.102:CT
GENERAL PUBLICATIONS.

Later HE 20.1202

FS 13.102:St 2   **• Item 475**
DIRECTORY, STATE OFFICIALS CHARGED WITH ENFORCEMENT OF FOOD, DRUG, COSMETIC, AND FEED LAWS. [Irregular]

FS 13.103/2   **• Item 475-D**
FOOD AND DRUG TECHNICAL BULLETINS. 1– [Irregular]

Later HE 20.4040

FS 13.104/2
INVESTIGATIONAL DRUG CIRCULARS.

FS 13.105:CT
LAWS.

FS 13.105:F 73   **• Item 475-B**
FEDERAL FOOD, DRUG, AND COSMETIC ACT, AS AMENDED, AND GENERAL REGULATIONS FOR ITS ENFORCEMENT. 1958– [Irregular]

FS 13.106:CT
REGULATIONS, RULES, AND INSTRUCTIONS.

Earlier FS 7.6
Later HE 20.4006

FS 13.106/2   **• Item 480**
F.D.C. REGS. [Food, Drug, and Cosmetic Regulations]. [Irregular]

Earlier designated Service and Regulatory Announcements and classified FS 13.115

FS 13.106/2:1/2   **• Item 480**
Part 1. GENERAL REGULATIONS FOR THE ENFORCEMENT OF THE FEDERAL FOOD, DRUG, AND COSMETIC ACT. [Irregular]

FS 13.107:v.nos.
FOOD AND DRUG REVIEW. [Monthly]

Earlier FS 7.7

FS 13.108   **• Item 477**
DRUG AND DEVICES, DDNJ(series). 1– 1940– [Irregular]

FS 13.109
FOODS, FNJ- (series). 1– 1940– [Irregular]

FS 13.110:nos.
SERVICE AND REGULATORY ANNOUNCEMENTS, CAUSTIC POISON.

Earlier A 46.13

FS 13.111   **• Item 475-A**
FDA PUBLICATIONS (series). 1– [Irregular]

Earlier FS 7.15
Later HE 20.4015

FS 13.112:nos.
NOTICES OF JUDGMENT UNDER CAUSTIC POISON ACT.

Earlier FS 7.9

FS 13.112/2
NOTICES OF JUDGMENT UNDER FEDERAL HAZARDOUS SUBSTANCES LABELING ACT. 1963–   [Irregular]

FS 13.113:nos.
NOTICES OF JUDGMENT UNDER FEDERAL FOOD, DRUG AND COSMETIC ACT: COSMETICS.

Earlier FS 7.13

FS 13.114:nos.
SERVICE AND REGULATORY ANNOUNCEMENTS, IMPORT MILK.

Earlier A 46.11

FS 13.115:nos.
SERVICE AND REGULATORY ANNOUNCEMENTS: FOOD, DRUG, AND COSMETIC.

Earlier FS 7

FS 13.116   **• Item 477**
NOTICES OF JUDGMENT, SUMMARIZING JUDICIAL REVIEW OF ORDERS UNDER SEC. 701 (f) OF THE FEDERAL FOOD, DRUG, AND COSMETIC ACT. 1– 1944–   [Irregular]

Earlier FS 7.17

FS 13.117
LEAFLETS. 1–   [Irregular]

FS 13.118   **• Item 478-A**
REPORT ON ENFORCEMENT AND COMPLIANCE. [Monthly]

FS 13.119:CT
HANDBOOKS, MANUALS, GUIDES.

Later HE 20.1208

FS 13.120
COMMERCIAL IMPORT DETENTIONS. [Monthly]

Later HE 20.1212, HE 20.4017

FS 13.120
REPORT OF IMPORT DETENTIONS. 1963– [Biweekly]

FS 13.121
FDA MEMO FOR CONSUMERS, CM- (series). 1– 1962–   [Irregular]

FS 13.122   **• Item 480-A**
STUDENT REFERENCE SHEETS, SR- (series). 1– 1965–   [Irregular]

FS 13.123
MONTHLY REPORT ON ADVERSE REACTIONS TO DRUGS AND THERAPEUTIC DEVICES.

FS 13.124
RADIO-TV PACKET. [Quarterly]

FS 13.125:CT
BIBLIOGRAPHIES AND LISTS OF PUBLICATIONS.

Later HE 20.4016

FS 13.126:v.nos.&nos.
INTERBUREAU BYLINES.

FS 13.127
FDA POSTERS. 1– 1966– [Irregular]

FS 13.128   **• Item 475-H**
FDA PAPERS. v. 1– 1967– [10 times a year]

Later HE 20.1210, HE 20.4010

FS 13.129   **• Item 475-I**
FDA'S LIFE PROTECTION SERIES. 1967– [Irregular]

FS 13.130   **• Item 475-J**
FACT SHEETS. 1– 1966– [Irregular]

FS 13.130/2:date
BDAC BULLETIN.

FS 13.131:CT
ADDRESSES.

FS 13.132   **• Item 475-L**
FDA CLINICAL EXPERIENCE ABSTRACTS. [Biweekly]
Later HE 20.1209, HE 20.4009

FS 13.133:v.nos.&nos.
HEALTH ASPECTS OF PESTICIDES, ABSTRACT BULLETIN.
Later HE 20.1209

FS 13.134:date   **• Item 475-N**
NATIONAL DRUG CODE DIRECTORY
Later HE 20.4012

FS 13.135:date
INTERSTATE SHELLFISH SHIPPERS LIST. [Monthly]

Earlier FS 2.16
Later HE 20.1213

VOCATIONAL REHABILITATION ADMINISTRATION (1962– 1967)

CREATION AND AUTHORITY

The Office of Vocational Rehabilitation (FS 10) was placed under the Office of Special Services by Reorganization Plan No. 2 of 1946, effective July 16, 1946. On April 11, 1953, it became a part of the newly created Department of Health, Education, and Welfare. In 1962 it was redesignated the Vocational Rehabilitation Administration. It was abolished on August 15, 1967.

FS 13.201:date
ANNUAL REPORTS.

Earlier FS 10.1

FS 13.202:CT
GENERAL PUBLICATIONS.

Earlier FS 10.2

FS 13.202:R 31/2   • Item 529
VOCATIONAL REHABILITATION ADMINISTRATION RESEARCH AND DEMONSTRATION PROJECTS. 1960–

FS 13.204:nos.
VR-ISC [Information Service Circular] (series).

FS 13.205:CT
LAWS.

FS 13.206:CT
REGULATIONS, RULES, AND INSTRUCTIONS.

Earlier FS 10.6

FS 13.207:nos.
REHABILITATION SERVICE SERIES.

FS 13.208:CT
ADDRESSES.

Earlier FS 10.8

FS 13.209:nos.
REHABILITATION STANDARDS MEMORANDUM.

FS 13.210:v.nos.
SELECTED REHABILITATION ABSTRACTS. [Bimonthly]

This is Rehabilitation Service series No. 26. See FS 13.207 for other numbers in the Rehabilitation Service series.

FS 13.211:nos.
INFORMATION SERVICE SERIES.

FS 13.212:nos.
ADMINISTRATIVE SERVICE SERIES.

FS 13.213:nos.
STATE EXCHANGE SERVICE ITEM SERIES. [Admin.]

FS 13.214:nos.
DIRECTOR'S LETTERS. [Admin.]

FS 13.215:nos.
GTP [Guidance, Training, and Placement] BULLETINS.

FS 13.216:v.nos.&nos.
REHABILITATION RECORD. [Bimonthly]

FS 13.217:date
HANDBOOK ON PROGRAMS OF OFFICE OF VOCATIONAL REHABILITATION.

FS 13.217/2:CT
HANDBOOKS, MANUALS, GUIDES.

FS 13.218:CT
BIBLIOGRAPHIES AND LISTS OF PUBLICATIONS.

FS 13.219:nos.
PROGRAM ADMINISTRATION REVIEW, PAR (nos). [Biennial]

FS 13.220:nos.
PUBLICITY POINTERS FOR STATE REHABILITATION DIRECTORS, LETTERS.

FS 13.221:v.nos.&nos.
VRA BULLETIN BOARD.

Earlier L 5.14

BUREAU OF EMPLOYEES' COMPENSATION (1946– 1950)

CREATION AND AUTHORITY

The Bureau of Employees' Compensation was established within the Federal Security Agency under Reorganization Plan No. 3 of 1946, effective July 16, 1946, to perform the functions of the United States Employee's Compensation Commission, which was abolished under the same reorganization plan. Reorganization Plan No. 19 of 1950, effective May 24, 1950, transferred the Bureau to the Department of Labor (L 26).

FS 13.301:date
ANNUAL REPORTS.

Earlier EC 1.1
Later L 26.1

FS 13.302:CT
GENERAL PUBLICATIONS.

Earlier EC 1.2
Later L 26.2

FS 13.305:CT
LAWS

Later L 26.5

FS 13.307:v.nos.
SAFETY BULLETIN.

WELFARE ADMINISTRATION (1963– 1967)

CREATION AND AUTHORITY

The Welfare Administration was established within the Department of Health, Education, and Welfare by the Secretary's reorganization of January 28, 1963. Components consisted of the Bureau of Family Services, Children's Bureau, Office of Juvenile Delinquency and Youth Development, and the Cuban Refugee Staff. Functions of the Administration reassigned to the Social and Rehabilitation Service (FS 17) by Department Reorganization of August 15, 1967.

FS 14.1:date
ANNUAL REPORTS.

FS 14.2:CT
GENERAL PUBLICATIONS.

FS 14.8:CT
HANDBOOKS, MANUALS, GUIDES.

FS 14.9:nos.
AGING. [Monthly]

Earlier FS 1.13
Later FS 15.10

FS 14.9/2:date
HIGHLIGHTS OF LEGISLATION ON AGING.

Earlier FS 1.13/4

FS 14.9/3:nos.
FACTS ON AGING.

Earlier FS 13.5

FS 14.9/4:CT
SELECTED REFERENCES ON AGING.

Earlier FS 1.18/2
Later FS 15.12/2

FS 14.9/5:nos.
PATTERNS FOR PROGRESS IN AGING, CASE STUDIES.

Earlier FS 1.13/3
Later FS 15.11

FS 14.10:v.nos.
WELFARE IN REVIEW. [Monthly]

FS 14.10/2:date
WELFARE IN REVIEW, STATISTICAL SUPPLEMENT.

FS 14.11:CT
ADDRESSES.

FS 14.12:CT
FEDERAL ASSISTANCE FOR PROJECTS IN AGING.

FS 14.13:CT
BIBLIOGRAPHIES AND LISTS OF PUBLICATIONS.

FS 14.14:nos.
WELFARE RESEARCH REPORTS.

FS 14.15:date
RESETTLEMENT RECAP, PERIODIC REPORT FROM CUBAN REFUGEE CENTER.

Administrative.

FS 14.16:nos.
PUBLIC INFORMATION COMMUNICATOR (series).

FS 14.17:CT
PAROLE SERIES.

FS 14.17/2:CT
CORRECTION SERIES.

FS 14.17/3:CT
LEGAL SERIES.

FS 14.17/4:CT
STUDIES IN DELINQUENCY.

CHILDREN'S BUREAU (1963– 1967)

CREATION AND AUTHORITY

The Children's Bureau (FS 3.200) was reassigned within the Department to the Welfare Department on January 28, 1963. The Bureau was placed under the newly created Social and Rehabilitation Service (FS 17.200) by Department reorganization on August 15, 1967.

FS 14.101:date
ANNUAL REPORT.
Earlier FS 3.201

FS 14.102:CT
GENERAL PUBLICATIONS.

Earlier FS 3.202

FS 14.102:T 68   • Item 452
DIRECTORY OF PUBLIC TRAINING SCHOOLS
SERVING DELINQUENT CHILDREN.
[Irregular]

FS 14.108:CT
HANDBOOKS, MANUALS, GUIDES.

Earlier FS 3.206/2

FS 14.109:v.nos.&nos.
CHILDREN, INTERDISCIPLINARY JOURNAL FOR
PROFESSIONS SERVING CHILDREN. [Bimonthly]

Earlier FS 3.207/2

FS 14.110:CT
ADDRESSES. [Irregular]

Earlier FS 3.225

FS 14.110/2:CT
JESSIE M. BIERMAN ANNUAL LECTURES IN
MATERNAL AND CHILD HEALTH.

FS 14.111:nos.
PUBLICATIONS (numbered).

Earlier FS 3.209

FS 14.112   • Item 450
BIBLIOGRAPHIES AND LISTS OF PUBLICATIONS.
[Annual]

Earlier FS 3.213/2

FS 14.113:nos.
STATISTICAL SERIES.

Earlier FS 3.214
Later FS 17.212

FS 14.114:nos.
RESEARCH RELATING TO CHILDREN.

Earlier FS 3.220
Later FS 17.211

FS 14.114/2   • Item 453-A
RESEARCH RELATING TO SPECIAL GROUPS OF
CHILDREN. 1–   1960–   [Irregular]

FS 14.115   • Item 452-A
JUVENILE DELINQUENCY: FACTS AND FACETS. 1–
1960–   [Irregular]

FS 14.116:nos.
WORK WITH CHILDREN COMING BEFORE COURTS.

Earlier FS 3.233

FS 14.117   • Item 452-B
HEADLINER SERIES. 1–   1962–   [Irregular]

FS 14.118:nos.
FOLDERS.

Earlier FS 3.210

FS 14.119:CT
FACTS ABOUT CHILDREN.

FS 14.120:date
PROJECT ON COST ANALYSIS IN CHILDREN'S IN-
STITUTIONS.

Earlier FS 14.102:In 7

FS 14.121:nos.
CHILD WELFARE REPORT.

Earlier FS 3.215

BUREAU OF FAMILY SERVICES
(1962–1967)

CREATION AND AUTHORITY

The Bureau of Family Services was established within the Welfare Administration of the
Department of Health, Education and Welfare by
administrative order effective January 1, 1962,
to succeed the Bureau of Public Assistance.
Abolished by Secretary's reorganization of August 15, 1967 and functions transferred to the
Social and Rehabilitation Service (FS 17).

FS 14.201:date
ANNUAL REPORTS.

FS 14.202:CT
GENERAL PUBLICATIONS.

Formerly in FS 3.2

FS 14.208:CT
HANDBOOKS, MANUALS, GUIDES.

FS 14.208/2:CT
MEDICAL CARE IN PUBLIC ASSISTANCE, GUIDES
AND RECOMMENDED STANDARDS.

Earlier FS 3.6/3:M 46 and FS 3.6/3:M 46/2

FS 14.208/3:CT
MENTAL HEALTH IN PUBLIC ASSISTANCE (series).

FS 14.208/4:CT
STAFF DEVELOPMENT SERIES.

FS 14.209:date
ADVANCE RELEASE OF STATISTICS ON PUBLIC
ASSISTANCE. [Monthly]

Earlier FS 3.14/2

FS 14.210:date
UNEMPLOYED-PARENT SEGMENT OF AID TO FAMI-
LIES WITH DEPENDENT CHILDREN. [Monthly]

Earlier FS 3.14/2

FS 14.211:date
STATE MAXIMUMS AND OTHER METHODS OF
LIMITING MONTHLY PAYMENTS OF RECIPIENTS
OF SPECIAL TYPES OF PUBLIC ASSISTANCE,
ANNUAL RELEASE.

FS 14.212:date
PUBLIC ASSISTANCE, ANNUAL STATISTICAL DATA,
CALENDAR YEAR.

FS 14.213:nos.
PUBLIC ASSISTANCE REPORTS.

Earlier FS 3.13

FS 14.213/2:nos.
PUBLIC ASSISTANCE INFORMATION, PAI (series).

Earlier FS 3.13/2

FS 14.214:date
REASONS FOR OPENING AND CLOSING PUBLIC
ASSISTANCE CASES.

Earlier FS 3.45

FS 14.215:date
SOURCE OF FUNDS EXPENDED FOR PUBLIC AS-
SISTANCE PAYMENTS.

Earlier FS 14.202:P 96

FS 14.216:CT
ADDRESSES.

FS 14.217:CT
BIBLIOGRAPHIES AND LISTS OF PUBLICATIONS.

FS 14.218:date
MEDICAL ASSISTANCE FOR THE AGED, FACT SHEET.
[Semiannual]

FS 14.219:date
IMPACT ON PUBLIC ASSISTANCE CASELOADS OF
(a) TRAINING PROGRAMS UNDER MANPOWER
DEVELOPMENT AND TRAINING ACT AND AREA
REDEVELOPMENT ACT, AND (b) PUBLIC AS-
SISTANCE WORK AND TRAINING PROGRAMS.
[Quarterly]

Earlier FS 14.202:P 96/6

FS 14.220:date
PROGRESS REPORT ON STAFF DEVELOPMENT.
[Annual]

FS 14.221:date
PUBLIC ASSISTANCE, VENDOR PAYMENTS FOR
MEDICAL CARE BY TYPE OF SERVICE, FISCAL
AND CALENDAR YEARS.

Earlier FS 14.202:M 46

ADMINISTRATION ON AGING
(1965–1967)

CREATION AND AUTHORITY

The Administration on Aging was established
by the Secretary of Health, Education, and Welfare on October 1, 1965, to carry out the provisions of the Older Americans Act of 1965 (79
Stat. 218; 42 U.S.C. 3001 note). The Administration was reassigned to the Social and Rehabilitation Service (FS 17.300) by Department reorganization order of August 15, 1967.

FS 15.1:date
ANNUAL REPORTS.

FS 15.2:CT
GENERAL PUBLICATIONS.

FS 15.8:CT
HANDBOOKS, MANUALS, GUIDES.

FS 15.9:CT
ADDRESSES.

FS 15.10:nos.
AGING.

Earlier FS 14.9

FS 15.11:nos.
PATTERNS FOR PROGRESS IN AGING.

Earlier FS 14.9/5

FS 15.12:CT
BIBLIOGRAPHIES AND LISTS OF PUBLICATIONS.

FS 15.12/2:CT
SELECTED REFERENCES ON AGING.

Earlier FS 14.9/4

FS 15.13:CT
FEDERAL FINANCIAL ASSISTANCE FOR PROJECTS
IN AGING.

FEDERAL WATER POLLUTION CONTROL ADMINISTRATION (1965– 1966)

CREATION AND AUTHORITY

The Federal Water Pollution Control Administration was established within the Department of Health, Education, and Welfare by section 2 of the Water Quality act of 1965 (79 Stat. 903), approved October 2, 1965, effective December 31, 1965. It became a bureau in the Department of the Interior (I 67) under Reorganization Plan 2 of 1966, effective May 1966.

FS 16.1:date
ANNUAL REPORTS.

Later I 67.1

FS 16.2:CT
GENERAL PUBLICATIONS.

Later I 67.2

FS 16.5:CT
LAWS.

FS 16.9:date
BUILDING FOR CLEAN WATER, REPORT ON FEDERAL INCENTIVE GRANTS FOR MUNICIPAL WASTE TREATMENT.

Earlier FS 2.64/6

SOCIAL AND REHABILITATION SERVICE (1967– 1969)

CREATION AND AUTHORITY

The Social and Rehabilitation Service was established within the Department of Health, Education and Welfare on August 15, 1967, to succeed the Welfare Administration (FS 14). [In 1970, the SuDocs class number became HE 17].

FS 17.1:date
ANNUAL REPORTS.

FS 17.2:CT
GENERAL PUBLICATIONS.

Later HE 17.2

FS 17.2:M 46/2
MEDICAL ASSISTANCE FINANCED UNDER PUBLIC ASSISTANCE TITLES OF SOCIAL SECURITY ACT. [Annual]

Later HE 17.2:M 46/2

FS 17.6:CT
REGULATIONS, RULES, AND INSTRUCTIONS.

Later HE 17.6

FS 17.8:CT
HANDBOOKS, MANUALS, GUIDES.

Later HE 17.8

FS 17.8/2:CT
MANUALS FOR VOLUNTEER PROBATION PROGRAMS.
Later HE 17.8/2

FS 17.9:v.nos.&nos.   • Item 532-A-2
WELFARE IN REVIEW. v. 1– 1963– [Bimonthly]

Later HE 17.9

FS 17.10:date
ADVANCE RELEASE OF STATISTICS ON PUBLIC ASSISTANCE. [Monthly]

Earlier FS 14.209

FS 17.11:date
UNEMPLOYED-PARENT SEGMENT OF AID TO FAMILIES WITH DEPENDENT CHILDREN. [Monthly]

Earlier FS 14.210

FS 17.12
STATISTICAL REPORT ON SOCIAL SERVICES, FORM FS-2069, QUARTER ENDED (date). [Quarterly]

FS 17.13:date
PUBLIC ASSISTANCE, ANNUAL STATISTICAL DATA.

FS 17.13/2
PUBLIC WELFARE PERSONNEL, ANNUAL STATISTICAL DATA, FISCAL YEAR (date). [Annual]

FS 17.14
ADDRESSES. [Irregular]

Later HE 17.14

FS 17.15:date
SOCIAL AND REHABILITATION SERVICE RESEARCH AND DEMONSTRATION PROJECTS.

Earlier FS 13.202:R 31/3
Later HE 17.15

FS 17.16:CT
PAROLE DECISION MAKING PAROLE SERIES.

Earlier FS 14.17
Later HE 17.16

FS 17.16/2:CT
CORRECTION SERIES.

Earlier FS 14.17/2
Later HE 17.16/2

FS 17.16/3:CT
LEGAL SERIES.

Earlier FS 14.17/3
Later HE 17.16/3

FS 17.16/4:CT
STUDIES IN DELINQUENCY.

Earlier FS 14.17/4
Later HE 17.16/4

FS 17.17:CT
BIBLIOGRAPHIES AND LISTS OF PUBLICATIONS.

Earlier FS 14.13
Later HE 17.17

FS 17.18
RESEARCH BRIEFS. [Irregular]

Later HE 17.18

FS 17.19   • Item 519
PUBLIC ASSISTANCE REPORTS. 1– [Irregular]

REHABILITATION SERVICES ADMINISTRATION (1967– 1969)

CREATION AND AUTHORITY

The Rehabilitation Services Administration was established within the Social and Rehabilitation Service on August 15, 1967 to succeed the Vocational Rehabilitation Administration (FS 13.200), which was abolished., [In 1970, the SuDocs class number became HE 17.100].

FS 17.101   • Item 528
ANNUAL REPORTS. [Annual]

Later HE 17.101

FS 17.102:CT
GENERAL PUBLICATIONS.

Later HE 17.102

FS 17.106:CT
REGULATIONS, RULES, AND INSTRUCTIONS.

Earlier FS 13.206
Later HE 17.106

FS 17.108:CT
HANDBOOKS, MANUALS, GUIDES.

Earlier FS 13.217/2
Later HE 17.108

FS 17.109:v.nos.&nos.   • Item 531-A
REHABILITATION RECORD. v. 1– 1960– [Bimonthly]

Earlier FS 13.216
Later HE 17.109

FS 17.110/2:nos.
INFORMATION SERVICE SERIES.

Earlier FS 13.211

FS 17.110/3   • Item 531
REHABILITATION SERVICES SERIES. 1– 1946– [Irregular]

Earlier FS 13.207
Later HE 17.110/3

FS 17.111
CASELOAD STATISTICS OF STATE VOCATIONAL REHABILITATION AGENCIES. [Annual]

Earlier FS 3.202:C 26

FS 17.112:CT
BIBLIOGRAPHIES AND LISTS OF PUBLICATIONS.

Earlier FS 13.218
Later HE 17.112

FS 17.113:v.nos.&nos.
MENTAL RETARDATION ABSTRACTS. [Quarterly]

Earlier FS 2.22/52
Later HE 17.113

CHILDREN'S BUREAU
(1967–1969)

CREATION AND AUTHORITY

The Children's Bureau (FS 14.100) was transferred to the Social and Rehabilitation Service on August 15, 1967. [In 1970, the SuDocs class number became HE 21.100]

FS 17.201:date
ANNUAL REPORT.

Earlier FS 14.101

FS 17.202:CT
GENERAL PUBLICATIONS.

Earlier FS 14.102
Later HE 21.102

FS 17.208:CT
HANDBOOKS, MANUALS, GUIDES.

Earlier FS 14.108

FS 17.209   • Item 499
CHILDREN. v. 1–   1954–   [Bimonthly]

Earlier FS 14.109
Later HE 21.9

FS 17.210   • Item 453
PUBLICATIONS (series). 1–   1912–   [Irregular]

Earlier FS 14.111
Later HE 21.100

FS 17.211   • Item 453-A
RESEARCH RELATING TO CHILDREN. 1–   1950–   [Irregular]

Earlier FS 14.114
Later HE 21.112

FS 17.212:CT
BIBLIOGRAPHIES AND LISTS OF PUBLICATIONS.

Earlier FS 14.112

FS 17.213   • Item 454
STATISTICAL SERIES. 1–   1947–

Later HE 17.23

FS 17.213:nos.   • Item 454
CHILD WELFARE STATISTICS. [Annual]

FS 17.213:nos.   • Item 454
CRIPPLED CHILDREN'S PROGRAM. [Annual]

FS 17.213:nos.   • Item 454
JUVENILE COURT STATISTICS. [Annual]

Later HE 17.23

FS 17.213:nos.   • Item 454
MATERNAL AND CHILD HEALTH SERVICES. [Irregular]

FS 17.213:nos.   • Item 454
PERSONNEL AND PERSONNEL PRACTICES IN PUBLIC INSTITUTIONS FOR DELINQUENT CHILDREN. [Annual]

Earlier FS 14.113

FS 17.214   • Item 453-B
RESEARCH REPORTS. 1–   1967–   [Irregular]

FS 17.215   • Item 451
FOLDERS. 1–   1923–   [Irregular]

Earlier FS 14.118
Later HE 21.111

FS 17.216:nos.
HEADLINER SERIES.

Earlier FS 14.117
Later HE 21.114

FS 17.217:CT
ADDRESSES.

Earlier FS 14.110

ADMINISTRATION ON AGING
(1967–1969)

CREATION AND AUTHORITY

The Administration on Aging (FS 15) was placed within the Social and Rehabilitation Service by Department reorganization of August 15, 1967. [In 1970, the SuDocs class number became HE 17.300].

FS 17.301:date
ANNUAL REPORTS.

Earlier FS 15.1
Later HE 17.301

FS 17.302:CT
GENERAL PUBLICATIONS.

Earlier FS 15.2
Later HE 17.302

FS 17.308:CT
HANDBOOKS, MANUALS, GUIDES.

Earlier FS 15.8
Later HE 17.308

FS 17.309   • Item 444-A
AGING. 1–   1951–   [Monthly]

Earlier FS 15.10
Later HE 17.309

FS 17.310   • Item 447-A-5
DESIGNS FOR ACTION FOR OLDER AMERICAN (series). 1967–   [Irregular]

Later HE 17.310

FS 17.310/2
FEDERAL FINANCIAL ASSISTANCE FOR PROJECTS IN AGING. 1967–   [Irregular]

Earlier FS 15.13

FS 17.311:CT
BIBLIOGRAPHIES AND LISTS OF PUBLICATIONS.

Earlier FS 15.12
Later HE 17.311

FS 17.312
ADDRESSES. [Irregular]

Earlier FS 15.9
Later HE 17.312

ASSISTANCE PAYMENTS ADMINISTRATION
(1967–1969)

CREATION AND AUTHORITY

The Assistance Payments Administration was established within the Social and Rehabilitation Service of the Department of Health, Education, and Welfare by the Secretary's reorganization plan of August 15, 1967. [In 1970, the SuDocs class number became HE 17.400].

FS 17.401:date
ANNUAL REPORT.

Later HE 17.401

FS 17.402:CT
GENERAL PUBLICATIONS.

Later HE 17.402

FS 17.408:CT
HANDBOOKS, MANUALS, GUIDES.

Later HE 17.408

FS 17.409:date
IMPACT ON PUBLIC ASSISTANCE CASELOADS OF: (a) PUBLIC ASSISTANCE WORK AND TRAINING PROGRAMS, AND (b) TRAINING PROGRAMS UNDER MANPOWER DEVELOPMENT AND TRAINING ACT. [Quarterly]

Earlier FS 14.219

FS 17.410:nos.
TREND REPORT, GRAPHIC PRESENTATION OF PUBLIC ASSISTANCE AND RELATED DATA. [Annual]

Later FS 17.612

FS 17.411:date
REASONS FOR OPENING AND CLOSING PUBLIC ASSISTANCE CASES. [Semiannual]

Earlier FS 14.214

MEDICAL SERVICES ADMINISTRATION
(1967–1969)

CREATION AND AUTHORITY

The Medical Services Administration, formerly the Mental Retardation Division of the Bureau of Health Services, was established within the Social and Rehabilitation Service by Secretary's reorganization of August 15, 1967. [In 1970, the SuDocs class number became HE 17.500].

FS 17.501:date
ANNUAL REPORT.

Later HE 17.501

FS 17.502:CT
GENERAL PUBLICATIONS.

Later HE 17.502

NATIONAL CENTER FOR SOCIAL STATISTICS
(1968– 1969)

CREATION AND AUTHORITY

The National Center for Social Statistics was established within the Social and Rehabilitation Service in 1968. [In 1970, the SuDocs class number became HE 17.600].

FS 17.601:date
ANNUAL REPORTS.

Later HE 17.601

FS 17.602:date
GENERAL PUBLICATIONS.

Later 17.602

FS 17.609:date
CHILD CARE ARRANGEMENTS OF AFDC RECIPIENTS UNDER THE WORK INCENTIVE PROGRAM, NCSS REPORT E-4.

Later HE 17.609

FS 17.610
ADVANCE RELEASE OF STATISTICS ON PUBLIC ASSISTANCE. [Monthly]

Earlier FS 17.10
Later HE 17.610

FS 17.611
UNEMPLOYED-PARENT SEGMENT OF AID TO FAMILIES WITH DEPENDENT CHILDREN. [Monthly]

Earlier FS 17.11

FS 17.612:nos.
TREND REPORT: GRAPHIC PRESENTATION OF PUBLIC ASSISTANCE AND RELATED DATA, NCSS REPORT A-4.

Earlier FS 17.410
Later HE 17.611

FS 17.613:date
REASONS FOR OPENING AND CLOSING PUBLIC ASSISTANCE CASES, NCSS REPORT A-5. [Semiannual]

Earlier FS 17.411

FS 17.614:nos.
PROGRAM FACTS ON FEDERALLY AIDED PUBLIC ASSISTANCE INCOME MAINTENANCE PROGRAM, NCSS REPORT A-6.

Later HE 17.614

FS 17.615:date
PUBLIC ASSISTANCE, ANNUAL STATISTICAL DATA, NCSS REPORT A-7.

Earlier FS 17.13

FS 17.616:date
MEDICAL ASSISTANCE FINANCED UNDER ASSISTANCE TITLES OF SOCIAL SECURITY ACT, NCSS REPORT B-1.

Earlier FS 17.2:M 46/2
Later HE 17.616

FS 17.617:date
PUBLIC ASSISTANCE, VENDOR PAYMENTS FOR MEDICAL CARE BY TYPE OF SERVICE, CALENDAR YEAR, NCSS REPORT B-2.

Earlier FS 14.221

FS 17.620:date
MEDICAID, FISCAL YEAR, NCSS REPORT B-5.

FS 17.621:date
MEDICAID AND OTHER MEDICAL FINANCED FROM PUBLIC ASSISTANCE FUNDS, NCSS REPORT B-6.

Later HE 17.621

FS 17.625:date
OAA AND AFDC, COST STANDARDS FOR BASIC NEEDS AND PERCENT OF SUCH STANDARDS MET FOR SPECIFIED TYPES OF CASES, NCSS REPORT D-2.

Earlier FS 17.2:OI 1

FS 17.626:date
STATE MAXIMUMS AND OTHER METHODS FOR LIMITING MONEY PAYMENTS TO RECIPIENTS OF SPECIAL TYPES OF PUBLIC ASSISTANCE, NCSS REPORT D-3.

Earlier FS 17.2:P 96

FS 17.627:date
MONEY PAYMENTS TO RECIPIENTS OF SPECIAL TYPES OF PUBLIC ASSISTANCE, NCSS REPORT D-4.

Earlier FS 14.202:P 96/4

FS 17.628:date
STATISTICAL REPORT ON SOCIAL SERVICES, FORM FS-2069, QUARTER ENDED, NCSS REPORT E-1.

Earlier FS 17.12

FS 17.629:date
PUBLIC WELFARE PERSONNEL, ANNUAL STATISTICAL DATA, NCSS REPORT E-2.
Earlier FS 17.13/2

FS 17.630:date
PROGRESS REPORT ON STAFF DEVELOPMENT FOR FISCAL YEAR, NCSS REPORT E-3.
Earlier FS 17.2:St 1

FS 17.631
SOURCE OF FUNDS EXPENDED FOR PUBLIC ASSISTANCE PAYMENTS. [Annual]
Earlier FS 14.215

FS 17.633:date
PUBLIC ASSISTANCE, COSTS OF STATE AND LOCAL ADMINISTRATION, SERVICES, AND TRAINING, FISCAL YEAR, NCSS REPORT F-3.
Earlier FS 14.202:P 96/7

FS 17.634:date
SOURCE OF FUNDS EXPENDED FOR PUBLIC ASSISTANCE PAYMENTS AND FOR COST OF ADMINISTRATION, SERVICE AND TRAINING, FISCAL YEAR, NCSS REPORT F-2.
Later HE 17.634

FS 17.635
IMPACT ON PUBLIC ASSISTANCE CASELOADS OF (a) PUBLIC ASSISTANCE WORK AND TRAINING PROGRAMS, AND (b) TRAINING PROGRAMS UNDER MANPOWER DEVELOPMENT AND TRAINING ACT. [Quarterly]
Earlier FS 17.409

FS 17.636:date
CONCURRENT RECEIPT OF PUBLIC ASSISTANCE MONEY PAYMENTS AND OLD-AGE, SURVIVORS, AND DISABILITY INSURANCE CASH BENEFITS BY PERSONS AGED 65 OR OVER.
Earlier FS 17.402:P 96

FS 17.638:date
CHILD WELFARE STATISTICS, NCSS REPORT CW-1
Later HE 17.638

FREEDMAN'S SAVINGS AND TRUST COMPANY
(1865– 1920)

CREATION AND AUTHORITY

The Freedmans' Savings and Trust Company was established by act of Congress, approved March 3, 1865. After having failed in 1874, the Company was administered for liquidation until 1920 by the Comptroller of the Currency.

FST 1.1:date
ANNUAL REPORTS.

FST 1.2:CT
GENERAL PUBLICATIONS.

FST 1.3:nos.
BULLETINS [none issued].

FST 1.4:nos.
CIRCULARS [none issued].

FEDERAL TRADE COMMISSION
(1914–   )

CREATION AND AUTHORITY

The Federal Trade Commission was established by the Federal Trade Commission Act of September 26, 1914 (38 Stat. 717).

INFORMATION

Federal Trade Commission
600 Pennsylvania Avenue, N.W.
Washington, D. C. 20580
(202) 326-2222
http://www.ftc.gov

FT 1.1   • **Item 533 (MF)**
ANNUAL REPORT. 1915–   [Annual]

Report submitted by the Commission to Congress for the fiscal year.
Covers activities of administration, investigation, hearing examiners, Office of the General Counsel, consultation.
Appendix contains list of FTC Commissioners (1915 to date), types of unfair methods and practices, statutes pertaining to the FTC, and general investigations by the Commission since 1915.
Also issued in the House Document series, 1915-1975.
ISSN 0083-0917

FT 1.1/2   • **Item 533-A-1 (EL)**
ANNUAL REPORT (FAIR DEBT COLLECTION PRACTICES).

FT 1.2:CT   • **Item 535**
GENERAL PUBLICATIONS.

FT 1.2:M 54/3   • **Item 535**
F.T.C. STATISTICAL REPORT ON MERGERS AND ACQUISITIONS. 1973–   [Annual] (Bureau of Economics)

Formed by the union of Large Mergers in Manufacturing and Mining [and] Current Trends in Merger Activity.
ISSN 0094-1662

FT 1.3:nos.
BULLETINS.

FT 1.3/2   • Item 533-A
CONSUMER BULLETINS. 1–   1968–   [Irregular]

FT 1.4:nos.   • Item 539
CIRCULARS.

FT 1.5:L-CT   • Item 539
LAWS.

FT 1.6:nos.
CONFERENCE RULINGS BULLETINS.

FT 1.7:date   • Item 538
RULES OF PRACTICE.

FT 1.8:date(CT)   • Item 537
RULES, REGULATIONS, AND INSTRUCTIONS (miscellaneous).

FT 1.8/2:CT   • Item 535-A
HANDBOOKS, MANUALS, GUIDES.

FT 1.8/3:nos.   • Item 536-C
CONSUMER SURVEY HANDBOOKS. 1–   1975–   [Irregular] (Seattle Regional Office)

FT 1.8/4:nos.
BUYER'S GUIDES.

FT 1.9:nos.
FOREIGN TRADE SERIES.

FT 1.10:CT
COST REPORTS.

FT 1.11:v.nos.   • Item 534
FEDERAL TRADE COMMISSION DECISIONS, FINDINGS, ORDERS AND STIPULATIONS. v. 1– 1915–   [Annual]

PURPOSE:– To report Commission decisions as required in Section 6(f) of the Federal Trade Commission Act.
During recent years, most volumes cover the fiscal year, or six-month period when material is voluminous.
Citation: F.T.C.

FT 1.11/a:v.nos.
– SEPARATES. T.P. IND. TABLES OF EASES & COMMODITIES.

FT 1.11/a 2:nos.
– SEPARATES. REPORT FINDINGS AND ORDER OF COMMISSION.

FT 1.11/a 3:CT
– SEPARATES. DECISIONS OF COURTS ON ORDERS OF COMMISSION.

FT 1.11/2:date
FEDERAL TRADE COMMISSION DECISIONS. [Monthly]

FT 1.11/3:nos.
STIPULATIONS.

FT 1.12:date
DIGEST OF DECISIONS.

FT 1.12/2:nos.   • Item 534-A
ADVISORY OPINION DIGESTS.

FT 1.13:date   • Item 539
STATUTES AND COURT DECISIONS. 1956/60– [Quinquennial] (Rules and Publications Branch)

Supersedes Statutes and Decisions Pertaining to the Federal Trade Commission, 1914/1929–1949/1955.

FT 1.13/2   • Item 539
STATUTES AND DECISIONS PERTAINING TO THE FEDERAL TRADE COMMISSION. [Annual & Quinquennial]

FT 1.14
ADDRESSES. [Irregular]

FT 1.15:date
MONTHLY SUMMARY OF WORK.

Slightly varying titles.

FT 1.16
TRADE PRACTICE RULES. [Irregular]

PURPOSE:– To enable industry as a unit, under the guidance of the Federal Trade Commission, to make its own rules of business conduct in order to maintain fair competitive conditions and establish ethical business practices in the industry.

FT 1.16:date
TRADE PRACTICE RULES (Compilations).

FT 1.16/2
PROPOSED TRADE PRACTICE RULES. [Irregular]

FT 1.17:CT
INDUSTRIAL CORPORATION REPORTS (by industries).

FT 1.18   • Item 536-A
QUARTERLY FINANCIAL REPORT FOR MANUFACTURING, MINING, AND TRADE CORPORATIONS. 1947–   [Quarterly]

Prior to 4th quarter, 1974, issued as Quarterly Financial Report for Manufacturing Corporations.
Later C 3.267
ISSN 0098-681X

FT 1.19
PRESS RELEASES. [Irregular]

Contains summaries of all FTC's major actions.

FT 1.19/2
NEWS SUMMARY. 1–   [Weekly]

PURPOSE:– To publish in pamphlet form a weekly compilation of pressreleases on Commission cases and miscellaneous activities.

FT 1.20:date
QUARTERLY FINANCIAL REPORT, UNITED STATES RETAIL AND WHOLESALE CORPORATIONS.

Previously classified FT 1.2:R 31/6

FT 1.21:date   • Item 536-B
REPORT OF FEDERAL TRADE COMMISSION ON RATES OF RETURN (after taxes) FOR IDENTICAL COMPANIES IN SELECTED MANUFACTURING INDUSTRIES.

Earlier FT 1.2:R 18

FT 1.22:date   • Item 535-A-1
LIST OF PUBLICATIONS.

Earlier FT 1.2:P 96/3

FT 1.22/2:nos.
SPECIAL REFERENCE LISTS.

FT 1.22/3:CT   • Item 535-A-1
BIBLIOGRAPHIES AND LISTS OF PUBLICATIONS. [Irregular]

FT 1.23:nos.
DOCKETS [Circuit Court of Appeals].

FT 1.24
ADVERTISING ALERT. 1–   1962–   [Irregular]

PURPOSE:– To alert the public generally to false and misleading advertising and other misrepresentation. Gives brief accounts of cases (with Docket numbers) coming before the Commission.

FT 1.24/2:v.nos.&nos.
CONSUMER ALERT. v. 1–   1971–   [Monthly]

PURPOSE:– To provide information of Federal programs and activities of interest to the consumer.

FT 1.25:date
CALENDAR. [Weekly] (Office of Public Information)

FT 1.26:nos.
FTC PACKETS.

FT 1.27:CT
BACKGROUND INFORMATION ON [various subjects].

FT 1.28:nos.
STATISTICAL REPORTS.

FT 1.29:v.nos./nos.   • Item 535-A-1 (MF)
LIBRARY BULLETIN.

FT 1.30:date   • Item 535 (MF)
ANNUAL LINE OF BUSINESS REPORT.

FT 1.31:CT   • Item 535-A-2
POSTERS. [Irregular]

FT 1.32   • Item 535-A-3 (EL)
FACTS FOR CONSUMERS (series). [Irregular]

Each issue contains facts for consumers on a different subject.

FT 1.32/2   • Item 535-A-4
FACTS FOR BUSINESS (Various Topics) (series).

FT 1.32/3:CT   • Item 535-A-4
FACTS FOR BUSINESS, DONATING TO PUBLIC SAFETY FUND RAISERS.

FT 1.33   • Item 535-B (EL)
FACTS FOR BUSINESS (series). [Irregular]

FT 1.34   • Item 535-C (E)
ELECTRONIC PRODUCTS.

FT 1.35:date   • Item 535-A-6 (MF)
TELEPHONE DIRECTORY. [Annual]

FT 1.36   • Item 535-A-7 (EL)
TAR, NICOTINE, AND CARBON DIOXIDE OF THE SMOKE OF...VARIETIES OF DOMESTIC CIGARETTES FOR THE YEAR.. [Annual]

FT 1.37   • Item 535-A-8 (MF) (EL)
BUREAU OF ECONOMICS STAFF REPORTS (series).

FOREIGN-TRADE ZONES BOARD
(1934–   )

CREATION AND AUTHORITY

The Foreign-Trade Zones Board was established by act of Congress approved June 18, 1934 (48 Stat. 998).

INFORMATION

Foreign-Trade Zones Board
U.S. Dept. of Commerce
FCB-Ste. 4100 W
1401 Constitution Ave.
Washington, DC 20230
(202) 482-2862
Fax: (202) 482-0002
http://ia.ita.doc.gov/ftzpage

FTZ 1.1   • Item 542 (MF)
ANNUAL REPORT. 1939–   [Annual]

Report submitted by the Board to Congress pursuant to section 16 of the Foreign-Trade Zones Act of June 18, 1934, as amended by Public Law 566, 81st Congress for the fiscal year.
Contains report of activities for each of the four zones. Appendix contains Board Orders, Memorandum Orders as the text of the Foreign-Trade Zones Act.
Reports issued prior to 1939 were included in the annual report of the Secretary of Commerce.

FTZ 1.2:CT • Item 542
GENERAL REPORTS.

FTZ 1.5:CT • Item 542
LAWS.

FTZ 1.7:
NEWS BULLETINS.

FTZ 1.8:nos.
GENERAL DESCRIPTION OF FOREIGN- TRADE ZONES.

FTZ 1.9:CT
ADDRESSES

FTZ 1.10:CT
ENVIRONMENTAL IMPACT STATEMENTS.

FEDERAL WORKS AGENCY
(1939– 1949)

CREATION AND AUTHORITY

The Federal Works Agency was established by Reorganization Plan No. 1 of 1939, effective July 1, 1939, to consolidate those agencies of the Federal Government dealing with public works. The agencies formed in the new Agency were the Public Buildings Administration, Public Roads Administration, Public Works Administration, Work Projects Administration, and the United States Housing Authority. The Agency was abolished by act of Congress, approved June 30, 1949 (63 Stat. 378) and its function transferred to General Services Administration (GS 1).

FW 1.1:date
ANNUAL REPORTS.

FW 1.2:CT
GENERAL PUBLICATIONS.

FW 1.5:CT
LAWS.

FW 1.6:CT
REGULATIONS, RULES, AND INSTRUCTIONS.

FW 1.6/2:nos.
FIELD OPERATION INSTRUCTIONS.

FW 1.7:CT
ADDRESSES.

FW 1.8:nos.
SPECIAL ORDERS.

Pub. desig. P.WA-nos.

FW 1.9:nos.
GENERAL CIRCULARS.

FW 1.10:nos.
GENERAL ORDERS.

FW 1.11:v.nos.
LIBRARY ACCESSIONS. [Biweekly]

Earlier FW 4.11

FW 1.12:nos.
TRAINING BULLETINS.

FW 1.13:nos.
DEFENSE HOUSING CONSTRUCTION BULLETINS. [Weekly]

FW 1.14:nos.
TRANSMITTAL LETTERS, MANUAL OF REGULATIONS AND PROCEDURE.

FW 1.15:v.nos.
PLANNING, CURRENT LITERATURE. [Weekly]

Later C 37.12

FW 1.16:nos.
CONSTRUCTION MATERIALS. [Monthly]

Earlier Pr 32.4827
Later GS 1.7

FW 1.17
STAFF MEMORANDUM. [Proc. Admin.]

FW 1.18
ADMINISTRATOR'S MEMORANDUMS. [Proc. Admin.]

FW 1.19
FIELD MEMORANDUM. [Proc. Admin.]

FW 1.20
OFFICE OF CHIEF ENGINEER, CIRCULAR LETTER. [Proc. Admin.]

FW 1.21
ADMINISTRATIVE PROCEDURE MEMORANDUM. [Admin.]

PUBLIC ROADS ADMINISTRATION
(1939– 1949)

CREATION AND AUTHORITY

The Bureau of Public Roads (A 22) was transferred from the Department of Agriculture to the Federal Works Agency and redesignated the Public Roads Administration by Reorganization Plan No. 1 of 1939, effective July 1, 1939. Under the Federal Property and Administrative Services Act of 1949 (63 Stat. 377, as amended), effective July 1, 1949, the Administration became a part of the newly created General Services Administration (GS 3) and its name returned to the Bureau of Public Roads.

FW 2.1:date
ANNUAL REPORTS.

Earlier A 22.1
Later GS 3.2

FW 2.2:CT
GENERAL PUBLICATIONS.

Earlier A 22.2
Later GS 3.2

FW 2.5:CT
LAWS.

Later C 37.5

FW 2.6:CT
REGULATIONS, RULES, AND INSTRUCTIONS.

Includes Handbooks and Manuals.

FW 2.7:v.nos.
PUBLIC ROADS, JOURNAL OF HIGHWAY RESEARCH. [Monthly]
Earlier A 22.6
Later GS 3.8

FW 2.8:v.nos.
HIGHWAYS, CURRENT LITERATURE. [Weekly]
Earlier A 22.10
Later C 37.10

FW 2.9:nos.
PLANNING SURVEY MEMORANDUM.
Earlier A 22.12

FW 2.10:nos.
STATEWIDE HIGHWAY PLANNING SURVEYS; NEWS BULLETINS.
Earlier A 22.13

FW 2.11:date
TRAFFIC VOLUME TRENDS. [Monthly]
Later FW 2.14

FW 2.12:CT
MAPS, PROGRESS.
Earlier A 22.9
Later C 37.13

FW 2.13:CT
MAPS, TRANSPORTATION.

Earlier A 22.9/2
Later C 37.11

FW 2.14:date
TRAFFIC VOLUME TRENDS. [Monthly]

Transferred to FW 2.16
Earlier FW 2.11

FW 2.15:CT
ADDRESSES.

FW 2.16:nos.
INFORMATIONAL MEMORANDUMS.

Later GS 3.7

FW 2.17:nos.
AUTOMOBILE REGISTRATION CHARACTERISTICS.

FW 2.18:CT
PRESIDENT'S HIGHWAY SAFETY CONFERENCE PUBLICATIONS.

Later C 37.7

FW 2.19:CA-nos.&date
HIGHWAY CONSTRUCTION CONTRACTS AWARDED BY STATE HIGHWAY DEPARTMENTS, TABLES.

HOUSING AUTHORITY
(1939– 1942)

CREATION AND AUTHORITY

The United States Housing Authority (I 40) was transferred to the Federal Works Agency by Reorganization Plan No. 1 of 1939, effective July 1, 1939. Under Executive Order 9070 of February 24, 1942, the Authority was consolidated with certain other agencies to form the Federal Public Housing Authority (NHA 4) of the National Housing Agency.

FW 3.1:date
ANNUAL REPORTS.
Earlier I 40.1
Later NHA 4.1

FW 3.2:CT
GENERAL PUBLICATIONS.
Earlier I 40.2
Later NHA 4.2

FW 3.5:CT
LAWS.
Earlier I 40.6

FW 3.7:vol
PUBLIC HOUSING. [Weekly]
Later NHA 4.8

FW 3.8:CT
ADDRESSES.
Earlier I 40.8

FW 3.9:nos.
BULLETINS ON POLICY AND PROCEDURE.
Earlier I 40.10

FW 3.10:nos.
MANAGEMENT EXPERIENCE NOTES.

FW 3.11:nos.
TECHNICAL INFORMATION NOTES.
Earlier I 40.11

WORK PROJECTS ADMINISTRATION (1939– 1943)

CREATION AND AUTHORITY

The Works Progress Administration (Y 3.W 89/2), an independent agency, was transferred to the Federal Works Agency and its name changed to Work Projects Administration by Reorganization Plan No. 1 of 1939, effective July 1, 1939. The Administration was abolished by June 30, 1943, by letter of the President to the Federal Works Administration, dated December 4, 1942.

FW 4.1:date
ANNUAL REPORTS.
Earlier Y 3.W 89/2:1

FW 4.2:CT
GENERAL PUBLICATIONS.
Earlier Y 3.W 89/2

FW 4.6:CT
REGULATIONS, RULES, AND INSTRUCTIONS.
Earlier Y 3.W 89/2:6

FW 4.7:letter-nos.
NATIONAL RESEARCH PROJECT, REPORTS.
Earlier Y 3.W 89/2:42

FW 4.8:nos.
OPERATING PROCEDURE MEMORANDUM.
Earlier Y 3.W 89/2:30

FW 4.9:nos.
HANDBOOK OF PROCEDURES LETTERS.
Earlier Y 3.W 89/2:29

FW 4.10:nos.
DIGEST OF PROCEDURES. [Monthly]
Earlier Y 3.W 89/2:10

FW 4.11:vol.
LIBRARY ACCESSIONS. [Weekly]
Earlier Y 3.W 89/2:41

FW 4.12:nos.
GENERAL LETTERS.
Earlier Y 3.W 89/2:23

FW 4.13:date
STATISTICAL BULLETINS. [Monthly]
Earlier Y 3.W 89/2:58

FW 4.14:CT
HISTORICAL RECORDS SURVEY.
Earlier Y 3.W 89/2:43

FW 4.15:nos.
INFORMATION SERVICE LETTERS.
Earlier Y 3.W 89/2:39

FW 4.16:nos.
GENERAL ORDERS.

FW 4.17:nos.
TECHNICAL SERIES: RESEARCH AND RECORDS PROJECTS CIRCULARS, LABORATORY CIRCULARS.
Earlier Y 3.W 89/2:59

FW 4.18:nos.
TECHNICAL SERIES: RESEARCH AND RECORDS PROJECTS CIRCULARS.

FW 4.19:nos.
SOCIAL PROBLEMS.
Earlier Y 3.W 89/2:57

FW 4.20:nos.
SAFETY BULLETINS.
Earlier Y 3.W 89/2:11

FW 4.21:nos.
TECHNICAL SERIES: RECREATION CIRCULARS.
Earlier Y 3.W 89/2:38

FW 4.22:nos.
TECHNICAL SERIES: RESEARCH, STATISTICAL AND SURVEY PROJECTS CIRCULARS.
Earlier Y 3.W 89/2:52

FW 4.23:nos.
TECHNICAL SERIES: RESEARCH AND RECORDS PROJECTS BIBLIOGRAPHIES.

FW 4.24:nos.
TECHNICAL SERIES: WORKERS' SERVICE CIRCULARS.

FW 4.25:CT
ADDRESSES.
Earlier Y 3.W 89/2:54

FW 4.26:nos.
TECHNICAL SERIES: COMMUNITY SERVICE CIRCULARS.

FW 4.27:nos.
TECHNICAL SERIES: LIBRARY.

FW 4.28:CT
WRITERS' PUBLICATIONS.
Earlier Y 3.W 89/2:24

FW 4.29:pt.nos.
BIBLIOGRAPHY OF AERONAUTICS. [Proc. Non-Government]
Earlier Y 3.W 89/2:60

FW 4.30:vol
MANUAL OF RULES AND REGULATIONS, TRANSMITTAL LETTERS.

FW 4.31:CT
PROJECTS OPERATED BY WORK PROJECTS ADMINISTRATION, ACCOMPLISHMENTS ON (by States).

FW 4.32:date
FEDERAL WORK PROGRAMS AND PUBLIC ASSISTANCE. [Monthly]

FW 4.33:date
FEDERAL WORK AND CONSTRUCTION PROJECTS. [Monthly]
Earlier Y 3.W 89/2:61

FW 4.34:nos.
TECHNICAL SERIES: ART CIRCULARS.
Earlier Y 3.W 89/2:48

FW 4.35:nos.
RESEARCH MONOGRAPHS.
Earlier Y 3.W 89/2:17

FW 4.36:vol
MARKETING LAWS SURVEY [publications].

FW 4.37:nos.
WPA WEEK IN NATIONAL DEFENSE.

FW 4.38:nos.
TECHNICAL SERIES: WELFARE CIRCULARS.

FW 4.39:nos.
COMMISSIONER'S LETTERS

FW 4.40:CT
POSTERS.

FW 4.41
COMMUNITY SERVICE LETTER. [Proc. Admin.]

PUBLIC WORKS ADMINISTRATION (1939– 1943)

CREATION AND AUTHORITY

The Federal Emergency Administration of Public Works (Y 3.F 31/4), and independent agency, was transferred to the Federal Works Agency and its name changed to Public Works Administration by Reorganization Plan No. 1 of 1939, effective July 1, 1939. The Administration was abolished by Executive Order 9357 of June 30, 1943, and its functions transferred to the Office of the Federal Works Administrator.

FW 5.1:date
ANNUAL REPORTS.
Earlier Y 3.F 31/4:1

FW 5.2:CT
GENERAL PUBLICATIONS.
Earlier Y 3.F 31/4:2

FW 5.5:CT
LAWS.
Earlier Y 3.F 31/4:5

FW 5.7:CT
ADDRESSES.
Earlier Y 3.F 31/4:9

FW 5.8:nos.
ADMINISTRATIVE ORDERS.
Earlier Y 3.F 31/4:22

FW 5.9
GENERAL ORDERS.

FW 5.10
ACCOUNTING DIVISION. [Proc.]

FW 5.11
ENGINEERING DIVISION ORDERS. [Proc. Admin.]

FW 5.12
LETTERS OF INSTRUCTIONS. [Admin.]

PUBLIC BUILDINGS ADMINISTRATION (1939– 1949)

CREATION AND AUTHORITY

The Public Buildings Administration was established within the Federal Works Agency by Reorganization Plan No. 1 of 1939, effective July 1, 1939. The Administration was abolished by act of Congress, approved June 30, 1949 (63 Stat. 378), and its functions transferred to the General Services Administration, under which agency the Public Buildings Service (GS 6) was established on December 11, 1949.

FW 6.1:date
ANNUAL REPORTS.

Later GS 6.1

FW 6.2:CT
GENERAL PUBLICATIONS.

Later GS 6.2

FW 6.6:CT
REGULATIONS, RULES, AND INSTRUCTIONS.

Later GS 6.6

FW 6.7:nos.
BULLETINS, SECTION OF FINE ARTS.

Earlier T 58.16

FW 6.8:date
TELEPHONE DIRECTORY, REPUBLIC 7500. [Monthly]

Later GS 6.7

FW 6.9:CT
PRESIDENT'S CONFERENCE ON FIRE PREVENTION PUBLICATIONS.

FW 6.10:nos.
ACCIDENT AND FIRE PREVENTION NEWS. [Bimonthly]

Nos. 1-6 entitled "Safety News."
The first 9 numbers were issued monthly.

BUREAU OF COMMUNITY FACILITIES (1939– 1949)

CREATION AND AUTHORITY

The Bureau of Community Facilities was established within the Federal Works Agency pursuant to Reorganization Plan No. 1 of 1939, dated April 25, 1939. The Bureau was transferred to the General Services Administration by the Federal Property and Administrative Services Act of 1949, approved June 30, 1949 (63 Stat. 377), where it became the Community Facilities Service (GS 1).

FW 7.1:date
ANNUAL REPORTS.

FW 7.2:CT
GENERAL PUBLICATIONS.

FW 7.6:CT
REGULATIONS, RULES, AND INSTRUCTIONS.

FW 7.7:date
REPORT ON PLAN PREPARATION OF STATE AND LOCAL PUBLIC WORKS. [Semiannual]

GENERAL ACCOUNTING OFFICE (1921–   )

CREATION AND AUTHORITY

The General Accounting Office was established by the Budget and Accounting Act, approved June 10, 1921 (42 Stat. 23).

INFORMATION

General Accounting Office
441 G Street, N.W.
Washington, D.C. 20548
(202) 512-3000
http://www.gao.gov

GA 1.1   • Item 543 (MF)
ANNUAL REPORT OF THE COMPTROLLER GENERAL OF THE UNITED STATES. 1922–   [Annual]

Also issued in the House Documents series.

GA 1.1/2:date   • Item 543-A (MF)
PERSONNEL APPEALS BOARD, ANNUAL REPORT.

GA 1.2:CT   • Item 545
GENERAL PUBLICATIONS.

GA 1.3:
BULLETINS.

GA 1.4:
CIRCULARS.

GA 1.5   • Item 544 (MF)
DECISIONS OF THE COMPTROLLER GENERAL OF THE UNITED STATES. [Bound Volumes] v. 1– 1922–   [Annual]

Each volume covers the fiscal year.
Citation: Comp. Gen.
ISSN 0011-7323

INDEXES.

The following cumulative indexes have been published.

INDEX TO THE PUBLISHED DECISIONS OF THE ACCOUNTING OFFICERS OF THE UNITED STATES.

Covers the period 1894 through June 30, 1919. Includes vols. 1– 27 of the Decisions of the Comptroller of the Treasury and vols. 1– 8 of the Decisions of the Comptroller General.

GA 1.5/a:v.nos.&nos.   • Item 544
– [Separates]. v. 1–   1922–   [Monthly]

Contains decisions by the Comptroller General's office on financial matters of the Federal Government. Later appears in bound volumes.
Index digests appear in the September, December, and March issues for previous quarter, cumulative tables and index-digest for fiscal year in June issues.

GA 1.5/a-2:letters-nos. • Item 546-D-1 (MF)
DECISIONS. [Irregular]

GA 1.5/2:date   • Item 546-D-1 (MF)
COMPTROLLER GENERAL OF THE UNITED STATES, DECISIONS, TESTIMONIES, REVIEWS.

Later, the more important decisions from standpoint of general application and precedent are selected and issued in the monthly pamphlet form (GA 1.5/2) and also in the annual bound volumes (GA 1.5).

GA 1.5/3   • Item 546
INDEX-DIGEST OF THE PUBLISHED DECISIONS OF THE COMPTROLLER GENERAL OF THE UNITED STATES. 1929/40–   [Quinquennial]

GA 1.5/4
DIGEST OF PUBLISHED DECISIONS OF THE COMPTROLLER GENERAL. 1921– 1976. [Irregular]

Digests have accompanied all of the published decisions of the Comptroller General. Formerly these advance sheets were referred to as Synopses of Published Decisions. They give the gist of the decisions including facts, legal question involved, holding, reason for holding, and citation to the law of regulations involved.

GA 1.5/5:v.nos.&nos.   • Item 546-C
QUARTERLY DIGESTS OF UNPUBLISHED DECISIONS OF THE COMPTROLLER GENERAL OF THE UNITED STATES: PERSONNEL LAW, CIVILIAN PERSONNEL. v. 1–   (Index-Digest Section)

ISSN 0360-2281

GA 1.5/6:v.nos.&nos.
– PAY AND ALLOCATIONS OF UNIFORMED SERVICE.

GA 1.5/7:v.nos.&nos.
CONTRACTS.

GA 1.5/8:v.nos.&nos.   • Item 546-G
DIGEST OF UNPUBLISHED DECISIONS OF THE COMPTROLLER GENERAL OF THE U.S. (Transportation)

GA 1.5/9:v.nos.&nos.   • Item 546-J
DIGEST OF UNPUBLISHED DECISIONS OF THE COMPTROLLER GENERAL OF THE UNITED STATES: APPROPRIATIONS AND MISCELLANEOUS SUBJECTS. [Quarterly]

ISSN 0145-1502
Combined with GA 1.5/10 and GA 1.5/13 to form GA 1.5/14

GA 1.5/10:v.nos.&nos.   • Item 546-F
QUARTERLY DIGEST OF UNPUBLISHED DECISIONS OF THE COMPTROLLER GENERAL OF THE UNITED STATES: PROCUREMENT LAW. v. 1– (Index- Digest Section, Office of the General Counsel)

ISSN 0092-8550
Combined with GA 1.5/9 and GA 1.5/13 to form GA 1.5/14

GA 1.5/11:v.nos.&nos.   • Item 546-H
QUARTERLY DIGEST OF UNPUBLISHED DECISIONS OF THE COMPTROLLER GENERAL OF THE UNITED STATES: PERSONNEL LAW, MILITARY PERSONNEL. v. 1–   (Index-Digest Section, Office of the General Counsel)

GA 1.5/12:v.nos.&nos.
DIGESTS OF UNPUBLISHED DECISIONS OF THE COMPTROLLER GENERAL OF THE UNITED STATES: GENERAL GOVERNMENT MATTERS, APPROPRIATIONS AND MISCELLANEOUS. [Semiannual]

GA 1.5/13:v.nos.&nos.
PERSONNEL LAW: CIVILIAN PERSONNEL AND MILITARY PERSONNEL. [Quarterly]

Combined with GA 1.5/9 and GA 1.5/10 to form GA 1.5/14

GA 1.5/14:v.nos.&nos. • Item 546-J
DIGESTS OF UNPUBLISHED DECISIONS OF THE COMPTROLLER GENERAL OF THE UNITED STATES. v. 1– 1984– [Monthly] (Index-Digest Section, Office of the General Counsel)

Formed by combining GA 1.5/9, GA 1.5/10, and GA 1.5/13.

GA 1.5/14-2:v.nos./nos. • Item 546-J
DIGESTS OF DECISIONS OF THE COMPTROLLER GENERAL OF THE UNITED STATES. [Monthly]

GA 1.6:nos.
GENERAL REGULATIONS. 1– 136. 1922– 1957.

GENERAL ACCOUNTING OFFICE POLICY AND PROCEDURES MANUAL FOR GUIDANCE OF FEDERAL AGENCIES. 1957– [Irregular]

Published in loose-leaf form and punched for 3-ring binder. Subscription includes basic volume plus supplementary material for an indefinite period.
Issued in the following parts:–

GA 1.6/1:date • Item 545-G-8
TITLE 1. THE U.S. GENERAL ACCOUNTING OFFICE.

Contains historical material relating to the General Accounting Office and describes its functions, responsibilities, and organization.
Formerly distributed to depository libraries under item number 545-G-1.

GA 1.6/2:date • Item 545-G-8
TITLE 2. ACCOUNTING PRINCIPLES AND STANDARDS OF INTERNAL AUDITING GUIDELINES.

Contains data on accounting principles and standards and their application. This section sold separately.
Formerly distributed to depository libraries under item number 545-G

GA 1.6/3:date • Item 545-G-8
TITLE 3. AUDIT.

Contains reference materials pertaining to the legal authorities for the audit and investigative activities of the General Accounting Office.
Formerly distributed to depository libraries under item number 545-G-2.

GA 1.6/4:date • Item 545-G-8
TITLE 4. CLAIMS-GENERAL.

Contains regulatory material relating to doubtful, administratively uncollectable, and general claims.
Formerly distributed to depository libraries under item number 545-G-3.

GA 1.6/5:date • Item 545-G-8
TITLE 5. TRANSPORTATION.

Contains data on the procurement, billing, and payment of freight and passenger transportation services furnished for the account of the United States. This section sold separately.
Formerly distributed to depository libraries under item number 545-G-4.

GA 1.6/6 • Item 545-G-8
GAO POLICY AND PROCEDURES MANUAL FOR GUIDANCE OF FEDERAL AGENCIES: TITLE 6, PAY, LEAVE, AND ALLOWANCES.

Prescribes principles and standards, and the forms, records, and procedures, for establishing and maintaining an adequate payroll system.

GA 1.6/7:date • Item 545-G-8
TITLE 7. FISCAL PROCEDURES.

Codifies the requirements and procedures having general application to accounting for appropriations, funds, and receipts of the Government.
This is a complete revision of Title 7 and reflects the new codification of title 31 of the U.S. Code effected by PL 97-258.
It is punched for a 3-ring binder, and will be periodically updated.
Formerly distributed to depository libraries under item number 545-G-6.

GA 1.6/8:date • Item 545-G-8
TITLE 8. RECORDS MANAGEMENT AND SERVICES.

Describes the responsibilities of the General Accounting Office in matters relating to the preservation and disposal of fiscal and accounting records of the Government.

GA 1.6/9:date
TITLE 9. ACCOUNTING FORMS.

Codifies the requirements and procedures for prescribing General Accounting Office standard forms and submitting accounting forms to the Comptroller General for review or approval.

GA 1.6/10:date • Item 545-G-8
TITLE 10. INTRODUCTION AND TABLE OF CONTENTS FOR TITLES 1-8.

Formerly distributed to depository libraries under item number 545-G-10.

GA 1.7:nos.
COMPTROLLER GENERAL'S SPECIAL REGULATIONS.

GA 1.8:nos.
GENERAL OFFICE ORDERS.

GA 1.9:CT
PAPERS IN RE.

GA 1.10:nos.
GENERAL ACCOUNTING OFFICE SALARY TABLES.

GA 1.11:nos.
ACCOUNTING SYSTEMS MEMORANDUM.

GA 1.11/2:nos.
ACCOUNTING PRINCIPLES MEMORANDUM.

GA 1.12 • Item 546-A
JOINT FINANCIAL MANAGEMENT IMPROVEMENT PROGRAM, ANNUAL REPORT FISCAL YEAR (date). [Annual]

GA 1.12/2:date • Item 546-B
FEDERAL FINANCIAL MANAGEMENT DIRECTORY. [Annual]

PURPOSE:– To facilitate the interchange of financial management information among agency officials in the Federal Government and thus aid in the development of intergovernmental cooperation among officials engaged in financial management activities.

GA 1.12/3:date
JFMIP NEWS. [Quarterly]

GA 1.13:CT • Item 546-D (EL)
REPORTS TO CONGRESS ON AUDITS, REVIEWS, AND EXAMINATIONS.

Also published in microfiche.

GA 1.13:L 81/2/date • Item 546-D
AUDIT OF PAYMENTS FROM SPECIAL BANK ACCOUNT TO LOCKHEED AIRCRAFT CORPORATION FOR C-5A AIRCRAFT PROGRAM, DEFENSE DEPARTMENT. 1st– 1971– [Quarterly] (B-162578)

Report to Congress made pursuant to

Public Laws 91-441, 92-156, 92-436, and 93-155.

GA 1.13/2:date
EXAMINATION OF THE INTER-AMERICAN FOUNDATION'S FINANCIAL STATEMENTS. [Annual]

GA 1.13/3:date • Item 546-D (MF)
STATUS OF STRATEGIC PETROLEUM RESERVE ACTIVITIES AS OF (date). [Quarterly]

GA 1.13/4: • Item 546-D (MF)
EXAMINATION OF THE FEDERAL FINANCING BANK'S FINANCIAL STATEMENTS FOR THE YEARS ENDED . . . [Annual]

GA 1.13/5: • Item 546-D (MF)
FINANCIAL AUDIT, SENATE RECORDING AND PHOTOGRAPHIC SUDIOS REVOLVING FUND. [Annual]

GA 1.13/5-2: • Item 546-D (MF)
FINANCIAL AUDIT, HOUSE RECORDING STUDIO REVOLVING FUND. [Annual]

GA 1.13/6: • Item 546-D (MF)
TAX POLICY AND ADMINISTRATION . . . ANNUAL REPORT ON GAO'S TAX- RELATED WORK. [Annual]

GA 1.13/7: • Item 546-D (MF)
FINANCIAL AUDIT, EXPORT-IMPORT BANK'S FINANCIAL STATEMENTS FOR ... [Annual]

GA 1.13/8: • Item 546-D (MF)
FINANCIAL AUDIT, HOUSE RESTAURANT REVOLVING FUND'S FINANCIAL STATEMENTS FOR . . . [Annual]

GA 1.13/8-2: • Item 546-D (MF)
FINANCIAL AUDIT, SENATE RESTAURANTS REVOLVING FUND FOR FISCAL YEARS. [Annual]

GA 1.13/9: • Item 546-D (MF)
NUCLEAR WASTE, QUARTERLY REPORT ON DOE'S NUCLEAR WASTE PROGRAM AS OF . . .

GA 1.13/10:date • Item 546-D (MF)
STATUS OF THE DEPARTMENT OF ENERGY'S IMPLEMENTATION OF NUCLEAR WASTE POLICY ACT.

GA 1.13/11: • Item 546-D (MF)
EXAMINATION OF THE PANAMA CANAL COMMISSION'S FINANCIAL STATEMENTS FOR THE YEARS ENDED ... [Annual]

GA 1.13/12: • Item 546-D (MF)
FINANCIAL AUDIT, FEDERAL SAVINGS AND LOAN INSURANCE CORPORATION'S . . . FINANCIAL STATEMENTS. [Annual]

GA 1.13/13: • Item 546-D (MF)
FINANCIAL AUDIT, FEDERAL HOME LOAN BANKS' FINANCIAL STATEMENTS FOR . . . [Annual]

GA 1.13/13-2:date • Item 546-D-2 (MF)
FINANCIAL AUDIT, FEDERAL HOME LOAN BANK BOARD'S FINANCIAL STATEMENTS FOR . . . [Annual]

GA 1.13/14: • Item 546-D (EL)
AGING, GAO ACTIVITIES IN FISCAL YEAR. [Annual]

GA 1.13/15: • Item 546-D (EL)
REPORT ON OPM, GAO'S ANNUAL REPORT ON ACTIVITIES OF OPM, FISCAL YEAR. [Annual]

GA 1.13/16: • Item 546-D (EL)
EXAMINATION OF THE FEDERAL DEPOSIT INSURANCE CORPORATION'S FINANCIAL STATEMENTS FOR THE YEARS ENDED . . . [Annual]

GA 1.13/17:date • Item 546-D-2
FINANCIAL AUDIT, ENVIRONMENTAL AND ENERGY STUDY CONFERENCE FINANCIAL STATEMENT FOR (date). [Annual]

GA 1.13/18: • Item 546-D-2 (MF)
STATUS OF OPEN RECOMMENDATIONS IMPROVING OPERATIONS OF FEDERAL DEPARTMENTS AND AGENCIES. [Annual]

Summarizes status of GAO's open recommendations for improving operations of federal departments and agencies. Summaries are presented in terms of budget functions.

GA 1.13/18-2:date/v.nos. • Item 546-D-3
GAO, STATUS OF OPEN RECOMMENDATIONS. [Annual]

Electronic version. Issued on floppy diskettes.

GA 1.13/19:date • Item 546-D-2
FINANCIAL AUDIT, HOUSE STATIONERY REVOLVING FUND STATEMENTS. [Annual]

GA 1.14:CT • Item 545-A
HANDBOOKS, MANUALS, GUIDES.

GA 1.14:C 15 • Item 545-A
MANUAL OF REGULATIONS AND INSTRUCTIONS RELATING TO THE DISCLOSURE OF FEDERAL CAMPAIGN FUNDS FOR CANDIDATES FOR THE OFFICE OF PRESIDENT OR VICE PRESIDENT OF THE UNITED STATES AND POLITICAL COMMITTEES SUPPORTING SUCH CANDIDATES. 1972. 66 p.

GA 1.15 • Item 544-A (MF)
GAO REVIEW. 1966– [Quarterly]

Contains articles on accounting generally and particularly on accounting and auditing activities of the General Accounting Office, its officials and employees.
Later GA 1.15/2
ISSN 0016-3414

GA 1.15/2:nos. • Item 544-A-1
THE G.A.O. JOURNAL. [Quarterly]

Intended for a broader readership than its predecessor, The GAO Review (GA 1.15).
Contains articles mainly in one of three categories: 1) public policy issues, 2) the inner workings of GAO as investigatory arm of the Congress, 3) spotlighting of people whose thoughts warrant such visibility.

GA 1.16:CT • Item 545
BIBLIOGRAPHIES AND LISTS OF PUBLICATIONS.

GA 1.16:P 96 • Item 545
LIST OF GAO PUBLICATIONS. v. 1– 1967– [Semiannual]

Later GA 1.16/2

GA 1.16/2:v.nos.&nos. • Item 546-E (MF)
LIST OF GAO PUBLICATIONS. v. 1– 1967– [Semiannual]

Earlier GA 1.16:P 96

GA 1.16/3:v.nos.&nos. • Item 546-E (EL)
MONTH IN REVIEW.

Previous titles: Reports Issued In . . .; Reports and Testimony
ISSN 0364-8265

GA 1.16/3-2: • Item 546-E
ANNUAL INDEX OF REPORTS ISSUED IN . . . [Annual]

GA 1.16/3-3:date • Item 546-E (EL)
ABSTRACTS OF REPORTS AND TESTIMONY, FISCAL YEAR . . .

GA 1.16/3-4:date • Item 546-E-1 (MF)
ABSTRACTS OF AND INDEXES FOR REPORTS AND TESTIMONY, FISCAL YEAR. [Annual]

GA 1.16/4:v.nos.&nos. • Item 546-E
GAO DOCUMENTS. v. 1– [Monthly]

Sub-title: A Catalog of Reports, Decisions and Opinions, Testimonies and Speeches.
A comprehensive record of current GAO publications and documents, including audit reports, staff studies, memoranda, opinions, speeches, testimony, and Comptroller General decisions.
ISSN 0193-0419

GA 1.16/5:date • Item 545
BIBLIOGRAPHY OF DOCUMENTS ISSUED BY GAO ON MATTERS RELATED TO: ADP.

GA 1.16/6:date • Item 545 (MF)
FOOD BIBLIOGRAPHY. [Annual]

GA 1.17:date
CONSOLIDATED LIST OF PERSONS OR FIRMS CURRENTLY DEBARRED FOR VIOLATIONS OF VARIOUS PUBLIC CONTRACTS ACTS INCORPORATING LABOR STANDARD PROVISIONS. 1971– [Quarterly]

ISSN 0364-7242

GA 1.17/2:date
INTERIM LIST OF PERSONS OR FIRMS CURRENTLY DEBARRED FOR VIOLATION OF VARIOUS PUBLIC CONTRACTS ACTS INCORPORATING LABOR STANDARDS PROVISIONS. [Monthly]

GA 1.18:CT • Item 545-C (MF)
ADDRESSES. [Irregular]

GA 1.19:nos. • Item 544-B
AUDIT STANDARDS, SUPPLEMENTAL SERIES. 1– 1973– [Irregular]

On August 1, 1972, the Comptroller General released Standards for Audit of Governmental Organizations, Programs, Activities & Functions, a set of standards that are designed to serve as a guide for improved auditing of Government programs. The standards provide for a scope of auditing of Government programs and activities that, properly applied, should result in much better information for managers, legislators, and the public on how public funds are administered and spent and whether results intended are being achieved. To further explain and interpret the standards and to demonstrate their application to the audit of programs at all levels of Government, the General Accounting Office intends to issue supplements to the standards from time to time as the need arises.

GA 1.20:date • Item 998-C
ALPHABETICAL LISTING OF (year) PRESIDENTIAL CAMPAIGN RECEIPTS. 1973– [Quadrennial]

Report compiled and submitted in accordance with Section (a)(7)(E) of the Federal Election Campaign Act of 1971.

GA 1.21:nos. • Item 545-D
DATA ANALYSIS NOTES. 1– [Irregular]

GA 1.22:CT • Item 545-E
CONGRESSIONAL SOURCEBOOK SERIES. [Irregular]

PURPOSE:– To facilitate identification, acquisitions, and compilation of relevant and reliable information which may be needed by the Congress in carrying out its oversight and budget control responsibilities.

GA 1.23 • Item 545-F
GC LEGISLATIVE HISTORY FILES. [Irregular] (Office of the General Counsel)

Legislative files containing laws and hearings, compiled in the Office of the General Counsel, and issued jointly under the auspices of the General Accounting Office and the Congressional Research Service of the Library of Congress.
Published in microfiche (48x).

GA 1.24:v.nos.&nos. • Item 545-H
OGC ADVISER. v. 1– 1976– [Quarterly] (Office of the General Counsel)

GA 1.25: • Item 544-C
ACCOUNTING SERIES. [Irregular]

Each publication is on a different subject.

GA 1.26 • Item 546-K (MF)
FINANCIAL MANAGEMENT PROFILE: DEPARTMENT OF HEALTH AND HUMAN SERVICES. [Irregular]

PURPOSE:– To profile the financial management structure of the Department of Health and Human Services as a test of a new audit approach called Control and Risk Evaluation. Describes financial management systems and the interrelationships of these systems.

GA 1.27:date • Item 545-G-7 (MF)
TELEPHONE DIRECTORY. [Irregular]

GA 1.28:CT • Item 544-D
DIRECTORIES. [Irregular]

GA 1.29:date • Item 545-J (MF)
ADVISORY COUNCIL ON CIVIL RIGHTS: ANNUAL REPORT.

PURPOSE:– To summarize Council activities in providing a medium for employees both to participate with and to improve communication with management in the area of civil rights.
Earlier HE 3.2:R 44

GA 1.30:date • Item 545-K (MF)
WOMEN'S ADVISORY COUNCIL: ANNUAL REPORT.

Summarizes activities of the Council, which addresses the interests of women in the General Accounting Office.

GA 1.33:nos. • Item 545
TRANSITION SERIES. [Irregular]

GA 1.34 • Item 545-L (EL)
GAO ONLINE SERVICE.

Available on Internet or via asynchronous connection.

GA 1.36 • Item 454-K-1 (MF)
LIBRARY FOCUS. [Bimonthly]

GA 1.37 • Item 546-D-4 (MF)
ACTIVE ASSIGNMENTS (series). [Quarterly]

GA 1.38: • Item 545-A-1 (MF)
INTERNATIONAL JOURNAL OF GOVERNMENT AUDITING (series).

GA 1.39 • Item 545-A-2 (MF)
GAO DOCUMENT (series).

GA 1.40 • Item 545-A-3(E)
ELECTRONIC PRODUCTS. (Misc.)

PERSONNEL APPEALS BOARD

GA 2.1:date • Item 543-A-1 (MF)
ANNUAL REPORT.

GA 2.2:CT • Item 543-A-2
GENERAL PUBLICATIONS

GEOGRAPHIC BOARD
(1906–1934)

CREATION AND AUTHORITY

The United States Board on Geographic Names was established as an independent agency by Executive Order 28 of September 4, 1890. Executive Order 493 of August 10, 1906, changed the name to United States Geographic Board, which existed until April 7, 1934, when Executive Order 6680 abolished the Board and transferred its functions to the Department of the Interior (I 33).

GB 1.1:date
ANNUAL REPORTS.

GB 1.2:CT
GENERAL PUBLICATIONS.

GB 1.3:nos.
BULLETINS.

GB 1.4:nos.
CIRCULARS [none issued].

GB 1.5:nos.
DECISIONS.

Later I 33.5

GB 1.5/2:nos.
DECISIONS.

Later I 33.5

GB 1.6:date
INDEX TO REPORTS AND SUPPLEMENTS.

GOVERNMENT PRINTING OFFICE
(1860–   )

CREATION AND AUTHORITY

The Government Printing Office was established by Congressional Joint Resolution 25, June 23, 1860.

INFORMATION

Government Printing Office
732 North Capital Street NW
Washington, D.C. 20401
(202) 512-0000
E-mail: gpoinfo@gpo.gov
http://www.gpo.gov

GP 1.1:date   • Item 548 (P) (EL)
ANNUAL REPORTS.

GP 1.1/2:date   • Item 556-C (EL)
GPO ACCESS. [Biennial]

GP 1.2:CT   • Item 548
GENERAL PUBLICATIONS.

GP 1.3:nos.
BULLETINS [none issued].

GP 1.3/2:nos.
ENGINEERING BULLETINS.

GP 1.4:nos.
CIRCULARS. [none issued].

GP 1.5:date
ALPHABETICAL LIST OF EMPLOYEES.

GP 1.6:date
GENERAL ORDERS.

GP 1.7:CT
SPECIFICATIONS, PROPOSALS, AND ADVERTISE-MENTS.

GP 1.8:nos.
DIVISION OF STORES, CIRCULAR ADVERTISE-MENTS OF SALE.

GP 1.9:nos.
TECHNICAL BULLETINS.

GP 1.10:nos.
APPRENTICE SERIES.

GP 1.11:CT   • Item 556-C
POSTERS. [Irregular]

GP 1.12:
DATED PUBLICATIONS.

For official use only.
GP 1.13:nos.
APPRENTICE LECTURES.

GP 1.14:v.nos.
AGPO.

GP 1.15:CT
ADDRESSES.

GP 1.16:nos.
ADMINISTRATIVE ORDERS.

GP 1.17:v.nos.
RECREATION AND WELFARE NEWS.

GP 1.18:nos.
SAFETY PAMPHLETS.

GP 1.19:v.nos.
G.P.O. BULLETIN.

Employee newspaper.

GP 1.20:nos.
PERSONNEL BULLETINS.

GP 1.21:nos.
PURCHASE CIRCULARS.

GP 1.22:date
DATED PERIODICAL SCHEDULES.

GP 1.23:CT
REGULATIONS, RULES, AND INSTRUCTIONS.

GP 1.23/2:nos.
SECURITY PROCEDURES. OFFICIAL USE.

GP 1.23/3:nos.
PLANNING DIVISION, INSTRUCTION AND PROCE-DURE.

Administrative.

GP 1.23/4:CT   • Item 548
HANDBOOKS, MANUALS, GUIDES. [Irregular]

GP 1.23/4:St 9   • Item 548
U.S. GOVERNMENT PRINTING OFFICE STYLE MANUAL. 1973. 548 p.

This manual was developed to facilitate Government printing through the standard-ization of grammar, punctuation, type size, and other printing techniques. It includes in-struction on capitalization, abbreviations, spelling, and other correct methods for writ-ing. Also included are several useful tables of scientific items, titles, and foreign money and measurements. A gift that can be used all year by teachers, authors, and students.

GP 1.24:nos.
SAFETY BULLETINS.

GP 1.25:nos.
GP-PIA JOINT RESEARCH BULLETINS.

GP 1.26:CT   • Item 548
APPRENTICE TRAINING SERIES.

GP 1.27:v.nos.
GENERAL MANAGEMENT SERIES.

GP 1.27/2:v.nos.
OFFICE MANAGEMENT SERIES.

GP 1.27/3:v.nos.
MANAGEMENT REVIEW [non Govt.-American Management Accociation]

GP 1.27/4:v.nos.
INTERNATIONAL MANAGEMENT SERIES. [non Govt.-American Management Association]

GP 1.27/5:v.nos.
FINANCIAL MANAGEMENT SERIES. [non Govt.-American Management Accociation]

GP 1.27/6:v.nos.
PERSONNEL. [Bimonthly] [non Govt.-American Man-agement Accociation]

GP 1.27/7:v.nos.
PERSONNEL SERIES. [non Govt.-American Manage-ment Accociation]

GP 1.27/8:v.nos.
INSURANCE SERIES. [non Govt.-American Manage-ment Accociation]

GP 1.27/9:nos.
MANUFACTURING SERIES. [non Govt.- American Management Accociation]

GP 1.27/10:nos.
MARKETING SERIES. [non Govt.-American Manage-ment Accociation]

GP 1.27/11:nos.
PACKAGING SERIES. [non Govt.-American Manage-ment Accociation]

GP 1.27/12:nos.
PRODUCTION SERIES. [non Govt.-American Man-agement Accociation]

GP 1.28:nos.
CIRCULAR LETTERS.

GP 1.29:nos.
CURRENT WORK, NEW PUBLICATIONS.

GP 1.30:nos.
EMPLOYEE LETTERS.

GP 1.31:nos.
TESTS AND TECHNICAL CONTROL DIVISION: IN-FORMATION BULLETINS.

GP 1.32:CT
BIBLIOGRAPHIES AND LISTS OF PUBLICATIONS.

GP 1.33:date
UNITED STATES GOVERNMENT PRINTING OFFICE PAPER CATALOG.

GP 1.34:v.nos.&nos.
GPO NEWSLETTER.

GP 1.35:date
DEPOSITORY LIBRARY COUNCIL REPORT TO THE PUBLIC PRINTER. [Annual]

GP 1.36:CT
DEPOSITORY LIBRARY COUNCIL TO THE PUBLIC PRINTER: ADDRESSES. [Irregular]

GP 1.37:nos.
TECHNICAL REPORTS. [Irregular] (Quality Control and Technical Department)

GP 1.38:nos. • Item 548-B
MARKETING MOVES, THE MARKETING BULLETIN FROM THE U.S. GOVERNMENT PRINTING OFFICE. [Irregular]

PURPOSE:– To provide news of Government Printing Office marketing activities to publishing Federal agencies on enhancing the marketability of their publications.

GP 1.39:date • Item 556-C
TELEPHONE DIRECTORY.
Earlier GP 1.2:T 23

GP 1.40 • Item 548-A-2 (EL)
ePUB ILLUSTRADED. (bimonthly)

GOVERNMENT PRINTING OFFICE

Library
GP 2.1:date
ANNUAL REPORTS.

GP 2.2:CT
GENERAL PUBLICATIONS.

GP 2.3:nos.
BULLETINS [none issued].

GP 2.4:nos.
CIRCULARS [none issued].

GP 2.5:date
LISTS OF BOOKS IN LIBRARY.

SUPERINTENDENT OF DOCUMENTS
(1895–   )

INFORMATION

Superintendent of Documents
Government Printing Office
732 N. Capital St. NW
Washington, D. C. 20401
http://www.gpo.gov/su_docs

GP 3.1:date
ANNUAL REPORT.

GP 3.1/2:date
– ORIGINAL SHEET [including] RECORD OF PUBLICATIONS DISTRIBUTED.

GP 3.2:CT • Item 551
GENERAL PUBLICATIONS.

GP 3.3:nos.
BULLETINS.

GP 3.4:nos.
CIRCULARS.

GP 3.5:nos.
BIBLIOGRAPHIES.

GP 3.6:nos.
DOCUMENT CATALOG.

GP 3.7:nos.
DOCUMENT INDEX.

Superseded by GP 3.7/2

GP 3.7/2 • Item 553
NUMERICAL LISTS AND SCHEDULE OF VOLUMES OF REPORTS AND DOCUMENTS OF CONGRESS. 73rd Cong.–   1933–   [Annual]

Separate list issued for each Session of Congress. Gives numerical list of Senate and House Reports and Documents, including the serial number for the Congressional Serial Set. A separate numerical list of the serial set volumes and the contents of each is also included.

GP 3.8 • Item 557-A (P)
• Item 557-B (MF)
MONTHLY CATALOG OF UNITED STATES GOVERNMENT PUBLICATIONS. [Annual]

Lists all Government publications, both printed and processed, GPO and non-GPO, received in the Division's library. Entries are arranged strictly by the SuDocs classification number and contain bibliographical information as entered in the OCLC data base. Each monthly issue contains the following indexes: Author, Title, Subject, Series/Report, Contract Number, Title Keyword. Indexes are cumulative semiannually Jan.– June and Jan.– Dec. A Series Supplement, issued separately, continues the Directory of U.S. Government Periodicals and Subscription Publications, formerly contained in the February issue. A list of Depository Libraries in contained in the September issue.

Beginning January 1986 the Registers of the Monthly Catalog, Periodicals Supplement, and Congressional Serial Set Supplement, and the indexes to each of them will be distributed to depositories in two formats, and depositories must select either paper or microfiche (not both).

GP 3.8/2
MONTHLY CATALOG INDEX. [Quarterly]

GP 3.8/3:date
CUMULATIVE INDEXES.

GP 3.8/4:date
GPO LIBRARY CATALOGING TRANSACTION TAPES. [Weekly]

GP 3.8/5: • Item 557-A (P)
• Item 557-B (MF)
MONTHLY CATALOG OF UNITED STATES GOVERNMENT PUBLICATIONS, PERIODICALS SUPPLEMENT. [Annual]

Former title: Serials Supplement.

GP 3.8/6: • Item 557-A (P)
• Item 557-B (MF)
– UNITED STATES CONGRESSIONAL SERIAL SET SUPPLEMENT. [Annual]

GP 3.8/6 • Item 557-N (P)
• Item 557-P (MF)
– UNITED STATES CONGRESSIONAL SERIAL SET SUPPLEMENT, INDEX.

GP 3.8/6 • Item 557-L (P)
• Item 557-M (MF)
REGISTER MONTHLY CATALOG OF UNITED STATES GOVERNMENT PUBLICATIONS, UNITED STATES CONGRESSIONAL SERIAL SET SUPPLEMENT. [Annual]

GP 3.8/7 • Item 557-C (CD)
MONTHLY CATALOG OF THE UNITED STATES GOVERNMENT PUBLICATIONS.

Issued on CD-ROM

GP 3.8/8 • Item 557-D
MONTHLY CATALOG OF THE UNITED STATES GOVERNMENT PUBLICATIONS. (Condensed version)

GP 3.8/8-8:date • Item 557-D-1
MONTHLY CATALOG OF UNITED STATES GOVERNMENT PUBLICATIONS, PERIODICAL SUPPLEMENT. [Annual]

GP 3.8/8-9 • Item 557-F (EL)
CATALOG OF U. S. GOVERNMENT PUBLICATIONS (online).

GP 3.9:nos. • Item 554
PRICE LISTS. 1898–   [Irregular]

With the exception of PL 36, superseded by Subject Bibliographies (GP 3.22/2).

36. GOVERNMENT PERIODICALS. Covers those periodicals for which subscriptions are taken by the Superintendent of Documents. Also includes manuals and similar materials sold on a subscription basis. Revised quarterly.

GP 3.10
BIBLIOGRAPHY OF UNITED STATES PUBLIC DOCUMENTS. DEPARTMENT LISTS.

GP 3.11:nos.
SCHEDULE OF VOLUMES (for document index).

GP 3.12:nos.
FREE LISTS.

GP 3.13:nos.
LEAFLETS.

GP 3.14:CT
ADVANCE SHEETS OF 3d EDITION OF CHECKLIST OF UNITED STATES PUBLIC DOCUMENTS.

GP 3.15:nos.
NUMERICAL TABLES AND SCHEDULE OF VOLUMES (for Document Index).

GP 3.16:nos.
DEPOSITORY INVOICES. [Monthly]

GP 3.16/2:nos.
GEOLOGICAL INVOICES, DEPOSITORY LIBRARIES.

GP 3.16/3:nos. • Item 566-C (EL)
DAILY DEPOSITORY SHIPPING LIST. 1–

ISSN 0145-0646

GP 3.16/3-2:v.nos.&nos. • Item 556-C (P) (EL)
ADMINISTRATIVE NOTES. [Irregular]

GP 3.16/3-3 • Item 556-C (P) (EL)
ADMINISTRATIVE NOTES TECHNICAL SUPPLEMENT. [Monthly]

GP 3.17:v.nos.&nos. • Item 556
SELECTED UNITED STATES GOVERNMENT PUBLICATIONS. v. 1– 11.   – 1982. [Monthly]

Provides an annotated guide to new publications available for sale by the Superintendent of Documents as well as important older publications still in stock.
Issued biweekly prior to January 1974.
Superseded by U.S. Government Books (GP 3.17/5).
ISSN 0566-8549

GP 3.17/2:CT
SELECTED UNITED STATES GOVERNMENT PUBLICATIONS.

GP 3.17/3:nos.
PERIODIC SUPPLEMENT, SELECTED UNITED STATES GOVERNMENT PUBLICATIONS. [Irregular]

GP 3.17/4:date
SELECTED U.S. GOVERNMENT PUBLICATIONS, SUPPLEMENTS.

GP 3.17/5:v.nos.&nos. • Item 556-A
U.S. GOVERNMENT BOOKS. v. 1–   1982– [Semiannual]

Each issue contains over 1,000 of the popular U.S. Government publications available from the Superintendent of Documents.
Supersedes Selected United States Government Publications (GP 3.17).

GP 3.17/6:v.nos.&nos.   • **Item 556-B**
NEW PRODUCTS FROM THE U.S. GOVERNMENT. v.
1–   1982–   [Bimonthly]

   PURPOSE:– To provide those who use government publications in a professional capacity with a list of the publications added to the Superintendent of Documents sales inventory for each two-month period.
   Earlier title: New Books.

GP 3.18:date
INFORMATION GOVERNING DISTRIBUTION OF GOVERNMENT PUBLICATIONS AND PRICE LISTS.

   Changed from GP 3.2

GP 3.19:date
PRICE LISTS OF GOVERNMENT PUBLICATIONS.

GP 3.20:nos.
DIVISION MEMORANDUMS.

GP 3.21:CT   • **Item 555-A**
PUBLICATIONS ANNOUNCEMENTS. [Irregular]

   Includes flyers, press releases and circulars announcing individual new publications, packets, or kits.

GP 3.21/2:CT   • **Item 551-A**
POSTERS. [Irregular]

GP 3.22:CT   • **Item 552**
LIST OF PUBLICATIONS (miscellaneous).

GP 3.22/2:nos.   • **Item 552-A (EL)**
SUBJECT BIBLIOGRAPHIES. 1–   1975– [Irregular]

   PURPOSE:– To provide the general public with an up-to-date list of publications available for sale by the Superintendent of Documents. Supersedes the Price Lists (GP 3.9).

GP 3.22/3:date   • **Item 552-B (MF)**
GPO SALES PUBLICATIONS REFERENCE FILE. [Bimonthly]

   PURPOSE:– To provide a catalog of all publications currently offered for sale by the Superintendent of Documents. The file is arranged by 1) GPO Stock Numbers, 2) Superintendent of Documents classification numbers, and 3) Alphabetical arrangement of subjects, titles, agency series and report numbers, key words and phrases, and personal authors.
   Published in microfiche (48x)

GP 3.22/3:manual
HOW TO USE THE MICROFICHE.

GP 3.22/3-2:date
GPO SALES PUBLICATIONS REFERENCE FILE, UPDATE. 1978–   [Bimonthly] (Subscription included with GP 3.22/3)

   Contains new items received in a month's period following issuance of the main reference file (GP 3.22/3). Items are listed by title only.
   Published in microfiche (48x).

GP 3.22/3-3:date   • **Item 552-B (MF)**
EXHAUSTED GPO SALES PUBLICATIONS REFERENCE FILE. [Annual]

   Published in microfiche (48x).

GP 3.22/3-4:date   • **Item 552-B (MF)**
CUMULATIVE PRICE AND STATUS CHANGE REPORT. [Biweekly]

GP 3.22/5   • **Item 552-A**
ELECTRONIC INFORMATION PRODUCTS AVAILABLE BY SPECIAL ORDER. [Semiannual]

GP 3.22/6   • **Item 522-C**
SIGCAT CD-ROM COMPENDIUM. [Quarterly]

GP 3.22/7   • **Item 552-B-1 (EL)**
SALES PRODUCT CATALOG (Online).

GP 3.23:nos.&date
CHECKLIST C (series).

GP 3.24:date   • **Item 556-C (P) (EL)**
LIST OF CLASSES IN 1950 REVISION OF CLASSIFIED LIST OF UNITED STATES GOVERNMENT PUBLICATIONS BY DEPARTMENTS AND BUREAUS. [Semiannual]

   GP 3.24:date/app.   All depository libraries
INACTIVE OR DISCONTINUED ITEMS FROM THE 1950 REVISION OF THE CLASSIFIED LIST. 1953–   [Annual]

   Issued as an appendix to the List of Classes of United States Government Publications Available for Selection by Depository Libraries.
   Frequency varies: 1953– 1976, irregular; 1977–   annual.

GP 3.24/2:date   • **Item 556-C**
INACTIVE OR DISCONTINUED ITEMS FROM THE 1950 REVISION OF THE CLASSIFIED LIST. [Annual]

GP 3.25:v.nos.&nos.
NEWSLETTER TO SALES AGENTS.

   Administrative.

GP 3.26:CT   • **Item 556-C**
REGULATIONS, RULES, AND INSTRUCTIONS.

GP 3.27:v.nos.&nos.
PUBLIC DOCUMENTS HIGHLIGHTS. [Irregular]

   ISSN 0145-062X

GP 3.27/2:nos.
PUBLIC DOCUMENTS HIGHLIGHTS, MICROFICHE CUMULATION. [Quinquennial]

GP 3.28:cong.sess.   • **Item 553-A**
FINAL CUMULATIVE FINDING AID, HOUSE AND SENATE BILLS. [Annual]

   Published in microfiche.

GP 3.29:CT   • **Item 556-C**
HANDBOOKS, MANUALS, GUIDES.

GP 3.29/2   • **Item 556-C (P) (EL)**
GPO ACCESS TRAINING MANUAL.

GP 3.30:date   • **Item 556-C (MF)**
TRANSCRIPTS OF PROCEEDINGS, MEETING OF DEPOSITORY COUNCIL TO THE PUBLIC PRINTER.

GP 3.30/2:date
SUMMARY OF MEETING DEPOSITORY LIBRARY COUNCIL TO THE PRINTER.

GP 3.30/3:date   • **Item 556-C (P) (EL)**
PROCEEDINGS OF THE ANNUAL FEDERAL DEPOSITORY LIBRARY CONFERENCE, . . . REGIONAL FEDERAL DEPOSITORY SEMINAR.

   Proceedings for the 1st and 2nd Annual Federal Depository Library Conference were included in Administrative Notes (GP 3.16/3-2).

GP 3.31:nos.   • **Item 556-C (EL)**
NEEDS AND OFFERS LIST. [Irregular]

GP 3.32:date
LIST OF ITEMS FOR SELECTION BY DEPOSITORY LIBRARIES. [Semiannual]

GP 3.32/2:date   • **Item 556-C (EL)**
GPO DEPOSITORY UNION LIST OF ITEM SELECTIONS. [Annual]

GP 3.33:date   • **Item 556-C (MF)**
BIENNIAL REPORT OF DEPOSITORY LIBRARIES, U.S. SUMMARY.

GP 3.33/2:date   • **Item 557-A (P)**
BIENNIAL REPORT OF DEPOSITORY LIBRARIES, SUMMARY REPORTS BY STATE.

GP 3.33/4   • **Item 556-C (P) (EL)**
BIENNIAL SURVEY OF DEPOSITORY LIBRARIES: RESULTS.

                                • **Item 557-A (P)**
GP 3.34:date   • **Item 557-B (MF)**
UNITED STATES CONGRESSIONAL SERIAL SET CATALOG: NUMERICAL LISTS AND SCHEDULE OF VOLUMES.

GP 3.35   • **Item 554-A**
THE FEDERAL BULLETIN BOARD.

   The Federal Bulletin Board provides Government Information from a variety of agencies in on-line files for downloading. Online service is available on the Internet or via asynchronous connection.

GP 3.36   • **Item 551-A-1**
DIRECTORIES.

GP 3.36/2   • **Item 556-C (P) (EL)**
FEDERAL DEPOSITORY LIBRARY DIRECTORY. [Annual]

GP 3.36/2-2   • **Item 552-D (EL)**
FEDERAL DEPOSITORY LIBRARY DIRECTORY (Online).

GP 3.37   • **Item 554-C**
GPO LOCATOR.

GP 3.38   • **Item 522-D (E)**
ELECTRONIC PRODUCTS.

GP 3.38/2:date/nos.   • **Item 522-D-1 (CD)**
THE FEDERAL ACQUISITION REGULATION.

GP 3.38/3   • **Item 522-D-2 (CD)**
FEDERAL TAX PRODUCTS. (annual)

GP 3.39   • **Item 556-C (EL)**
BEN'S GUIDE TO U.S. GOVERNMENT FOR KIDS.

GP 3.40   • **Item 556-C (EL)**
NET (NEW ELECTRONIC TITLES).

GENERAL SUPPLY COMMITTEE (1909– 1910)

CREATION AND AUTHORITY

   The General Supply Committee was established as an independent agency by Executive Order 1071 of May 13, 1909, pursuant to act of Congress, approved January 27, 1894 (28 Stat. 33). The Committee was abolished when a new General Supply Committee (T 45) was established within the Treasury Department by act of Congress, approved June 17, 1910 (36 Stat. 531).

GS 1.1:date   • **Item 558 (MF)**
ANNUAL REPORTS.

GS 1.2:CT   • **Item 559**
GENERAL PUBLICATIONS [none issued].

GS 1.3:nos.
BULLETINS [none issued].

GS 1.4:nos.
CIRCULARS [none issued].

GS 1.5/1:CT
GENERAL SCHEDULE OF SUPPLIES, FISCAL YEAR 1910.

GS 1.5/2:form letters or class nos.
GENERAL SCHEDULE OF SUPPLIES, FISCAL YEAR 1911.

GS 1.6:date
LIST OF AWARDS SHOWING CONTRACTORS AND PRICES FOR MATERIAL AND SUPPLIES CONTAINED IN GENERAL SCHEDULE, FISCAL YEAR.

NOTE:– GS-Letters reused for General Services Administration.

GENERAL SERVICES ADMINISTRATION (1949–   )

CREATION AND AUTHORITY

The General Services Administration was established by the Federal Property and Administrative Services Act of 1949 (63 Stat. 377, as amended), effective July 1, 1949, which transferred to the Administration the functions of the following agencies: Office of Contract Settlement (T 67), including the Contract Settlement Act Advisory Board and Contract Settlement Appeals Board; Bureau of Federal Supply (T 58); Federal Works Agency (FW 1), including Bureau of Community Facilities (FW 7) and Public Roads Administration (FW 2); National Archives Establishment (AE 1); and War Assets Administration (Y 3.W 19/8).

INFORMATION

Office of Citizens Services
and Communications
General Services Administration
18th and F Streets, NW
Washington, D. C. 20405
(202) 501-0705
Fax: (202) 501-1489
http//www.gsa.gov

GS 1.1   • Item 558
ANNUAL REPORT OF THE ADMINISTRATOR OF GENERAL SERVICES. 1949–   [Annual]

Report submitted by the Administrator to Congress pursuant to the Federal Property and Administrative Services Act of 1949, as amended, for the fiscal year.

GS 1.1/3:date   • Item 558-A-6
OFFICE OF INSPECTOR GENERAL, SEMIANNUAL REPORT TO THE CONGRESS.

Summarizes Office activities, which include responsibility for auditing and investigating administration programs for keeping the Administration and Congress informed of any deficiencies.

GS 1.2:CT   • Item 559
GENERAL PUBLICATIONS.

GS 1.4/2:letters-nos.
GENERAL SERVICES ADMINISTRTION CIRCULARS.

GS 1.4/3:nos.
FEDERAL MANAGEMENT CIRCULARS (numbered).

GS 1.5:CT   • Item 560
LAWS.

GS 1.6:CT   • Item 558-A-5
REGULATIONS, RULES, AND INSTRUCTIONS.

GS 1.6/2:CT
[SPECIAL REGULATIONS].

GS 1.6/3:
GENERAL REGULATIONS.

GS 1.6/4:trans.le.nos.
REGULATIONS OF GENERAL SERVICES ADMINISTRATION.

GS 1.6/5   • Item 558-A
FEDERAL PROCUREMENT REGULATIONS. [Irregular]

Subscription price includes supplementary material for an indefinite period. Issued in looseleaf form and punched for 3-ring binder.
Covers Federal Procurement Regulations prescribed by the Administrator of General Services under the Federal Property and Administrative Act of 1949.

GS 1.6/5-2:nos.
FEDERAL PROCUREMENT REGULATIONS, FPR NOTICES.

GS 1.6/5-3:nos.   • Item 558-A
GSA BULLETIN FPR, FEDERAL PROCUREMENT. [Irregular]

GS 1.6/6:CT   • Item 559-B
HANDBOOKS, MANUALS, GUIDES.

GS 1.6/6-2   • Item 558-A-1
COUNSELING GUIDES.

GS 1.6/7:nos.
DEFENSE MATERIAL REGULATIONS.

GS 1.6/8:letters-nos.   • Item 558-A-5
FEDERAL PROPERTY MANAGEMENT REGULATIONS, TEMPORARY REGULATIONS.

GS 1.6/8-2:letters-nos.   • Item 558-A-5
GSA BULLETIN. FPMR (series).

GS 1.6/8-2   • Item 558-A-5
FEDERAL TRAVEL REGULATIONS. (Includes basic manual plus supplementary material for an indefinite period) (FPMR 101-7)

PURPOSE:– To consolidate in one document the regulations on travel relocation allowances, and entitlements for Federal employees.

GS 1.6/8-3:letters-nos.   • Item 558-A-5
FEDERAL PROPERTY MANAGEMENT REGULATIONS AMENDMENTS. [Irregular]

GS 1.6/9:letters-nos.   • Item 599-D
GSA HANDBOOKS (numbered). [Irregular]

GSA Handbooks are issued by various branches of the Administration to inform the Federal Agencies about managerial procedures to be followed.

GS 1.6/10:date/v.nos.   • Item 559-K (EL)
FEDERAL ACQUISITION REGULATION (Online database).

GS 1.6/11   • Item 559-L
REGULATORY INFORMATION SERVICE CENTER: GENERAL PUBLICATION.

GS 1.6/11-2   • Item 559-L-1 (P) (EL)
DATABASES AND BROWSEABLE LISTS OF THE REGULATORY PLAN AND THE UNIFIED AGENDA OF FEDERAL REGULATORY AND DEREGULATORY ACTIONS. [Semiannual]

GS 1.6/12   • Item 558-B (EL)
FEDERAL ACQUISITION INSTITUTE: GENERAL PUBLICATIONS.

GS 1.7:nos.   • Item 559-B
PUBLIC CONSTRUCTION. [Monthly]

Earlier FW 1.16

GS 1.8:nos.
ADMINISTRATIVE ORDERS.

GS 1.9:nos.
SPECIFICATIONS.

GS 1.10:
FEDERAL SPECIFICATIONS ANNOUNCEMENTS.

GS 1.11:date
TELEPHONE DIRECTORY, GENERAL SERVICES ADMINISTRATION AND DEFENSE MATERIALS PROCUREMENT AGENCY. [Quarterly]

Later GS 12.12

GS 1.12:nos.
RELEASES.

GS 1.13   • Item 559-J (EL)
FORMS.

FEDERAL FIRE COUNCIL

GS 1.14:date
ANNUAL REPORTS.

GS 1.14/2
FEDERAL FIRE EXPERIENCE FOR FISCAL YEAR (date). [Annual]

PURPOSE:– To compile the fire experience of the Federal Government and to present the information for review by those who wish to profit from an analysis of this information. Includes textual summaries and statistical tables.

GS 1.14/2:date
FIRE LOSS TO GOVERNMENT PROPERTY. [Annual]

GS 1.14/3
MINUTES OF ANNUAL MEETING. [Annual]

Gives a brief abstract of the meeting, with portraits of the speakers, texts of topics presented, and annual committee reports.
Minutes of special meetings are also published.

GS 1.14/4:date
FEDERAL FIRE COUNCIL NEWS LETTER.

GS 1.14/5:CT
PUBLICATIONS.

GS 1.14/6:date
LIBRARY MATERIAL RECEIVED. [Monthly]

GS 1.14/7
RECOMMENDED PRACTICES. RP 1–   1962– [Irregular]

The objectives of the Federal Fire Council are to reduce Federal fire losses to life and property through a cooperative effort of all Federal agencies coordinated through the Council; to promote and assist in the establishment of adequate fire safety programs and criteria in all Federal Agencies; and to encourage fire research for the purpose of better understanding the phenomena of fire and to develop better techniques for fire control, suppression and prevention.
Recommendations of committees on fire prevention and related activities.

GS 1.14/8:date
FIRE SAFETY ACTIVITIES [list] ADMINISTRATIVE.

GS 1.14/9:nos.
CONSTRUCTION PROBLEMS RELATING TO FIRE PROTECTION.

Official use.

GS 1.14/10
ADDRESSES. [Irregular]

GS 1.14/11:nos.
SIGNIFICANT FIRE WRITEUP.

GS 1.14/12:nos.
RESEARCH REPORT DIGEST. Admin.

GS 1.14/13:nos.
PAMPHLETS.

GENERAL SERVICES ADMINISTRATION
(Continued)

GS 1.15   • Item 559-A (EL)
SUMMARY REPORT ON REAL PROPERTY OWNED
BY THE UNITED STATES THROUGHOUT THE
WORLD. 1955–   [Annual]

Report submitted by the Administrator to Congress for the fiscal year.
Contains a summary report accompanied by summary tables on Federal real property owned by the Federal government in the United States, outlying areas, and foreign countries.

GS 1.15/2   • Item 559-A (MF)
INVENTORY REPORT ON REAL PROPERTY LEASED
TO THE UNITED STATES THROUGHOUT THE
WORLD. 1956–   [Annual]

Report submitted by the Administrator to Congress for the fiscal year.
Companion volume to that listed above covering leased property.

GS 1.15/3   • Item 559-A
INVENTORY REPORT OF JURISDICTIONAL STATUS
OF FEDERAL AREAS WITHIN THE STATES, AS
OF JUNE 30. [Irregular]

GS 1.15/4:date   • Item 559-A
DETAILED LISTING OF REAL PROPERTY OWNED
BY THE UNITED STATES AND USED BY CIVIL
AGENCIES THROUGHOUT THE WORLD AS OF
SEPTEMBER 30 (year). [Annual]

GS 1.15/4-2:date   • Item 559-A (MF)
DETAILED LISTING OF REAL PROPERTY OWNED
BY THE UNITED STATES AND USED BY THE
DEPARTMENT OF DEFENSE FOR MILITARY FUNCTIONS THROUGHOUT THE WORLD, AS OF SEPTEMBER 30 (year). [Annual]

GS 1.15/5:date   • Item 559-A-1
U.S. REAL PROPERTY SALES LIST. [Quarterly]

This publication results from Executive Order 12348 to promote sale of surplus Federal real property for a wide range of uses, including industrial, commercial, and residential. Lists available property by state, city or county.

GS 1.16:date
DISABLING INJURIES, REPORT FOR YEAR.

GS 1.17:CT   • Item 559
BIBLIOGRAPHIES AND LISTS OF PUBLICATIONS.

GS 1.18:CT
ADDRESSES.

GS 1.19:nos.   • Item 558-A-2
CONSUMER INFORMATION SERIES. 1–   1971–
[Irregular]

GS 1.20:date
GSA NEWS. [Bimonthly]

GS 1.21:P-nos.
GSA STOCKPILE INFORMATION.

GS 1.22:date
STOCKPILE REPORT TO THE CONGRESS. [Semiannual]

Report submitted by the Office to Congress pursuant to section 4 of the Strategic and Critical Materials Stock Piling Act (Public Law 79-520).
Brief report, supported by statistical tables, concerning the conditions of the Nation's stockpile of strategic materials. Includes list of publications of the Bureau of Mines and Geological Survey which deal with such materials.
Earlier PrEx 4.9
Later FEM 1.12

GS 1.23:date
MANAGEMENT REPORTS.

GS 1.24:date
ANNUAL REPORT OF THE PUBLIC BUILDINGS
SERVICE VALUE ENGINEERING PROGRAM.

GS 1.25:CT   • Item 559-C (MF)
ENVIRONMENTAL IMPACT STATEMENT. [Irregular]

GS 1.26:date   • Item 559-E
GSA TRAINING CENTER CATALOG AND SCHEDULE.
[Annual]

Describes and lists, by region, courses available to Federal, State and local government employees.
Earlier: Calendar of Interagency Courses.

GS 1.26/2:CT   • Item 559-G
INTERAGENCY TRAINING PROGRAM (various subjects) (series). [Irregular] (GSA Training Center)

Series of brochures describing courses in various GSA mission areas such as procurement, supply, property management. They are expected to be updated on an annual basis.
Some subjects were offered by OPM and were classed PM 1.19/4.

GS 1.26/2-2:date   • Item 559-E
GSA TRAINING CENTER CATALOG AND SCHEDULE.
[Annual]

GS 1.26/3   • Item 559-J (E)
GSA INTERAGENCY TRAINING CENTER NEWSLETTER.

GS 1.27:CT
AUDIOVISUAL MATERIAL.

GS 1.28:date   • Item 559-F (MF)
LIST OF PARTIES EXCLUDED FROM FEDERAL
PROCUREMENT OR NONPROCUREMENT PROGRAMS. [Monthly]

Issued to notify Federal agency contracting officials of those contractors which are barred governmentwide from participating in Federal contracting programs. Also circulates information on contractors administratively debarred or suspended by agencies.
Earlier: Consolidate List of Debarred, Suspended, and Ineligible Contracts.

GS 1.29:nos.   • Item 580-A-3
FEDERAL TRAVEL DIRECTORY. [Monthly]

Earlier GS 2.21

GS 1.30   • Item 559-E-1
DIRECTORY OF ACADEMIC PROCUREMENT AND
RELATED PROGRAMS AND COURSES. [Annual]

GS 1.31:date   • Item 559-E-3 (MF)
GSA SUBCONTRACTING DIRECTORY. [Semiannual]

GS 1.32:CT   • Item 559-E-3
POSTERS. [Irregular]

GS 1.33   • Item 559-H (MF)
LABOR SURPLUS AREA ZIP CODE REFERENCE.
[Annual]

Lists the zip codes of all U.S. locations that have been classified as labor surplus areas by the Labor Department. Zip codes are listed numerically and identified by state.

GS 1.34   • Item 559-E-4 (EL)
WORLDWIDE GEOGRAPHIC LOCATION CODES.
[Annual]

Lists the standard numeric (number) and alpha (letter) codes federal agencies should use in designating geographic locations in automaticdata processing programs. Cities, counties, state, and countries are listed alphabetically.

GS 1.35   • Item 559-J (E)
ELECTRONIC PRODUCTS. [Irregular]

GS 1.36   • Item 559-J (EL)
U.S. PER DIEM RATES (CONUS).

GS 1.37   • Item 559-J (EL)
ICA NEWSLETTER.

GS 1.37/2   • Item 559-J (EL)
INFORMATION TECHNOLOGY NEWSLETTER.

GS 1.38   • Item 559-J (EL)
INTERGOVERNMENTAL SOLUTIONS NEWSLETTER.
[Quarterly]

GS 1.39   • Item 559-J (EL)
FEDWARE MAGAZINE.

GS 1.40   • Item 559-J-2 (EL)
FIRSTGOV.

GS 1.41   • Item 559-J-3 (EL)
FEDBIZOPPS (Federal Business Opportunities) (online database).

FEDERAL SUPPLY SERVICE
(1983–   )

CREATION AND AUTHORITY

The Federal Supply Service was established December 11, 1949, by the Administrator of General Services to supersede the Bureau of Federal Supply (T 58), which had been transferred from the Department of the Treasury under the Federal Property and Administrative Services Act of 1949 (63 Stat. 378), effective July 1, 1949. The name was changed to Office of Personal Property by GSA order, effective September 28, 1982; and later was changed to Office of Federal Supply and Services by GAS order of January 22, 1983.

INFORMATION

Federal Supply Service
General Services Administration
1941 Jefferson Davis Highway
Arlington, Virginia 22202
(703) 605-5400
Fax: (703) 305-6577
http://www.fss.gsa.gov

GS 2.1:date
ANNUAL REPORTS.

Earlier T 58.1

GS 2.2:CT   • Item 564
GENERAL PUBLICATIONS.

Earlier T 58.2

GS 2.4:nos.
FEDERAL SUPPLY CIRCULAR.

GS 2.4/2:nos.
CIRCULAR DC-NOS. WASHINGTON STORE.

GS 2.4/3:nos.
EXCESS PERSONAL PROPERTY AVAILABLE FOR
TRANSFER, CIRCULARS.

Earlier GS 2.2:P 43

GS 2.4/3-2:nos.
DEPARTMENT OF DEFENSE LIST OF EXCESS PERSONAL PROPERTY AVAILABLE FOR TRANSFER
TO FEDERAL CIVIL AGENCIES.

Supersedes GS 2.4/3

GS 2.4/4:nos.
CIRCULAR LETTER A (series)

Earlier T 58.11/2

GS 2.4/5:nos.
CIRCULAR LETTER E (series).

Earlier T 58.11/3

GS 2.6:CT • **Item 565-A**
REGULATIONS, RULES AND INSTRUCTIONS.

GS 2.6/2:nos.
FEDERAL HANDBOOK HB (series).

GS 2.6/3:CT • **Item 564-A**
HANDBOOKS, MANUALS, GUIDES (unnumbered).

Earlier GS 2.6

GS 2.6/4 • **Item 564-A**
SCIENTIFIC INVENTORY MANAGEMENT SERIES. [Irregular]

GS 2.7:class nos.&date
FEDERAL SUPPLY SCHEDULE.

Earlier T 58.8

GS 2.7/2:nos.
–AMENDMENTS.

Earlier T 58.8/4

GS 2.7/3
FEDERAL SUPPLY SCHEDULE, CHECKLIST AND GUIDE. [Quarterly]

GS 2.7/4:group nos.&date • **Item 564-B (EL)**
FEDERAL SUPPLY SCHEDULE (by groups). [Annual]

Earlier GS 2.7

GS 2.7/5:date • **Item 564-B (MF)**
FEDERAL SUPPLY SCHEDULE PROGRAM GUIDE.

PURPOSE:– To provide a comprehensive source of information that identifies supplies and services available.

GS 2.7/6:date • **Item 564-B (MF)**
MULTIPLE AWARD FEDERAL SUPPLY SCHEDULE.

GS 2.8 • **Item 563**
FEDERAL SPECIFICATIONS. [Irregular]

Specifications are clear and accurate descriptions of the technical requirements for materials, products, or services. They specify the minimum requirements for quality and construction of materials and equipment necessary for an acceptable product. Generally, specifications are in the form of written descriptions, drawings, prints commercial designations, industry standards, and other descriptive references. They are an integral part of the purchase contract.

The development of specifications involves extensive research and testing by trained and experienced technicians. Although developed for the use of Government buyers they are also available for general use. Some State, County, and Municipal governments, institutional and education organizations, and commercial firms use Government specifications for their own purchases.

Federal Specifications are those of a permanent nature, prepared for the use of two or more Federal agencies (at least one of which is a civil agency) for items of potential general application. They are promulgated by the General Services Administration and if applicable are mandatory for use by all Federal agencies, including the Department of Defense.

Interim Federal Specifications are those which are potentially Federal in nature but which are issued in interim form by individual agencies for optional use by all Federal agencies. This type of specification can eventually be changed to the permanent Federal type if sufficient interest in its use is demonstrated.

Other types of specifications include Military Specifications, published by the Department of Defense and listed in this guide under that agency, and Departmental Specifications, developed by the individual agencies in cases where the item is only of interest to that particular agency and no Federal or Interim Specification equivalent exists.

The Specification number used to designate a Federal specification has three component parts:

1) Group for Procurement to which the specification relates.
2) The initial letter of the title of the specification.
3) A serial number determined by the alphabetical location of the title.
Published in loose-leaf form and punched for ring binder.

GS 2.8/2 • **Item 565**
INDEX OF FEDERAL SPECIFICATIONS, STANDARDS, AND HANDBOOKS. [Irregular]

Lists Federal specifications alphabetically and numerically by procurement groupings. Also includes information concerning Federal standards, common-use military specifications, Federal qualified products lists, and related information.

Subscription includes basic volume issued as of January 1, and monthly cumulative supplements.

Information included in tabular presentation include title, number, FSC number, price, effective date.
ISSN 0364-1414.

GS 2.8/3 • **Item 563**
FEDERAL STANDARDS. [Irregular]

One of the most effective means of securing the proper quality and economy in Government supply operations is the standardization of supply items. Federal standards establish engineering or technical limitations and applications for materials, processes, methods and designs, including any related criteria considered essential to achieve the highest practical degree of uniformity in materials or products, or interchangeability of parts used in those products. Standards are for use in invitations for bids, proposals, and contracts.

Issued as Federal or Interim Standards, similar in nature to the specifications (listed above). Published in loose-leaf form and punched for ring binder.

GS 2.8/3-2 • **Item 563-A**
MILITARY SPECIFICATIONS.

GS 2.8/4:le-nos.
FEDERAL STANDARD STOCK CATALOG: SEC. 4, PT. 5, EMERGENCY FEDERAL SPECIFICATIONS.

GS 2.8/5:le-nos.
INTERIM FEDERAL SPECIFICATIONS.

GS 2.8/6:les-nos.
PROPOSED FEDERAL SPECIFICATIONS. PRELIMINARY.

GS 2.8/7 • **Item 563**
FEDERAL TEST METHOD STANDARDS. [Irregular]

Specifies and compiles for easy reference methods of testing which are applicable to a given product.

GS 2.9:nos.
TRAFFIC SERVICE LETTERS.

GS 2.9/2 • **Item 564-A-1 (P) (EL)**
BIBLIOGRAPHIES AND LISTS OF PUBLICATIONS.

GS 2.10:date
STORE STOCK CATALOG, GENERAL SERVICES ADMINISTRATION, ZONE PRICE LISTS, ZONE 1. [Quarterly]

Earlier T 58.2:St 6/3

GS 2.10/2:date
STORES STOCK CATALOG. [Semiannual]

Earlier GS 2.2:St 7
Later GS 2.10/6

GS 2.10/2-2 • **Item 565-B**
HANDTOOL SECTION (FSG 51 and FSG 52 items). [Irregular]

GS 2.10/3:date
STORES STOCK CATALOG, PRICE LISTS. REGION 3. OFFICIAL USE.

GS 2.10/4:date
STANDARD FORMS CATALOG.

Earlier GS 2.10/2
Later GS 2.10/6

GS 2.10/5 • **Item 565-B**
FEDERAL STOCK NUMBER REFERENCE CATALOG, NUMERICAL LISTING OF ITEMS AVAILABLE FROM GENERAL SERVICES ADMINISTRATION. [Annual]

GS 2.10/6: • **Item 565-B**
GSA SUPPLY CATALOG. [Annual and quarterly] (includes basic volume plus 3 quarterly supplements) (FSG 13-99)

Contains listings of items in general use throughout the Federal Government which are available from GSA supply distribution facilities. Includes descriptions, prices, units of issue, and other information relative to ordering these items.

Published in two volumes: Volume 1, issued annually, an alphabetical index, and Volume 2, issued quarterly, containing the National Stock Number Index with current prices and other ordering information.
ISSN 0095-5620

GS 2.10/6:C 96/date • **Item 565-B**
CUSTOMER ASSISTANCE GUIDE.

GS 2.10/6-2:date
SPECIAL SUPPLEMENT TO STOCK CATALOG.

GS 2.10/6-3:date • **Item 565-B**
GSA SUPPLY CATALOG CHANGE BULLETIN.

GS 2.10/6-4:date • **Item 565-B**
SUPPLY CATALOG PRICE LIST. [Semiannual]

GS 2.10/7:date • **Item 565-B**
FEDERAL SUPPLY CATALOG: NATIONAL SUPPLIER CHANGE INDEX. [Quarterly]

Discontinued with July 1974 issue. Information currently contained in quarterly issues of volume 2 of the GSA Supply Catalog (GS 2.10/6).

GS 2.11:
DEPARTMENT OF DEFENSE EXCHANGE SALE OF PERSONAL PROPERTY AVAILABLE FOR TRANSFER TO FEDERAL AGENCIES. ADMIN.

GS 2.12
TERM CONTRACT, TC- (series). [Irregular]

GS 2.13:date
THE SUPPLIER. Official use.

GS 2.14:date
ANNUAL MOTOR VEHICLE REPORT FOR FISCAL YEAR.

GS 2.15 • **Item 853-B**
INVENTORY OF AUTOMATIC DATA PROCESSING EQUIPMENT IN THE UNITED STATES GOVERNMENT. [Annual]

GS 2.16:nos. • **Item 558-A-2**
CONSUMER INFORMATION SERIES. 1– [Irregular]

GS 2.17:date • **Item 558-A-3 (EL)**
MARKETIPS. [Irregular]

GS 2.18:date • **Item 558-A-4 (MF) (EL)**
FEDERAL MOTOR VEHICLE FLEET REPORTS.

GS 2.19:nos.
LIFE CYCLE COSTING PROCUREMENT CASES.

GS 2.20:CT
POSTERS.

GS 2.21 • **Item 580-A-4**
FEDERAL TRAVEL DIRECTORY. [Monthly]
Earlier GS 8.10
Later GS 1.29

GS 2.21/2:date • Item 580-A-4 (MF)
FEDERAL HOTEL/MOTEL DISCOUNT DIRECTORY.
[Annual]

Earlier GS 8.10/2

GS 2.22:CT/nos. • Item 564-B
NEW ITEM INTRODUCTORY SCHEDULE. [Irregular]

GS 2.23:CT
CUSTOMER SUPPLY CENTER CATALOG.

GS 2.24/2: • Item 564-C
FSS P (Federal Supply Service Property) (series).

This series will include publications on miscellaneous topics pertaining to the work of the Office.

GS 2.26: • Item 564-C-1 (E)
ELECTRONIC PRODUCTS (misc.).

BUREAU OF PUBLIC ROADS
(1949)

CREATION AND AUTHORITY

The Public Roads Administration (FW 2) was transferred from the Federal Works Agency and placed in the newly created General Services Administration by the Federal Property and Administrative Services Act of 1949, effective July 1, 1949, and its name changed to the Bureau of Public Roads. Under Reorganization Plan No. 7 of 1949, effective August 20, 1949, the Bureau was transferred to the Department of Commerce (C 37).

GS 3.1:date
ANNUAL REPORTS.

Earlier FW 2.1
Later C 37.1

GS 3.2:CT
GENERAL PUBLICATIONS.

Earlier FW 2.2
Later C 37.2

GS 3.7:date
TRAFFIC VOLUME TRENDS. [Monthly]

Earlier FW 2.16
Later C 37.9

GS 3.8:v.nos.&nos.
PUBLIC ROADS, JOURNAL OF HIGHWAY RESEARCH.

Earlier FW 2.7
Later C 37.8

NATIONAL ARCHIVES AND RECORDS SERVICE
(1949–1985)

CREATION AND AUTHORITY

The National Archives and Records Service was established on December 11, 1949, by the Administrator of General Services to succeed the National Archives Establishment (AE 1) which had been transferred to the General Services Administration by the Federal Property and Administrative Services Act of 1949 (63 Stat. 378), effective July 1, 1949. The Service was made into the National Archives and Records Administration (AE 1.100) effective April 1, 1985.

GS 4.1:date
ANNUAL REPORTS.

Earlier AE 1.1

GS 4.2:CT • Item 569
GENERAL PUBLICATIONS. [Irregular]

Earlier AE 1.2
Later AE 1.102

GS 4.2:Au 2 • Item 569
REFERENCE LIST OF AUDIOVISUAL MATERIALS PRODUCED BY THE UNITED STATES GOVERNMENT. 1978. 396 p.

The Federal Government produces thousands of audiovisual materials that cover a wide range of subjects. These audiovisual materials are available to the public through sales, rentals, and free loans. The National Audiovisual Center serves as the central clearinghouse for all Federal audiovisual materials and makes them available through information and distribution services. The Reference List is a compilation of over 6000 audiovisual materials that have been produced by 175 Federal agencies. Materials are in the form of motion pictures, video formats, slide sets, audiotapes, and multimedia kits. Major subject areas in the collection include: medicine, dentistry, and allied health; education; science; social studies; industrial/technical training; safety; and the environmental sciences.
Materials in the Reference List arranged alphabetically by title, as well as under the various subject headings. Complete ordering information and a price list are included.

GS 4.2:C 76/2 • Item 569
INDEX/JOURNALS OF THE CONTINENTAL CONGRESS, 1774–1789. 1976. 429 p.

Consolidated index to the Library of Congress edition of the Journals of the Continental Congress.

GS 4.2:C 76/3 • Item 569
INDEX/PAPERS OF THE CONTINENTAL CONGRESS, 1774–1789. 1979. 5 v.

GS 4.4/2:nos.
NATIONAL ARCHIVES AND RECORDS SERVICE CIRCULAR.

GS 4.3:nos.
BULLETINS OF NATIONAL ARCHIVES.

Earlier AE 1.3

GS 4.6:CT • Item 570
REGULATIONS, RULES, AND INSTRUCTIONS.

Earlier AE 1.6

GS 4.6/2 • Item 569-B
RECORDS MANAGEMENT HANDBOOKS. [Irregular] (Subscription includes basic manual plus supplements for an indefinite period)

GS 4.6/2:F 31 • Item 569-B
FEDERAL REGISTER, WHAT IT IS AND HOW TO USE IT. 1978. 95 p.

The Federal Register system provides a uniform procedure for filing, publishing, and codifying Government documents. This handbook, which was developed for an educational workshop conducted by the Office of the Federal Register, explains the organization of the system, the procedures which result in the publication of the Federal Register, and the best way to find what you are looking for in the Register and the Code of Federal Regulations.

GS 4.6/2:N 21 • Item 569-B
GUIDE TO THE NATIONAL ARCHIVES OF THE UNITED STATES. 1974. 884 p.

Lists all official records of the U.S. Government received as of June 30, 1970, with the exception of Presidential papers. This is the first such guide published since 1948.

GS 4.6/3:date • Item 569-B
STANDARD AND OPTIONAL FORMS FACSIMILE HANDBOOK. (Subscription includes basic volume plus supplementary materials for an indefinite period)

GS 4.7 • Item 570-A (MF)
SPECIAL LISTS. 1– 1942– [Irregular]

Lists of material in the National Archives covering subjects rather than agencies as the Preliminary Inventories do. Covers all types of documents, films, maps, population schedules, etc., under the jurisdiction of the National Archives.
Later AE 1.115

GS 4.8
NATIONAL ARCHIVES ACCESSIONS. 1– 1940– [Irregular]

Serves as a supplement to National Archives Guide. Contains articles of interest; Accessions for the fiscal year; National Archives and Records Service announcements, including list of publications.
Published quarterly 1940– June 1952, irregular thereafter. Issues cover either one or two fiscal years.

GS 4.9:date
FRANKLIN D. ROOSEVELT LIBRARY, ANNUAL REPORT OF ARCHIVIST OF UNITED STATES.

Earlier AE 1.8

GS 4.10 • Item 570-D
PRELIMINARY INVENTORIES. 1– 1941– [Irregular]

Each publication devoted to a particular agency or phase within an agency. Detailed list and description of the records held.

GS 4.10/2:nos. • Item 570-B
NATIONAL ARCHIVES INVENTORY SERIES. 1– 1970– [Irregular]

Final inventories are issued as finding aids by the National Archives to help its staff render efficient reference service, to establish administrative control over the records in its custody, and to acquaint the public with its holdings. An inventory covers one of the 400 record groups (or an integral part of a record group) to which the holdings of the National Archives are allocated.

GS 4.11:nos.
FACSIMILES.

Earlier AE 1.21

GS 4.11/2:CT
FACSIMILES (unnumbered).

GS 4.12:nos. • **Item 571-A (MF)**
STAFF INFORMATION PAPERS. 1– [Irregular]

Formerly Staff Information Circulars.
Earlier AE 1.9

GS 4.13:v.nos. • **Item 571**
TERRITORIAL PAPERS OF UNITED STATES.

Earlier S 1.36

GS 4.14:CT • **Item 569-A**
NATIONAL HISTORICAL PUBLICATIONS COMMIS-
SION. [Publications].

GS 4.14/2:date
ANNOTATION, THE NEWSLETTER OF THE NATIONAL
HISTORICAL PUBLICATIONS AND RECORDS
COMMISSION. [Quarterly]

GS 4.14/3:date • **Item 569-A**
NHPRC (year) ANNUAL REPORT. (National Historical
Publications and Records Commission)

Later AE 1.114

GS 4.15
NATIONAL ARCHIVES REFERENCE INFORMATION
PAPERS. 1– 1942– [Irregular]

PURPOSE:– To list briefly in booklet form the
various records in the National Archives relating
to particular subjects such as transportation, the
Middle East, and the Independence of Latin American Nations.

GS 4.16:dt.&nos.
INTERAGENCY RECORDS ADMINISTRATION CON-
FERENCE, REPORTS OF MEETINGS.

GS 4.17 • **Item 569-C**
PUBLICATIONS OF NATIONAL ARCHIVES AND
RECORDS SERVICE. 1942– [Irregular]

List.

GS 4.17/2 • **Item 569-C**
LIST OF NATIONAL ARCHIVES MICROFILM PUBLI-
CATIONS. 1945– [Irregular]

GS 4.17/3:CT
BIBLIOGRAPHIES AND LISTS OF PUBLICATIONS.

Later AE 1.110

GS 4.17/4:nos.
MICROFILM LISTS.

GS 4.17/5:date • **Item 569-C-1**
SELECT LISTS. [Irregular] (National Audiovisual
Center)

PURPOSE:– To provide a list of materials
available for sale or rent from the Center.

GS 4.17/5-2:CT • **Item 569-C-1**
LIST OF AUDIOVISUAL MATERIALS PRODUCED BY
THE UNITED STATES GOVERNMENT (series).
[Irregular]

Each list is on a special subject.
Later AE 110/2

GS 4.17/5-3:date • **Item 569-C-1**
QUARTERLY UPDATE, A COMPREHENSIVE LISTING
OF NEW AUDIOVISUAL MATERIALS AND
SERVICES OFFERED BY THE AUDIOVISUAL
CENTER.

Later AE 1.109

GS 4.17/6:date • **Item 569-C-1**
MEDICAL CATALOG OF AUDIOVISUAL MATERIALS
PRODUCED BY THE UNITED STATES GOVERN-
MENT.

GS 4.17/7:CT • **Item 569-C-1**
SELECTED AUDIOVISUAL RECORDS, PHOTO-
GRAPHS OF (various subjects). [Irregular]

GS 4.18:nos. • **Item 570-C (MF)**
GUIDE TO GERMAN RECORDS MICROFILMED AT
ALEXANDRIA, VA. 1–

Later AE 1.112

GS 4.18/2:nos. • **Item 570-C**
GUIDES TO THE MICROFILMED RECORDS OF THE
GERMAN NAVY. 1– 1985– [Irregular]

Later AE 1.108

GS 4.19:date • **Item 569-F**
LIST OF RECORD GROUPS IN NATIONAL ARCHIVES
AND FEDERAL RECORDS CENTERS.

GS 4.20 • **Item 569-C**
NATIONAL ARCHIVES MICROFILM PUBLICATIONS:
PAMPHLETS ACCOMPANYING MICROCOPY.
[Irregular]

Each pamphlet describes the contents of the
microfilm publication, including a table of contents for individual rolls within the publication and
a detailed index to persons, agencies, etc. involved.
Later AE 1.119

GS 4.20/2:nos.
CONTENTS AND PRICE LIST FOR MICROFILM PUB-
LICATIONS. [Irregular]

GS 4.21:v.nos/fascicle nos. • **Item 569-D**
MILITARY OPERATIONS OF CIVIL WAR, GUIDE
INDEX TO OFFICIAL RECORDS OF UNION AND
CONFEDERATE ARMIES. 1861-65. v. 1– 1968–

GS 4.22 • **Item 569**
GENERAL INFORMATION LEAFLETS. 1– 1969–
[Irregular]

Later AE 1.113

GS 4.23:v.nos.&nos.
PROLOGUE, JOURNAL OF THE NATIONAL AR-
CHIVES. [Irregular]

Later AE 1.111
ISSN 0033-1031

GS 4.24:date • **Item 567-B (MF)**
DIRECTORY OF U.S. GOVERNMENT AUDIOVISUAL
PERSONNEL. (National Audiovisual Center)

GS 4.25:date
NEWS NOTES. [Irregular]

GS 4.26:CT • **Item 569-E**
POSTERS.

OFFICE OF THE FEDERAL REGISTER
(1949– 1985)

GS 4.101:date
ANNUAL REPORTS.

Earlier AE 2.1

GS 4.102:CT • **Item 574**
GENERAL PUBLICATIONS.

Earlier AE 2.2

GS 4.102:St 2 • **Item 574**
HOW TO FIND U.S. STATUTES AND U.S. CODE
CITATIONS. 1980. 9 p. il.

GS 4.107 • **Item 573**
FEDERAL REGISTER. v. 1– 1936– [Daily]

ISSN 0097-6326
Later AE 2.106

INDEXES.

ISSN 0364-1406

SUBJECT INDEX.

Monthly, cumulative quarterly and annually.

LIST OF CFR SECTIONS AFFECTED (codification guide).

Monthly, cumulative quarterly and annually.

GS 4.107/a:P 939/2 • **Item 573**
PRIVACY ACT ISSUANCES. 1976– [Annual]

Later AE 2.106/4

GS 4.107/a:R 245
GUIDE TO RECORD RETENTION REQUIRE-
MENTS. 1955– [Annual]

Published as part of the Federal Register, an index-digest of statutes and regulations requiring the keeping of records for possible audit by the Federal Government. Contains over 900 digests that describe the types
of records to be kept, who must keep them,
and how long they must be kept. An index
lists of ready reference the categories of
persons, companies, and products affected
by Federal record retention requirements.

GS 4.107/2:nos. • **Item 573-A**
FEDERAL REGISTER UPDATE. [Bimonthly]

PURPOSE:– To provide articles about new
developments in the printing and writing of documents published in the Federal Register and to
provide a forum for the exchange of ideas on how
to increase public participation in the rulemaking
process.

• **Item 572-B (P)**
GS 4.108 • **Item 572-C (MF)**
CODE OF FEDERAL REGULATIONS. 1938–
[Irregular]

Later AE 2.106/3

• **Item 572-B (P)**
GS 4.108/2 • **Item 572-C (MF)**
SUPPLEMENT TO TITLE 3, THE PRESIDENT. [An-
nual]

Contains the full text of Presidential documents– Presidential proclamations, Executive
Orders, and other Presidential documents.
Title 3 in the current edition of the Code of
Federal Regulations consists of reference tables
of Presidential documents cited or otherwise included in the Code of Federal Regulations, but
does not contain the text thereof. The full text of
Presidential documents is published only in the
daily issues of the Federal Register and in this
series of supplements.
The following compilations have been published:

1938– 1943
1943– 1948
1949– 1953
1954– 1958
1959– 1963
1964– 1965
1966– 1970
1971– 1975

GS 4.108/3:v.nos.&nos.
LIST OF CFR SECTIONS AFFECTED. [Monthly]

Includes U.S.C.-C.F.R. table of authorities.
ISSN 0363-8839

GS 4.108/4:date • Item 572
FINDING AIDS. 1973– [Annual]

PURPOSE:– To bring together in one volume the various finding aids that appeared formerly in other volumes of the Code of Federal Regulations. The primary finding aids are the Parallel Tables of Statutory Authorities and Rules, Presidential Documents Included or Cited in Currently Effective Rules, Guide to Federal Register Finding Aids, Acts Requiring Publication the Federal Register, and Guide to Record Retention Requirements. Also included are a List of Current CFR Volumes, List of Superseded CFR Volumes, Alphabetical List of CFR Subtitles and Chapters, and Table of CFR Titles and Chapters.

GS 4.109 • Item 577
UNITED STATES GOVERNMENT MANUAL. 1935– [Annual]
Later AE 2.108/2

GS 4.109/2:CT
GOVERNMENT ORGANIZATION HANDBOOKS.

GS 4.110 • Item 575
SLIP LAWS (public). [Irregular]

Note:– While compiled by the Federal Register Office and the series being classified in the SuDocs Classification scheme under this office, the laws are entered in the Monthly Catalog under Congress.
Later AE 2.110

GS 4.110/2:Cong.sess.&nos.
PUBLIC RESOLUTIONS.
Earlier S 7.5/2

GS 4.110/3:cong.sess.&nos. • Item 575-A
PRIVATE LAWS.

Earlier S 7.5/3
Later AE 2.110/2

GS 4.111 • Item 576
UNITED STATES STATUTES AT LARGE. v. 18–1873– [Annual]

The following special volumes have been published in recent years:

Vol. 68A Public Law 591, 83d Congress, Internal Revenue Code of 1954.
70A Title 10 and Title 32, United States Code.
76A Canal Zone Code.
77A Tariff Schedules.
Later AE 2.111

GS 4.111/2 • Item 576
TABLES OF LAWS AFFECTED.

The following compilations have been published:
Vol. 70-79 1956-1965
Cumulative index in each issue for current quarter, with separate indexes issued for January-June and January-December.

GS 4.112:v.nos.&nos.
ABSTRACTS OF DEFENSE REGULATIONS. [Monthly]

GS 4.113 • Item 574-A
PUBLIC PAPERS OF THE PRESIDENTS OF THE UNITED STATES. 1945– [Annual]

Begun in 1957 on the recommendation of the National Historical Publications Commission, this series is the first publication of Presidential papers by the Government since 1899. Now on a current basis, volumes have been published for each year of office for Presidents Truman, Eisenhower, Kennedy, Johnson, Nixon, Ford, Carter and Reagan.
Volumes contain messages to Congress, speeches, transcripts of news conferences, selected important press releases of the White House, to give an accurate record of the activities of the President in the year covered.
Similar Presidential material for the current year may be found in the Weekly Compilation of Presidential Documents.

In addition to the current series, the following volumes have been published for earlier presidents:–
Herbert Hoover. 1929– 1933.
Later AE 2.114

GS 4.113/2:CT • Item 574-A
PROCLAMATIONS AND EXECUTIVE ORDERS.

GS 4.113/2:H 76/v.1, 2 • Item 574-A
HERBERT HOOVER, MARCH 4, 1929– MARCH 4, 1953.

GS 4.113/3:date • Item 574-A
CODIFICATION OF PRESIDENTIAL PROCLAMATIONS AND EXECUTIVE ORDERS. [Irregular]

Later AE 2.113

GS 4.114 • Item 577-A
WEEKLY COMPILATION OF PRESIDENTIAL DOCUMENTS. v. 1– 1965– [Weekly]

ISSN 0511-4187
Later AE 2.109

GS 4.119:date • Item 573-B
DIRECTORY OF FEDERAL REGIONAL STRUCTURE. [Irregular]

PURPOSE:– To provide a directory of Federal agency regional structures designed to give practical information about regional offices of Federal departments and agencies. Included in the directory is a map showing the 10 standard Federal regions followed by tables listing the key personnel, addresses, and telephone numbers for agencies with offices in those regions. In addition, maps and tables are provided for those agencies with regional structures other than that of the standard regional system.

CONTRACT SETTLEMENT APPEAL BOARD
(1944– 1947, 1948– 1952)

CREATION AND AUTHORITY

The Contract Settlement Appeal Board was established by act of Congress, approved July 1, 1944 (58 Stat. 651). The Board was transferred to the Treasury Department (T 67) by Executive Order 9809 of December 12, 1946 and Reorganization Plan No. 1 of 1947, and again transferred to the General Services Administration (GS 5) by act of Congress, approved June 30, 1948 (63 Stat. 378). The Board was abolished by act of Congress, approved July 14, 1952 (66 Stat. 627).

GS 5.1:date
ANNUAL REPORTS.
Earlier T 67.1

GS 5.2:CT
GENERAL PUBLICATIONS.
Earlier T 67.2

GS 5.7:v.nos.
DECISIONS OF APPEAL BOARD (bound volumes).
Earlier T 67.8/2

GS 5.7/a:v.nos.&print nos.
– APPEAL BOARD PROCEEDINGS, PRINTS.
Earlier T 67.8/2a

PUBLIC BUILDINGS SERVICE
(1949–)

CREATION AND AUTHORITY

The Public Buildings Service was established December 11, 1949, by the Administrator of General Services, to supersede the Public Buildings Administration (FW 6) which was abolished by the Federal Property and Administrative Services Act of 1949 (63 Stat. 378), effective July 1, 1949.

INFORMATION

Public Buildings Service
General Services Administration
1800 F. Street
Washington, D. C. 20405
(202) 501-1100
Fax: (202) 501-2300

GS 6.1:date
ANNUAL REPORTS.
Earlier FW 6.1

GS 6.2:CT • Item 579
GENERAL PUBLICATIONS.
Earlier FW 6.2

GS 6.4:nos.
CIRCULARS.

GS 6.6:CT • Item 580
REGULATIONS, RULES, AND INSTRUCTIONS.
Earlier FW 6.7

GS 6.6/2:CT • Item 580
HANDBOOKS, MANUALS, GUIDES.

GS 6.7:date
TELEPHONE DIRECTORY, REPUBLIC 7500, EXECUTIVE 6300, DISTRICT 0525. [Quarterly]
Earlier FW 6.8

GS 6.8:nos. • Item 579-A
HISTORICAL STUDIES (numbered).

GS 6.9:CT • Item 579-B
ENVIRONMENTAL IMPACT STATEMENTS. [Irregular]

GS 6.10:date
VALUE ENGINEERING PROGRAM: ANNUAL REPORT.

FEDERAL FACILITIES CORPORATION
(1957– 1961)

CREATION AND AUTHORITY

The Federal Facilities Corporation (T 69) was transferred from the Treasury Department to the General Services Administration by Executive Order 10720 of July 11, 1957.

GS 7.1:date
ANNUAL REPORTS.

Earlier T 69.2

GS 7.2:CT
GENERAL PUBLICATIONS.

Earlier T 69.2

TRANSPORTATION AND COMMUNICATIONS SERVICE
(1961– 1972)

CREATION AND AUTHORITY

The Transportation and Public Utilities Service was established within the General Services Administration on July 1, 1955, to which were transferred the functions of the Public Utilities Division of the Federal Supply Service and the shipping functions from the Emergency Procurement Service Redesignated as the Transportation and Communications Service on October 19, 1961. Abolished by Administrator's order, effective July 15, 1972.

GS 8.1:date
ANNUAL REPORTS.

GS 8.2:CT   • Item 580-A-1
GENERAL PUBLICATIONS.

GS 8.6:CT   • Item 580-A-2
REGULATIONS, RULES, AND INSTRUCTIONS.

GS 8.6/2:CT   • Item 580-A
HANDBOOKS, MANUALS, GUIDES.

GS 8.8:CT
PUBLIC UTILITY SCHEDULES.

GS 8.9:date
ANNUAL MOTOR VEHICLE REPORT.

UTILIZATION AND DISPOSAL SERVICE
(1961– 1966)

CREATION AND AUTHORITY

The Utilization and Disposal Service was established by the Administrator of General Services on July 1, 1961. On July 29, 1966 the Service was abolished and its functions transferred to the Property Management and Disposal Service (GS 10).

GS 9.1:date
ANNUAL REPORT.

GS 9.2:CT
GENERAL PUBLICATIONS.

GS 9.3/2:nos.
EXCESS PROPERTY BULLETINS. 1 –   [Irregular]

GS 9.9:nos.
EXCESS PROPERTY CATALOG.

PROPERTY MANAGEMENT AND DISPOSAL SERVICE
(1966– 1973)

CREATION AND AUTHORITY

The Property Management and Disposal Service was established on July 29, 1966, by the Administrator of General Services. Transferred to the Service were functions formerly assigned to the Defense Materials Service and the Utilization and Disposal Service. Abolished on July 1, 1973 and functions transferred to the Federal Supply Service, Public Buildings Service, and the Office of Stockpile Disposal.

GS 10.1:date
ANNUAL REPORT.

GS 10.2:CT
GENERAL PUBLICATIONS.

GS 10.7/2:nos.
STOCKPILE INFORMATION. [Irregular]

ISSN 0364-8400

CONSUMER INFORMATION CENTER
(1970–   )

CREATION AND AUTHORITY

The Consumer Product Information Coordinating Center was established within the General Services Administration by Executive Order 11566, approved October 26, 1970. The name was later changed to Consumer Information Center.

INFORMATION

Consumer Information Center
General Services Administration
18th and F Streets, N.W.
Washington, D. C. 20405
Toll Free: (800) 688-9889

GS 11.1:date
ANNUAL REPORT.

GS 11.2:CT   • Item 580-B-3
GENERAL PUBLICATIONS.

GS 11.8:CT   • Item 508-B-2
HANDBOOKS, MANUALS, GUIDES. [Irregular]

GS 11.9:date   • Item 580-B (EL)
CONSUMER INFORMATION CATALOG. [Quarterly]

PURPOSE:– To provide an index of government publications on how to buy, use, and take care of consumer products. Prepared in cooperation with the Office of Consumer Affairs, Executive Office of the President.
Earlier: Consumer Product Information.

GS 11.9/2:nos.   • Item 580-B-4
NEW FOR CONSUMERS, HIGHLIGHTS OF NEW FEDERAL CONSUMER PUBLICATIONS. 1001– 1972–   [Irregular]

ISSN 0364-6777

GS 11.9/3:CT   • Item 580-B-5 (P) (EL)
CONSUMER'S ACTION.
Formerly: Consumer Resource Handbook
Previously: HE 1.508/2

GS 11.9/3-2   • Item 580-B-5 (EL)
CONSUMER FOCUS. [Irregular]

FEDERAL TECHNOLOGY SERVICE
(1982–   )

CREATION AND AUTHORITY

The Automated Data and Telecommunications Service was established within the General Services Administration in August 1972. The name was changed to Office of Information Resources Management by GSA order of August 17, 1982. Name changed to Federal Technology Service.

INFORMATION

Federal Technology Service
General Services Administration
10304 Eaton Pl.
Fairfax, VA 22030
(888) FTS-6397
Fax: (703) 306-6029
http://www.fts.gsa.gov

GS 12.1:date
ANNUAL REPORT.

GS 12.2:CT   • Item 580-C-2
GENERAL PUBLICATIONS.

GS 12.8:CT   • Item 580-C-2
HANDBOOKS, MANUALS, GUIDES. [Irregular]

GS 12.9:date   • Item 580-C-1 (MF)
SUMMARY OF FEDERAL ADP ACTIVITIES FOR FISCAL YEAR (date). 1974–   [Annual]

Contains summarized inventory, cost, manpower and utilization data relating to automatic data processing equipment (ADPE) used by the United States Government.
Volumes before 1972 called Inventory and Summary of Federal ADP Activities.
Companion volume to Inventory of Automatic Data Processing Equipment in the United States Government (GS 12.10).

GS 12.10:date   • Item 853-B (MF)
AUTOMATIC DATA PROCESSING EQUIPMENT INVENTORY IN THE UNITED STATES GOVERNMENT AS OF THE END OF THE FISCAL YEAR. [Annual]

Former title: Inventory of Automated Data Processing Equipment in the United States Government for Fiscal Year.
Earlier GS 2.15

GS 12.10/2:date   • Item 853-B
ADP AND TELECOMMUNICATIONS STANDARDS INDEX. [Annual]

GS 12.11:CT   • Item 580-C-2
NEW WAY OF SAVING (series). [Irregular]

GS 12.12:date   • Item 580-C-3 (MF)
TELEPHONE DIRECTORY, CENTRAL OFFICE AND REGIONS.

Earlier GS 1.11

GS 12.12/2:CT   • Item 580-C-3 (MF)
FTS DIRECTORIES [for various areas]. (Federal Telecommunications Service)

GS 12.12/2:1/date   • Item 580-C-3
TELEPHONE DIRECTORY, REGION 1.

GS 12.12/3:date   • Item 580-C-3
IRMS DIRECTORY OF ASSISTANCE. [Annual]

IRMS = Information Resources Management Services.

GS 12.13:date   • Item 580-C-4 (MF)
SPECIAL NOTICE CONCERNING BASIC AGREEMENTS TELEPROCESSING SERVICES PROGRAM (TSP) INDUSTRIAL GROUP 737, INDUSTRIAL CLASS 7374.

GS 12.14:nos.   • Item 580-C-5 (MF)
FEDERAL SOFTWARE EXCHANGE CATALOG, GSA/ADTS/C- (series).

PURPOSE:– To provide a means for identifying software that is already operational in the Federal Government.

GS 12.14/2:v.nos.&nos.   • Item 580-C-5 (MF)
FEDERAL SOFTWEAR EXCHANGE CATALOG, INFORMATION SUPPLEMENT. [Irregular]

GS 12.14/2-2:date   • Item 580-C-5 (MF)
FEDERAL SOFTWARE EXCHANGE CATALOG SUPPLEMENT. [Annual]

GS 12.15:CT   • Item 580-C-6
REGULATIONS, RULES, INSTRUCTIONS. [Irregular]

GS 12.15/2:date   • Item 559-J-1 (E)
GSA FIRMR/FAR REGULATIONS. [Quarterly]

Issued on CD-ROM.

GS 12.16   • Item 580-C-7 (MF)
OFFICE OF SOFTWARE DEVELOPMENT AND INFORMATION TECHNOLOGY: REPORTS (series). [Irregular]

Each report is on a different software development and information management subject.

GS 12.17:CT   • Item 580-C-2 (MF)
INFORMATION RESOURCES MANAGEMENT HANDBOOK (series). [Irregular]

GS 12.17/2:v.nos.&nos.
IRM FORUM. [Quarterly]

GS 12.17/3:   • Item 580-C-9
INFORMATION RESOURCES MANAGEMENT NEWSLETTER. [Bimonthly]

Presents short news items on GSA activities in the area of information resources management.

GS 12.18:date   • Item 569-B-1
STANDARD AND OPTIONAL FORMS FACSIMILE HANDBOOK.

GS 12.19   • Item 580-C-8
FEDERAL IRM DIRECTORY. [Annual]

IRM = Information Resources Management Developed by the Interagency Committee on Information Resources Management for the Federal IRM community. Contains organizational and alphabetical listings of IRM officials in various federal agencies.

FEDERAL PREPAREDNESS AGENCY (1976– 1979)

CREATION AND AUTHORITY

The Federal Preparedness Agency was established in 1976. The Agency was superseded by the Federal Emergency Management Agency, (FEM 1), pursuant to Reorganization Plan No. 3 of 1978 and Executive Orders 12127 (effective April 1, 1979) and 12148 (effective July 15, 1979).

GS 13.1:date   • Item 580-D-1
ANNUAL REPORT. 1st–   1976–

GS 13.2:CT
GENERAL PUBLICATIONS.

GS 13.9:date
NATIONAL HEALTH RESOURCES ADVISORY COMMITTEE: REPORTS OF MEETINGS.

JOINT FINANCIAL MANAGEMENT IMPROVEMENT PROGRAM

GS 14.2   • Item 580-D
GENERAL PUBLICATIONS.

GS 14.7   • Item 580-D-2 (EL)
JFMIP NEWS. [Quarterly]

GS 14.15   • Item 580-D-3 (EL)
CORE COMPETENCIES.

GS 14.16   • Item 580-D-4 (EL)
EXPOSURE DRAFTS.

GS 14.17   • Item 580-D-5 (EL)
SYSTEM REQUIREMENTS.

DEPARTMENT OF HEALTH AND HUMAN SERVICES (1980–   )

CREATION AND AUTHORITY

The Department of Health, Education, and Welfare was created by Reorganization Plan 1 of 1953. Under provisions of the act approved April 1, 1953 (67 Stat. 18; 5 U.S.C. 623), the Plan became effective on April 11, 1953. The Plan abolished the Federal Security Agency, created by Reorganization Plan 1 of 1939, and transferred all functions of the Federal Security Administrator (FS) to the Secretary of Health, Education, and Welfare and all components of the Agency to the Department. The Department was redesignated as the Department of Health and Human Services by Department of Education Organization Act (93 Stat. 695; 20 U.S.C. 3508) approved October 17, 1979.

NOTE:– During the period 1953 through 1969, FS SuDocs classes were used for HEW publications. Beginning January 1, 1970, the HE classes were assigned to HEW publications.

INFORMATION

Information Center
Department of Health and Human Services
200 Independence Avenue, S.W.
Washington, D. C. 20201
(202) 619-0257
Toll-Free: (877) 696-6775
http://www.dhhs.gov

HE 1.1:date   • Item 444
ANNUAL REPORT. [Annual]

Report submitted by the Secretary to the President and Congress for the fiscal year. Contains report of activities and programs of the Department of Health, Education, and Welfare and for each of its sub-agencies.
Earlier FS 1.1

HE 1.1/2:date   • Item 444-A-1 (MF) (EL)
OFFICE OF INSPECTOR GENERAL: ANNUAL REPORT.

Report submitted to Congress pursuant to section 204(a) of Public Law 94-505. Summarizes Office activities, which include responsibility for auditing and investigating the Department's programs and for keeping the Secretary and Congress informed of any deficiencies.

HE 1.1/2-2   • Item 444-A-3 (MF)
DIGEST OF SEMIANNUAL REPORTS AND FISCAL YEAR.

HE 1.1/3:date   • Item 444-A-1 (MF)
JUSTIFICATIONS OF APPROPRIATIONS ESTIMATES FOR COMMITTEE ON APPROPRIATIONS, FISCAL YEAR. [Annual]

HE 1.1/4   • Item 444-A-4 (EL)
INDICATORS OF WELFARE DEPENDENCE (annual report to congress).

HE 1.2:CT   • Item 445
GENERAL PUBLICATIONS. [Irregular]

Earlier FS 1.2

HE 1.2:ED 8/3   • Item 445
DHEW OBLIGATIONS TO INSTITUTIONS OF HIGHER LEARNING. 1967–   [Annual] (Office of Assistant Secretary for Health and Scientific Affairs)

Report covers fiscal year.
PURPOSE:– To serve as a directory function by reporting the amounts obligated during the fiscal year.

HE 1.6:CT   • Item 445-A
REGULATIONS, RULES AND INSTRUCTIONS.

HE 1.6/2:pt.nos.
AGENCY MANUAL. Loose-leaf. Admin.

HE 1.6/3:CT   • Item 445-A
HANDBOOKS, MANUALS, GUIDES.

Earlier FS 1.6/3

HE 1.6/5:   • Item 445-A
HANDBOOKS ON PROGRAMS OF DEPARTMENT OF HEALTH, EDUCATION AND WELFARE. [Annual]

Presents information about the program objectives of each major unit of the Department of Health, Education, and Welfare and the extent of the problem toward which the program is directed, the scope of the program, its legal basis, and related information. Provides for each program a five-year summary of fiscal, personnel, and other statistics showing program dimensions and trends.
Earlier FS 1.6/5

HE 1.6/6:date • Item 445-A
CATALOG OF HEW ASSISTANCE PROVIDING FINANCIAL SUPPORT AND SERVICE TO STATES, COMMUNITIES, ORGANIZATIONS, INDIVIDUALS. [Annual]

Provides facts on the background, purpose, financial aspects, and legal basis of the various financial assistance programs administered by the Department of Health, Education, and Welfare. Contains detailed information on the formulas used in distributing funds, State matching requirements, and figures on funds allocated under each program.
Earlier FS 1.6/6

HE 1.6/7:trans.nos. • Item 445-A-1 (EL)
GRANTS POLICY DIRECTIVES. 1968– [Irregular] (includes basic manual plus supplementary material for an indefinite period)

PURPOSE:– To provide guidelines on the fiscal and administrative aspects of grant management to all granting agencies of the Department of Health, Education and Welfare. It is intended to serve as a basic reference for those who are operationally engaged in the administrative and financial aspects of grants, as well as those program directors and others within the operating agencies who are involved in the award, review, or other program managements aspects of grants.
Price includes basic manual and supplementary material for an indefinite period.
Earlier FS 1.6/7
Formerly distributed to Documents Libraries under Item No. 445-A.

Former title: Grants Administration Manual

HE 1.6/7-2:nos. • Item 445-A-1
GRANTS ADMINISTRATION MANUAL CIRCULAR.

Included in price of subscription to Grants Administration Dept., staff manual.
Earlier FS 1.6/7-2
Formerly distributed to Documents Libraries under Item No. 445-A.

HE 1.6/7-3:nos. • Item 445-A
PHS GRANTS POLICY MEMORANDUM. 1– [Irregular]

Supplement to the DHEW Grants Administration Manual.

HE 1.6/8:date • Item 445-A
ACQUISITION REGULATION STAFF MANUAL. [Annual]

HE 1.7:CT • Item 445-I (MF)
ADDRESSES. [Irregular]

Earlier FS 1.7

HE 1.10:nos. • Item 447
TRAINING MANUALS.

Earlier FS 1.10

HE 1.15:letters-nos.
PRESS RELEASES. [Irregular]

HE 1.17:date • Item 444-D
FIELD DIRECTORY. [Annual]
PURPOSE:– Designed for use of Department personnel in addressing mail, in answering inquiries about field organization, and for other similar purposes.
Field units are listed alphabetically by State and city identified by organization and type of office or activity by means of organizational codes.
Earlier FS 1.17

HE 1.18:CT • Item 444-B (MF)
BIBLIOGRAPHIES AND LISTS OF PUBLICATIONS.

Earlier FS 1.2 FS 1.18

HE 1.18/2:nos.
SELECTED REFERENCES ON AGING.

Earlier FS 15.12/2

HE 1.18/3:date • Item 444-B
CATALOG, DEPARTMENT OF HEALTH, EDUCATION, AND WELFARE, PUBLICATIONS. [Quarterly and Annual] (Office of Public Affairs)

Earlier FS 1.18:P 96

HE 1.18/4:CT • Item 444-L-1 (MF)
HUMAN SERVICES, BIBLIOGRAPHY SERIES. 1976– [Irregular]

HE 1.19:date • Item 445-B
HEALTH, EDUCATION AND WELFARE TRENDS. 1959– [Annual]

Published as an annual supplement and companion volume to the Monthly Indicators.
Gives in chart and tabular form the annual data for the various series carried in the monthly publication.
Issued in two parts:
Part 1. National Trends.
Part 2. State Data and State Rankings in Health, Education, and Welfare.
Earlier FS 1.19

HE 1.21:date • Item 445-F
HEW FACTS AND FIGURES.

PURPOSE:– To acquaint the public with the general purpose and mission of Department of Health, Education, and Welfare, with statistical illustrations.
Earlier FS 1.21

HE 1.22:date-nos.
STATE SALARY RANGES OF SELECTED CLASSES OF POSITIONS IN EMPLOYMENT SECURITY, PUBLIC WELFARE, PUBLIC HEALTH, MENTAL HEALTH, CIVIL DEFENSE, VOCATIONAL REHABILITATION, (date).

HE 1.23:date • Item 445-G
PROPOSED MENTAL RETARDATION PROGRAMS. 1966– [Annual]

Title varies.
Earlier FS 1.2:M 52/3; FS 1.23

HE 1.23/3:date • Item 445-G
MENTAL RETARDATION GRANTS, FISCAL YEAR. 1964– [Annual]

Part 1. Construction, training, and Other Grants.
Part 2. Research and Demonstration.
Earlier FS 1.23/3

HE 1.23/4:nos. • Item 444-I
PROGRAMS FOR THE HANDICAPPED. 1965– [Irregular]

PURPOSE:– To present information on Department of Health, Education, and Welfare programs for the handicapped. Incidental information relating to the handicapped is also included. Certain issues are devoted to abstracts of mental retardation research projects sponsored by the Federal Government.
Previous title: Mental Retardation Reports.
ISSN 0565-2804
Earlier FS 1.23/4

HE 1.23/5:date • Item 445-G
MENTAL RETARDATION ACTIVITIES OF THE DEPARTMENT OF HEALTH, EDUCATION, AND WELFARE. [Annual]

Report covers calendar year.
Earlier FS 1.23/5

HE 1.23/6:date • Item 445-G
MENTAL RETARDATION SOURCE BOOK. 1972– [Irregular] (Office of Mental Retardation Coordination)

PURPOSE:– To coordinate the mental retardation statistics collected within the Department of Health, Education, and Welfare into one report.

HE 1.26:date • Item 444-C
EDUCATION AND TRAINING, ANNUAL REPORT OF SECRETARY OF HEALTH, EDUCATION AND WELFARE TO CONGRESS ON TRAINING ACTIVITIES UNDER MANPOWER DEVELOPMENT AND TRAINING ACT. 1st– 1962– [Annual]

Published as Office of Education publication OE-87020. Sub-title varies.
Report submitted by the Secretary of Health, Education, and Welfare to Congress for the calendar year as required by Part B of Title II of the Manpower Development and Training Act of 1962, as amended.
Report reviews accomplishments in the year, recommendations for improvements, and progress reports on the vocational training studies conducted under the supervision of the Secretary.
Earlier FS 1.2:Ed 8, FS 1.26

HE 1.27/2:date
HEW NOW. – 1979 [Monthly] (Office of Public Affairs) (HEW 391)

Published for the employees of the Department of Health, Education, and Welfare.
ISSN 0364-0949

HE 1.28:date • Item 444-H (MF)
TELEPHONE DIRECTORY. [Annual]

HE 1.28/2:CT • Item 444-H-1
DIRECTORIES. [Irregular]

HE 1.29:date-nos. • Item 445-H
PROGRAM ANALYSIS (series). 1966– [Irregular] Office of Assistant Secretary for Program Coordination.

PURPOSE:– To provide a cost-benefit analyses of Federal disease control and human investment programs to facilitate planning and budgeting.
Earlier FS 1.29

HE 1.31:nos. • Item 445-J
GRANTS ADMINISTRATION REPORTS. 1– 9. 1968– 1971. [Semiannual]

PURPOSE:– To provide a vehicle for communication to HEW grantees and Department grants administration personnel information on grants policies and procedures. Identifies and summarizes new policy issuances and procedures, provides background and rational for existing policies and, in general, reports on events of consequence to those in grants administration. From time to time, special reports on policy drafts are provided as inserts to the publication.
Issued quarterly prior to June 1971.
Earlier FS 1.31

HE 1.32:CT • Item 445
TASK FORCE ON PRESCRIPTION DRUGS. PUBLICATIONS.

Earlier FS 1.32

HE 1.33 • Item 445-K
REPORT OF CAREER SERVICE BOARD FOR SCIENCE. 1st– 1968–

PURPOSE:– To help establish a stimulating climate in which the professional HEW staff members can work, and also to help attract outstanding candidates to undertake assignments at HEW.
Earlier FS 1.33

HE 1.34:date
HEW NEWSLETTER.

Earlier FS 1.34

HE 1.34/2:nos. • Item 444-G
CONSUMER INFORMATION SERIES. 1– 1973– [Irregular]

HE 1.35:date
COST OF CLEAN AIR, REPORT OF SECRETARY OF HEALTH, EDUCATION, AND WELFARE.

Earlier FS 1.35

HE 1.36:   • Item 857-H-12
PROJECT HEAD START.

HE 1.37:nos.   • Item 445-M
FOOTNOTE, JOURNAL OF THE HEW AUDIT AGENCY.
1–   Dec. 1969–   [Annual]

PURPOSE:– To serve as a house organ for
the HEW Audit Agency.
Includes articles on accounting, auditing, management, personnel, human relations, and related
subjects.
ISSN 0533-1250

HE 1.38   • Item 444-B-1
DIRECTORY OF PUBLIC AND SECONDARY
SCHOOLS IN SELECTED DISTRICT, ENROLL-
MENT AND STAFF BY RACIAL/ETHNIC GROUP.
1968–   [Annual]

HE 1.39:date
PROGRESS REPORT ON NURSE TRAINING.

HE 1.40:date   • Item 445-D-1
HEALTH PROFESSIONS EDUCATION ASSISTANCE
PROGRAM, REPORT TO THE PRESIDENT AND
THE CONGRESS. 1967–   [Annual]

Report submitted by the Secretary of the Department of Health, Education, and Welfare to
the President and Congress pursuant to Title I,
Part D, of the Health Manpower Act of 1968 (PL
90-490).
Concerns Federal assitance in the education
of health professionals in medicine, osteopathic
medicine, dentistry, optometry, pediatric medicine,
pharmacy, and veterinary medicine. Includes background on legislation and funding, the different
levels and kinds of programs in the education
institutions representing the seven professional
fields, students' resources and attendant problems, and accomplishments of the HPEA Act
measured against its objectives.

HE 1.41:date-vols.   • Item 444-E
DHEW OBLIGATIONS TO [various institutions]. 1970–
[Annual]

Published in the following volumes:
v. 1. Institutions of Higher Education and
Other Nonprofit Organiza-
tions.
v. 2. Institutions of Higher Education.
v. 3. Health Professional Schools.
v. 4. Research Institutes and Other
Nonprofit Organizations.
v. 5. Hospitals.
Earlier HE 1.2:Ed 8/3 and HE 20.3002:M 46/
2

HE 1.42:CT   • Item 444-F
SYNCRISIS, THE DYNAMICS OF HEALTH. v. 1–
1972–   [Irregular] (Division of Planning and
Evaluation, Office of International Health)

PURPOSE:– To provide an analytic series on
interactions of health and socioeconomic development. Reports cover an individual country.
ISSN 0095-0351

HE 1.43:CT   • Item 444-K-5
POSTERS. [Irregular]

HE 1.43/2:CT
AUDIOVISUAL MATERIALS.

HE 1.45:v.nos.
REGION 7 NEWS ROUNDUP.

HE 1.46:date   • Item 444-J
NATIONAL PROFESSIONAL STANDARDS REVIEW
COUNCIL: ANNUAL REPORT. 1st–   1973–

HE 1.47:letters&nos.
INFORMATION MEMORANDUMS [issued by various
departments].

HE 1.47/2:letters&nos.
PROGRAM INSTRUCTIONS [issued by various de-
partments].

ISSN 0364-6823

HE 1.47/3:letters&nos.
PROGRAM REGULATION GUIDES [issued by various departments].

ISSN 0364-6815

HE 1.48:date   • Item 444-K
TOXICOLOGY RESEARCH PROJECTS DIRECTORY.
v. 1–5. 1976– 1980. [Quarterly] (Toxicology Information Subcommittee)

PURPOSE:– To provide an indexed directory
of current research project abstracts in toxicology and related fields as provided from the information received by the Smithsonian Science Information Exchange.
ISSN 0362-3211

HE 1.49:v.nos.&nos.   • Item 506-C-1
DEVELOPMENT DISABILITIES ABSTRACTS. v. 1–
13.   – 1978. [Quarterly]

Prior to 1977 entitled Mental Retardation and
Development Disabilities Abstracts.
Supersedes Mental Retardation Abstracts
(HE 17.113).

HE 1.50:v.nos.&nos.   • Item 444-L
JOURNAL OF HUMAN SERVICES ABSTRACTS. v. 1–
1976–   [Quarterly]

ISSN 0364-4782

HE 1.51:date   • Item 444-K-4
MENTAL RETARDATION AND THE LAW, A REPORT
ON THE STATUS OF CURRENT COURT CASES.

HE 1.52:nos.   • Item 444-K-1
TECHNICAL ANALYSIS PAPERS. 1–   1975–
[Irregular] (Office of Social Services and Human
Development)

HE 1.52/2:nos.
TECHNICAL ANALYSIS PAPERS. [Irregular] (Office
of Income Security Policy)

HE 1.53:date   • Item 444-K-2
ANNUAL REPORT TO CONGRESS ON CHILD SUP-
PORT ENFORCEMENT PROGRAM.

HE 1.54:nos.   • Item 444-K-3
HUMAN SERVICES, MONOGRAPH SERIES. 1–
[Irregular]

HE 1.55:date   • Item 444-K-6 (MF)
HEW REFUGEE TASK FORCE, REPORT TO THE CON-
GRESS.

HE 1.56:v.nos.&nos.   • Item 444-K-7
SHARING. v. 1–   1977–   [Quarterly]

PURPOSE:– To provide a clearinghouse for
improving the management of human services
and provide an exchange of ideas on projects
relating to human services.
ISSN 0162-6876

HE 1.57   • Item 444-M-1 (MF)
FINANCIAL ASSISTANCE BY GEOGRAPHIC AREA,
FISCAL YEAR. [Annual]

PURPOSE:– To provide a technical listing of
all HEW domestic assistance programs. Includes
funds obligated, identifies the recipient, the major components of HEW which obligated the funds,
and the Federal Domestic Assistance Program
for which the funds were obligated. Summarizes
the data for each county by the major components of HEW, HEW obligation, and total obligation in the county. Includes State summaries.
Issued for the following regions:–

REGION 1.   • Item 444-M-1 (MF)

Includes Connecticut, Maine, Massachusetts, New Hampshire, Rhode Island, and
Vermont.

REGION 2.   • Item 444-M-2 (MF)

Includes New York, New Jersey, Puerto
Rico, and the Virgin Islands.

REGION 3.   • Item 444-M-3 (MF)

Includes Delaware, District of Columbia,
Maryland, Pennsylvania, Virginia, and West
Virginia.

REGION 4.   • Item 444-M-4 (MF)

Includes Alabama, Florida, Georgia,
Kentucky, Mississippi, North Carolina, South
Carolina, and Tennessee.

REGION 5.   • Item 444-M-5 (MF)

Includes Illinois, Indiana, Michigan, Minnesota, Ohio, and Wisconsin.

REGION 6.   • Item 444-M-6 (MF)

Includes Arkansas, Louisiana, New
Mexico, Oklahoma, and Texas.

REGION 7.   • Item 444-M-7 (MF)

Includes Iowa, Kansas, Missouri, and
Nebraska.

REGION 8.   • Item 444-M-8 (MF)

Includes Colorado, Montana, North Dakota, South Dakota, Utah, and Wyoming.

REGION 9.   • Item 444-M-9 (MF)

Includes Arizona, California, Hawaii,
Nevada, and Guam.

REGION 10.   • Item 444-M-10 (MF)

Includes Alaska, Idaho, Oregon, and
Washington.

HE 1.58:date   • Item 444-K-8 (MF)
REPORT TO THE PRESIDENT AND CONGRESS ON
THE DRUG ABUSE, PREVENTION, AND TREAT-
MENT FUNCTIONS. 1st–   1978–   [Annual]

PURPOSE:– To summarize the activities, accomplishments, and prevention programs of the
Department. A description of the extent and health
consequences of drug abuse in the United States
is included.
Issued pursuant to section 3(b), Public Law
95-461, Drug Abuse and Treatment Amendments
of 1978.
Title varies.

HE 1.59:date   • Item 444-A-2 (MF)
HEALTH DATA INVENTORY. [Annual]

HE 1.60   • Item 444-P (E)
ELECTRONIC PRODUCTS. [Irregular]

HE 1.62:v.nos./nos.   • Item 445-M (EL)
PIC HIGHLIGHTS. [Quarterly]

HE 1.63:date   • Item 445-M-1 (P) (EL)
TRENDS IN THE WELL-BEING OF AMERICA'S CHIL-
DREN AND YOUTH.

HE 1.64:date   • Item 445-P
MEDICAL SUPPLY CATALOG. [Annual]

HE 1.65:date   • Item 445-M-2 (EL)
QUICK DRAW. [Quarterly].

FACILITIES ENGINEERING AND PROPERTY MANAGEMENT OFFICE (1971–   )

HE 1.101:date
ANNUAL REPORT.

HE 1.102:CT   • **Item 486-A-5**
GENERAL PUBLICATIONS.

HE 1.108:CT
HANDBOOKS, MANUALS, GUIDES.

HE 1.108/2:nos.   • **Item 486-A-4**
TECHNICAL HANDBOOK FOR FACILITIES ENGI-
NEERING AND CONSTRUCTION MANUALS.
[Irregular] (Office of Federally Assisted Construc-
tion)

The Office of Facilities Engineering and Property Management through the Regional Office of
Facilities Engineering and Construction, is responsible for furnishing architectural/engineering assistance and service during the design, bidding,
and construction phases of projects receiving
financial assistance from the Department of
Health, Education, and Welfare. The handbooks
provide information for project applicants and
State agencies.

HE 1.109:date   • **Item 486-A-1 (MF)**
REPRESENTATIVE CONSTRUCTION COSTS OF HOS-
PITALS AND RELATED HEALTH FACILITIES. 1948–
[Semiannual]

Compiles average cost of hospital and re-
lated health facilities of interest to HEW Regional
Offices, private architects, engineers, State
Health Agencies and area planning groups in all
States, and other Government agencies.
Earlier FS 1.74/6; HE 20.2510

ADMINISTRATION ON AGING (1973–1977)

CREATION AND AUTHORITY

The Administration of Aging (FS 15) was reassigned to the Social and Rehabilitation Service
(FS 17.300) by Departmental reorganization on
August 15, 1967. [The FS 17.300 SuDocs class
was used through 1969, becoming HE 17.300,
effective January 1, 1970.] The Administration
was transferred to the Office of Assistant Secretary for Human Development by Secretary's Order of June 15, 1973. In 1977, it became a part of
the Office of Human Development Services (HE
23.3000).

HE 1.201:date   • **Item 447-A-9**
ANNUAL REPORT.

Earlier HE 17.301
Later HE 23.3001

HE 1.202:CT   • **Item 447-A-1**
GENERAL PUBLICATIONS.

Earlier HE 17.302
Later HE 23.3002

HE 1.205:CT   • **Item 434-A-1**
LAWS.

Earlier HE 17.305
Later HE 23.3005

HE 1.208:CT   • **Item 447-A-3**
HANDBOOKS, MANUALS, GUIDES.

Later HE 23.3008

HE 1.208/2:CT   • **Item 447-A-3**
INFORMATION AND REFERRAL SERVICES (series).
[Irregular]

Earlier HE 17.308/2

HE 1.209:nos.   • **Item 447-A-7**
FACTS AND FIGURES ON OLDER AMERICANS. 1–
1972–   [Irregular]

Statistical studies.

HE 1.210:nos.   • **Item 444-A**
AGING. 1–   1951–   [Bimonthly]

Indexed by:–
Index to U.S. Government Periodicals
Public Affairs Information Service
Reader's Guide to Periodical Literature
ISSN 0002-0966
Earlier HE 17.309
Later HE 23.3110

HE 1.211:CT   • **Item 445-E-1**
PATTERNS FOR PROGRESS IN AGING. [Irregular]

Series of booklets reporting in detail upon an
outstandingly successful project for older people
with sufficient information for other organizations
and communities to develop a similar project
adapted to their particular circumstances.
Earlier HE 17.313

HE 1.212:CT   • **Item 447-A-6**
BIBLIOGRAPHIES AND LISTS OF PUBLICATIONS.
[Irregular]

HE 1.213:CT   • **Item 447-A-1**
HEW FACT SHEETS.

Later HE 23.3109

HE 1.214:date   • **Item 445-E-2**
NATIONAL DIRECTORY OF EDUCATION PROGRAMS
IN GERONTOLOGY. 1st ed.–   1976–   [Bien-
nial]

YOUTH DEVELOPMENT AND DELINQUENCY PREVENTION ADMINISTRATION (1974–1977)

CREATION AND AUTHORITY

The Youth Development and Delinquency Prevention Administration (HE 17.800) was transferred from the Social and Rehabilitation Service
to the Office of Assistant Secretary for Human
Development in 1974. In 1977, the Administration
was placed within the Office of Human Development Services (HE 23.1300).

HE 1.301:date
ANNUAL REPORT.

Earlier HE 17.801

HE 1.302:CT   • **Item 532-C-2**
GENERAL PUBLICATIONS. [Irregular]

Earlier HE 17.802

HE 1.308:CT   • **Item 532-D-1**
HANDBOOKS, MANUALS, GUIDES.

Later HE 23.1308

HE 1.309:CT   • **Item 532-C-4**
BIBLIOGRAPHIES AND LISTS OF PUBLICATIONS.

Earlier HE 17.809

HE 1.310:date   • **Item 532-D-3**
GRANTS, PREVENTIVE SERVICES, TRAINING,
TECHNICAL ASSISTANCE AND INFORMATION
SERVICES.

HE 1.311:date   • **Item 532-D-4**
YOUTH REPORTER.   – Feb. 1975. [Monthly, except
November] (Office of Public Information)

PURPOSE:– To provide a central source of
news, notes, and highlights of local and national
activities in the field of youth development.
ISSN 0092-5438

HE 1.312:nos.   • **Item 532-D-5**
SOURCE CATALOG ON YOUTH PARTICIPATION
(series). 1–   [Irregular]

OFFICE OF CHILD DEVELOPMENT (1975–1977)

CREATION AND AUTHORITY

The Office of Child Development (HE 21) was
placed directly under the Secretary of Health,
Education, and Welfare in 1975. In 1977, its functions were transferred to the Children, Youth and
Families Administration (HE 23.1000).

HE 1.401:date
ANNUAL REPORT.

Earlier HE 21.1

HE 1.402:CT   • **Item 454-C-1**
GENERAL PUBLICATIONS.

Earlier HE 21.2

HE 1.402:C 43/9   • **Item 454-C-1**
200 YEARS OF CHILDREN. 1977. 486 p.

PURPOSE:– To provide a look into the
lives and lifestyles of children over the last
200 years, documenting the remarkable
changes that have occurred and identifying
some current issues that have implications
for the future. Written about children but not
for them, 200 Years of Children is concerned
with the condition of, and changes in, children's
lives, their needs in health, education, and
welfare, the growing interest in children's recreation and literature, and the more recent
focus on the rights of children to develop to
their full potential.

HE 1.402:R 31   • **Item 454-C-1**
RESEARCH, DEMONSTRATION, AND EVALUA-
TION STUDIES. [Annual] (Research and Evalu-
ation Division)

Report covers fiscal year.

HE 1.408:CT   • **Item 454-C-4**
HANDBOOKS, MANUALS, GUIDES.

Earlier HE 21.8

HE 1.409:date   • **Item 454-C-5**
ANNUAL REPORT OF THE DEPARTMENT OF HEALTH,
EDUCATION, AND WELFARE TO CONGRESS ON
SERVICES PROVIDED TO HANDICAPPED CHIL-
DREN IN PROJECT HEAD START. 1st–   1973–

Earlier HE 21.8
Later HE 23.1012

HE 1.410:nos.   • Item 454-C-5
DAY CARE USA [publications]. 1–   [Irregular]

     Earlier HE 21.11

HE 1.411:CT   • Item 454-C-6
BIBLIOGRAPHIES AND LISTS OF PUBLICATIONS.
[Irregular]

CHILDREN'S BUREAU
(1975– 1977)

CREATION AND AUTHORITY

     The Children's Bureau (HE 21.100) was placed directly under the Secretary of Health, Education, and Welfare in 1975. In 1977, the Bureau was transferred to the newly established Children, Youth and Families Administration (HE 23.1200).

HE 1.451:date
ANNUAL REPORT.

     Earlier HE 21.101
     Later HE 23.1201

HE 1.452:CT   • Item 425
GENERAL PUBLICATIONS.

     Earlier HE 21.102
     Later HE 23.1202

HE 1.452:F 81/4   • Item 425
FOSTER FAMILY SERVICES SELECTED READING LIST. 1976. 78 p.

     Suggests books dealing with foster parents and children.

HE 1.458:CT   • Item 452-C
HANDBOOKS, MANUALS, GUIDES. [Irregular]

     Earlier HE 21.108
     Later HE 23.1208

HE 1.459:v.nos.&nos.   • Item 449
CHILDREN TODAY. [Bimonthly]

     Indexed by:–
       Education Index
       Index to U.S. Government Periodicals
       Nursing Literature Index
       Hospital Literature Index
       ISSN 0361-4336
       Supersedes Children (HE 21.9).
       Earlier HE 21.9/2
       Later HE 23.1209

BUREAU OF
CHILD DEVELOPMENT SERVICES

HE 1.461:date
ANNUAL REPORT.

HE 1.462:CT   • Item 445-N-2
GENERAL PUBLICATIONS.

HE 1.468:CT   • Item 445-N-1
HANDBOOKS, MANUALS, GUIDES.

HE 1.469:nos.   • Item 857-H-12
PROJECT HEAD START SERIES.

HE 1.470:CT
POSTERS. [Irregular]

CHILDREN'S BUREAU (Continued)

HE 1.480:CT   • Item 445-L-1
CHILD ABUSE AND NEGLECT (series). [Irregular]

HE 1.480/2:date   • Item 445-L-2
CHILD ABUSE AND NEGLECT REPORTS. Feb. 1976– [Quarterly]

     ISSN 0145-1383
     Later HE 23.1212

HE 1.480/3:date
CHILD ABUSE AND NEGLECT RESEARCH: PROJECTS AND PUBLICATIONS. [Semiannual]

     An extensive collection of information on child abuse and neglect research includes information abstracts of over 1,000 published documents and descriptions of on-going research projects. The publications abstracted represent medical, legal, psychological, sociological, and many over viewpoints of the child abuse and neglect problems.

HE 1.480/4:date   • Item 445-L-1
CHILD ABUSE AND NEGLECT PROGRAMS. [Semiannual]

     Later HE 23.1211

HE 1.480/5:date   • Item 445-L-1
NATIONAL CONFERENCE ON CHILD ABUSE AND NEGLECT: PROCEEDINGS. 1st– 1976–

OFFICE OF CONSUMER AFFAIRS
(1973–)

CREATION AND AUTHORITY

     The Office of Consumer Affairs (PrEx 16) was established within the Executive Office of the President by Executive Order 11583 of February 24, 1971. The Office was transferred to the Department of Health, Education, and Welfare by Executive Order 11702 of January 25, 1973.

HE 1.501:date
ANNUAL REPORT.

     Earlier PrEx 16.1

HE 1.502:CT   • Item 857-I-5
GENERAL PUBLICATIONS.

     Earlier PrEx 16.2

HE 1.502:St 2   • Item 857-I-5
DIRECTORY: FEDERAL, STATE AND LOCAL GOVERNMENT CONSUMER OFFICES. [Annual]

     PURPOSE:– To provide a basic source of information on government involvement in consumer protection for consumers, businessmen, and consumer organizations. Includes the address, phone number, and name of responsible officials in each office.
     Title varies.

HE 1.508:CT   • Item 857-I-2
HANDBOOKS, MANUALS, GUIDES.

     Earlier PrEx 16.8

HE 1.508/2:date   • Item 857-I-2
CONSUMER'S RESOURCE HANDBOOK.

     Later: GS 11.9/3

HE 1.509:v.nos.&nos.   • Item 857-I-1
CONSUMER NEWS. v. 1– 9, no. 12. April 1971– June 15, 1979. [Semimonthly]

     PURPOSE:– To keep the public informed on what the Government is doing to protect the consumer. Highlights the consumer activities of all Federal agencies, and covers unsafe products, unfair sales practices, air and water pollution and other issues.

     Indexed by: Index to U.S. Government Periodicals
     ISSN 0045-8260
     Issued by the Executive Office of the President (PrEx 16.9) prior to v. 3, no. 14, Oct. 15, 1973.

HE 1.509/2:date
DIRECTORY OF CONSUMER OFFICES.

     Issued as a supplement to Consumer News (HE 1.509).

HE 1.510:date   • Item 857-I-4
CONSUMER LEGISLATIVE MONTHLY REPORT. v. 1– 12. [Monthly while Congress is in session]

     PURPOSE:– To provide a comprehensive listing of consumer bills introduced in Congress, giving the status of each bill, index of bills by topic and bill number, description of each consumer act passed by Congress and signed by the President.
     Each issue is cumulative.
     Issued by the Executive Office of the President (PrEx 16.11) prior to August 1973.
     Prior to v. 2, no. 10, May-July 1974, unnumbered.

REHABILITATION SERVICES
ADMINISTRATION
(1975– 1977)

CREATION AND AUTHORITY

     The Rehabilitation Services Administration (HE 17.100) was placed directly under the Secretary of Health, Education, and Welfare in 1975. In 1977, the Administration was transferred to the newly established Office of Human Development Services (HE 23.4100).

HE 1.601:date
ANNUAL REPORT.

     Later HE 23.4101

HE 1.602:CT
GENERAL PUBLICATIONS.

     Later HE 23.4102

HE 1.608:CT
HANDBOOKS, MANUALS, GUIDES.

     Earlier HE 17.108

HE 1.609:date   • Item 529-D
ANNUAL REPORT OF THE DEPARTMENT OF HEALTH, EDUCATION, AND WELFARE TO THE PRESIDENT AND THE CONGRESS ON FEDERAL ACTIVITIES RELATED TO THE ADMINISTRATION OF THE REHABILITATION ACT OF 1973.

     ISSN 0098-4930

HE 1.610:date   • Item 506-C-2
FACT SHEET BOOKLETS, FISCAL YEAR (date). [Annual] (State Vocational Rehabilitation Agency)

     ISSN 0098-7964
     Earlier HE 17.119/2

HE 1.610/2:date
PROGRAM AND FINANCIAL PLAN, BASIC ASSUMPTIONS AND GUIDELINES. [Annual] (State Vocational Rehabilitation Agency)

     Earlier HE 17.102:St 2/6
     Later HE 23.4110

HE 1.610/3:date   • Item 506-C-2
PROGRAM DATA. [Annual] (State Vocational Rehabilitation Agency)

     Later HE 23.4110/2

HE 1.611:date   • Item 529-C
CASELOAD STATISTICS. [Annual] (State Vocational
   Rehabilitation Agency)

    ISSN 0566-0009
    Later HE 23.4109

HE 1.612:date   • Item 506-C-4
AMERICAN REHABILITATION. v. 1–   1975–
   [Bimonthly]

    Indexed by: Index to U.S. Government Peri-
    odicals.
    ISSN 0362-4048
    Later ED 1.211

OFFICE OF HUMAN DEVELOPMENT (1976–1977)

CREATION AND AUTHORITY

    The Office of Human Development was es-
tablished within the Department of Health, Education, and Welfare in 1976. It was redesignated
the Office of Human Development Services (HE
23) and reorganized by the Secretary's reorganization order of July 26, 1977.

HE 1.701:date   • Item 529-B-2
ANNUAL REPORT. 1st–   1976–

HE 1.702:CT   • Item 529-B-3
GENERAL PUBLICATIONS. [Irregular]

    Later HE 23.2

HE 1.706:CT   • Item 529-B-4
REGULATIONS, RULES, INSTRUCTIONS. [Irregular]

HE 1.709:nos.   • Item 529-B-1
OHD, GRANTS ADMINISTRATION MANUAL, TN- (se-
ries). [Irregular]

HE 1.710:date
NATIVE AMERICAN. [Bimonthly]

HEAD START BUREAU (1977)

CREATION AND AUTHORITY

    The Head Start Bureau (HE 21.200) was placed
directly under the Secretary of Health, Education, and Welfare in 1977. In the same year, it
was again transferred to the newly established
Office of Human Development Services (HE
23.1100).

HE 1.801:date
ANNUAL REPORT.

    Earlier HE 21.201

HE 1.802:CT
GENERAL PUBLICATIONS.

    Earlier HE 21.202
    Later HE 23.1102

HE 1.808:CT   • Item 499-G-1
HANDBOOKS, MANUALS, GUIDES. [Irregular]

    Earlier HE 21.208
    Later HE 23.1108

PUBLIC SERVICES ADMINISTRATION (1977)

CREATION AND AUTHORITY

    The Community Services Administration
(HE 17.700) was redesignated the Public Services
Administration and placed under the Secretary of
Health, Education, and Welfare in 1976. In 1977,
the Administration was transferred to the newly
established Office of Human Development Services (HE 23.2000).

HE 1.901:date
ANNUAL REPORT.

    Earlier HE 17.701
    Later HE 23.2001

HE 1.902:CT
GENERAL PUBLICATIONS.

    Earlier HE 17.702
    Later HE 23.2002

AGING ADMINISTRATION (1991–   )

CREATION AND AUTHORITY

    The Aging Administration was removed from
the Human Development Services Office in August 1991 by Secretarial Order and placed directly under the Health and Human Services Department as class HE 1.1000.

INFORMATION

    Administration on Aging
    Department of Health and Human Services
    300 Independence Ave., SW
    Washington, D.C. 20201
    (202) 619-7501
    http://www.aoa.gov

HE 1.1001:date   • Item 447-A-9 (MF)
ANNUAL REPORT.

    Earlier HE 23.3001

HE 1.1002:CT   • Item 447-A-1
GENERAL PUBLICATIONS.

    Earlier HE 23.3002.

HE 1.1005:CT   • Item 447-A-8
LAWS.

    Earlier HE 23.3005

HE 1.1008:CT   • Item 447-A-3
HANDBOOKS, MANUALS, GUIDES.

    Earlier HE 23.3008

HE 1.1009:CT   • Item 447-A-3
SOMEONE WHO CARES, A GUIDE TO HIRING AN
   IN-HOME CAREGIVER.

HE 1.1011:CT   • Item 447-A-6
BIBLIOGRAPHIES AND LISTS OF PUBLICATIONS.

    Earlier HE 23.3011

HE 1.1013:nos.   • Item 447-A-18 (EL)
INFORMATION MEMORANDUMS.

    Information memorandums to state agencies
administering plans related to older Americans.
Earlier HE 23.3013

HE 1.1014:CT   • Item 447-A-20 (MF)
DIRECTORIES.

HE 1.1015:nos.   • Item 444-A
AGING. 1–   1951–   [Quarterly]

    PURPOSE:- To present in condensed form
news of developments, programs, activities in
research and publications related to all aspects
of aging and the aged.
    Departments: News of State Commissions;
the Way the Wind Blows (announcements of conferences, seminars, courses, etc.); Books, Pamphlets and reports (annotated items).
    Indexed by:–
      Public Affairs Information Service
      Reader's Guide to Periodical Literature
    ISSN 0002-0966
    Earlier HE 23.3015

HE 1.1016   • Item 447-A-24
AOA REPORTS. [Quarterly]

HE 1.1017:   • Item 447-A-27 (EL)
AOA UPDATE.

HE 1.1018:   • Item 447-A-27 (E)
ELECTRONIC PRODUCTS (misc.).

SOCIAL SECURITY ADMINISTRATION (1970–1995)

CREATION AND AUTHORITY

    The Social Security Administration was es-
tablished and its predecessor, the Social Security Board was abolished by Federal Security
Agency Reorganization Plan 11, effective July
16, 1946.
    By Reorganization Plan 1, effective April 11,
1953, the Social Security Administration was
transferred from the Federal Security Agency (FS
3) to the Department of Health, Education, and
Welfare.
    [The SuDocs class FS 3 was used during the
period 1953–1969.]
    The Social Security Administration became
an independent agency (SSA) in the executive
branch by act of August 15, 1994 (108 Stat.
1464), effective March 31, 1995.

HE 3.1:date   • Item 513-A (MF)
ANNUAL REPORT.

    Earlier SS 1.1 FS 3.1

HE 3.2:CT   • Item 516
GENERAL PUBLICATIONS.

    Earlier SS 1.2 FS 3.2
    Later SSA 1.2

HE 3.3:v.nos.&nos.   • **Item 523**
SOCIAL SECURITY BULLETIN. v. 1–   1938–
[Monthly]

Official monthly publication of the Social Security Administration. Contains articles on the various programs of the Administration.
Departments: Social Security in Review; Notes and Brief Reports; Recent Publications; Current Operating Statistics.
Indexed by:–
Business Periodicals Index
Index to U.S. Government Periodicals
Public Affairs Information Service
ISSN 0037-7910
Earlier SS 1.25, FS 3.3
Later SS 1.22

HE 3.3/a:CT   • **Item 523-A-3**
SEPARATES. [Irregular]

HE 3.3/3:date   • **Item 523-A-1**
SOCIAL SECURITY BULLETIN, STATISTICAL SUPPLEMENT. [Annual]

Detailed annual data, issued separately beginning with the data for the calendar year 1955. Prior to that, data appeared in the September issues. Monthly data is contained in the Current Operating Statistics section of the monthly Bulletins.
Earlier FS 3.3/3
Later SSA 1.22/2

HE 3.3/5:date   • **Item 523**
AUTHOR, TITLE, AND SUBJECT INDEX TO THE SOCIAL SECURITY BULLETIN. [Irregular]

1938– 1979. 1982.

HE 3.3/6:v.nos.&nos.   • **Item 523-A-2**
CENTRAL OFFICE BULLETIN. [Biweekly]

Contains news items on SSA activities and employees.

HE 3.4:nos.   • **Item 517**
INFORMATION SERVICE CIRCULARS. ISC 1–   1957–
[Irregular]

Correspondence aids.
Earlier SS 1.4 FS 3.4

HE 3.4/2:nos.
SSA PROGRAM CIRCULARS: GENERAL SERIES. [Irregular]

HE 3.4/3:nos.
SSA PROGRAM CIRCULARS: PUBLIC INFORMATION. [Irregular]

HE 3.4/4:nos.
SSA PROGRAM CIRCULARS: DISABILITY. [Irregular]

Earlier HE 3.4/2

HE 3.4/5:nos.
SSA PROGRAM CIRCULAR: RETIREMENT AND SURVIVORS INSURANCE. [Irregular]

Earlier HE 3.4/2

HE 3.4/6:nos.
SSA PROGRAM CIRCULAR: SUPPLEMENTAL SECURITY INCOME. [Irregular]

Earlier HE 3.4/2

HE 3.4/7:v.nos.&nos.
ACCESS: A TECHNICAL CIRCULAR FOR THE END-USER COMPUTING COMMUNITY. [Monthly]

HE 3.5:CT   • **Item 518**
LAWS.

Earlier SS 1.5 FS 3.5

HE 3.5/2:nos.   • **Item 518**
LAWS AND REGULATIONS (numbered). 1–
[Irregular]

HE 3.5/3:date   • **Item 518-B (MF)**
LEGISLATIVE HISTORY OF TITLES I-XX OF THE SOCIAL SECURITY ACT. [Biennial]

Earlier HE 3.2:L 52/2

HE 3.6:CT   • **Item 520**
REGULATIONS, RULES, AND INSTRUCTIONS.

Earlier SS 1.6 FS 3.6
Later SSA 1.6

HE 3.6/2-2   • **Item 520-A-1**
ACQUIESCENCE RULING (series).

Later SSA 1.6/2

HE 3.6/3:CT   • **Item 516-C**
HANDBOOKS, MANUALS, AND GUIDES.

Earlier FS 3.6/3
Later SS 1.8

HE 3.6/3:So 1/3   • **Item 516-C**
SOCIAL SECURITY HANDBOOKS. 1978. 525 p.

PURPOSE:– To outline the provisions of the Social Security Act and related laws, covering information on Federal retirement, survivors disability, health insurance, black lung benefits, and supplemental security income programs.

HE 3.6/4:nos.   • **Item 516-C**
HEALTH INSURANCE FOR THE AGED. 1–   1966–
[Irregular]

Earlier FS 3.6/4

HE 3.6/5:nos.   • **Item 516-S**
PROGRAM OPERATIONS MANUAL SYSTEM. [Irregular]

Later SSA 1.8/2

                                         • **Item 516-S (P)**
HE 3.6/5   • **Item 516-X-1 (E)**
PROGRAM OPERATIONS MANUAL SYSTEM (POMS) AND MODERNIZED SYSTEM OPERATIONS MANUAL (MSOM) MONTHLY.

Issued on CD-ROM

HE 3.6/6:date   • **Item 516-C (MF)**
POST ENTITLEMENT MANUAL. [Irregular]

HE 3.6/7:nos.   • **Item 516-C-1**
OFFICE OF HEARINGS AND APPEALS HANDBOOK. [Irregular]

HE 3.6/8
SOCIAL SECURITY HANDBOOK. [Irregular]

PURPOSE:– To explain the Federal retirement, survivors, disability, and black lung benefits, supplemental security income programs, health insurance, and public assistance.
Earlier HE 3.6/3:So 1/3
Later SSA 1.8/3

HE 3.16/3:nos.   • **Item 512-D-11**
APPLICATIONS AND CASE DISPOSITIONS FOR PUBLIC ASSISTANCE, NCSS REPORT A-12.

HE 3.19:nos.   • **Item 516-F-1 (MF)**
ACTUARIAL STUDIES. 1–   [Irregular]

HE 3.19/2:nos.   • **Item 516-F (MF)**
ACTUARIAL NOTES. 1–   1962–   [Irregular]

Indexed by: Index to U.S. Government Periodicals
Earlier FS 3.19/2

HE 3.21/2:   • **Item 516-W**
FACT SHEET (VARIOUS TOPICS).

Each fact sheet will relate to a different topic, such as the retirement earnings test and earnings from self-employment.
Later SSA 1.19

HE 3.22:CT   • **Item 516-K**
POSTERS AND CHARTS. [Irregular]

HE 3.22/2:CT   • **Item 516-K-1**
AUDIOVISUAL MATERIALS. [Irregular]

HE 3.25/2:date&nos.   • **Item 527-A**
AMENDMENTS TO SOCIAL SECURITY LAWS, SSI.

Earlier FS 3.25/2

HE 3.28/2:nos.   • **Item 516-G**
RESEARCH AND STATISTICS NOTES. 1–   1978–

PURPOSE:– To get information quickly into the hands of users. The Notes may report on ongoing research, summarize preliminary findings or provide addenda to material already published. Includes subjects such as mortality of alcoholics, social welfare expenditures, and age differences in health care spending.
Issued in microfiche (24x).
Indexed by: Index to U.S. Government Periodicals.
Earlier FS 3.28/4

HE 3.28/4:nos.
HEALTH INSURANCE STATISTICS: CURRENT MEDICARE SURVEY REPORT. CMS 1–

Earlier FS 3.28/4

HE 3.28/5:nos.
HEALTH INSURANCE STATISTICS. HI 1–   1967–
[Irregular]

Earlier FS 3.28/5

HE 3.28/6:date&nos.   • **Item 516-G-1**
MONTHLY BENEFIT STATISTICS: OLD- AGE, SURVIVORS, DISABILITY, AND HEALTH INSURANCE, SUMMARY BENEFIT DATA. [Monthly] (Office of Research and Statistics.)

Tables summarize program data on Old- Age, Survivors, Disability, and Health Insurance; Supplemental Security Income; Aid to Families With Dependent Children; and General Assistance programs.
Calendar year benefit data issued separately.
ISSN 0364-040X
Earlier FS 3.28/6

HE 3.28/6-2:date   • **Item 516-G-1**
MONTHLY BENEFIT STATISTICS, SUMMARY PROGRAM DATA, CALENDAR YEAR (date). [Annual]

HE 3.28/6-3:date   • **Item 516-G-1**
MONTHLY BENEFIT STATISTICS: OLD-AGE, SURVIVORS, DISABILITY, AND HEALTH INSURANCE, FISCAL YEAR BENEFIT DATA.

Earlier FS 3.28/6-3

HE 3.28/6-4:date
INSURANCE PROGRAM QUALITY. [Quarterly]

HE 3.28/7:date
MONTHLY WORKLOAD TREND REPORT. [Monthly]

HE 3.28/7-2:date
MONTHLY WORKLOAD TREND REPORT, QUARTERLY SUMMARY. [Quarterly]

HE 3.28/8:date
RSI QUALITY APPRAISAL POSTADJUDICATIVE MONTHLY STATISTICAL SUMMARY. [Monthly]

HE 3.28/9:date   • **Item 516-G-1 (MF)**
RSI QUALITY APPRAISAL AWARDS AND DISALLOWANCES MONTHLY STATISTICAL SUMMARY. [Monthly]

HE 3.33:nos.   • **Item 517-A**
INTERNATIONAL TECHNICAL COOPERATION SERIES.

Earlier FS 3.33

HE 3.37:CT   • **Item 512-B-2**
INCOME MAINTENANCE TRAINING PROGRAM (series). [Irregular]

HE 3.38:CT   • **Item 516-B (MF)**
BIBLIOGRAPHIES AND LISTS OF PUBLICATIONS.

Earlier FS 3.38
Later SSA 1.10

HE 3.38/2:v.nos.&nos.
LIBRARY NOTES. [Monthly]

HE 3.38/3:date   • **Item 516-B**
SOCIAL SECURITY ADMINISTRATION PUBLICATIONS CATALOG. [Annual]

HE 3.38/4:date   • **Item 516-B**
STATISTICS RESEARCH ANALYSIS MICROFILES CATALOG. [Annual]

HE 3.38/5:date   • **Item 516-B**
PUBLICATIONS CATALOG, U.S. DEPARTMENT OF HEALTH AND HUMAN SERVICES.

HE 3.40:date   • **Item 516-A**
ANNUAL STATISTICS ON WORKERS UNDER SOCIAL SECURITY. 1937–   [Annual]

Contains statistics on employment earnings, insurance status under old-age, survivors, disability, and health insurance.
Earlier title: Handbook of Old-Age, Survivors, and Disability Insurance Statistics, (FS 3.2:01 1/3 and FS 3.40).

HE 3.41:date   • **Item 520-A**
REPORT OF ADVISORY COUNCIL ON SOCIAL SECURITY FINANCING. [Quinquennial]

1965 Report: Status of Social Security Program and Recommendations for its Improvement.
Earlier FS 3.41

HE 3.44:date/nos.   • **Item 523-A (MF)**
SOCIAL SECURITY RULINGS ON FEDERAL OLD-AGE, SURVIVORS, DISABILITY, AND HEALTH INSURANCE. [Quarterly]

PURPOSE:– To provide the public with official rulings relating to the Federal old-age, survivors, and disability insurance program in order to promote understanding of the provisions and administration of title II of the Social Security Act and related laws.
Social Security Rulings are divided into three parts: 1) interpretations and decisions of the Social Security Administration. Court decisions of particular significance may also be published in this section. 2) information regarding changes in title II of the Social Security Act and related regulations. 3) information regarding miscellaneous matters of general interest which do not fall into any of the categories mentioned above.
The rulings contained in Part I are cumulated annually in the Cumulative Bulletins (listed below).
Issued quarterly prior to 1968.
ISSN 0364-6750
Earlier FS 3.44

HE 3.44/2:date   • **Item 523-A (MF)**
SOCIAL SECURITY RULINGS, CUMULATIVE BULLETINS. [Annual]

Earlier FS 3.44/2

HE 3.46/2:nos.
PRELIMINARY FINDINGS FROM SURVEY OF NEW BENEFICIARIES, REPORT.

HE 3.49:nos.   • **Item 522-A (MF)**
RESEARCH REPORTS. [Irregular]

Earlier FS 3.49

HE 3.49:31
SOCIAL SECURITY PROGRAMS THROUGHOUT THE WORLD. 1969. 1970. 249 p.

Presents an analysis of the principal provisions of social security programs in all countries of the world. Countries are listed alphabetically and a separate summary is given for each country. The larger part of the programs covered are social insurance measures but several related types of social security programs are also included.

HE 3.49/3:date   • **Item 522-A (MF)**
SOCIAL SECURITY PROGRAMS THROUGHOUT THE WORLD. [Biennial]

Later SSA 1.24

HE 3.51:date   • **Item 515-A**
DIRECTORY OF PROVIDERS OF SERVICES: HOME HEALTH SERVICES. 1966–   [Irregular]

Earlier FS 3.51

HE 3.51/2:date   • **Item 515-A**
DIRECTORY OF PROVIDERS OF SERVICES: HOSPITALS. 1966–   [Irregular]

Earlier FS 3.51/2

HE 3.51/3:date   • **Item 515-A**
DIRECTORY OF PROVIDERS OF SERVICES: EXTENDED CARE FACILITIES. 1967–   [Irregular]

Earlier FS 3.51/3

HE 3.51/4:date   • **Item 515-A**
DIRECTORY OF PROVIDERS OF SERVICES: INDEPENDENT LABORATORIES.

Earlier FS 3.51/4

HE 3.51/5:date   • **Item 515-A**
DIRECTORY OF MEDICARE PROVIDERS AND SUPPLIERS OF SERVICES. 1st ed.–

Covers hospitals, extended care facilities, home health agencies, outpatient physical therapy, independent laboratories, Title 18, Health Insurance for the aged.

HE 3.51/6   • **Item 515-A (MF)**
OHA TELEPHONE DIRECTORY. [Annual]

HE 3.52:nos.   • **Item 523-B**
SOCIAL SECURITY INFORMATION SSI (series). 1– 1967–   [Irregular]

General explanation of the social security program.
Supersedes OASI series (FS 3.35).
Earlier FS 3.52

HE 3.52/2:nos.   • **Item 523-C**
TIB [Technical Information Bulletin] (series). 1– 1965–

PURPOSE:– To provide technical information on promulgation of the social security program.
Earlier FS 3.52/2

HE 3.54/2:nos.
FROM THE SOCIAL SECURITY SURVEY OF THE DISABLED, REPORTS.

PURPOSE:– To present analyses from a series of surveys of the disabled population aged 18-64 of the United States. Includes analyses of demographic characteristics, program relations, health care utilization and costs, income and income sources, work experience, rehabilitation and related areas of interest. Major disabling conditions, functional limitations, duration of disability and socio-economic characteristics are also studies in relation to their effect on the nature and severity of disability and labor force participation.

HE 3.54/3:nos.
FROM SOCIAL SECURITY SURVEY OF INSTITUTIONALIZED ADULTS, REPORTS. 1–   1971–   [Irregular]

Reports based on the 1967 Survey of Institutionalized Adults. The data for this survey were obtained through a multistage area probability sample of patients in long-term care institutions, excluding nursing homes, but including long-term wards of short-stay general hospitals. Data were collected on approximately 6,000 patients in Aug.- Oct., 1967, and included information on the limitations and treatment of institutionalized persons, their economic and social circumstances, charges and payments for their care, and the activities of financial administrators.

HE 3.55
HIR (series).

HE 3.56:nos.   • **Item 522-B (MF)**
OFFICE OF RESEARCH AND STATISTICS: STAFF PAPERS. 1–

HE 3.57:date/sec.nos.   • **Item 516-D**
HEALTH INSURANCE FOR THE AGED. [Annual, by sections]

HE 3.57/2:date
RETIREMENT AND SURVIVORS INSURANCE SEMI-ANNUAL ANALYSIS.

HE 3.58:date
TELEPHONE DIRECTORY.

HE 3.58/2:date   • **Item 516-C-2**
SOCIAL SECURITY ADMINISTRATION BALTIMORE DIRECTORY. [Annual]

PURPOSE– To provide organizational listings by office, and an alphabetical listing of Baltimore SSA employees. Lists Baltimore and Washington, D.C. metropolitan exchanges, and Washington D.C. federal agencies, etc.

HE 3.59:v.nos.&nos.   • **Item 516-E**
SOCIAL SECURITY STUDENT GAZETTE. v. 1–

HE 3.60:date   • **Item 512-D-10**
PUBLIC ASSISTANCE STATISTICS. [Monthly] (ORS Report A-2)

ISSN 0145-952X
Earlier HE 17.610
Superseded by Quarterly Public Assistance Statistics (HE 3.60/4).

HE 3.60/2:date   • **Item 512-D-9**
REQUESTS FOR AFDC HEARINGS IN PUBLIC ASSISTANCE, FISCAL YEAR (date). [Annual] (ORS Report E-8)

Former title: Requests for Hearings in Public Assistance.
Earlier HE 17.644

HE 3.60/3:date   • **Item 512-D-11**
APPLICATIONS AND CASE DISCONTINUANCES FOR AFDC. [Quarterly]

AFDC = Assistance for Dependent Children
Former title: Applications and Case Discontinuances for Public Assistance.

HE 3.60/4:date
QUARTERLY PUBLIC ASSISTANCE STATISTICS.

Continues and supersedes Public Assistance Statistics (HE 3.60).

HE 3.61:date   • **Item 512-D-12**
PUBLIC ASSISTANCE RECIPIENTS AND CASH PAYMENTS. [Annual]

Earlier HE 17.627/2

HE 3.61/2:date   • **Item 512-D-12 (MF)**
PUBLIC ASSISTANCE RECIPIENTS IN STANDARD METROPOLITAN STATISTICAL AREAS. [Annual]

HE 3.62   • **Item 523-D**
STUDIES FROM INTERAGENCY DATA LINKAGES. [Irregular]

HE 3.63:date   • **Item 512-D-13**
DISPOSITION OF PUBLIC ASSISTANCE CASES INVOLVING QUESTION OF FRAUD. (ORS Report E-7)

Earlier HE 17.642

HE 3.64:   • **Item 512-D-16**
AFDC STANDARDS FOR BASIC NEEDS. (ORS Report D-2).

HE 3.65:CT • Item 512-D-19
AID TO FAMILIES WITH DEPENDENT CHILDREN.
(series). [Irregular]

HE 3.65/2:date • Item 512-D-19
CHARACTERISTICS OF STATE PLANS FOR AID TO
FAMILIES WITH DEPENDENT CHILDREN UNDER
THE SOCIAL SECURITY ACT TITLE IV-A. [An-
nual]

　　　Formerly HE 3.2:C 43/6

HE 3.65/3 • Item 512-D-19
AID TO FAMILIES WITH DEPENDENT CHILDREN
(AFDC) INFORMATION MEMORANDUM. [Irregular]
(SSA-IM)

HE 3.65/4:nos.
AID TO FAMILIES WITH DEPENDENT CHILDREN,
ACTION TRANSMITTALS SSA-AT- (series).
[Irregular]

HE 3.66:v.nos.&nos. • Item 516-N (MF)
OHA LAW REPORTER. [Quarterly] (Office of Hearings and Appeals)

　　　Intended to serve as an unofficial informational guide to current developments in the laws
and policies pertaining to the Social Security
Administration and the issuing office.

HE 3.66/2:date
OHA NEWSLETTER. [Monthly]

HE 3.66/3 • Item 516-N (MF)
THE OHA LAW JOURNAL. [Quarterly]

　　　Later SSA 1.5/3

HE 3.67:CT
AFDC AND RELATED INCOME MAINTENANCE STUD-
IES. [Irregular]

HE 3.67/2:nos. • Item 516
STUDIES IN INCOME DISTRIBUTION (series). [Ir-
regular]

HE 3.68:nos.
SSA ADMINISTRATIVE DIRECTIVES SYSTEM
TRANSMITTAL NOTICE.

HE 3.68/2:v.nos.&nos.
SSA MANAGEMENT NEWSLETTER FOR SUPERVI-
SORS AND MANAGEMENT PERSONNEL.
[Bimonthly]

HE 3.68/3:nos.
LABOR AND EMPLOYEE RELATIONS BULLETIN FOR
SSA SUPERVISORY PERSONNEL.

HE 3.68/4 • Item 523-E
SYSTEMS INFORMATION NEWSLETTER. [Quarterly]

　　　PURPOSE:– To present information on SSA
computer systems in the form of short news items
and questions and answers.

HE 3.68/5:nos.
DIRECT LINE TO YOU. [Irregular]

HE 3.69:date
EXPENDITURES FOR PUBLIC ASSISTANCE PRO-
GRAMS. [Annual]

HE 3.69/2:letters-nos.
SSA TRAINING (series): TECHNICAL CORE CUR-
RICULUM.

HE 3.69/3:ltrs.
SSA TRAINING DATA REVIEW TECHNICIAN, BASIC
TRAINING COURSE.

HE 3.70:date • Item 512-D-20 (MF)
EXPENDITURES FOR PUBLIC ASSISTANCE PRO-
GRAM. [Annual]

　　　Tables present expenditures for such public
assistance programs as Aid to Families With De-
pendent Children, Supplementary Security Income,
Medicaid, and Social Services under Title XX and
Child Welfare Service under Title IV-B.
Report issued for fiscal year.

HE 3.71:date • Item 516-H (MF)
SSI RECIPIENTS BY STATE AND COUNTY. [Annual]

　　　Earlier title: Supplemental Security Income,
State and County Data.
Earlier HE 3.2:Se 2/7
Later SSA 1.17

HE 3.71/2:date
PROGRAM AND DEMOGRAPHIC CHARACTERISTICS
OF SUPPLEMENTAL SECURITY INCOME BEN-
EFICIARIES. [Annual]

HE 3.72:date • Item 516-J
REFUGEE RESETTLEMENT PROGRAM, REPORT TO
CONGRESS. [Annual]

　　　Report submitted to Congress pursuant to
the Immigration and Neutrality Act. Contains tables,
Federal agency reports, and resettlement agency
report. Lists state refugee coordinators, State
Purchase-of-Service contracts, and Refugee
Health Program grants.
Earlier HE 3.2:R 25

HE 3.73:(CT)/date
SOCIAL SECURITY BENEFICIARIES BY ZIP CODE
AREA. [Annual]

HE 3.73/2:date • Item 516-L (MF)
SOCIAL SECURITY BENEFICIARIES BY STATE AND
COUNTY. [Annual]

　　　Tables show the number of persons receiving
benefits and monthly payments being paid. Data
are shown for the retirement, survivor, and disability programs, and by sex for those age 62 and
over.

HE 3.73/3:date • Item 516-L
SOCIAL SECURITY BENEFICIARIES IN METROPOLI-
TAN AREAS. [Annual]

HE 3.74:nos.
QUICKLIST (series). [Irregular]

HE 3.75:date • Item 516-M
INCOME OF THE POPULATION 55 AND OVER.
[Annual]

　　　Tables break down income of the population
55 and over by earnings, retirement benefits,
interest and dividends, and veterans' benefits.

HE 3.76:date • Item 516-P (MF)
LOW INCOME HOME ENERGY ASSISTANCE PRO-
GRAM, REPORT TO CONGRESS. [Annual]

　　　This program (LIHEAP) is authorized by Title
26 of the Omnibus Budget Reconciliation Act of
1981 (PL 97-35). Its purpose is to assist low
income households to meet the costs of home
energy.

HE 3.77:date • Item 516-H-1
SUPPLEMENTAL SECURITY INCOME PROGRAM
FOR THE AGED, BLIND, AND DISABLED. [Annual]

　　　Subtitle: Characteristics of State Assistance
Programs for SSI Recipients.
PURPOSE:– To summarize additional assis-
tance provided by each State to complement the
Federal SSI payments to the aged, blind, and
disabled.
Earlier HE 3.2:Se 2/4

HE 3.78:nos. • Item 523-A-4
NEW BENEFICIARY SURVEY (series). 1–　[Irregu-
lar]

HE 3.79:date • Item 516-G-2 (MF)
SSA WORKLOAD ANALYSIS REPORT. [10 times a
year]

　　　Compares workloads, work-year to budget
plan. Tables summarize the workload of the Administration and also of its various offices.

HE 3.80:date
SYSTEMS TECHNOLOGY INFORMATION UPDATE.
[Monthly]

HE 3.81:date
MANAGER'S CALENDAR. [Quarterly]

HE 3.82:date
SOCIAL SECURITY INFORMATION ITEMS. [Monthly]

HE 3.83:nos.
CLAIMS REPRESENTATIVE (TITLE XVI) BASIC
TRAINING COURSE. [Irregular]

HE 3.84 • Item 516-R (MF)
FISCAL YEAR PLAN, AUTOMATED DATA PROCESS-
ING UPDATE. [Quarterly]

　　　Lists and describes Administration automatic
data processing projects showing start, finish,
and system release dates.

HE 3.86:date
STECS DATA LINK. [Quarterly]

HE 3.87:date • Item 516-T (MF)
BUDGET PROGRESS REPORT. [Quarterly]

　　　Progress report prepared by the Office of
Central Operation's Financial Management staff
to provide OCO's executive staff with an analysis of OCO workloads and resources.

HE 3.88:date • Item 516-A-1
YOUR SOCIAL SECURITY RIGHTS AND RESPONSI-
BILITIES, DISABILITY BENEFITS. [Annual]

　　　PURPOSE:– To explain the Social Security
rights of recipients of disability benefits. Includes
information on disability checks, disability reviews,
etc.
Earlier HE 3.2:D 63/3

HE 3.88/2:date • Item 516-A-1
YOUR SOCIAL SECURITY RIGHTS AND RESPONSI-
BILITIES, RETIREMENT AND SURVIVORS.
[Annual]

　　　PURPOSE:– To explain the Social Security
rights and responsibilities of those who receive
retirement and survivors benefits.

HE 3.89:date • Item 516-A-4
YOUR SOCIAL SECURITY. [Annual]

　　　Provides general information on Social Security including applying for benefits, financing of
the system, right of appeal, etc.
Earlier HE 3.2:So 13/25

HE 3.90:date • Item 516-A-3
WHAT YOU HAVE TO KNOW ABOUT SSI. [Annual]

　　　SSI = Supplemental Security Income.
PURPOSE– To provide information needed
by recipients of SSI concerning their checks,
reporting changes in their financial situation, and
their right to question a decision or be represented.
Earlier HE 3.2:So 13/32

HE 3.91:date • Item 516-L-1 (MF)
CHARACTERISTICS OF SOCIAL SECURITY DISABIL-
ITY INSURANCE BENEFICIARIES. [Annual]

　　　PURPOSE:– To present data that identify and
highlight basic characteristics of those disabled
workers whose claims for benefits were allowed.
Data include age, sex, occupation, diagnosis,
mobility, and state residence. Chiefly tables.

HE 3.93:date • Item 516-A-2
YOUR SOCIAL SECURITY RIGHTS & RESPONSI-
BILITIES, RETIREMENT & SURVIVORS BEN-
EFITS.

HE 3.94:date • Item 516
FAST FACTS & FIGURES ABOUT SOCIAL SECURITY.
[Annual]

　　　Later SSA 1.26

HE 3.95   • Item 516-L (MF)
EARNINGS AND EMPLOYMENT DATA FOR WAGE AND SALARY WORKERS COVERED UNDER SOCIAL SECURITY BY STATE AND COUNTY. [Annual]

Later SSA 1.17/3

HE 3.96:nos.   • Item 518
FORMS.

BUREAU OF FEDERAL CREDIT UNIONS (1970)

CREATION AND AUTHORITY

The Bureau of Federal Credit Unions was established within the Federal Security Agency by act of Congress approved June 29, 1948, and effective July 29, 1948. By agency order, it was made a part of the Social Security Administration. On April 11, 1953, the Social Security Administration became a part of the newly created Department of Health, Education, and Welfare by Reorganization Plan No. 1 of 1953. The Bureau was abolished and its functions transferred to the National Credit Union Administration (NCU 1) upon its establishment on March 10, 1970.
[During the period from 1953 through 1969, the SuDocs class continued under FS 3.300.]

HE 3.301:date
ANNUAL REPORTS.

Earlier FS 3.301
Later NCU 1.1

HE 3.302:CT
GENERAL PUBLICATIONS.

Earlier FS 3.303
Later NCU 1.3

HE 3.303:v.nos.&nos.
BULLETIN.

HE 3.305:CT
LAWS.

Earlier FS 3.315

HE 3.306/2:CT
HANDBOOKS, MANUALS, GUIDES.

Earlier FS 3.306/2
Later NCU 1.3

HE 3.309:nos.
RESEARCH REPORTS.

Earlier FS 3.309
Later NCU 1.10

HE 3.310:date
CREDIT UNION STATISTICS. [Monthly]

Earlier FS 3.310

ASSISTANCE PAYMENTS ADMINISTRATION (1977–   )

CREATION AND AUTHORITY

The Assistance Payments Administration (HE 17.400) was transferred by the Secretary's reorganization of March 8, 1977 (42 FR 13262) from the Social and Rehabilitation Service to the Social Security Administration.

HE 3.401:date
ANNUAL REPORT.

Earlier HE 17.401

HE 3.402:CT   • Item 512-B-2
GENERAL PUBLICATIONS. [Irregular]

Earlier HE 17.402

HE 3.408:CT   • Item 512-C-1
HANDBOOKS, MANUALS, GUIDES.

Earlier HE 17.408

OFFICE OF CHILD SUPPORT ENFORCEMENT (1977–1980)

CREATION AND AUTHORITY

The Office of Child Support Enforcement was established within the Social Security Administration pursuant to act of August 9, 1975 (89 Stat. 433). The Office was established as a separate organization by the Secretary's reorganization of March 8, 1977 (HE 24).
[Note:– The agency class, HE 24, was not established until 1980.]

HE 3.501:date
ANNUAL REPORT.

Earlier HE 1.53
Later HE 24.1

HE 3.502:CT   • Item 524-A-1
GENERAL PUBLICATIONS.

HE 3.508:CT   • Item 524-A
HANDBOOKS, MANUALS, GUIDES. [Irregular]

Later HE 24.8

OFFICE OF EDUCATION (1970–1975)

CREATION AND AUTHORITY

The Office of Education (I 16) became a part of the Federal Security Agency upon its establishment in 1939 (FS 5) and later in the Department of Health, Education, and Welfare in 1953. [During the period from 1953 through 1969, the SuDocs class FS 5 was continued to be used.] The Office was placed under the Education Division (HE 19.100) by authority of the Education Amendments of 1972, effective June 23, 1972 (86 Stat. 327).

HE 5.1:date   • Item 455
ANNUAL REPORT OF THE COMMISSIONER OF EDUCATION.

HE 5.1/2:date   • Item 460-A-22
ADMINISTRATION OF PUBLIC LAW 81-874 AND 81-815. 1st–   1951–

Later HE 19.101/2

HE 5.2:CT   • Item 461
GENERAL PUBLICATIONS.

Earlier I 16.2 and FS 5.2

HE 5.2:As 7/rp.(nos.)   • Item 461
NATIONAL ASSESSMENT OF EDUCATIONAL PROGRESS, PROJECT OF EDUCATION COMMISSION OF THE STATES: REPORTS. [Irregular]

National Assessment is a new venture in educational evaluation. It is designed to gather census-like data describing what groups of Americans know and can do, and over a period of time, to determine whether there is progress in educational attainments. The plan calls for a periodic assessment of ten subject areas at four age levels. In addition to the detailed reports of National Assessment, brief summaries of the results and commentaries by a panel of reviewers will be available.

HE 5.2:J 27   • Item 461
FILM RESOURCES ON JAPAN. 1975. 55 p.

This directory lists more than 500 films helpful in the study of Japan. The films cover almost every aspect of Japanese life and culture. Agriculture, animal life, dance, fishing, handicrafts, and women are but a few of the themes. Each entry includes a summary of the film's contents, running time, format, producer and/or distributor, and year of production.

HE 5.2:P 84/5   • Item 461
ACCREDITED POSTSECONDARY INSTITUTIONS AND PROGRAMS. 1971–   [Annual]

PURPOSE:– To provide a list of postsecondary institutions and programs which are accredited by, or which have preaccreditted status awarded by regional and national specialized agencies recognized by the U.S. Commissioner of Education.

HE 5.2:W 89/2   • Item 461
DIRECTORY OF REPRESENTATIVE WORK EDUCATION PROGRAMS, 1972–73. 1973. 338 p.

This Directory is the result of a study of existing school-supervised work education programs to describe different organizational patterns, and to identify constraints on program expansion and to examine incentives to increase employer participation. The programs included are listed alphabetically by State and by educational level, with all secondary level programs appearing first, postsecondary programs next, and programs operating at varied educational levels appearing last. For each program listed, a synopsis of its characteristics, as supplied by program personnel, is included.

HE 5.6:CT   • Item 461-A
RULES, REGULATIONS, AND INSTRUCTIONS.

Earlier FS 5.6
Later HE 19.106

HE 5.6/2:CT   • Item 461-A
HANDBOOKS, MANUALS, GUIDES.

Earlier FS 5.6 FS 5.6/2
Later HE 19.108

HE 5.8:CT   • Item 455-C
ADDRESSES. [Irregular]

Earlier FS 5.8

HE 5.10:CT   • **Item 455-D**
BIBLIOGRAPHIES AND LISTS OF PUBLICATIONS.

   Later HE 19.128 and HE 19.317

HE 5.20:CT
POSTERS.

   Earlier FS 5.20

HE 5.25:nos.   • **Item 460**
EDUCATION DIRECTORY. [Annual]

   Earlier FS 5.3, FS 5.25
   Later HE 19.113, HE 19.324, HE 19.324/2,
HE 19.324/3

HE 5.44/2:CT
EDUCATION BRIEFING PAPERS. [Irregular]

   Later HE 19.123

HE 5.73:date   • **Item 460-A-22**
PUBLIC SCHOOL FINANCE PROGRAMS. 1947/48–
   [Biennial]

   Earlier FS 5.73

   HE 5.73/2:date   • **Item 460-A-22**
   – STATE COMPILATIONS. 1953–   [Biennial]

      Earlier FS 5.73/2
      Later HE 19.126

HE 5.75:v.nos.&nos.   • **Item 455-B**
AMERICAN EDUCATION. [10 times a year]

HE 5.76
MANPOWER DEVELOPMENT AND TRAINING,
   PROJECTS APPROVED.

HE 5.77:nos.   • **Item 466-A**
RESEARCH IN EDUCATION. v. 1–   1966–
   [Monthly]

   The Educational Resources Information Center (ERIC) of the Office of Education publishes a
monthly abstract journal, Research in Education,
which announces newly funded Bureau of Research projects and recently completed research
or research related reports of interest to the educational community. Reports and projects are
abstracted and indexed by subject, author, or
investigator, and responsible institution.
   The monthly issues are cumulated annually
and published in two volumes on a Project Resume Index and the other a Report Resume Index.
   The ERIC is a nationwide information network
consisting of a central staff at the Office of Education and 19 clearinghouses, each of which focuses on a specific field of education.
   Reports cited in Research in Education may
be secured in microfiche or hard copy from ERIC
Document Reproduction Service, National Cash
Register Company, 4936 Fairmont Avenue,
Bethesda, Maryland 20014.
   Reports of research for the period 1956–1965
may be found in the two-volume Office of Education Reports, 1956–1965, Resumes (OE-12029)
and Indexes (OE-12028).
   Cumulative index issued semiannual.
   Earlier FS 5.77

HE 5.77/2:date
ERIC PRODUCTS, BIBLIOGRAPHY OF INFORMA-
TION ANALYSIS PUBLICATIONS OF ERIC CLEAR-
INGHOUSES.

HE 5.78
COMMUNITY SERVICES AND CONTINUING EDUCA-
TION, TITLE 1, HIGHER EDUCATION ACT OF
1965.

HE 5.79:date   • **Item 467-D**
TITLE 1, ELEMENTARY AND SECONDARY EDUCA-
TION ACT OF 1965, STATES REPORT. 1st–
1966–   [Annual]

   PURPOSE:– To report on the activities and
accomplishments under Title 1 of the Elementary
and Secondary Education Act of 1965, a program

designed to provide financial assistance to
schools serving areas with large concentrations
of children from low-income families.
   Earlier FS 5.79

HE 5.79/2:date   • **Item 467-D**
TITLE II, ELEMENTARY AND SECONDARY EDUCA-
TION ACT OF 1965, ANNUAL REPORT. 1st–
1966–   [Annual] (Education Division)

   PURPOSE:– To provide an annual compilation and analysis of data on the program of Title
II of the Elementary and Secondary Education
Act which provides direct Federal assistance for
the acquisition of school library resources, textbooks, and other instructional materials.
   Earlier HE 5.220:20108

HE 5.80:nos.   • **Item 467-C**
STATUS OF COMPLIANCE, PUBLIC SCHOOL DIS-
TRICTS, 17 SOUTHERN AND BORDER STATES,
REPORTS. 1–   1965–   [Monthly]

   Equal Educational Opportunities Programs.
Office for Civil Rights.
   PURPOSE:– To report the status of compliance, under Title VI of the Civil Rights Act of
1964, and certain related information with respect
to public school districts in the seventeen Southern and Border States.
   Gives in tabular form, by States and school
districts coded information on applicable assurance, assurance status, inadequate steps to
desegregate, General Counsel's Docket number,
and State code and District identifying number.
   Issued as of January, May, and September.
   Earlier FS 5.80

HE 5.81:date   • **Item 462-A**
HIGHER EDUCATION REPORTS.

   Earlier FS 5.81

HE 5.82:date   • **Item 467-A**
REPORT ON COOPERATIVE RESEARCH TO
IMPROVE THE NATION'S SCHOOLS. 1957–
[Annual]

   Report submitted to Congress of the education research projects and programs administered
by the Office of Education as required by the
Cooperative Research Act (P L 83-531), as
amended. Each annual report summarizes the
range and scope of the Federal investment in
educational research and related activities conducted outside the Office of Education and gives
examples of specific projects and programs.
   Covers the fiscal year.
   Earlier FS 5.82

HE 5.83:date   • **Item 459-A**
COMPOSITE LIST OF ELIGIBLE INSTITUTIONS FOR
GUARANTEED LOANS FOR COLLEGE
STUDENTS, HIGHER EDUCATION ACT OF 1965.
[Irregular] (Bureau of Higher Education, Division
of Student Financial Aid)

   PURPOSE:– To inform leaders, guarantee
agencies and students of schools that have established eligibility to participate in the Guaranteed Loan Program established by the Higher
Education Act of 1965.
   Issued in looseleaf form, punched for 3-ring
binders.
   Earlier FS 5.83

HE 5.83/2:date   • **Item 459-A**
COMPOSITE LIST OF ELIGIBLE INSTITUTIONS,
NATIONAL VOCATION STUDENT LOAN INSUR-
ANCE ACT OF 1965. [Irregular] (Bureau of Higher
Education, Division of Student Financial Aid)

   PURPOSE:– To inform lenders, guarantee
agencies and students of schools that have established eligibility to participate in the Guaranteed Loan Program established by the National
Vocational Student Loan Insurance Act of 1965.
   Earlier FS 5.83/2

HE 5.84:CT   • **Item 460-A-58**
INSTITUTE PROGRAMS FOR ADVANCED STUDIES.

   Earlier FS 5.84

HE 5.84:El 2   • **Item 460-A-58**
– ELEMENTARY SCHOOL PERSONNEL. 1968/
   69–   [Annual]

HE 5.84:Se 2   • **Item 460-A-58**
– SECONDARY SCHOOL PERSONNEL. 1968/69–
   [Annual]

   Earlier FS 5.84:Se 2

HE 5.84:T 22   • **Item 460-A-58**
– TRAINERS OF TEACHERS AND OTHER
   EDUCATION PERSONNEL AND UNDER-
   GRADUATES. 1968/69–   [Annual]

   Earlier FS 5.84:T 22

HE 5.85:date   • **Item 462-B**
NATIONAL ADVISORY COUNCIL ON VOCATIONAL
EDUCATION ANNUAL REPORT. 1st–   1969–

   Pursuant to Vocational Education Amendments of 1968, Public Law 90-576.
   Earlier FS 5.85

HE 5.86:date   • **Item 461-B**
BETTER EDUCATION FOR HANDICAPPED
CHILDREN, ANNUAL REPORT. [Annual]

   Review of program activities under Public Law
89-313, amendment to title 1, Elementary and
secondary education act, and title VI-A Elementary and Secondary Education Act.
   Earlier FS 5.86

HE 5.86/2:date   • **Item 461-B**
NATIONAL ADVISORY COMMITTEE ON THE HANDI-
CAPPED: ANNUAL REPORTS.

   Later HE 19.117

HE 5.87:CT   • **Item 461**
ELEMENTARY TEACHER EDUCATION PROGRAM,
FEASIBILITY STUDIES. [Irregular]

HE 5.88:date   • **Item 461**
FOCUS ON FOLLOW THROUGH. Nov. 1970–
[Monthly]

HE 5.89:nos.   • **Item 461-C**
PREP [Putting Research into Educational Practice]
REPORTS. 1–   1969–   [Monthly]

   PURPOSE:– To provide a series of monthly
reports on topics of interest and concern to educators. Written in non-technical language and targeted to specific audiences, summarizes and in-
terprets the significant findings of current research
and development and identifies exemplary programs and practices operating throughout the
Nation.

HE 5.90:nos.
ANALYTICAL NOTE.

HE 5.91:nos.   • **Item 461-E**
PARENTS AND BEGINNING READERS (series). 1–
1973–   [Irregular] (National Reader Center)

HE 5.92:date   • **Item 461**
HIGHER EDUCATION PERSONNEL TRAINING PRO-
GRAMS (year), FELLOWSHIP PROGRAMS.
[Annual]

HE 5.92/2   • **Item 455-E**
AWARDS, HIGHER EDUCATION ACT OF 1965 (P.L.
89-329) AS AMENDED, TITLE 3, STRENGTHEN-
ING DEVELOPING INSTITUTIONS.

   Later HE 10.139

HE 5.92/3:date   • **Item 460-A-51**
INVENTORY OF PHYSICAL FACILITIES IN INSTITU-
TIONS OF HIGHER EDUCATION, FALL (year).
[Annual]

   Earlier HE 5.251:51007
   Later HE 19.310

HE 5.92/4:date • Item 460-A-50
INDEX OF INSTITUTIONS OF HIGHER EDUCATION
BY STATE AND CONGRESSIONAL DISTRICT.
[Annual] (National Center for Educational Statistics)

Earlier HE 5.250:50060
Later HE 19.322

HE 5.92/4-2:CT
HEGIX IX REQUIREMENTS AND SPECIFICATIONS
FOR SURVEY. [Annual]

Later HE 19.309

HE 5.92/5:date • Item 460-A-54
EARNED DEGREES CONFERRED (year). [Annual]

Earlier HE 5.254:54013
Later HE 19.329

HE 5.92/6:date • Item 460-A-54
FALL ENROLLMENT IN HIGHER EDUCATION (year).

Publication first issued in 1946. Title varies,
1946– 1957.
Earlier HE 5.254:54023
Later HE 19.325

HE 5.92/7:year • Item 460-A-15
LIBRARY STATISTICS OF COLLEGES AND UNIVERSITIES, FALL (year). PART C, ANALYTIC REPORT.
[Annual]

PURPOSE:– To provide an analytic summary
of management and salary data on libraries of
higher education institutions, by type of institution and control, and by enrollment size and control.
Data for individual libraries are contained in
the companion volume, Institutional Data (listed
above).
Earlier HE 5.215:15031
Later HE 19.338

HE 5.92/8:date • Item 560-A-54
ASSOCIATE DEGREES AND OTHER FORMAL
AWARDS BELOW THE BACCALAUREATE (year).
[Annual]

Earlier HE 5.254:54045
Later HE 19.333

HE 5.92/9:date • Item 460-A-58
EDUCATION PROFESSION SERIES.

HE 5.92/10:date • Item 460-A-52
FINANCIAL STATISTICS OF INSTITUTIONS OF
HIGHER EDUCATION: CURRENT FUNDS, REVENUES AND EXPENDITURES, (year).

Earlier HE 5.250:50023
Later HE 19.316/2

HE 5.92/10-2:date • Item 460-A-52
FINANCIAL STATISTICS OF INSTITUTIONS OF
HIGHER EDUCATION: PROPERTY. [Annual]

Later HE 19.316

HE 5.92/11:date
EPDA HIGHER EDUCATIONAL PERSONNEL TRAINING INSTITUTES, SHORT TERM TRAINING PROGRAMS.

Earlier HE 5.258:58028-72-A

HE 5.92/12:date • Item 460-A-54
STUDENTS ENROLLED FOR ADVANCED DEGREES,
FALL (year). [Annual] (National Center for Educational Statistics)

Later HE 19.330

HE 5.93:date • Item 460-A-20
STATISTICS OF PUBLIC ELEMENTARY AND SECONDARY DAY SCHOOLS. 1954– [Annual]

Earlier HE 5.220:20007
Later HE 19.326

HE 5.93/2:date • Item 460-A-22
BOND SALES FOR PUBLIC SCHOOL PURPOSES.
1959/60– [Annual]

PURPOSE:– To provide a series of State- by-
State summary of new bond sales for public school
purposes, based on monthly listings of the Investment Bankers' Association of America.
The Summary includes the number and amount
of sales with average net interest costs, by issuing agencies and by Moody ratings. Quarterly
summaries are given for total sales and rated
bond issues by terms of maturity.
Earlier HE 5.222:22009
Later HE 19.323

HE 5.93/3:date
EXPENDITURES AND REVENUES FOR PUBLIC
ELEMENTARY AND SECONDARY EDUCATION.

Later HE 19.313

HE 5.93/4:date • Item 460-A-20
PRELIMINARY STATISTICS OF STATE SCHOOL SYSTEMS. [Biennial]

Earlier HE 5.220:20006

HE 5.93/5:date • Item 460-A-20
FALL (year) STATISTICS OF PUBLIC SCHOOLS,
ADVANCE REPORT. 1st– [Annual]

Earlier HE 5.220:20119
Later HE 19.318

HE 5.93/6:date • Item 460-A-24
PUPIL MOBILITY IN PUBLIC ELEMENTARY AND
SECONDARY SCHOOLS DURING THE (date)
SCHOOL YEAR.

HE 5.93/7:date • Item 460-A-20
PREPRIMARY ENROLLMENT. [Annual]

Earlier HE 5.220:20079
Later HE 19.327

HE 5.93/8:date • Item 460-A-20
STATISTICS OF LOCAL PUBLIC SCHOOL SYSTEMS,
FALL (year). [Annual]

Earlier HE 5.210:20112

HE 5.93/8-2:date
STATISTICS OF LOCAL PUBLIC SCHOOL SYSTEMS,
FINANCE, (year). 1st– 1967– [Annual]

Later HE 19.318/2

HE 5.93/9:date • Item 460-A-20
STATISTICS OF NONPUBLIC ELEMENTARY AND
SECONDARY SCHOOLS, (year). [Annual]

Supersedes Statistics of Nonpublic Elementary Schools (HE 5.220:20064) and Statistics of
Nonpublic Secondary Schools (HE 5.220:20050).

HE 5.93/10:date • Item 460-A-20
STATISTICS OF STATE SCHOOL SYSTEMS. 1959/
60– [Biennial]

Earlier HE 5.220:20022
Later HE 19.318/3

HE 5.93/11:date • Item 460-A-20
NONPUBLIC SCHOOLS IN LARGE CITIES.

On cover: Elementary and Secondary Education.

HE 5.94:CT • Item 460-A-14
RECENT EDUCATIONAL POLICY AND LEGISLATIVE
DEVELOPMENTS ABROAD (series). [Irregular]

Earlier HE 5.214

HE 5.94/2:date
INSTITUTIONS OF HIGHER EDUCATION INDEX BY
STATES AND CONGRESSIONAL DISTRICTS.

Earlier HE 5.250:50060

HE 5.95:date
ADVISORY COUNCIL ON ENVIRONMENTAL
EDUCATION: ANNUAL REPORT.

HE 5.96:date • Item 455-F
DIRECTORY OF SECONDARY SCHOOLS WITH
OCCUPATIONAL CURRICULUMS, PUBLIC AND
NONPUBLIC.

Later HE 19.337

HE 5.96/2:date • Item 455-F
DIRECTORY OF POSTSECONDARY SCHOOLS WITH
OCCUPATIONAL PROGRAMS, (year) (Public and
Private).

PURPOSE:– To provide a comprehensive listing of postsecondary schools and institutions
offering career-related programs, i.e. vocational
schools. Two-year and four-year colleges and
universities are listed if they offer occupational
programs that lead to a certificate or degree at
less than the baccalaureate level.

HE 5.96/3:date • Item 460-A-50
ACCREDITED POSTSECONDARY INSTITUTIONS AND
PROGRAMS. [Annual]

Earlier HE 5.250:50066-S

HE 5.97:date • Item 460-A-13
ADULT BASIS EDUCATION PROGRAM STATISTICS
(series).

Earlier HE 5.213:13037
Later HE 19.319

HE 5.98:date • Item 460-A-10
DIGEST OF EDUCATIONAL STATISTICS. 1962–
[Annual]

Earlier HE 5.210:10024
Later HE 19.315

HE 5.99:date • Item 460-A-14
RESEARCH AND TRAINING OPPORTUNITIES
ABROAD, (year), EDUCATIONAL PROGRAMS IN
FOREIGN LANGUAGE AND AREA STUDIES. [Annual] (Institute of International Studies)

Earlier HE 5.214:14134

HE 5.99/2:date • Item 460-A-14
OPPORTUNITIES ABROAD FOR TEACHERS (series).

Earlier HE 5.214:14047
Later HE 19.112

NUMBERED PUBLICATIONS

During the period 1959– 1971, Office of Education publications have been given OE- identification numbers consisting of five digits. The first two numbers designate the general or specific subject of the publication according to the classification scheme designed by the Office of Education to meet its publications. An outline of this scheme is reproduced below. Publications in each subject grouping are reproduced below. Publications in each subject grouping are numbered consecutively from 0 on as published. Annual publications are distinguished by an additional two digit number designating the year of coverage (not the year of publication).

For the period 1959– 1966, the publications previously published in the Bulletin, Circular, Miscellaneous, and Special Publication series were assigned numbers in these series as well as the appropriate OE number. In 1966, this practice was discontinued with the following numbers:

    Bulletin 1966, No. 18
    Circular 979
    Miscellaneous 54
    Special Publication 12
    Classification numbers HE 5.210 through HE 5.287 were assigned to correspond to the OE publication numbers.

In 1971, this numbering system was discontinued when a Department-wide system of publication numbering was established.

General Publications
  Miscellaneous 10000– 10999
  OE Publications 11000– 11999
  Research 12000– 12999
  Adult Education 13000– 13999
  International 14000– 14999
  Library Services 15000– 15999

Elementary and Secondary Education
  Administration and Statistics:
    General 20000– 20999
    Buildings, Equipment 21000– 21999
    Finances 22000– 22999
    Staff, Salaries 23000– 23999
    Students:
    Enrollment, Retention, Graduation 24000– 24999
    Guidance, Counseling, Testing 25000– 25999
    Careers 26000– 26999
    Curriculum and Activities:
    Foreign Languages 27000– 27999
    Health, Physical Education, Recreation . 28000– 28999
    Mathematics, Science 29000– 29999
    Language Arts 30000– 30999
    Social Studies 31000– 31999
    Other Subjects and Activities, General
      Teaching Methods 32000– 33999
      Audiovisual Aids 34000– 34999
    Exceptional Children,
      Special Education 35000– 35999
    Rural Education 36000– 36999
    Education of the Disadvantaged . 37000– 37999
    Equal Education Opportunities 38000– 38999

Higher Education
  Administration and Statistics:
    General 50000– 50999
    Building, Equipment 51000– 51999
    Finances 52000– 52999
    Faculties, Salaries 53000– 53999
  Students:
    Admission, Enrollment, Degrees 54000– 54999
    Costs and Financial Assistance 55000– 55999
    Curriculum 56000– 56999
  Special Institutions and Education:
    Junior Colleges, Community Colleges, Post-High
      School Courses 57000– 57999
      Teacher Education 58000– 58999
    Vocational Education
    General and Area Programs 80000– 80999
    Agriculture 81000– 81999
    Distributive Education 82000– 82999

    Home Economics 83000– 83999
    Trade and Industrial Education 84000– 84999
    Practical Nurse Education 85000– 85999
    Office Education 86000– 86999

HE 5.210:nos.   ● **Item 460-A-10**
MISCELLANEOUS PUBLICATIONS: GENERAL, OE 10,000– 10,999.

  Earlier FS 5.210

HE 5.210:10004   ● **Item 460-A-10**
REPORT ON THE NATIONAL DEFENSE EDUCATION ACT. 1959– [Annual] (OE-10004)

Report submitted by Commissioner of Education to Congress pursuant to section 1001 (c) of Public Law 864, 85th Congress for the fiscal year.

Provides a summary of the operation of the program administered by the Office of Education under the provisions authorized by the National Defense Education Act of 1958. Some of these provisions include loans to students in institutions of higher education, financial assistance for strengthening science, mathematics, and modern foreign language instruction, national defense fellowships, research and experimentation.
  Earlier FS 5.210:10004

HE 5.210:10005   ● **Item 460-A-10**
PROGRESS OF PUBLIC EDUCATION IN THE UNITED STATES OF AMERICA. [Annual] (OE-10005-A, B, C, & D)
  PURPOSE:– To present a summary report of the Office of Education to the International Conferences on Public Education, Geneva, Switzerland, jointly sponsored by the United Nations Educational, Scientific, and Cultural Organization and the International Bureau of Education.

The reports are presented in a non-technical style with plenty of illustrations, charts, and tables to supplement the text. While intended primarily for the International Conference, this annual report would serve equally well as a progress report on education to the Nation.

Issued for the years 1955/56– 1958/59 as Miscellaneous 81.

Published in four editions: English, French, Spanish, and Russian.
  Earlier FS 5.210:10005

HE 5.210:10024   ● **Item 460-A-10**
DIGEST OF EDUCATIONAL STATISTICS. 1962– [Annual] (OE-10024)

  Earlier FS 5.210:10024
  Later HE 5.98

HE 5.210:10030   ● **Item 460-A-10**
PROJECTIONS OF EDUCATIONAL STATISTICS TO [year]. [Annual] (OE-10030)

Companion volume to Digest of Education Statistics (OE-10024). Contains articles.
  Earlier FS 5.210:10030

HE 5.210:10064   ● **Item 460-A-10**
PROGRESS IN AMERICAN EDUCATION. [Annual] (OE-10064)

Reprint of the monthly feature, Research Report, appearing in American Education. The articles were developed from final research reports filed with the Office's National Center for Educational Research and Development.

HE 5.211:nos.   ● **Item 460-A-11**
MISCELLANEOUS PUBLICATIONS: PUBLICATIONS ABOUT OE AND HEW, OE 11,000– 11,999.

  Earlier FS 5.211
HE 5.211:11000   ● **Item 460-A-11**
PUBLICATIONS OF THE OFFICE OF EDUCATION. [Irregular] (OE-11000)

  Earlier FS 5.211:11000

HE 5.211:11002   ● **Item 460-A-11**
HANDBOOK OFFICE OF EDUCATION. [Irregular] (OE-11002)

  Earlier FS 5.211:11002

HE 5.211:11015   ● **Item 460-A-11**
AMERICAN EDUCATION'S ANNUAL GUIDE TO OE PROGRAMS. (Reprinted from American Education)

HE 5.212:nos.   ● **Item 460-A-12**
MISCELLANEOUS PUBLICATIONS: RESEARCH, OE 12,000– 12,999.

  Earlier FS 5.212

HE 5.212:[nos.]   ● **Item 460-A-12**
STUDIES IN COMPARATIVE EDUCATION, EDUCATION IN [country]. [Irregular]

Previously published in the Bulletin series, these studies are now issued in the OE-14000 series with an individual number for each publication.

Each study includes background summary information on the country, its people, historical development, government and administration, economic factors. In covering the educational systems of a country, the study covers various aspects from preprimary to post graduate work. Includes bibliographies.
  Earlier FS 5.212

HE 5.212:12014   ● **Item 460-A-12**
NATIONAL DEFENSE LANGUAGE DEVELOPMENT RESEARCH AND STUDIES. 1st– 1958/59– [Irregular] (OE 12014)

  Earlier FS 5.212:12014

HE 5.212:12016   ● **Item 460-A-12**
NATIONAL DEFENSE LANGUAGE DEVELOPMENT PROGRAM: COMPLETED RESEARCH, STUDIES, AND INSTRUCTIONAL MATERIALS, LISTS. 1– [Irregular] (OE-12016)

  Earlier FS 5.212:12016

HE 5.212:12051   ● **Item 460-A-12**
RESEARCH FOR PROGRESS IN EDUCATION, ANNUAL REPORT.

HE 5.213:nos.   ● **Item 460-A-13**
MISCELLANEOUS PUBLICATIONS: ADULT EDUCATION, OE 13,000– 13,999.

  Earlier FS 5.213

HE 5.214:nos.   ● **Item 460-A-14**
MISCELLANEOUS PUBLICATIONS: INTERNATIONAL EDUCATION, OE 14,000– 14,999.

  Earlier FS 5.214

HE 5.214:[nos.]   ● **Item 460-A-14**
STUDIES IN COMPARATIVE EDUCATION BIBLIOGRAPHY: [year] PUBLICATIONS. 1958– [Annual]

PURPOSE:– To present an extensive and useful listing of timely materials concerned with education in other countries (material for the U.S. is not included).

The first part gives listings of a general comparative nature as well as materials on individual countries in different geographical areas. The second part gives listings of publications wholly or partly devoted to specific areas or countries. Both parts include listings of some other bibliographies of current use in comparative education.

Prepared as a cooperative project of the staff of the International Education Relations Branch of the Division of International Education.
  Earlier FS 5.214

HE 5.214:14003 • Item 460-A-14
INTERNATIONAL TEACHER DEVELOPMENT PROGRAM, ANNUAL REPORT TO BUREAU OF EDUCATIONAL AND CULTURAL AFFAIRS, DEPT. OF STATE. 1956/57– [Annual] (OE-14003)

An illustrated report of the activities under the International Teacher Development Program, administered by the Office of Education in cooperation with the Department of State.
Earlier FS 5.214:14003

HE 5.214:14031 • Item 460-A-14
EDUCATIONAL MATERIALS LABORATORY REPORT. v. 1– [Irregular] (OE 14031)

PURPOSE:– To provide information service for teachers and librarians about the nature and availability of new materials related to various curricular areas.
Earlier FS 5.214:14031

HE 5.214:14031 • Item 460-A-14
PROGRAM AND SERVICES, REPORT OF EDUCATIONAL MATERIALS LABORATORY, DIVISION OF INTERNATIONAL STUDIES AND SERVICES. [Irregular] (OE-14031)

Earlier FS 5.214:14031

HE 5.214:14034 • Item 460-A-14
INFORMATION ON EDUCATION AROUND THE WORLD. 1– 1958– [Irregular] (OE-14034).

PURPOSE:– To supply basic data in concise form on matters of current interest in international education, including basic data on the educational systems and patterns of foreign countries. Includes bibliographies.
Earlier FS 5.214:14035

HE 5.214:14035 • Item 460-A-14
NEWSNOTE ON EDUCATION AROUND THE WORLD. 1956– [Irregular] (OE 14035)

HE 5.214:14046 • Item 460-A-14
ANNUAL REPORT ON THE TECHNICAL ASSISTANCE TRAINING PROGRAM IN EDUCATION. 1955– [Annual] (OE- 14046)

Prepared by the Technical Assistance Section, Educational Exchange and Training Branch, Division of International Education.
Since 1951, the Office of Education, by agreement with the International Cooperation Administration and its predecessor agencies, has exercised responsibility for the training of foreign nationals in the field of education. This annual report records the activities of this particular part of the Mutual Security Program.
Earlier FS 5.214:14046

HE 5.214:14047 • Item 460-A-14
TEACHER EXCHANGE OPPORTUNITIES UNDER THE INTERNATIONAL EDUCATIONAL EXCHANGE PROGRAM. [Annual] (OE-14047)

Gives information about teaching opportunities overseas– a description of the program, the basic requirements, types of exchange arrangements, important facts concerning awards, and when and where to apply.

HE 5.215:nos. • Item 460-A-15
MISCELLANEOUS PUBLICATIONS: LIBRARY SERVICES, OE 15,000– 15,999.

Earlier FS 5.215

HE 5.215:15023 • Item 460-A-15
LIBRARY STATISTICS OF COLLEGES AND UNIVERSITIES, INSTITUTIONAL DATA. 1950/60– [Annual] (OE-15023)

PURPOSE:– To gather and report basic data on library operations and staff salaries of use to administrators, chief librarians, and others concerned with planning library budgets and the development of library service to higher education in the United States.
Arrangement is by State and institution with the following items covered: collections, staff, expenditures, and salaries.
Replaces the annual statistics formerly published in the January issues of College and Research Libraries published by the American Library Association. 1962 Circ. 729
Earlier FS 5.215:15023

HE 5.215:15031 • Item 460-A-15
LIBRARY STATISTICS OF COLLEGES AND UNIVERSITIES, ANALYTIC REPORT. [Annual] (OE-15031)

Earlier FS 5.215:15031
Later HE 5.92/7

HE 5.215:15033 • Item 460-A-15
STATISTICS OF PUBLIC LIBRARY SYSTEMS SERVING POPULATIONS OF 100,000 OR MORE. [Irregular] (OE-15033)

Earlier FS 5.215:15033

HE 5.215:15034 • Item 460-A-15
STATISTICS OF PUBLIC LIBRARY SYSTEMS SERVING POPULATIONS OF 50,000– 99,999. 1950– [Irregular] (OE-15034)

Earlier FS 5.215:15034

HE 5.215:15035 • Item 460-A-15
STATISTICS OF LIBRARY SYSTEMS SERVING POPULATIONS OF 35,000– 49,999. 1956/57– [Irregular] (OE-15043)

Earlier FS 5.215:15035

HE 5.215:15046 • Item 460-A-15
LIBRARY EDUCATION DIRECTORY. [Biennial] (OE-15046)

1962-63 Misc. 43
1964-65 Misc. 51
Earlier FS 5.215:15046

HE 5.215:15049 • Item 460-A-15
STATISTICS OF PUBLIC SCHOOL LIBRARIES. [Irregular]

Part 1. Basic Tables.
Earlier FS 5.215:15049

HE 5.216:nos. • Item 460-A-16
MISCELLANEOUS PUBLICATIONS: NURSERY SCHOOLS AND KINDERGARTENS, OE 16,000– 16,999.

Earlier FS 5.216

HE 5.220:nos. • Item 460-A-20
ELEMENTARY AND SECONDARY EDUCATION: MISC. GENERAL STATISTICS.

Earlier FS 5.220

HE 5.220:20002A • Item 460-A-20
SELECTED REFERENCES. 1– 1947– [Irregular] (OE-20002A)

PURPOSE:– To provide recent reference materials, usually covering a five-year period, that will assist students and others making a survey of study of a problem area in education. The References deal with those items that are most frequently requested from the Office of Education by correspondents.
Earlier FS 5.200:20002A

HE 5.220:20006 • Item 460-A-20
PRELIMINARY STATISTICS OF STATE SCHOOL SYSTEMS. [Biennial] (OE-20006)

Presents the more important data which will appear later in the Statistics of State School Systems.
Earlier FS 5.220:20006
Later HE 5.93/4

HE 5.220:20007 • Item 460-A-20
FALL [year] ENROLLMENT, TEACHERS, AND SCHOOL-HOUSING IN FULL-TIME PUBLIC ELEMENTARY AND SECONDARY DAY SCHOOLS. 1954– [Annual] (OE-20007)

HE 5.220:20020 • Item 460-A-20
STATISTICS OF STATE SCHOOL SYSTEMS. 1959/60– [Biennial] (OE-20020)

Earlier FS 5.220:20022
Later HE 5.93/10

HE 5.220:20022 • Item 460-A-20
STATISTICS ON PUPIL TRANSPORTATION. 1947/48– [Irregular] (OE-20022)

Earlier FS 5.220:20022

HE 5.220:20032 • Item 460-A-20
STATISTICS OF EDUCATION IN THE UNITED STATES. 1958/59– [Annual] (OE-20032)

This series basically continues the former Biennial Survey of Education, published from 1917-18 through 1957-58. Except for the final number, which summarized the material in the previous numbers of the series as well as statistical material from sources outside the Office of Education, each publication in this annual series covers a particular area of educational statistics for a school year. The areas covered may differ from year to year.
1958-1959 Series:
1. Public Secondary Schools. Earlier FS 5.220:20032

HE 5.220:20050 • Item 460-A-20
STATISTICS OF NONPUBLIC SECONDARY SCHOOLS. 1960/61– [Irregular] (OE-20050)

Presents basic statistical information concerning the non-public secondary schools operating in the United States, covering organizational patterns, enrollment, teaching staff patterns, size classification, and graduates.
Earlier FS 5.220:200520
Superseded by Statistics of Nonpublic Elementary and Secondary Schools (HE 5.93/9).

HE 5.220:20064 • Item 460-A-20
STATISTICS OF NONPUBLIC ELEMENTARY SCHOOLS. [Irregular] (OE-20064)

1961/62 Circ. 753
Earlier FS 5.220:20064
Superseded by Statistics of Nonpublic Elementary and Secondary Schools (HE 5.93/9).

HE 5.220:20103 • Item 460-A-20
PACESETTERS IN INNOVATION. v. 1– 1966– [Annual]

PURPOSE:– To present information on Projects to Advance Creativity in Education (PACE) approved during the fiscal year under Title III, Supplementary Centers and Services, of the Elementary and Secondary Education Act of 1965.
Includes subjects local education agency, and project number indexes, and project resumes.
Reports cited may be secured in microfiche or hard copy from the ERIC Document Reproduction Service, National Cash Register Company, 4936 Fairmont Avenue, Bethesda, Maryland 20014.
Earlier FS 5.220:20103.

HE 5.220:20108 • Item 460-A-20
ANNUAL REPORT, TITLE 2, ELEMENTARY AND SECONDARY EDUCATION ACT OF 1965, SCHOOL LIBRARY RESOURCES, TEXTBOOKS, AND OTHER INSTRUCTIONAL MATERIALS. 1st– 1966– [Annual] (OE-20108)

Report is for the fiscal year.
Earlier FS 5.220:20108
Later HE 5.79/2

HE 5.220:20119   • **Item 460-A-20**
FALL [year] STATISTICS OF PUBLIC SCHOOLS, ADVANCE REPORT. 1st–   [Annual] (OE-20119)

    PURPOSE:– To make available at an early date some of the data obtained in the annual fall survey of elementary and secondary day schools. Includes data on pupils, teachers, school districts, schools, schoolhousing, and anticipated expenditures for the 50 States, the District of Columbia, and the outlying areas of the United States.

HE 5.221:nos.   • **Item 460-A-21**
ELEMENTARY AND SECONDARY EDUCATION PUBLICATIONS: BUILDINGS, EQUIPMENT, OE 21,000– 21,999.

    Earlier FS 5.221

HE 5.221:21033   • **Item 460-A-21**
CONDITION OF PUBLIC SCHOOL PLANTS. [Irregular] (OE-21033)

    Earlier FS 5.221:21033

HE 5.222:nos.   • **Item 460-A-22**
ELEMENTARY AND SECONDARY EDUCATION PUBLICATIONS: FINANCES, RECEIPTS, EXPENDITURES, OE 22,000– 22,999.

    Earlier FS 5.222

HE 5.222:22000   • **Item 460-A-22**
CURRENT EXPENDITURES PER PUPIL IN PUBLIC SCHOOL SYSTEMS. 1921/22– [Annual] (OE-22000)

    PURPOSE:– To furnish school officials, particularly superintendents and members of their administrative staffs, with current information on the spending patterns and trends in expenditures of public school systems.

    The various expense items include administration, instruction, fixed charges, attendance and health services, operation of plant, maintenance of plant, instruction by organizational level, with sub-items for most of the categories.

    For the years 1952/53– 1956/57, data were published in two volumes, one for Large Cities (25,000+) and the second for Small- and Medium-Sized Cities (2,500– 24,999).

    Prior to 1939/40, the data in this study were limited in scope to the presentation of total expenditures only, for each of the six major current accounts. Beginning with the 1939/40 report, the series was expanded to give, in detail, the principal sub-items composing the major current expenditure schedules.

    Title varies: 1921/22– 1938/39, Per Capita Costs in City Schools: 1939/40– 1950/51, Expenditure Per Pupil in City School Systems: 1951/52, Current Expenditures Per Pupil in City School Systems: 1952/53– 1956/57, Current Expenditures Per Pupil in Public School Systems (2 vols.), Large Cities, Small- and Medium-Sized Cities; 1957/58– 1958/59, Current Expenditures Per Pupil in Public School Systems; Urban School Systems; 1959/60– Current Expenditures Per Pupil in Large Public School Systems.

    Earlier FS 5.222:22000

HE 5.222:22003   • **Item 460-A-22**
ADMINISTRATION OF PUBLIC LAWS 874 AND 815, ANNUAL REPORT. 1st– 1951– [Annual] (OE-22003)

    Report submitted by Commissioner of Education to Congress pursuant to subsection 7(c) of Public Law 874 and subsection 12(c) of Public Law 815. Report covers fiscal year.

    Public Laws 874 and 815 authorize financial assistance to local educational agencies in federally affected areas for current operating expenses and for construction of school facilities.

    Report covers major program trends and accomplishments. It also presents a series of tables showing receipts, disbursements, and other data for each program for the fiscal year.

    Earlier FS 5.222:22003

HE 5.222:22009   • **Item 460-A-22**
BOND SALES FOR PUBLIC SCHOOL PURPOSES. 1959/60– [Annual] (OE- 22009)

    Earlier FS 5.222:22009
    Later HE 5.93/2

HE 5.222:22013   • **Item 460-A-22**
REVENUE PROGRAMS FOR THE PUBLIC SCHOOLS IN THE UNITED STATES. 1949/50– [Irregular] (OE-22013)

    PURPOSE:– To provide authoritative summaries on financing public education for the Nation and for the individual states. In these publications, State school finance programs may be examined, school revenue trends observed, and new provisions of State legislative enactments for schools noted. They are intended as a planning aid rather than a measuring stick of standards.

    The first study in this series, The Forty-Eight State School Systems, provide information for the 1948/49 school year and was published by the Council of State Governments. The Office of Education has since published the following studies:

    1949/50 Public School Finance Programs of the Forty-Eight States (Circ. 274)

    1953/54 Public School Finance Programs of the United States (Misc. 22)

    1957/58 Public School Finance Programs of the United States (Misc. 33)

    1959/60 Revenue Programs for the Public Schools in the United States (Misc. 38) [OE- 22013]

    Gives for each State descriptions of revenue provisions for State and local financing of public education, including sources of funds, schools indebtedness, assessment, budget and audit procedures, and trends in public school support.

    Earlier FS 5.222:22013

HE 5.222:22022   • **Item 460-A-22**
PROFILES IN SCHOOL SUPPORT, DECENNIAL OVERVIEW. (OE-22022)

    Earlier FS 5.222:22022

HE 5.222:22023   • **Item 460-A-22**
STATE PROGRAMS FOR PUBLIC SCHOOL SUPPORT. (OE-22023)

    Earlier FS 5.222:22023

HE 5.223:nos.   • **Item 460-A-23**
ELEMENTARY AND SECONDARY EDUCATION PUBLICATIONS: ADMINISTRATION, FACULTIES, SALARIES.

    Earlier FS 5.223

HE 5.223:23050   • **Item 460-A-23**
ADVISORY COUNCIL ON STATE DEPARTMENTS OF EDUCATION, ANNUAL REPORT. 1st– [Annual]

    Earlier FS 5.223:23050

HE 5.224:nos.   • **Item 460-A-24**
ELEMENTARY AND SECONDARY EDUCATION PUBLICATIONS: ENROLLMENT, RETENTION, GRADES, OE 24,000– 24,999.

    Earlier FS 5.224

HE 5.224:[nos.]   • **Item 460-A-24**
HEADLINER SERIES. 1– 1962– [Irregular]

    Earlier FS 5.224

HE 5.224:24012   • **Item 460-A-24**
SUBJECT OFFERINGS AND ENROLLMENTS, GRADES 9-12, NONPUBLIC SECONDARY SCHOOLS. (OE-24012)

    Earlier FS 5.224:24012

HE 5.225:nos.   • **Item 460-A-25**
ELEMENTARY AND SECONDARY EDUCATION PUBLICATIONS: GUIDANCE, TESTING, COUNSELING. (OE 25,000– 25,999)

    Earlier FS 5.225

HE 5.225:25015   • **Item 460-A-25**
NDEA COUNSELING AND GUIDANCE INSTITUTES. [Irregular] (OE-25015)

    Earlier FS 5.225:25015

HE 5.225:25036   • **Item 460-A-25**
DIRECTORY OF COUNSELOR EDUCATORS. 1962– [Irregular] (OE-25036)

    Earlier FS 5.225:25036

HE 5.225:25037A   • **Item 460-A-25**
DIRECTORY, STATE DEPARTMENT OF EDUCATION PERSONNEL FOR GUIDANCE, COUNSELING, AND TESTING. [Irregular] (OE-25037A)

    Earlier FS 5.225:25037

HE 5.226:nos.   • **Item 460-A-26**
ELEMENTARY AND SECONDARY EDUCATION PUBLICATIONS: CAREERS, OE 26,000– 26,999.

    Earlier FS 5.226

HE 5.226:26000   • **Item 460-A-26**
TEACHING OPPORTUNITIES, DIRECTORY OF PLACEMENT INFORMATION. 1955– [Irregular] (OE-26000)

    Earlier FS 5.226:26000

HE 5.227:nos.   • **Item 460-A-27**
ELEMENTARY AND SECONDARY EDUCATION PUBLICATIONS: FOREIGN LANGUAGES, OE 27,000– 27,999.

    Earlier FS 5.227

HE 5.228:nos.   • **Item 460-A-28**
ELEMENTARY AND SECONDARY EDUCATION PUBLICATIONS: HEALTH, PHYSICAL EDUCATION, RECREATION, OE 28,000– 28,999.

    Earlier FS 5.228

HE 5.229:nos.   • **Item 460-A-29**
ELEMENTARY AND SECONDARY EDUCATION PUBLICATIONS: MATHEMATICS, SCIENCE, OE 29,000– 29,999.

    Earlier FS 5.229

HE 5.229:29000   • **Item 460-A-29**
ANALYSIS OF RESEARCH IN THE TEACHING OF SCIENCE. 1950– [Annual] (OE-29000)
    This series of annual bulletins began in 1950 as a cooperative undertaking between the National Association for Research in Science Teaching and the Office of Education.

    PURPOSE:– To assemble the research findings in science education in such a form as to be most useful in the improvement of teaching of science.

    Section 1 gives an examination of the research; section 2, the interpretations and recommendations; and section 3, a bibliographical list of the studies.

    Earlier FS 5.229:29000

HE 5.229:29000   • **Item 460-A-29**
RESEARCH IN THE TEACHING OF SCIENCE. 1957/59– [Biennial] (OE- 29000)

    PURPOSE:– To make available summaries of selected research in the teaching of science to school personnel and research workers.

    Annotations of each project include problem, procedures, and findings. A list of the studies is included as a separate section in the publication.

    Earlier FS 5.229:29000

HE 5.229:29007 • Item 460-A-29
ANALYSIS OF RESEARCH IN THE TEACHING OF MATHEMATICS. 1952– [Biennial] (OE-290007)

PURPOSE:– To help implement research findings by making available the results of research in the teaching of mathematics that have been reported to the Office of Education.

The report is divided into two parts: The first is an overall analysis and the second is the Summary of Research Studies, with brief summaries of each study as to the problems, procedure, major findings and conclusions.
Earlier FS 5.229:29007

HE 5.230:nos. • Item 460-A-30
ELEMENTARY AND SECONDARY EDUCATION PUBLICATIONS: LANGUAGE ARTS, READING, WRITING, SPEAKING, OE 30,000– 30,999.

Earlier FS 5.230

HE 5.231:nos. • Item 460-A-31
ELEMENTARY AND SECONDARY EDUCATION PUBLICATIONS: SOCIAL STUDIES, OE 31,000– 31,999.

Earlier FS 5.213

HE 5.232:nos. • Item 460-A-32
ELEMENTARY AND SECONDARY EDUCATION PUBLICATIONS: CURRICULUMS, SUBJECTS, ACTIVITIES (elementary only), OE 32,000– 32,999.

Earlier FS 5.232

HE 5.233:nos. • Item 460-A-33
ELEMENTARY AND SECONDARY EDUCATION PUBLICATIONS: CURRICULUMS, SUBJECTS, ACTIVITIES (Secondary and Elementary-Secondary only), OE 33,000– 33,999.

Earlier FS 5.233

HE 5.234:nos. • Item 460-A-34
ELEMENTARY AND SECONDARY EDUCATION PUBLICATIONS: AUDIOVISUAL, OE 34,000– 34,999.

Earlier FS 5.234

HE 5.234:34002 • Item 460-A-34
TITLE VII– NEW EDUCATIONAL MEDIA NEWS AND REPORTS. 1959– [Irregular] (OE-34002)

Title VII of the National Defense Education Act provides for research, experimentation, and dissemination of information for more effective utilization of television, radio, motion pictures, and related media for educational purposes.
Gives news items and descriptions of reports.
Earlier FS 5.234:34002

HE 5.234:34006 • Item 460-A-34
U.S. GOVERNMENT FILMS FOR PUBLIC EDUCATIONAL USE. 1955– [Irregular] (OE-34006)

Earlier FS 5.234:34006

HE 5.234:34013 • Item 460-A-34
PROJECTS INITIATED UNDER TITLE VII, NATIONAL DEFENSE EDUCATION ACT. 1962– [Annual] (OE-34013)

PURPOSE:– To provide a list of projects supported under Title VII, Part A, National Defense Education Act which authorizes Federal support for research grants and contracts in the education uses of various mass media (television, film, radio) as well as programmed instruction, computer technology and simulation.

Lists all grants and contracts for research from the beginning of the Program. Projects are identified by serial number, the institution or agency, the name of the principal investigator, the project title, and the inclusive dates

of the grant or contract. The appendices index the projects by the names of the principal investigator and by State and grantee or contractor.

Earlier FS 5.234:34013

HE 5.234:34015 • Item 460-A-34
PROGRAMS, (year), GUIDE TO PROGRAMMED INSTRUCTIONAL MATERIALS AVAILABLE TO EDUCATORS BY (date). 1962– (OE-34015)

Earlier FS 5.234:34015

HE 5.234:34016 • Item 460-A-34
EDUCATIONAL AM AND FM RADIO AND EDUCATION TELEVISION STATIONS, BY STATE AND CITY. [Irregular] (OE- 34016)

Earlier FS 5.234:34016

HE 5.234:34021 • Item 460-A-34
PROJECTS INITIATED UNDER TITLE VII, NATIONAL DEFENSE ACT (continued). [Annual] (OE-34021)

PURPOSE:– To disseminate information concerning new education media (including the results of research and experimentation conducted under Part A of Title VII).
Lists all contracts initiated since the beginning of the program in September 1958. Contracts are identified by the project number, contractor, project director, the inclusive dates of the contract, and the funds committed. Appendices contain lists of project directors, contractors by location and by program area, and addresses of project directors.

Earlier FS 5.234:34021

HE 5.234:34039 • Item 460-A-34
CATALOG OF CAPTIONED FILMS FOR THE DEAF. [Irregular] (OE-34039)

Earlier edition issued as OE-34035.
Earlier FS 5.234:34039

HE 5.235:nos. • Item 460-A-35
ELEMENTARY AND SECONDARY EDUCATION PUBLICATIONS: SPECIAL EDUCATION, EXCEPTIONAL CHILDREN, OE 35,000– 35,999.

Earlier FS 5.234

HE 5.235:35003 • Item 460-A-35
EDUCATION OF EXCEPTIONAL CHILDREN AND YOUTH: SPECIAL EDUCATION PERSONNEL IN STATE EDUCATION DEPARTMENTS. 1955– [Irregular] (OE-35003)

Earlier FS 5.235:35003

HE 5.235:35051 • Item 460-A-35
SPECIAL EDUCATION PERSONNEL IN STATE EDUCATION DEPARTMENTS. 1955– [Irregular] (OE-35051)

Directory.
Earlier FS 5.235:35051

HE 5.235:35097 • Item 460-A-35
BETTER EDUCATION FOR HANDICAPPED CHILDREN, ANNUAL REPORT. 1st– 1968– [Annual] (OE- 35097)

Report submitted pursuant to Public Law 89-313, amendment to Title I and Title VI- A, Elementary and Secondary Education Act, for the fiscal year.
PURPOSE:– To present a graphic and narrative account of educational services provided handicapped children, ages 3– 19 years, through the two programs. Contains charts.
Earlier FS 5.86

HE 5.236:nos. • Item 460-A-36
ELEMENTARY AND SECONDARY EDUCATION PUBLICATIONS: RURAL SCHOOLS, RURAL EDUCATION, OE 36,000– 36,999.

Earlier FS 5.236

HE 5.237:nos. • Item 460-A-37
ELEMENTARY AND SECONDARY EDUCATION PUBLICATIONS: EDUCATION OF THE DISADVANTAGED, OE 37,000– 37,999.

Earlier FS 5.237

HE 5.237:37013 • Item 460-A-37
TITLE I OF ELEMENTARY AND SECONDARY EDUCATION ACT OF 1965, ANNUAL REPORT. 1st– 1965/66– [Annual]

Earlier FS 5.237:37013

HE 5.238:nos. • Item 460-A-38
ELEMENTARY AND SECONDARY EDUCATION OPPORTUNITIES, OE 38,000– 38,999.

Earlier FS 5.238

HE 5.250:nos. • Item 460-A-50
HIGHER EDUCATION PUBLICATIONS: MISCELLANEOUS, GENERAL STATISTICS, OE 50,000– 50,999.

Earlier FS 5.250

HE 5.250:nos. • Item 460-A-50
NEW DIMENSIONS IN HIGHER EDUCATION. 1– 1966– [Irregular]

Prepared by Clearinghouse of Studies on Higher Education, Division of Higher Education.
PURPOSE:– To present the findings of research and the experience bearing upon them in the various fields of education of concern to the colleges and universities.
Each publication in the series deals with a particular educational problem and attempts to present evidence assembled to describe practices which appear promising, and to direct the reader to useful sources of additional information and counsel.
Earlier FS 5.250

HE 5.250:50002 • Item 460-A-50
STATISTICS OF LAND-GRANT COLLEGES AND UNIVERSITIES. 1895/96– [Annual] (OE-50002)

Presents statistical data on faculty, students, degrees, income, expenditures, endowment, and plant facilities, etc., of the 68 land-grant colleges.
The Land-grant colleges and universities are so called because public land, or funds in lieu of public lands, were granted to the States for their establishment and support.

The scope of the information provided had gradually evolved from the primary purpose of accounting for funds appropriated under Federal legislation to its present form. Data is for the fiscal year. The basic tables are broken down by institution, with several tables further subdivided by student classification.

Earlier FS 5.250:50002

HE 5.250:50004 • Item 460-A-50
CLEARINGHOUSE OF STUDIES ON HIGHER EDUCATION: REPORTER. 1959– [Irregular] (OE-50004)

Annotated list of studies received by the Clearinghouse from institutions and agencies of higher education published since 1950 on various aspects as administration, alumni, extension, extracurricular activities, facilities, faculty, finance, degree requirements, libraries, research, work-study programs, etc. Arranged by subjects. Contains a list of contributors.
First three issues were published in the Circular series (562, 611, and 622).
Earlier FS 5.250:50004

HE 5.250:50008   • **Item 460-A-50**
SURVEY OF STATE LEGISLATION RELATING TO
HIGHER EDUCATION. 1956/57–   [Annual]
(OE-50008)

PURPOSE:– To disseminate information
on the status of education in the States and
Territories likely to be useful in planning future programs and budgets in higher education. In general, the legislation reported is
limited to that directly affecting colleges and
universities or that establishing policies in
the field of post-high school education. The
survey is made primarily for information or for
administrative use and does not attempt to
serve the purpose of a legal analysis.
Earlier FS 5.550:50008

HE 5.250:50012   • **Item 460-A-50**
ACCREDITED HIGHER INSTITUTIONS. 1917–
[Quadrennial] (OE-50012)

Published at approximately 4-year intervals, consists of lists of institutions of higher
education accredited by nationally reorganized regional and professional accrediting
agencies and by State agencies responsible
for accrediting with the various States.
Part 1 contains lists by regional associations; part 2, professional and technical
schools or departments accredited by nationally recognized agencies; part 3, institutions accredited and approved by State Departments of Education, State Accrediting
Commissions and State Universities. A general index by institution is also included.
Earlier FS 5.250:50012

HE 5.250:50023   • **Item 460-A-50**
FINANCIAL STATISTICS OF INSTITUTIONS OF
HIGHER EDUCATION. (OE- 50023)

Earlier FS 5.250:50023
Later HE 5.92/10

HE 5.250:50025   • **Item 460-A-50**
LAND-GRANT COLLEGES AND UNIVERSITIES,
PRELIMINARY REPORT FOR YEAR ENDED
JUNE 30, [year]. (Annual) (OE-50025)

Gives preliminary data on opening fall
enrollment, faculty and other professional
staff, current-fund income and expenditures,
Federal Appropriations.
Earlier FS 5.250:50025

HE 5.250:50052   • **Item 460-A-50**
DIRECTORY OF U.S. INSTITUTIONS OF HIGHER
EDUCATION, FALL [year]. 1967–   (OE-
50052)

PURPOSE:– To provide a directory of colleges and universities before the beginning
of the school year to which it pertains, or as
soon as possible after the opening of the fall
term. To do this, this publication is reproduced from computer print-out. This publication is not to be confused with the Education
Directory, Part 3, Higher Education, which is
the official directory produced by the Office
of Education.
Earlier FS 5.250:50052

HE 5.251:nos.   • **Item 460-A-51**
HIGHER EDUCATION PUBLICATIONS: BUILDINGS,
EQUIPMENT, OE 51,000– 51,999.

Earlier FS 5.251

HE 5.251:51016   • **Item 460-A-51**
HIGHER EDUCATION FACILITIES CLASSIFICA-
TION AND PROCEDURES MANUAL. 1968–
[Irregular] (OE-51016)

Higher Education Studies Branch, National
Center for Educational Statistics.
Earlier FS 5.251:51016

HE 5.252:nos.   • **Item 460-A-52**
HIGHER EDUCATION PUBLICATIONS: FINANCE,
RECEIPTS, EXPENDITURES, OE 52,000–
52,999.

Earlier FS 5.252

HE 5.252:52004   • **Item 460-A-52**
BOND SALES FOR HIGHER EDUCATION. [An-
nual] (OE-52004)

Published in College and University Finance Series.
Earlier FS 5.252:52004

HE 5.252:52005   • **Item 460-A-52**
HIGHER EDUCATION, BASIC STUDENT
CHARGES. 1962–   [Annual] (OE-52005)

Part 1, Institutional Data.
Earlier FS 5.252:52005

HE 5.253:nos.   • **Item 460-A-53**
HIGHER EDUCATION PUBLICATIONS: ADMINISTRA-
TION, FACULTIES, SALARIES, OE 53,000–
53,999.

Earlier FS 5.253

HE 5.253:53000   • **Item 460-A-53**
FACULTY AND OTHER PROFESSIONAL STAFF
IN INSTITUTIONS OF HIGHER EDUCATION.
1955–   [Biennial] (OE- 53000)

Presents data concerning the faculty and
other professional staff in all of the Nation's
institutions of higher education during the first
term.
The Office of Education has collected
statistics on college faculty and other professional staff since 1869/70 (annually
through 1961 and biennially thereafter). Data
from these surveys appear in the Biennial
Survey of Education in the United States from
1917/18 through 1957/58. Data from 1955,
1957/58 and 1959/60 were also published as
separates in the Circular series.
Preliminary data is published in the advance release, Summary Report, Faculty and
Other Professional Staff in Institutions of
Higher Education (OE-53012).
Earlier FS 5.253:53000.

HE 5.253:53004   • **Item 460-A-53**
HIGHER EDUCATION PLANNING AND
MANAGEMENT DATA. 1958–   [Annual] (OE-
53004)

PURPOSE:– Increasing enrollments in
higher education have generated new interest from college and university administrators in normative data with regard to institutional salaries, tuition and fees, and board
and room. In 1955 the National Federation of
College and University Business Officers Association requested that the Office of Education assume responsibility for an annual compilation and study of data concerning these
factors. Accordingly, the Office of Education
initiated this series in 1958 for the purpose of
disseminating comparative information which
may be useful in budget-making and other
planning activities.

Basis of comparison for each of the financial areas of study (salaries, tuition and
fees, and board and room) were established
as follows: 1) control-public or private; 2)
geographical region– North Atlantic, Great
Lakes and Plains, Southeast, and West and
Southwest; 3) type of institution-university,
liberal arts college, teachers college,
technological institute, theological school,
separately organized professional school, and
junior college; and 4) size of enrollment.
Covers fiscal year.
Earlier FS 5.253:53004

HE 5.253:53014   • **Item 460-A-53**
SUMMARY REPORT, FACULTY AND OTHER PRO-
FESSIONAL STAFF IN INSTITUTIONS OF
HIGHER EDUCATION. 1955–   [Biennial]
(OE-523014)

Summarizes data collected in the Office
of Education's regular biennial survey of faculty and other professional staff in institutions of higher education for the first term of
the academic year.
Earlier FS 5.253:53014

HE 5.253:53015   • **Item 460-A-53**
HIGHER EDUCATION SALARIES. 1962–
[Annual] (OE-53015)

Earlier FS 5.253:53015

HE 5.253:53023   • **Item 460-A-53**
FACULTY SALARIES IN LAND-GRANT COLLEGES
AND STATE UNIVERSITIES. 1935–   [An-
nual] (OE-53023)

Earlier FS 5.253:53023

HE 5.254:nos.   • **Item 460-A-54**
HIGHER EDUCATION PUBLICATIONS: ADMISSION,
ENROLLMENT, RETENTION, DEGREES, GRADU-
ATES, OE 54,000– 54,999.

Earlier FS 5.254

HE 5.254:54000   • **Item 460-A-54**
RESIDENT, EXTENSION, AND OTHER ENROLL-
MENTS IN INSTITUTIONS OF HIGHER LEARN-
ING. 1953–   [Irregular] (OE-54000)

PURPOSE:– To provide a series of comprehensive surveys of first-term enrollment
in institutions of higher education.
Figures are as of November for years
1953 through 1955 and for the end of the first
semester or first quarter for 1957/58.
Earlier FS 5.254:54000

HE 5.254:54001   • **Item 460-A-54**
JUNIOR-YEAR SCIENCE, MATHEMATICS, AND
FOREIGN LANGUAGE STUDENTS, FIRST-
TERM. 1957–   (OE- 54001)

1962/63 Circ. 731
Earlier FS 5.254:54001

HE 5.254:54003   • **Item 460-A-54**
INSTITUTIONAL DATA. 1958–   [Annual] (OE-
54003)

Earlier FS 5.254:54003

HE 5.254:54004   • **Item 460-A-54**
ADVANCE REPORT ON ENGINEERING ENROLL-
MENT AND DEGREES, [year]. 1949–
[Annual] (OE-54004)

Contains a summary of the data collected
in the annual survey of engineering enrollments and degrees conducted by the Office
of Education in cooperation with the American Society for Engineering Education. It is
issued in advance of the complete reports in
order to make available certain summary statistics as early as possible.
Data later appears in Engineering Enrollments and Degrees.
Earlier FS 5.254:54004

HE 5.254:54006   • **Item 460-A-54**
ENGINEERING ENROLLMENTS AND DEGREES.
1949–   [Annual] (OE-54006)

The surveys which provide the data for
these reports are conducted under the joint
auspices of the Office of Education and the
American Society for Engineering Education.
The data on engineering enrollments in
this series of reports are limited to enrollments in institutions of higher education which
confer engineering degrees in the United
States and Puerto Rico. Tables give number
of enrollments (fall) and degrees conferred
(previous year) for B.S., M.S., and PhD degrees.
Earlier FS 5.254:54006

HE 5.254:54007   • **Item 460-A-54**
ANALYTIC REPORT. 1958–   [Annual] (OE-54007)

Earlier FS 5.254:54007

HE 5.254:54009 • Item 460-A-54
SUMMARY REPORT ON SURVEY OF STUDENTS ENROLLED FOR ADVANCE DEGREES: FALL [year]. 1959– [Annual] (OE-54009)

Advanced summary report on the series of nationwide surveys of students enrolled for advanced degrees. A comprehensive analysis and presentation of detailed data from this survey is published later as Enrollment for Advanced Degrees: Fall (year).
Earlier FS 5.254:54009

HE 5.254:54010 • Item 460-A-54
SUMMARY REPORT ON BACHELOR'S AND HIGHER DEGREES CONFERRED DURING [school year]. [Annual] (OE- 54010)

Gives number of earned degrees conferred, by field, level, and sex, with percent change from previous school year.
Earlier FS 5.254:54010.

HE 5.254:54012 • Item 460-A-54
GUIDE TO ORGANIZED OCCUPATIONAL CURRICULUMS IN HIGHER EDUCATION. (OE-54012)

Covers graduates for fiscal year period and enrollments as of Oct. 1, institutional data.
Earlier FS 5.254:54012

HE 5.254:54013 • Item 460-A-54
EARNED DEGREES CONFERRED. 1948– [Annual] (OE-54013)

The main table is arranged by State and institution and gives number of earned degrees for each institution by level and by sex. General tables give analysis of data collected by general grouping.
Earlier FS 5.254:54013
Later HE 5.92/5

HE 5.254:54019 • Item 460-A-54
ENROLLMENT FOR MASTERS AND HIGHER DEGREES, FALL [year], FINAL REPORT. 1959– [Annual] (OE-54019)

PURPOSE:– To meet the need for data bearing on the expected flow of graduate students into the world of employment. The data are needed by the National Science Foundation, the National Institutes of Health, and the Office of Education for planning fellowship, training, research, and facilities programs. These data will also be useful to other public and nonpublic organizations with an interest in graduate education and to those responsible for administration of colleges and universities.
The initial survey on enrollment for advance degrees in the fall of 1959 was confined primarily to the fields of science, mathematics, and health professions. The survey in the fall of 1960 was expanded so as to collect enrollment data on all fields in which advanced degrees are conferred.
Main table gives enrollment for advanced degrees, by major field of study, State and institution, level, and full- and part-time status.

An advanced summary is released in Summary Report on Survey of Students Enrolled for Advanced Degrees, Fall (year).
Previous title: Enrollment for Advance Degrees, Fall (year).
Earlier FS 5.254:54019.

HE 5.254:54023 • Item 460-A-54
OPENING FALL ENROLLMENT IN HIGHER EDUCATION. [Annual]

Earlier FS 5.254:54023
Later HE 5.92/6

HE 5.255:nos. • Item 460-A-55
HIGHER EDUCATION PUBLICATIONS: STUDENT FINANCIAL ASSISTANCE, OE 55,000– 55,999.

Earlier FS 5.255

HE 5.255:55001 • Item 460-A-55
NATIONAL DEFENSE STUDENT LOAN PROGRAM, INCLUDING PARTICIPATING INSTITUTIONS. 1958/59– [Irregular] (OE-55001)

Lists by State of participating institutions of the National Defense Student Loan Program.
Earlier FS 5.255:55001

HE 5.255:55017 • Item 460-A-55
NATIONAL DEFENSE GRADUATE FELLOWSHIPS, GRADUATE PROGRAMS. (OE-55017)

Earlier FS 5.255:55017

HE 5.255:55027 • Item 460-A-55
FINANCIAL ASSISTANCE FOR COLLEGE STUDENTS, UNDERGRADUATE AND 1st-PROFESSIONAL. (OE-55027)

Earlier FS 5.255:55027

HE 5.255:55034 • Item 460-A-55
MODERN FOREIGN LANGUAGE FELLOWSHIP PROGRAM, NATIONAL DEFENSE EDUCATION ACT, TITLE 6 AND NDEA RELATED AWARDS UNDER FULLBRIGHT-HAYS ACT. [Annual] (OE-55034)

Earlier FS 5.255:55034

HE 5.256:nos. • Item 460-A-56
HIGHER EDUCATION PUBLICATIONS: COURSES OF STUDY, SUBJECTS. (OE 56,000– 56,999)

Earlier FS 5.256

HE 5.257:nos. • Item 460-A-57
HIGHER EDUCATION PUBLICATIONS: JUNIOR COLLEGES, COMMUNITY COLLEGES, POST HIGH SCHOOL COURSES, OE 57,000– 57,999.

Earlier FS 5.257

HE 5.258:nos. • Item 460-A-58
HIGHER EDUCATION PUBLICATIONS: TEACHER EDUCATION, OE 58,000– 58,999.

Earlier FS 5.258

HE 5.258:58028 • Item 460-A-58
EPDA [Education Professions Development Act] HIGHER EDUCATION PERSONNEL TRAINING PROGRAMS (year). [Annual] (OE-58028)

The Education Professions Development Act training programs are designed to assist institutions of higher education in meeting critical shortages of highly qualified personnel who are serving or are preparing to serve as teachers, administrators, or educational specialists in colleges and universities.
Directory, by State and Institution, gives program title and number, program director's name and title; type of personnel trained, degree awarded, educational level for which fellows are trained; and number of fellowships.

HE 5.258:58032 • Item 460-A-58
EDUCATION PROFESSIONS. 1st– 1969– [Annual] (OE-58032)

Report submitted by the Commissioner of Education pursuant to the Education Professions Development Act on the state of the education professions and plans for allocating funds authorized by the act.

HE 5.280:nos. • Item 460-A-80
VOCATIONAL EDUCATIONAL PUBLICATIONS: MISCELLANEOUS, OE 80,000– 80,999.

Earlier FS 5.280

HE 5.280:[nos.] • Item 460-A-80
AREA VOCATIONAL EDUCATION PROGRAM SERIES. 1– 1960– [Irregular] (OE-80)

Includes subjects such as 2-year post high school curriculum for electrical technology and for electronics technology.
Earlier FS 5.280

HE 5.280:80008 • Item 460-A-80
DIGEST OF ANNUAL REPORTS OF STATE BOARDS FOR VOCATIONAL EDUCATION TO THE OFFICE OF EDUCATION, DIVISION OF VOCATIONAL EDUCATION. 1933– [Annual] (OE-80008)

Each State submits a Financial and Statistical Report and a Descriptive Report to the Office of Education at the close of the fiscal year and provided in the basic vocational education act (Smith-Hughes Act). These annual reports furnish the Office of Education with complete information about enrollments in, and expenditures for, vocational programs which meet the standards under the Federal vocational education acts.
The data and information collected from these individual reports are consolidated and presented in charts, tables, and brief summaries in this annual publication.
Earlier FS 5.280:80008

HE 5.281:nos. • Item 460-A-81
VOCATIONAL EDUCATION PUBLICATIONS: AGRICULTURAL EDUCATION, OE 81,000– 81,999.

Earlier FS 5.281
HE 5.281:81002 • Item 460-A-81
SUMMARIES OF STUDIES IN AGRICULTURAL EDUCATION, SUPPLEMENTS, 1– 1943– [Annual] (OE-81002)

PURPOSE:-To encourage the implementation of the findings of research conducted by agricultural educators at the State level, the American Vocational Association, in co-operation with the Agricultural Education Branch of the Office of Education, initiated project 1932, which has made available summaries of numerous studies in agricultural education.
The first publication was issued in 1935 as Vocational Education Bulletin 180, Summaries of Studies in Agricultural Education. From 1942 to date, this has been kept up-to-date by supplements.
Earlier FS 5.281:81002

HE 5.282:nos. • Item 460-A-82
VOCATIONAL EDUCATION PUBLICATIONS: DISTRIBUTIVE EDUCATION, OE 82,000– 82,999.

Earlier FS 5.282

HE 5.283:nos. • Item 460-A-83
VOCATIONAL EDUCATION PUBLICATIONS: HOME ECONOMICS EDUCATION, OE 83,000– 83,999.

Earlier FS 5.283

HE 5.283:83008 • Item 460-A-83
HOME ECONOMICS IN INSTITUTIONS GRANTING BACHELOR'S OR HIGHER DEGREES. [Biennial] (OE-83008)

PURPOSE:-To publish the results of a biennial survey to determine the status of home economics degree-granting programs in the United States.
Main Feature is the statistical information covering enrollment, faculty, courses offered, credits required for a bachelor's degree.
Surveys to determine the status of home economics in 4-year college and universities have been conducted biennially in the Home Economics Education Branch of the Office of Education since 1947. Previous survey reports were issued under the title Home Economics in Degree-Granting Institutions.
Earlier FS 5.283:83008

HE 5.284:nos. • Item 460-A-84
VOCATIONAL EDUCATION PUBLICATIONS: TRADE AND INDUSTRIAL EDUCATION, OE 84,000– 84,999.
Earlier FS 5.284

HE 5.285:nos. • Item 460-A-85
VOCATIONAL EDUCATIONAL PUBLICATIONS: PRACTICAL NURSE EDUCATION, OE 85,000– 85,999.
Earlier FS 5.285

HE 5.286:nos. • Item 460-A-86
VOCATIONAL EDUCATION PUBLICATIONS: BUSI-
NESS EDUCATION, OE 86,000– 86,999.

   Earlier FS 5.286

HE 5.287:nos.
VOCATIONAL EDUCATION PUBLICATIONS: MAN-
POWER DEVELOPMENT AND TRAINING, OE
87,000– 87,999.

   Earlier FS 5.287

HE 5.288:nos.
FASHION INDUSTRY SERIES.

HE 5.289 • Item 459-B
NATIONAL ADVISORY COMMITTEE ON EDUCATION
OF THE DEAF: ANNUAL REPORT.

HE 5.290
SURVEY OF FEDERAL LIBRARIES. [Irregular]

   Later HE 19.311:L 61

HE 5.291:date • Item 460-A-10
PROJECTIONS OF EDUCATIONAL STATISTICS TO
(dates).

   Later HE 19.320

SOCIAL AND REHABILITATION
SERVICE
(1967– 1977)

CREATION AND AUTHORITY

   The Social and Rehabilitation Service was
established within the Department of Health, Education, and Welfare by the Secretary's reorganization of August 15, 1967. [During the period
from 1967 through 1969, the SuDocs class FS 17
was used.] The Service was abolished by
Secretary's reorganization of March 8, 1977 (42
FR 13262) and its constituent units transferred.

HE 17.1:date
ANNUAL REPORT.
   Earlier FS 17.1

HE 17.2:CT • Item 512-A-1
GENERAL PUBLICATIONS.

   Earlier FS 17.2

HE 17.2:M 46/2 • Item 512-A-1
MEDICAL ASSISTANCE FINANCED UNDER PUB-
LIC ASSISTANCE TITLES OF SOCIAL SECU-
RITY ACT. [Annual] (National Center for So-
cial Statistics) (NCSS Report B-1)

   Earlier FS 17.2:M 46/2
   Later HE 22.8

HE 17.2:St 2/2/date • Item 512-A-1
STATE EXPENDITURES FOR PUBLIC ASSIS-
TANCE PROGRAMS. [Annual] (Office of
Financial Management, Division of Finance)

   Covers programs approved under titles I,
IV-A, X, XVI, XIX, and XX of the Social Secu-
rity Act.
   Report is for the fiscal year.
   ISSN 0147-4170

HE 17.6:CT • Item 512-A-3
REGULATIONS, RULES AND INSTRUCTIONS.

HE 17.8:CT • Item 512-A-3
HANDBOOKS, MANUALS, GUIDES.

   Earlier FS 17.8

HE 17.8/2:CT • Item 512-A-4
MANUALS FOR VOLUNTEER PROBATION PRO-
GRAMS.
   Earlier FS 17.8/2

HE 17.9:v.nos.&nos. • Item 532-A-2
WELFARE IN REVIEW. v. 1– 10. 1963– 1972. [6 times
a year]

   PURPOSE:– To make available research reports on statistics prepared in the Welfare Administration on public assistance programs, child
health and welfare, juvenile delinquency, aging,
and Cuban refugee resettlement.
   In addition to the signed articles, includes
Publications of Interest, listing both Government
and private publications. Statistical data contained
in the Program and Operating Statistics section.
   Subject and author index contained in the
December issue.
   An annual statistical supplement is published
early each year.
   Earlier FS 17.9
   Superseded by Human Needs (HE 17.26).

HE 17.10:CT
BIBLIOGRAPHIES AND LISTS OF PUBLICATIONS.

HE 17.14:CT • Item 532-A-6
ADDRESSES. [Irregular]
   Earlier FS 17.14

HE 17.15:date • Item 512-A-2
RESEARCH (year), ANNOTATED LIST OF RESEARCH
AND DEMONSTRATION GRANTS. [Annual]

   PURPOSE:– To list all research and demonstration grants and research and training grants,
both current and completed, that have been
awarded by the Social and Rehabilitation Service
from the beginning of each program to date, with
the exception of grants awarded by the Division
of Mental Retardation. It is designed to meet the
needs of scholars, students, researchers, program planners, and administrators in the field of
social welfare and rehabilitation.
   Former title: Social and Rehabilitation Service Research and Demonstration Projects.
   Earlier FS 17.15, FS 13.202:R 32/3

HE 17.16: • Item 532-A-7
PAROLE SERIES.

HE 17.16/2: • Item 532-A-7
CORRECTION SERIES.

HE 17.16/3: • Item 532-A-7
LEGAL SERIES.

HE 17.16/4: • Item 532-A-7
STUDIES IN DELINQUENCY.

HE 17.17:CT • Item 532-A-3
BIBLIOGRAPHIES AND LISTS OF PUBLICATIONS.
   Earlier FS 17.17 FS 14.13

HE 17.18:v.nos.&nos.
RESEARCH AND DEMONSTRATIONS BRIEF [Bring
Research into Effective Focus]. v. 1, no. 1–
Aug. 15, 1967– [Irregular] (Research Utiliza-
tion Branch, Division of Research Demonstra-
tions)

   PURPOSE:– To disseminate in readable form
concise information about selected research
projects of interest to administrators and practitioners in the field of social welfare and rehabilitation.

HE 17.19:nos. • Item 519
PUBLIC ASSISTANCE REPORTS. 1–

HE 17.19/2:date • Item 519-A
SOURCE OF FUNDS EXPENDED FOR PUBLIC AS-
SISTANCE PAYMENTS. [Semiannual] (NCSS Re-
port F-1)

   Data presented for each State of sources
(Federal, State, and local) of public assistance
funds, arranged by special type of assistance.
   Separate reports issued for calendar and fis-
cal years.
   Earlier HE 17.617/4

HE 17.20:CT • Item 532-A-8
NATIONAL CITIZENS CONFERENCE ON REHABILI-
TATION OF THE DISABLED AND DISADVAN-
TAGED [publications].

HE 17.21:date • Item 532-A-9
GRANTS, JUVENILE DELINQUENCY PREVENTION
AND CONTROL ACT.
   Later HE 17.811

HE 17.22:date
JUVENILE DELINQUENCY REPORTER. – April 1970.

   Superseded by Delinquency Prevention Reporter, HE 17.810.

HE 17.23:nos. • Item 454
STATISTICAL SERIES (numbered). 1–   1947–

   Individual reports are issued for the various
programs of the Children's Bureau and cooperating State and local health and welfare agencies.
The following sub-series are currently being issued on a regular schedule. Titles may vary from
year-to-year and some issues may be expanded
to include special data.
   Earlier FS 17.213
JUVENILE COURT STATISTICS. [Annual]

      Includes data on delinquency cases (ex-
cluding traffic offenses); traffic cases; and
other cases (dependency, neglect or special
proceedings disposed of officially by juvenile
courts).
      Earlier FS 17.213
      Later J 1.53

HE 17.24:nos. • Item 532-A-10
WORKING PAPERS. 1–   1971–   [Irregular]

   Compilation of papers prepared as background
information, initial working papers, and beginning
work plans for the first research steps in three
areas of special interest: worker job mobility,
employment of subprofessionals; and impact of
organizational climate and structure on workers.

HE 17.25:nos. • Item 532-A-11
RESEARCH REPORTS. 1–   1971–   [Irregular]

HE 17.25/2:nos. • Item 532-A-11 (MF)
PROGRAM APPLICATION REPORTS. 1–   1973–
[Irregular]

HE 17.26:v.nos.&nos. • Item 532-A-12
HUMAN NEEDS. v. 1, nos.1– 11. 1972– April- May
1973. [Monthly]

   PURPOSE:– To provide editorial coverage of
all Federally-supported social and rehabilitation
services, such as child care, aging, delinquency
prevention, welfare, vocational rehabilitation, etc.
   Supersedes Welfare in Review (HE 17.9)

HE 17.27:v.nos.&nos. • Item 532-A-13
SOCIAL AND REHABILITATION RECORD. v. 1– 4.
1974– 1977. [10 times a year]

   PURPOSE:– To serve as a means of improving the management of human service programs,
such as assistance payments, individual and family social services, and vocational rehabilitation.
As a management tool, the magazine aids administrative personnel in State and local agencies,
public and private, to carry out their responsibilities more effectively.
   Indexed by: Index to U.S. Government Periodicals.
   ISSN 0092-7759
   Superseded by Record (HE 22.8).

HE 17.28:date • Item 519-B (MF)
ANNUAL REPORT OF WELFARE PROGRAMS.

HE 17.29:date • Item 532-A-14
REPORTS BULLETIN. [Semiannual]

   PURPOSE:– To serve as an official SRS list
of reports for use by SRS components and State
agencies, for information and control purposes.

REHABILITATION SERVICES ADMINISTRATION
(1970– 1975)

CREATION AND AUTHORITY

The Rehabilitation Services Administration was established within the Social and Rehabilitation Service (FS 17.100) by the Departmental reorganization of August 15, 1967 to succeed the Vocational Rehabilitation Administration (FS 13.200) which was abolished. [During the period from 1967 through 1969, the SuDocs class FS 17.100 was used.] In 1975, the Administration was placed directly under the supervision of the Secretary of Health, Education, and Welfare (HE 1.600).

HE 17.101:date • Item 528
ANNUAL REPORT. [Annual]

Reprint from the report of the Secretary of Health, Education and Welfare.
Earlier FS 17.101

HE 17.102:CT • Item 529
GENERAL PUBLICATIONS.

Earlier FS 17.102

HE 17.106:CT • Item 530
REGULATIONS, RULES, AND INSTRUCTIONS.

HE 17.108:CT • Item 529-B
HANDBOOKS, MANUALS, GUIDES.

Earlier FS 17.108 FS 13.217/2
Later HE 1.608

HE 17.109:v.nos.&nos. • Item 530-A
REHABILITATION RECORD. v. 1– 14, no. 5. 1960– Sept./Oct. 1973. [Bimonthly]
PURPOSE:– To disseminate basic information on new projects and findings in vocational rehabilitation to people who are providing such services and to those working directly with handicapped persons.
Contains signed articles by leading authorities in both the public and private spheres of rehabilitation and related fields. Includes annotated list of new publications.
Includes annual index.
Earlier FS 13.216, FS 13.17.109

HE 17.110/3:nos. • Item 531
REHABILITATION SERVICE SERIES. 1– 1946– [Irregular]

PURPOSE:– To make available to State agency personnel suggested information on methods and operating aids which is not classifiable as basic instructions.
Earlier FS 17.110/3

HE 17.111:date
CASELOAD STATISTICS STATE VOCATIONAL REHABILITATION AGENCIES. [Annual] (Division of Statistics and Studies)

PURPOSE:– To furnish both State agency administrative personnel and the Rehabilitation Services Administration with summary information on the caseload composition of the Program of Vocation Rehabilitation at National and State levels. Provides a comparative body of analytical data to afford a better perspective of the current proportions of the Federal-State rehabilitation effort, and serves as a factual base for planning for the future growth and expansion of the program.

HE 17.112:CT • Item 528-A
BIBLIOGRAPHIES AND LISTS OF PUBLICATIONS.

HE 17.113:v.nos.&nos. • Item 506-C-1
MENTAL RETARDATION ABSTRACTS. v. 1– 9. 1964– 1972. [Quarterly]

PURPOSE:– To provide a specialized information service designed to assist the Division in meeting its obligation to plan, direct, and coordinate a comprehensive nationwide program for those with mental retardation and related handicaps. It is intended to meet the needs of investigators and other workers in the field of mental retardation for rapid and comprehensive information about new developments and research results and to foster maximum utilization of these results.
Vol. 1, nos. 1-4 published in one volume.
Author and subject index included.
Earlier FS 2.22/52 prior to v. 6, no. 4

HE 17.114:nos.
STATISTICAL NOTES. 1–

HE 17.115:nos.
COMMISSIONERS LETTERS (numbered).

HE 17.116:nos.
REHABILITATION MEMORANDUM.

HE 17.117:CT • Item 491-A
MENTAL HEALTH STATISTICS: CURRENT FACILITY REPORTS. [Irregular]

PURPOSE:– To provide summary patient movement and administrative data on a current basis. The series contains data for the public mental hospitals which include state and county mental hospitals, and data for the public institutions for the mentally retarded.
Earlier FS 2.53/2, HE 20.2415/2

HE 17.117:H 79 • Item 491-A
MENTAL HEALTH STATISTICS: CURRENT FACILITY REPORTS. PROVISIONAL PATIENT MOVEMENT AND ADMINISTRATIVE DATA, STATE AND COUNTY MENTAL HOSPITALS, UNITED STATES. [Annual]

Covers fiscal year.
Earlier HE 20.2415/2:H 79

HE 17.118:date
DIRECTORY OF STATE AGENCIES FOR THE BLIND.

HE 17.118/2:date-reg.
NATIONAL DIRECTORY OF REHABILITATION FACILITIES. 1970– [Irregular] (Division of Rehabilitation Facilities)

Consists of 12 volumes, one for each HEW region, listing rehabilitation facilities which the State vocational rehabilitation agencies of that region utilize for rehabilitation services to clients.

HE 17.119:date • Item 506-C-2
STATE VOCATIONAL REHABILITATION AGENCY PROGRAM DATA, FISCAL YEAR (date). [Annual]

HE 17.119/2:date • Item 506-C-2
STATE VOCATIONAL REHABILITATION AGENCY: FACT SHEET BOOKLETS. [Annual]

HE 17.120:date
REHABILITATION SERVICES ADMINISTRATION, QUARTERLY INDICES.

HE 17.121:date-nos. • Item 506-C-3
SPECIAL REPORTS. 1972– [Irregular]

HE 17.122:date
STATE REHABILITATION FACILITIES SPECIALIST EXCHANGE. 1972– 1973. [Irregular] (Division of Service Systems, Office of Program Development)

PURPOSE:– To serve as a medium of exchange of information between the Rehabilitation Services Administration and the State rehabilitation facilities specialists.

ADMINISTRATION ON AGING
(1970– 1973)

CREATION AND AUTHORITY

The Administration on Aging (FS 15) was reassigned to the Social and Rehabilitation Service (FS 17.300) by Departmental reorganization of August 15, 1967. [During the period 1967 through 1969, SuDocs class FS 17.300 was used.] The Administration was transferred to the Office of the Assistant Secretary for Human Development (HE 1.200) by Secretary's Order of June 15, 1973.

HE 17.301:date
ANNUAL REPORT.

Earlier FS 17.301
Later HE 1.201

HE 17.302:CT • Item 447-A-1
GENERAL PUBLICATIONS.

Earlier FS 15.2, FS 17.302

HE 17.305:CT • Item 447-A-1
LAWS.

HE 17.308:CT • Item 447-A-3
HANDBOOKS, MANUALS, GUIDES.

Earlier FS 15.8, FS 17.308
Later HE 1.208

HE 17.308/2:CT • Item 447-A-3
INFORMATION AND REFERRAL SERVICES (series).

Later HE 1.208/2

HE 17.309:nos. • Item 444-A
AGING. 1– 1951– [Bimonthly]

Earlier FS 17.309, FS 15.10
Changed to HE 1.210 with no. 224

HE 17.310:CT • Item 447-A-5
DESIGNS FOR ACTION FOR OLDER AMERICANS. 1967– [Irregular]

A series of reports on successful projects being conducted by or in behalf of older people. The Administration on Aging collects and published these reports analyzing projects which are meeting some of the problems of older people. The project reports contain sufficient details for those interested to determine whether a similar project, adapted to the situation in a local community, should be undertaken. Names of individuals from whom additional information may be obtained are included.
Punched for 3-ring binder.
Earlier FS 17.310

HE 17.311:CT • Item 447-A-6
BIBLIOGRAPHIES AND LISTS OF PUBLICATIONS.

Earlier FS 17.311 and FS 15.12

HE 17.312:CT • Item 447-A-2
ADDRESSES.

Earlier FS 17.312 and FS 15.9
HE 17.313:CT • Item 447-A-3
PATTERNS FOR PROGRESS IN AGING. [Irregular]

Later HE 1.211

HE 17.314:nos.
FACTS AND FIGURES FOR OLDER AMERICANS.

Later HE 1.209

ASSISTANCE PAYMENTS ADMINISTRATION (1970– 1977)

CREATION AND AUTHORITY

The Assistance Payments Administration was established within the Social and Rehabilitation Service (FS 17.400) by the Departmental reorganization of August 15, 1967. [During the period from 1967 through 1969, the SuDocs class FS 17.400 was used.] The Administration was transferred to the Social Security Administration (HE 3.400) by the Secretary's reorganization of March 8, 1977.

HE 17.401:date
ANNUAL REPORT.

Earlier FS 17.401

HE 17.402:CT   • **Item 512-B-2**
GENERAL PUBLICATIONS.

Earlier FS 17.402
Later HE 3.402

HE 17.408   • **Item 512-B-1**
HANDBOOKS, MANUALS, GUIDES.

Earlier 17.408
Later HE 3.408

HE 17.408/2:CT   • **Item 512-B-2**
HOW THEY DO IT, ILLUSTRATIONS OF PRACTICE IN ADMINISTRATION OF AFDC (series).

Earlier FS 3.37
Later HE 3.37

MEDICAL SERVICES ADMINISTRATION (1970– 1977)

CREATION AND AUTHORITY

The Medical Services Administration was established within the Social and Rehabilitation Service (FS 17.500) by Departmental reorganization of August 15, 1967. [During the period from 1967 through 1969, the SuDocs class was FS 17.500 was used.] The Administration was transferred to the Health Care Financing Administration (HE 22.100) by the Secretary's reorganization of March 8, 1977.

HE 17.501:date
ANNUAL REPORT.

Earlier FS 17.501
Later HE 22.101

HE 17.502:CT   • **Item 512-C**
GENERAL PUBLICATIONS.

Earlier FS 17.502
Later HE 22.102

HE 17.508:CT   • **Item 512-C-1**
HANDBOOKS, MANUALS, GUIDES.

NATIONAL CENTER FOR SOCIAL STATISTICS (1970–   )

CREATION AND AUTHORITY

The National Center for Social Statistics was established within the Social and Rehabilitation Service (FS 17.600) by Departmental reorganization of August 15, 1967. [During the period from 1967 through 1969, the SuDocs class FS 17.600 was used.]

HE 17.601:date
ANNUAL REPORT.

Earlier FS 17.601

HE 17.602:date   • **Item 512-D-3**
GENERAL PUBLICATIONS.

Earlier FS 17.602

HE 17.609:date
CHILD CARE ARRANGEMENTS OF AFDC RECIPIENTS UNDER THE WORK INCENTIVE PROGRAM. [Quarterly] (NCSS Report E-4)

Tables give number of mothers of other caretakers who began enrollment in the WIN Program and number of their children who were provided care, by age group and by State; Child care arrangements, by age group and by State, of mothers or other caretakers who began enrollment in the WIN Program; and Number of mothers or other caretakers who were not referred for enrollment in the WIN Program for the sole reason that adequate child and arrangements were not available, and number of their children requiring child care, by age group and by State, for month or quarter.
Quarterly issues through July 1970.
ISSN 0091-813X

HE 17.610:date
PUBLIC ASSISTANCE STATISTICS. [Monthly]

Gives number, amount, and change from previous month and month a year ago of the various aid programs, such as old-age assistance, aid to dependent children, aid to the blind, aid to the permanently and totally disabled and general assistance.
ISSN 0145-952X
Earlier FS 17.610

HE 17.611:date
UNEMPLOYED PARENT SEGMENT OF AID TO FAMILIES WITH DEPENDENT CHILDREN (NCSS Report A-3).

Earlier FS 17.611

HE 17.612:date   • **Item 512-B**
TREND REPORT: GRAPHIC PRESENTATION OF PUBLIC ASSISTANCE AND RELATED DATA. [Annual] (NCSS Report A-4)

PURPOSE:– To provide information on the development of the public assistance programs under the Social Security Act and under State and local general assistance programs that are financed without Federal financial participation.
Earlier FS 17.410

HE 17.613:date-nos.
REASONS FOR OPENING PUBLIC ASSISTANCE CASES. [Semiannual] (NCSS Report A-5)

PURPOSE:– To summarize data on primary reasons for opening cases to receive assistance payments under Federally aided public assistance programs.

HE 17.613/2:date
REASONS FOR DISCONTINUING MONEY PAYMENTS TO PUBLIC ASSISTANCE CASES. [Quarterly] (NCSS Report A-11)

Statistical data by State for discontinuing money payments to cases, by reasons, for old-age assistance, aid to the blind, aid to permanently and totally disabled, and aid to families with dependent children.

HE 17.613/3:date   • **Item 512-D-11**
APPLICATIONS AND CASE DISPOSITIONS FOR PUBLIC ASSISTANCE. [Quarterly] (NCSS Report A-12)

ISSN 0360-6848
Later HE 3.60/3

HE 17.614:date   • **Item 512-D-1**
PROGRAM FACTS ON FEDERALLY AIDED PUBLIC ASSISTANCE INCOME MAINTENANCE PROGRAMS. (NCSS Report A-6)

PURPOSE:– To describe the four maintenance assistance programs operated under titles of the Social Security Act, as amended– Old Age Assistance, Aid to Families with Dependent Children, Aid to the Blind, and Aid to the Permanently and Totally Disabled.

HE 17.615
PUBLIC ASSISTANCE, ANNUAL STATISTICAL DATA. [Annual] (NCSS Report A-7)

Presents annual data in tabular form for the the recipients and expenditures of public assistance, by general categories and special types.

HE 17.616:date   • **Item 512-D-4**
MEDICAL ASSISTANCE (Medicaid) FINANCED UNDER TITLE XIX OF SOCIAL SECURITY ACT. 1967– [Quarterly] (NCSS Report B-1)

Previous title: Medical Assistance Financed under Public Assistance Titles of the Social Security Act.
ISSN 0147-309X
Earlier FS 17.616
Later HE 22.110

HE 17.617:date
PUBLIC ASSISTANCE: VENDOR PAYMENTS FOR MEDICAL CARE BY TYPE OF SERVICE, FISCAL YEAR ENDED (date). [Annual] (NCSS Report B-2)

Presents tabular data for each State on vendor payments for medical care by type of service for each special type of public assistance.

HE 17.617/2:date   • **Item 512-D-6**
RECIPIENTS AND AMOUNTS OF MEDICAL VENDOR PAYMENTS UNDER PUBLIC ASSISTANCE PROGRAMS. [Semiannual] (NCSS Report B-3)

Contains tables giving State data on number of recipients with vendor payments for medical or remedial care and the amounts of such payments, by type of care, for the period specified, including inpatient hospital, nursing home, physicians, dental and other practitioners, out- patient hospital, clinic, laboratory and radiological, home health, and prescribed drugs.

HE 17.617/3:date   • **Item 512-D-2**
NUMBER OF RECIPIENTS AND AMOUNTS OF PAYMENTS UNDER MEDICAID AND OTHER MEDICAL PROGRAMS FINANCED FROM PUBLIC ASSISTANCE FUNDS. [Annual] (NCSS Report B-4)

ISSN 0091-5920
Later HE 22.12

HE 17.617/4:date
VENDOR PAYMENTS FOR MEDICAL CARE UNDER PUBLIC ASSISTANCE, BY PROGRAM AND TYPE OF SERVICE, FISCAL YEAR (date). [Annual] (NCSS Report B-7)

HE 17.618:date
SOCIAL SERVICES FOR FAMILIES AND CHILDREN.
[Semiannual] (NCSS Report E-6)

PURPOSE:– To summarize data submitted by States reporting social services for families and children provided by public welfare agencies and the effects of such services.

HE 17.619:date
ASSESSMENTS COMPLETED AND REFERRALS TO MANPOWER AGENCIES BY WELFARE AGENCIES UNDER WORK INCENTIVE PROGRAM FOR AFDC RECIPIENTS.   – April-June 1972. [Quarterly] (NCSS Report E-5)

PURPOSE:– To provide data on specified welfare aspects of the WIN Program for AFDC dependents.
Continued as Work Incentive Program (HE 17.619/2)

HE 17.619/2:date   • Item 512-D-14
WORK INCENTIVE PROGRAM. (NCSS Report E-5)

HE 17.620:date   • Item 512-D-15
MEDICAID AND OTHER MEDICAL CARE FINANCED FROM PUBLIC ASSISTANCE FUNDS. [Semiannual] (NCSS Report B-5)

Separate reports issued for calendar and fiscal years.

HE 17.621:date   • Item 512-D-2
MEDICAID AND OTHER MEDICAL CARE FINANCED FROM PUBLIC ASSISTANCE FUNDS. [Irregular] (NCSS Report B-6)

Statistics cover national data; expenditures, aggregate and per inhabitant; recipients, total and number per 1,000 population; and average monthly amount of medical bills paid per recipient.
1951– 1969. 75 p. 1970.

HE 17.625:date   • Item 512-D-16
AID TO FAMILIES WITH DEPENDENT CHILDREN. [Annual] (NCSS Report D-2)

PURPOSE:– To present tabular data for each State on standards for basic needs for Old Age Assistance and Aid to Families with Dependent Children. The monthly amounts cited represent 1) the full standard, 2) the payment standard, and 3) the largest amount paid for basic needs.
Title varies.
Continues Public Assistance Programs, Standards for Basic Needs (ISSN 0098-8197).
Continued by Characteristics of State Plans for Aid to Families with Dependent Children (ISSN 0149-1792).
ISSN 0363-5686

HE 17.626:date
STATE MAXIMUMS AND OTHER METHODS OF LIMITING MONEY PAYMENTS TO RECIPIENTS OF SPECIAL TYPES OF PUBLIC ASSISTANCE. [Annual] (NCSS Report D-3)

HE 17.627:date
MONEY PAYMENTS TO RECIPIENTS OF SPECIAL TYPES OF PUBLIC ASSISTANCE. [Annual] (NCSS Report D-4)

HE 17.627/2:date   • Item 512-D-12
RECIPIENTS OF PUBLIC ASSISTANCE MONEY PAYMENTS AND AMOUNTS OF SUCH PAYMENTS, BY PROGRAM, STATE, AND COUNTY. [Annual] (NCSS Report A-8)
Later HE 3.61

HE 17.628:date
STATISTICAL REPORT ON SOCIAL SERVICES, QUARTER ENDING.

Earlier FS 17.628

HE 17.629:date   • Item 512-D-8
PUBLIC WELFARE PERSONNEL, ANNUAL STATISTICAL DATA. (NCSS Report E-2)

HE 17.630:date
EXPENDITURES FOR STAFF DEVELOPMENT AND TRAINING ACTIVITIES.

Former title: Progress Report on Staff Development for Fiscal Year (date).

HE 17.631:date
SOURCE OF FUNDS EXPENDED FOR PUBLIC ASSISTANCE PAYMENTS. [Semiannual] (NCSS Report F-1)

Later HE 17.19/2

HE 17.632:date
EXPENDITURES FOR PUBLIC ASSISTANCE PAYMENTS AND FOR ADMINISTRATIVE COSTS, BY PROGRAM AND SOURCE OF FUNDS. [Irregular] (NCSS Report F-5)

HE 17.633:date
PUBLIC ASSISTANCE: COSTS OF STATE AND LOCAL ADMINISTRATION, SERVICES, AND TRAINING. [Semiannual] (NCSS Report F-3)

Separate reports issued for calendar and fiscal years.

HE 17.634:date
SOURCE OF FUNDS EXPENDED FOR PUBLIC ASSISTANCE PAYMENTS AND FOR COST OF ADMINISTRATION, SERVICES, AND TRAINING. [Semiannual] (NCSS Report F-2)

Separate reports issued for calendar and fiscal years.

HE 17.635:date
IMPACT ON PUBLIC ASSISTANCE CASELOADS OF (a) PUBLIC ASSISTANCE WORK AND TRAINING PROGRAMS, AND (b) TRAINING PROGRAMS UNDER MANPOWER DEVELOPMENT AND TRIANING ACT. NCSS Report G-1.

Earlier FS 17.635

HE 17.636:date
CONCURRENT RECEIPT OF PUBLIC ASSISTANCE MONEY PAYMENTS AND OLD-AGE SURVIVORS, AND DISABILITY INSURANCE CASH BENEFITS 65 YEARS OR OVER. [Irregular] (NCSS Report G-2)

HE 17.638:date   • Item 512-D
CHILD WELFARE STATISTICS. [Annual] (NCSS Report CW-1)

Includes data for the United States and each reporting State on children receiving services from public and voluntary child welfare agencies and institutions; facilities for day care and foster care of children; personnel employed in public child welfare agencies, and those granted education leave; and expenditures for public child welfare services.
Statistics on adoption of children are published annually in a special supplement.
Earlier FS 17.638, FS 17.213

HE 17.639:date
PRELIMINARY REPORT OF FINDINGS, (year) AFDC STUDY.

HE 17.639/2:date
PRELIMINARY REPORT OF FINDINGS FROM MAIL QUESTIONNAIRE. AFDC Study, NCSS Report AFDC-2.

Earlier FS 17.602

HE 17.639/3:date   • Item 512-D-5
REPORT OF FINDINGS, AFDC STUDY. (NCSS AFDC-3)

PURPOSE:– To provide information on selected demographic and program characteristics of families and children who were receiving aid to families with dependent children.

HE 17.639/4:date   • Item 512-D-5
FINDINGS OF (year) AB [Aid to the Blind] STUDY. 1970–   (NCSS Report AB-1)

PURPOSE:– To provide statistical data from a sample survey of persons who received assistance payments in the aid to the blind (AB) program.
Issued in two parts:

Part 1. Demographic and Program Characteristics.
Part 2. Financial Circumstances.

HE 17.640:nos.   • Item 512-D-7
NCSS REPORT, H- (series). 1–

Reports on various aspects of public assistance.

HE 17.641:date
APPLICATIONS, CASES APPROVED, AND CASES DISCONTINUED FOR PUBLIC ASSISTANCE. [Quarterly] (Report A-9)

HE 17.642:date   • Item 512-D-13
REPORT ON DISPOSITION OF PUBLIC ASSISTANCE CASES INVOLVING QUESTIONS OF FRAUD, FISCAL YEAR. [Annual]

Later HE 3.63

HE 17.643:date
REASONS FOR DISPOSITION OF APPLICANTS OTHER THAN BY APPROVAL.   –1972. [Quarterly] (NCSS Report A-10)

Statistical data by state for disposition of applicants, by reasons, for old-age assistance, aid to the blind, aid to the permanently and totally disabled, and aid to families with dependent children.
Information continued in Applications and Case Dispositions for Public Assistance (NCSS Report A-12) (HE 17.613/3).

HE 17.643/2
REASONS FOR DISCONTINUING MONEY PAYMENTS TO PUBLIC ASSISTANCE CASES.   –1972. [Quarterly]

Information continued in Applications and Case Dispositions for Public Assistance (NCSS Report A-12) (HE 17.613/3).

HE 17.644:date   • Item 512-D-9
HEARINGS IN PUBLIC ASSISTANCE. [Semiannual] (NCSS Report E-8)

Continues Fair Hearings in Public Assistance (ISSN 0145-9422).
ISSN 0145-9449
Later HE 3.60/2

HE 17.645:date
CHILDREN SAVED BY PUBLIC WELFARE AGENCIES AND VOLUNTARY CHILD WELFARE AGENCIES AND INSTITUTIONS. (NCSS Report E-9)

ISSN 0145-9449

HE 17.646:date   • Item 512-D-17
ADOPTIONS IN (year). 1957–   [Annual] (NCSS Report E-10)

PURPOSE:– To provide information on the number of adoption petitions granted during the calendar year. Data are presented by State, by relationship of the petitioner to the child, race of the child, and birth status of the child for all children adopted. For children adopted by unrelated petitioners, data are presented by type of placement, age at time of placement, and birth status.

HE 17.647:date   • Item 512-D-18
SOCIAL SERVICES USA. [Quarterly]

Sub-title: Statistical Tables, Summaries and Analysis of Services Under the Social Security Act.
ISSN 0145-3041
Later HE 23.2010

PUBLIC SERVICES ADMINISTRATION (1976– 1977)

CREATION AND AUTHORITY

The Community Services Administration was established within the Social and Rehabilitation Service in 1970. Name changed to Public Services Administration and placed under supervision of the Secretary of Health, Education, and Welfare (HE 1.900) by Departmental notice of November 3, 1976.

HE 17.701:date
ANNUAL REPORT.

HE 17.702:CT   • Item 532-B-1
GENERAL PUBLICATIONS.

HE 17.708:CT   • Item 532-B-3
HANDBOOKS, MANUALS, GUIDES.

HE 17.709:date   • Item 532-B-2
SERVICES TO AFDC FAMILIES, ANNUAL REPORT TO CONGRESS.

HE 17.710:CT   • Item 532-B-4
BIBLIOGRAPHIES AND LISTS OF PUBLICATIONS. [Irregular]
        Later HE 23.2011

YOUTH DEVELOPMENT AND DELINQUENCY PREVENTION ADMINISTRATION (1970– 1974)

CREATION AND AUTHORITY

The Youth Development and Delinquency Prevention Administration was established within the Social and Rehabilitation Service in 1970. In 1974, the Administration was transferred to the Office of Assistant Secretary for Human Development (HE 1.300).

HE 17.801:date
ANNUAL REPORT.

HE 17.802:CT   • Item 532-C-2
GENERAL PUBLICATIONS.
        Later HE 1.302

HE 17.808:CT   • Item 532-C-3
HANDBOOKS, MANUALS, GUIDES.

HE 17.809:CT   • Item 532-C-4
BIBLIOGRAPHIES AND LISTS OF PUBLICATIONS.
        Later HE 1.309

HE 17.810:date
DELINQUENCY PREVENTION REPORTER. June-July 1970– [Irregular]

        Contains articles, reports, book reviews, and list of new publications in the field of juvenile delinquency.
        Supersedes Juvenile Delinquency Reporter. Classified HE 17.22 prior to June-July 1970 issue.

HE 17.811:date   • Item 523-A-9
JUVENILE DELINQUENCY PREVENTION AND CONTROL ACT OF 1968, GRANTS. [Annual]
        Earlier HE 17.21

NATIONAL INSTITUTE OF EDUCATION (1972– 1975)

CREATION AND AUTHORITY

The National Institute of Education was established within the Education Division by the Education Amendments of 1972, effective June 23, 1972 (86 Stat. 327).
        In 1975 the new SuDocs class HE 19.200 was established for the Institute.

HE 18.1:date
ANNUAL REPORT.

HE 18.2:CT   • Item 461-D-5
GENERAL PUBLICATIONS. [Irregular]

HE 18.9:nos.   • Item 461-C
PREP [Putting Research into Educational Practice] REPORTS. 1–   1969–

        Earlier HE 5.89

HE 18.10:v.nos.&nos.   • Item 466-A
RESOURCES IN EDUCATION. [Monthly] (Educational Resources Information Center)

        Prior to 1975, issued as Research in Education.
        Earlier HE 5.77
        Later HE 19.210

HE 18.11:nos.   • Item 461-D-1
CENTER FOR VOCATIONAL AND TECHNICAL EDUCATION, OHIO STATE UNIVERSITY: RESEARCH AND DEVELOPMENT SERIES. 1–   [Irregular]

        Earlier HE 5.2:CT

HE 18.11/2:nos.   • Item 461-D-2
CENTER FOR VOCATIONAL AND TECHNICAL EDUCATION, OHIO STATE UNIVERSITY: INFORMATION SERIES. 1–   [Irregular]

HE 18.12   • Item 461-D-3
MODEL PROGRAMS, TITLE III, ELEMENTARY AND SECONDARY EDUCATION ACT.

HE 18.13:nos.   • Item 461-D-4
ERIC CLEARINGHOUSE FOR SOCIAL STUDIES, SOCIAL SCIENCE EDUCATION: INTERPRETIVE STUDIES. 1–   [Irregular]

        Earlier HE 5 classes

EDUCATION DIVISION (1972– 1979)

CREATION AND AUTHORITY

The Education Division was established within the Department of Health, Education, and Welfare by the Education Amendments of 1972, effective June 23, 1972 (86 Stat. 327; 20 U.S.C. 1221e). The Division was abolished and its functions transferred to the Department of Education (ED 1) by the Department of Education Organization Act (93 Stat. 668), approved October 17, 1979.

HE 19.1:date
ANNUAL REPORT.

HE 19.2:CT   • Item 461-F
GENERAL PUBLICATIONS. [Irregular]

HE 19.8:CT   • Item 461-A
HANDBOOKS, MANUALS, GUIDES. [Irregular]

HE 19.9:CT   • Item 461
FUND FOR THE IMPROVEMENT OF POSTSECONDARY EDUCATION: PUBLICATIONS (series).

        Later ED 1.23

HE 19.9:R 31/date   • Item 461
RESOURCES FOR CHANGE, A GUIDE TO PROJECTS. [Annual]

        Report covers fiscal year.
        Later ED 1.23:R 31

OFFICE OF EDUCATION (1972– 1979)

CREATION AND AUTHORITY

The Office of Education (HE 5) was placed within the Education Division by the Education Amendments of 1972, effective June 23, 1972 (86 Stat. 327). The Office was abolished and its functions transferred to the Department of Education (ED 1) by the Department of Education Organization Act (93 Stat. 668), approved October 17, 1979.
        For the period 1972– 1975, the Office's publications continued to be assigned to the HE 5 class.

HE 19.101:date   • Item 455
ANNUAL REPORT.

        Earlier HE 5.1

HE 19.101/2:date   • Item 455
ADMINISTRATION OF PUBLIC LAW 81-874 and 81-815. 1st–   [Annual]

        Earlier HE 5.1/2
        Later ED 1.1/2

HE 19.101/3:date   • Item 461-C-3
ANNUAL EVALUATION REPORT ON PROGRAMS ADMINISTERED BY THE U.S. OFFICE OF EDUCATION.

        Later ED 1.39

HE 19.102:CT   • Item 461
GENERAL PUBLICATIONS.

        Earlier HE 5.2

HE 19.106:CT   • Item 461-A
REGULATIONS, RULES AND INSTRUCTIONS. [Irregular]

        Earlier HE 5.6

HE 19.108:CT   • Item 461-B-1
HANDBOOKS, MANUALS, GUIDES. [Irregular]

        Formerly distributed to depository libraries under Item 461-A.
        Earlier HE 5.6/2
        EXPLORING CAREERS, A STUDENT GUIDEBOOK (subseries).

        PURPOSE:– To help secondary school students appraise the pros and cons of a variety of careers. Each booklet provides readers with advice from working professionals, answers to frequently-asked questions, information on qualifications, duties and responsibilities, and down-to-earth advice on employment opportunities and salaries. With the benefit of this guidance on the arts and humanities professions, a high school student is much better equipped to make a long-range decision, and begin shaping education and experience to meet the requirements of a career.

HE 19.108:Ex 7 • Item 461-B-1
EXPLORING DANCE CAREERS. 1976. 23 p. il.

HE 19.108:Ex 7/2 • Item 461-B-1
EXPLORING WRITING CAREERS. 1976. 74 p. il.

HE 19.108:Ex 7/4 • Item 461-B-1
EXPLORING VISUAL ARTS AND CRAFTS
CAREERS. 1976. 162 p. il.

HE 19.108:Ex 7/6 • Item 461-B-1
EXPLORING THEATER AND MEDIA CAREERS.
1976. 138 p. il.

HE 19.108:Ex 7/8 • Item 461-B-1
EXPLORING CAREERS IN THE HUMANITIES.
1976. 175 p. il.

HE 19.108:Ex 7/10 • Item 461-B-1
EXPLORING MUSIC CAREERS. 1976. 67 p. il.

HE 19.108/2:CT • Item 461-A-4
CONSTRUCTION INDUSTRY SERIES. [Irregular]

HE 19.108/3:CT • Item 461-A
CURRICULUM GUIDE SERIES. [Irregular]

HE 19.108/4:date • Item 461-A-13
BASIC EDUCATIONAL OPPORTUNITY GRANT PRO-
GRAM HANDBOOK.

HE 19.109:CT • Item 460-A-14
EDUCATION AROUND THE WORLD (series). [Irregu-
lar]

    Indexed by: Index to U.S. Government Peri-
    odicals.
    Later ED 1.36

HE 19.110:CT • Item 455-C
ADDRESSES. [Irregular]

    Earlier HE 5.8

HE 19.111:nos. • Item 461-A-5
MONOGRAPHS ON EVALUATION IN EDUCATION. 1–
[Irregular]

    Later ED 1.15

HE 19.111/2:CT • Item 461-A-7
MONOGRAPHS ON CAREER EDUCATION (series).
[Irregular]

HE 19.112:date • Item 460-A-14
OPPORTUNITIES FOR TEACHERS ABROAD.

    Continues Teacher Exchange Opportunities
    under the International Educational Exchange
    Program (HE 5.214:14047).
    ISSN 0078-5458

HE 19.113:date • Item 460
EDUCATION DIRECTORY: EDUCATION ASSOCIA-
TIONS. [Annual]

    The first section covers, in a single alphabet,
    the following types of associations:

    1) Associations of educators and other persons
       directly concerned with schools and colleges.
    2) Community health, service, or social welfare
       groups that relate certain of their activities to
       school and college programs.
    3) Historical, learned, professional, research and
       scientific organizations growing out of or re-
       lated to school and college activities.
    4) Library and museum associations.
    5) Organizations sponsoring youth activities in
       schools and colleges or supplementing school
       or college programs.
       The other sections list:
    6) College professional fraternities, honor societ-
       ies, and recognized societies (national).
    7) State education associations.
    8) Foundations.
    9) Religious education associations.
    10) International education associations.
       Subject Index.
       ISSN 0160-0508
       Earlier HE 5.25
       Later ED 1.30

HE 19.114:date • Item 456-A
INSTRUCTIONAL EQUIPMENT GRANTS TITLE VI-A,
HIGHER EDUCATION ACT OF 1975, PL 89-329.
(Office of Libraries and Learning Resources) [An-
nual]

HE 19.115:v.nos.&nos. • Item 455-B
AMERICAN EDUCATION. [10 times a year]

    ISSN 0002-8304
    Prior to November 1974 classified HE 5.75
    Later ED 1.10

    INDEX.

        v. 1– 3. December 1964– November 1967.
    4 p. il.

HE 19.116:CT • Item 456-B
NATIONAL ADVISORY COUNCIL FOR CAREER EDU-
CATION: PUBLICATIONS. [Irregular]

HE 19.117:date • Item 461-B
NATIONAL ADVISORY COMMITTEE ON THE HANDI-
CAPPED: ANNUAL REPORT. 1st–   1974–

    Earlier HE 5.86/2

HE 19.117/2:date • Item 461-B
REPORT TO CONGRESS ON IMPLEMENTATION OF
PUBLIC LAW 94-142. [Annual]

    Report made by the Office of Education to
    Congress pursuant to the Education for All Handi-
    capped Children Act of 1975 (P.L. 94-142; 89
    Stat. 795). Report covers activities of the estab-
    lished centers on educational media and materi-
    als for the handicapped at various institutions of
    higher education, State and local educational
    agencies, and other appropriate non-profit agen-
    cies. These centers are contracted to design,
    develop, and adapt instructional materials to al-
    low handicapped persons to use new educational
    technology.

HE 19.118:CT
SUGGESTED TWO-YEAR POST-HIGH SCHOOL CUR-
RICULUMS (series).

    Earlier HE 5.6/2

HE 19.119:date • Item 461-C-1
CLOSER LOOK. [Semiannual] (National Information
Center for the Handicapped)

    Later ED 1.22

HE 19.120:nos. • Item 453-A
RESEARCH RELATING TO CHILDREN, BULLETINS.
1–   1949–

    Each issue covers a particular subject, list-
    ing all research projects which have been re-
    ported to the Children's Bureau Clearinghouse for
    Research in Child Life since 1948. Abstracts of
    most of the projects listed were included in the
    Clearinghouse publication, Research Relating to
    Children.
    Earlier HE 21.112

HE 19.121:nos. • Item 461-C-2
VOCATIONAL EDUCATION INFORMATION (series).

HE 19.122:date • Item 455-A-1 (MF)
USES OF STATE ADMINISTERED FEDERAL EDUCA-
TION FUNDS. 1st–   1975–   [Annual]

    Issued in 3 volumes: v. 1, State Administra-
    tion and Uses of Federal Grants for Education; v.
    2, Summary Presentation of Data on State Uses
    of Federal Grants for Education; and v. 3, Indi-
    vidual State Reports on Uses of Federal Grants
    for Education.
    Former title: State Administered Federal Edu-
    cation Funds.

HE 19.123:CT
EDUCATION BRIEFING PAPERS.

    Earlier HE 5.44/2

HE 19.124:date • Item 460-A-58
COMMISSIONER'S REPORT ON THE EDUCATION
PROFESSIONS.

    Each volume also has a distinctive title.
    ISSN 0148-5415

HE 19.125:date • Item 455-A-2
IGHT TO READ. [Annual]

    1976 Independence Through Literacy.
    Later ED 1.12

HE 19.126:date • Item 460-A-22
PUBLIC SCHOOL FINANCE PROGRAMS. [Annual]

    Earlier HE 5.73/2

HE 19.127:date • Item 455-A-3
CATALOG OF FEDERAL EDUCATION ASSISTANCE
PROGRAMS. [Biennial]

    Later ED 1.29
    ISSN 0097-7802

HE 19.128:CT • Item 455-D
BIBLIOGRAPHIES AND LISTS OF PUBLICATIONS.
[Irregular]

    Earlier HE 5.10
    Later ED 1.117

HE 19.128:W 84/2/v.nos.&nos. • Item 455-D
RESOURCES IN WOMEN'S EDUCATION EQUITY.
v. 1–   1977–   [Irregular] (Far West Laboratory for Educational Research and Development)

    Later ED 1.17/2

HE 19.129:nos. • Item 455-A-4
WS [Work-Study] REPORTS.

    College Work Study Program awards.
    Later ED 1.74

HE 19.130:date • Item 455-A-5
ADVISORY COMMITTEE ON ACCREDITATION AND
INSTITUTIONAL ELIGIBILITY: ANNUAL REPORT.
1st–

    Later ED 1.13

HE 19.131:date • Item 455-I (MF)
ADVISORY COUNCIL ON FINANCIAL AID TO
STUDENTS: ANNUAL REPORT.

HE 19.132:date • Item 455-A-6
COMMUNITY EDUCATION PROJECT DESCRIPTION
FOR FISCAL YEAR. [Annual]

    Superseded by Directory of Community Edu-
    cation Projects (HE 19.132/3).
    ISSN 0148-7116

HE 19.132/2:nos. • Item 455-A-7
COMMUNITY EDUCATION ADVISORY COUNCIL:
REPORTS. 1–   [Irregular]

HE 19.132/3:date • Item 455-A-13
DIRECTORY OF COMMUNITY EDUCATION
PROJECTS. [Annual]

    PURPOSE:– To identify and summarize com-
    munity education projects funded during the year.
    Continues: Community Education Project De-
    scriptions (HE 19.132).
    ISSN 0161-9047
    Later ED 1.20

HE 19.133:date • Item 455-J
PROGRESS OF EDUCATION IN THE U.S. OF
AMERICA.

    Report for the Conference of Education, spon-
    sored by the United Nations Educational, Scien-
    tific, and Cultural Organization, International Bu-
    reau of Education.
    Earlier HE 19.102:P 94
    Later ED 1.41

HE 19.134:CT • **Item 455-A-8**
OCCUPATIONAL HOME ECONOMICS EDUCATION SERIES. [Irregular]

HE 19.135:date • **Item 455-A-9**
HIGHER EDUCATION ACT TITLE 2-B, LIBRARY RESEARCH AND DEMONSTRATION PROGRAM, ABSTRACTS, FISCAL YEAR (date). [Annual]

HE 19.136:date • **Item 455-A-10**
WOMEN'S EDUCATIONAL EQUITY ACT. 1st– 1976–
[Annual]

Later ED 1.44
ISSN 0161-066X

HE 19.137:nos. • **Item 455-A-11**
TECHNICAL REPORTS FROM THE STUDY OF THE SUSTAINING EFFECTS OF COMPENSATORY EDUCATION ON BASIC SKILLS. 1– 1977–
[Irregular]

HE 19.138:date • **Item 455-A-12**
BFSA BULLETIN. 1978– [Monthly] (Bureau of Student Financial Assistance)

PURPOSE:– To provide a newsletter covering legislation and Federal programs related to student financial assistance.
Later ED 1.3/2

HE 19.139:date • **Item 455-A-14**
AWARDS, HIGHER EDUCATION ACT OF 1965 (P.L. 89-329) AS AMENDED TITLE 3, STRENGTHENING DEVELOPING INSTITUTIONS. [Annual]

Lists the Basic International Development Program awards for the fiscal year, giving the name of institution and amount of the grant.
Earlier HE 5.92/2

HE 19.139/2:date • **Item 455-A-17**
STRENGTHENING DEVELOPING INSTITUTIONS, TITLE 3 OF THE HIGHER EDUCATION ACT OF 1965, ANNUAL REPORT. (Advisory Council on Developing Institutions)

ISSN 0094-1751

HE 19.140:date • **Item 455-A-15**
NATIONAL ADVISORY COMMITTEE ON BLACK HIGHER EDUCATION AND BLACK COLLEGES AND UNIVERSITIES: ANNUAL REPORT. 1st– 1977–

Later ED 1.21

HE 19.141:CT • **Item 461**
IMPLEMENTING TITLE IX AND ATTAINING SEX-EQUITY: A WORKSHOP PACKAGE FOR POST-SECONDARY EDUCATORS. [Irregular]

HE 19.141/2:CT • **Item 461**
IMPLEMENTING TITLE IX AND ATTAINING SEX-EQUITY: A WORKSHOP FOR ELEMENTARY- SECONDARY EDUCATORS. [Irregular]

HE 19.142:date • **Item 455-A-16**
CATALOG OF ADULT EDUCATION PROJECTS. [Annual]

PURPOSE:– To provide information about the adult education programs funded under Section 306(a)(4) and 309 of the Adult Education Act of 1966, as amended.

HE 19.143:nos. • **Item 461-D-2**
INFORMATION SERIES. 1– [Irregular]

Earlier HE 18.11/2

HE 19.144:nos.
PAPERS IN EDUCATION FINANCE.

HE 19.145:date • **Item 455-F**
ACCREDITED POSTSECONDARY INSTITUTIONS AND PROGRAMS, (year). [Annual]

Earlier HE 5.96/3
Later ED 1.38

HE 19.146:CT
AUDIOVISUAL MATERIALS. [Irregular]

NATIONAL INSTITUTE OF EDUCATION (1972– 1979)

CREATION AND AUTHORITY

The National Institute of Education was established within the Education Division by the Education Amendments of 1972, effective June 23, 1972 (86 Stat. 327).

For the period 1972– 1975, the Institute's publications were assigned to the HE 18 class.

The Institute was transferred to the Department of Education (ED 1.300) pursuant to the Department of Education Organization Act (93 Stat. 668), approved October 17, 1979.

HE 19.201:date
ANNUAL REPORT.

Later ED 1.301

HE 19.202:CT • **Item 461-D-5**
GENERAL PUBLICATIONS.

Later ED 1.302

HE 19.208:CT • **Item 455-G-4**
HANDBOOKS, MANUALS, GUIDES. [Irregular]

Later ED 1.308

HE 19.208:H 53 • **Item 455-G-4**
HIGHER EDUCATION PLANNING, A BIBLIOGRAPHIC HANDBOOK. [Irregular]

Basic volumes kept up-to-date by supplements.

HE 19.209:v.nos.&nos. • **Item 455-G-1 (MF)**
INFORMATION, QUARTERLY NEWSLETTER OF THE NATIONAL INSTITUTE OF EDUCATION. v. 1– 1974–

Later ED 1.318

HE 19.209/2:v.nos.&nos.
NAEP NEWSLETTER. [Quarterly]

NAEP = National Assessment of Educational Progress.
Later ED 1.316

HE 19.210:v.nos.&nos. • **Item 466-A**
RESOURCES IN EDUCATION. [Monthly]

ISSN 0098-0897
Earlier HE 18.10
Later ED 1.11

HE 19.211:nos. • **Item 455-G-3**
INTERPRETIVE REPORTS. 1– 1975–

HE 19.212:nos. • **Item 455-G-5**
NIE PAPERS IN EDUCATION AND WORK. 1– 1976– [Irregular]

HE 19.213:CT • **Item 455-G-6**
BIBLIOGRAPHIES AND LISTS OF PUBLICATIONS. [Irregular]

Later ED 1.317

HE 19.214:date • **Item 455-G-7**
NATIONAL COUNCIL ON EDUCATION RESEARCH: ANNUAL REPORT.

Later ED 1.315

HE 19.215:nos. • **Item 455-G-8**
R AND D SYSTEMS STUDIES: TECHNICAL REPORTS. 1– [Irregular]

HE 19.216:date • **Item 455-G-9**
GRANTS COMPETITIONS AND RFPS: PLANNED NIE ACTIVITIES DURING THE FISCAL YEAR. [Annual]

HE 19.125:date • **Item 455-A-2**
RPURPOSE:– To provide information on who may receive awards, and eligible areas of research. Lists funding activities being planned during the year, with name and telephone numbers of persons to contact for more information, and announcement date of request for proposal.

HE 19.216/2:date • **Item 455-G-9**
FUNDING OPPORTUNITIES AT NIE, GRANTS COMPETITIONS AND REQUESTS FOR PROPOSALS IN FISCAL YEAR. [Annual]

Later ED 1.321

HE 19.218:nos. • **Item 461-D-1 (MF)**
RESEARCH AND DEVELOPMENT SERIES. 1– [Irregular] (Center for Vocational and Technical Education)

Earlier HE 18.11

HE 19.219:nos. • **Item 455-G-10**
VOCATIONAL EDUCATION STUDY PUBLICATIONS. 1– 1979– [Irregular]

Later ED 1.314

HE 19.220:CT • **Item 461-D-5**
WOMEN'S STUDIES, MONOGRAPH SERIES. [Irregular]

Later ED 1.312

NATIONAL CENTER FOR EDUCATIONAL STATISTICS (1972– 1979)

CREATION AND AUTHORITY

The National Center for Educational Statistics was established within the Education Division by the Education Amendments of 1972, effective June 23, 1972 (86 Stat. 327).

For the period 1972– 1975, the Center's publications were assigned to the HE 5 class.

The Center was transferred to the Department of Education (ED 1.100) Pursuant to the Department of Education Organization Act (93 Stat. 668), approved on October 17, 1979.

HE 19.301:date
ANNUAL REPORT.

HE 19.302:CT • **Item 461-A-1**
GENERAL PUBLICATIONS. [Irregular]

HE 19.302:St 2/2/date • **Item 461-A-1**
STATISTICS OF TRENDS IN EDUCATION. [Annual]

HE 19.303 • **Item 461-A-14**
BULLETINS.

HE 19.308:CT • **Item 461-A-3**
HANDBOOKS, MANUALS, GUIDES.

HE 19.308/2 • **Item 460-A-23**
STATE EDUCATIONAL RECORDS AND REPORTS SERIES. HANDBOOKS. 1– [Irregular]
Earlier FS 5.223

HE 19.309:CT • **Item 461-A-2**
HEGIS [Higher Education General Information Survey] IX REQUIREMENTS AND SPECIFICATIONS FOR SURVEYS OF [various subjects]. [Irregular]

HE 19.310:date • **Item 460-A-51**
INVENTORY OF PHYSICAL FACILITIES IN INSTITUTIONS OF HIGHER EDUCATION, FALL (year). [Annual]

Earlier HE 5.92/3

HE 19.311:CT • Item 455-H
SPONSORED REPORTS SERIES.

Earlier HE 5.290

HE 19.311:L 61 • Item 455-H
SURVEY OF FEDERAL LIBRARIES. [Irregular]

PURPOSE:– To provide a uniform and comprehensive statistical reporting system for Federal libraries. Contains data on operating expenditures, adequacy of holdings, size of staff, types of services, scope of users, organizational patterns, and other data essential for management decisions.
Earlier HE 5.290

HE 19.312:nos. • Item 461-A-8
NATIONAL ASSESSMENT OF EDUCATION PROGRESS: REPORTS.

Earlier HE 5.2:As 7
Later ED 1.118

HE 19.312:08-BLS (nos.) • Item 461-A-8
BASIC LIFE SKILLS REPORTS. 1– [Irregular] (National Assessment of Educational Progress, Suite 700, 1860 Lincoln Street, Denver, Colorado 80295)

HE 19.312/2:CT • Item 461-A-8
NATIONAL ASSESSMENT OF EDUCATIONAL PROGRESS [reports] (unnumbered).

Later ED 1.309

HE 19.313:date • Item 460-A-22
EXPENDITURES AND REVENUES FOR PUBLIC ELEMENTARY AND SECONDARY EDUCATION. 1973– [Annual] (Division of Survey Planning and Analysis, Elementary and Secondary Surveys Branch)

At head of title: Elementary and Secondary Education.
More detailed expenditure and revenue data published in Statistics of State School Systems (HE 19.318/3).
Title varies.
Earlier HE 5.93/3
Later ED 1.119

HE 19.314:date • Item 461-A-12
CONDITION OF EDUCATION. 1st– 1975– [Annual]

The report on the condition of education in America is submitted by the Secretary of Health, Education, and Welfare to Congress in accordance with section 406(d)(1) of the Education Amendments of 1974. The report includes a statistical examination of the Condition of Education and a programmatic review of the activities of the National Center for Education Statistics.
ISSN 0098-4752
Later E 1.109

HE 19.315:date • Item 460-A-10
DIGEST OF EDUCATIONAL STATISTICS. 1962– [Annual]

Earlier HE 5.98
Later ED 1.113

HE 19.316:date • Item 460-A-52
FINANCIAL STATISTICS OF INSTITUTIONS OF HIGHER EDUCATION: PROPERTY. [Annual]

ISSN 0566-5744
Earlier HE 5.92/10-2

HE 19.316/2:date • Item 460-A-52
FINANCIAL STATISTICS OF INSTITUTIONS OF HIGHER EDUCATION, CURRENT FUNDS, REVENUES, AND EXPENDITURES. [Annual] (Division of Survey Planning and Analysis, Higher Education Surveys Branch)

At head of title: Higher Education.
ISSN 0148-9305
Earlier HE 5.92/10
Later ED 1.116

HE 19.316/2-2:date • Item 460-A-52
FINANCIAL STATISTICS OF INSTITUTIONS OF HIGHER EDUCATION, FY 1977.

This class has been cancelled. See HE 19.316/ 2 .

HE 19.317:CT • Item 455-D
BIBLIOGRAPHIES AND LISTS OF PUBLICATIONS. [Irregular]

Earlier HE 5.10
Later ED 1.114

HE 19.317:P 96 • Item 455-D
PUBLICATIONS OF THE NATIONAL CENTER FOR EDUCATION STATISTICS. [List]. [Irregular]

HE 19.318:date • Item 460-A-20
STATISTICS OF PUBLIC SCHOOLS, ADVANCE REPORT, FALL. 1st– [Annual]

PURPOSE:– To make available at an early date some of the data obtained in the annual fall survey of elementary and secondary day schools. Includes data on pupils, teachers, school districts, schools, schoolhousing, and anticipated expenditures for the 50 States, the District of Columbia, and the outlying areas of the United States.
Earlier HE 5.93/5

HE 19.318/2:date • Item 460-A-22
STATISTICS OF LOCAL PUBLIC SCHOOL SYSTEMS, FINANCE, (year). 1st– 1967– [Annual]

PURPOSE:– To present reliable quantitative financial data on individual local public school systems for planning, policy, and research purposes.
Earlier HE 5.93/8-2

HE 19.318/3:date • Item 460-A-20
STATISTICS OF STATE SCHOOL SYSTEMS. [Annual]

Presents basic data on the organization, staffing, enrollment, and financing of public elementary and secondary day schools.
Periodic statistical reports on elementary and secondary education by the Office of Education began with the school year 1869/70. Statistics for the school years 1869/70 through 1915/16 were included as part of the Annual Report of the United States Commissioner of Education. For years 1917/18 through 1957/58, a report was issued biennially for each school year ending in an even number as Chapter 2 of the Biennial Survey of Education in the United States.
Preliminary summary data are published earlier in Preliminary Statistics of State School Systems.
Earlier HE 5.93/10

HE 19.318/4:date • Item 460-A-20
STATISTICS OF LOCAL PUBLIC SCHOOL SYSTEMS: PUPILS AND STAFF. [Annual]

Earlier HE 5.93/8

HE 19.319:date • Item 460-A-13
ADULT BASIC AND SECONDARY LEVEL PROGRAM STATISTICS, STUDENTS AND STAFF DATA. [Annual]

Earlier HE 5.97

HE 19.320:date • Item 460-A-10
PROJECTIONS OF EDUCATIONAL STATISTICS. 1st– 1964– [Annual]

PURPOSE:– To provide a 10-year projection of statistics for elementary and secondary schools and institutions of higher education. These statistics include enrollments, graduates, teachers, and expenditures.
Earlier HE 5.291

HE 19.321:date • Item 455-F
VOCATIONAL EDUCATION: SCHOOLS FOR CAREERS, AN ANALYSIS OF OCCUPATIONAL COURSES OFFERED BY SECONDARY AND POSTSECONDARY SCHOOLS.

HE 19.322:date • Item 460-A-50
INSTITUTIONS OF HIGHER EDUCATION, INDEX BY STATE AND CONGRESSIONAL DISTRICT. [Annual

Earlier HE 5.92/4
Later ED 1.116/2

HE 19.323:date • Item 460-A-22
BOND SALES FOR PUBLIC SCHOOL PURPOSES. [Annual]

Earlier HE 5.93/2

HE 19.324:date • Item 460
EDUCATION DIRECTORY: COLLEGES AND UNIVERSITIES. 1974/75– [Annual] (Division of Survey Planning and Analysis, Higher Education Surveys Branch)

Lists institutions in the United States and its outlying areas that offer at least a 2-year program of college-level studies in residence or, if nonresident in nature, that are accredited or pre-accredited by an accrediting agency recognized for such purpose by the U.S. Commission of Education.
Previous title: Education Directory, Higher Education
Also available on computer tape.
Earlier HE 5.25

HE 19.324/2:date • Item 460
EDUCATION DIRECTORY: PUBLIC SCHOOL SYSTEMS. [Annual]

PURPOSE:– To list all local agencies providing free public elementary and secondary education in the United States, by State.
ISSN 0083-2677
Earlier HE 5.25

HE 19.324/3:date • Item 460
EDUCATION DIRECTORY: STATE EDUCATION AGENCY OFFICIALS.

At head of title: Elementary and Secondary Education.
Earlier HE 5.25
Later ED 1.111/3

HE 19.325:date • Item 460-A-54
FALL ENROLLMENT IN HIGHER EDUCATION (year). [Annual]

At head of title: Higher Education.
Publication first issued in 1946. Title varies, 1946–1957.
Earlier HE 5.92/6
Later ED 1.124

HE 19.325/2:date • Item 460-A-54
POSTSECONDARY EDUCATION FALL ENROLLMENT IN HIGHER EDUCATION (year): INSTITUTIONAL DATA. [Annual]

ISSN 0095-8182
Earlier HE 5.92/6

HE 19.326:date • Item 460-A-20
STATISTICS OF PUBLIC ELEMENTARY AND SECONDARY DAY SCHOOLS. 1954– [Annual]

Earlier HE 5.93
Later ED 1.112

HE 19.327:date • Item 460-A-20
PREPRIMARY ENROLLMENT, OCTOBER (year). [Annual]

Earlier HE 593/7
Later ED 1.112/5

HE 19.328:date • Item 455-G-2
HIGHER EDUCATION BASIC STUDENT CHARGES. [Annual]

HE 19.329:date • Item 460-A-54
EARNED DEGREES CONFERRED. [Annual]

Earlier HE 5.92/5
Later ED 1.117

HE 19.330:date   • **Item 460-A-54**
STUDENTS ENROLLED FOR ADVANCED DEGREES.
1st–   1959–   [Annual] (Division of Survey
Planning and Analysis, Higher Education Surveys
Branch)

Presents student enrollment data for advanced degrees in over 300 discipline specialties
intended to cover the entire range of instructional
programs in higher education.
At head of title: Higher Education.
Earlier HE 5.92/12

HE 19.331:date   • **Item 461-A-9**
ANNUAL CONFERENCE ON HIGHER EDUCATION,
GENERAL INFORMATION SURVEY (HEGIS). 1st–

11th. June 2-4, 1975. Arlington, Va.

HE 19.332:date   • **Item 460-A-53**
SALARIES AND FRINGE BENEFITS. [Annual]

Earlier HE 5.253:53015

HE 19.333:date   • **Item 460-A-54**
ASSOCIATE DEGREES AND OTHER FORMAL
AWARDS BELOW THE BACCALAUREATE.
[Annual]

Earlier HE 5.92/8

HE 19.334:date   • **Item 461-A-10**
SUMMARY OF OFFERINGS AND ENROLLMENTS IN
PUBLIC AND SECONDARY SCHOOLS. [Annual]

HE 19.334/2:date   • **Item 461-A-10**
COURSE OFFERING, ENROLLMENTS, AND CUR-
RICULUM, PRACTICES IN PUBLIC SECONDARY
SCHOOLS.

HE 19.335:date   • **Item 461-A-11**
NEGLECTED OR DELINQUENT CHILDREN LIVING
IN STATE OPERATED OR SUPPORTED INSTITU-
TIONS. [Annual]

HE 19.336:date
SOCIAL AND ECONOMIC CHARACTERISTICS OF U.S.
SCHOOL DISTRICTS. [Annual]

HE 19.337:date   • **Item 455-F**
DIRECTORY OF POSTSECONDARY SCHOOLS WITH
OCCUPATIONAL PROGRAMS. 1971–   [Bien-
nial]

PURPOSE:– To provide a comprehensive listing of postsecondary schools and institutions
offering career-related programs, i.e. vocational
schools. Two-year and four-year colleges and
universities are listed if they offer occupational
programs that lead to a certificate or degree at
less than the baccalaureate level.
ISSN 0190-0420
Earlier HE 5.96/2

HE 19.337/2:date   • **Item 455-F**
OCCUPATIONAL EDUCATION ENROLLMENTS AND
PROGRAMS IN NONCOLLEGIATE POST
SECONDARY SCHOOLS. [Annual]

ISSN 0146-6496
Later ED 1.110

HE 19.338:date   • **Item 460-A-15**
LIBRARY STATISTICS OF COLLEGES AND UNIVER-
SITIES. [Annual]

Earlier HE 5.92/7
Later ED 1.122

OFFICE OF PUBLIC HEALTH AND SCIENCE
(1970–   )

CREATION AND AUTHORITY

The Public Health Service (FS 2) was transferred from the Federal Security Agency to the
newly established Department of Health, Education, and Welfare, effective April 11, 1953. [Dur-
ing the period 1953 through 1969, SuDocs class
FS 2 was used.]

INFORMATION

Office of the Secretary
Office of Public Health and Science
Department of Health and Human Services
200 Independence Ave., SW, Rm. 716-G
Washington, D. C. 20201
(202) 690-7694
http://www.osophs.dhhs.gov/ophs

HE 20.1:date
ANNUAL REPORT.

Earlier FS 2.1

HE 20.1/2:date   • **Item 483-A-17**
ADMINISTRATION OF PUBLIC HEALTH SERVICE:
REPORT TO CONGRESS. [Annual]

HE 20.1/3:date   • **Item 485-A-1 (MF) (EL)**
OFFICE OF RESEARCH INTEGRITY, ANNUAL RE-
PORT.

HE 20.2:CT   • **Item 485**
GENERAL PUBLICATIONS.

Earlier FS 5.2

HE 20.2:Ad 9/2   • **Item 485**
PHS PUBLIC ADVISORY GROUPS, AUTHORITY,
STRUCTURES, FUNCTIONS. [Irregular] Office
of the Surgeon General, Committee Management Office.

Earlier FS 2.2:Ad 9/2

HE 20.2:Ad 9/3   • **Item 485**
ROSTER OF MEMBERS OF PHS PUBLIC ADVI-
SORY GROUPS, COUNCILS, COM- MITTEES,
BOARDS, PANELS, STUDY SECTIONS.
[Irregular]

Earlier FS 2.2:Ad 9/3

HE 20.2:C 16/5   • **Item 485**
CANCER SERVICES, FACILITIES AND PRO-
GRAMS IN UNITED STATES. 1950– 1968.
[Irregular] (Publication 14)

Earlier FS 2.2:C 16/5

HE 20.2:D 54/7   • **Item 485**
DIGEST OF PREPAID DENTAL CARE PLANS.
1957–   [Irregular]

(Publication 585)
Earlier FS 2.2:D 54/7

HE 20.2:F 67/8   • **Item 485**
ANNUAL FLUORIDATION CENSUS REPORT.
[Annual]

Division of Dental Public Health and Resources.
Earlier FS 2.2:F 67/8

HE 20.2:In 25/9   • **Item 485**
INDIAN HEALTH HIGHLIGHTS.

Bureau of Medical Services, Division of
Indian Health.
Earlier FS 2.2:In 25/9

HE 20.2:M 31   • **Item 485**
HEALTH MANPOWER SOURCE BOOK. 1–
1952–   [Irregular]

Earlier FS 2.2:M 31

HE 20.2:P 75/2   • **Item 485**
DIRECTORY, POISON CONTROL CENTERS.
[Irregular]

National Clearinghouse for Poison Control Centers.
Earlier FS 2.2:P 75/2

HE 20.2:T 68/6   • **Item 485**
NATIONAL CONFERENCE ON PUBLIC HEALTH
TRAINING, REPORT TO THE SURGEON
GENERAL. 1st–   (Publication 1728)

Report submitted in pursuance of section
306(e) of the Public Health Service Act by
the chairman to the Surgeon General.
Contains conference recommendations.
Appendix contains legislation, conference organization, selected statistical data, list of
conferees, and conference personnel.
Earlier FS 2.2:T 68/6

HE 20.2:T 69   • **Item 485**
HEALTH INFORMATION FOR TRAVEL IN [area].
[Irregular]

Issued for the following areas:
Europe. (Publication 748)
Mexico, Central & South America,
Caribbean. (Publication
748B)
Asia, including Japan, Indonesia,
Philippines, Australia, New
Zealand. (Publication 748C)
Africa, including Malagasy Republic
and neighboring islands.
(Publication 748D)
Earlier FS 2.2:T 69

HE 20.3/2:v.nos./nos.   • **Item 483-I (EL)**
COMMISSIONED CORPS BULLETIN. [Monthly]

HE 20.5:CT
LAWS.

Earlier FS 2.5

HE 20.6:CT   • **Item 499**
REGULATIONS, RULES, INSTRUCTIONS. [Irregular]

HE 20.8:CT   • **Item 496-A**
HANDBOOKS, MANUALS, GUIDES. [Irregular]

HE 20.8/2:date/trans nos.   • **Item 496-A**
PHS GRANTS ADMINISTRATION MANUAL. [Irregular]

HE 20.8/3:nos.   • **Item 496-A**
PHS GRANTS POLICY MEMORANDUM.

HE 20.8/4:date/nos.   • **Item 485-B-2**
PHS DENTAL NOTES. [Quarterly]

PURPOSE:– To present notes and news on
dental activities, research, accomplishments from
the Chief Dental Officer and various components
of the Public Health Service.

HE 20.9:date
LIST OF PUBLICTIONS ISSUED BY PUBLIC HEALTH
SERVICE.

Earlier FS 2.24/2

HE 20.10:nos.   • **Item 486**
HEALTH INFORMATION SERIES (numbered). 1–
1945–   [Irregular]

Popular leaflets on various diseases, illnesses, and health problems. Used as correspondence aids, they average from 4 to 8 pages in
length.
This series is listed in PHS Publication 323, A
List of Health Information Leaflets and Pamphlets
of the Public Health Service.
Supersedes Health Leaflets and Health Education Series.

HE 20.11:nos. • **Item 481-A**
BIBLIOGRAPHY SERIES (numbered). 1– [Irregular]

Earlier FS 2.21

HE 20.11:45 • **Item 481-A**
BILIOGRAPHY ON SMOKING AND HEALTH. [Annual] (National Clearinghouse for Smoking and Health)

HE 20.11/2:CT • **Item 481-A**
BIBLIOGRAPHIES AND LISTS OF PUBLICATIONS. [Irregular]

HE 20.11/3: • **Item 481-A**
ODPHP PUBLICATIONS LIST. [Annual]

ODPHP = Office of Disease Prevention and Health Promotion

HE 20.12:CT • **Item 485-C**
POSTERS. [Irregular]

HE 20.12/2:CT
AUDIOVISUAL MATERIALS.

HE 20.13:nos. • **Item 483-I**
CCPM PAMPHLETS [Commissioned Corps Personnel Manual]. 1– (Office of Personnel)

Earlier FS 2.308

HE 20.13/2:nos. • **Item 483-I**
CC PAMPHLETS. 1– 1969– [Irregular] (Division of Emergency Health Services, Health Services and Mental Health Administration) (Publication 1071-D-8)

PURPOSE:– To help solve the research problems for emergency health and medical planners. Contains summaries of selected current articles on pertinent programs from professional journals and other periodicals, giving original source. Each issue contains a cumulative index.
CC = Commissioned Corps.
Earlier FS 2.320

HE 20.13/3:nos. • **Item 483-I (MF)**
COMMISSIONED CORPS PERSONNEL MANUAL. [Irregular]

HE 20.14:date • **Item 494-A (MF)**
CONFERENCE OF STATE SANITARY ENGINEERS, REPORT OF PROCEEDINGS. 1st– 1920– [Annual]

Earlier HE 20.1010

HE 20.15
JOINT MONOGRAPHS.

HE 20.16:date • **Item 494-F (MF)**
HEALTH STATISTICS PLAN. [Annual]
Each report covers a 5-year plan.
ISSN 0147-0949

HE 20.16/2:date • **Item 494-F**
HEALTH STATISTICS REPORT, FISCAL YEAR (date). [Annual]

HE 20.17:date • **Item 483-A-1 (MF)**
ANNUAL REPORT OF THE HEALTH INSURANCE BENEFITS ADVISORY COUNCIL.

HE 20.18:date • **Item 483-A-2**
FORWARD PLAN FOR HEALTH. [Annual]

HE 20.19:date • **Item 483-A-3 (MF)**
REPORT OF THE UNITED STATES DELEGATION TO THE WORLD HEALTH ASSEMBLY. 1st– 1948– [Annual]

Earlier HE 20.2:H 34/3

HE 20.20:date • **Item 483-A-4 (MF)**
HEALTH MAINTENANCE ORGANIZATIONS. 1st– 1975– [Annual]
Annual report submitted to Congress pursuant to Sec. 1315, Title 13, Public Health Service Act, gives information, statistical tables and charts on grants, contracts, loans, etc., to qualified health maintenance organizations.

HE 20.20/2:v.nos.&nos. • **Item 483-A-5**
FOCUS ON HEALTH MAINTENANCE ORGANIZATIONS. v. 1– 4. 1978– 1981. [10 times year]

PURPOSE:– To help keep health care decision makers and planners abreast of developments concerning Health Maintenance Organizations. Newsletter type of format.

HE 20.21:date • **Item 483-A-8**
HEALTH, UNITED STATES. [Annual]
Earlier HE 20.6018
Later HE 20.6223

HE 20.22:nos. • **Item 485 (MF)**
INTERNATIONAL HEALTH PLANNING METHOD SERIES. 1– 1979– [Irregular]

HE 20.22/2:nos. • **Item 483-A-7**
INTERNATIONAL HEALTH PLANNING REFERENCE SERIES. 1– 1980– [Irregular]

HE 20.23:date • **Item 483-A-6 (MF)**
NATIONAL TOXICOLOGY PROGRAM, REVIEW OF CURRENT DHHS, DOE, AND EPA RESEARCH RELATED TO TOXICOLOGY FISCAL YEAR (date). [Annual]
PURPOSE:– To review the toxicology research, testing, and methods development in progress during the fiscal year.

HE 20.23/2:date • **Item 483-A-6 (MF)**
NATIONAL TOXICOLOGY PROGRAM, ANNUAL PLAN, FISCAL YEAR (date).

PURPOSE:– To present the annual plan for developing scientific information for use in protecting the health of the public from damage by exposure to environmental chemicals.

HE 20.23/3:nos.&nos. • **Item 483-A-9 (MF)**
NTP TECHNICAL BULLETIN. [Quarterly] (National Toxicology Program)

PURPOSE:– To present results of tests performed to protect the public from exposure to harmful environmental chemicals.

HE 20.23/4:date • **Item 483-A-10 (MF)**
ANNUAL REPORT ON CARCINOGENS. 1– 1980–

Highly technical report prepared by the National Toxicology Program, consisting of both narrative and many tales listing substances either presently or expected to be considered carcinogens and to which a significant number of U.S. residents are exposed.

HE 20.24:CT • **Item 483-B-1 (MF)**
CASE STUDIES OF IPA'S [in various cities]. [Irregular]

Each issue presents a case study of a different IPA (Individual Practice Association) health maintenance organization which offers health care insurance.

HE 20.25:date • **Item 483-L-4 (MF)**
DIRECTORY OF ON-GOING RESEARCH IN SMOKING AND HEALTH. 1967– [Annual]

PURPOSE:– To provide a compilation of research studies dealing with the relationship between smoking and health, for use primarily for researchers in the field. Descriptions of on- going activities in the biomedical, behavioral, psychological, and other fields in both the United States and abroad.
For each research project, information includes title, principal investigators, objective, research methodology; results to date, future plans, project dates, source of financial support, and references.
Earlier HE 20.7015 prior to 1980 report.

HE 20.25/2:date • **Item 483-L-6**
HEALTH CONSEQUENCES OF SMOKING. [Annual]

Earlier HE 20.7016

HE 20.25/3:date • **Item 494-H-13 (MF)**
STATE LEGISLATION ON SMOKING AND HEALTH. [Annual]

HE 20.25/4:date • **Item 483-L-7**
STATE AND LOCAL PROGRAMS ON SMOKING AND HEALTH. [Biennial]

PURPOSE:– To list and describe state and local programs designed to reduce smoking among Americans. Includes such programs as cessation clinics, school-based programs, community and patient education.

HE 20.26:CT • **Item 483-A-11**
NCHCT MONOGRAPH SERIES. [Irregular] (National Center for Health Care Technology)

HE 20.27:date • **Item 483-A-12**
NATIONAL HMO CENSUS OF PREPAID PLANS. [Annual]

Consists mainly of tables on the number of prepaid health plans showing such information as total prepaid enrollment, family premiums, and annualized plans, etc.

HE 20.28 • **Item 483-B-2**
OMNIBUS SOLICITATION FOR THE SMALL BUSINESS INNOVATIVE RESEARCH. [Annual]

Later HE 20.3047/2

HE 20.28/2:date • **Item 483-B-2 (MF)**
SOLICITATION OF THE PUBLIC HEALTH SERVICE FOR SMALL BUSINESS RESEARCH (SBIR) CONTRACT PROPOSALS. [Annual]

HE 20.29: • **Item 495-A-1 (MF)**
PREVENTION. [Irregular]

Describes an agenda for national health promotion and disease prevention. Includes health status trends and agency innovations. Contains tables on prevention inventories.
Earlier HE 20.2:P 92

HE 20.29/2:date
PREVENTION REPORT. [Monthly]

HE 20.30:v.nos.&nos. • **Item 497**
PUBLIC HEALTH REPORTS. [Bimonthly]
PURPOSE:– To provide a forum for scientific, technical, administrative and analytical articles of interest to the public health profession.
Earlier HE 20.6011

HE 20.30/a • **Item 497**
– SEPARATES.

HE 20.31:nos. • **Item 483-A-15 (MF)**
PARKLAWN COMPUTER CENTER TECHNICAL NEWS. [Quarterly]

HE 20.32 • **Item 483-A-16 (MF)**
PARKLAWN TRAINING CENTER: TRAINING CATALOG. [Annual]

Training catalog of courses available to PHS employees and managers in such areas as executive-managerial-supervisory communication skills and data technology.

HE 20.32/2:date • **Item 483-A-16**
PARKLAWN TRAINING CENTER, QUARTERLY CALENDAR.

No longer a depository item. For internal/administrative use only, under 44 U.S.C. section 1902.

HE 20.33:date • **Item 532-E-9**
FAMILY PLANNING GRANTEES, DELEGATES, AND
CLINICS DIRECTORY. [Annual]

Earlier HE 20.5119/3

HE 20.34 • **Item 485-B**
ODPHP MONOGRAPH SERIES. [Irregular]

ODPHP = Office of Disease Prevention and
Health Promotion.

HE 20.34/2:date • **Item 485-B-1 (MF)**
ODPHP-HEALTHFINDER. [6 times a year]

ODPHP = Office of Disease Prevention and
Health Promotion.
Each issue contains an annotated bibliography in a different health area.

HE 20.35:ltrs./nos. • **Item 485-D**
FORMS. [Irregular]

HE 20.36:date
MEMORANDUM TO ALL NURSES IN THE PUBLIC
HEALTH SERVICE. [Quarterly]

HE 20.36/2: • **Item 485-E**
THE PHYSICIANS MEMORANDUM. [Irregular]

Memorandum from the Chief Physician Officer of the Public Health Service to PHS physicians on miscellaneous topics.
Discontinued.

HE 20.37: • **Item 485-F (MF)**
HEALTH INFORMATION RESOURCES IN THE FEDERAL GOVERNMENT. [Irregular]

This directory encompasses selected federal
and federally sponsored health information resources. Although not a comprehensive listing, it
will direct the user to a central source of information for each agency or department cited. Contains a resource and a subject index.

HE 20.38: • **Item 485-G**
FACT SHEET (series).
An individual issue may present facts on the
Public Health Service as a whole or on a particular component, such as the National Institute of
Health.

HE 20.38/2:CT • **Item 485-H**
NATIONAL ACTION PLAN ON BREAST CANCER FACT
SHEETS (series).

HE 20.39:CT • **Item 483-L-4**
DIRECTORIES.

HE 20.40:date • **Item 485-A-2 (EL)**
CLOSING THE GAP, WAGING WAR ON VIOLENCE.
[Bimonthly]

HE 20.40/2 • **Item 485-A-3 (EL)**
HIV IMPACT. [Quarterly]

HE 20.41/2 • **Item 485-A-4**
OFFICE ON WOMEN'S HEALTH-GENERAL PUBLICATIONS.

PRESIDENT'S COUNCIL ON PHYSICAL FITNESS AND SPORTS (1978–   )

INFORMATION

President's Council on Physical
Fitness and Sports
Department of Health and Human Services
Department W
200 Independence Avenue, SW, Rm. 738-H
Washington, DC 20201-0004
(202) 690-9000
Fax: (202) 690-5211
http://www.fitness.gov

HE 20.102:CT • **Item 484-D-3**
GENERAL PUBLICATIONS. [Irregular]

Earlier Pr 37.8:P 56/2

HE 20.108:CT • **Item 484-D-3**
HANDBOOKS, MANUALS, GUIDES.

Earlier Pr 37.8:P 56/2

HE 20.109:date • **Item 484-D-2**
NEWSLETTER. 1963–   [Bimonthly]

PURPOSE:– To keep persons involved in fitness, sports, athletic and recreation programs
informed about Council activities and programs,
and to report and inform readers of other developments in the fitness, sports and recreation
fields.
ISSN 0364-8079
Earlier Pr 37.8:P 56/2/N 47

HE 20.110:series nos.&nos. • **Item 585-D-1**
PHYSICAL FITNESS RESEARCH DIGEST. Series 1–
[Quarterly]

Each issue includes a detailed article with list
of references on a subject related to physical
fitness, such as jogging, swimming, muscular
power of the legs, etc.
ISSN 0094-9108
Earlier Pr 37.8:P 56/2/4 31/2

HE 20.111:v.nos.&nos. • **Item 484-D-2**
PHYSICAL FITNESS/SPORTS MEDICINE BIBLIOGRAPHY. v. 1–   [Quarterly]

PURPOSE:– To present bibliographic listings
on exercise physiology, sport injuries, physical
conditioning, and other medical aspects of exercise.
ISSN 0163-2582

HE 20.112:CT • **Item 484-D-4**
BIBLIOGRAPHIES AND LISTS OF PUBLICATIONS.
[Irregular]

HE 20.113:CT • **Item 484-D-5**
POSTERS.

HE 20.114 • **Item 484-D-6 (EL)**
PRESIDENT'S COUNCIL ON PHYSICAL FITNESS AND
SPORTS: RESEARCH DIGESTS.

NATIONAL CENTER FOR HEALTH CARE TECHNOLOGY

INFORMATION

National Center for Health Care Technology
Department of Health and Human Services
Room 310
5600 Fishers Lane
Rockville, Maryland 20857
(301) 443-4990

HE 20.201:date
ANNUAL REPORT.

HE 20.202:CT • **Item 483-A-14**
GENERAL PUBLICATIONS. [Irregular]

HE 20.209:CT • **Item 483-A-11 (MF)**
MONOGRAPH SERIES. [Irregular]

HE 20.210:v.nos.&nos. • **Item 483-A-13**
FACT SHEETS. v. 1–   1981–   [Irregular]

Single sheets, each devoted to a single subject.

INDIAN HEALTH SERVICE (1991–   )

INFORMATION

Communications Office
Indian Health Service
Department of Health and Human Services
The Reyes Bldg.
801 Thompson Ave., Ste. 400
Rockville, MD 20852-1627
(301) 443-3593
Fax: (301) 443-4794
http://www.ihs.gov

HE 20.302:CT • **Item 486-I-2**
GENERAL PUBLICATIONS.

Earlier HE 20.9402

HE 20.308:CT • **Item 486-K-1**
HANDBOOKS, MANUALS, GUIDES. [Irregular]

Earlier HE 20.9408

HE 20.309 • **Item 486-S-2**
BIBLIOGRAPHIES AND LISTS OF PUBLICATIONS.

HE 20.310: • **Item 486-S-3**
DIRECTORIES.

HE 20.310/2 • **Item 486-M-1 (MF)**
INDIAN HEALTH SERVICE DIRECTORY. [Semiannual]
Earlier HE 20.9412/2

HE 20.310/3: • **Item 486-S-7**
NAVAJO NATION & REGIONAL AREAS RESOURCE
DIRECTORY. [Biennial].

HE 20.311: • **Item 486-S-5**
MAPS.

HE 20.312: • **Item 486-S-4**
POSTERS.

HE 20.313: • **Item 486-S-6**
FORMS.

HE 20.315 • **Item 486-M-2 (MF)**
MONOGRAPH SERIES.

HE 20.316 • Item 486-I-3 (MF) (EL)
TRENDS IN INDIAN HEALTH. [Annual]
Earlier HE 20.9421

HE 20.317:date • Item 486-S-1
SCHOLARSHIP PROGRAM, APPLICANT INFORMATION INSTRUCTION BOOKLET. [Annual]

Explains the terms of Indian Health Scholarships received during the school year. The purpose of the Scholarship Program is to obtain health professional to meet the staffing needs of the Indian Health Service. Includes required application forms.
Earlier HE 20.9418

HE 20.317/2:date • Item 486-I-8
APPLICATION KIT TRIBAL MANAGEMENT GRANTS, ETC., FY [DATE] TRIBAL MANAGEMENT GRANT PROGRAM ANNOUNCEMENT.

HE 20.318 • Item 486-I-7 (MF)
CHR PROGRAM UPDATE. [Quarterly]

HE 20.319:date • Item 486-T-1 (P) (EL)
REGIONAL DIFFERENCES IN INDIAN HEALTH.

HE 20.320 • Item 486-S-1 (EL)
THE IHS PRIMARY CARE PROVIDER. [Monthly]

SUBSTANCE ABUSE AND MENTAL HEALTH SERVICES ADMINISTRATION (1995–   )

INFORMATION

Office of Communications
Substance Abuse and
    Mental Health Services Administration
5600 Fishers Lane
Rockville, Maryland 20857
(301) 443-8956
Fax: (301) 443-9050
http://www.samhsa.gov

HE 20.402:CT • Item 497-D-1
GENERAL PUBLICATIONS. [Irregular]

Earlier HE 20.8002

HE 20.408:CT • Item 497-D-3
HANDBOOKS, MANUALS, GUIDES.

Earlier HE 20.8008

HE 20.409 • Item 497-D-5 (MF)
BIBLIOGRAPHIES AND LISTS OF PUBLICATIONS.

HE 20.409/2:CT • Item 497-D-25
CSAP SUBSTANCE ABUSE RESOURCE GUIDE (series), (Various Topics).

HE 20.410: • Item 497-D-30
DIRECTORIES.

HE 20.410/2 • Item 497-D-20 (MF)
MENTAL HEALTH DIRECTORY. [Irregular]

PURPOSE:—To provide a listing of State mental health services and facilities, which include pubic and private agencies and institutions which provide direct mental health services to the mentally ill and emotionally disturbed. Information is given on the geographic area served, the type of operating agency, and the type of services provided by each facility. A listing of regional mental health offices of NIMH, state and Territorial mental and health authorities, voluntary mental health associations and national mental health agencies is also included.
Earlier HE 20.8123

HE 20.410/3:date • Item 498-C-15 (EL)
NATIONAL DIRECTORY OF DRUG ABUSE AND ALCOHOLISM TREATMENT AND PREVENTION PROGRAMS (Online database). [Annual] (Office of Applied Studies)

HE 20.414: • Item 497-D-31
POSTERS.

HE 20.415 • Item 497-D-16 (MF)
TECHNICAL ASSISTANCE PUBLICATION SERIES.

Earlier HE 20.8025

HE 20.415/2:CT • Item 497-D-27
TECHNICAL ASSISTANCE BULLETINS.

HE 20.415/3:nos. • Item 497-D-32 (MF)
CSAP TECHNICAL REPORT (series).

HE 20.416 • Item 467-A-29
STATISTICAL SERIES, ANNUAL DATA, DATA FROM THE DRUG ABUSE WARNING NETWORK (DAWN) (series).

Earlier HE 20.8212/11

HE 20.416/2 • Item 497-D-21 (MF)
ANNUAL EMERGENCY ROOM DATA SERIES.

HE 20.416/3:nos. • Item 497-D-33 (MF) (EL)
DRUG ABUSE WARNING NETWORK SERIES: D-(nos.).

HE 20.417:date • Item 497-D-17 (MF)
NATIONAL HOUSEHOLD SURVEY ON DRUG ABUSE: RACE/ETHNICITY, . . . [Annual]

HE 20.417/2:date • Item 497-D-24
NATIONAL HOUSEHOLD SURVEY ON DRUG ABUSE: POPULATION ESTIMATES. [Annual]

HE 20.417/3 • Item 497-D-26
NATIONAL HOUSEHOLD SURVEY ON DRUG ABUSE: MAIN FINDINGS. [Annual]

HE 20.417/4 • Item 497-D-36
NATIONAL HOUSEHOLD SURVEY ON DRUG ABUSE: PRELIMINARY RESULTS. [Annual]

HE 20.417/5 • Item 497-D-39 (P) (EL)
NATIONAL HOUSEHOLD SURVEY ON DRUG ABUSE: SUMMARY OF FINDINGS. [Annual]

HE 20.418:nos. • Item 497-D-18 (MF) (EL)
TREATMENT IMPROVEMENT PROTOCOL (TIP) SERIES.

Earlier HE 20.8029.

HE 20.419 • Item 497-D-19 (MF)
NCADI PUBLICATIONS CATALOG. [Semiannual]

Earlier HE 20.8012/2

HE 20.420 • Item 497-D-22 (MF)
CSAP CULTURAL COMPETENCE SERIES.
Earlier HE 20.8018/5

HE 20.421:nos. • Item 497-D-23
OFFICE OF APPLIED STUDIES, ADVANCE REPORT.

HE 20.422:nos. • Item 497-D-28
METHODOLOGICAL SERIES. (Office of Applied Studies).

HE 20.423:date • Item 497-D-29
UNIFORM FACILITY DATA SET (UFDS): DATA FOR.... [Annual]

HE 20.423/2:date • Item 497-D-35
THE TREATMENT EPISODE DATA SET (TEDS). [Annual]

HE 20.424:nos. • Item 497-D-34
ANALYTIC SERIES: A.

HE 20.425:v.nos./nos. • Item 497-D-37 (P) (EL)
SAMHSA NEWS. [Quarterly]

Formerly HE 20.8026:v./nos.
Continues ADAMHA NEWS
HE 20.8013:v./nos.

HE 20.426 • Item 497-D-38 (MF)
CSAP PREVENTION MONOGRAPH. (series)

HE 20.427 • Item 497-D-40
CENTER FOR METAL HEALTH SERVICES. (general publications)

HE 20.426 • Item 497-D-38 (MF)
CSAP PREVENTION MONOGRAPH. (series)

HE 20.427 • Item 497-D-40
CENTER FOR MENTAL HEALTH SERVICES. (general publication)

HE 20.427/2 • Item 497-D-41(EL)
CONSUMER INFORMATION SERIES. (various topics) (numbered)

HE 20.428 • Item 497-D-6 (P) (EL)
PREVENTION PIPELINE. [Monthly]

TOXIC SUBSTANCES AND DISEASE REGISTRY AGENCY

INFORMATION

Toxic Substances and Disease Registry Agency
1600 Clifton Rd.
Atlanta, GA 30333
(404) 498-0110
Toll-Free: (888) 422-8737
http://www.atsdr.cdc.gov

HE 20.501/2: • Item 504-R-3 (MF) (EL)
AGENCY FOR TOXIC SUBSTANCES AND DISEASE REGISTRY ANNUAL REPORT (MF).

HE 20.502:CT • Item 504-R-1
GENERAL PUBLICATIONS.
Earlier HE 20.7902

HE 20.508:CT • Item 504-R-2
HANDBOOKS, MANUALS, GUIDES.
Earlier HE 20.7908

HE 20.516 • Item 504-S-1 (EL)
HAZARDOUS SUBSTANCES & PUBLIC HEALTH. [Quarterly]
Earlier HE 20.7915

HE 20.517 • Item 444-P-5 (CD)
ATSDR, CD-ROM SERIES.
Earlier HE 20.7919

HE 20.518 • Item 504-R-4 (MF) (EL)
TOXICOLOGICAL PROFILES (Drafts, Updates and Finals).

HE 20.519 • Item 504-R-5 (MF) (EL)
CASE STUDIES IN ENVIRONMENTAL MANAGEMENT.

ENVIRONMENTAL HEALTH SERVICE
(1970)

HE 20.1001:date
ANNUAL REPORT.

HE 20.1002:CT
GENERAL PUBLICATIONS.

Earlier FS 2.2

HE 20.1009:date   • Item 499-E-1
PUBLIC ADVISORY COMMITTEES: AUTHORITY, STRUCTURE, FUNCTIONS, MEMBERS.

HE 20.1010:date   • Item 494-A
CONFERENCE OF STATE SANITARY ENGINEERS, REPORT OF PROCEEDINGS. 1st–   1920–
[Annual]

Earlier FS 2.83/4
Later HE 20.14

HE 20.1011:letters-nos.   • Item 483-F
ENVIRONMENTAL HEALTH SERIES.

Earlier FS 2.300

HE 20.1011:AH-nos.   • Item 483-F
AH. ARCTIC HEALTH. 1–   1965–   [Irregular]

Prepared by the Arctic Health Research Center.
Earlier FS 2.300:AH

HE 20.1011:AP-nos.   • Item 483-F
AP. AIR POLLUTION. 1–   [Irregular]

Earlier FS 2.300:AP

HE 20.1011:RH-nos.   • Item 483-F
RH. RADIOLOGICAL HEALTH. 1–   1962–
[Irregular]

PURPOSE:– To make available technical information on radiological health involving various aspects of methodology, studies of mechanisms, relationship of environmental factors to biological systems, and other scientific material that may be useful sources of reference in the field of radiological health.
Earlier FS 2.300:RH

ENVIRONMENTAL CONTROL ADMINISTRATION
(1970)

HE 20.1101:date
ANNUAL REPORT.

HE 20.1102:CT   • Item 468-A-8
GENERAL PUBLICATIONS.

Earlier FS 2.2

HE 20.1108:CT   • Item 468-A-2
HANDBOOKS, MANUALS, GUIDES.

Earlier FS 2.6/2 and FS 2.6
Later HE 20.1408

HE 20.1109:nos.   • Item 468-A-1
SELECTED PAPERS FROM BUREAU OF RADIOLOGICAL HEALTH SEMINAR PROGRAM (numbered). 1–   1969–   [Irregular]

The Bureau of Radiological Health's Office of Information disseminates information about the significant events occurring in the field of radio-

logical health. In pursuit of this mission, the Office conducts a program of seminars and symposia. When a presentation is believed to be of special interest, the speaker is invited to publish in this series.

HE 20.1110:v.nos.&nos.   • Item 498-B
RADIOLOGICAL HEALTH DATA AND REPORTS.
[Monthly]

Earlier FS 2.90
Later HE 20.1509, beginning with v. 11, no. 2.

HE 20.1111:nos.   • Item 468-A-3
RADIATION EXPOSURE OVERVIEWS, OCS [Office of Criteria and Standards] (series). 69-a–   1969–
[Annual]

The significance of a specific source of radiation and whether efforts directed towards its control are effective, depend, in large part, on an assessment of the magnitude of radiation exposure received by a population from that source. The process of assessment includes comparing estimates of exposure against pertinent guidance or standards. These comparisons provide reference points for radiation control programs.

Radiation exposure overviews are designed both to highlight these points of reference as well as identify needed information. Developed from available, salient information, each overview seeks to relate an observed or potential radiation source. Relevant guidance or standards and the status of exposure control efforts, where such data are available, are also incorporated.
Prepared by the Office of Criteria and Standards with the assistance of the Bureau of Radiological Health.

HE 20.1112:nos.   • Item 468-A-4
ORO [Office of Regional Operations] (series). 69-1–   1969–   [Irregular]

Later HE 20.1512
HE 20.1112:[nos.]   • Item 468-A-4
DIRECTORY OF PERSONNEL RESPONSIBLE FOR RADIOLOGICAL HEALTH PROGRAMS.
1969–   [Irregular]

Feb. 1970 70-1
Bureau of Radiological Health.

HE 20.1112:[nos.]   • Item 468-A-4
STATE RADIATION CONTROL LEGISLATION.
1969–   [Annual]

PURPOSE:– To present a review of State radiation control legislation. Gives legislation approved, legislation defeated or pending, and existing laws or statutes governing ionizing radiation, nonionizing radiation and radiologic technology. An index and a brief description of each bill introduced are included. Covers the calendar year.

HE 20.1113:nos.   • Item 483-F
ANALYTICAL REFERENCE SERVICE STUDIES. 1–   1954–   [Irregular]

The Analytical Reference Service is conducted by the Bureau of Water Hygiene of the Environmental Control Administration to evaluate laboratory methods in the environmental field. Now primarily directed toward examination of water, in the past studies have included methods for analysis of air, milk, and food. Some studies are periodically repeated for the advantage of new members, the evaluation of new methods or the re-evaluation of existing methods. The selection of studies is guided by requests from standard methods committees and the responses to questionnaires periodically circulated among the membership.

The following sub-series have been published:
Air
  Inorganics. 1–   1958–
    Lead. 1–   1961–
  Particulates. 1–   1964–
  Sulfur Dioxide. 1–   1963–
Food

  Pesticides. 1–   1961–
  Pesticides. 1–   1962–
  Freshwater Plankton. 1–   1964–
Water
  Chlorine. 1–   1969–
  Cyanides. 1–   1967–
  Fluoride. 1–   1958–
  Metals. 1–   1958–
  Minerals. 1–   1956–
  Nutrients. 1–   1966–
  Oxygen Demand. 1–   1960–
  Pesticides. 1–   1965–
  Phenols. 1–   1966–
  Surfactant. 1–   1959–
  Trace Elements. 1–   1962–

HE 20.1114:nos.   • Item 468-A-5
DEP [Division of Electronic Products] (series). 1969–
[Irregular]

The Division of Electronic Products (1) develops and administers performance standards for radiation emissions from electronic products; (2) studies and evaluates emissions of and conditions of exposure to electronic product [dhradiation and intense magnetic fields; (3) conducts or supports research, training, development and inspections to control and minimize such hazards, and (4) tests and evaluates the effectiveness of procedures and techniques for minimizing such exposures.
The technical reports of such studies and research are published in this series.

HE 20.1115:nos.   • Item 486-A-6
DBE [Division of Biological Effects] (series). 1969–
[Irregular]

Later HE 20.1514

HE 20.1115:[nos.]
RADIATION BIO-EFFECTS SUMMARY REPORT.
1965/66–   [Annual]

Annual report of progress and activities for the calendar year.
Report for the period July 1965– December 1966 entitled, Radiological Health Research, Summary Report.

HE 20.1116:nos.   • Item 483-0
INJURY CONTROL RESEARCH LABORATORY: RESEARCH REPORT, ICRL-RR (series). 68-1–
1968–

Earlier FS 2.316
Later HE 20.1809

HE 20.1117:CT   • Item 468-A-7
COMMUNITY ENVIRONMENTAL MANAGEMENT SERIES. 1970–   [Irregular] (Bureau of Community Environmental Management).

The following sub-series have been issued:
Community Organization Techniques. 1–   1970–
Housing and Hygiene. 1–   1970–
Environmental Health Planning. 1–   1971–

FOOD AND DRUG
ADMINISTRATION
(1970)

CREATION AND AUTHORITY

The Food and Drug Administration (FS 13.100) was transferred from the Federal Security Agency to the newly created Department of Health, Education, and Welfare in 1953. [During the period 1953 through 1969, the SuDocs class FS 13.100 was used.] In 1970, the SuDocs class was changed to HE 20.4000.

HE 20.1201:date
ANNUAL REPORT.

Reprint of section from Annual Report of the Department of Health, Education and Welfare.
Earlier FS 13.101 and FS 7.1
Later HE 20.4001

HE 20.1202:CT
GENERAL PUBLICATIONS.
Earlier FS 13.102
Later HE 20.4002

HE 20.1203/2:date
NATIONAL CLEARINGHOUSE FOR POISON CONTROL CENTERS, BULLETIN. 1957– [Monthly]
Earlier FS 2.96
Later HE 20.4003/2

HE 20.1205:CT
LAWS.
Earlier FS 13.105
Later HE 20.4005

HE 20.1206:CT
REGULATIONS, RULES, AND INSTRUCTIONS.
Earlier FS 13.106
Later HE 20.4006

HE 20.1208:CT • Item 475-G
HANDBOOKS, MANUALS, GUIDES.

Earlier FS 13.119

HE 20.1209:v.nos.&nos. • Item 475-L
FDA CLINICAL EXPERIENCE ABSTRACTS. [Biweekly]
Earlier FS 13.132 prior to v. 27, no. 7.
Later HE 20.4009 beginning with v. 28, no. 6.

HE 20.1210:v.nos.&nos. • Item 475-H
FDA PAPERS. v. 1– 1967– [Monthly]
Earlier FS 13.128 prior to v. 3, no. 11.
Later HE 20.4010

HE 20.1211:v/nos.&nos. • Item 475-M
HEALTH ASPECTS OF PESTICIDES, ABSTRACT BULLETIN. v. 1– 1968– [Monthly]

PURPOSE:– To foster current awareness of the major worldwide literature pertaining to the effects of pesticides on humans. It represents a monthly review of more than 500 domestic and foreign journals.
Consumers Protection and Environmental Health Service, Pesticides Program, Chamblee, Ga.
Annual index issued separately.
Earlier FS 13.133
Later HE 20.4011

HE 20.1212:nos.
COMMERCIAL IMPORT DETENTIONS. [Monthly]

Limited to food, drug, and cosmetic trade only.
Earlier FS 13.120
Later HE 20.4017

HE 20.1213:date
INTERSTATE SHELLFISH SHIPPERS LIST. [Monthly]

Earlier FS 13.135 and FS 2.16
Later HE 20.4014

HE 20.1214:CT
BIBLIOGRAPHIES AND LISTS OF PUBLICATIONS.

Earlier FS 13.125
Later HE 20.4016

NATIONAL AIR POLLUTION
CONTROL ADMINISTRATION
(1970)

HE 20.1301:date
ANNUAL REPORT.

HE 20.1302:CT • Item 483-E
GENERAL PUBLICATIONS.

Earlier FS 2.2

HE 20.1303/2:v.nos.&nos. • Item 483-S
APTIC [Air Pollution Technical Information Center] BULLETIN. [Irregular]

Office of Technical Information
and Publications
Air Pollution Technical Information Center
Raleigh, North Carolina 17065
Earlier FS 2.93/6, prior to v. 2, no. 9

HE 20.1303/3:v.nos.&nos. • Item 483-E-3
NAPCA ABSTRACT BULLETIN. v. 1– 1970– [Monthly]

HE 20.1303/4:date
BULLETIN OF AIR POLLUTION TRAINING COURSES.

HE 20.1308:CT • Item 483-E-2
HANDBOOKS, MANUAL, GUIDES.

Earlier FS 2.6/2

HE 20.1309 • Item 483-E
NATIONAL AIR POLLUTION CONTROL ADMINISTRATION PUBLICATION, AP (series).

Earlier FS 2.93/3

HE 20.1309/2:nos. • Item 483-E
NATIONAL AIR POLLUTION CONTROL ADMINISTRATION PUBLICATION, APTD (series).

Earlier FS 2.93/6

HE 20.1310:CT • Item 483-E
REPORTS FOR CONSULTATION ON INTERSTATE AIR QUALITY CONTROL REGIONS.

Earlier FS 2193/5

HE 20.1310/2:CT
AIR POLLUTION REPORT, FEDERAL FACILITIES, AIR QUALITY CONTROL REGIONS.

Later EP 4.10

HE 20.1311:date • Item 483-E-5
COMMUNITY AFFAIRS BULLETIN. [Irregular]

Title varies.

HE 20.1312:CT • Item 483-E-4
ADDRESSES.

Earlier FS 2.30 and T 27.31

BUREAU OF SOLID WASTE
MANAGEMENT
(1970)

HE 20.1401:date
ANNUAL REPORT.

HE 20.1402:CT • Item 487-A-1
GENERAL PUBLICATIONS.

HE 20.1408:CT • Item 487-A-2
HANDBOOKS, MANUALS, GUIDES.

Earlier HE 20.1108
Later EP 1.17

HE 20.1409:date
NATIONAL SURVEY OF COMMUNITY SOLID WASTE PRACTICES.

Later EP 1.17

HE 20.1410:CT
ADDRESSES.

BUREAU OF RADIOLOGICAL
HEALTH
(1970)

HE 20.1501:date
ANNUAL REPORT.

HE 20.1502:CT
GENERAL PUBLICATIONS.

HE 20.1508:CT
HANDBOOKS, MANUALS, GUIDES.

HE 20.1509:v.nos.&nos. • Item 498-B
RADIOLOGICAL HEALTH DATA AND REPORTS. 1– 1960– [Monthly]

PURPOSE:– To bring together in one concise volume, the most pertinent month by month statistical information on radiation in the environment.
Prepared by the Division of Radiological Health, December issues contain index. Each third issue expanded somewhat into quarterly report. Issues for the period April 1960 through March 1961 released by the Office of Technical Services as PB 161371.
Includes data and reports provided by Federal agencies, State health departments, universities, and foreign governmental agencies, subject to review by Departments of Defense, Interior, Agriculture, Commerce, Health, Education and Welfare, and Atomic Energy Commission.
Earlier HE 20.1110, prior to v. 11, no. 2.
Includes annual index.

HE 20.1510:nos.
SELECTED PAPERS FROM BUREAU OF RADIO-LOGICAL HEALTH SEMINAR PROGRAM. (numbered)

Earlier HE 20.1109

HE 20.1511:nos.
RADIATION EXPOSURE OVERVIEW, OCS [Office of Criteria and Standards] (series).

Earlier HE 20.1111

HE 20.1512:nos. • Item 468-A-4
ORD [Office of Regional Operations] (series).

The Office of Regional Operations assists and advises the Bureau of Radiological Health on regional and State radiological health activities. This office coordinates all radiological health activities for our active Federal-State partnership to achieve and maintain comprehensive radiological health control. The Office also guides and directs the state participation in Public Law 90-602.
Earlier HE 20.1112

HE 20.1513:nos.
DEP [Division of Electronic Products] (series).

Earlier HE 20.1115
Later HE 30.4110

HE 20.1514:nos.
DBE [Division of Biological Effects] (series).

Earlier HE 20.1115
Later HE 20.4114

HE 20.1515:nos.
BRH/OBD (series).

HE 20.1516:nos.
BRH/DMRE (series).

Earlier FS 2.314, FS 2.314/2
Later HE 20.4112

BUREAU OF OCCUPATIONAL SAFETY AND HEALTH (1970)

HE 20.1601:date
ANNUAL REPORT.

HE 20.1602:CT • Item 499-F-2
GENERAL PUBLICATIONS.

HE 20.1608:CT • Item 499-F-1
HANDBOOKS, MANUALS AND GUIDES.

OFFICE OF WATER HYGIENE (1970)

HE 20.1701:
ANNUAL REPORT.

HE 20.1702:
GENERAL PUBLICATIONS.

HE 20.1709: • Item 483-F
ANALYTICAL REFERENCE SERVICE STUDIES.

BUREAU OF COMMUNITY ENVIRONMENTAL MANAGEMENT (1970– 1972)

NOTE:– Effective 1972, the SuDocs class for the Bureau became HE 20.2850.

HE 20.1801:date
ANNUAL REPORT.

HE 20.1802:CT • Item 468-A-8
GENERAL PUBLICATIONS.

HE 20.1809:nos. • Item 483-0
INJURY CONTROL RESEARCH LABORATORY: RESEARCH REPORTS. ICRL- RR-68-1– 1968– [Irregular]

The Injury Control Research Laboratory conducts experimental studies of a person's ability to detect and appreciate hazards in his environment and protect himself from injury. The results of these studies are published in this series whenever a particular investigation, connected series of investigations, or technological development in injury control research methodology has been completed.
Earlier HE 20.1116 and FS 2.316

HE 20.1810:CT • Item 468-A-7
COMMUNITY ENVIRONMENTAL MANAGEMENT SERIES.

HE 20.1811:CT • Item 512-F-1
ENVIRONMENTAL HEALTH SERVICE SERIES ON COMMUNITY ORGANIZATION TECHNIQUES.

HEALTH SERVICES AND MENTAL HEALTH ADMINISTRATION (1968– 1973)

CREATION AND AUTHORITY

The Health Services and Mental Health Administration was established within the Public Health Service in 1968. The Administration was abolished by reorganization order, effective July 1, 1973, with functions transferred to the Center for Disease Control (HE 20.7000), the Health Resources Administration (H E 20.6000), and the Health Services Administration (HE 20.5000).

HE 20.2001:date
ANNUAL REPORT.

HE 20.2002:CT • Item 483-T-1
GENERAL PUBLICATIONS.

Earlier FS 2.2

HE 20.2005:CT • Item 483-T-5
LAWS.

HE 20.2008:CT • Item 483-T-2
HANDBOOKS, MANUALS, GUIDES.

HE 20.2009:date
18-MONTH CALENDAR OF NATIONAL MEETINGS. [Quarterly]

PURPOSE:– To serve as an informational guide, based on information selected from scientific publications and other sources.
Part A gives an alphabetical listing and Part B, a chronological listing. State and local meetings are not included.
Prior to Oct. 1, 1969, classified FS 2.315

HE 20.2010:v.nos.&nos. • Item 497
PUBLIC HEALTH REPORTS. [Monthly]

Includes annual index.
Discontinued with v. 85, no. 12. Replaced by HSMHA Health Reports, (HE 20.2010/2).
Earlier FS 2.7, prior to v. 84, no. 12.

HE 20.2010/2:v.nos.&nos. • Item 497
HEALTH SERVICES REPORTS. v. 86– 1971– [Monthly]

Former title: HSMAH Health Reports.
Continues Public Health Reports (HE 20.2010).
Later HE 20.5009

HE 20.2011:v.nos. • Item 483-T
HSMHA PUBLIC ADVISORY COMMITTEES: AUTHORITY, STRUCTURE, FUNCTIONS.
Earlier FS 2.321

HE 20.2011/2:v.nos. • Item 483-T
HSMHA PUBLIC ADVISORY COMMITTEES: ROSTER OF MEMBERS.

HE 20.2012:date • Item 481-A
LIST OF PUBLICATIONS. [Semiannual]

Covers period January-June and June- December.
Earlier FS 2.24/2

HE 20.2012/2:CT • Item 483-T-4
BIBLIOGRAPHIES AND LISTS OF PUBLICATIONS.

HE 20.2013:letters-nos. • Item 486-E
EMERGENCY HEALTH SERIES. 1963– [Irregular]

PURPOSE:– To provide in one series all publications relating to health mobilization.
Publications are numbered numerically within the following categories:

A. Emergency Health Services Planning
B. Environmental Health
C. Medical Care and Treatment
D. Training
E. Health Resources Evaluation
F. Civil Defense Emergency Hospitals
G. Health Facilities
H. Supplies, Equipment
I. Health Manpower
J. Public Water Supply
Former title: Health Mobilization Series
Earlier FS 2.302

HE 20.2013/2:nos. • Item 483-R
EMERGENCY HEALTH SERVICES DIGEST. 1– (Division of Emergency Health Services)

HE 20.2014:date • Item 483-T-3
INDIAN HEALTH PROGRAM. 1965– [Annual] (Publication 1394)

Capsule report of history, purpose, activities, progress and goals of the Indian Health Service.

HE 20.2014/2:date • Item 486-I
TO THE FIRST AMERICANS, ANNUAL REPORT ON INDIAN HEALTH PROGRAM TO PUBLIC HEALTH SERVICE. 1– 1967– [Annual]

PURPOSE:– To provide a report to the American Indian people on plans and progress in conducting the Public Health Service program of health services to Indians living on reservations, in Pueblos, and villages, and to Alaska natives most of whom live in small remote villages.
Earlier FS 2.86/4
Later HE 20.5312

HE 20.2015:date • Item 483-C
DIRECTORY OF LOCAL HEALTH AND MENTAL HEALTH UNITS. 1942– [Irregular] (PHS publication 118) (Office of Grants Management)
Earlier FS 2.77 and FS 2.2:L 78.

HE 20.2015/2:date • Item 483-B
DIRECTORY OF STATE, TERRITORIAL, AND REGIONAL HEALTH AUTHORITIES. [Annual] (PHS publication 75)
Earlier FS 2.77/2 and FS 2.2:H 34/5.

HE 20.2016:date • Item 483-P
GRANTS-IN-AID AND OTHER FINANCIAL ASSISTANCE PROGRAMS. [Annual]

Lists and describes the various forms of financial aid administered by the Health Service and Mental Health Administration.
Description includes purpose, financing, method for determining how Federal funds are allocated, matching requirements, who may receive Federal funds, how application for funds is made, recent development, legal basis on which funds are made available, and the office of the Administration from which additional information may be obtained.
Earlier FS 2.317

HE 20.2017:CT
POSTERS.

HE 20.2018:nos. • Item 500-A
PUBLIC HEALTH MONOGRAPH SERIES. 1– 1950–
[Irregular]

PURPOSE:– To present contributions to knowledge in the fields of public health, particularly
material that is extensive, detailed, or specialized and thus not practical for inclusion in HSMHA
Health Reports.

HE 20.2019:date • Item 485-A
HEALTH CONSEQUENCES OF SMOKING, REPORT
TO THE SURGEON GENERAL.

Earlier FS 2.309

HE 20.2020:date • Item 483-T-6
FEDERAL COAL MINE HEALTH PROGRAM, ANNUAL
REPORT OF THE FEDERAL COAL MINE HEALTH
AND SAFETY ACT.

Later HE 20.7109

HEALTH MAINTENANCE
ORGANIZATION SERVICE
(1972)

HE 20.2051:date
ANNUAL REPORT.

HE 20.2052:CT • Item 483-H-1
GENERAL PUBLICATIONS.

HE 20.2058:CT • Item 483-H-2
HANDBOOKS, MANUALS, GUIDES.

HE 20.2059:CT
POSTERS.

NATIONAL CENTER FOR HEALTH
SERVICES RESEARCH AND
DEVELOPMENT
(1970– 1973)

HE 20.2101:date
ANNUAL REPORTS.

HE 20.2102:CT • Item 491-B-1
GENERAL PUBLICATIONS.

Earlier FS 2.2
Later HE 20.6502

HE 20.2108:CT • Item 491-B-5
HANDBOOKS, MANUALS, GUIDES.

Later HE 20.6508

HE 20.2109:nos. • Item 491-B-7
FOCUS. [Quarterly]

HE 20.2110:nos. • Item 491-B-2
NCHS-RD (series). [Irregular]

HE 20.2111:nos. • Item 491-B-3
HSRD BRIEFS.

HE 20.2112:nos. • Item 491-B-4
REPRINT SERIES (numbered).

HE 20.2113:nos. • Item 491-B-6
PUBLICATIONS REPORTS (numbered). 1– 1970–
[Irregular]

HE 20.2113/2:CT • Item 491-B-10
BIBLIOGRAPHIES AND LISTS OF PUBLICATIONS.

HE 20.2114:CT • Item 491-B-8
CONFERENCE SERIES.

HE 20.2115:CT
CASE STUDY SERIES.

HE 20.2116:date • Item 491-B-11
SUMMARY OF GRANTS AND CONTRACTS ADMINIS-
TERED BY THE NATIONAL CENTER FOR HEALTH
SERVICES RESEARCH AND DEVELOP- MENT.
(Office of Inter-Organization Relations)

Later HE 20.6510

NATIONAL CENTER FOR HEALTH
STATISTICS
(1970– 1973)

CREATION AND AUTHORITY

The National Center for Health Statistics was
established within the Public Health Service in
1970. In 1973 the Center was placed under the
Health Resources Administration (HE 20.6200).

HE 20.2201:date • Item 508-A-1
ANNUAL REPORT.

Earlier FS 2.101
Later HE 20.6201

HE 20.2202:CT • Item 508
GENERAL PUBLICATIONS.

Earlier FS 2.102
Later HE 20.6202

HE 20.2202:V 83/962-71
CURRENT LISTING AND TOPICAL INDEX TO THE
VITAL AND HEALTH STATISTICS SERIES,
1962– 1972. May 1973. 19 p. (DHEW Publication No. (HSM) 73-1301 (Revised))

Provides a subject index and listing for
the Vital and Health Statistics Series (HE
20.2210).

HE 20.2206 • Item 509
REGULATIONS, RULES, AND INSTRUCTIONS.

HE 20.2208: • Item 509
HANDBOOKS, MANUALS, GUIDES.

Later HE 20.6208

HE 20.2209:v.nos.&nos. • Item 508-B
MONTHLY VITAL STATISTICS REPORT. [Monthly]

Earlier FS 2.116
Later HE 20.6009

HE 20.2210:nos. • Item 500-E
VITAL AND HEALTH STATISTICS. 1963– [Irregular]
(PHS publication 1000)

Earlier FS 2.85/2
Later HE 20.6209

HE 20.2211:date • Item 492-A
ANNUAL REPORT OF THE UNITED STATES
NATIONAL COMMITTEE ON VITAL AND HEALTH
STATISTICS. 1956–

Earlier FS 2.120, FS 2.63
Later HE 20.6211

HE 20.2212:date • Item 510
VITAL STATISTICS OF THE UNITED STATES. 1937–
[Annual]

Earlier FS 2.112
Later HE 20.6210

HE 20.2213: • Item 508-G
BIBLIOGRAPHIES AND LISTS OF PUBLICATIONS.

Later HE 20.6216

HE 20.2214:date • Item 509-A
PROCEEDINGS OF THE PUBLIC HEALTH CONFER-
ENCE ON RECORDS AND STATISTICS. 9th–
1962– [Biennial]

Later HE 20.6214

HE 20.2215:date • Item 509-B
HEALTH RESOURCES STATISTICS. 1965– [An-
nual]

Earlier FS 2.123
Later HE 20.6212

HE 20.2216:v.nos.
THE REGISTRAR AND STATISTICIAN.

Earlier FS 2.111
Later HE 20.6213

CENTER FOR DISEASE CONTROL
(1971– 1973)

NOTE:– The Center for Disease Control was
assigned a new class number (HE 20.7000) in
1973.

HE 20.2301:date
ANNUAL REPORT.

HE 20.2302:CT • Item 504
GENERAL PUBLICATIONS.

Earlier FS 2.60/2
Later HE 20.7008

HE 20.2308:CT • Item 505-A
HANDBOOKS, MANUALS, GUIDES.

Earlier FS 2.60/8

HE 20.2308:Sy 7/2 • Item 505-A
SEROLOGIC TESTS FOR SYPHILIS. [Irregular]

Earlier FS 2.60/7:Sy 7/2

HE 20.2308:pt.nos. • Item 505-A
TRAINING GUIDE, INSECT CONTROL SERIES.
pt. 1– [Irregular]

Earlier FS 2.60/7

HE 20.2308/2:nos.
ADVISORY MEMOS. [Irregular]

HE 20.2309:nos.
SALMONELLA SURVEILLANCE, REPORTS. 1–
1962– [Monthly]

PURPOSE:– To present a monthly compilation of the results of national salmonella surveillance and serve as a reference source of epidemiologic data for individuals interested in or working with the problem of salmonellosis. Emphasis
is on recent developments and articles are included describing specific outbreaks and their
epidemiologic investigation.
Earlier FS 2.60/12, FS 2.60/2:Sa 3/3

HE 20.2309/2:date
SALMONELLA SURVEILLANCE, ANNUAL SUMMARY.
1964–

Earlier FS 2.60/12-2
Later HE 20.7011/15

HE 20.2309/3:nos.
SHIGELLA SURVEILLANCE, REPORTS. 1–   1966–
[Quarterly]

PURPOSE:– To provide a record of the results of surveillance on shigella for circulation to the reporting states and a medium for special reports and discussions concerning shigellosis epidemics. Also serves as a reference for new discoveries about shigella as they are published elsewhere.
Yearly summary contained in report for fourth quarter.
Earlier FS 2.60/16 prior to no. 21.

HE 20.2309/4:nos.
MEASLES SURVEILLANCE, REPORTS. 1–

Later HE 20.7011

HE 20.2309/5:nos.
CENTER FOR DISEASE CONTROL, HEPATITIS SURVEILLANCE, REPORTS. [Irregular]

Earlier FS 2.60/13
Later HE 20.7011/6

HE 20.2309/6:date
FOODBORNE OUTBREAKS, ANNUAL SUMMARY. 1966–

Earlier FS 2.60/18
Later HE 20.7011/13

HE 20.2309/7:nos.
RUBELLA SURVEILLANCE, [Reports]. 1– 1969–
[Irregular]

Earlier FS 2.60/17
Later HE 20.2011/12

HE 20.2309/8:CT
NEUROTROPIC VIRAL DISEASES SURVEILLANCE [Reports].

Earlier FS 2.60/14
Later HE 20.7011/5

HE 20.2309/8:En 1/date
– ANNUAL ENCHALITIS SUMMARY.

Earlier FS 2.60/14:En 1
Later HE 20.7011/5:En 1

HE 20.2309/8:En 8/date.
– ENTEROVIRUS INFECTIONS, ANNUAL SUMMARY.

Earlier FS 2.60/14:En 8

HE 20.2309/9:CT
CENTER FOR DISEASE CONTROL ZOONOSES SURVEILLANCE [Reports].

Earlier FS 2.60/15

HE 20.2309/10:nos.
INFLUENZA-RESPIRATORY DISEASE SURVEILLANCE, REPORTS. 1–

HE 20.2309/12:date
TRICHINOSIS SURVEILLANCE, ANNUAL SUMMARY.

Later HE 20.7011/4

HE 20.2309/13:date
MALARIA SURVEILLANCE, ANNUAL REPORT.

Later HE 20.7011/8

HE 20.2309/14:nos.
DIPTHERIA SURVEILLANCE, REPORTS. 1–
[Annual]

HE 20.2309/15:date
CENTER FOR DISEASE CONTROL FAMILY PLANNING EVALUATION, ABORTION SURVEILLANCE REPORT, LEGAL ABORTIONS, U.S.

HE 20.2309/15-2:date
ABORTION SURVEILLANCE, ANNUAL SUMMARY.

Later HE 20.7011/20

HE 20.2310:v.nos.&nos.   • Item 508-A
MORBIDITY AND MORTALITY WEEKLY REPORT. v. 1– 1952–

Earlier FS 2.107/2; FS 2.60/9, prior to v. 18, no. 49.
Later HE 20.7009

HE 20.2311:date-nos.
CURRENT LITERATURE ON VENEREAL DISEASE, ABSTRACTS AND BIBLIOGRAPHY. 1952– [2-3 times a year] (Venereal Disease Branch, State and Community Services Division)

PURPOSE:– To present a survey of recently published worldwide literature regarding venereal diseases. Abstracts are taken from MEDLARS.
Last issue of each year contains subject and author indexes.
ISSN 0001-3544
Earlier FS 2.11/2

HE 20.2312:date
CDC VETERINARY PUBLIC HEALTH NOTES. 1958–
[Monthly] (Venereal Disease Branch, State and Community Services Division)

Later HE 20.7010

HE 20.2313:date   • Item 500-D
REPORTED TUBERCULOSIS DATA (year). 1958–
[Annual] (Tuberculosis Branch)

Earlier FS 2.42/3
Later HE 20.7017

HE 20.2314:date
UNITED STATES IMMUNIZATION SURVEY (date). [Annual] (Immunization Branch)

Later HE 20.7313

HE 20.2315
BIBLIOGRAPHIES AND LISTS OF PUBLICATIONS.

HE 20.2316:date   • Item 504-A
SMOKING AND HEALTH BULLETIN. 1970–
[Irregular] (National Clearinghouse for Smoking and Health)
Classified HE 20.2609 prior to April-May 1972 issue.
Later HE 20.7012

HE 20.2317   • Item 483-L-4
DIRECTORY OF ON-GOING RESEARCH IN SMOKING AND HEALTH, 1967– [Annual]

Earlier FS 2.2:Sm 7/5 and HE 20.2612
Later HE 20.7015

NATIONAL INSTITUTE OF MENTAL HEALTH
(1970– 1973)

HE 20.2401:date
ANNUAL REPORT.
Later HE 20.3801

HE 20.2402:CT   • Item 507-B-5
GENERAL PUBLICATIONS.

Earlier FS 2.22
Later HE 20.3802

HE 20.2402:H 13   • Item 507-B-5
DIRECTORY OF HALFWAY HOUSES FOR THE MENTALLY ILL AND ALCOHOLICS. 1973. 133 p.

The halfway houses are arranged alphabetically by State, and are grouped by primary resident group served. Each listing gives pertinent information such as capacity, age restriction, sex restriction, persons served, maximum stay permitted, and admission requirements.

HE 20.2402:N 16/3   • Item 507-B-5
DIRECTORY OF NARCOTIC ADDICTION TREATMENT AGENCIES IN THE UNITED STATES. 1970. 162 p.

This directory is limited to programs focused specifically on the treatment of narcotic addiction. It is a report of a study that has examined treatment in depth, and contains information on approximately 150 treatment programs.

HE 20.2402:Of 2/2   • Item 507-B-5
DIRECTORY OF INSTITUTIONS FOR MENTALLY DISORDERED OFFENDERS. 1972. 24 p.

Contains a listing of mental health and correctional institutions providing psychiatric care for adult mentally disordered offenders. Includes Federal, State, and municipal facilities.

HE 20.2408:CT   • Item 507-B-10
HANDBOOKS, MANUALS, GUIDES.

Later HE 20.3808

HE 20.2408/2:CT   • Item 507-B-10
SOCIAL SEMINAR DISCUSSION GUIDES. [Irregular]

HE 20.2409:v.nos.&nos.   • Item 507-Z-1
PSYCHOPHARMACOLOGY BULLETIN. v. 1– 1959–
[Quarterly]

Issued irregularly prior to 1969.
Earlier title: Psychopharmacology Service Center Bulletins.
Earlier FS 2.22/29, prior to v. 5, n. 3.
Later HE 20.8109

HE 20.2409/2:v.nos.&nos.   • Item 507-Z
PSYCHOPHARMACOLOGY ABSTRACTS. v. 1–
1961– [Monthly] (National Clearinghouse for Mental Health Information)

Issues prior to v. 2, no. 7 published by the Psychopharmacology Service Center.
Annual index issued separately.
Earlier FS 2.22/29-2
Later HE 20.8109/2

HE 20.2410:v.nos.&nos.   • Item 507-T
MENTAL HEALTH DIGEST. v. 1– 1969– [Monthly] (National Clearinghouse for Mental Health Information)

Issued as an unnumbered publication 1967–1968.
Earlier FS 2.22/40-5, prior to v. 1. no. 12.
Later HE 20.8009

HE 20.2411:date   • Item 507-B-3
OCCUPATIONAL MENTAL HEALTH NOTES. 1965–
[Bimonthly] (National Clearinghouse for Mental Health Information)

Directed to psychiatrists, psychologists, social workers, and others working with problems of mental health in industrial settings.
Contains notes and reviews on and announcements of national and international conferences on industrial mental health problems, plus occasional articles on various aspects of occupational mental health by professional working in this area. Each issue has a section devoted to abstracts of recent literature on the mental health of industrial workers.
Earlier FS 2.22/50-3 prior to Apr. 1969.

HE 20.2412:date   • Item 507-B-6
NATIONAL INSTITUTE OF MENTAL HEALTH SUPPORT PROGRAMS. [Irregular] (National Clearinghouse for Mental Health Information (PHS Publication 1700)

PURPOSE:– To provide information on grants programs administered by the National Institute of Mental Health, with directions on how to apply and to which division.
Earlier FS 2.22:N 21/8

HE 20.2413:date • Item 507-B-4
BULLETIN OF SUICIDOLOGY. 1967– [Irregular]

PURPOSE:– To provide a single focus for the publication of research findings in the areas of suicide prevention, crisis intervention, self- destructive behavior, and death and dying.
Consists of original articles, reprints of classic articles, news notes on suicide prevention activities of the Institute and throughout the United States, and an annotated bibliography of the recent literature on suicide.
It is a convenient source of information for the professional who would not have time to review the many journals in which relevant articles might otherwise be found.
Prepared jointly by the Center for Studies of Suicide Prevention and the National Clearinghouse for Mental Health Information.
Earlier FS 2.22/50-6 and FS 2.22:Su 3.

HE 20.2413/2:CT • Item 507-B-4
BULLETIN OF SUICIDOLOGY, SUPPLEMENTS. 1969– [Irregular]

Studies devoted to a single subject, such as suicide among youth.

HE 20.2414:date • Item 507-B-7
SCHIZOPHRENIA BULLETIN. (National Clearinghouse for Mental Health Information)
Later HE 20.8115

HE 20.2415:letters-nos. • Item 491-A
MENTAL HEALTH STATISTICS SERIES. 1968– [Irregular] (National Clearinghouse for Mental Health Information)

Earlier FS 2.53/2-2
Later HE 20.8110

HE 20.2415/2:H 79 • Item 491-A
MENTAL HEALTH STATISTICS: CURRENT FACILITY REPORTS. PROVISIONAL PATIENT MOVEMENT AND ADMINISTRATIVE DATA. STATE AND COUNTY MENTAL HOSPITALS, UNITED STATES.
Later HE 17.117:H 79.

HE 20.2416:nos. • Item 507-B-8
DRUG DEPENDENCE. 1– 1969– [Irregular] (National Clearinghouse for Mental Health Information)

PURPOSE:– To facilitate the dissemination and exchange of information in the field of drug dependence and abuse and to provide abstracts of the current literature in that general field.
Contains general article on current drug abuse problems and methods of treatment, drug articles of historical interest, and categorized abstracts of the current literature on drugs of abuse.

HE 20.2417:CT • Item 507-B-9
BIBLIOGRAPHIES AND LISTS OF PUBLICATIONS.

Earlier FS 2.22/13
Later HE 20.8113

HE 20.2417:Et 3 • Item 507-B-9
BIBLIOGRAPHY OF ETHNICITY AND ETHNIC GROUPS. 1973. 250 p.

Lists material related to the social, cultural, and psychological consequences of membership in a minority or ethnic group. Emphasis is given to two major subject areas: materials dealing with the situation of immigrant ethnic groups, their psychological adjustment and conditions affecting acculturation; and materials dealing with patterns of ethnic behavior, identity, family life, and communication structure.

HE 20.2417:Su 3 • Item 507-B-9
BIBLIOGRAPHY ON SUICIDE AND SUICIDE PREVENTION. 1972. 143 p.

Serves as a reference source of all the publications now available on suicide and suicide prevention, published from 1897 through 1970.

HE 20.2417:Ur 1 • Item 507-B-9
BIBLIOGRAPHY ON THE URBAN CRISIS. 1969. 452 p.

Provides a comprehensive and extensive listing of behavioral, psychological, and sociological literature, both academic and popular, on various aspects of life in our cities and on the causes, effects, and responses to urban disorders.

HE 20.2418:date • Item 506-C
MENTAL HEALTH DIRECTORY. [Irregular]

Earlier FS 2.22/49
Later HE 20.8123

HE 20.2419:nos. • Item 507-B-2
MENTAL HEALTH PROGRAM REPORTS. 1– 1967– [Annual] (PHS publication 1568) (National Clearinghouse for Mental Health Information)

Earlier FS 2.22/50-4
Later HE 20.8117

HE 20.2420:v.nos.&nos. • Item 506-B
CRIME AND DELINQUENCY ABSTRACTS. v. 1– 8, no. 6. – Nov. 1972. [Bimonthly] (National Clearinghouse for Mental Health Information)

Includes current projects and international bibliography.
Cumulative index issued separately.
Prepared under contract by Information Center on Crime Delinquency.
Discontinued with Volume 8, no. 6, November 1972.
Earlier FS 2.22/13-4

HE 20.2420/2:CT • Item 507-B-13
CRIME AND DELINQUENCY ISSUES, MONOGRAPH SERIES.

HE 20.2420/3:CT • Item 507-B-13
CRIME AND DELINQUENCY TOPICS, MONOGRAPH SERIES. (Center for Studies of Crime and Delinquency)

Later HE 20.3809

HE 20.2420/4:nos. • Item 507-B-20
RESEARCH REPORTS. 1– 1973– [Irregular] (Center for Studies of Crime and Delinquency)

Later HE 20.8114/2

HE 20.2421:CT
POSTERS. [Irregular]

HE 20.2422:CT • Item 512
SAINT ELIZABETH'S HOSPITAL, PUBLICATIONS.

Earlier FS 11.2
Later HE 11.2

HE 20.2423:date • Item 507-B-11
MENTAL HEALTH RESEARCH GRANT AWARDS, FISCAL YEAR. [Annual]

HE 20.2424:nos. • Item 507-B-12
SURVEY AND REPORTS SECTION STATISTICAL NOTES. 1– [Irregular]

Later HE 20.3812

HE 20.2425:nos. • Item 507-B-14
INNOVATIONS, MENTAL HEALTH SERVICES, PROGRESS REPORTS. 1– 1971–

HE 20.2426:date • Item 507-B-15
MENTAL HEALTH RESOURCES IN THE GREATER WASHINGTON AREA.

Later HE 20.8119

HE 20.2427:date • Item 507-B-16
ADMINISTRATION IN MENTAL HEALTH.

Later HE 20.8112

HE 20.2428:date • Item 507-B-17
ALCOHOL AND HEALTH NOTES. v. 1– Dec. 1972– [Monthly] (National Clearinghouse for Alcohol Information, National Institute on Alcohol Abuse and Alcoholism, Box 2345, Rockville, Maryland 20852)

Later HE 20.3811

HE 20.2429:CT • Item 507-B-18
NATIONAL CLEARINGHOUSE FOR MENTAL HEALTH INFORMATION ABSTRACTS. [Irregular]

HE 20.2430:v.nos.&nos. • Item 507-B-19
ALCOHOL HEALTH AND RESEARCH WORLD. v. 1– 1973– [Quarterly]

Later HE 20.3813

HE 20.2430/2:date • Item 507-B-5
PROCEEDINGS OF THE ANNUAL ALCOHOLISM CONFERENCE OF THE NATIONAL INSTITUTE ON ALCOHOL ABUSE AND ALCOHOLISM. 1st– 1971–

Later HE 20.8314

HEALTH CARE FACILITIES SERVICE
(1971– 1973)

HE 20.2501:date
ANNUAL REPORT.

Later HE 20.6401

HE 20.2502:CT • Item 486-A-2
GENERAL PUBLICATIONS.

Earlier FS 2.2
Later HE 20.6402

HE 20.2508:CT
HANDBOOKS, MANUALS, GUIDES.

HE 20.2509:date • Item 486-C
HILL-BURTON PROJECT REGISTER. [Annual]

Lists all Hill-Burton projects approved since the enactment of the Program, giving name and location of facility, project number, type of control, status of construction, type of facility, beds provided, type of construction, total cost and Federal share. Also includes national and State summaries of the number of projects approved since the beginning of the Program and during the latest fiscal year.
Formerly issued monthly.
Earlier FS 2.74

HE 20.2509/2:date • Item 486-C
HILL-BURTON PROGRAM PROGRESS REPORT. [Annual]

Summarized the projects approved under the Hospital and Medical Facilities (Hill-Burton) Program from July 1, 1947 through the current fiscal year. An annual report which includes highlights of the program, annual Hill-Burton appropriations, summary data on projects, facilities provided, costs, obligated funds, and status of construction. Appendix tables present detailed State data.
Earlier FS 2.95

HE 20.2510:date • Item 486-A-1
REPRESENTATIVE CONSTRUCTION COST OF HILL-BURTON HOSPITALS AND RELATED HEALTH FACILITIES. [Biannual]

Later title: Representative Construction Cost of Hospitals and Related Health Facilities.
Earlier FS 2.74/6
Later HE 1.109

HE 20.2511:letters-nos. • Item 486-D
HEALTH FACILITIES SERIES. [Irregular]

PURPOSE:– To provide guidelines for the planning, design, construction, equipping, and operations of hospitals and related health facilities.
Issued and numbered separately under the following categories:

A. Regulations.
B. Community Planning.
C. Organization and Administration.
D. Design and Equipment.
E. Research and Demonstration.
F. Reports and Analyses.
G. Bibliography.

HE 20.2512:CT • Item 486-A-3
BIBLIOGRAPHIES AND LISTS OF PUBLICATIONS. [Irregular]

COMMUNITY HEALTH SERVICE
(1970– 1973)

HE 20.2551:date
ANNUAL REPORT.

HE 20.2552:CT • Item 512-E-1
GENERAL PUBLICATIONS.

Earlier FS 2.2

HE 20.2557/2:date
CHScene, NOTES FROM THE COMMUNITY HEALTH SERVICE. 1970– [Irregular]

PURPOSE:– To serve as a forum for all members of the partnership for health. Supersedes Partnership for Health News (HE 20.2559).

HE 20.2558:CT • Item 512-E-2
HANDBOOKS, MANUALS, GUIDES.

Earlier FS 2.6/3
Later HE 20.5108

HE 20.2559:date
PARTNERSHIP FOR HEALTH NEWS. – 1970. [Irregular]

Earlier FS 2.319
Superseded by CHScene (HE 20.2557/2).

HE 20.2560:date
PUBLICATIONS CATALOG.

COMPREHENSIVE HEALTH
PLANNING SERVICE
(1970– 1973)

HE 20.2581:date
ANNUAL REPORT.

HE 20.2582:CT • Item 486-D-1
GENERAL PUBLICATIONS. [Irregular]

HE 20.2588/2:date • Item 486-D-2
MANUAL FOR REVIEW AND COMMENT. (Technical Assistance Branch)

PURPOSE:– To provide direction and guidance for comprehensive health planning agencies involved in review and comment of new and expanded health facilities or services in their area. It is helpful to health providers and the public in understanding the reasons for review and the process which planning agencies might undertake in carrying out this responsibility.

REGIONAL MEDICAL PROGRAMS
SERVICE
(1970– 1973)

HE 20.2601:date
ANNUAL REPORT.

Later HE 20.6301

HE 20.2602:CT • Item 483-L-1
GENERAL PUBLICATIONS.

Earlier FS 2.2
Later HE 20.6302

HE 20.2608:CT • Item 483-L-2
HANDBOOKS, MANUALS, GUIDES.

Earlier FS 2.6/2

HE 20.2609:date
SMOKING AND HEALTH BULLETIN. 1970– [Irregular] (National Clearinghouse for Smoking and Health)

Supersedes Smoking and Health Bibliographical Bulletin.
Earlier FS 2.24/4, prior to Dec. 1969.
Later HE 20.2316, after April-May 1972.

HE 20.2610:date
PROGRESS REPORTS, REGIONAL MEDICAL PROGRAMS FOR HEART DISEASE, CANCER, STROKE AND RELATED DISORDERS.

Earlier FS 2.313

HE 20.2611:date • Item 483-L-3
SELECTED BIBLIOGRAPHY OF REGIONAL MEDICAL PROGRAMS. [Irregular]

Earlier FS 2.24:M 46/2

HE 20.2612:date • Item 483-L-4
DIRECTORY OF ON-GOING RESEARCH IN SMOKING AND HEALTH. 1st– 1967– [Annual] (PHS publication 1665) (National Clearinghouse for Smoking and Health)

Earlier FS 2.2:Sm 7/5
Later HE 20.2317

INDIAN HEALTH SERVICE
(1970– 1973)

CREATION AND AUTHORITY

The Indian Health Service was transferred to the Health Services Administration (HE 20.5300) by reorganization order, effective July 1, 1973.

HE 20.2651:date
ANNUAL REPORT.
Later HE 20.5301

HE 20.2651/2:date
HEALTH PROGRAM SYSTEMS CENTER: ANNUAL REPORT.

HE 20.2652:CT • Item 486-I-2
GENERAL PUBLICATIONS.

Earlier FS 2.2
Later 20.5302

HE 20.2658:CT • Item 486-I-1
HANDBOOKS, MANUALS, GUIDES.
Earlier FS 2.6/2

HE 20.2658/2:nos.
OEH [Office of Environmental Health] GUIDELINES. 1– 1970– [Irregular]

This series consists of both the technical and administrative publications of the Office of Environmental Health and serves to amplify and further define the statements of policy within the operational framework contained in the Environmental Health Chapter of the Indian Health Service Manual.

HE 20.2659:date • Item 486-F
DENTAL SERVICES FOR NATIVE AMERICAN INDIANS AND ALASKA NATIVES. 1957– [Annual] (PHS publication 1870)

Earlier FS 2.86/3
Later HE 20.5309

HE 20.2660:CT/date
INDIAN VITAL STATISTICS [by area]. 1967–

Earlier FS 2.86/5

HE 20.2661:date • Item 486-I-3
INDIAN HEALTH TRENDS AND SERVICES. [Irregular] (Office of Program Planning and Evaluation, Program Analysis and Statistics Branch) (PHS Publication 2092)

Supersedes Indian Health Highlights (FS 2.2:In 25/9).
Earlier FS 2.2:In 25/18
Later HE 20.5310

FEDERAL HEALTH PROGRAM
SERVICE
(1970– 1973)

HE 20.2701:date
ANNUAL REPORT.

Later HE 20.5201

HE 20.2702:CT • Item 494-C-1
GENERAL PUBLICATIONS.

Earlier FS 2.2
Later HE 20.5202

HE 20.2708:CT
HANDBOOKS, MANUALS, GUIDES.

HE 20.2709:date • Item 494-C
ANNUAL STATISTICAL SUMMARY, FISCAL YEAR. 1959–

Later HE 20.5409

HE 20.2710:v.nos.&nos. • Item 494-C-2
AUTOMATED MULTIPHASIC HEALTH TESTING BIBLIOGRAPHY. v. 1. 1970. [Irregular]

HE 20.2710/2:CT • Item 494-C-3
BIBLIOGRAPHIES AND LISTS OF PUBLICATIONS.

HE 20.2711:date • Item 494-C-4
ALCOHOL AND YOU, HSMHA EMPLOYEE HEALTH PROGRAM ON ALCOHOLISM. 1972– 1973. [Bimonthly] (Federal Health Programs Service)

The HSMHA Employee Health Program on Alcoholism was established for the benefit of all HSMHA employees. The Program intends to develop educational programs so that all employees will be made aware that alcoholism is a progressive illness, usually involving a large intake of alcohol over several years before its symptoms become manifest to others.
Each issue provides a background discussion guide to a particular subject.

NATIONAL INSTITUTES OF HEALTH

HE 20.3001/2:C 16/11

MATERNAL AND CHILD HEALTH SERVICE
(1970– 1973)

HE 20.2751:date • Item 483-V-6
ANNUAL REPORT.

Later HE 20.5401

HE 20.2752:CT • Item 483-V-1
GENERAL PUBLICATIONS.

HE 20.2755:CT • Item 483-V-5
LAWS.

HE 20.2758:CT • Item 483-V-3
HANDBOOKS, MANUALS, GUIDES.

HE 20.2759:CT • Item 483-V-2
BIBLIOGRAPHIES AND LISTS OF PUBLICATIONS.

HE 20.2760:nos. • Item 483-V-4
MCHS STATISTICAL SERIES. 1– 1971– [Irregular]

Later HE 20.5113

HE 20.2761:nos.
MATERNAL AND CHILD HEALTH INFORMATION. 1970– 1973. [Monthly]

Superseded by the Community Health Scene (HE 20.5109).

NATIONAL INSTITUTE FOR OCCUPATIONAL SAFETY AND HEALTH
(1971– 1974)

HE 20.2801:date
ANNUAL REPORT.

HE 20.2802:CT
GENERAL PUBLICATIONS.

HE 20.2809:date • Item 494-D-1
TOXIC SUBSTANCES LIST. [Annual]

Later HE 20.7112

HE 20.2810:nos. • Item 494-D-3
OH [Occupational Health] (series).

HE 20.2811:CT • Item 494-D-4
CRITERIA FOR A RECOMMENDED STANDARD, OC-CUPATIONAL EXPOSURE TO [various subjects]. 1972– [Irregular]

Later HE 20.7110

HE 20.2812:CT
BIBLIOGRAPHIES AND LISTS OF PUBLICATIONS.

BUREAU OF COMMUNITY ENVIRONMENTAL MANAGEMENT
(1972– 1974)

HE 20.2851:date
ANNUAL REPORT.

Earlier HE 20.1801

HE 20.2852:CT • Item 512-F
GENERAL PUBLICATIONS.

Earlier HE 20.1802

HE 20.2859:nos. • Item 483-O
INJURY CONTROL RESEARCH LABORATORY: RESEARCH REPORTS, ICRL-RR- (series). [Irregular]

HE 20.2860:CT
POSTERS. [Irregular]

NATIONAL CENTER FOR FAMILY PLANNING SERVICE
(1972– 1973)

HE 20.2909:v.nos.&nos. • Item 494-E-1
FAMILY PLANNING DIGEST. v. 1– 1972– [Bimonthly]

Later HE 20.5111

NATIONAL INSTITUTES OF HEALTH
(1970–   )

INFORMATION

National Institutes of Health
9000 Rockville Pike
Bethesda, Maryland 20892
(301) 496-6000
http://www.nih.gov

HE 20.3001:date • Item 506-G (MF)
ANNUAL REPORT.

HE 20.3001/2:CT • Item 506-G (MF)
ANNUAL REPORTS OF COMMITTEES, STUDY SECTIONS, ETC.

HE 20.3001/2:Ad 9/date
ADULT DEVELOPMENT AND AGING RESEARCH COMMITTEE.

HE 20.3001/2:Ag 4/2/date
AGING REVIEW COMMITTEE.

HE 20.3001/2:Al 5/date
ALLERGY AND IMMUNOLOGY STUDY SECTION.

HE 20.3001/2:An 5/date
ANIMAL RESOURCES ADVISORY COMMITTEE.

HE 20.3001/2:Ar 7/2/date
NATIONAL ARTHRITIS, METABOLISM, AND DI-GESTIVE DISEASES ADVISORY COUNCIL.

HE 20.3001/2:Au 8/date
AUTOMATION IN THE MEDICAL LABORATORY SCIENCES REVIEW COMMITTEE.

HE 20.3001/2:B 13/date
BACTERIOLOGY AND MYCOLOGY STUDY SECTION.

HE 20.3001/2:B 39/date
BEHAVIORAL SCIENCES RESEARCH CONTRACT REVIEW COMMITTEE.

HE 20.3001/2:B 39/2/date
DEVELOPMENTAL BEHAVIORAL SCIENCES STUDY SECTION.

HE 20.3001/2:B 52/date
BIOPHYSICS AND BIOPHYSICAL CHEMISTRY A STUDY SECTION.

HE 20.3001/2:B 52/2/date
BIOPHYSICS AND BIOPHYSICAL CHEMISTRY B STUDY SECTION.

HE 20.3001/2:B 52/3/date
BIOMEDICAL COMMUNICATIONS STUDY SECTION.

HE 20.3001/2:B 52/4/date
BIOCHEMISTRY STUDY SECTION.

HE 20.3001/2:B 52/5/date
BIOMEDICAL LIBRARY REVIEW COMMITTEE.

HE 20.3001/2:B 52/6/date
BIOMETRY AND EPIDEMIOLOGY CONTRACT REVIEW COMMITTEE.

HE 20.3001/2:B 62/date
BLOOD DISEASES AND RESOURCES ADVISORY COMMITTEE.

HE 20.3001/2:B 62/2/date
NATIONAL BLOOD RESOURCE PROGRAM ADVISORY COMMITTEE.

HE 20.3001/2:B 74/date
BREAST CANCER EXPERIMENTAL BIOLOGY COMMITTEE.

HE 20.3001/2:B 74/2/date
BREAST CANCER DIAGNOSIS COMMITTEE.

HE 20.3001/2:B 74/3/date
BREAST CANCER TREATMENT COMMITTEE.

HE 20.3001/2:C 16/date
CANCER CLINICAL INVESTIGATION REVIEW COMMITTEE.

HE 20.3001/2:C 16/2/date
CANCER CONTROL COMMUNITY ACTIVITIES REVIEW COMMITTEE.

HE 20.3001/2:C 16/3/date
CANCER CONTROL AND REHABILITATION AD-VISORY COMMITTEE.

HE 20.3001/2:C 16/4/date
CANCER IMMUNOTHERAPY COMMITTEE.

HE 20.3001/2:C 16/5/date
CANCER IMMUNOBIOLOGY COMMITTEE.

HE 20.3001/2:C 16/6/date
CANCER IMMUNODIAGNOSIS COMMITTEE.

HE 20.3001/2:C 16/7/date
THIRD NATIONAL CANCER SURVEY UTILIZATION ADVISORY COMMITTEE.

HE 20.3001/2:C 16/8/date
CANCER CONTROL, PREVENTION, AND DETEC-TION REVIEW COMMITTEE.

HE 20.3001/2:C 16/9/date
CANCER SPECIAL PROGRAM ADVISORY COM-MITTEE.

HE 20.3001/2:C 16/10/date
CANCER RESEARCH CENTER REVIEW COMMIT-TEE.

HE 20.3001/2:C 16/11/date
CANCER TREATMENT ADVISORY COMMITTEE.

Guide to U.S. Government Publications 413

HE 20.3001/2:C 16/12/date
CANCER CONTROL GRANT REVIEW COMMITTEE.

HE 20.3001/2:C 16/13/date
CANCER CONTROL ADVISORY COMMITTEE.

HE 20.3001/2:C 16/14/date
CANCER CONTROL EDUCATION REVIEW COMMITTEE.

HE 20.3001/2:C 16/15/date
CANCER CONTROL TREATMENT AND REHABILITATION REVIEW COMMITTEE.

HE 20.3001/2:C 17/date
CARDIOLOGY ADVISORY COMMITTEE.

HE 20.3001/2:C 17/2/date
CARCINOGENESIS PROGRAM SCIENTIFIC REVIEW COMMITTEE A.

HE 20.3001/2:C 17/3/date
CARCINOGENESIS PROGRAM SCIENTIFIC REVIEW COMMITTEE B.

HE 20.3001/2:C 17/4/date
CARCINOGENESIS PROGRAM SCIENTIFIC REVIEW COMMITTEE C.

HE 20.3001/2:C 17/5/date
CARDIOVASCULAR AND RENAL STUDY SECTION.

HE 20.3001/2:C 17/6/date
CARDIOVASCULAR AND PULMONARY STUDY SECTION.

HE 20.3001/2:C 33/date
CELL BIOLOGY STUDY SECTION.

HE 20.3001/2:C 42/date
CHEMICAL/BIOLOGICAL INFORMATION HANDLING REVIEW COMMITTEE.

HE 20.3001/2:C 43/date
NATIONAL ADVISORY CHILD HEALTH AND HUMAN DEVELOPMENT COUNCIL.

HE 20.3001/2:C 61/date
CLINICAL APPLICATIONS AND PREVENTION ADVISORY COMMITTEE.

HE 20.3001/2:C 61/2/date
GENERAL CLINICAL RESEARCH CENTERS COMMITTEE.

HE 20.3001/2:C 73/date
COMPUTER AND BIOMATHEMATICAL SCIENCES STUDY SECTION.

HE 20.3001/2:C 73/2/date
COMMUNICATIVE SCIENCES STUDY SECTION.

HE 20.3001/2:C 73/3/date
COMMUNICATIVE DISORDERS REVIEW COMMITTEE.

HE 20.3001/2:C 76/date
CONTRACEPTIVE DEVELOPMENT CONTRACT REVIEW COMMITTEE.

HE 20.3001/2:C 76/2/date
CONTRACEPTIVE EVALUATION RESEARCH CONTRACT REVIEW COMMITTEE.

HE 20.3001/2:D 43/date
NATIONAL ADVISORY DENTAL RESEARCH COUNCIL.

HE 20.3001/2:D 43/2/date
DENTAL CARIES PROGRAM ADVISORY COMMITTEE.

HE 20.3001/2:D 43/3/date
DIVISION OF RESEARCH GRANTS: DENTAL STUDY SECTION.

HE 20.3001/2:D 43/4/date
DENTAL RESEARCH INSTITUTES AND SPECIAL PROGRAMS ADVISORY COMMITTEE.

HE 20.3001/2:D 56/date
DIGESTIVE DISEASES COORDINATING COMMITTEE.

HE 20.3001/2:Em 1/date
HUMAN EMBRYOLOGY AND DEVELOPMENT STUDY SECTION.

HE 20.3001/2:En 2/date
ENDOCRINOLOGY STUDY SECTION.

HE 20.3001/2:En 8/date
NATIONAL ADVISORY ENVIRONMENTAL HEALTH SCIENCES COUNCIL.

HE 20.3001/2:Ep 4/2/date
EPIDEMIOLOGY AND DISEASE CONTROL STUDY SECTION.

HE 20.3001/2:Ep 4/3/date
EPIDEMIOLOGY AND BIOMETRY ADVISORY COMMITTEE.

HE 20.3001/2:Ey 3/date
NATIONAL ADVISORY EYE COUNCIL.

HE 20.3001/2:G 28/date
GENETICS STUDY SECTION.

HE 20.3001/2:H 35/date
INTERAGENCY TECHNICAL COMMITTEE ON HEART, BLOOD VESSEL, LUNG, AND BLOOD DISEASES; AND BLOOD RESOURCES.

HE 20.3001/2:H 35/2/date
HEART AND LUNG PROGRAM PROJECT COMMITTEE.

HE 20.3001/2:H 37/date
HEMATOLOGY STUDY SECTION.

HE 20.3001/2:H 99/date
HYPERTENSION RESEARCH CENTERS ADVISORY COMMITTEE.

HE 20.3001/2:Im 6/date
IMMUNOLOGICAL SCIENCES STUDY SECTION.

HE 20.3001/2:Im 6/2/date
IMMUNOBIOLOGY STUDY SECTION.

HE 20.3001/2:In 3/date
INFECTIOUS DISEASE COMMITTEE.

HE 20.3001/2:K 54/date
ARTIFICIAL KIDNEY-CHRONIC UREMIA ADVISORY COMMITTEE.

HE 20.3001/2:M 31/date
MAMMALIAN MUTANT CELL LINES COMMITTEE.

HE 20.3001/2:M 46/date
NATIONAL ADVISORY GENERAL MEDICAL SCIENCES COUNCIL.

HE 20.3001/2:M 46/2/date
GENERAL MEDICINE A STUDY SECTION.

HE 20.3001/2:M 46/3/date
GENERAL MEDICINE B STUDY SECTION.

HE 20.3001/2:M 46/5/date
MEDICINAL CHEMISTRY A STUDY SECTION.

HE 20.3001/2:M 46/6/date
MEDICINAL CHEMISTRY B STUDY SECTION.

HE 20.3001/2:M 46/7/date
TROPICAL MEDICINE AND PARASITOLOGY STUDY SECTION.

HE 20.3001/2:M 46/8/date
NATIONAL MEDICAL LIBRARIES ASSISTANCE ADVISORY BOARD.

HE 20.3001/2:M 52/date
MENTAL RETARDATION RESEARCH COMMITTEE.

HE 20.3001/2:M 56/2/date
METABOLISM STUDY SECTION.

HE 20.3001/2:M 58/date
MICROBIAL CHEMISTRY STUDY SECTION.

HE 20.3001/2:M 73/date
MOLECULAR CONTROL WORKING GROUP.

HE 20.3001/2:M 73/2/date
MOLECULAR BIOLOGY STUDY SECTION.

HE 20.3001/2:N 39/date
NEUROLOGY A STUDY SECTION.

HE 20.3001/2:N 39/2/date
NEUROLOGY B STUDY SECTION.

HE 20.3001/2:N 39/3/date
NEUROLOGICAL DISORDERS PROGRAM-PROJECT REVIEW A COMMITTEE.

HE 20.3001/2:N 39/4/date
NEUROLOGICAL DISORDERS PROGRAM-PROJECT REVIEW B COMMITTEE.

HE 20.3001/2:N 39/5/date
NATIONAL ADVISORY NEUROLOGICAL AND COMMUNICATIVE DISORDERS AND STROKE COUNCIL.

HE 20.3001/2:N 39/6/date
NEUROLOGICAL DISEASES AND STROKE SCIENCE INFORMATION PROGRAM ADVISORY COMMITTEE.

HE 20.3001/2:N 95/date
NUTRITION STUDY SECTION.

HE 20.3001/2:Or 1/date
ORAL BIOLOGY AND MEDICINE STUDY SECTION.

HE 20.3001/2:P 27/date
PATHOLOGY A STUDY SECTION.

HE 20.3001/2:P 27/2/date
PATHOLOGY B STUDY SECTION.
HE 20.3001/2:P 41/date
PERIODONTAL DISEASES ADVISORY COMMITTEE.

HE 20.3001/2:P 49/date
PHARMACOLOGY STUDY SECTION.

HE 20.3001/2:P 49/2/date
PHARMACOLOGY-TOXICOLOGY PROGRAM COMMITTEE.

HE 20.3001/2:P 56/date
APPLIED PHYSIOLOGY AND BIOENGINEERING STUDY SECTION.

HE 20.3001/2:P 56/2/date
PHYSIOLOGY STUDY SECTION.

HE 20.3001/2:P 56/3/date
PHYSIOLOGICAL CHEMISTRY, STUDY SECTION.

HE 20.3001/2:P 81/date
POPULATION RESEARCH COMMITTEE.

HE 20.3001/2:P 81/2/date
POPULATION RESEARCH STUDY SECTION.

HE 20.3001/2:P 93/date
PRIMATE RESEARCH CENTERS ADVISORY COMMITTEE.

HE 20.3001/2:P 95/date
EXPERIMENTAL PSYCHOLOGY STUDY SECTION.

HE 20.3001/2:R 11/date
RADIATION STUDY SECTION.

HE 20.3001/2:R 11/2/date
ULTRAVIOLET RADIATION AND SKIN CANCER WORKING GROUP.

HE 20.3001/2:R 11/3/date
DIAGNOSTIC RADIOLOGY COMMITTEE.

HE 20.3001/2:R 26/date
BOARD OF REGENTS.

HE 20.3001/2:R 31/2/date
GENERAL RESEARCH SUPPORT PROGRAM ADVISORY COMMITTEE.

HE 20.3001/2:Sci 2/2/date
BOARD OF SCIENTIFIC COUNSELORS (National Eye Institute).

HE 20.3001/2:Sci 2/3/date
BOARD OF SCIENTIFIC COUNSELORS (Division of Cancer Treatment).

HE 20.3001/2:Sci 2/4/date
BOARD OF SCIENTIFIC COUNSELORS (Division of Cancer Biology and Diagnosis).

HE 20.3001/2:Sci 2/5/date
BOARD OF SCIENTIFIC COUNSELORS (National Institute of Arthritis, Metabolism, and Digestive Diseases).

HE 20.3001/2:Sci 2/6/date
BOARD OF SCIENTIFIC COUNSELORS (National Institute of Child Health and Human Development).

HE 20.3001/2:Sci 2/7/date
BOARD OF SCIENTIFIC COUNSELORS (National Institute of Allergy and Infectious Diseases).

HE 20.3001/2:Sci 2/8/date
BOARD OF SCIENTIFIC COUNSELORS (National Institute of Dental Research).

HE 20.3001/2:Sci 2/9/date
BOARD OF SCIENTIFIC COUNSELORS (National Institute on Drug Abuse).

HE 20.3001/2:Sci 2/10/date
BOARD OF SCIENTIFIC COUNSELORS (National Institute of Environmental Health Sciences).

HE 20.3001/2:Si 1/date
SICKLE CELL DISEASE ADVISORY COMMITTEE.

HE 20.3001/2:Su 7/date
SURGERY A STUDY SECTION.

HE 20.3001/2:Su 7/2/date
SURGERY B STUDY SECTION.

HE 20.3001/2:T 34/date
THERAPEUTIC EVALUATIONS COMMITTEE.

HE 20.3001/2:T 34/2/date
EXPERIMENTAL THERAPEUTICS STUDY SECTION.

HE 20.3001/2:T 66/date
TOXICOLOGY STUDY SECTION.

HE 20.3001/2:T 68/date
TRANSPLANTATION AND IMMUNOLOGY COMMITTEE.

HE 20.3001/2:T 83/date
TUMOR VIRUS DETECTION WORKING GROUP.

HE 20.3001/2:T 83/2/date
SOLID TUMOR VIRUS WORKING GROUP.

HE 20.3001/2:V 81/date
VIROLOGY STUDY SECTION.

HE 20.3001/2:V 81/2/date
VIRUS CANCER PROGRAM SCIENTIFIC REVIEW COMMITTEE A.

HE 20.3001/2:V 81/3/date
VIRUS CANCER PROGRAM SCIENTIFIC REVIEW COMMITTEE B.

HE 20.3001/2:V 81/4/date
VIRUS CANCER PROGRAM ADVISORY COMMITTEE.

HE 20.3001/2:V 81/5/date
AD HOC COMMITTEE FOR REVIEW OF THE SPECIAL VIRUS CANCER PROGRAM.

HE 20.3001/2:V 82/date
VISUAL SCIENCES A STUDY SECTION.

HE 20.3001/2:V 82/2/date
VISUAL SCIENCES B STUDY SECTION.

HE 20.3001/2:V 82/3/date
VISION RESEARCH PROGRAM COMMITTEE.

HE 20.3001/3:date/v.nos.   • Item 506-C (MF)
BIENNIAL REPORT OF THE NATIONAL INSTITUTES OF HEALTH.

HE 20.3002:CT   • Item 507
GENERAL PUBLICATIONS.

> Earlier FS 2.22

HE 20.3002:Au 2   • Item 507
CATALOG OF AUDIOVISUAL MATERIALS. [Irregular] (Library Branch, Nonprint Media Center)

HE 20.3002:B 52/4/date   • Item 507
BIOTECHNOLOGY RESOURCES. [Irregular] (Research Resources Information Center)

> Sub-title: A Research Resources Directory.

HE 20.3002:B 62/13   • Item 507
DIRECTORY OF COMMUNITY HIGH BLOOD PRESSURE CONTROL ACTIVITIES. [Irregular]

HE 20.3002:M 46/4   • Item 507
CLINICAL CENTER: MEDICAL STAFF DIRECTORY. [Annual] (Office of Medical Staff Affairs)

HE 20.3002:N 21/4/date   • Item 507
BASIC DATA RELATING TO THE NATIONAL INSTITUTES OF HEALTH. [Annual] (Office of Program Planning and Evaluation)

> Later HE 20.3041

HE 20.3006:CT   • Item 507-A-21
REGULATIONS, RULES, AND INSTRUCTIONS.

HE 20.3007:CT
PRESS RELEASES.

HE 20.3007/2:nos.   • Item 507-A-27
NEWS AND FEATURES FROM NIH, PORTFOLIO SERIES. 1–   [Irregular]

HE 20.3007/3:v.nos./nos.   • Item 507-A-27 (EL)
THE NIH RECORD. [Biweekly]

HE 20.3008:CT   • Item 507-H
HANDBOOKS, MANUALS, GUIDES.

> Earlier FS 2.22/15, FS 2.22

HE 20.3008/2:v.nos.&nos.   • Item 507-A-29 (EL)
NIH GUIDE FOR GRANTS AND CONTRACTS. v. 1– 1970–   [Irregular]

> PURPOSE:– To provide policy and administrative information to individuals and organizations who need to be kept informed of requirements and changes in grants and contracts activities administered by the National Institutes of Health.
> Provides dissemination of scientific program announcements, receipt dates for applications, dates of review cycles, and policies and procedures affecting grants.

HE 20.3008/2 a: • Item 507-A-29
– SEPARATES.

> Consists of reprints or extracts from NIH Guide for Grants and Contracts (HE 20.3008/2).

HE 20.3008/2-2:nos.   • Item 507-A-29
NIH GUIDE FOR GRANTS AND CONTRACTS. SUPPLEMENT.

HE 20.3008/3:nos.
NIH ADMINISTRATIVE MANUAL.

> Also called NIH Manual.
> For internal use, not sent to depositories.

HE 20.3008/4:date   • Item 507-A-56
REFERRAL GUIDELINES FOR FUNDING COMPONENTS OF PHS. [Biennial]

HE 20.3009:date   • Item 506-A
NIH PUBLICATIONS LIST. 1969–   [Semiannual]

> PURPOSE:– To provide an indexed reference source of all publications published by the National Institutes of Health.
> Former Title: NIH Quarterly Publication List.
> Earlier FS 2.22/13-9

HE 20.3009/2:date
RECENT TRANSLATION, SELECTED LIST. [Monthly]

> Earlier FS 2.22/130-2, prior to Dec. 1969.

HE 20.3009/3:date   • Item 506-A
CURRENT AND NON-CURRENT PERIODICALS IN THE NIH LIBRARY. 1965–   [Annual]

> Title and subject indexes to periodicals received in the NIH library.
> Former title: Periodicals Currently Received in the NIH Library.
> Earlier FS 2.22/13-3

HE 20.3010:date   • Item 507
CLINICAL CENTER, CURRENT CLINICAL STUDIES AND PATIENT REFERRAL PROCEDURES. 1953– [Semiannual]

> PURPOSE:– To provide brief descriptive material about major current clinical studies and an explanation of patient referral procedures. The Clinical Center is a laboratory-hospital facility that is shared by the eight National Institutes of Health that conduct combined laboratory and clinical study programs and the National Institute of Mental Health.
> Previously distributed to Depository Libraries under item No. 507-A-22.
> Earlier FS 2.22:C 61/3

HE 20.3011:nos.   • Item 483-U
COMPUTER RESEARCH AND TECHNOLOGY DIVISIONS: TECHNICAL REPORTS. 1–   1968– [Irregular]

> PURPOSE:– To provide technical documents of particular interest in the biomedical community. These reports include detailed descriptions of relevant computer programs and instructions in the use, as well as some theoretical background, in hopes that interested scientists will be encouraged to gain first-hand experience in applying them. In some cases, such reports may serve as foci around which DCRT will structure training courses to expand the knowledge and experience of NIH staff in applying computer science to problems of research and management.
> Earlier FS 2.22/64

HE 20.3011/2:date   • Item 506-G-2 (MF)
DIVISION OF COMPUTER RESEARCH AND TECHNOLOGY: ANNUAL REPORT.

HE 20.3012:CT   • Item 506-A (MF)
BIBLIOGRAPHIES AND LISTS OF PUBLICATIONS.

> Earlier FS 2.22/13

HE 20.3013:date   • Item 507-D
PUBLIC HEALTH SERVICE GRANTS AND AWARDS. [Annual]

> PURPOSE:– To provide information about grant and award programs supporting institutions, associations and foundations, State and local governments, and individuals.
> Issued in three volumes:

> Part 1. National Institutes of Health, Research Grants, Research Contracts.
> Part 2. National Institutes of Health, Training, Construction, Medical Libraries, and Summary Tables (including Research).
> Part 3. Health Services and Mental Health Administration, Food and Drug Administration, and Environmental Health Service.
> ISSN 0502-4749
> Earlier FS 2.22/7

HE 20.3013/2:date   • Item 507-D-9
BIOMEDICAL INDEX TO PHS-SUPPORTED RE-
SEARCH. 1961–   [Annual]

PURPOSE:– To disseminate information about
the current research in the biomedical sciences
being conducted by investigators with the aid of
Public Health Service research grant support.
Earlier titled: Research Awards Index.
Earlier: Research Grants Index.
Earlier FS 2.22/7-2

HE 20.3013/2-2:date   • Item 507-D-11 (MF)
NATIONAL INSTITUTES OF HEALTH RESEARCH
GRANTS: FISCAL YEAR (date) FUNDS. [Annual]

HE 20.3013/2-3:date   • Item 507-E-5
INDEX OF FEDERALLY SUPPORTED PROGRAMS IN
HEART, BLOOD VESSEL, LUNG, AND BLOOD
DISORDERS. [Annual]

Covers the fiscal year.

HE 20.3013/2-4:date   • Item 500-E-4 (EL)
CRISP BIOLOGICAL RESEARCH INFORMATION.

Issued on CD-ROM.

HE 20.3013/3:date
NATIONAL INSTITUTE OF HEALTH GRANTS AND
AWARDS, ARRANGED BY STATE, CITY AND IN-
STITUTION, REPORT 19M. [Monthly]

Information appears in HE 20.3013

HE 20.3013/4:date   • Item 507-D-10 (MF)
RESEARCH AND DEVELOPMENT CONTRACTS,
FISCAL YEAR FUNDS. [Annual]

Supersedes in part: Public Health Service
Grants and Awards (HE 20.3013).

HE 20.3013/4-2:date   • Item 507-D-14 (MF)
ANNUAL REPORT, DATA CAPTURED IN THE IMPAC
SYSTEM FOR RESEARCH AND DEVELOPMENT
CONTRACTS RECORDED DURING FY ....

HE 20.3013/5:date   • Item 507-D-12 (MF)
GRANTS FOR TRAINING, CONSTRUCTION, CANCER
CONTROL, MEDICAL LIBRARIES. [Annual]
(Statistics and Analysis Branch, Division of Re-
search Grants)

Continues: Grants for Training, Construction,
Medical Libraries (ISSN 1047-6955); and in part,
Public Health Service Grants and Awards (ISSN
0502-4749) (HE 20.3013).

HE 20.3013/6:v.nos.&nos.   • Item 507-A-30 (EL)
RESEARCH RESOURCES REPORTER. v. 1–
[Monthly]

ISSN 0160-807X

HE 20.3013/6 a   • Item 507-A-30
RESEARCH RESOURCES REPORTS (separates).

HE 20.3014:nos.   • Item 507-U
RESOURCES FOR BIOMEDICAL RESEARCH AND
EDUCATION, REPORTS. 1–   1962–   [Irregu-
lar]

Prepared by the Resources Analysis Branch,
Office of Program Planning.
PURPOSE:– To provide reference data on
significant developments relating to the Nation's
resources and requirements for medical and
health- related research and education. It is devoted to analyses of key resource variables including research manpower, expenditures,
facilities, and the economic, social, and institutional factors bearing upon such resources.
Former title: Resources for Medical Research
and Education, Reports.

HE 20.3014/2:nos.   • Item 507-W
RESOURCES ANALYSIS MEMOS. 1–   1959–
[Irregular]

Earlier FS 2.22/35

HE 20.3015:date   • Item 507-A-24 (MF)
MEDICAL STAFF FELLOWSHIP AT THE NATIONAL
INSTITUTES OF HEALTH.

Continues: Associated Training Programs in
Medical and Biological Sciences at National Insti-
tutes of Health.
Earlier FS 2.22:M 46/4

HE 20.3015/2:date   • Item 507-A-44 (MF)
SUMMER RESEARCH FELLOWSHIP PROGRAM AT
THE NATIONAL INSTITUTES OF HEALTH.
[Annual]

PURPOSE:– To provide a catalog of courses
open to all students of U.S. medical and dental
schools. Gives information on application and
selection procedures for the program and highlights current areas of study to which students
may be assigned.

HE 20.3015/3   • Item 506-A-9
SUMMER JOBS AT NIH, CATALOG. [Annual]

HE 20.3016:date   • Item 507-A-23 (EL)
NIH ALMANAC. 1964–   [Annual] (Office of Information)

PURPOSE:– To provide important historical
data and other reference material, updated annually. Contains pertinent facts about the National
Institutes of Health for biomedical research, research training, health professions manpower
resources, and biomedical communications.
Earlier FS 2.22:Al 6

HE 20.3017:date   • Item 506-A-5 (MF)
SCIENTIFIC DIRECTORY AND ANNUAL BIBLIO-
GRAPHY. 1956–   [Annual] (Office of Informa-
tion)

PURPOSE:– Intended for reference use by
research workers in the biomedical sciences. It
presents the broad outlines of NIH organizational
structure, the professional staff, and their scientific and technical publications covering work done
at NIH. Material is arranged by components, with
the directory and bibliography entries presented
together at the laboratory or branch level within
each component. The Directory includes the
names of scientific staff members, other key individuals, and visiting scientists and guest workers with tenure of a year or more.
ISSN 0083-2197
Earlier FS 2.22/13-8

HE 20.3018:date   • Item 507-N (MF)
NIH PUBLIC ADVISORY GROUPS: AUTHORITY,
STRUCTURE, FUNCTIONS. 1969–   [Semiannual]
(Committee Management Staff)

ISSN 0566-8301
Earlier FS 2.22/22-2

HE 20.3019:   • Item 507-A-17 (MF)
ADDRESSES.

HE 20.3020:CT   • Item 506-J
POSTERS.

HE 20.3020/2:CT
AUDIOVISUAL MATERIALS.

HE 20.3021:CT   • Item 507-A-19 (MF)
NURSING CLINICAL CONFERENCES PRESENTED
BY THE NURSING DEPARTMENT OF CLINICAL
CENTER.

Earlier FS 2.22/60

HE 20.3022:v.nos.&nos.   • Item 506-E
DRG [Division of Research Grants] NEWSLETTER.
[Irregular]

HE 20.3023:date   • Item 506-F
MEDICAL AND HEALTH RELATED SCIENCES THE-
SAURUS. 1963–   [Annual] (Division of Research
Grants)

This thesaurus is an indexing authority list
maintained by the Research Documentation Section for the annual Research grants index (HE
20.2013/2) a subject-matter index of research

projects supported by the Public Health Service.
It is an integral component of a comprehensive
computer search and retrieval system in the Division of Research Grants of the NIH, and is intended to aid the efforts of individuals and organizations who have the responsibility for developing scientific communications systems.

HE 20.3024:date   • Item 507-G
PROGRESS AGAINST CANCER, REPORT BY
NATIONAL ADVISORY CANCER COUNCIL. (PHS
Publication 1720)

Report of the National Advisory Cancer Council on progress in research against cancer conducted during the year.
Former title: Progress in Research on Cancer.
Earlier FS 2.22/14-2, FS 2.22:C 16/1

HE 20.3025:date   • Item 507-A-28
INVENTORY OF FEDERAL POPULATION RESEARCH,
FISCAL YEAR. 1970–   [Annual] (Interagency
Committee on Population Research)

PURPOSE:– To facilitate the exchange of information among those concerned with the population research activities funded by the various
Federal agencies and to encourage the coordination of research efforts. The scope of the Inventory, which lists all Federally supported research
projects in the field of population sciences,
encompasses a broad spectrum of research in
the biological, medical, social, and behavioral
sciences.
Previous title: Analysis of Federal Population
Research (ISSN 0092-850X).
Superseded by Inventory and Analysis of Federal Population Research (HE 20.3362/2).
ISSN 0092-7457

HE 20.3026:CT   • Item 507-A-31 (MF)
ENVIRONMENTAL IMPACT STATEMENTS. [Irregular]

HE 20.3027:date   • Item 507-A-32 (MF)
NATIONAL DIABETES ADVISORY BOARD: ANNUAL
REPORT. 1st–   1978–

Report to Congress on progress made in diabetes research treatment during the year.

HE 20.3027/2:date   • Item 506-A-12 (MF)
NATIONAL ARTHRITIS ADVISORY BOARD: ANNUAL
REPORT.

HE 20.3027/3:date   • Item 507-A-46 (MF)
NATIONAL CANCER ADVISORY BOARD: ANNUAL
REPORT.

Summarizes the Board's activities and recommendations regarding cancer research, planning, policy, and programs.

HE 20.3027/4:date   • Item 507-A-49 (MF)
ANNUAL REPORT OF THE NATIONAL DIGESTIVE
DISEASES ADVISORY BOARD. [Annual]

HE 20.3028:date   • Item 506-A-9 (MF)
DIABETES MELLITUS COORDINATING COMMITTEE,
ANNUAL REPORT TO THE DIRECTOR, NATIONAL
INSTITUTES OF HEALTH, FISCAL YEAR (date).
1st–   1974–

Earlier HE 20.3317

HE 20.3029:CT   • Item 507-A-33 (MF)
NATIONAL DIABETES ADVISORY BOARD: PUBLI-
CATIONS. [Irregular]

HE 20.3030:date   • Item 507-A-36 (MF)
NATIONAL INSTITUTES OF HEALTH CONSENSUS
DEVELOPMENT CONFERENCE SUMMARIES.
[Annual]

HE 20.3030/a:CT   • Item 507-A-36
– SEPARATES. [Irregular]

HE 20.3030/2
[REPRINTS OF ARTICLES PUBLISHED CONCERN-
ING NIH CONSENSUS DEVELOPMENT CONFER-
ENCES.] [Irregular]

HE 20.3031:CT • Item 506-A-13
MEDICINE FOR THE PUBLIC (series). [Irregular]

Intended for the general public, each publication is devoted to a specific topic, such as high blood pressure, ulcers, cancer, allergies, and other areas of biomedical research.

HE 20.3032:date • Item 507-A-35 (MF)
ARTHRITIS INTERAGENCY COORDINATING COMMITTEE: ANNUAL REPORT TO THE SECRETARY, FISCAL YEAR (date).

PURPOSE:– To present reports by individual Federal agencies on their research and activities in the field of arthritis. Intended as a reference and useful resource for Federal, State, and local agencies, the biomedical community and others involved in various aspects of rheumatic diseases.

HE 20.3033:date • Item 507-A-37 (MF)
PROGRAM HIGHLIGHTS. [Annual] (National Center for Research Resources)

Summarizes activities of the Division programs such as general clinical research centers, biomedical research and of projects designed to strengthen minority biomedical research.

HE 20.3034:date • Item 508-P (MF)
NEW GRANTS AND AWARDS, REPORT 19M. [Quarterly]

Lists by area and institution, new research training, construction, and medical library grants; new research contracts; and new research fellowship and research career program awards.

HE 20.3035:date • Item 507-A-38 (MF)
DIVISION OF RESEARCH SERVICE: ANNUAL REPORT.

Summarizes Division activities which include supporting biomedical research projects through planning, providing models and substrates, doing research, and recording and communicating research results.

HE 20.3036 • Item 507-A-39 (MF)
PROGRAM IN BIOMEDICAL AND BEHAVIORAL NUTRITION RESEARCH AND TRAINING, FISCAL YEAR. [Annual]

Presents reports on the nutrition program conducted through the various NIH institutes.

HE 20.3036/2:date • Item 507-A-39
PERSONNEL NEEDS AND TRAINING FOR BIOMEDICAL AND BEHAVIORAL RESEARCH. [Biennial]

HE 20.3036/3:date • Item 506-G (MF)
BIOMEDICAL ENGINEERING AND INSTRUMENTATION BRANCH, DIVISION OF RESEARCH BRANCH: ANNUAL REPORT.

HE 20.3036/4 • Item 507-A-57
RESEARCH AND DISCOVERY, ADVANCES IN BEHAVIORAL AND SOCIAL SCIENCES RESEARCH. [Semiannual]

HE 20.3037:date • Item 506-A-16 (EL)
TELEPHONE AND SERVICE DIRECTORY.

HE 20.3037/2:CT • Item 506-A-19 (MF)
DIRECTORIES.

HE 20.3037/3:date • Item 506-A-20
DIRECTORY FORMER GRANTS ASSOCIATES. [Irregular]

HE 20.3037/4:date • Item 506-A-21 (MF)
GENERAL CLINICAL RESEARCH CENTERS: A RESEARCH RESOURCES DIRECTORY. [Annual]

A guide to the clinical research projects, inpatient and outpatient facilities, and special assay services, tests, and instrument savailable at the general clinical research centers supported by NIH's National Center for Research Resources.

HE 20.3037/5: • Item 506-A-22 (MF)
DIRECTORY, EXTRAMURAL ASSOCIATES. [Annual]

Directory of Associates of NIH's Extramural Associates Program, by states. Extramural Associates are located at various universities and colleges throughout the U.S. and its territories.

HE 20.3037/6: • Item 506-A-23 (MF)
BIOMEDICAL RESEARCH TECHNOLOGY RESOURCES: A RESEARCH RESOURCES DIRECTORY. [Biennial]

A directory of resources available under the Biomedical Research Technology Program, which applies the physical sciences, mathematics, computers science, and engineering to biology and medicine. Organized by program area, then by type and by title under the type.

HE 20.3037/7 • Item 506-A-23 (MF)
MINORITY BIOMEDICAL RESEARCH SUPPORT PROGRAM, A RESEARCH RESOURCES DIRECTORY.

HE 20.3038:CT • Item 506-H
SEARCH FOR HEALTH (series). [Irregular]

Each issue deals with the treatment and prevention of a specific disease. Co-published in English and Spanish.

HE 20.3038/2: • Item 506-H-1
HEALTHLINE. [Irregular]

Contains short articles on the prevention of disease and the promotion of health through knowledge derived from research.

HE 20.3039:letters/year-nos. • Item 507-A-40
NIH PROGRAM EVALUATION REPORTS. [Irregular]

Published in microfiche.

HE 20.3040:date • Item 507-A-41 (MF)
SCHEDULE OF NIH CONFERENCES. [Quarterly]

Consists of two parts; The first lists and describes coming conferences, the second summarizes results of conferences already held. A calendar of biomedical meetings for the academic year may also be included in certain issues.
Also published in microfiche.

HE 20.3041:CT • Item 507-A-42
NIH DATA BOOK, BASIC DATA RELATING TO THE NATIONAL INSTITUTES OF HEALTH. [Annual]

Tables present statistics on NIH activities in research and development, appropriations, obligations, and awards.
Earlier HE 20.3002:N 21/4

HE 20.3042:date • Item 507-A-43 (MF)
CLINICAL ELECTIVES FOR MEDICAL AND DENTAL STUDENTS AT THE NATIONAL INSTITUTES OF HEALTH, CATALOG. [Annual]

Catalog of elective courses at the National Institutes of Health which are open to students from any U.S. medical or dental school.

HE 20.3043: • Item 507-A-45 (MF)
RECOMBINANT DNA RESEARCH (series). [Irregular]

DNA = deoxyribonucleic acid.
Each volume covers activities in regard to NIH guidelines for recombinant DNA research over a state period of time.
Earlier HE 20.3002:R 24

HE 20.3043/2:date • Item 507-A-45 (MF)
RECOMBINANT DNA ADVISORY COMMITTEE, MINUTES OF MEETING. [Annual]

HE 20.3044:date • Item 507-H (EL)
HANDBOOK FOR STAFF PHYSICIANS. [Annual] [Irregular]

HE 20.3045: • Item 507-A-47 (MF)
NIH PEER REVIEW NOTES. [Irregular] (Division of Research Grants)

Issued by the Division to inform NIH consultants and staff of developments on grant review policies and procedures.

HE 20.3045/2:date • Item 507-A-47 (MF)
DRG PEER REVIEW TRENDS. [Annual] (Division of Research Grants)

HE 20.3046:v.nos.&nos. • Item 507-A-36
NATIONAL INSTITUTES OF HEALTH CONSENSUS DEVELOPMENT CONFERENCE STATEMENTS.

HE 20.3047:date • Item 506-K (MF)
ABSTRACTS OF SMALL BUSINESS INNOVATION RESEARCH, PHASE I AND II PROJECTS. [Annual]

Abstracts of SBIR projects, organized by funding agency within the Department and by awarding component within each agency. Awards are made on the basis of scientific and technical merit, program relevance, potential for commercial application, and availability of funds.

HE 20.3047/2:date • Item 506-K (MF)
OMNIBUS SOLICITATION OF THE PUBLIC HEALTH SERVICE FOR SMALL BUSINESS INNOVATION RESEARCH (SBIR) GRANT APPLICATIONS. [Annual]

Earlier HE 20.28

HE 20.3048:date • Item 507-A-50 (MF)
DRG ANNUAL REPORT.

DRG = Division of Research Grants.

HE 20.3050:date • Item 507-A-48 (MF)
INSTRUCTIONS AND DATA SPECIFICATIONS FOR REPORTING DHHS OBLIGATIONS TO INSTITUTIONS OF HIGHER EDUCATION AND OTHER NONPROFIT ORGANIZATIONS. [Annual]

Instructions and specifications for reporting DHHS oblications to institutions of higher education and other nonprofit organizations.

HE 20.3051 • Item 506-G-3
DIVISION OF LEGISLATIVE ANALYSIS HIGHLIGHTS. [Irregular]

Each issue deals with various highlights of a session of the current Congress.
Earlier HE 20.3002:L 52/3

HE 20.3052:date • Item 506-G-4
WARREN G. MAGNUSON CLINICAL CENTER: ANNUAL REPORT.

PURPOSE:– To summarize activities of the Center, which is the world's largest hospital devoted exclusively to clinical research. Areas include hospital epidemiology, nuclear medicine, rehabilitation medicine, etc.

HE 20.3052/2:date • Item 506-G-4 (MF)
THE WARREN GRANT MAGNUSON CLINICAL CENTER (ANNUAL BROCHURE).

HE 20.3053:date
STAFF TRAINING IN EXTRAMURAL PROGRAMS. [Irregular]

HE 20.3053/2 • Item 507-D-10 (MF)
NIH EXTRAMURAL PROGRAMS, FUNDING FOR RESEARCH AND RESEARCH TRAINING.

HE 20.3054:v.nos.&nos. • Item 507-A-51 (EL)
PHARMACY NEWSLETTER. [Bimonthly] (Pharmacy Department, Clinical Center of NIH)

The newsletter contains short items on current concepts, pharmacy news, pharmacy department highlights, and formulary additions and deletions.
No longer a depository item. For internal/administrative use only, under 44 U.S.C. section 1902.

HE 20.3055: • Item 507-A-52 (MF)
EXTRAMURAL TRENDS. [Annual]

Presents data on extramural activities, awards in connection with which now account for 84 percent of the total NIH budget.

HE 20.3055/2 • Item 507-A-52 (EL)
NIH EXTRAMURAL DATA AND TRENDS. [Annual]

HE 20.3057: • Item 506-A-24
THE BEAR ESSENTIALS. [Irregular]

The newsletter contains information from the various disciplines within the pediatric branch of NIH.

HE 20.3058:date • Item 507-A-38 (MF)
NATIONAL INSTITUTES OF HEALTH DISEASE PREVENTION REPORT. [Annual]

HE 20.3059:nos. • Item 506-L
FORMS.

HE 20.3060 • Item 506-A-19
NIH TRAINING CENTER CATALOG AND CALENDAR. [Annual]

HE 20.3061:v.nos./nos • Item 506-A-19
THE NIH CATALYST. [Monthly]

HE 20.3062:CT • Item 507-A-54
FACT SHEET, NATIONAL INSTITUTES OF HEALTH

HE 20.3063 • Item 507-A-55 (MF)
THE HUMAN GENOME PROJECT PROGRESS REPORT, FISCAL YEARS . . . [Biennial]

HE 20.3064: • Item 506-M (E)
ELECTRONIC PRODUCTS (misc.).

HE 20.3065: • Item 507-A-58
NIH CURRICULUM SUPPLEMENT SERIES.
Issued on CD-ROM.

BUREAU OF HEALTH MANPOWER EDUCATION
(1970– 1973)

HE 20.3101:date
ANNUAL REPORT.

HE 20.3102:CT • Item 507-D-1
GENERAL PUBLICATIONS.
Earlier FS 2.22

HE 20.3108:CT • Item 507-D-3
HANDBOOKS, MANUALS, GUIDES.
Earlier FS 2.6/2

HE 20.3108/2:nos.
PRACTICAL GUIDE SERIES. 1– 1972– [Irregular] (Dental Health Center, Division of Dental Health)

HE 20.3109:sec.nos. • Item 507-D-2
HEALTH MANPOWER SOURCE BOOK. 1– 1952– [Irregular]

A miscellaneous collection of reports on various aspects of health manpower. Some sections deal with a single profession or occupation, some with several, and some with both health occupations and the health service industry data from decennial census.
The first 19 sections were issued by the former Division of Public Health Methods.
Earlier HE 20.2:M 31, FS 2.2:M 31

HE 20.3110:date • Item 493-C
NURSES IN PUBLIC HEALTH. [Irregular]

Reports the census of nurses employed in public health; analyzes trends in public health nursing manpower in the United States over a period of 30 years. Describes number, types, and other pertinent characteristics of National, State, and local agencies employing nurses for public health.
Earlier FS 2.81

HE 20.3111:date • Item 507-D-4
CURRENT RESEARCH PROJECT GRANTS. [Annual]

PURPOSE:– To list current nursing research project grants supported by Division of Nursing. Gives State, grant number, investigator, institution, and title of project.
Earlier FS 2.22:N 93/8.

HE 20.3112:date • Item 483-G
FLUORIDATION CENSUS. [Annual]
Earlier FS 2.304

HE 20.3113:CT • Item 507-D-5
BIBLIOGRAPHIES AND LISTS OF PUBLICATIONS.
Earlier FS 2.22/13

HE 20.3114:CT • Item 507-D-6
DMI [Division of Manpower Intelligence] REPORTS.
Later HE 20.6109

HE 20.3114/2:CT • Item 507-D-7
HEALTH MANPOWER DATA SERIES.

HE 20.3114/3:CT • Item 507-D-7
HEALTH MANPOWER CLEARINGHOUSE SERIES.
1971– [Irregular] (Division of Manpower Intelligence, National Clearinghouse for Health Manpower Information)

HE 20.3114/4:CT • Item 507-D-6
DMI ANALYTIC STUDIES (series). [Irregular]
Later HE 20.6109/2

HE 20.3116:CT • Item 507-D-8
YOU-IN [Youth Opportunities Unlimited in Nursing] (series). 1972– [Irregular]

NATIONAL CANCER INSTITUTE
(1970–   )

INFORMATION

National Cancer Institute
Department of Health and Human Services
National Institutes of Health
9000 Rockville Pike
Bethesda, Maryland 20892
(301) 435-3848
Toll Free: (800) 422-6237
http://www.cancer.gov

HE 20.3151:date • Item 507-G-18 (MF)
ANNUAL REPORT.

HE 20.3151/2:date • Item 507-G-17 (MF)
DIVISION OF CANCER RESEARCH RESOURCES AND CENTERS: ANNUAL REPORT.

HE 20.3151/3 • Item 507-G-19
DIVISION OF CANCER ETIOLOGY: ANNUAL REPORT.

Earlier: Division of Cancer Cause and Prevention: Annual Report.

HE 20.3151/4:date • Item 507-G-20
DIVISION OF CANCER PREVENTION AND CONTROL: ANNUAL REPORT.

Earlier: Division of Cancer Control and Rehabilitation: Annual Report.

HE 20.3151/5:date • Item 507-G-21 (MF)
DIVISION OF CANCER TREATMENT: ANNUAL REPORT.

HE 20.3151/6:date • Item 507-G-23
DIVISION OF CANCER BIOLOGY AND DIAGNOSIS: ANNUAL REPORT.

HE 20.3151/7:date • Item 507-G-35 (MF)
DIVISION OF EXTRAMURAL ACTIVITIES: ANNUAL REPORT.

Also published in microfiche.

HE 20.3151/8:date • Item 507-G-48 (MF)
DIVISION OF BASIC SCIENCES DIRECTORY. [Annual]

HE 20.3151/9 • Item 507-G-48 (MF)
DIVISION OF CLINICAL SCIENCES. ANNUAL RESEARCH DIRECTORY.

HE 20.3152:CT • Item 507-G-2
GENERAL PUBLICATIONS.
Earlier FS 2.22

A 20.3152/a:CT • Item 507-G-2
GENERAL PUBLICATIONS (separates).

E 20.3152/15 • Item 507-G-62 (EL)
THE NEALON REPORT (series). [Biannual]

HE 20.3153/2:date • Item 507-G-4
INFORMATION BULLETIN. 1966–   [Annual]

PURPOSE:– To describe for potential clinical, research, or staff associate applicants the work of the various units of the National Cancer Institute.

HE 20.3153/3:date • Item 507-G-29
DCT BULLETIN. [Irregular] (Division of Cancer Treatment)

PURPOSE:– To present brief summaries and announcements about conferences, research, policies, and other activities of the Division of Cancer Treatment.

HE 20.3158:CT • Item 507-G-6
HANDBOOKS, MANUALS, GUIDES.

HE 20.3159:v.nos.&nos. • Item 507-A-1
CARCINOGENESIS ABSTRACTS. v. 1–   1963–
[Monthly]

PURPOSE:– To provide an alerting service covering the literature pertinent to the induction of cancer in animals and human beings.
ISSN 0008-6258
Earlier FS 2.22/39, prior to v. 7, no. 12.

HE 20.3159/2:nos. • Item 507-G-12 (MF)
CARCINOGENESIS TECHNICAL REPORT SERIES, NCI-CG-TR- (series). 1–   [Irregular]

HE 20.3160:v.nos.&nos. • Item 507-A-9
CANCER CHEMOTHERAPY REPORTS, PT. 1. v. 1–
1959–   [Bimonthly] (Includes 10 monthly issues and approximately four supplements which are issued as Parts 2 or 3).

PURPOSE:– To provide an informal journal for the prompt publication of preliminary preclinical and clinical reports on cancer chemotherapy. Includes original contributions on all aspects of the treatment of cancer, preliminary reports of work in progress, appropriate commentaries and reviews, letters of pertinent to published articles, and the proceedings of symposia of interest to cancer chemotherapists.
Indexed by:–
Chemical Abstracts
Index to U.S. Government Periodicals
ISSN 0361-5960
Earlier FS 2.22/30

HE 20.3160/2:v.nos.&nos. • Item 507-A-9
CANCER CHEMOTHERAPY REPORTS, PT. 2. v. 1–
1968– [Irregular] (Subscription included with Pt. 1)

Contains the results of extensive but well defined studies in the field of cancer chemotherapy requiring the presentation of a large volume of data. Emphasis is on the publication of positive data both in tabular form as well as articles reviewing structure-activity relationships. Certain special studies carried out to augment the screening program are presented here. Part 2 was established to help fill the void created when Cancer Chemotherapy Screening Data was discontinued in 1968.
Indexed by: Index to U.S. Government Periodicals.
Earlier FS 2.22/30-3

HE 20.3160/3:v.nos.&nos.   **• Item 509-A-9**
CANCER CHEMOTHERAPY REPORTS. PT. 3. v. 1–
1968–   [Irregular] (Subscription included with
Pt. 1)

     Contains chemotherapy program information
(such as clinical brochures) of interest to chemotherapists.
     Indexed by: Index to U.S. Government Peri-
odicals.
     Earlier FS 2.22/30-4

HE 20.3160/4:v.nos.&nos.   **• Item 507-A-10**
CANCER CHEMOTHERAPY ABSTRACTS. v. 1– 12.
1960– 1972. [Bimonthly]

     PURPOSE:– To make available abstracts,
annotations, or citations of significant cancer chemotherapy articles collected from the current major
biomedical sources of the world literature.
     Annual index issued separately.
     Earlier FS 2.22/30-2

HE 20.3161:v.nos.&nos.   **• Item 488 (P) (EL)**
JOURNAL OF THE NATIONAL CANCER INSTITUTE.
v. 1– 1940– [Bimonthly]

     PURPOSE:– To publish original observations
in laboratory and clinical research in cancer. Articles include studies in laboratory and clinical
research epidemiology, and cancer control. Occasionally entire issues are devoted to the proceedings of scientific conferences or symposiums.
     Title page, list of contents, and index con-
tained in the June and December issues.
     Indexed by:
       Biological Abstracts
       Chemical Abstracts
       Index to U.S. Government Periodicals
       Index Medicus
       International Aerospace Abstracts
       Nuclear Science Abstracts
       ISSN 0027-8874

INDEXES.

     Cumulative index for v. 1– 16, 1940– 56,
was published in October 1957.

HE 20.3161/a:CT   **• Item 488**
SEPARATES. [Irregular]

HE 20.3161/2:date   **• Item 507-G-49**
NEWS FROM THE NATIONAL CANCER INSTITUTE.

     Previously: HE 20.3152:N47

HE 20.3161/3   **• Item 507-G-56**
NEWS FROM THE NATIONAL 5 A DAY PROGRAM.
[Semiannual]

HE 20.3162   **• Item 507-L**
NCI MONOGRAPHS. 1– 1959– [Irregular]

     Includes proceedings of scientific meetings
related to cancer and important collections of
interest.

HE 20.3162/2:v.nos.   **• Item 507-G-11**
CANCER RESEARCH SAFETY MONOGRAPH SERIES.
v. 1– [Irregular]

HE 20.3162/3:nos.   **• Item 507-L**
NCI MONOGRAPHS. [Irregular]

HE 20.3162/4:nos.   **• Item 507-L-15**
NATIVE AMERICAN MONOGRAPH (series).

HE 20.3162/5:CT   **• Item 507-L-16**
SEER MONOGRAPH.

HE 20.3163:   **• Item 507-G**
PROGRESS AGAINST CANCER, REPORT BY
NATIONAL ADVISORY CANCER COUNCIL.

HE 20.3164:CT   **• Item 507-G-1**
CHEMOTHERAPY FACT SHEETS. 1968– [Irregular]

     Contains information on preliminary preclini-
cal and clinical drug trials, the work reported not
being considered suitable for formal publication.
Results of work in progress, including negative
results, are also included.

HE 20.3165:CT   **• Item 507-G-3 (MF)**
BIBLIOGRAPHIES AND LISTS OF PUBLICATIONS.

HE 20.3165/2:nos.   **• Item 507-G-22**
OCC/SB (series). [Irregular] (Cancer Information Clearinghouse, Office of Cancer Communications)

     PURPOSE:– To provide bibliographies of
materials that present a variety of approaches to
cancer education.

HE 20.3165/3:date
CANCER INFORMATION CLEARINGHOUSE, QUAR-
TERLY ACCESSIONS LIST.

HE 20.3166:CT   **• Item 507-V**
RESEARCH REPORTS. [Irregular]

     Earlier FS 2.22/32-2

HE 20.3167:v.nos.&nos.   **• Item 507-G-5**
VIRAL TUMORIGENESIS REPORT. v. 1– v. 10, no. 2.
– 1972. [Semiannual]

HE 20.3168:date   **• Item 507-G-7**
NATIONAL CANCER PROGRAM: REPORT OF THE
NATIONAL CANCER ADVISORY BOARD. 1st–
[Annual]

     Report submitted by the Board to the Presi-
dent and Congress pursuant to the National Cancer Act of December 23, 1971, to report on its
activities in advising and assisting the Director of
the National Cancer Institute with respect to the
National Cancer Program.

HE 20.3168/2:date   **• Item 507-G-2**
NATIONAL CANCER PROGRAM, STRATEGIC PLAN
SERIES. 1973–

HE 20.3168/3:CT   **• Item 507-G-2**
NATIONAL CANCER PROGRAM PUBLICATIONS SE-
RIES.

HE 20.3168/4:date   **• Item 507-G-8 (MF)**
NATIONAL CANCER PROGRAM, REPORT OF THE
DIRECTOR. [Annual]

HE 20.3168/5:date   **• Item 507-G-9 (EL)**
NATIONAL CANCER PROGRAM: REPORT OF THE
PRESIDENT'S CANCER PANEL. [Annual]

HE 20.3168/6:date   **• Item 507-G-15**
NATIONAL CANCER PROGRAM REVIEW FOR COM-
MUNICATORS. [Irregular]

     Discontinued with issue for May 1979.

HE 20.3169:CT   **• Item 507-G-2**
PROGRESS AGAINST CANCER (series). 1974–
[Irregular] (Office of Cancer Communication, Na-
tional Cancer Program)

     PURPOSE:– To provide general information
to the public on causes, symptoms, diagnosis,
treatment and research of cancer. Individual leaflets are published for specific area or organs in
which cancer occurs.

HE 20.3170:CT   **• Item 507-G-10 (MF)**
INTERNATIONAL CANCER RESEARCH DATA BANK
PROGRAM [Publications].

HE 20.3171:nos.   **• Item 507-G-13**
NATIONAL CANCER INSTITUTE SMOKING AND
HEALTH PROGRAM [reports].

HE 20.3172:date   **• Item 507-G-14 (MF)**
REPORT OF THE DIVISION OF CANCER TREATMENT,
NCI.

HE 20.3172/2:date   **• Item 507-G-38**
CANCER TREATMENT SYMPOSIA. [Semiannual]

     Each volume presents proceedings of one or
more cancer symposia dealing with such areas
as surgery, radiotherapy, chemotherapy, supportive care, and medicinal chemistry. Manuscripts
are illustrated with tables, diagrams, graphs, elec-
tron micrographs, and photomicrographs. So far,
only two or three volumes have been issued a
year, consisting of 100 to 120 pages.

HE 20.3172/3   **• Item 507-G-61 (P) (EL)**
CANCER PROGRESS REPORT.

HE 20.3173:nos.   **• Item 507-G-16 (MF)**
INTERNATIONAL CANCER RESEARCH DATA BANK
PROGRAM: SPECIAL LISTING (series). 1–

HE 20.3173/2:letters-nos.
ICRDB CANCERGRAM. [Irregular] (International Cancer
Research Data Bank)

     PURPOSE:– To provide an abstracting ser-
vice for researchers on various aspects of cancer.
     Issued in the following sub-series:–

HE 20.3173/2:date
ORGAN SITE CARCINOGENESIS SKIN. [Monthly]

HE 20.3173/2:CB-(nos.) • Item 507-G-28 (MF)
CANCER BIOLOGY. [Irregular]

HE 20.3173/2:CK-(nos.) • Item 507-G-27 (MF)
CHEMICAL, ENVIRONMENTAL, AND RADIATION
CARCINOGENESIS. [Irregular]

HE 20.3173/2:CT-(nos.) • Item 507-G-26 (MF)
DIAGNOSIS AND THERAPY. [Irregular]

HE 20.3173/2-2:date   **• Item 507-G-28 (MF)**
RECENT REVIEWS, CARCINOGENESIS. [Annual]

     Supplement to the Cancergrams.

HE 20.3173/2-3:date   **• Item 507-G-28**
RECENT REVIEWS, CANCER DIAGNOSIS AND
THERAPY, SUPPLEMENT TO THE CANCER-
GRAMS. [Annual]

HE 20.3173/2-4:date   **• Item 507-G-28**
RECENT REVIEWS, CANCER VIROLOGY AND BIO-
LOGY, SUPPLEMENT TO THE CANCER- GRAMS.
[Annual]

HE 20.3173/3:letters-nos. • Item 507-G-16 (MF)
ONCOLOGY OVERVIEW, NCI/ICRDB (series).
[Irregular]

HE 20.3174:date   **• Item 507-G-25 (MF) (EL)**
NATIONAL CANCER INSTITUTE FACT BOOK. [Annual]

     PURPOSE:– To provide the Institute staff,
advisory groups, and others involved in management of National Cancer Programs with general
information, budget data, grants and contracts
information, and historical data about the National Cancer Institute.
     Cover title: NCI Fact Book.

HE 20.3175:CT   **• Item 507-G-24**
POSTERS. [Irregular]

HE 20.3175/2:CT
AUDIOVISUAL MATERIALS. [Irregular]

HE 20.3176:date   **• Item 507-G-30 (MF)**
NCI GRANTS AWARDED, FISCAL YEAR (date).

     PURPOSE:– To provide a directory of re-
search grants awarded by the National Cancer
Institute in the United States and abroad. Arrangement is by State, city, institution, and grant
number.

HE 20.3176/2
NCI GRANTS AWARDED, BY PRINCIPAL INVESTI-
GATOR.

HE 20.3176/3:date   **• Item 507-G-30 (MF)**
EXTRAMURAL GRANT AND CONTRACT AWARDS BY
PRINCIPAL INVESTIGATOR/CONTRACTOR. [An-
nual]

HE 20.3176/4:date   **• Item 507-G-30 (MF)**
EXTRAMURAL GRANT AND CONTRACT AWARDS BY
STATE, CITY INSTITUTION AND NUMBER. [An-
nual]

HE 20.3177:date • Item 507-G-31 (MF)
ANNUAL REPORT ON NATIONAL CANCER INSTI-
TUTE AND ENVIRONMENTAL PROTECTION
AGENCY PROJECTS.

Highly technical progress reports on projects
undertaken under the collaborative program between the National Cancer Institute and the Environmental Protection Agency concerning environmental cancer.

HE 20.3178:date • Item 507-G-32 (MF)
FIELD STUDIES AND STATISTICS PROGRAM. [Annual]
(Cancer Cause and Prevention Division)

Summarizes Program activities in its primary
function of intramural research into cancer epidemiology and biometry.

HE 20.3179:date
NCI GRANT SUPPORTED LITERATURE INDEX.
[Monthly]

HE 20.3180:date • Item 507-G-34 (MF)
NCI INVESTIGATIONAL DRUGS, PHARMACEUTICAL
DATA. [Annual]

PURPOSE:– To provide product information.
Drugs commercially available in the U.S. are excluded.

HE 20.3180/2:date • Item 507-G-34 (MF)
NCI INVESTIGATIONAL DRUGS, CHEMICAL INFOR-
MATION. [Annual]

HE 20.3180/2-2 • Item 507-G-34 (EL)
NCI INVESTIGATIONAL DRUGS, CHEMICAL INFOR-
MATION (database).

HE 20.3180/3:date • Item 507-G-39 (MF)
CCPDS PUBLIC REPORT. [Annual]

CCPDS = Centralized Cancer Patient Data
Systems.
PURPOSE:– To present historical background
for and accomplishments of the Centralized Cancer Patient Data System.

HE 20.3181: • Item 507-G-36
CHILDREN WITH CANCER (series). [Irregular]

Posters issued by the Institute.

HE 20.3182: • Item 507-G-37
CANCER FACTS (series). [Irregular]

Covers miscellaneous cancer subjects.
Former title: Fact Sheets (series).

HE 20.3182/2:CT • Item 507-G-37
BACKGROUNDER (series). [Irregular]

HE 20.3182/3:CT • Item 507-G-37
UPDATE (various topics). [Irregular]

HE 20.3182/4:nos. • Item 507-G-37
PARTNERS IN PREVENTION UPDATE. [Quarterly]

HE 20.3182/5:date • Item 507-G-37
NIH ALMANAC UPDATE. [Annual]

HE 20.3182/6: • Item 507-G-45
DATOS SOBRE TIPOS DE CANCER (series) (FACTS
ON CANCER SITES).

Each of these Spanish publications deals with
a different site in the body at which cancer may
occur. The agency has advised that they will not
be offered in English and may be revised from
time to time.

HE 20.3182/6-2:CT • Item 507-G-37
DATOS SOBRE EL CANCER (Cancer Facts).

HE 20.3182/7:CT • Item 507-G-37
FACT SHEET.

HE 20.3182/8: • Item 507-G-46
STATEMENT (various topics).

HE 20.3182/9: • Item 507-G-50 (EL)
SCLD UPDATES INDEX (database).

HE 20.3182/9-2:date • Item 507-G-55 (EL)
SCLD (State Legislative Database) Update.

HE 20.3182/9-3 • Item 507-G-50 (EL)
SCLD FACT SHEETS.

HE 20.3183:date • Item 507-G-3
PUBLICATIONS LIST FOR THE PUBLIC AND PA-
TIENTS. [Quarterly]

HE 20.3183/2:date • Item 507-G-3
PUBLICATIONS LIST FOR HEALTH PROFESSION-
ALS .[Quarterly]

HE 20.3183/3:date • Item 507-G-3
PUBLICATION CATALOGUE AND ORDER FORM. [An-
nual]

HE 20.3184:date • Item 507-G-40 (MF)
SMOKING, TOBACCO, AND CANCER PROGRAM,
ANNUAL REPORT.

PURPOSE:– To describe the goals, activities, and plans of the Smoking, Tobacco, and
Cancer Program and to reflect a more refined,
targeted, and aggressive intervention research
strategy toward control of smoking and tobacco.

HE 20.3184/2:nos. • Item 507-G-40 (MF)
SMOKING AND TOBACCO CONTROL MONOGRAPHS
(Series).

HE 20.3185:CT • Item 507-G-41
FORMS. [Irregular]

HE 20.3186:date • Item 507-G-42 (MF) (EL)
CANCER STATISTICS REVIEW.

PURPOSE:– To present data on cancer incidence, mortality, and survival in the U.S.; to analyze trends, and to show where progress has
been made, and where future efforts need to be
directed.
Earlier titled: Annual Cancer Statistics Review.

HE 20.3186/2 • Item 507-G-58 (EL)
THE RESEARCHERS' TOOLBOX.[Irregular]

HE 20.3187:date • Item 507-G-2
TITLE SURVEY OF COMPOUNDS WHICH HAVE BEEN
TESTED FOR CARCINOGENIC ACTIVITY. [Irregu-
lar]

Earlier HE 20.3152:C 17
HE 20.3188:CT • Item 507-G-43 (MF)
DIRECTORIES. [Irregular]

HE 20.3188/2:date • Item 507-G-52
DIVISION OF CANCER EPIDEMIOLOGY AND GE-
NETICS, ANNUAL RESEARCH DIRECTORY. [An-
nual]

HE 20.3189:date • Item 507-G-18 (MF)
OFFICE OF THE DIRECTORY, ANNUAL REPORT.

HE 20.3190:date • Item 507-G-44 (MF)
NATIONAL CANCER INSTITUTE BUDGET ESTIMATE.
[Annual]

PURPOSE– To present by-pass budget funding highlights, funding trends in cancer research,
areas of scientific opportunity, program accomplishments, and program plans.

HE 20.3191:nos. • Item 507-G-37
THE BEAR ESSENTIALS. [Quarterly]

Also issued as HE 20.3057

HE 20.3192 • Item 507-G-50 (E)
PROTOCALL.

HE 20.3193 • Item 507-G-50 (E)
ELECTRONIC PRODUCTS.

HE 20.3194:v.nos./nos. • Item 507-G-53 (EL)
PLCO NEWS. [Semiannual]

HE 20.3195:v.nos./nos. • Item 507-G-51
NBLIC (National Black Leadership Initiative on Cancer) NEWS. [Quarterly].

HE 20.3196:date • Item 507-G-54
DCEG (Division of Cancer Epidemiology and Genetics) LINKAGE. [Quarterly].

HE 20.3197:date • Item 512-G-52
CONVERSION OF NEOPLASMS BY TOPOGRAPHY
AND MORPHOLOGY ICD-0-2 TO ICD-10.

HE 20.3197/2:date • Item 512-G-52
CONVERSION OF NEOPLASMS BY TOPOGRAPHY
AND MORPHOLOGY ICD-0-2 TO ICD-9.

HE 20.3197/3:date • Item 512-G-52
CONVERSION OF NEOPLASMS BY TOPOGRAPHY
AND MORPHOLOGY ICD-0-1 TO ICD—2.

HE 20.3197/4:date • Item 512-G-52
CONVERSION OF NEOPLASMS BY TOPOGRAPHY
AND MORPHOLOGY ICD-0-2 TO ICD—1.

HE 20.3198 • Item 507-G-50 (EL)
PROTOCALL.

HE 20.3199:v.nos./nos. • Item 507-G-57 (P)
CANCER CONSORTIUM. (series)

HE 20.3199/2 • Item 507-G-59
RADIOLOGIC TECHNOLOGISTS HEALTH STUDY,
UPDATE. [Quarterly]

NATIONAL HEART, LUNG, AND BLOOD INSTITUTE
(1975–   )

INFORMATION

National Heart, Lung, and Blood Institute
Department of Health and Human Services
National Institutes of Health -31
9000 Rockville Pike
Bethesda, Maryland 20892
(301) 496-2411
Fax: (301) 402-0818
http://nhlbi.nih.gov

HE 20.3201:date • Item 507-E-13 (MF)
ANNUAL REPORT.

HE 20.3202:CT • Item 507-E-1
GENERAL PUBLICATIONS.
Earlier FS 2.22

HE 20.3202:P 96/2/date • Item 507-E-1
ANALYSIS OF CURRENT PULMONARY RE-
SEARCH PROGRAMS SUPPORTED BY THE
NATIONAL HEART, LUNG, AND BLOOD IN-
STITUTE. [Annual] (Division of Lung Diseases)

Report covers fiscal year.
Continues: Analysis of Current Pulmonary
Research Programs.
ISSN 0160-0591

HE 20.3208:CT • Item 507-E-2
HANDBOOKS, MANUALS, GUIDES.
Earlier FS 2.22/15

HE 20.3209:date • Item 506-A-3
FIBRINOLYSIS, THROMBOLYSIS, AND BLOOD CLOT-
TING BIBLIOGRAPHY. 1966–   [Annual] (Com-
mittee on Thrombolytic Agents)
Prepared in cooperation with National Library
of Medicine.
Earlier FS 2.22/13-6

HE 20.3209/2:v.nos.&nos. • Item 506-A-3
HEMOSTASIS AND THROMBOSIS, BIBLIOGRAPHY.
v. 1–   1966–   [Monthly and annual] (Division
of Blood Diseases and Resources)

Annual cumulation issued separately.
Prior to v. 11, no. 1 issued as Fibrinolysis,
Thrombolysis and Blood Clotting, Bibliography.
ISSN 0360-7607

HE 20.3210:date   • Item 507-E-3
MEDICAL DEVICES APPLICATION PROGRAM, ANNUAL REPORT.

    Entitled Artificial Heart Program, prior to July 29, 1970.

HE 20.3211:date   • Item 507-E-4 (MF)
NATIONAL HEART, BLOOD VESSEL, LUNG, AND BLOOD PROGRAM: ANNUAL REPORT OF THE DIRECTOR OF THE NATIONAL HEART AND LUNG INSTITUTE. 1st– 1974–

HE 20.3211/2:date   • Item 507-E-4 (MF)
NATIONAL HEART, BLOOD VESSEL, LUNG, AND BLOOD PROGRAM, ANNUAL REPORT OF THE DIRECTOR OR THE NATIONAL HEART AND LUNG INSTITUTE. 1st– 1974–

    Report submitted to the President for transmittal to Congress in accordance with P.L. 92-423.

HE 20.3211/2-2   • Item 507-E-4 (MF)
REPORT OF THE DIRECTOR, REPORT OF THE NATIONAL HEART, LUNG, AND BLOOD INSTITUTE.

HE 20.3211/3:date   • Item 507-E-11 (MF)
INTRAMURAL RESEARCH, ANNUAL REPORT.

    Consists of highly technical annual and project reports by the various laboratories and branches of the Institute.

HE 20.3211/4   • Item 505-A-21 (MF)
NHLBI NATIONAL RESEARCH SERVICE AWARD PROGRAMS SUMMARY DESCRIPTIONS.

HE 20.3212:date   • Item 507-E-5 (MF)
SUBJECT INDEX OF CURRENT RESEARCH GRANTS AND CONTRACTS ADMINISTERED BY THE NATIONAL HEART, LUNG, AND BLOOD INSTITUTE.

HE 20.3213:date   • Item 507-E-6 (MF)
MULTIPLE RISK INTERVENTION TRIAL, PUBLIC ANNUAL REPORT.

HE 20.3214:nos.   • Item 507-E-7
NATIONAL HIGH BLOOD PRESSURE EDUCATION PROGRAM: INFOMEMO (series). 1–

HE 20.3214/2:date
INFO MEMO BULLETIN. [Every 6 weeks]
    Now included in Heart Memo, HE 20.3225

HE 20.3214/3:date/nos.   • Item 507-E-15
INFOLINE. [Irregular]

    PURPOSE– To provide updates from the NHLBI on various topics such as disease prevention, education, and control activities in the area of blood resources. It also contains a calendar of upcoming medical events.

HE 20.3215:CT   • Item 507-E-8 (MF)
BIBLIOGRAPHIES AND LISTS OF PUBLICATIONS. [Irregular]

HE 20.3216:date   • Item 507-E-9
NATIONAL HEART, LUNG, AND BLOOD INSTITUTE'S FACT BOOK FOR FISCAL YEAR (date). [Annual]

    PURPOSE:– To provide descriptive text and statistics relating to the work of the Institute during the fiscal year.
    Continues: National Heart and Lung Institute Fact Book.
    ISSN 0363-8995

HE 20.3217:CT   • Item 507-E-10
POSTERS. [Irregular]

HE 20.3218:CT   • Item 507-E-1
FACT SHEETS. [Irregular]

HE 20.3219:date   • Item 507-E-12 (MF)
DEVICES AND TECHNOLOGY BRANCH CONTRACTORS MEETING, SUMMARY AND ABSTRACTS. [Annual]

    Earlier HE 20.3202:C 76

HE 20.3220:date   • Item 505-A-21
REQUEST FOR GRANT APPLICATIONS (series). [Irregular]

    Each request for grant application pertains to research in a different area.

HE 20.3221:date   • Item 507-E-13 (MF)
DIVISION OF LUNG DISEASES, PROGRAM REPORT. [Annual]

HE 20.3222:date/nos.   • Item 507-E-14
RESEARCH UPDATE. [Irregular]

    Published by the Institute's Office of Prevention, Education, and Control. Presents findings from research on diseases of the heart, blood, and lungs.

HE 20.3223:CT   • Item 507-E-8
DIRECTORIES. [Irregular]

HE 20.3224:date   • Item 507-E-13 (MF)
MINORITY PROGRAMS OF THE NATIONAL HEART, LUNG, AND BLOOD INSTITUTE. [Annual]

HE 20.3225:date   • Item 507-E-16 (P) (EL)
HEARTMEMO. [Quarterly]

HE 20.3225/2:date   • Item 507-E-17
ASTHMA MEMO. [3 times a yr.]

NATIONAL INSTITUTE OF ALLERGY AND INFECTIOUS DISEASES (1970–   )

INFORMATION

    National Institute of Allergy and
      Infectious Diseases
    Department of Health and Human Services
    National Institutes of Health -31
    Rm. 7A-50
    31 Center Dr., MSC 2520
    Bethesda, Maryland 20892-2520
    (301) 496-1521
    Fax: (301) 496-4409
    http://www.niaid.nih.gov

HE 20.3251:date
ANNUAL REPORT.

HE 20.3252:CT   • Item 505-A-1
GENERAL PUBLICATIONS.

HE 20.3258:CT   • Item 505-A-2
HANDBOOKS, MANUALS, GUIDES.

HE 20.3259:CT   • Item 505-A-4
BIBLIOGRAPHIES AND LISTS OF PUBLICATIONS.

HE 20.3260:CT   • Item 505-A-3
ADDRESSES. [Irregular]

HE 20.3261:date   • Item 505-A-5
ANNUAL WORKSHOP OF THE ASTHMA AND ALLERGIC DISEASE CENTERS.
    Contains proceedings of the workshop.

HE 20.3262:CT   • Item 505-A-1
ALLERGIC DISEASES RESEARCH (series). [Irregular]

HE 20.3262/2:CT   • Item 505-A-1
INFECTIOUS DISEASE RESEARCH SERIES. [Irregular]

HE 20.3263:date   • Item 505-A-6 (MF)
MICROBIOLOGY AND INFECTIOUS DISEASES PROGRAM, ANNUAL REPORT.

HE 20.3264:v.nos.&nos.   • Item 497-C-4
RECOMBINANT DNA TECHNICAL BULLETIN. v. 1– 1987– [Quarterly]
    Earlier HE 20.3460

HE 20.3265:CT
AUDIOVISUAL MATERIALS. [Irregular]

HE 20.3266:date   • Item 505-A-20 (MF)
NIAID AWARDS. [Annual]

    PURPOSE:– To provide an itemized listing of the extramural grants and contracts of the Institute.

HE 20.3267:   • Item 505-A-22 (MF)
ANNUAL REPORT OF INTRAMURAL ACTIVITIES.

    Summarizes activities and describes research undertaken by the various components of the Institute.

NATIONAL INSTITUTE OF DIABETES AND DIGESTIVE AND KIDNEY DISEASES (1985–   )

CREATION AND AUTHORITY

    Formerly National Institute of Arthritis and Metabolic Diseases; and National Institute of Arthritis, Diabetes, and Digestive and Kidney Diseases. The name was changed to National Institute of Diabetes and Digestive and Kidney Diseases by the Health Research Extension Act of 1985 (99 Stat. 820; 42 U.S.C. 201 note).

INFORMATION

    Office of Communications and Public Liaison
    National Institiute of Diabetes and Digestive
      and Kidney Diseases
    Department of Health and Human Services
    National Institutes of Health - 31
    31 Center Dr., Rm 9A04, MSC 2560
    Bethesda, Maryland 20892-2560
    (301) 496-5741
    http://www.niddk.nih.gov

HE 20.3301:date   • Item 506-A-17 (MF)
ANNUAL REPORT.

HE 20.3302:CT   • Item 507-A-25
GENERAL PUBLICATIONS.

    Earlier FS 2.22

HE 20.3308:CT   • Item 507-A-26
HANDBOOKS, MANUALS, GUIDES.

HE 20.3309:v.nos.&nos.   • Item 507-A-20
ENDOCRINOLOGY INDEX. [Bimonthly]

    PURPOSE:– To provide a current awareness tool for scientists working in the field of endocrinology and to help facilitate greater integration of research and clinical efforts in this field.
    This selected bibliography is produced from the National Library of Medicine's Medical Literature Analysis and Retrieval System (MEDLARS).
    The index includes a subject section, review section, method section, author section, subject index, and an author index.
    ISSN 0013-7235
    Earlier FS 2.22/48-2, prior to v. 2, no. 6

HE 20.3310:v.nos.&nos.   • Item 507-A-15 (EL)
DIABETES LITERATURE INDEX. v. 1– 1966– [Monthly]

    PURPOSE:– To fill an existing need in the field of diabetes and to assist the Institute in meeting its obligations to foster and support laboratory and clinical research into the nature, causes, and therapy for diabetes.
    Annual cumulations.
    ISSN 0012-1819

HE 20.3310/2:v.nos.&nos. • **Item 507-A-15**
DIABETES LITERATURE INDEX, ANNUAL INDEX IS-
SUE. [Annual]

    Earlier FS 2.22/53-2

HE 20.3310/3:v.nos.&nos. • **Item 506-A-15 (EL)**
DIABETES DATELINE, THE NATIONAL DIABETES
INFORMATION CLEARINGHOUSE BULLETIN. v.
1–   1980–   [Bimonthly]

    PURPOSE:– To provide a newsletter contain-
ing information on diabetes of interest to professionals, diabetics, and the general public. Covers
such topics as results of studies on diabetics
and their offspring, referral services and information exchanges for diabetics, and a calendar of
meetings of diabetes-related organizations.

HE 20.3311:v.nos.&nos. • **Item 506-A-2**
ARTIFICIAL KIDNEY BIBLIOGRAPHY. v. 1– 8. 1967–
1974. [Quarterly]

    PURPOSE:– To provide an information me-
dium particularly for contractors and grantees in
the areas of renal failure, artificial kidney transplantation.
    Contains literature citations relevant to the
artificial kidney and related areas selected through
MEDLARS, the computerized literature storage
and retrieval system of the National Library of
Medicine.
    Earlier FS 2.22/13-5

HE 20.3312:v.nos.&nos. • **Item 507-A-13**
ARTHRITIS AND RHEUMATIC DISEASES AB-
STRACTS. v. 1– 6. 1964– 1971. [Monthly]

    PURPOSE:– To make available abstracts of
current papers relevant to this field from virtually
every medical journal published throughout the
world and provide the rheumatologist and allied
professional investigators with a readily system-
atized compilation of current published work.
    Annual index issued separately.
    Discontinued with the completion of v. 6, since
Excerpta Medica's Arthritis and Rheumatism is
available commercially and serves the same
needs.
    Earlier FS 2.22/47

HE 20.3313:v.nos.&nos. • **Item 507-A-14**
GASTROENTEROLOGY ABSTRACTS AND CITA-
TIONS. v. 1– 12. 1966– 1982. [Monthly]

    PURPOSE:– To provide the clinician and
researcher in this field with a readily systemitized
compilation of current published work, and aid in
fostering and supporting laboratory and clinical
research into the nature, causes and therapy of
the diseases of the gastrointestinal tract.
    Makes available to scientists and clinicians
citations of all current papers relevant to this
field from medical journals published throughout
the world; approximately one-third of the citations dealing with the major aspects of gastroenterology have accompanying abstracts.
    Annual index issued separately.
    ISSN 0016-5093
    Earlier FS 2.22/54

HE 20.3314:date • **Item 506-A-6 (MF)**
ANNUAL CONTRACTORS' CONFERENCE ON ARTI-
FICIAL KIDNEY PROGRAM, PROCEEDINGS. 1st–
1968–   [Annual]

    Earlier FS 2.22:K 54.

HE 20.3315:v.nos.&nos. • **Item 506-A-7**
INDEX OF DERMATOLOGY. v. 1–   1969–   [Monthly]

    PURPOSE:– To provide a monthly guide to
the literature in clinical dermatology, investigative dermatology, and dermatopathology.
    Prepared in cooperation with the staff of the
National Library of Medicine.
    ISSN 0090-1245

HE 20.3316:CT • **Item 506-A-8 (MF)**
BIBLIOGRAPHIES AND LISTS OF PUBLICATIONS.

HE 20.3317:date • **Item 506-A-9**
DIABETES MELLITUS COORDINATING COMMITTEE:
ANNUAL REPORT. 1st–   1974–

    Later HE 20.3028

HE 20.3318:v.nos.&nos. • **Item 506-A-10**
KIDNEY DISEASE AND NEPHROLOGY INDEX. v. 1–
1975–   [Bimonthly]

    PURPOSE:– To provide a guide to literature
in experimental, pathological nephrology, clinical
urology. Includes the Artificial Kidney Bibliography.
    ISSN 0363-2369

HE 20.3319:date
ORGANIZATION AND FACT BOOK. [Annual]

HE 20.3320:CT • **Item 506-A-11 (MF)**
NIAMDD RESEARCH ADVANCES (on various
diseases). [Irregular]

    Each issue covers the research efforts, pro-
grams, etc. for a particular disease.

HE 20.3320/2:date • **Item 506-A-11 (MF)**
ARTHRITIS, RHEUMATIC DISEASES, AND RELATED
DISORDERS. [Annual]

    Earlier HE 20.3320:Ar 7

HE 20.3320/2-2:date • **Item 506-A-11 (MF)**
CYSTIC FIBROSIS. [Annual]

    Earlier HE 20.3320:C 99

HE 20.3320/2-3:date • **Item 506-A-11 (MF)**
DIGESTIVE DISEASES. [Annual]

    Earlier HE 20.3320:D 56

HE 20.3320/2-4:date • **Item 506-A-11 (MF)**
DIABETES MELLITUS. [Annual]

    Earlier HE 20.3320:D 54

HE 20.3320/2-5:date • **Item 506-A-11 (MF)**
KIDNEY, UROLOGY AND HEMATOLOGY. [Annual]

HE 20.3321:date • **Item 506-A-14 (MF)**
ARTHRITIS PROGRAM, ANNUAL REPORT TO THE
DIRECTOR. 1st–   1977–

    Report submitted to the President and Con-
gress pursuant to the National Arthritis Act. Describes activities of the Institute in meeting the
goals of the Arthritis Plan concerning progress in
related musculoskeletal diseases.

HE 20.3322:date • **Item 506-A-18 (MF)**
MULTIPURPOSE ARTHRITIS CENTERS PERSONNEL
DIRECTORY. [Annual]

HE 20.3322/2 • **Item 506-A-18 (MF)**
DIRECTORIES.

HE 20.3323:CT • **Item 505-B**
DIGESTIVE DISEASES CLEARINGHOUSE (fact
sheets).

    Each fact sheet concerns a different topic.

HE 20.3323/2:CT • **Item 505-B-1 (P) (EL)**
NATIONAL DIABETES INFORMATION CLEARING-
HOUSE (fact sheets).

HE 20.3323/3:CT • **Item 505-B-2**
FACT SHEETS NATIONAL KIDNEY AND UROLOGIC
DISEASES INFORMATION CLEARINGHOUSE.

HE 20.3324 • **Item 506-A-25**
KU (Kidney/Urologic) NOTES (series). [Irregular]

    Produced by the National Kidney and Uro-
logic Diseases Information Clearinghouse for the
Institute, Presents information/treatment of kidney and urologic diseases.

HE 20.3324/2 • **Item 506-A-27 (EL)**
RESEARCH UPDATES IN KIDNEY AND UROLOGIC
HEALTH. [Semiannual]

HE 20.3325:date • **Item 506-A-11 (CD)**
UNITED STATES RENAL DATA SYSTEM, ANNUAL DATA
REPORT.

HE 20.3325/2 • **Item 506-A-26 (E)**
ELECTRONIC PRODUCTS (misc.).

HE 20.3326 • **Item 506-A-28 (EL)**
PREVENT DIABETES PROBLEMS.

NATIONAL INSTITUTE OF CHILD HEALTH AND HUMAN DEVELOPMENT (1970–   )

INFORMATION

    National Institute of Child Health and
    Human Development
    Department of Health and Human Services
    NIH-3, Rm. 2A32, MSC 2425
    31 Center Dr.
    Bethesda, Maryland 20892
    (301) 496-5133
    Fax: (301) 402-1104
    http://www.nichd.nih.gov

HE 20.3351:date • **Item 506-D-7 (MF)**
ANNUAL REPORT.

HE 20.3351/2:date • **Item 506-D-7 (MF)**
CENTER FOR RESEARCH FOR MOTHERS AND CHIL-
DREN, PROGRESS REPORT. [Annual]

HE 20.3351/3:date • **Item 506-D-5 (MF)**
CENTER FOR POPULATION RESEARCH, PROGRESS
REPORT. [Annual]

HE 20.3352:CT • **Item 506-D-2**
GENERAL PUBLICATIONS.

    Earlier FS 2.22

HE 20.3358: • **Item 506-D-10**
HANDBOOKS, MANUALS, GUIDES. [Irregular]

HE 20.3359:nos. • **Item 506-D**
HUMAN DEVELOPMENT ABSTRACTS. 1–   1968–
[Irregular]

    PURPOSE:– To provide researchers with an
appropriate current awareness service that they
may be appraised of the results of research and
to establish better communication and greater
integration of the research effort in human development.
    Earlier FS 2.22/25-3

HE 20.3360:nos. • **Item 506-D-1**
POPULATION AND REPRODUCTION RESEARCH
ABSTRACTS. [Irregular]

    Title varies.

HE 20.3361:CT • **Item 506-D-3 (MF)**
BIBLIOGRAPHIES AND LISTS OF PUBLICATIONS.

HE 20.3362:nos. • **Item 506-A-4**
POPULATION RESEARCH REPORTS. 1–   [Irregular]
(Scientific Information Centers Branch)

    Earlier FS 2.22/61

HE 20.3362/2:date • Item 506-D-4
INVENTORY AND ANALYSIS OF FEDERAL POPULA-
TION RESEARCH. 1969–   [Annual] (Interagency
Committee on Population Research)

PURPOSE:– To provide timely and comprehensive information on current Federally supported
population research activities in order to meet
the need of those concerned with this growing
and increasingly significant field.
Lists research projects in the field of population research submitted by 13 Federal agencies
as well as institutional program grants. They are
arranged according to a classification system
comprised of four major groupings: 1) Biological
Sciences, 2) Animal Behavior and Ecology, 3)
Social Sciences, and 4) Institutional Programs.
Supersedes Inventory of Federal Population
Research [ISSN 0092-7457] (HE 20.3025), and
Analysis of Federal Population Research [ISSN
0092-850X].
ISSN 0160-6247

HE 20.3362/2-2:date • Item 506-D-4 (MF)
POPULATION SCIENCES, INVENTORY OF PRIVATE
AGENCY POPULATION RESEARCH. [Annual]
(Program Statistics Analysis Branch)

HE 20.3362/3:CT • Item 506-D-5
CPR POPULATION RESEARCH. [Irregular]

HE 20.3362/4:date • Item 506-D-6
ANNUAL SUMMARY PROGRESS REPORTS OF
POPULATION RESEARCH CENTERS AND PRO-
GRAM PROJECTS.

HE 20.3362/5:v.nos.&nos. • Item 506-D-5
POPULATION SCIENCES, INDEX OF BIOMEDICAL
RESEARCH. v. 1– 7. 1973– 1979. [Monthly] (Cen-
ter for Population Research)

PURPOSE:– To provide a useful resource to
those concerned with keeping informed of the
biomedical research literature in the population
sciences.
The Index is based on citations selected from
the corresponding monthly issues of the Index
Medicus. Compiled with the assistance and cooperation of the staff of the National Library of
Medicine.
Each bibliographic citation includes the title
in English, author, abbreviation of the journal title,
volume number, inclusive pagination, date of issue, and an abbreviation of the language of the
article if other than English. Review articles list
the number of references in parentheses.
Author index contains the authors' names
limited to three for any citation with cross references from second and third names to the first
author, where the full citation appears.
ISSN 0093-7398

HE 20.3362/6:CT • Item 506-D-5
CPR MONOGRAPH SERIES. [Irregular] (Center for
Population Research)

HE 20.3362/7:date • Item 506-D-2 (MF)
REPORT TO THE ADVISORY CHILD HEALTH AND
HUMAN DEVELOPMENT COUNCIL. [Annual] (Section on Nutrition and Growth, Clinical Nutrition
and Early Development Branch)

HE 20.3363:date • Item 506-D-8 (MF)
INVENTORY AND ANALYSIS OF NIH MATERNAL AND
CHILD HEALTH RESEARCH. [Annual]

Identifies and lists the research conducted
at the various National Institutes of Health in the
areas of child and maternal health.

HE 20.3364 • Item 506-D-9
NICHD RESEARCH HIGHLIGHTS AND TOPICS OF
INTEREST. [Irregular]

HE 20.3364/2: • Item 506-D-11
RESEARCH REPORT FROM THE NICHD. [Irregular]

This publication brings research news and
announcements from NICHD to members of the
American College of Obstetricians and Gynecolo-
gists. Areas covered include fertility and infertil-
ity, pregnancy, and contraception.

HE 20.3364/3: • Item 506-D-12
NICHD NEWS NOTES. [Irregular]

The News Notes are expected to be six-page
folders containing short items on such topics as;
prenatal care, contraception, and Anorexia
Nervosa. Articles may be reprinted from the NIH
Research Resources Reporter (HE 20.3013/6).

HE 20.3365:date • Item 506-D-11 (MF)
NATIONAL INSTITUTE OF CHILD HEALTH AND HU-
MAN DEVELOPMENT INTRAMURAL RESEARCH
PROGRAM: ANNUAL REPORT OF THE SCIEN-
TIFIC DIRECTOR.

NATIONAL INSTITUTE OF DENTAL AND CRANIOFACIAL RESEARCH
(1970–   )

INFORMATION

Public Information and Liaison Branch
National Institute of Dental
    and Craniofacial Research
Department of Health and Human Services
NIH-31
45 Center Dr., MSC 6400
Bethesda, Maryland 20892-6400
(301) 496-4261
Fax: (301) 402-3288
http://www.nidcr.nih.gov

HE 20.3401:date • Item 507-N-2 (MF)
ANNUAL REPORT.

HE 20.3401/2:date • Item 507-N-2 (MF)
NATIONAL INSTITUTE OF DENTAL RESEARCH
INDEXES. [Annual]

HE 20.3401/3:date • Item 507-N-2 (MF)
NATIONAL INSTITUTE OF DENTAL RESEARCH, PRO-
GRAMS. [Annual]

HE 20.3402:CT • Item 507-O-1
GENERAL PUBLICATIONS.

Earlier FS 2.22

HE 20.3402:C 58/2 • Item 507-O-1
CLEFT PALATE TEAM DIRECTORY. 1976. 132 p.

Compiled from a survey conducted by
the American Cleft Palate Association.

HE 20.3402:D 43 • Item 507-O-1
DENTAL RESEARCH IN THE UNITED STATES,
CANADA AND GREAT BRITAIN, FISCAL YEAR
(Date). [Annual] (Dental Research Data Of-
ficer)

A catalog of dental research projects sponsored during the fiscal year by Federal and
non-Federal organizations.
Previous title: Dental Research in the
United States and Canada.
Continued by National Institute of Dental
Research Programs, Grants, Awards, Contracts, and Intramural Projects (HE 20.3402:D
43/5).

HE 20.3402:D 43/5 • Item 507-O-1
NATIONAL INSTITUTE OF DENTAL RESEARCH
PROGRAMS, GRANTS, AWARDS, CON-
TRACTS, AND INTRAMURAL PROJECTS.
1973–   [Annual]

Continues: National Institute of Dental Research Grants and Awards (HE 20.3402:D
43).
ISSN 0360-7763

HE 20.3402:T 68/date • Item 507-O-1
TRAINEES AND FELLOWS SUPPORTED BY THE
NATIONAL INSTITUTE OF DENTAL RE-
SEARCH AND TRAINED DURING FISCAL
YEAR. 1968–   [Annual] (Dental Research
Data Officer)

PURPOSE:– To aid administrators and investigators in identifying and locating young
scientific talent that may be recruited for programs or careers in dental research.
Separate listings of trainees and fellows
given grants and awards.

HE 20.3407:CT • Item 507-N-7
RESEARCH NEWS (press releases).

HE 20.3408:CT • Item 507-O-2
HANDBOOKS, MANUALS, GUIDES.

Earlier FS 2.22/15

HE 20.3409:date • Item 507-O-3
DENTAL CARIES RESEARCH, FISCAL YEAR (date).
[Annual]

A catalog of dental caries research projects
sponsored during the fiscal year by Federal and
non-Federal organizations.

HE 20.3410:date • Item 507-N-1 (MF)
TRAINEES AND FELLOWS SUPPORTED BY THE
NATIONAL INSTITUTE OF DENTAL RESEARCH
AND TRAINED DURING FISCAL YEAR. [Annual]

Lists trainees and fellows supported through
grants and awards made by the National Institute
of Dental Research to assist administrators and
investigators in recruiting scientific talent for dental research.
Earlier HE 20.3402:T 68

HE 20.3411:CT
AUDIOVISUAL MATERIALS. [Irregular]

HE 20.3412:date • Item 507-N-3
SELECTED LIST OF TECHNICAL REPORTS IN DEN-
TISTRY. [Annual]

HE 20.3413:date • Item 507-N-4 (P) (EL)
NIDR RESEARCH DIGEST. [Irregular]

HE 20.3414:CT • Item 497-C-11
POSTERS. [Irregular]

HE 20.3415:CT • Item 497-C-12
FACT SHEETS (series). [Irregular]

Earlier HE 20.3402

HE 20.3416:date • Item 507-N-5 (MF)
NATIONAL ADVISORY DENTAL RESEARCH COUN-
CIL, SUMMARY MINUTES. [3 times a year]

Each issue presents the minutes of a different meeting of the National Advisory Dental Research Council.
Earlier HE 20.3402:Ad 9

HE 20.3417: • Item 507-O-4 (P) (EL)
SPECTRUM SERIES (various topics).

NATIONAL INSTITUTE OF GENERAL MEDICAL SCIENCES (1970–)

INFORMATION

National Institute of General Medical Sciences
National Institutes of Health
45 Center Dr., MSC 6200
Bethesda, Maryland 20892-6200
(301) 496-7301
http://www.nigms.nih.gov

HE 20.3451:date • **Item 497-C-3 (MF)**
ANNUAL REPORT.

Previously distributed to Depository Libraries under Item No. 497-B.

HE 20.3452:CT • **Item 497-C-1**
GENERAL PUBLICATIONS.
Earlier FS 2.22

HE 20.3459:CT • **Item 497-C-2**
NEW MEDICAL SCIENCE FOR THE 21st CENTURY. [Irregular]

HE 20.3460:v.nos.&nos. • **Item 497-C-4**
RECOMBINANT DNA TECHNICAL BULLETIN. v. 1–
1978– [Quarterly]

PURPOSE:– To link investigators involved in recombinant DNA research in the United States and abroad with the advisory groups and organizations active in this area and to provide prompt notification of certified-host vector systems to a broad community. Includes scientific information, news and comments, and bibliographies.

HE 20.3461:date • **Item 497-C-5 (MF)**
PHARMACOLOGY SCIENCES PROGRAM. [Annual]

Highly technical report containing highlights of selected research accomplishments in the field of pharmacology and toxicology during the fiscal year
Former title: Pharmacology-Toxicology Program.

HE 20.3461/2:date • **Item 497-C-7 (MF)**
PHARMACOLOGY RESEARCH ASSOCIATE PROGRAM. [Annual]

The goal of this Program is to develop leaders in pharmacological research for key positions in academic, industrial, and Federal research laboratories.
Earlier HE 20.3452

HE 20.3461/3 • **Item 497-E (MF)**
PHARMACOLOGY AND BIORELATED CHEMISTRY PROGRAM: BIENNIAL REPORT.

HE 20.3462:date • **Item 497-C-6**
FACT BOOK. [Annual]

PURPOSE:– To describe the organization and operation of the National Institute of General Medical Sciences and its individual programs.

HE 20.3463:date • **Item 497-C-8 (MF)**
NOBEL PRIZE LAUREATES. [Annual]

A roster of NIH scientists and grantees who have received the Nobel Prize.

HE 20.3464: • **Item 497-C-15 (EL)**
CATALOG OF CELL CULTURES AND DNA SAMPLES.

Earier title Cataog of Cell Lines.
Lists cell culture information from the NIGMS Human Genetic Mutant Cell Repository for use in genetic research.
Former title: Human Genetic Mutant Cell Repository (HE 20.3452:G 28/4).

HE 20.3465:date • **Item 497-C-10 (MF)**
NIGMS RESEARCH GRANTS. [Annual]

NIGMS = National Institute of General Medical Sciences.

HE 20.3465/2: • **Item 497-C-13 (MF)**
NIGMS RESEARCH REPORTS. [Irregular]

HE 20.3466:date • **Item 507-N-6**
CELLULAR AND MOLECULAR BASIS OF DISEASE PROGRAM, ANNUAL REPORT. [Annual]
Presents results of research into the cellular and molecular basis of disease (CMBD). The CMBD Program is concerned with the basic questions about the functions of cells and their components.
Formerly classified HE 20.3452:C 33/2

HE 20.3467:CT • **Item 497-C-14**
POSTERS. [Irregular]

HE 20.3468 • **Item 497-C-10 (MF)**
NIGMS TRAINING GRANTS. [Annual]

HE 20.3469 • **Item 497-C-16 (EL)**
NIGMS MINORITY PROGRAMS UPDATE. [Annual]

NATIONAL INSTITUTE OF NEUROLOGICAL DISORDERS AND STROKE (1975–)

INFORMATION

National Institute of Neurological
Disorders and Stroke
Department of Health and Human Services
NIH-31
9000 Rockville Pike
Bethesda, Maryland 20892
(301) 496-5924
Toll-Free: (800) 352-9424
http://www.ninds.nih.gov

HE 20.3501:date • **Item 507-L-9 (MF)**
ANNUAL REPORT.

HE 20.3502:CT • **Item 507-L-2**
GENERAL PUBLICATIONS.

Earlier FS 2.22

HE 20.3502:Am 9/2/date • **Item 507-L-2**
NINCDS AMYOTROPHIC LATERAL SCLEROSIS RESEARCH PROGRAM. [Annual]

HE 20.3502:C 33/3/date • **Item 507-L-2**
NINCDS CEREBRAL PALSY RESEARCH PROGRAM. [Annual]

ISSN 0161-2980

HE 20.3502:Ep 4/2/date • **Item 507-L-2**
NINCDS EPILEPSY RESEARCH PROGRAM. [Annual]

ISSN 0161-3014

HE 20.3502:H 35/3/date • **Item 507-L-2**
NINCDS HEARING, SPEECH, AND LANGUAGE RESEARCH PROGRAM. [Annual]

ISSN 0161-2999

HE 20.3502:H 92/2/date • **Item 507-L-2**
NINCDS HUNTINGTON'S DISEASE RESEARCH PROGRAM. [Annual]

HE 20.3502:M 91/date • **Item 507-L-2**
NINCDS MULTIPLE SCLEROSIS RESEARCH PROGRAM. [Annual]

ISSN 0161-3030

HE 20.3502:N 39/3/date • **Item 507-L-2**
NINCDS NEUROMUSCULAR DISORDERS RESEARCH PROGRAM. [Annual]

Supersedes NINCDS Muscular Dystrophy and the Neuromuscular Disorders Research Program (ISSN 0161-3057).

HE 20.3502:P 22/date • **Item 507-L-2**
NINCDS PARKINSON'S DISEASE RESEARCH PROGRAM. [Annual]

ISSN 0161-3022

HE 20.3502:Sp 4/2/date • **Item 507-L-2**
NNCDS SPINAL CORD INJURY RESEARCH PROGRAM. [Annual]

ISSN 0161-3049

HE 20.3502:St 8/date • **Item 507-L-2**
NINCDS STROKE RESEARCH PROGRAM. [Annual]

ISSN 0161-3006

HE 20.3508:CT • **Item 507-L-7**
HANDBOOKS, MANUALS, GUIDES. [Irregular]

HE 20.3509:v.nos.&nos. • **Item 507-A-18**
EPILEPSY ABSTRACTS. v. 1– 1967– [Monthly]

PURPOSE:– To keep physicians, scientists, and other workers in the field of epilepsy informed about projects and other developments reported in the medical literature.
Index for each volume published at the end of the year.
Earlier FS 2.22/59

HE 20.3509/2:date • **Item 507-A-18**
– COMPILATIONS.

1947– 1967. 2 v. [1969]
Vol. 1. Abstracts.
Vol. 2. Indexes.

HE 20.3510:nos. • **Item 507-L-1 (MF)**
NINCDS MONOGRAPHS. 1– 1965– [Irregular]

A series of scientific contributions by the Institute staff and consultants on specific subjects within the field of neurological and sensory disease research.
Previous title: NINDB [National Institute of Neurological Diseases and Blindness] Monographs.
Earlier FS 2.22/55

HE 20.3511:v.nos.&nos. • **Item 507-L-3**
PARKINSON'S DISEASE AND RELATED DISORDERS, CITATIONS FROM THE LITERATURE. v. 1– 11.
– 1980. [Monthly]

PURPOSE:– To provide current, selected, categorized bibliographical citations from the literature in a sizable but limited area of interest. Contains subject and author sections.

HE 20.3511/2:date • **Item 507-L-5**
PARKINSON'S DISEASE AND RELATED DISORDERS, INTERNATIONAL DIRECTORY OF SCIENTISTS. 1970– [Annual]

PURPOSE:– To serve as an aid to communication among those engaged in research on Parkinson's Disease and related neurological movement disorders.
Arranged by country, name, and institution. Each entry in the Geographical section shows the scientist's name, Directory entry no., specialty, department, institution, city and subject interests. The Name Directory is an alphabetic listing of institutions, locations, and affiliated scientists together with their entry number.

HE 20.3511/3:v.nos.&nos. • **Item 507-L-3**
PARKINSON'S DISEASE AND RELATED DISORDERS: CUMULATIVE BIBLIOGRAPHY. [Annual]

Prepared by Parkinson Information Center, College of Physicians and Surgeons, Columbia University.

HE 20.3512:date • **Item 507-A-6**
NINDS RESEARCH PROFILES. 1963–   [Annual]

PURPOSE:– To present a summary of research at the Institute performed during the year. Earlier FS 2.22/43

HE 20.3512/2:date • **Item 507-L-14**
NINCDS RESEARCH PROGRAM, STROKE. [Annual]

PURPOSE:– To compare stroke statistics for the past six years. Contains information on various stroke studies and clinical research centers. Earlier HE 20.3502:St 8

HE 20.3513:CT • **Item 507-L-4 (MF)**
BIBLIOGRAPHIES AND LISTS OF PUBLICATIONS.

HE 20.3513:Ep 4 • **Item 507-L-4**
EPILEPSY BIBLIOGRAPHY, 1950– 1975. 1976. 1860 p.
Includes key-word and author indexes. Serves as a cumulative index for the nine volumes of Epilepsy Abstracts (HE 20.3509) published through 1975.

HE 20.3513/2:nos. • **Item 507-L-4 (MF)**
BIBLIO-PROFILE ON HUMAN COMMUNICATION AND ITS DISORDERS, A CAPSULE STATE-OF-THE-ART REPORT AND BIBLIOGRAPHY. 1–   1971–   [Irregular]

HE 20.3513/3:nos. • **Item 507-L-6**
NINDS BIBLIOGRAPHY SERIES. 1–   1972–   [Irregular]

HE 20.3513/4:v.nos.&nos. • **Item 507-L-4**
CEREBROVASCULAR BIBLIOGRAPHY. v. 1–   [Quarterly]

HE 20.3516:date • **Item 507-L-8 (MF)**
NINDS INDEX TO RESEARCH GRANTS AND CONTRACTS. [Annual]

PURPOSE:– To provide information on biomedical research grants and contracts supported by the Institute during the fiscal year. Information includes subject, project number, and investigator, with descriptive title, Institute project area code, Institution, animals used, etc.

HE 20.3516/2:date • **Item 507-L-10 (MF)**
RESEARCH GRANTS, DATA BOOK. [Semiannual]

Separate sections contain lists of principal investigators active Institute grants, disorder classification, and program area. Earlier HE 20.2502:R 31/4

HE 20.3516/3:date • **Item 507-L-10 (MF)**
RESEARCH GRANTS, TRAINING AWARDS, SUMMARY TABLES. [Annual]

Earlier HE 20.3502:R 31/5

HE 20.3516/4:date • **Item 507-L-10 (MF)**
INTRAMURAL RESEARCH ANNUAL REPORT. [Annual]

HE 20.3517:CT • **Item 507-L-2**
REPORT OF THE PANEL ON PAIN TO THE NATIONAL ADVISORY NEUROLOGICAL AND COMMUNICATIVE DISORDERS AND STROKE COUNCIL. 1979–   [Irregular]
NOTE:– To be published in 7 volumes.

HE 20.3518:date • **Item 507-L-11**
FACT BOOKS (series). [Irregular]

PURPOSE:– To present the history, organizational structure, and activities of the Institute in carrying out the mission of research on the causes, prevention, diagnosis, and treatment of neurological and communicative disorders and stroke. Earlier HE 20.3502:F 11

HE 20.3519:date • **Item 507-L-12 (MF)**
MINUTES OF MEETING. [3 times a year]

Minutes of the National Advisory Neurological and Communicative Disorders and Stroke Council, concerning the Institute's research interests.

HE 20.3520 • **Item 507-L-13 (P) (EL)**
FACT SHEETS (various topics). [Irregular]

NATIONAL INSTITUTE OF ENVIRONMENTAL HEALTH SCIENCES
(1970–   )

INFORMATION

National Institute of Environmental Health Sciences
Department of Health and Human Services
PO Box 12233
111 Alexander Dr.
Research Triangle Park
NC 27709
(919) 541-1919
http://www.niehs.nih.gov

HE 20.3551:date • **Item 507-P-4 (MF)**
ANNUAL REPORT.

ISSN 0160-2187

HE 20.3551/2 • **Item 507-P-6 (MF) (EL)**
NATIONAL TOXICOLOGY PROGRAM, ANNUAL PLAN, FISCAL YEAR.

HE 20.3552:CT • **Item 507-P-1**
GENERAL PUBLICATIONS.

HE 20.3559:v.nos./nos. • **Item 507-P-2 (P) (EL)**
ENVIRONMENTAL HEALTH PERSPECTIVES. [Quarterly]

PURPOSE:– To provide communication of scientific information important to the understanding of chemically-induced disease. Provides a vehicle for rapid publication of conference and workshop proceedings on timely environmental health issues as well as published perspective-review articles important to the understanding of the impact of environmental agents on human health, including "State of the Art Reviews" prepared through a joint publication arrangement with the Toxicology Infor mation Program (National Library of Medicine).
Indexed by: Index to U.S. Government Periodicals.
ISSN 0091-6765

HE 20.3560:CT • **Item 507-P-3 (MF)**
BIBLIOGRAPHIES AND LISTS OF PUBLICATIONS. [Irregular]

HE 20.3561: • **Item 507-P-5**
NATIONAL INSTITUTE OF ENVIRONMENTAL HEALTH SCIENCES RESEARCH PROGRAMS.

Summarizes activities of institute research programs, which are aimed at understanding and ultimately preventing adverse effects of environmental agents.

HE 20.3562:date • **Item 507-P-5 (MF) (EL)**
ANNUAL REPORT ON CARCINOGENS.

HE 20.3563: • **Item 507-P-7 (MF)**
REVIEW OF CURRENT DHHS, DOE, AND EPA RESEARCH RELATED TO TOXICOLOGY. [Biennial]

HE 20.3564: • **Item 507-P-8 (MF) (EL)**
NATIONAL TOXICOLOGY PROGRAM, TECHNICAL REPORT SERIES.

HE 20.3564/2: • **Item 507-P-9 (MF) (EL)**
NATIONAL TOXICOLOGY PROGRAM, TOXICITY REPORT SERIES.

NATIONAL LIBRARY OF MEDICINE
(1970–   )

CREATION AND AUTHORITY

The National Library of Medicine (FS 2.200) was established in 1956 within the Public Health Service by act of Congress, approved August 3, 1956 (70 Stat. 960). [During the period from 1956 through 1969, the SuDocs class FS 2.200 was used.]

INFORMATION

National Library of Medicine
Department of Health and Human Services
NIH-38
8600 Rockville Pike
Bethesda, Maryland 20892
(301) 594-5983
Toll Free: (888) FIND-NLM
http://www.nlm.nih.gov

HE 20.3601:date • **Item 508-L**
ANNUAL REPORT. 1st–   [Annual]

Earlier FS 2.201

HE 20.3602:CT • **Item 508-D**
GENERAL PUBLICATIONS.

Earlier FS 2.202

HE 20.3602:H 34/date • **Item 508-D**
MEDICAL SUBJECT HEADINGS, ANNOTATED ALPHABETICAL LIST. [Annual]

Companion volume to: Medical Subject Headings, Tree Structures (HE 20.3602:H 34/2).
ISSN 0147-5711

HE 20.3602:H 34/2/date • **Item 508-D**
MEDICAL SUBJECT HEADINGS, TREE STRUCTURES.

Companion volume to: Medical Subject Headings, Annotated Alphabetical List (HE 20.3602:H 34).
ISSN 0147-099X

HE 20.3603/2:nos. • **Item 508-H-8 (EL)**
NLM TECHNICAL BULLETIN. [Monthly]

HE 20.3608:CT • **Item 508-K**
HANDBOOKS, MANUALS, GUIDES.

Earlier FS 2.217

HE 20.3608/2:date • **Item 508-H**
FILM REFERENCE GUIDE FOR MEDICINE AND ALLIED SCIENCES. 1956–   [Annual]

Published for the Federal Advisory Council on Medical Training Aids. Contains information on over 2,700 films related to medicine and allied sciences.

HE 20.3608/3:CT
FILM GUIDES.

HE 20.3608/4:date • **Item 508-H-5**
NATIONAL MEDICAL AUDIOVISUAL CENTER CATALOG. 1951–   [Annual]

Lists audiovisual materials available on short-term, free loan to health professionals from the National Library of Medicine's Atlanta-based National Medical Audiovisual Center.
Former title: Public Health Service Film Catalog.
Previously distributed to Depository Libraries under Item 497-A.
Earlier FS 2.2:F 48/2, FS 2.36/2

HE 20.3609:v.nos.&nos. • **Item 508-J**
NATIONAL LIBRARY OF MEDICINE CURRENT CATA-
LOG, MONTHLY LISTING. [Monthly]

Supersedes National Library of Medicine Cata-
log (LC 30.13).
Biweekly, prior to v. 5, no. 1.
Earlier FS 2.216

HE 20.3609/2:date • **Item 508-J**
NATIONAL LIBRARY OF MEDICINE CURRENT CATA-
LOG, CUMULATIVE LISTING. [Quarterly]

Prior to Jan.-Mar. 1967 classified and sold as
part of the subscription to the biweekly cumulation, FS 2.216.
Earlier FS 2.216/2

HE 20.3609/3:date • **Item 508-J**
NATIONAL LIBRARY OF MEDICINE CURRENT CATA-
LOG: ANNUAL CUMULATION. 1966– [Annual]

ISSN 0090-3124
Earlier FS 2.216/3

HE 20.3609/3-2:date • **Item 508-J (MF)**
NATIONAL LIBRARY OF MEDICINE CATALOG.

HE 20.3609/3-3:date • **Item 508-J (MF)**
NLM CATALOG SUPPLEMENT. [Quarterly]

HE 20.3609/4:date • **Item 508-H-5**
NATIONAL LIBRARY OF MEDICINE AUDIOVISUALS
CATALOG. [Quarterly, with 4th issue being cumu-
lative for the year]

Formerly a part of National Library of Medicine Current Catalog (HE 20.3609).
ISSN 0149-9939

HE 20.3609/4-2:CT
AUDIOVISUAL MATERIALS.

HE 20.3609/5:date
NLM NAME AND SERIES AUTHORITIES. [Quarterly]

HE 20.3610:v.nos.&nos. • **Item 508-F**
MONTHLY BIBLIOGRAPHY OF MEDICAL REVIEWS.
v. 1– 1967– 1977.

PURPOSE:– To provide quick guidance to
the latest reviews in the journal literature of bio-
medicine. Each monthly issue duplicates the
material appearing in the Bibliography of Medical
Reviews section of the corresponding issue of
Index Medicus.
ISSN 0027-0202
Earlier FS 2.209/2-2
Beginning in 1978, material contained in the
Monthly Bibliography of Medical Reviews is included in the monthly Index Medicus (HE 20.3612)
as a separate section and cumulated in the Cumulated Index Medicus (HE 20.3612/3).

HE 20.3610/2:date • **Item 508-F**
BIBLIOGRAPHY OF MEDICAL REVIEWS: CUMULA-
TIONS. [Quinquennial]
Annual, 1957– 1967
Quinquennial, 1966– 1975
The following quinquennial volumes were pub-
lished:
1967– 1970. 1970. 576 p.
1971– 1975. 1977. 1095 p.

HE 20.3611:nos. • **Item 508-E-2**
NOTES FOR MEDICAL CATALOGERS. v. 1– 1965–
[Irregular]

PURPOSE:– To provide additions and changes
to the schedules listed in the National Library of
Medicine classification.

HE 20.3612:v.nos.&nos. • **Item 508-E**
INDEX MEDICUS, INCLUDING BIBLIOGRAPHY OF
MEDICAL REVIEWS. v. 1– 1960– [Monthly]

PURPOSE:– To provide an accurate, up-to-
date index of the world's biomedical literature on
a monthly basis for use by librarians and health
professionals throughout the world.
Each issue contains a subject and name section and a separate Bibliography of Medical Re-

views (Also published separately [HE 20.3610]).
The subject section of each issue is quite de-
tailed in subject approach and lengthy in content.
January issues contain a list of journals in-
dexed with additions listed in the other issues.
Medical Subject Headings issued as Part 2 of
the January issue.
Annual cumulative volumes published sepa-
rately (HE 20.3612/3).
Supersedes Current List of Medical Litera-
ture.
ISSN 0019-3879
Earlier FS 2.208/2

HE 20.3612/2 • **Item 508-E-1**
ABRIDGED INDEX MEDICUS. v. 1– 1970–
[Monthly]

PURPOSE:– To provide a selected bibliogra-
phy, based on articles from approximately 100
English-language journals, designed for the needs
of the individual practitioner and libraries of small
hospitals and clinics.
Cumulative annual volumes issued separately
(HE 20.3612/2-2).
ISSN 0001-3331

HE 20.3612/2-2:date • **Item 508-E-1**
– CUMULATIVE ABRIDGED INDEX MEDICUS.
1970– [Annual]

PURPOSE:– To provide an annual cumulation of citations appearing in the monthly
Abridged Index Medicus (HE 20.3612/2) to
articles in approximately 100 English- language journals on clinical medicine.

HE 20.3612/3:v.nos. • **Item 508-E**
CUMULATED INDEX MEDICUS. v. 1– 1960–
[Annual]

Bound volumes.
Earlier FS 2.208/4

HE 20.3612/3-2 • **Item 508-E-4**
CUMULATED LIST OF NEW MEDICAL SUBJECT HEAD-
INGS.

HE 20.3612/3-3 • **Item 508-E-5**
PERMUTED MEDICAL SUBJECT HEADINGS.

HE 20.3612/3-4 • **Item 508-E-5**
MEDICAL SUBJECT HEADINGS: ANNOTATED
ALPHABETIC LIST.

HE 20.3612/3-5 • **Item 508-E-5**
MEDICAL SUBJECT HEADINGS: TREE STRUCTURES.

HE 20.3612/3-6 • **Item 508-E-5**
MEDICAL SUBJECT HEADINGS: TREE ANNOTA-
TIONS.

HE 20.3612/3-7 • **Item 508-E-6**
MEDICAL SUBJECT HEADINGS: SUPPLEMENTARY
CHEMICAL RECORDS.

HE 20.3612/3-8 • **Item 508-E-7**
MEDICAL SUBJECT HEADINGS: SUPPLEMENT TO
INDEX MEDICUS.

HE 20.3612/3-9 • **Item 508-E-5**
MEDICAL SUBJECT HEADINGS. [Annual]

HE 20.3612/4:date • **Item 508-E-3**
LIST OF JOURNALS INDEXED IN INDEX MEDICUS.

HE 20.3613:v.nos.&nos. • **Item 508-M**
TOXICITY BIBLIOGRAPHY. v. 1– 1968– 1977.
[Quarterly]

PURPOSE:– To provide health professionals
working in the field of toxicology and related disciplines with access to the world's relevant and
significant journal literature in this field.
The publication is a product of the Toxicology
Information Program, instituted in 1967, and is
based on the Library's computer-based MEDLARS
(Medical Literature Analysis and Retrieval System).
Covers the adverse and toxic effects of drugs
and chemicals reported in approximately 2,300
biomedical journals.

References on toxicity may be found in the
main body of Index Medicus (HE 20.3612).
Earlier FS 2.218

HE 20.3614:CT • **Item 508-F**
BIBLIOGRAPHIES AND LISTS OF PUBLICATIONS.

HE 20.3614/2:nos. • **Item 508-H-1**
LITERATURE SEARCHERS (numbered). 66-1–
1966– [Irregular]

PURPOSE:– To disseminate references to the
recent biomedical journal literature on single topics of widespread interest. Updated lists appear
each month in Index Medicus (HE 20.3612).

HE 20.3614/3:date • **Item 508-H-6 (MF)**
HEALTH SCIENCES SERIALS. [Quarterly]

Produced from the NLM serials data base,
this series is intended for inter-library loan and
serials management activities. Each new issue
fully supersedes the previous issue.
Published in microfiche.

HE 20.3614/4:v.nos.&nos. • **Item 508-H-7 (MF)**
QUARTERLY BIBLIOGRAPHY OF MAJOR TROPICAL
DISEASES. v. 1– 1978–

PURPOSE:– To provide an annotated bibliography of international scientific research literature on topics concerning filariases, leishmania-
sis, leprosy, malaria, etc. Intended for scientists
and institutions to foster the transfer of information to developing tropical nations.
Published in microfiche (24x).

HE 20.3614/5:date • **Item 508-H-5 (MF)**
HEALTH SCIENCES AUDIOVISUALS. [Quarterly]

Lists audiovisuals cataloged by the National
Library of Medicine since 1975, excluding
cataloging- in-publication titles and citations for
audiovisuals withdrawn from the library's collections.

HE 20.3614/6:nos. • **Item 508-F (MF)**
SPECIALIZED BIBLIOGRAPHY SERIES. [Irregular]

HE 20.3614/7:CT • **Item 508-F**
REFERENCE INFORMATION SERIES. [Irregular]

HE 20.3615:nos. • **Item 508-F**
BIBLIOGRAPHY OF THE HISTORY OF MEDICINE.
1– 1980– [Annual & Quinquennial]

Series of bibliographies of materials within
the NLM's History of Medicine Division on the
history of medicine and related sciences, professions, and institutions.
Earlier FS 2.209/4

HE 20.3615/2:date-nos. • **Item 508-H-1 (EL)**
CURRENT BIBLIOGRAPHIES IN MEDICINE (series).

HE 20.3615/3:v.nos./nos. • **Item 508-F-2**
AIDS BIBLIOGRAPHY. [Quarterly]

Contains citations to all preclinical, clinical,
epidemiologic, diagnostic, and prevention areas
added to NLM's MEDLINE and CATLINE data
bases for the period covered.

HE 20.3616:v.nos.&nos. • **Item 508-H-2**
SELECTED REFERENCES ON ENVIRONMENTAL
QUALITY AS IT RELATES TO HEALTH. v. 1–
1971– 1977. [Monthly]

PURPOSE:– To provide a subject/author index to journal articles covering aspects of environmental pollution which concern health.
References on environmental quality may be
found in the main body of Index Medicus (HE
20.3612).
ISSN 0049-0105

HE 20.3617:v.nos.&nos.   • Item 508-H-3
CURRENT BIBLIOGRAPHY OF EPIDEMIOLOGY. v.
1–   1969– 1977. [Monthly]

   PURPOSE:– To provide a monthly bibliography of articles concerning etiology, epidemiology
may be found in the main body of Index Medicus
(HE 20.3612).
   ISSN 0011-3247

HE 20.3617/2:v.nos.   • Item 508-H-3
– ANNUAL CUMULATIONS.

HE 20.3618:date   • Item 508-J
INDEX OF NLM SERIAL TITLES.

   PURPOSE:– To provide a keyword listing of
serial titles currently received by the National
Library of Medicine.

HE 20.3618/2:date   • Item 508-J (EL)
LIST OF SERIALS INDEXED FOR ONLINE USERS.
[Annual]

   Formerly HE 20.3602:Se 6

HE 20.3619:v.nos.&nos.• Item 508-F-1 (MF) (EL)
NATIONAL LIBRARY OF MEDICINE NEWSLINE.
[Bimonthly]

   Earlier FS 2.213
   Formerly National Library of Medicine News.

HE 20.3619/2:date   • Item 508-F-1 (MF)
A CATALOG OF PUBLICATIONS, AUDIOVISUALS,
AND SOFTWARE. [Irregular]

   PURPOSE:– To provide current ordering information for such library publications as those
available from the Government Printing Office,
from the National Technical Information Service;
reprinted publications; recurring bibliographies;
and brochures and fact sheets.
   Earlier titled: National Library of Medicine News:
NLM Publications.
   Earlier issued annually.

HE 20.3619/3:date   • Item 508-F-1 (MF)
NATIONAL LIBRARY OF MEDICINE STAFF DIREC-
TORY. [Annual]

HE 20.3620:nos.   • Item 508-H-4
TOX-TIPS, TOXICOLOGY TESTING IN PROGRESS.
1–   1976–   [Monthly]

   PURPOSE:– To provide a monthly current
awareness bulletin on long-term toxicity testing
begun.
   ISSN 0146-1559

HE 20.3621:CT   • Item 508-L (EL)
NATIONAL LIBRARY OF MEDICINE FACT SHEETS.
[Irregular]

HE 20.3622:CT   • Item 508-S
POSTERS.

HE 20.3623:   • Item 508-H-9
DIRECTORIES.

HE 20.3624:date/nos.   • Item 508-V (EL)
ENTREZ: DOCUMENT RETRIEVAL SYSTEM.

   Earlier titles: Entrez References and Entrez
Sequences
   Issued on CD-ROM.

HE 20.3624/2   • Item 508-D-2 (EL)
NCBI NEWSLETTER.

HE 20.3624/3:CT   • Item 508-D-3 (E)
ELECTRONIC PRODUCTS.

HE 20.3625   • Item 508-D-1
GREATFULLY YOURS.

HE 20.3626   • Item 508-F-3 (EL)
NLM LOCATORPLUS.

HE 20.3627   • Item 508-F-4 (EL)
PUBMED.

NATIONAL INSTITUTE ON DEAFNESS AND OTHER COMMUNICATION DISORDERS

INFORMATION

   National Institute on Deafness and
      Other Communication Disorders
   Department of Health and Human Services
   National Institutes of Health-31
   31 Center Dr., MSC 2320
   Bethesda, MD 20892-2320
   (301) 402-0252
   http://www.nidcd.nih.gov

HE 20.3652:   • Item 507-D-15
GENERAL PUBLICATIONS.

HE 20.3658:   • Item 507-D-17
HANDBOOKS, MANUALS, GUIDES.

HE 20.3659/2:date   • Item 507-D-16
PUBLICATIONS LIST. [Semiannual]

HE 20.3660:   • Item 507-D-20
DIRECTORIES.

HE 20.3660/2:   • Item 507-D-18 (EL)
RESOURCE DIRECTORY.

HE 20.3666:date   • Item 507-D-19 (P) (EL)
INSIDE NIDCD INFORMATION CLEARINGHOUSE
(newsletter). [Semiannual]

HE 20.3667:   • Item 507-D-18 (E)
ELECTRONIC PRODUCTS (misc.).

JOHN E. FOGARTY INTERNATIONAL CENTER FOR ADVANCED STUDY IN THE HEALTH SCIENCES (1970–   )

INFORMATION

   Office of Communications
   Fogarty International Center
   Department of Health and Human Services
   National Institutes of Health
   Bldg. 31, Rm. B2C29
   31 Center Dr. MSC 2220
   Bethesda, Maryland 20892-2220
   (301) 496-2075
   Fax: (301) 594-1211
   http://www.nih.gov/fic

HE 20.3701:date
ANNUAL REPORT.

HE 20.3701/2:date   • Item 507-C-4 (MF)
NATIONAL INSTITUTES OF HEALTH ANNUAL
REPORT OF INTERNATIONAL ACTIVITIES, FIS-
CAL YEAR. 1969–

   An annual report of international activities
published by the John E. Fogarty International
Center for Advanced Study in the Health Sciences. Its purpose is to list some of the more
representative examples of international cooperation being undertaken by the National Institutes of Health.
   Its narrative section describes how research
resources involving 53 countries were utilized or
shared by the National Institutes of Health to
carry out its primary objective of advancing medi-

cal sciences and the health of the American
people.
   Contains a listing of individual awards made
under various NIH programs which include research grants and contracts to foreign research
institutions; fellowships for foreign scientists to
train in the United States and for American scientists to train in outstanding foreign laboratories,
collaborative research agreements; and support
of international conferences.

HE 20.3702:CT   • Item 507-C-1
GENERAL PUBLICATIONS.

   Earlier FS 2.22

HE 20.3708:CT   • Item 507-C-11
HANDBOOKS, MANUALS, GUIDES. [Irregular]

HE 20.3709:date
PUBLIC HEALTH SERVICE INTERNATIONAL
POSTDOCTORATE RESEARCH FELLOWSHIPS
AWARDS FOR STUDY IN THE UNITED STATES.
[Annual]

   Earlier FS 2.22:F 33/10

HE 20.3709/2:date   • Item 507-C-5 (MF)
NATIONAL INSTITUTES OF HEALTH INTERNATIONAL
AWARDS FOR BIOMEDICAL RESEARCH AND
RESEARCH TRAINING, FISCAL YEAR (date).
1969–   [Annual] (International Cooperation and
Geographic Studies Branch)

   PURPOSE:– To list research grants to foreign investigators, contracts and agreements with
foreign research institutions, fellowships for foreign graduates to undertake research in the United
States and for Americans to work in outstanding
foreign laboratories, and foreign scientists and
scholars working at National Institutes of Health.

HE 20.3710:nos.   • Item 507-C-3 (MF)
FOGARTY INTERNATIONAL CENTER PROCEEDINGS.
1–   1969–

HE 20.3711:CT   • Item 507-C-7 (MF)
BIBLIOGRAPHIES AND LISTS OF PUBLICATIONS.

HE 20.3711:So 8/2   • Item 507-C-7
BIBLIOGRAPHY OF SOVIET SOURCES ON MEDI-
CINE AND PUBLIC HEALTH IN THE U.S.S.R.
1975. 235 p.

   This new bibliography serves as a comprehensive reference source to articles translated from Soviet medical journals, with principal emphasis on the period 1965– 1972.
About 95% of all items translated from Soviet
medical journals during that period are listed
here. They show the path of Russian progress
in such areas as cardiovascular disease,
psychiatry and psychology, toxicology, public health, biomedical research, hermatology,
infectious disease, and many other clinical
and health-related areas.

HE 20.3712:date   • Item 507-C-4 (MF)
STATISTICAL REFERENCE BOOK OF INTER-
NATIONAL ACTIVITIES. 1969–   [Annual] (Inter-
national Cooperation and Geographical Studies
Branch)

   PURPOSE:– Issued as a companion volume
to Annual Report of International Activities
(HE 20.3701/2) and International Awards for Biomedical Research and Research Training (HE
20.3709/2). These three publications present a
picture of past trends and current support of
international biomedical activities and are used
extensively by other Government agencies such
as the Department of State, the Congress as well
as senior officials in foreign countries, health
administrators and the general public.

HE 20.3713:v.nos.   • Item 507-C-8
FOGARTY INTERNATIONAL CENTER SERIES ON
PREVENTIVE MEDICINE. v. 1–

HE 20.3714:v.nos.   • Item 507-C-10
FOGARTY INTERNATIONAL CENTER SERIES ON THE
TEACHING OF PREVENTATIVE MEDICINE. v. 1–
1974–   [Irregular]

HE 20.3715:CT • Item 507-C-12
POSTERS. [Irregular]

HE 20.3717:date • Item 507-C-5
DIRECTORY OF INTERNATIONAL GRANTS AND FEL-
LOWSHIPS IN THE HEALTH SCIENCES. [Annual]

NATIONAL EYE INSTITUTE
(1970–   )

INFORMATION

National Eye Institute
Department of Health and Human Services
National Institutes of Health-31
2020 Vision Pl.
Bethesda, Maryland 20892-3655
(301) 496-5248
Fax: (301) 496-9970
http://www.nei.nih.gov

HE 20.3751:date • Item 507-Y-3 (MF)
ANNUAL REPORT.

HE 20.3752:CT • Item 507-Y-1
GENERAL PUBLICATIONS.

HE 20.3752:R 31/4/date • Item 507-Y-1
NATIONAL ADVISORY EYE COUNCIL: ANNUAL
REPORT ON VISION RESEARCH
PROJECTS. 1st–   1975–

HE 20.3758:CT • Item 507-Y-2
HANDBOOKS, MANUALS, GUIDES. [Irregular]

HE 20.3759:date • Item 507-Y
STATISTICS FOR (year) ON BLINDNESS IN THE
MODEL REPORTING AREA. 1962–   [Annual]

PURPOSE:– To provide statistics on annual
additions to registers of blind persons in 16 member states, population in these registers at end of
year, and population removed from registers during the year.
Data are reported as an aid to estimation of
the size of the blindness problem in a portion of
the United States.
Earlier FS 2.22/37-2

HE 20.3759/2:date • Item 507-Y
CONFERENCE OF MODEL REPORTING AREA FOR
BLINDNESS, PROCEEDINGS. 1st–   1962.
[Annual]

Earlier FS 2.22/37

HE 20.3760:date • Item 507-Y-5
DIRECTORIES.

HE 20.3766:date • Item 507-Y-4 (EL)
OUTLOOK. [Semiannual]

NATIONAL INSTITUTE OF
MENTAL HEALTH
(1970– 1974)

HE 20.3801:date
ANNUAL REPORTS.

Earlier HE 20.2401

HE 20.3802:CT • Item 507-B-5
GENERAL PUBLICATIONS.

Earlier HE 20.2402
Later HE 20.8102

HE 20.3808:CT • Item 507-B-10
HANDBOOKS, MANUALS, GUIDES.

Earlier HE 20.2408

HE 20.3808/2:CT • Item 507-B-21
COMMUNITY HANDBOOK SERIES. 1973–
[Irregular]

PURPOSE:– To aid youth in initiating counter-
culture service projects, and aid communities in
establishing their own community service delivery system.

HE 20.3809:CT • Item 507-B-13
CRIME AND DELINQUENCY ISSUES, MONOGRAPH
SERIES. [Irregular] (Center for Studies of Crime
and Delinquency)

Earlier HE 20.2420/2
Later HE 20.8114

HE 20.3810:CT • Item 507-B-22
ADDRESSES. [Irregular]

HE 20.3811:date • Item 507-B-17
ALCOHOL AND HEALTH NOTES. v. 1–   Dec. 1972–
[Monthly] (National Clearinghouse for Alcohol
Information, National Institute on Alcohol Abuse
and Alcoholism, Box 2345, Rockville, Maryland
20852)

Earlier HE 20.2428
Later HE 20.8309/2

HE 20.3812:nos. • Item 507-B-12
STATISTICAL NOTES. 1–   1969–   [Irregular] (Survey and Reports Section)

Earlier HE 20.2424
Later HE 20.8116

HE 20.3813:v.nos.&nos. • Item 507-B-19
ALCOHOL HEALTH AND RESEARCH WORLD. v. 1–
1973–   [Quarterly]

Earlier HE 20.2430
Later HE 20.8309

NATIONAL INSTITUTE ON AGING
(1976–   )

INFORMATION

National Institute on Aging
National Institutes of Health
NIH-31
Rm. 5C27
31 Center Dr., MSC 2292
Bethesda, MD 20892
(301) 496-1752
Fax: (301) 402-3442
http://www.nia.nih.gov

HE 20.3851:date • Item 447-A-10 (MF)
ANNUAL REPORT.

HE 20.3851/2:date • Item 447-A-10 (MF)
BIENNIAL REPORT TO THE CONGRESS.

HE 20.3852:CT • Item 447-A-26
GENERAL PUBLICATIONS.

Formerly issued under Item number 447-A-13.

HE 20.3858 • Item 447-B-4
HANDBOOKS, MANUALS, GUIDES.

Formerly issued under Item number 447-B.

HE 20.3859 • Item 447-A-11
SCIENCE WRITER SEMINAR SERIES. [Irregular]

HE 20.3860:date • Item 447-B-1 (MF)
NIA REPORT TO COUNCIL ON PROGRAM. [Annual]

HE 20.3861:CT • Item 447-A-12 (P) (EL)
AGE PAGE (series). [Irregular]
Single-page fact sheets on various concerns
of aging.

HE 20.3862:date • Item 447-A-16 (MF)
SPECIAL REPORT ON AGING. [Annual]

PURPOSE:– To present the results of exploration of a wide range of medical and psychoso-
cial issues affecting the growing older population
of the United States.
Earlier HE 20.3852:Ag 4/2

HE 20.3863 • Item 447-B-5
BIBLIOGRAPHIES AND LISTS OF PUBLICATIONS.

Formerly issued under Item number 447-B-2.

HE 20.3864 • Item 447-A-19
REQUEST FOR RESEARCH GRANT APPLICATIONS
(series). [Irregular]

The grant applications requested deal with
such areas as mechanisms of age-related changes
in blood pressure. They contain such information
as purpose, discipline and expertise, background,
and research goals.

HE 20.3865: • Item 447-B-3
NEWS NOTES.

News releases pertaining to aging.

HE 20.3866: • Item 447-A-21 (MF)
INTRAMURAL ANNUAL REPORT, NATIONAL INSTI-
TUTE OF AGING. [Annual]

PURPOSE– To provide information on all
National Institute of Aging-supported intramural
programs. Summarizes activities under the epidemiology, demography, and biometry programs
as well as of the various components of the Gerontology Research Center.

HE 20.3867: • Item 447-A-22
POSTERS.

HE 20.3868:CT • Item 447-A-23
DIRECTORIES.

HE 20.3869:date • Item 447-A-25 (PL)
PROGRESS REPORT ON ALZHEIMER'S DISEASE.
[Annual]

NATIONAL INSTITUTE OF
ARTHRITIS AND
MUSCULOSKELETAL AND SKIN
DISEASES

CREATION AND AUTHORITY

The National Institute of Arthritis and Musculoskeletal and Skin Diseases was established by
Public Law 99-158.

INFORMATION

Office of Communication and Public Liaison
National Institute of Arthritis and
Musculoskeletal and Skin Diseases
Bldg. 31, Rm. 4C05
31 Center Dr., MSC 2350
Bethesda, Maryland 20892-2350
(301) 496-8190
Fax: (301) 480-2814
http://www.niams.nih.gov

HE 20.3902:CT • Item 508-T
GENERAL PUBLICATIONS. [Irregular]

HE 20.3908 • Item 508-T-2
HANDBOOKS, MANUALS, AND GUIDES

HE 20.3915:date • Item 508-T-1
MEMO. [Irregular]

Includes new subjects on disorders of the musculoskeletal system, including bone and muscle diseases, sports medicine, and skin disorders.

HE 20.3916:CT • Item 508-T-2 (P) (EL)
HANDOUTS ON HEALTH (series). (various topics)

Includes Rheumatoid Arthritis and Atopic Dermatitis.

HE 20.3917 • Item 508-T-4 (P) (EL)
QUESTIONS AND ANSWERS ABOUT... (various topics).

NATIONAL INSTITUTE ON DRUG ABUSE
(1994–   )

INFORMATION

National Institute on Drug Abuse
Neuroscience Center Bldg.
6001 Executive Blvd.
Bethesda, MD 20892
443-6480
Fax: (301) 443-8908
http://www.nida.nih.gov

HE 20.3952:CT • Item 467-A-1
GENERAL PUBLICATIONS.

Earlier HE 20.8202

HE 20.3958 • Item 467-A-2
HANDBOOKS, MANUALS, GUIDES.

Earlier HE 20.8208

HE 20.3958/2:nos. • Item 467-A-31
THERAPY MANUALS FOR DRUG ADDICTION (series) (various titles).

HE 20.3959: • Item 467-A-3
BIBLIOGRAPHIES AND LISTS OF PUBLICATIONS.

HE 20.3960: • Item 467-A-28
DIRECTORIES.

HE 20.3961: • Item 467-A-22
POSTERS.

HE 20.3962: • Item 467-A-16 (MF)
ADDRESSES.

HE 20.3965:nos. • Item 831-C-12 (P) (EL)
RESEARCH MONOGRAPH SERIES. 1–   1975–

Earlier HE 20.8216

HE 20.3965/2:CT • Item 467-A-30 (EL)
NIDA RESEARCH REPORT SERIES.

HE 20.3965/3 • Item 467-A-34 (EL)
MIND OVER MATTER (series). [Irregular]

HE 20.3966:date • Item 831-C-13 (MF)
PROBLEMS OF DRUG DEPENDENCE. [Annual]

Earlier HE 20.8216/5

HE 20.3967:v.nos./nos. • Item 467-A-10 (P) (EL)
NIDA NOTES. [Bimonthly]

HE 20.3967/2: • Item 467-A-10 (EL)
NIDA CAPSULES.

HE 20.3968:date/v.nos. • Item 467-A-32 (P) (EL)
NATIONAL SURVEY RESULTS ON DRUG USE FROM THE MONITORING THE FUTURE STUDY. [Annual]

HE 20.3969:date/v.nos. • Item 467-A-33 (P) (EL)
EPIDEMIOLOGIC TRENDS IN DRUG ABUSE. [Semiannual]

HE 20.3970 • Item 467-A-34 (E)
ELECTRONIC PRODUCTS. (Misc.)

HE 20.3971 • Item 467-A-35 (EL)
COMMUNITY DRUG ALERT BULLETIN. [Monthly]

FOOD AND DRUG ADMINISTRATION
(1970–   )

CREATION AND AUTHORITY

The Food and Drug Administration (FS 13.100) was transferred from the Federal Security Agency to the newly created Department of Health, Education, and Welfare in 1953. [During the period from 1953 through 1969, the SuDocs class FS 13.100 was used. For a brief period in 1970, SuDocs HE 20.1200 was used prior to its present class.]

INFORMATION

Food and Drug Administration
Room 1261, Parklawn Bldg.
5600 Fishers Lane
Rockville, Maryland 20857-0001
(301) 443-1544
Fax: (301) 443-3100
Toll Free: 1-(888) INFO-FDA
http://www.fda.gov

HE 20.4001:date • Item 474 (MF)
ANNUAL REPORT.

Reprint of section from Annual Report of the Department of Health, Education, and Welfare.
Earlier HE 20.1201, FS 13.1001

HE 20.4001/2:date • Item 474 (MF)
PMS BLUE BOOK. [Annual]
PMS = Program Management System

HE 20.4001/3:date • Item 474-A-20
OFFICE OF MANAGEMENT AND SYSTEMS ANNUAL PERFORMACE REPORT. [Annual]

HE 20.4002:CT • Item 475
GENERAL PUBLICATIONS.
Earlier HE 20.1202, FS 13.102

HE 20.4002:B 62 • Item 475
DIRECTORY OF BLOOD ESTABLISHMENTS REGISTERED UNDER SECTION 510 OF THE FOOD, DRUG, AND COSMETIC ACT. 1976. 750 p. (Bureau of Biologics)

HE 20.4002:P 75 • Item 475
DIRECTORY, POISON CONTROL CENTERS. Rev. 1971. 50 p.

Gives the name, address, and director of the facilities, alphabetically by State, which provide for the medical profession, on a 24-hour basis, information concerning the treatment and prevention of accidents involving ingestion of poisonous and potentially poisonous substances.

HE 20.4003:date • Item 475-Q
FDA DRUG BULLETIN. [Irregular]

HE 20.4003/2:date • Item 475-Q
NATIONAL CLEARINGHOUSE FOR POISON CONTROL CENTERS, BULLETIN. 1–26. 1957–1982. [Bimonthly]
Published for poison control centers and selected organizations interested in the activities of prevention and treatment of accidental poisoning. The items included are both statistical and

technical oriented at the problems of acute poisoning.
Earlier HE 20.1203/2
ISSN 0049-5484

HE 20.4003/2-2:date • Item 480-B
DIRECTORY OF UNITED STATES POISON CONTROL CENTERS AND SERVICES. [Annual] (National Clearinghouse for Poison Control Centers)

Lists poison control centers and State coordinators for them, by State and city.

HE 20.4003/3:v.nos./nos. • Item 475-Q
FDA MEDICAL BULLETIN.

PURPOSE:– To inform the medical profession of pertinent drug information. Distribution to practicing M.D.'s, pharmacies, hospital administrators, osteopaths, podiatrists, various professional societies and journals, state health officers, FDA personnel, and individual requestors.
Earlier titled: FDA Drug Bulletin.
ISSN 0361-4344

HE 20.4003/4:v.nos.&nos. • Item 475-Q-1
LABORATORY INFORMATION BULLETIN. [Monthly]

HE 20.4003/5: • Item 475-P-1
ASSOCIATION OF FOOD AND DRUG OFFICIALS QUARTERLY BULLETIN. [Quarterly]

HE 20.4005:CT • Item 475-B
LAWS.

Earlier 20.1205

HE 20.4006:CT • Item 478
REGULATIONS, RULES, AND INSTRUCTIONS.

Earlier HE 20.1206

HE 20.4006/2:date • Item 478 (MF)
PREAMBLE COMPILATION, RADIOLOGICAL HEALTH.

Updated annually with a cumulative pocket supplement.

HE 20.4008:CT • Item 475-G
HANDBOOKS, MANUALS, GUIDES.

Earlier HE 20.1208

HE 20.4008/2:nos. • Item 475-G
INSPECTION OPERATIONS MANUAL TRANSMITTAL NOTICES.

Earlier HE 20.4008

HE 20.4008/4:nos. • Item 475-G
STAFF MANUAL GUIDE.

HE 20.4008/5:nos. • Item 475-G
COMPLIANCE POLICY GUIDES.

Earlier classed under HE 20.4008.

HE 20.4008/6:nos. • Item 475-G
REGULATORY PROCEDURES MANUAL.

HE 20.4008/7:nos. • Item 475-G
COMPLIANCE PROGRAM GUIDE MANUAL.

HE 20.4009:v.nos.&nos. • Item 475-L
FDA CLINICAL EXPERIENCE ABSTRACTS. v. 1– 45, no. 4. 1962– Oct. 1976. [Monthly] (Medical Library, Bureau of Drugs)

PURPOSE:– To provide an abstracting- indexing service covering 275 U.S. and foreign biomedical periodicals, principally in clinical medicine. Includes all titles appearing in Abridged Index Medicus and represents a distillation of significant human data on adverse effects, hazards, and efficacy of drugs, devices, and nutrients, and on adverse effects of cosmetics, household chemicals, pesticides, and food additives. Suspected as well as confirmed cases are included. Animal studies on teratogenicity and carcinogenicity are also within scope. Original case reports, clinical trials, authoritative reviews, editorials, letters to the editor, questions and answers, meeting reports, and original abstracts are scanned. Serves as literature support for FDA's Drug monitoring program. Also for use of physicians, medical schools and libraries, hospitals, pharmacists, and others concerned with or responsible for safe use of drugs.

Title varies: 1962– 1963, Adverse Effects of Drugs, Devices, Cosmetics; 1963, Reports in the Literature on Adverse Reactions to Drugs and Therapeutic Devices; 1964, MRL Journal of Literature Abstracts; 1965– 1966, MLB Journal of Literature Abstracts.
Issued biweekly prior to July 1971.
ISSN 0429-9442
Earlier FS 13.132, HE 20.1209

HE 20.4010:v.nos.&nos. • Item 475-H (P) (EL)
FDA CONSUMER. 1967– [10 times a year]

PURPOSE:– To encourage compliance with the laws and regulations administered by the FDA on the part of the regulated industries, and to provide information about their activities for the use of State, local and other Federal agencies in the same or allied fields and to the public, interested consumer and health education organizations, educational and health institutions, and the medical and scientific communities.
Formerly FDA Papers.
Indexed by: Index to U.S. Government Periodicals.
ISSN 0362-1332
Earlier HE 20.1212

HE 20.4010/a:CT • Item 475-H-1 (P) (EL)
FDA CONSUMER (separates).

HE 20.4010/2 • Item 475-W
FDA CONSUMER MEMOS. [Irregular]

PURPOSE:– To provide consumers with current and useful information on foods and drugs.

HE 20.4010/3:nos. • Item 475-H
CONSUMER UPDATE. [Irregular]

HE 20.4010/4: • Item 475-H-2
FDA CONSUMER SPECIAL REPORT (various topics).

HE 20.4010/5 • Item 475-H-2
CQ, CONSUMER QUARTERLY.

HE 20.4011:v.nos.&nos. • Item 475-M
HEALTH ASPECTS OF PESTICIDES, ABSTRACTS BULLETIN. v. 1– 1968– [Monthly] (Consumer Protection and Environmental Health Service)

PURPOSE:– To foster current awareness of the major worldwide literature pertaining to the effects of pesticides on humans. It represents a monthly review of more than 500 domestic and foreign journals.
Annual index issued separately.
Earlier FS 13.133, HE 20.1211

HE 20.4012:date • Item 475-N
NATIONAL DRUG CODE DIRECTORY. 1969– [Irregular] (Office of Scientific Coordination, Bureau of Drugs)

This publication contains descriptions of approximately 23,000 prescription and over- the-counter products. This Directory is composed of a main Directory section which is organized alphabetically by product name, and within product name (in case of certain generically labeled products which are produced by several manufacturers) alphabetically by an abbreviated form of the labeler's name. An index of Established Names is organized alphabetically and will lead the user back to the branded, single-ingredient products described in the main portion of the Directory. The National Drug Code Index is a list of codes in ascending sequence. Appendix 1 is a listing which relates the abbreviated labeler's name to the 3-character labeler codes and the labeler's full name and address.

HE 20.4013:date • Item 475-A
FDA CURRENT DRUG INFORMATION. [Irregular]

HE 20.4014:date • Item 478-E (P) (EL)
INTERSTATE CERTIFIED SHELLFISH SHIPPERS LIST. [Monthly] (Shellfish Sanitation Branch)

PURPOSE:– To provide a list of shellfish shippers (oysters, clams and mussels) of the United States, Canada, and Japan who have been certified by their respective states or countries as having grown, harvested, processed and marketed shellfish in compliance with standards of the National Shellfish Sanitation Program Manual of Operations.
Issues dated Feb. 1– Nov. 1, 1969 classified FS 13.135 and those prior to Feb. 1, 1969 were published by the Public Health Service (FS 2.16).
Prior to February 1975 issued biweekly.
Former title: Interstate Shellfish Shippers List.
ISSN 0364-7048
Earlier HE 20.1213, prior to April 1, 1970.

HE 20.4014/2:date • Item 478-E-1 (MF)
IMS LIST SANITATION COMPLIANCE AND ENFORCEMENT RATINGS OF INTERSTATE MILK SHIPPERS. [Quarterly]

HE 20.4015:nos. • Item 475-A
FDA PUBLICATIONS (numbered). 1– [Irregular]

Popular pamphlets on the work of the Food and Drug Administration, information about the U.S. Food, Drug and Cosmetic Act, information for the consumer on items covered by the above act.
Earlier FS 13.111

HE 20.4016:CT • Item 475-F
BIBLIOGRAPHIES AND LISTS OF PUBLICATIONS.
Earlier FS 13.125

HE 20.4016:C 46 • Item 475-F
FDA FEDERAL REGISTER DOCUMENTS, CHRONOLOGICAL DOCUMENT LISTING, 1936– 1976. 1977. 529 p.

Lists all published Federal Register documents relating to the activities of the Food and Drug Administration. Listings contain a subject area code, a subject description, and a citation to the Federal Register publication date and page number.

HE 20.4016/2:date • Item 478-G (MF)
CATALOG OF COURSES AND TRAINING MATERIALS. [Annual]

PURPOSE:– To describe short courses and workshops on miscellaneous food and drug- related topics which are offered by FDA's Division of Federal-State Relations.

HE 20.4017:nos. • Item 475-X (MF)
MONTHLY IMPORT DETENTION LIST. 1960–

Limited distribution to food, drug, and cosmetic trade.
PURPOSE:– To supply information concerning the occurrence of violations of the F.D.& C. and F.P.L. Acts involving imports, the nature of the violations and the commodities involved, and the sources of the violative shipments. Furnishes information to the constituent offices of FDA and

to the importing trade, as well as other government agencies and representatives of exporting countries.
Former title: Commercial Import Detentions.
ISSN 0363-6852
Earlier HE 20.1212, FS 13.120

HE 20.4018:nos.
OF SPECIAL INTEREST TO LABORATORIES.

HE 20.4019:date • Item 494-B-6 (MF)
POISON CONTROL STATISTICS. 1969– [Annual] (National Clearinghouse for Poison Control Centers)

Consists of several compilations taken from Poison Control Reports (Form FDA 2291). Includes information on trade-names and classes of products and is used as a quick reference by regulatory offices on the reported human toxicity experience with trade-name products. Distribution limited to Government agencies.

HE 20.4020:date • Item 475-Q
FLAMMABLE FABRICS, ANNUAL REPORT. 1st– 1969– (Bureau of Products Safety)

PURPOSE:– To report on studies made by the Food and Drug Administration Injury Study Units on the deaths, injuries, and economic losses resulting from accidental burning of products, fabrics, or related materials, as authorized by the Flammable Fabrics Act of 1953, as amended.
First report covered period September 1965– February 1968, second report covered period March 1969– June 1970.

HE 20.4021:nos. • Item 478-D
POSTERS. 1– [Irregular]
Earlier FS 13.127

HE 20.4021/2:nos.
FOOD STORAGE SANITATON SERIES POSTER.

HE 20.4021/3:CT
AUDIOVISUAL MATERIALS. [Irregular]

HE 20.4022:date • Item 475-P (MF)
PUBLIC ADVISORY COMMITTEES: AUTHORITY, STRUCTURE, FUNCTIONS. 1971– [Irregular]

HE 20.4023:nos. • Item 475-R (MF)
SELECTED TECHNICAL PUBLICATIONS. 1– 1965– [Semiannual]

PURPOSE:– To compile, in a single collection, reprints of scientific papers published by FDA personnel during the relevant period. Author and subject indexes have been provided starting with vol. 6 (July-Dec. 1967).

HE 20.4024:date • Item 475-S
BANNED TOY LIST.

HE 20.4025:v.nos.
FDA BY-LINES.

Earlier Interbureau By-line, FS 13.216

HE 20.4026:date • Item 475-T
NEISS [National Electronic Injury Surveillance System] NEWS, PRODUCT SAFETY. v. 1– (Bureau of Product Safety, Injury and Data Control Center)

Later Y 3.C 76/3:7-2

HE 20.4027:date • Item 475-U
FDA COMPILATION OF CASE STUDIES OF DRUG RECALLS.

HE 20.4028:date
BUREAU OF VETERINARY MEDICINE MEMO, BVMM- (series).

HE 20.4029:CT
FACTS FROM FDA, CURRENT AND USEFUL INFORMATION FROM FOOD AND DRUG ADMINISTRATION. [Irregular]

HE 20.4030:date • Item 475-Z
NATIONAL HEALTH RELATED ITEMS CODE DIRECTORY. 1974– [Irregular]

A computer-produced listing which is the result of a four year cooperative effort by government and private industry to establish a standardized identification system for processing of health-related items information. Included in the directory are coded identifications of medical and surgical treatment products and other health-related items generally used in the diagnosis, care, and treatment of patients.

HE 20.4031:v.nos.&nos. • Item 475-Y (MF)
EDRO RESEARCH PROGRESS REPORTS. [Semiannual] (Executive Director of Regional Operations)

Other title: EDRO Research Reports.

HE 20.4031/2:v.nos. • Item 494-B-5 (MF)
EDRO SARAP RESEARCH TECHNICAL REPORTS. [Annual]

HE 20.4032:date • Item 494-B-1
NATIONAL SHELLFISH SANITATION WORKSHOP, PROCEEDINGS. 1st– 1954– [Irregular] (Shellfish Sanitation Branch)

PURPOSE:– To provide Workshop participants and others interested in shellfish sanitation with a written record of each Workshop. The proceedings include a verbatim transcript of the general sessions, task force reports and recommendations, and prepared papers presented at the Workshop.
National Workshops are held every one to three years, to afford the federal-State-industry National Shellfish Sanitation Program (NSSP) participants the opportunity to meet together to discuss scientific and engineering advances in shellfish sanitation and technical and administrative changes affecting the shellfish industry and the NSSP.
Earlier FS 2.16/2
8th. January 16– 18, 1974. New Orleans, La.

HE 20.4033:date • Item 478-H (MF)
FDA QUARTERLY ACTIVITIES REPORT.

Highlights for FDA managers, significant activities, accomplishments, and decisions. summarizes FDA activities in such areas as progrm direction, animal drugs and feeds, human drugs and biologics, and food.
ISSN 0145-126X
Discontinued.

HE 20.4034:nos. • Item 494-B-3
OPE REPORTS. (Office of Planning and Evaluation)

HE 20.4035:date • Item 494-B-4
MEDICAL DEVICES AND DIAGNOSTIC PRODUCTS STANDARDS SURVEY, INTERNATIONAL EDITION.

Later HE 20.4309

HE 20.4035/2:date
MEDICAL DEVICES AND DIAGNOSTIC PRODUCTS STANDARDS SURVEY, NATIONAL EDITION.

Later HE 20.4309/2

HE 20.4036:date • Item 494-B-7 (MF)
PARKLAWN COMPUTER CENTER: ANNUAL REPORT.

HE 20.4036/2:date • Item 494-B-11 (MF)
PARKLAWN COMPUTER CENTER: COMPUTER TRAINING COURSES. [Annual]

PURPOSE:– To describe courses available to users of Parklawn Computer Center.
Earlier HE 20.4002:T 69

HE 20.4037:date • Item 494-B-8 (MF)
LOCATION DIRECTORY. 1979– [Annual]

Includes names, addresses, telephone numbers, and other data, about persons and organizations within the Food and Drug Administration.
Other title: Food and Drug Administration Location Directory.

HE 20.4014/2:date • Item 478-E-1
IMS LIST SANITATION COMPLIANCE AND ENFORCEMENT RATINGS OF INTERSTATE MILK SHIPPERS.

HE 20.4037/2:date • Item 494-B-8 (MF)
DIRECTORY OF STATE OFFICIALS. [Annual]

HE 20.4037/3:CT • Item 494-B-12
DIRECTORIES. [Irregular]

HE 20.4038:date • Item 494-B-9
FOOD AND DRUG ADMINISTRATION AND THE CONGRESS. 94th Congress– 1975/76– [Biennial] (Office of Legislative Affairs)

PURPOSE:– To provide the staff of the Food and Drug Administration with a narrative summary and charts on FDA Congressional activities, legislation, bills, hearings, etc., covering an entire Congress.

HE 20.4039:date • Item 494-B-10 (EL)
FDA ENFORCEMENT REPORT. [Weekly]
Contains information on prosecutions, seizures, injunctions, and recalls of products in violation of the law. Lists recalled products, complaints for injunction, seizure actions, and dispositions of prosecutions.

HE 20.4039/2:date • Item 494-B-13
THE ENFORCEMENT STORY.

HE 20.4040:nos. • Item 478-B (MF)
FDA TECHNICAL BULLETINS. 1– 1981– [Irregular]

Earlier FS 13.103/2

HE 20.4041:v.nos.&nos.
FDA BY-LINES. v. 1– 12. 1970– 1982. [Quarterly]

HE 20.4042:date • Item 478-C (MF)
ESTABLISHMENTS AND PRODUCTS LICENSED UNDER SECTION 351 OF THE PUBLIC HEALTH SERVICE ACT.

Licensed establishments are listed alphabetically and also by license number with the products each establishment is licensed to manufacture. Biological products are listed alphabetically with license number and name of each establishment licensed to manufacture each product.

HE 20.4043: • Item 480-B-1
HHS NEWS, FOOD AND DRUG ADMINISTRATION. [Irregular]

Consists of FDA news releases.

HE 20.4044 • Item 478-F
FORMS. [Irregular]

HE 20.4045: • Item 478-J (MF)
DISCUSSION OF FDA PRIORITIES. [Annual]

This booklet summarizes the votes of the consumers on FDA priorities plus the votes of other participants representing health professionals, state officials, trade associations, small business groups, and FDA Policy Board alumni.

HE 20.4046:date • Item 474
FOOD AND DRUG ADMINISTRATION, SUMMARY OF SIGNIFICANT ACCOMPLISHMENT AND ACTIVITIES IN FISCAL YEAR (date). [Annual]

HE 20.4047 • Item 494-B-8 (MF)
FDA ALMANAC.

HE 20.4048:date • Item 474-D (MF)
ANNUAL AFFIRMATIVE EMPLOYMENT ACCOMPLISHMENT AND ACTIVITIES IN FISCAL . . . [Annual]

HE 20.4049:v.nos./nos. • Item 475-H-3
SMART UPDATE. [Quarterly]

HE 20.4050:CT • Item 494-B-14
PAMPHLETS

BUREAU OF RADIOLOGICAL HEALTH (1971– 1983)

CREATION AND AUTHORITY

The Administration was transferred to the Department of Education (ED 1.200) pursuant to the Department of Education Organization Act (93 Stat. 668), approved on October 17, 1979. The Bureau was merged on March 9, 1984 with the Medical Devices Bureau to become The Center for Devices and Radiological Health (HE 20.4600).

HE 20.4101:date
ANNUAL REPORT.

Earlier HE 20.1501

HE 20.4102:CT • Item 498-B-2
GENERAL PUBLICATIONS.

Earlier HE 20.1502

HE 20.4102:R 31/date • Item 498-B-2
RESOURCES AND STAFFING. 1970– [Irregular] (Office of Associate Director for Administration)

ISSN 0098-6852

HE 20.4103:v.nos.&nos. • Item 498-B-14
BRH BULLETIN. v. 1– 1967– [Biweekly]

PURPOSE:– To provide a semi-technical newsletter, intended as a communications tool for transmitting information on significant Bureau activities relating to its mission of reducing unnecessary radiation exposure. In general, Bulletin stories focus on Bureau-initiated actions and programs and Bureau input to outside efforts. In rare instances stories may report on general radiological health matters to which the Bureau had no input– for example, Congressional actions regarding technologist licensure or State programs.

The Bulletin audience is primarily professionals with an interest in radiological health, including Federal, State, and international radiation control workers and public health officials; regulated industries; educational and research institutions; physicians, dentists, and other medical personnel; professional and industry associations; and members of the news media. It is not aimed at the consumer directly.
Later HE 20.4612
ISSN 0364-1023

HE 20.4103/2:date
BRH TECHNICAL INFORMATION ACCESSION BULLETIN. 1970– 1974. [Quarterly] (Bureau of Radiological Health)

PURPOSE:– To inform Bureau of Radiological Health personnel and State radiological health program staff of currently accessioned technical literature in BRH document retrieval systems. A section is also included for accessions to the BRH Publications Index and for publications of Bureau grantees. Bureau publications listed in the BRH Publications Index portion may also be accessioned into the other document retrieval system listings as appropriate.

HE 20.4106:CT • Item 498-B-8
REGULATIONS, RULES, AND INSTRUCTIONS. [Irregular]

HE 20.4108:CT • Item 498-B-1
HANDBOOKS, MANUALS, GUIDES.

Earlier HE 20.1508

HE 20.4108/2:CT   • Item 498-B-16
RADIOLOGICAL HEALTH QUALITY ASSURANCE
SERIES. [Irregular]

Consists of highly technical manuals written
for clinical users of medical radiation such as
diagnostic ultrasound B-scanning equipment.
Later HE 20.4611

HE 20.4109:date-nos.   • Item 498-B-5 (MF)
NORTHEASTERN RADIOLOGICAL HEALTH LABORA-
TORY, BRH/NERHL-(series). [Irregular]

HE 20.4110:nos.   • Item 468-A-5
BRH/DEP (series). (Division of Electronic Products)

Earlier HE 20.1513

HE 20.4111:nos.   • Item 498-B-4
BRH/OBD (series).

Earlier HE 20.1515

HE 20.4112:nos.   • Item 483-M
BRH/DMRE (series). (Division of Medical Radiation
Exposure)

Earlier HE 20.1516

HE 20.4113:nos.   • Item 468-A-4
ORO- (series). [Irregular]

Earlier HE 20.1512

HE 20.4114:nos.   • Item 468-A-6
BRH/DBE- (series). [Irregular] (Division of Biological
Effects)

The technical reports published by the Division of Biological Effects contain information generated by the Division staff which is timely and
useful to the radiological health program. Subjects covered by these reports are varied, for the
Division is charged with developing, through animal investigations and population studies, knowledge of the biological effects of radiation delivered to man from his environment and use of
substances and devices which emit radiation.
Earlier HE 20.1514

HE 20.4114/2:date   • Item 498-B-11 (MF)
REPORT OF THE DIVISION OF BIOLOGICAL
EFFECTS.

HE 20.4115:date   • Item 468-A-9
FEDERAL/STATE RADIATION CONTROL LEGISLA-
TION.

Earlier HE 20.4111:73-2

HE 20.4116:date   • Item 498-B-6 (MF)
BUREAU OF RADIOLOGICAL HEALTH RESEARCH
GRANTS PROGRAM, FISCAL YEAR, (date).
[Annual]

PURPOSE:– To describe research projects
supported by grants from the Bureau of Radiological Health for the fiscal year. Research grants
are listed by title, grant number, principal investigator, and institution.

HE 20.4117:date
PROGRESS IN RADIATION PROTECTION. 1973–
[Annual]

PURPOSE:– To present the year's progress
and activities in the radiological health activities
of the Food and Drug Administration. Material originally published in the Food and Drug
Administration's Annual Report.

HE 20.4118:date   • Item 498-B-7 (MF)
NATIONAL CONFERENCE ON RADIATION CONTROL.
[Proceedings] 1st– 1969– [Annual]

ISSN 0160-2136

HE 20.4119:date   • Item 498-B-9
CSU-PHS [Colorado State University-Public Health
Service] COLLABORATIVE RADIOLOGICAL
HEALTH LABORATORY: ANNUAL REPORT. 1st–
1962–

Later HE 20.4613

HE 20.4120:date   • Item 498-B-4
BRH PUBLICATIONS INDEX. 1970–   [Annual] (Technical Information Staff)

The Index is a vital tool to the Technical Information Staff, OADA, for management of its publication distribution and supply system. The Index is updated quarterly through publication of
the BRH Technical Information Accession Bulletin (HE 20.4103/2), and once a year reproduced
for distribution to the Bureau staff, State and
local radiological health programs and for use in
answering public inquiries for a list of publications.
ISSN 0090-8495
Earlier HE 20.4111:73-4

HE 20.4120/2:CT   • Item 498-B-13
BIBLIOGRAPHIES AND LISTS OF PUBLICATIONS.
[Irregular]

HE 20.4121:date   • Item 498-B-10
REPORT OF STATE AND LOCAL RADIOLOGICAL
HEALTH PROGRAMS. [Annual]

Earlier HE 20.4102:St 2

HE 20.4122:date   • Item 498-B-12 (MF)
DIRECTORY OF PERSONNEL RESPONSIBLE FOR
RADIOLOGICAL HEALTH PROGRAMS. [Semi-
annual]

ISSN 0149-8304
Earlier HE 20.1112

HE 20.4123:CT   • Item 458-B-15 (MF)
RADIATION RECOMMENDATIONS (series).
Later HE 20.4615

HE 20.4124:CT
AUDIOVISUAL MATERIALS. [Irregular]

CENTER FOR DRUGS AND BIOLOGICS
(1984– 1987)

CREATION AND AUTHORITY

The Center for Drugs and Biologics was formerly named the Bureau of Drugs and Biologics
and the National Center for Drugs and Biologics.
The name was changed to Center for Drugs and
Biologics by FDA notice dated March 9, 1984 (49
FR 10166). Functions were transferred to the Center
for Drug Evaluation and Research (HE 20.4700)
and Center for Biologics Evaluation and Research
by Secretary's notice of October 6, 1987 (52 FR
38275).

HE 20.4201:date
ANNUAL REPORT.

HE 20.4202:CT   • Item 499-K-1
GENERAL PUBLICATIONS.

HE 20.4208:CT   • Item 499-K-2
HANDBOOKS, MANUALS, GUIDES. [Irregular]

HE 20.4208/2:CT   • Item 499-K (MF)
GUIDELINES FOR THE CLINICAL EVALUATION OF
[various drugs]. [Irregular]

HE 20.4209:date
FDA DRUG AND DEVICE PRODUCTS APPROVALS,
FDA/BD- (nos). [Monthly]

HE 20.4210:date   • Item 499-K-3
APPROVED DRUG PRODUCTS WITH THERAPEUTIC
EQUIVALENCE EVALUATIONS. [Annual]

Lists currently marketed prescription drug products approved as safe and effective by FDA and
those pending approval. Contains trade name and
application holder indexes to approved drug products.

Consists of an annual basic volume updated
by periodic supplements.
Former title: Approved Prescription Drug Products with Therapeutic Equivalence Evaluations.

HE 20.4211:date   • Item 499-K-1
NEW DRUG EVALUATION STATISTICAL REPORT.

BUREAU OF MEDICAL DEVICES
(1977– 1984)

CREATION AND AUTHORITY

The Bureau was merged on March 9, 1984
with the Radiological Health Bureau to become
The Center for Devices and Radiological Health
(HE 20.4600).

HE 20.4301:date
ANNUAL REPORT.

HE 20.4302:CT   • Item 499-L
GENERAL PUBLICATIONS. [Irregular]

HE 20.4306:CT   • Item 499-L-1
RULES, REGULATIONS AND INSTRUCTIONS.

HE 20.4308:CT   • Item 499-L-3
HANDBOOKS, MANUALS, GUIDES. [Irregular]

HE 20.4309:date   • Item 494-B-4 (MF)
BUREAU OF MEDICAL DEVICES STANDARDS
SURVEY, INTERNATIONAL EDITION. [Annual]

Formerly published by the Food and Drug
Administration under the title Medical Devices
and Diagnostic Products Standards Survey, International Edition (HE 20.4035).

HE 20.4309/2:date   • Item 494-B-4 (MF)
BUREAU OF MEDICAL DEVICES STANDARDS
SURVEY, NATIONAL EDITION. [Annual]

Formerly published by the Food and Drug
Administration under the title Medical Devices
and Diagnostic Products Standards Survey, National Edition (HE 204035/2).

HE 20.4310:nos.   • Item 499-L-2 (MF)
FDA MEDICAL DEVICE STANDARDS PUBLICATIONS,
MDS (series). [Irregular]

HE 20.4310/2:nos.   • Item 499-L-2 (MF)
FDA MEDICAL DEVICE STANDARDS PUBLICATION,
TECHNICAL REPORTS, FDA-T- (series). 1–
[Irregular]

CENTER FOR VETERINARY MEDICINE
(1984–   )

INFORMATION

> Communications Staff
> Center for Veterinary Medicine
> Food and Drug Administration
> 7519 Standish Pl., HFV-12
> Rockville, Maryland 20855
> (301) 827-3800
> Fax: (301) 827-4401
> htttp://www.fda.gov/cvm/default.html

HE 20.4401:date
ANNUAL REPORT.

HE 20.4402:CT   • Item 499-D-2
GENERAL PUBLICATIONS.

HE 20.4408:CT   • Item 499-D-3
HANDBOOKS, MANUALS, GUIDES. [Irregular]

HE 20.4409:CT   • Item 499-D-1 (MF)
DRAFT ENVIRONMENTAL IMPACT STATEMENT. [Irregular]

HE 20.4410   • Item 499-D-4 (EL)
FDA VETERINARIAN. [Bimonthly]

> PURPOSE:– To provide information on veterinary medicine and the regulations governing the animal drug and feeds industries.

CENTER FOR FOOD SAFETY AND APPLIED NUTRITION
(1979–   )

CREATION AND AUTHORITY

> The Bureau of Foods was renamed the Center for Food Safety and Applied Nutrition By Food and Drug Administration notice March 9, 1984 (49 FR 10166).

INFORMATION

> Center for Food Safety and Applied Nutrition
> Food and Drug Administration
> 5100 Paint Branch Pkwy.
> College Park, MD 20740-3835
> (301) 436-1600
> Toll Free: (888) SAFEFOOD
> Fax: (301) 205-4733
> http://vm.cfsan.fda.gov

HE 20.4501:date
ANNUAL REPORTS.

HE 20.4502:CT   • Item 495-B-1
GENERAL PUBLICATIONS. [Irregular]

HE 20.4508:CT   • Item 495-B-2
HANDBOOKS, MANUALS, GUIDES. [Irregular]

HE 20.4509:CT   • Item 495-B-3
BIBLIOGRAPHIES AND LISTS OF PUBLICATIONS. [Irregular]

HE 20.4515:   • Item 495-B-4 (MF)
CENTER FOR FOOD SAFETY AND APPLIED NUTRITION TECHNICAL PLAN. [Annual]

> Consists of two volumes, Volume 1 concerning technical plan project descriptions and volume 2 technical plan positions and contract dollars.

CENTER FOR DEVICES AND RADIOLOGICAL HEALTH
(1984–   )

CREATION AND AUTHORITY

> The National Center for Devices and Radiological Health was formed by the merger of the Bureau of Radiological Health (HE 20.4100) and the Bureau of Medical Devices (HE 20.4300) in 1983. The name was changed to Center for Devices and Radiological Health by FDA notice dated March 9, 1984 (49 FR 10166).

INFORMATION

> Center for Devices and Radiological Health
> Food and Drug Administration
> 9200 Corporate Blvd.
> Rockville, Maryland 20850
> (301) 443-4690
> Fax: (301) 594-1320
> http://www.fda.gov/cdrh/index.html

HE 20.4601:date
ANNUAL REPORT.

HE 20.4602:CT   • Item 499-L-7
GENERAL PUBLICATIONS. [Irregular]

HE 20.4606:CT   • Item 499-L-4
REGULATIONS, RULES, INSTRUCTIONS. [Irregular]

HE 20.4606/2:   • Item 499-L-12
REGULATIONS FOR THE ADMINISTRATION AND ENFORCEMENT OF THE RADIATION CONTROL FOR HEALTH AND SAFETY ACT OF 1968. [Irregular]

> Regulations for administration and enforcement of the Radiation Control for Health and Safety Act of 1968, whose purpose is to protect the public from unnecessary exposure to radiation from electronic products.
> Earlier HE 20.4106:R 11

HE 20.4608:CT   • Item 499-L-8
HANDBOOKS, MANUALS, GUIDES. [Irregular]

HE 20.4608/2:CT   • Item 499-L-8
COMPLIANCE GUIDANCE SERIES.

HE 20.4609:CT   • Item 499-L-6 (MF)
BIBLIOGRAPHIES AND LISTS OF PUBLICATIONS. [Irregular]

HE 20.4609/2:date   • Item 498-B-4 (MF)
CENTER FOR DEVICES AND RADIOLOGICAL HEALTH PUBLICATIONS INDEX. [Biennial]

> Earlier: HE 20.4120

HE 20.4610:date   • Item 499-L-5 (MF)
RADIOLOGICAL HEALTH TRAINING RESOURCES CATALOG. [Biennial]

> Earlier HE 20.4102:T 68

HE 20.4611:CT   • Item 498-B-16 (MF)
JOINT NCDRH AND STATE QUALITY ASSURANCE SURVEYS IN NUCLEAR MEDICINE. [Irregular]

> Earlier HE 20.4108/2

HE 20.4612:v.nos./nos.   • Item 498-B-14
DRH RADIOLOGICAL HEALTH BULLETIN. v. 1– [Monthly]

> Earlier HE 20.4103

HE 20.4612/2:v.nos.&nos.   • Item 498-B-14
MEDICAL DEVICES BULLETIN. v. 1–   1983– [Monthly]

HE 20.4613:date   • Item 498-B-9 (MF)
CSU-PHS COLLABORATIVE RADIOLOGICAL HEALTH

LABORATORY. ANNUAL REPORT. 1st–   1962–

> CSU-PHS = Colorado State University- Public Health Service
> Earlier HE 20.4119

HE 20.4614:date   • Item 499-L-9
SMA MEMO. [Quarterly]

> Provides marketing and other information of interest to small manufacturers of medical devices. Memos are in the newsletter format.
> SMA = Small Manufacturers Assistance.

HE 20.4615:CT   • Item 498-B-15 (MF)
RADIATION RECOMMENDATIONS (series). [Irregular]

> Recommendations developed to encourage practices to help reduce unnecessary radiation exposure in situations where regulations would not be effective or desirable.
> Earlier HE 20.4123

HE 20.4616:CT   • Item 499-L-10
FDA SAFETY ALERTS (on various subjects). [Irregular]

> Each Alert covers a single topic.

HE 20.4617:CT   • Item 499-L-11 (MF)
SELECTION OF PATIENTS FOR X-RAY EXAMINATIONS (series). [Irregular]

> Each issue concerns a different topic related to selection of patients for X-ray examinations.

HE 20.4618   • Item 499-L-13 (EL)
OFFICE OF SCIENCE AND TECHNOLOGY ANNUAL REPORT.

HE 20.4618/2   • Item 499-L-15 (EL)
OFFICE OF DEVICE EVALUATION (ODE), ANNUAL REPORT. (Annual)

HE 20.4619:v.nos./nos.   • Item 499-L-14
MAMMOGRAPHY MATTERS. [Quarterly]

CENTER FOR DRUG EVALUATION AND RESEARCH
(1987–   )

CREATION AND AUTHORITY

> The Center for Drug Evaluation and Research was established November 1987 and replaces, in part, the Center for Drugs and Biologics (HE 20.4200) by Secretary's notice of October 6, 1987 (52 FR 38275). The name was changed to Center for Biologics Evaluation and Research in 1996.

INFORMATION

> Center for Drug Evaluation and Research
> Food and Drug Administration
> Woodmont Bldg. Two
> 1451 Rockville Pike
> Rockville, Maryland 20825
> (301) 594-5401
> http://www.fda.gov/cder

HE 20.4701   • Item 499-T-1 (MF)
ANNUAL REPORT.

HE 20.4702:CT   • Item 499-T
GENERAL PUBLICATIONS.

HE 20.4708:CT   • Item 499-P
HANDBOOKS, MANUALS, GUIDES.

HE 20.4709:   • Item 499-P-1
BIBLIOGRAPHIES & LISTS OF PUBLICATIONS.

HE 20.4715:date   • **Item 499-K-3 (EL)**
APPROVED DRUG PRODUCTS WITH THERAPEUTIC
EQUIVALENCE EVALUATIONS.

CENTER FOR BIOLOGICS
EVALUATION AND RESEARCH

INFORMATION

> Center for Biologics Evaluation and Research
> Food and Drug Administration
> 1401 Rockville Pike
> Bethesda, MD 20852-1448
> (301) 827-1800
> Fax: (301) 827-0440
> Toll Free: (800) 835-4709
> http://www.fda.gov/cber

HE 20.4801   • **Item 499-T-1 (MF) (EL)**
ANNUAL REPORT.

HE 20.4802:CT   • **Item 499-T-2**
GENERAL PUBLICATIONS.

HEALTH SERVICES
ADMINISTRATION
(1973– 1982)

CREATION AND AUTHORITY

> The Health Services Administration was
established within the Public Health Service by
reorganization order, effective July 1, 1973. The
Administration was superseded by the Health Resources and Services Administration (HE 20.9000)
by Secretarial reorganization of August 20, 1982,
effective September 1, 1982 (47 FR 38409).

HE 20.5001:date
ANNUAL REPORT.

HE 20.5001/2:CT
ANNUAL REPORTS OF COMMITTEES, COUNCILS,
ETC.

HE 20.5001/3:date   • **Item 486-E-3**
REPORT OF THE ADMINISTRATOR. [Annual]

HE 20.5002:CT   • **Item 486-E-1**
GENERAL PUBLICATIONS.

HE 20.5008:CT   • **Item 486-E-2**
HANDBOOKS, MANUALS, GUIDES. [Irregular]

HE 20.5009:v.nos.&nos.   • **Item 497**
HEALTH SERVICES REPORTS. v. 86– 89, no. 4. 1971–
1974. [Bimonthly]

> Monthly prior to 1974.
> Issued by the Health Services and Mental
Health Administration (HE 20.2010/2) prior to v.
88, no. 7.
> Redesignated Public Health Reports and pub-
lished by the Health Resources Administration
(HE 20.6011).

HE 20.5010:date   • **Item 444-J**
NATIONAL PROFESSIONAL STANDARDS REVIEW
COUNCIL: ANNUAL REPORT. 1st–   1973–
Earlier HE 1.46

HE 20.5011:date   • **Item 486-E-4**
NATIONAL HEALTH SERVICE CORPS SCHOLARSHIP
PROGRAM INFORMATION BULLETIN FOR
STUDENTS OF ALLOPATHIC MEDICINE, OSTEO-
PATHIC MEDICINE, AND DENTISTRY.

BUREAU OF HEALTH CARE
DELIVERY AND ASSISTANCE
(1973– 1983)

CREATION AND AUTHORITY

> The Bureau of Community Health Services
was established within the Health Services Administration by reorganization order, effective July
1, 1973. The Bureau was transferred in 1983 to
the Health Resources and Services Administration (HE 20.9100).

HE 20.5101:date
ANNUAL REPORT.

HE 20.5102:CT   • **Item 532-E-1**
GENERAL PUBLICATIONS.

HE 20.5108:CT   • **Item 512-E-2**
HANDBOOKS, MANUALS, GUIDES. [Irregular]
Earlier HE 20.2558

HE 20.5109:nos.
COMMUNITY HEALTH SCENE (series). 1–   1973–
[Irregular] ([HSA] 74-5051)

> PURPOSE:– To report on developments af-
fecting all Bureau of Community Health Services.
> Issue No. 1 was published as Information
(series).

HE 20.5110:CT   • **Item 512-E-3**
BIBLIOGRAPHIES AND LISTS OF PUBLICATIONS.

HE 20.5110:P 96   • **Item 512-E-3**
PUBLICATIONS OF THE BUREAU OF COMMU-
NITY HEALTH SERVICES. [Annual]

HE 20.5111:v.nos.&nos.   • **Item 494-E-1**
FAMILY PLANNING DIGEST. v. 1– 3. 1972– 1975.
[Bimonthly]

> PURPOSE:– To provide a digest of key ar-
ticles, papers and events from the field of family
planning for use by family planning workers.
> ISSN 0046-3213
> Prior to v. 2, no. 6, Nov. 1973, issued by the
National Center for Family Planning Service (HE
20.2909).

HE 20.5112:nos.   • **Item 512-E-4**
COMMUNITY HEALTH SCENE. 1–   1970–
[Irregular]

> PURPOSE:– To serve as a forum for all mem-
bers of the partnership for health. Supersedes
Partnership for Health News (HE 20.2559).
> Earlier HE 20.2557/2

HE 20.5113:nos.   • **Item 483-V-4**
MCH STATISTICAL SERIES. 1–   1971–   [Irregu-
lar]

> PURPOSE:– To present data on various pro-
grams authorized by Title V of the Social Security
Act.
> Continuation of statistical data contained in
the Statistical Series issued by the Children's
Bureau when the program was administered by
that agency.
> Earlier HE 20.2760

HE 20.5114:nos.   • **Item 532-E-3**
MCHS RESEARCH SERIES. 1–   [Irregular]
> PURPOSE:– To present summaries of final
reports of research projects concerned with improving the operation, functioning, and effectiveness of maternal and child health and crippled
children's services.

HE 20.5114/2:CT   • **Item 532-E-3**
RESEARCH TO IMPROVE HEALTH SERVICES FOR
MOTHERS AND CHILDREN. [Irregular]
Earlier HE 20.5114/2

HE 20.5115:nos.   • **Item 532-E-2**
NEIGHBORHOOD HEALTH CENTERS, SUMMARY OF
PROJECT DATA. 1–   [Quarterly] (Division of
Monitoring and Analysis)

> Prior to report no. 9 issued as Comprehen-
sive Health Service Projects.

HE 20.5116:date   • **Item 512-E-5**
MIGRANT HEALTH PROJECTS, SUMMARY OF
PROJECT DATA. [Quarterly]

> ISSN 0145-1340

HE 20.5117:date   • **Item 532-E-7**
HUMAN GENETICS INFORMATIONAL AND EDUCA-
TIONAL MATERIALS. 1979–   [Irregular]

> PURPOSE:– To provide an annotated bibliog-
raphy of print and non-print educational and informational materials in the field of human genetics
and genetic diseases. Intended for professionals, patients, students, etc.

HE 20.5118:CT   • **Item 532-E-8**
POSTERS AND CHARTS. [Irregular]

HE 20.5119/3:date   • **Item 532-E-9**
FAMILY PLANNING GRANTEES AND CLINICS,
DIRECTORY. [Annual]

> Later HE 20.33

FEDERAL HEALTH PROGRAMS
SERVICE
(1973– 1974)

HE 20.5201:date
ANNUAL REPORT.

> Earlier HE 20.2701

HE 20.5202:CT   • **Item 494-C-1**
GENERAL PUBLICATIONS.

> Earlier HE 20.2702

INDIAN HEALTH SERVICE
(1973– 1983)

CREATION AND AUTHORITY

> The Indian Health Service (HE 20.2700) was
transferred to the Health Services Administration
by reorganization order, effective July 1, 1973.
The Service was transferred in 1983 to the Health
Resources and Services Administration (HE
20.9400).

HE 20.5301:date   • **Item 486-F-2 (MF)**
ANNUAL REPORT.

> Earlier HE 20.2651
> Later HE 20.9401

HE 20.5301:date   • **Item 486-F-2 (MF)**
INDIAN HEALTH CARE IMPROVEMENT ACT,
ANNUAL REPORT.

> PURPOSE:– To describe progress made
by the Department in achieving the purposes
of the Act, which are to insure that the health
status of Indian people is at parity with that
of the general U.S. population and to achieve
maximum participation of Indian people in Indian health programs.
> Also published in microfiche.

HE 20.5301/2:date • Item 486-F-1 (MF)
NAVAJO AREA INDIAN HEALTH SERVICE, OFFICE
OF ENVIRONMENTAL HEALTH AND ENGINEER-
ING: ANNUAL REPORT.

Also published in microfiche.
Later HE 20.9413

HE 20.5302:CT • Item 486-I-2
GENERAL PUBLICATIONS. [Irregular]

Earlier HE 20.2652
Later HE 20.9402

HE 20.5308:CT • Item 486-K-1
HANDBOOKS, MANUALS, GUIDES. [Irregular]

Later HE 20.9408

HE 20.5309:date • Item 486-F (MF)
DENTAL SERVICE FOR AMERICAN INDIANS AND
ALASKAN NATIVES. [Annual]

PURPOSE:– To document and evaluate
progress of the dental program during the previous year and provide accurate data for future
program planning.
Earlier HE 20.2659

HE 20.5310:date • Item 486-I-3
INDIAN HEALTH TRENDS AND SERVICES. [Annual]
(Office of Program Planning and Evaluation, Program Analysis and Statistics Branch) (PHS Publication 2092)

PURPOSE:– To present current and trend information about the demographic characteristics
and the health status of Indians and Alaska Natives, as revealed by vital statistics, notifiable
disease data, selected health facility workloads,
and program services information.
Earlier HE 20.2661

HE 20.5311:date • Item 486-I-4
ALASKA NATIVE MEDICAL CENTER: ANNUAL RE-
PORT.

HE 20.5312:date • Item 486-I (MF)
TO THE FIRST AMERICANS, ANNUAL REPORT OF
THE INDIAN HEALTH PROGRAM. 1st–   1967–

Earlier HE 20.2014/2

BUREAU OF MEDICAL SERVICES
(1974–   )

CREATION AND AUTHORITY

The Bureau of Medical Services was established in 1974 within the Health Resources and
Services Administration.

HE 20.5401:date • Item 483-V-6
ANNUAL REPORT.

Earlier HE 20.2751

HE 20.5402:CT • Item 493-C-1
GENERAL PUBLICATIONS. [Irregular]

HE 20.5408:CT • Item 493-C-2
HANDBOOKS, MANUALS, GUIDES. [Irregular]

HE 20.5409:date • Item 494-C
ANNUAL STATISTICAL SUMMARY, FISCAL YEAR.
1959–

PURPOSE:– To impart information on inpa-
tient and outpatient medical care furnished in
U.S. Public Health Service facilities.
Issued in two parts:
Part 1. Management Data
Part 2. Diagnostic and Demographic Data.
Earlier HE 20.2709

HE 20.5410:v.nos.&nos. • Item 486
FEDERAL EMPLOYEE HEALTH SERIES. 1–
[Irregular]

Earlier FS 2.50/3

HE 20.5411:CT • Item 493-C-3
BIBLIOGRAPHIES AND LISTS OF PUBLICATIONS.
[Irregular]

HE 20.5412:nos.-v. • Item 484-B
RENAL DISEASE AND HYPERTENSION, PRO-
CEEDINGS, ANNUAL CONFERENCE. 1st–

13th May 1974 San Francisco, California
15th Nov. 1976 Miami Beach, Florida
Earlier HE 20.2702:R 29

BUREAU OF QUALITY
ASSURANCE
(1974–   )

HE 20.5501:date
ANNUAL REPORT.

HE 20.5502:CT • Item 494-G-1
GENERAL PUBLICATIONS.

HE 20.5508:CT • Item 494-G-2
HANDBOOKS, MANUALS, GUIDES. [Irregular]

BUREAU OF HEALTH
PERSONNEL DEVELOPMENT
AND SERVICE
(1980–   )

HE 20.5601:date
ANNUAL REPORT.

HE 20.5602:CT • Item 494-M
GENERAL PUBLICATIONS.

HEALTH RESOURCES
ADMINISTRATION
(1973– 1982)

CREATION AND AUTHORITY

The Health Resources Administration was
established within the Public Health Service by
reorganization order, effective July 1, 1973. The
Administration was merged with the Health Services Administration to form the Health Resources
and Services Administration (HE 20.9000) by
Secretarial reorganization of August 20, 1982,
effective September 1, 1982 (47 FR 38409).

HE 20.6001:date • Item 507-H-5
ANNUAL REPORTS.

Indexed by: Index to U.S. Government Periodicals.

HE 20.6001/2:date • Item 507-H-5
ENERGY ACTION STAFF: ANNUAL REPORT.

HE 20.6001/3:date • Item 507-H-6
HEALTH RESOURCES OPPORTUNITY OFFICE:
ANNUAL REPORT.

HE 20.6001/4:date • Item 507-H-8
DIVISION OF LONG-TERM CARE: ANNUAL REPORT.

HE 20.6001/5:CT • Item 507-H-12
ANNUAL REPORTS OF COMMITTEES, COUNCILS,
ETC.

HE 20.6001/5:H 34 • Item 507-H-12
NATIONAL COUNCIL ON HEALTH PLANNING AND
DEVELOPMENT.

HE 20.6002:CT • Item 507-H-1
GENERAL PUBLICATIONS.

HE 20.6007:CT • Item 507-H-2
HANDBOOKS, MANUALS, GUIDES. [Irregular]

HE 20.6009:v.nos.&nos. • Item 508-B
MONTHLY VITAL STATISTICS REPORT.

Issued by the Health Services and Mental
Health Administration (HE 20.2209) prior to v. 22,
no. 5, July 25, 1973.
ISSN 0364-0396
Later HE 20.6217

HE 20.6010:CT
HILL-BURTON HEALTH FACILITIES SERIES.

Later HE 20.30

HE 20.6011:v.nos.&nos. • Item 497
PUBLIC HEALTH REPORTS. v. 89, no. 5–   Sept.-
Oct. 1974–   [Bimonthly]

ISSN 0033-3549
Continues Health Services Reports (HE
20.5009).

HE 20.6012:CT • Item 507-H-7
HEALTH RESOURCES STUDIES. 1974–   [Irregular]

PURPOSE:– To acquaint a wide audience with
summaries of contract studies which are considered good examples of research in areas supported by the Health Resources Administration.

HE 20.6013:date • Item 483-T
HRA, HSA, CDS, ADAMHA PUBLIC ADVISORY COM-
MITTEES. [Quarterly]

Contains the roster of members, authority,
structure, and functions of the public advisory
councils, committees, boards, panels, and study
sections to the four agencies of the Public Health
Service most directly concerned with the organization, development, and delivery of health care
and services, as well as related research activities. The agencies are the Health Resources Administration (HRA), Health Services Administration (HSA), Center for Disease Control (CDS),
and the Alcohol, Drug Abuse, and Mental Health
Administration (ADAMHA).
Discontinued with the March 1981 issue.

HE 20.6014:v.nos.&nos.
HEALTH RESOURCES NEWS. [Monthly]

ISSN 0093-8785

HE 20.6015:v.nos.&nos. • Item 507-H-3
COMMITMENT. v. 1–   1976– 1978. [Quarterly]

This magazine is designed to describe the
people who practice in underserved areas, and
the programs and methods they use to serve
their patients better.
Indexed by: Index to U.S. Government Periodicals.
ISSN 0145-8698

HE 20.6016:CT • Item 507-H-4
BIBLIOGRAPHIES AND LISTS OF PUBLICATIONS.
[Irregular]

HE 20.6016:C 28 • Item 507-H-4
CATALOG OF PUBLICATIONS. [Irregular]

HE 20.6017:CT • Item 507-H-9
CHARTBOOKS. [Irregular] (Office of Health Resources
Opportunity)

HE 20.6018:date • Item 508
HEALTH, UNITED STATES. 1975– [Annual]

ISSN 0361-4468
Earlier HE 20.6202:H 34/3
Later HE 20.21

HE 20.6019:CT • Item 507-H-10
OHRO DIGEST. [Irregular] (Office of Health Resources
Opportunity)

PURPOSE:– To inform the public of developments and activities in Health Resources Administration that impact on health career opportunities and services for the disadvantaged.

HE 20.6020:CT • Item 507-H-11
PAPERS ON THE NATIONAL HEALTH GUIDELINES.
[Irregular]

Earlier HE 20.6002:P 19

HE 20.6021:date • Item 507-H-9
ACTION FOR THE DISADVANTAGED, ANNUAL RE-
PORT. [Annual]

HE 20.6022:date • Item 507-H-13
HEALTH PLANNING NEWSLETTER FOR GOVERN-
ING BODY MEMBERS. 1– 20. 1979– 1981.
[Monthly]

PURPOSE:– To provide an information exchange for participants in the health planning
activities authorized under the National Health
Planning and Resources Development Act. Includes short articles, illustrations, and other newsletter features.

HE 20.6023:date • Item 507-H-14
SCHOLARSHIP PROGRAM, APPLICANT INFOR-
MATION BULLETIN. [Annual] (National Health
Service Corps)

Contains the official description of the National Health Service Corps Scholarship Program,
including information on eligibility, benefits, rank-
ing procedure and other miscellaneous information.
Earlier HE 20.6002:Sch 6

HE 20.6024:CT/date
PHYSICIAN REQUIREMENTS FOR [various subjects]
(series). [Irregular]

BUREAU OF HEALTH PLANNING
(1978–   )

HE 20.6101:date • Item 509-C
ANNUAL REPORT. 1st– 1974–

HE 20.6102:CT • Item 509-A-1
GENERAL PUBLICATIONS.

HE 20.6108:CT • Item 509-A-2
HANDBOOKS, MANUALS, GUIDES. [Irregular]

HE 20.6109:CT • Item 507-D-6
DMI HEALTH MANPOWER INFORMATION EXCHANGE
REPORTS. (Division of Manpower Intelligence)

Earlier HE 20.3114

HE 20.6109/2:CT • Item 507-D-6
DMI ANALYTIC STUDIES (series). [Irregular] (Division of Manpower Intelligence)

Earlier HE 20.3114/4

HE 20.6110:CT • Item 509-A-3 (MF)
MONOGRAPHS AND DATA FOR HEALTH RESOURCES
PLANNING SERIES. [Irregular]

HE 20.6110/2:nos. • Item 509-A-6 (MF)
HEALTH PLANNING INFORMATION SERIES.

HE 20.6110/3:nos. • Item 509-A-6 (MF)
HEALTH PLANNING METHODS AND TECHNOLOGY
SERIES.

HE 20.6110/4:nos. • Item 509-A-6 (MF)
INTERNATIONAL HEALTH PLANNING SERIES. 1–
1979– [Irregular]

HE 20.6110/5:CT • Item 509-A-6
HEALTH PLANNING IN ACTION (series). [Irregular]

HE 20.6111:date • Item 509-A-4
DIRECTORY OF GRANTS, AWARDS, AND LOANS.
[Annual]

Earlier HE 20.3114:G 76
Later HE 20.6612

HE 20.6112:CT • Item 509-A-5
BIBLIOGRAPHIES AND LISTS OF PUBLICATIONS.

HE 20.6112/2:nos. • Item 509-A-7
HEALTH PLANNING BIBLIOGRAPHY SERIES. 1–
[Irregular]

HE 20.6113:CT • Item 486-D
HILL-BURTON HEALTH FACILITIES SERIES.

Earlier HE 20.6010

HE 20.6114:date • Item 509-A-8
ASSEMBLING THE HEALTH PLANNING STRUCTURE.
[Annual]

NATIONAL CENTER FOR HEALTH
STATISTICS
(1973–   )

CREATION AND AUTHORITY

The National Center for Health Statistics (HE
20.2200) was placed within the Health Resources
Administration in 1973.

INFORMATION

National Center for Health Statistics
Centers for Disease Control and Prevention
Division of Data
6525 Belcrest Rd.
Hyattsville, MD 20782-2003
(301) 458-4636
Fax: (301) 458-4020
http://www.cdc.gov/nchs

HE 20.6201:date • Item 508-A-1 (MF)
ANNUAL REPORT.

Earlier HE 20.2201

HE 20.6202:CT • Item 508
GENERAL PUBLICATIONS. [Irregular]

Earlier HE 20.2202

HE 20.6202:N 93 •|>Item 508
DIRECTORY OF NURSING HOME FACILITIES.

Provides a source of information for the
names, locations, and admission policies of
all inpatient nursing homes in the United
States. The directory lists 21,218 nursing
homes in four separate volumes:

HE 20.6202:N 93 NC
NORTH CENTRAL VOLUME. 1975. 332 p.

HE 20.6202:N 93 NE
NORTHEAST VOLUME. 1975. 227 p.

HE 20.6202:N 93 S
SOUTH VOLUME. 1975. 267 p.

HE 20.6202:N 93 W
WESTERN VOLUME.

HE 20.6208:CT • Item 509
HANDBOOKS, MANUALS, GUIDES.

Earlier HE 20.2208

HE 20.6208/2:date • Item 509
EXAMINATION STAFF PROCEDURES MANUAL FOR
THE HISPANIC HEALTH AND NUTRITION EXAMI-
NATION SURVEY.

HE 20.6208/2-2:date • Item 509 (MF)
INSTRUCTION MANUAL, PART 15f, DIETARY
INTERVIEWER'S MANUAL FOR THE HISPANIC
HEALTH AND NUTRITION EXAMINATION SUR-
VEY. [Annual]

HE 20.6208/2-3:date • Item 509 (MF)
INSTRUCTION MANUAL, PART 15e, PHYSICIAN'S
EXAMINATION MANUAL FOR THE HISPANIC
HEALTH AND NUTRITION EXAMINATION SUR-
VEY. [Annual]

HE 20.6208/2-4:date • Item 509 (MF)
INSTRUCTION MANUAL, PART 15g, MOBILE EXAMI-
NATION CENTER INTERVIEWER'S MANUAL FOR
THE HISPANIC HEALTH AND NUTRITION EXAMI-
NATION SURVEY. [Annual]

HE 20.6208/2-5:date • Item 509
INSTRUCTION MANUAL, PART 15b, FIELD STAFF
OPERATIONS FOR THE HISPANIC HEALTH AND
NUTRITION EXAMINATION SURVEY. [Annual]

HE 20.6208/2-6:date • Item 509-D
INSTRUCTION MANUAL PART 15d, DENTAL
EXAMINER'S MANUAL FOR THE HISPANIC
HEALTH AND NUTRITION SURVEY. [Annual]

HE 20.6208/3:date • Item 509 (MF)
INSTRUCTION MANUAL, PART 8, VITAL RECORDS
GEOGRAPHIC CLASSIFICATION. [Annual]

HE 20.6208/4:date • Item 509 (MF)
INSTRUCTION MANUAL, PART 2e, NONINDEXED
TERMS, STANDARD ABBREVIATIONS, AND
STATE GEOGRAPHIC CODES USED IN MOR-
TALITY DATA CLASSIFICATION. [Annual]

Earlier HE 20.6208:D 26

HE 20.6208/4-2:date • Item 509 (MF)
INSTRUCTION MANUAL, PART 2c, ICD 9 ACME
DECISION TABLES FOR CLASSIFYING UNDER-
LYING CAUSES OF DEATH. [Annual]

HE 20.6208/4-3:date • Item 509 (MF)
INSTRUCTION MANUAL PART 2b, INSTRUCTIONS
FOR CLASSIFYING MULTIPLE CAUSES OF
DEATH. [Annual]

HE 20.6208/4-4:date • Item 509-D (MF)
INSTRUCTION MANUAL PART 2a, INSTRUCTIONS
FOR CLASSIFYING THE UNDERLYING CAUSE
OF DEATH. [Annual]

HE 20.6208/4-5:date • Item 509-D (MF)
INSTRUCTION MANUAL PART 2a, ICDA EIGHTH
REVISION OF DECISION TABLES FOR CLASSI-
FYING UNDERLYING CAUSES OF DEATH. [An-
nual]

HE 20.6208/4-6:date • Item 509-D (MF)
INSTRUCTION MANUAL PART 2D, NCHS PROCE-
DURES FOR MORTALITY MEDICAL DATA
SYSTEM FILE PREPARATION AND MAINTE-
NANCE. [Annual]

HE 20.6208/4-7:date • Item 509-D (MF)
INSTRUCTION MANUAL PART 2G, DATA ENTRY IN-
STRUCTIONS FOR THE MORTALITY MEDICAL
INDEXING, CLASSIFICATION, AND RETRIEVAL
SYSTEM (MICAR). [Annual]

HE 20.6208/4-8:date • **Item 509-D (MF)**
INSTRUCTION MANUAL PART 2H, DICTIONARY OF VALID TERMS FOR THE MORTALITY MEDICAL INDEXING, CLASSIFICATION, AND RETRIEVAL SYSTEM (MICAR). [Annual]

HE 20.6208/5:date • **Item 509 (MF)**
INSTRUCTION MANUAL, PART 4, DEMOGRAPHIC CLASSIFICATION AND CODING INSTRUCTIONS FOR DEATH RECORDS. [Annual]

HE 20.6208/6:date • **Item 509 (MF)**
INSTRUCTION MANUAL PART 3a, CLASSIFICATION AND CODING INSTRUCTIONS FOR LIVE BIRTH RECORDS. [Annual]

HE 20.6208/6-2:date • **Item 509 (MF)**
INSTRUCTION MANUAL, PART 3b, CLASSIFICATION AND CODING INSTRUCTIONS FOR FETAL DEATH RECORDS. [Annual]

HE 20.6208/7:date • **Item 509 (MF)**
INSTRUCTION MANUAL, PART 6, CLASSIFICATION AND CODING INSTRUCTIONS FOR MARRIAGE RECORDS. [Annual]

HE 20.6208/8:date • **Item 509 (MF)**
INSTRUCTION MANUAL, PART 10, CLASSIFICATION AND CODING INSTRUCTIONS FOR INDUCED TERMINATION OF PREGNANCY RECORDS. [Annual]

HE 20.6208/9:date • **Item 509 (MF)**
INSTRUCTION MANUAL, PART 5, DATA PREPARATION OF THE CURRENT SAMPLE. [Annual]

HE 20.6208/10:date • **Item 509-D (MF)**
INSTRUCTION MANUAL PART 7, CLASSIFICATION AND CODING INSTRUCTIONS FOR DIVORCE RECORDS. [Annual]

HE 20.6208/11:date • **Item 509-D (MF)**
INSTRUCTION MANUAL PART 1, SOURCE RECORDS AND CONTROL SPECIFICATIONS. [Annual]

Earlier HE 20.6208:D 26

HE 20.6208/13: • **Item 509-E**
INTERNATIONAL HEALTH DATA REFERENCE GUIDE. [Annual]

A table covering one side of the guide shows data on vital statistics, hospital statistics, health manpower statistics, and national population-based surveys for 29 countries, from Australia to Yugoslavia.

HE 20.6208/14:date • **Item 509-D (MF)**
INSTRUCTION MANUAL PART 11, COMPUTER EDITS FOR MORTALITY DATA. [Annual]

HE 20.6208/15 • **Item 509-D (MF)**
INSTRUCTION MANUAL PART 12, COMPUTER EDITS FOR NATALITY DATA. [Annual]

HE 20.6208/16 • **Item 509-D (MF)**
INSTRUCTION MANUAL PART 18, GUIDELINES FOR IMPLEMENTING FIELD AND QUERY PROGRAMS FOR REGISTRATION OF BIRTHS AND DEATHS.

HE 20.6209 • **Item 500-E**
VITAL AND HEALTH STATISTICS. 1963– [Irregular]

Series 1-4 replace series A and D of Health Statistics from the U.S. National Health Survey (FS 2.85); Series 10-12 replace series B and C of that publication; and series 20-30 replace Vital Statistics– Special Reports (FS 2.109). Issued in the following sub-series:

GENERAL SERIES.

1. PROGRAMS, DEFINITIONS, PROCEDURES.

Reports which describe the general programs of the National Center for health Statistics and its offices and divisions, data collection methods used, definitions, and other material necessary for understanding the technical characteristics of published data.

2. RESEARCH ON STATISTICAL METHODOLOGY.

Studies of new statistical methodology including: experimental tests of new survey methods, studies of vital statistics collection methods, new analytical techniques, objective evaluation of reliability of collected data, contributions to statistical theory.

3. ANALYTICAL STUDIES.

Comprises reports presenting analytical or interpretive studies based on vital and health statistics. The primary aim is not to publish new tabulations of data, but to carry the analysis of data further than the expository type analyses given in other series, not limiting the type of statistical analysis to be covered.

4. COMMITTEE REPORTS AND DOCUMENTS.

Final reports of major committees concerned with vital and health statistics. Documents such as recommended model vital registration laws and revised birth and death certificates will be published in this series. Committee working papers and reports of limited or temporary interest are not included.

5. AMBULATORY CARE.

6. QUESTIONNAIRE DESIGN IN THE COGNITIVE RESEARCH LABORATORY.

HEALTH SURVEY SERIES.

10. HEALTH INTERVIEW SURVEY STATISTICS.

Statistics of illness, accidental injuries, disability, use of hospital, medical, dental, and other services, and other health-related topics, based on data collected in a continuing national household interview survey.

11. HEALTH EXAMINATION SURVEY STATISTICS.

Data from the direct examination, testing, and measurement of national samples of the population of the United States, including the medically defined prevalence of specific diseases, and distributions of the population with respect to various physical and physiological measurements.

12. HEALTH RECORDS SURVEY STATISTICS.

Reports on the health characteristics of person in institutions, and on hospital, medical nursing, and personal care received, based on national samples of establishments providing these services and samples of the residents or patients, or of records of the establishments.

13. HOSPITAL DISCHARGE SURVEY STATISTICS.

Statistics relating to discharged patients in short-stay hospitals, based on a sample of patient records in a national sample of hospitals.

14. HEALTH RESOURCES DATA: MANPOWER AND FACILITIES.

Statistics on the numbers, geographic distribution, and characteristics of health resources including physicians, dentists, nurses, other health manpower occupations, hospitals, nursing homes, and outpatient and other inpatient facilities.

16. ADVANCE DATA FROM VITAL AND HEALTH STATISTICS.

VITAL STATISTICS SERIES.

20. MORTALITY DATA.

Various special reports on mortality giving data other than that in the annual volume Vital Statistics of the United States or in the Monthly Vital Statistics Reports. Covers tabulations by cause of death, age, etc., time series of rates, data for geographic areas, State, cities, etc.

21. NATALITY DATA.

Data on birth by age of mother, birth order, geographic areas, States, cities, time series of rates, etc., compilations of data not included in the annual or monthly publications mentioned in Series 20 (above).

22. MARRIAGE AND DIVORCE STATISTICS.

Tabulations of data on marriage and divorce by various demographic factors, geographic areas, etc.

23. DATA FROM VITAL STATISTICS SURVEYS.

Includes tabulations based on a special program of sample surveys related to vital records. The subjects being covered in these surveys are varied including such topics as mortality by socioeconomic classes, hospitalization in the last year of life, X-ray exposure during pregnancy, etc.
Earlier HE 20.2210

24. SUPPLEMENTS TO THE MONTHLY VITAL STATISTICS REPORT.

HE 20.6209:1/nos. • **Item 500-E**
VITAL AND HEALTH STATISTICS, SERIES 1.

HE 20.6209/2:date • **Item 508-G**
CURRENT LISTING AND TOPICAL INDEX. [Annual]

Earlier HE 20.2202:V 83

HE 20.6209/3:nos. • **Item 500-E (EL)**
ADVANCE DATA FROM THE VITAL AND HEALTH STATISTICS OF NCHS. 1– 1976 [Irregular]

ISSN 0147-3956

HE 20.6209/4:date • **Item 500-E (MF)**
CURRENT ESTIMATES FROM THE NATIONAL HEALTH INTERVIEW SURVEY. [Annual]

Earlier HE 20.6209:10

HE 20.6209/4-2:date • **Item 500-E (MF)**
NATIONAL HEALTH INTERVIEW SURVEY, COMPUTER PROCESSING PROCEDURES, CALENDAR YEAR. [Annual]

HE 20.6209/4-3 • **Item 500-E-1 (CD)**
NATIONAL HEALTH INTERVIEW SURVEY, (NHIS).

HE 20.6209/4-4:nos. • **Item 500-E-2 (E)**
DISKETTE SERIES.

Issued on floppy diskettes.

HE 20.6209/4-5:nos. • **Item 500-E-5 (CD)**
NATIONAL AMBULATORY MEDICAL CARE SURVEY.

HE 20.6209/4-6 • **Item 500-E-6 (E)**
CATALOG OF ELECTRONIC DATA PRODUCTS. [Annual]

Issued on computer diskettes.

HE 20.6209/4-7:nos. • **Item 500-E-7 (CD)**
1987 BIRTH COHORT LINKED BIRTH/INFANT DEATH DATA SET SERIES 20.

HE 20.6209/4-8:v.nos./nos. • **Item 500-E-12 (CD)**
NATIONAL HEALTH AND NUTRITION EXAMINATION SURVEY, SERIES 11

HE 20.6209/5:date
DISABILITY DAYS, UNITED STATES. [Annual]

Earlier HE 20.6209:10/158

HE 20.6209/6:date • **Item 500-E (MF)**
SURGICAL AND NONSURGICAL PROCEDURES IN SHORTSTAY HOSPITALS, UNITED STATES. [Annual]

Earlier HE 20.6209

HE 20.6209/7:date   • Item 500-E (EL)
NATIONAL HOSPITAL DISCHARGE SURVEY: ANNUAL
SUMMARY.

Earlier titled: Utilization of Short-Stay Hospitals United States, Annual Summary.

HE 20.6209/7-2   • Item 500-E-3 (CD)
NATIONAL HOSPITAL DISCHARGE SURVEY.

HE 20.6209/8:date   • Item 500-E
INPATIENT UTILIZATION OF SHORT-STAY HOSPITALS BY DIAGNOSIS, UNITED STATES. [Annual]

HE 20.6209/9:date   • Item 509
DETAILED DIAGNOSES AND PROCEDURES FOR PATIENTS DISCHARGED FROM SHORT-STAY HOSPITALS, UNITED STATES. [Annual]

HE 20.6209/10   • Item 500-E-8 (CD)
NCHS CD-ROM Series (23).

HE 20.6209/11:v.nos./nos.   • Item 500-E-9 (CD)
NATIONAL CENTER FOR HEALTH STATISTICS, SERIES 21, CD-ROM.

HE 20.6209/12:nos.   • Item 506-W (CD)
NCHS ATLAS CD-ROM (series).

HE 20.6210:date   • Item 510
VITAL STATISTICS OF THE UNITED STATES. 1937–
[Annual]

Definite publication of vital statistics, containing extensive basic data and analysis on marriage, divorce, natality, fetal mortality, and mortality.
Issuing agency varies: 1937– 44, Bureau of the Census, Vital Statistics Division: 1945– 59, National Office of Vital Statistics; 1959– 62, National Center for Health Statistics, National Vital Statics Division; 1963–   , National Center for Health Statistics, Division of Vital Statistics.
Published in three volumes:
Vol. 1. Natality. [ISSN 0083-6710]
Vol. 2. Mortality.
Vol. 3. Marriage and Divorce.
Earlier HE 20.2212

HE 20.6210/a:date/v.nos.   • Item 510
TECHNICAL APPENDIX FROM VITAL STATISTICS OF THE UNITED STATES.

HE 20.6210/2:   • Item 510-A-1 (EL)
WHERE TO WRITE FOR VITAL RECORDS. [Irregular]

PURPOSE– To provide information on individual vital records maintained only on file in state or local vital statistics offices. Includes address, cost per copy, and remarks.
Earlier HE 20.6202:V 83

HE 20.6211:date   • Item 492-A (EL)
ANNUAL REPORT OF THE UNITED STATES NATIONAL COMMITTEE ON VITAL AND HEALTH STATISTICS FISCAL YEAR. 1956–

PURPOSE:– To report on the activities of the Committee, established in 1948 to advise on matters related to vital and health statistics and to promote and secure technical developments in the field.
Earlier HE 20.2211

HE 20.6212:date   • Item 509-B
HEALTH RESOURCES STATISTICS. [Annual]

PURPOSE:– To provide comprehensive statistical utilization, education and training, and recruitment of professional, technical, and auxiliary workers; and on health facilities providing inpatient care, including hospitals, nursing care and related homes, and other inpatient health facilities.
Earlier HE 20.2215

HE 20.6213:v.nos.&nos.   • Item 508-G-4
NEWS OF THE COOPERATIVE HEALTH STATISTICS SYSTEM. v. 1–   [3-5 times a year]

Four-page newsletter on the Cooperative

Health Statistics program which supports the development of State systems that collect uniform information to meet the needs of data users at local. State and Federal levels.
ISSN 0094-3045

HE 20.6213/2:date   • Item 508-G-3
DIRECTORY, UNITED STATES, TERRITORIES, AND CANADA. [Annual] (Division of the Cooperative Health Statistics System)

Lists addresses and telephone numbers for State health officers, registrars, principal statisticians, research directors, NCHS officials, and project directors of the Cooperative Health Statistics System.
Supplement to: News of the Cooperative Health Statistics System [ISSN 0094-3045] (HE 20.6213).

HE 20.6213/3   • Item 508-G-8
NEWS OF THE HISPANIC HEALTH AND NUTRITION EXAMINATION SURVEY. [Irregular]

PURPOSE:– To provide news information of the Survey (HHANES) considered the most comprehensive Hispanic health data ever created in the U.S.

HE 20.6214:date   • Item 509-A (P) (EL)
PROCEEDINGS OF THE PUBLIC HEALTH CONFERENCE ON RECORDS AND STATISTICS. 9th–
1962–   [Annual]

PURPOSE:– To provide to Conference participants and other interested users, a summary and presentation of the papers, discussions and workshops in each Conference. With editing and revision by outside speakers and NCHS staff, the original papers and speeches and included to provide as full as possible coverage of the meeting. The Conference draws together vital and health statisticians and health planners from the State, local and Federal Government agencies and from private groups in the health field to discuss mutual problems, programs and plans concerning the collection and use of vital and health data.
Earlier HE 20.2214

HE 20.6214/2:date   • Item 509-A
PUBLIC HEALTH CONFERENCE ON RECORDS AND STATISTICS, NATIONAL MEETING ANOUNCEMENT. [Annual]

HE 20.6215:v.nos.&nos.   • Item 500-E
U.S. DECENNIAL LIFE TABLES.

Earlier FS 2.85/3

HE 20.6216:CT   • Item 508-G
BIBLIOGRAPHIES AND LISTS OF PUBLICATIONS.

Earlier HE 20.2213

HE 20.6216:C 29   • Item 508-G
CATALOGUE OF PUBLICATIONS OF THE NATIONAL CENTER FOR HEALTH STATISTICS.

HE 20.6216/2:date   • Item 508-N (MF)
CLEARINGHOUSE ON HEALTH INDEXES: CUMULATED ANNOTATIONS. [Annual]

ISSN 0145-1294

HE 20.6216/2-2:date   • Item 508-N (MF)
CLEARINGHOUSE ON HEALTH INDEXES. [Quarterly]

HE 20.6216/3:date   • Item 508-G
PUBLICATION NOTE SERIES. [Quarterly]

HE 20.6216/4:date   • Item 508-G (MF)
CATALOG OF PUBLICATIONS OF THE NATIONAL CENTER FOR HEALTH STATISTICS. [Annual]

HE 20.6216/5:   • Item 508-G
NCHS HEALTH INTERVIEW STATISTICS, PUBLICATIONS FROM THE NATIONAL HEALTH INTERVIEW SURVEY, ADVANCE DATA REPORTS. [Annual]

HE 20.6216/6:date   • Item 508-G-9
REVIEWS OF NEW REPORTS FROM THE CENTERS FOR DISEASE CONTROL AND PREVENTION/ NATIONAL CENTER FOR HEALTH STATISTICS.

HE 20.6217:v.nos.&nos.   • Item 508-B (EL)
MONTHLY VITAL STATISTICS REPORT.

PURPOSE:– To provide provisional statistics on births, marriages, divorces, and deaths. Tables include live birth and marriages, each reporting area; marriage licenses in major city areas; death and infant deaths, each reporting area; deaths in the sample and estimated infant mortality rates, by age and cause, United States; deaths in the sample and estimated death rates, by age, color, and sex, United States; divorces, each reporting area. Tables give data for month and month a year ago, with cumulative totals for each of three years. Time lag is about 13 weeks for death data, 8 weeks for other data.
Supplements with varying titles issued irregularly.
ISSN 0364-0936
Earlier HE 20.6009

HE 20.6217/2:v.nos./nos.   • Item 500-E-10
MONTHLY VITAL STATISTICS REPORT FROM THE NATIONAL CENTER FOR HEALTH STATISTICS, ADVANCE REPORT OF FINAL NATALITY STATISTICS.

Issued on floppy diskettes.

HE 20.6218:nos.   • Item 508-G-1 (MF)
STATISTICAL NOTES FOR HEALTH PLANNERS. 1–
[Irregular]

HE 20.6219:date   • Item 508-G-2 (MF)
NATIONAL REPORTING SYSTEM FOR FAMILY PLANNING SERVICES: ANNUAL REPORT. 1st–

HE 20.6220:nos.   • Item 508-G-5
NCHS PUBLICATIONS ON [various subjects]. 1–
1979–   [Irregular]

PURPOSE:– To provide lists of statistical publications issued by NCHS on various subjects.

HE 20.6221:CT   • Item 508
DATA ON LICENSED PHARMACISTS (place).

HE 20.6222:date   • Item 508-G-6 (MF)
DETAILED DIAGNOSES AND SURGICAL PROCEDURES FOR PATIENTS DISCHARGED FROM SHORT-STAY HOSPITALS. [Annual]

Provides statistical data from the Center's National Hospital Discharge Survey. Tables show conditions diagnosed and procedures performed by diagnostic class and by age, sex and race for persons discharged from short-stay, non-Federal hospitals.
Also published in microfiche.

HE 20.6223:date   • Item 483-A-18
HEALTH, UNITED STATES. [Annual]

PURPOSE:– To present a report on the health status of the nation. Presents statistics concerning recent trends in the health care sector and detailed discussions of selected current health issues.
Also issued on floppy diskettes.
Earlier HE 29.21

HE 20.6223/3   • Item 483-A-8
HEALTHY PEOPLE 2000 REVIEW. [Annual]

HE 20.6224   • Item 510-A (MF)
NATIONAL DEATH INDEX ANNOUNCEMENTS (numbered). [Irregular]

Miscellaneous announcements pertaining to the National Death Index, which is a computerized central file of death record information.

HE 20.6225:date   • Item 508-R (MF) (EL)
NCHS CATALOG OF UNIVERSITY PRESENTATIONS. [Annual]

Briefly describes various topics covered by presentations through the NCHS University Visitation Program. The purpose of the presentations is to foster communication between NCHS and the University community.
Earlier HE 20.6202

HE 20.6226:date   • Item 508-G-7 (MF)
PUBLIC USE DATA TAPE DOCUMENTATION, NATAL-
ITY STATE SUMMARY. [Annual]

HE 20.6226/2:date   • Item 508-G-7 (MF)
PUBLIC USE DATA TAPE DOCUMENTATION, DETAIL
NATALITY. [Annual]

HE 20.6226/3:date   • Item 508-G-7 (MF)
PUBLIC USE DATA TAPE DOCUMENTATION, NATAL-
ITY LOCAL AREA SUMMARY. [Annual]

HE 20.6226/4:date   • Item 508-G-7
PUBLIC USE DATA TAPE DOCUMENTATION, DIVORCE
DATA, DETAIL. [Annual]

HE 20.6226/5:date
PUBLIC USE DATA TAPE DOCUMENTATION, MEDI-
CAL HISTORY, AGES 12-74 YEARS. [Irregular]

   For internal use, not sent to depositories.

HE 20.6226/5-2:date
PUBLIC USE DATA TAPE DOCUMENTATION, CHEST
X-RAY, PULMONARY DIFFUSION, AND TUBER-
CULIN TEST RESULTS AGES 25-74.

HE 20.6226/6:date
PUBLIC USE DATA TAPE DOCUMENTATION, MOR-
TALITY CAUSE-OF-DEATH SUMMARY DATA. [An-
nual]

   For internal use, not sent to depositories.

HE 20.6226/7:date
PUBLIC USE DATA TAPE DOCUMENTATION, MOR-
TALITY LOCAL AREA SUMMARY. [Annual]

   For internal use, not sent to depositories.

HE 20.6226/8:date
PUBLIC USE DATA TAPE DOCUMENTATION, PART 2,
INTERVIEWER'S MANUAL NATIONAL INTER-
VIEW SURVEY. [Annual]

   For internal use, not sent to depositories.

HE 20.6226/9:date
PUBLIC USE DATA TAPE DOCUMENTATION, PART 3,
MEDICAL CODING MANUAL AND SHORT INDEX.
[Annual]

HE 20.6226/10:date
PUBLIC USE DATA TAPE DOCUMENTATION, PART 1,
NATIONAL HEALTH INTERVIEW SURVEY.
[Annual]

   For internal use, not sent to depositories.

HE 20.6226/11:date
PUBLIC USE DATA TAPE DOCUMENTATION, FETAL
DEATHS DETAIL RECORDS. [Annual]

   For internal use, not sent to depositories.

HE 20.6228:CT   • Item 508-G-3
DIRECTORIES.

HE 20.6229:CT   • Item 508-G
REVIEWS OF NEW REPORTS (News Releases).

HE 20.6230:nos.   • Item 508-G-5 (EL)
HEALTHY PEOPLE 2000, STATISTICAL NOTES.

HE 20.6231:CT   • Item 500-E-11 (E)
ELECTRONIC PRODUCTS (misc.).

HE 20.6232:   • Item 508-G-10 (CD)
SECOND SUPPLEMENT ON AGING, VERSION 2 (series).

HE 20.6233   • Item 508-G-11 (EL)
AGING TRENDS (series).

REGIONAL MEDICAL PROGRAMS SERVICE
(1973)

HE 20.6301:date
ANNUAL REPORTS.

   Earlier HE 20.2601

HE 20.6302:CT   • Item 483-L-1
GENERAL PUBLICATIONS.

   Earlier HE 20.2602

HEALTH CARE FACILITIES SERVICE
(1973)

HE 20.6401:date
ANNUAL REPORTS.

   Earlier HE 20.2501

HE 20.6402:CT   • Item 486-A-2
GENERAL PUBLICATIONS.

   Earlier HE 20.2502

HE 20.6409:CT
HEALTH FACILITIES SERIES.

   Earlier HE 20.2511

AGENCY FOR HEALTHCARE RESEARCH AND QUALITY
(1989–   )

CREATION AND AUTHORITY

   FORMERLY National Center for Health Services Research and Health Care Technology Assessment; Agency for Health Care Policy and
Research.

INFORMATION
   Agency for Healthcare Research
      and Quality
   2101 E. Jefferson St., Ste. 501
   Rockville, MD 20852
   (301) 594-1364
   http://www.ahrq.gov

HE 20.6501:date
ANNUAL REPORTS.

   Earlier HE 20.2101

HE 20.6502:CT   • Item 507-I-1
GENERAL PUBLICATIONS.

   Earlier HE 20.2102

HE 20.6508:CT   • Item 491-B-5
HANDBOOKS, MANUALS, GUIDES.

   Earlier HE 20.2108

HE 20.6509:CT   • Item 491-B-10 (MF)
BIBLIOGRAPHIES AND LISTS OF PUBLICATIONS.

HE 20.6509/2:date   • Item 491-B-10 (MF)
BIBLIOGRAPHY OF PUBLICATIONS RESULTING
FROM EXTRAMURAL RESEARCH. [Annual]

   Earlier HE 20.6509:Ex 8

HE 20.6509/3   • Item 491-B-27 (EL)
AHRQ PUBLICATIONS CATALOG. [Semiannual] Formerly: AHCPR Publications Catalog

HE 20.6510:date   • Item 491-B-11 (MF)
SUMMARY OF GRANTS AND CONTRACTS ACTIVE
ON JUNE 30, (year). [Annual]

   Title varies.
   Earlier HE 20.2116

HE 20.6511:CT   • Item 491-B-12 (MF)
NCHSR RESEARCH DIGEST SERIES.

HE 20.6512:CT   • Item 491-B-13 (MF)
AHRQ RESEARCH REPORT SERIES.

   Formerly: NCHSR Research Reports Series.

HE 20.6512/2:CT   • Item 491-B-13 (MF)
AHCPR RESEARCH SUMMARY SERIES. Formerly:
NCHSR Research Summary Series.

HE 20.6512/3:CT   • Item 491-B-15 (MF)
NCHSR RESEARCH PROCEEDINGS SERIES. [Irregu-
lar] (National Center for Health Services Research)

   PURPOSE:– To extend availability of results
of new research announced at conferences, symposia, and seminars sponsored by the Center.
Includes key appearances given at meetings,
and discussions and responses. Intended to help
meet information needs of health services, researchers, etc.

HE 20.6512/4:CT   • Item 491-B-14 (MF)
NCHSR RESEARCH MANAGEMENT (series). [Irregu-
lar] (National Center for Health Services Research)

   PURPOSE:– To describe programmatic aspects of NCHSR research efforts with information
on NCHSR goals, research objectives, and priorities; administrative information on funding grants
and contracts. Intended for research planners,
administrators, and others who are involved with
allocation of research resources.

HE 20.6512/5:nos.   • Item 491-B-13 (EL)
AHRQ RESEARCH ACTIVITIES. [Monthly]

   Formerly: NCHSR Research Activities; AHCPR
Research Activities.

HE 20.6512/6:CT   • Item 491-B-13
PROGRAM NOTES. [Irregular]

HE 20.6512/7:date/nos.   • Item 491-B-18 (MF)
HEALTH TECHNOLOGY ASSESSMENT REPORTS
(series). [Irregular]

HE 20.6512/8:date   • Item 491-B-19
NCHSR PROGRAM SOLICITATION, INDIVIDUAL AND
INSTITUTIONAL. [Annual]

HE 20.6512/8-2:date   • Item 491-B-20
NCHSR PROGRAM SOLICITATION, GRANTS FOR
HEALTH SERVICES DISSERTATION RESEARCH.
[Annual]

   Announces grant support for research undertaken in conjunction with preparation of a doctoral dissertation.
   Earlier HE 20.6502:G 76/4

HE 20.6512/9:CT   • Item 491-B-19
NCHSR PROGRAM SOLICITATION (series).

HE 20.6513:nos. • Item 491-B-16
NATIONAL HEALTH CARE EXPENDITURES, DATA PREVIEW (series). 1– 1980– [Irregular] (National Center for Health Services Research)

PURPOSE:– To provide government agencies, legislative bodies, health professionals, and others concerned with health care policies with analytical reports on critical national health policy issues. Contains both narrative text and tables.

HE 20.6513/2:nos. • Item 991-B-16
NATIONAL HEALTH CARE EXPENDITURE STUDY (series). [Irregular]

HE 20.6514:nos. • Item 491-B-17
PROVIDER STUDIES RESEARCH NOTE.

PURPOSE:– To provide information to administrators, policymakers, health care professionals, and researchers on such issues as hospital costs and utilization.
Earlier title: Hospital Studies Program, Hospital Cost and Utilization Project, Research Notes.

HE 20.6514/2:CT • Item 491-B-17
NCHSR HEALTH CARE FOR THE AGING. [Annual]

HE 20.6514/3:nos. • Item 491-B-26
HCUP-3 (Healthcare Cost and Utilization Project) RESEARCH NOTE (series).

HE 20.6514/4 • Item 491-B-33 (EL)
HCUP FACTBOOK. [Semiannual]

HE 20.6515: • Item 491-B-21
FORMS.

HE 20.6516: • Item 491-B-22 (MF)
PUBLIC HEALTH SERVICE PROSPECTIVE PAYMENT ACTIVITY. [Annual]

PURPOSE– To summarize continuing and recently funded workon the effect of the prospective payment system on various PHS programs.Includes grants and contracts, work group and task force activity, and special analyses on prospective payment.

HE 20.6517:nos. • Item 491-B-16
NATIONAL MEDICAL EXPENDITURE SURVEY, RESEARCH FINDINGS (Series).

HE 20.6517/2:nos. • Item 491-B-16 (MF)
AHCPR NATIONAL MEDICAL EXPENDITURE SURVEY DATA SUMMARY (Series).

HE 20.6517/3:nos. • Item 491-B-16 (MF)
NATIONAL MEDICAL EXPENDITURE SURVEY METHODS (Series).

HE 20.6517/4 • Item 491-B-16 (MF)
INTRAMURAL RESEARCH HIGHLIGHTS, NATIONAL MEDICAL EXPENDITURE SURVEY.

HE 20.6517/5 • Item 491-B-25 (EL)
MEDTEP (Medical Treatment Effectiveness Program) UPDATE. [Semiannual]

HE 20.6517/6:nos. • Item 491-B-28 (P) (EL)
MEPS (Medical Expenditure Panel Survey) HIGHLIGHTS (nos.).

HE 20.6517/7:nos. • Item 491-B-29
MEPS, (Medical Expenditure Panel Survey), CHARTBOOK (series).

HE 20.6517/8 • Item 491-B-31 (EL)
METHODOLOGY REPORT (series).

HE 20.6517/9 • Item 491-B-34 (EL)
MEPS (MEDICAL EXPENDITURE PANEL SURVEY) RESEARCH FINDINGS (series).

HE 20.6518:CT • Item 491-B-13 (MF)
CONFERENCE SUMMARY REPORT (Series).

HE 20.6519:CT • Item 491-B-17
AHCPR LONG-TERM CARE STUDIES (Series).

HE 20.6519/2:CT • Item 491-B-17
AHCPR GRANT ANNOUNCEMENT.

HE 20.6520:nos. • Item 491-B-17 (MF)
CLINICAL PRACTICE GUIDELINE (Series).

HE 20.6520/2 • Item 491-B-17 (MF)
QUICK REFERENCE GUIDE FOR CLINICIANS (Series).

HE 20.6520/3 • Item 491-B-24 (CD)
CLINICAL PRACTICE GUIDELINES.

HE 20.6520/4 • Item 491-B-3 (MF) (EL)
GUIDELINE TECHNICAL REPORT(series).

HE 20.6521 • Item 491-B-23 (MF)
ACSUS REPORT (Aids Cost and Services Utilization Survey) (series).

HE 20.6522 • Item 507-I-2
HEALTH TECHNOLOGY REVIEW. [Irregular]

HE 20.6523 • Item 491-B-31 (E)
ELECTRONIC PRODUCTS. (Misc.)

HE 20.6524 • Item 491-B-31 (EL)
EVIDENCE REPORT/TECHNOLOGY ASSESSMENT. (series)

BUREAU OF HEALTH PROFESSIONS (1975– 1983)

CREATION AND AUTHORITY

The Bureau of Health Professions was transferred to the Health Resources and Services Administration (HE 20.9300) in 1983.

HE 20.6601:date • Item 507-J-3
ANNUAL REPORT.

HE 20.6602:CT • Item 507-J-1
GENERAL PUBLICATIONS. [Irregular]

Later HE 20.9302

HE 20.6608:CT • Item 507-J-5
HANDBOOKS, MANUALS, GUIDES. [Irregular]

HE 20.6609:CT • Item 507-J-2
BIBLIOGRAPHIES AND LISTS OF PUBLICATIONS.

Later HE 20.9309

HE 20.6610:date • Item 507-J-4
DIRECTORY OF PROGRAMS PREPARING REGISTERED NURSES FOR EXPANDED ROLES. [Annual]

Earlier HE 20.6102:N 93/3

HE 20.6611:CT • Item 507-J-6
BACKGROUND PAPERS.

HE 20.6612:date • Item 509-A-4
DIRECTORY OF GRANTS, AWARDS, AND LOANS. [Annual]

Earlier HE 20.6111

HE 20.6613:nos. • Item 507-J-7
NURSE PLANNING INFORMATION SERIES. 1– 1977– [Irregular]

Contains monographs and bibliographies relative to health planning.

HE 20.6614:nos. • Item 507-J-8 (MF)
GMENAC STAFF PAPERS. 1– 1977– [Irregular] (Graduate Medical Education National Advisory Committee)

HE 20.6615:date • Item 507-J-9 (MF)
NURSE TRAINING ACT OF 1975, REPORT TO CONGRESS. 1st– 1978– [Annual] (Division of Nursing)

Report made by the Secretary of Health, Education, and Welfare on the supply and distribution of, and requirements for nurses as required by section 951, Nurses Training Act of 1975, Title IX, Public Law 94-63.
ISSN 0161-8210

HE 20.6616:date • Item 507-J-10 (MF)
NATIONAL HEALTH SERVICE CORPS SCHOLARSHIP PROGRAM, REPORT BY SECRETARY OF HEALTH, EDUCATION, AND WELFARE TO CONGRESS. [Annual]

Tables show number of scholarships by discipline, educational institution, and State.

HE 20.6617:CT • Item 507-J-1 (MF)
CHARACTERISTICS OF PHYSICIANS: (by State). [Irregular]

Series consists of one report for each State and D.C. with no definite plans for updating.

HE 20.6618:date • Item 507-J-11
TRAINING HEALTH PROFESSIONALS. [Annual]

HE 20.6619:date • Item 507-J-12 (MF)
REPORT TO THE PRESIDENT AND CONGRESS ON THE STATUS OF HEALTH PROFESSIONS PERSONNEL IN THE UNITED STATES. [Biennial]

Later HE 20.9310

HE 20.6621:CT
DATA ON LICENSED PHARMACISTS SERIES BY STATE.

BUREAU OF HEALTH FACILITIES (1978–   )

HE 20.6701:date • Item 486-B-2
ANNUAL REPORT.

HE 20.6702:CT • Item 486-B-1
GENERAL PUBLICATIONS. [Irregular]

HE 20.6706:CT • Item 486-B-3
REGULATIONS, RULES, INSTRUCTIONS. [Irregular]

CENTERS FOR DISEASE CONTROL AND PREVENTION (1980–   )

CREATION AND AUTHORITY

The name was changed from Center for Disease Control pursuant to Secretary's notice of October 1, 1980 (45 FR 67772).
NOTE:– During the period 1970– 1973, SuDocs class HE 20.2300 was used for the Center's publications.

INFORMATION
Centers for Disease Control and Prevention
1600 Clifton Road, NE
Atlanta, Georgia 30333
(404) 639-3535
Fax: (888) 232-3299
http://www.cdc.gov

HE 20.7000
FORMS.

HE 20.7001:date
ANNUAL REPORT.

Earlier HE 20.2301

HE 20.7001/2:date   • Item 504-M (MF)
CONSOLIDATED ANNUAL REPORT ON STATE AND
TERRITORIAL PUBLIC HEALTH LABORATORIES.

HE 20.7001/3:date
VECTOR-BORNE DISEASES DIVISION ANNUAL
REPORT. [Annual]

HE 20.7002:CT   • Item 504
GENERAL PUBLICATIONS.
Earlier HE 20.2302

HE 20.7008:CT   • Item 505-A
HANDBOOKS, MANUALS, GUIDES.

Earlier HE 20.2308
Later HE 20.7808

HE 20.7008/2:CT   • Item 505-A
CDC LAB MANUAL. [Irregular]

HE 20.7008/3:nos.   • Item 494-L-1 (MF)
IMMUNOLOGY SERIES. 1–   [Irregular]

Earlier HE 20.7409

HE 20.7009:v.nos.&nos.   • Item 508-A (EL)
MORBIDITY AND MORTALITY WEEKLY REPORT. v.
1–   1952–

Provisional information on selected notifiable
diseases in the United States and on deaths in
selected cities for the week. Tables include cases
of specified notifiable diseases for the United
States and for each State, for the week, week a
year ago, and cumulative for the year; deaths in
selected cities, by geographic regions, and for
122 major cities for current week, previous week,
cumulative totals for year and year ago. Time lag
one week. Textual summary.
Earlier HE 20.2310
HEALTH INFORMATION FOR INTERNATIONAL
TRAVEL. [Annual] (Bureau of Epidemiology)

PURPOSE:– To provide the necessary
information on required vaccination, U.S. Public Health Service recommendations, International Certificates of Vaccinations, and health
hints, so that transmission of internationally
quarantinable diseases can be prevented.
Published as a supplement to Morbidity
and Mortality, Weekly Report.
Supersedes Vaccination Certificate Requirements for International Travel.
ISSN 0095-3539

HE 20.7009/a:CT   • Item 508-A-5
SEPARATES. [Irregular]

HE 20.7009/2   • Item 508-A (EL)
MMWR CDC SURVEILLANCE SUMMARIES. [Quarterly]

Earlier title: Surveillance Summaries.

HE 20.7009/2 a   • Item 508-A-5
– SEPARATES.

HE 20.7009/2-2:date/v.nos./nos.• Item 508-A-4 (EL)
MMWR RECOMMENDATIONS AND REPORTS.
[Irregular]

HE 20.7009/2-3:date   • Item 508-A-5
MMWR SURVEILLANCE SUMMARIES FROM THE
CENTER FOR INFECTIOUS DISEASES.

HE 20.7009/3:date   • Item 508-A-2 (MF)
INJURY EPIDEMIOLOGY AND CONTROL REPRINTS.
[Annual]

Each issue is a set of reprints of articles
related to injury epidemiology and control which
appeared in the CDC Morbidity and Mortality
Weekly Report (HE 20.7009).
Earlier HE 20.7009/a:In 5

HE 20.7009/4   • Item 508-A-3 (MF)
MORBIDITY WEEKLY REPORT, INJURY PREVEN-
TION REPRINTS. [Annual]

Each issue is a set of reprints of articles
related to injury prevention which appeared in the
CDC Morbidity and Mortality Weekly Report (HE
20.7009).

HE 20.7009/5   • Item 508-A-6
MMWR REPORTS ON AIDS. [Annual]

MMWR = Morbidity and Mortality Weekly Report
Contains all articles related to AIDS that appeared in the MMWR. Articlesare arranged chronologically and track the reporting of information
on AIDS.

HE 20.7009/6:   • Item 508-A-7
CHRONIC DISEASES NOTES AND REPORT.
[Irregular]

The CDC refers to this publication as a new
feature of the Morbidity and Mortality Weekly
Report (HE 20.7009) on chronic disease prevention activities in the states, at CDC, and in other
federal and private agencies.

HE 20.7009/7   • Item 504-C-3
EMERGING INFECTIOUS DISEASES. [Quarterly]

HE 20.7010:date
CDC VETERINARY PUBLIC HEALTH NOTES. 1958–
[Monthly] (Venereal Disease Branch, State and
Community Services Division)

PURPOSE:– To serve as a mechanism of
informally distributing general information on veterinary public health activities to all interested
individuals in the U.S. and throughout the world.
Contains information on viral, bacterial, fungal,
and parasitic diseases shared by animals and
man and has general information of interest to
those concerned with the control of the zooneses.
ISSN 0360-7836
Issued by the Health Services and Mental
Health Administration (HE 20.2312) prior to June
1973.

HE 20.7011:nos.
MEASLES SURVEILLANCE, REPORTS. 1–
[Irregular]

Earlier HE 20.2309/4

HE 20.7011/2:date   • Item 505-A-10 (MF)
CONGENITAL MALFORMATIONS SURVEILLANCE,
REPORTS. [Annual]

PURPOSE:– To provide information for those
interested in the epidemiology of congenital malformations.
ISSN 0092-5594

HE 20.7011/3:nos.
MYCOSES SURVEILLANCE, REPORTS. 1–
[Irregular]

HE 20.7011/4:date   • Item 505-A-11 (MF)
TRICHINOSIS SURVEILLANCE, ANNUAL SUMMARY.

Earlier HE 20.2309/12

HE 20.7011/5:CT   • Item 505-A-12 (MF)
NEUROTROPIC VIRAL DISEASES SURVEILLANCE.
[Annual]

Following titles are included in this series:–

HE 20.7011/5:En 1/date
ANNUAL ENCEPHALITIS SUMMARY (year).

Earlier HE 20.2309/8:En 1

HE 20.7011/6:nos.   • Item 505-A-17 (MF)
HEPATITIS SURVEILLANCE, REPORTS. 1–   [An-
nual]

ISSN 0566-991X
Earlier HE 20.2309/5

HE 20.7011/7:date   • Item 505-A-13 (MF)
PSITTACOSIS, ANNUAL SUMMARY.

ISSN 0091-0325

HE 20.7011/8:date   • Item 505-A-8 (MF)
MALARIA SURVEILLANCE, ANNUAL SUMMARY.

Earlier HE 20.2309/13

HE 20.7011/9:nos.
PRIMATE ZOONOSES SURVEILLANCE, REPORTS,
ANNUAL SUMMARY. 1–

HE 20.7011/10:date   • Item 505-A-7 (MF)
NATIONAL NOSOCOMIAL INFECTIONS STUDY, RE-
PORTS. [Annual]

PURPOSE:– To provide a technical report
summarizing information received from hospitals
voluntarily cooperating with the Center. Information is preliminary and is intended for the use of
those with an interest in and a responsibility for
control of infections associated with hospitalization.
ISSN 0146-7417

HE 20.7011/11:date   • Item 505-A-8 (MF)
RABIES, ZOONOSIS SURVEILLANCE, SUMMARY.
[Annual]

ISSN 0091-0317
Earlier HE 20.2309/9:R 11

HE 20.7011/12:date
RUBELLA SURVEILLANCE, [Reports]. 1–   1969–
[Irregular]

PURPOSE:– To review the available surveillance information on rubella, congenital rubella
syndrome, and rubella vaccine.
Describes data regarding vaccine distribution, utilization, safety, efficacy, and
reactogenicity that have been submitted to the
Center for Disease Control.
Earlier HE 20.2309/7

HE 20.7011/13:date   • Item 505-A-8 (MF)
FOODBORNE AND WATERBORNE DISEASE OUT-
BREAKS, ANNUAL SUMMARY. (Bureau of
Epidemiology, Bacterial Diseases Division, En-
teric Diseases Branch)

PURPOSE:– To summarize information received from State and city health departments,
the Food and Drug Administration, the Department of Agriculture, and other pertinent sources.
The information is preliminary and is
intendedprimarily for use by those with responsibility for disease control activities.
Earlier HE 20.2309/6

HE 20.7011/14:nos.   • Item 505-A-8 (MF)
INFLUENZA-RESPIRATORY DISEASE SURVEIL-
LANCE. [Annual]

Earlier HE 20.2309/6

HE 20.7011/15:date   • Item 505-A-14 (MF)
SALMONELLA SURVEILLANCE, ANNUAL SUMMARY.
1964–

PURPOSE:– To present a yearly compilation
of the results of national salmonella surveillance
and serve as a reference source of epidemiologic
data for individuals interested in or working with
the problem of salmonellosis.
Earlier HE 20.2309/2

HE 20.7011/16
BRUCELLOSIS SURVEILLANCE. [Annual]

ISSN 0090-1156

HE 20.7011/17:date
LEPTOSPIROSIS SURVEILLANCE, ANNUAL SUM-
MARY.

ISSN 0091-0295

HE 20.7011/18:nos.
SHIGELLA SURVEILLANCE, REPORTS.

    Earlier HE 20.2309/3

HE 20.7011/19:date
Rh HEMOLYTIC DISEASE SURVEILLANCE. [Annual]

HE 20.7011/20:date • Item 505-A-15 (MF)
ABORTION SURVEILLANCE, ANNUAL SUMMARY.

    ISSN 0094-0923

HE 20.7011/21:date
FAMILY PLANNING SERVICES. [Annual]

HE 20.7011/24:date • Item 505-A-16 (MF)
NUTRITION SURVEILLANCE, ANNUAL SUMMARY.

HE 20.7011/25:date • Item 505-A-8 (MF)
ENCEPHALITIS SURVEILLANCE, ANNUAL SUMMARY.

HE 20.7011/26:date
ASEPTIC MENINGITIS SURVEILLANCE, ANNUAL SUMMARY.

HE 20.7011/27:nos.
RICKETTSIAL DISEASE SURVEILLANCE. [Annual]

HE 20.7011/28:date
INTESTINAL PARASITE SURVEILLANCE. [Annual]

HE 20.7011/30:date • Item 505-A-8 (MF)
SURGICAL STERILIZATION SURVEILLANCE, TUBAL STERILIZATION.

HE 20.7011/30-2:date
SURGICAL STERILIZATION SURVEILLANCE, HYSTERECTOMY (series). [Annual]

HE 20.7011/31:date • Item 505-A-8 (MF)
POLIOMYELITIS SURVEILLANCE SUMMARY. [Annual]

HE 20.7011/32:date
GUILLAIN BARRE SYNDROME SURVEILLANCE.

HE 20.7011/33:date • Item 505-A-8 (MF)
WATER-RELATED DISEASE OUTBREAKS SURVEILLANCE. [Annual]

HE 20.7011/34:date
MUMPS SURVEILLANCE.

HE 20.7011/35:date • Item 505-A-8 (MF)
ENTEROVIRUS SURVEILLANCE. [Annual]

HE 20.7011/36:date • Item 505-A-18 (MF)
ADVERSE EVENTS FOLLOWING IMMUNIZATION SURVEILLANCE. [Irregular]

    Provides the public health community with information based on reports of adverse events following immunization.

HE 20.7011/37 • Item 504-N-1
BIOLOGICS SURVEILLANCE. [Semiannual]

    Intended primarily for those concerned with the national use and application of immunizing agents. Contains tables on net distribution of immunizing agents for various diseases in the United States.

HE 20.7011/38:date • Item 504-P
HIV/AIDS SURVEILLANCE. [Monthly]

HE 20.7011/39 • Item 504-P (MF)
NREVSS MONTHLY REPORT.
    Earlier title: NRVSS Monthly Report.

HE 20.7012:date • Item 504-A
SMOKING AND HEALTH BULLETIN. 1970– [Irregular] (National Clearinghouse for Smoking and Health)

    ISSN 0081-0364
    Earlier HE 20.2316
    Later HE 20.7211

HE 20.7013:date • Item 504-B (MF)
TUBERCULOSIS STATISTICS, (year), STATES AND CITIES (date). [Annual] (Tuberculosis Branch, State and Community Services Division)

    Companion volume to: Tuberculosis in the United States (HE 20.7310).
    ISSN 0090-9351

HE 20.7013/2:date • Item 504-B (MF)
TB NOTES.

    Earlier HE 20.7026:T 79/2

HE 20.7014:CT • Item 504-E
POSTERS. [Irregular]

HE 20.7015:date • Item 483-L-4
DIRECTORY OF ON-GOING RESEARCH IN SMOKING AND HEALTH. 1967– [Annual]

    PURPOSE:– To provide a compilation of research studies dealing with the relationship between smoking and health, for use primarily for researchers in the field. Descriptions of on-going activities in the biomedical, behavioral, psychological, and other fields in both the United States and abroad.
    For each research project, information includes title, principal investigators, objective, research methodology, results to date, future plans, project dates, source of financial support, and references.
    Earlier HE 20.2317
    Later HE 20.25

HE 20.7016:date • Item 485-A
HEALTH CONSEQUENCES OF SMOKING. [Annual]

    Earlier HE 20.2019
    Later HE 20.25/2

HE 20.7017:date • Item 500-D
REPORTED TUBERCULOSIS DATA. 1958– [Annual]

    PURPOSE:– To provide yearly national data on tuberculosis morbidity and mortality, and to furnish the public and health professionals throughout the nation with detailed information on the extent, concentration and trends in tuberculosis in the U.S.
    Covers tuberculosis X-ray casefinding activities, newly reported tuberculosis cases, form and extent of disease of newly reported active and probably active cases, source of report of newly reported cases, race and sex of newly reported cases, age distribution, public health nursing visits, and mortality.
    ISSN 0095-1226
    Earlier HE 20.2313
    Combined with Tuberculosis Programs to form Tuberculosis in the United States (HE 20.7310)

HE 20.7018:date • Item 505-A-9
STD FACT SHEETS. [Irregular]

    Presents facts and statistics on the sexually transmitted problem in the United States in text, tables, and graphs.
    Former title: VD Fact Sheet.
    STD = Sexually Transmitted Disease.
    Also published in microfiche.

HE 20.7018/2:nos.
VD STATISTICAL LETTER.

    ISSN 0363-2032
    Earlier FS 2.11/3
    Later HE 20.7309

HE 20.7019:CT • Item 483-L-5
BIBLIOGRAPHIES AND LISTS OF PUBLICATIONS. [Irregular]

HE 20.7019:Se 6 • Item 483-L-5
SERIAL HOLDINGS. (Library)

HE 20.7021 • Item 504-C (MF)
HOMESTUDY COURSES: COMMUNITY HYGIENE. [Irregular]

    Published in microfiche.

HE 20.7021/2:nos. • Item 504-C
HOMESTUDY COURSES: COMMUNICABLE DISEASE CONTROL. [Irregular]

    Published in microfiche.

HE 20.7021/3:nos. • Item 504-C (MF)
HOMESTUDY COURSES: PRINCIPLES OF EPIDEMIOLOGY.

HE 20.7021/3-2:nos. • Item 504-C (MF)
HOMESTUDY COURSES: MANUALS. [Irregular]

    Published in microfiche.

HE 20.7021/4:nos. • Item 504-C (MF)
HOMESTUDY COURSES: WATERBORNE DISEASE CONTROL. [Irregular]

    Published in microfiche.

HE 20.7021/4-2 • Item 504-C
SELF-STUDY COURSE 3014-G, WATERBORNE DISEASE CONTROL MANUALS.

HE 20.7021/5:nos. • Item 504-C (MF)
HOMESTUDY COURSES: BASIC MATHEMATICS. [Irregular]

    Published in microfiche.

HE 20.7021/6:nos. • Item 504-C (MF)
HOMESTUDY COURSES: FOODBORNE DISEASE CONTROL. [Irregular]

    Published in microfiche.

HE 20.7021/7:nos. • Item 504-C
HOMESTUDY COURSES: VECTORBORNE DISEASE CONTROL. [Irregular]

HE 20.7021/7-2:nos. • Item 504-C
HOMESTUDY COURSE 3013-G, VECTORBORNE DISEASE CONTROL (series). [Irregular]

HE 20.7021/8:nos. • Item 504-C (MF)
HOMESTUDY COURSE 3020-G, COMMUNITY HEALTH ANALYSIS (series). [Irregular]

HE 20.7021/8-2:CT • Item 504-C
HOMESTUDY COURSE 3020-G COMMUNITY HEALTH ANALYSIS– I MANUALS.

HE 20.7021/8-3:lesson nos. • Item 504-C
HOMESTUDY COURSE COMMUNITY HEALTH ANALYSIS– II.

HE 20.7021/9:nos. • Item 504-C
HOMESTUDY COURSES: WATER FLUORIDATION. [Irregular]

HE 20.7021/9-2:nos. • Item 504-C
HOMESTUDY COURSE 3017G, WATER FLUORIDATION.

HE 20.7021/9-3:lesson nos. • Item 504-C
HOMESTUDY COURSE 3017-G WATER FLUORIDATION TEST EXERCISE.

HE 20.7021/10:nos. • Item 504-C (MF)
HOMESTUDY COURSES: 3015-G, ENVIRONMENTAL PROTECTION. [Irregular]

HE 20.7021/11: • Item 504-C-2 (MF)
SELF-STUDY COURSE 3010-G, ENVIRONMENTAL HEALTH SCIENCES (series).

    The manuals that accompany the course are classified HE20.7021/11-2

HE 20.7021/11-2 • Item 504-C-2
– MANUALS (series).

    The manuals that accompany the Self-Study Course 3010-G (HE 20.7021/11).

HE 20.7022:nos.
CDC LABORATORY UPDATE (series). [Irregular]

HE 20.7022/3:date
PROFICIENCY TESTING SUMMARY ANALYSIS: GENERAL IMMUNOLOGY. [Irregular]
    Earlier HE 20.7412

HE 20.7022/3-3:date
PROFICIENCY TESTING SUMMARY ANALYSIS, PUBLIC HEALTH IMMUNOLOGY.

Internal, not sent to depository libraries.

HE 20.7022/3-4:date
PROFICIENCY TESTING SUMMARY ANALYSIS, PARASITOLOGY.

HE 20.7022/4:date
FLUORIDATED DRINKING WATER. [Monthly]
Earlier HE 20.7412/3

HE 20.7022/5:date
BLOOD LEAD. [Monthly]
Earlier HE 20.7412/2

HE 20.7022/6:date
ERTHROCYTE PROTOPORPHYRIN. [Monthly]
Earlier HE 20.7412/4

HE 20.7023:date
WEEKLY SUMMARY OF HEALTH INFORMATION FOR INTERNATIONAL TRAVEL.

HE 20.7024:CT   • Item 504 (MF)
TEENAGE HEALTH TEACHING MODULES (series).

HE 20.7025:date   • Item 504-D (MF)
EIS DIRECTORY. [Annual]

EIS = Epidemic Intelligence Service

HE 20.7026:CT   • Item 504-F (MF)
MEMORANDUM SERIES. [Irregular]

HE 20.7027:nos.
ADVISORY MEMORANDUMS. [Irregular]

HE 20.7028:date
STATE CLINICAL AND ENVIRONMENTAL LABORATORY LEGISLATION. [4 times a year]

Cumulative, with end of year issue subtitled: Final Disposition.

HE 20.7029:CT   • Item 505-A
VISITORS– REPORT TO NURSES' STATION BEFORE ENTERING ROOM (precautionary cards). [Irregular]

HE 20.7030:nos.   • Item 504-C (MF)
MODULE (series). [Irregular]

HE 20.7032:date   • Item 504-G
MONTHLY REPORT OF REAGENTS EVALUATION.

Lists commercial reagents submitted to the Center's Biological Products Program for evaluation and which meet performance specifications.

Later HE 20.7810

HE 20.7033:date   • Item 504-H (MF)
COMPUTER TRAINING COURSES. [Annual]

Lists and describes computer courses available to employees of the Center for Disease Control, such as Data Processing Fundamentals as well as more advanced courses.

HE 20.7034:nos.
CDC COURSE ANNOUNCEMENTS. [Irregular]

HE 20.7035:date   • Item 504-L
DEAR COLLEAGUE (letter). [Quarterly]

Intended to inform a wide variety of individuals and organizations about matters of interest in dental public health.

HE 20.7036:date   • Item 504-N-2 (MF)
ARTHROPOD-BORNE VIRUS INFORMATION EXCHANGE. [Semiannual]

Issued for the purpose of timely exchange of information among investigators of arthropod-borne viruses. Contains reports, summaries, observations, and comments submitted voluntarily by qualified investigators.

HE 20.7036/2:date   • Item 504-N (MF)
RABIES INFORMATION EXCHANGE. [Semiannual]

Contains articles on various studies, surveys, and other research on rabies worldwide.

HE 20.7037:date
PERFORMANCE EVALUATION SUMMARY ANALYSIS MYCOLOGY. [Quarterly]

HE 20.7037/2:date
PERFORMANCE EVALUATION SUMMARY ANALYSIS, BACTERIOLOGY. [Quarterly]

HE 20.7037/3:date
PERFORMANCE EVALUATION SUMMARY ANALYSIS, PARASITOLOGY. [Quarterly]

HE 20.7038:   • Item 504-P
FACTS ABOUT AIDS. [Semiannual]

Answers questions on the risk of contracting AIDS, actions individuals can take to reduce the spread of AIDS, and current research and related activities under way in the Public Health Service.
Earlier HE 20.2:AC 7

HE 20.7038/2   • Item 504-P
HIV/AIDS PREVENTION NEWSLETTER. [Quarterly]

HE 20.7038/3:v.nos./nos.   • Item 504-P
CDC, HIV/AIDS PREVENTION. [Quarterly]

HE 20.7039:nos.   • Item 444-P-1 (CD)
NATIONAL CENTER FOR CHRONIC DISEASE PREVENTION AND HEALTH PROMOTION (NCCDPHP) (numbered).

Later HE 20.7616

HE 20.7039/2   • Item 504-W (E)
ELECTRONIC PRODUCTS.

HE 20.7039/3:date   • Item 504-W-1 (CD)
MMWR, MORBIDITY AND MORALITY WEEKLY REPORT.

HE 20.7040:v.nos./nos.   • Item 504-L
HEALTHY PEOPLE 2000 STATISTICS AND SURVEILLANCE. [Quarterly]

HE 20.7041   • Item 505-C (CD)
LSOA.
LSOA = Longitudinal Study of Aging.

HE 20.7042   • Item 483-A-18
HEALTH UNITED STATES AND HEALTHY PEOPLE 2000 REVIEW. [Annual]

HE 20.7042/2   • Item 483-A-18 (E)
HEALTH UNITED STATES AND HEALTHY PEOPLE 2000 REVIEW FOR WINDOWS.

Issued on Floppy disks.

HE 20.7042/3   • Item 483-A-18 (E)
HEALTH UNITED STATES AND HEALTHY PEOPLE 2000 REVIEW.

Issued on Floppy disks.

HE 20.7042/4   • Item 483-A-18
HEALTH UNITED STATES AND HEALTHY PEOPLE 2000 REVIEW, STATISTICAL TABLES ON LOTUS SPREADSHEETS.

Issued on diskettes.

HE 20.7042/5   • Item 483-A-18
HEALTHY PEOPLE 2000 REVIEW.

HE 20.7042/6:date   • Item 483-A-19 (P) (EL)
HEALTH UNITED STATES. [Annual]

HE 20.7042/7:v.nos./nos.   • Item 483-A-20 (CD)
PUBLICATIONS FROM THE NATIONAL CENTER FOR HEALTH STATISTICS. [Annual]

HE 20.7043/1—51:date • Item 504-X-1—52 (MF)
STATE HEALTH PROFILE - [State]. [Annual]

HE 20.7044   • Item 504-W-2
CDC WONDER. (online database)

NATIONAL INSTITUTE FOR OCCUPATIONAL SAFETY AND HEALTH (1974–   )

INFORMATION

National Institute for
Occupational Safety and Health
Hurbert H. Humphrey Bldg.
200 Independence Ave., SW, Rm 715H
Washington, DC 20201
(202) 401-6997
Fax: (202) 205-2207
Toll Free: (800) 356-4674
http://www.cdc.gov/niosh/homepage.html

HE 20.7101:date   • Item 499-F-13 (MF)
ANNUAL REPORT.

HE 20.7102:CT   • Item 499-F-2
GENERAL PUBLICATIONS.

Earlier HE 20.2802

HE 20.7108:CT   • Item 499-F-3
HANDBOOKS, MANUALS, GUIDES. [Irregular]

HE 20.7108:H 34/2   • Item 499-F-3
RESOURCE GUIDE FOR HEALTH SCIENCE STUDENTS: OCCUPATIONAL AND ENVIRONMENTAL HEALTH. 1980. 59 p.
A directory of 139 government agencies and private firms engaged in occupational and environmental health projects.

HE 20.7108/2:CT   • Item 499-F-5
NIOSH HEALTH AND SAFETY GUIDES FOR [various businesses].

HE 20.7109:date   • Item 483-T-6 (MF)
FEDERAL MINE HEALTH PROGRAM FOR (year). [Annual]

PURPOSE:– To report the annual health activities conducted under the Federal Coal Mine Health and Safety Act of 1969.
Former title: Federal Mine Health Program in (year).
Earlier HE 20.2020

HE 20.7110:CT   • Item 494-D-4
CRITERIA FOR A RECOMMENDED STANDARD, OCCUPATIONAL EXPOSURE TO [various subjects]. 1972–   [Irregular]

PURPOSE:– To make recommendations to the Department of Labor for standards to protect workers from hazardous chemical and physical agents. Each criteria document provides, when appropriate, an environmental workplace limit, recommendations for medical examination and clinical tests, record keeping, engineering and control procedures, personal protective clothing and devices, and methods for informing the employee of the workplace hazard.
Earlier HE 20.2811

HE 20.7110/2:CT   • Item 494-D-4
RECOMMENDED STANDARDS. [Irregular]

HE 20.7111:CT   • Item 499-F-4 (MF)
NIOSH RESEARCH REPORTS. [Irregular]

HE 20.7111/2:CT   • Item 499-F-6 (MF)
NIOSH TECHNICAL REPORTS. [Irregular]

PURPOSE:– To provide basic an clinical researchers, legislators, occupational safety and health professionals, students, teachers, and others with data from which valid criteria and effective standards can be deduced to protect health and safety of workers exposed to potential hazards at their workplace.

HE 20.7111/3:   • Item 499-F-12 (MF)
NIOSH SURVEILLANCE REPORTS. [Irregular]
Each issue concerns place hazards in a different occupational area.

HE 20.7112:date   • Item 494-D-1 (MF)
TOXIC SUBSTANCE LIST. [Annual]

PURPOSE:– To identify all known toxic substances that may exist in our environment and to provide pertinent data on the toxic effects from known doses entering the body by any route described.
List contains over 25,000 listings of chemical substances, 11,000 being names of different chemicals with applicable toxic doses information, and 14,000 consisting of synonymous names and codes taken largely from listing of the Chemical Abstract Service.
Earlier HE 20.2809

HE 20.7112/2:CT   • Item 494-D-1
SUBFILE OF THE REGISTRY OF TOXIC EFFECTS OF CHEMICAL SUBSTANCES.

Earlier: Subfiles of the NIOSH Toxic Substances List.

HE 20.7112/3:date   • Item 494-D-1 (MF)
REGISTRY OF TOXIC EFFECTS OF CHEMICAL SUBSTANCES. [Quarterly]

Issued in microfiche edition.

HE 20.7112/4:date   • Item 494-D-1
REGISTRY OF TOXIC EFFECTS OF CHEMICAL SUBSTANCES, PERMUTED MOLECULAR FORMULA, INDEX. [Annual]

Issued in microfiche edition.

HE 20.7112/5:date   • Item 494-D-1 (MF)
REGISTRY OF TOXIC EFFECTS OF CHEMICAL SUBSTANCES (CUMULATIVE) SUPPLEMENT. [Annual]

HE 20.7113:CT   • Item 494-D-5 (MF)
SPECIAL HAZARD REVIEW. [Irregular]

PURPOSE:– To provide occupational health community with information concerning the adverse effects of widely used chemical or physical agents, and recommendations for the implementation of engineering controls and work practices for the protection of employees.
Earlier title: Special Occupational Hazard Review With Control Recommendations.

HE 20.7114:CT   • Item 499-F-7
BIBLIOGRAPHIES AND LISTS OF PUBLICATIONS. [Irregular]

HE 20.7114/2:date   • Item 499-F-21
NIOSH PUBLICATIONS CATALOG. [Annual]

HE 20.7115:nos.   • Item 499-F-8
CURRENT INTELLIGENCE BULLETIN. 1–   [Irregular]

Each issue contains technical articles relating to occupational hazards.
Nos. 1–18, reprinted in a single volume. 1978. 125 p. il.

HE 20.7115/2:date   • Item 499-F-8
CURRENT INTELLIGENCE BULLETINS, SUMMARIES. [Annual]

HE 20.7116:CT   • Item 499-F-9
SELF-EVALUATION INSTRUMENT (series). [Irregular]

Each issue consists of questionnaires to be used by management in a different industry to evaluate the safety of various on-the-job operations.

HE 20.7117:CT   • Item 499-F-10
OCCUPATIONAL SAFETY AND HEALTH HAZARDS (series). [Irregular]

Each issue deals with safety and health hazards of a different kind of occupational facility.

HE 20.7117/2:CT   • Item 499-F-10
NIOSH WORKER BULLETIN (series). [Irregular]

HE 20.7121:date   • Item 499-F-11 (MF)
PROGRAM PLAN BY PROGRAM AREAS FOR FISCAL YEAR. [Annual]

Outlines the Institute's program plan for inhouse and extramural projects and serves as a tool for ongoing planning and control by Institute management.

HE 20.7122:CT
AUDIOVISUAL MATERIALS. [Irregular]

HE 20.7123:CT   • Item 499-F-14
NIOSH ALERT. [Irregular]

PURPOSE:– To describe serious or fatal accidents that occur in commercial establishments and makes specific recommendations for safeguards to eliminate most of the hazards that cause them.

HE 20.7124   • Item 499-F-15 (EL)
NIOSH CERTIFIED EQUIPMENT LIST. [Irregular] (Diskettes)

Lists NIOSH certified (or approved) equipment.

HE 20.7125:date
HEALTH HAZARD EVALUATION SUMMARIES. [Irregular]

Earlier HE 20.7102:H 34

HE 20.7125/2:nos.   • Item 499-F-16
NIOSH HEALTH HAZARD EVALUATION REPORT (Series).

HE 20.7126:date   • Item 499-F-16 (MF)
NIOSH RESEARCH AND DEMONSTRATION GRANTS. [Annual]

PURPOSE:– To provide information on the status and scope of NIOSH research grants. Describes all active grants during the fiscal year and lists publications resulting from the research.
Earlier HE 20.7102:G 76

HE 20.7127:date   • Item 499-F-11 (MF)
NIOSH PROJECTS FOR (Fiscal Year).

Earlier titled: Program Plan of the National Institute for Occupational Safety and Health.

HE 20.7128:   • Item 499-F-17 (MF)
NIOSH SCHEDULE OF COURSES. [Annual]

Contains information for applicants, and application form, and a schedule of NIOSH courses at its headquarters and various centers throughout the country.
Earlier HE 20.6102:C 83

HE 20.7129:CT   • Item 499-F-19 (E)
ELECTRONIC PRODUCTS (misc.).

HE 20.7130:nos.   • Item 499-F-20 (MF)
INFORMATION CIRCULARS.

HE 20.7131:nos.   • Item 499-F-22 (MF)
REPORT OF INVESTIGATIONS (RI series).

BUREAU OF HEALTH EDUCATION (1973–1984)

CREATION AND AUTHORITY

The Bureau was abolished and its functions transferred to the Center for Health Promotion and Education (HE 20.7600) in 1984.

HE 20.7201:date
ANNUAL REPORT.

HE 20.7202:CT   • Item 494-H-4
GENERAL PUBLICATIONS.

HE 20.7208:CT   • Item 494-H-2
HANDBOOKS, MANUALS, GUIDES. [Irregular]

HE 20.7209:CT   • Item 494-H-1
BIBLIOGRAPHIES AND LISTS OF PUBLICATIONS. [Irregular]

HE 20.7209/2:date   • Item 494-H-5
CURRENT AWARENESS IN HEALTH EDUCATION. [Monthly]
Later HE 20.7609

HE 20.7210:date   • Item 494-H-3
STATE LEGISLATION ON SMOKING AND HEALTH. 1977–   [Annual]

PURPOSE:– To give tabulation by subject and State of smoking and health resolutions and bills introduced in State legislatures during the year.
ISSN 0146-017X

HE 20.7211:date   • Item 504-A
SMOKING AND HEALTH BULLETIN. 1970– [Irregular]

PURPOSE:– To disseminate extensive, detailed information in the field of smoking and health. Includes abstracts of items in many languages and includes articles from the late 1950's to date. All abstracts are in English.
All items appearing in the Bulletin will become part of the permanent collection of the Technical Information Center of the Clearinghouse and can be referred to by their accession numbers.
ISSN 0081-0363
Prior to 1978, published by the Center for Disease Control (HE 20.7012)

HE 20.7212:date   • Item 504-A-1
FOCAL POINTS. [Monthly] (Office of Health Information and Health Promotion)

PURPOSE:– To provide a newsletter for those engaged in health education activities to exchange ideas and information concerning health education programs and projects being carried out a local, State, regional and international levels. Also includes information on current activities and concerns of the Office of Health Information and Health Promotion.

CENTER FOR HIV, STD, AND TB (1973–   )

CREATION AND AUTHORITY
Formerly: Center for Prevention Services.

INFORMATION

National Center for HIV, STD
and TB Prevention
1600 Clifton Rd.
Atlanta, GA 30333
Toll Free: (800) 311-3435
(404) 639-3534
Fax: (404) 639-8600
http://www.cdc.gov/nchstp/od/nchstp.html

HE 20.7301:date
ANNUAL REPORT.

HE 20.7302:CT   • Item 494-K-1
GENERAL PUBLICATIONS. [Irregular]

HE 20.7308:CT   • Item 494-K-4
HANDBOOKS, MANUALS, GUIDES.

HE 20.7309:nos.   • Item 494-K-2
SEXUALLY TRANSMITTED DISEASE STATISTICS. 1– [Irregular]

Former title: VD Statistical Letter.
ISSN 0363-2032
Earlier HE 20.7018/2

HE 20.7309/2:date • **Item 494-K-2 (MF)**
SEXUALLY TRANSMITTED DISEASE SURVEIL-
LANCE. [Annual]

HE 20.7310:date • **Item 494-K-3 (EL)**
TUBERCULOSIS IN THE UNITED STATES. [Annual]

PURPOSE:– To provide a review of tubercu-
losis morbidity, mortality, and performance of tu-
berculosis programs, and to present an analysis
of the current status of the disease in the United
States.
Formed by the union of Reported Tuberculo-
sis Data (HE 20.7017) and Tuberculosis Programs.
Companion volume to Tuberculosis Statistics,
States and Cities (HE 20.7013).
ISSN 0146-7298

HE 20.7311:date • **Item 494-K-6**
SEXUALLY TRANSMITTED DISEASES, ABSTRACTS
AND BIBLIOGRAPHIES. [Irregular]

Consists of abstracts and selected bibliographies on clinical, laboratory diagnosis, and therapy
aspects of such diseases as syphilis, gonor-
rhea, genital herpes infection, trichomoniasis, etc.
Former title: CLVD (Current Literature on
Venereal Disease) Abstracts and Bibliographies.

HE 20.7311/2:date • **Item 494-K-5 (MF)**
IMMUNIZATION ABSTRACTS AND BIBLIOGRAPHY.
[Irregular]

PURPOSE:– To present a survey of recently
published periodical literature in the field of vaccine preventable disease. Consists of abstracts
from the publication, author index, subject index,
etc.

HE 20.7312:CT • **Item 494-K-7 (MF)**
BIBLIOGRAPHIES AND LISTS OF PUBLICATIONS.
[Irregular]

HE 20.7313:date
UNITED STATES IMMUNIZATION SURVEY. [Annual]

PURPOSE:– To report immunization levels for
specified diseases (polio, DPT, measles, rubella,
and smallpox) for the United States and certain
geographic, race, and age groups in the United
States.
Earlier HE 20.2314

HE 20.7314:CT
DIABETES CONTROL PROGRAM UPDATE.

HE 20.7315:date • **Item 494-K-8**
HEALTH INFORMATION FOR INTERNATIONAL
TRAVEL. [Annual]

PURPOSE:– To provide health information for
international travelers in such areas as vaccination, immunization, prophylaxis, and health hazards in specific localities. Also includes general
health hints for international travelers.
Formerly issued as an annual supplement to
Morbidity and Mortality Weekly Report (HE
20.7009).

HE 20.7315/2:date • **Item 494-K-8**
SUMMARY OF HEALTH INFORMATION FOR INTER-
NATIONAL TRAVEL. [Biweekly]

HE 20.7316: • **Item 494-K-9 (MF)**
DIRECTORY OF STD CLINICS.

STD = Sexually Transmitted Disease.
Directory of Sexually Transmitted Disease
Clinics in all 50 states plus Guam and Puerto
Rico. Arranged alphabetically by states and by
cities in each state. An abbreviated list of sexually transmitted diseases treated appears in the
services part for each treatment facility.

HE 20.7317:nos. • **Item 494-K-3 (MF)**
FLUORIDATION CENSUS. [Annual]

HE 20.7318: • **Item 494-K-10 (EL)**
CDC HIB/STD/TB PREVENTION NEWS UPDATE
(AIDS Daily Summaries).
Formerly: CDC NCHSTP: daily news up-
date.

HE 20.7319: • **Item 494-K-10 (E)**
ELECTRONIC PRODUCTS (misc.).

HE 20.7320:v.nos./nos. • **Item 494-K-11 (EL)**
HIV/AIDS SURVEILLANCE REPORT. [Semiannually]

HE 20.7320/2: • **Item 494-K-11 (EL)**
HIV/AIDS PREVENTION NEWSLETTER. [Quarterly].

HE 20.7320/3: • **Item 494-K-12 (EL)**
FACT SHEETS (NCHSTP-HIV/AIDS PREVENTION
DIVISION).

BUREAU OF LABORATORIES
(1973– 1984)

HE 20.7401:date
ANNUAL REPORT.

HE 20.7402:CT
GENERAL PUBLICATIONS. [Irregular]

HE 20.7408:CT • **Item 494-L**
HANDBOOKS, MANUALS, GUIDES. [Irregular]

HE 20.7409:nos. • **Item 494-L-1**
IMMUNOLOGY SERIES. 1– [Irregular]
Later HE 20.7008/3

HE 20.7410:CT • **Item 494-L-2**
BIBLIOGRAPHIES AND LISTS OF PUBLICATIONS.
[Irregular]

HE 20.7412:date
PROFICIENCY TESTING SUMMARY ANALYSIS: GEN-
ERAL IMMUNOLOGY. [Irregular]
Later HE 20.7022/3

HE 20.7412/2:date
BLOOD LEAD, PROFICIENCY TESTING. [Monthly]
Later HE 20.7022/5

HE 20.7412/3:date
FLUORIDATED DRINKING WATER, PROFICIENCY
TESTING. [Monthly]
Later HE 20.7022/4

HE 20.7412/4:date
ERYTHROCYTE PROTOPORPHYRIN, PROFICIENCY
TESTING. [Monthly]
Later HE 20.7022/6

HE 20.7413:nos. • **Item 494-L-4 (MF)**
POSITION CLASSIFICATION AND PAY IN STATE AND
TERRITORIAL PUBLIC HEALTH LABORATORIES.
[Annual]

Tables reflect pay changes and current classifications as reported by state and territorial
public health laboratories. Average annual salaries and percent of increase in salaries are compared for various periods.
Also published in microfiche.

NATIONAL CENTER FOR ENVIRONMENTAL HEALTH
(1984–   )

INFORMATION

National Center for Environmental Health
Centers for Disease Control and Prevention
1600 Clifton Rd. NE
Atlanta, GA 30333
(770) 488-7000
Toll Free: (888) 232-6789
Fax: (770) 488-7015
http://www.cdc.gov/nceh/default.htm

HE 20.7501:date
ANNUAL REPORT.

HE 20.7502:CT • **Item 494-L-6**
GENERAL PUBLICATIONS.

HE 20.7509:CT • **Item 494-L-5 (MF)**
BIBLIOGRAPHIES AND LISTS OF PUBLICATIONS.
[Irregular]

HE 20.7511:date • **Item 494-L-5 (P) (EL)**
SUMMARY OF SANITATION INSPECTION OF INTER-
NATIONAL CRUISE SHIPS.

HE 20.7512: • **Item 494-L-10 (E)**
ELECTRONIC PRODUCTS (misc.).

HE 20.7513: • **Item 494-L-10 (P) (EL)**
BROCHURES.

NATIONAL CENTER FOR CHRONIC DISEASE PREVENTION AND HEALTH PROMOTION
(1984–   )

INFORMATION

National Center for Chronic
Disease Prevention and Health Promotion
Centers for Disease Control and Prevention
Columbia Bldg.
2900 Woodcock Blvd.
Atlanta, GA 30341
(770) 488-5401
Fax: (770) 488-5971
http://www.cdc.gov/nccdphp/index.htm

HE 20.7601:date
ANNUAL REPORT.

HE 20.7602:CT • **Item 494-H-4**
GENERAL PUBLICATIONS. [Irregular]

HE 20.7608:CT • **Item 494-H-2**
HANDBOOKS, MANUALS, GUIDES. [Irregular]

HE 20.7609:date • **Item 494-H-5**
CURRENT AWARENESS IN HEALTH EDUCATION.
[Monthly]
Earlier HE 20.7209/2

HE 20.7610:CT • **Item 494-H-1 (MF)**
BIBLIOGRAPHIES AND LISTS OF PUBLICATIONS.
[Irregular]
Earlier HE 20.7209

HE 20.7610/2: • **Item 494-H-8 (MF)**
SMOKING AND HEALTH BULLETIN. [Annual]

Annotated bibliography on smoking and health.
Includes a cumulative author and subject index.
Earlier HE 20.11

HE 20.7611:date • Item 505-A-19 (MF)
SUICIDE SURVEILLANCE SUMMARY. [Biennial]

HE 20.7611/2: • Item 505-A-23 (MF)
HOMICIDE SURVEILLANCE.

Analyzes mortality data on victims of homicide over an eighty year period. Intended for use by clinicians, health planners and evaluators, and other public health professionals interested in the numbers and characteristics of homicide victims.

HE 20.7611/3:date • Item 505-A-24 (CD)
BEHAVIORAL RISK FACTOR SURVEILLANCE SYSTEM. [Biennial]

HE 20.7612:date • Item 494-H-6 (MF)
SECRETARY'S COMMUNITY HEALTH PROMOTION AWARDS. [Biennial]

PURPOSE:– To describe the efforts of communities throughout the nation that participated in the Community Health Promotion Awards Program.

Earlier HE 20.7002:Se 2

HE 20.7613:date • Item 494-H-7 (MF)
SMOKING AND HEALTH, A NATIONAL STATUS REPORT. [Biennial]

PURPOSE:–To describe progress being made to combat the health burden caused by smoking. Presents an inventory of activities at the national, state and local levels aimed at reducing cigarette smoking.

HE 20.7613/2: • Item 504-A
SMOKING AND HEALTH BULLETIN. [Irregular]

HE 20.7614:date • Item 483-L-6
THE HEALTH CONSEQUENCES OF INVOLUNTARY SMOKING. [Annual]

HE 20.7615:CT • Item 483-L-6
REPORTS OF THE SURGEON GENERAL.

HE 20.7616:nos. • Item 444-P-1 (CD)
NATIONAL CENTER FOR CHRONIC DISEASE PREVENTION AND HEALTH PROMOTION (NCCDPHP) (numbered).

Earlier HE 20.7039

HE 20.7617: • Item 494-H-9 (EL)
CHRONIC DISEASE NOTES & REPORTS. [Irregular].

CENTER FOR PROFESSIONAL DEVELOPMENT AND TRAINING (1984–   )

HE 20.7701:date
ANNUAL REPORT.

HE 20.7702:CT • Item 494-L-9
GENERAL PUBLICATIONS. [Irregular]

HE 20.7708:CT
HANDBOOKS, MANUALS, GUIDES. [Irregular]

HE 20.7709:CT • Item 494-L-8
REGULATIONS, RULES, INSTRUCTIONS.

HE 20.7710:lesson nos. • Item 504-C-1 (MF)
HOMESTUDY COURSE 3012-G, COMMUNICABLE DISEASE CONTROL.

NATIONAL CENTER FOR INFECTIOUS DISEASES (1984–   )

INFORMATION

Office of Health Communication
National Center for Infectious Diseases
Centers for Disease Control and Prevention
Mailstop C-14
1600 Clifton Rd.
Atlanta, GA 30333
(404) 639-3401
Fax: (400) 639-3039
http://www.cdc.gov/ncidod/index.htm

HE 20.7801:date
ANNUAL REPORT.

HE 20.7802:CT • Item 494-L-7
GENERAL PUBLICATIONS. [Irregular]

HE 20.7808:CT • Item 504-K
HANDBOOKS, MANUALS, GUIDES. [Irregular]

Earlier HE 20.7008

HE 20.7809:nos.
REAGENTS EVALUATION PROGRAM. [Irregular]

Later HE 20.7810/2

HE 20.7810 • Item 504-G
MONTHLY REPORT OF REAGENTS EVALUATION.

Lists commercial reagents submitted to the Center's Biological Products Program of evaluation and which meet performance specifications. Earlier HE 20.7032

HE 20.7810/2:Supp.nos. • Item 504-G (MF)
REAGENTS EVALUATION PROGRAM. [Irregular]

Earlier HE 20.7809
Discontinued.

HE 20.7811:date • Item 504-E-1 (MF)
ARBOVIRUS SURVEILLANCE, REFERENCE, AND RESEARCH. [Annual]

Includes information on arbovirus surveillance, reference, and research and on World Health Organization Reference Center activities.

HE 20.7816:nos. • Item 504-K-1 (P) (EL)
ADVISORY MEMO (series).

HE 20.7817:v.nos./nos. • Item 504-K-2 (EL)
EMERGING INFECTIOUS DISEASES.[Monthly].

HE 20.7818:date • Item 494-K-3 (P) (EL)
HEALTH INFORMATION FOR INTERNATIONAL TRAVEL. [Biennial].

Previously HE 20.7315

HE 20.7818/2:date • Item 504-K-4 (P) (EL)
SUMMARY OF HEALTH INFORMATION FOR INTERNATIONAL TRAVEL.

TOXIC SUBSTANCES AND DISEASE REGISTRY AGENCY (1992– 1995)

HE 20.7901:date • Item 504-R (MF)
AGENCY FOR TOXIC SUBSTANCES AND DISEASE BIENNIAL REPORT.

HE 20.7901/2 • Item 504-R (MF)
AGENCY FOR TOXIC SUBSTANCES AND DISEASE REGISTRY ANNUAL REPORT.

HE 20.7902:CT • Item 504-R
GENERAL PUBLICATIONS.
Later HE 20.502

HE 20.7908:CT • Item 504-R
HANDBOOKS, MANUALS, AND GUIDES. [Irregular]
Later HE 20.508

HE 20.7915:v.nos./nos. • Item 504-S
HAZARDOUS SUBSTANCES AND PUBLIC HEALTH. [Quarterly]
Later HE 20.516

HE 20.7916:CT • Item 504-T
FACT SHEETS.

HE 20.7917:nos. • Item 504-U
CASE STUDIES IN ENVIRONMENTAL MEDICINE.

HE 20.7918:nos. • Item 504-V (MF)
TOXICOLOGICAL PROFILE (TP) (Series).

HE 20.7919 • Item 444-P-5 (E)
ATSDR, CD-ROM SERIES.
Later HE 20.517

NATIONAL CENTER FOR INJURY PREVENTION AND CONTROL

INFORMATION

National Center for Injury
   Prevention and Control
Centers for Disease Control and Prevention
Mailstop K65
4770 Buford Hwy. NE
Atlanta, GA 30341-3724
(770) 488-1506
Fax: (770) 488-1667
http://www.cdc.gov/ncipc

HE 20.7952:CT • Item 494-N
GENERAL PUBLICATIONS.

HE 20.7956 • Item 494-N-4 (EL)
INJURY CONTROL UPDATE (series)

HE 20.7957:nos. • Item 494-N-2 (MF)
VIOLENCE SURVEILLANCE SUMMARY SERIES.

HE 20.7958 • Item 494-N-1
HANDBOOKS, MANUALS, GUIDES.

HE 20.7959 • Item 494-N-3 (EL)
ELECTRONIC PRODUCTS. (misc.)

NATIONAL IMMUNIZATION PROGRAM

HE 20.7962:　　• Item 494-P
GENERAL PUBLICATIONS.

HE 20.7968:　　• Item 494-P-1
HANDBOOKS, MANUALS, GUIDES.

SUBSTANCE ABUSE AND MENTAL HEALTH SERVICES ADMINISTRATION (1992–1995)

CREATION AND AUTHORITY

The Alcohol, Drug Abuse, and Mental Health Administration was established by Health, Education, and Welfare Secretary by Act of May 21, 1972 (88 Stat. 134). Functions were transferred to Health and Human Services Department by act of October 17, 1979 (93 Stat. 695). It was established as an agency of the Public Health Service by act of October 27, 1986 (100 Stat. 3207-106). It was renamed Substance Abuse and Mental Health Services Administration by act of July 10, 1992 (106 Stat. 325). Beginning in 1995 publications are classified by SuDocs numbers HE 20.400.

HE 20.8001:date　　• Item 497-D-4 (MF)
ANNUAL REPORT.

HE 20.8002:CT　　• Item 497-D-1
GENERAL PUBLICATIONS. [Irregular]

Later HE 20.402

HE 20.8008:CT　　• Item 497-D-3
HANDBOOKS, MANUALS, GUIDES. [Irregular]

Later HE 20.408

HE 20.8009:v.nos.&nos.　　• Item 507-T
MENTAL HEALTH DIGEST. v. 1– v. 5. 1969– 1973. [Monthly] (National Clearinghouse for Mental Health Information)

PURPOSE:– To reflect the whole spectrum of mental health and to present a broad sampling of subject matter and professional points of view. Contains condensations of journal articles, review, Federal and State program documents, and other pertinent material.
Issued as an unnumbered publication 1967–1968.
Earlier HE 20.2410

HE 20.8010:nos.　　• Item 831-C-1
REPORT SERIES.

HE 20.8010:33/nos.　　• Item 831-C-1
DRUG ABUSE PREVENTION REPORT. 1–1975–

HE 20.8011:date　　• Item 497-D-2 (MF)
SUMMARY PROCEEDINGS OF ADAMHA ANNUAL CONFERENCE OF THE STATE AND TERRITORIAL ALCOHOL, DRUG ABUSE, AND MENTAL HEALTH AUTHORITIES.

PURPOSE:– To provide summary proceedings of conferences covering matters of mutual interest and concern related to the planning, development, and administration of alcohol, drug abuse, and mental health programs.

HE 20.8012:CT　　• Item 497-D-5 (MF)
BIBLIOGRAPHIES AND LISTS OF PUBLICATIONS. [Irregular]

HE 20.8012/2:date　　• Item 497-D-5
NCADI PUBLICATIONS CATALOG.

Later HE 20.419

HE 20.8012/3　　• Item 497-D-6 (MF)
PREVENTION PIPELINE. [Bimonthly]

HE 20.8013:v.nos.&nos.　　• Item 497-D-6
ADAMHA NEWS. v. 1–　1975–　[Monthly]

PURPOSE:– To provide a newsletter on issues and events in the areas of abuse and alcoholism, drug abuse, and mental health.

HE 20.8013/a　　• Item 497-D-6
– SEPARATES.

HE 20.8013/2:　　• Item 497-D-13
ADAMHA UPDATE. [Quarterly]

Presents facts and figures on the nation's alcohol, drug abuse, and mental health problems, and ADAMHA's response to them. Designed for use of federal and state officials. Issues contain epidemiological data, results of selected studies, etc.

HE 20.8014:CT　　• Item 497-D-7
POSTERS. [Irregular]

HE 20.8015:CT　　• Item 497-D-6
HHS NEWS. [Irregular]

News releases.

HE 20.8016:date　　• Item 507-B-26 (MF)
ALCOHOL, DRUG ABUSE, MENTAL HEALTH RESEARCH GRANT AWARDS. [Annual]

Earlier HE 20.8118

HE 20.8017:date　　• Item 497-D-8 (MF)
ADAMHA WOMEN'S COUNCIL REPORT TO THE ADMINISTRATOR. [Annual]

Report analyzes the employment status of women in relation to men in each of the component parts of the Administration.

HE 20.8018:date　　• Item 497-D-9 (MF)
PREVENTION ACTIVITIES OF THE ALCOHOL, DRUG ABUSE, AND MENTAL HEALTH ADMINISTRATION. [Annual]

PURPOSE:– To summarize Administration activities directed toward prevention of alcohol, drug abuse, and mental health disorders.

HE 20.8018/2:nos.　　• Item 497-D-9 (MF)
OSAP PREVENTION MONOGRAPH (Series).

OSAP = Office for Substance Abuse Prevention.

HE 20.8018/3:nos.　　• Item 497-D-9 (MF)
OSAP TECHNICAL REPORT (Series).

HE 20.8018/4:date　　• Item 497-D-9
OSAP PUT ON THE BRAKES BULLETIN. [Semiannual]

HE 20.8018/5:nos.　　• Item 497-D-9 (MF)
OSAP CULTURAL COMPETENCE SERIES.

Later HE 20.420

HE 20.8019:date　　• Item 497-D-10
MEMORANDUM ON WOMEN'S ALCOHOL, DRUG ABUSE, AND MENTAL HEALTH ISSUES. [Quarterly]

Contains ADAMHA Research Highlights. Discontinued.

HE 20.8020:　　• Item 497-D-11 (MF)
ALCOHOL AND DRUG ABUSE AND MENTAL HEALTH SERVICES BLOCK GRANT, REPORT TO CONGRESS. [Annual]

Reports on activities of the states which have received funding under the Alcohol and Drug Abuse and Mental Health Services Block Grant.

HE 20.8021:　　• Item 497-D-12 (MF)
NDATUS INSTRUCTION MANUAL. [Biennial]

NDATUS = National Drug and Alcoholism Treatment Unit Survey
PURPOSE– To provide instructions for planning and conducting the NDATU survey at the state and unit levels. The data files that result from the survey serve as the main repository of information on drug abuse and alcoholism treatment units throughout the country.

HE 20.8022:　　• Item 497-D-14 (MF)
ADAMHA PUBLIC ADVISORY COMMITTEES, AUTHORITY, STRUCTURE, FUNCTIONS, MEMBERS. [Annual]

Contains information on the function, structure, and membership of public advisory committees in ADAMHA. The table of contents lists the committees according to organizational structures and the index lists the committees and members alphabetically.

HE 20.8023:CT　　• Item 497-D-15
DIRECTORIES.

HE 20.8024:date　　• Item 497-D-9 (MF)
REPORT OF THE ADVISORY PANEL ON ALZHEIMER'S DISEASE. [Annual]

HE 20.8025:nos.　　• Item 497-D-9 (MF)
TECHNICAL ASSISTANCE PUBLICATION SERIES.

HE 20.8026:v.nos./nos.　　• Item 497-D-6
SAMHSA NEWS.

HE 20.8027:nos.　　• Item 497-D-6
CSAP SPECIAL REPORTS.

HE 20.8028:v.nos./nos.　　• Item 497-D-6
CSAP HEALTHY DELIVERY.

HE 20.8029:nos.　　• Item 497-D-6
TREATMENT IMPROVEMENT PROTOCOL (TIP) (series).

NATIONAL INSTITUTE OF MENTAL HEALTH (1973–　)

INFORMATION

Public Inquiries
National Institute of Mental Health
6001 Executive Blvd., Rm. 8184, MSC 9663
Bethesda, MD 20892
(301) 443-4513
Fax: (301) 443-4279
http://www.nimh.nih.gov

HE 20.8101:date
ANNUAL REPORT.

Earlier HE 20.3801

HE 20.8102:CT　　• Item 507-B-5
GENERAL PUBLICATIONS.

Earlier HE 20.3802

HE 20.8103/2:　　• Item 507-B-37
IRG BULLETIN. [Quarterly]

IRG = Initiative Research Group
Published by the Division of Extramural Activities to inform NIMH consultants of developments related to Institute extramural programs and to review policies and procedures.
Discontinued.

HE 20.8107:CT • Item 507-B-5
ANNOUNCEMENT (Press Releases).

HE 20.8108:CT • Item 507-B-10
HANDBOOKS, MANUALS, GUIDES. [Irregular]

HE 20.8109:v.nos.&nos. • Item 507-Z-1
PSYCHOPHARMACOLOGY BULLETIN. v. 1– 1959–
[Quarterly]

PURPOSE:– To facilitate the dissemination and exchange of information among scientists in the field of psychopharmacology. The Bulletin includes material which is either not destined to appear in the more formal scientific literature or requires rapid release of information due to its timeliness. Special emphasis is on rapid informal reporting of work and news in the field which facilitates particularly the communication of the latest psychotropic drug information to the far-flung Regional and Collaborative Reference Centers which comprise the International Reference Center network.

Issued irregularly prior to 1969. Earlier title: Psychopharmacology Service Center Bulletins.
Indexed by:–
Biological Abstracts
Chemical Abstracts
Index to U.S. Government Periodicals
Index Medicus
ISSN 0048-5764
Earlier HE 20.2409

HE 20.8109/a • Item 507-Z-1
– SEPARATES.

HE 20.8109/2:v.nos.&nos. • Item 507-Z
PSYCHOPHARMACOLOGY ABSTRACTS. v. 1– 19. 1961– 1982. [Monthly] (National Clearinghouse for Mental Health Information)

PURPOSE:– To provide a specialized information medium designed to assist the Institute to meet its obligation to foster and support laboratory and clinical research into the nature and causes of mental disorders and methods of treatment and prevention. Specifically, this information service is designed to meet the needs of investigators in the field of psychopharmacology for rapid and comprehensive information about new developments and research results.

Formerly arranged under six broad categories, the abstracts are now listed in sequential order by the National Clearinghouse for Mental Informations processing numbers. Gaps in the numbers indicate non-psychopharmacology abstracts related to other areas of mental health and are omitted from the journal.

Issued prior to v. 2, no. 7 by the Psychopharmacology Service Center.
Annual index issued separately.
ISSN 0033-3166
Earlier HE 20.2409/2

HE 20.8110:letters-nos. • Item 491-A
MENTAL HEALTH STATISTICS SERIES. 1968– [Irregular] (National Clearinghouse for Mental Health Information)

Information in the following sub-series:

Series A. Mental Health Facility Reports: Descriptive data on mental health facilities, patients served, staffing and expenditures.
Series B. Analytical and Special Study Reports: Special purposes studies or detailed analytical and interpretive reports.
Series C. Methodology Reports: New statistical methodology, data collection procedures or models, new analytical techniques, evaluation of data collection procedures.
Series D. Conference and Committee Reports: Conference and committee reports on subjects of general interest to the field.
Earlier HE 20.2415

HE 20.8110/2:lets.-nos. • Item 491-A
MENTAL HEALTH SERVICE SYSTEM REPORTS. [Irregular]

Supersedes Mental Health Statistics Services (HE 20.8110).

HE 20.8111:nos. • Item 507-B-23
NIMH REPORT TO PHYSICIANS (series). 1– 1974– [Irregular]

HE 20.8112:date • Item 507-B-16
ADMINISTRATION IN MENTAL HEALTH.
Earlier HE 20.2427

HE 20.8113:CT • Item 507-B-9
BIBLIOGRAPHIES AND LISTS OF PUBLICATIONS. [Irregular]
Earlier HE 20.2417

HE 20.8113:Se 9 • Item 507-B-9
SEX ROLES: A RESEARCH BIBLIOGRAPHY. 1975. 362 p.

A bibliography for researchers, scientists, and students conducting investigations into the influence of sex roles on individual behavior and on societal institutions. The bibliography is organized by subjects and covers literature on an international level. Each entry includes a brief description of the research project and/or resulting publications. Subjects covered by this bibliography include sex differences, development of sex differences and sex roles, specialized sex roles in institutional settings, and cross-cultural overviews of the status of the sexes.

HE 20.8113:W 84 • Item 507-B-9
WOMAN AND MENTAL HEALTH: A BIBLIOGRAPHY. 1973. 247 p.

This bibliography is designed to provide information on the social, economic, and psychological pressures on women. The material was selected from behavioral science literature and audiovisual resources written between 1970 and 1973. It is intended to serve as a background and reference source for mental health professionals, behavioral scientists, and community action groups.

HE 20.8113/2:nos. • Item 507-B-24
MENTAL HEALTH EMERGENCIES ALERT. 1– 1974– [Irregular]

PURPOSE:– To provide periodic listings of annotations from current literature related to mental health emergencies provided by the NIMH Mental Health Emergencies Section, involving the mental health components of suicide, medical emergencies, drug overdose, acute alcoholism, rape and child abuse.

HE 20.8113/3:date • Item 507-B-9
PUBLICATIONS OF THE NATIONAL INSTITUTE OF MENTAL HEALTH. [Annual] (Public Inquiries Section, National Clearinghouse for Mental Health Information)

HE 20.8113/4:nos.
NIMH LIBRARY ACQUISITION LIST. [Monthly]

HE 20.8113/5:date • Item 507-B-9
MENTAL HEALTH SERVICE SYSTEM REPORTS AND STATISTICAL NOTES PUBLICATION LISTING. [Quarterly]

HE 20.8113/6:CT • Item 507-B-9
NEW PUBLICATIONS FROM THE NATIONAL INSTITUTE OF MENTAL HEALTH.

HE 20.8114:CT • Item 507-B-13
CRIME AND DELINQUENCY TOPICS: MONOGRAPH SERIES. [Irregular] (Center for Studies of Crime and Delinquency)
Earlier HE 20.3809

HE 20.8114/2:nos. • Item 507-B-20
RESEARCH REPORTS. 1– 1973– [Irregular] (Center for Studies of Crime and Delinquency)
Earlier HE 20.2420/4

HE 20.8114/3:CT • Item 507-B-13
CRIME AND DELINQUENCY TOPICS, MONOGRAPH SERIES. [Irregular] (Center for Studies of Crime and Delinquency)

PURPOSE:– To provide a series of monographs on current issues and direction in the area of crime and delinquency. The series is being sponsored by the Center for Studies of Crime and Delinquency to encourage the exchange of views of recognized authorities in the subject matter fields on issues and to promote in-depth analyses and development of insights and recommendations pertaining to them.
Former title: Crime and Delinquency Issues, Monograph Series.

HE 20.8115:v.nos./nos. • Item 507-B-7
SCHIZOPHRENIA BULLETIN. 1– [Quarterly] (National Clearinghouse for Mental Health Information)

Nos. 1-11 were issued on an irregular basis.
Indexed by: Index to U.S. Government Periodicals.
ISSN 0586-7614
Earlier HE 20.2414

HE 20.8115/a • Item 507-B-7
– SEPARATES.

HE 20.8116:nos. • Item 507-B-12
STATISTICAL NOTES. 1– 1969– [Irregular] (Survey and Reports Section)

PURPOSE:– To provide brief presentations of data, generally 4-10 pages, dealing with specific topics, such as length of stay in general hospital psychiatric inpatient units, source of funds for community mental health centers, educational level of admissions to State mental hospitals. Content usually includes tabular presentations of data and a brief description of the highlights of these data.
ISSN 0361-9311
Earlier HE 20.2424 and HE 20.3812

HE 20.8117:nos. • Item 507-B-2
MENTAL HEALTH PROGRAM REPORTS. 1– 1967– [Irregular] (PHS publication 1568) (National Clearinghouse for Mental Health Information)

PURPOSE:– To provide detailed descriptions of accomplishments achieved within the various programs of the National Institute of Mental Health. The series, an outgrowth of an earlier one devoted solely to studies supported through NIMH research grants, includes reports that span the broad range of substantive emphases and administrative mechanisms of the Institute.
Earlier HE 20.2419

HE 20.8118:date • Item 507-B-26
ALCOHOL, DRUG ABUSE, MENTAL HEALTH, RESEARCH GRANT AWARDS, FISCAL YEAR. 1973– [Annual] (Division of Extramural Research Programs, Program Analysis and Evaluation Section)

Continues: Mental Health Research Grant Awards (HE 20.2423).
Later HE 20.8016
ISSN 0096-1485

HE 20.8119:date • Item 507-B-15 (MF)
MENTAL HEALTH RESOURCES IN THE GREATER WASHINGTON AREA. [Annual]

ISSN 0092-5403
Earlier HE 20.2426

HE 20.8121 • Item 507-B-39
POSTERS, N.I.M.H.

Earlier HE 20.2421

HE 20.8121/2:CT
AUDIOVISUAL MATERIAL. [Irregular]

HE 20.8122 • Item 507-B-25
NEW DIMENSIONS IN MENTAL HEALTH. 1– 1974– [Irregular]

HE 20.8122/2:CT • Item 507-B-25
NEW DIMENSIONS IN MENTAL HEALTH, REPORT FROM THE DIRECTOR (series). [Irregular]

ISSN 0146-1451

HE 20.8123 • Item 506-C (MF)
MENTAL HEALTH DIRECTORY. [Irregular]

PURPOSE:– To provide a listing of State mental health services and facilities, which include public and private agencies and institutions which provide direct mental health services to the mentally ill and emotionally disturbed. Information is given on the geographic area served, the type of operating agency, and the type of services provided by each facility. A listing of regional mental health offices of NIMH, State and Territorial mental and health authorities, voluntary mental health associations and national mental health agencies is also included.
Earlier HE 20.2418
Later HE 20.410/2

HE 20.8123/2:CT • Item 506-C-6 (MF)
DIRECTORIES. [Irregular]

HE 20.8124:CT • Item 507-B-27
MENTAL HEALTH MATTERS. [Irregular]

Sub-title: A transcript of a Community Service Radio Program with guests from the Alcohol, Drug Abuse, and Mental Health Administration.

HE 20.8125:CT • Item 507-B-35
PRIMARY PREVENTION PUBLICATION SERIES. [Irregular]

HE 20.8126:CT • Item 507-B-28
TRENDS IN MENTAL HEALTH (series). [Irregular]
Discontinued.

HE 20.8127:nos. • Item 507-B-29
MENTAL HEALTH IN DEAFNESS. 1– 1977– [Irregular]

HE 20.8128:CT • Item 507-B-30
PLAIN TALK ABOUT [various subjects]. [Irregular]

PURPOSE:– Designed for the general public, contains leaflets on matters relating to mental health.

HE 20.8129:date • Item 507-B-33
DIRECTORY OF HALFWAY HOUSES AND COMMUNITY RESIDENCES FOR THE MENTALLY ILL. 1977– [Irregular]

Directory includes name of facility, address, phone number, services provided, number of beds, sexes and ages served, auspices of facility, and admission requirements.
Former title: Directory of Halfway Houses for the Mentally Ill and Alcoholics.

HE 20.8130:CT • Item 507-B-31
CARING ABOUT KIDS (series). [Irregular]

PURPOSE:– To provide a series of flyers produced to help parents care for their children and themselves in ways that foster good mental health.

HE 20.8131:CT • Item 507-B-32
SCIENCE REPORTS (series). [Irregular] (Division of Scientific and Public Information)

PURPOSE:– To present a report on scientific research on a particular mental health problem written for the layman.

HE 20.8131/2:CT • Item 507-B-32
SCIENCE MONOGRAPHS (series). [Irregular]

HE 20.8132: • Item 507-B-2
STUDIES IN SOCIAL CHANGE.

HE 20.8133:nos.
MENTAL HEALTH DEMOGRAPHIC PROFILE SYSTEM. MHDPS WORKING PAPERS. [Irregular]

HE 20.8134:nos. • Item 507-B-34
LITERATURE SURVEY SERIES. 1– 1981– [Irregular]

PURPOSE:– To provide annotated bibliographies on various diseases. Each issue is devoted to a single subject.

HE 20.8136:date • Item 507-B-36 (MF)
DIVISION OF INTRAMURAL RESEARCH PROGRAMS: ANNUAL REPORT.

HE 20.8137:date • Item 506-C
MENTAL HEALTH, UNITED STATES. [Annual]

HE 20.8138: • Item 507-B-38
FORMS.

HE 20.8139 • Item 507-B-40 (EL)
RESEARCH FACT SHEETS (various topics) (series).

NATIONAL INSTITUTE ON DRUG ABUSE
(1973–   )

CREATION AND AUTHORITY
The National Institute of Drug Abuse was transferred from the Alcohol, Drug Abuse and Mental Health Administration to the National Institutes of Health (HE 20.3950).

HE 20.8201:date
ANNUAL REPORT.

HE 20.8202:CT • Item 467-A-1
GENERAL PUBLICATIONS.

Later HE 20.3952

HE 20.8208:CT • Item 467-A-2
HANDBOOKS, MANUALS, GUIDES. [Irregular]

Later HE 20.3958

HE 20.8209:v.nos.&nos.
DACAS [Drug Abuse Current Awareness System]. v. 1– 4. 1972– 1976. [Biweekly] (National Clearinghouse for Drug Abuse Information)

PURPOSE:– To provide a comprehensive listing of citations of recent drug abuse literature. Classified PrEx 13.12 prior to v. 2, no. 5.

HE 20.8210:date • Item 483-F-1 (MF)
MARIHUANA AND HEALTH, ANNUAL REPORT TO THE CONGRESS FROM THE SECRETARY OF HEALTH, EDUCATION, AND WELFARE. 1st– 1971–

PURPOSE:– To serve as a widely available, up-to-date compendium of scientific information bearing on the issue of marihuana and health. Submitted by the Secretary of Health, Education, and Welfare pursuant to Title V of the Marihuana and Health Reporting Act (PL 91-296)

Earlier HE 20.2402:M 33/3

HE 20.8211:CT • Item 467-A-3
BIBLIOGRAPHIES AND LISTS OF PUBLICATIONS. [Irregular]

HE 20.8211/2:nos. • Item 467-A-3
SPECIAL BIBLIOGRAPHIES.

HE 20.8212:nos. • Item 467-A-6
STATISTICAL SERIES, QUARTERLY REPORT. 1– 6. 1975– 1976.

ISSN 0145-1065

HE 20.8212/2:nos. • Item 467-A-6 (MF)
STATISTICAL SERIES, SEMIANNUAL REPORT, SERIES D. [Irregular]

HE 20.8212/3:nos. • Item 467-A-6 (MF)
STATISTICAL SERIES, SERIES E. 1– [Annual] (Division of Scientific and Program Information)

ANNUAL DATA.

ANNUAL SUMMARY REPORT.

SMSA STATISTICS.

STATE STATISTICS.

HE 20.8212/4:date
QUARTERLY STATISTICAL BROCHURE.

Later HE 20.8212/2

HE 20.8212/5:nos. • Item 467-A-9 (MF)
STATISTICAL SERIES, SERIES A. 1– 1977– [Irregular]

HE 20.8212/6:nos. • Item 467-A-9 (MF)
STATISTICAL SERIES, SERIES F. 1– 1976– [Irregular]

HE 20.8212/7:nos. • Item 467-A-6 (MF)
STATISTICAL SERIES. SERIES G. 1– 1979–

HE 20.8212/8:nos. • Item 467-A-17 (MF)
STATISTICAL SERIES, SERIES B. 1–

Gives data on all known drug abuse and alcohol treatment units throughout the United States, with information derived from the National Drug and Alcoholism Treatment Utilization Survey.

HE 20.8212/9:nos. • Item 467-A-18 (MF)
STATISTICAL SERIES, SERIES C. 1– 1980– [Irregular]

HE 20.8212/10:nos. • Item 467-A-6 (MF)
STATISTICAL SERIES, SERIES H. 1– [Irregular]

Also published in microfiche.

HE 20.8212/11:date • Item 467-A-6 (MF)
STATISTICAL SERIES ANNUAL DATA, DATA FROM THE DRUG ABUSE WARNING NETWORK (DAWN) SERIES I.

Later HE 20.416

HE 20.8213:nos. • Item 467-A-4 (MF)
TECHNICAL PAPERS.

HE 20.8214:nos. • Item 467-A-5
RESEARCH ISSUES. 1– [Irregular]

HE 20.8215:v.nos.&nos. • Item 831-C-1
REPORT SERIES. [Irregular]

Indexed by: Index to U.S. Government Periodicals.
Earlier HE 20.8010

HE 20.8215/2:series nos.&nos. • Item 831-C-3
SELECTED REFERENCE SERIES. 1. no. 1– 1971–

Each bibliography in this series is a short, representative listing of citations of subjects of topical interest. The selection of literature is based on its currency, its significance in the field, and its availability in local bookstores or research libraries. The scope of the material is directed toward students writing research papers, special interest groups, such as educators, lawyers and physicians, and the general public requiring more resources than public information materials can provide. Each reference series is meant to present an overview of the existing literature, but is not meant to be comprehensive nor definite in scope.
Earlier PrEx 13.10/2

HE 20.8216:nos. • Item 831-C-8
RESEARCH MONOGRAPH SERIES. 1– 1975–

Later HE 20.3965

HE 20.8216/2:nos. • Item 831-C-9
SERVICES RESEARCH MONOGRAPH SERIES, NATIONAL POLYDRUG COLLABORATIVE PROJECT, TREATMENT MANUALS. 1– 1976– [Irregular]

HE 20.8216/2-2:CT • Item 831-C-11
SERVICES RESEARCH MONOGRAPH SERIES.
[Irregular]

HE 20.8216/3:nos. • Item 831-C-10
SERVICES RESEARCH REPORTS. [Irregular]

HE 20.8216/4:date • Item 467-A-14
SERVICES RESEARCH BRANCH NOTES. [Irregular]

PURPOSE:– To give persons concerned with provision of drug abuse service, information that can be significant to their treatment efforts prior to publication of a project's total findings.
Previously issued to depository libraries under Item 467-A-1.

HE 20.8216/5:date • Item 831-C-8 (MF)
PROBLEMS OF DRUG DEPENDENCE. [Annual]
Earlier HE 20.8216
Later HE 20.3966

HE 20.8217:CT • Item 467-A-7
TREATMENT PROGRAM MONOGRAPH (series). [Irregular]

PURPOSE:– To provide simple, staightforward presentations relevant to the operational aspects of the clinical setting. Intended for the Treatment Program Manager in the field.

HE 20.8217/2:CT • Item 467-A-7
TREATMENT RESEARCH MONOGRAPH (series). [Irregular]

HE 20.8217/3:CT • Item 467-A-7
TREATMENT RESEARCH REPORTS. [Irregular]

HE 20.8217/4:v.nos./nos. • Item 467-A-7
NIDA NOTES. [Quarterly]

Former title: Treatment Research Notes.

HE 20.8217/5 • Item 467-A-7
PREVENTION RESEARCH REPORTS.

HE 20.8217/6 • Item 467-A-7
NIDA RESEARCH REPORT SERIES.

HE 20.8218:date • Item 467-A-8
RESOURCES (series). [Irregular]

HE 20.8219:date • Item 467-A-11
DRUG USE AMONG AMERICAN HIGH SCHOOL STUDENTS. [Annual]

PURPOSE:– To provide detailed statistics on the prevalence and trends of drug use among American high school seniors.

HE 20.8219/2:date • Item 467-A-11
HIGHLIGHTS FROM STUDENT DRUG ABUSE IN AMERICA. [Annual]

HE 20.8220:date • Item 467-A-12
DRUG ABUSE RESEARCH AND DEVELOPMENT, FEDERALLY SUPPORTED DRUG ABUSE AND TOBACCO RESEARCH AND DEVELOPMENT, FISCAL YEAR (date).

PURPOSE:– To provide an inventory and analysis of research, and directories of individual projects by drug studies and by research area as well as an alphabetical list of investigations.

HE 20.8220/2: • Item 467-A-26 (MF)
DRUG ABUSE AND DRUG ABUSE RESEARCH. [Triennial]

Issues contain articles by various members of the scientific community on prevention and treatment research on drug abuse.

HE 20.8221:date • Item 467-A-13
CONNECTION. v. 1– 4. 1978– 1981. [Quarterly]

PURPOSE:– To provide a series of short articles, in newsletter format, in which policy, developments, and programs relating to the interface between justice and drug abuse treatment are discussed.
Prior to the Fall 1980 issue, published irregu-

larly and designated by volume and issue number.

HE 20.8221/2:nos. • Item 467-A-13
PROJECT CONNECTION: BEST STRATEGY (series). [Irregular]

HE 20.8222:date
DRUG ABUSE AMONG AMERICAN SCHOOL STUDENTS. [Annual]

HE 20.8223:nos. • Item 831-C-8 (MF)
MEDICAL MONOGRAPHS. 1– [Irregular]

HE 20.8224:v.nos.&nos. • Item 467-A-7
PREVENTION RESOURCES SERIES. v. 1– [Quarterly]

HE 20.8224/2:date • Item 467-A-25
PREVENTION NETWORKS. [Quarterly]

HE 20.8225:CT • Item 467-A-22
POSTERS.
Later HE 20.415

HE 20.8226:CT • Item 467-A-16 (MF)
ADDRESSES. [Irregular]

HE 20.8227:v.nos.&nos. • Item 467-A-19
DIRECTIONS. v. 1, no. 1. Fall 1980. [Quarterly]

Issued as an experimental bulletin, intended to help unify the substance abuse field by sharing among all of its disciplines ideas, resources and strategies for dealing with drug and alcohol problems. Contains short news items, photographs, and tables.
Note:– v. 1, no. 1, Fall 1980 only issue published.

HE 20.8228:CT • Item 467-A-20
DRUG ABUSE PREVENTION MONOGRAPH SERIES. [Irregular]

HE 20.8229:date • Item 467-A-21 (MF)
SOURCE BOOK. [Annual]

Contains descriptions of National Drug Abuse Center and National Center for Alcohol Education courses. Lists state and local training providers who present the courses, and lists other professional development resources in the U.S., by state.

HE 20.8230 • Item 467-A-23
CLINICAL AND BEHAVIORAL PHARMACOLOGY RESEARCH REPORT (series). [Irregular]

Each report deals with a different topic.

HE 20.8230/2:CT • Item 467-A-23 (MF)
CLINICAL REPORT SERIES.

HE 20.8231:date • Item 467-A-24 (MF)
DEMOGRAPHIC CHARACTERISTICS AND PATTERNS OF DRUG USE OF CLIENTS ADMITTED TO DRUG ABUSE TREATMENT PROGRAMS IN SELECTED SITES. [Annual]

PURPOSE:– To present data on clients admitted to state-monitored drug abuse treatment clinics. Compares characteristics of clients with different primary drug problems. Examines selected groups of clients by sex, race, and age differentials.

HE 20.8231/2 • Item 467-A-24 (MF)
DEMOGRAPHIC CHARACTERISTICS AND PATTERNS OF DRUG USE OF CLIENTS ADMITTED TO DRUG ABUSE TREATMENT PROGRAMS IN SELECTED STATES, TREND DATA. [Biennial]

HE 20.8232: • Item 467-A-27 (MF)
OFFICE OF SCIENCE MONOGRAPH SERIES.

Each issue will deal with a different topic, one example of which is drug abuse among ethnic minorities.

HE 20.8233:CT • Item 467-A-28
DIRECTORIES. [Irregular]

HE 20.8234:nos. • Item 831-C-1 (MF)
NIDA CAPSULES (SERIES).

HE 20.8235:nos. • Item 831-C-1
DRUG ABUSE SERVICES RESEARCH SERIES. [Irregular]

HE 20.8236:nos. • Item 467-A-5
TECHNICAL REPORTS (Series).

NATIONAL INSTITUTE ON ALCOHOL ABUSE AND ALCOHOLISM
(1973–)

INFORMATION

National Institute on Alcohol Abuse and Alcoholism
Willco Bldg.
6000 Executive Blvd.
Bethesda, Maryland 20892-7003
(301) 443-3885
http://www.niaaa.nih.gov

HE 20.8301:date • Item 483-G-3 (MF)
ANNUAL REPORT. 1st– 1972–

HE 20.8302:CT • Item 498-C-1
GENERAL PUBLICATIONS. [Irregular]

HE 20.8308:CT • Item 483-G-2
HANDBOOKS, MANUALS, GUIDES.

HE 20.8308/2:nos. • Item 483-G-2
NIAAA TREATMENT HANDBOOK SERIES. [Irregular]

HE 20.8308/3:CT • Item 483-G-5
U.S. ALCOHOL EPIDEMOLOGIC DATA REFERENCE MANUAL (series).

HE 20.8309:v.nos./nos. • Item 507-B-19 (EL)
ALCOHOL AND HEALTH RESEARCH . [Quarterly] (National Clearinghouse for Alcohol Information)

PURPOSE:– To provide persons engaged in research, treatment, or prevention work in alcohol abuse and alcoholism, and others involved in the field with current information on programs and research.
Issued by the National Institute of Mental Health (HE 20.3813) prior to the Fall 1973 issue.
Indexed by:–
Chemical Abstracts
Index to U.S. Government Periodicals
ISSN 0090-838X
Formerly: Alchol Health and Research World

HE 20.8309/2:date
ALCOHOL AND HEALTH NOTES. v. 1– 1972–1974. [Monthly] (National Clearinghouse for Alcohol Information)

PURPOSE:– To provide a newsletter of activities in the field of alcohol abuse and alcoholism. Includes listing of recent publications, grants issued by the Institute and meetings of groups and associations.
Earlier HE 20.3813

HE 20.8310:CT • Item 498-C-9
POSTERS. [Irregular]

HE 20.8311:CT • Item 498-C-2
BIBLIOGRAPHIES AND LISTS OF PUBLICATIONS.

HE 20.8311/2:nos. • Item 498-C-2
SUBJECT AREA BIBLIOGRAPHIES.

HE 20.8311/3:nos. • Item 498-C-8
NATIONAL CLEARINGHOUSE FOR ALCOHOL INFORMATION: GROUPED INTEREST GUIDES.

HE 20.8312:nos. • Item 498-C-5
NIAA INFORMATION AND FEATURE SERVICE. IFS-1– 107. 1974– 1983. [Irregular] (National Clearinghouse for Alcohol Information)

PURPOSE:– To provide coverage of developments in the alcoholism field for a broad audience of interested persons, such as health care workers, educators, criminal justice personnel, and researchers. Articles cover various aspects of alcoholism, including treatment, prevention, training, research, government programs, and local initiatives among other areas. Articles and pictures are prepared for easy reproduction by local publications in the field wishing to use the material.
ISSN 0364-0531

HE 20.8313:nos. • Item 498-C-6
SPECIAL REPORT TO THE U.S. CONGRESS ON ALCOHOL AND HEALTH. 1st–

Earlier HE 20.2402:Al 1/8

HE 20.8314:date • Item 498-C-7
ANNUAL ALCOHOLISM CONFERENCE OF THE NATIONAL INSTITUTE ON ALCOHOL ABUSE AND ALCOHOLISM, PROCEEDINGS. 1st– 1971–

Earlier HE 20.2430/2

HE 20.8315:nos. • Item 498-C-10 (MF)
RESEARCH MONOGRAPHS. 1– [Irregular]

PURPOSE:– To provide current information on a number of topics relevant to alcohol abuse and alcoholism.

HE 20.8316:date • Item 498-C-11 (MF)
REPORT TO THE UNITED STATES CONGRESS ON FEDERAL ACTIVITIES ON ALCOHOL ABUSE AND ALCOHOLISM. [Annual]

Issued pursuant to the Comprehensive Alcohol Abuse and Alcoholism Prevention, Treatment, and Rehabilitation Act of 1970, as amended (PL 91-616).

HE 20.8317:date • Item 498-C-12
STATISTICAL COMPENDIUM ON ALCOHOL AND HEALTH. [Annual]
Presents in tabular form data on alcohol consumption and its health and social consequences; financing, utilization, and effectiveness of treatment services, etc.

HE 20.8318 • Item 498-C-13
ANNOUNCEMENT, NATIONAL INSTITUTE ON ALCOHOL ABUSE AND ALCOHOLISM. [Irregular]

The announcements provide information needed to apply for grants to study the various aspects of alcoholism. Each announcement relates to a specific topic.

HE 20.8318/2:date • Item 498-C-13
SPECIAL ANNOUNCEMENTS (series). [Irregular]

HE 20.8319:date • Item 498-C-14 (MF)
STATE RESOURCES AND SERVICES FOR ALCOHOL AND DRUG ABUSE PROBLEMS. [Annual]

PURPOSE:– To present and analyze the results of the State Alcohol and Drug Abuse Profile data from 50 states, D.C., and Puerto Rico. Discusses such matters as funding levels and sources, and unmet treatment and services needs.

HE 20.8320:date • Item 498-C-15
NATIONAL DIRECTORY OF DRUG ABUSE AND ALCOHOLISM TREATMENT AND PREVENTION PROGRAMS. [Annual]

Directory of alcoholism and drug abuse service units by states and territories.
Earlier HE 20.8302:D 84

HE 20.8321: • Item 483-G-4
ANNUAL REPORT OF INTRAMURAL RESEARCH PROGRAM ACTVITIES FY.

HE 20.8322:nos. • Item 483-G-2 (P) (EL)
ALCOHOL ALERT (series).

HE 20.8323 • Item 483-G-2
PROJECT MATCH MONOGRAPH (series).

HE 20.8324 • Item 498-D (EL)
SURVEILLANCE REPORTS. [Irregular]

HEALTH RESOURCES AND SERVICES ADMINISTRATION (1982–   )

CREATION AND AUTHORITY

The Health Resources and Services Administration was formed by the merger of the Health Services Administration (HE 20.5000) and the Health Resources Administration (HE 20.6000) on September 1, 1982.

INFORMATION

Office of Communications
Health Resources and Services
Administration
5600 Fishers Lane
Rockville, Maryland 20857
(301) 443-3376
Fax: (301) 443-1989
http://www.hrsa.gov

HE 20.9001:date
ANNUAL REPORT.

HE 20.9002:CT • Item 507-H-17
GENERAL PUBLICATIONS.

HE 20.9008 • Item 507-H-15
HANDBOOKS, MANUALS, GUIDES.

HE 20.9009 • Item 507-H-16 (MF)
BIBLIOGRAPHIES AND LISTS OF PUBLICATIONS.

HE 20.9009/2:date • Item 507-H-16
CURRENT PUBLICATIONS. [Annual]

HE 20.9010 • Item 507-H-18 (MF)
HRSA SUMMARIES, PROGRAM EVALUATION STUDIES. [Irregular]

HE 20.9012:CT • Item 507-H-19
POSTERS. [Irregular]

HE 20.9013:date
HEALTH FACILITIES CONSTRUCTION PROGRAM LOAN, LOAN GUARANTEE AND MORTGAGE QUARTERLY STATUS REPORT. [Quarterly]

HE 20.9015: • Item 507-H-20 (EL)
HSRA DIRECTORY. [Semiannual]
HSRA = Health Resources and Services Administration
Contains organizational and alphabetical listings plus organizational charts.

HE 20.9015/2 • Item 507-H-24
DIRECTORIES.

HE 20.9016:date • Item 507-H-20 (MF)
A PROFILE. [Semiannual]

HE 20.9017:date • Item 507-H-21
THE RECRUITER: A NEWSLETTER FOR THE HEALTH PROFESSIONAL RECRUITER.

HE 20.9018:v.nos./nos. • Item 507-H-22 (P) (EL)
PREVIEW (vols./nos.). [Quarterly].

HE 20.9019:CT • Item 507-H-23
COUNCIL ON GRADUATE MEDICAL EDUCATION: GENERAL PUBLICATIONS.

BUREAU OF PRIMARY HEALTH CARE (1983–   )

CREATION AND AUTHORITY

The Bureau was transferred in 1983 from the Health Services Administration (HE 20.5100). Name changed to Bureau of Primary Health Care.

INFORMATION
Bureau of Primary Health Care
U.S. Dept. of Health and Human Services
East West Towers
4350 East West Hwy
Bethesda, MD 20814
(301) 594-4110
Fax: (301) 594-4075
http://www.bphc.hrsa.gov

HE 20.9101:date
ANNUAL REPORT.

HE 20.9102:CT • Item 532-E-10
GENERAL PUBLICATIONS. [Irregular]

HE 20.9108:CT • Item 532-E-12
HANDBOOKS, MANUALS, GUIDES. [Irregular]

HE 20.9109:CT • Item 532-E-11 (MF)
BIBLIOGRAPHIES AND LISTS OF PUBLICATIONS. [Irregular]

HE 20.9109/2: • Item 532-E-11
THE DEVELOPMENT AND MANAGEMENT OF AMBULATORY CARE PROGRAMS. [Annual]
Discontinued.

HE 20.9110 • Item 532-E-13 (MF)
NATIONAL HEALTH SERVICE CORPS INFORMATION BULLETINS (series). [Irregular]

Each Bulletin covers a single subject pertaining to the National Health Service Corps.

HE 20.9110/2:date • Item 532-E-13 (MF)
NATIONAL HEALTH SERVICE CORPS SCHOLARSHIP PROGRAM APPLICANT INFORMATION BULLETIN. [Annual]

HE 20.9110/3:date • Item 532-E-13
EXECUTIVE CORRESPONDENCE INFORMATION BULLETIN, NATIONAL HEALTH SERVICE CORPS. Discontinued.

HE 20.9110/4:v.nos.&nos. • Item 532-E-16
NHSC NOTES. [Bimonthly]
Discontinued.

NHSC = National Health Service Corps.
Each issue consists of a single folded sheet of news items about various activities of the Corps. Discontinued.

HE 20.9110/5:date • Item 532-E-13
NHSC FACT SHEETS. [Semiannual]

HE 20.9110/6:date • Item 532-E-13
NATIONAL HEALTH SERVICE CORPS INFORMATION BULLETIN, PRIVATE PRACTICE OPTION. [Annual]

HE 20.9110/7:date • Item 532-E-13 (MF)
NATIONAL HEALTH SERVICE CORPS INFORMATION BULLETIN, PRIVATE PRACTICE START UP LOAN PROGRAM. [Annual]

HE 20.9110/8:date • Item 532-E-13 (MF)
NATIONAL HEALTH SERVICE CORPS INFORMATION BULLETIN, PRIVATE PRACTICE LOAN PROGRAM FOR FORMER CORPS MEMBERS. [Annual]

HE 20.9110/9:date • Item 532-F (EL)
NHSC IN TOUCH, FREE ON-LINE SERVICE OPEN TO PRIMARY CARE PROVIDERS. [Quarterly]

HE 20.9110/10 • **Item 532-E-23 (MF)**
NATIONAL HEALTH SERVICE CORPS REPORT TO THE CONGRESS. [Annual]

HE 20.9111:CT • **Item 532-E-14**
INFORMATION BULLETIN, DIVISION OF MATERNAL AND CHILD HEALTH. [Irregular]

> Bulletins on miscellaneous topics pertaining to the work of the Division.
> Discontinued.

HE 20.9111/2:date/nos. • **Item 532-E-14**
MATERNAL AND CHILD HEALTH TECHNICAL INFORMATION SERIES. [Quaterly]
> Discontinued.

HE 20.9112:CT • **Item 532-E-15 (MF)**
DIRECTORIES. [Irregular]

HE 20.9112/2:date • **Item 532-E-17 (MF)**
330-FUNDED COMMUNITY HEALTH CENTERS DIRECTORY. [Annual]
> PURPOSE:– To list by region and states the community health centers authorized under Section 330 of the Public Health Service Act as amended. Such health centers provide comprehensive health services to urban and rural areas where there are shortages of medical personnel and services.

HE 20.9112/3:date
COMPREHENSIVE CLINICAL AND GENETIC SERVICES CENTERS, A NATIONAL DIRECTORY. [Irregular]
> Earlier HE 20.5102:G 28/3 and HE 20.9112:C 73

HE 20.9113:date
IMPAIRED PROFESSIONALS' RESOURCE GUIDE. [Bimonthly]

HE 20.9113/2:date
EMPLOYEE COUNSELING SERVICE PROGRAM MEMO. [Bimonthly]

HE 20.9113/3:date • **Item 532-E-18**
EMPLOYEE COUNSELING SERVICE PROGRAM, ANNUAL REPORT.

> PURPOSE:– To summarize activities of the Employee Counseling Service Program, which seeks to maximize the productivity of PHS employees within the Parklawn complex.
> Discontinued.

HE 20.9114 • **Item 532-E-19 (MF)**
ABSTRACTS OF ACTIVE PROJECTS.

> Contains abstracts of active projects in such areas as maternal and child health improvement. See HE 20.9211

HE 20.9115: • **Item 532-E-20 (MF)**
MEMORANDUM (series).

> Memorandums from the Bureau Director to Regional Health Administrators to provide guidance on such matters as Need/Demand Assessment to determine need for services in the case of continuation grants.

HE 20.9116:v.nos./nos. • **Item 532-E-22 (P) (EL)**
FEDERAL OCCUPATIONAL HEALTH MEMO SERIES. [Quarterly]

HE 20.9117 • **Item 532-E-21**
NETWORK NEWS. [Quarterly]
> Discontinued.

HE 20.9118 • **Item 532-E-24**
POLICY INFORMATION NOTICE (series).

HE 20.9120:v.nos./nos. • **Item 532-G (P) (EL)**
OPENING DOORS.

HE 20.9121: • **Item 532-E-25**
PHPC (Public Housing Primary Care Program) BULLETIN. [Quarterly]

HE 20.9122: • **Item 532-E-26**
EVALUATION BULLETIN (series).

MATERNAL AND CHILD HEALTH BUREAU
(1988–   )

CREATION AND AUTHORITY

> In 1983 the Health Maintenance Organizations and Resources Development Bureau was established in the Health Resources and Services Administration. In 1986 the name was changed to Bureau of Resources Development. The name was change again in 1988 to Maternal and Child Health and Resources Development Bureau. Name changed to Maternal and Child Health Bureau.

INFORMATION

> Information Officer
> Maternal and Child Health Bureau
> Health Resources and
>   Services Administration
> 18-05 Parklawn Bldg.
> 5600 Fishers Ln.
> Rockville, MD 20857
> (301) 443-2170
> Fax: (301) 443-1797
> http://www.mchb.hrsa.gov

HE 20.9201:date • **Item 486-A-10 (MF)**
ANNUAL REPORT.

HE 20.9202:CT • **Item 486-A-6**
GENERAL PUBLICATIONS. [Irregular]

HE 20.9203/2:CT • **Item 486-A-11**
INFORMATION BULLETIN, YOUTH 2000 (series). [Irregular]

> PURPOSE:– To deal with miscellaneous issues that will affect American youth as we move toward the 21st century.
> Discontinued.

HE 20.9208:CT • **Item 486-A-7**
HANDBOOKS, MANUALS, GUIDES. [Irregular]

HE 20.9209:date • **Item 486-A-8 (MF)**
DIRECTORY OF FACILITIES OBLIGATED TO PROVIDE UNCOMPENSATED SERVICES BY STATE AND CITY. [Annual]

> Lists health care facilities obligated to give uncompensated services under Titles VI and XVI of the Public Health Service Act. Data include type of facility, type of control (such as private nonprofit, city-county), and expiration date of uncompensated service obligation.

HE 20.9210:CT • **Item 486-A-9 (MF)**
BIBLIOGRAPHIES AND LISTS OF PUBLICATIONS. [Irregular]

HE 20.9211:date • **Item 532-E-19 (MF)**
ABSTRACTS OF ACTIVE PROJECTS. [Annual]

HE 20.9212:v.nos./nos. • **Item 486-A-12 (EL)**
EMSC (Emergency Medical Services for Children) NEWS. [Quarterly]

HE 20.9213:date • **Item 486-A-13**
CHILD HEALTH USA. [Annual]

HE 20.9214 • **Item 486-A-14 (E)**
ELECTRONIC PRODUCTS. (Misc.)

HE 20.9215 • **Item 486-A-14 (EL)**
TITLE V TODAY.

HE 20.9316: • **Item 507-J-17**
NPDP (National Practitioner Data Bank) NEWS. [Irregular].
> Cooperative Publication.

HEALTH PROFESSIONS BUREAU
(1983–   )

CREATION AND AUTHORITY

> The Bureu of Health Professions was transferred from the Health Resources Administration (HE 20.6600) in 1983.

INFORMATION
> Information Officer
> Bureau of Health Professions
> 5600 Fishers Lane
> Rockville, Maryland 20857
> (301) 443-2060
> Fax: (301) 443-0463
> http://www.bhpr.hrsa.gov

HE 20.9301:date
ANNUAL REPORT.

HE 20.9302:CT • **Item 507-J-1**
GENERAL PUBLICATIONS. [Irregular]
> Earlier HE 20.6602

HE 20.9308:CT • **Item 507-J-5**
HANDBOOKS, MANUALS, GUIDES. [Irregular]

HE 20.9309:CT • **Item 507-J-2 (MF)**
BIBLIOGRAPHIES AND LISTS OF PUBLICATIONS. [Irregular]
> Earlier HE 20.6609

HE 20.9309/2:date • **Item 507-J-2**
CURRENT PUBLICATIONS, DIVISION OF MEDICINE. [Annual]
> Earlier HE 20.9309:C 98

HE 20.9310:date • **Item 507-J-12 (MF)**
REPORT TO THE PRESIDENT AND CONGRESS, ON THE STATUS OF HEALTH PERSONNEL IN THE UNITED STATES. [Biennial]
> PURPOSE:– To present data in narrative, tables, and graphs on the status of the supply of physicians, dentists, optometrists, pharmacists, podiatrists, and veterinarians.
> Earlier HE 20.6619

HE 20.9311:date
QUARTERLY DEBT MANAGEMENT REPORT.

HE 20.9312:date • **Item 507-J-13 (MF)**
DIRECTORY OF AWARDS, BHPR SUPPORT. [Annual]

> Tables list awards by region, state, city, institution, and grant number.

HE 20.9313:date • **Item 507-J-14 (MF)**
TRENDS IN HOSPITAL PERSONNEL. [Irregular]

> Presents trends in U.S. hospital personnel for the past three years, based on the American Hospital Association annual surveys. Tables show total and full-time-equivalent hospital personnel in more than 5 occupations by state and region.

HE 20.9314: • **Item 507-J-15 (MF)**
MINORITIES AND WOMEN IN UNDERGRADUATE EDUCATION, GEOGRAPHIC DISTRIBUTIONS FOR ACADEMIC YEAR. [Annual]

> PURPOSE– To present data that highlight the distribution of total undergraduate enrollment by race/ethnicity and gender, and by state in which the institutions of higher education are located.

HE 20.9315 • **Item 507-J-16**
HEALTH WORKFORCE NEWSLINK. [Quarterly]

HE 20.9317 • **Item 507-J-19 (EL)**
HSRA STATE HEALTH WORKFORCE PROFILES.

HE 20.9317/2 • **Item 507-J-20 (EL)**
HRSA STATE HEALTHFORCE PROFILES. (database w/50 states)

INDIAN HEALTH SERVICE
(1983– 1991)

CREATION AND AUTHORITY

The Indian Health Service (HE 20.5300) was transferred from the Health Services Administration in 1983.

HE 20.9401:date
ANNUAL REPORT.

Earlier HE 20.5301

HE 20.9402:CT   • Item 486-I-2
GENERAL PUBLICATIONS.

Earlier HE 20.5302
Later HE 20.302

HE 20.9403/2:   • Item 486-W
TRIBAL ACTIVITIES BULLETIN. [Bimonthly]

Reports on IHS activities directed toward promoting the health and safety of American Indians.
No longer a depository item. For internal/administrative use only,under 44 U.S.C. section 1902.
Official Use Only.

HE 20.9408:CT   • Item 486-K-1
HANDBOOKS, MANUALS, GUIDES. [Irregular]

Earlier HE 20.5308
Later HE 20.308

HE 20.9409:date   • Item 486-I-5
CHART SERIES BOOK. [Annual]

Tables and charts include data on health status, demography, and patient care of American Indians and Alaska Natives.
Discontinued.

HE 20.9410:date   • Item 486-I-4 (MF)
PHARMACY BRANCH: ANNUAL REPORT.
Discontinued.

HE 20.9411   • Item 486-L
BIBLIOGRAPHIES AND LISTS OF PUBLICATIONS.
See HE 20.309

HE 20.9412:CT   • Item 486-M
DIRECTORIES. [Irregular]
See HE 20.310

HE 20.9412/2:date   • Item 486-M
INDIAN HEALTH SERVICE DIRECTORY. [Semiannual]

Later HE 20.310/2

HE 20.9413:date   • Item 486-F-1 (MF)
NAVAJO AREA INDIAN HEALTH SERVICE, OFFICE OF ENVIRONMENTAL HEALTH AND ENGINEERING, ANNUAL REPORT (fiscal year).

Summarizes Office activities in providing for the health of the Navajo Indians.
Earlier HE 20.5301/2

HE 20.9414:date   • Item 486-N (MF)
ANNUAL REPORT TO CONGRESS, INDIAN CIVIL SERVICE RETIREMENT ACT, PL 96-135.

HE 20.9415:CT   • Item 486-P
POSTERS. [Irregular]
Earlier A 21.7/4
See HE 20.312

HE 20.9416:date   • Item 486-R (MF)
STATUS REPORT OF THE OPERATION AND MAINTENANCE OF SANITATION FACILITIES SERVING AMERICAN INDIANS AND ALASKA NATIVES. [Annual]
Discontinued.

HE 20.9417:date   • Item 486-T (MF)
TRENDS IN UTILIZATION OF INDIAN HEALTH SERVICE AND CONTRACT HOSPITALS. [Annual]

PURPOSE– To summarize and analyze inpatient utilization of IHS direct and contract hospitals. Compares current data to that of five years ago and to five years before that and examines the trend over the 10 year period.

HE 20.9418:date   • Item 486-S
INDIAN HEALTH SERVICE SCHOLARSHIP PROGRAM: APPLICANT INFORMATION INSTRUCTION BOOKLET. [Annual]

Later HE 20.317

HE 20.9418/2:date   • Item 486-S
INDIAN HEALTH SERVICE SCHOLARSHIP PROGRAM STUDENT HANDBOOK. [Annual]

HE 20.9419:   • Item 486-P-1
MAPS.

Includes miscellaneous maps on various topics pertaining to the work of the Service.
See HE 20.311

HE 20.9420:CT   • Item 486-P-2
FORMS.
See HE 20.313

HE 20.9421:date   • Item 486-I-3
TRENDS IN INDIAN HEALTH. [Annual]

Later HE 20.316

HE 20.9422:date   • Item 486-T
INDIAN HEALTH SERVICE REGIONAL DIFFERENCES IN INDIAN HEALTH. [Annual]
See HE 20.319

HE 20.9423:v.nos./nos.   • Item 486-S
THE IHS PRIMARY CARE PROVIDER. [Monthly]
See HE 20.320

HIV/AIDS BUREAU

HE 20.9502:CT   • Item 507-K-1
GENERAL PUBLICATIONS.

HE 20.9508:   • Item 507-K-3
HANDBOOKS, MANUALS, GUIDES.

HE 20.9515:nos.   • Item 507-K-2
HIV/AIDS EVALUATION MONOGRAPH SERIES.

HE 20.9516   • Item 507-K-4 (EL)
HRSA CARE ACTION. (Monthly)

OFFICE OF CHILD DEVELOPMENT
(1970– 1975)

HE 21.1:date
ANNUAL REPORT.
Later HE 1.401

HE 21.2:CT   • Item 454-C-1
GENERAL PUBLICATIONS.
Later HE 1.402

HE 21.8:CT   • Item 454-C-4
HANDBOOKS, MANUALS, GUIDES.
Later HE 1.408
Inactive.

HE 21.8/2   • Item 445-L
MANUALS (numbered)

Earlier FS 1.36/2

HE 21.9:v.nos.&nos.   • Item 449
CHILDREN. [6 times a year with separate volume index]

Sub-title: An Interdisciplinary Journal for the Professions Serving Children.
PURPOSE:– To improve the quality and extend the availability of care given to children by professional health and welfare personnel. It provides a means of communication between them on the needs of children, on methods of meeting these needs, and on successes and failures in the applications of programs and techniques of care.

Contains signed articles. Annotated bibliography of new guides and reports included in some issues, as well as new government publications for professional workers in all issues.
Index issued separately.
Issued by Children's Bureau, Social and Rehabilitation Service, prior to v. 16, no. 6.
Earlier FS 17.209

HE 21.9/2:v.nos.&nos.   • Item 449
CHILDREN TODAY. 1972–   [Bimonthly]

PURPOSE:– To tell about Federal, State, and local services for children, child development, health and welfare laws, and other news pertinent to child welfare in the United States.
Indexed by: Guide to U.S. Government Periodicals
Supersedes Children (HE 21.9).

HE 21.10:date   • Item 454-C-2
PUBLICATIONS OF OFFICE OF CHILD DEVELOPMENT.
Discontinued.

HE 21.11:nos.   • Item 454-C-3
DAY CARE USA [publications]. 1–

HE 21.12:date   • Item 454-C-5
ANNUAL REPORT OF THE DEPARTMENT OF HEALTH, EDUCATION, AND WELFARE TO CONGRESS ON SERVICES PROVIDED TO HANDICAPPED CHILDREN IN PROJECT HEAD START. 1st–   1973–
Later HE 1.409

CHILDREN'S BUREAU
(1970– 1975)

HE 21.101:date
ANNUAL REPORT.
Later HE 1.451

HE 21.102:CT   • Item 452
GENERAL PUBLICATIONS.
Earlier FS 17.202, FS 14.102
Later HE 1.452

HE 21.108:CT   • Item 452-C
HANDBOOKS, MANUALS, GUIDES. [Irregular]
Later HE 1.458

HE 21.109:   • Item 454-B
YOUTH REPORTS. 1–   1970–   [Irregular]

PURPOSE:– To present a qualitative analysis of the opinions of high school youth on a variety of current topics. These studies are designed to deepen the understanding of this age group, and to make its opinions, values, goals, etc. available to the various government and voluntary agencies which deal with youth.
The opinion studies represent those of a limited but important segment of youth: urban and suburban high school students enrolled in college preparatory courses.
Discontinued.

HE 21.110:nos.   • **Item 453**
PUBLICATIONS (numbered). 1–   1912–   [Irregular]

More permanent studies and information are contained in this series, including the popular Infant Care and Prenatal Care publications.
Earlier FS 17.210
Discontinued.

HE 21.111:nos.   • **Item 451**
FOLDERS. 1–   1923–   [Irregular]

Small-sized pamphlets, ranging in length from 12 to 62 pages, written in a popular style and intended for wide distribution. Covers various diseases and defects of children, homemaker services, adoption, etc.
Earlier FS 17.215
Discontinued.

HE 21.112:nos.   • **Item 453-A**
RESEARCH RELATING TO CHILDREN, BULLETINS (numbered). 1–   1950–   [Irregular]

Each issue covers a particular subject, listing all research projects which have been reported to the Children's Bureau Clearinghouse for Research in Child Life since 1948. Abstracts of most of the projects listed were included in the Clearinghouse publication, Research Relating to Children.
Earlier FS 17.211, FS 14.114

HE 21.113:CT   • **Item 450**
BIBLIOGRAPHIES AND LISTS OF PUBLICATIONS.
Earlier FS 17.212
Discontinued.

HE 21.114:nos   • **Item 452-B**
HEADLINER SERIES
Earlier FS 17.216
Discontinued.

HE 21.115:date
ADVOCACY FOR CHILDREN

BUREAU OF HEAD START AND CHILD SERVICE PROGRAMS (1970–1977)

HE 21.201:date
ANNUAL REPORT.

HE 21.202:CT   • **Item 445-N-2**
GENERAL PUBLICATIONS.

HE 21.208:CT   • **Item 445-N-1**
HANDBOOKS, MANUALS, GUIDES.
Later HE 1.4687

HE 21.208/2:nos. or CT   • **Item 445-N-1**
HEALTHY THAT'S ME, PARENTS' HANDBOOKS. 1–   1971–   [Irregular]
Issued in comic book form.

HE 21.209:v.nosl&nos.
HEAD START NEWSLETTER. v. 1–   1965–   [Irregular]

ISSN 0017-8721
Earlier PrEx 10.12/2
Later HE 23.1014

HE 21.210:nos.   • **Item 445-N-3**
CARING FOR CHILDREN (series).
Discontinued.

HE 21.211:CT   • **Item 445-N-4**
BIBLIOGRAPHIES AND LISTS OF PUBLICATIONS.
Discontinued.

HE 21.212:nos.-letters   • **Item 857-H-12**
PROJECT HEAD START (series). 1–   1965–   [Irregular]
PURPOSE:– To provide the basic program component booklets for Head Start. Contains information on career development, medical and dental services, nutrition, volunteers, parents, daily activities, the psychologist, and equipment.
Earlier PrEx 10.12, FS 1.36

HE 21.213:CT
POSTERS.

HEALTH CARE FINANCING ADMINISTRATION (1977–   )

CREATION AND AUTHORITY

The Health Care Financing Administration was established within the Department of Health, Education, and Welfare by the Secretary's reorganization of March 8, 1977.

INFORMATION

Health Care Financing Administration
Department of Health and Human Services
200 Independence Avenue, S.W.
Washington, D. C. 20201
(410) 786-7843
http://www.ncfa.gov

HE 22.1:date
ANNUAL REPORT.

HE 22.2:CT   • **Item 512-A-1**
GENERAL PUBLICATIONS.
Earlier HE 17.2

HE 22.3:v.nos.&nos.   • **Item 532-A-13.**
RECORD. v. 1–   1977–   [Monthly]

Indexed by: Index to U.S. Government Periodicals.
Supersedes Social and Rehabilitation record (HE 17.27).
Continued by Forum (HE 22.10).

HE 22.8:CT   • **Item 512-A-3**
HANDBOOKS, MANUALS, GUIDES. [Irregular]
Earlier HE 17.8

HE 22.8/2:nos.   • **Item 512-A-21**
MEDICARE HOSPITAL MANUAL. [Irregular]
Din paper.

HE 22.8/2-2:   • **Item 512-A-21**
MEDICARE CHRISTIAN SCIENCE SANATORIUM HOSPITAL MANUAL SUPPLEMENT.
Din paper.

HE 22.8/3:nos.   • **Item 512-A-23**
MEDICARE SKILLED NURSING FACILITY MANUAL. [Annual]
Din paper.

PURPOSE:– To provide guidelines for skilled nursing facilities on procedures for payment, admission, billing, etc., under the Health Insurance of the Aged Act of 1965, as amended.

HE 22.8/4:nos.   • **Item 512-A-22**
MEDICARE PROVIDER REIMBURSEMENT MANUAL. [Annual]
Din paper.

PURPOSE:– To provide guidelines for implementing Medicare regulations on determining reasonable cost of provider services furnished under the Health Insurance for the Aged Act of 1965, as amended.

HE 22.8/5:nos.   • **Item 512-A-25**
MEDICARE HOME HEALTH AGENCY MANUAL. [Irregular]
Din paper.

PURPOSE:– To provide procedures on Home Health services for the aged, including coverage, start of care, and billing.
Consists of a basic manual and updating supplements.

HE 22.8/6:nos.   • **Item 512-A-25**
MEDICARE INTERMEDIARY MANUAL, PART 3, CLAIMS PROCESS.
Din paper.

HE 22.8/6-2:date   • **Item 512-A-25**
MEDICARE INTERMEDIARY MANUAL, PART 2, AUDITS-REIMBURSEMENT PROGRAM ADMINISTRATION.
Din paper.

HE 22.8/6-3:date   • **Item 512-A-25**
MEDICARE PART A INTERMEDIARY MANUAL, PART 1, FISCAL ADMINISTRATION.
Din paper.

HE 22.8/6-4:date   • **Item 512-A-25**
MEDICARE PART A INTERMEDIARY MANUAL, PART 4, AUDIT PROCEDURES.
Din paper.

HE 22.8/6-5:nos.   • **Item 512-A-25**
PROGRAM MEMORANDUM INTERMEDIARIES/CARRIERS. [Irregular]
Din paper.
Former title: Medicare Intermediary Letters.

HE 22.8/7:nos.   • **Item 512-A-25**
MEDICARE CARRIERS MANUAL, PART 3, CLAIMS PROCESS.
Din paper.

HE 22.8/7-2:date   • **Item 512-A-25**
MEDICARE CARRIERS MANUAL, PART 1, FISCAL ADMINISTRATION.
Din paper.

HE 22.8/7-3:date   • **Item 512-A-25**
MEDICARE CARRIERS MANUAL, PART 2, PROGRAM ADMINISTRATION.
Din paper.

HE 22.8/7-4   • **Item 512-A-25**
MEDICARE CARRIERS MANUAL, PART 4, PROFESSIONAL RELATIONS.
Din paper.

HE 22.8/7-5:nos.   • **Item 512-A-25**
MEDICARE CARRIER QUALITY ASSURANCE HANDBOOK.
Din paper.

HE 22.8/8:date   • **Item 512-A-25**
HCFA REGIONAL OFFICE MANUAL.
Din paper.

HE 22.8/8:date   • **Item 512-A-25**
PART 2, MEDICAID.

HE 22.8/8-2:date   • **Item 512-A-25**
PART 3, PROGRAM INTEGRITY. (HCFA Pub. 23-3)
Din paper.

HE 22.8/8-3:date   • **Item 512-A-25**
PART 4, STANDARDS AND CERTIFICATION GUIDELINES. (HCFA Pub. 23-4)
Din paper.

HE 22.8/8-4:date   • **Item 512-A-25**
PART 6, MEDICADE. (HCFA Pub. 23-6)

HE 22.8/8-5:date   • **Item 512-A-25**
PART 1, GENERAL. (HCFA Pub. 23-1)
Din paper.

HE 22.8/9:nos.   • **Item 512-A-22**
MEDICARE OUTPATIENT PHYSICAL THERAPY AND COMPREHENSIVE OUTPATIENT REHABILITATION FACILITY MANUAL. [Irregular]
Din paper.

Earlier titled: Medicare Outpatient Physical Therapy Provider Manual.

HE 22.8/10:date • Item 512-A-22
STATE MEDICAID MANUAL.
Din paper.

HE 22.8/11:date • Item 512-A-23
STATE BUY-IN MANUAL. (HCFA Pub. 24) [Irregular]
Din paper.

HE 22.8/12:date • Item 512-A-22
MEDICARE, MEDICAID, STATE OPERATIONS MANUAL, PROVIDER CERTIFICATION. (HCFA Pub. 7)
Din paper.

HE 22.8/13:date • Item 512-A-21
MEDICARE RENAL DIALYSIS FACILITY MANUAL.
Din paper.

HE 22.8/14:nos. • Item 512-A-21
MEDICARE COVERAGE ISSUES MANUAL. (HCFA Pub. 6) [Irregular]
Din paper.

HE 22.8/15:date • Item 512-A-21
MEDICARE PEER REVIEW ORGANIZATIONAL MANUAL.
Din paper.

HE 22.8/16:date • Item 512-A-39 (P) (EL)
YOUR MEDICARE HANDBOOK. [Annual]

Explains Medicare, hospital insurance, and medical insurance to Medicare recipients.
Earlier HE 22.8:M 46/4/

HE 22.8/17:date • Item 512-A-3
GUIDE TO HEALTH INSURANCE FOR PEOPLE WITH MEDICARE. [Annual]

HE 22.8/18 • Item 512-A-21
MEDICARE HOSPICE MANUAL.
Din paper.

HE 22.8/19:date • Item 512-A-21
MEDICARE RURAL HEALTH CLINIC MANUAL.

HE 22.8/20:date • Item 512-A-48 (MF)
EXECUTIVE/MANAGEMENT TRAINING HAND-BOOK. [Annual]
Din paper.

This handbook provides HCFA managers and executives with a summary of the FY programs that will be centrally funded. The handbooks provide advance information for planning purposes.

HE 22.8/21:date • Item 512-A-3
MEDICARE HEALTH MAINTENANCE ORGANIZATION/COMPETITIVE MEDICAL PLAN MANUAL.
Din paper.

HE 22.8/22:date • Item 444-P-3 (E)
HCFA'S LAWS, REGULATIONS, MANUALS. [Monthly]
See HE 22.8/23
Issued on CD-ROM.

HE 22.8/23 • Item 444-P-3 (EL)
MEDICARE AND MEDICAID PROGRAM MANUALS, TRANSMITTALS AND PROGRAM MEMOS.

HE 22.9:CT • Item 512-A-5 (MF)
END-STAGE RENAL DISEASE MEDICAL INFORMATION SYSTEM FACILITY REPORTS. [Irregular]

HE 22.9/2:date • Item 512-A-5 (MF)
END-STAGE RENAL DISEASE PROGRAM, ANNUAL REPORT TO CONGRESS.
Discontinued.

HE 22.9/3:date • Item 512-A-5
END-STAGE RENAL DISEASE PROGRAM MEDICAL INFORMATION SYSTEM, FACILITY SURVEY TABLES (year). [Annual]

HE 22.9/4:date • Item 512-A-5
END-STAGE RENAL DISEASE PROGRAM INSTRUCTION MANUAL FOR RENAL PROVIDERS. [Biennial]

HE 22.10:v.nos.&nos. • Item 532-A-13
FORUM. v. 1–5. – 1981. [Monthly]
Continues Record (HE 22.3).
Discontinued October 1981.

HE 22.11:CT • Item 512-A-6
HEALTH INSURANCE STUDIES: CONTRACT RESEARCH SERIES. [Irregular]

PURPOSE:– To present reports of studies done by contractors on various matters related to health insurance.
Discontinued.

HE 22.12:date • Item 512-D-2
STATE TABLES FISCAL YEAR (date), MEDICAID: RECIPIENTS, PAYMENTS AND SERVICES. [Annual]

Formed by the union of Numbers of Recipients and Amounts of Payments under Medicaid and Other Medical Programs Financed from Public Assistance Funds (HE 17.617/3) [ISSN 0091-5920] and Medicaid Recipient Characteristics and Units of Selected Medical Service [ISSN 0098-3616].

HE 22.12/2:date • Item 512-D-2
MEDICAID SERVICES STATE BY STATE. [Annual]

HE 22.12/3:date • Item 512-C-3
NATIONAL SUMMARY OF STATE MEDICAID MANAGED CARE PROGRAMS, PROGRAM DESCRIPTIONS.

HE 22.13:date • Item 512-D-4
MEDICAID STATISTICS. [Monthly] (Medicaid Report B-1)

PURPOSE:– To present summaries of data reported, by State agencies receiving grants- in- aid for medical assistance under Title XIX of the Social Security Act, of the number of people who received medical assistance and the amount of payments to medical vendors or to health-insuring agencies.
Earlier HE 22.110
Discontinued.

HE 22.13/2 • Item 512-A-62 (EL)
MEDICAID MANAGED CARE ENROLLMENT REPORT. [Annual]

HE 22.14:date • Item 512-A-8
HCFA COMMUNICATIONS DIRECTORY.

Former Title: HCFA Telephone Directory.
Discontinued.

HE 22.15 • Item 512-A-24 (MF)
HEALTH CARE FINANCING ADMINISTRATION RULINGS ON MEDICARE, MEDICAID, PROFESSIONAL STANDARDS REVIEW AND RELATED MATTERS. [Irregular]
Discontinued.

PURPOSE:– To provide rulings relating to the Medicare, Medicaid, Professional Standards Review Organizations and other programs under the jurisdiction of the Administration.
Former title: Health Care Financing Administration Rulings.

HE 22.16:nos. • Item 512-A-9
HEALTH CARE FINANCING RESEARCH AND DEMONSTRATION SERIES. 1– [Irregular]

PURPOSE:– To provide highly technical reports of research and demonstration projects funded by the Administration, including studies on health care administration, finance, costs, etc., intended to enable the Administration to develop standards for regulation of the industry.
Discontinued.

HE 22.16/2:date • Item 512-A-28 (MF)
RESEARCH AND DEMONSTRATIONS IN HEALTH CARE FINANCING. [Biennial]

Presents information on health care financing research and demonstrations conducted at various health care organizations throughout the country.

HE 22.17:date/nos.
RESEARCH AND STATISTICS NOTES.

HE 22.18:v.nos.&nos. • Item 512-A-10
HEALTH CARE FINANCING REVIEW. [Quarterly]
See HE 22.512

HE 22.18/a • Item 512-A-10
– SEPARATES.
See HE 22.512/2A

HE 22.18/2: • Item 512-A-10
HEALTH CARE FINANCING REVIEW ANNUAL SUPPLEMENT.
See HE 22.512/2

HE 22.19:CT • Item 512-A-11 (MF)
HEALTH CARE FINANCING, GRANTS AND CONTRACTS REPORTS. [Irregular]

PURPOSE:– To provide final reports of selected extra-mural research, demonstration, and evaluation projects supported by the Administration in the areas pertaining to health services finance, organization, and delivery.
Discontinued.

HE 22.19 • Item 512-A-11 (MF)
HEALTH CARE FINANCING EXTRAMURAL REPORTS (series). [Irregular]

HE 22.19/2:CT • Item 512-A-12 (MF)
HEALTH CARE FINANCING, RESEARCH REPORTS. [Irregular]

PURPOSE:– To provide reports of major studies, or research conducted by the staff of the Administration. Topics include health care financing, policy, planning, etc.

HE 22.19/3:date • Item 512-A-13 (MF)
HEALTH CARE FINANCING: GRANTS FOR RESEARCH AND DEMONSTRATIONS, FISCAL YEAR. [Annual]

PURPOSE:– To describe the grant program, types of grants considered, priority areas of interest, criteria for funding new projects, grant review process and grant application procedures.
Discontinued.

HE 22.19/4:CT • Item 512-A-14 (MF)
HEALTH CARE FINANCING NOTES. [Irregular]

PURPOSE:– To provide the public, as soon as it becomes available, with program data or information concerning health care financing. Mainly statistical tables with narrative summaries.
Discontinued.

HE 22.19/4-2:CT • Item 512-A-14 (MF)
HEALTH CARE FINANCING PROGRAM STATISTICS.
Discontinued December 1978.

HE 22.19/4-3:date • Item 512-A-14
HEALTH CARE FINANCING PROGRAM STATISTICS, MEDICARE AND MEDICAID DATA BOOK. [Annual]

Discontinued with the 1991 issue. Information contained in this publication appears in the HCFA Review (HE 22.18).
Earlier HE 22.19/4-2:D 26

HE 22.19/4-4:date • Item 512-A-14 (MF)
HEALTH CARE FINANCING PROGRAM STATISTICS, ANALYSIS OF STATE MEDICAID PROGRAM CHARACTERISTICS. [Annual]
Discontinued.

HE 22.19/5:CT • Item 512-A-18
HEALTH CARE FINANCING (series). [Irregular]

Each issue contains narrative and tables on a different area of health care financing such as Medicare patients 65 years and over.

HE 22.19/6:CT • Item 512-A-20 (MF)
HEALTH CARE FINANCING CONFERENCE PROCEEDINGS. [Irregular]

HE 22.19/7:CT
HEALTH CARE FINANCING MONOGRAPHS. [Irregular]

HE 22.19/8:CT • **Item 512-A-1**
HEALTH CARE FINANCING ISSUES, HMO- (series).
[Irregular]

HE 22.19/9:CT • **Item 512-A-37 (MF)**
HEALTH CARE FINANCING, EXTRAMURAL REPORT
(series).

HE 22.19/10: • **Item 512-A-40 (MF)**
HEALTH CARE FINANCING SPECIAL REPORT
(series).

HE 22.20:v.nos.&nos. • **Item 512-A-15**
HEALTH CARE FINANCING TRENDS. v. 1–   1979–
[Quarterly] (Children, Youth and Families Admin-
istration)

Contains tables and analyses highlighting economic developments in the health care sector.
Data are presented on national health expenditures; community hospitals statistics; consumer
price indexes; employment, hours, and earnings
of health workers; and a variety of national economic indicators.
Discontinued.

HE 22.21:date • **Item 512-A-16 (MF)**
MEDICARE ANNUAL REPORT.

Summarizes Administration activities in ex-
ecuting the Medicare program, which includes
payment of hospital and medical insurance benefits, claims processing, program funding, and
monitoring the performance of Medicare contractors.

HE 22.21/2:date • **Item 512-A-35**
MEDICARE PROGRAM STATISTICS. [Annual]

Tables present Medicare enrollment, reimbursement, and utilization statistics, by age, race,
sex, and area of residence.
Discontinued.

HE 22.21/2-2: • **Item 512-A-35**
MEDICARE PROGRAM STATISTICS, MEDICARE UTI-
LIZATION. [Annual]
Discontinued.

HE 22.21/3:date • **Item 512-A-38 (MF)**
IMPACT OF THE MEDICARE HOSPITAL PROSPEC-
TIVE PAYMENT SYSTEM, REPORT TO
CONGRESS. [Annual]
Discontinued.

HE 22.21/4 • **Item 512-A-58 (MF)**
INFLUENZA IMMUNIZATIONS PAID FOR BY MEDI-
CARE. [Annual]

HE 22.21/5 • **Item 512-A-60 (EL)**
MEDICARE HOSPICE BENEFITS. [Annual]

HE 22.22:CT • **Item 512-A-19 (MF)**
BIBLIOGRAPHIES AND LISTS OF PUBLICATIONS.
[Irregular]

HE 22.22/2 • **Item 512-A-59 (MF)**
OFFICE OF RESEARCH AND DEMONSTRATIONS
PUBLICATIONS CATALOG. [Biennial]

HE 22.23:CT
AUDIOVISUAL MATERIALS.

HE 22.24:date • **Item 512-A-26**
DENTAL CARE CHARGES. [Semiannual]
Discontinued.

HE 22.25:date • **Item 512-A-27 (MF)**
NATIONAL LISTING OF PROVIDERS FURNISHING
KIDNEY DIALYSIS AND TRANSPLANT SERVICES.
[Annual]

Tables list suppliers of End Stage Renal Disease services and approved dialysis stations by
service type and facility location. Approved ESRD
facilities are listed in State, city sequence.

HE 22.25/2:date • **Item 512-A-27 (MF)**
NATIONAL LISTING OF PROVIDERS FURNISHING
KIDNEY DIALYSIS AND TRANSPLANT SERVICES.
[Quarterly]

HE 22.26:nos. • **Item 512-A-29**
NATIONAL MEDICAL CARE UTILIZATION AND EX-
PENDITURE SURVEY, PRELIMINARY DATA RE-
PORTS (series). [Irregular]
Designed to collect data about the U.S. civil-
ian noninstitutionalized population and to produce
a data base to help analyze expenditures and
health services provided under the Medicaid and
Medicare programs.
Discontinued.

HE 22.26/2:nos. • **Item 512-A-29**
NATIONAL MEDICAL CARE UTILIZATION AND
EXPENDITURE SURVEY SERIES A, METHOD-
OLOGICAL REPORT. [Irregular]
Discontinued.

HE 22.26/3:nos. • **Item 512-A-29**
NATIONAL MEDICAL CARE UTILIZATION AND
EXPENDITURE SURVEY, SERIES B. [Irregular]
Discontinued.

HE 22.26/4:nos. • **Item 512-A-29**
NATIONAL MEDICAL CARE UTILIZATION AND
EXPENDITURE SURVEY, SERIES C. 1–   1986–
[Irregular]
Discontinued.

HE 22.27:CT • **Item 512-A-30**
POSTERS. [Irregular]

HE 22.28:nos. • **Item 512-A-22**
PROGRAM MEMORANDUM MEDICAID STATE AGEN-
CIES. [Irregular] (HCFA Pub. 17)

Former title: Medicaid Action Transmittals.
Din paper.

HE 22.28/2 • **Item 512-A-22**
PROGRAM MEMORANDUM HEALTH MAIN-TENANCE
ORGANIZATION/COMPETITIVE MEDICAL PLAN.
Din paper.

HE 22.28/3 • **Item 512-A-22**
PROGRAM MEMORANDUM QUALITY ASSURANCE.
Din paper.

HE 22.28/4 • **Item 512-A-22**
PROGRAM MEMORANDUM STATE SURVEY AGEN-
CIES.
Din paper.

HE 22.29:date • **Item 512-A-31**
MEDICARE DIRECTORY OF PREVAILING CHARGES.
[Annual]

Tabular presentation by states of prevailing
physician charges submitted to Medicare.
Earlier HE 22.2:C 37/2

HE 22.29/2:CT • **Item 512-A-31**
DIRECTORIES. [Irregular]

HE 22.30:date • **Item 512-A-33 (MF)**
BUDGET AND LEGISLATIVE PROGRAM, FISCAL
YEAR (date). [Annual]

HE 22.30/2:date • **Item 512-A-33**
JUSTIFICATION OF BUDGET AND LEGISLATIVE
PROGRAM FOR OFFICE OF MANAGEMENT AND
BUDGET. [Annual]

Earlier HE 22.30/2

HE 22.31:date • **Item 512-A-34 (MF)**
SOLICITATION OF THE PUBLIC HEALTH SERVICE
AND THE HEALTH CARE FINANCING
ADMINISTRATION FOR SMALL BUSINESS
INNOVATION RESEARCH CONTRACT
PROPOSALS. [Annual]
Discontinued.

HE 22.32:nos. • **Item 512-A-32**
FORMS. [Irregular]

HE 22.32/2 • **Item 512-A-32 (MF)**
HCFA FORMS INFORMATION CATALOG. [Annual]

HE 22.33:date • **Item 512-A-36**
JUSTIFICATIONS OF APPROPRIATION ESTIMATES
FOR COMMITTEE ON APPROPRIATIONS.
[Annual]

Justifications of appropriation estimates for
the Committee on Appropriations in the areas of
grants to States for Medicaid, payments to health
care trust funds, and program management.

HE 22.34: • **Item 512-A-41 (MF)**
MEDICARE HOSPITAL INFORMATION REPORT. [An-
nual]

Earlier title: Medicare Mortality Information.

HE 22.34:v. 1 • **Item 512-A-41**
– VOL. 1, ALABAMA - CALIFORNIA. [Annual]

Presents narrative and tabular information on Medicare hospital mortality for Alabama, Alaska, Arizona, Arkansas, and California.

HE 22.34:v. 2 • **Item 512-A-42**
– VOL. 2, COLORADO - ILLINOIS. [Annual]

Presents narrative and tabular information on Medicare hospital mortality for Colorado, Connecticut, Delaware, District of Columbia, Florida, Georgia, Hawaii, Idaho, and
Illinois.

HE 22.34:v. 3 • **Item 512-A-43**
– VOL. 3, INDIANA - MARYLAND. [Annual]

Presents narrative and tabular information on Medicare hospital mortality for Indiana, Iowa, Kansas, Kentucky, Louisiana,
Maine, and Maryland.
Cancelled.

HE 22.34:v. 4 • **Item 512-A-44**
– VOL. 4, MASSACHUSETTS - NEVADA. [Annual]

Presents narrative and tabular information on Medicare hospital mortality for Massachusetts, Michigan, Minnesota, Mississippi,
Missouri, Montana, Nebraska, and Nevada.
Cancelled.

HE 22.34:v. 5 • **Item 512-A-45**
– VOL. 5, NEW HAMPSHIRE - OHIO. [Annual]

Presents narrative and tabular informa-
tion on Medicare hospital mortality for New
Hampshire, New Jersey, New Mexico, New
York, North Carolina, North Dakota, and Ohio.
Cancelled

HE 22.34:v. 6 • **Item 512-A-46**
– VOL. 6, OKLAHOMA - TENNESSEE. [Annual]

Presents narrative and tabular information on Medicare hospital mortality for Oklahoma, Oregon, Pennsylvania, Puerto Rico,
Rhode Island, South Carolina, South Dakota,
and Tennessee.
Cancelled.

HE 22.34:v. 7 • **Item 512-A-47**
– VOL. 7, TEXAS - GUAM. [Annual]

Presents narrative and tabular informa-
tion on Medicare hospital mortality for Texas,
Utah, Vermont, Virgin Islands, Virginia, Wash-
ington, West Virginia, Wisconsin, Wyoming,
American Samoa, and Guam.
Cancelled.

HE 22.35:CT/date • **Item 512-G-1– G-51**
MEDICARE/MEDICAID NURSING HOME INFORMA-
TION (State). [Annual]

The Health Care Financing Administration provides information to the public on nursing homes
in this set and focuses mainly on the Medicare/
Medicaid programs. The information in this set
provides a valuable source of background materials on federal and state enforcement programs.

HE 22.35/nos.:date • **Item 512-G-1– 51 (MF)**
MEDICARE/MEDICAID NURSING HOME INFOR-
MATION [State]. [Annual]

HE 22.36:trans. nos. • **Item 512-A-22**
MEDICARE/MEDICAID SANCTION, REINSTATEMENT REPORT. [Irregular]
Discontinued.

HE 22.37:date • **Item 512-A-24**
HCFA COMMON PROCEDURE CODING SYSTEM (HCPCS) (Non-CPT-4 Portion). [Annual]

HE 22.38 • **Item 512-A-24 (P) (EL)**
HCFA RULINGS.

HE 22.39 • **Item 512-A-8 (MF)**
EMPLOYEE TRAINING AND CAREER DEVELOPMENT CATALOG.
Discontinued.

HE 22.40:CT • **Item 512-A-24**
HCFA FACT SHEET (Series).

HE 22.41 • **Item 512-A-1**
THE INTERNATIONAL CLASSIFICATION OF DISEASES, 9TH REVISION, CLINICAL MODIFI CATION. [Annual]

Earlier HE 22.2:In 8/2

HE 22.41/2:date • **Item 444-P-4 (CD) (EL)**
ICD.9.CM INTERNATIONAL CLASSIFICATION OF DISEASES. [Annual]

HE 22.42:date • **Item 512-A-49 (MF)**
FINANCIAL REPORT. [Annual]

HE 22.43:v.nos./nos. • **Item 512-A-57 (EL)**
HCFA HEALTH WATCH.

HE 22.44: • **Item 512-A-60 (E)**
ELECTRONIC PRODUCTS (misc.).

HE 22.45: • **Item 512-E**
BRAILLE PUBLICATIONS.

CENTER FOR MEDICAID AND STATE OPERATIONS
(1977–   )

CREATION AND AUTHORITY

The Medicaid Bureau was established within the Health Care Financing Administration by Secretary's reorganization of March 8, 1977.
Name changed to Center for Medicaid and State Operations.

INFORMATION

Center for Medicaid and State Operations
Centers for Medicare and Medicaid Services
7500 Security Blvd.
Baltimore, MD 21244-1850
(410) 786-3870

HE 22.101:date
ANNUAL REPORT.

Earlier HE 17.501

HE 22.102:CT • **Item 512-C**
GENERAL PUBLICATIONS. [Irregular]

Earlier HE 17.502

HE 22.108:CT • **Item 512-C-1**
HANDBOOKS, MANUALS, GUIDES.

HE 22.109:v.nos.&nos. • **Item 532-E-4**
JOURNAL FOR MEDICAID MANAGEMENT. [Quarterly]

ISSN 0147-6726
Later HE 22.411

HE 22.109/2:date • **Item 499-H**
MEDICAID MANAGEMENT REPORTS. [Quarterly]

Later HE 22.410

HE 22.110:date • **Item 512-D-4**
MEDICAID DATA. (Medicaid Report B-1)

Supersedes Medical Assistance Financed under Title XIX of the Social Security Act (HE 17.616), published by the National Center for Social Statistics.
ISSN 0147-2623
Later HE 22.13

HE 22.111:CT • **Item 532-E-5 (MF)**
ADVANCED TRAINING FOR WORKERS IN THE EARLY AND PERIODIC SCREENING, DIAGNOSIS AND TREATMENT PROGRAM: PUBLICATIONS. [Irregular]
Discontinued.

HE 22.112:CT • **Item 532-E-6 (MF)**
INSTITUTE FOR MEDICAID MANAGEMENT: PUBLICATIONS. [Irregular]
Discontinued.

HE 22.113:date
PRICE INFORMATION FOR DRUG PRODUCTS, INVOICE LEVEL PRICES. [Monthly]

HE 22.114:CT • **Item 512-C-2**
DIRECTORIES.

HE 22.115 • **Item 512-C-2 (MF)**
MEDICAID STATISTICS, PROGRAM AND FINANCIAL STATISTICS, FISCAL YEAR.

HE 22.116: • **Item 512-C-3**
NATIONAL SUMMARY OF STATE MEDICAID MANAGED CARE PROGRAMS. [Annual]

CLINICAL STANDARDS AND QUALITY OFFICE
(1977–   )

CREATION AND AUTHORITY

Formerly Health Standards and Quality Bureau.

INFORMATION

Clinical Standards and Quality Office
Centers for Medicare and Medicaid Services
7500 Security Blvd.
Baltimore, MD 21244-1850
(410) 786-6841

HE 22.201:date
ANNUAL REPORT.

HE 22.202:CT • **Item 499-J-1**
GENERAL PUBLICATIONS. [Irregular]

HE 22.202:Ad 9 • **Item 499-J-1**
DIRECTORY OF ADULT DAY CARE CENTERS. 1980. 162 p. il.

HE 22.208:CT • **Item 512-A-7**
HANDBOOKS, MANUALS, GUIDES.

HE 22.209:nos.
LONG-TERM CARE INFORMATION SERIES.

HE 22.210:date • **Item 499-J-1 (MF)**
PROFESSIONAL STANDARDS REVIEW ORGANIZATION, ANNUAL REPORT. 1st–   1977–
Discontinued.

HE 22.211:CT • **Item 499-J-2 (MF)**
BIBLIOGRAPHIES AND LISTS OF PUBLICATIONS. [Irregular]

HE 22.212:date • **Item 499-J-3 (MF)**
NHSQIC ANNUAL BIBLIOGRAPHY. (National Health Standards and Quality Information Clearinghouse)

Lists document accessions related to the mandate of the Health Standards and Quality Bureau. Contains bibliographic listings with author and subject indexes.
Discontinued.

HE 22.213:nos./yr. • **Item 499-J-4**
MEDICARE/MEDICAID DIRECTORY OF MEDICAL FACILITIES. [Annual]

Directory with facilities listed by section, State and city. Contains a numerical index.
Discontinued.

HE 22.216 • **Item 499-J-F (MF)**
NATIONAL LISTING OF MEDICARE PROVIDERS FURNISHING KIDNEY DIALYSIS & TRANSPLANT SERVICES. [Annual]

BUREAU OF PROGRAM POLICY
(1979–   )

HE 22.301:date
ANNUAL REPORT.

HE 22.302:CT
GENERAL PUBLICATIONS. [Irregular]

HE 22.309:date • **Item 499-H-1**
PRICE INFORMATION FOR DRUG PRODUCTS, INVOICE LEVEL PRICES. [Monthly]

PURPOSE:– To provide technical listings of drug product information supplied to the Food and Drug Administration under the provisions of the Drug Listing Act. Contains tables of price information, discontinued products, new submissions, etc. Also lists trade names, forms, and prescription or over-the-counter status.
Discontinued with the December 1980 issue.

CENTER FOR MEDICARE MANAGEMENT
(1979–   )

CREATION AND AUTHORITY

Formerly Bureau of Program Operations.

INFORMATION

Center for Medicare Management
Centers for Medicare and Medicaid Services
7500 Security Blvd.
Baltimore, MD 21244-1850
(410) 786-4164

HE 22.401:date
ANNUAL REPORTS.

HE 22.402:CT • **Item 499-N-2**
GENERAL PUBLICATIONS.

HE 22.408:CT • **Item 499-N-1**
HANDBOOKS, MANUALS, GUIDES. [Irregular]

HE 22.409:nos.
MEDICAID MEDICARE EXCHANGE. [Irregular]
(Medicaid/Medicare Management Institute)

HE 22.410:date • **Item 499-H**
MEDICAID MANAGEMENT REPORTS. [Quarterly]
Earlier HE 22.109/2
Discontinued 1978/3.

HE 22.410/2:date • **Item 499-H (MF)**
MEDICAID MANAGEMENT REPORTS. [Annual]

Earlier HE 22.109/2

HE 22.411:date   • Item 532-E-4
PERSPECTIVES ON MEDICAID AND MEDICARE
MANAGEMENT. [Quarterly]

    Former title: Journal for Medicaid Manage-
ment.
      Earlier HE 22.109
      Discontinued.

HE 22.412:CT   • Item 499-A-1 (MF)
BIBLIOGRAPHIES AND LISTS OF PUBLICATIONS.
[Irregular]

HE 22.414   • Item 499-H
MEDICARE UNIQUE PHYSICIAN IDENTIFICATION
   NUMBER DIRECTORY.
   Discontinued.

HE 22.414/2   • Item 499-H-2 (P) (CD)
(HCFA) MEDICAR E UNIQUE PHYSICIAN IDENTIFI-
CATION NUMBER (Directory).

HE 22.415   • Item 499-H (MF)
CARRIER QUALITY ASSURANCE REPORT. [Annual]
   Discontinued.

STRATEGIC PLANNING OFFICE

CREATION AND AUTHORITY

    Formerly Data Managemnet and Strategy
Bureau.

HE 22.502:CT   • Item 499-S-1
GENERAL PUBLICATIONS.

HE 22.508:CT   • Item 499-S
HANDBOOKS, MANUALS, GUIDES.

HE 22.508/2   • Item 499-S (MF)
HEALTH CARE FINANCING ADMINISTRATION
   INFORMATION SYSTEMS DEVELOPMENT
   GUIDE.

HE 22.509:date   • Item 499-R
HCFA STATISTICS. [Annual]

HE 22.510:date   • Item 512-A-56
NATIONAL LISTING OF MEDICARE PROVIDERS
   FURNISHING KIDNEY DIALYSIS AND TRANS-
   PLANT SERVICES. [Annual]

HE 22.510/2:date   • Item 499-R-2 (MF)
NATIONAL LISTING OF RENAL PROVIDERS
   FURNISHING KIDNEY DIALYSIS AND TRANS-
   PLANT SERVICES. [Semiannual]

HE 22.511   • Item 499-R-1 (MF)
DATA COMPENDIUM.

HE 22.512:v.nos./nos.   • Item 512-A-10
HEALTH CARE FINANCING REVIEW. [Quarterly].

HE 22.512/2A   • Item 512-A-10
HEALTH CARE FINANCING REVIEW (Seperates).

HE 22.513:date   • Item 512-A-61 (P) (EL)
ACTIVE PROJECTS REPORTS. [Annual].

OFFICE OF INFORMATION SERVICES

INFORMATION

    Office of Information Services
    Centers for Medicare and Medicaid Services
    7500 Security Blvd.
    Baltimore, MD 21244-1850
    (410) 786-1800
    Fax: (410) 786-1810
    http://www.cms.gov/about/agency/fbb.asp

HE 22.602:CT   • Item 512-H-2
GENERAL PUBLICATIONS.

HE 22.615:CT   • Item 512-H-1 (E)
ELECTRONIC PRODUCTS.

HE 22.616:   • Item 512-H (P) (EL)
PUBLIC USE FILES CATALOG. [Annual]

OFFICE OF HUMAN DEVELOPMENT SERVICES (1977–   )

CREATION AND AUTHORITY

    The Office of Human Development (HE 1.700)
was redesignated the Office of Human Development Services by Secretary's reorganization order of July 26, 1977.

INFORMATION

    Office of Human Development Services
    Department of Health and Human Services
    Washington, D. C. 20201
    (202) 472-7257

HE 23.1:date   • Item 529-B-2 (MF)
ANNUAL REPORT.

HE 23.2:CT   • Item 529-B-6
GENERAL PUBLICATIONS. [Irregular]

    Earlier HE 1.702

HE 23.8:CT   • Item 529-B-7
HANDBOOKS, MANUALS, GUIDES. [Irregular]

HE 23.9:CT   • Item 529-B-5
BIBLIOGRAPHIES AND LISTS OF PUBLICATIONS.
[Irregular]

HE 23.10:date   • Item 529-A-1
HUMAN DEVELOPMENT NEWS. [Bimonthly]

    PURPOSE:– To provide news of the Office of
Human Development Services in its aim of working with State and local agencies to create caring
communities.
    Non-depository.

HE 23.11:date   • Item 529-A-2 (MF)
OHDS TELEPHONE DIRECTORY. [Quarterly]

HE 23.12:v.nos.&nos.   • Item 449
CHILDREN TODAY. [Bimonthly]
    Earlier HE 23.1209
    Discontinued.

HE 23.13:date   • Item 529-A-3 (MF)
OFFICE OF HUMAN DEVELOPMENT SERVICES BUD-
   GET REQUEST. [Annual]
   Discontinued.

PRESIDENT'S COMMITTEE ON MENTAL RETARDATION (1978–   )

INFORMATION

    President's Committee
      on Mental Retardation
    370 L'Enfant Promenade, SW, Ste. 701
    Washington, DC 20447-0001
    (202) 619-0634
    Fax: (202) 205-9519
    http://www.acf.dhhs.gov/programs/pcmr

HE 23.101:date   • Item 528-B-1
ANNUAL REPORT.

HE 23.102:CT   • Item 529-B-8
GENERAL PUBLICATIONS.

HE 23.108:CT   • Item 528-B-2
HANDBOOKS, MANUALS, GUIDES. [Irregular]

HE 23.109:v.nos.&nos.   • Item 529-B-9
PCMR NEWSBREAK. v. 1, nos. 1– 9. Jan.– Nov. 1979.
   [Quarterly]

    PURPOSE:– To provide an up-to-date re-
source on key developments in broad mental retardation fields.
    Discontinued.

HE 23.110:date   • Item 444-K-4
MENTAL RETARDATION AND THE LAW, A REPORT
   ON STATUS OF CURRENT COURT CASES.
   [Annual]
    Earlier HE 1.51
    Discontinued.

ADMINISTRATION FOR CHILDREN AND FAMILIES (1977–   )

CREATION AND AUTHORITY

    The Administration for Children, Youth, and
Families was established within the Office of Human Development Services by Secretary's reorganization order of July 26, 1977. Name changed
to Administration for Children and Families.

INFORMATION

    Administration for Children,
      and Families
    Washington, D. C. 20201
    (202) 205-8347
    http://www.acf.dhhs.gov

HE 23.1001:date
ANNUAL REPORT.

HE 23.1002:CT   • Item 530-B-1
GENERAL PUBLICATIONS.

HE 23.1005:CT   • Item 530-B-6
LAWS. [Irregular]

HE 23.1008:CT   • Item 530-B-3
HANDBOOKS, MANUALS, GUIDES.

HE 23.1009:date   • Item 530-B-2
STATUS OF CHILDREN. 1977–1978   [Biennial]

    PURPOSE:– To present statistics from a wide
variety of both federal and nonfederal sources
pertaining to children, and to the conditions,
trends, and programs that affect them.

HE 23.1010:date • **Item 530-B-4**
RESEARCH DEMONSTRATION AND EVALUATION
STUDIES. 1977– [Annual]
    PURPOSE:– To describe the projects funded
by the Administration for Children, Youth, and
Families. Projects are listed under broad categories such as Head Start, Child Welfare, Day Care,
and Youth Development, and includes current
grant or contract period and amounts of awards.
    Earlier HE 1.402:R 31
    Discontinued 1979.

HE 23.1011:CT • **Item 499-M (MF)**
BIBLIOGRAPHIES AND LISTS OF PUBLICATIONS.
[Irregular]

HE 23.1012:date • **Item 454-C-5 (MF)**
STATUS OF HANDICAPPED CHILDREN IN HEAD
START PROGRAMS. 1st– 1973– [Annual]
Annual report submitted to Congress.
    Earlier HE 1.409
    Discontinued.

HE 23.1013:date • **Item 499-M-1**
TOWARD INTERAGENCY COORDINATION, FY
FEDERAL RESEARCH AND DEVELOPMENT ON
ADOLESCENCE. [Annual]

    PURPOSE:– To provide a comprehensive
overview of ongoing adolescence research activities across major funding agencies at the Federal level.
    Discontinued 1977.

HE 23.1013/2:date • **Item 499-M-2 (MF)**
TOWARD INTERAGENCY COORDINATION: FY
FEDERAL RESEARCH AND DEVELOPMENT ON
EARLY CHILDHOOD. [Annual]

    PURPOSE:– To provide a comprehensive
overview of ongoing childhood research activities across major funding agencies at the Federal
level.

HE 23.1014: • **Item 530-B-5**
HEAD START NEWSLETTER. [Bimonthly]

    PURPOSE:– To inform local grantees, del-
egate agency personnel of headquarters decisions, legislation, trends, plans and directions;
to present developments, ideas and methods of
local programs for use by other programs; to tell
individual success stories, human interest features; to offer unusual daily activity ideas; to
present the Director's point of view about the
program and social changes; to keep program
participants up to date on rules, regulations, conferences, how to order publications; and to sug-
gest publicity ideas.
    Earlier HE 21.209
    Discontinued 1978.

HE 23.1015:nos. • **Item 530-B-7 (MF)**
DOMESTIC VIOLENCE INFORMATION SERIES. 1–
1980– [Irregular] (National Clearinghouse
on Domestic Violence, Domestic Violence Office)

    PURPOSE:– To provide information and manu-
als on such subjects as programs serving bat-
tered women, effective use of volunteers in such
programs, counseling, and State domestic violence laws and how to pass them.
    Discontinued.

HE 23.1015/2: • **Item 530-B-7 (MF)**
DOMESTIC VIOLENCE MONOGRAPH SERIES.
[Irregular] (National Clearinghouse on Domestic
Violence, Domestic Violence Office)
    Discontinued.

HE 23.1016:CT • **Item 530-B-8**
FORMS. [Irregular]

HE 23.1017:date/nos. • **Item 530-B-9**
CHILD CARE BULLETIN.
    See HE 23.1415

HE 23.1018:date • **Item 530-B-10 (EL)**
CHILD MALTREATMENT: REPORTS FROM THE
STATES TO THE NATIONAL CHILD ABUSE AND
NEGLECT DATA SYSTEM. [Annual]

HEAD START BUREAU
(1977–   )

CREATION AND AUTHORITY

    The Head Start Bureau (HE 1.800) was placed
within the Office of Human Development Services
by Secretary's reorganization order of July 26,
1977.

INFORMATION

    Head Start Bureau
    Administration for Children and Families
    Department of Health and Human Services
    Mary E. Switzer Bldg.
    330 C Street, SW
    Washington, D. C. 20447
    (202) 205-8572
    http//www2.acf.dhhs.gov/programs/hsb

HE 23.1102:CT • **Item 499-G-2**
GENERAL PUBLICATIONS.

    Earlier HE 1.802

HE 23.1108:CT • **Item 499-G-1**
HANDBOOKS, MANUALS, GUIDES. [Irregular]

HE 23.1109:v.nos.&nos. • **Item 499-G-3**
CDA TRAINING AND RESOURCE BULLETIN. v. 1–
1978–

    PURPOSE:– To provide information on the
Child Development Associate Training Program
which was developed to improve programs for
young children by focusing on the competence of
the staff.
    Discontinued.

HE 23.1110:CT • **Item 499-G-1**
MAINSTREAMING PRESCHOOLERS (series).
[Irregular]

HE 23.1111:CT • **Item 499-G-4**
BIBLIOGRAPHIES AND LISTS OF PUBLICATIONS.
[Irregular]

HE 23.1111/2:v.nos.&nos. • **Item 499-G-5**
ANNOTATED BIBLIOGRAPHY OF CDA CURRICULUM
    MATERIALS. v. 1– 1978– [Irregular]

    PURPOSE:– To provide an annotated biblio-
graphy of the Child Development Associate curricula and supplemental resource materials arranged by competency areas with separate section of related resource materials.
    Discontinued.

HE 23.1112:CT • **Item 499-G-2**
GETTING INVOLVED (various subjects) (series).
[Irregular]

HE 23.1113:CT • **Item 499-G- (MF)**
DIRECTORIES. [Irregular]

HE 23.1114:nos.
INFORMATION MEMORANDUM (series). [Irregular]

HE 23.1115:date • **Item 499-G-4 (MF)**
HEAD START, PROGRAM DATA. [Annual]

CHILDREN'S BUREAU
(1977–   )

CREATION AND AUTHORITY

    The Children's Bureau (HE 1.450) was placed
within the Office of Human Development Services
by Secretary's reorganization order of July 26,
1977.

INFORMATION

    Children's Bureau
    Department of Health and Human Services
    Mary E. Switzer Bldg.
    330 C. Street, SW
    Washington, D.C. 20201
    (202) 205-8618
    Fax: (202)260-9345
    http://www.acf.dhhs.gov/programs/cb/

HE 23.1201:date
ANNUAL REPORT.

    Earlier HE 1.451

HE 23.1202:CT • **Item 452**
GENERAL PUBLICATIONS. [Irregular]

    Earlier HE 1.452

HE 23.1208:CT • **Item 452-C**
HANDBOOKS, MANUALS, GUIDES. [Irregular]

    Earlier HE 1.458

HE 23.1209:v.nos.&nos. • **Item 449**
CHILDREN TODAY. v. 1– 1972– [Bimonthly]

    PURPOSE:– To tell about Federal, State and
local services for children, child development,
health and welfare laws, and other news pertinent
to child welfare in the United States.
    Indexed by:–
        Education Index
        Hospital Literature Index
        Nursing Literature Index
    ISSN 0361-4336
    Earlier HE 1.459

HE 23.1210:CT • **Item 445-L-1 (MF)**
CHILD ABUSE AND NEGLECT (series). [Irregular]

    Earlier HE 1.480

HE 23.1210:G 51 • **Item 445-L-1**
INTERDISCIPLINARY GLOSSARY ON CHILD
ABUSE AND NEGLECT: LEGAL, MEDICAL,
SOCIAL WORK TERMS. [Irregular]

HE 23.1210/2:date • **Item 445-L-5 (MF)**
CHILD ABUSE AND NEGLECT RESEARCH,
PROJECTS AND PUBLICATIONS. [List] [Semi-
annual]

    Title varies.
    ISSN 0145-3025
    Earlier HE 1.480/3
    Discontinued.

HE 23.1210/3:date • **Item 445-L-3**
ANNUAL REVIEW OF CHILD ABUSE AND NEGLECT
    RESEARCH. 1978– (National Center on Child
Abuse and Neglect)

    PURPOSE:– To report on child abuse and
neglect during the previous year. Activities include a broad overview on the status of research,
based on the abstracts of completed and ongoing research studies contained in the computerized data base of the NCCAN Information Clearinghouse.
    Discontinued.

HE 23.1210/4:CT • **Item 445-L-4**
USER MANUAL SERIES. [Irregular] (National Center on Child Abuse and Neglect)

PURPOSE:– To provide information for personnel engaged in protection of children endangered by abuse or neglect.

HE 23.1211:date • **Item 445-L-1**
CHILD ABUSE AND NEGLECT PROGRAMS. [Semiannual]
Earlier HE 1.480/4
Discontinued.

HE 23.1212:date • **Item 445-L-2**
CHILD ABUSE AND NEGLECT REPORTS. Feb. 1976–Aug.1979. [Quarterly] 1980
ISSN 0145-1383
Earlier HE 1.480/2
Discontinued.

HE 23.1213:CT
CHILD WELFARE TRAINING (series). [Irregular]

HE 23.1214:CT
POSTERS.

HE 23.1215 • **Item 445-L-6 (MF)**
DIRECTORIES.

HE 23.1216: • **Item 445-L-7**
BIBLIOGRAHPIES & LIST OF PUBLICATIONS.

HE 23.1216/2: • **Item 445-L-8 (P&E)**
NATIONAL CLEARINGHOUSE ON CHILD ABUSE AND NEGLECT INFORMATION CATALOG. [Annual]

FAMILY AND YOUTH SERVICES BUREAU
(1977–   )

CREATION AND AUTHORITY

The Youth Development Office was transferred from the Office of Assistant Secretary for Human Development (HE 1.300) by order of July 26, 1977. Formerly: Youth Development Office.

INFORMATION

Family and Youth Services Bureau
Department of Health and Human Services
Mary E. Switzer Bldg., Rm. 2040
330 C. Street, SW
Washington, DC 20201
(202) 205-8102
Fax: (202) 205-9721
http://www.acf.dhhs.gov/programs/fysb

HE 23.1301:date • **Item 498-D-1 (MF)**
ANNUAL REPORT.

HE 23.1302:CT • **Item 532-C-2**
GENERAL PUBLICATIONS. [Irregular]

HE 23.1308:CT • **Item 532-D-1**
HANDBOOKS, MANUALS, GUIDES. [Irregular]

Earlier HE 1.308

HE 23.1309:date • **Item 498-D-1**
ANNUAL REPORT ON ACTIVITIES CONDUCTED TO IMPLEMENT THE RUNAWAY YOUTH ACT.

Report submitted pursuant to Section 315 of the Runaway Youth Act.
Covers fiscal year.
See HE 23.1309/2

HE 23.1309/2:date • **Item 498-D-1 (MF)**
RUNAWAY AND OTHERWISE HOMELESS YOUTH FISCAL YEAR, ANNUAL REPORT ON THE RUNAWAY YOUTH ACT.

CHILD CARE BUREAU

INFORMATION

Child Care Bureau
Department of Health and Human Services
Mary E. Switzer Bldg., Rm. 2046A
330 C. Street, SW
Washington, DC 20201
(202) 260-2309
http://www.acf.dhhs.gov/programs/ccb

HE 23.1402: • **Item 530-C**
GENERAL PUBLICATIONS.

HE 23.1415: • **Item 530-B-9 (EL)**
CHILD CARE BULLETIN.

HE 23.1415/2: • **Item 530-C-1**
TRIBAL CHILD CARE BULLETIN. [Semiannual]

ADMINISTRATION FOR PUBLIC SERVICES
(1977–   )

CREATION AND AUTHORITY

The Administration for Public Services (HE 1.900) was placed within the Office of Human Development Services by Secretary's reorganization order of July 26, 1977.

INFORMATION

Administration for Public Services
Office of Human Development Services
Department of Health and Human Services
Washington, D.C. 20201

HE 23.2001:date
ANNUAL REPORT.
Earlier HE 1.901

HE 23.2002:CT • **Item 532-B-1**
GENERAL PUBLICATIONS.
Earlier HE 1.902
Discontinued.

HE 23.2008:CT • **Item 532-B-3**
HANDBOOKS, MANUALS, GUIDES.
Discontinued.

HE 23.2009:date • **Item 502-A-1 (MF)**
REPORT TO CONGRESS ON TITLE 20 OF THE SOCIAL SECURITY ACT. 1st–   1977– [Annual]
Discontinued.

HE 23.2010:date • **Item 512-D-18**
SOCIAL SERVICES U.S.A. [Quarterly]

Sub-title: Statistical Tables, Summaries and Analysis of Service under Social Security Act.
ISSN 0145-3041
Earlier HE 17.647
Discontinued.

HE 23.2011:CT • **Item 532-B-4**
BIBLIOGRAPHIES AND LISTS OF PUBLICATIONS.
Earlier HE 17.710
Discontinued.

ADMINISTRATION ON AGING
(1977– 1991)

CREATION AND AUTHORITY

The Aging Administration was removed from the Human Development Services Office in August 1991 by Secretarial Order and placed directly under the Health and Human Services Department as class HE 1.1000.

HE 23.3001:date • **Item 447-A-9 (MF)**
ANNUAL REPORT.
Earlier HE 1.201
Later HE 1.1001

HE 23.3002:CT • **Item 447-A-1**
GENERAL PUBLICATIONS.

Earlier HE 1.202
Later HE 1.1002

HE 23.3002:T 68/2/date • **Item 447-A-1**
TRAINING AND MANPOWER DEVELOPMENT ACTIVITIES SUPPORTED BY THE ADMINISTRATION ON AGING UNDER TITLE IV-A OF THE OLDER AMERICANS ACT OF 1965, AS AMENDED, DESCRIPTIONS OF FUNDED PROJECTS. [Annual] (Office of Human Development Services.)

Report covers the fiscal year.
ISSN 0161-8288

HE 23.3005:CT • **Item 447-A-8**
LAWS. [Irregular]
Earlier HE 1.205
Later HE 1.1005

HE 23.3008:CT • **Item 447-A-3**
HANDBOOKS, MANUALS, GUIDES.
Earlier HE 1.208
Later HE 1.1008

HE 23.3009:CT • **Item 447-A-6**
BIBLIOGRAPHIES AND LISTS OF PUBLICATIONS. [Irregular]

HE 23.3011 • **Item 447-A-6**
BIBLIOGRAPHIES AND LISTS OF PUBLICATIONS.
Later HE 1.1011

HE 23.3012:nos.
USES OF RESEARCH SPONSORED BY THE ADMINISTRATION ON AGING, CASE STUDIES (numbered). [Irregular]

Each case study deals with uses of Administration research in a different subject area.
Discontinued No. 6.

HE 23.3013:nos. • **Item 447-A-18**
INFORMATION MEMORANDUMS. [Irregular]

Information memorandums to state agencies administering plans related to older Americans.
Later HE 1.1013

HE 23.3014:CT • **Item 447-A-20 (MF)**
DIRECTORIES. [Irregular]
See HE 1.1014

HE 23.3015:nos. • **Item 444-A**
AGING. 1–   1951–   [Quarterly]
Earlier HE 23.3110
Later HE 1.1015

NATIONAL CLEARINGHOUSE ON AGING
(1977–   )

CREATION AND AUTHORITY

The National Clearinghouse on Aging was placed within the Office of Human Development Services by Secretary's reorganization order of July 26, 1977.

INFORMATION

National Clearinghouse on Aging
Office of Human Development Services
Department of Health and Human Services
Washington, D.C. 20201

HE 23.3101:date
ANNUAL REPORT.

HE 23.3102:CT   • Item 502-A-2
GENERAL PUBLICATIONS. [Irregular]

HE 23.3108:CT   • Item 447-A-15
HANDBOOKS, MANUALS, GUIDES.

HE 23.3109:CT   • Item 447-A-14
HEW FACT SHEETS. [Irregular]
Earlier HE 1.213

HE 23.3110:nos.   • Item 444-A
AGING. 1– 1951– [Bimonthly]
Earlier HE 1.210
Later HE 23.3015

HE 23.3111:nos.   • Item 447-A-14
AOA OCCASIONAL PAPERS IN GERONTOLOGY. 1–
[Irregular]

HE 23.3112:nos.   • Item 502-A-3
STATISTICAL NOTES. 1– 1978– [Irregular]

PURPOSE:- To provide a series of newsletters describing the statistical programs and publications of interest to organizations and persons working in the field of aging.
Discontinued.

HE 23.3112/2:nos.   • Item 502-A-4
STATISTICAL REPORTS ON OLDER AMERICANS. [Irregular]

Reports on older Americans, particularly those 60 or more years old, who are entitled to services under the Older Americans Act. Reports may cover the American elderly in general or with particular segments of the aged population.

HANDICAPPED ADMINISTRATION FOR INDIVIDUALS
(1977–   )

CREATION AND AUTHORITY

The Administration for Handicapped Individuals was established within the Office of Human Development Services by Secretary's order of July 26, 1977.

INFORMATION

Administration for Handicapped Individuals
Office of Human Development Services
Department of Health and Human Services
Washington, D.C. 20201

HE 23.4001:date
ANNUAL REPORT.

HE 23.4002:CT
GENERAL PUBLICATIONS. [Irregular]

REHABILITATION SERVICES ADMINISTRATION
(1977– 1979)

CREATION AND AUTHORITY

The Rehabilitation Services Administration (HE 1.600) was placed within the Office of Human Development Services by Secretary's reorganization order of July 26, 1977. The Administration was transferred to the Department of Education (ED 1.200) pursuant to the Department of Education Organization Act (93 Stat. 668), approved on October 1979

HE 23.4101:date
ANNUAL REPORT.
Earlier HE 1.601
Later ED 1.201

HE 23.4102:CT   • Item 529
GENERAL PUBLICATIONS. [Irregular]
Earlier HE 1.602
Later ED 1.202

HE 23.4108:CT   • Item 529-B
HANDBOOKS, MANUALS, GUIDES. [Irregular]
Earlier HE 1.608

HE 23.4109:date   • Item 529-C
CASELOAD STATISTICS, STATE VOCATIONAL REHABILITATION AGENCIES. [Annual]

ISSN 0566-0009
Earlier HE 1.611
Discontinued.

HE 23.4110:date   • Item 529-E
STATE VOCATIONAL REHABILITATION AGENCY PROGRAM AND FINANCIAL PLAN. [Annual]

PURPOSE:– To provide State agencies with basic assumptions and guidelines for their use in developing program and financial plans for future fiscal years.
Earlier HE 1.610/2
Discontinued.

HE 23.4110/2:date   • Item 506-C-2
STATE VOCATIONAL REHABILITATION AGENCY: PROGRAM DATA. [Annual]

PURPOSE:– To provide public accountability for funds appropriated for the fiscal year and basic data for evaluating program performances and goal attainment.
ISSN 0147-0914
Earlier HE 1.610/3
Discontinued.

ADMINISTRATION FOR NATIVE AMERICANS
(1978–   )

INFORMATION

Administration for Native Americans
Mail Stop 348F
370 L'Enfant Promenade, SW
Washington, DC 20447-0002
(202) 690-7776
Fax: 690-7441
http://www.acf.dhhs.gov/programs/ana

HE 23.5001:date
ANNUAL REPORT.

HE 23.5002:CT   • Item 529-B-10
GENERAL PUBLICATIONS. [Irregular]

HE 23.5009:CT   • Item 529-B-6
ADDRESSES. [Irregular]

ADMINISTRATION ON DEVELOPMENTAL DISABILITIES

INFORMATION

Administration on Developmental
   Disabilities
Administration for Children and Families
Mail Stop HHH 300-F
370 L'Enfant Promenade, SW
Washington, DC 20447
(202) 690-6590
http://www.acf.dhhs.gov/programs/add

HE 23.6001:   • Item 529-F (MF)
ANNUAL REPORT.

Summarizes activities of the Administration, which is committed to expanding life opportunities for Americans with developmentaldisabilities through four grants programs authorized by the Developmental Disabilities Assistance and Bill of Rights Act.

OFFICE OF CHILD SUPPORT ENFORCEMENT
(1980–   )

CREATION AND AUTHORITY

The Office of Child Support Enforcement was established within the Social Security Administration (HE 3.500) pursuant to the act of January 4, 1975 (88 Stat. 2351). The Office was continued as a separate organization by the Secretary's reorganization of March 8, 1977. The Commissioner of Social Security Administration also serves as Director of OSE.
[Note:- the agency class, HE 24, was not established until 1980.]

INFORMATION

Office of Child Support Enforcement
Department of Health and Human Services
370 L'Enfant Promenade SW
4th Floor
(202) 401-9370
Fax: (202) 401-5559
http://www.acf.dhhs.gov/programs/cse

HE 24.1:date   • Item 524-A-5 (MF)
ANNUAL REPORT.

    Earlier HE 3.501

HE 24.2:CT   • Item 524-A-1
GENERAL PUBLICATIONS.

    Earlier HE 3.502

HE 24.8:CT   • Item 524-A
HANDBOOKS, MANUALS, GUIDES. [Irregular]

    Earlier HE 3.508

HE 24.9:v.nos.&nos.   • Item 524-A-6 (EL)
CHILD SUPPORT REPORT. [Monthly] (National Child
Support Enforcement Reference Center)

    Contains news items on child support en-
forcement in the U.S.
    Discontinued.

HE 24.9/2:date   • Item 524-A-6
CHILD SUPPORT ENFORCEMENT STATISTICS. [Semi-
annual]
    Discontinued.

HE 24.10:nos.   • Item 524-A-3 (MF)
MONOGRAPH SERIES. [Irregular]
    Discontinued.

HE 24.11:nos.
ABSTRACTS OF CHILD SUPPORT TECHNIQUES
(series). [Irregular]
    Discontinued.

HE 24.12:date   • Item 524-A-4 (MF)
INFORMATION SHARING INDEX. [Annual]

    Lists and annotates publications and audio-
visual materials on enforcement of child support.
Each section concerns a different area such as
history, legislation, establishment and enforcement of the support obligation, and operating techniques.
    Discontinued.

HE 24.13:CT   • Item 524-A-7 (MF)
BIBLIOGRAPHIES AND LISTS OF PUBLICATIONS.
[Irregular]

HE 24.14   • Item 524-A-9
ACTION TRANSMITTALS, OCSE-AT- (series). [Irregu-
lar]

    Each transmittal has a different subject such
as family support, child custody, and paternity
and transmits the applicable regulations to state
agencies administering child support enforcement
under Title 4-D of the Social Security Act.

HE 24.15   • Item 524-A-10
INFORMATION MEMORANDUMS, OCSE- IM- (series).
[Irregular]

    Each memorandum transmits information on
child support enforcement to state agencies administering child support enforcement plans approved under Title 4-D of the Social Security Act.

HE 24.16:   • Item 524-A-11 (MF)
STATE LEGISLATIVE SUMMARY, CHILDREN AND
YOUTH ISSUES. [Annual]

    Issued by the National Conference of State
Legislatures with partial support from HHS's Child
Support Enforcement Office. A compilation of
summaries of state legislation enacted during the
year.
    Discontinued.

CENTERS FOR MEDICARE AND MEDICAID SERVICES
(1986–   )

CREATION AND AUTHORITY

    The Family Support Administration was es-
tablished April 4, 1986. Now Centers for Medicare
and Medicaid Services.

INFORMATION

    Centers for Medicare and Medicaid Services
    7500 Security Blvd.
    Baltimore, MD 21244-1850
    (410) 786-3000
    http://www.cms.hhs.gov

HE 25.2:   • Item 524-A-12
GENERAL PUBLICATIONS.

HE 25.8:CT   • Item 516-V
HANDBOOKS, MANUALS, GUIDES.

HE 25.10   • Item 516-P (MF)
DIRECTORIES.

HE 25.15   • Item 512-D-10
QUARTERLY PUBLIC ASSISTANCE STATISTICS.
    Discontinued.

HE 25.16:date   • Item 516-J
REFUGEE RESETTLEMENT PROGRAM, REPORT TO
THE CONGRESS. [Annual]
    Discontinued.

HE 25.17:date   • Item 516-P
LOW INCOME HOME ENERGY ASSISTANCE
PROGRAM, REPORT TO CONGRESS. [Annual]
    Discontinued.

DEPARTMENT OF HOUSING AND URBAN DEVELOPMENT
(1965–   )

CREATION AND AUTHORITY

    The Housing and Home Finance Agency was
established by Reorganization Plan No. 3 of 1947,
effective July 27, 1947, which transferred the
functions of the Home Owner's Loan Corporation,
the Federal Savings and Loan Insurance Corporation, the Federal Housing Administration, the
United States Housing Authority, the Defense
Homes Corporation, and Federal Home Loan Bank
Board. Plan 3 provided for the constituent agencies to be the Home Loan Bank Board, the Federal Housing Administration, and the Public Housing Administration.
    The Department of Housing and Urban Devel-
opment was established by the Department of
Housing and Urban Development Act of September 9, 1965 (79 Stat. 667; 5 U.S.C. 642). The act,
which became effective November 9, 1965, transferred to and vested in the Secretary of Housing
and Urban Development all of the functions, powers, and duties of the Housing and Home Finance
Agency (including the Community Facilities Administration and the Urban Renewal Administration), of the heads and other officers and offices
of those agencies. The act also transferred to the
Department of Federal National Mortgage Association.

INFORMATION

    Public Affairs
    Department of Housing and
    Urban Development
    451 Seventh Street, S.W.
    Washington, D.C. 20410
    (202) 708-0865
    http://www.hud.gov

HH 1.1   • Item 581 (MF)
ANNUAL REPORT. 1st–   1965–   [Annual]

    Includes reports for the subordinate bureaus.
Report covers the calendar year.

HH 1.1/2:date   • Item 581-H (MF)
OFFICE OF INSPECTOR GENERAL: REPORT TO THE
CONGRESS. [Semiannual]

    Summarizes Office's activities, which include
responsiblity for auditing and investigating Department programs and for keeping the Secretary
and Congress informed of any deficiencies.

HH 1.1/3:date   • Item 582-A-2 (MF)
SOLAR ENERGY AND ENERGY CONSERVATION
BANK: ANNUAL REPORT.

    PURPOSE:- To summarize Bank activities in
subsidizing loans and providing grants for solar
energy and energy conservation measures in residential dwellings.

HH 1.1/4:date   • Item 581-J (MF)
BUDGET ESTIMATES, EXCERPTS FROM THE UNITED
STATES GOVERNMENT BUDGET. [Annual]

    Contains excerpts for the U. S. Government
budget pertaining to budget estimates for the
Department of Housing and Urban Development.
    Discontinued.

HH 1.1/4-2:date   • Item 581-J (MF)
FY BUDGET, SUMMARY. [Annual]

HH 1.1/5:date   • Item 581-J (MF)
ANNUAL AUDIT PLAN.

HH 1.1/6   • Item 581-H (MF)
THE SECRETARY'S SEMIANNUAL REPORT TO THE
CONGRESS.

HH 1.1/7:date   • Item 581
GOVERNMENT NATIONAL MORTGAGE ASSOCIA-
TION, GNMA, ANNUAL REPORT.

HH 1.1/8   • Item 581-H (MF)
IPS @ HUD.
    Discontinued.

HH 1.1/9   • Item 581-A-3 (MF)
THE STATE OF FAIR HOUSING, REPORT TO THE
CONGRESS. [Annual]

HH 1.1/10   • Item 581-L-1 (EL)
CONSOLIDATED ANNUAL REPORT FOR THE OF-
FICE OF COMMUNITY PLANNING AND DEVEL-
OPMENT.

HH 1.1/11   • Item 581-J-1 (MF)
CONSOLIDATED FINANCIAL REPORT FY.

HH 1.1/12   • Item 581-J-2 (EL)
PERFORMANCE PLAN FY...[Annual]

HH 1.2:CT   • Item 582
GENERAL PUBLICATIONS.

HH 1.3/2:nos.
STAFF BULLETIN. Admin.

HH 1.3/3:CT   • Item 584-A-1 (MF)
URBAN CONSORTIUM INFORMATION BULLETINS.

    PURPOSE:– To provide non-technical over-
views from the local government perspective, of
issues, problems and current approaches for
dealing with important community development
concerns.
    Discontinued.

HH 1.3/5 • Item 584-A-2
PROGRAM INTEGRITY BULLETIN. [Irregular]
Each bulletin covers a different program integrity topic.

HH 1.4:letters-nos.
CIRCULARS. Admin.

HH 1.5:CT • Item 583
LAWS.

Earlier NHA 1.5

HH 1.5/2:date
DETAILED SUMMARY OF HOUSING AMENDMENTS. [Annual]

HH 1.6:CT • Item 584
REGULATIONS, RULES, AND INSTRUCTIONS.

HH 1.6/2:v.nos.bk.nos.,date
OA MANUAL

HH 1.6/3:CT • Item 582-E
HANDBOOKS, MANUALS, GUIDES.

HH 1.6/3:En 8 • Item 582-E
INTERIM GUIDE FOR ENVIRONMENT ASSESSMENT. [Irregular] (Subscription includes basic volume plus supplements for an indefinite period)

HH 1.6/3-2:nos.
HUD SELLING LIST. [Biweekly]

HH 1.6/4:nos.
WORKABLE PROGRAM FOR COMMUNITY IMPROVEMENT, PROGRAM GUIDES.

HH 1.6/5 • Item 582-F
HUD PROGRAM GUIDES. [Irregular]

HH 1.6/6:nos. • Item 582-E
HUD HANDBOOKS (numbered). [Irregular]
ISSN 0364-2836

HH 1.6/6:RHA 7200.0 • Item 582-E
URBAN RENEWAL HANDBOOKS. (Subscription includes basic volume plus supplementary material for an indefinite period)

This Handbook, the official statement of the Department of Housing and Urban Development (HUD) which establishes the policies and requirements for the administration of Federally assisted urban renewal programs, is the basic issuance used to promulgate permanent policy and requirements for local administrative officials, and to establish broad national objectives and detailed requirements. It is also oriented to the user, i.e., the Local Public Agency (LPA), or other public body, that admisters the urban renewal program at the local level.

HH 1.6/6-2:nos.
HUD TRAINING HANDBOOKS. [Irregular]

HH 1.6/7 • Item 582-E
HUD GUIDES (numbered). [Irregular]

HH 1.6/8:nos.
HUD PERSONNEL PAMPHLET.

HH 1.6/9:CT • Item 582-E
HUD MINIMUM PROPERTY STANDARDS. [Irregular]

Issued in the following volumes:–

1. ONE AND TWO FAMILY DWELLINGS. 1973. ed. (includes basic volume plus supplementary material for an indefinite period)

2. MULTIFAMILY HOUSING. 1973 ed. (includes basic volume plus supplementary material for an indefinite period)

3. CARE-TYPE HOUSING. 1973. ed (includes basic volume plus supplementary material for an indefinite period)

4. MANUAL OF ACCEPTABLE PRACTICES.

(basic volume plus supplements for an indefintie period) Supplements volumes 1-3.

HH 1.6/9:So 4 • Item 582-E
INTERMEDIATE MINIMUM PROPERTY STANDARDS FOR SOLAR HEATING AND DOMESTIC HOT WATER SYSTEM. (Basic volume plus supplements for an indefinite period)

HH 1.6/10:nos. • Item 582-E-1
COMMUNITY PLANNING AND DEVELOPMENT, PROGRAM GUIDES.
Discontinued.

HH 1.6/11:CT • Item 582-E
PLANNING FOR HOUSING SECURITY (series).

HH 1.7 • Item 581-C (MF)
ADDRESSES. [Irregular]
Discontinued.

HH 1.8:nos.
TECHNICAL PAPERS.
Discontinued.

HH 1.9:nos.
TECHNICAL BULLETINS.
Discontinued.

HH 1.9/2:nos.
HOUSING RESEARCH. [Quarterly]

Replaces HH 1.9

HH 1.10:date
CURRENT FACTS ON HOUSING. [Monthly]

HH 1.11:nos.
STATISTICS BULLETINS.

HH 1.12:nos.
PUBLIC RELATIONS.

HH 1.13:nos.
MONTHLY REPORT ON HOUSING.

Restricted

HH 1.14 • Item 581-E-10
HOUSING AND URBAN DEVELOPMENT TRENDS 1968– [date]. v. 1– 33. 1948– 1980. [Quarterly]

Compilation of Statistics from various Government agencies on Housing production, construction costs, home financing, and public housing supplementing data contained in Housing Statistics Handbook (1948).
Annual data issued separately.
Prior to 1968 entitled Housing Statistics.
ISSN 0018-6619
Discontinued June 1980

HH 1.14/2
HISTORICAL SUPPLEMENT. [Annual]

HH 1.15
PRESS RELEASES. [Irregular]

HH 1.15/2:nos.
NEWS SUMMARY.

HH 1.15/3
CONSUMER RELATIONS NEWSLETTER. v. 1– 1966– [Monthly]

PURPOSE:– To present news of the Department of Housing and Urban Development and availability of new publications.

HH 1.15/4:v.nos.&nos. • Item 582-L
HUD NEWSLETTER. 1– 13. 1969– 1982. [Weekly]

PURPOSE:– To give timely reports on significant happenings in housing, urban development, and related fields, with specific emphasis on HUD-associated activities and programs.
Issued biweekly prior to v. 2, no. 1, Mar. 1, 1971.
ISSN 0017-6311
Discontinued March 1982.

HH 1.15/5:date
HUD ARTICLES IN PERIODICALS.

HH 1.16:CT
HOUSING RESEARCH DIVISION PUBLICATIONS.

This class has been cancelled and publications changed to HH 1.2.

HH 1.17 • Item 584-B-1
WATER AND SEWER FACILITIES GRANT PROGRAM, HUD INFORMATION SERIES. 1– 1966– [Irregular]
Discontinued.

HH 1.18:nos.
CONSTRUCTION AIDS.
Discontinued.

HH 1.18/2:nos.
IDEAS AND METHODS EXCHANGE NOS. (series).

HH 1.19:nos.
URBAN RENEWAL BULLETINS.

Changed to HH 7.2

HH 1.20:CT
POSTERS.

HH 1.21:date
CURRENT PROGRAMS AND OPERATIONS OF HOUSING AND HOME FINANCE AGENCY, FACTUAL SUMMARY FOR PUBLIC INTEREST ORGANIZATIONS. [Irregular]

HH 1.22:nos. • Item 584-B
[RENEWAL] R– SERIES.
Discontinued.

HH 1.23:CT • Item 581-D
BIBLIOGRAPHIES AND LISTS OF PUBLICATIONS.

Earlier HH 1.2
HH 1.23/2:nos.
HOUSING REFERENCES. [Bimonthly]

HH 1.23/3 • Item 582-D
HOUSING AND PLANNING REFERENCES, NEW SERIES. [Bimonthly]

Bibliographies.
ISSN 0018-6570
Discontinued No. 109

HH 1.23/4:nos. • Item 581-E-13
FOREIGN PUBLICATIONS ACCESSIONS LIST. 1– 1970– [Irregular] (Office of International Affairs)

PURPOSE:– To supply the U.S. Government and representatives of the U.S. housing and building industry with an ongoing bibliography of foreign housing, building, and urban development information.
ISSN 0364-0930
Discontinued.

HH 1.23/5:nos.
HUD LIBRARY RECENT ACQUISITIONS. [Semi-monthly]

HH 1.23/6:CT • Item 581-D
SOLAR BIBLIOGRAPHY (series). [Irregular]

HH 1.23/7:CT • Item 581-D-1
HUD USER BIBLIOGRAPHY SERIES. [Irregular]

Includes miscellaneous bibliographies covering topics concerning the work of the HUD Offices of Policy Development and of Research and International Affairs.
Discontinued.

HH 1.23/8:v.nos./nos. • Item 581-D-3 (EL)
URBAN RESEARCH MONITOR. [Bimonthly]

HH 1.24:date • Item 582-C
HOUSING IN THE ECONOMY. [Annual]
Earlier HH 1.2:H 81/26
Discontinued.

HH 1.25:date   • **Item 581-B**
ANNUAL REPORT, VOLUNTARY HOME MORTGAGE
CREDIT PROGRAM.
　　Earlier HH 1.2:V 88/2
　　Discontinued.

HH 1.26   • **Item 584-F**
URBAN PLANNING ASSISTANCE PROGRAM,
PROJECT DIRECTORY. [Irregular]
　　Discontinued.

HH 1.27   • **Item 582-G**
HUD-IP- (series). 1–   1966–   [Irregular]
　　Discontinued.

HH 1.28   • **Item 582-H**
HUD-MP- (series). 1–   [Irregular]
　　Discontinued.

HH 1.29   • **Item 582-F**
HUD-PG- (series). 1–   1966–   [Irregular]
　　Discontinued.

HH 1.30
HOUSING AND URBAN DEVELOPMENT NOTES. [Bi-
monthly]

　　A digest pointing to good techniques and
unusual local approaches and successes. Also
summarized pertinent information regarding urban renewal and other HUD programs, lists new
publications, etc.
　　Supersedes Urban Renewal Notes (HH 7.12).

HH 1.31   • **Item 593-C**
HUD-TS- (series). 1–   1966–   [Irregular]
　　Discontinued.

HH 1.32   • **Item 581-E-3 (MF)**
COUNTRY REPORT SERIES. [Irregular]
　　Each report covers housing in an individual
country. Includes bibliographies.
　　Discontinued.

HH 1.33   • **Item 582-I**
PR (series). 1–   [Irregular]
　　Discontinued.

HH 1.34:letters-nos.
NOTICES.

HH 1.35:letters-nos.   • **Item 582-J**
HUD CLEARINGHOUSE SERVICE, HCS-(series).
1969–   [Irregular]
　　Discontinued.

HH 1.36:v.nos.&nos.   • **Item 582-K**
HUD CHALLENGE. v. 1–   1969–   [Monthly]

　　PURPOSE:– To serve as the official journal
of the Department of Housing and Urban Development. Provides an authoritative source of information for persons who plan, administer, or
participate in housing and community development programs.
　　Issued bimonthly prior to the Jan. 1971 issue.
　　Indexed by: Index to U.S. Government Periodicals.
　　Discontinued.

HH 1.36/a:CT
HUD CHALLENGE REPRINTS.

HH 1.37:date   • **Item 582-A-1 (MF)**
GOVERNMENTAL NATIONAL MORTGAGE ASSOCIA-
TIONS. ANNUAL REPORT.

HH 1.37/2:date   • **Item 582-A-1**
– ANNUAL FINANCIAL AND STATISTICAL EX-
　　HIBITS.

　　　　　　　　　　　　　　• **Item 581-L (P)**
HH 1.37/3   • **Item 581-L-2 (EL)**
ALL PARTICIPANTS MEMORANDA.

HH 1.37/4:date   • **Item 581-L (P) (EL)**
ALL PARTICIPANTS MEMORANDA (Ginnie Mae)

HH 1.38:date   • **Item 582-M**
STATISTICAL YEARBOOK. 1966–

　　The Statistical Yearbook provides an annual
statistical summary of activities and operations
of the Department of Housing and Urban Development including characteristics of the properties, projects, communities, and people assisted
under Departmental programs. The Yearbook
serves as a data source book as well as an
analytical tool for persons in the Department, the
Congress, other government agencies, libraries,
research organizations, etc.
　　Federal Housing Administration data includes
tables on volume, financing by type of institution,
termination, disposition, default, claims paid, and
finance and accounting statements. Data on characteristics of purchasers and their homes include
age of mortgagor, income, fixed obligations, down
payments and costs, lot size, number of rooms,
etc.
　　Data on Low Rent Public Housing, College
Housing, Elderly and Handicapped Housing, Urban Renewal, and such Metropolitan Planning and
Development programs as Comprehensive Planning, Public Facilities, and Open Space Land are
in summary, State distribution, and annual series
tables. Considerable data are presented on characteristics of tenants of Low Rent Public Housing. Government National Mortgage Association
activities are included, as are other HUD programs such as Model Cities and Urban Research
and Technology. The Yearbook contains a section
of general statistics related to housing and urban
development. Selected data on population, households, income, housing quality, housing occupancy, vacancy, and sales, construction expenditures and costs, and residential mortgage
financing are presented.
　　Discontinued.

HH 1.39:CT   • **Item 581-E**
ENVIRONMENTAL PLANNING PAPERS.
　　Discontinued.

HH 1.40:nos.
HUD INTERNATIONAL INFORMATION SERIES. 1–
April 30, 1970–   [Irregular]
　　PURPOSE:– To bring significant foreign innovations in the housing industry to professional
societies, planners, universities research centers, city and municipal officials, other Federal
agencies, etc. in the U.S.
　　Discontinued.

HH 1.40/2:nos.   • **Item 581-E-1**
HUD INTERNATIONAL BRIEFS. 1–   1971–
[Irregular]

　　PURPOSE:– To promote the exchange of
housing and urban development information from
both foreign and domestic sources. Its content,
as the name implies, touches only on highlights
and pertinent information. Where information is
digested from a large paper, availability of the
complete work is indicated on the last page of
this issue.

HH 1.40/3:date   • **Item 581-E-1 (MF)**
HUD INTERNATIONAL SUPPLEMENTS. 1971–
[Irregular] (Office of International Affairs)

　　PURPOSE:– The supplement is a compilation
of pertinent articles in the field of housing and
urban development, from foreign publications
which are not readily available in the United States.
The material presented does not necessarily represent the views or policy of the Department of
Housing and Urban Development, nor does it im-
ply an endorsement of the policies of other nations.

HH 1.40/3-2:nos.
HUD INTERNATIONAL SPECIAL SUPPLEMENTS. 1–
1917–   [Irregular] (Office of International
Affairs)

　　PURPOSE:- To bring to the attention of the
American reader articles from foreign publications
which are not readily available in the United States.
Nos. 1-4 were unnumbered on title pages.

HH 1.40/4:CT   • **Item 481-E-1**
HUD INTERNATIONAL INFORMATION SOURCES
SERIES.

HH 1.40/5:CT   • **Item 581-E-9 (MF)**
HUD INTERNATIONAL SPECIAL REPORTS. [Irregular]
　　Discontinued.

HH 1.40/6:nos.
INTERNATIONAL BULLETIN. [Irregular]

　　Former title: HUD International Bulletin.

HH 1.40/7:nos.
INTERNATIONAL REVIEW. v. 1.   – 1980. [Irregular]
(Office of International Affairs.)

HH 1.41:nos.   • **Item 581-E-2 (MF)**
BIENNIAL HUD AWARDS FOR DESIGN EXCELLENCE
(numbered).
　　Earlier HH 1.28
　　Discontinued.

HH 1.42:nos.   • **Item 581-E-4**
MODEL CITIES MANAGEMENT SERIES, BULLETINS.
1–   1971–   [Irregular]
　　Discontinued.

HH 1.43:date
MONTHLY FACT SHEET.

HH 1.43/2:nos.   • **Item 582-S**
MAJOR PROGRAMS OF THE U.S. DEPARTMENT OF
HOUSING AND URBAN DEVELOPMENT, FACT
SHEETS. 1–   1979–   [Irregular] (HUD-523-
nos.)

　　PURPOSE:– To provide a series of fact sheets
on the major programs of the department.
　　Each issue devoted to a single subject.

HH 1.44:v.nos.
HUDDLE. [Monthly]

HH 1.44/2:   • **Item 581-K**
HOUSELINES. [3 times a year]

　　A minority affairs newsletter pertaining particularly to housing for blacks and Hispanics.
　　Discontinued.

HH 1.44/3:date   • **Item 581-K**
CDP NOTES. [Monthly]

HH 1.45:date
JOB FAIR JOURNAL.

HH 1.46:nos.   • **Item 581-E-5**
COMMUNITY DEVELOPMENT EVALUATION SERIES.
1–   [Irregular]
　　Discontinued.

HH 1.46/2:v.nos.&nos.
COMMUNITY DEVELOPMENT. v. 1–   1972–
(National League of Cities-U.S. Conference of
Mayors, 1612 K Street, N.W., Washington, D.C.
20006)

HH 1.46/3:date   • **Item 581-E-11 (MF)**
COMMUNITY DEVELOPMENT BLOCK GRANT PRO-
GRAM ANNUAL REPORTS. 1st–   1976–

　　Combined with Urban Development Action
Grant Program Annual Report (HH 1.46/5) to form
Consolidated Annual Report to Congress on Com-
munity Development Programs (HH 1.46/6).

HH 1.46/4:CT
COMMUNITY PLANNING AND DEVELOPMENT
EVALUATION: EVALUATION SERIES.

HH 1.46/5   • **Item 581-E-11 (MF)**
URBAN DEVELOPMENT ACTION GRANT PROGRAM.
[Annual]

　　Combined with Community Block Grant Pro-
gram (HH 1.46/3) to form Consolidated Annual
Report to Congress on Community Development
Programs (HH 1.46/6).

HH 1.46/6:date • Item 581-E-11 (MF)
CONSOLIDATED ANNUAL REPORT TO CONGRESS ON COMMUNITY DEVELOPMENT PROGRAMS.

Consolidates Community Development Block Grant Program (HH 1.46/3) and Urban Development Action Grant Program (HH 1.46/5) Annual Reports.

HH 1.46/6-2:date • Item 581-E-11 (MF)
COMMUNITY DEVELOPMENT BLOCK GRANT PROGRAM, DIRECTORY OF ALLOCATIONS FOR FISCAL YEARS (dates). [Annual]
Earlier HH 1.2:G 76/13

HH 1.47:date
STATUS REPORT:WORKABLE PROGRAM FOR COMMUNITY IMPROVEMENT. [Quarterly]

HH 1.48:CT
OPERATION BREAKTHROUGH, SITE PLANNER'S REPORT (series). [Irregular]

HH 1.49:date
ANNUAL REPORT OF HUD ACTIVITIES UNDER THE UNIFORM RELOCATION ASSISTANCE POLICIES ACT OF 1970. – 1974.

Statutory requirement for this report expired January 15, 1975.

HH 1.50:date • Item 581-E-6 (MF)
DIRECTORY OF MULTIFAMILY PROJECT MORTGAGE INSURANCE PROGRAMS BY PROJECT STATUS. [Quarterly] (Multifamily Activities Branch, Management Information Systems Division)

Previous title: Selected Multifamily Status Reports, Mortgage Insurance Programs by Name and Location of Each Project.
ISSN 0364-5827
Discontinued.

HH 1.51:date • Item 581-E-15 (MF)
LOCAL AUTHORITIES PARTICIPATING IN LOW-RENT HOUSING PROGRAMS. 1971– [Annual]

PURPOSE:- To provide summary data on HAA program status, by local housing authority and by locality.
This directory lists all local housing authorities with low-cost public housing project under the jurisdiction of the Housing Act of 1949. For each local authority, the directory indicates the city in which the authority is headquartered, the places in which the authority is headquartered, the places in which it has PHA low-rent programs, the number of such units and projects, the number of such units and projects, and the low-rent programs with which the authority is concerned.
Earlier HH 3.9
Discontinued.

HH 1.52:date • Item 581-E-8
ANNUAL HOUSING SURVEY.
Discontinued.

HH 1.53:CT
EXECUTIVE SUMMARY OF HUD RESEARCH PROJECT REPORT (series).

HH 1.54:date • Item 581-E-7 (MF)
EXPERIMENTAL HOUSING ALLOWANCE PROGRAM, ANNUAL REPORT. 1st– 1973– [Annual]
Discontinued.

HH 1.55:CT • Item 581-E-21 (MF)
FINAL ENVIRONMENTAL IMPACT STATEMENT.

HH 1.56:nos.
HUD RESEARCH.

HH 1.56/2:date • Item 581-D-2
HUD RESEARCH THESAURUS.

PURPOSE:- To provide a uniform classification scheme which permits information to be communicated or stored by one person and to be understood or retrieved by another. Contains about 2,500 terms representing concepts used to index the literature in the HUD user data base.
Discontinued January 1982.

HH 1.57:date
HPMC PERFORMANCE INDICATORS. 1975– [Monthly]
ISSN 0145-1359

HH 1.58:nos.
DEPARTMENTAL WEEKLY REPORTS.

HH 1.59:date
FINANCIAL STATEMENTS. [Quarterly]
ISSN 0145-1081

HH 1.60:date • Item 581-E-26 (MF)
MINORITY BUSINESS ENTERPRISE IN HUD PROGRAMS, ANNUAL REPORT.

PURPOSE:- To present development information on all low-rent projects administered by FHA.

HH 1.62:CT • Item 581-E-12
CHALLENGE/RESPONSE [papers]. [Irregular]
Discontinued.

HH 1.63:nos. • Item 581-E-14
PUBLIC HOUSING MANAGEMENT IMPROVEMENT PROGRAM: TECHNICAL MEMORANDUMS. 1– [Irregular]
Discontinued.

HH 1.64:date
REPORT TO CONGRESS ON THE EMERGENCY HOMEOWNER'S RELIEF ACT.

HH 1.65:nos. • Item 581-E-16 (MF)
FOOTNOTES. 1– 1976–
Discontinued.

HH 1.66:v.nos. • Item 581-E-17 (MF)
UTILITIES DEMONSTRATION SERIES. v. 1– 1977– [Irregular]
Discontinued.

HH 1.67:nos. • Item 581-E-18 (MF)
COMMUNITY STABILIZATION CASE STUDIES. 1– 1977– [Irregular]
Discontinued.

HH 1.68:date
UPDATE. [Irregular]

HH 1.69:date • Item 581-E-19 (MF)
HUD SOLAR STATUS.
Discontinued.

HH 1.70:CT • Item 581-E-20 (MF)
VICTIMIZATION, FEAR OF CRIME AND ALTERED BEHAVIOR (series). [Irregular]
Discontinued.

HH 1.71:date
HOUSING AUTHORITY PROJECT NOTE OFFERINGS ON (date). [Monthly]

HH 1.71/2:date
TABULATION OF PROJECT NOTE SALES FOR LOW-INCOME HOUSING. [Monthly]

HH 1.72:CT • Item 581-E-22 (MF)
HUD BUILDING TECHNOLOGY REPORTS. [Irregular]

HH 1.73:date • Item 581-E-23 (MF)
EVALUATION OF THE URBAN HOMESTEADING DEMONSTRATION PROGRAM. 1st– 1977– [Annual]
Discontinued.

PURPOSE:- To provide a progress report on all aspects of the urban homesteading program including description of the program, impact on different kinds of neighborhoods, etc.

HH 1.74:nos. • Item 581-E-24 (MF)
RESIDENTIAL SOLAR PROGRAM REPORTS. 1– 1978– [Irregular]

PURPOSE:- To disseminate information about the use of solar energy in residences, and provide practical guidance to the Nation's housing industry as it searches for ways to reduce homeowners dependence on conventional sources of energy.
Discontinued.

HH 1.75:date • Item 581-E-25 (MF)
PRESIDENT'S NATIONAL URBAN POLICY REPORT. 1st– 1978– [Biennial]

Report submitted to Congress on the overview of the National growth and development trends, describing progress and problems in the States, metropolitan areas, and nonmetropolitan communities.
Ceased in 1991.

HH 1.75/2:v.nos./nos. • Item 581-E-38 (EL)
CITYSCAPE - A JOURNAL OF POLICY DEVELOPMENT AND RESEARCH. [Issued 3 times a year]

HH 1.75/3:date • Item 581-D-4 (EL)
FIELD WORKS, IDEAS FOR HOUSING AND COMMUNITY DEVELOPMENT. [Bimonthly]

HH 1.76:nos. • Item 581-E-27 (MF)
METHODS OF URBAN IMPACT ANALYSIS (series). 1– 1979– [Irregular]

PURPOSE:- To explore a variety of methodological approaches to analysis of the urban impact of Federal programs, including such topics as welfare reform, neighborhood selfhelp programs, etc. Includes statistical data.
Discontinued.

HH 1.77:nos. • Item 581-E-28 (MF)
NSHCIC BULLETINS. 1– [Irregular] (National Solar Heating and Cooling Information Center)

HH 1.78:nos. • Item 581-A-2
ANNUAL HOUSING SURVEY STUDIES. 1st– 1978– Discontinued.

HH 1.79:date • Item 581 (MF)
ANNUAL REPORT ON THE NATIONAL HOUSING GOAL. 1st– 1970–

Report submitted by the Department of Housing and Urban Development pursuant to the Housing and Urban Development Act of 1968 (82 Stat. 602).
Includes information on the progress achieved by the Department toward meeting the housing goal, the outlook for the residential mortgage market in the coming year, and recommendations.
Also published in the House Document series.
Replaced by National Housing Production Report (HH 1.79/2).
Discontinued.

HH 1.79/2:date • Item 581 (MF)
NATIONAL HOUSING PRODUCTION REPORT. [Annual] (Office of Policy Development and Research)

Replaces Annual Report on the National Housing Goal (HH 1.79)

HH 1.80:date • Item 581-E-29 (MF)
INDIAN AND ALASKA NATIVE HOUSING AND COMMUNITY DEVELOPMENT PROGRAMS, ANNUAL REPORT TO CONGRESS.

PURPOSE:- To describe the Department's activities in delivering housing and community development assistance to eligible recipients and in improving program design and regulations. Includes projected costs for the next fiscal year and statistical tables.
Discontinued.

HH 1.80/2 • Item 581-G-1 (MF)
PUBLIC AND INDIAN HOUSING FY . . . PROGRAM FUNGINS PLAN. [Annual]

HH 1.81:nos.
CONSUMER NOTICE. [Monthly]

HH 1.82:date   • Item 581-A-1 (MF)
FINANCIAL MANAGEMENT CAPACITY SHARING
PROGRAM. [Annual]

PURPOSE:- To provide an annual report of
the Department's program to promote sharing of
successful approaches to financial management
problems among State and local governments
having and needing solutions. Emphasizes linking of budgeting, accounting, auditing, and performance measurement.

HH 1.83:date
HUD SCORECARD, QUALITY ASSURANCE PRO-
GRAM. [Quarterly]

HH 1.84:nos.   • Item 581-D (EL)
RECENT RESEARCH RESULTS. [Issued 10 times a
year]

HH 1.85:date   • Item 581-E-31
INTERAGENCY URBAN INITIATIVES ANTI-CRIME
PROGRAM, REPORT TO CONGRESS. 1st–
1980–   [Annual]

Summarizes Program activities, which are directed toward alleviating crime and fear in subsidized housing.
        Discontinued 1979/80.

HH 1.86:date   • Item 581-E-30 (EL)
LEGAL OPINIONS OF THE OFFICE OF GENERAL
COUNSEL. [Annual]

Consists of memorandum responses to Housing and Urban Development officials and others
giving legal opinions on various matters within
the purview of the Department. Contains a subject index plus indexes to citations of Federal
statutes, State statutes, the U.S. Constitution
and U.S. Code, and the Code of Federal Regulations.
        Issued in two volumes, each covering a six-
month period.

HH 1.87:date   • Item 581-F (MF)
ANNUAL REPORT TO CONGRESS ON THE SEC-
TION 312 REHABILITATION LOAN PROGRAM,
FISCAL YEAR (date). [Annual]
        See HE 1.46/6

HH 1.88:date   • Item 581-E-32
RESEARCH AND TECHNOLOGY PROGRAM, FISCAL
YEAR (date). [Annual]
        Discontinued.

HH 1.89:CT   • Item 581-G (MF)
STATE AND URBAN STRATEGIES (various States)
(series). [Irregular]

Consists of case studies of various States'
urban strategies for dealing with growth in an
orderly fashion.

HH 1.91:nos.   • Item 582-R (MF)
CONSOLIDATED SUPPLY PROGRAM. [Irregular]

Each catalog of supplies (for HUD contracts)
deals with a different group of supplies.
        Discontinued.

HH 1.92:date   • Item 581-E-33 (MF)
TELEPHONE DIRECTORY. [Irregular]

HH 1.93:letters-nos.
INSPECTOR GENERAL BULLETIN.

HH 1.94:nos.
TRUSS CONNECTOR BULLETIN.

HH 1.95:nos.
STRUCTURAL ENGINEERING BULLETIN.

HH 1.96:CT   • Item 582
MANAGEMENT DESIGN AND DEVELOPMENT TECH-
NICAL BULLETINS. [Irregular]

HH 1.97:   • Item 581-E-34 (MF)
AFFORDABLE HOUSING DEMONSTRATION, CASE
STUDIES. [Irregular]

Each study presents an affordable housing
demonstration in a different part of the United
States. Such demonstrations are underway in 20
states.
        Discontinued.

HH 1.97/2   • Item 581-E-34
CITIZEN ACTION FOR AFFORDABLE HOUSING,
CASE STUDIES.
        Discontinued.

HH 1.98:CT   • Item 581-E-35
POSTERS. [Irregular]

HH 1.99:date   • Item 582-T
SURVEY OF MORTGAGE LENDING ACTIVITY.
[Quarterly]

Tables present mortgage lending activity by
banks and other major lending institutions.

HH 1.99/2   • Item 582-T
SURVEY OF MORTGAGE LENDING ACTIVITY.
[Quarterly]

Earlier HH 1.99

HH 1.99/2-2:date   • Item 582-T
SURVEY OF MORTGAGE LENDING ACTIVITY STATE
ESTIMATES. [Annual]

HH 1.99/2-3:date   • Item 582-T
SURVEY OF MORTGAGE LENDING ACTIVITY.
[Annual]

HH 1.99/3   • Item 582-T (EL)
SECONDARY MARKET PRICES AND YIELDS AND
INTEREST RATES FOR HOME LOANS. [Monthly]

HH 1.99/4:date   • Item 582-T
SURVEY OF PENSION FUND INVESTMENT IN MORT-
GAGE INSTRUMENTS. [Quarterly]

HH 1.99/4-2:date   • Item 582-T
SURVEY OF MORTGAGE-RELATED SECURITY
HOLDINGS OF MAJOR INSTITUTIONS. [Quarterly]

HH 1.99/5:date   • Item 582-T
UDAG GRANTS TOTAL FOR SMALLER COM-
MUNITIES. [Bimonthly]
        Discontinued.

HH 1.99/5-2   • Item 582-T
UDAG GRANTS TOTAL FOR LARGE AND SMALL
COMMUNITIES. [Biennial]
        Discontinued.

HH 1.99/6:nos.   • Item 582-T (EL)
NEWS RELEASES (series). [Irregular]

HH 1.99/7:date
HUD SURVEY REVEALS LARGE INCREASE IN
PENSION FUND INVESTMENT IN MORTGAGE
INSTRUMENTS. [Annual]

HH 1.99/8:date   • Item 582-T
NEW PRIVATE MORTGAGE INSURANCE ACTIVITY.
[Monthly]
        Discontinued.

HH 1.100   • Item 582-N (MF)
PROGRAMS OF HUD. [Irregular]

Earlier HH 1.2:P 94/8
        Discontinued.

HH 1.101   • Item 582-P (MF)
ANALYSIS OF HUD-ACQUIRED HOME MORTGAGE
PROPERTIES. [Monthly]

Tabular analysis of HUD-acquired home mortgage properties by cities showing sales closed,
unsold properties, sales data, sales financing,
and aging of inventory.
        Discontinued.

HH 1.102:date
CONSOLIDATED LIST OF DEBARRED, SUSPENDED
AND INELIGIBLE CONTRACTORS AND GRANT-
EES. [Quarterly]

HH 1.102/2
– SUPPLEMENT. [Monthly]

HH 1.103:CT   • Item 582-W
FORMS. [Irregular]
        Non-depository.

HH 1.104   • Item 582-N-1
ELDERLY NEWS UPDATES. [Semiannual]

Contains news items that concern the elderly
in such areas as home equity conversion mechanisms and state property tax relief programs for
the elderly.
        Non-depository.

HH 1.105:   • Item 581-E-36 (MF)
CONGRESSIONAL JUSTIFICATION FOR ESTIMATES.
[Annual]

Presents the budget estimates for the Housing and Urban Development Department.

HH 1.107:   • Item 581-E-37 (MF)
PRODUCTIVITY IMPROVEMENT PROGRAM. [Annual]

Outlines actions which the Department will
take to increase the efficiency, quality, and timeliness of its program operations. This plan has
been submitted to the Office of Management and
Budget under the requirement of EO 12552.
        Discontinued.

HH 1.108:   • Item 582-E-2
COMMUNITY DEVELOPMENT PROGRAMS: STATE
REPORTS.

Describes how states, local governments, and
private partners are using the federal government's
community development programs.For all 50
states, DC, and PR, summarizes local efforts to
revitalize America's communities and neighborhoods.
        Discontinued.

HH 1.108/a: • Item 582-E-3
COMMUNITY DEVELOPMENT (separates by
state).

Each issue extracts community development program information for an individual
state from Community Development Programs,
State Reports (HH 1.108).
        Discontinued.

HH 1.108/2:date   • Item 582-E-4
COMMUNITY CONNECTIONS. [Annual]

HH 1.108/3:v.nos./nos.   • Item 582-E-4
EZ/EC NEWS. [Quarterly]

HH 1.109:date/nos.   • Item 582-T
OIG COMMUNIQUE.
        Discontinued.

HH 1.110   • Item 582-T (MF)
URBAN DEVELOPMENT ACTION GRANTS.
        Discontinued.

HH 1.113:date   • Item 581-K
HOME FRONT. [Quarterly]

HH 1.113/2:date   • Item 581-K
THE RESIDENT LEADER. [Quarterly]

HH 1.114   • Item 581-L (E)
ELECTRONIC PRODUCTS. [Irregular]

HH 1.114/2   • Item 581-L-4 (EL)
PATHWAYS (series).

HH 1.114/3   • Item 581-L-5 (EL)
HOMEFIRES: POLICY NEWSLETTER OF THE
HOME INVESTMENT PARTNERSHIP PROGRAM.

HH 1.115:v.nos./nos.   • Item 582-T
THE HUD SALES CONNECTION. [Quarterly]

HH 1.116:date   • Item 581-E-32 (MF)
FORECAST OF CONTRACT OPPORTUNITIES, FIS-
CAL YEAR . . . [Annual]

HH 1.117:nos. • Item 581-K
LABOR RELATIONS LETTERS.

HH 1.120:date/nos. • Item 582-X
HUD WELLNESS NEWSLETTER. [Quarterly]

HH 1.120/2:date/nos. • Item 581-K-1 (EL)
U.S. HOUSING MARKET CONDITIONS. [Quarterly]

HH 1.121:date • Item 582-A-3
KEYNOTES.
Discontinued.

HH 1.122:v.nos./nos. • Item 582-A-4
THE LEAD POST.

HH 1.123:date • Item 582-A-5
COUNSELOR'S CONNECTION. [Quarterly]

HH 1.124: • Item 581-L (EL)
PICTURE OF SUBSIDIZED HOUSEHOLDS.

HH 1.125:date • Item 582-T-2
SERVICE COORDINATORS CHRONICLE. [Semiannual]

HH 1.126: • Item 581-L (EL)
INCOME LIMITS AND SECTION 8 FAIR MARKET RENTS (FMRs).

HH 1.127: • Item 581-L (E)
NEIGHBORHOOD NETWORKS NEWS BRIEF. [Quarterly]
See HH 12.16/3

HH 1.127/2: • Item 581-L (E)
NEIGHBORHOOD NETWORKS NEWSLINE.
See HH 13.16/2

HH 1.128:nos • Item 581-L (EL)
HUD HOUSING TODAY. [Quarterly]

HH 1.129 • Item 582-T-3 (P)
CLUB NOTES.

HH 1.130 • Item 582-A-6 (EL)
GLOBAL OUTLOOK. [Quarterly]

FEDERAL HOUSING ADMINISTRATION
(1947–   )

CREATION AND AUTHORITY

The Federal Housing Administration (NHA 2) was transferred to the Housing and Home Finance Agency by Reorganization Plan 3, effective July 27, 1947. By act approved September 9, 1965 (79 Stat. 667), the Administration became a part of the newly established Department of Housing and Urban Development.

INFORMATION

Federal Housing Administration
Department of Housing and
Urban Development
451 Seventh St., SW
Washington, D.C. 20410
(800) 483-7342 (loans)

HH 2.1 • Item 593-F
FEDERAL HOUSING ADMINISTRATION ANNUAL REPORT.

Reprint of report published in the Annual Report of the Administrator. Includes section of Statistics of Insuring Operations and also includes a list of FHA publications issued during the year. Issued for the calendar year.

HH 2.2:CT • Item 589
GENERAL PUBLICATIONS. [Irregular]

HH 2.5:CT • Item 592
LAWS.

Earlier NHA 2.15

HH 2.6:[CT] • Item 594
FHA REGULATIONS. [Irregular]

HH 2.6/2:nos.
ADMINISTRATIVE RULES AND REGULATIONS UNDER SECTIONS OF NATIONAL HOUSING ACT.

HH 2.6/4:nos.
ALL APPROVED MORTGAGES, LETTERS TO ADMIN.

HH 2.6/6:CT • Item 589-A
HANDBOOKS, MANUALS, GUIDES.

HH 2.6/6:M 84 • Item 589-A
Vol. 10. MORTGAGEE'S HANDBOOK. [Irregular]

PURPOSE:–   To assist approved mortgages operating under the home mortgage sections of the National Housing Act. Looseleaf.

HH 2.6/6:Un 2 • Item 589-A
Vol. 7. FHA UNDERWRITING HANDBOOK, HOME MORTGAGES. [Irregular]

Looseleaf

HH 2.6/7:nos. • Item 589-A
TECHNICAL STANDARDS TRAINING GUIDES. 1– 1968–   [Irregular]

PURPOSE:–   To provide training guides on various subjects of interest to HUD-FHA field offices and the general public. The guides contain information which supplements the minimum property standards.

HH 2.7:nos. • Item 591-A (MF)
LAND PLANNING BULLETINS.

HH 2.8:nos.
COMPTROLLER CIRCULAR LETTERS.

Earlier NHA 2.14

HH 2.9/2:nos.
MECHANICAL ENGINEERING BULLETIN. ME–   (series).

HH 2.10:v.nos.
INSURED MORTGAGE PORTFOLIO. [Quarterly]

Earlier NHA 2.18

HH 2.11:CT
REQUIREMENTS FOR INDIVIDUAL WATER-SUPPLY AND SEWAGE-DISPOSAL SYSTEMS (by States).

Earlier NHA 2.17

HH 2.12:nos. • Item 593-A
TECHNICAL CIRCULARS.

Earlier NHA 2.12

HH 2.13:CT
ADDRESSES.

Earlier NHA 2.7

HH 2.14:nos.
USE OF MATERIALS BULLETINS.

HH 2.14/2:nos.
MATERIALS RELEASE.

HH 2.15:CT
POSTERS AND MAPS.

Earlier NHA 2.13

HH 2.16:date
TRENDS IN SELECTED ECONOMIC FACTORS, UNITED STATES. [Semiannual]

HH 2.17:CT
MINIMUM PROPERTY REQUIREMENTS FOR PROPERTIES OF ONE OR TWO LIVING UNITS LOCATED IN THE [various States].

Earlier NHA 2.18

HH 2.17/2:nos.
MPR REVISIONS.

HH 2.17/3 • Item 593
MINIMUM PROPERTY STANDARDS. [Irregular]

Minimum property standards were established to obtain those characteristics in a property which will assure present and continuing utility, durability and desirability as well as compliance with basic safety and health requirements. To provide this assurance, these standards set forth the minimum qualities considered necessary in the planning, construction and development of the property which is to serve as a security for an insured mortgage.
Includes illustrations. Loose-leaf and punched for 3-ring binder.
Minimum Property Standards issued for the following:
Low Cost Housing.
Nursing Homes.
One and Two Living Units.
Three or More Living Units.

HH 2.17/4 • Item 593
MINIMUM PROPERTY STANDARDS FOR 1 AND 2 LIVING UNITS. [Irregular] (Publication FHA 300)

Issued in loose-leaf form. Kept up-to-date by revisions.

HH 2.18
PRESS RELEASES. [Irregular]

HH 2.18/2:date
FHA SPECIAL FEATURES FOR USE AT ANY TIME.

HH 2.18/3:nos.
FHA RESEARCH AND STATISTICS RELEASE. [Irregular]

HH 2.18/4:nos.
FHA NEWS FILLERS FOR USE AT ANY TIME.

HH 2.19:
COMMENTS ON ECONOMIC AND HOUSING SITUATION. ADMIN.

HH 2.20:
CURRENT HOUSING SITUATION. [Monthly]

HH 2.21:nos.
OPERATORS LETTERS. ADMIN.

HH 2.22 • Item 593-B
STATEMENT OF FINANCIAL CONDITION. [Annual]

Four-page folder giving summary of financial statement as of December 31 of the Federal Housing Administration. Figures also contained in the Annual Report.

HH 2.22/2:date
TECHNICAL STATEMENTS. [Monthly] Admin.

HH 2.23:CT
TECHNICAL STUDIES REPORTS.

HH 2.23/2:date
LIST OF TECHNICAL STUDIES.

HH 2.24
FHA TRENDS, CHARACTERISTICS OF HOME MORTGAGES INSURED BY FHA. [Quarterly]

Statistical tables.
Previous title: Quarterly Report on FHA Trends.
ISSN 0364-2666

HH 2.24/2
– STATE TRENDS. [Quarterly]

HH 2.24/3
– AREA TRENDS. [Quarterly]

HH 2.24/4:date • **Item 593-F (MF)**
FHA HOMES, DATA FOR STATES, ON CHARAC-
TERISTICS OF FHA OPERATIONS UNDER SEC.
203. [Irregular] (Division of Research and Statistics)

> ISSN 0091-4932
> Earlier HH 2.2:H 75/13

HH 2.24/4-2:date • **Item 593-F (MF)**
DATA FOR STATES AND SELECTED AREAS ON CHAR-
ACTERISTICS OF FHA OPERATIONS UNDER
SECTION 245.

HH 2.24/5:date • **Item 593-F**
SUMMARY OF MORTGAGE INSURANCE OPERA-
TIONS AND CONTRACT AUTHORITY. [Monthly]
(Financial Analysis and Investment Division, Of-
fice of Finance and Accounting)

> ISSN 0364-8419

HH 2.24/6:date
SERIES DATA HANDBOOK. [Annual] (RR-25)

> Issued as a supplement to FHA Trends (HH
> 2.24)

HH 2.24/7:date • **Item 593-F (MF)**
CHARACTERISTICS OF FHA SINGLE- FAMILY MORT-
GAGES. [Annual] (RR-255)

HH 2.24/8 • **Item 593-F (MF)**
FHA HOME MORTGAGE INSURANCE OPERA-
TIONS, STATE, COUNTY AND MSA/PMSA. [Annual]

HH 2.25:date
FHA HONOR AWARDS FOR PRESIDENTIAL DESIGN.

HH 2.26:date
FHA LOW COST HOUSING TRENDS OF 1-FAMILY
HOMES INSURED BY FHA UNDER SEC. 221(d)(2).
1969– [Quarterly] (Division of Research and
Statistics) (RR-252)

> PURPOSE:– To highlight characteristics com-
> mon to homes of low and moderate income fami-
> lies that have had their mortgages insured under
> section 221(d)2 of the National Housing Act. One-
> page statistical summary.

HH 2.27:date
FHA MONTHLY REPORT OF OPERATIONS: PROJECT
MORGAGE INSURANCE PROGRAMS. 1935–
[Monthly] (Divison of Research and Statistics)
(RR-301)

> PURPOSE:– To provide Congress and the
> public with a statistical summary of the activities
> of the Federal Housing Administration.
> Prior to July 1969, the FHS Monthly Report of
> Operations was issued as one publication. From
> July 1969 until January 1975, issued in the fol-
> lowing parts:
> 1. Project Mortgage Programs.
> 2. Home Mortgage Programs.
> 3. Summary of Activities Under All Sec-
> tions.
> Beginning March 1975, part two issued sepa-
> rately (HH 2.27/2).
> ISSN 0145-5656

HH 2.27/2:date
FHA MONTHLY REPORT OF OPERATIONS: HOME
MORTGAGE PROGRAMS. 1975– [Quarterly]

> Prior to March 1975 issued as part 2 of the
> FHA Monthly Report of Operations (HH 2.27).
> ISSN 0145-5648

HH 2.28:CT • **Item 593-E (MF)**
ANALYSIS OF [city] HOUSING MARKET AS OF [date].
[Irregular]

HH 2.28/2:CT
CURRENT HOUSING MARKET SITUATION, REPORT
[various localities]. 1971– [Irregular] (Economic
and Market Analysis Division)

> PURPOSE:– To assist and guide the Depart-
> ment of Housing and Urban Development in its
> operations. the factual information, findings, and

conclusions may be useful also to builders, mort-
gagees, and others concerned with local housing
problems and trends. The reports do not purport
to make determinations with respect to the ac-
ceptability of any particular mortgage insurance
proposals that may be under consideration in the
subject locality.

HH 2.29:date • **Item 589-A-1**
HOUSING/FHA NEWS. [Biweekly]

HOUSING ASSISTANCE
ADMINISTRATION
(1965– 1969)

CREATION AND AUTHORITY

> The Public Housing Administration was es-
> tablished as a constituent agency of the Housing
> and Home Finance Agency under Reorganization
> Plan No. 3 of 1947, effective July 27, 1947. The
> Administration was abolished and its functions
> transferred to the Housing Assistance Adminis-
> tration of the newly established Department of
> Housing and Urban Development by the act of
> September 9, 1965 (79 Stat. 667), effective No-
> vember 9, 1965.

HH 3.1 • **Item 599**
ANNUAL REPORT. [Annual]

> Reprint of excerpts from the Annual Report of
> the Administrator.

HH 3.2:CT • **Item 599**
GENERAL PUBLICATIONS.

HH 3.3:v.nos.
PHA BULLETIN. [Monthly]

> Earlier EPHA Bulletin (NHA 4.3).

HH 3.3/2:nos.
BULLETINS.

> Earlier NHA 4.3/2

HH 3.3/3:nos.
DEFENSE HOUSING BULLETIN DH (series).

HH 3.3/4:nos.
PHA LOW-RENT HOUSING BULLETINS. [Irregular]

HH 3.4:date
CIRCULARS. [Admin.]

HH 3.5:CT
LAWS.

HH 3.6:CT
REGULATIONS, RULES AND INSTRUCTIONS.

HH 3.6/2:CT
HANDBOOKS, MANUALS, GUIDES.

HH 3.6/3:pt.nos.
LOCAL HOUSING AUTHORITY MANAGEMENT HAND-
BOOK.

HH 3.7:
RELEASES.

HH 3.8:nos.
TRENDS TOWARD OPEN OCCUPANCY IN HOUSING
PROGRAMS OF PUBLIC HOUSING ADMINIS-
TRATION.

> Earlier HH 3.2:Oc 1/2

HH 3.9
LOCAL AUTHORITIES PARTICIPATING IN HAA LOW-
RENT PROGRAMS. [Quarterly]

> Later HH 1.51

HH 3.10:date
PHA HONOR AWARDS FOR DESIGN EXCELLENCE.

HH 3.11:CT
BIBLIOGRAPHIES AND LISTS OF PUBLICATIONS.

HH 3.12
ADDRESSES. [Irregular]

FEDERAL HOME LOAN BANK
BOARD
(1947– 1955)

CREATION AND AUTHORITY

> The Home Loan Bank Board was established
> as a constituent agency of the Housing and Home
> Finance Agency by Reorganization Plan No. 3 of
> 1947, effective July 27, 1947. The Board as-
> sumed the functions of the Federal Home Loan
> Bank Board, the Board of Directors of the Home
> Owners' Loan Corporation, and the Board of Trust-
> ees of the Federal Savings and Loan Insurance
> Corporation. Under the Housing Amendments of
> 1955 (69 Stat. 640), the Board was made an
> independent agency and redesignated the Fed-
> eral Home Loan Bank Board (FHL 1).

HH 4.1:date
ANNUAL REPORTS.
> Earlier NHA 3.1
> Later FHL 1.1

HH 4.2:CT
GENERAL PUBLICATIONS.
> Earlier NHA 3.2
> Later FHL 1.2

HH 4.6:CT
REGULATIONS, RULES, AND INSTRUCTIONS.
> Earlier NHA 3.6
> Later FHL 1.6

HH 4.7:date
NONFARM REAL ESTATE FORECLOSURE REPORT.
[Quarterly]
> Earlier NHA 3.9
> Later FHL 1.8

HH 4.8:
RELEASES.

> Later FHL 1.7

HH 4.8/2:date
ESTIMATED FLOW OF SAVINGS IN SAVINGS AND
LOAN ASSOCIATIONS. [Monthly]

HH 4.8/3:date
ESTIMATED MORTGAGE LENDING ACTIVITY OF
SAVINGS AND LOAN ASSOCIATIONS. [Monthly]

> Later FHL 1.7/2

HH 4.8/4:date
ESTIMATED AMOUNT OF NONFARM MORTGAGES
OF $20,000 OR LESS RECORDED. [Monthly]

HH 4.9:date
MORTGAGE RECORDING LETTER. [Monthly]

> Later FHL 1.9

HH 4.10:date
SAVINGS AND MORTGAGE FINANCING DATA.
[Monthly]

> Later FHL 1.10

LAND AND FACILITIES DEVELOPMENT ADMINISTRATION (1965– 1969)

CREATION AND AUTHORITY

The Community Facilities Service was transferred from the General Services Administration to the Housing and Home Finance Agency. In 1965, Service redesignated the Land and Facilities Development Administration when it was transferred to the newly established Department of Housing and Urban Development.

HH 5.1:date
ANNUAL REPORT.

Earlier FW 7.1

HH 5.2:CT　　　　　　　　　　　　　　• Item 586
GENERAL PUBLICATIONS.

HH 5.6:CT
REGULATIONS, RULES, AND INSTRUCTIONS.

HH 5.7:
RELEASES.

HH 5.7/2:nos.
COMMUNITY FACILITIES ADMINISTRATION NEWS ABOUT NEW ACCELERATED PUBLIC WORKS PROGRAM.

HH 5.8:CT
ADDRESSES.

HH 5.9:CT
HANDBOOKS, MANUALS, GUIDES.

HH 5.10:date
CFA DESIGN AWARDS PROGRAM. [Annual]

FEDERAL NATIONAL MORTGAGE ASSOCIATION (1950– 1968)

CREATION AND AUTHORITY

The Federal National Mortgage Association was transferred from the Reconstruction Finance Agency to the Housing and Home Finance Agency by Reorganization Plan No. 22 of 1950. The Association continued under the Department of Housing and Urban development until 1968 when the 1968 Housing and Urban Development Act established two separate corporations– one, the Federal National Mortgage Association, became a Government-sponsored private corporation; the other, the Government National Mortgage Association remained in the Department of Housing and Urban Development to exercise the functions of the original FNMA.

HH 6.1:date
SEMI-ANNUAL REPORT.
Earlier Y 3.R 24:2 F 31n

HH 6.2:CT　　　　　　　　　　　　　• Item 594-A
GENERAL PUBLICATIONS.
Earlier Y 3.R 24:2

HH 6.5:CT　　　　　　　　　　　　　　• Item 583
LAWS.

HH 6.7:nos.
FHA AND VA MORTGAGES OWNED AND AVAILABLE FOR SALE BY FEDERAL NATIONAL MORTGAGE ASSOCIATION.
Earlier Y 3.R 24:14

HH 6.8:nos.
RELEASES.

HH 6.8/2:date
FEDERAL NATIONAL MORTGAGE ASSOCIATION NEWS. [Irregular]

RENEWAL ASSISTANCE ADMINISTRATION (1965– 1969)

CREATION AND AUTHORITY

The Urban Renewal Administration was established within the Housing and Home Finance Agency by Administrator's Reorganization Order No. 1, dated December 23, 1954, to succeed the Division of Slum Clearance and Urban Redevelopment. The Administration was abolished and its functions transferred to the Renewal Assistance Administration of the Department of Housing and Urban Development by act of September 9, 1965 (79 Stat. 667), effective November 9, 1965.

HH 7.1:date
ANNUAL REPORTS.

HH 7.2:CT　　　　　　　　　　　　• Item 584-C
GENERAL PUBLICATIONS.

HH 7.2:G 76　　　　　　　　　　　• Item 584-C
URBAN RENEWAL DEMONSTRATION GRANT PROGRAM, PROJECT DIRECTORY. [Irregular]

Describes the Urban Renewal Demonstration Grant Program (section 314 of the Housing Act of 1954, as amended) and describes briefly each of the projects supported under the program, both completed and still in execution.

HH 7.3:nos.
URBAN RENEWAL BULLETINS.

Changed from HH 1.19

HH 7.3/2:nos.
ADVISORY BULLETIN (series).

HH 7.3/3　　　　　　　　　　　　• Item 584-A
URBAN RENEWAL SERVICE BULLETINS. 1– [Irregular]

HH 7.3/4:nos.
URBAN PLANNING BULLETINS.

HH 7.6:CT
REGULATIONS, RULES, AND INSTRUCTIONS.

HH 7.6/2　　　　　　　　　　　　• Item 584-D
TECHNICAL GUIDES. 1–　1960–　[Irregular]

HH 7.6/3:CT　　　　　　　　　　• Item 584-E
HANDBOOKS, MANUALS, GUIDES.

HH 7.6/4
COMMUNITY RENEWAL PROGRAM GUIDES. CRP 1–　1963–　[Irregular]

HH 7.7:nos.
RELEASES. [Irregular]

HH 7.8
URBAN RENEWAL PROJECT CHARACTERISTICS. 1954–　[Irregular]

PURPOSE:– To provide summary characteristics of local slum clearance and urban renewal projects approved under title 3, Housing Act of 1954 and title 1 of the Housing Act of 1949.

HH 7.8/2:date
URBAN RENEWAL PROJECT DIRECTORY. [Quarterly]

Earlier HH 7.2:P 94

HH 7.8/3:date
URBAN PLANNING ASSISTANCE PROGRAM PROJECT DIRECTORY.

Later HH 1.26
HH 7.9
URBAN RENEWAL MANUAL, POLICIES AND REQUIREMENTS FOR LOCAL PUBLIC AGENCIES. [Irregular]

Prescribes the Federal policies, procedures, and requirements applicable to Local Public Agencies carrying out slum clearance and urban renewal projects under Title I of the Housing Act of 1949, as amended.
Subscription includes basic manual, binder, and supplementary service for approximately 2 years.

HH 7.9/2:nos.
LOCAL PUBLIC AGENCY LETTERS.

HH 7.10
REPORT OF URBAN RENEWAL OPERATIONS. 1956– [Monthly]

PURPOSE:– To provide updated summary statistics on the Urban Renewal Operations.

HH 7.11
REPORT OF URBAN PLANNING ASSISTANCE PROGRAM. 1957–　[Monthly]

PURPOSE:– To provide updated summary statistics on the Urban Planning Assistance Program.

HH 7.13:CT
ADDRESSES.

HH 7.14:date
RELOCATION FROM URBAN RENEWAL PROJECT AREAS. [Semiannual]

HH 7.15　　　　　　　　　　　　　• Item 584-I
LISTING OF LAND IN URBAN RENEWAL PROJECT AREAS AVAILABLE FOR PRIVATE REDEVELOPMENT.
PURPOSE:– To insure maximum participation in urban renewal by private enterprise; to help speed up disposition of land acquired by localities in their urban renewal project areas by making known the availability and location of this land to prospective redevelopers; and to answer inquiries from business firms and associations in the building, banking and financing, and real estate industries.
Lists in tabular form, by State, city, and project number: number of square feet for residential (single-family, multi-family, and total), commercial, and industrial use; local public agency address.

HH 7.16:date
URA HONOR AWARDS PROGRAM IN URBAN RENEWAL DESIGN.

HH 7.17:CT　　　　　　　　　　　• Item 584-K
BIBLIOGRAPHIES AND LISTS OF PUBLICATIONS.

HH 7.18
URA DEMONSTRATION GRANT SUMMARIES. 1965– [Irregular]

Each issue summarizes a single urban renewal demonstration report published with an urban renewal demonstration grant made under section 314 of the Housing Act of 1954, as amended. Highlights of the report are presented so that the reader can decide quickly whether he could profitably consult the complete report. Directions for obtaining the report are included.

HH 7.19:nos.
NEIGHBORHOOD FACILITIES GRANT PROGRAM LETTERS.

Pubs. Desig. NF-(nos).

URBAN MANAGEMENT ASSISTANCE ADMINISTRATION (1969–1974)

HH 8.1:date
ANNUAL REPORT.

HH 8.2:CT   • **Item 854-O**
GENERAL PUBLICATIONS.

HH 8.8:CT
HANDBOOKS, MANUALS, GUIDES.

HH 8.9:date   • **Item 584-N**
SELECTED ABSTRACTS OF PLANNING REPORTS. 1969– [Quarterly] (Office of Metropolitan Development)

PURPOSE:– To make the results of federally supported studies widely available to others.
Contains summaries of planning studies supported by HUD throughout the country. The studies range from general planning studies to specific development of implementation plans for the use of human, technical or physical resources.
Earlier title: Abstracts of "701" planning reports.

HH 8.10:nos.   • **Item 584-N-1**
HOUSING PLANNING INFORMATION SERIES. 1– [Irregular] (Office of Planning Assistance and Standards)

PURPOSE:– To make available information on how other agencies and organizations have helped to improve the supply and quality of housing and stimulate greater involvement of planners and public officials in the provision of housing, particularly for low-income and minority families.
Contains notes identifying some of the national organizations working in the housing field as well as recent reports, studies, and other housing information sources.

COMMUNITY DEVELOPMENT OFFICE

HH 9.1:date
ANNUAL REPORTS.

HH 9.2:CT
GENERAL PUBLICATIONS.

HH 9.9:date
REPORT OF URBAN RENEWAL OPERATIONS, TITLE 1, HOUSING ACT OF 1949 AS AMENDED. 1954–1974. [Monthly] (Community Planning and Development, Office of Management)

PURPOSE:– To provide cumulative and current fiscal year summary statistics for local urban renewal programs approved for federal assistance under Title I of Housing Act of 1949, as amended. These activities include Urban Renewal Projects, Neighborhood Development Programs, Code Enforcement Projects, Demolition Projects, Interim Assistance Programs, Certified Area Programs, Fair Program Grants, General Neighborhood Renewal Plans, and Feasibility Surveys. Statistics are summarized by project or program activities on a national and regional basis. New approvals, changes and terminations which occurred during the report month are also listed.

FEDERAL INSURANCE ADMINISTRATION

INFORMATION

Federal Insurance Administration
Department of Housing and
Urban Development
Washington, D.C. 20410

HH 10.1:date
ANNUAL REPORTS.

HH 10.2:CT   • **Item 594-A-1**
GENERAL PUBLICATIONS.

HH 10.8:CT   • **Item 594-A-3**
HANDBOOKS, MANUALS AND GUIDES.

HH 10.9:CT   • **Item 594-C-1 C-55**
FLOOD INSURANCE STUDIES (by State). [Irregular]

Previously issued to Depository Libraries under Item No. 594-A-2.

HH 10.10   • **Item 594-A-3**
COMMUNITY ASSISTANCE SERIES.

NEW COMMUNITIES ADMINISTRATION

HH 11.1:date
ANNUAL REPORT.

HH 11.2:CT   • **Item 599-A-1**
GENERAL PUBLICATIONS.

FEDERAL DISASTER ASSISTANCE ADMINISTRATION (–1979)

HH 12.1:date
ANNUAL REPORT.

HH 12.2:CT   • **Item 599-A-2**
GENERAL PUBLICATIONS. [Irregular]

HH 12.8:CT   • **Item 599-A-3**
HANDBOOKS, MANUALS, GUIDES. [Irregular]

HH 12.9:date
DISASTER INFORMATION. [Irregular]

Later FEM 1.9

HH 12.10:CT
AUDIOVISUAL MATERIALS. [Irregular]

MULTI-FAMILY HOUSING OFFICE

INFORMATION

Multi-Family Housing Office
Department of Housing & Urban Development
451 Seventh St., SW
Washington, DC 20410
708-2495
Fax: (202) 708-2583
http://www.hud.gov/groups/multifamily.cfm

HH 13.2:   • **Item 599-P-1**
GENERAL PUBLICATIONS.

HH 13.8:   • **Item 599-P-2**
HANDBOOKS, MANUALS, AND GUIDES

HH 13.15:   • **Item 599-P-3 (E)**
ELECTRONIC PRODUCTS (misc.).

HH 13.16:v.nos.   • **Item 599-P-4 (P) (EL)**
NEIGHBORHOOD NETWORKS NEWS. [Quarterly]

HH 13.16/2   • **Item 599-P-3 (EL)**
NEIGHBORHOOD NETWORKS NEWSLINE. [Bi-monthly]

HH 13.16/4: CT   • **Item 599-P-5**
NEIGHBORHOOD NETWORKS

HH 13.16/5   • **Item 599-P-6 (EL)**
NEIGHBORHOOD NETWORKS FACT SHEET.

DEPARTMENT OF THE INTERIOR (1849–   )

CREATION AND AUTHORITY

The Department of the Interior was created by act of March 3, 1849 (9 Stat. 395; 5 U.S.C. 481), which transferred to it the General Land Office, the Office of Indian Affairs, the Pension Office, and the Patent Office. The Department also had responsibility for supervision of the commissioner of Public buildings, the board of Inspectors and the Warden of the Penitentiary of the District of Columbia, the census of the United States, and the accounts of marshals and other officers of the United States courts, and of lead and other mines in the United States.

INFORMATION

Department of the Interior
1849 C Street, NW
Washington, D.C. 20240
(202) 208-3171
Fax: (202) 208-5048
http://www.doi.gov

I 1.1:date   • **Item 600-C**
ANNUAL REPORT.

I 1.1/2:date
RESEARCH AND ACTIVITIES UNDER SALTONSTALL-KENNEDY ACT, ANNUAL REPORT OF SECRETARY OF INTERIOR.

Later I 49.48

I 1.1/3 • Item 604-A
SALINE WATER CONVERSION REPORT FOR (year). 1952– [Annual]

A complete resume of the activities of the Office of Saline Water for the calendar year. Includes lists of Research and Development Progress Reports.
Report made by the Secretary of the Interior to the President and Congress as required by PL 82-448.

I 1.1/4 • Item 601-B (MF)
COOPERATIVE WATER RESOURCES, RESEARCH AND TRAINING. 1965– [Annual]

I 1.1/5:date • Item 601-G (MF)
OFFICE OF WATER RESEARCH AND TECHNOLOGY: ANNUAL REPORT. 1st– 1964– [Annual]

Report submitted by the Secretary of the Interior to the President and Congress showing particulars of the program of the Office of Water Research and Technology for the preceding year. It describes success of the research, new directions for the program, information dissemination and technology transfer, State water resources institute activities, OWRT activities, and training and manpower.

I 1.1/6:date • Item 600-C (MF)
INTERIOR BUDGET IN BRIEF, FISCAL YEAR HIGHLIGHTS. [Annual]

I 1.1/7:date • Item 600-C (MF)
OFFICE OF INSPECTOR GENERAL, SEMIANNUAL REPORT.

I 1.1/7-2:date • Item 600-C (MF)
OIG HIGHLIGHTS. [Semiannual]

OIG = Office of Inspector General

I 1.1/7-2:CT
– GENERAL PUBLICATIONS.

Later Y 3.Ar 2

I 1.2:CT • Item 603
GENERAL PUBLICATIONS.

I 1.3:nos.
BULLETINS [none issued].

I 1.3/2:nos.
EMPLOYEE INFORMATION BULLETIN. Admin.

I 1.3/3:date • Item 603-M
ENJOY OUTDOORS AMERICA BULLETIN. [Monthly]

I 1.4:nos.
CIRCULARS.

I 1.5 • Item 603-L
LAWS.

I 1.6:date
ARIZONA, GOVERNOR, ANNUAL REPORTS, 1878– 1912.

I 1.7:date
CAPITAL BUILDINGS AND GROUNDS, SUPERINTENDENT, ANNUAL REPORTS.

Later Y 3.Ar 2

I 1.8:date
COLUMBIA INSTITUTION FOR INSTRUCTION OF DEAF AND DUMB. ANNUAL REPORTS.

I 1.8/2:CT
– GENERAL PUBLICATIONS.

I 1.8/3:date
REPORT OF PROCEEDINGS OF CONVENTION OF AMERICAN INSTRUCTORS OF THE DEAF.

I 1.9:date
COLUMBIA RAILWAY COMPANY, ANNUAL REPORTS.

I 1.10:date
DAKOTA, GOVERNOR, ANNUAL REPORTS, 1878– 1912.

I 1.11:date
FIVE CIVILIZED TRIBES COMMISSIONER. ANNUAL REPORTS.

I 1.11/2:CT
– GENERAL PUBLICATIONS.

I 1.12:date
FREEDMAN'S HOSPITAL. ANNUAL REPORTS.

Later FS 2.54

I 1.12/2:CT
– GENERAL PUBLICATIONS.

Later FS 2.54/2

I 1.13:date
GAS AND METER INSPECTION. ANNUAL REPORT.

I 1.14:date
GOVERNMENT HOSPITAL FOR THE INSANE. ANNUAL REPORTS.

Later FS 11.1

I 1.14/2:CT
– GENERAL PUBLICATIONS.

Later FS 11.2

I 1.14/3:nos.
CIRCULARS. [none issued]

I 1.14/5:vol.
ST. ELIZABETH'S HOSPITAL, SUN DIAL.

I 1.15:date
HOT SPRINGS RESERVATION COMMISSION. ANNUAL REPORTS.

I 1.16:date
HOT SPRINGS RESERVATION IMPROVEMENT OFFICE, ANNUAL REPORTS.

I 1.17:date
HOT SPRINGS RESERVATION. ANNUAL REPORTS.

I 1.17/2:CT
– GENERAL PUBLICATIONS.

I 1.17/3:nos.
– BULLETINS.

I 1.17/4:nos.
– CIRCULARS.

I 1.17/5:date
– MEDICAL DIRECTOR, ANNUAL REPORTS.

I 1.18:date
HOWARD UNIVERSITY, ANNUAL REPORTS.

Later FS 5.40

I 1.19:date
IDAHO, GOVERNOR, ANNUAL REPORTS, 1878– 90.

I 1.20:date
MINE INSPECTOR FOR INDIAN TERRITORY, ANNUAL REPORTS, 1894– 1907.

I 1.20/2:date
INDIAN INSPECTOR FOR INDIAN TERRITORY. ANNUAL REPORTS.

I 1.21:date
MARITIME CANAL COMPANY OF NICARAGUA, ANNUAL REPORTS.

I 1.22:date
MONTANA, GOVERNOR, ANNUAL REPORT, 1878– 89.

I 1.23:date
MINE INSPECTOR FOR THE TERRITORY OF NEW MEXICO, ANNUAL REPORTS, 1895– 1912.

I 1.24:date
NEW MEXICO, GOVERNOR, ANNUAL REPORTS, 1878– 1912.

I 1.24/2:date
NEW MEXICO, TRAVELING AUDITOR AND BANK EXAMINER, ANNUAL REPORTS.

I 1.25:date
OFFICIAL REGISTER (or Blue Book) BIENNIAL.

Earlier S 1.11
Later CS 1.31

I 1.26:date
OKLAHOMA, GOVERNOR, ANNUAL REPORTS, 1891– 1907.

I 1.27:date
ANNUAL REPORTS ON CONSTRUCTION OF PENSION BUILDING, 1883– 87.

I 1.28:date
REGISTER OF THE DEPARTMENT OF THE INTERIOR.

I 1.29:date
SEQUOIA AND GENERAL GRANT NATIONAL PARKS, ANNUAL REPORTS.

I 1.30:date
UNION PACIFIC RAILWAY, GOVERNMENT DIRECTORS, ANNUAL REPORTS, 1864– 1898.

I 1.31:date
UTAH COMMISSION, ANNUAL REPORTS, 1882– 96.

I 1.32:date
UTAH, GOVERNOR, ANNUAL REPORTS, 1878– 96.

I 1.33:date
MINE INSPECTOR FOR THE TERRITORY OF UTAH, ANNUAL REPORTS, 1893– 95.

I 1.34:date
WASHINGTON HOSPITAL FOR FOUNDLINGS, ANNUAL REPORTS.

I 1.35:date
WASHINGTON, GOVERNOR, ANNUAL REPORTS, 1878– 90.

I 1.36:date
WYOMING, GOVERNOR, ANNUAL REPORTS, 1878– 90.

I 1.37:date
YELLOWSTONE NATIONAL PARK, ANNUAL REPORTS, 1898– 90.

I 1.38:date
YOSEMITE NATIONAL PARK, ANNUAL REPORTS.

I 1.39:date
PUERTO RICO, EDUCATION DEPT. ANNUAL REPORTS.

Later W 75.7

I 1.40:date
PUERTO RICO, INTERIOR DEPT. ANNUAL REPORTS.

Later W 75.9

I 1.41:date
HAWAII, GOVERNOR. ANNUAL REPORTS.

Later I 35.11/1

I 1.42:date
CRATER LAKE NATIONAL PARK, ANNUAL REPORTS.

I 1.43:date
MOUNT RAINIER NATIONAL PARK, ANNUAL REPORTS.

I 1.44:Cong.
LAWS RELATING TO THE DEPT. OF THE INTERIOR.

I 1.45:date
WASHINGTON AQUEDUCT, ANNUAL REPORTS.

I 1.46:CT
SPECIFICATIONS.

I 1.47:CT
LAWS AND REGULATIONS RELATING TO NATIONAL PARKS, RESERVATIONS, ETC.

I 1.47/2:CT
RULES AND REGULATIONS OF NATIONAL PARKS.

I 1.48:date
MESA VERDE NATIONAL PARK, ANNUAL REPORTS.

I 1.49:CT
PUBLIC NOTICES (concerning irrigation projects of reclamation service).

I 1.50:CT
MAPS OF STATES SHOWING LANDS DESIGNATED BY SECRETARY OF INTERIOR AS SUBJECT TO ENTRY UNDER ENLARGED HOMESTEAD ACT OF FEBRUARY 19, 1909.

I 1.51:date
COMMISSIONER OF PUBLIC BUILDINGS, ANNUAL REPORTS.

> Later W 38.1

I 1.52:date
GLACIER NATIONAL PARK, REPORTS.

I 1.53:CT
[INFORMATION REGARDING NATIONAL PARKS].

I 1.54:date
PLATT NATIONAL PARK, ANNUAL REPORTS.

I 1.55:CT
PENSION CASES, DECISIONS.

I 1.56:date
WIND CAVE NATIONAL PARK, ANNUAL REPORTS.

I 1.57:date
ROCKY MOUNTAIN NATNIONAL PARK. ANNUAL REPORTS.

I 1.58:date
GENERAL SUPERINTENDENT AND LANDSCAPE ENGINEER OF NATIONAL PARKS, ANNUAL REPORTS.

I 1.59:date
ALASKAN ENGINEERING COMMISSION, ALASKAN RAILROAD.

I 1.59/2:CT
– GENERAL PUBLICATIONS.

I 1.59/3:
– BULLETINS.

I 1.59/4:
– CIRCULARS.

I 1.59/5:v.nos.
– ALASKA RAILROAD RECORD.

I 1.60:date
CHIEF CLERK AND SUPERINTENDENT OF BUILDINGS, ANNUAL REPORT.

I 1.61:date
PAN PACIFIC CONFERENCE ON EDUCATION, REHABILITATION, RECLAMATION AND RECREATION. ANNUAL REPORTS.

I 1.61/2:CT
– GENERAL PUBLICATIONS.

I 1.61/3:nos.
– BULLETINS.

I 1.61/4:
– CIRCULARS.

1.62:date
PERRY'S VICTORY MEMORIAL COMMISSION. ANNUAL REPORTS.

I 1.62/2:CT
– GENERAL PUBLICATIONS.

I 1.62/3:nos.
– BULLETINS.

I 1.62/4:
– CIRCULARS.

I 1.62/5:
– LAWS.

I 1.62/6:
– REGULATIONS.

I 1.62/7:date
– ANNUAL MEETINGS.

I 1.63:nos.
ORDERS.

I 1.64:CT
ARCHAEOLOGIST FOR INTERIOR DEPT. ANNUAL REPORTS.

I 1.65:date
VIRGIN ISLANDS. ANNUAL REPORTS.

> After 1935 see I 35.13/1

I 1.65/2:CT
– GENERAL PUBLICATIONS.

> Later I 35.13/2

I 1.65/3:
– BULLETINS.

> Later I 35.13/3

I 1.65/4:
– CIRCULARS.

I 1.66:nos.
PURCHASING OFFICE CIRCULARS.

I 66/2:nos.
PURCHASING OFFICE ORDERS.

I 1.67:date
FEDERAL OIL CONSERVATION BOARD. ANNUAL REPORTS.

I 1.67/2:CT
– GENERAL PUBLICATIONS.

I 1.67/3:
– BULLETINS.

I 1.67/4:
– CIRCULARS.

I 1.67/5:CT
– LAWS.

I 1.68
ADDRESSES. [Irregular]

I 1.69:v.nos.   • Item 602
DECISIONS OF THE DEPARTMENT OF THE INTERIOR. v. 1–   1881–   [Irregular]

PURPOSE:– To make available to Government officials and to members of the public the leading administrative decisions of the Secretary of the Interior, his Assistant Secretaries, and the Solicitor, together with the leading opinions of the solicitor relating to matters within the jurisdiction of the Department of the Interior.

The first volume was issued in 1883, covering the period from January 1881 to June 1883. Prior to that time the decisions were published by private reporters.

While the majority of the decisions relates to cases concerning public lands, beginning in 1930, the Decisions contained all subjects coming under the Department's administration. Beginning in January 1955, the Decisions have been published in a monthly preprint form (I 1.69/a), with the bound volumes (I 1.69) being published at the end of each calendar year.

Each volume bears a number and each preprint bears the volume number and the individual preprint number, the numbers running in numerical sequence.

I 1.69/a:v.nos.&nos.   • Item 602-A
DECISIONS OF THE DEPARTMENT OF THE INTERIOR, SEPARATE PREPRINTS. [Monthly]

Decisions by the Department of the Interior on appeals, claims, and acts. Final number of each volume includes index-digest for that volume.

I 1.69/2:date   • Item 602-C
INDEX-DIGEST, PUBLISHED AND IMPORTANT UNPUBLISHED DECISIONS. [Quarterly] (Office of the Solicitor)

– CUMULATIVE INDEX-DIGEST. [Quinquennial and Decennial] 1955– 1964.

I 1.69/2-2:date
TOPICAL INDEXES TO DECISIONS AND OPINIONS OF THE DEPARTMENT OF THE INTERIOR. [Irregular]

> v. 52– 61. 1927– 1954. Issued in 2 parts.
> Earlier I 21.6

I 1.69/2-3:date   • Item 602
CUMULATIVE INDEX-DIGEST OF UNPUBLISHED DECISIONS. [Irregular]

> 1943– 1954.
> 1955– 1964.
> 1965– 1974. 1978. 1052 p.
> ISSN 0098-1087

I 1.69/3:v.nos.
DIGEST OF DECISIONS OF DEPARTMENT OF INTERIOR IN CASES RELATING TO PUBLIC LANDS.

> Earlier I 21.6

I 1.69/4:nos.   • Item 665-E
DECISIONS, SOLICITOR'S OPINIONS. M-1– [Irregular] (Office of the Solicitor)

I 1.69/5:nos.   • Item 665-D
DECISIONS OF LAND APPEALS. A-1–   [Irregular]

I 1.69/6:nos.   • Item 665-C
DECISIONS ON INDIAN APPEALS. IA-1–   [Irregular] (Office of the Solicitor)

I 1.69/7:nos.   • Item 665-A
DECISIONS ON CONTRACT APPEALS. IBCA-1– [Irregular] (Board of Contract Appeals)

I 1.69/8:nos.   • Item 665-F
DECISIONS ON TORT AND IRRIGATION CLAIMS. [Irregular]

I 69/9:date   • Item 602-B (MF)
OPINIONS OF THE SOLICITOR OF THE DEPARTMENT OF THE INTERIOR RELATING TO INDIAN AFFAIRS. [Irregular]

I 1.70:date
GENERAL INFORMATION REGARDING DEPT. OF THE INTERIOR.

> Changed from I 1.2:In 3/1-14

I 1.71:nos.
PROJECT TRAINING SERIES.

> Changed from I 29.28
> Later FS 4.9

I 1.72   • Item 601 (MF)
CONSERVATION BULLETINS. 1–   [Irregular]

Attractive, well-illustrated pamphlets on various aspects of conservation.

I 1.73:nos.
PERSONNEL BULLETINS.

I 1.73/2 • Item 603-D (MF)
PERSONNEL MANAGEMENT PUBLICATIONS. 1–
1964– [Irregular]

PURPOSE:– To provide non-regulatory personnel management material to personnel administrators and technicians, such as general outlines and guides, general information, and suggested procedures and techniques.

I 1.73/2:3 • Item 603
3. CAREERS IN THE UNITED STATES DEPART-
MENT OF THE INTERIOR. [Irregular]

A directory for college students covering
employment information activites of the Department of the Interior and its bureaus, and
recruitment needs.

I 1.74:dt.nos.&v.nos.&nos.
LAW LIBRARY REPORTER. [Bimonthly]

I 1.75:v.nos.&nos.
INSIDE INTERIOR. [Monthly]

ISSN 0364-6688

I 1.76:CT
POSTERS.

I 1.77:CT • Item 604
REGULATIONS, RULES, AND INSTRUCTIONS.

I 1.77/2:CT • Item 603-B
HANDBOOKS, MANUALS, GUIDES.

I 1.77/3 • Item 603-B
POLLUTION PREVENTION HANDBOOK (series).

I 1.77/4:nos. • Item 604
FINAL REGULATORY ANALYSIS, OSM- RA-(series).
Replaces I 70.14

I 1.77/5:nos.
DEPARTMENT OF THE INTERIOR ACQUISITION
REGULATION.

I 1.78:CT
MISSOURI BASIN INTER-AGENCY COMMITTEE PUB-
LICATIONS.
Later Y 3.M 59:2

I 1.79:date
DEPARTMENT OF INTERIOR IN MISSOURI RIVER
BASIN PROGRESS REPORT. [Annual]

I 1.80
PROGRESS, MISSOURI RIVER BASIN. 1945– 1970.
[Quarterly]

PURPOSE:– To assist in the coordination of
Federal, State, and local programs of resources
development within the Missouri River Basin.
April-June issue contains the annual report;
July- September issue includes a description of
the program for the coming fiscal year.

I 1.81:CT
FEDERAL INTER-AGENCY RIVER BASIN COM-
MITTEE PUBLICATIONS.
Later Y 3.F 31/13/2

I 1.82
[PRESS RELEASES]. [Irregular]

I 1.82/2:nos.
– ALASKA RAILROAD.

I 1.82/3
OFFICE OF SALINE WATER. [Irregular]

Discontinued December 1974.

I 1.83:CT
SALINE WATER CONSERVATION PROGRAM, RE-
PORTS AND PUBLICATIONS.

I 1.84:CT • Item 603-E
INDIAN ARTS AND CRAFTS BOARD PUBLICATIONS.

I 1.84/2:nos.
SMOKE SIGNALS.

I 1.84/3 • Item 603-E
FACT SHEETS: SOURCES OF INDIAN AND ESKIMO

ARTS AND CRAFTS. 1– 1967– [Irregular]

I 1.84/4 • Item 603-E
NATIVE AMERICAN ARTS (series). 1– 1968–
[Irregular]

PURPOSE:– To document, interpret, and promote contemporary arts by Indian, Eskimo, and
Aleut artists and craftsmen of the United States.

I 1.84/5
BIBLIOGRAPHY (series). 1– 1967– [Irregular]

I 1.85:date
REPORT OF SECRETARY TO PRESIDENT AND
CONGRESS ON MINERAL EXPLORATION PRO-
GRAM.

I 1.86 • Item 601-C (MF)
TELEPHONE DIRECTORY. [Semiannual]

ISSN 0160-080X

I 1.87:CT • Item 604-A
SEA WATER CONVERSION, SOLAR RESEARCH
STATION (series).

I 1.87/2:CT • Item 604-A
SALINE WATER CONVERSION DEMONSTRATION
PLANT.

I 1.87/3:CT • Item 604-A
CONCEPTUAL DESIGN OF 50 MGD DESALINATION
PLANTS.

I 1.87/4 • Item 604-A-2
DESALTING PLANTS INVENTORY REPORTS. 1–
1968– [Annual]

Inventory of world-wide land based desalting
plants in operation and under construction capable of producing 25,000 gallons or more of
fresh water daily, and projections of future desalting development.

OFFICE OF SALINE WATER

I 1.88 • Item 604-A-1
RESEARCH AND DEVELOPMENT PROGRESS
REPORTS. 1– 1952– [Irregular]

Series of reports designed to present accounts of progress on saline water conversion
with the expectation that the exchange of such
data will contribute to the long-range development of economical process applicable to large-
scale, low-cost demineralization of sea or other
saline waters.

I 1.88/2:date • Item 604-A-3 (MF)
CATALOG OF RESEARCH PROJECTS.

DEPARTMENT OF THE INTERIOR
(Continued)

I 1.89:CT • Item 600-A
BIBLIOGRAPHIES AND LISTS OF PUBLICATIONS.

I 1.89/2:nos.
ENVIRONMENTAL AWARENESS READING LIST,
EARL (series).

I 1.90:date
INTERIOR MUSEUM NEWS.

I 1.91 • Item 603-C
NATURAL RESOURCES OF [State]. 1963– [Irregu-
lar]

Separate publication for each State. Illustrated
capsule tour of the State's scenic beauty; varied
natural resources; mineral, water, and land development; and park and recreational opportunities. Major outdoor recreation areas in the State
are listed with facilities available to the fisherman, hunter, camper, or picnicker. Each booklet
outlines historical background, present development, and future plans of the State, and summarized Federal agency programs devoted to natural resources.

I 1.92:nos.
MANAGEMENT HIGHLIGHTS RELEASES. ADMINIS-
TRATIVE.

I 1.93:nos.
AREA REDEVELOPMENT TECHNICAL LEAFLETS.
(Resources Program Staff in cooperation with Area
Redevelopment Administration, Commerce Depart-
ment)

I 1.94 • Item 604-B
WATER RESOURCES RESEARCH CATALOG. v. 1–
1965– [Irregular]

PURPOSE:– To provide a summary of research in progress on eight subdivisions in water
research, useful as a source book to eliminate
duplication of research projects. Includes abstracts of research in both Federal and non- Federal programs. Index by author, subject, supporting agency, and principal investigator.

I 1.94/2:v.nos./nos. • Item 604-B-1 (MF)
SELECTED WATER RESOURCES ABSTRACTS. v. 1–
1968– [Monthly] (Water Resources Scientific Information Center)

Compilation of all abstract cards provided to
participants in the WRSIC Selective Dissemination of Information Program.
ISSN 0037-136X

I 1.95 • Item 601-A
CONSERVATION YEARBOOKS. 1– 1965–
[Annual]

PURPOSE:– To outline the problems confronting a rapidly-growing America, in the challenge of
guarding and preserving our natural resources–
land, water, air, and people. The informative, viv-
idly illustrated booklets urge a look at both current and future aspects of maintaining the quality
of our environment, with a view of tomorrow's
needs and demands.
In essence, the Yearbooks take the place of
the Department's annual report.

I 1.96:date • Item 603-F (MF)
TOWARDS IMPROVED HEALTH AND SAFETY FOR
AMERICA'S COAL MINERS, ANNUAL REPORT
OF THE SECRETARY OF THE INTERIOR.

I 1.96/2:date • Item 603-F (MF)
ADMINISTRATION OF FEDERAL METAL AND
NONMETALLIC MINE SAFETY ACT, ANNUAL RE-
PORT OF THE SECRETARY OF THE INTERIOR.
1st– 1970–

I 1.96/3:date • Item 603-F (MF)
ANNUAL REPORT OF THE SECRETARY OF THE IN-
TERIOR UNDER THE MINING AND MINERALS
POLICY ACT OF 1970. 1st– 1971–

I 1.96/4:date • Item 603-F (MF)
FEDERAL COAL MANAGEMENT REPORT. [Annual]

Report submitted by the Secretary of the In-
terior to Congress pursuant to Section 8 of the
Federal Coal Leasing Amendments Act of 1976.
Report covers fiscal year.

I 1.96/5:date • Item 603-F (MF)
ANNUAL REPORT OF THE SECRETARY OF INTE-
RIOR UNDER THE SURFACE MINING CONTROL
AND RECLAMATION ACT OF 1977.

I 1.96/6 • Item 603-F (MF)
THE FEDERAL MANAGERS' FINANCIAL INTEGRITY
ACT, SECRETARY'S ANNUAL STATEMENT AND
REPORT TO THE PRESIDENT AND THE CON-
GRESS.

WATER RESOURCES SCIENTIFIC
INFORMATION CENTER
Office of Water Resources Research

I 1.97:nos.
WATER RESOURCES SCIENTIFIC INFORMATION
CENTER, WRSIC- (series). [Irregular]

PURPOSE:– To provide bibliographies on current literature of water resources.

I 1.97/2:date   **• Item 601-H (MF)**
RESEARCH REPORTS SUPPORTED BY OFFICE OF WATER RESOURCES RESEARCH UNDER THE WATER RESOURCES RESEARCH ACT OF 1964 RECEIVED DURING THE PERIOD (date). [Semi-annual]

Lists reports and theses of research supported by the Office of Water Resources Research, proceedings of OWRR conferences, publications of the OWRR staff, state-of-the-art reports, etc.
Quarterly issues cumulative to annual.
ISSN 0145-9287

I 1.97/3:year-nos.   **• Item 603-G-1 (MF)**
WATER REUSE, OWRT/RU- (series). [Irregular]

PURPOSE:– To present technical studies on various phases of recycling and reuse of wastewater.

I 1.97/4:CT   **• Item 603-G-1 (MF)**
OWRT WATER REUSE RESEARCH AND DEVELOPMENT PROGRAM (series). [Irregular] (Office of Water Research and Technology)

I 1.97/5:nos.   **• Item 603-C-2 (MF)**
TECHNOLOGY, OWRT-TT- (series) [Irregular] (Office of Water Research and Technology)

PURPOSE:– To provide consulting engineers and others involved in supplying and improving water for municipal systems with reports and manuals on desalting research and development in the United States.

DEPARTMENT OF THE INTERIOR
(Continued)

I 1.98:CT   **• Item 603-G**
FINAL ENVIRONMENTAL IMPACT STATEMENTS. [Irregular]

I 1.98/2:nos.   **• Item 603-G (MF)**
POCS REFERENCE PAPERS (series). [Irregular]

Later I 53.29

I 1.98/3:nos.
POCS TECHNICAL PAPER.

Later I 53.29/2

I 1.99:date   **• Item 601-D (MF)**
OUTER CONTINENTAL SHELF RESEARCH MANAGEMENT ADVISORY BOARD: ANNUAL REPORT.

I 1.99/2:CT   **• Item 601-F**
OUTER CONTINENTAL SHELF ENVIRONMENTAL STUDIES ADVISORY COMMITTEE: PUBLICATIONS.

I 1.100:date   **• Item 601-J (MF)**
REPORT TO CONGRESS BY THE SECRETARY OF THE INTERIOR AND THE SECRETARY OF AGRICULTURE ON ADMINISTRATION OF THE WILD FREE- ROAMING HORSES AND BURRO ACT. 1st– [Irregular]

The Wild Free-Roaming Horse and Burro Act (PL 92-195), approved December 15, 1971, delegated to the Secretary of the Interior and the Secretary of Agriculture the authority and responsiblity for protection, managment, and control of wild free-roaming horses and burros on public lands administered by the Bureau of Land Management and the Forest Service.
The report is submitted by the Secretaries in compliance with section 10 of the Act, which presents the progress made and the problems encountered in the adminsitration of the purpose of the act of 1971.

I 1.101:CT   **• Item 601-E (MF)**
JOHNNY HORIZON ENVIRONMENTAL PROGRAM: ACTION BOOKLETS.

I 1.102:CT   **• Item 603-H (MF)**
HISTORICAL VIGNETTES, 1776-1976.

I 1.103:CT   **• Item 603-J (MF)**
WATER RESEARCH CAPSULE REPORT (series). [Irregular]

PURPOSE:– To give national recognition to successful water resources research and make available the usable research results and applications to potential users.

I 1.104:nos.
EMRIA [Energy Mineral Rehabilitation Inventory and Analysis] REPORTS. [Irregular]

I 1.105/2:date   **• Item 631-A (MF)**
YOUTH CONSERVATION REPORT. [Quarterly]

PURPOSE:– To provide a newsletter containing short articles on various subjects relating to the activities and personnel of the Youth Conservation Corps, Job Corps, an the Young Adults Conservation Corps.

I 1.105/3:date   **• Item 631-A (MF)**
YOUTH CONSERVATION CORPS, ANNUAL REPORT TO THE PRESIDENT AND THE CONGRESS. [Annual] (Youth Conservation Corps)

Published jointly with the Department of Agriculture.
Former title: Program Year.
Earlier A 13.2:Y 8/2

I 1.106:v.nos.   **• Item 603-K (MF)**
NATIONAL PETROLEUM RESERVE IN ALASKA TASK FORCE STUDY REPROTS. v. 1–   [Irregular]

I 1.107:v.nos.   **• Item 627-J**
INDIAN AFFAIRS, LAWS AND TREATIES. v 6– [Irregular]

Clothbound compilations of all treaties, laws, executive orders, and regulations relating to Indian affairs.
Volume 1– 5 were published by the Senate Committee on Indian Affairs (Y 4.In 2/2:L 44).
Commonly known as Kappler's Compilation of Indian Laws and Treaties.
Supplemental volumes will be published at intervals sufficient to keep the compilation reasonably current.

I 1.108
AUDIOVISUAL MATERIALS.

I 1.109:CT   **• Item 603-L**
LAWS.

I 1.110:date   **• Item 603-M**
TAKE PRIDE IN AMERICA, AWARDS PROGRAM. [Annual]

PURPOSE:– To announce the Take Pride in America awards program, which is aimed at encouraging a sense of stewardship and responsibility for our nation's public lands and natural resources. Includes eligibility criteria, entry procedures, and an application form.

I 1.110/2:date   **• Item 603-M**
TAKE PRIDE IN AMERICA, NATIONAL AWARDS CEREMONY. [Annual]

I 1.110/3:date   **• Item 603-M**
AMERICAN SPIRIT.

Earlier titled: National Campaign News.

I 1.111:   **• Item 603-G-5**
POSTERS.

I 1.112:date/nos.   **• Item 603-M**
UPDATE. [Irregular]

I 1.114   **• Item 600-D (E)**
ELECTRONIC PRODUCTS. [Irregular]

I 1.115   **• Item 603 (MF)**
THE DEPARTMENT OF EVERYTHING ELSE, HIGHLIGHTS OF INTERIOR HISTORY.

I 1.116:v.nos./nos.   **• Item 603-B-1 (P) (EL)**
PEOPLE LAND AND WATER. [Monthly]

I 2
FIRST CENSUS, 1790.

I 3
SECOND CENSUS, 1800.

I 4
THIRD CENSUS, 1810.

I 5
FOURTH CENSUS, 1820.

I 6
FIFTH CENSUS, 1830.

I 7
SIXTH CENSUS, 1840.

I 8
SEVENTH CENSUS, 1850.

I 9
EIGHTH CENSUS, 1860.

I 10
NINTH CENSUS, 1870.

I 11
TENTH CENSUS, 1880.

I 12
ELEVENTH CENSUS, 1890.

I 13
TWELFTH CENSUS, 1900.

CENSUS OFFICE
(1902– 1903)

CREATION AND AUTHORITY

The United States Census Office was established within the Department of the Interior on July 1, 1902, pursuant to act of Congress, approved March 6, 1902 (32 Stat. 51). On July 1, 1903, it was transferred to the Department of Commerce and Labor under the name of Bureau of the Census (C 3).

I 14.1:date
ANNUAL REPORTS.
Later C 3.1

I 14.2:CT
GENERAL PUBLICATIONS.

I 14.3:nos.
BULLETINS.

I 14.4:nos.
CIRCULARS. [None issued]

I 14.5:nos.
SPECIAL BULLETINS.

DIVISION OF PUBLIC DOCUMENTS
(1869– 1895)

I 15.1:date
ANNUAL REPORTS.

I 15.2:CT
GENERAL PUBLICATIONS.

I 15.3:nos.
BULLETINS. [None issued]

I 15.4
CIRCULARS. [none issued]

OFFICE OF EDUCATION
(1929– 1939)

CREATION AND AUTHORITY

The Bureau of Education was transferred from the independent agency known as the Department of Education to the Department of the Interior on July 1, 1869, under act of Congress, approved July 20, 1868. From October 1929, it has been known as the Office of Education. By Reorganization Plan No. 1 of 1939, effective July 1, 1939, the Office was transferred to the Federal Security Agency (FS 5).

I 16.1/1:date
ANNUAL REPORTS.

> Later FS 5.1

I 16.1/2:date
STATEMENT.

I 16.2:CT
GENERAL PUBLICATIONS.

> Later FS 5.2

I 16.3:dt.&nos.
BULLETINS.

> Later FS 5.3

I 16.4:nos.
CIRCULARS.

I 16.5:date
CIRCULARS OF INFORMATION.

I 16.6:nos.
SPECIAL CIRCULARS.

I 16.7:pt.nos.
ART AND INDUSTRY, EDUCATION IN INDUSTRIAL AND FINE ARTS IN UNITED STATES.

I 16.8:date
INTRODUCTION OF DOMESTIC REINDEER INTO ALASKA.

I 16.9:nos.
OFFICE CIRCULARS.

Library

I 16.10/1:date
ANNUAL REPORTS.

I 16.10/2:CT
GENERAL PUBLICATIONS.

I 16.10/3:nos.
BULLETINS.

I 16.10/4:nos.
CIRCULARS.

I 16.10/5:nos.
LIBRARY LEAFLETS.

Alaska Division

Includes Alaska School Service and Alaska Reindeer Service.

I 16.11/1:date
ANNUAL REPORTS.

I 16.11/2:CT
GENERAL PUBLICATIONS.

I 16.11/3:nos.
BULLETINS.

I 16.11/4:nos.
CIRCULARS.

Office of Education (Continued)

I 16.12:nos.
READING COURSES.

I 16.13:nos.
HOME EDUCATION CIRCULARS.

I 16.14:date
LIST OF PUBLICATIONS OF THE OFFICE OF EDUCATION.

I 16.14/2:CT
PUBLICATIONS OF BUREAU OF EDUCATION (misc. list).
> Later FS 5.10

I 16.15:v.nos.
CONTRIBUTIONS OF AMERICAN EDUCATIONAL HISTORY.

I 16.16:nos.
SCHOOL HOME-GARDEN CIRCULARS.

I 16.17:date
HIGHER EDUCATION CIRCULARS.

Kindergarten Division

I 16.18/1:date
ANNUAL REPORTS.

I 16.18/2:CT
GENERAL PUBLICATIONS.

I 16.18/3
BULLETINS.

I 16.18/4
CIRCULARS.

I 16.18/5:nos.
KINDERGARTEN EXTENSION SERIES.

Office of Education (Continued)

I 16.19:date
ELEMENTARY EDUCATION CIRCULARS.

I 16.20:date
TEACHERS' LEAFLETS.

I 16.21:nos.
COMMUNITY LEAFLETS.

I 16.21/2:let.
LESSONS IN COMMUNITY AND NATIONAL LIFE.

I 16.22:nos.
SECONDARY SCHOOL CIRCULARS.

I 16.23:nos.
VOCATIONAL EDUCATION LETTERS.

I 16.24:nos.
SCHOOL SANITATION LEAFLETS.

I 16.25:nos.
HOME ECONOMICS CIRCULARS.

I 16.26:vol.
SCHOOL LIFE.
> Later FS 5.7

I 16.26/2:nos.
– SUPPLEMENTS.

I 16.26/3:nos.
MARCH OF EDUCATION, NEWS LETTER FOR SCHOOL OFFICERS. [Monthly]

> Supplementary to School life, published between issues.
> Later FS 5.19

I 16.24/4:date
NEWS LETTERS. [Monthly]

> Supersedes I 16.26/3

I 16.27:CT
POSTERS AND CHARTS.
> Later FS 5.20

United States School Garden Army

I 16.28/1:date
ANNUAL REPORTS.

I 16.28/2:CT
GENERAL PUBLICATIONS.

I 16.28/3
BULLETINS.

I 16.28/4
CIRCULARS.

I 16.28/5:letters-nos.
LEAFLETS.

I 16.28/6:nos.
SCHOOL GARDEN ARMY LEAFLETS (general).

Office of Education (Continued)

I 16.29:nos.
HEALTH EDUCATION.

Americanization Division

I 16.30/1:date
ANNUAL REPORTS.

I 16.30/2:CT
GENERAL PUBLICATIONS.

I 16.30/3
BULLETINS.

I 16.30/4
CIRCULARS.

I 16.30/5:v.nos.
AMERICANIZATION.

Educational Extension Division

I 16.31/1:date
ANNUAL REPORTS.

I 16.31/2:CT
GENERAL PUBLICATIONS.

I 16.31/3
BULLETINS.

I 16.31/4
CIRCULARS.

I 16.31/5:date
NATIONAL LIBRARY SERVICE BULLETIN.

I 16.31/6:v.nos.
NATIONAL SCHOOL SERVICE.

> Nos. 1-8 issued by Public Information Committee Y 3.P 96/3:16.

I 16.31/7:nos.
EXTENSION LEAFLETS.

Office of Education (Continued)

I 16.32:nos.
COMMUNITY CENTER CIRCULARS.

I 16.33:nos.
INDUSTRIAL EDUCATION CIRCULARS.

I 16.34:CT or dt.
PRESS BULLETINS.

I 16.35:nos.
RURAL SCHOOL LEAFLETS.

I 16.36:nos.
CITY SCHOOL LEAFLETS.

I 16.37:nos.
COMMERCIAL EDUCATION LEAFLETS.

I 16.38:nos.
SCHOOL HEALTH STUDIES.

I 16.39:nos.
STATISTICAL CIRCULARS.

I 16.40:nos.
PHYSICAL EDUCATION SERIES.

I 16.41:nos.
FOREIGN EDUCATION LEAFLETS.

I 16.42:nos.
RURAL SCHOOL CIRCULARS.

I 16.43:nos.
PAMPHLETS.

> Later FS 5.17

I 16.44:nos.
LEAFLETS.

> Later FS 5.18

I 16.45:nos.
PROGRESS REPORTS.

I 16.46:nos.
BIBLIOGRAPHIES.

> Later FS 5.16

I 16.46/2:CT
BIBLIOGRAPHIES.

I 16.47:nos.
HOME EDUCATION LETTERS.

I 16.48:nos.
PARENT EDUCATION LETTERS.

I 16.49:nos.
COMMERCIAL EDUCATION CIRCULARS.

I 16.50:nos.
FOREIGN EDUCATION CIRCULARS.

I 16.51:nos.
HOME ECONOMICS LETTERS.

I 16.52:nos.
EMERGENCY BULLETINS.

I 16.53:nos.
MEMORANDUM TO ALL ADMINISTRATORS OF EMERGENCY EDUCATIONAL PROGRAMS.

Vocational Education Division

I 16.54/1:date
ANNUAL REPORTS.

I 16.54/2:CT
GENERAL PUBLICATIONS.

> Later FS 5.122

I 16.54/3:nos.
BULLETINS.

> Earlier VE 1.3
> Later FS 5.123

I 16.54/5:nos.
[MISCELLANEOUS SERIES]

> Earlier VE 1.15
> Later FS 5.11

I 16.54/6:CT
CIVILIAN CONSERVATION CORPS: VOCATIONAL SERIES.

> I 16.54/6:nos.
> – NUMBERED.

I 16.54/7:nos.
MISCELLANEOUS CIRCULARS.

> Later FS 5.127

I 16.54/8:nos.
LEAFLETS.

> Headings vary slightly
> Earlier VE 1.14
> Later FS 5.129

I 16.54/9:nos.
MONOGRAPHS.

> Earlier VE 1.11
> Later FS 5.128

Office of Education (Continued)

I 16.55:CT
ADDRESSES.

I 16.56:date
THE WORLD IS YOURS. [Monthly]

> Radio programs.

I 16.56/2:nos.
THE WORLD IS YOURS. [Weekly]

> Radio scripts.
> Later FS 5.14/1

I 16.56/3:nos.
OUR WONDER WORLD.

> 30 minute scripts.

I 16.57:nos.
AMERICAN YESTERDAYS, HISTORICAL RADIO SCRIPTS.

> 15 minute scripts.

I 16.57/1:nos.
ANSWER ME THIS: AMERICAN CITIES SERIES.

> 15 minute scripts.

I 16.58/2
QUESTIONS (and answers) FROM ANSWER ME THIS, RADIO PROGRAM. [Weekly]

I 16.58/3:nos.
ANSWER ME THIS, MISC. SERIES.

> 15 minute scripts.

I 16.58/4:nos.
ANSWER ME THIS, SONG SERIES.

> 15 minute scripts.

I 16.58/5:nos.
ANSWER ME THIS, HISTORICAL SERIES.

> 15 minute scripts.

I 16.59/1:date
EDUCATION IN THE NEWS. [Weekly]

> Radio scripts.

I 16.59/2:CT
EDUCATION IN THE NEWS.

> Supplementary material for broadcast.

I 16.60/1:nos.
HAVE YOU HEARD?

> 10 minute scripts.

I 16.60/2:nos.
HAVE YOU HEARD?

> 15 minute scripts.

I 16.60/3:CT.
HAVE YOU HEARD?

> Supplementary material to broadcasts. [Weekly]

I 16.61:nos.
INTERVIEWS WITH THE PAST.

> 15 minute programs.

I 16.62/1:nos.
LET FREEDOM RING. [Weekly]

> Radio scripts.

I 16.62/2:CT
LET FREEDOM RING.

> Supplements to broadcasts.

I 16.63:nos.
SAFETY MUSKETEERS.

> 15 minute scripts.

I 16.64:nos.
SYMPHONIE HALL.

> 30 minute scripts.

I 16.65/1:date
TREASURES NEXT DOOR. [Weekly]

> Radio scripts.

I 16.65/2:CT
TREASURES NEXT DOOR, SUPPLEMENTARY MATERIAL TO BROADCASTS.

I 16.65/3:nos.
TREASURES NEXT DOOR.

> 15 minute scripts.

I 16.66:nos.
EPOCH DISCOVERIES OF THE PAST, SCIENTIFIC RADIO SCRIPTS.

> 15 minute scripts.

I 16.67:nos.
PLANNING YOUR CAREER, VOCATIONAL GUIDANCE SERIES.

> 15 minute scripts.

I 16.68:nos.
PAN-AMERICAN SERIES.

> Radio programs.

I 16.69:nos.
CITY SCHOOL CIRCULARS.

I 16.70:CT
RADIO SCRIPTS: MISCELLANEOUS.

I 16.71:nos.
BULLETINS, MISCELLANEOUS.

> Later FS 5.30

I 16.72:nos.
AMERICANS ALL, IMMIGRANTS ALL. [Weekly]

Radio scripts.

I 16.73:nos.
WINGS FOR THE MARTINS. [Weekly]

Radio scripts.

I 16.74:nos.
DEMOCRACY IN ACTION. [Weekly]

Radio scripts.

I 16.75:nos.
LANGUAGE USAGE SERIES.

Later FS 5.12

I 16.76:nos.
CIRCULAR LETTERS.

Later FS 5.15

GEOGRAPHICAL AND GEOLOGICAL SURVEY OF THE ROCKY MOUNTAIN REGION (1874–1879)

CREATION AND AUTHORITY

The United States Geographical and Geological Survey of the Rocky Mountain Region, known also as the Powell Survey, originated in an appropriation in 1874 for a geological survey of Utah and continued by annual appropriations until 1879. The work of the Survey was carried on by the Geological Survey (I 19) in 1879.

I 17.1:date
ANNUAL REPORTS.

I 17.2:CT
GENERAL PUBLICATIONS.

I 17.3:nos.
BULLETINS. [None issued]

I 17.4:nos.
CIRCULARS. [None issued]

I 17.5:v.nos.
CONTRIBUTIONS TO NORTH AMERICAN ETHNOLOGY.

GEOLOGICAL AND GEOGRAPHICAL SURVEY OF THE TERRITORIES (1872–1879)

CREATION AND AUTHORITY

The Geological Survey of the Territories was established under an appropriation act in 1867 for the geological survey of Nebraska, under the direction of the General Land Office. In 1869, it was placed under the Secretary of the Interior. The Survey continued as the Geological and Geographical Survey of the Territories from 1872 until 1879 when its functions were transferred to the newly established Geological Survey.

I 18.1:date
ANNUAL REPORTS.

I 18.2:CT
GENERAL PUBLICATIONS.

I 18.3:v.nos.
BULLETINS.

I 18.4:nos.
CIRCULARS. [none issued]

I 18.5:v.nos.
FINAL REPORTS ON MONOGRAPHS.

I 18.6:nos.
MISCELLANEOUS PUBLICATIONS.

I 18.7:CT
MAPS.

GEOLOGICAL SURVEY (1878–   )

CREATION AND AUTHORITY

The Geological Survey was established by the act of March 3, 1879 (20 Stat. 394: 43 U.S.C. 31), which provided for "the classification of the public lands and the examination of the geological structure, mineral resources, and products of the national domain." The act of September 5, 1962 (76 Stat. 427; 43 U.S.C. 31 (b)), expanded this authorization to include such examinations outside the national domain. Topographic mapping and chemical and physical research were recognized as an essential part of the investigations and studies authorized by the organic act, and specific provision was made for them by Congress in the act of October 2, 1888 (25 Stat. 505, 526).

INFORMATION

Geological Survey
U.S. Geological Survey National Center
12201 Sunrise Valley Drive
Reston, VA 20192
(703) 648-4000
Fax: (703) 648-4454
http://www.usgs.gov

I 19.1:date   • Item 621-C (MF)
UNITED STATES GEOLOGICAL SURVEY YEARBOOK. 1977–   [Annual]

Continues: Annual Report (ISSN 0147-8478). ISSN 0162-9484

I 19.1/2:date   • Item 621-C-1 (E)
U.S. GEOLOGICAL SURVEY, FISCAL YEAR YEARBOOK. [Annual]

Issued on CD-ROM.

I 19.2:CT   • Item 621
GENERAL PUBLICATIONS.

I 19.2:C 72/2   • Item 621
BASE FLOWS AS OF [date] AT SELECTED GAGING STATIONS IN THE COLUMBIA RIVER BASIN. (Current Records Center, Water Resources Division)

I 19.2:El 3/2   • Item 621
ELEVATIONS AND DISTANCES. 1973. 23 p. il.

The data, determined from surveys and topographic maps, includes elevations of our major cities, high and low elevations of the U.S., elevations of U.S. summits, geographic centers, etc.

I 19.2:M 32/12   • Item 621
MAPS FOR AMERICA. 1979. 265 p. il.

PURPOSE:– To present the background of the American mapping effort as a whole and to provide a detailed presentation of information about the maps produced by the Survey. It explains the meaning of lines, colors, images, symbols, numbers, captions, and notes that appear on maps; the possible errors and anomalies affecting the reliability and interpretation of maps; the different kinds of maps and map data; and the various sources of maps and related information.

I 19.2:N 21 a   • Item 621
NATIONAL ATLAS OF THE UNITED STATES. 1970. 417 p.

PURPOSE:– To be of practical use to decision makers in government and business, planners, research scholars and others needing to visualize country-wide distributional patterns and relationships between environmental phenomena and human activities.
Contains 756 maps under the headings general reference, physical, historical, economic, socio-cultural, administrative, mapping and charting, and the world. Also contains a detailed subject index and a place- name index of over 41,000 entries.

I 19.3:nos.   • Item 620 (P) (EL)
BULLETINS. 1–   1883–   [Irregular]

Technical papers on all phases of geology and its allied sciences. Many of the bulletins consist of related papers on a single subject by various authors with each paper issued as a separate chapter within specific Bulletins.

BIBLIOGRAPHY OF NORTH AMERICAN GEOLOGY. [Annual]

Lists publications issued during the year on the geology of the continental United States, including Alaska and Hawaii as well as the rest of North American continent, Greenland, the West Indies and other adjacent islands, Guam, and other island possessions. Lists papers and books by American and foreign authors, regardless of place of publication.
Superseded by Bibliography and Index of Geology, published by the American Geological Institute.
In addition, the following compilations have been published.

I 19.3:222   • Item 620
CATALOGUE AND INDEX OF THE PUBLICATIONS OF THE HAYDEN, KING, POWELL, AND WHEELER SURVEYS. 1904. 208 p. (Bulletin 222)

I 19.3:274   • Item 620
DICTIONARY OF ALTITUDES IN THE UNITED STATES. 4th ed. 1906. 1072 p.

Supersedes Bulletins 5, 76, and 160.
Also issued as House Document 207 (59-1).

I 19.3:896   • Item 620
LEXICON OF GEOLOGIC NAMES OF THE UNITED STATES, INCLUDING ALASKA. 1938. 2 pts.

Lists geologic names with additional data such as age, thickness, formations, and bibliographical citations.
Includes names and ages, but not definitions of named geologic units of Canada, Mexico, West Indies, Central America, and Hawaii.
Supplemented by Geologic Names of North America (Bulletin 1056-A), and Bulletins 1200 and 1350.

I 19.3:1013   • Item 620
INDEX OF GENERIC NAMES OF FOSSIL PLANTS, 1820–1950. 1955. 262 p.

Based on Compendium Index of Paleobotany. Includes bibliography giving the full citations of the references in the index.

I 19.3:1056 • Item 620
PT. A. GEOLOGIC NAMES OF NORTH AMERICA INTRODUCED IN 1936– 1955. 1957. 405 p.

Compilation of new geologic names of North America, including Greenland, West Indies, Pacific Island Possessions, and the Trust Territory of the Pacific.

PT. B. INDEX TO GEOLOGIC NAMES OF NORTH AMERICA. 1959. p. 407– 622.

Gives geologic names arranged by age and by area containing type of locality. Supplements Lexicon of Geologic Names of the United States (Bulletin 896).

I 19.3:1200 • Item 620
LEXICON OF GEOLOGIC NAMES OF THE UNITED STATES, 1936– 1960. 1966. 3 pts.

Supplements Bulletin 896.
Supplemented by Bulletin 1350.

I 19.3:1212 • Item 620
BOUNDARIES OF THE UNITED STATES AND THE SEVERAL STATES. 1966. 291 p. il. pl.

Gives information on areas, boundaries, altitudes, and geographic centers.
Supersedes Bulletin 817.

I 19.3:1350 • Item 620
LEXICON OF GEOLOGIC NAMES OF THE UNITED STATES, 1961– 1967. 1970. 848 p.

Supplements Bulletins 896 and 1200.

I.19.3:1412 • Item 620
COAL RESOURCES OF THE UNITED STATES, January 1, 1974. 1974. 140 p. il.

I 19.3/2:date
WRD BULLEITN. (Water Resources Division) Admin.

I 19.3/3:nos. • Item 624-B (MF)
WATER-RESOURCES BULLETINS. [Irregular]

I 19.3/4:date
WATER RESOURCES DIVISIONS BULLETIN OF TRAINING.

I 19.3/5:nos. • Item 625
WATER SUPPLY BULLETINS. 1– [Irregular]

Earlier I 19.2:Se 1

I 19.3/6: • Item 620
STRATIGRAPHIC NOTES. [Annual]

I 19.4:nos. • Item 620-A
CIRCULARS.

I 19.4/2:nos. • Item 620-A
CIRCULARS. 1– 1933– [Irregular]

Brief technical and semitechnical studies, ranging from 5 to 25 pages in length.

EARTHQUAKES IN THE UNITED STATES. [Irregular]

No longer published in the Circulars series. Now classed separately (I 19.4/2-2).

INDEX OF SURFACE-WATER RECORDS TO (date). 1957– [Irregular]

PURPOSE:– To make available an index that shows all stream-flow and reservoir stations for which records have been or are to be published in reports of the Geological Survey.
Basic data on surface-water supply have been published in the series, Surface Water Supply of the United States, issued by the Geological Survey in its Water Supply Papers. Prior to 1961, the data were published annually, but effective with that date, it now will be published on a 5-year basis.
The index gives in tabular form for each station, the station number, drainage area,

periods of records for daily or monthly figures, annual peaks, and low-flow measurements.
Separate indexes are issued for each of the 14 drainage basins of the continental United States, plus Alaska and Hawaii. For a list, see page 356 of Volume 1.
Index is updated every 3 to 5 years.
Data to September 30, 1970 contained in Circulars 651 to 666.

REPORTS AND MAPS OF THE GEOLOGICAL SURVEY RELEASED ONLY IN THE OPEN FILES. [Annual]

As of May 1, 1974, the Geological Survey began announcing its open-file reports in the monthly list, New Publications of the Geological Survey (I 19.14/4), and discontinued issuing the annual list in the Circular series.

I 19.4/2-2:date • Item 620-A
EARTHQUAKES IN THE UNITED STATES. [Quarterly]

Published in Circular series (I 19.4/2).

I 19.4/3:date • Item 620-A
GEOLOGICAL STUDIES IN ALASKA BY THE U.S. GEOLOGICAL SURVEY DURING (date). Discontinued.

I 19.4/4:date • Item 620-A
ANNUAL REPORT ON ALASKA'S MINERAL RESOURCES.
Earlier I 19.4/2

I 19.4/5:nos. • Item 620-A
USGS RESEARCH ON ENERGY RESOURCES, PROGRAM AND ABSTRACTS. [Annual]

I 19.4/6:date • Item 620-A
STRONG-MOTION PROGRAM REPORT. [Annual]
Earlier I 19.4/2

I 19.4/7:date • Item 620-A
USGS RESEARCH ON MINERAL RESOURCES, PROGRAM AND ABSTRACTS. [Annual]Earlier I 19.4/2

I 19.4/8:date • Item 620-A
GEOLOGIC STUDIES IN ALASKA BY THE U.S. GEOLOGICAL SURVEY DURING (date). [Annual]

I 19.4/9 • Item 620-A
ESTIMATED USE OF WATER IN THE UNITED STATES. [Quinquennial]

I 19.5/1:nos.
GEOLOGIC ATLAS OF THE UNITED STATES. LIBRARY EDITION.
Later I 19.38

I 19.5/2:nos.
GEOLOGIC ATLAS OF THE UNITED STATES. FIELD EDITION.

I 19.5/3:CT
SHEETS OF NATIONAL ATLAS OF THE UNITED STATES.

I 19.5/4:nos.
HYDROLOGIC INVESTIGATION ATLAS, HA (series).

I 19.6:nos.
HYDROGRAPHY DIVISION CIRCULARS.

I 19.7:date
MINERAL PRODUCTS OF THE UNITED STATES.

I 19.8:date
MINERAL RESOURCES OF THE UNITED STATES.

Later C 22.8

I 19.9:v.nos.
MONOGRAPHS.

I 19.10:nos.
TOPOGRAPHIC ATLAS OF THE UNITED STATES.

I 19.11:le.
TOPOGRAPHIC MAPS CIRCULARS.

I 19.12:nos.
TOPOGRAPHIC MAP OF THE UNITED STATES.

I 19.13:nos. • Item 625 (P) (EL)
WATER SUPPLY PAPERS. 1– 1896– [Irregular]

Technical papers on various aspects of hydrogeology. In addition to the individual papers, the following sub-series are issued on a recurring basis:

BIBLIOGRAPHY OF HYDROLOGY AND SEDIMENTATION OF THE UNITED STATES AND CANADA. [Irregular]

Title varies.

COMPILATION OF THE RECORDS OF SURFACE WATERS OF THE UNITED STATES. 1963– [Irregular]

Separate reports issued for each drainage basin. Data up to September 1950 contained in Water Supply Papers 1301– 1319, 1372; data for period October 1950 to September 1960 contained in Water Supply Papers 1721– 1740.

GROUND-WATER LEVELS IN THE UNITED STATES. 1935– [Quinquennial]

Gives water levels for specified dates by States, Counties, and stations.
For the period 1935– 1939, published in single volumes (WSP 777, 817, 840, 845, and 886). From 1940 on, published in six parts, each part covering a geographical section of the United States. From 1940 through 1955, published annually.
The present publishing program calls for each section to be published on a quinquennial basis, with one or two reports issued each year, with a definite rotation sequence. The accompanying table at the end of this entry gives the individual Water Supply Paper numbers for the period 1940, to the present, with indications of the new program of rotation.

Pt. 1. Northeastern States. 1956/57– [Quinquennial]

Covers Connecticut, Delaware, Indiana, Massachusetts, Michigan, New Jersey, New York, Ohio, Pennsylvania, and Rhode Island.

Pt. 2. Southeastern States. 1956/58– [Quinquennial]

Covers Alabama, Florida, Georgia, Kentucky, Maryland, Mississippi, North Carolina, South Carolina, Tennessee, Virginia, and West Virginia.

Pt. 3. North-Central States. 1956– [Quinquennial]

Covers Iowa, Kansas, Minnesota, Nebraska, North Dakota, and Wisconsin.

Pt. 4. South-Central States. 1956/59– [Quinquennial]

Covers Arkansas, Louisiana, Oklahoma, and Texas.

Pt. 5. Northwestern States. 1956/60– [Quinquennial]

Covers Alaska, Colorado, Idaho, Montana, Oregon, Utah, Washington, and Wyoming.

Pt. 6. Southwestern States. 1956/60– [Quinquennial]

Covers Arizona, California, Hawaii, Nevada, and New Mexico.

QUALITY OF SURFACE WATERS OF THE UNITED STATES. 1941– [Annual]

Tables give chemical analysis, in parts per million, temperature of water, suspended sediment, and particle-size analyses of suspended sediment. Figures are for the water year (October 1– September 30).

Beginning in 1948, issued in two volumes, in 1950 in four, in 1957 in five, and in 1959 in six. Parts correspond to drainage basins as used in Surface Water Supply of the United States, a list being given under that entry below.

REPORT OF QUALITY OF SURFACE WATERS FOR IRRIGATION, WESTERN UNITED STATES. 1951– [Annual]

SUMMARY OF FLOODS IN THE UNITED STATES. [Annual]

SURFACE WATER SUPPLY OF THE UNITED STATES. 1901– [Quinquennial]

Gives measurements of stage, discharge, and content of streams, lakes, and reservoirs in the United States during the water year (Oct. 1– Sept. 30). Additional tables for certain stations give height at 12 PM in feet. Published annually 1901– 1960; quinquennially 1961/65– [ ].

In order to meet interim requirements, local offices will issue reports annually containing streamflow records only for the State or States within the local district beginning with records for the water year ending September 30, 1961.

North Atlantic Slope Basins.
1A Maine to Connecticut.
1B New York to Delaware.
1C Maryland to York River.

South Atlantic Slope and Eastern Gulf of Mexico Basins.
2A James River to Savannah River.
2B Ogeechee River to Carrabelle River.
2C Apalachicola River to Pearl River.

Ohio River Basin.
3A Above the Kanawha River.
3B Kanawha River to Louisville, Ky.
3C Louisville, Ky. to Wabash River.
3D Below the Wabash River.

St. Lawrence River Basin.
4A Streams Tributary to Lakes Superior, Michigan and Huron.
4B Below Lake Huron.
Hudson Bay and Upper Mississippi River Basins.
5A Hudson Bay Region.
5B Upper Mississippi River Basin above Keokuk, Ill.
5C Upper Mississippi River Basin below Keokuk, Ill.

Missouri River Basin.
6A Above Williston, N. Dak.
6B Williston, N. Dak. to Sioux City, Iowa.
6C Sioux City, Iowa to Nebraska City, Neb.
6D Below Nebraska City, Neb.
Lower Mississippi River Basin.
7A Lower Mississippi River Basin (except Arkansas River Basin).
7B Arkansas River Basin.

Western Gulf of Mexico Basins.
8A Mermentau River to Colorado River.
8B Lavaca River to Rio Grande.

Colorado River Basin.
9A Above the Green River.
9B Green River to Compact Point.
9C Lower Colorado River Basin.

10 Great Basin.

Pacific Slope Basins in California.
11A Tia Juana River to Santa Maria River.
11B Arroyo Grande to Oregon State Line (except Central Valley Basins).
11C Southern Central Valley Basins.
11D North Central Valley Basins.

Pacific Slope Basins in Washington.
12A Pacific Slope in Washington (except Columbia River Basin).
12B Upper Columbia River Basin.
13 Snake River Basin.
14 Pacific Slope Basins in Oregon and Lower Columbia River Basin.
15 Alaska.
16 Hawaii and Other Pacific Areas.

I 19.13:995 • **Item 625**
INDEX TO RIVER SURVEYS MADE BY THE GEOLOGICAL SURVEY AND OTHER AGENCIES, REVISED TO JULY 1, 1947. 1948. 145 p.

I 19.13/2:date • **Item 625**
SELECTED PAPERS IN THE HYDROLOGIC SCIENCES. [Irregular]

I 19.13/3:date • **Item 625**
NATIONAL WATER SUMMARY. [Annual]

I 19.14:date • **Item 623**
LIST OF PUBLICATIONS. [Annual]

I 19.14/2:CT • **Item 619-B**
LISTS OF PUBLICATIONS. MISCELLANEOUS.

I 19.14/3:nos.
LISTS OF PUBLICATIONS (numbered).

I 19.14/4:nos. • **Item 622-A**
NEW PUBLICATIONS OF GEOLOGICAL SURVEY (List). [Quarterly]
Annotated list of all publications, maps, and charts issued during the month by the Geological Survey. Cumulated quinquennially into complete lists of publications without annotations.
Formerly issued under item number 622.
ISSN 0364-2461

I 19.14/4-2 • **Item 621-J (EL)**
NEW PUBLICATIONS OF THE GEOLOGICAL SURVEY (List). [Monthly]

I 19.14/5:date
NEW REPORTS BY GEOLOGICAL SURVEY ABOUT WATER IN THE PACIFIC NORTHWEST. – 1974. [Irregular] (New Water Resources Data Center, Water Resources Division, Portland, Oregon) Earlier I 19.14/2:W 29/10

I 19.14/6:CT • **Item 619-G**
CATALOG OF PUBLISHED [State] MAPS. [Irregular]
Primarily an order form for the topographical map series published for the individual States.

I 19.14/7:nos.
TECHNICAL PUBLICATIONS (series). [Irregular]

I 19.15:date
REGULATIONS AND INSTRUCTIONS.

I 19.15/2:CT
REGULATIONS, RULES, AND INSTRUCTIONS, MISCELLANEOUS.

I 19.15/3:CT • **Item 619-F**
HANDBOOKS, MANUALS, GUIDES.

I 19.15/4:bk.nos./chap.no. • **Item 624-A (MF)**
TOPOGRAPHIC INSTRUCTIONS. [Irregular]

I 19.15/5 • **Item 624-A (MF)**
TECHNIQUES OF WATER-RESOURCES INVESTIGATIONS. [Irregular]

I 19.15/5:BK.5/chap.4 • **Item 624-A**
METHODS FOR THE COLLECTION AND ANALYSIS OF AQUATIC BIOLOGICAL AND MICROBIOLOGICAL SAMPLES. (basic volume plus supplementary material for an indefinite period) (Chapter 4, Book 5)
Contains methods the U.S. Geological Survey uses to collect, preserve, and analyze waters to determine their biological and microbiological properties. Pt. 1, discusses biological sampling and sample statistics; Pt. 2, consists of description of more than 45 methods; Pt. 3, consists of a glossary; Pt. 4, list of taxonic references.
ISSN 0565-596X

I 19.15/5:BK.5/chap.A5 • **Item 624-A**
METHODS FOR DETERMINATION OF RADIOACTIVE SUBSTANCES IN WATER AND FLUVIAL SEDIMENTS. (basic volume plus supplementary material for an indefinite period)
Gives analytical procedures as well as sources and significance of radioactive substance in water.
ISSN 0565-596X

I 19.15/6:[CT]
WATER RESOURCES DATA. [Annual]

Data for individual States are issued by the local offices.

I 19.16:nos. • **Item 624**
PROFESSIONAL PAPERS. 1– 1902– [Irregular]

Technical papers on all phases of geology. The following sub-series is issued on a recurring basis:

I 19.16 • **Item 624-A-1**
NATIONAL GAZETTEER OF THE UNITED STATES.

GEOLOGICAL SURVEY RESEARCH. [Annual]

Chapter A
Summary of recent significant scientific and economic results, accompanied by a list of geologic and hydrologic investigations in progress, and report on status of topographic mapping.

Chapters B+
Contains scientific notes and summaries of investigations prepared by members of Geologic Conservation, Water Resources, and Topographic Divisions in geology, hydrology, topographic mapping, and related fields.
Superseded by Journal of Research (I 19.61).

I 19.16/2: date • **Item 621-J (CD) (EL)**
GEOGRAPHIC NAMES INFORMATION SYSTEMS (GNIS). [Annual]

I 19.16:567 • **Item 624**
DICTIONARY OF ALASKA PLACE NAMES. 1967. 1,084 p.

I 19.16:820 • **Item 624**
UNITED STATES MINERAL RESOURCES. 1973. 722 p. il.
The Geological Survey provides in this volume the first overall assessment of mineral resources since that of the President's Materials Policy Commission in 1952. Each chapter contains not only a synthesis of the state of knowledge of the geology of a mineral commodity, but also an appraisal of the known resources and an examination of the geologic possibilities for finding additional deposits. Bibliographic material is cited at the tables and diagrams present comparisons of statistics.

I 19.16:929   • Item 624
ERTS-1, A NEW WINDOW ON OUR PLANET. 1976.
362 p. il.
    The launch of the Earth Resources Tech-
nology Satellite (ERTS-1) in 1972 was a major
step forward in extending man's ability to inventory the Earth's resources and to evaluate objectively his impact on the environment. This spacecraft represents the first
steps in merging space and remote-sensing
technologies into a system for inventorying
and managing the Earth's resources. It is a
good example of applying the scientific and
technological methodology gained from the
Nation's space program to the solution of
global environmental, natural-resources, food,
and energy problems. Examples presented in
this book show ERTS' vast potential for inventorying resources, monitoring environmental conditions, and measuring changes. Also
discussed are applications to cartography,
geophysics, oceanography, agriculture and
much more.

I 19.16:950   • Item 624
NATURE TO BE COMMANDED. 1978. 95 p. il.
    PURPOSE:– To demonstrate the value of
earth-science information in land and water
management by showing how earth-science
maps have been used in making plans and
decisions in a variety of urban settings.

I 19.17:
RECLAMATION SERVICE.

    I 19.17/1:date
    ANNUAL REPORTS.
        Later I 27.1

    I 19.17/2:CT
    GENERAL PUBLICATIONS.
        Later I 27.2

    I 19.17/3:nos.
    BULLETINS.

    I 19.17/4:nos.
    CIRCULARS.

    I 19.17/5:CT
    MAPS.
        Later I 27.7

    I 19.17/6:nos.
    SPECIFICATIONS.
        Later I 27.8

    I 19.17/7:specif.nos.
    DRAWINGS ACCOMPANYING SPECIFICATIONS.
        Later I 27.9

I 19.18:date
CLAY PRODUCTS OF UNITED STATES.

I 19.19:date
PRODUCTION OF COAL IN UNITED STATES FROM
1814 TO CLOSE OF CALENDAR YEAR.

I 19.20:nos.
EXPLOSIVES CIRCULARS.

I 19.21:CT
INTERNATIONAL MAP OF THE WORLD.

    I 19.21/1:CT
    – INDEX MAPS, GENERAL DESCRIPTIONS, ETC.

    I 19.21/2:13&nos.
    – SHEETS BY SECTIONS, NORTHERN HEMI-
        SPHERE AND SOUTHERN HEMISPHERE.

I 19.21/3:CT
STATE MAPS.

I 19.22:date
PRODUCTION OF SMELTER IN UNITED STATES (mid
year statements and annual statements, calendar years).

I 19.23:date
ADVANCE STATEMENTS OF PRODUCTIONS OF COP-
PER IN UNITED STATES (calendar year).

I 19.24:date
PRODUCTION OF LEAD IN UNITED STATES, CALEN-
DAR YEAR.

I 19.25:CT
MAPS.

I 19.25/2:nos.
GEOPHYSICAL INVESTIGATIONS MAPS.

I 19.25/3:nos.
COAL INVESTIGATIONS MAPS.

I 19.25/4:nos.
OIL AND GAS INVESTIGATIONS MAP OM (series).

I 19.25/5:nos.
OIL AND GAS INVESTIGATIONS CHARTS.

I 19.25/6:nos.
MISCELLANEOUS GEOLOGIC INVESTIGATIONS
MAPS. I-nos.

I 19.25/7:nos.
MISCELLANEOUS FIELD STUDIES MAPS, MF
(series).

I 19.25/8:nos.   • Item 619-G-19
ANTARCTIC RESEARCH PROGRAM MAPS. 1–
    [Irregular]

I 19.26:date
SERVICE BULLETIN.

I 19.27:CT
BASE MAPS, BY STATES.

I 19.28:v.nos.
MONTHLY BULLETIN OF HAWAIIAN VOLCANO OB-
SERVATORY.
    Earlier A 29.40

I 19.29:nos.
VOLCANO LETTER. [Weekly]
    Published by Hawaiian Volcano Research As-
sociation.
    Later I 29.19 and I 29.22

I 19.29/2
HAWAIIAN VOLCANO OBSERVATORY SUMMARY.
    [Quarterly]

I 19.30:nos.
WEEKLY REPORT ON PRODUCTION OF BITUMINOUS
COAL, ETC.

        Later C 22.14

I 19.31:date
COMMERCIAL STOCKS OF COAL.

I 19.32:date
PRODUCTION OF ELECTRICITY FOR PUBLIC USE
IN THE U.S. [Monthly & Annual]

I 19.33:date
PRODUCTION OF ELECTRICITY FOR PUBLIC USE
IN THE U.S. [Monthly]
    Later FP 1.11

I 19.34:nos.
INTERNATIONAL GEOLOGIC CONGRESS, 16th
WASHINGTON, D.C., July 22-29, 1933. GUIDE
BOOKS.

I 19.35:nos.
BIBLIOGRAPHICAL LISTS.

I 19.36:CT
[MINERAL DEPOSITS REPORTS.]

I 19.37:nos.
INDEX TO GEOLOGIC MAPPING IN UNITED STATES
(by State) MAPS.

I 19.38:CT
GEOLOGIC QUADRANGLE MAPS.
    Replaces folios of Geologic Atlas of United
States, 1894– 1945 (I 19.5/1).

I 19.39:nos.
MINERAL INVESTIGATIONS, FIELD STUDIES MAPS.

I 19.39/2:nos.
MINERAL INVESTIGATION RESOURCES APPRAISAL
MAS, MR-nos.

I 19.40:le-nos.
TOPOGRAPHIC MAPS.

I 19.41:CT
ALASKA RECONNAISSANCE TOPOGRAPHIC
SERIES.

I 19.41/6-2:CT   • Item 619-M-1– 53
CATALOG OF TOPOGRAPHIC AND OTHER PUB-
LISHED MAPS (by State).

I 19.41/6-3:CT   • Item 619-M-1– 53
INDEX TO TOPOGRAPHIC AND OTHER MAP
COVERAGE (series). [Irregular]
    Issued separately for each State.

I 19.41/7:CT   • Item 619-G
LIST OF GEOLOGICAL SURVEY GEOLOGIC AND
WATER-SUPPLY REPORTS AND MAPS FOR
(various States). [Irregular]

I 19.41/8:CT   • Item 619-G
GEOLOGIC MAP INDEX OF (various States).
    [Irregular]

I 19.41/9:date   • Item 623
PRICE AND AVAILABILITY LIST OF U.S. GEOLOGI-
CAL SURVEY PUBLICATIONS. [Annual]

                              • Item 619-J (MF)
I 19.42   • Item 624-B (EL)
NATIONAL WATER CONDITIONS
    PURPOSE:– To give information on streamflow
and ground-water levels each month for the United
States and most of Canada.
    Each issue has a map showing whether
streamflow for the past month was deficient, excessive, or in the normal range. The 30-year reference period 1931– 1960 is the standard with
which present data are compared. The map is
based on report from 1947 streamflow index stations. The map also shows ground-water levels in
1950 index wells; shows whether water levels
rose or declined and how current levels compare
with average levels for the same month. The textual portion of the report summarizes the conditions in various sections of the country. Included
on the back page of each issue is a list of new
reports of the Geological Survey about water.
    The May issues give summary for six-month
period, October 1– March 31; the November issue gives summary for the water year, October
1– September 31.
    Also published in microfiche.
    Former title: Water Resources Review.
    ISSN 0043-1400

I 19.42/2:date
WATER RESOURCES REVIEW, ANNUAL SUMMARY,
WATER YEAR.

I 19.42/3:CT   • Item 624-G-1– G-51
WATER RESOURCES INVESTIGATIONS IN [States].
    Beginning in 1978, published in the Open-
File Report series (I 19.76).

I 19.42/4:nos.   • Item 624-B (P) (EL)
WATER RESOURCES INVESTIGATIONS (numbered).
    1–   1973–   [Irregular] (Water Resources
Division)
    Includes reports that are of purely local inter-
est and other reports of limited interest, not intended for publication in a formal series of the
U.S. Geological Survey. They are duplicated
through the U.S. Government Printing Office in
small numbers for official use of Federal agencies and of cooperating State and local governments, and for distribution to local depositories.
Reports that contain only black and white illustrations are available for sale to the public by the
National Technical Information Service.

I 19.42/4-2:CT   • Item 624-B
WATER RESOURCES INVESTIGATIONS (various districts).

I 19.42/4-3:date   • Item 624-B (MF)
WATER RESOURCES RESEARCH PROGRAM OF THE
U.S. GEOLOGICAL SURVEY. [Annual]

I 19.42/5:nos. • Item 621 (MF)
CATALOG OF INFORMATION ON WATER DATA.
[Biennial] (Office of Water Data Coordination)
PURPOSE:– To publish the information contained in a computerized file of information about water-data-acquisitions activities in the United States and its territories and possessions. The catalog is not a file of actual water data, which must be obtained from the reporting agencies. The Catalog is published in 21 volumes, each covering streamflow and stage, quality of surface water, and quality of ground water.
The 1974 edition supersedes the 21 volumes of the previous edition (1972), the Index to Surface Water and Index to Water Quality Sections, 1970 edition, and all previous editions of these two indexes.
Each volume corresponds to a Water Resources Region (as designated by the Water Resources Council):–

1 New England Region
2 Mid Atlantic Region
3 South Atlantic-Gulf Region
4 Great Lakes Region
5 Ohio Region
6 Tennessee Region
7 Upper Mississippi Region
8 Lower Mississippi Region
9 Souris-Red-Rainy Region
10 Missouri Basin Region
11 Arkansas-White-Red Region
12 Texas-Gulf Region
13 Rio Grande Region
14 Upper Colorado Region
15 Lower Colorado Region
16 Great Basin Region
17 Pacific Northwest Region
18 California Region
19 Alaska Region
20 Hawaii Region
21 Caribbean Region (Includes both Puerto Rico and the Virgin Islands)

I 19.42/6:CT • Item 621 (MF)
CATALOG OF INFORMATION ON WATER DATA: INDEX TO STATIONS IN COASTAL AREAS.

I 19.42/7 • Item 624-B-1 (EL)
WATER-RESOURCES ABSTRACTS (database).

I 19.43 • Item 621-A
GEOPHYSICAL ABSTRACTS. 1– 1929– [Monthly]
Abstracts of current world literature pertaining to the physics of the solid earth and to geophysical exploration.
Each issue contains its own author index. Author and subject index for entire year issued separately, beginning with 1957. Prior to that date, it appeared in the October– December issues.
Geophysical Abstracts 1 to 86 were issued in Information Circulars by the Geophysical Section of the Bureau of Mines. That section was transferred to the Geological Survey on July 1, 1936, which issued abstracts 87-111. By Departmental Order of October 5, 1942, the geophysical work was again placed within the Bureau of Mines, during which time abstracts 112-127 were published. Beginning July 1, 1947, with abstract 128, the publication was again issued by the Geological Survey in the Bulletin series.
Prior to 1963, four issues were published each calendar year and assigned one bulletin number, with letter designations A-D for the quarterly issues (chapters) and the letter E for the annual index, this is in addition to the separate numbering of the abstracts.

I 19.44
[PRESS RELEASES]. [Irregular]

GEOLOGICAL SURVEY
Box 3202
Portland, Oregon 97208

I 19.45:date
CURRENT DISCHARGE AT SELECTED STATIONS IN PACIFIC NORTHWEST. [Weekly]

I 19.45/2:date
ACCURACY OF MONTHLY MEAN FLOW IN CURRENT RELEASES. ADMIN.

I 19.45/3
ANNUAL PEAK DISCHARGE AT SELECTED GAGING STATIONS IN PACIFIC NORTHWEST. [Annual] (Water Resources Division)

I 19.45/3-2:date
AVERAGE MONTHLY DISCHARGE FOR 15-YEAR BASE PERIOD AT SELECTED GAGING STATIONS AND CHANGE OF STORAGE IN CERTAIN LAKES AND RESERVOIRS IN PACIFIC NORTHWEST.
Earlier I 19.2:P 11

CURRENT RECORDS CENTER
Box 3621
Portland, Oregon 97208

I 19.46
PACIFIC NORTHWEST WATER RESOURCES SUMMARY. [Monthly]
Tables give estimated mean total discharge in cfs for month; reservoir storage; and quality of water. Charts give monthly streamflow at key gaging stations; month-end ground-water levels in key wells. Map gives streamflow and ground-water in relation to the average for the month. Textual summaries.
A separate release, Pacific Northwest Monthly Precipitation and Temperature, prepared by the Weather Bureau is mailed as a supplement to the Summary. It contains a weather map and a review of weather conditions.
ISSN 0499-5228

I 19.46/2
WEEKLY RUNOFF REPORT, PACIFIC NORTHWEST WATER RESOURCES. [Weekly]
Main table gives daily current discharge at selected stations in the Pacific Northwest. Second table gives storage in major reservoirs in the Pacific Northwest. Monthly data for both tables are contained in the release listed above, Storage in Major Power Reservoirs in the Columbia River Basin.
ISSN 0364-2607

I 19.46/2-2 & I 19.46/2-3
RIVER TEMPERATURE AT SELECTED STATIONS IN THE PACIFIC NORTHWEST. [Weekly & Monthly]

I 19.46/2-3:date
RIVER TEMPERATURES (degree F.) AT SELECTED STATIONS IN PACIFIC NORTHWEST. [Monthly]

I 19.46/3:date
ANNUAL SUMMARY OF WATER QUALITY DATA FOR SELECTED SITES IN THE PACIFIC NORTHWEST.
Earlier I 19.2:P 11/5

I 19.46/4:date • Item 621-G
PACIFIC NORTHWEST MONTHLY STREAMFLOW SUMMARY. [Monthly]
PURPOSE:– To present streamflow of Pacific Northwestern streams through tables, maps, and diagrams.
Disconnected.

GEOLOGICAL SUVEY (Continued)

I 19.47:date
MONTHLY MEAN DISCHARGE AT SELECTED GAGING STATIONS AND CHANGE OF STORAGE IN CERTAIN LAKES AND RESERVOIRS IN COLUMBIA RIVER BASIN.

I 19.47/2
CURRENT DISCHARGE AT SELECTED STATIONS IN THE PACIFIC NORTHWEST. [Monthly] (Water Resources Division, NW Water Resources Data Center, Box 3202, Portland, Oregon 97208)
Includes current discharge at selected stations in the Pacific Northwest; monthly mean discharge at selected gaging stations and change of storage in certain lakes and reservoirs in the Columbia River basin; month-end storage in major reservoirs in the Pacific Northwest; flood season flow, Columbia River near the Dalles.
Former title: Storage in Major Power Reservoirs in the Columbia River Basin.
ISSN 0364-4901

I 19.48
ANNOUNCEMENT OF WATER-RESOURCES REPORTS RELEASED FOR PUBLIC INSPECTION. [Irregular]
Prepared by the Water Resources Division. Reports listed, commonly known as Open-file reports, are those of too limited interest to warrant publication in a regular series but which should be made available to the public and reports containing data that are urgently needed for administrative reasons or for use by the public, prior to publication.

I 19.49:date
WATER LEVELS IN OBSERVATION WELLS IN SANTA BARBARA COUNTY, CALIFORNIA. [Annual]
Earlier I 19.2:W 46/3

I 19.50:CT
ADDRESSES.

I 19.51:nos.
[MAP INFORMATION OFFICE] MIO (series).

I 19.52:date
FLOOD SEASON FLOW COLUMBIA RIVER NEAR THE DALLES.
Earlier I 19.2:C 72/3
Later I 19.47/2

I 19.53:CT/date
SURFACE WATER RECORDS OF [States].

I 19.53/2:CT • Item 619-E-1– 619-E-53 (MF)
WATER RESOURCES DATA FOR [State]. [Annual]

Data collected in cooperation with State agencies and published in the following parts:–

1. Surface Water Records.
2. Water Quality Records.
3. Ground Water Records.
Information and requests for publications should be addressed to District Chief, Water Resources Division, U.S. Geological Survey at the following Addresses:–

ARIZONA
Box 4070
Tucson, Arizona 85717

ARKANSAS
2301 Federal Office Building
Little Rock, Arkansas 72201

CALIFORNIA
855 Oak Grove Avenue
Menlo Park, California 94025

COLORADO
Denver Federal Center
Denver, Colorado 80225

DELAWARE (Included with Maryland)

FLORIDA
903 West Tennessee Street
Tallahassee, Florida 32304

HAWAII
1100 Ward Avenue
Honolulu, Hawaii 96814

IDAHO
365 Federal Building
550 West Fort Street
Boise, Idaho 83702

ILLINOIS
Box 1026
Champaign, Illinois

IOWA
1041 Arthur Street
Iowa City, Iowa 52240

KANSAS

Box 3267
Lawrence, Kansas 66044

KENTUCKY

572 Federal Building
600 Federal Place
Louisville, Kentucky 40202

MARYLAND and DELAWARE

8809 Satyr Hill Road
Parkville, Maryland 21234

MICHIGAN

700 Capitol Savings and Loan Building
Lansing, Michigan 48933

MINNESOTA

1033 Post Office Building
St. Paul, Minnesota 55101

MISSOURI

103 W. 10th Street
Rolla, Missouri 65401

MONTANA

Box 1696
Helena, Montana 59601

NEBRASKA

127 Nebraska Hall
901 North 17th Street
Lincoln, Nebraska 68508

NEVADA

222 East Washington Street
Carson City, Nevada 89701

NEW JERSEY

420 Federal Building
Box 1238
Trenton, New Jersey 08607

NEW MEXICO

Box 4369
Albuquerque, New Mexico 87106

NORTH DAKOTA

Room 348, Federal Building
Bismarck, North Dakota 58501

OHIO

975 W. Third Avenue
Columbus, Ohio 43212

OREGON

Box 3203
Portland, Oregon 97208

TEXAS

Federal Building
300 East 8th Street
Austin, Texas 78701

WASHINGTON

Room 300
1305 Tacoma Avenue, South
Tacoma, Washington 98402

WEST VIRGINIA

3303 New Federal Office Building
Charleston, West Virginia 25301

WISCONSIN

1815 University Avenue
Madison, Wisconsin 53706

WYOMING

215 East 18th Avenue
Cheyenne, Wyoming 82001

I 19.53/3:date
NATIONAL REFERENCE LIST OF WATER QUALITY STATIONS, WATER YEAR (date).

I 19.53/4:nos.
WATER INFORMATION SERIES REPORTS. 1– 1971–   [Irregular]

I 19.53/5:CT   • Item 619-H
WATER RESOURCES ACTIVITIES IN [various States]. Each report covers water resources activities of a different State.

I 19.54   • Item 619-A
ABSTRACTS OF NORTH AMERICAN GEOLOGY. 1966–   [Monthly]
Serves as a supplement to Bibliography of North American Geology. Contains abstracts of technical papers and books and also citations of maps on the geology of North America, including Greenland, West Indies, Hawaii, Guam, and other U.S. island possessions. Articles of a general nature by North American authors appearing in foreign journals are also included. Arrangement by author with subject index.

WATER RESOURCES DIVISION
Menlo Park, California

I 19.55
ACTIVITIES OF WATER RESOURCES DIVISION, CALIFORNIA DISTRICT. 1963–   [Annual]
Report summarizes the scheduled activities of the California District, Water Resources Division, for the fiscal year. Also includes list of reports published or released to the open file.

I 19.55/2:date
PROGRAM OF WATER RESOURCES DIVISION, TEXAS DISTRICT, AND SUMMARY OF DISTRICT ACTIVITIES, FISCAL YEAR.

I 19.55/3:date   • Item 619-E-12 (MF)
ACTIVITIES OF THE U.S. GEOLOGICAL SURVEY, WATER RESOURCES DIVISION, STATUS OF IDAHO PROJECTS. [Biennial]

I 19.55/5:date   • Item 619-H (MF)
WATER RESOURCES ACTIVITIES IN ILLINOIS. [Annual]

I 19.55/6:date   • Item 619-E-35 (MF)
INDEX OF CURRENT WATER RESOURCES ACTIVITIES IN OHIO. [Annual]

I 19.55/7:date   • Item 619-E-11 (MF)
ACTIVITIES OF THE U.S. GEOLOGICAL SURVEY WATER RESOURCES DIVISION, HAWAII. [Annual]

GEOLOGICAL SURVEY (Continued)

I 19.56   • Item 619-C
RIVER BASINS OF THE UNITED STATES. 1968–   [Irregular]

I 19.57:nos.
INVESTIGATIONS OF FLOODS IN HAWAII, PROGRESS REPORTS. 1–   1958–   [Annual]
A basic data release presenting annual peak stage and discharge from a network of gaging stations. All previous data are included in each progress report for stations retained in the flood-peak network. A discussion of flood events during the reporting year and plans for the following year are included.

I 19.58:CT
COMPILATION OF HYDROLOGIC DATA [by area].

I 19.59:CT
PROPOSED STREAMFLOW DATA PROGRAM FOR [State].

I 19.59/2:CT
EVALUATION OF STREAMFLOW-DATA PROGRAM IN [various States].
Earlier I 19.2:St 8/4

I 19.60:nos.
GLACIOLOGICAL NOTES. (World Data Center A: Glaciology, 1305 Tacoma Avenue South, Tacoma, Washington 98402)
Acquisitions list.
Superseded by Glaciological Data Report (I 19.60).

I 19.61:v.nos.&nos.   • Item 619-D
JOURNAL OF RESEARCH OF THE U.S. GEOLOGICAL SURVEY. v. 1–   1973–   [6 times a year]
Contains papers written by members of the Geological Survey and their professional colleagues on various subjects in geology, hydrology, topography, and related earth sciences. Also contains a listing of recently released Geological Survey publications.
Supersedes the short-papers chapters of the former Geological Survey Research (Annual Review) issued in the Professional Papers series (I 19.16).
Indexed by: Index to U.S. Government Periodicals.
ISSN 0091-374X

I 19.62:nos.
BASIC-DATA CONTRIBUTIONS.

I 19.63:nos.
INTERAGENCY REPORTS.

I 19.64:nos.
USGS-TD- (series). [Irregular] (Topographic Division)

I 19.64/2:nos.
USGS-GD (series).

I 19.65:v.nos.&nos.   • Item 191-A
EARTHQUAKES AND VOLCANOES. v. 1–   1967–   [Bimonthly]
PURPOSE:– To provide current information on earthquake and seismological activities of interest to both general and specialized readers.
Issued by the Environmental Research Laboratories prior to v. 5, no. 4, July– August 1973 (C 55.611).
Earlier title: Earthquake Information Bulletin.
Indexed by: Index to U.S. Government Periodicals.

I 19.65/2:date   • Item 208
UNITED STATES EARTHQUAKES. [Annual]
PURPOSE:– To provide a summary of earthquake activity in the United States and regions outside the U.S. under its jurisdiction for the calendar year. Technical in nature, this annual report contains narrative and tabular summaries pertaining to geodetic work of seismological interest, tidal disturbances of seismic origin, fluctuations in well-water levels, and narrative summaries of the characteristics and effects of the principal earthquakes experienced during the year.
A history of the more important shocks of the country appears in Earthquake History of the United States (Pub. 41-1), issued in two parts. Part 1 covers the continental United States and Alaska (exclusive of California and western Nevada).
A summary of the earthquake program as carried out in the United States is outlined briefly in Earthquake Investigation in the United States (S.P. 282).
Current data may be found in the Quarterly Engineering Seismology Bulletin.
Time lag of publication is about 2 years (information for calendar year 1959 was published in 1961).
Prior to the 1981 issue, published by Environmental Data Service (C 55.226).

I 19.66:date • **Item 192-C (MF) (EL)**
PRELIMINARY DETERMINATION OF EPICENTERS, MONTHLY LISTINGS. (National Earthquake Information Center)
Provides a chronological listing of all earthquakes located by the National Ocean Survey to scientific and general users. Contains date and time of each shock, its geographic location, the region in which it centered and damage comments, its depth and magnitude, and the number of seismic stations used in computing these data.
ISSN 0364-7072
Earlier C 55.690

I 19.66/2:nos.
PRELIMINARY DETERMINATION OF EPICENTERS. [Weekly]

I 19.67:nos.
COMPUTER CONTRIBUTION (series). [Irregular] (Branch of Computer Information)
Projects are undertaken in the USGS which result in reports that warrant acknowledgment of their contribution to the use of computers in various fields. These reports are computer program descriptions and computer related documents published as Computer Contributions.

I 19.68:CT
MONTHLY WATER SUMMARY [By State].

I 19.69:nos.
ABSTRACTS OF EARTHQUAKE REPORTS FOR THE UNITED STATES. MSA 1– [Quarterly] (Open File Report) (National Center for Earthquake Research)
Prepared jointly by the Seismic Engineering Office of Earthquake Studies, San Francisco, California, and Environmental Data Service, National Geophysical and Solcar-Terrestrial Data Center, Boulder, Colorado.
Issued by Environmental Data Service (C 55.223) prior to MSA-149.

I 19.70:CT • **Item 624-C**
FLOOD-PRONE AREAS OF [various cities].

I 19.71:nos. • **Item 624-E**
NATIONAL CARTOGRAPHIC INFORMATION CENTER: NEWSLETTER. 1– 1975– [Quarterly]
ISSN 0364-7064

I 19.72:date
GEOLOGICAL SURVEY NATIONAL CENTER TELEPHONE DIRECTORY.

I 19.73:nos. • **Item 624-D**
OUTER CONTINENTAL SHELF STANDARD, GSS-OCS (series). 1– 1976– [Irregular] (Branch of Marine Oil and Gas Operations)
PURPOSE:– To provide technical standards delineating procedures, specifications, and requirements for a wide variety of Outer Continental Shelf oil field operations and equipment. These documents are for the use of Lessees and Operators of Outer Continental Shelf, in compliance with the requirements of the Outer Continental Shelf Orders, which reference the standards.

I 19.74:date • **Item 624-F (EL)**
INTERAGENCY ADVISORY COMMITTEE ON WATER DATA: SUMMARY OF MEETINGS. 1st– 1964– [Annual] (Office of Water Data Coordination)
10th. December 16, 1975.

I 19.74/2:date • **Item 624-F-1 (MF)**
NOTES ON SEDIMENTATION ACTIVITIES. [Annual] (Interagency Committee on Water Data)
PURPOSE:– To present information on sedimentation investigations being made by various Federal agencies, including work planned or in progress, research, publications, etc.

I 19.74/3:date • **Item 624-F (MF)**
FEDERAL PLAN FOR WATER-DATA ACQUISITION. [Annual]

I 19.75:date
REPORT OF WATER RESOURCES RESEARCH.

I 19.76:yr.-nos. • **Item 624-H (MF) (CD) (EL)**
OPEN-FILE REPORTS.
Also issued on diskettes.
Included with the Open File Reports as a finding aid is New Publications List (I 19.14/4).

I 19.77:nos. • **Item 625-A**
AERIAL PHOTOGRAPHY SUMMARY RECORD SYSTEM, APSRS- (series). [Irregular]
Consists of 34 publications covering all areas of the United States, each issued twice a year. Consists of maps with codes and keys, showing various aerial mapping projects of the different agencies.

I 19.78:nos. • **Item 619-F-1**
LANDSAT DATA USERS NOTES. 1– [Bimonthly] (Earth Resources Observation Satellite Data Center)
Later C 55.45

I 19.79:letters&nos. • **Item 619-G-1**
MAPS AND POSTERS.

I 19.80:CT • **Item 619-G-2**
NATIONAL MAPPING PROGRAM (series). [Irregular]
Correspondence-aids, fact-sheets designed to help the general public in locating and purchasing various government maps.

I 19.80/2 • **Item 619-G-29**
NEWSLETTER. [Irregular]
Newsletter of the National Cartographic Information Center. Contains articles on National Mapping Program activities.

I 19.80/3:nos.
DATA USERS GUIDE.

I 19.81:State CT • **Item 619-M-01– 53**
TOPOGRAPHICAL QUADRANGLE MAPS. 7.5' SERIES [Irregular]
A topographical map is a graphic representation of selected manmade and natural features of a part of the earth's surface plotted to a definite scale. They record in convenient, readable form the physical characteristics of the terrain as determined by precise engineering surveys and measurements. They show the location and shape of the mountains, valleys, and plains; the network of streams and rivers, and the principal works of man.
The 7.5' quadrangle has a scale of 1:24,000 (1 inch 2,000 feet), covers from 49 to 70 square miles, and is printed on sheets 22 x 27 inches.

I 19.81/2:nos. • **Item 619-M-1–53**
TOPOGRAPHICAL QUADRANGLE MAPS, 15' SERIES.

I 19.81/3:nos.-letters-nos. • **Item 619-M-3**
COLOR IMAGE MAP.

I 19.82:nos.
BASIC DATA SERIES GROUND-WATER RELEASES (series). [Irregular]

I 19.83:nos.
COOPERATIVE INVESTIGATIONS REPORTS (series). [Irregular]

I 19.84:date • **Item 620-B (MF)**
TELEPHONE DIRECTORY.

I 19.84/2:date
TELEPHONE DIRECTORY CENTRAL REGION.

I 19.85:nos. • **Item 619-G-3**
COAL INVESTIGATION MAPS. C-1– 1950– [Irregular]
Geologic maps on topographic of planimetric bases; various scales; show bedrock geology, stratigraphy, and structural relations in certain coal-resource areas.

I 19.86: • **Item 619-G-28**
INDEX TO GEOLOGIC MAPPING OF THE UNITED STATES. [Irregular]
Computer-generated State maps on planimetric bases; show location and scale of geologic maps published by Federal, State and private agencies.

I 19.87:nos. • **Item 619-G-4**
GEOPHYSICAL INVESTIGATIONS MAPS. GP-1– 1946– [Irregular]
Maps on topographic or planimetric bases; various scales; show results of surveys using geophysical techniques, such as gravity, magnetic, seismic, or radioactivity, which reflect subsurface structures that are of economic or geologic significance. Many maps are correlated with the surface geology.

I 19.88:nos. • **Item 619-G-5**
GEOLOGICAL QUADRANGLE MAPS. GQ-1– 1949– [Irregular]
Multicolor geologic maps on topographic bases in 7.5- or 15-minute quadrangle units; scales mainly 1:24,000 or 1:62,500; show bedrock, surficial, or engineering geology. Maps are accompanied by brief texts and some maps by structure and columnar sections also.

I 19.89:nos. • **Item 619-G-6**
HYDROLOGIC INVESTIGATION ATLASES (maps). HA-1– 1954– [Irregular]
Multicolor or black and white maps on topographic or planimetric bases presenting a wide range of geohydrologic data; both regular and irregular areas; principal scale 1:24,000, regional studies at 1:250,000 scale or smaller.

I 19.89/2: • **Item 619-G-6**
HYDROLOGIC UNIT MAP.

I 19.90:nos. • **Item 619-G-7**
MINERAL INVESTIGATIONS RESOURCE MAPS. MR-1– 1952– [Irregular]
Mineral distribution and classification maps; scales from 1:250,000 to 1:5,000,000; show geographic distribution and grade of mineral- resource commodities. Brief accompanying text may include a general description of the geologic occurrences, a locality index, and a bibliography.

I 19.91:nos. • **Item 619-G-8**
MISCELLANEOUS GEOLOGIC INVESTIGATIONS MAPS. I-1– 1955– [Irregular]
Maps on planimetric or topographic bases; regular and irregular areas; various scales; a wide variety of format and subject matter. The series also include 7.5-minute quadrangle photogeologic maps on planimetric bases which show geology as interpreted from aerial photographs. Series also include maps of Mars and the Moon.

I 19.91/2 • **Item 619-G-8**
CIRCUM-PACIFIC (CP) MAP SERIES.

I 19.92:nos. • **Item 619-G-9**
OIL AND GAS INVESTIGATION CHARTS. OC-1– 1944– [Irregular]
Charts show stratigraphic information for certain oil and gas fields and other hydrocarbon potential.

I 19.93:nos. • **Item 619-G-10**
OIL AND GAS INVESTIGATIONS MAPS. OM-1– 1943– [Irregular]
Maps on planimetric or topographic bases of oil and gas fields or other areas having hydrocarbon potential; various scales; show geology and sub-surface geological structure.

I 19.94:CT
WATER RESOURCES INVESTIGATIONS FOLDERS. [Irregular]
Single folder for each State. Maps show location of stream-gaging stations, observation wells, quality-of-water sampling sites, and investigation in progress. Small maps show other significant hydrologic aspects.

I 19.95:date • **Item 619-G-12**
TOPOGRAPHIC MAPPING, STATUS AND PROGRESS OF OPERATIONS. [Annual]
U.S. Map shows published topographic quadrangle maps and status of work in progress for 7.5- and 15- minute series mapping by the USGS and other Federal agencies.

I 19.96:date • **Item 619-G-13**
INDEX TO INTERMEDIATE SCALE MAPPING. [Semi-annual]
U.S. Map shows published and status of work in progress, including availability of advance materials and feature separates, for both topographic and planimetric 1:100,000-scale quadrangle maps by the USGS and other Federal agencies; U.S. Map on reverse side shows published and status of work in progress for both topographic and planimetric county maps in 1:50,000- and 1:100,000-scale.

I 19.97:date • **Item 619-G-14**
INDEX TO ORTHOPHOTOQUAD MAPPING. [Semiannual]
U.S. map shows published and status of work progress, including availability of advance materials, for orthophotoquads (monocolor photographic image maps in standard 7.5-minute quadrangle format without topographic detail).

I 19.97/2:date • **Item 619-G-14**
INDEX TO USGS/DMA 1:50,000-SCALE, 15 MINUTE QUADRANGLE MAPPING. [Semiannual]
U.S. map shows published USGS/DMA topographic quadrangle maps and quadrangle for which work is in progress. USGS/DMA maps are prepared and published selected areas of the U.S. on a cooperative basis by the U.S. Geological Survey and the Defense Mapping Agency.

I 19.97/3:date • **Item 619-G-14**
INDEX TO LAND USE AND LAND COVER MAPS AND DIGITAL DATA.
U.S. map shows published and open filed land use and land cover maps and filed associated maps (political units, hydrologic units, census county sub-divisions, Federal land ownership, and State land ownership) for 1:100,000 and 1:250,000-scale quadrangle; U.S. map on reverse side shows quadrangle for which digital data, derived from land use and land cover and associated maps, are available.

I 19.97/4 • **Item 619-G-31**
INDEX TO NATIONAL AERIAL PHOTOGRAPHY (Map).

I 19.97/5 • **Item 619-G-32**
INDEX TO DIGITAL LINE GRAPHS (DLG), (Map).

I 19.98: • **Item 619-G-17**
UNITED STATES SERIES OF TOPOGRAPHIC MAPS. [Irregular]
Conventional line topographic maps (Transverse Mercator projection) in 1° of latitude by 2° of longitude. Contour interval ranges from 50 feet in relatively flat areas to 200 feet in mountainous regions. 25-30 titles are expected each year.

I 19.99: • **Item 619-G-18**
ALASKA 1:250,000-SCALE SERIES (maps). [Irregular]
Alaska is covered by 153 maps; many are also printed in a shaded-relief edition on which the topography is made to appear three-dimensional by use of shadow effects. Conventional line topographic maps (Transverse Mercator projection) in 1° of latitude by 2° of longitude. Contour interval ranges from 50 feet in relatively flat areas to 200 feet in mountainous regions.

ANTARCTICAL TOPOGRAPHIC SERIES.

I 19.100: • **Item 619-G-19**
1:50,000-SCALE MAPS. [Irregular]
1:50,000 scale maps cover 15-minutes of latitude and 60 minutes oflongitude; contour interval 50 meters.

I 19.100/2 • **Item 619-G-19**
1:250,000-SCALE MAPS. [Irregular]
Reconnaissance maps with shaded relief at 1:250,000 scale; contour interval 20 meters.

I 19.100/3 • **Item 619-G-19**
1:500,000-SCALE MAPS. [Irregular]
Reconnaissance maps with shaded relief at 1:500,000 scale; contour interval 1,000 feet.

I 19.100/4 • **Item 619-G-19**
1:500,000-SCALE MAPS. [Irregular]
A sketch map series also with shaded relief but without contours at 1:500,000 is available. There is also a series of satellite image maps (Landsat) published; future satellite image maps will replace the sketch maps series.

I 19.100/5 • **Item 619-G-19**
1:1,000,000-SCALE MAPS. [Irregular]
1:1,000,000 scale maps on the specifications of the International Map of the World (IMW) series; map dimensions are 4° of latitude but degrees of longitude vary as meridians converge toward the South Pole. Also includes shaded relief maps at 1:2,188,800 scale.

I 19.100/6 • **Item 619-G-19**
ANTARCTIC PHOTOMAP (series). [Irregular]

I 19.101: • **Item 619-G-20**
UNITED STATES TOPOGRAPHIC/BATHYMETRIC MAPS. [Irregular]
Maps combine data previously shown separately on the USGS topographic map and the NOS (National Ocean Survey) bathymetric map. Portray both topographic (showing the showing water depths, portrayed by various colors or contour lines) information; scales vary depending on series, general 1:24,000 (7.5-minute) series; 1:100,000 (intermediate scale) series, and 1:250,000 (small scale) series.

I 19.102: • **Item 619-H-1– 53**
STATE MAP SERIES, PANIMETRIC, 1:500,00-SCALE. [Irregular]
Map shows counties, location and names of cities and towns, smaller settlements, railroads, township and range lines (in black); rivers, many small streams, and other water features (in blue); no contours are shown.

I 19.102/nos. • **Item 619-H-1– 53**
STATE MAP SERIES: PLANIMETRIC, TOPOGRAPHIC AND SHADED RELIEF (Various Scales) [State].

I 19.103: • **Item 619-J-1– 53**
STATE MAP SERIES, TOPOGRAPHIC, 1:500,000-SCALE. [Irregular]
This map, in addition to the information shown on the planimetric map described directly above, shows contours in brown, highways in purple, and selected Federal recreation areas (parks, monuments, wildlife refuges, etc.) by color patterns.

I 19.104: • **Item 619-K-1– 53**
STATE MAP SERIES, SHADED RELIEF, 1:500,00-SCALE. [Irregular]
This map is a modified version of the planimetric map described above (shows State capitals, county seats, and State and county boundaries in black, and water features in blue). The maps' physical features are brought out by shaded relief in color. Newer maps in this series show contours; older ones do not.

I 19.105: • **Item 619-L-1– 53**
STATE MAP SERIES, PLANIMETRIC, 1:1,000,000-SCALE. [Irregular]
Maps contain similar information and features as are on the 500,000-scale planimetric maps (I 19.102) with the exception that the size has been reduced and all features are printed in black.

I 19.106: • **Item 619-G-21**
NATIONAL PARK SERIES. [Irregular]
Topographic maps at various scales; shows national park, monuments, historic sites, etc. Many are printed in shaded relief editions. Special emphasis is placed on map detail pertaining to recreational opportunities.

I 19.107: • **Item 619-G-22**
UNITED STATES 1:1,000,000-SCALE MAPS. [Irregular]
Printed in two editions– 1) the U.S. contribution to the International Mapof the World (IMW); 2) a series that does not conform to the IMW specifications in all respects but satisfy the same

general purpose. Dimensions are 4° latitude by 6° longitude (12° longitude for Alaska). Shows principal cities and towns, railroads, and political boundaries in black; water features in blue, etc.

I 19.108:nos.&letrs. • **Item 619-P-1– 53**
COUNTY MAP SERIES. [Irregular]
Maps of the U.S. in county format at 1:50,000 scale, and some counties at 1:100,000 scale. Some counties may require more than one sheet, depending on size of the county. The 1:50,000-scale maps correspond closely in content with the 1:62,500-scale (15-minute) quadrangle maps. Reference systems shown include a full State plane coordinate grid, public land net, and UTM grid ticks. Less detail is shown on the 1:100,000-scale maps.

I 19.109: • **Item 619-G-24**
SLOPE MAPS. [Irregular]
The USGS does not produce slope maps as a standard series, but rather for selected areas based on need for such maps. Slope zones are particularly useful in studies related to land use, such as soil, drainage, vegetation and construction. On USGS maps, slope is indicated as a percentage; the legend indicates the angle of inclination and the gradient ratio.

I 19.110:letters-nos. • **Item 619-G-25**
UNITED STATES 1:1,000,000-SCALE SERIES. (Intermediate Scale Maps) [Irregular]
Topographic maps in 30- by 60-minute quadrangle format. Normally, they are derivative products of standard 1:24,000-scale (7.5-minute) publications. Produced in metric units with a contour interval of 5, 10, 20, or 50m. depending on terrain relief, and includes a full fine-line UTM grid.

I 19.111 • **Item 619-G-26 (EL)**
NATIONAL ATLAS (also online databases).

I 19.111/a:CT • **Item 619-G-26**
SEPARATE SHEETS OF SELECTED THEMATIC AND GENERAL REFERENCE MAPS FROM THE NATIONAL ATLAS OF THE UNITED STATES OF AMERICA. [Irregular]
Many maps included in the 1970 National Atlas are available separately from the USGS; economic, social, and cultural data in cartographic form, as well as maps and charts showing physical features such as climate, land forms, geology, soil, and vegetation are available in sets and singly.

I 19.112 • **Item 619-G-27**
LAND USE AND LAND COVER AND ASSOCIATED MAPS. [Irregular]
Compiled using USGS Level I and II classification system depicting land cover and man's activities. Associated maps include political units, hydrologic units, census county sub-divisions, and federal land ownership. Scale 1:250,000 or 1:100,000.

I 19.113:nos. • **Item 619-G-11**
MISCELLANEOUS FIELD STUDIES MAPS. MF-1– 1950– [Irregular]
Maps on topographic or planimetric bases; quadrangle or irregular areas; various scales; show preliminary results on various subjects such as environmental studies or wilderness mineral investigations.

I 19.114 • **Item 621-D**
WATER FACT SHEETS (series). [Irregular]

I 19.115 • **Item 621-E (MF)**
FEDERAL DIGITAL CARTOGRAPHY NEWSLETTER. [Irregular]
The purpose of the newsletter is to establish a forum to exchange information on Federal digital cartographic activities for people who work with, use, or are simply interested in digital cartographic data.

I 19.115/3 • **Item 621-E (MF)**
MINERAL RESOURCES NEWSLETTER. [Quarterly]

I 19.115/4 • **Item 621-E (EL)**
FGD (Federal Geographic Data) NEWSLETTER. [Irregular]

I 19.116:v.nos.&nos. • **Item 621-F**
TOPOGRAPHICALLY SPEAKING. [Monthly]
Newsletter of the Mid-Continent Mapping Center of the Geological Survey at Rolla, Missouri. No longer a depository item. For internal/administrative use only, under 44 U.S.C. section 1902.

I 19.118: • **Item 621-H (MF)**
WATER DATA COORDINATION DIRECTORY. [Annual]
Issued by USGS's Office of Water Data Coordination. A directory of the Interagency Advisory Committee (Federal) and the Advisory Committee on Water Data for Public Use (Non-Federal).

I 19.120 • **Item 621-J (E)**
ELECTRONIC PRODUCTS. [Irregular]

I 19.120/2 • **Item 621-J-1 (CD)**
USGS/NGIC GEOMAGNETIC OBSERVATORY DATA. [Annual]

I 19.120/3:date • **Item 621-J-3 (CD)**
CONTERMINOUS U.S. AVHRR BIWEEKLY COMPOSITES.

I 19.120/4:date • **Item 639-J (CD)**
MINERALS AND MATERIALS INFORMATION.

I 19.121:nos. • **Item 621-K (CD)**
DIGITAL DATA SERIES. DDS-1– 1991– [Irregular]

I 19.123 • **Item 619-G-30**
UNITED STATES: BASE MAPS (various scales).

I 19.124/nos. • **Item 626-B-2– 51**
DIGITAL ORTHOPHOTOQUADS DOQ FOR [State].
Issued on CD-ROM.

I 19.125:v.nos/nos. • **Item 621-H-1 (EL)**
NATIONAL WATER QUALITY LABORATORY NEWSLETTER.

I 19.127:nos. • **Item 621-L (P) (EL)**
FACT SHEET (series).

I 19.127/2 • **Item 621-L-1**
U.S.-MEXICO BORDER FIELD COORDINATING COMMITTEE FACT SHEET(series).

I 19.128 • **Item 621-J-1 (E)**
DRG DIGITAL RASTER GRAPHIC (series).

I 19.128 • **Item 619-R-7– R-53 (CD)**
DIGITAL RASTER GRAPHICS (DRG) FOR [State].

I 19.128/2:nos. • **Item 621-J-4 (CD)**
FDSN EARTHQUAKE DIGITAL DATA.

I 19.129 • **Item 639-H-3 (EL)**
METAL INDUSTRY INDICATORS. [Monthly]
Earlier I 28.173

I 19.130 • **Item 639-H-4 (MF)**
MINERAL INDUSTRY SURVEYS, ALUMINUM IN . . . [Monthly]
Earlier I 28.85

I 19.131 • **Item 639-H-5 (MF)**
MINERAL INDUSTRY SURVEYS, ANTIMONY IN THE . . . [Quarterly]
Earlier I 28.95

I 19.132 • **Item 639-G-1 (MF)**
MINERAL INDUSTRY SURVEYS, BAUXITE AND ALUMINA IN THE . . . [Quarterly]
Earlier I 28.80

I 19.133 • **Item 639-F-4 (MF)**
MINERAL INDUSTRY SURVEYS, BISMUTH IN . . . [Monthly]

I 19.134 • **Item 639-F-3 (MF)**
MINERAL INDUSTRY SURVEYS, CEMENT IN . . . [Monthly]
Earlier I 28.29

I 19.135 • **Item 639-H-6 (MF)**
MINERAL INDUSTRY SURVEYS, CHROMIUM IN . . . [Monthly]
Earlier I 28.84

I 19.136 • **Item 639-G-2 (MF)**
MINERAL INDUSTRY SURVEYS, COBALT IN . . . [Monthly]
Earlier I 28.76

I 19.137 • **Item 639-H-7 (MF)**
MINERAL INDUSTRY SURVEYS, COPPER IN . . . [Monthly]
Earlier I 28.59/2

I 19.138 • **Item 639-D-1 (MF)**
MINERAL INDUSTRY SURVEYS, CRUSHED STONE AND SAND IN . . . [Quarterly]
Earlier I 28.118/4

I 19.138/3:date • **Item 639-E**
MINERAL INDUSTRY SURVEYS, DIRECTORY OF PRINCIPAL CONSTRUCTION SAND AND GRAVEL PRODUCERS IN THE . . . , ANNUAL ADVANCED SUMMARY SUPPLEMENT.

I 19.139 • **Item 639-G-3 (MF)**
MINERAL INDUSTRY SURVEYS, FLUORSPAR IN THE . . . [Quarterly]
Earlier I 28.70

I 19.140 • **Item 639-F-5 (MF)**
MINERAL INDUSTRY SURVEYS, GYPSUM IN . . . [Monthly]
Earlier I 28.32

I 19.141 • **Item 639-F-6 (MF)**
MINERAL INDUSTRY SURVEYS, IRON AND STEEL SCRAP IN . . . [Monthly]
Earlier I 28.53

I 19.142 • **Item 639-F-7 (MF)**
MINERAL INDUSTRY SURVEYS, IRON ORE IN . . . [Monthly]
Earlier I 28.66

I 19.143 • **Item 639-F-8 (MF)**
MINERAL INDUSTRY SURVEYS, LEAD IN . . . [Monthly]
Earlier I 28.87

I 19.144 • **Item 639-F-9 (MF)**
MINERAL INDUSTRY SURVEYS, LIME IN . . . [Monthly]
Earlier I 28.28

I 19.145 • **Item 639-H-8 (MF)**
MINERAL INDUSTRY SURVEYS, MAGNESIUM IN . . . [Quarterly]
Earlier I 28.101

I 19.146 • **Item 639-H-9 (MF)**
MINERAL INDUSTRY SURVEYS, MANUFACTURED ABRASIVES. [Quarterly]
Earlier I 28.171

I 19.147 • **Item 639-E-2 (MF)**
MINERAL INDUSTRY SURVEYS, MARKETABLE PHOSPHATE ROCK. [Monthly]
Earlier I 28.119/3

I 19.148 • **Item 639-H-10 (MF)**
MINERAL INDUSTRY SURVEYS, NICKEL IN . . . [Monthly]
Earlier I 28.92

I 19.149 • **Item 639-F-10 (MF)**
MINERAL INDUSTRY SURVEYS, PRECIOUS METALS IN . . . [Monthly]

I 19.150 • **Item 639-G-4 (MF)**
MINERAL INDUSTRY SURVEYS, SILICON IN . . . [Monthly]
Earlier I 28.75

I 19.151 • **Item 639-E-3 (MF)**
MINERAL INDUSTRY SURVEYS, SODA ASH AND SODIUM SULFATE IN . . . [Monthly]
Earlier I 28.135/2

I 19.152 • **Item 639-F-11 (MF)**
MINERAL INDUSTRY SURVEYS, SULFUR IN . . . [Monthly]
Earlier I 28.63

I 19.153 • **Item 639-H-11 (MF)**
MINERAL INDUSTRY SURVEYS, TIN IN . . . [Monthly]
Earlier I 28.96

I 19.154 • **Item 639-G-5 (MF)**
MINERAL INDUSTRY SURVEYS, TITANIUM IN . . . [Monthly]
Earlier I 28.82/2

I 19.155 • **Item 639-G-6 (MF)**
MINERAL INDUSTRY SURVEYS, TUNGSTEN IN . . . [Monthly]
Earlier I 28.73

I 19.156 • **Item 639-G-7 (MF)**
MINERAL INDUSTRY SURVEYS, VANADIUM IN . . . [Monthly]
Earlier I 28.78

I 19.157 • **Item 639-G-8 (MF)**
MINERAL INDUSTRY SURVEYS, ZINC IN . . . [Monthly]
Earlier I 28.69

I 19.158 • **Item 639-F-13 (MF)**
MINERAL INDUSTRY SURVEYS, MANGANESE IN . . . [Monthly]
Earlier I 28.54

I 19.159 • **Item 639-F-12 (MF)**
MINERAL INDUSTRY SURVEYS, MOLYBDENUM IN . . . [Monthly]
Earlier I 28.58/2

I 19.160 • **Item 621-J (EL)**
MINERAL INDUSTRY SURVEYS. [Monthly & Quarterly].

I 19.161 • **Item 621-J (EL)**
MINERAL INDUSTRY SURVEYS. [Annual]

I 19.162:CT • **Item 621-J (EL)**
MINERAL INDUSTRY SURVEYS, MINERAL INDUSTRY OF [State] MINERALS. [Annual]

I 19.163 • **Item 621-J (EL)**
MINERAL INDUSTRY SURVEYS, MINERAL INDUSTRY OF [Country] MINERALS. [Annual]

I 19.164 • **Item 621-J (E)**
NEWSLETTER, FEDERAL GEOGRAPHIC DATA COMMITTEE.

I 19.165:date/v.nos. • **Item 639 (P) (EL)**
MINERALS YEARBOOK.

I 19.166 • **Item 621-J (EL)**
MINERAL COMMODITY SUMMARIES. [Annual]

HH 13.167 • **Item 620-C-2 (P) (EL)**
CONTAMINANT HAZARD REVIES (series).

HH 13.168 • **Item 621-M (EL)**
NATIONAL LAND COVER DATASET.

BIOLOGICAL RESOURCES DIVISION

I 19.202:CT • **Item 626-C**
GENERAL PUBLICATIONS.

I 19.208: • **Item 626-C-1**
HANDBOOKS, MANUALS, GUIDES.

I 19.209:nos. • **Item 626-C-2 (MF) (EL)**
BIOLOGICAL SCIENCE REPORT (series).

I 19.210:nos. • **Item 626-C-3 (MF)**
INFORMATION AND TECHNOLOGY REPORT (series).

I 19.211:   • **Item 626-C-4 (MF)**
NWHC TECHNICAL REPORT (National Wildlife Health Center) (series).

I 19.212:   • **Item 626-D-1-52**
GAP ANALYSIS PROGRAM.
    Issued on CD-ROM

I 19.212/1   • **Item 626-D-1-D-52 (CD)**
GAP ANALYSIS PROGRAM (GAP). (States)

BUREAU OF INDIAN AFFAIRS
(1947–   )

CREATION AND AUTHORITY

The Bureau of Indian Affairs was created in the War Department in 1824 and transferred to the Department of the Interior at the time of its establishment in 1849. The Snyder Act of 1921 (42 Stat. 208; 25 U.S.C. 13) provided substantive law for appropriations covering the conduct of activities by the Bureau of Indian Affairs. The scope and character of the authorizations contained in this act were broadened by the Indian Reorganization Act of 1934 (48 Stat. 984; 25 U.S.C. 461 et seq.).

INFORMATION

Office of Public Affairs
Bureau of Indian Affairs
1849 C Street, NW
Washington, DC 20240
(202) 208-3710
Fax: (202) 501-1516
http://www.doi.gov/bureau-indian-affairs.html

I 20.1   • **Item 626-A**
INDIAN AFFAIRS, (year), PROGRESS REPORT FROM THE COMMISSIONER OF INDIAN AFFAIRS. [Annual]

I 20.1/2:date
ANNUAL CREDIT REPORT.

I 20.1/3:date
NORTHWEST INDIAN FISHERIES COMMISSION. [Annual]

I 20.1/4   • **Item 627-A-2 (MF)**
ANNUAL EDUCATION REPORT.

I 20.2:CT   • **Item 627**
GENERAL PUBLICATIONS.

I 20.2:C 1/2   • **Item 627**
AMERICAN INDIAN CALENDAR. [Annual]
    PURPOSE:– To acquaint tourists with interesting events scheduled on Indian reservations during the year, such as ceremonials, dances, feats, and celebrations.

I 20.2:In 2/nos.   • **Item 627**
INFORMATION RESPECTING THE HISTORY, CONDITIONS, AND PROSPECTS OF THE INDIAN TRIBES OF THE UNITED STATES, Philadelphia, Lippincott, Grambo & Co. 1851– 57. 6 v. il.

I 20.2:In 2/26   • **Item 627**
FAMOUS INDIANS, A COLLECTION OF SHORT BIOGRAPHIES. 1975. 52 p. il.

I 20.2:In 2/27   • **Item 627**
BIOGRAPHICAL SKETCHES AND ANECDOTES OF 95 OF 120 PRINCIPAL CHIEFS FROM INDIAN TRIBES OF NORTH AMERICA. 1967. 452 p.

    Originally published in 1838.

I 20.2:P 75/6   • **Item 627**
HISTORY OF INDIAN POLICY. 1973. 328 p. il.
    This examination of the history of United States Indian policy is not intended to be a general history of the American Indian or a history of all interaction between the United States and Indians. This is a study of the Indian policies of the Spanish, French, Dutch, and the Indian policies of the Spanish, French, Dutch, and English colonial governments, as well as that of the United States since 1789. Also discussed are the assimilation, removal, allotment, the establishment of reservations, and the extension of local laws over tribes within the established States in America. Over 50 illustrations accompany the text: with an appendix of dates significant in the development of Indian Policy.

I 20.2:St 2/3   • **Item 627**
STATES AND THEIR INDIAN CITIZENS. Rev. 1973. 307 p. il.
    Presents the American Indians, their relationship to the land, their neighbors, State, local, and Federal governments. The appendix contains an analysis of the special messages on Indians to the Congress by Presidents Johnson and Nixon and a table that shows by State the acres of Indian land, Indian population, and whether Indian children are educated by public or Federal schools.

I 20.3:nos.
BULLETINS.

I 20.3/2:nos.
BULLETINS, MIMEOGRAPHED SERIES.

I 20.4:nos.
CIRCULARS.

I 20.5:date
INDIAN COMMISSIONERS BOARD, ANNUAL REPORTS.

I 20.6:CT
REPORTS OF SPECIAL AGENTS AND COMMISSIONS.

I 20.7:date
INDIAN SCHOOLS SUPERINTENDENT, ANNUAL REPORT.

I 20.8:CT
INDIAN SCHOOLS, (misc. publications).

I 20.9/1:date
LAWS (general).

I 20.9/2:CT   • **Item 628-C**
LAWS (special).

I 20.10:date
ROSTER OF OFFICERS OF INDIAN SERVICE.

I 20.11:date
(Proposals Received and Contracts Awarded for) SUPPLIES FOR INDIAN SERVICE.

I 20.12:CT
RULES, REGULATIONS AND INSTRUCTIONS.

I 20.12/2:CT   • **Item 627-D**
HANDBOOKS, MANUALS, GUIDES.

I 20.13/1:date
REGULATIONS OF INDIAN OFFICE (general).
    I 20.13/2:date&nos.
    – AMENDMENTS.

I 20.14:CT
PROPOSALS (and specifications for supplies) FOR INDIAN SERVICE.

I 20.15:date
REPORTS OF AGENTS AND SUPERINTENDENTS IN CHARGE OF INDIANS.

I 20.16:
CARLISLE INDIAN SCHOOL.
    Established at Carlisle, Pa., 1879.

I 20.16/1:CT
ANNUAL REPORTS.

I 20.16/2:CT
GENERAL PUBLICATIONS.

I 20.16/3:nos.
BULLETINS [none issued].

I 20.16/4:nos.
CIRCULARS [none issued].

I 20.16/5:nos.
INDIAN CRAFTSMAN.

I 20.16/6:date
ANNUAL SCHOOL CALENDAR.

I 20.17:
HAMPTON NORMAL AND AGRICULTURAL INSTITUTE.

I 20.17/1:date
ANNUAL REPORTS.

I 20.17/2:CT
GENERAL PUBLICATIONS.

I 20.17/3:nos.
BULLETINS [none issued].

I 20.17/4:nos.
CIRCULARS [none issued].

I 20.18:nos.
TREATIES AND AGREEMENTS.

I 20.19:date
ROUTES TO INDIAN AGENCIES AND SCHOOLS.

I 20.20:nos.
ORDERS.

I 20.21:date
FIVE CIVILIZED TRIBES, SUPERINTENDENT, ANNUAL REPORTS.

I 20.22:vol.
INDIANS AT WORK.

I 20.23:nos.
CIRCULAR LETTERS RELATED TO INDIAN EMERGENCY CONSERVATION WORK.

I 20.24:nos.
ROADS CIRCULAR.

I 20.25:nos.
ANNOUNCEMENTS OF EXAMINATIONS.

I 20.26:nos.
INDIAN EDUCATION.

I 20.27   • **Item 628-B (MF)**
ADDRESSES. [Irregular]

I 20.28:nos.
PERSONNEL BULLETINS. [Monthly]

I 20.29:CT
NATIONAL INDIAN INSTITUTE PUBLICATIONS.

I 20.30:nos.
SHERMAN PAMPHLETS.

I 20.31:nos.
INDIAN HANDICRAFT PAMPHLETS.

I 20.32:nos.
HOME IMPROVEMENT PAMPHLETS.

I 20.33:CT
INDIAN LIFE READERS.

I 20.34:nos.
INFORMATION PAMPHLETS.

I 20.35:nos.
TRANSMITTAL LETTERS [for Indian Service Manual].

I 20.36:CT
INDIAN CHILDREN'S OWN WRITINGS.

I 20.37:v.nos.
ADAHOONILIGII, NAVAHO LANGUAGE MONTHLY.
[Monthly]

I 20.38:date
DIRECTORY OF INDIAN SERVICE UNITS. [Quarterly]

I 20.39   • **Item 627-A-1**
INDIAN LEADER. [Semimonthly during school year]
    A newsletter on activities at the Bureau's
Haskell Indian Junior College.
    No longer a depository item. For internal/
administrative use only,under 44 U.S.C. section
1902.
    ISSN 0364-8028

I 20.40:nos.
NAVAHO HISTORICAL SERIES.

I 20.41:v.nos.&nos.
INDIAN SCHOOL JOURNAL. [Weekly (Oct.- May)].
    ISSN 0364-7056
I 20.42:
CHEMAWA AMERICAN. [Frequency varies some
    weekly, monthly]

I 20.43:CT
ADULT EDUCATION SERIES.

I 20.44:rp.nos.
NAVAJO YEARBOOK OF PLANNING IN ACTION.
    [Annual]
        Earlier I 20.2:N 22/2/9

I 20.44/2:CT
NAVAJO TRIBAL COUNCIL PUBLICATIONS.

I 20.45:nos.
PRESS RELEASES.

I 20.45/2:date
CONGRESSIONAL HEARINGS SCHEDULED. [Weekly]
    (Congressional and Legislative Affairs Staff)

I 20.46   • **Item 627-K-1**
ANNUAL EDUCATION REPORT, BUREAU OF INDIAN
    AFFAIRS.
        Earlier title: Statistics Concerning Indian Edu-
    cation.
        Formerly issued under item number 627-K.
        Data covers Bureau day schools, boarding
    schools, higher education, adult education pro-
    grams, and funding.
        Report covers fiscal year.

I 20.47:CT   • **Item 627-C**
MAPS.

I 20.48:CT   • **Item 627-F**
BIBLIOGRAPHIES AND LISTS OF PUBLICATIONS.
    [Irregular]

I 20.49:nos.
ORIENTATION MATERIAL, TRIBAL OPERATIONS,
    ADMINISTRATIVE.

I 20.50:nos.
STUDIES IN PLAINS ANTHROPOLOGY AND HISTORY.

I 20.51   • **Item 627-A (MF)**
INDIANS OF [States or Areas]. [Irregular]

I 20.51/2:CT   • **Item 627-A (MF)**
INDIANS: [various subjects]. [Irregular]
    Brief articles on individual Indian tribes or
subjects, such as Indian history, legends and
myths, language, etc.

I 20.52:nos.
MISSOURI RIVER BASIN INVESTIGATIONS
    PROJECT REPORTS.

I 20.53
DOWNDRAFT. v. 1–   1967–   [Irregular]
    PURPOSE:– To keep teachers and adminis-
trators in Bureau of Indian Affairs schools aware
of Title 1 activities.

I 20.54:v.nos.&nos.
FIRE, FORWARDING INDIAN RESPONSIBILITY IN
    EDUCATION.

I 20.55:date   • **Item 627-B**
INDIAN RECORDS.   – March 1973. [Monthly]

I 20.56:nos.   • **Item 627-E**
FINAL ENVIRONMENTAL IMPACT STATEMENTS. [Ir-
    regular]

I 20.56/2:CT   • **Item 627-E**
DRAFT ENVIRONMENTAL IMPACT STATEMENTS. [Ir-
    regular]

I 20.57:v.nos.&nos.
BIA EDUCATION RESEARCH BULLETIN.
    ISSN 0147-4391

I 20.58:date   • **Item 627-G (MF)**
COMBINED TRIBAL AND BUREAU LAW ENFORCE-
    MENT SERVICES: ANNUAL REPORT.
        Alternate title: Annual Law Enforcement Ser-
    vices Report.

I 20.59:v.nos.&nos.
IERC BULLETIN. [Monthly] (Indian Education
    Resources Center)
        Discontinued with issues for 1978.

I 20.60:v.nos.&nos.
EDUCATION PROFILE. [3 times a year]

I 20.61:date   • **Item 627-H (MF)**
ANNUAL REPORT OF INDIAN LAND.

I 20.61/2:date   • **Item 627-H (MF)**
ANNUAL REPORT OF INDIAN LAND AND INCOME
    FROM SURFACE.
        PURPOSE:– To present statistical data on
    the status of acreage under the jurisdiction of the
    Bureau, and income from leases. Includes extent
    of acreage, tribal agency ownership, location,
    types of leases, and income from them.

I 20.61/3:date   • **Item 627-H**
INDIAN FOREST MANAGEMENT. [Biennial]

I 20.61/4   • **Item 627-N (MF)**
MINERAL FRONTIERS ON INDIAN LANDS. [Annual]

I 20.61/5   • **Item 627-A-4 (EL)**
DIVISION OF ENERGY AND MINERAL RESOURCES
    ANNUAL REPORT.

I 20.62:CT   • **Item 627-C**
POSTERS AND MAPS. [Irregular]

I 20.63:nos.
ART AND INDIAN CHILDREN OF THE DAKOTAS (se-
    ries). [Irregular]

I 20.64:date   • **Item 627-L**
SPAWNING THE MEDICINE RIVER. [3 times a year]
    This numbered series according to the Bu-
reau, is one of the leading publications in the
country that publish writings of Native Americans.
Contains poetry, fiction, and plays. May be used
as a supplementary text in creative writing
courses.

I 20.65:nos.   • **Item 627-M (MF)**
BIA ADMINISTRATIVE REPORTS (series).

I 20.66:date   • **Item 627-F**
SOUTHWESTERN INDIAN POLYTECHNIC INSTITUTE,
    CATALOG.

I 20.67:v.nos./nos.   • **Item 627-H (MF)**
HORIZONS, INDIAN MINERAL RESOURCE. [Semian-
    nual]

I 20.68   • **Item 627-A-3 (E)**
ELECTRONIC PRODUCTS.

GENERAL LAND OFFICE
(1849– 1946)

CREATION AND AUTHORITY

    The General Land Office was established
within the Treasury Department by act of Congress, approved April 25, 1812. By act of Congress, approved March 3, 1849 (9 Stat. 395), the
Office was transferred to the newly created Department of the Interior. By Reorganization Plan
No. 3 of 1946, effective July 16, 1946, the General Land Office merged with the Grazing Service
to form the Bureau of Land Management (I 53).

I 21.1:date
ANNUAL REPORTS.

I 21.2:CT
GENERAL PUBLICATIONS.

I 21.3:nos.
BULLETINS. [None issued]

I 21.4:nos.
CIRCULARS.

I 21.5:v.nos.
LAND DECISIONS.
    Later I 1.69

I 21.6:CT
DIGEST OF [Land] DECISIONS.
    Later I 1.69/3

I 21.7:date
LAND LAWS (general).

I 21.8:CT
LAND LAWS (special).

I 21.9:date
RULES OF PRACTICE.

I 21.10:date
REGULATIONS, RULES, AND INSTRUCTIONS.
    By subjects.

I 21.11/1:date
MANUAL OF SURVEYING INSTRUCTIONS (general).
    Later I 53.7

I 21.11/2:date
EPHEMERIS OF SUN AND POLARIS. MANUAL OF
    SURVEYING INSTRUCTIONS, SUPPLEMENTARY.
    Later I 53.8

I 21.11/3:CT
TABLES AND FORMULAS FOR USE OF SURVEYORS
    AND ENGINEERS ON PUBLIC LAND SURVEYS.
    Later I 53.10

I 21.11/4:date
MANUAL OF INSTRUCTIONS FOR SURVEY OF MIN-
    ERAL LANDS IN UNITED STATES.

I 21.12:date
CIRCULAR SHOWING MANNER OF PROCEEDING
    TO OBTAIN TITLE TO LAND.

I 21.13:CT
MAPS.
    Later I 53.11

I 21.14:CT
OPENING INDIAN RESERVATIONS.

I 21.15:date
ROSTER OF FIELD OFFICERS.

I 21.16:nos.
LAND SERVICE BULLETIN.

I 21.17:dt.&nos.
INFORMATION BULLETINS.
    Earlier I 21.17
    Later I 53.9

I 21.18:nos.
ORDERS.

NATURAL RESOURCES LIBRARY
(1849–   )

INFORMATION

    Information Services Branch
    Natural Resources Library
    Department of the Interior
    Washington, D.C. 20240
    (202) 343-5815

I 22.1:date
ANNUAL REPORTS.

I 22.2:CT
GENERAL PUBLICATIONS.

I 22.3:nos.
BULLETINS.

I 22.4:nos.
CIRCULARS. [none issued]

I 22.5:date
CATALOGUES.

I 22.8:nos.
LIBRARY LIST OF ACCESSION. [Irregular] Proc.

I 22.8/2:date
ACCESSIONS LISTS.

I 22.9:CT
BIBLIOGRAPHIES AND LISTS OF PUBLICATIONS.

I 22.9/2:nos.   • Item 600-B
BIBLIOGRAPHY (series). 1–

I 22.10:v.nos.&nos.
POPULATION TRENDS AND ENVIRONMENTAL
    POLICY. v. 1– v. 2, no. 2. April 1969– May 1970.
    [Monthly]
        PURPOSE:– To provide informative abstract
    (with full bibliographic information) of current books,
    articles, reports, and other papers about popula-
    tion trends and their effects on the environment
    and natural resources.

PATENT OFFICE
(1849– 1925)

CREATION AND AUTHORITY

    The Patent Office was established within the
Department of State by act of Congress, approved July 4, 1836. Upon creation of the Department of the Interior in 1849, the Patent Office
was transferred to that Department. By Executive Order of April 1, 1925, it was transferred to
the Department of Commerce (C 21).

I 23.1/1:date
ANNUAL REPORTS TO CONGRESS (calendar year).
    Later C 21.1/1

I 23.1/2:date
ANNUAL REPORTS TO SECRETARY OF THE
    INTERIOR (fiscal year).

I 23.2:CT
GENERAL PUBLICATIONS.
    Later C 21.2

I 23.3:nos.
BULLETINS, CLASSIFICATION.
    Later C 21.3

I 23.4:nos.
CIRCULARS. [none issued]

I 23.5:CT
INDEXES TO PATENTS (special).

I 23.6:date
LIBRARY CATALOGS.

I 23.7:date
GENERAL INDEXES AND LISTS OF PATENTS.

I 23.8:v.nos
OFFICIAL GAZETTE
    Later C 21.5

    I 23.8/a 7:v.nos.
    – INDEX.
        Later C 21.5/a 4

    I 23.8/b:date
    –SUPPLEMENT.

I 23.9:nos.
ORDERS.

I 23.10:date
DECISIONS OF COMMISSIONER OF PATENTS
    (calendar year).
        Later C 21.6

I 23.11/1:date
PATENT LAWS (general).

I 23.11/2:date
U.S. STATUTES CONCERNING THE REGISTRATION
    OF TRADE-MARKS.
        Later C 21.7/2

I 23.11/3:date
U.S. STATUTES CONCERNING REGISTRATION OF
    PRINTS AND LABELS.
        Later C 21.7/3

I 23.12:date
RULES OF PRACTICE.
    Later C 21.9

I 23.13:date
RULES OF PRACTICE.
    Later C 21.8

I 23.14:date
SPECIFICATIONS AND DRAWINGS OF PATENTS.
    Later C 21.11

I 23.15:CT
BRIEFS.
    Later C 21.10

I 23.16:date
PRICE LISTS.

I 23.17:v.nos.
SPECIFICATIONS AND DRAWINGS OF PATENTS
    RELATING TO ELECTRICITY.

BUREAU OF PENSIONS
(1849– 1930)

CREATION AND AUTHORITY

    The Office of the Commissioner of Pensions
was established within the War Department by
act of Congress, approved March 2, 1833 (4 Stat.
622). By 1840, the Commissioner was under the
supervision of the Secretary of War and the Secretary of the Navy. Upon the establishment of the
Department of the Interior, in 1849, the Office of
the Commissioner of Pensions was transferred to
that Department by act of Congress, approved
March 3, 1949. From 1890, the Office was known
as the Bureau of Pensions. By act of Congress,
approved July 3, 1930, the Bureau of Pensions
was consolidated with the Veteran's Bureau to
form the Veterans' Administration (VA 1).

I 24.1:date
ANNUAL REPORTS.
    Later VA 2.1

I 24.2:CT
GENERAL PUBLICATIONS.
    Later VA 2.2

I 24.3:nos.
BULLETINS. [None issued]

I 24.4:nos.
CIRCULARS.

I 24.5:date
ANNUAL REPORTS OF ASSISTANTS SECRETARY
    OF THE INTERIOR ON WORK OF PENSION AP-
    PEALS BOARD.

I 24.6:date
LIST OF PENSIONERS.

I 24.7:date
LAWS, RULINGS AND REGULATIONS.
    Later VA 2.5

I 24.8:vol.
(PENSION) DECISIONS.

I 24.9:date
DIGEST OF LAWS, DECISIONS AND RULINGS.

I 24.10:date
ROSTER OF EXAMINING SURGEONS.

I 24.11/1:nos.
ORDERS, 1st SERIES, 1865– 1880.

I 24.11/2:nos.
ORDERS, 2nd SERIES, 1881– 1901.

I 24.11/3:nos.
ORDERS, 3rd SERIES, 1901–

I 24.12:date
ROSTER OF DISQUALIFIED ATTORNEYS.

I 24.13:date
INSTRUCTIONS TO EXAMINING SURGEONS.

I 24.14:date
LAWS GOVERNING GRANTING OF ARMY AND NAVY PENSIONS AND BOUNTY LAND.
　　Later VA 2.5/2

I 24.15:date
RULES OF PRACTICE.

I 24.16:nos.
FIELD REVIEW.

　　I 24.16/2:v.nos.
　　– INDEX.

COMMISSIONER OF RAILROADS
(1880– 1904)

CREATION AND AUTHORITY

　　The Office of the Auditor of Railroad Accounts was established in the Department of the Interior by Congress in 1878. An Act of March 3, 1881 changed the name to Office of the Commissioner of Railroads. The Office was terminated by Congress on June 30, 1904.

I 25.1:date
ANNUAL REPORTS.

I 25.2:CT
GENERAL PUBLICATIONS.

I 25.3
BULLETINS. [None issued]

I 25.4
CIRCULARS. [None issued]

ENTOMOLOGICAL COMMISSION
(1877– 1880)

CREATION AND AUTHORITY

　　The Entomological Commission was established within the Department of the Interior by act of Congress, approved March 3, 1877 (19 Stat. 357). The Commission was transferred to the Department of Agriculture (A 8) by acts of Congress, approved June 16, 1880 (21 Stat. 276), and March 3, 1881 (21 Stat. 383)

I 26.1:nos.
ANNUAL REPORTS.
　　Later A 8.1

I 26.2:CT
GENERAL PUBLICATIONS. [None issued]

I 26.3:nos.
BULLETINS.

I 26.4:nos.
CIRCULARS.

BUREAU OF RECLAMATION
(1902–　　　)

CREATION AND AUTHORITY

　　The Reclamation Act of 1902 (43 U.S.C. 391 et seq.), authorized the Secretary of the Interior to locate, construct, operate, and maintain works for the storage, diversion, and development of waters for the reclamation of arid and semiarid lands in the Western States. To perform these functions, the Secretary in July 1902 approved an organization plan for a Reclamation Service in the Geological Survey. In March 1907 the Reclamation Service was removed from the Survey and established under a Director. In June 1923 the Secretary created the position of Commissioner of Reclamation and changed the name Reclamation Service to Bureau of Reclamation. Power marketing function, including construction, operation, and maintenance of transmission lines and attendant facilities, were transferred to the Department of Energy by act of August 4, 1977 (91 Stat. 565), effective October 1, 1977. The Bureau was renamed the Water and Power Resources Service by Secretarial Order 3042 of November 6, 1979. The name was changed back to Bureau of Reclamation by Secretarial Order 3064 of May 18, 1981.

INFORMATION

　　Public Affairs Group
　　Bureau of Reclamation
　　Department of the Interior
　　1849 C Street, NW
　　Washington, DC 20240
　　(202) 513-0575
　　Fax: (202) 513-0314
　　http://www.usbr.gov

I 27.1:date　　　　　　• Item 663-A (MF) (EL)
ANNUAL REPORTS.
　　Earlier I 19.17/1

I 27.1/2:date　　　　　　• Item 663-A (MF)
SUMMARY REPORT OF THE COMMISSIONER, BUREAU OF RECLAMATION [and] STATISTICAL APPENDIX. [Annual]
　　PURPOSE:– To make available a summary of the Commissioner's report to the Secretary of the Interior with additional tables of frequency sought statistical data.
　　The statistical appendix includes: Part 1, General information: Part 2, data on Bureau operation: Part 3, table on economic data, obtained form outside sources, pertinent to the bureau programs; and Part 4, Project data, published as a separate volume, giving detailed information on each project.

I 27.1/3:date　　　　　　• Item 662-A
SUMMARY REPORT OF BUREAU'S FINANCIAL CONDITION AND OPERATIONS FOR FISCAL YEAR.

I 27.1/4:date　　　　　　• Item 663-A (MF)
SUMMARY STATISTICS, WATER, LAND AND RELATED DATA. 1982–　　[Annual]
　　Supersedes Appendix 1, Crop and Related Data.

I 27.1/4-2:date　　　　　　• Item 663-A
SUMMARY STATISTICS PROJECT DATA. [Annual]

I 27.1/4-3:date　　　　　　• Item 663-A
SUMMARY STATISTICS, FINANCES AND PHYSICAL FEATURES. [Annual]

I 27.1/5　　　　　　• Item 663-A-1 (EL)
BUREAU OF RECLAIMATION FY ANNUAL PERFORMANCE PLAN.

I 27.2:CT　　　　　　• Item 660
GENERAL PUBLICATIONS.

I 27.3:nos.
BULLETINS.

I 27.3/2
ADVANCE CONSTRUCTION BULLETINS. [Monthly]

I 27.3/3
ADVANCE EQUIPMENT BULLETIN. [Monthly]

I 27.4:nos.
CIRCULARS.

I 27.5　　　　　　• Item 663
RECLAMATION ERA. v. 1– 76. 1908– 1983. [Quarterly]
　　Presents articles written in a popular style on land reclamation, irrigation, crops, pasturing, and land recovery.
　　Title varies. 1908– 1924, Reclamation Record; 1924– 1931. New Reclamation Era; 1932–　Reclamation Era. Suspended June 1933– December 1934, May 1942– April 1946.
　　Indexed by:–
　　　　Bibliography of Agriculture
　　　　Biological Abstracts
　　　　Index to U.S. Government Periodicals
　　　　Selected Water Resources Abstracts
　　　　ISSN 0034-141X
　　I 27.5/a:nos.
　　– REPRINTS.

I 27.6:CT
STANDARD DESIGNS.

I 27.7:CT
MAPS.
　　Earlier I 29.17/5

I 27.7/2:date
LISTS OF MAPS, TOWNSITE, AND FARM UNIT PLOTS.

I 27.7/3:CT　　　　　　• Item 664-C
POSTERS. [Irregular]

I 27.7/3-2:CT
AUDIOVISUAL MATERIALS. [Irregular]

I 27.7/4:CT　　　　　　• Item 664-C
MAPS (miscellaneous).

I 27.8:nos.
SPECIFICATIONS.
　　Earlier I 19.17/6

I 27.9:specif.nos.
DRAWINGS ACCOMPANYING SPECIFICATIONS.
　　Earlier I 19.17/7

I 27.10
PUBLICATIONS AVAILABLE FOR FREE DISTRIBUTION. [Semiannual]

I 27.10/1:nos.
LISTS OF PUBLICATIONS.

I 27.10/2:date　　　　　　• Item 660-F
PUBLICATIONS FOR SALE. [Annual]
　　Previously issued semiannually.
　　Previous title: Publications Available for Sale.

I 27.10/3:CT
BIBLIOGRAPHIES.

I 27.10/4　　　　　　• Item 660-F
RECENT LIBRARY ADDITIONS. [Monthly]
　　Previous title: Selected List of Library Accessions.

I 27.10/5
BIBLIOGRAPHY (series). 1–　[Irregular]

I 27.11:CT
STANDARD SPECIFICATION.

I 27.12:CT
TOWNSITE PLATS.

I 27.13:CT
FARM UNIT PLATS.

I 27.14:CT
FREIGHT TARIFFS.

I 27.15:nos.
BOULDER CANYON PROJECT, CITY ORDERS.

I 27.16:date
HYDRAULIC AND EXCAVATION TABLES.
Changed from I 27.2:R 29/1-5

I 27.17
ADDRESSES. [Irregular]

I 27.18 • Item 660-G
RECLAMATION SAFETY NEWS. [Quarterly]
PURPOSE:– Published in the interest of accident prevention, contains safety performance
of both Government and contractor forces associated with reclamation projects. It also contains
photographs anditems of general interest pertinent to health and safety.
ISSN 0034-1436

I 27.19:CT • Item 664
REGULATIONS, RULES AND INSTRUCTIONS.
Changed from I 27.2

I 27.19/2:CT • Item 660-B
HANDBOOKS, MANUALS, GUIDES.
Earlier I 27.19

I 27.19/3:nos.
RECLAMATION INSTRUCTIONS SERIES.

I 27.20:date, later vol. and date
MANUAL OF THE BUREAU OF RECLAMATION.
Changed from I 27.2:M 31/1-4

I 27.20/2 • Item 660-B
DESIGN STANDARDS. 1–   [Irregular]

I 27.21:nos.
CONSERVATION BULLETINS.
Changed to I 1.72

I 27.21:pt.nos.&nos.
BOULDER CANYON PROJECT, FINAL REPORTS,
BULLETINS.

I 27.21/2:date
BOULDER CANYON PROJECT, ANNUAL REPORTS.

I 27.22:nos.
INFORMATION CIRCULARS.
Earlier I 27.2

I 27.23:nos.
COLUMBIA BASIN JOINT INVESTIGATIONS [Reports
on Problems].
See for charter and scope of investigations,
(I 27.2:C 72/5)

I 27.24:
IRRIGATION PHOTOGRAPHS.

I 27.25:CT
OUR RIVERS.

I 27.26:nos.
CENTRAL VALLEY PROJECT STUDIES [Reports on
Problems].

I 27.26/2
CENTRAL VALLEY PROJECT. ANNUAL REPORT.
[Annual]

I 27.27:CT • Item 661
LAWS.

I 27.27:L 44 • Item 661
FEDERAL RECLAMATION LAWS. v. 1–   1958–
[Irregular]

Vol.1. March 2, 1961–
August 14, 1964. 1958.
2. April 20. 1947–
September 2, 1958. 1959.
3. June 23, 1959–
November 8, 1965. 1966.

I 27.27/2 • Item 661-B (MF)
THE RECLAMATION REFORM ACT OF 1982, ANNUAL
REPORT TO THE CONGRESS. [Annual]

I 27.28:date
OFFICE AND PROJECT DIRECTORY. [Quarterly]
Earlier I 27.2:Of 2/2

I 27.29:nos.
STRUCTURAL RESEARCH LABORATORY REPORT,
SP- (series).

I 27.30:nos.
TECHNICAL MEMORANDUMS.

I 27.31:nos.
MATERIALS LABORATORIES REPORT, C- (series).

I 27.31/2:nos.
TECHNICAL MEMORANDUM (series). [Irregular]

I 27.32:nos.
HYDRAULIC LABORATORY REPORT, HYD- (series).

I 27.33:nos.
PHOTOELASTIC GROUP REPORTS.

I 27.34 • Item 664-B (MF)
ENGINEERING MONOGRAPHS. 1–   [Irregular]

I 27.35:
METALS LABORATORY UNIT REPORT, M- (series).
(Concrete Laboratory Section)

I 27.35/2:nos.
CONCRETE LABORATORY SECTION, DENVER:
MATERIALS INVESTIGATION UNIT REPORT (MI)
(series).

I 27.35/3:nos.
CONCRETE LABORATORY REPORT SP-(nos).

I 27.36:
BITUMINOUS LABORATORY UNIT REPORT, B-
(series). (Chemical Laboratory Section)

I 27.36/2:nos.
CHEMICAL LABORATORY SECTION, DENVER:
CHEMICAL LABORATORY UNIT REPORT (B) (se-
ries).

I 27.36/2:nos.
CHEMICAL LABORATORY SECTION, DENVER:
CHEMICAL LABORATORY UNIT REPORT (CH)
(series)

I 27.36/3:nos.
CHEMICAL LABORATORY UNIT REPORT (P) (series).

I 27.36/4:nos.
CHEMICAL LABORATORY SECTION, DENVER: PET-
ROGRAPHIC LABORATORY UNIT REPORT (PET)
(series).

I 27.37:
EARTH LABORATORY REPORT, EM-(series). (Earth
Laboratory Section)

I 27.37/a:date • Item 639-F-1
– PREPRINTS.

I 27.38:
GEOLOGICAL REPORTS, G (series). (Engineering
Geology Branch)

I 27.39:
MATHEMATICAL ANALYSIS GROUPS REPORTS. (Special Assignments Section, Dams Division)

I 27.39/2:nos.
DIVISION OF DESIGN, DAMS BRANCH REPORT, DD
(nos.).

I 27.39/3:nos.
REPORTS, HM- (series).

I 27.40:CT
PUBLIC NOTICES [concerning irrigation projects].
Earlier I 1.49

I 27.41:nos. • Item 660-E (EL)
WATER OPERATION AND MAINTENANCE BULLETIN.
[Quarterly] (Division of Water Operation and Main-
tenance, Engineering and Research Center, Den-
ver, Colorado)
Published for the benefit of those operating

water supply systems and serves as a medium of
exchanging operation and maintenance information. Presents information on labor- saving devices, less costly equipment and procedures that
will result in improved efficiency and reduced costs
of these systems.
Cumulative indexes issued separately.
Former title: Irrigation Operation and Maintenance Bulletin.
ISSN 0145-2800

I 27.42:date
REPORT ON FLOWS AND DIVERSIONS AT IMPERIAL
DAM AND ALL ACTIONS AFFECTING COORDI-
NATION THEREOF. [Monthly]

I 27.43:date
SUMMARY OF WATERSHED CONDITIONS AFFECT-
ING WATER SUPPLY OF THE LOWER COLO-
RADO RIVER. [Monthly, Jan.-June]
Former title: Lake Mead Water Supply Out-
look.

I 27.44:
PROJECT PLANNING REPORTS.

I 27.45 • Item 660-E (MF)
POWER O. AND M. BULLETINS. 1–   [Irregular]

I 27.45/2
POWER O. AND M. REPORT, FIELD REVIEW OF
MAINTENANCE. [Irregular]

I 27.45/3:CT
POWER O. AND M. REPORTS, FIELD REVIEW OF
OPERATION AND MAINTENANCE. [Irregular]
(Division of Power Operation and Maintenance,
Engineering and Research Center, Denver, Colo-
rado)

I 27.46:nos.
LABORATORY REPORT, SI- (series). [Semiannual].

I 27.47:
LIBRARY ACQUISITION LISTS. [Bimonthly]

I 27.48:
CONSTRUCTION TRENDS. [Quarterly]

I 27.49:date
SETTLEMENT OPPORTUNITIES ON RECLAMATION
PROJECTS. [Annual]
Earlier I 27.2:Se 7/3

I 27.50
PRESS RELEASES. [Irregular]

I 27.51:date
STORAGE DAMS. [Annual]

I 27.51/2:date
DIVERSION DAMS. [Annual]

I 27.51/3:date
STORAGE RESERVOIRS. [Annual]

I 27.52:v.nos.&nos.
RECAP, RECLAMATION'S CURRENT AWARENESS
PROGRAM.

I 27.53:nos.
WATER CONSERVATION REPORT, WC-(series).

I 27.54:nos. • Item 664-B (MF)
RESEARCH REPORTS. 1–   [Irregular]

Water Resources technical publications.

ANNUAL REPORT OF PROGRESS ON ENGI-
NEERING RESEARCH. [Annual]

I 27.55 • Item 663-A (MF)
FEDERAL RECLAMATION PROJECTS, WATER AND
LAND RESOURCE ACCOMPLISHMENTS.
[Summary Report]. [Annual]
Former title: Federal Reclamation Projects,
Crop Report.
The Summary Report, which at one time had
only one appendix containing statistical data, now
has three appendices:

App. 1.Accomplishments–
Statistical Data.
App. 2.Finances and Physical Features–
Statistical Data.
App. 3.Project Data.

I 27.55/2:CT • Item 660 (MF)
BUREAU OF RECLAMATION PROJECTS (by States).

I 27.56
BUREAU OF RECLAMATION PROGRESS. 1967–
[Quarterly] (Division of Program Coordination and
Finance)

I 27.57 • Item 664-G
PROJECT SKYWATER, ANNUAL REPORT. 1st–
1967– [Annual]
Presents the history, current activities, and
future plans of the Bureau of Reclamation's Atmospheric Water Resources Program, called
Project Skywater.
Issued in two volumes: Volume 1, Summary,
summarized the historical development of Project
Skywater, presents the major activities and results of the fiscal year in each of 11 program
activity items, and outlines the requirements and
plans for future research. Volume 2, Contractor
Reports, gives the fiscal year activities of each
Project Skywater contractor.

I 27.57/2:date • Item 664-G (MF)
PROJECT SKYWATER DATA INVENTORY SCPP
SEASON. [Annual]

I 27.57/3:date • Item 664-G (MF)
PROJECT SKYWATER, CRADP DAT INVENTORY.
[Annual]
CRADP = Colorado River Augmentation Dem-
onstration Program.

I 27.58:nos.
CANALS BRANCH REPORT CB (series).

I 27.59:nos.
GENERAL REPORTS.

I 27.60:nos. • Item 664-F (MF)
REC-ERC (series). [Irregular] (Engineering and Re-
search Center)
Formerly REC-OEC (series) published by the
Office of Chief Engineer.

I 27.61:date
WESTERN U.S. WATER PLAN, (year) PROGRESS
REPORT. 1st– 1971– [Biennial]
Report made pursuant to the Colorado River
Basin Project Act (P.L. 90-537) of 1968. This Act
directs the Secretary of the Interior to conduct
reconnaissance investigations for the purpose
of developing a general plan to meet the future
water needs of the 11 Western States lying wholly
or in part west of the Continental Divide, and to
report progress biennially to the President, the
National Water Commission, the Water Resources
Council, and the Congress.

I 27.62:CT
ANNUAL OPERATING PLANS.
Gives operating plans for individual projects.

I 27.66:nos.
PROJECT INVESTIGATION REPORTS.

I 27.68:v.nos.
POWER AND THE ENVIRONMENT, EVENTS OF IN-
TEREST OF NAVAJO POWER PROJECT.
[Monthly]

I 27.68:nos.
TRANSLATIONS.

I 27.69:CT
CONDITIONS OF MAJOR WATER SYSTEM
STRUCTURES AND FACILITIES, REVIEW OF
MAINTENANCE, REPORT OF EXAMINATION,
[various regions and projects]. [Irregular] (Office
of Design and Construction, Engineering and
Research Center, Denver, Colorado)
Compilation of Bureau of Reclamation draw-
ings, memorandum notes, etc., for internal use
by operation and maintenance personnel only.
Normally only one copy is prepared.

I 27.70:nos.
FINAL ENVIRONMENTAL STATEMENTS. [Irregular]

I 27.70/2:nos.
DATA ENVIRONMENTAL STATEMENTS. [Irregular]

I 27.71:date • Item 664-D (MF)
OPERATION OF THE COLORADO RIVER BASIN,
PROJECTED OPERATIONS, ANNUAL REPORT.

I 27.71/2 • Item 664-D (MF)
ANNUAL REPORT COLORADO RIVER STORAGE
PROJECT AND PARTICIPATING PROJECTS FOR
FISCAL YEAR (date). 1st– 1957–

I 27.71/3:date • Item 664-E (MF)
COLORADO RIVER BASIN PROJECT, ANNUAL
REPORT.

I 27.72:nos. • Item 664-B-1 (MF)
GENERAL RESEARCH, GR- (series). [Irregular] (Division of General Research, Engineering and Research Center)

I 27.73:CT • Item 660
HISTORICAL SITE [brochures]. [Irregular]

I 27.74:CT • Item 664-H (MF)
STATUS REPORT ON WATER AND POWER
RESOURCES SERVICE PROGRAMS WITHIN
(various States). [Annual]
Describes Service programs for conservation of soil and moisture, construction of dams
and irrigation systems, etc., in such States as
Wyoming, Montana, and North and South Dakota.

I 27.75:nos. • Item 660-D (MF)
ACER TECHNICAL MEMORANDUM (series). [Irregular]
(Assistant Commissioner Engineering and Re-
search)

I 27.76:nos. • Item 664-B-2 (MF)
WATER RESOURCES TEACHING GUIDE (series).
[Irregular]
Each guide is a single folded sheet on a
different subject. Guides are designed to teach
basic concepts to students and include background information, recommended activities, and
illustrative drawings.

I 27.77:date • Item 660-C (MF)
TELEPHONE DIRECTORY. [Irregular]

I 27.78:date • Item 660-H (MF)
WATER MANAGEMENT AND CONSERVATION PRO-
GRAM. [Annual]
The purposes of this report are to document
the Water Management and Conservation
Program's accomplishments, to help evaluate its
various activities, and to review the program's
future needs.

I 27.79:nos. • Item 664-B-1 (MF)
R (Series). (Research and Laboratory Services Division)

I 27.80:date • Item 660-E
GROUNDWATER RECHARGE ADVISORY. [Quarterly]

I 27.81:CT • Item 660-A-1 (E)
ELECTRONIC PRODUCTS. (Misc.)

I 27.82 • Item 660-I (MF)
ENVIRONMENTAL IMPACT STATEMENTS.

I 27.98:CT
PROJECT HISTORIES. [Annual]
Class made for Reclamation Bureau Library
Later I 27.2

I 27.99:CT
PROJECT AND RIVER BASIN REPORTS.
Class made for Reclamation Bureau Library

BUREAU OF MINES
(1910– 1925, 1934–)

CREATION AND AUTHORITY

The Bureau of Mines was established July 1,
1910, in the Department of the Interior by act of
May 16, 1910, as amended (30 U.S.C. 1, 3, 5-7);
was transferred to the Department of Commerce
in 1925 and returned to the Department of the
Interior in 1934 under the President's reorganization powers. The 1910 act, as amended, has been
supplemented by statutes authorizing the production and sale of helium, and helium research
(50 U.S.C. 167); inspection of coal mines (30
U.S.C. 451-460, as amended); activities leading
to the prevention of major disasters in coal mines
(30 U.S.C. 471-483); and responsibilities as set
forth in the Federal Metal and Nonmetallic Mine
Safety Act (80 Stat. 772; 30 U.S.C. 721 note).

INFORMATION

Office of Surface Mining
Reclamation and Enforcement, D.D.I.
1951 Constitution Ave., NW
Washington, DC 20240
(202) 208-2719
http://www.osmre.gov

I 28.1 • Item 604-C-1
ANNUAL REPORT. 1st– 1911–
Reprinted from the Annual Report of the Secretary of the Interior. No longer issued as a separate.

I 28.1:date • Item 637-A-4 (MF)
BUREAU OF MINES, ANNUAL FINANCIAL REPORT.

I 28.2:CT • Item 637
GENERAL PUBLICATIONS.

I 28.2:C 73/2 • Item 637
COMMODITY DATA SUMMARIES. [Annual]
(Division of Minerals)
Later I 28.148

I 28.2:M 66/6 • Item 637
MINERALS IN THE U.S. ECONOMY. [Annual]
(Mineral and Material Supply/Demand Analy-
sis)
Includes a ten-year supply-demand pro-
files for mineral and fuel commodities.

I 28.3:nos. • Item 636
BULLETINS. 1– 1910– [Irregular]

Technical studies describing major investigations conducted by the Bureau of Mines and are
considered to have permanent value. Usually report of major investigation or completed projects,
but may cover a significant phase of continuing
long-range project.
Material formerly presented in the Technical
Papers, Economic Papers, and Miners Circulars
are now published as Bulletins. However, those
volumes revised and still in demand retain the old
series designation upon revision.

MINERAL FACTS AND PROBLEMS. 1956–
[Irregular]
Gives up-to-date, comprehensive information on all important minerals-metals, nonmetals, and fuels. This one-volume encyclopedia discusses individual mineral commodities under such topics as history; geology
and mineralogy; prospecting and exploration;
mining and processing; uses and substitutes;
reserves, production, and consumption; word
trade; prices, costs, and taxes; employment;
transportation; and research and outlook.

I 28.3/b:CT
PREPRINTS FROM BULLETIN 556, MINERAL FACTS AND PROBLEMS.

I 28.3/c:CT • Item 636
PREPRINTS FROM MINERAL FACTS AND PROBLEMS.
Preprints from Bulletin 585 and subsequent editions are assigned to the class.

I 28.3/2:date • Item 636
MINERAL FACTS AND PROBLEMS. [Quinquennial]

I 28.4:nos.
CIRCULARS.

I 28.5:nos. • Item 638
LISTS OF PUBLICATIONS. SP 1– 1960–
[Irregular]
Supersedes Bureau of Mines Publications, BMP- (series).
Includes comprehensive lists of Bureau publications and articles writtenby Bureau of Mines personnel and published in technical journals outside the Bureau.

ADMINISTRATION OF THE FEDERAL METAL AND NONMETALLIC MINE SAFETY ACT. 1st–
1970– [Annual]
PURPOSE:– To report on development of standards, application, education and training, research and technical support, and State plans for developing and enforcing health and safety standards, as required under the Federal Metal and Nonmetallic Mine Safety Act of 1970.

BUREAU OF MINES RESEARCH IN (year). 1st–
1971– [Annual]
PURPOSE:– To present a summary of significant results in mining, metallurgy, and energy research conducted by the Bureau of Mines during the calendar year.

LIST OF BUREAU OF MINES PUBLICATIONS AND ARTICLES. [Annual & Quinquennial]
Annotated list of publications issued by the Bureau of Mines and articles that appear in scientific, technical, and trade journals. Contains a subject and author index.
Annual and quinquennial volumes serve as a supplement to: List of Publications issued by the Bureau of Mines from July 1, 1910 to January 1, 1960.
List of Journal Articles by Bureau of Mines Authors published July 1, 1910 to January 1, 1960.

I 28.5/1:date
(LISTS OF) PUBLICATIONS OF BUREAU OF MINES.

I 28.5/2 • Item 642
NEW PUBLICATIONS. 1– [Monthly]
Monthly list of publications issued by the Bureau of Mines. Cumulative lists issued in the Special Publications series.
ISSN 0364-1376

I 28.5/3:CT • Item 638
LIST OF PUBLICATIONS OF BUREAU OF MINES (miscellaneous).

I 28.5/3-2: • Item 638-H
BIBLIOGRAPHIES AND LISTS OF PUBLICATIONS.

I 28.5/4:date
INDEXES TO BUREAU OF MINES PUBLICATIONS.

I 28.6:nos. • Item 640
MINERS CIRCULARS. 2– 61. 1911– 1946.

I 28.7:nos.
TECHNICAL PAPERS. 1– 727. 1911– 1949.
Earlier C 22.5

I 28.8:nos.
SCHEDULE OF LISTS FOR PERMISSIBLE MINE EQUIPMENT. 1– 23. 1911– 1945.

I 28.9:date
MINE INSPECTOR FOR TERRITORY OF ALASKA, ANNUAL REPORTS. 1912– 1914.

I 28.10/1:
MONTHLY STATEMENT OF COAL-MINE FATALITIES IN UNITED STATES.

I 28.10/2:date
COAL MINE FATALITIES. [Monthly] (Mineral Industry Surveys)
Effective with April 1974 issue, published by the Mining and Enforcement and Safety Administration (I 69.10).
Earlier C 22.19/2

I 28.11:date
MANUAL OF REGULATIONS.

I 28.12:date
LIST OF MEMBERS OF BUREAU OF MINES.

I 28.13:nos.
MINERAL INVESTIGATIONS SERIES. 1– 18. 1918–
1919.
Nos. 1-12, War Minerals Investigation Series.

I 28.14:CT
POSTERS.

I 28.15:nos.
STANDARDIZATION OF PETROLEUM SPECIFICATIONS COMMITTEE, BULLETINS. 1– 4. 1919.

I 28.16:CT • Item 644
RULES, REGULATIONS AND INSTRUCTIONS.
Earlier C 22.18

I 28.16/2:CT • Item 637-B
HANDBOOKS, MANUALS, GUIDES.

I 28.16/3:CT • Item 637-B
BUREAU OF MINES HANDBOOKS (series).

I 28.17:date
PETROLEUM REFINERY STATISTICS. [Monthly]

I 28.17/2:date
PETROLEUM REFINERIES IN THE UNITED STATES AND PUERTO RICO. [Annual] (Mineral Industry Surveys)
Later E 3.11/5-4

I 28.18:date
PETROLEUM REFINERY STATISTICS. [Monthly]

I 28.18/2:date
PETROLEUM STATEMENT. [Monthly] (Mineral Industry Surveys)

I 28.18/3 • Item 642-A
PETROLEUM PRODUCTS SURVEY, PPS-(series).
1– 1957– (Mineral Industry Surveys)
The following four reports are issued on a recurring basis under a cooperative agreement between the American Petroleum Institute and the Bureau of Mines. Reports give summary and analytical data on the properties of the various types of fuels tested during the year, with subdivisions according to geographic marketing distribution. Data prior to 1957 were published either in the Information Circulars or Reports of Investigations series.

AVIATION TURBINE FUELS. 1947– [Annual]
Covers five grades of aviation gasoline plus aviation jet fuel. Published semiannually 1947– 1949 in cooperation with the Coordinating Research Council and annually since 1950 in cooperation with the American Petroleum Institute.

BURNER FUEL OILS. 1955– [Annual]
Covers six grades of burner fuel oils.

DIESEL FUEL OILS. 1950– [2 times a year]
Covers four classes of diesel fuel. Summer and winter reports issued separately beginning with data for 1969.

MOTOR GASOLINES. 1949– [2 times a year]
Summer and winter reports issued separately.

I 28.18/4:date
PETROLEUM STATEMENT. [Annual] (Mineral Industry Surveys)
Sub-title: Crude Petroleum Products, and Natural-gas-liquids, (year).

I 28.18/5:date
WORLD CRUDE OIL PRODUCTION ANNUAL (year). (Mineral Industry Surveys)

I 28.18/6:date
P.A.D. DISTRICTS SUPPLY/DEMAND. [Monthly]
Later E 3.11/6-4

I 28.18/7:date
P.A.D. DISTRICTS SUPPLY/DEMAND. [Quarterly] (Division of Petroleum and Natural Gas) (Mineral Industry Surveys)
Alternate title; Supply, Demand, and Stocks of All Oils by P.A.D. Districts, and Imports of All Oils by Country.
Later E 3.11/6-3

I 28.19:date
OUTPUT OF REFINERIES IN UNITED STATES. [Monthly beginning 1918]

I 28.20:date
STOCKS ON HAND AT REFINERIES. [Monthly]

I 28.21:date
STOCK ON HAND AT REFINERIES. [Annual]
See also I 28.17

I 28.22:date
RECENT ARTICLES ON PETROLEUM AND ALLIED SUBSTANCES. [Monthly]

I 28.23 • Item 637-A (MF)
REPORTS OF INVESTIGATIONS. 2000– 1919–
[Irregular]
Studies describing the principal features and results of minor investigations or phases of major investigations, keeping the mineral industries and the public advised on the current progress of original research. Reports on large research projects or on completed studies are published in the Bulletin series.

I 28.24:nos.
DISTRIBUTION OF COAL SHIPMENTS.
Earlier C 22.32
Later I 34.16

I 28.25:nos.
GEOPHYSICAL ABSTRACTS. [Monthly]
Earlier C 22.32

I 28.26:nos.
HEALTH AND SAFETY STATISTICS.
Earlier C 22.31

I 28.26/2:date
SAFETY COMPETITION, NATIONAL SAND AND GRAVEL. [Annual]
Earlier I 28.26

I 28.26/3:date
SAFETY COMPETITION, NATIONAL LIME ASSOCIATION. [Annual]
Formerly in I 28.26

I 28.26/4:date
SAFETY COMPETITION, NATIONAL CRUSHED STONE ASSOCIATION. [Annual]
Earlier I 28.26

I 28.26/5:date
NATIONAL FIRST-AID AND MINE RESCUE CONTEST. [Biennial]

I 28.26/6:nos. • Item 637-A (MF)
TECHNICAL PROGRESS REPORTS. 1– 1968–
[Irregular]
PURPOSE:– To make known new or improved systems and techniques in mining and metallurgy developed by the Bureau of Mines.

I 28.26/7:date
SAFETY COMPETITIONS, NATIONAL LIMESTONE INSTITUTE. [Annual] (Mineral Industry Surveys)

I 28.27:nos. • Item 637-A (MF)
INFORMATION CIRCULARS. 6000– 1925– [Irregular]
Digests, reviews, abstracts, and discussions of activities and developments in all phases of the mineral industries. Although they may contain references to Bureau research, they are intended primarily as general treatises on particular minerals, specific mineralized areas, methods and practices at representative mines and plants, economic developments, or industrial health and safety programs. Resource studies and materials surveys also are covered in this series.
Beginning in 1962, certain annual publications containing statistical data were transferred to the unnumbered Mineral Industry Survey series.

ANALYSES OF NATURAL GASES OF THE UNITED STATES. 1961– [Annual]
Gives routine analyses and related source data for gas samples collected during the calendar year as part of the continuous survey for the occurrence of helium in natural gas.
The report for 1961 is the first in this series which supplements Bulletins 486, published in 1951; 576, published in 1958, and 617, published in 1963.
FUELS AND ENERGY DATA.

HELIUM: BIBLIOGRAPHY OF TECHNICAL AND SCIENTIFIC LITERATURE, (year), INCLUDING PAPERS ON ALPHA-PARTICLES. [Annual]
Lists citations to the technical and scientific literature of helium and alpha-particles as abstracted by 12 abstract service publications.

INJURY EXPERIENCE IN COAL MINING. 1948– [Annual]
Beginning with data for 1971, published by the Mining Enforcement and Safety Administration in its MESA Information Report series (I 69.9).
Published 1948– 1952 in the Bulletin series.

INJURY EXPERIENCE IN QUARRYING. [Biennial]
Subsequently published by the Mining Enforcement and Safety Administration in its MESA Information Report series (I 69.9).

INJURY EXPERIENCE IN THE METALLIC MINERAL INDUSTRIES. 1956-57– [Annual]
Previous title: Injury Experience in the Metal Industries.
Supersedes, in part, Injury Experience in the Metal and Nonmetal Industries.
Subsequently published by the Mining Enforcement and Safety Administration in its MESA Information Report series (I 69.9).

INJURY EXPERIENCE IN THE NONMETALLIC INDUSTRIES. 1956-57– [Biennial]
Previous title: Injury Experience in the Nonmetal Industries.
Supersedes, in part, Injury Experience in the Metal and Nonmetal Industries.
Subsequently published by the Mining Enforcement and Safety Administration in its MESA Information Report series (I 69.9).

RESEARCH AND TECHNOLOGIC WORK ON EXPLOSIVES, EXPLOSIONS, AND FLAMES. [Annual]
Summarizes the research conducted by the Bureau's Explosives Research Laboratory during the fiscal year. Covers such items as ignition, structure, and behavior of flames; explosions and combustion processes; fundamental detonation problems; new explosive formulations; and the safety and performance of commercial explosives.

REVIEW OF BUREAU OF MINES COAL PROGRAM. 1937– [Annual]
Briefly describes the broad program of research and technologic work conducted by the Bureau of Mines on coal and related subjects during the calendar year. In addition to a description of investigations on mining, preparation, and utilization of coal, an account is given of the Bureau's work in mine health and safety, coal resources, mine explosives, and environmental conditions relating to coal mining and utilization.

REVIEW OF BUREAU OF MINES ENERGY PROGRAM. 1st– 1970– [Annual]
PURPOSE:– To report on research and progress accomplished during the calendar year on various aspects of the energy program.

SUMMARY OF MINING AND PETROLEUM LAWS OF THE WORLD. [Irregular]
Includes identification of the controlling laws or statutes governing minerals acquisition: reference to the administrative authority; analysis of the laws governing mines and quarries and their products; and analysis of laws applicable to natural gas, petroleum, and related materials.

v. 1. Western Hemisphere. 1970. 159 p. (IC 8489)
v. 2. East Asia and the Pacific. 1971. 104 p. (IC 8514)
v. 3. Near East and South Asia. 1972. 82 p. il. (IC 8544)
v. 4. Africa. 1974. 210 p. (IC 8610)
v. 5. Europe. 1974. 90 p. (IC 8631)

TECHNOLOGIC AND RELATED TRENDS IN THE MINERAL INDUSTRIES. 1st– 1970– [Annual]
PURPOSE:– To outline recent trends and developments in the minerals industry. Discusses new methods, equipment, techniques, and systems used to extract and process minerals more effectively.
Title varies: 1970, Trends in the Mineral Industry; 1971, Technologic Trends in the Minerals Industry.

I 28.27/2:date • Item 637-A (MF)
ANALYSES OF NATURAL GASES. [Annual]
Earlier I 28.27

I 28.28:nos.
MINERAL MARKET REPORTS.
Earlier C 22.28
Later I 19.144

I 28.28/2:date • Item 639-F (MF)
LIME. [Monthly] (Mineral Industry Surveys)

I 28.28/3:date • Item 639-F (MF)
LIME IN (year). [Annual] (Mineral Industry Surveys)

I 28.28/4:date • Item 639-G (MF)
LIME PLANTS IN THE UNITED STATES. [Annual]

I 28.29:date • Item 639-F (MF)
CEMENT. [Monthly] (Mineral Industry Surveys)
Previous title: Monthly Cement Statement.
ISSN 0364-0876
Earlier C 22.29
Later I 19.134

I 28.29/2:date • Item 639-F (MF)
CEMENT IN (year). [Annual] (Mineral Industry Surveys)

I 28.29/3:date • Item 639-G (MF)
DIRECTORY OF CEMENT PRODUCERS IN (year). [Annual] (Mineral Industry Surveys)

I 28.30:nos.
COKE AND COAL CHEMICAL. [Monthly] (Mineral Industry Surveys)
Previous title: Monthly Coke Report.
Later E 3.11/9

I 28.30/2:date
COKE PRODUCERS IN THE UNITED STATES IN (year). [Annual] (Mineral Industry Surveys)
Later E 3.11/16-2

I 28.30/3:date
COKE DISTRIBUTION, MANUAL. (Mineral Industry Surveys)
Later E 3.11/16

I 28.30/4:date
COKE AND COAL CHEMICALS IN (year). [Annual] (Mineral Industry Surveys)

I 28.31:date
PRELIMINARY ESTIMATES OF PRODUCTION OF COAL AND BEEHIVE COKE. [Monthly]
Recompilation of weekly statistics published in Weekly Coal Report (I 28.23).
Earlier C 22.17
Later I 34.15

I 28.32:date • Item 639-F (MF)
GYPSUM. [Monthly] (Mineral Industry Surveys)
Previous title: Quarterly Gypsum Reports.
Earlier C 22.33
Later I 19.140

I 28.32/2:date • Item 639-F (MF)
GYPSUM IN (year). [Annual] (Mineral Industry Surveys)

I 28.33:nos.
WEEKLY COAL REPORT. (Mineral Industry Surveys)
Later E 3.11/4

I 28.33/2:date
BITUMINOUS COAL AND LIGNITE DISTRIBUTION. [Quarterly] (Mineral Industry Surveys)
Annual summary issued separately.
Formerly in I 28.28
Later E 3.11/7

I 28.33/2-2:date
BITUMINOUS COAL AND LIGNITE MINE OPENINGS AND CLOSINGS IN CONTINENTAL UNITED STATES, (dates). [Irregular] (Mineral Industry Surveys)

I 28.33/3:date
COAL CHRONICLE. 1962– [Irregular]
Recently published items about coal and related subjects, summarized by the staff of the Division of Bituminous Coal.

I 28.34:date
STATISTICS OF BITUMINOUS COAL LOADED FOR SHIPMENT ON RAILROADS AND WATERWAYS AS REPORTED BY OPERATORS. [Annual]
Earlier C 22.34

I 28.35:date • Item 641
MOTION PICTURE FILMS OF THE BUREAU OF MINES. [Annual]
Earlier C 22.26/2

I 28.36:date
COKE AND BYPRODUCTS TABLES. – 1938. [Annual]
Earlier C 22.7

I 28.37 • Item 639
MINERALS YEARBOOK. 1932– [Annual]
Supersedes Mineral resources of the United States.

Annual statistical volumes, reviewing the mineral industries of the United States and foreign countries. Contains official Government statistics on metals, minerals, and mineral products, together with a factual record of economic and technological developments and trends. Beginning with the volume for 1952, issued in three volumes; for 1963, in four volumes:

Vols. 1 & 2. Metals, Minerals and Fuels.
Chapters on mineral commodities, metals, nonmetals, and mineral fuels, a review of the mineral industries, statistical summary and recapitulation, mining technology, metallurgical technology, and employment and injuries. Chapters for individual commodities, which are arranged alphabetically in the volume, give annual statistics on domestic production, consumption and uses, stocks, prices, foreign trade, reserves, and world production. Index. Charts.

Prior to 1966, Volumes 1 and 2 were published separately with Volume 2 devoted to mineral fuels.

Vol. 3. Area Reports: Domestic.
Chapters covering each of the 50 States and possessions of the United States. In addition, a chapter recapitulating the statistics in summary form on a regional basis and a chapter on employment and injuries are included.

Vol. 4. Area Reports: International.
Summary chapter reviews minerals in the world economy. Individual chapters, arranged by area and country, give data on production and trade (exports and imports).

I 28.37/a:CT • Item 639-F-1
MINERALS YEARBOOK (Preprint).

I 28.37/a 2:CT • Item 639-F-1
MINERALS YEARBOOK (Separates from Volumes 3 and 4).
Chapters which will later be included in the bound volumes are issued as preprints in advance of publication as they are completed.

I 28.37/2:nos. • Item 639-A (MF)
MINERAL PERSPECTIVES. MP 1– 1977– [Irregular]

I 28.37/3:nos. or CT • Item 639-B (MF)
MINERAL COMMODITY PROFILES, MCP-(series).

I 28.37/4:nos. • Item 639-C (MF)
STATE MINERAL PROFILES. SMP 1– [Annual]
PURPOSE:– To provide current information on the mining and mineral economy of single State. Includes tables, diagrams, and bibliographies.

I 28.37/6:date • Item 639-I (E)
STATISTICAL COMPENDIUM.
Issued on CD-ROM.

I 28.37/7:date • Item 639-J
U.S. BUREAU OF MINES, MINERALS AND MATERIALS INFORMATION.
Issued on CD-ROM.

I 28.38:nos.
ECONOMIC PAPERS. 1–21. –1940.
Earlier C 22.13

I 28.39 • Item 638-B
MINERAL TRADE NOTES. v. 1– 1935– [Monthly]
A monthly inventory of information from U.S. Government Foreign Service Offices and other sources that may not otherwise be made available promptly.
Brief news articles arranged by commodity bases on Foreign Service dispatches.
Annual index contained in the December issue.
Discontinued.
ISSN 0364-0191

I 28.39/2:nos.
– SPECIAL SUPPLEMENTS. 1– 1955–

I 28.40:nos.
MONOGRAPHS. 1– 8. – 1948.
Earlier C 22.24

I 28.41:nos.
PETROLEUM FORECAST. 1– 1935– Nov. 1973. [Monthly] (Mineral Industry Surveys)

I 28.42 • Item 637-C
INTERNATIONAL COAL TRADE. v. 1– 1931– [Monthly]
Subtitle:– A monthly inventory of information from United States Government Foreign Service Offices and other sources that may not otherwise be made available promptly.
Gives in textual summaries, supported by table and maps, the highlights of the solid fuels industry, by geographic areas and selected tables. Part II of each issue contains statistical tables on a coal trade-ocean freight rates, production, consumption, imports and exports for selected countries.
Index issued separately.
ISSN 0364-054X
Earlier C 18.100

I 28.42/2:date
ADVANCE DATA ON COAL, BITUMINOUS AND LIGNITE.

I 28.42/3:date
COAL BITUMINOUS AND LIGNITE IN (year). [Annual] (Mineral Industry Surveys)
Later E 3.11/7-2

I 28.43:v.nos.&nos.
INTERNATIONAL PETROLEUM TRADE. v. 1–33. 1932–1964. [Monthly]
Earlier C 18.102
Beginning July 1964, consolidated into International Petroleum Quarterly (I 28.43/2).

I 28.43/2:date
INTERNATIONAL PETROLEUM QUARTERLY. 1964–1966.
Consolidation of International Petroleum Trade (I 28.43), World Petroleum Statistics (I 28.91), and World Retail Prices on Gasoline, Kerosine, and Motor Lubricating Oil, (I 28.44).

I 28.43/3:date • Item 642-A
INTERNATIONAL PETROLEUM ANNUAL. 1965– [Annual]
Later E 3.11/5-3

I 28.44:vol.
WORLD RETAIL PRICES AND TAXES ON GASOLINE, KEROSENE, AND MOTOR LUBRICATING OILS. – 1964. [Annual]
Beginning July 1964, consolidated into International Petroleum Quarterly (I 28.43/2).

I 28.45:nos.
CRUDE PETROLEUM REPORTS BY REFINERIES. [Monthly]
Earlier I 32.9

I 28.45/2:date
CRUDE-OIL AND REFINED-PRODUCTS PIPELINE MILEAGE IN THE UNITED STATES. [Triennial] (Mineral Industry Surveys)
Later E 3.11/12

I 28.45/3:date
DISTRICT V PETROLEUM STATEMENT. [Monthly] (Mineral Industry Surveys)
Later E 3.11/6

I 28.45/4:date
FUEL OILS BY SULFUR CONTENT. 1972– [Monthly] (Mineral Industry Surveys)
Later E 3.11/8

I 28.45/5:date
SALES OF FUEL OIL AND KEROSENE IN (year). [Annual] (Mineral Industry Surveys)
Later E 3.11/11

I 28.46:date
WEEKLY CRUDE OIL STOCK REPORTS. 1– 1933–1963.
Earlier I 32.9

I 28.47:date
NATURAL GAS LIQUIDS. – 1967. [Monthly] (Mineral Industry Surveys)
Beginning May 1967, issued as supplement to Petroleum Statement (I 28.18/2).
Later E 3.11/2

I 28.48:nos.
QUESTION AND ANSWER HANDBOOKS.
Earlier C 22.35

I 28.48/2:CT • Item 643
QUESTION AND ANSWER HANDBOOKS.

I 28.49:nos.
WEEKLY ANTHRACITE AND BEEHIVE COKE REPORTS.
Earlier I 28.33

I 28.49/2:date
PENNSYLVANIA ANTHRACITE. [Weekly] (Mineral Industry Surveys)
Later E 3.11/3

I 28.50:date
PRELIMINARY ESTIMATES OF PRODUCTION OF PENNSYLVANIA ANTHRACITE AND BEEHIVE COKE. [Monthly] (Mineral Industry Surveys)
Earlier I 28.31

I 28.50/2:nos.
– MONTHLY PRELIMINARY ESTIMATES. – 1963. (Mineral Industry Surveys)
Note:– Statistics formerly in I 28.50

I 28.50/3:date
DISTRIBUTION OF PENNSYLVANIA ANTHRACITE FOR COAL YEAR (date). 1962– [Annual] (Mineral Industry Surveys)
Later E 3.11/3-3

I 28.50/4:date
COAL, PENNSYLVANIA ANTHRACITE IN (year). [Annual] (Mineral Industry Surveys)
Later E 3.11/3-2

I 28.51:vol.
FOREIGN MINERALS QUARTERLY. v. 1– 1938–1941. [Quarterly]
Superseded by Foreign Minerals Survey (I 28.81).

I 28.52 • Item 637-L
ADDRESSES. [Irregular]

I 28.53:nos. • Item 639-F (MF)
IRON AND STEEL SCRAP. [Monthly] (Mineral Industry Surveys)
Earlier 28.28
Later I 19.141

I 28.53/2:nos.
MINERAL MARKET REPORTS, I.S.P. (series). [Monthly]

I 28.53/2-2:date
IRON AND STEEL SCRAP IN (year). [Annual] (Mineral Industry Surveys)

I 28.53/3:nos.
IRON AND STEEL REPORT. [Monthly]

I 28.53/4:date • Item 639-F (MF)
IRON AND STEEL IN (year). [Annual] (Mineral Industry Surveys)

I 28.53/5:date • Item 639-F (MF)
IRON AND STEEL SLAG. [Annual] (Mineral Industry Surveys)
Earlier title: Slag-Iron and Steel in (year).

I 28.54:date • Item 639-E (MF)
MANGANESE. [Monthly] (Mineral Industry Surveys)
ISSN 0364-7900
Earlier I 28.28
Later I 19.158

I 28.54/2:date • Item 639-B (MF)
MANGANESE IN (year). [Annual] (Mineral Industry Surveys)

I 28.55:date • Item 639-G (MF)
MERCURY. [Quarterly] (Mineral Industry Surveys)
ISSN 0364-7919

I 28.55/2:date • Item 639-B (MF)
MERCURY IN (year). [Annual] (Mineral Industry
Surveys)

I 28.56:nos.
MONTHLY SLAB ZINC REPORTS. 1– 15. – 1941.
(Mineral Industry Surveys)
Superseded April 1944, by Monthly Zinc Reports (I 28.69).

I 28.57:nos.
ZINC MINE PRODUCTION.   –1968. [Monthly] (Mineral
Industry Surveys)
Incorporated into Zinc Industry (I 28.69).

I 28.58:nos.
MOLYBDENUM REPORTS. 1– 6. 1941– 1942. [Monthly]

I 28.58/2:nos. • Item 639-F (MF)
MOLYBDENUM REPORTS [new series]. 1–   1945–
[Monthly] (Mineral Industry Surveys)
Issued quarterly 1945– 1953.
ISSN 0364-7927
Later I 19.159
I 28.58/3:date
MOLYBDENUM. [Annual]
(Mineral Industry Surveys)

I 28.59:nos.
MINE PRODUCTION OF COPPER. [Monthly] (Mineral
Industry Surveys)
Superseded by I 28.59/2

I 28.59/2:date • Item 639-H
COPPER IN THE UNITED STATES. [Monthly]
Provides data on domestic mine, smelter, and
refinery production of copper as well as consumption, stocks, imports and exports. Chiefly
tables.
Supersedes Mine Production of Copper (I
28.59).
Incorporates Brass Hill Report (I 28.79/2) beginning May 1968.
Title varies.
ISSN 0364-0914
Later I 19.137

I 28.59/3:date
COPPER IN (year). [Annual] (Mineral Industry Surveys)

I 28.59/4:date
COPPER IN (year). [Preliminary] [Annual] (Mineral
Industry Surveys)

I 28.59/5:date
COPPER PRODUCTION. [Monthly] (Division of Nonferrous Metals) (Mineral Industry Surveys)
ISSN 0364-782X

I 28.60:nos.
LEAD MINE PRODUCTION. 1–   1941– 1968.
[Monthly] (Mineral Industry Surveys)

Information incorporated into Lead Industry
(I 28.87).

I 28.61:nos.
GOLD REPORT [Mine Production]. 1–   1943– 1968.
[Monthly] (Mineral Industry Surveys)
Previous title: Mine Production of Gold
Incorporated into Gold and Silver (I 28.61/2).

I 28.61/2:date • Item 639-F (MF)
GOLD AND SILVER. 1968–   [Monthly and Quarterly] (Mineral Industry Surveys)
Incorporates Gold (I 28.61) and Silver (I
28.62).
ISSN 0364-7862

I 28.61/3:date
GOLD AND SILVER IN (year). [Annual] (Mineral Industry Surveys)

I 28.62:nos.
SILVER [Mine Production]. 1–   1943– 1968. [Monthly]
(Mineral Industry Surveys)
Previous title: Mine Production of Silver.
Incorporated into Gold and Silver (I 28.61/2).

I 28.63:nos. • Item 639-F (MF)
SULFUR. [Monthly] (Mineral Industry Surveys)
Previous title: Native Sulfur.
Earlier I 28.29
Later I 19.152

I 28.63/2:date • Item 639-F (MF)
SULFUR. [Annual] (Mineral Industry Surveys)

I 28.63/3:date • Item 639-G (MF)
SULFUR IN (year), ADVANCE SUMMARY. [Annual]
(Mineral Industry Surveys)

I 28.63/4:date • Item 639-F (MF)
END USES OF SULFUR AND SULFURIC ACID IN
(year). [Annual] (Mineral Industry Surveys)

I 28.64:date
PRELIMINARY ESTIMATES ON PRODUCTION OF
BITUMINOUS COAL AND LIGNITE. [Monthly]
Earlier I 28.64

I 28.65:nos.
NONFERROUS SCRAP DEALERS REPORTS.
[Monthly]

I 28.66:date • Item 639-F (MF)
IRON ORE. [Monthly] (Mineral Industry Surveys)
ISSN 0364-7870
Later I 19.142
I 28.66/2:date • Item 639-F (MF)
IRON ORE IN (year). [Annual] (Mineral Industry
Surveys)

I 28.67:nos.
LEAD SCRAP CONSUMERS REPORTS. [Monthly]

I 28.68:date
ZINC SCRAP.   – 1968. [Monthly] (Mineral Industry
Surveys)
Incorporated in Zinc Industry (I 28.69).

I 28.69:date • Item 639-G (MF)
ZINC INDUSTRY. [Monthly] (Mineral Industry Surveys)
Provides data on consumption of slab zinc,
zinc mine production, smelter production, and
U.S. producers' price for High Grade zinc.
Later I 19.157

I 28.69/2:date
ZINC INDUSTRY IN (year). [Annual] (Mineral Industry
Surveys)

I 28.70:date • Item 639-G (MF)
FLUORSPAR. [Quarterly] (Mineral Industry Surveys)
ISSN 0364-7854
Later I 19.139

I 28.70/2:date • Item 639-G (MF)
FLUOSPAR. [Annual] (Mineral Industry Surveys)

I 28.71:nos.
ALUMINUM ALLOY INGOT, MONTHLY REPORTS.

I 28.71/2:date
ALUMINUM SCRAP AND SECONDARY INGOT.
[Monthly]

I 28.71/3:date
SECONDARY ALUMINUM.   – 1967. [Monthly] (Mineral
Industry Surveys)
Combined with Primary Aluminum (I 28.85)
beginning with May 1967 issue.

I 28.72:CT
MAPS.

I 28.73:date • Item 639-G (MF)
TUNGSTEN. [Monthly] (Mineral Industry Surveys)
Later I 19.155

I 28.73/2:date • Item 639-G (MF)
TUNGSTEN. [Annual] (Mineral Industry Surveys)

I 28.74:nos.
SOLID FUELS DISTRIBUTION REPORTS.

I 28.75:date • Item 639-G (MF)
SILICON. [Monthly] (Mineral Industry Surveys)
Earlier title: Ferrosilicon.
ISSN 0364-7846
Later I 19.150

I 28.75/2:date • Item 639-G (MF)
SILICON IN (year). [Annual] (Mineral Industry Surveys)
Earlier title: Ferrosilicon in (year).

I 28.75/3:date
FERROSILICON. [Quarterly]
ISSN 0364-7846

I 28.76:date • Item 639-G (MF)
COBALT [consumption]. [Monthly] (Mineral Industry
Surveys)
ISSN 0364-0892
Later I 19.136

I 28.76/2:date
COLBALT [refiners]. [Quarterly] (Mineral Industry
Surveys)
ISSN 0364-0906

I 28.76/3:date • Item 639-G (MF)
COBALT ANNUAL REVIEW. [Annual] (Mineral Industry Surveys)
Earlier title: Cobalt in (year).

I 28.77:date • Item 639-G
PLATINUM-GROUP METALS IN . . . [Quarterly]
Title varies.

I 28.77/2:date
PLATINUM-GROUP METALS IN (year). (Mineral Industry Surveys)

I 28.78:date • Item 639-G (MF)
VANADIUM. [Monthly] (Mineral Industry Surveys)
ISSN 0364-7951
Later I 19.156

I 28.78/2:date
VANADIUM IN (year). [Annual] (Mineral Industry
Surveys)

I 28.79:date
COPPER SCRAP CONSUMERS.   – 1967. [Monthly]
(Mineral Industry Surveys)
Combined in Copper Industry (I 28.59/2) beginning with June 1967 issue.

I 28.79/2:date
BRASS MILL SCRAP AND METAL CONSUMPTION
AND STOCKS AT BRASS AND WIRE MILLS.
–1968 [Monthly] (Mineral Industry Surveys)
Incorporated in Copper Industry (I 28.59/3).

I 28.80:nos. • Item 639-G
BAUXITE. 1–   1945–   [Quarterly] (Mineral Industry Surveys)
Previous title: Quarterly Bauxite Report.
Later I 19.132

I 28.80/2:date
ALUMINUM AND BAUXITE IN (year). [Annual] (Mineral
Industry Surveys)

I 28.81:nos.
FOREIGN MINERALS SURVEY.
Supersedes Foreign Minerals Quarterly I 28.51

I 28.81/2:date
WORLD MINERAL PRODUCTION IN (year). [Annual]
(Mineral Industry Surveys)

I 28.82:nos.
TITANIUM REPORTS. [Quarterly]

I 28.82/2:date • Item 639-G
TITANIUM. [Quarterly] (Mineral Industry Surveys)
ISSN 0364-7943
Later I 19.154

I 28.82/3:date
TITANIUM IN (year). [Annual] (Mineral Industry Surveys)

I 28.83:nos.
ZIRCONIUM REPORTS. [Quarterly]

I 28.83/2:date
ZIRCONIUM AND HAFNIUM IN (year). [Annual] (Mineral
Industry Surveys)

I 28.84:date   • **Item 639-H (MF)**
CHROMIUM. [Monthly] (Mineral Industry Surveys)
    ISSN 0364-0884
    Later I 19.135

I 28.84/2:date   • **Item 639-B (MF)**
CHROMIUM IN (year). [Annual] (Mineral Industry
  Surveys)

I 28.85:date   • **Item 639-H (MF)**
ALUMINUM. [Monthly] (Mineral Industry Surveys)
    ISSN 0364-085X
    Later I 19.130

I 28.86:v.nos.
ETIC LIQUID FUELS ABSTRACTS. [Bimonthly]

I 28.87:date   • **Item 639-F**
LEAD INDUSTRY IN . . . [Monthly]
    Former title: Lead Industry.
    ISSN 0364-7889
    Later I 19.143

I 28.87/2:date
LEAD IN (year). [Annual] (Mineral Industry Surveys)

I 28.87/3:date
LEAD PRODUCTION. [Monthly] (Division of Nonferrous Metals) (Mineral Industry Surveys)
    ISSN 0364-7897

I 28.88:date
CARBON BLACK. [Quarterly] (Mineral Industry
  Surveys)
    Issued monthly prior to October 1967.
    Later E 3.11/10

I 28.88/2:date
CARBON BLACK IN (year). [Annual] (Mineral Industry
  Surveys)
    Later E 3.11/10-2

I 28.89:date
COAL MINE INJURIES AND WORKTIME. [Monthly]
  (Mineral Industry Surveys)
    Effective with February 1974 issue, published
    by the Mining Enforcement and Safety Adminis-
    tration (I 69.10/2).

I 28.90:date
ZINC OXIDE. [Monthly] (Mineral Industry Surveys)

I 28.91:nos.
WORLD PETROLEUM STATISTICS. [Monthly]

I 28.92:nos.   • **Item 639-H (MF)**
NICKEL. [Monthly] (Mineral Industry Surveys)
    Later I 19.148

I 28.92/2:date
NICKEL IN (year). [Annual] (Mineral Industry Surveys)

I 28.93:date
COPPER SULFATE. [Quarterly] (Mineral Industry
  Surveys)
    ISSN 0364-7838

I 28.94:nos.
ANNUAL AREA REPORT, ADVANCE SUMMARY.

I 28.95:date   • **Item 639-H (MF)**
ANTIMONY. [Quarterly] (Mineral Industry Surveys)
    Later I 19.131

I 28.95/2:date   • **Item 639-B (MF)**
ANTIMONY IN (year). [Annual] (Mineral Industry Surveys)

I 28.96:date   • **Item 639-H (MF)**
TIN. [Monthly] (Mineral Industry Surveys)
    Later I 19.153

I 28.96/2:date
TIN IN (year). [Annual] (Mineral Industry Surveys)

I 28.97:CT
MATERIALS SURVEY.
    See also C 40.17 and A 13.2:L 97/16

I 28.98:nos.
NATURAL GAS. [Quarterly] (Mineral Industry Surveys)

I 28.98/2:nos.
UNDERGROUND STOCKS OF LP-GASES. [Monthly]

I 28.98/3:date
NATURAL GAS PROCESSING PLANTS IN UNITED
  STATES. [Biennial]
    Earlier I 28.27

I 28.98/4:date
NATURAL GAS IN (year). [Annual] (Mineral Industry
  Surveys)
    Later E 3.11

I 28.98/5:date
SHIPMENT OF LIQUEFIED PETROLEUM GASES AND
  METHANE IN (year). [Annual] (Mineral Industry
  Surveys)

I 28.98/6:date
NATURAL GAS PRODUCTION AND CONSUMPTION.
  [Annual] (Mineral Industry Surveys)
    Later E 3.11/2-2

I 28.98/7:date
WORLD NATURAL GAS IN (year). [Annual] (Mineral
  Industry Surveys)

I 28.99:nos.
WAR MINERALS REPORTS.
    Confidential during World War II.

I 28.100
[PRESS RELEASES]. [Irregular]

I 28.101:date   • **Item 639-H (MF)**
PRIMARY MAGNESIUM. [Quarterly] (Mineral Indus-
  try Surveys)
    Later I 19.145

I 28.101/2:date
MAGNESIUM AND MAGNESIUM COMPOUNDS IN
  (year). [Annual] (Mineral Industry Surveys)

I 28.101/2-2:date
MAGNESIUM AND MAGNESIUM COMPOUNDS IN
  (year). [Annual] (Mineral Industry Surveys)

I 28.101/3:date
CALCIUM-MAGNESIUM CHLORIDE IN (year). [Annual]
  (Mineral Industry Surveys)

I 28.101/4:date
CALCIUM AND CALCIUM COMPOUNDS IN (year).
  [Annual] (Mineral Industry Surveys)

I 28.102:date   • **Item 639-H**
CADMIUM. [Quarterly] (Mineral Industry Surveys)

I 28.102/2:date   • **Item 639-H-2 (MF)**
CADMIUM IN (year). [Annual] (Mineral Industry Surveys)

I 28.103:date   • **Item 639-F (MF)**
BISMUTH. [Quarterly] (Mineral Industry Surveys)

I 28.103/2:date   • **Item 639-F (MF)**
BISMUTH IN (year). [Annual] (Mineral Industry Surveys)

I 28.104:date
SELENIUM. [Quarterly] (Mineral Industry Surveys)

I 28.104/2:date   • **Item 693-H (MF)**
SELENIUM AND TELLURIUM IN (year).
  [Annual](Mineral Industry Surveys)

I 28.105:nos.
CONTRIBUTIONS FROM THERMODYNAMICS LABO-
  RATORY, PETROLEUM EXPERIMENT STATION,
  BARTLESVILLE, OKLAHOMA.

I 28.106:nos.
SILICON REPORT. [Quarterly]

I 28.107:date   • **Item 639-E (MF)**
PEAT PRODUCERS IN UNITED STATES. [Annual]
    Statistics formerly carried in I 28.27

I 28.107/2:date   • **Item 639-B**
PEAT. [Annual] (Mineral Industry Surveys)
    Earlier title: Advance Data on Peat in (year).

I 28.108:date
INJURY EXPERIENCE IN OIL AND GAS INDUSTRY
  OF UNITED STATES.
    Statistics formerly included in H.S.C series I
    28.26

I 28.108/2:date
INJURY EXPERIENCE AND RELATED EMPLOYMENT
  DATA FOR SAND AND GRAVEL INDUSTRY. [An-
  nual]

I 28.109:date
FUEL-BRIQUETS AND PACKAGED-FUEL PRO-
  DUCERS, ANNUAL. [Annual] (Mineral Industry
  Surveys)
    Formerly in I 28.27

I 28.110:date
ASPHALT SHIPMENTS IN (year). [Annual] (Mineral
  Industry Surveys)

I 28.110/2:date
ASPHALT SALES IN (year). [Annual] (Mineral Industry Surveys)
    Later E 2.11/18

I 28.111:date   • **Item 639-H (MF)**
FELDSPAR IN (year). [Annual] (Mineral Industry
  Surveys)

I 28.111/2:date   • **Item 639-H (MF)**
FELDSPAR. [Quarterly]

I 28.112:date   • **Item 639-H**
APPARENT CONSUMPTION OF INDUSTRIAL EXPLO-
  SIVES AND BLASTING AGENTS IN THE UNITED
  STATES. [Annual]
    Sub-title: apparent Consumption of Industrial
    Explosives and Blasting Agents in the United
    States, (year).
    Earlier: Explosives.

I 28.113:date
SAFETY IN MINERAL INDUSTRIES. [Annual] (Office
  of Accident Analysis) (Mineral Industry Surveys)
    Sub-title: Injury Experience and Worktime in
    Mineral Industries.

I 28.114:CT   • **Item 637-E**
LAWS.

I 28.115:date   • **Item 637-F**
BUREAU OF MINES RESEARCH (year), SUMMARY
  OF SIGNIFICANT RESULTS IN MINERAL TECH-
  NOLOGY AND ECONOMICS. 1971–   [Annual]
    PURPOSE:– To present summaries of the sig-
  nificant research projects and mineral intelligence
  studies including the development, through scientific and engineering investigations, of technology sufficient to increase the percentage of
  recovery of oil, coal, natural gas, copper, and
  other mineral products from the country's deposits; the improvement of the economics of recycling
  scrap metals; the achievement of more efficient
  utilization of virgin metals and minerals by extending their normal lifespan; and the finding of
  industrial uses for the many wastes of mineral
  processing that constitute unsightly dumps and
  contribute to air, water, and land pollution.

I 28.116:date
ABRASIVE MATERIALS IN (year). [Annual] (Mineral
  Industry Surveys)

I 28.117:date   • **Item 639-B (MF)**
DIRECTORY OF PRINCIPAL U.S. GEMSTONE
  PRODUCERS (Annual Advance Summary). (Min-
  eral Industry Surveys)
    Earlier title: Gem Stones in (year).

I 28.118:date
STONE IN (year). [Annual] (Mineral Industry Surveys)

I 28.118/2:date
DIRECTORY OF PRINCIPAL CRUSHED STONE
  PRODUCERS IN THE UNITED STATES IN (year).
  [Annual] (Mineral Industry Surveys)

I 28.118/2-2:date   • **Item 639-H (MF)**
CRUSHED STONE IN (year). [Annual]

I 28.118/3:date • Item 639-E (MF)
DIRECTORY OF PRINCIPAL DIMENSION STONE
PRODUCERS IN THE UNITED STATES. [Annual]
(Mineral Industry Surveys)

I 28.118/3-2:date • Item 639-H (MF)
DIMENSION STONE IN (year). [Annual]

I 28.118/4 • Item 639-D (MF)
CRUSHED STONE AND SAND AND GRAVEL IN THE
QUARTER OF . . . [Quarterly]
Later I 19.138

I 28.119:date • Item 639-H (MF)
PHOSPHATE ROCK IN (year). [Annual] (Mineral Industry Surveys)

I 28.119/2:date • Item 639-E (MF)
PHOSPHATE CROP YEAR. [Annual] (Mineral Industry
Surveys)

I 28.119/3:date • Item 639-E
MARKETABLE PHOSPHATE ROCK. [Monthly]
Earlier: Phosphate Rock.
Later I 19.147

I 28.119/4:date • Item 639-E (MF)
DIRECTORY OF COMPANIES PRODUCING PHOS-
PHATE ROCK IN THE UNITED STATES. [Annual]

I 28.120:date
POTASH IN (year). [Annual] (Mineral Industry Surveys)

I 28.120/2:date • Item 639-H (MF)
POTASH IN CROP YEAR (date). [Annual] (Mineral
Industry Surveys)

I 28.120/3:date • Item 639-H (MF)
POTASH IN (year). [Preliminary] [Annual] (Mineral
Industry Surveys)

I 28.121:date
MINOR NONMETALS IN (year), ANNUAL ADVANCE
SUMMARY. (Mineral Industry Surveys)

I 28.122:date • Item 639-B (MF)
PUMICE AND PUMICITE IN (year). [Annual] (Mineral
Industry Surveys)
Earlier title: Pumice and Volcanic Cinder in
(year).

I 28.123:date • Item 639-B (MF)
ASBESTOS IN (year). [Annual] (Mineral Industry Surveys)

I 28.124:date
BARITE IN (year). [Annual] (Mineral Industry Surveys)

I 28.125:date
BORON IN (year). [Annual] (Mineral Industry Surveys)

I 28.126:date
BROMINE IN (year). [Annual] (Mineral Industry Surveys)

I 28.127:date • Item 639-E (MF)
DIATOMITE IN (year). [Annual] (Mineral Industry Surveys)

I 28.128:date • Item 639-H (MF)
NATURAL GRAPHITE IN (year). [Annual] (Mineral
Industry Surveys)

I 28.128/2:date • Item 639-E (MF)
GRAPHITE IN (year). [Annual] (Mineral Industry Surveys)

I 28.129:date • Item 639-H (MF)
IODINE IN (year). [Annual] (Mineral Industry Surveys)

I 28.130:date • Item 639-B (MF)
MICA IN (year). [Annual] (Mineral Industry Surveys)

I 28.131:date • Item 639-E (MF)
KYANITE AND RELATED MINERALS IN (year). [Annual]
(Mineral Industry Surveys)

I 28.132:date • Item 639-E (MF)
NITROGEN IN (year). [Annual] (Mineral Industry Sur-

I 28.133:date • Item 639-B (MF)
PERLITE IN (year). [Annual] (Mineral Industry Surveys)

I 28.134:date • Item 639-E (MF)
SALT IN (year). [Annual] (Mineral Industry Surveys)

I 28.134/2:date • Item 639-E (MF)
DIRECTORY OF COMPANIES PRODUCING SALT IN
THE UNITED STATES. [Annual] (Mineral Industry
Surveys)

I 28.135:date • Item 639-B (MF)
SODIUM COMPOUNDS IN (year). [Annual] (Mineral
Industry Surveys)

I 28.135/2:date • Item 639-E
SODA ASH AND SODIUM SULFATE: U.S. PRODUC-
TION, TRADE AND CONSUMPTION. [Monthly]
Earlier: Sodium Compounds.
Later I 19.151

I 28.135/3:date • Item 639-E
SODIUM CARBONATE IN (year). [Annual] (Mineral
Industry Surveys)

I 28.135/4:date
SODIUM SULFATE IN (year). [Annual] (Mineral Industry Surveys)

I 28.136:date • Item 639-B (MF)
TALC. [Annual] (Mineral Industry Surveys)
Earlier title: Talc, Soapstone, and Pyrophyl-
lite in (year).

I 28.137:date • Item 639-B (MF)
VERMICULITE IN (year). [Annual] (Mineral Industry
Surveys)

I 28.138:date • Item 639-B-2 (MF)
BERYLLIUM IN (year). [Annual] (Mineral Industry Surveys)

I 28.139:date
CESIUM AND RUBIDIUM IN (year). [Annual] (Mineral
Industry Surveys)

I 28.140:date • Item 639-E (MF)
CLAYS IN (year). [Annual] (Mineral Industry Surveys)

I 28.141:date • Item 639-E-1 (MF)
COLUMBIUM AND TANTALUM IN (year). [Annual] (Mineral Industry Surveys)

I 28.142:date
FERROALLOYS IN (year). [Annual] (Mineral Industry
Surveys)

I 28.143:date • Item 639-E (MF)
LITHIUM IN (year). [Annual] (Mineral Industry Surveys)

I 28.144:date
RARE ELEMENTS AND THORIUM IN (year). [Annual]
(Mineral Industry Surveys)

I 28.145:date • Item 639-B (MF)
RHENIUM IN (year). [Annual] (Mineral Industry Surveys)

I 28.146:date • Item 639-E (MF)
SAND AND GRAVEL IN (year). [Annual] (Mineral Industry Surveys)

I 28.146/2 • Item 639-E (MF)
SAND AND GRAVEL (CONSTRUCTION) IN . . . [Annual]

I 28.147:date
URANIUM IN (year). [Annual] (Mineral Industry
Surveys)

I 28.148:date • Item 639-B-1 (MF)
MINERAL COMMODITIES SUMMARIES. [Annual]
For each commodity gives domestic industry,
salient statistics for the U.S., import sources,
tariff, depletion allowance, government incentive
and procurement, primary mental production and
capacity for U.S. and leading countries, and economic factors.
Former title: Commodity Data Summaries.
ISSN 0082-9137
Earlier I 28.2:C 73/2

I 28.149:date • Item 638-C
MINERALS AND MATERIALS, A BIMONTHLY SUR-
VEY.
PURPOSE:– To present data series for twelve
commodities and fossil fuels aggregate. The statistics collected cover production, consumption,
exports, imports, inventories, and price. Technical notes on the individual commodities supply
detailed descriptions of the data given. Charts
describe U.S. imports and exports of raw and
processed minerals. The "Highlights" section focuses on recent developments of interest in the
mineral industry. There is also an article concerning some aspects of the minerals industry.
Former title: Minerals and Materials, a Monthly
Survey

I 28.149/2:date • Item 638-C
MINERALS TODAY. [Bimonthly]

I 28.150:CT • Item 638-D
ENVIRONMENTAL STATEMENTS. [Irregular]

I 28.151:CT • Item 638-E (MF) (CD)
SPECIAL PUBLICATIONS (series). [Irregular]

I 28.151/2:date • Item 638-E
TECHNICAL HIGHLIGHTS MINING RESEARCH.
[Annual]

I 28.151/3 • Item 638-E-1 (MF)
TECHNOLOGY TRANSFER UPDATE. [Quarterly]

I 28.152:nos. • Item 637-A-3
TECHNOLOGY NEWS FROM THE BUREAU OF MINES.
[Irregular]
Describes tested developments from the Bu-
reau of Mines Research Programs.

I 28.153:date • Item 638-F (MF)
MINING RESEARCH REVIEW. [Annual]
PURPOSE:– To report on selected mining
research activities of the Bureau, covering such
subjects as safety, health, technology, environment and technology transfer.

I 28.154:v.nos.&nos. • Item 638-G (MF)
MINING RESEARCH CONTRACT REVIEW. v. 1–
[Semiannual]
PURPOSE:– To present a listing of current
Mining Research Programs administered by the
Bureau of Mines. Lists active contracts by con-
tract numbers within research areas, with con-
tractor name. Includes reports on completed re-
search.

I 28.154/2 • Item 638-G (MF)
ROLLA RESEARCH CENTER ANNUAL PROGRESS
REPORT FY.

I 28.155:nos. • Item 637-A (MF)
OPEN FILE REPORTS.

I 28.156:CT • Item 639-D (MF)
MINERAL ISSUES, AN ANALYTICAL SERIES.
[Irregular]
Each report analyzes issues related to a dif-
ferent metals industry.

I 28.156/2 • Item 639-D (MF)
MINERAL ISSUES. [Annual]

I 28.156/3:date • Item 639-D (MF)
MINERAL IN . . . [Annual]

I 28.157:CT
MAPS.

I 28.157:CT
AUDIOVISUAL MATERIALS. [Irregular]

I 28.159:date
CORUNDUM IN (year). [Annual] (Mineral Industry
Surveys)

I 28.160:date
GALLIUM IN (year). [Annual] (Mineral Industry Surveys)

I 28.161:date • Item 639-B (MF)
GARNET IN (year). [Annual] (Mineral Industry Surveys)

I 28.162:date
INDUSTRIAL DIAMOND IN (year). [Annual] (Mineral Industry Surveys)

I 28.163:date • **Item 639-B (MF)**
IRON OXIDE PIGMENTS IN (year). [Annual] (Mineral Industry Surveys)

I 28.164:date • **Item 639-E (MF)**
QUARTZ CRYSTALS IN (year). [Annual] (Mineral Industry Surveys)

I 28.165:date
RAW NONFUEL MINERAL PRODUCTION IN (year). [Annual] (Mineral Industry Surveys)

I 28.166:date • **Item 639-E (MF)**
STRONTIUM IN (year). [Annual] (Mineral Industry Surveys)

I 28.167 • **Item 637-A (MF)**
HELIUM RESOURCES OF THE U.S. [Biennial]

I 28.168:date • **Item 639-E (MF)**
TELLURIUM IN (year). [Annual]

I 28.169:date • **Item 639-E (MF)**
FERROUS METALS SUPPLY/DEMAND DATA. [Annual]

I 28.169/2:date • **Item 639-E**
INDUSTRIAL MINERALS SUPPLY/DEMAND DATA. [Annual]

I 28.169/3:date • **Item 636 (MF)**
NONFERROUS METALS SUPPLY, DEMAND DATA. [Annual]

I 28.170:date • **Item 637-A-2**
FEDERAL WOMEN'S PROGRAM NEWSLETTER. [Quarterly]
Contains short news items on the general status of women in the economic and occupational areas. Also focuses on particular women employees of the Bureau.

I 28.171:date • **Item 639-H**
MANUFACTURED ABRASIVES. [Quarterly]
Later I 19.146

I 28.173:nos. • **Item 639-H**
METAL INDUSTRY INDICATORS. [Monthly]
Later I 19.129

I 28.174 • **Item 639-H-1 (MF)**
FROTH FLOTATION IN THE UNITED STATES.

I 28.174/2 • **Item 639-F-2 (MF)**
GALLIUM IN . . . [Annual]

MINERAL INDUSTRY SURVEYS.
Mineral Industry Surveys is the title assigned to the periodic releases issued by the Bureau of Mines. These reports are available from the Publications distribution Branch, 4800 Forbes Avenue, Pittsburgh, Pennsylvania, 15212, except for District V Petroleum Demand Reports and Petroleum Statements, which may be obtained from the Office of Mineral Resources, 450 Golden Gate Avenue, Box 36012, San Francisco, California, 94102.
The majority of the releases in this series contains statistical data on production, consumption, stocks, etc., on the individual metals, nonmetals, and fuels. Releases are also issued on fatal and nonfatal injuries, man-hours worked in mineral industries, and timely reports on developments in industrial health and safety programs.
The statistical data in the weekly, monthly, and quarterly reports are usually replaced by preliminary annual data. The final annual data later appear in the Minerals Yearbook (I 28.37).

Prior to 1962, the Mineral Industry Surveys series contained three sub-series:

Mineral Market Reports, MMS [Mineral Market Statistics]. 1– 3305. (I 28.28)

Health and Safety Surveys, HHS [Health and Safety Statistics]. 1– 498. (I 28.26)

Petroleum Products Surveys. PPS 1–

Beginning in 1962, the sub-series title and numerical designation were dropped from the Mineral Market Reports and Health and Safety Surveys.

NATIONAL PARK SERVICE
(1916–   )

CREATION AND AUTHORITY

The National Park Service was established in the Department of the Interior by the act of August 25, 1916 (39 Stat. 535; 16 U.S.C. 1). Subsequent acts, Executive Orders, and proclamations have added to the National Park System and expanded the activities of the Service.

INFORMATION

Office of Communications
National Park Service
Department of the Interior
1849 C Street, NW
Washington, DC 20240
(202) 208-6843
Fax: (202) 219-0910
http://www.nps.gov

I 29.1:date • **Item 653-A (MF)**
ANNUAL REPORTS.

I 29.1/2:date • **Item 653-A (MF)**
OFFICE OF THE CHIEF SCIENTIST: ANNUAL REPORT.
Earlier: Advisory Council on Historic Preservation: Annual Report.

I 29.1/2:date • **Item 653-A**
ANNUAL REPORT OF THE CHIEF SCIENTIST OF THE NATIONAL PARK SERVICE. 1st–   1968– (Chief Scientist)
PURPOSE:– To provide a listing of natural and social science projects that were ongoing in the park system during the calendar year and also to present brief accounts of progress made during the year for a percentage of the listed projects.

I 29.1/3:date • **Item 653-A (MF)**
NATIONAL PARK SERVICE ANNUAL SCIENCE REPORT.

I 29.1/4:date • **Item 653-A-1 (MF) (EL)**
NATURAL RESOURCE YEAR IN REVIEW. [Annual]

I 29.2:CT • **Item 648**
GENERAL PUBLICATIONS.

I 29.3:vol.
PARK SERVICE BULLETINS. v. 1– v. 11, no. 6.   – 1941. [Monthly],
Superseded by I 29.3/2

I 29.3/2:v.nos.&nos.
NATIONAL PARK SERVICE BULLETIN. v. 12, no. 1– v. 15, no. 5. 1942– 1945. [Irregular]
Supersedes I 29.3, beginning with v. 12, no. 1, 1942.
Earlier title: Memorandum Regarding Personnel and Policy Changes, v. 12, no. 1– v. 14, no. 2.

I 29.3/3:nos. • **Item 646-H**
ECOLOGICAL SERVICES BULLETINS. 1–   [Irregular]

I 29.3/4: • **Item 646-H-1**
PARK SCIENCE, RESOURCE MANAGEMENT BULLETIN. [Quarterly]
Contains articles and features on scientific research that has important park management implications.

I 29.3/4-2 • **Item 646-H-2 (CD)**
PARK SCIENCE.

I 29.4:
CIRCULARS.

I 29.5:date
NATIONAL PARK CONFERENCES.

I 29.6:CT • **Item 651**
DESCRIPTIVE BOOKLETS AND FOLDERS ON THE INDIVIDUAL NATIONAL PARKS, MONUMENTS, ETC. [Irregular]
The National Park Service, in its information program, publishes two types of publications telling about the various national parks and monuments.
1. Folders. Issued as hand-outs to the visitors as they enter the particular area covered by the folder. These contain brief historical background and information for visitors with several illustrations. these are sold by the Superintendent of Documents for 5c each.
2. Pamphlets. For the more important and popular national parks and monuments, the pamphlets, ranging from 16 to 32 pages in length, give more complete information than the folders and have more permanent value in libraries.

I 29.6/2:CT • **Item 651-B**
NATIONAL SEASHORE [Information Circulars].

I 29.6/3:CT • **Item 651-B-1**
NATIONAL LAKESHORES [Information Circulars]. v. 1– 5.

I 29.6/3-2:v.nos.&nos.
SINGING SANDS ALMANAC. [Bimonthly] (Indian Dunes National Lakeside)

I 29.6/4:CT • **Item 651-B-2**
NATIONAL RIVERS [Information circulars]. 1969– [Irregular]
Brief description of the riverway including man and his relationship with the area, flora and fauna, the geological story, etc. Includes a map showing campgrounds, campsites, access points, picnic areas, and trails.

I 29.6/5:CT • **Item 651**
NATIONAL SCENIC TRAILS INFORMATION CIRCULARS. [Irregular]

I 29.6/6:CT • **Item 651-B-4**
NATIONAL HISTORIC SITES INFORMATION CIRCULARS. [Irregular]

I 29.6/7:date • **Item 654**
OUTDOORS IN THE SANTA MONICA MOUNTAINS NATIONAL RECREATION AREA. [Quarterly]
Earlier title: [Various Seasons] in the Santa Monica Mountains and Seashore.

I 29.7:CT
LIST OF PUBLICATIONS.

I 29.8:CT • **Item 651-A**
MAPS.

I 29.9:CT • **Item 656**
RULES, REGULATIONS AND INSTRUCTIONS.

I 29.9/2:CT • **Item 648-A**
HANDBOOKS, MANUALS, GUIDES.

I 29.9/2:Am 3 • **Item 648-A**
NATIONAL PARK SERVICE GUIDE TO THE HISTORIC PLACES OF THE AMERICAN REVOLUTION. 1974. 137 p. il. maps.
A handy guide to hundreds of sites and landmarks– the obscure and out-of-the-way as well as the important and well-known– which serve as living illustrations of the American Revolution. The book summarizes the course of the war in 18 States and along the Western Frontier and describes and locates the major surviving battlefields, skirmish sites, monuments, historic houses and buildings, and the memorable art and artifacts of the era.

I 29.9/3:CT
IN-SERVICE TRAINING SERIES.

I 29.9/3-2 • Item 648-A
VISITOR SERVICES TRAINING SERIES. 1968–
[Irregular]
Originally the series consisted of mimeographed booklets prepared for in-service use during the 1950's. During 1968, three of the five titles have been printed and offered for sale by the Superintendent of Documents.
PURPOSE:– Intended for use by uniformed employees of the National Park Service engaged in the various programs of the Service. The Booklets are useful also for instructors in the field of outdoor recreation as guidelines on how to interpret the environment.

I 29.9/4:CT • Item 648-C (MF)
COMPILATION OF ADMINISTRATIVE POLICIES.

I 29.9/4:N 21 • Item 648-C
COMPILATION OF ADMINISTRATIVE POLICIES FOR NATIONAL PARKS AND NATIONAL MONUMENTS OF SCIENTIFIC SIGNIFICANCE (Natural Area Category). 1967– [Irregular]
PURPOSE:– To state the administrative policies of the National Park Service for the management of the natural areas of the National Park system; to contribute to better public understanding of the management programs.

I 29.9/4:R 24/date • Item 648-C
COMPILATION OF ADMINISTRATIVE POLICIES FOR NATIONAL RECREATION AREAS, NATIONAL SEASHORES, NATIONAL LAKESHORES, NATIONAL PARKWAYS, NATIONAL SCENIC RIVERWAYS (Recreational Area Category). 1968–

I 29.9/5:nos. • Item 649
NATIONAL PARK SERVICE HANDBOOKS (numbered). [Irregular]

I 29.10:nos.
MARKING OF AMERICAN SCENERY.

I 29.11:nos.
EDUCATIONAL LEAFLETS. 1– 1931–

I 29.12:nos.
GUIDE LEAFLETS. 1– 1933–

I 29.12/2:CT
GUIDE LEAFLETS.

I 29.13 • Item 647
FAUNA SERIES. 1– 1933– [Irregular]

I 29.14:nos. • Item 646-I
OCCASIONAL PAPERS (Contribution of Wild Life Division). 1– 1933–

I 29.14/2:nos. • Item 646-I
OCCASIONAL REPORTS. [Irregular]

I 29.14/3 • Item 646-I-2
OCCASIONAL PAPERS (series): INTERAGENCY ARCHAEOLOGICAL SERIES, DENVER.

I 29.15/1:date
SOUTHWESTERN MONUMENTS, MONTHLY REPORTS.

I 29.15/2:date
SOUTHWESTERN MONUMENTS, SPECIAL REPORTS.

I 29.15/3:nos.
SOUTHWESTERN MONUMENTS. MUSEUM AND EDUCATION SERIES, LETTERS. 1–3. 1933–1935.

I 29.15/4:nos.
SOUTHWESTERN MONUMENTS, SPECIAL REPORTS. 1– 1936–

I 29.16:nos.
HISTORICAL SERIES, INDEPENDENT RADIO STATIONS (programs). 1–16. 1935.

I 29.17:nos.
NATIONAL PARKS PROGRAM [Radio Broadcasts]. 1– 1935–

I 29.18:nos.
RADIO (Independents) NATURAL SCIENCE SERIES TALKS. 1– 1935–

I 29.19:nos.
VOLCANO LETTER. –498. –1947. [Quarterly]

I 29.20:CT • Item 646-S
POSTERS.

I 29.20/2:CT
NATIONAL PARKS, USA [poster series].

I 29.20/3:CT
AUDIOVISUAL MATERIALS. [Irregular]

I 29.21:CT • Item 650
NATIONAL MONUMENTS AND NATIONAL MILITARY PARKS: INFORMATION CIRCULARS.
Earlier issues vary in titles.

I 29.22:date
NATURE NOTES, CLIP SHEETS. [Monthly]
Earlier I 19.29
Superseded by I 29.42

I 29.23:date
FACTS AND ARTIFACTS. [Monthly]
Superseded by I 29.42

I 29.24:CT
MOTORISTS GUIDES.

I 29.25:nos.
ART AND ARTISTS IN NATIONAL PARKS. 1–13. 1937. [Monthly]

I 29.26:nos. • Item 656-A
TREE PRESERVATION BULLETINS. 1– 1935–

I 29.27:CT
CHECK LIST OF BIRDS OF NATIONAL PARKS.

I 29.28:nos.
EMERGENCY CONSERVATION WORK, PROJECT TRAINING PUBLICATIONS.
Desig. P. T. Changed to I 1.71

I 29.29:CT
PHOTOGRAPHS OF SCENES OF NATIONAL PARKS, etc.

I 29.30:nos.
AMERICA'S HOUR OF DESTINY, RADIO SERIES. 1–26. 1938. [Weekly]

I 29.30/2:nos.
AMERICA'S HOUR OF DESTINY, RADIO SERIES. 1–13. 1938–1939.

I 29.31:nos.
CELEBRATED CONSERVATIONISTS IN OUR NATIONAL PARKS. 1–12. 1938. [Monthly]

I 29.32:CT
PHOTOGRAPHS OF SCENES IN NATIONAL PARKS (by name of park).

I 29.33:CT
SCHEDULES OF BASIC RATES (by name of park or monument).

I 29.34:nos.
TREASURE TRAILS. RADIO SCRIPTS. 1–13. 1936. [Weekly]

I 29.35
ADDRESSES. [Irregular]

I 29.36:vol.
REGIONAL REVIEW, REGION 1. v. 1– [ ]. 1938–1941. [Monthly]

I 29.37:
U.S. TRAVEL BUREAU.

I 29.37/1:date
ANNUAL REPORTS.

I 29.37/2:CT
GENERAL PUBLICATIONS.

I 29.37/5:date
OFFICIAL BULLETINS. v. 1– v. 3, no. 3. 1938–1942. [Monthly]

I 29.37/6:CT
ADDRESSES.

I 29.37/7:nos.
TRAVEL AND RECREATION NEWS LETTERS. 1–1939– [Biweekly]

I 29.37/8:date
CALENDAR OF EVENTS. –1942.

I 29.37/9:v.nos.&nos.
EASTERN TRAVEL TODAY.

I 29.38:vol.
COUNCIL RING. v. 1– v. 1, no. 37. 1938– 1941. [Monthly]

I 29.39:CT • Item 654
NATIONAL RECREATION AREA (Information Circulars).
Formerly: Recreational Demonstration Area

I 29.40:arts nos.
OUR OWN SPANISH-AMERICAN CITIZENS AND THE SOUTHWEST WHICH THEY COLONIZED. 1–12. 1939.

I 29.40/2
SIGNIFICANCE OF CORONADO CUARTO CENTENNIAL. Proc.

I 29.41:nos.
OCCASIONAL FORESTRY PAPERS. 1–6. 1938–1940.

I 29.42:date
PATROLS WITH PARK RANGERS. –1940.
Combines and supersedes I 29.22 and I 29.23

I 29.43:nos.
TWO ON A TRIP; RADIO SERIES, SCRIPTS. 1–13. 1940.

I 29.44:date
YEARBOOK, PARK AND RECREATION PROGRESS.
Changed from I 29.2

I 29.45:nos.
POPULAR STUDY SERIES: HISTORIES. 1– 1941–

I 29.46:CT • Item 653
LAWS.

I 29.46:L 44 • Item 653
LAWS RELATING TO THE NATIONAL PARK SERVICE. 1933– [Irregular]

I 29.47:nos.
ADVENTURES OF CUTHBERT (radio scripts). 1–15. 1941.

I 29.48:nos.
WHAT WE DEFEND (radio scripts). [1–4] [1941/42]

I 29.49:nos.
CONSERVATION MAN (radio scripts). 1–6.

I 29.50 • Item 657
SOURCE BOOK SERIES. 1– 1941– [Irregular]
PURPOSE:– To present basic documents and contemporary accounts relating to subjects comprehended by the areas of the National Park System.
Supplements the Historical Handbook series with compilations of selections of contemporary source material.

I 29.51:CT
MINIATURE PORTRAITS, WILDLIFE AT NATIONAL PARKS.

I 29.52 • Item 652
INTERPRETIVE SERIES. 1–3. 1942–1949. [Irregular]
PURPOSE:– To provide guides on historical subjects of a supplemental nature.
Each booklet covers a single subject, such as the history of the first legislative assembly at Jamestown, Va., the history of artillery, etc.

I 29.53:nos.
NATIONAL PARK LOCATION MAPS. 1– 1944–

I 29.54:nos.
SAFETY POST CARDS.

I 29.55:v.nos.
TRAVEL USA BULLETIN. v. 1, nos. 1– 12. 1948/49.
[Monthly]

I 29.56:nos.
SOURCES OF TRAVEL INFORMATION SERIES. 1– 4.
1948– 1949.

I 29.57:v.nos.
NATIONAL CALENDAR OF EVENTS. v. 1, no. 1. 1949.
[Quarterly]

I 29.58   • Item 649
HISTORICAL HANDBOOK SERIES. 1–   1950–
[Irregular]
    PURPOSE:– To provide the general public
with interpretive surveys concerning historical and
archaeological areas of the National Park System.
    These booklets provide excellent supplemen-
tal history texts in all periods of our United States
history, from early settlements and Indian tribal
areas of the Civil War, including such historic
landmarks as the Statue of Liberty, George
Washington's birthplace, Independence Hall, etc.
Well illustrated and documented with maps and
diagrams.

I 29.58/2:CT   • Item 649
NATIONAL PARK SERVICE HISTORY SERIES.

I 29.58/3:CT   • Item 649 (MF)
HISTORIC RESOURCE STUDIES. [Irregular]

I 29.58/4:CT   • Item 649-A
SPECIAL RESOURCE STUDY (series).

I 29.59   • Item 646-A
PUBLICATIONS IN ARCHEOLOGY. 1–   1951–
[Irregular]
    PURPOSE:– To provide the results of research
studies made in the National Park System archeological areas or in historical areas where
archeological research techniques are applicable.
    Each study covers a particular site or loca-
tion.
    Formerly Archeology Research Series.

I 29.59/2:nos.   • Item 646-A
ARCHEOLOGICAL COMPLETION REPORT SERIES.
1–   [Irregular]

I 29.59/3:date   • Item 646-V
ANNUAL REPORT ON THE ARCHEOLOGICAL PRO-
GRAMS OF THE WESTERN REGION.

I 29.59/4:date   • Item 646-A-1
ARCHEOLOGICAL AND HISTORICAL DATA RECOV-
ERY PROGRAM. [Annual]
    PURPOSE:– To present information on fed-
eral archeological data recovery activities by Interior and other federal departments that is required by section 5(c) of Public Law 93-291. Includes reports of such activities by states.
    Earlier I 70.2:Ar 2

I 29.59/5:v.nos./nos.   • Item 646-A-1
FEDERAL ARCHEOLOGY REPORT. [Bimonthly]

I 29.59/5-2:date   • Item 646-A-3
COMMON GROUND ARCHAEOLOGY AND
ETHMOGRAPHY IN THE PUBLIC INTEREST.
[Quarterly]
    Continues Federal Archeology Report.

I 29.59/6:nos.   • Item 646-A-1 (EL)
ARCHEOLOGICAL ASSISTANCE PROGRAM, TECH-
NICAL BRIEF (Series).

I 29.59/7:date   • Item 646-A-1
LISTING OF EDUCATION IN ARCHEOLOGICAL PRO-
GRAMS (LEAP).

I 29.59/8:nos.   • Item 646-A-1
ARCHEOLOGICAL ASSISTANCE STUDY (Series).

I 29.60:date
NATURALIST PROGRAM, ARCADIA NATIONAL PARK.
    Changed from I 29.6:Ac 1/3

I 29.60/2:date
NATURALIST PROGRAM, GREAT SMOKEY MOUN-
TAINS NATIONAL PARK.
    Changed from I 29.6:G 79/8

I 29.60/3:date
NATURALIST PROGRAM, MOUNT RAINIER NATIONAL
PARK.
    Changed from I 29.6:M 86/12

I 29.60/4:date
NATURALIST PROGRAM, SHENANDOAH NATIONAL
PARK.
    Changed from I 29.6:Sh 4/4

I 29.61:nos.
SELF-GUIDING NATURE TRAIL LEAFLETS, GLACIER
NATIONAL PARK. 1–   1952–

I 29.61/2:nos.
SELF-GUIDING NATURE TRAIL LEAFLETS, MOUNT
RAINIER NATIONAL PARK.

I 29.62:nos.   • Item 654-A
NATURAL HISTORY HANDBOOK SERIES. 1–   1954–
[Irregular]
    PURPOSE:– To provide guides to the flora
and fauna of the National Park System.
    Each booklet is devoted to one national park
or national monument area. Well illustrated. Gives
in addition to the information on wildlife and plants,
favorable time to visit the area, climate, etc.

I 29.62/2:nos.   • Item 646-L
NATURAL HISTORY THEME STUDIES. 1–   [Irregular]

I 29.63:date   • Item 654-C
PUBLIC USE OF NATIONAL PARKS, STATISTICAL
REPORT.   – 1972. [Monthly]
    Gives number of visitors, by types of areas
and by place. Issued in the following schedule:
    Winter Report: Summary of January-March
visitors (issued in April).
    Spring Report: Summary of April-May visitors
(issued in June).
    Summer Reports:
        June visitors, (issued in July).
        July visitors, (issued in August).
        August visitors, (issued in September).
        September visitors, (issued in October).
    Fall Report: Summary of October-December
visitors (issued in January).
    Irregular, prior to 1958.
    Earlier titles: Public Use, National Parks and
Related Areas, prior to 1962; Public Use, Tabulations of Visitors to Areas Administered by National Park Service 1953– 1962.

I 29.64:nos.
[PRESS RELEASES]. [Irregular]

I 29.65:date   • Item 646-D
ACTIVITIES IN THE NATIONAL CAPITAL REGION.
[Annual]
    Calendar of events from the Washington, D.C.,
area.

I 29.66:date   • Item 646-B
NATIONAL PARKS AND LANDMARKS. [Annual]
    Gives in tabular form the acreage, outstand-
ing characteristics and pertinent data, post office address for each of the areas administrated
by the National Park Service. Data is as of January 1, Includes a list of national historic sites
administrated but not owned by the Federal Government.
    Earlier title: Areas Administered by National
Park Service.

I 29.66/2:date
CALENDAR OF EVENTS IN AREAS ADMINISTERED
BY NATIONAL PARK SERVICE.
    Earlier I 29.2:Ev 2

I 29.67:
SHENANDOAH NATIONAL PARK CHIPS. [Monthly]

I 29.68
STATE PARK STATISTICS. [Annual]
    Tables cover expenditures, sources of funds,
attendance, areas and acreages, personnel, anticipated expenditures.

I 29.69:CT/date
ANNUAL PROSPECTUS OF WINTER USE AND
FACILITIES [various parks].

I 29.70:date
VISITOR ACCOMMODATIONS FURNISHED BY
CONCESSIONERS IN AREAS ADMINISTERED BY
NATIONAL PARK SERVICE. [Annual]

I 29.71:date   • Item 646-C
NATIONAL PARKS: CAMPING GUIDE. 1965–
[Annual]
    Title varies.
    Earlier I 29.2:C 15/3

I 29.72:v.nos.&nos.   • Item 646-C
PARK PRACTICE GRIST. [Bimonthly]
    Issued by National Conference on State
Parks, Inc. in cooperation with National Park Ser-
vice and American Inst. of Park Executives.
    See also I 70.22/2

I 29.72/2:date
DESIGN. [Quarterly] (Park Practice Program)
    See also I 70.22/3

I 29.73:nos.
PLOWBACK. 1–   1965–

I 29.74:CT   • Item 648-B
HISTORIC AMERICAN BUILDINGS SURVEY. [Irregular]

I 29.74/2:date   • Item 648-B
HISTORIC AMERICAN BUILDINGS SURVEY,
HISTORIC AMERICAN ENGINEERING RECORD
DIVISION, ANNUAL REPORT.

I 29.74/3:date   • Item 648-B-1
HABS/HAER REVIEW. [Annual]

I 29.75:CT
NATIONAL PARK SERVICE GOVERNOR'S BOOKS
[by State].

I 29.76:date   • Item 648-D
NATIONAL REGISTER OF HISTORIC PLACES. 1959–
    See also I 70.17

I 29.76/2:date   • Item 648-D
ADVISORY LIST OF NATIONAL REGISTER OF
HISTORIC PLACES.

I 29.76/3:nos.   • Item 648-D
NATIONAL REGISTER OF HISTORIC PLACES
BULLETINS. 1–   [Irregular]

I 29.76/4   • Item 648-D-1 (EL)
NATIONAL REGISTER INFORMATION SYSTEM. (online
database)

I 29.77:nos.   • Item 648-E
ANTHROPOLOGICAL PAPERS (numbered). 1–

I 29.78:nos.   • Item 646-F
URBAN ECOLOGY SERIES. 1–   1971–   [Irregu-
lar]

I 29.79:CT
WILDERNESS RECOMMENDATIONS FOR [various
areas]. [Irregular]
    PURPOSE:– To presents recommendations
sent by the President to Congress with respect
to the designation as wilderness of lands within
units of the National Park System in accordance
with provisions of the Wilderness Act of 1964.

I 29.79/2:CT
INTERPRETIVE PROSPECTUS (series). [Irregular]
    PURPOSE:– To provide interpretive concepts
of a particular National Park Service area or areas.

I 29.79/3:CT   • Item 651-B-5
GENERAL MANAGEMENT PLAN (and/or) DEVELOP-
MENT CONCEPT PLAN.
    Previously: General Management Plan.

I 29.79/4:CT
HISTORICAL BASE MAPS (series). [Irregular]

I 29.79/5   • Item 651-B-5 (MF)
ENVIRONMENTAL ASSESSMENT (Series).

I 29.79/6:CT • **Item 651-B-8 (MF)**
ENVIRONMENTAL IMPACT STATEMENT.

I 29.80:nos. • **Item 646-G**
SCIENTIFIC MONOGRAPH SERIES. 1– 1973–
[Irregular]

I 29.81:nos.
FINAL ENVIRONMENTAL STATEMENTS.

I 29.81/2:nos.
DRAFT ENVIRONMENTAL STATEMENTS.

I 29.82:CT • **Item 646-K**
BIBLIOGRAPHIES AND LISTS OF PUBLICATIONS.

29.83:date • **Item 646-M**
GRANTS-IN-AID CATALOGUE. [Annual]

I 29.84:nos. • **Item 646-J (P) (EL)**
PRESERVATION BRIEFS. 1– 1975– [Irregular]
See also I 70.12

I 29.84/2:CT • **Item 646-P**
HISTORIC AMERICAN ENGINEERING RECORD PUB-
LICATIONS. [Irregular]
Later I 70.9

I 29.84/2:C 28/976 • **Item 646-P**
HISTORIC AMERICAN ENGINEERING RECORD
CATALOG, 1976. 193 p. il.
Covers the period January 1, 1969 through
December 31, 1975.

I 29.84/3:nos. • **Item 646-J-1**
PRESERVATION TECH NOTES (series). 1–
[Irregular]
Series concerns the protection of significant
interior features of historic buildings during con-
struction.

I 29.84/3-2:nos. • **Item 646-J-1**
PRESERVATION TECH NOTES, HISTORIC INTERIOR
SPACES (series).

I 29.84/3-3:nos. • **Item 646-J-1**
PRESERVATION TECH NOTES, MUSEUM COLLEC-
TION STORAGE (series).

I 29.84/3-4:nos. • **Item 646-J-1**
PRESERVATION TECH NOTES, WINDOWS (series).

I 29.84/3-5:nos. • **Item 646-J-1**
PRESERVATION TECH NOTES, TEMPORARY PRO-
TECTION (series).

I 29.84/3-6:nos. • **Item 646-J-1**
PRESERVATION TECH NOTES, EXTERIOR WOOD-
WORK. [Irregular]

I 29.84/3-7 • **Item 646-J-1**
PRESERVATION TECH NOTES, MASONRY.

I 29.84/3-8:nos. • **Item 646-J-1**
PRESERVATION TECH NOTES, METALS.

I 29.84/3-9:nos. • **Item 646-J-1**
PRESERVATION TECH NOTES, MECHANICAL SYS-
TEMS.

I 29.84/3-10 • **Item 646-J-1 (MF)**
PRESERVATION TECH NOTES, DOORS.

I 29.84/3-11:nos. • **Item 868-J-1**
PRESERVATION TECH NOTES SITE (series).

I 29.84/3-12 • **Item 546-J-2**
PRESIDENT'S PARK NOTES, STATUES (series).

I 29.85:v.nos.&nos.
PARKS. v. 1– [Quarterly]
Sub-title: An International Journal for Manag-
ers of National Parks, Historic Sites, and Other
Projected Areas.
ISSN 0363-0617

I 29.86:CT • **Item 646-N-3**
CULTURAL RESOURCE MANAGEMENT STUDIES. [Ir-
regular]
See also I 70.11

I 29.86/2:v.nos.&nos. • **Item 646-N (EL)**
CULTURAL RESOURCES MANAGEMENT BULLETIN.
v. 1–

I 29.86/3 • **Item 646-N-3 (MF)**
CULTURAL RESOURCES REPORTS.

I 29.86/4 • **Item 646-N-3**
CULTURAL LANDSCAPE PUBLICATION. [Irregular]

I 29.87:v.nos.
EXPONENT. [Quarterly]
Sub-title: A Quarterly Publication of Planning
and Design Activities in the National Park Service.

29.88:CT • **Item 624-E-1**
HISTORIC STRUCTURE REPORTS.
See also I 70.10

I 29.88/2:CT
HISTORIC FURNISHING STUDY (series). [Irregular]

I 29.88/2-2:CT • **Item 624-E-1**
HISTORIC FURNISHINGS REPORT.

I 29.88/3:CT • **Item 648-E**
NATIONAL HISTORIC TRAILS (series). [Irregular]
Each issue is devoted to a single trail designated under the National Trails System Act. Contains a comprehensive plan for the trail's management and use through narrative, tables, charts,
and illustrations.

I 29.88/4:CT
HISTORIC STRUCTURE AND GROUNDS REPORT
(series). [Irregular]

I 29.88/5:CT • **Item 648-N**
SPECIAL HISTORY STUDIES (series). [Irregular]

I 29.88/6:CT • **Item 651**
NATIONAL HISTORIC PARK (series). [Irregular]

I 29.89:nos. • **Item 646-R**
NATURAL RESOURCES REPORTS. 1– [Irregular]

I 29.90:nos. • **Item 646-Q (MF)**
REPORTS OF THE CHACO CENTER. 1– 1977–
[Irregular]

I 29.91:nos. • **Item 646-W (MF)**
TRANSACTIONS AND PROCEEDINGS SERIES.
[Irregular]
Contains addresses and papers presented at
various symposiums and proceedings sponsored
by the National Park Service.

I 29.92:nos. • **Item 646-E**
PUBLICATIONS IN ANTHROPOLOGY (series). 1–
[Irregular] (Western Archeology Center)

I 29.93:v.nos.&nos. • **Item 646-T**
TRENDS. [Quarterly]
PURPOSE:– To provide topics of general in-
terest in park and recreation management and
programming.
See also I 70.22

I 29.94:date • **Item 646-L (MF)**
YELLOWSTONE GRIZZLY BEAR INVESTIGATIONS,
ANNUAL REPORT OF THE INTERAGENCY STUDY
TEAM.

I 29.94/2: • **Item 646-L-1 (MF)**
BEAR BIOLOGY ASSOCIATION: CONFERENCE SE-
RIES. [Irregular]

I 29.94/3: • **Item 646-L-1 (MF)**
BEAR BIOLOGY ASSOCIATION: MONOGRAPH SE-
RIES. [Irregular]

I 29.95:letters & nos. • **Item 646-Y (MF)**
REPORT (series). [Irregular] (South Florida Research
Center)

I 29.96:v.nos./nos. • **Item 648-T (MF)**
COURIER, THE NEWSMAGAZINE OF THE NATIONAL
PARK SERVICE. [Quarterly]
Contains features and articles on the activi-
ties, personnel, and historical aspects of the
National Park system.
Previous title: Courier, the National Park Ser-
vice Newsletter.

I 29.96/2:v.nos.&nos.
IN TOUCH, INTERPRETERS INFORMATION EX-
CHANGE. [Quarterly]

I 29.96/3:date • **Item 654**
GATEWAY NATIONAL RECREATION AREA PROGRAM
GUIDE. [Bimonthly]
Previous title: Gateway Outlook.

I 29.97:CT • **Item 650-A (MF)**
NATIONAL PRESERVES (series). [Irregular]
Consists of informational folders on individual
preserves. The preserve concept of the preserve
protects the resources but allows controlled extraction of minerals and other uses not normally
permitted in the National Park Service.

I 29.98:date • **Item 654-D (MF)**
GLEN ECHO PARK. [Quarterly]
Brochure on recreational activities.

I 29.99:nos.
CONTRIBUTIONS FROM THE CENTER FOR NORTH-
ERN STUDIES. [Irregular]

I 29.100:date • **Item 648-W (EL)**
CONSERVE-O-GRAM. [Irregular]

I 29.101:CT
ENVIRONMENTAL OVERVIEW AND ANALYSIS OF
MINING EFFECTS.

I 29.102:date • **Item 648-F (MF)**
PRESERVATION PLANNING SERIES, STATE PRO-
GRAM OVERVIEWS. [Annual]
Contains Program Overviews by region that
the States are required to prepare as part of their
Historic Preservation Fund grant applications.

I 29.103:date • **Item 648-G**
NATIONAL PARK SYSTEM AND RELATED AREAS,
INDEX. [Irregular]
Lists and briefly describes national parks,
monuments, historical sites, and related areas.

I 29.104:CT • **Item 624-E-7 (MF)**
PRESERVATION CASE STUDIES. [Irregular]
PURPOSE:– To provide a series of studies of
successful historic preservation projects, including economic benefits, energy savings, and other
aspects of interest to those concerned with the
preservation of historic structures.
Earlier I 70.12/2

I 29.104/2:CT • **Item 624-E-9 (MF)**
PRESERVATION PLANNING SERIES. [Irregular]
Earlier I 70.12/3

I 29.104/3:CT • **Item 624-E-7**
LOCAL PRESERVATION. [Irregular]

I 29.105:nos. • **Item 646-N-4 (MF)**
RESEARCH/RESOURCES MANAGEMENT REPORTS.
1– [Irregular] (Southern Region)

I 29.105/2:nos. • **Item 646-N-4 (MF)**
MIDWEST REGION: RESEARCH/RESOURCES MAN-
AGEMENT REPORTS.

I 29.106:CT • **Item 646-N-2 (MF)**
MANAGEMENT SERIES. [Irregular]
Earlier I 70.11/3

I 29.107:date • **Item 657-B-3**
LAND AND WATER CONSERVATION FUND GRANTS
MANUAL. [Irregular]
Subscription service includes basic manual
and supplementary material for an indeterminate
period.
Former title: Outdoor Recreation Grants-in-
Aid Manual.
Earlier I 66.8/2

I 29.107/2:date • **Item 657-B-3 (MF)**
LAND AND WATER CONSERVATION FUND, GRANTS-
IN-AID PROGRAM, ANNUAL REPORT. [Annual]

I 29.108:date • **Item 657-B-10**
FEDERAL RECREATION FEE REPORT. [Annual]
Earlier I 70.18

I 29.109:nos. • Item 648-K (MF)
TECHNICAL REPORTS. [Irregular]

I 29.110:date • Item 648-H (MF)
PARK AREAS AND EMPLOYMENT OPPORTUNITIES
FOR SUMMER. [Annual]
    PURPOSE:– To list by region, the park areas
and the approximate number of seasonal posi-
tions to be filled under such position options as
Interpretation, Law Enforcement, and General.

I 29.111:CT • Item 648-J (MF)
LAND PROTECTION PLAN (series). [Irregular]

I 29.112:nos. • Item 646-A-2
ARCHEOLOGICAL COLLECTION MANAGEMENT
PROJECT (ACMP) (series).
    Each numbered report is expected to con-
cern the Archeological Management Project for a
different historical site, such as the Minute Man
Historical Park in Massachusetts, and may consist of more than one volume.

I 29.113:date • Item 646-N-4
MIDWEST REGION ANNUAL SCIENCE REPORT.

I 29.114:date • Item 648-L (MF)
NATIONAL PARK STATISTICAL ABSTRACT. [Annual]
    Tables give number of visits and of overnight
stays at national parks over the last few years.
Also presents data on the public use of National
Park Service facilities by states.
    Earlier I 29.2:St 2/8

I 29.115:CT • Item 648-M
FORMS. [Irregular]

I 29.116:nos. • Item 646-N-5
SOUTHWEST CULTURAL RESOURCES CENTER:
PROFESSIONAL PAPERS. [Irregular]
    Includes professional papers on submerged
cultural resources throughout the National Park
System with an emphasis on historic shipwrecks,
such as Noquebay.

I 29.117:CT • Item 648-P
U.S. CONSTITUTION, A NATIONAL HISTORIC LAND-
MARK THEME STUDY. [Irregular]
    Commemorates the 1987 Bicentennial of the
Constitution.Identifies sites associated with land-
mark decisions of the Supreme Court and also
sites associated with giants of the Court.

I 29.117/2: • Item 648-P-1
DAMAGED AND THREATENED NATIONAL HISTORIC
LANDMARKS. [Annual]
    Describes those landmarks which are threat-
ened or damaged to such an extent that the
nationally significant features for which the sites
were designated are in danger of being irrevers-
ibly damaged or destroyed. Includes selected
photographs of endangered structures and sites.

I 29.117/3:CT • Item 648-P-1
LANDMARKS AT RISK. [Irregular]
I 29.117/4:date • Item 648-P-1
DAMAGED AND THREATENED NATIONAL NATURAL
LANDMARKS. [Annual]

I 29.118:date • Item 648-R (MF)
FEDERAL SURPLUS REAL PROPERTY PUBLIC
BENEFIT DISCOUNT PROGRAM, PARKS AND
RECREATION, REPORT TO CONGRESS. [Annual]
    Annual report concerning disposal of surplus
federal real property under the public benefit dis-
count program for parks and recreation purposes.
Lists number of properties by states.

I 29.119: • Item 646-R-1
HIGHLIGHTS OF NATURAL RESOURCES MANAGE-
MENT. [Annual]
    PURPOSE– To present highlights of a wide
range of NPS activities in managing its natural
resources programs. Contains articles on topics
as diverse as the Grizzly population in Yellowstone
National Park and use of prescribed fires to rep-
licate the natural cycle of fire and to help prevent
major uncontrolled fires.

I 29.120: • Item 648-S (MF)
CATALOG OF NATIONAL HISTORIC LANDMARKS.
[Biennial]
    Lists all National Historic Landmarks by state,

including buildings, structures, sites, and objects
of national significance.
    Earlier I 29.2:H 62/23

I 29.121: • Item 651-B-6
BUFFALO NATIONAL RIVER CURRENTS. [Annual]
    An annual publication in newspaper format
that informs visitors and others on the portion of
public lands managed by the staff of the Buffalo
National River. Contains information such as safety
tips, float trip planning, trails, things to see and
where to stay.

I 29.122: • Item 651-B-7
NATIONAL HERITAGE CORRIDOR JOURNAL. [Semi-
annual]
    A newspaper providing information about spe-
cial events and activities in the National Heritage
Corridor.

I 29.123:CT • Item 648-E
NATIONAL TRAILS DIRECTORY SERIES.

I 29.124:date • Item 646-R-1 (MF)
ANNUAL REPORT OF THE RIVERS AND TRAILS
CONSERVATION PROGRAMS.

I 29.125:date • Item 648-F
STATE OF THE ROCKY MOUNTAIN REGION. [An-
nual]

I 29.126:CT • Item 648-V
DIRECTORIES.

I 29.127:date • Item 646-K
CLEARINGHOUSE CLASSIFIEDS.

I 29.128:nos. • Item 648-T
TIMUCUAN TODAY AND TOMORROW, A NEWSLET-
TER FROM THE NATIONAL PARK SERVICE.

I 29.129 • Item 648-T (MF)
INTERPRETATION. [Quarterly]

I 29.130:date • Item 646-R-1
REPORT ON AMERICA'S NATIONAL SCENIC,
NATIONAL HISTORIC, AND NATIONAL RECRE-
ATION TRAILS (Fiscal Year).

I 29.131:nos. • Item 648-T
NEW ORLEANS JAZZ STUDY NEWSLETTER.

I 29.132 • Item 648-T
NPS STRATEGIC PLANNING, NATIONAL PARK SCAN.

I 29.133 • Item 648-T
THREE RIVERS REVIEW.

I 29.134:nos. • Item 648-T-2 (EL)
BATTLEFIELD UPDATE. [Monthly]

I 29.135:date/nos. • Item 648-T-1
OUTDOORS IN THE SANTA MONICA MOUNTAINS
NATIONAL RECREATION AREA.

I 29.136:no. • Item 648-T-3 (P) (EL)
NCPTT NOTES.

I 29.137 • Item 648-A-1 (E)
ELECTRONIC PRODUCTS. (Misc.)

I 29.138 • Item 653-A-2 (EL)
YELLOWSTONE WOLF PROJECT ANNUAL REPORT.

I 29.138/2 • Item 648-A-2 (EL)
YELLOWSTONE CENTER FOR RESOURCES. [An-
nual]

SOIL EROSION SERVICE
(1933–1935)

CREATION AND AUTHORITY

    The Soil Erosion Service was established
within the Department of the Interior in August
1933 pursuant to the National Industrial Recovery Act, approved June 16, 1933 (48 Stat. 201).
On March 25, 1935, the Service was transferred
to the Department of Agriculture (A 57).

I 30.1:date
ANNUAL REPORTS.

I 30.2:CT
GENERAL PUBLICATIONS.

I 30.3
BULLETINS.

I 30.4
CIRCULARS.

I 30.5
LAWS.

I 30.6
REGULATIONS.

I 30.7
MAPS.

I 30.8
POSTERS.

I 30.9:vol.
THE LAND, TODAY AND TOMORROW. [Monthly]

DIVISION OF SUBSISTENCE
HOMESTEADS
(1933–1935)

CREATION AND AUTHORITY

    The Division of Subsistence Homesteads was
established within the Department of the Interior
by Executive Order 6209 of July 21, 1933. The
Division was transferred to the Resettlement Administration (Y 3.R 31) on May 15, 1935.

I 31.1:date
ANNUAL REPORTS.

I 31.2:CT
GENERAL PUBLICATIONS.

I 31.3
BULLETINS.

I 31.4:nos.
CIRCULARS.

PETROLEUM ADMINISTRATIVE BOARD
(1933– 1935)

CREATION AND AUTHORITY

The Petroleum Administrative Board was established within the Department of the Interior by the Secretary of the Interior on September 11, 1933. The Board was terminated by Executive Order 7076 of June 15, 1935.

I 32.1:date
ANNUAL REPORTS.

I 32.2:CT
GENERAL PUBLICATIONS.

I 32.3
BULLETINS.

I 32.4
CIRCULARS.

I 32.5
LAWS.

I 32.6
REGULATIONS.

I 32.7
MAPS.

I 32.8
POSTERS.

I 32.9:nos.
CRUDE PETROLEUM REPORT BY REFINERIES.
[Monthly]
Later I 28.45

I 32.10:nos.
WEEKLY CRUDE OIL STOCK REPORT.
Later I 28.46

BOARD ON GEOGRAPHIC NAMES
(1934–)

CREATION AND AUTHORITY

The Board on Geographic Names was first established as the United States Board on Geographic Names by Executive Order 28 of September 4, 1890, as an independent agency. By Executive Order 493 of August 10, 1906, the name was changed to United States Geographic Board, which existed until April 17, 1934, when Executive Order 6680 abolished the Board and transferred its functions to the Department of the Interior. Departmental Order 1010, dated December 10, 1935, combined the functions of the Division of Geographic Names and the Advisory Committee on Geographic Names into one unit, called the United States Board on Geographic Names. The present Board on Geographic Names was established under the act of Congress, approved July 25, 1947 (61 Stat. 456).

INFORMATION

Board on Geographic Names
U.S. Geological Survey
12201 Sunrise Valley Dr.
523 National Center
Reston, VA 20192
(703) 648-4544
Fax: (703) 648-4549
http://geonames.usgs.gov/bgn.htm/

I 33.1:date
ANNUAL REPORTS.

I 33.2:CT   • Item 618
GENERAL PUBLICATIONS.

I 33.3:nos.
BULLETINS.

I 33.3/2   • Item 618-A (EL)
FOREIGN NAMES INFORMATION BULLETIN.

I 33.5:date
DECISIONS.
Earlier GB 1.5 and GB 1.5/2

I 33.5/2:nos.   • Item 617-A
DECISIONS OF GEOGRAPHIC NAMES IN THE UNITED STATES. [Annual]
The lists are designated by a composite numbering system, and first two digits denoting the year of publication, the next two digits the issue within the year.
Earlier: Decision Lists.
ISSN 0363-6828

I 33.5/3:nos.
RECOMMENDED LISTS.
These are lists of place names recommended by Division of Geography. Names approved by Board on Geographical Names are carried in Decisions, I 33.5/2.

I 33.6:CT
DECISIONS.

I 33.7:nos.
SPECIAL PUBLICATIONS. 1– 1943–

I 33.8   • Item 617
GAZETTEERS. 1– 1955– [Irregular]
Publication assumed by the Defense Mapping Agency (D 5.319).

I 33.8/2:CT   • Item 617
GAZETTEER SUPPLEMENTS. 1971– [Irregular]

PURPOSE:– To enable holders of published BGN gazetteers to update the entries that have been changed.

NATIONAL BITUMINOUS COAL COMMISSION
(1935– 1939)

CREATION AND AUTHORITY

The National Bituminous Coal Commission was established on September 21, 1935, pursuant to the Bituminous Coal Conservation Act of 1935, approved August 30, 1935. The Commission was abolished by Reorganization Plan No. 2 of 1939, effective July 1, 1939, and its functions transferred to the Bituminous Coal Division (I 46) of the Department of Interior.

I 34.1:date
ANNUAL REPORTS.
Later I 46.1

I 34.2:CT
GENERAL PUBLICATIONS.
Later I 46.2

I 34.6:CT
REGULATIONS, RULES, AND INSTRUCTIONS.

I 34.7:CT
MAPS.

I 34.9:nos.
GENERAL ORDERS (printed and processed).

I 34.10:nos.
SPECIAL ORDERS.

I 34.11:nos.
MEMORANDA.

I 34.12:nos.
OPINIONS.

I 34.13:nos.
ORDERS.
Later I 46.10

I 34.14:nos.
WEEKLY COAL REPORTS.
Earlier I 28.33
Later I 46.7

I 34.15:date
PRELIMINARY ESTIMATES OF PRODUCTION OF BITUMINOUS COAL. [Monthly]
Earlier I 28.31
Later I 46.11

I 34.16:nos.
DISTRIBUTION OF COAL SHIPMENTS. [Monthly]
Earlier I 28.24
Later I 46.8

I 34.17:dist.nos.
LIST OF BITUMINOUS COAL PRODUCERS WHO HAVE ACCEPTED BITUMINOUS COAL CODE PROMULGATED JUNE 21, 1937.
Later I 46.9

I 34.18:nos.
CLASSIFICATION SCHEDULES.
Class by schedule nos. with dist. nos. below.

I 34.19:nos.
PRICE SCHEDULES.
Class by schedule nos. with district numbers below.

I 34.20:CT
PAPERS IN RE.

I 34.21:date
BITUMINOUS COAL TABLES.
Earlier I 28.2:C 63/2
Later I 46.13

I 34.22:dist.nos.date
LIST OF CODE NUMBER PRODUCERS OF BITUMINOUS COAL.

OFFICE OF TERRITORIES
(1950– 1971)

CREATION AND AUTHORITY

The Office of Territories was established by the Secretary of the Interior on July 28, 1950, to assist in carrying out certain of his responsibilities pertaining to noncontiguous areas under the jurisdiction of the Government of the United States. Prior to that time territorial functions were performed by the Division of Territories and Island Possessions, which was established by a 1934 Executive order as a part of the Office of the Secretary. Abolished by Secretarial Order 2942, effective July 1, 1971, and powers, functions, and responsibilities transferred to the Deputy Assistant Secretary for Territorial Affairs in the Office of the Assistant Secretary-Public Land Management.

I 35.1:date
ANNUAL REPORTS.

I 35.2:CT   • Item 666
GENERAL PUBLICATIONS.

I 35.6:CT
REGULATIONS, RULES, AND INSTRUCTIONS.

I 35.7
PRESS RELEASES. [Irregular]

Territory of Alaska

I 35.10/1:date
ANNUAL REPORTS.
    Earlier I 1.5

I 35.10/2:CT
GENERAL PUBLICATIONS.

I 35.10/7:nos.
ALASKA RAILROAD, LOCAL PASSENGER TARIFFS.

I 35.10/8
RAILBELT REPORTER.

I 35.10/9
ALASKA RAILROAD, LOCAL FREIGHT TARIFFS.

I 35.10/11
PASSENGER CIRCULAR, ALASKA RAILROAD.

I 35.10/21
ALASKA ROAD COMMISSION. ANNUAL REPORTS.
    Earlier W 74.1

I 35.10/22
GENERAL PUBLICATIONS.
    Earlier W 74.2

Territory of Hawaii

I 35.11/1:date
ANNUAL REPORTS.
    Earlier I 1.41
I 35.11/2:CT
GENERAL PUBLICATIONS.

Puerto Rico

I 35.12/1:date
ANNUAL REPORTS OF THE GOVERNOR.
    Earlier W 75.1

I 35.12/2:CT
GENERAL PUBLICATIONS.

I 35.12/5:letters-nos.
ACTS AND RESOLUTIONS OF LEGISLATURE.
    Earlier W 75.12

Virgin Islands
I 35.13/1:date   • Item 671
GOVERNOR OF THE VIRGIN ISLANDS. [Annual]

I 35.13/2:CT   • Item 672
GENERAL PUBLICATIONS.
    Earlier I 1.65/2

I 35.13/3:nos.
BULLETINS.
    Earlier I 1.65/3

I 35.13/4:CT
LAWS ADMINISTERED BY GOVERNOR OF VIRGIN
    ISLANDS.

I 35.13/5:CT
LAWS ADMINISTERED BY GOVERNOR OF VIRGIN
    ISLANDS.

Dominican Customs Receivership

I 35.14/1:date
ANNUAL REPORTS.
    Earlier W 6.13/1

I 35.14/5:CT
LAWS.

Guam

I 35.15/1:date   • Item 672-A
ANNUAL REPORTS, GOVERNOR OF GUAM. [Annual]

I 35.15/2:CT
GENERAL PUBLICATIONS.

I 35.15/5:CT
LAWS.

High Commissioner of Trust Territory of Pacific Islands

I 35.16/1:date   • Item 670-A
ANNUAL REPORTS. 1952–   [Annual]

I 35.16/2:CT
GENERAL PUBLICATIONS.

I 35.16/8:date
REPORT OF TRUST TERRITORY OF PACIFIC IS-
LANDS TRANSMITTED TO UNITED NATIONS.

American Samoa

I 35.17/1   • Item 668-A
ANNUAL REPORT OF GOVERNOR TO SECRETARY
   OF INTERIOR. 1951–   [Annual]

I 35.17/2:CT
GENERAL PUBLICATIONS.

PUERTO RICO RECONSTRUCTION ADMINISTRATION
(1935– 1955)

CREATION AND AUTHORITY

    The Puerto Rico Reconstruction Administra-
tion was established within the Department of the
Interior by Executive Order 7057 of May 28, 1935.
The Administration was abolished effective Feb-
ruary 15, 1955, pursuant to Joint Resolution of
Congress, approved August 15, 1953 (67 Stat.
584), and its records transferred to the Office of
Territories (I 35).

I 36.1:date
ANNUAL REPORTS.

I 36.2:CT
GENERAL PUBLICATIONS.

I 36.3:nos.
BULLETINS.

MOTION PICTURES DIVISION
(1935– 1939)

I 37.1:date
ANNUAL REPORTS.

I 37.2:CT
GENERAL PUBLICATIONS.

GRAZING SERVICE
(1939– 1946)

CREATION AND AUTHORITY

    The Division of Grazing Control was estab-
lished within the Department of the Interior pursuant to the Taylor Grazing Act, approved June 28,
1934 (48 Stat. 1269). The name was changed to
Grazing Service by Departmental Order 1416,
effective August 26, 1939. Reorganization Plan
No. 3 of 1946, merged the Grazing Service with
the General Land Office to form the Bureau of
Land Management (I 53).

I 38.1:date
ANNUAL REPORTS.

I 38.2:CT
GENERAL PUBLICATIONS.

I 38.3:vol.
GRAZING BULLETINS. [Quarterly]

I 38.4:nos.
CIRCULARS.

I 38.6:CT
REGULATIONS, RULES, AND INSTRUCTIONS.

I 38.7:nos.
FIRE FIGHTING BULLETINS.

OFFICE OF CONSUMERS' COUNSEL
(1935– 1939)

CREATION AND AUTHORITY

    The Office of Consumers' Counsel was es-
tablished within the National Bituminous Coal
Commission (I 34) by the Bituminous Coal Conservation Act of 1935, approved August 30, 1935
(49 Stat. 993). The Office was abolished by Reorganization Plan No. 2, of 1939, effective July 1,
1939, and its functions transferred to the Office
of the Solicitor (I 48.50) of the Department of the
Interior.

I 39.1:date
ANNUAL REPORTS.
    Later I 48.51

I 39.2:CT
GENERAL PUBLICATIONS.
    Later I 48.52

I 39.3:letters-nos.
BULLETINS.

I 39.7:nos.
CONSUMER IDEAS.

I 39.8:vol.
COAL CONSUMERS' DIGEST.
    Later I 48.58

HOUSING AUTHORITY
(1937– 1939)

CREATION AND AUTHORITY

    The United States Housing Authority was es-
tablished within the Department of the Interior by
the United States Housing Act, approved September 1, 1937 (50 Stat. 888). The Authority was
transferred to the Federal Works Agency (FW 3)
by Reorganization Plan No. 1 of 1939, effective
July 1, 1939.

I 40.1:date
ANNUAL REPORTS.
    Later FW 3.1

I 40.2:CT
GENERAL PUBLICATIONS.
    Later FW 3.2

I 40.6:CT
LAWS.
    Later FW 3.5

I 40.7:date
STATUS OF SLUM-CLEARANCE AND LOW-RENT HOUSING PROJECTS. [Monthly]
Earlier Y 3.F 31/4:P 92/2

I 40.8:CT
ADDRESSES.
Later FW 3.8

I 40.9:nos.
REVIEW OF SOME RECENT MAGAZINE ARTICLES RELATING TO HOUSING.

I 40.10:nos.
BULLETINS ON POLICY AND PROCEDURE.
Later FW 3.9

I 40.11:nos.
TECHNICAL INFORMATION NOTES.
Later FW 3.11

PETROLEUM CONSERVATION DIVISION
(1936– 1946)

This class (I 41) was assigned to the SuDocs Classification Scheme but apparently never was used.

CIVILIAN CONSERVATION DIVISION

This class (I 42) was assigned to the SuDocs Classification Scheme but apparently never was used.

INFORMATION DIVISION
(1938– 1945)

I 43.1:date
ANNUAL REPORTS.

I 43.2:CT
GENERAL PUBLICATIONS.

I 43.7:vol.
CURRENT CONSERVATION. [Monthly]

I 43.8:nos.
WHAT PRICE AMERICA. [Weekly]
Radio scripts.

I 43.9:date
MOTION PICTURES DISTRIBUTED BY PHOTO-GRAPHIC SECTION.
Earlier I 37.2:M 85/3

BONNEVILLE POWER ADMINISTRATION
(1937– 1977)

CREATION AND AUTHORITY
    The Bonneville Power Administration was created pursuant to the act of August 20, 1937 (50 Stat. 731, as amended; 16 U.S.C. 832 et seq.). The Administration was transferred to the Department of Energy by act of August 4, 1977 (91 Stat. 565), effective October 1, 1977.

I 44.1:date
ANNUAL REPORTS.

I 44.2:CT   • Item 606-A-1
GENERAL PUBLICATIONS.

I 44.5:CT   • Item 606-A
LAWS.

I 44.6:CT
REGULATIONS, RULES, AND INSTRUCTIONS.

I 44.7:nos.
BONNEVILLE POWER NEWS. 1-1–   1939– 1940.
(PH nos.)

I 44.8
GENERATION AND SALES STATISTICS. 1938/39– [Semiannual]

    One release published for calendar year and one for fiscal year.
    Tables include summary of sales by calendar (or fiscal) years; electric energy account; summary of sales by classes of customers and by rate schedules; sales of electric energy by the Bonneville Power Administration, giving maximum KW demand, energy deliveries, and revenue, by purchaser. Charts.

I 44.9:CT
ECONOMIC BASE FOR POWER MARKETS.

I 44.10:nos.
RELEASES.

I 44.11:CT
BIBLIOGRAPHIES AND LISTS OF PUBLICATIONS.

I 44.12:date
ADVANCE PROGRAM. [Annual]

BUREAU OF FISHERIES
(1939– 1940)

CREATION AND AUTHORITY
    The Bureau of Fisheries (C 6) was transferred from the Department of Commerce to the Department of the Interior by Reorganization Plan No. 2 of 1939, effective July 1, 1939. Reorganization Plan No. 3 of 1940 merged the Bureau of Fisheries with the Bureau of Biological Survey (I 47) to form the Fish and Wildlife Service (I 49).

I 45.1:date
ANNUAL REPORTS.
Earlier C 6.1
Later I 49.1

I 45.2:CT
GENERAL PUBLICATIONS.
Earlier C 6.2
Later I 49.2

I 45.3:nos.
BULLETINS.
Earlier C 6.3/2
Later I 49.27

I 45.7:nos.
FISHERIES SERVICE BULLETINS. [Monthly]
Earlier C 6.9
Later I 49.7

I 45.8:nos.
STATISTICAL BULLETINS.
Earlier C 6.5
Later I 49.8

I 45.9:vol.
FISHERY MARKET NEWS. [Monthly]
Earlier C 6.18
Later I 49.10

I 45.10:date&nos.
LIBRARY BULLETINS, RECENT ACCESSIONS.
Earlier C 6.16
Later I 49.38

I 45.11:date
LAWS AND REGULATIONS FOR PROTECTION OF COMMERCIAL FISHERIES OF ALASKA.
Earlier C 1.4:241/1-25
Later I 49.24

I 45.12:nos.
MEMORANDUM [Inquiry].
Pubs. desig. 1-nos.
Earlier C 6.14
Later I 49.11

I 45.13:nos.
[MEMORANDUM, SCIENTIFIC].
Pubs. desig. Memo-S-nos.
Earlier C 6.15
Later I 49.20

I 45.14:CT
ADDRESSES.
Later I 49.25

I 45.15:date
PACIFIC SALMON PACK.
Earlier C 6.11
Later I 49.23

I 45.16:nos.
PUBLICATIONS (lists of).
Pubs. desig. A-no.

I 45.17:nos.
[PUBLICATIONS OF INTEREST TO SPORT FISHERMAN.]
Publications designated BB-no.
Earlier C 6.17

I 45.18:nos.
SPECIAL SCIENTIFIC REPORTS.
Later I 49.15

I 45.19:nos.
INVESTIGATIONAL REPORTS.
Earlier C 6.12

I 45.20:nos.
CIRCULAR ORDERS. INTER-OFFICE SERIES.

I 45.21:nos.
SPECIAL MEMORANDUM SERIES. [Proc.]

BITUMINOUS COAL DIVISION
(1939– 1943)

CREATION AND AUTHORITY
    The Bituminous Coal Division was established within the Department of the Interior on July 1, 1939, by Secretary's Order 1394 of June 16, 1939, pursuant to Reorganization Act of 1939 and Reorganization Plan No. 2 of 1939, to succeed the National Bituminous Coal Commission (I 34). The Division was abolished on August 24, 1943.

I 46.1:date
ANNUAL REPORTS.
Earlier I 34.1
Later I 51.1

I 46.2:CT
GENERAL PUBLICATIONS.
Earlier I 34.2
Later I 52.2

I 46.6:CT
REGULATIONS, RULES, AND INSTRUCTIONS.
Later I 50.6

I 46.7:nos.
COAL REPORTS. [Weekly]
Earlier I 34.14
Later I 51.7

I 46.8:nos.
DISTRIBUTION OF COAL SHIPMENTS. [Monthly]
Earlier I 34.16
Later I 51.8

I 46.9:district nos.&pt.nos.
LIST OF BITUMINOUS COAL PRODUCERS WHO
HAVE ACCEPTED BITUMINOUS COAL CODE
PROMULGATED JUNE 21, 1927.
Earlier I 34.17

I 46.10:nos.
ORDERS.
Earlier I 34.13

I 46.11:date
PRELIMINARY ESTIMATES OF PRODUCTION OF
BITUMINOUS COAL. [Monthly]
Earlier I 34.15
Later I 51.9

I 46.12:CT
BITUMINOUS COAL DIVISION, PAPERS IN RE.

I 46.13:date
BITUMINOUS COAL TABLES.
Earlier I 34.21

I 46.14:date
REGISTERED DISTRIBUTORS UNDER BITUMINOUS
COAL ACT OF 1937 [lists].

I 46.15:date
REGISTERED BONA FIDE AND LEGITIMATE FARM-
ERS' COOPERATIVE ORGANIZATIONS UNDER
BITUMINOUS COAL ACT OF 1937.

I 46.16:vol.
DECISIONS AND ORDERS.

I 46.17
DOCKETS.

BUREAU OF BIOLOGICAL
SURVEY
(1939– 1940)

CREATION AND AUTHORITY

The Bureau of Biological Survey (A 5) was
transferred from the Department of Agriculture to
the Department of the Interior by Reorganization
Plan No. 2 of 1939, effective July 1, 1939. Reorganization Plan No. 3 of 1940, effective June 30,
1940, consolidated the Bureau of Biological Survey with the Bureau of Fisheries (I 45) to form the
Fish and Wildlife Service (I 49).

I 47.1:date
ANNUAL REPORTS.
Earlier A 5.1

I 47.2:CT
GENERAL PUBLICATIONS.
Earlier A 5.2

I 47.6:CT
REGULATIONS, RULES, AND INSTRUCTIONS.
Later I 49.6

I 47.7:nos.
WILDLIFE LEAFLETS.
Earlier A 5.11
Later I 49.13

I 47.8:nos.
POSTERS (numbered).
Earlier A 5.9
Later I 49.14

I 47.9:nos.
WILDLIFE REVIEW.
Earlier A 5.12
Later I 49.17

I 47.10:v.nos.
BIRD BANDING NOTES.
Earlier A 5.15
Later I 49.21

I 47.11:nos.
WILDLIFE CIRCULARS.
Later I 49.16

I 47.12:CT
LISTS OF PUBLICATIONS
Earlier A 5.13
Later I 49.18

I 47.13:CT
ADDRESSES.
Earlier A 5.14
Later I 49.25

I 47.14:nos.
WILDLIFE RESEARCH BULLETINS.
Later I 49.19

SOLICITOR
(1941–   )

INFORMATION

Information Services
Office of the Solicitor
Department of the Interior
1849 C St. NW
Washington, D. C. 20240
(202) 208-5763
Fax: (202) 208-5584
http://www.doi.gov/sol/

I 48.1:date
ANNUAL REPORTS.

I 48.2:CT
GENERAL PUBLICATIONS.

I 48.6:CT   • Item 665
LAWS.

I 48.8:CT
ADDRESSES.

I 48.9:nos.
DIGEST OF TTEMS IN CONGRESSIONAL RECORD
OF APPARENT INTEREST TO DEPARTMENT OF
INTERIOR.

CONSUMERS' COUNSEL
DIVISION
(1939– 1941)

CREATION AND AUTHORITY

The Consumers' Counsel Division was established within the Office of the Solicitor of the
Department of the Interior by Departmental Order
1400, effective July 1, 1939, to succeed the
Office of Consumers' Counsel (I 39) of the National Bituminous Coal Commission. The Division
was abolished by act of Congress, approved April
11, 1941, and its functions transferred to the
Office of the Bituminous Coal Consumers's Counsel (Y 3.B 54/2).

I 48.51:date
ANNUAL REPORTS.
Earlier I 39.1

I 48.52:CT
GENERAL PUBLICATIONS.
Earlier I 39.2

I 48.57:CT
PAPERS IN RE.

I 48.58:vol.
COAL CONSUMERS' DIGEST. [Monthly]
Earlier I 39.8

FISH AND WILDLIFE SERVICE
(1940–   )

CREATION AND AUTHORITY

The Fish and Wildlife Service was established
within the Department of the Interior under Reorganization Plan No. 3 of 1940, effective June 30,
1940, by the consolidation of the Bureau of Fisheries (I 45) and the Bureau of Biological Survey (I
47). Pursuant to the Fish and Wildlife Act of 1956
(70 Stat. 1119), the United States Fish and Wildlife Service was established by the Secretary of
the Interior to succeed and replace the Fish and
Wildlife Service, effective November 5, 1956

INFORMATION

Fish and Wildlife Service
Department of the Interior
1849 C St. NW
Washington, D. C. 20240
Fax: (202) 208-6965
Toll Free: (800) 344-9453
http://www.fws.gov

I 49.1:date   • Item 613-C (MF)
ANNUAL REPORTS.
Earlier Biological Survey, Annual Reports I
47.1 and Fisheries Bureau, Annual Reports, C
6.1.

I 49.1/2   • Item 613-A
REPORT OF BUREAU OF COMMERCIAL FISHERIES
FOR CALENDAR YEAR (date). 1957–   [Annual]

I 49.1/3:date
ANNUAL REPORT, BUREAU OF SPORT FISHERIES
AND WILDLIFE. (Division of Wildlife Services,
Carolinas District)

I 49.1/4:date
REGION 4: ANNUAL REPORT.

I 49.1/5:date   • Item 614-E (MF)
COOPERATIVE FISHERY UNITS ANNUAL REPORT.

I 49.1/6:date   • Item 616-E (MF)
SPORT FISHERY AND WILDLIFE RESEARCH. 1972–
[Annual] (Box 25486, Denver Federal Center,
Denver, Colorado 80225) (Division of Research)
PURPOSE:– To provide information on the
activities of the Division of Research during the
fiscal year.
Formed by the union of the Progress is Sport
Fishery Research, with Wildlife Research Prob-
lems, Programs, Progress published in the Re-
source Publications (series) (I 49.66).
ISSN 0362-0700

I 49.1/7:   • Item 613-C-1 (MF)
ANNUAL REPORT, DIVISION OF LAW ENFORCE-
MENT.

I 49.1/8:date   • Item 613-C-2
BIENNIAL REPORT TO THE PRESIDENT OF THE
UNITED STATES.

I 49.2:CT   • Item 612
GENERAL PUBLICATIONS.

I 49.2:B 52   • Item 612
BIOLOGICAL SERVICES PROGRAM. [Annual]
ISSN 0148-5563

I 49.4:nos.   • Item 609
CIRCULARS.
See also C 55.304

I 49.4:16 • **Item 602**
MIGRATION OF BIRDS. 1950. 102 p. il. (Circular 16)

I 49.6:CT • **Item 612-E-1**
REGULATIONS, RULES AND INSTRUCTIONS.
[Irregular]
Earlier I 47.6

I 49.6/2:CT • **Item 612-E**
HANDBOOKS, MANUALS, GUIDES.

I 49.6/3
YOUR GUIDE TO FEDERAL WATERFOWL PRODUCTION AREAS. 1967– [Irregular]
Separate release for each State. Includes road map for the State over-printed showing location of waterfowl areas. Also includes a list of thelocations with directions from the nearest towns.

I 49.6/4:trans. nos.
LAW ENFORCEMENT MANUAL.

I 49.6/5 • **Item 612-E**
COAST ECOLOGICAL INVENTORY.

I 49.6/6:nos. • **Item 612-J (MF)**
FLORIDA COASTAL ECOLOGICAL INVENTORY CHARACTERIZATION, FWS/OBS– (series). [Irregular] (Division of Biological Services)

I 49.6/7:CT • **Item 612-K**
NATIONAL WETLANDS INVENTORY (various locations). [Irregular]

Issues describe and picture in black and white or color, various plant communities of the Wetlands.

I 49.6/7-nos. • **Item 611-W-1– 53 (MF)**
NATIONAL WETLANDS INVENTORY (maps) BY STATES, [State]. [Irregular]

I 49.6/7-2:nos. • **Item 611-W-1– 53 (MF)**
NATIONAL WETLANDS INVENTORY (maps, by States). [Irregular]

I 49.6/8:nos. • **Item 612-E (MF)**
IMPORT/EXPORT MANUAL, TRANSMITTAL LETTERS. 1– [Irregular]

I 49.7:nos.
FISHERIES SERVICE BULLETINS. 1– 307. [ ]–1940. [Monthly]

Earlier I 45.7
Later I 49.22

I 49.7/2: • **Item 612-N**
INFORMATION, REGION 6. [Irregular]
Bulletins may be technical in nature and contain drawings, diagrams, graphs, and tables.

I 49.8:nos.
STATISTICAL BULLETINS.
Superseded by I 49.8/2
Earlier I 45.8

I 49.8/2
CURRENT FISHERY STATISTICS.
See C 55.309/2

I 49.8/3
FROZEN FISH REPORT.

See C 55.309

I 49.8/4:
COLD STORAGE HOLDINGS OF FISHERY PRODUCTS.

I 49.8/5
HISTORICAL STATISTICS (series). HS 1– 1960– [Irregular]
Brief summaries giving annual data.

I 49.8/6
FOOD FISH, SITUATION AND OUTLOOKS, CEA-F- (series).
See C 55.309/5

I 49.8/7:v.nos.&nos.
FOOD FISH SITUATION AND OUTLOOK, ANNUAL REVIEW ISSUE. v. 1– 1964–

I 49.8/8:nos.
SHELLFISH SITUATION AND OUTLOOK, CEA-S (series).
See C 55.309/4

I 49.8/9
INDUSTRIAL FISHERY PRODUCTS, SITUATION AND OUTLOOK, CEA-I- (series).
See C 55.309/3

I 49.9:CT • **Item 612**
MAPS AND CHARTS.

I 49.10
COMMERCIAL FISHERIES REVIEW.
See C 55.310/2

I 49.11:nos.
MEMORANDUM (inquiry).
Pubs. desig. I-nos.
Earlier I 45.12

I 49.12:nos.
ALASKA GAME COMMISSION, CIRCULARS.
Earlier A 5.10/4

I 49.13 • **Item 616-B**
WILDLIFE LEAFLETS. I 41– 1939– [Irregular]
Correspondence aids, written in popular style on animals, birds, conservation, control of wildlife, predators and rodents, refuges, wildlife training and employment.
Leaflets 1– 140 were published by the Biological Survey and designated as BS-numbers.

BIG GAME INVENTORY FOR (year). [Annual]
Tables give, by State and species, kill and population estimation.
FUR CATCH IN THE UNITED STATES (year). [Annual]
Table gives fur catch, by State and species.
WILDLIFE IMPORTED INTO THE UNITED STATES. [Annual]

I 49.13/2:nos.
WILDLIFE MANAGEMENT SERIES LEAFLETS.

I 49.13/3:nos. • **Item 616-B**
WILDLIFE SERVICE LEAFLETS.
Issued by Wildlife Service Division.

I 49.13/4:nos. • **Item 616-B-1**
WILDLIFE LEAFLETS. 513– 1981– [Irregular]
Continues: Wildlife Service Leaflets (I 49.13/3), formerly distributed to Depository Libraries under Item 616-B.

I 49.13/5:nos. • **Item 616-B-1**
FISH AND WILDLIFE LEAFLETS. 1– 1984– [Irregular]

I 49.14:nos. • **Item 611-K**
POSTERS.
Earlier I 47.8

I 49.14/2:CT
AUDIOVISUAL MATERIALS. [Irregular]

I 49.15:nos.
SPECIAL SCIENTIFIC REPORTS.
Earlier I 45.18

I 49.15/2 • **Item 614-B**
– FISHERIES. 1– 1949–
Later C 55.312

MOURNING DOVE STATUS REPORT. [Annual]

WATERFOWL STATUS REPORT. [Annual]

WOODCOCK STATUS REPORT. [Annual]

I 49.15/3 • **Item 614-C (MF)**
– WILDLIFE. 1– 1949–
Merged with Technical Papers of U.S. Fish and Wildlife Service (I 49.68) to form Fish and Wildlife Technical Reports (I 49.100).

I 49.16:nos.
WILDLIFE CIRCULARS.
Superseded by I 49.4
Earlier I 47.11

I 49.17 • **Item 616-A**
WILDLIFE REVIEW. 1– 1935– [Quarterly]
Abstracting service for wildlife management, issued for the information of cooperators.
Indexed by: Biological Abstracts.
ISSN 0043-5511

I 49.17/2:date • **Item 616-A**
WILDLIFE ABSTRACTS.

I 49.18:CT • **Item 616-A-1**
BIBLIOGRAPHIES AND LISTS OF PUBLICATIONS. [Irregular]
Earlier I 47.12

I 49.18/2:nos.
NEW PUBLICATION LISTS (numbered). 1– 1942–

I 49.18/3:date
FISH AND WILDLIFE SERVICE PUBLICATIONS, PRINTED AND DUPLICATED MATERIAL. – 1969. [Monthly]

I 49.18/4:date
MONTHLY LIST OF OUTSIDE PUBLICATIONS AND ADDRESSES.

I 49.18/5 • **Item 611-C**
FISHERY AND OCEANOGRAPHY TRANSLATIONS. 1– 1964– [Irregular]
Prepared by the Bureau of Commercial Fisheries.
PURPOSE:– To provide information about translations of fishery and oceanography literature. It includes lists of translated Russian current titles, journal tables of content and short translations of articles.

I 49.18/6
PUBLICATIONS OF BUREAU OF SPORT FISHERIES AND WILDLIFE. [Annual]

I 49.18/8 • **Item 616-A-2**
FISH AND WILDLIFE REFERENCE SERVICE NEWSLETTER. [Quarterly]

I 49.18/9 • **Item 616-A-3**
PUBLICATIONS AVAILABLE FROM NORTHERN PRAIRIE SCIENCE CENTER. [Annual]

I 49.19:nos.
WILDLIFE RESEARCH BULLETINS.
Earlier I 47.14

I 49.20:nos.
[MEMORANDUM, SCIENTIFIC].
Pubs. desig. Memo. S-nos.
Earlier I 45.13

I 49.21:vol.
BIRD BANDING NOTES.
Earlier I 47.10

I 49.22:vol.
SERVICE SURVEY. v. 1– 1941– [Monthly]

I 49.23:date
PACIFIC SALMON PACK. –1941.
Earlier I 45.15

I 49.24:nos. • **Item 613 (MF)**
HUNTING REGULATIONS. 1– 1941–1975. [Irregular]
Informational pamphlets containing the text of current regulations.

I 49.24/2:date • **Item 613 (MF)**
SUMMARY OF FEDERAL HUNTING REGULATIONS
FOR (year). 1976– [Annual]
PURPOSE:– To inform hunters and all other
interested parties of the season dates, shooting
hours, daily bag and possession limits, and other
restrictions for hunting migratory game birds in
the United States under provisions of the Migratory Bird Treaty Act of July 3, 1918, as amended
(40 Stat. 755; 16 U.S.C. 703 et seq.).
The Secretary of the Interior annually adopts
hunting regulations to permit a reasonable harvest of migratory game birds and to leave an
adequate breeding stock for subsequent years.
To provide a sound basis for the regulations,
information is assembled each year on current
populations of birds and on numbers available for
harvesting. With a year's accumulation of data,
the Secretary establishes a framework of proposed hunting regulations, including season
lengths, bag and possession limits and the earliest opening and latest closing dates within which
the State conservation agencies recommend hunting seasons best suited to conditions in their
States. The resulting regulations under 50 CFR
20 are then pub lished in the FederalRegister and
a Summary prepared for distribution to Federal
and State conservation agencies who make the
Summaries available to hunters and other interested parties.
Covers the hunting, possession, transportation, and importation of mourning and white-winged
doves, wild pigeons, rails, woodcock, common
snipe, sea ducks, teal in September, and gallinules in the contiguous United States, Canada
geese in Wisconsin, and migratory birds in Alaska,
Hawaii, Puerto Rico, and the Virgin Islands.
Supersedes the former numbered regulatory
announcements (I 49.24).
Besides this general summary, separate summaries are issued for the following flyways:

I 49.24/3:date • **Item 613 (MF)**
ATLANTIC FLYWAY. [Annual]
Covers the hunting, possession, transportation and importation of ducks, geese, coots, gallinules, rails, woodcock, and snipe.

I 49.24/4:date • **Item 613 (MF)**
CENTRAL FLYWAY. [Annual]

Covers hunting, possession, transportation,
and importation of ducks, geese, coots, cranes,
gallinules, rails, woodcock, and snipe.

I 49.24/5:date • **Item 613 (MF)**
PACIFIC FLYWAY. [Annual]
Covers the hunting, possession, transportation, and importation of ducks, geese, brant,
swans, coots, gallinules, and snipe.

I 49.24/6:date • **Item 613 (MF)**
MISSISSIPPI FLYWAY. [Annual]
Covers hunting, possession, transportation,
and importation of ducks, geese, coots, gallinules,
rails, woodcock, and snipe.

I 49.25
ADDRESSES. [Irregular]

I 49.26 • **Item 614-A-1 (MF)**
RESEARCH REPORTS. 1– 1941– [Irregular]
Technical papers reporting the results of sci-
entific investigations. Publications issued in this
series are intended for a wider distribution than
those issued as Special Scientific Reports.
Formerly sent to depository libraries under
Item 614.

I 49.26/2
FISHERY INDUSTRY RESEARCH.
See C 55.311

I 49.26/2a
FIR [Fishery Industrial Research] REPRINTS. 1–
[Irregular]

I 49.27
FISHERY BULLETINS.
See C 55.313

I 49.28:nos.
FISHERY LEAFLETS. 1– 1941–

I 49.28/2 • **Item 610-B**
FISHERIES CENTER LEAFLETS. 1– 1965–

I 49.28/3 • **Item 611-J (MF)**
FISH DISEASE LEAFLETS, FDL- (series). FDL 1–
1966– [Irregular] (Bureau of Sport Fisheries
and Wildlife)

I 49.29:v.nos.-nos.
PITMAN-ROBERTSON QUARTERLY. v. 1– v. 14, no. 4.
1941– 1954.

I 49.29/2:v.nos.
DINGELL-JOHNSON QUARTERLY [Review of Accomplishments of Federal Aid in Fish Restoration Pro-
gram]. v. 1– 1953–

I 49.29/3:date • **Item 616-M-1 (MF)**
FEDERAL AID IN FISH AND WILDLIFE RESTORA-
TION. (Wildlife Management Institute and Sport
Fishing Institute) [Annual]

I 49.29/4:date • **Item 616-M-2**
STATISTICAL SUMMARY FOR FISH AND WILDLIFE
RESTORATION. [Annual]

All tabular presentation of statistics on fish
and wildlife restoration for 1939 to present.

I 49.30 • **Item 612-A (MF)**
NORTH AMERICAN FAUNA (series). 1– [Irregular]
Earlier A 5.5

I 49.31:nos.
BIRD MIGRATION MEMORANDUM.
Earlier A 5.16

I 49.32 • **Item 615**
STATISTICAL DIGESTS. 1– 1942–
Supersedes Administrative Reports. Consists
of the following sub-series.

ALASKA FISHERY AND FUR-SEAL INDUSTRIES.
[Annual]
Covers the fisheries of Alaska and the
fur-seal industry of the Pribilof Islands.

FISHERY STATISTICS OF THE UNITED STATES.
1939– [Annual]
Contains detailed statistics, analytic textual reviews, and graphic presentations on
the commercial fisheries of the United States.
Includes historical tables.
Published in the Statistical Digest since
1939. Data for 1958 were published in the
Administrative Report series of the Department of the Interior. Data prior to 1938 were
published in the Administrative Report Series
of the former Bureau of Fisheries.
Beginning with data for 1968, issued by
the National Marine Fisheries Service (C
55.316).

I 49.33:nos.
COMMERCIAL FISHERIES [market development lists].
1– 1944–

I 49.34:date
MONTHLY SUMMARY OF FISHERY TRADE, LAND-
INGS, RECEIPTS, PROCESSING, AND STOR-
AGE. 1– [ ]. 1943– 1945.

I 49.35:v.nos. • **Item 612-B**
PROGRESSIVE FISH CULTURIST. v. 1– 1934–
[Quarterly]
Contains articles of interest to fishery biolo-
gists and fish culturists.
Index contained in October issues.
Issued monthly, 1934– 1938; bimonthly 1939–
1941; suspended, 1941– 1946; quarterly 1947–
Indexed by:–
Biological Abstracts
Chemical Abstracts
Index to U.S. Government Periodicals
Nuclear Science Abstracts
ISSN 0033-0779

INDEXES.
Cumulative Subject and Author Index,
nos. 1– 56, 1934– 1941. (Resource Publication 24).

I 49.36 • **Item 610**
CONSERVATION IN ACTION. 1– 1947– [Irregu-
lar]
Popular, attractive booklets on various phases
of conservation.

I 49.36/2 • **Item 610**
CONSERVATION NOTES. 1– 1963– [Irregular]
PURPOSE:– To promote interest in the conservation and good use of our fish and wildlife
resources. Designed for school use, the leaflets
range in length from four to eight pages, and
punched for ring binder, and are illustrated with
line drawings.

I 49.37:nos.
COMMERCIAL FISHERIES [education leaflets]. 1–
1947–

I 49.38:v.nos.
LIBRARY BULLETINS. v. 1– v. 4, no. 12. 1946– 1949.
[Bimonthly]
Earlier I 45.10

I 49.39 • **Item 616**
TEST KITCHEN SERIES. 1– 1950– [Irregular]
Pamphlets on buying and cooking fish and
shellfish.

I 49.40 • **Item 609-B**
COMMERCIAL FISHERIES ABSTRACTS. v. 1– 1948–
[Monthly]
Monthly summary of important developments
for fishery industries.
Later C 55.310/2

I 49.40/2:v.nos.&nos. • **Item 614-A**
FISHERIES REVIEW. v. 1– 1955– [Quarterly]
Former title: Sport Fishery Abstract.
ISSN 0038-786X

I 49.41:nos.
COMMERCIAL FISHERIES [Economics Cooperative
Marketing Leaflets]. 1– 1946–

I 49.42:nos./date • **Item 614-A**
SL [Statistical Lists] (series). 1– 1962– [Irregu-
lar] (Bureau of Commercial Fisheries)

I 49.43:
SPECIAL MEMORANDUM SERIES.

I 49.44 • **Item 612-C**
REFUGE LEAFLETS. 1– 1953– [Irregular]
Each leaflet is 4-pages and describes a par-
ticular National Wildlife Refuge.

I 49.44/2:CT • **Item 612-C**
NATIONAL WILDLIFE REFUGES [Information Circulars,
Bird Lists, Etc.] (unnumbered).

I 49.44/3:CT   • **Item 612-C (MF)**
NATIONAL WILDLIFE REFUGES PLANNING UPDATE
(various locations). [Irregular]

I 49.44/4   • **Item 612-C**
REFUGES 2003: A PLAN FOR THE FUTURE OF THE
NATIONAL WILDLIFE REFUGE SYSTEM. [Irregular]

I 49.45
[PRESS RELEASES]. [Irregular]

I 49.46
COMMERCIAL FISHERIES TECHNOLOGY LEAFLETS.
TL 1–   [Irregular]

I 49.47:date
QUARTERLY PROGRESS REPORTS, WILDLIFE RE-
SEARCH LABORATORY, DENVER, COLORADO.

I 49.47/2:nos.
RESEARCH ON BIRD REPELLENTS, PROGRESS RE-
PORTS. 1–   1956–

I 49.47/3:nos.
WILDLIFE RESEARCH LABORATORY: TECHNICAL
NOTES. 1–   1959–

I 49.47/4:nos.   • **Item 614-D (MF)**
WILDLIFE RESEARCH REPORTS. 1–   1972–
[Irregular] See I 49.99

I 49.47/5:date
WILDLIFE RESEARCH CENTER, DENVER, COLO-
RADO: ANNUAL REPORT.

I 49.48
OPERATIONS OF THE BUREAU OF COMMERCIAL
FISHERIES UNDER THE SALTONSTALL-
KENNEDY ACT. 1955–   [Annual]

   Submitted by the Bureau to Congress pursuant to provisions of the Act of July 1, 1954 (68
Stat. 376), as amended by the Fish and Wildlife
Act of 1956 (70 Stat. 1119) for the fiscal year.
   The Act makes available funds from import
duties collected on foreign fishery products for
the promotion of the free flow in commerce of
domestic fishery products and provides for a wide
range of research and services supporting the
development and utilization of the nation's fishery resources and stabilization of the domestic
fishing industry.
   Reports covers the operations conducted by
or under contract with the Bureau of Commercial
Fisheries to encourage the distribution of domes-
tically produced fishery products.

I 49.49:CT   • **Item 611-A**
FISHERIES MARKETING BULLETINS, SPECIAL.
   Discontinued.

I 49.49/2:nos.   • **Item 611-F**
FISHERY MARKETING DEVELOPMENT SERIES. 1–
1966–   [Irregular]

I 49.50:date
MOURNING DOVE NEWSLETTER. [Annual]

I 49.50/2:date
BUREAU OF SPORT AND FISHERIES AND WILD-
LIFE'S IN-SIGHT.
   Discontinued.

I 49.51
SOMETHING ABOUT (series). SA 1–   1962–
[Irregular]

   Two-page correspondence aids, aimed at answering questions children might have concerning fish and wildlife conservation.

I 49.52
MARKET NEWS LEAFLETS. 1–   [Irregular]

   Concerns the fishing industries of foreign
countries, each leaflet devoted to a particular
country or a particular type of fishing in a group
of countries.

I 49.52/2:CT/date
MARKET NEWS SERVICE (Regional) PUBLICATIONS.

I 49.53
BRANCH OF FISHERY MANAGEMENT. ANNUAL RE-
PORT. 1961–   [Irregular]

49.53/2:CT/date
ANNUAL PROJECT REPORT, FISHERY MANAGE-
MENT PROGRAM.

I 49.53/3:date
DIVISION OF FISHERY SERVICES, REGION 4:
ANNUAL REPORT.

I 49.54
EDUCATIONAL AIDS. 1–   1962–   [Irregular]

   Posters.

I 49.55:date
ANNUAL WATERFOWL REPORT, ALASKA.

I 49.55/2:nos.
PACIFIC WATERFOWL FLYWAY REPORT.

I 49.56:date
FISH AND WILDLIFE REPORT.
   Issued as administrative aid.

I 49.57:nos.
MANUSCRIPT REPORTS, MR- (series).
   Issued by Biological Laboratory, Auke Bay,
   Alaska [not considered a publication].

I 49.58:nos.
FISH PROTEIN CONCENTRATE, REPORTS. 1–
1962–

I 49.59:nos.
DATA REPORT. 1–   1964–

   Microfiche only.
   Later C 55.324

I 49.60:date
GULF COAST SHRIMP DATA. [Monthly]
   Later I 49.8/2

I 49.61:date
ANNUAL REPORT OF THE SOUTHWESTERN
DISTRICT BRANCH OF PREDATOR & RODENT
CONTROL.

I 49.62:nos.
WOODS HOLE LABORATORY. REPORT.

I 49.63:nos.
FISH-PASSAGE RESEARCH PROGRAM PROGRESS
REPORTS. OFFICIAL USE.

I 49.64:CT
WETLANDS INVENTORIES.

I 49.65:   • **Item 611-E**
FISHERY PRODUCTS REPORT. [Daily, Monthly, and
Annual]
   Discontinued.

I 49.66   • **Item 613-B (MF)**
RESOURCE PUBLICATIONS. 1–   1965–   [Irregu-
lar]

   COOPERATIVE FISHERY UNIT REPORT. [An-
   nual] (Division of Fishery Services, Branch of
   Cooperative Fishery Units)

   DIVISION OF FISHERIES SERVICES ANNUAL
   REPORT.

   NATIONAL SURVEY OF FISHING AND HUNT-
   ING. [Irregular]

   NATIONAL WILDLIFE REFUGES. [Annual]

   PROGRESS IN SPORT FISHERY RESEARCH.
   [Annual]

      Covers pathology, nutrition, husbandry,
   public waters, environment. Also includes list
   of publications, manuscripts in press, special reports and major addresses.
      Prior to 1965, published as Circulars.
   WILDLIFE RESEARCH PROBLEMS, PRO-
   GRAMS, PROGRESS, (year). [Annual]
      Activities of the Division of Wildlife Re-

search of the Bureau of Sport Fisheries and
Wildlife for the calendar year.
Previously issued in Circular series.

I 49.66/2:   • **Item 613-B**
NEW PUBLICATIONS. [Quarterly] See I 49.66/3

I 49.66/3   • **Item 613-B (MF)**
NEW PUBLICATIONS, DENVER OFFICE. (Research
and Development) [Annual]

I 49.67
RESOURCE STATUS REPORTS. 1–

   DIVISION OF FISHERY MANAGEMENT
   SERVICE. ANNUAL REPORT. 1961–
   [Annual]
      Report for 1963 issued as Circular 194.

I 49.68   • **Item 615-A (MF)**
TECHNICAL PAPERS. 1–   1966–   [Irregular]
(Bureau of Sport Fisheries and Wildlife)

   Papers 1-3 published together.
   Merged with Special Scientific Reports: Wild-
life (I 49.15/3) to form Fish and Wildlife Technical
Reports (I 49.100).

I 49.69   • **Item 610-C (MF)**
FISH DISTRIBUTION REPORTS. 1–   1967–
[Irregular]

I 49.70:nos.   • **Item 610-D (MF)**
INVESTIGATIONS IN FISH CONTROL. 1–   1964–
[Irregular] (Fish Control Laboratories, Bureau
of Sports Fisheries and Wildlife)

   PURPOSE:– To publish results of work at the
Bureau's Fish Control Laboratories at La Crosse,
Wisconsin and War Springs, Georgia, and other
studies related to that work.
   For economic reasons, two or more reports
may be issued under a single cover.

I 49.71:nos.   • **Item 616-C-1**
WILDLIFE PORTRAIT SERIES. 1–   1969–
[Irregular]

   PURPOSE:– To provide colored illustrations,
suitable for framing, of our wild animal life. Sets
consist of 10 illustrations, 17 x 14 inches, accompanied by descriptive sheets for each illustration. Discontinued No. 5.

I 49.71/2:CT
POSTERS.

I 49.72:nos.
FTA [Field Training Aids] (series).

I 49.73:date   • **Item 611-H**
ACCIDENT CONTROL REPORTS. [Annual] (Bureau
of Sport Fisheries and Wildlife)

   Presents statistics in tabular and graphic form
concerning work injuries, traffic accidents, injury
frequency and patterns, accident causes and
prevention. Discontinued.

I 49.74:nos.   • **Item 611-G**
FOREIGN GAME LEAFLETS (numbered). FGL 1–
1970–   [Irregular] (Bureau of Sport Fisheries
and Wildlife)

   Each leaflet describes one species of foreign
game, including information on identification, habitat, climate, food, behavior and general habits,
abundance, interbreeding and competition, relation to agriculture, sporting characteristics, introductions and propagation, and bibliographical references.
   Punched for 3-ring binder.
   Discontinued.

I 49.75:date
QUARTERLY REPORT OF PROGRESS AT FISH CON-
TROL LABORATORY, LA CROSSE, WISCONSIN,
SOUTHEASTERN FISH CONTROL LABORATORY,
WARM SPRINGS, GEORGIA, AND HAMMOND
BAY BIOLOGICAL STATION, MILLERSBURG,
MICHIGAN.

I 49.76:nos.   • Item 611-I
FINAL ENVIRONMENTAL STATEMENTS. [Irregular]

I 49.77:v.nos.&nos.   • Item 611-L (EL)
ENDANGERED SPECIES BULLETIN. v. 1–   1976–
[Monthly] (Endangered Species Program)

   PURPOSE:– To provide monthly documentation of activities undertaken by the Fish and Wildlife Service and other Federal Agencies to implement the Endangered Species Act of 1973, the
Convention on International Trade in Endangered
Species, and similar protective legislation. Includes
Summaries of all Federal Register notices determining which species of animals and plants are
endangered and identifying their critical habitats;
discussion of court cases, interagency consultations, and other legal aspects of endangered
species conservation; and feature articles on the
biology and management of endangered species.
   ISSN 0145-9236
   Formerly: Endangered Species Technical Bulletin.

I 49.77/3:date   • Item 614-D
REPORT TO CONGRESS, ENDANGERED AND
THREATENED SPECIES RECOVERY PROGRAM.

I 49.77/4   • Item 611-L-1 (MF)
RECOVERY PROGRAM FOR THE ENDANGERED
FISHES OF THE UPPER COLORADO. [Quarterly]

I 49.77/5:CT   • Item 611-L-2 (P) (MF)
RECOVERY PLANS (various topics)

I 49.77/6:   • Item 611-L-3
FEDERAL AND STATE ENDANGERED SPECIES EX-
PENDITURES. [Annual]

I 49.78:nos.   • Item 611-M (MF)
TOPICAL BRIEFS: FISH AND WILDLIFE RESOURCES
AND ELECTRIC POWER GENERATION. 1–   [Ir-
regular]

I 49.79:v.nos.&nos.   • Item 611-P
FISH HEALTH NEWS. v. 1–   1972–   [Quarterly]

   PURPOSE:– To provide up-to-date communication of new research findings, book reviews
and other information on fish health.

I 49.79/2:nos.   • Item 616-B-1
FISH HEALTH BULLETIN (series).

I 49.81:v.nos.   • Item 611-R
BULLETIN, BIOLOGICAL SERVICES PROGRAM
NEWS. v. 1–   1977–   [Quarterly]

   PURPOSE:– To provide a newsletter type of
publication, containing short, illustrated articles
on a specific subject. Includes addresses for
obtaining more information about each article,
and reviews of publications relating to the subject covered.

I 49.82:v.nos.&nos.   • Item 611-T
WILDLIFE UPDATE. [Bimonthly] (Alaska Area Office)

   Consists of news notes on activities, programs, personnel, etc., pertaining to the Alaska
Area Office and the resources unders its jurisdiction.

I 49.83:nos.   • Item 611-S (MF)
INSTREAM FLOW INFORMATION PAPERS. 1–   [Ir-
regular]

   PURPOSE:– To provide results of studies,
written in a highly technical style, on probability
of use criteria for various species of fish.

I 49.83/2:   • Item 611-S-1
INSTREAM FLOW STRATEGIES [various States].

I 49.84:date   • Item 610-F (MF)
ADMINISTRATION OF THE MARINE MAMMAL
PROTECTION ACT OF 1972, REPORT OF THE
SECRETARY OF THE INTERIOR. [Annual]

I 49.85:date   • Item 624-J (MF)
CONVENTION ON INTERNATIONAL TRADE IN EN-
DANGERED SPECIES OF WILD FAUNA AND
FLORA, ANNUAL REPORT. 1st–   1977–
[Annual]

   PURPOSE:– To provide information and statistical tables on U.S. participation in the convention agreement through enforcement of the Endangered Species Act.

I 49.86:CT   • Item 610-C
NATIONAL FISH HATCHERY LEAFLETS [various
locations]. [Irregular]

I 49.87:date   • Item 610-E (MF)
FISHERY RESOURCES, FISCAL YEAR (date). [An-
nual]

   PURPOSE:– To summarize the activities of
the Service under the Fishery Resources Program, which is a cooperative State and Federal
effort dedicated to restoring, improving, and maintaining the quality, use, etc. of our recreational
and commercial fisheries resources.
   Earlier I 49.2:R 31/5

I 49.87/2:   • Item 610-E-1 (MF)
FISHERY AND AQUATIC MANAGEMENT PROGRAM,
YELLOWSTONE NATIONAL PARK. [Annual]

   Summarizes activities under the Fishery and
aquatic management programs in Yellowstone National Park, one of America's few remaining pris-
tine aquatic ecosystsms.

I 49.88:date   • Item 611-P-1
FISH AND WILDLIFE NEWS. [Quarterly]

   PURPOSE:– To serve as a newsletter of activities of the Service such as protection of endangered and threatened species, through establishment of wildlife refuges, etc.
   Earlier issued Bimonthly

I 49.89:nos.   • Item 611-R-1 (MF)
BIOLOGICAL SERVICES PROGRAM, FWS/OBS 80/
40- (series). [Irregular]

   Technical reports concerned with environmental issues that impact fish and wildlife resources
and their supporting ecosystems, such as the
effects of air emissions on wildlife resources.
   Issued jointly with the Environmental Protection Agency.
   Also known as Air Pollution and Acid Rain
Reports.

I 49.89/2:nos.   • Item 611-R-1
BIOLOGICAL REPORTS (series). 1–   [Irregular]

   Earlier I 49.89

I 49.90:nos.   • Item 616-C-2 (MF)
FERRET REPORTS. (series) [Irregular]

   Reports on searches of areas of potential
habitat of the endangered ferret, such as surveys for black-footed ferrets on coal occurrence
areas in Wyoming. Such surveys are required
before Final Environmental Impact Statements
can be issued.

I 49.91:CT   • Item 610-C-1 (MF)
IMPORTANT FISH AND WILDLIFE HABITATS OF (various States). [Irregular]

   Each issue identifies important fish and wildlife habitats in a different State with a view toward
encouraging action to perpetuate them.

I 49.92:date   • Item 614-D-1 (MF)
FISHERIES AND WILDLIFE RESEARCH. [Annual]

   Summarizes Service research into such areas as animal damage control and endangered
species, much of which is done with various Federal and State agencies and private organizations.
   Reports covers the fiscal year.

I 49.93:date   • Item 612-F
DUCK STAMP DATA. [Annual] (Includes basic manual
and supplementary material for an indefinite period)

   Provides reproductions of sketches from
which the annual Duck Stamps, beginning with
the 1934-35 stamp, were designed.
   Basic volume (3-ring looseleaf binder) kept
current by annual supplemental pages.

I 49.94:date   • Item 616-M (MF)
CURRENT FEDERAL RESEARCH REPORTS, FISH.
[Annual]

   Lists and describes Federal aid research
projects on fish in various States.

I 49.94/2:date   • Item 616-M (MF)
CURRENT FEDERAL AID RESEARCH REPORT, WILD-
LIFE.

I 49.95:State/CT
RARE AND ENDANGERED VASCULAR PLANT SPE-
CIES IN (various States). [Irregular]

I 49.96:date   • Item 612-G (MF)
PROGRESS IN FISHERY RESEARCH. [Annual] (Great
Lakes Fishery Laboratory)

   PURPOSE:– To present Laboratory accomplishments for the year such as surveying sport,
food, and forage fish populations; evaluating lake
trout restoration efforts; and helping develop interagency plans for managing fish populations.

I 49.97:date   • Item 612-H (MF)
HABITAT SUITABILITY INDEX MODELS (series). [Ir-
regular]

   Also published in microfiche.
   Each model concerns a different species of
fish or wildlife and is intended for use in impact
assessment and habitat management. Models are
hypotheses of species habitat, not statements
of proved caused and effect relationships.

I 49.97/2:nos.   • Item 612-H (MF)
HABITAT SUITABILITY INFORMATION. [Irregular]

I 49.98:date   • Item 611-B-52 (MF)
NATIONAL SURVEY OF FISHING, HUNTING, AND
WILDLIFE-ASSOCIATED RECREATION, U.S.
SUMMARY. [Quinquennial]

   PURPOSE:– To present survey results of
human uses of fish and wildlife, by States, for
such activities as fishing, hunting, and wildlife
observation.

I 49.98/2:CT/date   • Item 611-M-1– 53 (MF)
STATE REPORTS. [Quinquennial]

I 49.98/2-nos.   • Item 611-M-1– 52 (MF)
NATIONAL SURVEY OF FISHING, HUNTING, AND
WILDLIFE: ASSOCIATED RECREATION (by
States) [State]. [Quinquennial]

I 49.98/3:date-nos.   • Item 611-M-52 (MF)
ANALYSIS OF THE 1985 NATIONAL SURVEY OF
FISHING, HUNTING AND WILDLIFE ASSOCIATED
RECREATION REPORTS.

I 49.98/4   • Item 614-D-3 (CD)
NATIONAL SURVEY OF FISHING, HUNTING AND
WILDLIFE-ASSOCIATED RECREATION.

I 49.99:nos.   • Item 614-D (MF)
FISH AND WILDLIFE RESEARCH (series). 1–

I 49.100:nos.   • Item 614-C
FISH AND WILDLIFE TECHNICAL REPORTS (series).
1–   1984–   [Irregular]

   Formed by the merger of Special Scientific
Reports: Wildlife (I 49.15/3) and Technical Papers of U.S. Fish and Wildlife Service (I 49.68).

I 49.100/2:   • Item 614-C
WATERFOWL STATUS REPORT. [Annual]

I 49.100/3:date • **Item 612-L**
WATERFOWL, POPULATION STATUS, [date]. [Annual]

Previous title: Status of Waterfowl & Fall Flight Forecast.

I 49.100/4 • **Item 612-L (P) (EL)**
WATERFOWL 2000.

I 49.101:nos. • **Item 614-F**
ANIMAL DAMAGE CONTROL, ADC- (series). [Irregular]

Each issue deals with controlling damage done by a different kind of animal.

I 49.102:date • **Item 612-L**
ANNUAL REPORT OF LANDS UNDER CONTROL OF THE U.S. FISH AND WILDLIFE SERVICE. [Annual]

Presents statistical information by states on lands under control of the Service, which include national wildlife refuges, national waterfowl production areas, and national fish hatcheries.

I 49.103:date • **Item 614-D-2**
EMERGENCY STRIPED BASS RESEARCH STUDY. [Annual]

PURPOSE:– To summarize results of research on the status of stocks of striped bass on the Atlantic Coast as required by Section 7 of the Anadromous Fish Conservation Act.

I 49.104:CT • **Item 612-M**
DIRECTORIES.

I 49.105:date • **Item 616-A-1**
FISHERIES ACADEMY, COURSE CATALOG.

I 49.106 • **Item 612-L (MF)**
PRELIMINARY ESTIMATES OF WATERFOWL HARVEST AND HUNTER ACTIVITY IN THE UNITED STATES DURING THE HUNTING SEASON. [Annual]

I 49.106/2 • **Item 612-L (MF)**
TRENDS IN DUCK BREEDING POPULATIONS, 1955– [date]. [Annual]

I 49.106/3 • **Item 612-L (MF)**
PRELIMINARY ESTIMATES OF AGE AND SEX COMPOSITIONS OF DUCKS AND GEESE HARVESTED IN THE HUNTING SEASON IN COMPARISON WITH PRIOR YEARS. [Annual]

I 49.106/4 • **Item 612-L (MF)**
SANDHILL CRANE HARVEST AND HUNTER ACTIVITY IN THE CENTRAL FLYWAY DURING THE HUNTING SEASON. [Annual]

I 49.106/5 • **Item 600-D-2 (EL)**
MOURNING DOVE, BREEDING POPULATION STATUS. [Annual]

I 49.106/6 • **Item 600-D-2 (EL)**
AMERICAN WOODCOCK HARVEST AND BREEDING POPULATION STATUS. [Annual]

I 49.106/7 • **Item 616-A-1**
CATALOG OF TRAINING (Fiscal Year).

I 49.106/7-2:date/nos. • **Item 616-A-1**
NOTES, NATIONAL CONSERVATION TRAINING CENTER. [Quarterly]

I 49.107 • **Item 614-D-1 (MF)**
KLAMATH RIVER FISHERIES ASSESSMENT PROGRAM (Series).

I 49.108 • **Item 600-D-2 (E)**
ELECTRONIC PRODUCTS.

I 49.109:nos. • **Item 612-A-1 (MF)**
LONG TERM RESOURCE MONITORING PROGRAM, PROGRAM REPORT (series).

I 49.109/2:nos. • **Item 612-A-2 (MF)**
LONG TERM RESOURCE MONITORING PROGRAM, REPRINT (series).

I 49.109/3:nos. • **Item 614-D-4 (MF)**
LONG TERM RESOURCE MONITORING PROGRAM, SPECIAL REPORT (series).

I 49.109/4:nos. • **Item 614-D-5 (MF)**
LONG TERM RESOURCE MONITORING PROGRAM, TECHNICAL REPORT (series).

I 49.110:CT • **Item 614-D-6**
GALVESTON BAY FACT SHEET SERIES.

I 49.111 • **Item 612-P**
CULTURAL RESOURCE SERIES. [Irregular]

I 49.112 • **Item 600-D-2 (EL)**
MAT UPDATE.

I 49.113:CT • **Item 612-A-3**
ENVIRONMENTAL ASSESSMENT.

OFFICE OF THE PETROLEUM COORDINATOR FOR WAR (1942)

CREATION AND AUTHORITY

The Office of the Petroleum Coordinator for National Defense was established within the Department of the Interior pursuant to letter of the President, dated May 28, 1941. The Office was redesignated as the Office of the Petroleum Coordinator for War by letter of the President, dated April 20, 1942. The Office was abolished by Executive Order 9276 of December 2, 1942, and its functions transferred to the Petroleum Administration for War (Y 3.P 44).

I 50.1:date
ANNUAL REPORTS.

Later Y 3.P 44:1

I 50.2:CT
GENERAL PUBLICATIONS.

Later Y 3.P 44:2

I 50.6:CT
REGULATIONS, RULES, AND INSTRUCTIONS.

I 50.7:CT
PAPERS IN RE.

SOLID FUELS ADMINISTRATION FOR WAR (1943– 1947)

CREATION AND AUTHORITY

The Solid Fuels Administration for War was established within the Department of the Interior by Executive Order 9332 of April 19, 1943, to succeed the Office of Solid Fuels Coordinator for War, which was abolished. The Administration was terminated by Executive Order 9847 of May 6, 1947, effective June 30, 1947.

I 51.1:date
ANNUAL REPORTS.

Earlier I 46.1

I 51.2:CT
GENERAL PUBLICATIONS.
Earlier I 46.2

I 51.6:CT
REGULATIONS, RULES, AND INSTRUCTIONS.

Earlier I 46.6

I 51.7:nos.
COAL REPORTS. [Weekly]

Earlier I 46.7

I 51.8:nos.
DISTRIBUTION OF COAL SHIPMENTS. [Monthly]

Earlier I 46.8

I 51.9:date
PRELIMINARY ESTIMATES OF PRODUCTION OF BITUMINOUS COALS AND LIGNITE. [Monthly]

Earlier I 46.11
Later I 28.64

I 51.10:CT
POSTERS.

WAR RELOCATION AUTHORITY (1944– 1946)

CREATION AND AUTHORITY

The War Relocation Authority (Pr 32.5400) was transferred to the Department of the Interior by Executive Order 9423 of February 16, 1944. The Authority was terminated by Executive Order 9742 of June 25, 1946, effective June 30, 1946.

I 52.1:date
ANNUAL REPORTS.

Earlier Pr 32.5401

I 52.2:CT
GENERAL PUBLICATIONS.

Earlier Pr 32.5402

I 52.7:date
REPORTS. [Semiannual]

Earlier Pr 32.5407

I 52.8:CT
ADDRESSES.

I 52.9:nos.
COMMUNITY ANALYSIS REPORTS.

Earlier Pr 32.5401

I 52.10:nos.
PROJECT ANALYSIS SERIES.

Earlier Pr 32.5411

I 52.11:nos.
COMMUNITY ANALYSIS NOTES.

I 52.12
FAVORABLE CLIPS. [Proc.]

BUREAU OF LAND MANAGEMENT
(1946–   )

CREATION AND AUTHORITY

The Bureau of Land Management was established on July 16, 1946, through the consolidation of the General Land Office (I 21) and the Grazing Service (I 38) in accordance with the provisions of sections 402 and 403 of the President's Reorganization Plan 3 of 1946 (4 U.S.C. 1336-16).

INFORMATION

Office of Public Affairs
Bureau of Land Management
Department of the Interior
1849 C Street, NW
Washington, D. C. 20240
(202) 452-5125
Fax: (202) 452-5124
http://www.blm.gov

I 53.1:date   • **Item 600-D-4 (EL)**
BUREAU OF LAND MANAGEMENT ANNUAL REPORT.

Earlier I 21.1 and I 38.1

I 53.1/2:date   • **Item 633-C**
PUBLIC LAND STATISTICS. 1962–   [Annual]

Prior to 1962, issued as Statistical Appendix to the Annual Report.
Gives area of States, territories, and possessions; the public lands; Bureau of Land Management activities; financial transactions; summary statistics of acquisition of the public domain; disposals under various laws, mineral lease filings, cash receipts, permitted use of grazing districts, range development projects.

I 53.2:CT   • **Item 631**
GENERAL PUBLICATIONS.

Earlier I 21.2 and I 38.2

I 53.3/2   • **Item 634-B**
TECHNICAL BULLETINS. 1–   1968–   [Irregular]

I 53.4:nos.
CIRCULARS.

Earlier I 21.4

I 53.5:CT   • **Item 632-A**
LAWS (Administered by the Bureau).

I 53.6:CT
RULES, REGULATIONS, AND INSTRUCTIONS.

I 53.7:date
OF PUBLIC LANDS OF UNITED STATES.

Earlier I 21.11/1

I 53.7/2:CT   • **Item 633**
MANUALS AND HANDBOOKS (miscellaneous).

I 53.8   • **Item 630**
EPHEMERIS OF THE SUN, POLARIS AND OTHER SELECTED STARS WITH COMPANION DATA AND TABLES FOR THE YEAR [date]. 1910–   [Annual]

Prepared by the Nautical Almanac Office, Naval Observatory.
Presents information relating to daily declinations of the sun, and hourly changes in declinations, upper culminations and elongations of Polaris, and semimonthly positions of 28 selected stars. Published one year in advance of data covered.

I 53.9   • **Item 632 (MF)**
INFORMATION BULLETINS. 1–   1958–   [Irregular]
Popular guides for the general public.

I 53.10:date
STANDARD FIELD TABLES.

Earlier I 21.11/3

I 53.11:CT   • **Item 629-B**
MAPS AND MAP FOLDERS.

Earlier I 21.13

I 53.11/2:CT
CHARTS. [Irregular]

I 53.11/3:CT
AUDIOVISUAL MATERIALS. [Irregular]

I 53.11/3-2:CT   • **Item 631-E**
POSTERS. [Irregular]

I 53.11/4:   • **Item 619-G-16**
BUREAU OF LAND MANAGEMENT 1:100,000- SCALE MAPS. [Irregular]

Includes both the surface management and surface-minerals management BLM editions. Surface management edition shows public lands administered by BLM, other Federal lands, State lands and private lands. Restrictions on the management of Federal lands established by withdrawals are also shown. The surface-minerals management edition has the extent of Federally-owned mineral rights overprinted on the surface management edition.

I 53.11/4-2:nos.letrs.   • **Item 619-G-16**
BUREAU OF LAND MANAGEMENT MAPS, SURFACE AND MINERALS MANAGEMENT STATUS, SCALE 1:100,000. [Irregular]

I 53.11/5:letters-nos.   • **Item 629-B**
SURFACE MANAGEMENT QUADRANGLES (maps). [Irregular]

I 53.11/6:letters-nos.   • **Item 629-B**
MINERALS MANAGEMENT QUAD (maps). [Irregular]

I 53.12:v.nos.&nos.   • **Item 633-A**
OUR PUBLIC LANDS. v. 1–   1951–   [Quarterly]

PURPOSE:– To provide a forum for the exchange of information and ideas on the conservation, management, and development of the Nation's public land and resource base.
Subject matter, written in a non-technical language, includes articles on forest conservation, wildlife and livestock range management, minerals exploration and development, land use and management.
Issued in January, April, July and October.
Indexed by: Index to U.S. Government Periodicals.
ISSN 0030-6940

I 53.12/2:date   • **Item 633-A-1**
MANAGING THE NATION'S PUBLIC LANDS. [Annual]

Each section presents goals and accomplishments for a separate BLM operating program.

I 53.13
ADDRESSES. [Irregular]

I 53.14
[PRESS RELEASES]. [Irregular]

I 53.15:date   • **Item 632-A**
DIGEST OF GRAZING DECISIONS. [Issued every 20 years]

Latest volume issued covers 1959– 1978.

I 53.16   • **Item 633-B**
NATIONAL ADVISORY BOARD COUNCIL FOR GRAZING DISTRICTS. PROCEEDINGS OF ANNUAL MEETINGS. [Annual]

Verbatim report of the proceedings.

I 53.17:CT   • **Item 629-A-2**
BIBLIOGRAPHIES AND LISTS OF PUBLICATIONS.

I 53.17/2:date/nos.   • **Item 629-A-1 (MF)**
BLM MONTHLY ALERT.

I 53.18:date
ANNUAL FIRE REPORT.

Contains narrative and table of statistics, by states, on the year's fire season: causes, losses, classes of fires, etc.

I 53.19:nos.   • **Item 629-C**
DRAFT ENVIRONMENTAL STATEMENTS. [Irregular]

I 53.19/2:CT   • **Item 629-C**
FINAL ENVIRONMENTAL IMPACT STATEMENTS. [Irregular]

I 53.19/3:CT   • **Item 629-C (MF)**
ENVIRONMENTAL ANALYSIS RECORDS (series) [various areas]. [Irregular]

PURPOSE:– To determine impacts on the environment and identify methods to minimize these impacts. Some EARs may recommend an Environmental Statement be prepared. Environmental Analysis Records are prepared in BLM District Offices prior to project development. Approximately 11,000 EARs were prepared in fiscal year 1976.

I 53.20:nos.   • **Item 629-E-1**
TECHNICAL NOTES.

I 53.21:date   • **Item 629-D**
BLM NEWSLETTER.

I 53.22:nos.   • **Item 629-E (MF)**
CULTURAL RESOURCES SERIES (Colorado). 1–   [Irregular]

I 53.22/2:nos.   • **Item 629-E (MF)**
CULTURAL RESOURCE SERIES (Utah). [Irregular]

I 53.22/3:nos.   • **Item 629-E (MF)**
CULTURAL RESOURCES SERIES (Nevada). 1–   [Irregular]

I 53.22/4:CT   • **Item 629-E-5**
CULTURAL RESOURCES PUBLICATIONS (series). [Irregular]

Includes cultural resources overview, archeological investigations, cultural resource management plans, etc., for lands administered by the Bureau of Land Management.

I 53.22/5:nos.   • **Item 629-E**
CULTURAL RESOURCES SERIES (Montana). 1–   1985–   [Irregular]

I 53.22/6:nos.   • **Item 629-E**
CULTURAL RESOURCE SERIES. [Irregular] (Eastern States Office)

I 53.22/7:nos.   • **Item 629-E**
CULTURAL RESOURCE SERIES (Wyoming). 1–   [Irregular]

I 53.22/8:nos.   • **Item 629-E**
CULTURAL RESOURCE SERIES (Arizona). 1–   [Irregular]

I 53.22/9:   • **Item 629-E**
CULTURAL RESOURCES SERIES (NEW MEXICO).

I 53.22/10:nos.   • **Item 629-E (MF)**
CULTURAL RESOURCES SERIES (Oregon).

I 53.22/11:nos.   • **Item 629-E-5 (MF)**
CULTURAL RESOURCES INFORMATION SERIES.

I 53.23:CT   • **Item 629-E-2 (MF)**
WYOMING LAND USE DECISIONS (series). [Irregular]

I 53.23/2:CT   • **Item 629-E-2**
LAND USE DECISIONS AND RANGELAND PROGRAM SUMMARY (various locations). [Irregular]

Title varies.

I 53.23/3:CT • Item 629-E-2 (MF)
HERD MANAGEMENT AREA PLAN (various locations). [Irregular]

I 53.24:nos. • Item 632
RESOURCE INVENTORY NOTES. 1– [Irregular]

Superseded by Resources Evaluation Newsletter (A 13.69/14).

I 53.25:date
LAND. [Quarterly]

I 53.26:nos.
IS (series). [Quarterly]

I 53.27:nos. • Item 629-E-4
BIOLOGICAL SCIENCES SERIES. 1– 1979– [Irregular]

Highly technical reports.

I 53.28:nos.
ALASKA TECHNICAL REPORT.

I 53.29:nos.
POCS REFERENCE PAPERS. [Irregular]

POCS = Pacific Outer Continental Shelf
Earlier I 1.98/2

I 53.29/2:nos. • Item 603-G-3 (MF)
POCS TECHNICAL PAPERS. [Irregular]

POCS = Pacific Outer Continental Shelf.
Earlier I 1.98/3

I 53.30:nos. • Item 629-E-6 (MF)
TECHNICAL PAPERS. 1– (Alaska Outer Continental Shelf Office)

Papers present environmental descriptions, summaries of which will appear in future Environmental Impact Statements (I 53.19/2).

I 53.31:nos.
RESOURCE AND POTENTIAL RECLAMATION EVALUATION REPORTS.

I 53.32:date • Item 633-A-2 (MF)
OREGON AND WASHINGTON PLANNED LAND SALES. [Quarterly]

PURPOSE:– To provide land sale data including legal description, location, and sale date, with map of verso of single sheet.

I 53.32/2:CT • Item 633-A-2 (MF)
LAND SALE (brochure). [Irregular]

I 53.33:CT • Item 633-A-3 (MF)
WILDERNESS REPORT.

I 53.34:nos. • Item 629-E-7
WYOMING BLM WILDLIFE TECHNICAL BULLETINS. [Irregular]

I 53.35:nos. • Item 629-E-1
TECHNICAL REFERENCE (series). [Irregular]

I 53.36:v.nos.&nos. • Item 603-G-4 (MF)
CALIFORNIA DESERT DISTRICT PLANNING NEWSLETTER. v. 1– [Quarterly]

I 53.37:v.nos.&nos.
ALASKA CONVEYANCE NEWS. [5 times a year]

No longer a depository item.

I 53.38:letters-nos.
BLM CONTRACT SOLICITATION.

I 53.39:date • Item 631-C (MF)
SNAKE RIVER BIRDS OF PREY RESEARCH PROJECT, ANNUAL REPORT.

I 53.40:date • Item 631-B (MF)
SAVAL RANCH RESEARCH AND EVALUATION PROJECT, PROGRESS REPORT. [Annual]

PURPOSE:– To summarize progress in evaluating effects of range improvement practices on livestock production, vegetation, fish and wildlife, watershed hydrology, water quality, economic factors, and other resource values.

I 53.41 • Item 631-D
ALASKA PEOPLE. [Monthly]

Published for the employees of BLM, contains articles on BLM activities, and published in newsletter format.

I 53.41/2 • Item 629-E-11 (EL)
BLM-ALASKA FRONTIERS (6 times a year).

I 53.42:date
ENERGY. [Quarterly]

I 53.43:date • Item 631-G-1 (MF)
BLM FACTS AND FIGURES FOR UTAH. [Annual]

I 53.43/2:date • Item 631-G
BLM FACTS, OREGON AND WASHINGTON. [Annual]

PURPOSE:– To summarize Bureau accomplishments in Oregon and Washington.

I 53.43/3:date • Item 631-G-3 (MF)
BLM IN WYOMING. [Annual]

PURPOSE:– To summarize Bureau of Land Management activities in Wyoming.
Earlier I 53.2:W 98

I 53.43/4:date • Item 631-G-2 (MF)
NEVADA PROGRESS REPORT. [Annual]

PURPOSE:– To summarize Bureau of Land Management activities related to its management, conservation, protection, use, and disposal of Nevada's public lands.

I 53.43/5 • Item 631-G-3 (MF)
BLM IN NEW MEXICO, OKLAHOMA, TEXAS AND KANSAS. [Annual]

I 53.44:date
ANNUAL WATER QUALITY ANALYSES REPORT FOR NEVADA. [Annual]

I 53.45 • Item 631-F (MF)
WASHINGTON OFFICE TELEPHONE DIRECTORY. [Quarterly]

I 53.45/2 • Item 631-F (MF)
BUREAU OF LAND MANAGEMENT OFFICE DIRECTORY. [Annual]

I 53.46:CT • Item 631-G-4
FORMS. [Irregular]

I 53.47:date • Item 631-G-5 (MF)
PLAN OF WORK FOR COOPERATIVE HYDROLOGY INVESTIGATIONS. [Annual]

PURPOSE:– To present the plan of work for the hydrology investigations undertaken by BLM in cooperation with the Geological Survey. The purpose of the plan is to specify the nature and amount of assistance to be provided by the GS to BLM.

I 53.48:date • Item 631-G-3
RECREATION FUTURES FOR COLORADO. [Biennial]

I 53.49 • Item 629-E-1 (MF)
BLM-ALASKA TECHNICAL REPORTS.

I 53.50:date • Item 629-E-2 (MF)
RESOURCES MANAGEMENT PLAN ANNUAL UPDATE.

I 53.51:CT • Item 629-E-4 (MF)
HRW (series).

I 53.52:nos. • Item 629-E-4
RECREATION INFORMATION SERIES.

I 53.53 • Item 631-D-1 (MF)
COMPETITIVE OIL AND GAS LEASE SALE RESULTS, DATE OF SALE. [Six issues a year]

I 53.54/2 • Item 629-E-8 (MF)
ARIZONA DESERT DIGEST. [Quarterly]

I 53.55 • Item 629-E-2 (MF)
CHALLENGE COST SHARE REPORT. [Annual]

I 53.56:date • Item 631
STATE OF THE PUBLIC RANGE IN WYOMING. [Annual]

I 53.57 • Item 600-D-1 (CD)
GENERAL LAND OFFICE, AUTOMATED RECORDS PROJECT, PRE-1908 HOMESTEAD & CASH ENTRY PATENTS.

I 53.58 • Item 600-D-4 (E)
ELECTRONIC PRODUCTS.

I 53.59:CT • Item 629-E-9 (MF)
ENVIRONMENTAL IMPACT STATEMENT.

I 53.59/2:CT • Item 629-E-10
MANAGEMENT PLAN & ENVIRONMENTAL ASSESSMENT.

DEFENSE FISHERIES ADMINISTRATION (1950– 1953)

CREATION AND AUTHORITY

The Defense Fisheries Administration was established within the Department of the Interior by Departmental Order 2605, dated December 4, 1950, pursuant to the Defense Production Act of 1950 (64 Stat. 798) and Executive Order 10161 of September 9, 1950. The Administration was abolished by Department Order 2722 of May 13, 1953, effective June 30, 1953.

I 54.1:date
ANNUAL REPORTS.

I 54.2:CT
GENERAL PUBLICATIONS.

I 54.7
RELEASES.

OFFICE OF MINERALS EXPLORATION (1958– 1965)

CREATION AND AUTHORITY

The Defense Minerals Administration was established within the Department of the Interior by Departmental Order 2605, dated December 4, 1950, pursuant to the Defense Production Act of 1950 (64 Stat. 798) and Executive Order 10161 of September 9, 1950. The name was changed to Defense Minerals Exploration Administration by Departmental Order 2605, amendment 6, dated November 21, 1951. Termination of the program was announced by the Secretary of the Interior on June 6, 1958. The Office of Minerals Exploration was established pursuant to the act of August 21, 1958 (72 Stat. 700), to succeed the Defense Minerals Exploration Administration. The Office was abolished and its functions transferred to the Geological Survey (I 19) by Secretary's order 2886 of February 26, 1965, to be effective July 1, 1965.

I 55.1:date
ANNUAL REPORTS.

I 55.2:CT
GENERAL PUBLICATIONS.

I 55.6:CT
REGULATIONS, RULES, AND INSTRUCTIONS.

I 55.6/2:nos.
MINERAL ORDERS MO (series).

I 55.7
PRESS RELEASES. [Irregular]

I 55.9
ADDRESSES. [Irregular]

I 55.10
ANNUAL REPORT, LEAD AND ZINC MINING STABILIZATION PROGRAM, YEAR ENDING DECEMBER 31. 1962– [Annual]

Prepared and transmitted to Congress pursuant to Section 8 of Public Law 347, 87th Congress

The program to stabilize the mining of lead and zinc by small domestic procedures was authorized October 3, 1961, funds were appropriated July 25, 1962, and regulations published July 28, 1962. Report covering year ending December 31, 1962, was first in the series.

Textual summary supported by statistical tables.

DEFENSE ELECTRIC POWER ADMINISTRATION
(1951– 1953)

CREATION AND AUTHORITY

The Defense Power Administration was established within the Department of the Interior by Departmental Order 2605, dated December 4, 1950. The name was changed to Defense Electric Power Administration by Amendment 1, dated February 5, 1951. The Administration was abolished June 30, 1953 by Departmental Order 2721, dated May 7, 1953.

I 56.1:date
ANNUAL REPORTS.

I 56.2:CT
GENERAL PUBLICATIONS.

I 56.7
RELEASES.

I 56.8:CT
HANDBOOKS, MANUALS, GUIDES.

DEFENSE SOLID FUELS ADMINISTRATION
(1950– 1954)

CREATION AND AUTHORITY

The Defense Solid Fuels Administration was established within the Department of the Interior by Departmental Order 2605, dated December 4, 1950, pursuant to the Defense Production Act of 1950 (64 Stat. 816). It was abolished on June 29, 1954, by Departmental Order 2764.

I 57.1:date
ANNUAL REPORTS.

I 57.2:CT
GENERAL PUBLICATIONS.

I 57.6:CT
REGULATIONS, RULES, AND INSTRUCTIONS.

I 57.6/2:nos.
SOLID FUELS ORDERS SFO (series).

I 57.6/3:nos.
DSFA DELEGATIONS DEL (series).

I 57.7:
RELEASES.

I 57.7/2:nos.
DSFA MEMORANDUMS.

I 57.8:CT
ADDRESSES.

PETROLEUM ADMINISTRATION FOR DEFENSE
(1950– 1954)

CREATION AND AUTHORITY

The Petroleum Administration for Defense was established within the Department of the Interior by Departmental Order 2591, dated October 3, 1950, pursuant to the Defense Production Act of 1950 (64 Stat. 798) and Executive Order 10161 of September 9, 1950. The Administration was abolished by Departmental Order 2755, dated April 23, 1954.

I 58.1:date
ANNUAL REPORTS.

I 58.2:CT
GENERAL PUBLICATIONS.

I 58.7
RELEASES.

SOUTHWESTERN POWER ADMINISTRATION
(1943– 1977)

CREATION AND AUTHORITY

The Southwestern Power Administration was established by the Secretary of the Interior in 1943, to carry out the Secretary's responsibility for the sale and disposition of electric power and energy generated at certain projects constructed and operated by the Department of the Army. For these projects, the Administration carries out the functions assigned to the Secretary by the Flood Control Act 1944 (58 Stat 890) in the States of Kansas, Missouri, Oklahoma, Arkansas, Texas, and Louisiana. The Administration was transferred to the Department of Energy by act of August 4, 1977 (91 Stat. 565), effective October 1, 1977.

I 59.1:date
ANNUAL REPORT.

I 59.2:CT
GENERAL PUBLICATIONS. [Irregular]

I 59.8:date
REPORT OF PROGRESS. [Monthly]

I 59.9:CT
ADDRESSES. [Irregular]

OFFICE OF MINERALS AND SOLID FUELS
(1962– 1971)

CREATION AND AUTHORITY

The Office of Minerals and Solid Fuels was established within the Department of the Interior on November 2, 1962 to succeed the Office of Minerals Mobilization. Abolished on October 22, 1971 and its functions, powers, and responsibilities reassigned to the Deputy Assistant Secretary (Minerals and Energy Policy) in the Office of the Assistant Secretary– Mineral Resources.

I 60.1:date   • Item 634-A
REPORTS

I 60.2:CT   • Item 634-A
GENERAL PUBLICATIONS.

OIL IMPORT ADMINISTRATION
(1959– 1971)

CREATION AND AUTHORITY

The Oil Import Administration was established by Proclamation 3279 of March 10, 1959. On October 22, 1971, the Administration was merged with the Office of Oil and Gas (I 64)

I 61.1:date
REPORTS.

I 61.2:CT
GENERAL PUBLICATIONS.

I 61.7
PRESS RELEASES. [Irregular]

I 61.9
ADDRESSES. [Irregular]

OIL IMPORT APPEALS BOARD
(1959– 1971)

CREATION AND AUTHORITY

The Oil Import Appeals Board was established within the Department of the Interior on March 13, 1959. On December 23, 1971, the Board was made a part of the Office of Hearings and Appeals.

I 62.1:date
REPORTS.

I 62.2:CT
GENERAL PUBLICATIONS.

I 62.7
PRESS RELEASES. [Irregular]

I 62.9
DECISIONS. [Irregular]

Report on decisions handed down on petitions presented to the Oil Import Appeals Board.

OFFICE OF COAL RESEARCH
(1960– 1974)

CREATION AND AUTHORITY

The Office of Coal Research was established within the Department of the Interior by the Coal Research Act of July 7, 1960 (74 Stat. 336). Functions of the Office were transferred to the Energy Research and Development Administration by the Energy Reorganization Act of 1974, approved October 11, 1974 (88 Stat. 1237).

I 63.1   • **Item 606-C-1**
ANNUAL REPORTS. 1–   [Annual]

Report for the calendar year made by the Director to the Secretary of the Interior for submission to the President and Congress as required by section 7 of PL 86-599.

I 63.2:CT   • **Item 606-C-2**
GENERAL PUBLICATIONS.

I 63.7
PRESS RELEASES.   – Jan. 1975. [Irregular]

I 63.9
ADDRESSES. [Irregular]

I 63.10   • **Item 606-C-2**
RESEARCH AND DEVELOPMENT REPORTS. 1–
    1962–   [Irregular]

I 63.11:nos.
DESIGNS AND SPECIFICATIONS.

OFFICE OF OIL AND GAS
(1946– 1974)

CREATION AND AUTHORITY

The Office of Oil and Gas was established by the Secretary of the Interior on May 6, 1946, in response to a Presidential letter of May 3, 1946. Functions of the Office were transferred to the Federal Energy Administration by act of May 7, 1974 (88 Stat. 100).

I 64.1:date   • **Item 657-C**
ANNUAL REPORTS.

I 64.2:CT   • **Item 657-C**
GENERAL PUBLICATIONS.

I 64.7:date
PRESS RELEASES.

Discontinued June 28, 1974.

I 64.8:CT   • **Item 657-C**
HANDBOOKS, MANUALS, GUIDES.

I 64.9:CT
ADDRESSES.

I 64.10:nos.
TECHNICAL REPORTS. [Irregular]

I 64.11:date
OIL IMPORT TOTALS. [Monthly]

I 64.12:date
FEE LICENSES ISSUED FOR THE MONTH (date).
    1973– 1974. [Monthly]

Gives name of company, amount issued in barrels, and license period, for crude oil, motor gasoline, and unfinished oils and finished petroleum products.

SOUTHEASTERN POWER
ADMINISTRATION
(1950– 1977)

CREATION AND AUTHORITY

The Southeastern Power Administration was created by the Secretary of the Interior in 1950, to carry out functions assigned to the Secretary by the Flood Control Act of 1944 (58 Stat. 890), which pertain to the transmission and disposition of surplus electric power and energy generated at reservoir projects which are or may be under the control of the Department of the Army in the States of West Virginia, Virginia, North Carolina, South Carolina, Georgia, Florida, Alabama, Mississippi, Tennessee, and Kentucky. The Administration was transferred to the Department of Energy by act of August 4, 1977 (91 Stat. 565).

I 65.1
ANNUAL REPORT. [Annual]

I 65.2:CT
GENERAL PUBLICATIONS.

I 65.9
QUARTERLY REPORT. [Quarterly]

Issued monthly, prior to first quarter, 1964.

BUREAU OF OUTDOOR
RECREATION
(1963– 1978)

CREATION AND AUTHORITY

The Bureau of Outdoor Recreation was created April 2, 1963 by act of May 28, 1963 (16 U.S.C. 4601). The Bureau was terminated and its functions transferred to the Heritage Conservation and Recreation Service (I 70) by Secretary's Order of January 25, 1978.

I 66.1:date
ANNUAL REPORTS.

I 66.2:CT   • **Item 657-B-1**
GENERAL PUBLICATIONS.

I 66.6:CT
REGULATIONS, RULES, AND INSTRUCTIONS.

I 66.7
PRESS RELEASES. [Irregular]

I 66.8:CT   • **Item 657-B-7**
HANDBOOKS, MANUALS, GUIDES. [Irregular]

I 66.8/2:CT   • **Item 657-B-3**
OUTDOOR RECREATION GRANTS-IN-AID MANUAL.
    1965–   [Irregular]

Subscription includes basic manual plus supplementary material for an indefinite period.
    Later I 29.107

I 66.9
ADDRESSES. [Irregular]

I 66.10:v.nos.&nos.
BOR NEWS. ADMINISTRATIVE.

I 66.11   • **Item 657-B-2**
PUBLICATIONS (series). [Irregular]
I 66.12:nos.
STATISTICAL SERIES, REPORTS. 1–   1963–

I 66.13
TOURIST AND RECREATION POTENTIAL [by areas].
    [Irregular]

I 66.14:nos.
COORDINATION MEMORANDUMS. 1–   1965–

I 66.15:CT   • **Item 657-B-4**
BIBLIOGRAPHIES AND LISTS OF PUBLICATIONS.

   I 66.15:G 94   • **Item 657-B-4**
   CATALOG OF GUIDES TO OUTDOOR RECREATION AREAS AND FACILITIES. 1973. 79 p.

Guides to National, regional, and State recreation areas, published by private, State, and Federal organizations are listed, indicating title of guide, price, and ordering address. The catalog includes a cross-reference section presenting guides broken down by categories: camping, canoeing, fishing, hiking, and hunting.

   I 66.15:L 71   • **Item 657-B-4**
   INDEX TO SELECTED OUTDOOR RECREATION LITERATURE. v. 1–   1966–   [Annual]

Prepared in cooperation with the Department of the Interior Library.
Covers the calendar year.

I 66.16   • **Item 657-B-6**
OPERATION GOLDEN EAGLE, DIRECTORY OF FEDERAL RECREATION AREAS CHANGING ENTRANCE, ADMISSION AND USER FEES. [Annual]

I 66.17   • **Item 657-B-5**
OUTDOOR RECREATION ACTION. v. 1–   1966–
[Quarterly]

Reports major Federal, State, local and private actions affecting outdoor recreation, natural beauty, and related conservation matters. This publication should help to keep professionals, public, and private leaders in outdoor recreation abreast of significant developments.
Indexed by: Index to U.S. Government Periodicals.
ISSN 0030-7130

I 66.18   • **Item 657-B-8**
OUTDOOR RECREATION RESEARCH. 1–   1966–
[Irregular]

PURPOSE:– To promote the coordination and development of effective programs relating to outdoor recreation. Gives summaries of currently active research projects on outdoor recreation and environmental quality problems.

I 66.19:date
BALANCE, A DISCUSSION OF CONSERVATION ISSUES. 1968–   [Irregular; about 4 times a year] (Outdoor Recreation Bureau, Mid-Continent Region, Denver, Colorado)

A monograph devoting each issue to one facet of our environment. Includes contributions of both Bureau of Outdoor Recreation employees and outside authorities and is concerned with conservation issues, many of which are closely related to outdoor recreation.

I 66.19/2:date
CONTINENTAL DIVIDE TRAIL STUDY PROGRESS REPORTS. 1968–   [Irregular] (Mid-Continent Region, Denver, Colorado)

I 66.19/3:date
MID-CONTINENT MEMO. 1968–   [6 times a year]

A newsletter featuring articles on recreation and environmental subjects, with emphasis on the Rocky Mountain and Central Plains regions. Covers Federal, State, and local activities, as well as items relating to environmental education and research.

I 66.20
SERO SHORTS.

I 66.21:date
NORTHEAST REGION OUTDOOR MEMO. (Northeast Region, Philadelphia, Pennsylvania)

I 66.22:nos.   • **Item 657-B-9**
TECHNICAL ASSISTANCE BULLETINS. 1–
[Irregular]

I 66.23:date   • **Item 657-B-10**
FEDERAL RECREATION FEES. 1st–   1972–
[Annual]

Later I 70.18

I 66.24:CT   • **Item 657-B-1**
NATIONAL URBAN RECREATION STUDY (series).
[Irregular]

FEDERAL WATER QUALITY ADMINISTRATION (1970)

CREATION AND AUTHORITY

The Federal Water Pollution Control Administration (FS 16) was transferred to the Department of the Interior by Reorganization Plan No. 2 of February 18, 1966. The name was changed to Federal Water Quality Administration pursuant to the Water Quality Improvement Act of 1970 (84 Stat. 113), of 1970, effective April 3, 1970. Under Reorganization Plan No. 3, of 1970, effective December 20, 1970, the Administration was transferred to the Office of Water Quality (EP 2) of the Environmental Protection Agency.

I 67.1:date
ANNUAL REPORT.

Earlier FS 16.1

I 67.1/2   • **Item 473-A-1**
WATER POLLUTION CONTROL, FEDERAL COSTS, REPORT TO CONGRESS. 1969–   [Annual]

Reports submitted by the Administration to Congress pursuant to section 16 (a) of the Federal Water Pollution Control Act of 1966 (PL 84-660), as amended.

I 67.2:CT
GENERAL PUBLICATIONS.

Earlier FS 16.2

I 67.5:CT
LAWS.

Earlier FS 16.5

I 67.7
PRESS RELEASES. [Irregular]

I 67.8:CT
HANDBOOKS, MANUALS, GUIDES.

I 67.8/2:CT
INDUSTRIAL WASTE GUIDES.

Earlier FS 2.71

I 67.9   • **Item 496-C**
POLLUTION-CAUSED FISH KILLS IN (year). 1–
1960–   [Annual] WP-12

Formerly published by the Public Health Service as its Publication 847.
Summary report supplemented by statistical data.

I 67.10   • **Item 498-A**
WATER AND SEWER BOND SALES IN THE UNITED STATES. 1956/59–   [Annual]

PURPOSE:– To present data which are basic and necessary to the orderly and efficient management of water supply and pollution control programs.
Tables supplement the annual publication of contract award data, Sewage and Water Works Construction (I 67.11).
Previously published by the Public Health Service as its Publication 965 (FS 2.56/4).
First issued covered period July 1956– June 1959. Beginning with data for 1959, issued for the calendar year.

I 67.11   • **Item 498-A**
SEWAGE AND WATER WORKS CONSTRUCTION. 1952–   [Annual] WP-15

Data covers sewage treatment works, collec-

tion sewer, waterworks, and combination construction.
Published 1952– 1964 by the Public Health Service as its Publications 608, 633, 673, and 758 (FS 2.56/2).

I 67.12   • **Item 502-A**
SELECTED SUMMARIES OF WATER RESEARCH.
[Irregular]

Gives one paragraph summations of current research.

I 67.13   • **Item 502-A**
WATER POLLUTION CONTROL RESEARCH AND TRAINING GRANTS. [Annual]

Covers grant awards, research grants, demonstration grants, training grants, and research fellowships.

I 67.13/2:date
WATER POLLUTION CONTROL RESEARCH AND TRAINING GRANTS, INDEX.

Earlier FS 16.2:R 31

I 67.13/3:letters-nos.
WATER POLLUTION CONTROL RESEARCH SERIES, WP-20.

I 67.13/4:letters-nos.
WATER POLLUTION CONTROL RESEARCH SERIES.

Later EP 2.10

I 67.13/5:CT
MAPS.

I 67.14:CT
BIBLIOGRAPHIES AND LISTS OF PUBLICATIONS.

Later EP 2.27

I 67.14/2:v.nos.
ENVIRONMENTAL FACTORS IN COASTAL AND ESTUARINE WATERS, BIBLIOGRAPHIC SERIES.

I 67.15:date
BUILDING FOR CLEAN WATER. [Annual]

Earlier FS 16.9

I 67.16:date
PROJECT REGISTER, DISTRIBUTION BY RIVER BASIN OF PROJECTS APPROVED UNDER SEC. 8 OF FEDERAL WATER POLLUTION CONTROL ACT (Public law 660, 84th Cong.) AS AMENDED.

Later EP 2.13

I 67.16/2:date
PROJECT REGISTER, PROJECTS APPROVED, MONTHLY SUMMARY.

Later EP 1.9

I 67.17:date
BULLETIN OF COURSES, WATER POLLUTION CONTROL TRAINING PROGRAM.

I 67.18:CT
ADDRESSES

I 67.19:nos.
ROBERT A. TAFT WATER RESEARCH CENTER: REPORT TWRC- (series).

I 67.20:CT
POSTERS.

I 67.19:nos.
ESTUARINE POLLUTION STUDY SERIES.

Later EP 2.19

I 67.22:date
STATISTICAL SUMMARY. . .INVENTORY, MUNICIPAL WASTE FACILITIES.

Earlier FS 2.71/2
Later EP 2.17

I 67.23:nos.
WORKING PAPERS (numbered).

Later EP 2.23

ALASKA POWER ADMINISTRATION (1967– 1977)

CREATION AND AUTHORITY

The Alaska Power Administration was created by Secretary of the Interior order of June 16, 1967, to carry out functions assigned to the Secretary by the statutes cited therein, including among others the Eklutna Project Act (64 Stat. 382), and the Flood Control Acts of 1944 and 1962 (58 Stat. 890, 76 Stat. 1193; 16 U.S.C. 825s, 43 U.S.C. 390), as they relate to the State of Alaska. The Administration was transferred to the Department of Energy by act of August 4, 1977 (91 Stat. 565), effective October 1, 1977.

I 68.1:date   • **Item 604-C-1**
ANNUAL REPORT.

I 68.2:CT   • **Item 604-C-1**
GENERAL PUBLICATIONS.

I 68.9:CT
ALASKA RESOURCES DEVELOPMENT STUDIES. 1970–

MINING ENFORCEMENT AND SAFETY ADMINISTRATION (1973– 1978)

CREATION AND AUTHORITY

The Mining Enforcement and Safety Administration was established within the Department of the Interior by Secretary's Order 2953, effective May 7, 1973. The Administration was abolished by departmental directive of March 9, 1978, and its functions transferred to the newly established Mine Safety and Health Administration (L 38) in the Department of Labor.

I 69.1:date
ANNUAL REPORT.

I 69.2:CT   • **Item 637-H**
GENERAL PUBLICATIONS.

I 69.6:CT   • **Item 644**
REGULATIONS, RULES, AND INSTRUCTIONS.

I 69.7:date
NEWS RELEASES. [Irregular]

I 69.8:CT   • **Item 637-B**
HANDBOOKS, MANUALS, GUIDES.

I 69.8/2:nos.   • **Item 644-A**
SAFETY MANUALS. 1–   [Irregular]

Later L 38.8/2

I 69.9:nos.   • **Item 637-A**
MESA INFORMATION REPORT, IR- (series). 1–

Earlier I 28.27
Later L 38.10

I 69.10:date
MESA SAFETY REVIEWS: COAL-MINE FATALITIES. [Monthly] (Technical Support, 4015 Wilson Blvd., Arlington, Virginia 22203)

Prior to April 1974, issued in Mineral Industry Surveys series (I 28.10/2).
ISSN 0097-9368

I 69.10/2:date
MESA SAFETY REVIEWS: COAL-MINE INJURIES AND WORKTIME. [Monthly] (Health Safety Analysis Center, Box 25367, Denver, Colorado 80225)

Prior to February 1974, issued in Mineral Industry Surveys series (I 28.89).
ISSN 0097-9368

I 69.10/3:date   • **Item 637-G**
MESA SAFETY REVIEWS: INJURIES AT SAND AND GRAVEL PLANTS. [Annual]

Booklets on a variety of mine health and safety topics written in nontechnical terms.

I 69.11:v.nos.&nos.   • **Item 637-I**
MESA, THE MAGAZINE OF MINING HEALTH AND SAFETY. v. 1–   1975–   [Bimonthly]

Deals with mining health and safety topics and focuses on new MESA regulations, new developments in mine health and safety, and the technology available to make mines safe and healthful.
Indexed by: Index to U.S. Government Periodicals.
ISSN 0362-370X
Later L 38.9

I 69.12:date
NEWS RELEASES.

HERITAGE CONSERVATION AND RECREATION SERVICE (1978– 1981)

CREATION AND AUTHORITY

The Heritage Conservation and Recreation Service was established within the Department of the Interior by the Secretary on January 25, 1978, in accordance with provisions of section 2 of the Reorganization Plan No. 3 of 1950 (64 Stat. 1262). The Service was abolished by Secretarial Order 3060 of February 19, 1981, effective May 31, 1981, and its functions returned to the National Park Service (I 29).

I 70.1:date
ANNUAL REPORT.

I 70.2:CT   • **Item 647-B-1**
GENERAL PUBLICATIONS. [Irregular]

I 70.2:H 62/2/date   • **Item 648-D**
NATIONAL REGISTER OF HISTORIC PLACES. 1959–   [Irregular]

Earlier I 29.76
Later I 70.17

I 70.5:CT   • **Item 624-E-6**
LAWS.

I 70.8:CT   • **Item 624-E-2**
HANDBOOKS, MANUALS, GUIDES. [Irregular]

I 70.9:CT   • **Item 646-P**
HISTORIC AMERICAN ENGINEERING RECORDS PUBLICATIONS. [Irregular]

The Historic American Engineering Record (HAER) is an organization that prepares original measured drawings, historical reports, photographs, technical analyses, and other documentation on important historic structures. The documentation is deposited permanently in the Library of Congress for the use of the public.
Earlier I 29.84/2

I 70.10:CT   • **Item 624-E-1**
HISTORIC STRUCTURE REPORTS. [Irregular]

Each report pertains to one structure which is to be preserved, and analyzes the construction and alterations, documents current physical state of the building; selects appropriate treatment for preservation, establishes priority for work items; and makes an estimate of project costs. The completed report becomes the planning document for preservation of the structure.
See also I 29.88

I 70.11:CT   • **Item 646-N**
CULTURAL RESOURCE MANAGEMENT STUDIES. [Irregular]

See also I 29.86

I 70.11/2:CT   • **Item 646-N-1 (MF)**
CULTURAL RESOURCE MANAGEMENT SERIES.

Consists of highly technical publications directed mainly to archeologists.

I 70.11/3:CT   • **Item 646-N-2**
MANAGEMENT SERIES. [Irregular]

Later I 29.106

I 70.12:nos.   • **Item 646-J**
PRESERVATION BRIEFS. 1–   1975–   [Irregular]

See also I 29.84

I 70.12/2:CT   • **Item 624-E-7**
PRESERVATION CASE STUDIES. [Irregular]

Later I 29.104

I 70.12/3:CT   • **Item 624-E-9**
PRESERVATION PLANNING SERIES. [Irregular]

Later I 29.104/2

I 70.13:CT   • **Item 624-E-3**
MAPS. [Irregular]

I 70.14:nos.   • **Item 604**
FINAL REGULATORY ANALYSIS. OSM- RA-1- 1979–   [Irregular] (Office of Surface Mining, Reclamation, and Enforcement)

I 70.15:CT   • **Item 657-B-4**
BIBLIOGRAPHIES AND LISTS OF PUBLICATIONS. [Irregular]

I 70.15/2:CT   • **Item 657-B-4**
TECHNICAL PRESERVATION SERVICES READING LISTS.

I 70.16:CT   • **Item 624-E-4**
POSTERS. [Irregular]

I 70.17:date   • **Item 648-D**
NATIONAL REGISTER OF HISTORIC PLACES. 1959– [Irregular]

PURPOSE:– To provide a register of the buildings, structures, objects, sites, districts deemed of historical value and worthy of preservation. Arranged by State and county.
See also I 70.2:H 62/2

I 70.18:date   • **Item 657-B-10**
FEDERAL RECREATION FEE PROGRAM (year), INCLUDING FEDERAL RECREATION VISITATION DATA, A REPORT TO THE CONGRESS. [Annual]

Continues Federal Recreation Fees (I 66.23).
Later I 29.108

I 70.19:date • **Item 624-E-5 (MF)**
CULTURAL PROPERTIES PROGRAMS, YEAR-END REPORT. 1st– 1978– [Annual] (Office of Archeology and Historic Preservation)

PURPOSE:– To review the activities for the calendar year of the Office of Archeology and Historic Preservation in resource identification and documentation, preservation assistance, technical advice, and interagency assistance.

I 70.20:date • **Item 657-D**
NATIONWIDE OUTDOOR RECREATION PLAN. [Quinquennial]

Plan coordinates the development of recreation policy and programs. Sets forth needs and demands for public recreation. Suggested actions are also given for each level of government and private interests.

I 70.21:date
POPPIES AND PORTICOS, A HCRS HERITAGE NEWSLETTER. [Quarterly]

Discontinued in 1980/81.

I 70.22:v.nos.&nos. • **Item 646-T**
TRENDS. v. 1– [Quarterly] (Park Practice Program)

See also I 29.93

I 70.22/2:v.nos.&nos. • **Item 646-T-2**
GRIST. v. 1– [Bimonthly]

Purpose:– To provide, in newsletter format, information on practical solutions to various everyday problems in parks and recreational facilities.
Former title: Park Practice Grist.
See also I 29.72

I 70.22/3:date • **Item 646-T-1**
DESIGN. [Quarterly] (Park Practice Program)

PURPOSE:– To provide a compendium of plans for park and recreation structures such as picnic shelters, etc., which demonstrate quality design and intelligent use of materials.
See also I 29.72/2

I 70.22/4:date
INDEX TO DESIGN, GRIST, TRENDS. [Annual]

Provides an index for the Park Practice Program publications, Design (I 70.22/3), Grist (I 70.22/2), and Trends (I 70.22).

I 70.23:nos. • **Item 647-B-3 (MF)**
TECHNICAL NOTES. 1–

I 70.24:CT • **Item 624-E-8 (MF)**
IAS INVESTIGATION REPORTS. [Irregular]

Consists of highly technical reports on projects which are coordinated by Interagency Archeological Services and result from compliance with historic preservation law.
ISA Interagency Archeological Services.

I 70.25:nos. • **Item 647-B-2 (MF)**
NOTIFICATIONS, HCRS INFORMATION EXCHANGE (series). 1– [Irregular]

Announces and provides abstracts of documents and audiovisual aids to help managers, practitioners, and planners to provide recreation services and preserve natural and cultural resources.

OFFICE OF SURFACE MINING RECLAMATION AND ENFORCEMENT
(1977–   )

CREATION AND AUTHORITY

The Office of Surface Mining Reclamation and Enforcement was established within the Department of the Interior by the Surface Mining Control and Reclamation Act of 1977 (91 Stat. 4450), August 3, 1977.

INFORMATION

Office of Communications
Office of Surface Mining Reclamation
and Enforcement
Department of the Interior
1849 C Street, NW
Washington, D.C. 20240
(202) 208-2534
Fax: (202) 501-0549
http://www.osmre.gov

I 71.1:date • **Item 669-C (MF)**
ANNUAL REPORT.

I 71.2:CT • **Item 669-B**
GENERAL PUBLICATIONS. [Irregular]

I 71.3:nos. • **Item 669-A (MF)**
TECHNICAL SERVICES RESEARCH, OSM- TR- (series). [Irregular]

I 71.3/2:nos. • **Item 669-A (MF)**
TECHNICAL SERVICES AND RESEARCH, OSM/TM-(series). [Irregular]

I 71.4:CT • **Item 669-D**
HANDBOOKS, MANUALS, GUIDES. [Irregular]

I 71.5:CT • **Item 669-E**
LAWS. [Irregular]

I 71.11:nos. • **Item 671-D**
REFERENCE PAPERS (series). [Irregular] (Alaska Outer Continental Shelf Region)

Each paper concerns a different subject.

I 71.15:date • **Item 669-F (MF)**
TECHNICAP TRAINING COURSES, TECHNICAL TRAINING PROGRAM. [Annual]

Provides information on continuous technical training program activities to be offered by the Office. Courses relate to such areas as applied hydrology and blasting and inspection.

I 71.16:date • **Item 669-F (MF)**
EXCELLENCE IN SURFACE COAL MINING AND REC-LAMATION AWARDS. [Annual]

MINERALS MANAGEMENT SERVICE
(1982–   )

CREATION AND AUTHORITY

The Minerals Management Service was established on January 19, 1982, by Secretarial Order No. 3071, under the authority provided by section 2 of Reorganization Plan No. 3 of 1950 (64 Stat. 1262).

INFORMATION

Public Affairs Office
Minerals Management Service
Department of the Interior
1849 C Street, NW
Washington, DC 20240
(202) 208-3985
Fax: (202) 208-3968
http://www.mms.gov

I 72.1:date
ANNUAL REPORT.

I 72.2:CT • **Item 671-C**
GENERAL PUBLICATIONS. [Irregular]

I 72.3/2 • **Item 671-K (MF)**
RMP BULLETIN. [Irregular]

I 72.8:CT • **Item 671-G**
HANDBOOKS, MANUALS, GUIDES. [Irregular]

I 72.9:CT • **Item 671-A (MF)**
OUTER CONTINENTAL SHELF OIL AND GAS INFOR-MATION PROGRAM, SUMMARY REPORTS (various regions). [Irregular]

Each report summarizes outer continental shelf oil and gas activities in a different region, such as Mid-Atlantic, South Atlantic, etc., and their onshore impacts.

I 72.9/2:date • **Item 671-A-1**
ATLANTIC INDEX. [Annual]

I 72.9/3:date • **Item 671-A-2**
ALASKA INDEX. [Annual]

I 72.9/3-2:date
ALASKA SUMMARY REPORT. [Irregular]

I 72.9/4:date • **Item 671-A-3**
GULF OF MEXICO INDEX. [Annual]

I 72.9/5:date • **Item 671-A-3**
GULF OF MEXICO SUMMARY REPORT/INDEX. [Annual]

Earlier I 72.9 and I 72.9/4

I 72.9/6:date • **Item 671-F**
ALASKA SUMMARY/INDEX. [Annual]

I 72.9/7: • **Item 671-A**
PACIFIC SUMMARY/INDEX. [Annual]

I 72.10:date • **Item 671-B (EL)**
FEDERAL OFFSHORE STATISTICS, LEASING, EXPLORATION, PRODUCTION, REVENUE. [Annual]

PURPOSE:-To document statistically what has happened since the Federal government began leasing on the Outer Continental Shelf in 1954. Tabular data include the status, production, and summation of revenue from Federal offshore oil and gas operations.

I 72.11:nos. • **Item 671-D (MF)**
REFERENCE PAPERS.

I 72.12   • **Item 671-F (MF)**
OCS MONOGRAPHS (series). [Irregular]

     Each monograph will be concerned with a different subject and will be issued by the various regional offices and by the central office.
OCS = Outer Continental Shelf

I 72.12/2:date/nos.   • **Item 671-F (MF)**
OCS STUDIES (series). [Irregular]

     OCS = Outer Continental Shelf.

I 72.12/3:nos.   • **Item 671-F (MF)**
OCS REPORTS. [Irregular]

     OCS = Outer Continental Shelf

I 72.12/3-2:date   • **Item 671-F (MF)**
OUTER CONTINENTAL SHELF OIL AND GAS LEAS-ING AND PRODUCTION PROGRAM ANNUAL REPORT.

I 72.12/3-3:date   • **Item 671-F (MF)**
OUTER CONTINENTAL SHELF STATISTICAL SUM-MARY. [Annual]

I 72.12/3-4:nos.   • **Item 671-F-1 (MF)**
PACIFIC OUTER CONTINENTAL SHELF STUDIES PROGRAM (OCS) STATISTICAL REPORTS.

I 72.12/4:date   • **Item 671-A-4**
OCS MAP SERIES. [Irregular]

     Includes miscellaneous maps pertaining to outer continental shelf oil and gas activities.

I 72.12/5:date   • **Item 671-A-1 (MF)**
REGIONAL STUDIES PLAN, FISCAL YEAR, ATLAN-TIC OCS REGION. [Annual]

I 72.12/6:date
POCS EVENTS. [Monthly]

     POCS = Pacific Outer Continental Shelf
PURPOSE– To summarize news highlights re-lated to gas and oil leasing and development in the Pacific Outer Continental Shelf Region.
No longer a depository item.

I 72.12/7:date   • **Item 671-F (MF)**
ESTIMATED OIL AND GAS RESERVES. [Annual]

     Earlier I 72.12/3

I 72.12/8:date   • **Item 671-F (MF)**
DRAFT ENVIRONMENTAL STUDIES PLAN. [Annual]

I 72.12/9:nos.   • **Item 671-F**
OCS STATISTICAL SERIES.

I 72.12/10:nos.   • **Item 671-F (MF)**
OCS INFORMATION REPORT.

I 72.12/11:nos.   • **Item 671-F (MF)**
OCS EIS/EA (Environmental Assessment) (Series).

I 72.12/12:date/nos.   • **Item 671-F-2 (MF) (EL)**
OCS ACTIVITIES REPORT. [Semiannual]

I 72.13:date   • **Item 671-E (EL)**
MINERAL REVENUES, THE REPORT ON RECEIPTS FROM FEDERAL AND INDIAN LEASES. [Annual]

     PURPOSE:– To present data by states on royalties and other revenues from Federal and Indian offshore and onshore mineral leases.

I 72.14:date   • **Item 671-H**
OFFSHORE SCIENTIFIC AND TECHNICAL PUBLICA-TIONS. [Quarterly]

     PURPOSE:– To list all MMS offshore scien-tific and technical publications available to the public.

I 72.14/2:date   • **Item 671-H**
OFFSHORE SCIENTIFIC AND TECHNICAL PUBLICA-TIONS. [Annual]

I 72.15:CT   • **Item 671-J**
FORMS.

I 72.16:CT   • **Item 671-A-4**
POSTERS.

I 72.17:v.nos./nos.   • **Item 671-K (EL)**
MMS TODAY. [Quarterly]

I 72.18   • **Item 671-H (EL)**
OFFSHORE STATS. [Quarterly]

I 72.19:CT   • **Item 600-D-3 (E)**
ELECTRONIC PRODUCTS. [Irregular]

NATIONAL BIOLOGICAL SERVICE

I 73.2:CT   • **Item 615-B**
GENERAL PUBLICATIONS.

I 73.8   • **Item 615-B-1**
HANDBOOKS, MANUALS, GUIDES.

I 73.9   • **Item 615-B-2 (MF)**
RESEARCH PUBLICATIONS OF THE NATIONAL BIO-LOGICAL SERVICE.

I 73.10   • **Item 615-B-3 (MF)**
BIOLOGICAL SCIENCE REPORT (SERIES).

I 73.11   • **Item 615-B-4 (MF)**
INFORMATION AND TECHNOLOGY REPORT (SE-RIES).

UNITED STATES INFORMATION AGENCY
(1953– 1978, 1982– 1999)

CREATION AND AUTHORITY

     The United States Information Agency was established by Reorganization Plan 8 of 1953, effective August 1, 1953, and Executive Order 10477 of August 1, 1953, to carry out interna-tional information activities as authorized by the United States Information and Educational Ex-change Act of 1948, as amended (62 Stat. 6; 22 U.S.C. 1431). The international educational and cultural activities of the Agency are authorized by the United States Mutual Educational and Cultural Exchange Act of 1961 (75 Stat. 527, as amended; 22 U.S.C. 2451), implemented by Ex-ecutive Order 11034 of June 25, 1962. The Agency was abolished and its functions transferred to the International Communication Agency (ICA 1) by Executive Order 12048 of March 27, 1978. The name of the Agency was changed back to United States Information Agency by Public Law 97-241 (96 Stat. 291), approved August 24, 1982.
     Agency was abolished in 1999 and most of its functions were transferred to the Department of State.

IA 1.1:date   • **Item 672-B**
REPORT TO CONGRESS. 1st– 1953– [Semian-nual]

     Report submitted by the Agency to Congress on a semiannual basis.
     Describes the work the Agency is doing in its various activities– the Voice of America broad-casts, motion pictures, exhibits, overseas librar-ies, etc., with emphasis on the critical current conflicts and how USIA is telling America's story to the world.
     The semiannual report is published in an iden-tical edition under the title, Review of Operations (IA 1.1/2).
     Later ICA 1.1

IA 1.1/2:nos.
REVIEW OF OPERATIONS. [Semiannual]

     See IA 1.1

IA 1.1/3   • **Item 672-M (MF)**
OFFICE OF INSPECTOR GENERAL, SEMIANNUAL REPORT TO THE CONGRESS.

IA 1.2:CT   • **Item 672-B**
GENERAL PUBLICATIONS.

     See also ICA 1.2

IA 1.6:CT   • **Item 672-B**
REGULATIONS, RULES, AND INSTRUCTIONS.

     Later ICA 1.6

IA 1.6/2:CT   • **Item 672-D**
HANDBOOKS, MANUALS, GUIDES.

     See also ICA 1.8

IA 1.6/3:date/nos.   • **Item 672-D-1**
VOA, VOICE OF AMERICA, ENGLISH BROADCAST GUIDE. [Irregular]

IA 1.6/4:date/nos.   • **Item 672-D-2**
VOA, VOICE OF AMERICA, BROADCAST SCHED-ULE FOR LANGUAGES OTHER THAN ENGLISH.

IA 1.7:nos.
TELLING AMERICA'S STORY TO THE WORLD. RELEASE.

IA 1.8:v.nos.&nos.   • **Item 672-C**
PROBLEMS OF COMMUNISM. v. 1– 1952– [Bimonthly]

     Indexed by:–
        Index to U.S. Government Periodicals
        Public Affairs Information Service
        Social Sciences and Humanities Index
        ISSN 0032-941X
     See also ICA 1.9

IA 1.8/2:date
WORLDWIDE COMMUNIST PROPAGANDA ACTIVI-TIES.

IA 1.9:
USIS FEATURE.

IA 1.10:nos.
MAGAZINE REPRINT MR (series). [Weekly]

     Earlier S 1.78

IA 1.11:date
INTERNATIONAL BROADCASTING OF ALL NATIONS. [Annual]

IA 1.12:date
WORLDWIDE DISTRIBUTION OF RADIO RECEIVER SETS. [Annual]

IA 1.12/2:date
GEOGRAPHIC DISTRIBUTION OF RADIO SETS AND CHARACTERISTICS OF RADIO OWNERS IN COUNTRIES OF THE WORLD. [Annual]

IA 1.13:CT   • **Item 672-B**
ADDRESSES.

IA 1.13/2:CT
LECTURES (series).

IA 1.14:nos.
AMERICAN ILLUSTRATED. 1– 1956– [Monthly]

     Formerly entitled America, and classed S 1.55
     Later ICA 1.10

IA 1.14/2:
AMERICAN ILLUSTRATED (Polish language).

IA 1.15:v.nos.&nos.
SOVIET ORBIT PROPAGANDA.

IA 1.16:date
OVERSEAS TELEVISION DEVELOPMENTS. [Annual]

IA 1.16/2 • **Item 672-L**
TELECOMMUNICATIONS UPDATE. [Biweekly]

IA 1.17:v.nos.&nos. • **Item 672-F**
ENGLISH TEACHING FORUM. v. 1–   1963–
[Quarterly]

See also ICA 1.11
ISSN 0041-1434

IA 1.17/2:nos.
SELECTED ENGLISH TEACHING MATERIALS
CATALOGUE. 1–

IA 1.17/3:CT
ENGLISH TEACHING STUDY UNITS.

IA 1.18 • **Item 672-E**
SPECIAL LISTS. [Irregular]

IA 1.19:
VOICE OF AMERICA FORUM LECTURES: MASS
COMMUNICATION SERIES.

IA 1.19/2:
VOICE OF AMERICA FORUM LECTURES: SPACE
SCIENCE SERIES.

IA 1.19/3:
VOICE OF AMERICA FORUM LECTURES: MUSIC
SERIES.

IA 1.19/4:
VOICE OF AMERICA FORUM LECTURES: UNIVER-
SITY SERIES.

IA 1.20:v.nos.&nos.
USIA CORRESPONDENT. v. 1–

IA 1.21:date • **Item 672-B**
AGENCY IN BRIEF. [Annual]

PURPOSE:– For use as a training document
for new employees and to provide background
information on the Agency and its functions. It
summarizes the historical developments leading
to the establishment of the Agency, outlines the
organization and responsibilities of its major elements, briefly describes methods of programming
and budgeting for its continuing and special activities, and explains its personnel systems and
internal and external relationships.

IA 1.22:date
SPECIAL INTERNATIONAL EXHIBITIONS, ANNUAL
REPORT. 1st–   1963–

IA 1.23:CT
EXTERNAL INFORMATION AND CULTURAL RELA-
TIONS PROGRAMS: [various countries]. [Irregu-
lar] (Research Service, Office of Research and
Assessment)

IA 1.24:nos.
RESEARCH MEMORANDUM, M- (series).

IA 1.24/2:nos.
RESEARCH NOTES, N- (series).

IA 1.24/3:letters-nos.
OFFICE OF RESEARCH [Reports]. [Irregular]

Earlier reports classified IA 1.2

IA 1.25:v.nos.&nos. • **Item 672-J**
USIA WORLD. [Monthly]

Supersedes USICA World (ICA 1.13/2).
Published by the Agency for its employees at
home and abroad. Contains articles on USIA activities.

IA 1.26:date • **Item 672-G (MF)**
USIA TELEPHONE DIRECTORY. [Semiannual]

Earlier ICA 1.15

IA 1.27:CT • **Item 672-H**
BIBLIOGRAPHIES AND LISTS OF PUBLICATIONS.
[Irregular]

IA 1.27/2:date • **Item 672-H**
VCR AND FILM CATALOG. [Annual]

Earlier IA 1.27:F 48

IA 1.28:date • **Item 672-K (MF)**
USIA PRIVATE SECTOR COMMITTEES ANNUAL RE-
PORT.

IA 1.29:date • **Item 672-M (MF)**
OPPORTUNITIES ABROAD FOR EDUCATORS.
[Annual]

PURPOSE:– To present information on op-
portunities abroad for educators under the
Fulbright Program.
Earlier ED 1.19

IA 1.30:date • **Item 672-H**
USIA VIDEO LIBRARY CATALOG. [Annual]

IA 1.31 • **Item 672-N**
POSTERS.

IA 1.32 • **Item 672-B-3 (CD)**
USIA INFO BASE (Quick Reference Guide).

IA 1.32/2:CT • **Item 672-B-2 (E)**
ELECTRONIC PRODUCTS.

IA 1.33 • **Item 672-M (MF)**
USIA STRATEGIC INFORMATION RESOURCES MAN-
AGEMENT (IRM) PLAN, FISCAL YEAR.

IA 1.34 • **Item 672-B-2 (E)**
USIA WORLD.

IA 1.35: • **Item 672-B-2 (E)**
U.S. SOCIETY & VALUES (various languages).

IA 1.36: • **Item 672-B-2 (E)**
ISSUES OF DEMOCRACY (various languages).

IA 1.37: • **Item 672-B-2 (E)**
ECONOMIC PERSPECTIVES (various languages).

IA 1.38: • **Item 672-B-2 (E)**
U.S. FOREIGN POLICY AGENDA (various languages).

IA 1.39: • **Item 672-B-2 (E)**
GLOBAL ISSUES (various languages).

INTERSTATE COMMERCE
COMMISSION
(1887– 1995)

CREATION AND AUTHORITY

The Interstate Commerce Commission was
created as an independent establishment by the
Act to Regulate Commerce, of February 4, 1887
(24 Stat. 379, 383; 49 U.S.C. 1-22), as the Interstate Commerce Act. The Commission's authority
was strengthened and the scope of its jurisdiction has been broadened by subsequent legislation, such as the Hepburn Act, the Panama Canal
Act, the Motor Carrier Act of 1935, and the Transportation Acts of 1920, 1940, and 1958. Commission was abolished by an act of December 29,
1995 (109 stat. 932) and most funtions transferred to the Surface Transportation Board, Department of Transportation.

IC 1.1:date • **Item 673 (MF)**
ANNUAL REPORT. 1st–   1887–   [Annual]

Report submitted by the Commission to Congress for the fiscal year.
Includes transportation highlights; accounting, cost funding and valuation; economic research and statistics; mobilization planning for
defense; management activities; litigation involving Commission Orders; legislation and legislative activities; and legislative recommendations.

IC 1.2:CT • **Item 674**
GENERAL PUBLICATIONS.

IC 1.3:nos.
BULLETINS. 1– 4, 1895– 1899.

IC 1.3/2:nos. • **Item 674-J**
INFORMATION BULLETINS. 1–   1958–   [Irregu-
lar]

IC 1.3/2-2:date • **Item 674-J (MF)**
STATE REGULATORY COMMISSIONS AND FUEL TAX
DIVISIONS. [Annual]

IC 1.4/1:nos.
CIRCULARS. 1–

IC 1.4/2:date
CIRCULAR LETTERS.

IC 1.4/3:nos.
STATISTICAL SERIES CIRCULARS. 1–   1913–

IC 1.4/4:nos.
SPECIAL REPORT SERIES CIRCULARS. 1–   1906–

IC 1.5:nos.
SPECIAL REPORTS. 1–   1908–

IC 1.6:v.nos. • **Item 667**
INTERSTATE COMMERCE COMMISSION REPORTS.
DECISIONS OF THE INTERSTATE COMMERCE
COMMISSION OF THE UNITED STATES. v. 1–
1887–   [Irregular]

Covers traffic, finance, water carrier and freight
forwarder reports.
Vols. 1– 11 were printed privately. Prior to
1929, valuation reports were issued in this series, by since that date have been issued separately.
Individual volumes covering the period 1950
to date are not being listed here. However, the
finance and water carrier volumes are noted below:
Citation: I.C.C.
Classified IC 1.6/1, prior to v. 280.

IC 1.6/a
TRAFFIC, DECISIONS. 1–   [Irregular]

Includes water carrier and freight forwarder cases.
IC 1.6/1a, prior to v. 280.

IC 1.6/a:F
FINANCE DECISIONS. F 1–   [Irregular]

IC 1.6/1a, prior to F 8860.

IC 1.6/a:WC-nos.
WATER CARRIER DECISIONS. WC 1– WC 528.

Later cases included in Traffic Decisions.

IC 1.6/1a:v.nos.
– SEPARATES, INDEXES TO VOLUMES, AND
TABLE OF CASES.

IC 1.6/1a:CT
– SEPARATES: REPORT OF COMMISSION,
REPORT AND OPINION OF COMMISSION:
REPORT AND ORDER OF COMMISSION,
ETC.

IC 1.6/1a:v.nos.
– SEPARATES; VALUATION DECISIONS.

IC 1.6/1b:CT
– REPORT AND ORDER OF COMMISSION.

IC 1.6/2:nos.
TABLES OF CASES AND OPINIONS. v. 1– 1897–

IC 1.6/3:nos.
TABLE OF CASES CITED IN OPINIONS. v. 1–
1901–

IC 1.6/4:v.nos.
TABLE OF DEFENDANTS BEFORE INTERSTATE COM-
MERCE COMMISSION. v. 1–   1901–

IC 1.6/5:v.nos.
TABLE OF CASES IN BOTH ICC REPORTS AND ICC REPORTS.

IC 1.6/6:vol.
ICC REPORTS, CASES CITED. v. 1–   1907–

IC 1.6/7:vol.
TABLE OF COMMODITIES IN THE DECISIONS.

IC 1.6/8:
TABLE OF CASES ON FORMAL DOCKET OF ICC NOT DISPOSED OF IN PRINTED REPORTS.

IC 1.6/9:date
ICC CASES IN FEDERAL COURTS.

IC 1.6/10:   • Item 677
INTERSTATE COMMERCE COMMISSION REPORTS (2nd series).

IC 1.7/1:nos.
UNREPORTED OPINIONS. no.1–   1909–

IC 1.7/2:v.nos.
UNREPORTED OPINIONS, REPARATION [indexes]. v. 1–   1910–

IC 1.7/3:A-nos.
UNREPORTED OPINIONS [Reparation, new series].

IC 1.7/4:vol.
UNREPORTED OPINIONS, INDEXES [to. nox. 1-2249].

IC 1.8:nos.
CONFERENCE RULINGS BULLETINS. 1–   1908–

IC 1.9:CT
ORDERS [unnumbered].

IC 1.10:nos.
SPECIAL ORDERS. 1– 13. 1909– 1911.

IC 1.11:date   • Item 679
RULES OF PRACTICE. 1877–

IC 1.12/1:date
RULES AND REGULATIONS OF SERVICE.

IC 1.12/2:CT   • Item 678
RULES, REGULATIONS AND INSTRUCTIONS [miscellaneous].

IC 1.12/3:CT   • Item 678
HANDBOOKS, MANUALS, GUIDES.

IC 1.13/1:CT
PAPERS IN RE.

IC 1.13/2:CT by subject word.
PAPERS IN RE [proceedings of inquiry, general investigations, etc.].

IC 1.14:date
PRELIMINARY ABSTRACT OF STATISTICS OF RAILWAY STATISTICS.

IC 1.15:nos.
LIST OF CORPORATE NAMES OF COMMON CARRIERS.

IC 1.16
ADDRESSES. [Irregular]

IC 1.17
TRANSPORT ECONOMICS. 1951–   [Monthly]

PURPOSE:– To present current statistics and certain other material that is not readily available from other sources. The appendix tables show condensed statistics of Class I railroads and are intended to provide current statistics on a continuing basis, and includes net railway operating income, net income, working capital, employees, service hours and compensation.
ISSN 0041-1434

IC 1.18:date
PERSONS FURNISHING CARS TO OR ON BEHALF OF CARRIERS BY RAILROAD OR EXPRESS COMPANIES, SUMMARY OF QUARTERLY REPORTS.

IC 1.19:date   • Item 682-A-1 (MF)
REVENUES, EXPENSES AND STATISTICS OF FREIGHT FORWARDERS. 1943–   [Quarterly] (Statement 950)

Summary table gives quarterly and current year to date figures. Main table gives selected items for individual companies. two year comparisons.

IC 1.20:date
CARLOAD WAYBILL ANALYSES, DISTRIBUTION OF FREIGHT TRAFFIC AND REVENUE AVERAGES BY COMMODITY GROUPS AND RATE TERRITORIES. [Quarterly]

Note: 1947 series originally IC 1.2:C 17/5/947 to 947-4.

IC 1.21:date
CARLOAD WAYBILL ANALYSES, STATE BY STATE DISTRIBUTION OF TONNAGE BY COMMODITY GROUPS. [Quarterly]

Note: 1947 issues originally classified IC 1.2:C 17/7/947 to 1947-2.

IC 1.22:date
CARLOAD WAYBILL ANALYSES, TERRITORIAL DISTRIBUTION, TRAFFIC AND REVENUE BY COMMODITY GROUPS. [Quarterly]

IC 1.23:date
CARLOAD WAYBILL STATISTICS, QUARTERLY COMPARISONS, TRAFFIC AND REVENUE BY COMMODITY CLASSES. [Quarterly]

Gives for each commodity class the number of carloads, tons, revenue, average tons per car, short-line haul per ton haul per car, average revenue per 100 pounds, car, car-mile, and ton-mile. Two year comparisons.

IC 1.23/2:date
MILEAGE BLOCK DISTRIBUTION, TRAFFIC AND REVENUE BY COMMODITY CLASS, TERRITORIAL MOVEMENT, AND TYPE OF RATE, PRODUCTS OF AGRICULTURE, 1 PERCENT SAMPLE OF TERMINATIONS IN... STATEMENT MB- 1. [Annual]

Earlier IC 1.2:C 17/44

IC 1.23/3:date
CARLOAD WAYBILL STATISTICS ...MILEAGE BLOCK DISTRIBUTION, TRAFFIC AND REVENUE BY COMMODITY CLASS, TERRITORIAL MOVEMENT, AND TYPE OF RATE, ANIMALS AND PRODUCTS, 1 PERCENT SAMPLE OF TERMINATIONS IN... STATEMENT MB- 2. 1947–   [Annual]

Earlier IC 1.2:C 17/45

IC 1.23/4:date
CARLOAD WAYBILL STATISTICS ...MILEAGE BLOCK DISTRIBUTION, TRAFFIC AND REVENUE BY COMMODITY CLASS, TERRITORIAL MOVEMENT, AND TYPE OF RATE, PRODUCTS OF MINES, 1 PERCENT SAMPLE OF TERMINATIONS IN... STATEMENT MB-3. [Annual]

Earlier IC 1.2:C 17/47

IC 1.23/5:date
CARLOAD WAYBILL STATISTICS ...MILEAGE BLOCK DISTRIBUTION, TRAFFIC AND REVENUE BY COMMODITY CLASS, TERRITORIAL MOVEMENT, AND TYPE OF RATE, PRODUCTS OF FORESTS, 1 PERCENT SAMPLE OF TERMINATIONS IN... STATEMENT MB-4. [Annual]

Earlier IC 1.2:C 17/46

IC 1.23/6:date
CARLOAD WAYBILL STATISTICS, MILEAGE BLOCK DISTRIBUTION, TRAFFIC AND REVENUE BY COMMODITY CLASS, TERRITORIAL MOVEMENT, AND TYPE OF RATE, MANUFACTURERS AND MISCELLANEOUS FORWARDER TRAFFIC, ONE PERCENT SAMPLING OF TERMINATIONS.. . STATEMENT MB-5. 1947–   [Annual]

Earlier IC 1.2:C 17/43

IC 1.23/7:date
CARLOAD WAYBILL STATISTICS, TRAFFIC AND REVENUE PROGRESSIONS BY SPECIFIED MILEAGE BLOCKS FOR COMMODITY GROUPS AND CLASSES, 1 PERCENT SAMPLE OF CARLOAD TERMINATIONS IN YEAR, STATEMENT MB-6. 1947–   [Annual]

Gives progression by specified mileage blocks for number of carloads, average load per car, average haul per ton, revenue per hundred weight, per carload, car-mile, ton-mile, percent of first-class rate, and transit, rebilled, 1.c.1., and any quantity shipments not included in averages, by commodity groups and classes.
Earlier IC 1.2:C 17/50

IC 1.23/8:date
CARLOAD WAYBILL STATISTICS, DISTRIBUTION OF FREIGHT TRAFFIC AND REVENUE AVERAGES BY COMMODITY CLASSES. 1954–   [Annual]

Gives for each of the commodity classes the number of carloads, tons, revenue, average tons per car, short-line haul per ton and haul per car, average revenue per 100 pounds, per car, short-line car-mile and ton-mile.

SS STATE-TO-STATE DISTRIBUTION, TRAFFIC AND REVENUE.

Gives for each State-to-State movement, number of car-loads, tons, revenue, short-line haul per ton, and average revenue per 100 pounds. The following are in the SS- (series):

IC 1.23/9:SS-1
ALL COMMODITIES. 1949–   [Annual]

IC 1.23/10:SS-2
PRODUCTS OF AGRICULTURE. 1948–   [Annual]

IC 1.23/11:SS-3
ANIMALS AND PRODUCTS. [Annual]

IC 1.23/12:SS-4
PRODUCT OF MINES. 1947–   [Annual]

IC 1.23/13:SS-5
PRODUCTS OF FOREST. [Annual]

IC 1.23/14:SS-6
MANUFACTURES AND MISCELLANEOUS AND FORWARDER TRAFFIC. 1948–   [Annual]

IC 1.23/15:SS-7
TONS OF REVENUE FREIGHT ORIGINATED AND TONS TERMINATED BY STATES AND BY COMMODITY CLASS. 1951–   [Annual]

TC TYPE OF CAR.

IC 1.23/16:TC-1
MILEAGE DISTRIBUTION OF CARLOADS FOR EACH COMMODITY CLASS BY TYPE OF CAR. 1954–   [Annual]

Gives number of carloads by mileage block indicated for commodity class by type of car for traffic terminated in year.

IC 1.23/16:TC-2
WEIGHT DISTRIBUTION OF CARLOADS FOR EACH COMMODITY CLASS BY TYPE OF CAR. 1947–   [Annual]

Gives number of carloads for specified weight brackets by commodity class and type of car.

IC 1.23/19:TC-3
TERRITORIAL DISTRIBUTION OF CARLOADS FOR EACH COMMODITY CLASS BY TYPE OF CAR. [Annual]

Gives number of carloads by territorial movement indicated, by commodity class and type of car.

TD TERRITORIAL DISTRIBUTION.

IC 1.23/18:TD-1
TERRITORIAL DISTRIBUTION, TRAFFIC AND
REVENUE BY COMMODITY CLASSES. 1947–
[Annual]

The first table shows for all commodity
groups, and for each of the individual commodity classes composing those groups, the
territorial movements of traffic together with
the associated revenues, short-line ton-miles
and car-miles, average tons per car, short-
line haul per ton and haul per car, average
revenue per 100 pounds, per car, per car-
mile and ton-mile. the second table shows the
progressions of average revenue per hundred weight by specified mileage blocks for
interterritorial traffic by territory.

IC 1.23/20:date
SUPPLEMENT TO CARLOAD WAYBILL STATISTICS.

IC 1.24:date
DISTRIBUTION OF PETROLEUM PRODUCTS BY
PETROLEUM ADMINISTRATION DISTRICTS.
[Quarterly]

Gives the flow of crude petroleum, gasoline,
distillate fuel oils, residual fuel oils, and kerosene
within and between the Petroleum Administration
Districts.

IC 1.25:date&pt.nos. • Item 699 (MF)
TRANSPORT STATISTICS IN THE UNITED STATES.
88th– 1954– [Annual]

Beginning with data for 1954, issued under
present title and releases in seven separate section. Supersedes Annual Report on the Statistics
of Railways in the United States, 1st-87th Annual
Reports, 1888-1953, and other publications.
Separate parts are released as the data are
collected, compiled, and published. The complete
set of statistics consists of the following parts:

1. Railroads, their Lessors and Proprietary Companies, The Pullman Company, and Railway
Express Agency, Inc.
4. Electric Railways.
5. Carriers by Water.
6. Oil Pipe Lines.
7. Motor Carriers.
8. Freight Forwarders.
9. Private Car Lines.

Parts 2 and 3, covering the Pullman Company and Railway Express Agency have been
consolidated into part 1.

IC 1.26:date
COMPENSATION OF OFFICERS, DIRECTORS, ETC.,
CLASS 1 RAILROADS, LINE-HAUL AND SWITCH-
ING AND TERMINAL COMPANIES. 1933– [An-
nual]

Title varies.
Lists by name of company, the title of position and salary per annum as of close of year and
other compensation for positions paid $20,000 or
more per year. Also contains summary tables.

IC 1.27:date
INDEXES OF AVERAGE FREIGHT RATES ON RAIL-
ROAD CARLOAD TRAFFIC. 1947/50– [Annual]

Tables include indexes (1950 100) of average
freight rates for commodity groups and selected
commodity classes, for territorial movement in
total and by commodity group, for intraand interstate rates by commodity group, by commodity
groupings corresponding to Bureau of Labor Statistics classification for wholesale commodity price
index; bituminous coal at commodity rates in official territory.

IC 1.28
PRESS RELEASES. [Irregular]

IC 1.29
FREIGHT REVENUE AND WHOLESALE VALUE AT
DESTINATION OF COMMODITIES TRANS-
PORTED BY BY CLASS I LINE-HAUL RAILROADS.
[Irregular]

PURPOSE:– To show for selective years estimates of the relation between gross freight revenues of Class I line-haul railroads and the wholesale value at destination of commodities transported by them.
The latest study was made for 1959 (Statement 6112) with previous studies being made for
1929, 1930, 1933, 1936, 1939, 1941, 1946, 1950,
1953, and 1956.

IC 1.30:CT
SHEETS OF NATIONAL ATLAS OF UNITED STATES.

IC 1.31:nos. • Item 674-A (MF)
PUBLIC ADVISORIES. 1– 1972–

IC 1.32:CT • Item 674-B (MF)
ENVIRONMENTAL IMPACT STATEMENTS. [Irregular]

IC 1.33:CT • Item 674-C
BIBLIOGRAPHIES AND LISTS OF PUBLICATIONS.
[Irregular]

IC 1.34:date • Item 674-D (MF)
REPORT TO THE PRESIDENT AND THE CONGRESS
ON THE EFFECTIVENESS OF THE RAIL PAS-
SENGER SERVICES ACT. [Annual]

ISSN 0147-2178
Earlier TD 1.10/5

IC 1.35:v.nos.&nos. • Item 678-A
ICC REGISTER. [Daily]

IC 1.36: • Item 674-H (MF)
CONTRACT ADVISORY SERVICE SUMMARIES. [Quar-
terly]

Issued in accordance with the Staggers Rail
Act of 1980, which permanently established a
Contract Advisory Service within the Commission
to advise interested parties about contract
ratemaking and to disseminate summaries on
contracts filed with the Commission.

IC 1.37: • Item 674-G (MF)
TELEPHONE DIRECTORY. [Quarterly]

Discontinued.

IC 1.38:date • Item 674-K (MF)
MINORITY AND FEMALE MOTOR CARRIER LIST-
INGS. [Biennial]

PURPOSE:– To list separately by state, female and minority owned motor carriers holding
interstate operating authority.

IC 1.39:date • Item 674-F (MF)
ANNUAL REPORT TO THE INTERSTATE COMMERCE
COMMISSION, CLASS I AND CLASS II MOTOR
CARRIERS OF PROPERTY. [Annual]

IC 1.39/2:date • Item 674-F (MF)
ANNUAL REPORT TO THE INTERSTATE COMMERCE
COMMISSION, CLASS I PASSENGER. [Annual]

IC 1.39/3:date • Item 674-F (MF)
ANNUAL REPORT TO THE INTERSTATE COMMERCE
COMMISSION, CLASS I AND CLASS II MOTOR
CARRIERS OF HOUSEHOLD GOODS. [Annual]

IC 1.40:ltrs-nos. • Item 674-F
FORMS. [Irregular]

[ACCIDENT INVESTIGATION DIVISION]

IC 1 acci.1:date
ANNUAL REPORTS.

IC 1 acci.2:CT
GENERAL PUBLICATIONS.

IC 1 acci.3 • Item 681
ACCIDENT BULLETIN. 1– 1901– [Annual]

Summary and analysis of accidents on railroads in the United States subject to the Interstate Commerce Act.
Part I, Introductory Comments, gives brief
tables on casualties to persons of all classes of
passengers, to employee, to trespassers; high-

way grade-crossing accidents, and train accidents. Part II, General summaries and Tables,
gives further breakdown of accidents by individual
railway.
Since 1922, issued annually with single Bulletin number assigned to each year.

IC 1 acci.4:nos.
CIRCULARS.

IC 1 acci.5:invest.nos.
REPORTS ON INVESTIGATIONS OF INDIVIDUAL
ACCIDENTS.

IC 1 acci.6:date
RULES GOVERNING MONTHLY REPORTS OF RAIL-
WAY ACCIDENTS.

IC 1 acci.7:nos.
SUMMARY OF ACCIDENT INVESTIGATION REPORTS.
1-84. –1940.

IC 1 acci.8
RAIL-HIGHWAY GRADE-CROSSING ACCIDENTS FOR
YEAR-ENDED DEC. 31, 1935– [Annual]

Gives time of accidents, type, kind of crossing protection, types and speeds of vehicle and
trains involved weather conditions. Figures also
appear in Accident Bulletin.

IC 1 acci.9:date
ACCIDENTS REPORTED BY RAILROAD COMPANIES,
PRELIMINARY SUMMARY. [Monthly]

[BUREAU OF ACCOUNTS]

IC 1 acco.1:date
ANNUAL REPORTS.

IC 1 acco.2:CT • Item 682-A (MF)
GENERAL PUBLICATIONS.

IC 1 acco.2:F 88 • Item 682-A
COST OF TRANSPORTING FREIGHT BY CLASS I
AND CLASS II MOTOR COMMON CARRIERS OF
GENERAL COMMODITIES. [Irregular]

Title and regions covered vary.
PURPOSE:– To provide the Commission with
information on motor carrier costs for use in its
various functions, and to make available to the
public cost information useful to carriers, shippers, traffic organizations, rate bureaus, educators, and others.
Series of territorial motor carrier cost and
traffic studies that show unit costs, operating
factors and cost scales.
The following reports are being published
currently:–

IC 1 acco.2:F 88/2 • Item 682-A
– MIDDLEWEST REGION. 1953– [Annual]
(Statement 2C10)

IC 1 acco.2:F 88/3 • Item 682-A
– SOUTHWEST REGION. 1953– [Annual]
(Statement 2C11)

IC 1 acco.2:F 88/4 • Item 682-A
– ROCKY MOUNTAIN REGION. 1955– [An-
nual] (Statement 2C12)

IC 1 acco.2:F 88/5 • Item 682-A
– PACIFIC REGION. 1955– [Annual] (Statement 2C13)

IC 1 acco.2:F 88/6 • Item 682-A
– MIDDLE ATLANTIC REGION. [Annual] (Statement 2C4)

IC 1 acco.2:F 88/8 • Item 682-A
– EASTERN-CENTRAL REGION. [Annual] (Statement 2C8)

IC 1 acco.2:F 88/9 • Item 682-A
– NEW ENGLAND REGION, GROUP 2, BETWEEN
NEW ENGLAND AND NEW YORK CITY AREA
AND BEYOND. [Annual] (Statement 2C3)

IC 1 acco.2:F 88/10 • Item 682-A
– EAST-SOUTH TERRITORY. 1957– [Annual]
(Statement 2C6)

IC 1 acco.2:F 88/11 • Item 682-A
– SOUTH-CENTRAL TERRITORY. [Annual] (Statement 2C7)

IC 1 acco.2:F 88/12 • Item 682-A
– SOUTHERN REGION. 1957– [Annual] (Statement 2C5)

IC 1 acco.2:F 88/13 • Item 682-A
– CENTRAL REGION. [Annual] (Statement 2C9)

IC 1 acco.2:F 88/14 • Item 682-A
– PERFORMING TRANSCONTINENTAL SERVICE. 1959– [Annual] (Statement 2C14)

IC 1 acco.2:F 88/15 • Item 682-A
– NEW ENGLAND REGION, GROUP 1, WITHIN NEW ENGLAND REGION. [Annual] (Statement 2C2)

IC 1 acco.2:F 88/16 • Item 682-A
– BY REGIONS FOR TERRITORIES FOR YEAR (date). 1963– [Annual] (Statement 2C1)

IC 1 acco.3:nos.
ACCOUNTING BULLETINS. 1– 15. 1908– 1918.

IC 1 acco.4:nos.
ACCOUNTING SERIES CIRCULARS. 1– 1906–

IC 1 acco.5:nos.
DEPRECIATION SECTION SERIES CIRCULARS. 1– 1921–

IC 1 acco.7 • Item 682-C (MF)
RAIL CARLOAD COST SCALES BY TERRITORIES FOR YEAR (date). 1948– [Annual]

Based on year (two years previous to date of study) operations with adjustment to reflect wage and price levels as of January 1. Principal tables include carload mileage cost scales, in cents per 100 pounds, by district or region and by type of car; carload unit costs for various weight loads by type of equipment, adjusted and unadjusted.

IC 1 acco.8:date
RAILROAD CONSTRUCTION INDICES. [Annual]

Earlier IC 1 acco.2:R 13/5

IC 1 acco.9:date
DISTRIBUTION OF RAIL REVENUE CONTRIBUTION BY COMMODITY GROUPS. [Annual]

Earlier IC 1.2:R 13/5

IC 1 acco.10:date
SCHEDULE OF ANNUAL AND PERIOD INDICES FOR CARRIERS BY PIPELINE. [Annual]

IC 1 acco.11:date • Item 682-E
QUARTERLY FREIGHT LOSS AND DAMAGE CLAIMS REPORTED BY COMMON AND CONTRACT MOTOR CARRIERS OF PROPERTY. (Bureau of Accounts)

ISSN 0364-2283

IC 1 acco.12:date-nos.
QUARTERLY FREIGHT LOSS AND DAMAGE CLAIMS, CLASS 1, LINE-HAUL RAILROADS.

IC 1 acco.13:date • Item 682-F (MF)
COST OF TRANSPORTING FREIGHT, CLASS 1 AND CLASS 2 MOTOR COMMON CARRIERS OF GENERAL FREIGHT. [Annual]

[ACTS TO REGULATE COMMERCE]

IC act.1:date
ANNUAL REPORTS.

IC 1 act.2:
GENERAL PUBLICATIONS.

IC 1 act.5:date • Item 675 (MF)
INTERSTATE COMMERCE ACT, INCLUDING TEXT OR RELATED SECTIONS OF OTHER ACTS.

IC 1 act.5/2:vol. • Item 676
INTERSTATE COMMERCE ACTS ANNOTATED. [Irregular]

Compilation of Federal laws relating to the Interstate Commerce Act, with digest of pertinent decisions of Federal courts and the Interstate Commerce Commission and text of or reference to general rules and regulations.
Volumes 1– 5, published in 1930, from the basic set, with volumes 6– as supplements. During recent years, supplements have been issued triennially.

IC 1 act.5/3:v.nos.&nos.
ADVANCE BULLETIN OF INTERSTATE COMMERCE ACTS ANNOTATED. v. 1– 3. – 1981. [Irregular]

Supplements Interstate Commerce Acts Annotated. Bulletins are issued at frequent intervals in order to provide annotations covering legislation, regulations and court and commission decisions as currently as possible.
Index is cumulative for current volume.

IC 1 act.5/3-2:v.nos.&nos. • Item 674-E
ADVANCE BULLETIN OF INTERSTATE COMMERCE ACTS ANNOTATED [2d series]. v. 1– [Bimonthly]

ISSN 0083-1506

IC 1 act.6:CT
PROSECUTIONS UNDER ACT TO REGULATE COMMERCE.

IC 1 act.7:CT
DECISIONS UNDER ACT TO REGULATE COMMERCE.

IC 1 act.8:CT
DECISION UNDER ELKINS [anti-rebate] ACT.

[AIR MAIL CARRIERS]

IC 1 air.1
ANNUAL REPORTS.

IC 1 air.2:CT
GENERAL PUBLICATIONS.

IC 1 air.3:nos.
BULLETINS.

IC 1 air.4:nos.
CIRCULARS.

IC 1 air.7:date
ABSTRACT OF REPORTS OF FREE AND REDUCED-FARE TRANSPORTATION RENDERED BY AIRMAIL CARRIERS. [Semiannual]

[BLOCK SIGNALS AND TRAIN CONTROL BOARD]

IC 1 blo.1:date
ANNUAL REPORTS.

IC 1 blo.2:CT
GENERAL PUBLICATIONS.

IC 1 blo.3:nos.
BULLETINS.

IC 1 blo.4:nos.
CIRCULARS.

IC 1 blo.5:date
TABULATION OF STATISTICS PERTAINING TO BLOCK SIGNALS AND TELEGRAPH AND TELEPHONE FOR TRANSMISSION OF TRAIN ORDERS.

Later IC 1 saf.10

[DEFENSE TRANSPORT ADMINISTRATION]

IC 1 def.1:date
ANNUAL REPORTS.

IC 1 def.2:CT
GENERAL PUBLICATIONS.

IC 1 def.6:CT
REGULATIONS, RULES, AND INSTRUCTIONS.

IC 1 def.6/2:nos.
GENERAL ORDERS.

IC 1 def.6/3:nos.
DTA DELEGATIONS.

IC 1 def.6/4:nos.
ADMINISTRATIVE ORDER DTA (series).

IC 1 def.7
RELEASES.

[ELECTRIC RAILWAYS]

IC 1 eler.1:date
ANNUAL REPORTS.

IC 1 eler.2:CT
GENERAL PUBLICATIONS.

IC 1 eler.3:
BULLETINS.

IC 1 eler.4:
CIRCULARS.

IC 1 eler.5:date
ANNUAL REPORTS ON STREET RAILROADS IN DISTRICT OF COLUMBIA [including reports of District Electric Railway Commission, calendar years].

IC 1 eler.6:date
CLASSIFICATION OF EXPENDITURES FOR ROADS AND EQUIPMENT OF ELECTRIC RAILWAYS.

Superseded by IC 1 eler.9

IC 1 eler.7:date
CLASSIFICATION OF OPERATING EXPENSES OF ELECTRIC RAILWAYS.

Superseded by IC 1 eler.9

IC 1.eler.8:date
CLASSIFICATION OF OPERATING REVENUES OF ELECTRIC RAILWAYS.

Superseded by IC 1 eler.9

IC 1 eler.9:date
UNIFORM SYSTEM OF ACCOUNTS FOR ELECTRIC RAILWAYS.

This publication is a revision and consolidation of the different issues classed IC 1 eler.6, IC 1 eler.7, IC 1 eler.8.

[EXPRESS COMPANIES]

IC 1 exp.1:date
ANNUAL REPORTS ON STATISTICS OF EXPRESS COMPANIES IN THE UNITED STATES.

IC 1 exp.2:CT
GENERAL PUBLICATIONS.

IC 1 exp.3
BULLETINS.

IC 1 exp.4:nos.
SPECIAL EXPRESS COMPANY CIRCULARS.

IC 1 exp.5:date
CLASSIFICATION OF EXPENDITURES FOR REAL PROPERTY AND EQUIPMENT OF EXPRESS COMPANIES.
Superseded by IC 1 exp.9

IC 1 exp.6:date
CLASSIFICATION OF OPERATING EXPENSES OF EXPRESS COMPANIES.
Superseded by IC 1 exp.9

IC 1 exp.7:date
CLASSIFICATION OF OPERATING REVENUES OF EXPRESS COMPANIES.
Superseded by IC 1 exp.9

IC 1 exp.8:date
FORM OF GENERAL BALANCE SHEET STATEMENT FOR EXPRESS COMPANIES.

Superseded by IC 1 exp.9

IC 1 exp.9:date
UNIFORM SYSTEM OF ACCOUNTS FOR EXPRESS COMPANIES.

This publication is a revision and consolidation of the different issues classed under IC1 exp.5, IC1 exp.6, IC1 exp.7, IC1 exp.8.

[GAS CORPORATIONS]

IC 1 gas.1:date
ANNUAL REPORTS.

IC 1 gas.2:CT
GENERAL PUBLICATIONS.

IC 1 gas.3:
BULLETINS.

IC 1 gas.4:
CIRCULARS.

IC 1 gas.5:date
UNIFORM SYSTEM OF ACCOUNTS FOR GAS CORPORATIONS AND ELECTRIC CORPORATIONS IN THE DISTRICT OF COLUMBIA.

[HOURS OF SERVICE]

IC 1 hou.1:date
ANNUAL REPORTS.

IC 1 hou.2:CT
GENERAL PUBLICATIONS.

IC 1 hou.3:
BULLETINS.

IC 1 hou.4:
CIRCULARS.

IC 1 hou.5:date
HOURS OF SERVICE ACT TEXT OF ACT.

IC 1 hou.6:nos.
ADMINISTRATIVE RULINGS [under house of service act].

Formerly IC 4.17

IC 1 hou.7:CT
DECISIONS UNDER HOURS OF SERVICE ACT [individual cases].

IC 1 hou.8:date
DECISIONS UNDER HOURS OF SERVICE ACT [compilations].

Formerly IC 1.2:H 81/5
See also IC 1 saf.9:915

IC 1 hou.9:date
STATISTICAL ANALYSIS OF CARRIER'S MONTHLY HOURS OF SERVICE REPORTS.

[LOCOMOTIVE INSPECTION BUREAU]

IC 1 loc.1   • Item 686
ANNUAL REPORT OF THE DIRECTOR OF LOCOMOTIVE INSPECTION. 1st–   1912–   [Annual]

Report made to the Interstate Commerce Commission for the fiscal year.

IC 1 loc.2:CT
GENERAL PUBLICATIONS.

IC 1 loc.3:nos.
BULLETINS.

IC 1 loc.4:nos.
CIRCULARS.

IC 1 loc.5:date   • Item 687
LAWS, RULINGS, AND INSTRUCTIONS FOR INSPECTION AND TESTING OF LOCOMOTIVES AND TENDERS AND THEIR APPURTENANCES.

IC 1 loc.6:date   • Item 687
INTERPRETATIONS, RULINGS AND EXPLANATIONS REGARDING LAWS, RULINGS, AND INSTRUCTIONS.

IC 1 loc.7:CT
DECISIONS UNDER LOCOMOTIVE INSPECTION ACT [individual cases].

IC 1 loc.8:date
LAWS, RULES, AND INSTRUCTIONS FOR INSPECTION AND TESTING OF LOCOMOTIVES OTHER THAN STEAM.

[MOTOR CARRIERS BUREAU]

IC 1 mot.1:date
ANNUAL REPORTS.

IC 1 mot.2:CT
GENERAL PUBLICATIONS.

IC 1 mot.3:nos.
BULLETINS.

IC 1 mot.4:nos.
CIRCULARS.

IC 1 mot.5:CT
LAWS.

IC 1 mot.6:CT   • Item 689
REGULATIONS, RULES, AND INSTRUCTIONS.

IC 1 mot.7:letters-nos.
TARIFF CIRCULARS.

IC 1 mot.8   • Item 688 (MF)
MOTOR CARRIER CASES. 1–   1936–   [Irregular]

Citation: M.C.C.
Reports for finance cases issued in separate volumes, those since 1950 as follows:
Discontinued.

IC 1 mot.8/a:M
MOTOR CARRIER. M 1–   [Irregular]

IC 1 mot.8/a 2
MOTOR CARRIER, FINANCE. MF 1–   [Irregular]

IC 1 mot.9:CT
PAPERS IN RE.

IC 1 mot.10:nos.
SAFETY SERIES, BULLETINS. 1. 1938.

Superseded by IC 1 mot.6

IC 1 mot.11:date
REVENUES, EXPENSES, AND STATISTICS OF CLASS 1 MOTOR CARRIERS OF PASSENGERS. 1938– 1945. [Monthly]

IC 1 mot.12:date   • Item 690 (MF)
REVENUES, EXPENSES, OTHER INCOME, AND STATISTICS OF CLASS 1 MOTOR CARRIERS OF PASSENGERS. [Semiannual] (Bureau of Accounts) (Statement 750)

Table 1 gives summary by districts and region for inter-city and local or suburban carriers. Table 2 gives selected statistics for individual carriers by districts and regions. Two year comparisons.
Formerly quarterly.
ISSN 0363-406X

IC 1 mot.13:date   • Item 691 (MF)
REVENUES, EXPENSES, OTHER INCOME, AND STATISTICS OF LARGE MOTOR CARRIERS OF PROPERTY. 1939–   [Annual] (Bureau of Accounts) (Statement 800)

Gives for carriers with operating revenues of $1,000,000 or more; revenues, expenses, other income, and selected items, by districts and regions, or intercity and local carriers, intercity common carriers of general commodities, intercity common carriers of special commodities and intercity contract carriers. Two year comparisons. Formerly quarterly.
ISSN 0360-988X

IC 1 mot.13/2:date   • Item 691
SELECTED REVENUES, EXPENSES, OTHER INCOME, AND STATISTICS OF CLASS II CARRIERS OF PROPERTY. [Quarterly] (Statement 850-X)

Covers carriers having average gross operating revenues of $200,000 or more, but less than $1,000,000.
Gives freight revenue, operating expenses, net operating revenue, net income before and after income taxes for intercity and local carriers, intercity common carriers of general and special commodities, and intercity contract carriers.

IC 1 mot.14:date
STATISTICS OF CLASS I MOTOR CARRIERS.

IC 1 mot.14/2:date
SELECTED STATISTICS FOR CLASS 3 MOTOR CARRIERS OF PROPERTY. [Annual]

Earlier IC 1 mot.2:St 2/4

IC 1 mot.15:m-nos.
MOTOR CARRIERS, SPECIAL CIRCULARS.

IC 1 mot.16:CT
TERRITORIAL STUDIES OF MOTOR CARRIER COSTS, TRAFFIC AND RATE STRUCTURE.

IC 1 mot.17:letters-nos.   • Item 689 (MF)
ACCOUNTING CIRCULARS. 1–

IC 1 mot.18:nos.
MOTOR CARRIER INVESTIGATION REPORTS. 1– 1952–

IC 1 mot.19:
REPORTS AND ORDERS RECOMMENDED BY JOINT BOARDS.

IC 1 mot.20:date
ANALYSIS OF DEFECTIVE VEHICLE ACCIDENTS OF MOTOR CARRIERS. [Annual]

Earlier IC 1 mot.2:AC 2/3

IC 1 mot.21:date
MOTOR CARRIERS OF PROPERTY, ACCIDENT DATA. [Quarterly]

IC 1 mot.21/2:date
MOTOR CARRIERS OF PASSENGERS, CLASS 1 ACCIDENT DATA. [Quarterly]

IC 1 mot.21/3:date
SUMMARY OF MOTOR CARRIER ACCIDENTS. – 1960.

IC 1 mot.22:date   • Item 687-A (MF)
MOTOR CARRIER FREIGHT COMMODITY STATISTICS CLASS 1 COMMON AND CONTRACT CARRIERS OF PROPERTY. [Annual] (Bureau of Accounts)

[PIPE LINE COMPANIES]

IC 1 pip.1:date
ANNUAL REPORTS.

IC 1 pip.2:CT
GENERAL PUBLICATIONS.

IC 1 pip.3:
BULLETINS.

IC 1 pip.4:
CIRCULARS.

IC 1 pip.5:date
UNIFORM SYSTEM OF ACCOUNTS FOR PIPE LINES.

IC 1 pip.6:date   • Item 692-A
UNIFORM SYSTEM OF ACCOUNTS FOR PIPE LINES.

Prior to 1935 see IC 1 pip.5

IC 1 pip.7:date
TRANSPORTATION REVENUE AND TRAFFIC OF LARGE OIL PIPE LINE COMPANIES. 1938– [Semiannual] (Statement 600)

Gives for carriers having annual operating revenue of more than $500,000; transportation, number of barrels of oil originated on line and received for connections, by companies, for quarter. Two year comparisons.
Formerly quarterly.

IC 1 pip.8:
DEPRECIATION RATES FOR PROPERTY OF CARRIERS BY PIPE LINES.

IC 1 pip.9:date
PIPE LINE CARRIERS, ANNUAL GUIDE PRICES AND INDICES.

[RATE SECTION]

IC 1 rat.1:date
ANNUAL REPORTS.

IC 1 rat.2:CT
GENERAL PUBLICATIONS.

IC 1 rat.3:nos.
BULLETINS.

IC 1 rat.4:nos.
TARIFF CIRCULARS.

IC 1 rat.5:nos.
SPECIAL CIRCULARS. 1–   1902.

Changed from IC 1.10

IC 1 rat.6:nos.
FOURTH SECTION CIRCULARS. 1–   1911–

Changed from IC 1.54

IC 1 rat.7:nos.
FOURTH SECTION ORDERS. 5–   1911–

IC 1 rat.8:date
SCHEDULE OF SAILINGS OF STEAM VESSELS REGISTERED UNDER LAWS OF UNITED STATES AND INTENDED TO LOAD GENERAL CARGO AT PORTS IN UNITED STATES FOR FOREIGN DESTINATIONS.

[BUREAU OF SAFETY]

IC 1 saf.1:date   **• Item 693**
ANNUAL REPORT DIRECTOR OF THE BUREAU OF SAFETY.

IC 1 saf.2:CT
GENERAL PUBLICATIONS.

IC 1 saf.3:
BULLETINS.

IC 1 saf.4:
CIRCULARS.

IC 1 saf.5:date   **• Item 693-A**
SAFETY APPLIANCES ACT [text].

IC 1 saf.5/2:CT   **• Item 693-A**
LAWS.

IC 1 saf.6:date
RULES FOR INSPECTION OF SAFETY APPLIANCES.

IC 1 saf.7:CT
DECISIONS UNDER SAFETY APPLIANCE ACTS [individual cases].

IC 1 saf.8:date
DECISIONS UNDER SAFETY APPLIANCE ACTS [compilations].

IC 1 saf.9:date
INDEX-DIGEST OF DECISIONS UNDER FEDERAL SAFETY APPLIANCE ACTS.

IC 1 saf.10:date   **• Item 694**
TABULATIONS OF STATISTICS PERTAINING TO SIGNALS, INTERLOCKING, AUTOMATIC, TRAIN CONTROL, TELEGRAPH AND TELEPHONE FOR TRANSMISSION OF TRAIN ORDERS, AND SPRING SWITCHES AS USED ON RAILROADS OF UNITED STATES.

Earlier IC 1 bloc.5

[SLEEPING CAR COMPANIES]

IC 1 sle.1:date
ANNUAL REPORTS.

IC 1 sle.2:CT
GENERAL PUBLICATIONS.

IC 1 sle.5:date
CLASSIFICATION OF REVENUES AND EXPENSES OF SLEEPING CAR OPERATIONS, OF AUXILIARY OPERATIONS AND OF OTHER PROPERTIES FOR SLEEPING CAR COMPANIES. 1912–

Earlier IC 1.59

[BUREAU OF STEAM ROADS]

IC 1 ste.1
BUREAU OF STEAM ROADS.

IC 1 ste.2:CT   **• Item 696**
GENERAL PUBLICATIONS.

IC 1 ste.3:
BULLETINS OF REVENUES AND EXPENSES OF STEAM ROADS. 1– 69. 1909– 1914.

IC 1 ste.4:
CIRCULARS.

IC 1 ste.5/1:date
NATIONAL ASSOCIATION OF RAILWAY COMMISSIONERS. PROCEEDINGS OF ANNUAL CONVENTION. 1st– 24th. 1889– 1912.

IC 1 ste.5/2:CT
– GENERAL PUBLICATIONS.

IC 1 ste.6:date
PRELIMINARY REPORTS OF INCOME ACCOUNTING OF RAILWAYS IN UNITED STATES. 1892– 1907.

IC 1 ste.7:date
CLASSIFICATION OF OPERATING EXPENSES.

Changed from IC 1.16:889-908/2, 193.
Superseded by IC 1 ste.17

IC 1 ste.8:date
CLASSIFICATION OF EXPENDITURES FOR ROAD AND EQUIPMENT.

Changed from IC 1.15:897-909
Superseded by IC 1 ste.16

IC 1 ste.9:date
CLASSIFICATION OF OPERATING REVENUES.

Changed from IC 1.19:907, 908.
Superseded by IC 1 ste.17

IC 1 ste.10:date
CLASSIFICATION OF REVENUES AND EXPENSES BY OUTSIDE OPERATIONS.

Earlier IC 1.29/1, 2:
Superseded by IC 1 ste.16

IC 1 ste.11:date
ANNUAL REPORTS ON STATISTICS OF RAILWAYS IN UNITED STATES. 1st–   1888– OF TRAIN-MILES LOCOMOTIVE-MILES AND CAR-MILES.

Earlier IC 1.21

IC 1 ste.12:date
CLASSIFICATION OF EXPENDITURES FOR ADDITIONS AND BETTERMENTS.

Earlier IC 1.42:
Superseded by IC 1 ste.16

IC 1 ste.13:date
FORM OF GENERAL BALANCE SHEET STATEMENT.

Changed from IC 1.43:909, 910
Superseded by IC 1 ste.15

IC 1 ste.14:date
FORM OF INCOME AND PROFIT AND LOSS STATEMENT.

Changed from IC 1.60
Superseded by IC 1 ste.15

IC 1 ste.15:date
CLASSIFICATION OF INCOME, PROFIT & LOSS, AND GENERAL BALANCE SHEET ACCOUNTS.

Changed from IC 1.43:914
Superseded IC 1 ste.13 and IC 1 ste.14

IC 1 ste.16:date
CLASSIFICATION OF INVESTMENT IN ROAD EQUIPMENT.

Earlier IC 1.19:914
Supersedes IC 1 ste.8 and IC 1 ste.12

IC 1 ste.17:date
CLASSIFICATION OF OPERATING REVENUES AND OPERATING EXPENSES.

Changed from IC 1.19:914
Supersedes IC 1 ste.7, 9, and 10.

IC 1 ste.18:date
CONDENSED CLASSIFICATION OF OPERATING EXPENSES.

Changed from IC 1.16:908/3, 4; 914.

IC 1 ste.19:date
OPERATING REVENUES AND OPERATING EXPENSES CLASS 1 STEAM RAILWAY IN UNITED STATES.   – 1967. [Monthly]

IC 1 ste.19/2:date
ADVANCE SUMMARY OF REVENUES, EXPENSES, AND NET RAILWAY OPERATING INCOME, CLASS 1 STEAM RAILWAYS. [Monthly]

IC 1 ste.19/3:date   **• Item 709**
OPERATING REVENUES AND OPERATING EXPENSES OF CLASS I RAILROADS IN THE UNITED STATES. 1920–   [Quarterly] (Statement 100)

Tables include miles of road operated, revenue, expenses, taxes, for U.S. and by region and district, for quarter. Switching and terminal companies not included. Two year comparisons.
Beginning 1968 absorbed IC 1 ste.19, IC 1 ste.19/2, IC 1 ste.20.
Effective with July– December 1972 data, consolidated with other statements into Financial and Operating Statistics, Class I Railroads (IC 1 ste.19/4).

IC 1 ste.19/4:date   **• Item 698 (MF)**
FINANCIAL AND OPERATING STATISTICS, CLASS I RAILROADS. [Semiannual] (Bureau of Accounts) (Statement 100)

Effective with July– December 1972 data, replaces statements Q-100 (IC 1 ste.19/3); Q-125 (IC 1 ste.34); Q-200 (IC 1 ste.22); Q-210 (IC 1 ste.38/2): Q-220 (IC 1 ste.24); and Q-240 (IC 1 ste.36)

IC 1 ste.20:date
OPERATING REVENUES AND OPERATING EXPENSES OF LARGE STEAM ROADS WITH ANNUAL OPERATING REVENUES ABOVE $25,000,000.   – 1967.

IC 1 ste.21:date
OPERATING STATISTICS OF CLASS 1 STEAM ROADS, FREIGHT AND PASSENGERS SERVICE.

IC 1 ste.22:date   **• Item 698 (MF)**
OPERATING STATISTICS OF LARGE RAILROADS, SELECTED ITEMS. 1920– [Quarterly] (Statement 200)

Table gives selected items for freight and passenger service by region for individual railroad for quarter and quarter and a year ago. Fourth quarter reports give data for calendar year.
Tables in the following six items (Q–211– Q–240) give aggregates and averages for selected items or quarter and quarter a year ago.
Effective with July– December 1972 data, consolidated with other statements in Financial and Operating Statistics, Class I Railroads (IC 1 ste.19/4).

IC 1 ste.23:date
UNIT COSTS (selected expense accounts) OF CLASS 1 STEAM ROADS. [Freight and Passenger Train Service]. 1921–

IC 1 ste.24:date   **• Item 711 (MF)**
REVENUE TRAFFIC STATISTICS OF CLASS I RAILROADS IN THE UNITED STATES. 1921– [Quarterly] (Statement 220)

Switching and terminal companies not included.

IC 1 ste.25:date   **• Item 714 (MF)**
WAGE STATISTICS OF CLASS I RAILROADS IN THE UNITED STATES. 1921– [Annual] (Bureau of Accounts) (Statement 300)

Tables give number of employees, service hours, and compensation by occupation, with recapitulation by groups of employees. Switching and terminal companies not included.
Formerly monthly.

IC 1 ste.25/2:
NUMBER OF EMPLOYEES AT MIDDLE OF MONTH.

IC 1 ste.25/3:date
PRELIMINARY REPORT OF RAILROAD EMPLOYMENT, CLASS 1 LINE-HAUL RAILROADS. (Statement 350)

IC 1 ste.25/3-2:date
REPORT OF RAILROAD EMPLOYMENT, CLASS 1 LINE-HAUL RAILROADS. [Monthly]

IC 1 ste.26:date   **• Item 705**
FREIGHT COMMODITY STATISTICS OF CLASS I RAILROADS IN THE UNITED STATES. 1920– [Quarterly] (Statement 500)

Cover table gives tons of revenue carried and freight revenue of large Class I railroads. Additional tables give freight traffic originated, freight traffic terminated, total freight carried, and freight revenue, by class of commodities and by regions.

IC 1 ste.27:date
COMPARATIVE STATEMENT OF OPERATING AVERAGES, CLASS I STEAM RAILWAYS IN UNITED STATES.

IC 1 ste.28:date
PRELIMINARY STATEMENT OF CAPITALIZATION AND INCOME, CLASS I STEAM RAILWAYS IN UNITED STATES. 1924– 1931.

IC 1 ste.29:date   **• Item 704**
FREIGHT COMMODITY STATISTICS, CLASS I RAILROADS IN THE UNITED STATES FOR YEAR ENDED DECEMBER 31 (date). 1924– [Annual]

Tables give tons originated and freight revenue, by groups of commodities and by districts; number of tons revenue freight originated, by groups of commodities and by regions and districts; freight traffic originated, freight traffic terminated, total freight traffic carried, and freight revenue, by individual classes of commodities and by regions; average load per car originated, by individual classes of commodities and by regions; average revenue per ton originated or per ton terminated by classes of commodities; relative importance of the various groups of com-

modities, ratios of group totals to grand total, tons carried, and freight revenue, by individual railways; and tons of revenue freight and freight revenue for each Class I railway by individual classes of commodities.

IC 1 ste.30:date
FUEL AND POWER FOR LOCOMOTIVES AND RAIL MOTOR CARS OF CLASS I STEAM RAILWAYS IN UNITED STATES. 1925– 1963. (Statement 230)

IC 1 ste.31:date
SUMMARY OF ACCIDENTS REPORTED BY STEAM RAILWAYS. 1924– 1966. [Monthly]

IC 1 ste.32:date
OPERATING REVENUES AND OPERATING EXPENSES BY CLASS OF SERVICE, CLASS 1 STEAM RAILWAYS IN UNITED STATES. 1927– 1935.

IC 1 ste.33:date
GRAPHICAL SUPPLEMENT TO MONTHLY REPORTS. – 1941.

IC 1 ste.34:date   **• Item 712 (MF)**
SELECTED INCOME AND BALANCE SHEET ITEMS OF CLASS I RAILROADS IN THE UNITED STATES. 1932– [Quarterly] (Statement 125)

Table give for U.S. and regions selected income items; for U.S. selected expenditures and asset items, Two year comparisons. Second table gives selected income items by regions and district.
Effective with July– December 1972 data, consolidated with other statements into Financial and Operating Statistics, Class I Railroads (IC ste.19/4).

IC 1 ste.35:date   **• Item 706**
FREIGHT TRAIN PERFORMANCE OF CLASS I RAILROADS IN THE UNITED STATES. 1936– 1963. [Quarterly] (Statement 211)

Switching and terminal companies not included.
Replaced by IC 1 ste.38/2.

IC 1 ste.36:date   **• Item 708 (MF)**
MOTIVE POWER AND CAR EQUIPMENT OF CLASS I RAILROADS IN THE UNITED STATES. 1936– [Quarterly] (Statement 240)

Switch and terminal companies are included.
Effective with July– December 1972 data, consolidated with other statements into Financial and Operating Statistics, Class Railroads (IC1 ste.19/4).

IC 1 ste.37:date   **• Item 710**
PASSENGER TRAIN PERFORMANCE OF CLASS I RAILROADS IN THE UNITED STATES. 1936– 1963. [Quarterly] (Statement 213)

Switching and terminal companies not included.
Replaced by IC 1 ste.38/2

IC 1 ste.38:date   **• Item 715**
YARD SERVICE PERFORMANCE OF CLASS I RAILROADS IN THE UNITED STATES. 1936– 1963 [Quarterly] (Statement 215)

Replaced by IC 1 ste.38/2

IC 1 ste.38/2:date   **• Item 710 (MF)**
TRAIN AND YARD SERVICE OF CLASS I RAILROADS IN THE UNITED STATES. 1964– [Quarterly] (Statement 210)

Gives train and year service for U.S. and regions for freight and passenger trains.
Replaces IC 1 ste.35, IC 1 ste.37, and IC 1 ste.38
Effective with July– December 1972 data, consolidated with other statements into Financial and Operating Statistics, Class I Railroads (IC1 ste.19/4).

IC 1 ste.39:date
PASSENGER TRAFFIC STATISTICS (other than commutation) OF CLASS I STEAM RAILWAYS IN THE UNITED STATES SEPARATED BETWEEN COACH TRAFFIC AND PARLOR AND SLEEPING CAR TRAFFIC. – 1938. [Quarterly] (Statement 250)

IC 1 ste.40:date
PASSENGER TRAFFIC STATEMENTS (other than commutation) OF CLASS 1 STEAM RAILWAYS IN UNITED STATES SEPARATED BETWEEN COACH TRAFFIC AND PARLOR AND SLEEPING CAR TRAFFIC. 1938– 1963. [Monthly]

Incorporated in IC 1 ste.24

IC 1 ste.41:date
RAILWAYS FREIGHT AND PASSENGER TRAFFIC HANDLED ON HIGHWAYS, CLASS 1 STEAM RAILWAYS. 1939– 1942. [Quarterly] (Statement 225)

IC 1 ste.42:date
TONS OF REVENUE FREIGHT ORIGINATED AND TONS TERMINATED IN CARLOADS BY CLASSES OF COMMODITIES AND BY GEOGRAPHIC AREAS, CLASS 1 STEAM RAILWAYS. – 1950. [Quarterly] (Statement 550)

IC 1 ste.43:date
NUMBER OF FEMALES EMPLOYED BY CLASS 1 STEAMS RAILWAYS. – 1948. [Quarterly]

IC 1 ste.44:date   **• Item 702 (MF)**
UNIFORM SYSTEM OF ACCOUNTS FOR STEAM RAILWAYS. [Irregular]

IC 1 ste.45:date
STEAM RAILWAYS IN HANDS OF RECEIVERS AND TRUSTEES, AND CHANGES IN LIST OF COMPANIES AFFECTED BY RECEIVER SHIP OF TRUSTEESHIP.

1942 changed from IC 1 ste.2:R 24 and 1943 changed from IC 1 ste.2:R 24/943

IC 1 ste.46:date
CONDENSED CONSOLIDATED STATISTICAL STATEMENTS, CLASS 1 RAILWAYS HAVING ANNUAL RAILWAY OPERATING REVENUES OF $10,000,000 OR MORE.

IC 1 ste.47:
DEPRECIATION RATES FOR EQUIPMENT OF STEAM RAILROAD COMPANIES.

[TELEGRAPH COMPANIES]

IC 1 telg.1:date
ANNUAL REPORTS.

IC 1 telg.2:CT
GENERAL PUBLICATIONS.

IC 1 telg.3:
BULLETINS.

IC 1 telg.4:
CIRCULARS.

IC 1 telg.5:date
UNIFORM SYSTEM OF ACCOUNTS FOR TELEGRAPH AND CABLE COMPANIES. 1913–

[TELEPHONE DIVISION]

IC 1 telp.2:CT
GENERAL PUBLICATIONS.

IC 1 telp.3:
BULLETINS.

IC 1 telp.4:
CIRCULARS.

IC 1 telp.5:date
UNIFORM SYSTEM OF ACCOUNTS FOR TELEPHONE COMPANIES.

IC 1 telp.6:date
SUMMARY OF MONTHLY REPORTS OF LARGE TELEPHONE COMPANIES. – 1934.

IC 1 telp.7:date
TELEPHONE COMPANIES, SELECTED FINANCIAL AND OPERATING DATA FROM ANNUAL REPORTS.

Previous to 1924 title reads: Statement of Selected Items From Annual Reports of Telephone Companies.

[BUREAU OF VALUATION]

IC 1 val.1:date
ANNUAL REPORT.

IC 1 val.2:CT
GENERAL PUBLICATIONS.

IC 1 val.3:nos.
BULLETINS.

IC 1 val.4:nos.
CIRCULARS.

IC 1 val.5:nos.
VALUATION ORDERS.

IC 1 val.6:CT
INSTRUCTIONS FOR FIELD WORK.

IC 1 val.7:vol.
VALUATION REPORTS.

IC 1 val.7/a:CT
VALUATION DOCKETS.

IC 1 val.8:CT
PAPERS IN RE.

IC 1 val.9:vol.
VALUATION REPORTS.

Earlier IC 1.6/1

IC 1 val.9/a:B-nos.
VALUATION REPORTS (separates). 1– 2148. 1929– 1964.

Earlier IC 1.6/1a:B-nos.

IC 1 val.10:date
SELECTED ELEMENTS OF VALUE OF PROPERTY USED IN COMMON CARRIER SERVICE, BEFORE AND AFTER RECORDED DEPRECIATION AND AMORTIZATION, CLASS I LINE HAUL RAILWAYS, INCLUDING THEIR LESSORS AND PROPRIETARY COMPANIES. [Annual]

Earlier IC 1 val.2:C 23/3

IC 1 val.11:date
ELEMENTS OF VALUE OF PROPERTY, CLASS I SWITCHING AND TERMINAL COMPANIES USED IN COMMON CARRIER SERVICE. [Annual]

Earlier IC 1 val.2:C 23

IC 1 val.12:date
ELEMENTS OF VALUE OF PROPERTY, CLASS I SWITCHING AND TERMINAL COMPANIES USED IN COMMON CARRIER SERVICE. [Annual]

Earlier IC 1 asso.2:C 23

[BUREAU OF WATER CARRIERS]

IC 1 wat.1:date
ANNUAL REPORTS.

IC 1 wat.2:CT
GENERAL PUBLICATIONS.

IC 1 wat.3:
BULLETINS.

IC 1 wat.4:
CIRCULARS.

IC 1 wat.5:date
CLASSIFICATION OF OPERATING EXPENSES.

IC 1 wat.7:date
CLASSIFICATION OF OPERATING REVENUES.

IC 1 wat.7:date
CLASSIFICATION OF EXPENDITURES FOR REAL PROPERTY AND EQUIPMENT.

IC 1 wat.8:date
CLASSIFICATION OF INCOME AND PROFIT AND LOSS ACCOUNTS.

IC 1 wat.9:date
FORM OF GENERAL BALANCE SHEET STATEMENT.

IC 1 wat.10:date
CARRIERS BY WATER, SELECTED FINANCIAL AND OPERATING DATA FORM ANNUAL REPORTS.

IC 1 wat.11:date • Item 682-D (MF)
REVENUE AND TRAFFIC OF CLASS A AND B WATER CARRIERS. 1938– [Semiannual] (Statement 650)

Gives freight revenue, number of tons of revenue freight carried, passenger revenue, and number of revenue passengers carried, by company, for quarter. Two year comparisons.
Former title: Revenue and Traffic Carriers by Water.
Formerly quarterly.

IC 1 wat.12:
DEPRECIATION RATES OF CARRIERS BY WATER ADMINISTRATIVE.

IC 1 wat.13:
DEPRECIATION RATE FOR CARRIERS BY INLAND AND COASTAL WATERWAYS; SUB-ADV.

IC 1 wat.14:date • Item 715-C (MF)
UNIFORM SYSTEM OF ACCOUNTS FOR CARRIERS BY INLAND AND COASTAL WATERWAYS.

Earlier IC 1 wat.2:Ac 2

INTERNATIONAL COMMUNICATION AGENCY (1978– 1982)

CREATION AND AUTHORITY

The International Communication Agency was established as an independent agency by Executive Order 12048 of March 27, 1978 to succeed the United States Information Agency. The name of the Agency was changed back to United States Information Agency (IA) by Public Law 97-241 (96 Stat. 291), approved August 24, 1982.

ICA 1.1:date
ANNUAL REPORT.

Earlier IA 1.1

CA 1.2:CT • Item 672-B
GENERAL PUBLICATIONS.

See also IA 1.2

ICA 1.6:CT • Item 672-B
REGULATIONS, RULES, AND INSTRUCTIONS. [Irregular]

Earlier IA 1.6

ICA 1.8:CT • Item 672-D
HANDBOOKS, MANUALS, GUIDES. [Irregular]

See also IA 1.6/2

ICA 1.9:v.nos.&nos. • Item 672-C
PROBLEMS OF COMMUNISM. v. 1– 1952– [Bimonthly]

PURPOSE:– To make readily available significant background information and documentary material on the theoretical and political aspects of world communism today, with particular emphasis on the policies and aims of the Soviet Union and Communist China. Contains book reviews.
Index contained in the November-December issues.
See also IA 1.8
Indexed by:–
Public Affairs Information Service
Social Sciences Abstracts
ISSN 0032-941X

ICA 1.10:nos.
AMERICAN ILLUSTRATED [Russian Edition]. [Monthly]

Earlier IA 1.14

ICA 1.11:v.nos.&nos. • Item 672-F
ENGLISH TEACHING FORUM. v. 1– 1963– [Quarterly]

PURPOSE:– To provide a journal for those teaching the English language in foreign countries. Contains short articles on teaching techniques, news and ideas, textbook reviews, letters to the editor, etc.
ISSN 0041-1434
See also IA 1.17

ICA 1.12 • Item 672-F-1
DIRECTORY OF RESOURCES FOR CULTURAL AND EDUCATIONAL EXCHANGES AND INTERNATIONAL COMMUNICATION.

Earlier S 1.67/4

ICA 1.13:v.nos.&nos.
USICA WORLD. v. 1– 1979– 1981.

Superseded by publication with the same title (ICA 1.13/2).

ICA 1.13/2:v.nos.&nos.
USICA WORLD. v. 1– 1981– [Bimonthly]

Continues USIC World (ICA 1.13) in a redesigned format.
Superseded by USIA WORLD (IA 1.25).

ICA 1.14:CT
RESEARCH REPORT (series). [Irregular]

ICA 1.15:date • Item 672-G
TELEPHONE DIRECTORY. [Semiannual]

Later IA 1.26

ICA 1.16:CT
AUDIOVISUAL MATERIALS. [Irregular]

UNITED STATES INTERNATIONAL TRADE COMMISSION (1981–)

CREATION AND AUTHORITY

The United States Tariff Commission was created by act of Congress approved September 8, 1916 (39 Stat. 795). The Commission's present powers and duties are provided for largely by the Tariff Act of 1930; the Antidumping Act of 1921; and the Agricultural Adjustment Act; and the Trade Expansion Act of 1962. The name was changed to United States International Trade Commission by section 171 of the Trade Act of 1974 (88 Stat. 2009) [SuDocs agency class number changed to ITC 1 in November 1981.]

INFORMATION

United States International
Trade Commission
500 E Street, SW
Washington, D.C. 20436
(202) 205-2000
Fax: (202) 205-2798
http://www.usitc.gov

ITC 1.1:date   • **Item 977 (MF)**
ANNUAL REPORTS.

Earlier TC 1.1

ITC 1.2:CT   • **Item 978**
GENERAL PUBLICATIONS. [Irregular]

Earlier TC 1.2

ITC 1.3
BULLETINS.

ITC 1.4:nos.
CIRCULARS.

ITC 1.5:CT
LAWS.

Earlier TC 1.30

ITC 1.6:CT
REGULATIONS, RULES, AND INSTRUCTIONS. [Irregular]

Earlier TC 1.16

ITC 1.7:CT
RELEASES.

Earlier TC 1.29

ITC 1.8:CT   • **Item 978-A**
HANDBOOKS, MANUALS, GUIDES. [Irregular]

Earlier TC 1.16/2

ITC 1.9:nos.
BIBLIOGRAPHIES AND LISTS OF PUBLICATIONS. [Irregular]

Earlier TC 1.34

ITC 1.9/2:date   • **Item 980-F (MF)**
OUR LIBRARY PRESENTS. [Monthly]

Earlier TC 1.34/2

ITC 1.9/3:date   • **Item 980-F-1**
SELECTED PUBLICATIONS OF THE UNITED STATES INTERNATIONAL TRADE COMMISSION. [Annual]

Lists selected ITC publications issued from 1951 to date.

ITC 1.10:date   • **Item 982-B-2 (P) (EL)**
HARMONIZED TARIFF SCHEDULE OF THE U.S. ANNOTATED FOR STATISTICAL REPORTING PURPOSES.

(Includes basic volume plus supplementary material for an indefinite period)
PURPOSE:– To enable importers, customs brokers, customs officers, and other interested persons to determine the rates of duty applicable to imported articles, and the requirements for reporting statistical data with respect to such imports.
Earlier title: Tariff Schedules of the U.S. Annotated.
Earlier TC 1.35/2

ITC 1.10/2:date   • **Item 982-B-1**
HISTORY OF THE TARIFF SCHEDULES OF THE UNITED STATES ANNOTATED. 1981–   [Irregular] (Includes basic volume plus supplementary material for an indefinite period)

PURPOSE:– To provide a compilation that includes the Staged Rates, Amendments and Modifications, and Statistical Notes to the Tariff Schedules of the United States Annotated (ITC 1.10).
Basic volume kept current by the three supplements a year.

ITC 1.10/3   • **Item 980-E-11 (MF)**
IMPORTS UNDER ITEMS 806.30 AND 807.00 OF THE TARIFF SCHEDULES OF THE UNITED STATES. [Annual]

PURPOSE– To present and analyze statistical data on item 806.30 imports (US metal articles processed abroad and returned for further processing) and 807 imports (US articles assembled abroad).

ITC 1.10/4:date   • **Item 982-B-3 (CD)**
HARMONIZED TARIFF SCHEDULE OF THE UNITED STATES.

ITC 1.11:nos.   • **Item 982-B (MF)**
SUMMARY OF TRADE AND TARIFF INFORMATION (series). [Irregular]

Earlier TC 1.26/2

ITC 1.12:nos.   • **Item 980-E (MF)**
INVESTIGATIONS (series). [Irregular]

Contains all Investigation reports under various Tariff Acts that are not established as separate classes.
Earlier TC 1.31; TC 1.31/2; and TC 1.39

ITC 1.13:nos.   • **Item 980-G (MF)**
REPORT TO THE CONGRESS AND THE TRADE POLICY COMMITTEE ON TRADE BETWEEN THE U.S. AND THE NONMARKET ECONOMY COUNTRIES. [Quarterly]

Also published in microfiche.
Earlier TC 1.38

ITC 1.14:date   • **Item 982-A**
SYNTHETIC ORGANIC CHEMICALS, U.S. PRODUCTION AND SALES. [Annual]

Report prepared under the general provisions of sections 332 and 333 of the Tariff Act of 1930. Part 1 gives statistical data on production and sales of tars, tar crudes, and crudes derived from petroleum and natural gas. Part 2 gives statistical data on production and sales of intermediates and finished synthetic organic chemicals, by groups. Part 3 contains an alphabetical list of individual products, by groups, and names of manufactures, both by code name and alphabetical list with addresses. Appendix contains a glossary of synonymous names of cyclic intermediates and a cross-reference list of Color Index and common names of toners and lakes.
Earlier TC 1.33

ITC 1.14/2:nos.
PRELIMINARY REPORT ON U.S. PRODUCTION OF SELECTED SYNTHETIC ORGANIC CHEMICALS. [Monthly]

ITC 1.15:date   • **Item 980-E-7 (MF)**
U.S. TRADE SHIFTS IN SELECTED COMMODITY AREAS. [Quarterly]

ITC 1.15/2:date   • **Item 980-E-7 (EL)**
U.S. TRADE SHIFT SELECTED COMMODITY AREAS. [Annual]

ITC 1.15/3   • **Item 980-E-12 (EL)**
RECENT TRENDS IN U.S. SERVICES TRADE. [Annual]

ITC 1.16:date
U.S. AUTOMOTIVE TRADE STATISTICS, SERIES A: MOTOR VEHICLES. [Annual]

Earlier TC 1.2:Au 8/23

ITC 1.16/2:date
U.S. AUTOMOTIVE TRADE STATISTICS, SERIES B, PASSENGER AUTOMOBILES. [Annual]

Earlier TC 1.2:Au 8/23

ITC 1.16/3:date   • **Item 980-E-6**
U.S. AUTOMOBILE INDUSTRY: MONTHLY REPORT ON SELECTED ECONOMIC INDICATORS. [Monthly]

ITC 1.16/4:date   • **Item 980-E-6 (MF)**
U.S. AUTO INDUSTRY. [Annual]

Statistical data covers U.S. Factory Sales, Retail Sales, Imports, Exports, Apparent Consumption, Suggested Retail Prices, and Trade Balances with Selected Countries for Motor Vehicles.
Also published in microfiche.

ITC 1.17:date   • **Item 980-E-4 (MF)**
BOLTS, NUTS, AND LARGE SCREWS OF IRON OR STEEL. [Annual]

Earlier TC 1.2:B 63

ITC 1.17/2:date   • **Item 980-E-4 (MF)**
BOLTS, NUTS, AND LARGE SCREWS OF IRON OR STEEL. [Quarterly]
Earlier TC 1.2:B 63

ITC 1.18:date   • **Item 980-E-1 (MF)**
COLOR TELEVISION RECEIVERS. [Annual]

ITC 1.18/2:date   • **Item 980-E-1 (MF)**
COLOR TELEVISION RECEIVERS. [Quarterly]

Gives data on U.S. production, shipments, inventories, exports, employment, man-hours and prices.

ITC 1.19:date   • **Item 980-E-5 (MF)**
IMPORTS OF BENZENOID CHEMICALS AND PRODUCTS. [Annual]

Covers United States general imports of intermediates, dyes, medicinal, flavor and perfume material, and other finished benzenoid products entered during the year under schedule 4, pt. 1, of the Tariff Schedules of the United States.
Earlier TC 1.36

ITC 1.20:date   • **Item 980-E-3 (MF)**
PROCESSED MUSHROOMS. [Quarterly]

Gives data on U.S. producers, products, sales and inventories, U.S. imports, exports and apparent consumption.
Earlier TC 1.2:M 97/6

ITC 1.21:date   • **Item 980-E-2 (MF)**
NONRUBBER FOOTWARE. [Annual]
Earlier TC 1.2:F 73/80

ITC 1.21/2:date   • **Item 980-E-2 (MF)**
NONRUBBER FOOTWEAR. [Quarterly]

Gives data on U.S. products, exports, imports for consumption producers, price index and consumer price index.

ITC 1.22:nos.   • **Item 980-H (MF)**
STAFF RESEARCH STUDIES (series). 1–   [Irregular]
Each study concerns a different subject.

ITC 1.23:date   • **Item 980-E-8 (MF)**
U.S. TRADE SHIFT SELECTED COMMODITY AREAS. [Annual]

ITC 1.23:date   • **Item 980-E-8 (MF)**
BROOM CORN BROOMS: PRODUCERS' SHIPMENTS, IMPORTS FOR CONSUMPTION, EXPORTS, AND APPARENT CONSUMPTION. [Annual]

ITC 1.24:date   • **Item 980-A**
OPERATIONS OF THE TRADE AGREEMENTS PROGRAM. [Annual]
Report submitted by the Commission to Congress pursuant to section 350 (e) (2) of the Tariff Act of 1930, as amended, which requires the Tariff Commission to submit to Congress, at least once a year, a factual report of the operation of the Trade Agreements Program. Before the passage of the Trade Agreements Extension of 1955, various Executive Orders had directed the Commission to prepare similar annual reports and submit them to the President and to Congress.
Report covers U.S. trade agreements legislation, developments relating to the operation of the General Agreement of Tariffs and Trade, actions of the United States relating to its trade agreements program, and major commercial policy developments in countries with which the United States has trade agreements.
Also published in microfiche.
Earlier TC 1.14/3

ITC 1.25   • **Item 980-E-9 (MF)**
QUARTERLY SURVEY ON CERTAIN STAINLESS STEEL AND ALLOY TOOL STEEL. [Quarterly]

PURPOSE:– To compare U.S. production and shipments of certain steel and alloy steel products. Also contains data on employment, pricing, unfilled orders, and inventories.

ITC 1.25/2:date • Item 980-E-9 (MF)
ANNUAL SURVEY ON CERTAIN STAINLESS STEEL AND ALLOY TOOL STEEL.

ITC 1.26 • Item 980-E-10
HEAVYWEIGHT MOTORCYCLES: SELECTED ECONOMIC INDICATORS. [Quarterly]

ITC 1.26/2:date • Item 980-E-10
HEAVYWEIGHT MOTORCYCLES: ANNUAL REPORT ON SELECTED ECONOMIC INDICATORS. [Annual]

ITC 1.27:date • Item 980-E-9
MONTHLY REPORT ON SELECTED STEEL INDUSTRY DATA.

ITC 1.28:date • Item 980
SPECIAL AND ADMINISTRATIVE PROVISIONS. [Biennial]

Former title: Special and Administrative Provisions of Tariff Act (TC 1.10/2).

ITC 1.29 • Item 980-J (EL)
INTERNATIONAL ECONOMIC REVIEW. [Monthly]

Produced to keep the Commission informed about significant developments in international economics and trade and to maintain its readiness to inform and advise Congressional and Executive Branch policymakers on international trade matters.

ITC 1.29/2 • Item 980-J (MF)
INTERNATIONAL ECONOMIC REVIEW, SPECIAL EDITION, CHARTBOOK. [Annual]

ITC 1.30:date • Item 980-L (MF)
U.S. IMPORTS OF TEXTILES AND APPAREL UNDER THE MULTIFIBER ARRANGEMENT, STATISTICAL REPORT. [Annual]

PURPOSE– To present statistical tables on U.S. imports of cotton, wool, and manmade fiber textiles that may make comparisons over a period of several years.

ITC 1.31:date • Item 980-K (MF)
RUM: ANNUAL REPORT ON SELECTED ECONOMIC INDICATORS. [Annual]

Contains statistical information on rum in such areas as U.S. production, U.S. exports, and U.S. imports for consumption.

ITC 1.32:date • Item 980-M (MF)
ANNUAL REPORT ON THE IMPACT OF THE CARIBBEAN BASIN ECONOMIC RECOVERY ACT ON U.S. INDUSTRIES AND CONSUMERS. [Annual]

Reports on the impact of the Caribbean Basin Economic Recovery Act, which granted duty-free treatment of imports from designated Caribbean Basin countries. The initial report covers two years.

ITC 1.33 • Item 978-A-1 (MF)
INDUSTRY AND TRADE SUMMARY.

ITC 1.33/2:date • Item 978-A-2 (EL)
INDUSTRY TRADE AND TECHNOLOGY REVIEW.

DEPARTMENT OF JUSTICE
(1870–   )

CREATION AND AUTHORITY

The Department of Justice was established by the act of June 22, 1870 (16 Stat. 162; 28 U.S.C. 501, 503), with the Attorney General at its head. Prior to 1870 the Attorney General was a member of the President's Cabinet, but not the head of a department, the office having been created under authority of the act of September 24, 1789, as amended (1 Stat. 92, 16 Stat. 162; 28 U.S.C. 503).

INFORMATION

Department of Justice
900 Pennsylvania Ave., NW
Washington, D. C. 20530-0001
(202) 514-2007
Fax: (202) 514-4371
http://www.usdoj.gov

J 1.1:date • Item 717-C-1 (MF)
ANNUAL REPORT OF THE ATTORNEY GENERAL OF THE UNITED STATES. 1870–   [Annual]

Report submitted by the Attorney General to Congress for the fiscal year.
Also contains reports of subordinate bureaus.

J 1.1/2:date • Item 717-C
ANNUAL REPORT OF THE LAW ENFORCEMENT ASSISTANCE ADMINISTRATION. 1st–   1969–

Later J 26.1/3

J 1.1/2-2:date • Item 717-C-6
LEAA [Activities]. [Annual]

Text of the publication is identical to Annual Report of LEAA, (J 1.1/2).

J 1.1/3:date • Item 717-C
NATIONAL INSTITUTE OF LAW ENFORCEMENT AND CRIMINAL JUSTICE: ANNUAL REPORT. 1st– 1974–   (Law Enforcement Assistance Administration)
Report submitted to the President and Congress pursuant to provisions of the Omnibus Crime Control and Safe Streets Act of 1968 and Part D of the Crime Control Act of 1973 (P.L. 93-83).
Report Covers fiscal year.
ISSN 0097-8981

J 1.1/4:date • Item 717-C-9
REPORT OF THE UNITED STATES ATTORNEY FOR THE DISTRICT OF COLUMBIA. [Annual]

Report covers fiscal year, summarizing the activities and operations of the Office of the United States Attorney for the District.

J 1.1/5:date • Item 717-C-11 (MF)
ANNUAL REPORT TO THE PRESIDENT AND THE CONGRESS ON THE ACTIVITIES OF THE REHABILITATION ACT INTERAGENCY COORDINATING COUNCIL.

Report submitted to the President and Congress pursuant to Title V of the Rehabilitation Act of 1973, summarizing the Council's activities in protecting handicapped persons' rights in accordance with the Act.

J 1.1/6:date • Item 1063-C (MF)
FOREIGN CLAIMS SETTLEMENT COMMISSION OF THE UNITED STATES: ANNUAL REPORT.

Earlier Y 3.F 76/3:1

J 1.1/7:date • Item 717-C-1 (MF)
FINANCIAL LITIGATION ANNUAL REPORT.

• Item 717-C-1 (MF)
THE ATTORNEY GENERAL'S ADVISORY COMMITTEE OF UNITED STATES ATTORNEYS ANNUAL REPORT.

J 1.1/8:date

J 1.1/9:date • Item 717-C-19 (MF)
OFFICE OF THE INSPECTOR GENERAL SEMI-ANNUAL REPORT TO CONGRESS.

J 1.1/10 • Item 717-C-22 (MF)
STATISTICAL REPORT (Environment and Natural Resources Division).

J 1.1/11: • Item 717-C-24 (EL)
FOIA ANNUAL REPORT (Freedom of Information Act).

J 1.1/12 • Item 717-C-28 (EL)
REPORT OF THE OFFICE OF THE UNITED STATES ATTORNEY FOR THE SOUTHERN DISTRICT OF TEXAS, YEAR IN REVIEW. [Annual]

J 1.2:CT • Item 717
GENERAL PUBLICATIONS.

J 1.3: • Item 717-A-4 (MF)
BULLETINS.

J 1.3 • Item 717-A-4
BULLETIN ON ECONOMIC CRIME ENFORCEMENT. [4 to 6 times annually]

J 1.4:nos.
CIRCULARS.

J 1.5:nos • Item 717-C-23
OFFICIAL OPINIONS OF THE ATTORNEYS GENERAL OF THE UNITED STATES. [Irregular]

Opinions are issued separately as released (J 1.5/a) and later appear in bound volumes. Cumulative indexes to the opinions (J 1.5/2) are issued. The latest one published covers the period Jan. 1, 1941-Aug. 1, 1958.
Citation: A.G.
Earlier title: Opinions of the Attorney General.
Earlier issued under item number 718.

J 1.5/a:v.nos.&nos. • Item 718
OPINIONS OF ATTORNEY GENERAL [separate opinions].

J 1.5/2:date
– INDEX.

J 1.5/3:date • Item 717-C-4
LEGAL OPINIONS OF THE OFFICE OF GENERAL COUNSEL OF THE LAW ENFORCEMENT ASSISTANCE ADMINISTRATION. [Semiannual]

ISSN 0098-3926

J 1.5/4:v.nos. • Item 717-C-4
OPINIONS OF THE OFFICE OF LEGAL COUNSEL. v. 1–   1970–

J 1.6:date
DIGEST OF OFFICIAL OPINIONS OF ATTORNEY GENERAL.

J 1.7:nos. • Item 717-A-1 (MF)
REGISTER, DEPARTMENT OF JUSTICE AND THE COURTS OF THE UNITED STATES. 1st ed.– 1871–   [Annual]

Lists the principal officers of the Department of Justice in Washington, officers of the Administrative Office in the United States Courts, United States attorneys and marshals, by districts, and the United States penal and correctional institutions.

J 1.8:CT • Item 717-A
RULES, REGULATIONS AND INSTRUCTIONS.
Later Ju 10.7

J 1.8/2:CT • Item 717-A-1
HANDBOOKS, MANUALS, GUIDES.
Later J 26.8

J 1.8/3:CT • Item 717-A
PRESCRIPTIVE PACKAGE SERIES. [Irregular]
Later J 26.13

J 1.8/3:R 18 • Item 717-A
RAPE AND ITS VICTIMS: A REPORT FOR CITIZENS, HEALTH FACILITIES, AND CRIMINAL JUSTICE AGENCIES. 1975. 356 p. il.

This book looks at the way rape is currently viewed and treated in the United States. It analyzes current legal and medical procedures for handling rape, and recommends changes in certain crucial areas. The material in the book is based on findings of national surveys conducted in 1974 among police departments, medical facilities, prosecutors' offices, and citizens' action groups. Among the many important topics are how police interview a rape victim, counseling for rape victims, and legal issues being raised by rape law reformists.

J 1.8/4:date&nos. • Item 717-A-1
TECHNICAL ASSISTANCE GUIDE (series). [Irregular]

J 1.9:date
REPORTS OF BANKRUPTCY MATTERS.

J 1.10:
COMMISSION TO REVISE THE LAWS OF THE UNITED STATES: PUBLICATIONS.

NOTE:– This class was not used. See Y 3.L 44

J 1.10:CT • Item 717-O
NATIONAL INSTITUTE OF LAW ENFORCEMENT AND CRIMINAL JUSTICE: EXEMPLARY PROJECT REPORTS. [Irregular]

Later J 26.22

J 1.12:date
LIST OF U.S. JUDGES, ATTORNEYS AND MARSHALS.

J 1.12:date
REGISTER OF OFFICE OF ATTORNEY GENERAL.

J 1.13:CT
PAPERS IN RE.

J 1.13/2:CT
PAPERS IN RE. WORLD WAR RISK INSURANCE.

J 1.13/3:dates
PAPERS IN RE, INDEXES.

FEDERAL BUREAU OF INVESTIGATION

J 1.14/1 • Item 721-A (MF)
ANNUAL REPORT. [Annual]

J 1.14/2:CT • Item 721
GENERAL PUBLICATIONS.

J 1.14/2:F 49 • Item 721
SCIENCE OF FINGERPRINTS, CLASSIFICATION AND USES. 1973. 198 p. il.

This booklet was prepared by the Federal Bureau of Investigation for the use of law enforcement officers and agencies interested in starting fingerprint identification files. It is based on the FBI's experience in fingerprint identification work, which has resulted in the largest collection of classified fingerprints in the world.

J 1.14/3:nos.
BULLETINS [none issued].

J 1.14/4:nos.
CIRCULARS [none issued].

J 1.14/5:nos.
CIRCULAR LETTERS.

J 1.14/6:date
MANUAL OF INSTRUCTIONS.

J 1.14/7:date • Item 722
UNIFORM CRIME REPORTS FOR THE UNITED STATES. v. 1– 1930– [Annual]

PURPOSE:– To present in one volume the annual statistical data on crime trends, crime rate, offenses in individual areas (cities over 25,000), police employee data, offenses cleared and persons arrested, classification of offenses. Includes charts.

Later in 1957, the FBI employed a Consultant Committee on Uniform Crime Reporting to make an independent analysis of the Uniform Crime Reporting program. A special issue of Uniform Crime Reports were issued in November 1958 to publish the report and related papers of the Consultant Committee. Upon its recommendations, certain changes were incorporated into the new series of reports, the first of which was the annual report for 1958, issued in September 1959. A preliminary release Uniform Crime Reporting is issued quarterly and cumulative for each quarterly issue during the year. This release contains a summary chart of offenses known to the police for cities 100,000 population and over.

Published quarterly 1930– 1940; semiannually 1941– 1957; annually 1958–

J 1.14/7-2
UNIFORM CRIME REPORTING. [Quarterly]

Lists number of offenses known to the police, for quarter, by type of offense for each city with population of 100,000 and over. Two year comparisons. An annual publication, Uniform Crime Reports for the United States, gives data on crime in cities of 25,000 population and over.

J 1.14/7-3:date • Item 722-A
ASSAULTS ON FEDERAL OFFICERS. 1972– [Annual] (FBI Uniform Crime Reports)

PURPOSE:– To present statistical data on attacks upon officers of the Federal criminal justice systems as well as other Federal agencies, such as the Department of the Treasury and the U.S. Postal Service.

Prior to 1976, entitled Analysis of Assaults on Federal Officers.

Consolidated with Law Enforcement Officers Killed (J 1.14/7-5) to form Law Enforcement Officers Killed and Assaulted (J 1.14/7-6).
ISSN 0148-4257

J 1.14/7-4:CT • Item 722-A
FBI UNIFORM CRIME REPORTS [on various subjects].

J 1.14/7-4:B 63 • Item 722-A
BOMB SURVEY. [Annual]

Volumes for 1973– issued in cooperation with the National Bomb DataCenter.
Later J 1.14/7-7
ISSN 0363-3245

J 1.14/7-5:date • Item 722-A
FBI UNIFORM CRIME REPORTS: LAW ENFORCEMENT OFFICERS KILLED. [Annual]

Consolidated with Law Enforcement Officers Assaulted (J 1.14/7-3) to form Law Enforcement Officers Killed and Assaulted (J 1.14/7-6).
Earlier J 1.14/2:L 41/6

J 1.14/7-6:date • Item 722-A
LAW ENFORCEMENT OFFICERS KILLED AND ASSAULTED, UNIFORM CRIME REPORT. [Annual]

Consolidation of Assaults on Federal Officers (J 1.14/7-3) and Law Enforcement Officers Killed (J 1.14/7-5).

J 1.14/7-7:date • Item 722-A
UNIFORM CRIME REPORTS BOMB SUMMARY. [Annual]

PURPOSE:– To present a comprehensive report of incidents involving explosive and incendiary devices in the nation.
Volumes for 1973– issued in cooperation with the National Bomb Data Center.
Earlier J 1.14/7-4:B 63

J 1.14/7-8:date • Item 722-A-3 (CD)
CRIME IN THE UNITED STATES.

J 1.14/8:vol. • Item 717-C-5 (EL)
FBI LAW ENFORCEMENT BULLETIN. v. 1– 1932– [Monthly]

Indexed by: Index to U.S. Government Periodicals.
ISSN 0014-5688

J 1.14/8 a:CT • Item 717-C-5
REPRINTS (Separates). [Irregular]

J 1.14/8-2:nos. • Item 717-C-7
FBI BOMB DATA PROGRAM, GENERAL INFORMATION BULLETINS.

J 1.14/9:nos.
IDENTIFICATION ORDERS.

J 1.14/10:nos.
APPREHENSION ORDERS.

J 1.14/11:CT
POSTERS.

J 1.14/12:CT
REGULATIONS, RULES, AND INSTRUCTIONS.

J 1.14/13:nos.
WANTED FLYERS. 1– 1944–

J 1.14/14:nos.
WANTED FLYER APPREHENSION ORDERS.

J 1.14/15:nos.
CHECK CIRCULARS.

J 1.14/16:CT • Item 722-A-1
HANDBOOKS, MANUALS, GUIDES.

J 1.14/17
ADDRESSES. [Irregular]

J 1.14/18:v.nos.&nos. • Item 717-C-17
CRIME LABORATORY DIGEST. [Quarterly]

J 1.14/18/2 • Item 717-C-26 (EL)
FORENSIC SCIENCE AND COMMUNICATIONS. [Quarterly]

J 1.14/19:nos. • Item 722-A-2
NCIC NEWSLETTER. [Quarterly]

NCIC = National Crime Information Center
Presents news items on National Crime Information Center activities.

J 1.14/20:date • Item 722-A-2
FBI NATIONAL ACADEMY ASSOCIATES NEWSLETTER. [Quarterly]

J 1.14/21:CT • Item 722-B
POSTERS.

J 1.14/22:date • Item 717-C-17 (P) (EL)
TERRORISM IN THE UNITED STATES. [Annual]

J 1.14/23: • Item 717-C-25 (E)
ELECTRONIC PRODUCTS (misc.).

J 1.14/23-2 • Item 717-C-27 (EL)
CYBERNOTES. [Biweekly]

J 1.14/23-3 • Item 721-A-6 (EL)
HIGHLIGHTS (NATIONAL INFRASTRUCTURE PROTECTION CENTER). [Monthly]

J 1.14/24: • Item 721-A-1
CJIS, NEWSLETTER FOR THE CRIMINAL JUSTICE COMMUNITY.

J 1.14/25-2 • Item 721-A-2
NATIONAL DOMESTIC PREPAREDNESS OFFICE-GENERAL PUBLICATIONS.

J 1.14/25-3 • Item 721-A-3 (EL)
NDPO-INFORMATION BULLETINS.

J 1.14/25-4 • Item 721-A-4 (EL)
NDPO-FACT SHEET.

J 1.14/25-5 • Item 721-A-5 (EL)
THE BEACON (NDPO-MONTHLY NEWSLETTER).

BOARD OF PAROLE

J 1.15/1:date   • Item 717-C-2 (MF)
ANNUAL REPORT. 1st–   1911–
    Formerly annual.

J 1.15/2:CT
GENERAL PUBLICATIONS.

J 1.15/5:date
RULES AND REGULATIONS GOVERNING PAROL-
ING OF PRISONERS FROM PENITENTIARIES,
STATE INSTITUTIONS, [ETC.] (General).

J 1.15/6:CT
RULES AND REGULATIONS GOVERNING PAROL-
ING OF PRISONERS FROM U.S. PENITENTIA-
RIES [etc.] (special).

DEPARTMENT OF JUSTICE (Continued)

J 1.16:CT
RULES AND REGULATIONS FOR GOVERNMENT AND
DISCIPLINE OF UNITED STATES PENITENTIA-
RIES.

J 1.17:nos.
INTERPRETATION OF WAR STATUTES, BULLETINS.
1– 204. 1917– 1919.

J 1.18:date
REGISTER OF U.S. COMMISSIONERS.   –1929.

J 1.19:date
RECORDS AND BRIEFS IN U.S. CASES DECIDED
BY SUPREME COURT OF UNITED STATES.

J 1.19/1:t.p.&ind.
INDEXES FOR COMPILATIONS OF RECORDS,
BRIEFS, ETC.

J 1.19/2:date.t.p.&ind.
IN SUPREME COURT OF U.S., BRIEFS, PETITIONS,
AND MOTIONS OF WM. MARSHALL BULLETT,
SOLICITOR GENERAL.

J 1.19/3:date.ind.
U.S. SUPREME COURT, GOVT. BRIEFS IN CASES
ARGUED BY SOLICITOR GENERAL, INDEXES.

J 1.19/4:date.ind.
U.S. SUPREME COURT, GOVERNMENT BRIEFS IN
CASES ARGUED, INDEXES.

J 1.19/5:v.nos.t.p.&ind.
RECORDS AND BRIEFS IN CIRCUIT COURTS OF
APPEALS AND COURT OF APPEALS, DISTRICT
OF COLUMBIA.

J 1.19/6:v.nos.t.p.&ind.
PETITIONS FOR CERTIORARI AND BRIEFS ON
MERITS AND IN OPPOSITION FOR U.S. IN
SUPREME COURT OF U.S.

J 1.19/7:v.nos.t.p.&ind.
RECORDS AND BRIEFS IN CASES ARISING UNDER
AGRICULTURAL ADJUSTMENT ACT, BANKHEAD
ACT, AND KERR-SMITH TOBACCO ACT.

J 1.19/8:v.nos.t.p.&ind.
BRIEFS IN COURT OF CLAIMS, CASES PREPARED
OR ARGUED BY TAX DIVISION, DEPARTMENT
OF JUSTICE [title pages and indexes].

J 1.20:CT
BIBLIOGRAPHIES.

J 1.20/2:CT   • Item 717-G
BIBLIOGRAPHIES AND LISTS OF PUBLICATIONS.

J 1.20/3:date/sec.nos.   • Item 717-G (MF)
LIBRARY BOOK CATALOG. 1972–   [2 times per
year] (Technical Information Staff, Law Enforcement Assistance Administration)

    PURPOSE:– To provide knowledge regarding
the books, documents, and periodicals that are
available in the broad areas of law enforcement
and criminal justice. This information is considered to be of value to librarians, students, researchers, practitioners and to the general public.

    The catalog contains the holdings of the li-
braries of the Law Enforcement Assistance Administration, the Drug Enforcement Administration (formerly the Bureau of Narcotics and Dangerous Drugs), and the Federal Bureau of Prisons.

    The catalog is divided into the following sec-
tions:–
        Section 1, Author Catalog.
        Section 2, Title Catalog.
        Section 3, Subject Catalog.

J 1.20/4:nos.   • Item 717-Q
NCJRS DOCUMENT LOAN PROGRAM, DOCUMENT
LISTS. 1–   (National Institute of Law Enforce-
ment and Criminal Justice)

J 1.20/5:nos.   • Item 717-S (MF)
EVALUATION DOCUMENT LOAN LISTS. 1–
[Quarterly]

J 1.20/6:v.nos.&nos.   • Item 717-G
LIBRARY BULLETIN. [Quarterly]

J 1.21:CT
ATTORNEY GENERAL'S COMMITTEE ON
ADMINISTRATIVE PROCEDURE, GENERAL PUB-
LICATIONS.

J 1.22:nos.
ATTORNEY GENERAL'S COMMITTEE ON ADMINIS-
TRATIVE PROCEDURE, MONOGRAPHS. 1– 27.
1939– 1940.

J 1.23:nos.
DECISIONS ON FEDERAL RULES OF CIVIL PROCE-
DURE, BULLETINS. 1– 167. 1938– 1944. [Gener-
ally weekly]

J 1.24:nos.
NATIONAL CONFERENCE OF PREVENTION AND
CONTROL OF JUVENILE DELINQUENCY. 1–
1974–

J 1.25:v.nos.&nos.
U.S.A. CITIZENSHIP– KNOW IT, CHERISH IT, LIVE
IT. [Quarterly]

J 1.26   • Item 719-A
REPORT OF THE ATTORNEY GENERAL ON COMPE-
TITION IN THE SYNTHETIC RUBBER INDUSTRY.
1st–   1956–   [Annual]

    Report submitted by the Attorney General to
Congress pursuant to provisions of the rubber
Producing Facilities Disposal Act of 1953, for the
calendar year.
    This series of reports is made at the request
of the Senate Banking and Currency Committee.
When reporting its approval of the plan for the
disposal of Government synthetic rubber plants
after World War II, the Committee sought assurance of continuing antitrust surveillance of industry to be comprised of leading rubber, chemical and oil companies, in the main the only bidders on the properties. Accordingly, the Department of Justice was requested to report annually
during the first 10 years of private operation.
    Report describe activities during the year ac-
companied by statistical tables on production,
supply and demand, and prices.

J 1.27   • Item 719-B
REPORT OF THE ATTORNEY GENERAL PURSUANT
TO SECTION 2 OF THE JOINT RESOLUTION OF
JULY 28, 1955. CONSENTING TO AN INTERSTATE
COMPACT TO CONSERVE OIL AND GAS. 1st–
1956–   [Annual]

    Pursuant to section 2 of the Joint Resolution
of July 28, 1955, the Attorney General is authorized to make an annual report to Congress for
the duration of the Interstate Compact to Conserve Oil and Gas as to whether or not the activities of the States under the provisions of such
compact have been consistent with the purpose
as set out in article V of such compact.
    In addition to the textual summary, each re-
port contains a series of statistical tables on
crude oil production, capacity of refining companies, indexes of prices, reserves of crude oil.
    At present, the Compact is authorized to ex-
ist until September 1, 1963.

J 1.27/2:date   • Item 717-Z (MF)
REPORT OF THE ATTORNEY GENERAL, PURSUANT
TO SECTION 252(i) OF THE ENERGY POLICY
AND CONSERVATION ACT. 1st–   1976–
[Semiannual]

J 1.27/3:date   • Item 717-N-3 (MF)
REPORT OF THE U.S. DEPARTMENT OF JUSTICE
PURSUANT TO SECTION 8 OF THE FEDERAL
COAL LEASING AMENDMENTS ACT OF 1975.
[Annual]

    PURPOSE:– To report the results of studies
by the Attorney General on competition in the
coal and energy industries, and the adequacy of
antitrust provisions and laws in this area.
    Subtitle: Competition in the Coal Industry.
    ISSN 0162-5624

J 1.28:v.nos.   • Item 716-A
ADJUDICATIONS OF ATTORNEY GENERAL OF
UNITED STATES.

J 1.29   • Item 716-B
OFFICE OF ADMINISTRATIVE PROCEDURE. ANNUAL
REPORT. 1st–   1957–   [Annual]

    The Office of Administrative Procedure was
established within the Office of Legal Counsel of
the Department of Justice by Departmental Order
142-57, effective February 6, 1957, for purpose
of achieving improvements in administrative procedures within the executive department and
agencies of the Government.
    Reports cover activities of the Office and
statistical tables on administrative proceedings
of the various Government agencies.

J 1.30:date   • Item 719-C (EL)
REPORT OF THE ATTORNEY GENERAL TO THE CON-
GRESS OF THE UNITED STATES ON THE AD-
MINISTRATION OF THE FOREIGN AGENTS REG-
ISTRATION ACT OF 1938, AS AMENDED. 1942/
44–   [Semiannual]

    Report submitted by the Attorney General to
Congress pursuant to the Foreign Agents Registration Act of 1938, as amended, for the calendar
year.
    The Foreign Agents Registration Act requires
the Attorney General from time to time to report
to Congress concerning the administration of the
Act as well as the nature, sources and content of
political propaganda disseminated or distributed
by agents of foreign principals registered under
the terms of the statute.
    Includes alphabetical list of registrants whose
statements were filed during the year. Some reports cover more than one year.

J 1.31   • Item 719-D (MF)
IDENTICAL BIDDING IN PUBLIC PROCUREMENT
REPORT OF ATTORNEY GENERAL UNDER
EXECUTIVE ORDER 10936. 1st–   1961/62–
[Annual]
    ISSN 0501-9575

J 1.32   • Item 716-C
ANNUAL REPORT TO THE PRESIDENT AND
CONGRESS OF ACTIVITIES UNDER THE LAW
ENFORCEMENT ASSISTANCE ACT OF 1965. 1st–
1966–   [Annual]

    Report submitted by the Attorney General to
the President and Congress pursuant to provisions of Section 11 of the Law Enforcement Assistance Act of 1965 (PL 89-197) for the calendar
year.
    Appendix contains list of projects.

J 1.32/2:date   • Item 716-C (MF)
ATTORNEY GENERAL'S ANNUAL REPORT, FEDERAL
LAW ENFORCEMENT AND CRIMINAL JUSTICE
ASSISTANCE ACTIVITIES. 1st–   1972–

PURPOSE:– To provide a comprehensive report to the Congress and to the American people
on what the Federal Government is doing to make
the United States a safer and more just Nation.
The report is required by the Congress for a public accounting of the "law enforcement" and "criminal justice assistance" activities of the Federal
Government.
The report summarizes for the individual department and agencies on such activities.

J 1.33   • Item 717 (MF)
LEAA GRANTS AND CONTRACTS. (Law Enforcement
Assistance Administration)

List of grants and contracts awarded under
the Law Enforcement Assistance Act.

J 1.33/2   • Item 717 (MF)
LEAA GRANTS AND CONTRACTS: DISSEMINATION
DOCUMENT. [Irregular] (Law Enforcement Assis-
tance Administration)

Text of project reports submitted to the Department of Justice.

J 1.33/3:v.nos.&nos.   • Item 717-B-1
LEAA NEWSLETTER. v. 1–   1970–   [10 times a
year] (Law Enforcement Assistance Administration)

Later J 26.12

J 1.33/4:date
LEAA NEWS RELEASES. [Irregular] (Law Enforcement Assistance Administration)

ISSN 0145-3270

J 1.33/5:letters-nos.
NATIONAL PRISONER STATISTICS BULLETIN, SD-
NPS, (series).

Earlier J 16.23

J 1.34:CT
ADDRESSES. [Irregular]

J 1.34:CT   • Item 717-B-2 (MF)
BICENTENNIAL LECTURE SERIES. [Irregular]

J 1.35   • Item 717-B-1
LEEP AWARD LISTS. [Irregular] (Law Enforcement
Education Program)

J 1.35/2   • Item 717-B
LEEP NEWSLETTER. 1–   1969–   [Monthly] (Law
Enforcement Education Program)

J 1.35/3:nos.
LEEP ADMINISTRATION MEMOS.

J 1.35/4:date   • Item 717-B
AWARD, LEEP PARTICIPATING INSTITUTIONS, PRO-
GRAM YEAR. [Annual] (Law Enforcement Educa-
tion Program)

J 1.36:nos.   • Item 717-D (MF)
PR- (series). (Law Enforcement Assistance Adminis-
tration, National Institute of Law Enforcement and
Criminal Justice)

J 1.36/2:nos.   • Item 717-D
ICR- (series). (Law Enforcement Assistance Adminis-
tration, National Institute of Law Enforcement and
Criminal Justice)

J 1.37:nos.   • Item 717-E
NATIONAL CRIMINAL JUSTICE INFORMATION AND
STATISTICS SERVICE, SERIES. SC-EE 1–
1969–   [Irregular] (Law Enforcement Assistance
Administration)

PURPOSE:– To provide national estimates of
employment and expenditures by level of government (Federal, State and local) for law enforcement, legal and correctional activities. Individual
data are displayed for a number of large coun-

ties, cities and SMSA's. This knowledge of the
distribution of human and financial resources will
aid the States in establishing priorities for assistance and will make possible a better determination of the capabilities of different elements of
the system.

J 1.37/2:nos.   • Item 717-E
NATIONAL CRIMINAL JUSTICE INFORMATION AND
STATISTICS SERVICE, STATISTICS CENTER
REPORT. SC 1–   1970–   [Irregular] (Law En-
forcement Assistance Administration)

J 1.37/3:CT   • Item 717-E
CRIMINAL JUSTICE MONOGRAPH SERIES.
[Irregular] (National Institute of Law Enforcement
and Criminal Justice)

J 1.37/4:CT   • Item 717-E
CRIMINAL JUSTICE RESEARCH SERIES.

Later J 28.17

J 1.37/5:CT   • Item 717-B-8
CRIMINAL JUSTICE RESEARCH SOLICITATIONS.
[Irregular]

Later J 26.18

J 1.38:date   • Item 717-F
PROGRAM AND PROJECT PLAN FOR FISCAL YEAR
(date). 1971–   [Annual] (National Institute of
Law Enforcement and Criminal Justice, Law Enforcement Assistance Administration)

PURPOSE:– To serve as both a summariza-
tion of fiscal year activities of the National Institute of Law Enforcement and Criminal Justice
and as a guide to potential grantees and contractors, with the aim to provide information which will
lead first to an initial interchange of information
and ultimately, to a close working relationship
between LEAA, the Institute, and the research
and development resources of our nation.

J 1.39:CT   • Item 717-H (MF)
CRIMINAL JUSTICE AGENCIES. 1971–   (Statistics
Division, Law Enforcement Assistance Adminis-
tration)

J 1.40:nos.   • Item 717-I
STATISTICS TECHNICAL REPORTS. 1–   1972–
[Irregular] (Statistics Division, National Institute
of Law Enforcement and Criminal Justice, Law
Enforcement Assistance Administration)

J 1.41:nos.   • Item 717-J
LAW ENFORCEMENT STANDARDS PROGRAM,
LESP-RPT- (series). [Irregular] (National Institute
of Law Enforcement and Criminal Justice, Law
Enforcement Assistance Administration)

J 1.41/2:nos.   • Item 717-J
LAW ENFORCEMENT STANDARDS PROGRAM,
NILECJ-STD- (series). 1972–   [Irregular] (Na-
tional Institute of Law Enforcement and Criminal
Justice, Law Enforcement Assistance Adminis-
tration)

Later J 26.20

J 1.41/3:nos.   • Item 717-P (MF)
NILECJ-GUIDES.

J 1.42:v.nos.&nos.   • Item 717-K
NATIONAL CRIMINAL JUSTICE: DOCUMENT
RETRIEVAL INDEX. v. 1–   1972–   [Irregular]
(National Criminal Justice Reference Service, Law
Enforcement Assistance Administration)

J 1.42/2:nos.   • Item 717-M (MF)
SELECTED TOPIC DIGESTS. 1–   [Irregular]
PURPOSE:– To provide abridged summaries
of existing literature covering selected subjects
in a discipline related to police, corrections, or
court activities. The digest may contain highlights
of new technology, systems, methods, or equipment in the fields under review.

J 1.42/3:CT   • Item 717
NATIONAL CRIMINAL JUSTICE REFERENCE
SERVICE: MISCELLANEOUS PUBLICATIONS
SERIES.

J 1.42/3:SD-NCS-N   • Item 717-P
CRIMINAL VICTIMIZATION IN THE UNITED STATES.
v. 1–   1973–   [Annual] (National Criminal Justice Information and Statistics Service) (National
Crime Survey Report)

ISSN 0095-5833

J 1.42/3:SD-SB-(nos.)   • Item 717
SOURCEBOOK OF CRIMINAL JUSTICE STATISTICS.
1–   1973–   [Annual]

PURPOSE:– To provide a compilation of national criminal justice statistics culled from the
publications of various Governmental and private
agencies. Data is in the areas of public attitudes
toward crime, nature of offenses, types of persons arrested, and others.

J 1.43:date   • Item 717-L (MF)
LISTS OF PARTICIPATING INSTITUTIONS, FISCAL
YEAR (date). [Annual] (Law Enforcement Assis-
tance Administration)

PURPOSE:– To provide a list of those colleges and universities which are participating in
the Law Enforcement Education Program (LEEP)
as provided by Section 406 of Omnibus Crime
Control and Safe Streets Act of 1968 (Public Law
90-351), as amended.

J 1.44:CT   • Item 717
RESEARCH SERIES. [Irregular] (National Institute of
Law Enforcement and Criminal Justice, Law En-
forcement Assistance Administration)
Later J 26.15

J 1.44/2:CT   • Item 717-N-1
MONOGRAPH SERIES. [Irregular] (National Institute
of Law Enforcement Assistance Administration)

Later J 26.15/2

J 1.45:nos.   • Item 717-N (MF)
ENERGY REPORTS. (Emergency Energy Committee,
Law Enforcement Assistance Administration)

J 1.46:series-nos.   • Item 717-R
NATIONAL EVALUATION PROGRAM. A-1–   1975–

Later J 26.21

J 1.46/2:CT   • Item 717-R
NILECJ EVALUATION SERIES. [Irregular] (National
Institute of Law Enforcement and Criminal Jus-
tice)

Later J 26.21/2

J 1.47:date   • Item 717-W (MF)
OFFICE OF JUVENILE JUSTICE AND DELINQUENCY
PREVENTION: ANNUAL REPORT. 1st–   1975–

J 1.48:date   • Item 717-U
REPORTS OF THE ADVISORY COMMITTEE TO THE
ADMINISTRATOR ON STANDARDS FOR THE
ADMINISTRATION OF JUVENILE JUSTICE.

Discontinued.

J 1.48/2:date   • Item 717-B-12
NATIONAL ADVISORY COMMITTEE FOR JUVENILE
JUSTICE AND DELINQUENCY PREVENTION:
ANNUAL REPORT. 1st–   1976–

Later J 26.1/4

J 1.49:v.nos.&nos.   • Item 717-V (MF)
COST ANALYSIS OF CORRECTIONAL STANDARDS,
[various subjects].

J 1.50:CT
COURTHOUSE REORGANIZATION AND RENOVATION
PROGRAM [Publications].

J 1.51:date   • Item 717-N-2 (MF)
PROGRAM RESULTS INVENTORY. [Annual] (Law Enforcement Assistance Administration)

J 1.52:nos. • **Item 717-B-3 (MF)**
PROMIS [Prosecutor's Management Information System] RESEARCH PROJECT PUBLICATIONS. 1– [Irregular] (National Institute of Law Enforcement and Criminal Justice)

J 1.53:date • **Item 717-B-4**
JUVENILE COURT STATISTICS. 1974– [Annual] (National Center for Juvenile Justice)

Continues a publication of the same name issued by the Office of Youth Development, HEW (HE 17.23).
Later J 32.15

J 1.54:CT • **Item 717-B-5**
PROGRAM MODELS.

Later 26.16

J 1.55:date • **Item 717-B-6 (MF)**
STATISTICAL REPORT. (United States Attorney's Office)

PURPOSE:– To present charts and tables showing work handled by the United States Attorney's Office during the fiscal year. Includes criminal and civil cases pending, filed, and terminated, and type of offenses involved.
Later J 31.10

J 1.56:date • **Item 717-B-7**
FREEDOM OF INFORMATION CASE LIST. 1978– [Biennial]

PURPOSE:– To provide an alphabetical list of court decisions on the Freedom of Information Act, 5 U.S.C. 552, including cases with opinions not yet reported, with notations as to the exemptions or other issues involved in each case, and with topical index and other aids to users.
ISSN 0163-9390

J 1.57:date • **Item 717-B-9 (MF)**
EMPLOYMENT FACT BOOK. [Annual]

PURPOSE:– To provide statistical tables and graphs showing the Justice Department labor force by particular categories.

J 1.58:v.nos.&nos. • **Item 717-B-11**
FOIA [Freedom of Information Act] UPDATE. v. 1– 1979– [Quarterly]

PURPOSE:– To provide a newsletter to encourage agency compliance with the Freedom of Information Act by giving information, news, guidelines, reference material, training information, etc.

J 1.58/1 • **Item 717-B-16 (EL)**
FOIA POST.

J 1.59:v.nos.&nos. • **Item 717-B-1**
JUSTICE ASSISTANCE NEWS. v. 1– 1980– [10 times a year]

Supersedes LEEA Newsletter (J 26.12).

J 1.75:CT
PAPERS IN RE IN DISTRICT COURTS.

Formerly J 1.13

J 1.76:CT
PAPERS IN RE IN CIRCUIT COURTS.

Formerly J 1.13

J 1.76/2:nos.
PAPERS IN RE IN COURT OF APPEALS FOR SECOND CIRCUIT.

J 1.77:CT
PAPERS IN RE IN COURT OF APPEALS.

Formerly J 1.13

J 1.78:CT
PAPERS IN RE IN SUPREME COURT.

Formerly J 1.13

J 1.79:CT
PAPERS IN RE IN COURT OF CUSTOMS AND PATENT APPEALS.

J 1.80:CT
PAPERS IN RE IN COURT OF CLAIMS.

Formerly J 1.13

J 1.81:CT
PAPERS IN RE IN PATENT OFFICE (Interferences).

J 1.82:CT
PAPERS IN RE IN STATE SUPREME COURTS.

J 1.83:CT
PAPERS IN RE IN STATE COURTS OF APPEAL.

J 1.84:CT
PAPERS IN RE (miscellaneous).

J 1.85:CT
PAPERS IN RE INDIAN CLAIMS COMMISSION.

J 1.86:date • **Item 717-B-10 (MF)**
PROGRAM AND RESOURCE DIGEST. [Annual]

PURPOSE:– To report briefly on the activities, organization, and allocation of resources of the Department of Justice. Includes statistical data.

J 1.87:date • **Item 717-B-13 (MF)**
ANNUAL REPORT OF JUSTICE SYSTEM IMPROVEMENT ACT AGENCIES.

Summarizes the activities of the four Justice System Improvement Act Agencies: Law Enforcement Assistance Administration; National Institute of Justice; Justice Statistics Bureau; and the Office of Justice Assistance, Research, and Statistics.

J 1.88:date • **Item 717-B-14**
LEGAL ACTIVITIES. [Annual]

Summarizes only those Justice Department activities that are of a legal nature, in such operating units as its Antitrust Division and Civil Division.

J 1.89:date • **Item 717-A-2 (MF)**
TELEPHONE DIRECTORY. [Annual]

J 1.89/2:date • **Item 717-A-2 (MF)**
CIVIL DIVISION TELEPHONE DIRECTORY.

J 1.89/3:date • **Item 717-A-11**
DIRECTORIES.

J 1.90: • **Item 717-A-3**
NARCOTIC AND DANGEROUS DRUG SECTION MONOGRAPHS (series). [Irregular]

Each monograph is on an individual subject.

J 1.91:date • **Item 718-A-10**
TRAINING COURSE CALENDAR. [Annual]

PURPOSE:– To describe and give pertinent information on courses offered to department employees in various areas including management, professional development, and secretarial/clerical.

J 1.92:date • **Item 717-B-15 (MF)**
CIVIL DIVISION. [Annual]

PURPOSE:– To provide an overview of Division activites with emphasis on the opportunities available.
Earlier J 1.2:C 49/10

J 1.93:date • **Item 718-A-13**
ANNUAL REPORT OF THE ORGANIZED CRIME DRUG ENFORCEMENT TASK FORCE PROGRAM.

PURPOSE:– To describe how federal law enforcement agencies working together wage an ongoing battle with organized criminal groups to combat drug trafficking.

J 1.94:v.nos./nos. • **Item 716-C-1**
OBSCENITY ENFORCEMENT REPORTER. [Bimonthly]

Published by the National Obscenity Enforcement Unit, Criminal Division of the Justice Department. Reports on obscenity enforcement,including selected case law and federal sentencing guidelines.
Earlier: Obscenity Reporter.

J 1.95: • **Item 718-A-21**
TRUTH IN CRIMINAL JUSTICE SERIES.

J 1.96: • **Item 718-A-22**
REPORT TO THE ATTORNEY GENERAL (series).

Each report deals with a different topic.

J 1.98:nos. • **Item 718-A-23**
FORMS.

J 1.99:CT • **Item 717-A-10**
POSTERS.

J 1.100 • **Item 718-B (E)**
ELECTRONIC PRODUCTS. [Irregular]

J 1.101:v.nos./nos. • **Item 718-A-22**
JUSTICE. [Semiannual]

J 1.102:nos. • **Item 723-A-1**
OFFICE OF THE CHIEF ADMINISTRATIVE HEARING OFFICER (OCAHO) CASES.

J 1.102/2 • **Item 723-A-1**
OFFICE OF THE CHIEF ADMINISTRATIVE HEARING OFFICER (OCAHO) FILES.

J 1.102/3:nos. • **Item 723-A-1**
QUARTERLY UPDATE.

J 1.102/4:nos. • **Item 723-A-1**
OFFICE OF THE CHIEF ADMINISTRATIVE HEARING OFFICER (OCAHO) SUBPOENAS.

J 1.102/5:nos. • **Item 723-A-1**
INTERIM DECISIONS.

J 1.103 • **Item 717-C-20**
ADMINISTRATIVE DECISIONS UNDER EMPLOYER SANCTIONS AND UNFAIR IMMIGRATION-RELATED EMPLOYMENT PRACTICES LAW OF THE UNITED STATES.

J 1.104:v.nos./nos. • **Item 723-A-3 (EL)**
CIVIL RIGHTS FORUM.

J 1.105:v.nos./nos. • **Item 717-A-5**
NATION TO NATION.

J 1.106:date • **Item 717-A-6 (P) (EL)**
ENFORCING THE ADA, A STATUS REPORT FROM THE DEPARTMENT OF JUSTICE.

J 1.107:nos. • **Item 717-A-8**
ON THE BEAT: COMMUNITY ORIENTED POLICING SERVICES.
Formerly: Community Cops.

J 1.108 • **Item 718-B (E)**
NCIC 2000 NEWSLETTER.

J 1.109:date • **Item 717-A-30**
LEGAL ACTIVITIES. [Annual]

Issued in Braille.

J 1.109/2: • **Item 717-A-31**
BRAILLE PUBLICATIONS.

J 1.110 • **Item 717-A-32 (EL)**
WEED & SEED IN-SITES. [Quarterly]

J 1.111 • **Item 717-A-33 (P)**
REENTRY REPORT (THE NEWSLETTER OF THE REENTRY COURTS AND PARTNERSHIPS INITIATIVES).

J 1.112 • **Item 717-A-34 (EL)**
NATIONAL DRUG INTELLIGENCE CENTER (NDIC): GENERAL PUBLICATIONS.

ASSISTANT ATTORNEY GENERAL FOR COURT OF CLAIMS (1893–1934)

J 2.1:date
ANNUAL REPORTS.

J 2.2:CT
GENERAL PUBLICATIONS.

J 2.3:nos.
BULLETINS.

J 2.4:nos.
CIRCULARS.

J 2.7:CT
PAPERS IN RE.

    Earlier J 18.7

ASSISTANT ATTORNEY GENERAL FOR INDIAN DEPRECIATION CLAIMS (1894–1907)

J 3.1:date
ANNUAL REPORTS.

J 3.2:CT
GENERAL PUBLICATIONS.
J 3.3:nos.
BULLETINS.

J 3.4:nos.
CIRCULARS.

LIBRARY (1873–   )

INFORMATION

    Office of the Director
    Library
    Department of Justice
    Rm. 5400, Robert F. Kennedy
        Justice Bldg. (Main)
    950 Pennsylvania Ave., NW
    Washington, DC 20530
    (202) 514-3775
    http://www.usdoj.gov/jmd/ls/index.htm/

J 4.1:date
ANNUAL REPORTS.

J 4.2:CT
GENERAL PUBLICATIONS.

J 4.3
BULLETINS.

J 4.4
CIRCULARS.

J 4.5:date
CATALOGUES.

J 4.6:CT
REGULATION RULES, AND INSTRUCTIONS OF
    LIBRARY OF DEPARTMENT OF JUSTICE.

J 4.7:vol.
JUSTICE LIBRARY REVIEW. [Bimonthly]

SOLICITOR OF TREASURY (1880–1912)

J 5.1:date
ANNUAL REPORTS.

    Earlier T 44.1

J 5.2:CT
GENERAL PUBLICATIONS.

    Earlier T 44.2

J 5.3:nos.
BULLETINS.

J 5.4:nos.
CIRCULARS.

J 5.5:date
DIGEST OF OPINIONS.

J 5.6:date
REGULATIONS, RULES, AND INSTRUCTIONS.

    Earlier T 44.5

PENITENTIARY FORT LEAVENWORTH (1895–1926)

J 6.1:date
ANNUAL REPORTS.

J 6.2:CT
GENERAL PUBLICATIONS.

J 6.3:nos.
BULLETINS.

J 6.4:nos.
CIRCULARS.

PORTO RICO, ATTORNEY GENERAL (1901–1903)

J 7.1:date
ANNUAL REPORTS.

J 7.2:CT
GENERAL PUBLICATIONS.

J 7.3:nos.
BULLETINS.

J 7.4:nos.
CIRCULARS.

NATIONAL TRAINING SCHOOL FOR BOYS (1908–1939)

J 8.1:date
ANNUAL REPORTS.

    See also DC 19.1
J 8.2:CT
GENERAL PUBLICATIONS.

J 8.3
BULLETINS.

J 8.4:nos.
CIRCULARS.

NATIONAL TRAINING SCHOOL FOR GIRLS (1912–1926)

J 9.1:date
ANNUAL REPORTS.

J 9.2:CT
GENERAL PUBLICATIONS.

J 9.3
BULLETINS.

J 9.4:nos.
CIRCULARS.

ASSISTANT ATTORNEY GENERAL FOR SPANISH TREATY CLAIMS COMMISSION (1898–1910)

J 10.1:date
ANNUAL REPORTS.

J 10.2:CT
GENERAL PUBLICATIONS.

J 10.3:nos.
BULLETINS.

J 10.4:nos.
CIRCULARS.

J 10.5/1:docket nos.
STATEMENTS OF FACTS, AND BRIEFS.

J 10.5/2:v.nos.
BRIEFS, BOUND VOLUMES.

SOLICITOR GENERAL
(1909– 1939)

J 11.1:date
ANNUAL REPORTS.

J 11.2:CT
GENERAL PUBLICATIONS.

J 11.3:nos.
BULLETINS.

J 11.4:nos.
CIRCULARS.

ASSISTANT ATTORNEY GENERAL
FOR CUSTOMS MATTERS
(1909– 1923)

J 12.1:date
ANNUAL REPORTS.

J 12.2:CT
GENERAL PUBLICATIONS.

J 12.3:nos.
BULLETINS.

J 12.4:nos.
CIRCULARS.

PENITENTIARY McNEIL ISLAND
(1910– 1926)

J 13.1:date
ANNUAL REPORTS.

J 13.2:CT
GENERAL PUBLICATIONS.

J 13.3:nos.
BULLETINS.

J 13.4:nos.
CIRCULARS.

PENITENTIARY ATLANTA,
GEORGIA
(1910– 1926)

J 14.1:date
ANNUAL REPORTS.

J 14.2:CT
GENERAL PUBLICATIONS.

J 14.3:nos.
BULLETINS.

J 14.4:nos.
CIRCULARS.

BUREAU OF CRIMINAL
IDENTIFICATION
(1910– 1923)

J 15.1:date
ANNUAL REPORTS.

J 15.2:CT
GENERAL PUBLICATIONS.

J 15.3
BULLETINS.

J 15.4
CIRCULARS.

FEDERAL BUREAU OF PRISONS
(1930–   )

CREATION AND AUTHORITY

The Bureau of Prisons was established within the Department of Justice by Act of Congress, approved May 14, 1930.

INFORMATION

Office of Public Affairs
Federal Bureau of Prisons
Department of Justice
320 First St., NW
Washington, D.C. 20534
(202) 307-3198
Fax: (202) 514-6878
http://www.bop.gov

J 16.1:date   • **Item 726-C-5 (MF)**
ANNUAL REPORT. 1930–   [Annual]

J 16.2:CT   • **Item 726-C-1**
GENERAL PUBLICATIONS.

   J 16.2:P 93/3   • **Item 726-C-1**
   STATISTICAL REPORT, FISCAL YEAR (date). [Annual]

Research, Statistics and Development Branch, Division of Management and Planning.

J 16.3:nos.
BULLETINS.

J 16.4:nos.
CIRCULARS.

J 16.6:CT
REGULATIONS, RULES, AND INSTRUCTIONS.

J 16.6/2:CT   • **Item 726-C-2**
HANDBOOKS, MANUALS, GUIDES.

J 16.7:CT
SOCIAL SERVICE RESOURCE DIRECTORIES.

J 16.8:vol.
FEDERAL PROBATION.

J 16.9:nos.
RECENT PUBLICATIONS OF CRIMINOLOGY AND PENOLOGY. 1– 4. 1938.

J 16.10:CT
BIBLIOGRAPHIES, REFERENCE LISTS, ETC.

J 16.11:v.nos.&nos.
NEW ERA. v. 1– v. 54. 1944– 1968. Reinstated 1970– (U.S. Penitentiary, Leavenworth, Kansas)

J 16.12
BULLETIN BOARD.

J 16.13:v.nos.&nos.
ATLANTIAN. v.1– v. 26, no.4. 1938– 1967. [Quarterly] (United States Penitentiary, Atlanta, Georgia)

J 16.14:v.nos.&nos.
OUTLOOK. v. 1– v. 23, no. 2.   – 1957. (Federal Reformatory, El Reno, Oklahoma)

J 16.15:date
NUTMEG GUIDON. (Federal Correctional Institution, Danbury, Connecticut)

J 16.16:v.nos.&nos.
PERISCOPE. v. 1– v. 21. [   ]– 1953. (United States Penitentiary, Lewisburg, Pa.)

J 16.17:v.nos.&nos.
BORDER SENTINEL. v. 1–   [Monthly or Bimonthly] (Federal Correctional Institution, La Tuna, Texas)

J 16.17/2:date
BORDER SENTINEL COMMENT. [Monthly]

J 16.18:v.nos.&nos.
EAGLE. v. 1– v. 35. [   ]– 1968. (Federal Reformatory for Women, Alderson, West Virginia)

J 16.19:date
BEAM. 1948. (United States Federal Prison Camp, Maxwell Field, Alabama)

J 16.20:v.nos.&nos.
ISLAND LANTERN. v. 1– 56. 1939– 1980. [Bimonthly] (U.S. Penitentiary, McNeil Island, Washington)

Frequency varies.

J 16.21:v.nos&nos.
CHILIARCH. (Federal Reformatory, Chillicothe, Ohio)

J 16.22:date
PROGRESS REPORT.

J 16.23:nos.
NATIONAL PRISONER STATISTICS. 1–   1950–

EXECUTIONS. [Annual]

PURPOSE:– To list prisoners executed under civil authority, by race and offense; by age, race, offense and State; by State; by offense, race, and State. Issued each Spring covering the previous calendar year.

PRISONERS IN STATE AND FEDERAL INSTITUTIONS. [Annual]

PURPOSE:– To present summaries of sentenced prisoners received from court and present at the end of the year in State and Federal institutions for adult offenders, by institution and sex, by State; movement of sentenced prisoners, by regions and States. Issued each Summer covering preceding calendar year.

J 16.23/2
STATE PRISONERS: ADMISSIONS AND RELEASES. [Annual]

PURPOSE:– To present detailed data on the characteristics of adult felony prisoners admitted to and released from State correctional institutions for adult offenders in the United States during the calendar year.

J 16.23/3
CHARACTERISTICS OF STATE PRISONERS. [Annual]

PURPOSE:– To present characteristics of admissions, releases, and year-end population for State correctional institutions for adult felony offenders. Data are for the calendar year.

J 16.23/4
FEDERAL BUREAU OF PRISONS STATISTICAL
TABLES. [Annual]

Statistical tables cover population, commitments, discharges. Parole Board actions, and medical activities.

J 16.23/5:date   • Item 726-C-3 (MF)
STATISTICAL REPORT. 1967–   [Annual]

PURPOSE:– To present trend tables, volume summaries, inmate characteristics distributions, and Parole Board action summaries.
Statistical tables cover population, commitments, discharges, Parole Board actions, and medical activities.
Biennial 1967– 1972; annual, 1973–
Published in microfiche (24x).
Earlier J 16.23/4

J 16.24
BASIC DATA BOOK. 1st–   [Annual]

PURPOSE:– To present data on the Federal Prison System. It includes trends in population, costs, and employment, as well as brief resumes of various programs and objectives.

J 16.25:v.nos.&nos.
COMMUNITY EXCHANGE.

J 16.26:date   • Item 726-C-4
ANNUAL PROGRAM PLAN AND ACADEMY TRAINING SCHEDULE FOR FISCAL YEAR (date). [Annual]

PURPOSE:– To present the Institute program plan for rendering assistancein the field of corrections. Reflects the Institute's activities in areas of training, technical assistance, information dissemination, and policy/ program development.

J 16.27:CT
AUDIOVISUAL MATERIALS. [Irregular]

J 16.28:date
REQUEST FOR PROPOSALS. [Annual]

J 16.29:   • Item 726-C-6
MONDAY MORNING HIGHLIGHTS. [Weekly]

This weekly publication highlights activities of the Prisons Bureau such as personnel actions, retirements, and the current populations and capacities of various federal prisons.

J 16.30::v.nos./nos.   • Item 726-C-7 (MF)
FEDERAL PRISONS JOURNAL. [Quarterly]

J 16.31:date   • Item 726-C-3 (MF)
FACILITIES. [Annual]

J 16.32   • Item 726-C-8 (EL)
WEEKLY POPULATION REPORT.

J 16.33   • Item 726-C-8 (E)
ELECTRONIC PRODUCTS.

FEDERAL PRISON INDUSTRIES, INC.

J 16.51
ANNUAL REPORT.

Report submitted to Congress pursuant to provisions of sec. 4127 of title 18, U.S. Code for the fiscal year.

J 16.52:CT
GENERAL PUBLICATIONS.

J 16.55:nos.
REPORTS.

J 16.55/2:nos.
REPORT LETTERS.

J 16.56:CT
REGULATIONS, RULES, AND INSTRUCTIONS.

NATIONAL INSTITUTE OF CORRECTIONS

INFORMATION

National Institute of Corrections
Federal Bureau of Prisons
U.S. Department of Justice
320 First St., NW
Washington, DC 20534
(202) 307-3106
Toll Free: (800) 995-6423
http://www.nicic.org

J 16.102:CT   • Item 726-D
GENERAL PUBLICATIONS.

J 16.108:CT   • Item 726-D
HANDBOOKS, MANUALS, AND GUIDES. [Irregular]

J 16.109   • Item 726-E (MF)
SCHEDULE OF TRAINING AND SERVICES FOR FISCAL YEAR.

J 16.110:date   • Item 726-C-4 (MF)
NATIONAL INSTITUTE OF CORRECTIONS, ANNUAL PROGRAM PLAN, FISCAL YEAR.

J 16.111   • Item 726-D-1
BIBLIOGRAPHIES AND LISTS OF PUBLICATIONS.

BUREAU OF PROHIBITION
(1930– 1933)

CREATION AND AUTHORITY

The Bureau of Prohibition was established within the Department of Justice by the Prohibition Reorganization Act of 1930, approved May 27, 1930 (46 Stat. 427). The Bureau was abolished under Executive Orders 6166 of June 10, 1933, and 6639 of March 10, 1934, and its funcions transferred to the Bureau of Investigation (J 1.14).

J 17.1:date
ANNUAL REPORTS.

J 17.2:CT
GENERAL PUBLICATIONS.

J 17.3
BULLETINS.

J 17.4
CIRCULARS.

J 17.5:CT
LAWS.

J 17.6
REGULATIONS.

BUREAU OF WAR RISK LITIGATION
(1933– 1945)

CREATION AND AUTHORITY

The Bureau of War Risk Litigation was established within the Department of Justice on September 11, 1933, pursuant to Executive Order 6616 of June 10, 1933. The Bureau was abol-

ished on June 30, 1945, and its functions transferred to the Claims Division of the Department of Justice.

J 18.1:date
ANNUAL REPORTS.

J 18.2:CT
GENERAL PUBLICATIONS.

J 18.3
BULLETINS.

J 18.4
CIRCULARS.

J 18.5
LAWS.

J 18.6
REGULATIONS.

J 18.7:CT
PAPERS IN RE.

Later J 2.7

ALIEN PROPERTY DIVISION
(1941– 1942)

CREATION AND AUTHORITY

The Office of Alien Property Custodian (Y 3.Al 4) was abolished and its functions and records transferred to the newly established Alien Property Bureau in the Claims Division of the Department of Justice on May 1, 1934. On December 9, 1941, the Bureau was replaced by the Alien Property Division. On March 11, 1942, under authority of the Trading with the Enemy Act of 1917 and the First War Powers Act of December 18, 1941, the functions, personnel, and property of the Alien Property Division were transferred to the Office of Alien Property Custodian (Pr 32.5700) in the Office for Emergency Management.

J 19.1:date
ANNUAL REPORTS.
Earlier Y 3.Al 4:1
Later Pr 32.5701

J 19.2:CT
GENERAL PUBLICATIONS.
Earlier Y 3.Al 4:2
Later Pr 32.5702

ANTITRUST DIVISION
(1903– 1947)

CREATION AND AUTHORITY

The Antitrust Division was established within the Department of Justice by act of Congress, approved March 3, 1903 (32 Stat. 1062).

J 20.1:date
ANNUAL REPORTS.

J 20.2:CT
GENERAL PUBLICATIONS.

J 20.7:CT
PUBLIC STATEMENTS.

J 20.8:CT
PAPERS IN RE.

IMMIGRATION AND NATURALIZATION SERVICE
(1940–   )

CREATION AND AUTHORITY

The Immigration and Naturalization Service (L 15) was transferred from the Department of Labor to the Department of Justice by Reorganization Plan No. 5 of 1940, effective June 14, 1940.

INFORMATION

Immigration and Naturalization Service
Department of Justice
Washington, DC 20536
(202) 514-4316
Fax: (202) 514-3296
http://www.ins.usdoj.gov

J 21.1   • Item 723-A (MF)
ANNUAL REPORT. 1st–   1892–   [Annual]

Covers the fields of immigration, naturalization, patrol of the land borders, and the location and investigation of aliens illegally in the United States, and the resultant deportation of aliens. An appendix contains approximately 90 tables giving details by countries, legal classes admission, age, sex, occupations of aliens admitted or naturalized, investigations and apprehensions, passengers examined at ports of entry, and other miscellaneous tables.

J 21.2:CT   • Item 725
GENERAL PUBLICATIONS.

Earlier L 15.2

J 21.2:N 15   • Item 725
FOREIGN VERSIONS, VARIATIONS, AND DIMINUTIVES OF ENGLISH NAMES AND FOREIGN EQUIVALENTS OF U.S. MILITARY AND CIVILIAN TITLES. 1973. 54 p.

PURPOSE:– To aid personnel of the Immigration and Naturalization Service in their dealings with citizens of foreign countries. The information, provided in chart form, will be handy as a quick reference for anyone with an interest in foreign names and titles.

J 21.2:St 2/year   • Item 725
STATISTICAL YEARBOOK OF THE IMMIGRATION AND NATURALIZATION SERVICE. [Annual]

J 21.2/2:date   • Item 725-B
STATISTICAL YEARBOOK OF THE IMMIGRATION AND NATURALIZATION SERVICE. [Annual]

Data given for immigrants, refugees, nonimmigrants, nationality, enforcement, entries, litigation/legal activity and legislation.

J 21.2/10:date   • Item 725-B (EL)
STATISTICAL YEARBOOK OF THE IMMIGRATION AND NATURALIZATION SERVICE. [Annual]

Earlier J 21.2:St 2

J 21.2/10-2:date   • Item 725-B
QUARTERLY NONIMMIGRANT STATISTICS.

J 21.2/11:date   • Item 725-B
INS FACT BOOK. [Annual]

J 21.5   • Item 726
LAWS APPLICABLE TO IMMIGRATION AND NATIONALITY. 1953–   [Irregular]

Covers statutes of a permanent character, treaties, Proclamations, Executive Orders, and reorganization plans affecting the Immigration and Naturalization Service. Basic volume kept up-to-date by supplements.

1953 edition. 1557 p.
Supp. 1. July 1, 1952-Dec. 31, 1953. 53 p.
Supp. 2. 1954. 52 p.
Supp. 3. 1955-1959. 152 p.
Supp. 4. 1960-1962. 189 p.

J 21.5/2:CT   • Item 726
UNITED STATES IMMIGRATION LAWS, GENERAL INFORMATION.

Earlier J 21.2:Im 5/2

J 21.5/2:Im 6
UNITED STATES IMMIGRATION LAWS, GENERAL INFORMATION. [Irregular]

J 21.5/3:v.nos./nos.   • Item 726
OSC UPDATE. [Quarterly]

J 21.6:CT   • Item 727-A
REGULATIONS, RULES, AND INSTRUCTIONS. [Irregular]

Earlier L 15.6

J 21.6/2:date   • Item 726-A
OPERATIONS, INSTRUCTIONS, REGULATIONS, AND INTERPRETATIONS. [Irregular] (Includes basic manual and supplements for an indefinite period)

Consolidated reprint 1979 updates the original 1952 edition.
Kept up-to-date by Operations, Instructions, and Interpretations Transmittal Memos and Regulations Transmittal Memos.
Note:– Numbers 65 through 97 have been omitted for regulations and transmittals. Beginning with No. 98, transmittals and regulations will have the same number [DDSL 15,849, April 10, 1981]

J 21.6/2-2:nos.   • Item 726-A
OPERATIONS INSTRUCTIONS (series).

J 21.6/3:CT   • Item 725-A
HANDBOOKS, MANUALS, GUIDES.

J 21.7:letter-nos.
GENERAL ORDERS.

Earlier L 15.9/2

J 21.8:date
ESSENTIAL PROCEDURE AND REQUIREMENTS FOR NATURALIZATION UNDER GENERAL LAW (Form C-59).

Earlier L 15.13

J 21.9:CT   • Item 724
FEDERAL TEXTBOOK ON CITIZENSHIP.

Earlier L 15.11

J 21.10:vol.
MONTHLY REVIEW. v. 1– v.9, no.12. 1943– 1952.

Superseded by I & N Reporter (J 21.10/2).

J 21.10/2:v.nos.&nos.   • Item 724-A
INS REPORTER. v. 1–   1952–   [Quarterly]

Official organ of the Immigration and Naturalization Service. Contains articles of interest to members of the Service, professional workers interested in immigration and naturalization problems.
Departments: Changes in Regulations; Highlights of Selected Recent Court Decisions; Recent Administrative Decisions.
A statistical table is featured on the back cover of each issue. Index issued separately.
Prior to Fall 1976 issue entitled I & N Reporter (ISSN 0018-8514).
Supersedes Monthly Review (J 21.10).
ISSN 0147-0647

J 21.11   • Item 723
ADMINISTRATIVE DECISIONS UNDER IMMIGRATION AND NATIONALITY LAWS. v. 1–   1940/44–   [Irregular]

PURPOSE:– To present decisions of the At-
torney General, the Commissioner of Immigration and Naturalization, Board of Immigration Appeals, and other designated officials of the Immigration and Naturalization Service. Decisions published are those of a precedent-creating nature and published in this series in accordance with the Administrative Procedure Act of June 11, 1946 (60 Stat. 237).
Each volume includes cumulative index for all volumes issued to date.
Citation: I. & N. Dec.

J 21.11/2:nos.   • Item 723-A-5 (EL)
INTERIM ADMINISTRATIVE DECISIONS UNDER IMMIGRATION AND NATIONALITY LAWS.

PURPOSE:– To provide preliminary publications of the Presidential Board of Immigration Appeals decisions which are binding on all Immigration and Naturalization Offices. Later appear in the bound volumes (listed above).
Earlier title: Interim Decisions of the Department of Justice.
Earlier issued to Depository libraries under item number 723-A-1.

J 21.11/3:CT
POSTERS.

Earlier J 21.1:Al 4/4 and J 21.9:C 76/fig. 1-60

J 21.12:CT   • Item 725-C
POSTERS.

Earlier J 21.2:Al 4/4 and J 21.9:C 76

J 21.13:date
PASSENGER TRAVEL BETWEEN UNITED STATES AND FOREIGN COUNTRIES. [Annual Summary Reports]. – Jan. 1, 1976.

(Includes monthly, separate annual reports for fiscal and calendar years)

J 21.13/2
– [MONTHLY REPORTS].   – Jan. 1, 1976.

Gives data on alien and U.S. citizen passengers arrived and departed, by sea and by air, by U.S. and foreign flag, by U.S. ports of arrival and departure, and by countries of embarkation and debarkation.
The semiannual releases summarize the monthly issues for the fiscal and calendar years.
Superseded by U.S. International Air Traffic Statistics.
ISSN 0499-5708

J 21.14   • Item 723-B (MF)
CITIZENSHIP DAY AND CONSTITUTION WEEK BULLETINS. 1959–   [Annual]

A proclamation is issued annually by the President calling for observances of Citizenship Day and Constitution Week throughout the United States. Such observances are designed to honor native-born citizens newly arrived at voting age and persons who became naturalized citizens during the year, and to afford an opportunity for all citizens to rededicate themselves to the ideals and principles upon which the Nation was founded.
PURPOSE:– To provide a practical guide to methods and techniques which can be effectively used by communities and groups in planning appropriate observances during the commemorative period, and in assurance of the greatest active participation.
The Bulletin is generally made available in July or August in time for Citizenship Day (September 17) and Constitution Week (week beginning September 17).

J 21.15:date   • Item 723-C
ANNUAL INDICATORS OF IN-MIGRATION INTO THE UNITED STATES OF ALIENS IN PROFESSIONAL AND RELATED OCCUPATIONS. 1967–

Covers fiscal year.

J 21.16:CT • Item 726-A-1
BIBLIOGRAPHIES AND LISTS OF PUBLICATIONS. [Irregular]

J 21.17:date • Item 724-B
WESTERN REGIONAL NEWSLETTER. [Monthly]

J 21.18:v.nos.&nos.
CORAPORTER. [Irregular]

J 21.19:ltrs.nos. • Item 723-A-2 (EL)
FORMS.

J 21.20:date • Item 723-B (MF)
ADVANCE REPORT IMMIGRATION STATISTICS: FISCAL YEAR.

J 21.21:date • Item 723-B (MF)
THE PRESIDENT'S COMPREHENSIVE TRIENNIAL REPORT ON IMMIGRATION.

J 21.22:nos. • Item 723
IMMIGRATION ISSUES (Series).

J 21.23:case nos. • Item 723-A-1
OFFICE OF THE CHIEF ADMINISTRATIVE HEARING OFFICER (OCAHO) CASES.

J 21.23/2 • Item 723-A-1
QUARTERLY UPDATE, INDEX OF ADMINISTRATIVE LAW JUDGE AND CHIEF ADMINISTRATIVE HEARING OFFICER DECISIONS.

J 21.24: • Item 723-B-1 (E)
ELECTRONIC PRODUCTS (misc.).

J 21.25:v.nos/nos. • Item 723-B-1 (EL)
INS COMMUNIQUE. [Monthly]

OFFICE OF ALIEN PROPERTY
(1946– 1966)

CREATION AND AUTHORITY

The Office of Alien Property Custodian (Pr 32.5700) was terminated by an Executive Order on October 14, 1946, and transferred its functions to the Office of Alien Property in the Department of Justice. The Office was placed under the Civil Division on September 1, 1961. The Office was terminated on June 30, 1966.

J 22.1:date
ANNUAL REPORTS.

Earlier Pr 32.5701

J 22.2:CT
GENERAL PUBLICATIONS.

Earlier Pr 32.5702

J 22.7:CT
PAPERS IN RE.

COMMUNITY RELATIONS SERVICE
(1966–   )

CREATION AND AUTHORITY

The Community Relations Service (C 50) was transferred from the Department of Commerce to the Department of Justice by Reorganization Plan No. 6 of 1966.

INFORMATION

Community Relations Service
Department of Justice
600 E. Street, NW Ste-6000
Washington, DC 20530
(202) 305-2935
Fax: (202) 305-3009
http://www.usdoj.gov/crs

J 23.1 • Item 208-A (MF)
ANNUAL REPORT. 1st– 1966– [Annual]

Report submitted to Congress on the activities of the Community Relations Service pursuant to Section 1004 of the Civil Rights Act of 1964, covering the fiscal year.

J 23.2:CT • Item 208-A-1
GENERAL PUBLICATIONS.

Earlier C 50.2

J 23.3:CT • Item 208-A-3
HATE CRIME: THE VIOLENCE OF INTOLERANCE, CRS BULLETIN.

J 23.7
CRS MEDIA RELATIONS, NEWSPAPERS, MAGAZINE, RADIO, TELEVISION, INFORMATIONAL MONITORING SERVICE. [Weekly]

PURPOSE:– To list magazine articles, newspaper articles, and when possible radio and television programs for the coming week, which would be of interest to persons wishing information in civil rights or areas related to human relations.

J 23.8:CT • Item 208-A-2
HANDBOOKS, MANUALS, GUIDES.

Earlier C 50.8

J 23.9:CT
ADDRESSES.

Earlier C 50.9

DRUG ENFORCEMENT ADMINISTRATION
(1973–   )

CREATION AND AUTHORITY

On April 8, 1968, Reorganization Plan 1 of 1968 transferred the Bureau of Narcotics (T 56) from the Department of the Treasury and the Bureau of Drug Abuse Control from the Food and Drug Administration (FS 17.100) of the Department of Health, Education, and Welfare to the Department of Justice and created the Bureau of Narcotics and Dangerous Drugs. The Bureau was abolished by Reorganization Plan No. 2 of 1973, effective July 1, 1973, which also established the Drug Enforcement Administration to supersede it.

INFORMATION

Office of Public Affairs
Drug Enforcement Administration
Department of Justice
Mailstop AXS
2401 Jefferson Davis Hwy.
Alexandria, VA 22301
(202) 307-7967
http://www.usdoj.gov/dea

J 24.1:date • Item 967-D
ANNUAL REPORT.

Earlier T 56.1

J 24.1/2:date • Item 967-C (MF)
ANNUAL REPORT, OFFICE OF THE DEPUTY DIRECTOR– OPERATIONS.

J 24.1/3:date • Item 967-C (MF)
ANNUAL STATISTICAL REPORT.

J 24.2:CT • Item 967
GENERAL PUBLICATIONS.

Earlier T 56.2

J 24.3:v.nos.&nos. • Item 968-B
BNDD BULLETIN. v. 1– 1969–1973. [Bimonthly]

Superseded by Drug Enforcement (J 24.3/2).

J 24.3/2:v.nos.&nos. • Item 968-B
DRUG ENFORCEMENT. [3 times a year]

Indexed by: Index to U.S. Government Periodicals.
ISSN 0098-3470
Continues BNDD Bulletin (J 24.3)

J 24.6 • Item 968
REGULATIONS. 1– [Irregular]

Reprint of material published in Code of Federal Regulations.

J 24.8:CT • Item 968-A
HANDBOOKS, MANUALS, GUIDES.

J 24.9:date • Item 969
TRAFFIC IN OPIUM AND OTHER DANGEROUS DRUGS. 1912– [Annual]

Report submitted by the Commissioner of Narcotics and transmitted to Congress by the Secretary of the Treasury pursuant to the Act of June 14, 1930. Report also submitted through the Secretary of State to the nations signatory to the International Drug Conventions of 1912 and 1931.
Covers participation in international treaties; legislative measures; control of international trade, domestic trade, and manufacture; abuse of drugs (drug addictions); illicit traffic. Supplemented by statistical tables.

J 24.10:nos. • Item 475-J
FACT SHEETS. 1– 1969–

Nos. 1-18 published in one publication.
Earlier FS 13.130

J 24.11:CT • Item 968-J
POSTERS.

J 24.12:CT • Item 967-A
BIBLIOGRAPHIES AND LISTS OF PUBLICATIONS.

J 24.13:CT • Item 967-B
COMMUNITY DRUG ABUSE PREVENTION PROGRAM SERIES. [Irregular]

PURPOSE:– To provide suggestions in outline form for community groups engaged in drug abuse prevention.

J 24.14:nos. • Item 968-D (MF)
RTP-TR- (series). 1– 1971– [Irregular]

J 24.15:CT • Item 968-C (MF)
ADDRESSES. [Irregular]

J 24.16:nos.   • **Item 968-E (MF)**
DEA PERSONNEL MANAGEMENT SERIES. 1–
1972– [Irregular]

J 24.17:v.nos.&nos.   • **Item 967-E (MF)**
REGISTRANT FACTS. v.1– 1974– [Biannual]

ISSN 0364-8435

J 24.18:date   • **Item 968-F (MF)**
GEO-DRUG ENFORCEMENT PROGRAM SIX-MONTH
STATISTICS. [Semiannual]

J 24.18/2:date
DEA DRUG ENFORCEMENT STATISTICS REPORT.

J 24.18/3:date   • **Item 968-F**
QUARTERLY STATISTICAL REPORT.

J 24.18/4   • **Item 968-F-1**
QUARTERLY INTELLIGENCE TRENDS. [Quarterly]

PURPOSE:– To assess illicit drug production, trafficking, and use of cannabis, cocaine,
dangerous drugs, and opiates. Provides information essential to formulation of drug control programs in the U.S. and abroad.
Discontinued.

J 24.19:date   • **Item 968-G**
DAWN [Drug Abuse Warning Network] QUARTERLY
REPORT.

J 24.19/2:date   • **Item 968-G (MF)**
PROJECT DAWN [Drug Abuse Warning Network],
ANNUAL REPORT. 1st– 1978–

J 24.20:date   • **Item 967-A-1**
DEA WORLD. [Monthly]

PURPOSE:– To provide an illustrated newsletter containing information about the Drug Enforcement Administration and its staff.
Effective February 21, 1980, this publication
ceased to be distributed to depository libraries
under Item No. 968-G-1, at the request of the
issuing agency due to the "then sensitivity of its
contents."

J 24.21:date   • **Item 967 (MF)**
APPROPRIATION HEARINGS. [Annual]

J 24.22:date   • **Item 1093 (EL)**
NARCOTICS INTELLIGENCE ESTIMATE (year).
[Annual]

Earlier Y 3.N 16:2 N 16

J 24.23:CT   • **Item 967-F (MF)**
DRAFT ENVIRONMENTAL IMPACT STATEMENTS. [Ir-
regular]

Each statement examines the effects on the
environment of a different problem related to drug
enforcement.

J 24.24:   • **Item 967-G (MF)**
PROJECT LABEL, ALPHABETICAL LISTINGS BY
DRUG LABELER. [Triennial]

Project Label provides comprehensive listings of all manufacturers, packagers, labelers, or
distributors of any compound, mixture, or preparation containing any controlled substance.

J 24.24/2:   • **Item 967-G-1 (MF)**
PROJECT LABEL, ALPHABETICAL LISTINGS BY
CONTROLLED GENERIC DRUG INGREDIENTS.
[Triennial]

Project Label provides comprehensive listings of all manufacturers, packagers, labelers, or
distributors of any compound, mixture,or preparation containing any controlled substance. This
listing is by controlled generic drug ingredients.

J 24.24/3:   • **Item 967-G-2 (MF)**
PROJECT LABEL, ALPHABETICAL LISTINGS BY
DRUG LABELER OF DISCONTINUED PRODUCTS.
[Triennial]

Project Label provides comprehensive list-

ings of all manufacturers, packagers, labelers, or
distributors of any compound, mixture,or preparation containing any controlled substance. This
listing is by drug labeler of discontinued products.

J 24.24/4:   • **Item 967-G-3 (MF)**
PROJECT LABEL, ALPHABETICAL LISTINGS BY
DRUG PRODUCT. [Triennial]

Project Label provides comprehensive listings of all manufacturers, packagers, labelers, or
distributors of any compound, mixture, or preparation containing any controlled substance. This
listing is by drug product.

J 24.25:   • **Item 967-H**
DOMESTIC CANNABIS ERADICATION/SUPPRESSION
PROGRAM. [Annual]

This program was established to ensure a
coordinated effort between federal, state, and
local agencies aimed at eradication of domesti-
cally cultivated cannabis in the U.S.

J 24.26   • **Item 475-J**
THE FINANCIER, SPECIALIZING IN HOSTILE TAKE-
OVERS. [Irregular]

Discontinued.

J 24.27:nos.   • **Item 967-I**
FORMS.

J 24.29   • **Item 967-J- (EL)**
DRUG TRAFFICKING IN THE UNITED STATES. [Bien-
nial]

UNITED STATES MARSHALS SERVICE
(1789–   )

CREATION AND AUTHORITY

The United States Marshals Service was established pursuant to the first Judiciary Act of
September 24, 1789 (1 Stat. 73).

INFORMATION

U.S. Marshals Service
Department of Justice
Crystal Square Bldg. 3
1735 Jefferson-Davis Hwy.
Arlington, VA 22202
(202) 307-9000
Toll Free: (800) 336-0102
Fax: (202) 307-9177
http://www.usdoj.gov/marshals

J 25.1:date   • **Item 969-A-5 (MF)**
ANNUAL REPORT.

J 25.2:CT   • **Item 969-A-1**
GENERAL PUBLICATIONS. [Irregular]

J 25.8:CT   • **Item 969-A-2**
HANDBOOKS, MANUALS, GUIDES. [Irregular]

J 25.10   • **Item 969-A-6**
DIRECTORIES.

J 25.12:CT   • **Item 969-A-3**
POSTERS. [Irregular]

J 25.13:   • **Item 969-A-4 (MF)**
MASTER AGREEMENT. [Triennial]

Master agreement between the U.S. Marshals
Service and the American Federation of Government Employees, AFL-CIO.

J 25.15:   • **Item 969-A-7 (EL)**
U.S. MARSHALS SERVICE FACT SHEETS.

BUREAU OF JUSTICE ASSISTANCE

CREATION AND AUTHORITY

The Law Enforcement Assitance Administration was established within the Department of
Justice on June 19, 1968 pursuant to the Omni-
bus Crime Control and Safe Streets Act of 1968
(84 Stat. 197) as amended. The Law Enforcement
Assistance Administration was abolished and its
functions transferred to the Office of Justice
Assistance, Research, and Statistics by act of
December 27, 1979 (93 Stat. 1201; 42 U.S.C.
3781). The Office was abolished by section 609B
of act of October 12, 1984 (98 Stat. 2091; 42
U.S.C. 3781).
Formerly the Office of Justice Assistance,
Research, and Statistics

INFORMATION

Bureau of Justice Assistance
Department of Justice
810 Seventh St., NW, 4th Fl.
Washington, DC 20531
(202) 616-6500
Fax: (202) 305-1367
http://www.ojp.usdoj.gov/bja

J 26.1:date   • **Item 968-H-29 (MF)**
ANNUAL REPORT.

Earlier issued under Item number 717-C

J 26.1/2:date   • **Item 717-C (MF)**
NATIONAL INSTITUTE FOR JUVENILE JUSTICE AND
DELINQUENCY PREVENTION: ANNUAL REPORT.

J 26.1/3:date   • **Item 717-C**
NATIONAL INSTITUTE OF LAW ENFORCEMENT AND
CRIMINAL JUSTICE: ANNUAL REPORT.

Earlier J 1.1/2

J 26.1/4:date   • **Item 717-B-12**
NATIONAL ADVISORY COMMITTEE FOR JUVENILE
JUSTICE AND DELINQUENCY PREVENTION:
ANNUAL REPORT. 1st– 1976–

Earlier J 1.48/2

J 26.1/5:date   • **Item 968-H-30**
BJA PROGRAM PLAN.

J 26.2:CT   • **Item 968-H-1**
GENERAL PUBLICATIONS. [Irregular]

J 26.2:In 3   • **Item 968-H-1**
DIRECTORY OF CRIMINAL JUSTICE INFORMA-
TION SOURCES. [Irregular]

Later J 28.20

J 26.8:CT   • **Item 968-H-5**
HANDBOOKS, MANUALS, GUIDES. [Irregular]

Earlier J 1.8/2

J 26.8/2:nos.   • **Item 968-H-4**
GUIDELINE MANUALS, M- (series). [Irregular]

PURPOSE:– To provide information about
major categorical programs of the Law Enforcement Assistance Administration, including topics
such as discretionary grant programs, selected
program field tests, technical assitance and training.
Earlier J 1.8/2

J 26.9:CT   • **Item 968-H-2**
BIBLIOGRAPHIES AND LISTS OF PUBLICATIONS.
[Irregular]

Earlier J 1.20/2

J 26.9/2:date/nos. • **Item 968-H-2**
BUREAU OF JUSTICE ASSISTANCE PUBLICATIONS
LIST. [Quarterly]

J 26.10:letters & nos. • **Item 968-H-6**
NATIONAL CRIMINAL JUSTICE INFORMATION AND
STATISTICS SERVICE: [REPORTS]. [Irregular]

Includes reports on such subjects as victimization surveys, national crime surveys, national
prisoner statistics, and utilization of criminal justice statistics.
Earlier J 1.42/3
Later J 29.9

J 26.11:CT • **Item 968-H-8 (MF)**
VISITING FELLOWSHIP PROGRAM REPORTS. [Ir-
regular]

PURPOSE:– To report on a project in the
criminal justice field that was supported by a
grant from the National Institute of Law Enforcement and Criminal Justice.

J 26.12:v.nos.&nos. • **Item 717-B-1**
LEAA NEWSLETTER. v. 1– 1970– [10 times a
year]

PURPOSE:– To provide up-to-date reliable information of innovativeprograms, research developments, and new equipment and techniques
of value to the criminal justice community. Contains information on the LEAA program itself, as
well as significant programs developed by State
and local governments with the use of LEAA funds.
Earlier J 1.33/3

J 26.13:CT • **Item 968-H-3 (MF)**
PRESCRIPTIVE PACKAGE (series). [Irregular]

PURPOSE:– To provide a series of publications on possible methods and techniques for
improving various elements in the criminal justice
system.
Earlier J 1.8/3

J 26.14:CT • **Item 968-H-9**
CRIMINAL JUSTICE PERSPECTIVES (series).
[Irregular]

PURPOSE:– To present the implications of
significant research on basic issues facing the
criminal justice system.

J 26.15:CT • **Item 717-N-1 (MF)**
RESEARCH SERIES. [Irregular] (National Institute of
Law Enforcement and Criminal Justice)

Earlier J 1.44

J 26.15/2:CT • **Item 717-N-1 (MF)**
MONOGRAPH (series). [Irregular]

Earlier J 1.44/2
Later J 28.18

J 26.16:CT • **Item 717-B-5**
PROGRAM MODELS. [Irregular]

Earlier J 1.54
Later J 28.9

J 26.17:v.nos. • **Item 968-H-7**
INTERNATIONAL SUMMARIES. v. 1– 1978–
[Irregular] (National Criminal Justice Reference
Service)

Collection of selected translations in law enforcement and criminal justice on topics of current interest to researchers and practitioners.
Later J 28.16

J 26.18:CT • **Item 717-B-8 (MF)**
CRIMINAL JUSTICE RESEARCH SOLICITATION.
[Irregular]

Contains miscellaneous information sent out
to solicit bids for people to do research for the
National Institute of Law Enforcement and Criminal Justice.
Later J 1.37/5

J 26.19:nos. • **Item 968-H-10**
SELECTIVE NOTIFICATION OF INFORMATION. SNI
1– [Monthly] (National Criminal Justice Reference Service)

PURPOSE:– To provide citations and abstracts of recently acquired documents on criminology.

J 26.20:nos. • **Item 717-J**
LAW ENFORCEMENT STANDARDS PROGRAM.
NILECJ-STD- (series). 1972– 1980 [Irregular] (Na-
tional Institute of Law Enforcement and Criminal
Justice)

The objective of the Law Enforcement Standards Program is to develop voluntary performance standards, specifications and procurement
guidelines for equipment used by U.S. Federal,
State and local law enforcement and criminal justice agencies. In the course of standards development the program is defining minimum performance levels and developing methods for measuring the actual performance levels of the equipment. Equipment areas are: protective equipment
and clothing, communications, security systems,
weapons, emergency equipment, investigative
aids and vehicles. Continued by Technology Assessment Program, NIC Standard- (series) (J
28.15).

Earlier J 1.41/2

J 26.21:letters-nos. • **Item 717-R**
NATIONAL EVALUATION PROGRAM (series). A 1–
1975– [Irregular]

Earlier J 1.46

J 26.21/2:CT • **Item 717-R-3 (MF)**
NATIONAL INSTITUTE OF LAW ENFORCEMENT AND
CRIMINAL JUSTICE EVALUATION SERIES.

Earlier J 1.46/2

J 26.22:CT • **Item 717-O**
EXEMPLARY PROJECT REPORTS. [Irregular] (Na-
tional Institute of Law Enforcement and Criminal
Justice)

Earlier J 1.10
Later J 28.10

J 26.23:date • **Item 717-B (MF)**
AWARDS, LEEP PARTICIPATING INSTITUTIONS,
PROGRAM YEAR. [Annual] (Law Enforcement
Education Program)
Earlier J 1.35/4

J 26.24:date • **Item 717-N-4 (MF)**
PROGRAM PLAN, FISCAL YEAR (date).

PURPOSE:– To outline the National Institute
of Law Enforcement and Criminal Justice's priorities for law enforcement and criminal justice research and spell out other programs and projects
to be carried out during the coming year.

J 26.25:date • **Item 717-C-10 (MF)**
ANALYSIS AND EVALUATION, FEDERAL JUVENILE
DELINQUENCY PROGRAMS. 1st– 1977–
[Annual] (Office of Juvenile Justice and Delin-
quency Prevention)

PURPOSE:– To present an analysis and
evaluation of the Federal delinquency programs
administered by the Office of Juvenile Justice
and Delinquency. The Office serves as a focal
point for Federal efforts to control delinquency.
Earlier J 1.2:J 98/8

J 26.26: • **Item 717-K-1 (MF)**
NATIONAL CRIMINAL JUSTICE REFERENCE SER-
VICE: DOCUMENT RETRIEVAL INDEX.
Published in microfiche (24x).
Later J 28.22

J 26.27:CT • **Item 717-N-5 (MF)**
REPORTS OF THE NATIONAL JUVENILE JUSTICE
ASSESSMENT CENTERS (series). [Irregular]

Reports submitted pursuant to the Juvenile
Justice and Delinquency prevention Act of 1974,
as amended, to collect and synthesize knowledge and information from available literature on
all aspects of juvenile delinquency.

J 26.28:CT
SLIM SELECTED LIBRARY IN MICROFICHE.

J 26.29:nos. • **Item 717-N-5**
ASSET FORFEITURE (Series).

J 26.30:CT • **Item 717-N-1**
MONOGRAPHS (Series).

J 26.30/2:nos. • **Item 717-N-10**
EFFECTIVE PROGRAMS MONOGRAPH (series).

J 26.31:CT • **Item 717-N-1**
PROGRAM BRIEF (Series).

J 26.32:v.nos./nos. • **Item 717-N-1**
BUREAU OF JUSTICE ASSISTANCE BULLETIN.

J 26.32/2:CT • **Item 717-N-7**
BULLETIN, COMMUNITY PARTNERSHIPS.

J 26.33:CT • **Item 717-N-5**
FACT SHEETS (series).

UNITED STATES PAROLE COMMISSION

INFORMATION

United States Parole Commission
Department of Justice
5550 Friendship Boulevard, Ste. 420
Chevy Chase, Maryland 20815-7286
(301) 492-5990
Fax: (301) 492-6694
http://www.usdoj.gov/uspc

J 27.1:date • **Item 717-C-15 (MF)**
ANNUAL REPORT.

J 27.2:CT • **Item 717-C-8**
GENERAL PUBLICATIONS. [Irregular]

J 27.6:CT • **Item 717-C-16**
REGULATIONS, RULES, INSTRUCTIONS. [Irregular]

J 27.8:CT • **Item 717-C-12**
HANDBOOKS, MANUALS, GUIDES. [Irregular]

J 27.8/2 • **Item 717-C-3 (EL)**
RULES AND PROCEDURES MANUAL. [Irregular]

J 27.9:v.nos. • **Item 717-C-8**
FEDERAL PAROLE DECISION-MAKING: SELECTED
REPRINTS. v. 1– 1978– [Irregular]

PURPOSE:– To provide compilations of technical research papers reprinted from various government and non-government criminal justice publications on topics pertaining to Federal parole
decision-making.
v. 1. 1974-1977.

NATIONAL INSTITUTE OF JUSTICE
(1979–   )

CREATION AND AUTHORITY

The National Institute of Justice was established pursuant to the Justice System Improvement Act of 1979, approved December 27, 1979 (93 Stat. 1167).

INFORMATION

National Institute of Justice
Department of Justice
810 Seventh St., NW
Washington, DC 20531
(202) 307-2942
Fax: (202) 307-6394
http://www.ojp.usdoj.gov/nij

J 28.1:date • Item 718-C (MF)
ANNUAL REPORT.

J 28.2:CT • Item 718-A
GENERAL PUBLICATIONS. [Irregular]

J 28.3/2 • Item 718-A-12
CONSTRUCTION BULLETIN (series). [Irregular]

Each Bulletin deals with a different construction topic.

J 28.3/3: • Item 718-A-18
AIDS BULLETIN (series).

Presents information in such areas as the cause, transmission, and incidence of AIDS.

J 28.3/4:v.nos./nos. • Item 718-A-12
BJA BULLETIN.

J 28.8:CT • Item 968-H-11
HANDBOOKS, MANUALS, GUIDES. [Irregular]

J 28.8/2:CT • Item 718-A-1
POLICY BRIEFS. [Irregular]

J 28.8/3:nos./v.nos. • Item 968-H-36 (P) (EL)
NIJ GUIDE. [Irregular]

Subtitle: Action Guides for Legislators and Government Executives.

J 28.9:CT • Item 717-B-5 (MF)
PROGRAM MODELS. [Irregular]

PURPOSE:– To provide a synthesis of research and evaluation of the findings in a criminal justice topic area. Each report presents a series of programmatic options and analyzes the advantages and disadvantages of each.
Earlier J 26.16

J 28.10:CT • Item 717-O (MF)
EXEMPLARY PROJECT REPORTS. [Irregular]

Earlier J 26.22

J 28.11:CT • Item 968-H-15
BIBLIOGRAPHIES AND LISTS OF PUBLICATIONS. [Irregular]

J 28.12:CT • Item 718-A-2 (MF)
TEST DESIGN (series). [Irregular]

Each issue describes a field test to determine effectiveness of various approaches to different criminal justice concerns such as supervised pre-trial release and employment service for ex-offenders.

J 28.13:CT • Item 718-A-4 (MF)
CRIMINAL JUSTICE RESEARCH UTILIZATION PROGRAM (series).

J 28.14:nos. • Item 968-H-10
NATIONAL INSTITUTE OF JUSTICE REPORTS. [Bimonthly]

Earlier titled: NIJ Reports, A Bimonthly Journal of the National Institute of Justice.
Replaced by National Institute of Justice Catalog (J 28.14/2).
Earlier J 26.19

J 28.14/a:CT • Item 968-H-10
NIJ REPORTS/SNI (reprints). [Irregular]

J 28.14/2:nos. • Item 968-H-10
NATIONAL INSTITUTE OF JUSTICE CATALOG. [Bimonthly]

Included with the NIJ Journal.
Replaces NIJ Reports (J 28.14).

J 28.14/2-2:nos. • Item 968-H-10
NATIONAL INSTITUTE OF JUSTICE JOURNAL. [Monthly]

J 28.15:nos. • Item 717-J
TECHNOLOGY ASSESSMENT PROGRAM, NIJ STANDARD- (nos.). 1980– [Irregular]

Continues: Law Enforcement Standards Program, NILEC-STD- (series) (J 26.20).

J 28.15/2:nos. • Item 717-J
NIJ REPORTS (series). [Irregular]

J 28.15/2:date • Item 717-J-2
NATIONAL INSTITUTE OF JUSTICE, RESEARCH REPORT. [Annual]

J 28.15/2-2:CT • Item 717-J-1 (MF) (EL)
RESEARCH IN ACTION (series).

This series reprints selected articles from NIJ Reports (J 28.15/2) on miscellaneous topics.

J 28.15/2-3:date • Item 717-J-1 (P) (EL)
DUF: DRUG USE FORECASTING. [Quarterly]

J 28.15/2-4 • Item 717-J-2 (P) (EL)
ANNUAL REPORT ON OPIATE USE AMONG ARRESTEES.

J 28.15/2-5 • Item 717-J-3
ANNUAL REPORT ON COCAINE USE AMONG ARRESTEES.

J 28.15/2-6 • Item 717-J-4
ANNUAL REPORT ON MARIJUANA USE AMONG ARRESTEES.

J 28.15/2-7 • Item 717-J-5
ANNUAL REPORT ON METHAMPHETAMINE USE AMONG ARRESTEES.

J 28.16:nos. • Item 968-H-7 (MF)
INTERNATIONAL SUMMARIES. v. 1– 1978– [Irregular]

Earlier J 26.17

J 28.16/2:date • Item 718-A-15
EXECUTIVE SUMMARY (series). [Irregular]

Executive Summaries on crime, its causes and control, such as a summary on the enforcement of fines as criminal sanctions.
Earlier J 28.2

J 28.17:date • Item 717-E
CRIMINAL JUSTICE RESEARCH. [Annual]

Earlier J 1.37/4

J 28.18:CT • Item 717-N-6 (MF)
MONOGRAPHS (series). [Irregular]

Earlier J 26.15/2

J 28.19:CT • Item 718-A-3 (MF)
RESEARCH BULLETINS. [Irregular]

PURPOSE:– To report on Institute research in criminal justice.

J 28.20 • Item 718-A-14
DIRECTORY OF CRIMINAL JUSTICE INFORMATION SOURCES.

A reference tool on resources provided by various government and nongovernment organizations nationwide to assist law enforcement and criminal justice professionals. Directories are expected to contain about 200 pages. Their frequency cannot be predicted.
Earlier title: A Network of Knowledge, Directory of Criminal Justice Information Sources.
Earlier J 26.2:In 3

J 28.20/2:date • Item 718-A-16 (MF)
CRIMINAL JUSTICE INFORMATION EXCHANGE DIRECTORY. [Annual]

Provides quick access to the locations, holdings, and service of Criminal Justice Information Exchange libraries. Lists CJIE libraries alphabetically by state and by province, and alphabetically by city within state.

J 28.21 • Item 717-R
NATIONAL EVALUATION PROGRAM (series).

J 28.22:date • Item 717-K-1 (MF)
DOCUMENTS RETRIEVAL INDEX. [Annual]

Includes bibliographic citations, brief descriptive annotations, and availability information for documents in the collection. Published in five individual parts: document citation, title index, personal name and index, and a thesaurus.
Basic index covers year 1972-1978, with supplements issued annually.
Published in microfiche (24x).
Earlier J 26.26

J 28.23:CT • Item 718-A-7
ISSUES AND PRACTICES. [Irregular]

Designed for the criminal justice professional. Each report presents the program options and management issues in a different topic area, such as compensating victims of crimes.

J 28.23/2 • Item 718-A-40
ISSUES IN INTERNATIONAL CRIME.

J 28.24:CT • Item 718-A-3 (EL)
RESEARCH IN BRIEF (series). [Irregular]

J 28.24/2:date • Item 718-A-3
SPONSORED RESEARCH PROGRAMS. [Annual]

J 28.24/3:CT • Item 718-A-3
RESEARCH REPORTS (series). [Irregular]

J 28.24/3-2:CT • Item 718-A-33
PERSPECTIVES ON CRIME AND JUSTICE, LECTURE SERIES. [Annual]Perspectives on Crime and Justice, Lecture Series]

J 28.24/4: • Item 718-A-19
RESEARCH ABSTRACTS (series).

Contains abstracts of miscellaneous National Institute of Justice research.

J 28.24/5:date • Item 718-A-26
ANNUAL REPORT ON ADULT ARRESTEES.

J 28.24/6:date • Item 718-A-27
ANNUAL REPORT ON JUVENILE ARRESTEES/ DETAINEES.

J 28.24/7:CT • Item 718-A-29
RESEARCH PREVIEW (series).

J 28.24/9 • Item 718-A-38
PROGRAM BRIEF.

J 28.24/10 • Item 718-A-38 (EL)
THE NIJ RESEARCH REVIEW. [Quarterly]

J 28.25:date • Item 718-A-11
PROGRAM ANNOUNCEMENT, GRADUATE RE-
SEARCH FELLOWSHIP PROGRAM. [Annual]

J 28.25/2:date • Item 718-A-11
PROGRAM ANNOUNCEMENT, VISITING FELLOW-
SHIP PROGRAM. [Annual]

J 28.25/3:date • Item 718-A-11
RESEARCH PLAN. [Annual]

Merged with Evaluation Plan (J 28.25/4) to
form Research and Evaluation Plan (J 28.25/5).
Earlier titled: Research Program Plan.

J 28.25/4:date • Item 718-A-11
EVALUATION PLAN. [Annual]

Merged with Research Plan (J 28.25/3) to
form Research and Evaluation Plan (J 28.25/5).

J 28.25/5:date • Item 718-A-11
RESEARCH AND EVALUATION PLAN. [Annual]

Formed by the union of Research Plan (J
28.25/3) and Evaluation Plan (J 28.25/4).

J 28.26:CT • Item 968-H-11
CRIME FILE (series). [Irregular]

J 28.27 • Item 718-A-20
PERSPECTIVES ON POLICING (series).
This series will deal with miscellaneous top-
ics on policing.

J 28.28:date • Item 718-A-14
NATIONAL CRIMINAL JUSTICE THESAURUS. [Irregu-
lar]

J 28.29 • Item 718-A-7
ANNUAL EVALUATION REPORT ON DRUGS AND
CRIME: A REPORT TO THE PRESIDENT, THE
ATTORNEY GENERAL, AND THE CONGRESS.

J 28.30:CT • Item 718-A-11
PROGRAM FOCUS (series).

J 28.31 • Item 718-D (E)
ELECTRONIC PRODUCTS. [Irregular]

J 28.31/2:date • Item 718-D-1 (EL)
NATIONAL CRIMINAL JUSTICE REFERENCE
SERVICE DOCUMENT DATA BASE. [Semiannual]

Issued on CD-ROM.

J 28.31/2-2 • Item 718-D-1 (EL)
NCRJS ABSTRACT DATABASE.

J 28.32 • Item 718-D-2
NATIONAL INSTITUTE OF JUSTICE UPDATE.

J 28.33:CT • Item 718-E-1
SOLICITATION (series).

J 28.34 • Item 718-F
FELLOWSHIP PROGRAM ANNOUNCEMENT.

J 28.35: • Item 718-F-1
NIJ RESEARCH FORUM (series).

J 28.36:date • Item 718-A-37 (P) (EL)
BUILDING KNOWLEDGE ABOUT CRIME & JUSTICE.
[Annual]

J 28.37 • Item 718-D (EL)
TECHBEAT.

BUREAU OF JUSTICE STATISTICS
(1979–   )

CREATION AND AUTHORITY

The Bureau of Justice Statistics was established pursuant to the Justice System Improvement Act of 1979, approved December 27, 1979
(3 Stat. 1167).

INFORMATION

Bureau of Justice Statistics
Office of Justice Programs
Department of Justice
633 Indiana Avenue, N.W.
Washington, D.C. 20531
(202) 307-0765
Fax: (202) 307-5846
Toll Free: (800) 732-3277
http://www.ojp.usdoj.gov/bjs

J 29.1:date • Item 968-H-20 (MF)
ANNUAL REPORTS.

PURPOSE– To summarize Bureau activities
and presents statistical information on a variety
of criminal justice topics.

J 29.1/2:date • Item 717-R-7
BUREAU OF JUSTICE STATISTICS FISCAL YEAR: AT
A GLANCE.

J 29.2:CT • Item 717-R-1
GENERAL PUBLICATIONS. [Irregular]

J 29.8:CT • Item 717-R-2
HANDBOOKS, MANUALS, GUIDES. [Irregular]

J 29.8/2:date • Item 968-H-19 (MF)
DIRECTORY OF AUTOMATED CRIMINAL JUSTICE
INFORMATION SYSTEMS. [Irregular]

PURPOSE:– To describe over 1,000 criminal
justice information systems in state and local
agencies throughout the United States. Also identifies the statistical and communications capabilities of the systems.
Earlier J 29.8:C 86

J 29.9:letters-nos. • Item 968-H-6
BUREAU OF JUSTICE STATISTICS TECHNICAL RE-
PORTS. [Irregular]
Former title: Bureau of Justice Statistics Re-
ports.
Earlier J 26.10

J 29.9/2:date • Item 968-H-6
CRIMINAL VICTIMIZATION IN THE UNITED STATES.
[Annual]

J 29.9/2-2 • Item 968-H-27
CRIMINAL VICTIMIZATION IN THE UNITED STATES:
TRENDS. [Biennial]

J 29.9/3:date • Item 968-H-6
SUPPLEMENT TO STATE COURT MODEL STATISTI-
CAL DICTIONARY. [Irregular]
Earlier J 29.2:P 94/2

J 29.9/4:date • Item 968-H-6
PROSECUTION OF FELONY ARREST. [Annual]
Earlier J 29.9

J 29.9/5:date • Item 968-H-18
CHILDREN IN CUSTODY. [Biennial]

PURPOSE:– To provide information on public
and private residential facilities holding juveniles
in custody across the country. Also presents data
on the juveniles they hold.
Earlier J 26.10

J 29.9/6:date • Item 968-H-6 (P) (EL)
SOURCEBOOK OF CRIMINAL JUSTICE STATISTICS.
[Annual]
Earlier J 29.9

J 29.9/6-2:date • Item 968-H-31 (CD)
SOURCEBOOK OF CRIMINAL JUSTICE STATISTICS.

J 29.9/7:date • Item 968-H-22
PRISONERS IN STATE AND FEDERAL INSTITUTIONS
ON (date). [Annual]

PURPOSE– To present data on the number
and movement of prisoners in all state and federal correctional institutions. Examines changes
in geographic distribution of prisoners, composition of the prison population by race, sex.
Earlier J 29.9

J 29.9/8 • Item 968-H-12 (MF)
CRIMINAL JUSTICE INFORMATION POLICY (series).

J 29.10:CT • Item 968-H-12 (MF)
PRIVACY AND SECURITY OF CRIMINAL HISTORY
INFORMATION (series).

PURPOSE:– To resolve the conflict between
privacy and security in criminal justice cases
through titles on such subjects an analysis of
privacy issues, administrative security, and pertinent State legislation.

J 29.11:date • Item 968-H-13 (EL)
BUREAU OF JUSTICE STATISTICS BULLETIN.
[Monthly]

Presents issues and facts in crime and justice statistics aimed at decision-makers.

J 29.11/2:date • Item 968-H-13
JUSTICE EXPENDITURE AND EMPLOYMENT.
[Annual]

J 29.11/2-2:date • Item 968-H-13
JUSTICE EXPENDITURE AND EMPLOYMENT
EXTRACTS. [Annual]

J 29.11/2-3:date • Item 968-H-13
JUSTICE EXPENDITURE AND EMPLOYMENT IN THE
U.S. [Annual]

J 29.11/3 • Item 968-H-38 (EL)
JAILS IN INDIAN COUNTRY. [Annual]

J 29.11/3:date • Item 968-H-13
CAPITAL PUNISHMENT. [Annual]
Earlier J 29.11

J 29.11/4:date • Item 968-H-13
TELEPHONE CONTRACTS. [Irregular]
Earlier J 29.11

J 29.11/5:date • Item 968-H-13 (P) (EL)
JAIL INMATES. [Irregular]
Earlier J 29.11

J 29.11/5-2 • Item 968-H-33 (P) (EL)
PRISON AND JAIL INMATES AT MIDYEAR. [Annual]

J 29.11/6:date • Item 968-H-13
PROBATION AND PAROLE. [Annual]
Earlier J 29.11

J 29.11/7:date • Item 968-H-13 (P) (EL)
PRISONERS. [Annual]

J 29.11/8:date • Item 968-H-13
CRIME IN THE NATION HOUSEHOLD. [Annual]
Earlier title: Households Touched by Crime.

J 29.11/9 • Item 968-H-13
TRACKING OFFENDERS. [Irregular]

J 29.11/10:date • Item 968-H-13 (P) (EL)
BUREAU OF JUSTICE STATISTICS BULLETIN, CRIMI-
NAL VICTIMIZATION.

J 29.11/11:date • Item 968-H-13
FELONY SENTENCES IN STATE COURTS. [Annual]

J 29.11/11-2:date • Item 968-H-28
FELONY SENTENCES IN THE UNITED STATES.
[Annual]

J 29.11/11-3 • Item 968-H-32
STATE COURT SENTENCING OF CONVICTED FEL-
ONS. [Biennial]

J 29.11/12:date • **Item 968-H-13**
FELONS SENTENCED TO PROBATION IN STATE COURTS.

J 29.11/13-2:date • **Item 968-H-34 (CD) (EL)**
NATIONAL CORRECTIONS REPORTING PROGRAM. [Annual]

J 29.11/14:date • **Item 968-H-13**
PRETRIAL RELEASE OF FELONY DEFENDANTS. [Triennial]

J 29.11/15 • **Item 968-H-13 (EL)**
PROSECUTORS IN STATE COURTS. [Irregular]

J 29.11/16 • **Item 968-H-37 (EL)**
STATE COURT PROSECUTORS IN LARGE DISTRICTS. [Biennial]

J 29.12:nos. • **Item 968-H-14**
UNIFORM PAROLE REPORTS. Series 1–
Each report covers a different subject.

J 29.12/2:date • **Item 968-H-14**
PAROLE IN THE UNITED STATES. [Annual]
Earlier J 29.2:P 24/2

J 29.13:CT • **Item 968-H-16 (EL)**
SPECIAL REPORTS (series). [Irregular]

Timely reports of the most current justice data on such subjects as family violence and habeas corpus.

J 29.13/2:date • **Item 968-H-16**
PROFILE OF JAIL INMATES. [Quinquennial]

J 29.13/3 • **Item 968-H-16**
DRUGS AND JAIL INMATES. [Quinquennial]

J 29.14:CT • **Item 968-H-17**
BIBLIOGRAPHIES AND LISTS OF PUBLICATIONS. [Irregular]

J 29.14/2:date • **Item 968-H-26**
BUREAU OF JUSTICE STATISTICS PUBLICATIONS CATALOG.

J 29.15: • **Item 968-H-21 (EL)**
TECHNICAL REPORTS (series). [Irregular]

J 29.16: • **Item 968-H-23 (MF)**
CENSUS OF STATE ADULT CORRECTIONAL FACILITIES. [Quinquennial]
PURPOSE– To provide data on facilities, inmates, programs, staff, and expenditures for state-operated confinement and community-based correctional facilities throughout the U.S. tables present census data for the country as a whole and also by states.

J 29.17:date • **Item 968-H-24 (P) (EL)**
CORRECTIONAL POPULATIONS IN THE UNITED STATES. [Annual]

Consolidates in one volume data on correctional populations gathered in various statistical program of the Bureau. Designed for comparison of detailed information. Narrative and tables present data by states in such areas as jail inmates, probation, terms, and capital punishment.

J 29.18: • **Item 968-H-25**
FELONY LAWS OF THE FIFTY STATES AND THE DISTRICT OF COLUMBIA. [Irregular]

Presents results of the National Survey of State Felony Laws. The survey's principal objective was to provide a condensed listing of felony statutes and the sentencing and classification information necessary for their interpretation.

J 29.19: • **Item 717-R-4**
BJS DATA REPORT. [Annual]

PURPOSE– To present data on crime, drugs an crime, cost of crime, corrections.
Earlier J 29.2:D 26/3

J 29.20:date • **Item 968-H-16 (P) (EL)**
COMPENDIUM OF FEDERAL JUSTICE STATISTICS. [Annual]

J 29.21:date • **Item 968-H-23**
CENSUS OF LOCAL JAILS. [Quinquennial]

J 29.22:date • **Item 717-R-4 (MF)**
BJS STATISTICAL PROGRAMS, FY.

Formerly titled: BJS Program Application Kit, Fiscal Year.

J 29.23:date • **Item 968-H-14**
TEENAGE VICTIMS, A NATIONAL CRIME SURVEY REPORT. [Quinquennial]

J 29.24 • **Item 968-H-14**
NATIONAL UPDATE. [Quarterly]

J 29.25:date • **Item 968-H-14**
SURVEY OF STATE PRISON INMATES.

J 29.26:CT • **Item 968-H-14**
BJS DICUSSION PAPER.

J 29.27 • **Item 968-H-14**
CRIME DATA BRIEF.

J 29.28: • **Item 717-R-5**
SELECTED FINDINGS.

J 29.29: • **Item 717-R-2 (E)**
ELECTRONIC PRODUCTS.

J 29.30:date • **Item 717-R-9 (P) (EL)**
FEDERAL JUSTICE STATISTICS PROGRAM.

J 29.31 • **Item 968-H-35 (P) (EL)**
FACT SHEET.

ENVIRONMENT AND NATURAL RESOURCES DIVISION (1965–   )

CREATION AND AUTHORITY

Public Lands Division of the Department of Justice was created on Nov. 16, 1909 by Attorney General Geo. Wickersham.

INFORMATION

Environment and Natural Resources Division
Department of Justice
Tenth Street and Constitution Avenue, N.W.
Washington, D.C. 20530
(202) 514-2701
Fax: (202) 514-0557
http://www.usdoj.gov/enrd

J 30.1:date
ANNUAL REPORT.

J 30.2:CT
GENERAL PUBLICATIONS.

J 30.9:v.nos.&nos.
LAND AND NATURAL RESOURCES DIVISION JOURNAL. [Bimonthly]

J 30.9/2:v.nos.&nos.
WILDLIFE NEWSLETTER.
Published as a supplement to the Journal (J 30.9).

EXECUTIVE OFFICE FOR UNITED STATES ATTORNEYS

CREATION AND AUTHORITY

EOUSA was created April 6, 1953 by AG Order No. 8-53 to provice close liaison between the Department of Justice in Washington, DC and

the 93 U.S. Attorneys located throughout the 50 states and territories.

INFORMATION

Executive Office for U.S. Attorneys
Department of Justice
950 Pennsylvania Ave., NW, Rm. 2261
Washington, D.C. 20530
(202) 514-2121
Fax: 616-2278
http://www.usdoj.gov/usao

J 31.1:date
ANNUAL REPORT.

J 31.2:CT • **Item 717-C-13**
GENERAL PUBLICATIONS.

J 31.8:CT • **Item 717-C-18**
HANDBOOKS, MANUALS, GUIDES.

J 31.9:CT • **Item 717-C-9**
REPORT OF THE U.S. ATTORNEY GENERAL FOR THE DISTRICT OF (area) TO THE ATTORNEY GENERAL. [Annual]

District of Columbia Report earlier J 1.1/4.

J 31.10:date • **Item 717-B-6 (MF)**
STATISTICAL REPORT. [Annual]

Earlier J 1.55
Discontinued.

J 31.11:v.nos.&nos.
LECC NETWORK NEWS. [Quarterly]

J 31.12:v.nos.&nos. • **Item 717-C-14 (EL)**
UNITED STATES ATTORNEY'S BULLETINS. v. 1–
[6 times/yr.]
Bulletins on commendations, points to remember, and case notes for use by Justice Department attorneys. Includes comments on current legislation, court cases, rulings, and decisions.

J 31.13 • **Item 717-C-21 (MF)**
DIRECTORIES.

OFFICE OF JUVENILE JUSTICE AND DELINQUENCY PREVENTION (1974–   )

CREATION AND AUTHORITY

The Office of Juvenile Justice and Delinquency Prevention was established by the Juvenile Justice and Delinquency Prevention Act of 1974 (88 Stat. 1109; 42 U.S.C. 5601).

INFORMATION

Office of Juvenile Justice
and Deliquency Prevention
Office of Justice Programs
Department of Justice
810 Seventh St., NW
Washington, DC 20531
(202) 307-5911
Fax: (202) 307-2093
http://ojjdp.ncjrs.org

J 32.1:date • **Item 718-A-8 (MF)**
ANNUAL REPORT.

J 32.2:CT • **Item 718-A-5**
GENERAL PUBLICATIONS. [Irregular]

J 32.8:CT • **Item 718-A-6**
HANDBOOKS, MANUALS, GUIDES. [Irregular]

J 32.10:   **• Item 718-A-9 (EL)**
JUVENILE JUSTICE BULLETINS. [Irregular]

   Contains condensations of reports from various U.S. cities regarding juvenile justice concerns.

J 32.10/2:date   **• Item 718-A-9 (MF)**
OJJDP FISCAL YEAR, PROGRAM PLAN. [Annual]

J 32.10/3:date   **• Item 718-E (MF)**
REPORT TO CONGRESS, TITLE V INCENTIVE GRANTS FOR LOCAL DELINQUENCY PREVENTION PROGRAMS. [Annual]

J 32.11   **• Item 718-A-32**
BIBLIOGRAPHIES AND LISTS OF PUBLICATIONS.

J 32.15:date   **• Item 717-B-4**
JUVENILE COURT STATISTICS. [Annual]

   Earlier J 1.53

J 32.16:date   **• Item 718-A-17 (MF)**
DELINQUENCY IN THE UNITED STATES. [Annual]

   PURPOSE– To describe the volume and characteristics of delinquency and status offense cases disposed of by courts with juvenile jurisdiction.

J 32.17:date   **• Item 718-A-17 (MF)**
OJJDP ANNUAL REPORT ON MISSING CHILDREN.

J 32.18   **• Item 718-A-17 (MF) (EL)**
JUVENILES TAKEN INTO CUSTODY (FY).

J 32.19:v.nos.-nos.   **• Item 718-A-5**
JUVENILE JUSTICE CONDITIONS OF CONFINEMENT. [Quarterly]

J 32.20   **• Item 718-A-24**
OJJDP SUMMARY & RESEARCH SUMMARY (series).

J 32.20/2   **• Item 718-A-25**
OJJDP SUMMARY & PROGRAM SUMMARY (series).

J 32.20/3   **• Item 718-A-28 (MF)**
OJJDP REPORT & RESEARCH REPORT (series).

J 32.20/4:v.nos./nos.   **• Item 718-A-30**
JUVENILE JUSTICE, DEINSTITUTIONALIZING STATUS OFFENDERS: A RECORD OF PROGRESS.

J 32.21:date/nos.   **• Item 718-G**
OJJDP FACT SHEET (series). (Office of Juvenile Justice and Delinquency Prevention)

J 32.21/2:date/nos.   **• Item 718-G-1**
OJJDP YOUTH IN ACTION FACT SHEET.

J 32.21/2-2:date/nos   **• Item 718-G-2**
YOUTH IN ACTION BULLETIN (series).

J 32.21/3   **• Item 718-G-3 (EL)**
HIGHLIGHTS OF THE NATIONAL YOUTH GANG SURVEY. [Annual]

J 32.22:date   **• Item 718-A-34 (P) (EL)**
OJJDP DISCRETIONARY PROGRAM ANNOUNCEMENT. [Annual]

J 32.23:   **• Item 718-A-36 (E)**
ELECTRONIC PRODUCTS (misc.).

J 32.24:   **• Item 718-A-35 (EL)**
EASY ACCESS.

J 32.25   **• Item 718-A-41(EL)**
OJJDP NEWS @ A GLANCE. [Bimonthly]

OFFICE OF ATTORNEY PERSONNEL MANAGEMENT

J 33.1:date
ANNUAL REPORT.

J 33.2:CT
GENERAL PUBLICATIONS.

J 33.8:CT
HANDBOOKS, MANUALS, GUIDES. [Irregular]

J 33.9:CT   **• Item 716-B-1**
POSTERS. [Irregular]

OFFICE FOR VICTIMS OF CRIME

INFORMATION

   Office for Victims of Crime
   Office of Justice Programs
   Department of Justice
   810 Seventh St., NW
   Washington, DC 20531
   (202) 307-5983
   Fax: (202) 514-6383
   http://www.ojp.usdoj.gov/ovc

J 34.2:CT   **• Item 720-B**
GENERAL PUBLICATIONS.

J 34.3:date   **• Item 720-B-3 (P) (EL)**
OVC BULLETIN. [Irregular]

J 34.3/3   **• Item 720-B-6 (EL)**
OVC'S LEGAL SERIES BULLETINS.

J 34.4:   **• Item 720-B-1 (P) (EL)**
OVC FACT SHEETS (various topics).

J 34.8:   **• Item 720-B-5**
HANDBOOKS, MANUALS, GUIDES.

J 34.10:date   **• Item 720-B-4**
DIRECTORIES.

VIOLENCE AGAINST WOMEN OFFICE
(1995–   )

INFORMATION

   Violence Against Women Office
   Office of Justice Programs
   U.S. Dept. of Justice
   810 Seventh St., NW
   Washington, DC 20531
   (202) 307-6026
   Fax: 307-3911
   http://www.ojp.gov/vawo

J 35.2:CT   **• Item 719-A-2**
GENERAL PUBLICATIONS.

J 35.5:   **• Item 719-A-1 (EL)**
LAWS.

J 35.7:   **• Item 719-A-1 (EL)**
PRESS RELEASES.

J 35.8:   **• Item 719-A-1 (EL)**
HANDBOOK, MANUALS, AND GUIDES.

J 35.19:   **• Item 719-A-1 (EL)**
ELECTRONIC PRODUCTS (misc.)

J 35.20:   **• Item 719-A-1 (EL)**
VIOLENCE AGAINST WOMEN ACT NEWS.

J 35.21:   **• Item 719-A-3 (P) (EL)**
DOMESTIC VIOLENCE AND STALKING. [Annual]

OFFICE OF COMMUNITY ORIENTED POLICING SERVICES

INFORMATION

   Office of Community Oriented
      Policing Services
   1100 Vermont Avenue
   NW, Washington, DC 20530
   (202) 514-2058
   Toll Free: (800) 421-6770
   http://www.usdoj.gov/cops/home.htm

J 36.2   **• Item 720-C**
GENERAL PUBLICATIONS.

J 36.6   **• Item 720-C-2**
REGULATIONS, RULES, INSTRUCTIONS.

J 36.8   **• Item 720-C-1**
HANDBOOKS, MANUALS, GUIDES.

J 36.15   **• Item 720-C-3 (EL)**
PROBLEM-ORIENTED GUIDES FOR POLICE SERIES. (numbered)

CIRCUIT COURTS

   This Class (Ju 1) was assigned to the SuDocs Classification Scheme but apparently was never used.

U. S. CIRCUIT COURTS OF APPEALS

Ju 2.2:CT   **• Item 743-D**
GENERAL PUBLICATIONS.

Ju 2.9:v.nos.&nos.   **• Item 743-D**
SEVENTH CIRCUIT DIGEST. [Monthly]

   Digest of the U.S. Court of Appeals for the Seventh Circuit. The Digest is composed of four parts: a topical index, alphabetical case index, federal rules index, and a synopses section which covers the holdings of the cases decided by the Court.

Ju 2.10   **• Item 743-D**
DC CIRCUIT UPDATE. [Quarterly]

COURT OF CLAIMS
(1855– 1982)

CREATION AND AUTHORITY

This court was established on February 25, 1855 (10 Stat. 612; 28 U.S.C. 171), and its jurisdiction is set forth in 28 U.S.C. 1491-1506. The court has original jurisdiction to render judgment upon any claim against the United States founded upon the Constitution, upon any act of Congress, upon any regulation of an executive department, upon any expressed or implied contracts with United States, and for liquidated or unliquidated damages in case not sounding in court. The court also has jurisdiction over other specific types of claims against the United States, foremost of which is jurisdiction to render judgment for reasonable and entire compensation in cases where the United States in its governmental capacity had manufactured or used an invention covered by a patent without the license of its owner. The court also exercises appellate jurisdiction over decisions rendered by the Indian Claims Commission on claims by the various Indian tribes (25 U.S.C. 70s). Judgments of the court are final and conclusive on both the private citizen and the United States unless reviewed by the Supreme Court on writ of certiorari.

Ju 3.1:date
ANNUAL REPORTS.

Ju 3.2:CT   **• Item 731**
GENERAL PUBLICATIONS.

Ju 3.3:nos.
BULLETINS.

Ju 3.4:nos.
CIRCULARS.

Ju 3.5
CALENDAR. [Monthly (Oct.-June)]

Ju 3.6:date
JUDGEMENTS RENDERED BY COURT OF CLAIMS.

Ju 3.7:CT
OPINIONS.

Ju 3.8:CT
PAPERS IN RE.

Ju 3.9   **• Item 731**
CASES DECIDED IN THE COURT OF CLAIMS OF THE UNITED STATES. v. 1–   1863–   [Irregular]

In addition to the decisions of the Court of Claims are abstracts of the decisions of the Supreme Court in the Court of Claims cases.
Citation: C Cla.
Beginning with Volume 110, indexes are contained in every tenth volume (those ending in 0) and cover the preceding ten volumes. Index in Volume 110 covers Volume 100-109, Volume 120 covers Volumes 110-119, etc.

Ju 3.10:date   **• Item 731-B**
RULES.

Ju 3.10/2:CT   **• Item 732**
ORDERS AS TO PROCEDURE.

Ju 3.10/3:CT   **• Item 731-B**
REGULATIONS AND INSTRUCTIONS.
Earlier Ju 3.2

Ju 3.10/4:CT   **• Item 731-B**
HANDBOOKS, MANUALS, GUIDES.

Ju 3.11:CT
INDEX (general).

Ju 3.11/2:date
[INDEX TO] PRINTED RECORDS [miscellaneous cases].

Ju 3.11/3:date
[INDEX TO] PRINTED RECORDS, FRENCH SPOILATION CASES.

Ju 3.11/4:Cong.
[INDEX TO] REPORTS OF COURT OF CLAIMS IN FRENCH SPOILATION CASES.

Ju 3.11/5:Cong.
[INDEX TO] REPORTS OF COURT OF CLAIMS IN CONGRESSIONAL CASES.

Ju 3.12:date
DOCKET OF CASES PENDING IN COURT OF CLAIMS. GENERAL JURISDICTION.

DISTRICT COURTS

Ju 4.2:   **• Item 732-A**
GENERAL PUBLICATIONS (U.S. District Courts)

COURT OF PRIVATE LAND
CLAIMS
(1891– 1904)

CREATION AND AUTHORITY

The Court of Private Land Claims was established on July 1, 1891, pursuant to act of Congress, approved March 3, 1891. It was abolished on June 30, 1904.

Ju 5.1:date
ANNUAL REPORTS.

Ju 5.2:CT
GENERAL PUBLICATIONS.

Ju 5.3:nos.
BULLETINS.

Ju 5.4:nos.
CIRCULARS.

SUPREME COURT
(1790–   )

CREATION AND AUTHORITY

Article III, Section 1, of the Constitution of the United States provides that "The judicial power of the United States, shall be vested on one supreme Court, and in such inferior Courts as the Congress may from time to time ordain and establish." The Supreme Court of the United States was created in accordance with this provision and by authority of the Judiciary Act of September 24, 1789 (1 Stat. 73). It was organized on February 2, 1790.

INFORMATION

United States Supreme Court Building
Public Information Office
1 First Street, N.E.
Washington, D.C. 20543
(202) 479-3211
http://www.supremecourtus.gov

Ju 6.1:date
ANNUAL REPORTS.

Ju 6.2:CT   **• Item 738**
GENERAL PUBLICATIONS.

Ju 6.3:nos.
BULLETINS.

Ju 6.4:nos.
CIRCULARS.

Ju 6.5:date   **• Item 740-A-1**
JOURNAL. 1890–   [Daily]

Gives account of Court's proceedings for the day. Full texts of the decisions and orders are presented, but not the opinions. Also contains a list of the Justices present on the Bench during each day, announcements made by the Chief Justice, and names of counsel admitted to the Bar.

Ju 6.6:CT
OPINIONS.

Ju 6.7:CT
PAPERS IN RE.

Ju 6.8:vol.   **• Item 741**
UNITED STATES REPORTS, CASES ADJUDGED IN SUPREME COURT AT OCTOBER TERM. v. 1– 1970–   [Irregular]

Contains same material as in the Preliminary Prints, but in bound form and plus comprehensive tables of cases reported, cases cited and statutes cited, a subject index, and other miscellaneous materials. Approximately two to five volumes issued per Term (October to June or July).
Citation: U.S.
Classified Ju 6.8/1, prior to v. 346, 1953.

Ju 6.8/a:nos.   **• Item 740-B**
OFFICIAL REPORTS OF THE SUPREME COURT, PRELIMINARY PRINTS.

Ju 6.8/b:nos.   **• Item 740-A (EL)**
SLIP OPINIONS. [Irregular]

Published as the individual opinions are announced, with headnotes but without other editorial material which appear in the Preliminary Prints and bound volumes. Issued three days after opinions are announced.
Class changed from Ju 6.8/1b, effective 1954.

Ju 6.8/1:v.nos.&nos.   **• Item 740-B**
PRELIMINARY PRINTS. [Irregular]

Also known as Advance Sheets. Contains official text of all opinions of the Court, with headnotes and other editorial material prepared by the official Reporter. Also contains texts of all decisions per curiam and orders. The pagination of the Prints is the same as that which will appear in the bound volumes, thereby making early citations permissible. The Prints are issued from 12 to 18 months after the decisions have been announced. Each number contains a cumulative table of cases reported in the volume.
ISSN 0364-0973
Classified Ju 6.8/1a, prior to v. 348, 1955.

Ju 6.8/2:nos.
DIGESTS OF UNITED STATES REPORTS.

Ju 6.8/3:v.nos.&nos.
CONDENSED REPORTS OF CASES IN SUPREME COURT OF UNITED STATES. v. 1–   1791–
Unofficial edition.

Ju 6.8/4:dock.nos.
CASES ARGUED AND DECIDED IN SUPREME COURT OF UNITED STATES. 2–   1801/1808–
Unofficial edition.

Ju 6.8/5:v.nos.
DIGESTS OF U.S. SUPREME COURT REPORTS. v. 1–   1885–
Unofficial editions.

Ju 6.9:date • **Item 739**
RULES AND ORDERS.

Ju 6.9/2:date • **Item 739**
GENERAL ORDERS IN BANKRUPTCY.

Ju 6.9/3:date
RULES OF CIVIL PROCEDURE FOR DISTRICT
COURTS IN U.S.

Ju 6.10:date of term • **Item 739**
DOCKET OF SUPREME COURT.

Ju 6.11:CT • **Item 740**
REGULATIONS, RULES, AND INSTRUCTIONS.
    Note: Includes Handbooks and Manuals.
    See also Ju 6.9 and Ju 6.9/3

Ju 6.12:v.nos.&nos. • **Item 738-A (MF)**
DOCKET SHEET. [Bimonthly]

    Newsletter containing short articles on various subjects relating to the activities and personnel of the Supreme Court.
    A microfiche edition, issued on an annual basis, distributed to depository libraries under Item 738-A.

Ju 6.13:yr.&nos.
IN THE SUPREME COURT OF THE UNITED STATES
(series).

UNITED STATES COURT OF
APPEALS FOR THE FEDERAL
CIRCUIT
(1982–   )

CREATION AND AUTHORITY

    This court was created by the Act of August 5, 1909 (36 Stat. 91; 28 U.S.C. ch. 9) to decide certain questions arising under the customs laws, and in 1929 was given jurisdiction to review certain patent and trademark cases. It reviews decisions of the Customs Court on classifications and duties upon imported merchandise, decisions of the Patent Office of applications and interferences as to patents and trademarks, and legal questions in the findings of the Tariff Commission as to unfair practices in import trade (28 U.S.C. 1541-1543). The court consists of chief judge and four associate judges, a clerk, a marshal, a reporter, and their assistants. The court sits en banc with all judges present. The Court of Customs and Patent Appeals and the Court of Claims were superseded by the United States Court of Appeals for the Federal Circuit pursuant to the Federal Courts Improvement Act of 1982 (96 Stat. 25; 28 U.S.C. 41).

INFORMATION

    Clerk
    United States Court of Appeals
      for the Federal Circuit
    717 Madison Place, N.W.
    Washington, D.C. 20439
    (202) 633-6550
    http://www.uscourts.gov/courtsofappeals.html

Ju 7.1:date
ANNUAL REPORTS.

Ju 7.2:CT • **Item 734**
GENERAL PUBLICATIONS.

Ju 7.3:nos.
BULLETINS.

Ju 7.4:nos.
CIRCULARS.

Ju 7.5:nos. • **Item 733**
CASES DECIDED IN UNITED STATES COURT OF
APPEALS FOR THE FEDERAL CIRCUIT. v. 1–
1911–   [Annual]

    Vols. 1-16 issued by the Court of Customs Appeals. On March 2, 1929, the name of the Court of Customs Appeals was changed to the Court of Customs and Patent Appeals and beginning with volume 17, each volume of the Reports have been issued in two separate volumes, one titled Custom Cases Adjudged in the United States Court of Customs and Patent Appeals and the other, Patent Cases Adjudged in the United States Court of Customs and Patent Appeals.
    Period coverd by both volumes October to October [period for Customs Cases prior to 1955 were from April to April].
    Former title: Reports of Cases Adjudged in the Court of Customs and Patent Appeals.
    Citation: C.C.P.A.

Ju 7.5/2:v.nos.&nos. • **Item 733**
CASES DECIDED IN UNITED STATES COURT OF
APPEALS FOR THE FEDERAL CIRCUIT:
CUSTOMS CASES ADJUDGED IN THE COURT
OF APPEALS FOR THE FEDERAL CIRCUIT.
[Irregular]

Ju 7.6:CT
PAPERS IN RE.

Ju 7.7:date
CALENDAR.
    Changed from Ju 7.2:C 12/1-10

Ju 7.7/2:date
PATENT CALENDAR.

Ju 7.8:date • **Item 735**
RULES OF UNITED STATES COURT OF CUSTOMS
AND PATENT APPEALS.

Ju 7.8/2: • **Item 735-A**
REGULATIONS, RULES, INSTRUCTIONS.

Ju 7.9:nos.
APPEALS (series). [Irregular]

Ju 7.10:CT • **Item 735-B**
HANDBOOKS, MANUALS, GUIDES.

COMMERCE COURT
(1910– 1913)

CREATION AND AUTHORITY

    The United States Commerce Court was established by Mann-Elkins Act, approved June 18, 1910 (36 Stat. 539). The Court was abolished by act of Congress, approved October 22, 1913, effective December 31, 1913, and its functions transferred to the United States District Courts.

Ju 8.1:date
ANNUAL REPORTS.

Ju 8.2:CT
GENERAL PUBLICATIONS.

Ju 8.3:nos.
BULLETINS.

Ju 8.4:nos.
CIRCULARS.

Ju 8.5:nos.
OPINIONS.

Ju 8.6:v.nos.
[TITLE PAGE AND INDEX TO] OPINIONS.

UNITED STATES COURT OF
INTERNATIONAL TRADE
(1980–   )

CREATION AND AUTHORITY

    This court was established as the Board of United States General Appraisers by Act of June 10, 1890, which conferred upon it jurisdiction theretofore held by the U.S. district and circuit courts in actions arising under the tariff acts (26 Stat. 136; 19 U.S.C. ch. 4). The act of May 28, 1926 (44 Stat. 669; 19 U.S.C. 504a), created the United States Customs Court to supersede the board; by act of June 25, 1948 (62 Stat. 943; 28 U.S.C. 1582, 1583), the court was integrated into the United States courts structure, organization, and procedure. The act of July 14, 1956 (70 Stat. 532; 28 U.S.C. 251), established the court as a court of record of the United States under Article III of the Constitution of the United States.

INFORMATION

    Office of the Clerk
    United States Court of International Trade
    1 Federal Plaza
    New York, New York 10278-0001
    (212) 264-2814
    Fax: (212) 264-4138
    http://www.uscit.gov

Ju 9.1:date
ANNUAL REPORTS.

Ju 9.2:CT
GENERAL PUBLICATIONS.

Ju 9.3:
BULLETINS.

Ju 9.4:nos.
REAPPRAISEMENT CIRCULARS.   –1932.
    Earlier T 20.4/3
    Later T 1.11/21

Ju 9.4/2:date
INDEX TO REAPPRAISEMENT CIRCULARS.

Ju 9.5:date • **Item 736 (MF)**
UNITED STATES CUSTOMS COURT REPORTS. v. 1–
    1938–   [Semiannual]

    Decisions prior to June 1938 appeared in both the weekly (T 1.11/2) and bound volumes (T 1.11/1) of Treasury Decisions.

Ju 9.5/2:v.nos. • **Item 736**
UNITED STATES COURT OF INTERNATIONAL TRADE
REPORTS. v. 1–
    Continues United States Customs Court Reports (Ju 9.5).

ADMINISTRATIVE OFFICE OF THE UNITED STATES COURTS
(1939–   )

CREATION AND AUTHORITY

The Administrative Office of the United States Courts was created by Act of Congress approved August 7, 1939 (53 Stat. 1223; 28 U.S.C. 601). The Office was established November 6, 1939. The Director and the Deputy Director are appointed by the Supreme Court of the United States.

INFORMATION

Public Affairs Office
Administrative Office of the
    United States Courts
United States Supreme Court Building
Washington, D.C. 20544
(202) 502-2600

Ju 10.1:date   • **Item 728 (MF)**
ANNUAL REPORT OF THE PROCEEDINGS OF THE JUDICIAL CONFERENCE OF THE UNITED STATES [and] SEMIANNUAL REPORT OF THE DIRECTOR OF THE ADMINISTRATIVE OFFICE OF THE UNITED STATES COURTS. 1940–   [Annual]

Report submitted annually by the Chief Justice to Congress pursuant to 28 U.S.C. 331.
Judicial Conference of the United States. The Chief Justice of the United States shall summon annually the chief judge of each judicial circuit, the chief judge of the Court of Claims and a district judge from each judicial circuit to a conference at such time and place in the United States as he may designate [usually held in Washington, D.C. in September]. Special sessions of the conference may be called by the Chief Justice at such times and places as he may designate. 28 U.S.C. 331.
Reports of the proceedings of any special sessions held are included in the annual report of the Conference as appendices to the Report.
The report of the Director of the Administrative Office is a report of the activities of that office for the fiscal year. A substantial portion of his report is devoted to statistical data on various aspects of the courts and their work loads.
Frequency varies: 1940– 1974, annual; 1975– semiannual.
ISSN 0095-7836

Ju 10.1/2:date   • **Item 728 (MF)**
UNITED STATES COURTS: SELECTED REPORTS. [Annual]

Formerly titled: Reports of the Proceedings of the Judicial Conference of the United States [and] Annual Report of the Director of the Administrative Office of the U.S. Courts.

Ju 10.1/3   • **Item 728-C (MF)**
REPORT OF THE DIRECTOR: ACTIVITIES OF THE ADMINISTRATIVE OFFICE. [Annual]

Ju 10.1/4   • **Item 728-C-1 (MF)**
JUDICIAL BUSINESS OF THE UNITED STATES COURTS. [Annual]

Ju 10.2:CT   • **Item 729**
GENERAL PUBLICATIONS.

Ju 10.2:W 89   • **Item 729**
FEDERAL JUDICIAL WORKLOAD STATISTICS. [3 times a year] (Statistical Analysis and Reports Division)
Each issue covers a 12 month period.

Ju 10.3/2:v.nos.&nos.   • **Item 728-B (EL)**
THIRD BRANCH, A BULLETIN OF THE FEDERAL COURTS. v. 1–   1968–   [Monthly] (Federal Judicial Center, 1520 H Street N.W., Washington, D.C. 20005)

PURPOSE:– To serve as an exchange of information for judges and other court personnel.
ISSN 0040-6120

Ju 10.6:CT   • **Item 729-A**
REGULATIONS, RULES, AND INSTRUCTIONS.

Ju 10.6/2:CT   • **Item 729-B**
HANDBOOKS, MANUALS, GUIDES.

Ju 10.7:CT   • **Item 729-A**
RULES OF COURTS (by States).
Earlier J 1.8

Ju 10.8:v.nos.&nos.   • **Item 717-T**
FEDERAL PROBATION. 1937–   [Semiannual]

PURPOSE:– To present constructively worthwhile points of view relating to all phases of preventive and correctional activities in delinquency and crime.
Indexed by: Index to U.S. Government Periodicals.
ISSN 0014-9128

Ju 10.9   • **Item 729-C (MF)**
TABLES OF BANKRUPTCY STATISTICS. 1941–   [Annual]

PURPOSE:– To present statistical data with reference to bankruptcy cases commenced and terminated in the United States District Courts during the fiscal year. Prepared in accordance with section 53 of the Bankruptcy Act (11 U.S.C. 81).

Ju 10.10:date   • **Item 729 (MF)**
REPORT OF PROCEEDINGS OF REGULAR ANNUAL MEETING OF JUDICIAL CONFERENCE OF THE UNITED STATES. 1948–   [Annual]
Earlier Ju 10.2:J 89/2

Ju 10.10/2:date   • **Item 729**
REPORT OF PROCEEDINGS OF SPECIAL SESSION OF JUDICIAL CONFERENCE OF THE UNITED STATES.
Earlier Ju 10.2:J 89/3

Ju 10.11:date   • **Item 728-A**
FEDERAL OFFENDERS IN THE UNITED STATES COURTS. 1964–   [Annual]

Ju 10.12:date   • **Item 717-Y-5**
UNITED STATES COURTS, PICTORIAL SUMMARY. [Annual]
Consists of statistics in tabular and graphic form, together with narrative summaries on U.S. Courts of Appeals, District Courts, Criminal Justice Act, and personnel.

Ju 10.13:date   • **Item 717-Y**
GRAND AND PETIT JUROR SERVICE IN U.S. DISTRICT COURTS. [Annual]
Former title: Juror Utilization in United States District Courts.

Ju 10.14:date   • **Item 717-X (MF)**
MANAGEMENT STATISTICS FOR UNITED STATES COURTS.

Ju 10.15:date   • **Item 717-X-1**
DIRECTORY OF UNITED STATES PROBATION AND PRETRIAL SERVICES OFFICERS. [Quarterly]
Previous title: Directory of United States Probation Officers.

Ju 10.16:date   • **Item 717-Y-1 (MF)**
REPORT ON THE IMPLEMENTATION TO TITLE 1 AND TITLE 2 OF THE SPEEDY TRIAL ACT OF 1974. 1st–   [Annual]

Ju 10.17:date   • **Item 717-Y-2**
UNITED STATES COURT DIRECTORY. [Annual]
PURPOSE:– To provide a list of the names and addresses of all justices, judges, and clerks of all United States Courts.

Ju 10.18:date   • **Item 717-Y-4**
UNITED STATES DISTRICT COURTS SENTENCES IMPOSED CHART. [Annual]
PURPOSE:– To aid Federal Probation Officers in their presentence investigation report. Con-

sists of a computer print-out of sentences imposed by United States District Courts.

Ju 10.19:date   • **Item 717-Y-3 (EL)**
REPORT ON APPLICATIONS FOR ORDERS AUTHORIZING OR APPROVING THE INTERCEPTION OF WIRE, ORAL, OR ELECTRONIC COMMUNICATIONS, (WIRETAP REPORT). [Annual]
Earlier: Report on Applications for Orders Authorizing or Approving the Interception of Wire or Oral Communications.
Earlier Ju 10.2:C 73

Ju 10.20:date   • **Item 717-Y-6 (MF)**
TELEPHONE DIRECTORY.

Ju 10.21:date   • **Item 729-D**
FEDERAL JUDICIAL CASELOAD STATISTICS. [Annual]
Formerly: Federal Judicial Caseload Statistics.
Gives data on the workload of U.S. Courts, including Courts of Appeals, District Courts, and Bankruptcy Courts for the 12 month period ending with current quarter.

JU 10.21/2:date   • **Item 729-D-1**
STATISTICAL TABLES FOR THE FEDERAL JUDICIARY. [Semiannual]

Ju 10.22:date   • **Item 729-E (MF)**
EQUAL EMPLOYMENT OPPORTUNITY IN THE FEDERAL COURTS. [Annual]

Summarizes the Federal courts' continuing efforts to provide equality of employment opportunity in their personnel practices. Statistical reports present data on personnel activities of each Federal court with particular reference to sex and ethnic background of court employees. A separate appendix consists of the courts' own evaluation of their activities.
Also published in microfiche.

Ju 10.23:v.nos.&nos.   • **Item 729-F**
NEWS AND VIEWS. v. 1–   [Biweekly]
PURPOSE:– To present news and views of probation officers and others in the U.S. probation system. Contains short news items, articles, and regular features on shop talk, personnel changes, retirements, field notes, legislative update, etc.

Ju 10.24:nos.   • **Item 729-G**
JUDGES INFORMATION SERIES.

Ju 10.25   • **Item 729-G-1 (CD)**
COURT TESTIMONY AND MISCELLANEOUS INFORMATION.

TAX COURT OF THE UNITED STATES
(1942–   )

CREATION AND AUTHORITY

The Tax Court of the United States, which was the U.S. Board of Tax Appeals (Y 3.T 19), is an independent executive agency, (see sec. 7441, Internal Revenue Code of 1954, 68A Stat. 879). The change in name to the Tax Court was made by the Revenue Act of 1942 (56 Stat. 957).

INFORMATION

Administrative Office
United States Tax Court
400 Second Street, N.W.
Washington, D.C. 20217
(202) 606-8751

Ju 11.1:date
ANNUAL REPORTS.
Earlier Y 3.T 19/1

Ju 11.2:CT   • **Item 742-A**
GENERAL PUBLICATIONS.
    Earlier Y 3.T 19/2

Ju 11.7:v.nos.   • **Item 742**
REPORTS OF THE TAX COURT. v. 1–   1942–
    [Semiannual]
    Bound volumes.
    Supersedes Reports of the Board of Tax Ap-
peals (Y 3.T 9.6).
    Citation: T.C.

Ju 11.7/a:v.nos./nos.   • **Item 742**
[DECISIONS OF TAX COURT OF UNITED STATES
(Advance Sheet)]. v.1– v. 39, no. 114. [ ]–1963.
    Earlier Y 3.T 19/5

Ju 11.7/a2:v.nos./nos.   • **Item 742**
REPORTS, CONSOLIDATED PAMPHLETS. v. 1–
1942–   [Monthly]
    Final issue of each volume includes table of
cases reported in the volume.
    Citation: T.C.

Ju 11.7/2:date-nos.   • **Item 742-B (MF)**
TAX COURT MEMORANDA. 1–   [Irregular]
    Each memorandum summarizes and gives dis-
position of a different taxpayer case brought
against the Commissioner of Internal Revenue.
Published in microfiche (24x).

Ju 11.8   • **Item 743**
RULES OF PRACTICE. 1924–   [Irregular]
    PURPOSE:– To apprise litigants before the
Tax Court of the proper procedure for bringing
cases before the Court and of the Court's requirement for the conduct of litigation in the Court
when cases have been brought before it.

Ju 11.8/2:CT   • **Item 743**
REGULATIONS, RULES, AND INSTRUCTIONS.

EMERGENCY COURT OF APPEALS
(1942–   )

CREATION AND AUTHORITY

    The Emergency Court of Appeals was estab-
lished by the Emergency Price Control Act of
1942, approved January 30, 1942. It was continued under the Housing and Rent Act of 1948 and
the Defense Production Act of 1950.

INFORMATION

    Clerk
    Emergency Court of Appeals
    United States Courthouse
    Room 2400
    Washington, D.C. 20001
    (202) 535-3390

Ju 12.1:date
ANNUAL REPORTS.

Ju 12.2:CT
GENERAL PUBLICATIONS.

Ju 12.6:CT
REGULATIONS, RULES, AND INSTRUCTIONS.

Ju 12.7:CT
OPINIONS.
    Papers in re published by Price Administra-
tion Office and classified Pr 32.4217

FEDERAL JUDICIAL CENTER
(1967–   )

CREATION AND AUTHORITY

    The Federal Judicial Center was established
by act of Congress, approved December 20, 1967
(81 Stat. 664; U.S.C. 620).

INFORMATION

    Information Specialist
    Federal Judicial Center
    1520 H Street, N.W.
    Washington, D.C. 20005
    (202) 502-4181

Ju 13.1:date   • **Item 742-A-1 (MF)**
ANNUAL REPORTS.

Ju 13.2:CT   • **Item 743-C-1**
GENERAL PUBLICATIONS.

Ju 13.8:CT   • **Item 743-C-2**
HANDBOOKS, MANUALS, GUIDES.

Ju 13.8/2:date   • **Item 743-C-2**
BENCH COMMENT, A PERIODIC GUIDE TO RECENT
APPELLATE TREATMENT OF PRACTICAL PRO-
CEDURAL ISSUES.

Ju 13.8/3:v.nos./nos.   • **Item 743-C-7 (EL)**
GUIDELINE SENTENCING UPDATE. [Irregular]

Ju 13.8/4:nos.   • **Item 743-C-9 (P) (EL)**
HABEAS & PRISON LITIGATION CASE LAW UPDATE.

Ju 13.9:nos.   • **Item 743-C-4**
EDUCATION AND TRAINING SERIES.

Ju 13.9/2:date   • **Item 743-C-4**
CATALOGUE OF AUDIOVISUAL MEDIA PROGRAMS.
    [Annual]

Ju 13.9/3:date/nos.   • **Item 743-C-4**
CONNECTIONS. [Quarterly]

Ju 13.10:nos.   • **Item 743-C-3**
REPORT FJC-R (series). [Irregular]

Ju 13.10/2:nos.   • **Item 743-C-3**
STAFF PAPERS, FJC-SP- (series).

Ju 13.10/3:nos.   • **Item 743-C-3**
REPORT FJC-M- (series).

Ju 13.10/4:date   • **Item 743-C-3**
FJC-SES (series).

Ju 13.11:CT   • **Item 743-C-5**
BIBLIOGRAPHIES AND LISTS OF PUBLICATIONS.

Ju 13.11/2:date   • **Item 743-C-5 (P) (EL)**
CATALOG OF PUBLICATIONS. [Annual]

Ju 13.12:CT   • **Item 743-C-6**
INNOVATIONS IN THE COURTS: SERIES ON COURT
ADMINISTRATION. [Irregular]
    Series on court administration dealing with
areas such as mediation in different district courts.

Ju 13.13:nos.   • **Item 743-C-3**
FJC DIRECTIONS, A PUBLICATION OF THE FEDERAL
JUDICIAL CENTER. [Irregular]

Ju 13.13/2:date/nos.   • **Item 743-C-3 (EL)**
STATE – FEDERAL JUDICIAL OBSERVER. [Quar-
terly]

Ju 13.13/2-3   • **Item 743-C-3 (EL)**
INTERNATIONAL JUDICIAL OBSERVER. [Quarterly]

Ju 13.14:CT   • **Item 743-C-3 (MF)**
DIRECTORIES.

Ju 13.15:nos.   • **Item 746-C-6 (EL)**
THE COURT HISTORIAN.

Ju 13.16   • **Item 743-C-8 (MF)**
LONG-RANGE PLANNING SERIES.

Ju 13.17:nos.   • **Item 743-C-10**
SPECIAL NEEDS OFFENDERS, BULLETIN.

Ju 13.18   • **Item 743-C-11(E)**
ELECTRONIC PRODUCTS. (Misc.)

UNITED STATES BANKRUPTCY COURT

Ju 14.6:CT   • **Item 742-C**
REGULATIONS, RULES, AND INSTRUCTIONS.
    [Irregular]

U.S. COURT OF VETERANS APPEALS
(1992–   )

Ju 15.9:nos.   • **Item 742-D (MF)**
SLIP OPINIONS.

DEPARTMENT OF LABOR
(1913–   )

CREATION AND AUTHORITY

    The Department of Labor, ninth executive de-
partment, was created by act approved March 4,
1913 (37 Stat. 736; 5 U.S.C. 611) which divided
the Department of Commerce and Labor (C 1) into
two separate departments.

INFORMATION

    Department of Labor
    200 Constitution Ave., N.W.
    Washington, D.C. 20210
    (202) 219-7316
    Fax: (202) 219-7312
    http://www.dol.gov

L 1.1   • **Item 744 (MF)**
ANNUAL REPORTS. 1st– 1914– [Annual]
    Includes reports of subordinate bureaus.

L 1.1/2:date   • **Item 744-D**
OFFICE OF CONSTRUCTION INDUSTRY SERVICES:
ANNUAL REPORT.
    PURPOSE:– To report on activities during the
year covered, providing information on topical
subjects of interest to the construction industry,
with focus on effect the Federal Government,
through spending, legislation, regulation, research
and demonstration projects, may be having on
the industry.

L 1.1/2-2:2-8   • **Item 745-A**
    OCCUPANT EMERGENCY PLAN HANDBOOK
    FOR THE FRANCES PERKINS BUILDING.

L 1.1/3:date   • **Item 744 (MF)**
SECRETARY'S SEMIANNUAL MANAGEMENT RE-
PORT, U.S. DEPARTMENT OF LABOR.

L 1.1/4   • **Item 744-H (MF)**
U.S. DEPT. OF LABOR, ACCOUNTABILITY REPORT.
    [Annual]

L 1.1/5 • Item 744-H-1 (EL)
NSSB (NATIONAL SKILLS STANDARDS BOARD)
ANNUAL REPORT.

L 1.2:CT • Item 745
GENERAL PUBLICATIONS.

L 1.3:v.nos.
BULLETINS.

L 1.3/2:nos.
PERSONNEL BULLETINS.

L 1.3/3 • Item 747-A
BULLETINS. [Secretary's], S- (series). 1– 1959–
[Irregular]

L 1.3/4 • Item 746-D
MANPOWER RESEARCH BULLETINS. 1– 1963–
[Irregular]

L 1.4:nos.
CIRCULARS.

L 1.5:nos.
DECISIONS. 1– 1913–

L 1.5/2:v.nos./nos. • Item 745-G
DECISIONS OF THE OFFICE OF ADMINISTRATIVE
LAW JUDGES AND OFFICE OF ADMINISTRA-
TIVE APPEALS. [Bimonthly]
Decisions and orders in labor cases involving
but not limited to labor certification of aliens.

L 1.6:date
REGULATIONS (general).

L 1.7:CT • Item 747
RULES, REGULATIONS, AND INSTRUCTIONS (miscellaneous).

L 1.7/2:CT • Item 745-A
HANDBOOKS, MANUALS, GUIDES.

CURRENT BIBLIOGRAPHIES PREPARED BY THE
LIBRARY (series). 1– 1967– [Irregular]

L 1.7/2-2:nos. • Item 745-A
DLMS HANDBOOKS (series). [Irregular]

L 1.7/2-3 • Item 745-A
DLMS MANUAL (series).

L 1.7/3:nos.
EMPLOYEE DEVELOPMENT GUIDES. 1– 1961–

L 1.7/4:CT • Item 747
REGULATIONS AND INTERPRETIVE BULLETINS.

L 1.7/5:nos. • Item 745-C
OCCUPATIONAL GUIDES. 1– 1969– [Irregular]
PURPOSE:– To provide descriptions of and
job market information on various occupations
for use by counselors and placement officers in
professional placement offices of U.S. Training
and Employment Service and others dealing with
professional applicants.
Previously issued by Bureau of Employment
Security (L 7.32).

L 1.7/6:date • Item 756-B
JOB GUIDE FOR YOUNG WORKERS. 1st ed.–
1969/70– [Irregular]
Gives information on usual duties, characteristics of the job, qualifications, employment prospects, advancement opportunities, and where to
obtain additional information for various occupations. Of special use to young jobseekers, counselors in high schools and elsewhere, and secondary school teachers. Also discusses how financial aid may be obtained to further education
and also the many job-training programs available.
Earlier L 7.25/2

L 1.7/7:CT • Item 756-A
INTERVIEWING GUIDES FOR SPECIFIC DISABILI-
TIES. [Irregular]
Later L 37.8/4

L 1.7/8:nos. • Item 747-B
MA HANDBOOKS. [Irregular] (Manpower Administration)

Superseded by ET [Employment Training]
Handbooks (L 37.8/2).

L 1.7/9:CT • Item 745-A
ACT CAREER PLANNING GUIDE SERIES. [Irregular]

L 1.7/10 • Item 745-A
LIFT AWARDS, NOMINATION GUIDELINES. [Annual]

L 1.8:
NEGRO ECONOMICS DIVISION.

L 1.8/1:date
ANNUAL REPORTS.

L 1.8/2:CT
GENERAL PUBLICATIONS.

L 1.8/3:
BULLETINS.

L 1.8/4:
CIRCULARS.

L 1.9:CT
POSTERS.

L 1.9/2:CT
MAPS AND CHARTS.

L 1.9/3:date
LABOR CHARTS. – 1965. [Monthly]
Earlier L 1.9/2:L 11

L 1.9/4:CT
AUDIOVISUAL MATERIALS. [Irregular]

L 1.10:
INTERNATIONAL LABOR CONFERENCE, 1st, WASH-
INGTON, 1919.

L 1.10/1:date
[PROCEEDINGS, FINAL RECORD].

L 1.10/1:nos.
[PROCEEDINGS, PROVISIONAL RECORD].

L 1.10/2:CT
GENERAL PUBLICATIONS.

L 1.10/3:
BULLETINS.

L 1.10/4:
CIRCULARS.

L 1.10/5:nos.
REPORTS [on agenda].

L 1.11:
EMERGENCY CONSERVATION WORK BULLETINS.
1– 1933–

L 1.12:CT
DECISIONS OF SECRETARY [of Labor] IN MATTER
OF DETERMINATION OF PREVAILING MINIMUM
WAGE IN INDUSTRIES.
Later 18.9

L 1.13
ADDRESSES. [Irregular]

L 1.14:nos.
THIS MIGHT BE YOU (radio scripts). 1– 13. 1940.
[Weekly]

L 1.15:vol.
LABOR INFORMATION BULLETINS. v. 1– v. 20, no. 4.
[ ]– 1953. [Monthly]
Earlier L 2.10

L 1.16:CT
REPORT AND RECOMMENDATIONS OF FACT-
FINDING BOARDS.

L 1.17:CT
PUBLICATIONS OF NATIONAL WAGE STABILIZATION
BOARD.

L 1.18:nos.
GENERAL ORDERS.

L 1.19:series/nos.
SELECTED LIST OF RECENT ADDITIONS TO THE
LIBRARY. [Weekly]

L 1.20
PRESS RELEASES. [Irregular]

L 1.20/2:
COMBINED EMPLOYMENT AND UNEMPLOYMENT
RELEASES. [Monthly]

L 1.20/3:date
EMPLOYMENT, HOURS AND EARNINGS. [Monthly]

L 1.20/4:date
FILLER FACT SHEET.

L 1.20/5:date
MEMORANDUM TO EDITORS [wholesale prices selected fruits and vegetables].

L 1.20/6:date • Item 768-F-2
BLACK NEWS DIGEST. [Weekly] (Office of Information, Publications and Reports)

Contains news articles on the labor situation
as it relates to black workers.
Indexed by: Index to U.S. Government Periodicals.
ISSN 0045-2238

L 1.20/7:date • Item 768-F-3
NOTICIAS DE LA SEMANA, A NEWS SUMMARY FOR
HISPANICS. 1971– [Weekly]
Provides news about people, programs, and
economic matters of interest to Hispanics.
ISSN 0364-8451

L 1.20/8:date • Item 768-F-4
WOMEN AND WORK. 1973– [Monthly] (Office of
Information, Publications and Reports)

Contains news of particular interest to women,
with emphasis on economic matters such as employment and advancement.
Indexed by: Index to U.S. Government Periodicals.

L 1.21:
OILA MEMORANDUM MONTHLY SERVICE OF OFFICE
OF INTERNATIONAL LABOR AFFAIRS.

L 1.22:
SECRETARY'S INSTRUCTIONS.

L 1.22/2:nos.
SECRETARY'S ORDERS.

L 1.22/3:nos.
MANPOWER ADMINISTRATION ORDERS.

L 1.22/4:nos.
MANPOWER ADMINISTRATION NOTICE.

L 1.22/5:nos.
SECRETARY'S NOTICE.

L 1.23:
BUDGET AND MANAGEMENT CIRCULARS.

L 1.24:
SUPERVISOR'S BULLETINS (occasional). 1–
1952–

L 1.24/2:nos.
SUPERVISOR'S GUIDE SERIES. 1– 1959–

L 1.25:
PERSONNEL INSTRUCTIONS.

L 1.26:
ADMINISTRATIVE HANDBOOK, TRANSMITTAL
SHEETS.

L 1.27:nos.
LABOR YEARBOOK. 1– 1951–

L 1.28:v.nos.
WEEKLY LABOR NEWS DIGEST. v. 1– v. 10, no.4.
[ ]– 1954.
Earlier L 1.50

L 1.29:
FIELD LETTER, NATIONAL COMMITTEE FOR CONSERVATION OF MANPOWER IN WAR INDUSTRIES.

L 1.30:
PROGRESS REPORT ON PRESIDENT'S LABOR MANAGEMENT CONFERENCE, JOB NO.

L 1.31:
FACTS AND SERVICES FROM THE U.S. DEPARTMENT OF LABOR. [Biweekly]

L 1.32:nos.
CHARACTERISTICS OF THE INSURED UNEMPLOYED, MONTHLY REPORT.

L 1.33:
STAFF MEMO FROM U.S. SECRETARY OF LABOR.

L 1.34:CT • Item 744-A
BIBLIOGRAPHIES AND LISTS OF PUBLICATIONS.

L 1.34:M 31/4 • Item 744-A
INDEX TO PUBLICATIONS OF THE MANPOWER ADMINISTRATION. [Irregular] (Manpower Administration)

L 1.34/2:date
SELECTED REFERENCES FOR LABOR ATTACHES, LIST OF READILY AVAILABLE MATERIALS. [Annual]

L 1.34/3
NEW PUBLICATIONS. [Monthly] (Office of Information, Publications, and Reports)

Lists by subjects, giving title, pagination, price, issuing office, and series designation.
ISSN 0364-7528

L 1.34/4:nos.
CURRENT BIBLIOGRAPHIES PREPARED BY THE LIBRARY. 1– 1967–

L 1.34/5:v.nos.&nos. • Item 762-D-7
LABOR LITERATURE, RECENT ADDITIONS TO THE DEPARTMENT OF LABOR LIBRARY. v. 1– 6. – 1981. [Bimonthly]

L 1.34/6: • Item 744-A
PUBLICATIONS OF THE U.S. DEPARTMENT OF LABOR. [Annual]

L 1.35:nos.
AWARDS ROUND UP.

L 1.36:CT
NATIONAL STAY-IN-SCHOOL CAMPAIGN MAY– SEPTEMBER 1958 [release].

L 1.37:nos.
UNDERSECRETARY'S REPORT TO THE FIELD, NEWSLETTER FOR DEPARTMENT OF LABOR FIELD REPRESENTATIVES.

L 1.38:nos.
PERSONNEL MANAGEMENT TRAINING UNITS. 1– 1957–

MANPOWER ADMINISTRATION

L 1.39:nos.
MANPOWER REPORTS. 1– 1962– [Irregular]

L 1.39/2:nos. • Item 746-F
MANPOWER EVALUATION REPORTS. 1– 1963– [Irregular]

PURPOSE:– To inform government agencies, officials, and the public of the progress and problems of the training programs carried out under the Manpower Development and Training Act of 1962.

L 1.39/3:nos. • Item 746-H
MANPOWER/AUTOMATION RESEARCH MONOGRAPHS. 1– 1964– [Irregular]
PURPOSE:– To provide digests of manpower and automation research conducted for the Department of Labor under contractual arrangements, as authorized by title 1 of the Manpower Development and Training Act.
Copies of the full reports are made available to the libraries subscribing to the Documents Expediting Project, a list of which is contained at the end of each monograph.
Later L 37.14

L 1.39/4:contract nos.
MANPOWER/AUTOMATION RESEARCH NOTICES. 1964– [Irregular]

PURPOSE:– To inform the public of the availability of the research studies performed under contractual agreement with the Department of Labor as authorized under title I of the Manpower Development and Training Act.
Copies of the full report are digested in the Monographs, listed above, and are available in libraries subscribing to the Documents Expediting Project. They are also available for inspection at the field offices of the Department of Labor.

L 1.39/5:date • Item 746-I
MANPOWER AND AUTOMATION RESEARCH. 1963– [Annual]

Lists research and information projects undertaken and research reports issued during the fiscal year under the authority of title I of the Manpower Development and Training Act of 1962, and in the area of automation, under authority contained in the Department of Labor Appropriations Acts.
Gives project title, contractor, objectives and procedures, and status of project.

L 1.39/6:date • Item 746-I
MANPOWER RESEARCH PROJECTS, SPONSORED BY THE MANPOWER ADMINISTRATION THROUGH (date). [Annual]

Information for each project includes name of institution, doctoral candidate, sponsor, dissertation, brief description of objectives and procedures, and estimated completion date.

L 1.39/7:date
MANPOWER DAILY REPORTER.

L 1.39/8:CT • Item 745
SEMINAR OF MANPOWER POLICY AND PROGRAM.

Earlier L 1.2:M 31

L 1.39/9:v.nos.&nos. • Item 746-N
MANPOWER. v. 1– 1969– [Monthly]

Supersedes Employment Service Review (L 7.18/2) and Unemployment Insurance Review (L 7.18/3).
Superseded by Worklife (L 37.10).
Indexed by: Index to U.S. Government Periodicals.

L 1.39/10:date
MANPOWER TECHNICAL EXCHANGE. 1969– [Biweekly]

DEPARTMENT OF LABOR (Continued)

L 1.40:nos.
TRAINING FACTS, REPORTS. 1–

L 1.40/2:date
MANPOWER TRAINING FACTS. 1965–

L 1.41:nos.
OMAT-O-GRAM, FOR STAFF MEMBERS OF OFFICE OF MANPOWER, AUTOMATION, AND TRAINING. v. 1– 1962–

L 1.42 • Item 746-B
REPORT OF SECRETARY OF LABOR TO CONGRESS ON RESEARCH AND TRAINING ACTIVITIES. 1963– [Annual]

Prepared in accordance with section 309 of the Manpower Development and Training Act, giving report and evaluation of research, trainees, training programs, and training activities. Prepared in Office of Manpower Automation, and Training.

L 1.42/2:date • Item 746-C
EMPLOYMENT AND TRAINING REPORT OF THE PRESIDENT. 1963– [Annual]

Includes reports: Report on Employment and Training Requirements, Resources and Utilization by the Department of Labor and the Department of Health, Education, and Welfare; and the Report on Veterans Services by the Department of Labor.
Prior to 1976 entitled Manpower Report to the President and Report on Manpower Requirements, Resources, Utilization, and Training by the U.S. Department of Labor. Both reports were submitted pursuant to sec. 107 of the Manpower Development and Training Act of 1962, as amended.
Manpower Report of the President is a brief introductory report. Report of the Department of Labor is more detailed. Statistical Appendix contains detailed data on employment and unemployment, labor force, and other pertinent information.
Also published in the House Document series.
ISSN 0145-2444

L 1.42/2
INDEXES. 1963– 1972. 1973. 46 p.

L 1.42/2-2:date • Item 746-C (MF)
STATISTICS ON MANPOWER, SUPPLEMENT TO MANPOWER REPORT OF THE PRESIDENT.

L 1.42/2-3:CT • Item 762-D-8 (MF)
SUPPLEMENTS TO THE EMPLOYMENT AND TRAINING REPORT OF THE PRESIDENT. [Irregular]

L 1.43:nos.
WHAT'S NEW, TIPS FOR SUPERVISORS FROM OAAS. 1– 1963–

L 1.44
REPRINTS. 1– 1963– [Irregular]

L 1.45:nos.
MANPOWER PROGRAM EVALUATION. 1– 1963–

L 1.45/2:nos.
DEMONSTRATION NOTES, EXPERIMENTAL AND DEMONSTRATION MANPOWER PROGRAMS. 1– 1964– [Irregular]

The Demonstration Manpower Program conducted under the Manpower Development and Training Act is an attempt to reach and provide necessary services to those persons most in need of development and training– the hard-core unemployed, the uneducated, the culturally disadvantaged.
PURPOSE:– To provide digests of first-hand reports, on-the-spot studies and findings of workers in the field connected with the programs.

L 1.46:nos.
LMWP [Labor Management and Welfare-Pension] REPORTER.

L 1.47:CT • Item 746-E
LAWS.

L 1.48 • Item 762-D-10 (MF)
TECHNICAL ASSISTANCE AIDS. 1– 1960– [Irregular]

Each issue provides technical assistance on a different subject such as electing union officers and employer and consulting with periodic updating.
Formerly distributed to depository libraries under Item 762-D-2.

L 1.49:CT
NEIGHBORHOOD YOUTH CORPS PUBLICATIONS.

L 1.49/2:nos.
TECHNICAL AIDS. (Neighborhood Youth Corps)

L 1.50:CT
MANPOWER UTILIZATION-JOB SECURITY IN LONGSHORE INDUSTRY [by port].

L 1.51 • Item 762-D-3 (MF)
SUMMARY OF OPERATIONS, LABOR-MANAGEMENT REPORTING AND DISCLOSURE ACT. 1964– [Annual]

Covers the activities of the Office of Labor-Management and Welfare-Pension Reports with respect to the administration of the Labor-Management Reporting and Disclosure Act. Appendices include civil and criminal actions under the act and private litigation. List of publications of the Office.
Supersedes Summary of Operations issued by the Bureau of Labor-Management Reports.

L 1.51/2:date
LABOR-MANAGEMENT REPORTING AND DISCLOSURES ACT, AS AMENDED, REGULATIONS AND INTERPRETATIVE BULLETINS.

Class changed to L 1.7/4:L 11

L 1.51/3:date • Item 762-D-3
DIGEST AND INDEX OF PUBLISHED DECISIONS OF THE ASSISTANT SECRETARY OF LABOR FOR LABOR-MANAGEMENT RELATIONS PURSUANT TO EXECUTIVE ORDER 11491, AS AMENDED. [Irregular] (Labor-Management Services Administration, Office of Federal-Management Relations)

L 1.51/4:v.nos.&nos. • Item 762-D-3
DECISIONS AND REPORTS ON RULINGS OF THE ASSISTANT SECRETARY OF LABOR FOR LABOR-MANAGEMENT RELATIONS PURSUANT TO EXECUTIVE ORDER 11491. v. 1– 1970– 1971– (Office of Federal Labor-Management Relations, Labor-Management Services Administration)

Beginning with volume for 1978-1979, published by the Federal Labor Relations Authority (Y 3.F 31/21-3:10-2).

L 1.51/5:nos. • Item 762-D-6
PBGC [Pension Benefit Guaranty Corporation] FACT SHEETS. [Irregular]

L 1.51/6:v.nos. • Item 762-D-3 (MF)
RULINGS ON REQUESTS FOR REVIEW OF THE ASSISTANT SECRETARY OF LABOR FOR LABOR-MANAGEMENT RELATIONS PURSUANT TO EXECUTIVE ORDER 11491, AS AMENDED. v. 1– 1970– [Irregular]

v. 1. January 1, 1970– June 30, 1975.

L 1.52 • Item 746-J
REPORT OF OCCUPATIONAL TRAINING UNDER AREA REDEVELOPMENT ACT FOR FISCAL YEAR. 1962– [Annual]

Title varies. Covers fiscal year.

L 1.53:date
REGISTER OF PROJECTS APPROVED UNDER MANPOWER DEVELOPMENT AND TRAINING ACT. [Semiannual]

L 1.54:CT • Item 746-L
PLANS FOR PROGRESS PUBLICATIONS.

L 1.54/2:date
INFORMATION FROM PLANS FOR PROGRESS.

L 1.54/3:nos. • Item 745-B
INFORMATION NEWS LETTER.

L 1.55:date • Item 744-B
ADMINISTRATION ON WELFARE AND PENSION PLANS DISCLOSURE ACT. 1962– [Annual]

Report for the calendar year made by the Secretary of Labor to the Senate and House of Representatives pursuant to the act.

L 1.56:nos. • Item 746-M
RESEARCH AND DEVELOPMENT FINDINGS. 1– 1967– [Irregular]

Previous title: MDTA Experimental and Demonstration Findings, prior to no. 11.

L 1.57:nos.
DEPARTMENT OF LABOR PROGRAM REPORTS. 1– 1967– [Irregular]

Illustrated summaries of special programs sponsored by the Department of Labor.

L 1.58:nos. • Item 857-H-1
JCH [Job Corps Handbooks] (series).

Earlier PrEx 10.10
Later L 37.11/3

L 1.58/2:nos. • Item 744-C
PM (series). 1– (Manpower Administration, Job Corps) (Issued by Job Corps)

L 1.58/3:v.nos.&nos.
CORPSMAN, PUBLISHED FOR MEN AND WOMEN OF JOB CORPS.

L 1.59:date • Item 753-A
DIRECTORY OF LOCAL EMPLOYMENT SECURITY OFFICES. [Irregular] (Manpower Administration)

PURPOSE:– To provide a directory of local employment security offices, giving functions and occupational groups served.
Earlier L 7.68
Later L 37.18

L 1.60:date • Item 754
EMPLOYMENT SERVICE STATISTICS. 1974– 1972. [Monthly] (Manpower Administration)

PURPOSE:– To provide statistics on number of applicants, openings, placements, counseling interviews, and enrollments in selected training programs for the purpose of analysis, evaluation of the program, and improvement of performance.
Published as a supplement to Employment Service Review (L 7.18/2) by the Bureau of Employment Security, prior to May 1969

L 1.61:date • Item 754-B
EMPLOYMENT AND WAGES OF WORKERS COVERED BY STATE UNEMPLOYMENT INSURANCE LAWS AND UNEMPLOYMENT COMPENSATION FOR FEDERAL EMPLOYEES. 1938– [Quarterly] (Manpower Administration)
Prior to 3rd quarter, 1967, issued by Bureau of Employment Security (L 7.20/3).
Later L 2.104

L 1.62:v.nos.&nos. • Item 761-B
UNEMPLOYMENT INSURANCE CLAIMS. v. 1– 1945– [Weekly]
ISSN 0097-8841
Prior to April 1969, issued by the Bureau of Employment Security (L 7.18/4).
Beginning with v. 31, no. 19, dated November 17, 1975, issued by the Employment and Training Administration (L 37.12/2).

L 1.62/2:date • Item 758
UNEMPLOYMENT INSURANCE STATISTICS. 1964– [Monthly] (Manpower Administration)

Published as a supplement to Unemployment Insurance Review by the Bureau of Employment Security prior to the April 1969 issue (L 7.18/4).
Later L 37.12

L 1.63:date • Item 754-A
RURAL MANPOWER DEVELOPMENTS. 1953– Fall 1973. [Irregular] (Manpower Administration)

PURPOSE:– To provide employment data for seasonal hired farm labor and described the supply and demand situation for seasonal labor. Information is based on farm labor reports submitted by affiliated State employment security agencies and summarized on a National basis. Includes statistical information detailing data on seasonal farm worker employment and wage rate data for farm activities employing contract foreign or Puerto Rican workers, and special articles on topics of interest in the field of farm labor or related manpower.
Formerly Farm Labor Developments.
Issued by Bureau of Employment Security prior to October 1969 (L 7.55).

L 1.64:nos.
COOPERATIVE AREA MANPOWER PLANNING SYSTEM, INTERAGENCY COOPERATIVE ISSUANCES.

L 1.65:CT
JOB DESCRIPTIONS.
Earlier L 7.16

L 1.66:CT • Item 754-C (MF)
PUBLIC SECTOR LABOR RELATIONS INFORMATION EXCHANGE [Publications]. [Irregular] (Labor-Management Services Administration, Division of Public Employee Labor Relations)
Earlier in L 1.2 and L 1.7/2 classes.

L 1.66/2:date
PUBLIC SECTOR LABOR RELATIONS INFORMATION EXCHANGE: CALENDAR OF EVENTS. [Quarterly]

L 1.66/3: • Item 754-C (MF)
LABOR RELATIONS TODAY. [Bimonthly]
A newsletter for labor relations practitioners.

L 1.67 • Item 754-E (MF)
TELEPHONE DIRECTORY.

L 1.68:date • Item 754-D
PUBLIC EMPLOYMENT PROGRAM, ANNUAL REPORT TO CONGRESS.

L 1.69:v.nos.&nos. • Item 754-F
INTERCHANGE. v. 1– 1975– [Monthly]
Beginning with v. 1, no. 2, issued by the Bureau of Employment and Training (L 37.9) under title Manpower Interchange.

L 1.70:letters-nos.
EMPLOYMENT SERVICE TECHNICAL REPORTS.

L 1.71:date • Item 762-D-9 (MF)
WORK INCENTIVE PROGRAM: ANNUAL REPORT TO CONGRESS. 1st– 1970– [Annual]
Reports on employment and training under Title IV of the Social Security Act.
Published jointly with the Department of Health, Education, and Welfare.
1st– 4th reports issued by the House Ways and Means Committee as Committee Prints.
Some reports have distinctive titles.

L 1.72:nos.
CONSUMER INFORMATION LEAFLETS. [Irregular]

L 1.74:date • Item 744-E (MF) (EL)
SEMIANNUAL REPORT OF THE INSPECTOR GENERAL.

L 1.74/2:date • Item 744-E-1 (MF)
ANNUAL AUDIT PLAN FY, OFFICE OF INSPECTOR GENERAL.

L 1.75:CT • Item 744-D-1 (MF)
CONSTRUCTION COMMITTEES [various cities]. PUBLIC SECTOR BID CALENDARS BY AGENCIES. [Annual]
Consists mainly of projected public construction such as street maintenance, sewer reconstruction, etc. Separate report for each city.

L 1.76:date • Item 744-F (MF)
EMPLOYEE RETIREMENT INCOME SECURITY ACT, REPORT TO CONGRESS. [Annual]
PURPOSE:– To summarize department activities complying with PL 93-406, whose primary objective is to safeguard the financial security of the aged during retirement.
Earlier L 1.2:Em 7/16

L 1.76/2:date-nos. • Item 744-F-1
ERISA TECHNICAL RELEASE.
The releases announce the agency's enforcement policies under the Employee Retirement Income Security Act.

L 1.77:date • Item 771-F-1
WEEKLY NEWSPAPER SERVICE.
Presents brief releases on miscellaneous topics such as state and metropolitan area employment and unemployment, producer price indexes.

L 1.78:date • Item 771-F-2
LABOR PRESS SERVICE. [Weekly]
Each issue is expected to contain short news releases on miscellaneous activities of the Labor Derpement. Examples are certification of more labor surplus areas and the consumer price index.

L 1.78/2:date/nos. • Item 771-F-2
BUSINESS PRESS SERVICE. [Weekly]

• Item 771-F (P)
L 1.79. • Item 744-G (EL)
NEWS.
Press releases on various topics pertaining to the work of the Labor Department.

L 1.79/2:date • Item 771-F
REPORT ON QUALITY CHANGES FOR (year) MODEL PASSENGER CARS. [Annual]

L 1.79/2-2:date • Item 771-F
COLLECTIVE BARGAINING IN (year). [Annual]

L 1.79/2-3:date • Item 771-F
CONTINUED INCREASES IN INDUSTRY PRODUCTIVITY IN (year) REPORTED BY BLS. [Annual]

L 1.79/2-4:date • Item 771-F
OCCUPATIONAL INJURIES AND ILLNESSES IN (year). [Annual]

L 1.79/3 • Item 771-F
TECHNICAL NOTE.

L 1.80:CT • Item 745-A-2
POSTERS. [Irregular]

L 1.81:date • Item 745-D (MF)
REGISTER OF REPORTING EMPLOYERS. [Biennial]

PURPOSE:– To provide names of companies and individuals which have filed employer reports with the Labor Department from 1959 through current year, listed by employer and by state.

L 1.82:date • Item 745-E (MF)
REGISTER OF REPORTING SURETY COMPANIES. [Biennial]

PURPOSE:– To provide the names of surety, insurance, and bonding companies and other firms which have filed surety company reports with the Labor Department.

L 1.83:CT • Item 745-A-3
FORMS. [Irregular]

L 1.84:date • Item 745-F (MF)
REGISTER OF REPORTING LABOR ORGANIZATIONS. [Triennial]

PURPOSE:– To list labor organizations which have filed reports with the Department under the provisions of the Labor-Management reporting and Disclosure Act of 1959 or the Civil Service Reform Act of 1978. Arranged by states, territories, and foreign countries.
Earlier L 1.2:R 26

L 1.85 • Item 745-A-4
LABOR-MANAGEMENT COOPERATION BRIEF. [Irregular]

PURPOSE:– To inform Government officials, news media, unions, business firms, and other interested parties of conventions to be held.

L 1.86:date • Item 744-A
CATALOG OF COURSES FISCAL YEAR . . . [Annual]

L 1.86/2 • Item 744-A (MF)
MICROCOMPUTER TRAINING CATALOG, THE DOL ACADEMY, ETC.

L 1.87:nos. • Item 745-A-4
BLM (Series).

L 1.88:nos. • Item 745-A-4 (MF)
U.S. DEPARTMENT OF LABOR PROGRAM HIGHLIGHTS, FACT SHEET (Series).

L 1.89 • Item 744-G (E)
ELECTRONIC PRODUCTS. [Irregular]

L 1.90:v.nos./nos. • Item 745
AMERICAN WORKPLACE.

L 1.90/2:date • Item 768-C-18 (P) (EL)
REPORT ON THE AMERICAN WORKFORCE. [Annual]

L 1.91:date • Item 745-A-5
DEPARTMENT OF LABOR ACADEMY: ANNUAL REPORT.

L 1.92 • Item 745-J
BRAILLE BOOKS.

L 1.93:date/nos. • Item 745-H
LABOR EXCHANGE. [Quarterly]

L 1.94:date/v.nos. • Item 745-K (EL)
NSSB, SKILLS TODAY. [Quarterly]
Formerly: NSSB, Work Wise.

L 1.95 • Item 745-K-1 (EL)
SENIOR EXECUTIVE SERVICE, FORUM SERIES. (Annual)

L 1.96 • Item 745-K-2 (EL)
O-NET* (ONLINE DATABASE).

BUREAU OF LABOR STATISTICS
(1913–   )

CREATION AND AUTHORITY

The Bureau of Labor, (C 8) the predecessor of the Bureau of Labor Statistics, was established in the Department of the Interior, by act of June 27, 1884. In 1913, after several changes in status, it became the Bureau of Labor Statistics in the newly created Department of Labor. BLS is the Government's principal factfinding agency in the field of labor economics, particularly with respect to the collection and analysis of data on employment and manpower, productivity and technological developments, wages, industrial relations, work injuries, prices, and costs and standards of living.

INFORMATION

Bureau of Labor Statistics
Department of Labor
Postal Square Bldg.
Two Massachusetts Ave., NE
Washington, DC 20212
(202) 691-7800
Fax: (202) 691-6325
http://www.bls.gov

L 2.1:date
ANNUAL REPORTS.

Earlier C 8.1

L 2.2:CT • Item 769
GENERAL PUBLICATIONS.
Earlier C 8.2

L 2.2:Ou 8/8 • Item 769
INDEXES OF OUTPUT PER MAN-HOUR, HOURLY COMPENSATION, AND UNIT LABOR COSTS IN THE PRIVATE SECTOR OF THE ECONOMY AND THE NONFARM SECTOR. [Annual]

PURPOSE:– To provide information on hourly compensation, unit labor costs and nonlabor payments, prices, and output per man-hour for the private sector of the economy and the nonfarm sector. These data are useful in studying the relationship between prices, costs, and productivity.

L 2.2:P 93/19 • Item 769
CONSUMER PRICE INDEX, A SHORT DESCRIPTION. 1971. 1972. 11 p.

L 2.2:Un 33/9/date • Item 769
DIRECTORY OF NATIONAL UNIONS AND EMPLOYEES ASSOCIATIONS. [Irregular] (Includes basic manual plus supplementary material for indefinite period)

L 2.2/10:date • Item 769-G
NATIONAL SURVEY OF PROFESSIONAL, ADMINISTRATIVE, TECHNICAL AND CLERICAL PAY. [Annual]

PURPOSE:– To define various professional, administrative, technical, and clerical occupations at different levels in such terms as general characteristics, direction received, and typical duties and responsibilities.

L 2.3:nos. • Item 768-A-1
BULLETINS. 112– 1913– [Irregular]

Covers one-time studies on all phases of labor, directories, handbooks, occupational guides, statistical compilations.
Bulletins 1-111 were issued by a preceding agency, the Labor Bureau.
ANALYSIS OF WORK STOPPAGES. 1941– [Annual]

Gives strike activity as measured by the number of workers involved and total mandays of idleness. Includes in addition to overall data on work stoppages, such items as major stoppages, issues involved, industries and unions affected, geographic patterns, size and duration of stoppages, method of termination, and disposition of issues.

• Item 768-B-1– 768-B-52
AREA WAGE SURVEYS. 1950– [Annual]

The Bureau of Labor Statistics instituted in 1948 a program of surveys in which occupations common to a variety of manufacturing and nonmanufacturing industries are studied on a community-wide basis. The earlier studies were limited to office workers but were expanded by 1951 to include also professional and technical, maintenance and powerplant, and custodial and material movement occupations. In addition to all-industry occupational averages and distributions, data are provided wherever possible for the six major divisions studies; manufacturing, public utilities, wholesale trade, retail trade, finance, and services. The survey reports also provide summaries of work schedules and supplementary benefits.
Individual bulletins are published for each area surveyed. Data for each locality is brought together in part 1 of an annual 2-part summary bulletin; projections of the data to national and regional estimates are provided inpart 2 of the summary.
Each survey shows occupational earnings, establishment practice, and supplementary wage provisions, such as shift differentials, minimum entrance rates for women office workers scheduled weekly hours, overtime pay, wage structure characteristics and labor-management agreements, paid holidays and vacations, and health, insurance, and pension plans.
Former title: Occupational Wage Surveys.

• Item 768-B-1
METROPOLITAN AREAS, UNITED STATES AND REGIONAL SUMMARIES. [Annual]

Projects occupational earnings data from the individual wage surveys conducted during the previous July-June period to all metropolitan areas combined. Presents U.S. summaries by industry and region and provides analyses of wage trends and wage differences.
Title varies.

BLS PUBLICATIONS. [Irregular]

PURPOSE:– To provide in one volume a complete catalog of the major publications of the Bureau of Labor Statistics: numbered bulletins, numbered reports, and periodicals. Contains a numerical listing and a subject index.

Title varies.

DIGEST OF SELECTED PENSION PLANS UNDER COLLECTIVE BARGAINING. [Irregular]
Later L 2.99

DIRECTORY OF NATIONAL AND INTERNATIONAL LABOR UNIONS IN THE UNITED STATES. 1947– [Biennial]

Lists national and international unions, State labor organization, developments, structure and memberships.

Prior to 1955 entitled Directory of Labor Unions in the United States.

EMPLOYMENT AND EARNINGS STATISTICS FOR STATES AND AREAS, 1939– [date]. 1939/62– [Annual]

Gives for all States and 202 major areas annual averages for more than 7,500 series on payroll employment by industry and 3,300 series on hours and earnings of production workers by industry from the earliest date of availability. Also contains summary and analytical tables comparing employment and earnings trends by region, State, and major area. Map and charts also facilitate regional and State comparisons. Provides background information for economic forecasting, community and plant location planning, labor cost analysis, market research, personnel management, and economic and social studies.

For monthly data to supplement the annual compilations, see Employment and Earnings and Monthly Report on the Labor Force.

EMPLOYMENT AND EARNINGS STATISTICS FOR THE UNITED STATES, 1909– [date]. 1909/60– [Annual]

Gives national data from the earliest date of availability for over 400 industries. Includes monthly and annual averages for employment, hours and labor turnover; seasonally adjusted data, indexes of weekly hours and weekly payrolls, net spendable earnings, hourly earnings excluding overtime, summary and analytical items, all data adjusted to 1966 benchmarks.

For monthly data to supplement the annual compilations, see Employment and Earnings and Monthly Report on the Labor Force.

• Item 768-C-3
HANDBOOK OF LABOR STATISTICS. 1924/26– [Annual]

Presents in one volume the major series produced by the Bureau of Labor Statistics and related series from other governmental agencies and foreign.

In general, the tables start at the earliest time from which a continuous, reliable, and consistent series can be carried. Data for the last two years is given monthly in a majority of the tables and annual prior to that.

INDEXES OF OUTPUT PER MAN-HOUR, SELECTED INDUSTRIES, 1939 AND 1947– [year]. [Annual]

Gives indexes of output per man-hour, output per employee, and unit labor requirements for selected manufacturing and nonmanufacturing industries.

INDUSTRY WAGE SURVEYS.

• Item 768-C-1
NATIONAL SURVEY OF PROFESSIONAL, ADMINISTRATIVE, TECHNICAL, AND CLERICAL PAY. 1960– [Annual]

Provides averages and distributions of salary rates for about 80 professional, administrative, technical, and clerical work levels, in private industry. The data are presented nationally and for combined metropolitan areas. Trends from 1961 are provided.
ISSN 0501-7041

OCCUPATIONAL OUTLOOK FOR COLLEGE GRADUATES. [Irregular]
• Item 768-C-2
OCCUPATIONAL OUTLOOK HANDBOOK. 1949– [Biennial]

PURPOSE:– To provide comprehensive coverage of the major occupations of interest in guidance, with reports on over 700 occupations and 30 major industries, including, in addition to professional and white collar fields and the major types of farming, many of the industrial occupations in which most young people will find jobs.

Trends and outlook are emphasized to show the changing nature of occupational and industrial life, and to help on long-range educational and career planning. Each report shows what the job is like, what qualifications are required for a beginning position, prospects for advancement, employment outlook, location of the job, and earnings and working conditions.

Aids to the user include an introduction on using the Handbook in Guidance Service and a chapter on interpreting the information and obtaining additional facts about occupations, with cross-references.

Kept up-to-date by the Occupational Outlook Quarterly (L 2.70/4).

OCCUPATIONAL OUTLOOK REPORT SERIES.

Chapters from the Occupational Outlook Handbook are reprinted as separates for individual occupations or groups of occupations and published as sub-parts of the Bulletin numbers assigned to the Handbooks.

PRODUCTIVITY INDEXES FOR SELECTED INDUSTRIES. [Annual]

Continues: Indexes of Output per Man-Hour, Selected Industries (ISSN 0363-809X).
ISSN 0362-6946

RETAIL PRICES ON FOOD. 1941– [Quinquennial]

Gives indexes by commodity group, indexes and average prices of principal foods, for the United States; and indexes by commodity group and annual average prices of principal foods for each of 23 cities.

SELECTED METROPOLITAN AREAS. [Annual]

An annual summary of the results of the individual area wage surveys conducted during the previous July-June period. Covers occupational earnings, establishment practices, and supplementary wage provision.
• Item 768-C-4
UNION WAGES AND HOURS.

Gives data as of July 1 with trend from 1907 to date for the following industries:

BUILDING TRADES. 1936– [Annual]
LOCAL TRANSIT OPERATING EMPLOYEES. 1936– [Annual]
MOTORTRUCK DRIVERS AND HELPERS. 1936– [Annual]
PRINTING TRADES. 1936– [Annual]

• Item 768-C-5 (MF)
WAGE CHRONOLOGIES.

L 2.3:604 **• Item 768-A-1**
HISTORY OF WAGES IN THE UNITED STATES FROM COLONIAL TIMES TO 1928. [Revision of Bull. 499 with Supplement, 1929– 1933] 1934. 574 p. (Bulletin 604)

A picture of American wages in repre-

sentative occupations and industries from early colonial times to 1933. Part 1, largely text, deals with the period prior to 1840. Methods of age payments as well as the wages paid during these years are interpreted against the background of customs, system of labor (indenture and redemption), and working conditions peculiar to colonization. Part 2, which covers the period 1840 to 1933, is entirely statistical in presentation.

L 2.3:651 **• Item 768-A-1**
STRIKES IN THE UNITED STATES, 1880– 1936. 1938. 183 p. il.

PURPOSE:– To present the major statistical data available on strikes and lockouts from the earliest recorded date through 1936, with the principal portion covering the period 1927– 36.

L 2.3:1000 **• Item 768-A-1**
BRIEF HISTORY OF THE AMERICAN LABOR MOVEMENT. 1970. 143 p. il. (Bulletin 1000)

Introduces the reader to the mainstream of trade unionism in the United States. It presents simply and in general terms the role of labor organizations in American history and economic life. An appendix covering important events in American labor history from 1778 through 1969 is also included.

L 2.3:1977 **• Item 768-A-1**
U.S. WORKING WOMEN: A DATABOOK. 1977. 67 p.

A statistical report on the changing role of women in the labor force. Brief text gives highlights of 61 tables and 7 charts on the labor force participation of women– their employment and unemployment marital status, income, education, job tenure, work life expectancy, and other social and demographic characteristics.

L 2.3:2001 **• Item 768-A-1**
EXPLORING CAREERS. 1979. 547 p. il.

Prepared especially for junior high school students, this career education guide discusses different kinds of work, and includes stories, puzzles, questions and answers, and many photographs.

L 2.3/a 2:CT
OCCUPATIONAL OUTLOOK BRIEFS [excerpts from Occupational Outlook Handbook].

L 2.3/3:CT **• Item 768-C-1**
INDUSTRY WAGE SURVEY: (Various Industries).

L 2.3/3-2:CT **• Item 768-D-1**
INDUSTRY WAGE SURVEY SUMMARIES.

L 2.3/3-3:date **• Item 768-D-1 (EL)**
WAGE SURVEY SUMMARIES.

L 2.3/4:date **• Item 768-C-2 (P) (EL)**
OCCUPATIONAL OUTLOOK HANDBOOK.

L 2.3/4 a: **• Item 768-C-16**
REPRINTS FROM THE OCCUPATIONAL OUTLOOK HANDBOOK, BULLETINS.

Each reprint deals with a different occupational area.

L 2.3/4-2:date **• Item 768-A-10 (MF)**
OCCUPATIONAL PROJECTIONS AND TRAINING DATA. [Biennial]

Earlier L 2.3

L 2.3/4-3:date **• Item 768-A-1**
CAREER GUIDE TO INDUSTRIES. [Annual]

L 2.3/4-4:date **• Item 744-G-2 (CD)**
OCCUPATIONAL OUTLOOK HANDBOOK. [Biennial]

L 2.3/5:date **• Item 768-C-3**
HANDBOOK OF LABOR STATISTICS.

L 2.3/6   • Item 768-C-4
UNION WAGES AND BENEFITS.

L 2.3/8:date   • Item 768-C-17
BARGAINING CALENDAR, (year). [Annual]
    Issued in the Bulletin series.

L 2.3/9:date   • Item 768-A-4 (MF) (EL)
RELATIVE IMPORTANCE OF COMPONENTS IN THE
CONSUMER PRICE INDEXES. [Annual]

L 2.3/10:date   • Item 768-A-5 (MF) (EL)
EMPLOYEE BENEFITS IN MEDIUM AND LARGE PRI-
VATE ESTABLISHMENTS. [Biennial]
    Formerly: Employee Benefits in Medium and
Large Firms.

L 2.3/10-2:date   • Item 768-A-13 (P) (EL)
EMPLOYEE BENEFITS IN STATE AND LOCAL GOV-
ERNMENTS. [Biennial]

    PURPOSE– To present results of a BLS sur-
vey of the incidence and provisions of employee
benefit plans in state and local governments. Provides a detailed description of the scope and
statistical procedures used in the survey.

L 2.3/11:date   • Item 768-A-3
OCCUPATIONAL INJURIES AND ILLNESSES IN THE
UNITED STATES BY INDUSTRY. [Annual]

L 2.3/12:date   • Item 768-A-6 (MF) (EL)
GEOGRAPHIC PROFILE OF EMPLOYMENT AND
UNEMPLOYMENT. [Annual]

L 2.3/13:date   • Item 768-A-7
NATIONAL SURVEY OF PROFESSIONAL, ADMINIS-
TRATIVE, TECHNICAL, AND CLERICAL PAY.
[Annual]
    Earlier L 2.3
    Also classed L 2.2/10

L 2.3/13-2:   • Item 768-A-7
NATIONAL SURVEY OF PROFESSIONAL, ADMINIS-
TRATIVE, TECHNICAL, AND CLERICAL PAY: PRI-
VATE SERVICE INDUSTRIES. [Biennial]

L 2.3/14   • Item 768-C-6
INDUSTRY WAGE SURVEY: MILLWORK. [Irregular]

L 2.3/15:date   • Item 768-C-1
INDUSTRY WAGE SURVEY: MEAT PRODUCTS (year).
[Annual]

L 2.3/16:date   • Item 768-A-8
OCCUPATIONAL EMPLOYMENT IN MANUFACTURING
INDUSTRIES. [Triennial]

L 2.3/16-2:   • Item 768-A-12
OCCUPATIONAL EMPLOYMENT IN SELECTED
NONMANUFACTURING INDUSTRIES. [Annual]

    PURPOSE– To provide data from a survey of
occupational employment in such industries as
transportation, communications, utilities, trade,
educational services, and state and local government.

L 2.3/18:date   • Item 768-A-1
CONSUMER EXPENDITURE SURVEY: INTERVIEW
SURVEY, 1982-83. [Annual]
    Earlier L 2.3

L 2.3/18-2:date
CONSUMER EXPENDITURE SURVEY: DIARY SUR-
VEY. [Biennial]
    Earlier L 2.3

L 2.3/18-3   • Item 768-A-15 (MF)
CONSUMER EXPENDITURE SURVEY: QUARTERLY
DATA FROM THE INTERVIEW SURVEY.

L 2.3/19:date   • Item 768-C-1 (MF)
INDUSTRY WAGE SURVEY: PETROLEUM REFINING.
[Irregular]
    Earlier L 2.3/3

L 2.3/20:date   • Item 768-A-9 (MF)
PRODUCTIVITY MEASURES FOR SELECTED INDUS-
TRIES AND GOVERNMENT SERVICES. [Annual]
    Earlier: Productivity Measures for Selected
Industries.

L 2.3/21:date   • Item 768-C-1 (MF)
INDUSTRY WAGE SURVEY: SYNTHETIC FIBERS.
[Irregular]

L 2.3/22:date   • Item 768-C-1 (MF)
INDUSTRY WAGE SURVEY: BANKING. [Annual]
    Earlier L 2.3/3 and L 2.3

L 2.3/23:date   • Item 768-C-1 (MF)
INDUSTRY WAGE SURVEY: TEXTILE MILLS. [Irregu-
lar]
    Earlier L 2.3

L 2.3/24:date   • Item 768-C-1 (MF)
INDUSTRY WAGE SURVEY: HOSPITALS. [Irregular]
    Earlier L 2.3

L 2.3/25   • Item 768-C-1
INDUSTRY WAGE SURVEY: NURSING AND PER-
SONAL CARE FACILITIES.

L 2.3/26:   • Item 768-C-7
INDUSTRY WAGE SURVEY: CIGARETTE MANUFAC-
TURING. [Quinquennial]
    PURPOSE– To summarize the results of a
BLS survey of wages and employee benefits in
the cigarette manufacturing industry.

L 2.3/27:   • Item 768-C-8
INDUSTRY WAGE SURVEY: WOOD HOUSEHOLD
FURNITURE. [Annual]

    PURPOSE– To summarize results of a BLS
survey of occupational earnings and employee
benefits in the upholstered and nonupholstered
wood household furniture industries.

L 2.3/28:   • Item 768-A-11 (MF)
LINKING EMPLOYMENT PROBLEMS TO ECONOMIC
STATUS. [Annual]
    PURPOSE– To provide narrative and tabular
data on employment problems faced by American
workers and the impact of those problems on the
economic status of their families.
    Earlier L 2.3

L 2.3/29:   • Item 768-C-9 (MF)
INDUSTRY WAGE SURVEY: PRESSED OR BLOWN
GLASSWARE.

    PURPOSE– To summarize the results of a
BLS survey of occupational wages and employee
benefits in the pressed or blown glass and glassware industries.

L 2.3/30:   • Item 768-C-10 (MF)
INDUSTRY WAGE SURVEY: STRUCTURAL CLAY
PRODUCTS. [Irregular]
    PURPOSE– To summarize results of a BLS
survey of wages and related benefits in the structural clay products industries.

L 2.3/31:   • Item 768-C-11 (MF)
INDUSTRY WAGE SURVEY: INDUSTRIAL CHEMI-
CALS. [Quinquennial]
    This bulletin summarizes the results of a BLS
survey of wages and employment benefits in industrial chemicals in narrative and tables.
    Earlier L 2.3/3

L 2.3/32:   • Item 768-C-12 (MF)
INDUSTRY WAGE SURVEY: IRON AND STEEL
FOUNDRIES.
    PURPOSE– To summarize results of a BLS
survey of occupational wages and employee benefits in the iron and steel foundry industries. Chiefly
tables.

L 2.3/33:   • Item 768-C-13 (MF)
INDUSTRY WAGE SURVEY: CONTRACT CLEANING
SERVICES. [Quinquennial]
    PURPOSE– To summarize results of a BLS
survey of wages and related benefits in the contract cleaning services industries.

L 2.3/34:   • Item 768-C-14
INDUSTRY WAGE SURVEY: SHIPBUILDING AND
REPAIRING. [Triennial]
    PURPOSE– To summarize results of a BLS
survey of occupational wages and employee ben-
efits in the shipbuilding and repairing industry.
Designated Bulletins (nos.).

L 2.3/35:   • Item 768-C-15
INDUSTRY WAGE SURVEY: MEN'S AND BOY'S
SHIRTS AND NIGHTWEAR.

    PURPOSE– To summarize results of a BLS
survey of occupational earnings and employee
benefits in the men's and boy's shirt and nightwear
industry.
    Earlier L 2.3/3

L 2.3/36:date   • Item 768-A-14
PERMANENT MASS LAYOFFS AND PLANT
CLOSINGS. [Annual]
    PURPOSE:– To present narrative and tabular
data on permanent mass layoffs and plant closings by states.

L 2.3/37:date   • Item 768-C-1 (MF)
INDUSTRY WAGE SURVEY: DEPARTMENT STORES.
[Irregular]

L 2.3/38:date   • Item 768-C-1
INDUSTRY WAGE SURVEY: TEMPORARY HELP SUR-
VEY. [Irregular]

L 2.4:
CIRCULARS.

L 2.5:date
LIST OF PUBLICATIONS, BUREAU OF LABOR
STATISTICS.

L 2.6:v.nos.&nos.   • Item 770 (P) (EL)
MONTHLY LABOR REVIEW. v. 1–   1915–   [Monthly]
    PURPOSE:– To serve as the official journal
of the Bureau of Labor Statistics, and in effect,
the Department of Labor.
    Carries articles on labor economics and in-
dustrial relations, summaries of studies and reports, and technical notes.
    Departments: This Issue in Brief, The Labor
Month in Review, Foreign Labor Briefs, Significant Decisions in Labor Cases, Major Agreements
Expirations, Chronology of Recent Labor Events,
Developments in Industrial Relations, Book Review and Notes, and Current Labor Statistics.
    Current Labor Statistics section contains all
current BLS statistical series covering employment, labor turnover, earnings and hours, consumer and wholesale prices, work stoppages,
and productivity.
    Index to volume contained in the December
issues.
    Indexed by:–
        Business Periodicals Index
        Index to U.S. Government Periodicals
        Industrial Arts Index
        Public Affairs Information Service
        Readers' Guide to Periodical Literature
        ISSN 0098-1818

L 2.6/a:CT   • Item 770
– SEPARATES. [Irregular]

L 2.6/a 2:date
RETAIL PRICES. [Monthly]

L 2.6/a 3:date
LABOR OFFICES IN U.S. AND FOREIGN COUN-
TRIES.

L 2.6/a 4:date
BUILDING CONSTRUCTION.   – 1944. [Monthly]

L 2.6/a 5:date
CHANGES IN COST OF LIVING.

L 2.6/a 6:date
ANALYSIS OF STRIKES. [Monthly]

    Early issues read, with slight variations,
    Strikes and Lockouts.

L 2.6/a 7:nos.
LATIN AMERICAN SERIES. 1–   1939–

L 2.6/a 8:date
COURT DECISIONS OF INTEREST TO LABOR.

    Changed from L 2.6/a:C 835

L 2.6/a 9:date
PRICES. [Quarterly]

L 2.6/a 10:nos.
WAGE CHRONOLOGY SERIES.
Later 2.64

L 2.6/1:CT
REPRINTS. R 1–   [Irregular]

Important articles from Monthly Labor Review are available as reprints as long as the limited supply lasts.

L 2.6/1:L 524
STATE LABOR LEGISLATION IN (year). [Annual]
Reprinted from Monthly Labor Review.

L 2.6/2:date
MONTHLY LABOR REVIEW, STATISTICAL SUPPLE-MENTS.

L 2.7:CT
DESCRIPTIONS OF OCCUPATIONS.

Earlier L 7.6

L 2.8:date
WHOLESALE PRICES 1922– 1966. [Monthly]

L 2.9:date
EMPLOYMENT AND PAYROLLS. 1923– 1954. [Monthly]

L 2.9/2:date
TREND OF EMPLOYMENT IN U.S. (Monthly summary statements).   – 1933.

L 2.10:vol.
LABOR INFORMATION BULLETIN. v. 1– v. 9, no. 6. 1934– 1942. [Monthly]
Later L 1.15

L 2.11:nos.&CT
INDEXES OF RENTS BY TYPE OF DWELLING.

L 2.12:nos.
BUILDING PERMIT SURVEY.

L 2.13:nos.
STATE, COUNTY AND MUNICIPAL SURVEY [of 2 employment and payrolls].
Pubs. design, SCM-nos.

L 2.14:vol.
CHART SERIES. [Quarterly]

L 2.15:nos.
HISTORICAL STUDIES. 1– 78. 1941– 1945.

L 2.16:nos.
INDUSTRIAL AREA STUDIES. 1– [ ]. 1943– [ ].

L 2.17:date
SUMMARY OF TECHNOLOGICAL DEVELOPMENTS AFFECTING WAR PRODUCTION. 1941– 1946. [Monthly]

L 2.18:nos.
INDUSTRIAL AREA STATISTICAL SUMMARIES. 1– 1943–

L 2.19:CT
PRODUCTIVITY AND TECHNOLOGICAL DEVELOP-MENT DIVISION PUBLICATIONS.

L 2.20:CT
EFFECTS ON SELECTED COMMUNITIES OF WAR CONTRACT CUTBACKS AND CANCELLATIONS [Confidential].

L 2.21:nos.
LABOR NEWS. 1– [ ]. 1944– 1946. [Monthly]

L 2.22:date
CONSTRUCTION, MONTHLY SUMMARY OF CURRENT DEVELOPMENTS. 1944– 1954.
Replaced by C 41.30/3

L 2.22/2:date
CONSTRUCTION ACTIVITY [Monthly] Proc.
Later C 3.215/3

L 2.23:nos.
MEMORANDUM [of Industrial Relations Division] Proc.

L 2.24:date
INDEXES OF PRODUCTION WORKER EMPLOYMENT IN MANUFACTURING INDUSTRIES BY METRO-POLITAN AREA. 1940– 1947. [Monthly]

L 2.25:nos.
OCCUPATION WAGE RELATIONSHIPS, SERIES 1. 1– [11]. 1945– [1947].

L 2.26
ADDRESSES. [Irregular]

L 2.27:nos.
WAGE STRUCTURE, SERIES 2. 1–   1945.

Series 1:– see Occupational Wage Relation-ships, L 2.25
Series 3:– see Wage Movements, L 2.47

L 2.28:nos.
WORK AND WAGE EXPERIENCE STUDIES, RE-PORTS. 1– [7]. 1945– [1947].

L 2.29:CT
UNION WAGE SCALE STUDIES.

L 2.30:CT
SURVEY OF WORLD WAR II VETERANS AND DWELL-ING UNIT VACANCY AND OCCUPANCY [in city areas].

L 2.31:CT
SURVEY OF NEGRO WORLD WAR II VETERANS AND VACANCY AND OCCUPANCY OF DWELLING UNITS AVAILABLE TO NEGROES [in city areas].

L 2.32:nos.
NOTES ON LABOR ABROAD. 1–   1942. [Irregular]

L 2.32/2:v.nos.&nos.   **• Item 769-B**
LABOR DEVELOPMENTS ABROAD. v. 1– 17. 1956– 1972. [Monthly]

PURPOSE:– To present research information on recent labor developments in foreign coun-tries.
The primary sources are reports from Ameri-can Foreign Service posts, publications of for-eign governments, the foreign press, and ex-perts in international labor developments. Arrange-ment is by region and country.
Contains articles on the labor situation, trends in labor welfare, new labor laws; statistical tables on manpower, wages, and prices; comparative statistics on such subjects as price trends, wages, and work stoppages in foreign industrial coun-tries; indexes of living costs in foreign cities com-pared with Washington, D.C.
Annual index in December issue.

INDEXES.

CUMULATIVE INDEX. 1956– 1963. Rpt. 292

L 2.33:date   **• Item 768-E**
AVERAGE WHOLESALE PRICES AND INDEX NUM-BERS OF INDIVIDUAL COMMODITIES. [Monthly]

L 2.34:date   **• Item 768-E**
BUREAU OF LABOR STATISTICS CATALOG OF PUB-LICATIONS, BULLETINS, REPORTS, RELEASES, AND PERIODICALS. 1946–   [Semiannual]

Annotated list of publications of the Bureau of Labor Statistics, including those of the field offices as well as the Washington office.

L 2.34/2:CT   **• Item 768-E**
BIBLIOGRAPHIES AND LISTS OF PUBLICATIONS.
Formerly in L 2.2

L 2.34/3:date
PUBLICATIONS FOR SALE.

L 2.35:nos.
CONVERSION LISTS. 1–   1947–

L 2.36:nos.
BUILDING CONSTRUCTION IN URBAN AREAS IN UNITED STATES. [Monthly]

L 2.37:date   **• Item 768-I**
ESTIMATED RETAIL FOOD PRICES BY CITIES. [Monthly & Annual]

Gives U.S. indexes and percent change for food subgroups and individual items: city aver-age retail prices of food for U.S. and individual cities by subgroups and individual items.
The monthly average prices and indexes of individual foods are computed for the United States and for each of 23 large cities. The U.S. average prices are based upon a sample of 56 cities se-lected to represent all urbanized areas, cities and suburbs of the U.S. ranging from small cities of 2,500 population to cities the size of New York. Of the 56 cities used for the U.S. average, 23 of the large cities are also reported individually.
Annual summary issued separately.
Former title: Retail Food Prices by Cities.
ISSN 0091-0163

L 2.37/2:date
RETAIL FOOD PRICES IN LARGE CITIES, BY GROUPS. [Monthly]

L 2.38:date
CONSUMERS PRICE INDEX. [Monthly]

L 2.38/2:CT
CONSUMERS' PRICE INDEX FOR MODERATE-INCOME FAMILIES (adjusted series).

L 2.38/3:date   **• Item 768-F (P) (EL)**
CPI DETAILED REPORT, CONSUMER PRICE INDEX, U.S. CITY AVERAGE AND SELECTED AREAS. 1940–   [Monthly]

Gives U.S. city average for all items and com-modity groups; major groups indexes for selected dates, U.S. city average and 23 large cities; per-cent changes for U.S. city average and five large metropolitan areas; all items and major groups; U.S. city average and selected areas; food and its subgroups, U.S. city average and 23 large cities. Textual summaries. Most tables later ap-pear in Monthly Labor Review.
The Consumer Price Index measures aver-age changes in prices of goods and services usually brought by urban wage earners and cleri-cal workers, both families and single persons living alone. Index numbers are presented on the base 1957-59 100.
A description of the index is available in Bul-letin 1517, The Consumer Price Index, History and Techniques, in Bulletin 1168, Handbook of Methods for Surveys and Studies, and in the free pamphlet, The Consumer Price Index, A Short Description.
ISSN 0095-926X

L 2.38/3-2:date   **• Item 786-F (EL)**
NEWS, CONSUMER PRICE INDEX. [Monthly]

L 2.38/4:date
CONSUMER PRICE INDEX, PRICE INDEXES FOR SELECTED ITEMS AND GROUPS.   – 1967/ 68.
Earlier L 2.2:P 93/13
Later included in L 2.38/3

L 2.38/5:CT
CONSUMER PRICE INDEX [by individual cities and commodities].

L 2.38/6:date
CONSUMER PRICE INDEX, MOUNTAIN-PLAIN REGIONS. [Monthly]

L 2.38/7:date   **• Item 768-F-1**
CONSUMER PRICES: ENERGY AND FOOD. [Monthly]

Consists mainly of tables showing average retail prices for energy and food. Average retail energy prices are broken down into gasoline and fuel oil, electricity, and natural gas for U.S., cities and selected areas. Average retail food prices are broken down into specific commodities for U.S. and four regions.

L 2.38/8:date   **• Item 768-F**
CONSUMER PRICE INDEX, WASHINGTON, D.C. AREA. [Monthly]

L 2.38/8-2 • Item 768-F-5 (EL)
CONSUMER PRICE INDEX, CHICAGO. [Monthly]
This news release presents consumer price index information for the Chicago region. Tables include data for all urban workers and urban wage earners including clerical workers.

L 2.38/8-3:date/nos. • Item 768-F-6 (P) (EL)
NEWS, NEW YORK-NORTHEASTERN NEW JERSEY CPI. [Monthly]
CPI = Consumer Price Index
News release on the consumer price index for the New York-Northeastern New Jersey area.

L 2.38/8-4:date • Item 768-F-5
LATEST CONSUMER PRICE INDEX (Tables for U.S. and 6 Cities in Midwest). [Monthly]

L 2.38/9:date • Item 768-F
CONSUMER PRICE INDEX FOR ALL URBAN CONSUMERS. [Monthly]

L 2.38/10:date • Item 768-F (P) (EL)
SUMMARY OF CPI NEWS RELEASES.
CPI = Consumer Price Index
Earlier title: Consumer Price Index News Releases.

L 2.39:date
RETAIL FOOD PRICE INDEX. [Monthly]

L 2.39/2:date
INDEXES OF RETAIL PRICES ON MEATS IN LARGE CITIES. [Monthly]

L 2.39/3:date
RETAIL FOOD PRICE INDEX, WASHINGTON, D.C., AREA. [Monthly]

L 2.40:date • Item 769-F
RETAIL PRICES AND INDEXES OF FUELS AND UTILITIES. [Monthly]
Gives indexes of retail prices for gas, electricity and residential heating fuels, all cities combined; indexes of retail prices of gas and electricity, fuel oil and coal, by area; net monthly bills for specified amounts of gas, by area; average retail prices of residential heating gas and fuel oil by area.
Former title: Retail Prices and Indexes of Fuels and Electricity.

L 2.41:date
HOURS AND EARNINGS INDUSTRY REPORTS. – 1954. [Monthly]

L 2.41/2:v.nos./nos • Item 768-B
EMPLOYMENT AND EARNINGS AND MONTHLY REPORT ON LABOR FORCE. v. 1– 1954– [Monthly]
Formerly: Employment and Earnings and Monthly Report on Labor Force.

Data on employment and earnings include the number of wage and salary workers on payrolls of nonagricultural establishments, actual and seasonally adjusted, hours and earnings of production or nonsupervisory workers, labor turnover rates, man-hour and payroll indexes, and State and area data.

Data on the labor force include the employment status of the noninstitutional population, by age, sex and color; employed persons by occupational group, by type of industry, and hours of work; unemployed persons, by age, sex, and color; occupation of last job, and duration of unemployment; employment status of 14-15 year olds and selected seasonally adjusted data.
Indexed by: Index to U.S. Government Periodicals.
ISSN 0013-6840
Prior to February 1966, Monthly Report on Labor Force issued as a separate publication (L 2.84).

L 2.41/2-2:date • Item 768-B
SUPPLEMENT TO EMPLOYMENT AND EARNINGS. [Annual]
Earlier L 2.41/2

L 2.41/3:nos.
EMPLOYMENT, HOURS AND EARNINGS. [Monthly]
Replaced by L 2.84

L 2.41/4:date
STATE AND LOCAL GOVERNMENT EMPLOYMENT AND PAYROLLS. [Monthly]
Gives total figures for employment and payrolls.

L 2.41/5:date • Item 768-B
NATIONAL EMPLOYMENT, HOURS, AND EARNING INDUSTRY SUMMARIES [employees in nonagricultural establishments, by industry division]. [Annual]
Earlier L 2.2:Em 2/27

L 2.41/6:date
EMPLOYMENT IN THE MOUNTAIN STATES. [Monthly]
Combined with Employment in the Plains States (L 2.41/7) to form Employment and Earnings in the Mountain Plains Region (L 2.41/8).

L 2.41/7:date
EMPLOYMENT IN THE PLAINS STATES. [Monthly]
Combined with Employment in the Mountain States (L 2.41/6) to form Employment and Earnings in the Mountain Plains Region (L 2.41/8)

L 2.41/8:date
EMPLOYMENT AND EARNINGS IN THE MOUNTAIN PLAINS REGION. [Monthly]
Combines Employment in the Mountain States (L 2.41/6) and Employment in the Plains States (L 2.41/7).

L 2.41/9:date • Item 768-T (MF)
UNEMPLOYMENT IN STATES AND LOCAL AREAS. [Monthly]
Tables include data on labor force, employment, and unemployment, for States, labor market areas, counties, and cities of 25,000 population or more, pursuant to requirements of the Public Works and Economic Development Act of 1965, as amended.
Published in microfiche (48x).
Earlier title: Employment and Unemployment in State and Local Areas.

L 2.41/10 • Item 768-T (MF)
EMPLOYMENT AND UNEMPLOYMENT IN STATE AND LOCAL AREA. [Annual]
Annual summary of monthly data (L 2.41/9). Published in microfiche (48x).

L 2.41/11:date • Item 768-T
EMPLOYMENT IN PERSPECTIVE: WOMEN IN THE LABOR FORCE. [Quarterly]

L 2.41/11-2:date • Item 768-T
EMPLOYMENT IN PERSPECTIVE: MINORITY WORKERS. [Quarterly]

L 2.41/12:date • Item 768-T
NEWS, EMPLOYMENT AND WAGES IN FOREIGN-OWNED BUSINESSES IN THE UNITED STATES. [Quarterly]

L 2.42:date
LABOR TURNOVER. [ ]–1952. [Monthly]

L 2.42/2:date
FACTORY LABOR TURNOVER. [Monthly]
Table gives labor turnover rates in manufacturing, by major industry group, with total and new hires for accession rates; and total quits, layoffs for separation rates. Two month comparisons. Issued as a USDL release.
Previous title: Labor Turnover.

L 2.42/2-2:date
LABOR TURNOVER IN MANUFACTURING. [Monthly]

L 2.43:CT
OFFICE WORKERS, SALARIES, HOURS OF WORK, SUPPLEMENTARY BENEFITS (by cities).

L 2.43/2:date • Item 769-R
WHITE-COLLAR SALARIES. [Annual]
Relates to white-collar salaries in private industry in metropolitan and nonmetropolitan areas of the U.S. except Alaska and Hawaii.

L 2.43/3:date • Item 769-R
THE NATIONAL SURVEY OF WHITECOLLAR PAY. [Annual]

L 2.44:v.nos./nos. • Item 768-D
COMPENSATION AND WORKING CONDITIONS. [Monthly]
PURPOSE:– To list in tabular form wage changes negotiated or effective during the preceding month and coming to the attention of the Bureau of Labor Statistics. Information is compiled from newspaper reports and other secondary sources.
Information includes union, company or association, location, date effective, approximate number of workers, wage adjustment, and related information. Listings are limited to those cases involving 1,000 or more workers.
– Supplements. [Quarterly]
Gives major wage developments
Earlier titled: Current Wage Developments.

L 2.44/2:date • Item 771-D
WAGE DEVELOPMENTS IN MANUFACTURING, SUMMARY RELEASE. 1959– [Semiannual]
PURPOSE:– To provide a statistical summary of wage and benefit changes in the manufacturing industries.

L 2.44/3:date • Item 768-D (MF)
AVERAGE ANNUAL WAGES AND WAGE ADJUSTMENT INDEX FOR CETA PRIME SPONSORS. [Annual]

L 2.44/4:v.nos/nos. • Item 768-D (EL)
COMPENSATION AND WORKING CONDITIONS (numbered). [Quarterly]

L 2.45:v.nos.&nos.
COLLECTIVE BARGAINING AGREEMENTS RECEIVED BY BUREAU OF LABOR STATISTICS. [ ]–1951. [Monthly]

L 2.45/2:date • Item 769-H
MAJOR COLLECTIVE BARGAINING SETTLEMENTS IN PRIVATE INDUSTRY. [Quarterly]

L 2.45/2-2:date • Item 769-H
MAJOR COLLECTIVE BARGAINING SETTLEMENTS IN PRIVATE INDUSTRY. [Annual]
Earlier L 2.120

L 2.45/3:date • Item 769-H (P) (EL)
MAJOR WORK STOPPAGES. [Annual]

L 2.45/4:date • Item 769-H
STATE AND LOCAL GOVERNMENT COLLECTIVE BARGAINING SETTLEMENTS. [Annual]

L 2.46:CT • Item 771
REGULATIONS, RULES, AND INSTRUCTIONS.

L 2.46/2:
COMMODITIES AND SERVICES MANUAL.

L 2.46/3:CT • Item 769-A
HANDBOOKS, MANUALS, GUIDES.

L 2.46/4:date • Item 769-A (MF)
CURRENT EMPLOYMENT STATISTICS STATE OPERATING MANUAL.

L 2.46/5:date • Item 769-A (MF)
EMPLOYEE BENEFITS SURVEY HEALTH CODING MANUAL. [Annual]
Earlier L 2.46/3:Em 7/8

L 2.46/6:date • Item 769-A
EMPLOYEE BENEFITS SURVEY SICKNESS AND ACCIDENT CODING MANUAL. [Annual]

L 2.46/7:date • Item 769-A (MF)
EMPLOYEE BENEFITS SURVEY DEFINED BENEFIT PENSION CODING MANUAL. [Annual]
Earlier L 2.46/3:Em 7/7

L 2.46/8: • **Item 769-A (MF)**
EMPLOYEE BENEFITS SURVEY DEFINED CONTRI-
BUTION CODING MANUAL. [Annual]

L 2.46/9 • **Item 769-A (MF)**
EMPLOYEE BENEFITS SURVEY LIFE INSURANCE
CODING MANUAL. [Annual]

L 2.47:nos.
[INDUSTRY WAGE STUDIES], SERIES 3, WAGE
MOVEMENTS. 1–   1949–

Series 1:– see Occupational Wage Relationships, L 2.25
Series 2:– see Wage Structure, L 2.27

L 2.47/2:
INDUSTRY WAGE STUDIES MEMO.

L 2.48:nos.
SPECIAL SERIES. 1– 6. 1950– 1951.

L 2.49:CT
PRESS RELEASES. [Irregular]

Most releases covering activities of the Bureau of Labor Statistics are issued as Departmental releases rather than as Bureau releases.

L 2.49/2:dt.&nos.
PRICES FOR WEEK.

L 2.49/3:date
INDEX NUMBERS OF WHOLESALE PRICES BY
GROUPS AND SUBGROUPS OF COMMODITIES.
[Monthly]

L 2.49/4:
NEW ENGLAND ECONOMY, EMPLOYMENT, ETC.,
RELEASES.

L 2.49/5:
WAGE DEVELOPMENTS IN THE NEW ENGLAND
REGION.

L 2.50:v.nos.
WEEKLY LABOR NEWS DIGEST.
Later L 1.28

L 2.51:dt.&pt.nos.
NUMBER OF NEW DWELLING UNITS AND PERMIT
VALUATION OF BUILDING CONSTRUCTION AU-
THORIZED BY CLASS OF CONSTRUCTION IN
MOUNTAIN AND PACIFIC DIVISION BY CIVIL
DIVISION AND STATE. [Monthly]

L 2.51/2:dt.&pt.nos.
NUMBER OF NEW DWELLING UNITS AND PERMIT
VALUATION OF BUILDING CONSTRUCTION AU-
THORIZED BY CLASS OF CONSTRUCTION IN
NEW ENGLAND DIVISION BY CIVIL DIVISION
AND STATE. [Monthly]

L 2.51/3:date
NUMBER OF NEW DWELLING UNITS AND PERMIT
VALUATION OF BUILDING CONSTRUCTION AU-
THORIZED IN METROPOLITAN AREA OF WASH-
INGTON, D.C. [Monthly]
Later C 3.215/5

L 2.51/4:date
NUMBER OF NEW PERMANENT NONFARM DWELL-
ING UNITS STARTED BY URBAN OR RURAL
LOCATION, PUBLIC OR PRIVATE OWNERSHIP,
AND TYPE OF STRUCTURE CUMULATIVE YEAR-
TO-DATE. [Monthly]

L 2.51/5:date
NEW DWELLING UNITS AUTHORIZED BY LOCAL
BUILDING PERMITS. [Monthly]
Later C 3.215/4

L 2.51/6:date
CHARACTERISTICS OF NEW HOUSING. [Annual]

L 2.51/7:date
PERMIT VALUATION AND NUMBER OF NEW DWELL-
ING UNITS PROVIDED IN HOUSE-KEEPING AND
DWELLINGS AUTHORIZED IN METROPOLITAN
AREA OF WASHINGTON, D.C. BY TYPE OF
DWELLING AND SOURCE OF FUNDS. [Annual]
Earlier L 2.2:D 96/6

L 2.52:v.nos.&nos.
EMPLOYMENT HOURS, AND EARNINGS, STATE AND
AREA DATA. [Annual]

L 2.53:
SEMI-MONTHLY REPORT ON EMPLOYMENT SITUA-
TION.

L 2.53/2:date • **Item 768-T (EL)**
EMPLOYMENT SITUATION. [Monthly]

Issued as a USDL release. Tables and summary data on labor force, payroll employment,
hours and earnings, and unemployment rates.
Two month comparisons with change.
ISSN 0364-491X

L 2.53/2-2:date • **Item 768-T**
SUMMARY DATA FROM THE EMPLOYMENT SITUA-
TION NEWS RELEASE. [Monthly]

L 2.54:
WAGE OPERATIONS MANUAL OF PROCEDURES.

L 2.55:
UNION WAGE STUDIES MANUAL OF PROCEDURES.

L 2.56:
WEEKLY REVIEW OF RECENT DEVELOPMENTS.

L 2.57:nos.
MANPOWER REPORTS.

L 2.58:nos.
SPECIAL INDUSTRIAL RELATIONS REPORTS.

L 2.58/2:nos.
GUIDES TO INDUSTRIAL RELATIONS IN U.S.

L 2.59:
REVIEW OF MONTH.

L 2.60:date
TUESDAY SPOT MARKET PRICE INDEXES AND
PRICES. 1952–   [Weekly]
Former titles: Daily Indexes of Spot Market
Prices, Weekly Summary; and Daily Spot Market
Price Indexes and Prices, Weekly Summary.
ISSN 0364-2291

L 2.60/2:v.nos.
DAILY INDEXES AND SPOT MARKET PRICES 1–
[   ]. 1952– [1954].

L 2.60/3:date • **Item 771-G (EL)**
U.S. IMPORT AND EXPORT PRICE INDEXES. [Quar-
terly]

L 2.61:date/nos. • **Item 771-B (P) (EL)**
PRODUCER PRICE INDEXES. [Monthly]
Gives price index for month and preceding
month and price (in dollars) for current month for
individual commodities and groups. Arranged by
code numbers and abbreviated description. Also
includes industry-sector price indexes for the
output of selected industries and product classes,
textual summaries of price developments and
technical information.
Wholesale price index and special wholesale
price indexes appear in the Monthly Labor Review. For a detailed description of the index, see
BLS Handbook of Methods for Surveys and Studies (L 2.3:1458).
Prior to the March 1978 issue, entitled Wholesale Prices and Price Indexes [ISSN 0498-7667].
Former title: Producer Prices and Price Indexes.
ISSN 0161-7311

L 2.61/2:date
WHOLESALE PRICE INDEX (1947– 49=100), IN-
DEXES FOR GROUPS, SUBGROUPS, AND
PROJECT CLASSES OF COMMODITIES.
Changed from L 2.2:W 62/8

L 2.61/3:date
COMMODITIES INCLUDED IN (various) PRODUCTS
GROUP FOR REVISED WHOLESALE PRICE IN-
DEX.

L 2.61/4:date
CHANGES IN LIST OF COMMODITIES INCLUDED IN
WHOLESALE PRICE INDEX.

L 2.61/5:date
WHOLESALE (Preliminary Market) PRICE INDEX.
[Monthly]

L 2.61/6:group nos.
WHOLESALE PRICE INDEX (1947– 49=100), PRICES
AND PRICE RELATIVES FOR INDIVIDUAL COM-
MODITIES, 1951– 53.

L 2.61/6-2:nos.
WHOLESALE PRICE INDEX (1947– 49=100), PRICES
AND PRICE RELATIVES FOR INDIVIDUAL COM-
MODITIES IN REVISED INDEX 1947– 50 [by
group].

L 2.61/7:group nos.
WHOLESALE PRICE INDEX, MAJOR SPECIFICATION
CHANGES 1947– 53.

L 2.61/8:date
WHOLESALE PRICE INDEX SERIES 1947– 48=100:
ECONOMIC SECTOR INDEXES. [Monthly]

L 2.61/9:date
WHOLESALE PRICE INDEX, PRELIMINARY
ESTIMATE. 1967–   [Monthly]

L 2.61/10 • **Item 771-B (EL)**
NEWS, PRODUCER PRICE INDEXES. [Monthly]
Earlier title: Wholesale Price Indexes, Ad-
vance Summary.

L 2.61/10-2:date • **Item 771-B**
SUMMARY DATA FROM THE PRODUCER PRICE IN-
DEX NEWS RELEASE. [Monthly]

L 2.61/11:date • **Item 771-B**
PRODUCER PRICE INDEXES DATA FOR ... [Annual]
Formerly titled: Supplement to Producer Prices
and Price Indexes Data for (year).

L 2.62:nos.
WORK STOPPAGES, SERIES 5. 1–   1952–

L 2.62/2:date
WORK STOPPAGES. [Monthly]

Gives work stoppages by industry, affiliation
of unions involved, State, and by metropolitan
areas, Annual issue released in April. An analytical resume appears in the July issue of the
Monthly Labor Review, which in turn is followed
by more detailed statistical review in the Bulletin
series.

L 2.62/3:date
WORK STOPPAGES. [Annual]
Earlier L 2.2:W 89/2

L 2.63:date
PRESENT CHANGES IN GROSS HOURLY AND
WEEKLY EARNINGS OVER SELECTED
PERIODS.
Changed from L 2.2:Ea 7/5

L 2.63/2:date
PERCENT CHANGES IN GROSS AVERAGE HOURLY
EARNINGS OVER SELECTED PERIODS.
[Quarterly]

L 2.63/3:date
PERCENT CHANGES IN GROSS AVERAGE WEEKLY
EARNINGS OVER SELECTED PERIODS.
[Quarterly]

L 2.64:nos.
WAGE CHRONOLOGY SERIES 4. 1–   1953–
Earlier L 2.6/a 10

L 2.64/2:date • **Item 768-H**
DIRECTORY OF WAGE CHRONOLOGIES. [Annual]

L 2.65:
SPECIFICATIONS FOR RETAIL PRICES.

L 2.66:
MONTHLY DIGEST TO MEMBERS OF CONGRESS.

L 2.67:
SUPPLIES OF IMPORTANT FOODS IN RETAIL
STORES.

L 2.69:
STRIKES IN–

L 2.70:date
OCCUPATIONAL OUTLOOK PUBLICATIONS.
Changed from L 2.2:Oc 1

L 2.70/2:CT
OCCUPATIONAL OUTLOOK SUMMARY.
Changed from L 2.2

L 2.70/3:nos.
WALL CHARTS. 1– 1947– [Irregular]

Material based on previous editions of Occupational Outlook Handbook.

L 2.70/4:v.nos.&nos. • Item 770-A (P) (EL)
OCCUPATIONAL OUTLOOK QUARTERLY. v. 1– 1957– [4 times a year]

PURPOSE:– To provide current information on employment and outlook to keep readers up-to-date on developments between biennial issues of the Occupational Outlook Handbook (issued as a Bulletin).
Summarizes the results of new studies and reports the latest developments affecting occupations and industries covered in the Handbook. Also includes reports on related studies and projects conducted by other Governmental agencies.
Indexed by:–
Index to U.S. Government Periodicals
Public Affairs Information Service

L 2.70/4 a:CT • Item 770-A
SEPARATES. [Irregular]

L 2.71:nos. • Item 768-G
BLS REPORTS. 1– 1953–

Reports of a more specific nature are issued in this series, covering such topics as wage chronologies of individual companies, studies on the effect of the $1 minimum wage in various communities, wage structures of various industries, etc.

INJURY RATES BY INDUSTRY. 1958– [Annual]

Statistical tables give injury frequency rates, injury severity rates, average days of disability per case, and percent of disabling injuries resulting in death, permanent disability, or temporary disability, by industry. Two year comparisons.
1970 Rpt 406

LABOR LAW AND PRACTICE IN (Country). 1961– [Irregular]

PURPOSE:– To provide background material for U.S. businessmen and others who may be employing local workers abroad, trade union and labor specialists, consulting economists, and students.
Presents general information about the country and its workers, labor organizations, and employment conditions.

MAJOR PROGRAMS, BUREAU OF LABOR STATISTICS. [Annual]

PUBLICATIONS OF THE BUREAU OF LABOR STATISTICS. [Semiannual]

WORK INJURIES IN ATOMIC ENERGY. 1967– [Annual]
Title varies.

L 2.71/2:nos. • Item 768-P
REGIONAL REPORTS. 1– [Irregular] (Pacific Regional Office)

L 2.71/3:nos. • Item 768-P (MF)
REGIONAL REPORTS (numbered). (New England Regional Office, JFK Federal Building, Boston, Massachusetts 02003)

L 2.71/4:nos.
REGIONAL REPORTS (series). 1– [Irregular] (North Central Regional Office, 219 S. Dearborn Street, Chicago, Illinois 60604)

Covers Illinois, Indiana, Kentucky, Michigan, Minnesota, Ohio, and Wisconsin.

L 2.71/5 • Item 768-J (MF)
BLS STAFF PAPERS. 1– 1968– [Irregular]

PURPOSE:– To present original analytical papers by members of the Bureau of Labor Statistics staff which may include personal views of the results of independent work performed outside the office. The papers deal with economic, statistical, and other questions related to the work of the Bureau of Labor Statistics.

L 2.71/5-2 • Item 768-J-1 (EL)
NATIONAL LONGITUDINAL SURVEYS, DISCUSSION PAPER (series).

L 2.71/6:nos. • Item 768-P-1
REGIONAL REPORTS, MIDDLE ATLANTIC REGION. 1–

L 2.71/6-2:nos. • Item 768-P-1
NEWS, NYLS- (series). [Irregular]

L 2.71/6-3:date/nos. • Item 768-P-1
NEW YORK STATE UNEMPLOYMENT RATE. [Monthly]

L 2.71/6-4:date-nos. • Item 768-P-1
NEW JERSEY UNEMPLOYMENT RATE. [Monthly]

L 2.71/6-6:date • Item 768-P-1
REGIONAL DATA ON COMPENSATION SHOW WAGES, SALARIES AND BENEFITS COSTS IN THE NORTHEAST. [Quarterly]

L 2.71/6-7: • Item 768-P-1
JOBS IN NEW YORK-NORTHEASTERN NEW JERSEY. [Monthly]

L 2.71/6-8: • Item 768-P-1
NEW JERSEY UNEMPLOYMENT RATE . . . [Annual]

L 2.71/6-9: • Item 768-P-1
NEW YORK STATE UNEMPLOYMENT RATE . . . [Annual]

L 2.71/6-10: • Item 768-P-1
NEW YORK CITY'S UNEMPLOYMENT RATE . . . [Annual]

L 2.71/7:nos.
REGIONAL LABOR STATISTICS BULLETIN. 1– 1968–

L 2.71/8:nos. • Item 768-P-2 (MF)
SOUTHEASTERN REGIONAL OFFICE: REGIONAL REPORTS. 1– [Irregular]

L 2.71/9:nos. (MF) (EL)
REGION 6: REGIONAL REPORT SERIES. [Quarterly]

L 2.72:CT
LABOR STATISTICS SERIES.

L 2.72/2:CT
SOURCES OF INFORMATION REGARDING LABOR [various countries].

L 2.72/3:nos.
LABOR DIGEST. 1– 1963– [Irregular]

Notes prepared in the Division of Foreign Labor Conditions for inclusion in the Directory of Labor Organizations.
Brief reports (2-4 pages) on labor conditions in foreign countries including social and economic factors affecting labor, manpower, labor standards, and labor-management relations. Some reports include listing of labor organizations.

L 2.72/4:CT
DIRECTORY OF LABOR ORGANIZATIONS IN [various countries]. 1954– [Irregular]

With the formation of the International Confederation of Free Trade Unions in 1949, relationship between the United States and foreign labor unions increased. As a result, there was an increasing need for a source of reference on foreign labor developments, unions, officers, strength, political doctrine, etc. To fill this need, the directories were initiated in 1954.
The directories were compiled primarily for use by U.S. government agencies and U.S. labor organizations. Its audience soon expanded to include foreign government and labor organizations, universities, foundations, and private business concerns with interests abroad.
The series includes: Africa, Asia and Australia, Europe, and the Western Hemisphere. In addition, there is a series of directories relating to international labor organizations, which include: The International Trade Secretariats (ITS), the International Confederation of Free Trade Unions (ICFTU), the International Federation of Christian Trade Unions (CISC), and the World Federation of Trade Unions (WFTU).

L 2.73:
FREE MEN AT WORK. [Monthly]

L 2.74:nos.
ANNOUNCEMENTS [of reports published]. [Monthly]

L 2.74/2:nos.
NEW PUBLICATIONS IN WAGES AND INDUSTRIAL RELATIONS. 1954– [Irregular]

L 2.75:nos.
NET SPENDABLE EARNINGS. [Monthly]

PURPOSE:– To summarize current information on factory workers' pay. Gives gross average weekly earnings, spendable earnings and index of "real" spendable earnings for workers with no dependents and worker with 3 dependents for month, two preceding months, and month a year ago. Chart. Issued as a USDL release.

L 2.76:nos.
STUDIES OF AUTOMATIC TECHNOLOGY. 1– 1955–

L 2.77:date
INJURY-FREQUENCY RATES FOR SELECTED MANUFACTURING INDUSTRIES. [Quarterly]

L 2.77/2:date
INJURY RATES BY INDUSTRY. [Annual]

L 2.77/3:date
WORK INJURIES, CONTRACT CONSTRUCTION. [Annual]
Earlier L 2.2:In 5/3

L 2.77/4:date
WORK INJURIES, TRADE. [Annual]

L 2.77/5:date
ESTIMATED WORK INJURIES.

L 2.78:date
INDEXES OF PRICES FOR SELECTED MATERIALS, HYDRAULIC TURBINE INDUSTRY. [Quarterly]

L 2.78/2:date
INDEX OF STRAIGHT-TIME AVERAGE HOURLY EARNINGS FOR HYDRAULIC TURBINE OPERATIONS.

L 2.79:date
DEPARTMENT STORE INVENTORY PRICE INDEXES. 1949– [Semiannual]

Gives index figures (Jan. 1941 100) for U.S. by department groups for month with comparisons for month six months ago and a year ago. The January figures are published in March and the July figures in September.

L 2.80:date • Item 769-C (MF)
PROCEEDINGS OF THE INTERSTATE CONFERENCE ON LABOR STATISTICS. [Annual]

L 2.81:date
EMPLOYEES IN PRIVATE AND GOVERNMENT SHIPYARDS BY REGION. [Annual]
Earlier L 2.2:Sh 6/6

L 2.81/2:date
INDEXES OF CHANGE IN STRAIGHT-TIME AVERAGE HOURLY EARNINGS FOR SELECTED SHIPYARDS, BY TYPE OF CONSTRUCTION AND REGION. [Monthly]
Earlier L 2.2:Sh 6/7

L 2.82:nos.
EMPLOYMENT REPORTS. Proc.

L 2.83:date • **Item 768-N-1**
DIRECTORY, BUSINESS RESEARCH ADVISORY COUNCIL OF THE BUREAU OF LABOR STATISTICS. [Annual]

L 2.83/2:date
DIRECTORY OF LABOR RESEARCH ADVISORY COUNCIL TO THE BUREAU OF LABOR STATISTICS.

L 2.84:date
MONTHLY REPORT ON LABOR FORCE, EMPLOYMENT, UNEMPLOYMENT, HOURS AND EARNINGS.
Replaces C 3.186:P 57 and L 2.41/3

L 2.85:date
UNION CONVENTIONS, NATIONAL AND INTERNATIONAL UNIONS, STATE ORGANIZATIONS. [Annual]
Earlier L 2.2:Un 33/4

L 2.86:date • **Item 768-S**
OCCUPATIONAL EARNINGS AND WAGE TRENDS IN METROPOLITAN AREAS, SUMMARY. [3 times a year]

PURPOSE:– To present statistical data on average earnings and wage trends in specific areas.
Former title: Occupational Earnings in Major Labor Markets, Summary Release.
Earlier L 2.2:Oc 1/18

L 2.86/2:date
WAGE TRENDS FOR OCCUPATIONAL GROUPS IN METROPOLITAN AREAS, SUMMARY RELEASE. [Annual]

L 2.86/3:date & nos. • **Item 768-S (MF)**
OCCUPATIONAL EARNINGS IN SELECTED AREAS, SUMMARY. [Quarterly]

L 2.86/4:date • **Item 768-S**
OCCUPATIONAL EARNINGS IN BANKING, SELECTED METROPOLITAN AREAS SUMMARY. [Semiannual]

L 2.86/5:date • **Item 768-S**
OCCUPATIONAL EARNINGS IN ALL METROPOLITAN AREAS. [Annual]

L 2.87:date • **Item 769-E**
MAJOR BLS PROGRAMS. [Annual]
Earlier L 2.2:P 94/20

L 2.88:CT
INCOME, EDUCATION AND UNEMPLOYMENT IN NEIGHBORHOODS [by city].

L 2.89:date
INDEXES OF OUTPUT PER MAN-HOUR, SELECTED INDUSTRIES. [Annual]
Earlier L 2.2:Ou 8

L 2.89/2:date
INDEXES OF OUTPUT PER MAN-HOUR FOR THE PRIVATE ECONOMY. [Annual]

Gives data on the total private economy and the farm and nonfarm sectors. Within the nonfarm sector, separate measures are also included for manufacturing and nonmanufacturing industries. In addition to the output per man-hour measures, related indexes of output, employment, and man-hours are included.

L 2.90:date • **Item 771-E**
SUMMARY OF MANUFACTURING EARNINGS SERIES.
Earlier L 2.71:229

L 2.91:CT
EAST CENTRAL REGIONAL OFFICE PUBLICATIONS. (1365 Ontario Street, Cleveland, Ohio 44114)

Includes Kentucky, Michigan, Ohio, West Virginia.

L 2.92:CT
MIDDLE ATLANTIC REGIONAL OFFICE PUBLICATIONS. (341 9th Avenue, New York, New York 10001)

Includes Delaware, D.C., Maryland, New Jersey, New York, and Pennsylvania.

L 2.93:CT
NORTH EASTERN REGIONAL OFFICE PUBLICATIONS. (1603-A Federal Building, Boston, Massachusetts 02203)

Includes Connecticut, Maine, Massachusetts, New Hampshire, Rhode Island, and Vermont.

L 2.94:CT
NORTH CENTRAL REGIONAL OFFICE PUBLICATIONS. (219 S. Dearborn Street, Chicago, Illinois 60604)

Includes Illinois, Indiana, Iowa, Kansas, Nebraska, North Dakota, South Dakota, Wisconsin.

L 2.95:CT
SOUTHERN REGIONAL OFFICE PUBLICATIONS. (1371 Peachtree Street, N.E., Atlanta, Georgia 30309)

Includes Alabama, Arkansas, Florida, Georgia, Louisiana, Mississippi, North Carolina, Oklahoma, South Carolina, Tennessee, Texas, and Virginia.

L 2.96:CT
WESTERN REGIONAL OFFICE PUBLICATIONS.

L 2.97:nos.
URBAN EMPLOYMENT SURVEY: REPORTS (numbered). 1– 1970–

L 2.98:nos. • **Item 768-R**
SPECIAL LABOR FORCE REPORTS. 1– [Irregular]

Reprints from Monthly Labor Review, some with supplementary tables added.

L 2.98/2:CT
SUMMARY, SPECIAL LABOR FORCE REPORTS.

L 2.99:date • **Item 768-K**
DIGEST OF SELECTED PENSION PLANS. [Irregular] (Subscription includes basic volume plus supplementary changes for an indefinite period)

PURPOSE:– To summarize the principal features of selected pension plans for employees under collective bargaining and selected pension plans for salaried employees.
Earlier editions published as Bulletins (L 2.3).
Discontinued in 1980.

L 2.99/2:date • **Item 768-K**
DIGEST OF SELECTED HEALTH AND INSURANCE PLANS. [Irregular]

(Includes basic volume plus supplemental material for an indefinite period)
PURPOSE:– To summarize the principal features of selected pension plans for employees under collective bargaining and selected pension plans for salaried employees.
Former title: Digest of Health and Insurance Plans.
Earlier published as Bureau of Labor Statistics Bulletin 1629 (L 2.3:1629).
Latest edition: 1971 edition.
Issued in two volumes:
Vol. 1. Health Benefits.
Vol. 2. Insurance Benefits.
Discontinued in 1980.

L 2.100 • **Item 768-L**
PRICES, ESCALATION, AND ECONOMIC STABILITY (series). 1971– [Irregular]

PURPOSE:– To provide a series of interpretive publications on prices and inflation designed for a broader audience than that reached by the

technical bulletins, reports, and staff papers of the Bureau of Labor Statistics. The series is intended to contribute to an understanding of the Bureau's work and its relationship to the economic and social problems confronting American society.

L 2.101:date • **Item 768-M**
U.S. DEPARTMENT OF STATE INDEXES OF LIVING COSTS ABROAD, QUARTERLY ALLOWANCES, AND HARDSHIP DIFFERENTIALS. [Quarterly]

Former title: U.S. Department of State Indexes of Living Costs Abroad and Living Quarters Allowances.
Later S 1.76/4
ISSN 0364-9598

L 2.101/2:date
U.S. DEPARTMENT OF STATE INDEXES OF LIVING COSTS ABROAD AND QUARTERS ALLOWANCES, APRIL. [Annual]

L 2.102
QUARTERLY REVIEW OF PRODUCTIVITY, WAGES, AND PRICES. 1967– 1973.

L 2.102/2:v.nos.&nos. • **Item 768-O**
CHARTBOOK ON PRICES, WAGES, AND PRODUCTIVITY. v. 1– 6, no. 3. June 1974– Sept. 1979. [Monthly]

PURPOSE:– To present a comprehensive picture of current changes in prices, wages, costs, profits, and productivity in the U. S. economy, in their historical setting. Most of the charts show seasonally adjusted rates of change in prices and other factors, expressed at an annual rate. Includes charts and statistical tables.
Supplement to Quarterly Review of Productivity, Wages and Prices (L 2.102).
ISSN 0095-4837

L 2.102/2-2:v.nos.
CHARTBOOK ON PRICES, WAGES, AND PRODUCTIVITY.
Earlier L 2.102/2

L 2.103:date • **Item 768-N**
CONVENTIONS, (year): NATIONAL AND INTERNATIONAL UNIONS, STATE LABOR FEDERATIONS, PROFESSIONAL ASSOCIATIONS, STATE EMPLOYEE ASSOCIATION [list]. [Annual] (Office of Wages and Industrial Relations, Division of Industrial Relations)

L 2.104:date • **Item 754-B**
EMPLOYMENT AND WAGES, A QUARTERLY SUMMARY OF WORKERS COVERED BY STATE UNEMPLOYMENT INSURANCE LAWS AND UNEMPLOYMENT COMPENSATION FOR FEDERAL EMPLOYEES. 1938– (Office of Current Employment Analysis)

PURPOSE:– To provide national totals of employment and wage data in covered industries for 10 industry divisions, and by State and geographic region for 8 of the 10 industry divisions. A brief summary of trends and developments in covered employment and wages is included.
Previous title: Employment and Wages of Workers Covered by State Unemployment Insurance Laws and Unemployment Compensation for Federal Employees.
ISSN 0091-9403
Issued by Manpower Administration (L 1.61) prior to the 3rd quarter 1971 issue and the Bureau of Employment Security (L 7.20/3) prior to 3rd quarter 1967.

L 2.104/2:nos. • **Item 768-D (MF)**
EMPLOYMENT AND WAGES, ANNUAL AVERAGE.
Also published in microfiche.

L 2.105:CT • **Item 768-N-2 (MF)**
MUNICIPAL GOVERNMENT WAGE SURVEYS.

Contains occupational earnings, work practices, and supplementary benefits for the employees of municipal city governments. Each report is devoted to a single city government.

L 2.106:CT
INDUSTRY WAGE SURVEY REPORTS.

L 2.107:CT
AREA WAGE SURVEY REPORTS.

L 2.107/2:CT
AREA WAGE SURVEY ADVANCE REPORTS.

L 2.108:CT
COLLECTIVE BARGAINING SUMMARIES.

L 2.109:date   • **Item 768-N-1**
DIRECTORY OF THE LABOR RESEARCH ADVISORY COUNCIL TO THE BUREAU OF LABOR STATISTICS. 1978/80–   [Biennial]

     Lists members, title, organization, address, phone number, and committee membership.

L 2.110:date
CETA AREA EMPLOYMENT AND UNEMPLOYMENT. [Annual]
     Earlier L 2.2:Em 7/40

L 2.110/2:date-nos.
CETA AREA EMPLOYMENT AND UNEMPLOYMENT, BLS/CETA/MR- (series). [Monthly]

L 2.110/3:date-nos.
CETA AREA EMPLOYMENT AND UNEMPLOYMENT, SPECIAL REPORTS, BLS/CETA/SP- (series). [Irregular]

L 2.111:date
STATE, COUNTY AND SELECTED CITY EMPLOYMENT AND UNEMPLOYMENT. [Annual]
     Earlier L 2.2:Em 7/41

L 2.111/2:date-nos.
STATE, COUNTY AND SELECTED CITY EMPLOYMENT AND UNEMPLOYMENT, BLS/PWEDA/MR- (series). [Monthly]

L 2.111/3:date-nos.
UNEMPLOYMENT RATES FOR STATES AND LOCAL GOVERNMENTS, BLS/PWEDA/QR- (series). [Quarterly]
     Discontinued.

L 2.111/4:date-nos.
STATE, COUNTY AND SELECTED CITY EMPLOYMENT AND UNEMPLOYMENT, BLS/PWEDA/SP- (series). [Irregular]

L 2.111/5:date   • **Item 768-T-1 (EL)**
NEWS, METROPOLITAN AREA EMPLOYMENT AND UNEMPLOYMENT. [Monthly]
     Earlier title: State and Metropolitan Area Unemployment.
     Formerly: State and Metroplitan Area Employment and Unemployment.

L 2.111/5-2:date   • **Item 768-T-1**
STATE UNEMPLOYMENT. [Monthly]

L 2.111/6:date
UNEMPLOYMENT RATE BY RACE AND HISPANIC ORIGIN IN MAJOR METROPOLITAN AREAS. [Annual]

L 2.111/7:date   • **Item 768-T-3**
NEWS REGIONAL AND STATE EMPLOYMENT AND UNEMPLOYMENT.

L 2.112:CT
POSTERS.

L 2.113:CT   • **Item 768-B-1– B-52**
AREA WAGE SURVEY SUMMARIES BY CITIES.

L 2.113/2:CT
LAUNDRY AND DRY CLEANING WAGE SURVEY SUMMARIES BY CITIES.

L 2.113/3:CT
REFUSE HAULING WAGE SURVEY SUMMARIES BY CITIES.

L 2.113/4:CT
EATING AND DRINKING PLACES AND MOTELS WAGE SURVEY SUMMARIES BY CITIES.

L 2.113/5:CT   • **Item 768-B-1– B-52**
MOVING AND STORAGE WAGE SURVEY SUMMARIES BY CITIES.

L 2.113/5-2:date   • **Item 768-B-1– B-51**
MOVING AND STORAGE WAGE SURVEYS, SUMMARIES BY STATE. [Annual]

L 2.113/6:CT
AREA WAGE SURVEY SUMMARIES BY STATES.

L 2.113/7:CT   • **Item 768-B-2**
AIR TRANSPORTATION WAGE SURVEY.

L 2.113/8:CT   • **Item 768-W**
FORESTRY WAGE SURVEY (Summary) [various states].

     PURPOSE:– To present results of a survey of occupational wages in the forestry industry in a particular sate. These studies are conducted by BLS at the request of the Employment Standards Administration.

L 2.114:date   • **Item 768-A-2**
CATALOG OF SEMINARS, TRAINING PROGRAMS AND TECHNICAL ASSISTANCE IN LABOR STATISTICS. [Annual]

     Describes and presents a calendar of seminars on collecting and analyzing labor data, which are held in Washington, D.C., and are attended by statisticians, economists, and analysts from developing countries worldwide.

L 2.115:date   • **Item 768-T-2 (P) (EL)**
REAL EARNINGS. [Monthly]

L 2.117:date   • **Item 769-K (P) (EL)**
EMPLOYMENT COST INDEX. [Quarterly]

L 2.117/2:date   • **Item 769-K**
NORTHEAST EMPLOYMENT COST INDEX. [Quarterly]

L 2.118:date
EARNINGS OF WORKERS AND THEIR FAMILIES. [Quarterly]

L 2.118/2:date   • **Item 769-L**
EMPLOYMENT AND EARNINGS CHARACTERISTICS OF FAMILIES. [Annual]

     Tables present statistics on characteristics and extent of employment and earnings of various groups of U.S. families.

L 2.119:date   • **Item 769-J (P) (EL)**
PRODUCTIVITY AND COSTS. [Quarterly]

L 2.119/2:date   • **Item 769-J**
PRODUCTIVITY STATISTICS FOR FEDERAL GOVERNMENT FUNCTIONS, FISCAL YEAR.

L 2.120:date-nos.   • **Item 769-P (P) (EL)**
NEWS.

L 2.120/2:date   • **Item 769-P**
STATE AND REGIONAL UNEMPLOYMENT.
     Earlier: News, State Unemployment.

L 2.120/2-2:date   • **Item 769-P**
NEWS, AVERAGE ANNUAL PAY BY STATE AND STANDARD METROPOLITAN STATISTICAL AREA.

L 2.120/2-3:date   • **Item 769-P (P) (EL)**
NEWS, AVERAGE ANNUAL PAY BY STATE AND INDUSTRY.

L 2.120/2-4:date   • **Item 769-P**
NEWS, ANNUAL PAY LEVELS IN METROPOLITAN AREAS.

L 2.120/2-5:date   • **Item 769-P**
CONSUMER EXPENDITURE SURVEY RESULTS. [Annual]
     Earlier L 2.120

L 2.120/2-6:date   • **Item 769-P (P) (EL)**
INTERNATIONAL COMPARISONS OF MANUFACTURING PRODUCTIVITY AND LABOR COSTS TRENDS. [Annual]
     Earlier L 2.120

L 2.120/2-7:date   • **Item 769-P**
REPORT ON QUALITY CHANGES FOR (year) MODEL PASSENGER CARS. [Annual]

L 2.120/2-8:date   • **Item 769-P**
COLLECTIVE BARGAINING ACTIVITY IN (year). [Annual]

L 2.120/2-9:date   • **Item 769-P**
INDUSTRY PRODUCTIVITY IN (year) REPORTED BY BLS. [Annual]

L 2.120/2-10:date   • **Item 769-P**
MULTIFACTOR PRODUCTIVITY MEASURES. [Annual]
     Earlier L 2.120

L 2.120/2-11:date   • **Item 769-P (EL)**
OCCUPATIONAL INJURIES AND ILLNESSES IN (year). [Annual]
     Earlier L 1.79/2-4

L 2.120/2-12:   • **Item 769-P (EL)**
NEWS, UNION MEMBERS IN (DATE). [Annual]
     Formerly: Union Membership in (Date).

L 2.120/2-13:date   • **Item 769-P**
EMPLOYER COSTS FOR EMPLOYEE COMPENSATION. [Annual]

L 2.120/2-14:date   • **Item 769-J (P) (EL)**
BLS REPORTS ON MASS LAYOFFS IN THE . . . QUARTER. [Quarterly]

L 2.120/2-15:date   • **Item 769-J-1 (P) (EL)**
MONTHLY SERIES ON MASS LAYOFFS.

L 2.120/2-16   • **Item 769-P-1**
EMPLOYER COSTS FOR EMPLOYEE COMPENSATION, NORTHEAST REGION.

L 2.120/2-17:date   • **Item 769-P-2 (P) (EL)**
NEWS, EMPLOYMENT AND AVERAGE ANNUAL PAY FOR LARGE COUNTIES.

L 2.120/2-18   • **Item 769-P-2 (P) (EL)**
NEWS, WORK EXPERIENCE OF THE POPULATION. [Annual]

L 2.120/2-19   • **Item 769-P-3 (P) (EL)**
EXTENDED MASS LAYOFFS IN... [Annual]

L 2.121/
OCCUPATIONAL COMPENSATION SURVEY: PAY AND BENEFITS . . . METROPOLITAN AREA . . . BULLETIN.

     Starting in 1989 in order to reduce the number of classes, the Area Wage Surveys have been reclassified with a class stem for each state and cutter by city within that state. The first list below is the earlier classification. The current system follows.
     Earlier title: Area Wage Survey . . . Metropolitan Area . . . Bulletin.

L 2.121/1:CT/date   • **Item 768-B-1 (EL)**
OCCUPATIONAL COMPENSATION SURVEY: PAY AND BENEFITS, ALABAMA. [Annual]

L 2.121/2:CT/date   • **Item 768-B-2 (EL)**
OCCUPATIONAL COMPENSATION SURVEY: PAY AND BENEFITS, ALASKA. [Annual]

L 2.121/3:CT/date   • **Item 768-B-3 (EL)**
OCCUPATIONAL COMPENSATION SURVEY: PAY AND BENEFITS, ARIZONA. [Annual]

L 2.121/4:CT/date   • **Item 768-B-4 (EL)**
OCCUPATIONAL COMPENSATION SURVEY: PAY AND BENEFITS, ARKANSAS. [Annual]

L 2.121/5:CT/date   • **Item 768-B-5 (EL)**
OCCUPATIONAL COMPENSATION SURVEY: PAY AND BENEFITS, CALIFORNIA. [Annual]

L 2.121/6:CT/date   • **Item 768-B-6 (EL)**
OCCUPATIONAL COMPENSATION SURVEY: PAY AND BENEFITS, COLORADO. [Annual]

L 2.121/7:CT/date   • **Item 768-B-7 (EL)**
OCCUPATIONAL COMPENSATION SURVEY: PAY AND BENEFITS, CONNECTICUT. [Annual]

L 2.121/8:CT/date　　　• Item 768-B-8 (EL)
OCCUPATIONAL COMPENSATION SURVEY: PAY AND
BENEFITS, DELAWARE. [Annual]

L 2.121/9:CT/date　　　• Item 768-B-9 (EL)
OCCUPATIONAL COMPENSATION SURVEY: PAY AND
BENEFITS, FLORIDA. [Annual]

L 2.121/10:CT/date　　　• Item 768-B-10 (EL)
OCCUPATIONAL COMPENSATION SURVEY: PAY AND
BENEFITS, GEORGIA. [Annual]

L 2.121/11:CT/date　　　• Item 768-B-11 (EL)
OCCUPATIONAL COMPENSATION SURVEY: PAY AND
BENEFITS, HAWAII. [Annual]

L 2.121/12:CT/date　　　• Item 768-B-12 (EL)
OCCUPATIONAL COMPENSATION SURVEY: PAY AND
BENEFITS, IDAHO. [Annual]

L 2.121/13:CT/date　　　• Item 768-B-13 (EL)
OCCUPATIONAL COMPENSATION SURVEY: PAY AND
BENEFITS, ILLINOIS. [Annual]

L 2.121/14:CT/date　　　• Item 768-B-14 (EL)
OCCUPATIONAL COMPENSATION SURVEY: PAY AND
BENEFITS, INDIANA. [Annual]

L 2.121/15:CT/date　　　• Item 768-B-15 (EL)
OCCUPATIONAL COMPENSATION SURVEY: PAY AND
BENEFITS, IOWA. [Annual]

L 2.121/16:CT/date　　　• Item 768-B-16 (EL)
OCCUPATIONAL COMPENSATION SURVEY: PAY AND
BENEFITS, KANSAS. [Annual]

L 2.121/17:CT/date　　　• Item 768-B-17 (EL)
OCCUPATIONAL COMPENSATION SURVEY: PAY AND
BENEFITS, KENTUCKY. [Annual]

L 2.121/18:CT/date　　　• Item 768-B-18 (EL)
OCCUPATIONAL COMPENSATION SURVEY: PAY AND
BENEFITS, LOUISIANA. [Annual]

L 2.121/19:CT/date　　　• Item 768-B-19 (EL)
OCCUPATIONAL COMPENSATION SURVEY: PAY AND
BENEFITS, MAINE. [Annual]

L 2.121/20:CT/date　　　• Item 768-B-20 (EL)
OCCUPATIONAL COMPENSATION SURVEY: PAY AND
BENEFITS, MARYLAND. [Annual]

L 2.121/21:CT/date　　　• Item 768-B-21 (EL)
OCCUPATIONAL COMPENSATION SURVEY: PAY AND
BENEFITS, MASSACHUSETTS. [Annual]

L 2.121/22:CT/date　　　• Item 768-B-22 (EL)
OCCUPATIONAL COMPENSATION SURVEY: PAY AND
BENEFITS, MICHIGAN. [Annual]

L 2.121/23:CT/date　　　• Item 768-B-23 (EL)
OCCUPATIONAL COMPENSATION SURVEY: PAY AND
BENEFITS, MINNESOTA. [Annual]

L 2.121/24:CT/date　　　• Item 768-B-24 (EL)
OCCUPATIONAL COMPENSATION SURVEY: PAY AND
BENEFITS, MISSISSIPPI. [Annual]

L 2.121/25:CT/date　　　• Item 768-B-25 (EL)
OCCUPATIONAL COMPENSATION SURVEY: PAY AND
BENEFITS, MISSOURI. [Annual]

L 2.121/26:CT/date　　　• Item 768-B-26 (EL)
OCCUPATIONAL COMPENSATION SURVEY: PAY AND
BENEFITS, MONTANA. [Annual]

L 2.121/27:CT/date　　　• Item 768-B-27 (EL)
OCCUPATIONAL COMPENSATION SURVEY: PAY AND
BENEFITS, NEBRASKA. [Annual]

L 2.121/28:CT/date　　　• Item 768-B-28 (EL)
OCCUPATIONAL COMPENSATION SURVEY: PAY AND
BENEFITS, NEVADA. [Annual]

L 2.121/29:CT/date　　　• Item 768-B-29 (EL)
OCCUPATIONAL COMPENSATION SURVEY: PAY AND
BENEFITS, NEW HAMPSHIRE. [Annual]

L 2.121/30:CT/date　　　• Item 768-B-30 (EL)
OCCUPATIONAL COMPENSATION SURVEY: PAY AND
BENEFITS, NEW JERSEY. [Annual]

L 2.121/31:CT/date　　　• Item 768-B-31 (EL)
OCCUPATIONAL COMPENSATION SURVEY: PAY AND
BENEFITS, NEW MEXICO. [Annual]

L 2.121/32:CT/date　　　• Item 768-B-32 (EL)
OCCUPATIONAL COMPENSATION SURVEY: PAY AND
BENEFITS, NEW YORK. [Annual]

L 2.121/33:CT/date　　　• Item 768-B-33 (EL)
OCCUPATIONAL COMPENSATION SURVEY: PAY AND
BENEFITS, NORTH CAROLINA. [Annual]

L 2.121/34:CT/date　　　• Item 768-B-34 (EL)
OCCUPATIONAL COMPENSATION SURVEY: PAY AND
BENEFITS, NORTH DAKOTA. [Annual]

L 2.121/35:CT/date　　　• Item 768-B-35 (EL)
OCCUPATIONAL COMPENSATION SURVEY: PAY AND
BENEFITS, OHIO. [Annual]

L 2.121/36:CT/date　　　• Item 768-B-36 (EL)
OCCUPATIONAL COMPENSATION SURVEY: PAY AND
BENEFITS, OKLAHOMA. [Annual]

L 2.121/37:CT/date　　　• Item 768-B-37 (EL)
OCCUPATIONAL COMPENSATION SURVEY: PAY AND
BENEFITS, OREGON. [Annual]

L 2.121/38:CT/date　　　• Item 768-B-38 (EL)
OCCUPATIONAL COMPENSATION SURVEY: PAY AND
BENEFITS, PENNSYLVANIA. [Annual]

L 2.121/39:CT/date　　　• Item 768-B-39 (EL)
OCCUPATIONAL COMPENSATION SURVEY: PAY AND
BENEFITS, RHODE ISLAND. [Annual]

L 2.121/40:CT/date　　　• Item 768-B-40 (EL)
OCCUPATIONAL COMPENSATION SURVEY: PAY AND
BENEFITS, SOUTH CAROLINA. [Annual]

L 2.121/41:CT/date　　　• Item 768-B-41 (EL)
OCCUPATIONAL COMPENSATION SURVEY: PAY AND
BENEFITS, SOUTH DAKOTA. [Annual]

L 2.121/42:CT/date　　　• Item 768-B-42 (EL)
OCCUPATIONAL COMPENSATION SURVEY: PAY AND
BENEFITS, TENNESSEE. [Annual]

L 2.121/43:CT/date　　　• Item 768-B-43 (EL)
OCCUPATIONAL COMPENSATION SURVEY: PAY AND
BENEFITS, TEXAS. [Annual]

L 2.121/44:CT/date　　　• Item 768-B-44 (EL)
OCCUPATIONAL COMPENSATION SURVEY: PAY AND
BENEFITS, UTAH. [Annual]

L 2.121/45:CT/date　　　• Item 768-B-45 (EL)
OCCUPATIONAL COMPENSATION SURVEY: PAY AND
BENEFITS, VERMONT. [Annual]

L 2.121/46:CT/date　　　• Item 768-B-46 (EL)
OCCUPATIONAL COMPENSATION SURVEY: PAY AND
BENEFITS, VIRGINIA. [Annual]

L 2.121/47:CT/date　　　• Item 768-B-47 (EL)
OCCUPATIONAL COMPENSATION SURVEY: PAY AND
BENEFITS, WASHINGTON. [Annual]

L 2.121/48:CT/date　　　• Item 768-B-48 (EL)
OCCUPATIONAL COMPENSATION SURVEY: PAY AND
BENEFITS, WEST VIRGINIA. [Annual]

L 2.121/49:CT/date　　　• Item 768-B-49 (EL)
OCCUPATIONAL COMPENSATION SURVEY: PAY AND
BENEFITS, WISCONSIN. [Annual]

L 2.121/50:CT/date　　　• Item 768-B-50 (EL)
OCCUPATIONAL COMPENSATION SURVEY: PAY AND
BENEFITS, WYOMING. [Annual]

L 2.121/51:CT/date　　　• Item 768-B-51 (EL)
OCCUPATIONAL COMPENSATION SURVEY: PAY AND
BENEFITS, DISTRICT OF COLUMBIA. [Annual]

L 2.121/53　　　• Item 768-B-53
OCCUPATIONAL COMPENSATION SURVEY: PAY
ONLY (Outlying Areas), Consolidated Metropoli-
tan Areas.

L 2.121/54:CT/date　　　• Item 768-B-52
OCCUPATIONAL COMPENSATION SURVEY: PAY AND
BENEFITS, SELECTED METROPOLITAN AREAS.
[Annual]

L 2.121/56　　　• Item 768-B-54 (EL)
NATIONAL COMPENSATION SURVEY DIVISIONS.

L 2.121/57　　　• Item 768-B-55 (EL)
NATIONAL COMPENSATION SURVEY BULLETINS,
SUMMARIES, AND SUPPLEMENTAL TABLES FOR
NATIONAL. [Annual]

L 2.122　　　• Item 768-B-1– 52
AREA WAGE SURVEY SUMMARY (Series). [Annual]
　　　Starting in 1989 in order to reduce the number of classes, the Area Wage Surveys have
been reclassified with a class stem for each state
and cutter by city within that state. The first list
below is the earlier classification. The current
system follows.

L 2.122/1:CT/date　　　• Item 768-B-1
OCCUPATIONAL COMPENSATION SURVEY: PAY AND
BENEFITS, ALABAMA (Summary). [Annual]

L 2.122/2:CT/date　　　• Item 768-B-2
OCCUPATIONAL COMPENSATION SURVEY: PAY AND
BENEFITS, ALASKA (Summary). [Annual]

L 2.122/3:CT/date　　　• Item 768-B-3
OCCUPATIONAL COMPENSATION SURVEY: PAY AND
BENEFITS, ARIZONA (Summary). [Annual]

L 2.122/4:CT/date　　　• Item 768-B-4
OCCUPATIONAL COMPENSATION SURVEY: PAY AND
BENEFITS, ARKANSAS (Summary). [Annual]

L 2.122/5:CT/date　　　• Item 768-B-5
OCCUPATIONAL COMPENSATION SURVEY: PAY AND
BENEFITS, CALIFORNIA (Summary). [Annual]

L 2.122/6:CT/date　　　• Item 768-B-6
OCCUPATIONAL COMPENSATION SURVEY: PAY AND
BENEFITS, COLORADO (Summary). [Annual]

L 2.122/7:CT/date　　　• Item 768-B-7
OCCUPATIONAL COMPENSATION SURVEY: PAY AND
BENEFITS, CONNECTICUT (Summary). [Annual]

L 2.122/8:CT/date　　　• Item 768-B-8
OCCUPATIONAL COMPENSATION SURVEY: PAY AND
BENEFITS, DELAWARE (Summary). [Annual]

L 2.122/9:CT/date　　　• Item 768-B-9
OCCUPATIONAL COMPENSATION SURVEY: PAY AND
BENEFITS, FLORIDA (Summary). [Annual]

L 2.122/10:CT/date　　　• Item 768-B-10
OCCUPATIONAL COMPENSATION SURVEY: PAY AND
BENEFITS, GEORGIA (Summary). [Annual]

L 2.122/11:CT/date　　　• Item 768-B-11
OCCUPATIONAL COMPENSATION SURVEY: PAY AND
BENEFITS, HAWAII (Summary). [Annual]

L 2.122/12:CT/date　　　• Item 768-B-12
OCCUPATIONAL COMPENSATION SURVEY: PAY AND
BENEFITS, IDAHO (Summary). [Annual]

L 2.122/13:CT/date　　　• Item 768-B-13
OCCUPATIONAL COMPENSATION SURVEY: PAY AND
BENEFITS, ILLINOIS (Summary). [Annual]

L 2.122/14:CT/date　　　• Item 768-B-14
OCCUPATIONAL COMPENSATION SURVEY: PAY AND
BENEFITS, INDIANA (Summary). [Annual]

L 2.122/15:CT/date　　　• Item 768-B-15
OCCUPATIONAL COMPENSATION SURVEY: PAY AND
BENEFITS, IOWA (Summary). [Annual]

L 2.122/16:CT/date　　　• Item 768-B-16
OCCUPATIONAL COMPENSATION SURVEY: PAY AND
BENEFITS, KANSAS (Summary). [Annual]

L 2.122/17:CT/date　　　• Item 768-B-17
OCCUPATIONAL COMPENSATION SURVEY: PAY AND
BENEFITS, KENTUCKY (Summary). [Annual]

L 2.122/18:CT/date　　　• Item 768-B-18
OCCUPATIONAL COMPENSATION SURVEY: PAY AND
BENEFITS, LOUISIANA (Summary). [Annual]

L 2.122/19:CT/date　　　• Item 768-B-19
OCCUPATIONAL COMPENSATION SURVEY: PAY AND
BENEFITS, MAINE (Summary). [Annual]

L 2.122/20:CT/date   • Item 768-B-20
OCCUPATIONAL COMPENSATION SURVEY: PAY AND
BENEFITS, MARYLAND (Summary). [Annual]

L 2.122/21:CT/date   • Item 768-B-21
OCCUPATIONAL COMPENSATION SURVEY: PAY AND
BENEFITS, MASSACHUSETTS (Summary). [Annual]

L 2.122/22:CT/date   • Item 768-B-22
OCCUPATIONAL COMPENSATION SURVEY: PAY AND
BENEFITS, MICHIGAN (Summary). [Annual]

L 2.122/23:CT/date   • Item 768-B-23
OCCUPATIONAL COMPENSATION SURVEY: PAY AND
BENEFITS, MINNESOTA (Summary). [Annual]

L 2.122/24:CT/date   • Item 768-B-24
OCCUPATIONAL COMPENSATION SURVEY: PAY AND
BENEFITS, MISSISSIPPI (Summary). [Annual]

L 2.122/25:CT/date   • Item 768-B-25
OCCUPATIONAL COMPENSATION SURVEY: PAY AND
BENEFITS, MISSOURI (Summary). [Annual]

L 2.122/26:CT/date   • Item 768-B-26
OCCUPATIONAL COMPENSATION SURVEY: PAY AND
BENEFITS, MONTANA (Summary). [Annual]

L 2.122/27:CT/date   • Item 768-B-27
OCCUPATIONAL COMPENSATION SURVEY: PAY AND
BENEFITS, NEBRASKA (Summary). [Annual]

L 2.122/28:CT/date   • Item 768-B-28
OCCUPATIONAL COMPENSATION SURVEY: PAY AND
BENEFITS, NEVADA (Summary). [Annual]

L 2.122/29:CT/date   • Item 768-B-29
OCCUPATIONAL COMPENSATION SURVEY: PAY AND
BENEFITS, NEW HAMPSHIRE (Summary). [Annual]

L 2.122/30:CT/date   • Item 768-B-30
OCCUPATIONAL COMPENSATION SURVEY: PAY AND
BENEFITS, NEW JERSEY (Summary). [Annual]

L 2.122/31:CT/date   • Item 768-B-31
OCCUPATIONAL COMPENSATION SURVEY: PAY AND
BENEFITS, NEW MEXICO (Summary). [Annual]

L 2.122/32:CT/date   • Item 768-B-32
OCCUPATIONAL COMPENSATION SURVEY: PAY AND
BENEFITS, NEW YORK (Summary). [Annual]

L 2.122/33:CT/date   • Item 768-B-33
OCCUPATIONAL COMPENSATION SURVEY: PAY AND
BENEFITS, NORTH CAROLINA (Summary). [Annual]

L 2.122/34:CT/date   • Item 768-B-34
OCCUPATIONAL COMPENSATION SURVEY: PAY AND
BENEFITS, NORTH DAKOTA (Summary). [Annual]

L 2.122/35:CT/date   • Item 768-B-35
OCCUPATIONAL COMPENSATION SURVEY: PAY AND
BENEFITS, OHIO (Summary). [Annual]

L 2.122/36:CT/date   • Item 768-B-36
OCCUPATIONAL COMPENSATION SURVEY: PAY AND
BENEFITS, OKLAHOMA (Summary). [Annual]

L 2.122/37:CT/date   • Item 768-B-37
OCCUPATIONAL COMPENSATION SURVEY: PAY AND
BENEFITS, OREGON (Summary). [Annual]

L 2.122/38:CT/date   • Item 768-B-38
OCCUPATIONAL COMPENSATION SURVEY: PAY AND
BENEFITS, PENNSYLVANIA (Summary). [Annual]

L 2.122/39:CT/date   • Item 768-B-39
OCCUPATIONAL COMPENSATION SURVEY: PAY AND
BENEFITS, RHODE ISLAND (Summary). [Annual]

L 2.122/40:CT/date   • Item 768-B-40
OCCUPATIONAL COMPENSATION SURVEY: PAY AND
BENEFITS, SOUTH CAROLINA (Summary). [Annual]

L 2.122/41:CT/date   • Item 768-B-41
OCCUPATIONAL COMPENSATION SURVEY: PAY AND
BENEFITS, SOUTH DAKOTA (Summary). [Annual]

L 2.122/42:CT/date   • Item 768-B-42
OCCUPATIONAL COMPENSATION SURVEY: PAY AND
BENEFITS, TENNESSEE (Summary). [Annual]

L 2.122/43:CT/date   • Item 768-B-43
OCCUPATIONAL COMPENSATION SURVEY: PAY AND
BENEFITS, TEXAS (Summary). [Annual]

L 2.122/44:CT/date   • Item 768-B-44
OCCUPATIONAL COMPENSATION SURVEY: PAY AND
BENEFITS, UTAH (Summary). [Annual]

L 2.122/45:CT/date   • Item 768-B-45
OCCUPATIONAL COMPENSATION SURVEY: PAY AND
BENEFITS, VERMONT (Summary). [Annual]

L 2.122/46:CT/date   • Item 768-B-46
OCCUPATIONAL COMPENSATION SURVEY: PAY AND
BENEFITS, VIRGINIA (Summary). [Annual]

L 2.122/47:CT/date   • Item 768-B-47
OCCUPATIONAL COMPENSATION SURVEY: PAY AND
BENEFITS, WASHINGTON (Summary). [Annual]

L 2.122/48:CT/date   • Item 768-B-48
OCCUPATIONAL COMPENSATION SURVEY: PAY AND
BENEFITS, WEST VIRGINIA (Summary). [Annual]

L 2.122/49:CT/date   • Item 768-B-49
OCCUPATIONAL COMPENSATION SURVEY: PAY AND
BENEFITS, WISCONSIN (Summary). [Annual]

L 2.122/50:CT/date   • Item 768-B-50
OCCUPATIONAL COMPENSATION SURVEY: PAY AND
BENEFITS, WYOMING (Summary). [Annual]

L 2.122/51:CT/date   • Item 768-B-51
OCCUPATIONAL COMPENSATION SURVEY: PAY AND
BENEFITS, DISTRICT OF COLUMBIA (Summary).
[Annual]

L 2.122/53:CT/date   • Item 768-B-53
OCCUPATIONAL COMPENSATION SURVEY: PAY AND
BENEFITS, OUTLYING AREAS (Summary). [Annual]

L 2.122/54   • Item 768-G-1
OCCUPATIONAL COMPENSATION SURVEY: PAY AND
BENEFITS, STATE AND LOCAL GOVERNMENT, .
. . METROPOLITAN AREA (SUMMARIES).

Earlier title: Area Wage Survey, Selected Metropolitan Areas (Summary).

L 2.123/1–50   • Item 768-B-1– 50
MOVING AND STORAGE WAGE SURVEY SUMMARY
(series). [Annual]

L 2.123/1   • Item 768-B-1
MOBILE-PENSACOLA-PANAMA CITY, ALABAMA-
FLORIDA.

L 2.123/5   • Item 768-B-5
SAN FRANCISCO-OAKLAND, CALIFORNIA.

L 2.123/24   • Item 768-B-24
BILOXI-GULFPORT AND PASCAGOULA-MOSS
POINT, MISSISSIPPI.

L 2.123/30   • Item 768-B-30
PATERSON-CLIFTON-PASSAIC, NEW JERSEY.

L 2.124:date   • Item 768-G
SERIES AVAILABLE AND ESTIMATING METHODS,
BLS NATIONAL PAYROLL EMPLOYMENT PRO-
GRAM. [Annual]

Tabular presentation of the characteristics of
the National Employment, Hours, and Earnings
series published in Current Employment Statistics (L 2.71).

L 2.124/2:date   • Item 768-G-1
SERIES AVAILABLE AND ESTIMATING METHODS,
BLS CURRENT EMPLOYMENT STATISTICS PRO-
GRAM. [Annual]

L 2.125:date   • Item 768-G (MF)
MAJOR PROGRAMS, BUREAU OF LABOR STATIS-
TICS. [Annual]

Earlier L 2.71

L 2.126:date   • Item 769-M (P) (EL)
USUAL WEEKLY EARNINGS OF WAGE AND SAL-
ARY WORKERS. [Quarterly]

PURPOSE:– To present estimated median
weekly earnings of full-time and part-time U.S.
workers in such categories as race, age, and
sex.
Earlier: Weekly Earnings of Wage and Salary
Workers.

L 2.127:CT   • Item 769-N
FORMS. [Irregular]

L 2.128:date   • Item 769-S (MF)
INTERNATIONAL TRAINING PROGRAMS IN LABOR
STATISTICS. [Annual]

PURPOSE– To describe scheduled training
programs, giving seminar title, dates, participants,
objectives, and program content.

L 2.129:   • Item 769-T (MF)
RECORDKEEPING REQUIREMENTS FOR FIRMS
SELECTED TO PARTICIPATE IN THE ANNUAL
SURVEY OF OCCUPATIONAL INJURIES AND ILL-
NESSES. [Annual]

PURPOSE– To explain the requirements of
the Occupational Safety and Health Act of 1970
and Title 29 of the CFR, Part 1904, which requires
employers to prepare and maintain records of
occupational injuries and illnesses.

L 2.130:   • Item 768-G-2 (MF) (EL)
INTERNATIONAL COMPARISONS OF HOURLY
COMPENSATION COSTS FOR PRODUCTION
WORKERS IN MANUFACTURING. [3 times a year]

PURPOSE– To present highlights of preliminary measures of comparative levels and trends
in hourly compensation costs for production workers in manufacturing in various countries or areas.

L 2.131:date-nos.   • Item 768-E
BLS UPDATE. [Irregular]

L 2.132:date-nos.   • Item 768-E
ISSUES IN LABOR STATISTICS.

L 2.133   • Item 769-S
DESCRIPTION OF OUTPUT INDICATORS BY FUNC-
TION FOR THE FEDERAL GOVERNMENT, FISCAL
YEAR.

L 2.134   • Item 744-G-3 (E)
ELECTRONIC PRODUCTS. [Irregular]

L 2.135:nos.   • Item 769-A-1
NLS NEWS, NATIONAL LONGITUDINAL SURVEYS.

L 2.136:CT   • Item 769-A-2 (P) (EL)
BUREAU OF LABOR STATISTICS SURVEYS.

BUREAU OF IMMIGRATION
(1913– 1933)

CREATION AND AUTHORITY

The Bureau of Immigration and Naturalization
(C 7) was transferred from the Department of Commerce and Labor to the newly created Department of Labor and separated into two Bureaus (L
3 and L 6) by act of Congress approved March 4,
1913 (37 Stat. 736). Executive Order 6166 of
June 10, 1933 consolidated the two Bureaus into
the Immigration and Naturalization Service (L 15).

L 3.1:date
ANNUAL REPORTS.

Earlier C 7.1
Later L 15.1

L 3.2:CT
GENERAL PUBLICATIONS.

　　Earlier C 7.2

L 3.3
BULLETINS.

L 3.4
CIRCULARS.

　　Earlier C 7.4

L 3.5:date
IMMIGRATION LAWS AND REGULATIONS.

　　Earlier C 7.6
　　Later L 15.5/2

Information Division

L 3.6/1:date
ANNUAL REPORTS.

　　Earlier C 7.11

L 3.6/2:CT
GENERAL PUBLICATIONS.

L 3.6/5:nos.
AGRICULTURAL OPPORTUNITIES.

　　Earlier C 7.11/5

Bureau of Immigration (Continued)

L 3.7:date
TREATY, LAWS AND RULES GOVERNING ADMISSION OF CHINESE.

　　Earlier C 7.5
　　Later L 15.12

L 3.8:nos.
GENERAL ORDERS.

　　Later L 15.9

L 3.9:date
ANALYSIS OF STATISTICS. [Monthly]

DIVISION OF PUBLICATIONS AND SUPPLIES
(1913– 1948)

L 4.1:date
ANNUAL REPORTS.

L 4.2:CT
GENERAL PUBLICATIONS.

L 4.3
BULLETINS.

L 4.4
CIRCULARS.

L 4.5:date
LISTS OF PUBLICATIONS.

CHILDREN'S BUREAU
(1913– 1946)

CREATION AND AUTHORITY

　　The Children's Bureau (C 19) was transferred from the Department of Commerce and Labor to the newly created Department of Labor by act of Congress, approved March 4, 1913 (37 Stat. 736). The Bureau was transferred to the Federal Security Agency (FS 3.200) under the Social Security Administration by Reorganization Plan No. 2 of 1946.

L 5.1:date
ANNUAL REPORTS.
　　Earlier C 19.1
　　Later FS 3.201

L 5.2:CT
GENERAL PUBLICATIONS.
　　Earlier C 19.2
　　Later FS 3.202

L 5.3
BULLETINS.

L 5.4
CIRCULARS.

L 5.5
INFANT MORTALITY SERIES.

L 5.6
CARE OF CHILDREN SERIES.

L 5.7
DEPENDENT CHILDREN SERIES.

L 5.8
MONOGRAPHS.

　　Earlier C 19.5

L 5.9:nos.
INDUSTRIAL SERIES.

L 5.10:nos.
CHILD LABOR DIVISION, CIRCULARS.

L 5.11:nos.
RURAL CHILD WELFARE SERIES.

L 5.12:nos.
CHILDREN'S YEAR LEAFLETS.

L 5.13:nos.
LEGAL SERIES.

L 5.14:CT
POSTERS.
　　Later FS 3.221

L 5.15:nos.
CHILDREN'S YEAR FOLLOW-UP SERIES.

L 5.16:nos.
CONFERENCE SERIES.

L 5.17:nos.
DODGERS.

L 5.18:nos.
COMMUNITY CHILD-WELFARE SERIES.

L 5.19:nos.
CHARTS, MISCELLANEOUS.

L 5.19/2:CT
CHARTS, MISCELLANEOUS.

L 5.20:nos.
BUREAU PUBLICATIONS (numbered).
　　Later FS 3.209

L 5.21:nos.
LEGAL CHARTS.

L 5.22:nos.
FOLDERS.
　　Later FS 3.210

L 5.23:v.nos.
CHILD WELFARE NEWS SUMMARY. [Irregular]

L 5.24:date
PUBLICATIONS (lists of).
　　Later FS 3.213

L 5.25:nos.
STATISTICAL CARDS.

L 5.26:nos.
LESSON MATERIAL ON CARE OF PRE-SCHOOL CHILD.

L 5.27:form.nos.
SOCIAL STATISTICS IN CHILD WELFARE AND RELATED FIELDS.

L 5.28:date
MONTHLY EXPENDITURES FOR FAMILY RELIEF. [Quarterly]

L 5.29:vol.
MONTHLY RELIEF BULLETIN.
　　See L 5.32

L 5.30:date
MONTHLY MEMORANDUM FOR COOPERATING AGENCIES.

L 5.31:vol.
NEWS BULLETIN ON SOCIAL STATISTICS IN CHILD WELFARE AND RELATED FIELDS. [Monthly]
　　See L 5.32

L 5.32:vol.
MONTHLY BULLETIN ON SOCIAL STATISTICS.
　　Earlier L 5.29 and L 5.31.
　　Later L 5.36

L 5.33:date
CHANGES IN DIFFERENT TYPES OF PUBLIC AND PRIVATE RELIEF IN URBAN AREAS. [Monthly]
　　Later SS 1.10

L 5.34
MATERNAL AND CHILD WELFARE BULLETINS.

L 5.35:vol.
THE CHILD, MONTHLY NEWS SUMMARY.
　　Earlier L 5.23
　　Later FS 3.207

L 5.36:nos.
SOCIAL STATISTICS.

L 5.37:letters-nos.
TREND TABLES.

L 5.38:nos.
CHILD LABOR REGULATIONS, REGULATIONS.

L 5.39:nos.
CHILD LABOR REGULATIONS, ORDERS.

L 5.40:CT
LISTS OF REFERENCES.

L 5.41:nos.
DEFENSE OF CHILDREN SERIES.

L 5.42:nos.
RAISING A PRESIDENT. [Weekly]

　　Radio scripts.

L 5.43:nos.
CHILDREN IN WARTIME. [Weekly]

　　Radio scripts.

L 5.44:nos.
CHILDREN IN WARTIME. [Weekly]

　　Radio scripts.

L 5.45:nos.
WHICH JOBS FOR YOUNG WORKERS?

L 5.46:nos.
EMIC INFORMATION CIRCULARS.

L 5.47:CT
ADDRESSES.

L 5.48:CT
REGULATIONS, RULES, AND INSTRUCTIONS.

L 5.49:nos.
OUR NATION'S CHILDREN. [Bimonthly]

    Later FS 3.212

L 5.50:date
PRELIMINARY MONTHLY STATISTICAL REPORT ON
    EMIC PROGRAM.

    Later FS 3.208.

L 5.51:nos.
CHILD GUIDANCE LEAFLETS, SERIES ON EATING,
    FOR PARENTS.

    Later FS 3.211

L 5.51/2:nos.
CHILD GUIDANCE LEAFLETS, SERIES ON EATING,
    FOR STAFF.

L 5.52:nos.
CHILD WELFARE REPORTS.

    Later FS 3.215

BUREAU OF NATURALIZATION
(1913–1933)

CREATION AND AUTHORITY

    The Bureau of Immigration and Naturalization
(C 7) was transferred from the Department of Commerce and Labor to the newly created Department of Labor and separated into two Bureaus (L
3 and L 6) by act of Congress approved March 4,
1913 (37 Stat. 736). Executive Order 6166 of
June 10, 1933 consolidated the two Bureaus into
the Immigration and Naturalization Service (L 15)

L 6.1:date
ANNUAL REPORTS.

    Earlier C 7.10/1
    Later L 15.1

L 6.2:CT
GENERAL PUBLICATIONS.

    Earlier C 7.10/2

L 6.3:nos.
BULLETINS.

    Earlier C 7.10/3

L 6.4:nos.
CIRCULARS.

L 6.5:date
NATURALIZATION LAWS AND REGULATIONS.
    Earlier C 7.10/5

L 6.6:CT
COURT DECISIONS.

Citizenship Training Division

L 6.7/1:date
ANNUAL REPORTS.

L 6.7/2:CT
GENERAL PUBLICATIONS.

L 6.7/3
BULLETINS.

L 6.7/4
CIRCULARS.

L 6.7/5:CT
TEXTBOOKS AND MANUALS.

    Earlier L 6.7

Bureau of Naturalization (Continued)

L 6.8:CT
POSTERS.

L 6.9:nos.
GENERAL ORDERS.

    Later L 15.9

L 6.10:nos.
INSTRUCTIONS TO CLERKS OF COURTS EXER-
CISING NATURALIZATION JURISDICTION.

BUREAU OF EMPLOYMENT
SECURITY
(1949–1969)

CREATION AND AUTHORITY

    The United States Employment Service was
established within the Department of Labor by
Secretary's memorandum dated January 3, 1918.
On August 19, 1939, the Service merged with the
Bureau of Unemployment Compensation of the
Social Security Board (SS 1) to form the Bureau
of Employment Security as part of the Social
Security Administration (FS 3.100). The Bureau
was transferred back to the Department of Labor
(L 7) by Reorganization Plan No. 2 of 1949, effective August 20, 1949. The Bureau was abolished
by Secretary's order of March 14, 1969 and its
functions transferred to the Manpower Administration (L 1.39) in the Department of Labor.

L 7.1:date
ANNUAL REPORTS.

L 7.2:CT
GENERAL PUBLICATIONS.

L 7.2:D 62/9
DIRECTORY OF IMPORTANT LABOR AREAS.
[Irregular]

    PURPOSE:– To furnish information on
geographic boundaries of labor areas regularly classified by the Bureau of Employment
Security according to labor supply.
    Part 1 lists and defines the individual
areas in terms of countries and minor civil
subdivisions covered by the official U.S.
Employment Service's labor area definitions.
Part 2 lists alphabetically, by State, all counties, or parts of counties, included in any
area officially classified according to relative
adequacy of labor supply since July 1951.
    The directory may be used to find the
geographical boundaries of specific labor areas, the labor area covering a specific locality, or the labor supply classification for an
individual community if used in conjunction
with a current issue of "Area Trends in Employment and Unemployment."
    Issued in looseleaf form, punched for
ring binder. Latest edition: 6th ed. Oct 1, 1967.
Kept up-to-date by supplements issued from
time to time.

L 7.2:Oc 1   **• Item 755**
DICTIONARY OF OCCUPATIONAL TITLES.
    [Irregular]

    The following Supplements have also
been published.
    "Selected Characteristics of Occupations"
1966
    "Suffix Codes for Jobs Defined in Dictio-
nary of Occupational Titles." 1967
    Later L 37.302:Oc 1

L 7.3:v.nos.
BULLETINS.

L 7.3/2:nos.
BULLETINS.

L 7.3/3:nos.
BULLETINS (printed).

L 7.4
CIRCULARS.

L 7.5:v.nos.
BOY POWER.

L 7.6:CT
DESCRIPTIONS OF OCCUPATIONS.
    Later L 2.7
L 7.7:CT
POSTERS.

L 7.8:date
INDUSTRIAL EMPLOYMENT INFORMATION BULLE-
    TIN.

    L 7.8/a:CT
    – SEPARATES.

L 7.9:nos.
JUNIOR DIVISION NEWS-LETTER. [Bimonthly]

L 7.10:nos.
FIELD WORK SERIES.

L 7.11:date
MONTHLY REPORT OF ACTIVITIES.

Farm Labor Division

L 7.12/1:date
ANNUAL REPORTS.

L 7.12/2:CT
GENERAL PUBLICATIONS.

L 7.12/3:nos.
BULLETINS.

L 7.12/4:nos.
CIRCULARS.

Bureau of Employment Security
(Continued)

L 7.13:CT
NATIONAL EMPLOYMENT SERVICE (publications).

L 7.14:vol.
EMPLOYMENT SERVICE NEWS. [Monthly]

    Later FS 3.107

    L 7.14/a:CT
    – SEPARATES.
        Later FS 3.107/a

L 7.15:nos.
EMPLOYMENT OFFICE MANUAL SERIES (lettered).

L 7.15/2:letters
EMPLOYMENT OFFICE MANUAL SERIES (lettered).

L 7.16:CT
JOB SPECIFICATIONS.

L 7.17:CT
HANDBOOK OF DESCRIPTIONS OF SPECIALIZED
    FIELDS.
    Earlier Pr 32.5227

L 7.18:v.nos.
EMPLOYMENT SERVICE REVIEW. [Monthly]

Earlier Pr 32.5209
Later L 7.18/2, L 7.18/3

L 7.18/2:v.nos.&nos.
EMPLOYMENT SERVICE REVIEW. [Monthly]

Earlier L 7.18

L 7.18/2-2:date
EMPLOYMENT SERVICE STATISTICS, SUPPLEMENT TO EMPLOYMENT SERVICE REVIEW.

L 7.18/3:v.nos.&nos.
UNEMPLOYMENT INSURANCE REVIEW.

Supersedes L 7.18 and L 7.20

L 7.18/4:date
UNEMPLOYMENT INSURANCE STATISTICS. [Monthly]

L 7.19:date
CLASSIFICATION OF IMPORTANT LABOR MARKET AREAS. [Monthly]

L 7.19/2:date
CLASSIFICATION OF LABOR MARKET AREAS ACCORDING TO RELATIVE ADEQUACY OF LABOR SUPPLY. [Bimonthly]

Earlier L 7.2:C 56

L 7.19/2-2:date
EMPLOYMENT SERVICE STATISTICS. [Monthly]

Later L 1.60

L 7.20:date
LABOR MARKET. [Monthly]

Earlier Pr 32.5211
Later L 7.18/3

L 7.20/a:CT
– SEPARATES.

L 7.20/2:date
STATISTICAL SUPPLEMENT, LABOR MARKET AND EMPLOYMENT SECURITY. [Monthly]

L 7.20/3 • Item 754-B
EMPLOYMENT AND WAGES OF WORKERS COVERED BY STATE UNEMPLOYMENT INSURANCE LAWS AND UNEMPLOYMENT COMPENSATION FOR FEDERAL EMPLOYEES, BY INDUSTRY AND STATE. 1938– [Quarterly]

PURPOSE:– To furnish statistical data on employment and wages of workers covered by State unemployment insurance laws and by the program for Unemployment Compensation for Federal Employees.

L 7.20/4:date
FEDERAL CIVILIAN EMPLOYMENT AND WAGES OF WORKERS COVERED BY UNEMPLOYMENT COMPENSATION FOR FEDERAL EMPLOYEES, BY AGENCY, INDUSTRY AND STATE, SPECIAL ISSUE OF STATISTICAL SUPPLEMENT TO LABOR MARKET AND EMPLOYMENT SECURITY.

L 7.21:CT
NATIONAL ROSTER OF SCIENTIFIC AND SPECIALIZED PERSONNEL, MONOGRAPHS.

Earlier Pr 32.5219

L 7.22:date
LABOR MARKET INFORMATION AREA SERIES; BASIC STATEMENTS.

L 7.22/2:date
LABOR MARKET INFORMATION AREA SERIES, CURRENT SUPPLEMENTS. [Monthly]

Later FS 3.132

L 7.23:nos.
LABOR MARKET INFORMATION FOR USES COUNSELING: INDUSTRY SERIES.

Earlier Pr 32.5229
Later FS 3.131/2

L 7.23/2:date
– CURRENT SUPPLEMENTS. [Monthly]

Later FS 3.131

L 7.23/3:date
LABOR MARKET INFORMATION SERIES [compilations].

L 7.24:nos.
VOCATIONAL BOOKLETS.

L 7.25:CT
REGULATIONS, RULES, AND INSTRUCTIONS.

L 7.25/2:date
JOB GUIDE FOR YOUNG WORKERS. [Biennial]

Earlier L 7.2 J 57/4

L 7.25/3:CT
HANDBOOKS, MANUALS, GUIDES.

Earlier L 7.2, L 7.25

L 7.25/4 • Item 756-B
HANDBOOK SERIES. 1– 1963– [Irregular]

L 7.26:nos.
NATIONAL PHYSICAL DEMANDS INFORMATION SERIES.

L 7.27:CT
OCCUPATIONAL COMPOSITION PATTERNS.

L 7.28:unit nos.
EMPLOYMENT OFFICE TRAINING PROGRAM.

Earlier Pr 32.5220

L 7.29:date
VETERANS EMPLOYMENT NEWS. [Monthly]

L 7.30:nos.
VETERANS EMPLOYMENT SERVICE HANDBOOKS.

L 7.30/2 • Item 756-D
EMPLOYMENT SERVICES FOR VETERANS, ANNUAL REPORT. [Annual]

PURPOSE:– To describe services available to veterans through the public employment service and to promote the employment of veterans by employers.

L 7.31:nos.
DESCRIPTION OF PROFESSIONS SERIES, PAMPHLETS.

L 7.32:CT
OCCUPATIONAL GUIDE SERIES; JOB DESCRIPTIONS.

Later FS 3.133

L 7.32/2:CT
OCCUPATIONAL GUIDE SERIES; LABOR MARKET INFORMATION.

Later FS 3.133/2

L 7.33
ADDRESSES. [Irregular]

L 7.34:letters-nos.
JOB FAMILY SERIES.

Earlier Pr 32.5212

L 7.35:CT
LAWS.

L 7.36:nos.
REPORTS AND ANALYSIS HANDBOOK SERIES.

L 7.37 • Item 752
BENEFIT SERIES SERVICE, UNEMPLOYMENT INSURANCE REPORT. 1– 1950– [Monthly]

PURPOSE:– To bring together in one place in an organized way reference material useful to persons making nonmonetary determinations and those working on appeals.
Contains significant administrative and court decisions from the States that set forth new principles or new fact situations.
Issued in loose-leaf form with the necessary dividers.

L 7.38:v.nos.
INSURED UNEMPLOYMENT. [Weekly]

Earlier FS 3.128

L 7.38/2:date
INSURED UNEMPLOYED, PERSONAL AND ECONOMIC CHARACTERISTICS. [Monthly]

L 7.39:v.nos.
UNEMPLOYMENT INSURANCE CLAIMS. [Weekly]

Earlier FS 3.114

L 7.39/2:date
SIGNIFICANT PROVISIONS OF STATE UNEMPLOYMENT INSURANCE LAWS. [Annual]

Later L 33.10

L 7.40:v.nos.&nos.
EMPLOYMENT SECURITY ACTIVITIES. [Monthly]

Earlier FS 3.114

L 7.41
PRESS RELEASES. [Irregular]

L 7.42:date
TIME DISTRIBUTION SUMMARY. [Quarterly]

L 7.43
PRELIMINARY DATA ON UNEMPLOYMENT INSURANCE. [Monthly]

L 7.44
MANUAL TRANSMITTAL LETTER.

L 7.45
ADMINISTRATIVE REVIEW OUTLINE.

L 7.46
INSTRUCTOR'S WORK KIT.

L 7.47
BI-MONTHLY REPORT OF ACTIVITIES (Counseling, Selective Placement and Testing Division).

L 7.48
INTERSTATE APPEALS HANDBOOK.

L 7.49 • Item 756-E
INDUSTRY MANPOWERS SURVEYS. 1– [Irregular]

Presents analyses of manpower developments, current situation, and outlook with respect to the major industries of the country. They are based primarily upon establishment manpower information collected by local offices of the State agencies affiliated with the United States Employment Service, supplemented by information from other sources.
Each Survey is on a separate industry. Some industries have been surveyed more than once, with industries such as blast furnaces, steel works, and rolling mills surveyed almost annually.

L 7.50
UNEMPLOYMENT INSURANCE PROGRAM LETTERS.

L 7.51:date
BIMONTHLY SUMMARY OF LABOR MARKET DEVELOPMENTS IN MAJOR AREAS.

L 7.51/2
AREA CLASSIFICATION SUMMARY. [Bimonthly]

L 7.51/3 • Item 752-C
AREA TRENDS IN EMPLOYMENT AND UNEMPLOY-
MENT. [Monthly]

Prepared from area labor market reports from
State and local employment security offices affiliated with the Bureau of Employment Security.
As part of its area labor marketing program,
the Bureau of Employment Security rates or "clas-
sifies" 150 major production and employment centers, and a number of small areas, according to
the adequacy of their labor supply.
Presents a national round-up of area labor
market developments and outlook and separate
brief summaries for selected areas. Statistical
Supplement gives unemployment in major areas,
including work force, total employment and unemployment in 150 major employment centers.
Supersedes "Bimonthly Summary of Labor
Market Developments in Major Areas" (L 7.51)
and "Area Classification Summary" (L 7.51/2).
Previous title: "Area Labor Market Trends."

L 7.52
INTERVIEWING AID.

L 7.53
PHYSICAL CAPACITIES INFORMATION OUTLINE.

L 7.61 • Item 756-A
INTERVIEWING GUIDES FOR SPECIFIC DISABILI-
TIES. [Irregular]

PURPOSE:– To acquaint counselors with the
nature of disabilities and to assist him in understanding the medical and psychological aspects
of such disabilities.

L 7.55 • Item 754-A
FARM LABOR DEVELOPMENTS. 1954– [Monthly
(May-December)]

Presents for each month during the active
agricultural season (usually May-December) employment and the demand and supply situation
with respect to seasonal farm workers. Information is based primarily on farm labor reports submitted by affiliated State employment security
agencies. Theses reports on local areas are summarized on a national basis and by geographic
divisions.
Former title: "Farm Labor Market Developments."

L 7.55/2:date
EMPLOYMENT AND WAGE SUPPLEMENT, FARM
LABOR MARKET DEVELOPMENTS. [Monthly
(May– December)]

L 7.55/2-2:date
WAGE RATES IN SELECTED FARM ACTIVITIES.

Issued Monthly during active agricultural season.

L 7.55/3:nos.
FARM LABOR NEWSLETTERS.

L 7.56
EMPLOYMENT SECURITY EXCHANGE SERIES.

L 7.56/2:nos.
EMPLOYMENT SECURITY RESEARCH AND REPORT-
ING EXCHANGE SERIES. [Irregular]

L 7.56/3
EMPLOYMENT SECURITY RESEARCH EXCHANGE.
1– 1958– [Semiannual]

PURPOSE:– To serve as a clearinghouse for
information on the research, reporting, and labor
market information activities of the affiliated State
employment security agencies. It gives recognition to the research programs, focuses attention
on new and improved procedures and techniques,
and indicates trends in subject matter areas. It is
based on semiannual reports received from the
State agencies in April and October.
Covers research projects which, as of the
date of the State report, were recently completed,
in progress, or definitely planned.

L 7.57
BI-MONTHLY REPORT OF ACTIVITIES.

L 7.58
FOREIGN LABOR INTERPRETATION SERIES.

L 7.59:date
SELECTED AGRICULTURAL ACTIVITIES OF PUBLIC
EMPLOYMENT OFFICES. [Monthly]

L 7.60:date
KEY FACTS, EMPLOYMENT SECURITY OPERATIONS.
[Quarterly with monthly supplements]

L 7.61 • Item 752-B
BES (series). 1– [Irregular]

Includes handbooks, bibliographies, compilations of State laws, etc.
Publications in this series are numbered consecutively with letter prefixes designating the
office which prepared the publication. Those prefixes in use are.

E– U.S. Employment Service
ES–
R– Office of Program Review and Analy-
sis
U– Unemployment Insurance Service

L 7.62:CT
MAPS AND CHARTS.

L 7.63:date
LOCAL SHORTAGES IN SELECTED SCIENTIFIC AND
ENGINEERING OCCUPATIONS. [Bimonthly]

Earlier L 7.2:Sci 2

L 7.63/2 • Item 752-F
CURRENT EMPLOYMENT MARKET FOR ENGINEERS,
SCIENTISTS, AND TECHNICIANS. 1958– [Semi-
annual]

Presents an appraisal of trends in labor supply and demand for engineering, scientific, and
technical occupations in the major labor areas.
Previous title: "Current Labor Market Conditions in Engineering, Scientific, and Technical Occupations."

L 7.64:date
UNEMPLOYMENT IN MAJOR AREAS. [Bimonthly]

L 7.65:date
DEPARTMENT OF COMMERCE LIST OF CURRENTLY
ESSENTIAL ACTIVITIES, DEPARTMENT OF LA-
BOR LIST OF CURRENTLY CRITICAL OCCUPA-
TION.

Earlier C 1.2:Ac 8/3 and L 7.2:Oc 1/5

L 7.66:nos.
MANPOWER DEVELOPMENT PROGRAM HIGH-
LIGHTS. ADMINISTRATIVE.

L 7.66/2:CT
AREA REDEVELOPMENT MANPOWER REPORTS.

L 7.67:CT
BIBLIOGRAPHIES AND LISTS OF PUBLICATIONS.

L 7.68:date
DIRECTORY OF LOCAL EMPLOYMENT SECURITY
OFFICES. [Annual]

L 7.69:nos.
UNITED STATES EMPLOYMENT SERVICE TEST RE-
SEARCH REPORTS.

L 7.70:date
UNEMPLOYMENT INSURANCE TAX RATES BY
INDUSTRY. [Annual]

Earlier L 7.61:U-258

L 7.71
PROGRAM INFORMATION EXCHANGE. [Admin.]

L 7.72:nos.
MA/BES. [Admin.] (series)

L 7.73:nos.
SCHEDULE C PRECERTIFICATION LIST (numbered).

HOUSING CORPORATION
(1918– 1937)

CREATION AND AUTHORITY

The United States Housing Corporation was
established within the Bureau of Industrial Housing and Transportation of the Department of Labor on July 9, 1918, by the Secretary of Labor
pursuant to a directive of the President and the
acts of Congress, approved May 16 and June 4,
1918. The Corporation was transferred to the Procurement Division (T 58) of the Treasury Department by Executive Order 7841 of June 22, 1937.

L 8.1:date
ANNUAL REPORTS.

L 8.2:CT
GENERAL PUBLICATIONS.

L 8.3
BULLETINS.

L 8.4
CIRCULARS.

INFORMATION AND EDUCATION
SERVICE
(1918– 1919)

CREATION AND AUTHORITY

The Information and Education Service was
established within the War Labor Administration
of the Department of Labor on July 1, 1918. The
Service was terminated on June 30, 1919.

L 9.1:date
ANNUAL REPORTS.

L 9.2:CT
GENERAL PUBLICATIONS.

L 9.3
BULLETINS.

L 9.4
CIRCULARS.

L 9.5:nos. or CT
POSTERS.

NATIONAL WAR LABOR BOARD
(1918– 1919)

CREATION AND AUTHORITY

The National War Labor Board was estab-lished within the War Labor Administration of the Department of Labor on March 29, 1918, by the Secretary of Labor, and confirmed by the Presi-dent on April 8, 1918. The Board was formally dissolved on August 12, 1919.

L 10.1:date
ANNUAL REPORTS.

L 10.2:CT
GENERAL PUBLICATIONS.

L 10.3
BULLETINS.

L 10.4
CIRCULARS.

L 10.5:CT
FINDINGS.

WAR LABOR POLICIES BOARD
(1918– 1919)

CREATION AND AUTHORITY

The War Labor Policies Board was estab-lished within the War Labor Administration by the Secretary of Labor on May 13, 1918. The Board was discontinued in March 1919.

L 11.1:date
ANNUAL REPORTS.

L 11.2:CT
GENERAL PUBLICATIONS.

L 11.3
BULLETINS.

L 11.4
CIRCULARS.

TRAINING SERVICE
(1918– 1919)

CREATION AND AUTHORITY

The Training and Dilution Service, also known as the Training Service, was established within the War Labor Administration of the Department of Labor on July 16, 1918. The Service was termi-nated on July 30, 1919.

L 12.1:date
ANNUAL REPORTS.

L 12.2:CT
GENERAL PUBLICATIONS.

L 12.3:nos.
TRAINING BULLETINS.

L 12.4
CIRCULARS.

WOMEN'S BUREAU
(1920– 1971)

CREATION AND AUTHORITY

The Women's Bureau was established within the Department of Labor by act of Congress, approved June 5, 1920 (41 Stat. 987). Under Secretary's Order 13-71, effective April 28, 1971, the Bureau was transferred to the newly estab-lished Employment Standards Administration (L 36.100).

L 13.1:date
ANNUAL REPORTS.

See L 36.101

L 13.2:CT
GENERAL PUBLICATIONS.

See L 36.102

L 13.3   • Item 781
BULLETINS. 1–   1919–   [Irregular]

Popular guides on employment opportunities in various occupations and professions, social work, responsibilities of women workers, employ-ment of older women, civil and political status.

HANDBOOK ON WOMEN WORKERS. 1948– [Biennial]

PURPOSE:– To bring together basic in-formation on women's employment and occu-pations; the age and marital status of women workers; women's earnings and income; edu-cational status; and State laws affecting the employment and civil and political status of women.
Includes women in the labor force, laws governing women's employment and status, organizations of interest to women.
Title, 1948– 1952: Handbook of Facts on Women Workers.

LEGAL STATUS OF WOMEN IN THE UNITED STATES. [Irregular]

Issued as Bulletin 157. Separate report for each State.
Covers contracts and property, marriage and divorce, parents and children, and politi-cal rights of women.

L 13.4
CIRCULARS.

L 13.5:nos.
LAWS (charts, numbered). 1–   1920–

L 13.6:nos.
LAWS (maps, numbered). 1–   1921–

L 13.6/2:CT
LAWS (maps, miscellaneous).

L 13.6/3:CT
EQUAL PAY [Laws in various States]. [Irregular]

L 13.6/4:date   • Item 783-A-1
MARRIAGE LAWS AS OF (date). [Annual]

L 13.6/5:date   • Item 783-A-1
DIVORCE LAWS AS OF (date). [Annual]

L 13.7:nos.
FOLDERS. 1–   1923–

L 13.8:vol.
WOMAN WORKER. 1– 22. 1921– 1943. [Bimonthly]

L 13.9:CT
POSTERS.

L 13.10:nos.
SPECIAL BULLETINS. 1–   1940–

L 13.11:nos.   • Item 783
LEAFLETS. 1–   [Irregular]

Information and correspondence aids.
See L 36.110

L 13.12:CT
ADDRESSES. [Irregular]

L 13.13:nos.
UNION SERIES. 1–   1945–

L 13.14:CT   • Item 782-A
LABOR LAWS AFFECTING WOMEN, CAPSULE SUM-MARY. [Irregular]

Separate summary issued for each State. Digests current labor laws which are applicable to women, together with the extent of occupational coverage. Subjects include minimum wage, hours of work, plant facilities, and hazardous and un-healthful employment.

L 13.14/2:date   • Item 782-A
SUMMARY OF STATE LABOR LAWS FOR WOMEN. [Irregular]

All of the States have enacted some legisla-tions establishing standards for the employment of women. Principal areas of regulations are 1) Minimum wage, 2) Equal pay, 3) Hours, including maximum daily and weekly hours, day of rest, meal and rest periods, and nightwork, 4) Plant facilities, 5) Industrial homework, 6) Hazardous or unhealthful employment, 7) Employment be-fore and after childbirth. Not every State has enacted a law in each of the foregoing catego-ries, and the standards established vary from State to State.
A separate release is issued for each State and includes a summary of the provisions en-acted into law covering the categories listed above. Releases are revised as needed by legislative change.

L 13.14/3:date   • Item 782-A
DIGEST OF STATE LEGISLATION OF SPECIAL IN-TEREST TO WOMEN WORKERS. [Annual]

Digests State legislation enacted during the year on minimum wage, equal pay, hours to work, emergency relaxation, discrimination in employ-ment, State Commissions on the Status of Women, and industrial homework.

L 13.15:date
FACTS ON WOMEN WORKERS. 1946–   [Monthly]

L 13.16:CT
PRESS RELEASES. [Irregular]

L 13.17
FAMILY AND PROPERTY LAW [State] (date).

See L 36.109

L 13.18:date
CURRENT PUBLICATIONS OF THE WOMEN'S BUREAU.

Earlier L 13.2:P 96/5

L 13.18/2:CT
BIBLIOGRAPHIES AND LISTS OF PUBLICATIONS.

L 13.19:nos.   • **Item 783-A**
PAMPHLETS. 1–   1956– [Irregular]

   Informational studies on aspects of women workers.

L 13.20:date   • **Item 783-B**
WOMEN OF CONGRESS. 80th Cong. 1947– [Biennial]

   Contains photographs and brief biographies of the women elected to the Senate and House of Representatives. Includes table showing the number of women in each Congress, 1917 to date.

L 13.21:CT
EMPLOYMENT OUTLOOK FOR [various occupations].

L 13.22:CT   • **Item 783-C-1**
WOMEN WORKERS IN [State] (year). [Irregular]

   Separate releases issued for each State. Consists of a series of statistical tables on employment, age distribution, marital status, education, major occupational groups, industry groups, earnings and income.

L 13.22/2:date   • **Item 783-C-1**
BACKGROUND FACTS ON WOMEN WORKERS IN THE UNITED STATES. [Irregular]

   Earlier L 13.2:W 84/39

L 13.23:nos.   • **Item 783-C**
WOMEN IN THE WORLD TODAY, INTERNATIONAL REPORT. 1– 7. 1963 [Irregular]

   Presents comparative data and information on the international situation of such topics as political rights of women, equal pay, labor legislations, etc.
   Prepared in cooperation with the Bureau of International Labor Affairs.

WORKING CONDITIONS SERVICE (1918– 1919)

CREATION AND AUTHORITY

   The Working Conditions Service was established within the Department of Labor in August 1918. The Service was discontinued after June 30, 1919.

L 14.1:date
ANNUAL REPORTS.

L 14.2:CT
GENERAL PUBLICATIONS.

L 14.3
BULLETINS.

L 14.4
CIRCULARS.

IMMIGRATION AND NATURALIZATION SERVICE (1933– 1940)

CREATION AND AUTHORITY

   The Immigration and Naturalization Service was established within the Department of Labor by an Executive Order of June 10, 1933, combining the former Bureau of Immigration (L 3) and the Bureau of Naturalization (L 6). The Service was transferred to the Department of Justice by Reorganization Plan No. 5 of 1940, effective June 14, 1940.

L 15.1:date
ANNUAL REPORTS.

   Earlier L 3.2, L 6.2
   Later J 21.1

L 15.2:CT
GENERAL PUBLICATIONS.

   Later J 21.2

L 15.3
BULLETINS.

L 15.4
CIRCULARS.

L 15.5:nos.
LAWS.

L 15.5/2:date
IMMIGRATION LAWS AND RULES.

   Earlier C 7.6, L 3.5
   Later J 21.5

L 15.6:CT
REGULATIONS.

   Later J 21.6

L 15.7:nos.
MAPS.

L 15.8:CT
POSTERS.

L 15.9:nos.
GENERAL ORDERS.

   Earlier L 6.9, L 3.8

L 15.9/2:letters-nos.
GENERAL ORDERS (lettered-numbered).

   Later J 21.7

L 15.10:nos.
LECTURES.

L 15.11:CT
TEXTBOOKS AND MANUALS.

   Later J 21.9

L 15.12:date
TREATY, LAWS AND RULES GOVERNING ADMISSION OF CHINESE.

   Earlier L 3.7

L 15.13:date
ESSENTIAL PROCEDURE AND REQUIREMENTS FOR NATURALIZATION UNDER GENERAL LAW.

   Later J 21.8

BUREAU OF LABOR STANDARDS (1948– 1971)

CREATION AND AUTHORITY

   The Division of Labor Standards was established within the Department of Labor as a service agency by Departmental Order in 1934. The Division became the Bureau of Labor Standards by Departmental General Order 39, dated February 17, 1948. Upon establishment of Occupational Safety and Health Administration (L 35) by Public Law 91-596, approved April 28, 1971, the Bureau was abolished and its functions transferred to that agency.

L 16.1:date
ANNUAL REPORTS.

L 16.2:CT
GENERAL PUBLICATIONS.

L 16.3:nos.   • **Item 763**
BULLETINS. 1–   1935– [Irregular]

   Publications on safety, labor legislation and administration, child labor and youth employment.
   Later L 35.3
   Sub-series include:

ANNUAL DIGEST OF STATE AND FEDERAL LABOR LEGISLATION. 1935– [Annual]

   PURPOSE:– To present in layman's language the essential provisions of labor legislation enacted during the year by State legislatures and by the Congress of the United States. These digests are not official summaries.
   Digest on women's laws are based on summaries prepared by the Women's Bureau and digests of Federal acts on summaries prepared by the Labor Solicitor's Office. Digests are presented by State and topical heading. Also included is a summary of overall progress in labor legislation.

LABOR LAWS AND THEIR ADMINISTRATION. [Annual]

   Presents the proceedings of the conventions held by the International Association of Governmental Labor Officials. Includes only the major addresses, the statements of panel members, committee reports and resolutions.

LABOR OFFICES IN THE UNITED STATES AND CANADA. [Irregular]

   Latest edition: Jan. 1970 (Bulletin 177).
   Contains listings of Federal offices and agencies which deal with general labor problems, and such State and Provincial agencies in the United States and Canada as departments and bureau of labor, unemployment and accident compensation commissions, fair employment practices commissions, minimum wage boards, factory inspection services, and arbitration and conciliation boards.

OCCUPATIONAL HAZARDS TO YOUNG WORKERS. 1–   1942– [Irregular]

   Reports on findings of investigations made prior to the issuance of hazardous-occupations orders.
   Each pamphlet covers a single industry.

SAFETY IN INDUSTRY. 1959– [Irregular]

PURPOSE:– To present information necessary to prepare and implement an occupational safety and hygiene program in a workplace. Covers all aspects of safety planning, training, promotion, protection, enforcement, and accident and injury investigation, analysis, and evaluation.

L 16.3:212 • Item 763
STATE WORKMEN'S COMPENSATION LAWS, COMPARISON OF MAJOR PROVISIONS WITH RECOMMENDED STANDARDS, 1958– [Irregular]

Latest edition: Jan 1, 1967 (Bulletin 212)
PURPOSE:– To present a comparison of major provisions of State workmen's compensation laws, together with standards recommended by the U.S. Department of Labor, International Association of Industrial Accident Boards and Commissions, American College of Surgeons. American Medical Association, National Rehabilitation Association, or Council of State Governments.
Presented through a series of maps showing how each State meets or does not meet the requirements.

L 16.5:CT • Item 765-C
LAWS.

L 16.6:CT
REGULATIONS.

L 16.6/2:CT
HANDBOOKS, MANUALS, GUIDES.

L 16.6/3:v.nos. • Item 767-D
TODAY'S SAFETY GUIDE, ABSTRACTS.

Earlier L 16.6/2:Sa 1/2

L 16.7:CT
MAPS.

L 16.7/2:CT
COMPARISON OF STATE SAFETY CODES WITH ASA. [Irregular]

Printed as graphic charts (17 x 22"), the provisions of State safety codes are compared with like provisions of the American Standards Association's codes and recorded in symbol form as "same or similar to," "more restrictive to," or "less restrictive than the ASA standards." Charts are issued for individual types of machinery.

L 16.7/3:nos. • Item 765-D
HOW TO INSPECT CHARTS, HTIC LS-(series). 1964– [Irregular]

Illustrated charts on specific devices, operations, or machines showing suggested safe conditions and safe work methods. Sizes vary. Suitable for wall posters.

L 16.8:CT
POSTERS.

L 16.8/2:CT
SAFETY CHARTS.

L 16.8/2:Oc 1 • Item 765-G
OCCUPATIONAL SAFETY CHARTS. 1– [Irregular]

Notebook size (8 x 10") and punched for ring binder, these charts illustrate safety operation of common machines, tools, and equipment for use as posters, instruction guides, and promotion of safe work methods.

L 16.9:nos.
INDUSTRIAL HEALTH AND SAFETY SERIES. 1– 1935–

L 16.10:nos.
FOLDERS. 1– 1935–

L 16.11:dt.&nos.
LABOR STANDARDS. v. 1– 5, no. 2. 1936– 1942. [Monthly]

L 16.12:dt.&nos.
LEGISLATIVE REPORTS. [ ]– 1947. [Weekly]

L 16.12/2:nos.
LEGISLATIVE REPORTS, SUPPLEMENTARY BULLETINS. [ ]– 1943.

L 16.13:nos.
SPECIAL BULLETINS. 1– 18. 1940– 1945.

L 16.14:CT
APPRENTICESHIP STANDARDS.

L 16.15:CT
ADDRESSES. [Irregular]

L 16.16:nos.
TECHNICAL BULLETINS. 1– 1940–

Later Pr 32.5222

L 16.17:CT • Item 764
LIST OF PUBLICATIONS.

L 16.18:nos.
INDUSTRIAL SAFETY SUBJECTS. 1– 1943–

L 16.19:nos.
RUBBER SERIES. 1– 1944–

L 16.20:date
INDUSTRIAL SAFETY SUMMARIES. [ ]– 1945. [Monthly]

L 16.21:CT
STATE CHILD-LABOR STANDARDS (by States).

L 16.22:CT
WORKMEN'S COMPENSATION [employer edition] (by States).

L 16.22/2:CT
WORKMEN'S COMPENSATION [union edition] (by States).

L 16.23:CT
SAFETY AND HEALTH REQUIREMENTS (by States).

L 16.24:CT
WAGE PAYMENT (by States).

L 16.25:nos.
CONTROLLING CHEMICAL HAZARDS SERIES.

L 16.26:nos.
SERIES INTERAMERICAN. 1– 1946–

L 16.27:nos.
CHILD LABOR SERIES. 1– 28. 1946–

Superseded by Child-labor bulletins L 22.14

L 16.28:date
LABOR EDUCATION NEWS. – 1947.

L 16.29:date
STATE SAFETY DIGEST. – 1947.

L 16.30:date
PRESIDENT'S CONFERENCE ON INDUSTRIAL SAFETY, NEWS LETTER.

L 16.31:date
PERFORMANCE, STORY OF THE HANDICAPPED. [Monthly]

L 16.32:CT
SUMMARY OF MAJOR PROVISIONS OF CONVENTION AND OF LAW RELATING TO FACTORY INSPECTION (by States).

L 16.33:v.nos.
SAFETY BULLETIN. v. 1– 16, no. 1. – 1951. [Quarterly]

Earlier L 26.7

L 16.34:v.nos.&nos. • Item 766-A
SAFETY STANDARDS. v. 1– 1951– [Bimonthly]

Devoted to news and articles on developments in the field of industrial safety. Reports activities of the Federal Safety Council, the Federal agencies, the maritime industry, the President's Conference on Occupational Safety, State safety programs, and management and labor safety programs in general.
Later L 35.9

L 16.35
PRESS RELEASES. [Irregular]

L 16.35/2:nos.
NEWS FROM THE PRESIDENT'S CONFERENCE ON OCCUPATIONAL SAFETY.

L 16.35/3:nos.
NEWS FROM PRESIDENT'S CONFERENCE ON OCCUPATIONAL SAFETY, NEWSLETTERS.

L 16.36
PRESIDENT'S COMMITTEE ON EMPLOYMENT OF PHYSICALLY HANDICAPPED NEWS RELEASE. [Irregular]

Later PrEx 1.10/4

L 16.37:date
CASUALTIES AND INJURIES AMONG SHIPYARD AND DOCK WORKERS. 1953– [Quarterly]

L 16.38
CHILD LABOR AND YOUTH EMPLOYMENT BRANCH: MONTHLY REPORTS.

L 16.39
STATE SAFETY PROGRAM WORK SHEETS.

L 16.40
OCCUPATIONAL HAZARDS TO YOUNG WORKERS REPORTS.

L 16.41:nos.
YOUTH EMPLOYMENT TABLES TS (series). 1– 1954–

L 16.42:nos.
HOW TO USE INJURY STATISTICS TO PREVENT OCCUPATIONAL ACCIDENTS, SERIES PREPARED FOR PRESIDENT'S CONFERENCE ON OCCUPATIONAL SAFETY. 1– 4. 1955.

L 16.43:CT
PRESIDENT'S COMMITTEE ON MIGRATORY LABOR: PUBLICATIONS.

L 16.43/2:date
– MIGRATORY LABOR NOTES. [Irregular]

L 16.43/3:date
– PRESS RELEASES.

L 16.44
NEPH NEWSLETTERS.

L 16.44/2:CT
PUBLICATIONS.
Formerly in L 16.2

L 16.44/3:CT
ADDRESSES.

L 16.44/4:date
NEWSLETTER, TIPS AND TRENDS IN EMPLOYMENT OF MENTALLY HANDICAPPED.
Later PrEx 10.5

L 16.44/5:date
ANNUAL MEETING BULLETIN.

L 16.44/6:nos.
THE MICROPHONE, WOMEN'S COMMITTEE IDEA EXCHANGE.

L 16.45:nos. • Item 765-B
LEAFLETS. 1– 1959–

L 16.46:date
LABOR STANDARDS CLEARINGHOUSE.

MARITIME SAFETY DIGEST.

PURPOSE:– To report periodically to the maritime industry special items of interest to the industry.
Issued for the following:

L 16.47:date   • **Item 765-F**
– LONGSHORING. 1961–   [Irregular]

L 16.47/2:CT   • **Item 765-E**
– MARITIME SAFETY DATA FOR SHIPYARDS.

L 16.47/3:nos.   • **Item 765-F**
– SHIPYARDS. 1–   1964–   [Irregular]

L 16.47/4:CT
– MARITIME SAFETY DATA FOR SHIPYARD INDUSTRY.

L 16.47/5:CT   • **Item 765-E**
– MARITIME SAFETY DATA: LONGSHORING.

L 16.47/6:CT   • **Item 765-E**
– MARITIME SAFETY DATA FOR THE STEVEDORING INDUSTRY. [Irregular]

L 16.48   • **Item 766-E**
PUBLIC LAW 85-742, SAFETY AND HEALTH ADMINISTRATION, ANNUAL REPORT. 1–   1960– [Annual]

Public law 742, 85th Congress, amending section 41 of the Longshoremen's and Harbor Workers' Compensation Act, provides for a system of safety and health regulations, training programs, special studies and investigations, standards development, cooperative State and Federal programs, physical inspections, and such other activities as deemed reasonably necessary to protect the life, safety and health of employees engaged in longshoring, ship repairing, and other related employment upon navigable waters.
Section 1 covers the national program analysis for both longshoring and ship repairing; section 2 covers longshoring alone; and section 3 covers ship repairing and other harbor work.
Text is supplemented by charts and tables.

L 16.48/2:date
MARITIME INJURY SUMMARY REPORT, PUBLIC LAW. 85-742.

L 16.49:CT   • **Item 765-G**
OCCUPATIONAL SAFETY AIDS, OSA-LS-(series).
See L 35.10

L 16.50:nos.   • **Item 764-B**
FACT SHEETS. 1–   1964–

L 16.50/2:nos.
LABOR LAW SERIES. 1–   1952–   [Irregular]

PURPOSE:– To communicate in simple language the essential provisions of, and facts relating to State labor laws. Each booklet covers one subject area, and is revised as volume of law changes requires. Although these publications are accurate reflections of the law content, they should not be construed as binding administrative or judicial interpretations.
Previous title: Brief Summaries– Fact Sheets (L 16.50).

L 16.51:nos.
STUDENT WORK SHEETS, DEPARTMENT OF LABOR SAFETY TRAINING PROGRAMS, SWS-LS-(series). 1–   [Irregular]

L 16.51/2:nos.   • **Item 764-C**
SAFE WORK GUIDES, SWS LS- (series). 1– [Irregular]
Folders, each 4 pages, describing safety precautions for certain construction trades.
Later L 35.11

L 16.51/3:nos.   • **Item 767-C**
SUGGESTED SAFE PRACTICES FOR SHIPYARD WORKERS. 1–   1966–

L 16.51/3-2:nos.   • **Item 767-C**
SUGGESTED SAFE PRACTICES FOR LONGSHOREMEN. 1–   [Irregular]

L 16.51/4:nos.   • **Item 764-C**
STUDENT REFERENCE, DEPARTMENT OF LABOR SAFETY TRAINING PROGRAMS, SR LS-(series). 1–   [Irregular]

L 16.51/5:nos.   • **Item 767-B**
SAFEGUARD OUR NATION'S YOUTH ON THE JOB. 1–   1966–   [Irregular]

L 16.51/6:nos.   • **Item 764-C**
TECHNICAL REFERENCES, DEPT. OF LABOR SAFETY TRAINING PROGRAMS, TR-LS- (series). 1–   1964–   [Irregular]

PURPOSE:– To provide essential information on materials, equipment, practices, standards, and conditions which may affect the safety of health of workers. Content varies with subject, but may include good work and environmental practices and applications; data on injury, health and fire names to assist in identification; listings of typical packagings; measures needed to protect personnel in normal work situations; procedures for repair or cleanup in the event of breakdown or spillage.

L 16.51/7:nos.   • **Item 764-C**
CHEMICAL SAFETY DATA SHEETS, EDS- LS- (series). 1–   [Irregular]

L 16.51/8:nos.
STUDENT QUIZ, DEPARTMENT OF LABOR SAFETY TRAINING PROGRAMS, SQ-IS-(series).

L 16.51/9
OFF THE JOB SAFETY, OJS-LS- (series). 1–   1967– [Irregular]

PURPOSE:– To provide general promotional flyers, written in a popular style. Covers safety problems frequently encountered in non-employment situations. States nature of hazards involved, and makes recommendations for practices and equipment necessary to control or eliminate the hazards.

L 16.52:date   • **Item 764-E**
HIGHLIGHTS (year) SAFETY STANDARDS ACTIVITY. 1966–   [Biennial]

PURPOSE:– To report important changes in safety standards issued by Federal agencies, and voluntary national standards making organizations, principally the United States of American Standards Institute, the National Fire Protection Association, and the Underwriters' Laboratories, Inc.
Issued for even-numbered years.

CONSUMERS' PROJECT
(1936– 1938)

CREATION AND AUTHORITY

The Consumers' Division was transferred from the National Recovery Administration (Y 3.N 21/8) to the Department of Labor by Executive Order 7252 of December 21, 1935, and continued under emergency relief funds until June 30, 1938. On April 1, 1936, the name was changed to Consumers' Project. By letter of Secretary of Labor to the Secretary of Agriculture, the files and records were transferred to the Division of Consumers' Counsel of the Agricultural Adjustment Administration (A 55).

L 17.1:date
ANNUAL REPORTS.

L 17.2:CT
GENERAL PUBLICATIONS.

L 17.5:CT
LAWS.

L 17.9:vol
CONSUMER. [Bimonthly]
Earlier Y 3.N 21/8:22

L 17.10:nos.
REPORTS.

PUBLIC CONTRACTS DIVISION
(1936– 1942)

CREATION AND AUTHORITY

The Public Contracts Division was established within the Department of Labor by act of Congress approved June 30, 1936 (49 Stat. 2036). By order of the Secretary of Labor, effective October 15, 1942, the Public Contracts Division merged with the Wage and Hour Division (L 20) to form the Wage and Hour and Public Contracts Divisions (L 22).

L 18.1:date
ANNUAL REPORTS.
Later L 22.1

L 18.2:CT
GENERAL PUBLICATIONS.

L 18.3:nos.
BULLETINS. [Weekly]
Later L 22.3

L 18.6:CT
REGULATIONS, RULES, AND INSTRUCTIONS.

L 18.8:CT
POSTERS.

L 18.9:CT
(DECISIONS OF SECRETARY OF LABOR) IN MATTERS OF DETERMINATION OF PREVAILING MINIMUM WAGES IN INDUSTRIES.
Earlier L 1.12

CONCILIATION SERVICE
(1938– 1947)

CREATION AND AUTHORITY

The Division of Conciliation was established within the Department of Labor by the act of Congress, approved March 4, 1913 (37 Stat. 736), which established that Department. In July 1918, it became known as the Labor Adjustment Service until after the war when it became the Division of Conciliation again. In 1926, it was redesignated as the United States Conciliation Service. The Service was abolished by act of Congress, approved June 23, 1947 (61 Stat. 153), and its functions transferred to the newly established Federal Mediation and Conciliation Service (FM 1).
Note:– SuDocs class L 19 was established in 1938.

L 19.1:date
ANNUAL REPORTS.
Later FM 1.1

L 19.2:CT
GENERAL PUBLICATIONS.
Later FM 1.2

L 19.7:CT
ADDRESSES.

WAGE AND HOUR DIVISION
(1938–1942)

CREATION AND AUTHORITY

The Wage and Hour Division was established within the Department of Labor by the Fair Labor Standards Act, approved June 25, 1938 (52 Stat. 1060). On October 15, 1942, the Wage and Hour Division was consolidated with the Public Contracts Division (L 18) to form the Wage and Hour and Public Contracts Divisions (L 22).

L 20.1:date
ANNUAL REPORTS.
Later L 22.1

L 20.2:CT
GENERAL PUBLICATIONS.

L 20.5:CT
LAWS.

L 20.6:CT
REGULATIONS, RULES, AND INSTRUCTIONS.
Later L 22.6

L 20.7:nos.
INTERPRETATIVE BULLETINS.
Later L 22.10

L 20.8:pt.nos.
REGULATIONS.
Later L 22.9

L 20.9:CT
POSTERS.
Later L 22.8

L 20.10:CT
PAPERS IN RE.

L 20.11:CT
ADDRESSES.

L 20.12:CT
REPORTS ON INDUSTRIES.
Later L 22.7

OFFICE OF THE SOLICITOR
(1913–   )

CREATION AND AUTHORITY

The Office of the Solicitor was established within the Department of Labor by the act of March 4, 1913.
Note:– SuDocs class L 21 was established in 1942.

INFORMATION

Office of the Solicitor
Bureau of Labor
52002 Frances Perkins Bldg.
200 Constitution Ave., NW
Washington, DC 20210
(202) 693-5260
Fax: (202) 693-5278
http://www.dol.gov/sol/welcome.html

L 21.1:date
ANNUAL REPORTS.

L 21.2:CT   • Item 772
GENERAL PUBLICATIONS.

L 21.2:In 2   • Item 772
ADMINISTRATIVE DECISIONS, WALSH-HEALEY PUBLIC CONTRACTS ACT, INDEX-DIGEST. [Irregular]

Basic volume covers period 1942 through December 1964 and covers decisions in nearly 1,000 cases. The digest is arranged topically in general accord with the numbering system used by the Office of the Solicitor of Labor. It will be kept up-to-date by periodic additions referring to recent cases.

L 21.5:CT   • Item 772-C
LAWS.

L 21.6:CT   • Item 772-A
REGULATIONS, RULES, AND INSTRUCTIONS.

L 21.6/2:CT   • Item 772-B
HANDBOOKS, MANUALS, GUIDES.

L 21.7:CT
PAPERS IN RE.

L 21.8:nos.
VETERANS REEMPLOYMENT RIGHTS DIVISION CASES. 1–   1957–

L 21.9:
LEGAL FIELD LETTERS.

L 21.10:nos.
CASE ANALYSES.

L 21.11:
WEEKLY SUMMARY OF LEGISLATIVE WORK (by Congress).

L 21.12:nos.
LEGAL OPINION LETTER.

L 21.13:
COURT LITIGATION CASES CLOSED DURING (date).

L 21.14:
FINDINGS OF FACT AND RECOMMENDATIONS OF REFERENCE.

WAGE AND HOUR AND PUBLIC
CONTRACTS DIVISIONS
(1942–1971)

CREATION AND AUTHORITY

The Wage and Hour Division (L 20) and the Public Contracts Division (L 18) were consolidated to form the Wage and Hour and Public Contracts Divisions on August 21, 1942. The Divisions were redesignated the Wage and Hour Division and placed in the newly established Employment Standards Administration (L 36.200) by Secretary's Order 13-71, effective April 28, 1971.

L 22.1:date
ANNUAL REPORTS.
Earlier Wage and Hour Division (L 20.1) and Public Contracts Division (L 18.1)
Later L 36.201

L 22.2:CT   • Item 777
GENERAL PUBLICATIONS.
Later L 36.202

L 22.3:dt.&nos.
BULLETINS. [Weekly]
Earlier L 18.3

L 22.5:CT   • Item 778-B
LAWS.

L 22.5/2:date
FEDERAL LABOR LAWS.
Later L 36.205/2

L 22.6:CT   • Item 779
REGULATIONS, RULES, AND INSTRUCTIONS.
Earlier L 20.6

L 22.6/2
STATE LAWS AND REGULATIONS PROHIBITING EMPLOYMENT OF MINORS IN HAZARDOUS OCCUPATIONS. [Administrative]

L 22.6/3
CHILD LABOR REGULATIONS. [Irregular]
Earlier L 20.12

L 22.8:CT
POSTERS.
Earlier L 20.9

L 22.9:pt.nos.   • Item 780
REGULATIONS AND INTERPRETATIONS. 1–   1968. [Irregular]

L 22.10:nos.   • Item 778
INTERPRETATIVE BULLETINS. [Irregular]

L 22.10/2   • Item 778
EXPLANATORY BULLETINS. [Irregular]

L 22.11:nos.
RULINGS AND INTERPRETATIONS.

Earlier L 18.7

L 22.12:nos.
[DECISIONS UNDER WALSH-HEALEY PUBLIC CONTRACTS ACT.]

L 22.13:dt.nos.
CIRCULAR LETTERS.

L 22.14:nos.   • Item 776
CHILD-LABOR BULLETINS. 101–   1948– [Irregular]

Popular guides on provisions of the Fair Labor Standards Act in regard to child-labor.

L 22.15:CT
ADDRESSES. [Irregular]

L 22.16:CT
PRESS RELEASES. [Irregular]

L 22.17
WAGE STABILIZATION BULLETIN.

L 22.18
FIELD OPERATIONS HANDBOOK.

L 22.19:CT
WALSH-HEALEY PUBLIC CONTRACTS ACT MINIMUM WAGE DETERMINATION (for various industries).

L 22.20
QUARTERLY SUMMARY OF STATISTICS OF OPERATIONS.

L 22.21
MONTHLY SUMMARY OF STATISTICS OF OPERATIONS.

L 22.22
REGULATIONS UNDER FAIR LABOR STANDARDS ACT.

L 22.23
WALSH-HEALY PUBLIC CONTRACTS ACT, DECISIONS.

L 22.24
MANAGEMENT PROCEDURE NOTICES.

L 22.25
INCENTIVE AWARDS BULLETINS.

L 22.26:nos.
HAZARDOUS OCCUPATIONS ORDERS.

Earlier L 5.39

L 22.27:nos.
WAGE-HOUR TRAINING MEMORANDUM.

L 22.27/2:date
WAGE-HOUR NEWS LETTER.

L 22.28:CT
SPOT ANNOUNCEMENTS.

L 22.29:nos.   • Item 777-A
INDUSTRY PAMPHLETS. 1–   1958–   [Irregular]

Tells how Federal wage-hour laws apply to various industries.

L 22.30:nos.   • Item 778-C
QUESTIONS AND ANSWERS, QA-IND-(series).

L 22.31:date   • Item 780-A
REPORT OF THE SECRETARY OF LABOR SUBMITTED TO CONGRESS IN ACCORDANCE WITH REQUIREMENTS OF SEC. 4(d) OF THE FAIR LABOR STANDARDS ACT. 1958–   [Annual]

PURPOSE:– To submit annually to Congress an evaluation and appraisal by the Secretary of Labor of the minimum wages established by the Fair Labor Standards Act, together with his recommendations.

L 22.32:CT   • Item 775-A
BIBLIOGRAPHIES AND LISTS OF PUBLICATIONS.

L 22.33:CT   • Item 777-B
HANDBOOKS, MANUALS, GUIDES.

BUREAU OF APPRENTICESHIP AND TRAINING (1956– 1975)

CREATION AND AUTHORITY

The Apprentice Training Service was transferred from the War Manpower Commission and returned to the Department of Labor by Executive Order 9617 of September 19, 1945. The name was changed to Bureau of Apprenticeship by General Order 39 of February 17, 1948, and again to Bureau of Apprenticeship and Training by General Order 91 of December 11, 1956. By Secretary's Order 14-75 of November 12, 1975, the Bureau was placed under the newly established Employment and Training Administration (L 37.100).

L 23.1:date
ANNUAL REPORTS.

Later L 37.101

L 23.2:CT   • Item 748
GENERAL PUBLICATIONS.

Later L 37.102

L 23.2:Ap 6:date   • Item 748
NATIONAL APPRENTICESHIP PROGRAM. 1945–

Earlier Pr 32.5203:Ap 6/2/945

L 23.2:C 22   • Item 748
NATIONAL CARPENTRY APPRENTICESHIP AND TRAINING STANDARDS. [Irregular]

L 23.2:M 66   • Item 748
DIRECTORY FOR REACHING MINORITY GROUPS. 1973. 214 p.

A Department of Labor publication listing organization and individuals who are able to reach minority groups and are interested in supplying minority groups with information on job opportunities and job training. This directory lists concerned organizations and individuals by State and city, with names addresses, and telephone numbers included. It includes a listing of black colleges, universi-

ties, fraternities, and sororities. The National Association for the Advancement of Colored People, the National Urban League, and the Bureau of Indian Affairs are examples of organizations listed.

L 23.2:P 16   • Item 748
NATIONAL PAINTING AND DECORATING APPRENTICESHIP AND TRAINING STANDARDS ADOPTED BY THE NATIONAL JOINT PAINTING AND DECORATING APPRENTICESHIP AND TRAINING COMMITTEE. 1939– [Irregular]

L 23.3:nos.
BULLETINS.

L 23.4:nos.
CIRCULARS.

L 23.6:CT   • Item 749
REGULATIONS, RULES, AND INSTRUCTIONS.

L 23.6/2:CT   • Item 748-C
HANDBOOKS, MANUALS, GUIDES.

Later L 37.108

L 23.7:CT
POSTERS.

L 23.8:CT
ADDRESSES. [Irregular]

L 23.9:CT
REGISTERED GROUP-JOINT APPRENTICESHIP PROGRAMS IN CONSTRUCTION INDUSTRY (by trades).

L 23.10:nos.   • Item 748-B
BULLETINS [technical] T- (series). 1–   [Irregular]

L 23.11:nos.
REPORTS OF APPRENTICE SECTION PROGRAMS.

L 23.12:dt.&nos.
APPRENTICESHIP DIGEST.

Issued 3 times a year.
Earlier Apprenticeship Bibliography L 23.2:B 47

L 23.13:CT
RELEASES.

L 23.13/2:date
TRAINING INFORMATION RELEASES.

L 23.14
REPORT TO FIELD STAFF.

L 23.15:v.nos.&nos.
BUREAU OF APPRENTICESHIP AND TRAINING NEWS.

L 23.16:nos.
TRADE AND INDUSTRY PUBLICATIONS. 1– [Irregular]

L 23.17:nos.
APPRENTICESHIP COORDINATORS, BOOKLETS. 1– 1960–

L 23.18:CT   • Item 748-D
BIBLIOGRAPHIES AND LISTS OF PUBLICATIONS.

L 23.19:nos.
RESEARCH DIVISION REPORTS. 1–   1964–

L 23.20   • Item 748-F
TECHNICAL REPORTS. 1–   [Irregular]

RETRAINING AND REEMPLOYMENT ADMINISTRATION (1945– 1947)

CREATION AND AUTHORITY

The Retraining and Reemployment Administration was transferred from the Office of War Mobilization and Reconversion (Y 3.W 19/7) to the Department of Labor by Executive Order 9617 of September 19, 1945. The Administration was terminated on June 30, 1947, as provided in the act which created it.

L 24.1:date
ANNUAL REPORTS.

L 24.2:CT
GENERAL PUBLICATIONS.

L 24.3:nos.
BULLETINS.

L 24.5:CT
LAWS.

L 24.7:CT
ADDRESSES.

L 24.8:nos.
INFORMATION MEMORANDUMS.

OFFICE OF VETERANS' REEMPLOYMENT RIGHTS (1964–   )

CREATION AND AUTHORITY

The Veterans' Reemployment Rights Division was established within the Department of Labor on May 21, 1947, by order of the Secretary. The name was changed to Bureau of Veterans' Reemployment Rights by General Order 39 of February 17, 1948. The name was changed again in 1964 to Office of Veterans' Reemployment Rights.

INFORMATION

Office of Veterans' Reemployment Rights
Department of Labor
200 Constitution Avenue, N.W.
Room N5414
Washington, D.C. 20210
(202) 523-8611

L 25.1:date
ANNUAL REPORTS.

L 25.2:CT   • Item 773
GENERAL PUBLICATIONS.

L 25.6:CT   • Item 774
REGULATIONS, RULES AND INSTRUCTIONS.

L 25.6/2:CT   • Item 773-A
HANDBOOKS, MANUALS, GUIDES.

L 25.6/2:L 52   • Item 773-A
LEGAL GUIDE AND CASE DIGEST, VETERANS' REEMPLOYMENT RIGHTS UNDER THE UNIVERSAL MILITARY TRAINING AND SERVICE ACT, AS AMENDED, AND RELATED ACTS. 1964. 1342 p.

– SUPPLEMENT. 1973. 239 p.

L 25.6/2:V 64 • Item 773-A
VETERANS' REEMPLOYMENT RIGHTS HAND-
BOOKS. 1970. 196 p.

Designed to assist those who are concerned
with the reemployment rights of veterans, their
counselors, their former employers, their unions
and others who may be affected by questions in
this field. It covers such subjects as an explanation of just who is eligible for reemployment rights;
applying for reemployment; applicant's qualifications; change in employer's circumstances;
position to be offered and rate of pay to be provided; seniority rights, and duration of rights;
vacations, and disabled applicants. Also covered
are: Effect of Collective Bargaining Relationships;
Reservists and Guardsmen, tours of training duty
and initial active duty for training; examination,
deferred entrance, and rejection; enforcement
procedures; waiver of rights, remedies or defenses; delay in asserting rights; and Supreme
Court decisions on reemployment rights. At the
conclusion of the text of each subject, several
examples are given which clearly explain the subject matter.

L 25.7:
RELEASES.

L 25.8
FIELD LETTER, INFORMATION, LEGISLATIVE,
COURT DECISIONS, OPINIONS. 1–   [Irregular]

BUREAU OF EMPLOYEES' COMPENSATION (1950–1972)

CREATION AND AUTHORITY

The Bureau of Employees' Compensation
(FS 13.300) was transferred from the Federal
Security Agency to the Department of Labor by
Reorganization Plan No. 19 of 1950, effective
May 24, 1950. On March 13, 1972, the functions
of the Bureau were absorbed by the Office of
Wage Compensation Programs (L 36.400).

L 26.1:date
ANNUAL REPORTS.

Earlier FS 13.301

L 26.2:CT • Item 750
GENERAL PUBLICATIONS.

Earlier FS 13.302

L 26.2:D 62 • Item 750
DIRECTORY OF COMPENSATION DISTRICT
OFFICES AND DEPUTY COMMISSIONERS.
[Irregular]

L 26.2:In 5/4 • Item 750
FEDERAL WORK INJURY FACTS. v. 1–   1960–
[Annual]

Gives number, duration, and direct cost
factors of work injuries to civilian Federal employees during the calendar year, as reported
under the Federal Employees' Compensation
Act.

L 26.5:CT • Item 750-A
LAWS.

Earlier FS 13.305

L 26.6:CT • Item 750-B
REGULATIONS, RULES, AND INSTRUCTIONS.

L 26.6/2:CT • Item 750-B
HANDBOOKS, MANUALS, GUIDES.

L 26.7:v.nos.&nos.
SAFETY BULLETINS. [Quarterly]

Earlier FS 13.307
Later L 16.13

L 26.7/2:date • Item 823-A-1 (MF)
LIBRARY OF CONGRESS SUBJECT HEADING IN
MICROFORM, QUARTERLY CUMULATION.

L 26.8:date • Item 750-C
FEDERAL WORK INJURIES SUSTAINED DURING
CALENDAR YEAR. [Annual]

L 26.8/2:date • Item 750-C
FEDERAL WORK INJURY FACTS.

Earlier L 26.2:In 5/4

L 26.8/2-2:date • Item 750-C
FEDERAL WORK INJURY FACTS, OCCUPATIONAL
DISTRIBUTION, DURATION AND DIRECT COST
FACTORS OF WORK INJURIES TO CIVILIAN FED-
ERAL EMPLOYEES DURING CALENDAR YEAR.
[Annual]

L 26.9:date
WORK INJURIES REPORTED BY LONGSHOREMEN
AND HARBOR WORKERS. [Quarterly]

DEFENSE MANPOWER ADMINISTRATION (1951–1953)

CREATION AND AUTHORITY

The Office of Defense Manpower was established by General Order 48 of the Secretary of
Labor, dated September 29, 1950. The name was
changed to Defense Manpower Administration by
Amendment 1, of March 10, 1951, to General
Order 48. The Administration was abolished by
General Order 63, dated August 25, 1953, which
established the Office of Manpower Administration (L 1.39) to succeed it.

L 27.1:date
ANNUAL REPORTS.

L 27.2:CT
GENERAL PUBLICATIONS.

L 27.4:nos.
CIRCULAR.

L 27.7
RELEASES.

L 27.7/2:nos.
POLICY STATEMENTS.

Earlier Pr 33.1010

L 27.8:CT
ADDRESSES.

L 27.9:nos.
MEMORANDUMS. [Admin.]

EMPLOYEES' COMPENSATION APPEALS BOARD (1950–   )

CREATION AND AUTHORITY

The Employees' Compensation Appeals Board
was created by Reorganization Plan No. 2 of 1946
(60 Stat 1095) effective July 16, 1946. It was
transferred from the Federal Security Agency to
the Department of Labor by Reorganization Plan
No. 19 of 1950, effective May 24, 1950.

INFORMATION

Employees' Compensation Appeals Board
Department of Labor
200 Constitution Ave., NW, Rm. N-2609
Washington, DC 20210
(202) 693-6420
Fax: (202) 693-6367
http://www.dol.gov/dol/ecab/welcome.html

L 28.1:date
ANNUAL REPORTS.

L 28.2:CT • Item 749-B-1
GENERAL PUBLICATIONS.

L 28.7:
RELEASES.

L 28.8:nos.
OPINIONS.

L 28.9:v.nos. • Item 749-B
DIGEST AND DECISIONS OF THE EMPLOYEES'
COMPENSATION APPEALS BOARD.

Decisions of the Board of appeals taken from
determinations and awards with respect to employees of the Federal Government and of the
District of Columbia in cases arising under the
Federal Employees' Compensation Act of September 7, 1916, as amended (5 U.S.C.A. 751-
795).
Earlier: Decisions of Employees' Compensation Appeals Board.

BUREAU OF INTERNATIONAL LABOR AFFAIRS (1959–   )

CREATION AND AUTHORITY

The Office of International Labor Affairs was
established within the Department of Labor by
General Order 33 of the Secretary, dated October 10, 1947. The name was changed to Bureau
of International Labor Affairs, effective December 31, 1959.

INFORMATION

Bureau of International Labor Affairs
Department of Labor
200 Constitution Avenue, NW, Rm. C-4325
Washington, D.C. 20210
(202) 693-4770
Fax: (202) 693-4780
http://www.dol.gov/ilab

L 29.1:date
ANNUAL REPORTS.

L 29.2:CT   • Item 745-A-1
GENERAL PUBLICATIONS.

L 29.7:date
RELEASES.

L 29.8:CT   • Item 762
INTERNATIONAL LABOR STUDIES. 1959–
[Irregular]

　　PURPOSE:– To provide factual information
on the history, structure, membership and activities of those international labor organizations
known collectively as International Trade Secretariats.

L 29.9:CT   • Item 762-H
DIRECTORIES OF LABOR ORGANIZATIONS.

L 29.9/2:pt.nos.
DIRECTORY OF INTERNATIONAL TRADE UNION
ORGANIZATIONS.

　　Earlier L 29.2:D 62

L 29.9/3:date
DIRECTORY OF WORLD FEDERATION OF TRADE
UNIONS.

　　Earlier L 29.2:D 62/2

L 29.10:CT
ADDRESSES.

L 29.11:nos.
MEMORANDUMS. 1–

L 29.12:v.nos.&nos.   • Item 762-B-1 (MF)
INTERNATIONAL LABOR. v. 1–　1960– 1975
[Bimonthly]

　　PURPOSE:– To inform interested persons of
current and pertinent developments in the international labor field in general, and to enable U.S.
Foreign Service Labor Attaches and Labor Reporting Officers to keep up with trends and events
occurring in this field throughout the world in particular.

L 29.13:nos.   • Item 750-B-1 (MF)
MONOGRAPH (series). 1–　1978–　[Irregular]

　　Series of occasional publications in which
the Department of Labor reports on international
labor matters to other countries that are pertinent
to developments in the United States.

L 29.14:CT   • Item 749-C
COUNTRY LABOR PROFILES. [Irregular]

　　Each publication presents detailed information about a specific country, including narrative,
tables, charts, and illustrations on the labor force,
organized workers, labor standards, working conditions, rates of pay, costs and standards of
living.
　　Former title: Profile of Labor Conditions.

L 29.15:nos.   • Item 749-D (MF)
ECONOMIC DISCUSSION PAPERS. 1–　1981–

　　Highly technical papers on various aspects
of U.S. foreign trade.
　　Published in microfiche (24x).

L 29.15/2:nos.   • Item 749-D (MF)
OCCASIONAL PAPER (Series). [Irregular]

L 29.16:CT   • Item 749-E (P) (EL)
FOREIGN LABOR TRENDS (VARIOUS COUNTRIES).
[Annual]

　　Each report describes and analyzes labor
trends in a different foreign country. Covers significant labor developments, including labor management relations, trade unions, employment and
unemployment, wages, and the economic and
political background.

L 29.17:date   • Item 749-D
THE PRESIDENT'S COMPREHENSIVE TRIENNIAL
REPORT ON IMMIGRATION.

FEDERAL SAFETY COUNCIL
(1950–　　)

CREATION AND AUTHORITY

　　The Federal Safety Council was established
by Executive Order 10194 of December 19, 1950
to supersede the Federal Interdepartmental Safety
Council (FIS 1). The Council was reestablished by
Executive Order 10990 of February 2, 1962.

INFORMATION
　　Federal Safety Council
　　Department of Labor
　　Washington, D.C. 20210

L 30.1:date   • Item 762-E
ANNUAL REPORTS.
　　Earlier FIS 1.1

L 30.2:CT   • Item 762-E
GENERAL PUBLICATIONS.
　　Earlier FIS 1.2

L 30.8:
SAFETY NEWS LETTER, CURRENT INFORMATION
IN THE FEDERAL SAFETY FIELD.

L 30.9:CT   • Item 816
ADDRESSES.

L 30.10:CT   • Item 762-E
HANDBOOKS, MANUALS, GUIDES.

BUREAU OF
LABOR-MANAGEMENT REPORTS
(1959– 1963)

CREATION AND AUTHORITY

　　The Bureau of Labor-Management Reports
was established in the Department of Labor, pursuant to the Labor-Management Reporting and
Disclosure Act of 1959 (Public Law 86-257, 73
Stat. 519), by General Order 102 of the Secretary
of Labor, September 24, 1959. The Bureau was
abolished in 1963.

L 31.1:date
ANNUAL REPORTS.
　　Later L 1.51

L 31.2:CT
GENERAL PUBLICATIONS.

L 31.4:nos.
BUREAU CIRCULARS. [Admin.]

L 31.6/2:nos.
BUREAU ORDERS. [Admin.]

L 31.7:nos.
PRESS RELEASES.

L 31.8:nos.
TECHNICAL ASSISTANCE AIDS.
　　Later L 1.48

L 31.8/2:nos.
TECHNICAL ASSISTANCE REMINDERS.

L 31.9:v.nos.&nos.
NEWS MEMO. [Official Use.]

L 31.10:CT
ADDRESSES.

L 31.11:CT
BLMR RESEARCH STUDIES.

L 31.12:CT
HANDBOOKS, MANUALS, GUIDES.

L 31.13:nos.
BLM REPORTER.

L 31.14:nos.
BLM CORRESPONDENCE CURRICULUM COURSES.
　　[Admin.]

BUREAU OF WORK-TRAINING
PROGRAMS
(1967– 1969)

CREATION AND AUTHORITY

　　The Bureau of Work Programs was established in 1967 within the Manpower Administration of the Department of Labor. The name was
changed to Bureau of Work-Training Programs.
The Bureau was abolished by reorganization of
the Manpower Administration, effective March 17,
1969, and functions transferred to the U.S. Training and Employment Service (L 34).

L 32.1:date
ANNUAL REPORT.

L 32.2:CT
GENERAL PUBLICATIONS.

L 32.8:CT
HANDBOOKS, MANUALS, GUIDES.

L 32.9:CT
ADDRESSES.

UNEMPLOYMENT INSURANCE
SERVICE
(1969– 1975)

CREATION AND AUTHORITY

　　The Unemployment Insurance Service was
established within the Manpower Administration
of the Department of Labor, effective March 17,
1969. In 1975, the Service was placed under the
newly established Employment and Training Administration (L 37.200).

L 33.1:date
ANNUAL REPORT.
　　Later L 37.201

L 33.2:CT   • Item 783-E-1
GENERAL PUBLICATIONS.
　　Later L 37.202

L 33.8:CT   • Item 783-E-2
HANDBOOKS, MANUALS, GUIDES.
　　Earlier L 1.7/2

L 33.9:nos.   • Item 752
BENEFIT SERIES SERVICE, UNEMPLOYMENT
INSURANCE REPORT. [Monthly]

　　Consists of recent decisions in cases arising
out of unemployment insurance claims.
　　ISSN 0005-8750
　　Earlier L 7.37
　　Later L 37.209

L 33.10:date • Item 761-A
SIGNIFICANT PROVISIONS OF STATE UNEMPLOY-
MENT INSURANCE LAWS. [Semiannual]

 Earlier L 7.39/2
 Later L 37.210

L 33.11:date • Item 752-B
UNEMPLOYMENT INSURANCE TAX RATES BY IN-
DUSTRIES.

 Earlier L 7.70

L 33.12:CT • Item 783-E-3
BIBLIOGRAPHIES AND LISTS OF PUBLICATIONS.

 Later L 37.211

TRAINING AND EMPLOYMENT SERVICE
(1969– 1971)

CREATION AND AUTHORITY

 The Training and Employment Service was
established within the Manpower Administration
on March 17, 1969. The Service was abolished by
Secretary's Letter of December 6, 1971 and its
functions transferred to the Office of Employment Development Programs and the reestablished United States Employment Service.

L 34.1:date
ANNUAL REPORT.

L 34.2:CT • Item 755
GENERAL PUBLICATIONS.

L 34.5:CT • Item 759
LAWS.

L 34.8:CT • Item 756-B
HANDBOOKS, MANUALS, GUIDES.

 Later L 37.308

L 34.9:date • Item 752-C
AREA TRENDS IN EMPLOYMENT AND UNEMPLOY-
MENT. [Monthly]

 Earlier L 7.51/3
 Later L 37.13

L 34.10 • Item 756-E
INDUSTRY MANPOWER SURVEYS.

 Earlier L 7.49

OCCUPATIONAL SAFETY AND HEALTH ADMINISTRATION
(1971–   )

CREATION AND AUTHORITY

 The Occupational Safety and Health Administration was established within the Department
of Labor by the Occupational Safety and Health
Act of 1970 (84 Stat. 1590), approved April 28,
1971.

INFORMATION

 Occupational Safety and
 Health Administration
 Department of Labor
 200 Constitution Avenue, N.W.
 Washington, D.C. 20210
 (202) 693-1999
 Fax: (202) 693-2106
 http://www.osha.gov

L 35.1:date • Item 766-F-4 (MF)
ANNUAL REPORT.

L 35.2:CT • Item 765
GENERAL PUBLICATIONS.

L 35.3:nos. • Item 763
BULLETINS.

 Earlier L 16.3

L 35.5:CT • Item 765-C
LAWS.

L 35.6:CT • Item 766-D
REGULATIONS, RULES AND INSTRUCTIONS.

L 35.6/2:CT • Item 766-D
OCCUPATIONAL SAFETY AND HEALTH REGULA-
TIONS. [Irregular]

 L 35.6/3:v.nos. • Item 766-F
 OSHA STANDARDS AND REGULATIONS.

 L 35.6/3-1:date • Item 766-F
 OCCUPATIONAL SAFETY AND HEALTH: VOL-
 UME 1, GENERAL INDUSTRY STANDARD
 AND INTERPRETATIONS.

 L 35.6/3-2:date • Item 766-F
 OCCUPATIONAL SAFETY AND HEALTH: VOL-
 UME 2, MARITIME STANDARDS AND
 INTERPRETATIONS.

 L 35.6/3-3:date • Item 766-F
 OCCUPATIONAL SAFETY AND HEALTH: VOL-
 UME 3, CONSTRUCTION STANDARDS AND
 INTERPRETATIONS.

 L 35.6/3-4:date • Item 766-F
 OCCUPATIONAL SAFETY AND HEALTH: VOL-
 UME 4, OTHER REGULATIONS AND
 PROCEDURES.

 L 35.6/3-5:date • Item 766-F
 OCCUPATIONAL SAFETY AND HEALTH: VOL-
 UME 5, FIELD OPERATIONS MANUAL.

 L 35.6/3-6:date • Item 766-F
 OCCUPATIONAL SAFETY AND HEALTH: VOL-
 UME 6, INDUSTRIAL HYGIENE FIELD
 OPERATIONS MANUAL.

L 35.6/4:CT • Item 766-D
OSHA SAFETY AND HEALTH STANDARDS DIGESTS.

L 35.8:CT • Item 745-C-1
HANDBOOKS, MANUALS, GUIDES.

L 35.8/2:nos.
CONSTRUCTION SAFETY AND HEALTH TRAINING
COURSE.

L 35.9:v.nos.&nos. • Item 766-A
SAFETY STANDARDS. v. 1– 21, no. 5. 1951– Sept./
Oct. 1972. [Bimonthly]
 Superseded by Job Safety and Health (L 35.9/
2).

L 35.9/2:v.nos.&nos. • Item 766-A
JOB SAFETY AND HEALTH. v. 1, no. 1– Nov./Dec.
1972– [Monthly]

 PURPOSE:– To provide a single source for
news and articles on developments in the field of
industrial safety.
 ISSN 0090-4589
 Supersedes Safety Standards (L 35.9).

L 35.9/3:v.nos./nos. • Item 766-O (EL)
JS&HQ (Job Safety & Health Quarterly).

L 35.10:nos. • Item 765-G
OCCUPATIONAL SAFETY AID, DEPARTMENT OF
LABOR SAFETY TRAINING PROGRAMS, OSA-
OSHA- (series). 1– [Irregular]

 Series of informational folders on specific
areas of safety programming. Suitable for safety
committee discussion or training. Covers mechanical and physical hazards.
 Earlier L 16.49

L 35.11:nos. • Item 764-C
SAFE WORK GUIDE, OSHA- (series).

 Earlier L 16.51/2

L 35.11/2:CT • Item 766-J
SAFE WORK PRACTICES SERIES. [Irregular]

L 35.11/3:nos. • Item 766-J
FATAL FACTS: ACCIDENT REPORT. [Quarterly]

L 35.12:nos. • Item 765-F
MARITIME SAFETY DIGEST: SHIPYARDS. [Irregular]

 Earlier L 16.47/3

L 35.13:date • Item 766-G (MF)
OCCUPATIONAL SAFETY AND HEALTH STATISTICS
OF THE FEDERAL GOVERNMENT. 1st– 1972–
[Annual]

 ISSN 0092-8712

L 35.14:date • Item 766-D-1
TECHNICAL NOTES. 1973– [Irregular]

 PURPOSE:– To supplement general interest
new releases and be of interest to trade and
technical publications, trade associations, and
trade unions.
 Each technical note deals with OSHA approval of standards supplements to job safety
and health plans of a different state.
 ISSN 0145-0263

L 35.15:CT
ADDRESSES.

L 35.16:CT • Item 766-L
BIBLIOGRAPHIES AND LISTS OF PUBLICATIONS.

L 35.17:CT • Item 766-H
POLICY AND PROGRAMS SERIES. [Irregular]

L 35.18:CT • Item 766-I
JOB HEALTH HAZARDS SERIES.

L 35.19:CT • Item 766-K
SAFETY MANAGEMENT SERIES.

L 35.20:v.nos. • Item 766-M
INFLATIONARY IMPACT STATEMENTS. [Irregular]

L 35.21:CT • Item 766-F-1
FINAL ENVIRONMENTAL IMPACT STATEMENTS.

L 35.22:CT   • **Item 766-F-2**
CANCER ALERT SERIES. [Irregular]

PURPOSE:– To provide a series of leaflets intended to inform industries about occupational cancer, respiratory diseases, etc., caused by exposure to toxic and hazardous substances.

L 35.23:CT   • **Item 766-F-3**
MAPS AND POSTERS. [Irregular]

L 35.23/2:CT
AUDIOVISUAL MATERIALS. [Irregular]

L 35.24   • **Item 766-F-5**
FACT SHEET.

Fact sheets present Labor Department highlights, each on a different topic, such as job safety and health, the OSHA consultation service, etc.

L 35.24/2:nos.   • **Item 766-F-5**
ALERT BULLETIN (series).

L 35.25:date   • **Item 766-D**
FISCAL YEAR…OSHA TRAINING INSTITUTE SCHEDULE OF COURSES AND REGISTRATION REQUIREMENTS. [Annual]

L 35.25/2:date   • **Item 766-D**
OSHA NATIONAL TRAINING INSTITUTE CATALOG OF COURSES. [Annual]

L 35.26:nos.   • **Item 744-G-1 (CD)**
OSHA DOCUMENTS AND FILES.

L 35.27:nos.   • **Item 766-I**
CHEM ALERT.

L 35.28:nos.   • **Item 766-F-6**
FORMS.

EMPLOYMENT STANDARDS ADMINISTRATION (1971–   )

CREATION AND AUTHORITY

The Employment Standards Administration was established within the Department of Labor by Secretary's Order 13-71, effective April 28, 1971.

INFORMATION

Office of Public Affairs
Employment Standards Administration
Department of Labor
200 Constitution Avenue, N.W.
Room 53321
Washington, D.C. 20210
(202) 693-0023
http://www.dol.gov/esa

L 36.1:date
ANNUAL REPORT.

L 36.2:CT   • **Item 746-C-1**
GENERAL PUBLICATIONS.

L 36.3:nos.   • **Item 763**
BULLETINS. 1–   [Irregular]

Earlier L 16.3

L 36.8:CT   • **Item 746-C-5**
HANDBOOKS, MANUALS, GUIDES. [Irregular]

L 36.9:date   • **Item 780-A (MF)**
MINIMUM WAGE AND MAXIMUM HOURS UNDER THE FAIR LABOR STANDARDS ACT. [Annual]

Earlier L 22.31

L 36.10:nos.   • **Item 764-B (MF)**
LABOR LAW SERIES. 1–   1952–   [Irregular]

PURPOSE:– To communicate in simple language the essential provisions of, and facts relating to State labor laws. Each booklet covers one subject area, and is revised as volume of law changes requires. Although these publications are accurate reflections of the law content, they should not be construed as binding administrative or judicial interpretations.
Previous title: Brief Summaries-Fact Sheets (L 16.50).
Earlier L 16.50/2

L 36.11:date   • **Item 746-C-2 (MF)**
AGE DISCRIMINATION IN EMPLOYMENT ACT OF 1967, REPORTS COVERING ACTIVITIES UNDER THE ACT DURING (year).

L 36.12:date   • **Item 746-C-3 (MF)**
GROUPS WITH HISTORICALLY HIGH INCIDENCES OF UNEMPLOYMENT. [Biennial]

Report to Congress as required by section 4(d)(3) of the Fair Labor Standards Act.

L 36.13:date   • **Item 746-C-4 (MF)**
BLACK LUNG BENEFITS ACT OF 1972, ANNUAL REPORT ON THE ADMINISTRATION OF THE ACT.

L 36.14:v.nos.&nos.   • **Item 766-N**
FARM LABOR CONTRACTOR REGISTRATION ACT, PUBLIC REGISTRY, NATIONAL LISTING OF CONTRACTORS AND EMPLOYEES REGISTERED.

L 36.15:date   • **Item 746-C-7 (MF)**
ESA DIRECTORY OF OFFICES. [Semiannual]

Directory of national and regional offices.

L 36.15/2   • **Item 746-C-10**
DIRECTORIES.

L 36.16:date   • **Item 746-C-9 (MF)**
STATE WORKERS' COMPENSATION: ADMINISTRATION PROFILES. [Annual]

A compilation of information on the administration of workers' compensation programs in each state and the District of Columbia. Includes data on organization/personnel, budget/finance, and insurance requirements.
Earlier L 36.16:W 89/6

L 36.17   • **Item 746-C-8**
FORMS.

Includes miscellaneous forms on various subjects pertaining to the work of the Administration.

L 36.18:date   • **Item 746-C-9 (MF)**
LONGSHORE AND HARBOR WORKERS' COMPENSATION ACT, ANNUAL REPORT ON ADMINISTRATION OF THE ACT DURING FISCAL YEAR . .

WOMEN'S BUREAU (1971–   )

CREATION AND AUTHORITY

The Women's Bureau (L 13) was established by Congress in 1920. It was transferred to the Employment Standards Administration by Secretary's Order 13-71, effective April 28, 1971.

INFORMATION

Women's Bureau
Department of Labor
Room S3002
200 Constitution Ave. NW
Washington, DC 20210
(202) 693-6710
Fax: (202) 693-6746
http://www.dol.gov/wb

L 36.101:date
ANNUAL REPORT.

Earlier L 13.1

L 36.102:CT   • **Item 782**
GENERAL PUBLICATIONS.

Earlier L 13.2

L 36.103:nos.   • **Item 781**
BULLETINS. 1–   1919–   [Irregular]

Popular guides on employment opportunities in various occupations and professions, social work, responsibilities of women workers, employment of older women, civil and political status.
Earlier L 13.3

HANDBOOK ON WOMEN WORKERS. 1948– [Irregular]

PURPOSE:– To bring together basic information on women's employment and occupations; the age and marital status of women workers; women's earnings and income; educational status; and State laws affecting the employment and civil and political status of women.
Includes women in the labor force, laws governing womens's employment and status, organizations of interest to women.
Title, 1948– 1952: Handbook of Facts on Women Workers.
Frequency varies: 1948– 1962, Biennial; 1965–   Irregular.

LEGAL STATUS OF WOMEN IN THE UNITED STATES. [Irregular]

Issued as Bulletin 157. Separate report for each State.
Covers contracts and property, marriage and divorce, parents and children, and political rights of women.

L 36.108:CT   • **Item 736-C-2**
HANDBOOKS, MANUALS, GUIDES.

L 36.109:CT   • **Item 781-A**
FAMILY AND PROPERTY LAW. [Irregular]

A separate release is issued for each State. Covers the law as applicable in specified State for such items as property rights of women, earnings, contracts, liability and family support, property acquired by joint efforts during marriage, inheritance rights, marriage and divorce, age of majority, guardianship, and political rights.
Earlier L 13.17

L 36.110:nos.   • **Item 783**
LEAFLETS. 1–   [Irregular]

This series includes leaflets on various career opportunities for women, containing information on education and training requirements, general job descriptions, salary expectations, etc.
Earlier L 13.11

L 36.111   • **Item 782-A**
LABOR LAWS AFFECTING WOMEN, CAPSULE SUMMARY. [Irregular]
Separate summary issued for each State. Digests current labor laws which are applicable to women, together with the extent of occupational coverage. Subjects include minimum wage, hours of work, plant facilities, and hazardous and unhealthful employment.
Earlier L 13.14

L 36.112:nos.   • **Item 783-C-3**
PAMPHLETS. 1–   1956–   [Irregular]

Earlier L 13.19
Formerly distributed to depository libraries under Item 783-A.

L 36.113:date • Item 783-A-1
MARRIAGE LAWS AS OF (date). [Annual]

Earlier L 13.6/4

L 36.113/2:date • Item 783-A-1
DIVORCE LAWS AS OF (date). [Annual]

Earlier L 13.6/5

L 36.114:CT • Item 783-C-1
WOMEN WORKERS IN [State] (year). [Irregular]

Separate release issued for each State. Consists of a series of statistical tables on employment, age distribution, marital status, education, major occupational groups, industry groups, earnings and income.
Earlier L 13.22

L 36.114/2:date • Item 783-C-1
BACKGROUND FACTS ON WOMEN WORKERS IN THE UNITED STATES. [Irregular]

Earlier L 13.22/2

L 36.114/3:nos. • Item 783-C-3
FACTS ON WORKING WOMEN. [Irregular]

L 36.115:nos.
LEGISLATIVE SERIES. 1–   1972–   [Irregular]

PURPOSE:– To provide brief summaries of new legislation covering women.

L 36.116 • Item 781-B
DIRECTORIES.

WAGE AND HOUR DIVISION
(1971–   )

CREATION AND AUTHORITY

The Wage and Hour Division (L 22) was placed within the Employment Standards Administration by Secretary's Order 13-71, effective April 28, 1971.

INFORMATION

Wage and Hour Division
Department of Labor
Room S-3502
200 Constitution Avenue, N.W.
Washington, D.C. 20210
(202) 693-0051
Fax: (202) 693-1406
http://www.dol.gov/esa/whd/

L 36.201:date
ANNUAL REPORT.

Earlier L 22.1

L 36.202:CT • Item 777
GENERAL PUBLICATIONS.

Earlier L 22.2

L 36.203/2:nos. • Item 777-A-1
CHILD LABOR BULLETINS. 101–   1948– [Irregular]

Earlier L 22.14

L 36.205:CT • Item 778-B
LAWS. [Irregular]

Earlier L 22.5

L 36.205/2:date • Item 778-B
FEDERAL LABOR LAWS. [Irregular] (includes basic volume plus supplementary material for an indefinite period)

Contains all acts, regulations, and interpretative bulletins relative to the Fair Labor Standards Act administered by the Wage and Hour Division.
Earlier L 22.5/3

L 36.205/8:date • Item 778-B
FEDERAL LABOR LAWS. [Irregular] (includes basic volume and supplementary material for an indefinite period)

Contains laws administered by the Wage and Hour Division with regulations and interpretations.

L 36.206:CT • Item 779
REGULATIONS, RULES, AND INSTRUCTIONS.

Earlier L 22.6

L 36.206/2 • Item 780
REGULATIONS, TITLE 29, CODE OF FEDERAL REGULATIONS. [Irregular]
Earlier L 22.9

L 36.208:CT • Item 777-B
HANDBOOKS, MANUALS, GUIDES.
Earlier L 22.33

L 36.209:nos. • Item 778
INTERPRETATIVE BULLETINS. [Irregular]
Earlier L 22.10

L 36.210:CT • Item 777-B-1
POSTERS. [Irregular]

L 36.211:date/v.1 • Item 777-B-5
GENERAL WAGE DETERMINATIONS ISSUED UNDER THE DAVIS-BACON AND RELATED ACTS, VOL. 1, NORTHEASTERN STATES.

Covers: Connecticut, Maine, Massachusetts, New Hampshire, New Jersey, New York, Puerto Rico, Virgin Islands, Vermont.

L 36.211:date/v.2 • Item 777-B-6
GENERAL WAGE DETERMINATIONS ISSUED UNDER THE DAVIS-BACON AND RELATED ACTS, VOL. 2, MID ATLANTIC STATES.

Covers: Delaware, District of Columbia, Maryland, Pennsylvania, Virginia, West Virginia.

L 36.211:date/v.3 • Item 777-B-7
GENERAL WAGE DETERMINATIONS ISSUED UNDER THE DAVIS-BACON AND RELATED ACTS, VOL. 3. SOUTHEASTERN STATES.

Covers: Alabama, Florida, Georgia, Kentucky, Mississippi, North Carolina, South Carolina, Tennessee.

L 36.211:date/v.4 • Item 777-B-8
GENERAL WAGE DETERMINATIONS ISSUED UNDER THE DAVIS-BACON AND RELATED ACTS, VOL. 4. NORTH CENTRAL STATES.
Covers: Illinois, Indiana, Michigan, Minnesota, Ohio, Wisconsin.

L 36.211:date/v.5 • Item 777-B-9
GENERAL WAGE DETERMINATIONS ISSUED UNDER THE DAVIS-BACON AND RELATED ACTS, VOL. 5. SOUTH CENTRAL STATES.

Covers: Arkansas, Iowa, Kansas, Louisiana, Mississippi, Nebraska, New Mexico, Oklahoma, Texas.

L 36.211:date/v.6 • Item 777-B-4
GENERAL WAGE DETERMINATIONS ISSUED UNDER THE DAVIS-BACON AND RELATED ACTS, VOL. 6. WESTERN STATES

Covers: Alaska, Arizona, California, Colorado, Guam, Hawaii, Idaho, Montana, Nevada, North Dakota, Oregon, South Dakota, Utah, Washington, Wyoming.

L 36.211:date/v.7 • Item 777-B-10
GENERAL WAGE DETERMINATIONS ISSUED UNDER THE DAVIS-BACON AND RELATED ACTS, VOL. 7.

Covers Arizona, California, Hawaii, Nevada.

L 36.211/2 • Item 777-B-11
DAVIS-BACON WAGE DETERMINATIONS (online database).

L 36.212:CT • Item 777-C
FORMS.

L 36.213: • Item 777-A-2 (EL)
FACT SHEETS.

L 36.214: • Item 777-A-2 (E)
ELECTRONIC PRODUCTS (misc.).

L 36.215: • Item 777-A-2 (EL)
GARMENT ENFORCEMENT REPORT.

OFFICE OF FEDERAL EMPLOYEES' COMPENSATION
(1971–   )

INFORMATION

Office of Federal Employees' Compensation
Department of Labor
Washington, D.C. 20210

L 36.301:date
ANNUAL REPORT.

L 36.302:CT • Item 750
GENERAL PUBLICATIONS.

L 36.309:letters-nos. • Item 763-A-1
PAMPHLETS.

OFFICE OF WORKERS' COMPENSATION PROGRAMS
(1975–   )

CREATION AND AUTHORITY

The Office Wage Copmpensation Programs was established within the Employment Standards Administration of the Department of Labor in 1971. In 1973 the name was changed to Office of Workmens' Compensation Programs. In 1975 the name was again changed to Office of Workers' Compensation Programs.

INFORMATION

Office of Workers' Compensation Program
Department of Labor
Room S3524
200 Constitution Ave. NW
Washington, DC 20210
(202) 693-0031
Fax: (202) 693-1378
http://www.dol/gov/esa/owcp_org.htm

L 36.401:date • Item 779-A-6 (MF)
OWCP ANNUAL REPORT.

L 36.402:CT • Item 779-A-3
GENERAL PUBLICATIONS.

L 36.408:CT • Item 779-A-2
HANDBOOKS, MANUALS, GUIDES.

L 36.409:nos. • Item 779-A-1
PAMPHLETS (numbered).

L 36.410 • Item 746-C-6
FORMS. [Irregular]

L 36.411 • Item 779-A-4 (MF)
STATE WORKERS' COMPENSATION ADMINISTRA-
TION PROFILES. [Annual]

L 36.412 • Item 779-A-5 (MF) (EL)
STATE WORKERS' COMPENSATION LAWS.
[Semiannual]

EMPLOYMENT AND TRAINING
ADMINISTRATION
(1975–   )

CREATION AND AUTHORITY

The Employment and Training Administration
was established within the Department of Labor
by Secretary's Order 14-75 of November 12, 1975
to succeed the Manpower Administration (L 1.39),
which abolished by the same order.

INFORMATION

Employment and Training Administration
Department of Labor
200 Constitution Ave. NW
Washington, DC 20210
(202) 693-2700
Fax: (202) 693-2725
http://www.doleta.gov

L 37.1:date
ANNUAL REPORT.

L 37.2:CT • Item 780-A-1
GENERAL PUBLICATIONS.

L 37.6:CT • Item 780-A-4
REGULATIONS, RULES AND INSTRUCTIONS.
[Irregular]

L 37.8:CT • Item 780-A-3
HANDBOOKS, MANUALS, GUIDES. [Irregular]

L 37.8/2:nos. • Item 747-B
ET [Employment Training] HANDBOOKS.

Supersedes MA [Manpower Administration]
Handbooks (L 1.7/8).

L 37.8/3:CT • Item 780-A-2
CETA TECHNICAL DOCUMENTS (series). [Irregular]

L 37.8/4:CT • Item 756-A
INTERVIEWING GUIDES FOR SPECIFIC DISABILI-
TIES.

PURPOSE:– To acquaint counselors with the
nature of disabilities and to assist him in understanding the medical and psychological aspects
of such disabilities.
Earlier L 1.7/7

L 37.8/6:CT • Item 780-A-7 (MF)
CETA PROGRAM MODELS (series). [Irregular]

PURPOSE:– Designed to make available to
prime sponsor staffs the lessons some of the
more experienced of their colleagues feel they
have learned from service in the Comprehensive
Employment and Training Act (CETA) and previous programs. Covers program activities and service, and innovative programs.

L 37.9:v.nos.&nos. • Item 754-F
ETA INTERCHANGE. v. 1– 7. 1975– 1981. [Monthly]

ISSN 0364-2011
Earlier L 1.69

L 37.10:v.nos.&nos. • Item 746-N
WORKLIFE. [Monthly]

Designed for officials in industry, labor and
Government who need authoritative information
on what is being done about employment and
why, where, and how for whom it is being done.
ISSN 0361-7718
Supersedes L 1.39/9

L 37.11:v.nos.&nos. • Item 746-N-1
JOB CORPS HAPPENINGS. v. 1– 18.   – 1982.
[Monthly]

ISSN 0095-0025

L 37.11/2:date • Item 746-N-1
JOB CORPS HAPPENINGS, SPECIAL EDITIONS.
[Irregular]

PURPOSE:– To recruit applicants for Job
Corps training and answer questions about job
course training opportunities, living conditions,
and facilities in Job Corps centers, and other
related matters.

L 37.11/3:nos. • Item 857-H-1
JOB CORPS HANDBOOKS, JCH- (series). [Irregular]

Earlier L 1.58

L 37.12:date • Item 752-C
UNEMPLOYMENT INSURANCE STATISTICS. 1964–
1980. [Monthly]

PURPOSE:– To produce data that are collected and reported under employment insurance
programs in the 50 States, the District of Columbia, Puerto Rico, and the Virgin Islands, and under Federal programs covering Federal civilian
employees and ex-servicemen. Information is
given on benefit payment activities, employer
contributions, appeals, decisions, and disqualifi-
cations by issues; for selected industries and
major occupational groups; and by claimant's age,
sex and duration of employment.
The data are compiled by cooperating State
employment security agencies and, in some
cases, come from interviews with a sample of
claimants in local office of the Federal-State employment security system.
ISSN 0146-6038
Earlier L 1.62/2

L 37.12/2:date • Item 780-A-12 (EL)
UNEMPLOYMENT INSURANCE WEEKLY CLAIMS
REPORTS. v. 1–   1945– [Weekly]

Contains weekly analysis of unemployment
insurance claims and includes most recent weekly
data by State on initial claims and on insured
unemployment. A supplement attached once a
month provides preliminary monthly data on ex-
haustions and data on total insured unemployment in the major labor market areas for the week
ended nearest the middle of the month. Weekly
data for the entire year are presented in an annual
summary.
Prior to v. 31, no. 19, dated November 17,
1975, issued by the Manpower Administration (L
1.62).
ISSN 0097-8841

L 37.12/2-2:date/nos. • Item 780-A-12
UNEMPLOYMENT INSURANCE WEEKLY CLAIMS
REPORT. [Weekly]

Contains data on State and Federal prorams,
and provides seasonally adjusted data and unadjusted data.

L 37.13:date • Item 752-C
AREA TRENDS IN EMPLOYMENT AND UNEMPLOY-
MENT. [Monthly]

Prepared from area labor market reports from
State and local employment security offices affiliated with Bureau of Employment Security.
As part of its area labor marketing program,
the Bureau of Employment Security rates or "clas-
sifies" 150 major production and employment centers, and a number of small areas, according to
the adequacy of their labor supply.

Presents a national round-up of area labor
market developments and outlook and separate
brief summaries for selected areas. Statistical
Supplement gives unemployment in major areas,
including work force, total employment and unemployment in 150 major employment centers.
ISSN 0004-0916
Earlier L 34.9

L 37.14:nos. • Item 746-H (MF)
R & D MONOGRAPHS. 1–   [Irregular]

Formerly issued by Manpower Research and
Development Administration (L 1.39/2).

L 37.14/2:nos. • Item 746-H-1
MONOGRAPHS. (series) 1–   [Irregular]

PURPOSE:– To provide Private Industry Council staff members and other Comprehensive Employment Training Act planners, etc., with labor
market information.

L 37.15:CT • Item 780-A-5
BIBLIOGRAPHIES AND LISTS OF PUBLICATIONS.
[Irregular]

L 37.16:nos. • Item 780-A-6
OCCUPATIONAL AND CAREER INFORMATION (series). 1–   1977–   [Irregular]

PURPOSE:– To provide an occupationally oriented overview of the field for employment and
career counselors, as well as students and other
interested readers. Contains detailed descriptions
of current occupations, educational and training
requirements, the worker traits necessary, and
material on how to acquire the needed education
and training for entry into the field.

L 37.17:date • Item 780-A-8
LISTING OF ELIGIBLE LABOR SURPLUS AREAS
UNDER DEFENSE MANPOWER POLICY NO. 4A
AND EXECUTIVE ORDER 10582. [Quarterly]

Includes the name of the area and the political jurisdiction encompassed by the area. Provides a separate listing of areas added and de-
leted since the previous quarter.

L 37.18:date • Item 753-A
DIRECTORY OF LOCAL EMPLOYMENT SECURITY
OFFICES. [Irregular]

Earlier L 1.59

L 37.19:date • Item 780-A-9
YOUTH PROGRAM MODELS AND INNOVATIONS.
[Monthly]

PURPOSE:– To provide descriptions and
evaluations of various innovative and model employment, training, etc., programs and projects,
both government and privately supported, for
youth.

L 37.19/2:nos. • Item 780-A-11 (MF)
YOUTH KNOWLEDGE DEVELOPMENT REPORTS. 1–
1980–   [Irregular]
PURPOSE:– To provide a firm informational
basis for public policy to address youth employment problems and mandated by the Youth Employment and Demonstration Projects Act.

L 37.20:nos. • Item 780-A-10
UNEMPLOYMENT INSURANCE OCCASIONAL
PAPERS. [Irregular]

PURPOSE:– To present technical research
findings and analyses of various topics pertaining to unemployment insurance.

L 37.20/2:nos. • Item 780-A-10
UNEMPLOYMENT INSURANCE, TECHNICAL STAFF
PAPERS. 1–   [Irregular]

L 37.20/3 • Item 780-A-10 (MF)
UNEMPLOYMENT INSURANCE QUALITY CONTROL,
ANNUAL REPORT.

L 37.21:CT • Item 780-A-13
FACT SHEET (series). [Irregular]

Fact sheets highlight Administration activities. Each relates to a different topic.

L 37.21/2-2:date • Item 780-A-12
UNEMPLOYMENT INSURANCE WEEKLY CLAIMS REPORT. [Weekly]

L 37.22: • Item 746-H-2 (MF)
RESEARCH, EVALUATION, AND DEMONSTRATION PROJECTS. [Annual]

PURPOSE– To summarize projects funded by the Administration's Office of Strategic Planning and Policy Development. The 1986 edition includes projects completed between 1978 and December 31, 1986. Contains title, keyword, personal author, contract/grant, and NTIS order number indexes.

L 37.22/2:nos. • Item 746-H-2 (MF) (EL)
RESEARCH AND EVALUATION REPORT SERIES.

L 37.23:date • Item 746-H-2
TRAINING AND EMPLOYMENT REPORT OF THE SECRETARY OF LABOR. [Annual]

L 37.24:CT • Item 780-B
POSTERS.

L 37.25:CT • Item 744-G-4 (E)
ELECTRONIC PRODUCTS.

L 37.26: • Item 780-A-14 (P) (EL)
IDEAS THAT WORK (series). [Irregular]

APPRENTICESHIP TRAINING, EMPLOYER AND LABOR SERVICES (1975–   )

CREATION AND AUTHORITY

The Bureau of Apprenticeship and Training (L 23) was placed within the Employment and Training Administration by Secretary's Order 14-75 of November 12, 1975. Name changed to Apprenticeship Training, Employer and Labor Services.

INFORMATION

Apprenticeship Training Employer
and Labor Services
Department of Labor
200 Constitution Ave., NW
Washington, DC 20210
(202) 693-2796
Fax: (202) 693-2808

L 37.101:date
ANNUAL REPORT.

Earlier L 23.1

L 37.102:CT • Item 748
GENERAL PUBLICATIONS.

Earlier L 23.2

L 37.106/2:CT • Item 748
NATIONAL APPRENTICESHIP AND TRAINING STANDARDS FOR [various occupations].

L 37.108:CT • Item 748-C
HANDBOOKS, MANUALS, GUIDES.

Earlier L 23.6/2

L 37.109 • Item 748-C (MF)
TELEPHONE DIRECTORY, BUREAU OF APPRENTICESHIP AND TRAINING.

WORKFORCE SECURITY OFFICE (1975–   )

CREATION AND AUTHORITY

The Unemployment Insurance Service (L 33) was placed within the Employment and Training Administration by Secretary's Order 14-75 of November 12, 1975.Name changed to Workforce Security Office.

INFORMATION

Workforce Security Office
Department of Labor
Washington, D.C. 20210
(202) 219-7831
http://www.ows.doleta.gov/ui.asp

L 37.201:date
ANNUAL REPORT.

Earlier L 33.1

L 37.202:CT • Item 783-E-1
GENERAL PUBLICATIONS.

Earlier L 33.2

L 37.208:CT • Item 783-E-2
HANDBOOKS, MANUALS, GUIDES.[Irregularl

L 37.209:nos. • Item 752
BENEFIT SERIES SERVICE, UNEMPLOYMENT INSURANCE REPORT. 1-333.   – 1981. [Irregular]

ISSN 0005-8750
Earlier L 33.9

L 37.210:date • Item 761-A (MF)
SIGNIFICANT PROVISIONS OF STATE UNEMPLOYMENT INSURANCE LAWS. [Semiannual]

Earlier L 33.10

L 37.211:CT • Item 783-E-3
BIBLIOGRAPY AND LISTS OF PUBLICATIONS. [Irregular]

Earlier L 33.12

L 37.212:date • Item 783-E-4 (EL)
COMPARISON OF STATE UNEMPLOYMENT INSURANCE LAWS. [Semiannual]

PURPOSE:-To report State by State the types of workers and employers that are covered under the State laws; the method of financing the program; the benefits that are payable; the conditions to be met for payment; and administrative organizations established to do the job.
Earlier L 33.2:St 2/2

L 37.213:date • Item 738-E-5 (MF)
UNEMPLOYMFNT INSURANCE QUALITY APPRAISAL RESULTS. [Annual]

PURPOSE:-To present results of monitoring and appraisal of the Unemployed Insurance program as it is administered by State agencies.

L 37.213/2 • Item 783-E-5 (MF)
UNEMPLOYMENT INSURANCE OCCASIONAL PAPER.

L 37.214:date • Item 783-E-5 (EI)
UI DATA SUMMARY. [Quarterly]

L 37.215:date • Item 783-E-6
UI OUTLOOK.

UNITED STATES EMPLOYMENT SERVICE (1933–   )

CREATION AND AUTHORITY FOR USES:

The U.S. Employment Service is a nationwide system of public employment offices established by the Wagner-Peyser Act of 1933. This act was amended by The Workforce Investment Act of 1988. The Employment Service has been known as The Job Service, Labor Board and Unemployment Office.

INFORMATION

U.S. Employment Service
Department of Labor
Washington, D.C. 20210
(202) 693-3428
http://workforce security.doleta.gov//
employ.asp

L 37.301:date
ANNUAL REPORT.

L 37.302:CT • Item 755
GENERAL PUBLICATIONS. [Irregularl

L 37.302-Oc 1 • Item 755
DICTIONARY OF OCCUPATIONAL TITLES. 1st ed- [Irregular]

A compendium of about 20,000 occupations in the American economy, this large volume contains an integrated arrangement of occupational definitions and the classification structure used to group such occupations in terms of related duties and activities. It includes sections on the purpose and history of the Dictionary and how to use it as an occupational reference source or as tool for job placement. It contains occupational titles arranged alphabetically and by industry, and a glossary of defined technical terms.
Earlier L 7.2:Oc 1

L 37.308:CT • Item 756-B
HANDBOOKS, MANUALS, GUIDES. [Irregular]

Earlier L 34.8

L 37.308/2:nos. • Item 754-L
TECHNICAL ASSISTANCE GUIDES. [Irregularl

L 37.309:nos. • Item 754-G (MF)
TECHNICAL REPORT (numbered). [Irregular]

L 37.310:nos. • Item 754-H
JOB OPENINGS. 1-7. June 1977-1983. [Monthly]
PURPOSE:-To identify occupations for which large numbers of job openings were listed with public employment services computerized job banks during the previous month.
Continues: Occupations in Demand at Job Service Offices.

L 37.310/2:nos. • Item 754-H
JOB OPENINGS, EXTRA EDITION FOR STUDENTS AND RECENT GRADUATES.

Former title: Occupations on Demand at Job Service Offices, Extra Edition for Students and Recent Graduates.

L 37.311:date • Item 754-J (MF)
JOB BANK, FREQUENTLY LISTED OPENINGS [JOB-FLO]. [Monthly]

PURPOSE—To provide information on occupations for which there is a relatively large number of job listings in the preceding month with the public employment service Job Bank System. Includes professional, clerical, service, structural, etc., occupations by geographical area.
Information guide to the use of the publication issued twice a year.
Published in microfiche (48x).

L 37.312:nos. • Item 754-G (MF)
USES TEST RESEARCH REPORTS (series). 1- [Irregular]

L 37.313:CT • Item 754-M
FORMS. [Irregular]

MINE SAFETY AND HEALTH ADMINISTRATION
(1978–   )

CREATION AND AUTHORITY

The Mine Safety and Health Administration was established within the Department of Labor pursuant to the Federal Mine Safety and Health Amendments Act of 1977 (91 Stat. 1290), superseding the Mining Enforcement and Safety Administration (I 69) which was abolished.

INFORMATION

Office of Public Affairs
Mine Safety and Health Administration
Department of Labor
1100 Wilson Boulevard
Arlington, Virginia 22203
(202) 693-9400
Fax: (202) 693-9421
http://www.msha.gov

L 38.1:date
ANNUAL REPORT.

L 38.2:CT • Item 637-H
GENERAL PUBLICATIONS. [Irregular]

L 38.4: • Item 637-J-3
CIRCULARS.

L 38.5:CT • Item 637-J-2
LAWS. [Irregular]

L 38.6:CT • Item 644
REGULATIONS, RULES, AND INSTRUCTIONS. [Irregular]

L 38.8:CT • Item 637-K-2
HANDBOOKS, MANUALS, GUIDES. [Irregular]

L 38.8/2:nos./date • Item 644-A (MF)
SAFETY MANUALS. [Irregular]

Earlier I 69.8/2

L 38.9:v.nos.&nos. • Item 637-I
MINE SAFETY AND HEALTH. v. 1–   1975– [Bimonthly]

Prior to the February-March 1978 issue, published as MESA, the Magazine of Mining Health and Safety by the Mining Enforcement and Safety Administration, (I 69.11).
ISSN 0161-651X

L 38.10:nos. • Item 637-K-1 (MF)
INFORMATION REPORTS, IR- (series). 1–   [Irregular]
Earlier I 69.9

INJURY EXPERIENCE IN COAL MINING. [Annual] (Health and Safety Analysis Center, Division of Mining Information Systems, Denver, Colorado)

PURPOSE:– To present injury data and related employment statistics under the following topics; general injury experience, selected injury experience, injury experience by States, major disasters, and historical coal-mine-facility experience.
Prior to 1971, published by the Bureau of Mines in its Information Circular Series (I 28.27).
ISSN 0094-0432

INJURY EXPERIENCE IN QUARRYING. [Annual] (Health and Safety Analysis Center, Division of Mining Information Systems, Denver, Colorado)

Previously published by the Bureau of Mines in its Information Circular series (I 28.27).
ISSN 0098-4906

INJURY EXPERIENCE IN THE METALLIC MINERAL INDUSTRIES. [Annual] (Health and Safety Analysis Center, Division of Mining Information Systems, Denver, Colorado)

PURPOSE:– To provide statistical data compiled and analyzed by the Bureau of Mines on the various aspects of injury experience at metal mines, mills, and primary nonferrous smelters, refineries, and reduction plants. The statistical data on employment, worktime, and operating activity of the same industrial areas, obtained as correlative information to the injury data, also are presented.
Previously published by the Bureau of Mines in its Information Circular series (I 28.27).
ISSN 0160-8452

INJURY EXPERIENCE IN THE NONMETALLIC INDUSTRIES, EXCEPT STONE AND COAL. [Annual] (Health and Safety Analysis Center, Division of Mining Information Systems, Denver, Colorado)

PURPOSE:– To present injury experience and employment data for the nonmetal mines and mills, by States, type of mining, and principal nonmetallic minerals extracted, such as abrasives, asbestos, barite, clay, feldspar, fluorspar, gypsum, magnesite, mica, phosphate rock, potash, pumic salt, sulfur, talc and soapstone, and miscellaneous nonmetals.
Previously published by the Bureau of Mines in its Information Circular series (I 28.27).
ISSN 0160-8452

INJURY EXPERIENCE IN THE SAND AND GRAVEL INDUSTRY. [Annual] (Health and Safety Analysis Center, Division of Mining Information Systems, Denver, Colorado)

Continues Injury Experience and Worktime Data for the Sand and Gravel Industry (ISSN 0364-3131) (I 69.10/3).

L 38.10/2: • Item 637-K-1
INJURY EXPERIENCE IN SAND AND GRAVEL MINING. [Annual]

L 38.10/3:date • Item 637-P (MF)
INJURY EXPERIENCE IN STONE MINING. [Annual]

L 38.10/4: • Item 637-P-1 (MF)
INJURY EXPERIENCE IN COAL MINING.

L 38.10/5: • Item 637-P-2 (MF)
INJURY EXPERIENCE IN NONMETALLIC MINING (EXCEPT STONE AND COAL).

L 38.11:CT • Item 637-J
BIBLIOGRAPHIES AND LISTS OF PUBLICATIONS. [Irregular]

L 38.11/2:date/nos. • Item 637-J
NEW PUBLICATIONS. [Quarterly]

L 38.11/3: • Item 637-J
CATALOG OF TRAINING PRODUCTS FOR THE MINING INDUSTRY. [Annual]

L 38.11/4:nos. • Item 637-J
COURSES OF MSHA AND THE MINING INDUSTRY. [Annual]

L 38.11/4-2:date/nos. • Item 637-J
QUARTERLY UPDATE OF COURSES AND PRODUCTS.

L 38.12:date • Item 637-K (EL)
HOLMES SAFETY ASSOCIATION BULLETIN. [Monthly]

PURPOSE:– To provide mine safety personnel, owners, and miners with information pertaining to safety in underground and surface mines.

L 38.13:date • Item 637-J-1 (MF)
ANNUAL REPORT AND ACHIEVEMENTS, FISCAL YEAR (date).

Summarizes Administration activities in its overall function of enforcing the Federal Mine Safety and Health Act of 1977.

L 38.14:CT
AUDIOVISUAL MATERIAL. [Irregular]

L 38.14/2:CT • Item 637-N
POSTERS.

L 38.15: • Item 637-M (EL)
FATALGRAMS (series). [Irregular]

Fatalgrams are issued by the Administration's Metal and Nonmetal Mine and Safety Health Activity as accidents occur. They are single sheets with narrative description and a drawing of the accident.

L 38.16:date • Item 637-P (MF)
MINE INJURIES AND WORKTIME. [Quarterly]

Contains a chart showing the number of fatal injuries in the U.S. for the last three years. Other tables present various data on the number of operator injuries and the number of contractor injuries.

L 38.17:nos.
MSHA POLICY MEMORANDUM (series).

L 38.17/2:nos. • Item 637-K-3
MSHA PROGRAM INFORMATION BULLETIN (series). [Irregular]

Each bulletin is expected to concern a different topic, such as the reporting obligations of mine operators under Title 30 CFR Part 50.

L 38.17/2-2 • Item 637-K-6 (MF)
(MSHA) PROGRAM POLICY LETTER (Series).

L 38.17/3:nos./date • Item 637-K-5 (MF)
MSHA INSTRUCTION GUIDE SERIES. [Irregular]

Instruction guides on miscellaneous topics pertaining to the work of the Mine Safety and Health Administration.

L 38.18 • Item 637-K-4 (MF)
PROGRAMMED INSTRUCTION WORKBOOKS (series). [Irregular]

Each workbook deals with a different topic, such as roof and rib control.
Earlier I 69.12

L 38.19: • Item 637-M-1
POWER HAULAGE FATALITIES, COAL AND METAL/NONMETAL MINES. [Annual]

Presents one page abstracts of investigations of powered haulage fatalities in mining states from Arizona to Wisconsin.

L 38.19/2:date • Item 637-M-1
METAL/NONMETAL-UNDERGROUND FATALITIES. [Bi-annual]

Combined with Metal/Nonmetal Surface Fatalities (L 38.19/3) to form Metal/Nonmetal, Surface and Underground Fatalities (L 38.19/4).

L 38.19/3:date • Item 637-M-1
METAL/NONMETAL-SURFACE FATALITIES. [Semiannual]

Combined with Metal/Nonmetal Underground Fatalities (L 38.19/2) to form Metal/Nonmetal, Surface and Underground Fatalities (L 38.19/4).

L 38.19/3-2 • Item 637-M-2
FATAL ACCIDENTS INVOLVING DROWNING AT COAL AND METAL/NONMETAL MINES.

L 38.19/4:date • Item 637-M-1
METAL/NONMETAL, SURFACE AND UNDERGROUND FATALITIES.

Combines Metal/Nonmetal Underground Fatalities (L 38.19/2) with Metal/Nonmetal Surface Fatalities (L 38.19/3).

L 38.20:date • Item 637-K-1
FATALITIES IN SMALL UNDERGROUND COAL MINES. [Annual]

L 38.20/2:date • Item 637-K-1
COAL: UNDERGROUND FATALITIES. [Biannual]

Combined with Coal Surface Fatalities (L 38.20/3) to form Coal, Surface and Underground Fatalities (L 38.20/5).

L 38.20/3:date • Item 637-K-1
COAL: SURFACE FATALITIES. [Biannual]

Combined with Coal Underground Fatalities (L 38.20/2) to form Coal, Surface and Underground Fatalities (L 38.20/5).

L 38.20/3-3 • Item 637-K-7
COAL FATALITIES. [Semiannual]

L 38.20/4:date • Item 637-M-1
CONTRACTOR FATALITIES COAL AND METAL/NON-METAL MINES. [Annual]

L 38.20/5:date • Item 637-K-1
COAL, SURFACE AND UNDERGROUND FATALITIES.

Combines Coal Underground Fatalities (L 38.20/2) with Coal Surface Fatalities (L 38.20/3).

L 38.20/6 • Item 637-H-1
OT SERIES.

L 38.21 • Item 637-H-1
MINE EMERGENCY OPERATIONS TELEPHONE BOOK. [Annual]

VETERANS' EMPLOYMENT & TRAINING SERVICE
(1981–)

CREATION AND AUTHORITY

The office of the Assistant Secretary for Veterans' Employment and Training (OASVET) was established by Secretary's Order No. 5-81 in December 1981.

INFORMATION

Veterans' Employment and Training Service
Department of Labor
Room S1313
200 Constitution Ave. NW
Washington, DC 20210
(202) 693-4700
Fax: (202) 693-4754
http://www.dol.gov/vets

L 39.2:CT • Item 773-B
GENERAL PUBLICATIONS.

L 39.8: • Item 773-B-1
HANDBOOKS, MANUALS, GUIDES.

L 39.8/2:date • Item 773-B-2 (MF)
TRANSITION ASSISTANCE PROGRAM MILITARY CIVILIAN ONE GOOD JOB DESERVES ANOTHER PARTICIPANT MANUAL. [Biennial]

PENSION AND WELFARE BENEFITS ADMINISTRATION
(1974–)

INFORMATION

Pension and Welfare Benefits Administration
Department of Labor
Room S2524
200 Constitution Ave. NW
Washington, DC 20210
(202) 693-8300
Fax: (202) 219-5526
http://www.dol.gov/pwba

L 40.2:CT • Item 773-C
GENERAL PUBLICATIONS.

L 40.8:CT • Item 773-C-1
HANDBOOKS, MANUALS, GUIDES.

L 40.15:date • Item 744-F (MF)
EMPLOYEE RETIREMENT INCOME SECURITY ACT, REPORT TO CONGRESS. [Annual]

L 40.16 • Item 773-C-2 (MF)
PRIVATE PENSION PLAN BULLETIN. [Semiannual]

DISABILITY EMPLOYMENT POLICY OFFICE

L 41.2 • Item 783-F
GENERAL PUBLICATIONS.

L 41.8 • Item 783-F-1
HANDBOOKS, MANUALS, GUIDES.

L 41.15 • Item 783-F-2
BRAILLE PUBLICATIONS.

BUREAU OF LABOR
(1888–1903)

CREATION AND AUTHORITY

The Bureau of Labor was first organized in January 1885 under act of Congress, approved June 27, 1884, as part of the Department of the Interior. By act of Congress approved June 13, 1888, it became an independent agency with the title of Department of Labor, but without executive rank. It returned to a bureau status and was transferred to the newly created Department of Commerce and Labor (C 8) by act of Congress, approved February 14, 1903 (32 Stat. 827).

La 1.1:date
ANNUAL REPORTS.

Later C 8.1

La 1.2:CT
GENERAL PUBLICATIONS.

Later C 8.2

La 1.3:v.nos.
BULLETINS. [Bimonthly]

Later C 8.3

La 1.4:nos.
CIRCULARS (none issued).

La 1.5:nos.
SPECIAL REPORTS.

Later C 8.5

La 1.6:nos.
MONOGRAPHS ON SOCIAL ECONOMICS.

La 1.7:date
REPORTS ON HAWAII.

LIBRARY OF CONGRESS
(1800–)

CREATION AND AUTHORITY

The Library of Congress was established under the law approved April 24, 1800, appropriating $5,000 "for the purchase of such books as may be necessary for the use of Congress" (2 Stat. 56). The subsequent act of January 26, 1802, provided that "a librarian to be appointed by the President of the United States solely, shall take charge of the said library" (2 Stat. 129). The law library was created and made a part of the Library of Congress by the act of July 14, 1832 (5 Stat. 579; 2 U.S.C. 132, 134, 135, 137); the library of the Smithsonian Institution was deposited in the Library of Congress under the act of April 5, 1866 (14 Stat. 13; 2 U.S.C. 151). The Appropriation Act of February 19, 1897, provided for the appointment of the Librarian by the President, by and with the advice and consent of the Senate; vested in the Librarian the authority to appoint all the members of the staff "solely with reference to their fitness for their fitness for their particular duties" (29 Stat. 544; 2 U.S.C. 140); gave him the authority also to "make rules and regulations for the government of the Library" (29 Stat. 545, 42 Stat. 715; 2 U.S.C. 136); and created in it various departments (subsequently entitled "divisions") to perform certain processes or administer certain groups of material, e.g., manuscripts, maps, etc.

INFORMATION

Library of Congress
James Madison Memorial Bldg.
101 Independence. Ave. SE
Washington, DC 20540-4000
(202) 707-5000
http://www.loc.gov

LC 1.1:date • Item 785 (MF)
ANNUAL REPORT OF THE LIBRARIAN OF CONGRESS. 1866– [Irregular]

Report submitted by the Librarian of Congress to Congress for the fiscal year. Covers activities and operations for the year of the various Departments of the Library, including the Copyright Office. Appendix contains tables.
ISSN 0083-1565

LC 1.1/2:date   • **Item 785 (MF)**
LIBRARY OF CONGRESS, A BRIEF SUMMARY OF MAJOR ACTIVITIES IN THE FISCAL YEAR.

    Earlier LC 1.2:L 61/18

LC 1.2:CT   • **Item 786**
GENERAL PUBLICATIONS.

LC 1.3:nos.
BULLETINS [none issued].

LC 1.4:nos.
CIRCULARS [none issued].

LC 1.5:date
CATALOGS. 1802–

LC 1.6:CT
REGULATIONS, RULES, AND INSTRUCTIONS.

LC 1.6/2:nos.
LIBRARY ORDERS. 1– 1897–

    Changed from LC 1.6

LC 1.6/3:nos.
SPECIAL ORDERS.

LC 1.6/4:CT   • **Item 786-A**
HANDBOOKS, MANUALS, GUIDES.

    LC 1.6/4:C 44   • **Item 786-A**
    GUIDE TO SELECTED LEGAL SOURCES OF MAINLAND CHINA. 1967. 357 p. il. (Far Eastern Law Division, Law Library)

    Covers laws and regulations and periodical legal literature with a brief survey of administration of justice.

    LC 1.6/4:M 18/update/date   • **Item 786-A**
    MARC SERIALS EDITING GUIDE, BIMONTHLY UPDATES.

    Prior to 1980, issued as Monthly Updates.

LC 1.6/4-2:date   • **Item 786-A-1**
CONSER EDITING GUIDE. [Semiannual]

LC 1.6/5:nos.   • **Item 786-A**
REFERENCE GUIDES (Series).

LC 1.7:letters
CLASSIFICATION.
    Later LC 26.9

LC 1.7/2:nos.
L.C. CLASSIFICATION, ADDITIONS AND CHANGES. 1– 41. 1928– 1940.

    Later LC 26.9/2

LC 1.8:nos.
NOTES FOR LOUISIANA PURCHASE EXPOSITION, ST. LOUIS, MO., 1904. 1– 5. 1904.

LC 1.9:date
ALA CATALOG.

LC 1.10:date
ALA PORTRAIT INDEX. 1906. 1601 p.

    Provides an index to over 120,000 portraits in 1181 sets (6216 volumes), including books and periodicals published through 1904.

LC 1.11:v.nos.
RECORDS OF VIRGINIA COMPANY OF LONDON. v. 1– 1906–

LC 1.12:date
PUBLICATIONS ISSUED SINCE 1897. 1902– 1935.

LC 1.12/2:CT   • **Item 785-A**
BIBLIOGRAPHIES AND LISTS OF PUBLICATIONS. [Irregular]

    Earlier LC 1.2

LC 1.12/2:Ar 1   • **Item 785-A**
AMERICAN DOCTORAL DISSERTATIONS ON THE ARAB WORLDS, 1883– 1968. 1970. 103 p. (Near East Section, Orientalia Division)

    List doctoral dissertations on all subjects related to the Arab World accepted by universities in the United States and Canada from 1883 through the academic year 1967/68.

LC 1.12/2:G 74   • **Item 785-A**
GOVERNMENT ORGANIZATION MANUALS, A BIBLIOGRAPHY. 1975. 105 p.

LC 1.12/2:P 75   • **Item 785-A**
CHILDREN AND POETRY. 1969. 67 p. il. (Children's Book Section, General Reference)

    This selective, annotated bibliography which comprises rhymes and more serious poetry, and old and the new works originating in English and translations from all over the world reflect the growing interest of today's children and young people in poetry.

LC 1.12/2:P 96/date   • **Item 785-A**
LIBRARY OF CONGRESS PUBLICATIONS IN PRINT. 1956– [Annual]

    ISSN 0083-1603

LC 1.12/2-2:date   • **Item 785-A**
LIBRARY OF CONGRESS SELECTED PUBLICATIONS. [Annual]

LC 1.12/2-3:date   • **Item 785-A**
PUBLICATIONS IN PRINT. [Biennial]

LC 1.13:CT
POSTERS.

LC 1.14:CT   • **Item 784**
ADDRESSES.

LC 1.14:L 71   • **Item 784**
LITERARY LECTURES PRESENTED AT THE LIBRARY OF CONGRESS. 1973. 602 p.

    Compilation of lectures given at the Library of Congress over the last thirty years by giants of the literary world.

LC 1.15:nos.
PUBLICATIONS CHECKLISTS. 1– 1942–

LC 1.16:nos.
LATIN AMERICAN SERIES. 1– 1942–

LC 1.17:v.nos.&nos.   • **Item 788**
QUARTERLY JOURNAL OF LIBRARY OF CONGRESS. v. 1– 40. 1943– 1983.

    Published as a supplement to Annual report of Librarians of Congress. Includes annual index and a separate title page for each volume.
    Earlier title: Quarterly Journal of Current Acquisitions, prior to v. 21.
    ISSN 0041-7939

LC 1.18:v.nos.&nos.   • **Item 785-C (EL)**
INFORMATION BULLETIN. v. 1– 1942– [Monthly]

    PURPOSE:– To provide a news medium of the activities of the Library of Congress for Library personnel and those interested in its activities. Includes news of new accessions, resumes of annual reports of the various divisions, list of vacant positions and announcements of new appointments.
    ISSN 0041-7904

LC 1.19   • **Item 785-R (EL)**
A PERIODIC REPORT FROM THE NATIONAL DIGITAL LIBRARY PROGRAM.

LC 1.20:v.nos.
UNITED STATES QUARTERLY BOOK LIST. v. 1– 1945–

LC 1.21:nos.
MANUALS. 1– 1954–

LC 1.22:date
EXHIBITIONS. [Monthly]

LC 1.22/2:date
CALENDAR OF EVENTS IN THE LIBRARY OF CONGRESS. [Monthly, except August]

    List of exhibits and activities currently being held at the Library of Congress or those to be held in the near future. Of interest to those visiting or planning to visit the Library.

LC 1.23:v.nos.
SERIAL TITLES NEWLY RECEIVED. [Monthly]

LC 1.23/2:date
– (ANNUAL CUMULATION).

    Superseded by L 1.23/4

LC 1.23/3:v.nos.&nos.   • **Item 785-A-4**
NEW SERIAL TITLES. 1953– [Monthly & Annual]

    Lists serials received by the Library of Congress and other cooperating libraries commencing publication after December 31, 1949, with title pages in languages using the Roman alphabet, and to serials with Cyrillic, Greek, Gaelic, and Behraic title pages, which are included in transliteration.
    Prepared by the Serial Record Division, Processing Department under the sponsorship of the Joint Committee on Union List of Serials.
    Subscription includes monthly issues and annual cumulative volume.
    A continuing supplement to the Union List of Serials. Presents entries in a traditional "catalog card" format. The fullness of the record, depends on the amount of data reported and carried in the CONSER record.
    ISSN 0028-6680

LC 1.23/4:date
– ANNUAL CUMULATION.

    Replaces LC 1.23/2

LC 1.23/5:date&nos.
CLASSED SUBJECT ARRANGEMENT. [Monthly]

    ISSN 0028-6699

LC 1.24:nos.
RELEASES.

LC 1.25:
SOME RECENT BOOKS ON PUBLIC AFFAIRS AVAILABLE FOR CIRCULATION IN THE BOOK FORMS.

LC 1.26:nos.
BIBLIOGRAPHY OF TRANSLATIONS FROM RUSSIAN SCIENTIFIC AND TECHNICAL LITERATURE. 1– 39. 1953– 1956. [Monthly]

LC 1.27:v.nos.&nos.
HIGHLIGHTS OF CURRENT LEGISLATION AND ACTIVITIES IN MID-EUROPE. [Monthly]

LC 1.28:nos.
FACSIMILES.

LC 1.29
LIBRARY OF CONGRESS PL 480 NEWSLETTER. 1– 26. 1961– 1974. [Irregular]

    Serves a news medium of the activities of the program to participating libraries within the program.
    Superseded by Foreign Acquisitions Program Newsletter (LC 30.17).

ACCESSION LISTS.

Provides a monthly record of the publications acquired by the U.S. Library of Congress American Libraries Book Procurement Centers located in the individual countries.

The Lists are arranged by language of publication with each language section separately alphabetized by author. Within each language section commercial and government monographs are listed in a single alphabet. Monographs in series and annual publications are also included with the monographs. Government publications are indicated by an asterisk preceding the code number. Beginning in 1963, newspapers and periodicals are listed in the January or July issues. Cumulative author index is included in the December issues.

LC 1.30:v.nos.&nos.
INDIA. v. 1– 1962– [Monthly]

ISSN 0041-7734

LC 1.30/1-2:date
INDIA, ACCESSIONS LIST, ANNUAL SUPPLEMENT, CUMULATIVE LIST OF SERIALS.

LC 1.30/2:v.nos.&nos.
PAKISTAN. v. 1– 1962– [Monthly]

ISSN 0041-7777

LC 1.30/2-2:date • **Item 785-B-1 (MF)**
– PAKISTAN, ANNUAL SUPPLEMENT, CUMULATIVE LIST OF SERIALS. [Annual]

LC 1.30/2-3:date
PAKISTAN, INDEX [cumulations].

LC 1.30/3:v.nos.&nos. • **Item 785-B-1 (MF)**
MIDDLE EAST [United Arab Republic]. v. 1–
1963– [Bimonthly]

ISSN 0041-7769

LC 1.30/4:v.nos.&nos.
ISRAEL. v. 1– 10, no. 4. 1964– April 1973. [Monthly]

Author index in June and December issues. Cumulative list of titles issued semiannually.

LC 1.30/5:v.nos.&nos.
INDONESIA. v. 1– 1964– [Monthly]

LC 1.30/5-2:date
INDONESIA, CUMULATIVE LIST OF SERIALS.

LC 1.30/6:v.nos.&nos.
NEPAL. v. 1– 1966– [3 times a year]

LC 1.30/7:v.nos.&nos.
CEYLON. v. 1– 1967– [Quarterly]

LC 1.30/8:v.nos.&nos. • **Item 785-B-1 (CD)**
EASTERN AFRICA. v. 1– 1968– [Bimonthly]

Libraries only.
Annual serial supplement issued also.
ISSN 0090-371X

LC 1.30/8-2 • **Item 785-B-1 (CD)**
ACCESSIONS LIST, EASTERN AFRICA, ANNUAL SERIAL SUPPLEMENT.

LC 1.30/8-3:date • **Item 785-B-1 (MF)**
EASTERN AFRICA, ANNUAL PUBLISHERS DIRECTORY.

LC 1.30/8-4 • **Item 785-B-1 (MF)**
QUARTERLY INDEX TO PERIODICAL LITERATURE, EASTERN AND SOUTHERN AFRICA. [Quarterly]

LC 1.30/9:v.nos.
BANGLADESH. v. 1– 1972– [Twice a year]

Issued in June and December. Annual index included in December issue.

LC 1.30/10:v.nos.&nos. • **Item 785-B-1 (MF)**
SOUTHEAST ASIA. v. 1– [Quarterly]

ISSN 0096-2341

LC 1.30/10-2:date • **Item 785-B-1 (MF)**
CUMULATIVE LIST OF MALAYSIA, SINGAPORE AND BRUNEI SERIALS.

LC 1.30/10-3:v.nos.&nos.• **Item 785-B-1 (MF)**
SOUTH ASIA. [Monthly]

LC 1.30/10-4:date • **Item 785-B-1 (MF)**
SOUTH AFRICA, SERIALS SUPPLEMENT. [Annual]

LC 1.30/10-5:date • **Item 785-B-1 (MF)**
SOUTHEAST ASIA, BURMA, THAILAND, AND LAOS.

LC 1.30/11:v.nos.&nos. • **Item 785-B-1 (MF)**
BRAZIL. [Bimonthly]

ISSN 0095-795X

LC 1.30/11-2:date
BRAZIL, CUMULATIVE LIST OF SERIALS.

LC 1.30/11-3:date • **Item 785-B-1 (MF)**
BRAZIL, ANNUAL LIST OF SERIALS.

LC 1.31:CT • **Item 787-A**
NATIONAL REFERRAL CENTER FOR SCIENCE AND TECHNOLOGY PUBLICATIONS.
DIRECTORY OF INFORMATION RESOURCES IN THE UNITED STATES.

The following directories are based on the register of information resources that have been built up since the Center was established in 1962. Entries include areas of interest, holdings, publications, and information services. The following have been published:–

LC 1.31:D 62 • **Item 787-A**
– PHYSICAL SCIENCES, BIOLOGICAL SCIENCES, ENGINEERING. 1965. 352 p.

Later LC 1.31:D 62/6 and LC 1.31:D 62/7

LC 1.31:D 62/2 • **Item 787-A**
– SOCIAL SCIENCES. 1965. 218 p.

LC 1.31:D 62/3 • **Item 787-A**
– WATER. 1966. 248 p.

LC 1.31:D 62/4 • **Item 787-A**
– FEDERAL GOVERNMENT. 1974. 416 p.

LC 1.31:D 62/5 • **Item 787-A**
– GENERAL TOXICOLOGY. 1969. 293 p.

LC 1.31:D 62/6 • **Item 787-A**
– PHYSICAL SCIENCES, ENGINEERING. 1971. 803 p.

Earlier LC 1.31:D 62

LC 1.31:D 62/7 • **Item 787-A**
– BIOLOGICAL SCIENCES. 1972. 577 p.

Earlier LC 1.31:D 62

LC 1.32:nos. • **Item 785-E (EL)**
FLICC NEWSLETTER. 1– [Irregular]

FLICC = Federal Library & Information Center Committee.
Earlier FLC Newsletter.

LC 1.32/2:CT • **Item 785-B**
GENERAL LIBRARY COMMITTEE PUBLICATIONS.

LC 1.32/3
LIBRARY VACANCY ROSTER. 1966– [Monthly]

Federal Library Committee.

LC 1.32/4 • **Item 785-A-5**
THE FEDERAL LIBRARY AND INFORMATION CENTER COMMITTEE: ANNUAL REPORT FY ... 1st– 1970–
Earlier title: Federal Library Committee: Annual Report.

LC 1.32/5:v.nos./nos. • **Item 785-E-1 (EL)**
FEDLINK TECHNICAL NOTES. [Bimonthly]

FEDLINK = Federal Library and Information Network.
Published by the Federal Library and Information Center Committee (FLICC); Federal Library and Information Network (FEDLINK). Contains news of FLICC/ FEDLINK, OCLC (Online Computer Library Center), NTIS, and a calendar of events.

LC 1.33:nos.
NEWS FROM THE CENTER [for the Coordination of Foreign Manuscript Copying]. 1– 7. 1967– 1970

LC 1.34:v.nos. • **Item 785-D**
LETTERS OF DELEGATES TO CONGRESS, 1774– 1789. v. 1– 1977– [Irregular]

LC 1.35:nos. • **Item 785-F**
PRESERVATION LEAFLETS. [Irregular]

PURPOSE:– To provide libraries, archivists, and others with limited experience guidance in the conservation of books, manuscripts, etc.

LC 1.36:v.nos.&nos.
NATIONAL PRESERVATION REPORT. [3 times a year]

Continues Newspaper and Gazette Report (LC 29.10).

LC 1.37:nos.
NETWORK PLANNING PAPERS (series). [Irregular] (Network Development Office)

LC 1.38:nos. • **Item 785-J**
CENTER FOR THE BOOK VIEWPOINT SERIES. 1– [Irregular] (Center for the Book)

Each issue deals with a different subject.

LC 1.39:CT • **Item 785-G**
LIBRARY OF CONGRESS ACQUISITIONS [various divisions]. [Irregular]
This class not used. See LC 4.9.

LC 1.40:date • **Item 785-H**
DIRECTORY. [Annual]
Telephone directory containing organization, services, and personnel sections.

LC 1.40/2 • **Item 785-H**
DIRECTORIES.

LC 1.41:nos.
INVENTORY OF KNOWLEDGE SERIES. [Irregular]

LC 1.42:nos. • **Item 785-K**
OCCASIONAL PAPERS OF THE COUNCIL OF SCHOLARS (series). 1– [Irregular]

LC 1.43:nos. • **Item 785-L**
PRESERVATION AND NEW TECHNOLOGY OCCASIONAL PAPERS. 1– [Irregular]

PURPOSE:– To explore the new dimensions and implications of preservation technology.

LC 1.44:nos. • **Item 785-M**
NEWS FROM THE LIBRARY OF CONGRESS. [Irregular]
Press release material.

LC 1.45:date • **Item 785-N**
SYMBOLS OF AMERICAN LIBRARIES. [Irregular]

A dictionary of the abbreviations used to identify libraries in union catalogs, bibliographies, and other compilations which require the naming of institutions in a brief space.

LC 1.46:date • Item 786-B-1
PERFORMING ARTS. [Annual]

PURPOSE:– To present, analyze, and explore LC collections on the performing arts and their relationship to the history and development of motion pictures, music, broadcasting, recording, theater, and dance.

LC 1.47 • Item 785-B-2 (EL)
ANNUAL FORUM, FEDERAL INFORMATION POLICIES. [Annual]

PURPOSE:– To summarize proceedings of the annual forum on federal information policies. Each forum deals with a different topic, such as implementation of federal information policies and the implication for information access.

LC 1.48:nos. • Item 785-A-2
FORMS.

LC 1.49 • Item 786
THE GAZETTE.

LC 1.50 • Item 785-F (MF)
OPINION PAPERS.

LC 1.51:CT • Item 785-P
POSTERS.

LC 1.53 • Item 786-A-4 (MF)
DECADE OF THE BRAIN (series).

LC 1.54/2 • Item 785-R (EL)
THOMAS: LEGISLATIVE INFORMATION ON THE INTERNET.

LC 1.54/3 • Item 785-A-R (EL)
AMERICAN MEMORY DIGITAL COLLECTIONS (various topics).

LC 1.54: • Item 786-A-4 (E)
ELECTRONIC PRODUCTS.

LC 1.55: • Item 786-A-5
JEFFERSON'S LEGACY.

LC 1.56:v.nos./nos • Item 786-A-5
JEFFERSON'S LEGACY.

GENERAL REFERENCE AND BIBLIOGRAPHY DIVISION
(1944–   )

LC 2.1:date
ANNUAL REPORTS (none issued).

LC 2.2:CT • Item 806-C
GENERAL PUBLICATIONS.

LC 2.3:nos.
BULLETINS [none issued].

LC 2.4:nos.
CIRCULARS [none issued].

LC 2.5:date
A.L.A. SUB-COMMITTEE ON FEDERAL PUBLICATIONS.

LC 2.6:CT
ELEMENTARY BOOKS [of interest in connection with industrial training for national defense, brief lists].

LC 2.7:nos.
COOPERATIVE BIBLIOGRAPHIES. 1–   1941–

LC 2.7/2:CT • Item 806-H-2
BIBLIOGRAPHIES AND LISTS OF PUBLICATIONS. [Irregular]

LC 2.8:CT • Item 806-B
MANUALS OF GENERAL REFERENCE AND BIBLIOGRAPHY DIVISION.

LC 2.8:Af 8/3 • Item 806-B
FRENCH-SPEAKING CENTRAL AFRICA, A GUIDE TO OFFICIAL PUBLICATIONS IN AMERICAN LIBRARIES. 1973. 314 p.

PURPOSE:– To list published government records held by American libraries. Includes documents of former Belgian and French possessions from the beginning of colonial rule to the time of independence, as well as publications of national governments and regional and provincial administrations from independence to 1970. Also included are League of Nations and United Nations documents on Ruanda-Urundi and Cameroon, and selections of Belgian and French official publications pertaining to their former territories.

LC 2.9:date • Item 806-D
WORLD LIST OF FUTURE INTERNATIONAL MEETINGS. 1959– 1969. [Bimonthly] (International Organizations Section)

PURPOSE:– To provide a comprehensive and systematic calendar of forthcoming international meetings in all subjects, both inter- and nongovernmental, being held throughout the world over a 3-year period. With entries based on standard cataloging of conference documents by libraries and other institutions and to provide guidance to researchers. the publication was conceived also as an aid to the scheduling of meetings and the planning of attendance.

Part 1. Science, Technology, Agriculture, Medicine.
Part 2. Social, Cultural, Commercial, Humanistic.
Parts issued separately 1959– 1966, combined, 1967– 1969.
Replaces NS 1.8

LC 2.9/2:date • Item 806-D
WORLD LIST OF FUTURE INTERNATIONAL MEETING: PT. 2, SOCIAL, CULTURAL, COMMERCIAL, HUMANISTIC. 1959– 1966. [Bimonthly]

Issued with part 1 beginning with January 1967 issue.

LC 2.10:v.nos.&nos. • Item 806-H
ARMS, CONTROL AND DISARMAMENT. v. 1– 9, no. 2. 1964– Spring 1973. [Quarterly]

Prepared by the Arms Control and Disarmament Bibliography Section, General Reference and Bibliography Division, Reference Department. Lists trade books, selected Federal and foreign government publications, some 100 periodicals, and publications of national and international organizations and societies. Author index in each issue with a subject index and cumulative author index in the Fall issue.

LC 2.11:date • Item 806-I
CHILDREN'S BOOKS. 1964–   [Annual] (Children's Book Section)

Lists under subject headings, current books for preschool through junior high school age. Annotated information for each entry includes: Author, title, publisher, number of pages, price, grade level, and brief synopsis of the work.

LC 2.12:CT • Item 806-H-1
MAKTABA AFRIKANA SERIES. [Irregular]

Later LC 41.11

COPYRIGHT OFFICE
(1897–   )

INFORMATION

Copyright Office
Library of Congress
Room LM-403
101 Independence Avenue, S.E.
Washington, D.C. 20559-6000
(202) 707-3000
http://www.copyright.gov

LC 3.Form • Item 785-A-2
FORMS. [Irregular]

LC 3.1 • Item 785-A-1 (MF)
ANNUAL REPORT OF THE REGISTER OF COPYRIGHTS. 1900–   [Annual]

Reprinted from Annual Report of the Librarian of Congress.

LC 3.2:CT • Item 803
GENERAL PUBLICATIONS.

LC 3.3:nos. • Item 790
BULLETINS.

DECISIONS OF THE UNITED STATES COURTS INVOLVING COPYRIGHT. 1– 1898– [Biennial]

Contains substantially all copyright cases, as well as many cases involving related subjects in the field of literary property, decided by the Federal Courts, including some decisions of the State Courts of the United States.

LC 3.3/2:nos. • Item 790
DECISIONS OF THE UNITED STATES COURTS INVOLVING COPYRIGHT AND LITERARY PROPERTY, 1789– 1909, BULLETINS. [Irregular]

LC 3.3/3:date • Item 790
DECISIONS OF THE UNITED STATES COURTS INVOLVING COPYRIGHT. [Annual]

LC 3.4:nos. • Item 802-A
CIRCULARS, INFORMATION CIRCULARS, ETC. 1– 1900–

LC 3.4/2:nos. • Item 802-A (P) (EL)
CIRCULARS. 1–   1968–   [Irregular]

LC 3.4/3 • Item 802-A-1 (EL)
NEWSNET

LC 3.5:nos.
CATALOG OF TITLE ENTRIES OF BOOKS AND OTHER ARTICLES. 1– 1892–

LC 3.6
CATALOGUE OF COPYRIGHT ENTRIES.

LC 3.6/1:v.nos.
PT. 1. BOOKS [etc.] v. 1–   1906–

LC 3.6/2:v.nos.
PT.2 PERIODICALS. v. 1–   1906–

LC 3.6/3:v.nos.
PT. 3. MUSICAL COMPOSITIONS. v. 1–   1906–

LC 3.6/4:v.nos.
PT. 4. ENGRAVINGS, CUTS AND PRINTS, CHROMOS AND LITHOGRAPHS, PHOTOGRAPHS, FINE ARTS. v. 1–   1906–

LC 3.6/5:v.nos.
CATALOG OF COPYRIGHT ENTRIES. THIRD SERIES.
v. 1– 31. 1947– 1977. [Semiannual]

Each part of the Catalog is published in semi-annual members covering the periods January–June and July– December. These catalogs contain the claims of copyright registered during the particular periods for which they are issued. Issued in the following parts:–

LC 3.6/5 • **Item 791**
PART 1, BOOKS AND PAMPHLETS, INCLUDING SERIALS AND CONTRIBUTIONS TO PERIODICALS. [Semiannual]

Lists domestic and foreign books, pamphlets, serials, and contributions to periodicals.
ISSN 0041-7815

LC 3.6/5 • **Item 793**
PART 2, PERIODICALS.

Lists domestic and foreign periodicals and newspapers.
ISSN 0041-784X

LC 3.6/5 • **Item 794**
PARTS 3-4, DRAMA AND WORKS PREPARED FOR ORAL DELIVERY. [Semiannual]

Lists dramas, dramatic-musicals, lectures, sermons, monologs, and radio, television, and recording scripts.
ISSN 0041-7858

LC 3.6/5 • **Item 795**
PART 5, MUSIC. [Semiannual]

Lists published and unpublished music materials.
ISSN 0041-7866

LC 3.6/5 • **Item 797**
PART 6, MAPS AND ATLASES. [Semiannual]

Lists domestic and foreign maps, atlases, and other cartographic works.
ISSN 0041-7874

LC 3.6/5 • **Item 798**
PARTS 7-11A, WORKS OF ART, REPRODUCTIONS OF WORKS OF ART, SCIENTIFIC AND TECHNICAL DRAWINGS, PHOTOGRAPHIC WORKS, PRINTS AND PICTORIAL ILLUSTRATIONS. [Semiannual]
ISSN 0041-7882

LC 3.6/5 • **Item 799**
PART 11B, COMMERCIAL PRINTS AND LABELS. [Semiannual]

Lists prints and labels published in connection with the sale or advertisement of articles of merchandise or of services.
ISSN 0041-7823

LC 3.6/5 • **Item 800**
PARTS 12-13, MOTION PICTURES AND FILMSTRIPS. [Semiannual]

Lists domestic and foreign motion pictures and filmstrips.
ISSN 0161-2808

LC 3.6/5 • **Item 795**
PART 14, SOUND RECORDINGS. [Semiannual]

ISSN 0094-3592

LC 3.6/6:v.nos. • **Item 791 (MF)**
CATALOG OF COPYRIGHT ENTRIES. FOURTH SERIES. v. 1– 1978– [Semiannual]

Issued in the following parts:–

LC 3.6/6:v.nos./Pt 1 • **Item 791**
PART 1. NON-DRAMATIC LITERARY WORKS. [Quarterly]

LC 3.6/6:v.nos./Pt 2 • **Item 793 (MF)**
PART 2. SERIALS AND PERIODICALS. [Semiannual]

LC 3.6/6:v.nos./Pt 3 • **Item 794 (MF)**
PART 3. PERFORMING ARTS [Excluding Motion Pictures]. [Quarterly]

LC 3.6/6:v.nos./Pt 4 • **Item 800 (MF)**
PART 4. MOTION PICTURES AND FILMSTRIPS. [Semiannual]

LC 3.6/6:v.nos./Pt 5 • **Item 798 (MF)**
PART 5. VISUAL ARTS. [Semiannual]

LC 3.6/6:v.nos./Pt 6 • **Item 797 (MF)**
PART 6. MAPS. [Semiannual]

LC 3.6/6:v.nos./Pt 7 • **Item 795 (MF)**
PART 7. SOUND RECORDINGS. [Semiannual]

LC 3.6/6:v.nos./Pt 8 • **Item 793 (MF)**
PART 8. RENEWALS. [Semiannual]

LC 3.7:CT
REGULATIONS, RULES, AND INSTRUCTIONS.

LC 3.7/2:CT • **Item 790-A**
HANDBOOKS, MANUALS, GUIDES. [Irregular]

LC 3.8:CT • **Item 803-A (MF)**
CATALOG OF COPYRIGHT ENTRIES, CUMULATIVE SERIES.

LC 3.9:nos.
COPYRIGHT LAW STUDIES.

LC 3.10:CT
LAWS.

LC 3.11:date • **Item 803-B**
COMPENDIUM OF COPYRIGHT OFFICE PRACTICES. [Irregular] (Includes basic manual and supplement material or an indefinite period)

A general guide to Copyright Office practices in representative situations arising in the conduct of registration and related functions of the Office. The Compendium contains definitions and examples of registrable material, discusses common copyright problems, and indicates the action the Copyright Office will take in such cases. Some parts of the Compendium have not yet been completed, and the practices and policies of the Copyright Office are a subject to review and modification in the light of new developments and experiences; thus additions, deletions, and revisions will be made from time to time.

LC 3.12:nos./date • **Item 790**
ANNOUNCEMENT FROM THE COPYRIGHT OFFICE, ML- (series). [Irregular]

PURPOSE:– To inform the copyright community of new publications or developments in the copyright field.
ISSN 0145-0638

LC 3.13:date • **Item 785-A-3 (MF)**
LABOR MANAGEMENT WORKING GROUP: ANNUAL REPORT.

PURPOSE:– To summarize Group activities aimed at fostering labor management cooperation in the Copyright Office, improving the quality of work life for all staff, and eliminating barriers to organizational effectiveness.

LC 3.14:CT • **Item 803-B (P) (EL)**
FORMS.

MANUSCRIPT DIVISION
(1897–   )

INFORMATION

Manuscript Division
Library of Congress
Room LM-102
101 Independence Ave. SE
Washington, D.C. 20540-4680
(202) 707-5383
Fax: (202) 707-6336
E-Mail: mss@loc.gov
http://www.lcweb.loc.gov./rr/mss/

LC 4.1:date
ANNUAL REPORTS.

LC 4.2:CT • **Item 811-B-1**
GENERAL PUBLICATIONS.

LC 4.3:nos.
BULLETINS [none issued].

LC 3.3/3:date • **Item 790**
DECISIONS OF THE U.S. COURTS INVOLVING COPYRIGHT. [Annual]

LC 4.4:nos.
CIRCULARS [none issued].

LC 4.5:vol.
JOURNALS OF THE CONTINENTAL CONGRESS.

LC 4.6:
JOURNALS OF CONTINENTAL CONGRESS, MISCELLANEOUS.

LC 4.7 • **Item 811-B**
PRESIDENTS' PAPERS INDEX SERIES. [Irregular]

Under Public Law 85-147, approved August 16, 1957, the Librarian of Congress was authorized and directed to arrange, index, and microfilm the papers of the Presidents of the United States in the collections of the Library of Congress, in order to preserve their contents against destruction by war or other calamity and for the purpose of making them more readily available for study and research to the fullest possible extent.

The resulting program, begun in August 1958, consisted of modern techniques of publication in microfilm and indexing by punched-card methods, which made available to scholars everywhere the papers of 23 Presidents of the United States from George Washington to Calvin Coolidge.

As each collection was organized for microfilming, an index to it was prepared giving the date and the name of the writer and of the recipient of each manuscript. These indexes are essentially name-indexes to correspondents with descriptive information about each document and a key to where on the microfilm it is reproduced.

One copy of each index is supplied free to purchasers of the microfilms of the Presidents' papers. Positive copies of the microfilms for sale by the Photoduplication Service, Library of Congress, Washington, D.C. 20540.

Work has been completed on the papers for the following Presidents and indexes and microfilm are available for:

George Washington. 294 p.
Thomas Jefferson. 155 p.
James Madison. 61 p.
James Monroe. 25 p.
Andrew Jackson. 111 p.
Martin Van Buren 757 p.
William H. Harrison. 10 p.
John Tyler. 10 p. (Out of Print)
James Polk 911 p.
Zachary Taylor. 9 p.
Franklin Pierce. 16 p.

Abraham Lincoln. 124 p. (Out of Print)
Andrew Johnson. 154 p.
Ulysses S. Grant. 83 p.
James A. Garfield. 422 p.
Chester A. Arthur. 13 p.
Grover Cleveland. 345 p.
Benjamin Harrison. 333 p.
William McKinley. 482 p.
Theodore Roosevelt. 1,322 p.
William Howard Taft. 2,483 p.
Woodrow Wilson. 1600 p.
Calvin Coolidge. 34 p.

LC 4.8:CT   • Item 811-B-2
HANDBOOKS, MANUALS, GUIDES. [Irregular]

LC 4.9:date   • Item 785-G (MF)
LIBRARY OF CONGRESS ACQUISITIONS, MANU-
SCRIPT DIVISION. [Annual]

LC 4.10:nos.&pts.   • Item 811-B-3
REGISTERS OF PAPERS IN THE MANUSCRIPT
DIVISION OF THE LIBRARY OF CONGRESS.
[Irregular]

GEOGRAPHY AND MAP DIVISION
(1897–   )

CREATION AND AUTHORITY

Created by appropriation act effective July 1,
1897.

INFORMATION

Geography and Map Division
Library of Congress
Room LM-B01
101 Independence Ave. SE
Washington, DC 20540-4650
(202) 707-6277
Fax: (202) 707-8531
E-Mail:maps@loc.gov
http://www.loc.gov/rr/geomap/gmpage.html

LC 5.1:date
ANNUAL REPORTS.

LC 5.2:CT   • Item 811-A
GENERAL PUBLICATIONS.

LC 5.3:nos.
BULLETINS [none issued].

LC 5.4:nos.
CIRCULARS [none issued].

LC 5.5:nos.
NOTEWORTHY MAPS. 1–   1926–

LC 5.6:date   • Item 811-A-1
LIBRARY OF CONGRESS ACQUISITIONS. [Annual]
(Geography and Map Division)

Each issue is expected to contain separate
articles publicizing selected acquisitions of the
Geography and Map Division.

LC 5.8:CT   • Item 811-A-2
HANDBOOKS, MANUALS, GUIDES. [Irregular]

SERIAL AND GOVERNMENT PUBLICATIONS DIVISION RESEARCH SERVICE
(1956–   )

INFORMATION

Serial and Government Publication Division
Library of Congress
Room LM-133
101 Independence Ave. SE
Washington, DC 20540
(202) 707-5647

LC 6.1:date
ANNUAL REPORTS.

LC 6.2:CT   • Item 818-F
GENERAL PUBLICATIONS.

LC 6.3:nos.
BULLETINS [none issued].

LC 6.4:nos.
CIRCULARS [none issued].

LC 6.4/2:nos.   • Item 818-D
INFORMATION CIRCULARS.

LC 6.4/3:nos.   • Item 818-D
REFERENCE CIRCULARS. 1–   1968–   [Irregular]
(Serial Division)

LC 6.5:letters
WANT LISTS (lettered).

LC 6.6:CT
WANT LISTS (unlettered and unnumbered).

LC 6.7:date   • Item 818-F
NEWSPAPERS CURRENTLY RECEIVED. [Annual]

Lists United States and foreign newspapers
which are received and retained in the Library of
Congress both on a permanent and temporary
basis.

LC 6.8:CT   • Item 818-F-1
HANDBOOKS, MANUALS, GUIDES. [Irregular]

LC 6.9:CT   • Item 818-F-2
BIBLIOGRAPHIES AND LISTS OF PUBLICATIONS.
[Irregular]

DOCUMENTS DIVISION
(1900–1943)

LC 7.1:date
ANNUAL REPORTS.

LC 7.2:CT
GENERAL PUBLICATIONS.

LC 7.3:nos.
BULLETINS [none issued].

LC 7.4:nos.
CIRCULARS. [none issued]

LC 7.5:nos.
EXCHANGE LISTS.

LC 7.6:date
MONTHLY LIST OF STATE PUBLICATIONS.

Later LC 27.7

LIBRARY BUILDINGS AND GROUNDS SUPERINTENDENT
(1897–1922)

LC 8.1:date
ANNUAL REPORTS.

LC 8.2:CT
GENERAL PUBLICATIONS.

LC 8.3:nos.
BULLETINS [none issued].

LC 8.4:nos.
CIRCULARS [none issued].

DESCRIPTIVE CATALOGING DIVISION
(1940–   )

LC 9.1:date
ANNUAL REPORTS.

LC 9.2:CT   • Item 804
GENERAL PUBLICATIONS.

LC 9.3:nos.
BULLETINS.

LC 9.4:nos.
CIRCULARS [none issued].

LC 9.5:CT
CLASSIFICATION OUTLINE SCHEME OF CLASSES.

LC 9.6/1:CT
SUBJECT HEADINGS.

LC 9.6/2:letters
[LIST OF SUBJECT HEADINGS] (Advance Prints).

LC 9.6/3:edition & nos. later edition & supply nos.
LIST OF SUBJECT HEADINGS, ADDITIONS, COR-
RECTIONS, AND SUPPLEMENTS.

LC 9.7:CT   • Item 805
REGULATIONS, RULES, AND INSTRUCTIONS.

LC 9.8
NATIONAL UNION CATALOG OF MANUSCRIPT COL-
LECTIONS. [Irregular]

– INDEX.

LC 9.15:   • Item 804-A
HANDBOOKS, MANUALS, GUIDES.

LC 9.15/2:   • Item 806-A-10
BOOKS FOR BLIND AND PHYSICALLY HANDI-
CAPPED INDIVIDUALS. [Annual]

LC 9.16   • Item 804-B (EL)
LC CATALOGING NEWSLINE.

LC 9.17   • Item 804-C (E)
ELECTRONIC PRODUCTS.

LAW LIBRARY
(1905– 1981)

Note:– This inactive agency class has been replaced by LC 42.

LC 10.1:date
ANNUAL REPORTS.

LC 10.2:CT
GENERAL PUBLICATIONS.

LC 10.3:nos.
BULLETINS.

LC 10.4:nos.
CIRCULARS.

LC 10.5:
INDEX ANALYSIS OF FEDERAL STATUTES.

LC 10.6:CT
HEADINGS AND SUBHEADS FOR INDEX TO FEDERAL STATUTES.

PRINTS AND PHOT0GRAPHS DIVISION
(1921–   )

INFORMATION

Prints and Photograps Division
Library of Congress
Room LM-339
101 Independence Ave. SE
Washington, DC 20540-4730
(202) 707-6394
Fax: (202) 707-6647
http://www.lcweb.loc.gov/rr/print

LC 11.1:date
ANNUAL REP0RTS.

LC 11.2:CT
GENERAL PUBLICATIONS.

LC 11.3:nos.
BULLETINS [none issued].

LC 11.4:nos.
CIRCULARS [none issued].

MUSIC DIVISION
(1896–   )

INFORMATION

Music Division
Library of Congress
Room LM-113
101 Independence Ave. SE
Washington, D.C. 20540-4710
(202) 707-5507
Fax: (202) 707-0621
http://www.lcweb.bc.gov//rr/perform

LC 12.1:date
ANNUAL REPORTS.

LC 12.2:CT
GENERAL PUBLICATIONS.

LC 12.3:nos.
BULLETINS [none issued].

LC 12.4:nos.
CIRCULARS [none issued].

LC 12.7:album nos.&nos.
FOLK MUSIC OF UNITED STATES.

LC 12.8:CT • Item 812-A
ADDRESSES.

Earlier LC 12.2

LC 12.9:date • Item 813
THE LIBRARY OF CONGRESS PRESENTS A SEASON OF CHAMBER MUSIC. [Semiannual]

ACCESSIONS DIVISION
(1924– 1943)

LC 13.1:date
ANNUAL REPORTS.

LC 13.2:CT
GENERAL PUBLICATIONS.

LC 13.3
BULLETINS

LC 13.4
CIRCULARS.

CONGRESSIONAL RESEARCH SERVICE
(1914–   )

CREATION AND AUTHORITY

Congressional Research Service was first established as the Legislative Reference Service in 1914. It was renamed the Congressional Research Service by the Legislative Reorganization Act of 1970.

INFORMATION

Congressional Research Service
Library of Congress
Room LM-203
101 Independence Ave. SE
Washington, DC 20540
http://www.cweb.loc.gov/cisinfo

LC 14.1:date
ANNUAL REPORTS. 1916–

LC 14.2:CT • Item 807-A-4
GENERAL PUBLICATIONS.

LC 14.3:
BULLETINS.

LC 14.4:
CIRCULARS.

LC 14.5:nos.
STATE LAW INDEX.

Later LC 21.9

• Item 813
GENERAL PUBLICATIONS. **LC 12.2:CT**

LC 14.6:cong.&nos. • Item 807
DIGEST OF PUBLIC GENERAL BILLS AND RELATED RESOLUTIONS, WITH INDEX. 74th Cong–1936–   [Irregular]

Five to six cumulative issues, including a final issue for each session of Congress. Gives brief digest of each bill and resolution introduced, arranged in numerical sequence. Shows status of bills acted upon and brief annotation of laws enacted.
ISSN 0012-2785

LC 14.7:nos.
SPECIAL REPORTS.

Publications on State law index.
Earlier LC 21.7

LC 14.8:nos.
STATE LAW DIGEST, REPORTS.
Earlier LC 21.8

LC 14.9:date&nos.
PUBLIC AFFAIRS BULLETIN.

LC 14.10:date&nos.
STATE LEGISLATION OF 1941: SUMMARIES OF LAWS CURRENTLY RECEIVED IN LIBRARY OF CONGRESS. [Monthly]

LC 14.11:series letter&nos.
NATIONAL DEFENSE BULLETINS.

LC 14.12:nos.
BIBLIOGRAPHIES OF THE WORLD AT WAR.

LC 14.13:ser.nos.&nos.
ATOMIC ENERGY: SIGNIFICANT REFERENCES COVERING VARIOUS ASPECTS OF SUBJECT, ARRANGED TOPICALLY. [Monthly]

LC 14.14:nos.
PUBLIC AFFAIRS ABSTRACTS (new series).

LC 14.15
SUMMARIES OF COMMITTEE HEARINGS.

LC 14.16:
POSTWAR ABSTRACTS.

LC 14.16/2:
ABSTRACTS OF POST WAR LITERATURE.

Supersedes Postwar Abstracts.
Superseded by Public Affairs Abstracts.

LC 14.16/3:
C.I.A.A. ABSTRACTS.

LC 14.17:nos.
LRS MULTILITHED REPORTS.

LC 14.18:Cong./nos. • Item 807-A-1
MAJOR LEGISLATION OF THE CONGRESS. [Monthly while Congress is in session]

PURPOSE:– To provide congressional offices with concise summaries of current congressional issues and major legislation introduced in Congress.
Depository Item 807-A cancelled and reinstated June 11, 1980.

LC 14.19:v.nos./nos. • Item 807-A-5
CONGRESSIONAL RESEARCH SERVICE REVIEW. [10 times a year]

LC 14.19/2:date
UPDATE.

Supplement to the Congressional Research Service Review (L C 14.19).

LC 14.20:date • Item 807-A-2
CRS STUDIES IN THE PUBLIC DOMAIN (series). [Semiannual]

Consists of an annotated subject listing primarily of CRS studies and reports such as congressional committee prints and hearings which have been printed by the Government Printing Office within the given six-month period.
CRS Congressional Research Service.

LC 14.21:CT • Item 807-A-3
HANDBOOKS, MANUALS, GUIDES. [Irregular]

AERONAUTICS DIVISION
(1930– 1940)

LC 15.1:date
ANNUAL REPORTS.

LC 15.2:CT
GENERAL PUBLICATIONS.

LC 15.3
BULLETINS.

LC 15.4
CIRCULARS.

LC 15.5
LAWS

LC 15.6
REGULATIONS.

SERVICE FOR THE BLIND
(1929– 1936)

LC 16.1:date
ANNUAL REPORTS.

LC 16.2:CT
GENERAL PUBLICATIONS.

LC 16.3
BULLETINS.

LC 16.4
CIRCULARS.

ASIAN DIVISION
(1932–   )

INFORMATION

Asian Division
Library of Congress
Room LJ-150
101 Independence Ave. SE
Washington, DC 20540-4810
(202) 707-3766
Fax: (202) 707-1724
E-Mail:asian@loc.gov
http://www.loc.gov/rr/asian

LC 17.1:date
ANNUAL REPORTS.

LC 17.2:CT • Item 806-G
GENERAL PUBLICATIONS.

LC 17.3:
BULLETINS.

LC 17.4:
CIRCULARS.

LC 17.7:v.nos.&nos.
SOUTHERN ASIA, PUBLICATIONS IN WESTERN LANGUAGES, QUARTERLY ACCESSIONS LIST. v. 1– v. 9, no. 12. 1952– 1960.

LC 17.9:CT • Item 806-G-1
BIBLIOGRAPHIES AND LISTS OF PUBLICATIONS. [Irregular]

LC 17.10:CT • Item 806-G-2
POSTERS. [Irregular]

UNION CATALOG DIVISION
(1936–   )

LC 18.1:date
ANNUAL REPORTS. 1936/37– 1940.

LC 18.2:CT • Item 823-A
GENERAL PUBLICATIONS.

LC 18.7:nos.
UNION CATALOG, SELECTED LIST OF UNLOCATED RESEARCH BOOKS. 2– 1938– [Annual]

NATIONAL LIBRARY SERVICE FOR THE BLIND AND PHYSICALLY HANDICAPPED
(1978–   )

INFORMATION

National Library Service for the
Blind and Physically Handicapped
Library of Congress
Washington, D.C. 20542
(202) 707-5100
Fax: (202) 707-0712
E-Mail:n/s@loc.gov
http://www.loc.gov/nls/

LC 19.1:date
ANNUAL REPORTS. 1937–

LC 19.2:CT • Item 806
GENERAL PUBLICATIONS.

LC 19.4/2:nos. • Item 806-A-11
REFERENCE CIRCULARS. [Irregular]

LC 19.6:CT
REGULATIONS, RULES, AND INSTRUCTIONS.

LC 19.6/2:CT • Item 806-A-12
HANDBOOKS, MANUALS, GUIDES.

LC 19.9:v.nos.&nos. • Item 806-A-1 (P) (EL)
BRAILLE BOOK REVIEW. (printed form). 1932– [Bimonthly]

PURPOSE:– To inform readers of developments and activities in library services for the blind and physically handicapped. Includes book annotations, feature stories, and general news articles. Published in print and in Braille. Free for the blind and physically handicapped readers.
Annual author-title index issued separately.
ISSN 0006-873X

LC 19.9/2:date • Item 806-A-7
BRAILLE BOOKS. [Annual]

Lists Braille books available to adult and young adult readers.

LC 19.10:v.nos.&nos. • Item 806-A-2 (P) (EL)
TALKING BOOK TOPICS. v. 1– 1935– [Bimonthly]

PURPOSE:– To inform readers of developments and activities in library services for the blind and physically handicapped. Includes book annotations, feature stories, and general news articles. Published in print and on a recorded flexible disc. Free for blind and physically handicapped readers.
ISSN 0039-9183

LC 19.10/2:date • Item 806-A-8
TALKING BOOKS ADULT. [Annual]

This catalog lists alphabetically within subject categories disc books produced for adult and young adult readers. A separate section lists books for young adults under nonfiction and fiction headings. An author-title index and forms for ordering books are provided.
Earlier LC 19.2:T 14/14

LC 19.10/3:date • Item 806-A-9
CASSETTE BOOKS. [Annual]

This catalog lists cassette books produced for adult and young adult readers, alphabetically within subject categories under nonfiction and fiction headings. Separate sections list books for young adults under nonfiction and fiction headings as well as books in Portuguese and Spanish. An author-title index and forms for ordering books are provided.

LC 19.11:CT • Item 806-A-13
BIBLIOGRAPHIES AND LISTS OF PUBLICATIONS.

LC 19.11/2:date • Item 806-A-13 (P) (EL)
FOR YOUNGER READERS, BRAILLE AND TALKING BOOKS. [Biennial]

Earlier LC 19.11:Y 8

LC 19.11/2-2:date • Item 806-A-17 (P) (EL)
MAGAZINES IN SPECIAL MEDIA. [Biennial]

A descriptive listing of periodicals available in special media to blind and physically handicapped persons throughout the country. Lists magazines produced by the service and also magazines available from other sources.

LC 19.11/3 • Item 806-A-15
INSTRUCTIONAL CASSETTE RECORDINGS.

LC 19.11/3-2 • Item 806-A-15
INSTRUCTIONAL DISC RECORDINGS.

LC 19.11/3-3 • Item 806-A-15
LARGE-PRINT SCORES AND BOOKS.

LC 19.11/4 • Item 806-A-13
FOREIGN LANGUAGE BOOKS. [Biennial]

LC 19.12:v.nos.&nos. • Item 806-A-3
MUSICAL MAINSTREAM. v. 1– 1977– [Bimonthly]

PURPOSE:– To provide articles and announcements in the field of music.
Produced in large print.
Supersedes The New Braille Musician (LC 19.12/2).
ISSN 0364-7501

LC 19.12/2:date
NEW BRAILLE MUSICIAN.

Superseded by Musical Mainstream (LC 19.12).

LC 19.13:v.nos.&nos. • Item 806-A-4 (EL)
DBPH NEWS. v. 1– 1970– [Quarterly]

ISSN 0160-9211

LC 19.13/2:v.nos.&nos.   • Item 806-A-4 (EL)
DBPH UPDATE. [Quarterly]

LC 19.13/3:v.nos.&nos.   • Item 806-A-5 (MF)
OVERSEAS OUTLOOK. v. 1–   1977–   [Semian-
nual]

    Large-print newsletter type of publication for
people of limited vision to help keep them up to
date on general program news and activities of
the Division of the Blind and the Physically Handicapped. Designed primarily for overseas readers,
but contains useful information for U.S. residents.

LC 19.13/4:date   • Item 806-A-4
PROJECTS AND EXPERIMENTS.

LC 19.14:nos.   • Item 806-A-6
MUSIC CIRCULARS. 1–   1980–   [Irregular]

    Each circular is devoted to a single service
for the blind and physically handicapped.

LC 19.15:   • Item 806-A-10
FACTS (series). [Irregular]

    PURPOSE:– To provide information about NLS
services.

LC 19.15/2:date   • Item 806-A-10
BOOKS FOR BLIND AND PHYSICALLY HANDI-
CAPPED INDIVIDUALS. [Annual]

LC 19.16:date   • Item 806-A-14
LIBRARY RESOURCES FOR THE BLIND AND PHYSI-
CALLY HANDICAPPED. [Annual]

    Directory lists libraries, by State and city,
which cooperate in a free national library service
which provides recorded and Braille materials to
the blind and physically handicapped persons.
Presents statistics on leadership, circulation,
budget, staff, and collections.

LC 19.17:date   • Item 806-A-14
ADDRESS LIST, REGIONAL AND SUBREGIONAL
LIBRARIES FOR THE BLIND AND PHYSICALLY
HANDICAPPED. [Semiannual]

LC 19.18:CT   • Item 806-A-16
POSTERS. [Irregular]

LC 19.19:CT
MUSIC AND MUSICIANS (series).

    Earlier LC 19.2:M 97/3

LC 19.20:CT   • Item 808-A-18
DIRECTORIES. [Irregular]

LC 19.21:date   • Item 806-A-18
VOLUNTEERS WHO PRODUCE BOOKS, BRAILLE,
TAPE, LARGE TYPE. [Biennial]

LC 19.22:date   • Item 806-A-19
BRAILLE SCORES CATALOG-ORGAN, MUSIC AND
MUSICIANS. [Annual]

LC 19.23:date/nos.   • Item 806-A-20
BRAILLE BOOK REVIEW, TALKING BOOK TOPICS.
[Bimonthly]

    Issued on diskettes.

LC 19.24:date   • Item 806-A-21 (CD)
CD BLIND, NATIONAL LIBRARY SERVICE FOR THE
BLIND AND PHYSICALLY HANDICAPPED.

SEMITIC LITERATURE DIVISION
(1937– 1939)

LC 20.1:date
ANNUAL REPORTS

STATE LAW INDEX
(1937– 1939)

LC 21.1:date
ANNUAL REPORTS.

LC 21.2:CT
GENERAL PUBLICATIONS.

LC 21.7:nos.
SPECIAL REPORTS.

    Later LC 14.7

LC 21.8:nos.
STATE LAW DIGEST REPORTS.

    Later LC 14.8

LC 21.9:v.nos.
INDEX TO LEGISLATION OF STATES OF U.S.
    ENACTED. [Biennial]

    Earlier LC 14.5

COOPERATIVE CATALOGING AND
CLASSIFICATION SERVICE
(1934– 1940)

LC 22.1
ANNUAL REPORTS.

LC 22.2:CT
GENERAL PUBLICATIONS.

LC 22.7:nos.
NOTES AND DECISIONS ON APPLICATION OF DECI-
    MAL CLASSIFICATION, EDITION 13.
    Later LC 26.8

RARE BOOK AND SPECIAL
COLLECTIONS DIVISION
(1977–   )

INFORMATION

    Rare Book and Special Collections Division
    Library of Congress
    Room LJ-239
    Thomas Jefferson Bldg.
    1st St. and Independence Ave., SE
    Washington, DC 20540-4740
    (202) 707-3448
    Fax: (202) 707-4142
    E-Mail:RBSC@loc.gov
    http://lcweb.loc.gov/rr/rarebook

LC 23.1
ANNUAL REPORTS.

LC 23.2:CT   • Item 818
GENERAL PUBLICATIONS.

LC 23.8:CT   • Item 818
HANDBOOKS, MANUALS, GUIDES.

LC 23.9:   • Item 818-L
LIBRARY OF CONGRESS ACQUISITIONS. [Irregu-
lar]

    Each issue contains articles publicizing se-
lected acquisitions of the Division.

LC 23.16:CT   • Item 818-P
BIBLIOGRAPHIES AND LISTS OF PUBLICATIONS.
[Irregular]

LATIN AMERICAN, PORTUGUESE,
AND SPANISH DIVISION
(1974–   )

LC 24.1:date
ANNUAL REPORTS.   –1940.

LC 24.2:CT   • Item 806-F
GENERAL PUBLICATIONS.

LC 24.7   • Item 806-F
BIBLIOGRAPHICAL SERIES. 1–   1942–   [Irregu-
lar]

LC 24.7/2   • Item 806-F
BIBLIOGRAPHIES AND LISTS OF PUBLICATIONS.

LC 24.8:nos.
HISPANIC FOUNDATION SURVEY REPORTS OF
TEACHING AND RESEARCH ACTIVITIES IN
UNITED STATES AND LATIN AMERICA.

LC 24.10:
HISPANIC FOCUS (series). [Irregular]

    PURPOSE:– To acquaint the reader with
materials in the Library's collections that bear on
contemporary relevance. Occasional series of
short bibliographies.

LC 24.11:CT   • Item 806-F-2
DIRECTORIES. [Irregular]

PRINTS AND PHOTOGRAPHS
DIVISION
(1949–   )

INFORMATION

    Prints and Photographs Division
    Library of Congress
    Room LM-337
    101 Independence Ave. SE
    Washington, D.C. 20540-4730
    (202) 707-6394
    Fax: (202) 707-6647
    http://www.lcweb.loc.gov/rr/print

LC 25.1:date
ANNUAL REPORTS.

LC 25.2:CT   • Item 813-A
GENERAL PUBLICATIONS.

LC 25.2:V 67 • **Item 813-A**
VIEWPOINTS, A SELECTION FROM THE PIC-
TORIAL COLLECTIONS OF THE LIBRARY OF
CONGRESS.

A catalog commemorating 75 years of
visual arts at the Library of Congress. The
prints and photographs in this book are some
of the best works from the Library's collection, spanning a period from the 1700's
through modern times. Most of the samples
illustrate the older pictorial arts, such as
printmaking and lithographing. Almost every
imaginable event is captured in the Library's
rich and varied collection, with themes ranging from disasters to triumphs, boxing to architecture, acting to Indians, to life in the big
city. For history buffs, the book contains an
entire section devoted to world and U.S. history.

LC 25.6:CT
REGULATIONS, RULES, AND INSTRUCTIONS.

LC 25.8:date • **Item 813-A**
CATALOG OF NATIONAL EXHIBITION OF PRINTS.
[Annual]

Earlier LC 1.2:P 93/2

LC 25.8/2:CT • **Item 813-A-2**
HANDBOOKS, MANUALS, GUIDES. [Irregular]

LC 25.9:CT • **Item 813-A-1**
BIBLIOGRAPHIES AND LISTS OF PUBLICATIONS.
[Irregular]

CATALOGING POLICY AND
SUPPORT OFFICE
(1940–   )

CREATION AND AUTHORITY

Formerly Subject Cataloging Division.

LC 26.1:date
ANNUAL REPORT.

LC 26.2:CT • **Item 820**
GENERAL PUBLICATIONS.

Item 823 (P)

LC 26.7:nos./v.nos. • **Item 823**
SUBJECT HEADINGS USED IN THE DICTIONARY
CATALOGS OF THE LIBRARY OF CONGRESS.
[Quarterly & Annual] (Processing Department)

LC 26.7/2:date • **Item 823-A-1 (MF)**
LIBRARY OF CONGRESS SUBJECT HEADING IN
MICROFORM, QUARTERLY CUMULATION.

LC 26.7/2-2:date • **Item 823 (MF)**
L.C. SUBJECT HEADINGS WEEKLY LISTS.

LC 26.8/4:date • **Item 820-A**
SUBJECT CATALOGING MANUAL: SUBJECT HEAD-
INGS. [Irregular]

PURPOSE:– To provide guidelines for cataloging library materials in the Subject Cataloging
Division of the Library of Congress.

LC 26.8/5:date • **Item 820-A**
SUBJECT CATALOGING MANUAL, SHELF LISTING.
[Irregular]

LC 26.9:letters/date • **Item 819**
LIBRARY OF CONGRESS CLASSIFICATION SCHED-
ULES. [Irregular] (Subject Cataloging Division, Pro-
cessing Department)

The following volumes constitute the complete Library of Congress classification scheme:

A. General works: Polygraphy. 3d ed. 1947,
reprinted with supplementary pages, 1963.
47, 7 p. [Z696.U5A 1963] Card 63-60038.

B. Philosophy and religion:

Pt. 1, B-BJ Philosophy. 2d ed. 1950,
reprinted with supplementary pages,
1968. 166, 101 p. [Z696.U5B1 1968]
Card 67-60098.Pt. 2, BL-BX. Religion.
2d ed. 1962. 639 p. [Z696.U5B2] Card
62-60072.

C. History: Auxiliary sciences of history. 2d
ed. 1948, reprinted with supplementary
pages, 1967. [Z696.U5CF1967] Card 67-
61606.

D. History: General and Old World. 2d ed.
1959, reprinted with supplementary pages,
1966. 747, 55 p. [Z696.U5D 1966] Card
65-62173.

E-F. History: American. 1958, reprinted with
supplementary pages, 1965. 607, 23 p.
[Z696.U5E 1965] Card 65-60005.

G. Geography, anthropology, folklore, man-
ners and customs, recreation. 3d ed. 1954,
reprinted with supplementary pages, 1966.
502. 77 p. [Z696.U5G 1966] Card 66-61847.

H. Social sciences. 3d ed. 1950, reprinted
with supplementary pages, 1965. 614, 173
p. [Z696.U5H 1965] Card 65-60024.

J. Political science. 2d ed. 1924, reprinted
with supplementary pages, 1966. 434, 161
p. [Z696.U5J 1966] Card 66-60021.

K. Law. In preparation.

L. Education. 3d ed. 1951, reprinted with
supplementary pages, 1966. 200, 69 p.
[Z696.U5L 1966] Card 66-61846.

M. Music and books on music. 2d ed. 1917,
reprinted with supplementary pages 1968.
157, 133 p. [Z696.U5M 1968] Card 68-
60011.

N. Fine arts. 3d ed. 1922, reprinted with supplementary pages, 1962. 165, 77 p.
[Z696.U5N 1962] Card 62-60073.

P. Philology and literature:

Subclasses P-PA. Philology,
linguistics, classical philology, classical
literature. 1928, reprinted with
supplementary pages,1968. 447, 47 p.
[Z696.U5P 1968] Card 67-61607
Subclass PA. Supplement.
Byzantine and modern Greek literature,
medieval and modern Latin literature.
1942, reprinted with supplementary
page, 1968. 24, 1 p. [Z696.U5P613
1968] Card 68-60095.
Subclasses PB-PH. Modern
European languages. 1933, reprinted
with supplementary pages, 1966. 226,
51 p. [Z696.U5P63 1966] Card 65-
62403.
Subclass PG (in part). Russian
literature. 1948, reprinted with
supplementary pages, 1965. 256, 15 p.
[Z696.U5P635 1965] Card 65-60025
Subclasses PJ-PM. Languages and
literatures of Asia, Africa, Ocenia,

America, mixed languages, artificial
languages. 1935, reprinted with
supplementary pages, 1965. 249, 191 p.
[Z696.U5P64 1965] Card 65-60071.
Subclasses PJ-PM. Supplement.
Index to languages and dialect. 2d ed.
1957, reprinted with supplementary
pages, 1965. 71, 5 p. [Z696.U5P65
1965] Card 65-61907.
Subclasses PN, PR, PS, PZ.
Literature (general), English and
American literatures, fiction in English,
juvenile literature. 1915, reprinted with
supplementary pages, 1964. 272, 277 p.
[Z696.U5P7 1964] Card 64-60069.
Subclass PQ, pt. 1. French
literature. 1936, reprinted with
supplementary pages, 1966. 185, 17 p.
[Z696.U5P8 1966] Card 66-61874.
Subclass PQ, pt 2, Italian, Spanish
and Portuguese literatures. 1937,
reprinted with supplementary pages,
1965. 223, 29 p. [Z696.U5P82 1965]
Card 61-60065
Subclass PT, pt. 1. German
Literature. 1938, reprinted with
supplementary pages, 1966, 312, 17 p.
[Z696.U5P85 1966] Card 66-60026.
Subclass PT, pt. 2. Dutch and
Scandinavian literatures. 1942,
reprinted with supplementary pages,
1965. 102, 27 p. [Z696.U5P87 1965]
Card 65-60061.

Q. Science. 5th ed. 1950, reprinted with supplementary pages, 1967. 215, 129 p.
[Z696.U5Q 1967] Card 67-60039.

R. Medicine, 3 ed. 1952, reprinted with supplementary pages, 1966. 240, 81 p.
[Z696.U5R 1966] Card 66-61845.

S. Agriculture, plant and animal industry, fish
culture and fisheries, hunting sports. 3d
ed. 1948, reprinted with supplementary
pages, 1965. 101, 63 p. [Z696.U5S 1956]
Card 65-60084.

T. Technology. 4 ed. 1948. 325 p. [Z696.U5T
1948] Card 48-46705Supplement. Additions and changes to October 1964. 1965.
119 p. [Z663.78.C5T 1948 Suppl.] Card
48-46705

U. Military science, 3d ed. 1952, reprinted
with supplementary pages, 1966. 86, 21
p. [Z696.U5U 1966] Card 66-61848.

V. Naval science. 2d ed. 1953, reprinted with
supplementary pages, 1966, 115, 39 p.
[Z696.U5V 1966] Card 65-62543.

Z. Bibliography and library science. 4th ed.
1959, reprinted with supplementary pages,
1965. 226, 61 p. [Z696.U5Z] Card 65-
60072.

LC 26.9:DT-DX • **Item 819**
HISTORY OF AFRICA, AUSTRALIA, NEW
ZEALAND, ETC. 1989.

LC 26.9/2:List-nos. • **Item 821**
L.C. CLASSIFICATON; ADDITIONS AND CHANGES.
[Quarterly]

Includes new additions and changes to the
Library of Congress Classification scheme.
ISSN 0041-7912
Earlier LC 1.7/2

LC 26.10:CT • **Item 821-A**
HANDBOOKS, MANUALS, GUIDES. [Irregular]

ACQUISITIONS DEPARTMENT
(1943–1947)

LC 27.1:date
ANNUAL REPORTS.

LC 27.2:CT
GENERAL PUBLICATIONS.

LC 27.7:vol.
MONTHLY CHECKLIST OF STATE PUBLICATIONS.

>   Earlier LC 7.6
>   Later LC 30.9

CARD DIVISION
(1940)

LC 28.1:date
ANNUAL REPORTS.

LC 28.2:CT
GENERAL PUBLICATIONS.

LC 28.7:date
HANDBOOKS OF CARD DISTRIBUTION.

>   Earlier LC 9.2:H 19/1-6

REFERENCE DEPARTMENT
(1944–   )

LC 29.1:date
ANNUAL REPORTS.

LC 29.2:CT   • Item 818-B
GENERAL PUBLICATIONS.

LC 29.6:CT
REGULATIONS, RULES, AND INSTRUCTIONS.

LC 29.7:CT
CENSUS LIBRARY PROJECT SERIES.

LC 29.8:div.nos.
CATALOG OF OSRD REPORTS.

>   Changed to LC 36.8

LC 29.9:CT   • Item 818-B-2 (MF)
ADDRESSES.

LC 29.10:v.nos.&nos.
FOREIGN NEWSPAPER AND GAZETTE REPORT.
1973– 1976. [Quarterly]

>   PURPOSE:– To provide current data about various foreign newspaper and gazette acquisition and microfilming programs, announcements of newly available titles and cooperative microfilming projects, information about bibliographic and technical standards in newspaper microfilming, and other news of interest to the research community.
>   Prior to 1974, titled Foreign Newspaper.
>   Continued by National Preservation Report (LC 1.36).
>   ISSN 0361-0152

PROCESSING DEPARTMENT
(1940–   )

LC 30.1:date
ANNUAL REPORTS.

LC 30.2:CT   • Item 815
GENERAL PUBLICATIONS.

LC 30.6:CT   • Item 815-B
REGULATIONS, RULES, AND INSTRUCTIONS.

LC 30.7:nos.
CATALOGING SERVCE BULLETIN. 1–   1945–
[Irregular] (car subs.)

>   Serves as a medium to the subscribers of the Library of Congress catalog cards. Includes information on Dewey Decimal Classification changes, additions, etc. from the Decimal Classification Office, housed in the Library.
>   ISSN 0041-7890

LC 30.7/2:nos.   • Item 814-B
CATALOGING SERVICE BULLETIN. [Quarterly]

>   Consists of Library of Congress rules and interpretations in such areas as descriptive cataloging, subject cataloging, LC classification, and decimal classification.
>   ISSN 0160-8029
>   Earlier LC 30.7

LC 30.8
NATIONAL UNION CATALOG. 1956–   [Monthly, Annual & Quarterly]

>   A cumulative author list representing Library of Congress printed cards and titles reported by other American libraries. Covers books, pamphlets, periodicals, and other serials written in the Roman, Cyrillic, Greek, or Hebrew alphabets.
>   Supersedes the Library of Congress Catalog, Books: Authors in 1956 when it became a union catalog.
>   Issued monthly, cumulated quarterly and annually.
>   ISSN 0028-0348
>   Replaced by NUC Books (LC 30.26).
>   Cumulative editions of the National Union Catalog and its predecessor are as follows:

A CATALOG OF BOOKS REPRESENTED BY LIBRARY OF CONGRESS PRINTED CARDS ISSUED TO JULY 31, 1942. 1942– 46. 167 v.

>   – SUPPLEMENT; CARDS ISSUED AUGUST 1, 1941– DECEMBER 31, 1947. 1948. 42. v.

THE LIBRARY OF CONGRESS AUTHOR CATALOG: A CUMULATIVE LIST OF WORKS REPRESENTED BY LIBRARY OF CONGRESS CARDS. 1948– 52. 1953. 24 v.
– v. 24, FILMS.

THE NATIONAL UNION CATALOG, 1953– 57. 28 v.

>   – v. 27, MUSIC AND PHONORECORDS.

>   – v. 28, MOTION PICTURES AND FILMSTRIPS.

LC 30.8/2:date
LIBRARY OF CONGRESS AUTHOR CATALOG, ANNUAL CUMULATION.

LIBRARY OF CONGRESS CATALOG.
>   Issued in the following sections:

LC 30.8/3:date
BOOKS, SUBJECTS. 1950–   [Quarterly & Annual]

>   A cumulative list of works represented by Library of Congress printed cards. Contains entries for books, pamphlets, periodi-

cals, and other serials in the Roman, Cyrillic, Greek, and Hebrew alphabets.
>   Issued quarterly with a cumulative annual volume.
>   For cumulative list of works by author, see National Union Catalog entry above.
>   Replaced by NUC Books (LC 30.26).
>   The following cumulative editions have been published:
>   Cumulation for
>   1950– 52. 20 v.
>   1955– 59. 22 v.
>   ISSN 0096-8803

LC 30.8/4:date
MOTION PICTURES AND FILMSTRIPS. [Quarterly & Annual]

>   A cumulative list of works represented by Library of Congress, printed cards. Attempts to cover all educational motion pictures and filmstrips released in the United States and Canada and current theatrical motion pictures copyrighted in the United States.
>   Issued January– March, April– June, July– September, and annual cumulation.
>   ISSN 0091-3294

LC 30.8/5:date
MAPS AND ATLASES (semiannual issue and annual cumulation).

LC 30.8/6:date
MUSIC AND PHONORECORDS. [Semiannual & Annual]

>   A cumulative list of works represented by Library of Congress printed cards. Includes music intended or performance and all types of sound recordings.
>   Issued January– June and annual cumulation.

LC 30.8/7:date
NATIONAL UNION CATALOG: REGISTER OF ADDITION LOCATIONS.

LC 30.8/8:date
NATIONAL REGISTER OF MICROFORM MASTERS. v. 1–   1965–

>   PURPOSE:– To report master microforms of foreign and domestic books, pamphlets, serials, and foreign doctoral dissertations, but excludes technical reports, typescript translations, foreign or domestic archival manuscript collections, U.S. doctoral dissertations, and masters' theses.

LC 30.8/9:date&v.nos.
LIBRARY OF CONGRESS CATALOGS: MONOGRAPHIC SERIES.

>   Replaced by NUC Books (LC 30.26).
>   ISSN 0093-0571

LC 30.9:v.nos.&nos.   • Item 816
MONTHLY CHECKLIST OF STATE PUBLICATIONS. v. 1–   1910–   [Monthly] (Exchange and Gift Division)

>   Lists all State documents received by the Library of Congress.
>   Annual index issued separately.
>   ISSN 0027-0288
>   Earlier LC 27.7

LC 30.10:v.nos.
MONTHLY INDEX OF RUSSIAN ACCESSIONS. v. 1– v. 22, no. 5. 1948– 1969.

LC 30.10/2:CT
– SPECIAL SUPPLEMENTS.

LC 30.11:date
SUBJECT CATALOG, CUMULATIVE LIST OF WORKS REPRESENTED BY LIBRARY OF CONGRESS PRINTED CARDS. [Quarterly]

LC 30.12:v.nos.&nos.
EAST EUROPEAN ACCESSIONS LIST. v. 1– v. 19, no. 11/12. 1951– 1961. [Bimonthly]

LC 30.13:date
NATIONAL LIBRARY OF MEDICINE CATALOG.
– 1966.

>   Supplement to Library of Congress author
catalog.
>   Earlier title: Army Medical Library Catalog.
>   Superseded by National Library of Medicine
Current Catalog, (FS 2.216), beginning Jan. 1966.

LC 30.14:date   • Item 817-B
PROCEEDINGS OF ASSEMBLY OF STATE LIBRAR-
IANS.

>   Earlier LC 30.2:L 61

LC 30.15:nos.
NATIONAL PROGRAM FOR ACQUISITIONS AND
CATALOGING: PROGRESS REPORTS. 1–
1966–

>   Merged with special Foreign Acquisitions pro-
gram Newsletter (LC 30.17) to form LC Acquisition Trends (LC 30.17/2).

LC 30.16:nos.
CIP CATALOGING IN PUBLICATION, PROGRESS
REPORT. 1–   1971–   [Semiannual] (Process-
ing Department)

LC 30.17:nos.
FOREIGN ACQUISITIONS PROGRAM NEWSLETTER.
1974–   [Irregular]

>   Supersedes Library of Congress PL 480 News-
letter (LC 1.29).
>   Merged with National Program for Acquisi-
tions and Cataloging Progress Report (LC 30.15)
to form LC Acquisition Trends (LC 30.17/2)

LC 30.17/2:nos.
LC ACQUISITION TRENDS.

>   Supersedes National Program for Acquisitions
and Cataloging Progress Report (LC 30.15) and
Special Foreign Acquisitions Program Newsletter
(LC 30.17).
>   ISSN 0146-8936

LC 30.18:date
LIBRARY OF CONGRESS CATALOGS: CHINESE
COOPERATIVE CATALOG. [Monthly]

>   Replaced by NUC Books (LC 30.26).
>   ISSN 0095-1072

LC 30.19:date
LIBRARY OF CONGRESS NAME HEADINGS WITH
REFERENCES. [Quarterly]

>   Annual cumulation issued separately.
>   ISSN 0093-0563

LC 30.20:date
NEWSPAPERS IN MICROFORM. 1975–   [Annual]
(Catalog Publication Division)
>   Lists reports for both domestic and foreign
newspapers.
>   Supplements Newspapers in Microform, 1948–
1972, United States (LC 30.2:N 47) and Newspapers in Microform, 1948-1972, Foreign Countries
(LC 30.2:N 47/2).

LC 30.20/2:date
NEWSPAPERS IN MICROFILM, FOREIGN COUN-
TRIES. [Annual]

LC 30.21:date   • Item 815-A (MF)
ME AUTHORITIES, CUMULATIVE EDITION. 1980–
[Quarterly]

>   Listing of name authorities from the Library of
Congress computerized master file starting in
1977, including those for personal and corporate
names, conference headings, geographic names
of political and civil jurisdictions, and uniform titles.
>   Each quarterly issue supersedes the previ-
ous quarterly.

LC 30.22:date   • Item 815-E
CONSER TABLES, (date).

>   Earlier LC 1.2:C 76/7

LC 30.22/2   • Item 815-M (EL)
CONSER LINE.

LC 30.23:CT   • Item 815-D (MF)
NATIONAL LEVEL BIBLIOGRAPHIC RECORDS.

>   Contains specifications for data elements to
be included when creating cataloging records in
machine-readable form for nation-wide data bases.

LC 30.24:nos.   • Item 815-C
NETWORK PLANNING PAPERS (series). 1–
[Irregular]

>   PURPOSE:– To provide information for a ra-
tional and cost-effective design for development
of a nationwide library data base.

LC 30.25:CT   • Item 815-G
HANDBOOKS, MANUALS, GUIDES. [Irregular]

LC 30.26:date
NUC BOOKS. [Monthly]

>   Replaces LC 30.8, LC 30.8/3, LC 30.8/9, and
LC 30.18.
>   NUC = National Union Catalog.

LC 30.27:CT   • Item 815-H
BIBLIOGRAPHIES AND LISTS OF PUBLICATIONS.
[Irregular]

LC 30.27/2:date   • Item 815-H (P) (EL)
COMPLETE CATALOG, CATALOGING DISTRIBUTION
SERVICE.
>   Earlier title: Access CDS.

LC 30.27/2-2:date
MACHINE READABLE CATALOGING. [Annual]
>   Earlier LC 30.27:M 18

LC 30.27/2-3:   • Item 815-J (MF)
THE ALERT SERVICE AND YOU. [Annual]

>   Manual on LC's Alert Service, which enables
you to order notices for any combination of more
than 1800 subject categories and any combination of the 21 broad subject categories listed,
from A (General Works) to Z (Bibliography and
Library Science).

LC 30.27/7:date   • Item 815-H
ACCESS, CATALOGS AND TECHNICAL PUBLICA-
TIONS. [Annual]

LC 30.28:date   • Item 815-H-1
MARC DISTRIBUTION SERVICES. [Annual]

>   MARC = Machine Readable Cataloging.
>   PURPOSE:– To list and annotate MARC dis-
tribution services by category, such as Books
All, Books U.S., Music, GPO Monthly Catalog,
etc. Also contains information on retrospective
and other distribution services.

LC 30.29:   • Item 815-K
POSTERS.

LC 30.30:date   • Item 815-H
CDS CONNECTION. [Semiannual]

>   CDS = Cataloging Distribution Service.

LC 30.31:nos.   • Item 815-C
SPECIAL RESOURCES FOR RESEARCH (Series).

LC 30.32:date   • Item 815-L
SYMBOLS OF AMERICAN LIBRARIES. [Irregular]

LC 30.33   • Item 804-D (E)
ELECTRONIC PRODUCTS.

EUROPEAN AFFAIRS DIVISION
(1948– 1952)

LC 31.1:date
ANNUAL REPORTS.

LC 31.2:CT
GENERAL PUBLICATIONS.

SCIENCE AND TECHNOLOGY
PROJECT
(1948– 1952)

LC 32.1:date
ANNUAL REPORTS.

LC 32.2:CT
GENERAL PUBLICATIONS.

SCIENCE AND TECHNOLOGY
DIVISION
(1960–   )

INFORMATION

>   Science and Technology Division
>   Business Reference Services
>   Library of Congress
>   Rm. LA-508
>   101 Independence Ave., SE
>   Washington, D.C. 20540-4750
>   (202) 707-1925

LC 33.1:date
ANNUAL REPORTS.

LC 33.2:CT   • Item 818-A
GENERAL PUBLICATIONS.

LC 33.8:CT
HANDBOOKS, MANUALS, GUIDES.

LC 33.9:v.nos.   • Item 818-A-1
ANTARCTIC BIBLIOGRAPHY. v. 1–   1965–
[Irregular] (Cold Regions Bibliographic Section)

>   PURPOSE:– To present abstracts and indexes
of current Antarctic literature since 1962 relating
to biological sciences, expeditions, geological sciences, logistics, equipment and supplies, atmospheric physics, and political geography.

LC 33.9:951– 61   • Item 818-A
ANTARCTIC BIBLIOGRAPHY, 1951–61. 1970. 349 p.

>   Supplements main volumes with litera-
ture from an earlier period.

LC 33.9/2:CT
SELECTED REFERENCES ON [various subjects].

LC 33.9/3:CT   • Item 818-A-1
BIBLIOGRAPHIES AND LISTS OF PUBLICATIONS.
[Irregular]

LC 33.10:nos. • Item 818-A-2
LC SCIENCE TRACER BULLETIN, TB (series). [Irregular]

Each issue is devoted to a specific subject and includes LC subject headings used for the subject; basic, additional, and related texts; handbooks, encyclopedias, dictionaries; bibliographies on the subject; Government publications, journal articles; and additional sources of information.

LC 33.11:nos.
NRC SWITCHBOARD, SL (series).

STACK AND READER DIVISION
(1954–   )

LC 34.1:date
ANNUAL REPORTS.

LC 34.2:CT • Item 818-C
GENERAL PUBLICATIONS.

SLAVIC AND CENTRAL
EUROPEAN DIVISION
(1956–1983)

INFORMATION

Library of Congress
Room LJ-G59
Thomas Jefferson Bldg.
10 First Street, SE
Washington, D.C. 20515
(202) 707-5510
Fax: (202) 707-2076

LC 35.1:date
ANNUAL REPORTS.

LC 35.2:CT • Item 818-E
GENERAL PUBLICATIONS.

LC 35.9:CT • Item 818-E-1
BIBLIOGRAPHIES AND LISTS OF PUBLICATIONS. [Irregular]

TECHNICAL INFORMATION
DIVISION
(1954–1961)

LC 36.1:date
ANNUAL REPORTS.

LC 36.2:CT
GENERAL PUBLICATIONS.

LC 36.8:nos.
CATALOG OF OSRD REPORTS.

Earlier LC 29.8

LC 36.9:date
AVIATION MEDICINE, ANNOTATED BIBLIOGRAPHY.[Annual]

LC 36.10:CT
BIBLIOGRAPHIES AND LISTS OF PUBLICATIONS.

DECIMAL CLASSIFICATION
OFFICE
(1959–   )

LC 37.1:date
REPORTS.

LC 37.2:CT
GENERAL PUBLICATIONS.

LC 37.8:v.nos.&nos.
DEWEY DECIMAL CLASSIFICATION, ADDISTIONS, NOTES AND DECISIONS, [Irregular]. (Processing Department)
ISSN 0083-1573

AEROSPACE TECHNOLOGY
DIVISION
(1965–1973)

LC 38.1:date
REPORTS.

LC 38.2:CT • Item 788-A
GENERAL PUBLICATIONS.

LC 38.9:nos.
AID REPORTS.

LC 38.10:date
SCIENTIFIC RESEARCH INSTITUTES OF THE USSR.

LC 38.11:v.nos.&nos.
FOREIGN SCIENCE BULLETIN.

LC 38.12:v.nos.&nos.
GEOSCIENCE AND TECHNOLOGY BULLETIN. v. 1–1966–

AMERICAN FOLKLIFE CENTER
(1976–   )

CREATION AND AUTHORITY

The American Folklife Center was established within the Library of Congress by the American Folklife Preservation Act (89 Stat. 1129), approved January 2, 1976.

INFORMATION

American Folklife Center
Library of Congress
101 Independence Ave., SE
Washington, D.C. 20540-4610
(202) 707-5510
Fax: 707- 2076
E mail: folklife@loc.gov
http://www.cweb.loc.gov/folklife

LC 39.1:date
ANNUAL REPORT.

LC 39.2:CT • Item 818-G-2
GENERAL PUBLICATIONS. [Irregular]

LC 39.9:nos. • Item 818-G-1
PUBLICATIONS OF THE AMERICAN FOLKLIFE CENTER. 1– 1978– [Irregular]

LC 39.10:v.nos.&nos. • Item 818-G-3
FOLKLIFE CENTER NEWS. v. 1– 1978– [Quarterly]

PURPOSE:– To provide a forum of information on the programs, projects, and activities of the Folklife Center. Contains brief illustrated articles.

LC 39.11:nos. • Item 818-G-4
STUDIES IN AMERICAN FOLKLIFE. 1– [Irregular]

Each issue is devoted to a single subject.

LC 39.12:date • Item 818-G-5
AMERICAN FOLK MUSIC AND FOLKLORE RECORDINGS, A SELECTED LIST. [Annual]

PURPOSE:– To inform the public about newly issued folk records and audio tapes. Provides a usable resource for educators, librarians, and others interested in currently available sound recordings and folk music. Includes both reissues from the 1920's and later and also more recent recordings.

LC 39.13:nos. • Item 818-G-6
LC FOLK ARCHIVE REFERENCE AIDS, LCFARA- (series). [Irregular]

LC 39.13/2:nos. • Item 818-C-6
LC FOLK ARCHIVE FINDING AID (numbered).

LC 39.14:date • Item 818-G-7
FOLKLIFE ANNUAL.

PURPOSE:– To present articles written by folklife specialists on the traditional expressive life and culture of the United States.

LC 39.15:CT • Item 818-G-8
POSTERS.

MOTION PICTURE,
BROADCASTING, AND
RECORDED SOUND DIVISION

INFORMATION

Motion Picture, Broadcasting, and
Recorded Sound Division
Library of Congress
Room LM-336
101 Independence Ave. SE
Washington, D.C. 20540
(202) 707-8572
Fax: (202) 707-2371
http://www/cweb.loc.gov/rr/mopic

LC 40.1:date
ANNUAL REPORT.

LC 40.2:CT • Item 813-B
GENERAL PUBLICATIONS. [Irregular]

LC 40.2:F 71 • Item 813
FOLK RECORDINGS, SELECTED FROM THE ARCHIVE OF FOLK SONG. [Irregular]

LC 40.8:CT • Item 813-C
HANDBOOKS, MANUALS, GUIDES. [Irregular]

LC 40.9:CT • Item 813-D
BIBLIOGRAPHIES AND LISTS OF PUBLICATIONS. [Irregular]

LC 40.10:date • Item 813-E
THE MARY PICKFORD THEATER IN THE LIBRARY OF CONGRESS. [Quarterly]

AFRICAN AND MIDDLE EASTERN DIVISION

INFORMATION

African and Middle Eastern Division
Area Studies
Library of Congress
Room LJ-220
Thomas Jefferson Bldg.
101 Independence Ave., SE
Washington, D.C. 20540-4820
(202) 707-7937
Fax: (202) 252-3180
E-Mail:amed@loc.gov
http://www.cweb.loc.gov/rr/amed/div.html

LC 41.1:date
ANNUAL REPORT.

LC 41.2:CT   • **Item 818-H**
GENERAL PUBLICATIONS. [Irregular]

LC 41.9:CT   • **Item 818-H-1**
NEAR EAST SERIES. [Irregular]

Consists of a listing of Near East publications held by the Library of Congress, each publication on a different subject, such as Arab-World Newspapers, etc.

LC 41.10:   • **Item 818-H-2**
MIDEAST DIRECTIONS (series). [Irregular]

Each issue provides a selected list of references on a different subject.

LC 41.11:CT   • **Item 806-H-1**
MAKTABA AFRIKANA SERIES. [Irregular]
Earlier LC 2.12

LC 41.12:CT   • **Item 818-H-3**
BIBLIOGRAPHIES AND LISTS OF PUBLICATIONS. [Irregular]

LC 41.12/2:date   • **Item 818-H-3**
U.S. IMPRINTS ON SUB-SAHARAN AFRICA.

A guide to publications cataloged at the Library of Congress.

LAW LIBRARY
(1832–   )

INFORMATION

Law Library
Library of Congress
Room LM-240
101 Independence Ave, S.E.
Washington, D.C. 20540-3000
(202) 707-5079
Fax: (202) 707-1820
E-Mail:law@loc.gov
http://www.cweb.loc.gov/rr/law/contact.html

LC 42.1:date
ANNUAL REPORT.

LC 42.2:CT   • **Item 818-J**
GENERAL PUBLICATIONS. [Irregular]

LC 42.8   • **Item 818-K-1**
HANDBOOKS, MANUALS, GUIDES.

LC 42.9:CT   • **Item 818-K**
BIBLIOGRAPHIES AND LISTS OF PUBLICATIONS.

LC 42.15   • **Item 818-J-1**
INTRODUCTIONS TO RESEARCH IN FOREIGN LAW (series).

EUROPEAN DIVISION
(1983–   )

INFORMATION

European Division
Library of Congress
Room LJ-250
Thomas Jefferson Bldg.
101 Independence Ave., SE
Washington, D.C. 20540-4830
(202) 707-5522
Fax: 707-8482
E mail: eurref@loc.gov
http://www.cweb.loc.gov/rr/european

LC 43.1:date
ANNUAL REPORT.

L 43.2:CT   • **Item 818-M**
GENERAL PUBLICATIONS. [Irregular]

LC 43.8:CT
HANDBOOKS, MANUALS, GUIDES. [Irregular]

LC 43.9:CT   • **Item 818-N**
BIBLIOGRAPHIES AND LISTS OF PUBLICATIONS. [Irregular]

NATIONAL LABOR RELATIONS BOARD
(1935–   )

CREATION AND AUTHORITY

The National Labor Relations Board is an independent agency created by the National Labor Relations Act of July 5, 1935 (49 Stat. 449; 29 U.S.C. 151-166), as amended by the acts of June 23, 1947 (61 Stat. 136; 29 U.S.C. 151-167), October 22, 1951 (65 Stat. 601; 29 U.S.C. 158, 159, 168), and September 14, 1959 (73 Stat. 519; 29 U.S.C. 141, et seq.)

INFORMATION

Information Division
National Labor Relations Board
1099 14th St. NW
Washington, D.C. 20570
(202)273-1991
Fax: (202) 273-1789
http://www.nlrb.gov

LR 1.1:date   • **Item 824 (MF)**
ANNUAL REPORT. 1st–   1936–   [Annual]

Report submitted by the Board to the President and Congress pursuant to section 3(c) of the Labor Management relations Act of 1947 for the fiscal year.
Includes operations for fiscal year, representation cases, unfair labor practices, Supreme Court rulings, enforcement litigations, injunction litigation, contempt litigation, and miscellaneous litigation. The appendix contains statistical tables for the fiscal year.

LR 1.1/2:date
SUMMARY OF OPERATIONS, OFFICE OF GENERAL COUNSEL.

LR 1.2:CT   • **Item 827**
GENERAL PUBLICATIONS.

Earlier Y 3.N 21/13:2

LR 1.3:nos.
BULLETINS. 1–   1936–

Earlier Y 3.N 21/13:3

LR 1.5:CT   • **Item 828**
LAWS.

Earlier Y 3.N 21/13:5

LR 1.5/2:nos.   • **Item 826-C**
WEEKLY SUMMARY OF NLRB CASES.

LR 1.6:CT   • **Item 829**
REGULATIONS, RULES, AND INSTRUCTIONS.

Earlier Y 3.N 21/13:6

LR 1.6:R 86
RULES AND REGULATIONS AND STATEMENTS OF PROCEDURE. [Irregular]

Subscription service includes supplements for an indefinite period.
Contains Part 101. Statements of Procedure: Part 102, Rules and Regulations; Topical Index; National Labor Relations Board Organization and Functions; and the text of the Labor Management Relations Act, 1947, as amended Sept. 14, 1959.

LR 1.6/2:CT   • **Item 827-A**
HANDBOOKS, MANUALS, GUIDES.

LR 1.6/2:C 26   • **Item 827-A**
CASEHANDLING MANUAL. (basic manual, issued in three parts, and irregular supplements for an indefinite period)

LR 1.6/3:date   • **Item 827-A**
NATIONAL LABOR RELATIONS BOARD FIELD MANUAL. 1967–   [Irregular]

Subscription includes basic manual plus supplementary materials for an indefinite period.
PURPOSE:– To establish procedural and operational instructions for the guidance of agency staff in administrating the National Labor Relations Act.

LR 1.7:CT
ADDRESSES. [Irregular]

LR 1.8:v.nos.&date   • **Item 826**
DECISIONS AND ORDERS OF THE NATIONAL LABOR RELATIONS BOARD. v. 1–   1935–   [Irregular]

PURPOSE:– To supply official and full-text copies of all Board decisions issued in all unfair labor practice cases and in major representation cases.
Citation: N.L.R.B.

LR 1.8/2:nos.   • **Item 826**
DIGEST & INDEX OF DECISIONS OF NLRB.

Earlier LR 1.8

LR 1.8/3:date   • **Item 826**
DIGEST OF DECISIONS OF THE NATIONAL LABOR RELATIONS BOARD, ANNUAL SUPPLEMENTS. 1951–   [Annual]

Title varies.

LR 1.8/4:nos.   • **Item 826**
INDEX OF BOARD DECISIONS, CUMULATIVE SUPPLEMENTS.

LR 1.8/5:date/nos.   • **Item 826-A**
DIGEST OF DECISIONS OF THE NATIONAL LABOR RELATIONS BOARD, CS- (series). [Bimonthly]

LR 1.8/5-2:nos.
DIGEST OF DECISIONS OF NATIONAL LABOR RE-
LATIONS BOARD BW- (series).

LR 1.8/6:date   • **Item 826**
CLASSIFIED INDEX OF THE NATIONAL LABOR RE-
LATIONS BOARD DECISIONS AND RELATED
COURT DECISIONS.

    ISSN 0092-4962

LR 1.8/6-2:date   • **Item 826**
CLASSIFIED INDEX OF DECISIONS OF REGIONAL
DIRECTORS OF NATIONAL LABOR RELATIONS
BOARD IN REPRESENTATION PROCEEDINGS.

LR 1.8/7:date   • **Item 826**
CLASSIFICATION OUTLINE WITH TOPICAL INDEX
FOR DECISIONS OF THE NATIONAL LABOR
RELATIONS BOARD AND RELATED COURT DE-
CISIONS.

    Earlier: Classification Outline for Decisions
of NLRB and Related Court Decisions.

LR 1.8/8:date   • **Item 826-B**
CLASSIFIED INDEX OF DISPOSITIONS OF ULP
[Unfair Labor Practices] CHARGES BY THE
GENERAL COUNSEL OF THE NATIONAL LABOR
RELATIONS BOARD.

    ISSN 0147-7250

LR 1.8/9:v.nos.   • **Item 826**
SUPPLEMENT TO TABLES OF CASES DECIDED.

LR 1.9:CT
PAPERS IN RE.

    Earlier Y 3.N 21/13:11

LR 1.10:nos.
RESEARCH MEMORANDUMS. 1–   1938–

LR 1.11:nos.
OUTLINES. 1–   1937–

LR 1.12:CT   • **Item 826-D**
POSTERS AND CHARTS.

LR 1.13:CT
LISTS OF NATIONAL LABOR RELATIONS BOARD,
PUBLICATIONS.

LR 1.14:vol.   • **Item 825**
COURT DECISIONS RELATING TO THE NATIONAL
LABOR RELATIONS ACT. v. 1–   1939–
[Irregular]

   LR 1.14:v.nos./Ind
   INDEXES.

       v. 1– 9.   – 1955. 1958. 164 p.
       10– 22. 1956– 1973. 1974. 592 p.

LR 1.15:nos.
PRESS RELEASES. R.1–   [Irregular] (press only)

LR 1.15/2:v.nos.   • **Item 826-C (EL)**
WEEKLY SUMMARY OF N.L.R.B. CASES. W 1–
[Weekly]

    Provides a digest of actions of the National
Labor Relations Board, including stipulated decisions, orders, denial of motions, dismissal of
petitions, direction of election, decisions of review, and intermediate reports.
    Detailed information of the cases listed (cop-
ies of reports of decisions if available) may be
requested from the Division of Information. Decisions are later published in bound volumes.
    ISSN 0364-8109

LR 1.15/3:nos.
N.L.R.B. STATISTICAL SUMMARY COVERING THE
THREE MONTH PERIOD. S 1–   [Quarterly]

    Tables give nature and results of collective
bargaining elections conducted in cases closed
during quarterly period. Textual summary.

LR 1.15/4:date
QUARTERLY REPORT ON CASE DEVELOPMENTS.
[Quarterly]

LR 1.16:nos.   • **Item 825-A**
N.L.R.B. ELECTION REPORTS. ER 1–   1962–
[Monthly]

    Lists the outcome of secret-ballot voting by
employees of NLRB-conducted representation
elections as officially certified following resolution of post-election objections and/or challenges.
Results are listed for all elections except those
processed under Section 8 (b) (7) (C) (expedited)
or Section 9(A) (union ship deauthorizations)
    Lists in tabular form, by union and employer,
city and State, case number, industry code, unit,
type election, number eligible employees in unit,
number of valid votes (for and against), and unit
size code.
    The Election Report Glossary, Permanent Ref-
erence Material, published in March 1962, provides a guide to users of election report and
gives definition of codes used to indicate type of
election, unit involved, type of case, region and
regional office location, State (location of employer), and unions in order of numerical code.

LR 1.17:nos.   • **Item 827-B**
FORMS.

NATIONAL MILITARY
ESTABLISHMENT
(1947– 1949)

CREATION AND AUTHORITY

    The National Military Establishment was es-
tablished by act of Congress, approved July 26,
1947 (61 Stat 495) and consisted of the Department of the Army (formerly the War Department)
the Department of the Navy, and the newly created Department of the Air Force. Department of
Defense (D 1) by the National Security Act Amendments of 1949 (63 Stat. 579), approved August
10, 1949.

M 1.1:date
ANNUAL REPORTS.

M 1.2:CT
GENERAL PUBLICATIONS.
    Later D 1.2

M 1.6:CT
REGULATIONS, RULES, AND INSTRUCTIONS.

M 1.7:date
TELEPHONE DIRECTORY, NATIONAL DEFENSE.
    Earlier W 1.19
    Later D 1.7

M 1.8:sec.nos.
ARMED SERVICES PROCUREMENT REGULATIONS.
    Later D 1.13

M 1.8/2:nos.
ARMED SERVICES PROCUREMENT REGULATION
REVISIONS.
    Later D 1.13/2

M 1.9:nos.
EDUCATION MANUALS.
    Earlier W 1.55
    Later D 1.10

JOINT CHIEFS OF STAFF
(1947– 1949)

CREATION AND AUTHORITY

    The Joint Chiefs of Staff was established
within the National Military Establishment by act
of congress, approved July 26, 1947 (61 Stat.
495). By authority of the National Security Act
Amendments of 1949 (63 Stat. 579) it became a
part of the newly established Department of Defense (D 5).
    NOTE:– No publications were assigned to this
class during the period 1947– 1949.

ARMED SERVICES EXPLOSIVES
SAFETY BOARD
(1948– 1949)

CREATION AND AUTHORITY

    The Joint Army-Navy Ammunition Storage
Board was established in 1928. In May 1945, it
was renamed the Army-Navy Explosives Board.
In 1948, the name was changed to Armed Services Explosives Safety Board.

M 3.1:date
ANNUAL REPORTS.

M 3.2:CT
GENERAL PUBLICATIONS.

M 3.7:nos.
TECHNICAL PAPERS.
    Earlier W 1.64.

MUNITIONS BOARD
(1947– 1949)

CREATION AND AUTHORITY

    The Munitions Board was established within
the National Military Establishment by the National Security Act of 1947 (61 Stat. 499). The
Board continued under the Department of Defense (D 3) upon its establihsment in 1949.

M 5.1:date
ANNUAL REPORTS.
    Earlier M 401.1
    Later D 3.1

M 5.2:CT
GENERAL PUBLICATIONS.
    Earlier M 401.2
    Later D 3.2

M 5.7:nos.
JOINT ARMY-NAVY STANDARDS.
    Replaced by National Military Establishment
    Standards (M 5.8).
    Earlier N 20.28

M 5.8:nos.
NATIONAL MILITARY ESTABLISHMENT STANDARDS.
    Later D 3.7

M 5.9:nos.
ANC DOCUMENTS.
    Earlier Y 3.Ae 8.8
    Later D 3.9

RESEARCH AND DEVELOPMENT BOARD
(1947–1949)

CREATION AND AUTHORITY

The Research and Development Board was established within the National Military Establishment by the National Security Act of 1947 (61 Stat. 499). The Board continued under the Department of Defense (D 4).

M 6.1:date
ANNUAL REPORTS.
Earlier M 501.2
Later D 4.2

M 6.2:CT
GENERAL PUBLICATIONS.

Earlier M 501.2
Later D 4.2

DEPARTMENT OF THE ARMY
(1947–1949)

CREATION AND AUTHORITY

The Department of War (W 1) was designated the Department of the Army by the National Security Act of 1947 (61 Stat. 499), which established the National Military Establishment. The National Secuity Act Amendments of 1949 (63 Stat. 578) established the Department of Defense as an executive department of the Government and made the Department of the Army (D 101) one of the three military departments within the Department of Defense.

M 101.1:date
ANNUAL REPORTS.
Earlier W 1.1
Later D 101.1

M 101.2:CT
GENERAL PUBLICATIONS.
Earlier W 1.2
Later D 101.2

M 101.3:date&nos.
BULLETINS.
Earlier W 1.3
Later D 101.3

M 101.4:date&nos.
CIRCULARS.
Earlier W 1.4/2
Later D 101.4

M 101.7:date&nos,
GENERAL ORDERS.
Earlier W 1.46
Later D 101.7

M 101.8:dt.&nos.
SPECIAL ORDERS.
Earlier W 1.48
Later D 101.8

M 101.9:nos.
ARMY REGULATIONS.
Earlier W 1.6
Later D 101.9

M 101.10:v.nos.
ARMY INFORMATION DIGEST. [Monthly]
Earlier W 1.66
Later D 101.12

M 101.11:date
ARMY PROCUREMENT REGULATIONS.
Earlier W 109.8

M 101.12:sec.nos& le. nos.
SUPPLY CATALOGS.
Earlier W 1.67
Later D 101.16

M 101.13:letters-nos.
TECHNICAL BULLETINS.

Earlier W 1.58
Later D 101.25

M 101.14:dt.&nos.
GENERAL COURT-MARTIAL ORDERS.
Earlier W 1.51
Later D 101.14

M 101.15:nos.
JOINT ARMY AND AIR FORCE REGULATIONS.

M 101.16:nos.
MILITARY GOVERNMENT WEEKLY INFORMATION
BULLETINS.
Earlier W 1.72./5
Later M 105.8

M 101.17:nos.
FIELD MANUALS.
Earlier W 1.33
Later D 101.20

M 101.18:nos.
TECHNICAL MANUALS
Earlier W 1.35
Later D 101.12   *D101.11;*

M 101.19:date
OFFICAL ARMY AND AIR FORCE REGISTER.
Earlier D 101.13

M 101.20:nos.
CIVILIAN PERSONNEL CIRCULARS.
Later D 101.26

M 101.21:nos.
TABLES OF ORGANIZATION AND EQUIPMENT.
Earlier W 1.44
Later D 101.24

M 101.23:date
INDEX OF UNITED STATES ARMY, JOINT ARMY-NAVY,
AND FEDERAL SPECIFICATIONS AND STANDARDS.
Earlier W 1.50

M 101.24:nos.
MEMORANDUMS.
Proc. and printed.
Earlier W 1.60
Later D 101.32

M 101.25:nos.
PAMPHLETS.
Earlier W 1.43
Later D 101.22

M 101.26:nos.
U.S. ARMY SPECIFICATIONS.
Earlier W 1.49
Later D 101.28

M 101.27:nos.
SUPPLY BULLETINS.
Printed and proc.
Earlier W 1.61
Later D 101.15

M 101.28:nos.
OCCUPATIONAL BRIEFS.
Earlier W 1.63

M 101.29:nos.
TABLES OF ALLOWANCES.
Earlier W 1.28
Later D 101.23

M 101.30:dt.&le.
ORDERS.
Earlier W 1.14

M 101.31:nos.
REDUCTION TABLES.
Later D 101.18

M 101.32:nos.
SPECIAL REGULATIONS
Later D 101.10

M 101.34:nos.
POSTERS.
Earlier W 1.59
Later D 101.35

M 101.35:nos.
CIVILIAN PERSONNEL PAMPHLETS.
Earlier W 1.57
Later D 101.37

MEDICAL DEPARTMENT
(1947–1949)

CREATION AND AUTHORITY

The Medical Department (W 44) was established as a separate branch of the Army, headed by a Surgeon General, by act of Congress, approved April 14, 1818 (3 Stat. 426). By the Army Organization Act of 1950 (64 Stat. 263), the Department was redesignated the Army Medical Service (D 104).

M 102.1:date
ANNUAL REPORTS OF THE SURGEON GENERAL.
Earlier W 44.1
Later D 104.1

M 102.2:CT
GENERAL PUBLICATIONS.
Earlier W 44.2
Later D 104.2

M 102.3:v.nos.
BULLETIN OF ARMY MEDICAL DEPARTMENT.
[Monthly]

W 44.21/7
Later D 104.3

M 102.7:nos.
CURRENT LIST OF MEDICAL LITERATURE. [Weekly]
Earlier W 44.30
Later D 104.7

M 102.8:v.nos.
INDEX-CATALOGUE OF LIBRARY OF SURGEON
GENERAL'S OFFICE, 4TH SERIES.
Earlier W 44.7/4
Later D 8.9

M 102.9:nos.
MEDICAL DEPARTMENT EQUIPMENT LIST.
Later D 104.9

HISTORICAL DIVISION
(1947–1949)

CREATION AND AUTHORITY

The Historical Division was established within the National Military Establishment in 1947. It became a part of the Department of Defense (D 114) in 1949.

M 103.1:date
ANNUAL REPORTS.
Earlier W 110.1

M 103.2:CT
GENERAL PUBLICATIONS.
Earlier W 110.2

M 103.7:CT
UNITED STATES ARMY IN WORLD WAR II.
Later D 114.7

M 103.8:CT
AMERICAN FORCES IN ACTION SERIES.
Earlier W 110.7
Later D 114.9

M 103.9:nos.
UNITED STATES ARMY IN WORLD WAR, 1917-1919.

TROOP INFORMATION AND EDUCATION DIVISION
(1947–1949)

CREATION AND AUTHORITY

The Information and Education Division (W 111) was established within the National Military Establishment in 1947 and redesignated the Troop Information and Education Division. In 1949 the Division was transferred to the Department of Defense (D 2) and the Department of the Army (D 107).

M 104.1:date
ANNUAL REPORTS.
Earlier W 111.1
Later D 107.1

M 104.2:CT
GENERAL PUBLICATIONS.
Earlier W 111.2
Later D 107.2

M 104.7:nos.
ARMED FORCES TALK.
Earlier W 111.7
Later D 2.7

M 104.7:v.nos.
REPORT TO ARMY. [Semimonthly]

Trial issue was classed M 104.2:R 29

CIVIL AFFAIRS DIVISION
(1947–1949)

M 105.1:date
ANNUAL REPORTS.

M 105.2:CT
GENERAL PUBLICATIONS.

M 105.7:nos.
MONTHLY REPORT OF THE MILITARY GOVERNOR FOR GERMANY (U.S.).

M 105.7/2:CT/date
FINANCIAL REPORTS.
Earlier W 1.72/10

M 105.8:nos.
MILITARY GOVERNMENT WEEKLY INFORMATION BULLETIN.
Earlier W 1.72/5
Later S 1.85

M 105.9:nos.
OFFICAL GAZETTE OF CONTROL COUNCIL FOR GERMANY.
Earlier W 1.73

M 105.10:nos.
REPORT OF UNITED STATES COMMISSIONER OF AUSTRIA MILITARY GOVERNMENT. [Monthly]
Earlier W 1.73
Later S 1.89 and S 1.89/2

M 105.11:nos.
SUMMATION OF NON-MILITARY ACTIVITIES IN JAPAN. [Monthly]
Earlier W 1.75

M 105.12:nos.
SUMMATION OF UNITED STATES ARMY MILITARY GOVERNMENT ACTIVITIES IN RYUKYU ISLANDS. [Bimonthly]
Earlier W 1.78

M 105.13:nos.
SOUTH KOREA INTERIM GOVERNMENT ACTIVITIES. [Monthly]

Continues and replaces summation of United States Army Military Government activities in Korea (W 1.76).

M 105.14:nos.
MILITARY GOVERNMENT FOR GERMANY, STATISTICAL REPORTS. [Quarterly]
Earlier W 1.72/3

M 105.15:dt&nos.
MONTHLY REPORT PREPARED BY TECHNICAL STAFF, FUEL COMMITTEE, ALLIED CONTROL AUTHORITY.
Earlier W 1.83

M 105.16:nos.
REPORT OF ACCESSIONS. [Monthly]
Later M 108.9

M 105.17:CT
MILITARY GOVERNMENT FOR GERMANY (U.S.) SPECIAL REPORT OF MILTARY GOVERNMENT.
Earlier W 1.72/2

M 105.18:nos.
EUROPEAN RECOVERY PROGRAM, JOINT REPORT OF UNITED STATES AND UNITED KINGDOM MILITARY GOVERNORS. [Quarterly]

M 105.19:nos.
VISITING EXPERT SERIES.
Later S 1.87

M 105.20:nos.
BAVARIAN ECONOMIST. [Monthly]

M 105.21:nos.
SEMI-MONTHLY MILITARY GOVERNMENT REPORT FOR U.S. OCCUPIED AREA OF GERMANY.

M 105.22:nos.
WEEKLY REPORT ON JAPAN.
Later D 102.13

M 105.23:nos.
MEMORANDUM FOR JAPANESE GOVERNMENT.
Later D 102.14

M 105.24:nos.
SCIENCE AND TECHNOLOGY IN JAPAN, REPORTS.
Later D 102.15

M 105.25:nos.
SUPREME COMMANDER FOR ALLIED POWERS: NATURAL RESOURCES SECTION REPORTS.
Earlier W 1.80
Later D 102.20

M 105.26:nos.
GAZETTE OF THE ALLIED COMMISSION FOR AUSTRIA.
Earlier W 1.82
Later D 102.22

M 105.27:date
JOINT REPORT IMPORT AGENCY, REPORTS. [Monthly]

M 105.28:nos.&sec.nos.
JAPANESE ECONOMIC STATISTICS.
Later D 102.18

INTELLIGENCE DIVISION
(1947–1949)

CREATION AND AUTHORITY

The Military Intelligence Division (W 100) was established within the National Military Establishment in 1947.

M 106.1:date
ANNUAL REPORTS.
Earlier W 100.1

M 106.2:CT
GENERAL PUBLICATIONS.
Earlier W 100.2

JUDGE ADVOCATE GENERAL OF THE ARMY
(1947–1949)

CREATION AND AUTHORITY

The Judge Advocate General's Department (W 10) was established within the National Military Establishment in 1947. In 1949 it was transferred to the Department of Defense (D 108).

M 107.1:date
ANNUAL REPORTS.
Earlier W 10.1
Later 108.1

M 107.2:CT
GENERAL PUBLICATIONS.
Earlier W 10.2
Later D 108.2

M 107.3:v.nos.
BULLETIN OF JUDGE ADVOCATE GENERAL OF ARMY.
Earlier W 10.3
Later D 108.3

M 107.7:date
MANUAL FOR COURTS-MARTIAL, ARMY.
Earlier W 10.5/1
Later D 1.14

ADJUTANT GENERAL'S OFFICE
(1947–1949)

CREATION AND AUTHORITY

The Adjutant General's Department (W 3) was established within the National Military Establishment in 1947 and redesignated the Adjutant General's Office. In 1949 it was transferred to the Department of Defense (D 102).

M 108.1:date
ANNUAL REPORTS.
Earlier W 3.11
Later D 102.1

M 108.2:CT
GENERAL PUBLICATIONS.

Earlier W 3.2
Later D 102.2

M 108.7:dt.&nos.
DEPOT INFORMATION BULLETIN. [Weekly]

Earlier W 3.82

M 108.7/2
INFORMATION BULLETIN. [Weekly]

Proc. Admin.

M 108.8:date
OFFICIAL ARMY AND AIR FORCE REGISTER. [Annual]

Earlier W 3.11
Later D 102.9

M 108.9:nos.
REPORT OF ACCESSIONS. [Monthly]

Earlier M 105.16
Later D 102.7

Recruiting Publicity Bureau

M 108.75:CT
PUBLICATIONS.

Later D 102.75

M 108.76:v.nos.
U.S. ARMY AND AIR FORCE RECRUITING SERVICE
LETTER.

Earlier U.S. Army Recruiting Service Letter.
(W 3.83)

M 108.77:v.nos.
ARMY LIFE AND UNITED STATES ARMY RECRUIT-
ING NEWS. [Monthly]

Earlier W 3.45
Later D 102.77

M 108.78:nos.
RECRUITING PUBLICITY BUREAU POSTERS.

Earlier W 3.46/8
Later D 102.78

M 108.79:film-nos.
MEETING LEADERS GUIDE.

Earlier W 3.84/2

M 108.80:v.nos.
RECRUITING JOURNAL.

Later D 102.76

MILITARY ACADEMY
(1947– 1949)

CREATION AND AUTHORITY

The Military Academy (W 12) was established
within the National Military Establishment in 1947.
In 1949 the Academy was transferred to the Department of Defense (D 109).

M 109.1:date
ANNUAL REPORTS.
Earlier W 12.1
Later D 109.1

M 109.2:CT
GENERAL PUBLICATIONS.
Earlier W 12.2
Later D 109.2

M 109.6:CT
REGULATIONS, RULES, AND INSTRUCTIONS.

Earlier W 12.6/2
Later D 109.6

M 109.6/2:date
REGULATIONS FOR UNITED STATES CORPS OF
CADETS PRESCRIBED BY COMMANDANT OF
CADETS.

Earlier W 12.6/2:C 11

M 109.7:dt.&nos.
GENERAL ORDERS.

Earlier W 12.10

M 109.8:dt.&nos.
SPECIAL ORDERS.

Earlier W 12.11

M 109.9:dt.&nos.
MEMORANDUM.

Earlier W 12.15

M 109.10:dt.&nos.
GENERAL COURT-MARTIAL ORDERS.

Earlier W 12.13

M 109.11:date
OFFICAL REGISTER OF OFFICERS AND CADETS.
[Annual]

Earlier W 12.5
Later D 109.7

ENGINEER DEPARTMENT
(1947– 1949)

CREATION AND AUTHORITY

The Engineer Department (W 7) was established within the National Military Establishment
in 1947. In 1949 it was redesignated the Corps of
Engineers and transferred to the Department of
Defense (D 103).

M 110.1:date
ANNUAL REPORTS.
Earlier W 7.1/1
Later D 103.1

M 119.1
GENERAL PUBLICATIONS.
Earlier W 7.2
Later D 103.2

M 110.6:CT
REGULATIONS, RULES, AND INSTRUCTIONS.
Earlier NHA 2.15
Later D 103.6

M 110.7:pt.nos.&chap.nos.
ENGINEERING MANUAL FOR CIVIL WORKS CON-
STRUCTION.
Earlier W 7.35
Later D 103.10

M 110.8:nos.
GUIDE SPECIFICATIONS, CIVIL WORKS CONSTRUC-
TION.
Earlier W 7.37

M 110.9:date
INDEX OF SPECIFICATIONS USED BY CORPS OF
ENGINEERS.
Earlier W 7.18/4
Later D 103.12

M 110.10:dt.&nos.
SPECIAL ORDERS.
Earlier W 7.9
Later D 103.14

M 110.11:nos.
PORT SERIES.

Earlier W 7.21/2
Later D 103.8

M 110.12:nos.
MISCELLANEOUS SERIES.

Earlier W 7.22
Later D 103.11

M 110.13:pt.nos&chap.nos.
ENGINEERING MANUAL MILITARY CONSTRUCTION.

Earlier W 7.36
Later D 103.9

M 110.14:dt.&nos.
GENERAL ORDERS.

Earlier W 7.8
Later D 103.7

M 110.15:v.nos.
BULLETIN OF BEACH EROSION BOARD. [Quarterly]
Earlier W 7.38

M 110.16:date
ST. MARY'S FALLS CANAL, MICHIGAN, STATISTI-
CAL REPORT OF LAKE COMMERCE PASSING
THROUGH CANALS AT SAULT STE. MARIE,
MICHIGAN, AND ONTARIO.
Earlier W 7.26
Later D 103.17

M 110.17:nos.
TRANSPORTATION SERIES.
Earlier W 7.23

M 110.18:nos.
WATERWAYS EXPERIMENT STATION: TECHNICAL
MEMORANDUMS.

M 110.19:nos.
WATERWAYS EXPERIMENT STATION, BULLETINS.

Later D 103.24

M 110.20:nos.
AMS BULLETINS.

Earlier W 7.33/4
Later Later D 103.20/3 and D 103.24/2

Lake Survey Office

M 110.101:date
ANNUAL REPORTS.

Earlier W 33.1
Later D 103.201

M 110.102:CT
GENERAL PUBLICATIONS.

Earlier W 33.2
Later D 103.202

M 110.103:nos.
BULLETINS.
Earlier W 31.3
Later D 103.203

Mississippi River Commission

M 110.201:date
ANNUAL REPORTS.

Earlier W 31.1
Later D 103.301

M 110.202:CT
GENERAL PUBLICATIONS.

Later D 103.302

M 110.207:date
STAGES AND DISCHARGES, MISSISSIPPI RIVER AND ITS OUTLETS AND TRIBUTARIES. [Annual]
Earlier W 31.5
Later D 103.309

M 110.208:CT
MAPS.
Earlier W 31.7
Later D 103.307

Beach Erosion Board

M 110.301:date
ANNUAL REPORTS.

M 110.302:CT
GENERAL PUBLICATIONS.

M 110.303:v.nos.
BULLETIN OF BEACH EROSION BOARD.
Earlier W 7.38
Later D 103.16

M 110.307:nos.
TECHNICAL REPORTS.
Earlier W 7.29
Later D 103.5

M 110.308:nos.
TECHNICAL MEMORANDUM.
Later D 103.19

Engineer School

M 110.401:date
ANNUAL REPORTS.
Earlier W 7.16/1
Later D 103.101

M 110.402:CT
GENERAL PUBLICATIONS.
Later D 103.102

M 110.407:nos.
ENGINEER SCHOOL LIBRARY BULLETIN.
Later D 103.107

M 110.408:nos.
WEEKLY PERIODICAL INDEX.
Later 103.108

ORDNANCE DEPARTMENT
(1947–1949)

CREATION AND AUTHORITY

The Ordnance Department (W 34) was established within the National Military Establishment in 1947. In 1949, it became a part of the Department of Defense (D 105).

M 111.1:date
ANNUAL REPORTS.
Earlier W 34.1/1
Later D 105.1

M 111.2:CT
GENERAL PUBLICATIONS.
Earlier W 34.2
Later D 105.2

M 111.7:nos.
ORDNANCE DEPARTMENT SAFETY BULLETINS.
Earlier W 34.35
Later D 105.7

M 111.8:dt.&nos.
ORDNANCE DEPARTMENT ORDERS.
Earlier W 34.9/2
Later D 105.8

QUARTERMASTER GENERAL OF THE ARMY
(1947–1949)

CREATION AND AUTHORITY

The Quartermaster General of the Army (W 77) was established within the National Military Establishment in 1947, in 1949, it became part of the Department of Defense (D 106).

M 112.1:date
ANNUAL REPORTS.
Earlier W 77.1
Later D 106.1

M 112.2:CT
GENERAL PUBLICATIONS.
Earlier W 77.2
Later D 106.2

M 112.4:dt.&nos.
OMG CIRCULARS.
Earlier W 77.22

M 112.6:CT
REGULATIONS, RULES, AND INSTRUCTIONS.
Earlier W 77.10/1
Later D 106.6

M 112.7:v.nos.
DEPOT AND MARKET CENTER OPERATIONS. [Monthly]
Restricted.
Earlier W 77.38
Later D 106.7

M 112.8:nos.
QUARTERMASTER CORPS MANUAL.
Earlier W 77.15/1
Later D 106.6/2

M 112.9:nos.
Q.M.C. HISTORICAL STUDIES.
Earlier W 77.36

M 112.10:nos.
TECHNICAL LIBRARY BIBLIOGRAPHIC SERIES.
Earlier W 77.39

GENERAL STAFF
(1947–1949)

CREATION AND AUTHORITY

The General Staff (W 2) was established within the National Military Establishment 1947. In 1949, it was transferred to the Department of Defense (D 5).

M 113.1:date
ANNUAL REPORTS.
Earlier W 2.1

M 113.2:CT
GENERAL PUBLICATIONS.
Earlier W 2.2

NATIONAL GUARD BUREAU
(1947–1949)

CREATION AND AUTHORITY

The National Guard Bureau (W 70) was established within the National Military Establishment in 1947. In 1949, it became a part of the Department of Defense (D 12).

M 114.1:date
ANNUAL REPORTS.
Earlier W 70.1
Later D 112.1

M 114.2:CT
GENERAL PUBLICATIONS.
Earlier W 70.2
Later D 112.2

M 114.4:CT.&nos.
NGB CIRCULARS.
Earlier W 70.4/2
Later D 112.4

M 114.6:nos.
NATIONAL GUARD REGULATIONS.
Printed and Proc.
Earlier W 70.7/4
Later D 112.6

M 114.7:nos.
ARMY FIELD FORCES SUBJECT SCHEDULE.
Printed and Proc.

M 114.8:nos.
SPECIAL TEXT.
Designated NG-nos.

PANAMA CANAL
(1947–1949)

CREATION AND AUTHORITY

The Panama Canal (W 79) was established within the National Military Establishment in 1947. In 1949, it became a part of the Department of Defense (D 113).

M 115.1:date
ANNUAL REPORTS.
Earlier W 79.1
Later D 113.1

M 115.2:CT
GENERAL PUBLICATIONS.
Earlier W 79.2
Later D 113.2

M 115.6:CT
REGULATIONS, RULES, AND INSTRUCTIONS.

M 115.7:date
TIDE TABLES, BALBOA AND CRISTOBAL, CANAL ZONE.
Earlier W 79.8
Later D 113.7

M 115.8:date
SCHEDULES.
 Earlier W 79.11/6

M 115.9:nos.
CANAL ZONE JUNIOR COLLEGE, CATALOGUES.
 Earlier W 79.10/8
 Later D 113.8

M 115.10:date
ANNUAL REPORT OF INSURANCE BUSINESS
 TRANSACTED IN CANAL ZONE.
 Earlier W 79.10/6
 Later D 113.10

FINANCE DEPARTMENT
(1947– 1949)

CREATION AND AUTHORITY

 The Finance Department (W 97) was established within the National Military Establishment
in 1947. (No SuDocs class was established in
1949 when the Department of Defense was created.)

M 116.1:date
ANNUAL REPORTS.
 Earlier W 97.1

M 116.2:CT
GENERAL PUBLICATIONS.
 Earlier W 97.2

M 116.3:CT&nos.
FINANCE BULLETINS.
 Earlier W 97.3

SPECIAL SERVICES DIVISION
(1947– 1949)

CREATION AND AUTHORITY

 The Special Services Division (W 109) was
established within the National Military Establishment in 1947. (No SuDocs class was established
in 1949 when the Department of Defense was
created.)

M 117.1:date
ANNUAL REPORTS.
 Earlier W 109.101

M 117.2:CT
GENERAL PUBLICATIONS.
 Earlier W 109.102

M 117.7:date
ARMY NAVY HIT KIT OF POPULAR SONGS. [Monthly]
 Earlier W 109.10
 Later D 102.10

PUBLIC INFORMATION DIVISION
(1947– 1949)

M 118.1:date
ANNUAL REPORTS.

M 118.2:CT
GENERAL PUBLICATIONS.

M 118.3:v.nos.&nos.
ARMY ADVISORY COMMITTEE, BULLETIN.

COMMAND AND GENERAL STAFF
COLLEGE
(1947– 1949)

CREATION AND AUTHORITY

 The Command and General Staff College (W
28) was established within the National Military
Establishment in 1947. In 1949, it became a part
of the Department of Defense (D 110).

M 119.1:date
ANNUAL REPORTS.
 Earlier W 28.1
 Later D 110.1

M 119.2:CT
GENERAL PUBLICATIONS.
 Earlier W 28.1
 Later D 110.2

M 119.7:v.nos.
MILITARY REVIEW. [Monthly]
 Earlier W 28.10
 Later D 110.7

DEPARTMENT OF THE NAVY
(1947– 1949)

CREATION AND AUTHORITY

 The Department of the Navy (N 1) was established within the National Military Establishment
in 1947. In 1949, it became a part of the Department of Defense (D 201).

M 201.1:date
ANNUAL REPORTS.
 Earlier N 1.1
 Later D 201.1

M 201.2:CT
GENERAL PUBLICATIONS.
 Earlier N 1.2
 Later D 201.2

M 201.7:nos.
GENERAL ORDERS, 7TH SERIES.
 Earlier N 1.13/7

M 201.7/2:nos.
GENERAL ORDERS, SERIES OF 1948.

M 201.8:date
TELEPHONE DIRECTORY.
 Earlier N 1.23

M 201.9:dt.&nos.
COURT-MARTIAL ORDERS.
 Earlier N 1.14
 Later D 201.8

M 201.10:date
LAWS RELATING CHIEFLY TO NAVY, NAVY DEPART-
 MENT, AND MARINE CORPS.
 Earlier N 1.7

M 201.11:nos.
NAVY REGULATIONS.
 Earlier N 1.11/1

HYDROGRAPHIC OFFICE
(1947– 1949)

CREATION AND AUTHORITY

 The Hydrographic Office (N 6) was established within the National Military Establishment
in 1947. In 1949, it was transferred along with the
Department of the Navy to the Department of
Defense (D 203).

M 202.1:date
ANNUAL REPORTS.
 Earlier N 1.1
 Later D 203.1

M 202.2:CT
GENERAL PUBLICATIONS.
 Earlier N 1.2
 Later D 203.2

M 202.3:nos.
HYDROGRAPHIC BULLETINS. [Weekly]
 Earlier N 6.3
 Later D 203.3

M 202.4:nos.
CIRCULARS.
 Earlier N 6.4
 Later D 203.4

M 202.7:dt.&nos.
NOTICE TO AVIATORS. [Biweekly]

 Earlier N 6.25
 Later D 203.7

M 202.8:dt.&nos.
NOTICE TO MARINERS. [Weekly]
 Earlier N 6.11
 Later D 203.8

M 202.8/2:dt.&nos.
NOTICE TO MARINERS (restricted). [Semimonthly]
 Earlier N 6.11/2

M 202.9:dt.&nos.
NOTICE TO MARINERS RELATING TO GREAT LAKES
 AND TRIBUTARY WATERS WEST OF MONTREAL.
 [Weekly]
 Earlier N 6.12/2
 Later D 203.9

M 202.10:dt.&nos.
NOTICE TO MARINERS, NORTH AMERICAN-
 CARIBBEAN EDITION. [Weekly]
 Earlier N 6.11/5
 Later D 203.10

M 202.11:dt.&nos.
MEMORANDUM FOR AVIATORS.
 Earlier N 6.31
 Later D 203.11

M 202.12:date
TIDE, MOON AND SUN CALENDAR, BALTIMORE,
 MARYLAND. [Monthly]
 Earlier N 6.22/2
 Later D 203.12

M 202.13:date
TIDE CALENDAR FOR HAMPTON ROADS (Swells
 Point), VIRGINIA. [Monthly]
 Later D 203.13

M 202.14:date
TIDE CALENDAR, SAVANNAH, GEORGIA. [Monthly]
    Earlier N 6.22/3
    Later D 203.14

M 202.15:date
PILOT CHART OF CENTRAL AMERICAN WATERS;
   NO. 3500. [Monthly]
    Earlier N 6.24
    Later D 203.15

M 202.16:date
PILOT CHART OF INDIAN OCEAN; NO. 2603. [Monthly]
    Earlier N 6.17
    Later D 203.16

M 202.17:date
PILOT CHART OF NORTH ATLANTIC OCEAN; NO.
   1400. [Monthly]
    Earlier N 6.15/1
    Later D 203.17

M 202.18:date
PILOT CHART OF SOUTH ATLANTIC OCEAN; NO.
   2600. [Monthly]
    Earlier N 6.20
    Later D 203.18

M 202.19:date
PILOT CHART OF NORTH PACIFIC OCEAN; NO. 1401.
   [Monthly]
    Earlier N 6.16
    Later D 203.19

M 202.20:date
PILOT CHART OF SOUTH PACIFIC OCEAN; NO. 2601.
   [Quarterly]
    Earlier N 6.21
    Later D 203.20

M 202.21:let. or nos.
MAPS AND CHARTS.
    Earlier N 6.18
    Later D 203.21

M 202.22:nos.
FIELD CHARTS.
    Earlier N 6.18/2

M 202.23:nos.
HYDROGRAPHIC OFFICE PUBLICATIONS (numbered).
    Earlier N 6.8
    Later D 203.22

M 202.24:date
HYDROPAC MESSAGE SUMMARY.
    Earlier N 6.34

BUREAU OF MEDICINE AND SURGERY
(1947– 1949)

CREATION AND AUTHORITY

    The Bureau of Medicine and Surgery (N 10) was established within the National Military Estabishment in 1947. In 1949, it was transferred along with the Department of the Navy to the Department of Defense (D 206).

M 203.1:date
ANNUAL REPORTS.
    Earlier N 10.1
    Later D 206.1

M 203.2:CT
GENERAL PUBLICATIONS.
    Earlier N 10.2
    Later 206.2

M 203.3:v.nos.
GENERAL PUBLICATIONS.
    Earlier N 10.11/1
    Later D 206.3

M 203.3/2:v.nos.
HOSPITAL CORPS QUARTERLY.
    Earlier N 10.11/2

M 203.6:CT
REGULATIONS, RULES, AND INSTRUCTIONS.
    Earlier N 10.13
    Later D 206.6

M 203.7:v.nos.
BUMED NEWS LETTERS. [Biweekly]
    Restricted.
    Earlier N 10.18
    Later D 106.7

M 203.8:project nos.&rep.nos.
NAVAL MEDICAL RESEARCH INSTITUTE REPORTS.
    Later D 206.9

M 203.9:dt.&nos.
BUMED CIRCULAR LETTERS.
    Some numbers are restricted
    Printed and proc.
    Earlier N 10.20/2

M 203.10:date
STATISTICS OF DISEASES AND INJURIES IN NAVY.
    Earlier N 10.15
    Later D 206.11

M 203.11:CT
NAVAL MEDICAL RESEARCH INSTITUTE PUBLICATIONS.

M 203.12:chap.nos.
MANUAL OF MEDICAL DEPARTMENT, NAVY.
    Earlier N 10.5/1
    Later D 206.8

M 203.13:nos.
[MEDICAL RESEARCH LABORATORY REPORT.]
    Earlier N 10.22
    Later D 206.10

OFFICE OF INDUSTRIAL RELATIONS
(1947– 1949)

CREATION AND AUTHORITY

    The Office of Industrial Relations was established within the Natoinal Military Establishement in 1947. In 1949, it was transferred along with the Department of the Navy to the Department of Defense (D 204)

M 204.1:date
ANNUAL REPORTS.
    Later D 204.1

M 204.2:CT
GENERAL PUBLICATIONS.
    Later D 204.2

M 204.7:v.nos.
SAFETY REVIEW. [Monthly]
    Earlier N 1.33
    Later D 204.7

M 204.8:v.nos.&nos.
CIVILIAN PERSONNEL OF NAVAL SHORE ESTABLISHMENT. [Quarterly]
    Later D 204.8

BUREAU OF YARDS AND DOCKS
(1947– 1949)

CREATION AND AUTHORITY

    The Bureau of Yards and Docks (N 21) was established within the National Military Establishment in 1947. In 1949, it was transferred along with the Department of the Navy to the Department of Defense (D 209).

M 205.1:date
ANNUAL REPORTS.
    Earlier N 21.1
    Later D 209.1

M 205.2:CT
GENERAL PUBLICATIONS.
    Earlier N 21.2
    Later D 209.2

M 205.6:CT
REGULATIONS, RULES, AND INSTRUCTIONS.
    Earlier N 21.15

M 205.7:v.nos.
U.S. NAVY CIVIL ENGINEERS CORPS BULLETIN.
   [Monthly]
    Earlier N 21.14
    Later D 209.7

M 205.8:nos.
TECHNICAL DIGEST.
    Later 209.8

BUREAU OF NAVAL PERSONNEL
(1947– 1949)

CREATION AND AUTHORITY

    The Bureau of Naval Personnel (N 17) was established within the National Military Establishment in 1947. In 1949, it was transferred along with the Department of Defense (D 208).

M 206.1:date
ANNUAL REPORTS.
    Earlier N 17.1
    Later D 208.1

M 206.2:CT
GENERAL PUBLICATIONS.
    Earlier N 17.2
    Later D 208.2

M 206.3:nos.
ALL HANDS, BUREAU OF NAVAL PERSONNEL INFORMATION BULLETIN. [Monthly]
    Earlier N 17.27
    Later D 208.3

M 206.6:CT
REGULATIONS, RULES, AND INSTRUCTIONS.
    Earlier N 17.16/1 and N 17.16/4
    Later D 208.6

M 206.7:nos.
NAVAL TRAINING BULLETINS. [Monthly]
    Earlier N 17.33
    Later D 208.7

M 206.8:nos.
SEA CLIPPER. [Weekly]
    Earlier N 17.39
    Later D 208.8

M 206.9:date
NAVAL RESERVIST. [Monthly]
    Earlier N 17.37
    Later D 208.10

M 206.10:date
REGISTER OF COMMISSIONED AND WARRANT
 OFFICERS OF UNITED STATES NAVY AND
 MARINE CORPS.
    Earlier N 1.10
    Later D 208.12

NAVAL ACADEMY
(1947– 1949)

CREATION AND AUTHORITY

    The Naval Academy (N 12) was established
within the National Military Establishment in 1947.
In 1949, it was transferred along with the Department of the Navy to the Department of Defense
(D 208.100).

M 206.101:date
REPORT OF BOARD OF VISTORS TO NAVAL ACAD-
 EMY. [Annual]
    Earlier N 12.1
    Later D 208.101

M 206.102:CT
GENERAL PUBLICATIONS.
    Earlier N 12.2
    Later D 208.102

M 206.107
ANNUAL REGISTER OF NAVAL ACADEMY.
    Earlier N 12.5
    Later D 208.107

M 206.108:date
REGULATIONS GOVERNING ADMISSION OF
 CANDIDATES INTO NAVAL ACADEMY AS MID-
 SHIPMEN AND SAMPLE EXAMINATION
 QUESTIONS. [Annual]
    Earlier N 12.7
    Later D 208.108

NAVAL WAR COLLEGE
(1947– 1949)

CREATION AND AUTHORITY

    The Naval War College (N 15) was estab-
lished within the National Military Establishment
in 1947. In 1949, it was transferred along with the
Department of the Navy to the Department of
Defense (D 208.200).

M 206.201:date
ANNUAL REPORTS.
    Earlier N 15.1
    Later D 208.201

M 206.202:CT
GENERAL PUBLICATIONS.
    Earlier N 15.2
    Later D 208.202

M 206.207:v.nos.
INTERNATIONAL LAW DOCUMENTS.
    Earlier N 15.7/1

OFFICE OF NAVAL OPERATIONS
(1947– 1949)

CREATION AND AUTHORITY

    The Office of Naval Operations (N 27) was
established within the National Military Establishment in 1947. In 1949, it was transferred along
with the Department of the Navy to the Department of Defense (D 207).

M 207.1:date
ANNUAL REPORTS.
    Earlier N 27.1
    Later D 207.1

M 207.2:CT
GENERAL PUBLICATIONS.
    Earlier N 27.2
    Later D 207.2

M 207.6:CT
REGULATIONS, RULES, AND INSTRUCTIONS.
    Earlier N 27.5
    Later D 207.6

M 207.7:nos.
NAVAL AVIATION NEWS. [Monthly]
    Earlier N 27.16/2
    Later D 207.7

M 207.7/2:nos.
NAVAL AVIATION NEWS [Restricted]. [Monthly]
    Restricted information is deleted from this
edition for the edition for the edition that is sold.
    Earlier N 27.16
    Later D 207.7/2

M 207.8:dt.&nos.
FLIGHT SAFETY BULLETINS.
    Earlier N 27.18
    Later D 202.10

BUREAU OF AERONAUTICS
(1947– 1949)

CREATION AND AUTHORITY

    The Bureau of Aeronautics (N 28) was estab-
lished within the National Military Establishment
in 1947. In 1949, it was transferred along with the
Department of the Navy to the Department of
Defense (D 202).

M 208.1:date
ANNUAL REPORTS.
    Earlier N 28.1
    Later D 202.1

M 208.2:CT
GENERAL PUBLICATIONS.
    Earlier N 28.2
    Later D 202.2

M 208.6:CT
REGULATIONS, RULES, AND INSTRUCTIONS.
    Earlier N 28.13
    Later D 202.6

M 208.7:dt.&nos.
TECHNICAL ORDERS.
    Earlier N 28.8/2
    Later D 202.8

M 208.8:dt.&nos.
AVIATION CIRCULAR LETTERS.
    Earlier N 28.12

M 208.9:dt.&nos.
AIRCRAFT INSTRUMENT BULLETINS.
    Earlier N 28.20

M 208.10:dt.&nos.
TECHNICAL NOTES.
    Earlier N 28.6/2
    Later D 202.7

M 208.11:date
NAVAL AERONAUTICS PUBLICATIONS INDEX.
 [Restricted.]
    Earlier N 28.17

MARINE CORPS
(1947–1949)

CREATION AND AUTHORITY

The Marine Corps (N 9) was established within the National Military Establishment in 1947. In 1949, it was transferred along with the Department of the Navy to the Department of Defense (D 214).

M 209.1:date
ANNUAL REPORTS.
Earlier N 9.1
Later D 214.1

M 209.2:CT
GENERAL PUBLICATIONS.
Earlier N 9.2
Later D 214.2

M 209.6:CT
REGULATIONS, RULES, AND INSTRUCTIONS.
Earlier N 9.16

M 209.7:dt.&nos.
MARKSMANSHIP QUALIFICATIONS, ORDERS.
[Monthly]
Earlier N 9.10

M 209.8:nos.
MARINE CORPS ORDERS.
Earlier N 9.9/3

M 209.9:date
MARINE CORPS MANUAL.
Earlier N 9.15
Later D 214.9

BUREAU OF SHIPS
(1947–1949)

CREATION AND AUTHORITY

The Bureau of Ships (N 4) was established within the National Military Establishment in 1947. In 1949, it was transferred along with the Department of the Navy to the Department of Defense (D 211).

M 220.1:date
ANNUAL REPORTS.
Earlier N 29.1
Later D 211.1

M 210.2:CT
GENERAL PUBLICATIONS.
Earlier N 29.2
Later D 211.2

M 210.3:nos.
BULLETIN OF INFORMATION [Restricted]. [Quarterly]
Earlier N 29.10
Later D 211.13

M 210.6:CT
REGULATIONS, RULES, AND INSTRUCTIONS.

M 210.7:sec.nos.
GENERAL SPECIFICATIONS FOR BUILDING VESSELS OF NAVY.
Earlier N 29.7

M 210.8:chap.nos.
BUREAU OF SHIPS MANUAL.
Earlier N 29.13
Later D 211.7

M 210.8/2:nos.
–CHANGES.
Later D 211.7/2

BUREAU OF ORDNANCE
(1947–1949)

CREATION AND AUTHORITY

The Bureau of Ordnance (N 18) was established within the National Military Establishment in 1947. In 1949, it was transferred along with the Department of the Navy to the Department of Defense (D 215).

M 211.1:date
ANNUAL REPORTS.
Earlier N 18.1
Later D 215.1

M 211.2:CT
GENERAL PUBLICATIONS.
Earlier N 18.2
Later D 215.2

M 211.6:CT
REGULATIONS, RULES, AND INSTRUCTIONS.
Later 215.6

M 211.6
NAVAL ORDNANCE LABORATORY MEMORANDUM.

NAVAL OBSERVATORY
(1947–1949)

CREATION AND AUTHORITY

The Naval Observatory (N 18) was established within the National Military Establishment in 1947. In 1949, it was transferred along with the Department of the Navy to the Department of Defense (D 213).

M 212.1:date
ANNUAL REPORTS.
Earlier N 14.1
Later D 213.1

M 212.2:CT
GENERAL PUBLICATIONS.
Earlier N 14.2
Later D 213.2

M 212.4:nos.
CIRCULARS.

M 212.7:date
AMERICAN AIR ALMANAC.
Earlier N 11.6/3
Later D 213.7

M 212.8:date
AMERICAN EPHEMERIS AND NAUTICAL ALMANAC.
Earlier N 11.5
Later D 213.8

M 212.9:date
AMERICAN NAUTICAL ALMANAC.
Earlier N 11.6
Later D 213.11

M 212.10:v.nos.
PUBLICATIONS, 2ND SERIES.
Earlier N 14.6
Later D 213.10

BUREAU OF SUPPLIES AND ACCOUNTS
(1947–1949)

CREATION AND AUTHORITY

The Bureau of Supplies and Accounts (N 20) was established within the National Military Establishment in 1947. In 1949, it was transferred along with the Department of the Navy to the Department of Defense (D 212).

M 213.1:date
ANNUAL REPORTS.
Earlier N 20.1
Later D 212.1

M 213.2:CT
GENERAL PUBLICATIONS.
Earlier N 20.2
Later D 212.2

M 213.6:CT
REGULATIONS, RULES, AND INSTRUCTIONS.
Later D 212.6

M 213.7:nos.
NAVY DEPARTMENT SPECIFICATIONS.
Earlier N 20.6/2
Later D 212.9

M 213.8:nos.
JOINT ARMY-NAVY SPECIFICATIONS.
Earlier N 20.23
Later Later D 1.12

M 213.9:dt.&pt.nos.
INDEX OF SPECIFICATIONS USED BY NAVY DEPARTMENT. [Quarterly]
Earlier N 20.6/3
Later D 212.7

M 213.10:date
NAVAL EXPENDITURES.
Earlier N 20.21
Later D 212.8

JUDGE ADVOCATE GENERAL
(1947–1949)

CREATION AND AUTHORITY

The Judge Advocate General (N 7) was established within the National Military Establishment in 1947. In 1949, it was transferred along with the Department of the Navy to the Department of Defense (D 205).

M 214.1:date
ANNUAL REPORTS.
Earlier N 7.1
Later D 205.1

M 214.2:CT
GENERAL PUBLICATIONS.
Earlier N 7.2
Later D 205.2

M 214.6:CT
REGULATIONS, RULES, AND INSTRUCTIONS.

M 214.7:date
JAG JOURNAL. [Monthly]
Later 205.7

M 214.8:date
LAWS RELATING TO NAVY, ANNOTATED.
Earlier N 7.7

OFFICE OF PUBLIC RELATIONS
(1947– 1949)

CREATION AND AUTHORITY

The Office of Public Relations was trasferred to the National Military Establishment in 1947. [No SuDocs class was established in 1949 when the Department of Defense was created.]

M 214.1:date
ANNUAL REPORTS.
Earlier N 31.1

M 214.2:CT
GENERAL PUBLICATIONS.
Earlier N 31.2

OFFICE OF NAVAL RESEARCH
(1947– 1949)

CREATION AND AUTHORITY

The Office of Naval Research (N 32) was established within the National Military Establishment in 1947. In 1949, it was transferred along with the Department of the Navy to the Department of Defense (D 210).

M 216.1:date
ANNUAL REPORTS.

Earlier N 32.1
Later D 210.1

M 216.2:CT
GENERAL PUBLICATIONS.

Earlier N 32.2
Later D 210.2

M 216.7:nos.
NAVAL RESEARCH LABORATORY REPORTS.

Earlier N 32.7
Later D 210.8

DEPARTMENT OF THE AIR FORCE
(1947– 1949)

CREATION AND AUTHORITY

The Army Air Force (W 109) upon tranfer to the National Military Establishment in 1947, became the Department of the Air Force. In 1949, it was transferred to the Department of Defense (D 301).

M 301.1:date
ANNUAL REPORTS.

Earlier N 108.1
Later D 301.1

M 301.2:CT
GENERAL PUBLICATIONS.

Earlier W 108.2
Later D 301.2

M 301.4
CIRCULARS.

M 301.6:nos.
AF REGULATIONS.

Printed and proc.
Earlier W 108.6
Later D 301.6

M 301.6:CT
REGULATIONS, RULES, AND INSTRUCTIONS.
Earlier W 108.6

M 301.7:nos.
TABLES OF ORGANIZATION AND EQUIPMENT.

M 301.8:nos.
TECHNICAL PUBLICATIONS FOR AIR FORCE TECHNICAL LIBRARIES. BOOK LISTS.

Earlier W 108.2:B 64/2
Later D 301.20

M 301.9:v.nos.&nos.
AIR TECHNICAL INTELLIGENCE TECHNICAL DATA DIGEST. [Monthly]

Earlier W 108.18
Later D 301.14

M 301.10:date
INDEX OF SPECIFICATIONS AND BULLETINS APPROVED FOR U.S. AIR FORCE PROCUREMENT. [Semiannual]
Earlier W 108.13/3
Later D 301.18

M 301.11:date
ALPHABETICAL LIST COVERING ARMY AIR FORCES AND ARMY-NAVY AERONAUTICAL STANDARD DRAWINGS. [Semiannual]

Earlier W 108.15/2
Later D 301.16

M 301.13:date
NUMERICAL INDEX OF TECHNICAL PUBLICATIONS.

Earlier W 108.8
Later D 301.17

M 301.14:date
U.S. AIR FORCE RADIO FACILITY CHARTS. NORTH PACIFIC AREA.

Earlier W 108.27
Later D 301.13

M 301.15:date
U.S. AIR FORCE RADIO FACILITY CHARTS, ATALNTIC AND CARIBBEAN AREA. [Monthly]

Earlier W 108.27
Later D 301.11

M 301.16:v.nos.
JOINT AIR FORCE & NAVY RADIO FACILITY CHARTS. [Monthly]

Earlier W 108.29
Later D 301.12

M 301.17:date
RADIO FACILITY CHARTS, EUROPE, AFRICA, MIDDLE EAST.

Earlier W 109.2:R 11/947
Later D 301.9

M 301.17/2:v.nos.
CORRECTION TO UNSAFE RADIO FACILITY CHART, WEEKLY NOTICES TO AIRMEN.

Later D 301.9/2

M 301.18:nos.
[AIR FORCE MANUAL].

Earlier W 108.19 and W 108.22
Later D 301.7

M 301.19:date
RADIO FACILITY CHARTS, CARIBBEAN AND SOUTH AMERICAN AREA. [Bimonthly]

NOTE:-Prior to August 15, 1948 this information was published in Radio Facility Charts, Atlantic and Caribbean Area (M 301.15).
Later D 301.10 and D 301.10/2

M 30.20:nos.
TABLE OF ALLOWANCES.

M 301.21:nos.
AIR WEATHER SERVICE MANUAL.

Later D 30.27

M 301.22:nos.
AIR WEATHER SERVICE TECHNICAL REPORTS.

Earlier W 108.34
Later D 301.30

M 301.22/2:date
HISTORICAL WEATHER MAP, NORTHERN HEMISHERE, SEA LEVEL AND 500 MILLIBAR.

Earlier W 108.30

AIR ADJUTANT GENERAL'S OFFICE
(1947– 1949)

M 302.1:CT
ANNUAL REPORTS.
Later D 303.2

M 302.2:CT
GENERAL PUBLICATIONS.
Later D 303.2

M 302.7:date
AIR FORCE REGISTER.
Later D 303.7

MUNITIONS BOARD

M 401.1:date
ANNUAL REPORTS.

M 401.2:CT
GENERAL PUBLICATIONS.

RESEARCH AND DEVELOPMENT BOARD

M 501.1:date
ANNUAL REPORTS.

M 501.2:CT
GENERAL PUBLICATIONS.

BOARD OF MEDIATION (1926–1934)

CREATION AND AUTHORITY

The United States Board of Mediation was established by the Railway Labor Act, approved May 20, 1926 (44 Stat. 577) to succeed the United States Railroad Labor Board (RL 1). The Board of Mediation was abolished by act of Congress approved June 21, 1934 (48 Stat. 1193) and superseded by the National Mediation Board (NMB 1).

MB 1.1:date
ANNUAL REPORTS.

MB 1.2:CT
GENERAL PUBLICATIONS.

MB 1.4
CIRCULARS.

MB 1.21:date
EMERGENCY BOARD (WESTERN CARRIERS, 1928).

MB 1.21/2:date
EMERGENCY BOARD (KANSAS CITY, MEXICO AND ORIENT RAILWAY).

MB 1.22:date
EMERGENCY BOARD (TEXAS AND PACIFIC RAILWAY, 1929).

MB 1.23:date
EMERGENCY BOARD (LOUISIANA AND ARKANSAS RAILWAY, 1931)

MB 1.24:date
EMERGENCY BOARD (LOUISIANA AND ARKANSAS RAILWAY AND LOUISIANA, ARKANSAS AND TEXAS RAILROAD, 1932)

MB 1.25
EMERGENCY BOARD (KANSAS CITY SOUTHERN RAILROAD, ARKANSAS WESTERN RAILROAD, TEXARKANA & FOR SMITH RAILROAD, 1933).

MB 1.26:date
EMERGENCY BOARD (LOUISIANA, ARKANSAS AND TEXAS RAILROAD, 1933).

MB 1.27:date
EMERGENCY BOARD (SOUTH PACIFIC LINES IN TEXAS AND LOUISIANA & TEXAS AND NEW ORLEANS RAILROAD, 1933).

MB 1.28:date
EMERGENCY BOARD (MOBILE & OHIO RAILROAD, 1933).

MB 1.29:date
EMERGENCY BOARD (DENVER & RIO RAND WESTERN RAILROAD, 1934).

MB 1.30:date
EMERGENCY BOARD (DELAWARE & HUDSON RAILROAD, 1934).

MARITIME COMMISSION (1936–1950)

CREATION AND AUTHORITY

The United States Maritime Commission was established by act of Congress, approved June 29, 1936 (49 Stat. 1985), to succeed the United States Shipping Board (SB 1) and the United States Shipping Board Merchant Fleet Corporation (SB 2). The Commission was abolished by Reorganization Plan No. 21 of 1950, effective May 24, 1950, and its functions transferred to the Maritime Administration (C 39.200) of the Department of Commerce.

MC 1.1:date
ANNUAL REPORTS.

Later C 39.201

MC 1.2:CT
GENERAL PUBLICATIONS.

Later C 39.202

MC 1.5:CT
LAWS.

Later C 39.205

MC 1.6:CT
REGULATIONS, RULES, AND INSTRUCTIONS.

Later C 39.206

MC 1.7:nos.
GENERAL ORDERS.

MC 1.8:date
QUARTERLY REPORT ON EMPLOYMENT OF AMERICAN STEAM AND MOTOR MERCHANT VESSELS.

Earlier C 27.9/7

MC 1.9:date
U.S. WATER BORNE INTERCOASTAL TRAFFIC BY PORTS OF ORIGIN AND DESTINATION AND PRINCIPAL COMMODITIES.

Earlier C 27.9/9

MC 1.10:date
COMPARATIVE STATEMENT, FOREIGN COMMERCE OF U.S. PORTS, BY STATES.

Earlier C 27.9/2

MC 1.11:date
IMPORTS AND EXPORTS OF COMMODITIES BY U.S. COASTAL DISTRICTS AND FOREIGN TRADE REGIONS. [Annual]

Later title, Water-Borne Foreign Commerce of the U.S. (in Cargo Tons) Calendar Year.
Earlier C 27.9/4
Later MC 1.23

MC 1.12:date
AMERICAN FLAG SERVICES IN FOREIGN TRADE AND WITH U.S. POSSESSIONS. [Annual]

Earlier C 27.9/1

MC 1.13:CT
ADDRESSES.

MC 1.14:CT
MAPS.

Earlier C 27.9/13

MC 1.15:date
WATERBORNE PASSENGER TRAFFIC OF U.S.
[Annual]

> Prior to 1936, C 27.9/12
> Superseded by MC 1.23

MC 1.16:date
OCEAN GOING MERCHANT FLEETS OF PRINCIPAL
MARITIME NATIONS, IRON AND STEEL, STEAM
AND MOTOR VESSELS OF 2,000 GROSS TONS
AND OVER. [Semiannual]
> Earlier C 27.9/6

MC 1.17:date
REPORT ON VOLUME OF WATER BORNE FOREIGN
COMMERCE OF U.S. BY PORTS OF ORIGIN AND
DESTINATION. [Annual]

> Earlier SB 7.2:C 73
> Later C 27.9/10

MC 1.18:CT
PAPERS IS RE.

MC 1.19:date
COMPARATIVE SUMMARY OF WATER BORNE FOR-
EIGN COMMERCE.

> Calendar and fiscal years
> Earlier SB 7.5/399
> Later C 27.9/3

MC 1.20:date
WATER BORNE FOREIGN AND DOMESTIC COM-
MERCE OF U.S. [Annual]

> Earlier SB 7.205
> Later C 27.9/11

MC 1.21:nos.
TARIFF CIRCULARS.

> Earlier SB 1.8

MC 1.22:v.nos.
MARITIME COMMISSION REPORTS.

> Later C 39.108 and FMC 1.10

MC 1.23:date
WATER-BORNE FOREIGN AND NONCONTIGUOUS
COMMERCE AND PASSENGER TRAFFIC OF
UNITED STATES (Report 2610).

> This new Report 2610 replaces material pre-
> viously published in Report 157 (MC 1.15) and
> Report 275 (MC 1.11) which have been discontin-
> ued.

MC 1.24:vol.
VICTORY FLEET. [Weekly]

MC 1.25:CT
POSTERS.

MC 1.26:v.nos.
MARINE SURPLUS SELLER. [Monthly]

> Later Pr 33.216

MC 1.27:nos.
SURPLUS MATERIALS BULLETINS.

MC 1.28:vol.
OUR MERCHANT FLEET. [Monthly]

MC 1.29:nos.
GENERAL INFORMATION LETTER.

MC 1.30:nos.
HISTORICAL REPORTS OF WAR ADMINISTRATION.

BOARD OF MEDIATION AND CONCILIATION
(1913–1921)

CREATION AND AUTHORITY

The United States Board of Mediation and
Concilation was established by act of Congress,
approved July 15, 1913. The Board ceased to
function in 1921 and officially was abolished in
1926.

MCB 1.1:date
ANNUAL REPORTS.

MCB 1.2
GENERAL PUBLICATIONS.

MARITIME LABOR BOARD
(1938–1942)

CREATION AND AUTHORITY

The Maritime Labor Board was established on
June 23, 1938, by an amendment to the Merchant Marine Act of 1938, approved June 23,
1938 (52 Stat. 968), and extended by act of Congress, approved June 23, 1941 (55 Stat. 259).
The Board ceased to function in February 1942.

ML 1.1:date
ANNUAL REPORTS.

ML 1.2:CT
GENERAL PUBLICATIONS.

MERIT SYSTEMS PROTECTION BOARD
(1979–   )

CREATION AND AUTHORITY

The Merit Systems protection Board was established to succeed the United States Civil Service Comnmission (CS 1), by Reorganization Plan
No. 2 of 1978, effective January 1, 1979, pursuant to Executive Order 12107 of December 28,
1978, which also transferred mnany of the Commission functions to the Office of Peronnel Management (PM 1), which is purely manmagerial and
not adjudicatory.

INFORMATION

Merit Systems Protection Board
1615 M Street, NW
Washington, DC 20419
(202) 653-7200
(800) 209-8960
Fax: (202) 653-7130
E-Mail:mspb@mspb.gov
http://www.mspb.gov

MS 1.1:date   • **Item 290-K-1 (EL)**
ANNUAL REPORT. 1–   1979–

MS 1.2   • **Item 290-K-5**
GENERAL PUBLICATIONS. [Irregular]

MS 1.8:CT   • **Item 290-K-10**
HANDBOOKS, MANUALS, GUIDES.

MS 1.9:nos.   • **Item 290-K-6**
PAMPHLETS. 1–   [Irregular]

MS 1.10:v.nos.   • **Item 290-K-3 (EL)**
DECISIONS OF U.S. MERIT SYSTEMS PROTECTION
BOARD. v. 1–   1980–   [Irregular]

Initial set consists of two volumes totaling
about 1200 pages and an 85 page index of both
Civil Service Commission and Board decisions in
cases involving constitutionality, descrimination,
performance-related actions, prohibited personnel practices, etc.

MS 1.11:v.nos.&nos.   • **Item 290-K-4**
DIGEST. v. 1– 2. 1980– 1981. [Monthly]

Presents summaries of Board orders issued
in connection with adverse actions brought by
various Federal employees against their agencies.

MS 1.12:CT   • **Item 290-K-7**
POSTERS. [Irregular]

MS 1.15:date   • **Item 290-K-3 (MF)**
STUDY OF MSPB APPEALS DECISIONS FOR FY
(year). [Annual]

MS 1.16:date   • **Item 290-K-1**
REPORT ON THE SIGNIFICANT ACTIONS OF THE
OFFICE OF PERSONNEL MANAGEMENT.
[Annual]

MS 1.17:date   • **Item 290-K-11 (EL)**
ISSUES OF MERIT. [Quarterly]

OFFICE OF THE SPECIAL COUNSEL
(1979–   )

INFORMATION

Office of the Special Counsel
Merit Systems Protection Board
1615 M Street, NW
Washington, DC 20419

MS 2.1:date   • **Item 290-K-2 (MF)**
ANNUAL REPORT TO CONGRESS ON ACTIVITIES
OF THE OFFICE OF THE SPECIAL COUNSEL.
1st–   1979–

Summarizes Office activities in performing
its twofold function: investigating alleged violations under the Civil Service Reform Act and providing a channel for Federal employees to "blow
the whistle" on Government wrongdoing without
fear of retaliation.

MS 2.2:CT   • **Item 290-K-9**
GENERAL PUBLICATIONS. [Irregular]

MS 2.9:CT   • **Item 290-K-8**
POSTERS. [Irregular]

INSTITUTE OF MUSEUM
SERVICES
(1976– 1981)

CREATION AND AUTHORITY

The Institute os Museum Services was created as an independent agency by the Museum
Services Act in 1976. In December 1981, pusuant
to title II of an act approved December 23, 1981
(95 Stat. 1414), the Institute was established as
an independent agency within the National Foundation on the Arts and Humanities (NF 4).

MuS 1.2:CT   • **Item 239-N-1**
GENERAL PUBLICATIONS. [Irregular]

Later NF 4.2

DEPARTMENT OF THE NAVY
(1798– 1947)

CREATION AND AUTHORITY

The Department of the Navy, together with
the Office of the Secretary of the Navy, was
established by act of Congress, approved April
30, 1798 (1 Stat. 553). For 9 years prior that date
by provision of act of Congress, approved August 7, 1789 (1 Stat. 49), the conduct of naval
affairs was under the Secretary for the Deprtment
of War. The Department of the Navy was incorporated in the National Military Establishment (M
201) by the National Security Act of 1947 (61
Stat. 499).

N 1.1:date
ANNUAL REPORTS.

Later M 201.1

N 1.2:CT
GENERAL PUBLICATIONS.

Later M 201.2

N 1.3:nos.
BULLETINS [none issued].

N 1.4:date
CIRCULARS (unnumbered).

N 1.4/2:nos.
CIRCULARS (numbered).

N 1.5/1:nos.
CIRCULARS (numbered) 1ST SERIES. 1865-1867.

N 1.5/2:nos.
CIRCULARS (numbered) 2ND SERIES. 1871-1876.

N 1.5/3:nos.
CIRCULARS (numbered) 3RD SERIES. 1877-1892.

N 1.5/4:nos.
CIRCULARS (numbered) 4TH SERIES. 1893-1895.

N 1.5/5:nos.
CIRCULARS (numbered) 5TH SERIES. 1897-1899.

N 1.6:nos.
ACTS AND RESOLUTIONS RELATING CHIEFLY TO
NAVY, NAVY DEPARTMENT AND MARINE CORPS,
PASSED AT [Session] OF [Congress].

Later M 201.10

N 1.8:CT
EXPLORATIONS AND SURVEYS.

N 1.9:date
COMPILATIONS OF LAWS.

Later N 7.7

N 1.10:date
NAVY REGISTER.

Later M 206.10

N 1.11/1:date
NAVY REGULATIONS.

Later M 206.10

N 1.11/2:date
CHANGES IN NAVY REGULATIONS.

N 1.11/3:date
NAVY REGUATIONS, PROPOSED CHANGES.

N 1.12:nos.
DEPARTMENTAL ORDERS.

N 1.12/2:nos.
– 2ND SERIES, 1901-1904

N 1.13
GENERAL ORDERS.

N 1.13/1:nos.
– 1ST SERIES, 1863-1900

N 1.13/3:nos.
– 3RD SERIES, 1905-1908.

N 1.13/4:nos.
– 4TH SERIES, 1909–

N 1.13/5:nos.
– 5TH SERIES.

N 1.13/6:nos.
– 6TH SERIES.

N 1.13/7:nos.
– 7TH SERIES, 1935–

N 1.14:date
GENERAL COURT MARTIAL ORDERS.

Later M 201.9

N 1.14:vol.
COMPILATIONS OF COURT MARTIAL ORDERS.

N 1.15:nos.
NAVY YARD ORDERS.

N 1.16/1:nos.
SPECIAL ORDERS, 1ST SERIES, 1891-1900.

N 1.16/2:nos.
– 2ND SERIES, 1900– 1905.

N 1.16/3:nos.
– 3RD SERIES, 1905– 1908.

N 1.16/4:nos.
– 4TH SERIES, 1909–

N 1.17:CT
PROPOSALS, ADVERTISEMENTS, GENERAL INFOR-
MATION, ETC.

N 1.18/1:date
REGULATIONS GOVERNING UNIFORM.

N 1.18/2:date
CHANGES IN UNIFORM REGULATIONS.

N 1.19:CT
REGULATIONS, RULES, AND INSTRUCTIONS.

Later D 201.6

N 1.20:date
OFFICERS OF NAVY AND MARINE CORPS IN DIS-
TRICT OF COLUMBIA.

N 1.21/1:vol.
SCHELEY COURT OF INQUIRY PROCEEDINGS.

N 1.21/2:date
MISCELLANEOUS CORRESPONDENCE OF NAVY
DEPARTMENT CONCERNING SCHELEY'S COURT
OF INQUIRY.

N 1.22:CT
SPECIFICATIONS.

N 1.23:date
TELEPHONE LIST.

Later M 201.8

N 1.23/2:date
LOCAL TELEPHONE SYSTEM.

N 1.24:date
NAVY AND MARINE CORPS LIST AND DIRECTORY.

N 1.24/a:date
ALPHABETICAL LIST OF OFFICERS AND
VESSELS.

N 1.25:nos.
(NAVY YARD) EXAMINATION ORDERS.

N 1.26:CT
TRANSIT OF VENUS COMMISSION, 1874.

Naval Militia Office

N 1.27/1:date
ANNUAL REPORTS.

N 1.27/2:CT
GENERAL PUBLICATIONS.

N 1.27/3:nos.
BULLETINS.

N 1.27/4:nos.
CIRCULARS.

N 1.27/5:date
TRANSACTIONS OF NAVAL MILITIA ASSOCIATION
OF THE UNITED STATES.

N 1.27/6:date
REGISTER OF COMMISSIONED AND WARRANT
OFFICERS OF NAVAL MILITIA.

N 1.27/7:nos.
PUBLICATIONS FOR INSTRUCTION, ETC. OF NAVAL
MILITIA.

Department of the Navy (Continued)

N 1.28:date
MOVEMENTS OF VESSELS (fiscal year).

Naval Counsiting Board

N 1.29/1:date
ANNUAL REPORTS.

N 1.29/2:CT
GENERAL PUBLICATIONS.

N 1.29/3:nos.
BULLETINS.

N 1.29/4
CIRCULARS.

Department of the Navy (Continued)

N 1.30:nos.
SELECTIVE SERVICE MEMORANDUMS TO ALL
NAVY CONTRACTORS.

Proc. and printed.

N 1.31:CT
POSTERS

N 1.31/2:nos.
SAFETY POSTERS.

N 1.32:nos.
ADMINISTRATIVE REFERENCE SERVICE REPORTS.

N 1.33:v.nos.
SAFETY REVIEW. [Monthly]

Printed and Proc.
Later M 204.7

N 1.34:CT
STATE SUMMARY OF WAR CASUALTIES

N 1.34/2:v.nos.
COMBAT CONNECTED NAVAL CASUALTIES, WORLD
WAR II, BY STATES.

ASSISTANT SECRETARY
(1898–1904)

N 2.1:date
ANNUAL REPORTS.

N 2.2:CT
GENERAL PUBLICATIONS.

N 2.3:nos.
BULLETINS [none issued].

N 2.4:nos.
CIRCULARS, NAVAL MILITIA.

N 2.5:date
GUAM ISLAND, NAVAL GOVERNOR, ANNUAL RE-
PORTS.

N 2.6:date
TUTUILA COMMANDANT, U.S. NAVAL STATION, AN-
NUAL REPORTS.

N 2.7:date
ANNUAL REPORTS ON NAVAL MILITIA

ADMIRAL OF THE NAVY
(1886–1888)

N 3.1:date
ANNUAL REPORTS.

N 3.2:CT
GENERAL PUBLICATIONS [none issued].

N 3.3:nos.
BULLETINS.

N 3.4:nos.
CIRCULARS.

BUREAU OF CONSTRUCTION AND
REPAIR
(1862–1940)

CREATION AND AUTHORITY

The Bureau of Construction, Equipment, and
Repair was established within the Department of
the Navy by act of Congress, approved August
31, 1842 (5 Stat. 579). It was succeeded by the
Bureau of Construction and Repair by act of Congress, approved July 5, 1862 (12 Stat. 510). The
Bureau was consolidated with the Bureau of Engineering (N 19) to form the Bureau of Ships (N
29) by act of Congress, approved June 20, 1940
(54 Stat. 527).

N 4.1:date
ANNUAL REPORTS.

Later N 29.1

N 4.2:CT
GENERAL PUBLICATIONS.

Later N 29.2

N 4.3:nos.
BULLETINS.

N 4.3/2:nos.
C & R BULLETINS.

Superseded by N 29.9

N 4.4:date
CIRCULARS (unnumbered).

N 4.5:date
ALLOWANCE OF ARTICLES UNDER COGNIZANCE
OF BUREAU OF CONSTRUCTION AND REPAIR
FOR VESSELS OF NAVY.

N 4.6:CT
SPECIFICATIONS.

N 4.6/2:nos.
SPECIFICATION [Chiefly blueprints, a few being
mimeogaphed].

Superseded by N 28.10 and N 29.8

N 4.6/3:nos.
GENERAL SPECIFICATIONS FOR BUILDING
VESSELS OF U.S. NAVY, APPENDICES.

N 4.6/4:sec.nos.
GENERAL SPECIFICATIONS FOR BUILDING
VESSELS OF NAVY (by sections).

Later N 29.7

N 4.7:nos.
STANDARD NUMBER SERIES.

N 4.8:date
ANALYSIS OF EXPENDITURES UNDER STANDING
JOB ORDERS AT NAVY YARDS.

N 4.9:nos.
AERONAUTICAL SPECIFICATIONS.

N 4.10:date
CIRCULAR LETTERS.

N 4.11:CT
HANDBOOKS.

N 4.12:date
MANUAL.

Later included in N 29.13.

N 4.13:dt.&nos.
TECHNICAL BULLETINS.

N 4.14:dt.&nos.
GENERAL INFORMATION BULLETIN

N 4.15:nos.
BUREAU NEWS LETTER.

BUREAU OF EQUIPMENT
(1890– 1910)

CREATION AND AUTHORITY

The Bureau of Equipment and Recruiting was established within the Department of the Navy by act of Congress approved July 5 1862 (12 Stat 510). In 1890, the name was changed to Bureau of Equipment. The Bureau was abolished July 1, 1910, by act of Congress, approved June 24, 1910 (36 Stat. 613).

N 5.1:date
ANNUAL REPORTS.

N 5.2:CT
GENERAL PUBLICATIONS.

N 5.3:nos.
BULLETINS [none issued].

N 5.4:date
CIRCULARS [none issued].

N 5.5:date
ALLOWANCES FOR VESSELS OF THE NAVY.

N 5.6:CT
CATALOGS OF SHIPS AND CREW'S LIBRARIES OF
    THE U.S.

N 5.7:CT
SPECIFICATIONS.

N 5.8:date
COAL NOTICE FOR FOREIGN PORTS.

HYDROGRAPHIC OFFICE
(1866– 1947)

CREATION AND AUTHORITY

The present Hydrographic Office was established within the Bureau of Navigation of the Department of the Navy by act of Congress, approved June 21, 1866 (14 Stat. 69). From 1898 until 1910, it was under the Bureau of Equipment, when it was returned to Bureau of Navigation. Executive Order 9126 of April 8, 1942 transferred it to the jurisdiction of Chief of Naval Operation. The Hydrographic Charts and Instruments for 1842 until 1854, the United States Naval Observatory and Hydrographic Office for 1854 until 1866. In 1947, the Office was transferred along with the Department of the Navy to the National Military Establishment (M 202).

N 6.1:date
ANNUAL REPORTS.

    Later M 202.1

N 6.2:CT
GENERAL PUBLICATIONS.

    Later M 202.2

N 6.3:nos.
BULLETINS, HYDROGRAPHIC. [Weekly]

    Later M 202.3

N 6.3/2:nos.
ICE SUPPLEMENT TO HYDROGRAPHIC BULLETINS.

N 6.4
CIRCULARS.

    Later M 202.4

N 6.4
CIRCULARS.

    Later N 202.4

N 6.5:date
GENERAL CATALOG OF MARINERS & AVIATORS'
    CHARTS AND BOOKS.

N 6.5/2:CT
CHART AND BOOK CATALOGS (miscellaneous lists).

N 6.5/2:CT
CATALOG OF CHARTS AND PLANS ISSUED TO VES-
    SELS OF NAVY ON ASIATIC STATION.

    N 6.5/4:date
    – ON ATLANTIC STATION.

    N 6.5/5:date
    – ON EUROPEAN STATION.

    N 6.5/6:date
    – ON PACIFIC STATION.

N 6.5/7:nos.
CATALOG OF CHARTS AND PLANS ISSUED TO VES-
    SELS OF NAVY, PORTFOLIOS.

N 6.5/8:date
NUMERICAL INDEX FOR STATION CATALOGS.

N 6.5/9:date
INDEX TO H.O. CHARTS ISSUE.

N 6.5/10:date
INTRODUCTION TO STATION CATALOGS.

N 6.6:CT
CORRECTION AND ADDITIONS TO PUBLICATIONS
    OF OFFICERS AT HOME AND ABROAD.

N 6.7:nos.
[PRACTICAL PAPERS.]

N 6.8:nos.
HYDROGRAPHIC OFFICE PUBLICATIONS.

    Later M 202.23

N 6.9:date
LIBRARY CATALOGS.

N 6.10:nos.
NAUTICAL MONOGRAPHS.

N 6.11:date
NOTICE TO MARINERS.

    Later M 202.8

N 6.11/2:date
NOTICE TO MARINERS. [Semimonthly]

    Restricted.
    Later M 202.8/2

N 6.11/3:CT
SUPPLEMENTARY NOTICES TO MARINERS,
    CORRECTION SHEETS FOR COAST PILOTS.

N 6.11/4:nos.
SUPPLEMENTARY NOTICES TO MARINERS,
    CORRECTION SHEETS FOR H.O. PUBLICATIONS.

N 6.11/5:dt.&nos.
NOTICE TO MARINERS, NORTH AMERICAN-
    CARIBBEAN EDITION. [Weekly]

    Later M 202.10

N 6.12:date
NOTICE TO MARINERS FOR GREAT LAKES.
    [Monthly]

N 6.12/2:date
NOTICE TO MARINERS RELATING TO GREAT LAKES
    AND TRIBUTARY WATERS WEST OF MONTREAL.
    [Weekly]

    Later M 202.9

N 6.13:CT
NOTICE TO MARINERS ON GREAT LAKES, SPE-
    CIAL.

N 6.14:date
HYDROGRAPHIC NOTICE.

N 6.15:date
PILOT CHART OF NORTH ATLANTIC OCEAN.

    Later M 202.17

N 6.15/2:date
ICE SUPPLEMENT TO NORTH ATLANTIC PILOT
    CHART.

N 6.15/3:date
PILOT CHART OF NORTHERN ATLANTIC OCEAN.
    [Monthly]

    No. 1400b, Restricted.

N 6.15/4:date
PILOT CHART OF GREENLAND AND BARNETS SEAS.
    [Quarterly]

    No. 1400c, Restricted.

N 6.16:date
PILOT CHART OF NORTH PACIFIC OCEAN.

    Later M 202.19

N 6.17:date
PILOT CHART OF INDIAN OCEAN.

    Later M 202.16

N 6.18:letters-nos.
MAPS AND CHARTS.

    Later M 202.21

N 6.18/2:CT
MAPS AND CHARTS (miscellaneous).

    Later M 202.22

N 6.19:nos.
REPRINT OF HYDROGRAPHIC INFORMATION.

N 6.20:date
PILOT CHART OF SOUTH ATLANTIC OCEAN.
    [Quarterly]

    Later M 202.18

N 6.21:date
PILOT CHART OF SOUTH PACIFIC OCEAN. [Quar-
    terly]

    Later M 202.20

N 6.22:date
TIDE CALENDARS, NORFOLK AND NEWPORT NEWS.
    [Monthly]

    Later M 202.13

N 6.22/2:date
TIDE CALENDAR, BALTIMORE AND CAPE HENRY.

    Later M 202.12

N 6.22/3:date
TIDE CALENDAR, SAVANNAH, GEORGIA. [Monthly]

    Later M 202.14

N 6.23:nos.
INFORMATION CIRCULARS.

N 6.24:date
PILOT CHARTS OF CENTRAL AMERICAN WATERS.
    [Monthly]

    Later M 202.15

N 6.25:date
NOTICE TO AVIATORS. [Monthly]

    Later M 202.7

N 6.26:CT
SUPPLEMENT TO PILOT CHARTS.

N 6.27:nos.
AVIATION CHARTS.

N 6.27/2:date
INDEX OF AVIATION CHARTS.

N 6.27/3:VC-nos.
AVIATION CHARTS, V-HEAVIER-THAN-AIR-CRAFT, C-COMPUTER.

N 6.27/4:VZ-nos.
AVIATION OPERATING CHARTS.

N 6.28:date
PILOT CHARTS OF UPPER AIR, NORTH ATLANTIC OCEAN. [Monthly]

N 6.29:date
PILOT CHARTS OF UPPER AIR, NORTH PACIFIC OCEAN. [Monthly]

N 6.30:VP-nos.
AIRCRAFT PLOTTING SHEETS.

N 6.31:dt.&nos.
MEMORANDUM TO AVIATIORS.

    Later M 202.11

N 6.32:CT
REGULATIONS, RULES, AND INSTRUCTIONS.

    Note:– Includes Handbooks and Manuals.

N 6.33:nos.
GAZETTEERS (unnumbered) [restricted].

N 6.34:date
HYDROPAC MESSAGE SUMMARY. [Monthly]

    Later M 202.24

N 6.35:nos.
TECHNICAL REPORTS.

JUDGE-ADVOCATE GENERAL
(1880– 1947)

N 7.1:date
ANNUAL REPORTS.

    Later M 214.1

N 7.2:CT
GENERAL PUBLICATIONS.

    Later M 214.2

N 7.3:nos.
BULLETINS. [none issued].

N 7.7:date
LAWS RELATING TO NAVY, ANNOTATED.

    Earlier N 1.9
    Later M 214.8

N 7.7/2:dt.&nos.
LAWS RELATING TO NAVY, ANNOTATED, BULLETINS. [Quarterly]

SOLICITOR OF NAVY DEPARTMENT
(1908– 1947)

N 8.1:date
ANNUAL REPORTS.

N 8.2:CT
GENERAL PUBLICATIONS.

N 8.3:nos.
BULLETINS [none issued].

N 8.4:nos.
CIRCULARS [none issued].

N 8.5:CT
PAPERS IN RE.

MARINE CORPS
(1798– 1947)

CREATION AND AUTHORITY

    The United States Marine Corps was established by act of Congress, approved July 11, 1798 (1 Stat. 594). In 1947, the Corps was transferred along with the Department of the Navy to the Military Establishment (M 209).

N 9.1:date
ANNUAL REPORTS.

    Later M 209.1

N 9.2:CT
GENERAL PUBLICATIONS.

    Later M 209.2

N 9.3:nos.
BULLETINS [none issued].

N 9.4:nos.
CIRCULARS [none issued].

N 9.5/1:date
GENERAL ORDERS, 1ST SERIES, 1877– 1894.

   N 9.5/2:nos.
   – 2ND SERIES. 1908–

N 9.6/1:date
SPECIAL ORDERS, 1ST SERIES, 1895.

   N 9.6/2:nos.
   – 2ND SERIES. 1908–

N 9.7:date
ORDERS AND CIRCULARS (unnumbered).

N 9.8:date
REGULATIONS GOVERNING UNIFORM AND EQUIPMENT OF OFFICERS AND ENLISTED MEN.

N 9.9:nos.
MARINE CORPS ORDERS.

   N 9.9/2:nos.
   – SERIES, 1914–

   N 9.9/3:nos.
   – SERIES, 1927–

    Later M 209.8
   N 9.9/4:inc.nos.
   – (COMPILATIONS).

N 9.10:date
MARKSMANSHIP QUALIFICATIONS.

    Later M 209.7

N 9.11:CT
SPECIFICATIONS AND PROPOSALS.

N 9.12
CHANGES IN MARINE CORPS PAMPHLETS.

N 9.13:nos.
ACCOUNTABILITY MEMORANDUM.

N 9.14:nos.
TRANSPORTATION MEMORANDUM.

N 9.15:date
MANUALS.

    Later M 202.9

N 9.16:CT
REGULATIONS, INSTRUCTIONS, AND MANUALS (special).

    Later M 209.6

N 9.17:CT
POSTERS.

N 9.18:CT
MARINE CORPS SPECIFICATIONS.

N 9.19:nos.
CIRCULAR LETTERS.

N 9.20:date
REGISTER OF COMMISSIONED AND WARRANT OFFICERS OF MARINE CORPS RESERVE.

BUREAU OF MEDICINE AND SURGERY
(1842– 1947)

CREATION AND AUTHORITY

    The Bureau of Medicine and Surgery was established within the Department of the Navy by act of Congress, approved August 13, 1842 (5 Stat. 579). In 1947, the Bureau was transferred along with the Department of the Navy to the National Military Establishment (M 203).

N 10.1:date
ANNUAL REPORTS OF SURGEON-GENERAL.

    Later M 203.1

N 10.2:CT
GENERAL PUBLICATIONS.

    Later M 203.2

N 10.3
BULLETINS.

N 10.4:date
CIRCULARS.

N 10.5:date
INSTRUCTIONS.

    Later M 203.12

   N 10.5/1a:CT
   MANUAL FOR MEDICAL DEPARTMENT, NAVY (separates).

N 10.52:dt.&nos.
CHANGES IN MANUAL FOR MEDICAL DEPARTMENT, NAVY.

N 10.6:CT
SPECIFICATIONS.

N 10.7:date
DRILL REGULATIONS FOR HOSPITAL CORPS.

N 10.8:date
SUPPLY TABLE OF MEDICAL DEPARTMENT, NAVY, WITH ALLOWANCE FOR SHIPS.

N 10.9:nos.
CONTRIBUTIONS TO MEDICAL SCIENCE.

Naval Medical School

N 10.10/1:date
ANNUAL REPORTS.

Later N 10.201

N 10.10/2:CT
GENERAL PUBLICATIONS.

Later N 10.202

Bureau of Medicine and Surgery (Continued)

N 10.11:v.nos.
UNITED STATES NAVAL MEDICAL BULLETIN. [Quarterly]

Later M 203.3

N 10.11/2:nos.
–SUPPLEMENTS.

Later M 203.3/2

N 10.11/3:CT
–SPECIAL NUMBERS.

N 10.11/4:nos.
–SPECIAL NUMBERS.

N 10.12:nos.
–SUPPLEMENTS TO CORRESPONDENCE COURSES FOR NAVAL PHARMACISTS.

N 10.12:nos.
PREVENTIVE MEDICINE DIVISION, BULLETINS.

N 10.13:CT
REGULATIONS, INSTRUCTIONS AND HANDBOOKS.

Later M 203.6

N 10.14:nos.
CIRCULAR LETTERS.

N 10.14/2:inc.nos.
CIRCULAR LETTERS (compilations).

N 10.15:date
STATISTICS OF DISEASE AND INJURIES IN THE NAVY.

Later N 201.10

N 10.16:class.nos.
INSTRUCTOR'S GUIDE FOR CLASSES, FIRST AID TRAINING COURSES.

N 10.17:CT
POSTERS.

N 10.18:v.nos.
BUMED NEWS LETTERS. [Biweekly]

Later M 203.7

N 10.19:nos.
NAVMED VD [Leaflets].

N 10.20:date
BULLETIN OF BUREAU OF MEDICINE AND SURGERY CIRCULAR LETTERS.

N 10.20.2:dt.&nos.
BUMED CIRCULAR LETTERS, [Restricted].

Later M 203.9

N 10.21:nos.&rp.nos.
PROJECT REPORTS.

Series designated NM-nos.

N 10.22:nos.
MEDICAL RESEARCH LABORATORY REPORT.

Later M 203.13

National Naval Medical Center, Bethesda

N 10.101:date
ANNUAL REPORTS.

N 10.102:CT
GENERAL PUBLICATIONS.

Naval Medical School, Bethesda

N 10.201:date
ANNUAL REPORTS.

Earlier N 10.10/1

N 10.202:CT
GENERAL PUBLICATIONS.

Earlier N 10.10/2

N 10.206:CT
REGULATIONS, RULES, AND INSTRUCTIONS.

Includes Handbooks and Manuals.

NAUTICAL ALMANAC OFFICE
(1849–1947)

N 11.1:date
ANNUAL REPORTS.

N 11.2:CT
GENERAL PUBLICATIONS.

N 11.3
BULLETINS [none issued].

N 11.4
CIRCULARS [none issued].

N 11.5:date
AMERICAN EPHEMERIS AND NAUTICAL ALMANAC.
Later M 212.8

N 11.6:date
AMERICAN NAUTICAL ALMANAC.

Later M 212.9

N 11.6/2:date
AERONAUTICAL SUPPLEMENT TO AMERICAN NAUTICAL ALMANAC.

N 11.6/3:date
AIR ALMANAC.
Later M 212.7

N 11.7:nos.
ASTRONOMICAL PAPERS FOR AMERICAN EPHEMERIS AND NAUTICAL ALMANAC.

Later D 213.9

N 11.8:date
PACIFIC COASTER'S NAUTICAL ALMANAC (discontinued with the 1906 issue).

N 11.9:CT
TABLES COMPUTED FOR THE AMERICAN EPHEMERIS AND NAUTICAL ALMANAC.

N 11.10:date
ATLANTIC COASTERS' NAUTICAL ALMANAC.
Discontinued with 1892 issue

N 11.11:date
SKY DIAGRAMS.

NAVAL ACADEMY
(1845–1947)

N 12.1/1:date
ANNUAL REPORTS OF BOARD OF VISITORS.

N 12.1/2:date
ANNUAL REPORTS OF SUPERINTENDENT.

N 12.2:CT
GENERAL PUBLICATIONS.

N 12.3
BULLETINS [none issued].

N 12.4
CIRCULARS.

N 12.5:date
ANNUAL REGISTER.

N 12.6:date
REGULATIONS (general).

N 12.7:date
REGULATIONS GOVERNING ADMISSION OF CANDIDATES INTO NAVAL ACADEMY AS MIDSHIPMEN.

Later M 206.108

N 12.8/1:date
EXAMINATION PAPERS FOR ADMISSION.

N 12.8/2:date
EXAMINATION PAPERS (for promotion).

N 12.9:date
STATION DIRECTORY.

OFFICE OF NAVAL
INTELLIGENCE
(1882–1947)

N 13.2:CT
GENERAL PUBLICATIONS.

N 13.3
BULLETINS [none issued].

N 13.4
CIRCULARS [none issued].

N 13.5:nos.
GENERAL INFORMATION SERIES, INFORMATION FROM ABROAD.

Discontinued with 1902 issue.

N 13.7:CT
INFORMATION FROM ABROAD (unnumbered).

N 13.7:nos.
WAR NOTES, INFORMATION FROM ABROAD.

Discontinued with issue no. 8.

N 13.8:nos.
WAR NOTES, INFORMATION FROM ABROAD.

Discontinued with issue for 1893.

N 13.9:nos.
O.N.I. PUBLICATIONS (confidential).

N 13.10:date
MONTHLY INFORMATION BULLETINS.

N 13.11:v.nos.&nos.
ONI. [Weekly]

NAVAL OBSERVATORY
(1842– 1947)

N 14.1/1:date
ANNUAL REPORTS OF SUPERINTENDENT.

Later M 212.1

N 14.1/2:date
ANNUAL REPORTS OF BOARD OF VISITORS.

N 14.2:CT
GENERAL PUBLICATIONS.

Later M 212.2

N 14.3
BULLETINS [none issued].

N 14.4
CIRCULARS [none issued].

N 14.5:date
WASHINGTON OBSERVATIONS, PUBLICATIONS OF NAVAL OBSERVATORY, 1ST SERIES.

N 14.6:v.nos.
PUBLICATIONS OF NAVAL OBSERVATORY, 2ND SERIES.

Later M 212.10

N 14.7:date
LIBRARY CATALOGS.

N 14.8:CT
MAPS AND CHARTS.

N 14.9:nos.
EXPLANATIONS AND SAILING DIRECTIONS TO ACCOMPANY WIND AND CURRENT CHARTS (Maury).

N 14.10/1:CT
WIND AND CURRENT CHARTS, SERIES A, TRACK CHARTS.

N 14.10/2:letters
– SERIES B, TRADE WIND CHARTS.

N 14.10/3:letters
– SERIES C, PILOT CHARTS.

N 14.10/4:letters
– SERIES D, THERMAL CHARTS.

N 14.10/5:letters
– SERIES E, STORM AND RAIN CHARTS.

N 14.10/6:letters
– SERIES F, WHALE CHARTS.

N 14.10/7:CT
– MISCELLANEOUS.

N 14.11:nos.
NAUTICAL MONOGRAPHS (Maury).

N 14.13:date
CATALOGS OF CHARTS.

NAVAL WAR COLLEGE
(1884– 1947)

N 15.1:date
ANNUAL REPORTS.

Later M 206.201

N 15.2:CT
GENERAL PUBLICATIONS.

Later M 206.202

N 15.3
BULLETINS [none issued].

N 15.4
CIRCULARS [none issued].

N 15.5:date
ABSTRACT OF COURSE.

Discontinued with 1903 issue.

N 15.6:CT
ADDRESSES AND LECTURES.

N 15.7:date
INTERNATIONAL LAW SITUATIONS (Annual Discussions).

Later M 206.207

N 15.7/2:inclusive date
GENERAL INDEX TO INTERNATIONAL LAW SITUATIONS.

N 15.8:CT
NAVAL WAR COLLEGE EXTENSION

N 15.9:nos.
MONOGRAPHS.

NAVAL RECORDS AND LIBRARY OFFICE
(1915– 1947)

N 16.1:date
ANNUAL REPORTS.

N 16.2:CT
GENERAL PUBLICATIONS.

N 16.3
BULLETINS [none issued].

N 16.4
CIRCULARS [none issued].

N 16.5:nos.
OFFICE MEMORANDA.

N 16.6:series&v.nos.
OFFICIAL RECORDS OF UNION AND CONFEDERATE NAVIES IN WAR OF REBELLION.

N 16.7:date
CATALOGS AND LISTS OF AMERICAN AND FOREIGN ANNUALS AND PERIODICALS.

N 16.8:nos.
ACCESSIONS TO NAVY DEPARTMENT LIBRARY. [Semiannual]

N 16.9:nos.
MONOGRAPHS, HISTORICAL SECTION PUBLI-CAT-IONS.

BUREAU OF NAVAL PERSONNEL
(1942– 1947)

CREATION AND AUTHORITY

The Bureau of Navigation was established within the Department of the Navy by act of Congress, approved July 5, 1862 (12 Stat. 51). By act of Congress, approved May 13, 1942 (56 Stat. 276) the name was changed to Bureau of Naval Personnel. In 1947, the Bureau was transferred along with the Department of the Navy to the National Military Establishment (M 206).

N 17.1:date
ANNUAL REPORTS.
Later M 206.1

N 17.2:CT
GENERAL PUBLICATIONS.
Later M 206.2

N 17.3
BULLETINS [none issued].

N 17.4:date
CIRCULARS.

N 17.5:nos.
NAVAL PROFESSIONAL PAPERS.

N 17.6:CT
SPECIFICATIONS.

N 17.7/1:date
NAVAL HOME, ANNUAL REPORTS.

N 17.7/2:CT
NAVAL HOME, GENERAL PUBLICATIONS.

N 17.8:date
MOVEMENTS OF VESSELS. [Daily, except Sundays and Holidays].

N 17.9:date
ORDERS TO OFFICERS, U.S.N. [Daily, except Sundays and Holidays]

N 17.10:date
NAVY TRANSPRTATION SCHEDULES.

N 17.11:date
INVITATION FOR BIDS FOR TRANSPORTATION OF ENLISTED MEN OF NAVY AND MARINE CORPS.

N 17.12/1:CT
DRILL BOOKS, SIGNAL BOOKS AND CODE LISTS.

N 17.12/2:nos.
CHANGES IN DRILL BOOKS.

N 17.12/3:CT
CHANGES IN DRILL BOOKS (miscellaneous).

N 17.13:date
LIST OF ADDRESSES OF NAVY RECRUITING STATIONS.

N 17.14:date
LEAVES OF ABSENCE GRANTED OFFICERS. [Monthly]

N 17.15:date
ANNUAL REPORT OF SMALL AMRS TARGET PRACTICE.

N 17.16:CT
CHANGES IN REGULATIONS.

N 17.17:CT
CIRCULARS AND ORDERS (miscellaneous, unnumbered).

N 17.18/1:date
NAVAL TRAINING STATION, NEWPORT, ANNUAL REPORTS.

N 17.18/2:CT
NAVAL TRAINING STATION, NEWPORT, GENERAL
PUBLICATIONS.

N 17.19:CT
CATALOGS OF SHIPS AND CREW'S LIBRARIES OF
THE U.S.

N 17.20:date
CIRCULAR LETTERS.

N 17.21:date
LIST OF ADDRESSES OF NAVY RECRUITING
STATIONS.

N 17.22:CT
PORTS OF THE WORLD, DITTY BOX GUIDE BOOK
SERIES.

N 17.23:nos.
POSTERS.

N 17.23/2:CT
POSTERS.

N 17.23/3:nos.
[AIRCRAFT] RECOGNITION TEST [posters].

N 17.24/1:date
MANUAL OF BUREAU OF NAVIGATION.

N 17.24/2:CT
CHANGES IN MANUAL OF BUREAU OF NAVIGA-
TION.

N 17.24/3:nos
BUREAU MANUAL CIRCULARS.

N 17.24/4:CT
MANUALS AND HANDBOOKS.
Later M 206.6

N 17.25:CT
NAVY TRAINING COURSES.
Later D 208.11

N 17.26:date
LIST OF BOOKS AVAILABLE FOR SHIP AND STA-
TION LIBRARIES, NAVY.

N 17.27:nos.
NAVAL RESERVE CIRCULAR LETTERS.

N 17.29:nos.
AVIATION TRAINING PAMPHLETS.

N 17.30:date
YEARBOOK OF ENLISTED TRAINING.

N 17.31:nos.
CASE INSTRUCTION.
Later D 206.13

N 17.32:CT
NAVAL RESERVE INSPECTION BOARD PUBLICA-
TIONS.

N 17.33:nos.
TRADIV LETTERS. [Monthly]
Later M 206.7

N 17.34:CT
INSTRUCTOR TRAINING. BULLETINS.

N 17.35:nos.
NAVY WAR MAPS.

N 17.36:nos.
NAVY V-12 BULLETINS.
Proc. and printed.

N 17.37:date
NAVAL RESERVIST. [Monthly]
Later M 206.9

N 17.38:date
REGISTER OF COMMISSIONED AND WARRANT
OFFICERS OF NAVAL RESERVE.
Earlier N 25.6
Later D 208.12/2

N 17.39:nos.
SEA CLIPPER. [Weekly]
Later M 206.8

BUREAU OF ORDNANCE
(1862– 1947)

CREATION AND AUTHORITY

The Bureau of Ordnance and Hydrography
was established within the Department of the Navy
by act of Congress, approved August 31, 1842 (5
Stat. 579). The name was changed to Bureau of
Ordnance by act of Congress approved July 5,
1862 (12 Stat 510). In 1947, the Bureau was
transferred along with the Department of the Navy
to the National Military Establishment (M 211).

N 18.1:date
ANNUAL REPORTS.
Later M 211.1

N 18.2:CT
GENERAL PUBLICATIONS.
Later M 211.2

N 18.3
BULLETINS [none issued].

N 18.4:date
CIRCULARS [none issued].

N 18.5:ed.nos.
ORDNANCE INSTRUCTIONS FOR NAVY.

N 18.6:CT
SPECIFICATIONS (unnumbered).

N 18.7:CT
ORDNANCE INSTRUCTIONS FOR NAVY.

N 18.8:CT
NAVAL ORDNANCE PAPERS.

N 18.9:date
ORDNANCE CIRCULAR LETTERS.

N 18.10:CT
PAPERS IN RE.

N 18.11:vol.
NAVAL ORDNANCE BULLETIN.

N 18.12:vol.
NAVAL FIREPOWER. [Monthly]

BUREAU OF ENGINEERING
(1920– 1940)

CREATION AND AUTHORITY

The Bureau of Steam Engineering was established within the Department of the Navy by act
of Congress, approved July 5, 1862 (12 Stat.
510). The name was changed to Bureau of Engineering by act of Congress, approved June 4,
1920. By act of Congress, approved June 20,
1940 (54 Stat. 493), the Bureau was consolidated
with the Bureau of Construction and Repair (N 4)
to form the Breau of Ships (N 29).

N 19.1:date
ANNUAL REPORTS.

Later N 29.1

N 19.2:CT
GENERAL PUBLICATIONS.

Later N 29.2

N 19.3
BULLETINS [none issued].

N 19.4:date
CIRCULARS [none issued].

N 19.5:CT
SPECIFICATIONS.

N 19.5/2:letters-nos.
GENERAL SPECIFICATIONS FOR MACHINERY.

N 19.6:date
LIST AND STATIONS OF NAVAL INSPECTORS OF
ENGINEERING MATERIAL, ETC. FOR NAVY.

N 19.6/2:date
NAVAL MATERIAL INSPECTION DISTRICTS UNDER
INSPECTORS OF NAVAL MATERIAL.

N 19.7:date
LIST OF WIRELESS TELEGRAPH STATIONS OF THE
WORLD.

N 19.8/1:date
MANUAL OF ENGINEERING INSTRUCTIONS.

N 19.8/2:chap.nos.
MANUAL OF ENGINEERING INSTRUCTIONS,
INDIVIDUAL CHAPTERS. 1922–

Later N 29.11

N 19.8/3:nos.
CHANGES IN MANUAL OF ENGINEERING INSTRUC-
TIONS.

N 19.8/4:letters
CHNAGES IN MANUAL OF ENGINEERING INSTRUC-
TIONS, LETTERED.

N 19.9/1:nos.
CONFIDENTIAL BULLETIN OF ENGINEERING INFOR-
MATION.

N 19.9/2:nos.
BULLETIN OF ENGINEERING INFORMATION.

Later N 29.10

N 19.10:nos.
RADIO COMPASS BULLETINS.

N 19.11:chap.nos.
INSTRUCTIONS TO INSPECTORS OF ENGINEER-
ING MATERIALS.

Later included in N 29.13

N 19.12:nos.
CIRCULAR LETTERS.

Later N 29.12

N 19.13:nos.
RADIO AND SOUND BULLETIN.

BUREAU OF SUPPLIES AND ACCOUNTS
(1892–1947)

CREATION AND AUTHORITY

The Bureau of Provisions and Clothing was established within the Department of the Navy by act of Congress, approved August 31, 1842 (5 Stat. 579). The name was changed to Bureau of Supplies and Accounts by act of Congress, approved July 19, 1892. In 1947, the Bureau was transferred along with the Department of the Navy to the National Military Establishment (M 213).

N 20.1:date
ANNUAL REPORTS OF PAYMASTERGENERAL.

Later M 213.1

N 20.2:CT
GENERAL PUBLICATIONS.

Later M 213.2

N 20.3
BULLETINS [none issued].

N 20.3/2:date
APPROPRIATION BULLETINS.

N 20.4:date
CIRCULARS (unnumbered).

N 20.4/2:nos.
CIRCULARS (numbered).

N 20.5:date
PAY TABLES FOR USE OF PAY OFFICERS.

N 20.6/1:CT
SPECIFICATIONS.

N 20.6/2:nos.
SPECIFICATIONS (numbered).

Later M 213.7

N 20.6/3:date
INDEX TO SPECIFICATIONS.

Later M 213.9

N 20.7/1:nos.
MEMORANDA FOR INFORMATION OF OFFICERS OF PAY CORPS, ETC.

N 20.7/2:date
– INDEX.

N 20.7/3:date
BUREAU OF SUPPLIES AND ACCOUNTS MEMORANDA.

The 1931 volume supersedes memorandum nos. 1-343 (N 20.7/1).

N 20.7/4:date
SELECTED DECISIONS OF COMPTROLLER GENERAL APPLICABLE TO NAVAL SERVICE. [Quarterly]

Supersedes N 20.7/3:1931/2

N 20.8:date
CIRCULAR LETTERS.

N 20.9:nos.
NOTICES OF PURCHASES (of Miscellaneous Materials, Etc.).

N 20.10:nos.
NOTICE OF PURCHASES (of Miscellaneous Materials, Etc., for Western States).

N 20.11:date
COAL NOTICES FOR FOREIGN PORTS, CALENDAR YEAR.

N 20.12:nos.
CONTRACT BULLETIN.

N 20.13/1:CT
MANUALS, INSTRUCTIONS, AND REGULATIONS.

N 20.13/2:CT
– CHANGES.

N 20.13/3:nos.
U.S. NAVY TRAVEL INSTRUCTIONS, INSTRUCTION MEMORANDA.

N 20.14:CT
CATALOGS AND ADVERTISEMENTS OF SURPLUS EQUIPMENT FOR SALE.

N 20.14/2:nos.
NAVY SURPLUS BY AUCTION CATALOGS.

N 20.14/3:v.nos.
NAVY SURPLUS SUPPLIES CATALOG.

N 20.15:date
STANDARD STOCK CATALOGS.

N 20.16:classes
STANDARD STOCK CATALOGS, CLASSES NUMBERED.

N 20.16/2:nos.
STANDARD STOCK CATALOGS, ADDENDA

N 20.17:nos.
NAVY SHPPING GUIDE.

N 20.17/2:nos.
NAVY SHIPPING GUIDE, CHANGES.

N 20.18:date
CONTRACT BULLETIN.

N 20.19:CT
SCHEDULES.

Changed from N 20.19.

N 20.20:date
NAVY DEPARTMENT SPECIFICATIONS AND FEDERAL SPECIFICATIONS, MONTHLY BULLETIN.

N 20.21:date
NAVAL EXPENDITURES.

N 20.22:date
FEDERAL INCOME TAX INFORMATION [for Persons in Naval Service].

Earlier N 20.2:In 2

N 20.23:nos.
JOINT ARMY-NAVY SPECIFICATIONS

Later M 213.8

N 20.24:CT
POSTERS.

N 20.25:date
FUNCTIONS AND ORGANIZATION OF BUREAU OF SUPPLIES AND ACCOUNTS, CONTROL RECORD.

N 20.26:CT
PAPERS IN RE.

N 20.27:nos.
ARMY-NAVY JOINT PACKAGING INSTRUCTIONS.

N 20.28:nos.
JOINT ARMY-NAVY STANDARDS.

Later M 5.7

BUREAU OF YARDS AND DOCKS
(1862–1947)

CREATION AND AUTHORITY

The Bureau of Navy Yards and Docks was established within the Department of the Navy by act of Congress approved August 31, 1842 (5 Stat. 579). By act of Congress, approved July 5, 1862, the name was changed to Bureau of Yards and Docks. In 1947, the Bureau was transferred along with the Department of the Navy to the National Military Establishment (M 205).

N 21.1:date
ANNUAL REPORTS.

Later M 205.1

N 21.2:CT
GENERAL PUBLICATIONS.

Later M 205.2

N 21.3
BULLETINS [none issued].

N 21.4:date
CIRCULARS (unnumbered).

N 21.5:CT
SPECIFCIATIONS (unnumbered).

N 21.6:nos.
SPECIFICATIONS (numbered).

N 21.7:CT
REGULATIONS (special).

N 21.8:nos.
CONFIDENTIAL BULLETINS.

N 21.9:date
MANUAL

N 21.9/2:chap.nos.
– [Individual Chapters]

N 21.10:nos.
STANDARD SPECIFICATIONS (numbered).

Later D 209.11

N 21.11:nos.
NEWS MEMORANDUM. [Semimonthly]

N 21.12:date
TELEPHONE DIRECTORY, NAVY YARD, WASHINGTON, D.C.

Earlier N 1.23/2

N 21.13:date
SEABEE ITEMS OF INTEREST. [Semimonthly]

N 21.14:v.nos.
U.S. NAVY CIVIL ENGINEERS CORPS BULLETINS. [Monthly]

Succeeds N 21.11
Later M 205.7

N 21.15:CT
REGULATIONS, RULES, AND INSTRUCTIONS.

Later M 205.6

NAVAL COMMUNICATIONS SERVICE
(1916– 1947)

N 22.1:date
ANNUAL REPORTS.

N 22.2:CT
GENERAL PUBLICATIONS.

N 22.3
BULLETINS.

N 22.4
CIRCULARS.

N 22.5:date
RADIO COMMUNICATION CHARTS. [Monthly]

> **N 22.5/2:nos.**
> – SUPPLEMENT.

N 22.6:v.nos.
DAILY SHIPPING BULLETIN.

> Later SB 1.2

N 22.7:date
NAVAL COMMUNICATION SERVICE, COASTAL RADIO AND LANDLINE RATE SHEETS OF UNITED STATES.

N 22.8:date
NAVAL COMMUNICATION SERVICE, TRAFFIC RATE SHEETS.

DIVISION OF NAVAL MILITIA AFFAIRS
(1914– 1918)

N 23.1:date
ANNUAL REPORTS.

N 23.2:CT
GENERAL PUBLICATIONS.

N 23.3
BULLETINS.

N 23.4
CIRCULARS.

N 23.5:date
REGISTER OF NAVAL MILITIA.

N 23.6:nos.
NAVAL MILITIA CIRCULAR LETTERS.

N 23.6/2:nos.
CIRCULAR LETTERS (mimeographed).

COAST GUARD
(1917– 1919, 1941– 1946)

CREATION AND AUTHORITY

The United States Coast Guard was established by the act of Congress, approved January 28, 1915, as amended, as a branch of the Armed Forces of the United States, operating as a service in the Treasury Department during times of peace and in the Navy Department during times of war or when the President directs. Accordingly, the Coast Guard was transferred from the Treasury Department to the Navy Department by Executive Order 2587 of April 7, 1917 and returned by Executive Order 3160 of August 28, 1919; likewise transferred by Executive Order 8929 of November 1, 1941 and returned by Executive Order 9666 of December 28, 1945, effective January 1, 1946. Pursuant to Public Law 89-670, approved October 15, 1966 (80 Stat. 932), it was transferred to the newly created Department of Transportation (TD 5).

N 24.1:date
ANNUAL REPORTS.

> See also T 47.1

N 24.2:CT
GENERAL PUBLICATIONS.

> See also T 47.2

N 24.3
BULLETINS.

N 24.4
CIRCULARS.

N 24.5:nos.
GENERAL ORDERS.

N 24.6:nos.
SPECIAL ORDERS.

N 24.7:nos.
CIRCULAR LETTERS.

N 24.8:CT
REGULATIONS, RULES, AND INSTRUCTIONS. (Miscellaneous).

> Earlier T 47.8

N 24.9:date
REGULATIONS (General).

> Earlier T 47.9

N 24.10:date
REGISTER.

> Earlier T 47.10

N 24.11:vol.
COAST GUARD BULLETINS. [Monthly]

> Earlier T 47.21

N 24.12:date
NOTICE TO MARINERS, AFFECTING LIGHTS, BUOYS, AND OTHER AIDS TO NAVIGATION. [Weekly]

> Earlier T 47.19

N 24.13:date
NOTICE TO MARINERS, GREAT LAKES, AFFECTING LIGHTS, BUOYS AND OTHER AIDS TO NAVIGATION. [Weekly]

> Earlier T 47.20
> Later included in N 16.12/2

N 24.14:CT
RADIOBEACON SYSTEM (maps).

> Earlier T 47.22

N 24.15:date
LIGHT LIST, ATLANTIC COAST OF UNITED STATES, NORTHERN PART.

> Earlier T 47.23

N 24.16:date
LIGHT LIST, ATLANTIC COAST OF UNITED STATES, SOUTHERN PART.

> Earlier T 47.24

N 24.17:date
LIGHT LIST, ATLANTIC COAST OF U.S. INTRACOASTAL WATERWAY, HAMPTON ROADS TO RIO GRANDE INCLUDING INSIDE WATERS.

> Earlier T 47.28

N 24.18:date
LIGHT LIST, MISSISSIPPI AND OHIO RIVERS AND TRIBUTARIES.

> Earlier T 47.27

N 24.19:date
LIGHT LIST, PACIFIC COAST OF UNITED STATES.

> Earlier T 47.25

N 24.20:date
LIGHT LIST, GREAT LAKES, UNITED STATES AND CANADA.

> Earlier T 47.26

N 24.21:date
ENGINEER'S DIGEST. [Monthly]

> Earlier T 47.30

N 24.22:nos.
HEADQUARTERS' CIRCULARS.

> Earlier T 47.7/3

N 24.23:nos.
PILOTING AND OCEAN NAVIGATION PAMPHLETS.

N 24.24:vol.
MARINE INSPECTION AND NAVIGATION BULLETINS. [Monthly]

> Earlier C 25.12

N 24.25:nos.
GENERAL ORDERS (6th series, August 12, 1940–).

> Earlier T 47.5/6

N 24.26:nos.
PAY AND SUPPLY INSTRUCTIONS, CIRCULARS.

> Earlier T 47.8/2

N 24.27:nos.
NAVIGATION AND VESSEL INSPECTION CIRCULARS.

> Supersedes Circular Letters (C 25.13)
> Later T 47.34

N 24.28:nos.
EDUCATIONAL SERIES.

> Later T 47.36

N 24.29:nos.
LAW BULLETINS. [Monthly]

> Earlier T 47.17

N 24.30:date
COASTS OF UNITED STATES.

> Later T 47.35

N 24.31:CT
LAWS.

> Later 47.44

N 24.32:vol.
PROCEEDINGS OF MERCHANT MARINE COUNCIL.
[Monthly]

> Later T 47.31

N 24.33:CT
POSTERS.

N 24.34:v.nos.
COAST GUARD WAR NEWS CLIPPER.

N 24.35:nos.
AIR SEA RESCUE BULLETIN, [Restricted]. [Monthly]

> Proc. & printed.

N 24.36:CT
FACT BOOKS.

N 24.37:nos.
SHIP CONSTRUCTION MANUALS.

> Later T 47.37

N 24.38:nos.
CIVIL READJUSTMENT BULLETINS.

> Later T 47.33

N 24.39:nos.
COAST GUARD AT WAR SERIES.

NAVAL RESERVE FORCE DIVISION
(1915– 1918)

N 25.1:date
ANNUAL REPORTS.

N 25.2:CT
GENERAL PUBLICATIONS.

N 25.3
BULLETINS.

N 25.4
CIRCULARS.

N 25.5:nos.
NAVAL RESERVE CIRCULAR LETTERS AND IN-
STRUCTIONS.

N 25.6:date
REGISTER OF COMMISSIONED AND WARRANT
OFFICERS OF NAVAL RESERVE FORCE.

> Later N 17.38 and D 208.12/2

N 25.7:date
INSTRUCTIONS AND REGULATIONS.

N 25.7/2:date
NAVAL RESERVE REGULATIONS.

N 25.8:CT
NAVAL RESERVE OFFICE, CIRCULARS.

COMMISSION ON TRAINING CAMP ACTIVITIES
(1917– 1919)

N 26.1:date
ANNUAL REPORTS.

N 26.2:CT
GENERAL PUBLICATIONS.

N 26.3
BULLETINS.

N 26.4
CIRCULARS.

OFFICE OF NAVAL OPERATIONS
(1915– 1947)

CREATION AND AUTHORITY

> The Office of Naval Operations was estab-
lished within the Department of the Navy by act
of Congress, approved March 3, 1915 (38 Stat.
929). In 1947, the Office was transferred along
with the Department of the Navy to the National
Military Establishment (M 207).

N 27.1:date
ANNUAL REPORTS.

> Later M 207.1

N 27.2:CT
GENERAL PUBLICATIONS.

> Later M 207.2

N 27.3
BULLETINS.

N 27.4
CIRCULARS.

N 27.5:CT
MANUALS.

> Later M 207.6

N 27.6:nos.
COMMUNICATION CIRCULAR LETTERS.

N 27.7:nos.
COMMUNICATION DIVISION BULLETIN.

N 27.8:CT
NAVAL RESERVE INSPECTION BOARD PUBLICA-
TIONS.

> Earlier N 17.32

N 27.9:CT
FLIGHT PREPARATION TRAINING SERIES.

N 27.10:nos.
POSTERS. [Operational Dilberts].

> Earlier N 28.16

N 27.11:CT
POSTERS.

N 27.12:nos.
FIXED GUNNERY AND COMBAT TACTICS SERIES.

N 27.13:nos.
AEROLOGY SERIES.

> Earlier N 28.14

N 27.14:CT
CIVIL AFFAIRS HANDBOOKS.

N 27.15:nos.
RADAR BULLETINS [Confidential or restricted].

N 27.16:nos.
NAVAL AVIATION NEWS. [Restricted]. [Monthly]

> Later M 207.7/2

N 27.16/2:nos.
NAVAL AVIATION NEWS (Naval Air Reserve Edition).
[Monthly]

> Later M 207.7/1

N 27.17:letters-nos.
CIRCULAR LETTERS. [Proc.]

N 27.18:nos.
PHOTOGRAPHIC INTELLIGENCE CENTER RE-
PORTS.

N 27.19:nos.
OEG REPORT. (Operations Evaluation Group).

BUREAU OF AERONAUTICS
(1921– 1947)

CREATION AND AUTHORITY

> The Bureau of Aeronautics was established
by act of July 12, 1921 (42 Stat. 140). In 1947,
the Bureau was transferred along with the Department of the Navy to the National Military Establishment (M 208).

N 28.1:date
ANNUAL REPORTS.

> Later M 208.1

N 28.2:CT
GENERAL PUBLICATIONS.

> Later M 208.2

N 28.3
BULLETINS.

N 28.3/2:nos.
NAVAL AVIATION TRAINING DIVISION BULLETINS.

N 28.4
CIRCULARS.

N 28.5:nos.
AERONAUTICAL SPECIFICATIONS.

N 28.6:nos.
TECHNICAL NOTES.

N 28.6/2:nos.
TECHNICAL NOTES (Series of 1930–   ). [Offical
use only].

> Later M 208.9

N 28.7:date
MANUALS.

> Later D 202.6/2

N 28.8:nos.
TECHNICAL ORDERS.

N 28.8/2:dt.&nos.
TECHNICAL ORDERS (Series 1930–   ).

> Later M 208.7

N 28.9:nos.
POWER PLANT NOTES.

N 28.10:nos.
SPECIFICATIONS (Chiefly blueprints, some being mimeographed).

Supersedes N 4.6/2

N 28.11:CT
NAVAL AVIATION TRAINING SCHOOLS.

N 28.11/2:CT
NAVAL AVIATION TRAINING SCHOOL PUBLICATIONS.

N 28.12:nos.
CIRCULAR LETTERS.

Later M 208.8

N 28.13:CT
REGULATIONS, RULES, AND INSTRUCTIONS.

Later M 208.11

N 28.14:nos.
AEROLOGY SERIES.

N 28.15:CT
BASIC TABLES OF COMMISSIONING ALLOWANCES.

Printed and processed.

N 28.16:nos.
POSTERS (Dilbert series).

Later N 27.10

N 28.16/2:CT
POSTERS (Miscellaneous).

N 28.16/3:nos.
POSTERS [Spoiler the Mech series].

N 28.17:date
NAVAER PUBLICATIONS INDEX [Restricted]. [Quarterly with monthly supplements]

Later M 208.11

N 28.18:nos.
FLIGHT SAFETY BULLETINS.

Later M 207.8

N 28.19:nos.
AIRCRAFT INSTRUMENT BULLETIN, FLOWMETER SERIES, FLOWMETER BULLETINS.

N 28.20:dt.&nos.
AIRCRAFT INSTRUMENT BULLETINS.

Later M 208.9

N 28.21:nos.
GENERAL ENGINE BULLETINS.

BUREAU OF SHIPS
(1940– 1947)

CREATION AND AUTHORITY

The Bureau of Ships was established within the Department of the Navy by act of Congress, approved June 20, 1940 (54 Sat. 492) by a consolidation of the Bureau of Construction and Repair (N 4) and the Bureau of Engineering (N 19) which were abolished. In 1947, the Bureau was transferred along with the Department of the Navy to the National Military Establishment (M 210).

N 29.1:date
ANNUAL REPORTS.

Earlier N 4.1
Later M 210.1

N 29.2:CT
GENERAL PUBLICATIONS.

Earlier N 4.2 and N 19.2
Later M 210.2

N 29.6:CT
REGULATIONS, RULES, AND INSTRUCTIONS.

N 29.7:sec.nos.
GENERAL SPECIFICATIONS FOR BUILDING VESSELS OF NAVY.

Earlier N 4.6/4
Later M 210.7

N 29.8:nos.
GENERAL SPECIFICATIONS FOR VESSELS OF NAVY, APPENDIXES.

Earlier N 4.6/2

N 29.9:nos.
TECHNICAL BULLETINS.

Supersedes N 4.3/2

N 29.10:nos.
BULLETINS OF ENGINEERING INFORMATION [Restricted].

Earlier N 19.9/2

N 29.11:chap. nos.
MANUAL OF ENGINEERING INSTRUCTIONS (by chapters).

Earlier N 19.8/2

N 29.12:nos.
CIRCULAR LETTERS.

Earlier N 19.12

N 29.12/2:nos.
CIRCULAR LETTERS. Sept. 1, 1942–

N 29.13:chap.nos.
MANUAL OF BUREAU OF SHIPS (by chapters).

A Consolidation of the Manual of Engineering Instructions (N 29.11) and Manual of Bureau of Construction & Repair (N 4.12). Later M 210.8

N 29.14:nos.
TRAINING PUBLICATIONS.

N 29.15:CT
POSTERS.

N 29.16:nos.
BUSHIPS SURPLUS MATERIAL LIST SERIES.

Processed and printed.

N 29.17:nos.
TECHNICAL LITERATURE RESEARCH SERIES.

N 29.18
SPECIFICATIONS, AD INTERIM.

OFFICE OF PROCUREMENT AND MATERIAL
(1942– 1945)

CREATION AND AUTHORITY

The Office of Procurement and Material was established within the Department of the Navy by General Order 166, dated January 30, 1942. The Office was abolished in 1945.

N 30.1:date
ANNUAL REPORTS.

N 30.2:CT
GENERAL PUBLICATIONS.

OFFICE OF PUBLIC RELATIONS
(1941– 1947)

N 31.1:date
ANNUAL REPORTS.

Later M 215.1

N 31.2:CT
GENERAL PUBLICATIONS.

Later M 215.2

OFFICE OF NAVAL RESEARCH
(1946– 1947)

CREATION AND AUTHORITY

The Office of Naval Research was established within the Department of the Navy by act of Congress, approved August 1, 1946 (60 Stat. 779), succeeding the Office of Research and Inventions. In 1947, the Office was transferred along with the Department of the Navy to the National Military Establishment (M 216).

N 32.1:date
ANNUAL REPORTS.

Later M 216.1

N 32.2:CT
GENERAL PUBLICATIONS.

Later M 216.2

N 32.7:nos.
NAVAL RESEARCH LABORATORY REPORTS.

Later M 216.7

N 32.8
NRL PILOT.

Proc. Admin.

NATIONAL ACADEMY OF SCIENCES
(1863–   )

CREATION AND AUTHORITY

The National Academy of Sciences was established by an act of Congress approved on March 3, 1863 (12 Stat. 806).

INFORMATION
National Academy of Sciences
Washington, D.C. 20418

NA 1.1:date   • Item 830
ANNUAL REPORT. 1863–   [Annual]

The Academy was established on March 3, 1863, by an act of Incorporation passed by Congress.

The Academy is a private, nonprofit organization of scientists and engineers devoted to the furtherance of science and its use for the general welfare. Although it is not a part of the U.S. Government, it has enjoyed, since its inception more than a century ago, a close relationship with the Federal government as an official adviser on matter of science and technology.

The Annual Report is made to Congress each year, and issued in both Departmental edition, sold by the GPO, and in the Congressional edition as a Senate Document.

NA 1.1/2:date
DIVISION OF EARTH SCIENCES: ANNUAL REPORT.

NA 1.2:CT   • **Item 830**
GENERAL PUBLICATIONS.

NA 1.3:
BULLETINS [none issued].

NA 1.4:
CIRCULARS [none issued].

NA 1.5:v.nos.
MEMOIRS.

NA 1.6:v.nos.
BIBLIOGRAPHICAL MEMOIRS.

NA 1.7:date
CONSTITUTION AND MEMBERSHIP.

NA 1.8:v.nos.
PROCEEDINGS.

NA 1.9:date
RELEASES, U.S. NATIONAL COMMITTEE FOR INTERNATIONAL GEOPHYSICAL YEAR.

NA 1.10:nos.
TRANSPORTATION RESEARCH RECORD (series). [Irregular]

NATIONAL RESEARCH COUNCIL (1916–   )

NA 2.1:date
ANNUAL REPORTS.

NA 2.2:CT
GENERAL PUBLICATIONS.

NA 2.3:
BULLETINS.

NA 2.4:
NATIONAL RESEARCH COUNCIL, CIRCULARS.

NA 2.5:nos.
REPRINT AND CIRCULAR SERIES.

NA 2.6:CT
SCIENTIFIC AIDS TO LEARNING COMMITTEE, PUBLICATIONS.

NA 2.7:nos.
CHEMICAL-BIOLOGICAL COORDINATION CENTER, REVIEWS.

NA 2.8:date
SURVEY OF FOOD AND NUTRITION RESEARCH IN UNITED STATES.

NA 2.9:CT
NRC COMMITTEE ON AVIATION PSYCHOLOGY PUBLICATIONS.

NA 2.10:CT
UNDERSEA WARFARE COMMITTEE PUBLICATIONS.

NA 2.11
NEWS REPORT. [Bimonthly]

NA 2.12:date
PUBLICATIONS.

NATIONAL AERONAUTICS AND SPACE ADMINISTRATION (1958–   )

CREATION AND AUTHORITY

The National Aeronautics and Space Administration was established by the National Aeronautics and Space Act of 1958 (72 Stat. 426; 42 U.S.C. 2451 et seq.), as amended.

INFORMATION

National Aeronautics
and Space Administration
Headquarters
Washington, DC 20546-0001
(202) 358-0000
Fax: 358-3251
E mail: info-center@hq.nasa.gov
http://www.nasa.gov

NAS 1.1:date   • **Item 830-A**
SEMIANNUAL REPORTS. 1st–   1959–

INDEXES. October 1958– December 1969. 1972. 245 p.

NAS 1.1/2:date
MAJOR ACTIVITIES IN PROGRAMS OF NATIONAL AERONAUTICS AND SPACE ADMINISTRATION. [Semiannual]

NAS 1.1/3:date   • **Item 830-R**
YEAR IN REVIEW AT GODDARD SPACE FLIGHT CENTER. [Annual]

NAS 1.1/4:date   • **Item 830-A-1 (MF)**
SPINOFF, ANNUAL REPORT.

NAS 1.1/5:date   • **Item 830-A-1 (MF)**
ANNUAL REPORT TO THE ADMINISTRATOR, THE OFFICE OF EXPLORATION. [Annual]

NAS 1.1/6   • **Item 830-A-1 (MF)**
HIGHLIGHTS OF EARTH SCIENCE AND APPLICATIONS DIVISION.

NAS 1.1/7:date   • **Item 830-C-8 (EL)**
AEROSPACE SAFETY ADVISORY PANEL, ANNUAL REPORT.

NAS 1.2:CT   • **Item 830-C**
GENERAL PUBLICATIONS.

NAS 1.5:CT   • **Item 830-W**
LAWS.

NAS 1.6:CT   • **Item 830-A-5**
REGULATIONS, RULES, INSTRUCTIONS. [Irregular]

NAS 1.6/2:date   • **Item 830-N**
NASA PROCUREMENT REGULATION (NHB 5100.2). [Irregular] (Includes basic volume plus supplementary material, including NASA Procurement Regulation Directive (NAS 1.6/3), for an indefinite period)

PURPOSE:– To establish for the National Aeronautics and Space Administration uniform policies and procedures relating to procurement of property and services under authority of the National Aeronautics and Space Act of 1958, as amended.

NAS 1.6/2-2:date   • **Item 830-N**
PROCUREMENT NOTICES (series).

NAS 1.6/3   • **Item 830-N**
NASA PROCUREMENT REGULATION DIRECTIVE. [Irregular]

NAS 1.7
PRESS RELEASES. [Irregular]

NAS 1.7/2:date
LANGLEY RESEARCH CENTER, LANGLEY FIELD, VA., RELEASES.

NAS 1.7/3:date
AERONAUTICS UPDATE. 1972–   [Irregular]

NAS 1.8:CT   • **Item 830-B**
DICTIONARIES, GLOSSARIES, ETC.

NAS 1.8:Ae 8   • **Item 830-B**
AERONAUTICAL DICTIONARY. 1959. 199 p.

NAS 1.9:nos.
PUBLICATION ANNOUNCEMENTS. 1–   1958–

NAS 1.9/2:CT   • **Item 830-J**
BIBLIOGRAPHIES AND LISTS OF PUBLICATIONS.

NAS 1.9/2:Sp 1/957-977   • **Item 830-J**
BIBLIOGRAPHY OF SPACE BOOKS AND ARTICLES FROM NON-AEROSPACE JOURNALS. 1979. 243 p.

NAS 1.9/3:v.nos.&nos.
TECHNICAL PUBLICATIONS ANNOUNCEMENTS WITH INDEXES.

Superseded by NAS 1.9/4

NAS 1.9/4:nos.   • **Item 830-K (EL)**
STAR, SCIENTIFIC AND TECHNICAL AEROSPACE REPORTS. [Biweekly]

Announces, abstracts, and indexes reports issued by the National Aeronautics and Space Administration, as well as by other Government agencies, universities, industry, and research organizations both in the United States and abroad.
ISSN 0036-8741

NAS 1.9/5:v.nos.&nos.   • **Item 830-K**
CUMULATIVE INDEXES. [Annual]

Subscription includes 3 quarterly indexes and an annual cumulation, printed in 4 volumes, which covers the entire year.

NAS 1.9/6
GUIDE TO SUBJECT INDEXES FOR SCIENTIFIC AND TECHNICAL AEROSPACE REPORTS. 1–   1964.

NAS 1.10:nos.
MEMORANDUMS. [Irregular]

NAS 1.11:CT
ADDRESSES. [Irregular]

NAS 1.12:nos.   • **Item 830-D**
TECHNICAL REPORTS, R- (series). R 1–   1959– [Irregular]

Presents the final results of completed program of research. The criteria for assigning a publication of report series are breadth of the research program, the completeness of the findings, and the significance of the research effort to the scientific community. The Reports are intended for a wide distribution to the public.
Continues, to a certain extent, the Reports series published by the National Advisory Committee of Aeronautics.
Superseded by Technical Papers (NAS 1.60).

NAS 1.12/2:v.nos.
NASA TECHNICAL REPORTS (bound volumes).

NAS 1.12/3:nos.
JET PROPULSION LABORATORY: TECHNICAL REPORTS.

NAS 1.12/4   • **Item 830-H-3 (MF)**
JET PROPULSION LABORATORY, JPL/HR- (series).

NAS 1.12/6:nos.   • **Item 830-H-3 (MF)**
JPL-SP (series). [Irregular] (Jet Propulsion Laboratory)

NAS 1.12/7   • **Item 830-H-9**
JET PROPULSION LABORATORY: JPL/HR- (Series).

NAS 1.12/7:410-33(nos.)   • **Item 830-H-9**
SATCOM QUARTERLY.

NAS 1.12/7-2:date
TELEPHONE DIRECTORY, JET PROPULSION LABO-
RATORY.

NAS 1.12/8:nos.   • **Item 830-Y (MF)**
MISSION STATUS BULLETINS. [Irregular] (Jet Propulsion Laboratory)

NAS 1.12/9:   • **Item 830-H-22**
JPL FACTS (various topics).

NAS 1.13:nos.
NASA REPUBLICATIONS.

    Replaced by NAS 1.13/2:

NAS 1.13/2:nos.
TECHNICAL TRANSLATIONS, TT- (series). F 1–
[Irregular]

    Presents information which has previously
been published in a foreign language and is judged
to merit distribution in English.

NAS 1.14:nos.   • **Item 830-H-13**
TECHNICAL NOTES, TN- (series). D 1–   [Irregular]

    Includes those publications that present a
body of information, but lack some of the characteristics of the Technical Reports (Completeness,
importance of permanence). The Notes are not
reissued as Reports, although the information in
a Technical Note is sometimes combined with
other information and presented as a Technical
Report.
    Published in microfiche.
    Superseded by Technical Papers (NAS 1.60).

NAS 1.15:nos.   • **Item 830-D (MF)**
TECHNICAL MEMORANDUMS, TM–   (series). X 1–
[Irregular]

    Presents information which is given limited
distribution because of the unconformed or preliminary nature of the materials, the inclusion of
proprietary information, or the sensitive nature of
the information. Declassified Technical Memorandums may be released to the public in this series
or may be reissued as Technical Notes or Technical Reports.

NAS 1.15/2:date   • **Item 830-J**
BIBLIOGRAPHY OF LEWIS RESEARCH CENTER
TECHNICAL PUBLICATIONS ANNOUNCED IN
(year). [Annual]
NAS 1.16:date
INTERNATIONAL SATELLITE AND SPACE PROBE
SUMMARY [and charts]. [Irregular]

    Provides ready reference information on the
various space shots made by the U.S. and the
U.S.S.R. Loose-leaf and punched for 3-ring binder.

NAS 1.17:date   • **Item 830-E**
NASA-INDUSTRY PROGRAM PLANS CONFERENCE.

NAS 1.18:CT   • **Item 830-F**
HANDBOOKS, MANUALS, GUIDES.

NAS 1.18/2:pt.nos./date   • **Item 830-F (MF)**
INDEX TO MANAGEMENT ISSUANCES.

NAS 1.18/3:date   • **Item 830-F (MF)**
PETITIONS FOR PATENT WAIVER. 1966–
[Irregular] (Includes basic manual plus supple-
mentary materials for an indefinite period)

    Gives findings of fact and recommendations
of NASA Inventions and Contributions Board.

NAS 1.19:nos.   • **Item 830-G (MF)**
EDUCATIONAL PROGRAM, EP- (series). 1–   1961–
[Irregular] (Office of Educational Programs and
Services)

    Includes handbooks, bibliographies, etc.

NAS 1.19/2:date   • **Item 830-G-1**
NASA AERONAUTICS RESEARCH AND TECHNOL-
OGY, ANNUAL REPORT. [Annual]

PURPOSE– To present research highlights
and technical accomplishments under the NASA
Aeronautics Research and Technology Program
as well as glimpses of future research.

NAS 1.19/3:nos.   • **Item 830-H-20**
EDUCATIONAL BRIEFS FOR THE MIDDLE AND
SECONDARY LEVEL CLASSROOM. [Irregular]

NAS 1.19/4   • **Item 830-G-2 (MF)**
EG (series).

NAS 1.20:letters   • **Item 830-H (EL)**
NASA FACTS. 1–   [Irregular]

    Each issue describes a NASA program (Apollo,
Lunar Orbiter, etc.) or discusses a technique
(The Laser, Living in Space, etc.). Some are wall
display sheets.

NAS 1.21:nos.   • **Item 830-I**
SPECIAL PUBLICATIONS. SP 1–   [Irregular]

NAS 1.21:7011   • **Item 830-J-1 (MF)**
AEROSPACE MEDICINE AND BIOLOGY, A CON-
TINUING BIBLIOGRAPHY WITH INDEXES.
[Monthly]

NAS 1.21:7037   • **Item 830-J-2**
AERONAUTICAL ENGINEERING, A CONTINUING
BIBLIOGRAPHY WITH INDEXES. [Monthly]

NAS 1.21:7038   • **Item 830-J-11 (MF)**
SIGNIFICANT NASA INVENTIONS AVAILABLE
FOR LICENSING IN FOREIGN COUNTRIES.

    Includes abstracts of those inventions in
which NASA owns the principal or exclusive
rights and which have been made available in
the countries indicated.

NAS 1.21:7039   • **Item 830-J-3**
NASA PATENT ABSTRACTS BIBLIOGRAPHY.
[Semiannual]

NAS 1.21:7041   • **Item 830-J-4**
EARTH RESOURCES, A CONTINUING BIBLIO-
GRAPHY WITH INDEXES. [Quarterly]

NAS 1.21:7046   • **Item 830-J-9**
TECHNOLOGY FOR LARGE SPACE SYSTEMS,
A BIBLIOGRAPHY WITH INDEXES. [Semian-
nual]

    A selection of annotated references to
unclassified reports and journal articles that
were introduced into the NASA scientific and
technical information system during the six
month period.

NAS 1.21:7048   • **Item 830-J-8**
DATA BASES AND DATA BASE SYSTEMS, A
BIBLIOGRAPHY WITH INDEXES. [Irregular]

    A selection of annotated references to
unclassified reports and journal articles introduced into the NASA scientific and technical
information system in Scientific and Technical Aerospace Reports and International Aerospace Abstracts.

NAS 1.21:7063:nos.   • **Item 830-J-12 (MF)**
NASA SCIENTIFIC AND TECHNICAL PUBLICA-
TIONS.

    A catalog of special publications, refer-
ence publications, conference publications
and technical papers. Presents citations for
each of these publications.

NAS 1.21:7064   • **Item 830-J-7**
NASA THESAURUS SUPPLEMENT.

NAS 1.21:7085   • **Item 830-J-9**
LARGE SPACE STRUCTURES AND SYSTEMS IN
THE SPACE STATION ERA, A BIBLIOGRAPHY
WITH INDEXES. [Semiannual]

    This publication merges two NASA Spe-
cial Publications, NASA SP-7046 and NASA
SP-7056.

NAS 1.21:7500   • **Item 830-J-6**
MANAGEMENT, A CONTINUING BIBLIOGRAPHY
WITH INDEXES. [Annual]

NAS 1.22:nos.   • **Item 830-M**
QUALITY PUBLICATIONS, NPC 200 (series). 1–
1962–   [Irregular]

NAS 1.22:343   • **Item 830-M**
RINGS OF SATURN. 1974. 232 p. il.

    Contains the proceedings of a sympo-
sium held in July and August, 1973, on the
nature, physical properties, and potential
danger to spacecraft from the rings around
the planet Saturn. The symposium was held
after new evidence was found concerning the
content and possible hazards of these rings.
Participants included scientists involved with
the Mariner Jupiter-Saturn team, which will
send a probe in 1977.

NAS 1.22/2:nos.   • **Item 830-M**
RELIABILITY PUBLICATIONS, NPC 250 (series). 1–
1963–   [Irregular]

NAS 1.22/3:nos.   • **Item 830-M (MF)**
RELIABILITY AND QUALITY ASSURANCE PUBLICA-
TIONS, NHB- (series). [Irregular]

NAS 1.23:Les-nos.   • **Item 830-L**
AEROSPACE LEAFLETS, AL- (series). [Irregular] (Office of Educational Programs and Services)

NAS 1.24:date   • **Item 830-L-1 (MF)**
TELEPHONE DIRECTORY. HEADQUARTERS, WASH-
INGTON, D.C. [Quarterly]

    ISSN 0364-2488

NAS 1.24/2:date
TELEPHONE DIRECTORY. GODDARD SPACE FLIGHT
CENTER, GREENBELT, MD. [Semiannual]

NAS 1.24/3:date   • **Item 830-L-1 (MF)**
TELEPHONE DIRECTORY, KENNEDY SPACE CEN-
TER. [Semiannual]

NAS 1.24/4:   • **Item 830-Z-1**
NASA STI DIRECTORY.

NAS 1.26:nos.   • **Item 830-H-14 (MF)**
CONTRACTOR REPORTS. CR 1–   [Irregular]

    Published in microfiche.

NAS 1.27:nos.
TECHNICAL REPRINTS, RP- (series). [Irregular]

    Reprints of technical articles appearing in tech-
nical journals.

NAS 1.28:v.nos.&nos.
GODDARD SPACE FLIGHT CENTER, TECHNICAL
ABSTRACTS.

NAS 1.28/2:date
GEORGE C. MARSHALL SPACE FLIGHT CENTER:
QUARTERLY ABSTRACTS.

NAS 1.29:nos.
NASA TECH BRIEFS. [Irregular]

    PURPOSE:– To acquaint industry with the
technical content of innovations derived from
NASA space program.

NAS 1.29/2:nos.
AEC-NASA TECH BRIEFS. 1966–   [Irregular]

    Descriptions of innovations resulting from re-
search and development program of the Atomic
Energy Commission or joint AEC- NASA research
efforts.

NAS 1.29/3:v.nos.&nos.   • **Item 830-L-2**
NASA TECH BRIEFS. v. 1–   1976–   [Quarterly]

    ISSN 0145-319X

NAS 1.29/3-2:date-nos.   • **Item 830-L-2 (MF)**
NASA TECH BRIEFS (condensed version). [Monthly]

NAS 1.30 • Item 830-A-3 (MF)
NASA ANNUAL PROCUREMENT REPORT. [Annual] (Office of Procurement)

NAS 1.31:nos.
NASA HISTORICAL REPORTS.

NAS 1.32:v.nos.&nos.
SPEAKING OF SPACE & AERONAUTICS. v. 1–
1965– [Irregular] (Office of Public Affairs, Education Programs and Services Office)

Current, significant material relating to U.S. program to provide information for the educational community and general public. Includes reprints of speeches given by NASA officials.

NAS 1.33:date • Item 830-P
SPACE SCIENCE AND APPLICATIONS PROGRAM. [Annual]

NAS 1.34:date • Item 830-Q
PUBLICATIONS OF GODDARD SPACE FLIGHT CENTER, 1959– 62. v. 1– 1966– [Irregular]

v. 1. Space Sciences. 1966.
v. 2. Space Technology. 1967.

NAS 1.35:v.nos.&nos.
RELIABILITY ABSTRACTS AND TECHNICAL REVIEWS. v. 1– [Monthly]

Technical reviews prepared by Research Triangle Institute and indexes prepared by NASA Scientific and Technical Information Facility operated by Documentation, Inc.

NAS 1.36:date • Item 830-S
NASA BITS [Brief Ideas, Thoughts, Suggestions]. 1967– [Semiannual]

NAS 1.37:nos. • Item 830-T (MF) (EL)
NATIONAL SPACE SCIENCE DATA CENTER, NSSDC- (series).

Earlier title: Data Catalog, Satellite and Rocket Experiments, SSDA-.

NAS 1.37/2:nos. • Item 830-Z-1 (EL)
NATIONAL SPACE SCIENCE DATA CENTER: NEWSLETTER. [Bimonthly]

NAS 1.38:nos.
C (series). [Irregular]

NAS 1.39:nos.
PLANS OFFICE TECHNICAL REPORTS. (Goddard Space Center)

NAS 1.40:v.nos.&nos. • Item 830-A-7 (MF)
SATELLITE SITUATION REPORT. v. 1– [Quarterly] (Goddard Space Flight Center)

Tables present data on objects in orbit computed at Goddard Space Flight Center, NORAD, Greenbelt, Maryland, or provided by satellite owners.
ISSN 0581-8540

NAS 1.41:date • Item 830-U
RESEARCH AND TECHNOLOGY PROGRAM DIGEST, FLASH INDEX. [Annual] (Advanced Research and Technology)

NAS 1.42:date • Item 830-V
NASA'S UNIVERSITY PROGRAM, QUARTERLY REPORT OF ACTIVE GRANTS AND RESEARCH CONTRACTS. [Annual]

Previous to FY 1973, issued quarterly.

NAS 1.42/2:date • Item 830-A-6 (MF)
GRADUATE STUDENT RESEARCHERS PROGRAM. [Annual]

PURPOSE:– To describe administrative procedures and research activities under the Graduate Student Researchers Program at NASA Headquarters and also at NASA Centers.

NAS 1.43:CT • Item 830-H-6
POSTERS. [Irregular]

Formerly distributed to Depository Libraries under Item Number 830-C

NAS 1.43/2:nos.
NASA PICTURE SETS. 1– 1969–

NAS 1.43/3:letters-nos.
LUNAR CHARTS.

Earlier D 301.49/4

NAS 1.43/4 • Item 830-H-2
SPACE PHOTOGRAPHY INDEX. [Annual]

NAS 1.43/5:nos. • Item 830-H-6
VIKING PICTURE SETS. [Irregular]

NAS 1.43/6:CT • Item 830-H-6
LITHOS (series). [Irregular]

NAS 1.43/7:CT
AUDIOVISUAL MATERIALS. [Irregular]

NAS 1.44:v.nos.&nos. • Item 830-X
COMPUTER PROGRAM ABSTRACTS. v. 1– 1969– [Quarterly] (Office of Technology Utilization)

PURPOSE:– To provide an indexed abstract journal listing documented computer programs developed by or for the National Aeronautics and Space Administration, the Department of Defense, and the Atomic Energy Commission, which are for sale through NASA-sponsored Regional Dissemination Centers and the Computer Software Management and Information Center.
Contains program citations and abstracts arranged in subject categories, and five indexes: subject, originating source, program number/accession number, accession number/program number, and equipment requirements.
ISSN 0045-785X

NAS 1.44/2 • Item 830-X
– CUMULATIVE ISSUES.

NAS 1.45:nos. • Item 830-Y
MISSION REPORTS. MR 1– 1968– [Irregular]

Informal description, written in non-technical style, to report on particular mission and its results.

NAS 1.46:v.nos.&nos. • Item 830-H-1
NASA ACTIVITIES. v. 1– 1970– [Monthly]

PURPOSE:– To provide a newsletter for all NASA personnel, especially at supervisory and administrative levels, to keep them informed of important developments in the space program.
Contents cover significant space statement, legislative affairs, and such general activity of NASA as agreements, key awards, radio-television programs, new films, new publications, press releases, personnel changes, calendar of events, current launch schedule, and month lists of tech briefs, patents resulting from NASA research, and monetary awards for inventions and contributions.
Discontinued.

NAS 1.47 • Item 830-Z
ANNUAL EARTH RESOURCES PROGRAM REVIEW.

EARTH RESOURCES TECHNOLOGY SATELLITE: STANDARD CATALOG.

PURPOSE:– To provide dissemination of information regarding the availability of Earth Resources Technology Satellite imagery. The catalogs identify imagery which has been processed and input to the data files during the preceding month.
In addition to the routine monthly catalogs, the NDPF periodically publishes a comprehensive U.S. and Non-U.S. Standard Catalog. These catalogs include information on all observations acquired and processed by the facility since launch and are normally published in lieu of one of the monthly catalogs.

A monthly U.S. and Non-U.S. Standard Catalogs are divided into four parts. Part 1 consists of annotated maps which graphically depict the geographic areas covered by imagery listed in the current catalog. Part 2 contains a computer generated listing organized by observation identification number (ID) and includes pertinent information about each image. Part 3 provides a computer listing of observations organized by longitude/latitude. Part 4 identifies observations which have had changes made to their catalog information since their original entry in the data base.

NAS 1.48:nos. • Item 830-H-7
LANDSAT: U.S. STANDARD CATALOG. [Monthly] (Goddard Space Flight Center)

Covers the continental United States, Alaska, and Hawaii.
Not numbered prior to U-3, November 30, 1972.
ISSN 0364-7560

NAS 1.48/2:nos. • Item 830-H-7
LANDSAT: NON-U.S. STANDARD CATALOG. [Monthly] (Goddard Space Flight Center)

Not numbered prior to N-3, November 30, 1972.
ISSN 0364-7587

NAS 1.48/3:date • Item 830-H-7
LANDSAT 2, WORLD STANDARD CATALOG. [Monthly]

Combines Landsat U.S. Standard Catalog (NAS 1.48) and Landsat Non-U.S. Standard Catalog (NAS 1.48/2).
Published in microfiche.

NAS 1.48/4:date • Item 830-H-7
LANDSAT 3, WORLD STANDARD CATALOG. [Monthly]

Combines Landsat U.S. Catalog (NAS 1.48) and Landsat Non-U.S. Standard Catalog (NAS 1.48/2).
Published in microfiche.

NAS 1.49:v.nos.&nos. • Item 830-H-4
NASA REPORT TO EDUCATORS. v. 1– 1973– [4 times a year]

ISSN 0092-346X
Discontinued.

NAS 1.49/2:nos. • Item 830-H-4
EDUCATIONAL HORIZONS. [Three times a year]

NAS 1.50:CT
MAPS.

NAS 1.51:v.nos.&nos.
SPACE SCIENCE AND TECHNOLOGY TODAY (series).

NAS 1.52:date • Item 856-D (P) (EL)
AERONAUTICS AND SPACE ACTIVITIES, REPORT TO CONGRESS. [Annual]

Also issued in House Documents series.
Earlier PrEx 5.9

NAS 1.53:nos. • Item 830-H-5 (MF)
ANNOUNCEMENT OF OPPORTUNITIES FOR PARTICIPATION. AO 1– 1974– [Irregular]

NAS 1.53/2:date • Item 830-H-5
SPACE SCIENCE NOTICES.

NAS 1.53/3:nos. • Item 830-H-5 (EL)
RESEARCH ANNOUNCEMENT.

NAS 1.54:date
MANNED SPACE FLIGHT RESOURCES SUMMARY, BUDGET ESTIMATES. [Annual]

NAS 1.55:nos. • Item 830-H-10 (MF)
CONFERENCE PUBLICATIONS, NASA CP-(series). [Irregular]

NAS 1.56:nos. • Item 830-H-8
NEW PRODUCT IDEAS, PROCESS IMPROVEMENTS, AND COST-SAVING TECHNIQUES, RELATING TO [various subjects], NASA/SBA FA- (series). 1– [Irregular]

NAS 1.57:date
NASA MISHAP AND INJURY DATA. [Annual]

Title varies: Report of Accident/Injury Statistics and Mishap recapitulation; and Accident and Injury Data.

NAS 1.58:date
REPORT TO THE ADMINISTRATOR BY THE NASA AEROSPACE SAFETY ADVISORY PANEL. [Annual]

NAS 1.59:CT • Item 830-H-17 (MF)
ENVIRONMENTAL IMPACT STATEMENTS. [Irregular]

NAS 1.60:nos. • Item 830-H-15 (MF)
TECHNICAL PAPERS. 1– [Irregular]

Published in microfiche.
Supersedes Technical Notes (NAS 1.14) and Technical Reports (NAS 1.12).

NAS 1.61:nos. • Item 830-H-11 (MF)
REFERENCE PUBLICATIONS, RP- (series). [Irregular]

NAS 1.62:nos. • Item 830-H-18
LIFE SCIENCES STATUS REPORTS. 1– [Irregular]

PURPOSE:– To present summaries of Life Science Division and NASA experiments, activities, etc., of interest to life scientists and others concerned with NASA research.

NAS 1.62/2:date • Item 830-C-5
LIFE SCIENCES ACCOMPLISHMENTS. [Annual]

PURPOSE:– To describe and illustrate accomplishments of NASA's multidisciplinary Life Sciences program in such areas as space physiology and medicine and biological research.
Earlier NAS 1.15

NAS 1.62/3: • Item 830-C-5
LIFE SCIENCES REPORT. [Annual]

NAS 1.63:nos. • Item 830-K-2
UPPER ATMOSPHERIC PROGRAMS BULLETIN. [Bimonthly]

Funded jointly by the NASA Upper Atmospheric Research Program and the Federal Aviation Administration, High Altitude Pollution Program.
Published to facilitate and encourage communications among the scientific experiments, conferences, and courses as well as abstracts of technical papers.

NAS 1.64:CT • Item 830-K-1 (MF)
EARTH RESOURCES SATELLITE DATA APPLICATIONS SERIES. [Irregular]

Provides information on the disciplinary, functional, and educational uses of earth resources satellites in modular form. For example, universal modules may relate to such subjects as processing and analyzing Landsat data; data use modules to mineral and petroleum resources exploration; and applications manuals, to geological resources, mapping and sitting.

NAS 1.65:date • Item 830-A-2
RESEARCH AND TECHNOLOGY, ANNUAL REPORT. (Earth Resources Laboratory)

Presents major accomplishments of the Earth Resources Laboratory for the preceding year.

NAS 1.65/2:date • Item 830-A-2 (EL)
RESEARCH AND TECHNOLOGY FISCAL YEAR (date) ANNUAL REPORT OF THE GODDARD SPACE FLIGHT CENTER.

NAS 1.65/3: • Item 830-A-8 (MF)
RESEARCH AND TECHNOLOGY, ANNUAL REPORT OF THE LANGLEY RESEARCH CENTER.

PURPOSE– To summarize activities and accomplishments of the Langley Research Center in its research on Aeronautics, Electronics, Flight Systems, Systems Engineering Operations, and technology utilization.

NAS 1.66:date • Item 830-L-53 (MF)
SPACE BENEFITS: SECONDARY APPLICATION OF AEROSPACE TECHNOLOGY IN OTHER SECTORS OF THE ECONOMY. [Annual]

NAS 1.67:nos.
LUNAR AND PLANETARY INSTITUTE: TECHNICAL REPORTS. [Irregular]

NAS 1.68:nos. • Item 830-H-19 (MF)
AIRBORNE INSTRUMENTATION RESEARCH PROJECT SUMMARY CATALOG.

NAS 1.69: • Item 830-H-20 (EL)
NASA EDUCATIONAL BRIEFS FOR THE CLASSROOM (series). [Irregular]

Single-page releases, each devoted to a single subject.

NAS 1.70:date • Item 830-A-4 (MF)
RENEWABLE RESOURCES REMOTE SENSING RESEARCH PROGRAM REPORT. [Annual]

Summarizes Renewable Resources Remote Sensing research and analysis activity, which encompasses a variety of remote sensing science and related discipline science investigations.

NAS 1.71: • Item 830-J-10 (MF)
NASA PATENTS

PURPOSE:– To present applications for patents within NASA.

NAS 1.72:date • Item 830-C-2 (MF)
INTERNATIONAL HALLEY WATCH NEWSLETTER. [Irregular]

Contains the International Halley Watch, which was established to maximize the scientific value of ground-based and space studies of Comet Halley.

NAS 1.73:nos. • Item 830-C-1
HEALTH BULLETINS (series). [Irregular]

Each bulletin covers a different subject. Issued in connection with NASA's Occupational Medicine Program.

NAS 1.74:nos. • Item 830-C-3
PUBLIC MAIL SERIES, PMS- (series). [Irregular]

Each Information Summary deals with a different NASA topic.

NAS 1.75 • Item 830-C-4
PAMPHLETS (series). [Irregular]

Pamphlets on miscellaneous topics pertaining to the NASA mission.

NAS 1.76 • Item 830-Z-1 (EL)
STI BULLETIN. [Monthly]

Earlier title: STI-Recon Bulletin and Tech Info News.

NAS 1.77: • Item 830-H-21 (MF)
TECHNICAL TRANSLATIONS (NUMBERED).

Translations of non-English reports, conference papers, and journal articles of interest to the NASA scientific and technical program.

NAS 1.78: • Item 830-C-6
NASA EXCELLENCE AWARD FOR QUALITY AND PRODUCTIVITY. [Annual]

PURPOSE:– To summarize activities in connection with the NASA Excellence Award for Quality and Productivity, which is designed to recognize those companies which have achieved and demonstrated accomplishments in quality and productivity.

NAS 1.79: • Item 830-C-7
KEY DATES. [Annual]

A calendar for the current year with each day referring to a space related historical event. The verso of each month shows key events of each year beginning with 1957, the beginning of the space age. The main themes of the 1988 calendar are discoverers and discoveries.

NAS 1.80:date • Item 830-H-23 (MF)
SPACE MICROELECTRONICS. [Semiannual]

PURPOSE– To summarizes the activities of the Jet Propulsion Laboratory's Center for Space Microelectronics Technology, which was established to meet the growing demands of NASA and DoD for new microelectronics technology for space missions.

NAS 1.81:date • Item 830-A-7
PAYLOAD FLIGHT ASSIGNMENTS NASA MIXED FLEET. [Quarterly]

NAS 1.82:nos. • Item 830-I (MF)
NASA STD (Series).

NAS 1.83:nos. • Item 830-I
NASA NP (series).

NAS 1.84 • Item 830-I
NASA PED (series). [Irregular]

NAS 1.85:date • Item 830-A-1 (MF)
NASA BUDGET ESTIMATES. [Annual]

NAS 1.86 • Item 830-Z-1 (E)
ELECTRONIC PRODUCTS. [Irregular]

NAS 1.86/2:nos. • Item 830-Z-2 (CD)
MAGELLAN FULL-RESOLUTION RADAR MOSAICS.

NAS 1.86/3:letters • Item 830-Z-3(CD) (EL)
INTERNATIONAL SOLAR-TERRESTRIAL PHYSICS PROGRAM.

NAS 1.87:date • Item 830-C-2 (MF)
NASA MAGAZINE. [Quarterly]

NAS 1.89:nos. • Item 830-C-5
CALLBACK FROM NASA'S AVIATION SAFETY REPORTING SYSTEM.

NAS 1.90:nos. • Item 830-C-7
NASA INFORMATION SUMMARIES.

NAS 1.90/2 • Item 830-C-10 (EL)
NASA INFORMATION SYSTEMS NEWSLETTER.

NAS 1.91 • Item 830-C-6
DISCOVERY, THE NEWSLETTER OF THE SOLAR SYSTEM EXPLORATION DIVISION.

NAS 1.92:v.nos./nos. • Item 830-C-9
MICROGRAVITY NEWS. [Quarterly]

NAS 1.93:date/nos. • Item 830-C-11
ACTS QUARTERLY, LEWIS RESEARCH CENTER.

ACTS = Advanced Communications Technology Satellite.

NAS 1.94:date • Item 830-C-12 (EL)
INSIGHTS, HIGH PERFORMANCE COMPUTER AND COMMUNICATIONS. [Quarterly]

NAS 1.95 • Item 830-Z-1 (EL)
AEROSPACE TECHNOLOGY INNOVATION.

NAS 1.96:date • Item 830-Z-1 (EL)
NASA HISTORY: NEWS AND NOTES. [Quarterly]

NAS 1.97 • Item 830-C-13 (EL)
GRIDPOINTS. (Quarterly)

NATIONAL CAPITAL PARK AND PLANNING COMMISSION
(1926– 1952)

CREATION AND AUTHORITY

The National Capital Park and Planning Commission was established by act of Congress approved April 30, 1926 (44 Stat. 374). The Commission was succeeded by the National Capital Planning Commission (NC 2), established by the act of Congress approved July 19, 1952 (66 Stat. 781).

NC 1.1:date
ANNUAL REPORTS.

NC 1.2:CT
GENERAL PUBLICATIONS.

NC 1.3
BULLETINS.

NC 1.4
CIRCULARS.

NC 1.7:nos.
MONOGRAPHS.

NATIONAL CAPITAL PLANNING COMMISSION
(1952–   )

CREATION AND AUTHORITY

The National Capital Planning Commission was created by Public Law 592, approved July 19, 1952, and designated as the central planning agency for the Federal and District Governments to plan the approximate and orderly development and redevelopment of the national capital and conservation of the important natural and historical features thereof. It is the successor to three earlier agencies: the Highway Commission of D.C., the National Capital Park Commission, and National Capital Park and Planning Commission (NC 1).

INFORMATION

Office of Public Affairs
National Capital Planning Commission
401 Ninth St. NW
North Lobby, Ste. 500
Washington, DC 20576
(202) 482-7200
Fax: (202) 482-7272
E-Mail:info@ncpc.gov
http://www.ncpc.gov

NC 2.1:date • Item 831-A-2 (MF) (EL)
ANNUAL REPORTS.

NC 2.2:CT • Item 831-A-1
GENERAL PUBLICATIONS.

NC 2.2:P 69/2/date • Item 831-A
COMPREHENSIVE PLAN FOR THE NATIONAL CAPITAL. [Irregular] (Includes basic manual plus supplementary material for an indefinite period)

NC 2.8:CT
HANDBOOKS, MANUALS, GUIDES. [Irregular]

NC 2.9:CT
BIBLIOGRAPHIES AND LISTS OF PUBLICATIONS.

NC 2.10:nos.
INFORMATIONAL SERIES, REPORTS.

NC 2.11:date • Item 831-A (EL)
QUARTERLY REVIEW OF COMMISSION PROCEEDINGS.

ISSN 0098-308X

NC 2.11/2 • Item 831-A-3 (EL)
NCPC QUARTERLY (NATIONAL CAPITAL PLANNING COMMISSION NEWSLETTER).

NC 2.12:date
TENTATIVE AGENDA ITEMS. [Monthly]

NATIONAL CAPITAL REGIONAL PLANNING COUNCIL
(1952– 1966)

CREATION AND AUTHORITY

The National Capital Regional Planning Council was established by Public Law 592, 83rd Congress, 2nd session, approved July 19, 1952. The Council was abolished by Reorganization Plan 5 of 1966, effective September 8, 1966.

NC 3.1:date • Item 831-A
REPORT.

NC 3.2:CT • Item 831-A
GENERAL PUBLICATIONS.

NC 3.8:CT • Item 831-A
HANDBOOKS, MANUALS, GUIDES.

NC 3.9:nos.
NATIONAL CAPITAL OPEN-SPACE PROJECT: TECHNICAL REPORTS. 1– 1963–

NC 3.9/2:nos.
NATIONAL CAPITAL OPEN SPACE PROGRAM: PLANNING REPORTS.

NATIONAL CREDIT UNION ADMINISTRATION
(1970–   )

CREATION AND AUTHORITY

The National Credit Union Administration was established as an independent agency by Public Law 91-206, approved March 10, 1970, to succeed the Bureau of Federal Credit Unions.

INFORMATION

Office of Public and Congressional Affairs
National Credit Union Administration
1775 Duke St.
Alexandria, VA 22314
(703) 518-6330

NCU 1.1:date • Item 525 (EL)
ANNUAL REPORT.

Earlier FS 3.301

NCU 1.1/2:date • Item 525-B (MF)
STATE CHARTERED CREDIT UNIONS, ANNUAL REPORT.

NCU 1.1/3:date • Item 525
ANNUAL REPORT OF ADMINISTRATOR.

NCU 1.1/4:date • Item 527-D (MF)
ADMINISTRATOR'S ANNUAL FINANCIAL REPORT.

NCU 1.2:CT • Item 526
GENERAL PUBLICATIONS.

Earlier FS 3.302

NCU 1.3:v.nos.&nos. • Item 525-A
BULLETIN. [Quarterly]

ISSN 0090-7863
Earlier FS 3.303
Superseded by NCUA Quarterly (NCU 1.3/2)

NCU 1.3/2:v.nos.&nos. • Item 525-A
NCUA QUARTERLY. v. 1– 1973–

PURPOSE:– To provide a source for notices of rulemaking, results of statistical analyses, and news of interest to officials of the National Credit Union Administration.
Supersedes NCUA Bulletin (NCU 1.3)
ISSN 0090-7863

NCU 1.5:CT • Item 526-A
LAWS.

NCU 1.6:CT • Item 527
REGULATIONS, RULES, AND INSTRUCTIONS.

Earlier FS 2.305

NCU 1.6:R 86 • Item 527
NATIONAL CREDIT UNION ADMINISTRATION RULES AND REGULATIONS. March 1972. (Includes basic manual plus supplemental material for an indefinite period)

NCU 1.6/a:nos. • Item 527
ADVANCE COPY PROPOSED RULES AND REGULATIONS.

NCU 1.6/2 • Item 526-D-1 (EL)
REGULATORY ALERT.

NCU 1.8:CT • Item 526-B
HANDBOOKS, MANUALS, GUIDES.

NCU 1.8:St 2/2 • Item 526-B
MANUAL OF LAWS AFFECTING FEDERALLY INSURED STATE CREDIT UNIONS. [Irregular] (Subscription includes basic manual plus supplementary service for an indefinite period)

NCU 1.8/2:date
MANUAL OF LAWS AFFECTING FEDERAL CREDIT UNIONS. [Irregular] (Subscription includes basic manual plus supplementary service for an indefinite period)

NCU 1.9:v.nos.&nos.
CREDIT UNION STATISTICS. [Monthly]

ISSN 0364-1384
Earlier FS 3.310

NCU 1.9/2:date • Item 527-F (MF)
ANNUAL STATISTICS.

Consists of separate statistical tables on Federal Credit Unions and on Federally insured State Credit Unions showing assets, liabilities, investments, etc., of each group by region and State, by age or asset size, and by type of membership.

NCU 1.9/3:date • Item 527-F (MF)
MID-YEAR STATISTICS. [Annual]

NCU 1.9/3-2 • Item 527-F (MF)
MIDYEAR FINANCIAL & STATISTICAL REPORT.

NCU 1.10:nos. • Item 527-B
RESEARCH REPORTS.

Earlier FS 3.309

NCU 1.11:nos. • Item 527-C
WORKING PAPERS. 1– 1976– [Irregular]

NCU 1.12:date
NCUA REPORT. [Monthly]

NCU 1.13:v.nos.&nos. • Item 527-E
NCUA DIGEST. v. 1. 1979. [Irregular]

PURPOSE:– To provide news notes on credit union operations, official statements to Congress, interpretive rulings, regulations, etc., pertaining to insured credit unions. Includes statistical data. Intended for managers, credit organizations, etc.

NCU 1.14:date • Item 527-G (MF)
TELEPHONE DIRECTORY. [Irregular]

Consists of an organizational and regional directory of the Administration as well as a telephone listing of Federal Credit Unions in various departments of the government.

NCU 1.15:date • Item 527-E-1
NCUA REVIEW. [Bimonthly]

PURPOSE:– To provide information on Administration policies and programs with the reasoning behind its critical rules, regulations, and legal opinions. Designed primarily for those responsible for managing credit unions.
Discontinued with Februrary 1982 issue.

NCU 1.16 • Item 527-H (EL)
DIRECTORY OF FEDERALLY INSURED CREDIT UNIONS. [Annual]

Lists credit unions by States and cities, including address, number of members amount of shares (savings), amount of loans, and asset size.
Earlier title: Credit Union Directory.

NCU 1.17:date • Item 525
CENTRAL LIQUIDITY FACILITY: ANNUAL REPORT.

NCU 1.18:date • Item 525
NATIONAL CREDIT UNION SHARE INSURANCE FUND: ANNUAL REPORT.

NCU 1.19 • Item 526-C
NCUA LETTER TO CREDIT UNIONS. [Irregular]

Each letter deals with a different credit union topic.

NCU 1.20:date • Item 526-D (EL)
NCUA NEWS. [Monthly]

Presents news of activities of the National Credit Union Administration.

NCU 1.21:nos. • Item 526-C
RESEARCH STUDY (series). [Irregular]

NCU 1.22:nos. • Item 526-C
NCUA INVESTMENT REPORT (Series).

NCU 1.23 • Item 526-D-1 (E)
ELECTRONIC PRODUCTS. (Misc.)

NATIONAL FOUNDATION ON THE ARTS AND THE HUMANITIES (1965–   )

INFORMATION

National Foundation on the Arts
and the Humanities
1100 Pennsylvania Ave. NW
Washington, DC 20506

CREATION AND AUTHORITY

The National Foundation on the Arts and the Humanities was created as an independent agency by the National Foundation on the Arts and the Humanities Act of 1965 (79 Stat. 845; 20 U.S.C. 951 note). The Foundation consists of a National Endowment for the Arts, a National Endowment for the Humanities, and a Federal Council on the Arts and the Humanities. Each Endowment has its own Council, composed of the Endowment Chairman and 26 other members, which advises the Chairman with respect to policies and procedures and reviews applications for financial support and makes recommendations thereon.

The Federal Council on the Arts and the Humanities consists of nine members including the two Endowment Chairmen and is designed to coordinate the activities of the two Endowments and related programs of other Federal agencies.

NF 1.1:date • Item 831-B-3
REPORTS.

NF 1.2:CT • Item 831-B-3
GENERAL PUBLICATIONS.

NF 1.5:CT
LAWS.

NATIONAL ENDOWMENT FOR THE ARTS (1965–   )

INFORMATION

National Endowment for the Arts
1100 Pennsylvania Ave. NW
Washington, DC 20506
(202) 682-5400
Fax: (202) 682-5617
http://www.arts.endow.gov

NF 2.1:date • Item 831-B-2
ANNUAL REPORT. 1st–   1967–   [Annual]

Covers the activities of the National Endowment for the Arts and the National Council on the Arts for the fiscal year. Also includes a list of grants and contracts awarded, by art form, and list of grantees.

NF 2.2:CT • Item 831-B-2
GENERAL PUBLICATIONS.

NF 2.8:CT • Item 831-B-2
HANDBOOKS, MANUALS, GUIDES.

NF 2.8/2:date • Item 831-B-2
ARTISTS IN EDUCATION. [Annual]

NF 2.8/2-2:date • Item 831-B-2
LITERATURE, APPLICATION GUIDELINES. [Annual]

NF 2.8/2-3:date • Item 831-B-2
CHALLENGE GRANTS APPLICATION GUIDELINES. [Annual]

NF 2.8/2-4:date • Item 831-B-2
DANCE, APPLICATION GUIDELINES. [Annual]

NF 2.8/2-5 • Item 831-B-2
MUSIC PROFESSIONAL TRAINING CAREER DEVELOPMENT ORGANIZATIONS MUSIC RECORDING SERVICES TO COMPOSERS SPECIAL PROJECTS MUSIC.

Formerly Music Professional Training Career Development Organizations Music Recording Services to Composers Center for New Music Resources Special Projects.

NF 2.8/2-6:date • Item 831-B-2
THEATER/APPLICATION GUIDELINES. [Annual]
Earlier NF 2.8:T 34/2

NF 2.8/2-7:date • Item 831-B-2
MUSEUMS, APPLICATION GUIDELINES FY (year). [Annual]

NF 2.8/2-8:date • Item 831-B-2
MUSIC FELLOWSHIPS: COMPOSERS, JAZZ, SOLO RECITALISTS, APPLICATIONS GUIDELINES.

NF 2.8/2-9:date • Item 831-B-2
PRESENTERS AND FESTIVALS JAZZ MANAGEMENT, JAZZ SPECIAL PROJECTS, MUSIC, APPLICATION GUIDELINES, FISCAL YEAR (date).

Earlier: Music Presenters and Festivals Jazz Management and Special Reports.

NF 2.8/2-10:date • Item 831-B-2
MEDIA ARTS: FILM/RADIO/TELEVISION, APPLICATION GUIDELINES. [Annual]

NF 2.8/2-11:date • Item 831-B-4
DESIGN ARTS, APPLICATION GUIDELINES, FISCAL YEAR. [Annual]
Earlier NF 2.8:D 46

NF 2.8/2-12:date • Item 831-B-2
OPERA-MUSICAL THEATER, APPLICATION GUIDELINES. [Annual]
Earlier NF 2.8:Op 2/2

NF 2.8/2-13:date • Item 831-B-4
VISUAL ARTISTS FELLOWSHIPS. [Annual]

Earlier NF 2.8/2-13

NF 2.8/2-14:date • Item 831-B-2
MUSIC ENSEMBLES CHAMBER MUSIC, NEW MUSIC/JAZZ ENSEMBLES, CHORUSES, ORCHESTRAS/COMPOSER IN RESIDENCE, CONSORTIUM COMMISSIONING, APPLICATION GUIDELINES. [Annual]

NF 2.8/2-15:date • Item 831-B-2
ORGANIZATIONS VISUAL ARTS, APPLICATION GUIDELINES. [Annual]

Earlier: Visual Arts Grants to Organizations.

NF 2.8/2-16:date • Item 831-B-2
FOLK ARTS. [Annual]

Earlier NF 2.8:F 71

NF 2.8/2-17:date • Item 831-B-4
STATE PROGRAMS. [Annual]

Earlier NF 2.8:St 2

NF 2.8/2-18:date • Item 831-B-2
EXPANSION ARTS. [Irregular]

Earlier NF 2.8:Ex 7

NF 2.8/2-19:date • Item 831-B-4
ADVANCEMENT, APPLICATION GUIDELINES. [Annual]

NF 2.8/2-20:date • Item 831-B-2
CHALLENGE III GRANTS, APPLICATION GUIDELINES. [Annual]

NF 2.8/2-21:date • Item 831-B-2
LOCAL PROGRAMS, APPLICATION GUIDELINES. [Annual]

NF 2.8/2-22:date
INITIATIVE FOR INTERDISCIPLINARY ARTISTS INTER-ARTS. [Annual]

NF 2.8/2-23:date • Item 831-B-4
INTER-ARTS, PRESENTING ORGANIZATIONS ARTIST COMMUNITIES SERVICES TO THE ARTS, APPLICATION GUIDELINES. [Annual]

NF 2.8/2-24:date • Item 831-B-10
ARTS ADMINISTRATION FELLOWS PROGRAM, APPLICATION GUIDELINE FOR FISCAL YEAR.

NF 2.8/2-26:date • Item 831-B-2
INTER-ARTS, ARTISTS' PROJECTS: NEW FORMS. [Annual]

NF 2.8/2-28 • Item 831-B-4
ARTS IN AMERICA.

NF 2.8/2-29:date • Item 831-B-4
GRANTS TO PRESENTING ORGANIZATIONS, SPECIAL TOURING INITIATIVES APPLICATION GUIDELINES (Fiscal Year).

NF 2.8/2-30:date • Item 831-B-4
THEATER, SUPPORT TO INDIVIDUALS. [Annual]

NF 2.8/2-31:date • Item 831-B-4
LOCAL ARTS AGENCIES PROGRAM, APPLICATION GUIDELINES.

NF 2.8/2-32:date • Item 831-B-4
INTERNATIONAL, APPLICATION GUIDELINES FOR FISCAL YEAR.

NF 2.8/2-33:date • Item 831-B-4
SUPPORT TO ORGANIZATIONS THEATER.

NF 2.8/2-34 • Item 831-B-4
INTERNATIONAL APPLICATION GUIDELINES, INTERNATIONAL PROGRAM: FELLOWSHIPS AND RESIDENCIES PARTNERSHIPS.

NF 2.8/2-35 • Item 831-B-4
INTERNATIONAL APPLICATION GUIDELINES, INTERNATIONAL PROGRAM: INTERNATIONAL PROJECTS INITIATIVE FOR ORGANIZATIONS PARTNERSHIPS.

NF 2.8/2-36:date • Item 831-B-11
FOLK AND TRADITIONAL ARTS, APPLICATION GUIDELINES FOR FISCAL YEARS.

NF 2.8/2-37:date • Item 831-B-12
ARTS IN EDUCATION, ARTS PLUS, APPLICATION GUIDELINES FOR FISCAL YEAR. [Annual]

NF 2.9:nos.
FEDERAL DESIGN MATTERS. 1– 26. 1974– 1981. [Irregular]

This service is a means of providing Federal agencies and design professionals in the private sector with information on the progress and accomplishments of the President's Federal Design Improvement Program.
Issn 0363-8812

NF 2.10:CT
FEDERAL DESIGN LIBRARY (series). [Irregular]

NF 2.11:v.nos.&nos.
CULTURAL POST. [Bimonthly]

Superseded by Arts Review (NF 2.13).

NF 2.12:nos.
RESEARCH DIVISION REPORTS. [Irregular]

NF 2.13:v.nos.&nos.
ARTS REVIEW. [Quarterly]

Covers the Endowment programs and policies, funding categories, activities of grantees, and issues in the arts.
Supersedes the Cultural Post (NF 2.11).

NF 2.14:v.nos/nos. • Item 831-B-2
ARTIFACTS. [Monthly]

NF 2.15 • Item 831-B-16
GRANTS TO ORGANIZATIONS, APPLICATION GUIDELINES. [Annual]

NF 2.15/2:date • Item 831-B-17
GRANTS TO ORGANIZATIONS, APPLICATION FORMS. [Annual]

NF 2.15/3:date • Item 831-B-22 (P) (EL)
ARTSREACH, APPLICATION GUIDELINES. [Annual]

NF 2.16:date • Item 831-B-18
LITERATURE FELLOWSHIP APPLICATION GUIDELINES. [Annual]

NF 2.17: • Item 831-B-21 (E)
ELECTRONIC PRODUCTS (misc.).

NATIONAL ENDOWMENT FOR THE HUMANITIES (1965–   )

INFORMATION
National Endowment for the Humanities
1100 Pennsylvania Ave. N.W.
Washington, D.C. 20506
(202) 606-8400
Toll-Free: (800) NEH-1121
E-Mail:info@neh.gov
http://www.neh.gov

NF 3.1 • Item 831-B-1
ANNUAL REPORT. 1st–   1966–   [Annual]

Gives a record of activities and accomplishments during the fiscal year. Also includes a directory of the National Council on the Humanities, the staff members of the Endowment, a financial report, and a list of grants and awards made during the year.

NF 3.2:CT • Item 831-B-1
GENERAL PUBLICATIONS.

NF 3.7:nos.
NEH NEWS.

NF 3.8:CT • Item 831-B-1
HANDBOOKS, MANUALS, GUIDES.

NF 3.8/2:date • Item 831-B-1
SUMMER STIPENDS, GUIDELINES AND APPLICATION FORMS. [Annual]

NF 3.8/2-2:date • Item 831-B-1
HUMANITIES PROJECTS IN LIBRARIES, GUIDELINES APPLICATION INSTRUCTIONS. [Annual]

NF 3.8/2-3:date • Item 831-B-1
PRESERVATION PROGRAMS GUIDELINES AND APPLICATION INSTRUCTIONS. [Annual]

NF 3.8/2-4:date • Item 831-B-1
CHALLENGE GRANTS PROGRAM GUIDELINES AND APPLICATION MATERIALS. [Annual]

Earlier NF 3.8:C 351

NF 3.8/2-5:date • Item 831-B-1
HUMANITIES PROJECTS IN MUSEUMS AND HISTORICAL ORGANIZATIONS. [Annual]

NF 3.8/2-6:date • Item 831-B-1
YOUNGER SCHOLARS. [Annual]

NF 3.8/2-7:date • Item 831-B-1
FACULTY GRADUATE STUDY PROGRAM FOR HISTORICALLY BLACK COLLEGES AND UNIVERSITIES. [Annual]

NF 3.8/2-8:date • Item 831-B-1
HISTORICALLY BLACK COLLEGES AND UNIVERSITIES, FACULTY PROJECTS, SUMMER COLLEGE HUMANITIES PROGRAMS FOR HIGH SCHOOL JUNIORS. [Annual]

NF 3.8/2-9:date • Item 831-B-1
PUBLIC HUMANITIES PROJECTS, GUIDELINES AND APPLICATION INSTRUCTIONS.

Earlier NF 3.2:P 96

NF 3.8/2-10:date • Item 831-B-1
HUMANITIES PROJECTS IN LIBRARIES AND ARCHIVES, GUIDELINES AND APPLICATIONS INSTRUCTIONS. [Annual]

NF 3.9:nos. • Item 831-B-1
OCCASIONAL PAPERS. 1–   1969–   [Irregular]

Includes surveys, studies, and programs in a particular field that have been supported by grants from the National Endowment for the Humanities.

NF 3.10:date • Item 831-B-1
HUMANITIES. 1969– 1978 [Quarterly]

Newsletter describing programs of special interest that the Endowment is supporting. It informs educators and others interested in the humanities of programs that might be adapted elsewhere, and stimulates the submission of meritorious proposals to the Endowment.

NF 3.11:v.nos.&nos. • Item 831-B-8 (EL)
HUMANITIES (2d series). January 1980–   [Bimonthly]

PURPOSE:– To describe National Endowment of the Humanities programs, projects, and issues in the humanities. Also gives information on recent grants, deadlines, and useful information for applicants seeking funds.
Replaces class NF 3.11, with title, Nonpartisan Review.

NF 3.12:CT • Item 831-B-5
POSTERS.

NF 3.13:CT • Item 831-B-1
SUMMER SEMINARS FOR COLLEGE TEACHERS, SEMINAR DESCRIPTIONS.

Previously classed in NF 3.2 and NF 3.8.

NF 3.13/2:date • Item 831-B-5
SUMMER SEMINARS FOR COLLEGE TEACHERS, GUIDELINES AND APPLICATION FORMS FOR DIRECTORS. [Annual]

NF 3.13/2-2:date • Item 831-B-5
SUMMER SEMINARS FOR COLLEGE TEACHERS GUIDELINES AND APPLICATION FORM FOR PARTICIPANTS. [Annual]

Earlier NF 3.13:C 68

NF 3.13/2-3:date • Item 831-B-5
SUMMER SEMINARS FOR COLLEGE TEACHERS. [Annual]

NF 3.13/3:date • Item 831-B-5
SUMMER SEMINARS FOR SECONDARY SCHOOL TEACHERS. [Annual]

Earlier NF 3.13:Se 2

NF 3.13/3-2:date • Item 831-B-7
SUMMER SEMINARS FOR SECONDARY SCHOOL TEACHERS GUIDELINES AND APPLICATIONS FORM FOR PARTICIPANTS. [Annual]

Earlier NF 3.13:Se 2

NF 3.13/3-3:date • Item 831-B-7
SUMMER SEMINARS FOR SECONDARY SCHOOL TEACHERS GUIDELINES AND APPLICATION FORM FOR DIRECTORS. [Annual]

NF 3.13/3-4:date • Item 831-B-5
SUMMER SEMINARS FOR SECONDARY SCHOOL TEACHERS, SEMINAR DESCRIPTIONS. [Annual]

NF 3.13/3-5:date • Item 831-B-13
SUMMER SEMINARS FOR DIRECTORS, FOR COLLEGE TEACHERS, FOR SCHOOL TEACHERS, GUIDELINES AND APPLICATION FORM FOR PARTICIPANTS. [Annual]

NF 3.13/3-6:date • Item 831-B-14
SUMMER SEMINARS PARTICIPANTS, FOR COLLEGE TEACHERS AND SCHOOL TEACHERS.

NF 3.13/4:date • Item 831-B-5
NEH FELLOWSHIPS UNIVERSITY TEACHERS, COLLEGE TEACHERS, AND INDEPENDENT SCHOLARS ANNIVERSARY AND COMMEMORATIVE INITIATIVES. [Annual]

NF 3.14:date • Item 831-B-5
INSTITUTES FOR COLLEGE AND UNIVERSITY FACULTY. [Annual]

NF 3.15:date • Item 831-B-5
OVERVIEW OF ENDOWMENT PROGRAMS. [Annual]

Earlier NF 3.2:Ov 2

NF 3.16:date • Item 831-B-5
HUMANITIES PROJECTS IN MEDIA. [Annual]

NF 3.17:date • Item 831-B-1
DIVISION OF EDUCATION PROGRAMS, APPLICATION, INSTRUCTIONS AND FORMS. [Annual]

    Earlier NF 3.8:Ed 8

NF 3.18:date • Item 831-B-7
NEH TEACHER-SCHOLAR PROGRAM FOR ELEMENTARY AND SECONDARY SCHOOL TEACHERS, GUIDELINES AND APPLICATION INSTRUCTIONS.

NF 3.19:date • Item 831-B-7
NEH TRAVEL TO COLLECTIONS, SMALL GRANTS FOR RESEARCH TRAVEL TO LIBRARIES, ARCHIVES, MUSEUMS, AND OTHER REPOSITORIES. [Annual]
    Previously classed NF 3.8:T 69

NF 3.21:date • Item 831-B-1
HUMANITIES IN AMERICA: A REPORT TO THE PRESIDENT, THE CONGRESS, AND THE AMERICAN PEOPLE.

NF 3.22 • Item 831-B-1
SUMMER STIPENDS.

NF 3.23:date/nos. • Item 831-B-7
UPDATE. [Quarterly]

NF 3.24:date • Item 831-B-1
NEH EXHIBITIONS TODAY. [Semiannual]

NF 3.25:date • Item 831-B-9
STUDY GRANTS FOR COLLEGE TEACHERS. [Annual]

NF 3.26:date • Item 831-B-19
PUBLIC PROGRAMS. [Annual]

NF 3.27:date • Item 831-B-20
EVENTS, EXHIBITIONS,AND PROGRAMS.

INSTITUTE OF MUSEUM AND LIBRARY SERVICES
(1981–   )

CREATION AND AUTHORITY

    The Institute of Museum Services (MuS 1) was created as an independent agency by the Museum Services Act in 1976. In December 1981, pursuant to title II of an act approved December 23, 1981, the Institute was established as an independent agency within the National Foundation on the Arts and the Humanities. Name changed to Institute of Museum and Library Services.

INFORMATION

    Institute of Museum and Library Services
    Room 609
    1100 Pennsylvania Avenue, N.W.
    Washington, D.C. 20506
    (202) 606-8536
    E mail: imlsinfo@imls.gov
    http://www.imls.gov

NF 4.1:date • Item 290-N-1 (EL)
ANNUAL REPORT.

NF 4.2:CT • Item 290-N-1
GENERAL PUBLICATIONS. [Irregular]
    Earlier MuS 1.2

NF 4.9:date • Item 290-N-1
GENERAL OPERATING SUPPORT GRANT APPLICATION AND INFORMATION. [Annual]

NF 4.10:date • Item 290-N-1
CONSERVATION PROJECT SUPPORT GRANT APPLICATION AND INFORMATION. [Annual]
    Earlier NF 4.2:C 76

NF 4.11:date • Item 290-N-1
MUSEUM ASSESSMENT PROGRAM, GRANT APPLICATION AND INFORMATION. [Annual]

NF 4.11/2 • Item 290-N-3
NATIONAL LEADERSHIP GRANTS, GRANT, APPLICATION AND GUIDELINES. [Annual]

NF 4.15 • Item 290-N-1
IMS ACESS.

NF 4.15/2 • Item 290-N-4 (EL)
PRIMARY SOURCE. [Monthly]

NATIONAL HOME FOR DISABLED VOLUNTEER SOLDIERS
(1866–1930)

NH 1.1:date
ANNUAL REPORTS OF BOARD OF MANAGERS.

NH 1.2:CT
GENERAL PUBLICATIONS.

NH 1.3:nos.
BULLETINS.

NH 1.4:nos.
CIRCULARS.

NH 1.5:date
INSPECTION OF STATE SOLDIERS AND SAILOR'S HOMES.

NH 1.6:date
RECORD OF CHANGES IN MEMBERSHIP OF NATIONAL HOME FOR DISABLED VOLUNTEER SOLDIERS.

NH 1.7:v.nos.
PROCEEDINGS OF BOARD OF MANAGERS.

NATIONAL HOUSING AGENCY
(1942–1947)

CREATION AND AUTHORITY

    The National Housing Agency was established by Executive Order 9070 of February 24, 1942, pursuant to the First War Powers Act of 1941. To it were transferred the Federal Housing Administration, the Federal Home Loan Bank Board, the Home Owners Loan Corporation, the Federal Savings and Loan Insurance Corporation, and the United States Housing Authority. The Agency was abolished upon the establishment of the Housing and Home Finance Agency (HH 1) by Reorganization Plan No. 3 of 1947, effective July 27, 1947.

NHA 1.1:date
ANNUAL REPORTS.

NHA 1.2:CT
GENERAL PUBLICATIONS.

NHA 1.3:nos.
NATIONAL HOUSING BULLETINS.

NHA 1.5:CT
LAWS.

NHA 1.7:nos.
URBAN STUDIES DIVISION BULLETINS.

NHA 1.8:nos.
CLIP SHEETS. [Monthly]
    Earlier NHA 2.10

NHA 1.9:nos.
TECHNICAL DIVISION BULLETINS.

NHA 1.10:CT
ADDRESSES.

NHA 1.11:CT
POSTERS.

NHA 1.12:v.nos.
VETERANS EMERGENCY HOUSING PROGRAM: COMMUNITY ACTION REPORT TO MAYOR'S EMERGENCY HOUSING COMMITTEE.

    Later Y 3.H 81/2:8

NHA 1.13:v.nos.
HOUSING. [Monthly]

    Later Y 3.H 81/2:7

NHA 1.14:nos.
VETERAN'S EMERGENCY HOUSING PROGRAM: COMMUNITY ACTION BULLETIN.

FEDERAL HOUSING ADMINISTRATION
(1942–1947)

CREATION AND AUTHORITY

    The Federal Housing Administration (FL 2) was transferred from the Federal Loan Agency to the newly created National Housing Agency by Executive Order 9070 of February 24, 1942. By Reorganization Plan No. 3 of 1947, effective July 27, 1947, it became one of three constituent agencies of the Housing and Home Finance Agency (HH 2).

NHA 2.1:date
ANNUAL REPORTS.

    Earlier FL 2.1
    Later HH 2.1

NHA 2.2:CT
GENERAL PUBLICATIONS.

    Earlier FL 2.2
    Later HH 2.2

NHA 2.5:CT
LAWS.

NHA 2.6:CT
REGULATIONS, RULES, AND INSTRUCTIONS.

    Earlier FL 2.6
    Later HH 2.6

NHA 2.7:CT
ADDRESSES.

    Later HH 2.13

NHA 2.8:vol.
INSURED MORTGAGE PORTFOLIO.

    Earlier FL 2.12
    Later HH 2.10

NHA 2.9:nos.
PRESS DIGEST.

    Earlier FL 2.9

NHA 2.10:vol.
CLIP SHEETS.

    Earlier FL 2.7
    Later NHA 1.8

NHA 2.11:nos.
COMPTROLLER CIRCULAR LETTERS.

      Earlier FL 2.19

NHA 2.12:nos.
TECHNICAL CIRCULARS.

      Earlier FL 2.17
      Later HH 2.12

NHA 2.13:CT
POSTERS.

      Later HH 2.15

NHA 2.14:nos.
ENGINEERING BULLETINS.

      Later HH 2.16

NHA 2.15:date
TRENDS IN SELECTED ECONOMIC AND REAL
ESTATE FACTORS IN UNITED STATES. [Monthly]

      Later HH 2.16

NHA 2.16:nos.
URBAN MORTGAGE FINANCE READING LISTS.

NHA 2.17:CT
REQUIREMENTS FOR INDIVIDUAL WATER-SUPPLY
AND SEWAGE-DISPOSAL SYSTEMS (by States).

      Later HH 2.11

NHA 2.18:CT
MINIMUM PROPERTY REQUIREMENTS FOR PROP-
ERTIES OF ONE OR TWO LIVING UNITS (by
States).

FEDERAL HOME LOAN BANK ADMINISTRATION
(1942– 1947)

CREATION AND AUTHORITY

      The Federal Home Loan Bank Board (FL 3)
was transferred from the Federal Loan Agency to
the National Housing Agency and its name
changed to the Federal Home Loan Bank Administration by Executive Order 9070 of February
24, 1942. The Administration was abolished by
Reorganization Plan No. 3 of 1947, effective July
27, 1947, and its functions transferred to the
Home Loan Bank Board (HH 4) within the Housing
and Home Finance Agency.

NHA 3.1:date
ANNUAL REPORTS.

      Earlier FL 3.1
      Later HH 4.1

NHA 3.2:CT
GENERAL PUBLICATIONS.

      Earlier FL 3.2
      Later HH 4.2

NHA 3.5:CT
LAWS.

NHA 3.6:CT
REGULATIONS, RULES, AND INSTRUCTIONS.

      Earlier FL 3.6
      Later HH 4.6

NHA 3.8:vol.
FEDERAL HOME LOAN BANK REVIEW. [Monthly]

      Earlier FL 3.7

NHA 3.8/2:date
– STATISTICAL SUPPLEMENT. [Annual]

NHA 3.9:date
NON-FARM REAL ESTATE FORECLOSURE REPORTS.
[Monthly]

      Earlier FL 3.8
      Later HH 4.7

NHA 3.10:date
ANNUAL REPORTS OF FEDERAL SAVINGS AND
LOAN ASSOCIATIONS.

      Earlier FL 3.2:Sa 9/2

NHA 3.11:CT
FEDERAL SAVINGS AND LOAN INSURANCE COR-
PORATION.

      Earlier Y 3.F 31/3:12 and FL 3

FEDERAL PUBLIC HOUSING AUTHORITY
(1942– 1947)

CREATION AND AUTHORITY

      The Federal Public Housing Authority was
established within the National Housing Agency
by Executive Order 9070 of February 24, 1942,
to which the functions of the Housing Authority
(FW 3) and other agencies were transferred. The
Authority was abolished by Reorganization Plan
No. 3 of 1947, effective July 27, 1947, and its
functions transferred to the Public Housing Administration (HH 3) within the Housing and Home
Finance Agency.

NHA 4.1:date
ANNUAL REPORTS.

      Earlier FW 3.1

NHA 4.2:CT
GENERAL PUBLICATIONS.

      Earlier FW 3.2

NHA 4.3:nos.
EPHA BULLETINS. [Weekly]

      Later PHA Bulletin (HH 3.3).

NHA 4.3/2:nos.
BULLETINS.

NHA 4.6:CT
REGULATIONS, RULES, AND INSTRUCTIONS.

      Includes Handbooks and Manuals.

NHA 4.8:vol.
PUBLIC HOUSING. [Monthly]

      Earlier FW 3.7

NHA 4.9:nos.
SAFETY POSTERS.

NHA 4.10:letters-nos.
WAR HOUSING TECHNICAL BULLETINS.

NATIONAL MEDIATION BOARD
(1934–   )

CREATION AND AUTHORITY

      The National Mediation Board was established
by an act to amend the Railway Labor Act, approved June 21, 1934 (48 Stat. 1185), succeeding the United States Board of Mediation, effective July 21, 1934.

INFORMATION

      National Mediation Board
      1301 K Street, NW, Ste. 250 East
      Washington, D.C. 20005-7011
      (202) 692-5050
      Fax: (202) 692-5082
      http://www.nmb.gov

NMB 1.1:date   **• Item 832 (MF) (EL)**
ANNUAL REPORT. 1st–   1935–   [Annual]

      Report submitted by the Board to Congress
pursuant to section 4 of Public Law 442, 73rd
Congress for the fiscal year.
      Includes annual report of the National Rail-
road Adjustment board.
      Covers summary and observation, record of
cases, mediation disputes, representation disputes, arbitration and emergency boards, wage
and rule agreements, interpretation and application of agreements, organization and finances of
the Board. Appendix contains statistical tables.

NMB 1.2:CT   **• Item 834**
GENERAL PUBLICATIONS.

NMB 1.5:CT   **• Item 833-A**
LAWS.

NMB 1.6:CT
REGULATIONS, RULES, AND INSTRUCTIONS.

NMB 1.7:CT   **• Item 833 (MF)**
REPORTS OF EMERGENCY BOARDS. [Irregular]

      In the event of a dispute between the rail-
roads, the express and Pullman companies, and
the airlines on the one hand and their employees
on the other over agreements on rates of pay,
rules or working conditions, the President of the
United States, pursuant to section 10 of the Railway Labor Act, as amended (45 U.S.C. 160) establishes an Emergency Board by Executive Order to investigate the disputes and report to him
within 30 days.
      Each Emergency Board is numbered consec-
utively as created. Upon conclusion of its hearings
and investigations, the final report of each board
is issued separately.
      Reports are listed in the Monthly Catalog un-
der Emergency Boards (under sec. 10, Railway
Labor Act) and not under National Mediation Board.
      Each report presents the background infor-
mation relative to the dispute, a summary of the
problems involved, and the recommendations or
findings of the Board.

NMB 1.8:nos.
CASES. [Irregular]

NMB 1.9:v.nos.   **• Item 834 (EL)**
DETERMINATIONS OF THE NATIONAL MEDIATION
      BOARD. v. 1–   [Irregular]

      Earlier NMB 1.2:C 84

NATIONAL MUNITIONS CONTROL BOARD
(1936–1940)

NMC 1.1:date
ANNUAL REPORTS.

NMC 1.2:CT
GENERAL PUBLICATIONS.

NATIONAL SCIENCE FOUNDATION
(1950–   )

CREATION AND AUTHORITY

The National Science Foundation was established by the National Science Foundation Act of 1950 (64 Stat. 149; 42 U.S.C. 1861-1875), and was given additional authority by the National Defense Education Act of 1958 (72 Stat. 1601; 42 U.S.C. 1876-1879) and by the National Sea Grant College and Program Act of 1966 (80 Stat. 998; 33 U.S.C. 1121-1124).

INFORMATION

National Science Foundation
4201 Wilson Blvd.
Arlington, VA 22230
(703) 292-5111
http://www.nsf.gov

NS 1.1:date   • **Item 834-B (MF)**
ANNUAL REPORT. 1st–   1951–   [Annual]

Report submitted by the Foundation to the President pursuant to the National Science Foundation Act of 1950 for the fiscal year.
This annual report should be in the collection of both large and small libraries. With the emphasis placed upon the role of science in American life, this publication offers a cross-section of the activities and programs being performed in the various fields of science. Covering the program activities of the National Science Foundation, the report includes items such as Government support of scientific research, institutional grants, education in the sciences, dissemination of scientific information, special international programs, measuring and appraising the national investment in science. Includes a series of photographs illustrating the various Foundation-supported activities in science.
The appendices include:
Directory of the National Science Board, Staff, Committees, and Advisory Panels.
Financial Report for Fiscal Year.
Patents Resulting from NSA-supported Activities.
NSA-Supported Scientific Conferences, Symposia, and Advanced Science Seminars.
Publications of the National Science Foundation.
Also published as a House Document.

NS 1.1/2:date
ANNUAL REPORTS. (Division of Graduate Eduction in Science)

NS 1.1/3:date
ANNUAL REPORTS. (Division of Pre-College Education in Science)

NS 1.1/4:date
ANNUAL REPORTS. (Ofice of National R & D Assessment)

NS 1.1/5   • **Item 834-B-2 (MF)**
OFFICE OF INSPECTOR GENERAL SEMIANNUAL REPORT TO THE CONGRESS.

NS 1.2:CT   • **Item 834-C**
GENERAL PUBLICATIONS.

NS 1.2:In 2/4   • **Item 834-C**
OCEANOGRAPHIC ATLAS OF THE INTERNATIONAL INDIAN OCEAN EXPEDITION. 1971. 531 p. il.

The International Indian Ocean Expedition was an intensive study of the 28 million-square-mile Indian Ocean by scientists of 28 cooperating nations working from shore stations and an extensive fleet of research vessels. Major areas of interest were biological factors, including possible fishery resources; the formation of the ocean basin and the forces that have shaped and are continuing to shape it; the chemical and physical description of the waters of the Indian Ocean, and the study of their motions; and the interaction between the ocean and the atmosphere particularly with respect to the monsoon winds. This Atlas contains 449 colored maps and diagrams. It provides information on water temperature, depth, density, temperature gradient, and transport, as well as the salt, oxygen, phosphate, nitrate, and silicate content of the water. To provide users of this Atlas with the greatest amount of information about relatively unknown Indian Ocean, and to help provide a picture of the Ocean as an entity, the volume includes almost all data collected in the Indian Ocean from the mid-1920's to 1966.

NS 1.3:v.nos.&nos.   • **Item 834-F-8 (EL)**
NSF BULLETIN. v. 1–   [11 issues a year]

Contains brief articles on NSF programs, policies, and activities.
ISSN 0145-0670

NS 1.3/2:nos.
SCIENTIFIC MANPOWER BULLETINS.

NS 1.3/3:v.nos.&nos.   • **Item 834-F-6**
ARCTIC BULLETIN. v. 1–   [Quarterly] (Interagency Arctic Research Coordinating Committee)

One issue each year devoted to annual report.
ISSN 0092-427X

NS 1.7:date
PRESS RELEASES. [Irregular]

NS 1.8:date
LIST OF INTERNATIONAL AND FOREIGN SCIENTIFIC AND TECHNICAL MEETINGS. [Quarterly]

Earlier NS 1.2:Sci 2
Later LC 2.9

NS 1.9:date
QUARTERLY REPORT, GOVERNMENT SPONSORED AND GOVERNMENT SUPPORTED RESEARCH, SOCIAL SCIENCES AND INTERDISCIPLINARY AREAS.

NS 1.10:date   • **Item 834-E**
FEDERAL GRANTS AND CONTRACTS FOR UNCLASSIFIED RESEARCH IN LIFE SCIENCES. [Annual]

Earlier NS 1.2:G 76/2

NS 1.10/2:date   • **Item 834-E**
FEDERAL GRANTS AND CONTRACTS FOR UNCLASSIFIED RESEARCH IN PHYSICAL SCIENCES. [Annual]

NS 1.10/3:date   • **Item 834-E**
INSTITUTIONAL GRANTS FOR SCIENCE.

NS 1.10/4:date   • **Item 834-E (MF)**
GRANTS AND AWARDS FOR FISCAL YEAR (date). [Annual]

Includes a list of grants including name of institution, individual, and amount of grant for the various NSF-sponsored programs; list of fellowship awards; and list of institutions chosen by fellowship awardees.

NS 1.10/5:date
DIVISION OF SOCIAL SCIENCES QUARTERLY GRANT LIST.

NS 1.10/6:date   • **Item 834-E-1 (MF)**
RECENT AWARDS IN ENGINEERING. [Quarterly]

PURPOSE:– To provide information on the research awards made by the Directorate for Engineering. This quarterly is amined at those researchers, educators, administrators, and usrs who wish to keep abreast in various technical areas.
Discontinued.

NS 1.10/7:nos.   • **Item 834-E (MF)**
SUMMARY OF AWARDS. [Annual]

NS 1.10/8:date
APPLIED SOCIAL AND BEHAVIORAL SCIENCES RESEARCH INITIATION GRANTS. [Annual]

NS 1.11:nos.
REVIEWS OF DATA ON RESEARCH AND DEVELOPMENT. 1–   1953–   [Irregular]

NS 1.11/2:nos.   • **Item 834-G**
REVIEWS OF DATA ON SCIENCE RESOURCES. v. 1– 1964–   [Irregular]

Provides preliminary findings, summaries, and other short reports of surveys of R & D expenditures and scientific manpower as well as special analytical studies.
Supersedes Reviews of Data on Research and Development (NS 1.11) and Scientific Manpower Bulletin (NS 1.3/2).

NS 1.11/3:date   • **Item 834-G (EL)**
SRS DATA BRIEF.

NS 1.12:date   • **Item 834-F**
ACADEMIC YEAR INSTITUTES FOR SECONDARY SCHOOL TEACHERS AND SUPERVISORS OF SCIENCE AND MATHEMATICS. [Annual]

The Academic Year Institute program of the National Science Foundation supports the efforts of colleges and universities in providing opportunities for teachers of science and mathematics to spend an entire academic year in fulltime study of the subject matter of their disciplines, supported financially by the Federal Government.
Gives brief descriptions of each institute to indicate the general nature of the academic offerings and the number and type of personnel eligible for participation.
Earlier NS 1.2:Sci 2/3

NS 1.12   • **Item 834-F**
PROGRAMS FOR COLLEGE TEACHERS OF SCIENCE, MATHEMATICS, AND ENGINEERING. [Annual]

Directory of institutions offering programs for college teachers, such as research participation, summer institutes, short courses, academic year institutes, in-service seminars.
Gives brief description of each institution's program and eligibility requirements.

NS 1.12/2:date
ANNOUNCEMENTS OF SUMMER CONFERENCES FOR COLLEGE TEACHERS.

NS 1.12/3:date
RESEARCH PARTICIPATION FOR TEACHERS OF SCIENCE AND MATHEMATICS.

NS 1.13:CT   • **Item 834-H**
BIBLIOGRAPHIES AND LISTS OF PUBLICATIONS.

NS 1.13/2:date   • **Item 834-F-2**
EXPLORATORY RESEARCH AND PROBLEM ASSESSMENT: ABSTRACTS OF NSF RESEARCH RESULTS.

NS 1.13/3:v.nos.&nos.
ENERGY RESEARCH AND TECHNOLOGY: AB-
STRACTS OF NSF/RANN RESEARCH RESULTS.

NS 1.13/3-2:nos.   • **Item 834-F-3**
ENERGY RESEARCH AND TECHNOLOGY: AB-
STRACTS OF NSF/RANN RESEARCH REPORTS.

NS 1.13/4:date   • **Item 834-F-4**
ABSTRACTS OF NSF/RANN RESEARCH REPORTS:
PRIVATE SECTOR PRODUCTIVITY. [Irregular]

NS 1.13/5:date   • **Item 834-H (MF)**
PUBLICATIONS OF THE NATIONAL SCIENCE FOUN-
DATION. [Annual]

NS 1.13/6:date   • **Item 834-H (MF)**
PUBLICATIONS LIST. [Annual] (Division of Science
Resources Studies)

NS 1.14:date   • **Item 834-I**
SCIENTIFIC MANPOWER, SIGNIFICANT DEVELOP-
MENTS, VIEWS AND STATISTICS. [Annual]

NS 1.14/2:date   • **Item 834-I**
AMERICAN SCIENCE MANPOWER. 1954/55–
[Biennial]

Report of the National Register of Scientific
and Technical Personnel.
Provides data on education, specialization
by work activity and field, type of employer, salary, age, sex, geographic location, and other
characteristics.

NS 1.14/3:date
FEDERAL SCIENTIFIC AND TECHNICAL WORKERS:
NUMBERS AND CHARACTERISTICS. [Biennial]

NS 1.15:nos.   • **Item 831-B-1**
CURRENT RESEARCH AND DEVELOPMENTS IN
SCIENTIFIC DOCUMENTATION. [Semiannual]

Later NS 2.10

NS 1.16:nos.   • **Item 834-J**
SCIENTIFIC INFORMATION ACTIVITIES OF FEDERAL
AGENCIES. 1–   1958–   [Irregular]

Describes the policies and practices of the
Federal agencies relative to their scientific and
technical information activities. Serves as a
supplement to an earlier report, Organization of
the Federal Government for Scientific activities.
Each issue covers an agency or group of
agencies within a Department. Includes the
Agency's research mission and function; types
of publications issued; bibliographies issued by
the Government listing the publications, and special aspects of the agency's scientific information program of interest to the scientific community.

NS 1.17:v.nos.&nos.
SCIENCE INFORMATION NEWS. v. 1– v. 10, no. 5/6.
1959– 1968. [Bimonthly]

NS 1.17/2:nos.
INTERNATIONAL SCIENCE NOTES. 1–   1963–
[Monthly]

Later S 1.122

NS 1.17/3:nos.
INTERNATIONAL SCIENCE NOTES, SUPPLEMENTS.
1–   1963–

NS 1.18:nos.   • **Item 834-N (MF)**
FEDERAL FUNDS FOR RESEARCH, DEVELOPMENT,
AND OTHER SCIENTIFIC ACTIVITIES. 1–
1952–   [Annual]

PURPOSE:– To present and analyze Federal
funds provided for research, development, and
other scientific activities. Based on information
furnished by each Federal agency supporting
basic research, applied research, development,
R & D plant or facilities, scientific information
work, and general-purpose data collection.
Includes separate data by agency on character
of work; performers, both domestic and foreign;
and fields of science. Each report covers three
fiscal years. For the latest of the three years,
summary information is on projected obligations,
based on Federal agencies, budget proposals to
Congress; for the two earlier years, reflect progressive stages of reported action.

NS 1.18/2:date   • **Item 834-N (MF)**
FEDERAL FUNDS FOR RESEARCH AND DEVELOP-
MENT, DETAILED HISTORICAL TABLES, FISCAL
YEARS. [Annual]

Also published in microfiche.

NS 1.18/3:date   • **Item 834-N (MF)**
FEDERAL FUNDS FOR RESEARCH AND DEVELOP-
MENT, FEDERAL OBLIGATIONS FOR RESEARCH
BY AGENCY AND DETAILED FIELD OF SCIENCE,
FISCAL YEARS. [Annual]

Also published in microfiche.

NS 1.18/4:date   • **Item 834-N (MF)**
FEDERAL R & D FUNDING BY BUDGET FUNCTION.
[Annual]

NS 1.19   • **Item 834-O**
GRADUATE FELLOWSHIP AWARDS ANNOUNCED BY
NATIONAL SCIENCE FOUNDATION. [Annual]

Issued as a press release.

NS 1.19/2:date
COOPERATIVE GRADUATE FELLOWSHIP PROGRAM
FOR FISCAL YEAR, FELLOWSHIP AWARDS [and]
PROGRAM OF SUMMER FELLOWSHIPS FOR
GRADUATE TEACHING ASSISTANTS FOR FIS-
CAL YEAR.

NS 1.20:CT   • **Item 834-P**
HANDBOOKS, MANUALS, GUIDES.

NS 1.20/2:letters-nos.   • **Item 834-F-5**
GUIDE FOR PREPARATION OF PROPOSALS AND
PROJECT OPERATION. [Irregular]

NS 1.21:date   • **Item 834-R**
WEATHER MODIFICATION, ANNUAL REPORT. 1st–
1959–   [Annual]
Also issued in the House Document series.
Later C 55.27

NS 1.22:CT   • **Item 834-T**
SURVEYS OF SCIENCE RESOURCES SERIES.

NS 1.22:C 83/3   • **Item 834-T**
SCIENTIFIC ACTIVITIES IN UNIVERSITIES AND
COLLEGES. [Biennial]

Provides general-purpose data on financial and manpower resources used for research, development, and instruction in the
sciences and engineering. Separate data are
shown for schools of agriculture (including
agricultural experiment stations), medical
schools, and Federally Funded Research and
Development Centers managed by educational
institutions.

NS 1.22:G 74   • **Item 834-T**
SCIENTIFIC AND TECHNICAL PERSONNEL IN
THE FEDERAL GOVERNMENT. [Biennial]

Presents information on the occupational
characteristics of professional and nonpro-
fessional scientific and technical workers
employed by the Federal Government.

NS 1.22:In 2   • **Item 834-T**
RESEARCH AND DEVELOPMENT IN INDUSTRY.
1957–   [Annual]

PURPOSE:– To summarize the results of
annual surveys conducted by the Bureau of
the Census for the National Science Foundation in cooperation with industries involved.
These industry surveys, together with comparable Foundations surveys in other sectors of the economy, yield trend data on the
magnitude of R & D funds, in terms of types
of work and fields of science, and other economic characteristics of research and development.
Each report contains a brief analysis and
an extensive section of detailed statistical
tables.
Title varies.

NS 1.22/2:date   • **Item 834-T (EL)**
NATIONAL PATTERNS OF SCIENCE AND TECHNOL-
OGY RESOURCES. [Biennial]

NS 1.22/3:date   • **Item 834-T (MF)**
ACADEMIC SCIENCE/ENGINEERING: R & D FUNDS,
FISCAL YEAR (date). [Annual]
Earlier NS 1.22

NS 1.22/3-2:date
ACADEMIC SCIENCE/ENGINEERING, R & D FUNDS
FEDERAL SUPPORT SCIENTISTS AND ENGI-
NEERS GRADUATE ENROLLMENT AND
SUPPORT. [Annual]
Earlier NS 1.2

NS 1.22/4:date   • **Item 834-T (MF)**
ACADEMIC SCIENCE/ENGINEERING, GRADUATE
ENROLLMENT AND SUPPORT, FALL, DETAILED
STATISTICAL TABLES. [Annual]
Earlier NS 1.2

NS 1.22/5:date   • **Item 834-T (MF)**
IMMIGRANT SCIENTISTS AND ENGINEERS. [Annual]
NS 1.22/6:date
ACADEMIC SCIENCE/ENGINEERS: SCIENTIST AND
ENGINEERS. [Annual]

NS 1.22/7:date   • **Item 834-T (MF)**
U.S. SCIENTISTS AND ENGINEERS. [Biennial]

NS 1.22/8:date   • **Item 834-T (MF)**
CHARACTERISTICS OF RECENT SCIENCE AND
ENGINEERING GRADUATES. [Biennial]

NS 1.22/9:date   • **Item 834-T (MF)**
FEDERAL SCIENTISTS AND ENGINEERS. [Annual]

NS 1.22/11   • **Item 834-T-2 (EL)**
GRADUATE STUDENTS AND POSTDOCTORATES IN
SCIENCE AND ENGINEERING. [Annual]

NS 1.22/10   • **Item 834-T-1 (EL)**
NSF ENGINEERING NEWS. [Quarterly]

NS 1.23:date   • **Item 834-V**
CURRENT PROJECTS ON ECONOMIC AND SOCIAL
IMPLICATIONS OF SCIENTIFIC RESEARCH AND
DEVELOPMENT. [Annual]
Earlier NS 1.2:R 31/13

NS 1.24:nos.   • **Item 834-X**
SCIENCE COURSE IMPROVEMENT PROJECTS. 1–
1962–   [Irregular]

NS 1.25:nos.   • **Item 834-W**
INTERNATIONAL SCIENCE REPORTS. 1–   1962–

NS 1.26:v.nos.&nos.   • **Item 834-Y (P) (EL)**
ANTARCTIC JOURNAL OF THE UNITED STATES. v.
1–   1966–   [Quarterly]

Prepared jointly by the Office of Antarctic
Programs, National Science Foundation and the
U.S. Naval Support Force, Antarctica, Defense
Department.

PURPOSE:– To provide a common outlet for
all information on the National U.S. Antarctic Program to a broad audience of participants and
interested observers. Includes scientific and logistic reports on the U.S. program in Antarctica,
accounts of collaborative activities undertaken
in the United States, authoritative discussions of
antarctic matters by qualified authors, and other
matters of current and historical significance.
ISSN 0003-5335

NS 1.27:CT
ADDRESSES.

NS 1.28 • Item 834-Z
NATIONAL SCIENCE BOARD, NSB- (series). 1969–
[Irregular]

PURPOSE:– To provide in-depth studies of various aspects of science and science education.

NS 1.28/2:date • Item 834-Z (MF)
SCIENCE INDICATORS. [Biennial]

NS 1.28/3: • Item 834-C-11
A MONTHLY REPORT ON SELECTED CONGRESSIONAL ACTIVITIES.

PURPOSE– To provide information on selected Congressional activities to the National Science Foundation and the National Science Board. Discontinued.

NS 1.29:v.nos.&nos. • Item 834-F-1
MOSAIC. v. 1– 1970– [Bimonthly]

PURPOSE:– To serve as a medium of communication to and among individuals and groups directly affected by the Foundation as well as interested parties including other Federal officials involved in scientific affairs, science writers, and others who share a concern for the progress of science.
ISSN 0027-1284

NS 1.30:date • Item 834-N-1
FEDERAL SUPPORT TO UNIVERSITIES, COLLEGES, AND SELECTED NONPROFIT INSTITUTIONS, FISCAL YEAR (date), REPORT TO THE PRESIDENT AND CONGRESS. 1st– 1968– [Annual]
PURPOSE:– To serve as an informational and analytical tool for the science policymaking branches of Government, as well as for general use by individuals interested in agency, geographic, and institutional patterns of Federal science support. Annual report to the President and Congress on current levels and trends in Federal funding of research, development, and other activities at universities, colleges, and other related nonprofit institutions as required by the 1968 amendment to the NSF Act of 1950.

NS 1.30/2:date • Item 834-N-1 (MF)
FEDERAL SUPPORT TO UNIVERSITIES, COLLEGES, AND SELECTED NONPROFIT INSTITUTIONS, FISCAL YEAR. [Annual]

PURPOSE:– To present information on Federal support in terms of field of science, geographic locality, and type of institution receiving assistance. A major theme in the report is Federal obligations to universities and colleges for research and development. Data on Federal funding for nonscience activities are also given to provide a total picture of Federal support of higher education.

NS 1.30/2-2 • Item 834-N-1 (MF)
SELECTED DATA ON FEDERAL SUPPORT TO UNIVERSITIES AND COLLEGES, FISCAL YEAR.

NS 1.31:CT • Item 834-C-3
SCIENCE RESOURCES STUDIES HIGHLIGHTS. [Irregular]

PURPOSE:– To provide findings of National Science Foundation surveys on such subjects as academic employment of scientists and engineers in doctoral institutions, federal obligations to universities and colleges, and research and development expenditures at doctoral institutions.

NS 1.31/3-2:date • Item 834-F-3
ENERGY RESEARCH AND TECHNOLOGY, ABSTRACTS OF NSF/RANN RESEARCH REPORTS. (RANN [Research Applied to National Needs] Documents Center)

NS 1.32:date • Item 834-N-2
OCEANOGRAPHIC DATA EXCHANGE. (World Data Center A, Oceanography)

NS 1.33:CT
PROGRAM SOLICITATION (series). [Irregular]

NS 1.34:date
DAILY CONGRESSIONAL NOTIFICATION OF GRANTS AND CONTRACTS AWARDED.

ISSN 0364-5460

NS 1.35:date • Item 834-C-5 (MF)
ACTIVITY REPORT TO CONGRESS. [Quarterly]

Describes Foundation's activities in the fields of mathematical, physical, biological, behavioral, and social sciences, as well as science and engineering educational programs.
Published also in microfiche.
Former title: National Science Foundation Quarterly Report to Congress.

NS 1.36:date • Item 834-F-7
LISTING OF PEER REVIEWERS USED BY NSF DIVISIONS. [Annual]

NS 1.37:v.nos.&nos. • Item 834-N-3 (MF)
PROGRAM REPORTS [various subjects]. v. 1– 1977–

NS 1.38:v.nos. • Item 834-C-1
INITIAL REPORTS OF THE DEEP SEA DRILLING PROJECT. v. 1–

Earlier NS 1.2:D 36/2

NS 1.38/2: • Item 834-C-10
PROCEEDINGS OF THE OCEAN DRILLING PROGRAM, PART A, INITIAL REPORTS. [Irregular]

PURPOSE– To present results of investigations formerly given in Initial Reports of the Deep Sea Drilling Project (NS 1.38). That project will be superseded by the Ocean Drilling Program. Each of six annual cruises by the ODP vessel are expected to result in a Part A volume about 15 months later.

NS 1.39:date • Item 834-N-4
SUMMARIES OF PROJECTS COMPLETED IN FISCAL YEAR. [Annual]

PURPOSE:– To present technical summaries of research performed under NSF grants that were officially completed in the fiscal year. Arrangement is by broad disciplinary areas to enable readers to focus on those general research topics of interest to them.

NS 1.39/2:date • Item 834-N-4
PROJECT SUMMARIES. [Annual] (Division of Science Resources Studies)

NS 1.40:date • Item 834-C-2
SCIENCE AND TECHNOLOGY, REPORT TO THE CONGRESS. 1st– [Biennial]

NS 1.40/2:date • Item 834-C-6
FIVE-YEAR OUTLOOK ON SCIENCE AND TECHNOLOGY. [Biennial]

Identifies emergent issues likely to concern American society and describes some problems, opportunities, and constraints associated with the use of science and technology.

NS 1.41:CT • Item 834-B-1
MAPS AND ATLASES.

NS 1.42:date • Item 834-C-4
SCIENCE AND ENGINEERING PERSONNEL: A NATIONAL OVERVIEW. [Biennial]

PURPOSE:– To provide a report on the utilization and supply of U.S. scientists and engineers in general, on doctorate scientists and engineers in particular, and also on the dynamics, or movement of personnel into and out of, the science and engineering field.

NS 1.43:CT
AUDIOVISUAL MATERIALS. [Irregular]

NS 1.44:date • Item 834-C-4 (MF)
SCIENCE AND ENGINEERING DOCTORATES. [Annual]

NS 1.44/2:date • Item 834-C-4
NATIONAL SCIENCE FOUNDATION, DIRECTORY OF NSF-SUPPORTED TEACHER ENHANCEMENT PROJECTS. [Semiannual]

NS 1.45:date • Item 834-C-7
MATHEMATICAL SCIENCES POSTDOCTORAL RESEARCH FELLOWSHIPS. [Annual]

PURPOSE:– To announce and provide information and forms for applying for postdoctoral research fellowships in the mathematical sciences.
Earlier NS 1.2:M 42/7

NS 1.46:date • Item 834-E-2
ABSTRACTS OF PHASE I AWARDS, SMALL BUSINESS INNOVATION RESEARCH. [Annual]

NS 1.47:date • Item 834-P (EL)
GUIDE TO PROGRAMS. [Annual]

Earlier NS 1.20:P 94

NS 1.47/2:date
ENGINEERING RESEARCH CENTERS: PROGRAM ANNOUNCEMENT. [Annual]

NS 1.48:date • Item 834-E-3
NSF VISITING PROFESSORSHIPS FOR WOMEN. [Annual]

NS 1.48/2:date
RESEARCH OPPORTUNITIES FOR WOMEN SCIENTISTS AND ENGINEERS. [Annual]

NS 1.49:date • Item 834-C-9 (MF)
WOMEN AND MINORITIES IN SCIENCE AND ENGINEERING. [Biennial]

Focuses on the status of women and minorities, and physically handicapped persons in science and engineering.

NS 1.50:CT • Item 834-C-8
DIRECTORIES. [Irregular]

NS 1.50/2:date • Item 834-C-8
DIRECTORY OF AWARDS. [Annual]

NS 1.50/3 • Item 834-C-8 (MF)
DIRECTORY OF AWARDS, DIRECTORATE FOR ENGINEERING.

NS 1.51: • Item 834-C-12
STATES ARCTIC RESEARCH PLAN. [Biennial]
The Plan is a comprehensive statement of national needs and priorities in the areas of national security, national resource development,and acquisition of new scientific knowledge of the Arctic. It was prepared in accordance with Section 109 of PL 98-373.

NS 1.51/2:date • Item 834-C-14 (MF) (EL)
ARCTIC RESEARCH OF THE UNITED STATES. [Semi-annual]

Intended for those interested in learning about U.S.Government-Financed Arctic research activities. Issued by NSF on behalf of theInteragency Arctic Research Policy committee. Contains articles on Arctic research activities of several federal agencies.

NS 1.52: • Item 834-C-13
INTERNATIONAL SCIENCE AND TECHNOLOGY DATA UPDATE. [Annual]

Updates international science and technology data in such areas as research and development expenditures, science and engineering personnel, and science and technology outputs and impacts.

NS 1.53:date • Item 834-T (MF)
SCIENTIFIC AND ENGINEERING RESEARCH FACILITIES AT UNIVERSITIES AND COLLEGES. [Biennial]

NS 1.54   • Item 834-F-1 (MF)
NSF DIRECTIONS. [Bimonthly]

NS 1.55:CT   • Item 834-N (MF)
SELECTED DATA ON . . .

NS 1.56   • Item 834-C-15 (MF)
SURVEY OF GRADUATE STUDENTS AND
POSTDOCTORATES IN SCIENCE ENGINEER.
[Annual]

NS 1.57   • Item 834-C-16 (EL)
FRONTIERS, NEWSLETTER OF THE NATIONAL SCI-
ENCE FOUNDATION. [Monthly]

NS 1.58   • Item 834-C-17
DUE NEWS. [Annual]

NS 1.59   • Item 834-Z-1 (EL)
TIPSHEET (NSF News Media Tips).

NS 1.60   • Item 834-Z-1 (E)
ELECTRONIC PRODUCTS.

NS 1.61   • Item 834-Z-1 (EL)
PROFESSIONAL OPPORTUNITIES FOR WOMEN IN
RESEARCH AND EDUCATION. (Annual)

OFFICE OF SCIENCE
INFORMATION SERVICE
(1958–   )

INFORMATION

    Office of Science Information Service
    National Science Foundation
    Room 336
    1800 G Street, N.W.
    Washington, D.C. 20550

NS 2.1:date
REPORTS.

NS 2.2:CT   • Item 834-U
GENERAL PUBLICATIONS.

NS 2.8:nos.   • Item 834-M
NONCONVENTIONAL TECHNICAL INFORMATION
SYSTEMS IN CURRENT USE.

    Earlier NS 1.2:T 22

NS 2.9:CT   • Item 834-S
BIBLIOGRAPHIES AND LISTS OF PUBLICATIONS.

NS 2.10:nos.   • Item 834-K
CURRENT RESEARCH AND DEVELOPMENT IN
SCIENTIFIC DOCUMENTATION. 1–   1957–
[Semiannual]

    Compiled by the Office of Science Informa-
tion Service.
    PURPOSE:– To report all pertinent activities
in the field of scientific documentation in the United
States which has come to the attention of the
National Science Foundation, as well as foreign
projects on which information could be obtained.
    Reports are issued each May and November.
Each issue updates all previous issues. The
projects are arranged under five main groups: 1)
Information Needs and Uses, 2) Information Storage and Retrieval, 3) Mechanical Translation, 4)
Equipment, and 5) Potentially Related Research.

NS 2.11:CT
ADDRESSES.

NS 2.12:date
FEDERAL SCIENTIFIC AND TECHNICAL COMMUNI-
CATION, PROGRESS REPORT. [Annual]

    Earlier Y 3.F 31/16:2 C 73/3

OVERSEAS PRIVATE
INVESTMENT CORPORATION
(1969–   )

CREATION AND AUTHORITY

    The Overseas Private Investment Corpora-
tion was established as an independent agency
by Act of December 30, 1969 (83 Stat. 805).

INFORMATION

    Information Office
    Overseas Private Investment Corporation
    12th Floor
    1100 New York Ave. NW
    Washington, D.C. 20527
    (202) 336-8400
    Fax: (202) 408-9859
    E-Mail:info@opic.gov
    http://www.opic.gov

OP 1.1:date   • Item 834-W-4 (MF)
ANNUAL REPORT.

OP 1.2:CT   • Item 834-W-2
GENERAL PUBLICATIONS.

OP 1.8:CT   • Item 834-W-1
HANDBOOKS, MANUALS, GUIDES.

OP 1.9:date   • Item 834-W-3
TOPICS. 1972–   [Quarterly]

    PURPOSE:– To inform the public about sig-
nificant developments in OPIC's programs to encourage and assist private U.S. investment in
developing countries.
    Contains information regarding investment cli-
mates and opportunities abroad; newsworthy
projects assisted by OPIC insurance and finance
incentives; significant meetings, seminars and
overseas missions; claims settlements; changes
in key OPIC personnel, etc. Also usually contains special supplement ("Spotlite on . . .") featuring a detailed description of the investment
climate in specific less developed country, with
information on that country's laws, regulations,
incentives and attitudes towards private U.S. investment.
    ISSN 0145-1375

OP 1.10   • Item 834-W-5 (EL)
OPICNEWS. [Irregular]

UNITED STATES POSTAL
SERVICE
(1970–   )

CREATION AND AUTHORITY

    The Office of the Postmaster General was
created by act of September 22, 1789, which
continued regulations that originated with the
appointment of Benjamin Franklin as Postmaster
General by the Continental Congress. The first
act to provide in detail for a Post Office Department was passed February 20, 1792. The Post
Office Department was established as an executive department by act of Congress, approved
June 8, 1872 (17 Stat. 283). By Public Law 91-
375, approved August 12, 1970, the Post Office
Department was succeeded by the United States
Postal Service.

INFORMATION

    United States Postal Service
    475 L'Enfant Plaza West SW
    Washington, DC 20260-0010
    (202) 268-2000
    Toll Free: (800) 562-8777
    http://www.usps.gov

P 1.1   • Item 835 (MF)
ANNUAL REPORT. 1823–   [Annual]

    Covers the activities and services of the U.S.
Post Office Department during the fiscal year.
Appendix contains statistical tables.

P 1.1/2:date
REPORT TO EMPLOYEES FY, WASHINGTON, D.C.
POST OFFICE. [Annual]

P 1.2:CT   • Item 837
GENERAL PUBLICATIONS.

P 1.3   • Item 837-C (EL)
POSTAL BULLETIN. v. 1–   1880–   [Weekly]

    Daily bulletin of orders, instructions, and in-
formation relative to the Postal Service, including
philatelic, airmail, money order, parcel post, post
office changes as to establishments and discontinuances. Published each Tuesday.
    ISSN 0364-863X

P 1.3/2:nos.   • Item 837-C
POSTAL INSPECTION SERVICE BULLETIN.
[Quarterly].

P 1.4:nos.
CIRCULARS (none issued).

P 1.5:CT
ADVERTISEMENTS INVITING PROPOSALS FOR
CARRYING MAILS (by States).

P 1.6:date
ADVERTISEMENTS INVITING PROPOSALS FOR
COVERED REGULATION WAGON MAIL-
MESSENGER, TRANSFERS, AND MAIL STATION
SERVICE (discontinued).

P 1.7:date
ADVERTISEMENTS INVITING PROPOSALS FOR
CARRYING MAILS IN REGULATION SCREEN
WAGONS.

P 1.8:CT
ADVERTISEMENTS INVITING PROPOSALS FOR
CARRYING MAIL (miscellaneous).

P 1.9:CT
POSTAL TREATIES AND CONVENTIONS.

P 1.10:date
U.S. OFFICIAL POSTAL GUIDE.

P 1.10/2:date
ABRIDGED UNITED STATES OFFICIAL POSTAL
GUIDE.

P 1.10/3:date
STATE LIST OF POST OFFICES.

P 1.10/4 • Item 839-A-1
DIRECTORY OF POST OFFICES. 1955– [Annual]
(POD Publication 26)

Includes list of postal delivery zone offices, list of all post offices, branch post offices, and stations arranged alphabetically by States, and alphabetical list of all post offices, branch post offices, and named stations; a list of post offices, by classes, in each State and territory as of July 1, a list of Army posts, camps, and stations, and Air Force bases, fields, and installations, and a list of post offices that have beendiscontinued or had their names changed during the past two years.

Beginning with the 1963 issue, includes ZIP code numbers for each post office and also a numerical list of post offices by ZIP code.

The Directory is used primarily in identifying post offices and can be used in computing parcel post rates if used in connection with a zone key supplied by the local postmaster.

Issued annually as of July 1. For those having need to keep these lists up-to-date can do so through posting changes from the weekly Postal Bulletin.

Paper bound and punched for 3-ring binder.

Supersedes information formerly contained in U.S. Official Postal Guide, Part 1.

Formerly distributed to depository libraries under Item No. 839.

Beginning with the 1979 issue, combined with National Zip Code Directory (P 1.10/8)

P 1.10/5 • Item 839-A-2 (EL)
IMM (International Mail Manual). 1955– [Irregular]
(Subscription includes the basic volume plus supplementary material for an indefinite period. Issued in loose-leaf form and punched for 3-ring binder) (POD Publication 42)

Contains detailed information about postage rates, services available, prohibitions, import restrictions, and other conditions governing mail to other countries. The countries are listed alphabetically with the specific requirements applicable to mail addressed to each of them.

Formerly distributed to depository libraries under Item 839.

Earlier: Directory of International Mail.

P 1.10/6
COUNTY LIST OF POST OFFICES. [Annual]
Former title: Post Offices by States and Counties. Reprinted from the Directory of Post Offices.

P 1.10/7:CT/date
ZIP CODE DIRECTORIES [by States].

P 1.10/8:date • Item 839-A-3
NATIONAL FIVE-DIGIT ZIP CODE & POST OFFICE DIRECTORY. [Annual]

ZIP Code is a five-digit national coding plan which identifies each postal delivery unit and links that unit with a major post office through which mail is routed for delivery.

The National ZIP Code Directory was issued to consolidate and update the information previously published in the State ZIP Code Directories (P 1.10/7) issued in 1963.

Lists cities alphabetically under each State. Those cities having mail delivery from branches and stations are arranged in the appendix following each State and have street listings.

Formerly distributed to depository libraries under Item No. 839.

Beginning with the 1979 issue, the National ZIP Code Directory was combined with the Directory of Post Offices (P 1.10/4).

Earlier: National ZIP Code Directory.

P 1.10/9:nos. • Item 839-A-5 (EL)
ZIP + 4, STATE DIRECTORIES. [Irregular]

P 1.11:date
POSTAL LAWS AND REGULATIONS (General).

P 1.11/2:date
INSERTS TO POSTAL LAWS AND REGULATIONS.

P 1.11/3 • Item 838
POSTAL LAWS. [Irregular]

Latest basic volume: Revised 1967. 500 p.

A complete revision and reprinting of the laws affecting the Post Office Department and the Postal Service, this publication contains all of title 39 of the United States Code, as well as pertinent parts of titles 5, 6, 16, 18, 28, 31, 38, and 41.

The first revision since 1872, this publication consolidates and simplifies the laws. Simple language has been substituted for awkward and obsolete terms; conflicts in laws have been resolved, where possible; ambiguous provisions have been revised to reflect Comptroller General intrepretations; superseded, obsolete, or executed laws have been eliminated; and similar provisions have been consolidated.

Issued in loose-leaf form and punched for 3-ring binder. Kept up-to-date by Transmittal Letters containing revised sheets.

P 1.12:CT
POSTAL LAWS AND REGULATIONS [Special].

P 1.12/2:date
POSTAL MANUAL.

Replaces material heretofore published in the Postal Laws and Regulations (P 1.12), Post Office Manual, Postal Guide (P 1.10), and the Book of Instructions of the Postal Transportation Service.

Subscription includes basic volume plus supplementary material for an indefinite period.
Later P 1.12/5

P 1.12/3:dt.&chap.nos. • Item 838-A
POSTAL MANUAL [Simplified Edition].

Contains Chapter 1, Post Office Services (Domestic) and Chapter 2, International Mail of the Postal Manual (P 1.12/2), for the use of the general public to explain the services available, prescribe rates and fees, and prescribe conditions under which postal services are available to the public.

P 1.12/4:date • Item 838-C
POSTAL MANUAL [Issues].

Contains Chapter 3, Postal Procedure and Chapter 7, Personnel of the Postal Manual (P 1.12/2)

P 1.12/5:issue no.
POSTAL SERVICE MANUAL. [Irregular] (Includes basic volume plus supplementary material for an indefinite period)

Earlier P 1.12/2
Later replaced by Postal Contracting Manual (P 1.12/6), Employee and Labor Relation (P 1.12/7), Postal Operations Manual (P 1.12/8), Financial Management Manual (P 1.12/9), Administrative Support Manual (P 1.12/10), and Domestic Mail Manual (P 1.12/11)

P 1.12/5a • Item 838-A
INSTRUCTIONS FOR MAILERS. [Irregular] (Includes basic volume plus supplementary pages for an indefinite period)

Contains excerpts from Chapter 1, Postal Service manual for the use of individuals, companies, or organizations who use the mailing services of the U.S. Postal Service more than the average person.

P 1.12/5b • Item 843-B
– CHAPTER 5, TRANSPORTATION. [Irregular] (Includes basic volume plus supplementary material for approximately one year)

P 1.12/5-2:nos.
POSTAL SERVICE ORDERS. 73-4. – May 30, 1973. [Irregular]

P 1.12/6:date • Item 838-E
POSTAL CONTRACTING MANUAL. 1971– [Annual] (Includes basic manual plus changes for one year) (Publication 41)

PURPOSE:– To establish uniform policies and procedures relating to the procurement of facilities, equipment, supplies and services under the authority of Chapter 4, Title 39, of the United States Code, and mail transportation services by contract under Part 5, Title 39, United States Code.

P 1.12/6-2:date-nos. • Item 838-E
PM CIRCULAR. [Irregular]

Earlier PM 1.12/6

P 1.12/7:trans.nos • Item 839-A-4
EMPLOYEE AND LABOR RELATIONS. [Irregular] (Includes basic manual plus updating supplements for an indefinite period)

PURPOSE:– To set forth the personnel policies and regulations governing employment with the Postal Service. Topics covered include organization management, job evaluation, employment and placement, pay administration, employee benefits, employee relations, training, safety and health and labor relations.

Supersedes Chapter 4 of the Postal Service Manual (P 1.12/5)

P 1.12/8:trans.nos. • Item 837-E
POSTAL OPERATIONS MANUAL. [Irregular] (Subscription service includes updating transmittal letters for an indeterminate period)

Sets forth policies for the internal operations of post offices. It includes retail services, mail processing, transportation, delivery services, and fleet management.

Issued in looseleaf format and punched for 3-ring binders.

Supersedes Chapters 3 and 5 of the Postal Service Manual (P 1.12/5)

P 1.12/9:trans.nos. • Item 843
FINANCIAL MANAGEMENT MANUAL. [Irregular] (Includes supplements for an indefinite period)

PURPOSE:– To present an overview of the financial activities of the Postal Service, summarizing such topics as general accounting, post office accounting, accounts receivable and accounts payable, budget and planning, payroll accounting and control of assets.

P 1.12/10:trans.nos. • Item 843-F
ADMINISTRATIVE SUPPORT MANUAL. [Irregular] (Includes supplementary material for an indefinite period)

PURPOSE:– To describe matters of internal administration in the Postal Service, including functional statements as well as policies and requirementsregarding security, communications (printing, directives, forms, records, newsletters), government relations, procurement and supply, data processing systems, maintenance, and engineering.

P 1.12/11:trans.nos. • Item 843-B (EL)
DOMESTIC MAIL MANUAL. [Irregular] (Includes supplementary material for an indefinite period)

PURPOSE:– To assist customers in obtaining maximum benefits from domestic postal services. It includes applicable regulations and information about rates and postage, classes of mail, special services, wrapping and mailing requirements, and collections and delivery services.

Supersedes Chapter 1 of the Postal Service Manual (P 1.12/5).

P 1.12/11 a • Item 843-B
– SEPARATES. [Irregular]

P 1.13:CT
PROPOSALS.

P 1.13/2:dt.nos.
PROPOSALS AND SPECIFICATIONS FOR SUPPLIES, SCHEDULES.

P 1.14:date
REGISTER OF EMPLOYEES.

P 1.15:date
U.S. GOVERNMENT SALARY TABLES, POST-OFFICE DEPT.

P 1.16:CT
SPECIFICATIONS.

P 1.17:date
CUBA, POST DEPT., ANNUAL REPORTS.

P 1.18:CT
SCHEME OF CITY DISTRIBUTION.

P 1.19:date
ORDERS.

P 1.19/2:nos.
ORDERS, SERIES 1930.

P 1.20:Cong.
PUBLIC ACTS AND RESOLUTIONS RELATING TO POST OFFICE DEPT. AND POSTAL SERVICE.

P 1.21:CT
SCHEMES FOR SEPARATION OF MAIL BY STATES.

P 1.22:CT
ADVERTISEMENTS INVITING PROPOSALS FOR CARRYING MAIL ON STAR ROUTES (by States).

P 1.23:CT
ADVERTISEMENTS INVITING PROPOSALS FOR CARRYING MAIL ON STEAMBOAT ROUTES (by States).

P 1.24:date
ADVERTISEMENTS INVITING PROPOSALS FOR CARRYING MAILS BY AIRPLANE OR SEAPLANE.

P 1.24/2:CT
ADVERTISEMENT FOR TEMPORARY AIRMAIL SERVICE.

P 1.24/3:CT
ADVERTISEMENT FOR AIRMAIL SERVICE.

P 1.25/1:nos.
OFFICIAL PARCEL POST ZONE KEYS, UNITED STATES.

P 1.25/2:nos.
OFFICIAL PARCEL POST ZONE KEYS, VIRGIN ISLANDS.

P 1.25/3:nos.
OFFICIAL PARCEL POST ZONE KEYS, PUERTO RICO.

P 1.25/4:nos.
OFFICIAL PARCEL POST ZONE KEYS, HAWAII.

P 1.26:CT   • Item 837-H
POSTERS.

P 1.26/2:CT   • Item 838-D-1
COMMEMORATIVE STAMP POSTERS. [Irregular]

Superseded by USPS Stamp Posters (P 1.26/3)

P 1.26/3:nos.
USPS STAMP POSTERS. [Irregular]

Released approximately three to four weeks in advance of the issue dates of the stamps, each poster (8 x 10") provides an enlarged illustration of the stamp being issued, date and place of issue, name of designer, number of copies to be printed, size and color, and instructions on how to obtain first-day cancellations.
Supersedes Commemorative Stamp Posters (P 1.26/2)

P 1.26/3-2:CT
AUDIOVISUAL MATERIALS. [Irregular]

P 1.26/4:date
MINT SET OF COMMEMORATIVE STAMPS. [Annual]

P 1.27
ADDRESSES. [Irregular]

P 1.28:date
BUDGET DIGEST.

P 1.29
PRESS RELEASES. [Irregular]

P 1.29/2   • Item 843-A
LAW ENFORCEMENT REPORT. [Quarterly] (Office of Public and Media Relations)

PURPOSE:– To provide postal inspectors and other affected Departmental officials, law enforcement agencies, and organizations specifically interested in consumer protection, such as the Better Business Bureaus, information on the many schemes used to defraud through the mails.
Prior to 1974 issued as Enforcement Report of Postal Inspection Service, Fraud, Obscenity, Extortion.
ISSN 0094-8338

P 1.29/3:nos.
PHILATELIC RELEASES.

P 1.30   • Item 838-B
POSTAL SERVICE NEWS. v. 1– 1955– [Monthly]

PURPOSE:– To provide means of economical and regular communication among all postal employees.

P 1.31:nos.
PERSONNEL HANDBOOK, SERIES P-1, POSITION DESCRIPTION AND SALARY SCHEDULES, TRANSMITTAL LETTERS.

P 1.31/2
ENGINEERING HANDBOOK SERIES. E 1– [Irregular]

P 1.31/3   • Item 843
FACILITIES HANDBOOKS. S 1– [Irregular]

P 1.31/4:CT   • Item 843
HANDBOOKS, MANUALS, GUIDES.

P 1.31/5   • Item 843-C
PERSONNEL HANDBOOKS. P 1– [Irregular]

P 1.31/6:nos.   • Item 843-D
MAINTENANCE HANDBOOK, MS- (series). 1–

P 1.31/7:nos.   • Item 843-E
METHODS HANDBOOK, M- (series). 1– [Irregular]

Earlier P 24.6/2

P 1.31/7:31/3
DOMESTIC AIR SERVICE INSTRUCTIONS. (Subscription includes basic manual plus supplementary material for an indefinite period)

The manual sets forth the United States Postal Service policies, rules, regulations, and instructions concerning the safe and expeditious transportation of mail by aircraft.

P 1.31/8:nos.   • Item 843
HANDBOOK RE (series). [Irregular]

RE = Real Estate

P 1.31/9:nos.   • Item 843
HANDBOOK EL- (series). [Irregular]

P 1.31/10:nos.   • Item 843
HANDBOOK AS (series). [Irregular]

P 1.31/11:nos.   • Item 843
HANDBOOKS, DM- (series). [Irregular]

P 1.31/12:nos.   • Item 843
FISCAL HANDBOOK, SERIES F. [Irregular]

P 1.31/13:nos.   • Item 843-G
HANDBOOKS, PO (series). [Irregular]
A revisable handbook containing procedures and guidelines for managing the Computer Forwarding System and for establishing and monitoring the CFS model and program.

P 1.31/14:nos.   • Item 843
HANDBOOK F (series).

P 1.31/15:   • Item 843
HANDBOOK IM (INTERNATIONAL MAIL) (series).

P 1.31/16:nos.   • Item 843-G
HANDBOOK T (series).

P 1.32:nos.
SPECIFICATIONS ADMIN.

P 1.33:nos.
PURCHASE DESCRIPTIONS. ADMIN.

P 1.34:date   • Item 837-F (MF)
TELEPHONE DIRECTORY.

Official use only.
Earlier P 1.2:T 23/2

P 1.35:CT/date
POSTAL ZONE DIRECTORIES, TITLE VARIES. ADMIN.

P 1.36   • Item 837-B
INFORMATION SERVICE, IS- (series). [Irregular]

Correspondence aids.

P 1.36/2:nos.   • Item 837-B
PUBLIC INFORMATION (series). PI 1– 1967– [Irregular]

Supersedes IS- (series) (P 1.36).

P 1.37:date
ESTIMATED VOLUME OF MAIL AND SPECIAL SERVICES AND POSTAL REVENUES.

P 1.38:date
ANNOUNCEMENTS.

P 1.39:CT
MAPS AND CHARTS.

P 1.39/2
STATE POSTAL MAPS. [Irregular]

P 1.40:CT
MANHOUR SUMMARY.

P 1.41:nos.
ORGANIZATIONAL REPORTS.

P 1.42:date
WEEKLY HIGHLIGHT REPORT OF THE POST OFFICE DEPARTMENT.

P 1.43   • Item 838-D
POSTAL LIFE, THE MAGAZINE FOR POSTAL EMPLOYEES. v. 1– 1967– [Bimonthly]

Articles of general interest on activities and personalities connected with postal operations.
Indexed by: Index to U.S. Government Periodicals.
ISSN 0032-5368

P 1.44:nos.   • Item 837-D
POSTAL SERVICE INSTITUTE BULLETIN.

P 1.45
POSTAL LEADER, NEWSPAPER FOR POSTAL MANAGERS.

P 1.46:nos.
MANAGEMENT DATA SERIES.

P 1.47:v.nos.&nos.   • Item 837-N (MF)
MEMO TO MAILERS. [Bimonthly]

Published for mailers originating large quantities of mail.

P 1.47/2   • Item 837-N-1 (EL)
MAIL ROOM COMPANION.

P 1.48:date   • Item 837-G (MF)
COMPETITORS AND COMPETITION OF THE U.S. POSTAL SERVICE. [Annual]

Analyzes competitive aspects of services offered by organizations other than the Postal Service, such as United Parcel Services, etc.

P 1.49:date   • Item 837-J
TREASURY OF STAMPS ALBUM, SCHOOL YEAR (date). [Annual]

P 1.50:date • **Item 837-J**
BENJAMIN FRANKLIN STAMP CLUB. [Annual]

P 1.51:date • **Item 837-K**
AUDIT WORKLOAD PLAN. [Annual]

PURPOSE:– To describe financial, operations, and other types of audits of Postal Service activities performed by the Postal Inspection Service.

P 1.52:CT • **Item 837-L**
DIRECTORIES. [Irregular]

P 1.52/2:date • **Item 837-L (MF)**
EXPRESS MAIL NEXT DAY SERVICE, DIRECTORY FOR MINNEAPOLIS 554. [Semiannual]

P 1.53:CT • **Item 837-M**
MANAGEMENT INSTRUCTION (series). [Irregular]

Instructions to management on miscellaneous topics.

P 1.54:date • **Item 837-J-1**
MINT SET OF COMMEMORATIVE STAMPS. [Annual]

Discusses and reproduces commemorative stamps celebrating great events, people, and issues that helped shape our nation.

P 1.54/2:date • **Item 837-J-1**
MINT SET OF DEFINITIVE STAMPS.

P 1.55: • **Item 837-P**
NOTICES (series). [Irregular]

P 1.56: • **Item 843-H**
DISABLED VETERANS, AFFIRMATIVE ACTION PLAN. [Annual]

PURPOSE– To present the Disabled Veterans Affirmative Action Plan, which is to be used as working guidelines for positive action in the employment and advancement of disabled veterans in the Postal Service.

P 1.57: • **Item 837-R**
PUBLICATION (series).

P 1.58:date/nos. • **Item 837-S**
NATIONAL ELECTRONIC CATALOG. [Quarterly]

Issued on CD-ROM

P 1.59 • **Item 837-S-1 (E)**
ELECTRONIC PRODUCTS.

P 1.60: • **Item 837-S-1 (EL)**
POSTAL FACTS.

FIRST ASSISTANT POSTMASTER GENERAL
(1881– 1949)

P 2.1:date
ANNUAL REPORTS.

P 2.2:CT
GENERAL PUBLICATIONS.

P 2.3:nos.
BULLETINS.

P 2.4:nos.
CIRCULARS.

P 2.7:CT
POSTERS.

SECOND ASSISTANT POSTMASTER GENERAL
(1879– 1949)

P 3.1:date
ANNUAL REPORTS.

P 3.2:CT
GENERAL PUBLICATIONS.

P 3.3:nos.
BULLETINS.

P 3.4:nos.
CIRCULARS.

BUREAU OF FINANCE
(1949–   )

P 4.1:date
ANNUAL REPORTS.

P 4.2:CT • **Item 845-A**
GENERAL PUBLICATIONS.

P 4.3:nos.
BULLETINS.

P 4.4:nos.
CIRCULARS.

P 4.5:letters
INSTRUCTION LETTERS.

P 4.6 • **Item 844**
COST ASCERTAINMENT REPORT. 1926–   [Annual]

Presents cost analysis of carrying and handling the various classes of mail matter and of performing the special services.

Gives for Revenue and Volume: stamp and permit revenue (mail and special services), publishers' second-class mail, summary of revenues and volumes; for Expenditures: postal operations, transportation of mails, claims and miscellaneous, summary of expenditures; for Mails and Special Services (historical tables): annual basis; mail revenues, expenditures, pieces, and weights, by classes; special services revenues, expenditures, and transactions; quarterly basis: revenues, weights, pieces and transactions. Charts. Textual summaries.

P 4.7:date
STOLEN MONEY-ORDER FORMS.

P 4.8:date
STATEMENT OF POSTAL RECEIPTS AT 50 INDUSTRIAL OFFICES. [Monthly]

P 4.9:date
STATEMENT OF POSTAL RECEIPTS AT 50 SELECTED OFFICES. [Monthly]

Changed from P 4.Z 2

P 4.10 • **Item 840**
POSTAGE STAMPS OF THE UNITED STATES. 1927– [Biennial] (POD Publication 9)

Provides a comprehensive review of all United States postage stamps, from the first adhesive stamp issued in 1847 to the present time. It contains for each stamp a black and white illustration of the stamp with detailed information as to why each stamp was issued, its exact dimensions and color, what or whom it pictures, when and where it was first placed on sale and other pertinent information that might serve to identify properly the stamp.

Also included are data on many other points of interest about stamps and other postal materials and services– when postal cards, stamped envelopes, etc., were first issued, the number of stamps printed for each of the commemorative issues and the number of plates used in printing them; a list of the designer and engravers of each stamp issued from February 1953 through period covered by the volume; and special information on first-day covers.

P 4.11:date
DESCRIPTION OF U.S. POSTAL STAMP, HISTORICAL AND COMMEMORATIVE ISSUES (Junior Edition).

P 4.12:CT • **Item 845-B**
REGULATIONS, RULES, AND INSTRUCTIONS.

P 4.13 • **Item 841**
REVENUES AND CLASSES OF POST OFFICES. 1947–   [Annual]

Gives receipts of post offices for previous fiscal year, class of office and salary level of postmaster as of July of the current year.

FOURTH ASSISTANT POSTMASTER GENERAL
(1892– 1970)

P 5.1:date
ANNUAL REPORTS.

P 5.2:CT
GENERAL PUBLICATIONS.

P 5.3:nos.
BULLETINS [none issued].

P 5.4:nos.
CIRCULARS [none issued].

SOLICITOR FOR POST OFFICE DEPARTMENT
(1913– 1952)

P 6.1:date
ANNUAL REPORTS.

P 6.2:CT
GENERAL PUBLICATIONS.

P 6.3:nos.
BULLETINS.

P 6.4:nos.
CIRCULARS.

P 6.5:v.nos.
OFFICIAL OPINIONS.

DIVISION OF DEAD LETTERS
(1825–1904)

P 7.1:date
ANNUAL REPORTS.

P 7.2:CT
GENERAL PUBLICATIONS.

P 7.3:nos.
BULLETINS.

P 7.4:nos.
CIRCULARS.

P 7.5:date
CATALOGUE OF ARTICLES TO BE SOLD AT
  AUCTION.

P 7.6:ed.nos.
STREET DIRECTORY OF PRINCIPAL CITIES OF
  UNITED STATES.

INTERNATIONAL POSTAL
TRANSPORT DIVISION
(1946–1970)

P 8.1:date
ANNUAL REPORTS.

P 8.2:CT
GENERAL PUBLICATIONS.

P 8.3:nos.
BULLETINS.

P 8.4:nos.
CIRCULARS.

P 8.5:date
SCHEDULE OF STEAMERS APPOINTED TO CON-
  VEY MAILS TO FOREIGN COUNTRIES. [Monthly]

P 8.6:date
FOREIGN AIR MAIL SERVICE.

P 8.7:date
POSTAL UNION TRANSIT STATISTICS.

MONEY ORDERS DIVISION
(1864–1951)

P 9.1:date
ANNUAL REPORTS.

P 9.2:CT
GENERAL PUBLICATIONS.

P 9.3:nos.
BULLETINS.

P 9.4:nos.
CIRCULARS.

P 9.5:date
REGISTER OF MONEY ORDER POST OFFICES IN
  UNITED STATES.

P 9.6:date
INTERNATIONAL LIST, MONEY ORDER OFFICES IN
  FOREIGN COUNTRIES.

P 9.7:date
REGULATIONS AND INSTRUCTIONS.

TRANSPORTATION BUREAU
(1949–1970)

P 10.1:date
ANNUAL REPORTS.

P 10.2:CT   • Item 845
GENERAL PUBLICATIONS.

P 10.3:v.nos.
DAILY BULLETIN OF ORDERS AFFECTING POSTAL
  SERVICE.

P 10.4:nos.
CIRCULARS.

P 10.5:nos.
SCHEDULES OF RAILWAY POST OFFICES.

P 10.6:CT
SCHEMES OF STATES (General).

P 10.7:CT
SCHEMES (Special or Local R.P.O. Routes).

P 10.8:CT
SCHEMES OF STATES (from Certain Standpoints).

P 10.9:CT
SCHEMES OF CITY DISTRIBUTION.

P 10.10:CT
SCHEMES OF STATES (for Use of Publishers in Distribution of 2nd Class Mail).

P 10.11:nos.
GENERAL ORDERS.

P 10.11/2:nos.
GENERAL ORDERS, PHILADELPHIA REGION.

P 10.11/3:nos.
GENERAL ORDERS, SAN FRANCISCO REGION.

P 10.12/1:nos.
SCHEDULE OF MAIL TRAINS, 1st DIVISION.

P 10.12/2:nos.
SCHEDULE OF MAIL TRAINS, 2nd DIVISION.

P 10.12/3:nos.
SCHEDULE OF MAIL TRAINS, 3rd DIVISION.

P 10.12/4:nos.
SCHEDULE OF MAIL TRAINS, 4th DIVISION.

P 10.12/5:nos.
SCHEDULE OF MAIL TRAINS, 5th DIVISION.

P 10.12/6:nos.
SCHEDULE OF MAIL TRAINS, 6th DIVISION.

P 10.12/7:nos.
SCHEDULE OF MAIL TRAINS, 7th DIVISION.

P 10.12/8:nos.
SCHEDULE OF MAIL TRAINS, 8th DIVISION.

P 10.12/9:nos.
SCHEDULE OF MAIL TRAINS, 9th DIVISION.

P 10.12/10:nos.
SCHEDULE OF MAIL TRAINS, 10th DIVISION.

P 10.12/11:nos.
SCHEDULE OF MAIL TRAINS, 11th DIVISION.

P 10.12/12:nos.
SCHEDULE OF MAIL TRAINS, 12th DIVISION.

P 10.12/13:nos.
SCHEDULE OF MAIL TRAINS, 13th DIVISION.

P 10.12/14:nos.
SCHEDULE OF MAIL TRAINS, 14th DIVISION.

P 10.12/15:nos.
SCHEDULE OF MAIL TRAINS, 15th DIVISION.

P 10.12/16:CT/date
SCHEDULE OF MAIL ROUTES (by Region).
  Earlier P 10.12/1-P 10.12/15

P 10.13:date
POSTAL LAWS AND REGULATIONS APPLICABLE
  TO RAILWAY MAIL SERVICE.
    Changed from P 10.2

TOPOGRAPHY DIVISION
(1885–1936)

P 11.1:date
ANNUAL REPORTS.

P 11.2:CT
GENERAL PUBLICATIONS.

P 11.3:nos.
BULLETINS.

P 11.4:nos.
CIRCULARS.

P 11.5:CT
POST ROUTE MAPS.

P 11.6:date
PRICE LIST OF POST ROUTE MAPS.

P 11.7:date
LIST OF RURAL DELIVERY COUNTY MAPS.

P 11.8:date
OFFICIAL POSTAL MAPS.
    Supersedes P 11.6 and P 11.7

SALARIES AND ALLOWANCES
DIVISION
(1900–1902)

P 12.1:date
ANNUAL REPORT.

P 12.2:CT
GENERAL PUBLICATIONS.

P 12.3:nos.
BULLETINS.

P 12.4:nos.
CIRCULARS.

FREE DELIVERY DIVISION
(1900–1903)

P 13.1:date
ANNUAL REPORTS.

P 13.2:CT
GENERAL PUBLICATIONS.

P 13.3:nos.
BULLETINS.

P 13.4:nos.
CIRCULARS.

P 13.5:CT
REGULATIONS AND INSTRUCTIONS FOR RURAL
  FREE DELIVERY SERVICE.

P 13.6:date
OFFICIAL LIST OF RURAL FREE DELIVERY
  OFFICES.

POST OFFICE INSPECTOR DIVISION
(1905– 1916)

P 14.1:date
ANNUAL REPORTS.

P 14.2:CT
GENERAL PUBLICATIONS.

P 14.3:nos.
BULLETINS.

P 14.4:nos.
CIRCULARS.

P 14.5:date
POSTAL DECISIONS OF UNITED STATES AND OTHER COURTS AFFECTING POST OFFICE DEPART-MENT AND POSTAL SERVICES.

P 14.5:vol.
DIGEST OF DECISIONS.

P 14.6:case nos.
POSTERS.

P 14.6/2:CT
POSTERS.

PURCHASING AGENT
(1904– 1949)

P 15.1:date
ANNUAL REPORTS.

P 15.2:CT
GENERAL PUBLICATIONS.

P 15.3:nos.
BULLETINS.

P 15.4:nos.
CIRCULARS.

DIVISION OF RURAL DELIVERY
(1905– 1928)

P 16.1:date
ANNUAL REPORTS.

P 16.2:CT
GENERAL PUBLICATIONS.

P 16.3:nos.
BULLETINS.

P 16.4:nos.
CIRCULARS.

PNEUMATIC TUBE COMMISSION
(1904– 1909)

P 17.1:date
ANNUAL REPORTS.

P 17.2:CT
GENERAL PUBLICATIONS.

P 17.3:nos.
BULLETINS.

P 17.4:nos.
CIRCULARS.

EQUIPMENT AND SUPPLIES DIVISION
(1915– 1970)

P 18.1:date
ANNUAL REPORTS.

P 18.2:CT
GENERAL PUBLICATIONS.

P 18.3:nos.
BULLETINS.

P 18.4:nos.
CIRCULARS.

POSTAL SAVINGS DIVISION
(1943– 1970)

P 19.1:date
ANNUAL REPORTS.

P 19.2:CT
GENERAL PUBLICATIONS.

P 19.3:nos.
BULLETINS.

P 19.4:nos.
CIRCULARS.

P 19.5:CT
REGULATIONS.

P 19.6:date
INSTRUCTIONS TO POSTMASTERS.

    Earlier PS 1.6

P 19.7/1:date
INFORMATION ABOUT POSTAL SAVINGS SYSTEM (General).

P 19.7/2:CT by language
INFORMATION ABOUT POSTAL SAVINGS SYSTEM (General; Foreign Language Prints).

P 19.7:CT
POSTERS.

AIR POSTAL TRANSPORT DIVISION
(1946– 1970)

P 20.1:date
ANNUAL REPORTS.

P 20.2:CT
GENERAL PUBLICATIONS.

P 20.3:nos.
BULLETINS.

P 20.4:nos.
CIRCULARS.

P 20.7:CT
MAPS.

P 20.8:nos.
AIR MAIL SCHEDULES.

MOTOR-VEHICLE SERVICE DIVISION
(1924– 1941)

P 21.1:date
ANNUAL REPORTS.

P 21.2:CT
GENERAL PUBLICATIONS.

P 21.3:nos.
BULLETINS.

P 21.4:nos.
CIRCULARS.

P 21.6:CT
REGULATIONS, RULES, AND INSTRUCTIONS.

    Includes Handbooks and Manuals.

BUREAU OF ACCOUNTS
(1921– 1949)

P 22.1:date
ANNUAL REPORTS.

P 22.2:CT
GENERAL PUBLICATIONS.

P 22.3:nos.
BULLETINS.

P 22.4:nos.
CIRCULARS.

P 22.7:date
COST ASCERTAINMENT REPORTS.
    Earlier P 4.6
    Later P 25.9

BUILDING OPERATIONS AND SUPPLIES DIVISION
(1933– 1940)

P 23.1:date
ANNUAL REPORTS.

P 23.2:CT
GENERAL PUBLICATIONS.

BUREAU OF CHIEF POSTAL INSPECTOR
(1963– 1970)

P 24.1:date
ANNUAL REPORTS.

P 24.2:CT
GENERAL PUBLICATIONS.

P 24.6:CT
REGULATIONS, RULES, AND INSTRUCTIONS.

P 24.6/2   **• Item 843**
METHODS HANDBOOKS. M 1–   [Irregular]
    Later P 1.31/7

P 24.6/3
CRITERIA FOR USE IN PLANNING NEW FACILITIES,
CR- (series). 1–   [Irregular]

P 24.7:date
RECEIPTS AND CLASSES OF POST OFFICES, WITH
BASIC SALARIES OF POSTMASTERS.

    Later P 25.8

P 24.8   • **Item 842**
FIRST CLASS POST OFFICES WITH NAMED
STATIONS AND BRANCHES. 1951–   [Annual]
(POD Publication 6)

    Contains a list of first-class post offices with
named stations and branches arranged alphabetically by States as of July 1.

CONTROLLER BUREAU
(1954)

P 25.1:date
ANNUAL REPORT.

P 25.2:CT
GENERAL PUBLICATIONS.

P 25.8:date
RECEIPTS AND CLASSES OF POST OFFICES WITH
BASIC SALARIES OF POSTMASTERS.

    Earlier P 24.7
    Later P 4.13

P 25.9:date   • **Item 844**
COST ASCERTAINMENT REPORTS. 1926–   [An-
nual]

    Earlier P 22.7
    Later P 4.6

OFFICE OF PUBLIC BUILDINGS
AND PUBLIC PARKS OF THE
NATIONAL CAPITAL
(1925–1932)

PB 1.1:date
ANNUAL REPORTS.

PB 1.2:CT
GENERAL PUBLICATIONS.

PB 1.3:nos.
BULLETINS.

PB 1.4:nos.
CIRCULARS.

PB 1.5:CT
INSTRUCTIONS TO BIDDERS AND GENERAL SPECI-
FICATIONS.

PB 1.6:CT
MANUALS AND REGULATIONS.

PERSONNEL CLASSIFICATION
BOARD
(1923–1932)

CREATION AND AUTHORITY

    The Personnel Classification Board was es-
tablished by act of Congress, approved March 4,
1923 (42 Stat. 1488). The Board was abolished by
act of Congress, approved June 30, 1932, and
its functions transferred to the Civil Service Commission (CS 1).

PC 1.1:date
ANNUAL REPORTS.

PC 1.2:CT
GENERAL PUBLICATIONS.

PC 1.4:nos.
CIRCULARS.

PC 1.5:nos.
FORMS.

PEACE CORPS
(1982–   )

CREATION AND AUTHORITY

    The Peace Corps, formerly a component of
ACTION (AA 4), was established as an indepen-
dent agency by the International Security and
Development Act of 1981 (95 Stat. 612), approved
February 21, 1982.

INFORMATION

    Office of Public Affairs
    Peace Corps
    1111 20th St. NW
    Washington, D.C. 20526
    (202) 692-2230
    Toll -Free (800) 424-8540
    http://www.peacecorps.gov

PE 1.1:date   • **Item 835 (MF)**
ANNUAL REPORT.

    Summarizes activities of the Peace Corps at
home and abroad.
    Earlier AA 4.1

PE 1.2:CT   • **Item 900-D**
GENERAL PUBLICATIONS. [Irregular]

PE 1.8   • **Item 74-E-2**
HANDBOOKS, MANUALS, GUIDES. [Irregular]

    Earlier AA 4.8

PE 1.9:date   • **Item 74-E-1**
PEACE CORPS TIMES. v. 1–   1978–   [Quarterly]

    Earlier issued monthly and bimonthly.

PE 1.10:nos.   • **Item 74-E (P) (EL)**
INFORMATION COLLECTION AND EXCHANGE (series).

    Former title: Appropriate Technologies for Development.
    Earlier AA 4.8/2

PE 1.11:CT   • **Item 74-E-2 (MF)**
CORE CURRICULUM.

PE 1.12:CT   • **Item 74-E-3**
POSTERS.

PE 1.13:CT   • **Item 900-D-1 (E)**
ELECTRONIC PRODUCTS (misc.).

PE 1.13:SH   • **Item 900-D-1 (CD)**
SHARING PROMISING PRACTICES.

PRESS INTELLIGENCE DIVISION
FOR THE U.S. GOVERNMENT
(1933–1939)

PI 1.1:date
ANNUAL REPORTS.

PI 1.2:CT
GENERAL PUBLICATIONS.

PI 1.3:nos.
PRESS INTELLIGENCE BULLETINS.

    Earlier Y 3.N 21/8:13/1-684

PI 1.7:vol.
MAGAZINE ABSTRACTS. [Weekly]

    Title varies.
    Later Pr 32.208

PI 1.8:date
INDEXES TO PAPERS OF PRESIDENT FRANKLIN
DELANO ROOSEVELT.

OFFICE OF PERSONNEL
MANAGEMENT
(1979–   )

CREATION AND AUTHORITY

    The Office of Personnel Management was
established by Reorganization Plan No. 2 of 1978,
effective January 1, 1979, pursuant to Executive
Order 12107 of December 28, 1978. Many of the
Functions of the Civil Service Commission (CS 1)
were transferred to the Office of Personnel Management. The Office's duties and authority are
specified in the Civil Service reform Act of 1978
(92 Stat. 1111, 5 U.S.C. 1101), approved October
13, 1978.

INFORMATION

    Office of Personnel Management
    1900 E. Street, N.W.
    Washington, D.C. 20415-0001
    (202) 606-1212
    Fax: (202) 606-2573
    http://www.opm.gov

PM 1.1:date   • **Item 290 (MF)**
OPM, THE YEAR IN REVIEW.

    Former title: Annual Report.

PM 1.2:CT   • **Item 295**
GENERAL PUBLICATIONS. [Irregular]

PM 1.8:CT   • **Item 296-B**
HANDBOOKS, MANUALS, GUIDES. [Irregular]
    Earlier CS 1.7/4

PM 1.8/2:date   • **Item 296**
HANDBOOK OF OCCUPATIONAL GROUPS AND SE-
RIES OF CLASSES. [Irregular] (subscription includes basic volume plus supplementary material
for an indefinite period)

    PURPOSE:– To outline the Office of Person-
nel Management position-classification plan and
occupational groups and classes.
    Earlier CS 1.44

PM 1.8/3:letters-nos. • Item 290-A (P) (EL)
HANDBOOKS. [Irregular]
Earlier CS 1.45

PM 1.8/3:X-118 • Item 290-A
QUALIFICATION STANDARDS FOR WHITE COL-
LAR POSITIONS UNDER THE GENERAL
SCHEDULE. [Irregular] (includes basic manual
plus monthly revised pages for an indefinite
period)

PURPOSE:– To furnish current qualification standards for various grade-level occupations in Civil Service, under the Classification Act of 1949.
Earlier CS 1.45:X-118

PM 1.8/4:date • Item 296-C
ENROLLMENT INFORMATION GUIDE AND PLAN
COMPARISON CHART (OPEN SEASON) FOR RE-
TIREMENT SYSTEMS PARTICIPATING IN THE
FEDERAL EMPLOYEES HEALTH BENEFITS PRO-
GRAM. [Annual]

PURPOSE– To provide enrollment information and a plancomparison chart for health insurance plans participating in the Federal Employees Health Benefits Program. This information
enables federal employees to compare health
plans and possibly change to a different one
during theannual open season.

PM 1.8/5: • Item 296-C
ENROLLMENT INFORMATION GUIDE AND PLAN
COMPARISON CHART (OPEN SEASON) FOR
U.S.POSTAL SERVICE EMPLOYEES. [Annual]

PM 1.8/6: • Item 296-C
ENROLLMENT INFORMATION GUIDE AND PLAN
COMPARISON CHART (OPEN SEASON) FOR
FEDERAL CIVILIAN EMPLOYEES. [Annual]

PM 1.8/7:date • Item 296-C
ENROLLMENT INFORMATION GUIDE AND PLAN
COMPARISON CHART FOR FORMER SPOUSES
ENROLLED IN THE FEDERAL EMPLOYEES
HEALTH BENEFITS PROGRAM. [Annual]

PM 1.8/8:date • Item 296-C
ENROLLMENT INFORMATION GUIDE AND PLAN
COMPARISON CHART FOR FEDERAL CIVILIAN
EMPLOYEES IN POSITIONS OUTSIDE THE CON-
TINENTAL U.S. (INCLUDING STATES OF
ALABAMA AND HAWAII, AND ISLANDS OF GUAM
AND PUERTO RICO. [Annual]

PM 1.8/9 • Item 296-C
A GUIDE TO SUBSTANCE ABUSE TREATMENT BEN-
EFITS UNDER THE FEDERAL EMPLOYEES
HEALTH BENEFITS PROGRAM. [Triennial]

PURPOSE:– To provide a news magazine for
the exchange of ideas, experiences, and problems among Peace Corps volunteers.
Earlier AA 4.10/2
Prior to the March/April 1984 issue, designated by volume and numbers.

PM 1.8/10:date • Item 296-C
ENROLLMENT INFORMATION GUIDE AND PLAN
COMPARISON CHART FOR CSRS/FERS ANNU-
ITANTS. [Annual]

PM 1.8/11:date • Item 296-C
ENROLLMENT INFORMATION GUIDE AND PLAN
COMPARISON CHART, (OPEN SEASON) FOR
INDIVIDUALS ELIGIBLE FOR TEMPORARY CON-
TINUATION OF COVERAGE AND . . . [Annual]

PM 1.8/12:date • Item 296-C
ENROLLMENT INFORMATION GUIDE AND PLAN
COMPARISON CHART, OPEN SEASON. [Annual]

PM 1.8/13:date • Item 296-C
ENROLLMENT INFORMATION GUIDE AND PLAN
COMPARISON CHART FOR INDIVIDUALS RE-
CEIVING COMPENSATION FROM THE OFFICE
OF WORKERS COMPENSATION PROGRAMS.
[Annual]

PM 1.8/14 • Item 290-A-1
OPERATING MANUAL FOR QUALIFICATION STAN-
DARDS FOR GENERAL SCHEDULE POSITIONS.

Earlier title: Qualification Standards Handbook.

PM 1.9:nos. • Item 290-F (P) (EL)
SALARY TABLES, EXECUTIVE BRANCH OF THE
GOVERNMENT. 1– [Irregular]
Earlier CS 1.73

PM 1.10:letters-nos. • Item 299 (P) (EL)
PAMPHLETS. 1– 1947– [Irregular]
Earlier CS 1.48

PM 1.10:Sm 56-13 • Item 299
FEDERAL CIVILIAN WORK FORCE STATISTICS,
OCCUPATIONS OF FEDERAL WHITE-COLLAR
WORKERS.
Earlier CS 1.48

PM 1.10:Sm 59-11 • Item 299
FEDERAL CIVILIAN WORK FORCE STATISTICS,
OCCUPATIONS OF FEDERAL BLUE-COLLAR
WORKERS.
Earlier CS 1.48

PM 1.10/2:CT • Item 299 (EL)
FEDERAL CIVILIAN WORK FORCE STATISTICS (series). [Irregular]

PM 1.10/2-2:date • Item 299 (EL)
OCCUPATIONS OF FEDERAL WHITE-COLLAR AND
BLUE-COLLAR WORKERS. [Biennial]

PM 1.10/2-3:date • Item 299 (EL)
AFFIRMATIVE EMPLOYMENT STATISTICS. [Biennial]

PM 1.10/2-4 • Item 299-A-1 (EL)
PAY STRUCTURE OF THE FEDERAL CIVIL SERVICE.
[Annual]

PM 1.10/3:date • Item 299 (MF)
EMPLOYMENT BY GEOGRAPHIC AREA. [Annual]

PM 1.10/4:date • Item 299 (EL)
WORK YEARS AND PERSONNEL COSTS. [Annual]

PM 1.11:v.nos.&nos. • Item 290-C
CIVIL SERVICE JOURNAL. v. 1– 1960– [Quar-
terly]

Each issue contains approximately four or
five articles on problems dealing with personnel
administration and management, the civil service
system, job training, the work of government,
employee achievements, etc.
Departments: Recruiters Roundup, Legal Decisions, A Look at Legislation, Employment Focus, Training Digest, The Awards Story, ADP Billboard, and Shelf-Help (recommended reading list).
Earlier CS 1.66

PM 1.11/2:v.nos.&nos. • Item 290-C
MANAGEMENT. v. 1– 1979– [Quarterly]
Supersedes Civil Service Journal (PM 1.11).

PM 1.11/3:v.nos.&nos. • Item 290-C-1
PERSONNEL MANAGEMENT REFORM, PROGRESS
IN STATE AND LOCAL GOVERNMENTS. v. 1–
1980– [Quarterly]

PURPOSE:– To provide an in-depth analysis
of personnel reform efforts in individual States.

PM 1.12:nos. • Item 293-B
FEDERAL NEWS CLIP SHEET. 1– [Monthly]

PURPOSE:– To help keep Federal employees
abreast of developments affecting their employment. It is designed mainly for use by editors and
field installation house organs.
Earlier CS 1.69

PM 1.13:nos. • Item 293-D
FEDERAL LABOR-MANAGEMENT AND EMPLOYEE
RELATIONS CONSULTANT. 71-1– 1971–
[Biweekly]

PURPOSE:– To provide information to agencies, labor organizations, and the public and to
relay current information on what's happening in
Federal labor-management relations. Features full-
page spreads (pages 3 and 4 of each issue) on
arbitration and decisional precedents– designed
to provide ongoing training in the art and practice
of third-party decision making in the program.
Former title: Federal Labor-Management Consultant.
Earlier CS 1.80

PM 1.14:nos. • Item 294
FEDERAL PERSONNEL MANUAL: TRANSMITTAL
SHEETS.
Earlier CS 1.41

PM 1.14/2:nos. • Item 294
FEDERAL PERSONNEL MANUAL: BULLETINS,
INSTALLMENTS AND LETTERS. [Irregular]
Earlier CS 1.41/3

PM 1.14/3:nos. • Item 294 (EL)
FEDERAL PERSONNEL MANUAL: SUPPLEMENTS.
[Irregular]

Official medium of the Office of Personnel
Management for issuing its personnel regulations,
instructions, and suggestions to other agencies.
Subscriptions can be placed for the entire
series of basic volumes plus supplementary material for an indefinite period or for the individual
supplements listed below.
[Note:– The numbering system for the supplements previously published by the Civil Service
Commission (CS 1.41/4) has been retained in this
new class. Supplements listed below in brackets
are classified under the CS class.]
Earlier CS 1.41/4

271-1 DEVELOPMENT OF QUALIFICATION
STANDARDS.
271-2 TESTS AND OTHER APPLICANTS
APPRAISAL PROCEDURES.
292-1 PERSONNEL DATA STANDARDS.
[293-31] BASIC PERSONNEL RECORDS
AND FILES SYSTEM.
[296-31] PROCESSING PERSONNEL
ACTIONS.
298-1 CENTRAL PERSONNEL DATA FILE.
[305-1] EXECUTIVE RESOURCES
MANAGEMENT.
[330-1] EXAMINING PRACTICES
[335-1] EVALUATION OF EMPLOYEES FOR
PROMOTION AND
INTERNAL PLACEMENT.
[339-31] REVIEWING AND ACTING ON
MEDICAL CERTIFICATES.
[512-1] JOB GRADING SYSTEM FOR
TRADES AND
LABORORGANIZATIONS.
532-1 FEDERAL WAGE SYSTEM.
[532-2] FEDERAL WAGE SYSTEM, NON-
APPROPRIATED EMPLOY-
EES.
[711-1] LABOR-MANAGEMENT RELATIONS
PROGRAM PROVISIONS
AND TECHNICAL
GUIDANCE.
[731-1] DETERMINING SUITABILITY FOR
FEDERAL EMPLOYMENT.
[792-1] OCCUPATIONAL HEALTH
SERVICES FOR FEDERAL
CIVILIAN EMPLOYEES.
[792-1] ALCOHOLISM AND DRUG ABUSE
PROGRAM.
[831-1] RETIREMENT.
[870-1] LIFE INSURANCE.
[890-1] FEDERAL EMPLOYEES HEALTH
BENEFITS.
[910-1] NATIONAL EMERGENCY
READINESS OF FEDERAL
PERSONNEL MANAGE-
MENT.
[990-1] CIVIL SERVICE LAWS, EXECUTIVE
ORDERS, RULES AND
REGULATIONS.
[990-22] HOURS OF DUTY, PAY, AND
LEAVE, ANNOTATED.
[990-3] NATIONAL EMERGENCY STANDBY
REGULATIONS AND
INSTRUCTIONS, PERSON-
NEL AND MANPOWER.

PM 1.14/3-2 • **Item 294**
OPERATING MANUAL UPDATE.

PM 1.14/3-3 • **Item 294-A**
CSRS AND FERS HANDBOOK FOR PERSONNEL AND PAYROLL.

PM 1.14/3-4 • **Item 294-B (EL)**
GUIDE TO PROCESSING PERSONNEL ACTIONS. (online database)

PM 1.14/4:nos. • **Item 294**
NOTICE AND POSTING SYSTEM.

PM 1.15 • **Item 293-E (EL)**
EMPLOYMENT AND TRENDS AS OF . . . [Bimonthly]
Formerly titled: Federal Civilian Work Force Statistics.

PM 1.16:v.nos.&nos. • **Item 300-D**
PERSONNEL LITERATURE. [Monthly]

PURPOSE:– To list selected books, pamphlets, and other publications received in the Library during the previous month. Also includes periodical articles, unpublished dissertations, and microfilms.
Annual index issued separately.
Earlier CS 1.62

PM 1.17:v.nos.&nos. • **Item 290-H-1**
FIRST LINE, NEWSLETTER FOR FEDERAL SUPERVISORS AND MIDMANAGERS. v. 1– 5. 1976–1981. [Bimonthly]

PURPOSE:– To provide information on important developments in laws, Executive orders, the Federal Personnel Manual, and court decisions that affect Federal employees; and to provide articles on personnel management responsibilities of Federal supervisors and midmanagers.
Earlier CS 1.91

PM 1.18:v.nos.&nos. • **Item 291-C**
SPOTLIGHT. v. 1– 13. – 1981. [Bimonthly]

Combined Women in Action (PM 1.20) to form Spotlight on Affirmative Employment Programs (P 1.18/3).

PM 1.18/2:nos. • **Item 290-L (MF)**
EEO INFORMATION ON EQUAL OPPORTUNITY FOR STATE AND LOCAL GOVERNMENTS. [Irregular]
Earlier CS 1.76/2

PM 1.18/3 • **Item 290-H-2**
SPOTLIGHT ON AFFIRMATIVE EMPLOYMENT PROGRAMS. v. 1– 1982– [Monthly]

Formed by the union of Spotlight (PM 1.18) and Women in Action (PM 1.20).
Superseded by PM 1.18/4

PM 1.18/4:v.nos.&nos. • **Item 290-H-2**
RECRUITING HIGHLIGHTS. [Quarterly]

Supersedes PM 1.18/3 with different format and new numbering system.
This publication has been incorporated into Federal Staffing Digest (PM 1.18/5).
Earlier: Spotlight on Affirmative Employment Programs.

PM 1.18/5:date • **Item 290-H-2**
FEDERAL STAFFING DIGEST. [Quarterly]

This publication has incorporated Recruiting Highlights (PM 1.18/4).
Earlier CS 1.65

PM 1.19:v.nos./nos. • **Item 296-A (MF)**
INTERAGENCY TRAINING CATALOG OF COURSES. [Irregular]

PURPOSE:– To provide information about training programs offered in the Washington, D.C. area on an inter-agency basis.

ANNUAL BULLETIN.

Published before the beginning of each fiscal year, gives complete course descriptions and nomination information listed by content, indices for subject and agency. This basic volume is updated by new course descriptions by monthly publications which are so designed that they may be clipped and the contents inserted into looseleaf copy of annual IATPB maintained by agency training office.
Includes Annual Calendar, previously published separately, gives titles, dates, and course numbers of all IATPB listings arranged chronologically.

MONTHLY CALENDAR.

Includes titles, dates, course numbers, and nomination deadlines for two months, arranged chronologically. Updates new courses, new dates, cancellations, and nomination deadlines.

PM 1.19/2:date • **Item 291-D**
INTERAGENCY TRAINING, CALENDAR OF COURSES. [Quarterly]
Earlier CS 1.65/4

PM 1.19/3:nos. • **Item 290-G**
FEDERAL TRAINER, AN INFORMATION EXCHANGE FOR THE FEDERAL TRAINING COMMUNITY. 1– [Quarterly]
Earlier CS 1.84

PM 1.19/4:CT • **Item 291-G (MF)**
CATALOGS OF TRAINING COURSES [on various subjects]. [Irregular]
Earlier CS 1.65/9

PM 1.19/4-2:date
TRAINING AND DEVELOPMENT SERVICES. [Annual]
Earlier PM 1.9/4:T 68/2

PM 1.19/4-3: • **Item 299-B**
EMPLOYEE TRAINING IN THE FEDERAL SERVICE. [Annual]

PURPOSE– To present information on training covered under the Government Employee Training Act, Chapter 41, Title 5, United States Code.Tables contain both government-wide and agency-by-agency training statistics.

PM 1.19/4-4: • **Item 291-G-2 (MF)**
GUIDE TO TRAINING COURSES, WASHINGTON TRAINING DEVELOPMENT SERVICES.[Annual]

Catalog of training and delivery services offered by the OPM organization, Washington Area Service Center. Lists courses in such areas asfinancial management, information technology, management and support occupations, and personnel management.

PM 1.20:v.nos.&nos. • **Item 290-H-2**
WOMEN IN ACTION, AN INFORMATION SUMMARY FOR THE FEDERAL WOMEN'S PROGRAM. v. 1– 11. 1971– 1981. [Monthly]

Earlier CS 1.74/2
Combined with Spotlight (PM 1.18) to form Spotlight on Affirmative Employment Programs (P 1.18/3).

PM 1.21:nos. • **Item 292**
CURRENT FEDERAL EXAMINATION ANNOUNCEMENTS. [Bimonthly]
Earlier CS 1.28

PM 1.21/2:nos. • **Item 292**
ANNOUNCEMENTS [of examinations].
Earlier CS 1.26

PM 1.22:CT • **Item 290-E**
BIBLIOGRAPHIES AND LISTS OF PUBLICATIONS. [Irregular]
Earlier CS 1.61

PM 1.22/2:nos. • **Item 300-A-1 (MF)**
PERSONNEL BIBLIOGRAPHY SERIES. 1– 1960– [Irregular] (Library)

A series of subject bibliographies compiled by the Office of Personnel Management Library comprehensively covering the fields of personnel administration and civil service. These are reviewed by subject matter experts prior to publication. The titles are updated biennially.
Earlier CS 1.61/3

PM 1.23:date • **Item 290-P-2**
FEDERAL FORECAST FOR ENGINEERS. [Irregular]
PURPOSE:– To provide a nationwide summary of Federal Government projected vacancies and employment for professional engineers. Information includes the engineering specialties, and agencies offering the best opportunities by geographical area.
Earlier CS 1.2:En 3/3

PM 1.24:date • **Item 290-H-7 (MF)**
FEDERAL AGENCY CLASSIFICATION CHIEFS WORKSHOP: REPORTS. [Annual]

PURPOSE:– To provide a record of proceedings of the workshops.

PM 1.25:nos. • **Item 293-A**
FED FACTS.
Earlier CS 1.59

PM 1.26:date • **Item 295-A**
ACHIEVEMENTS. [Annual]
PURPOSE:– To describe the activities for the year under the Federal Incentive Awards Program.

PM 1.27:date
INTERGOVERNMENTAL PERSONNEL NOTES. [Bimonthly]
Earlier CS 1.86

PM 1.27/2:v.nos.&nos. • **Item 295-C (MF)**
INCENTIVE AWARDS NOTES. [Bimonthly]
Earlier CS 1.83

PM 1.28:nos. • **Item 300-A**
PERSONNEL MANAGEMENT SERIES.
Earlier CS 1.54

PM 1.28/2:date • **Item 300-A**
PERSONNEL MANAGEMENT TRAINING DIVISION I. [Annual]

PM 1.29:date • **Item 301-A**
COMPENSATION REPORT. [Annual]
Earlier CS 1.29/3
Former title: Federal Frigne Benefit Facts.

PM 1.30:date • **Item 291**
POSITION CLASSIFICATION STANDARDS FOR POSITIONS SUBJECT TO THE CLASSIFICATION ACT OF 1949. [Bimonthly] (Basic volume plus changes for an indefinite period)
Earlier CS 1.39

PM 1.30/a • **Item 291**
– SEPARATES.

PM 1.31:date • **Item 290-N (MF)**
TELEPHONE DIRECTORY.
Earlier CS 1.88

PM 1.31/2:date/nos. • **Item 290-N-2**
ORGANIZATIONAL DIRECTORY OF KEY OFFICIALS. [Quarterly]
This is essentially an organizational chart showing organization, name, and telephone number.

PM 1.31/3:date • **Item 290-N**
CHICAGO FEDERAL EXECUTIVE BOARD DIRECTORY.

PM 1.32:v.nos.&nos. • **Item 295-B**
IN BRIEF. v. 1– 1979– [Quarterly]
PURPOSE:– To inform agency General Counsels and their staffs of the latest developments in federal personnel law. Sets forth matters before the Merit System Protection Board, Federal Labor Relations Authority, and follows significant personnel matters in the Federal Courts. The name and telephone number of the attorney assigned to each case is provided for additional information.

PM 1.33:v.nos.&nos. • Item 295-C
REPORTER. v. 1– 13. – 1982. [Monthly]

PURPOSE:– To provide a newsletter for the Federal Employee Health and Alcoholism/Drug Abuse Programs.
Continues: Occupational Health Reporter (CS 1.90)

PM 1.34:v.nos.&nos. • Item 300-E
PERFORMANCE. v. 1– 2. 1980– 1981. [Issued 8 times a year]

Contains overviews of productivity measurement documents published by the Office on subjects such as measuring common administrative services and assessing productivity of operating personnel offices.

PM 1.35:CT • Item 299-A
POSTERS. [Irregular]

Earlier CS 1.89

PM 1.36:nos. • Item 292-A (MF)
INTERN PROGRAM, IP (series). [Irregular]

Each issue deals with a different aspect of Presidential Management Intern Program. Includes IPP (nos.)

PM 1.37:CT • Item 292-A-1 (MF)
EXEMPLARY PRACTICES IN FEDERAL PRODUCTIVITY. [Irregular]

Each issue describes a different Federal facility's productivity improvement program for the purpose of informing managers and supervisors of successful techniques for improving productivity.

PM 1.38:date • Item 292-A-2
PRODUCTIVITY RESEARCH PROGRAM FOR FISCAL YEAR (date). 1– [Annual]

PM 1.39:date • Item 293-D-1
INDEX OF FEDERAL LABOR RELATIONS CASES. [3 times a year]

Consists predominantly of a computerized index by subject category of Federal labor relations case decisions by such Federal agencies as the Federal Labor Relations Authority, Federal Labor Council, Assistant Secretary for Labor-Management Relations, etc.

PM 1.40:date • Item 290-H-8
DIGEST OF SIGNIFICANT CLASSIFICATION DECISIONS AND OPINIONS. v. 1– 1981– [Semiannual]

PURPOSE:– To increase classification consistency government-wide by making available recent key Office decisions on specific classification issues. To be used in conjunction with OPM classification standards.

PM 1.41:CT • Item 290-C-2
PROJECT MANAGEMENT SERIES. [Irregular]

PM 1.41/2:nos. • Item 290-C-3
CASE MANAGEMENT INFORMATION SERIES. 1– [Irregular]

PM 1.41/4:931-1 • Item 294
FEDERAL PERSONNEL ADMINISTRATION CAREER PROGRAMS.

Basic volume updated by continuing installments cumulated irregularly.
Discontinued [PL-36, Winter 1980]

PM 1.42:date • Item 290-L-1 (MF)
ANNUAL REPORT ON IMPLEMENTATION OF FEDERAL EQUAL OPPORTUNITY RECRUITMENT PROGRAM, REPORT TO CONGRESS.

Issued pursuant to the Civil Service Reform Act of 1978. Reports on Program efforts to increase the numbers of minorities and women in given occupational and salary grade groupings in the Federal Government.

PM 1.43:nos. • Item 290-P-1
PERSONNEL RESEARCH REPORTS, PRR-(series).

Earlier CS 1.71/7

PM 1.44:date • Item 290-T
INDEX TO INFORMATION. [Annual with quarterly supplements]

Index of information required to be available under the Freedom of Information Act. Lists publications containing such information by subject areas and titles.

PM 1.45:date • Item 292-A-2 (MF)
FEDERAL PRODUCTIVITY MEASUREMENT. [Annual]

Issued in microfiche.

PM 1.46:date • Item 291-H (MF)
CURRICULUM CATALOG. [Annual] (Supervisory Training Institute)

PURPOSE:– To provide all information needed to apply for supervisory course offerings in such areas as Basic Management Techniques and Group Management Programs. Includes transportation information and a Washington area map.

PM 1.47:date • Item 293-D-2 (MF)
UNION RECOGNITION IN THE FEDERAL GOVERNMENT, STATISTICAL SUMMARY. [Annual]

Provides tabular statistics on exclusive recognitions and agreements negotiated by Federal agencies, under Executive Order 11491.

PM 1.48:nos.
PS (series). [Irregular]

PM 1.49:CT • Item 290-H-5
MANAGEMENT ANALYSIS SERIES. [Irregular]

PURPOSE:– To provide information for Government officials on ADP (automatic data processing) training, services, and sources of information.
Earlier CS 1.65/7

PM 1.51:date • Item 293-D-3
CENTER FOR INFORMATION MANAGEMENT AND AUTOMATION: CALENDAR FOR FISCAL YEAR. [Annual]

Lists courses given by the Center.

PM 1.52 • Item 291-G-1 (MF)
CHICAGO REGIONAL TRAINING CENTER, COURSE ANNOUNCEMENTS.

Each single sheet announcement describes a course on a different work effectiveness topic.

PM 1.53: • Item 290-J-1
FORMS.

PM 1.54:v.nos./nos. • Item 290-C
THE INSTITUTE. [3 times a year]

PM 1.55:v.nos./nos. • Item 290-V (EL)
FOCUS ON FEDERAL EMPLOYEE HEALTH ASSISTANCE PROGRAMS. [Bimonthly]

PM 1.56:date • Item 293-D-3
CURRENT INFORMATION RESOURCE REQUIREMENTS OF THE FEDERAL GOVERNMENT. [Annual]

Later PrEx 2.12/5

PM 1.57:v.nos.&nos. • Item 290-P-1
PERSONNEL RESEARCH HIGHLIGHTS. [Irregular]

PM 1.58v.nos./nos. • Item 293-A
FEDERAL QUALITY NEWS.

PM 1.59 • Item 295-D (E)
ELECTRONIC PRODUCTS.

PM 1.59/2:date • Item 295-D-1 (CD)
HRCD HUMAN RESOURCES COMPACT DISK. [Semiannual]

PM 1.61 • Item 293-D-4 (MF)
FEDERAL EMPLOYEE SUBSTANCE ABUSE EDUCATION AND TREATMENT ACT OF 1986. [Annual]

PM 1.62 • Item 295-F (P) (EL)
NEW DEVELOPMENTS IN EMPLOYEE AND LABOR RELATIONS. [Bimonthly]

PM 1.63 • Item 295-D (EL)
SIGNIFICANT CASES, FEDERAL EMPLOYEE AND LABOR-MANAGEMENT RELATIONS (series).

PM 1.64 • Item 295-D-2 (EL)
SENIOR EXECUTIVE SERVICE NEWSLETTER. [Quarterly]

PM 1.65 • Item 295-D-3 (EL)
INDEX OF DECISIONS, FEDERAL SERVICE IMPASSES PANEL. [Annual]

PRESIDENT OF THE UNITED STATES

The Following scheme applies to each of the Presidents from Washington through Hoover:

.1:date
ANNUAL MESSAGES.

.2:CT
GENERAL PUBLICATIONS.

.3:nos.
BULLETINS.

.4:nos.
CIRCULARS.

.5:CT
EXECUTIVE ORDERS.

.6:date
INAUGURAL ADDRESS.

.7:CT
PROCLAMATIONS.

.8:CT
SPECIAL MESSAGES.

Pr 1	George Washington (1789– 1797)
Pr 2	John Adams (1797– 1801)
Pr 3	Thomas Jefferson (1801– 1809)
Pr 4	James Madison (1809– 1817)
Pr 5	James Monroe (1817– 1825)
Pr 6	John Quincy Adams (1825– 1829)
Pr 7	Andrew Jackson (1829– 1837)
Pr 8	Martin Van Buren (1837– 1841)
Pr 9	William Henry Harrison (1841)
Pr 10	John Tyler (1841– 1845)
Pr 11	James Knox Polk (1845– 1849)
Pr 12	Zachary Taylor (1849– 1850)
Pr 13	Millard Fillmore (1850– 1853)
Pr 14	Franklin Pierce (1853– 1857)
Pr 15	James Buchanan (1857– 1861)
Pr 16	Abraham Lincoln (1861– 1865)
Pr 17	Andrew Johnson (1865– 1869)
Pr 18	Ulysses Simpson Grant (1869– 1877)
Pr 19	Rutherford Birchard Hayes (1877– 1881)
Pr 20	James Abram Garfield (1881)
Pr 21	Chester Alan Arthur (1881– 1885)
Pr 22	Grover Cleveland (1885– 1889, 1893– 1897)
Pr 23	Benjamin Harrison (1889– 1893)
Pr 24	Grover Cleveland (not used, see Pr 22)
Pr 25	William KcKinley (1897– 1901)
Pr 26	Theodore Roosevelt (1901– 1909)
Pr 27	William Howard Taft (1909– 1913)
Pr 28	Woodrow Wilson (1913– 1921)
Pr 29	Warren Gamaliel Harding (1921– 1923)
Pr 30	Calvin Coolidge (1923– 1929)
Pr 31	Herbert Hoover (1929– 1933)

PRESIDENT OF THE UNITED STATES FRANKLIN DELANO ROOSEVELT (1933– 1945)

Pr 32.1:date
ANNUAL MESSAGES.

Pr 32.2:CT
GENERAL PUBLICATIONS.

Pr 32.3
BULLETINS.

Pr 32.4
CIRCULARS.

Pr 32.5:CT
EXECUTIVE ORDERS.

Pr 32.6:date
INAUGURAL ADDRESS.

Pr 32.7:CT
PROCLAMATIONS.

Pr 32.8:CT
SPECIAL MESSAGES.

Pr 32.9
PRESS RELEASES. (Mimeographed)

Pr 32.10:CT
CONGESTED PRODUCTION AREAS COMMITTEE [publications].

Proc. & printed.

BUREAU OF THE BUDGET (1939– 1945)

CREATION AND AUTHORITY

The Bureau of the Budget (T 51) was transferred from the Department of the Treasury to the Executive Office of the President under Reorganization Plan 1 of 1939 (53 Stat. 1423).
Note:– Separate SuDocs classes were assigned under individual Presidential Administration: Pr 32.100 for Roosevelt (1939– 1945), Pr 33.100 for Truman (1945– 1952) and Pr 34.100 for Eisenhower (1952– 1961). In 1961 the SuDocs class PrEx 2 was assigned to the Bureau.

Pr 32.101:date
ANNUAL REPORTS.

Earlier T 51.1
Later Pr 33.101

Pr 32.102:CT
GENERAL PUBLICATIONS.

Earlier T 51.2
Later Pr 33.102

Pr 32.104:nos.
CIRCULARS.

Superseded by Pr 32.104/2
Earlier T 51.4

Pr 32.104/2:letters-nos.
BUDGET CIRCULARS.

Supersedes Pr 32.104
Later Pr 33.104

Pr 32.106:CT
REGULATIONS, RULES, AND INSTRUCTIONS.

Includes Handbooks, Manuals.
Later Pr 33.106, Pr 33.106/2

Pr 32.107:date
BUDGET OF UNITED STATES GOVERNMENT.

Earlier T 51.5
Later Pr 33.107

Pr 32.108:CT
MANAGEMENT BULLETINS.

Later Pr 33.108

OFFICE OF GOVERNMENT REPORTS (1939– 1945)

CREATION AND AUTHORITY

The Office of Government Reports was established on July 1, 1939, to perform certain functions formerly exercised by the National Emergency Council, which was abolished. Executive Order 8248 of September 8, 1939, established the Office as an administrative unit within the Executive Office of the President. Executive Order 9182 of June 13, 1942, abolished the Office and transferred its functions to the Office of War Information in the Office for Emergency Management. The Office of Government Reports (Pr 33.400) was reestablished within the Executive Office of the President by Executive Order 9809 of December 12, 1946. The Office was terminated on June 30, 1948, pursuant to act of Congress, approved July 30, 1947 (61 Stat. 588).

Pr 32.201:date
ANNUAL REPORTS.

Earlier Y 3.N 21/9:1

Pr 32.202:CT
GENERAL PUBLICATIONS.

Earlier Y 3.N 21/9:2

Pr 32.206:CT
REGULATIONS, RULES, AND INSTRUCTIONS.

Pr 32.207:CT
DIRECTORY OF FEDERAL AND STATE DEPARTMENTS AND AGENCIES.

Earlier Y 3.N 21/9:9

Pr 32.208:vol
MAGAZINE ABSTRACTS. [Weekly]

Earlier PI 1.7
Later Pr 32.5011

Pr 32.209:nos.
PRESS INTELLIGENCE BULLETINS. [Daily, except Sundays and holidays]

Later Pr 32.5012

Pr 32.210:date
UNITED STATES GOVERNMENT MANUAL.

Earlier Y 3.N 21/9:2 M 31/2
Later Pr 32.5016

Pr 32.211:nos.
REPORTS.

Earlier Y 3.N 21/9:10

Pr 32.212:nos.
NATIONAL DEFENSE PROGRAM, CONTRACTS AND EXPENDITURES AS REPORTED IN PRESS RELEASES: TABULATIONS. [Semimonthly]

Later Pr 32.4009

Pr 32.213:date
NATIONAL DEFENSE AND NEUTRALITY, PROCLAMATIONS, EXECUTIVE ORDERS, ETC. [Irregular]

Pr 32.214:nos.
INFORMATION DIGEST.

Later Pr 32.5010

Pr 32.215:date
THIS WEEK IN DEFENSE.

Pr 32.216:CT
REFERENCE LISTS.

Pr 32.220:CT
OFFICE OF GOVERNMENT REPORTS: PUBLICATIONS OF STATE OFFICES.

This classification original with Duke University Library.

NATIONAL RESOURCES PLANNING BOARD (1939– 1943)

CREATION AND AUTHORITY

The National Resources Committee (Y 3.N 21/12) was combined with the Federal Employment Stabilization Office (C 26) to form the National Resources Planning Board by Reorganization Plan 1, of 1939, effective July 1, 1939. The Board was abolished by act of Congress, approved June 26, 1943 (57 Stat. 169), effect August 31, 1943.

Pr 32.301:date
[ANNUAL REPORTS] PROGRESS REPORTS.

Earlier Y 3.N 21/12:1

Pr 32.302:CT
GENERAL PUBLICATIONS.

Pr 32.304:nos.
CIRCULARS.

Earlier Y 3.N 21/12:4

Pr 32.305:CT
LAWS.

Pr 32.306:CT
REGULATIONS, RULES, AND INSTRUCTIONS.

Pr 32.307:nos.
BIBLIOGRAPHY OF REPORTS BY STATE AND REGIONAL PLANNING ORGANIZATIONS.

Pr 32.308:date
MONTHLY REPORTS ON FEDERAL WATER RESOURCES INVESTIGATIONS AND CONSTRUCTION PROJECTS.

Earlier Y 3.N 21/12:16

Pr 32.309:nos.
TECHNICAL PAPERS.

OFFICE FOR EMERGENCY MANAGEMENT
(1940–1945)

CREATION AND AUTHORITY

The Office for Emergency Management was established within the Executive Office of the President by an administrative order dated May 25, 1940, pursuant to Executive Order 8248 of September 8, 1939. By 1944, the Office became inactive.

Pr 32.401:date
ANNUAL REPORTS.

Pr 32.402:CT
GENERAL PUBLICATIONS.

Pr 32.402:L 54/date
REPORTS TO CONGRESS ON LEND-LEASE OPERATIONS.

Later Pr 32.5507

Pr 32.406:CT
REGULATIONS, RULES, AND INSTRUCTIONS.

Pr 32.407:vol
DEFENSE, OFFICIAL WEEKLY BULLETINS.

Earlier Y 3.C 831:107
Later Pr 32.5008

Pr 32.407/2:vol.
– SUPPLEMENTS.

Pr 32.408:CT
ARSENAL OF DEMOCRACY SERIES.

Pr 32.409:CT
POSTERS.

Pr 32.410:date
PRIORITIES ORDERS IN FORCE.

These are orders of the War Production Board.
Later Pr 32.4814

Pr 32.411:CT
ADDRESSES.

Pr 32.412:CT
FAIR EMPLOYMENT PRACTICE COMMITTEE [publications].

Pr 32.413:CT
PUBLICATIONS OF SCIENTIFIC RESEARCH AND DEVELOPMENT OFFICE.

Pr 32.413/2:nos.
TROPICAL DISEASES REPORTS.

Pr 32.413/3:nos.
OSRD [reports].

Pr 32.413/4:nos.
RADIO CORPORATION DIVISION PUBLICATIONS.

Pr 32.413/5:nos.
RADIATION LABORATORY PUBLICATIONS.

Pr 32.413/6:nos.
WAVE PROPAGATION GROUP REPORTS.

Pr 32.413/7:nos.
INFORMAL COMMUNICATIONS.

Pr 32.413/8:nos.
APPLIED MATHEMATICS PANEL PUBLICATIONS.

Pr 32.413/9:CT
MEDICAL RESEARCH COMMITTEE PUBLICATIONS.

Pr 32.413/10:nos.
SUMMARY OF REPORTS RECEIVED BY COMMITTEE ON MEDICAL RESEARCH.

Pr 32.413/11:date
SUMMARY PROGRESS REPORT, TROPICAL DETERIORATION COMMITTEE. [Monthly]

Pr 32.413/12:div.nos.&nos.
SUMMARY TECHNICAL REPORT OF NATIONAL DEFENSE RESEARCH COMMITTEE.

OFFICE OF PRODUCTION MANAGEMENT
(1941–1942)

CREATION AND AUTHORITY

The Office of Production Management was established within the Office for Emergency Management by Executive Order 8629 of January 7, 1941. The Office was abolished by Executive Order 9040 of January 24, 1942, and its functions transferred to the War Production Board (Pr 32.4800).

Pr 32.4001:date
ANNUAL REPORTS.

Pr 32.4002:CT
GENERAL PUBLICATIONS.

Pr 32.4006:CT
REGULATIONS, RULES, AND INSTRUCTIONS.

Pr 32.4007:nos.
FARMING OUT BULLETINS.

Earlier Y 3.C 831:111

Pr 32.4008:CT
POSTERS.

Pr 32.4009:nos.
NATIONAL DEFENSE PROGRAM CONTRACT AND AWARD LISTING.

Earlier Pr 32.212

Pr 32.4010:nos.
PRIORITIES REGULATIONS.

Later Pr 32.4807

Pr 32.4011:nos.
TRAINING WITHIN INDUSTRY, BULLETINS.

Proc. and printed.
Publications of labor division.

Pr 32.4012:nos.
TRAINING WITHIN INDUSTRY, EXAMPLES.

Proc. and printed.
Publications of Labor Division.
Later Pr 32.4808

Pr 32.4013:date
STATE DISTRIBUTION OF DEFENSE CONTRACT AWARDS. [Monthly]

Earlier Y 3.C 831:102 C 76
Later Pr 32.4828

STATE AND LOCAL COOPERATION DIVISION
(1940–1941)

Pr 32.4101:date
ANNUAL REPORTS.

Pr 32.4102:CT
GENERAL PUBLICATIONS.

Pr 32.4107:nos.
FIRE SERIES BULLETINS.

Pr 32.4108:nos.
STRUCTURE SERIES BULLETIN.

OFFICE OF PRICE ADMINISTRATION
(1941–1946)

CREATION AND AUTHORITY

The Office of Price Administration and Civilian Supply was established within the Office for Emergency Management by Executive Order 8734 of April 11, 1941, assuming the functions formerly administered by the Price Stabilization and the Consumer Divisions of the Advisory Commission to the Council of National Defense. The Office was redesignated the Office of Price Administration by Executive Order 8875 of August 28, 1941, and the functions relating to civilian supply transferred to the Office of Production Management (Pr 32.4000). The Office was consolidated with certain other agencies to form the Office of Temporary Controls (Pr 33.300) by Executive Order 9809 of December 12, 1946.

Pr 32.4201:date
ANNUAL REPORTS.

Pr 32.4202:CT
GENERAL PUBLICATIONS.

Pr 32.4203/2
RENT CONTROL BULLETIN.

Processed.

Pr 32.4203/3
LEGISLATIVE REFERENCE BULLETINS. [Proc. Admin.]

Pr 32.4205:CT
LAWS.

Pr 32.4206:CT
REGULATIONS, RULES, AND INSTRUCTIONS.

Pr 32.4206/2
OPA FIELD MANUAL. [Proc. Admin.]

Pr 32.4207:nos.
PRICE SCHEDULES.

Earlier Y 3.C 831:102 P 93

Pr 32.4208:nos.
NEW PASSENGER AUTOMOBILE RATIONING REGULATIONS, ORDERS.

Pr 32.4209:nos.
PROCEDURAL REGULATIONS.

Pr 32.4210:nos.
MAXIMUM PRICE REGULATIONS.

Pr 32.4211:nos.
GENERAL MAXIMUM PRICE REGULATIONS, BULLETINS.

Pr 32.4212:CT
POSTERS.

Pr 32.4213:CT
ADDRESSES.

Pr 32.4214:nos.
MAXIMUM RENT REGULATIONS.

Pr 32.4215:nos.
MANUALS.

Pr 32.4216:date
QUARTERLY REPORTS.

Pr 32.4217:CT
PAPERS IN RE.

Later Pr 33.309

Pr 32.4218:CT
DIGESTS FOR RETAILERS.

Issued by Retail Trade and Services Division. Pubs. desig. RTD-nos.

Pr 32.4219:nos.
EXPLANATORY BULLETIN.

Pr 32.4220:nos.
TIRE RATIONING GUIDES.

Pr 32.4221:nos.
RETAILERS' BULLETINS.

Pr 32.4222:nos.
SERVICE TRADES BULLETINS.

Pr 32.4223:nos.
WHOLESALERS BULLETINS.

Pr 32.4224:nos.
O.P.A. BULLETINS FOR SCHOOLS AND COLLEGES.

Pr 32.4225:CT
INCOME AND EXPENSE UNDER RENT CONTROL (by States).

Pr 32.4226:nos.
FOREIGN INFORMATION SERIES.

Pr 32.4227:nos.
WAR PROFIT STUDIES.

Later Pr 33.312

Pr 32.4228:nos.
FUEL OIL INDUSTRY LETTERS. [Bimonthly]

Pr 32.4229:vol.
GOVERNMENT MILEAGE ADMINISTRATOR. [Monthly]

Pr 32.4230:vol
INDUSTRY INFORMATION. [Weekly]

Pr 32.4230/2:nos.
INDUSTRY NEWS LETTERS.

Earlier Pr 32.4230

Pr 32.4231:nos.
RECENT PRICE INTERPRETATIONS.

Pr 32.4232:nos.
GROUP SERVICES BULLETINS. [Bimonthly]

Pr 32.4233:nos.
PRICE POLICY SERIES.

Printed and Proc.

Pr 32.4234:nos.
PRICE CONTROL REPORTS.

Pr 32.4235:v.nos.
TRANSPORTATION COMMITTEE BULLETINS. [Monthly]

Superseded by Pr 32.4216

Pr 32.4236:nos.
COAL RATIONING INDUSTRY LETTERS.

Pr 32.4237:nos.
STOVE RATIONING INDUSTRY LETTERS. [Monthly]

Pr 32.4238:date
REPORTS OF AREA OFFICE OPERATIONS. [Monthly]

Pr 32.4239:CT
FOREIGN INFORMATION BRANCH PUBLICATIONS.

Pr 32.4240:nos.
OPA INFORMATION LEAFLETS FOR SCHOOLS AND COLLEGES.

Pr 32.4241:date
OPA FOOD GUIDE FOR RETAILERS. [Monthly]

Pr 32.4242:nos.
FACTS YOU SHOULD KNOW, STATEMENTS.

Pr 32.4243:nos.
TRANSPORTATION AND PUBLIC UTILITIES DIVISION, NEWS LETTERS. RESTRICTED. [Semimonthly]

Pr 32.4244:CT
OPA TRADE BULLETINS.

Pr 32.4245:nos.
POINT VALUE CHARTS. [Monthly]

Pr 32.4246:vol.
PRICE TRENDS AND CONTROLS IN LATIN AMERICA, FORTNIGHTLY REVIEW.

Pr 32.4247:nos.
MATERIALS DIGEST.

Pr 32.4248:nos.
OPA MANUAL NEWS LETTERS.

Pr 32.4248/2:nos.
OPA MANUAL NEWS LETTERS, RENT.

Pr 32.4248/3:nos.
OPA MANUAL NEWS LETTERS, ACCOUNTING.

Pr 32.4248/4:nos.
OPA MANUAL NEWS LETTERS, PRICE.

Pr 32.4248/5:nos.
OPA MANUAL NEWS LETTERS, BOARD OF OPERATIONS.

Pr 32.4248/6:nos.
OPA MANUAL NEWS LETTERS, BOARD MANAGEMENT.

Pr 32.4248/7:nos.
OPA MANUAL NEWS LETTERS, ENFORCEMENT.

Proc. & printed.

Pr 32.4248/8:nos.
OPA MANUAL NEWS LETTERS, CLERICAL.

Pr 32.4248/9:nos.
OPA MANUAL NEWS LETTERS, ADMINISTRATIVE MANAGEMENT.

Pr 32.4249:date
COORDINATION SERVICE, DIGESTS OF INTERPRETATIONS OF SPECIFIC PRICE SCHEDULES AND REGULATIONS.

Pr 32.4250:nos.
OPA CHART BOOK RELEASES. [Monthly]

Consumer Division

Pr 32.4251:date
ANNUAL REPORTS.

Pr 32.4252:CT
GENERAL PUBLICATIONS.

Pr 32.4253:nos.
BULLETINS.

Earlier Y 3.C 831:109

Pr 32.4256:CT
REGULATIONS, RULES, AND INSTRUCTIONS.

Pr 32.4257:CT
ADDRESSES.

Pr 32.4258:nos.
CONSUMER PRICES. [Monthly]

Earlier Y 3.C 831:110

Pr 32.4259:nos.
AMERICAN FAMILY SERIES.

Pr 32.4260:nos.
FOOD FACTS OF INTEREST TO THE TRADE. [Weekly]

Pr 32.4261:vol.
TRANSPORTATION COMMITTEE NEWS. [Monthly]

Supersedes Pr 32.4235

Pr 32.4262:nos.
FACTS FOR APPAREL TRADE. [Semimonthly]

Pr 32.4263:nos.
DOWN ON THE FARM.

Pr 32.4264:vol.
VOLUNTEERS, BULLETIN FOR THOSE WHO DIRECT THEIR ACTIVITIES. [Semimonthly]

Pr 32.4265:vol
LIBRARY REFERENCE LIST.

Pr 32.4266:nos.
MILEAGE CONSERVATION LETTER.

Pr 32.4267:nos.
FACTS FOR CONSUMER DURABLES TRADE. [Weekly]

Pr 32.4268:date
PRICE CONTROL FACT SHEETS. [Monthly]

Pr 32.4269:nos.
HOUSING BULLETINS.

Pr 32.4270
ENFORCEMENT CHARTS, CHART SERIES A.

Pr 32.4271
INSIDE OPA.
Proc. Admin.

Pr 32.4272
RATIONED FOODS LETTER.

Proc. Admin.

Pr 32.4273
LABOR ADVISORY COMMITTEE BULLETINS.

Proc.

Pr 32.4274
OPA AND CONGRESS. [Weekly]

Proc. Admin.

Pr 32.4275
OPA HIGHLIGHTS.

Pr 32.4276
PRICE ACTION HIGHLIGHTS.

Proc. Admin.

Pr 32.4277:nos.
SHOE INFORMATION MEMORANDUM.

Pr 32.4277/2
LOCAL BOARD SHOE RATIONING LETTERS.

Proc.

Pr 32.4278
PROGRESS REPORT FOR WEEK ENDING.

Proc.

Pr 32.4279
LOCAL BOARD LETTER.

Pr 32.4280
WHAT'S GOING ON IN BUSINESS PRESS.

Proc. Admin.
Formerly, What's Going On in Trade Journals.

Pr 32.4281
ENFORCEMENT STATISTICS.

Proc.

DIVISION OF DEFENSE HOUSING COORDINATION
(1941– 1943)

Pr 32.4301:date
ANNUAL REPORTS.

Pr 32.4302:CT
GENERAL PUBLICATIONS.

Pr 32.4306:CT
REGULATIONS, RULES, AND INSTRUCTIONS.

Pr 32.4307:date
DEFENSE HOUSING FINANCED BY PUBLIC FUNDS, SUMMARIES. [Weekly]

OFFICE OF CIVILIAN DEFENSE
(1941– 1945)

CREATION AND AUTHORITY

The Office of Civilian Defense was established within the Office for Emergency Management by Executive Order 8757 of May 20, 1941. The Office was abolished by Executive Order 9562 of June, 4, 1945, effective June 30, 1945.

Pr 32.4401:date
ANNUAL REPORTS.

Pr 32.4402:CT
GENERAL PUBLICATIONS.

Pr 32.4404:nos.
CIRCULARS, GENERAL SERIES.

Proc. & printed.

Pr 32.4406:CT
REGULATIONS, RULES, AND INSTRUCTIONS.

Pr 32.4406:nos.
REGULATIONS (numbered).

Pr 32.4407:nos.
MEDICAL DIVISION, BULLETINS.

Pr 32.4408:nos.
OCD NEWS LETTERS, OFFICIAL BULLETINS.

Pr 32.4409:nos.
PROTECTIVE CONSTRUCTION SERIES.

Pr 32.4410:nos.
FIRE DEFENSE SECTION, BULLETINS.

Pr 32.4411:series nos.
STANDARD SCHOOL LECTURES, CIVILIAN PROTECTION.

Pr 32.4412:nos.
CIVIL AIR PATROL TRAINING MANUALS.

Pr 32.4413:CT
ADDRESSES.

Pr 32.4414:CT
POSTERS.

Pr 32.4415:nos.
EVACUATION BULLETINS.

Pr 32.4416:nos.
TRANSPORTATION BULLETINS.

Pr 32.4417:nos.
MEDICAL DIVISION SANITARY ENGINEERING BULLETIN.

Pr 32.4418:nos.
OPERATIONS LETTERS.

Pr 32.4419:nos.
CIRCULARS, MEDICAL SERIES.

Proc. and printed.

Pr 32.4420:nos.
FACILITY SECURITY PROGRAM BULLETINS.

Pr 32.4421:nos.
CIRCULARS, FACILITY SECURITY SERVICE.

Pr 32.4422:nos.
CIRCULARS, PROTECTION SERIES.

Proc. and Printed.

Pr 32.4423:nos.
CIRCULARS, WAR SERVICE SERIES.

Pr 32.4424:v.nos.
CIVIL AIR PATROL BULLETINS. [Weekly]

Pr 32.4425:v.nos.
STATISTICAL BULLETINS. [Bimonthly]

Pr 32.4426:nos.
RESUME OF ACTIVITIES OF PROTECTION BRANCH. [Monthly]

Pr 32.4427:date
PROTECTION SERVICES DIVISION [reports]. [Monthly]

OFFICE OF DEFENSE HEALTH AND WELFARE SERVICES
(1941– 1943)

CREATION AND AUTHORITY

The Office of Defense Health and Welfare Service was established within the Office for Emergency Management by Executive Order 8890 of September 3, 1941, to succeed the Office of the Coordinator of Health, Welfare, and Related Defense Activities, established by the Council of National Defense. The Office was abolished by Executive Order 9338 of April 29, 1943, and its functions transferred to the Federal Security Agency (FS 1)

Pr 32.4501:date
ANNUAL REPORTS.

Later FS 9.1

Pr 32.4502:CT
GENERAL PUBLICATIONS.

Later FS 9.2

Pr 32.4506:CT
REGULATIONS, RULES, AND INSTRUCTIONS.

Later FS 9.6

Pr 32.4507:CT
ADDRESSES.

Pr 32.4508:CT
POSTERS.

Pr 32.4509:nos.
RECREATION BULLETINS.

Earlier FS 8.8
Later FS 9.7

Pr 32.4510:nos.
FAMILY SECURITY BULLETINS.

Earlier FS 8.9

Pr 32.4511:nos.
FAMILY SECURITY CIRCULARS.

Pr 32.4512
COUNTY NUTRITION NEWS LETTER. [Admin.]

Pr 32.4512/2
STATE NUTRITION NEWS LETTER. [Admin.]

OFFICE OF INTER-AMERICAN AFFAIRS
(1945– 1946)

CREATION AND AUTHORITY

The Office for Coordination of Commercial and Cultural Relations Between the American Republics was established within the Council of National Defense, approved by the President on August 16, 1940. This Office was succeeded by the Office of the Coordinator of Inter-American Affairs, which was established within the Office for Emergency Management by Executive Order 8840 of July 30, 1941. The name was changed to Office of Inter-American Affairs by Executive Order 9532 of March 23, 1945. The information functions of the Office were transferred to the Department of State (S 1) by Executive Order 9608 of August 31, 1945. The Office was abolished by Executive Order 9710 of April, 1946, and its functions transferred to the Department of State, effective May 20, 1946, where it was succeeded by the Institute of Inter-American Affairs.

Pr 32.4601:date
ANNUAL REPORTS.

Pr 32.4602:CT
GENERAL PUBLICATIONS.

Pr 32.4606:CT
REGULATIONS, RULES, AND INSTRUCTIONS.

Pr 32.4607:CT
POSTERS.

Pr 32.4607/2:f(nos) p.(nos), s(nos)
[THE WAR ILLUSTRATED, POSTERS]

Pr 32.4608:f.v.nos.
EN GARDE POUR LA DEFENSE DES AMERIQUES.

Pr 32.4608:p.v.nos.
EM GUARDA PARA A DEFESA DAS AMERICAS. [Monthly]

Pr 32.4608:s.v.nos.
EN GUARDIA PARA LA DEFENSA DE LAS AMERICAS. [Monthly]

Pr 32.4609:e(nos)
AMERICAN NEWS LETTERS. [Fortnightly]

Pr 32.4609:p(nos.)
CARTA INFORMATIVA AMERICANA. [Fortnightly]

Pr 32.4610:CT
POSTERS.

Pr 32.4610:nos.
HEALTH AND SANITATION DIVISION NEWSLETTERS [Restricted]. [Fortnightly]

Later S 1.51

Pr 32.4611:date
REPORT OF ACTIVITIES; WEEKLY [Restricted].

Pr 32.4612:nos.
COORDINATION COMMITTEE ACTIVITIES [Restricted].

Pr 32.4613:CT
PUBLICATIONS COMPILED FROM STRATEGIC INDEX OF THE AMERICAS.

Pr 32.4614:CT
ADDRESSES.

Pr 32.4615:CT
INSTITUTE OF INTER-AMERICAN AFFAIRS PUBLICATIONS.

Later S 1.64

OFFICE OF FACTS AND FIGURES
(1941–1942)

CREATION AND AUTHORITY

The Office of Facts and Figures was established within the Office for Emergency Management by Executive Order 8922 of October 24, 1941. Executive Order 9182 of June 13,1942, abolished the Office and transferred its functions to the Office of War Information (Pr 32.5000) in the Office for Emergency Management.

Pr 32.4701:date
ANNUAL REPORTS.

Pr 32.4702:CT
GENERAL PUBLICATIONS.

Pr 32.4707:CT
POSTERS.

CIVILIAN PRODUCTION
ADMINISTRATION
(1945–1946)

CREATION AND AUTHORITY

The War Production Board was established within the Office for Emergency Management by Executive Order 9024 of January 16, 1942, succeeding the Office of Production Management (Pr 32.4000) and the Supply Priorities and Allocations Board. The Board was abolished by Executive Order 9638 of October 4, 1945, effective November 3, 1945, and succeeded by the Civilian Production Administration. The Administration was consolidated with the other agencies to form the Office of Temporary Controls (Pr 33.300) by Executive Order 9809 of December 12, 1946.

Pr 32.4801:date
ANNUAL REPORTS.

Pr 32.4802:CT
GENERAL PUBLICATIONS.

Pr 32.4806:CT
REGULATIONS, RULES, AND INSTRUCTIONS.

Pr 32.4807:nos.
PRIORITIES REGULATIONS.

Earlier Pr 32.1010

Pr 32.4808:nos.
TRAINING WITHIN INDUSTRY, EXAMPLES.

Earlier Pr 32.4021

Pr 32.4809:CT
ADDRESSES.

Pr 32.4810:letters-nos.
ORDERS.

Pr 32.4811:date
DIRECTORY OF CONTRACT OPPORTUNITIES.

Pr 32.4812:letters-nos.
POSTERS.

Pr 32.4812/2:nos.
BULLETIN BOARD PLACARDS.

Pr 32.4813:date
PRIORITIES. [Weekly]

Pr 32.4814:date
PRIORITIES IN FORCE.

Earlier Pr 32.410

Pr 32.4815:nos.
WAR PRODUCTION DRIVE, PROGRESS REPORT.

Pr 32.4815/2:date
MONTHLY REPORT TO WAR PRODUCTION BOARD.

Pr 32.4815/3
STATISTICS OF WAR PRODUCTION.

Pr 32.4816:nos.
TRAINING WITHIN THE INDUSTRY; BULLETIN.

For Bulletins issued by Production Management Office, see Pr 32.4022. For Bulletins issued by War Manpower Commission, see Pr 32.5208.

Pr 32.4817:nos.
RUBBER DIRECTOR OFFICE, PROGRESS REPORTS.

Pr 32.4818:nos.
LEAFLETS.

Pr 32.4819:date
NEWS TO USE, WARTIME FACTS ABOUT GOODS YOU SELL. [Monthly]

Pr 32.4820:v.nos.
LABOR MANAGEMENT NEWS. [Weekly]

Pr 32.4820/a:nos.
– REPRINTS.

Pr 32.4820/2:nos.
– SUPPLEMENTS.

Pr 32.4821:nos.
INFORMATIVE TECHNICAL BULLETINS.

Proc. & Printed.

Pr 32.4822:nos.
TRAINING WITHIN INDUSTRY ABSTRACTS, BRITISH ENGINEERING BULLETINS.

Later Pr 32.5215

Pr 32.4823:nos.
SALVAGE NEWS LETTERS. [Bimonthly]

Pr 32.4824:nos.
GENERAL REPORTS, OFFICE OF ASSISTANT RUBBER DIRECTOR FOR RESEARCH AND DEVELOPMENT OF SYNTHETICS.

Pr 32.4825:nos.
SMALLER WAR PLANTS CORPORATION PROGRAM AND PROGRESS REPORTS. [Bimonthly]

Earlier reports issued as Senate documents.

Pr 32.4826:nos.
MATERIAL SUBSTITUTES AND SUPPLY LISTS. [Quarterly]

Pr 32.4827:date
PRODUCTION AND AVAILABILITY OF CONSTRUCTION MATERIALS. [Monthly]

Restricted, for official use only.

Pr 32.4828:date
SUMMARY OF WAR SUPPLY AND FACILITY CONTRACTS BY STATE AND INDUSTRIAL AREA. [Monthly]

Earlier Pr 32.4013

Pr 32.4829:nos.
SUMMARY OF CONSTRUCTION AND PLANT EXPANSION. [Monthly]

Pr 32.4830:date
ORGANIZATION DIRECTORY. [Monthly]

Pr 32.4831:CT
STUDIES OF LABOR-MANAGEMENT PRODUCTION COMMITTEES.

Pr 32.4832:CT
RUBBER BUREAU PUBLICATIONS.

Pr 32.4833:nos.
QUALITY CONTROL REPORTS.

Pr 32.4834:date
CUTBACKS REPORTED TO PRODUCTION READJUSTMENT COMMITTEE [Restricted]. [Monthly]

Pr 32.4835:nos.
QUALITY CONTROL NOTES.

Pr 32.4836:date
RADIO AND RADAR INFORMATION LETTERS. [Monthly]

Pr 32.4837:date
MONTHLY REPORT ON CIVILIAN PRODUCTION.

Pr 32.4838:nos.
HISTORICAL REPORTS ON WAR ADMINISTRATION; WAR PRODUCTION BOARD, SPECIAL STUDIES.

Pr 32.4839:nos.
HISTORICAL REPORTS ON WAR ADMINISTRATION, WAR PRODUCTION BOARD, MISCELLANEOUS PUBLICATIONS.

Pr 32.4840:nos.
HISTORICAL REPORTS ON WAR ADMINISTRATION, WAR PRODUCTION BOARD, DOCUMENTARY PUBLICATIONS.

Pr 32.4841:date
LISTING OF MAJOR WAR SUPPLY CONTRACTS BY STATE AND COUNTY.

Pr 32.4842:date
ALPHABETICAL LISTING OF MAJOR WAR SUPPLY CONTRACTS. [Quarterly, Monthly]

Pr 32.4842/2:date
ALPHABETICAL LISTING OF MAJOR WAR SUPPLY CONTRACTS (compilations).

Pr 32.4842/3:date
ALPHABETICAL LISTING OF COMPLETED WAR SUPPLY CONTRACTS (compilations).

Pr 32.4843:date
FACILITIES EXPANSIONS AUTHORIZED LISTED BY MAJOR TYPES OF PRODUCTS. [Monthly]

Pr 32.4843/2
WPB FACILITIES ACTIONS.

Pr 32.4844:date
SUMMARY OF TRANSPORTATION. [Monthly]

Pr 32.4845:date
SUMMARY OF ACTION ON APPEALS.

   Proc.

Pr 32.4846:date
WEEKLY MEMORANDUM ON DOMESTIC TRANSPORTATION.

OFFICE OF DEFENSE TRANSPORTATION (1941–1949)

CREATION AND AUTHORITY

   The Office of Defense Transportation was established within the Office for Emergency Management by Executive Order 8989 of December 18, 1941, assuming the functions formerly administered by the Transportation Division of the Advisory Commission to the Council of National Defense (Y 3.C 831). The Office was terminated by Executive Order 10065 of July 6, 1949, effective July 1, 1949 pursuant to the Second Decontrol Act of 1947, as amended (62 Stat. 342).

Pr 32.4901:date
ANNUAL REPORTS.

Pr 32.4901/2:date
PROGRESS REPORTS TO THE PRESIDENT.

Pr 32.4902:CT
GENERAL PUBLICATIONS.

Pr 32.4906:CT
REGULATIONS, RULES, AND INSTRUCTIONS.

Pr 32.4907:CT
ADDRESSES.

Pr 32.4908:nos.
GENERAL ORDERS.

Pr 32.4909:CT
POSTERS.

Pr 32.4910:nos.
FARM VEHICLE ACTIVITY MEMORANDUMS.

Pr 32.4911:date
TRANSPORTATION BY RAIL, SUMMARY ANALYSIS OF RAILROAD SITUATION CONDITION REPORTS.

   Admin.

OFFICE OF WAR INFORMATION (1942–1945)

CREATION AND AUTHORITY

   The Office of War Information was established within the Office for Emergency Management by Executive Order 9182 of June 13, 1942, consolidating the Office of Facts and Figures (Pr 32.4700), the Office of Government Reports (Pr 32.200), the Division of Information of the Office for Emergency Management, and the Foreign Information Service, Outpost, Publications, and Pictorial Branches of the Coordinator of Information. The Office was abolished by Executive Order 9608 of August 31, 1945.

Pr 32.5001:date
ANNUAL REPORTS.

Pr 32.5002:CT
GENERAL PUBLICATIONS.

Pr 32.5005:CT
LAWS.

Pr 32.5006:CT
REGULATIONS, RULES, AND INSTRUCTIONS.

Pr 32.5008:vol.
VICTORY; OFFICIAL WEEKLY BULLETINS.

   Earlier Pr 32.407

Pr 32.5009:nos.
RADIO WAR GUIDE.

Pr 32.5010:nos.
INFORMATION DIGEST. [Daily except Sundays and Saturdays]

   Prior to June 15, 1942, Pr 32.214

Pr 32.5011:vol.
MAGAZINE ABSTRACTS; CURRENT DISCUSSION OF PUBLIC AFFAIRS. [Weekly]

   Prepared for use of Government officials by Intelligence Bureau.
   Prior to June 17, 1942: Pr 32.208.

Pr 32.5012:nos.
PRESS INTELLIGENCE BULLETINS. [Daily except Sundays]

   Prepared for use of U.S. Government officials by Intelligence Bureau.
   Prior to June 13, 1942: Pr 32.209.

Pr 32.5013:CT
ADDRESSES.

Pr 32.5014:date
A WEEK OF THE WAR.

   Publications of News Bureau.
   Prior to June 13, 1942: Pr 32.215

Pr 32.5015:nos.
POSTERS (numbered).

Pr 32.5016:date
UNITED STATES GOVERNMENT MANUAL.

   Earlier Pr 32.210
   Later Pr 33.110

Pr 32.5017:date
VICTORY SPEAKER; AN ARSENAL OF INFORMATION FOR SPEAKERS.

Pr 32.5017/2:nos.
SPECIAL BULLETIN ADDRESSED TO VICTORY SPEAKERS.

Pr 32.5018:nos.
DISCUSSION GUIDES.

Pr 32.5019:bk.nos.
U.S. GOVERNMENT CAMPAIGN TO PROMOTE PRODUCTION, SHARING, AND PROPER USE OF FOOD.

Pr 32.5019/2:CT
U.S. GOVERNMENT PROGRAM TO PROMOTE PRODUCTION, SHARING, AND PROPER USE OF FOOD (miscellaneous).

Pr 32.5020:nos.
O.W.I. REPORTS.

Pr 32.5021:v.nos.
VICTORY.

Pr 32.5022:date
DIGEST OF FUNCTIONS OF FEDERAL AGENCIES.

   Earlier Pr 32.202:F 31

Pr 32.5023:nos.
TOWARD NEW HORIZONS.

Pr 32.5024:date
MAGAZINE WAR GUIDES. [Monthly]

Pr 32.5025:vol.
U.S.A. [Monthly]

Pr 32.5026:nos.
LIBRARY WAR GUIDES. [Bimonthly]

Pr 32.5027:date
ADVANCE BULLETINS OF NEW POSTERS. [Monthly]

Pr 32.5028:OWI serial nos.
ARMY-NAVY WAR CASUALTIES [Confidential until released].

Pr 32.5029
SECURITY ADVISORY BOARD MEMORANDUMS.
   Proc. Admin.

Pr 32.5030:nos.
MEMORANDUMS.

Pr 32.5031:nos.
SPECIAL MEMORANDUMS.

NATIONAL WAR LABOR BOARD (1942–1945)

CREATION AND AUTHORITY

   The National War Labor Board was established within the Office for Emergency Management by Executive Order 9017 of January 12, 1942, to succeed the National Defense Mediation Board. The Board was transferred to the Department of Labor (L 1.17) by Executive Order 9617 of September 19, 1945.

Pr 32.5101:date
ANNUAL REPORTS.

Pr 32.5102:CT
GENERAL PUBLICATIONS.

Pr 32.5106:CT
REGULATIONS, RULES, AND INSTRUCTIONS.

Pr 32.5107:CT
DIRECTIVE ORDERS AND OPINIONS.

Pr 32.5108:vol.
DECISIONS.

Pr 32.5109:v.nos.
SUMMARIES OF DECISIONS.

Pr 32.5110:nos.
MONTHLY REPORTS.

Pr 32.5111:CT
ADDRESSES.

Pr 32.5112:nos.
WAGE STABILIZATION, GENERAL ORDERS AND INTERPRETATIONS.

WAR MANPOWER COMMISSION
(1942–1945)

CREATION AND AUTHORITY

The War Manpower Commission was established within the Office of Emergency Management by Executive Order 9139 of April 18, 1942. The Commission was terminated by Executive Order 9617 of September 19, 1945, and its functions transferred to the Department of Labor.

Pr 32.5201:date
ANNUAL REPORTS.

Pr 32.5202:CT
GENERAL PUBLICATIONS.

Pr 32.5206:CT
REGULATIONS, RULES, AND INSTRUCTIONS.

Pr 32.5207:CT
ADDRESSES.

Pr 32.5208:nos.
TRAINING WITHIN THE INDUSTRY BULLETIN.

For Bulletins issued by Production Management Office, see Pr 32.4011. For Bulletins issued by War Production Board, see Pr 32.4816.

Pr 32.5208/2:CT
TRAINING WITHIN INDUSTRY BULLETIN SERIES.

Pr 32.5209:vol.
MANPOWER REVIEW. [Monthly]

Earlier Employment Security Review, (FS 3.107).
Later L 7.18

Pr 32.5210:date
SUMMARY OF WEEKLY AGRICULTURAL REPORTS.

Earlier FS 3.126

Pr 32.5211:date
LABOR MARKET. [Monthly]

Earlier FS 3.113/2
Later L 7.20

Pr 32.5212:letters-nos.
JOB FAMILY SERIES.

Earlier FS 3.124
Later L 7.34

Pr 32.5213:CT
POSTERS.

Pr 32.5214:nos.
[TRAINING PAMPHLETS.]

Pr 32.5215:nos.
TRAINING WITHIN INDUSTRY ABSTRACTS, BRITISH ENGINEERING BULLETINS.

Earlier Pr 32.4822

Pr 32.5216:pr.no.
LISTS OF ESSENTIAL ACTIVITIES AND OCCUPATIONS.

Pr 32.5217:date
ADEQUACY OF LABOR SUPPLY IN IMPORTANT LABOR MARKET AREAS. [Monthly]

Pr 32.5218:date
PLACEMENT ACTIVITIES. [Monthly]

Pr 32.5219:CT
NATIONAL ROSTER OF SCIENTIFIC AND SPECIALIZED PERSONNEL, MONOGRAPHS.

Later L 7.21

Pr 32.5220:unit nos.
EMPLOYMENT OFFICE TRAINING PROGRAMS.

Later L 7.28

Pr 32.5221:pt.&sec. nos.
EMPLOYMENT SERVICE MANUAL.

Pr 32.5221/2:nos.
EMPLOYMENT SERVICE MANUAL, SUPPLEMENTS.

Pr 32.5222:nos.
TECHNICAL BULLETINS.

Earlier L 16.16

Pr 32.5223:CT
CASE HISTORY REPORTS FOR INDUSTRIES.

Pr 32.5224:dt.&nos.
LUMBER AND TIMBER BASIC PRODUCTS INDUSTRY, WOODEN CONTAINER INDUSTRY, EMPLOYER REPORT OF EMPLOYMENT AND REQUIRED LABOR FORCE BY STANDARD LUMBER TYPE REGION [Restricted]. [Bimonthly]

Pr 32.5225:date
SUMMARY OF ES-270 REPORTS. [Bimonthly]

Pr 32.5226:nos.
NATIONAL ROSTER OF SCIENTIFIC AND SPECIALIZED PERSONNEL, BULLETINS.

Pr 32.5227:CT
HANDBOOK OF DESCRIPTION OF SPECIALIZED FIELDS.

Pr 32.5228:CT
JOB DESCRIPTIONS.

Pr 32.5229:nos.
LABOR MARKET INFORMATION FOR UNITED STATES EMPLOYMENT SERVICE COUNSELING: INDUSTRY SERIES.

Later L 7.23

Pr 32.5230:nos.
DOCUMENTS OF WAR MANPOWER PROGRAM IN UNITED STATES.

National Youth Administration

Pr 32.5251:date
ANNUAL REPORTS.

Earlier FS 6.1

Pr 32.5252:CT
GENERAL PUBLICATIONS.

Earlier FS 6.2

Pr 32.5253/2
SHOP BULLETIN.

Proc.

Pr 32.5256
REGULATIONS, RULES, AND INSTRUCTIONS. {Poole}

Pr 32.5257:nos.
HANDBOOK OF PROCEDURE MEMORANDUM.

Earlier FS 6.12

Pr 32.5258:nos.
MANUAL OF FINANCE AND STATISTICS MEMORANDUM OF NATIONAL YOUTH ADMINISTRATION.

Earlier FS 6.17

Pr 32.5259
YOUTH PERSONNEL LETTER.

Proc. Admin.

Pr 32.5259/2
CIRCULAR LETTER.

Proc. Admin.

Selective Service System

Pr 32.5271:date
ANNUAL REPORTS.

See also Y 3.Se 4:1

Pr 32.5272:CT
GENERAL PUBLICATIONS.

See also Y 3.Se 4:2

Pr 32.5275:CT
LAWS.

Pr 32.5276:CT
REGULATIONS, RULES, AND INSTRUCTIONS OF SELECTIVE SERVICE SYSTEM.

See also Y 3.Se 4:10

Pr 32.5277:nos.
LOCAL BOARD RELEASES.

See also Y 3.Se 4:11

Pr 32.5277/2:nos.
TRANSMITTAL MEMO FOR LOCAL BOARD MEMORANDUM.

Later Y 3.Se 4:13

Pr 32.5278:nos.
OCCUPATIONAL BULLETINS OF SELECTIVE SERVICE SYSTEM.

See also Y 3.Se 4:12

Pr 32.5279:vol
SELECTIVE SERVICE.

See also Y 3.Se 4:9

Pr 32.5280:date/packet nos.
SELECTIVE SERVICE MANUAL.

Later Y 3.Se 4:7

Pr 32.5281:nos.
MEDICAL CIRCULARS OF SELECTIVE SERVICE BUREAU.

See also Y 3.Se 4:8

Pr 32.5282:nos.
REEMPLOYMENT BULLETINS.

WAR SHIPPING ADMINISTRATION
(1942–1946)

CREATION AND AUTHORITY

The War Shipping Administration was established within the Office for Emergency Management by Executive Order 9054 of February 7, 1942. The Administration was abolished by act of Congress, approved July 8, 1946 (60 Stat. 501), effective September 1, 1946, and its functions transferred to the United States Maritime Commission (MC 1).

Pr 32.5301:date
ANNUAL REPORTS.

Pr 32.5302:CT
GENERAL PUBLICATIONS.

Pr 32.5306:CT
REGULATIONS, RULES, AND INSTRUCTIONS.

Pr 32.5307:nos.
GENERAL ORDERS.

Pr 32.5308:CT
POSTERS.

Pr 32.5309
ADMINISTRATIVE ORDERS.

    Proc.

WAR RELOCATION AUTHORITY
(1942– 1944)

CREATION AND AUTHORITY

    The War Relocation Authority was established within the Office for Emergency Management by Executive Order 9102 of March 18, 1942. The Authority was transferred to the Department of the Interior (I 52) by Executive Order 9423 of February 16, 1944.

Pr 32.5401:date
ANNUAL REPORTS.

    Later I 52.1

Pr 32.5402:CT
GENERAL PUBLICATIONS.

    Later I 52.2

Pr 32.5406:CT
REGULATIONS, RULES, AND INSTRUCTIONS.

Pr 32.5407:date
REPORTS. [Quarterly]

    Later I 52.7

Pr 32.5408:CT
FACTS ABOUT AMERICA SERIES.

Pr 32.5409:CT
ADDRESSES.

Pr 32.5410:nos.
COMMUNITY ANALYSIS REPORTS.

    Later I 52.9
Pr 32.5411:nos.
PROJECT ANALYSIS SERIES.

    Later I 52.10.

OFFICE OF LEND-LEASE
ADMINISTRATION
(1941– 1943)

CREATION AND AUTHORITY

    The Office of Lend-Lease Administration was established within the Office for Emergency Management by Executive Order 8926 of October 28, 1941, to succeed the Division of Defense Aid Reports. By Executive Order 9380 of September 25, 1943, the Administration was consolidated with certain other agencies to form the Foreign Economic Administration (Pr 32.5800) in the Office for Emergency Management.

Pr 32.5501:date
ANNUAL REPORTS.

Pr 32.5502:CT
GENERAL PUBLICATIONS.

Pr 32.5507:date
REPORTS TO CONGRESS ON LEND-LEASE OPERATIONS.

    Earlier Pr 32.402:L 54
    Later Pr 32.5809

BOARD OF WAR
COMMUNICATIONS
(1941– 1947)

CREATION AND AUTHORITY

    The Defense Communications Board was established by Executive Order 8546 of September 24, 1940. Executive Order 9183 of June 15, 1942 changed the name to the Board of War Communications. The Board was abolished by Executive Order 9831 of February 24, 1947, and its functions transferred to the Federal Communications Commission (CC 1).

Pr 32.5601:date
ANNUAL REPORTS.

Pr 32.5602:CT
GENERAL PUBLICATIONS.

OFFICE OF ALIEN PROPERTY
CUSTODIAN
(1942– 1946)

CREATION AND AUTHORITY

    The Office of Alien Property Custodian was established within the Office for Emergency Management by Executive Order 9095 of March 11, 1942, pursuant to the Trading with the Enemy Act of 1917 (40 Stat. 411). The Executive Order 9142 of April 21, 1942, transferred the functions of the Alien Property Division (J 19) of the Department of Justice to the Alien Property Custodian. The Office was terminated by Executive Order 9788 of October 13, 1946, terminated by Executive Order 9788 of October 13, 1946, and its functions transferred to the Department of Justice (J 22).

Pr 32.5701:date
ANNUAL REPORTS.

    Earlier J 19.1
    Later J 22.1

Pr 32.5702:CT
GENERAL PUBLICATIONS.

    Earlier J 19.2
    Later J 22.2

FOREIGN ECONOMIC
ADMINISTRATION
(1943– 1945)

CREATION AND AUTHORITY

    The Foreign Economic Administration was established by Executive Order 9380 of September 25, 1943, which consolidated the following agencies: Office of Lend-Lease Administration (Pr 32.5500), Office of Foreign Relief and Rehabilitation Operations, Office of Economic Warfare, and the foreign economic operations of the Office of Foreign Economic Coordination. The Administration was terminated by Executive Order 9630 of September 27, 1945, and its functions transferred to various agencies.

Pr 32.5801:date
ANNUAL REPORTS.

Pr 32.5802:CT
GENERAL PUBLICATIONS.

Pr 32.5803/2
SECURITY BULLETINS.

Pr 32.5806:CT
REGULATIONS, RULES, AND INSTRUCTIONS.

Pr 32.5807:nos.
CURRENT EXPORT BULLETINS.

    Earlier Y 3.Ec 74/2:109
    Later C 34.7

Pr 32.5808:nos.
COMPREHENSIVE EXPORT SCHEDULES.

    Earlier Y 3.Ec 74/2:108
    Later C 34.8

Pr 32.5809:nos.
REPORTS TO CONGRESS ON LEND-LEASE OPERATIONS.

    12th and 13th reports to be changed from Pr 32.5802:L 54/943-2
    Earlier Pr 32.5507
    Later S 1.43

Pr 32.5810:CT
EUROPEAN TRANSPORTATION SURVEY. [Confidential]

Pr 32.5811:CT
POSTERS.

Pr 32.5812:nos.
REPORTS TO CONGRESS ON UNITED STATES PARTICIPATION IN OPERATIONS OF UNRRA UNDER ACT OF MARCH 28, 1944. [Quarterly]

    Later S 1.44

Pr 32.5813:nos.
T.I.D.C. PROJECTS ON GERMAN INDUSTRIAL AND ECONOMIC DISARMAMENT.

OFFICE OF WAR MOBILIZATION
(1943– 1944)

CREATION AND AUTHORITY

The Office of War Mobilization was established within the Office for Emergency Management by Executive Order 9347 of May 27, 1943. The Office was succeeded by the Office of War Mobilization and Reconversion (Y 3.W 19/7) under Executive Order 9488 of October 3, 1944.

Pr 32.5901:date
ANNUAL REPORTS.

Pr 32.5902:CT
GENERAL PUBLICATIONS.

Pr 32.5906:CT
REGULATIONS, RULES, AND INSTRUCTIONS.

Pr 32.5907:CT
ADDRESSES.

Pr 32.5908:nos.
SURPLUS WAR PROPERTY ADMINISTRATION REGULATIONS.

OFFICE OF ECONOMIC STABILIZATION
(1942– 1945, 1946)

CREATION AND AUTHORITY

The Office of Economic Stabilization was established within the Office for Emergency Management by Executive Order 9250 of October 3, 1942. The Office was abolished by Executive Order 9620 of September 20, 1945, and its functions transferred to the Office of War Mobilization and Reconversion (Y 3.W 19/7). It was reestablished within the Office for Emergency Management by Executive Order 9699 of February 21, 1946. Executive Order 9762 of July 25, 1946, transferred the Office back to the Office of War Mobilization and Reconversion (Y 3.W 19/7).

Pr 32.6001:date
ANNUAL REPORTS.

Pr 32.6002:CT
GENERAL PUBLICATIONS.

Pr 32.6007:CT
POSTERS.

PRESIDENT OF THE UNITED STATES HARRY S. TRUMAN
(1945– 1953)

Pr 33.1:date
ANNUAL MESSAGES.

Pr 33.2:CT
GENERAL PUBLICATIONS.

Pr 33.3
BULLETINS.

Pr 33.4
CIRCULARS.

Pr 33.5:nos.
EXECUTIVE ORDERS.

Pr 33.6:date
INAUGURAL ADDRESS.

Pr 33.7:CT
PROCLAMATIONS.

Pr 33.8:CT
SPECIAL MESSAGES.

Pr 33.9:CT
COUNCIL OF ECONOMIC ADVISERS PUBLICATIONS.

Later Pr 34.9

Pr 33.10:date
ECONOMIC REPORT OF THE PRESIDENT.

Later Pr 34.10

Pr 33.11:CT
CITIZENS FOOD COMMITTEE PUBLICATIONS.

Printed and processed.

Pr 33.12:CT
PRESIDENT'S WATER RESOURCES POLICY COMMISSION PUBLICATIONS.

Pr 33.13:CT
PRESIDENT'S COMMUNICATIONS POLICY BOARD.

Pr 33.14:CT
PRESIDENT'S COMMISSION ON MIGRATORY LABOR.

Pr 33.15:v.nos.
RESOURCES FOR FREEDOM, REPORT TO THE PRESIDENT BY PRESIDENT'S MATERIALS POLICY COMMISSION.

Pr 33.16:date
REPORT OF PRESIDENT'S AIRPORT COMMISSION.

Pr 33.17
PRESIDENT'S COMMITTEE ON GOVERNMENT CONTRACT COMPLIANCE, RELEASES.

Pr 33.17/2:date
PRESIDENT'S COMMITTEE ON GOVERNMENT CONTRACT COMPLIANCE, REPORTS AND PUBLICATIONS.

Pr 33.18:CT
PRESIDENT'S COMMISSION ON IMMIGRATION AND NATURALIZATION, REPORTS AND PUBLICATIONS.

Pr 33.19:CT
PRESIDENT'S COMMISSION ON HEALTH NEEDS OF NATION: REPORTS AND PUBLICATIONS.

Pr 33.19/2
– RELEASES.

Pr 33.20:CT
PRESIDENT'S ADVISORY COMMITTEE ON MANAGEMENT, REPORTS AND PUBLICATIONS.

Pr 33.21
RELEASES.

Pr 33.22:CT
MISSOURI BASIN SURVEY COMMISSION, REPORTS AND PUBLICATIONS.

BUREAU OF THE BUDGET
(1945– 1952)

CREATION AND AUTHORITY

The Bureau of the Budget (T 51) was transferred from the Department of the Treasury to the Executive Office of the President under Reorganization Plan 1 of 1939 (53 Stat. 1423).
Note:– Separate SuDocs classes were assigned under individual Presidential Administrations: Pr 32.100 for Roosevelt (1939– 1945), Pr 33.100 for Truman (1945– 1952) and Pr 34.100 for Eisenhower (1952– 1961). In 1961 the SuDocs class PrEx 2 was assigned to the Bureau.

Pr 33.101:date
ANNUAL REPORTS.

Earlier Pr 32.101

Pr 33.102:CT
GENERAL PUBLICATIONS.

Earlier Pr 32.102

Pr 33.103:dt.-nos.
BULLETINS.

Later Pr 34.103

Pr 33.104:letters-nos.
CIRCULARS.

Earlier Pr 32.104/2

Pr 33.106:CT
REGULATIONS, RULES, AND INSTRUCTIONS.

Pr 33.106/2:nos.
BUDGET-TREASURY REGULATIONS.

Earlier Pr 32.106

Pr 33.107:date
BUDGET OF UNITED STATES GOVERNMENT.

Earlier Pr 32.107
Later Pr 34.107

Pr 33.108:CT
MANAGEMENT BULLETINS.

Earlier Pr 32.108
Later PrEx 2.3/2

Pr 33.109:v.nos.
PUBLIC MANAGEMENT SOURCES. [Monthly]

Later Pr 34.109

Pr 33.110:date
UNITED STATES GOVERNMENT MANUAL.

Earlier Pr 32.5016
Later Pr 33.407

Pr 33.111:nos.
HISTORICAL REPORTS ON WAR ADMINISTRATION.

Pr 33.112:date
MOTOR VEHICLE REPORT. [Annual]

Pr 33.113:date
RECEIPTS FROM AND PAYMENTS TO THE PUBLIC.

Pr 33.114:nos.
MANAGEMENT NOTES. [Irregular]

Pr 33.115:nos.
STATISTICAL REPORTER. [Monthly]

Processed.
Later Pr 34.112

WAR ASSETS ADMINISTRATION
(1946– 1947)

CREATION AND AUTHORITY

The War Assets Administration was established within the Office for Emergency Management by Executive Order 9689 of January 31, 1946, effective March 25, 1946. Reorganization Plan No. 1 of 1947, effective July 1, 1947, abolished the War Assets Administration and transferred its functions to the Surplus Property Administration.

Pr 33.201:date
ANNUAL REPORTS.

Pr 33.202:CT
GENERAL PUBLICATIONS.

Pr 33.207:date
SURPLUS PROPERTY NEWS.

Earlier FL 5.12

Pr 33.208:nos.
SURPLUS REPORTER.

Earlier FL 5.14

Pr 33.209:nos.
SURPLUS GOVERNMENT PROPERTY SPECIAL LISTINGS.

Earlier FL 5.13
Later Y 3.W 19/8:7

Pr 33.210:date
GENERAL SUMMARY OF INVENTORY STATUS AND MOVEMENT OF CAPITAL AND PRODUCERS GOODS, PLANTS, AIRCRAFT, AND INDUSTRY AGENT ITEMS.

Earlier FL 5.11

Pr 33.211:date
PROGRESS REPORT TO CONGRESS BY WAR ASSETS ADMINISTRATION. [Quarterly]

Later Y 3.W 19/8:11

Pr 33.212:date
REVIEW OF THE MONTH.

Superseded by Pr 33.214

Pr 33.213:date
SCHEDULE OF SALES OFFERINGS.
Earlier Y 3.W 19/8:8

Pr 33.214:date
PROGRESS ANALYSIS. [Monthly]

Supersedes Pr 33.212

Pr 33.215:sec.nos.&date
PROGRESS REPORTS. [Monthly]

Superseded by Progress analysis Pr 33.214

Pr 33.216:nos.
MARINE SURPLUS SELLER. [Monthly]

Earlier MC 1.26

Pr 33.217:v.nos.
TARGET. [Weekly]

Earlier Y 3.W 19/8:10

OFFICE OF TEMPORARY CONTROLS
(1946– 1947)

CREATION AND AUTHORITY

The Office of Temporary Controls was established within the Office for Emergency Management by Executive Order 9809 of December 12, 1946, consolidating the Office of War Mobilization and Reconversion (Y 3.W 19/7), the Office of Economic Stabilization (Pr 32.6000), the Office of Price Administration (Pr 32.4200), and the Civilian Production Administration (Pr 32.4800), Executive Order 9841 of April 23, 1947, provided for the termination of the Office of June 1, 1947.

Pr 33.301:date
ANNUAL REPORTS.

Pr 33.302:CT
GENERAL PUBLICATIONS.

Pr 33.307:nos.
OPA ECONOMIC DATA SERIES.

Pr 33.308:nos.
HISTORICAL REPORTS ON WAR ADMINISTRATION, OFFICE OF PRICE ADMINISTRATION, MISCELLANEOUS PUBLICATIONS.

Pr 33.309:CT
PAPERS IN RE.

Earlier Pr 32.4217

Pr 33.310:nos.
HISTORICAL REPORTS ON WAR ADMINISTRATION, OFFICE OF PRICE ADMINISTRATION, GENERAL PUBLICATIONS.

Pr 33.311:nos.
HISTORICAL REPORTS ON WAR ADMINISTRATION, WAR PRODUCTION BOARD, GENERAL STUDIES.

Pr 33.312:nos.
WAR PROFITS STUDIES.

Earlier Pr 32.4227

OFFICE OF GOVERNMENT REPORTS
(1946– 1948)

CREATION AND AUTHORITY

The Office of Government Reports (Pr 32.200) was reestablished within the Executive Office of the President by Executive Order 9809 of December 12, 1946. The Office was terminated on June 30, 1948, pursuant to act of Congress, approved July 30, 1947 (61 Stat. 588).

Pr 33.401:date
ANNUAL REPORTS.

Pr 33.402:CT
GENERAL PUBLICATIONS.

Pr 33.407:date
UNITED STATES GOVERNMENT MANUAL.

Earlier Pr 33.110
Later AE 2.11

PHILIPPINE ALIEN PROPERTY ADMINISTRATION
(1946– 1951)

CREATION AND AUTHORITY

The Philippine Alien Property Administration was established within the Office for Emergency Management by Executive Order 9789 of October 14, 1946. The Administration was abolished by Executive Order 10254 of June 15, 1951, effective June 29, 1951, and its functions transferred to the Department of Justice.

Pr 33.501:date
ANNUAL REPORTS.

Pr 33.502:CT
GENERAL PUBLICATIONS.

Pr 33.507:nos.
VESTING ORDERS.

NATIONAL SECURITY COUNCIL
(1949– 1953)

CREATION AND AUTHORITY

The National Security Council (Y 3.N 21/17) was established as an independent agency by the National Security Act of 1947, approved July 26, 1947 (61 Stat. 497). Reorganization Plan No. 4 of 1949, effective August 20, 1949, transferred it to the Executive Office of the President.

Pr 33.601:date
ANNUAL REPORTS.
Earlier Y 3.N 21/17:1

Pr 33.602:CT
GENERAL PUBLICATIONS.
Earlier Y 3.N 21/17:2
Pr 33.608:CT
INTERDEPARTMENTAL COMMITTEE ON INTERNAL SECURITY, REPORTS AND PUBLICATIONS.

Pr 33.609:CT
INTERDEPARTMENTAL INTELLIGENCE CONFERENCE REPORTS AND PUBLICATIONS.

CENTRAL INTELLIGENCE AGENCY
(1949– 1953)

CREATION AND AUTHORITY

The Central Intelligence Agency (Y 3.N 21/17:100) was established within the National Security Council on September 20, 1947, pursuant to the National Security Act of 1947, approved July 26, 1947 (61 Stat. 498), succeeding the National Intelligence Authority. Reorganization Plan No. 4 of 1949, effective August 20, 1949, transferred the Agency to the Executive Office of the President.
    Later SuDocs class: Pr 34.600

Pr 33.651:date
ANNUAL REPORTS.
    Earlier Y 3.N 21/17:101

Pr 33.652:CT
GENERAL PUBLICATIONS.

    Earlier Y 3.N 21/17:102

Pr 33.657:dt.&nos.
DAILY REPORT, FOREIGN RADIO BROADCASTS.

    For official use only.
    Earlier Y 3.N 21/17:107

Pr 33.658:CT
MAPS.

NATIONAL SECURITY RESOURCES BOARD
(1949– 1953)

CREATION AND AUTHORITY

The National Security Resources Board (Y 3.N 21/18) was transferred to the Executive Office of the President by Reorganization Plan No. 4 of 1949, effective August 20, 1949. The Board was abolished by Reorganization Plan No. 3 of 1953, effective June 12, 1953, and its functions transferred to the newly created Office of Defense Mobilization (Pr 34.200).

Pr 33.701:date
ANNUAL REPORTS.

    Earlier Y 3.N 21/18:1

Pr 33.702:CT
GENERAL PUBLICATIONS.

    Earlier Y 3.N 21/18:2

Pr 33.706:CT
REGULATIONS, RULES, AND INSTRUCTIONS.

Pr 33.707:nos.
CIVIL DEFENSE PLANNING ADVISORY BULLETINS.

    Processed or printed.

Pr 33.708:nos.
RELEASES.

FEDERAL CIVIL DEFENSE ADMINISTRATION
(1950– 1951)

CREATION AND AUTHORITY

The Federal Civil Defense Administration was established within the Office of Emergency Management by Executive Order 10186 of December 1, 1950. The Federal Civil Defense Act of 1950 (62 Stat. 1245), approved January 12, 1951, established the Administration as an independent agency (FCD 1).

Pr 33.801:date
ANNUAL REPORTS.

    Later FDC 1.1

Pr 33.802:CT
GENERAL PUBLICATIONS.

    Later FDC 1.2

Pr 33.807
RELEASES.

MUTUAL SECURITY AGENCY
(1951– 1953)

CREATION AND AUTHORITY

The Mutual Security Agency was established by the Mutual Security Act of 1951 (65 Stat. 373) to succeed the Economic Cooperation Administration (Y 3.Ec 74/3), which was abolished. The Agency was abolished by Reorganization Plan No. 7 of 1953, effective August 1, 1953, and was succeeded by the Foreign Operations Administration (FO 1).

Pr 33.901:date
SEMIANNUAL REPORTS.

Pr 33.901/2:nos.
SEMIANNUAL REPORTS UNDER MUTUAL DEFENSE ASSISTANCE CONTROL ACT.

    Later FO 1.1/2

Pr 33.902:CT
GENERAL PUBLICATIONS.

Pr 33.905:CT
LAWS.

Pr 33.906:CT
REGULATIONS, RULES, AND INSTRUCTIONS.

Pr 33.907
PRESS RELEASES.

Pr 33.908:date
PROCUREMENT AUTHORIZATION AND ALLOTMENTS. [Monthly]

    Earlier Y 3.Ec 74/3:14
    Later FO 1.8

Pr 33.909:date
PAID SHIPMENTS. [Monthly]

    Earlier Y 3.Ec 74/3:13
    Later FO 1.9

Pr 33.910:date
MONTHLY REPORT FOR PUBLIC ADVISORY BOARD.

    Earlier Y 3.Ec 74/3:7
    Later FO 1.10

Pr 33.911:date
EUROPEAN PROGRAM, LOCAL CURRENCY COUNTERPART FUNDS. [Monthly]

    Earlier Y 3.Ec 74/3:13
    Later FO 1.11

Pr 33.911/2:date
FAR EAST PROGRAM LOCAL CURRENCY COUNTERPART FUNDS. [Monthly]

    Later FO 1.11/2

Pr 33.912:nos.
PRIORITIES BULLETINS.

    Earlier Y 3.Ec 74/3:30

Pr 33.913
SMALL BUSINESS CIRCULAR MSA/CBC (series).

    Later FO 1.12

Pr 33.913/2:nos.
SMALL BUSINESS CIRCULAR TCA/SEC (series).

    Later FO 1.13/2

Pr 33.914
MEMO FOR SMALL BUSINESS MSA/SBM (series).

    Later FO 1.13
Pr 33.914/2:nos.
MEMO FOR SMALL BUSINESS TCA/SBM (series).

    Later FO 1.14

Pr 33.915:v.nos.
TRANS-ATLANTIC, FROM OFFICE OF LABOR ADVISORS, MSA LABOR NEWS LETTER. [Monthly]

    Earlier Y 3.Ec 74/3:31

Pr 33.916:nos.
CONTRACT CLEARING HOUSE SERVICE, SUMMARIES.

    Later FO 1.16

Pr 33.917:nos.
WEEKLY SUMMARY OF EXPORT OPPORTUNITIES FOR SMALL BUSINESS.

    Later FO 1.17

Pr 33.918:CT
SPECIAL MISSION TO FRANCE FOR ECONOMIC COOPERATION.

    Earlier Y 3.Ec 74/3:22

Pr 33.918/2:CT
SPECIAL MISSION TO GREECE FOR ECONOMIC COOPERATION.

    Earlier Y 3.Ec 74/3:37
Pr 33.918/3:CT
SPECIAL MISSION TO ITALY FOR ECONOMIC COOPERATIONS.

Pr 33.919:CT
MSA COUNTRY SERIES.

Pr 33.920
PRODUCT ANALYSIS SERVICE.

Pr 33.921
MUTUAL SECURITY MISSION TO CHINA.

    Later FO 1.27

Pr 33.921/2:v.nos.&nos.
CHINESE-AMERICAN ECONOMIC COOPERATION.

Pr 33.922:nos.
FAR EAST DATA BOOK.

Earlier Y 3.Ec 74/3:38

Pr 33.923:CT
SPECIAL MISSION TO PORTUGAL.

OFFICE OF DEFENSE MOBILIZATION (1950– 1953)

CREATION AND AUTHORITY

The first Office of Defense Mobilization was established within the Executive Office of the President by Executive Order 10193 of December 16, 1950. By Reorganization Plan No. 3. of 1953, its functions were transferred to the newly created Office of Defense Mobilization (Pr 34.200).

Pr 33.1001:date
ANNUAL REPORTS.

Pr 33.1002:CT
GENERAL PUBLICATIONS.

Later Pr 34.202

Pr 33.1006:CT
REGULATIONS, RULES, AND INSTRUCTIONS.

Pr 33.1006/2:nos.
DEFENSE MOBILIZATION ORDERS DMO (series).

Pr 33.1007
RELEASES.

Later Pr 34.207

Pr 33.1008:nos.
REPORT TO THE PRESIDENT BY DIRECTOR OF DEFENSE MOBILIZATION. [Quarterly]

Later Pr 34.201

Pr 33.1009:CT
ADDRESSES.

Pr 33.1010:nos.
DEFENSE MANPOWER POLICY STATEMENT.

Pr 33.1011
REPORT ON BORROWING AUTHORITY. [Quarterly]

Processed.

DEFENSE PRODUCTION ADMINISTRATION (1950– 1953)

CREATION AND AUTHORITY

The Defense Production Administration was established by Executive Order 10200 of January 3, 1951, pursuant to the Defense Production Act of 1950 (64 Stat. 798). Executive Order 10433 of February 4, 1953, abolished the Defense Production Administration and transferred its functions to the Office of Defense Mobilization (Pr 33.1000). SuDocs class Pr 33.1100 was cancelled and changed to DP 1.

Pr 33.1101:date
ANNUAL REPORTS.

Changed to DP 1.1

Pr 33.1102:CT
GENERAL PUBLICATIONS.

Changed to DP 1.2

Pr 33.1107
RELEASES.

PRESIDENT OF THE UNITED STATES DWIGHT D. EISENHOWER (1953– 1961)

Pr 34.2:CT
GENERAL PUBLICATIONS.

Later PrEx 1.2

Pr 34.6
INAUGURAL ADDRESS.

Pr 34.7
RELEASES.

Pr 34.8:CT • Item 851-J
COMMITTEES AND COMMISSIONS OF THE PRESIDENT.

The following are Committees and Commissions established by the President for which publications have been issued and classes established:

Pr 34.8:Ad 6/CT
ADMINISTRATIVE CONFERENCE (1953– 1954): PUBLICATIONS.

Pr 34.8:Av 5/CT
AVIATION FACILITIES PLANNING OFFICE (1957): PUBLICATIONS.

Pr 34.8:C 76/2/CT
COMMITTEE ON GOVERNMENT CONTRACTS (1953– 1960): PUBLICATIONS.

Pr 34.8:Ed 3/CT
PRESIDENT'S COMMITTEE ON EDUCATION BEYOND HIGH SCHOOL (1956– 1957): PUBLICATIONS.

Pr 34.8:Em 7/CT
PRESIDENT'S COMMITTEE ON GOVERNMENT EMPLOYMENT POLICY (1955– 1961): PUBLICATIONS.

Pr 34.8:En 3/CT
PRESIDENT'S COMMITTEE ON ENGINEERS AND SCIENTISTS FOR FEDERAL GOVERNMENT PROGRAMS (1957): PUBLICATIONS.

Pr 34.8:F 31/CT
JOINT FEDERAL STATE ACTION COMMITTEE (1957– 1960): PUBLICATIONS.

Pr 34.8:H 53/CT
PRESIDENT'S ADVISORY COMMITTEE ON NATIONAL HIGHWAY PROGRAM (1955): PUBLICATIONS.

Pr 34.8:H 81/CT
PRESIDENT'S ADVISORY COMMITTEE ON GOVERNMENT HOUSING POLICIES AND PROGRAMS (1953): PUBLICATIONS.

Pr 34.8:H 89/CT
PRESIDENT'S ADVISORY COMMITTEE ON HUNGARIAN REFUGEE RELIEF (1957): PUBLICATIONS.

Pr 34.8:M 59/CT
PRESIDENT'S COMMITTEE TO STUDY MILITARY ASSISTANCE PROGRAM (1959): PUBLICATIONS.

Pr 34.8:M 98/CT
PRESIDENT'S CITIZEN ADVISERS ON MUTUAL SECURITY PROGRAM (1957): PUBLICATIONS.

Pr 34.8:N 21a/CT
NATIONAL AGRICULTURAL ADVISORY COMMISSION (1953– 1965): PUBLICATIONS.

Pr 34.8:P 92/CT
PRESIDENT'S ADVISORY COMMISSION ON PRESIDENTIAL OFFICE SPACE (1957): PUBLICATIONS.

Pr 34.8:P 93/CT
PRESIDENT'S CABINET COMMITTEE ON PRICE STABILITY FOR ECONOMIC GROWTH (1959): PUBLICATIONS.

Pr 34.8:R 13/CT
PRESIDENTIAL RAILROAD COMMISSION: PUBLICATIONS.

Pr 34.8:Sci 2/CT
PRESIDENT'S SCIENCE ADVISORY COMMITTEE (1951– 1961): PUBLICATIONS.

Later Pr 35.8:Sci 2

Pr 34.8:Sci 27/CT
PRESIDENT'S COMMITTEE ON SCIENTISTS AND ENGINEERS (1958): PUBLICATIONS

Pr 34.8:Sm 1/CT
CABINET COMMITTEE ON SMALL BUSINESS (1956): PUBLICATIONS.

Pr 34.8:V 64/CT
PRESIDENT'S COMMISSION ON VETERANS PENSIONS (1955– 1956): PUBLICATIONS.

Pr 34.8:W 29/CT
PRESIDENTIAL ADVISORY COMMITTEE ON WATER RESOURCES POLICY (1955): PUBLICATIONS.

Pr 34.8:W 89/CT
WORLD ECONOMIC PRACTICES COMMITTEE (1959): PUBLICATIONS.

Pr 34.8:Y 8/CT
PRESIDENT'S COUNSEL ON YOUTH FITNESS (1956– 1963): PUBLICATIONS

Later Pr 35.8:P 56

Pr 34.9:CT
COUNCIL OF ECONOMIC ADVISORS: PUBLICATIONS.

Earlier Pr 33.9

Pr 34.10:date
ECONOMIC REPORT OF THE PRESIDENT.

> Earlier Pr 33.10
> Later Pr 35.9

Pr 34.11:CT
WHITE HOUSE DISARMAMENT STAFF PUBLI-
CATIONS.

Pr 34.11/2:date
DIGEST, DISARMAMENT INFORMATION SUM-
MARY.

Pr 34.11/3:letters-nos.
WHITE HOUSE DISARMAMENT STAFF, BACK-
GROUND SERIES.

Pr 34.11/4:CT
WHITE HOUSE DISARMAMENT STAFF, AD-
DRESSES.

BUREAU OF THE BUDGET
(1953– 1961)

CREATION AND AUTHORITY

> The Bureau of the Budget (T 51) was
transferred from the Department of the Treasury to the Executive Office of the President
under Reorganization Plan No. 1 of 1939 (53
Stat. 1423).
> Note:– Separate SuDocs classes were
assigned under individual Presidential Administrations: Pr 32.100 for Roosevelt (1939–
1945), Pr 33.100 for Truman (1945– 1952)
and Pr 34.100 for Eisenhower (1952– 1961).
In 1961 the SuDocs class PrEx 2 was assigned to the Bureau.

Pr 34.101:date
ANNUAL REPORTS.

> PrEx 2.1

Pr 34.102:CT
GENERAL PUBLICATIONS.

> Later PrEx 2.2

Pr 34.103:nos.
BULLETINS.

> Earlier Pr 33.103
> Later PrEx 2.3

Pr 34.104:letters-nos.
CIRCULARS.

> Earlier Pr 33.104
> Later PrEx 2.4

Pr 34.106:CT
REGULATIONS, RULES, AND INSTRUCTIONS.

> Earlier Pr 33.106
> Later PrEx 2.6

Pr 34.106/2:nos.
BUDGET TREASURY REGULATIONS.

> Earlier Pr 33.106/2

Pr 34.107:date
BUDGET OF UNITED STATES GOVERNMENT.

> Earlier Pr 33.107
> Later PrEx 2.8

Pr 34.107/2:date
FEDERAL BUDGET IN BRIEF. [Annual]

> Earlier Pr 34.102:B 85/2
> Later PrEx 2.8/2

Pr 34.107/3:date
REVIEW OF BUDGET. [Annual]

> Earlier Pr 34.102:B 85
> Later PrEx 2.8/3

Pr 34.107/4:date
YOUR FEDERAL BUDGET. [Annual]

> Earlier Pr 34.102:B 85/3

Pr 34.107/5:date
BUDGET OF UNITED STATES GOVERNMENT, DIS-
TRICT OF COLUMBIA. [Annual]

> Later PrEx 2.8/4

Pr 34.108
MANAGEMENT BULLETINS.

Pr 34.109:v.nos.
PUBLIC MANAGEMENT SOURCES. [Monthly]

Pr 34.110:CT
ADDRESSES.

Pr 34.111:date
FEDERAL STATISTICAL DIRECTORY.

> Earlier Pr 34.102:St 2
> Later PrEx 2.10

Pr 34.112
STATISTICAL REPORTER. [Monthly]

> Office of Statistical Standards.
> Later PrEx 2.11

Pr 34.113:nos.
STATISTICAL EVALUATION REPORTS.

Pr 34.114:CT
STAFF REPORTS.

OFFICE OF DEFENSE
MOBILIZATION
(1953– 1958)

CREATION AND AUTHORITY

> The first Office of Defense Mobilization
(Pr 33.1000) was established within the Executive Office of the President by Executive Order
10193 of December 16, 1950. By Reorganization
Plan No. 3 of 1953, its functions were transferred
to the newly created Office of Defense Mobilization. Under Reorganization Plan No. 1 of 1958,
effective July 1, 1958, the Office of Defense
Mobilization and the Federal Civil Defense Administration (FCD 1) were combined to form the Office of Defense and Civilian Mobilization (Pr
34.700).

Pr 34.201:date
REPORT TO THE PRESIDENT BY DIRECTOR OF
OFFICE OF DEFENSE MOBILIZATION. [Quarterly]

> Earlier Pr 33.1008
> Later Pr 34.701

Pr 34.202:CT
GENERAL PUBLICATIONS.

> Earlier Pr 33.1002
> Later Pr 34.702

Pr 34.205:CT
LAWS.

Pr 34.206:CT
REGULATIONS, RULES, AND INSTRUCTIONS.

Pr 34.206/2
DEFENSE MOBILIZATION ORDERS.

Pr 34.207:nos.
RELEASES.

> Earlier Pr 33.1007

Pr 34.208
DEFENSE MANPOWER POLICY (series).

Pr 34.209
LABOR-MANAGEMENT MANPOWER POLICY COM-
MITTEE, PUBLICATIONS.

Pr 34.210
STOCKPILE REPORT TO CONGRESS. [Semiannual]

> Earlier Pr 34.202:St 6
> Later Pr 34.709

CENTRAL INTELLIGENCE
AGENCY
(1953– 1961)

CREATION AND AUTHORITY

> The Central Intelligence Agency was estab-
lished within the National Security Council on
September 20, 1947, pursuant to the National
Security Act of 1947, approved July 26, 1947 (61
Stat. 498), succeeding the National Intelligence
Authority. Reorganization Plan No. 4 of 1949, ef-
fective August 20, 1949, transferred the Agency
to the Executive Office of the President.

Pr 34.601:date
ANNUAL REPORT.

> Earlier Pr 33.601

Pr 34.602:CT
GENERAL PUBLICATIONS.

> Earlier Pr 33.602

Pr 34.608
OPERATING COORDINATING BOARD, PUBLICATIONS.

Pr 34.609:nos.
SCIENTIFIC INFORMATION REPORT. [Semimonthly]

Pr 34.610:nos.
CONSOLIDATED TRANSLATION SURVEY.

Pr 34.611:CT
PUBLICATIONS.

FOREIGN BROADCAST INFORMATION SERVICE (1953– 1961)

Pr 34.651:date
ANNUAL REPORTS.

Pr 34.652:CT
GENERAL PUBLICATIONS.

Pr 34.659:date
BROADCASTING STATIONS OF THE WORLD.

    Later PrEx 7.9

Pr 34.660:dt.&nos.
DAILY REPORTS, FOREIGN RADIO BROADCASTS.

    Earlier Pr 33.657
    Later PrEx 7.10

  Pr 34.660/2:dt.&nos.
  – SUPPLEMENTS.

    Later PrEx 7.10/2

OFFICE OF DEFENSE AND CIVILIAN MOBILIZATION (1958– 1961)

CREATION AND AUTHORITY

The Office of Defense Civilian Mobilization was established by Reorganization Plan No. 1 of 1958 (72 Stat. 1799) for the purpose of centralizing authority of nonmilitary defense function in a single agency, consolidating functions of the Office of Defense Mobilization (Pr 34.200) and Federal Civil Defense Administration (FCD 1). The name was changed to Office of Civil and Defense Mobilization by act of August 26, 1958 (72 Stat. 861). Civil defense functions were transferred to the Secretary of Defense (D 13) by EO 10952 of July 20, 1961, and the remaining functions redesignated Office of Emergency Planning (PrEx 4) by act of September 22, 1961 (75 Stat. 630; 50 U.S.C. App. 2271 note).

Pr 34.701:date
REPORTS.

    Earlier FCD 1.1, Pr 34.201
    Later PrEx 4.1

Pr 34.702:CT
GENERAL PUBLICATIONS.

    Earlier FCD 1.2, Pr 34.202
    Later PrEx 4.2

Pr 34.703:nos.
BULLETINS. (Official use only)

    Later PrEx 4.3

Pr 34.704/2:nos.
INTERAGENCY CIRCULARS.

    Later PrEx 4.4/2

Pr 34.706:CT
REGULATIONS, RULES, AND INSTRUCTIONS.

    Later PrEx 4.6

Pr 34.706/2:nos.
INTERIM DIRECTIVES.

    Later PrEx 4.6/2

Pr 34.706/3:nos.
DEFENSE MOBILIZATION ORDERS.

    Earlier Pr34.206/3
    Later PrEx 4.6/3

Pr 34.706/4:nos.
OCDM REGULATIONS. [Irregular]

    Later PrEx 4.6/4

Pr 34.706/5:nos.
ADMINISTRATIVE ORDERS.

    Later PrEx 4.6/5

Pr 34.706/6:nos.
EMERGENCY OPERATIONS ORDERS.

    Later PrEx 4.6/6

Pr 34.707:nos.
RELEASES.

    Later PrEx 4.7

Pr 34.708:nos.
[LEAFLET] L-SERIES.

    Earlier FCD 1.20
    Later PrEx 4.8

Pr 34.708/2:date
CIVIL AND DEFENSE MOBILIZATION DIRECTORY.

    Later PrEx 4.8/2

Pr 34.709:date
STOCKPILE REPORT TO CONGRESS. [Semiannual]

    Earlier Pr 34.210
    Later PrEx 4.9

Pr 34.710:CT
ADDRESSES.

    Later PrEx 4.10

Pr 34.711:CT
BIBLIOGRAPHIES AND LISTS OF PUBLICATIONS.

Pr 34.712:nos.
ADMINISTRATIVE MANUALS, AM (series).

    Later PrEx 4.12/2

Pr 34.751:date
PROGRESS REPORT, INTERIM STATISTICAL REPORT. [Quarterly]

    Later PrEx 4.1/2

Pr 34.751/2:date
ANNUAL STATISTICAL REPORT.

    Earlier FCD 1.1/2
    Later PrEx 4.1/2

Pr 34.752:CT
GENERAL PUBLICATIONS (Civil Defense).

    Earlier FCD 1.2

Pr 34.753:nos.
CIVIL DEFENSE TECHNICAL BULLETINS.

    Earlier FCD 1.3
    Later PrEx 4.3/2

Pr 34.753/2:nos.
INFORMATION BULLETINS (Civil Defense).

    Earlier FCD 1.13/11
    Later PrEx 4.3/3

Pr 34.753/3:nos.
ADVISORY BULLETINS.

    Earlier FCD 1.3/2
    Later PrEx 4.3/4

Pr 34.753/4:nos.
SURPLUS PROPERTY: BULLETIN.

    Later PrEx 4.3/5

Pr 34.755:CT
LAWS [relating to Civil Defense].

Pr 34.757/2:nos.
NEWS RELEASES [Civil Defense]

    Later PrEx 4.7/2

Pr 34.757/3:nos.
SPECIAL PROMOTION SERIES FROM OFFICE OF CIVIL AND DEFENSE MOBILIZATION, BATTLE CREEK, MICHIGAN, BULLETINS.

    Earlier FCD 1.7/3

Pr 34.757/4:nos.
SPECIAL PROMOTION SERIES FROM OFFICE OF CIVIL AND DEFENSE MOBILIZATION, BATTLE CREEK MICHIGAN, NATIONAL CIVIL DEFENSE DAY [or Week] BULLETINS.

    Earlier FCD 1.7/3

Pr 34.758:nos.
LEAFLET L(series).

    Cancel Pr 34.708
    Earlier FCD 1.20
    Later PrEx 4.13

Pr 34.759:nos.
MISCELLANEOUS PUBLICATIONS MP-(series).

    Later D 13.9

Pr 34.760:v.nos.&nos.
NEWSPICTURES [Civil Defense].

    Earlier FCD 1.16/2
    Later PrEx 4.7/3, D 1.34/2

Pr 34.760/2:v.nos.
NEWS FEATURES. [Irregular]

    Earlier FCD 1.16
    Later PrEx 4.7/4

Pr 34.761:CT
HANDBOOKS AND MANUALS (Civil Defense) (unnumbered).

    Later PrEx 4.12

Pr 34.761/2:v.nos.
HANDBOOK H- (series).

    Later PrEx 4.12/3, D 13.8/3

Pr 34.761/3:nos.
TECHNICAL MANUALS.

    Earlier FCD 1.6/3
    Later PrEx 4.12/4

Pr 34.761/4:nos.
INSTRUCTORS GUIDE IG (series).

    Earlier FCD 1.6/5
    Later PrEx 4.12/5

Pr 34.761/5:nos.
POCKET MANUAL PM (series).

    Earlier FCD 1.6/8

Pr 34.761/6:nos.
ADMINISTRATIVE GUIDES, AG SERIES.

Pr 34.761/7:nos.
STUDENT MANUAL, SM (series).

    Later D 13.8/5

Pr 34.762:CT
NATIONAL CIVIL DEFENSE DAY (or Week) PUBLI-
CATIONS.

Earlier FCD 1.23

Pr 34.763:nos.
TECHNICAL REPORT TR (series).

Earlier FCD 1.14

Pr 34.764:nos.
PUBLIC BOOKLET PB (series).

Earlier FCD 2.27/2

Pr 34.764/2:nos.
PUBLIC AFFAIRS FLYER, PA-F (series).

Earlier FCD 1.17

Pr 34.765:nos.
POSTERS P- (series).

Pr 34.766:nos.
CD SKITS.

PRESIDENT OF THE UNITED STATES JOHN F. KENNEDY (1961– 1963)

Pr 35.2:CT
GENERAL PUBLICATIONS.

Pr 35.7:date
PRESS RELEASES.

Pr 35.8:CT   • Item 851-J
COMMITTEES AND COMMISSIONS OF THE PRESI-
DENT.

Following are the Committees and Commissions established by the President for which publications have been issued and classes established:

Pr 35.8:Ad 6/CT
ADMINISTRATIVE CONFERENCE OF UNITED
STATES (1961): PUBLICATIONS

Pr 35.8:Ag 4/CT
PRESIDENT'S COUNCIL ON AGING (1962– 1963):
PUBLICATIONS.

Pr 35.8:Ai 7/CT
COMMISSION TO INQUIRE INTO CONTROVERSY
BETWEEN CERTAIN AIR CARRIERS OF
THEIR EMPLOYEES (1961): PUBLICATIONS.

Pr 35.8:Ap 4/CT
PRESIDENT'S APPALACHIAN REGIONAL COM-
MISSION: PUBLICATIONS.

Pr 35.8:Ar 5/CT
PRESIDENT'S COMMITTEE ON EQUAL OPPOR-
TUNITY IN THE ARMED FORCES (1963):
PUBLICATIONS.

Pr 35.8:Ar 7/CT
PRESIDENT'S ADVISORY COUNCIL ON THE
ARTS (1963): PUBLICATIONS.

Pr 35.8:C 15/CT
PRESIDENT'S COMMISSION ON CAMPAIGN
COSTS (1961– 1962): PUBLICATIONS.

Pr 35.8:C 86/CT
COMMITTEE ON FEDERAL CREDIT PROGRAMS
(1963): PUBLICATIONS.

Pr 35.8:D 84/CT
AD HOC PANEL ON DRUG ABUSE (1962– 1963):
PUBLICATIONS.

Pr 35.8:Ed 8/CT
PRESIDENT'S COMMITTEE ON PUBLIC HIGHER
EDUCATION IN THE DISTRICT OF COLUM-
BIA: PUBLICATIONS.

Pr 35.8:Em 7/CT
PRESIDENT'S COMMITTEE ON EQUAL EMPLOY-
MENT OPPORTUNITY (1961– 1965): PUBLI-
CATIONS.

Pr 35.8:Em 7/2/CT
PRESIDENT'S TASK FORCE ON EMPLOYEE-
MANAGEMENT RELATIONS IN FEDERAL
SERVICE (1961): PUBLICATIONS.

Pr 35.8:Em 7/3/CT
PRESIDENT'S COMMITTEE TO APPRAISE
EMPLOYMENT AND UNEMPLOYMENT STA-
TISTICS (1962): PUBLICATIONS.

Pr 35.8:F 76/CT
PRESIDENT'S FOREIGN INTELLIGENCE ADVI-
SORY BOARD (1961): PUBLICATIONS.

Pr 35.8:F 76/2/CT
PRESIDENT'S ADVISORY PANEL ON NATIONAL
ACADEMY OF FOREIGN AFFAIRS: PUBLI-
CATIONS.

Pr 35.8:F 76/3/CT
TASK FORCE ON PROMOTING INCREASED
FOREIGN INVESTMENTS IN UNITED STATES
CORPORATE SECURITIES AND INCREASED
FOREIGN FINANCING FOR UNITED STATES
CORPORATIONS OPERATING ABROAD
(1964): PUBLICATIONS.

Pr 35.8:J 98/CT
PRESIDENT'S COMMITTEE ON JUVENILE DE-
LINQUENCY AND YOUTH CRIME (1961–
1970): PUBLICATIONS.

Pr 35.8:L 11/CT
PRESIDENT'S ADVISORY COMMITTEE ON
LABOR-MANAGEMENT POLICY (1961–
1963): PUBLICATIONS.

Pr 35.8:M 31/CT
PRESIDENT'S TASK FORCE ON MANPOWER
CONSERVATION: PUBLICATIONS.

Pr 35.8:M 46/CT
PRESIDENT'S COMMITTEE ON NATIONAL MEDAL
OF SCIENCE (1961): PUBLICATIONS.

Pr 35.8:M 52/CT
PRESIDENT'S PANEL ON MENTAL RETARDATION:
PUBLICATIONS.

Pr 35.8:M 69/CT
PRESIDENT'S MISSILE SITES LABOR COMMIS-
SION (1961– 1967): PUBLICATIONS.

Pr 35.8:M 97/CT
PRESIDENT'S MUSIC COMMITTEE ON PEOPLE
TO PEOPLE PROGRAM: PUBLICATIONS.

Pr 35.8:N 16/CT
PRESIDENT'S ADVISORY COMMISSION ON
NARCOTIC AND DRUG ABUSE (1963): PUB-
LICATIONS.

Pr 35.8:N 21/CT
KENNEDY-JOHNSON NATURAL RESOURCES
ADVISORY COMMITTEE (1961– 1964): PUB-
LICATIONS.

Pr 35.8:Of 2/CT
AD HOC COMMITTEE ON FEDERAL OFFICE
SPACE (1962): PUBLICATIONS.

Pr 35.8:P 38/CT
PRESIDENT'S COUNCIL ON PENNSYLVANIA
AVENUE: PUBLICATIONS.

Pr 35.8:P 38/2/CT
PRESIDENT'S COMMITTEE ON CORPORATE
PENSION FUNDS AND OTHER PRIVATE RE-
TIREMENT AND WELFARE PROGRAMS: PUB-
LICATIONS.

Pr 35.8:P 56/CT
PRESIDENT'S COUNCIL ON PHYSICAL FITNESS
(1963– 1968): PUBLICATIONS.

Earlier Pr 34.8:Y 8
Later Pr 36.8:P 56

Pr 35.8:R 13/CT
RAILROAD LIGHTER CAPTAINS COMMISSION
(1961): PUBLICATIONS.

Pr 35.8:R 24/CT
RECREATION ADVISORY COUNCIL: PUBLICA-
TIONS.

Pr 35.8:R 26/CT
PRESIDENT'S COMMISSION ON REGISTRATION
AND VOTING PARTICIPATION (1963): PUB-
LICATIONS.

Pr 35.8:Sci 2/CT
PRESIDENT'S SCIENCE ADVISORY COMMITTEE
(1961– 1963): PUBLICATIONS.

Earlier Pr 34.8:Sci 2

Pr 35.8:Sm 1/CT
WHITE HOUSE COMMITTEE ON SMALL BUSI-
NESS (1962– 1963): PUBLICATIONS.

Pr 35.8:T 31/CT
PRESIDENT'S CABINET TEXTILE ADVISORY
COMMITTEE (1962): PUBLICATIONS.

Pr 35.8:W 29/CT
WHITE HOUSE-DEPARTMENT OF THE INTERIOR
PANEL ON WATERLOGGING AND SALINITY
IN WEST PAKISTAN: PUBLICATIONS.

Pr 35.8:W 84/CT
PRESIDENT'S COMMISSION ON STATUS OF
WOMEN (1961– 1963): PUBLICATIONS.

Pr 35.8:Y 8/2/CT
PRESIDENT'S COMMITTEE ON YOUTH
EMPLOYMENT: PUBLICATIONS.

Pr 35.9:date
ECONOMIC REPORT OF THE PRESIDENT.

Earlier Pr 34.10
Later Pr 36.9

PRESIDENT OF THE UNITED STATES LYNDON B. JOHNSON (1963– 1969)

Pr 36.1:date
REPORT.

Pr 36.2:CT
GENERAL PUBLICATIONS.

Pr 36.7:date
PRESS RELEASES.

Pr 36.8:CT   • Item 851-J
COMMITTEES AND COMMISSIONS OF THE PRESI-
DENT.

Following are the Committees and Commissions established by the president for which publications have been issued and classes established:

Pr 36.8:Al 1/CT
PRESIDENT'S REVIEW COMMITTEE FOR DE-
VELOPMENT PLANNING IN ALASKA (1964):
PUBLICATIONS.

Pr 36.8:Ar 5/CT
PRESIDENT'S COMMISSION ON ALL-VOLUN-
TEER ARMED FORCES: PUBLICATIONS.

Pr 36.8:B 85/CT
PRESIDENT'S COMMISSION ON BUDGET CON-
CEPTS (1967– 1969): PUBLICATIONS.

Pr 36.8:C 18/CT
PRESIDENTIAL TASK FORCE ON CAREER
ADVANCEMENT (1967): PUBLICATIONS.

Pr 36.8:C 49/CT
NATIONAL ADVISORY COMMISSION ON CIVIL
DISORDERS (1967– 1968): PUBLICATIONS.

Pr 36.8:C 73/CT
PRESIDENT'S TASK FORCE ON COMMUNICA-
TIONS POLICY (1967– 1968): PUBLICA-
TIONS.

Pr 36.8:C 76/CT
PRESIDENT'S COMMITTEE ON CONSUMER
INTERESTS (1964– 1969): PUBLICATIONS.

Pr 36.8:C 86/CT
PRESIDENT'S COMMISSION ON CRIME IN THE
DISTRICT OF COLUMBIA (1965– 1969): PUB-
LICATIONS.

Pr 36.8:Ec 7/CT
COMMITTEE ON ECONOMIC IMPACT OF DE-
FENSE AND DISARMAMENT (1965– 1969):
PUBLICATIONS.

Pr 36.8:Eq 2/CT
PRESIDENT'S COUNCIL ON EQUAL OPPORTU-
NITY (1965): PUBLICATIONS.

Pr 36.8:F 73/CT
NATIONAL ADVISORY COMMISSION ON FOOD
AND FIBER (1965– 1969): PUBLICATIONS.

Pr 36.8:H 34/CT
NATIONAL ADVISORY COMMISSION ON HEALTH
MANPOWER (1966– 1969): PUBLICATIONS.

Pr 36.8:H 34/2/CT
PRESIDENT'S ADVISORY COMMISSION ON
HEALTH FACILITIES (1967– 1968): PUBLI-
CATIONS.

Pr 36.8:H 35/CT
PRESIDENT'S COMMISSION ON HEART
DISEASE, CANCER, AND STROKE (1965):
PUBLICATIONS.

Pr 36.8:H 88/CT
PRESIDENT'S COMMISSION FOR OBSERVANCE
OF HUMAN RIGHTS YEAR 1968 (1968): PUB-
LICATIONS.

Pr 36.8:In 2/CT
PRESIDENT'S COMMISSION ON INCOME MAIN-
TENANCE PROGRAMS: PUBLICATIONS.

Pr 36.8:K 38/CT
PRESIDENT'S COMMISSION ON ASSASSINA-
TION OF PRESIDENT JOHN F. KENNEDY
(1963– 1964): PUBLICATIONS.

Pr 36.8:L 41/CT
PRESIDENT'S COMMISSION OF LAW ENFORCE-
MENT AND ADMINISTRATION OF JUSTICE
(1965– 1969): PUBLICATIONS.

Pr 36.8:M 31/CT
PRESIDENT'S COMMITTEE ON MANPOWER
(1964): PUBLICATIONS.

Pr 36.8:M 33/CT
COMMISSION ON MARINE SCIENCE,
ENGINEERING AND RESOURCES: PUBLI-
CATIONS.

Pr 36.8:M 52/CT
PRESIDENT'S COMMITTEE ON MENTAL RETAR-
DATION: PUBLICATIONS.

Pr 36.8:N 21/CT
PRESIDENT'S TASK FORCE ON PRESERVATION
OF NATURAL BEAUTY (1965): PUBLICA-
TIONS.

Pr 36.8:P 27/CT
PRESIDENT'S COMMISSION ON THE PATENT
SYSTEM (1965): PUBLICATIONS.

Pr 36.8:P 38/CT
PRESIDENT'S TEMPORARY COMMISSION ON
PENNSYLVANIA AVENUE (1965): PUBLICA-
TIONS.

Pr 36.8:P 56/CT
PRESIDENT'S COUNCIL ON PHYSICAL FITNESS
AND SPORTS (1968– 1969): PUBLICATIONS.

    Earlier Pr 35.8:Y 8
    Later Pr 37.8:P 56/2

Pr 36.8:P 81/CT
PRESIDENT'S COMMITTEE ON POPULATION
AND FAMILY PLANNING (1968): PUBLICA-
TIONS.

Pr 36.8:P 84/CT
PRESIDENT'S COMMISSION ON POSTAL OR-
GANIZATION (1967– 1968): PUBLICATIONS.

Pr 36.8:P 93/CT
CABINET COMMITTEE ON PRICE STABILITY
(1968– 1969): PUBLICATIONS.

Pr 36.8:R 24/CT
CITIZENS' ADVISORY COMMITTEE ON RECRE-
ATION AND NATURAL BEAUTY (1966– 1969):
PUBLICATIONS.

Pr 36.8:R 29/CT
PRESIDENT'S COMMITTEE ON MENTAL RETAR-
DATION: PUBLICATIONS.

Pr 36.8:R 88/CT
NATIONAL ADVISORY COMMISSION ON RURAL
POVERTY (1966– 1967): PUBLICATIONS.

Pr 36.8:Sch 6/CT
COMMISSION ON PRESIDENTIAL SCHOLARS
(1964– 1969): PUBLICATIONS.

Pr 36.8:Se 4/CT
TASK FORCE ON STRUCTURE OF SELECTIVE
SERVICE SYSTEMS: PUBLICATIONS.

Pr 36.8:Se 4/2/CT
TASK FORCE ON STRUCTURE OF SELECTIVE
SERVICE SYSTEM (1967): PUBLICATIONS.

Pr 36.8:Sp 1/CT
SPACE TASK GROUP (1969): PUBLICATIONS.

Pr 36.8:Su 7/CT
NATIONAL ADVISORY COUNCIL ON SUPPLE-
MENTAL CENTERS AND SERVICE (1968–
1969): PUBLICATIONS.

Pr 36.8:Su 7/2/CT
PRESIDENT'S NATIONAL ADVISORY COUNCIL
ON SUPPLEMENTARY CENTERS AND SER-
VICES (1968– 1969): PUBLICATIONS.

Pr 36.8:T 67/CT
PRESIDENT'S SPECIAL COMMITTEE ON U.S.
TRADE RELATIONS WITH EAST EUROPEN
COUNTRIES AND THE SOVIET UNION: PUB-
LICATIONS.

Pr 36.8:T 69/CT
INDUSTRY-GOVERNMENT SPECIAL TASK
FORCE ON TRAVEL (1967– 1968): PUBLICA-
TIONS.

Pr 36.8:Ur 1/CT
NATIONAL COMMISSION ON URBAN PROB-
LEMS: PUBLICATIONS.

Pr 36.8:Ur 1/2/CT
NATIONAL COMMISSION ON URBAN PROBLEMS
(1968– 1969): PUBLICATIONS.

Pr 36.8:V 81/CT
NATIONAL COMMISSION ON THE CAUSES AND
PREVENTION OF VIOLENCE (1968– 1969):
PUBLICATIONS.

Pr 36.8:W 58/CT
PRESIDENT'S COMMISSION ON WHITE HOUSE
FELLOWS (1964– 1969): PUBLICATIONS.

Pr 36.8:Y 8/CT
PRESIDENT'S COUNCIL ON YOUTH OPPORTU-
NITY: PUBLICATIONS

Pr 36.9:date
ECONOMIC REPORT OF THE PRESIDENT.

    Earlier Pr 35.9
    Later Pr 37.9

Pr 36.10:date
ANNUAL REPORT OF THE PRESIDENT OF THE
UNITED STATES ON TRADE AGREEMENTS PRO-
GRAM.

PRESIDENT OF THE UNITED
STATES RICHARD M. NIXON
(1969– 1974)

Pr 37.1:date
REPORT.

Pr 37.2:CT   • Item 850
GENERAL PUBLICATIONS.

Pr 37.7:date
PRESS RELEASES.

Pr 37.8:CT   • Item 851-J
COMMITTEES AND COMMISSIONS OF THE PRESI-
DENT.

    Following are the committees and Commis-
sions established by the President for which publications have been issued and classes established:

Pr 37.8:Ag 4/CT   • Item 851-J
TASK FORCE ON THE PROBLEMS OF AGING.

Pr 37.8:Ag 8/CT   • Item 851-J
TASK FORCE ON AGING.

Pr 37.8:Ai 7/CT   • Item 851-J
TASK FORCE ON AIR POLLUTION.

Pr 37.8:Ar 5/CT   • Item 851-J
PRESIDENT'S COMMISSION ON ALL VOLUNTEER
ARMED FORCES.

Pr 37.8:B 96/CT   • Item 851-J
TASK FORCE ON BUSINESS TAXATION.

Pr 37.8:C 11   • Item 851-J
CABINET COMMITTEE ON CABLE COMMUNICA-
TIONS.

Pr 37.8:C 15/CT   • Item 851-J
PRESIDENT'S COMMISSION ON CAMPUS UN-
REST.

Pr 37.8:Ec 7/CT   • Item 851-J
TASK FORCE ON ECONOMIC GROWTH.

Pr 37.8:Ed 8/CT   • Item 851-J
TASK FORCE ON HIGHER EDUCATION.

Pr 37.8:En 2/2/CT   • Item 851-J
INTERAGENCY TASK FORCE ON SYNTHETIC
FUELS COMMERCIALIZATION.

Pr 37.8:En 8/CT   • Item 851-J
CITIZENS ADVISORY COMMITTEE ON ENVIRON-
MENTAL QUALITY.

    Item 1061-C

Pr 37.8:En 8/P 43/v.nos.&nos.
PESTICIDES MONITORING JOURNAL [Panel on Pesticide Monitoring]. [Quarterly] (Division of Pesticide Community Studies, FDA)

Earlier Y 3.F 31/18:9 prior to v. 4, no. 1, under the auspices of Federal Committee on Pest Control.
Later PrEx 14.9

Pr 37.8:Ex 3/CT   • Item 851-J
PRESIDENT'S ADVISORY COUNCIL ON EXECUTIVE ORGANIZATION.

Pr 37.8:Ex 7/CT   • Item 851-J
PRESIDENT'S EXPORT COUNCIL: PUBLICATIONS. [Irregular]

Pr 37.8:H 34/CT   • Item 851-J
PRESIDENT'S COMMITTEE ON HEALTH EDUCATION.

Pr 37.8:H 53/CT   • Item 851-J
TASK FORCE ON HIGHWAY SAFETY.

Pr 37.8:H 81/CT   • Item 851-J
TASK FORCE ON LOW-INCOME HOUSING.

Pr 37.8:In 8/2/CT   • Item 851-J
COMMISSION ON INTERNATIONAL TRADE AND INVESTMENT POLICY.

Pr 37.8:In 8/3/CT   • Item 851-J
COUNCIL ON INTERNATIONAL ECONOMIC POLICY.

Pr 37.8:In 8/3/R 29/2   • Item 851-J
INTERNATIONAL ECONOMIC REPORT OF THE PRESIDENT. 1–   1973–   [Annual]

Includes the annual report of the Council on International Economic Policy.

Pr 37.8:M 31/CT   • Item 851-J
PRESIDENT'S ADVISORY COUNCIL ON MANAGEMENT IMPROVEMENT.

Pr 37.8:M 52/CT   • Item 851-J
TASK FORCE ON THE MENTALLY HANDICAPPED.

Pr 37.8:M 72/CT   • Item 851-J
TASK FORCE ON MODEL CITIES.

Pr 37.8:N 21g/CT   • Item 851-J
NATIONAL GOALS RESEARCH STAFF.

Pr 37.8:Oc 2/CT   • Item 851-J
TASK FORCE ON OCEANOGRAPHY.

Pr 37.8:Oi 5/CT   • Item 851-J
CABINET TASK FORCE ON OIL IMPORT CONTROL.

Pr 37.8:P 43/CT   • Item 851-J
PRESIDENT'S COMMISSION ON PERSONNEL INTERCHANGE.

Pr 37.8:P 56/CT   • Item 851-J
TASK FORCE ON THE PHYSICALLY HANDICAPPED.

Pr 37.8:P 56/2/CT   • Item 851-J
PRESIDENT'S COUNCIL ON PHYSICAL FITNESS AND SPORTS.

Earlier Pr 36.8:P 56

Pr 37.8:P 56/2/N 47/date   • Item 851-J
NEWSLETTER. 1963–   [Irregular]

ISSN 0364-8079
Earlier Pr 37.8:P 56/N 47
Later HE 20.109

Pr 37.8:P 56/2/R 31/2   • Item 851-J
PHYSICAL FITNESS RESEARCH DIGEST. [Quarterly]

ISSN 0094-9108
Later HE 20.110

Pr 37.8:P 93/CT   • Item 851-J
TASK FORCE ON PRISONER REHABILITATION.

Pr 37.8:P 94/CT   • Item 851-J
NATIONAL COMMISSION ON PRODUCTIVITY AND WORK QUALITY: PUBLICATIONS.

Name varies: 1972– 1973, National Commission on Productivity; 1974– 1975, National Commission on Productivity and Work Quality.
Superseded by National Center Productivity and Quality of Working Life (Y 3.P 94:1).

Pr 37.8:P 94/R 29   • Item 851-J
PRODUCTIVITY, ANNUAL REPORT. 1st– 4th. 1972– 1975.

ISSN 0099-0841

Pr 37.8:P 96/CT   • Item 851-J
AD HOC ADVISORY GROUP ON PRESIDENTIAL VOTE FOR PUERTO RICO.

Pr 37.8:R 26/CT
FEDERAL REGIONAL COUNCIL.

Pr 37.8:R 88/CT   • Item 851-J
TASK FORCE ON RURAL DEVELOPMENT.

Pr 37.8:Sch 6/CT   • Item 851-J
PRESIDENT'S COMMISSION ON SCHOOL FINANCE.

Pr 37.8:Sci 2/CT   • Item 851-J
TASK FORCE ON SCIENCE POLICY.

Pr 37.8:Sm 1/CT   • Item 851-J
TASK FORCE ON IMPROVING AND PROSPECTS OF SMALL BUSINESS.

Pr 37.8:St 2/CT   • Item 851-J
PRESIDENT'S COMMISSION ON FEDERAL STATISTICS.

Pr 37.8:T 48   • Item 851-J
PRESIDENT'S ADVISORY PANEL ON TIMBER AND THE ENVIRONMENT.

Pr 37.8:Un 3/CT   • Item 851-J
PRESIDENT'S COMMISSION FOR OBSERVANCE OF 25th ANNIVERSARY OF THE UNITED NATIONS.

Pr 37.8:Ur 1/CT   • Item 851-J
TASK FORCE ON URBAN RENEWAL.

Pr 37.8:W 84/CT   • Item 851-J
TASK FORCE ON WOMEN'S RIGHTS AND RESPONSIBILITIES.

Pr 37.8:Y 8/CT   • Item 851-J
PRESIDENT'S COUNCIL ON YOUTH OPPORTUNITY.

Pr 37.9:date   • Item 848
ECONOMIC REPORT OF THE PRESIDENT.

Earlier Pr 36.9
Later Pr 38.9

Pr 37.10:date   • Item 848-A
ANNUAL REPORT OF THE PRESIDENT OF UNITED STATES ON TRADE AGREEMENTS PROGRAM.

Later Pr 38.13

Pr 37.11:date   • Item 848-B
FEDERAL OCEAN PROGRAM, ANNUAL REPORT TO CONGRESS.

Earlier PrEx 12.1
Later Pr 38.11

Pr 37.12:date   • Item 848-C
FEDERAL ADVISORY COMMITTEES, ANNUAL REPORT OF THE PRESIDENT. 1st–   1973–

Later Pr 38.10

Pr 37.13:date
PUBLIC LAW 480, AGRICULTURAL EXPORT ACTIVITIES, ANNUAL REPORT OF THE PRESIDENT.

Formerly published as House and Senate reports.

Pr 37.14:date
RURAL DEVELOPMENT GOALS. 1st–   1973–   [Annual]

Pursuant to Title VI, Section 603 (b), of the Rural Development Act of 1972, the Secretary of Agriculture is required to establish goals for rural development and to report annually on the progress in attaining those goals. Report covers the fiscal year.

PRESIDENT OF THE UNITED STATES GERALD R. FORD (1974– 1977)

Pr 38.2:CT   • Item 850
GENERAL PUBLICATIONS. [Irregular]

Pr 38.2:Oc 1/date   • Item 850
PRESIDENT'S REPORT ON OCCUPATIONAL SAFETY AND HEALTH. 1st–   1971–   [Annual]

Pr 38.7:date
PRESS RELEASES.

Pr 38.8:CT   • Item 851-J
COMMITTEES AND COMMISSIONS OF THE PRESIDENT. [Irregular]

The following are the Committees and Commissions established by the President for which publications have been issued and classes established.

Pr 38.8:C 33/CT   • Item 851-J
COMMISSION ON CIA ACTIVITIES WITHIN THE UNITED STATES: REPORT.

Pr 38.8:C 59/CT   • Item 851-J
PRESIDENTIAL CLEMENCY BOARD: PUBLICATIONS.

Pr 38.8:C 73/CT   • Item 851-J
PRESIDENT'S PANEL ON FEDERAL COMPENSATION.

Pr 38.8:In 8/CT   • Item 851-J
COUNCIL ON INTERNATIONAL ECONOMIC POLICY.

Pr 38.8:Oi 9   • Item 851-J
PRESIDENT'S COMMISSION ON OLYMPIC SPORTS.

Pr 38.8:R 25/CT   • Item 851-J
INTERAGENCY TASK FORCE FOR INDOCHINA REFUGEES.

Pr 38.8:R 26/CT   • Item 851-J
DOMESTIC COUNCIL REVIEW GROUP ON REGULATORY REFORM.

Pr 38.9:date   • Item 848
ECONOMIC REPORT OF THE PRESIDENT. [Annual]
Earlier Pr 37.9

Pr 38.10:date   • Item 848-C
FEDERAL ADVISORY COMMITTEE, ANNUAL REPORT OF THE PRESIDENT. 1st–   1973–
Earlier Pr 37.12

Pr 38.11:date   • Item 848-B
FEDERAL OCEAN PROGRAM, ANNUAL REPORT TO CONGRESS.
Earlier Pr 37.11
Later Pr 39.12

Pr 38.12:date • Item 848-D
FEDERAL PERSONAL DATA SYSTEMS SUBJECT TO THE PRIVACY ACT OF 1974, ANNUAL REPORT OF THE PRESIDENT. 1st–   1975–

Later Pr 39.11

Pr 38.13:date • Item 848-E
ANNUAL REPORT OF THE PRESIDENT ON THE TRADE AGREEMENTS PROGRAM.

Also issued in House Documents series.
Earlier Pr 37.10
Later Pr 39.13

PRESIDENT OF THE UNITED STATES JIMMY CARTER (1977–1981)

Pr 39.2:CT • Item 850
GENERAL PUBLICATIONS. [Irregular]

Pr 39.2:En 2 • Item 850
NATIONAL ENERGY PLAN. 128 p. il.

This is the text of President Carter's proposed energy program for the development and conservation of the nation's energy resources. The comprehensive plan details the energy policy outlined by the President during his "Fireside Chat" of April 18 and his address before the Joint Session of Congress on April 20. Aimed at assuring a continuous supply of adequate energy throughout the foreseeable future, the plan encompasses provisions on oil and natural gas pricing, conversions to coal, the future of nuclear and hydroelectric power, the importance of solar energy, the proposed Department of Energy, conservation tactics, and much more.

Pr 39.8:CT • Item 851-J
COMMITTEES AND COMMISSIONS OF THE PRESIDENT.

Pr 39.8:Ag 3/CT • Item 851-J
PRESIDENT'S COMMISSION FOR A NATIONAL AGENDA FOR THE EIGHTIES.

Pr 39.8:An 8/CT • Item 851-J
NATIONAL COMMISSION FOR THE REVIEW OF ANTI-TRUST LAWS AND PROCEDURES.

Pr 39.8:C 63 • Item 851-J
PRESIDENT'S COMMISSION ON COAL. [Irregular]

Pr 39.8:Ex 7/CT • Item 851-J
PRESIDENT'S EXPORT COUNCIL.

Pr 39.8:H 74/CT • Item 851-J
PRESIDENT'S COMMISSION ON THE HOLOCAUST.

Pr 39.8:M 52/CT • Item 851-J
PRESIDENT'S COMMISSION ON MENTAL HEALTH.

Pr 39.8:P 38 • Item 851-J
PRESIDENT'S COMMISSION ON PENSION POLICY.

Pr 39.8:W 89/CT • Item 851-J
WORLD HUNGER WORKING GROUP.

Pr 39.8:W 89/3 • Item 851-J
PRESIDENTIAL COMMISSION ON WORLD HUNGER.

Pr 39.9:date • Item 848
ECONOMIC REPORT OF THE PRESIDENT. [Annual]

Earlier Pr 38.9

Pr 39.10:date • Item 848-C
FEDERAL ADVISORY COMMITTEES ANNUAL REPORT OF THE PRESIDENT.

Earlier Pr 38.10
Later Pr 10.10

Pr 39.11:date • Item 848-D (MF)
REPORT OF THE PRESIDENT ON THE IMPLEMENTATION OF THE PRIVACY ACT OF 1974. [Annual]

Report covers the calendar year.
Former title: Federal Personal Data Systems Subject to the Privacy Act of 1974.
ISSN 0149-2845
Earlier Pr 38.12

Pr 39.12:date • Item 848-B
FEDERAL OCEAN PROGRAM, ANNUAL REPORT TO CONGRESS.

Earlier Pr 38.11

Pr 39.13:date • Item 848-E
ANNUAL REPORT OF THE PRESIDENT ON THE TRADE AGREEMENTS PROGRAM. (Trade Policy Staff Committee, 1800 G Street, N.W., Washington, D.C. 20506)

Earlier Pr 38.13

Pr 39.14:date • Item 851-J-2
NATIONAL CONSUMER BUYING ALERT. 1979–1981. [Monthly] (Office of the Special Assistant for Consumer Affairs)

PURPOSE:– To provide consumers with useful information about expected marketplace trends and conditions for items such as food, energy, housing, and health care. Contains brief articles.

Pr 39.15:CT • Item 850
HANDBOOKS, MANUALS, GUIDES. [Irregular]

Pr 39.15:C 76 • Item 850
CONSUMERS' RESOURCE HANDBOOK. [Irregular]

PRESIDENT OF THE UNITED STATES RONALD REAGAN (1981–1989)

Pr 40.2:CT • Item 850
GENERAL PUBLICATIONS.

Pr 40.8:CT • Item 851-J
COMMITTEES AND COMMISSIONS OF THE PRESIDENT.

Pr 40.8:Am 3/CT • Item 851-J
PRESIDENT'S COMMISSION ON AMERICANS OUTDOORS.

Pr 40.8:Ar 7 • Item 851-J
PRESIDENTIAL TASK FORCE ON THE ARTS AND HUMANITIES.

Pr 40.8:B 52 • Item 851-J
NATIONAL BIPARTISAN COMMISSION ON CENTRAL AMERICA.

Pr 40.8:B 96 • Item 851-J
PRESIDENTIAL ADVISORY COMMITTEE ON SMALL AND MINORITY BUSINESS OWNERSHIP.

Pr 40.8:Br 78 • Item 851-J
PRESIDENTIAL COMMISSION ON BROADCASTING TO CUBA.

Pr 40.8:C 73 • Item 851-J-3
PRESIDENT'S COMMISSION ON INDUSTRIAL COMPETITIVENESS.

Pr 40.8:C 82 • Item 851-J
PRESIDENT'S PRIVATE SECTOR SURVEY ON COST CONTROL.

Pr 40.8:C 86 • Item 851-J-3
PRESIDENT'S COMMISSION ON ORGANIZED CRIME.

Pr 40.8:D 36/CT • Item 851-J-3
PRESIDENT'S BLUE RIBBON COMMISSION ON DEFENSE MANAGEMENT.

The Commission was established in July 1985 to conduct a study of current defense management.

Pr 40.8:D 84 • Item 851-J
PRESIDENTIAL COMMISSION ON DRUNK DRIVING.

Pr 40.8:Et 3 • Item 851-J
PRESIDENT'S COMMISSION FOR THE STUDY OF ETHICAL PROBLEMS IN MEDICINE AND BIOMEDICAL AND BEHAVIORAL RESEARCH.

Pr 40.8:Ex 3 • Item 851-J-5
PRESIDENT'S COMMISSION ON EXECUTIVE EXCHANGE.

Includes miscellaneous publications issued by the Commission, which arranges temporary exchanges of executives between the federal government and private corporations.
Later Pr 40.8/2

Pr 40.8:Ex 7 • Item 851-J-3
PRESIDENT'S EXPORT COUNCIL.

Pr 40.8:F 49 • Item 851-J-3
TASK GROUP ON REGULATION OF FINANCIAL SERVICES.

Pr 40.8:H 79 • Item 851-J
PRESIDENT'S COMMISSION ON HOSTAGE COMPENSATION.

Pr 40.8:H 81 • Item 851-J
PRESIDENT'S COMMISSION ON HOUSING.

Pr 40.8:In 2 • Item 851-J-3
PRESIDENTIAL COMMISSION ON INDIAN RESERVATION ECONOMIES.

Pr 40.8:In 8 • Item 851-J
PRESIDENT'S COUNCIL ON INTEGRITY AND EFFICIENCY.

Pr 40.8:M 31 • Item 851-J
PRESIDENT'S COUNCIL ON MANAGEMENT IMPROVEMENT.

Pr 40.8:M 46/CT • Item 851-J
PRESIDENT'S ADVISORY COMMITTEE ON MEDIATION AND CONCILIATION.

Pr 40.8:M 59 • Item 851-J
MILITARY MANAGEMENT TASK FORCE.

Pr 40.8:N 88 • Item 851-J
PRESIDENT'S NUCLEAR SAFETY OVERSIGHT COMMITTEE.

Pr 40.8:P 38 • Item 851-J
PRESIDENT'S COMMISSION ON PENSION POLICY.

Pr 40.8:P 93 • Item 851-J-3
PRESIDENT'S TASK FORCE ON PRIVATE SECTOR INITIATIVES.

Pr 40.8:P 94 • Item 851-J-3
WHITE HOUSE CONFERENCE ON PRODUCTIVITY.

Pr 40.8:R 11/CT • Item 851-J-4
ADVISORY BOARD FOR RADIO BROADCASTING TO CUBA.

Pr 40.8:Sch 6   • Item 851-J-3 (MF)
COMMISSION ON PRESIDENTIAL SCHOLARS.

Pr 40.8:So 1   • Item 851-J-3
NATIONAL COMMISSION ON SOCIAL SECURITY.

Pr 40.8:Sp 1/CT   • Item 851-J
PRESIDENTIAL COMMISSION ON THE SPACE SHUTTLE CHALLENGER ACCIDENT.

Pr 40.8:Sp 3   • Item 851-J
PRESIDENT'S SPECIAL REVIEW BOARD.

Pr 40.8:V 66   • Item 851-J-3
PRESIDENT'S TASK FORCE ON VICTIMS OF CRIME.

Pr 40.8:W 58   • Item 851-J-3 (MF)
PRESIDENT'S COMMISSION ON WHITE HOUSE FELLOWSHIPS.

Pr 40.8:W 84   • Item 851-J
INTERAGENCY COMMITTEE ON WOMEN'S BUSINESS ENTERPRISE.

Pr 40.8:Y 8   • Item 851-J-3
PRESIDENT'S COUNCIL FOR INTERNATIONAL YOUTH EXCHANGE.

Pr 40.8/2:date   • Item 851-J-3
PRESIDENT'S COMMISSION ON EXECUTIVE EXCHANGE: THE FEDERAL SECTOR. [Annual]

    Earlier Pr 40.8:Ex 3

Pr 40.8/3:date   • Item 851-J
THE PRESIDENT'S COUNCIL ON INTEGRITY AND EFFICIENCY, A PROGRESS REPORT TO THE PRESIDENT. [Semiannual]

Pr 40.9:date   • Item 848
ECONOMIC REPORT OF THE PRESIDENT. [Annual]

    Earlier Pr 39.9

Pr 40.10:date   • Item 848-C
FEDERAL ADVISORY COMMITTEES, ANNUAL REPORT OF THE PRESIDENT. 1st–   1972–

    Earlier Pr 39.10

Pr 40.11:date   • Item 848-E
ANNUAL REPORT OF THE PRESIDENT OF THE UNITED STATES ON TRADE AGREEMENTS PROGRAM.

Pr 40.12:date   • Item 851-J-3
WHITE HOUSE FELLOWSHIPS. [Annual]

    Earlier Pr 40.8:W 58

PRESIDENT OF THE UNITED STATES GEORGE BUSH (1989– 1993)

Pr 41.2:CT   • Item 850
GENERAL PUBLICATIONS. [Irregular]

Pr 41.8:CT   • Item 851-J
COMMITTEES AND COMMISSIONS OF THE PRESIDENT.

Pr 41.8:B 52   • Item 851-J
THE PRESIDENT'S COUNCIL ON COMPETITIVENESS.

Pr 41.8:Br 78/date   • Item 851-J
PRESIDENT'S ADVISORY BOARD FOR CUBA BROADCASTING.

Pr 41.8:Et 3   • Item 851-J
PRESIDENT'S COMMISSION ON FEDERAL ETHICS LAW REFORM.

Pr 41.8:G 51   • Item 851-J
WHITE HOUSE CONFERENCE ON SCIENCE AND ECONOMICS RESEARCH RELATED TO GLOBAL CHANGE.

Pr 41.8:L 71   • Item 851-J
NATIONAL INSTITUTE FOR LITERACY.

Pr 41.8:R 26   • Item 851-J
PRESIDENT'S COUNCIL ON COMPETITIVENESS.

Pr 41.8/3:date   • Item 851-J
PRESIDENT'S COUNCIL ON INTEGRITY AND EFFICIENCY: REPORTS.

Pr 41.9   • Item 848
ECONOMIC REPORT OF THE PRESIDENT.

Pr 41.10:date   • Item 848-C
FEDERAL ADVISORY COMMITTEE ANNUAL REPORT OF THE PRESIDENT.

Pr 41.11:date   • Item 848-E
ANNUAL REPORT OF THE PRESIDENT ON TRADE AGREEMENTS PROGRAM.

Pr 41.12:date   • Item 851-J
THE WHITE HOUSE FELLOWSHIPS.

PRESIDENT OF THE UNITED STATES WILLIAM CLINTON (1993–2001)

Pr 42.2:CT   • Item 850
GENERAL PUBLICATIONS.

    Earlier Pr 41.2

Pr 42.8:CT   • Item 851-J
SPECIAL COMMITTEES AND COMMISSIONS.

    Earlier Pr 41.8

Pr 42.8:Ad 9   • Item 851-J
PRESIDENTIAL ADVISORY COMMITTEE ON GULF WAR VETERANS' ILLNESSES.

Pr 42.8:B 52/F 49   • Item 851-J
BIPARTISAN COMMISSION ON ENTITLEMENT AND TAX REFORM: REPORTS.

Pr 42.8:C 86/CT/date   • Item 851-J
THE PRESIDENT'S CRIME PREVENTION COUNCIL.

Pr 42.8:D 63   • Item 851-J
EXECUTIVE SUMMARY, REPORT OF THE NATIONAL COMMISSION ON JUDICIAL DISCIPLINE & REMOVAL.

Pr 42.8:W 84   • Item 556-C
AMERICA'S COMMITMENT: FEDERAL PROGRAMS BENEFITING WOMEN AND NEW INITIATIVES AS FOLLOW-UP TO THE U.N. FOURTH WORLD CONFERENCE ON WOMEN.

Pr 42.8/3:date   • Item 851-J
A PROGRESS REPORT TO THE PRESIDENT (Fiscal Year).

PR 42.8/4:date/nos.   • Item 851-J-13 (EL)
THE JOURNAL OF PUBLIC INQUIRY (Date). [Semiannual]

Pr 42.9:date   • Item 848
ECONOMIC REPORT OF THE PRESIDENT.

    Earlier Pr 41.9

Pr 42.10:date   • Item 848-C (EL)
FEDERAL ADVISORY COMMITTEE ANNUAL REPORT OF THE PRESIDENT.

    Earlier Pr 41.10

Pr 42.11:date   • Item 848-E
ANNUAL REPORT OF THE PRESIDENT ON TRADE AGREEMENTS PROGRAM.

Pr 42.12   • Item 848
THE WHITE HOUSE FELLOWSHIPS.

Pr 42.13   • Item 851-J-7 (E)
ELECTRONIC PRODUCTS.

PRESIDENT OF THE UNITED STATES GEORGE H. BUSH (2001–   )

Pr 43.2   • Item 850-A
GENERAL PUBLICATIONS.

Pr 43.8   • Item 851-J-16
SPECIAL COMMITTEES AND COMMISSIONS.

Pr 43.9   • Item 848-F (P)(EL)
ECONOMIC REPORT OF THE PRESIDENT.

Pr 43.13   • Item 851-J-15 (E)
ELECTRONIC PRODUCTS (misc.)

Pr 43.14   • Item 851-J-17
OFFICE OF HOMELAND SECURITY (GENERAL PUBLICATIONS).

EXECUTIVE OFFICE OF THE PRESIDENT (1961–   )

CREATION AND AUTHORITY

    The Executive Office of the President was established by Reorganization Plans 1 and 2 of 1939, effective July 1, 1939. Executive Order 8248 of September 8, 1939 established the various divisions of the Executive Office at the time.
    Note:– Beginning in January 1961, SuDocs classes PrEx were established for the various agencies within the Executive Office of the President. Prior to this date, agencies within the Executive Office which continued through the administration of more than one President were assigned separate SuDocs classes under each President. Purely personal documents of the President are assigned Pr classes.

INFORMATION

Executive Office of the President
1600 Pennyslvania Ave., NW
Washington, DC 20500
(202) 456-1414
Fax: (202) 456-2461
http://www.whitehouse.gov

PrEx 1.2:CT   • Item 766-C-3
GENERAL PUBLICATIONS. [Irregular]

    Earlier Pr 34.2

PrEx 1.3/2:nos.   • Item 766-C-16
ONDCP BULLETIN.

PrEx 1.3/3   • **Item 766-C-29**
ONDCP BRIEF (series).

PrEx 1.7:date
PRESS RELEASES.

PrEx 1.8:CT
HANDBOOKS, MANUALS, GUIDES.

PrEx 1.9:v.nos.&nos.
FOOD FOR PEACE BULLETIN.

    Superseded by Food for Peace Newsletter (PrEx 1.9/2)

PrEx 1.9/2:nos.
FOOD FOR PEACE, MONTHLY NEWSLETTER ABOUT ACTIVITIES UNDER PI 480.

    Replaces PrEx 1.9
    Later S 18.34

President's Committee on Employment of the Handicapped

PrEx 1.10:CT   • **Item 766-C**
GENERAL PUBLICATIONS.

    Earlier L 16.44/2

PrEx 1.10:M 66   • **Item 766-C**
MINUTES, ANNUAL MEETING. 1962–   [Annual]
PrEx 1.10/2:CT   • **Item 766-C (MF)**
ADDRESSES.

    Earlier L 16.44/3

PrEx 1.10/3   • **Item 766**
PERFORMANCE, STORY OF THE HANDICAPPED. 1977–   [Monthly]

    From 1977 through 1981, issues were assigned volume and issue numbers.
    Indexed by: Index to U.S. Government Periodicals.
    ISSN 0031-5214
    Later PrEx 1.10/3-2

PrEx 1.10/3-2:v.nos.&nos.   • **Item 766**
DISABLED USA. v. 1–   1977–   [Quarterly]

    ISSN 0148-5407
    Earlier PrEx 1.10/3

PrEx 1.10/3-3:v.nos./nos.   • **Item 766**
WORK LIFE. [Quarterly]

PrEx 1.10/4:date   • **Item 766-C-12**
PRESIDENT'S COMMITTEE ON EMPLOYMENT OF THE HANDICAPPED: PRESS RELEASES.

    Press releases on miscellaneous topics pertaining to the work of the President's Committee on Employment of the Handicapped.
    Earlier L 16.36

PrEx 1.10/4-2:date
SPECIAL REPORT, FRESH VIEWS ON EMPLOYMENT OF THE MENTALLY HANDICAPPED.

    ISSN 0145-0247

PrEx 1.10/4-3:date
INVOLVEMENT FOR COMMUNITY ORGANIZATIONS WITH EMPLOYMENT OF THE MENTALLY RESTORED.

PrEx 1.10/4-4:CT
NEWS AND CLUES FOR SHELTERED WORKSHOP. [Irregular]

PrEx 1.10/5:date
NEWSLETTER, TIPS AND TRENDS IN EMPLOYMENT OF THE MENTALLY HANDICAPPED.

    Earlier L 16.44/4

PrEx 1.10/6:date   • **Item 766-C-4**
ANNUAL NATIONAL ABILITY COUNTS CONTEST [announcement].

    Earlier L 16.44/2:Ab 4/2

PrEx 1.10/7:date   • **Item 766-C**
PROGRAM GUIDE.

    Earlier L 16.44/2:P 94

PrEx 1.10/8:CT   • **Item 766-C-5**
HANDBOOKS, MANUALS, GUIDES. [Irregular]

PrEx 1.10/9:CT   • **Item 766-C-1**
BIBLIOGRAPHIES AND LISTS OF PUBLICATIONS. [Irregular]

PrEx 1.10/10:CT   • **Item 766-C-2**
POSTERS. [Irregular]

PrEx 1.10/11:   • **Item 766-C-6**
EMPLOYER GUIDE (series). [Irregular]

    Each Guide concerns a different subject.

PrEx 1.10/12:date   • **Item 766-C**
ANNUAL WORK PLAN.

PrEx 1.10/13:date   • **Item 766-C-10**
ANNUAL REPORT TO MEMBERSHIP.

    Summarizes activities of the Committee in carrying out its mission to facilitate development of maximum employment opportunities for the handicapped.

PrEx 1.10/14:date   • **Item 766-C-11**
SPECIAL REPORTS (series). [Irregular]

PrEx 1.10/15:   • **Item 766-C-15**
PEOPLE WITH DISABILITIES IN OUR NATION'S JOB TRAINING PARTNERSHIP ACT PROGRAMS. [Annual]

    Tables present data on participation of people with disabilities in the U.S. Job Training Partnership Act programs. The appendix lists representatives of state governor's committees on employment of the handicapped.

PrEx 1.10/16:date   • **Item 766-C-15**
THE PRESIDENT'S COMMITTEE ON EMPLOYMENT OF PEOPLE WITH DISABILITIES REPORT. [Annual]

PrEx 1.10/16-2:date   • **Item 766-C-31**
PRESIDENT'S COMMITTEE ON EMPLOYMENT OF PEOPLE WITH DISABILITIES ANNUAL REPORT (Braille).

PrEx 1.10/17:date   • **Item 766-C-15**
THE PRESIDENT'S COMMITTEE ON EMPLOYMENT OF PEOPLE WITH DISABILITIES (Annual Meeting).

PrEx 1.10/17-2:date   • **Item 766-C-23**
PRESIDENT'S COMMITTEE ON EMPLOYMENT OF PEOPLE WITH DISABILITIES, ANNUAL NATIONAL CONFERENCE.

    Issued in Braille.

PrEx 1.10/18:v.nos./nos.   • **Item 766**
NEWSBRIEF. [Monthly]

PrEx 1.10/19   • **Item 766-C-20**
PRESIDENT'S COMMITTEE ON THE EMPLOYMENT OF PEOPLE WITH DISABILITIES, GENERAL PUBLICATIONS (Braille Version).

PrEx 1.10/20:v.nos./nos.   • **Item 766-C-21**
DISABILITY NETWORK NEWS.

PrEx 1.10/20-2:v.nos./nos.   • **Item 766-C-22**
DISABILITY NETWORK NEWS.

    Issued in Braille.

Executive Office of the President (Continued)

PrEx 1.11:CT   • **Item 850**
PRESIDENT'S REORGANIZATION PROJECT: PUBLICATIONS. [Irregular]

PrEx 1.12:date   • **Item 776-C-7**
WHITE HOUSE REPORT TO STUDENTS. [3 or 4 times a year]

PrEx 1.12/2:date   • **Item 766-C-24 (P) (EL)**
INSIDE THE WHITE HOUSE. [Semiannual]

PrEx 1.13   • **Item 766-C-8**
PSI HIGHLIGHTS. [Irregular]

    PURPOSE:– To present news of private sector initiatives and the President's Volunteer Action Awards to private organizations and individuals.
    PSI = Private Sector Initiatives.

PrEx 1.14:date   • **Item 766-C-9**
NATIONAL TRADE ESTIMATE, REPORT ON FOREIGN TRADE BARRIERS. [Annual]

    PURPOSE:– To identify and analyze the most important barriers of major U.S. trading partners to U.S. exports. Describes in detail, by country, and lists their distorting impacts.

PrEx 1.15:   • **Item 766-C-14 (MF)**
CIRRPC ANNUAL REPORT.

    CIRRPC = Committee on Interagency Radiation Research and Policy Coordination.
    Summarizes activities of the Committee, which coordinates radiation matters between agencies, evaluates radiation research, and advises on the formulation of radiation policy.

PrEx 1.16:   • **Item 766-C-13**
THE PRESIDENTIAL ADVISORY COMMITTEE ON SMALL AND MINORITY BUSINESS OWNERSHIP, ANNUAL REPORT.

    Summarizes results of the Committee's activities and makes recommendations as required by EO 12190. This Committee is expected to continue indefinitely. Therefore, its class has been changed from Pr 40.8:B 96 to PrEx 1.16 for the reason that Pr classes are numbered for the current president and PrEx classes are not.

PrEx 1.17:date   • **Item 766-C-18 (MF)**
NATIONAL COMMUNICATIONS SYSTEM ANNUAL REPORT.

PrEx 1.17/2   • **Item 766-C-17**
GENERAL PUBLICATIONS: NATIONAL COMMUNICATIONS SYSTEM.

PrEx 1.18:   • **Item 766-C-27 (EL)**
COASTAL AMERICA PROGRESS REPORT. [Annual]

PrEx 1.18/2:CT   • **Item 766-C-33**
COASTAL AMERICA: GENERAL PUBLICATIONS.

PrEx 1.18/3:v.nos./nos.   • **Item 766-C-26 (EL)**
COASTAL AMERICA UPDATE. [Quarterly]

PrEx 1.19   • **Item 766-C-28 (MF) (EL)**
SPECIAL APPOINTED COMMITTEES.

PrEx 1.20   • **Item 851-J-10 (E)**
THE WOMEN'S NEWSLETTER.

PrEx 1.21   • **Item 851-J-10 (E)**
ELECTRONIC PRODUCTS.

PrEx 1.22:date   • **Item 766-C-32 (MF)**
TELEPHONE DIRECTORY. [Annual]

OFFICE OF MANAGEMENT AND BUDGET (1970–   )

CREATION AND AUTHORITY

The Bureau of the Budget was reorganized by the Reorganization Plan 2 of 1970 and its functions transferred to the Bureau of Management and Budget.

INFORMATION

Office of Management and Budget
Eisenhower Executive Office Bldg.
725 17th St. NW
Washington, DC 20503
(202) 395-3080
Fax: (202) 395-3888
http://www.whitehouse.gov/omb

PrEx 2.1:date
ANNUAL REPORTS.

Earlier Pr 34.101

PrEx 2.2:CT • Item 854
GENERAL PUBLICATIONS.

Earlier Pr 34.102

PrEx 2.3:nos. • Item 854 -A-2 (MF) (EL)
BULLETINS.

Earlier Pr 34.103

PrEx 2.3/2:CT • Item 855
MANAGEMENT BULLETINS.

Earlier Pr 33.108

PrEx 2.3/3:CT • Item 855
EXECUTIVE MANAGEMENT BULLETIN (series). 1970– [Irregular]

PURPOSE:– To inform managers and staff personnel in the executive branch of management improvement techniques applicable to common areas of Government.

PrEx 2.4:nos. • Item 854-D
CIRCULARS. 1– [Irregular]

PURPOSE:– To provide guides on policy and procedure for the Bureau of the Budget and other Government agencies.
Earlier Pr 34.104

PrEx 2.6:CT • Item 856
REGULATIONS, RULES, AND INSTRUCTIONS.

Earlier Pr 34.106

PrEx 2.6/2:CT • Item 854-A
HANDBOOKS, MANUALS, GUIDES.

PrEx 2.6/2:In 27 • Item 854-A
STANDARD INDUSTRIAL CLASSIFICATION MANUAL. [Irregular] (Prepared by the Office of Statistical Standards)

Latest edition: 1967.

PrEx 2.6/3:date • Item 854-A-4
STANDARD OCCUPATIONAL CLASSIFICATION MANUAL. [Irregular]

PrEx 2.8:date • Item 853 (P) (EL)
BUDGET OF UNITED STATES GOVERNMENT, FISCAL YEAR . . .

Figures are for the fiscal year. In addition to the Budget Message of the President, contains a detailed account by Departments and Agencies of proposed budget items, giving previous year's actual figures, present year's estimated and coming year's proposed amounts. Also contains tables of estimates for trust funds and supplemental figures, including historical comparison of budget receipts and expenditures.

The following have been incorporated into this publication: The Budget of the United States Government, Appendix (PrEx 2.8:date/app.); United States Budget in Brief (PrEx 2.8/3); Special Analyses, Budget of the United States Government (PrEx 2.8/5); Historical Tables, Budget of the United States Government (PrEx 2.8/8); Management of the United States Government (PrEx 2.8/9); and Major Policy Initiatives (PrEx 2.8/10).

APPENDIX. [Annual] (Also published in the House Documents series)

This massive book, over 1000 pages long, is the most precise and detailed of all the budget documents. It contains the specific language of each proposal for each agency, and tells what functions each agency is expected to perform. It distinguishes funds appropriated for the President's use and for use by the judiciary. Supplementary appropriations, such as increased costs and salaries, and funds needed for emergency relief are discussed. The schedule of budgetary transactions for each agency is included, as well as explanations of funding for such Government-owned corporations as the PensionBenefit Guaranty Corporation, and for Government-sponsored private corporations, such as the Federal National Mortgage Corporation. Detailed budget estimates for each Federal agency and lists of the permanent positions in each agency (number and Federal grade level) complete the Appendix.

This publication has been incorporated into The Budget of the United States Government (PrEx 2.8).

PrEx 2.8/1:date • Item 853-C (CD) (EL)
BUDGET OF THE UNITED STATES GOVERNMENT. [Annual]

PrEx 2.8/a:date
– SEPARATE, BUDGET MESSAGE OF THE PRESIDENT AND SUMMARY BUDGET STATEMENTS.

Earlier Pr 34.107/a

PrEx 2.8/a2:date
SPECIAL ANALYSIS OF FEDERAL ACTIVITIES IN PUBLIC WORKS AND OTHER CONSTRUCTION IN BUDGET.

Earlier Pr 34.102:P 96

PrEx 2.8/a3:date
SPECIAL ANALYSIS OF FEDERAL AID TO STATE AND LOCAL GOVERNMENTS IN BUDGET.

Earlier Pr 34.102:Ai 2

PrEx 2.8/a4:date
SPECIAL ANALYSIS OF FEDERAL RESEARCH AND DEVELOPMENT PROGRAMS IN BUDGET.

Earlier Pr 34.102:R 31

PrEx 2.8/a5:date
SPECIAL ANALYSIS OF FEDERAL CREDIT PROGRAMS IN BUDGET.

Earlier Pr 34.102:C 86

PrEx 2.8/a6:date
SPECIAL ANALYSIS OF PRINCIPAL FEDERAL STATISTICAL PROGRAMS IN BUDGET.

Earlier Pr 34.102:St 2/3

PrEx 2.8/a7:date
FEDERAL GOVERNMENT RECEIPTS FROM AND PAYMENTS TO (public) SPECIAL ANALYSIS 4.

PrEx 2.8/a8:date
INVESTMENT, OPERATING AND OTHER BUDGET EXPENDITURES, SPECIAL ANALYSIS D.

PrEx 2.8/a9:date
FOREIGN CURRENCY AVAILABILITIES AND USES, SPECIAL ANALYSIS E.

PrEx 2.8/a10:date
HISTORICAL COMPARISON OF BUDGET RECEIPTS AND EXPENDITURES BY FUNCTION, SPECIAL ANALYSIS G.

PrEx 2.8/a11:date
CONTENTS, FORMAT AND CONCEPTS OF FEDERAL BUDGET, REPRINT OF SELECTED PAGES FROM BUDGET OF UNITED STATES GOVERNMENT.

PrEx 2.8/2:date • Item 855-A
FEDERAL BUDGET IN BRIEF. 1951– [Annual]

Published at the same time the Budget is presented to Congress in January. Summarizes the budget for the fiscal year. Also includes summary financial data of earlier years, results of Government activities in the previous fiscal year. Tables include budget totals, budget receipts, unspent balance authority carried forward at end of year, expenditures and new obligational authority by agency, budget and trust fund expenditures for public works, budget expenditures by function, historical table of budget receipts and expenditures, public debt and budget expenditures by function. Contains many charts.

PrEx 2.8/3:date
FEDERAL BUDGET, MIDYEAR REVIEW.

This publication has been incorporated into The Budget of the United States Government (PrEx 2.8).
Earlier Pr 34.107/3

PrEx 2.8/4:date • Item 853
BUDGET OF UNITED STATES GOVERNMENT, DISTRICT OF COLUMBIA. 1958/59– [Annual] (Also published in the House Documents series)

PrEx 2.8/5:date • Item 855-B (P) (EL)
SPECIAL ANALYSES, BUDGET OF UNITED STATES FISCAL YEAR. [Annual]

Contains special analyses that provide different aspects of the budget, such as current services and national income accounts, economical and financial analyses of the budget as a whole, and Government-wide information on a few specific programs financed by the Federal budget.

This publication has been incorporated into The Budget of the United States Government (PrEx 2.8).

PrEx 2.8/6 • Item 855-A
BUDGET HIGHLIGHTS. [Annual]

PrEx 2.8/7:date • Item 853
BUDGET REVISIONS.

PrEx 2.8/8:date • Item 853 (P) (EL)
HISTORICAL TABLES. [Annual]

This publication has been incorporated into The Budget of the United States Government (PrEx 2.8).

PrEx 2.8/9:date • Item 853
MANAGEMENT OF THE UNITED STATES GOVERNMENT, FISCAL YEAR (date). [Annual]

PrEx 2.8/10: • Item 855-A
MAJOR POLICY INITIATIVES. [Annual]

PrEx 2.8/11:date • Item 853
BUDGET OF THE U.S. GOVERNMENT: DIRECTOR'S INTRODUCTION AND OVERVIEW TABLES.

PrEx 2.8/12:date • Item 853 (P) (EL)
BUDGET SYSTEM AND CONCEPTS OF THE UNITED STATES GOVERNMENT. [Annual]

PrEx 2.9:v.nos.&nos. • Item 854-C
PUBLIC MANAGEMENT SOURCES. v. 1– 34. 1945–1978. [Monthly]

Annotated list of books received by the Library.
This publication has been incorporated into The Budget of the United States Government (PrEx 2.8).
ISSN 0364-2275

PrEx 2.10:date • Item 853-A
FEDERAL STATISTICAL DIRECTORY. 1st ed.–1955– [Irregular]

PURPOSE:– Designated to serve as a guide to facilitate communication with offices concerned with particular statistical functions.
Lists, by organizational units within each agency, the names, office addresses, and telephone numbers of professional, technical, and administrative personnel associated with statistical and related activities of the agencies of the executive branch of the Federal Government.
This publication has been incorporated into The Budget of the United States Government (PrEx 2.8).

PrEx 2.10/2:date • Item 853-A-6 (MF)
FEDERAL STATISTICS. [Annual]

PURPOSE:– To report on statistical programs and activities of the U.S. government. Discusses developments in organization and management of statistical programs.

PrEx 2.10/3:date • Item 853-A-6
STATISTICAL PROGRAMS OF THE UNITED STATES GOVERNMENT. [Annual]

PrEx 2.11:nos. • Item 855-C
STATISTICAL REPORTER. [Monthly] (Office of Statistical Standards)
Discontinued with Dec. 1981 issue.
ISSN 0039-050X
Earlier Pr 34.112
See also C 1.69

PrEx 2.12:date
INVENTORY OF AUTOMATIC DATA PROCESSING (ADP) EQUIPMENT IN FEDERAL GOVERNMENT. [Annual]

Earlier PrEx 2.2:Au 8

PrEx 2.12/2:nos.
DIRECTORY, EXECUTIVE ORIENTATION COURSES IN AUTOMATIC DATA PROCESSING. 1– 1960–

For continuation of this series, see CS 1.56/2.

PrEx 2.12/3:date
MAJOR DATA PROCESSING AND TELECOMMUNICATION ACQUISITION PLANS OF FEDERAL EXECUTIVE AGENCIES.

PrEx 2.12/4:date • Item 854-C-3
FIVE-YEAR PLAN FOR MEETING THE AUTOMATIC DATA PROCESSING AND TELECOMMUNICATIONS NEEDS OF THE FEDERAL GOVERNMENT. [Annual]

PURPOSE:– To provide Federal managers with information about current trends and issues in the fields of automatic data processing and telecommunications.
Earlier PrEx 2.2:Au 8/5

PrEx 2.12/5:date • Item 854-C-3
CURRENT INFORMATION TECHNOLOGY RESOURCES REQUIREMENTS OF THE FEDERAL GOVERNMENT. [Annual]

Earlier PM 1.56

PrEx 2.13:nos.
STATISTICAL EVALUATION REPORTS.

PrEx 2.14:CT • Item 854-E
BIBLIOGRAPHIES AND LISTS OF PUBLICATIONS.

PrEx 2.14/2:date • Item 854-I (MF)
FEDERAL INFORMATION LOCATOR SYSTEM (FILS).

PrEx 2.15:CT
ADDRESSES. [Irregular]

PrEx 2.16:nos.
COST REDUCTION NOTES.

PrEx 2.17:nos.
WORKING PAPERS. [Irregular] (prepared by the Office of Statistical Standards)

PrEx 2.18:date
SIMPLIFYING FEDERAL AID TO STATES AND COMMUNITIES, ANNUAL REPORT TO THE PRESIDENT OF AN INTERAGENCY PROGRAM. 1st– 1970– [Annual]

Report of progress made by the Urban Affairs Council agencies working with the Bureau of the Budget to streamline the delivery of Federal resources which assist States and communities in programs of service to people in its three-year effort.

PrEx 2.19:date • Item 854-B
FEDERAL MANAGEMENT IMPROVEMENT CONFERENCE. PROCEEDINGS. 1st– [Annual]

PrEx 2.20:date • Item 853-A-1 (P) (EL)
CATALOG OF FEDERAL DOMESTIC ASSISTANCE. 1971– [Irregular] (includes basic volume plus supplementary material for an indefinite period) (Binder)

PURPOSE:– To assist in identifying the types of Federal domestic assistance available, describing eligibility requirements for the particular assistance being sought, and providing guidance on how to apply for specific types of assistance. Also intended to improve coordination and communication between the Federal Government and State and local governments.
Supersedes Catalog of Federal Assistance Programs (PrEx 10.2:P 94).
ISSN 0097-7799

PrEx 2.21:date • Item 853-A-2
REPORT TO CONGRESS, OFFICE OF FEDERAL PROCUREMENT POLICY. 1st– 1975– [Annual]

PrEx 2.22:nos. • Item 853-A-3
OFPP PAMPHLETS. 1– 1976– [Irregular] (Office of Federal Procurement Policy)

PrEx 2.23:CT • Item 853-A-4 (MF)
FEDERAL ACQUISITIONS INSTITUTE: PUBLICATIONS.

PrEx 2.24:date • Item 854-C-1 (MF)
FEDERAL PROCUREMENT DATA SYSTEM. [Quarterly]

Consists mainly of tables showing Federal contract actions over $10,000 by State, by executive department and agency. Data can be used for geographical and market analysis, for information on minority small business enterprises, etc., for assessing the impact of Federal acquisition on the Nation's economy, for acquisition policy development and for management improvement.

PrEx 2.24/2:date • Item 854-C-1
FEDERAL PROCUREMENT DATA SYSTEM, ANNUAL ANALYSIS 2. 1– [Quarterly]

PrEx 2.24/3:date
FEDERAL PROCUREMENT DATA SYSTEM, SPECIAL ANALYSIS 3. [Quarterly]

Replaced by PrEx 2.24/13

PrEx 2.24/8:date
FEDERAL PROCUREMENT DATA SYSTEM, SPECIAL ANALYSIS 8. [Quarterly]

Replaced by PrEx 2.24/13

PrEx 2.24/10:date
FEDERAL PROCUREMENT DATA SYSTEM, SPECIAL ANALYSIS 10. [Quarterly]

Replaced by PrEx 2.24/13

PrEx 2.24/12:date • Item 854-C-1
FEDERAL PROCUREMENT DATA SYSTEM, COMBINED SPECIAL ANALYSES. [Quarterly]

Combines Special Analyses numbers 5, 6, 7, and 9.
Replaced by PrEx 2.24/13

PrEx 2.24/13:date • Item 854-C-1 (MF)
FEDERAL PROCUREMENT DATA SYSTEM, STANDARD REPORT, [Quarterly]

NOTE:– This class replaces all of the Special Analysis classes PrEx 2.24/2 through PrEx 2.24/12.

PrEx 2.24/14: • Item 854-C-4
FEDERAL PROCUREMENT DATA SYSTEM, CONTRACTOR IDENTIFICATION FILE, ALPHABETICAL LISTING. [Annual]

A ready reference for federal government procurement officials to determine contractor identification numbers for awards exceeding $25,000. The first section lists domestic contractors and the second section foreign contractors by country, and then by contractory within the country.

PrEx 2.24/15:nos. • Item 854-C-1
PROCUREMENT REGULATORY ACTIVITY REPORT.

PrEx 2.25:date • Item 853-A-5 (MF)
MANAGING FEDERAL INFORMATION RESOURCES. [Annual]

Summarizes Office activities in implementing the Paper Work Reduction Act of 1980 in such areas as improving Federal information management and reducing information collection burdens on the private sector and State and local governments.

PrEx 2.26:nos.
POLICY LETTERS (series). [Irregular]

PrEx 2.27:date • Item 854-C-2
MAJOR INFORMATION TECHNOLOGY SYSTEMS, ACQUISITION PLANS OF FEDERAL EXECUTIVE AGENCIES. [Annual]

Presents plans of Federal executive agencies to acquire information technology systems, facilities, and related services during the coming five years.

PrEx 2.28:nos. • Item 126-D-7 (MF)
STATISTICAL POLICY WORKING PAPERS. [Irregular]

Earlier C 1.70
PrEx 2.29:date • Item 854-F
INFORMATION COLLECTION BUDGET OF THE UNITED STATES. [Annual]

This "paper work budget" prepared under the Paperwork Reduction Act of 1980 is a process for measuring and controlling the costs of Federal Information collections.

PrEx 2.30:date • Item 854-G
REGULATORY PROGRAM OF THE UNITED STATES GOVERNMENT. [Annual]

PURPOSE:– To present a comprehensive program of regulatory policies, goals, and priorities. Includes an overview and significant regulatory actions of the executive departments of the government.

PrEx 2.31:date • Item 853 (P) (EL)
MID-SESSION REVIEW OF THE BUDGET. [Annual]

Earlier PrEx 2.2:B 85/4

PrEx 2.32:   • **Item 854-H**
POSTERS.

Includes miscellaneous posters on various subjects pertaining to the work of the Office.

PrEx 2.33:   • **Item 854-J**
FEDERAL FINANCIAL MANAGEMENT STATUS REPORT & FIVE-YEAR PLAN.

PrEx 2.34:nos.   • **Item 854-A-1**
AUDIT LEGAL LETTER GUIDANCE (series).

PrEx 2.35   • **Item 854-A-3 (P)**
STATEMENT OF FEDERAL FINANCIAL ACCOUNTING STANDARDS (series).

PrEx 2.35/2   • **Item 854-A-3 (P)**
STATEMENT OF FEDERAL FINANCIAL ACCOUNTING CONCEPTS (series).

NATIONAL SECURITY COUNCIL (1961–   )

CREATION AND AUTHORITY

The National Security Council was established by the National Security Act of 1947 (61 Stat. 496; 50 U.S.C. 402), amended by the National Security Act Amendments of 1949 (63 Stat. 579; 50 U.S.C. 401 et. seq.).

INFORMATION

Dep. Executive Secretary
National Security Council
Executive Office of the President
Eisenhower Executive Office Bldg.
17th St. and Pennsylvania Ave. NW
Washington, D.C. 20504
(202) 456-9301
Fax: (202) 456-9300
http://www.whitehouse.gov/nsc

PrEx 3.2:CT   • **Item 856-A-2**
GENERAL PUBLICATIONS. [Irregular]

PrEx 3.8   • **Item 856-A-15**
HANDBOOKS, MANUALS, GUIDES.

PrEx 3.10:CT   • **Item 856-A-2**
PUBLICATIONS. (Central Intelligence Agency)

PrEx 3.10:N 21   • **Item 856-A-2**
NATIONAL BASIC INTELLIGENCE FACTBOOK. [Semiannual] (Central Intelligence Agency)

PURPOSE:– To present information on 188 foreign countries such as type of government, economy, transportation system, defense forces and more.

PrEx 3.10/2:date
CONSOLIDATED TRANSLATION SURVEY. (Foreign Documents Division)
Earlier Pr 34.610

PrEx 3.10/3:nos.
CIA/RR ER (series). (Office of Research and Reports)

PrEx 3.10/4:CT   • **Item 856-A-1**
MAPS AND ATLASES. [Irregular] (Central Intelligence Agency)

PrEx 3.10/5:nos.   • **Item 856-A-4**
ER (series). [Irregular] (National Foreign Assessment Center)

PURPOSE:– To provide intelligence research papers covering such subjects as international trade, world shipbuilding, Soviet economy, nuclear energy, etc.
Superseded by National Foreign Assessment Center Publications (series) (PrEx 3.10/7).

PrEx 3.10/6:letters-nos.   • **Item 856-A-14**
RESEARCH PAPERS. [Irregular]

Superseded by National Foreign Assessment Center Publications (series) (PrEx 3.10/7).

PrEx 3.10/7:nos.   • **Item 856-A-4 (MF)**
DIRECTORATE OF INTELLIGENCE PUBLICATIONS (numbered).

Supersedes ER (series) (PrEx 3.10/5), Research Papers (PrEx 3.10/6), and Reference Aids (series) (PrEx 3.11).
Formerly titled: National Foreign Assessment Center Publications.

PrEx 3.10/7-2:date   • **Item 856-A-4**
APPEARANCES OF SOVIET LEADERS. [Annual]

Earlier PrEx 3.10/7

PrEx 3.10/7-3:date   • **Item 856-A-4**
DIRECTORY OF IRAQI OFFICIALS. [Irregular]

Earlier PrEx 3.10/7

PrEx 3.10/7-4:date   • **Item 856-A-4**
DIRECTORY OF SOVIET OFFICIALS, NATIONAL ORGANIZATIONS. [Irregular]

Earlier PrEx 3.10/7

PrEx 3.10/7-5:date   • **Item 856-A-4**
HANDBOOK OF ECONOMIC STATISTICS. [Annual]

Earlier PrEx 34.10/7:CPAS

PrEx 3.10/7-6:date   • **Item 856-A-4**
DIRECTORY OF OFFICIALS OF THE DEMOCRATIC PEOPLE'S REPUBLIC OF KOREA. [Annual]

Earlier PrEx 3.10/7:CR

PrEx 3.10/7-7:date   • **Item 856-A-4 (MF)**
DIRECTORY OF USSR FOREIGN TRADE ORGANIZATION AND OFFICIALS. [Annual]

Earlier PrEx 3.10/7:CR

PrEx 3.10/7-8   • **Item 856-A-4**
DIRECTORY OF YUGOSLAV OFFICIALS. [Irregular]

Earlier PrEx 3.10/7:CR 83-11848

PrEx 3.10/7-9:date
DIRECTORY OF CHINESE OFFICIALS, PROVINCIAL ORGANIZATIONS. [Annual]

PrEx 3.10/7-10:date   • **Item 856-A-8**
DIRECTORY OF CZECHOSLOVAK OFFICIALS, A REFERENCE AID.

PrEx 3.10/7-11:date   • **Item 856-A-4**
DIRECTORY OF USSR MINISTRY OF DEFENSE AND ARMED FORCES OFFICIALS. [Irregular]

Earlier PrEx 3.10/7:CR 83-13274

PrEx 3.10/7-12:date   • **Item 856-A-4**
DIRECTORY OF BULGARIAN OFFICIALS. [Irregular]

Earlier PrEx 3.10/7:CR

PrEx 3.10/7-13:date   • **Item 856-A-4**
DIRECTORY OF CHINESE OFFICIALS AND ORGANIZATIONS. [Monthly]
National Level Organizations, Provincial Organizations, andScientific and Educational Organizations.
Earlier PrEx 3.10/7

PrEx 3.10/7-14:date   • **Item 856-A-4**
DIRECTORY OF SOVIET OFFICIALS: REPUBLIC ORGANIZATIONS, A REFERENCE AID.

PrEx 3.10/7-15:   • **Item 856-A-4**
DIRECTORY OF POLISH OFFICIALS.

PrEx 3.10/7-16:date   • **Item 856-A-4 (MF)**
DIRECTORY OF SOVIET OFFICIALS: SCIENCE AND EDUCATION.

PrEx 3.10/7-17:   • **Item 856-A-8 (MF)**
DIRECTORY OF USSR MINISTRY OF FOREIGN AFFAIRS OFFICIALS.

Directory of USSR Ministry of Foreign Affairs Officials.

PrEx 3.10/7-18:date   • **Item 856-A-8**
DIRECTORY OF OFFICIALS OF THE REPUBLIC OF CUBA.

PrEx 3.10/7-19   • **Item 856-A-8**
DIRECTORY OF THE REPUBLIC OF NICARAGUA.

PrEx 3.10/7-22:date-nos.   • **Item 856-A-8**
DIRECTORY OF IRANIAN OFFICIALS.

PrEx 3.10/7-23   • **Item 856-A-4**
DIRECTORY OF ALBANIAN OFFICIALS.

PrEx 3.10/7-24:date   • **Item 856-A-8**
DIRECTORY OF ROMANIAN OFFICIALS, A REFERENCE AID.

PrEx 3.10/7-25:date   • **Item 856-A-8**
DIRECTORY OF OFFICIALS OF VIETNAM, A REFERENCE AID.

PrEx 3.10/8:nos.   • **Item 856-A-6 (MF)**
CHINA, INTERNATIONAL TRADE QUARTERLY REVIEW, ER-CIT (nos.).

Provides trade data on China. Predominantly statistical tables.
Issued in microfiche (24x).

PrEx 3.11:letters/nos.   • **Item 856-A-3**
REFERENCE AIDS.

Superseded by National Foreign Assessment Center Publications (series) (PrEx 3.10/7).

PrEx 3.11/2:nos.   • **Item 856-A-5 (EL)**
CHIEFS OF STATE AND CABINET MEMBERS OF FOREIGN GOVERNMENTS, CR CS(series). [Monthly] (Reference Aid)

PURPOSE:– To list current chiefs of state, cabinet members of most foreign governments, including those reorganized, not officially recognized, and those not yet fully independent. Each issue supersedes the previous issue.
Published in microfiche (24X).
ISSN 0162-2951

PrEx 3.12:date
USC/FAR CONSOLIDATED PLAN FOR FOREIGN AFFAIRS RESEARCH. 1st–   1971–   [Annual]

Covers fiscal year.

PrEx 3.13:date-nos.   • **Item 856-B-12**
ECONOMIC INDICATORS WEEKLY REVIEW, ER-EI (series).

PURPOSE:– To provide up-to-date information on changes in the domestic and external economic activities of major non-Communist developed countries. Consists of statistical data.
Also published in microfiche.

PrEx 3.14:nos.   • **Item 856-B-13 (MF)**
INTERNATIONAL ENERGY BIWEEKLY STATISTICAL REVIEW, ER-IEBSR (series).

Superseded by International Energy Statistical Review (PrEx 3.14/2).

PrEx 3.14/2:nos.   • **Item 856-B-12**
ECONOMIC AND ENERGY INDICATORS, DI EEI. [Biweekly]

PURPOSE:– To provide current information on changes in domestic and international energy activities, including oil and natural gas production.
Also published in microfiche.
Combines selected data from Economic Indicators Weekly Review (PrEx 3.13) and International Energy Statistical Review (PrEx 3.14).
Earlier: International Energy Statistical Review.

PrEx 3.15:date • **Item 856-A-7**
WORLD FACTBOOK. [Annual]

Provides basic data with maps on the land, water, people, government, economy, communications, and defense forces of all countries of the world.
Continues National Basic Intelligence Factbook (PrEx 3.10:N 31).

PrEx 3.15/2:date • **Item 856-A-10 (CD) (EL)**
THE WORLD FACTBOOK.

PrEx 3.16:date • **Item 856-A-9**
HANDBOOK OF INTERNATIONAL ECONOMIC STATISTICS. [Annual]

PrEx 3.17:CT • **Item 856-A-12 (MF) (EL)**
GENERAL PUBLICATIONS.

PrEx 3.18:CT • **Item 856-A-13 (MF) (EL)**
CENTER FOR THE STUDY OF INTELLIGENCE MONOGRAPHS.

PrEx 3.19:date/no. • **Item 856-A-14 (EL)**
STUDIES IN INTELLIGENCE.

PrEx 3.20 • **Item 856-A-16 (EL)**
CUBA, HANDBOOK OF TRADE STATISTICS. [Annual]

PrEx 3.21 • **Item 856-G (EL)**
NATIONAL INTELLIGENCE COUNCIL (NIC) GENERAL PUBLICATIONS.

OFFICE OF EMERGENCY PREPAREDNESS (1968–1973)

CREATION AND AUTHORITY

The Office of Emergency Preparedness, so designated by act of October 21, 1968 (82 Stat. 1194; 50 U.S.C. App. 2271 n.), is a redesignation of the Office of Emergency Planning. The responsibilities of the Office are prescribed by Executive Order 11051 of September 27, 1962. The Office was abolished by Reorganization Plan No. 1 of 1973 and its functions transferred to the Department of the Treasury, Department of Housing and Urban Development, and the General Services Administration, effective July 1, 1973.

PrEx 4.1:date • **Item 856-C-1**
ANNUAL REPORTS.

Earlier Pr 34.701

PrEx 4.1/2:date
PROGRESS REPORT, STATISTICAL REPORTS.

Earlier Pr 34.751, Pr 34.751/2
Later D 13.1/2

PrEx 4.2:CT • **Item 856-C-1**
GENERAL PUBLICATIONS.

Earlier Pr 34.702

PrEx 4.3:nos.
BULLETINS.

Official use only.
Earlier Pr 34.703

PrEx 4.3/2:nos.
CIVIL DEFENSE TECHNICAL BULLETINS.

Earlier Pr 34.753

PrEx 4.3/3:nos.
INFORMATION BULLETINS, IB– (series). – 1962.

Earlier Pr 34.753/2

PrEx 4.3/4:nos.
ADVISORY BULLETINS.

Earlier Pr 34.753/3

PrEx 4.3/5:nos.
SURPLUS PROPERTY BULLETINS.

Earlier Pr 34.753/4
Later D 13.3

PrEx 4.4
OEP CIRCULARS. [Irregular]

PrEx 4.4/2:nos
INTERAGENCY CIRCULARS.

Earlier Pr 34.704/2

PrEx 4.4/3:nos. • **Item 856-C-2**
OEP ECONOMIC STABILIZATION CIRCULARS. 1– [Irregular]

PrEx 4.5:CT
LAWS.

Earlier Pr 34.755

PrEx 4.6:CT
REGULATIONS, RULES, AND INSTRUCTIONS.

Earlier Pr 34.706

PrEx 4.6/2:nos.
INTERIM DIRECTIVES.

Earlier Pr 34.706/2

PrEx 4.6/3:nos.
DEFENSE MOBILIZATION ORDERS.

Earlier Pr 34.706/3

PrEx 4.6/4:nos.
OCDM REGULATIONS.

Reprint from Federal Register.
Earlier Pr 34.706/4

PrEx 4.6/5:nos.
ADMINISTRATIVE ORDERS.

Earlier Pr 34.706/5

PrEx 4.6/6:nos.
EMERGENCY OPERATION ORDERS.

Earlier Pr 34.706/6

PrEx 4.6/7:annex nos.
NATIONAL PLAN FOR CIVIL DEFENSE AND DEFENSE MOBILIZATION.

Earlier Pr 34.706:N 21

PrEx 4.6/8:chap.nos.
NATIONAL PLAN FOR EMERGENCY PREPAREDNESS.

PrEx 4.7:nos.
PRESS RELEASE.

Earlier Pr 34.707

PrEx 4.7/2:nos.
NEWS RELEASES.

Earlier Pr 34.757/2

PrEx 4.7/3:nos.
NEWSPICTURES.

Earlier Pr 34.760
Later 1.34/2

PrEx 4.7/4:v.nos.&nos.
NEWS FEATURE PAGE.

Earlier Pr 34.760/2
Later D 1.34

PrEx 4.8:date
OCDM TELEPHONE DIRECTORY.

Earlier Pr 34.708

PrEx 4.8/2:date
CIVIL AND DEFENSE MOBILIZATION DIRECTORY.

Earlier Pr 34.708/2

PrEx 4.9:date
STOCKPILE REPORT TO CONGRESS. [Semiannual]

Later GS 1.22

PrEx 4.10:CT
ADDRESSES.

Earlier Pr 34.710

PrEx 4.11:CT
BIBLIOGRAPHIES AND LISTS OF PUBLICATIONS.

PrEx 4.12:CT
HANDBOOKS, MANUALS, GUIDES.

Earlier Pr 34.761
Later D 13.8

PrEx 4.12/2:nos.
ADMINISTRATIVE MANUALS, AM (series).

PrEx 4.12/3:nos.
HANDBOOK H (series).

Earlier Pr 34.761/2
Later D 13.8/3

PrEx 4.12/4:nos.
TECHNICAL MANUALS.

Earlier Pr 34.761/3

PrEx 4.12/5:nos.
INSTRUCTOR'S GUIDE IG (series).

Earlier Pr 34.761/4
Later D 12.8/7

PrEx 4.12/5-2:CT
INTERIM INSTRUCTORS GUIDES.

Earlier FCD 1.6/5-2

PrEx 4.12/6:nos.
POCKET MANUALS PM (series).

Later D 13.8/2

PrEx 4.13:nos.
LEAFLET L (series).

Earlier Pr 34.758
Later D 13.15

PrEx 4.14:nos.
MISCELLANEOUS PUBLICATIONS MP SERIES.

Later D 13.9

PrEx 4.15:v.nos.&nos.
RESEARCH TECHNICAL LIBRARY BIWEEKLY ACCESSION LIST.

PrEx 4.16:v.nos.&nos.
NEWSLETTERS. [Irregular]

PrEx 4.17:date
DIRECTORY OF TELECOMMUNICATIONS MANAGEMENT, ANNUAL REPORT.

National Resources Evaluation Center

PrEx 4.18:nos.
NREC TECHNICAL REPORTS. 1– [Irregular]

PrEx 4.18/2:nos.
NREC ANALYSIS REPORTS. 1– [Irregular]

PrEx 4.18/3:nos.
NREC TECHNICAL MANUALS. 1–　[Irregular]

PrEx 4.18/4:CT
PUBLICATIONS (unnumbered).

National Resources Analysis Center

PrEx 4.19:nos.
SYSTEMS EVALUATION DIVISION: REPORT R (series). 1–　1968–　[Irregular]

　　　PURPOSE:– To report the results of a major study project and intended to be an authoritative contribution on its subject.

NATIONAL AERONAUTICS AND SPACE COUNCIL
(1961– 1973)

CREATION AND AUTHORITY

　　　The National Aeronautics and Space Council was established by the National Aeronautics and Space Act of 1958 (72 Stat. 427, as amended; 42 U.S.C. 2471). The Council was abolished by Reorganization Plan No. 1 of 1973, effective June 30, 1973.

PrEx 5.1:date
REPORTS.

PrEx 5.2:CT
GENERAL PUBLICATIONS.

PrEx 5.9　　　　　　　　　　　• Item 856-D
REPORT TO CONGRESS, UNITED STATES AERONAUTICS AND SPACE ACTIVITIES. [Annual]

　　　Also issued in the House Documents series.
Later NAS 1.52

PrEx 5.10:CT
ADDRESSES.

COUNCIL OF ECONOMIC ADVISERS
(1961–　　)

CREATION AND AUTHORITY

　　　The Council of Economic Advisers was established in the Executive Office of the President by the Employment act of 1946 (60 Stat. 24, U.S.C. 1023). It now functions under Reorganization Plan 9 of 1953, effective August 1, 1953.
　　　Note:– Publications of Council of Economic Advisers were formerly entered in the Monthly Catalog under President of United States.

INFORMATION

　　　Council of Economic Advisers
　　　Executive Office Building
　　　17th St. and Pennsylvania Ave. NW
　　　Washington, D.C. 20502
　　　(202) 395-5084
　　　Fax: (202) 395-6958
　　　http://www.whitehouse.gov/cea

PrEx 6.1:date
REPORTS.

PrEx 6.2:CT　　　　　　　　　　• Item 857-E-1
GENERAL PUBLICATIONS.

PrEx 6.9:CT
ADDRESSES.

　　　Earlier Pr 34.9

PrEx 6.10:date　　　　　　　　• Item 857-E-2
CONSUMER ADVISORY COUNCIL REPORT.

　　　Includes list of selected publications of Federal Government of interest to consumers.

FOREIGN BROADCAST INFORMATION SERVICE
(1961–　　)

PrEx 7.2:CT
GENERAL PUBLICATIONS.

PrEx 7.9:date　　　　　　　　　• Item 856-B
BROADCASTING STATIONS OF THE WORLD. 1st– 1946–　[Irregular]

　　　Lists all known radio broadcasting and television stations except those in the continental United States on domestic channels.
　　　Issued in the following parts:

　　　Part 1. According to Country and City
　　　Part 2. According to Frequency.
　　　Part 3. According to Call Letters and
　　　　　　　　　　Station Name or Slogan.
　　　Part 4. Frequency Modulation and Television
　　　　　　　　　　Stations.

PrEx 7.10:v.nos.&nos.
DAILY REPORT, FOREIGN RADIO BROADCASTS.

　　　PURPOSE:– To provide texts of current news and commentary monitored by the Foreign Broadcast Information Service from foreign broadcasts, news agency transmissions, newspapers, and periodicals.
　　　Published in microfiche.
　　　Issued for the following areas:–
　　　　　　　　　　　　• Item 856-B-6 (MF)
AFRICA (SUB-SAHARA).

　　　　　　　　　　　　• Item 856-B-3 (MF)
ASIA AND PACIFIC.

　　　　　　　　　　　　• Item 856-B-4 (MF)
EASTERN EUROPE. [ISSN 0565-551X]

　　　　　　　　　　　　• Item 856-B-5 (MF)
LATIN AMERICA.

　　　　　　　　　　　　• Item 856-B-6 (MF)
MIDDLE EAST AND NORTH AFRICA.

　　　　　　　　　　　　• Item 856-B-6 (MF)
NEAR EAST AND SOUTH ASIA.

　　　　　　　　　　　　• Item 856-B-7 (MF)
PEOPLE'S REPUBLIC OF CHINA.

　　　　　　　　　　　　• Item 856-B-8 (MF)
SOVIET UNION. [ISSN 0565-5560]

　　　　　　　　　　　　• Item 856-B-9 (MF)
SUB-SAHARAN AFRICA.

　　　　　　　　　　　　• Item 856-B-10 (MF)
WESTERN EUROPE.

PrEx 7.10:v.nos.&nos.
SPECIAL REPORTS.

PrEx 7.10/2:date
DIALY REPORTS, FOREIGN RADIO BROADCASTS, SUPPLEMENTS.

　　　Earlier Pr 34.660/2

PrEx 7.10/3:date/nos.　　　• Item 856-A-11 (CD)
FBIS PUBLICATIONS REPORTS.

PrEx 7.11:nos.
SPECIAL REPORTS.

PrEx 7.12:nos.　　　　　　　• Item 856-B-11
TRENDS IN COMMUNIST MEDIA. [Weekly]

　　　Analyzes Chinese, Soviet, and other Communists media output and behavior concerning key political issues.
　　　Published in microfiche (24x)

PrEx 7.13:nos.
JPRS [Joint Publications Research Service] (series).

　　　The Joint Publications Research Service translates and abstracts foreign language political and technical media for Federal agencies. More than 80,000 reports published since 1957, are available to the public.
　　　Most JPRS reports are concerned with publications in communist countries, through materials from all nations may be translated. About half the reports are in the scientific and technical fields.
　　　Regular use of JPRS translations give scientists, engineers, technicians, researchers and business people access to current foreign thought in many areas.
　　　Earlier Y 3.J 66:13
　　　Published in the following categories:–

PrEx 7.13　　　　　　　　• Item 1067-M-3 (MF)
ASIA.

PrEx 7.13　　　　　　　　• Item 1067-M-2 (MF)
CHINA.

PrEx 7.13　　　　　　　　• Item 1067-M-4 (MF)
EUROPE.

PrEx 7.13　　　　　　　　• Item 1067-M-5 (MF)
LATIN AMERICA.

PrEx 7.13　　　　　　　　• Item 1067-M-1 (MF)
MISCELLANEOUS.

PrEx 7.13　　　　　　　　• Item 1067-M-6 (MF)
NEAR EAST AND AFRICA.

PrEx 7.13　　　　　　　　• Item 1067-M-7 (MF)
USSR.
JPRS [INDEX].

　　　An index to JPRS translations is available from The Micro Photo Division of Bell & Howell, Old Mansfield Road, Wooster, Ohio 44691, entitled the Bell & Howell TRANSDEX Index. It has a keyword section, a names section, and a bibliographic listing section. In addition, the Index includes a brief section which correlates series titles with the specific document numbers.

PrEx 7.14
WORLDWIDE REPORTS.

PrEx 7.14:nos.　　　　　　　• Item 1067-L-2
ENVIRONMENTAL QUALITY. 1–　[Irregular]

　　　Issued in JPRS series (PrEx 7.13).
　　　Published in microfiche.

PrEx 7.14/2:nos.　　　　　• Item 1067-L-9 (MF)
EPIDEMIOLOGY. 1–　[Irregular]

　　　Issued in JPRS series (PrEx 7.13).
　　　Published in microfiche.

PrEx 7.14/3:nos.　　　　　• Item 1067-L-5
LAW OF THE SEA. 1–　[Irregular]

　　　Issued in JPRS series (PrEx 7.13).
　　　Published in microfiche.

PrEx 7.14/4:nos.　　　　• Item 1067-L-17 (MF)
NUCLEAR DEVELOPMENT AND PROLIFERATION. 1–　[Irregular]

　　　Issued in JPRS series (PrEx 7.13).
　　　Published in microfiche.

PrEx 7.14/5:nos. • **Item 1067-L-10 (MF)**
TELECOMMUNICATION POLICY, RESEARCH AND
DEVELOPMENT. 1– [Irregular]

Issued in JPRS series (PrEx 7.13).
Published in microfiche.

PrEx 7.14/6:nos.
TERRORISM.

PrEx 7.14/7:nos. • **Item 106-L-17 (MF)**
ARMS CONTROL. [Daily]

PrEx 7.15
CHINA REPORTS.

PrEx 7.15:nos. • **Item 1067-L-14 (MF)**
AGRICULTURE. 1– [Irregular]

Issued in JPRS series (PrEx 7.13).
Published in microfiche.

PrEx 7.15/2:nos. • **Item 1067-L-12**
ECONOMIC AFFAIRS. 1– [Irregular]

Issued in JPRS series (PrEx 7.13).
Published in microfiche.

PrEx 7.15/2-2 • **Item 1067-L-12**
CHINA. [Irregular]

PrEx 7.15/3:nos. • **Item 1067-L-14**
PLANT AND INSTALLATION DATA. 1–

Issued in JPRS series (PrEx 7.13).
Published in microfiche.

PrEx 7.15/4:nos. • **Item 1067-L-12**
POLITICAL, SOCIOLOGICAL AND MILITARY
AFFAIRS. 1– [Irregular]

Issued in JPRS series (PrEx 7.13).
Published in microfiche.

PrEx 7.15/4-2 • **Item 1067-L-12**
CHINA STATE COUNCIL BULLETIN. [Irregular]

PrEx 7.15/5:date/nos. • **Item 1067-L-15 (MF)**
RED FLAG. 1– [Irregular]

Issued in JPRS series (PrEx 7.13).
Published in microfiche.

PrEx 7.15/6:nos. • **Item 1067-L-13 (MF)**
SCIENCE AND TECHNOLOGY. 1– [Irregular]

Issued in JPRS series (PrEx 7.13).
Published in microfiche.

PrEx 7.15/6-2 • **Item 1067-L-13**
JPRS (series) SCIENCE & TECHNOLOGY, CHINA:
ENERGY. [Irregular]

PrEx 7.16
ASIA REPORTS.

PrEx 7.16:nos. • **Item 1067-L-3 (MF)**
JAPAN REPORT. 1– [Irregular]

Issued in JPRS series (PrEx 7.13).
Published in microfiche.

PrEx 7.16/2:nos. • **Item 1067-L-12 (MF)**
EAST ASIA, KOREA: KULLOJA. [Irregular]

Issued in JPRS series (PrEx 7.13).
Published in microfiche.

PrEx 7.16/2-2:nos. • **Item 1067-L-12 (MF)**
JPRS REPORT: EAST ASIA, KOREA. 1– 1987–
[Irregular]

PrEx 7.16/3:nos. • **Item 1067-L-12**
MONGOLIA REPORT. [Irregular]

Issued in JPRS series (PrEx 7.13).
Published in microfiche.

PrEx 7.16/4:nos. • **Item 1067-L-12 (MF)**
SOUTHEAST ASIA REPORT. 1– [Irregular]

Issued in JPRS series (PrEx 7.13).
Published in microfiche.
Former title: South and East Asia Report.

PrEx 7.16/4-2 • **Item 1067-L-2**
EAST ASIA, VIETNAM: TAP CHI CONG SAN.
[Irregular]

PrEx 7.16/5:nos. • **Item 1067-L-12**
VIETNAM REPORT. 1– [Irregular]

Issued in JPRS series (PrEx 7.13).
Published in microfiche.
Discontinued with the December 1982 is-
sue.

PrEx 7.16/6:nos. • **Item 1067-L-3 (MF)**
JAPAN REPORT. SCIENCE AND TECHNOLOGY.
[Irregular]

Earlier PrEx 7.16/6

PrEx 7.17
EASTERN EUROPE REPORTS.

PrEx 7.17:nos. • **Item 1067-L-1**
ECONOMIC AND INDUSTRIAL AFFAIRS. 1–
[Irregular]

Issued in JPRS series (PrEx 7.13).
Published in microfiche.

PrEx 7.17/2:nos. • **Item 1067-L-1**
POLITICAL, SOCIOLOGICAL, AND MILITARY
AFFAIRS. 1– [Irregular]

Issued in JPRS series (PrEx 7.13).
Published in microfiche.

PrEx 7.17/3:nos. • **Item 1067-L-1**
SCIENTIFIC AFFAIRS. [Irregular]

Issued in JPRS series (PrEx 7.13).
Published in microfiche.

PrEx 7.17/4:date/nos. • **Item 1067-L-4**
EUROPE AND LATIN AMERICA REPORT, SCIENCE
AND TECHNOLOGY.

Earlier PrEx 7.17/3 and PrEx 7.19

PrEx 7.17/5:date/nos. • **Item 1061-L-1**
EAST EUROPE. [Irregular]

PrEx 7.17/6:nos. • **Item 1067-L-4 (MF)**
JPRS REPORT: SCIENCE AND TECHNOLOGY,
EUROPE. 1– 1988– [Irregular]

PrEx 7.18
WESTERN EUROPE REPORTS.

PrEx 7.18:nos. • **Item 1067-L-8 (MF)**
WEST EUROPE REPORT. 1– [Irregular]

Issued in JPRS series (PrEx 7.13).
Published in microfiche.

PrEx 7.18/2:nos. • **Item 1067-L-8**
SCIENCE AND TECHNOLOGY. 1– [Irregular]

Issued in JPRS series (PrEx 7.13).
Published in microfiche.

PrEx 7.19:nos. • **Item 1067-L-4 (MF)**
LATIN AMERICA REPORT. [Irregular]

Issued in JPRS series (PrEx 7.13).
Published in microfiche.

PrEx 7.20:nos. • **Item 1067-L-7 (MF)**
NEAR EAST AND SOUTH ASIA REPORT. 1–
[Irregular]

Issued in JPRS series (PrEx 7.13).
Published in microfiche.
Former title: Near East and Africa Report.

PrEx 7.20/2:nos. • **Item 1067-L-7 (MF)**
SUB-SAHARAN AFRICA REPORT. 1– [Irregular]

Issued in JPRS series (PrEx 7.13).
Published in microfiche.

PrEx 7.21
USSR REPORTS (General).

PrEx 7.21:nos. • **Item 1067-L-1**
AGRICULTURE. 1– [Irregular]

Issued in JPRS series (PrEx 7.13).
Published in microfiche.

PrEx 7.21/2:nos. • **Item 1067-L-1**
ECONOMIC AFFAIRS. 1– [Irregular]

Issued in JPRS series (PrEx 7.13).
Published in microfiche.

PrEx 7.21/2-2:date/nos. • **Item 1067-L-1**
USSR REPORT: NATIONAL ECONOMY. [Irregu-
lar]

PrEx 7.21/2-3 • **Item 1067-L-1**
SOVIET UNION, FOREIGN MILITARY REVIEW.
[Irregular]

PrEx 7.21/3:nos. • **Item 1067-L-13**
CONSTRUCTION AND EQUIPMENT. 1–
[Irregular]

Issued in JPRS series (PrEx 7.13).
Published in microfiche.
No longer published.
Superseded by Construction and Related
Industry (PrEx 7.21/3-2) and Machine Tools
and Metal Working Equipment (PrEx 7.21/3-
3).

PrEx 7.21/3-3 • **Item 1067-L-18**
JPRS (series) USSR REPORTS, MACHINE TOOLS
AND METAL WORKING EQUIPMENT.

PrEx 7.21/4:nos. • **Item 1067-L-1 (MF)**
MILITARY AFFAIRS. 1– [Irregular]

Issued in JPRS series (PrEx 7.13).
Published in microfiche.

PrEx 7.21/4-2:date/nos. • **Item 1067-L-1**
SOVIET UNION, FOREIGN MILITARY REVIEW.
[Irregular]

PrEx 7.21/4-3:date-nos. • **Item 1067-L-1**
SOVIET UNION, FOREIGN MILITARY HISTORY
JOURNAL. [Irregular]

PrEx 7.21/5:nos. • **Item 1067-L-1 (MF)**
POLITICAL AND SOCIOLOGICAL AFFAIRS. 1–
[Irregular]

Issued in JPRS series (PrEx 7.13).
Published in microfiche.

PrEx 7.21/5-2 • **Item 1067-L-1 (MF)**
SOVIET UNION, POLITICAL AFFAIRS. [Irregular]

PrEx 7.21/6 • **Item 1067-L-13**
ENERGY. 1– [Irregular]

Issued in JPRS series (PrEx 7.13).
Published in microfiche.

PrEx 7.21/7 • **Item 1067-L-1**
INTERNATIONAL ECONOMIC RELATIONS. 1–
[Irregular]

Issued in JPRS series (PrEx 7.13).
Published in microfiche.

PrEx 7.21/7-2:nos. • **Item 1067-L-1 (MF)**
USSR REPORT INTERNATIONAL AFFAIRS.
[Irregular]

PrEx 7.21/7-3 • **Item 1067-L-1 (MF)**
SOVIET UNION, PEOPLE OF ASIA AND AFRICA.
[Irregular]

PrEx 7.21/8:nos.   • Item 1067-L-1
CONSUMER GOODS AND DOMESTIC TRADE.
1–   [Irregular]

   Issued in JPRS series (PrEx 7.13).
   Published in microfiche.

PrEx 7.21/9:nos.   • Item 1067-L-1
HUMAN RESOURCES. 1–   [Irregular]

   Issued in JPRS series (PrEx 7.13).
   Published in microfiche.

PrEx 7.21/9-2   • Item 1067-L-13
JPRS (series) SOVIET UNION, THE WORKING
CLASS & THE CONTEMPORARY WORLD. [Ir-
regular]

PrEx 7.21/10:nos.   • Item 1067-L-1
TRANSPORTATION. 1–   [Irregular]

   Issued in JPRS series (PrEx 7.13).
   Published in microfiche.

PrEx 7.21/10-2   • Item 1067-L-13
SOVIET UNION AVIATION AND COSMONAUTICS.
[Irregular]

PrEx 7.21/11:nos.   • Item 1067-L-1 (MF)
TRANSLATION FROM KOMMUNIST. 1–
[Irregular]

   Issued in JPRS series (PrEx 7.13).
   Published in microfiche.

PrEx 7.21/12:nos.   • Item 1067-L-12 (MF)
PROBLEMS OF THE FAR EAST. [Irregular]

   Issued in JPRS series (PrEx 7.13).
   Published in microfiche.

PrEx 7.21/13:nos.   • Item 1067-L-1
SOCIOLOGICAL STUDIES. 1–   [Irregular]

   Issued in JPRS series (PrEx 7.13).
   Published in microfiche.

PrEx 7.21/14:date/nos.• Item 1067-L-16 (MF)
ECONOMICS, POLITICS, IDEOLOGY. [Irregular]

   Issued in JPRS series (PrEx 7.13).
   Published in microfiche.

PrEx 7.21/14-2:nos.   • Item 1067-L-16 (MF)
JPRS REPORT: SCIENCE AND TECHNOLOGY,
USSR, LIFE SCIENCES. 1–   1987–
[Irregular]

PrEx 7.21/15:nos.   • Item 1067-L-13 (MF)
JPRS REPORT: SOVIET UNION, WORLD
ECONOMY AND INTERNATIONAL
RELATIONS. 1–   1987–   [Irregular]

PrEx 7.22
USSR REPORTS (Scientific and Technical).

PrEx 7.22:nos.   • Item 1067-L-13 (MF)
LIFE SCIENCES: BIOMEDICAL AND BEHAVIORAL
SCIENCES. 1–   [Irregular]

   Issued in JPRS series (PrEx 7.13).
   Published in microfiche.

PrEx 7.22/2:nos.   • Item 1067-L-13
LIFE SCIENCES: EFFECTS OF NONIONIZATION
ELECTROMAGNETIC RADIATION. 1–
[Irregular]

   Issued in JPRS series (PrEx 7.13).
   Published in microfiche.

PrEx 7.22/3:nos.   • Item 1067-L-13
LIFE SCIENCES: AGROTECHNOLOGY AND
FOOD RESOURCES. 1–   [Irregular]

   Issued in JPRS series (PrEx 7.13).
   Published in microfiche.
   Discontinued with the December 1982 is-
   sue.

PrEx 7.22/3-2:nos.   • Item 1067-L-13
CONSTRUCTION AND RELATED INDUSTRY. 1–
[Irregular]

   Issued in JPRS series (PrEx 7.13)
   Published in microfiche.

PrEx 7.22/3-3:nos.   • Item 1067-L-13
MACHINE TOOLS AND METAL WORKING EQUIP-
MENT. 1–   [Irregular]

   Issued in JPRS series (PrEx 7.13)
   Published in microfiche.

PrEx 7.22/4:nos.   • Item 1067-L-13 (MF)
CHEMISTRY. 1–   [Irregular]

   Issued in JPRS series (PrEx 7.13).
   Published in microfiche.

PrEx 7.22/5:nos.   • Item 1067-L-13 (MF)
CYBERNETICS, COMPUTERS, AND AUTO-
MATION TECHNOLOGY. 1–   [Irregular]

   Issued in JPRS series (PrEx 7.13).
   Published in microfiche.

PrEx 7.22/6:nos.   • Item 1067-L-13 (MF)
ELECTRONICS AND ELECTRICAL ENGINEER-
ING. 1–   [Irregular]

   Issued in JPRS series (PrEx 7.13).
   Published in microfiche.

PrEx 7.22/7:nos.   • Item 1067-L-13 (MF)
ENGINEERING AND EQUIPMENT. 1–   [Irregular]

   Issued in JPRS series (PrEx 7.13).
   Published in microfiche.

PrEx 7.22/8   • Item 1067-L-13 (MF)
EARTH SCIENCES. 1–   [Irregular]

   Issued in JPRS series (PrEx 7.13).
   Published in microfiche.

PrEx 7.22/9:nos.   • Item 1067-L-13 (MF)
SPACE. 1–   [Irregular]

   Issued in JPRS series (PrEx 7.13).
   Published in microfiche.

PrEx 7.22/10   • Item 1067-L-13 (MF)
MATERIALS SCIENCE AND METALLURGY. 1–
[Irregular]

   Issued in JPRS series (PrEx 7.13).
   Published in microfiche.

PrEx 7.22/11:nos.   • Item 1067-L-13 (MF)
PHYSICS AND MATHEMATICS. 1–   [Irregular]

   Issued in JPRS series (PrEx 7.13).
   Published in microfiche.

PrEx 7.22/12:nos.   • Item 1067-L-1 (MF)
BIOLOGY AND AEROSPACE MEDICINE. 1–
[Irregular]

   Issued in JPRS series (PrEx 7.13).
   Published in microfiche.

PrEx 7.22/13:nos.   • Item 1067-L-13
BIOMEDICAL AND BEHAVIORAL SCIENCES. 1–
[Irregular]

   Issued in JPRS series (PrEx 7.13).
   Published in microfiche.

PrEx 7.22/14:nos.   • Item 1067-L-13 (MF)
SCIENCE AND TECHNOLOGY POLICY.

   Issued in JPRS series (PrEx 7.13)
   Published in microfiche.

PrEx 7.23:CT   • Item 1067-L-11 (MF)
MISCELLANEOUS REPORTS. [Irregular]

   Issued in JPRS series (PrEx 7.13).
   Published in microfiche.

OFFICE OF SCIENCE AND TECHNOLOGY (1962–1973)

CREATION AND AUTHORITY

   The Office of Science and Technology was
established in the Executive Office of the President by Reorganization Plan 2, of 1962, effective
June 8, 1962. The Director and Deputy Director
are appointed by the President with the advice
and consent of the State. The Office was abolished by Reorganization Plan No. 1 of 1973, effective June 30, 1973.

PrEx 8.1:date
ANNUAL REPORTS.

PrEx 8.2:CT   • Item 857-F-1
GENERAL PUBLICATIONS.

PrEx 8.7
PRESS RELEASES. [Irregular]

PrEx 8.8
HANDBOOKS, MANUALS, GUIDES.

PrEx 8.9:date   • Item 857-F-2
FEDERAL WATER RESOURCES RESEARCH PRO-
GRAM FOR FISCAL YEAR. 1965–   [Annual]

FEDERAL COORDINATING COUNCIL FOR SCIENCE, ENGINEERING, AND TECHNOLOGY (1976–   )

CREATION AND AUTHORITY

   The Federal Coordinating Council for Science,
Engineering, and Technology was established by
act of May 11, 1976 (90 Stat. 471; 42 U.S.C.
6651). The Council was abolished and its functions transferred to the President by Reorganization Plan No. 1 of 1977, effective February 26,
1978. EO 12039 of February 24, 1978, redelegated
these functions to Director of the Office of Science and Technology Policy (PrEx 23) and established a new Federal Coordinating Council for
Science, Engineering, and Technology, effective
February 26, 1978.

PrEx 8.101:date
ANNUAL REPORT.

PrEx 8.102:CT   • Item 856-F
GENERAL PUBLICATIONS.

PrEx 8.108:CT   • Item 1061-B
HANDBOOKS, MANUALS, GUIDES. [Irregular]

PrEx 8.109:date   • Item 856-E-6
NATIONAL MARINE POLLUTION PROGRAM, FISCAL
YEARS (date).

   Earlier: Federal Plan for Ocean Pollution Research, Development, and Monitoring.

PrEx 8.109/2:nos.   • Item 856-E-6 (MF)
–WORKING PAPERS. 1–   1979–   [Irregular]

PrEx 8.110:date • **Item 856-E-7 (MF)**
NATIONAL ATMOSPHERIC SCIENCES PROGRAM.
[Biennial]

> Earlier Y 3.F 31/16

PrEx 8.111:date • **Item 856-E-6**
REPORT OF THE FCCSET COMMITTEE ON EDUCATION AND HUMAN RESOURCES. [Annual]

PrEx 8.111/2:date • **Item 856-E-6**
A REPORT BY THE FCCSET COMMITTEE ON LIFE SCIENCES AND HEALTH. [Annual]

OFFICE OF THE U.S. TRADE REPRESENTATIVE
(1974–)

CREATION AND AUTHORITY

The Office of the Special Representative for Trade Negotiations was established as an agency in the Executive Office of the President by Executive Order 11075 of January 15, 1963; as amended by Executive Order 11106 of April 18, 1963. The Office carries out its functions under the authority of the Trade Expansion Act of 1962 (19 U.S.C. 1801) and Executive Order 11075, as amended. The name was change in 1974 to Office of the U.S. Trade Representative.

INFORMATION

> Office of the U.S. Trade Representative
> 600 Seventeenth Street, N.W.
> Washington, D.C. 20508
> (202) 395-USTR
> Fax: (202) 395-3911
> Toll-Free: (888) 473-8787
> E mail: contactustr@ustr.gov
> http://www.ustr.gov

PrEx 9.1:date • **Item 857-G-1**
REPORTS.

PrEx 9.2:CT • **Item 857-G-1**
GENERAL PUBLICATIONS.

PrEx 9.7:date
PRESS RELEASES. [Irregular]

PrEx 9.9:CT
ADDRESSES. [Irregular]

PrEx 9.10:date • **Item 766-C-9 (P) (EL)**
NATIONAL TRADE ESTIMATE, REPORT ON FOREIGN TRADE BARRIERS. [Annual]

PrEx 9.11:date • **Item 857-G-1**
TRADE POLICY AGENDA AND ANNUAL REPORT OF THE PRESIDENT OF THE AGREEMENTS PROGRAM. [Annual]

PrEx 9.12:v.nos./nos. • **Item 857-J**
NAFTA REVIEW. [Quarterly]

OFFICE OF ECONOMIC OPPORTUNITY
(1964– 1975)

CREATION AND AUTHORITY

The Office of Economic Opportunity (OEO) was established within the Executive Office of the President by the Economic Opportunity Act of 1964 (78 Stat. 508; 42 U.S.C. 2701), as amended. The Office was abolished by Act of January 4, 1975 (88 Stat. 2310; 42 U.S.C. 2941) and its functions transferred to the Community Services Administration (CSA 1).

PrEx 10.1 • **Item 857-H-10**
ANNUAL REPORT. 1st– 1965– [Annual] (also issued in the House Document series)

> Individual reports published with distinctive titles.

PrEx 10.2:CT • **Item 857-H**
GENERAL PUBLICATIONS.

> **PrEx 10.2:C 73-3** • **Item 857-H**
> DIRECTORY CAP [Community Actions Programs] GRANTEES.

> **PrEx 10.2:P 86/9/v.nos.** • **Item 857-H**
> MAPS OF MAJOR CONCENTRATIONS OF POVERTY IN STANDARD METROPOLITAN STATISTICAL AREAS OF 250,000 OR MORE POPULATION. v. 1– 1966– [Irregular]

> **PrEx 10.2:P 94/date** • **Item 857-H**
> CATALOG OF FEDERAL ASSISTANCE PROGRAMS. 1965– [Quarterly]
> Superseded by Catalog of Federal Domestic Assistance (PrEx 2.20).

PrEx 10.5:CT • **Item 857-H-3**
LAWS.

PrEx 10.6:CT • **Item 857-H-2**
REGULATIONS, RULES, AND INSTRUCTIONS.

PrEx 10.7:date
PRESS RELEASES. [Irregular]

PrEx 10.7/2:v.nos.&nos.
NEWS SUMMARY OF WAR ON POVERTY. v. 1– 1966– [Weekly]

PrEx 10.7/3:date
OEO NEWS SUMMARY. [Irregular]

PrEx 10.8:CT • **Item 857-H-2**
HANDBOOKS, MANUALS, GUIDES.

> **PrEx 10.8:H 34/2** • **Item 857-H-2**
> HEAD START, CHILD DEVELOPMENT PROGRAM. MANUAL OF POLICIES AND INSTRUCTIONS. (Community Action Program)

> > Contains instructions to applicants for financial assistance for full year and summer child development program under title 11-A of the Economic Opportunity Act of 1964, as amended.
> > Issued in looseleaf form.

PrEx 10.8/2:nos.
VISTA MANUALS.

PrEx 10.8/3:nos.
OEO HANDBOOKS.

PrEx 10.8/4 • **Item 857-H-2**
OEO TRAINING MANUALS. [Irregular]

PrEx 10.8/5
OEO MANUALS. [Irregular]

PrEx 10.9:v.nos.&nos.
COMMUNITIES IN ACTION. v. 1– v. 1, no. 4, 1965.

PrEx 10.9/2:nos. • **Item 857-H-9**
COMMUNITIES IN ACTION. v. 1– v. 5, no. 3. 1966– 1969. [Irregular]

> Supersedes previous series with same title, which was discontinued with the August 1965 issue.

PrEx 10.9/3:CT • **Item 857-H-3**
COMMUNITY ACTION (series).

PrEx 10.9/4: • **Item 857-H-7**
C/HS PAMPHLETS. [Irregular]

> Earlier title CAP Pamphlets.

PrEx 10.9/5:CT
COMMUNITY PROFILES. 1967– [Irregular]

> PURPOSE:– To increase the scope, accessibility, accuracy and utility of information on the social, economic and demographic makeup of each county in the United States. Describes the social and economic characteristics of the United States at a local level.

PrEx 10.10:nos.
JCH (series).

PrEx 10.10/2:v.nos.&nos.
CORPSMAN, PUBLISHED FOR MEN AND WOMEN OF JOB CORPS.

PrEx 10.10/3:v.nos.&nos.
JOB CORPS STAFF NEWSLETTER.

PrEx 10.10/4:CT
JOB CORPS CENTERS [descriptive folders].

PrEx 10.11:CT
ADDRESSES.

PrEx 10.12:nos.
PROJECT HEAD START (series). 1– 1966– [Irregular]

PrEx 10.12/2
HEAD START NEWSLETTER. 1– 1966– [Irregular]

> Later HE 21.209

PrEx 10.13 • **Item 857-H-6**
VISTA. v. 1– 6. [Monthly]

> Entitled Vista Volunteer prior to October 1968.

PrEx 10.13/2 • **Item 857-H-14**
VISTA VOICE. [Irregular]

> Later Y 3.N 21/29:16-9

PrEx 10.13/3 • **Item 857-H**
VISTA PAMPHLETS. [Irregular]

PrEx 10.13/4:v.nos.&nos.
V-LINE, BULLETIN OF INFORMATION.

PrEx 10.14:v.nos.&nos. • **Item 857-H-5**
RURAL OPPORTUNITIES. v. 1– 1966– [Irregular]

> Published as an information service in the War on Poverty of the Office of Economic Opportunity, Community Action Program.

PrEx 10.15:CT • **Item 857-H-4**
BIBLIOGRAPHIES AND LISTS OF PUBLICATIONS.

PrEx 10.16:v.nos.&nos.
ADVISORY. v. 1– 1966– [Monthly]

> Monthly newsletter from the Office of National Councils and Organizations to advisory councils.

PrEx 10.17:v.nos.&nos. • **Item 1857-H-8**
LAW IN ACTION. v. 1– [Monthly]

> Monthly account of the Legal Services Program.

PrEx 10.18:date
ANNUAL REPORT OF LEGAL SERVICES PROGRAM OF OFFICE OF ECONOMIC OPPORTUNITY TO THE AMERICAN BAR ASSOCIATION. 1st– 1966–   [Annual]

PrEx 10.19:v.nos.&nos.
TRAVELER/EL VIAJERO, QUARTERLY NEWSLETTER FOR MIGRANT AND SEASONAL FARM WORKERS. v. 1–   1966–   [Quarterly]

Published in English and Spanish as information service by the Special Field Programs Division of CAP (Community Actions Programs].

PrEx 10.20:CT   • **Item 857-H-11**
SO . . . YOU WANT TO BE A [occupation] (series). 1967–   [Irregular] (Job Corps Center for Women)

PrEx 10.21:date   • **Item 857-H-13**
VISTA FACT BOOK. [Monthly]

Includes list of active projects, with directory of names of project contracts and local sponsors.

PrEx 10.22:date   • **Item 857-H-16**
NATIONAL ADVISORY COUNCIL ON ECONOMIC OPPORTUNITY, ANNUAL REPORT. [Annual]

Later Y 3.Ec 7:1

PrEx 10.23:nos.   • **Item 857-H-17**
OEO PAMPHLETS. [Irregular]

Later CSA 1.9

PrEx 10.24:CT
FEDERAL OUTLAYS. [Annual]

Later CSA 1.10

PrEx 10.25:v.nos.&nos.
DIGEST. v. 1–   1970–   [Monthly]

PrEx 10.26:v.nos.&nos.
COMMUNICATOR.

PrEx 10.27:v.nos.&nos.   • **Item 857-H-18**
OPPORTUNITY. v. 1–3, no. 1. 1971– January/February 1973. [Monthly.except January/February and August/ September]

PURPOSE:– To accurately and dramatically portray significant programs of the Office of Economic Opportunity and the people who benefit from such programs. Contains articles and graphs showing how basic problems of poverty are being acted upon and reduced through the activities of the Agency in carrying out its basic mandate from the President and Congress.

NATIONAL COUNCIL OF THE ARTS
(1964– 1965)

CREATION AND AUTHORITY

The National Council of the Arts was established by act of September 3, 1964 (78 Stat. 950; 20 U.S.C. 781 note). By act of September 29, 1965 (79 Stat. 845; 20 U.S.C. 951 note) it was transferred to the National Foundation on the Arts and Humanities (NF).

PrEx 11.1:date
ANNUAL REPORT.

PrEx 11.2:CT
GENERAL PUBLICATIONS.

NATIONAL COUNCIL ON MARINE RESOURCES AND ENGINEERING DEVELOPMENT
(1966– 1971)

CREATION AND AUTHORITY

The National Council on Marine Resources and Engineering Development was established in the Executive Office of the President by the Marine Resources and Development Act of 1966 (80 Stat. 203; 33 U.S.C. 1101), as amended by the acts of January 2, 1968 and May 23, 1969. Terminated in 1971 due to lack of funds.

PrEx 12.1:date   • **Item 1070-H**
ANNUAL REPORTS. 1–   1966–   [Annual]

Report submitted by the Chairman in accordance with the Marine Resources and Engineering Development Act of 1966 for the fiscal year. Individual reports have distinctive titles.

PrEx 12.2:CT
GENERAL PUBLICATIONS.

PrEx 12.8:CT
HANDBOOKS, MANUALS, GUIDES.

PrEx 12.9:nos.
CMREF [Committee on Marine Research, Education, and Facilities] PAMPHLETS. 1–   [Irregular]

PrEx 12.10:date   • **Item 1070-H**
MARINE RESEARCH, FISCAL YEAR. [Annual]

Catalog of unclassified marine research activities sponsored by Federal and non-Federal organizations.

PrEx 12.11:nos.
MSAS [Marine Sciences Affairs Staff] PUBLICATIONS. 1–   1969–

NATIONAL CLEARINGHOUSE FOR DRUG ABUSE INFORMATION
(1970– 1973)

PrEx 13.1:date
ANNUAL REPORT.

PrEx 13.2:CT   • **Item 831-C-5**
GENERAL PUBLICATIONS.

PrEx 13.2:D 84   • **Item 831-C-5**
DRUG ABUSE PREVENTION MATERIALS FOR SCHOOLS. 1971 48 p. il.

Provides facts and resources for the teacher on the latest education techniques of drug abuse prevention; how one becomes aware of his own and others' emotional reactions to drug abuse; various proven approaches used in drug prevention and education activities throughout communities in the U.S.; and beginning approaches or alternatives to drug abuse. Describes the materials to begin effective education about all aspects of drug abuse, particularly relative to elementary, junior, and senior high school students, Order forms are included for obtaining materials from the National Clearinghouse For Drug Abuse Information.

PrEx 13.8:CT   • **Item 831-C**
HANDBOOKS, MANUALS, GUIDES.

PrEx 13.9:v.nos.&nos.   • **Item 831-C-1**
REPORT SERIES. [Irregular]

Indexed by Guide to U.S. Government Periodicals.
Later HE 20.8010

PrEx 13.9/2:v.nos.&nos.   • **Item 831-C-7**
DRUG ABUSE PREVENTION REPORT. 1–2, no. 2. 1973– 1974. [Monthly]

Indexed by Guide to U.S. Government Periodicals.

PrEx 13.10:CT   • **Item 831-C-2**
BIBLIOGRAPHIES AND LIST OF PUBLICATIONS.

PrEx 13.10/2:series&nos.   • **Item 831-C-3**
SELECTED REFERENCE SERIES. 1, no. 1–   1971–

Later HE 20.8215/2

PrEx 13.11:date   • **Item 831-C-4**
TUNE IN, DRUG ABUSE NEWS.

PrEx 13.12:v.nos.&nos.   • **Item 831-C-6**
DACAS [Drug Abuse Current Awareness System]. 1– 1972–   [Biweekly]

Later HE 20.8209

COUNCIL ON ENVIRONMENTAL QUALITY
(1970–   )

CREATION AND AUTHORITY

The Council on Environmental Quality was established within the Executive Office of the President by Public Law 91-190, approved January 1, 1970.

INFORMATION

Communications Office
Council on Environmental Quality
722 Jackson Place, N.W.
Washington, D.C. 20503
(202) 456-6224
Fax: (202) 456-6546
http://www.whitehouse.gov/ceq

PrEx 14.1:date   • **Item 856-E-1 (MF)**
ANNUAL REPORTS. 1st–   1970–

PrEx 14.1/a:CT   • **Item 856-E-1**
– SEPARATES.

PrEx 14.1/2:date   • **Item 856-E-3**
CITIZENS' ADVISORY COMMITTEE ON ENVIRONMENTAL QUALITY: ANNUAL REPORT. 1st–

PrEx 14.2:CT   • **Item 856-E**
GENERAL PUBLICATIONS.

PrEx 14.6:CT   • **Item 856-E-5**
REGULATIONS, RULES, AND INSTRUCTIONS. [Irregular]

PrEx 14.8:CT   • **Item 856-E-4**
HANDBOOKS, MANUALS, GUIDES. [Irregular]

PrEx 14.9:v.nos.&nos. • Item 1061-C
PESTICIDES MONITORING JOURNAL. v. 1– 1967–
1981. [Quarterly]

PURPOSE:– To provide information on pesticide levels relative to man and his environment. Reports will be restricted to those dealing with data gathered from air, earth, water, food, and life, by the Federal Government, States, universities, hospitals, and non-Government research institutions.
Indexed by:–
Bibliography of Agriculture
Biological Abstracts
Chemical Abstracts
Index Medicus
Index to U.S. Government Periodicals
Selected Water Resources Abstracts
ISSN 0031-6156

PrEx 14.10:v.nos.&nos. • Item 856-E-2
102 MONITOR, ENVIRONMENTAL IMPACT STATEMENTS. v. 1, no. 1– Feb. 1970– [Monthly]

OFFICE OF POLICY DEVELOPMENT
(1970–   )

CREATION AND AUTHORITY

The Domestic Council was established by Reorganization Plan No. 2 of 1970, dated March 12, 1970, composed of Cabinet members. The Council was abolished and its functions transferred to the President, and the Domestic Policy Staff by Reorganization Plan No. 1 of 1977, effective March 26, 1978 pursuant to Executive Order 12045 of March 27, 1978. The Domestic Policy Staff was redesignated the Office of Policy Development in 1981.

INFORMATION

Domestic Policy Council
Office of Policy Development
Executive Office of the President
1600 Pennsylvania Avenue, N.W.
Washington, D.C. 20500
(202) 456-5594
Fax: (202) 456-5557
http://www.whitehouse.gov/dpc

PrEx 15.1:date
ANNUAL REPORT.

PrEx 15.2:CT • Item 856-B-1
GENERAL PUBLICATIONS.

PrEx 15.9:date • Item 856-B-2
REPORT ON NATIONAL GROWTH AND DEVELOPMENT. 1st– 1977– [Biennial] (Committee on Community Development)
Report submitted to Congress pursuant to section 703(a) of Title 7, Housing and Urban Development Act of 1970.

OFFICE OF CONSUMER AFFAIRS
(1971– 1973)

CREATION AND AUTHORITY

The Office of Consumer Affairs was established within the Executive Office of the President by Executive Order 11583 of February 24, 1971. Office was transferred to the Department of Health, Education, and Welfare (HE 1.500) by Executive Order 11702 of January 25, 1973.

PrEx 16.1:date
ANNUAL REPORT.

Later HE 1.501

PrEx 16.2:CT • Item 857-I-5
GENERAL PUBLICATIONS.

Later 1.502

PrEx 16.2:St 2/2 • Item 857-I-5
DIRECTORY OF STATE, COUNTY, AND CITY GOVERNMENT CONSUMER OFFICES. 1973. 35 p.

PrEx 16.8:CT • Item 857-I-2
HANDBOOKS, MANUALS, GUIDES.

Later HE 1.508

PrEx 16.8:Se 6 • Item 857-I-2
GUIDE TO FEDERAL CONSUMER SERVICES. 1971. 151 p.

Lists the consumer services of every Federal agency or bureau that is either directly or indirectly concerned with consumer issues.

PrEx 16.9:v.nos.&nos. • Item 857-I-1
CONSUMER NEWS. v. 1– 1971– [Semimonthly]

Later HE 1.509

PrEx 16.10:CT • Item 857-I-3
BIBLIOGRAPHIES AND LISTS OF PUBLICATIONS. [Irregular]

PrEx 16.10:Ed 8 • Item 857-I-3
CONSUMER EDUCATION BIBLIOGRAPHY. Rev 1971. 192 p.

This bibliography lists over 4,000 books, pamphlets, periodical articles, audio-visual aids, and teacher's materials relating to consumer interest and education.
Prepared in cooperation with the New York Public Library.

PrEx 16.11:date • Item 857-I-4
CONSUMER LEGISLATIVE MONTHLY REPORT. [Monthly]

Earlier Pr 36.8:C 76/L 52
Later HE 1.510

COST OF LIVING COUNCIL
(1971– 1974)

CREATION AND AUTHORITY

The Cost of Living Council was established within the Executive Office of the President by Executive Order 11615 of August 15, 1971. The Council was abolished by Executive Order 11788 of June 18, 1974, effective July 1, 1974.

PrEx 17.1:date
ANNUAL REPORT.

PrEx 17.2:CT • Item 857-L-2
GENERAL PUBLICATIONS.

PrEx 17.7:date
COST OF LIVING COUNCIL NEWS. 1971– [Irregular] (Office of Public Affairs)

PrEx 17.7/2:date
CONSTRUCTION INDUSTRY STABILIZATION COMMITTEE: PRESS RELEASES.

PrEx 17.8:CT • Item 857-L-3
HANDBOOKS, MANUALS, GUIDES.

PrEx 17.9:date • Item 857-L-1
ECONOMIC STABILIZATION PROGRAM QUARTERLY REPORT. 1971– 1974.

PrEx 17.9/2:nos.
ECONOMIC STABILIZATION PROGRAM, BI-WEEKLY SUMMARY. 1– 1973–

PrEx 17.10:nos. • Item 857-L-1
ECONOMIC STABILIZATION PROGRAM (series). 1– 1973–

Some issues unnumbered.

PrEx 17.11:CT
ADDRESSES.

PrEx 17.12:date • Item 857-L-4
TELEPHONE DIRECTORY.

OFFICE OF TELECOMMUNICATIONS POLICY
(1970– 1977)

CREATION AND AUTHORITY

The Office of Telecommunications Policy was established within the Executive Office of the President by Reorganization Plan 1 of 1970, effective April 20, 1970. The Office was abolished by Reorganization Plan 1 of 1977, effective March 26, 1978, with certain of its functions transferred to the President and all others to the Department of Commerce (C 1.59).

PrEx 18.1:date • Item 857-M-1
ACTIVITIES AND PROGRAMS. [Annual]

Annual report.

PrEx 18.2:CT • Item 857-M-1
GENERAL PUBLICATIONS.

PrEx 18.8:CT • Item 857-M-1
HANDBOOKS, MANUALS, GUIDES.

PrEx 18.8:R 11 • Item 857-M-1
MANUAL OF REGULATIONS AND PROCEDURES
FOR RADIO FREQUENCY MANAGEMENT. [Ir-
regular] (includes basic manual plus quarterly changes for an indefinite period)

PrEx 18.9:date • Item 857-M-1
ANNUAL REPORT ON ACTIVITIES AND ACCOM-
PLISHMENTS UNDER THE COMMUNICATIONS
SATELLITE ACT OF 1962.

Covers calendar year.

PAY BOARD
(1971– 1973)

CREATION AND AUTHORITY

The Pay Board was established within the
Cost of Living Council by Executive Order 11627
of October 15, 1971. The Board was abolished by
Executive Order 11695 of January 11, 1973.

PrEx 19.1:date
ANNUAL REPORTS.

PrEx 19.2:CT
GENERAL PUBLICATIONS.

SPECIAL ACTION OFFICE FOR
DRUG ABUSE PREVENTION
(1972– 1975)

CREATION AND AUTHORITY

The Special Action Office for Drug Abuse
Prevention was established within the Executive
Office of the President by Executive Order 11599
of June 17, 1971, and act of Congress, approved
March 21, 1972 (86 Stat. 65). The Office was
terminated on June 30, 1975, pursuant to terms
of establishing the act.

PrEx 20.1:date • Item 857-B-1
ANNUAL REPORT. 1–   1973–

PrEx 20.2:CT • Item 857-B-2
GENERAL PUBLICATIONS.

PrEx 20.8:CT • Item 857-B-4
HANDBOOKS, MANUALS, GUIDES.

PrEx 20.9:letters-nos. • Item 857-B-3 (MF)
SPECIAL ACTION OFFICE MONOGRAPH (series).

FEDERAL ENERGY OFFICE
(1973– 1977)

CREATION AND AUTHORITY

The Federal Energy Office was established
within the Executive Office of the President by
Executive Order 11748 of December 4, 1973.

PrEx 21.1:date
ANNUAL REPORT.

PrEx 21.2:CT
GENERAL PUBLICATIONS.

PrEx 21.7:date
PRESS RELEASES. [Irregular]

PrEx 21.8:CT
HANDBOOKS, MANUALS, GUIDES

Later FE 1.8

PrEx 21.9:date
PETROLEUM SITUATION REPORT.

Later FE 1.9

PrEx 21.10:CT
ADDRESSES. [Irregular]

PrEx 21.11:date
TELEPHONE DIRECTORY.

PrEx 21.13:date
PETROLEUM IMPORT REPORTING SYSTEM,
WEEKLY SITUATION REPORT.

Later FE 1.9/2

PrEx 21.14:date
WEEKLY PETROLEUM STATISTICAL REPORT.

COUNCIL ON WAGE AND PRICE
STABILITY
(1974– 1981)

CREATION AND AUTHORITY

The Council on Wage and Price Stability was
established within the Executive Office of the
President by Act of August 24, 1974 (88 Stat.
750). The Council was abolished by Executive
Order 12288 of January 29, 1981.

PrEx 22.1:date • Item 857-C-1
ANNUAL REPORT.

PrEx 22.2:CT • Item 857-C-1
GENERAL PUBLICATIONS.

PrEx 22.9:date&nos. • Item 857-O-1
QUARTERLY REPORT. 1975–

ISSN 0145-1286

PrEx 22.10:date
PRESS RELEASES.

OFFICE OF SCIENCE AND
TECHNOLOGY POLICY
(1976–   )

CREATION AND AUTHORITY

The Office of Science and Technology Policy
was established within the Executive Office of
the President by the National Science and Technology Policy, Organization, and Priorities Act of
1976 (90 Stat. 463), approved May 11, 1976,
superseding the Office of Science and Technology (PrEx 8).

INFORMATION

Office of Science and Technology Policy
Executive Office of the President
Washington, D.C. 20502--0001
(202) 395-7347
Fax: (202) 456-6021
E mail:ostpinfo@ostp.eop.gov
http://www.ostp.gov

PrEx 23.1:date
ANNUAL REPORT.

PrEx 23.2:CT • Item 857-P-2
GENERAL PUBLICATIONS. [Irregular]

PrEx 23.9:date • Item 857-F-1
ACTIVITIES OF THE FEDERAL COUNCIL FOR
SCIENCE AND TECHNOLOGY AND THE FED-
ERAL COORDINATING COUNCIL FOR SCIENCE,
ENGINEERING AND TECHNOLOGY, REPORT.
[Annual]

Earlier Y 3.F 31/16:1

PrEx 23.10:date • Item 857-P-1
DIRECTORY OF FEDERAL TECHNOLOGY TRANS-
FER.

Earlier Y 3.F 31/16:F 31

PrEx 23.11 • Item 857-P-3 (EL)
IITF ACTIVITY REPORTS.

PrEx 23.12 • Item 857-P-3 (E)
ELECTRONIC PRODUCTS.

PrEx 23.13 • Item 857-P-4 (EL)
HIGH PERFORMANCE COMPUTING AND COMMUNI-
CATIONS IMPLEMENTATION PLAN.

PrEx 23.14:CT • Item 857-P-5
NATIONAL SCIENCE AND TECHNOLOGY COUNCIL:
GENERAL PUBLICATIONS.

OFFICE OF DRUG ABUSE POLICY
(1976– 1978)

CREATION AND AUTHORITY

The Office of Drug Abuse Policy was established within the Executive Office of the President by act of March 19, 1976 (90 Stat. 242; 21
U.S.C. 1111). The Office was abolished and functions transferred to the President by Reorganization Plan No. 1 of 1977, effective March 26, 1978.

PrEx 24.1:date • Item 857-G-2
ANNUAL REPORT.

PrEx 24.2:CT • Item 857-G-3
GENERAL PUBLICATIONS.

REGULATORY INFORMATION SERVICE CENTER
(1982–)

INFORMATION

Regulatory Information Service Center
New Executive Office Building, Room 5216
726 Jackson Place, N.W.
Washington, D.C. 20530
(202) 395-4931

PrEx 25.1:date
ANNUAL REPORT.

PrEx 25.2:CT • **Item 857-A-1**
GENERAL PUBLICATIONS. [Irregular]

OFFICE OF NATIONAL DRUG CONTROL POLICY

INFORMATION

Office of National Drug Control Policy
750 17th Street, NW
Washington, DC 20006
(202) 395-6700
Fax: (202) 395-6708
http://www.whitehousedrugpolicy.gov

PrEx 26.1/2:date • **Item 857-R-3 (P) (EL)**
THE NATIONAL DRUG CONTROL POLICY. [Annual]

PrEx 26.1/4:date • **Item 857-R-4**
FY BUDGET HIGHLIGHTS FEDERAL DRUG CONTROL
PROGRAMS. [Annual]

PrEx 26.2:CT • **Item 857-R**
GENERAL PUBLICATIONS. [Irregular]

PrEx 26.8:CT • **Item 857-R-1**
HANDBOOKS, MANUALS, AND GUIDES. [Irregular]

PrEx 26.10:date • **Item 857-R-2 (EL)**
PULSE CHECK. [Semiannual]

VICE PRESIDENT OF THE UNITED STATES GEORGE BUSH
(1980– 1988)

PrVp 40.2:CT • **Item 851-J**
GENERAL PUBLICATIONS. [Irregular]

PrVp 40.2:T 27 • **Item 851-J**
PUBLIC REPORT OF THE VICE PRESIDENT'S
TASK FORCE ON COMBATTING TERRORISM.

VICE PRESIDENT OF THE UNITED STATES DAN QUAYLE
(1989– 1993)

INFORMATION

Office of the Vice President
Eisenhower Executive Office Bldg.
Washington, DC 20501
(202) 456-1414
http://www.whitehouse.gov/vicepresident

PrVp 41.2:CT • **Item 851-J-1**
GENERAL PUBLICATIONS.

PrVp 41.2:Sp 1 • **Item 851-J-1**
FINAL REPORT TO THE PRESIDENT ON THE
U.S. SPACE PROGRAM.

VICE PRESIDENT OF THE UNITED STATES ALBERT GORE
(1993–2001)

PrVp 42.2:CT • **Item 851**
GENERAL PUBLICATIONS.

PrVp 42.10 • **Item 851-J-14**
DIRECTORIES

PrVp 42.15 • **Item 851-J-6**
REINVENTION ROUNDTABLE, HELPING FEDERAL
WORKERS CREATE A GOVERNMENT THAT
WORKS BETTER AND COST LESS.

PrVp 42.16 • **Item 851-J-8 (EL)**
REINVENTION EXPRESS.

PrVp 42.17 • **Item 851-J-9 (E)**
ELECTRONIC PRODUCTS.

VICE PRESIDENT OF THE UNITED STATES RICHARD CHENEY
(2001–)

PrVp 43.2 • **Item 851-K**
GENERAL PUBLICATIONS.

PrVp 43.17 • **Item 851-K-1 (E)**
ELECTRONIC PRODUCTS.

POSTAL SAVINGS SYSTEM
(1910– 1966)

CREATION AND AUTHORITY

The Postal Savings System was established
by act of June 25, 1910 (39 U.S.C. 5203, 5205),
to provide facilities for deposit of savings at interest, with the security of the U.S. Government
for repayment. Act of March 28, 1966 (80 Stat.
92; 39 U.S.C. 5225-5229) provided for closing of
the System.

PS 1.1:date
ANNUAL REPORTS.

PS 1.2:CT
GENERAL PUBLICATIONS.

PS 1.3:nos.
BULLETINS.

PS 1.4:nos.
CIRCULARS.

PS 1.5/1:date
REGULATIONS (general).

PS 1.5/2:CT
REGULATIONS (special).

PS 1.6:CT
INSTRUCTIONS TO POSTMASTERS.

Later P 19.6

NATIONAL RAILROAD ADJUSTMENT BOARD
(1934–)

CREATION AND AUTHORITY

The National Railroad Adjustment Board was
established by act of Congress, approved June
21, 1934.

INFORMATION

National Railroad Adjustment Board
220 South State Street
Chicago, Illinois 60604
(312) 427-8383

RA 1.1:date
ANNUAL REPORTS.

RA 1.2:CT
GENERAL PUBLICATIONS.

RA 1.4:nos.
CIRCULARS.

RA 1.7:vol.
AWARDS, 1st DIVISION (bound edition) SEPARATES
NOT CLASSED.

RA 1.7/2:inc.nos.
AWARDS, 1st DIVISION. GENERAL INDEX.

RA 1.8:vol.
AWARDS, 2nd DIVISION (bound edition).

RA 1.9:vol.
AWARDS, 3rd DIVISION (bound edition).

RA 1.10:vol.
AWARDS, 4th DIVISION (bound edition).

NATIONAL RAILROAD ADJUSTMENT BOARD SECOND DIVISION

RA.2

This class (RA 2) was assigned to the SuDocs Classification Scheme but apparently never was used.

NATIONAL RAILROAD ADJUSTMENT BOARD THIRD DIVISION

RA 3.1:date
ANNUAL REPORTS.

Included in National Mediation Board Annual Reports, (NMB 1.1).

RA 3.2:CT
GENERAL PUBLICATIONS.

RA 3.7:vol.
AWARDS.

RESERVE BANK ORGANIZATION COMMITTEE
(1913– 1914)

CREATION AND AUTHORITY

The Reserve Bank Organization Committee was established by act of Congress, approved December 23, 1913 (38 Stat. 251). The Committee ceased to exist on October 31, 1914.

RB 1.1:date
ANNUAL REPORTS.

RB 1.2:CT
GENERAL PUBLICATIONS.

RB 1.3
BULLETINS.

RB 1.4
CIRCULARS.

RB 1.5:nos.
LIST OF MEMBER BANKS BY DISTRICTS.

RB 1.6:district
DISTRICT RESERVE ELECTORS FOR MEMBER BANKS IN DISTRICT.

RB 1.7:nos.
REGULATIONS.

FEDERAL RADIO COMMISSION
(1927– 1934)

CREATION AND AUTHORITY

The Federal Radio Commission was established by act of Congress, approved February 23, 1927 (44 Stat. 1162). The Commission was abolished by the Communications Act of 1934, approved June 19, 1934 (48 Stat. 1102), and its functions transferred to the Federal Communications Commission (CC).

RC 1.1:date
ANNUAL REPORTS.

Later CC 1.1

RC 1.2:CT
GENERAL PUBLICATIONS.

Later CC 1.2

RC 1.3:nos.
RADIO SERVICE BULLETINS. [Monthly]

Later CC 1.3/2

RC 1.4
CIRCULARS.

RC 1.5:nos.
OFFICIAL BULLETIN.

RC 1.6:nos.
GENERAL ORDERS.

RC 1.7:CT
PAPERS IN RE.

RC 1.8:date
PRACTICE AND PROCEDURE.

RC 1.9:date
BROADCASTING RADIO STATIONS OF THE UNITED STATES.

Later CC 2.10, CC 2.11, CC 2.12, CC 1.10

RC 1.10:date
RULES AND REGULATIONS.

RC 1.11:CT
MAPS.

RAILROAD LABOR BOARD
(1920– 1926)

CREATION AND AUTHORITY

The United States Railroad Labor Board was established by the Transportation Act, approved February 28, 1920. The Board was superseded by the United States Board of Mediation (MB 1), established by the Railway Labor Act, approved May 20, 1926.

RL 1.1:date
ANNUAL REPORTS.

RL 1.2:CT
GENERAL PUBLICATIONS.

RL 1.3
BULLETINS.

RL 1.4
CIRCULARS.

RL 1.5:nos.
ORDERS.

RL 1.6:nos.
DECISIONS.

RL 1.6/2:vol.
– COMPILATIONS.

RL 1.6/3:nos.
INDEX DIGEST OF DECISIONS.

RL 1.7:date
ANNOUNCEMENTS.

RL 1.8:nos.
WAGE SERIES REPORTS.

RL 1.9:v.nos.
MONTHLY AND ANNUAL EARNINGS OF TRAIN AND ENGINE SERVICE EMPLOYEES.

Mimeographed.

RL 1.10:date
RATES OF PAY OF SHOP CRAFTS.

Mimeographed.

RENEGOTIATION BOARD
(1951– 1979)

CREATION AND AUTHORITY

The Renegotiation Board was created by the Renegotiation Act of 1951 (65 Stat. 7; 50 U.S.C. App. 1211) as an independent establishment in the executive branch of the Government and was organized on October 3, 1951 to administer such act. The Renegotiation Act of 1951, transferred to the Renegotiation Board certain powers, functions, and duties conferred upon the War Contracts Price Adjustment Board by the Renegotiation Act of February 25, 1944 (58 Stat. 78, as amended; 50 U.S.C. App. 1191). In addition, the secretary of Defense delegated to the Renegotiation Board, effective January 20, 1952, all powers, functions, and duties conferred upon the Secretary of Defense by the Renegotiation Act of 1948 (62 Stat. 259, as amended and extended; 50 U.S.C. App 1193). The Board was terminated March 31, 1979 pursuant to act of October 10, 1978 (92 Stat. 1043).

RnB 1.1   • **Item 308**
ANNUAL REPORT. 1st–   1956–   [Annual]

Report submitted by the Board to Congress pursuant to section 144 of the Renegotiation Act of 1951, as amended, for the fiscal year.
Brief report of activities.

RnB 1.2:CT   • **Item 308**
GENERAL PUBLICATIONS.

RnB 1.5:CT   • **Item 308**
LAWS.

RnB 1.6:CT   • **Item 308**
REGULATIONS, RULES, AND INSTRUCTIONS.

RnB 1.6/2   • **Item 308**
RENEGOTIATION BOARD REGULATIONS. [Irregular] (Subscription includes basic regulations, supplements, and revisions for an indefinite period)

Contains regulations governing the recovery of excessive profits derived by contractors in connection with the national defense program contracts.
ISSN 0364-6726

RnB 1.6/3   • **Item 308**
RENEGOTIATION STAFF BULLETINS.

RnB 1.6/4:date • Item 308
MILITARY RENEGOTIATION REGULATIONS UNDER RENEGOTIATION ACT OF 1948.

Earlier D 1.8

RnB 1.6/5 • Item 308
RENEGOTIATION BOARD RULINGS. 1– [Irregular]

Subscription included with Renegotiation Board Regulations.

RAILROAD RETIREMENT BOARD
(1935–)

CREATION AND AUTHORITY

The Railroad Retirement Board was established by the Railroad Retirement Act of 1935, approved August 29, 1935 (49 Stat. 967, as amended; 45 U.S.C. 215-228). The Board derives authority also from the Railroad Unemployment Insurance Act, approved June 25, 1938 (52 Stat. 1094, as amended; 45 U.S.C. 351-367)

INFORMATION

Railroad Retirement Board
844 Rush Street
Chicago, Illinois 60611-2092
(312) 751-4500
Fax: (312) 751-7136
Toll-Free: (800) 808-0772
http://www.rrb.gov

RR 1.1:date • Item 858 (MF)
ANNUAL REPORT. 1st– 1936– [Annual] (also issued in the House Documents series)

RR 1.1:date/sup. • Item 858
– STATISTICAL SUPPLEMENT. [Annual]

RR 1.2:CT • Item 859
GENERAL PUBLICATIONS.

RR 1.5:CT • Item 860
LAWS.

RR 1.6:CT • Item 861
REGULATIONS, RULES, AND INSTRUCTIONS.

RR 1.6/2:CT • Item 859-A
HANDBOOKS, MANUALS, GUIDES.

RR 1.7:vol.
WEEKLY REVIEW.

RR 1.7/2:v.nos.
MONTHLY REVIEW.

Replaces RR 1.7

RR 1.7/3 • Item 859-B
RRB QUARTERLY REVIEW. [Quarterly] (Information Service, Office of Actuary and Research)

Contains articles on Board operations, on such topics as retirement-survivor and unemployment-sickness benefit programs for railroad employees and families.
Indexed by: Index to U.S. Government Periodicals.
ISSN 0565-9973
Prior to the April-June 1968 issue, entitled Monthly Review (RR 1.7/2)
Discontinued with No. 3 (June 1981).

RR 1.8:nos.
LAW BULLETINS.

RR 1.9:nos.
EMPLOYEES BOOKLETS.

RR 1.10:CT
PAPERS IN RE.

RR 1.11:date
STATISTICAL SUMMARY, RAILROAD RETIREMENT BOARD OPERATIONS. [Monthly]

RR 1.12:date • Item 860-A
LEGAL OPINIONS, RULINGS IN ADMINISTRATION OF RAILROAD RETIREMENT ACT AND RAILROAD UNEMPLOYMENT INSURANCE ACT.

RR 1.13
MONTHLY BENEFIT STATISTICS: RAILROAD RETIREMENT AND UNEMPLOYMENT INSURANCE PROGRAMS. 1st– 1968– [Monthly]

ISSN 0364-7129

RR 1.14:nos.
RRB ACTUARIAL STUDIES.

RR 1.15:date
RRB-SSA FINANCIAL INTERCHANGE: CALCULATIONS FOR FISCAL YEAR WITH RESPECT TO OASI, DI, AND HI TRUST FUNDS.

RR 1.16: • Item 859-A-1 (EL)
QUARTERLY BENEFIT STATISTICS REPORT.

RR 1.17: • Item 859-A-1 (E)
ELECTRONIC PRODUCTS (misc.).

DEPARTMENT OF STATE
(1789–)

CREATION AND AUTHORITY

The Department of State is the oldest executive department of the U.S. Government. Initially, the foreign affairs of the United States were conducted by the Continental Congress, whose first effort to establish a foreign service and a channel through which to conduct the Nations's limited international relations was made in 1775. At that time a Committee of Secret Correspondence, with Benjamin Franklin as chairman, was appointed for the "sole purpose of corresponding with our friends in Great Britain, Ireland, and other parts of the world." In 1777, this committee was succeeded by a Committee for Foreign Affairs, which had limited functions and little real power over our foreign relations.

INFORMATION

Department of State
Harry S. Truman Bldg.
2201 C Street, NW
Washington, DC 20520
(202) 647-4000
http://www.state.gov

• Item 872-B (P) (EL)
S 1.1:nos./v.nos. • Item 872-C (MF)
FOREIGN RELATIONS OF THE UNITED STATES. 1861– [Annual]

A collection of official papers relating to the foreign relations of the United States. One or more volumes have been published for each year since 1861, with the exception of 1869. There is a considerable time-lag between the date of the volume and the publication date.
Prior to 1931, entitled Papers Relating to Foreign Relations of the United States.
The following special supplements have been issued;–

1914– 1920, The Lansing Papers. 2 v. 1939– 1940 (S 1.1/c)
1916– 1918, The World War. 6 v. 1929– 1933.
1919, The Paris Peace Conference. 13 v. 1942– 1947.
1919, Russia. 1 v. 1937.
1931– 1939, The Soviet Union. 1 v. 1952.

1942, China. 1 v. 1956. (S 1.1/2:C 44)
1946, Council of Foreign Ministers. 1 v. 1970.
1947, Council of Foreign Ministers; Germany and Austria. 1 v. 1972. (S 1.1:947/v.2)

Special volumes devoted to Conferences are classified S 1.1/3

S 1.1 • Item 872-D (MF)
– MICROFICHE SUPPLEMENT.

S 1.1/b:date
– INDEXES.

S 1.1/c:v.nos.
LANSING PAPERS.

S 1.1/2:CT/date • Item 872
FOREIGN RELATIONS (by countries).

S 1.1/2:C 44 • Item 872
CHINA, 1942. 1956. 782 p. (Publication 6353)

CHINA, 1943. 1957. 908 p. (Publication 6459)

S 1.1/3:CT • Item 872
FOREIGN RELATIONS OF UNITED STATES, DIPLOMATIC PAPERS: CONFERENCES.

S 1.1/3:C 12 • Item 872
CONFERENCES AT CAIRO AND TEHRAN, 1943, 1961. 932 p. il. (Historical Office, Bureau of Public Affairs) (Publication 7187)

S 1.1/3:M 29 • Item 872
CONFERENCES AT MALTA AND YALTA, 1945. 1955. 1032 p. il. (Historical Office, Bureau of Public Affairs) (Publication 6199)

S 1.1/3:P 84 • Item 872
CONFERENCE OF BERLIN (Potsdam Conference), 1945. 2 v.

v. 1. 1960. 1088 p. (Historical Office, Bureau of Public Affairs) (Publication 7015)
v. 2. 1960. 1645 p. il. (Historical Office, Bureau of Public Affairs) (Publication 7163)

S 1.1/3:Q 3 • Item 872
CONFERENCE AT QUEBEC, 1944. 1972. 527 p. il. (Historical Office, Bureau of Public Affairs) (Publication 8627)

Presents documentation relating to the ninth conference participated in by President Roosevelt and Prime Minister Churchill after the United States became a belligerent in World War II, together with papers on the Roosevelt-Churchill conversations which took place at Hyde Park, New York, immediately following the Quebec Conference. The conversations concerned planning for the final stages of the war both in Europe and the Far East.

S 1.1/3:W 27 • Item 872
CONFERENCES AT WASHINGTON, 1941– 1942, AND CASABLANCA, 1943. 1968. 895 p. il (Historical Office, Bureau of Public Affairs) (Publication 8414)

The primary topic of discussion at these conferences was the formulation of American-British strategy for the war against Germany, Italy, and Japan. But important political subjects were also discussed. Documentation of high-level conversations and discussions are also included.

S 1.1/3:W 27/2 • Item 872
CONFERENCES AT WASHINGTON AND QUEBEC, 1943. 1970. 1382 p. il. (Historical Office, Bureau of Public Affairs) (Publication 8552)

Covers World War II conferences attended by President Roosevelt or President Truman, along with Prime Minister Churchill or Marshall Stalin, or both Churchill and Stalin. It contains extensive documentation on military subjects which were the predominant concerns of the conferences. Important political subjects were also discussed.

S 1.1/4:date   • **Item 863 (MF)**
ANNUAL REPORT OF THE VISA OFFICE. [Annual]
(Bureau of Security and Consular Affairs)

Brief summary of activities of the Office for
the fiscal year. Majority of the report of devoted
to statistical tables on immigrant and nonimmigrant visas issued.
Formerly distributed to Depository Libraries
under Item No. 862-D.

S 1.1/5:date
SUMMARY OF PASSPORT OFFICE ACCOMPLISH-
MENTS. [Annual]

S 1.1/6:date   • **Item 863 (MF)**
ANNUAL REPORT, INSPECTOR GENERAL DEPART-
MENT OF STATE AND FOREIGN SERVICE.

S 1.1/6-2   • **Item 863-D (MF)**
OFFICE OF INSPECTOR GENERAL, FY ANNUAL
PLAN.

S 1.1/7:date   • **Item 864-B-7 (MF)**
COUNTRY REPORTS ON THE WORLD REFUGEE
SITUATION, A REPORT TO CONGRESS. [Annual]

Focuses on overseas refugee assistance
rather than U.S. domestic programs for refugees.
Provides information on the major refugee situations in the world. Describes help being given
refugees by the U.S. and other countries.

S 1.1/7-2   • **Item 864-B-9 (P) (EL)**
U.S. REFUGEE ADMISSIONS PROGRAM FOR FY.
[Annual]

S 1.1/8:date   • **Item 876-A-5 (EL)**
REPORT TO CONGRESS ON VOTING PRACTICES
IN THE UNITED NATIONS. [Annual]

Reports on the activities of countries within
the UN in accordance with P.L. 99-190. Assesses
the degree of support of U.S. foreign policy within
the UN context by governments of UN member
nations. Presents UN members' voting records on
specific issues.
Earlier S 1.2:V 94

S 1.1/9:date/nos.   • **Item 863 (MF)**
THE SECRETARY'S SEMIANNUAL MANAGEMENT
REPORT TO THE CONGRESS.

S 1.2:CT   • **Item 876**
GENERAL PUBLICATIONS.

S 1.2:C 83/2/date   • **Item 876**
SCHEDULE OF COURSES. [Annual] (Foreign Ser-
vice Institute)

Description of courses given by the Institute for foreign affairs personnel.

S 1.2:En 3   • **Item 876**
ENGLISH-FRENCH GLOSSARY. 1976. 645 p. (Lan-
guage Services Division)

This glossary was compiled primarily as a
tool for State Department personnel and for
use in U.S. posts in francophone countries. It
contains selected terms and expressions not
readily available in dictionaries.

S 1.2:F 76a/4   • **Item 876**
FOREIGN AFFAIRS RESEARCH, A DIRECTORY
OF GOVERNMENT RESOURCES. 1969. 50 p.

Provides in one publication a broad, descriptive listing of the many Government resources accessible to the scholar who is
engaged in social and behavioral science research on foreign areas and international affairs.

S 1.2:N 23   • **Item 919**
NAZI-SOVIET RELATIONS, 1939– 41, DOCU-
MENTS FROM THE GERMAN FOREIGN
OFFICE. 1948. 362 p. (Publication 3023)

S 1.2:P 31/8   • **Item 876**
PEACE AND WAR, UNITED STATES FOREIGN
POLICY, 1931– 41. 1943. 874 p. (Publication
1983)

S 1.2:Un 3   • **Item 876**
UNIVERSITY CENTERS OF FOREIGN AFFAIRS
RESEARCH, SELECTIVE DIRECTORY. 1968.
139 p. (Publication 8378)

S 1.2:V 82/2   • **Item 876**
VISA REQUIREMENTS OF FOREIGN GOVERN-
MENTS. 1963–   [Irregular] (Passport Of-
fice) (M-264)

This pamphlet is prepared solely for the
information of United States citizens traveling as tourists, and does not apply to persons going as immigrants to foreign countries. It gives such information as: regulations, passport and visa requirements, fees
(U.S. currency only), vaccination and inocu-
lation, and where to write for specific requirements.
Previous title: Fees Charged by Foreign
Countries for the Visa of United States Passports.

S 1.3   • **Item 864**
DEPARTMENT OF STATE BULLETIN. v. 1–   1939–
[Monthly]

PURPOSE:– As the official weekly record, it
provides the public and interested Government
agencies with information on developments in the
field of foreign relations and on the work of the
Department of State and the Foreign Service.
Includes news conferences, speeches, and
statements of the President and the Secretary of
State, speeches of Departmental officials, selected press releases of the White House and the
U.S. Mission to the United Nations. Also includes
current actions on treaties, calendar of interna-
tional conferences and meetings, and listings of
Department of State press releases, publications
of the Department of State, congressional
documents relating to foreign policy, and current
United Nations documents.
Index for volume issued separately. Each is-
sue has been numbered consecutively since the
Bulletin began in 1939. Articles indexed in Reader's
Guide to Periodical Literature.
Issued weekly prior to January 1978.
Indexed by:–
Index to U.S. Government Periodicals
Public Affairs Information Service
Reader's Guide to Periodical Literature
ISSN 0041-7610

S 1.3/a:CT   • **Item 864**
SEPARATES. [Irregular]

S 1.3/s:CT
FILM BULLETINS.

S 1.3/2:CT
FILM BULLETINS.

S 1.3/3:nos.
FOREIGN CURRENCY BULLETIN.

S 1.3/4:v.nos./nos.   • **Item 863 (EL)**
VISA BULLETIN. [Monthly]

S 1.3/5:v.nos./nos.   • **Item 864**
U.S. DEPARTMENT OF STATE DISPATCH. 1990–
[Weekly]

ISSN 1051-7693

S 1.4/1:date
CIRCULARS (unnumbered).

S 1.4/2:nos.
CIRCULARS: GENERAL INSTRUCTIONS, CONSULAR
OR SPECIAL INSTRUCTIONS, CONSULAR.

S 1.4/3:date
DIGEST OF CIRCULAR INSTRUCTION TO CONSU-
LAR OFFICERS.

Changed from S 1.5

S 1.4/4:nos.
FOREIGN SERVICE FINANCE CIRCULARS.

S 1.4/5:nos.
FOREIGN SERVICE PERSONNEL CIRCULARS.

S 1.5:date
CONSULAR REGULATIONS.

See S 1.4/3

S 1.5/2:nos.
MEMORANDUM TRANSMITTING MIMEOGRAPHED
INSERTS FOR FOREIGN SERVICE REGULA-
TIONS.

S 1.5/3:chap.nos.
FOREIGN SERVICE REGULATIONS (by chapters).

S 1.5/4:le-nos.
FOREIGN SERVICE MANUAL, TRANSMITTAL
LETTERS.

S 1.5/5:letters-nos.
FOREIGN SERVICE HANDBOOK TRANSMITTAL LET-
TERS.

S 1.5/6:v.nos.
FOREIGN AFFAIRS MANUAL.

S 1.5/6-2:nos.
FOREIGN AFFAIRS MANUAL CIRCULARS.

S 1.6:date
REGISTER, DEPARTMENT OF STATE.

Later S 1.69

S 1.7   • **Item 873**
FOREIGN SERVICE LIST. 1929–   [3 times a year]
(Publication 7802)

Lists field staffs of the U.S. Foreign Service,
the U.S. Information Agency, the Agency for International Development, the Peace Corps, and
the Foreign Agricultural Service of the Department of Agriculture. Also includes totals of Foreign Service posts by rank and the most recent
post changes.
ISSN 0015-7287

S 1.7/2:date   • **Item 864-B-2**
FOREIGN SERVICE CLASSIFICATION LIST. [Annual]

Includes all changes in rank effective with
the date of the publication, for Foreign Service
personnel of the Department of State.

S 1.8   • **Item 865 (EL)**
DIPLOMATIC LIST. 1893–   [Quarterly]

List of foreign missions in Washington arranged alphabetically by countries, including
names and addresses of diplomats. Also lists the
Chiefs of Missions in their order of precedence.
ISSN 0012-3099

S 1.8/2:date   • **Item 868-C**
EMPLOYEES OF DIPLOMATIC MISSIONS. [Quarterly]
(Publication 8522)

PURPOSE:– To list the employees of foreign
mission in Washington.
ISSN 0501-9664

S 1.9:date
COMMERCIAL REGULATIONS OF FOREIGN COUN-
TRIES.

Later S 4.1

S 1.10:date   • **Item 901-E**
INSTRUCTIONS TO DIPLOMATIC AND CONSULAR
OFFICERS.

S 1.10   • **Item 876-B-2**
ENVIRONMENTAL DIPLOMACY. [Annual]

S 1.11:date
OFFICIAL REGISTER. [Biennial]

Later I 1.25

S 1.12:date
LIST OF FOREIGN CONSULAR OFFICERS IN UNITED
STATES.

S 1.13:CT
AMERICAN FOREIGN SERVICE.

S 1.14:nos. • Item 901-J
MONTHLY POLITICAL REPORTS, CONFIDENTIAL.
CHANGES IN FOREIGN SERVICE.

S 1.15:CT
BLANK FORMS.

S 1.16:date
HAITIAN CUSTOMS RECEIVERSHIP. ANNUAL RE-
PORTS.

S 1.17:nos.
RUSSIAN SERIES (confidential).

S 1.18:nos.
REGULATIONS FOR CLERKS OF COURTS WHO TAKE
PASSPORT APPLICATIONS.

S 1.19:date
MAILING LIST OF CONSULAR SERVICE OF UNITED
STATES.

S 1.20:nos.
MONTHLY POLITICAL REPORT. [confidential]

S 1.21 • Item 876-C (MF)
TELEPHONE DIRECTORY. (3 times/yr.)

Covers Department of State, Agency for
International Development, and Arms Control and
Disarmament Agency.

S 1.21/2:CT • Item 876-C-1
DIRECTORIES. [Irregular]

S 1.22
INTERNATIONAL SCIENCE NOTES. [Quarterly]

Information on selected scientific problems
and activities as they relate to U.S. foreign policy.

S 1.22:date
AMERICAN HIGH COMMISSIONER TO HAITI.

S 1.23:date
HAITI, ANNUAL REPORTS OF FINANCIAL ADVISER-
GENERAL RECEIVER.

S 1.24:CT
GENERAL RECEIVER OF CUSTOMS FOR LIBERIA.

S 1.25:nos. • Item 877-B
PRESS RELEASES. [Weekly]

S 1.25/2 • Item 877-B
PRESS RELEASES. [Irregular]

Covers activities of the Department, international conferences, treaties, visits of foreign dig-
nitaries, addresses and statements of Departmental officials.

S 1.25/3:date
FOREIGN POLICY OUTLINES. – October 1974.

Superseded by Gist (S 1.128).

S 1.25/4:date • Item 877-B (MF)
SECRETARY OF STATE PRESS CONFERENCES.
[Irregular]

S 1.25/5:date
INTERVIEWS. [Irregular]

S 1.25/6:date • Item 877-A
STATEMENTS.

S 1.26 • Item 877
INTER-AMERICAN SERIES. 1–   1929–   [Irregu-
lar]

S 1.27:nos.
PASSPORT SERIES.

S 1.27/2
SUMMARY OF PASSPORT STATISTICS. [Quarterly]

ISSN 0565-9566

S 1.27/3:date
PASSPORT OFFICE [NEWSLETTER].

S 1.28:nos.
WESTERN EUROPEAN SERIES.

S 1.29:CT
PERMANENT COURT OF INTERNATIONAL JUSTICE.

S 1.30:date
PUBLICATIONS OF THE DEPARTMENT OF STATE,
QUARTERLY LIST.

S 1.30/2:date
RECENT RELEASES, SELECTED INFORMATION
MATERIALS. [Quarterly] (Office of Media Service,
Bureau of Public Affairs)

PURPOSE:– To list the important publications
and audio-visual materials available to the general public.
Formerly Selected Publications and Audio-
Visual Materials.

S 1.30/3:CT • Item 876-B-1
BIBLIOGRAPHIES AND LISTS OF PUBLICATIONS.

Formerly distributed to depository libraries under Item No. 886.

S 1.30/3-2:date • Item 876-B-1
SELECTED STATE DEPARTMENT PUBLICATIONS.
[Semiannual]

Earlier S 1.30/3

S 1.30/4
INVENTORY OF RECENT PUBLICATIONS AND
RESEARCH STUDIES IN THE FIELD OF INTER-
NATIONAL AND CULTURAL AFFAIRS. 1–
[Irregular] (CU reference Center, Public Informa-
tion and reports Staff, Bureau of Educational and
Cultural Affairs)

S 1.30/5:date/nos. • Item 876-B-1 (MF)
LIBRARY OF THE DEPARTMENT OF STATE, NEW
ACQUISITIONS FOR . . . [Monthly]

S 1.31:nos.
NEAR EASTERN SERIES.

S 1.32:CT
SPECIFICATIONS.

S 1.33:nos.
MAP SERIES.

S 1.33/2:CT • Item 864-B-6
MAPS AND ATLASES.

S 1.34:date
FOREIGN CONSULAR OFFICES IN THE U.S.
[Quarterly]

S 1.35:nos.
EASTERN EUROPEAN SERIES.

S 1.36:vol.
TERRITORIAL PAPERS OF UNITED STATES.

Later GS 4.14

S 1.37 • Item 862 (MF)
COMMERCIAL POLICY SERIES. 1–   1934–
[Irregular]

S 1.38:nos. • Item 870 (MF)
EAST ASIAN AND PACIFIC SERIES. 1–   1932–
[Irregular]

Prior to no. 154, designated Far Eastern Series.

VIET-NAM INFORMATION NOTES. 1–   1967–
[Irregular]

Short, factual, quick-reference briefing papers, each of which summarizes the most
significant available material on one important aspect of the situation in Viet-Nam.

S 1.39:nos.
IMMIGRATION SERIES.

S 1.40:CT • Item 888
REGULATIONS, RULES, AND INSTRUCTIONS.

S 1.40/2 • Item 876-B
HANDBOOKS, MANUALS, GUIDES.

S 1.40/2:Of 2 • Item 876-B
KEY OFFICERS OF FOREIGN SERVICE POSTS,
GUIDE FOR BUSINESSMEN. 1964–
[Quarterly]

Pocket-sized directory, prepared as an
aid to Americans with business interests
abroad, listing key officers of embassies,
missions, consulates general, and consulates, with whom business people would most
likely deal.
ISSN 0023-0790

S 1.40/3
CLERK OF COURT HANDBOOK ON PASS PORTS.

S 1.40/4 • Item 865-C
DISCUSSION GUIDE, TAPE-RECORDED DEPART-
MENT OF STATE BRIEFINGS. [Irregular]

Gives brief purpose and contents of the tape
recording, some discussion questions, and list of
reference material and related audiovisual materials.
Punched for ring binder. Each guide is 3 or 4
pages in length.

S 1.40/4-2 • Item 865-C
DISCUSSION GUIDES [to films]. [Irregular] (Office of
Media Services, Bureau of Public Affairs)

Brief guide to the documentary films produced
by or for the Department of State. Includes suggested reading list and references, as well as
additional audiovisual materials.

S 1.40/5:date • Item 876-B (EL)
KEY OFFICERS OF FOREIGN SERVICE POSTS.
[Semiannual]

Sub-title: Guide for Business Representatives
Earlier S 1.40/2:Of 2

S 1.40/6: • Item 876-B
ESCORT INTERPRETER MANUAL.

S 1.40/7: • Item 863-B (EL)
COUNTRY COMMERCIAL GUIDES. [Annual]

S 1.41:CT • Item 846-B-6
POSTERS.

S 1.42:v.nos.
RECORD. [Monthly]

Replaced by S 1.42/2

S 1.42/2:v.nos.
FIELD REPORTER. [Bimonthly]

Replaces S 1.42

S 1.43:nos.
REPORT TO CONGRESS ON LEND-LEASE OPERA-
TIONS. [Quarterly]

Earlier Pr 23.5809

S 1.44:nos.
REPORT TO CONGRESS ON OPERATIONS OF
UNRRA UNDER ACT OF MAR. 28, 1944. [Quar-
terly]

Earlier Pr 32.5812

S 1.44/2
CUMULATIVE REPORT ON FISCAL RELATIONS.

S 1.45:nos.
EUROPEAN SERIES.

S 1.46:CT
INTERIM INTERNATIONAL INFORMATION SERVICE
PUBLICATIONS.

S 1.47:date
REPORT TO CONGRESS ON FOREIGN SURPLUS
DISPOSAL. [Quarterly]

Earlier Y 3.W 19/7:20

S 1.48:CT
FOREIGN LIQUIDATION OFFICE PUBLICATIONS.

S 1.49:nos.
UNITED STATES AND UNITED NATIONS REPORT
  SERIES.

> No. 1 in this series was issued as Conference
> Series 82 (S 5.30:82).

S 1.50:nos.
UNITED STATES-UNITED NATIONS INFORMATION
  SERIES.

S 1.51:nos.
NEWSLETTER, HEALTH AND SANITATION DIVISION,
  INSTITUTE OF INTER-AMERICAN AFFAIRS.
  [Monthly]

> Earlier Pr 32.4610

S 1.52:nos.
REGISTER OF VISITORS. [Weekly]

S 1.53:CT
FOREIGN AFFAIRS BACKGROUND SUMMARY.

S 1.54:CT
FOREIGN TRADE [reports by States].

S 1.55:nos.
AMEPNKA. THIS IS A RUSSIAN EDITION OF
  AMERICA.

S 1.56:CT
INTERNATIONAL INFORMATION AND CULTURAL
  AFFAIRS OFFICE PUBLICATIONS.

S 1.57:nos.
OIR REPORTS.

S 1.57/2:nos.
INTELLIGENCE INFORMATION BRIEFS, IIB–   (series).

S 1.58:dt.&nos.
WIRELESS BULLETIN. [Daily except Sunday]

S 1.58/2:
IPS WIRELESS FILE. [Daily except Sat.]

> Supersedes S 1.58

S 1.59:dt.&nos.
AIR BULLETIN.

S 1.59/2:v.nos.
– ECONOMICS. [Weekly]

S 1.59/3:v.nos.
– LABOR. [Weekly]

S 1.59/4:v.nos.
– **U.S.A. LIFE. [Weekly]**

S 1.59/5:v.nos.
–WORLD AFFAIRS. [Fortnightly]

S 1.59/6:v.nos.
– AGRICULTURE. [Weekly]

S 1.59/7:v.nos.
– SCIENCE. [Weekly]

S 1.59/8:v.nos.
– CULTURAL. [Weekly]

S 1.60:nos.
[INFORMATION ARTICLES].

S 1.61:dt.&nos.
NEWS DIGEST. [Daily Monday through Friday]

S 1.62:nos.
MEMORANDUM FOR INFORMATION.

S 1.63:date
REPORT TO CONGRESS ON UNITED STATES FOR-
  EIGN RELIEF PROGRAM. [Quarterly]

> Earlier Y 3.Ec 74/3:9

S 1.64:CT
INSTITUTE OF INTER-AMERICAN AFFAIRS PUBLI-
  CATIONS.

> Earlier Pr 32.4615

S 1.64/2:CT
READING PROGRAM.

S 1.64/3:nos.
INTER-AMERICAN AFFAIRS INSTITUTE. BUILDING
  A BETTER HEMISPHERE SERIES, POINT 4 IN
  ACTION.

S 1.64/4:date
EDUCATION NEWSLETTER.

S 1.64/5:date
MONTHLY REPORT, FOOD SUPPLY DIVISION.

S 1.64/6:date
PROGRESS IN AGRICULTURE.

S 1.64/7:CT
COOPERATIVE HEALTH PROGRAM REPORTS.

S 1.65   **• Item 868**
ECONOMIC COOPERATION SERIES. 1–   1948–
  [Irregular]

S 1.66:date
INFORMATION SHEET. [Monthly]

S 1.67   **• Item 878**
INTERNATIONAL INFORMATION AND CULTURAL
  SERIES. 1–   1948–   [Irregular]

> The following sub-series is published on a
> recurring basis:

CULTURAL PRESENTATIONS USA, (year),
  REPORT TO CONGRESS AND THE PUBLIC.
  [Annual]

> Report to Congress by the Advisory Com-
> mittee on the Arts. Covers the fiscal year.
> Previous title: Cultural Presentation Pro-
> gram of the Department of State.

INTERNATIONAL EXCHANGE.

> Prior to 1967 entitled Educational and Cul-
> tural Diplomacy.

S 1.67/2:date
EDUCATIONAL AND CULTURAL EXCHANGE PRO-
  GRAM FISCAL YEAR, AMERICAN GRANTEES.

S 1.67/3:date
INTERAGENCY DIRECTORY, KEY CONTRACTS FOR
  PLANNING, SCIENTIFIC AND TECHNICAL EX-
  CHANGE PROGRAMS, EDUCATIONAL TRAVEL,
  STUDENTS, TEACHERS, LECTURES, RE-
  SEARCH SCHOLARS, SPECIALISTS.

> Earlier S 1.2:G 76/962

S 1.67/4:date   **• Item 1049-F**
DIRECTORY OF CONTACTS FOR INTERNATIONAL
  EDUCATIONAL, CULTURAL AND SCIENTIFIC
  EXCHANGE PROGRAMS.

> Continues: Directory of Frequent Contacts
> for International Educational, Cultural, Scientific
> and Technical Exchange Programs.
> Later ICA 1.12

S 1.68:nos.
NEWS LETTER FROM DIRECTOR GENERAL OF FOR-
  EIGN SERVICE. Restricted.

S 1.68/2:date   **• Item 863**
FOREIGN CONSULAR OFFICES IN THE UNITED
  STATES. [Annual]

> Formerly published in Department of Foreign
> Service Series (S 1.69)

S 1.69   **• Item 863 (MF)**
DEPARTMENT AND FOREIGN SERVICE SERIES. 1–
  1948–   [Irregular]

> Recurring sub-series included.

S 1.69   **• Item 877 & 863**
BIOGRAPHIC REGISTER. 1860–   [Annual]

> PURPOSE:– To provide biographic infor-
> mation on personnel of the Department of
> State and other Federal Government agen-
> cies in the field of foreign affairs. Biographies
> are included for Ambassadors, Ministers,
> Chiefs of Missions, Foreign Service officers,
> Foreign Service Information officers, Foreign
> Service Reserve officers, Foreign Service
> Staff officers, classes 1 through 4, and Civil
> Service employees of grade GS-12 and above.
> Also included are biographies for personnel
> of the U.S. Mission to the United Nations,
> Agency for International Development, the
> Peace Corps, the U.S. Information Agency,
> the U.S. Arms Control and Disarmament
> Agency, and the Foreign Agricultural Service
> of the Department of Agriculture.
> Prior to 1950, classified S 1.6

S 1.69   **• Item 863 & 871**
FOREIGN CONSULAR OFFICES IN THE UNITED
  STATES. [Annual]

> PURPOSE:– To provide a complete and
> official listing of the foreign consular offices
> in the United States, together with their juris-
> dictions and recognized personnel.

S 1.69:147   **• Item 863**
UNITED STATES CHIEFS OF MISSION 1778–
  1973. 1973. 229 p.

> Lists approximately 2,000 Chiefs of Mis-
> sion from 1778 through March 31, 1973. Ar-
> rangement is chronologically under country
> with data included for each person such as
> name, residence, career status, title,
> appointment,presentation of credentials, and
> termination of mission. Alphabetically name
> list included.

S 1.69:161   **• Item 863**
EAGLE AND THE SHIELD. 1976. 637 p. il.

> PURPOSE:– To tell the story of the great
> Seal of the United States. Beginning with the
> first committee on the subject in 1776 and
> carrying through to the latest revisions and
> controversies concerning the design, this
> volume chronicles the surprisingly complex
> history of the Great Seal, illuminating its many
> little-known intertwinings with great Americans
> and great events.

S 1.69:162   **• Item 863**
SECRETARIES OF STATE, PORTRAITS AND
  BIOGRAPHICAL SKETCHES. 1978. 125 p. il

S 1.69/2:date   **• Item 863 (EL)**
FOREIGN CONSULAR OFFICES IN THE UNITED
  STATES. [Annual]

S 1.70 • **Item 882-B**
INTERNATIONAL ORGANIZATION AND CONFERENCE
SERIES (1959–). 1– 1959– [Irregular]

Effective February 1959, the sub-series breakdown was discontinued, with all subsequent publications grouped in this new numbered series.

TRUST TERRITORY OF THE PACIFIC ISLANDS.
ANNUAL REPORT ON ADMINISTRATION OF
THE TERRITORY OF THE PACIFIC ISLANDS.
1st– 1947/48– [Annual]

Report transmitted by the United States
to the United Nations pursuant to article 88 of
the charter of the United Nations for the fiscal year.
Published 1948– 51 by the Department of
the Navy; 1952– 53 by the Department of the
Interior; 1954– by the Department of State.
Material contained in the report is supplied by the Navy and Interior Departments.

U.S. PARTICIPATION IN THE UNITED NATIONS,
REPORT BY THE PRESIDENT TO CON-
GRESS. [Annual]

PURPOSE:– To provide a comprehensive
survey of United States participation in the
work of the United Nations and the specialized agencies for the calendar year.
Also issued in the House Document series.

UNITED STATES CONTRIBUTIONS TO INTERNA-
TIONAL ORGANIZATIONS. 1st– 1952–
[Annual] (Bureau of International Organiza-
tion Affairs)

Also issued in the House Documents series.

S 1.70/1:nos.
INTERNATIONAL ORGANIZATION AND CONFERENCE
SERIES, GENERAL.

S 1.70/2:nos.
INTERNATIONAL ORGANIZATION AND CONFERENCE
SERIES II, REGIONAL.

S 1.70/3:nos.
INTERNATIONAL ORGANIZATION AND CONFERENCE
SERIES III, UNITED NATIONAL (including com-
missions).

S 1.70/4:nos.
INTERNATIONAL ORGANIZATION AND CONFERENCE
SERIES IV, SPECIALIZED AGENCIES.

S 1.70/5 • **Item 882-C**
INTERNATIONAL ORGANIZATION SERIES. 1–
1968– [Irregular]

PURPOSE:– To provide the American public
with authentic information about international organization of particular interest to U.S. foreign
relations.
Each pamphlet provides information on the
origin of the organization; its membership and
administration; its principal accomplishments,
current problems and future plans; the extent
and nature of U.S. interest and/or participation;
and maps, charts, and other illustrative materials
as appropriate.

S 1.70/6:date
SCHEDULE OF INTERNATIONAL CONFERENCES.
[Quarterly] (Office of International Conferences,
Bureau of International Organization Affairs)

S 1.70/7:date • **Item 882-B (MF)**
TRUST TERRITORY OF THE PACIFIC ISLANDS.
[Annual]

S 1.70/8:date • **Item 882-B (MF)**
UNITED STATES PARTICIPATION IN THE UNITED
NATIONS. [Annual]

S 1.70/9:date • **Item 882-B**
UNITED STATES CONTRIBUTIONS TO INTER-
NATIONAL ORGANIZATIONS. [Annual]

S 1.71 • **Item 875**
GENERAL FOREIGN POLICY SERIES. 1– 1948–
[Irregular]

The following sub-series are published on a
recurring basis:

UNITED STATES FOREIGN POLICY. [Annual]

Annual report of the Secretary of State to
Congress covering the progress of U.S. diplomacy during the year. It includes sections
on international economic policy, disarmament, international social and scientific policy
and U.S. relations with Europe, Asia, the
Middle East, and Africa. The Secretary's report also discusses U.S. efforts to strengthen
international laws and institutions, including
the United Nations. It concludes with an annex comprised of the tests of selected documents, agreements, and policy statements
made.

S 1.71/2 • **Item 875**
AMERICAN FOREIGN POLICY, CURRENT DOCU-
MENTS. 1956– [Annual]

An annual, one-volume compilation of the principal published official papers, selected to indicate the scope, goals, and implementation of the
foreign policy of the United States.
The materials included in each volume are
arranged in 14 parts– one on overall policy, one
on the United Nations and international law, seven
on developments in particular regions and countries, one on disarmament, atomic energy, and
related developments, three on trade, foreign
assistance, international development, and educational and cultural exchange programs, and
one on the Department of State.
The following two publications provide compilations for years prior to 1956:–

A Decade of American Foreign Policy: Basic Document, 1941-49. (Senate Document 123, 81st
Congress) 1950.

American Foreign Policy, 1950-55: Basic Documents. 2 v. 1957. (publ. 6446)

S 1.71/2-2:date • **Item 875 (MF)**
AMERICAN FOREIGN POLICY CURRENT DOCU-
MENTS (Supplement). [Annual]

S 1.71/3:nos. • **Item 868-B**
ECONOMIC FOREIGN POLICY SERIES. 1– 1970–

S 1.71/4:nos. • **Item 877-C**
CURRENT POLICY (series). 1– [Irregular]

Individual issues of the Current Policy Series
are usually designated as a sub-series within the
major series issued by the Department of State.
This class number has been assigned for those
Current Policy publications not assigned to any
major series.

S 1.71/4-2:nos. • **Item 877-C**
CURRENT POLICY DIGEST. [Monthly]

S 1.71/5:CT • **Item 876-A-3**
PUBLIC INFORMATION SERIES. [Irregular]

Each issue concerns a different subject.

S 1.71/6 • **Item 877-C**
REGIONAL BRIEF.

S 1.72:nos.
CURRENT DEVELOPMENTS REPORT ON EUROPEAN
RECOVERY.

S 1.73:v.nos.
DOCUMENTS AND STATE PAPERS. [Monthly]

S 1.74 • **Item 869**
EUROPEAN AND BRITISH COMMONWEALTH SE-
RIES. 1– 1948– [Irregular]

S 1.75:date
FOREIGN AFFAIRS HIGHLIGHTS. [Monthly]

S 1.76:nos.
STANDARDIZED GOVERNMENT CIVILIAN ALLOW-
ANCE REGULATIONS, ALLOWANCE CIRCULARS.

S 1.76/2:
STANDARDIZED GOVERNMENT POST DIFFER-
ENTIAL REGULATIONS, DIFFERENTIAL
CIRCULARS.

S 1.76/3:nos. • **Item 888 (EL)**
STANDARDIZED REGULATIONS (Government Civilians, Foreign Areas). [Irregular]

S 1.76/3-2:supp.nos. • **Item 888 (EL)**
MAXIMUM TRAVEL PER DIEM ALLOWANCES FOR
FOREIGN AREAS. [Monthly]

S 1.76/4:date/nos. • **Item 768-M (EL)**
U.S. DEPARTMENT OF STATE INDEXES OF LIVING
COSTS ABROAD, ETC. [Quarterly]

Earlier L 2.101

S 1.77:nos.
PRESS FEATURE.

S 1.77/2:CT
SPECIAL PRESS FEATURE.

S 1.78:nos.
MAGAZINE REPRINTS.
Later IA 1.10

S 1.79:date
WEEK IN THE UNITED STATES.

S 1.80:date
WEEKLY ROUNDUPS, ECONOMIC LETTER.

S 1.81:nos.
CURRENT REVIEWS OF ECONOMIC AND SOCIAL
PROBLEMS IN UNITED NATIONS.

S 1.82:ser.le&v.nos. • **Item 866**
DOCUMENTS ON GERMAN POLICY 1918– 54.

S 1.82/2:ser.le&nos.
AKTEN ZUR DEUTSCHEN AUSWARTIGEN POLITIC,
1918– 45, GERMAN EDITION OF S 1.82.

S 1.83:nos.
NEGRO NOTES.

S 1.84:letters-nos.
INFORMATION NOTES.

S 1.85:date
INFORMATION BULLETIN, OFFICE OF U.S. HIGH
COMMISSIONER FOR GERMANY. [Monthly]
Earlier M 105.8

S 1.86 • **Item 883**
NEAR AND MIDDLE EASTERN SERIES. 1– 1948–
[Irregular]

S 1.86/2:nos. • **Item 883-A**
NEAR EAST AND SOUTH ASIAN SERIES. 1– 1973–
[Irregular]

S 1.87:nos.
VISITING EXPERT SERIES.

Earlier M 105.9

S 1.88:nos.
OFFICIAL GAZETTE OF ALLIED HIGH COMMISSION
FOR GERMANY.

S 1.89:nos.
REPORT OF UNITED STATES HIGH COMMIS-
SIONER, U.S. ELEMENT, ALLIED COMMISSION
FOR AUSTRIA. [Quarterly]

Earlier M 105.10

S 1.89/2:nos.
REPORT OF UNITED STATES HIGH COMMIS-
SIONER, STATISTICAL ANNEX, U.S. ELEMENT,
ALLIED COMMISSION FOR AUSTRIA. [Quarterly]

Earlier M 105.10

S 1.89/3:date
REPORT OF AUSTRIA, OFFICE OF U.S. HIGH COM-
MISSIONER FOR AUSTRIA.

S 1.89/4:CT
OFFICE OF UNITED STATES HIGH COMMISSIONER
FOR AUSTRIA. GENERAL PUBLICATIONS.

S 1.90:nos.
QUARTERLY REPORT ON GERMANY, OFFICE OF
U.S. HIGH COMMISSIONER FOR GERMANY.

S 1.91:CT
OFFICE OF U.S. HIGH COMMISSIONER FOR GER-
MAN PUBLICATIONS.

S 1.91/2:date
– QUARTERLY ECONOMIC AND FINANCIAL
REVIEW: FEDERAL REPUBLIC OF GERMANY &
WESTERN SECTORS OF BERLIN.

S 1.91/3:date
– HANDBOOK OF ECONOMIC STATISTICS.

S 1.91/4:nos.
GERMAN SCIENCE BULLETIN.

S 1.92:nos.
BIBLIOGRAPHY.

   Changed from S 1.2:B 47/2

S 1.92/2:nos.
SOVIET BIBLIOGRAPHY. [Fortnightly]

   Changed from S 1.2:B 47/2

S 1.92/3
BIBLIOGRAPHIC LISTS.

S 1.92/4
INTERNATIONAL POLITICS, SELECTIVE MONTHLY
BIBLIOGRAPHY. v. 1– 1956– [Monthly]

   Libraries only

S 1.93:date
UNITED STATES ADVISORY COMMISSION ON
INFORMATION, SEMIANNUAL REPORT TO
CONGRESS.

S 1.94:nos.
NEWS NOTES ON SPECIAL AREAS. [Monthly]

S 1.95:CT
HISTORICAL MONOGRAPHS OF OFFICE OF U.S.
HIGH COMMISSIONER FOR GERMANY.

S 1.96:
RESEARCH PROJECTS.

S 1.97:date
UNITED STATES POLICY TOWARD USSR AND
INTERNATIONAL COMMUNISM, MONTHLY DI-
GEST OF PERTINENT DATA APPEARING IN
DEPARTMENT OF STATE PUBLICATIONS.

S 1.98   • **Item 871-A**
FOREIGN POLICY BRIEFS. [Fortnightly]

   Concise, single-sheet summary of significant
foreign policy developments and background
material on current policy problems, drawing on
information sources of all foreign affairs agencies of the Government.

S 1.99:CT
ADVISORY COMMITTEE ON VOLUNTARY FOREIGN
AID PUBLICATIONS.

S 1.99/2:date
REPORT OF CLASSIFIED PROGRAM OF EXPORTS
AND VALUE BY AMERICAN AGENCIES VOLUN-
TARILY REGISTERED WITH ADVISORY
COMMITTEE ON VOLUNTARY FOREIGN AID.
[Quarterly]

   Changed from Y 3.Ad 9/4:4

S 1.99/3:date
SUMMARY STATEMENT OF INCOME AND EXPENDI-
TURES OF VOLUNTARY RELIEF AGENCIES REG-
ISTERED WITH ADVISORY COMMITTEE ON
VOLUNTARY FOREIGN AID. [Quarterly]
   Later FO 1.22

S 1.100:nos.
USIS FEATURE.

S 1.100/2:CT
USIS FEATURE, SPECIAL.

S 1.100/3:CT
USIS PUBLICATONS.

S 1.101:nos.
EXTERNAL RESEARCH REPORT, RESEARCH LISTS.

S 1.101/2:nos.
EXTERNAL RESEARCH REPORTS, ER-(series)
OFFICIAL USE.

S 1.101/3:nos.
EXTERNAL RESEARCH PAPERS.

S 1.101/4:nos.
EXTERNAL RESEARCH REPORT, MEMORANDUMS,
ERM(series). Official Use.

S 1.101/5:nos.
EXTERNAL RESEARCH REPORTS, POLICY RE-
SEARCH BRIEF, PRB- (series). Official Use.

S 1.101/6:nos.
LIST OF CURRENT STUDIES, BR (series).

S 1.101/7:nos.
RESEARCH MEMORANDUM RSB (series).

S 1.101/7-2
RESEARCH MEMORANDUMS. RES 1– [Irregular]

S 1.101/7-3:nos.
RESEARCH MEMORANDUM REU– (series).

S 1.101/7-4:nos.
RESEARCH MEMORANDUM FRE– (series).

S 1.101/8:CT
POLICY RESEARCH STUDIES.

S 1.101/9:date
GOVERNMENT-SUPPORTED RESEARCH, INTER-
NATIONAL AFFAIRS, RESEARCH COMPLETED
AND IN PROGRESS. [Annual fiscal year] (Office
of External Research)

S 1.101/10:date   • **Item 869-D**
GOVERNMENT-SUPPORTED RESEARCH ON
FOREIGN AFFAIRS, CURRENT PROJECT INFOR-
MATION. 1975– 1981. [Annual]

S 1.101/11:letters-nos.
EXTERNAL RESEARCH STUDIES.

S 1.101/12:letters-nos.
RESEARCH STUDIES.

S 1.102:nos.
SOVIET UNION AS REPORTED BY FORMER SO-
VIET CITIZENS, REPORTS.

S 1.102/2:nos.
SOVIET AFFAIRS NOTE.

S 1.102/3:nos.
REPORT ON EXCHANGE WITH SOVIET UNION AND
EASTERN EUROPE.

S 1.103:
CALENDAR FOR HEARINGS CONCERNING TRADE
AGREEMENTS.

S 1.104:date
CALENDAR OR TRADE AGREEMENTS.

S 1.105:CT
FACTS ABOUT POINT 4.

S 1.106   • **Item 877-A (MF)**
ADDRESSES. [Irregular]

S 1.106/2
PUBLIC SERVICE OFFICE, S- (series). 1– [Irregu-
lar]

   Reprints of speeches made by State Department officials, issued in printed pamphlet for wide
distribution.

S 1.107:CT
QUESTIONS AND ANSWERS.

S 1.108:nos.
BACKGROUND NOTES. [Irregular]

S 1.109:
FOREIGN SERVICE NEWS LETTER. [Monthly]

S 1.110:CT
REFUGEE RELIEF PROGRAM.

S 1.111
WORLD STRENGTH OF THE COMMUNIST PARTY
ORGANIZATIONS, ANNUAL REPORT. 1st–
1948– [Annual] (Bureau of Intelligence and
Research)

   PURPOSE:– To provide brief tabular and narrative account for each communist party.
   A checklist of communist parties precedes
the full regional tabulation so as to give the reader
a quick view of certain basic information.

S 1.112:
AMERICAN CONSULATE GENERAL, HONG KONG.
INDEX OF CHINESE MAINLAND PRESS.

S 1.112/2
AMERICAN CONSUALATE GENERAL, HONG KONG.

   Abstracts of Chinese Mainland Press.

S 1.112/3
AMERICAN CONSULATE GENERAL, HONG KONG.

   Surveys of Chinese Mainland Press.

S 1.113:nos.
BIOGRAPHIC DIRECTORIES.

S 1.113/2:nos.
BIOGRAPHIC REFERENCE AIDS, BA (series).

S 1.113/3:nos.
INTELLIGENCE RESEARCH AIDS.

   Later PrEx 3.11

S 1.114:
FOREIGN SERVICE INSTITUTE. QUARTERLY PRO-
JECTION OF COURSES.

S 1.114/2:CT   • **Item 872-A (MF)**
FOREIGN SERVICE INSTITUTE: BASIC COURSE SE-
RIES.

S 1.114/2-2:CT   • **Item 872-A (MF)**
FOREIGN SERVICE INSTITUTE, READERS.

S 1.114/3:CT   • **Item 872-A (MF)**
FOREIGN SERVICE INSTITUTE, GENERAL PUBLI-
CATIONS.

S 1.114/3-10:date   • **Item 872-A (MF)**
FOREIGN SERVICE INSTITUTE: SCHEDULE OF
COURSES. [Annual]

S 1.114/3-11:nos.   • **Item 872-A**
FOREIGN SERVICE INSTITUTE: BULLETIN.

S 1.114/3-12:nos.   • **Item 872-A**
FOREIGN SERVICE INSTITUTE: CENTER PAPER.

S 1.114/4:date
FOREIGN SERVICE INSTITUTE BULLETIN.

S 1.115:v.nos.&nos.
AMERICAN EMBASSY, ROME: QUARTERLY STATIS-
TICAL BULLETIN.

S 1.116   • **Item 862-A**
AFRICAN SERIES. 1– 1960– [Irregular]

S 1.117:date
DOCUMENTS ON DISARMAMENT.

Later AC 1.11/2

S 1.117/2:nos.
DISARMAMENT SERIES.

S 1.117/3:nos.
DISARMAMENT DOCUMENT SERIES. (Disarmament Administration)

Earlier publications entitled Disarmament Briefs.
Later AC 1.11

S 1.117/4:nos.
DISARMAMENT BRIEFS.

S 1.117/5:nos. • **Item 862-C**
ARMS CONTROL AND DISARMAMENT, STUDIES IN PROGRESS OR RECENTLY COMPLETED.

S 1.118:nos. • **Item 864-B (EL)**
STATE. [Monthly]

PURPOSE:– To acquaint the Department's personnel, both at home and abroad, with developments of interest which may affect operations or personnel.
Indexed by: Index to U.S. Government Periodicals.
Former title: Department of State Newsletter prior to the January 1981 issue.
ISSN 0041-7629

S 1.118/2: • **Item 864-B-8**
UPDATE FROM STATE. [Bimonthly]

PURPOSE– To provide a fresh look at the modern diplomacythat is leading the world into the 21st century. It informs about what Foreign Service and State Department Personnel are doing and thinking and to explorethe full range of international affairs through their eyes and ears.

S 1.119
GEOGRAPHIC REPORTS. 1– [Irregular] (Office of the Geographer)

S 1.119/2 • **Item 876-A**
GEOGRAPHIC BULLETINS. 1– 1963– [Irregular] (prepared by the Office of the Geographer)

Studies relative to the political entities of the world including factual information on the independence of political areas and pertinent information about them.

S 1.119/3 • **Item 876-A-2**
INTERNATIONAL BOUNDARY STUDIES. 1– 1961– [Irregular] (prepared by the Office of the Geographer)

PURPOSE:– To provide background information on international boundaries and act as guides to federal mapping agencies in representation of international boundaries in accordance with United States policy.

S 1.119/4:nos. • **Item 876-A-2**
GEOGRAPHIC AND GLOBAL ISSUES. 1– 1964– [Quarterly] (Prepared by the Office of the Geographer)

PURPOSE:– To provide information on the changes in the world sovereignty patterns– A newly independent country name, a change of capital, a change in first order civil divisions.
Earlier title: Geographic Notes, GE- (series).

S 1.119/5:nos. • **Item 876-A-4**
LIMITS IN THE SEAS (series). 1– [Irregular]

Issued by the Office of Geographer of the Department's Bureau of Intelligence and Research.
PURPOSE:– To to set forth the basis for national arrangements for the measurement of marine areas of the division of the maritime areas of coastal states.

S 1.120:nos.
ACQUISITIONS LIST OF ANTARCTIC CARTOGRAPHIC MATERIALS.

S 1.121:date
FORECAST OF CITIZEN DEPARTURES TO EUROPE. OFFICIAL USE.

S 1.122:date/nos.
INTERNATIONAL SCIENCE NOTES.

S 1.123 • **Item 862-B (EL)**
BACKGROUND NOTES. [Irregular]

Short, factual pamphlets about individual countries and territories, written by officers in the Department of State's geographic bureaus and edited and published by the General Publications Division.
Each Note includes information on the country's land, people, history, government, political conditions, economy, and foreign relations. Included also is a map and usually a brief bibliography.
There are about 150 "Notes" in the series with approximately 75 being revised each year.
The Superintendent of Documents provides the following subscription services for the Background Notes:
Complete set of all currently in stock (without binder).
One-year subscription to updated issues (without binder).
Binder.
Indexed by: Index to U.S. Government Periodicals.
ISSN 0501-9966

S 1.123/2:date • **Item 862-B (EL)**
BACKGROUND NOTES: INDEX. [Irregular]

S 1.123/3:date
BACKGROUND NOTES: INDEX. [Monthly Mailings]

This class established for sales purposes only. Individual publications will be classified S 1.123.

S 1.124:nos. • **Item 862-E**
CENTER FOR INTERNATIONAL SYSTEMS RESEARCH: OCCASIONAL PAPERS.

S 1.125 • **Item 869-A**
FAR [Far Area Research] HORIZONS. v. 1– 10. 1968– 1977. [Quarterly] (published by the Office of External Research for the Interagency Foreign Area Research Coordination Group)

PURPOSE:– To promote communications between U.S. Government agencies which sponsor science research in foreign affairs and the academic and other private individuals and institutions engaged in such research.
Includes list of recent publications of interest.
Indexed by: Index to U.S. Government Periodicals.
ISSN 0532-1255

S 1.126:date/nos. • **Item 869-B**
FOREIGN AFFAIRS RESEARCH PAPERS AVAILABLE. [Monthly] (Office of External Research)

PURPOSE:– To provide a monthly accessions list of foreign affairs research papers as received by the Foreign Affairs Research Documentation Center.
Temporarily discontinued with issue for Feb. 1979 [MC 80-1460].
ISSN 0092-9492

S 1.126/2:CT • **Item 869-B**
FOREIGN AFFAIRS RESEARCH SPECIAL PAPERS AVAILABLE. [Annual] (Foreign Affairs Research Documentation Center)

Issued for the Following areas:
American Republics (S 1.126/2:Am 3).
Near East, South Asia, and North Africa (S 1.126/2:Ea 7/3).

S 1.126/3: • **Item 869-B-1**
FOREIGN AFFAIRS NOTES. [Irregular]

S 1.127:CT • **Item 869-C**
POST REPORTS [Various Countries]. [Irregular]

Also published in microfiche.

S 1.128:CT • **Item 864-B-4**
GIST. [Irregular]

PURPOSE:– To provide a series of quick reference aids to U.S. foreign relations.
Supersedes Foreign Policy Outlines (S 1.25/3)
ISSN 0364-2623

S 1.128/2:date • **Item 864-B-4**
GIST INDEX. [Irregular]

S 1.129:nos. • **Item 864-B-1**
SPECIAL REPORTS. [Irregular]

SEMIANNUAL REPORT, IMPLEMENTATION OF HELSINKI ACCORD. 1st– 1975–

7th. June 1– Nov. 30, 1979. Sr 62

S 1.129/2:date • **Item 864-B-1 (MF)**
IMPLEMENTATION OF HELSINKI FINAL ACT. [Annual]

Earlier S 1.129

S 1.130:CT
SECRETARY OF STATE'S ADVISORY COMMITTEE ON PRIVATE INTERNATIONAL LAW: PUBLICATIONS. [Irregular]

S 1.130/2:CT
[ANNUAL REPORTS OF ADVISORY COMMITTEES.]

S 1.130/2:In 8
COMMITTEE ON INTERNATIONAL INTELLECTUAL PROPERTY.

S 1.130/2:L 41
PANEL OF INTERNATIONAL LAW.

S 1.130/2:Oc 2
OCEAN AFFAIRS ADVISORY COMMITTEE.

S 1.130/2:Sci 2
ADVISORY COMMITTEE ON SCIENCE AND FOREIGN AFFAIRS.

S 1.130/2:Sh 6
SHIPPING COORDINATING COMMITTEE.

S 1.131:nos. • **Item 876-A-1 (MF)**
SELECTED DOCUMENTS (series). 1– [Irregular]

Documents deal with foreign policy in such areas as human rights, the Panama Canal treaties, and policy toward China. Series includes only those selected documents that are not identified as being in other Department of State series.

S 1.132:date
ACTION IN THE UNITED STATES OF AMERICA RELATED TO STRATOSPHERIC MONITORING. [Semiannual]

S 1.133:CT • **Item 864-B-3 (MF)**
ENVIRONMENTAL IMPACT STATEMENTS. [Irregular]

S 1.134:v.nos.&nos.
AF PRESS CLIPS. [Irregular]

Consists of reprints of articles from non-government newspapers on subjects of concern to the Bureau of African Affairs in carrying out its work.

S 1.134/2:v.nos.&nos.
ARA NEWS ROUNDUP. (Bureau of Inter-American Affairs)

PURPOSE:– To present reprints of articles from non-government newspapers on subjects concerning the Bureau's work.

S 1.135:v.nos.&nos.
NATO REVIEW. [Bimonthly]

Published for U.S. distribution by the Atlantic Council of the United States and by the State Department. Contains articles intended to contribute to a constructive discussion of Atlantic problems.

S 1.136:CT
BOARD OF APPELLATE REVIEW.

S 1.137:   • Item 863-A
FOREIGN SERVICE WRITTEN EXAMINATION REGISTRATION AND APPLICATION FORM. [Irregular]

Contains registration information about the Foreign Service written examination and an application form for registering to take the examination. Designed for the Foreign Service Officer candidate only.
Earlier S 1.69

S 1.138:date   • Item 876-A-6 (P) (EL)
PATTERNS OF GLOBAL TERRORISM. [Annual]

Presents information on patterns of terrorism wherever it occurs throughout the world.

S 1.138/2:date   • Item 876-A-7 (P) (EL)
SIGNIFICANT INCIDENTS OF POLITICAL VIOLENCE AGAINST AMERICANS.

S 1.139:date   • Item 863-A (MF)
TRAINING OPPORTUNITIES, COURSE CURRICULUM CATALOG. [Annual]

S 1.139/2:date   • Item 863-A
DIPLOMATIC SECURITY TRAINING RESOURCES, ETC. FISCAL YEAR . . .

S 1.140:nos.   • Item 882-B
FOCUS ON CENTRAL AND EASTERN EUROPE. [Irregular]

S 1.141:v.nos./nos.   • Item 863-A-1
DEFENSE TRADE NEWS. [Quarterly]

S 1.142   • Item 863-B (E)
ELECTRONIC PRODUCTS. [Irregular]

S 1.142/2   • Item 863-B (E)
U.S. FOREIGN AFFAIRS ON CD-ROM. [Irregular]

Issued on CD-ROM.

S 1.143:nos.   • Item 863-C
FORMS. (Institute of Inter-American Affairs)

S 1.144:date   • Item 863-A-1 (MF)
GSO NEWSLINE. [Quarterly]

S 1.145:v.nos./nos.   • Item 863-A-1 (MF) (EL)
U.S. MAB BULLETIN. [Quarterly]

S 1.146   • Item 876-A-6 (EL)
INTERNATIONAL NARCOTICS CONTROL STRATEGY REPORT. [Annual]

S 1.147   • Item 864-B-1 (MF)
ANNUAL REPORTS TO THE GOVERNMENTS OF CANADA, U.S., SASKATCHEWAN AND MONTANA BY THE POPLAR RIVER BILATERAL MONITORING COMMITTEE.

S 1.148:date   • Item 876-A-8
HIDDEN KILLERS. [Irregular]

S 1.149:   • Item 876-A-9
GLOBAL CRIME. [Annual]

S 1.150   • Item 876-A-10 (P) (EL)
FORECAST CONTRACT OPPORTUNITIES. [Annual]

S 1.151   • Item 876-A-11 (EL)
ANNUAL REPORT ON INTERNATIONAL RELIGIOUS FREEDOM (Bureau for Democracy, Human Rights and Labor).

S 1.152   • Item 876-A-12 (EL)
VICTIMS OF TRAFFICKING AND VIOLENCE PROTECTION ACT: 2000, TRAFFICKING IN PERSONS REPORT. [Annual]

AMERICAN REPUBLIC BUREAU

This class (S 2) was assigned to the SuDocs Classification Scheme but apparently was never used.
See also AR

ARBITRATION AND MIXED COMMISSIONS TO SETTLE INTERNATIONAL DISPUTES

S 3.2:CT   • Item 889
GENERAL PUBLICATIONS.

S 3.5:CT
COMMISSION APPOINTED TO EXAMINE FRENCH SPOILATION CLAIMS PRESENTED UNDER TREATY WITH FRANCE OF JULY 4, 1831.

S 3.6:CT
FRENCH AND AMERICAN CLAIMS COMMISSION, 1880– 84.

S 3.7/1:nos.
FUR SEAL ARBITRATION, PARIS, 1893.

S 3.7/1a:CT
FUR SEAL ARBITRATION, PARIS, 1893 (separates).

S 3.7/2:CT
BERING SEA CLAIMS COMMISSION, 1896– 97.

S 3.8:CT
GREAT BRITAIN AND UNITED STATES CLAIMS COMMISSION.

S 3.9:CT
JOINT COMMISSION ON HUDSON'S BAY AND PUGET'S SOUND.

Agricultural Companies Claims.

S 3.10/1:CT
NORTHEASTERN BOUNDARY ARBITRATION.

S 3.10/2:CT
NORTHWESTERN BOUNDARY COMMISSION, 1957– 61.

S 3.10/3:CT
NORTHERN BOUNDARY COMMISSION, 1872– 76.

S 3.10/3a:CT
– SEPARATES.

S 3.11:CT
COMMISSION TO ARBITRATE CLAIMS OF VENEZUELA STEAM TRANSPORTATION COMPANY OF NEW YORK AGAINST VENEZUELA.

S 3.12:CT
UNITED STATES AND MEXICAN CLAIMS COMMISSION, 1869– 76.

S 3.13:
ARBITRATIONS UNDER TREATY OF WASHINGTON.

S 3.13/1:
GENEVA ARBITRATION (Alabama Claims).

S 3.13/2:CT
WASHINGTON ARBITRATION (American-British Mixed Claims Commission).

S 3.13/3:CT
BERLIN ARBITRATION (Northwestern Boundary).

S 3.13/4:CT
HALIFAX COMMISSION (Fishery Commission).

S 3.14:CT
U.S. v. SALVADOR ARBITRATION TRIBUNAL.

S 3.15:CT
COSTA RICA-NICARAGUA BOUNDARY ARBITRATION.

S 3.16/1:CT
ALASKAN-CANADIAN BOUNDARY COMMISSION, 1892– 95.

S 3.16/2:CT
ALASKAN BOUNDARY TRIBUNAL, 1903.

S 3.17:CT
VENEZUELAN MIXED CLAIMS COMMISSIONS, CARACAS 1902 AND 1903.

S 3.18:
PERMANENT COURT OF ARBITRATION, THE HAGUE.

S 3.18/1:CT
– PIOUS FUND OF THE CALIFORNIAS.

S 3.18/2:CT
– VENEZUELAN ARBITRATION.

S 3.18/3:CT
– NORTH ATLANTIC COAST FISHERIES ARBITRATION.

S 3.18/3a:CT
– SEPARATES.

S 3.18/4:CT
– UNITED STATES-VENEZUELA ARBITRATION ON BEHALF OF ORINOCO STEAMSHIP COMPANY.

S 3.18/5:CT
UNITED STATES-NORWAY ARBITRATION.

S 3.18/6:CT
– ISLAND OF PALMAS ARBITRATION.

S 3.19/1:CT
MEXICAN BOUNDARY SURVEY, 1882– 96.

S 3.19/2:CT
MEXICAN BOUNDARY COMMISSION, 1889–

S 3.19/3:CT
INTERNATIONAL BOUNDARY COMMISSION, U.S.-MEXICO. CHAMIZAL ARBITRATION.

S 3.19/4:CT
INTERNATIONAL COMMISSION FOR EQUITABLE DISTRIBUTION OF WATER OF RIO GRANDE.

S 3.20:CT
ARGENTINA-BRAZIL BOUNDARY ARBITRATION.

S 3.21/1:
UNITED STATES v. CHILE, ARBITRATION OF CASE OF BRIG. MACEDONIAN.

S 3.21/2:CT
UNITED STATES AND CHILEAN CLAIMS COMMISSION, 1892– 94.

S 3.21/3:CT
UNITED STATES AND CHILEAN CLAIMS COMMISSION, 1900– 01.

S 3.21/4:CT
UNITED STATES v. CHILE, ALSOP CLAIMS.

S 3.22:CT
SPANISH-AMERICAN PEACE COMMISSION.

S 3.23:CT
INTERNATIONAL JOINT COMMISSION ON BOUNDARY WATERS BETWEEN UNITED STATES AND CANADA, 1909.

S 3.24:CT
INTERNATIONAL (Canadian) BOUNDARY COMMISSIONS.

S 3.25:   • Item 889-A (MF)
ANNUAL REPORT.
        Annual Joint Report from the International
Boundary Commissioners of the Canadian Section and the U.S. Section of the Commission.
Summarizes activities of the Commission, which
keeps the U.S.- Canadian boundary clear and
well marked and makes regulatory decisions on
proposed projects that cross or adjoin the boundary.

S 3.26:CT
CANADIAN-AMERICAN FISHERIES COMMISSION,
1893– 96.

S 3.27:CT
AMERICAN-CANADIAN FISHERIES CONFERENCE,
1918.

S 3.28:CT
PEACE CONFERENCE, PARIS, 1919.

S 3.29:
CONFERENCE ON LIMITATION OF ARMAMENT, WASH-
INGTON, 1921– 22.

S 3.29/1:date
REPORT OF AMERICAN DELEGATION.

S 3.29/2:CT
GENERAL PUBLICATIONS.

S 3.29/3
BULLETINS.

S 3.29/4
CIRCULARS.

S 3.29/5:date
[FINAL PROCEEDINGS.]

S 3.29/5a:CT
– SEPARATES.

S 3.29/6:nos.
[PROCEEDINGS] (Individual sessions).

S 3.30:CT
LAND JOINT COMMISSION, UNITED STATES AND
PANAMA.

S 3.31:
MIXED CLAIMS COMMISSION, UNITED STATES AND
GERMANY.

S 3.31/1:date
ANNUAL REPORTS.

S 3.31/2:CT
GENERAL PUBLICATIONS.

S 3.31/3
BULLETINS.

S 3.31/4
CIRCULARS.

S 3.31/5:CT
PAPERS IN RE.

S 3.31/6:date
ADMINISTRATIVE DECISIONS.

S 3.31/7:nos.
AMERICAN COMMISSIONER, DECISION NO.
    (decisions fixing fees).

S 3.32:CT
INTERNATIONAL CONFERENCE ON MARITIME LAW.
    BRUSSELS, 1922.

S 3.33:CT
AMERICAN AND BRITISH CLAIMS ARBITRATION.

S 3.34:date
MIXED CLAIMS COMMISSIONS, UNITED STATES
AND MEXICO. ANNUAL REPORT.

S 3.34/1:date
ANNUAL REPORTS.

S 3.34/2:CT
GENERAL PUBLICATIONS.

S 3.34/3:
BULLETINS.

S 3.34/4:
CIRCULARS.

S 3.34/5:CT
PAPERS IN RE.

S 3.34/6:date
– OPINIONS AND DECISIONS.

S 3.34/6a:CT
– SEPARATES, DECISIONS OF SPECIAL
    MEXICAN CLAIMS COMMISSIONS.

S 3.35:CT
ARBITRATION BETWEEN REPUBLIC OF CHILE AND
    REPUBLIC OF PERU WITH RESPECT TO UN-
    FULFILLED PROVISIONS OF TREATY OF PEACE
    OF OCT. 20, 1883, UNDER PROTOCOL AND SUPP.
    ACT. SIG. WASH. JULY 20, 1922.

S 3.36:CT
COMMISSION ON EXTRATERRITORIAL JURISDIC-
    TION IN CHINA.

S 3.37:
TRIPARTITE CLAIMS COMMISSION (U.S., Austria,
    and Hungary).

S 3.37/1:date
REPORT.

S 3.37/2:CT
GENERAL PUBLICATIONS.

S 3.37/3:
BULLETINS.

S 3.37/4:
CIRCULARS.

S 3.37/5:CT
PAPERS IN RE.

S 3.37/6:nos.
ADMINISTRATIVE DECISIONS.

S 3.37/6a:CT
– SEPARATES.

S 3.38:CT
INTERNATIONAL CONFERENCE OF AMERICAN
    STATES ON CONCILIATION AND ARBITRATION,
    WASHINGTON, DEC. 10, 1928– Jan. 5, 1929.

S 3.39:nos.
ARBITRATION SERIES.

S 3.40:CT
COMMISSION OF INQUIRY AND CONCILIATION,
    BOLIVIA AND PARAGUAY; REPORT OF CHAIR-
    MAN.

    See S 1.26:1

S 3.41:CT
AMERICAN-TURKISH CLAIMS COMMISSION.

BUREAU OF FOREIGN COMMERCE (1897– 1903)

CREATION AND AUTHORITY

        The Bureau of Statistics was established within
the Department of State by act of Congress,
approved June 20, 1874 (18 Stat. 90). On July 1,
1897, the name was changed to Bureau of Foreign Commerce. On July 1, 1903, the Bureau was
consolidated with the Bureau of Statistics (T 37)
of the Treasury Department to form the Bureau of
Statistics (C 14) in the newly created Department
of Commerce and Labor.

S 4.1:date
ANNUAL REPORTS. COMMERCIAL RELATIONS.

    Earlier S 1.9
    Later C 14.5 and C 10.8

S 4.2:CT
GENERAL PUBLICATIONS.

S 4.3:nos.
BULLETINS.

S 4.4:nos.
CIRCULARS.

S 4.5:nos.
ADVANCE SHEETS OF CONSULAR REPORTS.

    Later C 14.6

S 4.6:date
INDEXES TO ADVANCE SHEETS OF CONSULAR
    REPORTS.

    Later C 14.7

S 4.7:v.nos.
CONSULAR REPORTS. [Monthly]

    Later C 14.8 and C 10.6

S 4.8:v.nos.
GENERAL INDEXES TO MONTHLY CONSULAR RE-
    PORTS.

    Later C 14.8

S 4.9:v.nos.
SPECIAL CONSULAR REPORTS.

    Later C 14.10 and C 10.7

S 4.10:CT
CONSULAR REPORTS (miscellaneous, unnumbered).

S 4.11:date
EXPORTS DECLARED FOR UNITED STATES.

S 4.12:date
REVIEW OF THE WORLD'S COMMERCE.

    Later C 14.15 and C 10.9

S 4.13:nos.
SPECIAL ISSUE, CONSULAR REPORTS.

INTERNATIONAL CONGRESSES, CONFERENCES, AND COMMISSIONS

S 5.1:date
ANNUAL REPORTS.

S 5.2:CT
GENERAL PUBLICATIONS.

S 5.5:date
INTERNATIONAL STATISTICAL CONGRESS.

S 5.6:date
INTERNATIONAL GEOGRAPHIC CONGRESS.

S 5.7:date
INTERNATIONAL GEOLOGICAL CONGRESS.

S 5.8:CT
INTERCONTINENTAL RAILWAY COMMISSION.

S 5.9:
INTERNATIONAL AMERICAN CONFERENCE.

S 5.9/1:CT
INTERNATIONAL AMERICAN CONFERENCE, 1st, WASHINGTON, 1889– 90.

   S 5.9/1a:CT
   – SEPARATES.

S 5.9/2:CT
INTERNATIONAL AMERICAN CONFERENCE, 2d. MEXICO CITY, 1901– 02.

S 5.9/3:CT
INTERNATIONAL AMERICAN CONFERENCE, 3d. RIO de JANEIRO, 1906.

S 5.9/4:
INTERNATIONAL AMERICAN CONFERENCE, 4th, BUENOS ARIES, 1910.

S 5.9/5:CT
INTERNATIONAL AMERICAN CONFERENCE, 5th, SANTIAGO, CHILE, MAR. 25– MAY 3, 1923.

S 5.9/6:CT
INTERNATIONAL AMERICAN CONFERENCE, 6th HAVANA, CUBA, JAN. 16– FEB. 20, 1928.

S 5.9/7:CT
INTERNATIONAL CONFERENCE OF AMERICAN STATES, 7th, Montevido, Uruguay, Dec. 3-26, 1933.

S 5.10:v.nos.
INTERNATIONAL MARINE CONFERENCE, WASHINGTON, 1889.

S 5.11:date
INTERNATIONAL SANITARY CONFERENCE, WASHINGTON, 1881.

S 5.12:CT
CENTRAL AMERICAN PEACE CONFERENCE, WASHINGTON, 1907.

S 5.13:date
MONETARY CONFERENCES.

S 5.14:date
PAN-AMERICAN SCIENTIFIC CONGRESS, SANTIAGO, CHILE, 1908– 09.

S 5.14/2:CT
PAN-AMERICAN SCIENTIFIC CONGRESS, 2d, WASHINGTON, D.C., 1915– 16.

S 5.14/3:CT
PAN AMERICAN SCIENTIFIC CONGRESS, 3d LIMA, PERU, 1924– 25.

S 5.14/4:CT
AMERICAN SCIENTIFIC CONGRESS, 7th, MEXICO CITY, SEPT. 8-17, 1935.

S 5.14/5:CT
AMERICAN SCIENTIFIC CONGRESS, 8th, WASHINGTON, D.C., May 10-18, 1940.

S 5.15:date
INTEROCEANIC CANAL CONGRESS, PARIS, 1879.

S 5.16:CT
PAN-AMERICAN MEDICAL CONGRESS, WASHINGTON, 1893.

S 5.17:CT
ELECTRICAL COMMISSION, 1884.

S 5.18/1:date
INTERNATIONAL PRISON CONGRESS.

S 5.18/2:CT
INTERNATIONAL PRISON COMMISSION.

S 5.19:vol.
15th INTERNATIONAL CONGRESS ON HYGIENE AND DEMOGRAPHY, WASHINGTON, SEPT. 23– 28, 1912.

S 5.20:CT
CANADIAN-AMERICAN FISHERIES COMMISSION.

S 5.20:date
INTERNATIONAL CONGRESS AGAINST ALCOHOLISM.

S 5.21/1:CT
PAN-PACIFIC SCIENTIFIC CONFERENCE, 1st HONOLULU, 1920.

S 5.21/2:CT
PAN-PACIFIC EDUCATIONAL CONFERENCE, 1st HONOLULU, AUGUST 1921.

S 5.21.3
PAN-PACIFIC PRESS CONFERENCE, OCT. 1921.

S 5.21/4
PAN-PACIFIC COMMERCIAL CONFERENCE, AUG. 1922.

S 5.22:CT
PAN-PACIFIC EDUCATIONAL CONFERENCE, 1st HONOLULU, AUGUST 1921.

S 5.23:CT
PAN-AMERICAN CONGRESS OF HIGHWAYS, 1st BUENOS AIRES, OCT. 3– 13, 1925.

S 5.23/2:CT
PAN-AMERICAN CONGRESS ON HIGHWAYS, 2d RIO de JANERIO, AUG. 16– 31, 1929.

S 5.24:date
CONFERENCE OF OIL POLLUTION OF NAVIGABLE WATERS.

S 5.25:CT
INTERNATIONAL RADIOTELEGRAPH CONFERENCE OF WASHINGTON, 1927.

   S 5.25/a:CT
   – SEPARATES.

S 5.26:CT
INTERNATIONAL RADIOTELEGRAPH CONFERENCE OF MADRID, 1932.

S 5.27:CT
INTERNATIONAL TELEGRAPH CONFERENCE, PARIS, 1925.

S 5.27/2:CT
INTERNATIONAL TELEGRAPH CONFERENCE, BRUSSELS, 1928.

S 5.28:CT
INTERNATIONAL CIVIL AERONAUTICS CONFERENCE, WASHINGTON, DEC. 12– 14, 1928.

S 5.29:CT
INTERNATIONAL CONFERENCE FOR REVISION OF CONVENTION OF 1914 FOR SAFETY OF LIFE AT SEA, LONDON, APR. 16– MAY 31, 1919.

S 5.30:nos.
CONFERENCE SERIES.

S 5.31:
PERMANENT INTERNATIONAL ASSOCIATION OF ROAD CONGRESS.

   S 5.31:1/date
   ANNUAL REPORTS.

   S 5.31:2/CT
   GENERAL PUBLICATIONS.

   S 5.31:3/nos.
   BULLETINS.

S 5.32:CT
INTER-AMERICAN CONFERENCE ON AGRICULTURE, FORESTRY, AND ANIMAL INDUSTRY, WASHINGTON, SEPT. 8– 20, 1930.

S 5.33:CT
INTERNATIONAL COMMISSION OF INQUIRY INTO EXISTENCE OF SLAVERY AND FORCED LABOR IN REPUBLIC OF LIBERIA.

S 5.34:CT
PAN AMERICAN CHILD CONGRESS, 6th LIMA. JULY 4– 11, 1930.

S 5.35:
INTERNATIONAL FISHERIES COMMISSION.

S 5.35:2/CT
GENERAL PUBLICATIONS.

   Changed from S 5.35

S 5.35:4/nos.
CIRCULARS.

S 5.35:5/date
PACIFIC HALIBUT FISHERY REGULATIONS.

S 5.35:6/nos.
INTERNATIONAL PACIFIC HALIBUT COMMISSION. TECHNICAL REPORTS. (non-Government).

S 5.36:CT
WORLD POWER CONFERENCE, 3d. WASHINGTON, D.C. SEPT. 7– 12, 1936.

S 5.37:CT
INTERNATIONAL COMMISSION ON LARGE DAMS OF WORLD POWER CONFERENCE.

   S 5.37/a:le-nos.
   – SEPARATES.

S 5.38:CT
INTER-AMERICAN CONFERENCE FOR MAINTENANCE OF PEACE, 1936.

S 5.39:CT
INTERNATIONAL CONGRESS OF MILITARY MEDICINE AND PHARMACY.

S 5.40:CT
INTER-AMERICAN TECHNICAL AVIATION CONFERENCE, 1st Sept. 15– 25, 1937, LIMA, PERU.

S 5.41:CT
UNITED NATIONS CONFERENCE ON FOOD AND AGRICULTURE.

S 5.42:CT
INTERNATIONAL COMMISSION FOR AIR NAVIGATION.

S 5.43:CT
INTER-AMERICAN DEVELOPMENT COMMISSION.

S 5.44:CT
UNITED NATIONS CONFERENCE ON INTERNATIONAL ORGANIZATION.

S 5.45:CT
INTER-AMERICAN DEFENSE BOARD.

S 5.46:doc.nos.
INTERNATIONAL MONETARY FUND AND INTERNATIONAL BANK FOR RECONSTRUCTION AND DEVELOPMENT.

S 5.47:CT
ANGLO-AMERICAN CARIBBEAN COMMISSION PUBLICATIONS.

S 5.48:CT   • **Item 894**
NATIONAL COMMISSION FOR UNITED NATIONS EDUCATIONAL, SCIENTIFIC AND CULTURAL ORGANIZATION PUBLICATIONS.

S 5.48/2:v.nos.
NATIONAL COMMISSION NEWS. [Monthly]

S 5.48/3:nos.
CONFERENCE NEWS. NON-GOVT.

Issued by UNESCO.

S 5.48/4:nos.
UNESCO CONFERENCE NEWSLETTER. NON-GOVT.

S 5.48/5:nos.
U.S. NATIONAL COMMISSION FOR UNESCO NEWSLETTER. [Biweekly]

S 5.48/6:nos.
UNESCO WORLD REVIEW WEEKLY RADIO NEWS FROM UNITED NATIONS EDUCATIONAL, SCIENTIFIC, AND CULTURAL ORGANIZATION, PARIS, FRANCE.

S 5.48/7:
U.S. NATIONAL COMMISSION FOR UNESCO [papers relating to discussions and recommendations, agenda, etc., concerning work of UNESCO prepared for meetings of U.S. National Commission].

S 5.48/8:nos.
UNESCO FACTS.

S 5.48/9:CT
NATIONAL COMMISSION FOR UNITED NATIONS EDUCATIONAL, SCIENTIFIC AND CULTURAL ORGANIZATION: ADDRESSES.

S 5.48/10:CT
NATIONAL COMMISSION FOR UNITED NATIONS EDUCATIONAL, SCIENTIFIC AND CULTURAL ORGANIZATION: MAPS AND POSTERS.

S 5.48/11:nos.
U.S. NATIONAL COMMISSION FOR UNESCO, EXECUTIVE COMMITTEE, SUMMARY OF NOTICE OF MEETINGS.

S 5.48/12:nos.
– SUMMARY MINUTES OF MEETING.

S 5.48/13:date
UNITED NATIONS EDUCATIONAL, SCIENTIFIC AND CULTURAL ORGANIZATION NEWS [releases].

S 5.48/14:CT
U.S. NATIONAL COMMISSION FOR UNESCO MEMOS.

S 5.49:nos.
LIST OF OFFICIAL INTERNATIONAL CONFERENCES AND MEETINGS. [Monthly]

S 5.50:CT
INTERNATIONAL TELECOMMUNICATION UNION.

S 5.50/2:CT
NORTH ATLANTIC TREATY ORGANIZATION PUBLICATIONS. (non-Government)

S 5.51
INTERNATIONAL BANK FOR RECONSTRUCTION AND DEVELOPMENT.

S 5.51/1:date
ANNUAL REPORTS.

S 5.51/2:CT
GENERAL PUBLICATIONS.

S 5.51/7:nos.
RELEASES.

S 5.51/8:CT
ADDRESSES.

S 5.52:nos.
INTERNATIONAL CIVIL AVIATION ORGANIZATION REPORT OF REPRESENTATIVES OF UNITED STATES. [Annual]

See for first 3 reports, S 1.70/4:In 85, nos. 1, 4, 5

S 5.53:CT
ALLIED HIGH COMMISSION, GERMANY, PUBLICATIONS. NON-GOVT.

S 5.54:CT
OFFICE OF UNITED STATES ECONOMIC COORDINATOR FOR CENTO AFFAIRS, NON-GOVT. CENTRAL TREATY ORGANIZATION.

S 5.55:nos.
UNITED STATES MISSION TO THE UNITED NATIONS PRESS RELEASES.

S 5.56:CT
U.S. NATIONAL COMMITTEE OF THE CCIR [Comite Consultatif International des Radiocommunication]: PUBLICATIONS. [Irregular]

INTERNATIONAL EXHIBITS AND EXPOSITIONS

S 6.5:
SANTIAGO, CHILE, INTERNATIONAL EXHIBITION, 1875.

S 6.6:
LONDON, INTERNATIONAL FISHERIES EXHIBITION, 1883.

S 6.7:CT
MANDRID, COLUMBIAN HISTORICAL EXPOSITION, 1892– 1893.

S 6.8/1:CT
MELBOURNE, INTERNATIONAL EXHIBITION, 1880.

S 6.8/2:CT
MELBOURNE INTERNATIONAL EXHIBITION, 1888.

S 6.9:CT
PARIS, UNIVERSAL EXPOSITION, 1867.

S 6.10:CT
PARIS, UNIVERSAL EXPOSITION, 1878.

S 6.11:CT
PARIS, UNIVERSAL EXPOSITION, 1889.

S 6.12:CT
PARIS, UNIVERSAL EXPOSITION, 1900.

S 6.13:CT
PHILADELPHIA, INTERNATIONAL EXHIBITION, 1876.

S 6.14:CT
VIENNA, INTERNATIONAL EXHIBITION, 1873.

S 6.15:CT
NASHVILLE, TENNESSEE, CENTENNIAL EXPOSITION, 1897.

S 6.16:CT
OMAHA, TRANS-MISSISSIPPI AND INTERNATIONAL EXPOSITION, 1898.

S 6.17:
CINCINNATI, CENTENNIAL EXPOSITION, 1897.

S 6.18:CT
ST. LOUIS, LOUISIANA PURCHASE EXPOSITION, 1904.

S 6.19:CT
CHICAGO, WORLD'S COLUMBIAN EXPOSITION, 1893.

S 6.20:CT
RIO DE JANEIRO, INTERNATIONAL EXPOSITION OF CENTENARY OF INDEPENDENCE OF BRAZIL, 1922– 23.

S 6.21:CT
SEVILLE, SPAIN, IBERO-AMERICAN EXPOSITION, OCTOBER 12, 1928–

S 6.22:CT
PHILADELPHIA, SESQUICENTENNIAL INTERNATIONAL EXPOSITION, 1926.

S 6.23:CT
GOLDEN GATE INTERNATIONAL EXPOSITION, 1939–

S 6.24:CT
NEW YORK CITY, NEW YORK'S WORLD'S FAIR, 1939– 40.

LAWS OF THE UNITED STATES

S 7.2:CT
GENERAL PUBLICATIONS.

S 7.5:C.S.&nos.
SLIP LAWS: PUBLIC LAWS.

Later GS 4.110/1

S 7.5/2:C.S.&nos.
PUBLIC RESOLUTIONS.

Later GS 4.110/2

S 7.5/3:C.S.&nos.
PUBLIC LAWS.

Later GS 4.110/3

S 7.6:C & S
SESSION LAWS OF PAMPHLET LAWS (State Department edition).

S 7.7:C
LOWELL EDITION.

S 7.8:v.
BIOREN AND DUANE EDITION.

S 7.9:v.
STATUTES AT LARGE.

Later GS 4.111
Later AE 2.111

S 7.9/2:date
CODE OF LAWS OF UNITED STATES AND SUPPLEMENTS.

S 7.10:v.
REVISED STATUTES.

S 7.11:date
INDEXES.

S 7.12:date
DIGESTS.

S 7.12:vol.
DIGEST OF INTERNATIONAL LAW.

S 7.12/2:v.nos.   • Item 864-A
DIGEST OF INTERNATIONAL LAWS, WHITEMAN
SERIES. v. 1– 15. 1963– 1973.

Prepared under the direction of Marjorie Millace
Whiteman.

Although the 15-volume collection is called
the Whiteman Digest, it is an official digest- and
in-depth collection of legal materials arranged
categorically and beginning, for the most part,
with the early 1940's. It deals with such subjects
as sovereignty, state's rights and responsibilities, asylum, jurisdiction, diplomatic privileges and
immunities, extradition, expropriation of property,
and civil strife and war.

The Whiteman Digest also treats a variety of
legal situations never encountered before in the
history of international law. Subsequent to the
last previous digest-the Hackworth Digest published in 1940-aviation law has greatly developed;
the United Nations has come into existence; and
there have been a number of important developments in the field of economics, such as the
creation of the International Monetary Fund (IMF).

The Whiteman Digest stresses the factual
and historical settings of cases and incidents
and quotes extensively from original sources. It
describes to the user how the law has been interpreted under certain circumstances by various
authorities on specific occasions. It is a tool to
be used in ascertaining the law, not a statement
of the law.

The Whiteman Digest of International Law is
the fifth digest published by the State Department. The others are by John L. Cadwalader
(1877); Dr. Francis Wharton (1886); John Bassett
Moore (1906); and Green H. Hackworth (1940). (S
7.12)

A comprehensive index is contained in volume 15.

S 7.12/3:date   • Item 864-A
DIGEST OF UNITED STATES PRACTICE IN INTER-
NATIONAL LAW. 1973–   [Annual]

PURPOSE:– To provide information relating
to international legal practice, treaties and executive agreements, Federal court decisions, testimony and statements before congressional and
international bodies, speeches, diplomatic notes,
correspondence, and internal memoranda. Covered areas include: human rights, international
waterways, treaty law, fisheries, economic law,
arms control, and more. This Digest is of interest
to members of the public as well as Government
officials, lawyers, and scholars.

S 7.13:C & S
SESSION LAWS, OR PAMPHLET LAWS (Little, Brown
and Company edition).

S 7.14:CT by subj.
STATE DEPARTMENT, INTERNATIONAL LAW (texts,
precedents and discussions published by the
State Department)

BUREAU OF ROLLS AND
LIBRARY
(1789– 1921)

S 8.1:date
ANNUAL REPORTS.

S 8.2:CT
GENERAL PUBLICATIONS.

S 8.3:
BULLETINS.

S 8.4:C&S
CIRCULAR [stating of what a set of laws of – Cong.,
–session consists].

S 8.5:date
CATALOGUES.

S 8.6:nos.
LIST OF BOOKS RECEIVED OLD SERIES.

S 8.7:nos.
LIST OF BOOKS, PAMPHLETS, AND MAPS
RECEIVED, NEW SERIES. [Quarterly (later Semi-
annual)]

TREATIES

S 9.2:CT   • Item 897
GENERAL PUBLICATIONS.

S 9.5/1:date
TREATIES AND OTHER INTERNATIONAL ACTS OF
U.S.

S 9.5/2:CT or nos.
TREATY SERIES.
Superseded by S 1.10

S 9.5/3:CT
POSTAL TREATIES AND CONVENTIONS.

S 9.6:CT by country
FOREIGN TREATIES AND CONVENTIONS (United
States not a Signatory).

S 9.7:nos.
TREATY INFORMATION BULLETIN.

S 9.8:nos.
EXECUTIVE AGREEMENT SERIES.
Superseded by S 9.10

S 9.9:nos.
LISTS OF COMMERCIAL TREATIES AND CONVEN-
TIONS, AND AGREEMENTS AFFECTED BY
EXCHANGE OF NOTES OR DECLARATIONS IN
FORCE BETWEEN UNITED STATES AND OTHER
COUNTRIES.

S 9.10:nos.   • Item 899
TREATIES AND OTHER INTERNATIONAL ACTS SE-
RIES. 1501–   1946–   [Irregular]

Texts of the individual treaties and international agreements are issued in this series. The
treaties and international agreements are later
collected together and published in bound form
under the title United States Treaties and Other
International Agreements (S 9.12).
ISSN 0083-0186

S 9.11:date
UNITED STATES TREATY DEVELOPMENTS.

S 9.11/2:nos.
UNITED STATES TREATY DEVELOPMENTS, TRANS-
MITTAL SHEETS.

S 9.11/3:date
NUMERICAL LIST OF TREATY SERIES, EXECUTIVE
AGREEMENT SERIES AND TREATIES AND
OTHER INTERNATIONAL ACTS SERIES.

S 9.12   • Item 899-A
UNITED STATES TREATIES AND OTHER INTER-
NATIONAL AGREEMENTS.

Compilation of treaties and other international
agreements. Formerly included in Statutes at
Large. Individual treaties are also published separately in the Treaties and Other International Acts
series (S 9.10).

S 9.12/2:v.nos.   • Item 899-A (MF)
TREATIES AND OTHER INTERNATIONAL AGREE-
MENTS OF UNITED STATES, 1776– 1949. v. 1–

S 9.13:
ADVANCE UNITED STATES SHORT WAVE BROAD-
CAST PROGRAMS.

S 9.14:date   • Item 900-A (P) (EL)
TREATIES IN FORCE. [Annual]

List of treaties and other international agreements to which the United States has become a
party and which are in force as of the date of
compilation.

S 9.14/2   • Item 900-A-1 (EL)
TREATY ACTION. [Annual]

PORTO RICO
(1909)

S 10.1:date
ANNUAL REPORT OF THE GOVERNOR.

Later W 75.1

S 10.2:CT
GENERAL PUBLICATIONS.

S 10.3:nos.
BULLETINS [none issued].

S 10.4:nos.
CIRCULARS [none issued].

BUREAU OF TRADE RELATIONS
(1903– 1912)

CREATION AND AUTHORITY

The Bureau of Trade Relations was established within the Department of State on July 1,
1903, by Departmental Order pursuant to the act
of Congress establishing the Department of Commerce and Labor. The Bureau was abolished on
September 12, 1912, and was succeeded by the
Office of the Foreign Trade Advisers, which was
established at the same time.

S 11.1:date
ANNUAL REPORTS.

S 11.2:CT
GENERAL PUBLICATIONS.

S 11.3:nos.
BULLETINS.

S 11.4:nos.
CIRCULARS.

STATE, WAR AND NAVY DEPARTMENT BUILDING OFFICE (1883–1925)

CREATION AND AUTHORITY

The State, War, and Navy Department was consolidated with the Public Buildings and Grounds Office (W 38) by Public Law 478-6 approved February 26, 1925 to be known as the Public Buildings and Public Parks of the National Capital Office.

S 12.1:date
ANNUAL REPORTS.

S 12.2:CT
GENERAL PUBLICATIONS.

S 12.3
BULLETINS.

S 12.4
CIRCULARS.

S 12.5:nos.
ORDERS.

WAR TRADE BOARD SECTION (1919–1924)

CREATION AND AUTHORITY

The War Trade Board Section was established within the Department of State by Departmental Order 143 of July 1, 1919 to succeed the War Trade Board (WT 1) which was abolished. The Section continued until January 24, 1924, when it was attached and made a part of the Solicitor's Office by Departmental Order 285.

S 13.1:date
ANNUAL REPORTS.

S 13.2:CT
GENERAL PUBLICATIONS.

S 13.3:
BULLETINS.

S 13.4:
CIRCULARS.

S 13.5:nos.
WAR TRADE BOARD JOURNAL.

Earlier WT 1.5

UNITED STATES COURT FOR CHINA (1906–1933)

CREATION AND AUTHORITY

United States Court for China was established by act of Congress, approved June 30, 1906 (34 Stat. 814).

S 14.1:date
ANNUAL REPORTS.

S 14.2:CT
GENERAL PUBLICATIONS.

S 14.3:
BULLETINS.

S 14.4:
CIRCULARS.

S 14.5:vol.nos.
EXTRATERRITORIAL CASES.

CULTURAL RELATIONS DIVISION (1938–1944)

CREATION AND AUTHORITY

The Division of Cultural Relations was established within the Department of State by Departmental Order 768, dated July 18, 1938. The Division was abolished by Departmental Order 1218, dated January 15, 1944, and its functions transferred to the Office of Public Information.

S 15.1:date
ANNUAL REPORTS.

S 15.2:CT
GENERAL PUBLICATIONS.

S 15.5:CT
CONFERENCES ON INTER-AMERICAN RELATIONS.

CENTRAL TRANSLATING OFFICE (1940–1944)

CREATION AND AUTHORITY

The Central Translating Office was established within the Department of State by Departmental Order 862, dated July 9, 1940. The Office was abolished by Departmental Order 1218, dated January 15, 1944, and its functions transferred to the Central Translating Division.

S 16.1:date
ANNUAL REPORTS.

S 16.2:CT
GENERAL PUBLICATIONS.

S 16.7:nos.
PUBLICATIONS [Spanish and Portuguese].

INTERNATIONAL COOPERATION ADMINISTRATION (1955–1961)

CREATION AND AUTHORITY

The International Cooperation Administration was established within the Department of State by Secretary of State, effective July 1, 1955, pursuant to Executive Order 10610 of May 9, 1955, to succeed the Foreign Operations Administration (FO), which was abolished. Transferred also under the Order were the Institute of Inter-American Affairs (S 1.64), the Office of Small Business, and the International Development Advisory Board (Y 3.In 85). The Administration was abolished by the Foreign Assistance Act of 1961 (75 Stat. 446) and its functions transferred to the newly established Agency for International Development (S 18).

S 17.1:date
REPORTS TO CONGRESS. [Semiannual]

Earlier FO 1.1

S 17.1/2:
SEMIANNUAL REPORTS ON OPERATIONS UNDER MUTUAL DEFENSE ASSISTANCE ACT.

Earlier FO 1.1/2

S 17.2:CT
GENERAL PUBLICATIONS.

Earlier FO 1.2

S 17.3:nos.
ICA BULLETINS (numbered).

Replaces Procurement Information Bulletins issued by FOA.
Earlier FO 1.3

S 17.3/2:date
TECHNICAL BULLETIN.

Earlier FO 1.3/2

S 17.5:CT
INTERNATIONAL COOPERATION ADMINISTRATION LAWS.

S 17.6:
REGULATIONS, RULES AND INSTRUCTIONS.

Earlier FO 1.6

S 17.6/2:nos.
REGULATIONS (numbered).

S 17.6/3:CT
HANDBOOKS, MANUALS, GUIDES.

Earlier S 17.6

S 17.6/4:nos.
TRAINING MANUAL.

Later S 18.8/2

S 17.7:date
RELEASES.

S 17.8:date
ECONOMIC FORCES IN UNITED STATES IN FACTS AND FIGURES.

Earlier FO 1.30

S 17.10:date
OPERATIONS REPORT. [Irregular]

Earlier FO 1.10

S 17.11/3:date
COUNTERPART FUNDS AND ICA FOREIGN CUR-
RENCY ACCOUNTS. [Quarterly]

    Earlier FO 1.11/3

S 17.13:
ICA SMALL BUSINESS CIRCULARS.

    Earlier FO 1.13
    Later S 18.4/2

S 17.14:
SMALL BUSINESS MEMO, ICA/SBM SERIES.

    Earlier FO 1.14

S 17.18:date
TRIAL PROJECTS BULLETIN. [Monthly]

    Earlier FO 1.18
    Later S 18.10

S 17.22:date
REPORT OF COMMODITIES AND FUNDS FOR RE-
LIEF AND REHABILITATION BY AMERICAN AGEN-
CIES REGISTERED WITH ADVISORY COMMIT-
TEE ON VOLUNTARY FOREIGN AID AS SHOWN
ON THEIR MONTHLY SCHEDULE C 200 REPORT
OF EXPORTS [and summary statement of in-
comes and expenditures of voluntary relief agen-
cies registered with Advisory Committee on For-
eign Aid as shown in their schedule C 100 re-
ports]. [Quarterly]

    Earlier FO 1.22
    Later S 18.19

S 17.22/2:date
ANNUAL REPORT OF ADVISORY COMMITTEE ON
VOLUNTARY FOREIGN AID COVERING RELIEF
SHIPMENTS MADE BY VOLUNTARY AGENCIES
TO COUNTRIES AND AREAS PARTICIPATING IN
OVERSEAS FREIGHT SUBSIDY PROGRAM,
FISCAL YEAR.

S 17.23:date
REPORT OF COMMODITIES AND FUNDS FOR RE-
LIEF AND REHABILITATION BY AMERICAN AGEN-
CIES REGISTERED WITH ADVISORY COMMIT-
TEE ON VOLUNTARY FOREIGN AID.

S 17.24:CT
ISC FACT SHEETS.

    See for FOA Fact Sheets FO 1.24

S 17.25:CT
COUNTRY SERIES.

    Earlier FO 1.25

S 17.26:nos.
ICA FINANCED AWARDS.

    Earlier FO 1.26
    Later S 18.11

S 17.26/2:nos.
ICA CONTRACTS NOTICE.

S 17.28:CT
PLANT REQUIREMENTS REPORTS (Small Industry
Series).

    Earlier FO 1.28
    Later S 18.22

S 17.29/1:
TRAINING FILMS.

    Earlier FO 1.29

S 17.29/2:CT
ANNOTATED BIBLIOGRAPHY OF TECHNICAL FILMS
[by subject].

S 17.29/3:CT
SUPPLEMENTS TO ICA FILM BIBLIOGRAPHIES.
Admin.

S 17.29/4:date
LISTING OF LOAN FILMS AVAILABLE.

S 17.31:
NEWSLETTER ON COMMUNITY DEVELOPMENT IN
TECHNICAL COOPERATION.

    Earlier FO 1.31

S 17.32:
TECHNICAL INQUIRY SERVICE.

S 17.32/2:CT
OPERATIONAL DATA.

S 17.33:
MULTIPLIER. [Bimonthly]

S 17.34:date
ICA HEALTH SUMMARY. [Monthly]

S 17.35:date
MUTUAL SECURITY PROGRAM, SUMMARY PRESEN-
TATION. [Annual]

    Earlier FO 1.2:M 98
    Later S 18.28

S 17.35/2:date
BACKGROUND FOR MUTUAL SECURITY, FISCAL
YEAR.
    Earlier S 17.2:M 98

S 17.36:nos.
COMMUNITY DEVELOPMENT BULLETINS.
    Later S 18.25

S 17.37:
SMALL INDUSTRY SERIES, COTTAGE INDUSTRIES
BULLETINS.

S 17.38:
PROGRAMS AND ITINERARIES.

S 17.39:date
INDUSTRIAL REPORTS AND PUBLICATIONS.
    Later S 18.20

S 17.39/2:CT
BIBLIOGRAPHIES AND LISTS OF PUBLICATIONS.

S 17.40:
COST SYSTEM OUTLINES.

S 17.41:date
ROSTER OF VOLUNTEER AND NON-PROFIT
GROUPS AND AGENCIES INTERESTED IN TECH-
NICAL COOPERATION ABROAD. [Irregular]

    Earlier S 17.2:V 88/2

S 17.41/2:date
STATUS REPORT, VOLUNTARY AND NON-PROFIT
AGENCY TECHNICAL CROP RATION CON-
TRACTS WITH INTERNATIONAL COOPERATION
ADMINISTRATION. [Irregular]

S 17.41/3:date
REGISTER OF VOLUNTARY AGENCIES.

    Earlier S 17.2:V 88

S 17.42:CT
LITERATURE RECOMMENDATIONS.

S 17.43:date
INVESTMENT GUARANTEES STAFF CIRCULAR LET-
TERS. [Official Use]

S 17.44:CT
UNITED STATES OPERATIONS MISSION TO VIET-
NAM, PUBLICATIONS.

    Later S 18.31/2

S 17.44/2:CT
JAPAN PRODUCTIVITY CENTER, UNITED STATES
OPERATIONS MISSION TO JAPAN, PUBLICA-
TION.

S 17.44/3:CT
UNITED STATES OPERATIONS MISSION TO THAI-
LAND.

S 17.45:v.nos.&nos.
TECHNICAL DIGEST. [Monthly]

    For use overseas.

S 17.45/2:nos.
TECHNICAL DIGEST SUPPLEMENTS.

S 17.45/3:v.nos.&nos.
TECHNICAL DIGEST SERVICE: INFORMATION KIT.

S 17.46:date
REVIEW OF MUTUAL COOPERATION IN PUBLIC
ADMINISTRATION. [Annual]

S 17.47:nos.
ICA DIGEST. [Biweekly]

AGENCY FOR INTERNATIONAL
DEVELOPMENT
(1961–   )

CREATION AND AUTHORITY

    Section 621 of the Foreign Assistance Act of
1961 (75 Stat. 445; 22 U.S.C. 2381), authorizes
the President to exercise his functions under
that act through such agency as he may direct.
Pursuant to direction and authority contained in
Executive Order 10973 of November 3, 1961, the
Agency for International Development (A.I.D.) was
established by State Department Delegation of
Authority 104 of November 3, 1961, as an agency
within the Department of State.

INFORMATION

    Agency for International Development
    Ronald Reagan Bldg.
    1300 Pennsylvania Ave. NW
    Washington, DC 20523-1000
    (202) 712-4810
    Fax: (202) 216-3524
    http://www.usaid.gov

S 18.1   ● Item 900-C-3
REPORT TO CONGRESS ON FOREIGN ASSISTANCE
PROGRAM. 1962–   [Annual]

    Report prepared under the direction of the
Administrator of the Agency for International Development, with the cooperation and participation
of the Department of State and the Department of
Defense. Transmitted to Congress by the President for the fiscal year.
    Discusses activities of the program by geo-
graphical areas. Also includes military assistance
as well as programs of other countries, international organizations, and private enterprise. Supersedes Report to Congress on the Mutual Security Program, published for the period 1951–
1961 and issued by the Department of State in its
General Foreign Policy series.
    Also published in the House Documents se-
ries.

S 18.1/2:date
OPERATIONS OF OFFICE OF PRIVATE RESOURCES.

S 18.1/3:date   ● Item 900-C-2 (MF)
IMPLEMENTATION OF SECTION 620(S) OF THE
FOREIGN ASSISTANCE ACT OF 1961, AS
AMENDED, A REPORT TO CONGRESS. [Annual]

S 18.2:CT   ● Item 900-C-2
GENERAL PUBLICATIONS.

S 18.3/2:nos.
AID PROCUREMENT INFORMATION BULLETIN.

S 18.3/3:nos.
IB– (series). (Information Bulletin).

S 18.4/2:nos.
AID SMALL BUSINESS CIRCULAR.

PURPOSE:– To make available to interested suppliers procurement data concerning specific proposed AID-financed purchases. Commodities are divided into 21 groups, listed below, so that individual firms may elect to receive only those circulars containing information of interest to them.

Most published items are invitations to bid or solicitations of offers by foreign private importers or governments desiring to utilize funds made available under the AID program for imports from the United States, or occasionally from wider free world sources.

Earlier S 17.13.

S 18.6:CT
REGULATIONS, RULES, AND INSTRUCTIONS.

S 18.6/2   • Item 900-C-5
PROCUREMENT REGULATIONS. 1965–   [Irregular]

Subscription includes basic regulations plus supplementary material for an indefinite period.

S 18.7
PRESS RELEASES. [Irregular]

S 18.8:CT   • Item 900-C-4
HANDBOOKS, MANUALS, GUIDES.

S 18.8/2:nos.
TRAINING MANUAL.

S 18.9:nos.
AID SMALL SUBINESS MEMO, TRADE INFORMA-TION FOR AMERICAN SUPPLIERS.

PURPOSE:– To make available to interested suppliers trade information andgeneral information regarding AID financed procurement proce-dures, practices and regulations.

S 18.10:date
INDUSTRIAL ACTIVITIES BULLETIN. [Bimonthly]

Earlier S 17.18

S 18.11:nos.
AID-FINANCED AWARDS.

Earlier S 17.26

S 18.12
REGISTER OF VOLUNTARY AGENCIES. [Irregular] (prepared by the Advisory Committee on Volun-tary Foreign Aid)

S 18.13:CT
PROGRAM AND ITINERARY. ADMINISTRATIVE.

S 18.14:date
COUNTERPART FUNDS AND AID FOREIGN CUR-RENCY ACCOUNTS. [Quarterly]

Earlier S 17.11

S 18.15   • Item 900-C-1 (MF)
ADDRESSES. [Irregular]

S 18.16
OPERATIONS REPORT. 1972–   [Annual]

Charts and tables provide summary informa-tion of official data on significant aspects of the AID program, commitments by regions, country, and type of program; loans by country, AID-fi-nanced commodity purchases and source of pro-curement; AID surplus agricultural commodity programs; project fields of activity; numbers of U.S. technicians abroad and participant trainees; and investment guarantees.

S 18.16/2:date
AGENCY FOR INTERNATONAL DEVELOPMENT PRO-CUREMENT REGULATIONS, AIDPR.

S 18.17:series/v.nos.
TRAINING MATERIAL.

S 18.17/2:series/v.nos.
COMMUNITY DEVELOPMENT: CASE STUDIES.

S 18.18:nos.
TECHNICAL DIGEST FEATURE, TD (series) OFFI-CIAL USE.

S 18.19
VOLUNTARY FOREIGN RELIEF PROGRAMS, ACTIVITIES OF REGISTERED AMERICAN VOL-UNTARY AGENCIES. [Semiannual] (prepared by the Advisory Committee on Voluntary Foreign Aid and issued to the public by the Statistics and Reports Division)

S 18.20:date
INDUSTRIAL REPORTS AND PUBLICATIONS.

Earlier S 17.39

S 18.21:nos.
B- [Bibliography].

S 18.21/2:CT
BIBLIOGRAPHIES AND LISTS OF PUBLICATIONS.

Earlier S 17.39/2

S 18.21/3:CT
A.I.D. BIBLIOGRAPHY SERIES. 1–

S 18.22:nos.
PLANT REQUIREMENTS.

Earlier S 17.28

S 18.23:nos.
TECHNICAL INQUIRY SERVICE. (Issued in coopera-tion with Office of Technical Service, Commerce Dept. Official use)

S 18.24:v.nos.&nos.
PUBLIC ADMINISTRATION PRACTICES AND PERSPECTIVES, DIGEST OF CURRENT MATER-IALS. [official use]

S 18.25:v.nos.&nos.
COMMUNITY DEVELOPMENT REVIEW.

Earlier S 17.36

S 18.26:date
QUARTERLY REPORT OF ALL INVESTMENT GUAR-ANTIES ISSUED.

S 18.26/2:date
QUARTERLY REPORT OF APPLICATIONS IN PRO-CESS.

S 18.26/3:date
CUMULATIVE REPORT OF ALL SPECIFIC RISK IN-VESTMENT GUARANTIES ISSUED SINCE THE BEGINNING OF THE PROGRAM THROUGH. [Quarterly]

S 18.27:date
U.S. BOOK EXCHANGE SERVICE.

S 18.28   • Item 1056-D
PROPOSED FOREIGN AID PROGRAM, SUMMARY PRESENTATION TO CONGRESS. FY 1963– [Annual]

PURPOSE:– To provide Members of Con-gress, Government agencies, and the general public with information regarding proposed pro-grams of the Agency for the coming fiscal year.

Presented jointly by the Agency for Interna-tional Development and the Department of De-fense covering the economic and military aspects.

Continues annual series of predecessor agen-cies.

S 18.28/a:CT
PROPOSED FOREIGN AID PROGRAM FISCAL YEAR, SUMMARY PRESENTATION TO CONGRESS (separates).

S 18.29   • Item 1056-D
PROJECTS, BY FIELD OF ACTIVITY AND COUNTY. FY 1956–   [Annual]

Title sometimes published as Projects, by Country and Field of Activity.

Continues annual series of predecessor agen-cies.

S 18.30:CT
A.I.D. BACKGROUND SERIES.

S 18.30/2:nos.   • Item 900-C-19
A.I.D. DISCUSSION PAPERS. 1–   [Irregular]

Prepared to improve knowledge of analytical studies, research results, and assistance poli-cies among Agency personnel, and to share such information with other interested persons.

S 18.31:CT
UNITED STATES OPERATIONS MISSION TO THE PHILIPPINES, PUBLICATIONS.

S 18.31/2:CT
UNITED STATES OPERATIONS MISSION TO VIET-NAM, PUBLICATIONS.

Earlier S 17.44

S 18.32:v.nos.&nos.
MULTIPLIER. [Administrative]

S 18.33   • Item 900-C-6
DEVELOPMENT DIGEST. v. 1–   1962–   [Quar-terly] (National Planning Association)

Includes selected excerpts, summaries, and reprints of current materials on economic and social development.

Previous titles: Development Research Di-gest and Development Research Review. Publi-cation suspended July 1964– July 1965.

Indexed by: Index to U.S. Government Peri-odicals.

ISSN 0012-1576

S 18.34   • Item 900-C-8
WAR ON HUNGER, MONTHLY NEW REPORT. v. 1–11.   – 1977. [Monthly] (Office of Material Re-sources)

Issued by Food and Peace Office, Executive Office of the President, prior to issue no. 29.

Previous titles: Food for Freedom and Food for Peace.

Indexed by: Index to U.S. Government Peri-odicals.

ISSN 0043-0269

Superseded by Agenda (S 18.34/2)

S 18.34/2:v.nos.&nos.   • Item 900-C-8
AGENDA. v. 1–   1978– 1982. [Monthly]

News reports on activities under PL 480

Supersedes War on Hunger (S 18.34)

Superseded by Horizons (S 18.58)

ISSN 0161-1976

S 18.35:date
INDEX TO CATALOG OF INVESTMENT INFORMA-TION AND OPPORTUNITIES.

S 18.35/2:nos.
CATALOG OF INVESTMENT INFORMATION AND OPPORTUNITIES, IP. SUPPLEMENTS.

S 18.35/3:CT
CATALOG OF INVESTMENT OPPORTUNITIES INDEX, SUPPLEMENTS.

S 18.36:nos.
INDUSTRY PROFILES, ACCESSION NOTICES.

S 18.37:CT
ECONOMIC GROWTH TRENDS [by region].

S 18.38:nos.
PUBLIC ADMINISTRATION BULLETIN [for Vietnam]. [Monthly]

S 18.39:nos.
PRIVATE DEVELOPMENT ASSISTANCE SERIES, REPORTS. (numbered).

S 18.40:date
SUMMARY OF MONTHLY ECONOMIC DATA FOR VIET-NAM.

S 18.41:date
INTERNATIONAL POLICE ACADEMY REVIEW. [Quarterly]

S 18.42:nos. • Item 900-C-7
APPLICATIONS OF MODERN TECHNOLOGIES TO INTERNATIONAL DEVELOPMENT, AID-OST– (series). [Quarterly] (Office of Science and Technology)

S 18.42/2:nos.
TA/OST- (series). [Irregular]

S 18.43:v.nos.&nos. • Item 900-C-7
A.I.D. MEMORY DOCUMENTS. [Quarterly] (A.I.D. Reference Center)

S 18.44:CT
SPRING REVIEW [of] NEW CEREAL VARIETIES.

S 18.45:nos. • Item 900-C-9 (MF)
AGRICULTURE TECHNOLOGY FOR DEVELOPING COUNTRIES, TECHNICAL SERIES PAPERS. 1– 1971–   [Irregular]

S 18.46:Cong. no./nos.
CONGRESSIONAL RECORD REVIEW. [Daily while Congress is in session]

ISSN 0364-8516

S 18.47:v.nos.&nos. • Item 900-C-17 (MF)
A.I.D. RESEARCH ABSTRACTS, TN-AAA-(series). v. 1–   [Quarterly]

Prior to v. 1, no. 4, issued as A.I.D. Research Abstracts.
Contains abstracts if AID publications on such subject areas as agriculture, development assistance, economics, environment and natural resources, health, nutrition, science and technology, and transportation.
ISSN 0096-1507

S 18.50:nos. • Item 900-C-9 (MF)
TECHNICAL SERIES BULLETINS. 1–   [Irregular]

Series includes information papers, bibliographies, etc., on agricultural technology for developing world areas such as Pacific and Indian Oceans islands and tropics in general, treating such subjects as rapid crop improvement using tissue culture technique.

S 18.51:CT
WORKING DOCUMENT SERVICES (various countries).

S 18.52:nos. • Item 900-C-10
AID PROJECT IMPACT EVALUATION REPORTS (numbered) SERIES. [Irregular]

S 18.52/2:nos. • Item 900-C-11 (MF)
DISCUSSION PAPERS.

S 18.52/3:nos. • Item 900-C-12 (MF)
SPECIAL STUDIES.

S 18.52/4:nos. • Item 900-C-13 (MF)
EVALUATION REPORTS.

S 18.52/5:CT • Item 900-C-13 (MF)
DESIGN AND EVALUATION METHODS (series).

S 18.53:CT • Item 900-C-14 (MF)
COUNTRY PROFILES. [Irregular]

Each report covers an individual country, giving information on government, disaster preparedness, population, etc. to support planning and relief operations of the Office of U.S. Foreign Disaster Assistance.
Published in microfiche.

S 18.54:CT • Item 900-C-15 (MF)
REGIONAL PROFILES. [Irregular]

Similar in nature to Country Profile series (S 18.53). Covers Regions, such as the Caribbean Community.
Published in microfiche.

S 18.55 • Item 900-C-16 (MF)
WOMEN IN DEVELOPMENT (series). [Irregular]

Publications deal with women's concerns worldwide in such areas as political action, education, employment, health, family, population, and housing.

S 18.56 • Item 900-C-18
SELECTED STATISTICAL DATA BY SEX. [Irregular]

Each issue presents statistical data in text and tables on status and roles of women in a different AID-participating country. Approximately 60 countries in the series.
Published in microfiche.

S 18.57:
OCCASIONAL PAPER SERIES.

S 18.58:v.nos.&nos. • Item 900-C-8
HORIZONS. v. 1–   1982–   [10 issues per year]

Supersedes Agenda (S 18.34/2), which has been discontinued.

S 18.59:nos.
DEVELOPMENT STUDIES PROGRAM OCCASIONAL PAPERS.

S 18.60:CT • Item 900-C-20
POSTERS. [Irregular]

S 18.60/2:CT
AUDIOVISUAL MATERIALS. [Irregular]

S 18.61:v.nos./nos. • Item 900-C-21
USAID HIGHLIGHTS.

Newsletter which explains AID programs.

S 18.62 • Item 900-C-14
PUBLICATIONS SERIES.

S 18.63 • Item 900-C-21 (EL)
FRONT LINES. [11 issues per year]

S 18.64:v.nos./nos. • Item 900-C-21
SCIENCE AND TECHNOLOGY AGRICULTURE REPORTER (STAR). [Quarterly]

S 18.65: • Item 900-C-22 (EL)
ELECTRONIC PRODUCTS (misc.).

S 18.66: • Item 900-C-22 (EL)
AFRICAN VOICES.

S 18.67: • Item 900-C-22 (EL)
SD DEVELOPMENTS.

S 18.68: • Item 900-C-22 (EL)
FEWS (Famine Early Warning System) BULLETIN.

S 18.68/2: • Item 900-C-22 (EL)
FEWS (Famine Early Warning System) SPECIAL REPORT.

S 18.69: • Item 900-C-22 (EL)
SPA UPDATE. [Semiannual]

PEACE CORPS
(1961– 1971)

CREATION AND AUTHORITY

Fulfilling a campaign promise which he first made in a speech to University of Michigan students, President John F. Kennedy created the Peace Corps by Executive Order 10924 on March 1, 1961. Later that year, Congress wrote the new agency into law by passing the Peace Corps Act of September 22, 1961. The Peace Corps now operates under the authority of this act, as amended (75 Stat. 612; 22 U.S.C. 2501 et seq.) The Corps was transferred to ACTION (AA 4) by Reorganization Plan 1 of 1971, effective July 1, 1971.

S 19.1
ANNUAL REPORT. 1st–   1961/62–   [Annual]

Fiscal year.

S 19.1/2:date
PEACE CORPS CONGRESSIONAL PRESENTATION, FISCAL YEAR.

Administrative.

S 19.2:CT
GENERAL PUBLICATIONS.

S 19.3/2:nos.
OPPORTUNITIES TO SERVE BULLETINS.

S 19.3/3:nos.
OPPORTUNITIES TO SERVE, P & T (series).

S 19.6/2:nos.
INTERIM POLICY DIRECTIONS.

S 19.7:nos.
PRESS RELEASES.

S 19.8:CT
HANDBOOKS, MANUAL, GUIDES.

S 19.9:v.nos.&nos.
PEACE CORPS NEWS. [Irregular]

S 19.9/2:v.nos.&nos.
PEACE CORPS NEWS, SPECIAL COLLEGE SUPPLEMENT.

S 19.9/3:date
PEACE CORPS NEWSLETTER.

S 19.10:v.nos.&nos.
THE VOLUNTEER.

Administrative.

S 19.11:date
PEACE CORPS VOLUNTEER, QUARTERLY STATISTICAL SUMMARY.

S 19.11/2
PEACE CORPS VOLUNTEER. v. 1–   1962–   [Monthly]

Serves as a news publication on the activities of the Peace Corps program. Well illustrated, this monthly "newsletter" should be in all libraries as an example of what the Good Americans are doing.
Supersedes Peace Corps News.

S 19.11/3:v.nos.&nos.
INFORMATIONAL VOLUNTEER.

S 19.12:date
BI-WEEKLY SUMMARY OF PEACE CORPS TRAINEES AND VOLUNTEERS.

S 19.12/2:date
BI-ANNUAL STATISTICAL SUMMARY. (Office of Administration and Finance)

Gives data on volunteers, trainees, and program analyses of the Peace Corps.

S 19.13:
PEACE CORPS OPPORTUNITY NEWSLETTER OF SPECIAL INTEREST TO PROFESSIONAL AND TECHNICAL PEOPLE.

S 19.14:CT
BIBLIOGRAPHIES AND LISTS OF PUBLICATIONS.

S 19.15:CT
PEACE CORPS PROGRAM DESCRIPTIONS.

Administrative.

S 19.16
PEACE CORPS PROGRAM DIRECTORY.

S 19.17
ADDRESSES. [Irregular]

S 19.18:nos.
PEACE CORPS FACULTY PAPER.

S 20.2   • Item 900-E
GENERAL PUBLICATIONS.

S 20.8   • Item 900-E-1
HANDBOOKS, MANUALS, GUIDES.

S 20.9   • Item 900-E-8
BIBLIOGRAPHIES AND LISTS OF PUBLICATIONS.

S 20.15   • Item 900-E-2-(E)
ELECTRONIC PRODUCTS (misc.).

S 20.16   • Item 900-E-5 (EL)
ECONOMIC PERSPECTIVES. (various languages) [Irregular]

S 20.17   • Item 900-E-6 (EL)
U.S. FOREIGN POLICY AGENDA. (various languages) [Irregular]

S 20.18   • Item 900-E-7 (EL)
GLOBAL ISSUES. (various languages) [Irregular]

S 20.19   • Item 900-E-3 (EL)
U.S. SOCIETY & VALUES. (various languages) [Irregular]

S 20.20   • Item 900-E-4
ISSUES OF DEMOCRACY. (various languages) [Irregular]

S 20.21   • Item 900-E-9
FREEDOM PAPERS.

EDUCATIONAL AND CULTURAL AFFAIRS BUREAU

S 21.2   • Item 900-F-1
GENERAL PUBLICATIONS.

S 21.15   • Item 900-F (P) (EL)
ENGLISH TEACHING FORUM. [Quarterly]

ARMS CONTROL AND INTERNATIONAL SECURITY

S 22.2   • Item 900-G
GENERAL PUBLICATIONS.

BUREAU OF ARMS CONTROL

S 22.102   • Item 900-H
GENERAL PUBLICATIONS.

S 22.106   • Item 900-H-1 (P) (EL)
WORLD MILITARY EXPENDITURES AND ARMS TRANSFER. [Annual]

SHIPPING BOARD (1916– 1933)

CREATION AND AUTHORITY

The United States Shipping Board was established by act of Congress, approved September 7, 1916 (39 Stat. 729) and organized on January 30, 1917. Executive Order 6166 of June 10, 1933, directed the abolition of the Shipping Board.

SB 1.1:date
ANNUAL REPORTS.
Later C 27.1

SB 1.2:CT
GENERAL PUBLICATIONS.
Later C 27.2

SB 1.3:
BULLETINS.

SB 1.4:
CIRCULARS.

SB 1.5:
SPECIFICATIONS.
Cancelled, see SB 2.5

SB 1.6:CT
REGULATIONS, MISCELLANEOUS.

SB 1.7:date
RULES OF PRACTICE.

SB 1.8:nos.
TARIFF CIRCULARS.
Later MC 1.21

SB 1.9:nos.
GENERAL ORDERS.

SB 1.10:v.nos.
UNITED STATES SHIPPING BOARD REPORTS.

SB 1.12:v.nos.
DAILY SHIPPING BULLETIN.
Earlier N 22.6

SB 1.13:CT
PAPERS IN RE.
Later C 27.10

SB 1.14:date
NATIONAL CONFERENCE ON MERCHANT MARINE.

SHIPPING BOARD MERCHANT FLEET CORPORATION (1927– 1936)

CREATION AND AUTHORITY

The Shipping Board Emergency Fleet Corporation was established on April 16, 1917, pursuant to the Shipping Act of September 7, 1916. By act of Congress, approved February 11, 1927 (44 Stat. 1083), the name was changed to United States Shipping Board Merchant Fleet Corporation. The Corporation was abolished on October 26, 1936, by the Merchant Marine Act, approved June 29, 1936 (49 Stat. 1985), and its functions transferred to the United States Maritime Commission (MC 1).

SB 2.1:date
ANNUAL REPORTS.

SB 2.2:CT
GENERAL PUBLICATIONS.

SB 2.3:
BULLETINS.

SB 2.4:
CIRCULARS.

SB 2.5:
SPECIFICATIONS.

SB 2.6:v.nos.
EMERGENCY FLEET NEWS.

SB 2.7:CT
POSTERS.

SB 2.8:v.nos.
SHIPYARD BULLETIN.

SB 2.9:v.nos.
SHIPBUILDERS BULLETIN.

SB 2.10:date
EXACT LOCATION OF ALL SHIPS IN WHICH SHIPPING BOARD IS INTERESTED.

SB 2.11:date
LIST OF AMERICAN AND FOREIGN SHIPS OWNED, UNDER REQUISITION OR CHARTERED TO SHIPPING BOARD.

SB 2.12:nos.
WEEKLY REPORT OF VESSELS UNDER JURISDICTION OF SHIPPING BOARD.

SB 2.13:date
CONTRACT AND REQUISITIONED STEAMSHIPS.

SB 2.14:date
SCHEDULE OF SAILINGS OF SHIPPING BOARD VESSELS IN GENERAL CARGO SERVICE.

SB 2.15:nos.
CATALOGUES (numbered).

SB 2.16:v.nos.
MERCHANT FLEET NEWS. [Monthly]

RECRUITING SERVICE
(1917– 1919)

SB 3.1:date
ANNUAL REPORTS.

SB 3.2:CT
GENERAL PUBLICATIONS.

SB 3.3:
BULLETINS.

SB 3.4:
CIRCULARS.

SB 3.5:vol.
MERCHANT MARINER, DEVOTED TO MEN OF AMERI-
CAN MERCHANT MARINE. [Weekly]

MARINE AND DOCK INDUSTRIAL
RELATIONS DIVISION
(1917– 1933)

SB 4.1:date
ANNUAL REPORTS.

SB 4.2:CT
GENERAL PUBLICATIONS.

SB 4.3:
BULLETINS.

SB 4.4:
CIRCULARS.

PLANNING AND STATISTICS
DIVISION
(1918– 1919)

SB 5.1:date
ANNUAL REPORTS.

SB 5.2:CT
GENERAL PUBLICATIONS.

SB 5.3:
BULLETINS.

SB 5.4:
CIRCULARS.

SB 5.5:date
REPORT ON VESSELS TRADING WITH UNITED
STATES.

SB 5.6:date
CONTROL AND EMPLOYMENT OF VESSELS
TRADING WITH UNITED STATES.

PORT AND HARBOR FACILITIES
COMMISSION
(1918– 1919)

SB 6.1:date
ANNUAL REPORTS.

SB 6.2:CT
GENERAL PUBLICATIONS.

SB 6.3:
BULLETINS.

SB 6.4:
CIRCULARS.

RESEARCH BUREAU
(1916– 1933)

SB 7.1:date
ANNUAL REPORTS.

SB 7.2:CT
GENERAL PUBLICATIONS.

SB 7.3:
BULLETINS.

SB 7.4:
CIRCULARS.

SB 7.5/100:date
OCEAN GOING MERCHANT FLEETS OF PRINCIPAL
MARITIME NATIONS, VESSELS OF 2,000 GROSS
TONS AND OVER. [Semi-annual]

   Later C 27.9/6

SB 7.5/157:a.date/1
WATER BORNE PASSENGER TRAFFIC OF THE
UNITED STATES, FISCAL YEAR. [Annual]

   Later C 27.9/12

SB 7.5/157:a.date/2
WATER BORNE PASSENGER TRAFFIC OF THE
UNITED STATES, CALENDAR YEAR. [Annual]

SB 7.5/157:q.date
WATER BORNE PASSENGER TRAFFIC OF THE
UNITED STATES. [Quarterly]

SB 7.5/158:a.date/1
INTERCOASTAL TRAFFIC, FISCAL YEAR. [Annual]

SB 7.5/158:a.date/2
INTERCOASTAL TRAFFIC, CALENDAR YEAR. [Annual]

SB 7.5/158:q.date
INTERCOASTAL TRAFFIC. [Quarterly]

SB 7.5/162:a.date
LUMBER SHIPMENTS FROM PACIFIC COAST TO
ATLANTIC COAST. [Annual]

SB 7.5/162:q.date
LUMBER SHIPMENTS FROM PACIFIC COAST TO
ATLANTIC COAST. [Quarterly]

SB 7.5/216:date
WATER BORNE FOREIGN COMMERCE OF UNITED
STATES, FISCAL YEAR.

SB 7.5/275:a.date/1
IMPORTS AND EXPORTS OF COMMODITIES BY
UNITED STATES COASTAL DISTRICTS AND FOR-
EIGN TRADE REGIONS, FISCAL YEAR. [Annual]

   Later C 27.9/4

SB 7.5/275:a.date/2
– (ANNUAL) CALENDAR YEAR.

SB 7.5/275:m.date
– (MONTHLY).

SB 7.5/275:q.date
– (QUARTERLY).

SB 7.5/295:date
WATER BORNE COMMERCE OF UNITED STATES
INCLUDING FOREIGN INTERCOASTAL AND
COASTWISE TRAFFIC AND COMMERCE OF U.S.
NONCONTIGUOUS TERRITORY. [Annual]

   Later C 27.9/11

SB 7.5/296:date
COMPARATIVE STATEMENT OF FOREIGN COM-
MERCE OF UNITED STATES PORTS HANDLING
CARGO TONNAGE OF 100,000 LONG TONS AND
OVER.

SB 7.5/298:date
COMPARATIVE STATEMENT OF FOREIGN COM-
MERCE OF UNITED STATES PORTS BY STATES.

SB 7.5/300:date
QUARTERLY REPORT ON EMPLOYMENT OF AMERI-
CAN MERCHANT VESSELS.

   Later C 27.9/7

SB 7.5/317:a.date/1
U.S. WATER BORNE INTERCOASTAL TRAFFIC BY
PORTS OF ORIGIN AND DESTINATION AND PRIN-
CIPAL COMMODITIES, FISCAL YEAR. [Annual]

   SB 7.5/317:a.date/2
   – (ANNUAL) CALENDAR YEAR.

      Later C 27.9/9

   SB 7.5/317:q.date
   – (QUARTERLY).

SB 7.5/399:date
COMPARATIVE SUMMARY OF WATER BORNE FOR-
EIGN COMMERCE. [Quarterly]

   Later C 27.9/3

SB 7.5/399-417:date
COMPARATIVE SUMMARY, IMPORTS & EXPORTS.
[Monthly (later Bimonthly)]

SB 7.5/1100:date
OCEAN GOING MERCHANT FLEETS OF THE PRIN-
CIPAL MARITIME NATIONS, 2,000 GROSS TONS
AND OVER. [Quarterly]

SB 7.5/1105:date
STATUS OF VESSEL CONSTRUCTION AND RECON-
DITIONING UNDER MERCHANT MARINE ACTS
OF 1920 and 1928.

   Later 27.9/8

SB 7.6:CT
MAPS.

   Later C 27.9/13

SB 7.7:date
WATER BORNE FOREIGN COMMERCE OF UNITED
STATES BY UNITED STATES COASTAL DIS-
TRICTS AND FOREIGN TRADE REGIONS
(reports).

SB 7.8:nos.
VESSELS RECEIVING BENEFITS OF CONSTRUC-
TION LOANS UNDER MERCHANT MARINE ACT
OF 1928.

LAW BUREAU
(1916– 1919)

SB 8.1:date
ANNUAL REPORTS.

SB 8.2:CT
GENERAL PUBLICATIONS.

SB 8.3:
BULLETINS.

SB 8.4:
CIRCULARS.

OPERATIONS BUREAU
(1917– 1920)

SB 9.1:date
ANNUAL REPORTS.

SB 9.2:CT
GENERAL PUBLICATIONS.

SB 9.3:
BULLETINS.

SB 9.4:
CIRCULARS

FINANCE BUREAU
(1918– 1920)

SB 10.1:date
ANNUAL REPORTS.

SB 10.2:CT
GENERAL PUBLICATIONS.

SB 10.3:
BULLETINS.

SB 10.4:
CIRCULARS.

SB 10.5:
LAWS.

SB 10.6:
REGULATIONS.

SB 10.7:date
ANNUAL REPORT AND GENERAL FINANCIAL STATE-MENT.

Later C 27.11

CONSTRUCTION BUREAU
(1918– 1934)

SB 11.1:
ANNUAL REPORTS.

SB 11.2:
GENERAL PUBLICATIONS.

SB 11.3:
BULLETINS.

SB 11.4:
CIRCULARS.

SMALL BUSINESS
ADMINISTRATION
(1953–   )

CREATION AND AUTHORITY

The Small Business Administration was eated by the Small Business Act of 1953 (67 Stat. 232), and derives its present existence and authority from the Small Business Act (72 Stat. 384; 15 U.S.C. 631 et seq.), as amended.

INFORMATION

Small Business Administration
409 Third St. SW
Washington, D.C. 20416
(202) 205-6600
Toll-Free: (800) UASK-SBA
http://www.sba.gov

SBA 1.1:date/v.nos   • **Item 901-A (MF)**
ANNUAL REPORT. 1st–   1953/54–

Report submitted by the Administration to the President and Congress pursuant to section 10(a) of the Small Business Act of 1958, as amended (P.L. 85-536) on an annual basis.
Covers such topics as economic position of small business, SBA financial assistance to small firms, assistance under the Small Business Investment Act, financing of SBA loan and investment programs, government contracts and technical assistance, management and research assistance, foreign trade assistance.
Appendix contains lists of certificates of competency under which contract awards were made and list of business loans approved during the six-month period. Also includes financial statements.
Some reports have distinctive titles.
Issued semiannually 1954– 1961, annually 1962–

SBA 1.1/2:date   • **Item 901-A**
STATE OF SMALL BUSINESS, A REPORT TO THE PRESIDENT. [Annual]

                              • **Item 901-A (EL)**
SBA 1.1/2-2:   • **Item 901-A-4 (MF)**
SMALL BUSINESS ECONOMIC INDICATORS.

SBA 1.1/3:date   • **Item 901-A (MF)**
SEMI-ANNUAL REPORT OF THE INSPECTOR GENERAL, U.S. SMALL BUSINESS ADMINISTRATION.

SBA 1.1/4:date   • **Item 901-B-4 (MF)**
RESULTS UNDER THE SMALL BUSINESS INNOVATION DEVELOPMENT ACT OF 1982. [Annual]

SBA 1.1/5:date   • **Item 901-B-4 (EL)**
ANNUAL REPORT OF THE CHIEF COUNSEL FOR ADVOCACY ON IMPLEMENTATION OF THE REGULATORY FLEXIBILITY ACT. [Annual]

SBA 1.1/6:date   • **Item 901-A-5 (MF)**
CHIEF FINANCIAL OFFICER ANNUAL REPORT.

SBA 1.2:CT   • **Item 901-B**
GENERAL PUBLICATIONS.

SBA 1.2:In 8   • **Item 901-B**
SMALL BUSINESS INVESTMENT COMPANIES LICENSED BY THE SMALL BUSINESS ADMINISTRATION AS OF (date). [Annual]

Directory with listing by States. Kept up-to-date with supplements.

SBA 1.2/2:date   • **Item 901-B-3**
SMALL BUSINESS SUBCONTRACTING DIRECTORY. [Annual]

Intended primarily as a marketing aid for small businesses. Lists the major prime contractors to the Federal government as those offering to small businesses the greatest potential for subcontracting.

SBA 1.2/10:date   • **Item 901-B-3**
SMALL BUSINESS SUBCONTRACTING DIRECTORY. [Annual]

SBA 1.3   • **Item 901-K**
SMALL BUSINESS BIBLIOGRAPHIES. 1–   1958–   [Irregular]

PURPOSE:– To provide bibliographies and descriptive summaries on particular types and lines of small business, such as handicrafts and home products, home businesses, and mail order selling.
Previous title: Small Business Bulletins.

SBA 1.4/2:nos.
PRODUCTS LIST CIRCULARS. [Monthly]

SBA 1.6:CT   • **Item 901-O**
REGULATIONS, RULES, AND INSTRUCTIONS.

SBA 1.7
PRESS RELEASES. [Irregular]

SBA 1.7/2:date   • **Item 901-B-9**
SBA NEWS. [Quarterly]

Issued by the Chicago District Office of the Administration. Contains short news items on SBA activities.

SBA 1.10   • **Item 901-E**
MANAGEMENT AIDS FOR SMALL MANUFACTURERS. 1–   1952–   [Irregular]

PURPOSE:– To aid owners and managers of small manufacturing companies in recognizing and solving functional management problems in such fields as financing, maintenance, personnel, and business-Government relations.
Articles are written by independent specialists and designed to be read by the chief operating executive of small manufacturing plants.

SBA 1.10/2   • **Item 901-E**
ANNUALS. 1–   1955–   [Annual]

PURPOSE:– To make available in one single volume a year's issue of Management Aids. Volumes are revised as needed.

SBA 1.11   • **Item 901-I**
TECHNICAL AIDS FOR SMALL MANUFACTURERS. 1–   1952–   [Irregular]

PURPOSE:– To aid the chief technical officers in small manufacturing companies in recognizing and solving problems in such fields as layout, materials handling, equipment, and material.

SBA 1.11/2:nos.
TECHNICAL AIDS FOR SMALL BUSINESS, ANNUALS.

SBA 1.12   • **Item 901-C (MF)**
SMALL BUSINESS MANAGEMENT SERIES. 1–
1952– [Irregular]

    PURPOSE:– To present a series of booklets
ranging in length from 15 to 100 pages, discussing functional management problems in small business.
    Authors are independent specialists from pri-
vate business and the professions.

SBA 1.12/2:nos.
MANAGEMENT RESEARCH SUMMARY (series).

SBA 1.13:date
U.S. GOVERNMENT SPECIFICATIONS DIRECTORY.
[Annual]

    Later SBA 1.13/3

SBA 1.13/2:date
U.S. GOVERNMENT SPECIFICATIONS DIRECTORY.
[Annual]

    Later SBA 1.13/3

SBA 1.13/3:date   • **Item 901-D**
U.S. GOVERNMENT PURCHASING AND SALES
DIRECTORY GUIDE FOR SELLING OR BUYING
IN THE GOVERNMENT MARKET. 1954–
[Irregular]

    Lists alphabetically the products and services
bought by Federal Government military departments and civilian agencies. It also includes an
explanation of the ways in which the Small Business Administration can help a business obtain
Government prime contracts and subcontracts,
comprehensive descriptions of the scope of the
increasingly important Government market for
research and development, and data on Government sales of surplus property.

SBA 1.13/4:CT   • **Item 901-D-1**
DIRECTORIES.

SBA 1.13/5:date   • **Item 901-D-1 (MF)**
TELEPHONE DIRECTORY. [Annual]

SBA 1.14   • **Item 901-J**
SMALL MARKETERS AIDS. 1– 1954– [Irregular]

    PURPOSE:– To aid owners and managers of
retail, wholesale, and service enterprises in recognizing and solving functional management problems in such fields as accounting and record
keeping, human relations, selling, and office management.
    Articles are written by independent special-
ists and designed to be ready by the chief operating executive in a small firm.

SBA 1.14/2   • **Item 901-J**
ANNUALS. 1– 1959– [Annual]

    PURPOSE:– To make available in one single
volume a year's issues of Marketers Aids. The
following Annuals have been issued:

SBA 1.15   • **Item 901-L**
STARTING AND MANAGING SERIES. 1– [Irregu-
lar]

    Series of booklets giving helpful hints on how
to start and operate various small businesses,
such as a print shop, establishing and operating
a bookkeeping and accounting service, etc. This
series was originally issued by the Department of
Commerce, but has since been taken over by the
Small Business Administration.

SBA 1.16:date
LIST OF SMALL COMPANIES FOR RESEARCH AND
DEVELOPMENT WORK.

SBA 1.17   • **Item 901-T (MF)**
ADDRESSES. [Irregular]

SBA 1.18:date   • **Item 901-N**
SMALL BUSINESS ADMINISTRATION PUBLICATIONS
[lists].

SBA 1.18/2:CT   • **Item 901-N**
BIBLIOGRAPHIES AND LISTS OF PUBLICATIONS.

SBA 1.18/3   • **Item 901-N**
SMALL BUSINESS ADMINISTRATION PUBLICA-
TIONS, CLASSIFICATION OF MANAGEMENT
PUBLICATIONS. [Annual]

SBA 1.18/4:date   • **Item 901-N**
SELECTED ABSTRACTS OF COMPLETED RE-
SEARCH STUDIES, FISCAL YEAR (date). [An-
nual]

SBA 1.19:CT   • **Item 901-P**
HANDBOOKS, MANUALS, GUIDES.

    SBA 1.19:L 78   • **Item 901-P**
HANDBOOK FOR PARTICIPATION LOANS WITH
THE SMALL BUSINESS ADMINISTRATION.
1960– [Irregular]

    SBA 1.19/2:nos.
PROCUREMENT AND TECHNICAL ASSISTANCE
HANDBOOKS (numbered).

SBA 1.20:nos.
SMALL BUSINESS RESEARCH SERIES.

SBA 1.20/2:date
SUGGESTED RESEARCH TOPICS.

SBA 1.20/3   • **Item 901-B-6**
RESEARCH SUMMARY (Series).

SBA 1.21:v.nos.&nos.
SELECTED LIBRARY ACQUISITIONS. [Monthly]

SBA 1.22:v.nos.&nos.
REPORTER.

SBA 1.23:date
SMALL BUSINESS INVESTMENT COMPANIES
LICENSED BY SMALL BUSINESS ADMINISTRA-
TION. [Quarterly]

    Earlier SBA 1.2:In 8

SBA 1.24   • **Item 901-S**
ADMINISTRATIVE MANAGEMENT COURSE PRO-
GRAM TOPICS. 1– [Irregular]

SBA 1.25   • **Item 901-U**
ENTERPRISE. v. 1– 1967– [Irregular]

SBA 1.26:date
ADVISORY COUNCIL NEWS.

SBA 1.27   • **Item 901-V**
SBA ECONOMIC REVIEW. v. 1– 1968– [Irregu-
lar] (Office of Planning, Research and Analysis)

    PURPOSE:– Designed to give Agency distri-
bution to studies, articles, statistics, and other
timely information which may be of interest and
help to the SBA central and field offices in planning, administration or evaluation of programs.

SBA 1.27/2:   • **Item 901-B-10**
QUARTERLY REVIEW, 503 AND 504 ECONOMIC
DEVELOPMENT LOAN PROGRAMS. [Quarterly]

    PURPOSE:– To provide tabular data on eco-
nomic development loans by state and by region.

SBA 1.28:date
SUMMARY OF SMALL BUSINESS FINANCING BY
SBIC'S. [Semiannual] (Office of Investment)

SBA 1.29:date
SBIC INDUSTRY REPORTS.

SBA 1.30:date   • **Item 910-W (MF)**
SBIC DIGEST, THE EQUITY FINANCING ARM OF
SBA.

    ISSN 0149-2500

SBA 1.31:date   • **Item 901-A-1 (MF)**
INTERAGENCY COMMITTEE ON WOMEN'S BUSI-
NESS ENTERPRISE, ANNUAL REPORT TO CON-
GRESS.

SBA 1.31/2:date   • **Item 901-A-2**
WOMEN ALONG BUSINESS LINES. [Quarterly]

    PURPOSE:– To provide a newsletter on fea-
tures of interest to women business owners, including SBA awards and grants.

SBA 1.32:nos.   • **Item 901-E**
MANAGEMENT AIDS. [Irregular]

SBA 1.32/2:nos.   • **Item 901-E**
BUSINESS DEVELOPMENT PUBLICATION. [Irregu-
lar]

SBA 1.32/3:CT   • **Item 901-E**
FINANCIAL MANAGEMENT SERIES. [Irregular]

SBA 1.33:CT
AUDIOVISUAL MATERIALS. [Irregular]

SBA 1.33/2:CT   • **Item 901-A-3**
POSTERS. [Irregular]

SBA 1.34:date   • **Item 901-Y**
STATES AND SMALL BUSINESS: PROGRAMS AND
ACTIVITIES. [Annual]

    PURPOSE:– To present information on state
programs supporting small business. Individually
describes small business programs and activities of the states, Puerto Rico, and the Virgin
Islands. A matrix and tables provide statistical
data and comparisons by state.

SBA 1.35:nos.   • **Item 901-L**
STARTING OUT SERIES. [Irregular]

SBA 1.36:date   • **Item 901-B-1**
FIRMS IN THE 8(a) BUSINESS DEVELOPMENT PRO-
GRAM. [Annual]

    Lists firms in the 8(a) Business Development
Program, by region, state, and SBA Servicing
Office.
    Earlier SBA 1.2:F 51

SBA 1.36/2:CT   • **Item 901-B-1 (MF)**
FISCAL YEAR . . . GUARANTEES AND 8(A) CON-
TRACTS.

SBA 1.37:date   • **Item 901-B-2 (EL)**
PRE-SOLICITATION ANNOUNCEMENTS, SMALL
BUSINESS INNOVATION PROGRAMS. [Quarterly]

    Announcements provide only advance infor-
mation about small business innovation research
opportunities.

SBA 1.38:v.nos.&nos.   • **Item 901-B-7**
NETWORK. [Monthly]

    Presents news of SBA activities.

SBA 1.39:date
INCUBATOR TIMES. [Quarterly]

SBA 1.40:CT   • **Item 901-B-5**
FORMS. [Irregular]

SBA 1.41   • **Item 901-B-6 (MF)**
ISSUES ALERT (series).

    Each report deals with a different topic.

SBA 1.42:date   • **Item 901-B-8 (MF)**
LISTING OF SBIR AWARDEES. [Irregular]

    SBIR = Small Business Innovation Research.
Earlier SBA 1.2:Sm 1/12

SBA 1.43:   • **Item 901-B-11 (MF)**
NOMINATE A SMALL BUSINESS PERSON OR
ADVOCATE OF THE YEAR. [Annual]

    PURPOSE– To provide information on how to
nominate a small business person or advocate
for Small Business Week. Outlines various award
categories and describes the criteria used in selecting award winners.

SBA 1.44:date   • **Item 901-A**
FIVE-YEAR INFORMATION RESOURCES MANAGE-
MENT PLAN, FISCAL YEARS . . . [Annual]

SBA 1.45:date • Item 901-Y (MF)
LOAN PROFILES, FISCAL YEAR . . .

SBA 1.46:date • Item 901-B-9
OUTREACH. [Quarterly]

SBA 1.47:nos. • Item 901-B-10 (MF)
OPINION DIGEST. [Quarterly]

SBA 1.48:date • Item 901-B-9
NATURAL RESOURCE DEVELOPMENT PROGRAM
ANNUAL REPORT.

SBA 1.49:CT • Item 901-B-9
FOCUS ON THE FACTS (series).

SBA 1.49/2:nos. • Item 901-B-13 (P) (EL)
THE FACTS ABOUT ... (series)

SBA 1.50:date • Item 901-B-11 (EL)
SMALL BUSINESS PROFILES. [Annual]

SBA 1.51:v.nos./nos. • Item 901-B-12 (P) (EL)
SMALL BUSINESS ADVOCATE. [Monthly]

SBA 1.52:date • Item 901-B-14 (MF) (EL)
SMALL BUSINESS LENDING IN THE UNITED STATES.
[Annual]

SMALL DEFENSE PLANTS ADMINISTRATION
(1951– 1953)

CREATION AND AUTHORITY

The Small Defense Plants Administration was
established by the Defense Production Act Amendments of 1951 (65 Stat. 131). The Administration
was terminated by the Defense Production Act
Amendments of 1953 (67 Stat. 131). Executive
Order 10504 of December 1, 1953, transferred its
functions to the Small Business Administration
(SBA 1).

SDP 1.1:date
QUARTERLY, REPORTS.

SDP 1.2:CT
GENERAL PUBLICATIONS.

SDP 1.7:
RELEASES.

SDP 1.8:nos.
ADMINISTRATIVE ORDERS.

SDP 1.9:CT
ADDRESSES.

SDP 1.10:nos.
MANAGEMENT AIDS FOR SMALL BUSINESS.

SDP 1.11:nos.
TECHNICAL AIDS FOR SMALL BUSINESS.

SDP 1.12:nos.
SMALL BUSINESS MANAGEMENT SERIES.

SDP 1.13:nos.
PRODUCTION NOTES.

SECURITIES AND EXCHANGE COMMISSION
(1934–   )

CREATION AND AUTHORITY

The Securities and Exchange Commission
was created under authority of the Securities
Exchange Act of 1934 (48 Stat. 881; 15 U.S.C.
78a to 78jj), and was organized on July 2, 1934.

INFORMATION

Office of Investor Education and Assistance
Securities and Exchange Commission
450 Fifth Street, N.W.
Washington, D.C. 20549
(202) 942-7040
E-Mail:help@sec.gov
http://www.sec.gov

SE 1.1 • Item 903 (EL)
ANNUAL REPORT. 1st–   1935–   [Annual]

Report submitted by the Commission to Congress pursuant to section 23(b) of the Securities
and Exchange Act of 1934; section 23 of the
Public Utility Holding Company Act of 1935; section 46(a) of the Investment Company Act of
1940; section 216 of the act of June 29, 1949,
amending the Bretton Woods Agreement Act; and
section 11(b) of the Inter-American Development
Bank Act. Report covers the fiscal year.
A separate report of activities is given for
each of the various laws the SEC is responsible
for administering. The appendix contains statistical tables as well as tabular summaries of actions taken, etc., of the Commission.

SE 1.2:CT • Item 904
GENERAL PUBLICATIONS. [Irregular]

SE 1.3:
BULLETINS.

SE 1.4:
CIRCULARS.

SE 1.5:CT • Item 906 MF)
LAWS.

SE 1.5:In 8/2 • Item 906
INVESTMENT ADVISERS ACT OF 1940 AND
GENERAL RULES AND REGULATIONS
THEREUNDER AS IN EFFECT (date). [Irregu-
lar]

Gives text of the Investment Advisors
Act of 1940. Appendix gives provisions of
Investment Company Act of 1940 incorpo-
rated into Section 202(a) (12) of Investment
Advisers Act of 1940. General Rules and
Regulations are reprinted from Title 17, Code
of Federal Regulations, part 275.

SE 1.5:Se 2/2 • Item 906
SECURITIES EXCHANGE ACT OF 1934, AS
AMENDED TO (date). [Irregular]

SE 1.5:Se 2/3 • Item 906
SECURITIES ACT OF 1933, AS AMENDED
TO (date). [Irregular]

SE 1.6:CT • Item 907 (MF)
REGULATIONS, RULES, AND INSTRUCTIONS.
(includes handbooks and manual).

SE 1.6:F 49 • Item 907
REGULATIONS S-X UNDER THE SECURITIES
ACT OF 1933, AS IN EFFECT (date). 1940–
[Irregular]

Covers Securities Exchange Act of 1934,
Public Utility Holding Company Act of 1935,
and Investment Company Act of 1940.

Title 17, part 210, Code of Federal Regulations.

SE 1.6:R 86/2 • Item 907
GENERAL RULES AND REGULATIONS UNDER
THE SECURITIES ACT OF 1933, AS IN
EFFECT (date). 1938–   [Irregular]

Title 17, part 230, Code of Federal Regulations.

SE 1.6:R 86/3 • Item 907
GENERAL RULES AND REGULATIONS UNDER
THE SECURITIES EXCHANGE ACT OF 1934,
AS IN EFFECT (date). [Irregular]

Title 17, part 240, Code of Federal Regulations.

SE 1.6:R 86/4 • Item 907
RULES OF PRACTICE AND RULES RELATING
TO INVESTIGATIONS AND CODE OF BEHAV-
IOR GOVERNING EXPARTE COMMUNICA-
TIONS BETWEEN PERSONS OUTSIDE THE
COMMISSION AND DECISIONAL EMPLOY-
EES. [Irregular]

Reprint of Title 17, Code of Federal Regulations, parts 201 and 203.

SE 1.6:R 86/9 • Item 907
GENERAL RULES AND REGULATIONS UNDER
THE INVESTMENT COMPANY ACT OF 1940,
AS IN EFFECT (date). 1941–   [Irregular]

Title 17, part 270, Code of Federal Regulations.

SE 1.7:CT
MAPS.

SE 1.8:
POSTERS.

SE 1.9:v.nos./nos. • Item 906-A
OFFICIAL SUMMARY OF SECURITY TRANSACTIONS
AND HOLDINGS. v. 1–   1935–   [Monthly]

Gives condensed and abbreviated information on security transactions and holdings reported under the provisions of the Security Exchange Act of 1934, the Public Utility Holding
Company Act of 1935 and the Investment Company Act of 1940, as reported by officers, directors, and certain other persons.
ISSN 0364-2267

SE 1.10:letters
SCHEDULES.

SE 1.11:v.nos. • Item 908
DECISIONS AND REPORTS. v. 1–   1934–   [Ir-
regular]

Completes texts of decisions and opinions.
Individual decisions or opinions are first issued
as press releases and later compiled into final,
bound form in this series.
Citation: S.E.C.

SE 1.11/2:date/supp. • Item 908
SUPPLEMENT TO INDEX TO COMMISSION DECI-
SIONS.

SE 1.12:CT
PAPERS IN RE.

SE 1.13/1:date
REGISTRATION RECORD, SECURITIES ACT OF 1933.

SE 1.13/2:date
REGISTRATION RECORD, SECURITIES ACT OF 1933,
INDEXES.

SE 1.13/3:date
HANDBOOK TO REGISTRATION RECORD, SECURI-
TIES ACT OF 1933.

SE 1.14:CT
ADDRESSES.

SE 1.15:date
OVER-THE-COUNTER BROKERS AND DEALERS REGISTERED WITH SECURITIES & EXCHANGE COMMISSION.
Changed from SE 1.2

SE 1.16 • **Item 907-B (MF)**
SECURITIES TRADED ON EXCHANGES UNDER THE SECURITIES EXCHANGE ACT, AS OF DEC. 31 (year). 1936– [Annual]

Annual directory, with quarterly supplements, containing an alphabetical list of all securities traded on national securities exchanges under the Securities Exchange Act of 1934.

SE 1.17:nos.
CENSUS OF AMERICAN LISTED CORPORATIONS, REPORTS.

SE 1.17/2:CT
SURVEY OF AMERICAN LISTED CORPORATIONS. GENERAL PUBLICATIONS.

SE 1.17/3:vol
STATISTICS OF AMERICAN LISTED CORPORATIONS.

SE 1.18:vol
SURVEY OF AMERICAN LISTED CORPORATIONS.

SE 1.18/2:nos.
SURVEY OF AMERICAN LISTED CORPORATIONS. REPORTED INFORMATION ON SELECTED DEFENSE INDUSTRIES.

SE 1.18/3:nos.
SURVEY OF AMERICAN LISTED CORPORATIONS. REPORTS.

SE 1.19 • **Item 905**
JUDICIAL DECISIONS. v. 1– 1934/39– [Irregular]

Contains all court decisions, reported and unreported, in civil and criminal cases involving statutes administered by the Securities and Exchange Commission.

SE 1.20 • **Item 908-A**
SEC MONTHLY STATISTICAL REVIEW. v. 1– 1942– [Monthly]

Presents data on new securities offerings, registrations, underwriters, trading on exchanges, stock price indexes, round-lot and odd-lot trading, special offerings, secondary distributions, and other financial series. Certain tables presented only quarterly.
Earlier title: Statistical Bulletin.
ISSN 0039-0410

SE 1.20/2:v.nos./nos. • **Item 907-B (MF)**
LITIGATION ACTIONS AND PROCEEDINGS BULLETINS.

SE 1.20/3:date • **Item 907-B (MF)**
SUPPLEMENT LITIGATION, ACTIONS AND PROCEEDINGS BULLETIN INDEX. [Annual]

SE 1.21:date
TABLE OF DECISIONS AND REPORTS. [Quarterly]

SE 1.22:date
SURVEY OF AMERICAN LISTED CORPORATIONS: QUARTERLY SALES DATA.

SE 1.23:v.nos.&nos.
REVIEW OF CURRENT PERIODICALS, NEW SERIES. [Semimonthly]

SE 1.24:nos. • **Item 902**
ACCOUNTING SERIES RELEASES.

SE 1.25/1:nos.
RELEASES. CORPORATE REORGANIZATION.

SE 1.25/2:nos.
RELEASES. HOLDING COMPANY ACT OF 1935.

SE 1.25/3:nos.
RELEASES. INVESTMENT COMPANY ACT OF 1940.

SE 1.25/4:nos.
RELEASES. SECURITIES ACT OF 1933.

SE 1.25/5:nos.
RELEASES. SECURITIES EXCHANGE ACT OF 1934.

SE 1.25/6
STATISTICAL SERIES. [Varies]

The following are issued on a regular basis:

CORPORATE PENSION FUNDS. [Annual]

Gives totals for U.S. only of receipts and expenditures, and distribution of assets.

CORPORATE SECURITIES OFFERED FOR CASH. [Quarterly]

Gives corporate securities offered for cash sale by type of security, offering and issue; proposed uses of estimated net proceeds from offerings of corporate securities. Tables appear later in Statistical Bulletin.

PLANT AND EQUIPMENT EXPENDITURES OF U.S. BUSINESS. [Quarterly]

Gives quarterly figures for a two-year period manufacturing, mining, railroad, transportation other than rail, public utilities, commercial and other, both actual and anticipated. Tables later appear in the Statistical Bulletin.
VOLUME AND COMPOSITION OF INDIVIDUALS' SAVINGS. [Quarterly]

Tables give saving by individuals, by type of savings. Figures later appear in the Statistical Bulletin.

WEEKLY TRADING DATA ON NEW YORK EXCHANGES. [Weekly]

Gives SEC indexes of weekly closing prices of common stocks on New York Stock Exchange, by type of industry, round-lot stock transactions on the New York Stock Exchange of shares for each trading date, stock transactions for odd-lot accounts of odd-lot dealers on the New York Stock Exchange of shares and value for each trading date, and round-lot and odd-lot stock transactions on the American Stock Exchange in shares for each trading date. Figures later appear in the Statistical Bulletin.

WORKING CAPITAL OF U.S. CORPORATIONS. [Quarterly]

Table gives current assets and liabilities of U.S. corporations on a quarterly basis for a two year period. Figures later appear in the Statistical Bulletin.

SE 1.25/7:nos.
RELEASES. TRUST INDENTURE ACT OF 1939.

SE 1.25/8
PRESS RELEASES. [Irregular]

Releases are issued under the following categories:

ACCOUNTING SERIES RELEASES (SE 1.24).

Compilations.
1– 77, amended to March 10, 1956. 1956.
313 p.
77– 89, amended to November 1961. 1962. 75 p.

ASIAN DEVELOPMENT BANK ACT (SE 1.25/14).

CORPORATE REORGANIZATION ACT RELEASES (SE 1.25/1).

HOLDING COMPANY ACT RELEASES (SE 1.25/2).

INVESTMENT ADVISERS ACT OF 1940 RELEASES (SE 1.25/9).

INVESTMENT COMPANY ACT RELEASES (SE 1.25/3).

LITIGATION RELEASES (SE 1.25/11).

QUARTERLY FINANCIAL REPORT FOR MANUFACTURING CORPORATIONS.

Published jointly with the Federal Trade Commission and listed under that agency (FT 1.18)

SECURITIES ACT OF 1933 RELEASES (SE 1.25/3).

SECURITIES EXCHANGE ACT OF 1934 RELEASES (SE 1.25/5).

SE 1.25/9:nos.
INVESTMENT ADVISERS ACT RELEASES.

SE 1.25/10:nos.
BRETTON WOODS AGREEMENTS ACT RELEASES.

SE 1.25/11:nos.
LITIGATION RELEASES.

SE 1.25/12:date-nos. • **Item 908-B (EL)**
NEWS DIGEST. [Daily]

Contains a brief resume of all financial proposals field with and important actions taken by the Commission.
ISSN 0364-6718

SE 1.25/13:nos.
INTER-AMERICAN DEVELOPMENT BANK RELEAESES.

SE 1.25/14:nos.
ASIAN DEVELOPMENT BANK ACT, RELEASES.

SE 1.26:date
COST OF FLOTATION. [Quarterly]

SE 1.27 • **Item 903-A (MF)**
DIRECTORY OF COMPANIES FILING ANNUAL REPORTS WITH THE SECURITIES AND EXCHANGE COMMISSION. 1976– [Annual]

Arrangement is alphabetically by companies and by industry groups.

SE 1.28:nos.
SPECIAL MARKET STUDY RELEASES.

SE 1.29:v.nos.&nos. • **Item 908-C (MF)**
SEC DOCKET. v. 1– 1973– [Weekly]

A compilation of releases from the Securities and Exchange Commission issued during the week.
ISSN 0091-4061

SE 1.30:nos. • **Item 908-D**
ECONOMIC STAFF PAPERS. [Irregular]

SE 1.31:nos. • **Item 908-E**
STAFF ACCOUNTING BULLETINS. 1– 1975– [Irregular]

SE 1.32:date
REPORT COORDINATING GROUP ANNUAL REPORT TO THE SECURITIES AND EXCHANGE COMMISSION.

SE 1.33:date
CURRENT TRENDS.

SE 1.34:date • **Item 908-F (MF)**
OFFICIAL LIST OF SECTION 13(f) SECURITIES. [Quarterly]

PURPOSE:– To provide a list of equity securities of $100 million or more aggregate value. Intended for institutional investment managers to facilitate determination of whether or not they have to file a report under the SEC rule.

SE 1.35:nos.
CAPITAL MARKET WORKING PAPERS.

SE 1.35/2:date • **Item 907-B (MF) (EL)**
FINAL REPORT OF THE SEC GOVERNMENT BUSINESS FORUM ON SMALL BUSINESS CAPITAL FORMATION. [Annual]

SE 1.36:CT • **Item 904-A**
HANDBOOKS, MANUALS, GUIDES. [Irregular]

SE 1.37:CT • **Item 908-G**
FORMS. [Irregular]

SE 1.38 • **Item 908-G-1 (EL)**
SEC SPECIAL STUDIES.

SMITHSONIAN INSTITUTION
(1846–   )

CREATION AND AUTHORITY

The Smithsonian Institution was created by act of Congress approved August 10, 1846 (9 Stat. 102; 20 U.S.C. 41 et seq.), under the terms of the will of James Smithson, of London, England, who in 1829 bequeathed his fortune to the United States to found, at Washington, under the name of the "Smithsonian Institution," an establishment for the "increase and diffusion of knowledge among men."

INFORMATION
Office of Public Affairs
Smithsonian Institution
1000 Jefferson Drive, S.W.
Washington, D.C. 20560
(202) 357-1300
E-Mail:info@si.edu
http://www.si.edu

SI 1.1:date • **Item 903 (EL)**
SMITHSONIAN YEAR (date) ANNUAL REPORT OF THE SMITHSONIAN INSTITUTION. [Annual]

Contains the administrative report of the Secretary of the Smithsonian Institution (listed above) together with a General Appendix, containing a collection of scientific articles, written in a popular style and illustrated with charts, plates, etc. The range of subjects is as diversified as the interest of mankind in science and the arts.

The objective of the General Appendix to the Annual Report of the Smithsonian Institution is to furnish brief accounts of scientific discovery in particular direction, reports of investigations made by staff members and collaborators of the Institution; and memoirs of a general character or on special topics that are of interest or value to the numerous correspondents of the Institution.

The method of presenting an annual report enriched by the series of articles has continued in its present form since 1889.

Copies of the individual articles are available as separates upon request to the Editorial and Publications Division as long as the supply lasts.

Also published in the House Documents series.

INDEXES.

AUTHOR-SUBJECT INDEX TO ARTICLES IN SMITHSONIAN ANNUAL REPORTS.

1849– 1961. 1963. 200 p. (Pub. 4503)

SI 1.1/a • **Item 909**
REPORT OF THE SECRETARY AND FINANCIAL REPORT OF THE EXECUTIVE COMMITTEE OF THE BOARD OF REGENTS. 1846–   [Annual]

Report submitted by the Secretary of the Smithsonian Institution to Congress pursuant to section 5593 of the revised Statutes of the United States for the fiscal year.

Contains a report of the Secretary of the overall activities during the year. Also included are the reports of the various subordinate bureaus, including the U.S. National Museum, Bureau of American Ethnology, Astrophysical Observatory, National Collection of Fine Arts, Freer Gallery of Art, National Air Museum, National Zoological Park, Canal Zone Biological Area, International Exchange Service, and National Gallery of Art. Reports are accompanied by plates illustrating activities of recent acquisitions to the various collections. The report of the executive committee of the Board of Regents is also included. Each report contains a list of publications issued during the fiscal year.

The report in this edition is issued in a paper cover and released shortly after the first of the year. The report also appears in a cloth bound edition (see below) released later in the year.

The U.S. National Museum issues its own annual report separately.

SI 1.1/a2:date
ASTROPHYSICAL OBSERVATORY, REPORTS.
Changed from SI 1.1/a:As 898/1.

SI 1.1/a3
SMITHSONIAN INTERNATIONAL EXCHANGE SERVICE ANNUAL REPORT. [Annual]
Reprint from Smithsonian Year.

SI 1.1/a4:date
NATIONAL ZOOLOGICAL PARK, REPORTS.
Earlier SI 1.1/a:N 213/4

SI 1.1/a5:date
RADIATION AND ORGANISMS DIVISION, REPORTS.
Changed from SI 1.1/2:R 118/15.

SI 1.1/a6:date
SMITHSONIAN INSTITUTION PRESS, ANNUAL REPORTS.
Reprinted from Smithsonian Year.

SI 1.1/2:date • **Item 910-J (MF)**
NATIONAL ZOOLOGICAL PARK: ANNUAL REPORT.

SI 1.1/3:date
CENTER FOR SHORT-LIVED PHENOMENA: ANNUAL REPORT.

SI 1.1/4:date • **Item 909 (MF)**
SMITHSONIAN YEAR (date), STATEMENT BY THE SECRETARY. [Annual]

SI 1.2:CT • **Item 910**
GENERAL PUBLICATIONS.

SI 1.2:St 1 • **Item 910**
PORTRAITS OF THE AMERICAN STAGE, 1771– 1971. 1971. 203 p. il

The National Portrait Gallery, Smithsonian Institution. Issued to conincide with an exhibition in celebration of the inaugural season of the John F. Kennedy Center for the Performing Arts, this publication portrays 92 personalities of the American stage, with a short biographical sketch of each. It spans 2 centuries of personalities of the American stage whose primary achievements have been in the drama, dance, opera, musical comedy, and on the concert stage. A photograph, sketch or bust of each personality is included.

SI 1.3:
BULLETINS [none issued].

SI 1.3/2 • **Item 910-X (EL)**
CWIHP (Cold War International History Project) BULLETIN. [Irregular]

SI 1.4:
CIRCULARS [none issued].

SI 1.5:date
LIST OF OFFICIAL PUBLICATIONS OF GOVERNMENT DISTRIBUTED FOR LIBRARY OF CONGRESS THROUGH SMITHSONIAN INSTITUTION.

SI 1.6:v.nos.
SMITHSONIAN CONTRIBUTIONS TO KNOWLEDGE. v. 1– 35. 1948– 1916.

First series published by the Smithsonian; presenting in quarto form memoirs and monographs on the physical and natural sciences.

SI 1.7
SMITHSONIAN MISCELLANEOUS COLLECTION. v. 1–   1856–

Contains papers relating to nearly every branch of science, with those in the fields of biology, geology, and anthropology predominating.

Papers are issued and numbered separately within each volume. A larger work will be assigned a single volume number. Title page and table of contents are issued separately.

WORLD WEATHER RECORDS.

– [To 1920.] 1927. 1199 p. (Smithsonian Miscellaneous Collections, v. 79) (Publication 2913)

– 1921– 30. 1934. 616 p. (Smithsonian Miscellaneous Collections, v. 90) (Publication 3218)

– 1931– 40. 1947. 646 p. (Smithsonian Miscellaneous Collections, v. 105) (Publication 3803)

SI 1.7:120
SMITHSONIAN PHYSICAL TABLES. 9th ed. 1954. 827 p. il. (Smithsonian Miscellaneous Collection, v. 120) (Publication 4169)

SI 1.8:date
LIST OF PUBLICATIONS.

SI 1.9:date
SPECIFICATIONS FOR SUPPLIES.

SI 1.10:v.nos.
BULLETIN OF THE PHILOSOPHICAL SOCIETY OF WASHINGTON.

SI 1.11:v.nos.
HARRIMAN ALASKA SERIES.

SI 1.12:v.nos.
ANNUALS OF ASTROPHYSICAL OBSERVATORY. v. 1–   1900–

Published about once every 10 years since 1900. Each volume contains summaries of research for the years covered by that volume, plus several papers, largely on solar radiation and instrumentation.

SI 1.12/2 • **Item 909-B**
SMITHSONIAN CONTRIBUTIONS TO ASTROPHYSICS. v. 1–   1956–

PURPOSE:– To communicate the results of research conducted at the Astrophysical Observatory of the Smithsonian Institution for the increase and diffusion of knowledge in the field of astrophysics, with particular emphasis on the problems of the sun, earth, and solar system.

Papers are numbered and published separately, but paged consecutively within each volume.

SI 1.12/3:nos.
RESEARCH IN SPACE SCIENCES, SPECIAL REPORT.

SI 1.12/4
ASTRONOMICAL PAPERS TRANSLATED FROM THE RUSSIAN. 1–   [Irregular] (Astrophysical Observatory, Cambridge, Mass.)

SI 1.12/5:date
SATELLITE SITUATION REPORT.

SI 1.13:date
EXPLORATIONS AND FIELD-WORK OF SMITHSONIAN INSTITUTION.

Changed from Si 1.2:Ex 7

SI 1.14
WAR BACKGROUND STUDIES.

SI 1.15:CT
REGULATIONS, RULES, AND INSTRUCTIONS.

SI 1.16:nos.
INSTITUTE OF SOCIAL ANTHROPOLOGY PUBLICATIONS.

SI 1.17:date
LIST OF SMITHSONIAN PUBLICATIONS AVAILABLE.

    Earlier SI 1.1/a:P 96 & SI 1.7/a:P 96

SI 1.17/2:CT   • **Item 909-C**
BIBLIOGRAPHIES AND LISTS OF PUBLICATIONS.

SI 1.17/3:nos.
SMITHSONIAN ANTHROPOLOGICAL BIBLIOGRAPHIES.

SI 1.17/4:date   • **Item 909-C**
SMITHSONIAN INSTITUTION PRESS, NEW TITLES. [Semiannual]

SI 1.18:date
TRAVELING EXHIBITIONS, ADMINISTRATIVE.

SI 1.19   • **Item 910**
[INFORMATIONAL LEAFLETS] SIL- (series).

SI 1.20:CT   • **Item 909-D**
HANDBOOKS, MANUALS, GUIDES.

SI 1.20/2:v.nos.   • **Item 909-D-1**
HANDBOOK OF NORTH AMERICAN INDIANS. v. 1–20. 1978–   [Irregular]

    The Smithsonian Institution is preparing a new 20-volume Handbook of North American Indians, edited by William C. Sturtevant, to be published over an extended period of years. This will be a completely new encyclopedia, not a revision of the 2-volume Handbook of American Indians North of Mexico which was edited by Frederick W. Hodge and published in 1907– 1910. The new Handbook will summarize scholarly knowledge of the history and the cultures of all North American Indians and Eskimos, from the earliest prehistoric times up to the present. The area covered is America north of Meso-America. This includes a good part of northern Mexico, all of the continental United States, Canada, Alaska and the Greenlandic and Siberian Eskimos. While most of the several hundred authors are academic scholars (especially anthropologists and historians), they are writing for a broader audience. The Handbook articles will be concise, exhaustive, accurate, and written for the educated general reader as well as for the specialist. The work should become a standard reference encyclopedia not only for university teachers and students, researchers, and writers in the social sciences and humanities, but also for the general public, including particularly Indian people and those whose jobs or interest relate to some aspect of Indian life and culture.

    Each volume will contain about 800 pages including an index. Each can be purchased and used independently of other Handbook volumes (except that volume 9 and 10 form a unit as do 18 and 19)

    The Handbook will be divided as follows:–

Vol. 1: Introduction.
Vol. 2: Indians in Contemporary Society.
Vol. 3: Environment, Origins, and Population.
Vol. 4: History of Indian-White Relations.
Vol. 5: Arctic.
Vol. 6: Subarctic.
Vol. 7: Northwest Coast.
Vol. 8: California.
Vol. 9: Southwest.
Vol. 10: Southwest.
Vol. 11: Great Basin.
Vol. 12: Plateau.
Vol. 13: Plains.
Vol. 14: Southeast.
Vol. 15: Northeast.
Vol. 16: Technology and Visual Arts.
Vol. 17: Languages.
Vol. 18: Biographical Dictionary.
Vol. 19: Biographical Dictionary.
Vol. 20: General Index.

SI 1.21
EDWIN A. LINK LECTURE SERIES. [Irregular]

SI 1.22
PUBLICATIONS IN SLAVAGE ARCHEOLOGY. 1– 1966– [Irregular]

SI 1.23
SMITHSONIAN JOURNAL OF HISTORY. v. 1– v. 3, no. 4. [Quarterly]

SI 1.24   • **Item 910-A**
SMITHSONIAN TORCH. 1–   [Irregular] (published by the Public Information Officer for the Smithsonian Institution personnel)

    ISSN 0037-7341

SI 1.25   • **Item 910-C**
ATOLL RESEARCH BULLETIN. 1–   1951– [Irregular]

    Issued by the Smithsonian Institution as part of its Tropical Biology Program, provides reports of original research, with the emphasis on basic rather than applied research, in the field of Atoll studies.

    Nos. 1– 117 were issued by the Pacific Science Board, National Academy of Sciences, with financial support from the Office of Naval Research. Its pages were largely devoted to reports resulting from the Pacific Science Board's Coral Atoll Program.

SI 1.26   • **Item 910-B**
SMITHSONIAN CONTRIBUTIONS TO EARTH SCIENCES. 1–   1969–   [Irregular]

    PURPOSE:– To provide reports of original research in subject fields of interest to Smithsonian scientists, especially those in the National Museum of Natural History, and to colleagues elsewhere. The emphasis is on basic rather than applied research in such fields as meteoritics, mineralogy, physical oceanography, and geology.

SI 1.27:nos.   • **Item 910-D**
SMITHSONIAN CONTRIBUTIONS TO ZOOLOGY.

SI 1.28:nos.   • **Item 910-F**
SMITHSONIAN STUDIES IN HISTORY AND TECHNOLOGY. 1–   1969–

SI 1.29:nos.   • **Item 910-E**
SMITHSONIAN CONTRIBUTIONS TO BOTANY.

SI 1.30:nos.   • **Item 910-G**
SMITHSONIAN CONTRIBUTIONS TO PALEOBIOLOGY.

SI 1.31:CT   • **Item 909-A-1**
ADDRESSES.

SI 1.32:v.nos.&nos.
SMITHSONIAN INSTITUTION INFORMATION SYSTEMS INNOVATIONS. v. 1–   1969–   [Irregular] (Information Systems Division)

    PURPOSE:– To make available to the academic and museum community what is taking place within the Institution in the way of innovative automation.

SI 1.33:nos.   • **Item 921-A**
SMITHSONIAN CONTRIBUTIONS TO ANTHROPOLOGY.

SI 1.34:nos.   • **Item 910-H**
ARCHIVES AND SPECIAL COLLECTIONS OF THE SMITHSONIAN INSTITUTION.

SI 1.35:date   • **Item 910-I**
CALENDAR OF THE SMITHSONIAN INSTITUTION. [Monthly] (Office of Public Affairs)

SI 1.36:v.nos.   • **Item 910-A-1**
RIF NEWSLETTER. v. 1–   1971–   [Quarterly]

    RIF = Reading is Fundamental.
    ISSN 0364-8389

SI 1.36/2:   • **Item 910-A-2**
READING IS FUNDAMENTAL, INC., BOOK SUPPLIER PROFILE. [Annual]

    Lists all the booksellers qualified to serve Reading is Fundamental projects. Lists are periodically updated by addenda which include the profiles of any newly qualified suppliers. Each complete new profile listing supersedes previous listings and addenda.

SI 1.37:nos.   • **Item 910-A-2**
RESEARCH REPORTS. 1–   1972–   [Quarterly] (Office of Public Affairs)

    PURPOSE:– To provide scientific researchers, academic institutions, and members of the public with information about scientific an other research underway or completed by the various components of the Smithsonian Institution, in a form comprehensible to persons without specialized knowledge.
    ISSN 0364-0175

SI 1.38:CT   • **Item 910-Y**
POSTERS. [Irregular]

SI 1.39:nos.   • **Item 910-K**
PUBLICATIONS IN MUSEUM BEHAVIOR. 1–   1974– [Irregular]

SI 1.40:nos.   • **Item 910-L (MF)**
RIIES BIBLIOGRAPHIC STUDIES. 1–   1976– [Irregular] (Research Institute on Immigration and Ethnic Studies)

SI 1.40/2:nos.   • **Item 910-R (MF)**
RIIES OCCASIONAL PAPERS. 1–   [Irregular] (Research Institute on Immigration and Ethnic Studies)

SI 1.40/3   • **Item 910-R (MF)**
RIIES RESEARCH NOTES.

SI 1.41:nos.   • **Item 910-M**
SMITHSONIAN CONTRIBUTIONS TO THE MARINE SCIENCES. 1–   1977–   [Irregular]

SI 1.42:nos.   • **Item 910-P**
SMITHSONIAN STUDIES IN AIR AND SPACE. 1– 1977–   [Irregular]

SI 1.43:nos.   • **Item 910-T**
SMITHSONIAN FOLKLIFE STUDIES. 1–   1980– [Irregular]

    Monographs present studies of "old ways" in music, food preparation, and crafts.

SI 1.43/2:date   • **Item 910-T**
FESTIVAL OF AMERICAN FOLKLIFE. [Annual]

SI 1.44:date   • **Item 910-W (MF) (EL)**
SMITHSONIAN OPPORTUNITIES FOR RESEARCH AND STUDY IN HISTORY, ART, SCIENCE. [Biennial]

    PURPOSE:– To describe opportunities for research and study under Smithsonian fellowships and grants, including in-residence appointments using Smithsonian facilities.
    Earlier SI 1.2:R 31

SI 1.45   • **Item 910-X (E)**
SMITHSONIAN (Web Magazine).

SI 1.46   • **Item 910-X (E)**
INCREASE & DIFFUSION.

SI 1.47   • **Item 910-X (E)**
ELECTRONIC PRODUCTS.

SI 1.48:   • **Item 910-X (EL)**
ANNALS OF THE SMITHSONIAN INSTITUTION.

SI 1.49:   • **Item 909-C-1 (CD)**
GLOBAL VOLCANISM PROGRAM, DIGITAL INFORMATION SERIES

BUREAU OF AMERICAN ETHNOLOGY

SI 2.1:date
ANNUAL REPORTS.

SI 2.2:CT
GENERAL PUBLICATIONS.

SI 2.3 • Item 913
BULLETINS. 1– 1887– [Irregular]

PURPOSE:– To make available publications of research in ethnology, archaeology, and general anthropology, particularly of the history, material culture, customs, and religious practices of the American Indian. Also included in this series are the studies on Eskimos and other ethnic groups living in lands under the jurisdiction of the United States.
Also published in the House Document series.

SI 2.3/a2:nos.
– SEPARATES, ANTHROPOLOGICAL PAPERS.

SI 2.4:nos.
CIRCULARS [none issued].

SI 2.5:date
LIST OF PUBLICATIONS.

NATIONAL MUSEUM OF AMERICAN HISTORY (1980–)

CREATION AND AUTHORITY

The National Museum of History and Technology was established in 1964. The name was changed to National Museum of American History by act of October 13, 1980 (94 Stat. 1884; 20 U.S.C. 59 note).

INFORMATION

National Museum of American History
Fourteenth Street and Constitution Ave., N.W.
Washington, D.C. 20560
(202) 357-4698
http://www.americanhistory.si.edu

SI 3.1:date • Item 918
ANNUAL REPORT. 1888– [Annual]

Report submitted by the Director of the U.S. National Museum to the Secretary of the Smithsonian Institution for the fiscal year.
Contains a report of the activities for the year together with a well-illustrated account of the various exhibits improved upon, recent accessions, care of the collections, etc. Includes a list of publications issued during the year and a detailed list of donors to the national collections.
Also published in the House Documents series.

SI 3.1/2
MUSEUM OF NATURAL HISTORY. ANNUAL REPORT. [Annual]

Reprinted from Smithsonian Year.

SI 3.2:CT • Item 921
GENERAL PUBLICATIONS.

SI 3.3 • Item 919
BULLETINS. 1– 1875– [Irregular]

PURPOSE:– To make available monographs of large zoological groups and other general systematic treatises, faunal works, reports of expeditions, catalogs of type specimens, special collections, and material of a similar nature. Most of the works are scholarly in nature, but a few are of interest to the layman.
Certain of the larger works are issued in separate parts with individual part numbers.

SI 3.3:[nos.] • Item 919
CONTRIBUTIONS FROM THE MUSEUM OF HISTORY AND TECHNOLOGY, PAPERS. 1– [Irregular]

SI 3.4:nos.
CIRCULARS.

SI 3.5:nos.
SPECIAL BULLETINS.

SI 3.6:nos.
PROCEEDINGS.

SI 3.7
PROCEEDINGS APPENDIXES.

Consolidtated with SI 3.4

SI 3.8 • Item 920
CONTRIBUTIONS FROM THE U.S. NATIONAL HERBARIUM. v. 1– 1902–

PURPOSE:– To publish general systematic treatises on floral groups, relating to the botanical collections of the U.S. National Herbarium and specific expeditions.

SI 3.9:CT • Item 918-A
BIBLIOGRAPHIES AND LISTS OF PUBLICATIONS.

SI 3.10:CT • Item 921
HANDBOOKS, MANUALS, GUIDES.

SI 3.11 • Item 921-A
SMITHSONIAN CONTRIBUTIONS TO ANTHROPOLOGY. v. 1– 1965– [Irregular]

SI 3.12 • Item 921-B
PHILATELIC DEDICATORY LECTURE SERIES.

SI 3.13:v.nos.&nos. • Item 921-A-1 (EL)
BULLETIN OF THE GLOBAL VOLCANISM NETWORK [Monthly] (National Museum of Natural History)

Provides alert information regarding earthquakes and volcanic and meteoric events worldwide.
Continues SEAN Bulletin. (Scientific Event Alert Network).

AMERICAN HISTORICAL ASSOCIATION (1889–)

SI 4.1:date • Item 915 (MF)
ANNUAL REPORT.

Vol. 1. Proceedings. 1889– [Annual]

Also published in the House Documents series.

Vol 2. WRITINGS OF AMERICAN HISTORY. 1902– [Annual]
This volume, a classified list of books and articles on United States history that were published during the year, continues a series begun with the issuance of a volume that listed writings published in 1902. Volumes for the years 1904– 1905 and 1941– 1947 have not been prepared.
Also published in the House Document series.

SI 4.2:CT
GENERAL PUBLICATIONS.

SI 4.3:
BULLETINS [none issued].

SI 4.4:
CIRCULARS [none issued].

SI 4.5:v.nos.
PAPERS OF AMERICAN HISTORICAL ASSOCIATION.

NATIONAL SOCIETY OF THE DAUGHTERS OF THE AMERICAN REVOLUTION (1896– 1948)

SI 5.1:date
ANNUAL REPORT.

Also published in Senate Documents series.

SI 5.2:CT
GENERAL PUBLICATIONS.

SI 5.3
BULLETINS.

SI 5.4
CIRCULARS.

NATIONAL MUSEUM OF AMERICAN ART (1980–)

CREATION AND AUTHORITY

The National Collection of Fine Arts was established in 1937. The name was changed to National Museum of American Art by act of October 13, 1980 (94 Stat. 1884; 20 U.S.C. 71 note).

INFORMATION

National Museum of American Art
750 Ninth Street, N.W.
Washington, D.C. 20560-0970
(202) 275-1500
http://www.nmaa.si.edu

SI 6.1:date
ANNUAL REPORTS.

SI 6.2:CT • Item 916
GENERAL PUBLICATIONS.

SI 6.2:B 23 • Item 916
AMERICAN ART IN THE BARBIZON MOOD. 1975. 191 p. il.

This catalog is a pictorial collection of the works of those mid-nineteenth century American artists who carried on the Barbizon style. Several of the works are shown in color. The book also compares the styles of French artists of the Barbizon school with the Americans' styles. A short biography of each artist whose works are reviewed is also provided.

SI 6.3:
BULLETINS.

SI 6.4:
CIRCULARS.

SI 6.5:nos.
CATALOGUE OF COLLECTIONS.

SI 6.8:CT   • **Item 916-A**
HANDBOOKS, MANUALS, GUIDES. [Irregular]

SI 6.9:CT
POSTERS.

FREER GALLERY OF ART AND ARTHUR M. SACKLER GALLERY
(1921–   )

INFORMATION

    Freer Gallery of Art and
        Arthur M. Sackler Gallery
    1050 Independence Ave. SW
    Washington, D.C. 20560
    (202) 357-4880
    Fax: (202) 357-4911
    www.asia.si.edu

SI 7.1:date
ANNUAL REPORTS.

SI 7.2:CT   • **Item 922-C**
GENERAL PUBLICATIONS.

SI 7.3
BULLETINS.

SI 7.4
CIRCULARS.

SI 7.5
LAWS.

SI 7.6
REGULATIONS.

SI 7.7:nos.
ORIENTAL STUDIES.

SI 7.8
OCCASIONAL PAPERS. v. 1–   1947–

    PURPOSE:– To provide a means of publishing papers on subjects relating to the arts of the Gallery, written by scholars.

NATIONAL GALLERY OF ART
(1937–   )

INFORMATION

    National Gallery of Art
    Smithsonian Institution
    Constitution Avenue and Sixth Street, NW
    Washington, D.C. 20565
    (202) 737-4215
    Fax: (202) 842-2356
    http://www.nga.gov

SI 8.1:date
ANNUAL REPORTS.

SI 8.2:CT   • **Item 917**
GENERAL PUBLICATIONS.

SI 8.8:CT   • **Item 917**
HANDBOOKS, MANUALS, GUIDES. [Irregular]

SI 8.9:   • **Item 917**
REPORT AND STUDIES IN THE HISTORY OF ART.
   1967–   [Annual]

    PURPOSE:– To publish scholarly articles and to report on the activities of the National Gallery, covering acquisitions exhibitions, publications, donors, visiting lecturers, music, paintings on extended loan, and other related activities. Includes black and white illustrations.

SI 8.10:CT   • **Item 917-A**
POSTERS. [Irregular]

SI 8.11   • **Item 917-B**
FILM CALENDAR. [Quarterly]

    A calendar of films to be shown at the National Gallery of Art.

SI 8.11/2:date/nos.   • **Item 917-B**
CALENDAR OF EVENTS. [Monthly]

NATIONAL AIR AND SPACE MUSEUM
(1967–   )

INFORMATION

    National Air and Space Museum
    Seventh Street & Independence
    Ave., SW
    Washington, D.C. 20560
    (202) 357-2700
    Fax: (202) 357-2426

SI 9.1:date
ANNUAL REPORTS.

SI 9.2:CT   • **Item 922-A-1**
GENERAL PUBLICATIONS.

SI 9.9:v.nos.&nos.   • **Item 922-A**
SMITHSONIAN ANNALS OF FLIGHT. v. 1–   1964–
   [Irregular]

    Papers and monographs on aeronautics and astronautics, on the history of aviation, and on related subjects, by staff members of the National Air and Space Museum and their collaborators.

SI 9.11:CT
AUDIOVISUAL MATERIALS. [Irregular]

JOHN F. KENNEDY CENTER FOR THE PERFORMING ARTS
(1963–   )

INFORMATION

    John F. Kennedy Center
    for the Performing Arts
    2700 F Street, N.W.
    Washington, D.C. 20566
    (202) 416-8000
    http://www.kennedy-center.org

SI 10.1:date
ANNUAL REPORTS.

SI 10.2:CT
GENERAL PUBLICATIONS.

SI 10.7:date
PRESS RELEASES.

SI 10.9:v.nos.&nos.
FOOTLIGHT. [Monthly]

NATIONAL PORTRAIT GALLERY
(1961–   )

INFORMATION

    Public Affairs Office
    National Portrait Gallery
    750 9th St., NW, Ste-8300
    Washington, D.C. 20560
    (202) 275-1738
    http://www.npg.si.edu

SI 11.1:date
ANNUAL REPORT.

SI 11.2:CT   • **Item 922-B**
GENERAL PUBLICATIONS.

SI 11.2:Am 3/5   • **Item 922-B**
FIFTY AMERICAN FACES. 1978. 256 p. il.

    PURPOSE:– To present a collection of fifty portraits of famous men and women who have made significant contributions to American history, development, and culture. Selections were reproduced from photography, the life mask, caricature, and folk art.

SI 11.2:L 62   • **Item 911-B**
FACING THE LIGHT, HISTORIC AMERICAN PORTRAIT DAGUERREOTYPES. 1978. 378 p. il.

    Contains 110 daguerreotypes from the collection of the National Portrait Gallery of persons occupying a place in the public eye during the middle nineteenth century. Each portrait is accompanied by a brief history of the subject and the portrait.

SI 11.2:M 75   • **Item 922-B**
PRESIDENT MONROE'S MESSAGE. 1974. 128 p. il.

    Portrays the events, people, and climate of the U.S. at the time of President James Monroe's address to Congress on December 2, 1823. This address contained the famous "Monroe Doctrine". The story of Monroe Doctrine's formulation, reception, and impact on world events is told through the lives of important statesmen from the United States and abroad.

SI 11.2:P 42   • **Item 922-B**
NATIONAL PORTRAIT GALLERY PERMANENT COLLECTION ILLUSTRATED CHECKLIST. 1978. 172 p. il.

    PURPOSE:– To list alphabetically by subject the holdings of the National Portrait Gallery. Each entry includes a cameo-size reference reproduction and lists artist, medium, size, and year of completion.

SI 11.2:P 92/2   • **Item 922-B**
'IF ELECTED…' UNSUCCESSFUL CANDIDATES FOR THE PRESIDENCY, 1796– 1972. 512 p. il.

    This roster of unsuccessful candidates for the presidency contains the names of those who were president, as well as those who never won the prize, including major-party candidates who tried twice or even three times, plus the even larger number of third-party candidates. Here are contenders who were greater than their opponents and also names which only studies such as this recall from near oblivion. There is a portrait of each candidate, and also interesting account of his life and philosophy.

SI 11.2:St 1/771-971 • Item 922-B
PORTRAITS OF THE AMERICAN STAGE, 1771–1971. 1971. 203 p.

Issued to coincide with an exhibition in celebration of the inaugural season of the John F. Kennedy Center for the Performing Arts, portrays 92 personalities of the American stage, including drama, dance, opera, musical comedy, and concert stage. A portrait, sketch or bust is included for each personality.

SI 11.15: • Item 922-E (EL)
THE NATIONAL PORTRAIT GALLERY CALENDAR OF EVENTS. [Quarterly]

Calendar of events at the National Portrait Gallery, including exhibitions and lectures.

SI 11.16: • Item 922-F (EL)
PROFILE: SMITHSONIAN NATIONAL PORTRAIT GALLERY NEWS. [Quarterly]

WOODROW WILSON INTERNATIONAL CENTER FOR SCHOLARS (1967–   )

INFORMATION

Woodrow Wilson International
Center for Scholars
1 Woodrow Wilson Plaza, South Bldg.
1300 Pennsylvania Ave. NW
Washington, DC 20004-3027
(202) 691-4000
Fax: (202) 691-4001

SI 12.1:date
ANNUAL REPORT.

SI 12.2:CT
GENERAL PUBLICATIONS.

SI 12.9:nos.
OCEAN SERIES.

SI 12.10:nos.
ENVIRONMENT SERIES. 1–   [Irregular]

SI 12.11:nos.
INTERNATIONAL AFFAIRS SERIES.

HIRSHHORN MUSEUM AND SCULPTURE GARDEN (1974–   )

INFORMATION

Hirshhorn Museum and Sculpture Garden
Seventh Street and Independence Ave. SW
Washington, D.C. 20560
(202) 357-4080
Fax: (202) 786-2682
E-Mail:inquiries@hmsg.si.edu
http://www.hirshhorn.si.edu

SI 13.1:date
ANNUAL REPORT.

SI 13.2:CT • Item 922-B-1
GENERAL PUBLICATIONS. [Irregular]

SI 13.8:CT
HANDBOOKS, MANUALS, GUIDES.

NATIONAL MUSEUM OF AFRICAN ART (1979–   )

CREATION AND AUTHORITY

The National Museum of African Art was established in 1964. It was incorporated as a bureau of the Smithsonian in 1979.

INFORMATION

Museum of African Art
950 Independence Avenue, S.W.
Washington, D.C. 20560-0708
(202) 357-4600
Fax: (202) 357-4879
http://www.nmafa.si.edu

SI 14.2: • Item 922-D-2
GENERAL PUBLICATIONS.

SI 14.15: • Item 922-D-1
CALENDAR OF EXHIBITIONS AND PROGRAMS. [Quarterly]

The museum's Calendar outlines programs–special tours,workshops, film series, lectures, and other events– presented in conjunction with special exhibits.

SI 14.16: • Item 922-D (MF)
EDUCATIONAL PROGRAMS AND RESOURCES. [Biennial]

PURPOSE– To describe programs and resources offered throughout the year. Most programs are associated with the museum's Permanent Collection, one gallery which is devoted to sculpture from various African regions south of the Sahara, and another to art from the famous Nigerian kingdom of Benin.

SOCIAL SECURITY BOARD (1935– 1939)

CREATION AND AUTHORITY

The Social Security Board was established as an independent agency by the Social Security Act, approved August 14, 1935 (49 Stat. 620). By Reorganization Plan No. 1 of 1939, effective July 1, 1939, the Board became a part of the Federal Security Agency (FS 3).

SS 1.1:date
ANNUAL REPORTS.

Later FS 3.1

SS 1.2:CT
GENERAL PUBLICATIONS.

Later FS 3.2

SS 1.4:nos.
INFORMATION SERVICE CIRCULARS.

Later FS 3.4

SS 1.5:CT
LAWS.

Later FS 3.5

SS 1.6:CT
REGULATIONS, RULES, AND INSTRUCTIONS.

Later FS 3.6

SS 1.6/2:nos.
REGULATIONS (numbered).

Later FS 3.6

SS 1.7:CT by states
UNEMPLOYMENT COMPENSATION LAWS.

SS 1.8:CT
ADDRESSES.

Later FS 3.10

SS 1.9:v.
PUBLIC ASSISTANCE, MONTHLY STATISTICS FOR U.S.

Later SS 1.25/al

SS 1.10:v.
RELIEF IN URBAN AREAS. [Monthly]

Earlier L 5.33
Later SS 1.25/a 3

SS 1.11:CT
POSTERS.

SS 1.12:nos.
UNEMPLOYMENT COMPENSATION CIRCULARS.

SS 1.13:v.
PUBLIC ASSISTANCE, QUARTERLY REVIEW OF STATISTICS FOR U.S.

Monthly rev. SS 1.9

SS 1.14:nos.
LABOR INFORMATION CIRCULARS.

SS 1.15:date
TREND OF URBAN RELIEF. [Monthly]

Prior to March-April 1937, Y 3.F 31/5:25

SS 1.16:date
SUMMARY OF PROGRESS. [Quarterly]

Prior to April-July 1937 issued monthly.

SS 1.17:v
WEEKLY ACCESSION LIST OF LIBRARY.

Later FS 3.8

SS 1.18:CT
WHAT SOCIAL SECURITY MEANS TO INDUSTRIES.

SS 1.19:date
SIGNIFICANT PROVISIONS OF STATE UNEMPLOYMENT COMPENSATION LAWS. [Quarterly]

SS 1.19/2:
SUMMARY OF STATE UNEMPLOYMENT COMPENSATION LAWS.

SS 1.20:pt.nos.
UNEMPLOYMENT COMPENSATION INTERPRETATION SERVICE, FEDERAL SERVICE, FEDERAL SERIES.

SS 1.21:pt.nos.
UNEMPLOYMENT COMPENSATION INTERPRETATION SERVICE, STATE SERVICE; STATE SERIES.

SS 1.22:v.
MONTHLY ACCESSION LIST OF LIBRARY, LEGAL REFERENCE SECTION.

Later FS 3.7

SS 1.23:v.
CURRENT STATISTICS OF RELIEF IN RURAL AND
TOWN AREAS. [Monthly]

Prior to v. 2, no. 7, Y 3.W 89/2:25

SS 1.24:v.
SOCIAL SECURITY BULLETINS; DESK BULLETINS.
[Monthly]

Early title: Selected Current Statistics.
Later SS 1.2

SS 1.25:v.
SOCIAL SECURITY BULLETINS. [Monthly]
Supersedes SS 1.24
Later FS 3.3

SS 1.25/al:date
PUBLIC ASSISTANCE, STATISTICS FOR U.S.
[Monthly]
Preprinted from Social Security Bulletins.
Earlier SS 1.9
Later FS 3.3/a 2

SS 1.25/a 2:date
RELIEF IN RURAL AND TOWN AREAS.
Preprinted from SS Bulletins.
Earlier SS 1.10

SS 1.25/a 3:date
RELIEF IN URBAN AREAS. [Monthly]

Preprinted from SS Bulletins.
Earlier SS 1.10

SS 1.25/a 4:CT
SOCIAL SECURITY BULLETINS, SEPARATES,
MISCELLANEOUS. [Monthly]

Later FS 3.3/a

SS 1.26:date
GENERAL RELIEF OPERATIONS OF LARGE CITY
PUBLIC WELFARE AGENCIES. [Monthly]

SS 1.27:nos.
BUREAU MEMORANDUMS.

Later FS 3.11

SS 1.28:nos.
RESEARCH MEMORANDUMS.

SS 1.29:nos.
STAFF MEMORANDUMS.

SS 1.30:nos.
BUREAU REPORTS.
Later FS 3.9

SS 1.31:date
COMPARISON OF STATE UNEMPLOYMENT COMPEN-
SATION LAWS.

SS 1.32:vol.
UNEMPLOYMENT COMPENSATION INTERPRE-
TATION SERVICE, BENEFIT SERIES.

SS 1.33:v.
OLD-AGE INSURANCE OPERATING STATISTICS
REVIEW. [Monthly]
Later FS 3.15

SS 1.34:nos.
ACTUARIAL STUDIES.
Later FS 3.19

SOCIAL SECURITY
ADMINISTRATION
(1995–   )

CREATION AND AUTHORITY

The Social Security Administration was transferred from the Department of Health and Human
Services (HE 3) as an independent agency in the
executive branch by act of August 15, 1994 (108
Stat. 1464), effective March 31, 1995.

INFORMATION
Social Security Administration
6401 Security Boulevard
Baltimore, Maryland 21235
Toll Free: (800) 772-1213
http://www.ssa.gov

SSA 1.1:   • Item 517-B-3 (MF)
ANNUAL REPORT.
Earlier HE 3.1

SSA 1.1/2   • Item 517-B-7 (EL)
SAA'S ACCOUNTABILITY REPORT FOR FY... [An-
nual]

SSA 1.1/3   • Item 517-B-7 (EL)
SAA'S   ACCOUNTABILITY   REPORT   FOR
FY...SUMMARY. [Annual]

SSA 1.1/4   • Item 517-B-8 (EL)
ANNUAL REPORT OF THE BOARD OF TRUSTEES
OF THE FEDERAL OLD-AGE AND SURVIVORS
INSURANCE AND DISABILITY TRUST FUNDS.

SSA 1.2:CT   • Item 517-B
GENERAL PUBLICATIONS. [Irregular]
Earlier HE 3.2

SSA 1.2:P41   • Item 517-B (EL)
PERFORMANCE PLAN, FISCAL YEAR...AND
REVISED FINAL FISCAL YEAR...PERFORMANCE
PLAN. [Annual]

SSA 1.2/15:CT   • Item 517-D
BRAILLE PUBLICATIONS.

SSA 1.5/3   • Item 516-N (MF)
THE OHA LAW JOURNAL. [Quarterly]
Earlier HE 3.66/3

SSA 1.6   • Item 520
REGULATIONS, RULES, INSTRUCTIONS.
Earlier HE 3.6

SSA 1.6/2:nos.   • Item 517-G
SOCIAL SECURITY ACQUIESCENCE RULING (Se-
ries).

Each ruling deals with the appeal of a different applicant for a particular kind of Social Security benefit, such as disability insurance, supplemental security income, etc.
Earlier HE 3.6/2-2

SSA 1.8:CT   • Item 517-C
HANDBOOKS, MANUALS, AND GUIDES. [Irregular]
Earlier HE 3.6/3

SSA 1.8/2:nos.   • Item 517-H
POMS PROGRAM OPERATIONS MANUAL SYSTEM.
Earlier HE 3.6/5

SSA 1.8/3:date   • Item 516-C-1
SOCIAL SECURITY HANDBOOK. [Irregular]

PURPOSE:—To explain the Federal retirement, survivors, disability, and black lung benefits, supplemental security income programs,
health insurance, and public assistance.
Earlier HE 3.6/8

SSA 1.8/4:date   • Item 516-X-1 (CD)
SSA PUBLICATIONS ON CD-ROM.

SSA 1.9   • Item 516-B-5
DIRECTORIES.

SSA 1.9/2   • Item 516-B-6
SSA BALTIMORE TELEPHONE DIRECTORY.

SSA 1.10:CT   • Item 516-B-1
BIBLIOGRAPHIES AND LISTS OF PUBLICATIONS.
Earlier HE 3.38

SSA 1.13:   • Item 517-B-4
FORMS.
Earlier HE 3.96

SSA 1.17:date   • Item 517-B-1 (EL)
SSI RECIPIENTS BY STATE AND COUNTY. [Annual]

PURPOSE:– To present tabular data on State
and County distribution of Federally administered
payments to persons receiving supplemental security income.
Earlier HE 3.71

SSA 1.17/2:date   • Item 517-H-2 (P) (EL)
STATE ASSISTANCE PROGRAMS FOR SSI RECIPI-
ENTS. [Annual]

SSA 1.17/3   • Item 516-L-2 (EL)
EARNINGS AND EMPLOYMENT DATA FOR WAGE
AND SALARY WORKERS COVERED UNDER
SOCIAL SECURITY, BY STATE AND COUNTY.
[Annual]
Earlier HE 3.95

SSA 1.17/4:date   • Item 516-L-3 (P) (EL)
OASDI BENEFICIARIES BY STATE AND COUNTY.
[Annual]

SSA 1.19:CT   • Item 517-E
FACT SHEET (various topics).
Earlier HE 3.21/2

SSA 1.19/2:date   • Item 517-B-2
SOCIAL SECURITY, FACTS AND FIGURES.

SSA 1.20:date   • Item 517-F (EL)
WHEN YOU GET SOCIAL SECURITY RETIREMENT
OR SURVIVORS BENEFITS, WHAT YOU NEED
TO KNOW. [Annual]

SSA 1.21   • Item 517-J
WHEN YOU GET SOCIAL SECURITY DISABILITY
BENEFITS, WHAT YOU NEED TO KNOW.

SSA 1.22:v.nos./nos.   • Item 523-A-5 (P) (EL)
SOCIAL SECURITY BULLETINS. v. 1— 1938—
[Quarterly]

Official publication of the Social Security Administration. Contains articles on the various programs of the Administration
Departments: Social Security in Review; Notes
and Brief Reports; Recent Publications; Current
Operation Statistics.
Earlier HE 3.3

SSA 1.22/2   • Item 523-A-1
ANNUAL STATISTICAL SUPPLEMENT TO THE
SOCIAL SECURITY BULLETIN.

Detailed annual data, issued separately beginning with the data for the calendar year 1955.
Prior to that, data appeared in the September
issues. Monthly data is contained in the Current
Operating Statistics section of the Social Security Bulletins (SSA 1.22).
Earlier HE 3.3/3

SSA 1.23   • Item 516-R (MF)
AUTOMATED DATA PROCESSING PLAN UPDATE.
[Semiannual]

SSA 1.24 • Item 522-A-1 (P) (EL)
SOCIAL SECURITY PROGRAMS THROUGHOUT THE WORLD. [Annual]

PURPOSE:–To present analysis of the principal provisions of social security programs in all countries of the world. Countries are listed alphabetically and a separate summary is given for each country. The larger part of the programs covered are social insurance measures but several related types of social security programs are also included.
Earlier HE 3.49/3

SSA 1.24/2:date • Item 517-B
SOCIAL SECURITY PROGRAMS IN THE UNITED STATES.

SSA 1.25:nos. • Item 516-F (EL)
ACTUARIAL NOTES.

SSA 1.25/2: • Item 516-X-3 (EL)
ACTUARIAL STUDIES.

SSA 1.26:date • Item 516-A-5 (EL)
FAST FACTS & FIGURES ABOUT SOCIAL SECURITY. [Annual]

Earlier HE 3.94

SSA 1.27: • Item 516-X-2 (E)
ELECTRONIC PRODUCTS (misc.).

SSA 1.28: • Item 516-X-2 (EL)
SOCIAL SECURITY TODAY.

SSA 1.29: • Item 517-B-6 (P) (EL)
SOCIAL SECURITY AGREEMENTS (various countries).

SSA 1.30 • Item 516-M (EL)
INCOME OF THE POPULATION 55 OR OLDER.

SSA 1.31: • Item 516-X-4 (EL)
DISABILITY NOTES.

DEPARTMENT OF THE TREASURY
(1789–   )

CREATION AND AUTHORITY

The Treasury Department was created by act of Congress approved September 2, 1789 (1 Stat. 65; 31 U.S.C. 1001). Many subsequent acts have figured in the development of the Department, delegating new duties to its charge and establishing the numerous bureaus and divisions which now compose the Treasury.

INFORMATION

Office of Public Correspondence
Department of the Treasury
1500 Pennsylvania Ave. NW
Washington, DC 20220
(202) 622-1260
Fax: (202) 622-6415
http://www.treas.gov

T 1.1 • Item 923
ANNUAL REPORT OF THE SECRETARY OF THE TREASURY ON THE STATE OF THE FINANCES. [Annual]

Contains a review of the activities of the Department and sub-agencies and statistical tables.
Also published in the House Documents series.

T 1.1/2:date • Item 923 (MF)
OFFICE OF REVENUE SHARING: ANNUAL REPORT.
1st–   1974–

T 1.1/3:date • Item 923
UNITED STATES GOVERNMENT, ANNUAL REPORT, APPENDIX.

Supersedes Combined Statement of Receipts Expenditures Balances of Government for Fiscal Year (date), (T 63.113).

T 1.1/4:date • Item 923 (MF)
TREASURY EXECUTIVE INSTITUTE: ANNUAL REPORT.

T 1.1/5 • Item 923 (MF)
SEMIANNUAL REPORT TO THE CONGRESS (Office of the Inspector General).

T 1.1/6 • Item 923-A-8 (EL)
TREASURY INSPECTOR GENERAL FOR TAX ADMINISTRATION. [Semiannual]

T 1.2:CT • Item 925
GENERAL PUBLICATIONS.

T 1.2/3 • Item 923-B-2 (EL)
TREASURY NEWS.

T 1.3 • Item 926-A
TREASURY BULLETIN. 1939–   [Quarterly]

PURPOSE:–To extend knowledge of the public finances, monetary developments and activities of the Treasury Department by making information available in a more compact and usable form. The data contained in this publication supplements or recapitulates that contained in the daily Treasury statements and other publications and press releases.
Gives summary of Federal fiscal operations, budget receipts and expenditures, trust account and other transactions, cash income and outgo, debt outstanding and Treasurer's account, statutory debt limitation, debt operations, U.S. savings bonds, Treasury savings notes, ownership of Federal securities, Treasury survey of ownership of Federal securities, market quotations on Treasury securities, average yields on long-term bonds, Internal Revenue collections, monetary statistics, Exchange Stabilization Fund, capital movements. Cumulative index. Charts.
Later T 63.103/2
ISSN 0041-2155

T 1.4:date
CIRCULARS.

T 1.4/2 • Item 924
DEPARTMENT CIRCULARS. 1–   1913–   [Irregular]

Regulations and instructions. Issued in an unnumbered series from 1789 to 1913.

T 1.4/3 • Item 924
DEPARTMENT CIRCULARS, PUBLIC DEBT SERIES. [Irregular]

T 1.5 • Item 923-A-2
DAILY STATEMENT OF THE TREASURY. 1895–   [Daily]

Gives account of Treasurer of the United States; cash deposits and withdrawals; changes in the public debt; effects of operations on public debt; memorandum on interfund transactions; U.S. savings bond program.

Gives account of Treasurer of the United States; cash deposits and withdrawals; changes in the public debt; effects of operations on public debt; memorandum on interfund transactions; U.S. savings bond program.
The last daily issue of each month gives additional tables on the public debt; U.S. savings bonds; summary of public debt and guaranteed obligations outstanding; statements of the public debt, guaranteed obligations, contingent liabilities, and obligation of government operations and other agencies, held by the Treasury; direct and guaranteed debt on significant days.

The deposits and withdrawals shown in these statements are those that affect the account of the Treasurer of the United States. Receipts and expenditures of the U.S. Government on a budgetary basis, showing surplus or deficit, reported on a daily basis prior to February 17, 1954, are nowpublished in the Monthly Statements (listed below), which are released shortly after the middle of the following month.
ISSN 0145-0239

T 1.5/2 • Item 923-A-2
MONTHLY STATEMENT OF RECEIPTS AND OUTLAYS OF THE UNITED STATES GOVERNMENT. [Monthly]

Includes summary table: budget summary (fiscal year to date); budget receipts and expenditures (in detail), trust accounts; sales and redemption of obligations of Government agencies in markets (net), in public debt securities (net), effect of operations on public debt; public enterprise funds; summary of budget receipts and expenditures, fiscal year, by month.
Prior to July 31, 1972, entitled Monthly Statement of Receipts and Expenditures of the United States Government.
Later T 63.113/2
ISSN 0364-1007

T 1.5/3:date • Item 923-A-2
MONTHLY STATEMENT OF PUBLIC DEBT OF THE UNITED STATES. (Subscription includes T 1.5 and T 1.5/2)

Prior to July 1974 included in Month End Daily Statement of the Treasury.
Later T 63.215
ISSN 0364-1015

T 1.6:date
REPORTS ON CONDITION OF BANKS IN U.S.

T 1.6/2 • Item 982-L (E)
APPLICATIONS, NOTICES, ORDERS.

T 1.7:date
LAWS, COMPILATIONS AND DIGESTS.

T 1.8:nos.
GENERAL PUBLICATIONS.

T 1.9/1:date
CUSTOMS REGULATIONS.

T 1.9/2:date
REVISED CUSTOMS REGULATIONS.

T 1.10:CT • Item 926
REGULATIONS, RULES, AND INSTRUCTIONS.

T 1.10/2 • Item 926-A-1
HANDBOOKS, MANUALS, GUIDES.

T 1.11/1:date
TREASURY DECISIONS.

T 1.11/1a:vol.
INDEX TO TREASURY DECISIONS UNDER CUSTOMS AND OTHER LAWS.

T 1.11/2:date
TREASURY DECISIONS. [Weekly]

T 1.11/2a:date
REAPPRAISEMENT DECISIONS, FOR REVIEW BY U.S. CUSTOMS COURT AS PUBLISHED IN WEEKLY TREASURY DECISIONS.

T 1.11/3 • Item 950-D
CUSTOMS BULLETIN. [Weekly]

ISSN 0011-4146
Bound volume T 1.11/4.
Supersedes Treasury Decisions Under Customs (T 1.11/2).
Later T 17.6/3-4

T 1.11/4:nos. • Item 927
CUSTOMS BULLETINS (bound volume).

Later T 17.6/3-5

T 1.12:date
DIGESTS AND INDEXES OF TREASURY DECISIONS.

T 1.13:date
TREASURY REGISTER.

T 1.14:nos.
SYNOPTICAL SERIES, 1869.

T 1.15:date
CIRCULAR LETTER.

T 1.16:CT
CUBA AND PUERTO RICO SPECIAL COMMISSIONER (Porter).

T 1.17:CT
PUERTO RICO SPECIAL COMMISSIONER (Carroll).

T 1.18/1:date
REVENUE COMMISSION, REPORTS (general).

T 1.18/2:nos.
REVENUE COMMISSION, SPECIAL REPORTS (numbered).

T 1.19:date
REVENUE, SPECIAL COMMISSIONER, ANNUAL REPORTS.

T 1.20:date
TREASURY CATTLE COMMISSION, REPORTS.

T 1.21:date
APPRAISEMENT COMMISSION, REPORTS.

T 1.22:CT
PAN AMERICAN FINANCIAL CONFERENCE, WASHINGTON, D.C., MAY 24, 1915.

T 1.22/2:CT
PAN AMERICAN FINANCIAL CONFERENCE, 2d, WASHINGTON, 1920.

T 1.23:
INTERNATIONAL HIGH COMMISSION.

T 1.23/1:date
ANNUAL REPORTS.

T 1.23/2:CT
GENERAL PUBLICATIONS.

T 1.23/3:
BULLETINS.

T 1.23/4:
CIRCULARS.

T 1.23/5:date
STATISTICAL BULLETINS.

T 1.23/6:date
CENTRAL EXECUTIVE COUNCIL, REPORTS OF MEETINGS.

T 1.23/7:date
UNITED STATES SECTION, REPORTS OF MEETINGS.

T 1.24:date
COMPANIES HOLDING CERTIFICATES OF AUTHORITY FROM SECRETARY OF TREASURY AS ACCEPTABLE SECURITIES ON FEDERAL BONDS. [Quarterly]

Later T 63.116

T 1.25:
PUBLICITY BUREAU, LIBERTY LOAN OF 1917.

T 1.25/1:date
ANNUAL REPORTS.

T 1.25/2   **• Item 982-C-1 (E)**
TRANSPO TOPICS.

T 1.25/3:
BULLETINS.

T 1.25/4:
CIRCULARS.

T 1.25/5:date
WOMAN'S LIBERTY LOAN COMMITTEE (miscellaneous publications).

T 1.25/6:date
PRESS NOTICES.

T 1.25/7:nos.
POSTERS.

T 1.25/8:CT
POSTERS, SMALL.

T 1.25/9:CT
POSTERS (miscellaneous).

T 1.26:
NATIONAL WAR SAVINGS COMMITTEE.

T 1.26/1:date
ANNUAL REPORTS.

T 1.26/3:
BULLETINS.

T 1.26/4:
CIRCULARS.

T 1.26/5:nos. or CT
POSTERS.

T 1.26/6:nos.
BLANK FORMS.

T 1.26/7:v.nos.
WAR SAVER.

T 1.26/8:v.nos.
SAVINGS LETTER.

T 1.27:
WAR LOAN ORGANIZATION.

T 1.27/1:date
ANNUAL REPORTS.

T 1.27/2:CT
GENERAL PUBLICATIONS.

T 1.27/3:
BULLETINS.

T 1.27/4:
CIRCULARS.

T 1.27/11-19
NATIONAL WOMAN'S LIBERTY LOAN COMMITTEE.

T 1.27/11:nos.
ANNUAL REPORTS.

T 1.27/12:CT
GENERAL PUBLICATIONS.

T 1.27/13:
BULLETINS.

T 1.27/14:
CIRCULARS.

T 1.27/21-29
PUBLICITY BUREAU.

T 1.27/21:date
ANNUAL REPORTS.

T 1.27/22:CT
GENERAL PUBLICATIONS.

T 1.27/23:
BULLETINS.

T 1.27/24:
CIRCULARS.

T 1.27/31-39
SAVINGS SYSTEM.

T 1.27/31:date
ANNUAL REPORTS.

T 1.27/32:CT
GENERAL PUBLICATIONS.

T 1.27/33:
BULLETINS.

T 1.27/34:
CIRCULARS.

T 1.27/35:nos. or CT
POSTERS.

T 1.27/36:vol. or nos.
SAVINGS LETTER.

T 1.27/37:date
THE DIRECTOR.

T 1.28:date   **• Item 924-A (MF)**
TELEPHONE DIRECTORY. [Semiannual]

ISSN 0364-1058

T 1.29:date
INTEREST-BEARING DEBT OUTSTANDING. [Monthly]

T 1.30:CT
PUBLIC WORKS OF ART PROJECT.

T 1.31   **• Item 926-B (MF)**
ADDRESSES. [Irregular]

T 1.32:CT   **• Item 925-H**
POSTERS. [Irregular]

T 1.33:nos.
PUBLIC CIRCULARS.

Later T 65.7

T 1.34:CT
PAPERS IN RE.

T 1.35:CT
INTERDEPARTMENTAL WAR SAVINGS BOND COMMITTEE PUBLICATIONS.

T 1.36:date
– MONTHLY BULLETINS.

T 1.37:CT
PRELIMINARY STUDY OF CERTAIN FINANCIAL LAWS AND INSTITUTIONS (by country).

T 1.38:nos.
TREASURY DEPARTMENT-GENERAL ACCOUNTING OFFICE JOINT REGULATIONS.

T 1.39
PRESS RELEASES. [Irregular]

T 1.40:date   **• Item 925-D**
FACTS ABOUT UNITED STATES MONEY. [Annual]

T 1.41:v.nos.&nos.
TREASURY SAFETY COUNCIL SAFETY BULLETIN. ADMINISTRATIVE.

T 1.41/2:date
MINUTES OF THE ANNUAL MEETING OF THE TREASURY SAFETY COUNCIL.

T 1.41/3:date   **• Item 925-F-1 (MF)**
ANNUAL REPORT OF SAFETY PROGRESS FOR (year). 1st–   1948–   (Treasury Occupational Safety and Health Council)

Summarizes the Council's activities and results in reducing the occurrence, severity, and costs of accidents and injuries in the Treasury Department.

T 1.42:nos.
MANAGEMENT IMPROVEMENT SERIES. ADMINISTRATIVE.

T 1.43   **• Item 925-A**
PROGRESS IN MANAGEMENT IMPROVEMENT. 1st– 1949–   [Annual]

T 1.44   **• Item 925-B (MF)**
TAX POLICY RESEARCH STUDIES. 1–   1968– [Irregular]

T 1.45 • Item 925-C (MF)
FOREIGN CREDITS BY UNITED STATES GOVERN-MENT, STATUS OF ACTIVE FOREIGN CREDITS OF UNITED STATES GOVERNMENT AND OF IN-TERNATIONAL ORGANIZATIONS. [Semiannual]

PURPOSE:– To provide a record of the sta-tus of foreign debts owed to the U.S. Government and to international organizations.

T 1.45/2:date • Item 925-G-6 (MF)
STATUS OF ACTIVE FOREIGN CREDITS OF THE UNITED STATES GOVERNMENT: FOREIGN CRED-ITS BY UNITED STATES GOVERNMENT AGEN-CIES. [Quarterly]

T 1.45/3:date • Item 925-G-6 (MF)
CONTINGENT FOREIGN LIABILITIES OF U.S. GOV-ERNMENT. [Quarterly]

T 1.45/4:date • Item 925-G-6 (MF)
ARREARAGE TABLES OF AMOUNTS DUE AND UNPAID, 90 DAYS OR MORE ON FOREIGN CREDITS OF THE UNITED STATES GOVERNMENT. [Quarterly]

T 1.45/5:date • Item 924-G-6 (MF)
SIGNIFICANT ARREARAGES DUE THE UNITED STATES GOVERNMENT AND UNPAID 90 DAYS OR MORE BY OFFICIAL FOREIGN OBLIGORS. [Quarterly]

T 1.46:v.nos. • Item 925-F
DOCUMENT LOCATOR, CROSS REFERENCE INDEX TO GOVERNMENT REPORTS. v. 1– 1974–

T 1.47:nos.
DISCUSSION PAPER SERIES. [Irregular]

T 1.48:v.nos.&nos.
TREASURY PAPERS. [Monthly]

ISSN 0364-6696

T 1.49:v.nos.&nos.
REVENUES, AND OFFICE OF REVENUE SHARING NEWSLETTER. (Office of Revenue Sharing)

T 1.50:date
INVENTORY OF NONPURCHASED FOREIGN CUR-RENCIES. [Annual]

Earlier T 63.117

T 1.51:nos. • Item 925-G
ANTIRECESSION PAYMENT SUMMARY. 1– 1976– [Quarterly]

Prior to No. 7, titled Antirecession Fiscal As-sistance to State and Local Governments.

T 1.52:date • Item 925-G-3 (MF)
HIGH INCOME TAX RETURNS. [Annual]

Report submitted to pursuant to Sec. 2123 of the Tax Reform Act of 1976. Contains statistical tables, charts, and other information on taxpay-ers (including those who do not pay any taxes) with income of $200,000 or more.

T 1.52/2:date
GENERAL REVENUE SHARING. [Annual]

T 1.53:date • Item 925-G-4
GENERAL REVENUE SHARING PAYMENTS. [Quarterly]

PURPOSE:– To list quarterly payments sched-uled to State and local governments eligible for general revenue sharing funds.
Earlier T 1.2:P 29
Superseded by Revenue Sharing Quarterly Payment (T 1.53/3).

T 1.53/2:date • Item 925-G-4
GENERAL REVENUE SHARING. [Annual]

T 1.53/3:date • Item 925-G-4
REVENUE SHARING QUARTERLY PAYMENT. [Quarterly]

Supersedes General Revenue Sharing Quar-terly Payment (T 1.53).

T 1.54:date • Item 925-G-1 (MF)
OPERATION AND EFFECT OF THE DOMESTIC INTERNATIONAL SALES CORPORATION LEG-ISLATION. [Annual]

Report submitted to Congress pursuant to provisions of Public Law 92-178, Revenue Act of 1971.
This report describes the operation and ef-fect of legislation authorizing the establishment of domestic international sales corporations and granting tax deferral on their profits.

T 1.55:date • Item 925-G-2 (MF)
OPERATION AND EFFECT OF THE POSSESSIONS CORPORATION SYSTEM OF TAXATION. 1st– 1978– [Annual]

Report to Congress containing an analysis of the operation and effect of the possessions cor-poration system of taxation, on Puerto Rico and other United States Possessions.

T 1.56:date • Item 925-G-5 (MF)
OPERATION AND EFFECT OF THE INTERNATIONAL BOYCOTT PROVISIONS OF THE INTERNAL REV-ENUE CODE, ANNUAL REPORT. 1st– 1978– [Annual]

PURPOSE:– To present an analysis of the international boycott provisions of the Internal Revenue Code and a summary of the activities of the Department in enforcing those provisions.

T 1.57:CT
MAPS AND CHARTS.

T 1.58:date • Item 923-A-4 (MF)
ANNUAL REPORT OF THE CHAIRMAN OF THE DE-VELOPMENT COORDINATION COMMITTEE, STA-TISTICAL ANNEX 3. 1st–

Presents statistical data showing repayments of the U.S. Government credits extended under the Foreign Assistance Act, contingent foreign liabilities, status of active foreign credits of the U.S. Government; and summaries of U.S. Gov-ernment net foreign assistance.

T 1.59:date • Item 923-A-3 (MF)
ANNUAL REPORT OF THE INSPECTOR GENERAL.

T 1.60:date • Item 923-A-5 (MF)
FEDERAL LAW ENFORCEMENT TRAINING CENTER: ANNUAL REPORT.

T 1.61 • Item 923-A-6
FINANCIAL REPORTS, A NEWSLETTER FROM THE FINANCIAL INVESTIGATIONS DIVISION. [Quarterly]

T 1.62:CT • Item 923-A-7
FACT SHEETS (series). [Irregular]
Issued by the Office of Revenue Sharing. Each Fact Sheet concerns a different revenue sharing topic.

T 1.63:date • Item 925-J
FORMS CATALOG. [Annual]

T 1.63/2: • Item 925-J-1
FORMS.

T 1.64/2:date • Item 925-G-4
FINAL STATE AND LOCAL DATA ELEMENTS. [Annual]

Earlier T 1.2:R 32/14

T 1.65:CT • Item 923-A-3 (MF)
REPORT TO THE CONGRESS ON . . . (Various Sub-jects).

T 1.66 • Item 923-B (E)
ELECTRONIC PRODUCTS. [Irregular]

T 1.67:date • Item 925-G-4
TRENDS IN MONEY LAUNDERING. [Quarterly]

T 1.67/2 • Item 923-B-4 (EL)
NATIONAL MONEY LAUNDERING STRATEGY. [An-nual]

WAR SAVINGS STAFF
(1942–1943)

CREATION AND AUTHORITY

The Defense Savings Staff was established within the Treasury Department by Departmental Order 39, dated March 19, 1941. In 1942, the name was changed to War Savings Staff. The Staff was succeeded by the War Finance Divi-sion (T 66) in 1943.

T 1.101:date
ANNUAL REPORTS.
Later T 66.1

T 1.102:CT
GENERAL PUBLICATIONS.
Later T 66.2

T 1.106:CT
REGULATIONS, RULES, AND INSTRUCTIONS.
Later T 66.6

T 1.107:CT
POSTERS.
Later T 66.8

T 1.108:vol.
DEFENSE SAVINGS STAFF NEWS.

T 1.109:nos.
PROGRAM AIDS.

T 1.110:nos.
FIELD ORGANIZATION NEWS LETTERS. [Weekly]
Later T 66.7

T 1.111:nos.
SCHOOLS AT WAR, WAR SAVINGS NEWS BULLE-TINS FOR TEACHERS.
Later T 66.9

T 1.112:nos.
SPECIAL PICTURE PAGES.
Later T 66.13

T 1.113:nos.
STARS IN SERVICE.
Later T 66.14

T 1.114:nos.
AMERICAN HEROES.
Later T 66.15

APPOINTMENTS DIVISION
(1875– 1940)

CREATION AND AUTHORITY

The Appointments Division was established within the Treasury Department by act of Congress, approved March 3, 1875 (18 Stat. 396). The Division was abolished in 1940, when it was succeeded by the Division of Personnel, established on July 1, 1940, pursuant to Executive Order 7916 of June 24, 1938.

T 2.1:date
ANNUAL REPORTS.

T 2.2:CT
GENERAL PUBLICATIONS.

T 2.3:nos.
BULLETINS [none issued].

T 2.4:nos.
CIRCULARS.

T 2.5:date
COMPANIES AUTHORIZED UNDER ACT OF AUGUST 13, 1894 TO BE ACCEPTED AS SURETIES ON FEDERAL BONDS.

AUDITOR FOR TREASURY DEPARTMENT
(1871– 1921)

T 3.1:date
ANNUAL REPORTS.

T 3.2:CT
GENERAL PUBLICATIONS.

T 3.3:nos.
BULLETINS [none issued].

T 3.4:nos.
CIRCULARS.

AUDITOR FOR WAR DEPARTMENT
(1867– 1921)

T 4.1:date
ANNUAL REPORTS.

T 4.2:CT
GENERAL PUBLICATIONS.

T 4.3:nos.
BULLETINS [none issued].

T 4.4:nos.
CIRCULARS.

AUDITOR FOR INTERIOR DEPARTMENT
(1894– 1921)

CREATION AND AUTHORITY

The Office of the Third Auditor of the Treasury Department was established within the Treasury Department by act of Congress, approved March 3, 1817. On October 1, 1894, the name was changed to Auditor for Interior Department. Under the Budget and Accounting Act of 1921, approved June 10, 1921, (42 Stat. 23), the Office was abolished and its functions transferred to the General Accounting Office (GA 1).

T 5.1:date
ANNUAL REPORTS.

T 5.2:CT
GENERAL PUBLICATIONS.

T 5.3:nos.
BULLETINS [none issued].

T 5.4:nos.
CIRCULARS.

AUDITOR FOR THE NAVY DEPARTMENT
(1894– 1921)

CREATION AND AUTHORITY

The Office of the Fourth Auditor of the Treasury Department was established within the Treasury Department by act of Congress, approved March 3, 1817. On October 1, 1894, the name was changed to Auditor for Navy Department. Under the Budget and Accounting Act of 1921, approved June 10, 1921 (43 Stat. 23), the Office was abolished and its functions transferred to the General Accounting Office (GA 1).

T 6.1:date
ANNUAL REPORTS.

T 6.2:CT
GENERAL PUBLICATIONS.

T 6.3:nos.
BULLETINS [none issued].

T 6.4:date
CIRCULARS.

T 6.5:date
DIGEST OF NAVAL APPROPRIATIONS FOR FISCAL YEAR.

AUDITOR FOR STATE AND OTHER DEPARTMENTS
(1894– 1921)

CREATION AND AUTHORITY

The Office of the Fifth Auditor for the Treasury Department was established within the Treasury Department by act of Congress, approved March 3, 1817. On October 1, 1894, the name was changed to Auditor for State and Other Departments. Under the Budget and Accounting Act of 1921, approved June 10, 1921 (42 Stat. 23), the Office was abolished and its functions transferred to the General Accounting Office (GA 1).

T 7.1:date
ANNUAL REPORTS.

T 7.2:CT
GENERAL PUBLICATIONS.

T 7.3:nos.
BULLETINS [none issued].

T 7.4:nos.
CIRCULARS.

AUDITOR FOR POST OFFICE DEPARTMENT
(1894– 1921)

CREATION AND AUTHORITY

The Office of the Sixth Auditor of the Treasury Department was established within the Treasury Department by act of Congress, approved July 2, 1836. On October 1, 1894, the name was changed to Auditor for Post Office Department. Under the Budget and Accounting Act of 1921, approved June 10, 1921 (43 Stat. 23), the Office was abolished and its functions transferred to the General Accounting Office (GA 1).

T 8.1:date
ANNUAL REPORTS.

T 8.2:CT
GENERAL PUBLICATIONS.

T 8.3
BULLETINS.

T 8.4
CIRCULARS.

T 8.5:date
FINANCIAL STATEMENT.

DIVISION OF BOOKKEEPING AND WARRANTS
(1894–1940)

CREATION AND AUTHORITY

The Division of Warrants, Estimates, and Appropriations was established within the Treasury Department about 1879. By act of Congress, approved July 31, 1894, effective October 1, 1894, the name was changed to Division of Bookkeeping and Warrants. Reorganization Plan No. 3 of 1940, effective June 30, 1940, placed the Division in the Bureau of Accounts (T 63.100) of the Fiscal Service.

T 9.1:date
ANNUAL REPORTS.

Later T 63.113

T 9.2:CT
GENERAL PUBLICATIONS.

T 9.3
BULLETINS.

T 9.4
CIRCULARS.

T 9.5:date
DIGEST OF APPROPRIATIONS.

Later T 63.115

T 9.6:date
ESTIMATES OF APPROPRIATIONS.

T 9.7:date
STATEMENT OF BALANCES, APPROPRIATIONS, AND DISBURSEMENTS.

T 9.8:date
STATEMENT OF TREASURY, DAILY.

T 9.9:date
PUBLIC DEBT AND CASH IN TREASURY.

T 9.10:date
COMPARATIVE STATEMENT OF RECEIPTS AND EXPENDITURES OF UNITED STATES.

T 9.11:last date covered
RECEIPTS AND DISBURSEMENTS OF GOVERNMENT CONSOLIDATED INTO BUREAU OF ACCOUNTS, FISCAL SERVICE IN TREASURY DEPARTMENT BY PRESIDENT'S REORGANIZATION PLAN NO. 3, EFFECTIVE JUNE 30, 1940.

CHIEF CLERK AND SUPERINTENDENT
(1897–1910)

T 10.1:date
ANNUAL REPORTS.

T 10.2:CT
GENERAL PUBLICATIONS.

T 10.3
BULLETINS.

T 10.4
CIRCULARS.

T 10.5:CT
SPECIFICATIONS AND INSTRUCTIONS TO BIDDERS.

COAST AND GEODETIC SURVEY
(1878–1903)

CREATION AND AUTHORITY

The Coast and Geodetic Survey traces its history to the Survey of the Coast, which was established within the Treasury Department in 1816. The Survey ceased to function, but was revived by act of Congress, approved July 10, 1832. On March 11, 1834, it was transferred to the Navy Department, where it remained until March 26, 1836, when it was returned to the Treasury Department. In 1836, the name was changed to Coast Survey. By act of Congress, approved June 20, 1878 (20 Stat. 206, 215), the name was again changed to Coast and Geodetic Survey. The Survey was transferred July 1, 1903 to the newly created Department of Commerce and Labor (C 4).

T 11.1:date
ANNUAL REPORTS.
Later C 4.1

T 11.1/b:date
– SUMMARY.

T 11.2:CT
GENERAL PUBLICATIONS.

T 11.3:v.nos.
BULLETINS.

T 11.4:nos.
CIRCULARS.

Later C 4.4

T 11.5:date
CATALOGUE OF CHARTS, COAST PILOTS, AND TIDE TABLES.

T 11.6:date
UNITED STATES COAST PILOT, ATLANTIC COAST.

Later C 4.6

T 11.7/1:date
PACIFIC COAST, COAST PILOT: CALIFORNIA, OREGON, AND WASHINGTON.

Later C 4.7/1

T 11.7/2:date
UNITED STATES COAST PILOT, PACIFIC COAST, ALASKA, PART 1, DIXON ENTRANCE TO YAKUTAT BAY.

Later C 4.7/2

T 11.8:date
LAWS RELATING TO COAST AND GEODETIC SURVEY.

T 11.9:nos.
MAPS AND CHARTS.

Later C 4.9

T 11.10:CT
MAPS AND CHARTS, MISCELLANEOUS.

T 11.11:date
NOTICE TO MARINERS.

Later C 4.11

T 11.12:CT
REGULATIONS, RULES, AND INSTRUCTIONS.

Later C 4.12

T 11.13:date
TIDE TABLES, ATLANTIC COAST [for calendar year].

Later C 4.13

T 11.14:date
TIDE TABLES, PACIFIC COAST [for calendar year].
Later C 4.14

T 11.15:date
TIDE TABLES [for calendar year].
Later C 4.15

T 11.16:nos.
SPECIAL PUBLICATIONS.

T 11.17:CT
SPECIFICATIONS.

T 11.18:CT
LEAFLETS ACCOMPANYING EXHIBIT TO COAST AND GEODETIC SURVEY AT PAN-AMERICAN EXPOSITION, BUFFALO, NEW YORK, 1901.

T 11.19/1:date
COAST AND GEODETIC SURVEY SUBOFFICE, MANILA, TIDE TABLES OF PHILIPPINE ISLANDS.
Later C 4.18/1

T 11.19/2:date
COAST AND GEODETIC SURVEY SUBOFFICE, MANILA, PHILIPPINE ISLANDS NOTICE TO MARINERS.
Later C 4.18/2

T 11.19/3:sec.nos.
COAST AND GEODETIC SURVEY SUBOFFICE, MANILA, PHILIPPINE ISLANDS SAILING DIRECTIONS.
Later C 4.18/3

T 11.20:CT
LEAFLETS ACCOMPANYING EXHIBIT OF COAST AND GEODETIC SURVEY AT WORLD'S FAIR, CHICAGO ILLINOIS, 1893.

COMPTROLLER OF THE CURRENCY
(1863–   )

CREATION AND AUTHORITY

The Office of the Comptroller of the Currency was established within the Department of the Treasury by act of Congress, approved February 25, 1863.

INFORMATION

Comptroller of the Currency
Independence Square, MS 3-2
250 E. Street, SW
Washington, D.C 20219-0001
(202) 874-4700
http://www.occ.treas.gov

T 12.1   • **Item 946**
COMPTROLLER OF CURRENCY ANNUAL REPORT.

Contains review of activities supplemented by statistical tables.
Also published in the House Documents series.
Incorporated into the Quarterly Journal (T 12.18).

T 12.1/a:date
– SEPARATES, TEST OF REPORT.

T 12.1/a:CT
– SEPARATES: MISCELLANEOUS.

T 12.2:CT   • **Item 947**
GENERAL PUBLICATIONS.

T 12.3:nos.
BULLETINS.

T 12.3/2:nos.
WEEKLY BULLETIN. Official Use.

T 12.4
CIRCULARS.

T 12.5 • **Item 945**
ABSTRACT OF REPORTS OF CONDITION OF NATIONAL BANKS. 1– 1897– [3 times a year or more]

Gives condition of national banks on selected dates; loans and U.S. Government obligation held by national banks; demand and time deposits, cash, balance with other banks, including reserve balances, and cash items in process of collection; condition of national banks, by classes, by States; loans and discounts of national banks, by States; loans and discounts of national banks, by States; U.S. government obligations held by national banks, by States; cash, balances with other banks, including reserve balances, and cash items in process of collection reported by national banks, by States; deposits of national banks, by States; condition of national banks in each Federal Reserve district; reserves of national banks. Comparative figures for five call dates.

T 12.5/2:nos.
– IN DISTRICT OF COLUMBIA.

T 12.6:date
NATIONAL-BANK ACT AS AMENDED.

T 12.7:date
DIGEST OF NATIONAL BANK DECISIONS.

T 12.7/2:vol.
DIGEST OF DECISIONS RELATING TO NATIONAL BANKS.

Changed from T 12.7

T 12.8:date
INSTRUCTIONS AND SUGGESTIONS RELATIVE TO ORGANIZATION, ETC., OF NATIONAL BANKS.

T 12.8/2
REGULATIONS. 1– [Irregular]

T 12.9:date
STATEMENT SHOWING AMOUNT OF NATIONAL BANK NOTES OUTSTANDING [etc.]. [Monthly]

T 12.10:date
LIST OF NATIONAL BANK EXAMINERS.

T 12.11/1:date
[CIRCULAR LETTERS TO PRESIDENTS OR CASHIERS OF NATIONAL BANKS ASKING FOR REPORT OF CONDITIONS OF BANKS].

T 12.11/2:date
CIRCULAR LETTER TRANSMITTING BLANK REPORTS.

T 12.11/3:CT
CIRCULAR LETTERS (miscellaneous).

T 12.11/4:nos.
CIRCULAR LETTERS [to conservators of national banks]. (Pubs. desig. CR-nos.)

T 12.10:date
DUTIES AND LIABILITIES OF DIRECTORS OF NATIONAL AND MEMBER BANKS OF FEDERAL RESERVE SYSTEM.
Changed from T 12.2:F 31

T 12.13:CT
ADDRESSES.
Changed from T 12.2

T 12.14:CT
SUMMARY OF ASSETS AND LIABILITIES.

T 12.15:nos.
EARNINGS, EXPENSES AND DIVIDENDS OF ACTIVE BANKS IN DISTRICT OF COLUMBIA, ABSTRACT. [Semiannual]

T 12.16:v./nos.
THE NATIONAL BANKING REVIEW. [Quarterly]

T 12.17:CT • **Item 946-A**
HANDBOOKS, MANUALS, GUIDES.

T 12.18: • **Item 946-B (MF) (EL)**
QUARTERLY JOURNAL, COMPTROLLER OF THE CURRENCY.
Journal of record for the most significant actions and policies of the Comptroller. Includes policy statements, decisions on banking structure, selected speeches and testimony, and articles.

T 12.19: • **Item 947-A-1 (E)**
ELECTRONIC PRODUCTS (misc.).

T 12.20: • **Item 947-A-1 (EL)**
OCC BULLETINS (series).

T 12.21: • **Item 947-A-1 (EL)**
OCC ALERTS (series).

T 12.22: • **Item 947-A-1 (EL)**
ECONOMIC WORKING PAPERS (series).

T 12.23: • **Item 947-A-1 (EL)**
OCC ADVISORY LETTERS (series).

T 12.24: • **Item 947-A-4**
LAWS.

T 12.25: • **Item 947-A-5**
REGULATIONS, RULES, INSTRUCTIONS.

FIRST COMPTROLLER
(1867– 1894)

T 13.1:date
ANNUAL REPORTS.

T 13.2:CT
GENERAL PUBLICATIONS.

T 13.3:nos.
BULLETINS [none issued].

T 13.4:nos.
CIRCULARS.

T 13.5:vol.
DECISIONS.

T 13.6:date
GOVERNMENT SALARY TABLES.

SECOND COMPTROLLER
(1880– 1894)

T 14.1:date
ANNUAL REPORTS.

T 14.2:CT
GENERAL PUBLICATIONS.

T 14.3:nos.
BULLETINS [none issued].

T 14.4:date
CIRCULARS.

T 14.5:vol.
DIGEST OF DECISIONS.

COMPTROLLER OF THE TREASURY
(1894– 1921)

CREATION AND AUTHORITY

The Office of the Comptroller of the Treasury was established by act of Congress approved July 31, 1894, effective October 1, 1894 (28 Stat. 205) which abolished the offices of the Second Comptroller and the Commissioner of Customs, transferred their functions to the First Comptroller, and renamed the office, the Comptroller of the Treasury. Under the Budget and Accounting Act of 1921, approved June 10, 1921 (42 Stat. 23), the Office was abolished and its functions transferred to the General Accounting Office (GA 1).

T 15.1:date
ANNUAL REPORTS.

T 15.2:CT
GENERAL PUBLICATIONS.

T 15.3:nos.
BULLETINS.

T 15.4:nos.
CIRCULARS.

T 15.5:vol.
DECISIONS.

T 15.6:nos.
DIGEST OF DECISIONS.

COMMISSIONER OF CUSTOMS
(1849– 1894)

T 16.1:date
ANNUAL REPORTS.

T 16.2:CT
GENERAL PUBLICATIONS [none issued].

T 16.3:nos.
BULLETINS [none issued].

T 16.4:nos.
CIRCULARS.

CUSTOMS SERVICE
(1927–   )

CREATION AND AUTHORITY

The Bureau of Customs was created by the act of March 3, 1927 (44 Stat. 1381; 19 U.S.C. 2071). Authority for the collection of customs revenue was established by the second, third, and fifth acts of the first Congress in 1789.

INFORMATION

Office of Public Affairs
U.S. Customs Service
1300 Constitution Ave. NW
Washington, D.C. 20229
(202) 927-1770
http://www.customs.treas.gov

T 17.1   • **Item 950-C (EL)**
ANNUAL REPORTS.

T 17.2:CT   • **Item 950**
GENERAL PUBLICATIONS.

T 17.3:nos.
BULLETINS [none issued].

T 17.4:nos.
CIRCULARS.

T 17.5:CT   • **Item 952-A**
REGULATIONS, RULES, INSTRUCTIONS.

T 17.5/2:CT   • **Item 950-A**
HANDBOOKS, MANUALS, GUIDES.

T 17.5/2:Ex 7   • **Item 950-A**
EXPORTING TO THE UNITED STATES. 1977. 101 p.

Summarizes the laws, regulations, and requirements that must be complied with by those who plan to export to the United States.

T 17.6:date
CUSTOMS LAWS (general).

T 17.6/2:date   • **Item 948**
LAWS AND REGULATIONS ENFORCED OR ADMINISTERED BY THE UNITED STATES CUSTOMS SERVICE.

T 17.6/3:date   • **Item 948-A-1 (MF)**
DECISIONS/RULINGS. [Quarterly]

T 17.6/3-2:date   •|>**Item 948-A-1 (MF)**
KEYWORD WORKSHEET. [Quarterly]

T 17.6/3-3:date   • **Item 948-A-1**
KEYWORD DIRECTORY. [Quarterly]

Decisions/Rulings contain full text of rulings, and a numerical index sheet.
Keyword Worksheet Directory together comprise the Legal Precedent Retrieval System, an index of selected Decisions and other documents.
Updates of the LPRS and cumulative; Decision/Rulings are not cumulative.
Published in microfiche (24x or 48x).

T 17.6/3-4:v.nos.&nos.   • **Item 950-D**
CUSTOMS BULLETIN AND DECISIONS. [Weekly]

Contains regulations, rulings, decisions and notices concerning customs and related matters and decisions of the U.S. Customs Court and the U.S. Court of Customs and Patent Appeals.
Earlier T 1.11/3

T 17.6/3-5:nos.   • **Item 927 (MF)**
CUSTOMS BULLETINS (bound volumes). v. 1– [Irregular]
Earlier T 1.11/4

T 17.6/3-6   • **Item 948-A-1**
CLASSIFICATION RULINGS AND DECISIONS: INDEX HARMONIZED TARIFF SCHEDULES OF THE UNITED STATES OF AMERICA. [Quarterly]

T 17.6/3-7   • **Item 948-A-3 (EL)**
LEGAL PRECEDENT RETRIEVAL SYSTEM. (online database)

T 17.6/4:v.nos./nos.   • **Item 950-F (MF)**
CUSTOMS LABORATORY BULLETIN. [Quarterly]

T 17.7:date
TARIFFS.

T 17.8:nos.
APPEALS PENDING BEFORE UNITED STATES COURTS IN CUSTOMS CASES.

T 17.9:date   • **Item 948-A**
CUSTOMS REGULATIONS OF U.S. REVISED PAGES. [Monthly]

Contains regulations made and published for the purpose of carrying out the customs laws administered by the Bureau of Customs.
Subscription includes basic volume plus supplementary service for a 2-year period. Published in loose-leaf form and punched for 3-ring binder.

T 17.9/2   • **Item 948**
MEASUREMENT OF VESSELS. [Irregular]

Issued as Part 2 of Customs Regulations.
Consists of regulations relating to and measurement of vessels, together with relevant laws of the United States, Suez Canal regulations, and Panama Canal rules.
Basic volume is kept up-to-date by revised pages.

T 17.9/3:   • **Item 948-A-2 (MF)**
COMMODITY CLASSIFICATIONS UNDER THE HARMONIZED SYSTEM, HARMONIZED SYSTEM RULINGS PACKET. [Monthly]

Contains tariff classification rulings for such commodities as textiles, shoes, foodstuffs, steel, etc.

T 17.10:date   • **Item 951**
MERCHANT MARINE STATISTICS.

T 17.11:date
MONTHLY SUPPLEMENT TO MERCHANT VESSELS OF UNITED STATES.

T 17.11/2:date
MERCHANT VESSELS OF UNITED STATES. [Annual]

Earlier T 17.2:V 63

T 17.12:nos.   • **Item 950-E**
CUSTOMS INFORMATION SERIES. [Irregular]

PURPOSE:– To provide general customs information as to practices and requirements of law for importers of goods and services.

T 17.13:CT   • **Item 950-E-1**
BIBLIOGRAPHIES AND LISTS OF PUBLICATIONS. [Irregular]

T 17.15:date   • **Item 948-B (MF)**
TELEPHONE DIRECTORY. [Annual]

T 17.15/2:   • **Item 948-B-1**
DIRECTORIES.

Includes miscellaneous directories.

T 17.16:v.nos.&nos.   • **Item 950-F (EL)**
CUSTOMS TODAY [Quarterly]

Official magazine of the Customs Service.

T 17.16/2:date/nos.   • **Item 950-F**
CUSTOMS TRADE QUARTERLY. [Quarterly]

T 17.17:date   • **Item 950-G (MF)**
IMPORTING INTO THE UNITED STATES. [Annual]

Sets forth procedures for both U.S. importers and foreign exporters. Includes information on organization of the Customs Service, entry of goods, invoices, assessment of duty, marking, fraud laws, and foreign trade zones.
Earlier T 17.5/2

T 17.18:date   • **Item 948-C (MF)**
COUNTERVAILING DUTY AND ANTIDUMPING CASE REFERENCE LIST. [Quarterly]

Tabular reference list of countervailing duty and antidumping cases, showing such information as exporting foreign country, company, commodity, rate, currency/ units, and case numbers.

T 17.19:date   • **Item 950-H (MF)**
CURRENT LISTINGS OF CARRIER'S BONDS. [Quarterly]

T 17.19/2:date   • **Item 950-H**
CURRENT LISTING OF AIRCRAFT BONDS. [Quarterly]

T 17.20:CT   • **Item 950-K**
FORMS. [Irregular]

T 17.21:CT   • **Item 950-J**
POSTERS. [Irregular]

T 17.22:date   • **Item 950-L**
CUSTOMS U.S.A. [Annual]

PURPOSE:– To summarize activities of the Customs Service.

T 17.23:date   • **Item 950-A (MF) (EL)**
U.S. CUSTOMS GUIDE FOR PRIVATE FLYERS (General Aviation Pilots). [Annual]
Earlier T 17.5/2

T 17.24:date   • **Item 950-N (MF)**
WORKFORCE PROFILE. [Annual]
Tables show the servicewide and regional profiles of the workforce in terms of race and sex and by distribution within pay levels.

T 17.25:   • **Item 950-M (MF)**
CUSTOMS PERFORMANCE REPORTS. [Annual]

PURPOSE– To provide Customs Service management with an informational reference and analysis tool. Presents workload and performance data in tables and graphs at regional and district levels of activity.

T 17.26:nos./date   • **Item 950-P**
CUSTOMS PUBLICATION (series).

T 17.27:nos.   • **Item 950-P**
HISTORICAL STUDY (series).

T 17.28:v.nos./nos.   • **Item 950-F**
GLOBAL TRADE TALK. [Bimonthly]

T 17.29:CT   • **Item 950-N**
INTERNATIONAL TRAINING AND ADVISORY ASSISTANCE PROGRAMS.

BUREAU OF ENGRAVING AND PRINTING
(1862–   )

CREATION AND AUTHORITY

The Bureau of Engraving and Printing was established within the Treasury Department by act of Congress, approved July 11, 1862 (12 Stat. 532). In the first few years of its existence, the Bureau was called the National Currency Bureau.

INFORMATION

Bureau of Engraving and Printing
Department of the Treasury
Fourteenth and C Streets, S.W.
Washington, D.C. 20228
(202) 874-3019
Fax: (202) 874-3177
http://www.bep.treas.gov

T 18.1:date
ANNUAL REPORTS.

T 18.2:CT   • Item 953
GENERAL PUBLICATIONS.

T 18.3:nos.
BULLETINS [none issued].

T 18.4:nos.
CIRCULARS.

T 18.5:CT
PROPOSALS AND SPECIFICATIONS.

T 18.6:date   • Item 953-A (MF)
TELEPHONE DIRECTORY.

T 18.8:CT
HANDBOOKS, MANUALS, GUIDES. [Irregular]

BOARD OF EXAMINERS
(1853–1909)

CREATION AND AUTHORITY

The Board of Examiners was established within the Treasury Department by act of Congress, approved March 3, 1853 (10 Stat. 211). The Board was abolished on February 10, 1909.

T 19.1:date
ANNUAL REPORTS, EXAMINATIONS IN THE TREASURY DEPARTMENT.

T 19.2:CT
GENERAL PUBLICATIONS.

T 19.3:nos.
BULLETINS [none issued].

T 19.4:nos.
CIRCULARS.

UNITED STATES CUSTOMS COURT
(1926–1930)

CREATION AND AUTHORITY

The Board of United States General Appraisers was established within the Treasury Department by act of Congress, approved June 10, 1890 (26 Stat. 136). The name was changed to the United States Customs Court by act of Congress, approved May 26, 1926. The Court was transferred from the Treasury Department by act of Congress, approved June 17, 1930 (Ju 9).

T 20.1:date
ANNUAL REPORTS OF BOARD OF GENERAL APPRAISERS.

T 20.2:CT
GENERAL PUBLICATIONS.

T 20.3:nos.
BULLETINS [none issued].

T 20.4/1:inclusive nos.
CIRCULARS, REAPPRAISEMENTS OF MERCHANDISE BY GENERAL APPRAISERS OR REAPPRAISEMENT CIRCULARS.

T 20.4/2:date
INDEX TO REAPPRAISEMENTS MADE BY BOARD OF GENERAL APPRAISERS.

T 20.4/3:nos.
REAPPRAISEMENT CIRCULARS. [Weekly]
        Later Ju 9.4

T 20.4/4:date
INDEX TO REAPPRAISEMENT CIRCULARS.

T 20.5:date
REPORT TO CONFERENCE OF LOCAL APPRAISERS HELD AT NEW YORK.

T 20.6:date
REGULATIONS, RULES, AND INSTRUCTIONS.

BUREAU OF IMMIGRATION
(1891–1903)

CREATION AND AUTHORITY

The Bureau of Immigration was established within the Treasury Department on July 12, 1891 pursuant to an act of Congress, approved March 3, 1891 (26 Stat. 1085). On July 1, 1903 the Bureau of Immigration was transferred to the newly created Department of Commerce and Labor (C 7).

T 21.1:date   • Item 955 (MF)
ANNUAL REPORTS.
        Later C 7.1

T 21.2:CT   • Item 955 (MF)
GENERAL PUBLICATIONS.
        Later C 7.2

T 21.3:nos.
BULLETINS [none issued].

T 21.4:nos.
CIRCULARS.
        Later C 7.4

T 21.5:date
LAWS AND REGULATIONS.
        Later C 7.5 and C 7.6

INTERNAL REVENUE SERVICE
(1953–   )

CREATION AND AUTHORITY

The Office of Commissioner of Internal Revenue was created by the act of July 1, 1862 (12 Stat. 432; 26 U.S.C. 3900).

INFORMATION

Internal Revenue Service Headquarters
Department of the Treasury
1111 Constitution Avenue, N.W.
Washington, D.C. 20224
(202) 622-5000
Fax: (202) 622-8653
http://www.irs.treas.gov

T 22.1   • Item 955 (MF)
ANNUAL REPORT. 1863–   [Annual]

Covers operations and activities of the Service for the fiscal year. Appendix contains statistical tables on Internal Revenue collections; alcohol and tobacco taxes; cases receiving appellate consideration or litigation, cost of administration.

Also published in the House Documents series.

T 22.1/2:date   • Item 955-D (MF)
CHIEF COUNSEL: ANNUAL REPORT.

T 22.2:CT   • Item 956
GENERAL PUBLICATIONS.

T 22.2:Or 3   • Item 956
CUMULATIVE LIST, ORGANIZATIONS DESCRIBED IN SECTION 170 (c) OF THE INTERNATIONAL REVENUE CODE OF 1954. [Irregular]

IRS Publication 78.
ISSN 0499-6453
Later T 22.2/11

T 22.2:T 72/date   • Item 956
TREND ANALYSES AND RELATED STATISTICS. [Annual]

Supersedes Economic Demographic and Related Tax Statistics (T 22.2:Ec 7/3/yr.)

T 22.2/3:date   • Item 956-B
PROPOSED MULTI-YEAR OPERATING PLAN, STATISTICS OF INCOME DIVISION. [Annual]

Projects Division budget expenditures for the current and succeeding six years. Volume 1 provides the direct and total costs by category for all Division projects. Volume 2 documents in detail the resource tables shown in Volume 1.

T 22.2/10:   • Item 956-B
PROPOSED MULTI-YEAR OPERATING PLAN, STATISTICS OF INCOME DIVISION, FISCAL YEAR.

T 22.2/11:date • **Item 956**
CUMULATIVE LIST OF ORGANIZATIONS. [Annual]

This list has been prepared as a source of reference material from which both taxpayers and Internal Revenue service personnel may avail themselves of current information pertaining to the names of those organizations contributions to which are deductible by donors for Federal income tax purposes.
Earlier T 22.2:Or 3

T 22.2/12:date • **Item 956**
PACKAGE X, INFORMATIONAL COPIES OF FEDERAL TAX FORMS. [Annual]

T 22.2/13:date • **Item 956 (MF)**
PROJECTIONS: NUMBER OF RETURNS TO BE FILED. [Annual]

Earlier T 22.2:P 94/7

T 22.2/14:date • **Item 956**
SPECIAL ENROLLMENT EXAMINATION. [Annual]

T 22.2/15: • **Item 956-J**
DOCUMENT (series).

T 22.2/15:5528/date • **Item 956-J**
QUARTERLY REPORT DISCIPLINARY AND RELATED ACTIONS.

T 22.2/15:6741 • **Item 956-J**
NEWS YOU COULD USE, A REPORT ON HRMS PROGRAMS. [Bimonthly]

T 22.2/15:7141/date • **Item 956-J**
ORDER POINT BULLETIN. [Bimonthly]

T 22.2/15:7177/date • **Item 956-J**
IRS INTERNATIONAL SPOTLIGHT. [Quarterly]

Earlier title: Update, IRS International.

T 22.2/15:7208/date • **Item 956-J**
FED STATE BULLETIN. [Quarterly]

T 22.2/15:7371 • **Item 956-J**
INSPECTION NATIONAL NEWS. [Bimonthly]

T 22.2/15:7375/date • **Item 916-J**
NETWORK. [Quarterly]

T 22.2/15:7446 • **Item 956-J**
CURRENCY & BANKING NEWS DIGEST. [Quarterly]

T 22.2/15:7583/date • **Item 956-J**
REFLECTIONS. [Quarterly]

T 22.2/15-2: • **Item 956-J-1**
COMPUTER SERVICES NEWSLETTER. [Quarterly]

A newsletter on IRS Computer Services activities, includingvarious systems, data bases, processes, and training programs.

T 22.2/15-3:date • **Item 923-B-3 (CD)**
INTERNAL REVENUE MANUAL.

T 22.3:CT • **Item 957-A**
BULLETINS.

This class is for miscellaneous bulletins and not for bulletins that belong in T 22.23, Internal Revenue Bulletin.

T 22.3/2:date • **Item 957-A**
FINCEN TRENDS. [Semiannual]

T 22.4:nos.
CIRCULARS.

T 22.5:date
COLLECTIONS OF CIRCULARS, ETC., ISSUED BY OFFICE OF INTERNAL REVENUE.

T 22.6:date
LIST OF COLLECTION DISTRICTS.

T 22.7:date
PRELIMINARY REPORT OF COMMISSIONER OF INTERNAL REVENUE. [Annual]

T 22.7/2:date
FEDERAL TAX COLLECTIONS, CALENDAR YEAR.

T 22.8:v.
TREASURY DECISIONS UNDER INTERNAL REVENUE LAWS.

T 22.8/2:date
DIGESTS OF DECISIONS AND REGULATIONS.

T 22.9:date
INTERNAL REVENUE LAW IN FORCE.

T 22.10:date
ABSTRACT OF INTERNAL REVENUE LAWS IN FORCE.

T 22.11:nos.
REGULATIONS. SERIES 1.

T 22.12:nos.
REGULATIONS. SERIES 2.

T 22.13:nos.
REGULATIONS. SERIES 3.

T 22.14:nos.
REGULATIONS. SERIES 4.

T 22.15:nos.
REGULATIONS. SERIES 5.

T 22.16:nos.
REGULATIONS. SERIES 6.

T 22.17:nos. • **Item 961**
REGULATIONS. SERIES 7.

T 22.17/2 • **Item 954**
REGULATIONS. ALCOHOL TAX UNIT.

Earlier T 59.6

T 22.17/3 • **Item 961**
TITLE 26, CODE OF FEDERAL REGULATIONS, PARTS. [Irregular]

Reprinted from the Code of Federal Regulations, individual chapters and subchapters are made available on the specific subjects pertaining to the Internal Revenue Service.

T 22.17/4:pt.nos. • **Item 954**
REGULATIONS (pt. nos. of Title 27 Code of Federal Regulations).
Later T 70.6/3

T 22.18:nos.
SPECIALS.

T 22.19:CT • **Item 961**
REGULATIONS AND INSTRUCTIONS.

T 22.19/2:CT • **Item 956-A**
HANDBOOKS, MANUALS, GUIDES.
Formerly in T 22.19

T 22.19/2:C 49 • **Item 956-A**
TAX GUIDE FOR U.S. CITIZENS ABROAD. [Annual] (IRS Publications No. 54)

T 22.19/2:Es 8 • **Item 956-A**
GUIDE TO FEDERAL ESTATE AND GIFT TAXATION.

T 22.19/2:F 22 • **Item 956-A**
FARMER'S TAX GUIDE, INCOME AND SELF EMPLOYMENT TAXES. 1955– [Annual] (Publication 225)

T 22.19/2:Sm 1 • **Item 956-A**
TAX GUIDE FOR SMALL BUSINESS. 1956– [Annual] (IRS Publication No. 334)

Covers individuals, corporations, partnerships, income, excise and employment taxes, with emphasis on the answers to Federal tax questions and problems common to most small businesses.

T 22.19/2-2:date
UNDERSTANDING TAXES, TEACHER'S GUIDE. [Annual]

T 22.19/2-3:date • **Item 956-A**
TAX GUIDE FOR SMALL BUSINESS. [Annual]

T 22.19/3:nos. • **Item 961**
LOOSELEAF REGULATIONS SYSTEM, SERVICE.

The Internal Revenue Service has established a system of looseleaf tax regulations, divided for distribution purposes into five individual services. These include all tax regulations issued by the Internal Revenue Service except those relating to alcohol, tobacco, and certain firearm taxes and those issued under tax conventions.
Supplements incorporated into the system additions and changes to the regulations within a few weeks following their publication in the Federal Register.
Subscriptions for each service include the basic material issued to date plus supplementary material for an indefinite period.
The services generally follow the arrangement of the subchapters in Chapter 1 of Title 26 of the Code of Federal Regulations.

T 22.19/3:1 • **Item 961**
1. INCOME TAX.

T 22.19/3:2 • **Item 961**
2. ESTATE AND GIFT TAX.

T 22.19/3:3 • **Item 961**
3. EMPLOYMENT TAX.

T 22.19/3:4 • **Item 961**
4. EXCISE TAXES.

T 22.19/3:5 • **Item 961**
5. PROCEDURE AND ADMINISTRATION.

T 22.19/4:nos.
INFORMATION GUIDE (series).

T 22.19/5 • **Item 956-A**
TOBACCO TAX GUIDE. 1964– [Irregular]

Publication 464 issued in looseleaf form. Subscription includes basic volume plus supplementary material for an indefinite period.
Establishes a system for maintaining current, in a single volume, the basic reference materials dealing with the Federal taxes on tobacco products and cigarette papers and tubes and the related procedures for production and handling of these articles.
Publication discontinued as a government publication. Information regarding federal regulations on firearms, explosives, and tobacco will be found in the commercial publication, Federal Reporter for Firearms, Explosives, and Tobacco, issued by the Commerce Clearing House, Inc. of Chicago, Illinois.

T 22.19/6
REVENUE PROCEDURES. [Irregular]

T 22.20/1:nos.
CIRCULAR LETTERS (numbered).

T 22.20/2 • **Item 955-A**
CIRCULARS. A– [Irregular]

T 22.21:date
LIST OF DISTILLERY WAREHOUSES.

T 22.22:letters
BULLETINS, INCOME TAX (lettered).

T 22.23:nos.   • ITEM 957 (P) (EL)
INTERNAL REVENUE BULLETIN. 1922–   [Weekly]

PURPOSE:– To provide an authoritative instrument of the Commissioner of Internal Revenue for the announcement of official rulings and procedures of the Internal Revenue Service, and for the publication of Treasury Decision, Executive Orders, tax conventions, legislation, and court decisions pertaining to internal revenue matters.

Other items included are announcements relating to proposed regulationspublished with notice of proposed rulemaking, announcements relating to decisions of the Tax Court of the United States, announcement of the disbarment and suspension of attorneys and agents from practice before the Treasury Department.
ISSN 0020-5761

T 22.23/a:CT   • Item 957
SEPARATES. [Irregular]

T 22.23/1:dt.&nos.
– MONTHLY.

T 22.23/2:dt.&nos.
INTERNAL REVENUE BULLETIN SERVICE, SPECIAL BULLETINS.

T 22.24:nos.
DIGEST OF INCOME TAX RULINGS. [Bimonthly]

T 22.24/2:nos.
INTERNAL REVENUE BULLETIN. BI-MONTHLY DIGEST.

T 22.25   • Item 960
CUMULATIVE BULLETIN. 1922–   [Semiannual]

Compilation of the material appearing in the monthly issues.

T 22.25/2:date
DIGEST OF INCOME TAX RULINGS.

T 22.25/3:trans.nos.
INTERNAL REVENUE BULLETIN INDEX-DIGEST QUARTERLY SYSTEM SERVICE 1, TAX MATTERS OTHER THAN ALCOHOL, TOBACCO, AND FIREARMS.

T 22.25/4:trans.nos.
INTERNAL REVENUE BULLETIN, INDEX-DIGEST QUARTERLY SYSTEM: SERVICE 2, ALCOHOL, TOBACCO, AND FIREARMS TAXES. (Designated Document 5379)

INDEX-DIGEST SUPPLEMENT SYSTEM.

T 22.25/5   • Item 960-A
1. INCOME TAX. 1968–   [Irregular] (Publication 641)

ISSN 0263-3594

T 22.25/6   • Item 960-A-1
2. ESTATE AND GIFT TAXES. 1968–   [Irregular] (Publication 642)

ISSN 0363-8456

T 22.25/7   • Item 960-A-2
3. EMPLOYMENT TAX. 1968–   [Irregular] (Publication 643)

ISSN 0363-8502

T 22.25/8   • Item 960-A-3
4. EXCISE TAXES. 1968–   [Irregular] (Publication 644)

ISSN 0363-8499

T 22.25/9   • Item 960
5. ALCOHOL, TOBACCO, AND FIREARMS. 1968–1974. [Irregular] (Publication 645)

Superseded by Alcohol, Tobacco and Firearms Cumulative Bulletin (T 70.7/2).

T 22.26:date
SALES TAX RULINGS.

T 22.27:date
SALES TAX RULINGS, CUMULATIVE BULLETIN.

T 22.28:date
MANUALS (general).

T 22.29:CT
INTERNAL REVENUE REGULATIONS AND INSTRUCTIONS.

T 22.30:CT
PRO-MIMEOGRAPHS.

T 22.31:nos.
FIELD ORDERS (numbered).

T 22.32:CT   • Item 961-A
LAWS (Miscellaneous).

T 22.33:vol.
INTERNAL REVENUE NEWS.

T 22.34:CT
PAPERS IN RE.

T 22.35:date
STATISTICS OF INCOME. [Annual]

Earlier T 22.2:In 2/1
Later T 22.35/2 and T 22.35/3

T 22.35/2   • Item 964
STATISTICS OF INCOME.

T 22.35/2:B 96   • Item 964
BUSINESS INCOME TAX RETURNS. [Annual] (Publication 438)

T 22.35/2:C 81   • Item 964
CORPORATION INCOME TAX RETURNS. [Annual] (Publication 16)

T 22.35/2:F 44/2   • Item 964
FIDUCIARY INCOME TAX RETURNS. [Annual] (Publication 808)

Supersedes Fiduciary, Gift, and Estate Tax Returns.
ISSN 0161-6803

T 22.35/2:F 76/date   • Item 964
FOREIGN TAX CREDIT CLAIMED ON CORPORATION INCOME TAX RETURNS. [Annual]

T 22.35/2:In 2   • Item 964
INDIVIDUAL INCOME TAX RETURNS. [Annual] (Publication 79)

T 22.35/3   • Item 964
STATISTICS OF INCOME. PRELIMINARY REPORTS. [Annual]

T 22.35/3:B 96   • Item 964
BUSINESS INCOME TAX RETURNS. [Annual] (Publication 453)

Superseded by SOI Bulletin (T 22.35/4).

T 22.35/3:C 81   • Item 964
CORPORATION INCOME TAX RETURNS. [Annual] (Publication 159)

Superseded by SOI Bulletin (T 22.35/4).

T 22.35/3:In 2   • Item 964
INDIVIDUAL INCOME TAX RETURNS. [Annual] (Publication 198).

Superseded by SOI Bulletin (T 22.35/4).

T 22.35/4:v.nos./nos.   • Item 964-C
SOI BULLETIN. [Quarterly]

Provides statistics in text, graphs, and tables from individual and business income tax returns for given years.
Also published in microfiche.
SOI Statistics of Income.
Replaces the following Preliminary Statistics of Income Reports: Business (T 22.35/3:B 96), Corporate (T 22.35/3:C 81), and Individual (T 22.35/3:In 2).

T 22.35/4 a   • Item 964-C
– SEPARATES.

T 22.35/5:date   • Item 964
STATISTICS OF INCOME, CORPORATION INCOME TAX RETURNS. [Annual]
Earlier T 22.35/2

T 22.35/5-2:date   • Item 964
CORPORATION INCOME TAX RETURNS, SOURCE BOOK. [Annual]

T 22.35/5-3:date   • Item 964
SOURCE BOOK SOLE PROPRIETORSHIP RETURNS. [Quinquennial]

T 22.35/6:date   • Item 964
STATISTICS OF INCOME, PARTNERSHIP RETURNS. [Quinquennial]
Earlier T 22.35/2

T 22.35/7:nos.   • Item 964
STATISTICS OF INCOME, CORPORATION INCOME TAX RETURNS DOCUMENTATION GUIDES. [Irregular]

T 22.35/8:date   • Item 964
INDIVIDUAL INCOME TAX RETURNS. [Annual]

T 22.36:date
INTERNAL REVENUE COLLECTION DISTRICTS (multigraphed).

T 22.37:nos.
INTERNAL REVENUE NEWS LETTER. [Monthly]

T 22.38:date
INCOME TAX BREVITIES FOR USE BY RADIO BROADCASTING STATIONS.
Formerly in T 22.2

T 22.39:date
LIST OF FORMS, RECORDS, LAWS, AND REGULATIONS PERTAINING TO INTERNAL REVENUE SERVICE.

T 22.40:date
INCOME TAX RETURNS: NUMBER OF INDIVIDUAL BY STATES, COUNTIES, CITIES, AND TOWNS. [Annual]

T 22.41:CT   • Item 955-E
POSTERS.

T 22.41/2:CT
AUDIOVISUAL MATERIAL. [Irregular]

T 22.42
PRESS RELEASES. [Irregular]

T 22.42/2:nos.
TECHNICAL INFORMATION RELEASE TIR (Series).

ISSN 0364-670X

T 22.43   • Item 964-A
ALCOHOL AND TOBACCO, SUMMARY STATISTICS. 1953–   [Annual] (IRS Publication No. 67)

Includes data on establishments and permits; comparative statistics, materials, production, stocks, withdrawals, losses, etc. for undenatured ethyl alcohol, denatured alcohol, distilled spirits; unrectified, rectified spirits and wines, distilled spirits bottled for consumption, denatured rum, fermented malt liquors and cereal beverages, wines, vinegar, tobacco; claims; label activity; collections. Figures are for the fiscal year. Index.
Previous title; Statistics Relating to the Alcohol and Tobacco Industries.

T 22.44:date   • Item 964-B
YOUR FEDERAL INCOME TAX. [Annual] (IRS Publication no. 17)

Written in plain layman's language with many examples and illustrations, it provides for the individual tax payer information on what is taxable and what is deductible. Covers all Federal tax questions and problems of concern to the majority of tax payers.

T 22.44/2:nos. • Item 964-B (P) (EL)
TAX INFORMATION, IRS PUBLICATIONS (numbered).
1968– [Annual]

Information leaflets designed to aid persons
filling out their tax forms. The majority of the
publications are revised annually to reflect any
new changes. Titles vary from year-to-year for
many of the publications.

T 22.44/3:date • Item 964-B
CATALOG AND QUICK INDEX TO TAXPAYER INFOR-
MATION PUBLICATIONS. (Publication 900)

T 22.46:nos.
PRESS RELEASES. [Irregular]

T 22.46/2:CT • Item 955-C
MEDIA FEATURE SERVICE. [Irregular]

PURPOSE:– To provide the news media with
background information on taxes for reprinting in
publications, especially those with small circulation or specialized interests.

T 22.48:date • Item 955-B (MF)
IRS PHONE BOOK, NATIONAL OFFICE. [Semiannual]

T 22.48:date • Item 955-B-2
IRS INTERNATIONAL TELEPHONE DIRECTORY.
[Semiannual]

Directory of the Office of the Assistant Commission (International). Contains alphabetical and
organizational listings. Also lists foreign posts.

T 22.48/2:date • Item 955-B
CHIEF COUNSEL OFFICE DIRECTORY. [Semiannual]

T 22.48/3 • Item 955-B-1 (MF)
TELEPHONE DIRECTORY, SALT LAKE CITY DIS-
TRICT. [Irregular]

T 22.48/4:date • Item 955-B-2 (MF)
INTERNATIONAL TELEPHONE DIRECTORY. [Semi-
annual]

T 22.48/5 • Item 955-B-1 (MF)
OGDEN SERVICE CENTER TELEPHONE USERS
GUIDE.

Earlier title: Telephone Users Guide.

T 22.48/6:date • Item 955-B-1 (MF)
MARTINSBURG COMPUTING CENTER TELEPHONE
USER'S GUIDE. [Quarterly]

T 22.49:date • Item 964-B-1
IRS CLIP-SHEET. [Annual]

T 22.50:nos. • Item 964-D
EXEMPT ORGANIZATIONS CURRENT DEVELOP-
MENTS. [Quarterly]

Contains separate sections on exempt organizations current developments in such areas as
proposed and enacted legislation, regulations and
proposed regulations, revenue rulings and procedures, and litigation.

T 22.51:CT • Item 964-E
FORMS.

T 22.51/2:date • Item 964-B
TAX PRACTITIONER REPRODUCIBLE KIT.

T 22.51/3:date • Item 964-B
TAX PRACTITIONER UPDATE.

T 22.51/4:date • Item 923-B-1 (CD) (EL)
FEDERAL TAX FORMS, INCLUDES NON-CALENDAR
YEAR PRODUCTS.

T 22.52:date
AUDIT DISCRIMINANT FUNCTION REPORTING SYS-
TEM. [Annual]

T 22.53:date • Item 955-F (MF)
REPORT ON INTERNAL AUDIT ACTIVITIES OF THE
INTERNAL REVENUE SERVICE. [Annual]

T 22.54 • Item 956-C
DIRECTORIES. [Irregular]

T 22.55 • Item 956-D
DIRECTOR'S NEWSLETTER, CHICAGO DISTRICT.
[Bimonthly]

T 22.55/2:date • Item 956-E
IRS NEWS. [Bimonthly]

T 22.55/2-2:date • Item 956-E
IRS SERVICE. [Quarterly]

T 22.57: • Item 956-F
REPRODUCIBLE TAX FORMS FOR USE IN
LIBRARIES. [Annual]

Published as an aid to taxpayers who have a
need for specific tax forms and find it more convenient to obtain photocopies at their local library. Reproduces selected tax forms for this
purpose.

T 22.59: • Item 956-G (MF)
LEADER'S DIGEST. [Quarterly]

Published by the IRS to provide IRS managers with a digest of creative management ideas
and techniques for assessing, and
developing skills in their employees.

T 22.60: • Item 956-A-1 (MF)
DISTRICT DIRECTOR'S RESPONSIBILITY AND
AUTHORITY FOR CID ACTIVITY. [Annual]

CID = Criminal Investigation Division
PURPOSE– To provide an overview of the
operations of IRS's Criminal Investigation Division
to assist in developing a better working
understanding of that function from a point of view.

T 22.62: • Item 956-H (MF)
TRAINING TIPS AND TRENDS. [Bimonthly]

An informal journal for training professionals
published by the Advanced Instructional Systems
section of the IRS.

T 22.63:nos. • Item 964-B-2
NOTICES. [Irregular]

T 22.64:v.nos./nos. • Item 956-E
TAXFAX. [Quarterly]

T 22.65:v.nos./nos. • Item 956-H
CAREER CONNECTIONS. [Quarterly]

T 22.66:CT • Item 964-B-1
IRS HISTORICAL STUDIES.

T 22.67 • Item 956-E (MF)
CONTROLLER'S MONTHLY FINANCIAL REPORT.

T 22.69 • Item 956-K (E)
ELECTRONIC PRODUCTS. (Misc.)

T 22.70 • Item 956-K (MSSP)
MARKET SEGMENT SPECIALIZATION PROGRAM.

LIBRARY
(1818–)

T 23.1:date
ANNUAL REPORTS [none issued].

T 23.2:CT
GENERAL PUBLICATIONS [none issued].

T 23.3:nos.
BULLETINS [none issued].

T 23.4:nos.
CIRCULARS [none issued].

T 23.5:date
CATALOGUES.

T 23.7:v.nos.
REVIEW OF CURRENT INFORMATION IN TREASURY
LIBRARY. [Semimonthly]

T 23.7/2:date
CONSOLIDATED REVIEW OF CURRENT INFORMA-
TION. [Annual]

LIFE-SAVING SERVICE
(1878– 1915)

CREATION AND AUTHORITY

The Life-Saving Service was established by
act of Congress June 18, 1878 (20 Stat. 164).
Under act of Congress, approved January 28,
1915, the Service merged with the Revenue-Cutter Service (T 33) to form the Coast Guard (T 47).

T 24.1:date
ANNUAL REPORTS.

T 24.2:CT
GENERAL PUBLICATIONS.

T 24.3:nos.
BULLETINS [none issued].

T 24.4:nos.
CIRCULARS.

T 24.5:date
OFFICIAL REGISTER OF LIFE-SAVING SERVICE,
WITH POST OFFICE ADDRESSES.

T 24.6:date
REGULATIONS (General).

T 24.7:CT
SPECIFICATIONS, PLANS, DRAWINGS, ETC.

Life-Saving Appliance Board

T 24.8/1:date
ANNUAL REPORTS.

Later T 47.12/1

T 24.8/2:CT
GENERAL PUBLICATIONS.

Later T 47.12/2

LIGHTHOUSE BOARD
(1852– 1903)

CREATION AND AUTHORITY

The Lighthouse Board was established within
the Treasury Department on October 9, 1852,
pursuant to act of Congress, approved August
31, 1852 (10 Stat. 119), although lighthouses had
been maintained by the Government as far back
as 1789, the work of which was sometimes referred to as the Lighthouse Establishment. Upon
the establishment of the Department of Commerce
and Labor on July 1, 1903, the Lighthouse Board
was transferred to that Department (C 9).

T 25.1:date
ANNUAL REPORTS.
Later C 9.1

T 25.2:CT
GENERAL PUBLICATIONS.
Later C 9.2

T 25.3:nos.
BULLETINS.

    Later C 9.3

T 25.4:date
CIRCULARS.

    Later C 9.4

T 25.5:date
BEACONS, BUOYS, AND DAYMARKS, 1ST DISTRICT.

    Later C 9.5

T 25.6:date
BEACONS, BUOYS, AND DAYMARKS, 2ND DISTRICT.

    Later C 9.6

T 25.7:date
BEACONS, BUOYS, AND DAYMARKS, 3RD DISTRICT.

    Later C 9.7

T 25.8:date
BEACONS, BUOYS, AND DAYMARKS, 4TH DISTRICT.

    Later C 9.8

T 25.9:date
BEACONS, BUOYS, AND DAYMARKS, 5TH DISTRICT.

    Later C 9.9

T 25.10:date
BEACONS, BUOYS, AND DAYMARKS, 6TH DISTRICT.

    Later C 9.10

T 25.11:date
BEACONS, BUOYS, AND DAYMARKS, 7TH DISTRICT.

    Later C 9.11

T 25.12:date
BEACONS, BUOYS, AND DAYMARKS, 8TH DISTRICT.

    Later C 9.12

T 25.13:district nos.&date
BEACONS, BUOYS, AND DAYMARKS, NORTHERN LAKES AND RIVERS [9th, 10th, and 11th districts].

    Later C 9.13

T 25.14:district nos.&date
BEACONS, BUOYS, AND DAYMARKS, PACIFIC COAST [12th and 13th districts].

    Later C 9.14

T 25.15:date
LAWS AND REGULATIONS.

    Later C 9.15 and C 9.16

T 25.16:date
LIGHTS AND FOG SIGNALS, ATLANTIC AND GULF COASTS.

    Later C 9.17

T 25.17:date
LIGHTS AND FOG SIGNALS, NORTHERN LAKES AND RIVERS AND CANADA.

    Later C 9.18

T 25.18:date
LIGHTS AND FOG SIGNALS, PACIFIC COAST AND BRITISH COLUMBIA.

T 25.19:date
NOTICE TO MARINERS.

    Later C 9.20

T 25.20:date
POST LIGHTS ON WESTERN RIVERS [14th, 15th, and 16th district].

    Later C 9.21

T 25.21:CT
SPECIFICATIONS.

    Later C 9.22

T 25.22:date
INSTRUCTIONS TO LIGHT KEEPERS.

    Later C 9.23

T 25.23:date
BEACONS, BUOYS, AND DAYMARKS IN 3RD SUBDISTRICT EMBRACING PORTO RICO AND ADJACENT ISLANDS.

    Later C 9.24

T 25.24:CT
RULES AND REGULATIONS.

    Later C 9.25

T 25.25:CT
MAPS.

DIVISION OF LOANS AND CURRENCY
(1876–1919)

CREATION AND AUTHORITY

    The Division of Loans and the Division of Currency were established within the Treasury Department by act of Congress, approved March 3, 1875 (18 Stat. 398). The two Divisions were consolidated into the Division of Loans and Currency by act of Congress, approved August 15, 1876 (19 Stat. 149). The Division was consolidated with the Register's Office and placed under the Commissioner of the Public Debt in 1919.

T 26.1:date
ANNUAL REPORTS [none issued].

T 26.2:CT
GENERAL PUBLICATIONS.

T 26.3:nos.
BULLETINS [none issued].

T 26.4:nos.
CIRCULARS.

T 26.5:date
CIRCULATION STATEMENT.

T 26.6/1:date
LAWS RELATING TO LOANS AND CURRENCY.

T 26.6/2:date
LAWS RELATING TO COINAGE.

T 26.7:date
CAVEAT LIST OF UNITED STATES REGISTERED BONDS. [Monthly]

PUBLIC HEALTH SERVICE
(1912–1939)

CREATION AND AUTHORITY

    The Marine Hospital Service was established within the Treasury Department by act of Congress, approved July 16, 1798 (1 Stat. 605). The name was changed to Public Health and Marine Hospital Service by Act of Congress, approved July 1, 1902 (32 Stat. 712). On August 14, 1912, the name was again changed to Public Health Service. The Service was transferred to the Federal Security Agency (FS 2) by Reorganization No. 1 of 1939, effective July 1, 1939.

T 27.1:date
ANNUAL REPORTS OF THE SURGEON-GENERAL.

    Later FS 2.1

T 27.2:CT
GENERAL PUBLICATIONS.

    Later FS 2.2

T 27.3:nos.
HYGIENIC LABORATORY BULLETINS, NATIONAL INSTITUTE OF HEALTH BULLETIN.

    Later FS 2.23

T 27.4:date
CIRCULARS.

T 27.5:date
OFFICIAL LIST OF COMMISSIONED AND OTHER OFFICERS OF U.S. PUBLIC HEALTH AND MARINE HOSPITAL SERVICE.

T 27.6:v.nos.
PUBLIC HEALTH REPORTS. [Weekly]

    Later FS 2.7

T 27.6/a:nos.
REPRINTS FROM PUBLIC HEALTH REPORTS.

    Later FS 2.7/a

T 27.6/2:nos.
SUPPLEMENTS TO PUBLIC HEALTH REPORTS.

    Later FS 2.8

T 27.7:date
REGULATIONS GOVERNING UNIFORMS.

T 27.8:date
REGULATIONS FOR GOVERNMENT OF PUBLIC HEALTH AND MARINE HOSPITAL SERVICE.

T 27.8/2:date
AMENDMENTS TO REGULATIONS, PUBLIC HEALTH SERVICE.

T 27.9/1:date
QUARANTINE LAWS AND REGULATIONS (General).

T 27.9/2:CT
QUARANTINE LAWS AND REGULATIONS (Miscellaneous).

T 27.10:nos.
YELLOW FEVER INSTITUTE, BULLETINS.

T 27.11:CT
SPECIFICATIONS.

T 27.12:nos.
PUBLIC HEALTH BULLETINS.

    Later FS 2.3

T 27.13:date
LIST OF CHANGES OF STATIONS, ETC.

Later FS 2.28

T 27.14:CT
REGULATIONS AND INSTRUCTIONS (Miscellaneous).

T 27.15:date
BUREAU CIRCULAR LETTERS.

T 27.15/2:date
BUREAU CIRCULAR LETTERS (Compilations).

T 27.15/3:nos.
BUREAU CIRCULARS.
Later FS 2.14

T 27.15/4:date
BUREAU CIRCULARS (unnumbered).

T 27.16:date
PUBLICATIONS OF PUBLIC HEALTH AND MARINE-HOSPITAL SERVICE.

T 27.17:nos.
MISCELLANEOUS PUBLICATIONS.
Later FS 2.29

T 27.18:date
MONTHLY LIST OF PUBLICATIONS.

T 27.19:CT
POSTERS.
Later FS 2.26

T 27.20:nos.
VENEREAL DISEASE BULLETINS.
Later FS 2.11

T 27.21:date
SOCIAL HYGIENE MONTHLY.

T 27.22:nos.
KEEP WELL SERIES.

T 27.23:nos.
OFFICIAL CIRCULARS, V.D.

T 27.24:nos.
HOSPITAL DIVISION CIRCULARS.
Later FS 2.12

T 27.25:date
CONFERENCES OF EDUCATORS ON SEX EDUCATION.

T 27.26:v.nos.
VENEREAL DISEASE INFORMATION.
Later FS 2.9

T 27.26/2:nos.
– SUPPLEMENTS.

Later FS 2.10

T 27.27:nos.
HOSPITAL DIVISION SIMILAR LETTERS.
Later FS 2.18

T 27.28:date
PUBLIC HEALTH ENGINEERING ABSTRACTS.
[Weekly]
Later FS 2.13

T 27.29:nos.
VENEREAL DISEASE DIVISION, COMPILATIONS.
Later FS 2.19

T 27.30:vol.
NATIONAL NEGRO HEALTH NEWS.
Later FS 2.19

T 27.31:CT
ADDRESSES.
Later FS 2.30

T 27.32:date
CONFERENCE OF STATE AND TERRITORIAL HEALTH OFFICERS WITH U.S. PUBLIC HEALTH SERVICE, TRANSACTIONS.
Earlier T 27.1 and T 27.12
Later FS 2.34

T 27.33:vol.
HOSPITAL NEWS. [Semimonthly]
Later FS 2.12

T 27.34:vol.
HEALTH OFFICER. [Monthly]
Later FS 2.15

T 27.35:nos.
PUBLIC HEALTH BROADCASTS. [Semimonthly]

Changed from T 27.Z/2

T 27.35/2:nos.
LEAFLETS.
Later FS 2.37

T 27.36:nos.
WEEKLY CENSUS REPORT OF U.S. MARINE AND CONTRACT HOSPITALS.

Changed from T 27.Z/2

T 27.37:letters
NATIONAL HEALTH SURVEY: POPULATION SERIES, BULLETINS, PRELIMINARY REPORTS.

T 27.38:nos.
NATIONAL HEALTH SURVEY: SICKNESS AND MEDICAL CARE SERIES, BULLETINS, PRELIMINARY REPORTS.

T 27.39:nos.
NATIONAL HEALTH SURVEY: HEARING STUDY SERIES, BULLETINS, PRELIMINARY REPORT.

T 27.40:CT
BIBLIOGRAPHIES, MISCELLANEOUS.
Later FS 2.24

T 27.41:nos.
CHILD HYGIENE [Letters].

Changed from T 27.39

T 27.42:date
OUTBREAKS OF DISEASE CAUSED BY MILK AND MILK PRODUCTS AS REPORTED BY HEALTH AUTHORITIES AS HAVING OCCURRED IN U.S.

T 27.43:nos.
FOLDERS.

Transferred from T 27.2
Later FS 2.25

UNITED STATES MINT
(1873–   )

CREATION AND AUTHORITY

The Mint of the United States was established by act of Congress April 2, 1792 (1 Stat. 246). The Bureau of the Mint was established by act of Congress February 12, 1873 (17 Stat. 424; 31 U.S.C. 251-287). The name was changed by Secretarial order dated January 9, 1984 (49 FR 5020).

INFORMATION

Public Affairs Office
United States Mint
Department of the Treasury
801 9th Street, NW
Washington, D.C. 20220
(202) 354-7227
Toll-Free: (800) 872-6468
http://www.usmint.gov

T 28.1   **• Item 965 (MF)**
ANNUAL REPORT. 1st– 1873– [Annual]

Review of the activities and operations of the Bureau. Contains statistical tables.

T 28.2:CT   **• Item 966**
GENERAL PUBLICATIONS.

T 28.3:nos.
BULLETINS [none issued].

T 28.4:nos.
CIRCULARS.

T 28.5:date
PROCEEDINGS OF ASSAY COMMISSION.

T 28.6:date
MINERAL RESOURCES WEST OF ROCKY MOUNTAINS.

T 28.7:date
PRODUCTION OF PRECIOUS METALS, CALENDAR YEAR.

T 28.8:date
CIRCULAR OF INQUIRY CONCERNING GOLD AND SILVER COINAGE AND CURRENCY OF FOREIGN COUNTRIES, INCLUDING PRODUCTION, IMPORT AND EXPORT, AND INDUSTRIAL CONSUMPTION OF GOLD AND SILVER.

T 28.9:date
GENERAL INSTRUCTIONS AND REGULATIONS IN RELATION TO TRANSACTION OF BUSINESS AT MINTS AND ASSAY OFFICES WITH COINAGE LAWS.

T 28.10:date
LAWS RELATING TO COINAGE.

T 28.11:CT
SPECIFICATIONS.

T 28.12:date
DOMESTIC COINAGE EXECUTED DURING (month).
[Monthly]

T 28.13:   **• Item 966-A**
POSTERS.

Includes miscellaneous posters on various subjectspertaining to the work of the Bureau.

T 28.14:date   **• Item 966 (MF)**
WORLD COINAGE REPORT.

NATIONAL BOARD OF HEALTH
(1879– 1886)

CREATION AND AUTHORITY

The National Board of Health was established within the Treasury Department by act of Congress, approved March 3, 1879 (20 Stat. 484). The Board was terminated in August 1886.

T 29.1:date
ANNUAL REPORTS.

T 29.2:CT
GENERAL PUBLICATIONS [none issued].

T 29.3/1:vol.
BULLETINS.

T 29.3/2:nos.
SUPPLEMENTS [to] BULLETINS.

T 29.4:nos.
CIRCULARS.

BUREAU OF NAVIGATION
(1884– 1903)

CREATION AND AUTHORITY

The Bureau of Navigation was established within the Treasury Department by act of Congress, approved July 5, 1884. The Bureau was transferred to the Department of Commerce (C 11) upon the establishment of that agency on July 1, 1903.

T 30.1:date
ANNUAL REPORTS.
Later C 11.1

T 30.2:CT
GENERAL PUBLICATIONS.
Later C 11.2

T 30.3:nos.
BULLETINS [none issued].

T 30.4:nos.
CIRCULARS.

T 30.5:date
LIST OF MERCHANT VESSELS.
Earlier T 37.11
Later C 11.5

T 30.6:date
NAVIGATION LAWS.
Later C 11.6

DIVISION OF PUBLIC MONEYS
(1875– 1921)

CREATION AND AUTHORITY

The Division of Public Moneys was established within the Treasury Department by act of Congress, approved March 3, 1875 (18 Stat. 396), effective July 1, 1875. In 1921, the division was absorbed by the Division of Bookkeeping and Warrants (T 9).

T 31.1:date
ANNUAL REPORTS.

T 31.2:CT
GENERAL PUBLICATIONS.

T 31.3:nos.
BULLETINS.

T 31.4:nos.
CIRCULARS.

REGISTER OF THE TREASURY
(1870– 1927)

T 32.1:date
ANNUAL REPORTS.

T 32.2:CT
GENERAL PUBLICATIONS.

T 32.3:nos.
BULLETINS [none issued].

T 32.4:nos.
CIRCULARS.

T 32.5:date
ACCOUNT OF RECEIPTS AND EXPENDITURES.

REVENUE-CUTTER SERVICE
(1894– 1915)

CREATION AND AUTHORITY

The Revenue-Cutter Service was established under an act of Congress, approved August 4, 1790. Customs collectors supervised the cutters from 1791 until 1843, when a Revenue Marine Division was established in the Office of the Secretary of the Treasury. In 1849 control of the cutters was again to the collectors. A new Revenue Marine Division was established in 1871. On July 31, 1894, the name was changed to Revenue-Cutter Service. On January 28, 1915, the Service merged with the Life-Saving Service (T 24) to form the newly established Coast Guard (T 47).

T 33.1:date
ANNUAL REPORTS.

T 33.2:CT
GENERAL PUBLICATIONS.

T 33.3:nos.
BULLETINS.

T 33.4:nos.
CIRCULARS.

T 33.5/1:nos.
GENERAL ORDERS [1st series]. 1895– 1906.

T 33.5/2:nos.
GENERAL ORDERS [2nd series]. 1970–

T 33.6:date
REGISTER OF OFFICERS AND VESSELS.

T 33.7:date
REGULATIONS FOR REVENUE-CUTTER SERVICE (General).

T 33.8:date
RULES, REGULATIONS, AND INSTRUCTIONS (Miscellaneous).

T 33.9:CT
SPECIFICATIONS.

T 33.10:date
LIST AND STATION OF COMMISSIONED OFFICERS.

T 33.11:date
SCHOOL OF INSTRUCTION.

T 33.12:nos.
SPECIAL ORDERS (Confidential).

T 33.13:nos.
CIRCULAR LETTERS

SECRET SERVICE
(1865–   )

CREATION AND AUTHORITY

The United States Secret Service, formerly the Secret Service Division, was established July 5, 1865, when the first Chief of the Secret Service was appointed. The Service derives its authority from the act of Congress, approved June 23, 1860 (12 Stat. 102) and the act of July 11, 1862 (12 Stat. 533). The Service was reorganized by act of August 5, 1882 (22 Stat. 230).

INFORMATION

Office of Government Liaison & Public Affairs
United States Secret Service
Department of the Treasury
950 H Street, NW, Ste. 8400
Washington, D.C. 20223
(202) 406-5708
http://www.secretservice.gov

T 34.1:date
ANNUAL REPORTS.

T 34.1/2:date   • Item 974
REPORT TO THE PUBLIC.

T 34.2:CT   • Item 974
GENERAL PUBLICATIONS.

T 34.3:nos.
BULLETINS [none issued].

T 34.4:nos.
CIRCULARS.

T 34.4/2:date
NEW COUNTERFEITS CIRCULAR LETTERS.

T 34.5:nos.
GENERAL ORDERS.

T 34.7:nos.
NEW CONTERFEITS (numbered).

See New Counterfeits, Circular Letter (T 34.4/2).

T 34.8:CT   • Item 974
HANDBOOKS, MANUALS, GUIDES.

T 34.9:date
ANNUAL STATISTICAL SUMMARY.

T 34.10:CT
AUDIOVISUAL MATERIALS. [Irregular]

T 34.10/2:CT   • Item 974-A
POSTERS. [Irregular]

SPECIAL AGENTS DIVISION
(1860–1915)

CREATION AND AUTHORITY

The Special Agents Division was established within the Treasury Department about 1860. The Division ceased to exist in 1915.

T 35.1:date
ANNUAL REPORTS.

T 35.2:CT
GENERAL PUBLICATIONS.

T 35.3:nos.
BULLETINS [none issued].

T 35.4:nos.
CIRCULARS.

T 35.5:date
MANUFACTURE OF TIN AND TERNE PLATES IN UNITED STATES (Year).

T 35.6:date
REPORT ON SALMON FISHERIES OF ALASKA. [Annual]
Later C 2.1

T 35.7:date
REPORTS AND STATISTICAL TABLES ON FUR-SEAL INVESTIGATIONS IN ALASKA.

PRINTING AND STATIONERY DIVISION
(1875–1927)

T 36.1:date
ANNUAL REPORTS.

T 36.2:CT
GENERAL PUBLICATIONS.

T 36.3:nos.
BULLETINS [none issued].

T 36.4:nos.
CIRCULARS.

T 36.5/1:date
CATALOGUE OF BOOKS AND BLANKS FOR USE BY CUSTOMS AND OTHER OFFICERS.

T 36.5/2:date
CATALOGUE OF BOOKS AND BLANKS USED BY OFFICERS OF CUSTOMS AT PORT OF NEW YORK.

T 36.5/3:date
CATALOGUE OF BOOKS AND BLANKS USED IN OFFICE OF ASSISTANT TREASURER, NEW YORK.

BUREAU OF STATISTICS
(1866–1903)

CREATION AND AUTHORITY

The Bureau of Statistics was established within the Treasury Department by act of Congress, approved July 28, 1866. The Bureau was consolidated with the Bureau of Statistics in the newly created Department of Commerce and Labor (C 14), effective July 1, 1903.

T 37.1:date
ANNUAL REPORTS, FOREIGN COMMERCE AND NAVIGATION.
Later C 14.1

T 37.2:CT
GENERAL PUBLICATIONS.

T 37.3/1:date
[BULLETINS] EXPORTS OF BREADSTUFFS. [Monthly]
Later T 37.3/4

T 37.3/2:date
[BULLETINS], EXPORTS OF MINERAL OILS AND COTTON. [Monthly]
Later T 37.3/4

T 37.3/3:date
[BULLETINS], EXPORTS OF PRINCIPAL ARTICLES OF DOMESTIC PROVISIONS. [Monthly]
Later T 37.3/4

T 37.3/4:date
[BULLETINS], EXPORTS OF DOMESTIC BREADSTUFFS, ETC. [Monthly]
Later C 14.3

T 37.4:nos.
CIRCULARS.

T 37.5:date
STATEMENT OF FOREIGN COMMERCE AND IMMIGRATION. [Monthly]

T 37.6:date
QUARTERLY REPORTS SHOWING IMPORTS AND EXPORTS.

T 37.7:date
TOTAL VALUES OF IMPORTS AND EXPORTS.
Later C 14.12

T 37.8:date
MONTHLY SUMMARY OF COMMERCE AND FINANCE.
Later C 14.14

T 37.9:date
ADVANCE SHEETS FROM MONTHLY SUMMARY OF COMMERCE AND FINANCE.
Later C 14.13

T 37.10:date
STATISTICAL ABSTRACT OF UNITED STATES.
Later C 14.16

T 37.11:date
LIST OF MERCHANT VESSELS.
Later T 30.5

STEAMBOAT INSPECTION SERVICE
(1852–1903)

CREATION AND AUTHORITY

The Steamboat Inspection Service was established within the Treasury Department by act of Congress, approved August 30, 1852. The Service was transferred to the newly created Department of Commerce and Labor (C 15) on July 1, 1903.

T 38.1:date
ANNUAL REPORT OF SUPERVISING INSPECTOR-GENERAL.
Later C 15.1

T 38.2:CT
GENERAL PUBLICATIONS.

T 38.3:nos.
BULLETINS [none issued].

T 38.4:nos.
CIRCULARS.
Later C 15.4

T 38.5/1:date
LAWS GOVERNING STEAMBOAT-INSPECTION SERVICE (General).
Later C 15.5

T 38.5/2:CT
LAWS, RULES, AND REGULATIONS (Special).

T 38.6:date
STEAMBOAT INSPECTORS' MANUAL.
Later C 15.6

T 38.7:date
LIST OF MASTERS, MATES [ETC.] OF MERCHANT STEAM, MOTOR, AND SAIL VESSELS, LICENSED DURING CALENDAR YEAR.
Later C 15.7

T 38.8:CT
PILOT RULES.
Later C 15.8

T 38.9:date
GENERAL RULES AND REGULATIONS PRESCRIBED BY BOARD OF SUPERVISING INSPECTORS OF STEAMBOATS.
Later C 15.9

T 38.10:date
PROCEEDINGS OF BOARD OF SUPERVISING INSPECTORS.

T 38.11:date
PROCEEDINGS OF BOARD OF SUPERVISING INSPECTORS, SPECIAL MEETINGS.

SUPERVISING ARCHITECT
(1867–1920)

T 39.1:date
ANNUAL REPORTS.

T 39.2:CT
GENERAL PUBLICATIONS.

T 39.3:nos.
BULLETINS [none issued].

T 39.4:nos.
CIRCULARS.

T 39.5:CT
REGULATIONS, RULES, AND INSTRUCTIONS.

T 39.6:CT
SPECIFICATIONS FOR PUBLIC BUILDINGS.

T 39.6/2:nos.
PLANS OF PUBLIC BUILDINGS.

T 39.7:CT
PROPOSALS FOR CONSTRUCTION OF PUBLIC BUILDINGS, SPECIFICATIONS AND PROPOSALS FOR REPAIRS, ETC. AT PUBLIC BUILDINGS.

T 39.8/1:date
SCHEDULE 1, CHAIRS, ETC. [for Public Buildings].

T 39.8/2:date
SCHEDULE 2, DESKS, ETC. [for Public Buildings].

T 39.8/3:date
SCHEDULE 3, SECTIONAL DEVICES.

T 39.8/4:date
SCHEDULE 4, CLOCKS.

T 39.8/5:date
SCHEDULE 5, METAL ARTICLES.

T 39.8/6:date
SCHEDULE 6, MISCELLANEOUS ARTICLES.

T 39.9:CT
ADVERTISEMENTS FOR BIDS, SPECIFICATIONS, ETC. FOR EQUIPMENT OF PUBLIC BUILDINGS.

T 39.10:CT by name of dept.
PROGRAMMER OF COMPETITION FOR SELECTION OF ARCHITECT FOR BUILDING FOR [ ] DEPARTMENT.

TREASURER OF THE UNITED STATES
(1789–1940)

CREATION AND AUTHORITY

The Office of the Treasurer was established within the Department of the Treasury by act of September 2, 1789 (1 Stat. 65). Reorganization Plan No. 3 of 1940, effective June 30, 1940, placed the Office within the newly established Fiscal Service (T 63.300).

T 40.1:date
ANNUAL REPORTS.

T 40.2:CT
GENERAL PUBLICATIONS.

T 40.3:nos.
BULLETINS [none issued].

T 40.4:nos.
CIRCULARS.

T 40.5:date
FUNDED INDEBTEDNESS OF DISTRICT OF COLUMBIA. [Quarterly]

T 40.6:date
ANNUAL REPORT ON SINKING FUND AND FUNDED DEBT OF DISTRICT OF COLUMBIA, FOR FISCAL YEAR.

T 40.7:nos.
MEMORANDA (numbered).

T 40.8:date
MONTHLY STATEMENT OF PAPER CURRENCY OF EACH DENOMINATION OUTSTANDING.
    Later T 63.307

T 40.9:date
WEEKLY STATEMENT OF BONDS HELD IN TRUST FOR NATIONAL BANKS.

T 40.10:date
CONTENTS OF VAULTS [OF] TREASURY DEPARTMENT.

NATIONAL BUREAU OF STANDARDS
(1901–1903)

CREATION AND AUTHORITY

The National Bureau of Standards traces its history to August 5, 1882, when the Office of Construction of Standard Weights and Measures was established within the Coast and Geodetic Survey. In 1891, it became the Office of Standard Weights and Measures. By act of Congress, approved March 3, 1901 (31 Stat. 1449), the National Bureau of Standards was established as a separate agency within the Treasury Department. On July 1, 1903, it was transferred to the newly created Department of Commerce and Labor (C 13).

T 41.1:date
ANNUAL REPORTS.
    Later C 13.1

T 41.2:CT
GENERAL PUBLICATIONS [none issued].

T 41.3:nos.
BULLETINS [none issued].

T 41.4:nos.
CIRCULARS [none issued].

T 41.5:nos.
CIRCULARS OF INFORMATION.
    Later C 13.5

MISCELLANEOUS DIVISION
(1888–1906)

CREATION AND AUTHORITY

The Division of Mercantile Marine and Internal Revenue was established within the Department of the Treasury by act of Congress, approved March 3, 1875 (18 Stat. 396). The name was changed in 1882 to the Division of Captured Property, Claims, and Lands. In 1888, the name was again changed to Miscellaneous Division. The Division ceased to exist on June 30, 1906.

T 42.1:date
ANNUAL REPORTS.

T 42.2:CT
GENERAL PUBLICATIONS [none issued].

T 42.3:nos.
BULLETINS [none issued].

T 42.4:nos.
CIRCULARS.

AUDITOR OF PORTO RICO
(1900–1909)

T 43.1:date
ANNUAL REPORTS.
    Later W 75.6/1

T 43.2:CT
GENERAL PUBLICATIONS.
    Later W 75.6/2

T 43.3:nos.
BULLETINS [none issued].

T 43.4:nos.
CIRCULARS [none issued].

OFFICE OF SOLICITOR OF TREASURY
(1830–1870)

CREATION AND AUTHORITY

The Office of Solicitor of Treasury was established within the Department of the Treasury by act of Congress, approved May 29, 1830. The Office was transferred to the Department of Justice (J 5) by act of June 22, 1870.

T 44.1:date
ANNUAL REPORTS.
    Later J 5.1

T 44.2:CT
GENERAL PUBLICATIONS.
    Later J 5.2

T 44.3:nos.
BULLETINS [none issued].

T 44.4:nos.
CIRCULARS.

T 44.5:date
INSTRUCTIONS, RULES, REGULATIONS, ETC.
    Later J 5.6

GENERAL SUPPLY COMMITTEE
(1910–1933)

CREATION AND AUTHORITY

The General Supply Committee was established within the Treasury Department by act of Congress, approved June 17, 1910 (36 Stat. 531), superseding the General Supply Committee which had been established in 1909. The Committee was abolished by Executive Order 6166 of June 10, 1933, and its functions transferred to the Procurement Division (T 58).

T 45.1:date
ANNUAL REPORTS.

T 45.2:CT
GENERAL PUBLICATIONS.

T 45.3:nos.
BULLETINS.

T 45.4:nos.
CIRCULARS.
Later T 58.4

T 45.5/1:form letters or class nos.
GENERAL SCHEDULE OF SUPPLIES, FISCAL YEAR
1912.
Later T 58.7

T 45.5/2:form letters or class nos.
GENERAL SCHEDULE OF SUPPLIES, FISCAL YEAR
1913.

T 45.5/3:class nos.
GENERAL SCHEDULE OF SUPPLIES, FISCAL YEAR
1914.

T 45.5/4:class nos.
GENERAL SCHEDULE OF SUPPLIES, FISCAL YEAR
1915.

T 45.5/5:class nos.
GENERAL SCHEDULE OF SUPPLIES, FISCAL YEAR
1916.

T 45.5/6:form letters or class nos.
SPECIFICATIONS AND PROPOSALS, FISCAL YEAR
1917.

T 45.5/7:form letters or class nos.
SPECIFICATIONS AND PROPOSALS, FISCAL YEAR
1918.

T 45.5/8:form letters or class nos.
SPECIFICATIONS AND PROPOSALS, FISCAL YEAR
1919.

T 45.5/9:form letters
SPECIFICATIONS AND PROPOSALS FOR SUPPLIES,
FISCAL YEAR 1920.

T 45.5/10:form letters or class nos.
SPECIFICATIONS AND PROPOSALS FOR SUPPLIES,
FISCAL YEAR 1921.

T 45.5/11:form letters or class nos.
SPECIFICATIONS AND PROPOSALS FOR SUPPLIES,
FISCAL YEAR 1922.

T 45.5/12:form letters or class nos.
SPECIFICATIONS AND PROPOSALS FOR SUPPLIES,
FISCAL YEAR 1923.

T 45.5/13:form letters or class nos.
SPECIFICATIONS AND PROPOSALS FOR SUPPLIES,
FISCAL YEAR 1924.

T 45.5/14:form letters or class nos.
SPECIFICATIONS AND PROPOSALS FOR SUPPLIES,
FISCAL YEAR 1925.

T 45.5/15:form letters or class nos.
SPECIFICATIONS AND PROPOSALS FOR SUPPLIES,
FISCAL YEAR 1926.

T 45.5/16:form letters or class nos.
SPECIFICATIONS AND PROPOSALS FOR SUPPLIES,
FISCAL YEAR 1927.

T 45.5/17:form letters or class nos.
SPECIFICATIONS AND PROPOSALS FOR SUPPLIES,
FISCAL YEAR 1928.

T 45.5/18:form letters or class nos.
SPECIFICATIONS AND PROPOSALS FOR SUPPLIES,
FISCAL YEAR 1929.

T 45.5/19:form letters or class nos.
SPECIFICATIONS AND PROPOSALS FOR SUPPLIES,
FISCAL YEAR 1930.

T 45.5/20:form letters or class nos.
SPECIFICATIONS AND PROPOSALS FOR SUPPLIES,
FISCAL YEAR 1931.

T 45.5/21:class nos.
SPECIFICATIONS AND PROPOSALS FOR SUPPLIES,
FISCAL YEAR 1932.

T 45.5/22:class nos.
SPECIFICATIONS AND PROPOSALS FOR SUPPLIES,
FISCAL YEAR 1933.

T 45.5/23:class nos.
SPECIFICATIONS AND PROPOSALS FOR SUPPLIES,
FISCAL YEAR 1934.
Later T 58.7

T 45.6:date or fiscal year
LIST OF AWARDS SHOWING CONTRACTORS AND
PRICES CONTAINED IN GENERAL SCHEDULE
OF SUPPLIES, FISCAL YEAR (date).
Later T 58.8

T 45.7:class nos. and date
REQUIREMENT FORMS.

T 45.8:class nos.
QUARTERLY PRICE LISTS.
Later T 58.9

T 45.9:date
SURPLUS PROPERTY LIST.

OFFICE OF THE SUPERVISING TEA EXAMINER
(1897–1920)

CREATION AND AUTHORITY

The Office of Supervising Tea Examiner was
established within the Department of the Treasury in 1912 pursuant to the Tea Act of March 2,
1897. On July 1, 1920, the administration of the
Tea Act was transferred to the Bureau of Chemistry (A 7).

T 46.1:date
ANNUAL REPORTS.

T 46.2:CT
GENERAL PUBLICATIONS.

T 46.3:nos.
BULLETINS.

T 46.4
CIRCULARS.

COAST GUARD
(1915–1917, 1919–1941, 1947–1966)

CREATION AND AUTHORITY

The United States Coast Guard was established by the act of Congress, approved January
28, 1915, as amended, as a branch of the Armed
Forces of the United States, operating as a service in the Treasury Department during times of
peace and in the Navy Department in times of war
or when the President directs. Accordingly, the
Coast Guard was transferred from the Treasury
Department to the Navy Department by Executive Order 2587 of April 7, 1917 and returned by
Executive Order 3160 of August 28, 1919; likewise transferred by Executive Order 8929 of November 1, 1941 and returned by Executive Order
9666 of December 28, 1945, effective January 1,
1946. Pursuant to Public Law 89-670, approved
October 15, 1966 (80 Stat. 932), it was transferred
to the newly created Department of Transportation (TD 5).

T 47.1:date
ANNUAL REPORTS.
Later N 24.1

T 47.2:CT
GENERAL PUBLICATIONS.
Later N 24.2

T 47.3:nos.
BULLETINS.

T 47.4
CIRCULARS.

T 47.4/2
INTELLIGENCE OFFICE CIRCULARS.

T 47.4/3
COMMUNICATIONS CIRCULARS.

T 47.4/4
MATERIAL DIVISION CIRCULARS.

T 47.5:date
GENERAL ORDERS.

T 47.5/2:nos.
GENERAL ORDERS [2nd series]. June 10, 1916–

T 47.5/3:nos.
GENERAL ORDERS [3rd series]. March 15, 1922–

T 47.5/4:nos.
GENERAL ORDERS [4th series]. March 15, 1923–

T 47.5/5:nos.
GENERAL ORDERS [5th series]. March 13, 1931–

T 47.5/5a
– EXTRACTS.

T 47.5/6:nos.
GENERAL ORDERS [6th series]. August 12, 1940–
Later N 24.25

T 47.5/6a
– EXTRACTS.

T 47.6:nos.
SPECIAL ORDERS.

T 47.7:nos.
CIRCULAR LETTERS.

T 47.7/2:nos.
CIRCULAR LETTERS [2nd series]. June 10, 1916–

T 47.7/3:nos.
CIRCULAR LETTERS [3rd series]. December 12,
1933–
Later N 24.22

T 47.8:CT
REGULATIONS, RULES, AND INSTRUCTIONS
(Miscellaneous).
Later N 24.8

T 47.8/2:nos.
PAY AND SUPPLY INSTRUCTIONS CIRCULARS.
Later N 24.26

T 47.8/3:CT
HANDBOOKS, MANUALS, GUIDES.

T 47.9:date
REGULATIONS, RULES, AND INSTRUCTIONS.

T 47.10:date
REGISTER OF COMMISSIONED AND WARRANT
OFFICERS AND CADETS AND SHIPS AND
STATIONS OF COAST GUARD.

T 47.10/2:date
REGISTER OF COMMISSIONED AND WARRANT
OFFICERS, COAST GUARD RESERVE.

T 47.11:CT
SPECIFICATIONS.

Life-Saving Appliance Board

T 47.12/1:date
ANNUAL REPORTS.
Earlier T 24.8/1

T 47.12/2:CT
GENERAL PUBLICATIONS.
Earlier T 24.8/2

Coast Guard (Continued)

T 47.13:nos.
INSTRUCTIONS (numbered).

T 47.14:date
STANDARD STOCK CATALOGUES.

T 47.15:dt.&nos.
PERSONNEL SECTION BULLETINS.

T 47.16:nos.
REPORT OF GUNNNERY EXERCISES [for official use only].

T 47.17:nos.
LAW BULLETINS. [Monthly]
    Later N 24.29

T 47.18:CT
ADDRESSES.

T 47.19:dt.&nos.
NOTICE TO MARINERS, AFFECTING LIGHTHOUSES AND OTHER NAVIGATIONAL AIDS. [Weekly]
    Earlier C 9.26
    Later N 42.12

T 47.20:dt.&nos.
NOTICE TO MARINERS, GREAT LAKES, AFFECTING LIGHTHOUSES AND OTHER NAVIGATIONAL AIDS. [Weekly]
    Earlier C 9.41
    Later N 42.13

T 47.20/2
LOCAL NOTICE TO MARINERS [Cleveland edition].

T 47.20/3
LOCAL NOTICE TO MARINERS [Sault Ste. Marie edition].

T 47.21:vol.
COAST GUARD BULLETINS. [Monthly]
    Formerly Lighthouse Service Bulletins (C 9.31).
    Later N 24.11

T 47.22:CT
RADIO BEACON SYSTEM (maps).
    Earlier C 9.53:R 11, C 9.53:R 11/2 and C 9.53:R 11/3
    Later N 24.14

T 47.23:date
LIGHT LIST, ATLANTIC COAST OF UNITED STATES, NORTHWEST PART.
    Earlier C 9.50
    Later N 24.15

T 47.24:date
LIGHT LIST, ATLANTIC COAST OF UNITED STATES, SOUTHERN PART.
    Earlier C 9.51
    Later N 24.16

T 47.25:date
LIGHT LIST, PACIFIC COAST OF UNITED STATES.

    Earlier C 9.1
    Later N 24,19, T 47.25, and T 47.52

T 47.25/2:dt.&v.nos.
LOCAL LIST OF LIGHTS AND OTHER MARINE AIDS, PACIFIC. [Annual]

T 47.26:date
LIGHT LIST, GREAT LAKES, UNITED STATES AND CANADA.
    Earlier C 9.30
    Later N 24.20, T 47.26 and T 47.52

T 47.26/2:date
RADIO AIDS TO NAVIGATION, GREAT LAKES, UNITED STATES AND CANADA.
    Earlier D 203.2:R 11

T 47.27:date
LIGHT LIST, MISSISSIPPI AND OHIO RIVERS AND TRIBUTARIES.
    Earlier C 9.29/2
    Later N 24,18, T 47.27, and T 47.52

T 47.28:date
LIGHT LIST, ATLANTIC COAST OF UNITED STATES, INTERCOASTAL WATERWAY, HAMPTON ROADS TO RIO GRANDE, INCLUDING INSIDE WATERS.
    Earlier C 9.52
    Later N 24.17

T 47.29:dt.&nos.
ENGINEERING CHARTS.

T 47.30:date
ENGINEER'S DIGEST. [Monthly]
    Later N 24.21

T 47.31:v.nos.
PROCEEDINGS OF THE MERCHANT MARINE COUNCIL. [Monthly]
    Earlier N 24.32

T 47.32:v.nos.
AIR SEA RESCUE BULLETIN [Restricted]. [Monthly]
    Earlier N 24.35

T 47.32/2:date
AIRCRAFT EMERGENCY PROCEDURES OVER WATER.

T 47.33:nos.
CIVIL READJUSTMENT BULLETINS.
    Earlier N 24.38

T 47.34:nos.
NAVIGATION AND VESSEL INSPECTION CIRCULARS.
    Earlier N 24.27

T 47.35:date
LIGHT LIST, ATLANTIC AND GULF COASTS OF UNITED STATES.
    Earlier N 24.30
    Later T 47.52

T 47.35/2:date. & vol. nos.
LIST OF LIGHTS AND OTHER MARINE AIDS, ATLANTIC COAST (by district).

T 47.36:nos.
EDUCATIONAL SERIES.
    Earlier N 24.28

T 47.37:nos.
SHIP CONSTRUCTION MANUALS.

    Earlier N 24.37

T 47.38:dt.&nos.
FINANCE AND SUPPLY CIRCULARS.

T 47.39:dt.&nos.
FINANCE AND SUPPLY MEMORANDUMS.

T 47.40:dt.&nos.
UNIFORM CIRCULARS.

T 47.41:nos.
ACTIVE PEACETIME SERVICE.
    Publications designated C.G. AP-nos.

T 47.42:nos.
ELECTRONICS ENGINEERING REPORTS.

T 47.42/2:nos.
CIVIL ENGINEERING REPORTS.

T 47.43:dt.&nos.
AVIATION TECHNICAL ORDERS.

T 47.44:CT
LAWS.
    Earlier N 24.31

T 47.45
AVIATION TECHNICAL LETTERS.

T 47.46
NAVAL ENGINEERING MEMORANDUM.

T 47.47:v.nos.
COAST GUARD RESERVIST. [Monthly]

T 47.48:CT
POSTERS.

T 47.49:date
MOTORBOAT SAFETY. [Irregular]
    Earlier T 47.2:M 85

T 47.50:date
DIRECTIVES, PUBLICATIONS AND REPORTS INDEX.

T 47.50/2:date
BIBLIOGRAPHY OF PUBLICATIONS FOR PUBLIC EDUCATION AND MEMBERSHIP TRAINING.

T 47.51:date
EQUIPMENT LISTS.

T 47.52:v.nos./date
LIST OF LIGHTS AND OTHER MARINE AIDS.

        Vol. 1-2 Atlantic Coast
        Vol. 3 Pacific Coast
        Vol. 4 Great Lakes
        Vol. 5 Mississippi River
    Earlier T 47.35, T 47.25, T 47.26, T 47.27

T 47.53:date
COAST GUARD ACADEMY CATALOG.

T 47.54:date
RECREATIONAL BOATING IN UNITED STATES, REPORT ON ACCIDENTS, NUMBERING AND RELATED ACTIVITIES. [Semiannual]

T 47.55:nos.
OCEANOGRAPHIC REPORTS.

FEDERAL FARM LOAN BUREAU (1916– 1933)

CREATION AND AUTHORITY

The Federal Farm Loan Bureau was established within the Treasury Department under supervision of the Federal Loan Board by the Federal Farm Loan Act, approved July 17, 1916 (39 Stat. 360). The Bureau was abolished and its functions transferred to the Farm Credit Administration (FCA 1) by Executive Order 6084 of March 27, 1933, effective May 27, 1933.

T 48.1:date
ANNUAL REPORTS.

T 48.2:CT
GENERAL PUBLICATIONS.

T 48.3:nos.
BULLETINS.

T 48.4:nos.
CIRCULARS.

T 48.5:v.nos.
BORROWERS' BULLETIN.

T 48.6:date
STATEMENTS OF CONDITION OF FEDERAL LAND BANKS, ETC.
    Later FCA 1.7

T 48.7
REGULATIONS (general).

T 48.7/2:CT
REGULATIONS (miscellaneous).

BUREAU OF WAR RISK INSURANCE
(1914– 1921)

CREATION AND AUTHORITY

The Bureau of War Risk Insurance was established within the Treasury Department by act of Congress, approved September 2, 1914. The Bureau was abolished by act of Congress, approved August 9, 1921, and its functions transferred to the Veterans' Bureau (VB 1).

T 49.1:date
ANNUAL REPORTS.

T 49.2:CT
GENERAL PUBLICATIONS.

T 49.3:nos.
BULLETINS.

T 49.4:nos.
CIRCULARS.

Military and Naval Insurance Division

T 49.5/1:date
ANNUAL REPORTS.

T 49.5/2:CT
GENERAL PUBLICATIONS.

T 49.5/3:nos.
BULLETINS.

T 49.5/4
CIRCULARS.

Marine and Seaman's Insurance Division

T 49.6/1:date
ANNUAL REPORTS.

T 49.6/2:CT
GENERAL PUBLICATIONS.

T 49.6/3:nos.
BULLETINS.

T 49.6/4
CIRCULARS.

Conservation Section

T 49.7/1:date
ANNUAL REPORTS.

T 49.7/2:CT
GENERAL PUBLICATIONS.

T 49.7/3
BULLETINS.

T 49.7/4
CIRCULARS.

Bureau of War Risk Insurance (Continued)

T 49.8:nos.
PUBLIC NOTICES.

T 49.9:nos.
INSURANCE BULLETINS.

T 49.10:nos.
REGULATIONS.

GOVERNMENT ACTUARY
(1919– 1935)

T 50.1:date
ANNUAL REPORTS.

T 50.2:CT
GENERAL PUBLICATIONS.

T 50.3
BULLETINS.

T 50.4
CIRCULARS.

T 50.5:date
MARKET PRICES AND INVESTMENT VALUES OF OUTSTANDING BONDS AND NOTES. [Monthly]

BUREAU OF THE BUDGET
(1921– 1939)

CREATION AND AUTHORITY

The Bureau and Accounting Act, approved June 10, 1921 (42 Stat. 20; 31 U.S.C. 11-16), provided that the President shall transmit to Congress the proposed annual budget of the United States, together with other budgetary information. The same act created the Bureau of the Budget, locating it in the Treasury Department, but placing it under the immediate direction of the President. Under Reorganization Plan 1 of 1939 (53 Stat. 1423), the Bureau was transferred from the Treasury Department to the Executive Office of the President (Pr 32.100), established at the same time.

T 51.1:date
ANNUAL REPORTS.
    Later Pr 32.101

T 51.2:CT
GENERAL PUBLICATIONS.
    Later Pr 32.102

T 51.3
BULLETINS.

T 51.4:nos.
CIRCULARS.
    Later Pr 32.104

T 51.5:date
BUDGET.
    Later Pr 32.107

T 51.6:date
ALTERNATIVE BUDGET.

Chief Coordinator for General Supply

T 51.7/1:date
ANNUAL REPORTS.

T 51.7/2:CT
GENERAL PUBLICATIONS.

T 51.7/3:nos.
BULLETINS.

T 51.7/4
CIRCULARS.

T 51.7/5
CIRCULAR LETTERS.

T 51.7/6:date&sec.nos.
FEDERAL STANDARD STOCK CATALOGS.
    Later T 58.10/3

T 51.7/7:classes
FEDERAL STANDARD STOCK CATALOGS, (Classes numbered).

T 51.7/8:letters
FEDERAL STANDARD STOCK CATALOGS.

T 51.7/9:letters
FEDERAL STANDARD STOCK CATALOGS, GROUPS FOR PROCUREMENT SEC. 3, PART 7, DETAILED DATA.
    Later T 58.10/4

T 51.7/10:nos.
FEDERAL STANDARD STOCK CATALOGS, ADDENDA.
    Later T 58.10/5

T 51.7/11
[Vacant].

T 51.7/12
[Vacant].

T 51.7/13-19
[Vacant].

T 51.7/20:nos.
ADDENDA AND ERRATA SHEETS TO FEDERAL SPECIFICATIONS.

T 51.7/21:CT
INDEX OF ACTIVITIES OF FEDERAL GOVERNMENT.

Permanent Conference on Printing

T 51.8/1:date
ANNUAL REPORTS.

T 51.8/2:CT
GENERAL PUBLICATIONS.

T 51.8/3
BULLETINS.

T 51.8/4
CIRCULARS.

T 51.8/5:date
MINUTES OF MEETINGS.

Interdepartmental Board of Contracts and Adjustments

T 51.9/1:date
ANNUAL REPORTS.

T 51.9/2:CT
GENERAL PUBLICATIONS.

T 51.9/3
BULLETINS.

T 51.9/4
CIRCULARS.

Federal Traffic Board

T 51.10/1:date
ANNUAL REPORTS.

T 51.10/2:CT
GENERAL PUBLICATIONS.

T 51.10/3
BULLETINS.

T 51.10/4
CIRCULARS.

T 51.10/5:nos.
FREIGHT CLASSIFICATION CIRCULARS.

Interdepartmental Board on Simplified Office Procedure

T 51.11/1:date
ANNUAL REPORTS.

T 51.11/2:CT
GENERAL PUBLICATIONS.

T 51.11/3
BULLETINS.

T 51.11/4
CIRCULARS.

T 51.11/5:nos. of meeting
PROCEEDINGS OF EXECUTIVE COMMITTEE MEETING.

T 51.11/6:nos.
MEMORANDUM.

T 51.11/7:nos.
UNITED STATES GOVERNMENT INTERDEPARTMENTAL STANDARDS.

BUREAU OF SUPPLY (1922–1927)

CREATION AND AUTHORITY

The Bureau of Supply was established within the Treasury Department by Departmental Order 283, dated May 28, 1922. The Bureau became the Division of Supply (T 55) on July 1, 1927, pursuant to act of Congress, approved January 26, 1927.

T 52.1:date
ANNUAL REPORTS.

T 52.2:CT
GENERAL PUBLICATIONS.

T 52.3
BULLETINS.

T 52.4
CIRCULARS.

T 52.5:CT
SPECIFICATIONS.

FEDERAL NARCOTICS CONTROL BOARD (1922–1930)

CREATION AND AUTHORITY

The Federal Narcotics Control Board was established by act of Congress, approved May 26, 1922. The Board was abolished by act of Congress, approved June 14, 1930, and its functions transferred to the newly created Bureau of Narcotics (T 56).

T 53.1:date
ANNUAL REPORTS.

T 53.2:CT
GENERAL PUBLICATIONS.

T 53.3
BULLETINS.

T 53.4
CIRCULARS.

BUREAU OF INDUSTRIAL ALCOHOL (1930–1933)

CREATION AND AUTHORITY

The Bureau of Industrial Alcohol was established within the Treasury Department by the Prohibition Reorganization Act of 1930, approved May 27, 1930 (46 Stat. 427). By Executive Order 6166 of June 10, 1933, the Bureau was abolished and its functions transferred to the Bureau of Internal Revenue (T 22).

T 54.1:date
ANNUAL REPORTS.

T 54.2:CT
GENERAL PUBLICATIONS.

T 54.4
BULLETINS.

T 54.4
CIRCULARS.

T 54.5:nos.
REGULATIONS.

T 54.6:date
DIGEST OF SUPREME COURT DECISIONS INTERPRETING NATIONAL PROHIBITION ACT.

T 54.7:CT
PRO-MONOGRAPHS.

     Supersedes T 22.30

T 54.9:nos.
INSPECTION MANUALS.

T 54.10:nos.
GENERAL CIRCULARS.

     Numbers 1-113 read: Circular Letters.

DIVISION OF SUPPLY (1927–1935)

CREATION AND AUTHORITY

The Bureau of Supply (T 52) became the Division of Supply on July 1, 1927, pursuant to act of Congress, approved January 26, 1927. The Division ceased to exist in 1935.

T 55.1:date
ANNUAL REPORTS.

T 55.2:CT
GENERAL PUBLICATIONS.

T 55.3
BULLETINS.

T 55.4
CIRCULARS.

T 55.5:CT
SPECIFICATIONS AND PROPOSALS.

BUREAU OF NARCOTICS (1930–1968)

CREATION AND AUTHORITY

The Bureau of Narcotics was established within the Treasury Department by an act of Congress, approved June 14, 1930 (46 Stat. 585). The Bureau was abolished by Reorganization Plan 1 of 1968, dated February 7, 1968 and its functions transferred to the Bureau of Narcotics and Dangerous Drugs (J 24), established by the same Plan within the Department of Justice.

T 56.1:date
ANNUAL REPORTS.

T 56.2:CT
GENERAL PUBLICATIONS.

T 56.3
BULLETINS.

T 56.4
CIRCULARS.

T 56.4/2
LEGAL INFORMATION CIRCULAR.

T 56.5
LAWS.

T 56.6:nos.
REGULATIONS (numbered).

T 56.6:CT
REGULATIONS, RULES, AND INSTRUCTIONS (miscellaneous).

T 56.7:nos.
CIRCULAR LETTERS.

T 56.7/2:nos.
BUREAU ORDERS. 1938–

T 56.8:date
TRAFFIC IN OPIUM AND OTHER DANGEROUS DRUGS.

T 56.9:date
TRAFFIC IN OPIUM AND OTHER DANGEROUS DRUGS, PHILIPPINE ISLANDS.

PUBLIC DEBT SERVICE (1920–1940)

CREATION AND AUTHORITY

The Public Debt Service was established within the Department of the Treasury in 1920, being a consolidation of the Division of Public Debt and Accounts, Division of Loans and Currency, and the Register's Office. Reorganization Plan No. 3 of 1940, redesignated the Service as the Bureau of the Public Debt (T 63.200) and placed it under the newly established Fiscal Service effective June 30, 1940.

T 57.1:date
ANNUAL REPORTS.

T 57.2:CT
GENERAL PUBLICATIONS.

T 57.3
BULLETINS.

T 57.4
CIRCULARS.

T 57.5:CT
LAWS.

T 57.6
REGULATIONS.

T 57.7:date
CIRCULATION STATEMENTS. [Monthly]

> Later T 63.207

BUREAU OF FEDERAL SUPPLY
(1947– 1949)

CREATION AND AUTHORITY

The Procurement Division was established within the Treasury Department by Executive Order 6166 of June 10, 1933, pursuant to act of Congress, approved March 3, 1933 (47 Stat. 1517). The name was changed to Bureau of Federal Supply, effective January 1, 1947, by Departmental Order 73, dated November 19, 1946. The Bureau was transferred to the General Services Administration by the Federal Property and Administration Services Act of 1949 (63 Stat. 378), effective July 1, 1949, where it became the Federal Supply Service (GS 2).

T 58.1:date
ANNUAL REPORTS.

> Later GS 2.1

T 58.2:CT
GENERAL PUBLICATIONS.
> Later GS 2.2

T 58.3:nos.
BULLETINS.

T 58.4:nos.
CIRCULARS
> Earlier T 45.4
> Later T 58.8/3

T 58.4/2:nos.
CIRCULARS [new series].

T 58.5
LAWS.

T 58.6:CT
REGULATIONS, RULES, AND INSTRUCTIONS.

T 58.7:date
SPECIFICATIONS AND PROPOSALS FOR SUPPLIES.
> Earlier T 45.5/1-23

T 58.8:date
GENERAL SCHEDULE OF SUPPLIES, CONTAINING AWARDS FOR MATERIALS, SUPPLIES AND EQUIPMENT.
> Earlier T 45.6
> Later GS 2.7

T 58.8/2:date
GENERAL SCHEDULE OF SUPPLIES: INDEX OF AWARDS.

T 58.8/3:nos.
GENERAL SCHEDULE OF SUPPLIES.
> Earlier T 58.4

T 58.8/4:nos.
FEDERAL SUPPLY SCHEDULE, AMENDMENTS.
> Later GS 2.7/2

T 58.9:class nos.
QUARTERLY PRICE LISTS.
> Earlier T 45.8

T 58.10
FEDERAL STANDARD STOCK CATALOG.

T 58.10/2:class nos.
– CLASS NUMBERS.

T 58.10/3:letter nos.
– OUTLINE OF FORM FOR FEDERAL SPECIFICATIONS.

> Is section 4, part 2 of Federal Standard Stock Catalog (T 58.10).
> Earlier T 51.7/6
> Later GS 2.8

T 58.10/3:add.nos.ch.no.ind.
FEDERAL SPECIFICATIONS, ADDENDA AND ERRATA SHEETS: CHANGES INDEXES.

T 58.10/4:letters
– GROUPS FOR PROCUREMENT, DETAILED DATA.

> Is Section 3, part 7 of Federal Standard Stock Catalog (T 58.10).
> Earlier T 51.7/9

T 58.10/5:nos.
– ADDENDA.

> Earlier T 57.7/10

T 58.10/6:nos.
– SUPPLIES. . .ADDENDA.

T 58.11:nos.
CIRCULAR LETTERS.

> Later T 58.11/2

T 58.11/2:nos.
CIRCULAR LETTERS, A SERIES.

T 58.11/3:letters-nos.
CIRCULAR LETTERS, B SERIES.

> Earlier T 58.1

T 58.11/4:nos.
CIRCULAR LETTERS, C SERIES.

T 58.12:nos.
TRAFFIC INFORMATION LETTERS.

T 58.13:nos.
SURPLUS LISTS.

T 58.13/2:nos.
SURPLUS PROPERTY CIRCULARS.

T 58.14:nos.
FIELD SURPLUS LISTS.

T 58.15:nos.
PROCUREMENT DIVISION BULLETINS.

T 58.16:nos.
AIR PROJECTS BULLETINS.

T 58.17:nos.
MEMORANDUM TO STATE PROCUREMENT OFFICERS.

T 58.18:CT
POSTERS.

T 58.19:date
QUARTERLY PRICE LIST.

T 58.20:nos.
TRAFFIC SERVICE LETTERS.

T 58.21:CT
NATIONAL ACADEMY FOR PUBLIC PURCHASING, PUBLICATIONS.

T 58.22:CT
ADDRESSES.

T 58.23:nos.
LIST OF AVAILABLE SURPLUS PROPERTY LOCATED IN DISTRICT OF COLUMBIA.

T 58.24
ADMINISTRATIVE AND PERSONNEL INSTRUCTIONS.

FEDERAL ALCOHOL
ADMINISTRATION
(1935– 1940)

CREATION AND AUTHORITY

The Federal Alcohol Administration (Y 3.F 31/ 10) was established as an independent agency by Executive Order 6474 of December 4, 1933. The Administration was abolished when the Federal Alcohol Administration Act, approved August 29, 1935 (49 Stat. 977) established within the Treasury Department a new Federal Alcohol Administration. The New Federal Alcohol Administration was in turn abolished by Reorganization Plan No. 3 of 1940, effective June 30, 1940, and its functions transferred to the Bureau of Internal Revenue (T 22).

T 59.1:date
ANNUAL REPORTS.

T 59.2:CT
GENERAL PUBLICATIONS.

T 59.5:CT
LAWS.

T 59.6:nos.
REGULATIONS.

> Later T 22.17/2

T 59.7:CT
ADDRESSES.

COMMISSIONER OF ACCOUNTS
AND DEPOSITS
(1920– 1940)

CREATION AND AUTHORITY

The Commissioner of Accounts and Deposits was established within the Department of the Treasury in January 1920. Under Reorganization Plan No. 3 of 1940, effective June 30, 1940, the office was placed under the newly established Fiscal Service and redesignated the Bureau of Accounts (T 63.100).

T 60.1:date
ANNUAL REPORTS.

T 60.2:CT
GENERAL PUBLICATIONS.

T 60.6:CT
REGULATIONS, RULES, AND INSTRUCTIONS.

T 60.7:nos.
FIELD OFFICE MEMORANDUM.

T 60.8:nos.
VOUCHER EXAMINATION MEMORANDUM

> Later T 63.111

T 60.9:nos.
ACCOUNTING PROCEDURE MEMORANDUM.

> Later T 63.110

T 60.10
ADMINISTRATIVE MEMORANDUM.

T 60.11:date
REPORTS SHOWING FINANCIAL STATUS OF FUNDS
   PROVIDED IN EMERGENCY RELIEF APPRO-
   PRIATION ACTS.
      Changed from T 60.2
      Later T 63.114

T 60.12:date
REPORTS SHOWING STATUS OF FUNDS PROVIDED
   IN EMERGENCY RELIEF APPROPRIATION ACTS.
   [Monthly]
      Later T 63.107

T 60.13:date
REPORTS SHOWING STATUS OF FUNDS AND ANALY-
   SES OF EXPENDITURES, EMERGENCY APPRO-
   PRIATION ACTS. [Quarterly]
      Later T 63.109

T 60.14:date
REPORTS SHOWING STATUS OF FUNDS AND ANALY-
   SES OF EXPENDITURES, PUBLIC WORKS AD-
   MINISTRATION OF FEDERAL WORKS AGENCY.
   [Monthly]
      Slightly varying titles.
      Later T 63.108

PROCESSING TAX BOARD OF REVIEW
(1936– 1942)

CREATION AND AUTHORITY

   The Processing Tax Board of Review was
established within the Treasury Department by
the Revenue Act of 1936 (49 Stat. 1652). The
Board was abolished by the Revenue Act of 1942
(56 Stat. 967), and its functions transferred to
the Tax Court of the United States (Ju11).

T 61.1:date
ANNUAL REPORTS.

T 61.2:CT
GENERAL PUBLICATIONS.

T 61.6:CT
REGULATIONS, RULES, AND INSTRUCTIONS.

DIVISION OF RESEARCH AND STATISTICS
(1934– 1947)

CREATION AND AUTHORITY

   The Division of Research and Statistics was
established within the Treasury Department by
Departmental Order 8, dated September 17, 1934.
The Division was abolished by Departmental Order 92, dated September 23, 1947, and was succeeded by the Office of Technical Staff (T 68).

T 62.1:date
ANNUAL REPORTS.
      Later T 68.1

T 62.2:CT
GENERAL PUBLICATIONS.
      Later T 68.2

T 62.7:date
MARKET PRICES AND YIELDS OF OUTSTANDING
   BONDS, NOTES AND BILLS OF U.S. [Monthly]
      Earlier T 50.5
      Later T 68.7

T 62.8:date
INTEREST BEARING DEBT OUTSTANDING. [Monthly]
      Earlier T 1.29

T 62.9:nos.
STATISTICS OF CAPITAL MOVEMENTS BETWEEN
   U.S. AND FOREIGN COUNTRIES.
      Superseded by T 1.3

FISCAL SERVICE
(1940–   )

CREATION AND AUTHORITY

   The Fiscal Service was established in the
Treasury Department by Reorganization Plan 3 of
1940, effective June 30, 1940, by joint resolution
(54 Stat. 321). It now consists of the Office of the
Fiscal Assistant Secretary, Bureau of the Public
Debt, and the Financial Management Service.

INFORMATION

   Fiscal Service
   Department of the Treasury
   Washington, D.C. 20226

T 63.1:date
ANNUAL REPORT.

T 63.2:CT   • **Item 925-E-1**
GENERAL PUBLICATIONS.

T 63.6:CT
REGULATIONS, RULES, AND INSTRUCTIONS.

T 63.7
UNITED STATES SAVINGS BONDS ISSUED AND
   REDEEMED THROUGH (date). [Monthly]

      Gives amount issued, redeemed, and out-
   standing, and percent outstanding of amount issued, by type of bonds.
      ISSN 0145-0697

T 63.8:nos.   • **Item 925-E**
CHECK PAYMENT AND RECONCILIATION MEMO-
   RANDA, CP & R (series).

T 63.9:CT   • **Item 925-E**
HANDBOOKS, MANUALS, GUIDES.

FINANCIAL MANAGEMENT SERVICE
(1984–   )

CREATION AND AUTHORITY

   The Bureau of Accounts was established as
a part of the Fiscal Service of the Treasury Department by Reorganization Plan No. 3 of 1940,
effective June 30, 1940. The Bureau succeeded
the Office of the Commissioner of Accounts and
Deposits (T 60). Functions of the Bureau of Accounts were transferred to the Bureau of Government Financial Operations by Treasury Order 229
of January 24, 1974. The name was changed to
Financial Management Service by Secretary's Order 145-21, effective October, 10, 1984.

INFORMATION

   Financial Management Service
   Dept. of the Treasury
   Liberty Center
   401 14th Street, SW
   Washington, DC 20227
   (202) 874-6740
   Fax: (202) 874-6743
   E-mail:webmaster@fms.treas.gov
   http://www.fms.treas.gov

T 63.101:date
ANNUAL REPORTS.

T 63.101/2:date   • **Item 928-F**
UNITED STATES GOVERNMENT ANNUAL REPORT.
   [Annual]

      PURPOSE:– To present an overview of the
   government's cash basic position and results of
   operations.
      Earlier T 1.1/3 and T 63.113

T 63.101/2-2:date   • **Item 928-F (MF)**
APPENDIX. [Annual]
      Earlier T 1.1/3

T 63.102:CT   • **Item 928-A**
GENERAL PUBLICATIONS.

T 63.102:Ex 2/date   • **Item 925**
TREASURY REPORTING RATES OF EXCHANGE
   AS OF (date). [Quarterly] (Foreign Currency
   Branch, Division of Central Accounts and Re-
   ports)

T 63.103/2:date/nos.   • **Item 928-A (EL)**
TREASURY BULLETIN. [Quarterly]

      PURPOSE:– To extend knowledge of the pub-
   lic finances, monetary developments and activities of the Treasury Department by making information available in a more compact and usable
   form. The data contained in this publication supplements or recapitulates that contained in the daily
   Treasury statements and other publications and
   press releases.
      Gives summary of Federal fiscal operations,
   budget receipts and expenditures, trust account
   and other transactions, cash income and outgo,
   debt outstanding and Treasurer's account, statutory debt limitation, debt operations, U.S. savings bonds, Treasury savings notes, ownership
   of Federal securities, Treasury survey of ownership
   of Federal securities, market quotations on Treasury securities, average yields on long-term bonds,
   Internal Revenue collections, monetary statistics, Exchange Stabilization Fund, capital movements. Cumulative index. Charts.
      Earlier T 1.3

T 63.106:CT
REGULATIONS, RULES, AND INSTRUCTIONS.

T 63.107:date
EMERGENCY RELIEF APPROPRIATION ACTS, RE-
   PORTS SHOWING STATUS OF FUNDS. [Monthly]
      Earlier T 60.12

T 63.108:date
PUBLIC WORKS ADMINISTRATION OF FEDERAL
   WORKS AGENCY, REPORTS SHOWING STATUS
   OF FUNDS AND ANALYSES OF EXPENDITURES.
   [Monthly]
      Earlier T 60.14

T 63.109:date
EMERGENCY RELIEF APPROPRIATION ACTS, RE-
   PORTS SHOWING STATUS OF FUNDS AND
   ANALYSES TO EXPENDITURES. [Quarterly]
      Earlier T 60.13

T 63.110:nos.
ACCOUNTING PROCEDURE MEMORANDUM.
      Earlier T 60.9

T 63.110/2:nos.
PROCEDURES MEMORANDUM.

T 63.111:nos.
VOUCHER EXAMINATION MEMORANDUM.
      Earlier T 60.8

T 63.112:date
STATEMENT OF PUBLIC DEBT OF UNITED STATES.
   [Monthly]

T 63.113:date   • **Item 928**
COMBINED STATEMENT OF RECEIPTS, EXPENDI-
   TURES, AND BALANCES OF UNITED STATES.
      Earlier T 9.1
      Superseded by United States Government,
   Annual Report, Appendix (T 1.1/3).

T 63.113/a:CT
COMBINED STATEMENT OF RECEIPTS, EXPEN-
DITURES, AND BALANCES OF UNITED
STATES GOVERNMENT (separates).

T 63.113/2:date   • **Item 923-A-2 (EL)**
MONTHLY TREASURY STATEMENT OF RECEIPTS
AND OUTLAYS OF THE UNITED STATES GOV-
ERNMENT. [Monthly]
    Earlier T 1.5/2

T 63.113/2-2:date   • **Item 923-A-2 (EL)**
DAILY TREASURY STATEMENT. [Daily]

T 63.113/3:date   • **Item 928 (MF) (EL)**
CONSOLIDATED FINANCIAL STATEMENTS OF THE
UNITED STATES GOVERNMENT, FISCAL YEAR.

T 63.114:date
REPORTS OF PRESIDENT TO CONGRESS SHOW-
ING STATUS OF FUNDS AND OPERATIONS UN-
DER EMERGENCY RELIEF APPROPRIATION
ACTS. [Annual]
    Earlier T 60.11

T 63.115:date
DIGEST OF APPROPRIATION.
    Earlier T 9.5

T 63.116:date
COMPANIES HOLDING CERTIFICATES OF AUTHOR-
ITY FROM SECRETARY OF TREASURY, AS
ACCEPTABLE SECURITIES ON FEDERAL BONDS.
    Earlier T 1.24

T 63.117:date
SEMIANNUAL CONSOLIDATED REPORT OF BAL-
ANCES OF FOREIGN CURRENCIES ACQUIRED
WITHOUT PAYMENT OF DOLLARS AS OF
DECEMBER 31 (year).

    Prepared in accordance with Section 613(c)
of the Foreign Assistance Act of 1962 (75 Stat.
443).
    Shows the balances of U.S.-owned foreign
currencies held in accounts of accountable officers of the United States, and the balances of
country-owned funds held in accounts of foreign
governments over which the United States exercises some control. The balances are stated in
units of foreign currency and United States dollar
equivalents broken down by country and the
agency having administrative control.
    Later T 1.50

T 63.118:date   • **Item 970**
STATEMENT OF UNITED STATES CURRENCY AND
COIN. 1887–   [Monthly]
    (Form 1028)

    One-page statistical summary, giving various
types of currency and coin outstanding and
amounts in circulation.
    Earlier T 63.308

T 63.118/2:date   • **Item 970-A-4 (MF)**
REPORTS ON FOREIGN CURRENCIES HELD BY THE
U.S. GOVERNMENT. [Semiannual]

    Separate tables present an analysis of total
foreign currencies held by the U.S. Government;
transactions and balances by category, agency,
and account; and transactions and balances by
country, agency, and account.
    Also published in microfiche.
    Earlier T 63.102:C 93

T 63.118/3:date
STATEMENT OF FOREIGN CURRENCIES PUR-
CHASED WITH DOLLARS. [Semiannual]
    Earlier T 63.102:C 93/3

T 63.119:CT   • **Item 928-B**
HANDBOOKS, MANUALS, GUIDES. [Irregular]

T 63.120:date   • **Item 928-C**
FEDERAL AID TO STATES, FISCAL YEAR. [Annual]

    Presents data on Federal grants-in-aid to State
and local governments, by States, and by granting Federal agencies.
    Earlier T 63.102:Ai 2

T 63.121:date   • **Item 928-A-1**
TREASURY REPORTING RATES OF EXCHANGE.
[Quarterly]

    Tables present rates of exchange of all for-
eign currencies to the dollar in which the U.S
government has an interest.

T 63.122:CT   • **Item 928-D**
POSTERS. [Irregular]

T 63.123:CT   • **Item 928-E**
FACT SHEETS (series). [Irregular]

    Fact sheets on miscellaneous topics pertain-
ing to the work of the Bureau.

T 63.124:nos.   • **Item 928-A**
NEWSGRAM. [Irregular]

    Supplements Green Book (T 63.102:G 82)

T 63.125:date
TACTICAL PLAN. [Annual]

T 63.126:   • **Item 928-H (MF)**
HEADQUARTERS TELEPHONE DIRECTORY. [Semi-
annual]

    Contains organizational and alphabetical list-
ings forHeadquarters, Financial Management Service.

T 63.127:   • **Item 928-G**
DIRECT DEPOSIT MARKETING. [Annual]

    Contains information on direct deposit mar-
keting, whichpromotes direct deposit participation by benefit payment participants via such
means as check inserts and messages on the
check envelope.

T 63.128   • **Item 928-G (EL)**
THE FINANCIAL CONNECTION. [Quarterly]

T 63.129:   • **Item 928-A-2 (EL)**
FINANCIAL REPORT TO THE CITIZENS.

T 63.130:   • **Item 928-A-2 (EL)**
ELECTRONIC PRODUCTS (misc.).

T 63.131   • **Item 928-A-3 (EL)**
STATUS REPORT OF U.S. TREASURY-OWNED GOLD.
[Monthly]

BUREAU OF THE PUBLIC DEBT
(1940–   )

CREATION AND AUTHORITY

    The Bureau of the Public Debt was estab-
lished as a part of the Fiscal Service of the Treasury Department by Reorganization Plan No. 3 of
1940, effective June 30, 1940, succeeding the
Public Debt Service (T 57).

INFORMATION

    Division of Comunications
    Bureau of the Public Debt
    Department of the Treasury
    999 E Street, NW
    Washington, DC 20239-0001
    (202) 480-6456
    Fax: (202) 480-7719
    http://www.publicdebt.treas.gov

T 63.201:date
ANNUAL REPORTS.

T 63.202:CT   • **Item 970-A-5**
GENERAL PUBLICATIONS. [Irregular]

    T 63.202/10:date   • **Item 970-A-5 (MF)**
    TELEPHONE LISTING, WASHINGTON AREA.
    [Irregular]

T 63.207:date
CIRCULAR STATEMENT OF UNITED STATES.
[Monthly]
    Earlier T 57.7
    Later T 63.308

T 63.208:
STATUTORY DEBT LIMITATION AS OF. . .

T 63.209   • **Item 970-A**
TABLES OF REDEMPTION VALUES FOR UNITED
STATES SAVINGS BONDS, SERIES A-E. [Semi-
annual]
    ISSN 0498-8752

T 63.209/2:date   • **Item 970-A**
TABLE OF REDEMPTION VALUES FOR UNITED
STATES SAVINGS BONDS, SERIES A TO E,
INCLUSIVE. [Semimonthly]

T 63.209/3
TABLES OF REDEMPTION VALUES FOR UNITED
STATES SAVINGS BONDS, SERIES J. [Semian-
nual]

T 63.209/4:date
COMPARISON OF REDEMPTION VALUE OF SERIES
E SAVINGS BONDS AS OF . . . Offical Use.

T 63.209/5:date   • **Item 970-A-1**
TABLES OF REDEMPTION VALUES OF $25 SERIES
E SAVINGS BONDS SERIES.

T 63.209/5-2:date   • **Item 970-A-1**
TABLES OF REDEMPTION VALUES FOR $50 SE-
RIES EE AND $25 SERIES E SAVINGS BOND.
[Semiannual]

T 63.209/6:date   • **Item 970-A-3**
TABLES OF REDEMPTION VALUES FOR UNITED
STATES SAVINGS BONDS, SERIES E. [Semian-
nual]

    Continues: Tables of Redemption Values for
United States Savings Bonds, (A-E series) (T
63.209).

T 63.209/7:date   • **Item 970-A-2**
TABLES OF REDEMPTION VALUES FOR UNITED
STATES SAVINGS BONDS, SERIES EE. [Semi-
annual]

    Continues: Tables of Redemption Values for
United States Savings Bonds (A-E series) (T
63.209).

T 63.209/8:date   • **Item 970-A-7**
UNITED STATES INDIVIDUAL RETIREMENT BONDS,
TABLES OF REDEMPTION VALUES FOR ALL
DENOMINATION BONDS. [Annual]

T 63.209/8-2:date   • **Item 970-A-7**
UNITED STATES RETIREMENT PLAN BONDS,
TABLES OF REDEMPTION VALUES FOR ALL
DENOMINATION BONDS. [Annual]

T 63.209/8-4   • **Item 970-A-7**
SERIES H/HH SAVINGS BONDS.

T 63.210:date   • **Item 970-A**
TABLES OF REDEMPTION VALUES FOR UNITED
STATES SAVINGS NOTES.

T 63.210/2:date   • **Item 970-A-13**
TABLES OF REDEMPTION VALUES FOR UNITED
STATES SERIES E SAVINGS BONDS AND SAV-
INGS NOTES.

T 63.210/3   • **Item 970-A-15 (EL)**
U.S. SAVINGS BOND COMPREHENSIVE SAVINGS
BOND VALUE TABLES (Series EE, I Bond, Series
E and Savings Notes). [Semiannual]

T 63.211:CT   • **Item 970-A-6**
HANDBOOKS, MANUALS, GUIDES. [Irregular]

T 63.212:CT   • **Item 970-A-8**
FORMS. [Irregular]

T 63.213 • **Item 970-A-9**
PD NEWS, SPECIAL EDITIONS. [Irregular]

PD = Public Debt
The News is issued in special editions on different topics, such as the Combined Federal Campaign.

T 63.214:date • **Item 970-A-10**
LONG RANGE PLANS. [Annual]

PURPOSE– To summarize the Bureau's long range plan for carrying out its mission, which is to borrow money needed to operate the federal government and to account for the remaining public debt.

T 63.215:date • **Item 970-A-11 (EL)**
MONTHLY STATEMENT OF THE PUBLIC DEBT OF THE UNITED STATES. [Monthly]

T 63.217:date • **Item 970-A-14 (CD)**
BONDPRO, U.S. SAVINGS BOND PRICING SYSTEM. [Semiannual]

OFFICE OF THE TREASURER OF THE UNITED STATES
(1940–   )

CREATION AND AUTHORITY

The Office of the Treasurer (T 40) was established under the act of September 2, 1789 (1 Stat. 65), which created the Treasury Department. Reorganization Plan No. 3 of 1940, effective June 30, 1940, established it as part of the Fiscal Service of the Treasury Department.

INFORMATION

Office of the Treasurer of the United States
Department of the Treasury
1500 Pennsylvania Avenue, NW
Washington, D.C. 20220
(202) 622-0100
Fax: (202) 622-2258

T 63.301:date
ANNUAL REPORTS

T 63.302:CT
GENERAL PUBLICATIONS.

T 63.306/2:nos.
TREASURER'S MEMORANDUMS.

T 63.307:date
PAPER CURRENCY OF EACH DENOMINATION OUTSTANDING, MONTHLY STATEMENTS.
Earlier T 40.8

T 63.308:date • **Item 970**
STATEMENT OF UNITED STATES CURRENCY AND COIN. 1887–   [Monthly] (Form 1028)

Former title: Circulation State of United States Money.
Later T 63.118

TAX ADVISORY STAFF
(1949– 1953)

CREATION AND AUTHORITY

The Division of Tax Research was established within the Treasury Department by Departmental Order 18, dated March 25, 1938, effective June 1, 1939. The name of the Division was changed to Tax Advisory Staff by Departmental Order 115, dated June 17, 1949. The Tax Advisory Staff was abolished by Departmental Order 170, dated March 1, 1953 and succeeded by the Analysis Staff.

T 64.1:date
ANNUAL REPORTS.

T 64.2:CT
GENERAL PUBLICATIONS.

T 64.7:CT
ADDRESSES.

FOREIGN FUNDS CONTROL
(1940– 1947)

CREATION AND AUTHORITY

The Foreign Funds Control was established within the Treasury Department in April 1940, pursuant to Executive Order 8389 of April 10, 1940. On September 11, 1940, the Control became an administrative unit of the Treasury Department. The Control was terminated on July 15, 1947, and its functions transferred to the Office of International Finance.

T 65.1:date
ANNUAL REPORTS.

T 65.2:CT
GENERAL PUBLICATIONS.

T 65.6:CT
REGULATIONS, RULES, AND INSTRUCTIONS.

T 65.7:nos.
PUBLIC CIRCULARS.
Earlier T 1.33

T 65.8:CT
ADDRESSES.

T 65.9
GENERAL RULINGS.

T 65.10
GENERAL LICENSES UNDER EXECUTIVE ORDER 8389.

SAVINGS BONDS DIVISION
(1945–   )

CREATION AND AUTHORITY

The War Finance Division was established within the Department of the Treasury by Departmental Order 50, dated June 25, 1943, to succeed the War Savings Staff (T 1.100). By Departmental Order 62, dated December 26, 1945, the Division was superseded by the Savings Bonds Division.

INFORMATION

Marketing Office
U.S. Savings Bonds
Department of the Treasury
999 E Street
Washington, D.C. 20239-0001
(202) 691-3535
Fax: (202) 208-1574
http://www.savingsbonds.gov

T 66.1:date
ANNUAL REPORTS.
Earlier T 1.101

T 66.2:CT • **Item 971**
GENERAL PUBLICATIONS.
Earlier T 102

T 66.3/2 • **Item 971-A-1**
SEMIANNUAL INTEREST RATE BULLETINS.

PURPOSE:– To present the interest rates for Series E and Series EE bonds May-October and November-April.

T 66.6:CT • **Item 972**
REGULATIONS, RULES, AND INSTRUCTIONS.

T 66.6/2:CT • **Item 971-A**
HANDBOOKS, MANUALS, GUIDES.

T 66.7:vol.
MINUTE MAN. [Semimonthly]
Earlier T 1.110

T 66.8:CT • **Item 971-A-2**
POSTERS. [Irregular]
Earlier T 1.107

T 66.9:nos.
SCHOOLS AT WAR, WAR SAVINGS NEWS BULLETINS FOR TEACHERS.
Earlier T 1.111

T 66.10:nos.
WOUNDED AMERICANS SERIES.

T 66.11:nos.
BOUNDS OVER AMERICA.

T 66.12:nos.
WAR BONDS IN ACTION.

T 66.13:nos.
FEATURE PICTURE PAGES.
Earlier T 1.112

T 66.14:nos.
STARS IN SERVICE.
Earlier T 1.113

T 66.15:nos.
AMERICAN HEROES.
Earlier T 1.114

T 66.16:date
P.S. PAYROLL SAVINGS BULLETIN. [Monthly]
Replaced by T 66.20

T 66.17:nos.
ANY BONDS TODAY?

T 66.18:CT
ADDRESSES.

T 66.19:nos.
UNCLE SAM SAYS. [Monthly]

T 66.20:v.nos.
NEWS AND QUOTES. [Monthly]

Replaces P.S. Payroll Savings Bulletin (T 66.16).

T 66.21:
EDUCATION SECTION NEWS LETTER.

T 66.22:date
U.S. TREASURY SAVINGS STAMP NEWS. [Irregular]

T 66.23:date
TABLE OF INVESTMENT YIELDS FOR UNITED STATES SAVINGS BONDS OF SERIES E. OFFICIAL USE.

T 66.24
BOND TIPS FROM YOU U.S. SAVINGS BOND REPORTER. [Quarterly]

T 66.24/2:v.nos.&nos.   **• Item 971-A-3 (EL)**
BOND TELLER. 1971–   [Semiannual]

Supersedes Bond Tips (T 66.24).
Published for banking personnel. Contains news items on U.S. savings bonds in areas such as interest rates paid, the status of E bonds, and general questions and answers.

T 66.25:v.nos.&nos.   **• Item 971-A-4**
COMMUNICATOR'S QUARTERLY. [Quarterly]

Contains informational and promotional material in narrative and pictorial form for the use of organizational U.S. savings bonds communicators.

CONTRACT SETTLEMENT OFFICE (1946–1948)

CREATION AND AUTHORITY

The Office of Contract Settlement (Y 3.W 19/7:100) was transferred to the Department of the Treasury by an Executive Order of December 12, 1946. The Office was again transferred to the newly established General Services Administration (GS 5) by the Federal Property and Administrative Services Act of 1949.

T 67.1:date
ANNUAL REPORTS.
Earlier Y 3.W 19/7:101
Later GS 5.1

T 67.2:CT
GENERAL PUBLICATIONS.
Earlier Y 3.W 19/7:102
Later GS 5.2

T 67.7:nos.
WAR CONTRACT TERMINATIONS AND SETTLEMENTS, REPORT TO CONGRESS. [Quarterly]
Earlier Y 3.W 19/7:107

T 67.8:nos.
APPEAL BOARD PROCEEDINGS.
Earlier Y 3.W 19/7:108

T 67.8/2:v.nos.
DECISIONS OF APPEAL BOARD (bound volumes).
Later GS 5.7

TECHNICAL STAFF OFFICE (1947–1953)

T 68.1:date
ANNUAL REPORTS.
Earlier T 62.1

T 68.2:CT
GENERAL PUBLICATIONS.
Earlier T 62.2

T 68.7:date
PRICES AND YIELDS OF PUBLIC MARKETABLE SECURITIES ISSUED BY UNITED STATES GOVERNMENT AND BY FEDERAL AGENCIES. [Monthly]
Earlier T 62.7

FEDERAL FACILITIES CORPORATION (1954–1957)

CREATION AND AUTHORITY

The Federal Facilities Corporation was established within the Treasury Department, effective July 1, 1954, pursuant to Executive Order 10539 of June 22, 1954, which transferred to the Corporation the rubber and tin programs of the Reconstruction Finance Corporation (Y 3.R 24), which was abolished. By Executive Order 10720 of July 11, 1957, the Corporation was transferred to the General Services Administration (GS 7).

T 69.1:date
ANNUAL REPORTS.

T 69.2:CT
GENERAL PUBLICATIONS.

T 69.7
RELEASES.

T 69.8:date
MEMORANDUM TO ALL RUBBER PURCHASERS.
Admin.

BUREAU OF ALCOHOL, TOBACCO AND FIREARMS (1972–   )

CREATION AND AUTHORITY

The Bureau of Alcohol, Tobacco and Firearms was established within the Department Order 221, effective July 1, 1972, which transferred to the Bureau those functions, powers, and duties of the Internal Revenue Service arising under laws relating to alcohol, tobacco, and explosives.

INFORMATION

Bureau of Alcohol, Tobacco and Firearms
Department of Treasury
650 Massachusetts Ave. NW
Washington, D.C. 20226
(202) 927-7777
Fax: (202) 927-7862
Http://www.atf.treas.gov

T 70.1:date   **• Item 971-D (MF)**
ANNUAL REPORT.

T 70.2:CT   **• Item 971-B**
GENERAL PUBLICATIONS.

T 70.5:CT   **• Item 961-A**
LAWS.

T 70.5:F 51   **• Item 961-A**
PUBLISHED ORDINANCES, FIREARMS. [Annual]

Lists State laws and local ordinances relevant to the Gun Control Act of 1968. Also includes information on Federal laws on firearms and ammunition, questions and answers on the Gun Control Act, and advice about importing firearms.

T 70.5/2:   **• Item 961-A-1**
LAW ENFORCEMENT LEGAL UPDATE. [Quarterly]

Each issue presents information on various BATF cases involving such matters as search and seizure, evidence, arrest, and firearms.

T 70.6:CT   **• Item 954**
REGULATIONS, RULES, AND INSTRUCTIONS. [Irregular]
Earlier T 22.17/2 and T 22.17/4

T 70.6/2:pt.nos.   **• Item 961 (MF)**
REGULATIONS (Part nos. of Title 26 of the Code of Federal Regulations).
Earlier T 22.17/3

T 70.6/3   **• Item 954 (MF)**
REGULATIONS (pt. nos. of Title 27 Code of Federal Regulations). [Irregular]
Earlier T 22.17/4

T 70.7:date-nos.   **• Item 961-C (EL)**
ALCOHOL, TOBACCO, AND FIREARMS. [Quarterly]

Lists all new laws, regulations, codes and rulings or changes with reference to alcohol, tobacco, and firearms.
ISSN 0098-0757

T 70.7/2:date   **• Item 961-B**
ALCOHOL, TOBACCO AND FIREARMS CUMULATIVE BULLETIN. [Annual]

PURPOSE:– To publish all substantive rulings necessary to promote a uniform application of all laws administered by the Bureau as well as all rulings that supersede, revoke, modify, or amend any of those previously published in the Bulletin (including those published prior to July 1, 1972, in the Internal Revenue Bulletin).
Covers Treasury decisions, Bureau rulings, Bureau procedures, legislations, administrative matters, and Court decisions.
Supersedes section 5 of the International Revenue Bulletin (T 22.25/9).

T 70.8:CT   **• Item 971-F**
HANDBOOKS, MANUALS, GUIDES. [Irregular]

T 70.9:date   **• Item 964-A**
ALCOHOL AND TOBACCO SUMMARY STATISTICS, DISTILLED SPIRITS, WINE, BEER, TOBACCO, ENFORCEMENT TAXES, FISCAL YEAR.

MONTHLY STATISTICAL RELEASES.

T 79.9/2:date
CIGARETTES AND CIGARS.

T 70.9/3:date
DISTILLED SPIRITS.

T 70.9/4:date   **• Item 971-B-7 (EL)**
BEER. [Monthly]

T 70.9/5:date   **• Item 971-B-8 (EL)**
WINES. [Monthly]

T 70.9/6:date
SEIZURES AND ARRESTS.

T 70.9/7:date   **• Item 971-E**
TOBACCO PRODUCTS. [Monthly]

T 70.10:nos.   • Item 971-E
INDUSTRY CIRCULARS. [Irregular]

ISSN 0364-5789

T 70.11:date   • Item 971-D-1 (MF)
EXPLOSIVES INCIDENTS, ANNUAL REPORT. 1st–
1976–

PURPOSE:– To provide text and tables on
explosives incidents throughout the United States
including bombings and such arsons as are under Bureau jurisdiction.

T 70.12:CT
AUDIOVISUAL MATERIALS.

T 70.13:CT   • Item 961-D
BIBLIOGRAPHIES AND LISTS OF PUBLICATIONS.
[Irregular]

T 70.14:date   • Item 971-B-1 (EL)
STATE LAWS AND PUBLISHED ORDINANCES.
[Annual]

PURPOSE:– To list by states, state laws and
ordinances regarding firearms. Also contains tables
on common elements in state firearms laws.

T 70.15:date   • Item 971-B (MF)
FIREARMS, CURIORS AND RELICS LIST. [Annual]

Continues: ATF Curios and Relics List.
Earlier titled: Firearms and Ammunition Cu-
rios and Relics List.
Earlier T 70.2:C 92

T 70.16:CT   • Item 954-A
DECISIONS AND ORDERS. [Irregular]

T 70.17:date&nos.   • Item 971-B-2
DIRECTOR'S MEMORANDUM. [Quarterly]

Contains black and white photographs of and
short news items concerning activities and employees of the Bureau.

T 70.18:date   • Item 961-C (EL)
FFL NEWSLETTER. [Annual]
Formerly titled: Federal Firearms Licensee
News.

T 70.18/2   • Item 961-E (EL)
ALCOHOL AND TOBACCO NEWSLETTER. [Monthly]

T 70.19:date   • Item 971-G (MF)
ANNUAL AWARDS BROCHURE. [Annual]

Lists bureau employees who received various kinds of awardsduring the reported year.

T 70.21:CT   • Item 971-H
POSTERS.

T 70.22:   • Item 971-B-3
FORMS.

T 70.24:dak   • Item 71-B-4
COMMERCE IN FIREARMS IN THE UNITED STATES.
[Annual]

T 70.25   • Item 971-B-5 (E)
ELECTRONIC PRODUCTS. (Misc.)

T 70.26   • Item 971-B-6 (EL)
CRIME GUN TRACE REPORTS. (Annual)

OFFICE OF THRIFT SUPERVISION
(1989–   )

INFORMATION

Office of Thrift Supervision
1700 G. St., NW
Washington, DC 20552
(202) 906-6000
http://www.ots.treas.gov

T 71.2   • Item 596
GENERAL PUBLICATIONS.
Earlier FHL 1.2

T 71.6   • Item 597
REGULATIONS, RULES, INSTRUCTIONS.
Earlier FHL 1.6

T 71.7:nos.   • Item 596-A (EL)
NEWS. (Office of Thrift Supervisor)
Earlier FHL 1.25/3

T 71.7/2:date-nos.   • Item 596-A (MF)
FHFM NEWS RELEASES.

T 71.8   • Item 597
HANDBOOKS, MANUALS, GUIDES.
Earlier FHL 1.6/2

T 71.15:v.nos./nos.   • Item 597-A-2
JOURNAL. [Monthly]
Earlier FHL 1.27

T 71.16:nos.   • Item 595-A-2
RESEARCH PAPERS (Series).

T 71.17:date   • Item 597-A-1
SAVINGS AND HOME FINANCING SOURCE BOOK.
1952–   [Annual]
Statistical tables on various aspects of savings and home financing with emphasis placed on
the institutions affiliated with the Federal Home
Loan Bank System and the Federal Savings and
Loan Insurance Corporation. Can be kept up-to-
date by use of the various periodic releases issued by the board.
Earlier FHL 1.11

T 71.18:date   • Item 597-A-5
ASSET AND LIABILITY TRENDS. [Annual]

T 71.19:date   • Item 597-A-2
COMBINED FINANCIAL STATEMENTS. [Annual]

T 71.20:date   • Item 597-A-2
RTC REVIEW. [Monthly]

T 71.21:date   • Item 597-A-2
MONTHLY THRIFT DATA.

T 71.22   • Item 597-A-2
THE SILVER LINING. [Bimonthly]

INTERNATIONAL TRADE
COMMISSION
(1974– 1981)

CREATION AND AUTHORITY

The United States Tariff Commission was
created by act of Congress approved September
8, 1916 (39 Stat. 795). The Commission's present
powers and duties are provided for largely by the
Tariff Act of 1930; the Antidumping Act, 1921;
and the Agricultural Adjustment Act; and the Trade
Expansion Act of 1962. The name was changed
to United States International Trade Commission
by section 171 of the Trade Act of 1974 (88 Stat.
2009). [SuDocs agency class number was
changed to ITC 1 in November 1981.]

TC 1.1   • Item 977
ANNUAL REPORT. 1st–   1917–   [Annual]

Report submitted by the commission to Congress pursuant to section 332 of the Tariff Act of
1930 for the fiscal year.
Includes information on current reports and
publications issued or revised during the year.
List of available reports printed on inside covers.
Later ITC 1.1

TC 1.2:CT   • Item 978 (MF)
GENERAL PUBLICATIONS.
Later ITC 1.2

TC 1.2:T 17/20   • Item 978
TWO CENTURIES OF TARIFFS, THE BACK-
GROUND AND EMERGENCE OF THE U.S.
INTERNATIONAL TRADE COMMISSION. 1976.
144 p. il.

TC 1.3:
BULLETINS.
Later ITC 1.3

TC 1.4:
CIRCULARS.
Later ITC 1.4

TC 1.5:nos.
TARIFF INFORMATION SERIES.

TC 1.6:le.&nos.
TARIFF INFORMATION SURVEYS.

TC 1.7:date
INDEXES.

TC 1.8:date
RULES OF PRACTICE AND PROCEDURE.

TC 1.9:nos.
REPORTS, 2d SERIES.

TC 1.10:CT
MANUALS.

TC 1.10:Im 7/4   • Item 980
UNITED STATES IMPORT DUTIES. 1946–
[Irregular]
Contains schedules of articles subject of
duty and articles free of duty.
Subscription includes basic volume plus
supplementary material for an indefinite period.
Special and Administrative Provisions of
the Tariff Act of 1930, previously issued as
part 2 of the 1952 edition, is now published
separately.

TC 1.10/2   • Item 980
SPECIAL AND ADMINISTRATIVE PROVISIONS OF
THE TARIFF ACT OF 1930, AS AMENDED, AS IN
EFFECT ON [date]. [Irregular]
Contains the text of Title III, Special Provi-
sions, and Title IV, Administrative Provisions, of
the Tariff Act of 1930.
Previously published as Part 2 of United States
Import Duties, 1952 edition, but now issued sepa-
rately.
Subscription includes basic volume plus
supplementary material for an indefinite period.
Issued in looseleaf form and punched for 3-ring
binder.

Later ITC 1.28

TC 1.11:CT
ANALYSIS OF TRADE.

TC 1.12:CT
ADDRESSES.

TC 1.13:CT
IMPORTS UNDER RECIPROCAL TRADE AGREE-
MENTS, BY COUNTRIES.

TC 1.14:CT
TRADE AGREEMENTS (by countries).

TC 1.14/2:CT
INTERDEPARTMENTAL TRADE AGREEMENTS
ORGANIZATION, PUBLICATIONS.

TC 1.14/3 • Item 980-A (MF)
OPERATIONS OF THE TRADE AGREEMENTS PRO-
GRAM. 1st– 1934/48– [Annual]
Later ITC 1.24

TC 1.15:CT
INDUSTRIES AND RECIPROCAL TRADE AGREE-
MENTS, REPORTS ON, BY INDUSTRIES.

TC 1.16:CT • Item 982
REGULATIONS, RULES, AND INSTRUCTIONS.
Later ITC 1.6

TC 1.16/2:CT • Item 978-A
HANDBOOKS, MANUALS, GUIDES.
Earlier TC 1.2 and TC 1.6
Later ITC 1.8

TC 1.17:date
ANALYSIS OF MISCELLANEOUS CHEMICAL
IMPORTS THROUGH NEW YORK.

TC 1.18:nos.
WAR CHANGES IN INDUSTRY SERIES, REPORTS.

TC 1.19:CT
AGRICULTURAL, PASTORAL, AND FOREST INDUS-
TRIES IN AMERICAN REPUBLICS.

TC 1.20:CT
ECONOMIC CONTROL AND COMMERCIAL POLICY
IN AMERICAN REPUBLICS.

TC 1.21:CT
MINING AND MANUFACTURING INDUSTRIES IN THE
AMERICAN REPUBLICS.

TC 1.22:CT
RECENT DEVELOPMENTS IN FOREIGN TRADE OF
AMERICAN REPUBLICS.

TC 1.23:CT
JAPANESE TRADE STUDIES.

TC 1.23/2:nos.
JAPANESE TRADE STUDIES, SPECIAL INDUSTRY
ANALYSES.

TC 1.24:v.nos.
TRADE AGREEMENT DIGEST.

TC 1.25:nos.
PRELIMINARY REPORT ON PRODUCTION ON
SPECIFIED SYNTHETIC ORGANIC CHEMICALS
IN UNITED STATES; FACTS FOR INDUSTRY SE-
RIES.

TC 1.25/2:nos.
FACTS FOR INDUSTRY SERIES 6-2 AND 6-10,
ORGANIC CHEMICALS AND PLASTIC MATERI-
ALS. [Monthly]

Previously issued as two publications and
classified TC 1.25

TC 1.25/3
S.O.C. [Synthetic Organic Chemicals] (series).

SERIES C. PRELIMINARY REPORT ON U.S.
PRODUCTION OF SELECTED SYNTHETIC
ORGANIC CHEMICALS. [Monthly]

TC 1.25/4
S.O.C. [Synthetic Organic Chemicals] (series).

SERIES P. PRELIMINARY REPORT ON U.S. PRO-
DUCTION AND SALES OF PLASTIC AND
RESIN MATERIALS. [Monthly]

TC 1.26:v.nos . Item 982-B (MF)
SUMMARIES OF TARIFF INFORMATION.

TC 1.26/2:sched.&v.nos.
SUMMARIES OF TRADE AND TARIFF INFORMATION.
Later ITC 1.11

TC 1.27:nos.
INDUSTRIAL MATERIALS SERIES: REPORT M (series).

TC 1.28
PUBLIC NOTICES. [Irregular]
ISSN 0145-0328

TC 1.29
PUBLIC INFORMATION [releases]. [Irregular]

ISSN 0145-0328
Later ITC 1.7

TC 1.30:CT
LAWS.
Later ITC 1.5

TC 1.31:CT • Item 980-C (MF)
DETERMINATION OF NO (material) INJURY (or threat
thereof) (series). [Irregular]

Consists of investigative reports which state
on the cover that there has been a determination
of no injury to a U.S. industry from the import of
the product. For reports that state an injury on
the cover, see TC 1.31/2.
Published in microfiche (24x).
Later ITC 1.12

TC 1.31/2:CT • Item 980-D (MF)
DETERMINATION OF INJURY (series). [Irregular]

Consists of investigative reports which state
on the cover a determination of injury or likelihood of injury to a U.S. industry. For reports that
state no injury on the cover, see TC 1.31.
Published in microfiche (24x)
Later ITC 1.12

TC 1.32
IMPORTS OF COAL-TAR PRODUCTS. 1944–
[Annual]

Gives quantity of imports of coal-tar intermediates, coal-tar products, coal-tar dyes, coal-tar
medicinals and pharmaceuticals, coal-tar flavor
and perfume materials.

TC 1.33 • Item 982-A
SYNTHETIC ORGANIC CHEMICALS, UNITED STATES
PRODUCTION AND SALES. 1917– [Annual]
Later ITC 1.14

TC 1.33/2
SYNTHETIC ORGANIC CHEMICALS, UNITED STATES
PRODUCTION AND SALES, PRELIMINARIES.
1966– [Annual]

Individual reports issued for separate products.

TC 1.34:date
PUBLICATIONS OF TARIFF COMMISSION.
Later ITC 1.9

TC 1.34/2:nos.
SELECTED-CURRENT ACQUISITIONS. [Monthly]
Later ITC 1.34/2

TC 1.35:date
UNITED STATES IMPORT DUTIES.
Earlier TC 1.10:Im 7/4

TC 1.35/2 • Item 982-B
TARIFF SCHEDULES OF THE UNITED STATES,
ANNOTATED. [Irregular] (includes basic manual
plus supplementary material for an indefinite pe-
riod) (Publication TC 103)
ISSN 0082-173X
Later ITC 1.10

TC 1.35/3 • Item 982-B
TARIFF SCHEDULES OF THE UNITED STATES.
[Irregular] (Publication TC 112) (Includes basic
volume plus supplementary material for an indefi-
nite period)
Issued in looseleaf form.

TC 1.36
IMPORTS OF BENZENOID CHEMICALS AND PROD-
UCTS. 1964– [Annual]
Later ITC 1.19

TC 1.37:nos.
STAFF RESEARCH STUDIES. 1– 1971–
[Irregular]

TC 1.38:nos.
REPORT TO CONGRESS AND AND EAST-WEST
FOREIGN TRADE BOARD ON TRADE BETWEEN
UNITED STATES AND NONMARKET ECONOMY
COUNTRIES. [Quarterly]
Later ITC 1.13

TC 1.38/2:CT
SPECIAL REPORTS TO CONGRESS AND EAST-
WEST FOREIGN TRADE BOARD.

TC 1.39:nos. • Item 980-B (MF)
REPORTS ON INVESTIGATIONS AND INQUIRIES
(series). [Irregular]

Consists of investigation reports which de-
termine whether a U.S. industry will be injured or
retarded because of imports of the product.
Published in microfiche (24x).
Reports in this series do not state "injury" or
"no injury" information on the cover. For reports
which state "injury" on the cover, see TC 1.31/2.
For reports which state "no injury" on cover, see
TC 1.31.
Later ITC 1.12

DEPARTMENT OF
TRANSPORTATION
(1966–   )

CREATION AND AUTHORITY

The Department of Transportation was established by the Department of Transportation Act of
October 15, 1966 (80 Stat. 931; 49 U.S.C. 1651
note.)

INFORMATION

Department of Transportation
400 Seventh Street, S.W.
Washington, D.C. 20590
(202) 366-4000
http://www.dot.gov

TD 1.1 • Item 982-C (MF)
ANNUAL REPORT. 1st– 1967– [Annual]

Also issued in the House Document series.

TD 1.1/3:date • Item 982-C-22 (EL)
OFFICE OF INSPECTOR GENERAL: SEMIANNUAL
REPORT TO CONGRESS.

Summarizes office activities, which include
responsibility for auditing and investigation Department programs and for keeping the Secretary
of Transportation and Congress informed of any
deficiencies.

TD 1.1/3-2 • Item 982-L (EL)
INSPECTOR GENERAL AUDIT REPORTS.

TD 1.1/3-3 • Item 982-L (EL)
INSPECTOR GENERAL INSPECTIONS & EVALUA-
TIONS REPORTS.

TD 1.1/4:date • Item 982-C-22 (MF)
THE SECRETARY'S SEMIANNUAL REPORT TO THE
CONGRESS.

TD 1.1/5 • Item 982-C-22 (MF)
A REPORT OF THE SECRETARY OF TRANSPORTA-
TION PURSUANT TO THE INTERMODAL
SURFACE TRANSPORTATION EFFICIENCY ACT
OF 1991.

TD 1.1/6 • Item 982-C-22 (MF)
CHIEF FINANCIAL OFFICER'S FINANCIAL STATE-
MENTS.

TD 1.1/7 • Item 982-C-32 (MF)
REPORT TO THE SECRETARY, FEDERAL
MANAGER'S FINANCIAL INTEGRITY ACT.

TD 1.2:CT • **Item 982-C-1**
GENERAL PUBLICATIONS.

TD 1.3/2:v.nos.&nos.
TECHNICAL INFORMATION CENTER: BULLETINS. [Quarterly]

TD 1.6:CT • **Item 982-C-3**
REGULATIONS, RULES, INSTRUCTIONS.

TD 1.6/2 • **Item 982-C-3 (EL)**
REGULATIONS OF THE OFFICE OF THE SECRETARY. 1967– [Irregular] (Includes basic manual plus supplementary material for an indefinite period)

TD 1.6/3:date • **Item 982-C-34 (EL)**
TRANSPORTATION ACQUISITION CIRCULAR, SUMMARY OF ITEMS. TAC-nos.

TD 1.7
PRESS RELEASES. 1967– [Irregular]

TD 1.8:CT • **Item 982-C-5**
HANDBOOKS, MANUALS, GUIDES.

TD 1.8/2:CT
ENVIRONMENTAL ASSESSMENT NOTEBOOK SERIES.

TD 1.9 • **Item 982-C-7 (MF)**
TELEPHONE DIRECTORY. 1968– [Semiannual]

TD 1.9/2
TELEPHONE DIRECTORY (alphabetical).

TD 1.9/3:date
TELEPHONE DIRECTORY, DIRECTORY OF SERVICES AND CLASSIFIED.

TD 1.9/4:CT • **Item 982-C-7 (MF)**
DIRECTORIES.

TD 1.10 • **Item 982-I-7**
REPORT ON HIGH SPEED GROUND TRANSPORTATION ACT OF 1965. IT– 1966– [Annual]

Report made by the Secretary of Transportation to the President and Congress pursuant to sec. 10 (a) of the act approved Sept. 30, 1965 (79 Stat. 895), as amended by act of Oct. 15, 1966 (80 Stat. 931).

TD 1.10/2
REPORT TO CONGRESS ON THE ADMINISTRATION OF THE NATIONAL TRAFFIC VEHICLE SAFETY ACT OF 1966. 1– 1966– [Annual]

Report submitted by Secretary of Transportation to the President and Congress pursuant to Section 102 of the National Traffic and Motor Vehicle Safety Act for the calendar year.

TD 1.10/3
REPORT TO CONGRESS ON THE ADMINISTRATION OF THE HIGHWAY SAFETY ACT OF 1966. 1st– 1966– [Annual]

Report submitted by the Secretary of Transportation to the President and Congress pursuant to Section 202 of the Highway Safety Act of 1966 for the calendar year.
The first report covered the period September 9, 1966 to December 31, 1967.
Each report is in two volumes. The first volume contains the texts and the second is made up of Appendixes including a statistical compilation of highway casualty and other date.
Also issued as a House Document.

TD 1.10/4:date
ANNUAL REPORT OF SECRETARY OF TRANSPORTATION OF ADMINISTRATION OF NATURAL GAS PIPELINES SAFETY ACT OF 1968.

TD 1.10/5:date
RAIL PASSENGER SERVICE ACT, REPORT TO CONGRESS. [Annual]
Later IC 1.34

TD 1.10/6:date
ANNUAL REPORT TO THE PRESIDENT AND THE CONGRESS SUBMITTED BY THE SECRETARY OF TRANSPORTATION UNDER THE EMERGENCY RAIL SERVICE ACT OF 1970.

TD 1.10/6-2:CT/date
FINANCIAL CONDITIONS OF [various railroads], ANNUAL REPORT TO THE PRESIDENT AND THE CONGRESS.

TD 1.10/7:date • **Item 982-C-23 (MF)**
ANNUAL REPORT BY THE PRESIDENT TO THE CONGRESS ON THE ADMINISTRATION OF THE FEDERAL RAILROAD SAFETY ACT OF 1970.

Contains tables on train accidents, casualties in accidents or incidents in rail-highway grade crossings, etc.

TD 1.10/8:date
ANNUAL REPORT ON ALASKA RAILROAD.

TD 1.11
ADDRESS. 1967– [Irregular]

TD 1.12:date
SUMMER YOUTH OPPORTUNITY PROGRAM ANNUAL REPORT.

TD 1.13:date
NATIONAL MOTOR VEHICLE SAFETY ADVISORY COUNCIL SUMMARY REPORT. [Annual]

TD 1.13/2:date
NATIONAL HIGHWAY SAFETY ADVISORY COMMITTEE: ANNUAL REPORT.

TD 1.14:CT
TRANSPORTATION FORECAST (series).

TD 1.15:nos. • **Item 982-C-9**
BIBLIOGRAPHIC LISTS (numbered). 1– 1969– (Office of Administrative Operations, Library Services Division)

TD 1.15/2:CT • **Item 982-C-12**
BIBLIOGRAPHIES AND LISTS OF PUBLICATIONS.

TD 1.15/3:date • **Item 982-C-21**
SELECTED LIBRARY ACQUISITIONS. [Monthly]

ISSN 0145-9309

CURRENT LITERATURE COMPILED BY THE LIBRARY STAFF.

TD 1.15/4:v.nos.&nos.
TRANSPORTATION.

TD 1.15/5:v.nos.&nos.
URBAN TRANSPORTATION AND PLANNING.

TD 1.15/6:v.nos.&nos.
ADMINISTRATION AND MANAGEMENT.

TD 1.16:date • **Item 982-C-4**
FEDERAL AIRCRAFT NOISE ABATEMENT PLAN, FISCAL YEAR. 1st– 1969–

TD 1.17:CT • **Item 982-C-1**
AUTOMOBILE INSURANCE AND COMPENSATION STUDIES.

TD 1.18:date
DOMESTIC AND INTERNATIONAL FACILITATION PROGRAM. [Annual] (Office of Facilitation)

PURPOSE:– To review the calendar year domestic and international facilitation program to be administered by the Office of Facilitation, Office of Assistant Secretary for Policy and International Affairs, DOT.
Includes list of various projects; identification of the professional staff members and their team assignments; facilitation research programs recently completed, underway, or planned; and projections of the anticipated facilitation progress expected during the calendar year.

TD 1.19:date • **Item 982-I-17 (MF)**
DEPARTMENT OF TRANSPORTATION NATIONAL PLAN FOR NAVIGATION. 1970– [Irregular] (Federal Aviation Administration and U.S. Coast Guard)

PURPOSE:– Issued for information and use in the management of civil navigation systems, including planning, programming, and implementation to meet validated requirements, and will be maintained current on periodic basis.

TD 1.20:yr.-nos. • **Item 982-I-5 (MF)**
DOT TST- (series). [Irregular] (Office of the Assistant Secretary for Systems Development and Technology)

Superseded by DOT-RSPD-DSP (series) (TD 1.20/7).

TD 1.20/2:nos. • **Item 982-I-5 (MF)**
DOT-TSC-OST- (series). [Irregular]

TD 1.20/3:nos.
OST/TST REPORTS.

TD 1.20/4:nos.
REPORT DOT/MTB/OHMO (series). [Irregular]

TD 1.20/5:nos.
DOT/OPS (series). [Irregular]

TD 1.20/6:nos. • **Item 982-C-10 (MF)**
REPORT DOT/OST/P (series). [Irregular]

TD 1.20/6-2:date • **Item 982-C-10 (MF)**
PROGRAM OF UNIVERSITY RESEARCH REPORT REPRINTED. [Annual]

Earlier TD 1.20/6

TD 1.20/7:nos. • **Item 982-I-13 (MF)**
DOT-RSPD-DPB (series). [Irregular] (Research and Special Programs Directorate)

Supersedes DOT-TST (series) (TD 1.20).

TD 1.20/8:nos. • **Item 982-I-15 (MF)**
REPORT DOT-I- (series). [Irregular] (Office of Assistant Director of Transportation for Intergovernmental Affairs)

TD 1.20/9:nos. • **Item 982-C-24 (MF)**
REPORT DOT-TSC-RSPD- (series). [Irregular] (Research and Special Programs Directorate)

Published in microfiche (24x).

TD 1.20/10:nos. • **Item 982-I-15 (MF)**
DOT-T (Series).

TD 1.21:date
ANNUAL REPORT ON HIGHWAY RELOCATION ASSISTANCE.

TD 1.22:date
CARLOAD WAYBILL STATISTICS, STATEMENT TD-1.
Earlier IC 1.23/18

TD 1.23:v.nos.
URBAN TRANSPORTATION RESEARCH AND PLANNING CURRENT LITERATURE.

TD 1.24:date • **Item 982-I-8 (MF)**
ANNUAL REPORT OF THE SECRETARY OF TRANSPORTATION ON HAZARDOUS MATERIALS CONTROL. 1st– 1970–
Later TD 9.15

TD 1.25:v.nos.&nos.
TRANSPORTATION TOPICS FOR CONSUMERS. v. 1– 27. 1972– 1981. [Quarterly] (Office of Consumer Affairs)

PURPOSE:– To establish a two-way communication between the Department of Transportation and consumers for a safer, more convenient and more efficient transportation system. Contains brief notices of new ideas, lists new publications of interest in the field of transportation.
Merged with Dialog to form Transpo Topics (TD 1.25/2).
ISSN 0364-6653

TD 1.25/2:date • **Item 982-C-1 (EL)**
TRANSPO TOPICS. [Quarterly]

Formed by the merger of Transportation Consumer (TD 1.25) and Dialog.

TD 1.25/3   • **Item 982-C-1 (EL)**
DOT TALK.

TD 1.25/4   • **Item 982-C-1 (EL)**
TRANSPORTATION LINK.

TD 1.26:date   • **Item 982-C-6 (MF)**
NATIONAL TRANSPORTATION REPORT. 1st–
1972–   [Annual]

PURPOSE:– To provide to the Congress a comprehensive reporting on the status of the nation's freight and passenger transportation systems as well as the capital investment needs through 1990 as reported by State and local officials. In addition, alternative capital investment programs from each of the States in response to three separate Federal capital assistance program alternatives. Finally, to report upon the analysis of several high priority urban and intercity transportation issues and recommendations for consideration in the development of future national transportation policy, legislation and programs.

TD 1.27:v.nos.&nos.   • **Item 982-C-8**
TRANSPORTATION USA. v. 1– 7.   – 1980. [Quarterly] (Office of Public Affairs)

Indexed by: Index to U.S. Government Periodicals.
ISSN 0094-9922

TD 1.28:date   • **Item 982-C-8**
IMPLEMENTING TRANSPORTATION POLICY. 1st–
1972–   [Annual]

Annual report on the implementation of the statement on National Transportation Policy.

TD 1.29:nos.
WORKING PAPERS.

TD 1.30:CT
ENERGY CONSERVATION FACT SHEETS.

TD 1.31:v.nos.&nos.
DOT NEWS. [Biweekly]

TD 1.32:v.nos.&nos.
AUDIT JOURNAL. (Office of Audits)

TD 1.33:date   • **Item 982-C-20 (MF)**
REPORT TO THE PRESIDENT ON NATIONAL CARGO SECURITY PROGRAM. [Annual]

PURPOSE:– To review and evaluate the status of the cooperative Federal-industry effort to reduce theft-related losses in transportation.

TD 1.34:date
BUDGET STATUS REPORT.

TD 1.34/2:nos.   • **Item 982-C-11 (MF)**
DEPARTMENT OF TRANSPORTATION BUDGET PROGRAM: ANALYSIS OF FISCAL YEAR DOT PROGRAM BY POLICY AND RD&D MANAGEMENT OBJECTIVES, DOT-OST- (series).

TD 1.34/3:date
BUDGET ESTIMATES. [Annual]
Earlier TS 1.2:B 85/2

TD 1.34/4:date   • **Item 982-C-15 (MF)**
DEPARTMENT OF TRANSPORTATION BUDGET, EXCERPTS FROM THE PRESIDENT'S BUDGET. [Annual]

TD 1.35:nos.   • **Item 982-C-13 (MF)**
REPORT TES (series).

TD 1.36:date
DIRECTORY OF INFORMATION SYSTEMS. [Semiannual]

TD 1.37:date
FACT SHEETS. (Office of Public Affairs)

TD 1.38:nos.
CLIMATIC IMPACT ASSESSMENT PROGRAM: TECHNICAL ABSTRACT REPORT, TAR- (series). [Monthly]

TD 1.38/2:nos.
CLIMATIC IMPACT ASSESSMENT PROGRAM: NEWSLETTER.

TD 1.39:date
GRANT AWARDS.

TD 1.40:date   • **Item 982-C-25 (MF)**
U.S. INTERNATIONAL AIR TRAVEL STATISTICS. [Monthly with quarterly cumulations]

Also published in microfiche.
ISSN 0145-9341

TD 1.40/2:date   • **Item 982-C-25 (MF)**
U.S. INTERNATIONAL AIR TRAVEL STATISTICS, FISCAL YEAR. [Annual]

Also published in microfiche.

TD 1.40/3:date   • **Item 982-C-25 (MF)**
U.S. INTERNATIONAL AIR TRAVEL STATISTICS, CALENDAR YEAR. [Annual]

Also published in microfiche.

TD 1.40/4:date   • **Item 982-C-33 (EL)**
U.S. INTERNATIONAL AIR PASSENGER AND FREIGHT STATISTICS, CALENDAR YEAR. [Quarterly]

TD 1.40/5   • **Item 982-C-38 (EL)**
INTERNATIONAL AVIATION DEVELOPMENTS SERIES.

TD 1.41:CT
ENVIRONMENTAL IMPACT STATEMENTS. [Irregular]

TD 1.42:v.nos.&nos.
CIVIL RIGHTS REVIEW. [Monthly]

TD 1.43:v.nos.&nos.
OST-NDER BULLETIN.

TD 1.45:date   • **Item 982-C-14 (MF)**
UNIVERSITY RESEARCH: SUMMARY OF AWARDS, PROGRAM OF UNIVERSITY RESEARCH. [Annual]

TD 1.46:date   • **Item 982-C-16 (MF)**
DoT EMPLOYMENT FACTS. [Semiannual]

TD 1.47:date   • **Item 982-C-17 (MF)**
DESIGN, ART, AND ARCHITECTURE IN TRANSPORTATION, ANNUAL REPORT TO THE SECRETARY OF TRANSPORTATION. 1st–

PURPOSE:– To provide a summary of progress made in implementing the secretary's program of encouraging good design, art, and architecture in air, rail, and highway transportation facilities and services.

TD 1.48:nos.   • **Item 982-C-18 (MF)**
TRANSPORTATION SAFETY INFORMATION REPORT. [Quarterly]

PURPOSE:– To summarize and compare selected national-level transportation safety statistics for all modes of transportation.

TD 1.49:CT   • **Item 982-C-19**
TECHNOLOGY SHARING REPRINT SERIES. [Irregular]

Includes miscellaneous publications on topics concerning transportation technology, research developments, etc., of interest to State and local agencies and planners, industry, etc.

TD 1.50:CT
AUDIOVISUAL MATERIALS. [Irregular]

TD 1.51:date   • **Item 982-C-26 (MF)**
SOURCES OF INFORMATION ON URBAN TRANSPORTATION PLANNING METHODS. [Annual]

Sourcebook intended for use of transportation planners in determining what publications, courses, etc., are available from Urban Mass Transportation Administration or Federal Highway Administration to help solve analysis problems related to urban transportation.

TD 1.52:CT   • **Item 982-C-27 (MF)**
MICROCOMPUTERS IN TRANSPORTATION (various titles). [Irregular]

PURPOSE:– To present information on microcomputers in transportation in terms of software and sources, getting started in microcomputers, and selecting a single user system.

TD 1.53:nos.   • **Item 177-A-1 (MF)**
AIRCRAFT OPERATING COST AND PERFORMANCE REPORT. [Annual]

TD 1.54:   • **Item 982-C-29 (EL)**
AIR TRAVEL CONSUMER REPORT. [Monthly]

Designed to provide consumers with information on the quality of services provided by the airlines. Narrative and tables present data on flight delays, mishandled baggage, oversales, and consumer complaints.

TD 1.56   • **Item 982-L (E)**
ELECTRONIC PRODUCTS. [Irregular]

TD 1.56/2   • **Item 982-L-2 (CD)**
1990 CENSUS TRANSPORTATION PLANNING PACKAGE.

TD 1.56/3:date   • **Item 982-L-4 (CD)**
TRAFFIC SAFETY DATA ASCII AND SAS VERSIONS. [Annual]

TD 1.56/4   • **Item 982-L-5 (CD)**
RAIL WAYBILL DATA.

TD 1.56/5:CD nos.   • **Item 982-L-6 (CD)**
TIGER/LINE.

TD 1.57:CT   • **Item 982-C-22**
SECRETARY'S TASK FORCE ON COMPETITION IN THE U.S. DOMESTIC AIRLINE INDUSTRY.

TD 1.59   • **Item 982-L (EL)**
THE DOTTED LINE.

TD 1.60   • **Item 982-L (EL)**
ITS UPDATE.

TD 1.61:   • **Item 982-C-36**
PORT SECURITY (series).

TD 1.62   • **Item 982-C-37 (MF) (EL)**
U.S. DEPARTMENT OF TRANSPORTATION FY…PROCUREMENT FORECAST. (Annual)

NATIONAL TRANSPORTATION SAFETY BOARD
(1966–   )

CREATION AND AUTHORITY

The National Transportation Safety Board was established within the Department of Transportation by the Department of Transportation Act of 1966 (80 Stat. 935). The Board became an independent agency of the Federal Government on April 1, 1975, by the Independent Safety Board Act of 1974 (88 Stat. 2156; 49 U.S.C. 1901).

INFORMATION

National Transportation Safety Board
490 L'Enfant Plaza, SW
Washington, D.C. 20594
(202) 314-6000
http://www.ntsb.gov

TD 1.101   • **Item 982-I-18 (MF) (EL)**
ANNUAL REPORT. 1967–   [Annual]

Report made by the Board to Congress covering its activities during the calendar year.
Formerly distributed to depository libraries under Item No. 982-I.

TD 1.102:CT   • **Item 982-I-27**
GENERAL PUBLICATIONS.

TD 1.106/2:date
PART 430, RULES PERTAINING TO AIRCRAFT ACCIDENTS, INCIDENTS, OVERDUE AIRCRAFT, AND SAFETY INVESTIGATIONS.

TD 1.106/3:nos.   • **Item 982-I-24**
SAFETY RECOMMENDATIONS. [Irregular]

TD 1.106/4:yr.nos.   • **Item 982-I-24 (MF)**
SAFETY REPORTS, NTSB-SR (series). [Irregular]

     PURPOSE:– To provide reports, each of which outline the board efforts to stimulate implementation of safety improvements, describe progress made toward safety in a specific area of transportation.

TD 1.107
PRESS RELEASES. 1967– [Irregular]

TD 1.108:CT   • **Item 982-I-12**
HANDBOOKS, MANUALS, GUIDES.

TD 1.109
BRIEFS OF ACCIDENTS, U.S. CIVIL AVIATION. 1967– [Monthly]

TD 1.109/2
BRIEFS OF ACCIDENTS INVOLVING (various) AIRCRAFT. 1964– [Annual]

     Separate brief issued for each individual type of aircraft. Contains the facts, conditions, circumstances and probable cause for each accident involving that aircraft make and model during the year. Several statistical tables relating to type of accident, kind of flying, probable cause and injuries are also provided.

TD 1.109/3
BRIEFS OF ACCIDENTS INVOLVING AIR TAXI OPERATIONS, U.S. GENERAL AVIATION. 1964– [Annual]

TD 1.109/4:date
BRIEFS OF ACCIDENTS INVOLVING AERIAL APPLICATIONS OPERATIONS, U.S. GENERAL AVIATION.

TD 1.109/5:date
BRIEFS OF ACCIDENTS INVOLVING ROTOCRAFT, U.S. GENERAL AVIATION.

TD 1.109/6:date
BRIEFS OF ACCIDENTS INVOLVING AMATEUR BUILT (homebuild) AIRCRAFT, U.S. GENERAL AVIATION.

TD 1.109/7:date
BRIEFS OF ACCIDENTS INVOLVING MID-AIR COLLISIONS, U.S. CIVIL AVIATION.

TD 1.109/8:date
BRIEFS OF ACCIDENTS INVOLVING MISSING AIRCRAFT, U.S. GENERAL AVIATION. (Bureau of Aviation Safety)

TD 1.109/9:date
BRIEFS OF ACCIDENTS INVOLVING ALCOHOL AS A CAUSE/FACTOR, U.S. GENERAL AVIATION. (Bureau of Aviation Safety)

TD 1.109/10:date
BRIEFS OF ACCIDENTS INVOLVING CORPORATE/ EXECUTIVE AIRCRAFT, U.S. GENERAL AVIATION. (Bureau of Aviation Safety)

TD 1.109/11:date
BRIEFS OF ACCIDENTS BY MAKE AND MODEL OF AIRCRAFT, U.S. GENERAL AVIATION (compilation).

TD 1.109/12:date
BRIEFS OF FATAL ACCIDENTS INVOLVING WEATHER AS A CAUSE/FACTOR, U.S. GENERAL AVIATION. [Annual]

     ISSN 0360-7127

TD 1.109/13:nos.   • **Item 982-I-3 (MF)**
AIRCRAFT ACCIDENT REPORTS, BRIEF FORMAT, U.S. CIVIL AVIATION, NTSB- BA– (series). [Irregular]

     ISSN 0363-8324
     Earlier TD 1.109

TD 1.109/14:nos.
BRIEFS OF AIRCRAFT ACCIDENTS INVOLVING TURBINE POWERED AIRCRAFT, U.S. GENERAL AVIATION, CALENDAR YEAR, NTSB-AMM- (series).

TD 1.109/15:date
LISTING OF AIRCRAFT ACCIDENTS/INCIDENTS BY MAKE AND MODEL, U.S. CIVIL AVIATION, NTSB-AMM- (nos.). [Irregular]

TD 1.109/16:nos.   • **Item 982-I-16 (MF)**
REPORT NTSB-AMM (series). [Annual]

     PURPOSE:– To provide briefs of aircraft accidents in civil and general aviation. Each publication covers a specific subject and each title is issued annually.

     The following sub-series are currently being published:–

BRIEFS OF ACCIDENTS INVOLVING AERIAL APPLICATION OF OPERATIONS, U.S. GENERAL AVIATION.

BRIEFS OF ACCIDENTS INVOLVING ALCOHOL AS A CAUSE/FACTOR, U.S. GENERAL AVIATION.

BRIEFS OF ACCIDENTS INVOLVING AMATEUR/ HOME BUILT AIRCRAFT, U.S. GENERAL AVIATION.

BRIEFS OF ACCIDENTS INVOLVING COMMUTER AIR CARRIERS AND ON-DEMAND AIR TAXI OPERATIONS, U.S. GENERAL AVIATION.

BRIEFS OF ACCIDENTS INVOLVING CORPORATE/ EXECUTIVE AIRCRAFT, U.S. GENERAL AVIATION.

BRIEFS OF ACCIDENTS INVOLVING MIDAIR COLLISIONS, U.S. GENERAL AVIATION.

BRIEFS OF ACCIDENTS INVOLVING MISSING AND MISSING LATER RECOVERED AIRCRAFT, U.S. GENERAL AVIATION.

BRIEFS OF ACCIDENTS INVOLVING ROTORCRAFT, U.S. GENERAL AVIATION.

BRIEFS OF ACCIDENTS INVOLVING TURBINE POWERED AIRCRAFT, U.S. GENERAL AVIATION.

BRIEFS OF FATAL ACCIDENTS INVOLVING WEATHER AS A CAUSE/FACTOR, U.S. GENERAL AVIATION.

LISTING OF AIRCRAFT ACCIDENTS/INCIDENTS BY MAKE AND MODEL, U.S. CIVIL AVIATION.

TD 1.110
ADDRESSES. 1967– [Irregular]

TD 1.111:nos.
ORDERS EA (nos.).

TD 1.112   • **Item 982-I-9 (MF)**
AIRCRAFT ACCIDENT REPORTS NTSB- AAR- (series). 1967– [Irregular]

TD 1.112/2:CT   • **Item 982-I-9 (MF)**
SPECIAL INVESTIGATION REPORTS. NTSB-SIR-NOS.

TD 1.112/3   • **Item 982-I-11 (MF)**
RAILROAD ACCIDENT REPORTS. NTSB-RAR-NOS. 1968– [Irregular]

     Detailed individual formal reports issued on the facts, circumstances, and probable cause of highly selected major railroad accidents. Separate report issued for each accident selected.

TD 1.112/4   • **Item 982-I-14 (MF)**
RAILROAD-HIGHWAY ACCIDENT REPORTS. 1968– [Irregular]

     Detailed individual formal reports issued on the facts, circumstances, and probable cause of highly selected major highway-railroad accidents. Separate report issued for each accident selected.

TD 1.112/5:nos.   • **Item 982-I-19 (MF)**
RAILROAD ACCIDENT REPORTS, BRIEF FORMAT, NTSB-RAB (series). [Irregular]

     PURPOSE:– To publish briefs of selected railroad accidents, covering basic facts, conditions, circumstances, and probable cause in each case.

TD 1.112/6:nos.   • **Item 982-I-9 (MF)**
AIRCRAFT ACCIDENT/INCIDENT SUMMARY REPORTS. [Irregular]

TD 1.112/7:date   • **Item 982-I-11 (MF)**
RAILROAD ACCIDENT/INCIDENT SUMMARY REPORTS. [Irregular]

TD 1.113:date   • **Item 982-I-6 (MF)**
ANNUAL REVIEW OF AIRCRAFT ACCIDENT DATA, U.S. GENERAL AVIATION, CALENDAR YEAR (date).

     Earlier: Annual Review of U.S. General Aviation Accidents.

TD 1.113/2
ANNUAL REVIEW OF U.S. AIR CARRIER ACCIDENTS OCCURRING IN CALENDAR YEAR (date). 1964– [Annual]

     Gives statistical data and briefs of accidents compiled from reports of U.S. Air, Carrier accidents that occurred during a calendar year. The briefs contain the facts, conditions, circumstances and probable cause for each accident. The record of individual U.S. Air Carriers, U.S. Certificated Route Air Carriers, and U.S. Supplemental Air Carriers is provided by several types of service. Other statistical data include aircraft hours and miles flown, passengers carried, accident rates total and fatal, causal factors, and injuries. In addition, an analysis of the data included in the review is enclosed as an insert.

TD 1.113/3
ANALYSIS OF AIRCRAFT ACCIDENT DATA, U.S. GENERAL AVIATION. [Annual]

TD 1.113/4
ANALYSIS OF ACCIDENTS INVOLVING AIR TAXI OPERATIONS, U.S. GENERAL AVIATION. 1966– [Annual]

TD 1.113/5:date   • **Item 982-I-6 (MF)**
ANNUAL REVIEW OF AIRCRAFT ACCIDENT DATA, U.S. AIR CARRIER OPERATIONS CALENDAR YEAR (date).

     Earlier: Analysis of Aircraft Accident Data, U.S. Air Carrier Operations.

TD 1.113/6
PRELIMINARY ANALYSIS OF AIRCRAFT ACCIDENT DATA, U.S. CIVIL AVIATION. 1967– [Annual]

TD 1.114:nos.
BUREAU OF AVIATION SAFETY REPORT, BASR (series).

TD 1.115:date   • **Item 982-I-1 (MF)**
LIST OF PUBLICATIONS.

TD 1.116:CT   • **Item 982-I-21 (MF)**
MARINE ACCIDENT REPORTS. [Irregular]

     Formerly entitled Marine Casualty Reports and issued by the Marine Board of Investigation. Later TD 5.49

TD 1.116/2   • **Item 982-I-21 (MF)**
MARINE ACCIDENT REPORTS, SUMMARY FORMAT ISSUES. 1– 1978– [Semiannual]

TD 1.116/3:nos. • Item 982-I-21 (MF)
MARINE ACCIDENT REPORTS, BRIEF FORMAT.
[Irregular]

TD 1.116/4:nos. • Item 982-I-21 (MF)
MARINE ACCIDENT/INCIDENT SUMMARY REPORTS
(series). [Irregular]

TD 1.117:CT • Item 982-I-20 (MF)
HIGHWAY ACCIDENT REPORTS. [Irregular] (Bureau
of Surface Transportation)

Series of illustrated reports of highway accident investigations with analyses, causes, and
hypotheses of causes involving automobiles,
trucks, buses, and railroad trains and including
safety recommendations.

TD 1.117/2:nos. • Item 982-I-20 (MF)
HIGHWAY ACCIDENT REPORTS, BRIEF FORMAT,
NTSB-HAB- (series). [Irregular]

TD 1.117/3:nos. • Item 982-I-20 (MF)
HIGHWAY ACCIDENT/INCIDENT SUMMARY RE-
PORTS. [Irregular]

TD 1.118:CT • Item 982-I-10 (MF)
PIPELINE ACCIDENT REPORTS. 1969– [Irregular]

PURPOSE:– To report facts developed in investigations conducted by the Safety Board, including circumstances and the determination of
probable cause of pipeline accidents.

TD 1.118/2:nos.
NTSS-PSS (series).

TD 1.118/3:nos. • Item 982-I-10 (MF)
PIPELINE ACCIDENT REPORTS: BRIEF FORMAT,
NTSB-PAB- (series). [Irregular]

TD 1.118/4:nos. • Item 982-I-10 (MF)
PIPELINE ACCIDENT/INCIDENT SUMMARY RE-
PORTS. [Irregular]

TD 1.119:v.nos.&nos.
THE SAFETY BOARD, MONTHLY EMPLOYEE PUBLI-
CATION.

TD 1.120:nos. • Item 982-I-23 (MF)
SPECIAL STUDY REPORT, NTSB-HSS– (series).
1969– [Irregular]

PURPOSE:– To present detailed studies published by the Safety Board on specific important
aspects of surface transportation safety. Contains information, conclusions and safety recommendations.

TD 1.121:year-nos. • Item 982-I-2
NTSB-AAS [National Transportation Safety Board, As-
pects of Aviation Safety] (series). 69-1– 1969–
[Irregular]

PURPOSE:– To provide detailed studies by
the Safety Board on specific important aspects
of aviation safety. Studies contain information,
conclusions, and safety recommendations.

TD 1.122:v.nos. • Item 982-I-4 (MF)
NATIONAL TRANSPORTATION SAFETY BOARD DE-
CISIONS. [Bound volumes] v. 1– 1967/1972–

v. 1. April 1, 1967– December 31, 1972.

TD 1.123:nos.
NTSB-PAM- (series).

TD 1.124:date
TELEPHONE DIRECTORY.

TD 1.125:date • Item 982-I-22 (MF)
SAFETY EFFECTIVENESS EVALUATION, NTSB-SEE-
(series). [Irregular]

PURPOSE:– To present assessment reports
on the effectiveness of selected programs administered by the various government agencies
pertaining to transportation safety and accident
prevention. Topics include accident data systems,
passive restraints, truck breaking systems, etc.

TD 1.126:nos.
OPINIONS AND ORDERS. [Irregular]

TD 1.127: • Item 982-I-25
SAFETY STUDIES, NTSB/SS- (series). [Irregular]

Each study deals with a different subject.

TD 1.128:nos. • Item 982-I-9 (MF)
HAZARDOUS MATERIALS ACCIDENT REPORTS,
NTSB/HZM.

TD 1.129 • Item 982-I-24 (MF)
NTSB SAFETY RECOMMENDATION (Series).

Reports contain briefs of aviation accidents
which involved alcohol use by the pilot-in-com-
mand. Presents facts, conditions, circumstances
and probable causes for each accident.

TD 1.130 • Item 982-L-3 (MF)
NTSB/RP (series).

TD 1.131 • Item 982-I-28 (MF)
NTSB NEWS DIGEST. [Irregular]

TD 1.132: • Item 982-I-29 (E)
ELECTRONIC PRODUCTS (misc.).

TRANSPORTATION SECURITY ADMINISTRATION

TD 1.202 • Item 982-R
GENERAL PUBLICATIONS.

FEDERAL HIGHWAY ADMINISTRATION (1966–   )

CREATION AND AUTHORITY

The Federal Highway Administration became
a component of the Department of Transportation
pursuant to the Department of Transportation Act
of October 15, 1966 (80 Stat. 932).

INFORMATION

Federal Highway Administration
Department of Transportation
400 Seventh Street, S.W.
Washington, D.C. 20590
(202) 366-0537
Fax: (202) 366-3244
http://www.fhwa.dot.gov

TD 2.1:date
ANNUAL REPORT.

TD 2.2:CT • Item 982-G-5
GENERAL PUBLICATIONS.

TD 2.3:date
FHWA BULLETINS.

TD 2.3/2:nos.
HIGHWAY COMMISSION MANAGEMENT BULLETIN.

TD 2.3/3: • Item 982-G-46 (MF)
BULLETINS (series).

TD 2.5:CT • Item 982-G-4
LAWS.

TD 2.6:CT
REGULATIONS, RULES, AND INSTRUCTIONS.

TD 2.7
PRESS RELEASES. 1967– [Irregular]

TD 2.8:CT • Item 982-G-2
HANDBOOKS, MANUALS, GUIDES.

TD 2.8:T 67 • Item 982-G-2
MANUAL ON UNIFORM CONTROL DEVICES FOR
STREETS AND HIGHWAYS. [Irregular]
(Includes basic manual and supplements for
an indefinite period) (National Advisory Com-
mittee on Uniform Traffic Control Devices)

PURPOSE:– To review the design and
placement of signs, signals, markings, and
devices placed on streets and highways to
regulated or guide traffic. Uniform standards
for traffic control devices are presented and
illustrations of proper sign placement are included. The growing use of symbols on traffic
signs and the employment of color coding
and pavement markings in traffic control are
also covered.
Spine title: Manual on Uniform Traffic Control Devices.

TD 2.8/2:v.nos.
MANUAL ON UNIFORM TRAFFIC CONTROL DEVICES
FOR STREETS AND HIGHWAYS: OFFICIAL RUL-
INGS ON REQUESTS FOR INTERPRETATIONS,
CHANGES, AND EXPERIMENTATIONS. [Annual]

TD 2.9:nos.
ROUNDUP OF FEDERAL HIGHWAY ADMINISTRATION
NEWS.
Earlier C 37.29

TD 2.10:CT
BIBLIOGRAPHIES AND LISTS OF PUBLICATIONS.

TD 2.11
ADDRESSES. 1967– [Irregular]

TD 2.12:v.nos.&nos.
FEDERAL HIGHWAY ADMINISTRTION NEWS.

TD 2.12/2:nos.
FEDERAL HIGHWAY ADMINISTRATION NEWSLET-
TER.

TD 2.13
HIGHWAY PLANNING NOTES. 1–   1962–
[Irregular]

PURPOSE:– To keep Bureau of Public Roads
employees and the public informed on current
developments in the highway planning field. Presented in a newsletter format.
Previously published by Bureau of Public
Roads (C 37.26 and TD 2.111).

TD 2.14:nos. • Item 982-G-3 (MF)
HIGHWAY AND ITS ENVIRONMENT, ANNUAL
AWARDS COMPETITION. 1st–   1968–   [An-
nual] (Scenic Enhancement Division, Office of
Environmental Policy)

Sponsored by the Department of Transportation, the annual Highway and Its Environment
Contest is designed to give public recognition to
agencies, organizations and business enterprises
that took action during the year to protect, preserve or enhance the highway environment. Each
booklet gives a picture and brief description of
each of the award winning entries for each of ten
categories.

TD 2.14/2:CT • Item 982-G-3
ANNUAL HIGHWAY AWARDS COMPETITION.

TD 2.15:date • Item 982-G-6
SUMMER YOUTH OPPORTUNITY CAMPAIGN. [An-
nual]

TD 2.16:date
ANNUAL REPORT TO THE SECRETARY OF TRANS-
PORTATION ON THE ACCIDENT INVESTIGATION
AND REPORTING ACTIVITIES OF THE FEDERAL
HIGHWAY ADMINISTRATION IN (year). 1st–
1968–

PURPOSE:– To report on the progress, problems, and results of the working relationship between the Federal Highway Administration and
the National Transportation Safety Board, and to
recommend steps that will promote mutual objectives.
Report submitted by the Federal Highway Administrator to the Secretary of Transportation in
accordance with DOT order 2000.1, dated October 1, 1968.

TD 2.17:date
ANNUAL REPORT ON THE STATUS OF EQUAL EM-
PLOYMENT OPPORTUNITY PROGRAM. 1st–
1969–   (Office of Civil Rights)

TD 2.18:date   • **Item 982-G-7**
HIGHWAY TRANSPORTATION. 1970–   [Irregular]
(Publications Office)

PURPOSE:– To describe programs of the
Federal Highway Administration and related operations. Contains brief, illustrated articles.
Indexed by: Index to U.S. Government Periodicals.

TD 2.19:v.nos./nos.   • **Item 268 (EL)**
PUBLIC ROADS, JOURNAL OF HIGHWAY RESEARCH.
v. 1–   1918–   [Quarterly]

PURPOSE:– To acquaint highway engineers
and others interested in highway matters with the
results of the Administration's research in high-
way planning, design, construction, finance, high-
way use, and in a wide variety of materials for
use in road construction.
Title page and list of contents issued sepa-
rately for each volume.
Indexed by:–
Chemical Abstracts
Engineering Index Annual
Engineering Index Monthly
Index to U.S. Government Periodicals
ISSN 0033-3735
Earlier TD 2.109, C 37.8

TD 2.20:date   • **Item 265-H (MF)**
FATAL AND INJURY ACCIDENTS RATES ON FED-
ERAL-AID AND OTHER HIGHWAY SYSTEMS.
1967–   [Annual]

Statistical data on fatal and personal injury
accidents on Federal-aid and other highway systems.

TD 2.21:date
HIGHWAY PROGRESS. [Annual]

TD 2.22:date
NEW DEVELOPMENTS IN HIGHWAYS. [Irregular]

PURPOSE:– To provide an announcement
service of available technical reports in the field
of highway development, such as design, economics, hydraulics, maintenance, management,
materials, right-of-way, structures, and traffic.
Information is given on availability of the reports
either from the National Technical Information
Service or other sources.
Earlier TD 1.24, prior to the September 1970
issue.

TD 2.23:date   • **Item 265-B (EL)**
HIGHWAY STATISTICS. 1st ed.–   1945–   [An-
nual] (Highway Statistics Division, Office of Highway Planning)

PURPOSE:– To present statistical and analytical tables of general interest on motor fuel,
motor vehicles, driver licensing, highway-user
taxation, State highway finance, highway mileage, and Federal aid for highways for current
year; and highway finance data for municipalities, counties, townships, and other units of local

government for previous year.
Historical data contained in Highway Statis-
tics, Summary to (year), (TD 2.23/3).
ISSN 0095-344X
Earlier TD 2.110

TD 2.23/2:date   • **Item 265-B (MF)**
HIGHWAY STATISTICS SUMMARY.

TD 2.23/3   • **Item 982-G-50 (MF)**
HIGHWAY TRUST FUND, FINANCIAL STATEMENT.
[Annual]

TD 2.23/4   • **Item 982-L-10 (EL)**
HIGHWAY INFORMATION QUARTERLY. [Quarterly]

TD 2.23/5   • **Item 982-L-10 (EL)**
HIGHWAY INFORMATION UPDATE.

TD 2.23/6   • **Item 982-L-12 (EL)**
OUR NATION'S HIGHWAYS: SELECTED FACTS AND
FIGURES. [Biennial]

TD 2.23/7   • **Item 982-G-55 (EL)**
HIGHWAY TRAFFIC NOISE IN THE UNITED STATES:
PROBLEM AND RESPONSE [Triennial]

TD 2.24:date   • **Item 982-G-8 (MF)**
R & D HIGHWAY & SAFETY TRANSPORTATION SYS-
TEM STUDIES. [Annual]
PURPOSE:– To provide a compilation of on-
going research and development activity being
sponsored or performed by the Federal Highway
Administration and the National Highway Safety
Administration.
ISSN 0363-7182
Continuation of Highway and Development
Studies (TD 2.113).

TD 2.25:nos.   • **Item 982-G-30 (MF)**
HIGHWAY PLANNING TECHNICAL REPORTS. 1–
1963–   [Irregular]

Previously distributed to Depository Libraries
under Item No. 265-D.
Earlier TD 2.120

TD 2.26:nos.   • **Item 982-G-14 (MF)**
REPORT FH- (series).

TD 2.27:nos.   • **Item 265-F (MF)**
HYDRAULIC ENGINEERING CIRCULARS. HEC 1–
[Irregular]

PURPOSE:– To provide design information,
as developed, for hydraulic structures for highways. Contains general design information, including methods and procedures, presented in a
simple manner for ready use by highway engineers.
Earlier TD 2.104, C 37.4/2

TD 2.28:date   • **Item 982-G-9 (MF)**
FEDERAL-AID HIGHWAY RELOCATION ASSISTANCE
AND PAYMENT STATISTICS. 1970–   [Annual]

TD 2.29:date (MF)
ANNUAL REPORT ON URBAN AREA TRAFFIC
OPERATIONS IMPROVEMENT. 1st–   1972–
(Office Traffic Operations)

Issued by the Secretary of Transportation to
Congress pursuant to sec. 10, Public Law 90-
495.

TD 2.30:nos.   • **Item 982-G-11 (MF) (EL)**
REPORT FHWA-RD- (series). [Irregular]

TD 2.30/2:nos.
FHWA-RDDP REPORTS.

TD 2.30/3:letters&nos.
REPORT DOT-TSC-FHWA (series).

TD 2.30/4:nos.   • **Item 982-G-19 (MF)**
REPORTS, FHWA-TS- (series). [Irregular]

TD 2.30/5:date-nos.   • **Item 982-G-21 (MF)**
REPORT FHWA/PL (series). [Irregular]

TD 2.30/6:year-nos.   • **Item 982-G-29 (MF)**
REPORTS, FHWA-HO (series). [Irregular] (Office of
Highway Operation)

Includes various reports on topics such as
R & D program for highway construction, foreign
projects, experimental construction projects, etc.

TD 2.30/7:nos.   • **Item 982-G-32 (MF)**
FHWA-OEP/HEV- (series) [Irregular]

Reports on highway-related subjects such as
the effectiveness of barriers against highway
noise.

TD 2.30/8:nos.   • **Item 982-G-33 (MF)**
REPORT FHWA-TO- (series). [Irregular] (Office of Traffic Operations)

TD 2.30/9:nos.
FHWA-CA- (series). [Irregular]

TD 2.30/10:nos.
FHWA-CA-TL- (series).

TD 2.30/11:nos.   • **Item 982-G-19**
REPORT FHWA-RT (Series).

TD 2.30/12:date-nos.   • **Item 982-G-11 (MF)**
FHWA-AD (Series).

TD 2.30/13:nos.   • **Item 982-G-11 (MF)**
FHWA-SA (Series).

TD 2.30/13-2   • **Item 982-G-49 (EL)**
FOCUS.

TD 2.30/14:nos.   • **Item 982-G-21 (MF)**
REPORT FHWA/MC (series).

TD 2.30/15:nos.   • **Item 982-G-29 (MF)**
REPORT FHWA/HI (series).

TD 2.30/16:nos.   • **Item 982-G-11 (MF)**
FHWA-PD (series).

TD 2.30/16-2   • **Item 982-G-51 (EL)**
GREEN ROADSIDES. [Quarterly]

TD 2.30/16-3:date   • **Item 982-Q (MF)**
PRICE TRENDS FOR FEDERAL-AID HIGHWAY CON-
STRUCTION. [Quarterly]

TD 2.30/17:nos.   • **Item 982-G-11 (MF)**
FHWA-FLP (series). [Annual]

TD 2.30/18:nos.   • **Item 982-G-48 (MF)**
FHWA-CR (series).

TD 2.30/19:   • **Item 982-G-53 (MF)**
FHWA-JPO (series).

TD 2.30/20:date   • **Item 982-G-54**
FHWA-MCRT (series).

TD 2.31:nos.   • **Item 982-G-12 (MF)**
NATIONWIDE PERSONAL TRANSPORTATION STUDY:
REPORTS. 1–   1972–   [Irregular]

TD 2.32:v.nos.   • **Item 982-G-10**
WATER SUPPLY AND WASTE DISPOSAL SERIES. v.
1–   [Irregular] (Hydraulics and Hydrology Group,
Office of Research)

TD 2.33:nos.   • **Item 982-G-27 (MF)**
HYDRAULIC DESIGN SERIES. 1–   [Irregular]

PURPOSE:– To provide technical information
concerning hydraulic designs related to roads
and highways, including bridge waterways, open-
channel flow, roadside drainage channels, etc.
Earlier TD 2.127

TD 2.34:v.nos.&nos.   • **Item 982-G-13**
HIGHWAY FOCUS. v. 1– 13. 1969– 1981. [Irregular]
(Office of Highway Operations)

ISSN 0363-7182

TD 2.35:CT   • **Item 982-G-18 (MF)**
FINAL ENVIRONMENTAL STATEMENTS.

TD 2.36:date-nos.   • **Item 982-G-15**
ENHANCED UTCS SOFTWARE OPERATOR'S
MANUAL, IMPLEMENTATION PACKAGE (series).

TD 2.36/2:date • **Item 982-G-35 (MF)**
IMPLEMENTATION DIVISION ACTIVITIES. [Annual]

Summarizes Division activities which include research and development on highway construction, traffic lane delineation, etc.

TD 2.36/3:date • **Item 982-G-24**
FHWA RESEARCH AND DEVELOPMENT IMPLEMENTATION CATALOG.

PURPOSE:– To provide a list of selected publications, visual aids, computer programs and training materials that are available as a part of the Federal Highway Administration implementation program.

TD 2.37:CT • **Item 982-G-28**
MAPS. [Irregular]

TD 2.38:nos.
HIGHWAY SAFETY PROGRAM STANDARDS.

TD 2.39:nos. • **Item 982-G-17 (MF)**
NATIONAL HIGHWAY INSTITUTE BULLETINS. 1– [Irregular]

TD 2.40:nos. • **Item 982-G-25 (MF)**
DEMONSTRATION PROJECTS DP (series).

TD 2.40/2:date
QUARTERLY REPORT, DEMONSTRATION PROJECTS PROGRAM. – Dec. 1973.

ISSN 0145-9279

TD 2.40/3:nos.
REPORT FHWA DP-PC- (series). [Irregular]

TD 2.40/4:nos. • **Item 982-G-25 (MF) (EL)**
EXPERIMENTAL PROJECTS (series). 1– 1985– [Irregular]

TD 2.41:nos. • **Item 265-J (MF)**
FHWA PROGRAM, HY- (series).

TD 2.42:date • **Item 982-G-16 (MF)**
FEDERALLY COORDINATED PROGRAM OF HIGHWAY RESEARCH AND DEVELOPMENT. [Annual]

TD 2.43:nos.
REPORT UCDP (series).

TD 2.44:nos. • **Item 982-G-31 (MF)**
ENVIRONMENTAL ACTION PLAN REPORTS (numbered).

TD 2.46:date • **Item 982-G-41**
MONTHLY MOTOR GASOLINE REPORTED BY STATES.

A cumulative tabulation by states of gross gallons of gasoline reported by wholesale distributors to state motor fuel tax agencies.

TD 2.46/2:date • **Item 982-G-41 (EL)**
MONTHLY MOTOR FUEL REPORTED BY STATES.

TD 2.47:date
BID OPENING REPORT, FEDERAL-AID HIGHWAY CONSTRUCTION CONTRACTS, CALENDAR YEAR.

TD 2.48:nos. • **Item 982-G-20 (MF)**
STRUCTURAL ENGINEERING SERIES. 1– [Irregular]

TD 2.49:date
PRICE TRENDS FOR FEDERAL-AID-HIGHWAY CONSTRUCTION. [Quarterly]
Earlier C 37.22

TD 2.50:date • **Item 982-G-41 (MF)**
TRAFFIC VOLUME TRENDS. [Monthly]
Earlier C 37.9

TD 2.51:date
MONTHLY HIGHWAY CONSTRUCTION CONTRACTS AWARDED BY STATE AND FEDERAL AGENCIES AND TOLL AUTHORITIES.

TD 2.52:date
BUDGET ESTIMATES. [Annual]

TD 2.53:nos. • **Item 982-G-22 (MF)**
NATIONAL EXPERIMENTAL AND EVALUATION PROGRAM PROJECTS, (Reports). [Irregular]

TD 2.54:CT • **Item 982-G-23 (MF)**
USER-ORIENTED MATERIALS FOR UTPS [Urban Transportation Planning System] (series). [Irregular]

PURPOSE:– To provide a series of user-oriented materials designed to aid planners in understanding and applying the computer package UTSP, the Urban Transportation Planning System.

TD 2.55:date • **Item 982-G-26 (MF)**
NATIONAL TRUCK CHARACTERISTIC REPORT. [Annual]

PURPOSE:– To provide a collection of key truck weight summary tables and graphs intended to meet the planning and programming needs for truck weight data at State regional, and national level.

TD 2.56:date • **Item 982-G-3 (MF)**
HIGHWAY JOINT DEVELOPMENT AND MULTIPLE USE.

TD 2.57 • **Item 987-H-1 (MF)**
STATEWIDE TRANSPORTATION PLANNING AND MANAGEMENT SERIES. 1– 1980– [Irregular]

Consists of papers by State planners sharing some of their transportation planning successes. Areas of interest are jurisdictional responsibility for transportation systems, financial planning, and coordination, economic development, public involvement, intermodal coordination, and others related to statewide planning efforts.

TD 2.58:date • **Item 982-G-34 (MF)**
HIGHWAY SAFETY STEWARDSHIP REPORT. [Annual]

Consists largely of tables and graphs interspersed with narrative on highway safety improvement programs, by State, in such areas as rail-highway crossings, pavement marking demonstrations, and hazard elimination.

TD 2.59:CT
AUDIOVISUAL MATERIALS. [Irregular]

TD 2.59/2:CT • **Item 982-G-38**
POSTERS. [Irregular]

TD 2.60:date • **Item 982-G-36**
COST OF OWNING AND OPERATING AUTOMOBILES AND VANS. [Triennial]

Presents owning and operating costs in tables and text. Traces the costs of personal ownership and operation of five cars ranging in size from large to subcompact and one van through a 12-year lifetime of 120,000 miles.

TD 2.61:date • **Item 982-G-37**
DRIVER LICENSE ADMINISTRATION REQUIREMENTS AND FEES. [Biennial]

PURPOSE:– To present tabular information by States, showing administrative requirements and qualifications needed to obtain U.S. driver licenses.

TD 2.62:nos. • **Item 982-G-39**
SAFETY EVALUATION SERIES. [Irregular]

TD 2.63:date • **Item 982-C-40**
LICENSE PLATES. [Annual]

Pictures in color and tabulated data on U.S., Canadian, and Mexican license plates for cars and trucks. Data on plates include colors, types, slogans, expiration, personalization, handicapped or disabled, expiration, enforcement, sale, and earliest display dates; and disposition on sale.
Earlier TD 2.2:L 61

TD 2.64 • **Item 982-G-42 (P) (EL)**
HIGHWAY TAXES AND FEES: HOW THEY ARE COLLECTED AND DISTRIBUTED. [Irregular]

Contains tables on such information as state laws that provide for taxation on motor vehicles, motor carriers, and licensed drivers, and the distribution of these taxes and fees.
Earlier TD 2.2:H 53/28

TD 2.64/2 • **Item 982-G-42**
GRADUATE FELLOWSHIP ANNOUNCEMENT.

TD 2.65:v.nos.&nos.
U.S. HIGHWAYS. [Quarterly]

TD 2.66:date • **Item 982-G-43 (MF)**
SUMMARY OF SAFETY MANAGEMENT AUDITS. [Annual]

PURPOSE:– To report results of Safety Management Audits on motor carrier/shipper operations, which are conducted to determine compliance with the Administration's safety requirements.

TD 2.67:date • **Item 982-G-44 (MF)**
CROSS-REFERENCE INDEX OF CURRENT FHWA DIRECTIVES. [Semiannual]

Each index cross-references FHWA directives and supersedes the preceding issue.
Earlier TD 2.2:F 31/14

TD 2.68: • **Item 982-G-47**
DIRECTORIES.

TD 2.69: • **Item 982-G-45 (MF)**
FHWA/DF (series).
Each report deals with a different topic.

TD 2.70:date • **Item 982-M (EL)**
RESEARCH AND TECHNOLOGY TRANSPORTER. [Monthly]

TD 2.71 • **Item 678-A**
FEDERAL HIGHWAY ADMINISTRATION REGISTER. [Daily]

TD 2.72 • **Item 982-G-52 (MF)**
CORPS CONNECTION. [Quarterly]

TD 2.73 • **Item 982-L-10 (E)**
ELECTRONIC PRODUCTS.

TD 2.74 • **Item 982-L-10 (EL)**
THE RED LIGHT REPORTER.

TD 2.75 • **Item 982-L-10 (EL)**
INNOVATIVE FINANCE QUARTERLY.

TD 2.75/2 • **Item 982-L-10 (EL)**
INNOVATIVE FINANCE.

BUREAU OF PUBLIC ROADS
(1967– 1969)

CREATION AND AUTHORITY

The Bureau of Public Roads (C 37) was transferred from the Department of Commerce to the newly created Department of Transportation by the Department of Transportation Act of October 15, 1966 (80 Stat. 931). In 1969 the Bureau was abolished and its functions absorbed by the Federal Highway Administration (TD 2).

TD 2.101:date
ANNUAL REPORT.
Earlier C 37.1

TD 2.102:CT
GENERAL PUBLICATIONS.
Earlier C 37.2

TD 2.104   • **Item 265-F**
HYDRAULIC ENGINEERING CIRCULARS. 1–
[Irregular]
    Prior to number 11, classified C 37.4/2.

TD 2.105:CT
LAWS.
    Earlier C 37.5

TD 2.106:CT
REGULATIONS, RULES, AND INSTRUCTIONS.
    Earlier C 37.6

TD 2.107
[PRESS RELEASES]. [Irregular]

TD 2.108:CT
HANDBOOKS, MANUALS, GUIDES.
    Earlier C 37.6/2

TD 2.109   • **Item 268**
PUBLIC ROADS, JOURNAL OF HIGHWAY RESEARCH.
v. 1–   1918–   [Bimonthly]

    PURPOSE:– To acquaint highway engineers
and others interested in highway matters with the
results of the Bureau's research in highway planning, design, construction, finance, highway use,
and in a wide variety of materials for use in road
construction.
    Index issued separately. Volume covers two
years.
    Prior to v. 34, no. 7 (April 1967) classified C
37.8

    TD 2.109/a:CT
    PUBLIC ROADS, JOURNAL OF HIGHWAY
    RESEARCH (Separates).
        Earlier C 37.8/a

TD 2.110   • **Item 265-B**
HIGHWAY STATISTICS. 1945–   [Annual]

    PURPOSE:– To present statistical data on
motor fuels, motor vehicles, highway finance,
mileage of public roads and streets, Federal aid.
Includes maps and charts.

TD 2.110/2
SUMMARY TO (year). 1945–   [Decennial]

    Contains historical statistics, some as far
back as 1904, of the more important series in the
annual volumes.

TD 2.111:nos.
HIGHWAY PLANNING NOTES.
    Earlier C 37.26

TD 2.112:v.nos.&nos.
HIGHWAYS, CURRENT LITERATURE.
    Earlier C 37.10

TD 2.112/2:v.nos.&nos.
URBAN TRANSPORTATION, RESEARCH AND PLAN-
NING, CURRENT LITERATURE.
    Earlier C 37.12/2

TD 2.113   • **Item 265-E**
HIGHWAY RESEARCH AND DEVELOPMENT
STUDIES USING FEDERAL-AID RESEARCH AND
PLANNING FUNDS. 1963–   [Annual]

TD 2.113/2
HIGHWAY RESEARCH AND DEVELOPMENT NEWS,
PLANT ECOLOGY AND ESTHETICS, PROGRESS
AND IMPLEMENTATION. 1–   1969–   [Irregu-
lar]

TD 2.114:v.nos.&nos.
BPR EMERGENCY READINESS NEWSLETTER.
    Earlier C 37.31

TD 2.115
TRAFFIC SPEED TRENDS. [Irregular]

TD 2.116:CT
MAPS.
    Earlier C 37.13

TD 2.117
BPR PROGRAM (series). 1965–   [Irregular]

TD 2.117/2:letters-nos.
TIES COMPUTER PROGRAM (series).

TD 2.118
INTERSTATE SYSTEM TRAVELED-WAY STUDY RE-
PORTS. 1–   1967–   [Irregular]

TD 2.119
ADDRESSES. [Irregular]

TD 2.120   • **Item 265-D**
HIGHWAY PLANNING TECHNICAL REPORTS. 1–
1963–   [Irregular]

TD 2.121:date
REPORT ON STATUS OF MULTIPLE USE AND JOINT
DEVELOPMENT.
    Later TD 2.56

TD 2.121/2:CT
DEVELOPMENT OF MULTIPLE USE FACILITIES ON
HIGHWAY RIGHT-OF-WAY [by area].

TD 2.122:date
TRAFFIC SYSTEMS REVIEWS AND ABSTRACTS.
[Monthly]

TD 2.123:CT
BIBLIOGRAPHIES AND LISTS OF PUBLICATIONS.

TD 2.124:date
NEW DEVELOPMENTS IN HIGHWAYS.

TD 2.125:date
CONFERENCE PROCEEDINGS [of] AASHO COMMIT-
TEE ON ELECTRONICS.

TD 2.126:date
FATAL AND INJURY ACCIDENT RATES OF FEDERAL-
AID AND OTHER HIGHWAY SYSTEMS. 1968–
[Annual]
    Earlier TD 2.103:Ac 2

TD 2.127:nos.
HYDRAULIC DESIGN SERIES (numbered).
    Earlier C 37.23
    Later TD 2.33

TD 2.128:CT
HIGHWAY CONSTRUCTION USAGE FACTORS FOR
[major highway construction materials].
    Earlier C 37.2

TD 2.129:date
HIGHWAY ACTIVITIES OF MUNICIPALITIES OF
50,000 OR MORE POPULATION. [Annual]

TD 2.130:v.nos.&nos.
HIGHWAY FOCUS.

NATIONAL HIGHWAY SAFETY
BUREAU
(1966– 1970)

CREATION AND AUTHORITY

    The National Highway Safety Bureau was es-
tablished within the Department of Transportation
by the Department of Transportation Act of October 15, 1966 (80 Stat. 931). The Bureau was
superseded by the National Highway Traffic Safety
Administration (TD 8) by the Highway Safety Act
of 1970 (84 Stat. 1739).

TD 2.201:date
ANNUAL REPORT.

TD 2.202:CT
GENERAL PUBLICATIONS.

TD 2.206:CT
REGULATIONS, RULES, AND INSTRUCTIONS.

TD 2.208:CT
HANDBOOKS, MANUALS, GUIDES.

TD 2.208/2:nos.
HIGHWAY SAFETY PROGRAM STANDARDS (numbered).
    Later TD 8.8/4

TD 2.209   • **Item 982-D-2**
MOTOR VEHICLE SAFETY DEFECT RECALL
CAMPAIGNS REPORTED TO THE DEPARTMENT
OF TRANSPORTATION BY DOMESTIC AND FOR-
EIGN VEHICLE MANUFACTURERS. 1967–
[Quarterly]

TD 2.210
HIGHWAY SAFETY LITERATURE, ANNOUNCEMENT
OF RECENT ACQUISITIONS. 1–   1967– [Semi-
monthly] (National Traffic Safety Institute, Documentation Center)

TD 2.210/2:nos.
HIGHWAY SAFETY BULLETIN.

TD 2.210/3:nos.
HIGHWAY SAFETY LITERATURE COMPILATIONS.

TD 2.210/4:nos.
HIGHWAY SAFETY LITERATURE INDEXES.

TD 2.210/4-2:nos.
HIGHWAY SAFETY LITERATURE INDEXES.
[Quarterly]

TD 2.211
ADDRESSES. 1967–   [Irregular]

TD 2.212:date
EXECUTIVE SUMMARIES, NATIONAL HIGHWAY
SAFETY BUREAU CONTRACTORS REPORT.
[Annual]

TD 2.213:v.nos.&nos.   • **Item 982-D-6**
CONSUMER INFORMATION SERIES. v. 1–   1970–

FEDERAL MOTOR CARRIER
SAFETY ADMINISTRATION
(1966–   )

CREATION AND AUTHORITY

    Formerly: Bureau of Motor Carrier Safety.

INFORMATION

    Federal Motor Carrier Safety Administration
    Department of Transportation
    400 Seventh Street, S.W.
    Washington, D.C. 20590
    (202) 366-0456
    Fax: (202) 366-7298
    http://www.fmcsa.dot.gov

TD 2.301:date
ANNUAL REPORT.
    Earlier IC 1 mot.1

TD 2.302:CT   • **Item 689-A-2**
GENERAL PUBLICATIONS.
    Earlier IC 1 mot.2

    TD 2.302:B 96/year   • **Item 689-A-2**
    SAFETY BUS CHECKS. 1969–   [Annual]

        PURPOSE:– To provide an indication of
    the extent of compliance with pertinent basic
    safety regulations; to identify specific limited
    areas of weak compliance, and to serve as a
    guide in improving conformity to safety regu-
    lations.

TD 2.303:v.nos.&nos.
ON GUARD, BUREAU OF MOTOR CARRIER SAFETY
BULLETIN.

TD 2.306:CT   • **Item 689-A-7 (MF)**
REGULATIONS, RULES, AND INSTRUCTIONS.

TD 2.308:CT • **Item 689-A-8**
HANDBOOKS, MANUALS, GUIDES. [Irregular]

TD 2.309:nos. • **Item 689-A-3 (MF)**
MOTOR CARRIER ACCIDENT INVESTIGATION
REPORTS. [Irregular]

TD 2.310 • **Item 689-A-4 (MF)**
ACCIDENTS OF LARGE MOTOR CARRIERS OF
PROPERTY. [Annual]

Covers interstate motor carriers with annual
operating revenues of $200,000 or more.

TD 2.310/2:date • **Item 689-A-6 (MF)**
ACCIDENTS OF CLASS 1 MOTOR CARRIERS OF
PASSENGERS. [Annual]

Contains statistical data on fatalities, injuries, property damage and type of accidents reported by motor carriers of passengers operating
in interstate or foreign commerce.

TD 2.311:date
SELECTED SAFETY ROAD CHECKS MOTOR
CARRIERS OF PROPERTY.
Earlier TD 2.302:R 53

TD 2.312:date • **Item 689-A-5 (MF)**
ANALYSIS OF MOTOR CARRIER ACCIDENTS INVOLV-
ING VEHICLE DEFECTS OF MECHANICAL FAIL-
URE.

PURPOSE:– To provide a summary of accidents concerning interstate, foreign, or intrast-
ate travel which resulted in the loss of life, bodily
injury requiring medical treatment away from the
accident, and total damage to all property was,
$2,000 or over.
Earlier IC 1 mot.20

TD 2.312/2:date
ANALYSIS OF ACCIDENT REPORTS INVOLVING
FIRE.
Earlier TD 2.302:Ac 2

TD 2.312/3:date • **Item 689-A-1 (MF)**
ANALYSIS AND SUMMARY OF ACCIDENT INVESTI-
GATIONS. [Annual] (Federal Highway Administra-
tion)

TD 2.313:date • **Item 689-B (MF)**
ROADSIDE VEHICLE INSPECTIONS. [Annual]

PURPOSE:– To provide a compilation of results of the Bureau's roadside vehicle inspections. Contains both narrative and tables on factors contributing to accidents such as defects
found inspected vehicles, driver violations, etc.

TD 2.313/2:date • **Item 689-B (MF)**
BMCS NATIONAL ROADSIDE INSPECTION. [Semi-
annual]

TD 2.314.6/4 • **Item 689-A (P)(EL)**
FEDERAL MOTOR CARRIER SAFETY ADMINISTRA-
TION, REGISTER. [Daily]

FEDERAL RAILROAD
ADMINISTRATION
(1966–   )

CREATION AND AUTHORITY

The Federal Railroad Administration was created pursuant to section 3(e)(1) of the Department of Transportation Act of 1966 (80 Stat. 932).
The act provided for the transfer to the Department of The Alaska Railroad, Department of the
Interior; the railroad and pipeline safety activities
of the Bureau of Railroad Safety and Service of
the Interstate Commerce Commission; and the
Office of High Speed Ground Transportation, Department of Commerce. These organizational
elements were assigned to the Federal Railroad
Administration by the Secretary of Transportation
under authority granted by the act.

INFORMATION
Public Affairs Officer
Federal Railroad Administration
Department of Transportation
1120 Vermont Ave.
Washington, D.C. 20590
(202) 493-6024
Fax: (202) 493-6009
http://www.fra.dot.gov

TD 3.1:date
ANNUAL REPORT.

TD 3.1/2:date • **Item 701-E-1 (MF)**
ANNUAL FINANCIAL STATEMENT.

TD 3.2:CT • **Item 701-B**
GENERAL PUBLICATIONS.

TD 3.5:CT • **Item 687**
LAWS.

TD 3.6:CT • **Item 701-A**
REGULATIONS, RULES, AND INSTRUCTIONS.

TD 3.7
PRESS RELEASES. 1967–   [Irregular]

TD 3.8:CT • **Item 701-F**
HANDBOOKS, MANUALS, GUIDES.

TD 3.8/2:nos. • **Item 701-D**
ORDERS (numbered).

TD 3.9 • **Item 701**
SUMMARY OF ACCIDENTS REPORTED BY ALL LINE-
HAUL AND SWITCHING AND TERMINAL RAIL-
ROAD COMPANIES. 1924–   [Monthly]

Table gives number killed or injured by type of
accident with breakdown by total persons, trespassers, nontrespassers, employees on duty,
passengers on train, and other nontrespassers.
ISSN 0565-5307
Prior to the November 1966 issue published
by Interstate Commerce Commission (IC 1 ste.31).
Statement M-400.

TD 3.9/2:date
PRELIMINARY REPORT OF RAILROAD ACCIDENTS
AND RESULTING CASUALTIES.

TD 3.10
RAILROAD ACCIDENT INVESTIGATION REPORTS.
[Irregular]
Earlier IC 1 acci.5
Later TD 3.110

TD 3.10/2:nos.
RAILROAD ACCIDENT INVESTIGATION SUMMARY
REPORTS (numbered).
Later TD 3.110/2

TD 3.11
ADDRESSES. [Irregular]

TD 3.12 • **Item 701-B-2**
BIBLIOGRAPHIES AND LISTS OF PUBLICATIONS.

TD 3.13:nos.
NECTP [Northeast Corridor Transportation Project]
(series). 1–

TD 3.13/2:nos. • **Item 701-C-5 (MF)**
REPORT FRA/NECPO- (series). (Northeast Corridor
Improvement Project)

Publications covering various aspects of railroad operation, such as safety, equipment specifications, passenger data, etc., with regard to
the Northeast Corridor Improvement Project.

TD 3.13/3:date • **Item 701-C-5 (MF)**
NORTHEAST CORRIDOR IMPROVEMENT PROJECT
ANNUAL REPORT.

Report submitted in accordance with Section
703(I)(D) of PL 94-210, the Railroad Revitalization and Regulatory Reform Act of 1976.

TD 3.13/4:nos. • **Item 701-C-4 (MF)**
FRA-RNC (series).

TD 3.14:date • **Item 701-E (MF)**
CARLOAD WAYBILL STATISTICS, TERRITORIAL DIS-
TRIBUTION TRAFFIC AND REVENUE BY COM-
MODITY CLASSES. [Annual] (Rail Systems Analy-
sis and Program Development Office)

TD 3.15:nos. • **Item 701-C**
FRA-ORD & D (series). [Irregular] (Office of Research,
Development and Demonstrations)

Reports published in microfiche.

TD 3.15/2:letters-nos.
REPORT FRA-RT (series).

TD 3.15/3:letters-nos.
REPORT DOT-TSC-FRA (series).

TD 3.15/4:nos.
REPORT, RP (series). [Irregular]

TD 3.15/5:yr.nos. • **Item 701-C-1 (MF)**
REPORT FRA-OPPD (series). [Irregular]

TD 3.15/6:nos. • **Item 701-C-3 (MF)**
REPORT FRA/RFA (series). [Irregular]

TD 3.15/7:nos. • **Item 701-D-1 (MF)**
REPORTS FRA/TTC- (series) [Irregular] (Transportation Test Center)

Highly technical reports by the Transportation Test Center.

TD 3.15/8:nos. • **Item 701-D-1**
FRA/TTC (series).

FRA/TTC = Federal Railroad Administration,
Transportation Test Center.

TD 3.16:CT • **Item 701-G**
MAPS AND CHARTS. [Irregular]

TD 3.17:CT • **Item 701-C-2 (MF)**
ENVIRONMENTAL IMPACT STATEMENT. [Irregular]

TD 3.18:v.nos./nos. • **Item 701-B-1**
TRAIN OF THOUGHT. [Monthly]

RAILROAD SAFETY OFFICE
(1966–   )

INFORMATION

Railroad Safety Office
Federal Railroad Administration
Department of Transportation
1120 Vermont Ave., NW
Washington, D.C. 20590
(202) 493-6300
http://www.fra.dot.gov/safety/index.htm

TD 3.101:date
ANNUAL REPORT.

TD 3.102:CT
GENERAL PUBLICATIONS.

TD 3.103:nos.   • **Item 681 (MF)**
ACCIDENT BULLETINS.
　　Earlier IC 1 acci.3

TD 3.106:CT   • **Item 681-A**
REGULATIONS, RULES, AND INSTRUCTIONS.

TD 3.108:CT   • **Item 681-E**
HANDBOOKS, MANUALS, GUIDES. [Irregular]

TD 3.109:date   • **Item 681-B (MF)**
RAIL-HIGHWAY CROSSING ACCIDENT/ INCIDENT
AND INVENTORY BULLETIN. [Annual]

　　Former title: Rail-Highway-Grade Crossing Ac-
cidents/Incidents Bulletin.
　　Earlier IC 1 acci.8

TD 3.110:nos.   • **Item 681-B (MF)**
RAILROAD ACCIDENT INVESTIGATION REPORTS.
1–   1911–   [Irregular]

　　PURPOSE:– To make public the causes of
serious railroad accidents and the circumstances
surrounding such accidents, in accordance with
the Accident Reports Act of 1910. They are distributed widely throughout the railroad industry
and serve an educational purpose related to the
promotion of the railroad safety.
　　Earlier TD 3.10, IC 1 acci.5

TD 3.110/2:nos.
SUMMARY OF ACCIDENTS INVESTIGATED BY THE
FEDERAL RAILROAD ADMINISTRATION IN THE
FISCAL YEAR (dates). 1970–   [Annual]

　　PURPOSE:– To provide essential information
necessary to ascertain the type of railroad operation involved, kind of accident investigated,
cost of the accident in terms of casualties and
railroad property damage, and apparent cause.
　　Earlier TD 3.10/2

TD 3.110/3:nos.
RAILROAD EMPLOYEE ACCIDENT INVESTIGATION
REPORTS.

TD 3.110/4:date   • **Item 681-B (MF)**
RAILROAD ACCIDENT INVESTIGATION REPORTS;
COMPILATIONS.

TD 3.110/5:date   • **Item 681-C (MF)**
RAILROAD EMPLOYEE FATALITIES INVESTIGATED
BY THE FEDERAL RAILROAD ADMINISTRATION
IN (year). [Annual]

TD 3.111:date   • **Item 681-C (MF)**
SUMMARY OF ACCIDENTS INVESTIGATED BY THE
FEDERAL RAILROAD ADMINISTRATION IN CAL-
ENDAR YEAR. [Annual]

TD 3.112:CT   • **Item 681-D**
LAWS. [Irregular]

FEDERAL AVIATION
ADMINISTRATION
(1966–   )

CREATION AND AUTHORITY

　　The Federal Aviation Administration, formerly
the Federal Aviation Agency, became a part of
the Department of Transportation in 1967 as a
result of the Department of Transportation Act of
October 15, 1966 (80 Stat. 932).

INFORMATION

Office of Public Affairs
Federal Aviation Administration
Department of Transportation
800 Independence Avenue, SW, Rm. 810
Washington, D.C. 20591
(202) 366-4000
Fax: (202) 267-3505
http://www.faa.gov

TD 4.1:date   • **Item 431-A-57 (MF)**
ANNUAL REPORT.

TD 4.2:CT   • **Item 431-C-8**
GENERAL PUBLICATIONS.
　　Earlier FAA 1.2

　　TD 4.2:H 62/926-71   • **Item 431-C-8**
　　FAA HISTORICAL FACT BOOK, A CHRONOLOGY,
　　1926– 1971. 1974. 315 p. il.

　　　　Outlines Federal contributions to the development of civil aviation during the 45 years
since the passage of the Air Commerce Act.
The chronology begins with the Air Commerce
Act of 1926, and focuses on the organizational evolution, legislative developments, and
program activities of the Federal Aviation
Administration and its predecessor agencies.

TD 4.2/10:date   • **Item 431-C-29**
NATIONAL AIRSPACE SYSTEM PLAN. [Annual]
　　Subtitle: Facilities, Equipment, and Associated Development.
　　PURPOSE:– To report on activities undertaken to accommodate safely the increasing demand for aviation services.

TD 4.2/11:date   • **Item 431-C-29 (MF)**
PARTS MANUFACTURER APPROVALS. [Annual]

TD 4.3/6:date   • **Item 431-D-7**
MINIMUM ENROUTE IFR ALTITUDES OVER
PARTICULAR ROUTES AND INTERSECTIONS.
[Semiannual]

　　Semiannual consolidation of Part 95, sub-
chapter F of the Federal Aviation Regulations (TD
4.6).
　　IFR = Instrument Flight Rules
　　Earlier TD 4.302:AI 7

TD 4.4/2:nos.
ADVISORY CIRCULARES (numbered). [Irregular]

TD 4.5:CT   • **Item 431-A-8**
LAWS.

TD 4.5/2:date   • **Item 431-A-8 (EL)**
FAA INTERCOM.
　　Previously titled: Headquarters Intercom.

TD 4.6:pt.nos.   • **Item 431-C-13**
FEDERAL AVIATION REGULATIONS. [Irregular]

　　Subscription of each service listed below includes basic volume plus supplementary changes
for an indefinite period.
　　Earlier FAA 1.6/8

　　Part 1. DEFINITIONS AND ABBREVIATIONS.
　　(Formerly Volume 1).

Part 11. GENERAL RULE-MAKING PROCE-
DURES. (Formerly in Volume 2).

Part 13. INVESTIGATION AND ENFORCE-
MENT PROCEDURES. (Formerly in Volume 2).

Part 21. CERTIFICATION PROCEDURES FOR
PRODUCTS AND PARTS. (Formerly contained in Volume 2).

Part 23. AIRWORTHINESS STANDARDS,
NORMAL, UTILITY, AND ACROBATIC CAT-
EGORY AIRPLANES. (Formerly contained
in Volume 3).

Part 25. AIRWORTHINESS STANDARDS,
TRANSPORT CATEGORY AIRPLANES.
(Formerly contained in Volume 3).

Part 27. AIRWORTHINESS STANDARDS,
NORMAL CATEGORY ROTORCRAFT. (Formerly contained in Volume 4).

Part 29. AIRWORTHINESS STANDARDS,
TRANSPORT CATEGORY ROTORCRAFT.
(Formerly contained in Volume 4).

Part 33. AIRWORTHINESS STANDARDS, AIR-
CRAFT ENGINES. (Formerly contained in
Volume 4).

Part 36. NOISE STANDARDS, AIRCRAFT TYPE
AND AIRWORTHINESS CERTIFICATION.
(Formerly contained in Volume 3).

Part 37. TECHNICAL STANDARD ORDER
AUTHORIZATIONS. (Formerly contained
in Volume 2).

Part 43. MAINTENANCE, PREVENTIVE MAIN-
TENANCE, REBUILDING AND ALTER-
ATIONS. (Formerly contained in Volume
5).

Part 47. AIRCRAFT REGISTRATION. (Formerly
contained in Volume 2).

Part 61. CERTIFICATION: PILOTS AND
FLIGHT INSTRUCTORS. (Formerly contained in Volume 9).

Part 63. CERTIFICATION: FLIGHT
CREWMEMBERS OTHER THAN PILOTS.
(Formerly contained in Volume 9).

Part 65. CERTIFICATION: AIRMEN OTHER
THAN FLIGHT CREWMEMBERS. (Formerly
contained in Volume 9).

Part 91. GENERAL OPERATING AND FLIGHT
RULES. (Formerly contained in Volume 6).

Part 93. SPECIAL AIR TRAFFIC RULES AND
AIRPORT TRAFFIC PATTERNS. (Formerly
contained in Volume 6).

Part 103. TRANSPORTATION OF DANGER-
OUS ARTICLES AND MAGNETIZED MA-
TERIALS. (Formerly contained in Volume
6).

Part 105. PARACHUTE JUMPING. (Formerly
contained in Volume 6).

Part 108. AIRPLANE OPERATOR SECURITY.

Part 121. CERTIFICATION AND OPERATIONS:
AIR CARRIERS AND COMMERCIAL
OPERATORS OF LARGE AIRCRAFT.
(Formerly contained in Volume 7).

Part 123. CERTIFICATION AND OPERATIONS:
AIR TRAVEL AND CLUBS USING LARGE
AIRPLANES. (Formerly contained in Vol-
ume 7).

Part 125. CERTIFICATION AND OPERATIONS:
AIRPLANES HAVING A SEATING CAPAC-
ITY OF 20 OR MORE PASSENGERS OR
A MAXIMUM PAYLOAD OF 6,000 POUNDS
OR MORE.

Part 127. CERTIFICATION AND OPERATIONS OF SCHEDULED AIR CARRIERS WITH HELICOPTERS. (Formerly contained in Volume 7).

Part 133. ROTORCRAFT EXTERNALLOAD OPERATIONS. (Formerly contained in Volume 8).

Part 135. AIR TAXI OPERATORS AND COMMERCIAL OPERATORS OF SMALL AIRCRAFT. (Formerly contained in Volume 8).

Part 139. CERTIFICATION AND OPERATIONS: LAND AIRPORTS SERVING CAB-CERTIFICATED SCHEDULED AIR CARRIERS OPERATING LARGE AIRCRAFT OTHER THAN HELICOPTERS. (Formerly contained in Volume 10).

Part 141. PILOT SCHOOLS. (Formerly contained in Volume 9).

Part 150. AIRPORT NOISE COMPATIBILITY PLANNING.

Part 152. AIRPORT AID PROGRAM. (Formerly contained in Volume 10).

Part 159. NATIONAL CAPITAL AIRPORTS. (Formerly contained in Volume 10).

TD 4.6/2:v.nos.&nos. • Item 431-C-13
REGULATIONS, RULES, AND INSTRUCTIONS. [Irregular]
Earlier FAA 1.6

TD 4.6/2-2:nos. • Item 431-C-13
INSTRUCTION BOOKS (series). [Irregular]

TD 4.6/3:v.nos. • Item 431-C-13
FEDERAL AVIATION REGULATIONS (by volume).

Subscriptions to the following parts include the basic volume plus supplemental material for an indefinite period.

TD 4.6/3:v. 1 • Item 431-C-13
Volume 1. 1969– [Irregular]

Contains FAR Part:
1. Definitions and Abbreviations.

TD 4.6/3:v. 2 • Item 431-C-13
Volume 2. 1969– [Irregular]

Contains FAR Parts:

11. General Rule Making Procedures.
13. Enforcement Procedures.
15. Nondiscrimination in Federally Assisted Programs of the Federal Aviation Administration
21. Certification Procedures for Products and Parts.
37. Technical Standard Order Authorizations.
39. Airworthiness Directives
45. Identification and Registration Marking.
47. Aircraft Registration.
49. Recording of Aircraft Titles and Security Documents.
189. Representatives of the Administrator.
185. Testimony by Employees and Production of Records in Legal Proceedings.
187. Fees.
189. Use of Federal Aviation Administration Communications System.

TD 4.6/3:v. 3 • Item 431-C-13
Volume 3. 1969– [Irregular]

Contains FAR Parts:

23. Airworthiness Standards: Normal, Utility, and Acrobatic Category Airplanes.
25. Airworthiness Standards: Transport Category Airplanes.
36. Noise Standards: Aircraft Type Certification.

TD 4.6/3:v. 4 • Item 431-C-13
Volume 4. 1969– [Irregular]

Contains FAR Parts:

27. Airworthiness Standards: Normal Category Rotorcraft.
29. Airworthiness Standards: Transport Category Rotorcraft.
31. Airworthiness Standards: Manned Free Balloons.
33. Airworthiness Standards: Aircraft Engines.
35. Airworthiness Standards: Propellers.

TD 4.6/3:v. 5 • Item 431-C-13
Volume 5. 1969– [Irregular]

Contains FAR Parts:

43. Maintenance, Preventive Maintenance, Rebuilding, and Alteration.
145. Repair Stations.
149. Parachute Lofts.

TD 4.6/3:v. 6 • Item 431-C-13
Volume 6. 1969– [Irregular]

Contains FAR Parts:

91. General Operating and Flights Rules.
93. Special Air Traffic Rules and Airport Traffic Patterns.
99. Security Control of Air Traffic.
101. Moored Balloons, Kites, Unmanned Rockets, and Unmanned Free Balloons.
103. Transportation of Dangerous Articles and Magnetized Materials.
105. Parachute Jumping.

TD 4.6/3:v. 7 • Item 431-C-13
Volume 7. 1969– [Irregular]

Contains FAR Parts:
121. Certification and Operation: Air Carriers and Commercial Operators of Large Aircraft.
123. Certification and Operations of Scheduled Air Carriers with Helicopters.
129. Operations of Foreign Air Carriers.

TD 4.6/3:v. 8 • Item 431-C-13
Volume 8. 1969– [Irregular]

Contains FAR Parts:

133. Rotorcraft External-Load Operations.
135. Air Taxi Operators and Commercial Operators of Small Aircraft.
137. Agricultural Aircraft Operations.

TD 4.6/3:v. 9 • Item 431-C-13
Volume 9. 1969– [Irregular]

Contains FAR Parts:

61. Certification: Pilots and Flight Instructors.
63. Certification: Flight Crewmembers Other Than Pilots.
65. Certification: Airmen Other Than Flight Crewmembers.
67. Medical Standards and Certification.
141. Pilot Schools.
143. Ground Instructors.
147. Mechanic Schools.

TD 4.6/3:v. 10 • Item 431-C-13
Volume 10. 1969– [Irregular]

Contains FAR Parts:

139. Certification and Operation: Land Airports Serving CAB Certificated Scheduled Air Carriers Operating Large Aircraft (Other than Helicopters).
151. Federal Aid to Airports.
152. Airport Aid Program.

153. Acquisitions of U.S. Land for Public Airports.
155. Release of Airport Property From Surplus Property Disposal Restrictions.
159. National Capital Airports.
165. Wake Island Code.
167. Annette Island, Alaska, Airport.

TD 4.6/3:v. 11 • Item 431-C-13
Volume 11. 1969– [Irregular]

Contains FAR Parts:

71. Designation of Federal Airways, Controlled Airspace, and Reporting Points.
73. Special Use Airspace.
75. Establishment of Jet Routes.
77. Objects Affecting Navigable Airspace.
95. IFR Altitudes.
97. Standard Instrument Approach Procedures.
157. Notice of Construction, Alteration, Activation, and Deactivation of Airports.
169. Expenditure of Federal Funds for Nonmilitary Airports or Air Navigation Facilities Thereon.
171. Non-Federal Navigation Facilities.

TD 4.8:CT • Item 431-C-4
HANDBOOKS, MANUALS, GUIDES.

Earlier FAA 1.8

TD 4.8/2:nos. • Item 431-C-4
FAA HANDBOOK. 1– [Irregular]

TD 4.8/3:date • Item 431-C-26 (MF)
FLIGHT STANDARDS INFORMATION MANUAL. [Semi-annual]
Presents summary statistics in tabular form on civil aviation and the Flight Standards program activities relating to engineering and manufacturing, general aviation, and air carriers.
Prior to February 1974, issued quarterly.
ISSN 0565-4866

TD 4.8/4:CT • Item 431-C
AIRPORT DESIGN STANDARDS.
Earlier TD 4.8:Ai 7/14

TD 4.8/5:nos. • Item 431-A-27
ADVISORY CIRCULARS, AC (series). [Irregular]
Later TD 4.44

TD 4.9:v.nos.&nos. • Item 431-A-11 (P) (EL)
FAA AVIATION NEWS. 1962– [Bimonthly]

A monthly safety magazine for airmen containing a variety of articles designed to save lives and protect aircraft. Illustrated features cover approved flight techniques and aircraft management on all types of weather and terrain. Also: the latest authoritative word on proposed and effective rule changes. Flight Forum (Letters Page) offers a direct communication channel with FAA headquarters in Washington.
Formerly FAA General Aviation News.
Indexed by: Index to U.S. Government Periodicals.
ISSN 0362-7942
Supersedes Aviation News, FAA 1.41.

TD 4.9/2:nos. • Item 431-A-55
FAA WORLD. [Monthly]

PURPOSE:– To provide an official publication of the news and activities of the Federal Aviation Administration for its employees.

TD 4.10
FAA AIRWORTHINESS DIRECTIVE. [Biweekly]

Issued in postal card form. Supersedes CAA Air worthiness Directive (C 31.147/2)

TD 4.10/2:nos.   • **Item 431-A-15 (MF)**
SUMMARY OF AIRWORTHINESS DIRECTIVES.

Vol 1. SMALL AIRCRAFT. [Irregular]

Latest edition: Jan. 1, 1967. Subscription includes basic volume plus annual supplements for an indefinite period.
Prescribes airworthiness directives for aircraft, aircraft engines, propellers, or appliances when an unsafe condition with respect to design feature, part, or characteristic is found in a product during service.
Current directives published in FAA Airworthiness Directive (TD 4.10).

TD 4.10/3:date   • **Item 431-A-15 (MF)**
SUMMARY OF AIRWORTHINESS DIRECTIVES. Vol. 2. LARGE AIRCRAFT. [Irregular]
Earlier FAA 1.28/3

TD 4.10/4:nos.   • **Item 431-A-15**
FEDERAL AVIATION ADMINISTRATION AIRWORTHINESS DIRECTIVES. [Biweekly]

TD 4.10/5:date   • **Item 431-A-15 (MF)**
INDEX AND USER GUIDE VOL. 1, AIRWORTHINESS DIRECTIVES SMALL AIRCRAFT. [Quarterly]

TD 4.10/5-2   • **Item 431-A-15 (MF)**
INDEX AND USER GUIDE VOL. 2, AIRWORTHINESS DIRECTIVES LARGE AIRCRAFT. [Quarterly]

TD 4.11   • **Item 431-A-9**
INTERNATIONAL NOTICES TO AIRMEN. v. 1–   1947– [Biweekly]

Provides biweekly Notice-to-Airmen service on a worldwide basis. Covers temporary hazardous conditions, changes in facility operational data, and foreign entry producers and regulations.
Supplements International Flight Information Manual.
Former Title: International Notams.
ISSN 0364-6742

TD 4.12   • **Item 431-C-5**
AIRMAN'S INFORMATION MANUAL.

Supersedes Airman's Guide, Directory of Airports and Seaplane Bases, and Flight Information Manual.
Issued in the Following parts:

Part 1. BASIC FLIGHT MANUAL AND ATC PROCEDURES. [Quarterly]
Later TD 4.12/3

Part 2. AIRPORT DIRECTORY. [Semiannual]

Part 3. OPERATIONAL DATA. [Every 56 days] (Subscription includes Part 3A)

Part 3A. NOTICE TO AIRMEN. [Biweekly between issues of Part 3] (Subscription included with Part 3)
Later TD 4.12/2

Part 4. GRAPHIC NOTICES AND SUPPLEMENTAL DATA. [Quarterly]
Later TD 4.12/4

TD 4.12/2:date   • **Item 431-C-5 (P) (EL)**
NOTICES TO AIRMEN. [Biweekly]

Prior to April 1978, published as Part 3A of the Airman's InformationManual (TD 4.12).

TD 4.12/3:date   • **Item 431-C-5 (MF) (EL)**
AIRMAN'S INFORMATION MANUAL. [Semiannual]

Prior to July 1978, published as part 1 of the Airman's Information Manual (TD 4.12)
Prior to 1982, issued semiannually.

TD 4.12/4:date   • **Item 431-C-5**
GRAPHIC NOTES AND SUPPLEMENTAL DATA. 1978–1982.

Prior to July 1978, published as part 4 of the Airman's Information Manual (TD 4.12).

TD 4.13   • **Item 431-C-13**
STATUS OF FEDERAL AVIATION REGULATIONS, NEW.

TD 4.14   • **Item 177-A (MF)**
AIRPORT ACTIVITY STATISTICS OF CERTIFICATED ROUTE AIR-CARRIERS. 1962–   [Annual]

PURPOSE:– To provide the air-transport industry and the public with basic statistics relating to passenger, freight, express, and mail traffic at each of the many airports served by the U.S. airlines.
One report issued for calendar year, one for fiscal. Published jointly by the Civil Aeronautics Board and the Federal Aviation Agency.
Supersedes Air Commerce Traffic Pattern (FAA 8.9) of the Federal Aviation Agency and Airport Activity Statistics of Certificated Route Air Carriers (C 31.251) of the Civil Aeronautics Board.

TD 4.15   • **Item 431-C-2**
AIRCRAFT TYPE CERTIFICATE DATA SHEETS AND SPECIFICATIONS.   – 1977. [Monthly] (Includes basic manual plus monthly supplements for an indefinite period)

Includes an alphabetical index and individual specifications for all aircraft of which there are more than 50 currently in service in the 3 weight groups and a condensed aircraft listing of specifications pertaining to older aircraft models of which not more than 50 individual aircraft are still in service.
Published in looseleaf form, punched for 3-ring binder.
Former title; Aircraft Specifications.
ISSN 0364-1244
Superseded by (TD 4.15/3– TD 4.15/7) Type Certificate Data Sheets and Specifications, Volumes 1– 5.

TD 4.15/2   • **Item 431-C-2**
AIRCRAFT ENGINE AND PROPELLER TYPE CERTIFICATE DATA SHEETS AND SPECIFICATIONS.   – 1977. [Monthly] (Includes basic manual plus monthly supplements for an indefinite period)

Includes alphabetical index specifications for all of the more active aircraft engines and propellers as well as condensed engine and propeller listings of specifications that are seldom revised.
Published in looseleaf form, punched for 3-ring binder.
Previous titles: Engine and Propeller Specifications, and Aircraft Engine and Propeller Specifications and type Certificate Data Sheets.
Superseded by (TD 4.15/2– TD 4.15/7) Type Certificate Data Sheets and Specifications, Volumes 1– 5.

TYPE CERTIFICATE DATA SHEETS AND SPECIFITIONS. 1977–   [Annual with monthly supplements]

Supersedes former subscription services. Aircraft Type Certificate Data Sheets and Specifications (TD 4.15) and Aircraft Engine and Propeller Certificate Data Sheets and Specifications (TD 4.15/2) effective March 1977.
Issued in the following five volumes, each of which is sold on an annual basis which includes the basic volume and monthly updating supplements:

TD 4.15/3:date   • **Item 431-C-2 (MF)**
VOLUME 1. SINGLE-ENGINE AIRPLANES. 1977–   [Annual and monthly] (Includes basic volume with monthly supplements)

TD 4.15/4:date   • **Item 431-C-2 (MF)**
VOLUME 2. SMALL MULTIENGINE AIRPLANES. 1977–   [Annual and monthly] (Includes basic volume plus monthly supplements)

TD 4.15/5:date   • **Item 431-C-2 (MF)**
VOLUME 3. LARGE MULTIENGINE AIRPLANES. 1977–   [Annual and monthly] (includes basic volume plus monthly supplements)

TD 4.15/6:date   • **Item 431-C-2 (MF)**
VOLUME 4. ROTORCRAFT, GLIDERS, AND BALLOONS. 1977–   [Annual and monthly] (includes basic volume plus monthly supplements)

TD 4.15/7:date   • **Item 431-C-2 (MF)**
VOLUME 5. AIRCRAFT ENGINES AND PROPELLERS. 1977–   [Annual and monthly] (includes basic volume plus monthly supplements)

TD 4.15/8:date   • **Item 431-C-2 (MF)**
VOLUME 6. AIRCRAFT LISTING AND AIRCRAFT ENGINE AND PROPELLER LISTING. 1977– [Annual]

TD 4.15/9:date   • **Item 431-C-2 (MF)**
INDEX AND USER GUIDE TO TYPE CERTIFICATE DATA SHEETS AND SPECIFICATIONS. [Monthly]

TD 4.15/10:date   • **Item 431-C-2 (MF)**
AMENDED TYPE CERTIFICATE DATA SHEETS AND SPECIFICATIONS. [Monthly]

TD 4.16
PACIFIC AIRMAN'S GUIDE AND CHART SUPPLEMENT. [Monthly]

Supersedes Airman's Guide, Pacific Supplement (FAA 1.25/3).

TD 4.16/2:v.nos.&nos.
ALASKA AIRMAN'S GUIDE AND CHART SUPPLEMENT. v. 1– v. 7, no. 8.   – Sept. 1969. [Issued every 28 days]

TD 4.17   • **Item 431-A-50**
FAA PUBLICATIONS.

List of Publications.

TD 4.17/2:nos.   • **Item 431-A-1**
SELECTED TECHNICAL REPORTS, INFORMATION RETRIEVAL BULLETIN.

TD 4.17/3:nos.
BIBLIOGRAPHIC LISTS. 1– 18. 1961– 1969.

Superseded by Bibliographic Lists (TD 1.15), beginning November 1969.
Earlier FAA 1.10/3.

TD 4.17/4:date
CURRENT LEGAL LITERATURE. 1962– 1968. [Bimonthly]

TD 4.17/5:CT   • **Item 431-A-50**
BIBLIOGRAPHIES AND LISTS OF PUBLICATIONS.

TD 4.17/6:nos.   • **Item 431-A-30**
GUIDE TO FEDERAL AVIATION ADMINISTRATION PUBLICATIONS. FAA-APA- PG-1–   1977– [Irregular]

TD 4.18:date   • **Item 431-A-16**
CENSUS OF U.S. CIVIL AIRCRAFT AS OF DECEMBER 31, (year). 1964–   [Annual] (Statistical Services Branch of the Data Systems Division, Office of Management Services)

Summarizes and analyzes annually all civil aircraft registered with FAA as of December 31. Data include detailed tabulations for (1) registered and eligible air carrier aircraft, (2) eligible general aviation aircraft, and (3) ten-year forecasts of aircraft counts. In addition, there are two master tabulations– (1) total eligible and ineligible aircraft by manufacturer and (2) eligible civil aircraft by type, by state, and by county. Several graphs showing trends in air craft counts are also included.
Supersedes Statistical Study of U.S. Civil Aircraft FAA 1.32/2, 1950– [ ], and U.S. Active Aircraft by State and County.
Issued 1950– 1958 by the U.S. Civil ?Aeronautics Administration.

TD 4.18/2:date • **Item 431-F-5**
UNITED STATES CIVIL AIRCRAFT REGISTER. [Semi-annual]

A register of active civil aircraft, listed by registration number, and showing name and address of owner, manufacturer's serial number, make, model, year of manufacturer, and type of aircraft.

TD 4.19 • **Item 431-C-1 (MF)**
FAA AIR TRAFFIC ACTIVITY. [Semiannual]

One release issued for calendar year, one for fiscal year.
Gives data on air traffic activity of the FAA Airways system as measured by fix postings, departures, and overs; aircraft operations; instrument approaches; aircraft contacted and flight plans originated; and intermediate field landings.
Companion volume to IRF Altitude Usage and Terminal Locations for Planning Purposes.
Former title: Federal Airways Air Traffic Activity.

TD 4.19/2 • **Item 431-C-1**
AIR TRAFFIC PATTERNS FOR IFR AND VFR AVIATION. CALENDAR YEAR. [Annual]

TD 4.19/3 • **Item 431-D-4 (MF)**
ENROUTE IFR AIR TRAFFIC SURVEY, PEAK DAY. [Semiannual]

One release issued for calendar year, one for fiscal year.
Provides basic information on peak day Instrument Flight Rule (IFR) air traffic between pairs of communities having significant IFR air traffic between them. Three analyses of IFR departures have been made, namely altitude, distance, and concentration. All three have value from an operational viewpoint. Arranged by centers and pairs of fixes having 20 or more aircraft on IFR peak day.

TD 4.19/4:date • **Item 431-C-1 (MF)**
MILITARY AIR TRAFFIC ACTIVITY REPORT.

TD 4.19/5:date
GREAT LAKES REGION AIR TRAFFIC ACTIVITY. [Semiannual]

Report for calendar and fiscal years.

TD 4.20 • **Item 431-C-14 (MF)**
FAA STATISTICAL HANDBOOK OF CIVIL AVIATION. 1944– [Annual]

A more general handbook of statistics on airports, Federal airways, aircraft and airmen certifications, general aviation flying, aeronautical production and exports, scheduled air carrier operations, accidents. Contains historical tables. Charts.
Earlier FAA 1.32

TD 4.21:date • **Item 431-A-14**
NATIONAL FIELD OFFICE DIRECTORY.

Earlier Field Facility Directory (FAA 1.43).

TD 4.22:date
ANNUAL REPORT OF OPERATIONS UNDER THE FEDERAL AIRPORT ACT. 1st– 1946– [Annual]

Prior to 1959, issued by the Civil Aeronautics Administration (C 31.145/3)

TD 4.22/2:date • **Item 177-B (MF)**
ANNUAL REPORT OF OPERATIONS UNDER THE AIRPORT AND AIRWAY DEVELOPMENT ACT. 1st– 1970–

Report covers fiscal year.

TD 4.23:nos.
REPORT RD (series).

TD 4.24:date • **Item 431-A-15**
STANDARDS FOR SPECIFYING CONSTRUCTION OF AIRPORTS. 1948– [Irregular]

Contains specifications for the construction of airports and airparks in the U.S. and its possessions. Items covered are clearing and grubbing, grading, drainage, paving, lighting, turfing, and incidental construction items.
Issued by Civil Aeronautics Administration prior to 1959. Now part of FAA's advisory circulars, AC 150/5370-IA
Former title: Standard Specifications for Construction of Airports.
Earlier FAA 4.10

TD 4.24/2:nos.
STANDARDS, FAA-STD (series).

TD 4.25:CT • **Item 431-A-21**
AVIATION EDUCATION (series).

TD 4.26:nos.
INTERCOM.

TD 4.26/2 • **Item 431-A-54**
GREAT LAKES INTERCOM. [Semimonthly]

Newsletter on FAA activities with particular emphasis on the Great Lakes Region.

TD 4.27:CT
MAPS AND CHARTS.
Earlier FAA 1.16

TD 4.28:date • **Item 431-F-6 (MF)**
ACCEPTABLE METHODS, TECHNIQUES, AND PRACTICES: AIRCRAFT ALTERATIONS. [Irregular] (Includes basic manual plus supplements for an indefinite period)

Contains methods, techniques, and practices acceptable to the Administrator for use in altering civil aircraft.
GPO subscription service discontinued December 15, 1977. To be superseded by an individual sales publication.
Earlier FAA 5.16

TD 4.28/2:date • **Item 431-F-7**
ACCEPTABLE METHODS, TECHNIQUES, AND PRACTICES: AIRCRAFT INSPECTION AND REPAIR. [Irregular] (Includes basic manual plus supplements for an indefinite period)

Contains methods, techniques, and practices acceptable to the Administrator for inspection and repair to civil aircraft.
Earlier FAA 5.15

TD 4.29:CT
ADDRESSES.
Earlier FAA 1.12

TD 4.30:nos.
SYSTEM PACKAGE PROGRAM, NS-SPP-(series).

TD 4.31:date
ANNUAL NATIONAL AVIATION SYSTEM PLANNING REVIEW CONFERENCE, SUMMARY REPORT.

TD 4.32:nos. • **Item 431-A-42 (MF)**
NATIONAL AVIATION FACILITIES EXPERIMENTAL CENTER, ATLANTIC CITY, NEW JERSEY: REPORT NA- (series).

TD 4.32/2:nos.
OFFICE OF NOISE ABATEMENT: REPORT FAA-NO (series).

TD 4.32/2-2:date
EXECUTIVE SUMMARY OF NATIONAL AVIATION SYSTEM POLICY SUMMARY AND TEN YEAR PLAN.

TD 4.32/3:nos.
REPORT FAA-NS– (series).

TD 4.32/4:nos.
OFFICE OF AVIATION POLICY AND PLANS: REPORT FAA-AV- (series). [Irregular]

TD 4.32/5:nos.
REPORT FAA-AT- (series).

TD 4.32/6:nos. • **Item 431-A-20 (MF)**
REPORT FAA-EM- (series).

TD 4.32/7:nos. • **Item 431-A-33 (MF)**
REPORT FAA-ED (series). [Irregular] (Office of System Engineering Management)

TD 4.32/8:nos. • **Item 431-A-20 (MF)**
REPORT FAA-EE- (series). [Irregular] (Office of Environment and Energy)

Supersedes FAA-EQ- (series) (Office of Environmental Quality).

TD 4.32/9:nos. • **Item 431-A-25 (MF)**
REPORT FAA-E- (series). [Irregular]

TD 4.32/10:nos. • **Item 431-A-19 (MF)**
REPORT FAA-QS- (series).

TD 4.32/11:nos. • **Item 431-A-24 (MF)**
REPORT FAA-AVP- (series). [Irregular] (Aviation Policy Office)

TD 4.32/12:nos. • **Item 431-A-22 (MF)**
REPORT FAA-C- (series).

TD 4.32/13:nos. • **Item 431-A-36 (MF)**
REPORT FAA-ER (series).

TD 4.32/14:nos. • **Item 431-A-29 (MF)**
REPORTS FAA-ASP (series). [Irregular]

TD 4.32/15:nos. • **Item 431-A-28 (MF)**
REPORT FAA-AP (series). [Irregular]

TD 4.32/16:nos.
REPORT FAA-AEM- (series). [Irregular]

TD 4.32/17:yr.-nos. • **Item 431-A-38 (MF)**
REPORT FAA-MS- (series). [Irregular]

TD 4.32/17-2: • **Item 431-A-38 (MF)**
GENERAL AVIATION ACTIVITY AND AVIONICS SURVEY. [Annual]

TD 4.32/18:letters-nos. • **Item 431-A-41 (MF)**
FAA-ASF- (series).

Highly technical papers dealing with aviation safety.

TD 4.32/19:nos. • **Item 431-A-43**
ACCIDENT PREVENTION PROGRAM, FAA-P- (series). 1– [Irregular]

PURPOSE:– To provide the flying public with safety information that is handy and each to review. Each report concerns a different accident prevention subject.

TD 4.32/20:nos. • **Item 431-A-45**
FAA-PM- (series). [Irregular]

Technical publications on miscellaneous subjects issued by FAA's Program Engineering and Maintenance Service.

TD 4.32/21:nos. • **Item 431-A-48**
FAA-T- (series). [Irregular]

Each publication is a written test required of applicants for a different pilot's or Aviation Mechanic's Certificate.

TD 4.32/22:nos. • **Item 431-A-49**
FAA-S- (series). [Irregular]

Consists of Practical Test Standards to be used by FAA inspectors and examiners when conducting airman practical oral and flight tests.

TD 4.32/23:nos. • **Item 431-C-29 (MF)**
FAA/AT- (series). [Irregular]

TD 4.32/24:nos. • **Item 431-A-53 (MF)**
FAA/CT- (series). [Irregular]

TD 4.32/25:nos. • **Item 431-A-48 (MF)**
DOT TSC (Series)

TD 4.32/26 • **Item 431-F-10 (MF)**
FAA-P (series).

TD 4.33:date • **Item 431-A-17 (MF)**
NATIONAL AVIATION SYSTEM PLAN.

Provides a factual statement of the funding of programs needed to meet aviation's requirements during the next ten years.

TD 4.33/2:date • **Item 431-A-17**
NATIONAL AVIATION SYSTEM-POLICY SUMMARY. [Annual]

Summarizes the policies, requirements, goals and criteria for development of National Aviation system (NAS) over the next ten years.

TD 4.33/2-2:date
EXECUTIVE SUMMARY OF NATIONAL AVIATION SYSTEM POLICY SUMMARY AND TEN YEAR PLAN.

TD 4.33/3:date • **Item 431-A-17 (EL)**
NATIONAL AIRPORT SYSTEM PLAN. 1972– [Biennial]

The Plan, a requirement of the Airport and Airway Development Act of 1970, sets forth approximately 4,000 airports, both existing and recommended new, which comprise the Nation's basic civil airport system. It itemizes the development recommended to make the system adequate to anticipate and meet the needs of civil aeronautics, to meet requirements in support of the national defense and to meet the special needs of the postal service. The cost of recommended improvements exceeds six billion dollars over the next ten years.

TD 4.33/4 • **Item 431-A-17 (MF)**
GREAT LAKES REGION AVIATION SYSTEMS, TEN YEAR PLAN.

TD 4.33/5:date • **Item 431-A-26 (MF)**
ROCKY MOUNTAIN REGIONAL AVIATION SYSTEM PLAN.

TD 4.33/6:date • **Item 431-A-51 (MF)**
INFORMATION RESOURCES MANAGEMENT PLAN (series). [Irregular]

TD 4.34:nos.
DATA REPORTS (numbered). 1–   1969–

TD 4.35:date • **Item 431-A-34 (MF)**
COMMUTER AIR CARRIER OPERATIONS AS OF (date). 1st–   1969–   [Annual] (Information and Statistics Division, Office of Management Systems)

Presents annual operations of commuter air carriers based on data obtained from the Civil Aeronautics Board reporting system. Continues data contained in Scheduled Air Taxi Operators (TD 4.2:T 19) prior to 1969.
Formerly distributed to depository libraries under Item 431-A-18.

TD 4.36:date • **Item 431-A-5**
SUMMARY OF SUPPLEMENTAL TYPE CERTIFICATES. 1971–   [Irregular] (Includes basic manual plus quarterly supplementary materials for an indefinite period)

PURPOSE:– To list all FAA supplemental type certificates issued which the holders have indicated will be made available to others.
Latest edition: Jan. 1, 1971.
ISSN 0364-6416

TD 4.37:nos.
NOISE ABATEMENT NEWSLETTER.

TD 4.38:nos.
EC BULLETIN. (Office of Aviation Economics)

TD 4.39:date
AV BULLETIN. AV-71-1–   1971–   [Irregular] (Office of Aviation Policy and Plans)

Background material consisting of charts and explanatory notes on policies and programs of the Administration.

TD 4.39/2:nos.
AVP BULLETIN. [Monthly] (Office of Aviation Policy)

Continues AV Bulletin (TD 4.39).

TD 4.40:date
FAA TRAINING PROGRAMS, ANNUAL REPORT. 1st– 1971–   (Office of Training)

Covers fiscal year.

TD 4.41:date • **Item 431-C-24 (MF)**
FINANCIAL REPORT (year). [Annual]

PURPOSE:– To provide a comprehensive financial picture of Administration operations for the fiscal year as well as comparative information for the previous year.

TD 4.42:date
NATIONAL AIRSPACE SYSTEM DOCUMENTATION FACILITY CATALOG. [Quarterly and annual]

TD 4.43:date
DENVER ARTC CENTER: ANNUAL REPORT (Rocky Mountain Region).

TD 4.44:date
PROFILES OF SCHEDULED AIR CARRIER AIRPORT OPERATIONS, TOP 100 U.S. AIRPORTS. [Semi-annual]

TD 4.44/2:date
PROFILES OF SCHEDULED AIR CARRIER PASSENGER TRAFFIC, TOP 100 U.S. AIRPORTS. [Annual]

TD 4.44/3:date • **Item 431-A-23**
PROFILES OF SCHEDULED AIR CARRIER OPERATIONS BY STAGE LENGTH. [Annual] (Aviation Forecast Branch, Office of Aviation Policy)

TD 4.44/4:date • **Item 431-A-23 (MF)**
PROFILES OF SCHEDULED AIR CARRIER AIRPORT OPERATIONS BY EQUIPMENT TYPE, TOP 100 U.S. AIRPORTS. [Annual]

TD 4.45:CT
FINAL ENVIRONMENTAL IMPACT STATEMENT.

TD 4.46:nos.
ARTS III COMPUTER PROGRAM FUNCTIONAL SPECIFICATIONS (CPFS).

TD 4.47:nos.
NOTICES (numbered).

TD 4.48:CT • **Item 431-A-35**
ENVIRONMENTAL IMPACT STATEMENTS.

Also issued in microfiche.

TD 4.49:date
CONCORDE MONITORING MONTHLY REPORT, DULLES INTERNATIONAL AIRPORT.

TD 4.49/2:date
CONCORDE MONITORING, JOHN F. KENNEDY INTERNATIONAL AIRPORT. [Monthly]

TD 4.50:date
BUDGET ESTIMATES. [Annual]

TD 4.51:date • **Item 431-A-32**
FAA CATALOG OF TRAINING COURSES. [Annual]

PURPOSE:– To provide general information to persons interested in the training programs of the Federal Aviation Administration.

TD 4.52:date • **Item 431-A-37 (MF)**
FAA DIRECTORY. [Semiannual]

Directory of addresses and telephone numbers of FAA headquarters and regional field facilities.

TD 4.52/2:CT • **Item 431-A-37 (MF)**
TELEPHONE DIRECTORY (by region). [Annual]

TD 4.52/3:date
AIRCRAFT CERTIFICATION DIRECTORY. [Annual]

TD 4.53:date • **Item 431-A-39**
MONTHLY MANAGEMENT REPORT.

Presents in charts and graphs current aviation information on safety, airmen, air traffic activity, etc., as well as budget, employment, and other administrative information of the Federal Aviation Administration.
Discontinued with March 1981 issue.

TD 4.54:date • **Item 531-A-40**
IFR AND VFR PILOT EXAM-O-GRAMS. [Irregular] (Subscription includes basic volume plus supplementary material for an indefinite period) (FAA-P-8080)

Basic volume contains numbered exam-o-grams aimed at correcting common misconceptions in areas critical to aviation safety such as area navigation, airport surveillance radar approaches, etc.
IFR = Instrument Flight Rules; VFR = Visual Flight Rules.

TD 4.55: • **Item 431-C-25**
FAA FORECAST CONFERENCE PROCEEDINGS. 1st– [Annual]

Provides proceedings of conferences held to review forecasts of aviation activity and to share implications of those forecasts.
Also published in microfiche.

TD 4.56:date • **Item 431-A-47**
ALASKA REGION-TEN YEAR PLAN. [Annual]

Intended for use by organizations involved in planning to meet Alaska's air transportation needs.

TD 4.57:yr.nos. • **Item 431-C-27**
FAA-APO- (series). [Irregular]

Published in microfiche.

TD 4.57/2:date • **Item 431-C-27 (MF)**
FAA AVIATION FORECASTS. [Annual]

TD 4.57/3:date • **Item 431-A-17 (MF)**
NATIONAL AIRWAY SYSTEM ANNUAL REPORT.

TD 4.58:CT
AUDIOVISUAL MATERIALS. [Irregular]

TD 4.59:date • **Item 431-A-44 (MF)**
AIRCRAFT UTILIZATION AND PROPULSION RELIABILITY REPORT. [Monthly]

TD 4.60:trans.-nos. • **Item 431-C-28**
STANDARD INSTRUMENT APPROACH PROCEDURES. [Biweekly]

Establishes, amends, suspends, or revokes Standard Instrument Approach procedures for operations at certain airports. Also provides information on take off minimums, departure procedures and fixed actions.

TD 4.61:date • **Item 431-A-46 (MF)**
ANNUAL REPORT OF ACCOMPLISHMENTS UNDER THE AIRPORT IMPROVEMENT PROGRAM.

Report submitted to Congress in accordance with Section 521 of the Airport and Airway Development Act of 1982 (PL 97-248). Describes accomplishments of the airport grant program.

TD 4.62:date • **Item 431-A-17 (MF)**
AVIATION WEATHER SYSTEM PLAN. [Annual]

TD 4.63:date • **Item 431-A-52 (MF)**
NATIONAL PLAN OF INTEGRATED AIRPORT SYSTEMS. [Biennial]

Report to Congress pursuant to P.L. 97-248 estimates costs related to establishing a system of airports in the U.S. to meet present and anticipated demands.

TD 4.64:date • Item 431-A-56 (MF)
FEDERAL AVIATION ADMINISTRATION PLAN FOR RESEARCH, ENGINEERING, AND DEVELOPMENT. [Annual]

PURPOSE– To provide the agency's view of the essential research, engineering, and development activities needed to assure that the National Airspace System keeps pace with anticipated demands through the year 2010.
Earlier TD 4.2:R 31

TD 4.65:date • Item 431-C-30 (MF)
DEMOGRAPHIC PROFILES OF THE AIRWAY FACILITIES WORK FORCE. [Annual]

PURPOSE– To present demographic profiles of the AF Airways Facilities force through tables and graphs. Includes age, length of service, funding source, education, etc.

TD 4.66:date • Item 431-A-26 (MF)
MONTANA PILOT BULLETIN.

TD 4.68:v.nos./nos. • Item 431-A-17
FAA AVIATION SAFETY JOURNAL. [Quarterly]

TD 4.69:CT • Item 431-S
POSTERS.

TD 4.70:v.nos./nos. • Item 431-A-17
AVIATION EDUCATION. [Quarterly]

TD 4.71 • Item 431-A-17 (MF)
ATMOSPHERIC PROGRAMS BULLETIN. [Quarterly]

TD 4.72 • Item 431-C-58 (MF)
FAA STRATEGIC PLAN.

TD 4.73:date • Item 431-C-59 (MF)
CURRENT FAA TELECOMMUNICATIONS, FISCAL YEAR . . . [Annual]

TD 4.75 • Item 982-L-8 (E)
ELECTRONIC PRODUCTS.

TD 4.76:CT • Item 982-L-9 (E)
ELECTRONIC PRODUCTS.

TD 4.77: • Item 982-L-9 (EL)
AVIATION CAPACITY ENHANCEMENT PLAN.

TD 4.78 • Item 982-L-9 (EL)
AIR TRAFFIC PUBLICATIONS LIBRARY.

TD 4.79 • Item 982-L-13
AIRPORT/FACILITY DIRECTORY.

TD 4.79/2 • Item 982-L-14
SUPPLEMENT ALASKA.

TD 4.79/3 • Item 982-L-15
CHART SUPPLEMENT PACIFIC.

TD 4.79/9 • Item 982-L-16
NORTH ATLANTIC ROUTE CHART.

TD 4.79/10 • Item 982-L-23
NORTH PACIFIC ROUTE CHART COMPOSITE.

TD 4.79/10-1 • Item 982-L-24
NORTH PACIFIC ROUTE CHART NORTHEAST AREA.

TD 4.79/11 • Item 982-L-27
SECTIONAL AERONAUTICAL CHARTS.

TD 4.79/12 • Item 982-L-17
TERMINAL AREA CHARTS (VRF).

TD 4.79/13 • Item 982-L-25
U.S. GULF COAST VFR AERONAUTICAL CHART.

TD 4.79/13-6 • Item 982-L-31
GRAND CANYON VFR AERONAUTICAL CHART (GENERAL AVIATION).

TD 4.79/14 • Item 982-L-26
WORLD AERONAUTICAL CHARTS.

TD 4.79/15 • Item 982-L-18
IFR ENROUTE LOW ALTITUDE (U.S.).

TD 4.79/16 • Item 982-L-19
IFR ENROUTE LOW ALTITUDE (ALASKA).

TD 4.79/16-2 • Item 982-L-21
IFR AREA CHARTS (U.S.).

TD 4.79/16-3 • Item 982-L-28
IFR/VFR LOW ALTITUDE PLANNING CHART.

TD 4.79/17 • Item 982-L-20
IFR ENROUTE HIGH ALTITUDE (U.S.).

TD 4.79/17-2 • Item 982-L-22
IFR ENROUTE HIGH ALTITUDE CHARTS (ALASKA).

TD 4.80 • Item 982-O (P)(EL)
U.S. TERMINAL PROCEDURES.

TD 4.81 • Item 982-L-29
FAA AERONAUTICAL CHARTS AND RELATED PRODUCTS.

TD 4.81/2 • Item 982-L-30
FAA AERONAUTICAL CHARTS AND RELATED PRODUCTS PRICE LIST.

TD 4.82:1 • Item 982-L-32
NIMA NAUTICAL CHARTS, PUBLIC SALE, REGION 1, UNITED STATES AND CANADA.

TD 4.82:2/ • Item 982-L-33
NIMA NAUTICAL CHARTS, PUBLIC SALE, REGION 2, CENTRAL AND SOUTH AMERICA AND ANTARCTICA.

TD 4.82:3 • Item 982-L-34
NIMA NAUTICAL CHARTS, PUBLIC SALE, REGION 3, WESTERN EUROPE, ICELAND, GREENLAND, AND THE ARCTIC.

TD 4.82:4 • Item 982-L-35
NIMA NAUTICAL CHARTS, PUBLIC SALE, REGION 4, SCANDINAVIA, BALTIC AND RUSSIA.

TD 4.82:5 • Item 982-L-36
NIMA NAUTICAL CHARTS, PUBLIC SALE, REGION 5, WESTERN AFRICA AND THE MEDITERRANEAN.

TD 4.82:6 • Item 982-L-37
NIMA NAUTICAL CHARTS, PUBLIC SALE, REGION 6, INDIAN OCEAN.

TD 4.82:7 • Item 982-L-38
NIMA NAUTICAL CHARTS, PUBLIC SALE, REGION 7, AUSTRALIA, INDONESIA, AND NEW ZEALAND.

TD 4.82:8 • Item 982-L-39
NIMA NAUTICAL CHARTS, PUBLIC SALE, REGION 8, OCEANIA.

TD 4.82:9 • Item 982-L-40
NIMA NAUTICAL CHARTS, PUBLIC SALE, REGION 9, EAST ASIA.

TD 4.83 • Item 431-C-60
FAA FUTURE TELECOMMUNICATIONS PLAN "FUCHSIA BOOK". [Annual]

TD 4.84 • Item 431-C-61
NIMA AERONAUTICAL CHARTS AND PUBLICATIONS.

AIRPORT PROGRAMS OFFICE

TD 4.101:date
ANNUAL REPORT.
Earlier FAA 8.1

TD 4.102:CT • Item 982-E-1
GENERAL PUBLICATIONS.
Earlier FAA 8.2

TD 4.108:CT • Item 431-H-2
HANDBOOKS, MANUALS, GUIDES.
Earlier 8.8

TD 4.109 • Item 431-C-7
NATIONAL AIRPORT PLAN, FISCAL YEARS [dates]. 1944–

TD 4.110:date • Item 431-H-3
INDEX OF ADVISORY CIRCULARS. [Annual] (Standards Division)

TD 4.111 • Item 431-C-4
AIRPORT DESIGN STANDARDS. [Irregular]

PURPOSE:– To provide engineering and design procedures and principles which should be followed to assure proper airport development. Airport design standards are published in the 5300 Series of the Advisory Circulars and listed in the Advisory Circular Checklist and Status of Regulations in the Federal Register.

TD 4.112:nos. • Item 431-H-4 (MF)
REPORTS, AS- (series).

TD 4.112/2:nos. • Item 431-H-5 (MF)
REPORT FAA-APP (series). [Irregular] (Airports Program Office)

AIRPORT SAFETY AND STANDARDS OFFICE

TD 1.152 • Item 431-E-10
GENERAL PUBLICATIONS.

TD 1.158 • Item 431-E-11 (P) (EL)
HANDBOOKS, MANUALS, GUIDES.

AVIATION MEDICINE OFFICE

TD 4.201:date
ANNUAL REPORT.
Earlier FAA 7.1

TD 4.202:CT • Item 431-E-3
GENERAL PUBLICATIONS.
Earlier FAA 7.2

TD 4.208:CT • Item 431-E-2
HANDBOOKS, MANUALS, GUIDES.

TD 4.209 • Item 431-E-6
AVIATION MEDICAL EDUCATION SERIES. 1– 1965– [Irregular]

TD 4.210 • Item 431-E-4 (EL)
AVIATION MEDICAL REPORT, AM- (series).

Reprints from professional journals.

TD 4.210/2 • Item 431-E-4 (MF)
AAM (Series).

TD 4.211:date • Item 431-E-1 (EL)
DIRECTORY, AVIATION MEDICAL EXAMINERS.
Earlier FAA 7.8

TD 4.212:CT
ADDRESSES.

TD 4.213:date • Item 982-L-7 (CD)
OFFICE OF AVIATION MEDICINE ENCYCLOPEDIA OF MEDICAL PROGRAM DATA. [Quarterly]

TD 4.214: • Item 431-E-1 (E)
ELECTRONIC PRODUCTS (misc.).

TD 4.215: • Item 431-E-1 (EL)
FEDERAL AIR SURGEONS MEDICAL BULLETIN.

AIR TRAFFIC OPERATIONS SERVICE

TD 4.301:date
ANNUAL REPORT.
Earlier FAA 3.1

TD 4.302:CT • Item 431-D-5
GENERAL PUBLICATIONS.
Earlier FAA 3.2

TD 4.308:CT • Item 431-D-1
HANDBOOKS, MANUALS, GUIDES.
Earlier FAA 3.8/2

TD 4.308:Ae 8 • Item 431-D-1
AERONAUTICAL INFORMATION PUBLICATION.
Later TD 4.308/2

TD 4.308:Ai 7/3 • Item 431-D-1
AIR TRAFFIC CONTROL HANDBOOK. [Quarterly] (Includes basic handbook and quarterly changes) (Handbook 7110.65)

TD 4.308:C 76   • Item 431-D-1
CONTRACTIONS. (includes basic manual plus
supplementary material for an indefinite period) (7340.1C)

PURPOSE:– To provide the approved word
and phrase contraction used by personnel of
the Federal Administration and other agencies that provide air traffic control, communications, weather, charting and associated
services.
Issued in looseleaf form, punched for 3-
ring binders.
Formerly Contracts Handbook

TD 4.308:En 1   • Item 431-D-1
EN ROUTE AIR TRAFFIC CONTROL. (includes
basic volume plus quarterly changes for an
indefinite period)

PURPOSE:– To prescribe air traffic control procedures and phraseology for use by
personnel providing en route air traffic control services.

TD 4.308:F 64   • Item 431-D-1
FLIGHT SERVICES HANDBOOK. (includes basic
manual plus supplementary material for an
indefinite period) (7110.10A)

Consists of two parts; part 1 prescribes
procedures and phraseology for use by personnel providing flight assistance and communications services, and part 2 includes
Service A and B teletypewriter operating procedures, and the conterminous U.S. Service
A weather schedules.
Issued in looseleaf form, punched for 3-
ring binder.

TD 4.308:T 27   • Item 431-D-1
TERMINAL AIR TRAFFIC CONTROL. [Irregular]
(includes basic volume plus quarterly changes
for an indefinite period)

Prescribes air traffic control procedures
and phraseology for use by personnel providing terminal air traffic control services. It is
one of the air traffic control manuals referred
to in Part 65 of the Federal Aviation Regulations.

TD 4.308/2:date   • Item 431-D-1
AERONAUTICAL INFORMATION PUBLICATION.
[Biennial]

Subscription includes quarterly amendments
for an indefinite period. A comprehensive aeronautical publication containing regulations and
data required for safe aircraft operations in the
National Airspace System (NAS).
Earlier TD 4.308:Ae 8

TD 4.309   • Item 431-C-18
INTERNATIONAL FLIGHT INFORMATION MANUAL.
[Annual & Quarterly]

Provides essential information to pilots in planning foreign flights. It contains a world-wide directory of airports, all airports of entry, and the normal foreign requirements for passports, visas,
health, and customs data. It also contains information on special flight restrictions and regulations, foreign entry and flight requirement, North
Atlantic and Pacific Ocean station vessels, U.S.
aeronautical telecommunications service, and the
International Civil Aviation organization.
Subscription includes basic manual plus quarterly supplement.
ISSN 0364-0418

AMENDMENTS. [Irregular]

Subscription includes basic manual plus
supplementary material for 1 year.

TD 4.310   • Item 431-D-3
LOCATION IDENTIFIERS. [3 times/yr.]

Lists location identifiers (3-letter code, suggesting whenever possible, the location name
that it represents) for the United States, and its
possessions, and indicates, by means of aster-
isks, the United States international place name
abbreviations (4-letter code used in international
communications).
Each issue supersedes previous edition.
ISSN 0364-5282

TD 4.311:date
NON COMPULSORY RADIO FIXES.

TD 4.312:date
INDEX OF STANDARD INSTRUMENT APPROACH
PROCEDURES. [Semiannual]

Gives in tabular form city, airport, type, procedure, amendment number, and effective date
as of specific dates.

TD 4.313:date
ENROUTE IFR PEAK CHARTS, FISCAL YEAR.
Earlier FAA 3.11/3

TD 4.314:nos.
NATIONAL FLIGHT DATA DIGEST. [Daily]

TD 4.315:date
ATS FACT BOOK. [Quarterly]
Earlier FAA 3.14

TD 4.316:date   • Item 431-D-7
MINIMUM ENROUTE IFR ALTITUDES OVER
PARTICULAR ROUTES AND INTERSECTIONS.
[Semiannual]
Earlier TD 4.302:Al 7

TD 4.317:sec.nos./date
CONTROLLER CHART SUPPLEMENT. [Semiannual]

FLIGHT STANDARDS SERVICE

TD 4.401:date   • Item 431-F-9
ANNUAL REPORTS.

TD 4.402:CT   • Item 431-F-4
GENERAL PUBLICATIONS.
Earlier FAA 5.2

TD 4.408:CT   • Item 431-F-3
HANDBOOKS, MANUALS, GUIDES.
Earlier FAA 5.8/2

TD 4.409   • Item 431-C-6
GENERAL AVIATION INSPECTION AIDS SUMMARY.
1959–   [Monthly]
Prepared for the use of mechanics, operators of repair stations, and others engaged in the
inspection and maintenance of general aircraft
and designed to provide an interchange of service experience to aid in the early detection of
service difficulties.
Grouped in two sections, the first section
titled Inspection Aids, is devoted to inspection
items which apply to specific models of aircraft,
engines, and components. The aircraft are arranged in alphabetical order, followed by engines,
propellers, and accessories. The second section
titled Maintenance Notes contains general information and in some instances may be applicable
to more than one specific aircraft.
Subscription includes basic manual plus 11
monthly supplements.
ISSN 0364-0159

TD 4.410:date
FAA AIRCRAFT PROGRAM DATA FEEDBACK.
[Quarterly]

TD 4.411:CT
TENTATIVE AIRWORTHINESS STANDARDS.

TD 4.412:CT
ADDRESSES.

TD 4.413:date
AVIATION ACCIDENT STATISTICAL SUMMARY, CAL-
ENDAR YEAR. [Annual]

TD 4.414:nos.   • Item 431-F-8 (EL)
GENERAL AVIATION AIRWORTHINESS ALERTS. AC-
1–   [Monthly]
Earlier TS 4.8/5

TD 4.415   • Item 431-F-11 (MF)
FLIGHT STANDARDS SERVICE DIRECTORY.
[Semiannual]

SYSTEMS RESEARCH AND DEVELOPMENT SERVICE

TD 4.501:date
ANNUAL REPORT.
Earlier FAA 2.1

TD 4.502:CT   • Item 431-B-2
GENERAL PUBLICATIONS.
Earlier FAA 2.2

TD 4.509:nos.   • Item 431-B-5 (MF)
REPORT, FAA-RD- (series). 64-1–   1963–   [Ir-
regular]
Technical reports.
Class replaces TD 4.23 with same title.

TD 4.509/2:nos.   • Item 431-B-6 (MF)
REPORT FAA-AEE (series).

TD 4.510:CT
ADDRESSES.

AIRCRAFT DEVELOPMENT SERVICE

TD 4.601:date
ANNUAL REPORT.

TD 4.602:CT
GENERAL PUBLICATIONS.

TD 4.609:CT
BIBLIOGRAPHIES AND LISTS OF PUBLICATIONS.

TD 4.610:CT
ADDRESSES.

TD 4.611:nos.
REPORT FAA DS- (series).

AIRWAY FACILITIES SERVICE

TD 4.701:date
ANNUAL REPORT.

TD 4.702:CT
GENERAL PUBLICATIONS. [Irregular]

TD 4.709:nos.   • Item 431-P (MF)
REPORT AAF (series). [Irregular]

TD 4.710:date
AIR NAVIGATION AND AIR TRAFFIC CONTROL FA-
CILITY PERFORMANCE AND AVAILABILITY RE-
PORT, CALENDAR YEAR. [Annual] (RIS:SM 6040-
20)

TD 4.710/2:date
FACILITY PERFORMANCE REPORT, CALENDAR
YEAR. [Annual] (RIS:SM 6040-49)

CIVIL AVIATION SECURITY SERVICE

TD 4.801:date   • Item 431-N-3
ANNUAL REPORT.

TD 4.802:CT   • Item 431-N-3
GENERAL PUBLICATIONS. [Irregular]

TD 4.809:date   • Item 431-N-1 (MF)
DIRECTORY, LOCAL LAW ENFORCEMENT ORGANI-
ZATIONS PARTICIPATING IN AVIATION
SECURITY.

TD 4.810:date   • **Item 431-N-2 (MF)**
SEMIANNUAL REPORT TO CONGRESS ON THE EFFECTIVENESS OF THE CIVIL AVIATION SECURITY PROGRAM.

Presents information in narrative and tables on hijackings and bomb threats against U.S. foreign aircraft in the U.S., and other threats to civil aviation security, making comparisons with earlier years.

TD 4.811   • **Item 431-N-4 (MF)**
ANNUAL REPORT.

AIRCRAFT CERTIFICATION SERVICE

TD 4.902:CT   • **Item 431-V**
GENERAL PUBLICATIONS. [Irregular]

TD 4.908:CT   • **Item 431-V-1**
HANDBOOKS, MANUALS, GUIDES. [Irregular]

TD 4.915:date   • **Item 431-V-2 (MF)**
AIRCRAFT CERTIFICATION SERVICE INTERNATIONAL STRATEGIC PLAN. [Annual]

COAST GUARD
(1966–   )

CREATION AND AUTHORITY

The United States Coast Guard (T 47) was transferred pursuant to Public Law 89-670, approved October 15, 1966 (80 Stat. 932) from the Treasury Department to the newly created Department of Transportation.

INFORMATION

United States Coast Guard
2100 Second Street, S.W.
Washington, D.C. 20593-0001
(202) 366-4000
Fax: (202) 267-4985
http://www.uscg.mil

TD 5.1:date
ANNUAL REPORT.
    Earlier T 47.1

TD 5.2:CT   • **Item 934**
GENERAL PUBLICATIONS.
    Earlier T 47.2

TD 5.3:nos.   • **Item 931-A (MF)**
BULLETINS. 1–

TD 5.3/2:nos.   • **Item 931-A-1 (MF)**
AIDS TO NAVIGATION BULLETIN. [Irregular]

TD 5.3/3:date   • **Item 931-A-16**
ELECTRONICS SYSTEMS INFORMATION BULLETINS. [Monthly]

    ISSN 0145-1316

TD 5.3/4:date   • **Item 941-B-1**
PORT SAFETY BULLETIN. [Quarterly]

    PURPOSE:– To serve as a forum on matters and problems common to U.S. Coast Guard Captains of the Port.
    ISSN 0145-1138

TD 5.3/5:nos.   • **Item 935-B**
COAST GUARD LAW BULLETIN. 1–   [Irregular]

Each issue consists of a compilation of memoranda that render decisions on matters of international and general law and military justice as they relate to the Coast Guard. Contains a topical index which lists such subject areas as civil penalties, navigable waters, offshore structures, etc.

TD 5.3/6:date
INFORMATION BULLETIN. (Master Chief Petty Officer of the Coast Guard)

TD 5.3/7:nos.   • **Item 931-A-7**
FLIGHT SAFETY BULLETIN. 1–   [Irregular]

Official medium for furnishing information and advice in the field of flight safety to Coast Guard Personnel. Includes short summaries of aircraft accidents and informal letters.

TD 5.3/8:nos.
TELECOMMUNICATIONS BULLETIN.

TD 5.3/9   • **Item 931-A-16**
COAST GUARDS. [Monthly]

TD 5.3/10   • **Item 931-A-16**
COAST GUARD MAGAZINE.

TD 5.3/11:date   • **Item 931-A-16 (EL)**
COAST GUARD [Monthly]
    Previous: Commandant's Bulletin

TD 5.4/2:nos.   • **Item 941-B (EL)**
NAVIGATION AND VESSEL INSPECTION CIRCULARS (numbered). [Irregular]
    Earlier T 47.34

TD 5.4/3:nos.   • **Item 941-B (MF)**
BOATING SAFETY CIRCULARS. 1– 69 1969– [Irregular]

    Limited distribution (Office of Boating Safety)

TD 5.5:CT   • **Item 935**
LAWS.

TD 5.6   • **Item 943**
RULES AND REGULATIONS. [Irregular]
    Reprints of rules and regulations originally published in the Code of Federal Regulations.

TD 5.6:V 63/7   • **Item 943**
RULES AND REGULATIONS FOR FOREIGN VESSELS OPERATING IN THE NAVIGABLE WATERS OF THE UNITED STATES. [Irregular]

Subscription services consists of a basic manual and changes for an indefinite period.

A direct reprint of selected United States regulations appearing in Titles 33 and 46 of the Code of Federal Regulations relating to foreign vessel design, equipment, and operation. It is prepared as a convenience for the operators, agents and owners of foreign flag vessels which operate in the United States waters.

TD 5.8:CT   • **Item 934-A**
HANDBOOKS, MANUALS, GUIDES.
    Earlier T 47.8/3

TD 5.8:B 63   • **Item 934-A**
RECREATIONAL BOATING GUIDE. 1971. 96 p. il.

This book is a handy reference to the principles of safe boating and is an excellent companion to Skipper's Course (TD 5.2:Sk 3). Whatever type of boat you operate, this book will tell you in simple and non-technical terms what you need to know about all phases of recreational boating. It includes information on equipment required, right of way, and emergency precautions.

TD 5.8/2:CT   • **Item 934-A**
BAR GUIDES [various areas]. [Irregular]

TD 5.9
LIGHT LISTS. [Annual]

PURPOSE:– To provide a compilation of lights, fog signals, buoys, day beacons, light ships, radio beacons, racons, and loran stations maintained by or under the authority of the U.S. Coast Guard. Designed for use in conjunction with nautical charts, the lists provide complete information about the various navigational aids. This data includes latitude, longitude, nominal range, height above water or ground, day marks, and miscella-

neous remarks (radio beacon frequencies, duration and frequency of horn blasts, etc.) Corrections or amendments, when they occur, will be listed in the "Notice to Mariners" and the "Local Notice to Mariners", available from the Coast Guard.

For areas other than the Continental United States, see the Lists of Lights and Fog Signals published by the Hydrographic Office of the Department of the Navy.
    Published in the following parts:

TD 5.9:1   • **Item 936-A-1**
ATLANTIC COAST OF THE UNITED STATES. 1943– [Annual] (Publication CG-158)

Covers 1st, 3rd, and 5th Coast Guard Districts.

TD 5.9:2   • **Item 936-A-2**
ATLANTIC AND GULF COAST OF THE UNITED STATES. [Annual] (Publication CG-160)

Covers 7th and 8th Coast Guard District.

TD 5.9:3   • **Item 936-A-3**
PACIFIC COAST AND PACIFIC ISLANDS. 1921– [Annual] (Publication CG-162)
    Covers 11th, 12th, 13th, 14th, and 17th Coast Guard Districts.

TD 5.9:4   • **Item 936-A-4**
GREAT LAKES. 1910–   [Annual] (Publication CG-159)

Covers the 9th Coast Guard District.

TD 5.9:5   • **Item 936-A-5**
MISSISSIPPI RIVER SYSTEM OF THE UNITED STATES. 1910–   [Annual] (Publication CG-161)

Covers the 2nd Coast Guard District.

TD 5.9:6/date   • **Item 936-A-6**
PACIFIC COAST AND PACIFIC ISLANDS.

TD 5.9:7   • **Item 936-A-7**
GREAT LAKES, UNITED STATES AND CANADA. [Annual]

TD 5.10
NOTICE TO MARINERS RELATING TO GREAT LAKES AND TRIBUTARY WATERS WEST OF MONTREAL. –1974. [Weekly (during season)] (Navy Oceanographic Office)

TD 5.11   • **Item 941-A (MF)**
BOATING STATISTICS. [Semiannual]

Report of accidents, numbering, and related activities.
    Previous title: Recreational Boating in the United States.

TD 5.11/2:nos.   • **Item 941-B-2 (MF)**
REPORT CG-B- (series). [Irregular]

Covers reports and statistical data relating to boating.

TD 5.12:date   • **Item 950-B (MF)**
SUPPLEMENT TO MERCHANT VESSELS OF UNITED STATES. [Bimonthly]

Gives changes occurring during the month to keep the annual volume up-to-date.
Information is given in tabular form covering ownership changes in steam, motor and sail vessels of 100 gross tons and over; changes of names of vessels; visual-signal letters assigned to reassigned to vessels; additions to the merchant marine (vessels obtaining first documents); redocumentation of vessels previously removed from records; documented vessels removed from the merchant marine; and changes in gross and net tonnages and home ports for steam motor and sail vessels of 500 gross tons and over.
    Prior to March 1, 1967, published by the Bureau of Customs (T 17.11).
    Prior to July 1973, issued as Monthly Supplement to Merchant Vessels of United States.
    ISSN 0364-0957

TD 5.12/2:date • **Item 931-A-4 (MF)**
MERCHANT VESSELS OF UNITED STATES. [Annual]

Contains the names of American merchant vessels and yachts which had uncancelled documents (register, enrollment and licenses, or license) on January 1, 1970. For each vessel listed, the official number, signal and radio-call letters, rig information, name of vessel, symbols used for signal and radio-call letters, classification, gross and net tonnage, dimensions of the vessel in register length, breadth an depth, year of build, place of build, trade or business in which the vessel is engaged, horsepower, name of owner and home port are provided.
Earlier T 17.11/2
Formerly distributed to depository libraries under Item number 950.

TD 5.12/3:date
VESSEL SAFETY REVIEW.

ISSN 0145-1146

TD 5.13:v.nos.nos. • **Item 941 (EL)**
MERCHANT MARINE COUNCIL, PROCEEDINGS. v. 1– 1944– [Quarterly] (Publication CG-129)
ISSN 0364-0981

TD 5.14:v.nos.nos. • **Item 931-F-1 (EL)**
COAST GUARD RESERVIST. v. 1– 1953– [Bimonthly] (Publication CG-298)

ISSN 0364-104X

TD 5.15 • **Item 982-F-1**
CADET PROFILE, UNITED STATES COAST GUARD ACADEMY. [Annual]

Prepared by Directory of Admissions for use of secondary school guidance counselors.

TD 5.16 • **Item 930-B**
COAST GUARD ACADEMY. CATALOGUE OF COURSES. [Annual]

TD 5.16/2:date • **Item 930-B**
UNITED STATES COAST GUARD ACADEMY, NEW LONDON, CONNECTICUT: BULLETIN OF INFORMATION. [Annual] (Publications CG-147)

TD 5.17:v.nos.&nos. • **Item 931-A-9**
ENGINEERS DIGEST. [Quarterly] (CG-133)

Includes research papers, special studies, and general interest articles.
ISSN 0013-8177

TD 5.18 • **Item 940-B (MF)**
OCEANOGRAPHIC REPORTS. 1– [Irregular]

TD 5.18/2:nos. • **Item 940-C (MF)**
OCEANOGRAPHIC UNIT TECHNICAL REPORTS.

TD 5.19 • **Item 942 (MF)**
REGISTER OF OFFICERS AND CADETS. 1915– [Annual] (Publication CG-111)

TD 5.19/2 • **Item 942 (MF)**
REGISTER OF RESERVE OFFICERS. 1950– [Annual] (Publication CG-238)

TD 5.19/3:date • **Item 942 (MF)**
REGISTER OF MILITARY PERSONNEL IN THE WASHINGTON, D.C. AREA. (Publication CG-141)

TD 5.19/4 • **Item 942 (MF)**
HISTORICAL REGISTER, U.S. REVENUE CUTTER SERVICE OFFICERS.

TD 5.20 • **Item 933-A (MF)**
EQUIPMENT LISTS. [Irregular] (CG-190)

Latest edition: Aug. 1, 1968.
All listings have been published either in the Federal Register or Proceedings of the Merchant Marine Council.

TD 5.21:CT • **Item 931-A-15**
RESERVE TRAINING PUBLICATIONS INDEX.
Earlier T 47.50

TD 5.21/2 • **Item 931-A-10**
COAST GUARD AUXILIARY BIBLIOGRAPHY OF PUBLICATIONS.

Previously distributed to depository libraries under Item 931-B

TD 5.21/3:date • **Item 931-A-15**
UNITED STATES COAST GUARD ANNOTATED BIBLIOGRAPHY

TD 5.21/4:CT • **Item 931-A-15**
BIBLIOGRAPHIES AND LISTS OF PUBLICATIONS.

TD 5.21/5:CT
COMTAC [Communications and Tactical] PUBLICATIONS INDEX. [Semiannual]

TD 5.21/6:date • **Item 931-A-12**
DIRECTIVES, PUBLICATIONS, AND REPORTS INDEX. [Semiannual]

PURPOSE:– To assist Coast Guard units in maintaining up-to-date files of directives and publications, and in identifying required reports. Identifies cancelled and effective Commandant Instructions, directives, and publications required to be maintained by Coast Guard units. Contains both a numerical and alphabetical cross index of publications.
Semiannual editions are cumulative.

TD 5.22
CIVIL ENGINEERING REPORTS. 1– [Irregular] (Civil Engineering Division, Office of Engineering)

TD 5.23:date • **Item 935-A**
PROCEEDINGS OF NATIONAL DATA BUOY SYSTEMS SCIENTIFIC ADVISORY MEETINGS.

TD 5.24:date • **Item 931-C**
ON SCENE, NATIONAL MARITIME SAR [Search and Rescue] REVIEW. 1970– [Bimonthly]

PURPOSE:– To present new methods, techniques and procedures in the field of Search and rescue. It is distributed to U.S. military and civilian agencies directly involved in Search and Rescue operations.
Issued quarterly prior to September 1971.
Former title: National Maritime SAR Review.
ISSN 0093-2124

TD 5.25:nos.
OFFICE OF RESEARCH AND DEVELOPMENT PROJECT [Reports].

TD 5.25/2:nos. • **Item 931-A-3 (MF)**
OFFICE OF RESEARCH AND DEVELOPMENT: REPORTS CG-D- (series). [Irregular]

TD 5.26
OCEAN ENGINEERING TECHNICAL MANUALS.

TD 5.27:v.nos.&nos. • **Item 931-D**
RIVER CURRENTS. 1947– [Bimonthly] (Office of Information, U.S. Coast Guard, St. Louis, Missouri 63103)

PURPOSE:– To provide information about the Coast Guard in general and the Second Coast Guard District, headquartered in St. Louis, specifically.
ISSN 0145-0689

TD 5.27/2:CT • **Item 931-D**
– SUPPLEMENTS.

TD 5.28:date • **Item 931-A-2 (MF)**
BOATING SAFETY NEWSLETTER. [Quarterly]
ISSN 0145-109X

TD 5.28/2:date
BOAT ENGINEERING NEWSLETTER.

PURPOSE:– To provide a forum for exchange of engineering information for small cutters and boats.
ISSN 0145-1154

TD 5.28/3:v.nos.&nos. • **Item 942-B**
ENVIRONMENTAL RESPONSE NEWSLETTER. [Semiannual]

Previous title: Environmental Protection Newsletter.

TD 5.28/4:date
RECREATION BOATING SAFETY R & D, ANNUAL REPORT.

TD 5.29:CT
U.S. COAST GUARD HISTORICAL MONOGRAPH PROGRAM.

TD 5.30:CT • **Item 931-A-18**
BICENTENNIAL SERIES.

The Bicentennial Series deals with the history of the U. S. Coast Guard.

TD 5.30/2:CT
HISTORICAL SERIES.

Continues Bicentennial Series (TD 5.30).

TD 5.31:date
DAILY OPERATIONS HIGHLIGHTS.

TD 5.32:CT
ENVIRONMENTAL IMPACT STATEMENTS.

TD 5.34:date • **Item 931-A-8 (MF)**
ACTIVITIES RELATING TO TITLE II, PORTS AND WATERWAYS SAFETY ACT OF 1972, REPORT TO CONGRESS. [Annual]
Contains a description of rules, regulations, international standards, conferences and other activities of the Secretary of Transportation and the Coast Guard related to the Act.

TD 5.34/2:date • **Item 931-A-13 (MF)**
ACTIVITIES RELATING TO THE PORT AND TANKER SAFETY ACT. [Annual]

Reports activities undertaken to comply with the Port and Tanker Safety Act, which includes standards for ship design and equipment, personnel and manning operations.

TD 5.35:nos. • **Item 931-A-6 (MF)**
OFFICE OF MERCHANT MARINE SAFETY, CG-M- (series).

TD 5.36:nos. • **Item 931-A-5 (MF)**
REPORT CG-WEP- (series). [Irregular]

TD 5.37:date
AERONAUTICAL ENGINEERING NEWSLETTER.

TD 5.38:date
CUTTER RADAR PROJECT NEWSLETTER. [Bimonthly]

TD 5.39:nos.
FOCUS, RECRUITING. [Monthly]

TD 5.40:date
HI-LINE, NEWSLETTER FOR ENLISTED PERSONNEL. [Quarterly]

TD 5.41:date
BUDGET ESTIMATES. [Annual]
Earlier TD 5.2:B 85

TD 5.43:nos.
TECHNICAL PUBLICATIONS (series). [Irregular]

TD 5.44:National/date • **Item 931-E**
NATIONAL CONTINGENCY PLAN, EMERGENCY RESPONSE CONTACTS LISTING DIRECTORY.

Separate reports issued for the following regional offices:

TD 5.44:1/date • **Item 931-E-1 (MF)**
FEDERAL REGION 1.

TD 5.44:2/date • **Item 931-E-2 (MF)**
FEDERAL REGION 2.

TD 5.44:3/date • **Item 931-E-3 (MF)**
FEDERAL REGION 3.

TD 5.44:4/date • **Item 931-E-4 (MF)**
FEDERAL REGION 4.

TD 5.44:5/date • **Item 931-E-5 (MF)**
FEDERAL REGION 5.

TD 5.44:6/date • **Item 931-E-6 (MF)**
FEDERAL REGION 6.

TD 5.44:7/date • **Item 931-E-7 (MF)**
FEDERAL REGION 7.

TD 5.44:8/date • **Item 931-E-8 (MF)**
FEDERAL REGION 8.

TD 5.44:9/date • **Item 931-E-9 (MF)**
FEDERAL REGION 9.

TD 5.44:10/date • **Item 931-E-10 (MF)**
FEDERAL REGION 10.

TD 5.45:date • **Item 931-F (MF)**
RETIREE NEWSLETTER. [Monthly]

Newsletter on developments of interest to Coast Guard retirees and their dependents.

TD 5.46:date
COAST GUARD DESCRIPTIVE STOCK LIST, BASIC EDITION. [Quarterly]

TD 5.47:CT • **Item 931-G**
MAPS AND POSTERS. [Irregular]

TD 5.47/2:CT
AUDIOVISUAL MATERIAL.

TD 5.48:nos. • **Item 931-A-14 (MF)**
COMMANDANT'S INTERNATIONAL TECHNICAL SERIES. [Irregular]

Each issue deals with a different subject such as maneuvering and stopping of ships, code of safety for fishermen and fishing vessels, regulations and guidelines for inert gas systems, etc. Published in microfiche.

TD 5.49:CT • **Item 931-A-17 (MF)**
MARINE CASUALTY REPORTS. [Irregular]

PURPOSE:– To present results of major marine accident investigations conducted by the National Transportation Safety Board and the Coast Guard. Each report consists of an accident description, analysis of the causes, with conclusions and recommendations.
Formerly entitled Marine Casualty Reports and issued by the Marine Board of Investigation.
Formerly classed TD 1.116 and distributed to Depository Libraries under Item 982-I-21.

TD 5.50:date • **Item 934-B (MF)**
SAR STATISTICS. [Annual]

Narrative and tabular presentation of data reported by U.S. Coast Guard operating facilities that conducted search and rescue operations.
SAR Search and Rescue
Earlier TD 5.2:Se 1

TD 5.51:date • **Item 934-C**
POLLUTING INCIDENTS IN AND AROUND U.S. WATERS. [Annual]

PURPOSE:– To present final data on pollution discharged into U.S. navigable waters for the first year reported and preliminary data for the second year.
Earlier TD 5.2:P 76

TD 5.52:date • **Item 934-D**
TELECOMMUNICATIONS PLAN. [Irregular]

PURPOSE:– To describe the near to mid-term telecommunications goals and objectives for Coast Guard Command, Control and Communications support.

TD 5.53:nos. • **Item 934-E (MF)**
FLIGHT LINES, USCG AVIATION NEWSLETTER. [Irregular]

PURPOSE:– To provide information and advice on aviation matters to Coast Guard personnel.

TD 5.54: • **Item 934-F**
FORMS.

TD 5.55: • **Item 934-G (MF)**
COAST GUARD TELEPHONE DIRECTORY. [3 times a year]

Contains USCG headquarters organizational listings pluslistings for USCG field and district offices.

TD 5.56:date • **Item 934-B (MF)**
SPECIAL NOTICE TO MARINERS. [Annual]

TD 5.57:nos. • **Item 934**
MERCHANT MARINE EXAMINATION QUESTIONS (Series).

Sent as related material.

TD 5.57/2 • **Item 982-L-1 (CD)**
OPERATING INSTRUCTION FOR MERCHANT MARINE EXAMINATION QUESTS BOOKS, NAVIGATION GENERAL BOOK.

TD 5.59:date • **Item 931-A-9 (MF)**
WOMEN IN THE COAST GUARD. [Quarterly]

TD 5.60:nos. • **Item 931-A-15**
CONSUMER FACT SHEET.

TD 5.61 • **Item 931-A-15 (EL)**
STANDARD DISTRIBUTION LIST. [Semiannual]

TD 5.62:date • **Item 935-A-1 (MF)**
BUDGET IN BRIEF.

TD 5.63 • **Item 934-A-1 (EL)**
SHIP STRUCTURE COMMITTEE.

TD 5.64:date • **Item 931-H (MF)**
FIVE YEAR INFORMATION RESOURCE MANAGEMENT PLAN (FYIRMP). [Annual]

TD 5.65:date • **Item 935-A-2 (MF)**
U.S. COAST GUARD CIVILIAN WORKFORCE REPORT, FISCAL YEAR. [Annual]

TD 5.66 • **Item 935-A-3 (EL)**
MARINE SAFETY NEWSLETTER.

TD 5.67 • **Item 935-A-3 (E)**
ELECTRONIC PRODUCTS.

TD 5.68 • **Item 935-A-3 (EL)**
SYSTEMS TIMES. (Quarterly)

SAINT LAWRENCE SEAWAY DEVELOPMENT CORPORATION (1966–   )

CREATION AND AUTHORITY

The Saint Lawrence Seaway Development Corporation (Y 3.Sa 2) was established by an act of Congress approved May 13, 1954 (68 Stat. 92; 33 U.S.C. 981). This was amended by the Department of Transportation Act (80 Stat. 943) and made the Corporation subject to the direction and supervision of the Secretary of Transportation with the Administrator of the Corporation reporting directly to the Secretary of Transportation.

INFORMATION

Saint Lawrence Seaway Development
Corporation
800 Independence Avenue, S.W.
Washington, D.C. 20591
(202) 366-4000
http://www.seaway.dot.gov

TD 6.1 • **Item 982-C-28 (MF)**
ANNUAL REPORT. 1st–   1954/55–   [Annual]

Report submitted by the Administrator of the Corporation and transmitted by the Secretary of Commerce to the President pursuant to section 10 of Public Law 358, 83rd Congress, for the calendar year.
Also published in the House Document series.
Formerly distributed to Depository Libraries under Items 1074-C and 982-C.

TD 6.2:CT
GENERAL PUBLICATIONS.
Earlier Y 3.Sa 2.2

TD 6.8:CT
HANDBOOKS, MANUALS, GUIDES.

TD 6.9
TRAFFIC REPORT OF THE ST. LAWRENCE SEAWAY. [Annual]

Published jointly with the Canadian St. Lawrence Seaway Authority. Statistical data on traffic, by type of vessel, type of cargo, origin of cargo, country of registry.

TD 6.10:date
U.S. GREAT LAKES PORTS, STATISTICS FOR OVERSEAS AND CANADIAN WATERBORNE COMMERCE. [Quarterly]

ISSN 0145-1308

FEDERAL TRANSIT ADMINISTRATION (1968–   )

CREATION AND AUTHORITY

The Urban Mass Transportation Administration was established as a component of the Department of Transportation by section 3 of the President's Reorganization Plan 2 of 1968, effective July 1, 1968, which transferred most of the functions and programs under the Urban Mass Transportation Act of 1964, as amended (78 Stat. 302; 49 U.S.C. 1601 et seq.). from the Department of Housing and Urban Development. Formerly: Urban Mass Transportation Administration.

INFORMATION

Office of Public Affairs
Federal Transit Administration
Department of Transportation
400 Seventh Street, S.W.
Washington, D.C. 20590
(202) 426-4043
http://www.fta.doc.gov

TD 7.1 • **Item 892-H-16 (MF)**
ANNUAL REPORT.

TD 7.2:CT • **Item 982-H-2**
GENERAL PUBLICATIONS.

TD 7.4:nos. • **Item 982-H-12**
CIRCULARS. [Irregular]

TD 7.5:CT • **Item 982-H-4**
LAWS.

TD 7.8:CT • **Item 982-H-3**
HANDBOOKS, MANUALS, GUIDES.

TD 7.9:date • Item 982-H-6 (MF)
DIRECTORY OF RESEARCH, DEVELOPMENT AND
DEMONSTRATION PROJECTS.

Summarizes the Research, Development and
Demonstration projects funded under Section 6
of the Urban Mass Transportation Act of 1964, as
amended. Also included are projects funded under an earlier pilot program of demonstration
grants, authorized by the Housing Act of 1961.
These projects have been grouped under the four
main program categories which constitute the
present structure of the RD&D program. Bus Program, Rail Program, New Systems Program, and
Technical Planning and Evaluation.
Issued in loose leaf form.
Previously distributed to Depository Libraries
under Item 982-H

TD 7.10:CT • Item 982-H-5
BIBLIOGRAPHIES AND LISTS OF PUBLICATIONS.

TD 7.10/2:date • Item 982-H-5
URBAN MASS TRANSPORTATION ABSTRACTS.
[Bimonthly]

TD 7.10/3:v.nos. • Item 982-H-7
URBAN MASS TRANSPORTATION ABSTRACTS. v. 1–
6. 1980– 1982. [Irregular]

Abstracts reports describing results of research, development, and demonstration Administration activities, for dissemination to government, state, and local transportation agencies,
private industry, and the general public.

TD 7.11:nos. • Item 982-H-8 (MF)
REPORTS, UMTA-PA- (series).

TD 7.11/2:date • Item 982-H-8
NATIONAL URBAN MASS TRANSPORTATION
STATISTICS. [Annual]
Earlier TD 7.11

TD 7.11/2-2 • Item 982-H-8 (EL)
COMPENDIUM OF NATIONAL URBAN MASS TRANS-
PORTATION STATISTICS FROM THE 1989 SEC-
TION 15 REPORT.

TD 7.12:CT
ADDRESSES.

TD 7.13:date
REPORT TO CONGRESS CONCERNING THE
DEMONSTRATION OF FARE-FREE MASS TRANS-
PORTATION. [Annual]

TD 7.14:v.nos.&nos.
UMTA TRANSCRIPT.
Formerly UMTA Newsnotes.

TD 7.15:CT • Item 982-H-9 (MF)
ENVIRONMENTAL IMPACT STATEMENTS. [Irregular]

TD 7.16:date
BUDGET ESTIMATES.

TD 7.17:nos. • Item 982-H-10 (MF)
DOT-TSC-UMTA- (series). [Irregular] (Transportation
Systems Center)

TD 7.17/2 • Item 982-H-15 (MF)
DOT-FTAMA (series).

TD 7.18:date • Item 982-H-11
STATUS OF THE NATION'S LOCAL PUBLIC
TRANSPORTATION, CONDITIONS AND PERFOR-
MANCE, REPORT TO CONGRESS. [Biennial]

PURPOSE:– To assess the current performance and condition of public mass transportation, in accordance with Section 310 of the Surface Transportation Assistance Act of 1982.

TD 7.19: • Item 982-H-13
DIRECTORIES.

TD 7.19/2 • Item 982-H-13
A DIRECTORY OF URBAN PUBLIC TRANSPORTA-
TION SERVICE.

TD 7.20:date • Item 982-H-14 (MF)
REPORT ON FUNDING LEVELS AND ALLOCATIONS
OF FUNDS

NATIONAL HIGHWAY TRAFFIC SAFETY ADMINISTRATION (1970–   )

CREATION AND AUTHORITY

The National Highway Traffic Safety Bureau
(TD 2.200) became the National Highway Traffic
Safety Administration effective December 31,
1970, pursuant to the Highway Safety Act of
1970 (84 Stat. 1739).

INFORMATION
National Highway Traffic
Safety Administration
Department of Transportation
400 Seventh Street, SW
Washington, D.C. 20590
(202) 366-9550
http://www.nhtsa.dot.gov

TD 8.1:date • Item 982-D-46 (P) (EL)
ANNUAL REPORT.
Earlier TD 2.201

TD 8.2:CT • Item 982-D-1
GENERAL PUBLICATIONS.
Earlier TD 2.202

TD 8.5/2:v.nos.&nos. • Item 982-D-11 (MF)
TRAFFIC LAWS COMMENTARY. v. 1–   1972–
[Irregular]

PURPOSE:– To cover, on a selective basis,
the development and status of State motor vehicle and traffic laws, particularly as they relate
to provisions in the Uniform Vehicle Code.
Continues a similar series published prior to
1972 by the National Committee on Uniform Traffic Laws and Ordinances, Suite 430, 1776 Massachusetts Avenue, N.W., Washington, D.C. 20036

TD 8.5/2:3/2 • Item 982-D-11
BICYCLING LAWS IN THE UNITED STATES. 1974.
212 p.

Reviews the laws relating to bicycles in
50 States and in 50 communities selected at
random. The material is arranged to permit
easy comparison of the laws of the different
jurisdictions for each regulated area. The laws
and ordinances are those adopted before
January 1, 1974.

TD 8.5/2:3/3 • Item 982-D-11
PEDESTRIAN LAWS IN THE UNITED STATES,
October 1974. 1974. 245 p.

The pedestrian laws of the 50 States and
of 50 communities are reviewed in this study
prepared by the National Highway Traffic
Safety Administration. Since pedestrians are
so vulnerable to serious injury or death when
involved in motor vehicle accidents, this study
can be a significant aid to those concerned
with safety on U.S. highways.

TD 8.5/3:date • Item 982-D-28
DRIVER LICENSING LAWS ANNOTATED. 1978–
[Annual]

Consists of basic volume plus annual supplements. Contains the section of the Uniform Vehicle Code pertaining to diver licensing, with annotations showing how the State laws conform to
the Code.

TD 8.6:CT • Item 982-D-31
REGULATIONS, RULES, AND INSTRUCTIONS.
Earlier TD 2.206

TD 8.6/2:date • Item 982-D-3
FEDERAL MOTOR VEHICLE SAFETY STANDARDS
AND REGULATIONS. [Basic Volumes] 1972–
[Irregular] (includes basic manual plus supple-
mentary material [TD 8.6/3] for an indefinite pe-
riod)

Contains all Federal motor vehicle safety standards and regulations issued from 1966 to date.
ISSN 0364-6858

TD 8.6/3:nos. • Item 982-D-32
SUPPLEMENTS. 1–   [Irregular] (included with
basic volume [TD 8.6/2])

Prior to number 26, Supplements were
classified TD 2.206:M 85.

TD 8.6/4:nos.
FEDERAL MOTOR VEHICLE SAFETY STANDARDS.
1–   [Irregular] (Office of Standards Enforcement)

TD 8.8:CT • Item 982-D-3
HANDBOOKS, MANUALS, GUIDES.

Earlier TD 2.208

TD 8.8/2:nos. • Item 982-D-8
COMMUNITY ACTION PROGRAM FOR TRAFFIC
SAFETY, GUIDES (numbered). 1–   1970–
[Irregular]

PURPOSE:– To assist local officials in implementing successful traffic safety programs in their
communities. The guides incorporate the concepts
outlined in the national highway safety program
standards which have particular relevance to local government responsibilities.

TD 8.8/3:nos. • Item 982-D-3
HIGHWAY SAFETY PROGRAM MANUAL. 1–

TD 8.8/4:nos.
HIGHWAY SAFETY PROGRAM STANDARDS. 1–
[Irregular]

TD 8.9:date • Item 982-D-2
MOTOR VEHICLE SAFETY DEFECT RECALL CAM-
PAIGNS. [Quarterly]

Summary of defect campaigns by domestic
and foreign manufactures, as reported to the
National Highway Traffic Safety Administration.
Full reports are contained in Motor Vehicle
Safety Defect Recall Campaigns, Detailed Re-
ports, obtainable from the National Technical In-
formation Service.
ISSN 0565-7717
Earlier TD 2.209

TD 8.9/2:date • Item 982-D-2 (MF)
SAFETY RELATED RECALL CAMPAIGNS FOR MOTOR
VEHICLES AND MOTOR VEHICLE EQUIPMENT,
INCLUDING TIRES. [Quarterly]

TD 8.9/3:date • Item 982-D-20 (MF)
SAFETY RELATED RECALL CAMPAIGNS FOR MOTOR
VEHICLES AND MOTOR VEHICLE EQUIPMENT
INCLUDING TIRES, DETAILED REPORTS. [Quar-
terly]

ISSN 0146-7026

TD 8.10:nos. • Item 982-D-4
HIGHWAY SAFETY LITERATURE. [Semimonthly]

PURPOSE:– To provide an abstract service
to the literature of the highway safety.
Former title: Announcement of Highway Safety
Literature.
Frequency varies. Formerly weekly and bi-
weekly.
ISSN 0300-6905
Earlier TD 2.210 prior to no. 70-18, dated July
30, 1970.

TD 8.10/2:nos. • Item 982-D-4
– INDEXES. [Annual]

Earlier TD 2.210/4
Includes Personal author index, Corporate author index, Subject (search term) index.

TD 8.10/3:date/letters • Item 982-D-4
HIGHWAY SAFETY LITERATURE ANNUAL CUMULATIONS.
Earlier TD 2.210/3
Issued in the following cumulation:–

ac Accident Bibliography
hf Human Factors Bibliography
hs Highway Safety Bibliography
ra Related Areas Bibliography
vs Vehicle Safety Bibliography

TD 8.10/4:CT
HIGHWAY SAFETY LITERATURE, SUPPLEMENTS.

TD 8.11:nos. • Item 982-D-21 (MF)
MULTIDISCIPLINARY ACCIDENT INVESTIGATIONS (numbered). [Irregular]

TD 8.11/2:v.nos.&nos. • Item 982-D-10 (MF)
MULTIDISCIPLINARY ACCIDENT INVESTIGATION SUMMARIES. v. 1– 1970– [Irregular]

PURPOSE:– To identify injury causation and all of the contributing factors in automobile crashes, to evaluate the effectiveness of countermeasures, and to provide early detection of design and functional problems of the vehicle and highway.
ISSN 0364-2445

TD 8.11/2-2:date • Item 982-D-7 (MF)
– CUMULATIONS. v. 1– 1968-70– [Irregular]

TD 8.12 • Item 982-D-7 (MF)
REPORT ON ACTIVITIES UNDER THE NATIONAL TRAFFIC AND MOTOR VEHICLE SAFETY ACT. [Annual]

TD 8.12/2 • Item 982-D-34 (MF)
REPORT ON ACTIVITIES UNDER HIGHWAY SAFETY ACT. [Annual]

Available in Document edition.
Report submitted by the Secretary of Transportation to the President and Congress pursuant to Section 202 of the Highway Safety Act of 1966 for the calendar year.
The first report covered the period September 9, 1966 to December 31, 1967.
Each report is in two volumes, The first volume contains the text and the second is made up of Appendixes including a statistical compilation of highway casualty and other data.
Also issued as a House Document.
Earlier TD 1.10/3

TD 8.12/3:date • Item 982-D-7 (MF)
HIGHWAY AND TRAFFIC SAFETY. [Annual]

PURPOSE:– To report on activities of the National Highway Traffic Safety Administration and the Federal Highway Administration under the Highway Safety Act of 1966 and the National Traffic and Motor Vehicle Act of 1966.
Also issued as a House Document.

TD 8.12/4:date • Item 982-D-17 (MF)
REPORT ON ADMINISTRATIVE ADJUDICATION OF TRAFFIC INFRACTIONS. [Annual]

TD 8.12/5:date
DRIVER EDUCATION EVALUATION PROGRAM (DEEP) STUDY, REPORT TO CONGRESS. [Annual]

TD 8.13:CT • Item 982-D-14
BIBLIOGRAPHIES AND LISTS OF PUBLICATIONS.

TD 8.13/2:nos.
SPECIAL BIBLIOGRAPHY (series).

TD 8.13/3:nos. • Item 982-D-22 (MF)
SUBJECT BIBLIOGRAPHIES FROM HIGHWAY SAFETY LITERATURE, SB- (series).

TD 8.14:v.nos.&nos. • Item 982-D-6
CONSUMER INFORMATION SERIES. v. 1– 1970– [Annual]

PURPOSE:– To help the consumer to know more about automobile safety performance and compare the safety performance of new cars in the American market. Data is provided by the individual auto manufacturers in response to regulations issued by the National Highway Traffic Safety Administration. Covers stopping distance, acceleration and passing ability, and tire reserve load.
Earlier TD 2.213

TD 8.14/2:v.nos.&nos. • Item 982-D-9
CONSUMER AID SERIES. v. 1– 1970– [Irregular]

PURPOSE:– To assist the consumer in comparing important aspects of motor vehicle safety performance. Compares items of safety performance on any single make and model with others, such as brakes or tires.

TD 8.14/3:CT • Item 982-D-9
CONSUMER AFFAIRS FACT SHEETS (series). 1973– [Irregular]

PURPOSE:– To present basic consumer information on automobiles and their accessories.

TD 8.15:date
NATIONAL HIGHWAY SAFETY BUREAU CONTRACTS.

Lists of contracts awards made during the fiscal year in excess of $5,000 related to a wide variety of program requirements for motor vehicle and highway safety and their administrative support.
Earlier TD 2.202:C 76

TD 8.15/2:date
CONTRACT RESEARCH REPORTS. [Annual]

Lists contract reports released to the public and available through the national Technical Information Service.

TD 8.16:date • Item 982-D-12 (MF)
REPORT ON THE INTERNATIONAL TECHNICAL CONFERENCE ON EXPERIMENTAL SAFETY VEHICLES. 1st– 1971–

Includes proceedings and special reports of the activities of the individual countries participating in the Conference.
1st Jan. 25-27, 1971. Paris, France
3rd May 30– June 2, 1972. Washington, D.C.
4th March 13– 16, 1973. Kyoto, Japan

TD 8.16/2:date
EXPERIMENTAL SAFETY VEHICLE PROGRAM AND VEHICLE SAFETY RESEARCH, PROGRESS REPORT. [Semiannual]

TD 8.17:date
ANNUAL REPORT TO THE SECRETARY ON ACCIDENT INVESTIGATION AND REPORTING ACTIVITIES.

TD 8.18:date • Item 982-D-36
TRAFFIC SAFETY NEWSLETTER. [Quarterly]

Designated TSP 134
Consists of news items on traffic safety in the United States.
Former title: National Traffice Safety Newsletter.
ISSN 0364-846X

TD 8.18/2:v.nos.&nos. • Item 982-D-36
TRAFFIC SAFETY EVALUATION RESEARCH REVIEW. [Bimonthly]

Supplement to Traffic Safety Newsletter (TD 8.18).

TD 8.19:v.nos.&nos. • Item 982-D-15 (MF)
TRI-LEVEL ACCIDENT INVESTIGATION SUMMARIES.

TD 8.20:date • Item 982-D-16 (MF)
ANNUAL REPORT ON PUBLIC INFORMATION AND EDUCATION COUNTERMEASURE OF ALCOHOL SAFETY ACTION PROJECTS. (Office of Driver and Pedestrian Traffic Safety Programs)

TD 8.21:date • Item 982-D-18 (MF)
INTERNATIONAL CONGRESS ON AUTOMOTIVE SAFETY: PROCEEDINGS.

TD 8.22:CT • Item 982-D-23 (MF)
NHTSA TECHNICAL REPORTS. [Irregular]

Formerly NHTSA Staff Reports.

TD 8.23:CT
NHTSA TECHNICAL NOTES.

TD 8.23/2:letters-nos.
MEMORANDUM REPORTS. [Irregular]

TD 8.24:CT
ADDRESSES.

TD 8.25:v.nos.&nos.
NHTSA NEWS. [Semimonthly] (Executive Secretariat)

TD 8.26:date • Item 982-D-29 (EL)
AUTOMOTIVE FUEL ECONOMY PROGRAM, ANNUAL REPORT TO CONGRESS.

TD 8.27:date • Item 982-D-19 (P) (EL)
FATAL ACCIDENT REPORTING SYSTEM ANNUAL REPORT.

PURPOSE:– To present data collected in the Fatal Accident Report System (FARS), a computerized data base containing information on fatal motor vehicle traffic accidents occurring in the 50 States, the District of Columbia, and Puerto Rico.

TD 8.27/2 • Item 982-D-42
NHTSA FACTS.

TD 8.28:date
BUDGET ESTIMATES. [Annual]

TD 8.29:nos. • Item 982-D-30 (MF)
REPORT DOT-TSC-NHTSA- (series).

Highly technical reports that analyze the U.S. automobile industry marketing methods and practices, performance characteristics of U.S. cars, etc.
Published in microfiche (24x).

TD 8.30:date • Item 982-D-24 (MF)
FACT BOOKS. [Annual]

PURPOSE:– To provide a compendium of highway traffic safety information presenting statistical data on factors related to motor vehicles and motor vehicle accidents.

TD 8.31:CT • Item 982-D-25
POSTERS. [Irregular]

TD 8.32:date • Item 892-D-35 (MF)
REPORT ON TRAFFIC ACCIDENTS AND INJURIES FOR (year). [Annual]

PURPOSE:– To present traffic accident and injury data collected nationwide through the National Accident Sampling System.
Also published in microfiche.

TD 8.33:date • Item 429-E-3
FUEL ECONOMY NEWS. 1980– [Quarterly]

PURPOSE:– To serve as the official newsletter of the Department's Voluntary Truck and Bus Fuel Economy Program.
Earlier E 1.79

TD 8.34:date • Item 982-D-37 (MF)
COMPLIANCE TESTING REPORTS (series). [Quarterly]

TD 8.35: • Item 982-D-38
DIRECTORIES.

TD 8.36:v.nos/nos. • Item 982-D-39
AUTO AND TRAFFIC SAFETY. [Semiannual]

TD 8.37 • Item 982-D-40
AUTOFACTS (series).

TD 8.38 • Item 982-D-1
MONTHLY TRAFFIC FATALITY REPORT.

TD 8.39:date • Item 982-D-43
YOUTH FATAL CRASH AND ALCOHOL FACTS. [Annual]

TD 8.40:date • Item 982-D-44 (EL)
TRAFFIC SAFETY DIGEST. [Quarterly].

TD 8.61:v.nos./nos. • Item 982-C-35 (MF) (EL)
CRASHWORTHINESS RESEARCH NEWS.

TD 8.62: • Item 982-D-45
STATE TRAFFIC SAFETY INFORMATION. [Annual]

TD 8.63: • Item 982-D-47(P)(EL)
TRAFFIC TECHS. [Series]

TD 8.64: • Item 982-D-48 (E)
ELECTRONIC PRODUCTS. [Misc.]

TD 8.65: • Item 982-D-48 (EL)
STATE LEGISLATIVE FACT SHEETS.

TD 8.66: • Item 982-D-49(EL)
BUYING A SAFER CAR FOR CHILD PASSENGERS.
[Annual]

OFFICE OF HAZARDOUS
MATERIALS TRANSPORTATION
(1975–   )

CREATION AND AUTHORITY

The Office of Hazardous Materials Transportation was established within the Department of Transportation in 1975. Formerly: Materials Transportation Bureau.

INFORMATION

Office of Hazardous Materials Transportation
Department of Transportation
2100 Second Street, S.W.
Washington, D.C. 20590
(202) 755-9260

TD 9.1:date
ANNUAL REPORT.

TD 9.2:CT • Item 982-J-1
GENERAL PUBLICATIONS.

TD 9.8:CT • Item 982-J-2
HANDBOOKS, MANUALS, GUIDES. [Irregular]

TD 9.9:CT
ADDRESSES.

TD 9.10:letters-nos. • Item 982-J-5 (MF)
REPORT DOT/MTB- (series). [Irregular]

TD 9.11:date • Item 982-J-3 (MF)
ANNUAL REPORT OF THE ADMINISTRATION OF THE NATURAL GAS PIPELINE SAFETY ACT. 1st–
1968–

PURPOSE:– To summarize the activities of the agency in administering the Act. Includes information on pipeline failures, casualties, regulations, research, and legislation.

TD 9.12:v.nos.&nos.
OHM NEWSLETTER. (Office of Hazardous Materials Operation)

TD 9.13:nos.
ADVISORY BULLETIN. (Office of Pipeline Safety Operations)

TD 9.14:date • Item 982-J-4 (MF)
OPERATIONS AND ENFORCEMENT OFFICE: ANNUAL REPORT.

Summarizes the activities of the Office, which functions to enforce regulations, distribute literature, and provide training in the safe handling and transportation of hazardous materials.

TD 9.15:date • Item 982-I-8 (MF)
ANNUAL REPORT OF THE SECRETARY OF TRANSPORTATION ON HAZARDOUS MATERIALS TRANSPORTATION. 1st–   1970–

Report submitted to Congress pursuant to the Transportation Safety Act of 1974 on the transportation of hazardous materials during the preceeding calendar year.
Also published in microfiche.
Earlier TD 1.24

RESEARCH AND SPECIAL
PROGRAMS ADMINISTRATION
(1977–   )

CREATION AND AUTHORITY

The Research and Special Programs Administration was established within the Department of Transportation on September 23, 1977.

INFORMATION

Research and Special Programs
Administration
Department of Transportation
400 Seventh Street, S.W.
Washington, D.C. 20590
(202) 366-4000
Fax: (202) 366-7432
http://www.rspa.dot.gov

TD 10.1:date
ANNUAL REPORT.

TD 10.1/1 • Item 982-K-9 (MF)
ANNUAL REPORT ON HAZARDOUS MATERIALS TRANSPORTATION.

TD 10.2:CT • Item 982-K-2
GENERAL PUBLICATIONS. [Irregular]

TD 10.6:CT • Item 982-K-6
RULES, REGULATIONS, AND INSTRUCTIONS. [Irregular]

TD 10.8:CT • Item 982-K-3
HANDBOOKS, MANUALS, GUIDES. [Irregular]

TD 10.9:date • Item 982-K-1 (MF)
NATIONAL TRANSPORTATION STATISTICS, ANNUAL REPORT.

PURPOSE:– To provide annual data for selected national transportation statistics, covering items such as cost, inventory, and performance data describing passenger and cargo operations.

TD 10.9/2:date • Item 177-A-17 (MF)
AIR CARRIER INDUSTRY SCHEDULED SERVICE TRAFFIC STATISTICS QUARTERLY.

TD 10.9/3:date • Item 982-K-8 (MF)
AIR CARRIER TRAFFIC STATISTICS MONTHLY.
Later TD 12.15/2

TD 10.9/4 • Item 982-K-8
AIR CARRIER FINANCIAL STATISTICS QUARTERLY.
Later TD 12.15/3

TD 10.10:CT • Item 982-K-4
BIBLIOGRAPHIES AND LISTS OF PUBLICATIONS.
[Irregular]

TD 10.11:date • Item 982-K-5 (MF)
OFFICE OF OPERATIONS AND ENFORCEMENT: ANNUAL REPORT.

TD 10.11/2:date • Item 982-K-7 (MF)
DoT AWARDS TO ACADEMIC INSTITUTIONS. [Annual]

PURPOSE– To list contracts and grants awarded by the Transportation Department to colleges and universities.
Earlier TD 10.11 and TD 1.20/7

TD 10.12:date • Item 982-J-3 (MF)
ANNUAL REPORT ON PIPELINE SAFETY. [Annual]

TD 10.13:date • Item 982-K-7 (MF)
SMALL BUSINESS INNOVATION RESEARCH PROGRAM SOLICITATION. [Annual]

TD 10.14:date • Item 982-K-7 (MF)
UNIVERSITY TRANSPORTATION CENTER PROJECT ABSTRACTS (FY).

TD 10.15 • Item 982-K-10 (EL)
VOLPE TRANSPORTATION JOURNAL. [Semiannual]

TD 10.16:date • Item 982-K-12 (CD)
HAZARDOUS MATERIALS TRANSPORTATION TRAINING MODULES. [Biennial]

TD 10.17 • Item 982-K-11 (E)
ELECTRONIC PRODUCTS. (Misc.)

MARITIME ADMINISTRATION
(1981–   )

CREATION AND AUTHORITY

The Maritime Administration was transferred from the Department of Commerce (C 39.200) by Public Law 97-31 of August 6, 1981 (95 Stat. 151).

INFORMATION

Office of Congressional and Public Affairs
Maritime Administration
Department of Transportation
400 Seventh Street, S.W.
Washington, D.C. 20590
(202) 366-5807
Toll Free: (800) 99MARAD
E-mail: pao.marad@marad.dot.gov
http://www.marad.dot.gov

TD 11.1:date • Item 233
ANNUAL REPORT.
Earlier C 39.201

TD 11.2:CT • Item 235
GENERAL PUBLICATIONS. [Irregular]

TD 11.6 • Item 235-A-1
LAWS.

TD 11.8:CT • Item 235-B
HANDBOOKS, MANUALS, GUIDES. [Irregular]
Earlier C 39.206/3

TD 11.8/2:date • Item 235-B (P) (EL)
MARITIME LABOR-MANAGEMENT AFFILIATIONS GUIDE.
Earlier TD 11.8:Se 1

TD 11.9:CT • Item 233-C
BIBLIOGRAPHIES AND LISTS OF PUBLICATIONS.
Earlier C 39.227

TD 11.9/2:date • Item 233-C
MARAD PUBLICATIONS. [Irregular]

TD 11.10:date
U.S. MERCHANT MARINE DATA SHEET. [Monthly]
Earlier C 39.238

TD 11.11:date • **Item 236-F (MF) (EL)**
VESSEL INVENTORY REPORT. [Quarterly]

Part I contains an alphabetical listing of all merchant-type ships in the United States Merchant fleet, whether privately-owned or Maritime Administration-owned, showing for each ship the name of owner and/or operator, the design, the type of operating agreement, the effective date of the operating agreement and the deadweight tonnage. Part II provides an alphabetical arrangement of owners and/or operators together with a list of the vessels controlled by each. Part III lists the Reserve Fleet sites maintained by the Maritime Administration and the vessels both merchant and military types, in lay-up at each site, together with design-type summaries for individual sites and for the Reserve Fleet as a whole.
Also published in microfiche.
Earlier C 39.217

TD 11.12:date • **Item 237-A**
STATISTICAL ANALYSIS OF THE WORLD'S MERCHANT FLEET. [Biennial]
Earlier C 39.224

TD 11.13:date • **Item 33-H (MF)**
U.S. OCEANBORNE, FOREIGN TRADE ROUTES. [Annual]
Earlier C 39.240

TD 11.13/2 • **Item 333-H**
U.S. OCEANBORNE FOREIGN TRADE FORECAST. Discontinued.

TD 11.14:date • **Item 236-B (MF) (EL)**
MERCHANT FLEETS OF THE WORLD, SEA-GOING STEAM AND MOTOR SHIPS OF 1,000 GROSS TONS AND OVER. [Annual]
Earlier C 39.212

TD 11.15:date • **Item 233-H**
NEW SHIP CONSTRUCTION. [Annual]
Earlier C 39.212/3

TD 11.15/2 • **Item 233-H (MF)**
RELATIVE COST OF SHIPBUILDING.

TD 11.16:date • **Item 233-E (MF)**
FOREIGN FLAG MERCHANT SHIPS OWNED BY U.S. PARENT COMPANIES. [Annual]
Earlier C 39.230

TD 11.17:nos. • **Item 233-L (MF)**
NMRC- (series). [Irregular] (National Maritime Research Center)
Earlier C 39.244

TD 11.18:nos. • **Item 233-K (MF)**
CAORF TECHNICAL REPORTS (series). [Irregular] (Computer Aided Operations Research Facility)

Highly technical reports.
Also published in microfiche (24x)
Earlier C 39.243

TD 11.19:date • **Item 233-B (MF)**
DOMESTIC WATERBORNE TRADE OF THE UNITED STATES.

Gives for dry cargo ships and tank ships: shipping areas to receiving areas and receiving areas from shipping areas, by commodity; shipping port to receiving port and receiving port from shipping port, total tonnage. Summary charts give historical data.
Former title: Domestic Oceanborne and Great Lakes Commerce of the United States.
Also published in microfiche.
Earlier C 39.222

TD 11.20:date • **Item 233-M (MF)**
BULK CARRIERS IN THE WORLD FLEET. [Annual]

Consists of statistical tables that provide the following information on bulk carriers by country and cargo category: year built, gross tonnage, deadweight tonnage, speed in knots, and draft in feet.
Earlier C 39.202:B 87

TD 11.21:date • **Item 233-D (MF)**
CONTAINERIZED CARGO STATISTICS. [Quarterly]

One of a statistical series of containerized cargo reports released for the information of industry and interested government agencies.
The report is designed to cover the trade areas which have the greatest concentration of container shipping– U.S. North Atlantic/United Kingdom and European Continent (Trade Route 5-7-8-9) and U.S. Pacific/Far East (Trade Route 29).
Formerly Foreign Oceanborne Trade of the United States Container Cargo, Selected Trade Routes.
Also published in microfiche.
Earlier C 39.233

TD 11.22:date • **Item 237**
INDEX OF CURRENT REGULATIONS OF THE MARITIME ADMINISTRATION, MARITIME SUBSIDY BOARD, NATIONAL SHIPPING AUTHORITY. [Annual]
Earlier C 39.206/4

TD 11.23:nos. • **Item 233-J (MF)**
TECHNICAL REPORTS, MA-RD- (series). [Irregular]

TD 11.24:date • **Item 333-J**
INTERNATIONAL SHIPBORNE BARGE REGISTER. [Annual]
Earlier C 39.241

TD 11.25: • **Item 233-N (MF) (EL)**
REPORT ON SURVEY OF U.S. SHIPBUILDING AND REPAIR FACILITIES. [Annual]

Report issued pursuant to the Merchant Marine Act of 1936, to determine if an adequate mobilization base exists for national defense and for use in a national emergency.
Earlier C 39.202:Sh 64/22

TD 11.26:v.nos.&nos. • **Item 233-J-1 (MF)**
MARATIC R & D TECHNOLOGY TRANSFER JOURNAL. v. 1– [Bimonthly]

Newsletter on Administration technological research and developments believed to have commercial and general maritime applications.
Earlier C 39.227/2

TD 11.27:date • **Item 233-P**
MARITIME SUBSIDIES. [Biennial]

Each report provides information on the economic backgrounds of a group of nationals of the world and on the extent to which they subsidize their merchant fleets.
Earlier C 39.202:Su 1/2

TD 11.28:date • **Item 235-B-1 (MF)**
U.S. EXPORTS AND IMPORTS TRANSSHIPPED VIA CANADIAN PORTS. [Annual]

PURPOSE:– To present dollar value and estimated tonnage for U.S. exports and imports transshipped via Canadian ports.
Earlier TD 1.2:Ex 7

TD 11.29:date • **Item 233-M (MF)**
TANKERS IN THE WORLD FLEET. [Annual]

TD 11.30:date • **Item 233-R (MF)**
REPORT TO THE CONGRESS ON THE STATUS OF THE PUBLIC PORTS OF THE UNITED STATES. [Annual]

Reports on the conditions of the U.S. public ports as required by PL 96-371. Includes the ports' economic and technological development, the extent to which they contribute to national security, and those factors which may impede the continued development of U.S. public ports.

TD 11.31:date • **Item 233-F (MF)**
INVENTORY OF AMERICAN INTERMODAL EQUIPMENT. [Annual]

TD 11.32:date • **Item 233-E**
ESTIMATED VESSEL OPERATING EXPENSES. [Annual]
Discontinued.

TD 11.33:date
MARITIME ADMINISTRATION UNIVERSITY RESEARCH PROGRAM. [Annual]
Earlier C 39.202:R 31/2

TD 11.34: • **Item 235-B-2**
FORMS.

TD 11.35 • **Item 235-B-3 (EL)**
U.S. FOREIGN WATERBORNE TRANSPORTATION STATISTICS QUARTERLY REPORT.

BUREAU OF TRANSPORTATION STATISTICS

INFORMATION

Bureau of Transportation Statistics
Dept. of Transportation
400 Seventh St. SW
Washington, DC 20590
(202) 366-DATA
Fax: (202) 366-3640
E-Mail:info@bts.gov
http://www.bts.gov

TD 12.1: • **Item 982-N (MF)**
TRANSPORTATION STATISTICS ANNUAL REPORT.

TD 12.1/2:date • **Item 982-K-1 (MF) (EL)**
NATIONAL TRANSPORTATION STATISTICS, ANNUAL REPORT.

TD 12.2 • **Item 982-N-1**
GENERAL PUBLICATIONS.

TD 12.10: • **Item 982-N-9 (P) (EL)**
DIRECTORIES.

TD 12.11: • **Item 982-N-11**
POSTERS.

TD 12.15 • **Item 982-N-5 (MF)**
AIR CARRIER INDUSTRY SCHEDULED SERIES: TRAFFIC STATISTICS QUARTERLY.
Earlier TD 10.9/2

TD 12.15/2:date • **Item 982-N-2 (MF)**
AIR CARRIER TRAFFIC STATISTICS MONTHLY.
Earlier TD 10.9/3

TD 12.15/3:date • **Item 982-N-3 (MF)**
AIR CARRIER FINANCIAL STATISTICS QUARTERLY.
Earlier TD 10.9/4

TD 12.16 • **Item 982-N-4**
TRANSPORTATION STATISTICS IN BRIEF. [Annual]

TD 12.17: • **Item 982-N-7 (E)**
ELECTRONIC PRODUCTS (misc.).

TD 12.18:v.nos./nos. • **Item 982-N-10 (EL)**
JOURNAL OF TRANSPORTATION AND STATISTICS.

TD 12.19: • **Item 982-N-7 (EL)**
TRANSTATS.

SURFACE TRANSPORTATION BOARD

INFORMATION

Surface Transportation Board
Dept. of Transportation
1925 K St. NW
Washington, DC 20423-0001
(202) 565-1674
http://www.stb.dot.gov

TD 13.2:   **• Item 982-P**
GENERAL PUBLICATIONS.

TD 13.6/2:v.nos.   **• Item 982-P-1**
SURFACE TRANSPORTATION BOARD REPORTS.

U.S. TRADE AND DEVELOPMENT AGENCY

TDA 1.1   **• Item 1100 (EL)**
ANNUAL REPORT.

TDA 1.2   **• Item 1100-A-1**
GENERAL PUBLICATIONS.

TDA 1.15   **• Item 1100-A-2 (EL)**
UPDATE. [Quarterly]

TDA 1.16   **• Item 1100-A-3 (E)**
ELECTRONIC PRODUCTS. (misc.)

DEPARTMENT OF VETERANS AFFAIRS
(1930–   )

CREATION AND AUTHORITY

The Veterans Administration was established as an independent agency under the President by Executive Order 5398, of July 21, 1930, in accordance with the act of July 3, 1930 (46 Stat. 1016). This act authorized the President to consolidate and coordinate Federal agencies especially created for or concerned in the administration of laws providing benefits for veterans. The Administration was renamed Veterans Affairs Department by Act of October 25, 1988 (102 Stat. 2635).

INFORMATION

Department of Vetrans Affairs
810 Vermont Avenue, NW
Washington, D.C. 20420
(202) 273-5400
Toll-Free: (800) 827-1000
http://www.va.gov

VA 1.1   **• Item 983 (MF)**
ANNUAL REPORT. 1931–   [Annual]

Report made by the Administrator of Veterans Affairs to Congress pursuant to provisions of 38 U.S.C. 214 for the fiscal year.

Reports cover the various types of programs administered by the Veterans Administration, such as medical care, compensation and pensions, automobiles and other conveyances for disabled veterans, vocational rehabilitation and education, guaranteed and insured loans, direct loans, grants to disabled veterans for specially adapted housing, insurance, guardianship, etc.

A special section of Statistical Tables is included in each report which gives detailed data on the various operations and programs of the agency.

Also published in the House Documents series.

VA 1.1/2:date   **• Item 983 (MF)**
ANNUAL REPORT OF THE SURGICAL SERVICE.

VA 1.1/3:date   **• Item 983 (MF)**
ANNUAL REPORT ON THE MANAGEMENT EFFICIENCY PILOT PROGRAM (MEPP).

VA 1.1/4:date   **• Item 983**
VA MEDICAL RESEARCH SERVICE, ANNUAL REPORT.

VA 1.1/5   **• Item 983-F (MF)**
REPORT OF THE CHAIRMAN, FY, BOARD OF VETERANS' APPEALS.

VA 1.1/7   **• Item 983-H (MF)**
VA HEALTH SERVICES RESEARCH & DEVELOPMENT SERVICE PROGRESS REPORTS. [Annual]

VA 1.2:CT   **• Item 985**
GENERAL PUBLICATIONS.

VA 1.2/2:date   **• Item 985-H**
DATA ON VIETNAM ERA VETERANS. [Biennial]

Tables present data on Vietnam era veterans in terms of their numbers, employment status, medical compensation and pensions, education, housing assistance, and VA expenditures.
Earlier classed in VA 1.2

VA 1.2/10:date   **• Item 985-H**
DATA ON VIETNAM ERA VETERANS. [Biennial]

VA 1.2/11   **• Item 985-K (MF) (EL)**
GEOGRAPHIC DISTRIBUTION OF VA EXPENDITURES, STATE, COUNTY, AND CONGRESSIONAL DISTRICT. [Annual]
Formerly VA 1.2:Ex 7

VA 1.2/12:date   **• Item 985-M**
DATA ON FEMALE VETERANS. [Annual]

PURPOSE:– To present data on female veterans in the four major areas of population, health care, compensation and pension, and education benefits.

VA 1.3:
BULLETINS.

VA 1.3/3:date   **• Item 983-C (EL)**
RECRUITMENT BULLETIN. [Monthly]

Lists nationwide opportunities for employment with the VA, showing position titles, locations, and grades.

VA 1.3/4:date
APPROVED RECURRING REPORTS BULLETIN 12-AY. [Annual]

VA 1.4:nos.
CIRCULARS.

VA 1.4/2:nos.
PERSONNEL CIRCULAR LETTERS. [Irregular]

VA 1.5:CT
LAWS.

VA 1.6:CT   **• Item 988-C**
REGULATIONS, RULES, AND INSTRUCTIONS. [Irregular]

VA 1.6:nos.   **• Item 989**
VA REGULATIONS.

    VA 1.6/2:nos.
    – GENERAL. TRANSMITTAL SHEETS.

    VA 1.6/3:nos.
    – CLAIMS. TRANSMITTAL SHEETS.

    VA 1.6/4:nos.
    – INSURANCE. TRANSMITTAL SHEETS.

    VA 1.6/5:nos.
    – LEGAL SERVICES. TRANSMITTAL SHEETS.

    VA 1.6/6:nos.
    – LOAN GUARANTY. TRANSMITTAL SHEETS.

    VA 1.6/7:nos.
    – VETERANS TUITION APPEALS BOARD. TRANSMITTAL SHEETS.

    VA 1.6/8:nos.
    – VOCATIONAL REHABILITATION AND EDUCATION. TRANSMITTAL SHEETS.

    VA 1.6/9:nos.
    – FINANCES. TRANSMITTAL SHEETS.

    VA 1.6/10:nos.
    – MEDICAL. TRANSMITTAL SHEETS.

VA 1.7:nos.
ADMINISTRATOR'S ORDERS.
    Superseded by VA 1.17

VA 1.8:nos.
ADMINISTRATOR'S DECISIONS.

VA 1.8/2:vol.
DECISIONS (bound volumes).

VA 1.8/3:v.nos.
DECISIONS OF ADMINISTRATOR (bound volumes).

VA 1.9:vol.
MEDICAL BULLETIN. [Monthly]
    Earlier VA 3.9

VA 1.10:CT   **• Item 987**
HANDBOOKS, MANUALS, GUIDES (unnumbered).

VA 1.10/2:nos.
MANUALS (numbered).

VA 1.10/3:nos.   **• Item 987**
PROGRAM GUIDE PG (series).

VA 1.10/4:nos.   **• Item 987**
GUIDE G (series).

VA 1.10/5   **• Item 987**
HANDBOOK (series). [Irregular]

    VA 1.10/5:232-68-1/2   **• Item 987**
    HANDBOOK FOR VETERANS ADMINISTRATION CONTRACT REPRESENTATIVES. Rev. 1971. 626 p. il. (Handbook 232-68-1)

    Contains complete information on all benefit subjects needed by those actively assisting veterans, their dependents and beneficiaries. It is a reference document for Veterans Administration employees and accredited representatives of veterans of service organizations.

VA 1.11:nos.
CLINICAL BULLETINS.
    Earlier VA 3.8

VA 1.12:CT
PAPERS IN RE.

VA 1.13:date
ANNUAL STATEMENTS, GOVERNMENT LIFE INSURANCE FUND.
    Earlier VB 1.17 and VA 3.2:L 62

VA 1.13/2:date
NATIONAL SERVICE LIFE INSURANCE ANNUAL STATEMENT FOR CALENDAR YEAR.

VA 1.14:date
LAWS AND EXECUTIVE ORDERS RELATING TO COMPENSATION, PENSION, EMERGENCY OFFICERS' RETIREMENT, ETC.

VA 1.15:nos.
VETERANS ADMINISTRATION INSTRUCTIONS.

VA 1.16:CT
POSTERS. [Irregular]   • **Item 985-N**

VA 1.16/2:CT
AUDIOVISUAL MATERIALS. [Irregular]

VA 1.17:nos.
ORGANIZATION ORDERS.

    Supersedes Administration Orders (VA 1.7).

VA 1.18   • **Item 987**
MANUALS, M- (series). [Irregular]

VA 1.19:nos.   • **Item 988**
PAMPHLETS. [Irregular]

VA 1.20:date   • **Item 986**
DEPARTMENT OF VETERANS AFFAIRS PUBLICA-
TIONS INDEX. [Annual]
    Earlier: Index to Veterans Administration Pub-
lications.

VA 1.20/2   • **Item 983-A**
BIBLIOGRAPHIES AND LISTS OF PUBLICATIONS.

VA 1.20/3:nos.   • **Item 983-A**
BIBLIOGRAPHIES (numbered).

VA 1.20/4:nos.   • **Item 983-A-1**
VA CATALOGS (numbered).

VA 1.21:CT
ADDRESSES.

VA 1.22   • **Item 986-A(MF)**
INFORMATION BULLETINS, IB- (series). [Irregular]

    SUREMENT DATA AND HEARING AID SELEC-
TION PROCEDURES, CONTRACT YEAR
(date). [Annual]

    Describes procedures and methods used
by the Veterans Administration in selecting
hearing aids to be placed on contract for
regular issue to hard-of-hearing veterans during the contract year. Also lists the names of
all the manufacturers solicited; those which
participated; names of the models submitted;
models selected for contract, along with the
raw test data and performance score or each
model measured.

VA 1.22:13-1/v.nos.&nos.   • **Item 986-A**
SAFETY, OCCUPATIONAL HEALTH AND FIRE
PROTECTION BULLETIN. v. 1– 18, no.
3.   – 1975. [Irregular] (Department of
Medicine and Surgery) (IB 13-1)

    PURPOSE:– To disseminate timely infor-
mation to all VA stations regarding safety,
occupational health and fire protection matters, the VA safety program and VA safety
award standings.

VA 1.22:15-5/v.nos.&nos.   • **Item 986-A**
NEWSLETTER FOR RESEARCH IN MENTAL
HEALTH AND BEHAVIORAL SCIENCES. v. 1–
18 [Quarterly] (Research Unit on Aging, Vet-
erans Administration Center, Bay Pines,
Florida) (IB 15-5)

    Entitled Newsletter for Research in Psy-
chology prior to v. 15, no. 1.
    Indexed by: Index to U.S. Government
Periodicals.
    ISSN 0092-394X

VA 1.22/2:v.nos.&nos.   • **Item 986-A (MF)**
INFORMATION BULLETINS. [Quarterly]

VA 1.22/3:date   • **Item 986-A**
HANDBOOK OF HEARING AID MEASUREMENT.
[Annual]

VA 1.23:nos.
TECHNICAL BULLETINS. (Pubs. desig. TB nos. & letter nos.)

VA 1.23/2   • **Item 987-A**
MEDICAL BULLETINS. MB 1–   [Irregular]

VA 1.23/3:nos.   • **Item 983-B(EL)**
JOURNAL OF REHABILITATION, RESEARCH AND
DEVELOPMENT. Spring 1964–   [Irregular]
(Bureau of Medicine and Surgery)

    PURPOSE:– To provide physicians, thera-
pists, prosthetists, orthotists, and others interested in the fields of prosthetics and sensory
aids information on bioengineering studies, new
techniques and devices, and other related aspects of the complex man-machine fields involving devices for disabled individuals.
    Earlier: Bulletin of Prosthetics Research.

VA 1.23/3-2:date   • **Item 983-B (MF)(EL)**
REHABILITATION R AND D PROGRESS REPORTS.
[Annual]

VA 1.23/4:date   • **Item 983-A-2 (MF)**
EXCHANGE OF MEDICAL INFORMATION PROGRAM,
ANNUAL REPORT.

    PURPOSE:– To describe the activities,
projects, etc., carried out under the Program which
supports projects facilitating the exchange of
medical information between academic and clinical enters, and remote Administration facilities.

VA 1.23/5:v.nos.&nos.   • **Item 983-A-9(EL)**
AGENT ORANGE REVIEW. v. 1–   [Irregular]

    Published as part of VA's expanded program
to provide information on Agent Orange to concerned veterans and their families.

VA 1.24:v.nos.&nos.
READJUSTMENT ALLOWANCE ACTIVITIES.

VA 1.25:v.nos.&nos.
QUARTERLY REVIEW.

VA 1.26:date
RESEARCH STUDIES.

VA 1.27:v.nos.&issue nos.
VA STATISTICAL SUMMARY. [Monthly]

VA 1.28:session nos.
CLERICAL WORKSHOP SERIES.

VA 1.29:date
ACCIDENT AND FIRE REPORT.

VA 1.30:nos.
VA CATALOG.

VA 1.31:nos.
CURRENT INFORMATION ON OCCUPATIONAL OUT-
LOOK.

VA 1.32:
ICE LETTERS.

VA 1.33:
HOSPITAL CONSTRUCTION AND ACTIVATION, SUM-
MARY.

VA 1.34   • **Item 989-B**
VA FACT SHEETS, IS- (series). [Irregular]

VA 1.34:1   • **Item 989-B**
FEDERAL BENEFITS FOR VETERANS AND
DEPENDENTS. [Irregular]

    PURPOSE:– To provide only general infor-
mation concerning most Federal benefits enacted by Congress of the United States for
veterans, their dependents, and beneficiaries. It discusses benefits for veterans of the
Spanish-American War, World Wars I and II,
Korean Conflict, Post-Korean Conflict, peacetime veterans and 6-month enlistees, and for
those in active service.

VA 1.35:
SELF-EMPLOYMENT CLAIMS AND PAYMENT BY
AGENCIES. [Monthly]

VA 1.36:
UNEMPLOYMENT ALLOWANCE CLAIMS AND PAY-
MENT DATA BY AGENCIES.

VA 1.37:
OCCUPATIONAL OUTLOOK REVIEW.

VA 1.38   • **Item 989-A**
TRAINING GUIDES, TG- (series). [Irregular]

VA 1.39:nos.
INTERIM ISSUES. ADMINISTRATIVE.

VA 1.40:v.nos.&nos.
QUARTERLY PROGRESS REPORT ON VETERANS
ADMINISTRATION-ARMED FORCES STUDY ON
CHEMOTHERAPY OF TUBERCULOSIS.

VA 1.40/2   • **Item 988-A**
TRANSACTION OF RESEARCH CONFERENCE IN
PULMONARY DISEASES.

    Formerly Conference on Chemotherapy of Tu-
berculosis.

    INDEX.

    Vols. 1– 19. 1946– 1960

VA 1.41:v.nos.   • **Item 989-C**
TRANSACTIONS OF RESEARCH CONFERENCES ON
COOPERATIVE CHEMOTHERAPY STUDIES IN
PSYCHIATRY AND RESEARCH APPROACHES TO
MENTAL ILLNESS.

VA 1.42:date   • **Item 989-C**
PROCEEDINGS OF ANNUAL CLINICAL SPINAL CORD
INJURY CONFERENCE.

VA 1.43   • **Item 987-B**
MEDICAL RESEARCH IN VETERANS ADMINISTRA-
TION, ANNUAL REPORT. [Annual]

VA 1.43/2:date   • **Item 987-B**
VA MEDICAL RESEARCH CONFERENCE ABSTRACTS.
[Annual]

VA 1.43/3   • **Item 987-B**
HIGHLIGHTS OF VA MEDICAL RESEARCH. [Annual]
(Research Service, Department of Medicine and
Surgery)

VA 1.43/4   • **Item 987-B**
MEDICAL RESEARCH PROGRAM, SYNOPSIS.
[Annual] (Research Service, Department of Medi-
cine and Surgery)

VA 1.43/5:date   • **Item 987-C (EL)**
SUMMARY OF MEDICAL PROGRAMS. [Monthly]

    Contains statistical data on various VA medi-
cal programs.
    Also published in microfiche.
    Continues: Veterans Administration Summary
of Medical Programs.
    Indexed by: American Statistics Index.

VA 1.44   • **Item 989-D**
VA BENEFITS IN BRIEF. 1958–   [Irregular]

    Title varies.

VA 1.45   • **Item 989-E**
TECHNICAL REPORT, TR- (series). [Irregular]

VA 1.46   • **Item 985-A(MF)**
GOVERNMENT LIFE INSURANCE PROGRAMS FOR
VETERANS AND SERVICEMEN. [Annual]

    Report for the calendar year.

VA 1.46/2   • **Item 983 (MF)**
SERVICEMEN'S GROUP LIFE INSURANCE
PROGRAM, ANNUAL REPORT. 1st–   1966–
[Annual]

VA 1.47:nos.   • **Item 988-B**
SEARCH, ADMINISTRATIVE RESEARCH BULLETINS,
ARB- (series).

VA 1.48:nos.   • **Item 989-F(MF)**
VA MONOGRAPHS. [Irregular]

VA 1.48/2:nos.   • **Item 989-F (MF)**
RESEARCH MONOGRAPHS.

VA 1.48/3:nos. • **Item 989-H**
CONTROLLER PATIENT CENSUS MONOGRAPHS. 1– [Irregular] (Department of Medicine and Surgery)

VA 1.48/4:nos. • **Item 989-H**
IM&S-M SERIES.

VA 1.49:nos. • **Item 989-G**
VETERANS EDUCATION NEWSLETTER. [Irregular]

ISSN 0145-0271

VA 1.50:nos. • **Item 989-I**
EXTENDED CARE CENSUS REPORTS. 1– [Irregular]

VA 1.51:date
WAGE COMMITTEE: ANNUAL REPORT OF ACTIVITIES.

VA 1.52:date • **Item 985-C**
VOLUNTARY SERVICE NATIONAL ADVISORY COMMITTEE: REPORT OF ANNUAL MEETING.
Earlier VA 1.2:V 88

VA 1.53:nos. • **Item 989-B**
VA-DMA-IS (series). (Department of Memorial Affairs)

VA 1.54:v.nos.&nos.
PULSE. [Monthly]

PURPOSE:– To serve as a newsletter for the Veterans Administration employees.

VA 1.55:nos. • **Item 938-A-3(EL)**
SEMIANNUAL REPORT OF THE INSPECTOR GENERAL. 1– 1978–

VA 1.55/2:nos. • **Item 983-A-3**
DIGEST, INSPECTOR GENERAL REPORT TO THE CONGRESS. [Semiannual]

VA 1.56:date
NEWSLETTER, RESEARCH AND DEVELOPMENT IN HEALTH CARE. [Quarterly]

VA 1.56/2:v.nos.&nos. • **Item 989-G-1**
NORTH CENTRAL REGIONAL MEDICAL EDUCATION CENTER: NEWSLETTER. v. 1– [Quarterly]

VA 1.56/3:v.nos. • **Item 989-G-2**
VA MEDICAL CENTER, PHOENIX, ARIZONA: NEWSLETTER. [Quarterly]

VA 1.56/4:nos.
MEDICAL INFORMATION RESOURCES MANAGEMENT OFFICE: NEWSLETTER. [Irregular]

VA 1.56/5 • **Item 989-G-3**
VA MEDICAL CENTER, ALLEN PARK, MICHIGAN: NEWSLETTER. [Monthly]

Newsletter published for employees, patients and volunteers of the Center.

VA 1.56/6: • **Item 989-G-4**
HINES SIGHT. [3 times a year]

Published by Nursing Service, Edward A. Hines, Jr. VAHospital, Hines, Illinois.
Contains articles and features on activities in the VA Hospital in Hines, Illinois.

VA 1.57:yr.-nos. • **Item 989-J**
SERIES W- (numbered). [Irregular]

Consists of studies regarding use by women veterans of VA benefit programs.
W = Women.

VA 1.58:date • **Item 985-B**
LEGISLATIVE STATUS REPORT. [Monthly] (Office of General Counsel)

Includes reports on the legislative status of bills under consideration, laws recently enacted, and Congressional hearings of interest to the Veterans Administration.

VA 1.59:CT • **Item 983-A-6**
ENVIRONMENTAL IMPACT STATEMENTS. [Irregular]

VA 1.60: • **Item 983-A-4 (MF)**
TELEPHONE DIRECTORY. [Irregular]

VA 1.61:v.nos.&nos. • **Item 983-A-5**
ROUNDS OF THE TEACHING STAFF. [2-4 issues per year]

Official journal of the Wadsworth Medical Center.

VA 1.62:date • **Item 983-A-7(MF)**
DIRECTORY OF VETERANS ORGANIZATIONS AND STATE DEPARTMENTS OF VETERANS AFFAIRS. [Annual]

Separately lists veterans service organizations including those Federally and not Federally chartered, State organizations recognized by the VA, and other organizations which provide valuable aid, assistance, or services to veterans.

VA 1.62/2:CT • **Item 983-A-10**
DIRECTORIES. [Irregular]

VA 1.62/2-2:date • **Item 983-A-10**
DIRECTORY OF VETERANS ADMINISTRATION FACILITIES. [Irregular]
Earlier VA 1.2:D 62

VA 1.63:CT • **Item 893-A-8**
VA HEALTH PROFESSIONAL SCHOLARSHIP PROGRAM: PUBLICATIONS. [Irregular]

Includes all publications pertaining to the VA Health Professional Scholarship Program.

VA 1.66:date
NEWSLETTER, RESEARCH AND DEVELOPMENT IN HEALTH CARE. [Quarterly]

VA 1.67:CT • **Item 987-D (MF)**
BIOMETRICS MONOGRAPH SERIES. [Irregular]

VA 1.68:date • **Item 987-E (MF)**
FIVE YEAR MEDICAL FACILITY CONSTRUCTION NEEDS ASSESSMENT. [Annual]

An assessment submitted to Congress of the need for facility improvements to support the health care mission of the VA. Lists construction needs for the coming five year period.

VA 1.68/2:date • **Item 987-E (MF)**
FIVE YEAR MEDICAL FACILITY DEVELOPMENT PLAN. [Quinquennial]

VA 1.69:nos. • **Item 983-A-4**
CONSOLIDATED ADDRESS AND TERRITORIAL BULLETIN, VA STATION ADDRESSES, IDENTIFICATION NUMBERS, AND TERRITORIAL JURISDICTIONS. [Annual]

VA 1.70:CT • **Item 987-F**
MAPS AND ATLASES. [Irregular]

VA 1.71:date • **Item 985-E (MF)**
TREND DATA. [Annual]

PURPOSE:– To present tabular and graphic data for the past 24 years on veteran population, expenditures and employment, VA facilities, veterans appeals, guardianship, compensation and pension, occupational rehabilitation and education, loan guaranty, life insurance, and health care.
Earlier VA 1.2:T 72

VA 1.72: • **Item 985-D**
NEWSLETTER, REGENERATION RESEARCH. [Irregular]

Contains short articles.

VA 1.73:date • **Item 985-F**
DRUG FORMULARY. [Annual] (Medical Center, Saginaw, Michigan)

VA 1.73/2:date • **Item 985-F**
DRUG INDEX, FORMULARY. [Annual]

VA 1.73/3:date • **Item 985-F-1**
FORMULARY. [Annual]

Lists various therapeutic agents available at the Lakeside Medical Center Pharmacy SVC by both generic and brand names.

VA 1.73/4:date • **Item 985-F-2**
FORMULARY, WEST SIDE MEDICAL CENTER, CHICAGO, ILLINOIS. [Annual]

The formulary is a system by which committees of members from the medical, pharmacy, nursing, and administrative staff of the medical center evaluate appraise and select those drug products considered useful and effective in patient care. Such products are listed in the formulary.

VA 1.73/5:date • **Item 985-F-3**
VETERANS ADMINISTRATION MEDICAL CENTER, TUCSON, ARIZONA, FORMULARY.

The formulary lists products considered useful and effective in patient care at the VA Medical Center at Tucson, Arizona.

VA 1.73/6:date/pts. • **Item 985-F-3**
FORMULARY, VA MEDICAL CENTER SEPULVEDA, GEORGIA. [Annual]

VA 1.74:nos. • **Item 989-F**
STATISTICAL BRIEFS (series). [Irregular]

VA 1.75: • **Item 985-G (MF)**
EMPLOYMENT DATA ON TITLE 38 PHYSICIANS, DENTISTS, AND NURSES. [Quarterly]

Tabular employment data on Veterans Administration Title 38 physicians, dentists, and nurses in a pay status. Includes such information as gains, losses, and promotions by assignment and by age.

VA 1.76:nos. • **Item 985-S**
INSTRUCTIONAL PROGRAM NOTES. [Irregular]

VA 1.77:date • **Item 985-J (MF)**
VA ADP AND TELECOMMUNICATIONS PLAN. [Annual]

VA 1.77/2:date • **Item 985-J (MF)**
DM&S ADP PLAN. [Annual]

DM&S = Department of Medicine and Surgery.
Issued as a supplement to the VA ADP and Telecommunications Plan (VA 1.77).

VA 1.78:date • **Item 985-F**
WEST SIDE VA MEDICAL CENTER FORMULARY. [Annual]

VA 1.79 • **Item 985-L**
IMPORTANT INFORMATION ABOUT YOU AND YOUR MEDICATION. [Irregular]

Each issue provides information on a single medication.

VA 1.80:date • **Item 985-P**
OFFICE OF PROCUREMENT AND SUPPLY LETTER. [Quarterly]

VA 1.81:date • **Item 985-R (MF)**
NETWORKED AUDIOVISUALS. [Annual]
Earlier VA 1.2:N 38

VA 1.82 • **Item 987-G**
ENERGY MANAGEMENT AND CONTROL QUARTERLY.

Tables show achievement of annual energy management targets by various VA facilities and medical districts as well as other data on VA energy consumption.

VA 1.83:date
OMB SUBMISSION. [Annual]

VA 1.83/2:date/v.nos. • **Item 987-K (MF)**
DEPARTMENT OF VETERANS AFFAIRS, FY BUDGET IN BRIEF AND BUDGET SUBMISSION. [Annual]

VA 1.84:date • Item 987-H (MF)
MANAGING CLINICAL COSTS. [Annual]

PURPOSE:– To present information and many graphs, tables, and charts on managing clinical costs so as to provide optimum patient care while maintaining cost effectiveness.

VA 1.85:CT • Item 987-J
FORMS. [Irregular]

VA 1.86: • Item 983-D
INFORMATION SYSTEMS STRATEGIC PLAN. [Annual]

PURPOSE– To report on the VA Information Systems Plan, which integrates the automation plans of each VA element into a single agency-wide plan.

VA 1.88: • Item 983-A-11 (MF)
SELECTED COMPENSATION AND PENSION DATA BY STATE OF RESIDENCE. [Annual]

PURPOSE– To report data on the magnitude and geographic distribution of beneficiaries and payments under the VA Compensation Pension programs. Provides information to the Administrator of Veterans Affairs, VA department heads, etc., and to the Congress.

VA 1.89: • Item 987-K
MANAGEMENT AND PRODUCTIVITY IMPROVEMENT REPORT. [Annual]

PURPOSE– To summarize VA activities in response to President Reagan's Productivity Improvement Program initiated in 1986.

VA 1.90:date • Item 987-L
CDE NEWS. [Quarterly]

VA 1.91:date • Item 983-A-2(MF)
MEDICAL RESEARCH SERVICE ADVISORY GROUPS. [Annual]

VA 1.92:date • Item 987-H
GERIATRIC RESEARCH, EDUCATION, AND CLINICAL CENTERS (GRECC'S) FISCAL YEAR . . . SUMMARY OF PROGRAM ACTIVITIES.

VA 1.93:vol.nos./nos. • Item 989-G
VANGUARD. [Bimonthly]

VA 1.94:date/nos. • Item 989-K(EL)
PTSD RESEARCH QUARTERLY.

VA 1.94/2 • Item 983-E(EL)
PTSD (POST-TRAUMATIC STRESS DISORDER) CLINICAL QUARTERLY.

VA 1.95 • Item 983-E(E)
ELECTRONIC PRODUCTS. [Irregular]

VA 1.95/2 • Item 983-E-1 (CD)
BOARD OF VETERANS' APPEALS DECISIONS. [Annual]

VA 1.95/3:date • Item 983-E-2 (CD)
AUTOMATED REFERENCE MATERIALS SYSTEM (ARMS). [Monthly]

VA 1.97 • Item 985-T (MF)
FACILITY-BASED HIV/AIDS EDUCATION DEMONSTRATION PROJECT FY.

VA 1.100: • Item 983-E (EL)
VHA EMPLOYEE NEWSLETTER.

VA 1.101: • Item 983-E(EL)
VHA HIGHLIGHTS.

VA 1.103 • Item 983-E (EL)
CIO INFORMATION IN THE NEWS.

VA 1.104:v.nos./nos. • Item 985-M-1 (P) (EL)
GULF WAR REVIEW.

BUREAU OF PENSIONS
(1930– 1931)

CREATION AND AUTHORITY

The Bureau of Pensions (I 24) was transferred from the Department of the Interior and consolidated with the Veterans' Bureau (VB 1) to form the Veterans' Administration, by act of Congress, approved July 3, 1930.

VA 2.1:date
ANNUAL REPORTS.
Earlier I 24.1

VA 2.2:CT
GENERAL PUBLICATIONS.
Earlier I 24.2

VA 2.3
BULLETINS.

VA 2.4
CIRCULARS.

VA 2.5
LAWS.
Earlier I 24.7

VA 2.5/2:date
LAWS GOVERNING GRANTING OF ARMY AND NAVY PENSIONS.
Earlier I 24.14

VA 2.6
REGULATIONS.

VETERANS BUREAU
(1930– 1931)

CREATION AND AUTHORITY

The Veterans' Bureau (VB 1) was consolidated with the Bureau of Pensions (I 24) and the National Home for Disabled Volunteer Soldiers to form the newly established Veterans' Administration by Executive Order 5398 of July 21, 1931, issued pursuant to act of Congress, approved July 3, 1930.

VA 3.1:date
ANNUAL REPORTS.
Earlier VB 1.1

VA 3.2:CT
GENERAL PUBLICATIONS.
Earlier VB 1.2

VA 3.3
BULLETINS.
Earlier VB 1.3

VA 3.4
CIRCULARS.

VA 3.5:CT
LAWS.
Earlier VB 1.6

VA 3.6
REGULATIONS.
Earlier VB 1.7

VA 3.7:nos.
GENERAL ORDERS.
Earlier VB 1.5

VA 3.8:nos.
CLINICAL BULLETINS.
Earlier VB 1.15
Later VA 1.11

VA 3.9:vol.
MEDICAL BULLETIN. [Monthly]
Earlier VB 1.16
Later VA 1.9

VA 3.10:CT
REGULATIONS, INSTRUCTIONS, AND MANUALS.
Earlier VB 1.10/2

VETERANS BUREAU
(1921– 1930)

CREATION AND AUTHORITY

The Veterans Bureau was established by act of Congress, approved August 9, 1921, consolidating the Bureau of War Risk Insurance (T 49) of the Treasury Department and the Rehabilitation Division of the Federal Board for Vocational Education (VE 1). By Executive Order 5398 of July 21, 1931, issued pursuant to act of Congress, approved July 3, 1930, the Veterans Bureau was transferred to the newly established Veterans Administration (VA 3).

VB 1.1:date
ANNUAL REPORTS.
Later VA 3.1

VB 1.2:CT
GENERAL PUBLICATIONS.
Later VA 3.2

VB 1.3
BULLETINS.
Later VA 3.3

VB 1.4
CIRCULARS.

VB 1.5:nos.
GENERAL ORDERS.
Later VA 3.7

VB 1.6:CT
LAWS.
Later VA 3.5

VB 1.7:nos.
REGULATIONS.
Later VA 3.6

VB 1.8:nos.
FIELD ORDERS.

VB 1.9:nos.
INSTRUCTIONS (numbered).

VB 1.10/1:date
REGULATIONS, RULES, AND INSTRUCTIONS (dated).

VB 1.10/2:CT
REGULATIONS, RULES, AND INSTRUCTIONS.
Later VA 3.10

VB 1.10/3:date
REGULATIONS AND PROCEDURE.

VB 1.10/4:CT
REGULATIONS AND PROCEDURE.

VB 1.11:nos.
HOSPITAL SECTION ORDERS.
Earlier T 27.24

VB 1.12:nos.
SPECIAL ORDERS.

VB 1.13:nos.
DIGEST OF LEGAL OPINIONS. [Monthly]

VB 1.13/2:vol.
DIGEST OF LEGAL OPINIONS (Compilations).

VB 1.14:nos.
PROPERTY REGULATIONS (numbered).

VB 1.15:nos.
CLINICAL BULLETINS. [Monthly]

    Later VA 3.8

VB 1.16:vol.
MEDICAL BULLETIN. [Monthly]

    Later VA 3.9

VB 1.17:date
ANNUAL STATEMENTS.

    Later VA 1.13

VB 1.18:CT
PAPERS IN RE.

FEDERAL BOARD FOR VOCATIONAL EDUCATION
(1917– 1933)

CREATION AND AUTHORITY

    The Federal Board for Vocational Education was established by the Smith-Hughes Act, approved February 23, 1917 (39 Stat. 929). The Board was transferred to the Office of Education (I 16) in the Department of the Interior by Executive Order 6166 of June 10, 1933.

VE 1.1:date
ANNUAL REPORTS.

VE 1.2:CT
GENERAL PUBLICATIONS.

VE 1.3
BULLETINS.
    Later I 16.54/3

VE 1.4
CIRCULARS.

VE 1.5:v.nos.
VOCATIONAL SUMMARY, CIRCULARS OF INFORMATION.

VE 1.6:nos.
VOCATIONAL REHABILITATION SERIES (Opportunity Monographs).

VE 1.7:nos.
REHABILITATION LEAFLETS.

VE 1.8:nos.
JOINT SERIES (Rehabilitation Monographs).

VE 1.9:nos.
INSTRUCTIONS.

VE 1.10:date
YEARBOOK.

VE 1.11:nos.
CIVILIAN VOCATIONAL REHABILITATION SERIES, MONOGRAPHS.
    Later I 16.54/9

VE 1.12:nos.
MISCELLANEOUS CIRCULARS.
    Later I 16.54/7

VE 1.13:date
NATIONAL CONFERENCE ON VOCATIONAL REHABILITATION.

VE 1.14:nos.
LEAFLETS.
    Later I 16.54/8

VE 1.15:nos.
MISCELLANEOUS SERIES.
    Later I 16.54/5

DEPARTMENT OF WAR
(1789– 1947)

CREATION AND AUTHORITY

    The Department of War was established as an executive department by act of Congress, approved Aug. 7, 1789 (1 Stat. 49). The Department of War was designated the Department of the Army by the National Security Act of 1947 (61 Stat. 499), which established the National Military Establishment. The National Security Act Amendments of 1949 (63 Stat. 578) established the Department of Defense as an executive department of the Government and made the Department of the Army one of the three military departments within the Department of Defense.

W 1.1:date
ANNUAL REPORTS.
    Later M 101.1

W 1.2:CT
GENERAL PUBLICATIONS.
    Later M 101.2

W 1.3:date & nos.
BULLETINS.
    Earlier W 3.3
    Later M 101.2

W 1.3/2
COMMERCIAL TRAFFIC BULLETIN.

W 1.4:date & nos.
CIRCULARS.

W 1.4/2:date & nos.
CIRCULARS. 1918–
    Later M 101.4

W 1.4/3:CT
CIRCULARS, BY SUBJECTS. Restricted.

W 1.5:v.nos.
ARMY AND NAVY OFFICIAL GAZETTE.

W 1.6:date
ARMY REGULATIONS.
    Later M 101.9

W 1.6/2:nos.
CHANGES IN ARMY REGULATIONS.

W 1.7:CT
CUSTOMS TARIFF AND REGULATION.

W 1.8:date
LAWS (general).
    Later D 108.5/2

W 1.8/2:CT
LAWS (miscellaneous).

W 1.8/3:CT & Sec.
ACTS AND RESOLUTIONS RELATING TO WAR DEPARTMENT.

    W 1.8/3a:CT & Sec.
    – CHRONOLOGICAL INDEX.

W 1.8/4:date & nos.
CHANGES IN MILITARY LAWS OF UNITED STATES.

W 1.9:date
LIST OF NEWSPAPERS DESIGNATED TO PUBLISH ADVERTISEMENTS OF WAR DEPARTMENT.

W 1.10:date
REGISTER OF WAR DEPARTMENT.

W 1.11:date
OFFICERS OF ARMY, THEIR FAMILIES AND FAMILIES OF DECEASED OFFICERS, RESIDING IN OR NEAR DISTRICT OF COLUMBIA.
    Later W 3.81

W 1.12:CT
REGULATIONS, RULES, AND INSTRUCTIONS (miscellaneous).

W 1.12/2
ADMINISTRATIVE MEMORANDUM.
    Processed.

W 1.12/3
LUBRICATION ORDERS, WDLO-nos.

W 1.12/4
CIVILIAN PERSONNEL PROCEDURES MANUAL.

W 1.13:nos.
TARIFF CIRCULARS.

W 1.14:letters-nos.
ORDERS AND CIRCULARS.
    Later M 101.30

W 1.15:date
INTERNATIONAL CONGRESS OF ENGINEERS, 1893.

W 1.16:date
CUBA, PROVISIONAL GOVERNOR, ANNUAL REPORTS.

W 1.17:date
ARMY OF CUBAN PACIFICATION, ANNUAL REPORTS.

W 1.18:nos.
SPECIAL REGULATIONS.

W 1.19:date
TELEPHONE DIRECTORY.
    Later M 1.7

W 1.20:cl.sec.&v.nos.
RECORDS OF WORLD WAR (class, sections, and volume numbers).

W 1.21:nos.
TRAINING REGULATIONS.

W 1.21/2:date
CHANGES IN TRAINING REGULATIONS.

W 1.21/3:date
TRAINING PUBLICATIONS: RECISIONS.

W 1.22:nos.
TECHNICAL REGULATIONS.

W 1.23:nos.
TRAINING MANUALS.

The Assistant Secretary of War

W 1.24/1:date
ANNUAL REPORTS.

W 1.24/2:CT
GENERAL PUBLICATIONS.

W 1.24/5:
PROCUREMENT CIRCULARS.
    Later W 1.31

W 1.24/6:
CURRENT PROCUREMENT NEWS DIGEST. [Monthly]

W 1.24/7:date
CHANGES IN U.S. ARMY AND FEDERAL SPECIFICATIONS.
    Later W 1.38

Department of War (Continued)

W 1.25:nos.
TABLES OF ORGANIZATION.

Superseded by W 1.44

W 1.25:date
LISTS OF TABLES OF ORGANIZATION.

W 1.25/2:date
TABLES OF ORGANIZATION, RECISIONS.

W 1.26:nos.
TABLES OF EQUIPMENT.

Superseded by W 1.44

W 1.27:nos.
TABLES OF BASIC ALLOWANCES.

W 1.28:CT
TABLES OF ALLOWANCES.
Later M 101.29

W 1.28:nos.
TABLES OF ALLOWANCES (numbered).

W 1.29:nos.
MOBILIZATION REGULATIONS.

W 1.30:nos.
CIVILIAN CONSERVATION CORPS CIRCULARS.

W 1.31:date&nos.
PROCUREMENT CIRCULARS PRINTED AND PRO-
CESSED.

Earlier W 1.24/5

W 1.32:CT
MILITARY RESERVATIONS.

W 1.33:nos.
FIELD MANUAL AND FIELD REGULATIONS.

Pubs. desig. FM-nos.
Earlier Basic Field Manuals (W 3.63), Field
Manuals (W 3.63/2), Field Service Regulations
(W 26/1:F 45/1-2).
Later M 101.17

W 1.34:nos.
TRAINING MEMORANDUMS.

W 1.35:nos.
TECHNICAL MANUALS.

Pubs. desig. TM-nos.
Later M 101.18

W 1.36:nos.
TRAINING CIRCULARS.

Pubs. desig. TC-no.
Later M 101.22

W 1.37:nos.
MOBILIZATION TRAINING PROGRAM.
Proc. and printed.

W 1.38:date
MONTHLY REPORTS ON CHANGES IN U.S. ARMY
SPECIFICATIONS, FEDERAL SPECIFICATIONS,
COMMERCIAL STANDARDS [and] SIMPLIFIED
PRACTICE RECOMMENDATIONS.
Earlier W 1.24/7
Later W 109.10

W 1.39:nos.
[WOMEN'S ARMY AUXILIARY CORPS] CIRCULARS.

Pubs. desig. WAAC Circulars.

W 1.40:nos.
PRE-INDUCTION TRAINING COURSE.

W 1.41:date
DIGEST OF WAR DEPARTMENT DIRECTIVES AND
INDEX OF GENERAL ORDERS, BULLETINS, AND
NUMBERED CIRCULARS. [Monthly]
Earlier W 3.22

W 1.42:nos.
CIVILIAN PERSONNEL REGULATIONS.

W 1.43:nos.
PAMPHLETS.
Later M 101.25

W 1.44:nos.
TABLES OF ORGANIZATION AND EQUIPMENT.

Supersedes W 1.25 and W 1.26 which gradually ceased as the new series came out to replace them.
Later M 101.21

W 1.45:nos.
ILLUSTRATED INSTRUCTOR'S REFERENCE [for film
strips].

Proc. and printed.

W 1.46:dt.&nos.
GENERAL ORDERS.

Earlier W 3.22
Later M 101.7

W 1.47:date
GENERAL ORDERS, BULLETINS AND NUMBERED
CIRCULARS; INDEXES.

W 1.48:dt.&nos.
SPECIAL ORDERS.

Earlier W 3.23
Later M 101.8

W 1.49:nos.
U.S. ARMY SPECIFICATIONS.

Later M 101.26

W 1.50:date
INDEXES OF U.S. ARMY AND FEDERAL SPECIFICA-
TIONS USED BY WAR DEPARTMENT.

Prior to 1944: W 3.48/2
Later M 101.23

W 1.51:dt.&nos.
GENERAL COURT MARTIAL ORDERS.

Earlier W 3.32
Later M 101.14

W 1.52:CT
GRAPHIC PORTFOLIOS, CHARTS, AND POSTERS.

W 1.53:nos.
GRAPHIC TRAINING AIDS.
Later D 101.21

W 1.54:nos.
CIVILIAN MEDICAL DIVISION HEALTH MESSAGES.

W 1.54/2:CT
CIVILIAN MEDICAL DIVISION PUBLICATIONS.

W 1.55:nos.
EDUCATIONAL MANUALS.
Later M 1.9

W 1.56:sec.&le-nos.
MODIFICATION WORK ORDERS.

Supersedes Field Service Modification Work
Orders, (W 34.33).
Later D 101.29

W 1.57:nos.
CIVILIAN PERSONNEL PAMPHLETS.

Proc. and printed.

W 1.58:sec.&nos.
TECHNICAL BULLETINS.
Later M 101.13

W 1.59:CT
POSTERS.

W 1.60:nos.
MEMORANDUMS.

Proc. & printed.
Later M 101.24

W 1.61:nos.
SUPPLY BULLETINS.

Proc. & printed.
Later M 101.27

W 1.62:nos.
READJUSTMENT REGULATIONS. Restricted.

W 1.63:nos.
OCCUPATIONAL BRIEFS.

Later M 101.28

W 1.64:nos.
TECHNICAL PAPERS OF ARMY-NAVY EXPLOSIVES
SAFETY BOARD.

Later M 3.7

W 1.65:nos.
WHAT THE SOLDIER THINKS, MONTHLY DIGEST OF
WAR DEPARTMENT STUDIES ON ATTITUDES OF
AMERICAN TROOPS.

W 1.66:v.no.
ARMY INFORMATION DIGEST. [Monthly]

Formerly I & E Digest, (W 109.210).
Later M 101.10

W 1.67:sec.nos.&le-nos.
WAR DEPARTMENT CATALOGS.

See prior to June 11, 1946, Army Service
Forces Catalogs, (W 109.14).
Later M 101.12

W 1.69:nos.
RECOGNITION JOURNAL. [Monthly]

W 1.70:CT
ARMY EXTENSION COURSES.

W 1.71:CT
STRATEGIC BOMBING SURVEY PUBLICATIONS.

W 1.71/2:nos.
STRATEGIC BOMBING SURVEY, CORPORATION
REPORTS.

W 1.72:nos.
MILITARY GOVERNMENT OF GERMANY, MONTHLY
REPORT OF MILITARY GOVERNOR, U.S. ZONE.

Later M 105.7

W 1.72:nos.&add.-nos.
[FUNCTIONAL REPORTS]. [Bimonthly]

W 1.72/2:CT
MILITARY GOVERNMENT OF GERMANY, SPECIAL
REPORT OF MILITARY GOVERNOR, U.S. ZONE.

Later M 105.17

W 1.72/3:nos.
REGISTRATION, EMPLOYMENT AND UNEMPLOY-
MENT, U.S. ZONE, STATISTICAL REPORT.

Later M 105.14

W 1.72/4:nos.
MILITARY GOVERNMENT REGULATIONS.

W 1.72/5:nos.
MILITARY GOVERNMENT WEEKLY INFORMATION
BULLETINS.

Later M 101.16 and M 105.8

W 1.72/6:nos.
MILITARY GOVERNMENT FOR GERMANY, FIAT RE-
PORTS.

W 1.72/7:nos.
MILITARY GOVERNMENT FOR GERMANY, FIAT TECH-
NICAL BULLETINS.

W 1.72/8:v.nos.
NEWS OF GERMANY.

W 1.72/9:nos.
[BRITISH INTERROGATION OF GERMAN SCIEN-
TISTS, REPORTS.]

W 1.72/10:CT/date
FUNCTIONAL REPORTS. [Monthly]

Later M 105.7/2

W 1.73:nos.
OFFICIAL GAZETTE OF CONTROL COUNCIL FOR
GERMANY.

Later M 105.9

W 1.74:nos.
MILITARY GOVERNMENT, AUSTRIA, REPORT OF
UNITED STATES COMMISSIONER. [Monthly]

Later M 105.10

W 1.75:nos.
SUMMATION OF NON-MILITARY ACTIVITIES IN JA-
PAN. [Monthly]

Later M 105.11

W 1.76:nos.
SUMMATION OF UNITED STATES ARMY MILITARY
GOVERNMENT ACTIVITIES IN KOREA. [Monthly]
Later M 105.13

W 1.76/2:CT
UNITED STATES ARMY MILITARY GOVERNMENT IN
KOREA PUBLICATIONS.

W 1.77:CT
ARMED FORCES INSTITUTE PUBLICATIONS.

W 1.78:nos.
SUMMATION OF UNITED STATES ARMY MILITARY
GOVERNMENT ACTIVITIES IN THE RYUKYU IS-
LANDS.
Later M 105.12

W 1.79:nos.
JOINT ARMY-NAVY PUBLICATIONS.

W 1.80:nos.
NATURAL RESOURCES SECTION REPORTS.
Later M 105.25 and D 102.20

W 1.80/2:nos.
NATURAL RESOURCES SECTION PRELIMINARY
STUDIES.

W 1.81:nos.
MILITARY GOVERNMENT WEEKLY FIELD REPORTS.

W 1.82:dt.&nos.
GAZETTE OF ALLIED COMMISSION FOR AUSTRIA.
[Monthly]
Later D 101.22
W 1.83:dt.&nos.
MONTHLY REPORT PREPARED BY TECHNICAL
STAFF, FUEL COMMITTEE ALLIED CONTROL
AUTHORITY.

Later M 105.15

W 1.84:CT
SUPREME COMMANDER FOR ALLIED POWERS:
GENERAL PUBLICATIONS.

Later D 102.11

W 1.84/2:nos.
CAPTURED AND SURRENDERED JAPANESE ARMY
AND NAVY SUPPLIES AND EQUIPMENT IN
JAPAN AND SOUTH KOREA, SUPREME COM-
MANDER FOR ALLIED POWERS.

GENERAL STAFF CORPS
(1903–1947)

W 2.1:date
ANNUAL REPORTS.

Later M 113.1

W 2.2:CT
GENERAL PUBLICATIONS.

Later M 113.2

W 2.3:
BULLETINS.

W 2.4:
CIRCULARS.

W 2.5:date
MEMORANDA.

W 2.6:CT
REGULATIONS AND INSTRUCTIONS.

W 2.6/2:CT
CHANGES IN REGULATIONS AND INSTRUCTIONS
(numbered).

W 2.7:date
EXTRACTS FROM REPORTS BY REGULAR AND MILI-
TARY OFFICERS ON JOINT ARMY AND MILITIA
COAST-DEFENSE EXERCISES.

W 2.8:nos.
GENERAL ORDERS.

W 2.9:v.nos.
OFFICIAL BULLETINS.

W 2.10:date
STOPPAGE CIRCULAR.

Formerly W 77.5

W 2.11:nos.
MORALE ITEMS. [Monthly]

W 2.12:CT
STRATEGIC SERVICES OFFICE PUBLICATIONS.

W 2.13:nos.
PUBLICATIONS OF RESEARCH AND ANALYSIS
BRANCH.

Earlier Y 3.C 78/3:7
Later S 1.57

ADJUTANT GENERAL'S
DEPARTMENT
(1913–1947)

CREATION AND AUTHORITY

The Adjutant General's Department was es-
tablished within the War Department by act of
Congress, approved Mar. 3, 1813. By act of Con-
gress, approved Apr. 23, 1904, the Adjutant
General's Office and the Record and Pension
Office were united to form the Military Secretary's
Office. This office was redesignated Adjutant
General's Office in 1907. Later renamed the Adju-
tant General's Department, it was designated the
Adjutant General's Corps by the Army Organiza-
tion Act of 1950 (64 Stat. 263).

W 3.1/1:date
ANNUAL REPORTS TO SECRETARY OF WAR.

Later M 108.1

W 3.1/2:date
ANNUAL REPORTS TO GENERAL OFFICER COM-
MANDING.

W 3.2:CT
GENERAL PUBLICATIONS.

Later M 108.2

W 3.3:nos.
BULLETINS.

Later W 1.3

W 3.4:date
CIRCULARS.

W 3.4/2:date
ADJUTANT GENERAL'S OFFICE CIRCULARS.

W 3.5/1:letters
ARTILLERY CIRCULARS.

Series begun 1892.

W 3.5/2:letters
ARTILLERY CIRCULARS.

Series begun 1893.

W 3.6:date
CIRCULARS RELATING TO THE WAR DEPARTMENT.

W 3.7:date
CIRCULARS (lettered).

W 3.8:date
GENERAL ORDERS EMBRACING LAWS AFFECTING
THE ARMY.

W 3.9:date
APPOINTMENTS, PROMOTIONS, RETIREMENTS,
ETC. [Weekly]

W 3.10:date
ARMY LIST AND DIRECTORY. [Monthly]

W 3.10/2:date
EMERGENCY OFFICERS, ARMY LIST AND DIREC-
TORY.

W 3.11:date
ARMY REGISTER.
Later M 108.8

W 3.11/2
REGISTER OF NON-COMMISSIONED STAFF.

W 3.12:pt.nos.
OFFICIAL ARMY REGISTER OF VOLUNTEER FORCE
OF U.S. ARMY, 1861-65.

W 3.13:date
COMPENDIUM OF GENERAL ORDERS AMENDING ARMY REGULATIONS.

W 3.14:date
COAST ARTILLERY MEMORANDA.

W 3.15:date
MONTHLY LIST OF OFFICERS ABSENT ON LEAVE IN EXCESS OF TIME.

W 3.16:CT
DRILL REGULATIONS.

W 3.16/1:CT
DRILL REGULATIONS, MANUALS, AND INSTRUCTIONS FOR ARMY.

W 3.16/2:CT
CHANGES IN DRILL REGULATIONS (numbered).

W 3.17/1:date
RECRUITING FOR LINE OF ARMY.

W 3.17/2:date
STATEMENT OF RECRUITING FOR LINE OF ARMY AT GENERAL RECRUITING STATIONS AND THEIR AUXILIARIES.

W 3.18:CT
EXAMINATION PAPERS.

W 3.19:CT
MEMORANDA (unnumbered).

W 3.20:date
MILITARY COMMANDS AND POSTS, ETC.

W 3.21:date
OFFICIAL REGISTER OF OFFICERS OF VOLUNTEERS IN SERVICE OF UNITED STATES.

W 3.22:date
GENERAL ORDERS.

Later W 1.46

W 3.23:date
SPECIAL ORDERS.

Later W 1.48

W 3.24:CT
ORDERS (Miscellaneous, unnumbered).

W 3.24/2
MEMORANDUMS.

Admin.

W 3.25:nos.
(PUBLIC MONEYS DEPOSITARIES) CIRCULARS.

W 3.26:date
(RECRUITING SERVICE CIRCULARS).

W 3.27:date
ROSTER OF GENERAL OFFICERS OF GENERAL STAFF, VOLUNTEERS, (War with Spain, 1898).

W 3.28:CT
RULES, REGULATIONS AND INSTRUCTIONS.

W 3.29:date
SOLDIER'S HANDBOOK.

W 3.30:date
STATIONS OF ARMY.

W 3.31:date
SPECIAL ORDERS, WAR DEPARTMENT.

W 3.32:date
GENERAL COURT MARTIAL ORDERS.

Later W 1.51

W 3.32/2:nos.
ORDNANCE FIELD SERVICE CIRCULARS, CUMULATIVE SERIAL LIST.

W 3.33:CT
MILITIA AFFAIRS DIVISION.

W 3.34:date
ROSTER OF OFFICERS, ADJUTANT-GENERAL'S DEPARTMENT.

W 3.35:date
REPORT ON THE MILITIA OF U.S.

W 3.36:CT
EQUIPMENT MANUAL.

W 3.36/2:CT
CHANGES IN EQUIPMENT MANUALS.

W 3.36/3
EQUIPMENT MANUAL FOR SERVICE IN EUROPE.

W 3.37:date
TECHNICAL NOTES OF COAST ARTILLERY TARGET PRACTICE.

W 3.38:date
SURRENDERS AND APPREHENSIONS REPORTED OF MEN CHARGED WITH DESERTION FROM ARMY. [Monthly]

W 3.39:nos.
U.S. ARMY TRAINING MANUALS.

See W 26.10 for Field Artillery Notes.

W 3.39/1:nos.
U.S. ARMY TRAINING MANUALS NUMBERED.

W 3.39/2:CT
UNITED STATES ARMY TRAINING PUBLICATIONS (misc.).

W 3.39/3:CT
TRAINING MANUALS, UNITED STATES ARMY (misc.).

W 3.40:date
EXTRACTS FROM GENERAL ORDERS AND BULLETINS, WAR DEPARTMENT RELATING TO REGIMENTAL AND COMPANY ADMINISTRATION.

W 3.40/2:date
INDEX TO MONTHLY EXTRACTS FROM GENERAL ORDERS AND BULLETINS.

W 3.41:CT
BLANK FORMS.

W 3.42:date
ORGANIZATION DIRECTORY [confidential].

W 3.42/2:nos.
CHANGE SHEETS APPLYING TO ORGANIZATION DIRECTORY.

W 3.43:v.nos.
PERSONNEL. (Committee on Classification of Personnel in Army).

W 3.44:date
OFFICIAL LIST OF OFFICERS RESERVE CORPS, ARMY.

W 3.45:vol.
U.S. ARMY RECRUITING NEWS.

W 3.46:CT
POSTERS (miscellaneous).

W 3.46/2:nos.
RECRUITING SERIES POSTERS.

W 3.46/3:nos.
SERVICE SERIES POSTERS.

W 3.46/4:CT
SERVICE SERIES SPECIAL POSTERS.

W 3.46/5:nos.
PICTORIALS, SERIES 1936.

W 3.46/6:nos.
PICTORIALS, SERIES 1937.

W 3.46/7:nos.
ARMY CONSERVATION PROJECT POSTERS.

Includes Tags and Posters.

W 3.46/8:nos.
RECRUITING PUBLICITY BUREAU POSTERS.

Later M 108.78

W 3.47:nos.
U.S. ARMY EDUCATIONAL MANUALS.

W 3.48/1:nos.
U.S. ARMY SPECIFICATIONS.

Later W 1.49

W 3.48/2:date
INDEX TO U.S. ARMY SPECIFICATIONS.

Superseded by W 1.50

W 3.49:date
COMPILATION OF OFFICE MEMORANDA.

W 3.50/1:date&lesson nos.
ARMY CORRESPONDENCE COURSES: SUBCOURSE, MOBILIZATION AND ADMINISTRATION, LESSON ASSIGNMENT SHEETS.

W 3.50/2:date&lesson nos.
ARMY CORRESPONDENCE COURSES: SUBCOURSE, MAP READING (or map reading and sketching) LESSON ASSIGNMENT SHEETS.

W 3.50/3:date&lesson nos.
ARMY CORRESPONDENCE COURSES: SUBCOURSE, MILITARY LAW, LESSON ASSIGNMENT SHEETS.

W 3.50/4:date&lesson nos.
ARMY CORRESPONDENCE COURSES: SUBCOURSE, MILITARY SANITATION AND FIRST AID.

W 3.50/5:date&lesson nos.
ARMY CORRESPONDENCE COURSES: SUBCOURSE, ASSOCIATED ARMS.

W 3.50/6:date&lesson nos.
ARMY CORRESPONDENCE COURSES: SUBCOURSE, PROPERTY, EMERGENCY PROCUREMENT AND FUNDS.

W 3.50/7:date&lesson nos.
ARMY CORRESPONDENCE COURSES: SUBCOURSE, INTERIOR GUARD DUTY, LESSON ASSIGNMENT SHEETS.

W 3.50/8:date&lesson nos.
ARMY CORRESPONDENCE COURSES: SUBCOURSE, SIGNAL COMMUNICATION FOR ALL ARMS AND SERVICES.

W 3.50/9:date&lesson nos.
ARMY CORRESPONDENCE COURSES: SUBCOURSE, CARE OF ANIMALS AND STABLE MANAGEMENT.

W 3.50/10:date&lesson nos.
ARMY CORRESPONDENCE COURSES: SUBCOURSE, ADMINISTRATION.

W 3.50/11:date&lesson nos.
ARMY CORRESPONDENCE COURSES: SUBCOURSE, DEFENSE AGAINST CHEMICAL WARFARE.

W 3.50/12:date&lesson nos.
ARMY CORRESPONDENCE COURSES: SUBCOURSE, MILITARY DISCIPLINE, COURTESIES, AND CUSTOMS OF SERVICE.

W 3.50/13:date&lesson nos.
ARMY CORRESPONDENCE COURSES: SUBCOURSE, MILITARY LAW, COURTS-MARTIAL.

W 3.50/14:date&lesson nos.
ARMY CORRESPONDENCE COURSES: SUBCOURSE, MILITARY LAW, LAW OF MILITARY OFFENSES.

W 3.50/15:date&lesson nos.
ARMY CORRESPONDENCE COURSES: SUBCOURSE, SUPPLY AND MESS MANAGEMENT.

W 3.50/16:date&lesson nos.
ARMY CORRESPONDENCE COURSES: SUBCOURSE, INDUSTRIAL MOBILIZATION.

W 3.50/17:date&lesson nos.
ARMY CORRESPONDENCE COURSES: SUBCOURSE, ORGANIZATION OF ARMY.

W 3.51:date&sec.no.
ARMY EXTENSION COURSES: ANNOUNCEMENTS.

W 3.52:nos.
ARMY EXTENSION COURSES: SPECIAL TEXT.

W 3.53/1:date&lesson no.
ARMY EXTENSION COURSES: SUBCOURSE NO 1 CALVARY.

W 3.53/2:date&lesson no.
ARMY EXTENSION COURSES: FIELD ARTILLERY.

W 3.53/3:date&lesson no.
ARMY EXTENSION COURSES: INFANTRY.

W 3.54:date&lesson no.
ARMY EXTENSION COURSES: SUBCOURSE 2. INFANTRY, BASIC COURSE ACCOUNTING AND PATROLLING, WEAPONS AND MUSKETRY.

W 3.54/2:date & lesson no.
– LESSON SOLUTIONS AND EXAMINATIONS.

W 3.55:date&lesson no.
ARMY EXTENSION COURSES: SUBCOURSE 3.

    Reserved.

W 3.56:date&lesson no.
ARMY EXTENSION COURSE: SUBCOURSE 4.

    Reserved.

W 3.57:date&lesson no.
ARMY EXTENSION COURSES: SUBCOURSE 5.

    Reserved.

W 3.58:date&lesson no.
ARMY EXTENSION COURSES: SUBCOURSE 6, GENERAL COURSE, PRACTICAL PROBLEMS.

W 3.59:date&lesson no.
ARMY CORRESPONDENCE COURSE: SUBCOURSE 7.

    Reserved.

W 3.60:date&lesson no.
ARMY CORRESPONDENCE COURSE: SUBCOURSE 8.

    Reserved.

W 3.61:date&lesson no.
ARMY CORRESPONDENCE COURSES: SUBCOURSE 9.

    Reserved.

W 3.62:date&lesson no.
ARMY CORRESPONDENCE COURSES: SUBCOURSE 10. MEDICAL, BASIC COURSE.

W 3.63:vol.
BASIC FIELD MANUAL.

    Later W 1.33

W 3.63/2:CT
FIELD MANUALS.

    Superseded by W 1.33

Army Extension Courses

W 3.64:subcourse no.&lesson no.
EXTENSION COURSE OF ADJUTANT GENERAL'S DEPARTMENT, LESSON ASSIGNMENT SHEETS.

    Later W 1.70

W 3.64/2:
EXTENSION COURSE OF ADJUTANT GENERAL'S DEPARTMENT, LESSON ASSIGNMENT SHEETS, 1932– 33.

W 3.65:subcourse no.&lesson no.
EXTENSION COURSE OF JUDGE ADVOCATE GENERAL'S DEPARTMENT, LESSON ASSIGNMENT SHEETS.

W 3.65/2
EXTENSION COURSE OF JUDGE ADVOCATE GENERAL'S DEPARTMENT, LESSON ASSIGNMENT SHEETS, 1935– 36.

W 3.66:subcourse no.&lesson no.
EXTENSION COURSE OF MILITARY INTELLIGENCE DIVISION, GENERAL STAFF, LESSON ASSIGNMENT SHEETS.

W 3.67:subcourse no.&lesson no.
EXTENSION COURSE OF AIR CORPS SCHOOLS, LESSON ASSIGNMENT SHEETS.

W 3.67/2:subcourse no.&lesson no.
EXTENSION COURSE OF AIR CORPS SCHOOLS, LESSON ASSIGNMENT SHEETS, 1932– 33.

W 3.67/3:subcourse no.&lesson no.
EXTENSION COURSE OF AIR CORPS SCHOOLS, LESSON ASSIGNMENT SHEETS, 1934– 35.

W 3.67/4:subcourse no.&lesson no.
EXTENSION COURSE OF AIR CORPS SCHOOLS, 1935– 1936.

W 3.68:subcourse no.&lesson no.
EXTENSION COURSE OF CAVALRY SCHOOL.

W 3.68/2:subcourse no.&lesson no.
EXTENSION COURSE OF CAVALRY SCHOOL, 1934– 35.

W 3.68/3:subcourse no.&lesson no.
EXTENSION COURSE OF CAVALRY SCHOOL, 1937– 38.

W 3.69:subcourse no.&lesson no.
EXTENSION COURSE OF COAST ARTILLERY SCHOOL.

W 3.69/2
EXTENSION COURSE OF COAST ARTILLERY SCHOOL, 1938– 39.

W 3.70:subcourse no.&lesson no.
EXTENSION COURSE OF FIELD ARTILLERY SCHOOL.

W 3.70/2
EXTENSION COURSE OF FIELD ARTILLERY SCHOOL, 1932– 33.

W 3.71:subcourse no.&lesson no.
EXTENSION COURSE OF MEDICAL FIELD SERVICE SCHOOL, LESSON ASSIGNMENT SHEETS.

W 3.71/2:subcourse no.&lesson no.
EXTENSION COURSE OF MEDICAL FIELD SERVICE SCHOOL, LESSON ASSIGNMENT SHEETS, 1932– 33.

W 3.71/3:subcourse no.&lesson no.
EXTENSION COURSE OF MEDICAL FIELD SERVICE SCHOOL, LESSON ASSIGNMENT SHEETS, 1933– 34.

W 3.71/4:subcourse no.&lesson no.
EXTENSION COURSE OF MEDICAL FIELD SERVICE SCHOOL, LESSON ASSIGNMENT SHEETS, 1934– 35.

W 3.71/5
EXTENSION COURSE OF MEDICAL FIELD SERVICE SCHOOL, LESSON ASSIGNMENT SHEETS, 1935– 36.

W 3.72:subcourse no.&lesson no.
EXTENSION COURSE OF QUARTERMASTER CORPS SCHOOL.

W 3.72/2
EXTENSION COURSE OF QUARTERMASTER CORPS SCHOOL, 1938– 39.

W 3.73:subcourse no.&lesson no.
EXTENSION COURSE OF SIGNAL SCHOOL.

W 3.73/2:subcourse no.&lesson no.
EXTENSION COURSE OF SIGNAL SCHOOL, 1932– 33.

W 3.74:subcourse no.&lesson no.
EXTENSION COURSE OF FINANCE SCHOOL, 1932– 33.

W 3.74/2:subcourse no.&lesson no.
EXTENSION COURSE OF FINANCE SCHOOL, 1933– 34.

W 3.74/3
EXTENSION COURSE OF FINANCE SCHOOL, 1935– 36.

W 3.75:subcourse no.&lesson no.
EXTENSION COURSE OF ENGINEER SCHOOL.

Adjutant-General's Department (Continued)

W 3.76:nos.
PRACTICE BOOKLETS.

W 3.77:v.nos.
ARMY POSTAL BULLETIN. [Semimonthly]

W 3.78:nos.
BOOKLETS.

W 3.79:nos.
CLASSIFICATION MEMORANDUM.

W 3.80:date
OUR WAR. [Monthly]

W 3.81:date
OFFICERS OF ARMY IN OR NEAR DISTRICT OF COLUMBIA.

    Earlier W 1.11

W 3.82:nos.
INFORMATION BULLETINS. [Weekly]

    Later M 108.7

W 3.83:v.nos.
U.S. ARMY RECRUITING SERVICE LETTER.
    Later M 108.76

W 3.84:film nos.
SELLING ARMY AND AIR FORCE CAREERS.
    Earlier M 108.79

W 3.84/2:film nos.
MEETING LEADERS GUIDE.
    Earlier M 108.79/2

CHICKAMAUGA AND CHATTANOOGA NATIONAL MILITARY PARK COMMISSION (1890– 1922)

W 4.1:date
ANNUAL REPORTS.

W 4.2:CT
GENERAL PUBLICATIONS.

W 4.3:
BULLETINS.

W 4.4:
CIRCULARS.

SUBSISTENCE DEPARTMENT
(1775– 1912)

W 5.1:date
ANNUAL REPORTS OF COMMISSARY GENERAL.

W 5.2:CT
GENERAL PUBLICATIONS.

W 5.3:
BULLETINS [none issued].

W 5.4:date
CIRCULARS.

W 5.5:date
MANUAL FOR ARMY COOKS.

W 5.6:date
MANUAL FOR SUBSISTENCE DEPARTMENT.

W 5.6/2:nos.
– CHANGES.

W 5.7:date
REGULATIONS FOR SUBSISTENCE DEPARTMENT.

W 5.8:date
ROSTER OF SUBSISTENCE DEPARTMENT.

BUREAU OF INSULAR AFFAIRS
(1902– 1939)

CREATION AND AUTHORITY

The Division of Customs and Insular Affairs was established within the War Department on Dec. 13, 1898. It became the Division of Insular Affairs on Dec. 10, 1900. By act of Congress, approved July 1, 1902 (32 Stat. 712), the name was changed to Bureau of Insular Affairs. The Bureau was abolished and its functions transferred to the Division of Territories and Island Possession of the Department of the Interior by Reorganization Plan No. 2 of 1939, effective July 1, 1939.

W 6.1:date
ANNUAL REPORTS.

W 6.2:CT
GENERAL PUBLICATIONS.

W 6.3:
BULLETINS.

W 6.4:nos.
CIRCULARS.

W 6.5:CT
IMMIGRATION REGULATIONS.

W 6.6:CT
TRANSLATIONS.

W 6.7:date
MONTHLY SUMMARY OF COMMERCE OF PORTO RICO.

W 6.8:date
QUARTERLY SUMMARY OF COMMERCE OF PHILIPPINE ISLANDS.

W 6.9:date
MONTHLY SUMMARY OF COMMERCE OF CUBA.

W 6.10:nos.
PHILIPPINE INSURGENT RECORDS.

W 6.11:date
PHILIPPINE TARIFFS.

W 6.12:Cong.
ACTS OF CONGRESS, TREATIES, AND PROCLAMATIONS RELATING TO NONCONTIGUOUS TERRITORY.

Dominican Customs Receivership

W 6.13/1:date
ANNUAL REPORTS.
Later I 35.14/1

W 6.13/2:CT
GENERAL PUBLICATIONS.

W 6.13/3:
BULLETINS.

W 6.13/4:
CIRCULARS.
W 6.13/5:date
SUMMARY OF COMMERCE OF DOMINICAN REPUBLIC.

Insular Affairs Bureau (Continued)

W 6.14:CT
PAPERS IN RE.

Haitian Customs Receivership

W 6.15/1:date
ANNUAL REPORTS.

W 6.15/2:CT
GENERAL PUBLICATIONS.

W 6.15/3:nos.
BULLETINS.

W 6.15/4:nos.
CIRCULARS.

ENGINEER DEPARTMENT
(1802– 1947)

CREATION AND AUTHORITY

The Corps of Engineers was established by act of Congress, approved March 16, 1802.

W 7.1:date
ANNUAL REPORTS.
Later M 110.1

W 7.1/2:date
INDEXES TO ANNUAL REPORTS.

W 7.2:CT
GENERAL PUBLICATIONS.
Later M 110.2

W 7.3:
BULLETINS [none issued].

W 7.4:date
CIRCULARS.

W 7.5:CT
EXPLORATIONS AND SURVEYS.

W 7.6/1:C.S.
LAWS AFFECTING CORPS OF ENGINEERS.

W 7.6/2:C.S.
LAWS RELATING TO CONSTRUCTION OF BRIDGES OVER NAVIGABLE WATERS, – CONGRESS, – SESSION.

W 7.6/3:CT
LAWS (compilations and miscellaneous).

W 7.7:date
STATEMENT SHOWING RANK DUTIES AND ADDRESSES OF OFFICERS OF CORPS OF ENGINEERS. [Quarterly]

W 7.8:date
GENERAL ORDERS.
Later M 110.14

W 7.8/2:chap.nos.
ORDERS AND REGULATIONS, SINCE 1933.

W 7.8/3:chap.nos.
ORDERS AND REGULATIONS, NEW EDITION.
Later D 103.6/2

W 7.9:date
SPECIAL ORDERS.
Later M 110.11

W 7.10:nos.
PROFESSIONAL PAPERS.

W 7.11/1:date
REGULATIONS (general).

W 7.11/2:CT
REGULATIONS AND INSTRUCTIONS (special).

W 7.11/3:date
COMPILATIONS AND DIGESTS OF ORDERS, CIRCULARS, REGULATIONS, AND DECISIONS.

W 7.11/4:date
CHANGES IN ENGINEER REGULATIONS.

W 7.12:date
INDEX TO RIVER AND HARBOR ACT APPROVED.

W 7.13:CT
MAPS AND DRAWINGS.

W 7.13/2:nos.
EEL RIVER CHARTS

W 7.13/3:nos.
OHIO RIVER CHARTS.

W 7.13/4:nos.
OHIO RIVER FLOOD PLAIN CHARTS.

W 7.13/5:nos.
WABASH RIVER CHARTS.

W 7.13/6:nos.
WHITE RIVER CHARTS.

W 7.14:v.nos.
EXPLORATIONS AND SURVEYS FOR RAILROAD FROM MISSISSIPPI RIVER TO PACIFIC OCEAN.

W 7.15:nos.
INFORMATION CIRCULAR.

Engineer School

W 7.16/1:date
ANNUAL REPORTS.

W 7.16/2:nos.
OCCASIONAL PAPERS.

W 7.16/3:nos.
BULLETINS.

W 7.16/4:nos.
CIRCULARS.

W 7.16/5:vol.
PROFESSIONAL MEMOIRS.

W 7.16/6:no.
– SUPPLEMENTS.

W 7.16/7:CT
BIBLIOGRAPHIES.

Engineer Department (Continued)

W 7.17:date
DATES OF RETIREMENT OF OFFICERS OF CORPS
OF ENGINEERS.

W 7.18:nos.
STANDARD SPECIFICATIONS.

W 7.18/2:CT
SPECIFICATIONS (miscellaneous).

W 7.18/3:nos.
GENERAL SPECIFICATIONS.

W 7.18/4:date
INDEXES OF GENERAL SPECIFICATIONS.

> Later M 110.10

W 7.19:nos.
INSTRUCTION BOOKS.

W 7.20:nos.
INSTRUCTION MANUALS.

W 7.21:nos.
PORT SERIES.

> See also W 7.34, Port and Terminal Facilities.

W 7.21/2:nos.
PORT SERIES (2d series).

W 7.22:nos.
MISCELLANEOUS SERIES.

> Later M 110.12

W 7.23:nos.
TRANSPORTATION SERIES.

> Later M 110.17

W 7.24:pts.
CORPS OF ENGINEERS SUPPLY CATALOGUES.

W 7.25:nos.
LAKE SERIES.

> Later D 103.18

W 7.26:date
ST. MARY'S FALLS CANAL, MICHIGAN, STATISTI-
CAL REPORT OF LAKE COMMERCE.

> Later M 110.16

W 7.27:nos.
HYDROLOGIC PAMPHLETS.

W 7.28:nos.
BEACH EROSION BOARD, PAPERS.

W 7.29:nos.
BEACH EROSION BOARD, TECHNICAL REPORTS.

> Later M 110.307

W 7.30:nos.
BLUE BOOKS.

W 7.31:CT
APPLICABLE DRAWINGS FOR ENGINEER EQUIP-
MENT.

W 7.31/2:CT
GENERAL DRAWINGS OF SNOW REMOVAL EQUIP-
MENT.

W 7.32:CT
POSTERS.

W 7.32/3:nos.
ARMY MAP SERVICE, A.M.S. MEMORANDUM.

W 7.33:CT
ARMY MAP SERVICE PUBLICATIONS.

W 7.33/2:nos.
AMS TECHNICAL MANUALS.
> Later D 103.20/2

W 7.33/4:nos.
ARMY MAP SERVICE BULLETINS.

> Later M 110.20

W 7.34:CT
PORT AND TERMINAL FACILITIES.

> Also see Port Series W 7.21

W 7.35:pt.nos.&chap.nos.
ENGINEERING MANUAL FOR CIVIL WORKS.

> Printed and proc.
> Later M 110.7

W 7.36:pt.nos.&chap.nos.
ENGINEERING MANUAL FOR WAR DEPARTMENT
CONSTRUCTION.

> Printed and proc.
> Later M 110.13

W 7.37:nos.
GUIDE SPECIFICATIONS FOR CIVIL WORKS.

> Later M 110.9

W 7.38:v.nos.
BULLETIN OF BEACH EROSION BOARD. [Quarterly]

> Later M 110.303

W 7.39:nos.
STRATEGIC ENGINEERING STUDIES, SES.

> Proc.

GEOGRAPHICAL SURVEYS WEST
OF 100th MERIDIAN
(1869–1884)

W 8.1:date
ANNUAL REPORTS.

W 8.2:CT
GENERAL PUBLICATIONS.

W 8.3:
BULLETINS.

W 8.4:
CIRCULARS.

W 8.5:v.nos.
FINAL REPORTS OR MONOGRAPHS.

INSPECTOR GENERAL'S
DEPARTMENT
(1874–1947)

W 9.1/1:date
ANNUAL REPORTS TO SECRETARY OF WAR.

W 9.1/2:date
ANNUAL REPORTS TO GENERAL COMMANDING
ARMY.

W 9.2:CT
GENERAL PUBLICATIONS.

W 9.3:
BULLETINS.

W 9.4:
CIRCULARS.

W 9.5:date
INSPECTION OF SEVERAL BRANCHES OF NATIONAL
HOME FOR DISABLED VOLUNTEER SOLDIERS.

W 9.6:nos.
INSPECTION STANDARDS. MIMEOGRAPHED.

W 9.7:nos.
INSPECTION GUIDES. MIMEOGRAPHED.

> Supersedes Inspection Standards (W 9.6).

W 9.8:v.nos.
INFORMATION CIRCULARS.

W 9.8/2:date
PRACTICAL CHECK LISTS. [Monthly]

> Supplement to W 9.8

JUDGE ADVOCATE GENERAL'S
DEPARTMENT
(1884– 1947)

CREATION AND AUTHORITY

> While the work of the Judge Advocate Gen-
eral can be traced back to 1775, the formal organization of a department did not occur until Mar.
2, 1849, when an act of Congress established
the office of the Judge Advocate General. The
act of Congress, approved July 17, 1862 reorganized the office and in 1864, the Bureau of Military Justice was established, to which the Judge
Advocate General and his functions were transferred. In 1884, the Bureau of military Justice and
the corps of judge advocates were merged into
the Judge Advocate General's Department.

W 10.1:date
ANNUAL REPORTS.
> Later M 107.1

W 10.2:CT
GENERAL PUBLICATIONS.
> Later M 107.2

W 10.3:vol.
BULLETINS. [Monthly]
> Prior to Jan.-June 1942, W 10.7
> Later M 107.3

W 10.4:
CIRCULARS.

W 10.5:date
MANUAL FOR COURTS-MARTIAL.
> Later M 107.7

W 10.5/2:date of edition
CHANGES [in] MANUAL FOR COURTSMARTIAL (numbered).

W 10.6:CT
COURTS-MARTIAL, COURTS OF INQUIRY, AND MILI-
TARY COMMISSIONS.

W 10.7:date
DIGEST OF OPINIONS OF JUDGE-ADVOCATE-
GENERAL.
> Later W 10.3

W 10.8:date
DIGEST OF OPINIONS OF JUDGE-ADVOCATE-
GENERAL, ARMY. [Monthly]

W 10.9:date
OPINIONS OF JUDGE ADVOCATE GENERAL, ARMY.
[Monthly]

W 10.10:incl.dates
CONSOLIDATED INDEX OF OPINIONS AND DIGESTS
OF OPINION OF JUDGE ADVOCATE GENERAL.

LIBRARY
(1880–1908)

W 11.1:date
ANNUAL REPORTS (none issued).

W 11.2:CT
GENERAL PUBLICATIONS.

W 11.3:
BULLETINS.

W 11.4:
CIRCULARS.

W 11.5:nos.
SUBJECT CATALOGUES.

W 11.6:date
CATALOGUES (miscellaneous).

W 11.7:date
ROUGH LIST OF MORE IMPORTANT ADDITIONS.

MILITARY ACADEMY
(1802–1947)

W 12.1/1:date
ANNUAL REPORT OF BOARD OF VISITORS.

> Later M 109.1

W 12.1/2:date
ANNUAL REPORT OF SUPERINTENDENT.

W 12.1/3:date
ANNUAL REPORT OF INSPECTOR.

W 12.2:CT
GENERAL PUBLICATIONS.

> Later M 100.2

W 12.3:
BULLETINS.

W 12.4:date
CIRCULARS.

W 12.5:date
OFFICIAL REGISTER OF OFFICERS AND CADETS.

> Later M 109.11

W 12.6/1:date
REGULATIONS FOR MILITARY ACADEMY (general).

W 12.6/2:CT
REGULATIONS (special).

> Later M 109.6

W 12.7:date
LIST OF CADETS ADMITTED (cumulative).

W 12.8:date
ROSTER OF OFFICERS AND TROOPS.

W 12.9:date
INFORMATION RELATIVE TO APPOINTMENT AND ADMISSION OF CADETS OF MILITARY ACADEMY.

W 12.10:date
GENERAL ORDERS.
> Later M 109.7

W 12.11:date
SPECIAL ORDERS.
> Later M 109.8

W 12.12:date
REGISTER OF OFFICERS AND GRADUATES (triennial).

W 12.13:date
GENERAL COURT-MARTIAL ORDERS.

> Later M 109.10

W 12.14:date
SPECIAL COURT-MARTIAL ORDERS.

W 12.15:date
MEMORANDUM.

> Later M 109.9

W 12.16:date
INDEX TO GENERAL ORDERS, SPECIAL ORDERS, SPECIAL AND GENERAL COURT-MARTIAL ORDERS AND MEMORANDA.

CALIFORNIA DEPARTMENT
(1858–1865, 1904–1907)

W 13.1:date
ANNUAL REPORTS.

W 13.2:CT
GENERAL PUBLICATIONS.

W 13.3:nos.
BULLETINS [none issued].

W 13.4:date
CIRCULARS.

W 13.5:date
GENERAL ORDERS.

W 13.6:date
SPECIAL ORDERS.

W 13.7:date
ROSTER OF TROOPS.

DEPARTMENT OF THE COLORADO
(1893–1903)

W 14.1:date
ANNUAL REPORTS.

W 14.2:CT
GENERAL PUBLICATIONS.

W 14.3:nos.
BULLETINS [none issued].

W 14.4:date
CIRCULARS [none issued].

W 14.5:date
GENERAL ORDERS.

W 14.6:date
SPECIAL ORDERS.

W 14.7:date
ROSTER OF TROOPS.

DEPARTMENT OF THE COLUMBIA
(1865–1904)

W 15.1:date
ANNUAL REPORTS.

W 15.2:CT
GENERAL PUBLICATIONS.

W 15.3:nos.
BULLETINS [none issued].

W 15.4:date
CIRCULARS [none issued].

W 15.5:date
GENERAL ORDERS.

W 15.6:date
SPECIAL ORDERS.

W 15.7:date
ROSTER OF TROOPS.

DEPARTMENT OF DAKOTA
(1867–1904)

W 16.1:date
ANNUAL REPORTS.

W 16.2:CT
GENERAL PUBLICATIONS.

W 16.3:nos.
BULLETINS [none issued].

W 16.4:date
CIRCULARS [none issued].

W 16.5:date
GENERAL ORDERS.

W 16.6:date
SPECIAL ORDERS.

W 16.7:date
ROSTER OF TROOPS.

DEPARTMENT OF THE EAST
(1853–1903)

W 17.1:date
ANNUAL REPORTS.

W 17.2:CT
GENERAL PUBLICATIONS.

W 17.3:
BULLETINS.

W 17.4:date
CIRCULARS.

W 17.5:date
GENERAL ORDERS.

W 17.6:date
SPECIAL ORDERS.

W 17.7:date
ROSTER OF TROOPS.

W 17.8:nos.
TRAINING CIRCULARS.

     See W 99.12/8 for later Training Circulars, issued by 2d. Corps Area.

W 17.9:
GENERAL COURT-MARTIAL ORDERS.

DEPARTMENT OF THE GULF
(1862– 1911)

W 18.1:date
ANNUAL REPORTS.

W 18.2:CT
GENERAL PUBLICATIONS.

W 18.3:nos.
BULLETINS [none issued].

W 18.4:date
CIRCULARS.

W 18.5:date
GENERAL ORDERS.

W 18.6:date
SPECIAL ORDERS.

W 18.7:date
ROSTER OF TROOPS.

DEPARTMENT OF THE LAKES
(1866– 1911)

W 19.1:date
ANNUAL REPORTS.

W 19.2:CT
GENERAL PUBLICATIONS.

W 19.3:nos.
BULLETINS [none issued].

W 19.4:date
CIRCULARS.

W 19.5:date
GENERAL ORDERS.

W 19.6:date
SPECIAL ORDERS.

W 19.7:date
ROSTER OF TROOPS.

DEPARTMENT OF THE MISSOURI
(1862– 1911)

W 20.1:date
ANNUAL REPORTS.

W 20.2:CT
GENERAL PUBLICATIONS.

W 20.3:nos.
BULLETINS [none issued].

W 20.4:date
CIRCULARS.

W 20.5:date
GENERAL ORDERS.

W 20.6:date
SPECIAL ORDERS.

W 20.7:date
ROSTER OF TROOPS.

PHILIPPINES DIVISION
(1900– 1912)

W 21.1:date
ANNUAL REPORTS.

W 21.2:CT
GENERAL PUBLICATIONS.

W 21.3:nos.
BULLETINS.

W 21.4:
CIRCULARS.

W 21.4/1:nos.
CIRCULARS, EXPEDITIONARY FORCES [none issued].

W 21.4/2:nos.
CIRCULARS, EXPEDITIONARY FORCES AND DEPARTMENT OF THE PACIFIC.

W 21.4/3:date
CIRCULARS, DEPARTMENT OF THE PACIFIC AND 8th ARMY CORPS.

W 21.4/4:nos.
CIRCULARS, DIVISION OF THE PHILIPPINES.

W 21.4/5:date
CIRCULARS, INDEPENDENT DIVISION 8th ARMY CORPS.

W 21.4/6:nos.
CIRCULARS, 8th ARMY CORPS.

W 21.4/7:nos.
CIRCULARS, DEPARTMENT OF THE PACIFIC [none issued].

W 21.4/8:nos.
CIRCULARS, DEPARTMENT OF THE PACIFIC AND OFFICE OF MILITARY GOVERNOR IN PHILIPPINE ISLANDS [none issued].

W 21.4/9:date
CIRCULARS, MILITARY GOVERNOR IN PHILIPPINE ISLANDS.

W 21.5:
GENERAL ORDERS.

W 21.5/1:nos.
GENERAL ORDERS, EXPEDITIONARY FORCES.

W 21.5/2:nos.
GENERAL ORDERS, EXPEDITIONARY FORCES AND DEPARTMENT OF THE PACIFIC.

W 21.5/3:date
GENERAL ORDERS, DEPARTMENT OF THE PACIFIC AND 8th ARMY CORPS.

W 21.5/4:nos.
GENERAL ORDERS, DIVISION OF THE PHILIPPINES.

W 21.5/5:nos.
GENERAL ORDERS, INDEPENDENT DIVISION 8th ARMY CORPS.

W 21.5/6:nos.
GENERAL ORDERS, 8th ARMY CORPS.

W 21.5/7:nos.
GENERAL ORDERS, DEPARTMENT OF THE PACIFIC.

W 21.5/8:nos.
GENERAL ORDERS, DEPARTMENT OF THE PACIFIC AND OFFICE OF MILITARY GOVERNOR IN PHILIPPINE ISLANDS.

W 21.5/9:date
GENERAL ORDERS, MILITARY GOVERNOR IN PHILIPPINE ISLANDS.

W 21.6:date
SPECIAL ORDERS.

W 21.7/1:date
ROSTER OF TROOPS.

W 21.7/2:date
OFFICERS OF ARMY, STATIONS OF TROOPS, AND LIST OF GARRISONED TOWNS.

W 21.8:nos.
MILITARY INFORMATION DIVISION GENERAL STAFF (Manila) BULLETINS.

DEPARTMENT OF THE PLATTE
(1866– 1898)

W 22.1:date
ANNUAL REPORTS.

W 22.2:CT
GENERAL PUBLICATIONS.

W 22.3:nos.
BULLETINS [none issued].

W 22.4:date
CIRCULARS.

W 22.5:date
GENERAL ORDERS.

W 22.6:
SPECIAL ORDERS.

W 22.7:date
ROSTER OF TROOPS.

DEPARTMENT OF PORTO RICO
(1898– 1900)

W 23.1:date
ANNUAL REPORTS.

W 23.2:CT
GENERAL PUBLICATIONS.

W 23.3:nos.
BULLETINS [none issued].

W 23.4:date
CIRCULARS.

W 23.5:date
GENERAL ORDERS.

W 23.6:date
SPECIAL ORDERS.

W 23.7:date
ROSTER OF TROOPS.

DEPARTMENT OF TEXAS
(1853– 1911)

W 24.1:date
ANNUAL REPORTS.

W 24.2:CT
GENERAL PUBLICATIONS.

W 24.3:nos.
BULLETINS [none issued].

W 24.4:date
CIRCULARS.

W 24.5:date
GENERAL ORDERS.

W 24.6:date
SPECIAL ORDERS.

W 24.7:date
ROSTER OF TROOPS.

W 24.8:date
STATION LIST.

DEPARTMENT OF CUBA
(1898– 1902)

W 25.1:date
ANNUAL REPORTS (military).

W 25.2:CT
GENERAL PUBLICATIONS.

W 25.3:nos.
BULLETINS.

W 25.4:date
CIRCULARS.

W 25.5:date
GENERAL ORDERS.

W 25.6:date
SPECIAL ORDERS.

W 25.7:date
ROSTER OF TROOPS.

W 25.8:date
CIVIL REPORTS.

W 25.9:date
[CIVIL ORDERS].

WAR PLANS DIVISION
(1892– 1903)

W 26.1:date
ANNUAL REPORTS.

W 26.2:CT
GENERAL PUBLICATIONS.

W 26.3/1:nos.
BULLETINS OLD SERIES.

W 26.3/2:nos.
BULLETINS NEW SERIES.

W 26.4:
CIRCULARS.

W 26.5:date
INDEX OF SPECIAL MILITARY SUBJECTS CONTAINED IN BOOKS, PAMPHLETS AND PERIODICALS RECEIVED DURING QUARTER ENDING [date].

W 26.6:CT
MAPS.

W 26.7:nos.
MONTHLY LIST OF MILITARY INFORMATION.

W 26.8:CT
STATEMENT OF A PROPER MILITARY POLICY FOR THE UNITED STATES.

W 26.9:CT
REGULATIONS AND INSTRUCTIONS.

W 26.9/2:CT
CHANGES IN REGULATIONS AND INSTRUCTIONS (numbered).

W 26.10:nos.
FIELD ARTILLERY NOTES.

Changes from W 3.39

W 26.11:nos.
TRAINING CIRCULAR.

W 26.12:CT
BLANK FORMS AND RECORD BOOKS.

Historical Branch

W 26.15/1:date
ANNUAL REPORTS.

W 26.15/2:CT
GENERAL PUBLICATIONS.

W 26.15/3:
BULLETINS.

W 26.15/4:
CIRCULARS.

W 26.15/5:nos.
MONOGRAPHS.

W 26.15/6:pt.nos.
MONOGRAPH SERIES ON AMERICAN MILITARY PARTICIPATION IN WORLD WAR.

Training and Instructions Branch

W 26.16/1:date
ANNUAL REPORTS.

W 26.16/2:CT
GENERAL PUBLICATIONS.

W 26.16/3:
BULLETINS.

W 26.16/4:
CIRCULARS.

W 26.16/5:nos.
MILITARY NOTES ON TRAINING AND INSTRUCTION.

Education and Special Training Committee

W 26.17/1:date
ANNUAL REPORTS.

W 26.17/2:CT
GENERAL PUBLICATIONS.

W 26.17/3:
BULLETINS.

W 26.17/4:
CIRCULARS.

W 26.17/5:date
INSTRUCTION MANUALS.

Education and Recreation Branch

W 26.18/1:date
ANNUAL REPORTS.

W 26.18/2:CT
GENERAL PUBLICATIONS.

W 26.18/3:
BULLETINS.

W 26.18/4:
CIRCULARS.

MILITARY PRISON, FORT LEAVENWORTH
(1874– 1909)

W 27.1:date
ANNUAL REPORTS.

W 27.2:CT
GENERAL PUBLICATIONS.

W 27.3:
BULLETINS.

W 27.4:
CIRCULARS.

GENERAL SERVICE SCHOOLS
(1881– 1947)

W 28.1:date
ANNUAL REPORTS.

W 28.2:CT
GENERAL PUBLICATIONS.

W 28.3:date
BULLETINS.

W 28.4:date
CIRCULARS.

W 28.5:date
GENERAL ORDERS.

W 28.6:date
SPECIAL ORDERS.

W 28.7:date
ROSTERS.

W 28.8:date&nos.
INSTRUCTION SHEETS.

W 28.9:date&nos.
COMBAT ORDERS.

W 28.10:vol.
QUARTERLY REVIEW OF MILITARY LITERATURE.

W 28.11:date
COMMAND AND GENERAL STAFF SCHOOL, FORT LEAVENWORTH, SCHEDULE.

W 28.11/2:nos.
SCHEDULE, GENERAL STAFF COURSE.
Early issues: Special Course.

W 28.11/3:nos.
PROGRAMS AND SCHEDULES, SERVICES OF SUPPLY STAFF COURSE.

W 28.12:date
LIBRARY BULLETIN.

W 28.13:incl.dts.&nos.
COMMAND AND GENERAL STAFF SCHOOL, FORT LEAVENWORTH, SCHOOL MEMORANDUM.

W 28.14:date&nos.
COMMAND AND GENERAL STAFF SCHOOL, FORT LEAVENWORTH, MEMORANDUM.

COAST ARTILLERY SCHOOL
(1867–1916)

W 29.1:date
ANNUAL REPORTS.

W 29.2:CT
GENERAL PUBLICATIONS.

W 29.3:
BULLETINS.

W 29.4:nos.
CIRCULARS.

W 29.5:v.nos.
JOURNAL OF UNITED STATES ARTILLERY. [Bimonthly]

W 29.6:date
REGULATIONS AND PROGRAMME OF INSTRUCTION.

W 29.7:nos.
ARTILLERY NOTES.

W 29.8:nos.
ARTILLERY MEMORANDA.

MOUNTED SERVICE SCHOOL
(1887–1947)

W 30.1:date
ANNUAL REPORTS.

W 30.2:CT
GENERAL PUBLICATIONS.

W 30.3:
BULLETINS.

W 30.4:date
CIRCULARS.

W 30.5/1:date
REGULATIONS (general).

W 30.5/2:CT
RULES, REGULATIONS AND INSTRUCTIONS.

W 30.6:date
GENERAL ORDERS.

W 30.7:date
SPECIAL ORDERS.

W 30.8:vol.
MAILING LIST. [Quarterly]

W 30.9:nos.
CAVALRY SCHOOL, FORT RILEY, MAP PROBLEMS, 1932–33.

W 30.9/2:nos.
MAP PROBLEMS, 1933–34.

W 30.9/3:nos.
MAP PROBLEMS, 1934–35.

W 30.9/4:nos.
MAP PROBLEMS, 1935–36.

W 30.9/5:nos.
MAP PROBLEMS, 1936–37.

W 30.9/6:nos.
MAP PROBLEMS, 1937–38.

W 30.10:nos.
CALVARY SCHOOL, FORT RILEY, TERRAIN EXERCISES, 1932–33.

W 30.10/2:nos.
CALVARY SCHOOL, FORT RILEY, TERRAIN EXERCISES, 1933–34.

W 30.10/3:nos.
CALVARY SCHOOL, FORT RILEY, TERRAIN EXERCISES, 1934–35.

W 30.10/4:nos.
CALVARY SCHOOL, FORT RILEY, TERRAIN EXERCISES, 1935–36.

W 30.10/5:nos.
CALVARY SCHOOL, FORT RILEY, TERRAIN EXERCISES, 1936–37.

W 30.10/6:nos.
CALVARY SCHOOL, FORT RILEY, TERRAIN EXERCISES, 1937–38.

W 30.11:CT
POSTERS.

MISSISSIPPI RIVER COMMISSION
(1879–1947)

CREATION AND AUTHORITY

The Mississippi River Commission was established by act of Congress, approved June 28, 1879 (21 Stat. 37), and placed under the supervision of the Chief of Engineers.

W 31.1:date
ANNUAL REPORTS.
Later M 110.201

W 31.2:CT
GENERAL PUBLICATIONS.
Later M 110.202

W 31.3:
BULLETINS.

W 31.4:
CIRCULARS.

W 31.5:date
STAGES OF THE MISSISSIPPI RIVER AND ITS PRINCIPAL TRIBUTARIES.
Later M 110.207

W 31.6:date
TABULATED RESULTS OF DISCHARGE MEASUREMENTS.

W 31.7:CT
MAPS.
Later M 110.208

W 31.7/2:le.
LOCATION SHEETS OF MAPS AND CHARTS.

W 31.8:nos.
WATERWAYS EXPERIMENT STATION, VICKSBURG– PAPERS.

W 31.9:CT
MAP OF ALLUVIAL VALLEY OF MISSISSIPPI RIVER, QUADRANGLES.
Later D 108.308

W 31.9/2:date
INDEX MAP OF QUADRANGLES.
Later D 108.308/2

W 31.10:v.nos.&nos.
THE EXPERIMENT STATION HYDRAULICS BULLETIN.

MISSOURI RIVER COMMISSION
(1884–1902)

W 32.1:date
ANNUAL REPORTS.

W 32.2:CT
GENERAL PUBLICATIONS.

W 32.3:
BULLETINS.

W 32.4:
CIRCULARS.

W 32.5:CT
MAPS.

W 32.6:date
STAGES OF MISSOURI RIVER.

NORTHERN AND NORTHWESTERN LAKES SURVEY
(1841–1947)

W 33.1:date
ANNUAL REPORTS.
Later M 110.101

W 33.2:CT
GENERAL PUBLICATIONS.
Later M 110.102

W 33.3:nos.
BULLETINS.
Later M 110.103

W 33.4:
CIRCULARS.

W 33.5:nos.
REGULATIONS FOR SALE OF LAKE SURVEY CHARTS.

W 33.6:chart nos.
CHARTS.
Earlier W 33.6/1 and W 33.8

W 33.6/1:nos.
CHARTS OF ST. LAWRENCE RIVER (numbered).
Changed to W 33.6

W 33.6/2:nos.
CHARTS OF ST. MARY'S RIVER.
Changed to W 33.6

W 33.7/1:date
GENERAL CHART OF NORTHERN AND NORTHWESTERN LAKES [and rivers].
Changed to W 33.6

W 33.7/2:letters
CHARTS OF GREAT LAKES.

Changed to W 33.6

W 33.7/3:letters&nos.
COAST CHARTS OF GREAT LAKES.

Changed to W 33.6

W 33.8:CT by names of places
HARBOR CHARTS AND CHARTS OF SPECIAL LOCALITIES.

W 33.9:chart nos.
NORTHERN AND NORTHWESTERN LAKES SURVEY, INTERNATIONAL BOUNDARY WATERS.

ORDNANCE DEPARTMENT
(1812– 1947)

CREATION AND AUTHORITY

The Ordnance Department was established within the War Department by act of Congress, approved May 14, 1812. During the period from 1821 to 1832, it was a part of the Artillery. The Army Reorganization Act of 1950 (64 Stat. 263) designated it the Ordnance Corps, although it is sometimes referred to as the Ordnance Department.

W 34.1/1:date
ANNUAL REPORTS.

Later M 111.1

W 34.1/2:date
INDEXES TO ANNUAL REPORTS.

W 34.2:CT
GENERAL PUBLICATIONS.

Later M 111.2

W 34.3:
BULLETINS.

W 34.4:date&nos.
CIRCULARS.

W 34.4/2:date
CIRCULARS [new series, 1913–].

W 34.4/3:nos.
ORDNANCE DEPARTMENT CIRCULARS (Oct. 20, 1930–).

Mimeographed.

W 34.4/4:nos.
ORDNANCE DEPARTMENT CIRCULARS (Jan. 1, 1943–).

W 34.5:CT
INSTRUCTIONS, DESCRIPTIONS AND HANDBOOKS.

W 34.6:date
LAWS.

W 34.7/1:date
ORDNANCE MANUAL.

W 34.7/2:date
ORDNANCE SUPPLY MANUAL.

W 34.7/3:date
MANUAL FOR USE OF INSPECTORS OF ORDNANCE.

W 34.7/4:CT
MANUAL FOR USE OF INSPECTORS OF ORDNANCE (miscellaneous).

W 34.8:v.nos.
NOTES ON CONSTRUCTION OF ORDNANCE.

W 34.9:date&nos.
ORDNANCE ORDERS.

W 34.9/2:nos.
ORDERS (August 15, 1930–).

Mimeographed.

W 34.9/3:nos.
ORDERS (Jan. 2, 1943–).

Later M 111.8

W 34.10:nos.
ORDNANCE MEMORANDA.

W 34.10/2
ORDNANCE OFFICE MEMORANDA.

W 34.11:v.nos.
ORDNANCE NOTES.

W 34.12/1:date
REGULATIONS FOR GOVERNMENT OF ORDNANCE DEPARTMENT (general).

Later D 105.6 and D 105.6/2

W 34.12/2:CT
RULES AND REGULATIONS (special).

Later D 105.6

W 34.13:CT
SPECIFICATIONS, INSTRUCTIONS TO BIDDERS, PROPOSALS.

W 34.14:date
TESTS OF METALS AT WATERTOWN ARSENAL.

W 34.14/2:inclusive dates covered
INDEX TO TESTS OF METALS AT WATERTOWN ARSENAL.

W 34.15:CT
SALES OF CONDEMNED ORDNANCE AND STORES.

W 34.16:CT
CATALOGUES OF MATERIALS AND SUPPLIES REQUIRED AT ARSENALS, ETC.

W 34.16/2:vol.nos.
STORAGE CATALOGUE.

W 34.16/3:vol.nos.
ARMY STORAGE CATALOGUE.

W 34.17:v.nos.
COLLECTION OF ORDNANCE REPORTS AND OTHER IMPORTANT PAPERS RELATING TO ORDNANCE DEPARTMENT.

W 34.18:CT
PRICE-LISTS.

W 34.19:date
GENERAL ORDERS.

W 34.20:date
SPECIAL ORDERS.

W 34.21:date
BOOKS AND PAMPHLETS CATALOGUED.

W 34.21/2:date
SELECTED LIST OF ARTICLES IN CURRENT PERIODICALS OF INTEREST TO ORDNANCE DEPARTMENT. [Monthly]
Changed from W 34.2:P 41

W 34.21/3:nos.&secs.
ORDNANCE TECHNICAL LIBRARY BULLETINS. [Monthly]
Earlier W 34.21/1 and W 34.21/2

W 34.21/4:nos.
SELECTED LIST OF PUBLICATIONS ADDED TO LIBRARY. [Monthly]
These are bulletins of the Ordnance Dept. Library.
Earlier W 34.21/3:1-17/sec.B

W 34.22:nos.
ORDNANCE RECRUITING BULLETINS.

W 34.22/2:letter
STANDARD NOMENCLATURE LISTS.

W 34.23:letter
ORDNANCE PROVISION SYSTEM, SCHEDULE OF REVIEW FOR GROUP.

Later, Schedule of Stores Reports.

W 34.23/2:date
INTRODUCTION TO ORDNANCE CATALOGUE.

W 34.23/3:date
ORDNANCE PUBLICATIONS FOR SUPPLY INDEX.

W 34.23/4:nos.
STANDARD NOMENCLATURE LISTS, OBSOLETE GENERAL SUPPLIES.

W 34.24:CT
INSPECTION AND PROOF REPORTS.

W 34.25:nos.
DESIGN MANUAL NOTES.

W 34.26:nos.
ORDNANCE FIELD SERVICE BULLETINS.

W 34.27:nos.
ORDNANCE TECHNICAL NOTES.

W 34.28:nos.
SPECIFICATIONS (numbered).

W 34.29/1:CT
POSTERS (miscellaneous).

W 34.29/2:nos.
ORDNANCE RECRUITING POSTERS.

W 34.29/3:A-nos.
JOE DOPE POSTERS (1st series).

W 34.29/4:nos.
JOE DOPE POSTERS (2d series).

W 34.30:nos.
ORDNANCE FISCAL BULLETIN.

W 34.31:nos.
OFFICE ORDERS.

Mimeographed.

W 34.32:nos.
ORDNANCE FIELD SERVICE CIRCULARS.

W 34.32/2:nos.
ORDNANCE FIELD SERVICE CIRCULARS, CUMULATIVE SERIAL LISTS.

Processed.

W 34.33:letter-nos.
FIELD SERVICE MODIFICATION WORK ORDERS.

Superseded by W 1.56

W 34.34:nos.
FIRING TABLES.

W 34.35:nos.
ORDNANCE DEPARTMENT SAFETY BULLETINS.

Later M 111.7

W 34.36:nos.
ORDNANCE FIELD SERVICE TECHNICAL BULLETINS.

W 34.37:nos.
SAFETY DIGEST.

W 34.38:letters
ORDNANCE STORAGE AND SHIPMENT CHARTS.

W 34.39:nos.
ORDNANCE EQUIPMENT CHARTS.

W 34.40:vol.
FIREPOWER. [Biweekly]

W 34.41:nos.
TREMENDOUS RIFLES SERIES.

W 34.42:date
REVIEW, STATISTICAL REVIEW OF ORDNANCE ACCIDENT EXPERIENCE. [Monthly]

ORDNANCE AND FORTIFICATION BOARD
(1888–1920)

W 35.1:date
ANNUAL REPORTS.

W 35.2:CT
GENERAL PUBLICATIONS.

W 35.3:
BULLETINS [none issued].

W 35.4:
CIRCULARS [none issued].

PAY DEPARTMENT
(1816–1912)

W 36.1:date
ANNUAL REPORTS.

W 36.2:CT
GENERAL PUBLICATIONS.

W 36.3:
BULLETINS [none issued].

W 36.4:nos.
CIRCULARS.

W 36.5:date
DISTANCE CIRCULARS.

W 36.6:date
STOPPAGE CIRCULARS.

W 36.7/1:date
MANUAL FOR PAY DEPARTMENT.

W 36.7/2:date
MANUAL AMENDMENT CIRCULARS.

W 36.8:date
MONTHLY STATION LIST OF OFFICERS.

W 36.9:date
OFFICIAL TABLE OF DISTANCES.

W 36.10:date
ARMY PAY TABLES.

PROVOST MARSHAL GENERAL
(1863–1947)

W 37.1:date
ANNUAL REPORTS.

W 37.2:CT
GENERAL PUBLICATIONS.

W 37.3:
BULLETINS [none issued].

W 37.4:date
CIRCULARS.

W 37.5:date
REGULATIONS.

W 37.6:CT
RULES, REGULATIONS AND INSTRUCTIONS (miscellaneous).

W 37.7:nos.
COMPILED RULINGS OF PROVOST MARSHAL GENERAL.

W 37.8:form nos.
BLANK FORMS.

W 37.9:nos.
BOARDS OF INSTRUCTION BULLETINS.

W 37.10:nos.
REGISTRATION REGULATIONS.

W 37.11:CT
POSTERS.

PUBLIC BUILDINGS AND GROUNDS OFFICE
(1867–1925)

W 38.1:date
ANNUAL REPORTS.

Earlier I 1.51

W 38.2:CT
GENERAL PUBLICATIONS.

W 38.3:
BULLETINS.

W 38.4:
CIRCULARS.

W 38.5:CT
SPECIFICATIONS.

QUARTERMASTER'S DEPARTMENT
(1812–1912)

CREATION AND AUTHORITY

The Quartermaster's Department was established within the Army by act of Congress, approved Mar. 28, 1812 (2 Stat. 696). An Act of Congress, approved Aug. 24, 1912, created the Quartermaster Corps, which consolidated the Pay Department, Quartermaster's Department, and the Subsistence Department.

W 39.1:date
ANNUAL REPORTS.

W 39.2:CT
GENERAL PUBLICATIONS.

W 39.3:
BULLETINS [none issued].

W 39.4:date
CIRCULARS.

W 39.5:date
INSPECTORS OF NATIONAL CEMETERIES, ANNUAL REPORTS.

W 39.6:date
GENERAL ORDERS.

W 39.7:nos.
ROLL OF HONOR.

W 39.8:v.nos.
ROLL OF HONOR, SUPPLEMENT; STATEMENT OF DISPOSITION OF BODIES OF DECEASED UNION SOLDIERS AND PRISONERS OF WAR REMOVED TO NATIONAL CEMETERIES IN SOUTHERN AND WESTERN UNITED STATES.

W 39.9/1:date
REGULATIONS FOR QUARTERMASTER'S DEPARTMENT (general).

W 39.9/2:date
MANUAL FOR QUARTERMASTER'S DEPARTMENT.

W 39.9/3:CT
RULES, REGULATIONS AND INSTRUCTIONS (special).

W 39.10:nos.
SPECIFICATIONS (numbered).

W 39.11:CT
SPECIFICATIONS (unnumbered).

W 39.12:date
ROSTER SHOWING STATIONS AND DUTIES OF OFFICERS. [Monthly]

RECORDS AND PENSION OFFICE
(1892–1907)

W 40.1:date
ANNUAL REPORTS.

W 40.2:CT
GENERAL PUBLICATIONS.

W 40.3:
BULLETINS [none issued].

W 40.4:
CIRCULARS.

W 40.5:date
STATIONS OF ARMY.

W 40.6:date
ARMY LIST AND DIRECTORY.

BUREAU OF REFUGEES, FREEDMEN, AND ABANDONED LANDS
(1865–1947)

W 41.1:date
ANNUAL REPORTS.

W 41.2:CT
GENERAL PUBLICATIONS.

W 41.3:
BULLETINS.

W 41.4:
CIRCULARS.

W 41.5:date
SEMI-ANNUAL REPORT ON SCHOOLS FOR FREED-MEN.

W 41.6:date
ANNUAL REPORT OF ASSISTANT COMMISSIONER.

SIGNAL OFFICE
(1860–1947)

CREATION AND AUTHORITY

The Signal Corps was established as a separate branch of the Army by act of Congress, approved Mar. 3, 1863. During its early history, it was known as the Signal Office and also the Signal Service.

W 42.1:date
ANNUAL REPORTS.

Later D 111.1

W 42.1/a:date
ANNUAL REPORTS (separates; miscellaneous extracts).

W 42.2:CT
GENERAL PUBLICATIONS.

Later D 111.2

W 42.3:nos.
SIGNAL CORPS BULLETIN.

W 42.4:nos.
CIRCULARS.

W 42.4/2:nos.
CIRCULARS, 1931–[date] CHANGES.

W 42.5:nos.
ARCTIC SERIES.

W 42.6:date
ARMY CODED CARD.

W 42.7/1:date
INTERNATIONAL METEOROLOGICAL OBSERVA-TIONS.

W 42.7/2:date
SUMMARY AND REVIEW OF INTERNATIONAL ME-TEOROLOGICAL OBSERVATIONS FOR MONTH OF.

W 42.8/1:date
DAILY BULLETIN OF SIMULTANEOUS WEATHER REPORTS WITH SYNOPSES INDICATIONS, AND FACTS FOR MONTH OF.

W 42.8/2:date
DAILY BULLETIN OF SIMULTANEOUS WEATHER REPORTS WITH SYNOPSES INDICATIONS, AND FACTS FOR MONTH OF [with maps].

W 42.8/3:date
TRI-DAILY METEOROLOGICAL RECORD [for] MONTH OF.

W 42.9:date
ROSTER AND STATION OF OFFICERS OF SIGNAL CORPS.

W 42.10:date
ORDERS.

W 42.11/1:nos.
PROFESSIONAL PAPERS OF SIGNAL SERVICE (numbered).

W 42.11/2:CT
PROFESSIONAL PAPERS OF SIGNAL CORPS (un-numbered).

W 42.12:date
RAIN AND DRY WINDS, COMPUTED FOR DIFFER-ENT GEOGRAPHICAL DISTRICTS.

W 42.13/1:CT
RULES, REGULATIONS AND INSTRUCTIONS.

W 42.13/2:CT
CHANGES IN DRILL REGULATIONS.

W 42.14:nos.
SIGNAL SERVICE NOTES.

W 42.15:CT
SPECIFICATIONS.

W 42.15/2:nos.
SPECIFICATIONS (numbered).

W 42.16:nos.
TORNADO CIRCULARS [old series].

W 42.17:nos.
TORNADO CIRCULARS [new series].

W 42.18:date
WEEKLY WEATHER CHRONICLE.

W 42.19:pt.nos.
[DAILY RIVER STAGES].

W 42.20:date
MONTHLY WEATHER REVIEW.

W 42.21:nos.
DIVISION OF TELEGRAMS AND REPORTS FOR BENEFIT OF COMMERCE AND AGRICULTURE, CIRCULAR.

W 42.22/1:CT
MANUALS.

W 42.22/2:nos.
MANUALS (numbered).

W 42.22/3:nos.
CHANGES IN SIGNAL CORPS MANUALS (numbered).

W 42.23:date
WEATHER MAPS.

W 42.24:date
METEOROLOGICAL RECORD.

W 42.25:CT
MAPS.

W 42.26:nos.
SIGNAL CORPS MEMORANDUM.

W 42.27:date
WEATHER-CORP BULLETIN.

W 42.28:nos.
BALLOON BULLETINS.

W 42.29:nos.
RADIO COMMUNICATION PAMPHLETS.

W 42.30:nos.
WIRE COMMUNICATION PAMPHLETS.

W 42.31:nos.
TRAINING PAMPHLETS.

W 42.32:nos.
FIELD PAMPHLETS.

W 42.33:CT
POSTERS.

Signal School, Army, Fort Monmouth, New Jersey

W 42.34/1:date
ANNUAL REPORTS.

W 42.34/2:CT
GENERAL PUBLICATIONS.

W 42.34/3:
BULLETINS.

W 42.34/4:
CIRCULARS.

W 42.34/5:nos.
PAMPHLETS.

Mimeographed.
Series desig. SP

W 42.34/6:nos.
SIGNAL SCHOOL PAMPHLETS.

Series desig. SS

W 42.34/7:incl.dates&nos.
INSTRUCTION CIRCULARS.

W 42.34/8:nos.
MAP PROBLEMS.

Equipment Division

W 42.35:nos.
BULLETINS.

W 42.36:nos.
GENERAL MEMORANDUM.

W 42.37:nos.
SPECIAL MEMORANDUM.

Signal Office (Continued)

W 42.38:CT
CATALOGS AND STOCK LISTS.

W 42.39:v.
SIGNAL CORPS LIBRARY RECORD. [Weekly]

W 42.40:nos.
SIGNAL CORPS TECHNICAL INFORMATION
LETTERS [Restricted]. [Monthly]

Early issues read Information letter.

W 42.41:v.
INFORMATION LETTERS [unrestricted]. [Monthly]

DISTRICT OF COLUMBIA
SOLDIERS HOME
(1851–1947)

W 43.1:date
ANNUAL REPORTS.

W 43.2:CT
GENERAL PUBLICATIONS.

W 43.3:
BULLETINS [none issued].

W 43.4:
CIRCULARS [none issued].

MEDICAL DEPARTMENT
(1818–1947)

CREATION AND AUTHORITY

The Medical Department was established as
a separate branch of the Army, headed by a
Surgeon General, by act of Congress, approved
Apr.14, 1818 (3 Stat. 426). By the Army Organization Act of 1950 (64 Stat. 263), the Department
was redesignated the Army Medical Service.

W 44.1:date
ANNUAL REPORTS.

Later M 102.1

W 44.2:CT
GENERAL PUBLICATIONS.

Later M 102.2

W 44.3:
BULLETINS.

W 44.4:date
CIRCULARS.

W 44.4/2:nos.
CIRCULARS, NEW SERIES.

W 44.5:CT
CIRCULARS OF INFORMATION.

Army Medical School

W 44.6/1:date
ANNUAL REPORTS.

W 44.6/2:CT
GENERAL PUBLICATIONS [none issued].

W 44.6/3:
BULLETINS [none issued].

W 44.6/4:
CIRCULARS [none issued].

W 44.6/5:date
ORDER OF DUTIES, ETC.

Medical Department (Continued)

W 44.7/1:v.
INDEX-CATALOGUE OF LIBRARY OF SURGEON-
GENERAL'S OFFICE [1st series].

W 44.7/2:v.
INDEX-CATALOGUE OF LIBRARY OF SURGEON-
GENERAL'S OFFICE [2d series].

W 44.7/3:v.
INDEX-CATALOGUE OF LIBRARY OF SURGEON-
GENERAL'S OFFICE [3d series].

W 44.7/4:v.
INDEX-CATALOGUE OF LIBRARY OF SURGEON-
GENERAL'S OFFICE [4th series].

Later M 102.8

W 44.8/1:
DRILL REGULATIONS, HOSPITAL CORPS.

W 44.8/2:date
CHANGES [in] HOSPITAL DRILL REGULATIONS.

W 44.9:date
MANUAL FOR MEDICAL DEPARTMENT.

W 44.9/2:date of edition
CHANGES IN MANUAL FOR MEDICAL DEPARTMENT
(numbered).

W 44.10:v.
MEDICAL AND SURGICAL HISTORY OF WAR OF
REBELLION, 1861–65.

W 44.11:date
ARMY METEOROLOGICAL REGISTER.

W 44.12:CT
SPECIFICATIONS.

W 44.13:date
STATION-LIST OF OFFICERS OF MEDICAL DEPART-
MENT.

W 44.14:date
CATALOGUES.

W 44.15:date
REGULATIONS FOR GOVERNMENT OF UNITED
STATES ARMY GENERAL HOSPITAL.

W 44.16:v.nos.
REVIEW OF WAR SURGERY AND MEDICINE.

W 44.17:v.nos.
CARRY ON.

W 44.18:nos.
MEDICAL WAR MANUAL.

W 44.19:v.nos.
MEDICAL DEPARTMENT OF UNITED STATES ARMY
IN WORLD WAR.

W 44.20/1:CT
POSTERS (miscellaneous).

W 44.20/2:nos.
RECRUITING POSTERS.

Medical Field Service School
Carlisle Barracks, Pennsylvania

W 44.21/1:date
ANNUAL REPORTS.

W 44.21/2:CT
GENERAL PUBLICATIONS.

W 44.21/3:date
BULLETINS– ARMY MEDICAL BULLETIN (unnumbered
series).

W 44.21/4:
CIRCULARS.

W 44.21/5:
LAWS.

W 44.21/7:date later nos.
ARMY MEDICAL BULLETIN.

Later M 102.3

W 44.21/8:vol.
VETERINARY BULLETINS. [Quarterly]

Supplement to Army Medical Bulletin. Mimeographed.

W 44.21/9:date
ARMY MEDICAL BULLETIN [unnumbered series].

W 44.21/10:vol.
ARMY MEDICAL BULLETIN [volumed series].

W 44.21/11:nos.
PAMPHLETS.

W 44.21/12:vol.
DENTAL BULLTIN. [Quarterly]

Supplement to Army Medical Bulletin.

Medical Department (Continued)

W 44.22:vol.nos.
MEDICO-MILITARY REVIEW FOR MEDICAL DEPART-
MENT, ARMY. [Semimonthly]

Mimeographed.

Army School of Nursing
Walter Reed General Hospital
Army Medical Center, Washington, D.C.

W 44.23/1:date
ANNUAL REPORTS.

W 44.23/2:CT
GENERAL PUBLICATIONS.

W 44.23/3:
BULLETINS.

W 44.23/4:
CIRCULARS.

W 44.23/5:date
ANNUAL COURSES.

W 44.23/6:date
ANNUAL TRAINING COURSES IN DIETETICS.

W 44.23/7:date
ANNUAL TRAINING COURSE IN PHYSIOTHERAPY.

W 44.23/8:date
ANNUAL TRAINING COURSE IN OCCUPATIONAL
THERAPY.

Medical Department (Continued)

W 44.24:date
CLASSIFICATION OF PERIODICALS, ARMY MEDI-
CAL LIBRARY.

W 44.25:vol.
FLIGHT SURGEON TOPICS. [Quarterly]

W 44.26:date
MEDICAL DEPARTMENT SUPPLY CATALOGUES.

W 44.27:date
CIRCULARS OF INFORMATION RELATIVE TO
APPOINTMENT AS FIRST LIEUTENANTS IN MEDI-
CAL CORPS OF REGULAR ARMY.

Changed from W 44.5:M 46c/2-29 (varying
titles).

W 44.28:date
DENTAL CORPS OF REGULAR ARMY, CIRCULARS OF INFORMATION RELATIVE TO APPOINTMENTS AS FIRST LIEUTENANTS IN.

Changed from W 44.5

W 44.29:v.nos.
ARMY NURSE. [Monthly]

W 44.30:v.nos.
CURRENT LIST OF MEDICAL LITERATURE. [Weekly]

Later M 102.7

WAR RECORDS OFFICE
(1878– 1899)

W 45.1:date
ANNUAL REPORTS.

W 45.2:CT
GENERAL PUBLICATIONS.

W 45.3:
BULLETINS.

W 45.4:date
CIRCULARS RELATING TO PLAN AND METHODS OF PUBLICATION OF OFFICIAL RECORDS OF UNION AND CONFEDERATE ARMIES (unnumbered).

W 45.5:serial nos.
WAR OF REBELLION, COMPILATION OF OFFICIAL RECORDS OF UNION AND CONFEDERATE ARMIES [or Rebellion Records].

W 45.5/2:v.nos.
– ADDITIONS AND CORRECTIONS.

W 45.6:CT
WAR OF REBELLION, COMPILATION OF OFFICIAL RECORDS OF UNION AND CONFEDERATE ARMIES [or Rebellion Records], INDEXES.

W 45.7:pt.nos.
ATLAS TO ACCOMPANY [War of Rebellion] OFFICIAL RECORDS OF UNION AND CONFEDERATE ARMIES [or Rebellion Records].

W 45.8:v.nos.
ATLAS TO ACCOMPANY [War of Rebellion] OFFICIAL RECORDS OF UNION AND CONFEDERATE ARMIES [or Rebellion Records].

W 45.8/2:CT
ADDITIONS AND CORRECTIONS TO ATLAS.

W 45.9:v.nos.
REPORTS OF MILITARY OPERATIONS DURING REBELLION, 1860– 65.

GETTYSBURG NATIONAL
MILITARY PARK COMMISSION
(1893– 1922)

W 46.1:date
ANNUAL REPORTS.

W 46.2:CT
GENERAL PUBLICATIONS

W 46.3:
BULLETINS [none issued].

W 46.4:
CIRCULARS [none issued].

CUBAN CENSUS OFFICE
(1899– 1900)

W 47.1:date
ANNUAL REPORTS.

W 47.2:CT
GENERAL PUBLICATIONS.

W 47.3:nos.
BULLETINS.

W 47.4:nos.
CIRCULARS.

PORTO RICO CENSUS OFFICE
(1899– 1900)

W 48.1:date
ANNUAL REPORTS.

W 48.2:CT
GENERAL PUBLICATIONS.

W 48.3:nos.
BULLETINS.

W 48.4:nos.
CIRCULARS.

PHILIPPINE ISLANDS
(1900– 1934)

W 49.1:date
ANNUAL REPORTS.

W 49.2:CT
GENERAL PUBLICATIONS.

W 49.3:
BULLETINS [none issued].

W 49.4:
CIRCULARS [none issued].

Civil Service Bureau

W 49.5/1:date
ANNUAL REPORTS.

W 49.5/2:CT
GENERAL PUBLICATIONS.

W 49.5/3:nos.
BULLETINS [none issued].

W 49.5/4:
CIRCULARS [none issued].

W 49.5/5:date
OFFICIAL ROSTER OF OFFICERS AND EMPLOYEES.

W 49.5/6:date
MANUAL OF INFORMATION.

Education Bureau

W 49.6/1:date
ANNUAL REPORTS.

W 49.6/2:CT
GENERAL PUBLICATIONS.

W 49.6/3:nos.
BULLETINS.

W 49.6/4:
CIRCULARS [none issued].

W 49.6/5:vol.
PHILIPPINE CRAFTSMAN.

Philippine Islands (Continued)

W 49.7/1:date
PUBLIC LAWS AND RESOLUTIONS. [Quarterly]

W 49.7/2:v.nos.
PUBLIC LAWS WITH AMENDMENTS. [Annual]

W 49.7/3:date
ACTS AND PUBLIC RESOLUTIONS.

W 49.7/4:date
COMPILATIONS OF ACTS.

W 49.8:CT
SLIP LAWS.

Forestry Bureau

W 49.9/1:date
ANNUAL REPORTS.

W 49.9/2:CT
GENERAL PUBLICATIONS.

W 49.9/3:nos.
BULLETINS.

W 49.9/4:nos.
CIRCULARS.

Customs Bureau

W 49.10/1:date
ANNUAL REPORTS.

W 49.10/2:
GENERAL PUBLICATIONS [none issued].

W 49.10/3:
BULLETINS [none issued].

W 49.10/4:
CIRCULARS [none issued].

W 49.10/5:v.nos.
CUSTOMS DECISIONS.

W 49.10/6:nos.
CUSTOMS ADMINISTRATIVE CIRCULARS.

W 49.10/7:nos.
MANILA CUSTOM-HOUSE GENERAL ORDERS.

W 49.10/8:v.
CHINESE AND IMMIGRATION CIRCULARS.

W 49.10/9:nos.
CUSTOMS MARINE CIRCULAR.

W 49.10/10:nos.
CUSTOMS ADMINISTRATIVE ORDERS.

W 49.10/11:nos.
CIRCULAR LETTERS.

Mimeographed.

Architecture and Construction of Public Buildings Bureau

W 49.11/1:date
ANNUAL REPORTS.

W 49.11/2:CT
GENERAL PUBLICATIONS.

W 49.11/3:
BULLETINS [none issued].

W 49.11/4:
CIRCULARS [none issued].

Engineering Bureau

W 49.12/1:date
ANNUAL REPORTS.

W 49.12/2:
GENERAL PUBLICATIONS [none issued].

W 49.12/3:
BULLETINS [none issued].

W 49.12/4:
CIRCULARS [none issued].

Weather Bureau

W 49.13/1:date
ANNUAL REPORT.

W 49.13/1-1:date
– ADMINISTRATIVE REPORT.

W 49.13/1-2:date
– SCIENTIFIC REPORT.

W 49.13/2:CT
GENERAL PUBLICATIONS.

W 49.13/3:date
BULLETINS.

W 49.13/4:
CIRCULARS [none issued].

W 49.13/5:nos.
INSTRUCTIONS (Spanish).

Exposition Board

W 49.14/1:date
ANNUAL REPORTS.

W 49.14/2:CT
GENERAL PUBLICATIONS.

W 49.14/3:
BULLETINS [none issued].

W 49.14/4:
CIRCULARS [none issued].

Health Bureau

W 49.15/1:date
ANNUAL REPORTS.

W 49.15/2:CT
GENERAL PUBLICATIONS.

W 49.15/3:nos.
BULLETINS.

W 49.15/4:
CIRCULARS [none issued].

W 49.15/5:date
QUARTERLY REPORTS.

W 49.15/6:v.nos.
PHILIPPINE HEALTH SERVICE, MONTHLY BULLETIN.

Phillippine Lslands (Continued)

W 49.16:v.nos.
OFFICIAL GAZETTE.

Government Laboratories Bureau

W 49.17/1:date
ANNUAL REPORTS.

W 49.17/2:CT
GENERAL PUBLICATIONS.

W 49.17/3:nos.
BULLETINS.

W 49.17/4:
CIRCULARS [none issued].

Finance and Justice Department

W 49.18/1:date
ANNUAL REPORTS.

W 49.18/2:
GENERAL PUBLICATIONS [none issued].

W 49.18/3:
BULLETINS [none issued].

W 49.18/4:
CIRCULARS [none issued].

Interior Department

W 49.19/1:date
ANNUAL REPORTS.

W 49.19/2:CT
GENERAL PUBLICATIONS.

W 49.19/3:
BULLETINS [none issued].

W 49.19/4:
CIRCULARS [none issued].

Audits Bureau

W 49.20/1:date
ANNUAL REPORTS.

W 49.20/2:
GENERAL PUBLICATIONS [none issued].

W 49.20/3:
BULLETINS [none issued].

W 49.20/4:
CIRCULARS [none issued].

Agriculture Bureau

W 49.21/1:date
ANNUAL REPORTS.

W 49.21/2:CT
GENERAL PUBLICATIONS.

W 49.21/3:nos.
BULLETINS.

W 49.21/4:
CIRCULARS [none issued].

W 49.21/5:nos.
FARMERS' BULLETINS.

W 49.21/6:nos.
PRESS BULLETINS.

W 49.21/7:v.nos.
PHILIPPINE AGRICULTURAL REVIEW. [Monthly]

W 49.21/8:nos.
POPULAR BULLETINS.

W 49.21/9:nos.
EXTENSION WORK CIRCULARS.

W 49.21/10:v.nos.
PHILIPPINE FARMER. [Monthly]

Mining Bureau

W 49.22/1:date
ANNUAL REPORTS.

W 49.22/2:CT
GENERAL PUBLICATIONS.

W 49.22/3:nos.
BULLETINS.

W 49.22/4:
CIRCULARS [none issued].

Justice Bureau

W 49.23/1:date
ANNUAL REPORTS OF ATTORNEY-GENERAL.

W 49.23/2:
GENERAL PUBLICATIONS [none issued].

W 49.23/3:
BULLETINS [none issued].

W 49.23/4:
CIRCULARS [none issued].

W 49.23/5:v.nos.
OFFICIAL OPINIONS OF ATTORNEY-GENERAL.

Navigation Bureau

W 49.24/1:date
ANNUAL REPORTS.

W 49.24/2:CT
GENERAL PUBLICATIONS.

W 49.24/3:
BULLETINS [none issued].

W 49.24/4:nos.
CIRCULARS.

Museum of Ethnology, Natural History and Commerce

W 49.25/1:date
ANNUAL REPORTS.

W 49.25/2:CT
GENERAL PUBLICATIONS.

W 49.25/3:nos.
BULLETINS.

W 49.25/4:
CIRCULARS [none issued].

Executive Bureau

W 49.26/1:date
ANNUAL REPORTS.

W 49.26/2:CT
GENERAL PUBLICATIONS.

W 49.26/3:
BULLETINS [none issued].

W 49.26/4:
CIRCULARS [none issued].

Lands Bureau

W 49.27/1:date
ANNUAL REPORTS.

W 49.27/2:CT
GENERAL PUBLICATIONS.

W 49.27/3:
BULLETINS [none issued].

W 49.27/4:
CIRCULARS [none issued].

Currency Division

W 49.28/1:date
ANNUAL REPORTS.

W 49.28/2:CT
GENERAL PUBLICATIONS.

W 49.28/3:
BULLETINS [none issued].

W 49.28/4:
CIRCULARS [none issued].

Ethnological Survey

W 49.29/1:date
ANNUAL REPORTS.

W 49.29/2:CT
GENERAL PUBLICATIONS [none issued].

W 49.29/3:
BULLETINS [none issued].

W 49.29/4:
CIRCULARS [none issued].

W 49.29/5:v.nos.
ETHNOLOGICAL SURVEY PUBLICATIONS.

Supply Bureau

W 49.30/1:
ANNUAL REPORTS.

W 49.30/2:
GENERAL PUBLICATIONS [none issued].

W 49.30/3:
BULLETINS [none issued].

W 49.30/4:
CIRCULARS [none issued].

Science Bureau

W 49.31/1:date
ANNUAL REPORTS.

W 49.31/2:CT
GENERAL PUBLICATIONS.

W 49.31/3:
BULLETINS [none issued].

W 49.31/4:
CIRCULARS [none issued].

W 49.31/5:vol.
PHILIPPINE JOURNAL OF SCIENCE.

Constabulary Bureau

W 49.32/1:date
ANNUAL REPORTS.

W 49.32/2:CT
GENERAL PUBLICATIONS [none issued].

W 49.32/3:
BULLETINS [none issued].

W 49.32/4:
CIRCULARS.

W 49.32/5:date
GENERAL ORDERS.

W 49.32/6:date
SPECIAL ORDERS.

W 49.32/7:date
CONSTABULARY NOTES.

Moro Province

W 49.33/1:date
ANNUAL REPORTS OF GOVERNOR.

W 49.33/2:CT
GENERAL PUBLICATIONS.

W 49.33/3:
BULLETINS [none issued].

W 49.33/4:
CIRCULARS [none issued].

Manila

W 49.34/1:date
ANNUAL REPORTS.

W 49.34/2:CT
GENERAL PUBLICATIONS.

W 49.34/3:
BULLETINS [none issued].

W 49.34/4:
CIRCULARS [none issued].

Governor General

W 49.35/1:date
ANNUAL REPORTS.

W 49.35/2:CT
GENERAL PUBLICATIONS.

W 49.35/3:
BULLETINS [none issued].

W 49.35/4:
CIRCULARS [none issued].

W 49.35/5:date
EXECUTIVE ORDERS AND PROCLAMATIONS.

Public Works Bureau

W 49.36/1:date
ANNUAL REPORTS.

W 49.36/2:
GENERAL PUBLICATIONS [none issued].

W 49.36/3:
BULLETINS [none issued].

W 49.36/4:
CIRCULARS [none issued].

Public Instruction Department

W 49.37/1:date
ANNUAL REPORTS.

W 49.37/2:CT
GENERAL PUBLICATIONS.

W 49.37/3:
BULLETINS.

W 49.37/4:
CIRCULARS.

Civil Sanitarium, Benguet

W 49.38/1:date
ANNUAL REPORTS.

W 49.38/2:CT
GENERAL PUBLICATIONS [none issued].

W 49.38/3:
BULLETINS [none issued].

W 49.38/4:
CIRCULARS [none issued].

Philippine Legislature

W 49.39/1:Leg.&Sess.
ACTS.

W 49.39/2:
GENERAL PUBLICATIONS [none issued].

Philippine Commission

W 49.40/1:L.&S.
JOURNAL.

W 49.40/2:
GENERAL PUBLICATIONS [none issued].

Philippine Assembly

W 49.41/1:L.&S.
JOURNAL.

W 49.41/2:CT
GENERAL PUBLICATIONS.

W 49.41/3:
BULLETINS [none issued].

W 49.41/4:
CIRCULARS [none issued].

W 49.41/5:vol.
ACTAS DE LA ASAMBLEA FILIPINA [Spanish only].

Internal Revenue Bureau

W 49.42/1:date
ANNUAL REPORTS.

W 49.42/2:CT
GENERAL PUBLICATIONS.

W 49.42/3:
BULLETINS [none issued].

W 49.42/4:
CIRCULARS [none issued].

Philippine Medical School

W 49.43/1:date
ANNUAL REPORTS.

W 49.43/2:CT
GENERAL PUBLICATIONS [none issued].

W 49.43/3:
BULLETINS [none issued].

W 49.43/4:
CIRCULARS [none issued].

W 49.43/5:date
ANNUAL ANNOUNCEMENTS.

Posts Bureau

W 49.44/1:date
ANNUAL REPORTS.

W 49.44/2:CT
GENERAL PUBLICATIONS [none issued].

W 49.44/3:
BULLETINS [none issued].

W 49.44/4:
CIRCULARS [none issued].

W 49.44/5:date
ANNUAL ANNOUNCEMENTS.

Printing Bureau

W 49.45/1:date
ANNUAL REPORTS.

W 49.45/2:CT
GENERAL PUBLICATIONS.

W 49.45/3:
BULLETINS [none issued].

W 49.45/4:
CIRCULARS [none issued].

Supreme Court

W 49.46/1:date
ANNUAL REPORTS.

W 49.46/2:CT
GENERAL PUBLICATIONS.

W 49.46/3:
BULLETINS [none issued].

W 49.46/4:
CIRCULARS [none issued].

Department of Commerce and Police

W 49.47/1:date
ANNUAL REPORTS.

W 49.47/2:CT
GENERAL PUBLICATIONS.

W 49.47/3:nos.
BULLETINS.

W 49.47/4:nos.
CIRCULARS.

Sales Agency

W 49.48/1:date
ANNUAL REPORTS.

W 49.48/2:CT
GENERAL PUBLICATIONS.

W 49.48/3:nos.
BULLETINS.

W 49.48/4:nos.
CIRCULARS.

W 49.48/5:CT
MAPS.

Coast and Geodetic Survey Bureau Commerce and Police Department

W 49.49/1:date
ANNUAL REPORTS.

W 49.49/2:CT
GENERAL PUBLICATIONS.

W 49.49/3:
BULLETINS.

W 49.49/4:
CIRCULARS.

W 49.49/5:nos.
MAPS.

Public Utility Commissioners Board

W 49.50/1:date
ANNUAL REPORTS.

W 49.50/2:CT
GENERAL PUBLICATIONS.

W 49.50/3:
BULLETINS.

W 49.50/4:
CIRCULARS.

Philippine Islands Census, 1918

W 49.51/1:date
ANNUAL REPORTS.

W 49.51/2:CT
GENERAL PUBLICATIONS.

W 49.51/3:
BULLETINS.

W 49.51/4:
CIRCULARS.

W 49.51/5:date and v.nos.
FINAL VOLUMES.

Commerce and Industry Bureau

W 49.52/1:date
ANNUAL REPORTS.

W 49.52/2:CT
GENERAL PUBLICATIONS.

W 49.52/3:
BULLETINS.

W 49.52/4:
CIRCULARS.

W 49.52/5:nos.
STATISTICAL BULLETINS.

Library and Museum

W 49.53/1:date
ANNUAL REPORTS.

W 49.53/2:CT
GENERAL PUBLICATIONS.

W 49.53/3:
BULLETINS.

W 49.53/4:
CIRCULARS.

Independence Commission

W 49.54:nos.
BULLETINS.

Plant Industry Bureau

W 49.55/1:date
ANNUAL REPORTS.

W 49.55/2:CT
GENERAL PUBLICATIONS.

W 49.55/3:
BULLETINS.

W 49.55/4:
CIRCULARS.

W 49.55/5:vol.
PHILIPPINE JOURNAL OF AGRICULTURE.

Department of Agriculture and Commerce Statistics Division

W 49.56/1:date
ANNUAL REPORTS.

W 49.56/2:CT
GENERAL PUBLICATIONS.

CALIFORNIA DEBRIS COMMISSION
(1893)

W 50.1:date
ANNUAL REPORTS.

W 50.2:CT
GENERAL PUBLICATIONS.

W 50.3:
BULLETINS [none issued].

W 50.4:
CIRCULARS [none issued].

PACIFIC DIVISION
(1847– 1907)

W 51.1:date
ANNUAL REPORTS.

W 51.2:CT
GENERAL PUBLICATIONS.

W 51.3:
BULLETINS [none issued].

W 51.4:
CIRCULARS [none issued].

W 51.5:date
GENERAL ORDERS.

W 51.6:date
SPECIAL ORDERS.

W 51.7:date
ROSTER OF TROOPS.

DEPARTMENT OF WASHINGTON
(1861– 1869)

W 52.1:date
ANNUAL REPORTS.

W 52.2:CT
GENERAL PUBLICATIONS.

W 52.3:
BULLETINS [none issued].

W 52.4:date
CIRCULARS.

W 52.5:nos.
GENERAL ORDERS.

W 52.6:date
SPECIAL ORDERS.

W 52.7:date
ROSTER OF TROOPS [none issued].

COAST ARTILLERY OFFICE
(1901– 1941)

W 53.1:date
ANNUAL REPORTS.

W 53.2:CT
GENERAL PUBLICATIONS.

W 53.3:
BULLETINS [none issued].

W 53.4:
CIRCULARS [none issued].

W 53.5:CT
RANGE TABLES.

W 53.6:nos.
COAST ARTILLERY MEMORANDUM.

VICKSBURG NATIONAL MILITARY PARK COMMISSION
(1899)

W 54.1:date
ANNUAL REPORTS.

W 54.2:CT
GENERAL PUBLICATIONS

W 54.3:
BULLETINS [none issued].

W 54.4:
CIRCULARS [none issued].

ARMY WAR COLLEGE
(1900– 1945)

W 55.1:date
ANNUAL REPORTS.

W 55.2:CT
GENERAL PUBLICATIONS.

W 55.3:
BULLETINS [none issued].

W 55.4:
CIRCULARS [none issued].

W 55.7:nos.
LIBRARY BULLETINS. [Monthly]

W 55.8:nos.
ABSTRACTS OF SELECTED PERIODICAL ARTICLES
OF MILITARY INTEREST. [Monthly]

DEPARTMENT OF LUZON
(1900– 1914)

W 56.1:date
ANNUAL REPORTS.

W 56.2:CT
GENERAL PUBLICATIONS [none issued].

W 56.3:
BULLETINS [none issued].

W 56.4:date
CIRCULARS.

W 56.5:date
GENERAL ORDERS.

W 56.6:date
SPECIAL ORDERS.

W 56.7:date
ROSTER OF TROOPS.

DEPARTMENT OF PINAR DEL RIO
(1898– 1900)

W 57.1:date
ANNUAL REPORTS.

W 57.2:
GENERAL PUBLICATIONS [none issued].

W 57.3:
BULLETINS [none issued].

W 57.4:date
CIRCULARS.

W 57.5:date
GENERAL ORDERS.

W 57.6:date
SPECIAL ORDERS.

W 57.7:date
ROSTER OF TROOPS.

W 57.8:date
CIVIL ORDERS.

DEPARTMENT OF MATANZAS AND SANTA CLARA
(1898– 1900)

W 58.1:date
ANNUAL REPORTS.

W 58.2:
GENERAL PUBLICATIONS [none issued].

W 58.3:
BULLETINS [none issued].

W 58.4:date
CIRCULARS.

W 58.5:date
GENERAL ORDERS.

W 58.6:date
SPECIAL ORDERS.

W 58.7:date
ROSTER OF TROOPS.

DEPARTMENT OF SANTIAGO AND PUERTO PRINCIPE
(1898– 1900)

W 59.1:date
ANNUAL REPORTS.

W 59.2:
GENERAL PUBLICATIONS [none issued].

W 59.3:
BULLETINS [none issued].

W 59.4:date
CIRCULARS.

W 59.5:date
GENERAL ORDERS.

W 59.6:date
SPECIAL ORDERS.

W 59.7:date
ROSTER OF TROOPS.

SUBMARINE DEFENSE SCHOOL
(1901– 1908)

W 61.1:date
ANNUAL REPORTS.

W 61.2:
GENERAL PUBLICATIONS [none issued].

W 61.3:
BULLETINS [none issued].

W 61.4:
CIRCULARS [none issued]

NORTHERN DIVISION
(1904– 1907)

W 62.1:date
ANNUAL REPORTS.

W 62.2:
GENERAL PUBLICATIONS [none issued].

W 62.3:
BULLETINS [none issued].

W 62.4:
CIRCULARS [none issued].

W 62.5:date
GENERAL ORDERS.

W 62.6:date
SPECIAL ORDERS.

W 62.7:date
ROSTER OF TROOPS.

SHILOAH NATIONAL MILITARY PARK COMMISSION
(1894)

W 63.1:date
ANNUAL REPORTS.

W 63.2:CT
GENERAL PUBLICATIONS.

W 63.3:
BULLETINS [none issued].

W 63.4:
CIRCULARS [none issued].

ATLANTIC DIVISION
(1865–1907)

W 64.1:date
ANNUAL REPORTS.

W 64.2:CT
GENERAL PUBLICATIONS.

W 64.3:
BULLETINS [none issued].

W 64.4:date
CIRCULARS.

W 64.5:date
GENERAL ORDERS.

W 64.6:
SPECIAL ORDERS.

W 64.7:date
ROSTER OF TROOPS.

DEPARTMENT OF ARIZONA
(1870–1893)

W 65.1:date
ANNUAL REPORTS.

W 65.2:CT
GENERAL PUBLICATIONS.

W 65.3:
BULLETINS [none issued].

W 65.4:date
CIRCULARS.

W 65.5:date
GENERAL ORDERS.

W 65.6:date
SPECIAL ORDERS.

W 65.7:date
ROSTER OF TROOPS.

DEPARTMENT OF THE SOUTH
(1862–1883)

W 66.1:date
ANNUAL REPORTS.

W 66.2:CT
GENERAL PUBLICATIONS.

W 66.3:
BULLETINS [none issued].

W 66.4:date
CIRCULARS.

W 66.5:date
GENERAL ORDERS.

W 66.6:date
SPECIAL ORDERS.

W 66.7:date
ROSTER OF TROOPS.

DEPARTMENT OF VIRGINIA AND NORTH CAROLINA
(1861–1870)

W 67.1:date
ANNUAL REPORTS [none issued].

W 67.2:CT
GENERAL PUBLICATIONS.

W 67.3:
BULLETINS [none issued].

W 67.4:date
CIRCULARS.

W 67.5/1:date
GENERAL ORDERS (Department of Virginia and North Carolina).

W 67.5/2:date
GENERAL ORDERS (Department of Virginia).

W 67.5/3:date
GENERAL ORDERS (Department of North Carolina).

W 67.5/4:date
GENERAL ORDERS (Division of the James).

W 67.6:date
SPECIAL ORDERS.

W 67.7:date
ROSTER OF TROOPS [none issued].

INTERNATIONAL WATERWAYS COMMISSION
(1902–1913)

W 68.1:date
ANNUAL REPORTS, PROGRESS REPORTS.

W 68.2:CT
GENERAL PUBLICATIONS.

W 68.3:
BULLETINS.

W 68.4:
CIRCULARS.

SOUTHEASTERN DIVISION
(1903–1907)

W 69.1:date
ANNUAL REPORTS.

W 69.2:CT
GENERAL PUBLICATIONS [none issued].

W 69.3:nos.
BULLETINS [none issued].

W 69.4:date
CIRCULARS.

W 69.5:date
GENERAL ORDERS.

W 69.6:date
SPECIAL ORDERS.

W 69.7:date
ROSTER OF TROOPS.

NATIONAL GUARD BUREAU
(1933–1947)

CREATION AND AUTHORITY

The Division of Militia Affairs was established Feb. 12, 1908, in the Office of Secretary of War. General Order No. 24, dated July 6, 1916, pursuant to the act of Congress, approved June 3, 1916, reorganized the Division, designating it the Militia Bureau. In 1933, the name was changed to National Guard Bureau.

W 70.1:date
ANNUAL REPORTS.
　　Later M 114.1

W 70.2:CT
GENERAL PUBLICATIONS.
　　Later M 114.2

W 70.3:
BULLETINS.

W 70.4:date
CIRCULARS.

W 70.4/2:dt.&nos.
MIMEOGRAPHED CIRCULARS, SERIES A AND B.

　　Supersedes W 70.10
　　Later M 114.4

W 70.5:date
ROSTER OF ORGANIZED MILITIA OF UNITED STATES, BY DIVISIONS, BRIGADES, REGIMENTS, COMPANIES, AND OTHER ORGANIZATIONS, WITH THEIR STATIONS.

　　Earlier W 3.33:R 73/1-6
　　Later D 112.8

W 70.6:CT
RULES, REGULATIONS AND INSTRUCTIONS.

W 70.7:date
MILITIA BUREAU REGULATIONS (general).

　　Earlier W 3.33:R 26

W 70.7/2:date&nos.
CHANGES IN REGULATIONS (general).

W 70.7/3:nos.
CHANGES IN REGULATIONS (compilation).

W 70.7/4:nos.
MILITIA BUREAU, NATIONAL GUARD REGULATIONS.

    Later M 114.6

W 70.8:nos.
NATIONAL GUARD BUREAU MANUALS.

    Series desig. NGB nos.

W 70.9:CT
QUESTIONS FOR NATIONAL GUARD OFFICERS.

W 70.10:date
CIRCULAR LETTERS (mimeographed).

    Superseded by W 70.4/2

W 70.11:date&nos.
TRAINING CIRCULARS.

    Mimeographed

W 70.12:nos.
TABLES OF ORGANIZATION, N.G.B.

    Changed from W 1.25

DEPARTMENT OF ALASKA
(1868– 1901)

W 71.1:date
ANNUAL REPORTS.

W 71.2:
GENERAL PUBLICATIONS.

W 71.3:
BULLETINS.

W 71.4:
CIRCULARS.

W 71.5:date
GENERAL ORDERS.

W 71.6:date
SPECIAL ORDERS.

W 71.7:date
ROSTER OF TROOPS.

DEPARTMENT OF MINDANAO
(1899– 1914)

W 72.1:date
ANNUAL REPORTS.

W 72.2:
GENERAL PUBLICATIONS.

W 72.3:
BULLETINS.

W 72.4:date
CIRCULARS.

W 72.5:date
GENERAL ORDERS.

W 72.6:date
SPECIAL ORDERS.

W 72.7:date
ROSTER OF TROOPS.

ISTHMIAN CANAL COMMISSION
(1902– 1905)

W 73.1:date
ANNUAL REPORTS.

W 73.2:CT
GENERAL PUBLICATIONS.

W 73.3:
BULLETINS.

W 73.4:nos.
CIRCULARS.

W 73.5:nos.
LAWS.

Sanitation Department

W 73.6/1:date
ANNUAL REPORTS.

W 73.6/2:CT
GENERAL PUBLICATIONS.

W 73.6/3:nos.
BULLETINS [of] LABORATORY OF BOARD OF HEALTH.

W 73.6/4:nos.
CIRCULARS.

W 73.6/5:date
(MONTHLY) REPORTS.

Isthmian Canal Commission (Continued)

W 73.7:CT
SPECIFICATIONS.

W 73.8:v.nos.
CANAL RECORD.

W 73.9/1:date
MINUTES OF MEETINGS (pamphlet form).

W 73.9/2:date
MINUTES OF MEETINGS (indexes and digests).

W 73.10/1:nos.
CIRCULARS [proposals for supplies].

W 73.10/2:nos.
PROPOSALS FOR [supplies to accompany Circular proposals].

W 73.11:date
MANUAL OF INFORMATION.

W 73.12:date
MISCELLANEOUS SPECIAL REPORTS OF CHAIRMAN, ENGINEERS, ETC.

ALASKA ROAD COMMISSION
(1905– 1932)

CREATION AND AUTHORITY

    The Alaska Road Commission was established within the War Department by act of Congress, approved Jan. 27, 1905 (33 Stat. 616). The Commission was transferred to the Department of the Interior by act of Congress, approved June 30, 1932 (47 Stat. 446). By Memorandum of Agreement between the Department of Commerce and the Department of the Interior, dated Aug. 14-15, 1956, pursuant to the Federal-Aid Highway Act of 1956, the Commission was transferred to the Department of Commerce.

W 74.1:date
ANNUAL REPORTS.

    Later I 35.10/21

W 74.2:
GENERAL PUBLICATIONS.

    Later I 35.10/22

W 74.3:
BULLETINS.

W 74.4:nos.
CIRCULARS.

PORTO RICO
(1909– 1934)

W 75.1:date
ANNUAL REPORTS OF GOVERNMENT.

    Earlier S 10.1
    Later I 35.12/1

W 75.2:CT
GENERAL PUBLICATIONS.

W 75.3:
BULLETINS.

W 75.4:
CIRCULARS.

Anemia Dispensary Service

W 75.5/1:date
ANNUAL REPORTS.

W 75.5/2:CT
GENERAL PUBLICATIONS.

W 75.5/3:
BULLETINS.

W 75.5/4:
CIRCULARS.

Auditor

W 75.6/1:date
ANNUAL REPORTS.

    Earlier T 43.1

W 75.6/2:
GENERAL PUBLICATIONS.

    Earlier T 43.2

W 75.6/3:
BULLETINS.

W 75.6/4:
CIRCULARS.

Education Department

W 75.7/1:date
ANNUAL REPORTS.
    Earlier I 1.39

W 75.7/2:CT
GENERAL PUBLICATIONS.

W 75.7/3:
BULLETINS.

W 76.7/4:
CIRCULARS.

Health, Charities, and Corrections Department

W 75.8/1:date
ANNUAL REPORTS.

W 75.8/2:CT
GENERAL PUBLICATIONS.

W 75.8/3:
BULLETINS.

W 75.8/4:
CIRCULARS.

Interior Department

W 75.9/1:date
ANNUAL REPORTS.
    Earlier I 1.40

W 75.9/2:CT
GENERAL PUBLICATIONS.

W 75.9/3:
BULLETINS.

W 75.9/4:
CIRCULARS.

Treasurer

W 75.10/1:date
ANNUAL REPORTS.

W 75.10/2:CT
GENERAL PUBLICATIONS.

W 75.10/3:
BULLETINS.

W 75.10/4:
CIRCULARS.

Justice Department

W 75.11/1:date
ANNUAL REPORTS.

W 75.11/2:CT
GENERAL PUBLICATIONS.

W 75.11/3:nos.
BULLETINS.

W 75.11/4:nos.
CIRCULARS.

Porto Rico (Continued)

W 75.12:Legis.&Sess.
ACTS AND RESOLUTIONS OF THE LEGISLATURE.
    Later I 35.12/5

Office of Director of Sanitation

W 75.13/1:date
ANNUAL REPORTS.

W 75.13/2:CT
GENERAL PUBLICATIONS.

W 75.13/3:nos.
BULLETINS.

W 75.13/4:nos.
CIRCULARS.

Labor Bureau

W 75.14/1:date
ANNUAL REPORTS.

W 75.14/2:CT
GENERAL PUBLICATIONS.

W 75.14/3:
BULLETINS.

W 75.14/4:
CIRCULARS.

W 75.14/5:date
SPECIAL REPORTS.

Civil Service Commission

W 75.15/1:date
ANNUAL REPORTS.

W 75.15/2:CT
GENERAL PUBLICATIONS.

Executive Secretary

W 75.16/1:date
ANNUAL REPORTS.

W 75.16/2:CT
GENERAL PUBLICATIONS.

W 75.16/3:
BULLETINS.

W 75.16/4:
CIRCULARS.

Agriculture and Labor Department

W 75.17/1:date
ANNUAL REPORTS.

W 75.17/2:CT
GENERAL PUBLICATIONS.

W 75.17/3:
BULLETINS.

W 75.17/4:
CIRCULARS.

WESTERN DIVISION
(1911– 1920)

W 76.1:date
ANNUAL REPORTS.

W 76.2:CT
GENERAL PUBLICATIONS.

W 76.3:nos.
BULLETINS.

W 76.4:nos.
CIRCULARS.

W 76.5:date
GENERAL ORDERS.

W 76.6:date
SPECIAL ORDERS.

W 76.7:date
ROSTER OF TROOPS.

QUARTERMASTER CORPS
(1912– 1947)

CREATION AND AUTHORITY

The Quartermaster's Department was established within the Army by act of Congress, approved Mar. 28, 1812 (2 Stat. 696). An act of Congress, approved Aug. 24, 1912, created the Quartermaster Corps, which consolidated the Pay Department, Quartermaster's Department, and the Subsistence Department.

W 77.1:date
ANNUAL REPORTS.
    Later M 112.1

W 77.2:CT
GENERAL PUBLICATIONS.
    Later M 112.2

W 77.3:nos.
BULLETINS.

W 77.4:nos.
CIRCULARS.

W 77.4/2:nos.
CHANGES [in] CIRCULARS.

W 77.4/3:nos.
CIRCULARS (numbered).

W 77.5:date
STOPPAGE CIRCULARS. [Monthly]
    Later W 2.10

W 77.6:date
ROSTER SHOWING STATIONS AND DUTIES OF OFFICERS.

W 77.7:date
ARMY PAY TABLES.

W 77.8:CT
SPECIFICATIONS.

W 77.8/2:nos.
SPECIFICATIONS.

W 77.8/3:date
INDEXES TO SPECIFICATIONS.

    Changed to W 3.48/2

W 77.8/4:nos.
SPECIFICATIONS NOTICES. [Monthly]

W 77.9:date
PRICE LIST OF SUBSISTENCE STORES IN WASH-INGTON BARRACKS, D.C. [Monthly]

W 77.10:CT
RULES, REGULATIONS, AND INSTRUCTIONS.

W 77.10/2:CT&nos.
CHANGES TO RULES, REGULATIONS AND INSTRUCTIONS.

W 77.11:date
LAWS.

W 77.12:date
RULES AND REGULATIONS.

W 77.13:date
SCHEDULES (numbered).

W 77.14:date
LIST OF AWARDS.

W 77.15:CT
MANUALS.
    Later M 112.8

W 77.15/2:CT
CHANGES IN MANUALS.

W 77.15/3:nos.
INSPECTION MANUAL BULLETINS.

W 77.16/1:date
MANUAL FOR QUARTERMASTER CORPS.

> **W 77.16/2:date**
> – CHANGES.

> **W 77.16/3:nos.**
> QUARTERMASTER CORPS MANUAL.

> Printed and processed.
> Later M 112.8

W 77.17:CT
LECTURES.

W 77.18:date
QUARTERMASTER GENERAL OF THE ARMY, OFFICIAL TABLE OF DISTANCES.

W 77.19:date
PURCHASE AND STORAGE NOTICES.

> Formerly W 89.8

W 77.20:nos.
MONTHLY COMMODITY STATEMENT OF SURPLUS.

W 77.21:vol.
QUARTERMASTER CORPS. RECRUITING NOTES.

W 77.22:date
CIRCULAR LETTERS.
> Mimeographed, with some exceptions.
> Later M 112.4

W 77.23/1:nos.
GENERAL SUPPLIES FIXED PRICE LISTS.

W 77.23/2:nos.
GENERAL SUPPLIES LISTS.

W 77.23/3:nos.
CLOTHING AND EQUIPAGE FIXED PRICE LISTS.

W 77.23/4:nos.
CLOTHING AND EQUIPAGE LISTS.

W 77.23/5:nos.
SURPLUS LEATHER AND HARNESS LISTS.

W 77.23/5-1:nos
LEATHER AND HARNESS FIXED PRICE LISTS.

W 77.23/5-2:nos
SURPLUS LEATHER AND HARNESS LISTS.

W 77.23/6:nos.
MACHINERY AND ENGINEERING MATERIALS FIXES PRICE LISTS.

W 77.23/7:nos.
MACHINERY AND ENGINEERING MATERIALS LISTS.

W 77.23/8:nos.
MEDICAL AND HOSPITAL LISTS.

W 77.23/9:nos.
MOTOR AND VEHICLES FIXED PRICE LISTS.

W 77.23/10:nos.
MOTOR AND VEHICLES LISTS.

W 77.23/11:nos.
SURPLUS SUBSISTENCE LISTS.

W 77.23/12:nos.
TEXTILE LISTS.

W 77.24:nos.
QUARTERMASTER CORPS SUBSISTENCE SCHOOL, CHICAGO, ILL., BULLETINS.

W 77.25:nos.
JOINT MILITARY PASSENGER AGREEMENT.

W 77.25/2:date
JOINT MILITARY PASSENGER AGREEMENT, SIDE AGREEMENT.

W 77.26:nos.
JOINT MILITARY PASSENGER EQUALIZATION AGREEMENT.

W 77.27:date&nos.
PURCHASE NOTICES. MIMEOGRAPHED.

W 77.27/2:nos.
CONTRACT BULLETINS.

> Formerly Purchase Notices (W 77.27).

W 77.28:CT
SALE OF UNITED STATES VESSELS.

W 77.29:date
SHIPS REGISTER.

W 77.30:date
HANDBOOK FOR QUARTERMASTER.

W 77.31:letter-nos.
MOTOR TRANSPORT, TECHNICAL SERVICE BULLETINS.

W 77.32:nos.
EXCESS PROPERTY NOTICES.

W 77.33:nos.
PERSONNEL BULLETINS.

W 77.34:vol.
QUARTERMASTER LIBRARY RECORD. [Weekly]

W 77.35:CT
POSTERS.

W 77.36:nos.
Q.M.C. HISTORICAL STUDIES.
> Later M 112.9

W 77.37:CT
PETROLEUM FACILITIES OF [foreign countries] [confidential].

W 77.38:v.nos.
DEPOT AND MARKET CENTER OPERATIONS. [Monthly]
> Later M 112.7

W 77.39:nos.
TECHNICAL LIBRARY BIBLIOGRAPHIC SERIES.
> Later M 112.10

CENTRAL DEPARTMENT
(1911– 1920)

W 78.1:date
ANNUAL REPORTS.

W 78.2:CT
GENERAL PUBLICATIONS.

W 78.3:
BULLETINS.

W 78.4:
CIRCULARS.

W 78.5:date
GENERAL ORDERS.

W 78.6:date
SPECIAL ORDERS.

W 78.7:
POSTERS (class reserved: none received).

W 78.8/1:date
ANNUAL REPORTS, 2d DIVISION.

W 78.8/2:CT
GENERAL PUBLICATIONS.

W 78.8/3:
BULLETINS.

W 78.8/4:
CIRCULARS.

W 78.8/5:date
GENERAL COURT-MARTIAL ORDERS.

W 78.8/6:date
GENERAL ORDERS.

W 78.9:date
GENERAL COURT MARTIAL ORDERS.

CANAL ZONE
(1912– 1945)

CREATION AND AUTHORITY

> The Canal Zone Government was established as an independent agency by the act of August 24, 1912 (37 Stat. 561), as amended by the act of September 26, 1950 (64 Stat. 1041), and codified in section 31 of title 2 of the Canal Zone Code (76 Stat. 7).

W 79.1:date
ANNUAL REPORT OF GOVERNORS.

> Later M 115.1

W 79.2:CT
GENERAL PUBLICATIONS.
> Later M 115.2

W 79.3:
BULLETINS.

W 79.4:
CIRCULARS.

W 79.5:vol.
CANAL RECORD.

W 79.6:nos.
TARIFFS.

W 79.7:nos.
CLASSIFICATION OF ACCOUNTS.

W 79.8:date
TIDE, MOON, AND SUNRISE TABLES, BALBOA, PANAMA, AND CRISTOBAL, COLONIES. [Annual]

> Later M 115.7

W 79.9:date
RULES & REGULATIONS GOVERNING CARRYING AND KEEPING OF ARMS, HUNTING, PROTECTION OF BIRDS AND THEIR NESTS, & FISHING IN CANAL ZONE.

> Changed from W 79.2

Executive Department

W 79.10/1:date
ANNUAL REPORTS.

W 79.10/2:CT
GENERAL PUBLICATIONS.

W 79.10/3:
BULLETINS.

W 79.10/4:
CIRCULARS.

W 79.10/5:date
CANAL ZONE OFFICIAL POSTAL GUIDE.

W 79.10/6:date
ANNUAL REPORT OF INSURANCE BUSINESS
TRANSACTED IN CANAL ZONE.
Later M 115.10

W 79.10/7:nos.
CURRICULUM MONOGRAPHS.

W 79.10/8:nos.
CANAL ZONE JUNIOR COLLEGE CATALOGUES.
Later M 115.7

W 79.10/9:nos.
CANAL ZONE JUNIOR COLLEGE, EXTENSION
DIVISION, CATALOGUES.

Washington Office

W 79.11/1:date
ANNUAL REPORT.

W 79.11/2:CT
GENERAL PUBLICATIONS.

W 79.11/3:
BULLETINS.

W 79.11/4:
CIRCULARS.

W 79.11/5:date
MANUAL OF INFORMATION.

W 79.11/6:nos.
W CIRCULAR [proposals for supplies].
Later M 115.8

W 79.11/7:nos.
PROPOSALS FOR [Supplies to Accompany Circular
Proposals].

W 79.11/8:date
EXECUTIVE ORDERS RELATING TO PANAMA
CANAL.

Health Department

W 79.12/1:date
ANNUAL REPORTS.
Later PaC 1.12

W 79.12/2:CT
GENERAL PUBLICATIONS.

W 79.12/3:
BULLETINS.

W 79.12/4:
CIRCULARS.

W 79.12/5:date
MONTHLY REPORTS OF DEPARTMENT OF HEALTH.

W 79.12/6:v.nos.
PROCEEDINGS OF MEDICAL ASSOCIATION OF ISTH-
MIAN CANAL ZONE.

Panama Railroad Company

W 79.13/1:date
ANNUAL REPORTS.

W 79.13/2:CT
GENERAL PUBLICATIONS.

W 79.13/3:
BULLETINS.

W 79.13/4:
CIRCULARS.

W 79.13/5:nos.
CLASSIFICATION OF ACCOUNTS.

W 79.13/6:nos.
SPECIAL TARIFFS.

Agronomist

W 79.14/1:date
ANNUAL REPORTS.

W 79.14/2:CT
GENERAL PUBLICATIONS.

W 79.14/3:
BULLETINS.

W 79.14/4:
CIRCULARS.

DEPARTMENT OF VISAYAS
(1911–1920)

W 80.1:date
ANNUAL REPORTS.

W 80.2:CT
GENERAL PUBLICATIONS.

W 80.3:
BULLETINS.

W 80.4:
CIRCULARS.

HAWAII DEPARTMENT
(1910–1920)

W 81.1:date
ANNUAL REPORTS.

W 81.2:CT
GENERAL PUBLICATIONS.
W 81.3:
BULLETINS.

W 81.4:
CIRCULARS.

W 81.5:date
ROSTER AND DIRECTORY OF TROOPS IN HAWAIIAN
DEPARTMENT.

W 81.6:date
HAWAII DISTRICT, HAWAII DEPARTMENT, AND HA-
WAIIAN DEPARTMENT GENERAL.

W 81.7:date
SPECIAL ORDERS.

W 81.8:date
GENERAL COURT-MARTIAL ORDERS.

W 81.9:date
MEMORANDUM.

NATIONAL BOARD FOR
PROMOTION OF RIFLE PRACTICE
(1914–1922)

W 82.1:date
ANNUAL REPORTS.

W 82.2:CT
GENERAL PUBLICATIONS.

W 82.3:
BULLETINS.

W 82.4:
CIRCULARS.

W 82.5:vol.
SHOOTING NEWS.

SOUTHERN DEPARTMENT
(1913–1920)

W 83.1:date
ANNUAL REPORTS.

W 83.2:CT
GENERAL PUBLICATIONS.

W 83.3:nos.
BULLETINS.

W 83.4:nos.
CIRCULARS.

W 83.5:date
GENERAL ORDERS.

W 83.6:date
SPECIAL ORDERS.

W 83.7:date
ROSTER.

SOUTHEASTERN DEPARTMENT
(1917–1920)

W 84.1:date
ANNUAL REPORTS.

W 84.2:CT
GENERAL PUBLICATIONS.

W 84.3:date
BULLETINS.

W 84.4:
CIRCULARS.

W 84.5:date
GENERAL ORDERS.

W 84.6:date
SPECIAL ORDERS.

W 84.7:date
INSTRUCTION BULLETINS.

TRAINING CAMP ACTIVITIES COMMISSION
(1917– 1919)

W 85.1:date
ANNUAL REPORTS.

W 85.2:CT
GENERAL PUBLICATIONS.

W 85.3:
BULLETINS.

W 85.4:
CIRCULARS.

W 85.5:CT
POSTERS.

NORTHEASTERN DEPARTMENT
(1917– 1920)

W 86.1:date
ANNUAL REPORTS.

W 86.2:CT
GENERAL PUBLICATIONS.

W 86.3:
BULLETINS.

W 86.4:
CIRCULARS.

W 86.5:date
GENERAL ORDERS.

W 86.6:date
SPECIAL ORDERS.

AIR SERVICE
(1918– 1941)

W 87.1:date
ANNUAL REPORTS.

Later W 108.101

W 87.1/2:date
ANNUAL REPORT OF DIRECTOR OF AIRCRAFT PRODUCTION.

W 87.1/3:date
ANNUAL REPORT OF DIRECTOR OF MILITARY AERONAUTICS.

W 87.2:CT
GENERAL PUBLICATIONS.

Later W 108.102

W 87.3:nos.
BULLETINS.

Later W 108.108

W 87.4:nos.
CIRCULARS.

Later W 108.104

W 87.5:CT
MANUALS (miscellaneous).

W 87.6:
BULLETIN OF EXPERIMENTAL DEPARTMENT, AIRPLANE ENGINEERING DIVISION.

W 87.7:CT
POSTERS.

W 87.8:nos.
TECHNICAL ORDERS.

W 87.9:date
NAME AND ADDRESS OF AIR SERVICE OFFICERS.

W 87.9/2:date
DIRECTORY OF AIR SERVICE STATIONS.

W 87.10:nos.
INFORMATION CIRCULARS.

W 87.11:vol.nos.
AIR SERVICE INFORMATION CIRCULAR.

W 87.11/1:vol.
– (AEROSTATION).

W 87.11/2:vol.
– (AVIATION).

Supersedes W 87.13, W 87.14, and W 87.15

W 87.11/3:nos.
CHANGES IN AIR SERVICE INFORMATION CIRCULAR.

W 87.12:nos.
AERONAUTIC INFORMATION BULLETINS.

W 87.13:
AERONAUTICAL INFORMATION LIST.

Superseded by Air Service Information Circular (W 87.11/2).

W 87.14:
PROGRESS REPORTS, ENGINEERING DIVISION, McCOOK FIELD.

Superseded by Air Service Information Circular (W 87.11/2).

W 87.15:nos.
REPORTS OF SECRETARY OF ENGINEERING DIVISION, McCOOK FIELD.

Superseded by Air Service Information Circular (W 87.11/2).

W 87.16:date
MEMORANDA.

W 87.17:
PERSONNEL ORDERS.

W 87.18:date
LETTERS OF INSTRUCTION.

W 87.19:vol.
AIR CORPS NEWSLETTER.

Later W 108.7

W 87.20:nos.
LIBERTY ENGINE SERVICE BULLETINS.

W 87.21:nos.
AERONAUTICAL BULLETINS.

Later C 23.5

W 87.21/2:nos.
ROUTE INFORMATION SERIES.

W 87.21/3:nos.
AERONAUTICAL BULLETINS, STATE SUMMARIES.

Superseded by C 23.7

W 87.22:CT
MAPS.

W 87.22/2:nos.
AIR NAVIGATION MAPS.

W 87.23:nos.
TECHNICAL ORDERS.

Later W 108.108

W 87.24:CT
AIR SERVICE TACTICAL SCHOOL, LANGLEY FIELD, VA.

W 87.25:class nos.
AIR CORPS CATALOGS, STOCK LISTS.

Later W 108.107

W 87.26:date
AIR CORPS TECHNICAL REPORTS.

Air Corps Primary Flying School Randolph Field, Texas

W 87.27/1:date
ANNUAL REPORTS.

W 87.27/2:CT
GENERAL PUBLICATIONS.

MOTOR TRANSPORT CORPS
(1918– 1920)

W 88.1:date
ANNUAL REPORTS.

W 88.2:CT
GENERAL PUBLICATIONS.

W 88.3:
BULLETINS.

W 88.4:
CIRCULARS.

PURCHASE, STORAGE, AND TRAFFIC DIVISION
(1918– 1919)

W 89.1:date
ANNUAL REPORTS.

W 89.2:CT
GENERAL PUBLICATIONS.

W 89.3:
BULLETINS.

W 89.4:
CIRCULARS.

W 89.5:nos.
SUPPLY BULLETINS.

W 89.6/1:nos.
SUPPLY CIRCULARS.

W 89.6/2:nos.
CHANGES [to] SUPPLY CIRCULARS AND SUPPLY BULLETINS.

W 89.6/3:date
COMPILATION OF SUPPLY CIRCULARS AND SUPPLY BULLETINS.

W 89.6/4:date and nos.
COMPILATION OF SUPPLY CIRCULARS AND SUPPLY BULLETINS, CHANGES.

W 89.7:nos.
WAR DEPARTMENT CATALOGUES (standard specifications).

W 89.8:date
PURCHASE AND STORAGE NOTICES.

Later W 77.19

TANK CORPS
(1918– 1919)

W 90.1:date
ANNUAL REPORTS.

W 90.2:CT
GENERAL PUBLICATIONS.

W 90.3:
BULLETINS.

W 90.4:
CIRCULARS.

CHEMICAL CORPS
(1946– 1947)

CREATION AND AUTHORITY

The Chemical Warfare Service was established within the War Department by General Order 62, dated June 28, 1918. In 1946, the Service was renamed the Chemical Corps.

W 91.1:date
ANNUAL REPORTS.

W 91.2:CT
GENERAL PUBLICATIONS.

W 91.3:vol.
CHEMICAL WARFARE BULLETINS, REVIEW OF DEVELOPMENTS IN APPLICATION OF CHEMICALS TO MILITARY EFFORT. [Quarterly]

W 91.4:
CIRCULARS.

W 91.6:CT
CHEMICAL WARFARE SCHOOL, EDGEWOOD ARSENAL, MARYLAND: REGULATIONS, RULES, AND INSTRUCTIONS.

W 91.7:nos.
CHEMICAL WARFARE FIELD SERVICE BULLETINS.

Chemical Warfare School
Edgewood Arsenal, Maryland

W 91.8/1:date
ANNUAL REPORTS.

W 91.8/2:CT
GENERAL PUBLICATIONS.

W 91.8/7:nos.
PAMPHLETS.

W 91.8/8:bk.nos.
CHEMICAL WARFARE SCHOOL TEXTS.

Chemical Corps (Continued)

W 91.9:nos.
CHEMICAL WARFARE TECHNICAL BULLETINS. [Restricted]

W 91.10:date
NEWS LETTERS. [Monthly]

CONSTRUCTION DIVISION
(1918– 1920)

W 92.1:date
ANNUAL REPORTS.

W 92.2:CT
GENERAL PUBLICATIONS.

W 92.3:
BULLETINS.

W 92.4:
CIRCULARS.

W 92.5:letters
MANUAL OF CONSTRUCTION DIVISION, ARMY.

WAR DEPARTMENT CLAIMS
BOARD
(1919– 1922)

W 93.1:date
ANNUAL REPORTS.

W 93.2:CT
GENERAL PUBLICATIONS.

W 93.3:
BULLETINS.

W 93.4:
CIRCULARS.

W 93.5:vol.
DECISIONS.

W 93.6:nos.
INFORMATION CIRCULARS.

REAL ESTATE SERVICE
(1918– 1920)

W 94.1:date
ANNUAL REPORTS.

W 94.2:CT
GENERAL PUBLICATIONS.

W 94.3:
BULLETINS.

W 94.5:
CIRCULARS.

AMERICAN EXPEDITIONARY
FORCES
(1914– 1920)

W 95.1:date
ANNUAL REPORTS.

W 95.2:CT
GENERAL PUBLICATIONS.

W 95.3:
BULLETINS.

W 95.3/2:nos.
MUSKETRY BULLETINS.

W 95.4:
CIRCULARS.

W 95.5:
GENERAL ORDERS.

W 95.6:
SPECIAL ORDERS.

W 95.7:
COURT MARTIAL ORDERS.

W 95.8:CT
REGULATIONS AND INSTRUCTIONS.

W 95.9:nos.
PRESS REVIEW.

W 95.10:date
SUMMARY OF INFORMATION.

W 95.11:nos.
SUMMARY OF AIR INFORMATION.

W 95.12:nos.
SUMMARY OF INTELLIGENCE.

W 95.13:nos.
NOTES ON RECENT OPERATIONS.

W 95.14:CT
BLANK FORMS AND RECORD BOOKS.

W 95.15:nos.
CITATION ORDERS.

W 95.16:nos.
GRAVES REGISTRATION SERVICE BULLETINS.

Air Service

W 95.21/1:date
ANNUAL REPORTS.

W 95.21/2:CT
GENERAL PUBLICATIONS.

W 95.21/3:
BULLETINS.

W 95.21/4:
CIRCULARS.

W 95.21/5:nos.
AIR SERVICE BULLETIN, A.E.F.

W 95.21/6:nos.
BALLOON NOTES. A.E.F.

W 95.21/7:nos.
TECHNICAL SECTION BULLETINS.

W 95.21/8:nos.
RADIO BULLETINS.

Artillery Office

W 95.22/1:date
ANNUAL REPORTS.

W 95.22/2:CT
GENERAL PUBLICATIONS.

W 95.22/3:
BULLETINS.

W 95.22/4:
CIRCULARS.

Engineer Department

W 95.23/1:date
ANNUAL REPORTS.

W 95.23/2:CT
GENERAL PUBLICATIONS.

W 95.23/3:
BULLETINS.

W 95.23/4:
CIRCULARS.

Army Heavy Artillery School
Angers, France

W 95.24/1:date
ANNUAL REPORTS.

W 95.24/2:CT
GENERAL PUBLICATIONS.

W 95.24/3:
BULLETINS.

W 95.24/4:
CIRCULARS.

Saumur Artillery School
Saumur, France

W 95.25/1:date
ANNUAL REPORTS.

W 95.25/2:CT
GENERAL PUBLICATIONS.

W 95.25/3:
BULLETINS.

W 95.25/4:
CIRCULARS.

FIELD ARTILLERY OFFICE
(1918– 1922)

W 96.1:date
ANNUAL REPORTS.

W 96.2:CT
GENERAL PUBLICATIONS.

W 96.3:
BULLETINS.

W 96.4:
CIRCULARS.

W 96.5:nos.
INFORMATION BULLETIN.

FINANCE DEPARTMENT
(1920– 1947)

W 97.1:date
ANNUAL REPORTS.
　　　Later M 116.1

W 97.2:CT
GENERAL PUBLICATIONS.
　　　Later M 116.2

W 97.3:date&nos.
BULLETINS– FINANCE BULLETINS.

　　　Replaced Finance Memorandums (W 97.6)
　　　Later M 116.3

W 97.4:
CIRCULARS.

W 97.5:date
FINANCE CIRCULARS.

W 97.5/2:nos.
FINANCE CIRCULARS, CHANGES.

W 97.5/3:letters&nos.
FINANCE CIRCULARS.

W 97.5/4:nos.
FINANCE CIRCULARS, LETTERED, CHANGES.

W 97.6:nos.
FINANCE MEMORANDUM.

W 97.7:date
STOPPAGE CIRCULAR. [Monthly]

　　　Mimeographed.

Finance School
Washington, D.C.

W 97.8/1:date
ANNUAL REPORTS.

W 97.8/2:CT
GENERAL PUBLICATIONS.

W 97.8/7:nos.
FINANCE SCHOOL TEXTS.

Army Service Forces
Fiscal Director's Office

W 97.101:date
ANNUAL REPORTS (Dependency Benefits Office).

W 97.102:CT
GENERAL PUBLICATIONS. (Dependency Benefits
　Office).

W 97.105:CT
LAWS.

TRANSPORTATION SERVICE
(1919– 1920)

W 98.1:date
ANNUAL REPORTS.

W 98.2:CT
GENERAL PUBLICATIONS.

W 98.3:
BULLETINS.

W 98.4:
CIRCULARS.

ARMY AND CORPS AREAS AND
DEPARTMENTS
(1920– 1934)

W 99.1:date
ANNUAL REPORTS.

W 99.2:CT
GENERAL PUBLICATIONS.

W 99.3:
BULLETINS.

W 99.4:
CIRCULARS.

1st Corps Area

Formerly Northeastern Department (W 86).

W 99.11/1:date
ANNUAL REPORTS.

W 99.11/2:CT
GENERAL PUBLICATIONS.

W 99.11/3:date
BULLETINS.

W 99.11/4:date
CIRCULARS.

W 99.11/5:date
GENERAL ORDERS.

W 99.11/6:date
SPECIAL ORDERS.

W 99.11/6:date
SPECIAL ORDERS.

W 99.11/7:date&nos.
GENERAL COURT-MARTIAL ORDERS.

W 99.11/8:date&nos.
TRAINING MEMORANDUM.

W 99.11/9:date&nos.
[CIVILIAN CONSERVATION CORPS] MEMORANDUM.

W 99.11/10:date&nos.
[CIVILIAN CONSERVATION CORPS] GENERAL
　ORDERS.

W 99.11/11:date&nos.
[REGULATIONS].

2d Corps Area

Formerly part of Eastern Department.

W 99.12/1:date
ANNUAL REPORTS.

W 99.12/2:CT
GENERAL PUBLICATIONS.

W 99.12/3:date
BULLETINS.

W 99.12/4:date
CIRCULARS.

W 99.12/5:date
GENERAL ORDERS.

W 99.12/6:date
SPECIAL ORDERS.

W 99.12/7:date
GENERAL COURT-MARTIAL ORDERS.

W 99.12/8:date
TRAINING CIRCULARS.

3d Corps Area

Formerly a part of Eastern Department.

W 99.13/1:date
ANNUAL REPORTS.

W 99.13/2:CT
GENERAL PUBLICATIONS.

W 99.13/3:date
BULLETINS.

W 99.13/4:date
CIRCULARS.

W 99.13/5:date
GENERAL ORDERS.

W 99.13/6:date
SPECIAL ORDERS.

W 99.13/7:date
GENERAL COURT-MARTIAL ORDERS.

W 99.13/8:date
TRAINING MEMORANDUM.

W 99.13/9:date&nos.
RECREATION MEMORANDUM.

W 99.13/10:date&nos.
R.O.T.C. MEMORANDUM.

W 99.13/11:date&nos.
HEADQUARTERS ORDERS.

W 99.13/12:date&nos.
QUARTERMASTER LETTERS OF INFORMATION.

W 99.13/13:date&nos.
NATIONAL GUARD MEMORANDUM.

W 99.13/14:date&nos.
EXTENSION SCHOOL MEMORANDUM.

4th Corps Area

Formerly part of the Southeastern Department, (W 84).

W 99.14/1:date
ANNUAL REPORTS.

W 99.14/2:CT
GENERAL PUBLICATIONS.

W 99.14/3:date
BULLETINS.

W 99.14/4:date
CIRCULARS.

W 99.14/5:date
GENERAL ORDERS.

W 99.14/6:date
SPECIAL ORDERS.

W 99.14/7:date
GENERAL COURT-MARTIAL ORDERS.

W 99.14/8:date&nos.
TRAINING MEMORANDUM.

W 99.14/9:date&nos.
NATIONAL GUARD MEMORANDUM.

W 99.14/10:date&nos.
GOLF BULLETINS.

W 99.14/11:date&nos.
TENNIS MEMORANDUM.

5th Corps Area

Formerly a part of the Central Department, (W 78) and the Eastern Department.

W 99.15/1:date
ANNUAL REPORTS.

W 99.15/2:CT
GENERAL PUBLICATIONS.

W 99.15/3:date
BULLETINS.

W 99.15/4:date
CIRCULARS.

W 99.15/5:date
GENERAL ORDERS.

W 99.15/6:date
SPECIAL ORDERS.

W 99.15/7:date
GENERAL COURT-MARTIAL ORDERS.

W 99.15/8:date&nos.
TRAINING MEMORANDUM.

W 99.15/9:date&nos.
HEADQUARTERS MEMORANDUM.

W 99.15/10:nos.
TENNIS BULLETINS.

W 99.15/11:nos.
GOLF BULLETIN.

W 99.15/12:nos.
CIVILIAN CONSERVATION CORPS: MEMORANDUM.

W 99.15/13:nos.
CIVILIAN CONSERVATION CORPS: CIRCULARS.

6th Corps Area

Formerly part of the Central Department, (W 78).

W 99.16/1:date
ANNUAL REPORTS.

W 99.16/2:CT
GENERAL PUBLICATIONS.

W 99.16/3:date
BULLETINS.

W 99.16/4:date
CIRCULARS.

W 99.16/5:date
GENERAL ORDERS.

W 99.16/6:date
SPECIAL ORDERS.

W 99.16/7:date
GENERAL COURT-MARTIAL ORDERS.

W 99.16/8:date&nos.
TRAINING MEMORANDUM.

W 99.16/9:date&nos.
GOLF BULLETIN.

W 99.16/10:date&nos.
ADMINISTRATIVE ORDERS.

W 99.16/11:date&nos.
SPECIAL COURT-MARTIAL ORDERS.

W 99.16/12:nos.
ORGANIZED RESERVES CIRCULAR.

7th Corps Area

Formerly part of the Central Department, (W 78).

W 99.17/1:date
ANNUAL REPORTS.

W 99.17/2:CT
GENERAL PUBLICATIONS.

W 99.17/3:date
BULLETINS.

W 99.17/4:date
CIRCULARS.

W 99.17/5:date
GENERAL ORDERS.

W 99.17/6:date
SPECIAL ORDERS.

W 99.17/7:date
GENERAL COURT-MARTIAL ORDERS.

W 99.17/8:date
TRAINING CIRCULARS.

W 99.17/9:date&nos.
RECRUITING MEMORANDUM.

W 99.17/10:date&nos.
RECRUITING BULLETINS.

W 99.17/11:date&nos.
TRAINING BULLETINS.

W 99.17/12:date&nos.
CHEMICAL WARFARE SERVICE BULLETIN.

W 99.17/13:date&nos.
[CITIZEN MILITARY TRAINING CAMPS] BULLETIN.

W 99.17/14:date&nos.
EXTENSION SCHOOL BULLETIN.

W 99.17/15:date&nos.
NATIONAL GUARD BULLETINS.

W 99.17/16:date&nos.
ORDNANCE BULLETINS.

W 99.17/17:date&nos.
ORGANIZED RESERVES BULLETIN.

W 99.17/18:date&nos.
RESERVE OFFICERS TRAINING CORPS BULLETIN.

W 99.17/19:nos.
MANEUVER MEMORANDUM.

8th Corps Area

Formerly part of the Southern Department (W 83), Central Department (W 78), Southeastern Department (W 84).

W 99.18/1:date
ANNUAL REPORTS.

W 99.18/2:CT
GENERAL PUBLICATIONS.

W 99.18/3:date
BULLETINS.

W 99.18/4:date
CIRCULARS.

W 99.18/5:date
GENERAL ORDERS.

W 99.18/6:date
SPECIAL ORDERS.

W 99.18/7:date&nos.
MEMORANDUM.

W 99.18/8:date&nos.
ORGANIZED RESERVES MEMORANDUM.

W 99.18/9:date&nos.
TENNIS BULLETIN.

W 99.18/10:date&nos.
TRAINING MEMORANDUM.

9th Corps Area

Formerly the Western Department (W 76) and part of the Southern Department (W 83).

W 99.19/1:date
ANNUAL REPORTS.

W 99.19/2:CT
GENERAL PUBLICATIONS.

W 99.19/3:date
BULLETINS.

W 99.19/4:date
CIRCULARS.

W 99.19/5:date
GENERAL ORDERS.

W 99.19/6:date
SPECIAL ORDERS.

W 99.19/7:date&nos.
GENERAL COURT-MARTIAL ORDERS.

W 99.19/8:date
COMPILATION OF ORDERS.

W 99.19/9:date&nos.
NATIONAL GUARD MEMORANDUM.

W 99.19/10:date&nos.
SUMMER TRAINING CAMP BULLETINS.
Changed from W 99.19/7

W 99.19/11:date&nos.
TRAINING MEMORANDUM.

W 99.19/12:date
CIVILIAN CONSERVATION CORPS UNIT.

10th Corps Area

Formerly Hawaii Department (W 81).

W 99.20/1:date
ANNUAL REPORTS.

W 99.20/2:CT
GENERAL PUBLICATIONS.

W 99.20/3:date
BULLETINS.

W 99.20/4:date
CIRCULARS.

W 99.20/5:date
GENERAL ORDERS.

W 99.20/6:date
SPECIAL ORDERS.

W 99.20/7:date&nos.
TRAINING MEMORANDUM.

W 99.20/8:date&nos.
MEMORANDUM.

W 99.20/9:nos.
REGULATIONS.

11th Corps Area

Panama Canal Department

W 99.21/2:CT
GENERAL PUBLICATIONS.

W 99.21/3:date
BULLETINS.

W 99.21/4:date
CIRCULARS.

W 99.21/5:date
GENERAL ORDERS.

W 99.21/6:date
SPECIAL ORDERS.

W 99.21/7:date
GENERAL COURT-MARTIAL ORDERS.

W 99.21/8:date
PANAMA CANAL DEPARTMENT, LIST AND DIREC-
TORY.

W 99.21/9:date&nos.
MEMORANDUM.

W 99.21/10:date & nos.
MEMORANDUM.

Processed.

12th Corps Area

Formerly Philippine Division (W 80).

W 99.22/1:date
ANNUAL REPORTS.

W 99.22/2:CT
GENERAL PUBLICATIONS.

W 99.22/3:date
BULLETINS.

W 99.22/4:date
CIRCULARS.

W 99.22/5:date
GENERAL ORDERS.

W 99.22/6:date
SPECIAL ORDERS.

MILITARY INTELLIGENCE
DIVISION
(1918– 1947)

W 100.1:date
ANNUAL REPORTS.
Later M 106.1

W 100.2:CT
GENERAL PUBLICATIONS.
Later M 106.2

W 100.3:
BULLETINS.

W 100.4:
CIRCULARS.

W 100.5:CT
MANUALS.

W 100.6:CT
MAPS.

W 100.7:nos.
SPECIAL SERIES.

W 100.8:nos.
STATION AND PROGRAM NOTES [of Foreign Broadcast Intelligence Service].

W 100.9:nos.
SPECIAL RELEASES [of Foreign Broadcast Intelligence Service].

W 100.10:date
DAILY REPORT, FOREIGN RADIO BROADCASTS,
TABLE OF CONTENTS. [Monthly]

W 100.11:nos.
DAILY REPORT, FOREIGN RADIO BROADCASTS,
EUROPEAN SECTION.

INLAND AND COASTWISE
WATERWAYS SERVICE
(1920– 1923)

W 101.1:date
ANNUAL REPORTS.

W 101.2:CT
GENERAL PUBLICATIONS.

W 101.3:
BULLETINS.

W 101.4:
CIRCULARS.

AMERICAN NATIONAL RED
CROSS
(1917– 1947)

W 102.1:date
ANNUAL REPORTS.
Later Y 3.Am 3/5:1

W 102.2:CT
GENERAL PUBLICATIONS.
Later Y 3.Am 3/5:2

W 102.3:
BULLETINS.

W 102.4:
CIRCULARS.

W 102.5:CT
POSTERS.

W 102.6:v.nos.
PRISONERS OF WAR BULLETINS. [Monthly]

W 102.7:CT
REGULATIONS, RULES AND INSTRUCTIONS.

Later Y 3.Am 3/5:6

INLAND WATERWAYS
CORPORATION
(1924– 1939)

CREATION AND AUTHORITY

The Inland Waterways Commission was established by the President on March 14, 1907.
The Commission submitted its report in 1908.

W 103.1:date
ANNUAL REPORTS.
Later C 29.1

W 103.2:CT
GENERAL PUBLICATIONS.
Later C 29.2

W 103.3:
BULLETINS.

W 103.4:
CIRCULARS.

ARMY INDUSTRIAL COLLEGE
(1924– 1947)

W 104.1:date
ANNUAL REPORTS.

W 104.2:CT
GENERAL PUBLICATIONS.

W 104.7:CT
[LECTURES] COURSES 1936– 37.

W 104.7/2:CT
[LECTURES] COURSES 1937– 38.

W 104.7/3:CT
[LECTURES] COURSES 1938– 39.

W 104.7/4:CT
[LECTURES] COURSES 1939– 40.

W 104.7/5:CT
[LECTURES] COURSES AUGUST– DECEMBER 1940.

W 104.7/6:CT
[LECTURES] COURSES 1941.

W 104.8:date
LIST OF BOOKS RECEIVED. [Quarterly]

U.S. HIGH COMMISSIONER TO
PHILIPPINE ISLANDS
(1934– 1942)

W 105.1:date
ANNUAL REPORTS.

PHILIPPINE ISLANDS,
PRESIDENT
(1934– 1941)

W 106.1:date
ANNUAL REPORTS.

PUBLIC RELATIONS DIVISION
(1946– 1947)

W 107.1:date
ANNUAL REPORTS.

W 107.2:CT
GENERAL PUBLICATIONS.

W 107.7:vol.
NEWSMAP. [Weekly]

Later W 109.107:

W 107.8:CT
POSTERS.

W 107.9:nos.
WAR REPORTS FOR LOGGERS AND MILL MEN.

W 107.10:nos.
[METAL PAMPHLETS].

W 107.11:BRP serial nos.
ARMY WAR CASUALTIES [Confidential until released].

W 107.12:serial nos.
CIVILIAN PERSONNEL LIBERATED FROM JAPANESE
CUSTODY.

W 107.13:CT
WORLD WAR II HONOR LIST OF DEAD AND MISSING
(by States).

ARMY AIR FORCE
(1941– 1947)

W 108.1:date
ANNUAL REPORTS.

Later M 301.1

W 108.2:CT
GENERAL PUBLICATIONS.

Later M 301.2

W 108.3:nos.
BULLETINS.

Earlier W 108.103

W 108.3/2:
READJUSTMENT BULLETIN.

W 108.6:CT
REGULATIONS, RULES, AND INSTRUCTIONS
(miscellaneous).

Later M 301.6

W 108.7:vol.
AIR FORCE NEWS LETTER. [Monthly]

W 108.8:nos.
TECHNICAL ORDERS. [Restricted]

Earlier W 108.108
Later M 301.13

W 108.9:class no.
STOCK LISTS.

Earlier W 108.107

W 108.9/2:class no.
ABBREVIATED STOCK LISTS.

W 108.10:nos.
TECHNICAL POSTERS (Pilot Safety Series).

W 108.11:nos.
A.A.F. MEMORANDUM.

W 108.12:nos.
ARMY AIR FORCES LIBRARY BULLETINS.

W 108.13:nos.
ARMY AIR FORCES SPECIFICATIONS.

W 108.13/2:date
– INDEX. [Monthly]

W 108.13/3:date
INDEX OF SPECIFICATIONS APPROVED FOR AAF
PROCUREMENT. [Semiannual]

Later M 301.11

W 108.14:CT
POSTERS.

W 108.15:date
NUMERICAL LIST COVERING ARMY AIR FORCES
AND ARMY-NAVY AERONAUTICAL STANDARD
PARTS. [Monthly]

Later M 301.12

W 108.15/2:date
ALPHABETICAL LIST COVERING ARMY AIR FORCES
AND ARMY-NAVY AERONAUTICAL STANDARD
PARTS. [Semiannual]

W 108.16:v.nos.
PUBLICATIONS OF WEATHER RESEARCH CENTER.

W 108.17:nos.
PUBLICATIONS OF DIRECTORATE OF WEATHER;
SPECIAL SERIES.

W 108.18:vol.
TECHNICAL DATA DIGEST. [Monthly]

Proc. & printed.
Later M 301.9

W 108.19:nos.
AIR FORCES MANUALS.

Later M 301.18

W 108.20:letter-nos.
DETAILED MOCK-UP INFORMATION.

W 108.21:nos.
INFORMATION LETTERS. [Monthly]

W 108.22:nos.
AAF MANUALS.

Later M 301.18

W 108.23:nos.
INFORMATIONAL BULLETINS.

W 108.24:nos.
WINGS AT WAR SERIES.

W 108.25:nos.
AVIATION PSYCHOLOGY PROGRAM RESEARCH
REPORTS.

W 108.26:date
ARMY AIR FORCES RADIO AND FACILITY CHARTS,
ATLANTIC AND CARIBBEAN AREAS. [Monthly]

W 108.27:date
ARMY AIR FORCES RADIO FACILITY CHARTS, NORTH
PACIFIC AREA.

Later M 301.14 and M 301.15

W 108.28:nos.
WEATHER DIVISION PUBLICATIONS, REPORTS.

W 108.29:v.nos.
JOINT ARMY & NAVY RADIO FACILITY CHARTS.

Later M 301.16

W 108.30:date
HISTORICAL WEATHER MAP, NORTHERN HEMI-
SPHERE.

W 108.31:nos.
TRANSLATIONS.

W 108.32:nos.
INFORMATION INTELLIGENCE SUMMARY.

W 108.33:v.nos.
IMPACT.

W 108.34:nos.
AIR WEATHER SERVICE TECHNICAL REPORTS.

Late M 301.22

W 108.35:v.nos.&nos.
WEATHER SERVICE BULLETIN.

W 108.36:nos.
AIR WEATHER SERVICE, SPECIAL STUDIES.

W 108.36/2:nos.
1st WEATHER WING, SPECIAL STUDY.

W 108.37:nos.
AAF BOMBING ACCURACY, REPORT NO.

Air Corps

W 108.101:date
ANNUAL REPORTS.

Earlier W 87.1/1

W 108.102:CT
GENERAL PUBLICATIONS.

Earlier W 87.2

W 108.103:nos.
BULLETINS.

Earlier W 87.3
Later W 108.3

W 108.104:nos.
CIRCULARS.

Earlier W 87.4

W 108.107:class nos.
STOCK LISTS.

Earlier W 87.25
Later W 108.9

W 108.108:nos.
TECHNICAL ORDERS. RESTRICTED.

Processed.
Earlier W 87.23
Later W 108.8

SERVICES OF SUPPLY
(1940– 1947)

W 109.1:date
ANNUAL REPORTS.

W 109.2:CT
GENERAL PUBLICATIONS.

W 109.4
ASF CIRCULARS. [Official]

W 109.5
LAWS.

W 109.6:CT
REGULATIONS, RULES AND INSTRUCTIONS.

W 109.7:nos.-letter
PROCUREMENT REGULATIONS (numbered-lettered).

[To be incorporated into W 109.9]

W 109.8:nos.
PROCUREMENT REGULATIONS (numbered), PERMANENT REGULATIONS.

Supersedes Army Regulations 5-series (W 1.6/1:5) and Procurement Circulars (W 1.31).
Later M 101.11

W 109.8/2:nos.
PROCUREMENT REGULATIONS.

W 109.9:nos.
GENERAL ORDERS.

W 109.10:date
U.S. ARMY SPECIFICATIONS, FEDERAL SPECIFICATIONS, COMMERCIAL STANDARDS, [and] SIMPLIFIED PRACTICE RECOMMENDATIONS; REPORTS ON CHANGES IN. [Monthly]

Early W 1.38

W 109.11:CT
POSTERS.

W 109.12:nos.
ARMY SERVICE FORCES MANUALS.

W 109.13:nos.
HYMNS FROM HOME.

W 109.14:sec.nos.&letter-nos.
ARMY SERVICES FORCES CATALOGS.

Earlier issues of Ordnance Supply Catalogs (W 34.23).

W 109.15:nos.
MEMORANDUM S-NOS.

Proc. Admin.

W 109.15/2
SOS CIVILIAN PERSONNEL MANUAL.

Proc. Admin.

W 109.15/3:nos.
ADMINISTRATIVE MEMORANDUM S-NOS.

Proc. Admin.

Special Services Division

W 109.101:date
ANNUAL REPORTS.

Later M 117.1

W 109.102:CT
GENERAL PUBLICATIONS.

Later M 117.2

W 109.107:vol.
NEWSMAP. [Weekly]

Prepared and distributed by Army Orientation Course.
Earlier W 107.7
Later W 109.207

W 109.107/2:v.nos.
– OVERSEAS EDITION. [Weekly]

Later W 109.208

W 109.107/3:v.nos.
– INDUSTRIAL EDITION. [Weekly]
Later W 109.209

W 109.108:v.
SPECIAL SERVICE DIGEST [For official use only]. [Monthly]

W 109.109:date
ARMY HIT KIT OF POPULAR SONGS. [Monthly]

Later M 117.7

W 109.110:CT
POCKET GUIDES [to foreign countries].

W 109.111:CT
LANGUAGE GUIDES.

W 109.112:CT
MAPS.

W 109.113:CT
POSTERS.

W 109.114:nos.
SOLDIER SHOWS, BLUEPRINT SPECIALS.

W 109.115:nos.
HOSPITAL ENTERTAINMENT GUIDES.

W 109.116:nos.
SOLDIER SHOWS, FOLIOS.

W 109.117
SPECIAL SERVICE TOPICS.

Morale Services Division

W 109.201:date
ANNUAL REPORTS.

Later W 111.1

W 109.202:CT
GENERAL PUBLICATIONS.

Later W 111.2

W 109.206:CT
REGULATIONS, RULES, AND INSTRUCTIONS.

W 109.207:v.nos.
NEWSMAP FOR ARMED FORCES. [Weekly]

Earlier W 109.107

W 109.207/2:v.nos.
NEWSMAP FOR ARMED FORCES, SPECIAL EDITION. [Weekly]

W 109.208:v.nos.
NEWSMAP, OVERSEAS EDITION. [Weekly]

Earlier W 109.107/2

W 109.209:v.nos.
NEWSMAP, INDUSTRIAL EDITION. [Weekly]

Earlier W 109.107/3

W 109.210:v.nos.
DIGEST FOR OFFICIAL USE ONLY. [Monthly]

Later Army Information Digest, (W 1.66).

W 190.211:CT
POSTERS.

W 109.211/2:nos.
[SAVINGS PROGRAM] POSTERS.

W 109.212:nos.
FACT SHEETS.

Later W 111.7

W 109.213:CT
MAPS.

W 109.214:letter– nos.
POST-WAR PLANS FOR SOLDIER SERIES, REPORTS.

W 109.215:CT
POCKET GUIDES [to foreign countries].

Earlier W 109.110
Later D 2.8

W 109.216
G.I. GALLEY.

Office of Chief of Transportation

W 109.301:date
ANNUAL REPORTS.

Later D 117.1

W 109.302:CT
GENERAL PUBLICATIONS.

W 109.307:nos.
TRANSPORTATION CORPS PAMPHLETS.

HISTORICAL DIVISION
(1946–1947)

W 110.1:date
ANNUAL REPORTS.

> Later M 103.1

W 110.2:CT
GENRAL PUBLICATIONS.

> Later M 103.2

W 110.7:CT
AMERICAN FORCES IN ACTION SERIES.

> Later M 103.8

INFORMATION AND EDUCATION DIVISION
(1944–1947)

W 111.1:date
ANNUAL REPORTS.

> Earlier W 109.201
> Later M 104.1

W 111.2:CT
GERNERAL PUBLICATIONS.

> Earlier W 109.202
> Later M 104.2

W 111.7:nos.
ARMY TALK [Weekly].

> Earlier W 109.212
> Later M 104.7

WAR TRADE BOARD
(1917–1919)

CREATION AND AUTHORITY

The War Trade Board was established by Executive Order 2729-A of Oct. 12, 1917, to succeed the Exports Administrative Board. The Board was termininated on June 30, 1919, and succeeded by the War Trade Board Section of the Department of State.

WT 1.1:date
ANNUAL REPORTS

WT 1.2:CT
GENERAL PUBLICATIONS.

WT 1.3
BULLETINS.

WT 1.4
CIRCULARS.

WT 1.5:nos.
JOURNAL OF WAR TRADE BOARD.

> Later S 13.5

WT 1.6:nos.
WAR TRADE BOARD PAMPHLETS.

WT 1.7:nos.
ENEMY TRADING LIST.

Transportation Bureau

WT 2.1:date
ANNUAL REPORTS

WT 2.2:CT
GENERAL PUBLICATIONS.

WT 2.3
BULLETINS

WT 2.4
CIRCULARS.

WT 2.5:nos.
GENERAL RULES.

WT 2.6:nos.
SPECIAL RULES.

Exports Bureau

WT 3.1:date
ANNUAL REPORTS.

WT 3.2:CT
GENERAL PUBLICATIONS.

WT 3.3
BULLETINS.

WT 3.4
CIRCULARS.

Imports Bureau

WT 4.1:date
ANNUAL REPORTS.

WT 4.2:CT
GENERAL PUBLICATIONS.

WT 4.3
BULLETINS.

WT 4.4
CIRCULARS.

WT 4.5:date
RULES AND REGULATIONS OF BUREAU OF IMPORTS.

Research Bureau

WT 5.1:date
ANNUAL REPORTS.

WT 5.2:CT
GENERAL PUBLICATIONS.

WT 5.3
BULLETINS.

WT 5.4
CIRCULARS.

CONGRESS

In accordance with recommendations from the Government Documents Round Table (ALA) and the Depository Library Council to the Public Printer, classes Y 1.1/2 through Y 1.1/8 and Y 1.4/1 through Y 1.4/9 have been implemented for Congressional publications, beginning with the 97th Congress, 1st Session (1981), and is in keeping with the expressed desirability of filing Congressional documents and reports in Serial Set order. [Daily Depository Shipping List 15,543, dated January 23, 1981]

X 1– X 42
ANNUALS OF CONGRESS.

X 43– X 71
REGISTER OF DEBATES.

X 72– X 180
CONGRESSIONAL GLOBE.

X 94-2:H.doc.661   • Item 995-G-1
DESCHLER'S PRECEDENTS OF THE U.S. HOUSE OF REPRESENTATIVES.

                          • Item 993 (P)
X   • Item 993-A (MF)
CONGRESSIONAL RECORD. [Bound volumes]

                          • Item 994-B (P)
X/a   • Item 994-C (MF)
CONGRESSIONAL RECORD. v. 1– 1873– [Daily]

Contains a verbatim record of the debates and proceedings of the Senate and the House of Representatives. Contents of the daily edition are edited, corrected, and sometimes rearranged, and republished in a bound edition.
Index, which includes History of Bills and Resolutions is issued fortnightly.
The Congressional Record is published daily while Congress is in session.
ISSN 0363-7239

X   • Item 993-A-1
CONGRESSIONAL RECORD (Bound) 1985 AND FORWARD.

X 1.1   • Item 993-A (MF)
CONGRESSIONAL RECORD.

X 1.1   • Item 993-A-1
CONGRESSIONAL RECORD; 1985 AND FORWARD. (Bound)

                          • Item 993-B (P)
X 1.1   • Item 993-C (MF)
CONGRESSIONAL RECORD, INDEX AND DAILY DIGEST.

                      • Item 994-B (P) (EL)
X 1.1/:v.nos./nos.   • Item 994-C (MF)
CONGRESSIONAL RECORD. [Daily]

X 1.1/a   • Item 994-D
CONGRESSIONAL RECORD PROCEEDINGS OF THE HOUSE AND SENATE, EXTENSIONS OF REMARKS, AND THE DAILY DIGEST, ALSO THE CRI.

Online service available on Internet or via asynchronous connection.

                      • Item 1030-A (P)
                • Item 1030-B (MF) (EL)
XJH   • Item 1030-B-1(CD)
JOURNAL OF THE HOUSE OF REPRESENTATIVES. [Annual]

Article I, Section 5 of the Constitution requires that "Each House shall keep a Journal of its proceedings, and from time to time publish the same, excepting such parts as may in their judgement require secrecy; and the yeas and nays of the members of each House on any question shall, at the desire of one fifth of those present be entered on the Journal."
Contains actions of the House in session, a list of bills and resolutions introduced each day, memorials and petitions to Congress, annual messages of the president, veto messages of the President. Includes a section on History of Bills and Resolutions, a numerical list showing the action taken upon each bill.

                         • Item 1047-A (P)

XJS • **Item 1047-B (MF)**
JOURNAL OF THE SENATE. [Annual]

Article I, Section 5 of the Constitution requires that "Each House shall keep a Journal of its proceedings, and from time to time publish the same, excepting such parts as may in their judgment require secrecy; and the yeas and nays of the members of each House on any question shall, at the desire of one fifth of those present, be entered on the Journal."

Contains actions of the Senate in session, a list of bills and resolutions introduced each day, memorials, and petitions to Congress, annual messages of the President, veto messages of the President, inaugural addresses and proceedings of impeachments trials in the Senate. Includes a section on History of Bills and Resolutions, and numerical list showing the action taken upon each bill.

Y 1
MISCELLANEOUS PUBLICATIONS OF CONGRESS.

Later Y 1.1/4 and Y 1.1/6

Y 1.Cong./sess:letters • **Item 1008-A-1**
SENATE EXECUTIVE REPORTS AND DOCUMENTS.

Reports and documents relative to treaties submitted to the U.S. Senate for ratification, nominations, etc. relative to executive session held by the Senate.

Y 1.1:CT
MISCELLANEOUS UNCLASSIFIED PUBLICATIONS OF BOTH HOUSE AND SENATE.

• **Item 996-C, 1008-E (P)**
Y 1.1/2:nos. • **Item 996-B, 1008-D (MF)**
SERIAL SET.

• **Item 996-A (P)**
Y 1.1/3:Cong.&nos. • **Item 996-B (MF)**
SENATE DOCUMENTS.

• **Item 996-A (P)**
Y 1.1/4:Cong.-nos. • **Item 996-B (MF)**
SENATE TREATY DOCUMENTS.

Deals with treaties submitted to the Senate for ratification, nominations, etc. relative to executive sessions held by the Senate.
Earlier Y 1.Cong./sess.-letters

• **Item 1008-C (P)**
Y 1.1/5:Cong.&nos. • **Item 1008-D (MF)**
SENATE REPORTS.

• **Item 1008-C (P)**
Y 1.1/6:Cong.&nos. • **Item 1008-D (MF)**
SENATE EXECUTIVE REPORTS.

Deals with treaties submitted to the Senate for ratification, nominations, etc., relative to executive sessions held by the Senate.

• **Item 996-A (P)**
Y 1.1/7:Cong.&nos. • **Item 996-B (MF)**
HOUSE DOCUMENTS.

• **Item 1008-C (P)**
Y 1.1/8:Cong.&nos. • **Item 1008-D (MF)**
HOUSE REPORTS.

Y 1.1/9:nos. • **Item 1008-D-1**
POLYMER DIVIDERS IMPRINTED WITH (SUDOCS) CLASSIFICATION NUMBER SYSTEM TO CONVERT MICROFICHE HOUSE AND SENATE REPORTS AND DOCUMENTS INTO THE CONGRESSIONAL SERIAL SET.

Y 1.1/10: • **Item 1008-D-2**
TITLE PAGE AND/OR TABLE OF CONTENTS.

The title page and/or table of contents to be used by libraries to bind Senate and House Documents and Reports to create a U.S. Congressional Serial set volume. Printed on acid free paper.

HOUSE OF REPRESENTATIVES

INFORMATION

U.S. House of Representatives
Washington, DC 20515
(202) 224-3121
http://www.house.gov

Y 1.2:CT • **Item 998**
HOUSE OF REPRESENTATIVES (miscellaneous publications).

Y 1.2:D 45/date • **Item 998**
DESCHLER'S PROCEDURE, A SUMMARY OF THE MODERN PRECEDENTS AND PRACTICES OF THE U.S. HOUSE OF REPRESENTATIVES.

Y 1.2:P 69 • **Item 998**
PLATFORMS OF THE DEMOCRATIC PARTY AND THE REPUBLICAN PARTY. [Quadrennial]

Prepared by the Clerk, House of Representatives.
Contains the text of the platforms adopted by the two major parties at their National Conventions held to nominate the Presidential candidates.

Y 1.2:T 23
TELEPHONE DIRECTORY.

ISSN 0147-8958

COMPILATIONS OF LAWS.

PURPOSE:– To provide in one volume all laws of a particular subject or groups of related subjects.
These pamphlets provide a handy reference service to the laws and their amendments which have been passed on the various subjects covered by the individual compilations. These compilations are made under the supervision of the Superintendent of the Document Room and are brought up-to-date as required.

Y 1.2:Ag 8/5 • **Item 998**
LAWS RELATING TO AGRICULTURE [February 18, 1922– date]. [Irregular]

Y 1.2:Ag 8/6 • **Item 998**
AGRICULTURAL TRADE DEVELOPMENT AND ASSISTANCE ACT OF 1954 AND AMENDMENTS [July 10, 1954– date.]. [Irregular]

Y 1.2:Ai 7
ARMY, POSTAL, AND NAVY AIR SERVICE LAWS [March 2, 1913– date]. [Irregular]

Y 1.2:Ai 7
LAWS RELATING TO COMMERCIAL AIR SERVICE AND MISCELLANEOUS AIR LAWS [May 10, 1916– date]. [Irregular]

Y 1.2:An 8 • **Item 998**
ANTITRUST LAWS WITH AMENDMENTS [1890– date]. [Irregular]

Covers Sherman Act, Clayton Act, Federal Trade Commission Act and amendments, Export Trade Act, Banking corporations authorized to do foreign banking business, National Industrial Recovery Act, Price discrimination.

Y 1.2:At 7 • **Item 998**
ATOMIC ENERGY ACT OF 1946 AND AMENDMENTS [August 1, 1946– date]. [Irregular]

Y 1.2:B 22/2 • **Item 998**
BANKRUPTCY LAWS OF THE UNITED STATES [July 1, 1898– date]. [Irregular]

Y 1.2:C 82 • **Item 998**
COTTON AND GRAIN FUTURES ACTS, COMMODITY EXCHANGE AND WAREHOUSE ACTS AND OTHER LAWS RELATING THERETO [August 7, 1916– date]. [Irregular]

Y 1.2:C 86 • **Item 998**
CRIME, KIDNAPPING, AND PRISON LAWS [June 21, 1902– date]. 1934– [Irregular]

Y 1.2:Em 7/6 • **Item 998**
COMPILATION OF LAWS RELATING TO MEDIATION, CONCILIATION, AND ARBITRATION BETWEEN EMPLOYERS AND EMPLOYEES, LAWS [on] DISPUTES BETWEEN CARRIERS AND EMPLOYERS AND SUBORDINATE OFFICIALS UNDER LABOR BOARD, EIGHT-HOUR LAWS, EMPLOYERS' LIABILITY LAWS, LABOR AND CHILD LABOR LAWS [October 1, 1888– date]. 1922– [Irregular]

Y 1.2:Es 6 • **Item 998**
LAWS RELATING TO ESPIONAGE, SABOTAGE, ETC. [June 15, 1917– date] 1920– [Irregular]

Y 1.2:F 22 • **Item 998**
FARM RELIEF AND AGRICULTURAL ADJUSTMENT ACTS [June 15, 1929– date]. [Irregular]

Y 1.2:F 31 • **Item 998**
FEDERAL FARM LOAN ACT WITH AMENDMENTS AND FARM MORTGAGE AND FARM CREDIT ACTS. [July 17, 1916– date]. 1923– [Irregular]

Y 1.2:F 31/2 • **Item 998**
FEDERAL RESERVE ACT OF 1913 WITH AMENDMENTS AND LAWS RELATING TO BANKING [December 23, 1913– date]. 1920– [Irregular]

Y 1.2:F 31/7 • **Item 998**
FEDERAL POWER COMMISSION LAWS AND HYDRO-ELECTRIC POWER DEVELOPMENT LAWS [June 10, 1920– date]. [Irregular]

Y 1.2:F 31/8 • **Item 998**
LAWS RELATING TO FEDERAL CORRUPT PRACTICES AND POLITICAL ACTIVITIES, FEDERAL CORRUPT PRACTICES ACT, HATCH POLITICAL ACTIVITIES ACT, MISCELLANEOUS RELATED ACTS AND REGULATIONS [February 28, 1925– date]. [Irregular]

Y 1.2:F 31/10 • **Item 998**
FEDERAL FOOD, DRUG, AND COSMETIC ACT. [Irregular]

Y 1.2:F 76/4 • **Item 998**
LAWS RELATING TO FORESTRY, GAME CONSERVATION, FLOOD CONTROL AND RELATED SUBJECTS [March 1, 1911– date]. 1936– [Irregular]

Y 1.2:H 75/3 • **Item 998**
HOME OWNER'S LOAN ACTS AND HOUSING ACTS [July 22, 1932– date]. [Irregular]

Y 1.2:H 79 • **Item 998**
HOSPITAL SURVEY AND CONSTRUCTION ACT WITH AMENDMENTS [August 13, 1946– date]. [Irregular]

Y 1.2:In 8/3 • **Item 998**
LAWS RELATING TO INTERSTATE COMMERCE AND TRANSPORTATION [August 29, 1916– date]. [Irregular]

Y 1.2:L 61 • **Item 998**
LIBERTY LOAN ACTS [April 24, 1917– date]. 1919– [Irregular]

Y 1.2:L 66 • **Item 998**
LIQUOR LAWS [August 8, 1890– date].

Y 1.2:M 46 • **Item 998**
LAWS AUTHORIZING ISSUANCE OF MEDALS AND COMMEMORATIVE COINS [June 20, 1974– date]. [Irregular]

Y 1.2:N 21/3 • **Item 998**
NATURALIZATION LAWS [May 9, 1918– date]. 1926– [Irregular]

Y 1.2:N 39 • **Item 998**
NATURALITY LAWS [August 31, 1935– date]. [Irregular]

Y 1.2:Oi 5 • **Item 998**
OIL LANDS LEASING ACT OF 1920 WITH AMEND-MENTS AND OTHER LAWS RELATING TO MINERAL LANDS [March 2, 1919– date]. 1934– [Irregular]

Y 1.2:Op 3 • **Item 998**
OPIUM AND NARCOTIC LAWS [February 9, 1909– date]. [Irregular]

Y 1.2:P 26 • **Item 998**
PASSPORT CONTROL ACTS [February 1, 1917– date]. [Irregular]

Y 1.2:P 38/2 • **Item 998**
PENSION LAWS [June 25, 1918– date]. [Irregular]

Y 1.2:P 96/3 • **Item 998**
PUBLIC BUILDINGS ACT OF 1926, WITH AMEND-MENTS, CONDEMNATION LAWS WITH AMENDMENTS, PUBLIC WORKS AND CONSTRUCTION LAWS [May 7, 1926– date]. [Irregular]

Y 1.2:R 11 • **Item 998**
RADIO LAWS OF THE UNITED STATES [June 24, 1910– date]. [Irregular]

Y 1.2:R 13 • **Item 998**
RAILROAD RETIREMENT AND UNEMPLOYMENT INSURANCE ACT, AS AMENDED [August 29, 1935– date]. [Irregular]

Y 1.2:R 24/2 • **Item 998**
RECONSTRUCTION FINANCE CORPORATION ACT WITH AMENDMENTS AND SMALL BUSINESS ADMINISTRATION ACT WITH AMENDMENTS INCLUDING RELATED ACTS ON SMALL BUSINESS [January 22, 1932– date]. 1933– [Irregular]

Y 1.2:R 53 • **Item 998**
LAWS RELATING TO FEDERAL AID AND CONSTRUCTION OF ROADS [August 24, 1912– date]. [Irregular]

Y 1.2:Sa 3/2 • **Item 998**
LAWS RELATING TO CIVIL SERVICE SALARY CLASSIFICATION, CIVIL SERVICE PREFERENCE, ETC. [August 23, 1912– date]. [Irregular]

Y 1.2:Se 1/2 • **Item 998**
SEAMEN'S ACT AS AMENDED AND OTHER LAWS RELATING TO SEAMEN [March 4, 1915– date]. 1927– [Irregular]

Y 1.2:Se 2 • **Item 998**
LAWS RELATING TO SECURITIES COMMISSION, EXCHANGES AND HOLDING COMPANIES [May 27, 1933– date]. [Irregular]

Y 1.2:Se 4 • **Item 998**
SELECTIVE SERVICE ACT AS AMENDED [May 18, 1917– date]. 1943– [Irregular]

Y 1.2:Sh 6 • **Item 998**
LAWS RELATING TO SHIPPING AND MERCHANT MARINE [September 7, 1916– date]. 1935– [Irregular]

Y 1.2:Sm 1 • **Item 998**
SMALL BUSINESS ADMINISTRATION AND INVESTMENT ACT, WITH AMENDMENTS [1953– date]. [Irregular]

Y 1.2:So 1 • **Item 998**
LAWS RELATING TO SOCIAL SECURITY AND UNEMPLOYMENT COMPENSATION [August 14, 1935– date]. [Irregular]

Y 1.2:So 4/7 • **Item 998**
SOLDIERS' AND SAILORS' CIVIL RELIEF ACT OF 1940 AND AMENDMENTS [October 17, 1940– date]. [Irregular]

Y 1.2:Su 7/date • **Item 998-A**
SURPLUS PROPERTY ACT OF 1944, AND AMENDMENTS. [Irregular]

Y 1.2:T 17/2 • **Item 998**
EMERGENCY TARIFF LAWS OF 1921 AND RE-CIPROCAL TRADE AGREEMENT ACT OF 1934, WITH ALL AMENDMENTS [May, 1934– date]. [Irregular]

Y 1.2:V 64 • **Item 998**
LAWS RELATING TO VETERANS. 1917– [Irregular]

Y 1.2:V 85/2 • **Item 998**
LAWS RELATING TO VOCATIONAL EDUCATION AND AGRICULTURAL EXTENSION WORK [May 8, 1914– date]. [Irregular]

Y 1.2/2:dt&nos. • **Item 998-A**
CALENDAR OF UNITED STATES HOUSE OF REPRESENTATIVES AND HISTORY OF LEGISLATION. [Weekly while Congress is in session]

ISSN 0364-0558

Y 1.2/4 • **Item 998-C**
ANNUAL REPORT OF POLITICAL COMMITTEES SUPPORTING CANDIDATES FOR HOUSE OF REPRESENTATIVES. (Clerk of House of Representatives)

Published pursuant to provisions of the Federal Election Campaign Act of 1971, Public Law 92-225, approved February 7, 1972.

• **Item 991-A (P) (EL)**
Y 1.2/5:date/nos./v.nos. • **Item 991-B (CD) (EL)**
UNITED STATES CODE. [Annual]

Contains the general and permanent laws of the United States.
Issues published prior to 1976 edition were classed Y 4.J 89/1:Un 3/3
The 1976 edition is kept up to date by annual supplements.
Citation: U.S.C.
Issued on CD-ROM.

Y 1.2/5-2 • **Item 991-B (E)**
UNITED STATES CODE. [Annual]

Issued on CD-ROM.

Y 1.2/6:CT • **Item 998-A-1 (MF)**
LIST OF STANDING COMMITTEES. [Irregular]

Y 1.2/7:date • **Item 998 (MF)**
TELEPHONE DIRECTORY. [Semiannual]

Earlier Y 1.2:T 23

Y 1.2/8:date • **Item 998**
CROSS-REFERENCES WITHIN THE INTERNAL REVENUE CODE AS OF (date). [Irregular]

Earlier Y 1.2:In 8/5

Y 1.2/9: • **Item 998-E**
HISTORY IN THE HOUSE. [Twice a year]

Newsletter on the past and present history of the House, such as Congress in Philadelphia and the 1987 celebration of the bicentennial of the "Great Compromise".

Y 1.2/10 • **Item 998-A-3 (EL)**
ELECTION STATISTICS.

SENATE

INFORMATION

U.S. Senate
Washington, DC 20510
(202) 224-3121
http://www.senate.gov

Y 1.3:CT • **Item 998-A-1**
MISCELLANEOUS PUBLICATIONS.

Y 1.3:Se 5/11 • **Item 998**
UNITED STATES SENATE, A HISTORICAL BIBLIOGRAPHY. 1977. 78 p. il.

A guide to significant studies on the Senate, its practices, customs, and former members. Includes approximately 1,000 citations to books, articles, and dissertations.

Y 1.3:T 23 • **Item 998**
TELEPHONE DIRECTORY.

Y 1.3:V 64/2/798-976 • **Item 998**
PRESIDENTIAL VETOES. 1978. 533 p.

A comprehensive listing of the Presidential vetoes of legislation enacted by the Congress from the first through the Ninety-Fourth Congress. The compilation is arranged chronologically by the administration in which the vetoes occurred and by Congresses within the administration.

Y 1.3/2:dt.&nos.
EXECUTIVE CALENDARS.

ISSN 0148-7515
Earlier Y 1.1

Y 1.3/3:dt.&nos. • **Item 998-B (MF)**
CALENDARS OF BUSINESS. [Daily]

ISSN 0364-5886
Earlier Y 1.3

• **Item 1047-C (P)**
Y 1.3/4 • **Item 1047-D (MF)**
JOURNAL OF EXECUTIVE PROCEEDINGS OF SENATE. v. 1– [Annual]

Contains parliamentary proceedings of executive sessions of the U.S. Senate. Includes supplement listing executive nominations and treaties received and action taken thereon by the Senate during the session of Congress.

Y 1.3/5: • **Item 998-C**
ANNUAL REPORTS OF POLICITICAL COMMITTEES SUPPORTING CANDIDATES FOR SENATE.

Y 1.3/7:nos. • **Item 955-R**
SENATE BUDGET SCOREKEEPING REPORT.

Y 1.3/8:nos. • **Item 998-D**
SENATE HISTORY (series). 1– [Irregular]

Newsletter on past and present items of general interest in the history of the Senate.

Y 1.3/9:nos. • **Item 998-A-1 (MF)**
LIST OF STANDING COMMITTEES.

Earlier Y 1.3:C 73/58

Y 1.3/10 • **Item 998-A-1 (MF)**
U.S. SENATE TELEPHONE DIRECTORY.

CONGRESSIONAL BILLS, RESOLUTIONS, AND AMENDMENTS

• **Item 1006 (P)**
Y 1.4/1:Cong.&nos. • **Item 1006-A (EL)**
SENATE BILLS.

Y 1.4/2:Cong.&nos. • **Item 1006-A (EL)**
SENATE RESOLUTIONS.

Y 1.4/3:Cong.&nos. • **Item 1006-A (EL)**
SENATE JOINT RESOLUTIONS.

Y 1.4/4:Cong.&nos. • **Item 1006-A (EL)**
SENATE CONCURRENT AMENDMENTS.

Y 1.4/5 • **Item 1006-A (EL)**
SENATE PRINTED AMENDMENTS.

Y 1.4/6:Cong.&nos. • **Item 1006-A (EL)**
HOUSE BILLS.

Y 1.4/7:Cong.&nos. • **Item 1006-A (EL)**
HOUSE RESOLUTIONS.

Y 1.4/8:Cong.&nos. • Item 1006-A (EL)
HOUSE JOINT RESOLUTIONS.

Y 1.4/9:Cong.&nos. • Item 1006-A (EL)
HOUSE CONCURRENT RESOLUTIONS.

Y 1.5 • Item 998-F (E)
ELECTRONIC PRODUCTS. [Irregular]

Y 1.6 • Item 1006-B (EL)
ALL ENROLLED BILLS OF THE 103RD CONGRESS
FROM THE BEGINNING OF THE 1ST SESSION,
1994.

    Online service updated on irregular basis as
bills are passed. Available on Internet or via asynchronous connection.

NATIONAL COMMISSION
ON AIDS

Y 3.Ac 7:1/date • Item 1089-M (MF)
ANNUAL REPORTS.

Y 3.Ac 7:2 CT • Item 1089-M
GENERAL PUBLICATIONS.

ADMINISTRATIVE CONFERENCE
OF THE UNITED STATES
(1964–)

CREATION AND AUTHORITY

    The Administrative Conference of the United
States was established as a permanent independent agency by the Administrative Conference
Act (5 U.S.C. 571-576) enacted in 1964. The statutory provisions prescribing the organization and
activities of the Conference are based in part
upon the experience of two temporary Conferences called by the President in 1953 and 1961,
each of which operated for a period of 18 months.

INFORMATION

    Administrative Conference of the United
States
    2120 L Street, N.W.
    Washington, D.C. 20037
    (202) 254-7020

Y 3.Ad 6:1/date • Item 1049-G (MF)
ANNUAL REPORT.

Y 3.Ad 6:2 CT • Item 1049-G-1
GENERAL PUBLICATIONS.

Y 3.Ad 6:8 CT • Item 1049-H-1
HANDBOOKS, MANUALS, GUIDES. [Irregular]

Y 3.Ad 6:9/vol.nos. • Item 1049-H
RECOMMENDATIONS AND REPORTS OF THE
ADMINISTRATIVE CONFERENCE OF THE UNITED
STATES. v. 1– 1970– [Annual]

    PURPOSE:– To publish the official recommendations of the Conference, the research reports in support thereof, and other important Conference documents.
    Contains all official documents, names of all
persons who have served as members of the
Conference and a detailed discussion of methods of operation and activities. The appendix includes the enabling statute, the bylaws, and a
list of all participating agencies.

Y 3.Ad 6:9-2/v.nos.&nos. • Item 1049-H
ADMINISTRATIVE CONFERENCE NEWS.

Y 3.Ad 6:10 • Item 1049-H
STUDIES IN ADMINISTRATIVE LAW AND PROCEDURE.

Y 3.Ad 6:11/CT • Item 1049-H
RESOURCE PAPERS IN ADMINISTRATIVE LAW.

ADVISORY COMMITTEE ON
FISCAL RELATIONS STUDY
(1936– 1937)

Y 3.Ad 9/1:1/date
REPORTS.

Y 3.Ad 9/1:2 CT
GENERAL PUBLICATIONS.

ADVISORY COMMITTEE ON
EDUCATION
(1937– 1939)

CREATION AND AUTHORITY

    The President's Committee on Vocational Education was established by letter of the President
on September 19, 1936. On April 19, 1937, the
Committee was enlarged and renamed the Advisory Committee on Education. The Committee
ceased to function in 1939.

Y 3.Ad 9/2:2 CT
GENERAL PUBLICATIONS.

Y 3.Ad 9/2:7/nos.
STAFF STUDIES.

ADVISORY COUNCIL ON
SOCIAL SECURITY
(1938)

Y 3.Ad 9/3:1 CT • Item 1049-I
REPORT.

ADVISORY COMMITTEE ON
VOLUNTARY FOREIGN AID
(1946– 1953)

CREATION AND AUTHORITY

    The Advisory Committee on Voluntary Foreign Aid was established under authority of similar letters of May 14, 1946, from the president to
the Secretaries of State and Agriculture, to succeed the President's War Relief Control Board.

Y 3.Ad 9/4:1/date
ANNUAL REPORTS.

Y 3.Ad 9/4:2 CT
GENERAL PUBLICATIONS.

Y 3.Ad 9/4:4/nos.
CIRCULARS.

    Later S 1.99/2

ADVISORY COMMISSION ON
UNIVERSAL TRAINING
(1946– 1948)

Y 3.Ad 9/5:1/date
ANNUAL REPORTS.

Y 3.Ad 9/5:2 CT
GENERAL PUBLICATIONS.

ADVISORY COMMITTEE ON
WEATHER CONTROL
(1953– 1957)

CREATION AND AUTHORITY

    The Advisory Committee on Weather Control
was established by act of August 13, 1953 (67
Stat. 559; 15 U.S.C. 311 note), to study and
evaluate public and private experiments in weather
control to determine extent to which the United
States should experiment with, engage in, or regulate pertinent activities. The Committee was terminated by act of August 28, 1957 (71 Stat. 426)
on December 31, 1957.

Y 3.Ad 9/6:1/date
ANNUAL REPORTS.

Y 3.Ad 9/6:2 CT
GENERAL PUBLICATIONS.

Y 3.Ad 9/6:7/date
RELEASES.

Y 3.Ad 9/6:8/nos.
TECHNICAL REPORTS.

ADVISORY COMMISSION ON
INFORMATION
(1948– 1968)

CREATION AND AUTHORITY

    The Advisory Commission on Information was
established by act of January 27, 1948 (62 Stat.
10, 22 U.S.C. 1466), to recommend to the Director, United States Information Agency, policies
and programs for carrying out the purposes of
the act concerning international informational
activities.

Y 3.Ad 9/7:1 • Item 1049-B
ANNUAL REPORT. 1– [Annual]

Y 3.Ad 9/7:2 CT • Item 1049-B
GENERAL PUBLICATIONS.

ADVISORY COMMISSION ON INTERGOVERNMENTAL RELATIONS
(1959–   )

CREATION AND AUTHORITY

The Commission was established by act of September 24, 1959, as amended by act of November 2, 1966 (73 Stat. 703, 80 Stat. 1162; 5 U.S.C. 2371).

INFORMATION

Advisory Commission on Intergovernmental Relations Suite 2000, Vanguard Building 1111 Twentieth Street, N.W. Washington, D.C. 20575 (202) 653-5640

Y 3.Ad 9/8:1   • **Item 1049-D**
ANNUAL REPORT. 1st–   1960–   [Annual]

Report submitted by the Chairman to the President and to Congress pursuant to Public Law 380, 86th Congress for the year, February 1– January 31.
Public Law 86-380, approved by the President September 24, 1959, provided for the establishment of a permanent, bipartisan body of twenty-six members, to give continuing study to the relationships among local, State, and National levels of government.
Beginning with report for 1981, the Annual Report is incorporated into the Winter issue of Intergovernmental Perspective (Y 3.Ad 9/8:11).

Y 3.Ad 9/8:2 CT   • **Item 1049-D**
GENERAL PUBLICATIONS.

Y 3.Ad 9/8:3/nos.
INFORMATION BULLETINS.

Y 3.Ad 9/8:7/date
PRESS RELEASES.

Y 3.Ad 9/8:8 CT   • **Item 1049-D**
HANDBOOKS, MANUALS, GUIDES.

Y 3.Ad 9/8:9 CT
ADDRESSES.

Y 3.Ad 9/8:10 CT   • **Item 1049-D**
BIBLIOGRAPHIES AND LISTS OF PUBLICATIONS.

Y 3.Ad 9/8:11/v.nos.&nos.   • **Item 1049-D**
INTERGOVERNMENTAL PERSPECTIVE. [Quarterly]

Beginning with report for 1981, the Annual Report is incorporated in the Winter issue.
Indexed by: Index to U.S. Government Periodicals.
ISSN 0362-8507

Y 3.Ad 9/8:12/nos.
FROM THE ACIR LIBRARY: ACCESSIONS LIST.

ISSN 0145-1332

Y 3.Ad 9/8:12-2/nos.
FROM THE ACIR LIBRARY: PERIODICAL INDEX.

ISSN 0145-1324

Y 3.Ad 9/8:13/nos.
CONGRESSIONAL WATCH.

Y 3.Ad 9/8:14/nos.
INFORMATION INTERCHANGE SERVICE.

Y 3.Ad 9/8:17   • **Item 1049-D**
CHANGING PUBLIC ATTITUDES ON GOVERNMENTS AND TAXES. [Annual]
Earlier Y 3.Ad 9/8:2 G 74/5

Y 3.Ad 9/8:18/date   • **Item 1049-D**
SIGNIFICANT FEATURES OF FISCAL FEDERALISM. [Annual]

Y 3.Ad 9/8:19/date
TAX CAPACITY OF THE STATES. [Annual]
Earlier Y 3.Ad 9/8:2 T 19/24

Y 3.Ad 9/8:20/date   • **Item 1049-D**
A CATALOG OF FEDERAL GRANT-IN-AID PROGRAMS TO STATE AND LOCAL GOVERNMENTS.

ADVISORY COMMISSION ON INTERNATIONAL EDUCATIONAL AND CULTURAL AFFAIRS
(1961–   )

CREATION AND AUTHORITY

The Advisory Commission on International Educational and Cultural Affairs was established by act of September 21, 1961 (75 Stat. 532; 22 U.S.C. 2456).

Y 3.Ad 9/9:1/date   • **Item 1049-F**
ANNUAL REPORTS.

Y 3.Ad 9/9:2 CT   • **Item 1049-F**
GENERAL PUBLICATIONS.

Y 3.Ad 9/9:9/date   • **Item 1049-F**
INTERNATIONAL EDUCATION AND CULTURAL EXCHANGE. [Quarterly]

PURPOSE:– To serve as a forum for the expression of divergent views on the most pressing issues in the field. Includes articles on various exchange programs, both government and private.
Indexed by: Index to U.S. Government Periodicals.
ISSN 0020-6601

Y 3.Ad 9/9:18/date
SIGNIFICANT FEATURES OF FISCAL FEDERALISM (year) EDITION. [Annual]

ADVISORY COMMITTEE ON THE ARTS
(1961– 1973)

CREATION AND AUTHORITY

The Advisory Committee on the Arts was established by act of September 21, 1961 (75 Stat. 532; 22 U.S.C. 2456), to advise and assist the U.S. Advisory Commission on International Educational and Cultural Affairs, the President, and other officers of the Government in the conduct of programs in the field of international educational exchange and cultural presentations with special reference to the role of the arts in such fields and other international activities concerned with the arts.

Y 3.Ad 9/10:1/date
ANNUAL REPORT.

Y 3.Ad 9/10:2 (CT)
GENERAL PUBLICATIONS.

ADVISORY COMMITTEE ON FEDERAL PAY

INFORMATION

Advisory Committee on Federal Pay 1730 K Street, N.W. Washington, D.C. 20006 (202) 653-6193

Y 3.Ad 9/11:1/date   • **Item 1089-F**
ANNUAL REPORT.

Y 3.Ad 9/11:2 CT   • **Item 1089-F**
GENERAL PUBLICATIONS.

UNITED STATES ADVISORY COMMISSION ON PUBLIC DIPLOMACY

Y 3.Ad 9/12:1/date   • **Item 1049-L**
ANNUAL REPORTS.

Y 3.Ad 9/12:2 CT   • **Item 1049-L**
GENERAL PUBLICATIONS. [Irregular]

AERONAUTICS BOARD
(1916– 1948)

CREATION AND AUTHORITY

The Aeronautical Board was established in 1916 by agreement of the Secretary of War and the Secretary of Navy. By military order of July 5, 1939, effective July 1, 1939, the Board was placed under the direction of the President as Commander-in-Chief of the Army and Navy. On July 27, 1948, the Secretary of Defense directed that the Board be dissolved and its functions transferred to the Munitions Board (M 5) and the Research and Development Board (M 6), effective August 1, 1948.

Y 3.Ae 8:1/date
ANNUAL REPORTS.

Y 3.Ae 8:2 CT
GENERAL PUBLICATIONS.

Y 3.Ae 8:6 CT
REGULATIONS, RULES, AND INSTRUCTIONS.

Y 3.Ae 8:7/date
ARMY-NAVY AERONAUTICAL STANDARDS, INDEX.

Y 3.Ae 8:8/nos.
AND BULLETINS.

Earlier Y 3.Ar 5/3:7
Later M 5.9

AFRICAN DEVELOPMENT FOUNDATION
(1984–)

CREATION AND AUTHORITY

The African Development Foundation was established by the African Development Foundation Act (22 U.S.C. 290h) in 1984.

INFORMATION

African Development Foundation
1400 I St., NW, 10th Fl.
Washington, D.C. 20036
(202) 673-3916
Fax: (202) 673-3810
Email:info@adf.gov
http://www.adf.gov

Y 3.Af 8:2 CT   • Item 1061-M
GENERAL PUBLICATIONS.

Issued on CD-ROM.

Y 3.Af 8:8 CT   • Item 1061-M
HANDBOOKS, MANUALS, AND GUIDES.

Y 3.Af 8:9/date   • Item 1061-M
ADVANCE, THE JOURNAL OF THE AFRICAN DEVELOPMENT FOUNDATION. [Annual]

An annual anthology of reports, essays and monographs ongrassroots economic development in Africa.

Y 3.Af 8:10   • Item 1061-M
BEYOND RELIEF.

COMMISSION TO INVESTIGATE AND STUDY AGRICULTURAL CREDITS IN EUROPE
(1913– 1916)

Y 3.Ag 8/1:CT
PUBLICATIONS.

JOINT COMMISSION OF AGRICULTURAL INQUIRY
(1921– 1922)

CREATION AND AUTHORITY

The Joint Commission on Agricultural Inquiry was established by Senate Concurrent Resolution of June 7, 1921 (42 Stat. 1807). Reports of the Commission were published in 1921 and 1922.

Y 3.Ag 8/2:2 CT
PUBLICATIONS.

AIRCRAFT BOARD
(1917– 1919)

CREATION AND AUTHORITY

The Aircraft Board was established by act of Congress, approved October 1, 1917, to succeed the Aircraft Production Board of the Council of National Defense. By Executive Order 3066 of March 19, 1919, the Board was terminated.

Y 3.Ai 7:2 CT
PUBLICATIONS.

JOINT COMMISSION ON AIRPORTS
(1929– 1930)

Y 3.Ai 7/2:2 CT
PUBLICATIONS.

AIR COORDINATING COMMITTEE
(1946– 1960)

CREATION AND AUTHORITY

The Air Coordinating Committee was established by Executive Order 9781 of September 19, 1946, and amended by Executive Order 10360 of June 11, 1952 and 10655 of January 28, 1956. The Committee was terminated by Executive Order 10883 of August 11, 1960.

Y 3.Ai 7/3:1/date
ANNUAL REPORTS.

Y 3.Ai 7/3:2 CT
GENERAL PUBLICATIONS.

Y 3.Ai 7/3:7/nos.
RELEASES.

Y 3.Ai 7/3:8/nos.
AIR TRAFFIC CONTROL & NAVIGATION PANEL MEMORANDUM.

Y 3.Ai 7/3:9/date
AIRPORT USE PANEL QUARTERLY REPORT.

Y 3.Ai 7/3:10/nos.
AIR COORDINATING COMMITTEE MEMORANDUM.

AIRWAYS MODERNIZATION BOARD
(1957– 1958)

CREATION AND AUTHORITY

The Airways Modernization Board was established by act of August 14, 1957 (71 Stat. 349; 49 U.S.C. 1211), to develop and select procedures, facilities, and devices required for safe civil and military aviation, with certain exceptions, and to promote maximum coordination of air traffic control and air defense systems. The Board was transferred to the Federal Aviation Agency by E.O. 10786 of November 1, 1958, pursuant to act of August 23, 1958 (72 Stat. 810).

Y 3.Ai 7/4:1/date
REPORTS.

Y 3.Ai 7/4:2 CT
GENERAL PUBLICATIONS.

Y 3.Ai 7/4:7/date
RELEASES.

NATIONAL COMMISSION ON AIR QUALITY

INFORMATION

National Commission on Air Quality
499 South Capitol Street, S.W.
Washington, D.C. 20003
(202) 245-2405

Y 3.Ai 7/5:1/date   • Item 1089
ANNUAL REPORT.

Y 3.Ai 7/5:2 CT   • Item 1089-E
GENERAL PUBLICATIONS.

Y 3.Ai 7/5:9/v.nos.&nos.
AIR WAVES. v. 1. 1980. [Monthly]

Y 3.Ai 7/5:10/nos.   • Item 1089
STUDIES (numbered). 1–

Y 3.Ai 7/5:12 CT   • Item 1089
BIBLIOGRAPHIES AND LISTS OF PUBLICATIONS.

SECOND COURT OF COMMISSIONERS OF ALABAMA CLAIMS
(1882– 1885)

Y 3.AI 1:1/v.nos.
REPORTS [of] CASES, 1882– 1885.

Y 3.AI 1:2 CT
GENERAL PUBLICATIONS.

NATIONAL ALCOHOL FUELS COMMISSION
(1978–   )

CREATION AND AUTHORITY

The National Alcohol Fuels Commission was established by Public Law 95-599 (92 Stat. 2724), approved November 6, 1978.

Y 3.AI 1/2:1/date   • Item 1089
ANNUAL REPORT.

Y 3.AI 1/2:2 CT   • Item 1089
GENERAL PUBLICATIONS. [Irregular]

Y 3.AI 1/2:9 CT   • Item 1089
PUBLIC HEARINGS (various cities).

ALASKA INTERNATIONAL RAIL AND HIGHWAY COMMISSION
(1956– 1961)

Y 3.AI 1s:1/date
ANNUAL REPORT.

Y 3.AI 1s:2 CT
GENERAL PUBLICATIONS.

TEMPORARY ALASKA CLAIMS COMMISSION
(1964)

Y 3.AI 1s/2:1/date
ANNUAL REPORT.

Y 3.AI 1s/2:2 CT
GENERAL PUBLICATIONS.

FEDERAL RECONSTRUCTION AND DEVELOPMENT PLANNING COMMISSION FOR ALASKA
(1964)

CREATION AND AUTHORITY

The Federal Reconstruction and Development Planning Commission for Alaska was established by Executive Order 11150 of April 2, 1964, to develop coordinated plans for Federal programs for reconstruction and economic and resources development in Alaska, following the earthquake of March 27, 1964, and to recommend appropriate action to carry out such plans.

Y 3.AI 1s/3:1/date
REPORT.

Y 3.AI 1s/3:2 CT
GENERAL PUBLICATIONS.

FEDERAL FIELD COMMITTEE FOR DEVELOPMENT PLANNING IN ALASKA
(1964– 1965)

CREATION AND AUTHORITY

The Federal Field Committee for Development Planning in Alaska was established by Executive Order 11182 of October 2, 1964. The Committee was abolished by Executive Order 11209 of March 25, 1965.

Y 3.AI 1s/4:1/date
REPORT.

Y 3.AI 1s/4:2/date
GENERAL PUBLICATIONS.

OFFICE OF ALIEN PROPERTY CUSTODIAN
(1917– 1934)

CREATION AND AUTHORITY

The Office of Alien Property Custodian was established under the Trading with Enemy Act of 1917, approved October 5, 1917 (40 Stat. 411). Executive Order 6694 of May 1, 1934, effective July 1, 1934 abolished the Office and transferred its functions to the Department of Justice, where the Alien Property Bureau (J 19) was established within the Claims Division to carry out the remaining functions of the Alien Property Custodian.

Y 3.AI 4:1/date
ANNUAL REPORTS.

Later J 19.1
Y 3.AI 4:2 CT
GENERAL PUBLICATIONS.

Later J 19.2

Y 3.AI 4:3
BULLETINS.

Y 3.AI 4:4
CIRCULARS.

Y 3.AI 4:5
BLANK FORMS.

COMMISSION ON DISPOSITION OF ALCATRAZ ISLAND

Y 3.AI 16:1/date
REPORT.

Y 3.AI 16:2 CT
GENERAL PUBLICATIONS.

AMERICAN BATTLE MONUMENTS COMMISSION
(1923–   )

CREATION AND AUTHORITY

The American Battle Monuments Commission was created by act of Congress approved March 4, 1923 (42 Stat. 1509; 36 U.S.C. 121). It derives its authority from this and subsequent acts and Executive orders (36 U.S.C. ch. 8; Executive Orders 6614 of February 26, 1934, 6690 of April 25, 1934, 9704 of March 14, 1946, and 10057 of May 14, 1949; and act approved June 26, 1946, as amended, 60 Stat. 317, 70 Stat. 642; 36 U.S.C. 121).

INFORMATION

American Battle Monuments Commission
Courthouse Plaza II, Ste. 500
2300 Clarendon Blvd.
Arlington, VA 22201-3367
(703) 696-6900
Fax: (703) 696-6666
http://www.abmc.gov

Y 3.Am 3:1/date   • Item 1050 (MF)
ANNUAL REPORT.

Y 3.Am 3:2 CT   • Item 1050
GENERAL PUBLICATIONS.

Y 3.Am 3/2   • Item 1089-N
REPORTS AND PUBLICATIONS.

AMERICAN SAMOAN COMMISSION
(1926– 1931)

Y 3.Am 3/2:2 CT
PUBLICATIONS.

AMERICAN RELIEF ADMINISTRATION
(1919– 1923)

CREATION AND AUTHORITY

The American Relief Administration was established by Executive Order 3055-B of February 24, 1919. Though the Administration ended its official status on June 28, 1919, it continued as an unofficial agency until 1923.

Y 3.Am 3/2:1/date
ANNUAL REPORTS.

Y 3.Am 3/2:2 CT
GENERAL PUBLICATIONS.

Y 3.Am 3/3:3/nos
BULLETINS.

AMERICAN COMMISSION FOR PROTECTION AND SALVAGE OF ARTISTIC AND HISTORIC MONUMENTS IN WAR AREAS
(1943–1946)

CREATION AND AUTHORITY

The American Commission for the Protection and Salvage of Artistic and Historic Monuments in War Areas was established by approval of the President on June 23, 1943, and announced by Secretary of State on August 20, 1943. The functions of the Commission were assumed by the Department of State as announced on August 16, 1946.

Y 3.Am 3/4:2 CT
PUBLICATIONS.

AMERICAN NATIONAL-RED CROSS
(1949–1952)

Y 3.Am 3/5:1/date
ANNUAL REPORTS.

Earlier W 102.1

Y 3.Am 3/5:2 CT
GENERAL PUBLICATIONS.

Earlier W 102.2

Y 3.Am 3/5:6 CT
REGULATIONS, RULES, AND INSTRUCTIONS.

Earlier W 102.7

AMERICAN REVOLUTION BICENTENNIAL ADMINISTRATION
(1973–1977)

CREATION AND AUTHORITY

The American Revolution Bicentennial Commission was established by act of July 4, 1966 (80 Stat. 259). The Commission was abolished by act of December 11, 1973 (87 Stat. 704), which created the American Revolution Bicentennial Administration. The Administration was abolished June 30, 1977 by terms of the act.

Y 3.Am 3/6:1/date
REPORTS. 1–

Report submitted pursuant to Public Law 93-179.

Y 3.Am 3/6:2 CT
GENERAL PUBLICATIONS.

Y 3.Am 3/6:7-2:v.nos.&nos.
BICENTENNIAL ERA.

Y 3.Am 3/6:8 CT   • Item 1089
HANDBOOKS, MANUALS, GUIDES.

Y 3.Am 3/6:9 CT
POSTERS. [Irregular]

Y 3.Am 3/6:10/v.nos.&nos.
BICENTENNIAL TIMES. [Monthly]

Supersedes Bicentennial Newsletter.
ISSN 0361-4905

Y 3.Am 3/6:11/date
BICENTENNIAL BULLETIN.   – 1975. [Irregular]

Y 3.Am 3/6:12/nos
CALL FOR ACHIEVEMENT BOOKLETS.

ANTHRACITE COAL STRIKE COMMISSION
(1902–1903)

CREATION AND AUTHORITY

The Anthracite Coal Commission was established by the President on October 16, 1902. The Commission submitted its report on March 18, 1903.

Y 3.An 8:2 CT
PUBLICATIONS

ANTHRACITE COAL COMMISSION
(1920)

CREATION AND AUTHORITY

The Anthracite Coal Commission was established by proclamation of the President on June 3, 1920 (41 Stat. 1796). The Commission submitted its report in 1920.

Y 3.An 8/2:2 CT
PUBLICATIONS.

FEDERAL DEVELOPMENT PLANNING COMMITTEE FOR APPALACHIA
(1964–1965)

CREATION AND AUTHORITY

The Federal Development Planning Committee for Appalachia was established by Executive Order 11186 of October 23, 1964. The Committee was abolished by Executive order 11209 of March 25, 1965 which established the Federal Development Committee for Appalachia to succeed it.

Y 3.Ap 4:1/date
REPORT

Y 3.Ap 4:2 CT
GENERAL PUBLICATIONS.

APPALACHIAN REGIONAL COMMISSION
(1965–   )

CREATION AND AUTHORITY

The Commission was established by the Appalachian Regional Development Act of 1965 (79 Stat. 5; 40 U.S.C. App 1) to develop plans for and coordinate the comprehensive programs for regional economic development authorized by the act.

INFORMATION

Public Affairs Office
Appalachian Regional Commission
1666 Connecticut Avenue, NW, Ste. 700
Washington, D.C. 20009-1068
(202) 884-7799
Email:info@arc.gov
http://www.arc.gov

Y 3.Ap 4/2:1   • Item 1050-A
ANNUAL REPORT. 1st–   1965–   [Annual]

Covers calendar year.

Y 3.Ap 4/2:2 CT   • Item 1050-A
GENERAL PUBLICATIONS.

Y 3.Ap 4/2:8 CT   • Item 1050-A
HANDBOOKS, MANUALS, GUIDES.

Y 3.Ap 4/2:9-2 (nos.)   • Item 1050-A (P) (EL)
APPALACHIA. v. 1–   [Quarterly]

Indexed by: Index to U.S. Government Periodicals.
ISSN 0003-6595

Y 3.Ap 4/2:10/nos.
RESEARCH REPORTS.

Y 3.Ap 4/2:11/v.nos.&nos.
APPALACHIAN REPORTER. [Semimonthly]

Y 3.Ap 4/2:12/nos.
APPALACHIAN EDUCATION SATELLITE PROJECT TECHNICAL REPORTS. 1–   [Irregular]

Y 3.Ap 4/2:16   • Item 1050-A-1 (E)
ELECTRONIC PRODUCTS.

COMMISSION ON REVISION OF THE FEDERAL COURT APPELLATE SYSTEM
(1972–1973)

CREATION AND AUTHORITY

The Commission on Revision of the Federal Court Appellate System was established in 1972 by Public Law 92-489. Its final report was submitted on December 18, 1973.

Y 3.Ap 4/3:1/date
REPORT.

Y 3.Ap 4/3:2 CT   • Item 1089
GENERAL PUBLICATIONS.

COMMISSION ON ERECTION OF MEMORIALS AND ENTOMBMENT OF BODIES IN ARLINGTON MEMORIAL AMPHITHEATER (1921– 1925)

Y 3.Ar 1:1/date
REPORT.

Y 3.Ar 1:2 CT
GENERAL PUBLICATIONS.

ARCHITECT OF THE CAPITOL (1793–   )

CREATION AND AUTHORITY

The first Architect of the Capitol was appointed by the president in 1793. From 1817 to March 3, 1843, there was an architect for the Capitol under the Commissioner of Public Buildings, under the title of Surveyor of the Capitol and also Architect of Public Buildings. By act of Congress, approved March 3, 1843, the Office was terminated. The Office of Architect of Extension of United States Capitol was established within the Department of the Interior on June 11, 1851. On March 23, 1853, the Office was transferred to the War Department and on April 16, 1862, returned to the Department of the Interior. The name was changed to Superintendent of Capitol Building and Grounds by act of Congress, approved February 14, 1902 (32 Stat. 20). In 1921 the name was changed to Architect of the Capitol.

INFORMATION

Office of the Architect of the Capitol
U.S. Capitol Building
Washington, D.C. 20515
(202) 255-1200
http://www.aoc.gov

Y 3.Ar 2:1/date   • Item 996
ANNUAL REPORT. 1st–   1804–

Y 3.Ar 2:2 CT.
PUBLICATIONS.
Earlier I 1.7/2-2

ARLINGTON MEMORIAL AMPHITHEATER COMMISSION (1921– 1960)

CREATION AND AUTHORITY

The Arlington Memorial Amphitheater Commission was created by act of March 4, 1921 (41 Stat. 1440; 24 U.S.C. 291-295), to report annually to Congress, through the President of the United States, on memorials to be erected and the bodies of certain deceased members of the Armed Forces to be entombed during the next ensuing year within the Amphitheater in Arlington National Cemetery in Virginia. The Commission was abolished by act approved September 2, 1960 (74 Stat. 739), and its functions transferred to the Secretary of Defense.

Y 3.Ar 5:2 CT
PUBLICATIONS.

ARLINGTON MEMORIAL BRIDGE COMMISSION (1913– 1933)

CREATION AND AUTHORITY

The Arlington Memorial Bridge Commission was created by act approved March 4, 1913 (37 Stat. 855; D.C. Code (1951 ed.) 8-158), to report to Congress a suitable design for a memorial bridge acrosss the Potomac River from the city of Washington to the Arlington estate. The Commission was abolished by EO 6166 of June 10, 1933, and functions transferred to the Office of National Parks, Buildings, and Reservations.

Y 3.Ar 5/2:2 CT
PUBLICATIONS.

AIR FORCE-NAVY CIVIL COMMITTEE ON AIRCRAFT DESIGN CRITERIA (1948)

Y 3.Ar 5/3:1/date
ANNUAL REPORTS.

Y 3.Ar 5/3:2 CT
GENERAL PUBLICATIONS.

Y 3.Ar 5/3:7/nos.
ANC [publications].

Later Y 3.Ac 8:8

NATIONAL COMMISSION ON ARTHRITIS AND RELATED MUSCULOSKELETAL DISEASES

Y 3.Ar 7:1/date
ANNUAL REPORTS.

Y 3.Ar 7:2 CT
GENERAL PUBLICATIONS. [Irregular]

Y 3.Ar 7:8 CT
HANDBOOKS, MANUALS, GUIDES. [Irregular]

ATLANTIC-PACIFIC INTEROCEANIC CANAL STUDY COMMISSION (1964– 1970)

CREATION AND AUTHORITY

The Atlantic-Pacific Interoceanic Canal Study Commission was established by Public law 88-609, approved September 22, 1964. The Commission ceased to exist on December, 1970, pursuant to law creating it.

Y 3.At 6:1/date
REPORT.

ATOMIC ENERGY COMMISSION (1946– 1974)

CREATION AND AUTHORITY

The Atomic Energy Commission was established by the Atomic Energy Act of 1946 (60 Stat. 755), as amended by the Atomic Energy Act of 1954, as amended (68 Stat. 919; 42 U.S.C. 2011 et seq.) The Atomic Energy Commission was abolished by the Energy Reorganization Act of 1974, approved October 11, 1974 (88 Stat. 1237: 42 U.S.C. 5814) and its functions transferred to the Energy Research and Development Administration and the Nuclear Regulatory Commission.

Y 3.At 7:1   • Item 1053
ANNUAL REPORT TO CONGRESS. [Annual]

Report submitted by the Commission to Congress pursuant to the Atomic Energy Act of 1954 for the calendar year.
Part 1 covers the atomic energy industry during the year and the related activities, including industry and Commission activities, the civilian nuclear power program, programs in support of industry. Part 2 covers nuclear power programs for the year. Part 3 covers the major activities in the atomic energy programs. Part 4 covers regulatory activities.
Some of the more important reference sources contained in the Appendix include:
Major Research and Development Installations
Commission-Owned Patents
Annotated List of Publications
Summary of Formal Hearings
Nuclear Reactors Built, Building or Planned in the U.S.
The annual report is sold by the Superintendent of Documents under the title, Major Activities in the Atomic Energy Program (Y 3.A t 7: 2P 94/2).
Reports were issued semiannually, 1st-25th, 1946-July/Dec. 1958; annually 1959–
Index for each annual report issued separately.
Also issued in the Senate Documents series.

INDEXES.

Cumulative Index to 25 Semiannual Reports of the Atomic Energy Commission to Congress. 1961. 321 p. (Y 3.At 7:17/2-15/ ind).

Y 3.At 7:2 CT   • Item 1051
GENERAL PUBLICATIONS.

Y 3.At 7:2 P 56/2   • Item 1051
STATISTICAL SUMMARY OF THE PHYSICAL RESEARCH PROGRAM AS OF JUNE 30 (year). [Annual]

Presents a statistical analysis of the physical research program administered by the Division of Research, U.S. Atomic Energy Commission. Included is information on funds budgeted for salaries and wages, materials and supplies, travel, communications, publications, indirect expenses, and equipment.

Y 3.At 7:2 P 94/2   • Item 1051
MAJOR ACTIVITIES IN THE ATOMIC ENERGY PROGRAMS. [Annual]

Presents highlights of the year's activities of the Atomic Energy Commission. The three sections of the book discuss regulatory activities, environmental safety; and operating and developmental functions.

Y 3.At 7:2 R 11/28 • **Item 1051 & 745**
STUDIES IN WORKMEN'S COMPENSATION AND RADIATION INJURY. v. 1– [Irregular]

Y 3.At 7:3 • **Item 1052-A**
SAFETY AND FIRE PROTECTION BULLETINS. 1– [Irregular]

Y 3.At 7:5/date • **Item 1051-D**
LAWS (relating to work of AEC).

Y 3.At 7:5-2/date
LEGISLATIVE HISTORIES OF ATOMIC ENERGY ACTS.

Y 3.At 7:6 CT • **Item 1052**
REGULATIONS, RULES, AND INSTRUCTIONS.

Y 3.At 7:6-2 • **Item 1052**
ATOMIC ENERGY COMMISSION RULES AND REGULATIONS. [Irregular]

Includes the rules and regulations promulgated under the Atomic Energy Act of 1954, as amended.
Subscription includes basic volume plus supplementary materials for an indefinite period.

Y 3.At 7:6-3 CT • **Item 1051-F**
HANDBOOKS, MANUALS, GUIDES.

Earlier Y 3.At 7:6

Y 3.At 7:6-4 CT • **Item 1051-F**
AEC LICENSING GUIDES.

Y 3.At 7:7/v.nos.
GUIDE TO PUBLISHED RESEARCH ON ATOMIC ENERGY. [Monthly]

Distribution restricted to persons employed by Atomic Energy Commission and its contractors.
Superseded by Y 3.At 7:16

Y 3.At 7:8/nos.
DECLASSIFIED DOCUMENTS.

Y 3.At 7:9/v.nos.nos.
LIST OF DECLASSIFIED DOCUMENTS. [Semimonthly]

Restricted.

Y 3.At 7:10/nos.
LIST OF DECLASSIFIED DOCUMENTS.

Publications carry Declassified Documents release number.

Y 3.At 7:11/v.nos.&nos.
ABSTRACTS OF DECLASSIFIED DOCUMENTS. [Semimonthly]

Superseded by Y 3.At 7:16

Y 3.At 7:12/le-nos.
ISOTOPES BRANCH CIRCULARS.

Y 3.At 7:13/v.nos
ATOMIC ENERGY IN FOREIGN COUNTRIES. [Monthly]

Y 3.At 7:14/nos.
INFORMATION LETTERS.

Y 3.At 7:15/nos.
LIST [of Atomic Energy Commission Documents Available for Sale]. [Monthly]

Later C 41.29

Y 3.At 7:16 • **Item 1051-A**
NUCLEAR SCIENCE ABSTRACTS. v.1– 1948– [Semimonthly]

Later ER 1.10

Y 3.At 7:16-2/v.nos.
– BOUND VOLUMES.

Y 3.At 7:16-3/date
NEW NUCLEAR DATA, ANNUAL CUMULATIONS.

Earlier in Nuclear Science Abstracts.
Superseded by Y 3.At 7:16-4

Y 3.At 7:16-4/date • **Item 1051-A**
NUCLEAR DATA TABLES. [Annual]

Supersedes Y 3.At 7:16-3

Y 3.At 7:16-5 • **Item 1051-A**
INDEX. 1948– [Semimonthly]

Issued quarterly, cumulative semiannually, annually, and quinquennially.
The following cumulative indexes have been published:
Vols. 1– 4.
1948– 1950 Cumulative Subject, Author and Number Index (In Vol. 4, No. 24B [Dec. 1950].
Vols 5– 10
1951– 1956 Subject and Author Indexes.
Vols. 11– 15
1957– 1961 Subject, Author and Corporate Author Indexes.
Vols. 16-20
1962– 1966 Subject, Author and Corporate Author Indexes.

CUMULATIVE REPORT NUMBER INDEX (Y 3.At 7:16-2)

Vols	1– 15	1947– 1961
Vols	16– 21	1962– 1967
Vols	22– 22	1967– 1973
Later ER 1.10/2		

Y 3.At 7:17/nos.
SEMIANNUAL REPORTS.

Y 3.At 7:18/nos
SECURITY PAMPHLETS.

Y 3.At 7:19/v.nos.
RA-DET. [Monthly]

For official use only.

Y 3.At 7:20/nos.
RADIATION INSTRUMENT CATALOG.

Y 3.At 7:21
NATIONAL NUCLEAR ENERGY SERIES.

Y 3.At 7:22 • **Item 1051-C**
AEC RESEARCH AND DEVELOPMENT REPORTS. [Irregular]

Later ER 1.11

Y 3.At 7:23/v.nos.
GUIDE TO RUSSIAN SCIENTIFIC PERIODICAL LITERATURE.

Y 3.At 7:24/nos.
TECHNICAL INFORMATION DIVISION PUBLICATIONS.

Y 3.At 7:25/v.nos.
OAK RIDGE INSTITUTE OF NUCLEAR STUDIES NEWS LETTER. [Monthly]

Y 3.At 7:25-2/date
OAK RIDGE INSTITUTE OF NUCLEAR STUDIES. ANNUAL REPORT.

Y 3.At 7:26/CT
POSTERS.

Y 3.At 7:27/v.nos.
ISOTOPICS. [Quarterly]

Y 3.At 7:27-1/nos.
ISOTOPE DEVELOPMENTS. [Irregular]

Y 3.At 7:28
TECHNICAL INFORMATION SERVICE: CATALOGING BULLETINS.

Y 3.At 7:28-2/nos.
TECHNICAL INFORMATION BULLETIN.

Y 3.At 7:28-3/nos.
AFC TECHNICAL INFORMATION BULLETIN.

Replaces Y 3.At 7:47, Y 3.At 7:28-2

Y 3.At 7:29
OAK RIDGE INSTITUTE OF NUCLEAR STUDIES, QUARTERLY PROGRESS REPORT.

Y 3.At 7:30
MICROCARD AVAILABILITY LISTS. [Semimonthly]

Y 3.At 7:31/nos.
AIRBORNE ANOMALY LOCATIONS MAPS.

Y 3.At 7:31-2/nos.
PRELIMINARY MAPS.

Y 3.At 7:32/date
NUCLEAR NOTES FOR INDUSTRY. [Monthly]

Y 3.At 7:33
PRESS RELEASES. [Irregular]

News items of Commission activities, license issuances, access permit issuances.

Y 3.At 7:33-2/v.nos.&nos.
AEC NEW RELEASES. [Weekly]

Y 3.At 7:33-3/date
AEC NEW RELEASE INDEX. [Irregular]

Y 3.At 7:34 • **Item 1051-N**
ADDRESSES. [Irregular]

Y 3.At 7:35 • **Item 1051-Q**
CATALOG AND PRICE LIST OF STABLE ISOTOPES INCLUDING RELATED MATERIALS AND SERVICES.

Y 3.At 7:36 • **Item 1051-E**
REACTOR AND FUEL PROCESSING TECHNOLOGY. v. 1– 15, no. 4. 1957– 1972. [Quarterly]

PURPOSE:– To keep scientists and engineers informed of recent progress in power reactor technology, including reactor physics, heat transfer, reactor dynamics and safety, fuel elements and processing, and reactor materials.
Pertinent information formerly published in Reactor Fuel Processing (Y 3.At 7:37), which has been discontinued, is now being issued in a separate section of this publication.

Y 3.At 7:37/v.nos. • **Item 1051-E**
REACTOR FUEL PROCESSING. [Quarterly]

Y 3.At 7:38 • **Item 1051-E**
REACTOR MATERIALS. v. 1– 1958– [Quarterly] (Battelle Memorial Institute)

PURPOSE:– To keep scientists and engineers informed of recent developments in materials for use in nuclear reactor cores, including fuel and fertile material, moderator materials, control materials, structural materials, and special fabrication techniques.
Previous title: Reactor Core Materials.

Y 3.At 7:39 • **Item 1051-M**
ANNUAL FINANCIAL REPORT. [Annual]
Report submitted by the Controller to the Atomic Energy Commissioners, setting forth the financial position of the Commission as of June 30, the results of operations for the fiscal year and other unclassified financial information.

Y 3.At 7:40-1/nos.
FIRST UNITED NATIONS CONFERENCE ON PEACEFUL USES OF ATOMIC ENERGY, PAPERS.

Y 3.At 7:40-2/nos.
SECOND UNITED NATIONS CONFERENCE ON PEACEFUL USES OF ATOMIC ENERGY, PAPERS.

Y 3.At 7:41
[RESERVED FOR U.N. CONFERENCES].

Y 3.At 7:42/date • **Item 1051**
TRILINEAR CHART OF NUCLIDES.

Y 3.At 7:43/pt.nos.
LIVING WITH RADIATION.

Y 3.At 7:44 CT
BIBLIOGRAPHIES AND LISTS OF PUBLICATIONS.

Y 3.At 7:44 N 47
AEC NEWS RELEASE INDEX. [Semiannual]

Y 3.At 7:44-2
TRANSLATION LISTS. [Irregular]

Later ER 1.18

Y 3.At 7:45 • Item 1051-H
NUCLEAR SAFETY. v. 1– 1959– (Oak Ridge National Laboratory).

PURPOSE:– To keep reactor designers, reactor builders, reactor fuel specialists, regulatory and public safety officials informed on the current developments in nuclear safety. Activities of the Commission's Advisory Committee on Reactor Safeguards and the Hazards Evaluation Branch are also summarized and recent safeguards reports are review.
Indexed by: Index to U.S. Government Periodicals.

Y 3.At 7:46/v.nos.
DOORWAY TO LEGAL NEWS.

Y 3.At 7:47/date
AEC DEPOSITORY LIBRARY BULLETIN. [Irregular]

Y 3.At 7:48/date
ATOMIC ENERGY RESEARCH IN LIFE AND PHYSICAL SCIENCES. [Annual]

Earlier Y 3.At 7:2 L 62

Y 3.At 7:48 • Item 1051-I
FUNDAMENTAL NUCLEAR ENERGY RESEARCH. [Annual]

PURPOSE:– To report on some of the more significant advancements made during the year in the basic research and exploratory development work conducted in the areas of biomedical and environmental sciences, the physical sciences, and nuclear reactor technology.
Issued as a supplement to the annual report.

Y 3.At 7:48 • Item 1051-I
[ATOMIC ENERGY RESEARCH REPORTS]. 1960– [Annual]

Issued as a supplement to the Commission's Annual Report to Congress. Each report covers a specialized field of science or basic research crossing many branches of science. Each report is well illustrated and a valuable reference tool.

Y 3.At 7:49 • Item 1051-J
ATOMIC ENERGY COMMISSION REPORTS, OPINIONS OF THE ATOMIC ENERGY COMMISSION WITH SELECTED ORDERS. v. 1– 1956/61– [Irregular]

Vol. 1 1956– 1961
Vol. 2 1962– 1964
Later Y 3.N 88:11

Y 3.At 7:50
EURATOM PUBLICATIONS, EUROPEAN ATOMIC ENERGY COMMUNITY, INTERNATIONAL ORGANIZATION.

Y 3.At 7:51/nos.
RESEARCH AND DEVELOPMENT ABSTRACTS OF USAEC, RDA (series).

Y 3.At 7:51-2/v.nos.&nos.
RESEARCH AND DEVELOPMENT IN PROGRESS.

Y 3.At 7:52 • Item 1051-L
ISOTOPES AND RADIATION TECHNOLOGY. v. 1– 9. 1963– 1972. [Quarterly] (Oak Ridge National Laboratory)

PURPOSE:– To provide a review of Atomic Energy Commission sponsored isotopes production and development, process radiation development, applications of isotopes, and materials and services in the isotopes and radiation field available from the Commission

TECHNICAL PROGRESS REVIEWS.

Staying abreast of important developments reported in the burgeoning atomic energy literature in one of the most pressing problems faced by scientists, engineers, and technical administrators. As one means of attacking this problem the Atomic Energy Commission initiated in 1957 the publication of quarterly Technical Progress Reviews. The Reviews, prepared under contract by recognized authorities, digest and evaluate significant developments in selected areas of nuclear science and technology. Besides providing concise summaries of information generated in unclassified programs, the Reviews serve as a mechanism for disseminating information derived from classified programs when the information can be dissociated from classified applications.

Y 3.At 7:53/date
NUCLEAR THEORY REFERENCE BOOK. [Biennial]

Y 3.At 7:54
UNDERSTANDING THE ATOM SERIES. 1963– [Irregular]

PURPOSE:– To orient students, teachers, and the general public on the significance of nuclear science developments in specific areas.

Y 3.At 7:54-2
WORLD OF THE ATOM SERIES BOOKLETS. 1970– [Irregular]

PURPOSE:– To describe various field of nuclear energy for the use of junior high school students and their teachers.

Y 3.At 7:55
TELEPHONE DIRECTORY, HEADQUARTERS, GERMANTOWN, MD.

Y 3.At 7:55-2 • Item 1051-Q
FEDERAL TELECOMMUNICATIONS SYSTEM TELEPHONE DIRECTORY.

Y 3.At 7:56/date • Item 1051-O
NUCLEAR INDUSTRY.

Earlier Y 3.At 7:2 N 88/13

Y 3.At 7:57/nos.
OPERATING EXPERIMENTS, REACTOR SAFETY ROE (series).

Y 3.At 7:58 • Item 1051-P
PUBLIC SAFETY NEWSLETTER. 1– [Irregular] (Division of Operational Safety).

Y 3.At 7:59/v.nos.&nos.
ENERGY ABSTRACTS FOR POLICY ANALYSIS.

Later ER 1.9

AVIATION ADVISORY COMMISSION (1970)

CREATION AND AUTHORITY

The Aviation Advisory Commission was established pursuant to Public Law 91-258, approved May 21, 1970.

Y 3.Av 5:1/date • Item 1089
REPORT.

AVIATION SAFETY COMMISSION

Y 3.Av 5/2:CT • Item 1089-A-1
REPORTS AND PUBLICATIONS.

COMMISSION ON BANKRUPTCY LAWS OF THE UNITED STATES (1970)

Y 3.B 22:1/date
REPORT.

Y 3.B 22:2/CT
GENERAL PUBLICATIONS.

ARCHITECTURAL AND TRANSPORTATION BARRIERS COMPLIANCE BOARD (1976–   )

INFORMATION

Architectural and Transportation Barriers and Compliance Board
1331 F Street, NW, Ste. 1000
Washington, DC 20004-1111
(202) 272-0080
Toll-Free: (800) 872-2253
Fax: (202) 272-0081
Email:info@access-board
http://www.access-board.gov

Y 3.B 27:1/date • Item 1062-D-1 (MF)
REPORT. [Annual]

Y 3.B 27:2 CT • Item 1062-D-1
GENERAL PUBLICATIONS.

Y 3.B 27:3-2/nos. • Item 1062-D-2
BULLETINS.

Y 3.B 27:5 • Item 1062-D-1
LAWS.

Y 3.B 27:8 CT • Item 1062-D-1
HANDBOOKS, MANUALS, GUIDES.

Y 3.B 27:9 CT • Item 1062-D-1
BIBLIOGRAPHIES AND LISTS OF PUBLICATIONS. [Irregular]

Y 3.B 27:15/date-nos. • Item 1062-D-1
ACCESS AMERICA. [Quarterly]

Y 3.B 27:16 • Item 1062-D-1 (EL)
ACCESS CURRENTS. [Bimonthly]

BATTLE OF NEW ORLEANS SESQUICENTENNIAL CELEBRATION COMMISSION (1962–1965)

CREATION AND AUTHORITY

The Battle of New Orleans Sesquicentennial Celebration Commission was established by Joint Resolution of October 9, 1962 (Public Law 87-759, 87th Congress, 76 Stat. 755).

Y 3.B 32:1/date
REPORTS.

BATTLE OF LAKE ERIE SESQUICENTENNIAL CELEBRATION COMMISSION

Y 3.B 32/2:1/date
REPORTS.

BERLIN SILVER COMMISSION (1894)

Y 3.B 45:2 CT
PUBLICATIONS.

COMMISSION ON THE BICENTENNIAL OF THE UNITED STATES CONSTITUTION (1986–)

Y 3.B 47/2:2 CT • Item 1089-A-2
GENERAL PUBLICATIONS. [Irregular]

Y 3.B 47/2:8 CT • Item 1089-A-2
HANDBOOKS, MANUALS, GUIDES.

Y 3.B 47/2:12 CT • Item 1089-A-2
POSTERS.

Y 3.B 47/2:15/v.nos.&nos. • Item 1089
NEWSLETTER. v. 1– 1986– [Monthly]

Y 3.B 47/2:16/date • Item 1089-A-2
CALENDAR. [Annual]

NATIONAL ADVISORY AND COORDINATING COUNCIL ON BILINGUAL EDUCATION

CREATION AND AUTHORITY

The National Advisory and Coordinating Council on Bilingual Education, was created by PL 98-511.

Y 3.B 49:1/date • Item 1063-J
ANNUAL REPORTS.

Y 3.B 49:2 CT • Item 1063-J
GENERAL PUBLICATIONS.

BITUMINOUS COAL COMMISSION (1919–1920)

CREATION AND AUTHORITY

The United States Bituminous Coal Commission was established by the President on December 19, 1919. The Commission was abolished by Executive Order 3249 of March 24, 1920.

Y 3.B 54:2 CT
PUBLICATIONS.

BITUMINOUS COAL CONSUMERS' COUNSEL (1941–1943)

Y 3.B 54/2:1/date
ANNUAL REPORTS.

Y 3.B 54/2:2 CT
GENERAL PUBLICATIONS.

Y 3.B 54/2:7/vol.
COAL CONSUMERS' DIGEST. [Monthly]

Earlier I 48.58

COMMITTEE FOR PURCHASE FROM PEOPLE WHO ARE BLIND OR SEVERELY DISABLED (1974–)

CREATION AND AUTHORITY

The Committee on Purchases of Blind-made Products was established by act of June 25, 1938 (52 Stat. 1196). The name was changed to Committee for Purchase of Products and Services of the Blind and Other Severely Handicapped (Y 3. P 97) by act of June 23, 1971 (85 Stat. 77). The name again was changed to Committee for Purchase from the Blind and Other Severely Handicapped by act of July 25, 1974 (88 Stat. 392) and classed Y 3.P 97.

INFORMATION

Committee for Purchase from People who are Blind or Severely Disabled
1421 Jefferson Davis Hwy.
Jefferson Plaza II, Ste. 10800
Arlington, VA 22202-3259
(703) 603-7740
Fax: (703) 603-0655
Email:info@jwod.gov
http://www.jwod.gov

Y 3.B 6:1/date
ANNUAL REPORT.

Later Y 3.P 97:1

Y 3.B 61:2 CT
GENERAL PUBLICATIONS.

Later Y 3.P 97:2

Y 3.B 61:6 CT
REGULATIONS, RULES, AND INSTRUCTIONS. [Irregular]

Y 3.B 61:8/date
SCHEDULE OF BLIND-MADE PRODUCTS. [Semi-annual]

Earlier Y 3.B 61:2 P 94
Superseded by Procurement List (Y 3.P 97:10).

BOSTON NATIONAL HISTORIC SITES COMMISSION (1955–1960)

CREATION AND AUTHORITY

The Boston National Historic Sites Commission was created by Public law 75, 84th Congress, approved June 16, 1955. The Commission ceased to exist on June 16, 1960, pursuant to act of February 19, 1957, as amended (71 Stat. 4, 72 State. 296, 73 Stat. 279).

Y 3.B 65:1/date
REPORTS.

Y 3.B 65:2 CT
GENERAL PUBLICATIONS.

BOARD FOR INTERNATIONAL BROADCASTING
(1973–   )

CREATION AND AUTHORITY

The Board for International Broadcasting was established by the Board for International Broadcasting Act 1973 (87 Stat. 456).

INFORMATION

Board for International Broadcasting
Suite 400
1201 Connecticut Avenue, N.W.
Washington, D.C. 20036
(202) 254-8040

Y 3.B 78:1/date   • Item 1062-B-1
ANNUAL REPORT. 1st–   1975–

Y 3.B 78:2 CT   • Item 1062-B-1
GENERAL PUBLICATIONS.

Y 3.B 78:9/date   • Item 1062-B-1
BUDGET. [Annual]

ADVISORY BOARD FOR CUBA BROADCASTING

Y 3.B 78/2:1/date   • Item 1089
REPORT BY THE ADVISORY BOARD FOR CUBA BROADCASTING.

JOINT COMMISSION ON PLANS FOR EXTENSION AND COMPLETION OF THE CAPITOL BUILDING
(1904)

Y 3.C 17:2 CT
PUBLICATIONS

CAPITAL ISSUES COMMITTEE
(1918– 1919)

CREATION AND AUTHORITY

The Capital Issues Committee was established within the Federal Reserve Board in January 1918, at the request of the Secretary of the Treasury. This Committee continued until May 1918, when it was superseded by a new Capital Issues Committee, appointed by the President under authority of the War Finance Corporation Act, approved April 5, 1918. The second Committee continued until December 31, 1918. A Presidential Proclamation of August 30, 1919, abolished the Committee and transferred its functions to the Federal Trade Commission.

Y 3.C 17/2:1/date
ANNUAL REPORTS.

Y 3.C 17/2:2 CT
GENERAL PUBLICATIONS.

Y 3.C 17/2:3
BULLETINS.

Y 3.C 17/2:4/nos
CIRCULARS.

CENTRAL AND SOUTH AMERICAN COMMISSION
(1885– 1886)

Y 3.C 33:2 CT
PUBLICATIONS.

CENTRAL STATISTICAL BOARD
(1933– 1940)

CREATION AND AUTHORITY

The Central Statistical Board was established as an independent agency by Executive Order 6255 of July 27, 1933, under authority of the National Industrial Recovery Act (48 Stat 195). The Board was transferred to the Bureau of the Budget by Reorganization Plan No. 1 of 1939, effective when its functions were assumed by the Division of Statistical Standards of the Bureau of the Budget.

Y 3.C 33/2:1/date
ANNUAL REPORTS.

Y 3.C 33/2:2 CT
GENERAL PUBLICATIONS.

CENTRAL HOUSING COMMITTEE
(1935– 1942)

CREATION AND AUTHORITY

The Central Housing Committee was established by the President on September 27, 1935. The Committee was abolished by Executive Order 9070 of February 24, 1942, and its functions transferred to the National Housing Agency.

Y 3.C 33/3:1/date
ANNUAL REPORTS.

Y 3.C 33/3:2 CT
GENERAL PUBLICATIONS.

Y 3.C 33/3:7/nos.
HOUSING INDEX-DIGEST. [Semimonthly except August]

Y 3.C 33/3:8/nos.
SELECTED REFERENCES ON HOUSING.

Y 3.C 33/3:9/nos.
SPECIAL REPORTS.

Y 3.C 33/3:10/nos.
HOUSING LEGAL DIGEST, DECISIONS, OPINIONS, LEGISLATION RELATING TO HOUSING CONSTRUCTION AND FINANCE. [Monthly]

Y 3.C 33/3:11/nos.
TECHNICAL BULLETINS. [Bimonthly]

CENTRAL STATISTICAL COMMITTEE
(1935– 1939)

CREATION AND AUTHORITY

The Central Statistical Committee was established by act of Congress, approved July 25, 1935 (49 Stat. 498). It was abolished by Reorganization Plan No. 1 of 1939, effective July 1, 1939, and its functions transferred to the Director of the Bureau of the Budget.

Y 3.C 33/4:1/date
ANNUAL REPORTS.

Y 3.C 33/4:2 CT
GENERAL PUBLICATIONS.

Y 3.C 33/4:6/nos.
REGULATIONS.

CENSUS OF PARTIAL EMPLOYMENT, UNEMPLOYMENT AND OCCUPATIONS
(1937– 1938)

CREATION AND AUTHORITY

The Census of Partial Employment, Unemployment, and Occupations was established as an independent agency by Executive Order 7711 of September 22, 1937, pursuant to act of Congress, approved August 30, 1937 (50 Stat. 883). The agency was abolished on October 31, 1938 and its records transferred to the Department of Commerce by Executive Order 7999 of October 31, 1938.

Y 3.C 33/5:1/date
ANNUAL REPORTS.

Y 3.C 33/5:2 CT
GENERAL PUBLICATIONS.

CENSORSHIP OFFICE
(1941– 1945)

CREATION AND AUTHORITY

The Censorship Office was established by EO 8985 of December 19, 1941, to censor communications by mail, cable, radio, or other means of transmission passing between the United States and any foreign country. The Office was terminated by EO 9631 of September 28, 1945, effective November 15, 1945.

Y 3.C 33/6:1/date
ANNUAL REPORTS.

Y 3.C 33/6:2 CT
GENERAL PUBLICATIONS.

Y 3.C 33/6:6 CT
REGULATIONS, RULES, AND INSTRUCTIONS.

U.S. CHEMICAL SAFETY AND HAZARD INVESTIGATION BOARD
(1990 -)

INFORMATION

U. S. Chemical Safety and
Hazard Investigation Board
2175 K. St., NW, Ste. 400
Washington, DC 20037-1809
(800) 424-8802
(202) 261-7600
Fax: (202) 261-7650
Email:info@csb.gov
http://www.chemsafety.gov

Y 3.C 42:CT   • Item 1093-A
GENERAL PUBLICATIONS.

Y 3.C 43:2 CT
PUBLICATIONS.

Y 3.C 42/2:2   • Item 1093-A
GENERAL PUBLICATIONS.

Y 3.C 42/2:15   • Item 1093-A-1 (E)
ELECTRONIC PRODUCTS. (Misc.)

Y 3.C 42/2:16   • Item 1093-A-2 (EL)
INVESTIGATIONS AND NEWS.

CHICAGO STRIKE COMMISSION
(1894)

CREATION AND AUTHORITY

The Chicago Strike Commission was established in 1894 and submitted its report the same year.

NATIONAL ADVISORY COUNCIL ON CHILD NUTRITION
(1971–)

Y 3.C 43/2:1/date   • Item 1062-C-1
ANNUAL REPORT. 1st–   1971–

Y 3.C 43/2:2 CT   • Item 1062-C-1
GENERAL PUBLICATIONS.

U.S. NATIONAL COMMISSION ON THE INTERNATIONAL YEAR OF THE CHILD

Y 3.C 43/3:1/date   • Item 1089
ANNUAL REPORT.

Y 3.C 43/3:2 CT
GENERAL PUBLICATIONS. [Irregular]

INTERAGENCY PANEL ON EARLY CHILDHOOD RESEARCH AND DEVELOPMENT

Y 3.C 43/4:1/date
ANNUAL REPORT.

NATIONAL COMMISSION ON CHILDREN

Y 3.C 43/5:2 CT   • Item 1089-O
GENERAL PUBLICATIONS.

CIVILIAN CONSERVATION CORPS
(1937– 1939)

CREATION AND AUTHORITY

The Civilian Conservation Corps was created by act approved June 28, 1937 (50 Stat. 319; 16 U.S.C. 584), as amended, to succeed Emergency Conservation Work established by EO 6101 of April 5, 1933, under act of March 31, 1933 (48 Stat. 22), as amended. The Corps was made a part of the Federal Security Agency (FS 4) by Reorganization Plan 1, effective July 1, 1939.

Y 3.C 49:1/date
ANNUAL REPORTS.

Y 3.C 49:2 CT
GENERAL PUBLICATIONS.

Y 3.C 49:6 CT
REGULATIONS, RULES, AND INSTRUCTIONS.

Y 3.C 49:7/date
MONTHLY SAFETY BULLETIN.

Earlier Y 3.Em 3.10
Later FS 4.8

Y 3.C 49:8/nos.
POSTERS.

Earlier Y 3.Em 3:9

Y 3.C 49:9/nos.
FORESTRY PUBLICATIONS.

Earlier Y 3.Em 3:7
Later FS 4.7

CIVIL WAR CENTENNIAL COMMISSION
(1957– 1966)

CREATION AND AUTHORITY

The Civil War Centennial Commission was established pursuant to Joint Resolution approved September 7, 1957 (71 Stat. 636; 36 U.S.C. 741), to prepare for the nationwide commemorations of the one hundredth anniversary of the Civil War. The Commission submitted its final report to Congress and was terminated May 1, 1966, pursuant to terms of the act.

Y 3.C 49/2:1/date
REPORTS.

Y 3.C 49/2:2 CT
GENERAL PUBLICATIONS.

Y 3.C 49/2:3/nos.
BULLETINS. [Official Use]

Y 3.C 49/2:6 CT
REGULATIONS, RULES, AND INSTRUCTIONS.

Y 3.C 49/2:8/v.nos.&nos.
100 YEARS AFTER [Newsletter]. [Monthly]

Y 3.C 49/2:9/v.nos.&nos.
MILITARY OPERATIONS OF THE CIVIL WAR, GUIDE INDEX TO OFFICIAL RECORDS OF THE UNION AND CONFEDERATE ARMIES, 1861– 65.

INTERAGENCY COMMITTEE ON UNIFORM CIVIL RIGHTS POLICIES AND PRACTICES
(1974)

Y 3.C 49/4:1/date
ANNUAL REPORT.

Y 3.C 49/4:2 CT
PUBLICATIONS.

FEDERAL INTERAGENCY COUNCIL ON CITIZEN PARTICIPATION
(1977–   )

Y 3.C 49/5:1/date
REPORT.

Y 3.C 49/5:2 CT
GENERAL PUBLICATIONS.

CLAIMS COMMISSION
(1871–1875)

Y 3.C 52:2 CT
PUBLICATIONS.

INTERAGENCY CLASSIFICATION REVIEW COMMITTEE
(1976–1978)

Y 3.C 56:1/date
PROGRESS REPORT.

Y 3.C 56:2 CT
GENERAL PUBLICATIONS.

COAL COMMISSION
(1922–1923)

CREATION AND AUTHORITY

The United States Coal Commission was established by act of Congress, approved September 22, 1922. The Commission was terminated on September 22, 1923, by statutory limitation.

Y 3.C 63:2 CT
PUBLICATIONS.

COASTAL PLAINS REGIONAL COMMISSION
(1967–1981)

CREATION AND AUTHORITY

Title V of the Public Works and Economic Development Act of 1965 (79 Stat. 552; 42 U.S.C. 3121) authorizes the Secretary of Commerce to designate economic development regions. Following such designation, the Secretary invites the States of the region to establish a regional commission. The Coastal Plains Region, consisting of 159 counties in North Carolina, South Carolina, and Georgia was designated on December 21, 1966. The Commission was formally organized on July 29, 1967. Members are the Federal chairman and the Coastal Plains Governors. The Governors elect one of their members to be the Commission State Co-chairman. The Federal role abolished through repeal of the Public Works and Economic Development Act by sec. 1821 of Public Law 97-35 of August 13, 1981 (95 Stat. 766), effective October 1, 1981.

Y 3.C 63/2:1/date
ANNUAL REPORT.

Y 3.C 63/2:2 CT
GENERAL PUBLICATIONS.

Y 3.C 63/2:7/nos.
PRESS RELEASES.

Y 3.C 63/2:9 CT
ADDRESSES.

COMMISSION ON FAIR MARKET VALUE POLICY FOR FEDERAL COAL LEASING

Y 3.C 63/3:1/date   • Item 1089-G
ANNUAL REPORTS.

Y 3.C 63/3:2/CT   • Item 1089-G
GENERAL PUBLICATIONS.

Y 3.C 63/3:8 CT
HANDBOOKS, MANUALS, GUIDES.

JOINT COMMISSION ON THE COINAGE
(1965–1975)

CREATION AND AUTHORITY

The Joint Commission on the Coinage was established by the Coinage Act of 1965 (79 Stat. 2580). The Commission expired January 4, 1975, under provisions of section 14 of Federal Advisory Committee Act of October 6, 1972 (88 Stat. 776).

Y 3.C 66:1/date
REPORT.

Y 3.C 66:2 CT
GENERAL PUBLICATIONS.

COLORADO RIVER INTERSTATE– GOVERNMENT COMMISSION
(1923)

Y 3.C 71:2 CT
PUBLICATIONS.

COLUMBIA BASIN INTER- AGENCY COMMITTEE
(1946–   )

CREATION AND AUTHORITY

The Columbia Basin Inter-Agency was established by the Federal Inter-Agency River Basin Committee on February 5, 1946, for the purpose of coordinating the planning, construction, and administration of the multiple-purpose development program of the Columbia River Basin and the coastal areas in Washington and Oregon which drain into the Pacific Ocean.

Y 3.C 72:1/date
ANNUAL REPORTS.

Y 3.C 72:2 CT
GENERAL PUBLICATIONS.

Y 3.C 72:9/date
REVIEW OF POSTWAR PLANNING IN PACIFIC NORTHWEST.

Later Y 3.P 11/4:9

COMMODITY CREDIT CORPORATION
(1933– 1939)

CREATION AND AUTHORITY

The Commodity Credit Corporation was established October 17, 1933, pursuant to Executive Order 6340 of October 15, 1933, under the laws of the State of Delaware as an agency of the United States. Reorganization Plan No. 1 of 1939, effective July 1, 1939, transferred the corporation to the Department of Agriculture (A 71).

Y 3.C 73:1/date
ANNUAL REPORTS.
   Later A 71.1

Y 3.C 73:2 CT
GENERAL PUBLICATIONS.
   Later A 71.2

Y 3.C 73:3
BULLETINS.

Y 3.C 73:4
CIRCULARS.

Y 3.C 73:5
LAWS.

Y 3.C 73:6
REGULATIONS.
   Later A 71.6

Y 3.C 73:8
POSTERS.

Y 3.C 73:9/nos.
CORN CIRCULAR LETTERS.

Y 3.C 73:10/nos.
COTTON CIRCULAR LETTERS.

Y 3.C 73:11/nos.
GUM TURPENTINE AND GUM ROSIN CIRCULAR LETTERS.

Y 3.C 73:12/date
CURRENT STATEMENT OF LOANS BY YEARS AND COMMODITIES. [Monthly]
   Later A 71.7

COMBINED RAW MATERIAL BOARD, UNITED STATES AND GREAT BRITAIN
(1942– 1945)

CREATION AND AUTHORITY

The Combined Raw Materials Board was established on January 26, 1942 by the governments of the United States and Great Britain. By agreement of both governments, the Board was abolished on December 31, 1945. Its work was carried on by the newly created Combined Tin Committee, established in January 1946.

Y 3.C 73/2:1/date
ANNUAL REPORTS.

Y 3.C 73/2:2 CT
GENERAL PUBLICATIONS.

COMBINED PRODUCTION AND RESOURCE BOARD, UNITED STATES, GREAT BRITAIN, AND CANADA
(1942– 1945)

Y 3.C 73/3:1/date
ANNUAL REPORTS.

Y 3.C 73/3:2 CT
GENERAL PUBLICATIONS.

INTERIM COMPLIANCE PANEL
(1972)

CREATION AND AUTHORITY

The Interim Compliance Panel was established by Public Law 92-500, approved October 18, 1972.

Y 3.C 73/4:1/date
ANNUAL REPORTS.

Y 3.C 73/4:2 CT
GENERAL PUBLICATIONS.

COMMODITY FUTURES TRADING COMMISSION
(1974–   )

CREATION AND AUTHORITY

The Commodity Futures Trading Commission was established as an independent agency by the Commodity Futures Trading Commission Act of 1974 (88 Stat. 1389; 7 U.S.C. 41), superseding the Commodity Exchange Authority (A 85) of the Department of Agriculture, which was abolished by the same act.

INFORMATION

Commodity Futures Trading Commission
3 Lafayette Centre
1155 21st St., NW
Washington, D.C. 20581
(202) 418-5000
Fax: 418-5521
http://www.cftc.gov

Y 3.C 73/5:1/date   • Item 39-B
ANNUAL REPORTS.

Y 3.C 73/5:2 CT   • Item 39
GENERAL PUBLICATIONS.

Y 3.C 73/5:3-2/nos.   • Item 39-C
ECONOMIC BULLETINS. 1–   1977–   [Irregular]

Y 3.C 73/5:9/date&nos.   • Item 39-D
COMMITMENTS OF TRADERS IN COMMODITY FUTURES WITH MARKET CONCENTRATION RATIOS. [Monthly] (New York City Office)

Includes data for cotton, frozen concentrated orange juice, potatoes, wool, and imported frozen fresh boneless beef. Tables present a breakdown of monthend open interest for markets in which five or more traders hold positions equal to or above the reporting levels established by the Commission. Tables shown open interest separately by reportable and nonreportable positions.
   Prior to April 30, 1975 issued by the Commodity Exchange Authority (A 85.9).
   Combined with Y 3.C 73/5:9/2 to form Y 3.C 73/5:9/3

Y 3.C 73/5:9/2/date&nos.
COMMITMENTS OF TRADERS IN COMMODITY FUTURES. [Monthly] (Chicago, Illinois Office)

Includes data for wheat, corn, oats, soybeans, soybean oil, soybean meal, coconut oil, crude palm oil, eggs, cattle, frozen pork bellies, and live hogs.
   Prior to April 30, 1975 issued by Commodity Exchange Authority.
   Combined with Y 3.C 73/5:9 to form Y 3.C 73/5:9/3

Y 3.C 73/5:9-3/date   • Item 39-D
COMMITMENTS OF TRADERS IN COMMODITY FUTURES. [Monthly]

Earlier Y 3.C 73/5:9 and Y 3.C 73/5:9-2
Combines New York and Chicago markets.

Y 3.C 73/5:9-4/date   • Item 39-D
COMMITMENTS OF TRADERS IN COMMODITY OPTIONS. [Bimonthly]

Y 3.C 73/5:10/date
STOCKS OF GRAIN IN DELIVERABLE POSITIONS FOR CHICAGO BOARD OF TRADE, FUTURES CONTRACTS IN EXCHANGE-APPROVED AND FEDERALLY LICENSED WAREHOUSES, AS REPORTED BY THOSE WAREHOUSES. [Weekly] (Commodity Exchange Authority, 141 West Jackson Blvd. Chicago, Illinois 60604)

Title varies.
Gives stocks represented by outstanding warehouse receipts as reported by licensed warehouses, by grain and grade, as of date (Friday), previous week, and previous years.
   ISSN 0145-2509
   Earlier A 85.14

Y 3.C 73/5:11/nos.
ON CALL POSITIONS IN SPOT COTTON BASED ON NEW YORK COTTON FUTURES REPORTED BY MERCHANTS IN SPECIAL ACCOUNT STATUS. [Weekly]

ISSN 0364-2224
Prior to May 1975 issued by Commodity Exchange Authority.

Y 3.C 73/5:12/nos.
CFTC STAFF INTERPRETATIVE LETTERS.

Y 3.C 73/5:13 CT
ADDRESSES.

COMPETITIVENESS POLICY COUNCIL

Y 3.C 73/6:1/date   • Item 1089-Z-1
ANNUAL REPORT.

Y 3.C 73/6:2 CT   • Item 1089-Z-1
GENERAL PUBLICATIONS.

CONSTRUCTION INDUSTRY COLLECTIVE BARGAINING COMMISSION
(1974–　　)

Y 3.C 76:1/date
ANNUAL REPORT.

Y 3.C 76:2 (CT)
GENERAL PUBLICATIONS.

NATIONAL COMMISSION ON CONSUMER FINANCE
(1968–　　)

CREATION AND AUTHORITY

The National Commission on Consumer Finance was established by Public Law 90-321, approved May 29, 1968.

Y 3.C 76/2:1/date　　　　　• **Item 1089**
REPORT.

Y 3.C 76/2:2 CT　　　　　• **Item 1089**
GENERAL PUBLICATIONS.

CONSUMER PRODUCT SAFETY COMMISSION
(1972–　　)

CREATION AND AUTHORITY

The Consumer Product Safety Commission was established as an independent Federal regulatory agency by the Consumer Product Safety Act of October 27, 1972 (86 Stat. 1207; U.S.C. 92-573).

INFORMATION

Consumer Product Safety Commission
4330 East-West Hwy.
Washington, D.C. 20207-0001
(301) 504-0990
Fax: 504-0124
Email:info@cpsc.gov
http://www.cpsc.gov

Y 3.C 76/3:1/date　　　　• **Item 1062-C-5 (EL)**
ANNUAL REPORT.

Y 3.C 76/3:2 CT　　　　　• **Item 1062-C**
GENERAL PUBLICATIONS.

Y 3.C 76/3:5 CT　　　　　• **Item 1062-C-4**
LAWS.

Y 3.C 76/3:6
REGULATIONS, RULES, AND INSTRUCTIONS.

Y 3.C 76/3:6-2/nos　　　　• **Item 1062-C-4**
ORDERS (numbered). [Irregular]

Y 3.C 76/3:7/nos.　　　　• **Item 1062-C-20**
PRESS RELEASES. [Irregular]

Y 3.C 76/3:7-2/v.nos.&nos.　　• **Item 475-T**
NEISS [National Electronic Surveillance System] NEWS, PRODUCT SAFETY. v. 1–　[Monthly]

ISSN 0364-6475
Earlier HE 20.4026

Y 3.C 76/3:7-3/v.nos./nos.　　• **Item 475-T-1 (MF)**
NEISS DATA HIGHLIGHTS. v. 1–　[Annual]

Y 3.C 76/3:8 CT　　　　　• **Item 1062-C-6**
HANDBOOKS, MANUALS, GUIDES. [Irregular]

Y 3.C 76/3:8-2/nos　　　　• **Item 1062-C-2**
CPSC TRAINING SERIES. 1–　[Irregular]

Y 3.C 76/3:8-3 CT　　　　• **Item 1062-C-6**
SPOT THE DANGER, USER'S GUIDE TO [various products] SAFETY SERIES.

Y 3.C 76/3:9/v.nos.&nos.　　• **Item 1064-B**
BANNED PRODUCTS [list]. v. 1, pt. 1–　1973–　[Monthly]

PURPOSE:– To provide a list of banned products so that they may be identified and removed from sale.
Under provisions of the Consumer Product Safety Act and the Federal Hazardous Substances Act, the Consumer Product Safety Commission has the responsibility to ban hazardous products.

Y 3.C 76/3:10 CT
ADDRESSES. [Irregular]

Y 3.C 76/3:11/nos　　　　• **Item 1062-C-7**
FACT SHEETS. 1–　[Irregular]

Y 3.C 76/3:11-2/nos.
TECHNICAL FACT SHEETS.

Y 3.C 76/3:11-3 CT　　　　• **Item 1062-C-15**
ALERT SHEETS. [Irregular]

PURPOSE:– To provide a series of 4- to 6-page publications, each explaining the potential hazards of particular product.

Y 3.C 76/3:11-4/date/nos.　　• **Item 1062-C-21**
SAFETY NEWS. [Bimonthly]

Y 3.C 76/3:12/date　　　　• **Item 1062-C-3**
NATIONAL POISON PREVENTION WEEK. 1st– 1962–　[Annual]

Y 3.C 76/3:13 CT　　　　　• **Item 1062-C-8**
BIBLIOGRAPHIES AND LISTS OF PUBLICATIONS.

Y 3.C 76/3:14　　　　　• **Item 1062-C-9**
POSTERS. [Irregular]

Y 3.C 76/3:14/2 CT
AUDIOVISUAL MATERIALS.

Y 3.C 76/3:15 CT　　　　• **Item 1062-C-10**
ENVIRONMENTAL IMPACT STATEMENTS. [Irregular]

Y 3.C 76/3:16/date　　　　• **Item 1061-C-11**
CPSC MEMO. [Monthly]

PURPOSE:– To provide product safety information such as warning labels, petition filing, recalls, safe use of products, potentially harmful products, etc. in a publication especially designed for consumers.
Discontinued with Aug.-Sept. 1981 issue.

Y 3.C 76/3:17 CT　　　　• **Item 1062-C-13**
HAZARD ANALYSIS REPORTS [on various subjects]. [Irregular]

PURPOSE:– To present comprehensive analyses of all available epidemiological data pertaining to specific product areas. Data from the National Electronic Injury Surveillance System, as well as information contained within the Death Certificate File, Injury Surveillance Desk data base, and non-CPSC data sources are utilized.
Earlier Y 3.C 76/3:2 H 34

Y 3.C 76/3:17-2 CT　　　　• **Item 1062-C-12**
HIA [Hazard Identification and Analysis] SPECIAL REPORTS. [Irregular]

PURPOSE:– To present the results of specific surveys, and responses to specific requests on data focused on a particular aspect of product's involvement in accidents.

Y 3.C 76/3:18/date　　　　• **Item 1062-C-17**
FLAMMABLE FABRICS REPORT. [Annual]

PURPOSE:– To provide an annual progress report on the Commission's activities, with priorities and data pertaining to injuries and deaths resulting from flammable fabrics fires.
Continues: Reports Required by the Flammable Fabrics Act.

Y 3.C 76/3:19/nos.-letters　　• **Item 1062-C-14**
PRODUCT SAFETY EDUCATION UNIT (series). [Irregular]

Each unit consists of two leaflets, one for the student and the other for the teacher, on subjects such as poison prevention, kitchen safety, bicycles, etc.
Previously distributed to Depository Libraries under Item no. 1062-C-6.

Y 3.C 76/3:20/date　　　　• **Item 1062-C-18**
CONSUMER COMPLAINT CONTACT SYSTEM, ANNUAL REPORT. 1st–　1978–

Y 3.C 76/3:22 CT　　　　• **Item 1062-C-16**
CONSUMER DEPUTY PROGRAM (series). [Irregular]

PURPOSE:– To provide results of household surveys on consumer products.

Y 3.C 76/3:23/date　　　• **Item 1062-C-19 (MF)**
CPSC TELEPHONE DIRECTORY. [Quarterly]

Y 3.C 76/3:24　　　　　• **Item 1062-C-21**
FIRE SAFETY FOCUS SHEETS. [Irregular]

Each focus sheet deals with a different kind of fire.

Y 3.C 76/3:26/v.nos.&nos.　　• **Item 1062-C-20**
CPSC PUBLIC CALENDAR. [Weekly]

Y 3.C 76/3:27/v.nos./nos.　　• **Item 1064-B**
MECAP NEWS. [Bimonthly]

Y 3.C 76/3:28/v.nos./nos.　　• **Item 1062-C-22**
CONSUMER PRODUCT SAFETY REVIEW. [Quarterly]

ADVISORY COMMITTEE ON THE RECORDS OF CONGRESS
(1990–   )

CREATION AND AUTHORITY

The Advisory Committee on the Records of Congress was established under Authority of Public Law 101-509, November 5, 1990.

INFORMATION

Advisory Committee on
the Records of Congress
National Archives & Records Administration
700 Pennsylvania Ave., NW
Washington, DC 20408
Toll-Free: (866) 272-6272
http://www.archives.gov/records_
of_congress/advisory_committee

Y 3.C 76/4:2 CT   • **Item 1089-Q**
GENERAL PUBLICATIONS.

ADVISORY COMMISSION ON CONFERENCES IN OCEAN SHIPPING

Y 3.C 76/5:CT   • **Item 1089**
REPORTS AND PUBLICATIONS.

COORDINATOR FOR INDUSTRIAL COOPERATION
(1935–1937)

CREATION AND AUTHORITY

The Office of the Coordinator for Industrial Cooperation was established by EO 7193 of September 26, 1935, to supervise the conference of representatives of industry, labor, and consumers, and to coordinate and report to the President on matters relating to appointment, discharge, compensation, and duties of officers and employees of the National Recovery Administration. Continued by EO 7324 of March 30, 1936. The Office ceased to Function on June 30, 1937.

Y 3.C 78:1/date
ANNUAL REPORTS.

Y 3.C 78:2 CT
GENERAL PUBLICATIONS.

Y 3.C 78:7/vol.
ANALYSIS OF PRODUCTION, WAGES AND EMPLOYMENT IN MANUFACTURING INDUSTRIES, 1914–1933.

COOPERATIVE ENTERPRISE IN EUROPE COMMITTEE
(1936–1937)

CREATION AND AUTHORITY

The Cooperative Enterprise in Europe Committee was established in 1936 and submitted its report in 1937.

Y 3.C 78/2:1
REPORT.

Y 3.C 78/2:2 CT
GENERAL PUBLICATIONS.

COORDINATOR FOR INFORMATION
(1941–1942)

Y 3.C 78/3:1/date
ANNUAL REPORTS.

Y 3.C 78/3:2 CT
GENERAL PUBLICATIONS.

Y 3.C 78/3:7/nos.
PUBLICATIONS OF RESEARCH AND ANALYSIS BRANCH.

Later W 2.13

NATIONAL COMMISSION ON NEW TECHNOLOGICAL USES OF COPYRIGHTED WORKS
(1974–1978)

CREATION AND AUTHORITY

The National Commission on New Technological Uses of Copyrighted Works was established in the Library of Congress by act of Congress, approved December, 31, 1974.

Y 3.C 79:1/date
REPORTS

Y 3.C 79:2 CT
GENERAL PUBLICATIONS.

Y 3.C 79:9/nos.
TRANSCRIPT CONTU MEETINGS (numbered).

COST ACCOUNTING STANDARDS BOARD
(1970–1981)

CREATION AND AUTHORITY

The Cost Accounting Standards Board was established by act of August 15, 1970 (84 Stat. 796; 50 U.S.C. App. 2166(a) as an agent of Congress and independent of the executive departments. Board was terminated in 1981 due to lack of funding.

Y 3.C 82:1/date   • **Item 1063-D-1**
ANNUAL REPORT.

Y 3.C 82:2 CT   • **Item 1063-D-1**
GENERAL PUBLICATIONS. [Irregular]

Y 3.C 82:6 CT   • **Item 1063-D-1**
REGULATIONS, RULES, AND INSTRUCTIONS.

COUNCIL OF NATIONAL DEFENSE
(1916–1918)

CREATION AND AUTHORITY

The Council of National Defense was established by act of Congress, approved August 29, 1916 (39 Stat. 649). Subsequent to 1918, the Council became inactive. The Council was reactivated on May 29, 1940 by the President when he appointed a new Advisory Commission (Y 3.C 831).

Y 3.C 83:1/date
ANNUAL REPORTS.

Y 3.C 83:2 CT
GENERAL PUBLICATIONS.

Y 3.C 83:3
BULLETINS.

Y 3.C 83:4
CIRCULARS.

Y 3.C 83:5/nos.
COMMUNITY COUNCIL CIRCULARS.

Y 3.C 83:6 CT
BLANK FORMS.

Commercial Economy Board

Y 3.C 83:11/date
ANNUAL REPORTS.

Y 3.C 83:12 CT
GENERAL PUBLICATIONS.

Y 3.C 83:13
BULLETINS

Y 3.C 83:14
CIRCULARS.

Highways Transport Committee

Y 3.C 83:21/date
ANNUAL REPORTS.

Y 3.C 83:22 CT
GENERAL PUBLICATIONS.

Y 3.C 83:23/nos.
BULLETINS.

Y 3.C 83:24
CIRCULARS.

Labor Committee

Y 3.C 83:31/date
ANNUAL REPORTS.

Y 3.C 83:32 CT
GENERAL PUBLICATIONS.

Y 3.C 83:33
BULLETINS.

Y 3.C 83:34
CIRCULARS.

Y 3.C 83:35/nos.
WELFARE WORK SERIES.

Medical Section

Y 3.C 83:41/date
ANNUAL REPORTS.

Y 3.C 83:42 CT
GENERAL PUBLICATIONS.

Y 3.C 83:43
BULLETINS.

Y 3.C 83:44
CIRCULARS.

War Industries Board

Y 3.C 83:51/date
ANNUAL REPORTS.

>   Later Y 3.W 19/2:1

Y 3.C 83:52 CT
GENERAL PUBLICATIONS.

>   Later Y 3.W 19/2:2

Y 3.C 83:53
BULLETINS.

Y 3.C 83:54
CIRCULARS.

>   Later Y 3.W 19/2:4

Woman's Committee

Y 3.C 83:61/date
ANNUAL REPORTS.

Y 3.C 83:62 CT
GENERAL PUBLICATIONS.

Y 3.C 83:63
BULLETINS.

Y 3.C 83:64/nos.
CIRCULARS.

Y 3.C 83:65/nos.
NEWS LETTER.

Y 3.C 83:66/nos.
TRUTH TELLER.

Y 3.C 83:67/nos.
NOTES FROM FOREIGN NEWS BUREAU.

State Councils Section

Y 3.C 83:71/date
ANNUAL REPORTS.

Y 3.C 83:72 CT
GENERAL PUBLICATIONS.

Y 3.C 83:73/nos.
BULLETINS.

Y 3.C 83:74
CIRCULARS.

Y 3.C 83:75/nos.
INFORMATION CIRCULARS.

Y 3.C 83:76/nos.
GENERAL LETTERS.

Field Division

Y 3.C 83:81/date
ANNUAL REPORTS.

Y 3.C 83:82 CT
GENERAL PUBLICATIONS.

Y 3.C 83:83/nos.
BULLETINS.

Y 3.C 83:84/nos.
CIRCULARS.

Y 3.C 83:85/nos.
INFORMATION CIRCULARS.

Y 3.C 83:86/nos.
GENERAL LETTERS.

Y 3.C 83:87/v.nos.
NATIONAL DEFENSE.

Reconstruction Research Division

Y 3.C 83:91/date
ANNUAL REPORTS.

Y 3.C 83:92 CT
GENERAL PUBLICATIONS.

Y 3.C 83:93
BULLETINS.

Y 3.C 83:94
CIRCULARS.

Y 3.C 83:95/nos
DAILY DIGEST OF RECONSTRUCTION NEWS.

OFFICE OF THE NATIONAL COUNTERINTELLIGENCE EXECUTIVE

Y 3.C 83/2:1-2   • **Item 1089-Q-1 (EL)**
FOREIGN ECONOMIC COLLECTION AND INDUS-
TRIAL ESPIONAGE. [Annual]

Y 3.C 83/2:2   • **Item 1089-Q-2**
GENERAL PUBLICATIONS.

COUNCIL OF NATIONAL DEFENSE (1940– 1941)

NOTE:– No publications were classified under the Y 3.C 831 class.

COUNCIL OF NATIONAL DEFENSE ADVISORY COMMISSION (1940– 1941)

CREATION AND AUTHORITY

The Council of National Defense (Y 3. C 831)
was reactivated on May 29, 1940 by the President when he appointed a new Advisory Commission. Administrative Order of January 7, 1941,
transferred the activities of the Council to the
Office for Emergency Management (Pr 32.400).

Y 3.C 831:101/date
ANNUAL REPORTS.

Y 3.C 831:102 CT
GENERAL PUBLICATIONS.

Y 3.C 831:106 CT
REGULATIONS, RULES, AND INSTRUCTIONS.

Y 3.C 831:107/v.nos.
DEFENSE, BULLETINS. [Weekly]

>   Later Pr 32.407

Y 3.C 831:109/nos.
CONSUMER DIVISION, BULLETINS.

>   Later Pr 32.4253

Y 3.C 831:110/nos.
CONSUMER DIVISION, CONSUMER PRICES.
[Biweekly]

>   Later Pr 32.4258

Y 3.C 831:111/nos.
FARMING OUT BULLETINS.

NATIONAL ADVISORY COMMISSION ON CRIMINAL JUSTICE STANDARDS AND GOALS
(1971–   )

CREATION AND AUTHORITY

The National Advisory Commission on Criminal Justice Standards and Goals was established by the Administrator of the Law Enforcement Assistance Administration, Department of Justice, on October 20, 1971, to formulate standards at State and local levels.

Y 3.C 86:1/date
ANNUAL REPORT.

Y 3.C 86:2 CT   • **Item 1089**
GENERAL PUBLICATIONS.

Y 3.C 86:2 J 98   • **Item 1089**
JUVENILE JUSTICE AND DELINQUENCY PREVENTION. 1976. 822 p.

PURPOSE:– To present the national standards for juvenile justice and delinquency prevention developed by the 1975 Task Force on Juvenile Justice and Delinquency Prevention. There are standards for preventing delinquency, providing health and education services, the roles of government, police, and the community, and more.

NATIONAL CRITICAL MATERIALS COUNCIL
(1984–   )

CREATION AND AUTHORITY

The National Critical Materials Council was established by the National Critical Materials Act of 1984 (30 U.S.C. 1801 et seq.)

INFORMATION

National Critical Materials Council
Eighteenth and C Streets, N.W.
Washington, D.C. 20240
(202) 347-1847

Y 3.C 86/2:2 CT   • **Item 1063-M**
GENERAL PUBLICATIONS. [Irregular]

COMMISSION FOR THE IMPROVEMENT OF THE FEDERAL CROP INSURANCE PROGRAM`

Y 3.C 88:1/date
ANNUAL REPORTS.

Y 3.C 88:2 CT   • **Item 1089**
GENERAL PUBLICATIONS.

DEFENSE MANPOWER COMMISSION
(1973–   )

CREATION AND AUTHORITY

The Defense Manpower Commission was established by PL 93-155, approved November 16, 1973.

Y 3.D 36:1/date
REPORT.

Y 3.D 36:2 CT
GENERAL PUBLICATIONS.

Y 3.D 36:9/v.nos.
DEFENSE MANPOWER COMMISSION STAFF STUDIES AND SUPPORTING PAPERS.

DEFENSE BASE CLOSURE AND REALIGNMENT COMMISSION

Y 3.D 36/2:1/date   • **Item 1089-R**
REPORT TO THE PRESIDENT. [Annual]

DEFENSE NUCLEAR FACILITIES SAFETY BOARD
(1988–   )

INFORMATION

Defense Nuclear Facilities Safety Board
625 Indiana Ave., NW, Ste. 700
Washington, DC 20004-2901
(202) 694-7000
Toll Free: (800) 788-4016
Email:mailbox@dnfsb.gov
http://www.dnfsb.gov

Y 3.D 36/3:1/date   • **Item 1089-R-1 (EL)**
ANNUAL REPORT.

Y 3.D 36/3:9/nos.   • **Item 1089-R-2**
TECHNICAL REPORT DNFSB/TECH- (series).

Y 3.D 36/3:10   • **Item 1089-R-3 (EL)**
RECOMMENDATIONS OF THE DNFSB (series).

Y 3.D 36/3:11   • **Item 1089-R-3 (EL)**
DNFSB SITE REPRESENTATIVES WEEKLY ACTIVITIES REPORTS.

Y 3.D 36/3:12   • **Item 1089-R-3 (EL)**
DNFSB STAFF ISSUE REPORTS.

Y 3.D 36/3:13   • **Item 1089-R-3 (E)**
ELECTRONIC PRODUCTS (misc.).

DELAWARE RIVER BASIN COMMISSION
(1961–   )

CREATION AND AUTHORITY

The Delaware River Basin Commission was created as a Federal-Interstate Compact establishment consisting of the U.S. Government and the States of Pennsylvania, New Jersey, New York, and Delaware, by act of Congress approved September 27, 1961 (75 Stat. 688).

INFORMATION

Delaware River Basin Commission
Department of Interior Building
25 State Police Dr.
West Trenton, NJ 08628-0360
(609) 883-9500
Fax (609) 883-9522
http://www.drbc.net

Y 3.D 37/2:1/date
REPORT.

Y 3.D 37/2:2 CT
GENERAL PUBLICATIONS.

COMMITTEE ON DEPARTMENT METHODS
(1903–1909)

CREATION AND AUTHORITY

The Committee on Department Methods, also known as the Keep Commission, was established by the President on March 12, 1903. The Committee functioned until 1909.

Y 3.D 44:1/date
ANNUAL REPORT.

Y 3.D 44:2 CT
GENERAL PUBLICATIONS.

DEVELOPMENT LOAN FUND
(1958–1961)

CREATION AND AUTHORITY

The Development Loan Fund was transferred from the International Cooperation Administration (S 17) when it became an independent corporation agency of the United States by the Mutual Security Act of 1958 (Public Law 85-577). It was abolished by the Foreign Assistance Act of 1961 (75 Stat. 445) and its functions redelegated to the Agency for International Development (S 18) pursuant to letter of the President dated September 30, 1961, and Executive Order 10973 of November 3, 1961.

Y 3.D 49:1/date
ANNUAL REPORTS.

Y 3.D 49:2 CT
GENERAL PUBLICATIONS.

COMMISSION TO INVESTIGATE TITLE OF UNITED STATES TO LANDS IN THE DISTRICT OF COLUMBIA
(1908–1916)

CREATION AND AUTHORITY

The Commission to Investigate Title of United States to Lands in the District of Columbia, also known as the Commission on Government Lands in the District of Columbia, was established by act of Congress, approved May 30, 1908 (35 Stat. 543). The Commission submitted its report in 1916.

Y 3.D 63:2 CT
PUBLICATIONS.

DISPLACED PERSONS COMMISSION
(1948–1952)

CREATION AND AUTHORITY

The Displaced Persons Commission was established by the Displaced Persons Act of 1948 (62 Stat. 1009), which provided that the Commission be terminated by August 31, 1952.

Y 3.D 63/2:1/date
SEMIANNUAL REPORT TO THE PRESIDENT AND THE CONGRESS.

Y 3.D 63/2:2 CT
GENERAL PUBLICATIONS.

Y 3.D 63/2:6 CT
REGULATIONS, RULES, AND INSTRUCTIONS.

Y 3.D 63/2:7/nos.
RESEARCH SERIES REPORTS.

NATIONAL COUNCIL ON DISABILITY

INFORMATION

National Council on Disability
1331 F Street, NW, Ste 850
Washington, DC 20004
(202) 272-2004
Fax: 272-2022
http://www.ncd.gov

Y 3.D 63/3:1 date   • **Item 1063-H-2 (MF)**
ANNUAL REPORT.

Y 3.D 63/3:1-2   • **Item 1063-H-3 (EL)**
NATIONAL DISABILITY POLICY: A PROGRESS REPORT. [Annual]

Y 3.D 63/3:2 CT   • **Item 1063-H**
GENERAL PUBLICATIONS.

Y 3.D 63/3:8 CT   • **Item 1063-H-1**
HANDBOOKS, MANUALS, AND GUIDES.

NATIONAL ADVISORY COUNCIL FOR DRUG ABUSE PREVENTION
(1976–   )

Y 3.D 84:1/date
REPORT.

Y 3.D 84:2 CT
GENERAL PUBLICATIONS.

NATIONAL DRUG POLICY BOARD
(1987–   )

CREATION AND AUTHORITY

The National Drug Policy Board is an extension of the National Drug Enforcement Policy Board established by the National Narcotics Act of 1984, as modified by Executive Order 12590 of March 26, 1987.

Y 3.D 84/2:1   • **Item 1062-J**
ANNUAL REPORT.

Y 3.D 84/2:2   • **Item 1062-J**
GENERAL PUBLICATIONS. [Irregular]

ECONOMY AND EFFICIENCY COMMISSION
(1910–1913)

Y 3.Ec 7:1/date
ANNUAL REPORTS.

Y 3.Ec 7:2 CT
GENERAL PUBLICATIONS.

Y 3.Ec 7:3/nos.
BULLETINS.

Y 3.Ec 7:4/nos.
CIRCULARS.

NATIONAL ADVISORY COUNCIL ON ECONOMIC OPPORTUNITY
(1964–1981)

Y 3.Ec 7/2:1/date   • **Item 857-H-16**
ANNUAL REPORT. 1st–   1968–

Also issued in the House Documents series. Earlier PrEx 10.22

Y 3.Ec 7/2:2 CT
GENERAL PUBLICATIONS.

NATIONAL ECONOMIC COMMISSION

Y 3.Ec 7/3:CT   • **Item 1089**
STAFF PAPERS, BACKGROUND PAPERS AND MAJOR TESTIMONY.

Y 3.Em 7/3:11/date   • **Item 1089-H**
MONOGRAPH SERIES.

ECONOMIC SECURITY COMMITTEE
(1934–1936)

Y 3.Ec 74:1/date
ANNUAL REPORTS.

Y 3.Ec 74:2 CT
GENERAL PUBLICATIONS

BOARD OF ECONOMIC WARFARE
(1941–1943)

CREATION AND AUTHORITY

The Economic Defense Board was established by Executive Order 8839 of July 30, 1941. Executive Order 8982 of December 17, 1941, changed the name to Board of Economic Warfare. Executive Order 9361 of July 15, 1943 abolished the Board and transferred its functions to the Office of Economic Warfare in the Office for Emergency Management (Pr 32.400).

Y 3.Ec 74/2:1/date
ANNUAL REPORTS.

Y 3.Ec 74/2:2 CT
GENERAL PUBLICATIONS.

Y 3.Ec 74/2:7 CT
LATIN AMERICAN PUBLIC UTILITIES SURVEY.

Y 3.Ec 74/2:8 CT
LATIN AMERICAN TRANSPORTATION SURVEY.

OFFICE OF EXPORTS
(1942–1943)

CREATION AND AUTHORITY

The Office of Export Control was established within the Economic Defense Board by Executive Order 8900 of September 15, 1941, succeeding the Office of the Administrator of Export Control (Y 3.Ex 7/2). The name was changed to Office of Exports on April 6, 1942. The Office was terminated by Executive Order 9361 of July 15, 1943, and functions transferred to the Office of Economic Warfare of the Office for Emergency Management (Pr 32.400).

Y 3.Ec 74/2:101/date
ANNUAL REPORTS.

Y 3.Ec 74/2:102 CT
GENERAL PUBLICATIONS.

Y 3.Ec 74/2:107/nos.
EXPORT CONTROL SCHEDULES (numbered).

Earlier Y 3.Ex 7/3:7

Y 3.Ec 74/2:108/nos.
COMPREHENSIVE EXPORT CONTROL SCHEDULES.
[Bimonthly]

Earlier Y 3.Ex 7/2
Later Pr 32.5808:86

Y 3.Ec 74/2:109/nos
CURRENT CONTROL BULLETINS.

Later Pr 32.580

ECONOMIC COOPERATION
ADMINISTRATION
(1948–1951)

CREATION AND AUTHORITY

The Economic Cooperation Administration was established by the Economic Cooperation Act of 1948, approved April 3, 1948 (62 Stat. 138). It was abolished by the act of Congress, approved October 10, 1951 (65 Stat. 373) and its functions transferred to the Mutual Security Agency (Pr 33.900), effective December 30, 1951, pursuant to Executive Order 10300 of November 1, 1951.

Y 3.Ec 74/3:1/date
ANNUAL REPORTS.

Y 3.Ec 74/3:2 CT
GENERAL PUBLICATIONS.

Y 3.Ec 74/3:6 CT
REGULATIONS, RULES, AND INSTRUCTIONS.

Y 3.Ec 74/3:7/nos
PUBLIC ADVISORY BOARD, REPORTS.

Later Pr 33.910

Y 3.Ec 74/3:8/nos.
REPORT TO CONGRESS ON ECONOMIC COOPERATION ADMINISTRATION. [Quarterly]

Y 3.Ec 74/3:9/nos.
REPORT TO CONGRESS ON UNITED STATES FOREIGN RELIEF PROGRAM. [Quarterly]

Earlier S 1.63
Later S 1.65

Y 3.Ec 74/3:10 CT
EUROPEAN RECOVERY PROGRAM, COUNTRY STUDY.

Y 3.Ec 74/3:10-2 CT
COUNTRY DATA BOOK.

Earlier Y 3.Ec 74/3:10

Y 3.Ec 74/3:11 CT
EUROPEAN RECOVERY PROGRAM, COMMODITY STUDY.

Y 3.Ec 74/3:12/date
LOCAL CURRENCY COUNTERPART FUNDS. [Monthly]

Later Pr 33.911

Y 3.Ec 74/3:13/date
PAID SHIPMENTS. [Monthly]

Later Pr 33.909

Y 3.Ec 74/3:13-2 CT
PAID SHIPMENTS (By country), SPECIAL STATEMENTS.

Y 3.Ec 74/3:14/date
PROCUREMENT AUTHORIZATIONS. [Monthly]

Later Pr 33.908

Y 3.Ec 74/3:15/nos.
CURRENT REPORT ON MARSHALL PLAN.

Y 3.Ec 74/3:16/nos.
RECOVERY GUIDES, PARTICIPATING COUNTRIES.
[Bimonthly]

Y 3.Ec 74/3:17/v.nos.&nos.
MARSHALL PLAN NEWS.

Y 3.Ec 74/3:18/v.nos.
INTERIM REPORT ON EUROPEAN RECOVERY PROGRAM.

Y 3.Ec 74/3:19/nos.
SMALL BUSINESS CIRCULARS.

Y 3.Ec 74/3:19-2/nos.
MEMO FOR SMALL BUSINESS.

Y 3.Ec 74/3:20 CT
SPECIAL MISSION TO GERMANY.

Y 3.Ec 74/3:21 CT
SPECIAL MISSION TO BELGIUM-LUXEMBOURG.

Y 3.Ec 74/3:22 CT
SPECIAL MISSION TO FRANCE.

Later Pr 33.918

Y 3.Ec 74/3:23 CT
SPECIAL MISSION TO TRIESTE.

Y 3.Ec 74/3:24 CT
EUROPEAN PROGRAM, SPECIAL STATEMENTS.

Y 3.Ec 74/3:25 CT
SPECIAL MISSION TO DENMARK.

Y 3.Ec 74/3:26 CT
SPECIAL MISSION TO PORTUGAL.

Y 3.Ec 74/3:27
RELEASES.

Y 3.Ec 74/3:28 CT
SPECIAL ECONOMIC AND TECHNICAL MISSION TO PHILIPPINES.

Y 3.Ec 74/3:29 CT
MISSION TO CHINA.

Y 3.Ec 74/3:30/nos.
PRIORITIES BULLETINS.

Later Pr 33.912

Y 3.Ec 74/3:31/nos.
TRANS-ATLANTIC, FROM OFFICE OF LABOR ADVISORS, ESC LABOR NEWS LETTER. [Monthly]

Later Pr 33.915

Y 3.Ec 74/3:32
PUBLICATIONS, SPECIAL MISSION TO ITALY.

Y 3.Ec 74/3:33
PUBLICATIONS, SPECIAL MISSION TO NETHER-LANDS.

Y 3.Ec 74/3:34
PUBLICATIONS, SPECIAL MISSION TO TURKEY.

Y 3.Ec 74/3:35
PUBLICATIONS, SPECIAL MISSION TO AUSTRIA.

Y 3.Ec 74/3:36
PUBLICATIONS, SPECIAL MISSION TO IRELAND.

Y 3.Ec 74/3:37 CT
MISSION TO GREECE.

Earlier Pr 33.918/2

Y 3.Ec 74/3:38/nos.
FAR EAST DATA BOOK.

Later Pr 33.922

Y 3.Ec 74/3:39 CT
SPECIAL MISSION TO UNITED KINGDOM.

FEDERAL INTERAGENCY COMMITTEE ON EDUCATION
(1964–   )

CREATION AND AUTHORITY

The Federal Interagency Committee on Education was established by Executive Order 11185 of Oct. 16, 1964.

INFORMATION

Federal Interagency Committee on Education
Room 2083 (FOB6)
Department of Education
400 Maryland Avenue, S.W.
Washington, D.C. 20202
(202) 447-7501

Y 3.Ed 8:1/date   • Item 1062-A
ANNUAL REPORTS.

Y 3.Ed 8:2 CT   • Item 1062-A
GENERAL PUBLICATIONS.

Y 3.Ed 8:9/v.nos.&nos.
FICE REPORT.

NATIONAL ADVISORY COUNCIL ON EDUCATION OF DISADVANTAGED CHILDREN
(1965– 1982)

CREATION AND AUTHORITY

The National Advisory Council on Education of Disadvantaged Children was established by Public Law 89-10, approved April 11, 1965. The Council was abolished in October 1982.

Y 3.Ed 8/2:1/date
ANNUAL REPORT.

Y 3.Ed 8/2:2 CT   • Item 1062-A-1
GENERAL PUBLICATIONS. [Irregular]

NATIONAL ADVISORY COUNCIL ON EDUCATION PROFESSIONS DEVELOPMENT
(1967–   )

Y 3.Ed 8/3:1/date   • Item 1091
ANNUAL REPORT.

Y 3.Ed 8/3:2 CT   • Item 1091
GENERAL PUBLICATIONS. [Irregular]

NATIONAL ADVISORY COUNCIL ON ADULT EDUCATION
(1974–   )

CREATION AND AUTHORITY

The National Advisory Council on Adult Education was established by the Adult Education Act of 1966, PL 89-750, enacted November 3, 1966 (84 Stat. 163; 20 U.S.C. 1209) and amended by PL 91-230, Title III.

INFORMATION

National Advisory Council on Adult Education
425 Thirteenth Street, N.W.
Washington, D.C. 20004
(202) 376-8892

Y 3.Ed 8/4:1/date   • Item 1062-A-2
ANNUAL REPORT. 1st–

Publications were previously distributed to Depository Libraries under Item 1089.

Y 3.Ed 8/4:2 CT   • Item 1062-A-2
GENERAL PUBLICATIONS.

Publications were previously distributed to Depository Libraries under Item 1089.

NATIONAL COMMISSION ON FINANCING OF POSTSECONDARY EDUCATION
(1973–   )

Y 3.Ed 8/5:1/date   • Item 1089
REPORT.

Y 3.Ed 8/5:2 CT   • Item 1089
GENERAL PUBLICATIONS. [Irregular]
Includes staff papers.

ADVISORY COUNCIL ON WOMEN'S EDUCATIONAL PROGRAMS
(1976–   )

INFORMATION

Advisory Council on Women's Educational Programs
425 Thirteenth Street, N.W.
Washington, D.C. 20005
(202) 376-1038

Y 3.Ed 8/6:1/date   • Item 1063-E-1
ANNUAL REPORTS.

Y 3.Ed 8/6:2 CT   • Item 1063-E-1
GENERAL PUBLICATIONS.

NATIONAL ADVISORY COUNCIL ON EQUALITY OF EDUCATIONAL OPPORTUNITY
(1972–   )

CREATION AND AUTHORITY

The National Advisory Council on Equality of Educational Opportunity was established by the Educational Amendments Act of June 23, 1972 (Public Law 92-318).

INFORMATION

National Advisory Council on Equality of Educational Opportunity
1325 G Street, N.W.
Washington, D.C. 20005
(202) 724-0221

Y 3.Ed 8/7:1/date
REPORTS.

Y 3.Ed 8/7:2 CT
GENERAL PUBLICATIONS.

NATIONAL ADVISORY COUNCIL ON CONTINUING EDUCATION

Y 3.Ed 8/8:1/date
CONTINUING EDUCATION IS WORK. [Annual]

INTERGOVERNMENTAL ADVISORY COUNCIL ON EDUCATION

Y 3.Ed 8/9:1/date
ANNUAL REPORTS.

Y 3.Ed 8/9:2 CT   • **Item 1063-N**
GENERAL PUBLICATIONS.

EIGHT HOUR COMMISSION (1916– 1917)

CREATION AND AUTHORITY

The Eight Hour Commission, also known as the Eight Hour Day Commission was established by act of Congress, approved September 5, 1916. The Commission completed its work in 1917.

Y 3.Ei 4:2 CT
PUBLICATIONS.

ELECTORAL COMMISSION OF 1877 (1877)

CREATION AND AUTHORITY

The Electoral Commission was established by act of Congress, approved January 29, 1877. Hearings were held and proceedings published in 1877.

Y 3.Ei 2:CT
PUBLICATIONS.

ELECTRIC HOME AND FARM AUTHORITY (1933– 1939)

CREATION AND AUTHORITY

The Electric Home and Farm Authority was incorporated under the laws of the District of Columbia, August 1, 1935, to succeed the Electric Home and Farm Authority, Inc., and made an agency of the Government by Executive Order 7139 of August 12, 1935. Reorganization Plan No. 1 of 1939, dated April 25, 1939, placed the Authority within the Federal Loan Agency (FL 4).

Y 3.Ei 2/2:1/date
ANNUAL REPORTS.

Later FL 4.1

Y 3.Ei 2/2:2 CT
GENERAL PUBLICATIONS.

Later FL 4.2

Y 3.Ei 2/2:4/nos.
CIRCULARS.

Later FL 4.4

FEDERAL ELECTION COMMISSION (1974–   )

CREATION AND AUTHORITY

The Federal Election Commission was established by the Federal Election Campaign Act Amendments of 1974 (88 Stat. 1280; 2 U.S.C. 437c).

INFORMATION

Federal Election Commission
999 E. St. NW
Washington, D.C. 20463
(202) 694-1100
Toll Free: (800) 424-9530
http://www.fec.gov

Y 3.Ei 2/3:1/date   • **Item 1091-A(MF)**
ANNUAL REPORT.

Y 3.Ei 2/3:2 CT   • **Item 1091-A**
GENERAL PUBLICATIONS.

Y 3.Ei 2/3:2 St 2   • **Item 1091-A**
FEDERAL-STATE ELECTION LAW SURVEY: AN ANALYSIS OF STATE LEGISLATION, FEDERAL LEGISLATION AND JUDICIAL DECISIONS. 1975– [Issued and cumulated monthly during election years; quarterly during non-election years]

Prepared by the American Law Division, Congressional Research Service, Library of Congress.
Previously published by Office of Federal Elections.

Y 3.Ei 2/3:2-10/date   • **Item 1091-A**
CAMPAIGN FINANCE LAW. [Annual]

Earlier Y 3.Ei 2/3:2 L 44/2

Y 3.Ei 2/3:5 CT   • **Item 1091-A**
LAWS. [Irregular]

Y 3.Ei 2/3:6 CT   • **Item 1091-A**
REGULATIONS, RULES, AND INSTRUCTIONS.

Y 3.Ei 2/3:8 CT   • **Item 1091-A**
HANDBOOKS, MANUALS, GUIDES. [Irregular]

Y 3.Ei 2/3:9/date
FEDERAL-STATE ELECTION LAW SURVEY. [Quarterly]

Sub-title: An Analysis of State Legislation, Federal Legislation, and Judicial Decision.
Superseded by Election Law Updates (Y 3.Ei 2.3:9-2)

Y 3.Ei 2/3:9-2/date   • **Item 1091-A**
ELECTION LAW UPDATES. [Quarterly cumulative to annual]

Provides a comprehensive legal synopses of all Federal and state election laws enacted during each respective year. Produced on a quarterly, cumulative basis in cooperation with the Ameri-

can Law Division of the Library of Congress, this publication has become the accepted source of information on changes in election law in the United States. Each edition is divided into appropriate sections with a comprehensive subject index and past editions have covered Federal and state campaign finance laws including contribution definitions and coverage, excess campaign funds, expenditures, political committees and depositories, public financing, reporting requirements and taxation. Past editions have also included information on state ballot access laws, absentee voting and registration provisions and voting devices and equipment.

Supersedes Federal-State Election Law Survey (Y 3.Ei 2/3:9).

Y 3.Ei 2/3:10/v.nos.&nos.   • **Item 1091-A**
FEC JOURNAL OF ELECTION ADMINISTRATION. v. 1–   1977–   . [Irregular]

ISSN 0148-740X

Y 3.Ei 2/3:11/v.nos.&nos.   • **Item 1091-A (EL)**
FEDERAL ELECTION COMMISSION RECORD.

ISSN 0145-8566

Y 3.Ei 2/3:11-2/date
FEDERAL ELECTION COMMISSION RECORD, INDEX.

Y 3.Ei 2/3:12/date   • **Item 1091-A**
ELECTION CASE LAW. [Quarterly]

Provides a comprehensive legal synopsis of all Federal and state election cases decided during each respective year. Also produced on a quarterly, cumulative basis in cooperation with the American Law Division of the Library of Congress, this series has become the accepted central reference resource on Federal and state election case decisions. Each edition is divided into appropriate sections with a comprehensive subject index and past editions have included case decisions on campaign financing, ballot access, corrupt practices, lobbying, election contests, voter residency requirements and qualifications and other areas of interest to those who monitor election activities at Federal and state levels.

Y 3.Ei 2/3:13 CT   • **Item 1091-A**
CAMPAIGN GUIDE. [Irregular]

Y 3.Ei 2/3:14/date   • **Item 1091-A**
ELECTION DIRECTORY. [Annual]

Y 3.Ei 2/3:14-2/date   • **Item 1091-A (MF) (EL)**
COMBINED FEDERAL/STATE DISCLOSURE DIRECTORY. [Annual]

Y 3.Ei 2/3:15/date   • **Item 1091-A (MF)**
FEC REPORTS ON FINANCIAL ACTIVITY.

Y 3.Ei 2/3:15-2/date
FEC INDEX OF COMMUNICATION COSTS.

Y 3.Ei 2/3:15-3/date
FEC INDEX OF INDEPENDENT EXPENDITURES.

Y 3.Ei 2/3:16/date   • **Item 1091-A (MF)**
FEDERAL ELECTIONS ..., ELECTION RESULTS FOR THE U.S. SENATE AND U.S. HOUSE OF REPRESENTATIVES. [Biennial]

Y 3.Ei 2/3:18/nos.   • **Item 1091-A**
INNOVATIONS IN ELECTION ADMINISTRATION.

Y 3.Ei 2/3:19/date   • **Item 1091-A-1**
SELECTED COURT CASE ABSTRACTS. [Annual]

NATIONAL COMMISSION ON ELECTRONIC FUND TRANSFERS
(1974–   )

CREATION AND AUTHORITY

The National Commission on Electronic Fund Transfers was established by Title II of Public Law 93-495 of October 28, 1974.

Y 3.El 2/4:1/date
ANNUAL REPORT.

Y 3.El 2/4:2 CT
GENERAL PUBLICATIONS.

EMERGENCY CONSERVATION WORK
(1933–1937)

CREATION AND AUTHORITY

The Emergency Conservation Work was established as an independent agency by Executive Order 6101 of April 5, 1933, pursuant to act of Congress, approved March 31, 1933 (48 Stat. 22). The agency was succeeded by the Civilian Conservation Corps (Y 3.C 49) by act of Congress, approved June 28, 1937 (50 Stat. 319).

Y 3.Em 3:1/date
ANNUAL REPORTS.

Y 3.Em 3:2 CT
GENERAL PUBLICATIONS.

Y 3.Em 3:3
BULLETINS.

Y 3.Em 3:4
CIRCULARS.

Y 3.Em 3:5
LAWS.

Y 3.Em 3:6 CT
REGULATIONS (includes rules).

Y 3.Em 3:7/nos
FORESTRY PUBLICATIONS.

Later Y 3.C 49:9

Y 3.Em 3:8/nos
SAFETY DIVISION BULLETINS.

Design. ECW-nos.

Y 3.Em 3:9/nos.
POSTERS. (Published by Safety Division)

Later Y 3.C 49:8

Y 3.Em 3:10/date
MONTHLY SAFETY BULLETINS.

Later Y 3.C 49:7

EMERGENCY LOAN GUARANTEE BOARD
(1972–   )

Y 3.Em 3/2:1/date • Item 1089
ANNUAL REPORT. 1st–   1972–

Y 3.Em 3/2:2 CT • Item 1089
GENERAL PUBLICATIONS.

EMPLOYER'S LIABILITY AND WORKMAN'S COMPENSATION COMMISSION
(1910–1912)

CREATION AND AUTHORITY

The Employer's Liability and Workmen's Compensation Commission was established on June 25, 1910. The Commission submitted its report in 1912.

Y 3.Em 7:1/date
ANNUAL REPORTS.

Y 3.Em 7:2 CT
GENERAL PUBLICATIONS.

Y 3.Em 7:3/nos.
BULLETINS.

Y 3.Em 7:4/nos.
CIRCULARS.

NATIONAL COMMISSION ON EMPLOYMENT AND UNEMPLOYMENT STATISTICS

Y 3.Em 7/2:1/date
REPORT.

Y 3.Em 7/2:2 CT
GENERAL PUBLICATIONS. [Irregular]

Y 3.Em 7/2:9/nos. • Item 1089
BACKGROUND PAPERS.

NATIONAL COMMISSION FOR EMPLOYMENT POLICY
(1978–   )

CREATION AND AUTHORITY

The National Commission for Employment Policy was established by Public Law 95-524 (92 Stat. 2002), approved October 27, 1978 to succeed the National Commission for Manpower Policy (Y 3. M 31).

Y 3.Em 7/3:1/date • Item 1089-H
ANNUAL REPORT.
Earlier Y 3.M 31:1

Y 3.Em 7/3:2 CT • Item 1089-H
GENERAL PUBLICATIONS.

Earlier Y 3.M 31:2

Y 3.Em 7/3:9/nos. • Item 1089-H
SPECIAL REPORTS (numbered).

Earlier Y 3.M 31:9

Y 3.Em 7/3:10/nos. • Item 1089-H
RESEARCH REPORTS (Series).

Y 3.Em 7/3:11 • Item 1089-H
MONOGRAPH SERIES.

UNITED STATES ENRICHMENT CORPORATION

Y 3.En 2:1/date • Item 1089-H-1 (MF)
ANNUAL REPORT.

Y 3.En 2:2 CT • Item 1089-H-1
GENERAL PUBLICATIONS.

EQUAL EMPLOYMENT OPPORTUNITY COMMISSION
(1965–   )

CREATION AND AUTHORITY

The Equal Employment Opportunity Commission was created by title VII of the Civil Rights Act of 1964 (78 Stat. 241; 42 U.S.C. 2000a), and became operational July 2, 1965.

INFORMATION

Equal Employment Opportunity Commission
1801 L St., NW
Washington, D.C. 20507
(202) 663-4900
Fax: 663-4494
http://www.eeoc.gov

Y 3.Eq 2:1/date • Item 1059-A-1 (EL)
ANNUAL REPORT. 1st–   1968–

Y 3.Eq 2:1-2 • Item 1059-A-4 (MF)
EEO SEMIANNUAL REPORT TO THE CONGRESS, OFFICE OF INSPECTOR GENERAL.

Y 3.Eq 2:2 CT • Item 1059-A-1
GENERAL PUBLICATIONS.

Y 3.Eq 2:6 CT • Item 1059-A-1
RULES, REGULATIONS, AND INSTRUCTIONS. [Irregular]

Y 3.Eq 2:6-2 • Item 1059-A-1
FIELD NOTES.

Y 3.Eq 2:7/date • Item 1059-A-1
PRESS RELEASES.

Y 3.Eq 2:7-2 • Item 1059-A-1
EEOC REPORTS, CLEARINGHOUSE SERVICE FOR BUSINESS NEWSLETTERS AND PERIODICALS. 1967–   [Irregular]

Y 3.Eq 2:8 CT • Item 1059-A-1
HANDBOOKS, MANUALS, GUIDES.

Y 3.Eq 2:9 • Item 1059-A-1
NEWSLETTER. [Irregular]

Y 3.Eq 2:10 • Item 1059-A-1
DIGEST OF LEGAL INTERPRETATIONS ISSUED OR
ADOPTED BY THE COMMISSION, COMPILATION.
1965– [Quarterly] (Office of General Counsel)

Y 3.Eq 2:10-2 • Item 1059-A-1
ANNUAL DIGEST OF LEGAL INTERPRETATIONS. 1st–
1966– [Annual] (Office of General Counsel)

Y 3.Eq 2:11 • Item 1059
RESEARCH REPORTS. 1967– [Irregular] (Office
of Research and Reports)

Y 3.Eq 2:12/nos. • Item 1059-A-1
EQUAL EMPLOYMENT OPPORTUNITY REPORTS. 1–
1968– [Annual]

Series of annual compilation of minority and
female employment statistics for 123 metropolitan areas, 50 States, and 60 major industries,
covering nine occupational categories.

Y 3.Eq 2:12-2/date
JOB PATTERNS FOR MINORITIES AND WOMEN IN
APPRENTICESHIP PROGRAMS AND REFERRAL
UNIONS. [Annual]

Y 3.Eq 2:12-3/date
MINORITIES AND WOMEN IN PUBLIC ELEMENTARY
AND SECONDARY SCHOOLS. [Annual]

Y 3.Eq 2:12-4/date • Item 1059-A-1
JOB PATTERNS FOR MINORITIES AND WOMEN IN
STATE AND LOCAL GOVERNMENT.

Issued biennially since 1991.
Formerly titled: Minorities and Women in State
and Local Government.

Y 3.Eq 2:12-5/date • Item 1059-A-1 (MF)
ANNUAL REPORT ON THE EMPLOYMENT OF
MINORITIES, WOMEN AND HANDICAPPED IN-
DIVIDUAL IN THE FEDERAL GOVERNMENT. [An-
nual]

Y 3.Eq 2:12-7/date • Item 1059-A-1 (MF)
JOB PATTERNS FOR MINORITIES AND WOMEN AND
PRIVATE INDUSTRY.

Y 3.Eq 2:13 CT • Item 1059-A-1
POSTERS.

Y 3.Eq 2:14/date/pt.nos. • Item 1059-A-1
STATE AND LOCAL GOVERNMENT FUNCTIONAL
PROFILE SERIES.

Y 3.Eq 2:15/v.nos.&nos. • Item 1059-A-7 (MF)
EEOC MISSION. [Quarterly]

Earlier issued Bimonthly.

Y 3.Eq 2:16/date • Item 1059-A-1
COORDINATION OF FEDERAL EQUAL EMPLOYMENT
OPPORTUNITY PROGRAMS. [Annual]

Y 3.Eq 2:17 CT
BIBLIOGRAPHIES AND LISTS OF PUBLICATIONS.

Y 3.Eq 2:18/date • Item 1059-A-2 (MF)
EQUAL EMPLOYMENT OPPORTUNITY COMMISSION
DECISIONS, FEDERAL SECTOR. [Bimonthly]

Y 3.Eq 2:18-2/ • Item 1059-A-2 (MF)
INDEXES ... EQUAL EMPLOYMENT OPPORTUNITY
COMMISSION DECISIONS. [Bimonthly]

Y 3.Eq 2:18-3/ • Item 1059-A-2 (MF)
RELATED PUBLICATIONS. [Bimonthly]

Y 3.Eq 2:18-4 • Item 1059-A-2 (MF)
EQUAL EMPLOYMENT OPPORTUNITY/CODE OF
FEDERAL REGULATIONS TITLE 29.

Y 3.Eq 2:18-5 • Item 1059-A-2 (MF)
EQUAL EMPLOYMENT OPPORTUNITY MANAGE-
MENT DIRECTIVES/BULLETINS.

Y 3.Eq 2:18-6 • Item 1059-A-2 (MF)
EQUAL EMPLOYMENT OPPORTUNITY FEDERAL
REGISTER.

Y 3.Eq 2:19/date-nos. • Item 1059-A-1
SEMI-ANNUAL CHECKLIST OF THE EEOC ORDERS.

Y 3.Eq 2:20 • Item 1059-A-5
BIBLIOGRAPHIES AND LISTS OF PUBLICATIONS.

Y 3.Eq 2:21 • Item 1059-A-6
BRAILLE PUBLICATIONS.

ERICSSON MEMORIAL COMMISSION
(1918)

Y 3.Er 4:CT
PUBLICATIONS.

OFFICE OF GOVERNMENT ETHICS
(1978–   )

CREATION AND AUTHORITY

The Office of Government Ethics was
established by the Ethics in Government Act of
1978. Originally part of the Office of Personnel
Management, OGE became a separate agency
on October 1, 1989, as part of the Office of
Government Ethics Reauthorization Act of 1988.

INFORMATION

Office of Government Ethics
1201 New York Ave., NW, Ste. 500
Washington, DC 20005-3917
(202) 208-8000
Fax: 208-8037
http://www.usoge.gov

Y 3.Et 3:1/date • Item 1089-T (MF)
BIENNIAL REPORT TO CONGRESS.

Y 3.Et 3:2 CT • Item 1089-T
GENERAL PUBLICATIONS.

Y 3.Et 3:8 CT • Item 1089-T
HANDBOOKS, MANUALS, GUIDES. [Irregular]

Y 3.Et 3:15/v.nos./nos. • Item 1089-T-1 (EL)
GOVERNMENT ETHICS NEWSGRAM. [Quarterly]

Y 3.Et 3:16 • Item 1089-T-2 (CD)
THE ETHICS CD. [Semiannual]

JOINT COMMISSION ON LAWS ORGANIZING EXECUTIVE DEPARTMENTS
(1893– 1894)

CREATION AND AUTHORITY

The Joint Commission on Laws Organizing
Executive Departments was established by act
of Congress, approved March 3, 1893. The Commission ceased to exist in 1894.

Y 3.Ex 3:CT
PUBLICATIONS.

EXECUTIVE COUNCIL
(1933– 1934)

CREATION AND AUTHORITY

The Executive Council was established by
Executive Order 6202-A of July 11, 1933. The
Council was consolidated with the National Emergency Council (Y 3.N 21/9) by Executive Order
6889-A of October 29, 1934.

Y 3.Ex 3/2:CT
PUBLICATIONS

COMMISSION ON EXECUTIVE, LEGISLATIVE AND JUDICIAL SALARIES
(1967–   )

CREATION AND AUTHORITY

The Commission on Executive, Legislative,
and Judicial Salaries was established by Public
Law 90-206 of December 16, 1967.

INFORMATION

Commission on Executive, Legislative
and Judicial Salaries
734 Jackson Place, N.W.
Washington, D.C. 20006
(202) 377-3914

Y 3.Ex 3/3:1/date • Item 1089
REPORT. [Irregular]

Y 3.Ex 3/3:2 CT
GENERAL PUBLICATIONS.

EXPORTS CONTROL COMMITTEE
(1918– 1919)

CREATION AND AUTHORITY

The Exports Control Committee was established jointly by the Secretaries of War and Navy
and the Director General of Railroads on June 11,
1918. The Committee was terminated on March 1,
1919.

Y 3.Ex 7:CT
PUBLICATIONS.

OFFICE OF THE ADMINISTRATOR OF EXPORT CONTROL
(1940–1941)

CREATION AND AUTHORITY

The Office of the Administrator of Export Control was established by Congress on July 2, 1940. Its functions were transferred to the Office of Export Control (Y 3.Ec 74/2:100) in the newly established Economic Defense Board on September 14, 1941.

Y 3.Ex 7/2:1/date
ANNUAL REPORTS.

Y 3.Ex 7/2:2 CT
GENERAL PUBLICATIONS.

Y 3.Ex 7/2:7/nos.
EXPORT CONTROL SCHEDULES (numbered).

Y 3.Ex 7/2:7/let.
EXPORT CONTROL SCHEDULES (lettered).

Y 3.Ex 7/2:8/nos.
COMPREHENSIVE EXPORT CONTROL SCHEDULES. [Monthly]

EXPORT-IMPORT BANK OF THE UNITED STATES
(1968–   )

CREATION AND AUTHORITY

The Export-Import Bank of Washington was authorized in 1934 as a banking corporation organized under the laws of the District of Columbia (Executive Order 6581, February 1, 1934). The Bank was continued as an agency of the United States by acts of Congress in 1935, 1937, 1939, and 1940. It was made an independent agency of the Government by the Export-Import Bank Act of 1945 (59 Stat. 526; 12 U.S.C. 635), subsequently amended in 1947 to reincorporate the Bank under Federal charter. The name was changed to Export-Import Bank of the United States by act of March 13, 1968 (82 Stat. 47).

INFORMATION

Public Affairs Office
Export-Import Bank of the United States
811 Vermont Avenue, N.W.
Washington, D.C. 20571
(202) 565-3946
Toll Free:(800) 565-3946
Fax: (202) 565-3380
http://www.exim.gov

Y 3.Ex 7/3　　　　　● Item 1061 (MF)
STATEMENT OF ACTIVE LOANS AND FINANCIAL GUARANTEES. [Semiannual]

Y 3.Ex 7/3:1　　　　● Item 1061 (MF)
REPORT TO CONGRESS. 1945–　[Annual]

Report submitted by the Bank to Congress for the fiscal year. Supplemented by a Quarterly Report.

Y 3.Ex 7/3:2 CT　　　● Item 1060 (MF)
GENERAL PUBLICATIONS.
Earlier Y 3.F 76:2 Ex 7/3

Y 3.Ex 7/3:5 CT　　　● Item 1060
LAWS.

Y 3.Ex 7/3:6 CT　　　● Item 1060
REGULATIONS, RULES, AND INSTRUCTIONS.

Y 3.Ex 7/3:8/nos
PUBLIC INFORMATION SERIES.

Y 3.Ex 7/3:9　　　　● Item 1060
ADDRESSES. [Irregular]

Y 3.Ex 7/3:10 CT　　　● Item 1060
HANDBOOKS, MANUALS, GUIDES.

Y 3.Ex 7/3:11/v.nos.&nos.
EXIMBANK RECORD. [Monthly]

Y 3.Ex 7/3:12/date　● Item 1060 (MF)
STATEMENT OF ACTIVE LOANS AND FINANCIAL GUARANTEES. [Semiannual]

NATIONAL ADVISORY COUNCIL ON CONTINUING EDUCATION
(1965–   )

CREATION AND AUTHORITY

The National Advisory Council on Extension and Continuing Education was established by Public Law 89-329, approved November 8, 1965. The name was changed to National Advisory Council on Continuing Education in 1982.

INFORMATION

National Advisory Council on
Continuing Education
425 Thirteenth Street, N.W.
Washington, D.C. 20004
(202) 376-8888

Y 3.Ex 8:1/date　　　● Item 1062-B
ANNUAL REPORT. 1st–

Y 3.Ex 8:2 CT　　　● Item 1062-B
GENERAL PUBLICATIONS.

FARM TENANCY SPECIAL COMMITTEE
(1937)

Y 3.F 22:2 CT
GENERAL PUBLICATIONS.

FARM CREDIT SYSTEM INSURANCE CORPORATION
(1987–   )

CREATION AND AUTHORITY

The Farm Credit System Insurance Corporation was established by the Agricultural Credit Act of 1987 as an independent U.S. government-controlled corporation.

INFORMATION

Federal Credit System Insurance Corporation
(703) 883-4380
http://www.fcsic.gov

Y 3.F 22/2:1 date　● Item 1089-N-1 (MF)
ANNUAL REPORT.

FEDERAL ELECTRIC RAILWAYS COMMISSION
(1919–1920)

CREATION AND AUTHORITY

The Federal Electric Railways Commission was established by the President on May 31, 1919. The Commission made its report on July 28, 1920.

Y 3.F 31:CT
PUBLICATIONS.

FEDERAL FUEL DISTRIBUTOR
(1922–1923)

CREATION AND AUTHORITY

The Office of the Federal Fuel Distributor was established by act of Congress, approved September 22, 1922. The Office was terminated on September 21, 1923 under statutory limitations.

Y 3.F 31/2:CT
PUBLICATIONS.

FEDERAL HOME LOAN BANK BOARD
(1932–1939)

CREATION AND AUTHORITY

The Federal Home Loan Bank Board was established by the Federal Home Loan Bank Act, approved July 22, 1932 (47 Stat. 725). Under Reorganization Plan No. 1 of 1939, effective July 1, 1939, the Board was transferred to the Federal Loan Agency (FL 3).

Y 3.F 31/3:1/date
ANNUAL REPORTS.
Later FL 3.1

Y 3.F 31/3:2 CT
GENERAL PUBLICATIONS.
Later FL 3.2

Y 3.F 31/3:3
BULLETINS.

Y 3.F 31/3:4
CIRCULARS.

Y 3.F 31/3:5
LAWS.

Y 3.F 31/3:6
REGULATIONS.

Y 3.F 31/3:7 CT
RULES AND REGULATIONS.

Y 3.F 31/3:8 CT
HOME OWNERS' LOAN CORPORATION PUBLICATIONS.
Later FL 3.9

Y 3.F 31/3:9/vol.
FEDERAL HOME LOAN BANK REVIEW. [Monthly]
Later FL 3.7

Y 3.F 31/3:10/date
NON-FARM REAL ESTATE FORECLOSURES.
[Monthly]
    Later FL 3.8

Y 3.F 31/3:11 CT
ADDRESSES.
    Changed from Y 3.F 31/3:2

Y 3.F 31/3:12 CT
FEDERAL SAVINGS AND LOAN INSURANCE
CORPORATION PUBLICATIONS.

Y 3.F 31/3:13
FEDERAL SAVINGS AND LOAN INSURANCE
CORPORATION ANNUAL REPORTS.
    Included in Y 3.F 31/3:1

FEDERAL EMERGENCY ADMINISTRATION OF PUBLIC WORKS (1933– 1939)

CREATION AND AUTHORITY

    The Federal Emergency Administration of
Public Works was established pursuant to the
National Industrial Recovery Act, approved June
16, 1933 (48 Stat. 200). Reorganization Plan No.
1 of 1939, effective July 1, 1939, transferred the
Administration to the Federal Works Agency and
changed its name to the Public Works Administration (FW 5).

Y 3.F 31/4:1/date
ANNUAL REPORTS.
    Later FW 5.1

Y 3.F 31/4:2 CT
GENERAL PUBLICATIONS.
    Later FW 5.2

Y 3.F 31/4:3/nos.
BULLETINS.

Y 3.F 31/4:4/nos.
CIRCULARS.

Y 3.F 31/4:5 CT
LAWS.
    Later FW 5.5

Y 3.F 31/4:6 CT
REGULATIONS.

Y 3.F 31/4:7/nos.
FEDERAL AND NON-FEDERAL PROJECTS
APPROVED. [Weekly]

Y 3.F 31/4:8/nos.
NATIONAL PLANNING BOARD CIRCULAR LETTERS.

Y 3.F 31/4:9 CT
ADDRESSES.
    Later FW 5.7

Housing Division

Y 3.F 31/4:10/date
ANNUAL REPORTS.

Y 3.F 31/4:11 CT
GENERAL PUBLICATIONS.

Y 3.F 31/4:12/nos.
BULLETINS.

Y 3.F 31/4:13
[Reserved].

Y 3.F 31/4:14/nos.
HOUSING DIGEST. [Quarterly]

Y 3.F 31/4:15
SPECIFICATIONS.

Y 3.F 31/4:16/date
HOUSING NEWS. [Monthly]

Y 3.F 31/4:17/nos.
RESEARCH BULLETINS.

Y 3.F 31/4:18
LIBRARY ACCESSION LIST.

Y 3.F 31/4:19
ADDRESSES.

Y 3.F 31/4:20
[Reserved].

Federal Emergency Administration of Public Works (Continued)

Y 3.F 31/4:21 CT
PAPERS IN RE.

Y 3.F 31/4:22/nos.
ADMINISTRATIVE ORDERS.
    Later FW 5.8

Y 3.F 31/4:23/letters
PWA CIRCULARS.

Y 3.F 31/4:24/nos.
PWA BULLETINS, FOR INFORMATION OF STAFF.

Y 3.F 31/4:25
ACCOUNTING DIVISION ORDERS.

Y 3.F 31/4:26
DIGEST OF CONGRESSIONAL RECORD AND FED-
ERAL REGISTER PERTAINING TO MATTERS
RELATING TO PUBLIC WORKS.

Y 3.F 31/4:27
ENGINEERING DIVISION ORDERS.
    Processed.

Y 3.F 31/4:28
INSPECTION SPECIAL FIELD ORDER. [Admin.]

Y 3.F 31/4:29
INSPECTION DIVISION ORDERS.

Y 3.F 31/4:30
ORDERS.

Y 3.F 31/4:31
OFFICE ORDERS.

Y 3.F 31/4:32
LETTERS OF INSTRUCTIONS.

FEDERAL EMERGENCY RELIEF ADMINISTRATION (1933– 1938)

CREATION AND AUTHORITY

    The Federal Emergency Relief Administration
was established by act of Congress, approved
May 12, 1933 (48 Stat. 55). The Administration
was terminated on June 30, 1938, pursuant to
provisions of the Emergency Relief Appropriation
Act of 1937 (50 Stat. 352).

Y 3.F 31/5:1/date
ANNUAL REPORTS.

Y 3.F 31/5:2 CT
GENERAL PUBLICATIONS.

Y 3.F 31/5:3
BULLETINS.

Y 3.F 31/5:4
CIRCULARS.

Y 3.F 31/5:5
LAWS.

Y 3.F 31/5:6
REGULATIONS.

Y 3.F 31/5:7/nos.
RULES AND REGULATIONS.

Y 3.F 31/5:8/date
MONTHLY REPORTS.

Y 3.F 31/5:9/nos.
ACCIDENT ANALYSIS (Confidential).
    Earlier Y 3.F 31/7:9/1-11

Y 3.F 31/5:10 CT
POSTERS.

Y 3.F 31/5:11/vol.
RURAL REHABILITATION. [Issued about every 60
days].
    Multigraphed with retroprinted illustrations.

Y 3.F 31/5:12/vol
CONCERNING WORKERS' EDUCATION. [Monthly and
Bimonthly]

Y 3.F 31/5:13/vol
THE PROJECT. [Monthly]

Y 3.F 31/5:14/nos.
SUMMARY OF POLICIES, REPORTS, AND OTHER
PUBLICATIONS. [Semimonthly]

Y 3.F 31/5:15/date
INDEX TO POLICIES, REPORTS, AND OTHER PUB-
LICATIONS.
    May 23, 1933– September 15, 1934 title
reads: Index to Bulletin.

Y 3.F 31/5:16/vol.
EMERGENCY PARENT EDUCATION BULLETINS.

Y 3.F 31/5:17/vol.
SAFETY NEWS LETTER. [Monthly]

Y 3.F 31/5:18 CT
BIBLIOGRAPHIES (miscellaneous).

Y 3.F 31/5:19 CT
BIBLIOGRAPHIES (Non-institutional relief measures
of States and territories).

Y 3.F 31/5:20/nos.
SELECTED LIST OF REFERENCES ON OLD-AGE
SECURITY.

Y 3.F 31/5:21/date
BIBLIOGRAPHIES (Social Recovery Plan).

Y 3.F 31/5:22/vol.
COOPERATIVE SELF-HELP.

Y 3.F 31/5:23/nos.
RELIEF NOTICES. [Weekly]

Y 3.F 31/5:24/nos.
SAFETY BULLETINS.
    Earlier Y 3.F 31/7:10

Y 3.F 31/5:25/date
TREND OF URBAN RELIEF. [Monthly]
    Later SS 1.15

Y 3.F 31/5:26/nos.
NEWS LETTER FOR STATE SUPERVISORS OF
RURAL RESEARCH. [Monthly]

Y 3.F 31/5:27/date
TRANSIENTS. [Monthly]

Y 3.F 31/5:28/series no. &nos.
RESEARCH BULLETINS.

Y 3.F 31/5:29/letters-nos.
RESEARCH BULLETINS.

Y 3.F 31/5:30/date
AVERAGE MONTHLY RELIEF BENEFITS PER FAMILY,
PRINCIPAL CITY AREAS AND REMAINDER OF
EACH STATE.

Y 3.F 31/5:31/date
EMPLOYMENT AND PAY ROLLS, EMERGENCY WORK
RELIEF PROGRAM. [Weekly]

Y 3.F 31/5:32/date
FEDERAL EMERGENCY RELIEF ADMINISTRATION GRANTS. [Monthly]

Y 3.F 31/5:33/date
FEDERAL EMERGENCY RELIEF ADMINISTRATION GRANTS DISTRIBUTED ACCORDING TO PROGRAMS AND PERIODS FOR WHICH GRANTS WERE MADE. [Monthly]

Y 3.F 31/5:34/date
SUMMARY OF EMERGENCY RELIEF STATISTICS. [Monthly]

Y 3.F 31/5:35/date
TOTAL OBLIGATIONS INCURRED FOR EMERGENCY RELIEF FROM ALL PUBLIC FUNDS BY STATE AND LOCAL RELIEF ADMINISTRATION IN CONTINENTAL UNITED STATES. [Quarterly]

Y 3.F 31/5:36/date
INTENSITY OF RELIEF MAPS. [Monthly]

Y 3.F 31/5:37/date
TREND OF RELIEF IN CONTINENTAL UNITED STATES.

Y 3.F 31/5:38/date
LIBRARY ACCESSIONS, RESEARCH LIBRARY. [Weekly]
Earlier Y 3.W 89/2:41

FEDERAL COORDINATOR OF TRANSPORTATION
(1933– 1936)

CREATION AND AUTHORITY

The Federal Coordinator of Transportation was established by the Emergency Railroad Transportation Act of June 16, 1933. The Office was terminated June 16, 1936.

Y 3.F 31/6:1/date
ANNUAL REPORTS.

Y 3.F 31/6:2 CT
GENERAL PUBLICATIONS.

Y 3.F 31/6:3
BULLETINS.

Y 3.F 31/6:4
CIRCULARS.

Y 3.F 31/6:5
LAWS.

Y 3.F 31/6:6
REGULATIONS.

Y 3.F 31/6:7 CT
MAPS.

FEDERAL CIVIL WORKS ADMINISTRATION
(1933– 1934)

CREATION AND AUTHORITY

The Federal Civil Works Administration was established by Executive Order 6420-B. The Administration was abolished in March 1934, and its functions transferred to the Federal Emergency Relief Administration (Y 3.F 31/5).

Y 3.F 31/7:1/date
ANNUAL REPORTS.

Y 3.F 31/7:2 CT
GENERAL PUBLICATIONS.

Y 3.F 31/7:3
BULLETINS.

Y 3.F 31/7:4
CIRCULARS.

Y 3.F 31/7:5
LAWS.

Y 3.F 31/7:6
REGULATIONS.

Y 3.F 31/7:7/nos.
RULES AND REGULATIONS.

Y 3.F 31/7:8 CT
POSTERS.

Y 3.F 31/7:9/nos.
ACCIDENT ANALYSIS.

Later Y 3.F 31/5:9/12

Y 3.F 31/7:10/nos.
SAFETY DEPARTMENT BULLETINS.

Later Y 3.F 31/5:24/19

FEDERAL DEPOSIT INSURANCE CORPORATION
(1933–   )

CREATION AND AUTHORITY

The Federal Deposit Insurance Corporation was organized under authority of section 12B of the Federal Reserve Act, approved June 16, 1933 (48 Stat. 162; 12 U.S.C. 264). By legislation approved September 21, 1950 (64 Stat. 873; 12 U.S.C. 1811-1833, section 12B of the Federal Reserve Act, as amended, was withdrawn as part of the Federal Reserve Act and made a separate law known as the "Federal Deposit Insurance Act." The act also made numerous amendments to the former deposit insurance statutes.

INFORMATION

Information Office
Federal Deposit Insurance Corporation
550 Seventeenth Street, N.W.
Washington, D.C. 20429-9990
(202) 393-8400
Toll Free: (800) 759-6596
http://www.fdic.gov

Y 3.F 31/8:1 • Item 1061-K (MF)
ANNUAL REPORT. 1934– [Annual]

Report of activities for the year. Contains statistical tables on banks and deposit insurance activities.

Y 3.F 31/8:1-2/date • Item 1061-K (MF)
FDIC STATISTICS ON BANKING. [Annual]

Y 3.F 31/8:1-3 • Item 1061-K-3
MERGER DECISIONS. [Annual]

Y 3.F 31/8:2:CT • Item 1061-K
GENERAL PUBLICATIONS.

Y 3.F 31/8:3/nos
BULLETINS.

Y 3.F 31/8:4/date
CIRCULARS.

Y 3.F 31/8:5/date
LAWS.

Y 3.F 31/8:6/letters
REGULATIONS.

Y 3.F 31/8:7
MAPS.

Y 3.F 31/8:8
POSTERS

Y 3.F 31/8:9
REPORT OF CALL. 1– 1934–

Contains the following recurring publications:

Y 3.F 31/8:9
ASSETS, LIABILITIES, AND CAPITAL ACCOUNTS, COMMERCIAL AND MUTUAL SAVINGS BANKS. [Semiannual]

Gives assets and liabilities of all operating banks by type of bank and by State, of operating insured commercial banks by class of bank and by State, of operating mutual savings banks by State.

Y 3.F 31/8:9-2/date
REPORT OF CALLS, ASSETS, LIABILITIES, CAPITAL, ACCOUNTS, COMMERCIAL AND MUTUAL SAVINGS BANKS (unnumbered).

Joint report of Federal Deposit Insurance Corporation, Board of Governors of Federal Reserve System, and Office of Comptroller of Currency.
Earlier Y 3.F 31/8:9

Y 3.F 31/8:10
ADDRESSES. [Irregular]

Y 3.F 31/8:11 CT
REGULATIONS, RULES, AND INSTRUCTIONS.

Y 3.F 31/8:12/vol.
COOPERATIVE SAVINGS WITH FEDERAL CREDIT UNIONS. [Bimonthly]
Earlier A 72.13

Y 3.F 31/8:13/date
FEDERAL CREDIT UNIONS, QUARTERLY REPORTS OF ORGANIZATION. Proc.
Earlier A 72.14
Later FS 3.307

Y 3.F 31/8:14/date
FEDERAL CREDIT UNIONS, ANNUAL REPORTS OF OPERATIONS.
Earlier A 72.19
Later FS 3.301

Y 3.F 31/8:15/dt.&nos.
BULLETIN ML– NOS.

Changes in list of operating banking offices insured by FDIC.

Y 3.F 31/8:16
PRESS RELEASES. [Irregular]

Y 3.F 31/8:17
REPORT TO INSURED BANKS. 1936– [Semiannual]

Provides a brief report of activities and a statement of financial condition (assets and liabilities). Also includes a statement of income and deposit insurance fund; analysis of disbursements, recoveries and losses in insurance transactions.

Y 3.F 31/8:18
OPERATING BANK OFFICES INSURED BY THE FEDERAL DEPOSIT INSURANCE CORPORATION, AS OF [date]. – 1973.

– CHANGES IN LIST OF OPERATING BANKING OFFICES INSURED BY THE FEDERAL DEPOSIT INSURANCE CORPORATION. [Monthly]

Y 3.F 31/8:19
BANK OPERATING STATISTICS. 1967–   [Annual]

    PURPOSE:– To supply meaningful banking statistics to insured banks and those interested in banking operations.
    The tables have been prepared from reports of condition and earnings submitted at year- end by all insured commercial banks. They are designed to allow comparisons of bank operations in each State and, whenever possible, in its more immediate area.

Y 3.F 31/8:20 CT
SUMMARY OF ACCOUNTS AND DEPOSITS IN ALL
    COMMERCIAL BANKS [by districts].
        Earlier Y 3.F 31/8:2 Ac 2

Y 3.F 31/8:21/date
SUMMARY OF ACCOUNTS AND DEPOSITS IN ALL
    MUTUAL SAVINGS BANKS.
        Earlier Y 3.F 31/8:2 AC 2/2

Y 3.F 31/8:22/date   • **Item 1061-K (MF)**
DATABOOK: OPERATING BANKS AND BRANCHES,
    SUMMARY OF DEPOSITS. 1971–   [Annual]
        Formerly titled: Banks and Branches Data
Book.

Y 3.F 31/8:23   • **Item 1061-K-13 (MF)**
TRUST ASSETS OF FINANCIAL INSTITUTIONS.
        Earlier title: Trust Assets of Insured Commercial Banks.

Y 3.F 31/8:24   • **Item 1061-K-5 (EL)**
FDIC CONSUMER NEWS. [Quarterly]

Y 3.F 31/8:25/date   • **Item 1061-K**
CHANGES AMONG OPERATING BANKS AND
    BRANCHES. [Annual]

Y 3.F 31/8:26/date   • **Item 1061-K (MF) (EL)**
HISTORICAL STATISTICS ON BANKING.

Y 3.F 31/8:27/v.nos./nos • **Item 1068-K-6 (P) (EL)**
FDIC BANKING REVIEW.

Y 3.F 31/8:28/date   • **Item 1061-K-7(P)(EL)**
SURVEY OF REAL ESTATE TRENDS.

Y 3.F 31/8:29/date   • **Item 1061-K-8 (P) (EL)**
FDIC QUARTERLY BANKING PROFILE. [Quarterly]

Y 3.F 31/8:30   • **Item 1061-K-9**
INVESTMENT PROPERTIES. [Quarterly]

Y 3.F 31/8:31   • **Item 1061-K-10**
REAL ESTATE ASSET INVENTORY. [Semiannual]

Y 3.F 31/8:32 CT   • **Item 1061-K-12**
HANDBOOKS, MANUALS, GUIDES.

Y 3.F 31/8:33   • **Item 1061-K-14 (E)**
ELECTRONIC PRODUCTS.

Y 3.F 31/8:34   • **Item 1061-K-14 (EL)**
FINANCIAL INSTITUTION LETTERS (FILS).

Y 3.F 31/8:35   • **Item 1061-K-14 (EL)**
REPORT ON UNDERWRITING PRACTICES. (semiannual)

FEDERAL SURPLUS RELIEF CORPORATION
(1933– 1935)

CREATION AND AUTHORITY

    The Federal Surplus Relief Corporation was established as an independent agency on October 4, 1933, under authority of the National Industrial Recovery Act, approved June 16, 1933 (48 Stat. 195). On November 18, 1935, the agency was placed under the Secretary of Agriculture as its administrator and the name was changed to Federal Surplus Commodities Corporation (A 69).

Y 3.F 31/9:1/date
ANNUAL REPORTS.
    Later A 69.1

Y 3.F 31/9:2 CT
GENERAL PUBLICATIONS.
    Later A 69.2

FEDERAL ALCOHOL CONTROL ADMINISTRATION
(1933– 1935)

CREATION AND AUTHORITY

    The Federal Alcohol Administration was established as an independent agency by Executive Order 6474 of December 4, 1933. The Administration was abolished when the Federal Alcohol Administration Act, approved August 29, 1935 (49 Stat. 977) established within the Treasury Department a new Federal Alcohol Administration (T 59).

Y 3.F 31/10:1/date
ANNUAL REPORTS.

Y 3.F 31/10:2 CT
GENERAL PUBLICATIONS.

Y 3.F 31/10:3
BULLETINS.

Y 3.F 31/10:4
CIRCULARS.

Y 3.F 31/10:5
LAWS.

Y 3.F 31/10:6 CT
REGULATIONS (miscellaneous).

Y 3.F 31/10:7/nos.
BREWERS' CODE REGULATIONS.

Y 3.F 31/10:8/nos.
BREWERS' CODE INTERPRETATIONS.

Y 3.F 31/10:9/nos.
CODE SERIES.

Y 3.F 31/10:10/nos.
MISBRANDING REGULATIONS.

Y 3.F 31/10:11/nos.
MISBRANDING RULINGS.

Y 3.F 31/10:12/nos.
GENERAL PUBLICATIONS.

Y 3.F 31/10:13/nos.
TEMPORARY REGULATIONS.

Y 3.F 31/10:14/nos.
TEMPORARY JOINT REGULATIONS.

Y 3.F 31/10:15/nos.
WHOLESALE CODE REGULATIONS.

FEDERAL HOUSING ADMINISTRATION
(1934– 1939)

CREATION AND AUTHORITY

    The Federal Housing Administration was established as an independent agency by the National Housing Act, approved June 27, 1934 (48 Stat. 1246). It was transferred to the Federal Loan Agency (FL 2) by Reorganization Plan No. 1, effective July 1, 1939.

Y 3.F 31/11:1/date
ANNUAL REPORTS.
    Later FL 2.1

Y 3.F 31/11:2 CT
GENERAL PUBLICATIONS.
    Later FL 2.2

Y 3.F 31/11:3
BULLETINS.

Y 3.F 31/11:4
CIRCULARS.
    Later FL 2.4

Y 3.F 31/11:5 CT
LAWS.
    Later FL 2.5

Y 3.F 31/11:6
REGULATIONS.

Y 3.F 31/11:7 CT
RULES AND REGULATIONS.
    Later FL 2.6

Y 3.F 31/11:8/nos.&CT
POSTERS.

Y 3.F 31/11:9/vol.
BETTER HOUSING (weekly newsletter).

Y 3.F 31/11:10 CT
ADDRESSES.
    Printed and mimeographed.
    Also numbered.
    Later FL 2.18

Y 3.F 31/11:11/nos.
LOCAL CHAIRMAN OF BETTER HOUSING PROGRAM
    COMMITTEE. [Irregular]

    Numbers assigned arbitrarily.

Y 3.F 31/11:12/nos.
MODERNIZATION CREDIT PLAN, BULLETINS.

Y 3.F 31/11:13/vol.
CLIP SHEETS (current issues, weekly).
    Later FL 2.7

Y 3.F 31/11:14/nos.
CLIP SHEETS.

Y 3.F 31/11:15/vol.
WOMEN'S PAGE CLIP SHEETS.

Y 3.F 31/11:16/nos.
GENERAL ORDERS.
    Later FL 2.14

Y 3.F 31/11:17/nos.
ADMINISTRATIVE BULLETINS.

Y 3.F 31/11:18/vol.
HOUSING PROMOTION POINTERS.

Y 3.F 31/11:19/dt.&nos.
TECHNICAL BULLETINS.
    Later FL 2.15

Y 3.F 31/11:20/nos.
PRESS DIGEST. [Daily except Sunday]
    Superseded by Y 3.F 31/11:38

Y 3.F 31/11:21/nos.
PRESS DIGEST, WEEKLY DIGEST OF PERIODICALS.
    Later FL 1.8

Y 3.F 31/11:22/nos.
SPOT NEWS FROM FIELD.

    Released daily to publicity writers.

Y 3.F 31/11:23/date
WHAT'S DOING IN YOUR TOWN. [Weekly]

Y 3.F 31/11:24/date
WEEKLY STATISTICAL REPORTS.

Y 3.F 31/11:25/nos.
WOMAN'S PAGE FEATURE. [Weekly]

Y 3.F 31/11:26/nos.
CLASS A LOAN BULLETINS.

Y 3.F 31/11:27/letters
BETTER HOUSING NEWS FLASHES SYNOPSIS.

Y 3.F 31/11:28/nos.
DIVISIONAL MEMORANDUM.

Y 3.F 31/11:29/nos.
FIELD NEWS. [Confidential Release] [Weekly]

Y 3.F 31/11:30/nos.
WEEKLY ADVERTISING DIGEST.

Y 3.F 31/11:31/nos.
INTER-OFFICE BULLETINS. [Confidential]

Y 3.F 31/11:32/vol.
INSURED MORTGAGE PORTFOLIO. [Monthly]
    Later FL 2.12

Y 3.F 31/11:33/nos.
MODEL TOWN HOME SELECTOR.

Y 3.F 31/11:34/nos.
TITLE I FALL PROGRAM, MODERNIZE FOR WINTER, SPECIAL FIELD BULLETINS. [Weekly]

Y 3.F 31/11:35/date
ADMINISTRATIVE AREAS.

    Areas called Regions in 1935 and Zones in 1936.

Y 3.F 31/11:36/date
AMORTIZATION SCHEDULES.
    Later FS 2.13

Y 3.F 31/11:36/nos.
AMORTIZATION SCHEDULES (individual).

Y 3.F 31/11:37/nos.
COMPTROLLER CIRCULAR LETTERS.
    Later FL 2.19

Y 3.F 31/11:38/nos.
PRESS DIGEST. [Daily except Sundays and Saturdays].

    Supersedes Y 3.F 31/11:20
    Later FL 2.9

Y 3.F 31/11:39/nos.
ADVERTISING DIGEST. [Weekly]
    Later FL 2.10

Y 3.F 31/11:40/nos.
TECHNICAL CIRCULARS.
    Later FL 2.17

Y 3.F 31/11:41
COST DATA LETTERS.

FEDERAL COMMITTEE ON APPRENTICE TRAINING
(1934– 1942)

CREATION AND AUTHORITY

    The Federal Committee on Apprentice Training was established by Executive Order 6750-C of June 27, 1934. It was later known as the Federal Committee on Apprenticeship. The Committee functioned within the Apprenticeship Section of the Division of Labor Standards of the Department of Labor from 1937 until 1942. Executive Order 9139 of April 18, 1942 transferred the Committee to the Federal Security Agency.

Y 3.F 31/12:1/date
ANNUAL REPORTS.

Y 3.F 31/12:2 CT
GENERAL PUBLICATIONS.

Y 3.F 31/12:3/nos.
BULLETINS.

Y 3.F 31/12:9/nos.
APPRENTICE TRAINING NEWS.

Y 3.F 31/12:10 CT
ADDRESSES.

FEDERAL INTER-AGENCY RIVER BASIN COMMITTEE
(1939– 1954)

CREATION AND AUTHORITY

    The Federal Interagency River Basin Committee was established on August 8, 1939, through a memorandum of understanding among the participating agencies. The Committee was superseded by the Interagency Committee on Water Resources, established by the President on May 26, 1954.

Y 3.F 31/13:1/date
ANNUAL REPORTS.

Y 3.F 31/13:2 CT
GENERAL PUBLICATIONS.

    Earlier I 1.18

Y 3.F 31/13:3/nos.
NOTES ON HYDROLOGIC ACTIVITIES, BULLETINS.

Y 3.F 31/13:8/nos.
SEDIMENTATION BULLETINS.

Y 3.F 31/13:9/nos.
STUDY OF METHODS USED IN MEASUREMENT AND ANALYSIS OF SEDIMENT LOADS IN STREAMS, REPORTS.

    Later Y 3.In 8/8:10

ARKANSAS-WHITE-RED BASINS INTER-AGENCY COMMITTEE
(1977–   )

Y 3.F 31/13-2:1/date
REPORTS.

Y 3.F 31/13-2:2 CT
GENERAL PUBLICATIONS. [Irregular]

    Y 3.F 31/13-2:2 M 66
    MINUTES OF MEETING. 1st–   1955–

FEDERAL INTER-AGENCY COMMITTEE ON RECREATION
(1946–   )

CREATION AND AUTHORITY

    The Federal Inter-Agency Committee on Recreation was organized in September 1946 by a group of Federal Agencies administering public recreation lands, facilities, and service programs.

Y 3.F 31/14:1/date
ANNUAL REPORTS.

Y 3.F 31/14:2 CT
GENERAL PUBLICATIONS.

FEDERAL COUNCIL ON AGING
(1956– 1962)

Y 3.F 31/15:1/date   • Item 1061-A-1
ANNUAL REPORTS.

Y 3.F 31/15:2 CT   • Item 1061-A-1
GENERAL PUBLICATIONS.

Y 3.F 31/15:8 CT   • Item 1061-A-1
BIBLIOGRAPHIES AND LISTS OF PUBLICATIONS.

Y 3.F 31/15:9 CT   • Item 1061-A-1
ADDRESSES.

Y 3.F 31/15:10/date   • Item 1061-A-1
STATUS REPORT. [Irregular]

FEDERAL COUNCIL FOR SCIENCE AND TECHNOLOGY
(1959– 1963)

CREATION AND AUTHORITY

    The Council was established by Executive Order 10807 of March 13, 1959, amended by Executive Order 11381 of November 8, 1967, to promote closer cooperation among Federal Agencies, to facilitate resolution of common problems and to improve planning and management in science and technology, and to advise and assist the President regarding Federal programs affecting more than one agency. Council was abolished by Reorganization Plan No. 1 of 1973, effective June 30, 1973.

Y 3.F 31/16:1/date • **Item 1061-B**
REPORTS.

Y 3.F 31/16:2 CT • **Item 1061-B**
GENERAL PUBLICATIONS.

Y 3.F 31/16:2 F 31 • **Item 1061-B**
DIRECTORY OF FEDERAL TECHNOLOGY
TRANSFER. 1975. 202 p. il.

The term "technology transfer" refers to
the transfer of existing research knowledge
into useful processes, products, or programs
that fulfill public or private needs. State and
local government officials and private industry will find this book useful in their efforts to
share the results on federal research programs more effectively. The book is an easy-
to-use index of programs, resources, and contact points. Each section gives a succinct
description of an agency's program, including the agency's research base, its technology transfer policy and objectives, areas of
responsibility, methods of implementation, accomplishments, and user organizations.

Y 3.F 31/16:2 M 33/2 • **Item 1061-B**
MARINE RESEARCH. 1973. 1180 p.

This volume, an update of the 1969 edition, gives basic information and brief descriptions of more than 4,500 scientific
projects in fields related to marine science,
sponsored by government and private agencies. It gives the findings of some of the
recently completed projects. Some topics
covered include meteorology, marine geology,
and non-human living systems.

Y 3.F 31/16:8 CT • **Item 1061-B**
HANDBOOKS, MANUALS, GUIDES.

Y 3.F 31/16:9 • **Item 1061-B**
ICO [Interagency Committee on Oceanography]
PAMPHLETS. 1– [Irregular]

Y 3.F 31/16:9-2 • **Item 1061-B**
ICO [Interagency Committee on Oceanography] IN-
FORMAL REPORTS. 1– [Irregular]

Y 3.F 31/16:10 • **Item 1061-B**
[PROCEEDINGS OF SYMPOSIUMS]. [Irregular]

Y 3.F 31/16:11 • **Item 1061-B**
ANNUAL REPORT ON GOVERNMENT PATENT
POLICY. [Annual]

Prepared in consultation with the Department
of Justice as required by sec. 3 of the Statement
of Government patent policy, issued by the President of the United States, October 10, 1963.

Y 3.F 31/16:12 • **Item 1061-B**
ICAS [Interdepartmental Committee for Atmospheric
Sciences] REPORTS. 1– 1960– [Irregular]
PURPOSE:– To present important aspects of
the Federal research program in the atmospheric
sciences that are of concern to the Federal Council
for Science and Technology, the President, and
Congress.

Y 3.F 31/16:13 CT • **Item 1061-B**
INTERDEPARTMENTAL COMMITTEE FOR METEORO-
LOGICAL SERVICES PUBLICATIONS.

Y 3.F 31/16:14/date • **Item 1061-B**
FEDERAL EXCAVATION TECHNOLOGY PROGRAM,
ANNUAL REPORT. 1– 1971– (Interagency
Committee on Excavation Technology).

PURPOSE:– To provide an opportunity of reporting on activities and accomplishments of the
Interagency Committee on Excavation Technology.

FEDERAL RADIATION COUNCIL
(1959–1970)

CREATION AND AUTHORITY

The Federal Radiation Council was established
by Executive Order 10831 of August 14, 1959,
and by section 274h of the Atomic Energy Act of
1954, as amended on September 23, 1959 (73
Stat. 690). The Council was abolished by Reorganization Plan 3 of 1970, effective December 2,
1970, and its functions transferred to the Environmental Protection Agency (EP 1).

Y 3.F 31/17:1/date • **Item 1063-E**
ANNUAL REPORTS.

Y 3.F 31/17:2 CT • **Item 1063-E**
GENERAL PUBLICATIONS.

Y 3.F 31/17:8 • **Item 1063-E**
REPORTS. 1– 1960– [Irregular]

PURPOSE:– To serve as a guidance for all
Federal agencies in the formulation of radiation
standards and in the establishment and execution of programs of cooperation with the States.

FEDERAL COMMITTEE ON PEST
CONTROL
(1964–   )

CREATION AND AUTHORITY

The Federal Committee on Pest Control was
established in August 1964 in response to a recommendation in the 1963 report of the President's
Science Advisory Committee. The Committee is
composed of representatives of the Departments
of Agriculture; Defense; Health, Education, and
Welfare; and Interior.

Y 3.F 31/18:1/date • **Item 1061-C**
ANNUAL REPORT.

Y 3.F 31/18:2 CT • **Item 1061-C**
GENERAL PUBLICATIONS.

Y 3.F 31/18:9 • **Item 1061-C**
PESTICIDES MONITORING JOURNAL. v. 1– 1967–
[Quarterly]
Later Pr 37.8:En 8/P 43

FEDERAL COMMITTEE ON
RESEARCH NATURAL AREAS
(1966–   )

CREATION AND AUTHORITY

The Federal Committee on Research Natural
Areas evolved from an information committee
established February 1966 within the Department
of Interior into an interagency committee to develop a classification system of natural area type
found in the United States. The Committee includes representatives of the various land managing bureaus of the Federal Government.

Y 3.F 31/19:1/date • **Item 1061-D**
REPORT.

Y 3.F 31/19:2 CT • **Item 1061-D**
GENERAL PUBLICATIONS.

Y 3.F 31/19:9/date • **Item 1061-D**
DIRECTORY OF RESEARCH NATURAL AREAS ON
FEDERAL LANDS OF UNITED STATES OF
AMERICA.

FEDERAL EXECUTIVE BOARD
(1961–   )

CREATION AND AUTHORITY

The Federal Executive Boards were established by Presidential Directive of John F.
Kennedy, November 13, 1961 to improve coordination among Federal activities and programs
outside Washington.

INFORMATION

Federal Executive Board
http://www.feb.gov

Y 3.F 31/20:1/date • **Item 1061-E**
ANNUAL REPORT.

Y 3.F 31/20:2 CT • **Item 1061-E**
GENERAL PUBLICATIONS.

Y 3.F 31/20:8 CT • **Item 1061-E**
HANDBOOKS, MANUALS AND GUIDES.

Y 3.F 31/20:8-2 • **Item 1061-E-1**
FISCAL YEAR DIRECTORY BALTIMORE FEDERAL
EXECUTIVE BOARD.

FEDERAL LABOR RELATIONS
COUNCIL
(1969–1979)

CREATION AND AUTHORITY

The Federal Labor Relations Council was established by Executive Order 11491 of October
29, 1969, as amended by Executive Order 11616
of August 26, 1971, Executive Order 11636 of
December 17, 1971, and Executive Order 11838
of February 6, 1975. The Council was abolished
and its functions transferred to the Federal Labor
Relations Authority (Y 3. F 31/12-3) by Reorganization Plan No. 2 of 1978, effective January 1,
1979, pursuant to Executive Order 12107 of December 28, 1978.

Y 3.F 31/21:1/date • **Item 1089-B**
ANNUAL REPORT.

Y 3.F 31/21:2 CT • **Item 1089-B**
GENERAL PUBLICATIONS.

Y 3.F 31/21:9/v.nos.
DECISIONS AND INTERPRETATIONS OF THE
FEDERAL LABOR RELATIONS COUNCIL.

Y 3.F 31/21:10/nos.
FLRC REPORT OF CASE DECISIONS AND FSIP
RELEASES.
Superseded by FLRA Report on Case Deci-
sions and FSIP Releases (Y 3.F 31/12-3:9).

Y 3.F 31/21:11/date
SUBJECT MATTER INDEX WITH CROSSREFERENCE
TABLE.

FEDERAL SERVICE IMPASSES
PANEL
(1969–   )

CREATION AND AUTHORITY

The Federal Impasses Panel was established by Executive Order 11491 of October 29, 1969, as amended by Executive Order 11616 of August 26, 1971; Executive Order 11636 of Dec. 17, 1971; and Executive Order 11838 of February 6, 1975.

Y 3.F 31/21-2:1/date   • **Item 1061-G-3**
REPORTS. [Irregular]

Y 3.F 31/21-2:2 CT   • **Item 1061-G-3**
GENERAL PUBLICATIONS. [Irregular]

Y 3.F 31/21-2:7/nos.
PRESS RELEASES.

Y 3.F 31/21-2:8 CT   • **Item 1061-G-3**
HANDBOOKS, MANUALS, GUIDES.

Y 3.F 31/21-2:9/date   • **Item 1061-G-3**
SUBJECT-MATTER INDEX AND TABLE OF CASES.
    [Annual]
        Earlier Y 3.F 31/21-2:2 Su 1

FEDERAL LABOR RELATIONS
AUTHORITY
(1979–   )

CREATION AND AUTHORITY

The Federal Labor Relations Authority was established by Reorganization Plan No. 2 of 1978, effective January 1, 1979, pursuant to Executive Order 12107 of December 28, 1978, to super-seded the Federal Labor Relations Council (Y 3. F 31/21) which was abolished.

INFORMATION

Federal Labor Relations Authority
607 14th St. NW
Washington, D.C. 20424-0001
(202) 482-6560
http://www.flra.gov

Y 3.F 31/21-3:1/date   • **Item 1062-H (MF) (EL)**
ANNUAL REPORT.

Summarizes Authority activities, which include setting policy and providing guidance on Federal labor-management relations and insuring that statutory rights and obligations of Federal agencies and Federal employees and their organizations, are fulfilled.

Y 3.F 31/21-3:2 CT   • **Item 1061-G-1**
GENERAL PUBLICATIONS. [Irregular]

Y 3.F 31/21-3:5 CT   • **Item 1062-G-2**
LAWS. [Irregular]

Y 3.F 31/21-3:8 CT   • **Item 1061-G-5**
HANDBOOKS, MANUALS, GUIDES. [Irregular]

Y 3.F 31/21-3:9   • **Item 1061-G-1**
FLRA REPORT ON CASE DECISIONS AND FSIP RELEASES.

Supersedes FIRC Report on Case Decisions and FSIP Releases (Y 3.F 31/21:10).

Y 3.F 31/21-3:9-2   • **Item 1061-G-1**
DIGESTS AND TABLES OF CASES, DECISIONS OF THE FEDERAL LABOR RELATIONS AUTHORITY. [Irregular]

Y 3.F 31/21-3:9-3   • **Item 1061-G-1**
DIGESTS AND TABLES OF CASES, DECISIONS OF THE FEDERAL LABOR RELATIONS AUTHORITY.

Y 3.F 31/21-3:9-4/date   • **Item 1061-G-1**
CITATOR, DECISIONS OF THE FEDERAL LABOR RELATIONS AUTHORITY.

Y 3.F 31/21-3:9-5/date   • **Item 1061-G-1**
FEDERAL REGISTER PROPOSED AMENDMENTS. [Irregular]

Y 3.F 31/21-3:10   • **Item 1061-G-6**
SUPPLEMENTAL DIGEST AND INDEX OF PUBLISHED DECISIONS OF THE ASSISTANT SECRETARY OF LABOR FOR LABOR-MANAGEMENT RELATIONS PURSUANT TO EXECUTIVE ORDER 11491.

    Earlier L 1.51/3

Y 3.F 31/21-3:10-2/nos.   • **Item 1061-G-6 (MF)**
DECISIONS AND REPORTS ON RULINGS OF THE ASSISTANT SECRETARY OF LABOR FOR LABOR-MANAGEMENT RELATIONS PURSUANT TO EXECUTIVE ORDER 11491, AS AMENDED. v. 1–   1970-71–   [Biennial]

Formerly published by the Department of Labor (L 1.51/4).

Y 3.F 31/21-3:10-3/date   • **Item 762-D-12**
SUBJECT MATTER INDEXES TO DECISIONS OF THE FEDERAL LABOR RELATIONS AUTHORITY. [Annual]

Lists FLRA Decisions by number and by subject.

Y 3.F 31/21-3:10-4/v. nos.   • **Item 1061-G-1 (MF)**
DECISIONS OF THE FEDERAL LABOR RELATIONS AUTHORITY.

Y 3.F 31/21-3:11/date   • **Item 762-D-11**
CLASSIFIED INDEX OF DISPOSITIONS OF ULP CHARGES BY THE GENERAL COUNSEL OF THE FEDERAL LABOR RELATIONS AUTHORITY. [Quarterly]

PURPOSE:– To provide a subject matter index to advice memoranda and appeal letters for unfair labor practice cases, by case number, type, and date.
ULP = unfair labor practices.

Y 3.F 31/21-3:12/date   • **Item 1061-G-4**
REPORTS ON CASE HANDLING DEVELOPMENTS OF THE OFFICE OF THE GENERAL COUNSEL. [Quarterly]

Summarizes individual cases brought before the Authority's General Counsel Office on such subjects as union fines and discipline of members, and agency right to file grievances, giving disposition, etc.

Y 3.F 31/21-3:13 CT   • **Item 1061-G-1**
RULES AND REGULATIONS. [Irregular]

Y 3.F 31/21-3:14/date   • **Item 1061-G-1**
FLRA REPORT OF CASE DECISIONS AND FSIP RELEASES, INFORMATION ANNOUNCEMENT.

Y 3.F 31/21-3:14-2/date   • **Item 1061-G-1**
FLRA REPORT OF CASE DECISIONS AND FSIP RELEASES, INFORMATION ANNOUNCEMENT.

Y 3.F 31/21-3:14-3/nos.   • **Item 1061-G-1**
FEDERAL SERVICE IMPASSES PANEL RELEASES.

Y 3.F 31/21-3:14-4/date   • **Item 1061-G-1**
FLRA REPORT OF CASE DECISIONS AND FSIP RELEASES, REPRESENTATION PETITIONS INDEX OF AUTHORITY ORDERS.

Y 3.F 31/21-3:14-5/date   • **Item 1061-G-1**
FLRA REPORT OF CASE DECISIONS AND FSIP RELEASES, REPRESENTATION PETITIONS INDEX OF OGC CASE NUMBERS, PART 2.

Y 3.F 31/21-3:14-6/date   • **Item 1061-G-1**
FLRA REPORT OF CASE DECISIONS AND FSIP RELEASES, UNFAIR LABOR PRACTICE CHARGES, INDEX OF AUTHORITY ORDERS, PART 1.

Y 3.F 31/21-3:14-7/date   • **Item 1061-G-1**
FLRA REPORT OF CASE DECISIONS AND FSIP RELEASES, UNFAIR LABOR PRACTICE CHARGES, INDEX OF UNNUMBERED AUTHORITY ORDERS, PART 2.

Y 3.F 31/21-3:14-8   • **Item 1061-G-1**
FLRA REPORT OF CASE DECISIONS AND FSIP RELEASES, UNFAIR LABOR PRACTICE CHARGES, INDEX OF ALJ DECISIONS, PART 3.

Y 3.F 31/21-3:14-9/date   • **Item 1061-G-1**
FLRA REPORT OF CASE DECISIONS AND FSIP RELEASES, UNFAIR LABOR PRACTICE CHARGES, INDEX OF OGC CASE NUMBERS, PART 5.

Y 3.F 31/21-3:14-10/date   • **Item 1061-G-1**
FLRA REPORT OF CASE DECISIONS AND FSIP RELEASES, UNFAIR LABOR PRACTICE CHARGES, INDEX OF SUPPLEMENTAL DECISIONS, PART 5.

Y 3.F 31/21-3:14-11/nos.   • **Item 1061-G-1**
CASE INFORMATION SHEETS.

Y 3.F 31/21-3:14-14   • **Item 1061-G-1(EL)**
FLRA NEWS.

Y 3.F 31/21-3:15/v.nos.&nos. • **Item 1061-G-8(EL)**
FLRA BULLETIN. [Irregular]

Previously: FLRA Quarterly Summary

FEDERAL COMMITTEE ON
ECOLOGICAL RESERVES

INFORMATION

Federal Committee on Ecological Reserves
National Science Foundation
1800 G Street, N.W.
Washington, D.C. 20550

Y 3.F 31/22:1/date   • **Item 1061-D**
ANNUAL REPORT.

Y 3.F 31/22:2 CT   • **Item 1061-D**
GENERAL PUBLICATIONS. [Irregular]

Y 3.F 31/22:9   • **Item 1061-D**
DIRECTORY OF RESEARCH NATURAL AREAS ON FEDERAL LANDS OF THE UNITED STATES OF AMERICA. [Irregular]

Compilation and computerization of data by the Nature Conservancy.

OFFICE OF THE FEDERAL INSPECTOR, ALASKA NATURAL GAS TRANSPORTATION SYSTEM
(1979–   )

CREATION AND AUTHORITY

The Office of the Federal Inspector for the Alaska Natural Gas Transportation System was established by Executive Order 12142 of June 21, 1979.

INFORMATION

Office of the Federal Inspector, Alaska
Natural Gas Transportation System
Room 3412, Post Office Building
1200 Pennsylvania Avenue, N.W.
Washington, D.C. 20044
(202) 275-1100

Y 3.F 31/23:1/date
ANNUAL REPORT.

Y 3.F 31/23:2 CT
GENERAL PUBLICATIONS. [Irregular]

Y 3.F 31/23:9/nos.
ALASKA GAS PIPELINE UPDATE. [Biweekly]

FEDERAL INTERAGENCY COMMITTEE ON THE INTERNATIONAL YEAR OF DISABLED PERSONS

Y 3.F 31/24:1/date
REPORTS.

FEDERAL RETIREMENT THRIFT INVESTMENT BOARD
(1986–   )

CREATION AND AUTHORITY

The Federal Retirement Thrift Investment Board was established as an independent agency by the Federal Employees' Retirement System Act of 1986 (5 U.S.C. 8472) to administer the Thrift Saving Plan that began April 1987.

INFORMATION

Federal Retirement Thrift Investment Board
1250 H Street, NW
Washington, D.C. 20005
(202) 942-1600
Fax: (202) 942-1676
http://www.frtib.gov

Y 3.F 31/25:2 CT   • **Item 1061-L**
GENERAL PUBLICATIONS.

Y 3.F 31/25:13 CT
FORMS.

NATIONAL COMMISSION ON FINANCIAL INSTITUTION REFORM, RECOVERY AND ENFORCEMENT

Y 3.F 32:2 CT   • **Item 1061-G-7**
GENERAL PUBLICATIONS.

FEDERAL FINANCIAL INSTITUTIONS EXAMINATION COUNCIL
(1979–   )

CREATION AND AUTHORITY

The Federal Financial Institutions Examination Council was established on March 10, 1979 pursuant to Public Law 95-630 (92 Stat. 3694), approved November 10, 1978.

INFORMATION

Federal Financial Institutions Examination
Council
Suite 701
1776 G Street, N.W.
Washington, D.C. 20006
(202) 356-0177

Y 3.F 49:1/date   • **Item 1061-J**
ANNUAL REPORT.

Y 3.F 49:2 CT
GENERAL PUBLICATIONS.

NATIONAL COMMISSION ON FIRE PREVENTION AND CONTROL
(–1973)

Y 3.F 51:1/date   • **Item 1089**
REPORT.

FOOD ADMINISTRATION
(1917–1920)

CREATION AND AUTHORITY

The United States Food Administration was established by Executive Order 2679-A of August 10, 1917, pursuant to the Food and Fuel Control (Lever) Act, approved August 10, 1917. The Administration was abolished by Executive Order 3320 of August 21, 1920.

Y 3.F 73:1/date
ANNUAL REPORTS.

Y 3.F 73:2 CT
GENERAL PUBLICATIONS.

Y 3.F 73:3/nos.
BULLETINS.

Y 3.F 73:4
CIRCULARS.

Y 3.F 73:5/vol.
WEEKLY BULLETINS.

Y 3.F 73:6/nos.
DIVISION OF COOPERATIVE ORGANIZATIONS.

Y 3.F 73:7 CT
REGULATIONS, RULES, AND INSTRUCTIONS (MISC).

Y 3.F 73:8/nos.
SPEAKERS' BULLETINS.

Y 3.F 73:9/vol.
FOOD NEWS NOTES FOR PUBLIC LIBRARIES.

Y 3.F 73:10 CT or nos.
POSTERS.

Y 3.F 73:11/nos
ON GUARD SERIES.

Y 3.F 73:12/vol.
BULLETIN FOR THE CLERGY.

Y 3.F 73:13/vol.
RELIGIOUS PRESS BULLETIN.

Y 3.F 73:14/nos.
CANNED FOODS DIVISION BULLETINS.

Y 3.F 73:15/nos.
MILLING DIVISION CIRCULARS.

Y 3.F 73:16/nos.
RETAIL STORES SECTION FLYERS.

Y 3.F 73:17/nos.
BULLETINS FOR RETAIL MERCHANTS.

Y 3.F 73:18/nos.
LICENSE REGULATIONS (numbered).

Y 3.F 73:19/nos.
OFFICIAL STATEMENT OF UNITED STATES FOOD ADMINISTRATION.

Y 3.F 73:20/nos.
CANNED FOODS BULLETINS.

Y 3.F 73:21/nos.
OPINIONS, INTERPRETATIONS AND RULINGS.

Y 3.F 73:22/nos.
TESTED RECIPES (numbered).

Y 3.F 73:23 CT
RECIPES (unnumbered).

Y 3.F 73:24/nos.
STEAMSHIP DEPARTMENT BULLETINS.

Y 3.F 73:25/nos.
FOOD CONSERVATION NOTES.

Y 3.F 73:26/nos.
DISPLAY POSTERS.

Y 3.F 73:27 CT
HOME CARDS.

SPECIAL ADVISER TO THE PRESIDENT ON FOREIGN TRADE
(1934– 1935)

CREATION AND AUTHORITY

The Office of the Special Adviser to the President on Foreign Trade was established by EO 6651 of March 23, 1934, to coordinate information and statistics on foreign trade collected by any department or agency of the Government. The Office ceased to function at the expiration of the National Recovery Administration.

Y 3.F 76:1/date
ANNUAL REPORTS.

Y 3.F 76:2 CT
GENERAL PUBLICATIONS.

FOREIGN ECONOMIC POLICY COMMISSION
(1953– 1954)

CREATION AND AUTHORITY

The Commission on Foreign Economic Policy was established by Public Law 215, 83rd Congress, approved August 7, 1953. Under Public Law 215, the Commission ceased to exist sixty days after its final report (January 23, 1954).

Y 3.F 76/2:1/date
REPORT.

Y 3.F 76/2:2 CT
GENERAL PUBLICATIONS.

FOREIGN CLAIMS SETTLEMENT COMMISSION OF THE UNITED STATES
(1954– 1980)

CREATION AND AUTHORITY

The Foreign Claims Settlement Commission of the United States is an independent agency created by Reorganization Plan 1 of 1954 (68 Stat. 1279), effective July 1, 1954. Its duties and authority are defined in the International Claims Settlement Act of 1949, as amended (64 Stat. 12; 22 U.S.C. 1621-1642) and the War Claims Act of 1948 (62 Stat. 1240; 50 U.S.C. 2001-2016). The Commission was transferred to the Department of Justice as a separate agency within the Department, effective March 14, 1980, by Public Law 96-209 (94 Stat. 96).

Y 3.F 76/3:1   **• Item 1063-C**
ANNUAL REPORT TO THE CONGRESS. 1st–   1954–

Report submitted by the Commission to Congress pursuant to provisions of section 9 of the War Claims Act of 1948 (62 Stat. 1240; 50 U.S.C. App. 2001-1016), as amended, and of section 3(c) of the International Claims Settlement Act of 1949 (64 Stat. 12; 22 U.S.C. 1621-1627), as amended. Periods covered end June and Dec. 31.

The 14th report covering the period ending June 30, 1961 constitutes the first complete report of the present Commission.

Semiannual 1954– 1966; annual, 1967–

Y 3.F 76/3:2 CT   **• Item 1063-C**
GENERAL PUBLICATIONS.

Y 3.F 76/3:3/nos.   **• Item 1063-C**
BULLETINS.

Y 3.F 76/3:4/nos.   **• Item 1063-C**
CIRCULARS.

Y 3.F 76/3:5 CT   **• Item 1063-C**
LAWS.

Y 3.F 76/3:6 CT   **• Item 1063-C**
REGULATIONS, RULES, AND INSTRUCTIONS.

Y 3.F 76/3:7   **• Item 1063-C**
RELEASES.

BOARD OF FOREIGN SCHOLARSHIPS
(1946–   )

CREATION AND AUTHORITY

The Board of foreign Scholarships was established within the Department of State by act of Congress, approved august 1, 1946 (60 Stat. 755).

INFORMATION

Board of Foreign Scholarships
United States Information Agency
Room 247
301 Fourth Street, S.W.
Washington, D.C. 20547
(202) 485-7290

Y 3.F 76/4:1   **• Item 1063-F**
ANNUAL REPORT. [Annual]

Y 3.F 76/4:2 CT   **• Item 1063-F**
GENERAL PUBLICATIONS.

COMMISSION ON ORGANIZATION OF THE GOVERNMENT FOR THE CONDUCT OF FOREIGN POLICY
(1972– 1974)

Y 3.F 76/5:1/date
REPORT.

Y 3.F 76/5:2 CT
GENERAL PUBLICATIONS.

BOARD ON FORTIFICATIONS AND OTHER DEFENSES
(1885– 1886)

CREATION AND AUTHORITY

The Board on Fortifications and Other Defenses was appointed by the President in 1885 pursuant to act of Congress, approved March 3, 1885. The Board submitted its report in 1886.

Y 3.F 77:CT
PUBLICATIONS.

FOUR CORNERS REGIONAL COMMISSION
(1965– 1981)

CREATION AND AUTHORITY

The Four Corners Regional Commission has been established by the Secretary of Commerce under authority of Public Law 89-136, approved August 26, 1965. The Federal role in this Commission was abolished through repeal of the Public Works and Economic Development Act of 1965, by section 1821 of Public Law 97-35 of August 13, 1981 (95 Stat. 766), effective October 1, 1981.

Y 3.F 82:1/date
REPORT.

Y 3.F 82:2 CT
GENERAL PUBLICATIONS.

Y 3.F 82:7/nos.
PRESS RELEASES.

Y 3.F 82:9 CT
ADDRESSES.

FUEL ADMINISTRATION
(1917– 1919)

CREATION AND AUTHORITY

The Fuel Administration was established as an emergency agency by Executive Order of August 23, 1917. The agency was discontinued in 1919.

Y 3.F 95:1/date
ANNUAL REPORTS.

Y 3.F 95:2 CT
GENERAL PUBLICATIONS.

Y 3.F 95:3
BULLETINS.

Y 3.F 95:4
CIRCULARS.

Y 3.F 95:5/nos.
PUBLICATIONS (numbered).

Y 3.F 95:6/nos. or CT
POSTERS.

Y 3.F 95:7/nos.
SPEAKERS SERIES.

Y 3.F 95:8/nos.
ENGINEERING BULLETINS.

Y 3.F 95:9/nos.
OIL DIVISION, BULLETINS.

COMMISSION ON REVIEW OF THE NATIONAL POLICY TOWARD GAMBLING
(1975–   )

Y 3.G 14:1/date   • Item 1089
REPORT. [Irregular]

Y 3.G 14:2 CT
GENERAL PUBLICATIONS.

GEORGE ROGERS CLARK SESQUICENTENNIAL COMMISSION
(1928– 1939)

CREATION AND AUTHORITY

The George Rogers Clark Sesquicentennial Commission was established by Public Resolution 51, approved May 23, 1928 (45 Stat. 723) The Commission was abolished on June 30, 1939.

Y 3.G 29:CT
PUBLICATIONS.

COMMISSION ON THE ROLE OF GOLD IN DOMESTIC AND INTERNATIONAL MONETARY SYSTEMS

Y 3.G 57:1/date
REPORTS.

GOVERNMENT PATENTS BOARD
(1950– 1961)

CREATION AND AUTHORITY

The Government Patents Board was established by Executive Order 10096 of January 23, 1950. The Board was abolished by Executive Order 10930 of March 24, 1961 and functions transferred to the Department of Commerce.

Y 3.G 74:1/date
ANNUAL REPORTS.

Y 3.G 74:2 CT
GENERAL PUBLICATIONS.

Y 3.G 74:7/nos.
ADMINISTRATIVE ORDERS.

GOVERNMENTS SECURITY COMMISSION
(1955– 1957)

CREATION AND AUTHORITY

The Commission on Government Security was established by act of Congress, approved August 9, 1955 (69 Stat. 595), and extended by act of Congress, approved July 25, 1956 (70 Stat. 634), to June 30, 1957. The Commission submitted its final report on June 21, 1957.

Y 3.G 74/2:1/date
REPORT.

Y 3.G 74/2:2 CT
GENERAL PUBLICATIONS.

GOVERNMENT ACTIVITIES AFFECTING PRICES AND COSTS COMMITTEE
(1959– 1961)

Y 3.G 74/3:1/date
ANNUAL REPORT.

Y 3.G 74/3:2 CT
GENERAL PUBLICATIONS.

COMMISSION ON GOVERNMENT PROCUREMENT
(1969–   )

CREATION AND AUTHORITY

The Commission on Government Procurement was established by act of November 26, 1969 (83 Stat. 269; 41 U.S.C. note), to study and investigate present statutes, policies, regulations, and practices followed by contracting agencies in the executive branch, and their procurement organizations, to determine to what extent these facilitate the policy set forth in section 1 of the act.

Y 3.G 74/4:1/date   • Item 1089
REPORTS.

Y 3.G 74/4:2 CT
GENERAL PUBLICATIONS.

Y 3.G 74/4:5 CT
LAWS.

GRADES AND SALARIES COMMITTEE
(1907– 1908)

CREATION AND AUTHORITY

The Committee on Grades and Salaries was established by Executive Order 651 of June 11, 1907.

Y 3.G 75:CT
PUBLICATIONS.

GRANT MEMORIAL COMMISSION
(1913)

Y 3.G 76:CT
PUBLICATIONS.

GREAT PLAINS DROUGHT AREA COMMITTEE
(1936)

CREATION AND AUTHORITY

The Great Plains Drought Area Committee was established by the President on July 22, 1936. The Committee made its report in August 1936. On September 17, 1936, the President established the Great Plains Committee (Y 3.G 79/2) to succeed this Committee.

Y 3.G 79:CT
PUBLICATIONS.

GREAT PLAINS COMMITTEE
(1936)

CREATION AND AUTHORITY

The Great Plains Committee was established by the President on September 17, 1936, to succeed the Great Plains Drought Area Committee (Y 3.G 79). The Committee made its report in December 1936.

Y 3.G 79/2:1/date
REPORT.

Y 3.G 79/2:2 CT
GENERAL PUBLICATIONS.

GREAT LAKES BASIN COMMISSION
(1967– 1981)

CREATION AND AUTHORITY

The Great Lakes Basin Commission was established by Executive Order 13345 of April 20, 1967 pursuant to the Water Resources Planning Act (79 Stat. 244). The Commission was abolished by Executive Order 12319, September 9, 1981.

Y 3.G 79/3:1/date   • **Item 1063-G**
REPORT.

Y 3.G 79/3:2 CT   • **Item 1063-G**
GENERAL PUBLICATIONS.

Y 3.G 79/3:9/v.nos.&nos.
COMMUNICATOR. v. 1– 11.   – 1981. [Monthly]

Y 3.G 79/3:10/nos.
MAUMEE RIVER BASIN, MRB- (series).

GUN FOUNDRY BOARD
(1883– 1884)

CREATION AND AUTHORITY

The Gun Foundry Board was established within the Navy Department pursuant to act of Congress, approved March 3, 1883. The Board submitted its report on February 16, 1884 and a supplemental report on December 20, 1884.

Y 3.G 95:CT
PUBLICATIONS.

ALEXANDER HAMILTON BICENTENNIAL COMMISSION
(1954– 1958)

CREATION AND AUTHORITY

The Alexander Hamilton Bicentennial Commission was established by act of Congress, approved August 20, 1954 (68 Stat. 746). The law stated that the Commission should expire upon the completion of its duties, but in no event later than January 11, 1958.

Y 3.H 18:1/date
ANNUAL REPORT.

Y 3.H 18:2 CT
GENERAL PUBLICATIONS.

NATIONAL COUNCIL ON THE HANDICAPPED
(1984–   )

CREATION AND AUTHORITY

The National Council on the Handicapped was established in the Health, Education and Welfare Department by act of November 6, 1978 (92 Stat. 2977). It was trasferred to the Education Department by act of October 17, 1979 (93 Stat. 677) and reorganized as independent agency by act of February 22, 1984 (98 Stat. 26).

INFORMATION

National Council on the Handicapped
Suite 814
800 Independence Avenue, S.W.
Washington, D.C. 20591
(202) 453-3846

Y 3.H 19:8 CT   • **Item 1063-H**
REPORTS AND PUBLICATIONS.

Includes all publications of the Council, which is the only Federal agency mandated to address, analyze, and make recommendations on issues of public policy regarding persons with disabilities regardless of age, disability type, or other individual circumstances.

HAWAIIAN COMMISSION
(1898– 1899)

CREATION AND AUTHORITY

The Hawaiian Commission was established by joint resolution of Congress, approved July 7, 1898. Reports were submitted in 1898 and 1899.

Y 3.H 31:CT
PUBLICATIONS.

NATIVE HAWAIIANS STUDY COMMISSION

Y 3.H 31/2:1/date
ANNUAL REPORT.

Y 3.H 31/2:2 CT
GENERAL PUBLICATIONS.

Y 3.H 31/2:8 CT
HANDBOOKS, MANUALS, GUIDES.

ADVISORY COUNCIL ON HISTORIC PRESERVATION
(1966–   )

CREATION AND AUTHORITY

The Advisory Council on Historic Preservation was established by Public Law 89-665, Title II, sec. 201 (a), approved October 15, 1966.

INFORMATION

Advisory Council on Historic Preservation
Room 809
1100 Pennsylvania Avenue, N.W.
Washington, D.C. 20004
(202) 786-0503
Email:achp@achp.gov
http://www.achp.gov

Y 3.H 62:1/date   • **Item 1064-A(MF)**
ANNUAL REPORT. 1st–   1969/70–

Y 3.H 62:2 CT   • **Item 1064-A**
GENERAL PUBLICATIONS.

Y 3.H 62:5   • **Item 1064-A**
NATIONAL HISTORIC PRESERVATION ACT OF 1966, AS AMENDED.

Y 3.H 62:6 CT
REGULATIONS, RULES, INSTRUCTIONS. [Irregular]

Y 3.H 62:8 CT   • **Item 1064-A**
HANDBOOKS, MANUALS, GUIDES. [Irregular]

UNITED STATES CAPITOL HISTORICAL SOCIETY

INFORMATION

United States Capitol Historical Society
200 Maryland Avenue, N.E.
Washington, D.C. 20515
(202) 543-8919

Y 3.H 62/2:8 CT   • **Item 1064-D**
HANDBOOKS, MANUALS, GUIDES. [Irregular]

Y 3.H 62/2:9/date   • **Item 1064-D**
WE THE PEOPLE' CALENDAR. [Annual]

Y 3.H 62/2:10 CT
POSTERS. [Irregular]

Y 3.H 62/2:11 CT
AUDIOVISUAL MATERIALS. [Irregular]

U.S. SUPREME COURT HISTORICAL SOCIETY

Y 3.H 62/3:2 CT   • **Item 1064-E**
GENERAL PUBLICATIONS.

WHITE HOUSE HISTORICAL ASSOCIATION

Y 3.H 62/4:2 CT • Item 1089-J
GENERAL PUBLICATIONS.

Y 3.H 62/4:8 CT • Item 1089-J
HANDBOOKS, MANUALS, AND GUIDES.

FEDERAL HOLIDAY COMMISSION

Y 3.H 71:1/date
ANNUAL REPORTS.

Y 3.H 71:2 CT • Item 1089
GENERAL PUBLICATIONS.

Y 3.H 71:12 CT • Item 1089
POSTERS.

PERMANENT COMMITTEE FOR THE OLIVER WENDELL HOLMES DEVISE
(1965–   )

CREATION AND AUTHORITY

The Permanent Committee for the Oliver Wendell Holmes Devise was established by Public Law 246, 84th Congress, 1st session, approved August 5, 1955.

INFORMATION

Permanent Committee for the
Oliver Wendell Holmes Devise
Library of Congress
Washington, D.C. 20540
(202) 287-5383

Y 3.H 73:1/date • Item 1063-D
ANNUAL REPORTS.

Y 3.H 73:2 CT • Item 1063-D
GENERAL PUBLICATIONS.

UNITED STATES HOLOCAUST MEMORIAL COUNCIL

INFORMATION

United States Holocaust Memorial Council
100 Raoul Wallenberg Pl., SW
Washington, DC 20024-2150
(202) 488-0400
Fax: (202) 488-2606
http://www.ushmm.gov

Y 3.H 74:1/date
ANNUAL REPORTS.

Y 3.H 74:2 CT • Item 1070-K-1
GENERAL PUBLICATIONS. [Irregular]

Y 3.H 74:8 CT • Item 1070-K-1
HANDBOOKS, MANUALS, GUIDES. [Irregular]

Y 3.H 74:9 CT • Item 1070-K-1
POSTERS. [Irregular]

Y 3.H 74:10/date-nos. • Item 1070-K-1
NEWSLETTER.

Y 3.H 74:11 • Item 1070-K-1
DIRECTORIES.

Y 3.H 74:12 CT • Item 1070-K-1
POSTERS.

Y 3.H 74:13 • Item 1070-K-1
BIBLIOGRAPHIES AND LISTS OF PUBLICATIONS.

HOMES COMMISSION
(1908)

Y 3.H 75:CT
PUBLICATIONS.

INTERGENCY COUNCIL ON THE HOMELESS

Y 3.H 75:1/date • Item 1089-S
ANNUAL REPORTS.

Y 3.H 75:2 CT • Item 1089-S
GENERAL PUBLICATIONS.

Y 3.H 75:8 CT • Item 1089-S
HANDBOOKS, MANUALS, GUIDES.

Y 3.H 75:15/date • Item 1089-S
COUNCIL COMMUNIQUE.

Y 3.H 75:16 • Item 1089-S
PROGRAM ALERT. [Irregular]

Y 3.H 75:17/nos. • Item 1089-S
FACT SHEETS.

COMMISSION TO SUPERVISE CONSTRUCTION OF BUILDING FOR THE OFFICES FOR THE HOUSE OF REPRESENTATIVES
(1905)

Y 3.H 81:CT
PUBLICATIONS.

OFFICE OF THE HOUSING EXPEDITER
(1947– 1951)

CREATION AND AUTHORITY

The Office of the Housing Expediter was established by Executive Order 9820 of January 11, 1947, pursuant to the Veterans Emergency Housing Act of 1946, approved May 22, 1946 (60 Stat. 208). The position of Housing Expediter was first created within the Office of War Mobilization and Reconversion (Y 3.W 19/7) on December 12, 1945. The Office of the Housing Expediter was abolished by Executive Order 10276 of July 31, 1951, and its functions transferred to the Economic Stabilization Agency (ES 1).

Y 3.H 81/2:1/date
ANNUAL REPORTS.

Y 3.H 81/2:2 CT
GENERAL PUBLICATIONS.

Y 3.H 81/2:5 CT
LAWS.

Y 3.H 81/2:6 CT
REGULATIONS, RULES, AND INSTRUCTIONS.

Y 3.H 81/2:7/date
REPORT, OFFICE OF HOUSING EXPEDITER. [Monthly]

Earlier NHA 1.13

Y 3.H 81/2:8/v.nos.
VETERANS EMERGENCY HOUSING PROGRAM: COMMUNITY ACTION REPORT TO MAYOR'S EMERGENCY HOUSING COMMITTEE.

Earlier NHA 1.12

Y 3.H 81/2:9 CT
PAPERS IN RE.

Y 3.H 81/2:10
RELEASES.

HUDSON-CHAMPLAIN CELEBRATION COMMISSION

Y 3.H 86:1/date
REPORTS.

Y 3.H 86:2 CT
GENERAL PUBLICATIONS.

NATIONAL COMMISSION FOR THE PROTECTION OF HUMAN SUBJECTS OF BIOMEDICAL AND BEHAVIORAL RESEARCH
(1977–   )

Y 3.H 88:1/date
REPORTS.

Y 3.H 88:2 CT • Item 1089
GENERAL PUBLICATIONS.

IMMIGRATION COMMISSION
(1907–1910)

CREATION AND AUTHORITY

The Joint Commission on Immigration, also known as the Immigration Commission, was established by act of Congress, approved February 20, 1907 (34 Stat. 909). By act of Congress, approved March 4, 1909 (35 Stat. 982), the termination date was set at March 1, 1910.

Y 3.Im 6:CT
PUBLICATIONS.

SELECT COMMISSION ON IMMIGRATION AND REFUGEE POLICY
(1978–1980)

CREATION AND AUTHORITY

The Select Commission on Immigration and Refugee Policy was established by Public Law 95-412, approved October 5, 1978. The final report is required to be submitted by September 30, 1980, after which the Commission will be terminated.

Y 3.Im 6/2:1/date • Item 1089
REPORT.

Y 3.Im 6/2:9/nos.
NEWSLETTER. [Monthly]
Discontinued in 1981.

INDIAN CURRENCY COMMISSION (GREAT BRITAIN)
(1893)

Y 3.In 2/1:CT
PUBLICATIONS.

INDUSTRIAL COMMISSION
(1899–1902)

Y 3.In 2/2:CT
PUBLICATIONS.

JOINT COMMISSION TO INVESTIGATE INDIAN AFFAIRS
(1914–1915)

CREATION AND AUTHORITY

The Joint Commission to Investigate Indian Affairs was established by act of Congress, approved June 30, 1913 (38 Stat. 81). The Commission ceased to function in 1915.

Y 3.In 2/3:CT
PUBLICATIONS.

COMMISSION ON INDUSTRIAL RELATIONS
(1913-1916)

CREATION AND AUTHORITY

The Commission on Industrial Relations was established by act of Congress, approved August 23, 1913 (37 Stat. 415). The Commission submitted its report in 1916.

Y 3.In 2/4:CT
GENERAL PUBLICATIONS.

COMMITTEE ON INDUSTRIAL ANALYSIS
(1936–1937)

CREATION AND AUTHORITY

The Committee on Industrial Analysis was established within the Department of Commerce by Executive Order 7323 of March 21, 1936, effective April 1, 1936, to complete the work of the Advisory Council, the Division of Business Cooperation, and the Division of Review, all of the National Recovery Administration (Y 3. N 21/8), which were abolished by the same Order. The Committee was terminated on February 17, 1937, when its final report was submitted to the President.

Y 3.In 2/5:1/date
REPORT.

Y 3.In 2/5:2 CT
GENERAL PUBLICATIONS.

INDIAN CLAIMS COMMISSION
(1946–1978)

CREATION AND AUTHORITY

The Indian Claims Commission was established by act of August 13, 1946 (60 Stat. 959). The Commission was terminated and the pending cases were transferred to the United States Court of Claims pursuant to act of October 8, 1976 (90 Stat. 1990) effective September 30, 1978.

Y 3.In 2/6:1/date • Item 1067
ANNUAL REPORTS.

Y 3.In 2/6:2 CT • Item 1067
GENERAL PUBLICATIONS.

COMMISSION ON INCREASED INDUSTRIAL USE OF AGRICULTURAL PRODUCTS
(1956)

Y 3.In 2/7:1/date
REPORTS.

Y 3.In 2/7:2 CT
GENERAL PUBLICATIONS.

NATIONAL INDUSTRIAL POLLUTION CONTROL COUNCIL
(1970–   )

CREATION AND AUTHORITY

The National Industrial Pollution Control Council was established by Executive Order 11523, dated April 9, 1970, pursuant to the National Environmental Policy Act of 1969 (P L 91-190), approved January 1, 1970.

Y 3.In 2/8:1/date • Item 1070-B-2
ANNUAL REPORT.

Y 3.In 2/8:2 CT • Item 1070-B-2
GENERAL PUBLICATIONS.

NATIONAL COUNCIL ON INDIAN OPPORTUNITY
(1968–1974)

CREATION AND AUTHORITY

The Council was established by Executive Order 11399 of March 6, 1968, to encourage and coordinate the use of Federal programs to benefit the American Indian population. It is also responsible for appraising the impact and progress of such programs and suggesting ways to improve them to fit the needs and desires of the Indian population.

Y 3.In 2/9:1/date
ANNUAL REPORT.

Y 3.In 2/9:2 CT
GENERAL PUBLICATIONS.

Y 3.In 2/9:9/v.nos.&nos.
NCIO NEWS. v. 1–   1970–   [Irregular]

Contains news of programs and meetings relative to the work of the National Council on Indian Opportunity, which provides a mechanism for involvement by the Indian people in the Federal policy and program formulation process.

NATIONAL ADVISORY COUNCIL ON INDIAN EDUCATION
(1965–   )

CREATION AND AUTHORITY

The National Advisory Council on Indian Education is authorized by section 9151 of the Elementary and Secondary Education Act of 1965, as amended.

INFORMATION

National Advisory Council on Indian Education
Office of Indian Education
Department of Education
400 Maryland Ave., SW
Washington, DC 20202
(202) 260-3774
http://www.ed.gov/offices/oese/oie/about_oie/nacie.html

Y 3.In 2/10:1/date   • **Item 1070-B-5 (MF)**
ANNUAL REPORT. 1st–   1974–

Y 3.In 2/10:2 CT   • **Item 1070-B-5**
GENERAL PUBLICATIONS.

Y 3.In 2/10:8 CT   • **Item 1070-B-5**
HANDBOOKS, MANUALS, AND GUIDES.

NATIONAL COMMISSION FOR INDUSTRIAL PEACE
(1974–   )

Y 3.In 2/11:1/date   • **Item 1070-B-4**
REPORT. 1st–   1974–

Y 3.In 2/11:2 CT
GENERAL PUBLICATIONS.

INTERNATIONAL EXCHANGE COMMISSION
(1903–1904)

CREATION AND AUTHORITY

The Commission on International Exchange was established by act of Congress, approved March 3, 1903 (32 Stat. 1138). By act of Congress, approved February 18, 1904 (33 Stat. 15), the Commission was terminated on November 1, 1904.

Y 3.In 8:CT
PUBLICATIONS.

INTERDEPARTMENTAL SOCIAL HYGIENE BOARD
(1918–1923)

CREATION AND AUTHORITY

The Interdepartmental Social Hygiene Board was established by act of Congress, approved July 9, 1918 (40 Stat. 886). By Executive Order 3874 of June 20, 1923, the Board was abolished and its functions transferred to the Public Health Service (T 27).

Y 3.In 8/2:CT
PUBLICATIONS.

INTERDEPARTMENTAL COMMITTEE TO COORDINATE HEALTH AND WELFARE ACTIVITIES
(1935–1939)

CREATION AND AUTHORITY

The Interdepartmental Committee to Coordinate Health and Welfare Activities was established by the President on August 15, 1935, and reestablished by Executive Order 7481 of October 27, 1936. The Committee ceased to function in 1939.

Y 3.In 8/3:1/date
REPORTS.

Y 3.In 8/3:2 CT
GENERAL PUBLICATIONS.

INTERDEPARTMENTAL COMMITTEE ON SCIENTIFIC RESEARCH AND DEVELOPMENT
(1947–1959)

CREATION AND AUTHORITY

The Interdepartmental Committee on Scientific Research and Development was established by Executive Order 9912 of December 24, 1947.

Y 3.In 8/4:1/date
ANNUAL REPORTS.

Y 3.In 8/4:2 CT
GENERAL PUBLICATIONS.

INTERNATIONAL DEVELOPMENT ADVISORY BOARD
(1950–1955)

CREATION AND AUTHORITY

The International Development Advisory Board was established by Executive Order 10159 of September 8, 1950, pursuant to section 409 of the Act for International Development, approved June 5, 1950. Under Executive Order 10610 of May 9, 1955, the Board was transferred to the International Cooperation Administration (S 17) in the Department of State, effective July 1, 1955.

Y 3.In 8/5:1/date
REPORTS.

Y 3.In 8/5:2 CT
GENERAL PUBLICATIONS.

INTERDEPARTMENTAL COMMITTEE ON CHILDREN AND YOUTH
(1948–   )

CREATION AND AUTHORITY

The Interdepartmental Committee on Children and Youth was organized in 1948 at the request of the President to aid in developing appropriate working relationships among Federal agencies having programs affecting the well being of children and youth and between the Federal Government and State agencies for children and youth.

Y 3.In 8/6:1   • **Item 1067-B**
ANNUAL REPORT. [Annual]

Y 3.In 8/6:2 CT   • **Item 1067-B**
GENERAL PUBLICATIONS.

INTERGOVERNMENTAL RELATIONS COMMISSION
(1953–1955)

CREATION AND AUTHORITY

The Commission on Intergovernmental Relations was established by act of Congress, approved July 10, 1953 (67 Stat. 145). The Commission was terminated by act of Congress, approved February 7, 1955 (69 Stat. 7), effective June 30, 1955.

Y 3.In 8/7:CT
PUBLICATIONS.

INTERAGENCY COMMITTEE ON WATER RESOURCES
(1954– 1956)

CREATION AND AUTHORITY

The Interagency Committee on Water Resources was established by the Interagency Agreement on Coordination of Water and Related Land Resources Activities, approved by the President on May 26, 1954 to replace the Federal Interagency River Basin Committee (Y 3. F 31/13).

Y 3.In 8/8:1/date
ANNUAL REPORTS.

Y 3.In 8/8:2 CT
GENERAL PUBLICATIONS.

Y 3.In 8/8:7/nos.
NOTES ON HYDROLOGIC ACTIVITIES, BULLETINS.
Earlier Y 3.F 31/13:3

Y 3.In 8/8:8/nos.
SEDIMENTATION BULLETIN.
Earlier Y 3.F 31/13:8

Y 3.In 8/8:9/nos.
JOINT HYDROLOGY-SEDIMENTATION BULLETINS.

Y 3.In 8/8:10/nos.
STUDY OF METHODS USED IN MEASUREMENT AND ANALYSIS OF SEDIMENT LOADS IN STREAMS, REPORTS.
Earlier Y 3.F 31/13:9

Y 3.In 8/8:11 CT
BIBLIOGRAPHIES AND LISTS OF PUBLICATIONS.

INTERDEPARTMENTAL COMMITTEE ON NARCOTICS
(1951– 1970)

CREATION AND AUTHORITY

The Interdepartmental Committee on Narcotics was established by Executive Order 10302, dated November 2, 1951. The Committee was abolished by Executive Order 11529, dated April 24, 1970.

Y 3.In 8/9:1/date
ANNUAL REPORTS.

Y 3.In 8/9:2 CT
GENERAL PUBLICATIONS.

INTERDEPARTMENTAL COMMITTEE FOR THE STUDY OF JURISDICTION OVER FEDERAL AREAS WITHIN THE STATES
(1954– 1957)

CREATION AND AUTHORITY

The Interdepartmental Committee for the Study of Jurisdiction over Federal Areas within the States was established on December 15, 1954, upon recommendation of the Attorney General, approved by the President and the Cabinet. Reports were submitted in 1956 and 1957.

Y 3.In 8/10:1/date
REPORTS.

Y 3.In 8/10:2 CT
GENERAL PUBLICATIONS.

INTERAGENCY COMMITTEE ON AGRICULTURAL SURPLUS DISPOSAL
(1954– 1956)

Y 3.In 8/11:1/date
REPORTS.

Y 3.In 8/11:2 CT
GENERAL PUBLICATIONS.

INTERDEPARTMENTAL COMMITTEE ON RADIATION PRESERVATION OF FOOD
(1956)

CREATION AND AUTHORITY

The Interdepartmental Committee on Radiation Preservation of Food was established upon the recommendation of the Secretary of Defense.

Y 3.In 8/12:1/date
REPORTS.

Y 3.In 8/12:2 CT
GENERAL PUBLICATIONS.

INTERDEPARTMENTAL COMMITTEE ON NUTRITION FOR NATIONAL DEFENSE
(1954)

CREATION AND AUTHORITY

The Interdepartmental Committee on Nutrition for National Defense was established in 1954.

Y 3.In 8/13:1/date
REPORTS.

Y 3.In 8/13:2 CT
GENERAL PUBLICATIONS.

Later FS 2.22/57

Y 3.In 8/13:6 CT
REGULATIONS, RULES, AND INSTRUCTIONS.

Y 3.In 8/13:6-2 CT
HANDBOOKS, MANUALS, GUIDES.

Y 3.In 8/13:9/date
ARMED FORCES INTERNATIONAL NUTRITION CONFERENCE [proceedings].

Earlier Y 3.In 8/13:2 Ar 5

INTERDEPARTMENTAL COMMITTEE ON CIVILIAN COMPENSATION
(1958)

CREATION AND AUTHORITY

The Interdepartmental Committee on Civilian Compensation was created by a steering committee established to make a study of civilian compensation in the Executive Branch of the Federal Government. The study was directed in a Cabinet Paper dated April 6, 1958.

Y 3.In 8/14:1/date
REPORTS.

Y 3.In 8/14:2 CT
GENERAL PUBLICATIONS.

COMMISSION ON INTERNATIONAL RULES OF JUDICIAL PROCEDURE
(1958)

CREATION AND AUTHORITY

The Commisson on International Rules of Judicial Procedure was established by Public Law 906, 85th Congress, second Session, approved September 2, 1958.

Y 3.In 8/15:1/date
ANNUAL REPORTS.

Y 3.In 8/15:2 CT
GENERAL PUBLICATIONS.

INTERAGENCY COMMITTEE ON AUTOMATIC DATA PROCESSING
(1960)

Y 3.In 8/16:1/date
REPORTS.

Y 3.In 8/16:2 CT
GENERAL PUBLICATIONS.

Y 3.In 8/16:9 CT
BIBLIOGRAPHIES AND LISTS OF PUBLICATIONS.

INTERDEPARTMENTAL COMMITTEE TO COORDINATE FEDERAL URBAN AREA ASSISTANCE PROGRAMS
(1959)

CREATION AND AUTHORITY

The Interdepartmental Committee to Coordinate Federal Urban Area Assistance Programs was established pursuant to a 1959 directive from the President.

Y 3.In 8/17:1/date
REPORTS.

Y 3.In 8/17:2 CT
GENERAL PUBLICATIONS.

INTERDEPARTMENTAL HIGHWAY SAFETY BOARD
(1960– 1970)

CREATION AND AUTHORITY

The Interdepartmental Safety Board was established by Executive Order 10898 of December 2, 1960, and amended by Executive Order 10986 of January 12, 1962. The Board was terminated by Executive Order 11515 of March 13, 1970.

Y 3.In 8/18:1/date
REPORTS.

Y 3.In 8/18:2 CT
GENERAL PUBLICATIONS.

INTERDEPARTMENTAL FEDERAL TORT CLAIMS COMMITTEE
(1960)

Y 3.In 8/19:1/date
REPORTS.

Y 3.In 8/19:2 CT
PUBLICATIONS.

INTERAGENCY COMMITTEE ON INTERNATIONAL ATHLETICS
(1963)

Y 3.In 8/20:1/date
REPORTS.

Y 3.In 8/20:2 CT
GENERAL PUBLICATIONS.

INTERDEPARTMENTAL COMMITTEE ON THE STATUS OF WOMEN
(1963– 1978)

CREATION AND AUTHORITY

The Committee was established by Executive Order 11126 of November 1, 1963, as amended by Executive Order 11221 of May 6, 1965. The Committee was terminated by Executive Order 12050 of January 15, 1978.

Y 3.In 8/21:1 • Item 1067-I
REPORT OF PROGRESS IN (year) ON THE STATUS OF WOMEN. 1st– 1964– [Annual]

Report made by the International Committee on the Status of Women and the Citizens' Advisory Council on the Status of Women to the President in accordance with Executive Order 11126, as amended. Report is for the calendar year.
Covers education, home and community, employment, labor standards, legal status of women, political and social action, and international developments. Includes a bibliography of publications mentioned in the text.

Y 3.In 8/21:2 CT • Item 1067-I
GENERAL PUBLICATIONS.

Y 3.In 8/21:7-2/date • Item 1067-I
PROGRESS-AMERICAN WOMEN.

INTERAGENCY COMMITTEE ON EXPORT EXPANSION
(1963– 1973)

CREATION AND AUTHORITY

The Interagency Committee on Export Expansion was established by Executive Order 11132 of December 12, 1963. The Committee was abolished by Executive Order 11753 of December 20, 1973 and superseded by the President's Interagency Committee on Export Expansion.

Y 3.In 8/22:1/date
ANNUAL REPORT.

Y 3.In 8/22:2 CT
GENERAL PUBLICATIONS.

INTERAGENCY COMMITTEE ON MEXICAN AMERICAN AFFAIRS
(1967)

Y 3.In 8/23:1/date • Item 1067-K
REPORTS.

Y 3.In 8/23:2 CT • Item 1067-K
GENERAL PUBLICATIONS.

Y 3.In 8/23:7/date
PRESS RELEASES.

Y 3.In 8/23:9 CT
ADDRESSES.

Y 3.In 8/23:10 CT
BIBLIOGRAPHIES AND LISTS OF PUBLICATIONS.

INTERSTATE COMMISSION ON THE POTOMAC RIVER BASIN
(1976–   )

Y 3.In 8/24:1/date
ANNUAL REPORT.

Y 3.In 8/24:2 CT
GENERAL PUBLICATIONS.

INTER-AMERICAN FOUNDATION
(1969–   )

CREATION AND AUTHORITY

The Inter-American Foundation was established as a Government corporation by act of December 30, 1969 (83 Stat. 821).

INFORMATION

Inter-American Foundation
901 Stuart St., 10th Fl.
Arlington, VA 22203
(703) 306-4301
Fax: (703) 306-4365
Email:info@iaf.gov
http://www.iaf.gov

Y 3.In 8/25 • Item 1051-D-1(P) (EL)
INTER-AMERICAN FOUNDATION. [Annual]

Y 3.In 8/25:1/date • Item 1051-D-1
ANNUAL REPORT.

Y 3.In 8/25:2 CT • Item 1051-D-1
GENERAL PUBLICATIONS. [Irregular]

Y 3.In 8/25:15/v.nos./nos. • Item 1051-D-1(P) (EL)
GRASSROOTS DEVELOPMENT: JOURNAL OF THE INTER-AMERICAN FOUNDATION. [Semiannual]

Also issued in Spanish and Portuguese.
ISSN 0733-6608

Y 3.In 8/25:16/nos. • Item 1051-D-1
COUNTRY FOCUS SERIES.

Y 3.In 8/25:17/nos. • Item 1051-D-1
SERIE DE ESTUDIOS DE PAISES. [Irregular]

INTERAGENCY COMMITTEE ON INTERMODAL CARGO
(1978–   )

Y 3.In 8/26:1/date • Item 1051-D-2
REPORT.

Y 3.In 8/26:2 CT • Item 1051-D-2
GENERAL PUBLICATIONS. [Irregular]

OFFICE OF THE FEDERAL INSPECTOR FOR THE ALASKA NATURAL GAS TRANSPORTATION SYSTEM
(1979–   )

CREATION AND AUTHORITY

The Office of the Federal Inspector for the Alaska Natural Gas Transportation System was established by Executive Order 12142 of June 21, 1979.

INFORMATION

Office of the Federal Inspector for the Alaska Natural Gas Transportation System
Room 3G064
1000 Independence Avenue, S.W.
Washington, D.C. 20585
(202) 252-4669

Y 3.In 8/27:2 CT   • Item 1089
GENERAL PUBLICATIONS.

INTERNATIONAL JOINT COMMISSION UNITED STATES AND CANADA
(1911–   )

CREATION AND AUTHORITY

The International Joint Commission was established in 1911 pursuant to the Treaty of January 11, 1909 between the United States and Great Britain.

INFORMATION

International Joint Commission
1250 23rd St., NW, Ste. 100
Washington, D.C. 20440
(202) 736-9024
Fax: (202) 467-0746
http://www.ijc.org

Y 3.In 8/28:CT   • Item 1061-F-2
REPORTS AND PUBLICATIONS.

Y 3.In 8/28:2 CT   • Item 1061-F-2
GENERAL PUBLICATIONS.

Y 3.In 8/28:8 CT
HANDBOOKS, MANUALS, GUIDES. [Irregular]

Y 3.In 8/28:9/date
GREAT LAKES WATER QUALITY BOARD REPORT. (Great Lakes Water Quality Board) [Biennial]

Y 3.In 8/28:10/date
GREAT LAKES RESEARCH ADVISORY BOARD: REPORT. [Biennial]

Y 3.In 8/28:11/date
BIENNIAL REPORT UNDER THE GREAT LAKES WATER QUALITY AGREEMENT OF 1978.

Y 3.In 8/28:12/date
GREAT LAKES SCIENCE ADVISORY BOARD: ANNUAL REPORT.

Y 3.In 8/28:13 CT
BIBLIOGRAPHIES AND LISTS OF PUBLICATIONS. [Irregular]

Y 3.In 8/28:14/date
INTERNATIONAL REFERENCE GROUP ON GREAT LAKES POLLUTION FROM LAND USE ACTIVITIES: ANNUAL PROGRESS REPORT.

Y 3.In 8/28:15/date
COMMITTEE ON THE ASSESSMENT OF HUMAN HEALTH EFFECTS OF GREAT LAKES WATER QUALITY: ANNUAL REPORT.

Y 3.In 8/28:16/date
GREAT LAKES SCIENCE ADVISORY BOARD: ANNUAL REPORT.

Y 3.In 8/28:17/v.nos.&nos.
FOCUS ON GREAT LAKES WATER QUALITY. v. 1– [Irregular]

INTERAGENCY TASK FORCE ON SMALL BUSINESS FINANCE

Y 3.In 8/29:2 CT
GENERAL PUBLICATIONS. [Irregular]

Y 3.In 8/29:9 CT
STUDIES OF SMALL BUSINESS FINANCE.

INTERPARLIAMENTARY UNION, UNITED STATES GROUP

Y 3.In 8/29-2:CT   • Item 1061-F-3
REPORTS AND PUBLICATIONS. [Irregular]

INTERAGENCY TASK FORCE ON ACID PRECIPITATION

CREATION AND AUTHORITY

The Interagency Task Force on Acid Precipitation coordinates the National Acid Precipitation Assessment Program mandated by PL 96-294.

Y 3.In 8/31:1/date   • Item 1063-L
ANNUAL REPORT.

Y 3.In 8/31:1-2   • Item 1063-L-1 (MF)
NATIONAL ACID PRECIPITATION ASSESSMENT PROGRAM, REPORT TO CONGRESS. [Biennial]

Y 3.In 8/31:2 CT   • Item 1063-L
GENERAL PUBLICATIONS.

Y 3.In 8/31:15   • Item 1063-L
NAPAP NEWSLETTER. [Quarterly]

BOARD FOR TESTING IRON, STEEL, AND OTHER METALS
(1875– 1881)

CREATION AND AUTHORITY

The Board for Testing Iron, Steel, and Other Metals was established by act of Congress, approved March 3, 1875. The Board submitted its final report in 1881.

Y 3.Ir 6:CT
PUBLICATIONS.

ISTHMIAN CANAL COMMISSION
(1899– 1902)

CREATION AND AUTHORITY

The Isthmian Canal Commission was first established on June 10, 1899, by the President under authorization from Congress on March 3, 1899. The first Commission ceased to operate in 1902. A second Isthmian Canal Commission (W 73) was established by the President in May 1904, pursuant to act of Congress, approved June 28, 1902 (32 Stat. 481).

Y 3.Is 7:CT
PUBLICATIONS.

JAMESTOWN–WILLIAMSBURG–YORKTOWN CELEBRATION COMMISSION
(1953)

CREATION AND AUTHORITY

The Jamestown-Williamsburg-Yorktown Celebration Commission was established by act of Congress, approved August 13, 1953 (67 Stat. 576), which states that the Commission will terminate upon submission of its final report.

Y 3.J 23:CT
PUBLICATIONS.

JAPAN-UNITED STATES FRIENDSHIP COMMISSION (1975–   )

CREATION AND AUTHORITY

The Japan-United States Friendship Commission was established by Public Law 94-118, approved October 20, 1975.

INFORMATION

Japan-United States Friendship Commission
1120 Vermont Ave., NW, Ste. 800
Washington, D.C. 20005
(202) 418-9800
Fax: (202) 418-9802
http://www.jusfc.gov/
commissn/commissn.html

Y 3.J 27:1/date   • Item 1061-F-1
ANNUAL REPORT.

Y 3.J 27:2 CT   • Item 1061-F-1
GENERAL PUBLICATIONS. [Irregular]

Y 3.J 27:7/v.nos./nos.   • Item 1061-F-4
THE COMMISSIONER.

JOINT PUBLICATIONS RESEARCH SERVICE (1949– 1979)

Y 3.J 66:1/date
ANNUAL REPORTS.

Y 3.J 66:2 CT
GENERAL PUBLICATIONS.

Y 3.J 66:8/nos.
JPRS (NY) REPORTS.

Y 3.J 66:9/nos.
JPRS/DC REPORTS.

Y 3.J 66:10/nos.
JPRS (DC) L- (series).

Y 3.J 66:11/nos.
JPRS (NY) L- (series).

Y 3.J 66:12/nos.
JPRS R (series).

Y 3.J 66:13/nos.
JPRS (series).

Supersedes Y 3.J 66:8 through Y 3.J 66:11. Effective July 2, 1979, the JPRS series of publications was transferred to the Foreign Broadcast Information Service and classed PrEx 7.13.
When the issuing office was changed, certain titles and sub-series also were changed.
The following sub-series were offered on an annual subscription basis:

ASIA SERIALS.

Translations on Mongolia.
Translations on North Korea.
Translations on North Vietnam.
Translations on South and East Asia.
Japan Science and Technology (U.S. Government Users Only).

COMMUNIST CHINA SERIALS.

Scientific Abstracts.
Translations on Communist China.

EASTERN EUROPE SERIALS.

Translations on Ececholslovakia (U.S. Government Users Only).
Translations on EE: Political Sociological, Military Affairs.
Translations on EE: Economic and Industrial Affairs.
Bio-Medical Sciences.
Chemistry.
Cybernetics, Computers, and Automation Technology.
Earth Sciences.
Electronics and Electrical Engineering.
Engineering and Equipment.
Materials Sciences and Metallurgy.
Physics and Mathematics.

INTERNATIONAL SERIALS.

Epidemiology Reports from the World Press.
Translations on Western Europe.
Index of LeMonde.
Translations on French Nuclear, Missile, Space and Related Military Development (U.S. Government Users Only).

LATIN AMERICA SERIALS.

Translations on Latin America.
NEAR EAST AND AFRICAN SERIALS.

ISSN 0145-9317
Translations on the Near East.
Translations on Africa.
Translations on Africa (U.S. Government users only).

USSR SERIALS.

General
Translations on USSR Political and Sociological Affairs.
Translations on USSR Military Affairs.
USA: Economics, Politics, Ideology.
Economy and Industry.
Translations on USSR Economic Affairs.
Translations on USSR Agriculture.
Translations on USSR Industrial Affairs.
Translations on USSR Resources.
Translations on USSR Trade and Services.
Scientific.
Soviet Bloc Research in Geophysics, Astronomy, and Space.
ISSN 0363-7220
Scientific Abstracts Bio-Medical Sciences.
ISSN 0145-9325
Chemistry.
Cybernetics, Computers and Automations Technology.
Electronics and Electrical Engineering.
Engineering Equipment.
Materials Science and Metallurgy.
Physics and Mathematics.
Cover-to-Cover Serials.
Herald of Communications.
Meteorology and Hydrology.
Space Biology and Medicine.
Soviet Public Health.
VESTNIK of the USSR Academy of Medical Sciences.
VESTNIK of the USSR Academy of Sciences.

Y 3.J 66:14/nos.
USSR AND EASTERN EUROPEAN SCIENTIFIC ABSTRACTS, GEOPHYSICS, ASTRONOMY, AND SPACE. [Biweekly]

Prior to 358 entitled Soviet-Bloc Research in Geophysics, Astronomy, and Space.
Supersedes C 41.40

Y 3.J 66:15/date
CATALOG OF CURRENT JOINT PUBLICATIONS RESEARCH PUBLICATIONS.

JOINT RESEARCH AND DEVELOPMENT BOARD (1946– 1947)

CREATION AND AUTHORITY

The Joint Research and Development Board was established by charter of Secretaries of War and Navy on June 6, 1946, to coordinate all research and development activities of joint interest to War and Navy Departments. The Board was abolished by the National Security Act of 1947 (61 Stat. 506) and its functions transferred to the newly created Research and Development Board (M 6).

Y 3.J 66/2:1/date
ANNUAL REPORT.

Y 3.J 66/2:2 CT
AL PUBLICATIONS.

INTERDEPARTMENTAL COUNCIL TO COORDINATE ALL FEDERAL JUVENILE DELINQUENCY PROGRAMS (1973–   )

Y 3.J 98:1/date   • Item 1089
ANNUAL REPORT.

Y 3.J 98:2 CT   • Item 1089
GENERAL PUBLICATIONS.

Y 3.J 98:8 CT
HANDBOOKS, MANUALS, GUIDES.

INTERAGENCY LAND ACQUISITION CONFERENCE (1971–   )

CREATION AND AUTHORITY

The Interagency Land Acquisition Conference was established on an informal basis and is composed of members of various Government agencies which work in land acquisition, or with real property.

Y 3.L 22:1/date
ANNUAL REPORTS.

Y 3.L 22:2 CT
GENERAL PUBLICATIONS.

Y 3.L 22:8 CT   • Item 1089
HANDBOOKS, MANUALS, GUIDES.

COMMISSION TO REVISE AND CODIFY THE LAWS OF THE UNITED STATES
(1899–1906)

CREATION AND AUTHORITY

The Commission to Revise and Codify Criminal and Penal Laws was established by act of Congress, approved June 4, 1897 (30 Stat. 58). By acts of Congress, approved March 3, 1899 (30 Stat. 1116) and March 3, 1901 (31 Stat. 1181), the duties were enlarged to the revision of all laws of a permanent or general nature. The name was changed to Commission to Revise and Codify the Laws of the United States when the duties were enlarged. The Commission submitted its final report on December 15, 1906.

Y 3.L 44:CT
PUBLICATIONS.

LEGAL SERVICES CORPORATION
(1974–   )

INFORMATION

Legal Services Corporation
750 First St., NE, 10th Fl.
Washington, DC 20002-4250
(202) 336-8800
Fax: (202) 336-8959
Email:info@lsc.gov
http://www.lsc.gov

Y 3.L 52:1   **• Item 1089-A-6 (EL)**
OFFICE OF INSPECTOR GENERAL, SEMIANNUAL REPORT TO THE CONGRESS.

Y 3.L 52:1/2   **• Item 1089-A-7 (EL)**
COMMENTS ON THE OFFICE OF INSPECTOR GENERAL'S SEMIANNUAL REPORT TO THE CONGRESS.

Y 3.L 52:2   **• Item 1089-A-5**
GENERAL PUBLICATIONS.

LEWIS AND CLARK TRAIL COMMISSION
(1964–1969)

CREATION AND AUTHORITY

The Lewis and Clark Trail Commission was established by act of October 6, 1964 (78 Stat. 1005). The Commission submitted its final report in October 1969 and ceased to exist.

Y 3.L 58:1/date
REPORTS.

Y 3.L 58:2 CT
GENERAL PUBLICATIONS.

Y 3.L 58:7
PRESS RELEASES.

NATIONAL COMMISSION ON LIBRARIES AND INFORMATION SCIENCE
(1970–   )

CREATION AND AUTHORITY

The National Commission on Libraries and Information Science was established by Public Law 91-345, approved July 20, 1970.

INFORMATION

National Commission on Libraries
and Information Science
1110 Vermont Ave., NW, Ste. 820
Washington, DC 20005-3552
(202) 606-9200
Fax: (202) 606-9203
http://www.nclis.gov

Y 3.L 61:1/date   **• Item 1061-F (EL)**
ANNUAL REPORTS. 1st–   1971-1972–

Y 3.L 61:2 CT   **• Item 1061-F**
GENERAL PUBLICATIONS.

FEDERAL INTERAGENCY FIELD LIBRARIANS WORKSHOP
(1972–1974)

Y 3.L 61/2:1/date
ANNUAL REPORT.

Y 3.L 61/2:2 CT
GENERAL PUBLICATIONS.

Y 3.L 61/2:9/date
PROCEEDINGS OF THE ANNUAL FEDERAL INTERAGENCY FIELD LIBRARIANS WORKSHOP. 1st–3rd. 1972–1974.

LINCOLN SESQUICENTENNIAL COMMISSION
(1957–1960)

CREATION AND AUTHORITY

The Lincoln Sesquicentennial Commission was established by act of Congress, approved September 2, 1957. The Commission terminated on March 1, 1960.

Y 3.L 63:1/date
REPORTS.

Y 3.L 63:2 CT
GENERAL PUBLICATIONS.

Y 3.L 63:7/date
PRESS RELEASES.

NATIONAL INSTITUTE FOR LITERACY
(1991–   )

CREATION AND AUTHORITY

The National Institute for Literacy was established by the National Literacy Act of 1991. It was reauthorized under the Workforce Investment Act of 1998.

INFORMATION

National Institute for Literacy
1775 I Street, NW, Ste. 730
Washington, DC 20006-2401
(202) 233-2025
Fax: (202) 233-2050
http://www.nifl.gov

Y 3.L 71:1 date   **• Item 1089-V (MF)**
ANNUAL REPORT.

Y 3.L 71:2 CT   **• Item 1089-V**
GENERAL PUBLICATIONS.

Y 3.L 71:8   **• Item 1089-V**
HANDBOOKS, MANUALS AND GUIDES.

Y 3.L 71:10 CT   **• Item 1089-V-1**
DIRECTORIES.

Y 3.L 71:15/v.nos.&nos.   **• Item 1089-V**
LITERACY NEWS. [Monthly]

Y 3.L 71:16/v.nos./nos.   **• Item 1089-V-2**
LITERACY LEADER FELLOWSHIP PROGRAM REPORTS (series).

Y 3.L 71:17   **• Item 1089-V-3 (EL)**
STATE POLICY UPDATES.

Y 3.L 71:18   **• Item 1089-V-3 (EL)**
POLICY UPDATES.

Y 3.L 71:19   **• Item 1089-V-3 (E)**
ELECTRONIC PRODUCTS. (Misc.)

Y 3.L 71:20   **• Item 1089-V-4 (EL)**
EFF HOT TOPICS. [Quarterly]

Y 3.L 71:21   **• Item 1089-V-5**
LINKAGES. [Semiannual]

LOWELL HISTORIC CANAL DISTRICT COMMISSION
(1975–1977)

CREATION AND AUTHORITY

The Lowell Historic Canal District Commission was established by act of January 4, 1975 (88 Stat. 2330). The Commission expired in January 1977 pursuant to terms of the act.

Y 3.L 95:1/date   **• Item 1089**
REPORT. 1st–   1977–

Y 3.L 95:2 CT   **• Item 1089**
GENERAL PUBLICATIONS. [Irregular]

JAMES MADISON MEMORIAL COMMISSION
(1960–   )

CREATION AND AUTHORITY

The James Madison Memorial Commission was established by Public Law 86-417, approved April, 8, 1960.

Y 3.M 26:1/date
REPORTS.

Y 3.M 26:2 CT
GENERAL PUBLICATIONS.

NATIONAL COMMISSION FOR MANPOWER POLICY
(1973– 1978)

CREATION AND AUTHORITY

The National Commission for Manpower Policy was succeeded by the National Commission for Employment Policy (Y 3.E c 7/3) established by Public Law 95-524 (92 Stat. 2002), approved October 27, 1978.

Y 3.M 31:1/nos.
ANNUAL REPORT. 1st–   1975–

Later Y 3.Em 7/3:1

Y 3.M 31:2 CT
GENERAL PUBLICATIONS.

Later Y 3.Em 7/3:2

Y 3.M 31:7/date
NEW RELEASES.

Y 3.M 31:9/nos.
SPECIAL REPORTS. 1–   [Irregular]

Later Y 3.Em 7/3:9

Y 3.M 31:10/nos.
REPORTS (numbered).

MARITIME ADVISORY COMMITTEE
(1964– 1968)

CREATION AND AUTHORITY

The Maritime Advisory Committee was established by Executive Order 11156 of June 17, 1964, to consider matters of Federal maritime policy, including those policies and practices which may be followed by labor, management, or the Government for strengthening the trade, national defense, manpower, and labor relations of the maritime industry. The Committee was terminated by Executive Order 11427 of September 4, 1968.

Y 3.M 33:1/date
REPORT.

Y 3.M 33:2/CT
GENERAL PUBLICATIONS.

MARIHUANA AND DRUG ABUSE COMMISSION
(1970–   )

CREATION AND AUTHORITY

The Marihuana and Drug Abuse Commission was established by Public Law 91-513, approved October 27, 1970.

Y 3.M 33/2:1/date   • **Item 1089**
REPORT.

Y 3.M 33/2:2 CT   • **Item 1089**
GENERAL PUBLICATIONS.

MARINE MAMMAL COMMISSION
(1972–   )

CREATION AND AUTHORITY

The Marine Mammal Commission was established by the Marine Mammal Protection Act of 1972 (P.L. 92-522).

INFORMATION

Marine Mammal Commission
4340 East West Highway, Ste. 905
Bethesda, MD 20814
(301) 504-0087
Fax: (301) 504-0099
http://www.mmc.gov

Y 3.M 33/3:1/date   • **Item 1064-C (MF)**
ANNUAL REPORT.

Y 3.M 33/3:2 CT   • **Item 1064-C**
GENERAL PUBLICATIONS. [Irregular]

Y 3.M 33/3:9/nos.   • **Item 1064-C (MF)**
REPORTS, MMC (series). [Irregular]

Y 3.M 33/3:9-2/date   • **Item 1064-C (MF)**
SURVEY OF FEDERALLY-FUNDED MARINE MAMMAL RESEARCH AND STUDIES. [Annual]

Earlier Y 3.M 33/3:9

JOHN MARSHALL BICENTENNIAL CELEBRATION COMMISSION
(1954– 1955)

CREATION AND AUTHORITY

The United States Commission for the Celebration of the Two Hundredth Anniversary of the Birth of John Marshall, also known as the John Marshall Bicentennial Celebration Commission, was established by act of Congress, approved August 13, 1954 (68 Stat. 702), which stated that the Commission was to expire on December 31, 1955.

Y 3.M 35:CT
PUBLICATIONS.

NATIONAL COMMISSION ON MATERIALS POLICY
(1970–   )

CREATION AND AUTHORITY

The National Commission on Materials Policy was established by Public Law 91-512, approved October 26, 1970.

Y 3.M 41:1/date
ANNUAL REPORT.

Y 3.M 41:2 CT   • **Item 1089**
GENERAL PUBLICATIONS.

MEDIATION COMMISSION
(1917– 1918)

Y 3.M 46:CT
PUBLICATIONS.

COUNCIL ON GRADUATE MEDICAL EDUCATION
(1987–   )

CREATION AND AUTHORITY

The Council on Graduate Medical Education was established by Title 7 of the PHS Act in Section 709 (H), as amended by PL 99-272, to advise and make recommendations to the Secretary of Health and Human Services on graduate medical education.

INFORMATION

Council on Graduate Medical Education
Division of Medicine & Dentistry
Bureau of Health Professions
Health Resources & Services Administration
U.S. Dept. of Health & Human Services
5600 Fishers Lane, Rm. 9A-21
Rockville, MD 20867
(301) 443-6326
Fax: 443-8890
http://www.cogme.gov

Y 3.M 46/2:1/date   • **Item 1061-P**
ANNUAL REPORT.

Y 3.M 46/2:2 CT   • **Item 1061-P**
GENERAL PUBLICATIONS. [Irregular]

MEDICARE PAYMENT ADVISORY COMMISSION
(1997–   )

CREATION AND AUTHORITY

The Medicare Payment Advisory Commission (Med PAC) was established by the Balanced Budget Act of 1997 (P.L. 105-33) as an independent federal body to advise the U.S. Congress on issues affecting the Medicare program.

INFORMATION

Medicare Payment Advisory Commission
601 New Jersey Ave., NW, Ste. 9000
Washington, DC 20001-2021
(202) 653-7220
http://www.medpac.gov

Y 3.M 46/3:1   • Item 1050 (EL)
MEDPAC REPORT TO CONGRESS. [Semiannual]

Y 3.M 46/3:2   • Item 1150-A
GENERAL PUBLICATIONS.

MERCHANT MARINE COMMISSION
(1904–1905)

CREATION AND AUTHORITY

The Merchant Marine Commission was established by act of Congress, approved April 28, 1904 (33 Stat. 561). The Commission submitted its report in 1905.

Y 3.M 53:CT
PUBLICATIONS.

MERCHANT MARINE AND DEFENSE COMMISSION

Y 3.M 53/2:2 CT   • Item 1061-N
GENERAL PUBLICATIONS.

UNITED STATES METRIC BOARD
(1975–1982)

CREATION AND AUTHORITY

The United States Metric Board was established by the Metric Conversion Act of 1975, P.L. 94-168 (89 Stat. 1007; 15 U.S.C. 205d). The Board was terminated on October 1, 1982 due to lack of funding.

Y 3.M 56:1/date
ANNUAL REPORT.

Y 3.M 56:2 CT   • Item 1089
GENERAL PUBLICATIONS. [Irregular]

MIGRATORY BIRD CONSERVATION COMMISSION
(1929–   )

CREATION AND AUTHORITY

The Migratory Bird Conservation Commission was established by the Migratory Bird Conservation Act of February 18, 1929 (45 Stat. 1222).

INFORMATION

Migratory Bird Conservation Commission
4401 North Fairfax Dr.
Mail Stop ARLSQ-622
Arlington, VA 22203-1610
(703) 358-1716
http://www.realty.fns.gov/mbcc.html

Y 3.M 58:1/date   • Item 1061-H-4
ANNUAL REPORT.

Y 3.M 58:2 CT   • Item 1061-H
GENERAL PUBLICATIONS.

COMMISSION FOR THE STUDY OF INTERNATIONAL MIGRATION AND COOPERATIVE ECONOMIC DEVELOPMENT

Y 3.M 58/2:1/date
ANNUAL REPORTS.

Y 3.M 58/2:2 CT   • Item 1089
GENERAL PUBLICATIONS.

COMMISSION TO EXAMINE THE MILITARY ACADEMY
(1860)

Y 3.M 59:CT
PUBLICATIONS.

FEDERAL MINE SAFETY AND HEALTH REVIEW COMMISSION
(1978–   )

INFORMATION

Federal Mine Safety and Health Review Commission
Sixth Floor
1730 K Street, N.W.
Washington, D.C. 20006
(202) 653-5633
Fax: (202) 653-5030
E-Mail:info@fmshrc.gov
http://www.fmshrc.gov

Y 3.M 66:1/date
ANNUAL REPORT.

Y 3.M 66:2 CT
GENERAL PUBLICATIONS. [Irregular]

Y 3.M 66:9/v.nos./nos.   • Item 1061-H-1
DECISIONS. [Monthly]

Y 3.M 66:9-2/date   • Item 1061-H-2
FEDERAL MINE SAFETY AND HEALTH REVIEW COMMISSION INDEX. [Quarterly]

Provides an index to the Decisions (Y 3. M 66:9).

MINIMUM WAGE STUDY COMMISSION

Y 3.M 66/2:1/date
ANNUAL REPORT.

Y 3.M 66/2:2 CT
GENERAL PUBLICATIONS. [Irregular]

MISSOURI BASIN INTER-AGENCY COMMITTEE
(1945–1972)

CREATION AND AUTHORITY

The Missouri Basin Inter-Agency Committee was established in April 1945, by the Federal Inter-Agency River Basin Committee. The Committee was absorbed by the Missouri River Basin Commission on March 22, 1972.

Y 3.M 69:1/date   • Item 607
ANNUAL REPORT ON PROGRESS. 1959–

Y 3.M 69:2 CT   • Item 607
GENERAL PUBLICATIONS.

Y 3.M 69:8/date   • Item 607
ANNUAL REPORT ON PROGRAMMING.

Earlier Y 3.M 69:2 L 22

Y 3.M 69:9/date   • Item 607
COMPREHENSIVE FRAMEWORK STUDY, MISSOURI RIVER BASIN.

MISSOURI RIVER BASIN COMMISSION
(1972–1981)

CREATION AND AUTHORITY

The Commission was abolished by Executive Order 12319, September 9, 1981.

Y 3.M 69/2:1/date   • Item 607
REPORT.

Y 3.M 69/2:2 CT   • Item 607
GENERAL PUBLICATIONS.

Y 3.M 69/2:3/v.nos.&nos.
MRBC BASIC BULLETIN.

MONETARY COMMISSION
(1876)

CREATION AND AUTHORITY

The United States Monetary Commission, also known as the Silver Commission of 1876, was established by joint resolution of Congress, approved August 15, 1876. The Commission submitted its report in 1876.

Y 3.M 74:CT
PUBLICATIONS

MONITORED RETRIEVABLE
STORAGE REVIEW COMMISSION

Y 3.M 74/2:1/date
ANNUAL REPORTS.

Y 3.M 74/2:2 CT   • **Item 1089**
GENERAL PUBLICATIONS.

MORTGAGE INTEREST RATES
COMMISSION
(1968– 1969)

CREATION AND AUTHORITY

The Mortgage Interest Rates Commission was established by Public Law 90-301, approved May 7, 1968.

Y 3.M 84:1   • **Item 1089**
REPORT. 1–   1969–   [Annual]

INTERAGENCY TASK FORCE ON
MOTOR VEHICLE GOALS
BEYOND 1980
(1977–   )

Y 3.M 85:1/date
ANNUAL REPORT.

Y 3.M 85:2 CT
GENERAL PUBLICATIONS.

MOTOR CARRIER RATEMAKING
STUDY COMMISSION

INFORMATION

Motor Carrier Ratemaking
  Study Commission
100 Indiana Avenue, N.W.
Washington, D.C. 20004
(202) 724-9600

Y 3.M 85/2:1/date
ANNUAL REPORT.

Y 3.M 85/2:2 CT
GENERAL PUBLICATIONS.

MUSCLE SHOALS COMMISSION
(1931)

CREATION AND AUTHORITY

The Muscle Shoals Commission was established in 1931. The Commission submitted its report on November 14, 1931.

Y 3.M 97:CT
PUBLICATIONS.

NATIONAL NARCOTICS
INTELLIGENCE CONSUMERS
COMMITTEE
(1978–   )

Y 3.N 16:1/date   • **Item 1093**
REPORT.

Y 3.N 16:2 CT   • **Item 1093**
GENERAL PUBLICATIONS. [Irregular]

COMMISSION ON
NATURALIZATION
(1905)

CREATION AND AUTHORITY

The Commission on Naturalization was established by Executive Order 296 of March 1, 1905. The Commission submitted its report on November 8, 1905.

Y 3.N 21/1:CT
PUBLICATIONS.

NATIONAL MONETARY
COMMISSION
(1908– 1912)

CREATION AND AUTHORITY

The National Monetary Commission was established by act of Congress, approved May 30, 1908 (35 Stat. 552). The Commission ceased to exist in 1912.

Y 3.N 21/2:CT
PUBLICATIONS.

NATIONAL WATERWAYS
COMMISSION
(1909– 1911)

CREATION AND AUTHORITY

The National Waterways Commission was established by act of Congress, approved March 3, 1909 (35 Stat. 818). By act of Congress, approved February 27, 1911, the Commission was terminated on November 4, 1911.

Y 3.N 21/3:CT
PUBLICATIONS.

NATIONAL COAST-DEFENSE
BOARD
(1905– 1906)

CREATION AND AUTHORITY

The National Coast Defense Board was established by the President on January 31, 1905. The Board submitted its final report on February 1, 1906.

Y 3.N 21/4:CT
PUBLICATIONS.

NATIONAL ADVISORY
COMMITTEE FOR AERONAUTICS
(1915– 1958)

CREATION AND AUTHORITY

The National Advisory Committee for Aeronautics was established by act of Congress, approved March 3, 1915 (38 Stat. 930), as amended. The Committee was abolished by act approved July 29, 1958 (72 Stat. 432) and its functions transferred to the newly established National Aeronautics and Space Administration (NAS 1).

Y 3.N 21/5:1/date
ANNUAL REPORTS.

Y 3.N 21/5:2 CT
GENERAL PUBLICATIONS.

Y 3.N 21/5:3
BULLETINS.

Y 3.N 21/5:4
CIRCULARS.

Y 3.N 21/5:5/nos.
REPORTS (technical: numbered).

Y 3.N 21/5:6/nos.
TECHNICAL NOTES.

Y 3.N 21/5:7/date
BIBLIOGRAPHY OF AERONAUTICS.

Y 3.N 21/5:8/nos.
TECHNICAL MEMORANDUMS.

Y 3.N 21/5:9/nos.
AIRCRAFT CIRCULARS.

Y 3.N 21/5:10/nos.
MISCELLANEOUS PAPERS.

Y 3.N 21/5:11/nos.
WARTIME REPORTS.

Y 3.N 21/5:12/nos.
WARTIME REPORT RELEASE LISTS. [Monthly]

Y 3.N 21/5:13/nos.
[LIST OF TECHNICAL NOTES AND TECHNICAL MEMO-
RANDUMS]. [Monthly]

Y 3.N 21/5:14/nos.
RESEARCH ABSTRACTS.

Y 3.N 21/5:15/nos.
RESEARCH MEMORANDUM, RM (series).

Y 3.N 21/5:16
AGARD PUBLICATIONS.

Y 3.N 21/5:17/date
INDEX OF NACA TECHNICAL PUBLICATIONS.
    [Annual]

    Earlier Y 3.N 21/5:2 T 22

NATIONAL FOREST
RESERVATION COMMISSION
(1911– 1976)

CREATION AND AUTHORITY

    The National Forest Commission was estab-
lished by the act of March 1, 1911 (36 Stat. 962).
The Commission was abolished by act of October
22, 1976 (90 Stat 2961) and its functions transferred to the Secretary of Agriculture.

Y 3.N 21/6:1/date
ANNUAL REPORTS.

Y 3.N 21/6:2 CT
GENERAL PUBLICATIONS.

NATIONAL COMMISSION ON LAW
OBSERVANCE AND
ENFORCEMENT
(1929– 1931)

CREATION AND AUTHORITY

    The National Commission on Law Observance
and Enforcement was established by the President pursuant to the act of Congress, approved
March 4, 1929. The Commission ceases to function in August 1931.

Y 3.N 21/7:1/date
REPORTS.

Y 3.N 21/7:2 CT
GENERAL PUBLICATIONS.

Y 3.N 21/7:3
BULLETINS.

Y 3.N 21/7:4
CIRCULARS.

Y 3.N 21/7:5/nos.
PUBLICATIONS.

Y 3.N 21/7:6/v.nos
REPORTS (compilation of publications).

    Limited edition.

NATIONAL RECOVERY
ADMINISTRATION
(1933– 1935)

CREATION AND AUTHORITY

    The National Recovery Administration was es-
tablished by the President on June 16, 1933,
pursuant to the National Industrial Recovery Act
(48 Stat. 194). The Administration was terminated
by Executive Order 7252 of December 21, 1935.

Y 3.N 21/8:1/date
ANNUAL REPORTS.

Y 3.N 21/8:2 CT
GENERAL PUBLICATIONS.

Y 3.N 21/8:3/nos.
BULLETINS.

Y 3.N 21/8:4
CIRCULARS.

Y 3.N 21/8:5
LAWS.

Y 3.N 21/8:6 CT
REGULATIONS.

    Includes rules.

Y 3.N 21/8:7 CT
CODES OF FAIR COMPETITION.

    Y 3.N 21/8:7 at (code nos.)
    – APPROVED CODES.

Y 3.N 21/8:8 CT
POSTERS.

Y 3.N 21/8:9/nos.
NRA NEWS. [Weekly]

Y 3.N 21/8:10/nos.
BLUE EAGLE LETTERS.

Y 3.N 21/8:11/nos.
COMPLIANCE BOARDS INSTRUCTIONS.
    Pubs. desig. CB-nos.

Y 3.N 21/8:12/nos.
RETAIL BULLETINS.

Y 3.N 21/8:13/nos.
PRESS INTELLIGENCE BULLETINS. [Daily]
    Later PI 1.3

Y 3.N 21/8:14 CT
ADDRESSES.

Y 3.N 21/8:15/nos.
FOOD AND GROCERY BULLETINS.

Y 3.N 21/8:16 CT
CONSUMERS' ADVISORY BOARD. GENERAL
PUBLICATIONS.

Y 3.N 21/8:17 (code nos.).
LABOR PROVISIONS FOR INDUSTRIES (Posters).

Y 3.N 21/8:18/nos.
MILESTONES ALONG RECOVERY HIGHWAY. [Semi-
weekly]

Y 3.N 21/8:19/vol.
BLUE EAGLE. [Weekly]

Y 3.N 21/8:20/nos.
LEGAL RESEARCH BULLETINS.

Y 3.N 21/8:21/date
NEWS LETTERS TO SALESMEN.
    Slightly varying titles.

Y 3.N 21/8:22/nos.
CONSUMER. [Biweekly]

    Successor to Consumer Notes, (Y 3. N 21/
9:8).
    Maps (Study of natural areas of trade) is
cancelled.

Y 3.N 21/8:23/nos.
EVIDENCE STUDIES.

Y 3.N 21/8:24/code nos.
STATISTICAL MATERIALS.

Y 3.N 21/8:25/nos.
WORK MATERIALS.

Y 3.N 21/8:26/nos.
CONSUMER DIVISION REPORTS.
    Processed. Confidential.

NATIONAL EMERGENCY
COUNCIL
(1933– 1939)

CREATION AND AUTHORITY

    The National Emergency Council was estab-
lished by Executive Order 6433-A of November
17, 1933. The Council was abolished by Reorganization Plan No. 2 of 1939, effective July 1,
1939.

Y 3.N 21/9:1/date
ANNUAL REPORTS.

Y 3.N 21/9:2 CT
GENERAL PUBLICATIONS.

Y 3.N 21/9:3/nos.
BULLETINS (Consumers' Division).

Y 3.N 21/9:7/nos.
NOTES AND SUGGESTIONS. [Monthly]

Y 3.N 21/9:8/vol.
CONSUMER NOTES. [Monthly]
Superseded by Y 3.N 21/8:22

Y 3.N 21/9:9 CT
DIRECTORY OF FEDERAL AGENCIES AND DEPART-
MENTS IN STATES.
Later Pr 32.207

Y 3.N 21/9:10 CT
STATE AND NATIONAL REPORTS.
Later Pr 32.211

Y 3.N 21/9:11 CT/date
REPORT OF COORDINATION MEETING OF FEDERAL
AGENCIES (by States).

Y 3.N 21/9:12 CT
NATIONAL EMERGENCY COUNCIL (States).

NATIONAL LABOR BOARD
(1933–1934)

CREATION AND AUTHORITY

The National Labor Board was established by
the President on August 5, 1933. The Board was
superseded by the first National Labor Relations
Board (Y 3.N 21/13), established by Executive
Order 6763 of June 29, 1934.

Y 3.N 21/10:1/date
ANNUAL REPORTS.

Y 3.N 21/10:2 CT
GENERAL PUBLICATIONS.

NATIONAL RECOVERY REVIEW
BOARD
(1934)

CREATION AND AUTHORITY

The National Review Board was established
by Executive Order 6632 of March 7, 1934. The
Board was abolished by Executive Order 6771 of
June 30, 1934.

Y 3.N 21/11:1/date
ANNUAL REPORTS.

Y 3.N 21/11:2 CT
GENERAL PUBLICATIONS.

NATIONAL RESOURCES
COMMITTEE
(1935–1939)

CREATION AND AUTHORITY

The National Resources Board was established by Executive Order 6777 of June 30, 1934,
to succeed the National Planning Board (Y 3.F
31/4:8) which was abolished. Executive Order
7065 of June 7, 1935, effective June 15, 1935,
replaced the National Resources Board with the
National Resources Committee. By Reorganization Plan No. 1 of 1939, effective July 1, 1939,
the National Resources Committee was combined
with the Federal Employment Stabilization Office
(C 26) of the Department of Commerce to form
the National Resources Planning Board (Pr
32.300).

Y 3.N 21/12:1/date
ANNUAL REPORTS. [Progress Reports]
Later Pr 32.301

Y 3.N 21/12:2 CT
GENERAL PUBLICATIONS.

Y 3.N 21/12:3 let.nos.
BULLETINS.

Y 3.N 21/12:4
CIRCULARS.
Later 32.304

Y 3.N 21/12:9/date and CT
STATE PLANNING ACTIVITIES PROGRESS RE-
PORTS.

Y 3.N 21/12:10 CT
INVENTORY OF WATER RESOURCES.

Y 3.N 21/12:11/nos.
BIBLIOGRAPHY OF REPORTS BY STATE AND
REGIONAL PLANNING ORGANIZAIONS: RE-
PORTS RECEIVED IN LIBRARY OF NATIONAL
RESOURCES COMMITTEE.

Y 3.N 21/12:12/nos
DRAINAGE BASIN COMMITTEE REPORTS.

Y 3.N 21/12:13 CT
ADDRESSES.

Y 3.N 21/12:14/nos.
HOUSING MONOGRAPH SERIES.

Y 3.N 21/12:15/nos.
WEEKLY SUMMARY OF FEDERAL LEGISLATION
RELATING TO NATIONAL RESOURCES COMMIT-
TEE, ACTIVITIES BULLETINS.

Y 3.N 21/12:16/date
MONTHLY REPORTS ON FEDERAL WATER
RESOURCES INVESTIGATIONS AND CON-
STRUCTION PROJECTS.
Later Pr 32.308

NATIONAL LABOR RELATIONS
BOARD
(1934–1935)

CREATION AND AUTHORITY

The National Labor Relations Board was established by Executive Order 6763 of June 29,
1934, pursuant to the public resolution of June
19, 1934 (48 Stat. 1183), to succeed the National
Labor Board (Y 3.N 21/10). The Board was superseded by a second National Labor Relations Board
(LR 1), established by the National Labor Relations Act, approved July 5, 1935 (49 Stat. 449).

Y 3.N 21/13:1/date
ANNUAL REPORTS.
Later LR 1.1

Y 3.N 21/13:2 CT
GENERAL PUBLICATIONS.
Later LR 1.2

Y 3.N 21/13:3/nos.
BULLETINS.
Later LR 1.3

Y 3.N 21/13:4
CIRCULARS.

Y 3.N 21/13:5 CT
LAWS.
Later LR 1.5

Y 3.N 21/13:6 CT
REGULATIONS.
Later LR 1.6

Y 3.N 21/13:7
MAPS.

Y 3.N 21/13:8
POSTERS.

Y 3.N 21/13:9/date
DECISIONS.

Later LR 1.8

Y 3.N 21/13:10/date
REPORTS. [Monthly]

Y 3.N 21/13:11 CT
PAPERS IN RE.

Later LR 1.9

NATIONAL YOUTH
ADMINISTRATION
(1935–1939)

CREATION AND AUTHORITY

The National Youth Administration was established within the Works Progress Administration
by Executive Order 7086 of June 26, 1935, pursuant to the Emergency Relief Appropriation Act
of 1935, approved April 8, 1935 (48 Stat. 115).
The Administration was transferred to the Federal
Security Agency (FS 6) by Reorganization Plan
No. 1 of 1939, effective July 1, 1939.

Y 3.N 21/14:1/date
ANNUAL REPORTS.

Later FS 6.1

Y 3.N 21/14:2 CT
GENERAL PUBLICATIONS.

Later FS 6.2

Y 3.N 21/14:3/nos.
BULLETINS.

Y 3.N 21/14:4/nos.
CIRCULARS.

Y 3.N 21/14:7/nos.
LETTERS TO STATE YOUTH DIRECTORS.

Pubs desig. Y-nos.
Later FS 6.7

Y 3.N 21/14:8/nos.
INFORMATION CIRCULARS.

Pubs. desig. NYA-nos.

Y 3.N 21/14:9/date
HANDBOOK OF PROCEDURES.

Y 3.N 21/14:10/nos
HANDBOOK OF PROCEDURES LETTERS.

Y 3.N 21/14:11/nos.
TECHNICAL INFORMATION CIRCULARS.

Later FS 6.14

NATIONAL INTERREGIONAL HIGHWAY COMMITTEE
(1941– 1944)

CREATION AND AUTHORITY

The National Interregional Highway Committee was established by the President on April 14, 1941. The Committee submitted its report in 1944.

Y 3.N 21/15:CT
PUBLICATIONS.

NATIONAL ADVISORY COUNCIL ON INTERNATIONAL MONETARY AND FINANCIAL POLICIES
(1966–   )

CREATION AND AUTHORITY

The National Advisory Council on International Monetary and Financial Problems was established originally as a statutory body by the Bretton Woods Agreements Act of July 31, 1945 and later defined in Executive Order 10033 of February 8, 1949. The Council was reestablished as the National Advisory Council on International Monetary and Financial Policies by Executive Order 11269 of February 14, 1966.
INFORMATION

National Advisory Council on International Monetary and Financial Policies
Room 5455, Main Treasury Building
Washington, D.C. 20220
(202) 566-5227

Y 3.N 21/16:1/date   • Item 1070-K
ANNUAL REPORTS.

Y 3.N 21/16:2 CT
GENERAL PUBLICATIONS.

NATIONAL SECURITY COUNCIL
(1947– 1949)

CREATION AND AUTHORITY

The National Security Council was established as an independent agency by the National Security Act of 1947, approved July 26, 1947 (61 Stat. 497). Reorganization Plan No. 4 of 1949, effective August 20, 1949, transferred it to the Executive Office of the President (Pr 33.600).

Y 3.N 21/17:1/date
ANNUAL REPORTS.

Later Pr 33.601

Y 3.N 21/17:2 CT
GENERAL PUBLICATIONS.

Later Pr 33.602

CENTRAL INTELLIGENCE AGENCY
(1947– 1949)

CREATION AND AUTHORITY

The Central Intelligence Agency was established within the National Security Council on September 20, 1947, pursuant to the National Security Act of 1947, approved July 26, 1947 (61 Stat. 498), succeeding the National Intelligence Authority. Reorganization Plan No. 4 of 1949, effective August 20, 1949, transferred the Agency to the Executive Office of the President (Pr 33.650).

Y 3.N 21/17:101/date
ANNUAL REPORTS.

Later Pr 33.651

Y 3.N 21/17:102 CT
GENERAL PUBLICATIONS.

Later Pr 33.652

Y 3.N 21/17:107/nos.
DAILY REPORT, FOREIGN RADIO BROADCASTS.

For official use only.
Later Pr 33.657

NATIONAL SECURITY RESOURCES BOARD
(1947– 1949)

CREATION AND AUTHORITY

The National Security Resources Board was established as an independent agency by the National Security Act of 1947, approved July 26, 1947 (61 Stat. 499). The Board was transferred to the Executive Office of the President (Pr 33.700) by Reorganization Plan No. 4 of 1949, effective August 20, 1949.

Y 3.N 21/18:1/date
ANNUAL REPORTS.

Later Pr 33.701

Y 3.N 21/18:2 CT
GENERAL PUBLICATIONS.

Later Pr 33.702

NATIONAL SECURITY TRAINING COMMISSION
(1951– 1957)

CREATION AND AUTHORITY

The National Security Training Commission was established by act of Congress, approved June 19, 1951 (65 Stat. 75). Upon its own recommendation the Commission expired June 30, 1957, pursuant to letter of the President of March 25, 1957.

Y 3.N 21/19:1/nos.
SEMIANNUAL REPORTS.

Y 3.N 21/19:2 CT
GENERAL PUBLICATIONS.

Y 3.N 21/19:7
RELEASES.

NATIONAL CAPITAL SESQUICENTENNIAL COMMISSION
(1947– 1952)

CREATION AND AUTHORITY

The National Capital Sesquicentennial Commission was established by act of Congress, approved July 18, 1947. The Commission ceased to function in 1952.

Y 3.N 21/20:1/date
REPORTS.

Y 3.N 21/20:2 CT
GENERAL PUBLICATIONS.

NATIONAL CAPITAL TRANSPORTATION AGENCY
(1960– 1967)

CREATION AND AUTHORITY

The National Capital Transportation Agency was established by the National Capital Transportation Act of 1960 (74 Stat. 537). By Executive Order 11373 of September 20, 1967, effective September 30, 1967, the Agency was abolished and its functions transferred to the Washington Metropolitan Area Transit Authority.

Y 3.N 21/21:1/date   • Item 1070-E
ANNUAL REPORTS.

Y 3.N 21/21:2 CT   • Item 1070-E
GENERAL PUBLICATIONS.

NATIONAL COMMISSION ON FOOD MARKETING
(1964)

Y 3.N 21/22:1/date • Item 1070-G
ANNUAL REPORTS.

Y 3.N 21/22:2/CT
GENERAL PUBLICATIONS.

Y 3.N 21/22:9/nos • Item 1070-G
TECHNICAL STUDIES.

NATIONAL VISITOR FACILITIES ADVISORY COMMISSION
(–1975)

CREATION AND AUTHORITY

The National Visitor Center Study Commission was established by act of March 12, 1968 (82 Stat. 45). Later, its names was changed to National Visitor Facilities Advisory Commission. The Commission was terminated on January 5, 1975, under the provisions of section 14, of the Federal Advisory Committee Act of October 6, 1972 (86 Stat. 776).

Y 3.N 21/23:1/date
REPORT.

NATIONAL WATER COMMISSION
(1968–1973)

CREATION AND AUTHORITY

The Commission was established by act of September 26, 1968 (82 Stat. 868, 42 U.S.C. 1962a note). The Commission was terminated September 26, 1973.

Y 3.N 21/24:1/date
REPORT.

Y 3.N 21/24:2 CT • Item 1089
GENERAL PUBLICATIONS.

Y 3.N 21/24:9/nos.
INTERIM REPORTS (numbered). 1–   1969–

NATIONAL COMMISSION ON PRODUCT SAFETY
(1967–1970)

CREATION AND AUTHORITY

The National Commission on Product Safety was established by Public Law 90-146, approved November 20, 1967. The Commission submitted its final report in June 1970.

Y 3.N 21/25:1/date
REPORTS.

Y 3.N 21/25:2 CT
GENERAL PUBLICATIONS.

NATIONAL COMMISSION ON REFORM OF FEDERAL CRIMINAL LAWS
(1966–1971)

CREATION AND AUTHORITY

The National Commission on Reform of Federal Criminal Laws was established by Public Law 89-801, approved November 8, 1966. The Commission ceased to exist in 1971.

Y 3.N 21/26:1/date • Item 1089
REPORT.

Y 3.N 21/26:2 CT • Item 1089
GENERAL PUBLICATIONS.

NATIONAL BUSINESS COUNCIL FOR CONSUMER AFFAIRS
(1971–1973)

CREATION AND AUTHORITY

The National Business Council for Consumer Affairs was established by Executive Order 11614 of August 4, 1971. The Council ceased to exist in 1973.

Y 3.N 21/27:1/date • Item 1070-I
ANNUAL REPORT.

Y 3.N 21/27:2 CT • Item 1070-I
GENERAL PUBLICATIONS.

Y 3.N 21/27:8 CT • Item 1070-I
HANDBOOKS, MANUALS, GUIDES.

NATIONAL ACADEMY OF PUBLIC ADMINISTRATION

A nonpartisan collegial society formed to advance the effectiveness of government at all levels through sound management and counsel on the practical implications of public policy.

Y 3.N 21/28:1/date • Item 1070-K-2
ANNUAL REPORT.

Y 3.N 21/28:2 CT • Item 1070-K-1
GENERAL PUBLICATIONS. [Irregular]

Y 3.N 21/28:8 CT • Item 1070-K-1
HANDBOOKS, MANUALS, GUIDES. [Irregular]

CORPORATION FOR NATIONAL AND COMMUNITY SERVICE

Previously Commission on National and Community Service.

INFORMATION

Senior Corps
Corporation for National and
    Community Service
1201 New York Ave., NW
Washington, DC 20525
(202) 606-5000
Toll Free: (800) 424-8867
http://www.seniorcorps.org

Y 3.N 21/29:1 date • Item 1089-U
ANNUAL REPORT.

Y 3.N 21/29:1-2/date-nos. • Item 1089-U-1
QUARTERLY REPORT.

Y 3.N 21/29:2 CT • Item 1089-U-3
GENERAL PUBLICATIONS.

Y 3.N 21/29:8 • Item 1089-U-2
HANDBOOKS, MANUALS, GUIDES.

Y 3.N 21/29:10 CT • Item 1089-U-10
DIRECTORIES.

Y 3.N 21/29:12 • Item 1089-U-22
POSTERS.

Y 3.N 21/29:15/date • Item 1089-U-4 (EL)
SCP EXCHANGE.

Y 3.N 21/29:16-1 • Item 1089-U-16 (MF)
AMERICORPS: USDA ANNUAL REPORT.

Y 3.N 21/29:16-2 CT • Item 1089-U-5
AMERICORPS: GENERAL PUBLICATIONS. [Irregular]

Y 3.N 21/29:16-3 CT • Item 1089-U-6
AMERICORPS: HANDBOOKS, MANUALS, GUIDES.

Y 3.N 21/29:16-9 • Item 1089-U-14
AMERICORPS: VISTA VOICE.

Earlier PrEx 10.13/2

Y 3.N 21/29:16-14 • Item 1089-U-13 (EL)
AMERICORPS NEWS.

Y 3.N 21/29:16-15 • Item 1089-U-17 (EL)
NATIONAL SERVICE NEWS.

Y 3.N 21/29:16-16/date • Item 1089-U-18
VISTA SOURCE. [Quarterly]

Y 3.N 21/29:16-17/CT • Item 1089-U-19
AMERICORPS LEADERS PROGRAM, A SERVICE
LEADERSHIP DEVELOPMENT PROGRAM OF THE
CORPORATION FOR NATIONAL SERVICE.

Y 3.N 21/29:16-18/v.nos./nos • Item 1089-U-21
GETTING TO THE CORPS. [Quarterly]

Y 3.N 21/29:17-2 • Item 1089-U-9
VISTA: GENERAL PUBLICATIONS. [Irregular]

Y 3.N 21/29:17-3/v.nos./nos. • Item 1089-U-7
VISTA NEWS FLASH. [Quarterly]

Y 3.N 21/29:17-4/nos. • Item 1089-U-8 (MF)
VISTA: FORMS.

Y 3.N 21/29:17-8 CT • Item 1089-U-11
VISTA: HANDBOOKS, MANUALS, GUIDES. [Irregular]

Y 3.N 21/29:17-16 CT • Item 1089-U-15
VISTA-DIRECTORIES.

Y 3.N 21/29:17-15/date/nos. • Item 1089-U-12
NATIONAL VISTA NEWS. [Quarterly]

Earlier AA 1.9/6

Y 3.N 21/29:18-1 • Item 1089-U-20
FACT SHEETS.

Y 3.N 21/29:18-8 • Item 1089-U-23
HANDBOOKS, MANUALS AND GUIDES.

NEAR EAST RELIEF
(1920)

Y 3.N 27:1/date
ANNUAL REPORTS.

NATIONAL COMMISSION ON NEIGHBORHOODS
(1977– 1979)

Y 3.N 31:1/date
REPORT.

Y 3.N 31:2 CT
GENERAL PUBLICATIONS. [Irregular]

NEW JERSEY TERCENTENARY CELEBRATION COMMISSION
(1960)

Y 3.N 42:1/date
REPORTS.

Y 3.N 42:2 CT
GENERAL PUBLICATIONS.

NEW ENGLAND REGIONAL COMMISSION
(1965– 1981)

CREATION AND AUTHORITY

Title V of the Public Works and Economic
Development Act of 1965 (79 Stat. 552: 42 U.S.C.
3121) authorizes the Secretary of Commerce to
designate economic development regions. Following such designation, the Secretary invites
the States of the region to establish a regional
commission. The New England Region, consisting of the entire States of Connecticut, Massachusetts, New Hampshire, Rhode Island, Vermont,
and Maine was designated on March 2, 1966. The
Commission was formally organized on March 20,
1967. Members are the Federal Cochairman and
the New England Governors. The Governors elect
one of their members to be the Commission State
Cochairman. The Federal role in this Commission
was abolished through repeal of the Public Works
and Economic Development Act by section 1821
of Public Law 97-35 of August 13, 1981 (95 Stat.
766) effective October 1, 1981.

Y 3.N 42/2:1/date
ANNUAL REPORT.

Y 3.N 42/2:2 CT
GENERAL PUBLICATIONS.

Y 3.N 42/2:7/date
PRESS RELEASES.

Y 3.N 42/2:9/nos.
ENERGY PROGRAM TECHNICAL REPORTS.

NEW ENGLAND RIVER BASINS COMMISSION
(1967– 1981)

Y 3.N 42/3:1/date
ANNUAL REPORT.

Y 3.N 42/3:2 CT
GENERAL PUBLICATIONS. [Irregular]

NICARAGUA CANAL COMMISSION
(1897– 1899)

CREATION AND AUTHORITY

The Nicaragua Canal Commission was established by act of Congress, approved June 4,
1897. The Commission made its report on May 9,
1899.

Y 3.N 51:CT
PUBLICATIONS.

NORTHWEST TERRITORY CELEBRATION COMMISSION
(1935– 1939)

CREATION AND AUTHORITY

The Northwest Territory Celebration Commission was established by joint resolution of Congress, approved August 2, 1935. The Commission ceased to exist in 1939.

Y 3.N 81:1/date
REPORT.

Y 3.N 81:2 CT
GENERAL PUBLICATIONS.

NORTH CAROLINA TERCENTENARY CELEBRATION COMMISSION
(1935– 1938)

Y 3.N 81/2:1/date
ANNUAL REPORT.

Y 3.N 81/2:2 CT
GENERAL PUBLICATIONS.

NORTH ATLANTIC REGIONAL WATER RESOURCES STUDY COORDINATING COMMITTEE
(1965–   )

CREATION AND AUTHORITY

The North Atlantic Regional Water Resources
Study Coordinating Committee was established
in 1965 under the authority of the Water Resources Planning Act (Public Law 89-80).

Y 3.N 81/3:1/date
REPORT.

NORTHERN GREAT PLAINS RESOURCES PROGRAM

Y 3.N 81/4:1/date
ANNUAL REPORTS.

Y 3.N 81/4:2 CT
GENERAL PUBLICATIONS. [Irregular]

NORTHWEST FEDERAL REGIONAL COUNCIL
(1977–   )

Y 3.N 81/5:1/date
ANNUAL REPORT.

Y 3.N 81/5:2 CT
GENERAL PUBLICATIONS. [Irregular]

NORTHERN MARIANA ISLANDS COMMISSION
(1976– 1985)

CREATION AND AUTHORITY

The Northern Mariana Islands Commission was created in 1976 by Public Law 94-241 (29 U.S.C. 206). The Commission was disbanded with the submission of its final report in August 1985.

Y 3.N 81/6:1/date
ANNUAL REPORT.

Y 3.N 81/6:2 CT
GENERAL PUBLICATIONS. [Irregular]

Y 3.N 81/6:9 CT
WELCOMING AMERICA'S NEWEST COMMONWEALTH: REPORTS. [Irregular]

NORTHWEST INDIAN FISHERIES COMMISSION

Y 3.N 81/7:date   • Item 1089-A-1 (MF)
ANNUAL REPORT.

NORTHWEST POWER PLANNING COUNCIL

Y 3.N 81/8:1   • Item 1089-W4-1 (EL)
ANNUAL REPORT.

Y 3.N 81/8:2   • Item 1089-W-4
GENERAL PUBLICATIONS.

Y 3.N 81/8:8   • Item 1089-W-2 (EL)
HANDBOOKS, MANUALS, GUIDES.

Y 3.N 81/8:10   • Item 1089-W-4 (EL)
DIRECTORY OF ORGANIZATIONS.

Y 3.N 81/8:15   • Item 1089-W-5 (EL)
INDEPENDENT ECONOMIC ANALYSIS BOARD (IEAB) DOCUMENTS.

Y 3.N 81/8:16   • Item 1089-W-6 (EL)
INDEPENDENT SCIENTIFIC ADVISORY BOARD (ISAB) DOCUMENTS.

Y 3.N 81/8:17   • Item 1089-W-7 (EL)
INDEPENDENT SCIENTIFIC REVIEW PANEL (ISRP) DOCUMENTS.

NUCLEAR REGULATORY COMMISSION
(1975–   )

CREATION AND AUTHORITY

The Nuclear Regulatory Commission was established as an independent regulatory agency under the provisions of the Energy reorganization Act of 1974 (88 Stat 1242; 42 U.S.C. 5841) and Executive Order 11834, of January 15, 1975, effective January 19, 1975.

INFORMATION

Nuclear Regulatory Commission
Washington, DC 20555
(301) 415-8200
Toll Free: (800) 368-5642
http://www.nrc.gov

Y 3.N 88:1/date   • Item 1053 (MF)
ANNUAL REPORT. 1st–   1975–

Y 3.N 88:2 CT   • Item 1051-H-1
GENERAL PUBLICATIONS.

Y 3.N 88:6/date   • Item 1052
RULES AND REGULATIONS, TITLE 10, CODE OF FEDERAL REGULATIONS, CHAPTER 1.

Earlier Y 3.At 7:6-2

Y 3.N 88:6-2/nos.   • Item 1051-R-1 (MF)
REGULATORY GUIDES.

PURPOSE:– To describe and make available to the public methods acceptable to the NRC staff of implementing specific parts of the Commission's regulations, to delineate techniques used by the staff in evaluating specific problems of postulated accidents, or to provide guidance to applicants. Highly technical.

Issued in the following parts:–

                              • Item 1051-R-1
1. POWER REACTORS.
                              • Item 1051-R-2
2. RESEARCH AND TEST REACTORS.
                              • Item 1051-R-3 (MF)
3. FUELS, AND MATERIALS FACILITIES.
                              • Item 1051-R-4 (MF)
4. ENVIRONMENTAL AND SITING.
                              • Item 1051-R-5 (MF)
5. MATERIALS AND PLANT PROTECTION.
                              • Item 1051-R-6 (MF)
6. PRODUCTS.
                              • Item 1057-R-7 (MF)
7. TRANSPORTATION.
                              • Item 1057-R-8 (MF)
8. OCCUPATIONAL HEALTH.
                              • Item 1051-R-9 (MF)
9. ANTITRUST AND FINANCIAL REVIEW.
                              • Item 1051-R-10 (MF)
10. GENERAL.

Y 3.N 88:6-3/nos.   • Item 1052 (MF)
DRAFT REGULATORY GUIDE, DG- (Series).

Y 3.N 88:6-4   • Item 1052 (MF)
REGULATORY GUIDE LIST.

Y 3.N 88:7/v.nos.&nos.   • Item 1051-H-26 (EL)
NEWS RELEASES. [Irregular]

Y 3.N 88:8 CT   • Item 1051-H-18
HANDBOOKS, MANUALS, GUIDES.

Y 3.N 88:9/v.nos.&nos.   • Item 1051-H
NUCLEAR SAFETY. v. 1–   1959–   (Oak Ridge National Laboratory)

PURPOSE:– To keep reactor designers, reactor builders, reactor fuel specialists, and regulatory and public safety officials informed on the current developments in nuclear safety. Activities of the Commission's Advisory Committee are also summarized and recent safeguards reports are reviewed.
Indexed by:–
   Biological Abstracts
   Chemical Abstracts
   Engineering Index Annual
   Engineering Index Monthly
   Index to U.S. Government Periodicals
   Nuclear Science Abstracts
   Selected Water Resources Abstracts.
Published by the Department of Energy (EEN1.93) subsequent to the May-June 1981 issue.
   ISSN 0029-5604
   Earlier Y 3.At 7:45

Y 3.N 88:9-2/v.nos.&nos.
NUCLEAR SAFETY INDEX.

Y 3.N 88:10/nos.   • Item 1051-H-2 (MF)
NUREG- (series).

Y 3.N 88:10-2/date/v.nos.   • Item 1051-H-2 (MF)
BUDGET ESTIMATES, FISCAL YEARS (dates). [Annual]
   Earlier Y 3.N 88:10/1100

Y 3.N 88:10-3/date   • Item 1051-H-2 (MF)
COMPILATION OF CONTRACT RESEARCH FOR THE MATERIALS BRANCH, DIVISION OF ENGINEERING SAFETY. [Annual]

   Earlier Y 3.N 88:10/0975/v.

Y 3.N 88:10-4/   • Item 1051-H-2 (MF)
COMPILATION OF CONTRACT RESEARCH FOR THE CHEMICAL ENGINEERING BRANCH, DIVISION OF ENGINEERING TECHNOLOGY.

Y 3.N 88:10-5/   • Item 1051-H-2 (MF)
OCCUPATIONAL RADIATION EXPOSURE AT COMMERCIAL NUCLEAR POWER REACTORS AND OTHER FACILITIES.

Y 3.N 88:10-6/   • Item 1052-B (EL)
INTERAGENCY STEERING COMMITTEE ON RADIATION STANDARDS. [Annual]

Y 3.N 88:11/v.nos.   • Item 1051-J (MF)
NUCLEAR REGULATORY COMMISSION ISSUANCES: OPINIONS AND DECISIONS OF THE NUCLEAR REGULATORY COMMISSION WITH SELECTED ORDERS. v. 1–   1975–   [Semiannual] (Office of Public Affairs, Technical Information Center)

Consists of the reprinted pages for the six monthly issues for each semiannual periods.
Continues: Atomic Energy Commission Reports; Opinions and Decisions of the Atomic Energy Commission with Selected Orders (Y 3.At 7:49).

Y 3.N 88:11-2/v.nos.&nos.   • Item 1051-J-1
NUCLEAR REGULATORY COMMISSION ISSUANCES. [Monthly]

Y 3.N 88:12/date
CURRENT EVENTS: POWER REACTORS. [Irregular]

   ISSN 0145-1111

Y 3.N 88:12-2/v.nos.&nos.   • Item 1051-H-35
POWER REACTOR EVENTS. [Bimonthly] (NUREG-BR-0051)

Compiles operating experience information about commercial nuclear power plants. Summarizes noteworthy events and listing of abstracts of the Commission and other documents on safety-related or possible generic issues. Intended as a feedback to various nuclear plan personnel, managers, etc.
   Earlier Y 3.N 88:12

Y 3.N 88:13 CT
OPERATING EXPERIENCE, BULLETIN INFORMATION REPORT.
   Earlier Y 3.At 7:57

Y 3.N 88:14/date   • Item 1051-H-19 (EL)
TELEPHONE DIRECTORY. [Irregular]

• Item 1051-H-4
Y 3.N 88:15/v.nos.&nos. • Item 1051-T (floppy)
LICENSED OPERATING REACTORS, STATUS SUM-
MARY REPORT. v. 1– 1977– [Annual]
(NUREG-0020)

PURPOSE:– To provide timely data on the
operation of nuclear units with as much accuracy
as possible within the time constraints.
Earlier title: Operating Units Status Report,
Licensed Operations Reactors, Data for Decisions.
Also issued annually on diskettes.

Y 3.N 88:16/v.nos.&nos. • Item 1051-H-5
CONSTRUCTIONS STATUS REPORT, NUCLEAR
POWER PLANTS, DATA FOR DECISIONS. v. 1–6.
1978– 1982. [Monthly] (NUREG-0030)

PURPOSE:– To provide the necessary information for monitoring the progress of construction of nuclear power plants.

Y 3.N 88:17/date • Item 1051-H-3
STEAM GENERATOR TUBE INTEGRITY PROGRAM.
[Quarterly] (NUREG-0359)

PURPOSE:– To provide progress review reports on the laboratory research program to investigate the behavioral characteristics of de-
fected tubing similar to those found in PWR steam
generators.

Y 3.N 88:18/v.nos.&nos. • Item 1051-H-6
WATER REACTOR SAFETY RESEARCH, BUFF BOOK
I. [Bimonthly]

Y 3.N 88:19/v.nos.&nos. • Item 1051-H-8
APPROVED TASK PLANS FOR CATEGORY "A"
GENERIC ACTIVITIES. v. 1– 1977– (NUREG-
0371)

Y 3.N 88:20/v.nos. • Item 1051-H-7
REPORT TO CONGRESS ON ABNORMAL OCCUR-
RENCES. 1– 1975– [Quarterly]

Y 3.N 88:21/v.nos.&nos.
PUBLICATIONS [list]. (NUREG-0304)

Y 3.N 88:21-2/v.nos.&nos. • Item 1051-H-14
TITLE LIST OF DOCUMENTS MADE PUBLICLY AVAIL-
ABLE. v. 1– 1979– [Monthly] (NUREG-0504)

PURPOSE:– To present an annotated list of
highly technical materials received and issued by
the Nuclear Regulatory Commission pertaining to
civilian nuclear power plants, radioactive materials, and the agency's regulatory duties. Indexed
by personal author, broad subject and corporate
source, and report number.

Y 3.N 88:21-3/v.nos. • Item 1051-H-14 (MF)
REGULATORY AND TECHNICAL REPORTS (Abstract
Index Journal).

Y 3.N 88:22 CT
BIBLIOGRAPHIES AND LISTS OF PUBLICATIONS.

Y 3.N 88:23 • Item 1051-H-9
STAFF PRACTICE AND PROCEDURE DIGEST.
(NUREG-0386) [Quarterly]

Y 3.N 88:24/v.nos./nos. • Item 1051-H-10 (MF)
LICENSE CONTRACTOR AND VENDOR INSPECTION
STATUS REPORT. v. 1– 1977– [Quarterly]
(NUREG-0040)

PURPOSE:– To provide information on inspection results. Contains information submitted by
licensees in accordance with NRC rules and regulations, covering events attributed by licensee to
design deficiencies and equipment malfunctions.

Y 3.N 88:25/nos. • Item 1051-H-11 (MF)
CONTRACTOR REPORTS, NUREG/CR-(series). 1–
[Irregular]

Y 3.N 88:25-2/letters-nos. • Item 1051-H-11 (MF)
CONTRACTOR REPORTS. [Irregular]

This class does not include NUREG-CR (reports) (Y 3.N 88:25).

Y 3.N 88:25-3/date • Item 1051-H-11 (MF)
REVIEW OF WASTE PACKAGE VERIFICATION TEST.
[Semiannual]

Y 3.N 88:25-4/date • Item 1051-H-11 (MF)
FUEL PERFORMANCE ANNUAL REPORT. [Annual]

Y 3.N 88:25-5/ • Item 1051-H-11 (MF)
LONG-TERM EMBRITTLEMENT OF CAST DUPLEX
STAINLESS STEELS IN LWR SYSTEMS.

Earlier Y 3.N 88:25

Y 3.N 88:25-6/date • Item 1051-H-11 (MF)
PRECURSORS TO POTENTIAL SEVERE CORE
DAMAGE ACCIDENTS. [Annual]

Earlier Y 3.N 88:25

Y 3.N 88:25-7/date • Item 1051-H-44 (MF)
UNIVERSITY OF MARYLAND COLLEGE PARK 2x4
LOOP TEST FACILITY. [Annual]
Annual report of the investigators of the Uni-
versity of Maryland at College Park (UMCP) 2x4
Loop Test Facility. Includes theoretical investiga-
tion and experimental investigation and contains
many mathematical formulas and diagrams.

Y 3.N 88:25-8/ • Item 1051-H-43 (MF)
LWR PRESSURE VESSEL SURVEILLANCE
DOSIMETRY IMPROVEMENT PROGRAM.
[Annual]

LWR = Light Water Reactor
Summarizes activities under this Program,
whose purposes is to test,improve, and stan-
dardize reactor analysis methods used to predict
the integrated effect of neutron exposure to LWR
pressure vessels.

Y 3.N 88:25-9/ • Item 1051-H-11 (MF)
NDE OF STAINLESS STEEL AND ON-LINE LEAK
MONITORING OF LWR'S, ANNUAL REPORT.

Y 3.N 88:25-10/ • Item 1051-H-11 (MF)
STEAM GENERATOR GROUP PROJECT. [Annual]

Y 3.N 88:25-11/ • Item 1051-H-11 (MF)
RADIONUCLIDE MIGRATION AROUND URANIUM ORE
BODIES– ANALOGUE OF RADIOACTIVE WASTE
REPOSITORIES. [Annual]

Y 3.N 88:25-12/ • Item 1051-H-11 (MF)
RADIOACTIVE MATERIALS RELEASED FROM
NUCLEAR POWER PLANTS. [Annual]

Y 3.N 88:26/v.nos.&nos. • Item 1051-H-12
PROGRAM SUMMARY REPORT. v. 1–4. – 1980.
[Every four weeks] (NUREG-0380)

PURPOSE:– To provide information on all
phases of nuclear regulations. intended as an
information and decision-making tool for middle
and upper level managements of the Nuclear
Regulatory Commission.
Discontinued. Superseded by Summary Information Report (Y 3.N 88:41).

Y 3.N 88:27/nos. • Item 1051-H-13 (MF)
NUREG/CP (series). [Irregular]
PURPOSE:– To provide conference proceedings and reports based on symposia sponsored
by the Commission and intended for the scientific
and technical community.

Y 3.N 88:28/v.nos.&nos. • Item 1051-H-15 (MF)
LICENSED FUEL FACILITY STATUS REPORT. v. 1–
1978– [Semiannual] (NUREG-0430)

PURPOSE:– To present statistical data and
information on licensed nuclear fuel facilities including inventory difference data, Commission
inspection results, licensee event report, radioactive effluent data, etc.

Y 3.N 88:29/v.nos.&nos. • Item 1051-H-16
SYSTEMATIC EVALUATION PROGRAM, STATUS SUM-
MARY REPORT. v. 1– 1978– [Quarterly]
(NUREG-0485)

PURPOSE:– To diagram the target for evaluations of currently operating power reactors concerning adequate safety of design and operation,
including seismicity, accident detection, etc. The
Program reviews operating power reactors with
respect to current licensing criteria, documents
results, and identifies the need for plant changes,
if necessary.
Former title: Regulatory Licensing Status Summary Report

Y 3.N 88:30/date • Item 1051-H-17
UNRESOLVED SAFETY ISSUES SUMMARY, AQUA
BOOK. [Quarterly]

Y 3.N 88:31/nos • Item 1051-H-20
BROCHURE REPORTS, NUREG-BR (series). [Irregu-
lar] (Fuel Facility and Materials Safety Inspection
Division)

Y 3.N 88:31/0083 • Item 1051-H-40 (MF)
COMPUTER CODES AND MATHEMATICAL MODELS.
[Quarterly]

Contains extracts from NUREG and NUREG/
CR reports dealing with design or use of computer codes for scientific, technical or technol-
ogy-related activities of NRC. Intended as a guide
for scientific and technical analysts on availability and content of NRC codes and code packages including documentation.

Y 3.N 88:31/0110 • Item 1051-H-20
TECHNICAL SPECIFICATION IMPROVEMENT PRO-
GRAM HIGHLIGHTS. [Irregular]

Y 3.N 88:32/v.nos.&nos. • Item 1051-H-22 (MF)
STANDARDS DEVELOPMENT STATUS SUMMARY
REPORT. v. 1– 1981– [Monthly] (NUREG-
0566)

Presents management information, in table
form, to be used by the Office of Standards Development in scheduling, monitoring, and controlling the process by which its regulatory standards, environment statements, etc., are written.
Summarizes schedule plans for development of
such publications.
Prior to 1982, issued monthly.

Y 3.N 88:33/v.nos.&nos. • Item 1051-H-24 (MF)
FACILITIES LICENSE APPLICATION RECORD. v. 1,
no. 1–3. 1981. [Bimonthly]

Lists central station nuclear power plants licenses in effect for operating reactors; construction permits in effect, pending, withdrawn, terminated or revoked; and research, test, and power
reactors for export.

Y 3.N 88:34/date • Item 1051-H-25 (MF)
TOPICAL REPORT REVIEW STATUS. [Semiannual]
(NUREG-0390)

PURPOSE:– To aid NRC personnel in managing the topical report program. Consists mainly of
tables that show the status of topical reports, by
NRC branches, industrial organizations, and titles.

Y 3.N 88:35/v.nos.&nos. • Item 1051-H-21
OPERATING REACTORS LICENSING ACTIONS SUM-
MARY. v. 1– 1981– [Monthly] (NUEEG-0748)

PURPOSE:– To provide the Commission with
a statistical overview of licensing actions dealing
with operating power and nonpower reactors.

Y 3.N 88:36/v.nos.&.nos. • Item 1051-H-23
RESEARCH RESULTS UTILIZATION, RESEARCH
PROJECT CONTROL SYSTEM, STATUS SUM-
MARY REPORT. [Quarterly] (NUREG-0435)

This publication, commonly called the "RILs
Book", provides status and control information
concerning the utilization of research results in
the regulatory policies and practices of the Nuclear
Regulatory Commission.

Y 3.N 88:37/date
WEEKLY INFORMATION REPORT.

Y 3.N 88:38 • **Item 1051-H-27 (MF)**
LICENSEE EVENT REPORT (LER) COMPILATION.
[Monthly] (NUREG/CR-2000)

Consists of summaries of Licensee Event
Reports furnished NRC by nuclear power plant
licensees, arranged alphabetically by facility name
and chronologically by event date. Summaries
indicate corrective actions taken.

Y 3.N 88:39/nos
TRANSLATION SERIES. [Irregular]

Y 3.N 88:40 CT
AUDIOVISUAL MATERIALS. [Irregular]

Y 3.N 88:41/v.nos.&nos.
SUMMARY INFORMATION REPORT. [Quarterly]
(NUREG-0871)

Contains summary data concerning the
Nuclear Regulatory Commission and its licens-
ees for general use by the Chairman, other Com-
missioners and Commission staff officers, the
Executive Director for Operations, and the Office
Directors. Consists Largely of tables, graphs, and
maps.
Also includes data that were formerly con-
tained in Program Summary Report [NUREG-0380]
(Y 3.N 88:26) which has been discontinued.

Y 3.N 88:42/v.nos.&nos. • **Item 1051-H-29**
INFORMATION REPORT ON STATE LEGISLATION.
[Monthly]

Presents a compilation of summaries of State
bills in nuclear areas that have been introduced
in the legislative sessions.

Y 3.N 88:43/v.nos.&nos. • **Item 1051-H-31 (MF)**
NRC-TLD DIRECT RADIATION MONITORING NET-
WORK. [Quarterly] [NUREG-0837]

PURPOSE:– To provide the status and re-
sults of the NRC thermoluminescent dosimeter
(TLD) direct radiation monitoring. It presents the
radiation levels measured in the vicinity of NRC
Licensed facility sites throughout the country.
Also published in microfiche.

Y 3.N 88:44/v.nos.&nos. • **Item 1051-H-30**
REGULATORY LICENSING STATUS SUMMARY RE-
PORTS. v. 1– 12.   – 1983. [Monthly]

Management report designed to provide information needed to control review processes for
central station nuclear reactor applications. Tables
present the status of such applications.
Published in microfiche.

Y 3.N 88:45/v.nos./nos. • **Item 1051-H-32 (MF)**
NRC REGULATORY AGENDA. [Quarterly] (NUREG-
0936)

A compilation of all rules on which the Commission has proposed or is considering action
and all petitions for rulemaking received and pending disposition by the Commission.

Y 3.N 88:46/v.nos.&nos. (MF)
LPDR UPDATE. [Quarterly]

Newsletter chiefly intended to enhance com-
munication between the Local Public Document
Room Branch Staff and the 130 LPDR Library
Staffs.

Y 3.N 88:47/v.nos.&nos. • **Item 1051-H-33(MF)**
ENFORCEMENT ACTIONS, SIGNIFICANT ACTIONS
RESOLVED. [Quarterly] (NUREG-0940)

Summarizes significant enforcement actions
resolved and includes copies of letters, notices,
licensees' responses, and orders sent by the
Commission to the licensee regarding enforcement action. Intended for dissemination to managers and employees engaged in activities licensed by NRC, in the interest of promoting public health and safety as well as common defense
and security.

Y 3.N 88:48/v.nos.&nos. • **Item 1051-H-36**
SAFETY RESEARCH PROGRAMS SPONSORED BY
OFFICE OF NUCLEAR REGULATORY RESEARCH.
[Semiannual]

Combines 1) Quarterly Technical Progress Report on Water Reactor Safety Programs Sponsored by NRC's Division of Reactor Safety Research, and 2) Water Reactor Research Division
Quarterly Progress Report, both previously
classed under Y 3.N 88:25.

Y 3.N 88:49/v.nos.&nos. • **Item 1051-H-37**
NEWS, REVIEWS, AND COMMENT. [Quarterly]

Y 3.N 88:50/date • **Item 1051-H-38 (EL)**
WEEKLY INFORMATION REPORT.

Contains a summary of key events of the
week for those who may prefer a more condensed
version and also a more detailed account.

Y 3.N 88:51/v.nos.&nos. • **Item 1051-H-26**
ITS NEWS. v. 1–   [Quarterly]

ITS = Information Technology Services.

Y 3.N 88:52/CT • **Item 1051-H-39**
DIRECTORIES.

Y 3.N 88:53 • **Item 1051-H-41**
INTERNATIONAL AGREEMENT REPORTS (series).
[Irregular]

Includes reports resulting from international
agreements between the United States and foreign countries.

Y 3.N 88:54/v.nos.&nos. • **Item 1051-H-42**
RESEARCH NEWS. [Quarterly]

PURPOSE:– To present news of nuclear research and activities.

Y 3.N 88:55/date • **Item 1051-H-38**
WEEKLY INFORMATION REPORT.

Y 3.N 88:56 • **Item 1051-H-8 (MF)**
GENERIC LETTER (Series).

Y 3.N 88:56-2/nos. • **Item 1051-H-8 (MF)**
NRC INFORMATION NOTICE.

• **Item 1051-H-27 (EL)**
Y 3.N 88:57 • **Item 1052-B (E)**
NMSS LICENSEE NEWSLETTER. [Quarterly]

Y 3.N 88:57-2 • **Item 1052-B (EL)**
SEALED SOURCE AND DEVICE NEWSLETTER
(SS&D).

Y 3.N 88:58/nos. • **Item 1051-H-13 (MF)**
NUREG/GR (Series).

Y 3.N 88:59/nos. • **Item 1051-S**
FORMS.

Y 3.N 88:60/date • **Item 1053-A-1 (MF)**
CHIEF FINANCIAL OFFICER'S ANNUAL REPORT.

Y 3.N 88:61 • **Item 1052-B (E)**
ELECTRONIC PRODUCTS.

Y 3.N 88:62 • **Item 1089-W (MF)**
NRC PUBLIC DOCUMENT ROOM COLLECTION.

NUCLEAR WASTE TECHNICAL REVIEW BOARD

CREATION AND AUTHORITY

The Nuclear Waste Technical Review Board
was established by the Nuclear Waste Policy
Amendments Act (1987) [Public Law 100-203-
December 22, 1987, Part].

INFORMATION

U. S. Nuclear Waste Technical Review Board
2300 Clarendon Blvd., Ste. 1300
Arlington, VA. 22201
(703) 235-4473
235-4495
http://www.nwtrb.gov

Y 3.N 88/2:1/date • **Item 1089-W (EL)**
REPORT TO THE U.S. CONGRESS AND THE U.S.
SECRETARY OF ENERGY FROM THE NUCLEAR
WASTE TECHNICAL REVIEW BOARD.

Y 3.N 88/2:2 CT • **Item 1089-W**
GENERAL PUBLICATIONS.

NATIONAL NUTRITION MONITORING ADVISORY COUNCIL

Y 3.N 95:2 CT • **Item 1089-A-2**
GENERAL PUBLICATIONS. [Irregular]

COMMISSION ON OBSCENITY AND PORNOGRAPHY (1967– 1970)

CREATION AND AUTHORITY

The Commission on Obscenity and Pornogra-
phy was established by Public Law 90-100, approved October 3, 1967 to investigate the relationship of obscene or pornographic materials to
anti-social behavior and to submit its report not
later than January 3, 1970.

Y 3.Ob 7:1/date
REPORT.

Y 3.Ob 7:2 CT
GENERAL PUBLICATIONS.

Y 3.Ob 7:9/date
PROGRESS REPORTS.

Y 3.Ob 7:10/v.nos.
TECHNICAL REPORTS.

OCCUPATIONAL SAFETY AND HEALTH REVIEW COMMISSION
(1970–   )

CREATION AND AUTHORITY

The Occupational Safety and Health Review Commission was established as an independent agency by the Occupational Safety and Health Act of 1970 (84 Stat. 1590).

INFORMATION

Public Information Office
Occupational Safety and
    Health Review Commission
1120 20th Street, NW, 9th Fl.
Washington, D.C. 20036-3457
(202) 606-5398
Fax: (202) 606-5050
http://www.oshrc.gov

Y 3.Oc 1:1/date   • **Item 1070-L**
ANNUAL REPORT.

Y 3.Oc 1:2 CT   • **Item 1070-L**
GENERAL PUBLICATIONS.

Y 3.Oc 1:6 CT   • **Item 1070-L**
REGULATIONS, RULES, AND INSTRUCTIONS.

Y 3.Oc 1:8 CT   • **Item 1070-L**
HANDBOOKS, MANUALS, GUIDES.

Y 3.Oc 1:9/date   • **Item 1070-L**
DECISIONS AND ORDERS. [Irregular]

   April 28, 1971– November 21, 1972. [1973]
256 p.

Y 3.Oc 1:10/v.nos.   • **Item 1070-L**
OSAHRC REPORTS: DECISIONS OF THE OCCUPA-
TIONAL SAFETY AND HEALTH REVIEW COM-
MISSION. v. 1–   1971–   [Irregular]

Y 3.Oc 1:10-2/v.nos.   • **Item 1070-L (EL)**
ADMINISTRATIVE LAW JUDGE AND COMMISSION
DECISIONS. v. 1–   1971–   [Monthly]

   ISSN 0094-7776

Y 3.Oc 1:10-3/date   • **Item 1070-L**
INDEX TO DECISIONS. 1979–   [Quarterly]

Y 3.Oc 1:10-4/date   • **Item 1070-L**
CITATOR TO DECISIONS OF THE OCCUPATIONAL
SAFETY AND HEALTH REVIEW COMMISSION.
[Quarterly]

Y 3.OC 1:10-5/   • **Item 1070-L-2 (EL)**
ALJ DECISIONS.

Y 3.OC 1:10-6   • **Item 1070-L-2 (EL)**
COMMISSION DECISIONS.

Y 3.OC 1:11   • **Item 1070-L-2 (E)**
ELECTRONIC PRODUCTS (misc.).

NATIONAL OCCUPATIONAL INFORMATION COORDINATING COMMITTEE
(1976–   )

CREATION AND AUTHORITY

The National Occupational Information Coordinating Committee was established by Public
Law 94-482 (90 Stat. 2198), approved October
12, 1976

Y 3.Oc 1/2:1/date
REPORT.

Y 3.Oc 1/2:2 CT
GENERAL PUBLICATIONS. [Irregular]

Y 3.Oc 1/2:8 CT
HANDBOOKS, MANUALS, GUIDES. [Irregular]

NATIONAL ADVISORY COMMITTEE ON OCEANS AND ATMOSPHERE
(1971–   )

CREATION AND AUTHORITY

The National Advisory Committee on Oceans
and Atmosphere was established by Public Law
92-125, approved August 16, 1971.

Y 3.Oc 2:1/date   • **Item 1070-J**
REPORTS. 1st–   1972–   [Annual]

Y 3.Oc 2:2 CT   • **Item 1070-J**
GENERAL PUBLICATIONS.

Y 3.Oc 2:8 CT   • **Item 1070-J**
HANDBOOKS, MANUALS, GUIDES.

OLD WEST REGIONAL ACTION PLANNING COMMISSION
(1965– 1981)

CREATION AND AUTHORITY

The Old West Regional Action Planning Commission was established pursuant to title V of the
Public Works and Economic Development Act of
1965, as amended. The Federal role in this Commission was abolished through repeal of the Public Works and Economic Development Act by
section 1821 of Public Law 97-35 of August 13,
1981 (95 Stat. 766) effective October 1, 1981.

Y 3.Ol 1:2 CT
GENERAL PUBLICATIONS.

COMMISSION ON ORGANIZATION OF THE EXECUTIVE BRANCH OF THE GOVERNMENT
(1947– 1949)

CREATION AND AUTHORITY

The Commission on Organization of the Executive Branch of the Government was established by act of Congress, approved July 7, 1947
(61 Stat. 246). By provisions of the same act, the
Commission ceased to exist on June 12, 1949.

Y 3.Or 3:1/date
ANNUAL REPORTS.

Y 3.Or 3:2 CT
GENERAL PUBLICATIONS.

Y 3.Or 3:7/letters
TASK FORCE REPORTS, APPENDIXES.

COMMISSION ON ORGANIZATION OF THE EXECUTIVE BRANCH OF THE GOVERNMENT
(1953– 1955)

CREATION AND AUTHORITY

The Commission on Organization of the Executive Branch of the Government was established by act of Congress, approved July 10,
1953 (67 Stat. 142). By act of Congress approved
May 23, 1955 (69 Stat. 64), the Commission was
terminated, effective June 30, 1955, with a liquidation period not to exceed ninety days thereafter.

Y 3.Or 3/2:1/date
REPORTS.

Y 3.Or 3/2:2 CT
PUBLICATIONS.

Y 3.Or 3/2:7
RELEASES.

Y 3.Or 3/2:8 CT
TASK FORCE REPORTS.

OUTDOOR RECREATION RESOURCES REVIEW COMMISSION
(1958– 1962)

CREATION AND AUTHORITY

The Outdoor Recreation Resources Review
Commission was created by act of June 28, 1958
(72 Stat. 238, as amended; 16 U.S.C. 17k note),
to conduct a nationwide inventory and evaluation
of outdoor recreation resources and opportunities, through Federal agencies, States, and private groups, and to determine from data compiled, necessary resources and opportunities to
meet future requirements. The Commission
submitted its final report to the President in January 1962 and was terminated on September 1,
1962.

Y 3.Ou 8:1/date
REPORTS.

Y 3.Ou 8:2 CT
GENERAL PUBLICATIONS.

Y 3.Ou 8:9/date
PROCEEDINGS OF JOINT MEETING WITH ITS ADVISORY COUNCIL. [Semiannual]

Y 3.Ou 8:10/nos.
ORRC STUDY REPORTS.

OZARKS REGIONAL COMMISSION
(1966– 1981)

CREATION AND AUTHORITY

Title V of the Public Works and Economic Development Act of 1965 (79 Stat. 552; 42 U.S.C. 3121) authorized the Secretary of Commerce to designate economic development regions. Following such designation, the Secretary invites the States of the region to establish a regional commission. The Ozarks Region, consisting of 134 counties in Missouri, Arkansas, Kansas, and Oklahoma was designated on March 1, 1966. The Commission was formally organized on September 7, 1966. Members are the Federal Cochairman and the Ozarks Governors. The Federal role in this Commission was abolished through repeal of the Public Works and Economic Development Act by section 1821 of Public Law 97-35 of August 13, 1981 (95 Stat. 766) effective October 1, 1981.

Y 3.Oz 1:1/date
ANNUAL REPORT.

Y 3.Oz 1:2 CT
GENERAL PUBLICATIONS.

Y 3.Oz 1:7/date
PRESS RELEASES.

PACIFIC RAILWAY COMMISSION
(1887)

CREATION AND AUTHORITY

The United States Pacific Railway Commission was established by act of Congress, approved March 3, 1887. The final report of the Commission was submitted to the President in December 1887.

Y 3.P 11:CT
PUBLICATIONS.

PACIFIC SOUTHWEST INTER-AGENCY COMMITTEE
(1955)

CREATION AND AUTHORITY

The Pacific Southwest Inter-Agency Committee was established in 1955, replacing the Pacific Southwest Inter-Agency Technical Committee (Y 3.P 11/3). By executive action of the President in 1966, PSIAC became a field committee.

Y 3.P 11/2:1/date
REPORT.

Y 3.P 11/2:2 CT
GENERAL PUBLICATIONS.

PACIFIC SOUTHWEST FEDERAL INTERAGENCY TECHNICAL COMMITTEE
(– 1955)

Y 3.P 11/3:1/date
ANNUAL REPORT.

Y 3.P 11/3:2 CT
GENERAL PUBLICATIONS.

Y 3.P 11/3:9/nos.
PAPERS. 1–   1950–   [Irregular]

PACIFIC NORTHWEST RIVER BASINS COMMISSION
(1967– 1981)

CREATION AND AUTHORITY

The Pacific Northwest River Basins Commission was established by Executive Order 11311, dated March 6, 1967, under provisions of Title II of the Water Resources Planning Act of 1965 (P.L. 89-80).

Y 3.P 11/4:1/date
REPORT.

Y 3.P 11/4:2 CT
GENERAL PUBLICATIONS.

Y 3.P 11/4:8 CT
HANDBOOKS, MANUALS, GUIDES.

Y 3.P 11/4:9/date
REVIEW OF POWER PLANNING IN PACIFIC NORTHWEST, CALENDAR YEAR.

Y 3.P 11/4:10 CT
RIVER MILE INDEX.

PACIFIC NORTHWEST REGIONAL COMMISSION
(1976– 1981)

Y 3.P 11/5:1/date
ANNUAL REPORT.

Y 3.P 11/5:2 CT
GENERAL PUBLICATIONS.

COMMISSION ON FEDERAL PAPERWORK
(1974– 1978)

CREATION AND AUTHORITY

The Commission on Federal Paperwork was established by act of December 27, 1974 (88 Stat. 1789). The Commission was terminated in January 1978.

Y 3.P 19:1/date   • Item 1072-B (MF)
REPORTS.

Y 3.P 19:2 CT   • Item 1072-B (MF)
GENERAL PUBLICATIONS.

Y 3.P 19:8 CT   • Item 1072-B
HANDBOOKS, MANUALS, GUIDES.

Y 3.P 19:9 CT   • Item 1072-B
POSTERS.

PANAMA CANAL COMMISSION
(1979–   )

CREATION AND AUTHORITY

The Panama Canal Commission was established as an independent agency by the Panama Canal Act of 1979 (93 Stat. 452), approved September 27, 1979, superseding the Canal Zone Government (C Z 1), which was abolished by the same act. The Commission will perform its designated functions until December 31, 1999, at which time the Canal will be turned over to the Republic of Panama, pursuant to the Panama Canal Treaty of 1977.

INFORMATION

Panama Canal Commission
1825 I St. NW
Washington, D.C. 20006
(202) 634-6441

Y 3.P 19/2:1/date   • Item 1089-K (MF)
ANNUAL REPORT.

Y 3.P 19/2:2 CT   • Item 1089-K
GENERAL PUBLICATIONS. [Irregular]

Y 3.P 19/2:9/v.nos.&nos.   • Item 1089-K
PANAMA CANAL SPILLWAY. [Weekly]
    Earlier CZ 1.11

Y 3.P 19/2:10/date   • Item 1089-K
PANAMA CANAL REVIEW. [Semiannual]
    Earlier CZ 1.8

PROSPECTIVE PAYMENT ASSESSMENT COMMISSION

CREATION AND AUTHORITY

The Commission was established by the Social Security Act as amended by PL 98-21.

Y 3.P 29:1/date • Item 1061-H-3
ANNUAL REPORT.

Y 3.P 29:1-2/date
TECHNICAL APPENDIXES TO THE REPORT AND RECOMMENDATIONS TO THE SECRETARY, U.S.DEPARTMENT OF HEALTH AND HUMAN SERVICES. [Annual]
Earlier Y 3.P 29:1

Y 3.P 29:2 CT • Item 1061-H-3
GENERAL PUBLICATIONS.

Y 3.P 29:3/date • Item 1061-H-3
MEDICARE PROSPECTIVE PAYMENT AND THE AMERICAN HEALTH CARE SYSTEM. [Annual]
Earlier Y 3.P 29:2 M 46

UNITED STATES INSTITUTE OF PEACE
(1984–   )

CREATION AND AUTHORITY

The United States Institute of Peace was established as an independent, Federal nonprofit corporation by act of October 19, 1984 (22 U.S.C. 4603).

INFORMATION

United States Institute of Peace
Suite 200
1200 7th St. NW
Washington, D.C. 20036-3011
(202) 457-1700
Fax: (202) 429-6063
E-Mail:usip_requests@usip.org
http//.www.usip.org

Y 3.P 31 • Item 1063-K- (E)
ELECTRONIC PRODUCTS. (misc.)

Y 3.P 31:1/date • Item 1063-K-1
BIENNIAL REPORT.

Y 3.P 31:2 CT • Item 1063-K-2
GENERAL PUBLICATIONS.

Y 3.P 31:3 CT • Item 1063-K
NATIONAL PEACE ESSAY CONTEST BROCHURES AVAILABLE.

Y 3.P 31:4/date • Item 1063-K
PEACE ESSAY CONTEST.

Y 3.P 31:8 CT • Item 1063-K-5
HANDBOOKS, MANUALS, GUIDES.

Y 3.P 31:10 • Item 1063-K-2 (MF)
DIRECTORIES.

Y 3.P 31:13 CT • Item 1063-K-6
FORMS.

Y 3.P 31:15/v.nos.& nos. • Item 1063-K-7
JOURNAL. [Bimonthly]

Y 3.P 31:15-2/v.nos.&nos. • Item 1063-K-7
PEACE WATCH.

Y 3.P 31:16/nos. • Item 1063-K-8
IN BRIEF (Series).

Y 3.P 31:17 CT • Item 1063-K-5
BIBLIOGRAPHIES.

Y 3.P 31:18 • Item 1063-K-9 (MF)
SERIES ON RELIGION NATIONALISM AND INTOLERANCE.

Y 3.P 31:19/nos. • Item 1063-K-11
PEACEWORKS (series).

Y 3.P 31:20 • Item 1063-K (EL)
SPECIAL REPORTS.

PENNSYLVANIA AVENUE DEVELOPMENT CORPORATION
(1972– 1996)

CREATION AND AUTHORITY

The Pennsylvania Avenue Development Corporation was established as a wholly owned Federal corporation by the Act of October 27, 1972 (86 Stat. 1266; 40 U.S.C. 871 et seq.), as amended. Terminated by P.L. 104-99, January 26, 1996.

Y 3.P 38:1/date • Item 1089-L
ANNUAL REPORT. 1st–   1974–
ISSN 0094-7059

Y 3.P 38:2 CT • Item 1089-L
GENERAL PUBLICATIONS. [Irregular]

Y 3.P 38:8 CT • Item 1089-L
HANDBOOKS, MANUALS, GUIDES. [Irregular]

Y 3.P 38:16/date • Item 1089-L-1
THE AVENUE REPORT.

PENSION BENEFIT GUARANTY CORPORATION
(1974–   )

CREATION AND AUTHORITY

The Pension Benefit Guaranty Corporation was established by Title IV of the Employee Retirement Income Security Act of 1974, approved September 2, 1974 (88 Stat. 1004; 29 U.S.C. 1302).

INFORMATION

Pension Benefit Guaranty Corporation
1200 K Street, N.W.
Washington, D.C. 20005-4026
(202) 326-4000
Fax: (202) 326-4153
http://www.pbgc.gov

Y 3.P 38/2:1/date • Item 1070-N (MF)
ANNUAL REPORT. 1st–   1975–

Y 3.P 38/2:2 CT • Item 1070-N
GENERAL PUBLICATIONS.

Y 3.P 38/2:8 CT • Item 1070-N-1
HANDBOOKS, MANUALS, GUIDES.

Y 3.P 38/2:9/date • Item 1070-N (MF)
TELEPHONE DIRECTORY. [Quarterly]

Y 3.P 38/2:11 CT • Item 1070-N
FORMS.

Y 3.P 38/2:12/ • Item 1070-N-2 (P) (EL)
PENSION INSURANCE DATA BOOK:PBGC SINGLE-EMPLOYER PROGRAM. [Annual]

Y 3.P 38/2:13/ • Item 1070-N-3 (E)
ELECTRONIC PRODUCTS (misc.).

Y 3.P 38/12:14/ • Item 1070-N-4 (EL)
FACT SHEETS (PENSION BENEFIT GUARANTY CORPORATION).

FEDERAL WORKING GROUP ON PEST MANAGEMENT
(1974–   )

Y 3.P 43:1/date
ANNUAL REPORT.

Y 3.P 43:2 CT • Item 1089
GENERAL PUBLICATIONS.

Y 3.P 43:8 CT
HANDBOOKS, MANUALS, GUIDES.

ADVISORY COUNCIL ON INTERGOVERNMENTAL PERSONNEL POLICY
(1973–   )

Y 3.P 43/2:1/date
ANNUAL REPORT. 1st–   1973–

Y 3.P 43/2:2 CT
GENERAL PUBLICATIONS.

PETROLEUM ADMINISTRATION FOR WAR
(1942– 1946)

CREATION AND AUTHORITY

The Petroleum Administration for War was established by Executive Order 9276 of December 2, 1942, to succeed the Office of Petroleum Coordinator for War (I 50). The Administration was abolished by Executive Order 9718 of May 3, 1946, effective May 8, 1946.

Y 3.P 44:1/date
ANNUAL REPORTS.

Earlier I 50.1

Y 3.P 44:2 CT
GENERAL PUBLICATIONS.

Earlier I 50.2

Y 3.P 44:6 CT
REGULATIONS, RULES, AND INSTRUCTIONS.

Includes Handbooks and Manuals.

PHILIPPINE COMMISSION
(1899–1900)

CREATION AND AUTHORITY

The first Philippine Commission was established by the President in January 1899. The Commission submitted its final report on January 31, 1900. The second Philippine Commission was established by the President in April 1900. That Commission was abolished by act of Congress, approved August 29, 1916 (39 Stat. 545).

Y 3.P 53:CT
PUBLICATIONS.

PHILIPPINE WAR DAMAGE COMMISSION
(1946–1951)

CREATION AND AUTHORITY

The Philippine War Damage Commission was established by the Philippine Rehabilitation Act, approved April 30, 1946 (60 Stat. 128). The Commission was terminated on March 31, 1951, pursuant to the General Appropriation Act of 1951 (64 Stat. 699).

Y 3.P 53/2:1/date
SEMIANNUAL REPORTS.

Y 3.P 53/2:2 CT
GENERAL PUBLICATIONS.

PHYSICIAN PAYMENT REVIEW COMMISSION

CREATION AND AUTHORITY

The Physician Payment Review Commission was created by Public Law 99-272 to review current methods for paying physicians under the Medicare program and to make recommendations for change.

Y 3.P 56:1/date   • Item 1070-K-3
ANNUAL REPORTS.

JOINT COMMISSION ON GOVERNMENT PURCHASES OF PNEUMATIC TUBES
(1912–1914)

Y 3.P 74:CT
PUBLICATIONS.

JOINT COMMISSION ON PNEUMATIC TUBE MAIL SERVICE
(1917)

Y 3.P 74/2:CT
PUBLICATIONS.

COMMISSION ON POLITICAL ACTIVITY OF GOVERNMENT PERSONNEL
(1966–)

CREATION AND AUTHORITY

The Commission on Political Activity of Government Personnel was established by Public Law 89-617, approved October 3, 1966.

Y 3.P 75:1/date
REPORT.

Y 3.P 75:2 CT
GENERAL PUBLICATIONS.

COMMISSION ON POPULATION GROWTH AND THE AMERICAN FUTURE
(1970)

CREATION AND AUTHORITY

The Commission on Population Growth and the American Future was established by Public Law 91-213, approved March 16, 1970.

Y 3.P 81:1/date   • Item 1089
REPORTS.

Y 3.P 81:2 CT   • Item 1089
GENERAL PUBLICATIONS.

Y 3.P 81:9/nos.   • Item 1089
RESEARCH REPORTS. 1– 1972– [Irregular]

NATIONAL COMMISSION FOR THE OBSERVANCE OF WORLD POPULATION YEAR
(1974)

CREATION AND AUTHORITY

The National Commission for the Observance of World Population Year, 1974, was established by Executive Order 11763 of January 17, 1974. The Commission was required to conclude its work by the end of 1974 and make its report to the President within thirty days there-after, at which time the Commission was deemed to be terminated.

Y 3.P 81/2:1/date
REPORT.

PORTO RICO LAWS COMMISSION
(1901)

Y 3.P 83:CT
PUBLICATIONS.

COMMISSION TO INVESTIGATE THE POSTAL SERVICE
(1898–1901)

CREATION AND AUTHORITY

The Commission to Investigate the Postal Service was established by act of Congress, approved June 13, 1898 (30 Stat. 445). The Commission ceased to exist in 1901.

Y 3.P 84/1:CT
PUBLICATIONS.

POSTAL COMMISSION
(1906–1907)

CREATION AND AUTHORITY

The Commission on Second-Class Mail Matter, also known as the Postal Commission, was established by act of Congress, approved June 26, 1906. The Commission held hearings in October-November 1906 and submitted its report in 1907.

Y 3.P 84/2:CT
PUBLICATIONS.

JOINT COMMISSION ON THE POSTAL SERVICE
(1920)

Y 3.P 84/3:CT
PUBLICATIONS.

POSTAL RATE COMMISSION
(1970–)

CREATION AND AUTHORITY

The Postal Rate commission was established as an independent agency by Chapter 36, sub-chapter 1 of the Postal Reorganization Act of August 12, 1970 (84 Stat. 759; 39 U.S.C. 3601-3604)

INFORMATION

Postal Rate Commission
1333 H Street, NW, Ste. 300
Washington, D.C. 20268-0001
(202) 789-6800
Fax: (202) 789-6861
E-Mail:prc-admin@prc.gov
http://www.prc.gov

Y 3.P 84/4:1/date • Item 1092-A (MF)
REPORTS. • Item 1092 (P)

Y 3.P 84/4:2 CT • Item 1092-A (MF)
GENERAL PUBLICATIONS. • Item 1092 (P)

Y 3.P 84/4:9/letters&nos. • Item 1092-A (MF)
[POSTAL RATE HEARINGS] DOCKETS. • Item 1092 (P)

COMMISSION ON POSTAL SERVICE
(1976– 1977)

CREATION AND AUTHORITY

The Commission on Postal Service was established by Public Law 94-421 of September 24, 1976. The Commission was instructed to submit its final report on or before March 15, 1977.

Y 3.P 84/5:1/date • Item 1089
ANNUAL REPORT.

Y 3.P 84/5:2 CT
GENERAL PUBLICATIONS.

PRESIDENT'S ORGANIZATION ON UNEMPLOYMENT RELIEF
(1931– 1932)

CREATION AND AUTHORITY

The President's Emergency Committee for Employment was established in October 1930. On August 19, 1931, the Committee was reorganized as the President's Organization on Unemployment Relief. The Organization ceased to exist on June 30, 1932.

Y 3.P 92:1/date
ANNUAL REPORTS.

Y 3.P 92:2 CT
GENERAL PUBLICATIONS.

Y 3.P 92:3
BULLETINS.

Y 3.P 92:4
CIRCULARS.

Y 3.P 92:5/nos.
COMMUNITY PLANS AND ACTIONS.

Y 3.P 92:6 CT
ADMINISTRATION OF RELIEF COMMITTEES.

Y 3.P 92:7 CT
EMPLOYMENT PLANS AND SUGGESTIONS COMMITTEE.

PRESIDENT'S COMMITTEE ON CROP INSURANCE
(1936)

CREATION AND AUTHORITY

The President's Committee on Crop Insurance was established in 1936. The Committee submitted its report in December 1936.

Y 3.P 92/2:2 CT
GENERAL PUBLICATIONS.

PRESIDENT'S COMMITTEE ON ADMINISTRATIVE MANAGEMENT
(1936– 1937)

CREATION AND AUTHORITY

The President's Committee on Administrative Management was established in 1936. The Committee submitted its report in January 1937.

Y 3.P 92/3:1/date
REPORT.

Y 3.P 92/3:2 CT
GENERAL PUBLICATIONS.

Y 3.P 92/3:7/nos.
STUDIES ON ADMINISTRATIVE MANAGEMENT IN GOVERNMENT OF U.S.

PRESIDENT'S COMMITTEE ON CIVIL SERVICE IMPROVEMENT
(1939– 1941)

CREATION AND AUTHORITY

The President's Committee on Civil Service Improvement was established by Executive Order 8044 of January 31, 1939. The Committee submitted its final report in February 1941.

Y 3.P 92/4:CT
PUBLICATIONS.

PRESIDENT'S COMMITTEE ON RELIGIOUS AND MORAL WELFARE AND PRESIDENT'S COMMITTEE ON RELIGION AND WELFARE IN THE ARMED FORCES
(1949– 1951)

CREATION AND AUTHORITY

The President's Committee on Religious and Moral Welfare and Character Guidance in the Armed Forces was established by Executive Order 11013 of October 27, 1948. By Executive Order 10043 of March 10, 1949, the name was changed to President's Committee on Religion and Welfare in the Armed Forces.

Y 3.P 92/5:1/date
ANNUAL REPORTS.

Y 3.P 92/5:2 CT
GENERAL PUBLICATIONS.

PRESIDENTIAL COMMISSION ON CATASTROPHIC NUCLEAR ACCIDENTS

Y 3.P 92/6:1/date
ANNUAL REPORTS.

Y 3.P 92/6:2 CT • Item 1089
GENERAL PUBLICATIONS.

PRINTING INVESTIGATION COMMISSION
(1905– 1907)

CREATION AND AUTHORITY

The Printing Investigation Commission was established by act of Congress, approved March 3, 1905. The Commission ceased to exist in 1907.

Y 3.P 93:CT
PUBLICATIONS.

PRIORITY IN TRANSPORTATION COMMISSIONER
(1917)

Y 3.P 93/2:1/date
ANNUAL REPORTS.

Y 3.P 93/2:2 CT
GENERAL PUBLICATIONS.

PRISON INDUSTRIES REORGANIZATION ADMINISTRATION
(1935– 1940)

CREATION AND AUTHORITY

The Prison Industries Reorganization Administration was established on September 26, 1935, by the Emergency Relief Administration Act of 1935 (49 Stat. 115). The Administration functioned until September 30, 1940.

Y 3.P 93/3:1/date
ANNUAL REPORTS.

Y 3.P 93/3:2 CT
GENERAL PUBLICATIONS.

Y 3.P 93/3:3
BULLETINS.

PRICE COMMISSION
(1971– 1973)

CREATION AND AUTHORITY

The Price Commission was established by Executive Order 11627, October 15, 1971, pursuant to the Economic Stabilization Act of 1970, as amended (84 Stat. 1468; 85 Stat. 13, 38, 743). The Commission was abolished by Executive Order 11695 of January 11, 1973.

Y 3.P 93/4:1/date
ANNUAL REPORTS.

Y 3.P 93/4:2 CT   • Item 1089
GENERAL PUBLICATIONS.

Y 3.P 93/4:7 (CT)
PRESS RELEASES.

Y 3.P 93/4:9
INFORMATION FOR BUSINESS EXECUTIVES [AND] FIRMS WITH RETAILING AND WHOLESALE INTERESTS.   – September 1972. [Irregular]

PRIVACY PROTECTION STUDY
COMMISSION
(1974)

Y 3.P 93/5:1/date
REPORT.

Y 3.P 93/5:2 CT
GENERAL PUBLICATIONS.

NATIONAL CENTER FOR
PRODUCTIVITY AND QUALITY OF
WORKING LIFE
(1977– 1978)

Y 3.P 94:1/date   • Item 1092-B
ANNUAL REPORT. 1st–   1976–

Supersedes Annual Report of the National Commission on Productivity and Work Quality (Pr 37.8:P 94/R 29).
ISSN 0149-063X

Y 3.P 94:2 CT   • Item 1092-B
GENERAL PUBLICATIONS. [Irregular]

Y 3.P 94:9 CT   • Item 1092-B
PRODUCTIVITY AND JOB SECURITY.

PUBLIC LAND COMMISSION
(1879– 1880)

CREATION AND AUTHORITY

The Public Land Commission was appointed by the President on July 1, 1879 pursuant to act of Congress, approved March 3, 1879 (20 Stat. 294). The Commission submitted its report in 1880.

Y 3.P 96/1:CT
PUBLICATIONS.

PUBLIC LANDS COMMISSION
(1903– 1905)

CREATION AND AUTHORITY

The Public Lands Commission was established by the President on October 22, 1903. The Commission submitted its report in 1905.

Y 3.P 96/2:CT
PUBLICATIONS.

COMMITTEE ON PUBLIC
INFORMATION
(1917– 1919)

CREATION AND AUTHORITY

The Committee on Public Information was established by Executive Order 2594 of April 13, 1917. The Committee ceased to function on June 30, 1919.

Y 3.P 96/3:1/date
ANNUAL REPORTS.

Y 3.P 96/3:2 CT
GENERAL PUBLICATIONS.

Y 3.P 96/3:3/v.nos.
OFFICIAL BULLETIN.

Y 3.P 96/3:4
CIRCULARS.

Y 3.P 96/3:5/nos.
FOUR-MINUTE MEN BULLETINS.

Y 3.P 96/3:6 CT
RED, WHITE, AND BLUE SERIES.

Y 3.P 96/3:7/nos.
WAR INFORMATION SERIES.

Y 3.P 96/3:8/date
SPECIAL FEATURES SERVICE.

Y 3.P 96/3:9/nos.
LOYALTY LEAFLETS.

Y 3.P 96/3:10/nos.
SPEAKING DIVISION BULLETINS.

Y 3.P 96/3:11/nos.
CATALOGUE OF PHOTOGRAPHS AND STEREOPTICON SLIDES.

Y 3.P 96/3:12 CT
POSTERS.

Y 3.P 96/3:13/letters
FOUR MINUTE MEN NEWS.

Y 3.P 96/3:14/nos.
FOUR MINUTE MEN, ARMY BULLETINS.

Y 3.P 96/3:15/nos.
INDUSTRIAL RELATIONS DIVISION, SPECIAL SERVICE FOR EMPLOYERS, BULLETINS.

Y 3.P 96/3:16/vol.nos.
NATIONAL SCHOOL SERVICE.
Later I 16.31/6

Y 3.P 96/3:17/nos.
FOUR MINUTE MEN DIVISION, SCHOOL BULLETINS.

Y 3.P 96/3:18/nos.
CARTOONS BUREAU, BULLETIN.

PUBLIC BUILDINGS
COMMISSION
(1919– 1933)

CREATION AND AUTHORITY

The Public Buildings Commission was established by act of Congress, approved March 1, 1919 (40 Stat. 1269). The Commission was abolished by Executive Order 6227 of July 27, 1933, and its functions transferred to the Office of National Parks, Buildings and Reservations.

Y 3.P 96/4:CT
PUBLICATIONS.

COMMISSION ON THE
CONSERVATION AND
ADMINISTRATION OF THE
PUBLIC DOMAIN
(1930– 1931)

CREATION AND AUTHORITY

The Commission on the Conservation and Administration of the Public Domain, popularly known as the Public Lands Commission, was established by authority of act of April 10, 1930. The Commission submitted its report on February 11, 1931.

Y 3.P 96/5:CT
PUBLICATIONS.

PUBLICATION BOARD
(1945)

CREATION AND AUTHORITY

The Publication Board was established by Executive Order 9568 of June 8, 1945. The Board was succeeded by the Office of the Publication Board (C 35) in the Department of Commerce

Y 3.P 96/6:1/date
ANNUAL REPORTS.

Y 3.P 96/6:2 CT
GENERAL PUBLICATIONS.

Y 3.P 96/6:6 CT
REGULATIONS, RULES, AND INSTRUCTIONS.

Y 3.P 96/6:7/nos.
REPORTS.

Y 3.P 96/6:8/nos.
OPB REPORTS.

Y 3.P 96/6:9/v.nos.
BIBLIOGRAPHY OF SCIENTIFIC AND INDUSTRIAL REPORTS DISTRIBUTED BY OFFICE OF PUBLICATION BOARD. [Weekly]

Y 3.P 96/6:10/nos.
[COMMUNICATIONS REPORTS.]

PUBLIC LAND LAW REVIEW COMMISSION (1964– 1970)

CREATION AND AUTHORITY

The Public Land Law Review Commission was established by act of September 19, 1964. The Commission submitted its report and recommendations to Congress and the President on June 30, 1970.

Y 3.P 96/7:1/date
REPORT.

Y 3.P 96/7:2 CT
GENERAL PUBLICATIONS.

NATIONAL COMMISSION ON SERERELY DISTRESSED PUBLIC HOUSING

Y 3.P 96/9:2 CT • Item 1089
GENERAL PUBLICATIONS.

COMMITTEE ON PURCHASE OF PRODUCTS AND SERVICES OF THE BLIND AND OTHER SEVERELY HANDICAPPED (1971– 1974, 1993–)

CREATION AND AUTHORITY

The Committee on Purchase of Products and Services of the Blind and Other Severely Handicapped was established in 1971 to direct procurement of selected commodities and services of the Federal Government to qualified nonprofit agencies that service blind and other severely handicapped individuals with the objective on increasing employment opportunities for these individuals (85 Stat. 77; 41 U.S.C. 46-48).

INFORMATION

Committee for Purchase from the Blind
  and Other Severely Handicapped
Jefferson Plaza II
1421 Jefferson Davis Hwy.
Arlington, Virginia 22202-3259
(703) 603-7740
http://www.jwod.gov

Y 3.P 97:1/date • Item 1089-X
REPORT.
  Earlier Y 3.B 61:1

Y 3.P 97:2 CT • Item 1089-X
GENERAL PUBLICATIONS.
  Earlier Y 3.B 61:2

Y 3.P 97:8 CT • Item 1089-X
HANDBOOKS, MANUALS, GUIDES.

Y 3.P 97:9/date
COMMITTEE DIGEST. [Bimonthly]

• Item 1089
Y 3.P 97:10/date • Item 1089-X
PROCUREMENT LIST. [Annual]
  Supersedes Schedule of Blind-Made Products (Y 3.B 61:8).

INTERAGENCY RACIAL DATA COMMITTEE (1970)

CREATION AND AUTHORITY

The Interagency Racial Data Committee was established in November 1970 at the request of the Office of Economic Opportunity Task Force on Uniform Civil Rights Policies and Practices.

Y 3.R 11:1/date
REPORT.

Y 3.R 11:2 CT
GENERAL PUBLICATIONS. [Irregular]

UNITED STATES RADIATION POLICY COUNCIL (1980– 1982)

CREATION AND AUTHORITY

The United States Radiation Policy Council was established by Executive Order 12194 of February 1980. The Council was abolished by Executive Order 12379 of August 17, 1982.

Y 3.R 11/2:1/date
ANNUAL REPORT.

Y 3.R 11/2:2 CT • Item 1070-R-1
GENERAL PUBLICATIONS. [Irregular]

RAILROAD SECURITIES COMMISSION (1910– 1911)

CREATION AND AUTHORITY

The Railroad Securities Commission was established by the President in August 1910, pursuant to act of Congress, approved June 18, 1910 (36 Stat. 556). The Commission submitted its report in 1911.

Y 3.R 13:CT
PUBLICATIONS.

RAILROAD ADMINISTRATION (1918– 1939)

CREATION AND AUTHORITY

The United States Railroad Administration was established on February 9, 1918, pursuant to Presidential Proclamation 1419 of December 26, 1917, and the act of Congress, approved August 29, 1916. An act of Congress, approved February 28, 1920, authorized the liquidation of the Administration, which was completed by 1939.

Y 3.R 13/2:1/date
ANNUAL REPORTS.

Y 3.R 13/2:1-b/date
  – ABSTRACTS.

Y 3.R 13/2:2 CT
GENERAL PUBLICATIONS.

Y 3.R 13/2:3
BULLETINS.

Y 3.R 13/2:4/nos.
CIRCULARS.

Y 3.R 13/2:5/nos.
GENERAL ORDERS AND ORDERS.

Y 3.R 13/2:6 CT
AGREEMENTS.

Y 3.R 13/2:7/nos.
SPECIFICATIONS.

Y 3.R 13/2:8 CT
PAPERS IN RE.

Y 3.R 13/2:9 CT
ANNUAL REPORTS OF REGIONS.

Finance Division

Y 3.R 13/2:11/date
ANNUAL REPORTS.

Y 3.R 13/2:12 CT
GENERAL PUBLICATIONS.

Y 3.R 13/2:13/nos.
BULLETINS.

Y 3.R 13/2:14/nos.
CIRCULARS.

Y 3.R 13/2:15/nos.
CENTRAL ADVISORY PURCHASING COMMITTEE, CIRCULARS.

Operation Division

Y 3.R 13/2:21/date
ANNUAL REPORTS.

Y 3.R 13/2:22 CT
GENERAL PUBLICATIONS.

Y 3.R 13/2:23/nos.
BULLETINS.

Y 3.R 13/2:24/nos.
CIRCULARS.

Y 3.R 13/2:25/nos.
MECHANICAL DEPARTMENT CIRCULARS.

Y 3.R 13/2:26/nos.
SAFETY SECTION CIRCULARS.

Y 3.R 13/2:27/nos.
CAR SERVICE SECTION, CIRCULARS.

Y 3.R 13/2:28/nos.
FUEL CONSERVATION CIRCULARS.

Y 3.R 13/2:29/nos.
CAR SERVICE SECTION, BULLETINS.

Comptroller

Y 3.R 13/2:31/date
ANNUAL REPORTS.

Y 3.R 13/2:32 CT
GENERAL PUBLICATIONS.

Y 3.R 13/2:33/nos.
ACCOUNTING BULLETINS.

Y 3.R 13/2:34/nos.
CIRCULARS.

Y 3.R 13/2:35/nos.
OVER CHANGE CLAIM CIRCULARS.

Traffic Division

Y 3.R 13/2:41/date
ANNUAL REPORTS.

Y 3.R 13/2:42 CT
GENERAL PUBLICATIONS.

Y 3.R 13/2:43/nos.
BULLETINS.

Y 3.R 13/2:44/nos.
CIRCULARS.

Y 3.R 13/2:45/nos.
AGRICULTURAL SECTION, CIRCULAR LETTERS.

Labor Division

Y 3.R 13/2:51/date
ANNUAL REPORTS.

Y 3.R 13/2:52 CT
GENERAL PUBLICATIONS.

Y 3.R 13/2:53/nos.
BULLETINS.

Y 3.R 13/2:54/nos.
CIRCULARS.

Y 3.R 13/2:55/case nos.
RAILWAY BOARD OF ADJUSTMENT NO. 1, DECISIONS (individual cases).

Y 3.R 13/2:56/case nos.
RAILWAY BOARD OF ADJUSTMENT NO. 2, DECISIONS (individual cases).

Y 3.R 13/2:56/date
RAILWAY BOARD OF ADJUSTMENT NO. 2, DECISIONS (compilations, quarterly).

Y 3.R 13/2:57/case nos.
RAILWAY BOARD OF ADJUSTMENT NO. 3, DECISIONS (individual cases).

Y 3.R 13/2:57/date
RAILWAY BOARD OF ADJUSTMENT NO. 3, DECISIONS (compilations).

Law Division

Y 3.R 13/2:61/date
ANNUAL REPORTS.

Y 3.R 13/2:62 CT
GENERAL PUBLICATIONS.

Y 3.R 13/2:63/nos.
BULLETINS.

Y 3.R 13/2:64/nos.
CIRCULARS.

Y 3.R 13/2:65/nos.
CLAIMS AND PROPERTY PROTECTION SECTION, CIRCULARS.

Suggestions and Complaints Bureau

Y 3.R 13/2:71/date
ANNUAL REPORTS.

Y 3.R 13/2:72 CT
GENERAL PUBLICATIONS.

Y 3.R 13/2:73
BULLETINS.

Y 3.R 13/2:74
CIRCULARS.

Public Service Division

Y 3.R 13/2:81/date
ANNUAL REPORTS.

Y 3.R 13/2:82 CT
GENERAL PUBLICATIONS.

Y 3.R 13/2:83/nos.
BULLETINS.

Y 3.R 13/2:84/nos.
CIRCULARS.

Liquidation Claims Division

Y 3.R 13/2:91/date
ANNUAL REPORTS.

Y 3.R 13/2:92 CT
GENERAL PUBLICATIONS.

Y 3.R 13/2:93/nos.
BULLETINS.

Y 3.R 13/2:94/nos.
CIRCULARS.

Capital Expenditures Division

Y 3.R 13/2:101/date
ANNUAL REPORTS.

Y 3.R 13/2:102 CT
GENERAL PUBLICATIONS.

Y 3.R 13/2:103
BULLETINS.

Y 3.R 13/2:104/nos.
CIRCULARS.

Purchases Division

Y 3.R 13/2:111/date
ANNUAL REPORTS.

Y 3.R 13/2:112 CT
GENERAL PUBLICATIONS.

Y 3.R 13/2:113
BULLETINS.

Y 3.R 13/2:114
CIRCULARS.

Troop Movement Section

Y 3.R 13/2:121/date
ANNUAL REPORTS.

Y 3.R 13/2:122 CT
GENERAL PUBLICATIONS.

Y 3.R 13/2:123
BULLETINS.

Y 3.R 13/2:124/nos. and letters & nos.
CIRCULARS (numbered and lettered & numbered).

Y 3.R 13/2:125/nos.
DEMOBILIZATION CIRCULAR LETTERS.

COMMISSION ON RAILROAD RETIREMENT
(1970– 1972)

CREATION AND AUTHORITY

The Commission on Railroad Retirement was established by Public Law 91-377, approved August 12, 1970. By Public Law 92-46, the Commission was required to transmit to the President and Congress its report, together with its recommendations, no later than July 1, 1972.

Y 3.R 13/3:1/date • Item 1089
REPORT.

Y 3.R 13/3:2 CT • Item 1089
GENERAL PUBLICATIONS.

UNITED STATES RAILWAY ASSOCIATION
(1974– 1987)

CREATION AND AUTHORITY

The United States Railway Association was established by Public Law 93-236 of January 2, 1974, to plan and finance a new rail system for the Northeastern region of the United States. The Association was terminated April 1, 1987 by act of October 21, 1986 (100 Stat. 1906).

Y 3.R 13/4:1/date • Item 1070-R
ANNUAL REPORT. 1st– 1974–

Y 3.R 13/4:2 CT • Item 1070-R
GENERAL PUBLICATIONS.

Y 3.R 13/4:7/date • Item 1070-R
PRESS RELEASES. [Irregular]

Y 3.R 13/4:9/date • Item 1070-R
REPORT TO CONGRESS ON CONRAIL PERFORMANCE. [Annual]

RECONSTRUCTION FINANCE CORPORATION
(1932– 1939, 1947– 1954)

CREATION AND AUTHORITY

The Reconstruction Finance Corporation was established by the Reconstruction Finance Corporation Act, approved January 22, 1932 (47 Stat. 5). Reorganization Plan No. 1 of 1939 grouped the Corporation with other agencies to form the Federal Loan Agency (FL 5), effective July 1, 1939. When the Federal Loan Agency was abolished by the act approved June 30, 1947 (61 Stat. 202), the Corporation returned to its independent status. The act of Congress, approved July 30, 1953 (67 Stat. 230) provided for its termination on June 30, 1954. Reorganization Plan No. 2 of 1954 and Executive Order 10539 of June 22, 1954 provided for the transfer of its functions to other agencies.

Y 3.R 24:1/date
ANNUAL REPORTS.
Later FL 5.1

Y 3.R 24:2 CT
GENERAL PUBLICATIONS.
Later FL 5.2 and HH 6.2

Y 3.R 24:3
BULLETINS.

Y 3.R 24:4/nos.
CIRCULARS.
Later FL 5.4

Y 3.R 24:5 CT
LAWS.
Later FL 5.5

Y 3.R 24:6 CT
REGULATIONS, RULES AND INSTRUCTIONS.

Y 3.R 24:7/date
QUARTERLY REPORTS.
Later FL 5.7

Y 3.R 24:8/nos.
EMERGENCY RELIEF BULLETINS.

Y 3.R 24:9/nos.
RFC MORTGAGE COMPANY, CIRCULARS.

Y 3.R 24:10 CT
PAPERS IN RE.
      Later FL 5.10

Y 3.R 24:11/date
[MONTHLY REPORTS].
      Later FL 5.8

Y 3.R 24:12 CT
ADDRESSES.
      Later FL 5.9

Y 3.R 24:13/nos.
FEDERAL NATIONAL MORTGAGE ASSOCIATION,
      CIRCULARS.

Y 3.R 24:14/nos.
FHA AND VA MORTGAGES OWNED AND AVAILABLE
      FOR SALE BY RECONSTRUCTION FINANCE
      CORPORATION AND FEDERAL NATIONAL MORT-
      GAGE ASSOCIATION.

Y 3.R 24:15
RELEASES.

Y 3.R 24:16/nos.
SPECIFICATIONS.

Y 3.R 24:17
MEMORANDUM TO ALL OPERATORS. [Admin.]

NATIONAL STUDY COMMISSION ON RECORDS AND DOCUMENTS OF FEDERAL OFFICIALS (1974–1976)

CREATION AND AUTHORITY

The National Study Commission on Records
and Documents of Federal Officials was established by the Presidential Recordings and Materials Preservation Act of December 19, 1974, Public Law 93-526. The Commission was instructed
to submit a report to the President and Congress
not later than March 31, 1976, and cease to exist
60 days thereafter.

Y 3.R 24/2:1/date   • **Item 1089**
REPORT.

REGULATORY COUNCIL

Y 3.R 26:1/date
REPORTS.

Y 3.R 26:2 CT   • **Item 1071-C**
GENERAL PUBLICATIONS. [Irregular]

Y 3.R 26:9/date
CALENDAR OF FEDERAL REGULATIONS. [Semi-
annual]

INTERAGENCY REGULATORY LIAISON GROUP

Y 3.R 26/2:1/date   • **Item 1071-B**
REPORTS.

Y 3.R 26/2:2 CT   • **Item 1071-B**
GENERAL PUBLICATIONS. [Irregular]

Y 3.R 26/2:8 CT
HANDBOOKS, MANUALS, GUIDES. [Irregular]

Y 3.R 26/2:9/v.nos.&nos.   • **Item 1071-B**
REGULATORY REPORTER. v. 1–   1979–

RENT COMMISSION OF DISTRICT OF COLUMBIA (1919–1925)

Y 3.R 29:CT
PUBLICATIONS.

COMMISSION ON RENOVATION OF THE EXECUTIVE MANSION (1949–1952)

Y 3.R 29/2:CT
REPORTS AND PUBLICATIONS.

RESETTLEMENT ADMINISTRATION (1935–1937)

CREATION AND AUTHORITY

The Resettlement Administration was established as an independent agency by Executive
Order 7020 of April 30, 1935. The Administration
was transferred to the Department of Agriculture
(A 61) by Executive Order 7530 of December 31,
1936, effective January 1, 1937.

Y 3.R 31:1/date
ANNUAL REPORTS.

Y 3.R 31:2 CT
GENERAL PUBLICATIONS.

Y 3.R 31:9
LAND POLICY CIRCULARS. [Monthly]
      Later A 61.9

Y 3.R 31:10 CT
ADDRESSES.

Y 3.R 31:11/nos.
ADMINISTRATIVE INSTRUCTIONS.

Y 3.R 31:12/nos.
ADMINISTRATIVE NOTICES.

Y 3.R 31:13/nos.
ADMINISTRATIVE ORDERS.

Y 3.R 31:14/nos.
COMPTROLLER GENERAL'S RULINGS.

Y 3.R 31:15/date
DIGEST OF PROCEDURE MANUAL MATERIALS.

Y 3.R 31:16/nos.
EXECUTIVE ORDERS (Affecting Resettlement Administration).

Y 3.R 31:17/nos.
EXECUTIVE ORDERS (Affecting Works Progress Administration).

Y 3.R 31:18/nos.
FLOW CHARTS.

Y 3.R 31:19/nos.
GRAPHS.

Y 3.R 31:20/nos.
ORGANIZATION CHARTS.

Y 3.R 31:21/nos.
WORKS PROGRESS ADMINISTRATION ORDERS.

Y 3.R 31:22/nos.
ADMINISTRATION DATA.

Y 3.R 31:23/nos.
LAND USE PLANNING PUBLICATIONS.
      Later A 61.8

Y 3.R 31:24/nos.
HANDBOOKS.

Y 3.R 31:25 CT
MAPS.

Y 3.R 31:26/letters-nos.
PROCEDURES INDEXES.

Y 3.R 31:27 CT
PROCEDURE MANUALS, TABLE OF CONTENTS BY
      SUBJECT.

Y 3.R 31:28/date
PROCEDURE MATERIAL INSERT RECORDS.

Y 3.R 31:29/date
RESEARCH-REFERENCE ACCESSIONS. [Semi-
monthly]
      Later A 61.15

RESOLUTION TRUST CORPORATION

Y 3.R 31/2:1/date   • **Item 1061-K-1**
ANNUAL REPORT.

Y 3.R 31/2:2 CT   • **Item 1061-K-1**
GENERAL PUBLICATIONS.

Y 3.R 31/2:15   • **Item 1061-K-10**
REAL ESTATE ASSET INVENTORY.

Y 3.R 31/2:16   • **Item 1061-K-4**
THE SILVER LINING. [Quarterly]

Y 3.R 31/2:17   • **Item 1061-K-11**
RTC REVIEW. [Monthly]

REVISION OF STATUTES COMMISSION (1872–1873)

Y 3.R 32:CT
PUBLICATIONS.

FRANKLIN DELANO ROOSEVELT MEMORIAL COMMISSION
(1955–   )

CREATION AND AUTHORITY

The Franklin Delano Roosevelt Memorial Commission was established by Public Law 372, 84th Congress, 1st session, approved Aug. 11, 1955. Terminated by act of Nov. 14, 1997 (III Stat.1601).

Y 3.R 67:1/date   • Item 1073-A
REPORTS.

Y 3.R 67:2 CT   • Item 1073-A
GENERAL PUBLICATIONS.

RUBBER PRODUCING FACILITIES DISPOSAL COMMISSION
(1953–1956)

CREATION AND AUTHORITY

The Rubber Producing Facilities Disposal Commission was established by act of Congress, approved August 7, 1953 (67 Stat. 408). Executive Order 10678 of September 20, 1956, abolished the Commission and transferred its functions to the Federal Facilities Corporation (T 69), effective September 24, 1956.

Y 3.R 82:1/date
REPORTS.

Y 3.R 82:2 CT
GENERAL PUBLICATIONS.

Y 3.R 82:7/nos.
RELEASES.

RURAL ELECTRIFICATION ADMINISTRATION
(1935–1939)

CREATION AND AUTHORITY

The Rural Electrification Administration was established by Executive Order 7037 of May 11, 1935 pursuant to the Emergency Relief Appropriation Act of 1935, approved April 8, 1935 (49 Stat. 115). Reorganization Plan No. 1 of 1939, effective July 1, 1939 transferred the Administration to the Department of Agriculture (A 68).

Y 3.R 88:1/date
ANNUAL REPORTS.
     Later A 68.1

Y 3.R 88:2 CT
GENERAL PUBLICATIONS.
     Later A 68.2

Y 3.R 88:6 CT
REGULATIONS, RULES, AND INSTRUCTIONS.

Y 3.R 88:8 CT
POSTERS.

Y 3.R 88:9/vol.
RURAL ELECTRIFICATION NEWS. [Monthly]
     Later A 68.9

Y 3.R 88:10 CT
ADDRESSES.

Y 3.R 88:11/nos.
SUGGESTED RURAL LINE CONSTRUCTION.

Y 3.R 88:12/nos.
GENERAL PROGRESS BULLETINS: NEW ALLOTMENTS. [Weekly]
     Supersedes Press Releases (not classified).
     Later A 68.8

Y 3.R 88:13/nos.
GENERAL CONSTRUCTION BULLETINS.
     Later A 68.7

Y 3.R 88:14/nos.
UTILIZATION POSTERS.

Y 3.R 88:15/nos.
DAILY INDEX OF REA NEWS.

Y 3.R 88:16/date
FARM POWER NEWS. [Weekly]

Y 3.R 88:17/date
[LIBRARY LIST OF PAMPHLETS, BOOKS, ETC.] [Weekly]
     Later A 68.10

Y 3.R 88:18/nos.
ENGINEERING BULLETINS.

Y 3.R 88:19
ADMINISTRATIVE ORDERS.
     Proc.

Y 3.R 88:20
GENERAL MEMORANDUM.
     Proc. Admin.

Y 3.R 88:21
GENERAL ORDERS.
     Proc. Admin.

RURAL DEVELOPMENT PROGRAM COMMITTEE
(1954–1963)

CREATION AND AUTHORITY

The Rural Development Program Committee was established in May 1954.

Y 3.R 88/2:1/date
ANNUAL REPORTS.

Y 3.R 88/2:2 CT
GENERAL PUBLICATIONS.

Y 3.R 88/2:8/nos.
RURAL RESOURCE LEAFLETS.

     Earlier A 21.25/2

Y 3.R 88/2:9/nos.
RURAL DEVELOPMENT PROGRAM NEWS. [Irregular]

     Earlier A 21.25

Y 3.R 88/2:10 CT
HANDBOOKS, MANUALS, GUIDES.

COMMITTEE ON RURAL DEVELOPMENT
(1963–1966)

CREATION AND AUTHORITY

The Committee on Rural Development was established by Executive Order 11122 of October 16, 1963. Executive Order 11307 of September 30, 1966 abolished the Committee and transferred its functions to the Secretary of Agriculture.

Y 3.R 88/3:1/date
REPORTS.

Y 3.R 88/3:2 CT
GENERAL PUBLICATIONS.

SAINT LAWRENCE SEAWAY DEVELOPMENT CORPORATION
(1954–1966)

CREATION AND AUTHORITY

The Saint Lawrence Seaway Development Corporation was established by act of Congress, approved May 13, 1954 (68 Stat. 92). Pursuant to Public Law 89-670, approved October 15, 1966 (80 Stat. 932), it was made a component of the newly established Department of Transportation (TD 6).

Y 3.Sa 2:1/date
ANNUAL REPORTS.

Y 3.Sa 2:2 CT
GENERAL PUBLICATIONS.

Y 3.Sa 2:7/date
RELEASES.

Y 3.Sa 2:8 CT
MAPS AND CHARTS.

Y 3.Sa 2:9 CT
BIBLIOGRAPHIES AND LISTS OF PUBLICATIONS.

Y 3.Sa 2:10 CT
ADDRESSES

SAINT AUGUSTINE QUADRICENTENNIAL COMMISSION
(1962)

Y 3.Sa 2/2:1/date
REPORTS.

Y 3.Sa 2/2:2 CT
GENERAL PUBLICATIONS.

SANTO DOMINGO COMMISSION
(1871)

Y 3.Sa 5:CT
PUBLICATIONS.

SELECTIVE SERVICE SYSTEM
(1948–   )

CREATION AND AUTHORITY

The Selective Service System was established by Executive Order of September 23, 1940, pursuant to the Selective Training and Service Act of September 16, 1940. Except between December 5, 1942 and December 5, 1943, when it was under the jurisdiction of the War Manpower Commission (Pr 23.5270), the System was responsible to the President. On March 31, 1947, when legislation authorizing selective service expired, the Office of Selective Service Records was established to liquidate the System and preserve and provide service on its records. The Selective Service System was reconstituted by an act of June 24, 1948.

INFORMATION

Selective Service System
1515 Wilson Blvd.
Arlington, VA 22209-2425
(703) 605-4100
Fax: (703) 605-4106
Email:information@sss.gov
http://www.sss.gov

Y 3.Se 4:1 • Item 1076 (EL)
ANNUAL REPORT TO THE CONGRESS OF THE UNITED STATES, FROM THE DIRECTOR.

Earlier issued semiannually.

Y 3.Se 4:2 CT • Item 1075
GENERAL PUBLICATIONS.
See also Pr 32.5272

Y 3.Se 4:4/nos
SELECTIVE SERVICE CIRCULARS.

Y 3.Se 4:5 CT
LAWS.

Y 3.Se 4:6/vol.
SELECTIVE SERVICE REGULATIONS.

Y 3.Se 4:6/date
SELECTIVE SERVICE REGULATIONS (date).

Y 3.Se 4:7 • Item 1077
SELECTIVE SERVICE REGULATIONS. – 1971. [Irregular]

Includes all official rules and regulations of the Selective Service System for local boards.
Subscription includes basic volume plus supplementary material for an indefinite period.

Y 3.Se 4:8/nos.
MEDICAL CIRCULARS.
See also Pr 32.5281

Y 3.Se 4:9/vol.
SELECTIVE SERVICE.
See also Pr 32.5297

Y 3.Se 4:10 CT
REGULATIONS, RULES, AND INSTRUCTIONS.
See also Pr 32.5276

Y 3.Se 4:10-2 CT • Item 1075
HANDBOOKS, MANUALS, GUIDES.

Y 3.Se 4:10-2 R 26 • Item 1075
REGISTRANTS PROCESSING MANUAL. [Irregular] (Includes basic manual plus supplementary material for an indefinite period) (SSR PM-600)

PURPOSE:– To disseminate directives which will govern the operational aspects of the Selective Service System at State and local levels. It contains all necessary information for registration, classification, examination, induction, allied subjects and procedures relating thereto.
This publication replaces Selective Service Regulations (SSRG) (Y 3.Se 4:7) and Local Board Memoranda (LBM) (Y 3.S e 4:13-2), which are discontinued.

Y 3.Se 4:11/nos.
LOCAL BOARD RELEASES.
See also Pr 32.5277

Y 3.Se 4:12/nos.
OCCUPATIONAL BULLETINS.
See also Pr 32.5278

Y 3.Se 4:13/nos.
TRANSMITTAL MEMO [for] LOCAL BOARD MEMORANDUMS.

Y 3.Se 4:13/date
LOCAL BOARD MEMORANDA (Compilations).

Y 3.Se 4:13-2 • Item 1079
LOCAL BOARD MEMORANDA. [Irregular]
Contains information relating to Selective Service and allied or related fields.
Subscription includes basic volume plus supplementary material for an indefinite period.

Y 3.Se 4:13-3/nos.
LOCAL BOARD MEMORANDUMS (numbered).
Earlier Y 3.Se 4:13-2

Y 3.Se 4:14/packet letters
[HISTORICAL NOTES].

Y 3.Se 4:15/nos.
MEDICAL STATISTICS BULLETINS.

Y 3.Se 4:16 nos.
MEDICAL TRANSMITTAL MEMORANDUMS.

Y 3.Se 4:17 • Item 1078
SPECIAL MONOGRAPHS. 1–   [Irregular]

Y 3.Se 4:18/nos.
VETERANS ASSISTANCE INFORMATION. PRINTED AND PROCESSED.

Y 3.Se 4:19/packet nos.
OFFICE OF SELECTIVE SERVICE RECORDS REGULATIONS.

Y 3.Se 4:20 • Item 1077-A
SELECTIVE SERVICE NEWS. v. 1–   1951– 1976. [Monthly]

PURPOSE:– To enhance the furtherance and exchange of employee morale and information, the dissemination of which does not come within the scope of the regular channels of instruction.
Each issue 4 pages. Departments: Savings Bond Report, Official Notices, and Classification Picture.
A similar publication was issued under the same title during the period 1941-1947. When resumed in August 1951, it was renumbered to begin with volume 1, number 1.
ISSN 0361-2716

Y 3.Se 4:21
MEMORANDUM TO STATE DIRECTORS.

Y 3.Se 4:22/date • Item 1077-B
SELECTIVE SERVICE COLLEGE QUALIFICATION TEST, BULLETIN OF INFORMATION. [Annual]
Earlier Y 3.Se 4:2 C 68

Y 3.Se 4:23
POSTERS.

Y 3.Se 4:24/date • Item 1079-B
LIST OF LOCAL BOARDS OF THE SELECTIVE SERVICE SYSTEM. [Irregular] (includes basic manual plus supplementary material for an indefinite period)

Gives local board number, county or area under which it has jurisdiction, address and State code number.

Y 3.Se 4:25 CT • Item 1077-C
DRAFT INFORMATION SERIES. [Irregular]

Y 3.Se 4:26/date • Item 1075-A (MF)
TELEPHONE DIRECTORY. [Irregular] 83-2

Y 3.Se 4:27/date • Item 1079-B
THE REGISTER. [Monthly]

UNITED STATES SENTENCING COMMISSION
(1987–   )

CREATION AND AUTHORITY

The United States Sentencing Commission was established by P.L. 98-473.

INFORMATION

Office of Public Affairs
U.S. Sentencing Commission
One Columbus Circle, NE
Washington, D.C. 20002-8002
(202) 502-4500
Email:pubaffairs@ussc.gov
http://www.ussc.gov

Y 3.Se 5:1 • Item 1094 (MF)
REPORTS AND PUBLICATIONS.

Y 3.Se 5:2 CT • Item 1094
GENERAL PUBLICATIONS.

Y 3.Se 5:8 CT • Item 1094
HANDBOOKS, MANUALS, GUIDES.

Y 3.Se 5:14 • Item 1094 (MF)
PUBLIC HEARINGS.

Y 3.Se 5:15 • Item 1094 (MF)
REPRINT SERIES. [Irregular]

Y 3.Se 5:16 • Item 1094-B (MF)
MINUTES OF U.S. SENTENCING COMMISSION MEETINGS.

Y 3.Se 5:17/date • Item 1094-C (MF) (EL)
GUIDE LINES.

NATIONAL ADVISORY COMMITTEE ON SEMICONDUCTORS
(1988–   )

Y 3.Se 5/3:1/date • Item 1094-A (MF)
REPORTS.

Y 3.Se 5/3:2 CT • Item 1094-A
GENERAL PUBLICATIONS.

SHIP STRUCTURE COMMITTEE
(1946–   )

CREATION AND AUTHORITY

The Ship Structure Committee was established by the Secretary of the Treasury in July 1946 to continue the work of a wartime board on improvement of hull structures. Its membership consists of various government agencies.

INFORMATION

Ship Structure Committee
U.S. Coast Guard (G-MSE/SSC)
2100 Second St., NW
Washington, D.C. 20593-0001
(202) 267-0148
Fax: (202) 267-4816
http://www.shipstructure.org

Y 3.Sh 6:2 CT   • Item 1072-A
GENERAL PUBLICATIONS.

Y 3.Sh 6:3 CT   • Item 1072-A
BIBLIOGRAPHIES AND LISTS OF PUBLICATIONS.
[Irregular]

Y 3.Sh 6:6/letters-nos.   • Item 1072-A
TECHNICAL REPORTS.

Y 3.Sh 6:6/SSC-nos.   • Item 1072
SSC [Ship Structure Committee]. 1–   [Irregular]

AMERICAN SHIPBUILDING
COMMISSION
(1973–   )

Y 3.Sh 6/2:1/date   • Item 1089
REPORT.

Y 3.Sh 6/2:2 CT
GENERAL PUBLICATIONS.

JOINT COMMISSION TO
CONSIDER THE PRESENT
ORGANIZATIONS OF THE SIGNAL
SERVICE, GEOLOGICAL SURVEY,
COAST AND GEODETIC SURVEY,
AND HYDROGRAPHIC OFFICE
(1886)

Y 3.Si 2:1/date
REPORTS.

Y 3.Si 2:2 CT
GENERAL PUBLICATIONS.

NATIONAL COMMISSION ON
SOCIAL SECURITY
(1977–   )

CREATION AND AUTHORITY

The National Commission on Social Security was established by Public Law 95-216, the Social Security Amendments of 1977.

Y 3.So 1:1/date   • Item 1089
ANNUAL REPORT.

Y 3.So 1:2 CT   • Item 1089
GENERAL PUBLICATIONS. [Irregular]

SOURIS-RED-RAINY RIVER
BASINS COMMISSION
(1967–1973)

CREATION AND AUTHORITY

The Souris-Red-Rainy River Basins Commission was established by Executive Order 11359 of June 20, 1967. Its life was extended from June 30, 1972 to June 30, 1973 by Executive Order 11635 of December 9, 1971. The Commission was abolished and its functions transferred to the Upper Mississippi River Basin Commission by Executive Order 11737 of September 7, 1973.

Y 3.So 8:1/date
ANNUAL REPORT.

Y 3.So 8:2 CT
GENERAL PUBLICATIONS.

SOUTHWEST BORDER
REGIONAL COMMISSION
(1965–1981)

CREATION AND AUTHORITY

The Southwest Border Regional Commission was established under Title V of the Public Works and Economic Development Act of 1965, as amended (42 U.S.C. 3121). The Federal role in this Commission was abolished through repeal of the Public Works and Economic Development Act by section 1821 of Public Law 97-35 of August 13, 1981 (95 Stat. 766) effective October 1, 1981.

Y 3.So 8/2:1/date
REPORT.

Y 3.So 8/2:2 CT
GENERAL PUBLICATIONS. [Irregular]

NATIONAL COMMISSION ON
SPACE

Y 3.Sp 1:CT
REPORTS AND PUBLICATIONS.

SPANISH TREATY CLAIMS
COMMISSION
(1901–1910)

CREATION AND AUTHORITY

The Spanish Treaty Claims Commission was established by act of Congress, approved March 2, 1901. The Commission ceased to exist on May 2, 1910.

Y 3.Sp 2:1/date
ANNUAL REPORTS.

Y 3.Sp 2:2 CT
GENERAL PUBLICATIONS.

Y 3.Sp 2:3
BULLETINS [none issued].

Y 3.Sp 2:4
CIRCULARS [none issued].

Y 3.Sp 2:5/docket nos.
PETITIONS.

Y 3.Sp 2:6/nos.
OPINIONS.

CABINET COMMITTEE ON
OPPORTUNITY FOR THE
SPANISH SPEAKING PEOPLES
(1970–1974)

CREATION AND AUTHORITY

The Cabinet Committee on Opportunities for Spanish-Speaking Peoples was established by Public Law 91-181, approved December 30, 1969. The Committee supersedes the Inter-Agency Committee on Mexican American Affairs. The Committee was terminated on December 30, 1974, pursuant to the terms of the act.

Y 3.Sp 2/7:1/date   • Item 1067-K
ANNUAL REPORT.

Y 3.Sp 2/7:2 CT   • Item 1067-K
GENERAL PUBLICATIONS.

Y 3.Sp 2/7:7 CT
PRESS RELEASES. [Irregular]

Y 3.Sp 2/7:9/v.nos.&nos.
HOY. v. 1– 3. 1972– 1974. [Semimonthly]

STRATEGY COUNCIL ON DRUG ABUSE
(1972–   )

CREATION AND AUTHORITY

The Strategy Council on Drug Abuse was established by Public Law 92-255, approved March 21, 1971.

Y 3.St 8:1/date   • Item 1089
REPORT.

Y 3.St 8:2 CT   • Item 1089
GENERAL PUBLICATIONS. [Irregular]

NATIONAL COMMISSION ON STUDENT FINANCIAL ASSISTANCE

Y 3.St 9:1/date
ANNUAL REPORTS.

Y 3.St 9:2 CT
GENERAL PUBLICATIONS. [Irregular]

Y 3.St 9:9/nos.
REPORTS. 1–   [Irregular]

SUBVERSIVE ACTIVITIES CONTROL BOARD
(1950–1973)

CREATION AND AUTHORITY

The Subversive Activities Control Board was established by the Subversive Activities Control Act of 1950 (64 Stat. 987, 50 U.S.C. 781 et seq.). The act was amended by the Communist Control Act of 1954 (68 Stat. 775) and by the act of January 2, 1968 (81 Stat. 765). Ceased to operate June 30, 1973, unfunded.

Y 3.Su 1:1   • Item 1079-A
REPORT. 1st–   1951–   [Annual]

Report submitted by the Board to the President and Congress pursuant to section 12(c) of the Subversive Activities Control Act of 1950 (P.L. 81-831) for the fiscal year.

Y 3.Su 1:2 CT   • Item 1079-A
GENERAL PUBLICATIONS.

Y 3.Su 1:6 CT   • Item 1079-A
REGULATIONS, RULES, AND INSTRUCTIONS.

Y 3.Su 1:8
DECISIONS, ORDERS AND REPORTS.

Y 3.Su 1:8-2:v.nos.   • Item 1079-A
REPORTS OF SUBVERSIVE ACTIVITIES CONTROL BOARD (bound volumes).

SUGAR EQUALIZATION BOARD
(1918–1926)

CREATION AND AUTHORITY

The United States Sugar Equalization Board was established by the Food Administrator as a Delaware corporation on July 11, 1918. The Board was terminated by Executive Order 4475 of July 10, 1926.

Y 3.Su 3:CT
PUBLICATIONS.

FEDERAL BOARD OF SURVEYS AND MAPS
(1936–1942)

CREATION AND AUTHORITY

The Board of Surveys and Maps of the Federal Government was established by Executive Order 3026 of December 30, 1919. The name was changed to Federal Board of Surveys and Maps by Executive Order 7262 of January 4, 1936. The Board was abolished by Executive Order 9094 of March 10, 1942, and its functions transferred to the Bureau of the Budget (Pr 32.100).

Y 3.Su 7:1/date
ANNUAL REPORTS.

Y 3.Su 7:2 CT
GENERAL PUBLICATIONS.

Y 3.Su 7:3
BULLETINS.

Y 3.Su 7:4
CIRCULARS.

Y 3.Su 7:5/date
MINUTES.

Y 3.Su 7:8/nos.
EDUCATIONAL SERIES.

Y 3.Su 7:9/nos.
INFORMATION SERIES.

NATIONAL COMMISSION ON SUPPLIES AND SHORTAGES
(1974–1977)

CREATION AND AUTHORITY

The National Commission on Supplies and Shortages was established by act of September 30, 1974 (88 Stat. 1168), as amended by act of August 5, 1975 (89 Stat. 399). The Commission was terminated March 31, 1977, pursuant to terms of the establishing act.

Y 3.Su 7/2:1/date
ANNUAL REPORT.

Y 3.Su 7/2:2 CT
GENERAL PUBLICATIONS.

NATIONAL COMMISSION ON SUPERCONDUCTIVITY

Y 3.Su 7/3:2 CT   • Item 1089
GENERAL PUBLICATIONS.

TARIFF COMMISSION
(1882)

CREATION AND AUTHORITY

The Tariff Commission was established by act of Congress, approved May 15, 1882. The Commission submitted its report in that year.

Y 3.T 17:CT
PUBLICATIONS.

TARIFF BOARD
(1909–1916)

CREATION AND AUTHORITY

The Tariff Board was established by the President pursuant to the act of Congress, approved August 5, 1909 (36 Stat. 83). The Board was abolished and its functions transferred to the United States Tariff Commission (TC 1), established by act of Congress, approved September 8, 1916.

Y 3.T 17/2:CT
PUBLICATIONS.

BOARD OF TAX APPEALS
(1924–1942)

CREATION AND AUTHORITY

The Board of Tax Appeals was established by act of Congress, approved June 2, 1924 (43 Stat. 336). The name was changed to the Tax Court of the United States (Ju 11) and placed within the Department of Justice by the Revenue Act of 1942 (56 Stat. 957).

Y 3.T 19:1/date
ANNUAL REPORTS.
    Later Ju 11.1

Y 3.T 19:2 CT
GENERAL PUBLICATIONS.
    Later Ju 11.2

Y 3.T 19:3
BULLETINS.

Y 3.T 19:4
CIRCULARS.

Y 3.T 19:5/v.nos.
REPORTS (individual opinions). [Weekly]
    Later Ju 11.7/a

Y 3.T 19:6/v.nos.
REPORTS.
    Later Ju 11.7

Y 3.T 19:7/date
RULES OF PRACTICE.
    Later Ju 11.8

Y 3.T 19:8/vol.
REPORTS, TABLE OF PROCEEDINGS REPORTED.

Y 3.T 19:9/vol.
REPORTS.
Later Ju 11.7/a2

NATIONAL COMMISSION OF TECHNOLOGY, AUTOMATION, AND ECONOMIC PROGRESS
(1964– 1966)

CREATION AND AUTHORITY

The National Commission of Technology, Automation, and Economic Progress was established by act of August 19, 1964 (78 Stat. 463). The Commission submitted its final report to the President and Congress on January 1, 1966, and was terminated pursuant to the act establishing it.

Y 3.T 22:1/date
REPORT.

Y 3.T 22:2 CT
GENERAL PUBLICATIONS.

OFFICE OF TECHNOLOGY ASSESSMENT
(1972– 1995)

CREATION AND AUTHORITY

The Office of Technology Assessment was established by the Technical Assessment Act of 1972 (86 Stat. 797) to help Congress anticipate, and plan for, the consequences of uses of technology. Became inactive September 30, 1995.

Y 3.T 22/2:1/date   • **Item 1070-M**
ANNUAL REPORTS.

Y 3.T 22/2:2 CT   • **Item 1070-M**
GENERAL PUBLICATIONS.

Y 3.T 22/2:7/date   • **Item 1070-M**
PRESS RELEASES. [Irregular]

Y 3.T 22/2:9 CT   • **Item 1070-M**
BIBLIOGRAPHIES AND LISTS OF PUBLICATIONS.

Y 3.T 22/2:9/date   • **Item 1070-M-1**
CATALOG, PUBLICATIONS OF THE OFFICE OF TECHNOLOGY ASSESSMENT. [Annual]

Y 3.T 22/2:10/date   • **Item 1070-M**
ASSESSMENT ACTIVITIES. [Irregular]

Y 3.T 22/2:11 CT
TECHNICAL MEMORANDUM (series).

Y 3.T 22/2:12   • **Item 1070-M-2**
BACKGROUND PAPER (series).

TENNESSEE VALLEY AUTHORITY
(1933–   )

CREATION AND AUTHORITY

The Tennessee Valley Authority is a corporation created by act of Congress May 18, 1933 (48 Stat. 58; 16 U.S.C. 831-831dd).

INFORMATION

Public Information Office
Tennessee Valley Authority
400 West Summit Hill Drive
Knoxville, Tennessee 37902-1499
(865) 632-2101
http://www.tva.gov

Y 3.T 25:1   • **Item 1080 (MF)**
ANNUAL REPORT. 1934–   [Annual]

Report submitted by the Authority to the President and Congress for the fiscal year.
Covers the activities of the Authority during the fiscal year for construction, multiple-use reservoir operations, electric power service, fertilizer development and farming, forest development, tributary watershed developments.
Appendix contains financial statements, statistical tables, and texts of power contracts and agreements.

Y 3.T 25:1a T 256/2
TVA (year). [Annual]

Contains principal text of annual report, intended for distribution to the public.

Y 3.T 25:1-2   • **Item 1080 (MF)**
FINANCIAL STATEMENTS FOR FISCAL YEAR (date). 1940–   [Annual]

Serves as a preliminary, as well as a separate, publication of the financial statements which later appear in the annual report.
Gives balance sheets; statements of operations and funds; schedules containing details of fixed assets, power expense, nonpower net expenses, operation of multiple-use facilities, and administrative and general expenses. Data are for the fiscal year.

Y 3.T 25:1-3   • **Item 1080 (MF)**
MUNICIPAL AND COOPERATIVE DISTRIBUTORS OF TVA POWER, (date) OPERATIONS. [Annual]

Covers the operations during the fiscal year of the municipal electric systems and rural electric cooperatives which purchased power at wholesale from TVA for distribution at standard TVA retail rates to their customers.
The data for this report were assembled by TVA from annual reports and other materials prepared by each of the independent, locally owned electric systems.
Merged with Power and Annual Report (Y 3.T 25:1-7) and OEDC Annual Report (Y 3.T 25:1-15) to form Power Program Summary (Y 3.T 25:1-16).

Y 3.T 25:1-4
DIVISION OF FORESTRY DEVELOPMENT, ANNUAL REPORT. [Annual]

Reviews activities of the Division for the fiscal year, covering such subjects as development of valley forests, reforestation, application of forest management, strip mine reclamation, use of valley forest, fish and wildlife.
Statistical appendix contains data on the various activities of the Division.
Issued by the Division of Forestry Development, Norris, Tennessee 37828.

Y 3.T 25:1-5
AGRICULTURAL AND CHEMICAL DEVELOPMENT, (date) ANNUAL REPORT. [Annual]

A non-technical report of the research activities of the TVA during the year in such subjects as fertilizers, agronomic research, forestry research, licenses, and patents, plant modernization, process improvement, educational programs, distributor demonstrations, tributary area development.

Y 3.T 25:1-6/date
REPORT OF CHIEF ENGINEER FOR FISCAL YEAR.

Y 3.T 25:1-7   • **Item 1082-A**
POWER ANNUAL REPORT. 1960– 1981. [Annual]

A non-technical report of the TVA's electric power activities for the fiscal year told in text, pictures, charts, tables, and maps.
Statistical tables cover financial statements; operating statistics; net power assets; system input, system output; consumer statistics; and coal statistics.
Merged with Municipal and Cooperative Distributors to TVA Power (Y 3.T 25:1-3) and OEDC Annual Report (Y 3.T 25:1-15) to form Power Program Summary (Y 3.T 25:1-16).

Y 3.T 25:1-8/date
NATIONAL FERTILIZER DEVELOPMENT CENTER, ANNUAL REPORT.

Y 3.T 25:1-9
DIVISION OF HEALTH AND SAFETY, ANNUAL REPORT.

Y 3.T 25:1-10/date
OFFICE OF HEALTH AND ENVIRONMENTAL SCIENCE: ANNUAL REPORT.

Y 3.T 25:1-11/date
DIVISION OF FORESTRY, FISHERIES, AND WILDLIFE DEVELOPMENT, ANNUAL REPORT.

Y 3.T 25:1-12/date
DIVISION OF WATER CONTROL PLANNING: ANNUAL REPORT.

Y 3.T 25:1-13/date
DIVISION OF ENVIRONMENTAL PLANNING: ANNUAL REPORT.

Y 3.T 25:1-14/date
TVA RETIREMENT SYSTEM: ANNUAL REPORT.

Y 3.T 25:1-15/date
OFFICE OF ENGINEERING DESIGN AND CONSTRUCTION: ANNUAL REPORT.

Merged with Power Annual Report (Y 3.T 25:1-7) and Municipal and Cooperative Distributors to TVA Power (Y 3.T 25:1-3) to form Power Summary (Y 3.T 25:1-16).

Y 3.T 25:1-16:date   • **Item 1082-A (MF)**
SUMMARY OF FINANCIAL STATEMENTS AND SALES STATISTICS, DISTRIBUTORS OF TVA POWER. [Annual]

Combines three publications: Power Annual Report (Y 3.T 25:1-7); OEDC Annual Report (Y 3.T 25:1-15); and Municipal and Cooperative Distributors to TVA Power (Y 3.T 25:1-3).
Formerly titled: Power Program Summary.

Y 3.T 25:1-17/date   • **Item 1083-B (MF)**
INTERNATIONAL DEVELOPMENT CENTER: ANNUAL REPORT.

Y 3.T 25:1-18   • **Item 1080 (MF)**
STATISTICS, DISTRIBUTORS OF TVA POWER FISCAL YEARS.

Y 3.T 25:1-19/   • **Item 1080 (MF)**
INSPECTOR GENERAL SEMIANNUAL REPORTS. [Semiannual]

Y 3.T 25:2 CT   • **Item 1082**
GENERAL PUBLICATIONS.

Y 3.T 25:2 OP 2 • Item 1082
FACTS ABOUT TVA OPERATION. [Annual]

PURPOSE:– To provide the facts which will answer the questions most often asked about the TVA and its operations.

Y 3.T 25:2 T 25/30 • Item 1082
TVA POWER (year). [Annual]

Y 3.T 25:3 • Item 1083-B (MF)
BULLETINS.

Y 3.T 25:3-2/letters-nos. • Item 1083-B (MF)
NATIONAL FERTILIZER DEVELOPMENT CENTER: BULLETINS. [Irregular]

Y 3.T 25:4 • Item 1083-C
CIRCULARS.

Y 3.T 25:4-2/letters-nos.
NATIONAL FERTILIZER DEVELOPMENT CENTER: CIRCULARS.

Y 3.T 25:5 CT
LAWS.

Y 3.T 25:6 CT
REGULATIONS, RULES, AND INSTRUCTIONS.

Y 3.T 25:6-2 CT • Item 1082-G
HANDBOOKS, MANUALS, GUIDES.

Y 3.T 25:6-3/nos.
LAND BETWEEN THE LAKES [field guides]. 1– 1971– [Irregular]

Y 3.T 25:6-4/CT • Item 1082-G
ENERGY DESIGN GUIDELINES (series). [Irregular]

Earlier Y 3.T 25:6-2/En 2

Y 3.T 25:7 CT • Item 1082-D
MAPS (Miscellaneous).

Y 3.T 25:7-2 CT
SHEETS OF NATIONAL ATLAS OF UNITED STATES.

Y 3.T 25:8 • Item 1082-K
POSTERS. [Irregular]

Y 3.T 25:9 CT
ELECTRIC HOME AND FARM AUTHORITY PUBLICATIONS.

Y 3.T 25:10/nos.
GEOLOGIC BULLETINS.

Y 3.T 25:11/nos.
LAND PLANNING AND HOUSE BULLETINS.

Y 3.T 25:12/nos.
STATISTICAL BULLETINS.

Y 3.T 25:13
ELECTRICITY SALES STATISTICS. [Monthly]

Retail distribution of electricity at TVA resale rates.
Annual summary issued separately.
ISSN 0364-0124

Y 3.T 25:13-2/date • Item 1082-B (MF)
ELECTRICITY SALES STATISTICS, DISTRIBUTION OF ELECTRICITY AT TVA WHOLESALE AND RETAIL RATES (calendar year). [Annual]

Y 3.T 25:13-3/date • Item 1080 (MF)
MONTHLY LOAN DATA REPORT. [Annual]

Y 3.T 25:14
PRECIPITATION IN TENNESSEE RIVER BASIN. 1936– 1980. [Monthly & Annual] (Hydraulic Data Branch, Division of Water Control Planning)

Monthly releases give daily data, annual summary, issued separately, gives monthly data.
ISSN 0362-7667

Y 3.T 25:15 CT
ADDRESSES.

Y 3.T 25:16 • Item 1083-A
TECHNICAL MONOGRAPHS. 1– 1934– [Irregular]

PURPOSE:– To serve both internal and external requests for information on special phases of TVA's engineering work. This includes manuals of technical information, for convenient reference, on the Tennessee Valley resources and special phases on TVA's multiple purpose hydro system and steam-electric plants. The Monograph series includes selected drawings on major projects, cofferdam design, geology and mineral resources of the Valley, engineering data on hydro and steam plants in the system, laboratory model studies, and structural behavior of dams.

Y 3.T 25:17 • Item 1083
TECHNICAL REPORTS. 1– 1940– [Irregular]

Reports consist mainly of the following subseries:

PROJECT REPORT SERIES.

PURPOSE:– To record under one cover, for convenient reference, a summary of the planning, design construction, initial operations, organization, labor rates, major purchases, and special tests on a major hydro or steam plant built by TVA.

SPECIAL REPORT SERIES.

PURPOSE:– To present TVA's experience in its principal phases of engineering research, including concrete; surveying and mapping; geology and foundation treatment; civil and structural, electrical and mechanical design of hydro plants; flood control and navigation.

Y 3.T 25:18/nos.
FORESTRY BULLETINS. 1–

Y 3.T 25:19 • Item 1081
CHEMICAL ENGINEERING REPORTS. 1– [Irregular]

Y 3.T 25:20/vol.
FIRE FACTS. [Monthly]

Y 3.T 25:21/nos.
MARGIN NOTES. [Monthly]

Y 3.T 25:22/v.nos.&nos.
TEAMWORK. [Monthly]

A newsletter published jointly by the Central Joint Cooperative Committee TVA and the Tennessee Valley Trades and Labor Council.
Distribution is within TVA only.

Y 3.T 25:23/nos.
AGRICULTURAL ENGINEERING PUBLICATIONS.

Y 3.T 25:24/letters-nos. • Item 1083 (MF)
TECHNICAL NOTES.

Y 3.T 25:25
CHEMICAL ENGINEERING BULLETINS. [Irregular]

PURPOSE:– To describe the chemical engineering activities of TVA, covering investigations in more detail than is possible in technical journal articles.

Y 3.T 25:26/nos.
REPORTS OF PROJECT ON RESEARCH IN AGRICULTURAL AND INDUSTRIAL DEVELOPMENT IN TENNESSEE VALLEY REGION.

Y 3.T 25:27 CT
FORESTRY RELATIONS DIVISION, PUBLICATIONS.

Y 3.T 25:27-2/date
WATERFOWL MONITORING INVESTIGATIONS.

Y 3.T 25:28 CT
LUMBER PRODUCTION NOTES.

Y 3.T 25:28-2/nos.
FOREST PRODUCTS INDUSTRY NOTES.

Y 3.T 25:29 CT
AGRICULTURAL RELATIONS DIVISION PUBLICATIONS.

Y 3.T 25:29 F 41/7
FERTILIZER SUMMARY DATA BY STATES AND GEOGRAPHIC AREAS. [Biennial]

PURPOSE:– To supply data in plant nutrient consumption and use of TVA fertilizer materials, by States and regions.

Y 3.T 25:29
FERTILIZER TRENDS. [Biennial]

PURPOSE:– To show in graphical and tabular form the changes that have occurred in the fertilizer industry during the last 20 to 30 years. It includes descriptions of the major agricultural and chemical development programs of the Tennessee Valley Authority; trends in the phosphorus, nitrogen, and potash fertilizer industries; trends in the consumption and production of fertilizer materials and mixtures; and trade in fertilizer materials with other countries.

Y 3.T 25:29-2
AGRICULTURAL ECONOMICS BRANCH REPORTS. [Irregular]

PURPOSE:– To provide useful information in regional development and fertilizer education programs.

Y 3.T 25:30 CT
POWER OFFICE, PUBLICATIONS.

Y 3.T 25:30 In 27
INDUSTRIAL DEVELOPMENT IN TVA AREA DURING (date). [Annual]

Covers industrial development activities reported in the TVA area during the calendar year.
Summaries of increased kilowatt demands, investment and employment by major industrial groups are provided for the entire TVA area and each of the five TVA power districts. Information for each power district is listed by State, country, and city, and gives location, company, SIC no., product or operation, type of development, estimated completion date, and estimated increases in demand, investment, and employment.

Y 3.T 25:30-2/date • Item 1082-E
INDUSTRIAL DEVELOPMENT IN THE TVA AREA. [Annual]

Reports in tabular form, new and expanding industrial plant activities in the Tennessee Valley area. Individual firms are listed in district tables alphabetically by state, county, and city showing kilowatt demand, investment, and employment figures. Contains maps and graphs comparing power demands, investments, and employments during recent calendar years.
Earlier Y 3.T 25:30 In 27

Y 3.T 25:31 CT • Item 1082-H
BIBLIOGRAPHIES AND LISTS OF PUBLICATIONS.

Y 3.T 25:31 T 25 • Item 1082-H
BIBLIOGRAPHY FOR THE TVA PROGRAM. [Annual]

While not admittedly a comprehensive bibliography of the Tennessee Valley Authority this list is quite adequate in its coverage of all aspects of the TVA, its history and its work. Includes trade books as well as government publications.
Prepared by the Technical Library.

Y 3.T 25:32/date
REPORT ON SCIENTIFIC RESEARCH PROJECTS CONDUCTED DURING FISCAL YEAR.

Y 3.T 25:33/date
TVA POWER, QUARTERLY REPORT.

Y 3.T 25:34/nos.
FORESTRY INVESTIGATION NOTES.

Y 3.T 25:35
ENGINEERING LABORATORY RESEARCH. [Annual]

Covers results of research in the fields of civil engineering, mechanical engineering, and instrumentation.

Y 3.T 25:36
FERTILIZER ABSTRACTS. v. 1–   1968– 1982. [Monthly]

Prepared by the Technical Library staff from technical journals and patents.
ISSN 0015-0290

Y 3.T 25:37
FISH MONITORING INVESTIGATIONS, BROWNS FERRY NUCLEAR PLANT, WHEELER RESERVOIR, ALABAMA. 1968–   [Quarterly]

ISSN 0364-6033

Y 3.T 25:37-2/date
FISH MONITORING INVESTIGATIONS, CUMBERLAND STEAM PLANT, CUMBERLAND RIVER, TENN. [Quarterly]

Y 3.T 25:37-3/date
FISH MONITORING INVESTIGATIONS: SEQUOYAH NUCLEAR PLANT, CHICKAMAUGA RESERVOIR, TENNESSEE. [Quarterly]

Y 3.T 25:38/nos.
DIVISION OF WATER CONTROL PLANNING: REPORTS.

Y 3.T 25:39/v.nos.&nos.
TENNESSEE VALLEY PERSPECTIVE. v. 1– 10. 1970– 1980. [Quarterly]

PURPOSE:– To report and interpret the changing nature of the Tennessee Valley Region– The region's uniqueness, vitality, strengths, and problems, and to help create a common awareness for its needs and opportunities.
It is a quarterly issue of a monthly publication for TVA employees and retirees.
Indexed by: Index to U.S. Government Periodicals.
ISSN 0364-2615

Y 3.T 25:40 CT
FISH INVENTORY DATA. [Annual]

Y 3.T 25:41 CT
TENNESSEE VALLEY STREAMS, THEIR FISH, BOTTOM FAUNA, AND AQUATIC HABITAT [by areas]. 1968–   [Irregular] (Division of Forestry, Fisheries, and Wildlife Development)

PURPOSE:– To evaluate the relative abundance (standing crop) and habitat of aquatic life of six streams tributary to the Tennessee River. Studies have been made for the following streams, with dates of the study:–

Emory River. 1968.
Powell River Drainage Basin. 1968.
Flint River Drainage Basin 1969.
Upper Little Tennessee River Drainage Basin. 1969.
Sequatchie River Drainage Basin. June 1970.
Buffalo River Drainage Basin. Sept.– Oct. 1971.

Y 3.T 25:42/nos.
RESEARCH PAPERS. 1–   [Irregular]

Y 3.T 25:43/date
BUDGET PROGRAM, JUSTIFICATION OF PROGRAMS AND ESTIMATES FOR FISCAL YEAR (date), SUBMITTED TO CONGRESS. [Annual]

Y 3.T 25:44/letters-nos.   • Item 1082-F (MF)
ENVIRONMENTAL RADIOACTIVITY LEVELS (series). [Annual] (Division of Environmental Planning)

Consists of annual reports, each on a different nuclear plant.

Y 3.T 25:45 CT   • Item 1082-F (MF)
FINAL ENVIRONMENTAL STATEMENTS. [Irregular]

Y 3.T 25:46/nos.
FLOOD REPORT, WM- (series). (Division of Water Management)

Y 3.T 25:47/v.nos.&nos.   • Item 1082-F-2
IMPACT. v. 1–   [Quarterly]

Newsletter published by TVA's Division of Environmenal Planning for employees and others interested in keeping informed about the environment of the Tennessee Valley Region.

Y 3.T 25:48/date   • Item 1082-A (MF)
DIVISION OF FOSSIL AND HYDRO POWER. MONTHLY REPORT.

Y 3.T 25:48-2/date   • Item 1082-F-1 (MF)
DIVISION OF NUCLEAR POWER: MONTHLY REPORT.

Y 3.T 25:49/CT   • Item 1082-J
POSTERS. [Irregular]

Y 3.T 25:50/CT
CLIMATIC DATA BASE.

Y 3.T 25:51/date   • Item 1082-F-1 (MF)
ENVIRONMENTAL RADIOACTIVITY LEVELS, WATTS BAR NUCLEAR PLANT. [Annual]

Y 3.T 25:52/date   • Item 1082-F-1 (MF)
ENVIRONMENTAL RADIOACTIVITY LEVELS, BELEFONTE NUCLEAR PLANT. [Annual]

Y 3.T 25:53/date   • Item 1082-F-1 (MF)
RADIOLOGICAL IMPACT ASSESSMENT, BROWNS FERRY NUCLEAR PLANT. [Annual]

Y 3.T 25:54/date   • Item 1082-F-1 (MF)
AQUATIC ENVIRONMENTAL CONDITIONS IN CHICKAMUGA RESERVOIR DURING OPERATION OF SEQUOYAH NUCLEAR PLANT. [Annual]

Y 3.T 25:55/date   • Item 1082-F-1 (MF)
ENVIRONMENTAL RADIOACTIVITY LEVELS, BROWNS FERRY NUCLEAR PLANT. [Annual]

Y 3.T 25:56/date   • Item 1082-F-1
ENVIRONMENTAL RADIOACTIVITY LEVELS, SEQUOYAH NUCLEAR PLAN. [Annual]

Y 3.T 25:57/date   • Item 1082-F-1 (MF)
ANNUAL RADIOLOGICAL ENVIRONMENTAL OPERATING REPORT, SEQUOYAH NUCLEAR PLANT.

Y 3.T 25:58/date   • Item 1082-A (MF)
LOAD FORECAST AND POWER SUPPLY SUMMARY PREPARED FOR FISCAL YEAR (date). [Annual]

Y 3.T 25:59/nos.   • Item 1083 (MF)
WATER RESOURCES REPORTS, WR-(series). [Irregular]

Y 3.T 25:59-2/nos.   • Item 1083 (MF)
WATER RESOURCES/WATER QUALITY, WR/WQ (series).

Y 3.T 25:60 CT
MARKETING RESEARCH.

Y 3.T 25:61/v.nos.&nos.
FORUM FOR APPLIED RESEARCH AND PUBLIC POLICY. [Quarterly]

Y 3.T 25:62/date
FOSSIL AND HYDRO POWER MONTHLY REPORT. [Monthly]

Y 3.T 25:63/date   • Item 1082-F-1
U.S. NUCLEAR PLANTS COST PER KW REPORT, OFFICE OF NUCLEAR POWER. [Semiannual]

Y 3.T 25:64/CT   • Item 1082-L
DIRECTORIES. [Irregular]

Y 3.T 25:65/date   • Item 1083-C
PROGRESS. [Annual]

Earlier Y 3.T 25:4

Y 3.T 25:66/date
FERTILIZER TRENDS, PRODUCTION, CONSUMPTION, AND TRADE. [Annual]

Earlier Y 3.T 25:3-2/Y-195

Y 3.T 25:67/date
INSPECTOR GENERAL: MASTER PLAN, FISCAL YEAR (date). [Annual]

Y 3.T 25:68/date   • Item 1082-F-1 (MF)
U.S. NUCLEAR PLANTS COST PER KW REPORT, OFFICE OF NUCLEAR POWER. [Semiannual]

Y 3.T 25:70/   • Item 1083-B (MF)
FERTILIZER SUMMARY DATA. [Annual]

Y 3.T 25:71   • Item 1082-M (MF)
TVA/WM (series).

Y 3.T 25:72   • Item 1082-A-1 (EL)
ECONOMIC EDGE.

Y 3.T 25:73   • Item 1082-A-1 (E)
ELECTRONIC PRODUCTS. (Misc.)

Y 3.T 25:74   • Item 1082-A-1 (EL)
TVA TODAY.

THOMAS JEFFERSON MEMORIAL COMMISSION (1936– 1939)

CREATION AND AUTHORITY

The Thomas Jefferson Memorial Commission was established in 1936. The Commission submitted its final report in 1939.

Y 3.T 36:CT
PUBLICATIONS.

COMMISSION TO INVESTIGATE PURCHASE OF AMERICAN-GROWN TOBACCO BY FOREIGN GOVERNMENTS (1912– 1914)

CREATION AND AUTHORITY

The Commission to Investigate Purchase of American-Grown Tobacco by Foreign Governments, also known as the Tobacco Commission, was established by act of Congress, approved August 24, 1912 (37 Stat. 504). The Commission held hearings in 1914.

Y 3.T 55:CT
PUBLICATIONS.

U.S STUDY COMMISSION ON THE SAVANNAH, ALTAMAHA, SAINT MARYS, APALACHICOLA-CHATTAHOOCHEE, AND PERDIDO-ESCAMBIA RIVER BASINS AND INTERVENING AREAS

Y 3.Un 3/4

NATIONAL TOURISM RESOURCES REVIEW COMMISSION
(1971–1973)

CREATION AND AUTHORITY

The National Tourism Resources Review Commission was established by Public Law 91-477, approved October 21, 1971. The Commission was terminated in August 1973.

Y 3.T 64:1/date • Item 1089
REPORT.

Y 3.T 64:2 CT • Item 1089
GENERAL PUBLICATIONS.

Y 3.T 64:9/nos.
NTRRC NEWS BULLETIN. [Monthly]

EAST-WEST FOREIGN TRADE BOARD
(1975–1981)

CREATION AND AUTHORITY

The East-West Foreign Trade Board was established by Executive Order 11846 of March 27, 1975. The board was abolished in 1981.

Y 3.T 67:1/date • Item 1081-A-1
EAST-WEST FOREIGN TRADE BOARD REPORT. [Quarterly]

ISSN 0145-966X

TRANSPORTATION INVESTIGATION AND RESEARCH BOARD
(1940–1944)

Y 3.T 68:1/date
ANNUAL REPORTS.

NATIONAL TRANSPORTATION POLICY STUDY COMMISSION
(1976–   )

CREATION AND AUTHORITY

The National Transportation Policy Study Commission was established by the Federal-Aid Highway Act of 1976 (PL 94-280)

Y 3.T 68/2:1/date
ANNUAL REPORT.

Y 3.T 68/2:2 CT
GENERAL PUBLICATIONS. [Irregular]

Y 3.T 68/2:9/nos. • Item 1089
NTPSC SPECIAL REPORTS. [Irregular]

Y 3.T 68/2:10/nos. • Item 1089
WORKING PAPERS.

TUBERCULOSIS COMMITTEE
(1906)

Y 3.T 79:CT
PUBLICATIONS.

NATIONAL COMMISSION ON UNEMPLOYMENT COMPENSATION
(1976–1980)

CREATION AND AUTHORITY

The National Commission on Unemployment Compensation was established by Public Law 94-566 (90 Stat. 2681), approved October 20, 1976. The Commission submitted its final report in 1980.

Y 3.Un 2:1/date
REPORT.

Y 3.Un 2:2 CT • Item 1089
GENERAL PUBLICATIONS. [Irregular]

Y 3.Un 2:9 CT
BIBLIOGRAPHIES AND LISTS OF PUBLICATIONS.

UNITED STATES CONSTITUTION SESQUICENTENNIAL COMMISSION
(1935–1941)

CREATION AND AUTHORITY

The United States Constitution Sesquicentennial Commission was established by Public Resolution 53, approved August 23, 1935 (49 Stat. 735). The Commission ceased to exist in 1941.

Y 3.Un 3:2 CT
GENERAL PUBLICATIONS.

Y 3.Un 3:6/nos.
INFORMATION SHEETS.

Y 3.Un 3:7 CT
POSTERS [includes certificates].

Y 3.Un 3:8 CT
MAPS.

U.S. STUDY COMMISSION ON NECHES, TRINITY, BRAZOS, AND SAN JACINTO RIVER BASINS AND INTERVENING AREAS
(1958–1962)

CREATION AND AUTHORITY

The U.S. Study Commission on the Neches, Trinity, Brazos, and San Jacinto River Basins and Intervening Areas, commonly known as the U.S. Study Commission– Texas, was established by act of August 28, 1958 (72 Stat. 1058, as amended). The Commission expired June 30, 1962, having completed the work for which it was established.

Y 3.Un 3/2:1/date
REPORTS.

Y 3.Un 3/2:2 CT
GENERAL PUBLICATIONS.

U.S.– FAO INTERAGENCY COMMITTEE
(1958)

Y 3.Un 3/3:CT
PUBLICATIONS.

U.S. STUDY COMMISSION ON THE SAVANNAH, ALTAMAHA, SAINT MARYS, APALACHICOLA-CHATTAHOOCHEE, AND PERDIDO-ESCAMBIA RIVER BASINS AND INTERVENING AREAS
(1958–1963)

CREATION AND AUTHORITY

The U.S. Study Commission on the Savannah, Altamaha, Saint Marys, Apalachicola-Chattahoochee, and Perdido-Escambia River Basins and Intervening Areas, commonly known as the U.S. Study Commission, Southeast River Basins, was established by act of August 28, 1958 (72 Stat. 1090). The Commission was deactivated on December 23, 1963, having completed the work for which it was established.

Y 3.Un 3/4:CT
PUBLICATIONS.

UNITED STATES-PUERTO RICO COMMISSION ON STATUS OF PUERTO RICO
(1964)

CREATION AND AUTHORITY

The United States-Puerto Rico Commission on the Status of Puerto Rico was established by Public Law 88-271, approved February 20, 1964. The Commission was terminated by terms of the act.

Y 3.Un 3/5:1
REPORT.

Y 3.Un 3/5:2
GENERAL PUBLICATIONS.

UPPER GREAT LAKES REGIONAL COMMISSION
(1967– 1981)

CREATION AND AUTHORITY

Title V of the Public Works and Economic Development Act of 1965 (79 Stat 552; 42 U.S.C. 3121) authorizes the Secretary of Commerce to designate economic development regions. Following such designation, the Secretary invites the States of the region to establish a regional commission. The Upper Great Lakes Region, consisting of 119 counties in Michigan, Minnesota, and Wisconsin was designated on March 3, 1966. The Commission was formally organized on April 11, 1967. Members are the Federal Cochairman and the Upper Great Lakes Governors. The Governors elect one of their members to be the Commission State Cochairman. The Federal role in this Commission was abolished through repeal of the Public Works and Economic Development Act by section 1821 of Public Law 97-35 of August 13, 1981 (95 Stat. 766) effective October 1, 1981.

Y 3.Up 6:1/date
ANNUAL REPORT.

Y 3.Up 6:2 CT
GENERAL PUBLICATIONS.

Y 3.Up 6:7/nos.
NEWS RELEASE.

No Longer published.

VENEZULEAN BOUNDARY COMMISSION
(1897)

Y 3.V 55:CT
PUBLICATIONS.

VETERANS' EDUCATION APPEALS BOARD
(1950– 1957)

CREATION AND AUTHORITY

The Veterans' Education Appeals Board was established by act approved July 13, 1950 (64 Stat. 336). The Board was terminated by act of August 28, 1957 (71 Stat. 474), effective October 28, 1957.

Y 3.V 64:1/date
REPORTS.

Y 3.V 64:2 CT
GENERAL PUBLICATIONS.

Y 3.V 64:7/date
SELECTED REPORTS OF CASES BEFORE VETERANS' EDUCATION APPEALS BOARD.

NATIONAL ADVISORY COUNCIL ON VOCATIONAL EDUCATION
(1968–   )

CREATION AND AUTHORITY

The National Advisory Council on Vocational Education was established under Title I of the Vocational Education Amendments Act of 1968 (Public Law 90-576).

Y 3.V 85:1/date   • Item 1070-B-1
ANNUAL REPORTS.

Y 3.V 85:2 CT   • Item 1070-B-1
GENERAL PUBLICATIONS.

Y 3.V 85:9/nos.   • Item 1070-B-1
NATIONAL POLICY ON CAREER EDUCATION, REPORTS. 1st–

WAR INVESTIGATING COMMISSION
(1899)

CREATION AND AUTHORITY

The War Investigating Commission was established in 1899, to investigate the conduct of War Department in the War with Spain. The Commission submitted its report in 1899.

Y 3.W 19:CT
PUBLICATIONS.

WAR INDUSTRIES BOARD
(1918)

CREATION AND AUTHORITY

The War Industries Board (Y 3.C 83:50) of the Council of National Defense was made an independent agency by Executive Order 3868 of May 28, 1918. By Executive Order 3019-A of December 31, 1918, the Board was abolished.

Y 3.W 19/2:1/date
ANNUAL REPORTS.

Earlier Y 3.C 83:51

Y 3.W 19/2:2 CT
GENERAL PUBLICATIONS.

Earlier Y 3.C 83:52

Y 3.W 19/2:3
BULLETINS.

Y 3.W 19/2:4
CIRCULARS.

Earlier Y 3.C 83:54

Y 3.W 19/2:5/date
DIRECTORY.

Y 3.W 19/2:6/nos.
WEEKLY REVIEW.

Priorities Division

Y 3.W 19/2:11/date
ANNUAL REPORTS.

Y 3.W 19/2:12 CT
GENERAL PUBLICATIONS.

Y 3.W 19/2:13
BULLETINS.

Y 3.W 19/2:14
CIRCULARS.

Y 3.W 19/2:15/nos.
BLANK FORMS.

Y 3.W 19/2:16/nos.
LABOR PRIORITY BULLETINS.

Y 3.W 19/2:17/nos.
OFFICE REVIEW.

Employment Management Section

Y 3.W 19/2:21/date
ANNUAL REPORTS.

Y 3.W 19/2:22 CT
GENERAL PUBLICATIONS.

Y 3.W 19/2:23
BULLETINS.

Y 3.W 19/2:24
CIRCULARS.

Planning and Statistics Division

Y 3.W 19/2:31/date
ANNUAL REPORTS.

Y 3.W 19/2:32 CT
GENERAL PUBLICATIONS.

Y 3.W 19/2:33/nos.
BULLETINS.

Y 3.W 19/2:34/nos.
CIRCULARS.

Y 3.W 19/2:35/nos.
WEEKLY BULLETIN ON RAW MATERIALS.

Y 3.W 19/2:36/nos.
WEEKLY STATISTICAL NEWS.

Y 3.W 19/2:37/nos.
COMMODITY BULLETINS. [Weekly]

Y 3.W 19/2:38/series and nos.
COMMODITY BULLETINS. [Monthly]

Price Section

Y 3.W 19/2:41/date
ANNUAL REPORTS.

Y 3.W 19/2:42 CT
GENERAL PUBLICATIONS.

Y 3.W 19/2:43/nos.
BULLETINS.

Y 3.W 19/2:44/nos.
CIRCULARS.

Y 3.W 19/2:45/date
BULLETIN OF MONTHLY PRICES DURING THE WAR.

Y 3.W 19/2:46/nos.
PRICE FIXING BULLETINS.

Y 3.W 19/2:47/nos.
W.I.B. PRICE BULLETINS.

Y 3.W 19/2:48
STORAGE BULLETINS.

WAR FINANCE CORPORATION
(1918– 1939)

CREATION AND AUTHORITY

The War Finance Corporation was established by act of Congress, approved April 5, 1918 (40 Stat. 506). By act of Congress, approved March 1, 1929, the liquidation was assigned to the Secretary of the Treasury. Under Reorganization Plan No. 2 of 1939, effective July 1, 1939, the Corporation was abolished.

Y 3.W 19/3:1/date
ANNUAL REPORTS.

Y 3.W 19/3:2 CT
GENERAL PUBLICATIONS.

Y 3.W 19/3:3
BULLETINS.

Y 3.W 19/3:4
CIRCULARS.

WAR CLAIMS ARBITER
(1928– 1931)

Y 3.W 19/4:1/date
ANNUAL REPORTS.

Y 3.W 19/4:2 CT
GENERAL PUBLICATIONS.

Y 3.W 19/4:3
BULLETINS.

Y 3.W 19/4:4
CIRCULARS.

Y 3.W 19/4:5
DECISIONS AND ORDERS.

WAR POLICIES COMMISSION
(1930– 1932)

CREATION AND AUTHORITY

The War Policies Commission was established by Public Resolution 98 of Congress, approved June 27, 1930. The Commission submitted its final report in 1932.

Y 3.W 19/5:CT
PUBLICATIONS.

WAR CONTRACTS PRICE
ADJUSTMENT BOARD
(1944– 1951)

CREATION AND AUTHORITY

The War Contracts Price Adjustment Board was established by the Renegotiation Act, approved February 25, 1944 (58 Stat. 85). The Board was abolished by act of Congress, approved March 23, 1951 (65 Stat. 7), and its functions transferred to the Renegotiation Board (RnB 1) and the General Services Administration (GS 1).

Y 3.W 19/6:1/date
ANNUAL REPORTS.

Y 3.W 19/6:2 CT
GENERAL PUBLICATIONS.

Y 3.W 19/6:5 CT
LAWS.

Y 3.W 19/6:6 CT
REGULATIONS, RULES, AND INSTRUCTIONS.

OFFICE OF
WAR MOBILIZATION AND
RECONVERSION
(1944– 1946)

CREATION AND AUTHORITY

The Office of War Mobilization and Reconversion was established by act of Congress, approved October 3, 1944 (58 Stat. 788), to succeed the Office of War Mobilization (Pr 32.5900). The Office was consolidated with certain other agencies to form the Office of Temporary Controls (Pr 33.300) by Executive Order 9809 of December 12, 1946.

Y 3.W 19/7:1/date
ANNUAL REPORTS.

Y 3.W 19/7:2 CT
GENERAL PUBLICATIONS.

Y 3.W 19/7:6 CT
REGULATIONS, RULES, AND INSTRUCTIONS.

Y 3.W 19/7:7 CT
ADDRESSES.

Y 3.W 19/7:8/date
PROBLEMS OF MOBILIZATION AND RECONVERSION, REPORTS TO THE PRESIDENT, SENATE, AND HOUSE OF REPRESENTATIVES BY DIRECTOR OF WAR MOBILIZATION AND RECONVERSION. [Quarterly]

Y 3.W 19/7:9 CT
INTERAGENCY COMMITTEE ON FOREIGN SHIPMENTS: PUBLICATIONS.

Y 3.W 19/7:10/nos.
REPORTS OF THE INTER-AGENCY POLICY COMMITTEE ON RUBBER.

OFFICE OF CONTRACT SETTLEMENT (1944– 1947)

CREATION AND AUTHORITY

The Office of Contract Settlement was established by act of Congress, approved July 1, 1944 (58 Stat. 651). The Office was transferred to the Office of War Mobilization and Reconversion by act of Congress, approved October 3, 1944 (58 Stat. 785). Executive Order 9809 of December 12, 1946, and Reorganization Plan 1 of 1947 placed the Office in the Treasury Department (T 67).

Y 3.W 19/7:101/date
ANNUAL REPORTS.

Later T 67.1

Y 3.W 19/7:102 CT
GENERAL PUBLICATIONS.

Later T 67.2

Y 3.W 19/2:106/nos.
REGULATIONS.

Y 3.W 19/7:107/date
WAR CONTRACT TERMINATIONS AND SETTLEMENTS, REPORT BY DIRECTOR OF CONTRACT SETTLEMENT TO CONGRESS. [Quarterly]

Later T 67.7

Y 3.W 19/7:108/nos.
APPEAL BOARD PROCEEDINGS.

Later T 67.8

SURPLUS PROPERTY ADMINISTRATION (1945– 1946)

CREATION AND AUTHORITY

The Surplus Property Administration was established within the Office of War Mobilization and Reconversion by act of Congress, approved September 18, 1945 (59 Stat. 533), to succeed the Surplus Property Board, which was abolished. The Administration was abolished by Executive Order 9689 of January 31, 1946, and its functions transferred to the War Assets Corporation and the Department of State.

Y 3.W 19/7:201/date
ANNUAL REPORTS.

Y 3.W 19/7:202 CT
GENERAL PUBLICATIONS.

Y 3.W 19/7:206 CT
REGULATIONS, RULES, AND INSTRUCTIONS.

Y 3.W 19/7:207/date
QUARTERLY PROGRESS REPORTS BY THE SURPLUS PROPERTY BOARD TO CONGRESS.

Later S 1.47

WAR ASSETS ADMINISTRATION (1947– 1949)

CREATION AND AUTHORITY

The War Assets Administration (Pr 33.200) was established within the Office for Emergency Management by Executive Order 9689 of January 31, 1946, effective March 25, 1946. Reorganization Plan No. 1 of 1947, effective July 1, 1947, abolished the War Assets Administration and transferred its functions to the Surplus Property Administration (Y 3.W 19:200), which in turn was redesignated the War Assets Administration as a statutory agency until the expiration of the Surplus Property Act. Under the Federal Property and Administrative Services Act, approved June 30, 1949, the Administration was placed under the General Services Administration for liquidation.

Y 3.W 19/8:1/date
ANNUAL REPORTS.

Y 3.W 19/8:2 CT
GENERAL PUBLICATIONS.

Y 3.W 19/8:7/nos.
SPECIAL LISTINGS.

Earlier Pr 33.209

Y 3.W 19/8:8/date
SCHEDULE OF SALES. [Weekly]

Earlier Pr 33.213

Y 3.W 19/8:9/nos.
SURPLUS GOVERNMENT PROPERTY SPECIAL OFFERINGS.

Y 3.W 19/8:10/v.nos.
TARGET. [Weekly]

Earlier Pr 33.217

Y 3.W 19/8:11/date
PROGRESS REPORT TO CONGRESS BY WAR ASSETS ADMINISTRATION. [Quarterly]

Earlier Pr 33.211

Y 3.W 19/8:12/date
OFFERINGS AND SALES OF OFFICE OF PERSONAL PROPERTY DISPOSAL. [Biweekly]

WAR CLAIMS COMMISSION (1948– 1954)

CREATION AND AUTHORITY

The War Claims Commission was established by the War Claims Act of 1948, approved July 3, 1948 (62 Stat. 1240). It was abolished by Reorganization Plan No. 1 of 1954, effective July 1, 1954, and its functions transferred to the Foreign Claims Settlement Commission of the United States (Y 3.F 76/3).

Y 3.W 19/9:1/nos.
SEMI-ANNUAL REPORT TO CONGRESS.

Y 3.W 19/9:2 CT
GENERAL PUBLICATIONS.

COMMISSION ON WARTIME RELOCATION

Y 3.W 19/10:CT
REPORTS.

WASHINGTON MONUMENT JOINT COMMISSION (1876– 1888)

Y 3.W 27:CT
PUBLICATIONS.

GEORGE WASHINGTON BICENTENNIAL COMMISSION (1924– 1932)

CREATION AND AUTHORITY

The George Washington Bicentennial Commission, also known as the United States Commission for the Celebration of the 200th Anniversary of the Birth of George Washington, was established by Senate Joint Resolution 85 (43 Stat. 671), approved December 2, 1924. The Commission submitted its final report in 1932.

Y 3.W 27/2:1/date
REPORTS.

Y 3.W 27/2:2 CT
GENERAL PUBLICATIONS.

Y 3.W 27/2:3
BULLETINS.

Y 3.W 27/2:4
CIRCULARS.

Y 3.W 27/2:5/nos.
GENERAL NEWSPAPER RELEASES.

Y 3.W 27/2:6/nos.
PAMPHLETS.

Y 3.W 27/2:7/nos.
CLIP SHEETS.

Y 3.W 27/2:8 CT
CLIP SHEETS (miscellaneous).

Y 3.W 27/2:9/nos.
PROGRAMS (numbered).

Y 3.W 27/2:10 CT
POSTERS.

Y 3.W 27/2:11/nos.
CLIP SHEETS (special educational issues).

Y 3.W 27/2:12 CT
PLAYS AND PAGEANTS.

Y 3.W 27/2:13/vol.
WRITINGS OF GEORGE WASHINGTON.

Y 3.W 27/2:14/vol.
LITERATURE SERIES.

Y 3.W 27/2:15 CT
HISTORY OF GEORGE WASHINGTON BICENTENNIAL CELEBRATION.

WATER RESOURCES COUNCIL
(1965– 1982)

CREATION AND AUTHORITY

The Water Resources Council was established by the Water Resources Planning Act of 1965, approved July 22, 1965 (79 Stat. 244).

Y 3.W 29:1/date • Item 1090
REPORT.

Y 3.W 29:2 CT • Item 1090
GENERAL PUBLICATIONS.

Y 3.W 29:3/nos. • Item 1090
BULLETINS.

Y 3.W 29:7/date • Item 1090
PRESS RELEASES.

Y 3.W 29:8 CT • Item 1090
HANDBOOKS, MANUALS, GUIDES.

Y 3.W 29:8-2/nos. • Item 1090
GUIDELINES.

Y 3.W 29:9/nos. • Item 1090
JOINT HYDROLOGY-SEDIMENTATION BULLETINS.

Earlier Y 3.In 8/8:9

Y 3.W 29:10/date • Item 1090
NOTES ON SEDIMENTATION ACTIVITIES.

Y 3.W 29:11/v.nos.
WRC REPORT.

Y 3.W 29:12 (CT) • Item 1090
BIBLIOGRAPHIES AND LISTS OF PUBLICATIONS.

Y 3.W 29:13/nos. • Item 1090
SUPPLEMENTAL REPORTS TO THE SECOND NATIONAL WATER ASSESSMENT.

NATIONAL COMMISSION ON WATER QUALITY
(1972)

CREATION AND AUTHORITY

The National Commission on Water Quality was established by the Water Pollution Control Act Amendments of 1972 (86 Stat. 875), approved October 18, 1972.

Y 3.W 29/2:1/date • Item 1089
REPORTS.

Y 3.W 29/2:2 CT • Item 1089
GENERAL PUBLICATIONS.

SELECT COMMISSION ON WESTERN HEMISPHERE IMMIGRATION
(1965)

CREATION AND AUTHORITY

The Select Commission on Western Hemisphere Immigration was established by Public Law 89-236, approved October 3, 1965.

Y 3.W 52:1/date
REPORT.

Y 3.W 52:2 CT
GENERAL PUBLICATIONS.

WESTERN WATER POLICY REVIEW ADVISORY COMMISSION
(1995–   )

CREATION AND AUTHORITY

The Western Water Policy Review Commission was established under the Western Water Policy Review Act of 1992 (P.L. 102-575, Title XXX). Commission was chartered by the Secretary of the Interior on September 15, 1995.

INFORMATION

Western Water Policy Review
   Advisory Commission
P.O. Box 25007, D-5010
Denver, CO 80225-0007
(303) 445-2100
(303) 445-6693
http://www.den.doi.gov/wwprac/index.html

Y 3.W 52/2:2 CT • Item 1089-A-3
GENERAL PUBLICATIONS.

WHEAT DIRECTOR
(1919– 1920)

Y 3.W 56:1/date
ANNUAL REPORTS.

Y 3.W 56:2 CT
GENERAL PUBLICATIONS.

Y 3.W 56:3/nos.
BULLETINS.

Y 3.W 56:4/nos.
CIRCULARS.

Y 3.W 56:5/nos.
OFFICIAL STATEMENT OF WHEAT DIRECTOR.

Succeeds Official Statement of Food Administrator.

Grain Corporation

Y 3.W 56:11/date
ANNUAL REPORTS.

Y 3.W 56:12 CT
GENERAL PUBLICATIONS.

Y 3.W 56:13/nos.
BULLETINS.

Y 3.W 56:14
CIRCULARS.

Y 3.W 56:15/date
PRESS NOTICES.

Y 3.W 56:16 CT
POSTERS.

Y 3.W 56:17/nos.
BULLETINS [Kansas City Office].

WHITE HOUSE CONFERENCE ON CHILD HEALTH AND PROTECTION
(1930)

Y 3.W 58:1/date • Item 1088
PROCEEDINGS.

Y 3.W 58:2 CT
GENERAL PUBLICATIONS.

Y 3.W 58:3
BULLETINS.

Y 3.W 58:4
CIRCULARS.

Y 3.W 58:5/nos.
CURRENT INFORMATION.

Y 3.W 58:6/nos.
WHITE HOUSE CONFERENCE HAPPENINGS.

WHITE HOUSE CONFERENCE ON EDUCATION
(1954– 1955)

CREATION AND AUTHORITY

The White House Conference on Education was established by act of Congress, approved July 26, 1954 (68 Stat. 532), and was held in Washington, D.C., November 28– December 1, 1955.

Y 3.W 58/2:1/date
ANNUAL REPORTS.

Y 3.W 58/2:2 CT
GENERAL PUBLICATIONS.

Y 3.W 58/2:7/date
RELEASES.

Y 3.W 58/2:8/date
NEWSLETTER.

Y 3.W 58/2:9/nos.
CONFERENCE NOTES. [Monthly]

Proc. Admin.

WHITE HOUSE CONFERENCE ON CHILDREN
(1960)

CREATION AND AUTHORITY

Every ten years during this century there has been a White House Conference concerned with the Nation's children and youth. The first such conference, called by President Theodore Roosevelt, was held in 1909.

In a letter dated May 27, 1958 and released May 28, 1958, to the Secretary of Health, Education, and Welfare, who is also chairman of the Interdepartmental Committee on Children and Youth, President Dwight D. Eisenhower directed that the sixth White House Conference on Children and Youth be held in March 1960.

Y 3.W 58/3:1/date
REPORTS.

Y 3.W 58/3:2 CT
GENERAL PUBLICATIONS.

WHITE HOUSE CONFERENCE ON CHILDREN
(1970)

Y 3.W 58/3-2:1/date
REPORTS.

Y 3.W 58/3-2:2 CT
GENERAL PUBLICATIONS.
Y 3.W 58/3-2:9 CT
BIBLIOGRAPHIES AND LISTS OF PUBLICATIONS.

WHITE HOUSE CONFERENCE ON YOUTH
(1970–1971)

Y 3.W 58/3-3:1/date
REPORTS.

Y 3.W 58/3-3:2 CT
GENERAL PUBLICATIONS.

WHITE HOUSE CONFERENCE ON AGING
(1958–1961)

CREATION AND AUTHORITY

The White House conference on Aging was called by the President of the United States in January 1961 in order to develop recommendations for further research and action in the field of aging, according to provisions of Public Law 908 of the 85th Congress, 2nd session, approved September 2, 1958. The law assigned responsibility for the planning and conduct of the Conference to the Secretary of Health, Education and Welfare with the cooperation of other Federal departments and agencies.

Y 3.W 58/4:1/date
REPORTS.

Y 3.W 58/4:2 CT
GENERAL PUBLICATIONS.

Y 3.W 58/4:8 CT
HANDBOOKS, MANUALS, GUIDES.

WHITE HOUSE CONFERENCE ON NARCOTIC AND DRUG ABUSE
(1962)

CREATION AND AUTHORITY

The first White House Conference on Narcotic and Drug Abuse was held in Washington, D.C., September 27-28, 1962, at the request of President Kennedy.

Y 3.W 58/5:1/date
REPORTS.

Y 3.W 58/5:2 CT
GENERAL PUBLICATIONS.

WHITE HOUSE CONFERENCE ON CONSERVATION
(1962)

CREATION AND AUTHORITY

The White House Conference on Conservation, held in Washington, D.C., on May 24 and 25, 1962, was proposed by President John F. Kennedy in his Message to Congress on Our Conservation Program, March 1, 1962.

Y 3.W 58/6:1/date
REPORTS.

Y 3.W 58/6:2 CT
GENERAL PUBLICATIONS.

WHITE HOUSE CONFERENCE ON NATIONAL ECONOMIC ISSUES
(1962)

CREATION AND AUTHORITY

The White House Conference on National Economic Issues, called by President Kennedy at the recommendation of his Advisory Committee on Labor-Management Policy, met in Washington, D.C., on May 21 and 22, 1962.

Y 3.W 58/7:1/date
REPORTS.

Y 3.W 58/7:2 CT
GENERAL PUBLICATIONS.

WHITE HOUSE CONFERENCE ON EXPORT EXPANSION
(1963)

CREATION AND AUTHORITY

President Kennedy in his balance of payments message to Congress on July 18, 1963, stated that in order to give momentum to the expansion of our export performance, he would convene a White House Conference on Export Expansion on September 17 and 18, 1963. On August 15, 1963, the White House announced plans for the conference and named chairman and speakers.

Y 3.W 58/8:1/date
REPORTS.

Y 3.W 58/8:2 CT
GENERAL PUBLICATIONS.

WHITE HOUSE CONFERENCE ON MENTAL RETARDATION
(1963)

CREATION AND AUTHORITY

The White House Conference on Mental Retardation was held in Warrenton, West Virginia, September 18–20, 1963, in response to the invitation of July 24, 1963 from President John F. Kennedy to the Governors of the States.

Y 3.W 58/9:1/date
REPORTS.

Y 3.W 58/9:2 CT
GENERAL PUBLICATIONS.

COMMITTEE FOR THE PRESERVATION OF THE WHITE HOUSE
(1964–   )

CREATION AND AUTHORITY

The Committee for the Preservation of the White House was established by Executive Order 11145 of March 7, 1964, to make recommendations to the President as to the articles of furniture, fixtures, and decorative objects which shall be used or displayed in the principal corridor on the ground floor and the principal public rooms on the first floor of the White House, and as to the decor and arrangements therein best suited to enhance the historic and artistic values of the White House and of such articles, fixtures, and objects. The Committee also advises the Director of the National Park Service with respect to the preservation and interpretation of the museum character of the areas in the White House mentioned above.

Y 3.W 58/10:1/date   • Item 1088
REPORT.

Y 3.W 58/10:2 CT
GENERAL PUBLICATIONS.

WHITE HOUSE CONFERENCE ON INTERNATIONAL COOPERATION
(1965)

CREATION AND AUTHORITY

The White House Conference on International Cooperation was held in Washington, D.C., November 19– December 1, 1965.

Y 3.W 58/11:1
REPORT.

Y 3.W 58/11:2
GENERAL PUBLICATIONS.

WHITE HOUSE CONFERENCE ON NATURAL BEAUTY
(1965)

CREATION AND AUTHORITY

The White House Conference on Natural Beauty, which was called by President Johnson, was held in Washington, D.C., May 24– 25, 1965.

Y 3.W 58/12:1/date
REPORT.

Y 3.W 58/12:2 CT
GENERAL PUBLICATIONS.

Y 3.W 58/12:7/date
PRESS RELEASES.

WHITE HOUSE CONFERENCE ON EQUAL EMPLOYMENT OPPORTUNITY
(1965)

CREATION AND AUTHORITY

The White House Conference on Equal Employment Opportunity was held in Washington, D.C., August 19 and 20, 1965.

Y 3.W 58/13:1/date
REPORT.

Y 3.W 58/13:2 CT
GENERAL PUBLICATIONS.

WHITE HOUSE CONFERENCE ON HEALTH
(1965)

CREATION AND AUTHORITY

The White House Conference on Health was held in Washington, D.C., November 3 and 4, 1965, at the invitation of President Johnson.

Y 3.W 58/14:1/date
REPORT.

Y 3.W 58/14:2 CT
GENERAL PUBLICATIONS.

WHITE HOUSE CONFERENCE "TO FULFILL THESE RIGHTS"
(1966)

CREATION AND AUTHORITY

The White House Conference "To Fulfill These Rights" was held in Washington, D.C., June 1– 2, 1966.

Y 3.W 58/15:1/date
REPORT.

Y 3.W 58/15:2 CT
GENERAL PUBLICATIONS.

WHITE HOUSE CONFERENCE ON FOOD, NUTRITION AND HEALTH
(1969– 1970)

CREATION AND AUTHORITY

The White House Conference on Food, Nutrition, and Health was held in Washington, D.C., December 2– 4, 1969 at the request of the President. Its final report was published in 1970.

Y 3.W 58/16:CT
PUBLICATIONS.

WHITE HOUSE CONFERENCE ON INDUSTRIAL WORLD AHEAD
(1971)

CREATION AND AUTHORITY

The White House Conference on Industrial World Ahead was held at Phoenix, Arizona on November 9, 1971.

Y 3.W 58/17:1/date   • Item 1088
REPORT.

Y 3.W 58/17:2 CT   • Item 1088
GENERAL PUBLICATIONS.

Y 3.W 58/17:7/nos.   • Item 1088
PRESS RELEASES. [Irregular]

Y 3.W 58/17:9 CT   • Item 1088
ADDRESSES.

WHITE HOUSE CONFERENCE ON HANDICAPPED INDIVIDUALS
(1976)

Y 3.W 58/18:1/date   • Item 1088
REPORT.

Y 3.W 58/18:2 CT   • Item 1088
GENERAL PUBLICATIONS.

Y 3.W 58/18:9/date   • Item 1088
NATIONAL NEWSLETTER. [Quarterly]

WHITE HOUSE CONFERENCE ON BALANCED NATIONAL GROWTH AND ECONOMIC DEVELOPMENT
(1978)

CREATION AND AUTHORITY

The White House Conference on Balanced National Growth and Economic Development was held on January 29 through February 2, 1978.

Y 3.W 58/19:1/date
REPORT. 1978.

Y 3.W 58/19:2 CT
GENERAL PUBLICATIONS.

WHITE HOUSE CONFERENCE ON LIBRARY AND INFORMATION SERVICES
(1978)

Y 3.W 58/20:1/date
ANNUAL REPORT.

Y 3.W 58/20:2 CT
GENERAL PUBLICATIONS.

Y 3.W 58/20:8 CT
HANDBOOKS, MANUALS, GUIDES.

Y 3.W 58/20:9 CT
POSTERS. [Irregular]

WHITE HOUSE CONFERENCE ON SMALL BUSINESS

Y 3.W 58/21:2 CT • Item 1088
GENERAL PUBLICATIONS. [Irregular]

WHITE HOUSE COMMISSION ON SMALL BUSINESS

Y 3.W 58/21-2:1/date • Item 1088
REPORT.

WHITE HOUSE CONFERENCE ON FAMILIES
(1979)

Y 3.W 58/22:1/date
REPORT.

Y 3.W 58/22:2 CT
GENERAL PUBLICATIONS.

Y 3.W 58/22:9/v.nos.&nos. • Item 1088-A-1
REPORT FROM THE WHITE HOUSE CONFERENCE ON FAMILIES. v. 1–　1979–　[Irregular]

WHITE HOUSE CONFERENCE ON INDIAN EDUCATION

Y 3.W 58/23:2 CT • Item 1088
GENERAL PUBLICATIONS.

INTER-DEPARTMENTAL BOARD ON WIRELESS TELEGRAPHY
(1904)

CREATION AND AUTHORITY

　　The Inter-departmental Board on Wireless Telegraphy was established by the President on June 24, 1904. The final report of the Board was submitted on July 12, 1904.

Y 3.W 74:CT
PUBLICATIONS.

NATIONAL COMMISSION FOR REVIEW OF FEDERAL AND STATE LAWS RELATING TO WIRETAPPING AND ELECTRONIC SURVEILLANCE
(1968)

Y 3.W 74/2:1/date
REPORT.

Y 3.W 74/2:2 CT
GENERAL PUBLICATIONS.

WOLF MANAGEMENT COMMITTEE

Y 3.W 83:CT • Item 1089-A-1
PUBLICATIONS AND REPORTS.

　Y 3.W 83:CT • Item 1089-A-1
　REINTRODUCTION AND MANAGEMENT OF WOLVES IN YELLOWSTONE NATIONAL PARK AND THE CENTRAL IDAHO WILDERNESS AREA.

NATIONAL COMMISSION ON THE OBSERVANCE OF INTERNATIONAL WOMAN'S YEAR, 1975
(1975– 1978)

CREATION AND AUTHORITY

　　The National Commission on the Observance of International Woman's Year, 1975, was established by Executive Order 11832 of January 9, 1975, as amended by Executive Order 11889 of November 25, 1975. The Commission continued by act of December 23, 1975 (89 Stat. 1003) and was terminated March 31, 1978, pursuant to terms of the act.

Y 3.W 84:1/date
REPORT.

Y 3.W 84:2 CT
GENERAL PUBLICATIONS.

Y 3.W 84:9/nos. • Item 1089
LEGAL STATUS OF HOMEMAKERS IN [various States]. [Irregular]

　　PURPOSE:– To outline the laws and judicial precedents affecting homemakers in States throughout the U.S. The booklets typically discuss: Recent revisions in the law; statutes affecting divorce, widowhood, and employment; and decisions on support, property ownership, credit, and rape.
　　Separate publication for each State.

Y 3.W 84:10
WORKSHOP GUIDES. W 1–　[Irregular]

Y 3.W 84:11/nos.
UPDATE.

NATIONAL ADVISORY COUNCIL ON WOMEN'S EDUCATIONAL PROGRAMS
(1977–　　)

Y 3.W 84/2:1/date • Item 1088-A
REPORTS.

Y 3.W 84/2:2 CT • Item 1088-A
GENERAL PUBLICATIONS. [Irregular]

TASK FORCE ON WOMEN, MINORITIES, AND THE HANDICAPPED IN SCIENCE AND TECHNOLOGY

Y 3.W 84/3:2 CT • Item 1089
GENERAL PUBLICATIONS. [Irregular]

WOODROW WILSON CENTENNIAL CELEBRATION COMMISSION (1954)

CREATION AND AUTHORITY

The Woodrow Wilson Centennial Celebration Commission was established by act of Congress, approved August 30, 1954 (68 Stat. 964). The Commission was terminated upon submission of its report to Congress by provisions of the act that created it.

Y 3.W 86:1/date
REPORT.

Y 3.W 86:2 CT
GENERAL PUBLICATIONS.

WOODROW WILSON MEMORIAL COMMISSION (1961–1966)

CREATION AND AUTHORITY

The Woodrow Wilson Memorial Commission was established by act of October 4, 1961 (75 Stat. 783). The Commission ceased to function upon the submittal of its final report to the President and Congress on September 29, 1966.

Y 3.W 86/2:1/date
ANNUAL REPORTS.

Y 3.W 86/2:2 CT
GENERAL PUBLICATIONS.

WORLD WAR FOREIGN DEBT COMMISSION (1922–1927)

CREATION AND AUTHORITY

The World War Foreign Debt Commission was established by act of Congress, approved February 9, 1922 (42 Stat. 363). The Commission ceased to function in 1927.

Y 3.W 89:CT
PUBLICATIONS.

WORKS PROGRESS ADMINISTRATION (1935–1939)

CREATION AND AUTHORITY

The Works Progress Administration was established as an independent agency by Executive Order 7034 of May 6, 1935, pursuant to the Emergency Relief Appropriation Act of 1935, and continued by subsequent yearly Emergency Relief Appropriation Acts. Reorganization Plan No. 1 of 1939, effective July 1, 1939, changed the name to Works Projects Administration (FW 4) and placed it in the Federal Works Agency.

Y 3.W 89/2:1/date
ANNUAL REPORTS.

Later FW 4.1

Y 3.W 89/2:2 CT
GENERAL PUBLICATIONS.

Later FW 4.2

Y 3.W 89/2:3/nos.
BULLETINS.

Y 3.W 89/2:4/nos.
CIRCULARS.

Y 3.W 89/2:5 CT
LAWS.

Y 3.W 89/2:6 CT
REGULATIONS, RULES, AND INSTRUCTIONS.

Later FW 4.6

Y 3.W 89/2:7
MAPS.

Y 3.W 89/2:8 CT
POSTERS.

Y 3.W 89/2:9/nos.
ADMINISTRATIVE ORDERS.

Y 3.W 89/2:10/nos.
DIGEST OF POLICIES, REPORTS, AND OTHER PUBLICATIONS. [Semimonthly]

Later FW 4.10

Y 3.W 89/2:11/nos.
SAFETY BULLETINS.

Later FW 4.20

Y 3.W 89/2:12/nos.
ADJUSTMENT ORDERS.

Y 3.W 89/2:13/series nos.&nos. and letters-nos.
RESEARCH BULLETINS.

Y 3.W 89/2:13 CT
RESEARCH BULLETINS, CATALOG AND SUBJECT INDEX.

Y 3.W 89/2:14/nos.
GUIDE TO ELIGIBILITY OF W.P.A. PROJECTS.

Y 3.W 89/2:15/date
EMPLOYMENT UNDER WORKS PROGRAM, EXCLUSIVE OF ADMINISTRATIVE EMPLOYEES. [Weekly]

Y 3.W 89/2:16/nos.
NEWS LETTER FOR STATE SUPERVISORS OF RURAL RESEARCH. [Monthly]

Y 3.W 89/2:17/nos.
RESEARCH MONOGRAPHS.

Later FW 4.35

Y 3.W 89/2:18/series nos.&nos.
WORKING PROCEDURES.

Y 3.W 89/2:19/date
RESEARCH LIBRARY ABSTRACTS: FOREIGN. [Monthly]

Y 3.W 89/2:20/date
RESEARCH LIBRARY ABSTRACTS: DOMESTIC.

Y 3.W 89/2:21/nos.
[LETTERS] TO STATE WORKS PROGRESS ADMINISTRATORS.

Y 3.W 89/2:22/vol.
FEDERAL THEATRE PROJECT PUBLICATIONS.

Y 3.W 89/2:23/nos.
GENERAL LETTERS TO STATE WORKS PROGRESS ADMINISTRATORS.

Later FW 4.12

Y 3.W 89/2:24 CT
FEDERAL WRITERS' PROJECT.

Includes American Guide Series.
Later FW 4.28

Y 3.W 89/2:25/vol.
CURRENT STATISTICS OF RELIEF IN RURAL AND TOWN AREAS.

Later SS 1.23

Y 3.W 89/2:26/date
EMPLOYMENT HOURS AND EARNINGS ON PROJECTS OPERATED BY WPA. [Semimonthly]

Y 3.W 89/2:27/date
EMPLOYMENT HOURS AND EARNINGS ON STUDENT AID PROJECTS OF NYA. [Monthly]

Y 3.W 89/2:28/nos.
COMMUNITY ORGANIZATION FOR LEISURE, SERIALS.

Y 3.W 89/2:29/nos.
HANDBOOK OF PROCEDURES LETTERS.

Later FW 4.9

Y 3.W 89/2:30/letter-nos. or nos.
OPERATING PROCEDURE MEMORANDUM.

Later FW 4.8

Y 3.W 89/2:31 CT
FEDERAL MUSIC PROJECT.

Y 3.W 89/2:32/date
REPORT ON PROGRESS OF WORKS PROGRAM. [Monthly]

Y 3.W 89/2:33/vol.
SEMIMONTHLY NEWS LETTER, FEDERAL THEATRE PROJECT.

Y 3.W 89/2:34/date
REPORT ON PROGRESS ON WORKS PROGRAM.

Y 3.W 89/2:35 CT
DIGEST OF PUBLIC WELFARE PROVISIONS UNDER LAWS OF STATES.

Y 3.W 89/2:36 CT
ANALYSIS OF CONSTITUTIONAL PROVISIONS AFFECTING PUBLIC WELFARE IN STATES.

Y 3.W 89/2:37/nos.
TECHNICAL SERIES: EDUCATION CIRCULARS.

Y 3.W 89/2:38/nos.
TECHNICAL SERIES: RECREATION CIRCULARS.

Later FW 4.21

Y 3.W 89/2:39/nos.
INFORMATION SERVICE LETTERS.

Later FW 4.15

Y 3.W 89/2:40 CT
FEDERAL ART PROJECT.

Y 3.W 89/2:41/date
LIBRARY ACCESSIONS, RESEARCH LIBRARY.
[Weekly]

Earlier Y 3.F 31/5:38
Later FW 4.11

Y 3.W 89/2:42/letters-nos.
NATIONAL RESEARCH PROJECT REPORTS:
MINERAL TECHNOLOGY AND OUTPUT PER MAN
STUDIES, REPORTS.

Later FW 4.7

Y 3.W 89/2:43 CT
HISTORICAL RECORDS SURVEY.

Y 3.W 89/2:44/nos.
TECHNICAL SERIES: HOUSEHOLD SERVICE
DEMONSTRATION CIRCULARS.

Y 3.W 89/2:45/nos.
TECHNICAL SERIES: HOUSEKEEPING AID
CIRCULARS.

Y 3.W 89/2:46/nos.
TECHNICAL SERIES: PUBLIC ADMINISTRATION
CIRCULARS.

Y 3.W 89/2:47/nos.
NATIONAL RESEARCH PROJECT: STUDIES OF
CHANGING TECHNIQUES AND EMPLOYMENT IN
AGRICULTURE, REPORTS.

Y 3.W 89/2:48/nos.
TECHNICAL SERIES: ART CIRCULARS.

Later FW 4.34

Y 3.W 89/2:49/nos.
TECHNICAL SERIES: SCHOOL LUNCH CIRCULARS.

Y 3.W 89/2:50/letters-nos.
NATIONAL RESEARCH PROJECT: REPORTS,
STUDIES IN CHANGING LABOR PRODUCTIVITY,
REPORTS.

Y 3.W 89/2:51/letters-nos.
NATIONAL RESEARCH PROJECT: REPORTS, STUD-
IES OF EFFECTS OF INDUSTRIAL CHANGE ON
LABOR MARKETS, REPORTS.

Y 3.W 89/2:52/nos.
TECHNICAL SERIES: RESEARCH, STATISTICAL, AND
SURVEY PROJECT CIRCULARS.

Later FW 4.22

Y 3.W 89/2:53/letters-nos.
NATIONAL RESEARCH PROJECT: REPORTS, PHILA-
DELPHIA LABOR MARKET STUDIES, REPORTS.

Y 3.W 89/2:54 CT
ADDRESSES.

Later FW 4.25

Y 3.W 89/2:55/letters-nos.
NATIONAL RESEARCH PROJECT: REPORTS, PRO-
DUCTIVITY AND EMPLOYMENT IN SELECTED
INDUSTRIES, REPORTS.

Y 3.W 89/2:56/letters-nos.
NATIONAL RESEARCH PROJECT: REPORTS,
STUDIES IN EQUIPMENT CHANGES AND
INDUSTRIAL TECHNIQUES, REPORTS.

Y 3.W 89/2:57/nos.
SOCIAL PROBLEMS.

Later FW 4.19

Y 3.W 89/2:58/date
STATISTICAL BULLETINS. [Monthly]

Later FW 4.13

Y 3.W 89/2:59/nos.
TECHNICAL SERIES: TECHNICAL SERVICES LABO-
RATORY CIRCULARS.

Later FW 4.17

Y 3.W 89/2:60
REGIONAL RESEARCH BULLETINS, NEW YORK AND
NEW ENGLAND.

Y 3.W 89/2:61/date
FEDERAL WORK AND CONSTRUCTION PROJECTS.
[Monthly]

Later FW 4.33

NATIONAL COMMISSION ON STATE WORKMEN'S COMPENSATION LAWS
(1970–   )

CREATION AND AUTHORITY

The National Commission of State Workmen's
Compensation Laws was established by Public
Law 91-596, approved December 17, 1970.

Y 3.W 89/3:1/date   • Item 1089
REPORT.

Y 3.W 89/3:2 CT   • Item 1089

GENERAL PUBLICATIONS. YORKTOWN CENTENNIAL COMMISSION
(1881–1883)

CREATION AND AUTHORITY

The Yorktown Centennial Commission, also
known as the Yorktown Monument Commission,
was established by act of Congress, approved
March 3, 1881. The Commission submitted its
report in 1883.

Y 3.Y 8:CT
PUBLICATIONS.

YORKTOWN SESQUICENTENNIAL COMMISSION
(1928–1930)

CREATION AND AUTHORITY

The Yorktown Sesquicentennial Commission
was established by House Concurrent Resolution
No. 43, passed May 28, 1928 (45 Stat. 2393). The
report of the Commission was made in 1930.

Y 3.Y 8/2:CT
PUBLICATIONS.

COMMISSIONS, COMMITTEES, AND BOARDS

Y 3.2:CT   • Item 1089
REPORTS AND PUBLICATIONS.

Y 3.2:AD 9/CT   • Item 1089
SOCIAL SECURITY ADVISORY BOARD, PUBLI-
CATIONS.

Y 3.2:AS 7/R 29   • Item 1089
ASSASSINATION RECORDS REVIEW BOARD,
REPORTS.

Y 3.2:B 22/B 22/v.nos.   • Item 1089
NATIONAL BANKRUPTCY REVIEW COMMIS-
SION, PUBLICATIONS.

Y 3.2:C 73   • Item 1089
U.S. COMMISSION ON THE BICENTENNIAL OF
THE U.S. CONSTITUTION.

Y 3.2:C 76/B 49   • Item 1089
CONSUMER BILL OF RIGHTS AND RESPONSI-
BILITIES COMMISSION.

Y 3.2:D 56/R 29   • Item 1089
COMMISSION ON DIETARY SUPPLEMENT
LABELS, PUBLICATIONS.

Y 3.2:IM 6/AM 3   • Item 1089
IMMIGRATION AND IMMIGRANT POLICY.

Y 3.2:K 12/CT   • Item 1089
KAHO'OLAWE ISLAND CONVEYANCE COMMIS-
SION: REPORTS.

Y 3.2:M 66/H 62   • Item 1089
UNITED STATES COMMISSION ON MINORITY
BUSINESS DEVELOPMENT, FINAL REPORT.

Y 3.2:Un 2/CT   • Item 1089
ADVISORY COUNCIL ON UNEMPLOYMENT COM-
PENSATION.

SPECIAL COMMITTEE ON THE YEAR 2000 TECHNOLOGY PROBLEM
(Senate)

Y 4.3:T:CT   • Item 1009-B-12
GENERAL PUBLICATIONS.

COMMITTEE ON ACCOUNTS
(House)

Y 4.Ac 2:CT
PUBLICATIONS.

COMMISSION ON ADMINISTRATIVE REVIEW
(House)

CREATION AND AUTHORITY

The Commission on Administrative Review was established by H. Res. 1368, 94th Congress.

Y 4.Ad 6:CT • Item 1009
PUBLICATIONS.

COMMITTEE ON AERONAUTICAL AND SPACE SCIENCES
(Senate)

CREATION AND AUTHORITY

The Senate Committee on Aeronautical and Space Sciences was replaced by the Senate Committee on Commerce, Science, and Transportation (Y 4.C 73/7).

Y 4.Ae 8:CT • Item 1032
HEARINGS. [Irregular]

Issued as monographs.

Y 4.Ae 8:Cong./cal.nos.
LEGISLATIVE CALENDAR. 86th Cong.– 1959/60– [Irregular]

Includes author index; measures enacted into public law vetoed; hearings on nominations referred to committee; chronology; alphabetical list of witnesses and dates appearing; publications of the committee.
ISSN 0498-9945

SPECIAL COMMITTEE ON AGING
(Senate)

INFORMATION

Senate Special Committee on Aging
Dirksen Senate Office Building, Rm. G-31
Washington, D.C. 20510
(202) 224-5364
Fax: (202) 224-9926
http://aging.senate.gov

Y 4.Ag 4:nos. • Item 1009-B-1 (P)
HEARINGS. • Item 1009-C-1 (MF)

Y 4.Ag 4:CT • Item 1009-B (P)
PUBLICATIONS. • Item 1009-C (MF)

Y 4.Ag 4:Cong.-nos. • Item 1009-B-1 (P)
COMMITTEE PRINTS. [Irregular] • Item 1009-C-1 (MF)

Y 4.Ag 4:P 96/date • Item 1009
PUBLICATIONS LIST. [Biennial]

Issued as a Committee Print.
Contains list of publications 87th Congress, February 1961, through the current Congress.

SELECT COMMITTEE ON AGING
(House)

INFORMATION

House Select Committee on Aging
712 House Office Building Annex No. 1
300 New Jersey Avenue, S.E.
Washington, D.C. 20515
(202) 226-3375

Y 4.Ag 4/2:CT • Item 1009-B-2 (P)
HEARINGS. [Irregular] • Item 1009-C-2 (MF)

Y 4.Ag 4/2:CT • Item 1009-B (P)
PUBLICATIONS. • Item 1009-C (MF)

Y 4.Ag 4/2:CT • Item 1009-B-2 (P)
COMMITTEE PRINTS. [Irregular] • Item 1009-C-2 (MF)
Earlier Y 4.Ag 4/2:R 86/9
Later Y 4.Ag 4/2-12

Y 4.Ag 4/2:date
RULES OF PROCEDURE. [Biennial]

Y 4.Ag 4/2:Ag 4/5 • Item 1009
PROGRESS IN AGING. 95th– 1977-78– [Biennial]
Issued as a Committee Print.
Report for each Congress.

Y 4.Ag 4/2-10:date • Item 1009-B-2 (P)
ACTIVITIES OF AGING COMMITTEE. [Annual] • Item 1009-C-2 (MF)

Y 4.Ag 4/2-11:date • Item 1009-B-2 (P)
FEDERAL INCOME TAX GUIDE FOR OLDER AMERICANS. [Annual] • Item 1009-C-2 (MF)
Earlier Y 4.Ag 4/2/6

Y 4.Ag 4/2-12:date • Item 1009-B-2 (P)
RULES OF PROCEDURE. [Biennial] • Item 1009-C-2 (MF)

COMMITTEE ON AGRICULTURE
(House)

INFORMATION

House Committee on Agriculture
1301 Longworth House Office Building
Washington, D.C. 20515
(202) 225-2171
Email:agriculture@mail.house.gov
http://agriculture.house.gov

Y 4.Ag 8/1:nos. • Item 1010-A (P)
HEARINGS. [Irregular] • Item 1010-B (MF)

Alphabetical designations are given the hearings for each Congress: A– Z, AA– ZZ, AAA–ZZZ, etc., as required, Hearings held by the full committee and the various sub-committee are included in the designation scheme.

Y 4.Ag 8/1:Cong./cal.nos.
LEGISLATIVE CALENDAR. [Irregular]

Includes house resolutions, concurrent resolutions, and joint resolutions with docket numbers; Senate bills and resolutions with docket numbers; report numbers on House bills; public and private laws; status of House and Senate bills; bills referred to subcommittees; subject and author indexes; hearings printed; hearings on watershed projects and action taken; hearings not printed; special reports; President's messages.

Y 4.Ag 8/1:CT • Item 1010-A (P)
COMMITTEE PRINTS. • Item 1010-B (MF)

Y 4.Ag 8/1:L 52
AGRICULTURAL LEGISLATION IN THE CONGRESS. [Biennial]

Y 4.Ag 8/1-2:date
NEWS RELEASES AND MISCELLANEOUS PUBLICATIONS. [Irregular]

Y 4.Ag 8/1-11:date • Item 1010-A (P)
RULES OF THE COMMITTEE ON AGRICULTURE. • Item 1010-B (MF)
Earlier Y 4.Ag 8/1:R 86

Y 4.Ag 8/1-12:date • Item 1010-A (P)
LEGISLATIVE CALENDAR. [Annual] • Item 1010-B (MF)
Earlier Y 4.Ag 8/1

COMMITTEE ON AGRICULTURE AND FORESTRY
(Senate)

Superseded by the Committee on Agriculture, Nutrition and Forestry (Y 4.Ag 8/3)

Y 4.Ag 8/2:CT • Item 1032
HEARINGS. [Irregular]

Issued as monographs.

Y 4.Ag 8/2:Cong./cal.nos.
LEGISLATIVE CALENDAR. [Irregular]

Includes list of nominations; hearings; index by author and by subject.
ISSN 0364-4170

COMMITTEE ON AGRICULTURE, NUTRITION, AND FORESTRY
(Senate)

Supersedes Senate Committee on Agriculture and Forestry (Y 4.A g 8/2) and the Select Committee on Nutrition and Human Needs (Y 4.N 95).

INFORMATION

Senate Committee on Agriculture, Nutrition and Forestry
328A Russell Senate Office Building
Washington, D.C. 20510-6000
(202) 244-2035
http://agriculture.senate.gov

Y 4.Ag 8/3:CT • Item 1032-C (P)
PUBLICATIONS. • Item 1032-D (MF)

Y 4.Ag 8/3:Cong.-nos. • Item 1032-C (P)
COMMITTEE PRINTS. [Irregular] • Item 1032-D (MF)

Y 4.Ag 8/3:hrg.nos. • Item 1032-C (P)
HEARINGS. • Item 1032-D (MF)

Y 4.Ag 8/3-2:date
NEWS RELEASES AND MISCELLANEOUS PUBLICATIONS. [Irregular]

SELECT COMMITTEE OF INQUIRY INTO OPERATIONS OF AIR SERVICES
(House)

Y 4.Ai 7:CT
PUBLICATIONS.

SPECIAL COMMITTEE ON INVESTIGATION OF AIR MAIL AND OCEAN MAIL CONTRACTS
(Senate)

Y 4.Ai 7/2:CT
PUBLICATIONS.

JOINT SELECT COMMITTEE ON ALCOHOL IN MANUFACTURES AND ARTS

Y 4.Al 1/1:CT
PUBLICATIONS.

COMMITTEE ON ALCOHOL LIQUOR TRAFFIC
(House)

Y 4.Al 1/2:CT
PUBLICATIONS.

COMMITTEE ON AMERICAN SHIP-BUILDING
(House)

Y 4.Am 3/1:CT
PUBLICATIONS.

SPECIAL COMMITTEE ON INVESTIGATION OF AMERICAN SUGAR REFINING COMPANY
(House)

Y 4.Am 3/2:CT
PUBLICATIONS.

SPECIAL COMMITTEE TO INVESTIGATE AMERICAN RETAIL FEDERATION

Y 4.Am 3/3:CT
PUBLICATIONS.

SPECIAL COMMITTEE TO INVESTIGATE CONDITIONS IN THE AMERICAN MERCHANT MARINE

Y 4.Am 3/4:CT
PUBLICATIONS.

SPECIAL COMMITTEE TO STUDY PROBLEMS OF AMERICAN SMALL BUSINESS
(Senate)

Y 4.Am 3/5:CT
PUBLICATIONS.

COMMITTEE ON APPROPRIATIONS
(House)

INFORMATION

House Committee on Appropriations
H 218 The Capitol
Washington, D.C. 20515
(202) 225-2771
http://www.house.gov/appropriations

                • **Item 1011 (P)**
Y 4.Ap 6/1:CT   • **Item 1011-A (MF)**
HEARINGS. [Irregular]

     Hearings are published individually by the full committee and the various subcommittees. Each subcommittee has the responsibility of a certain agency or group of related agencies. Titles and general coverage of the hearings are usually repeated each year and in that sense form continuations. The Library of Congress catalogs each

hearing separately as a monograph rather than as a continuation.

     In addition to the annual hearings on the fiscal budgets, additional hearings are held for supplemental or deficiency appropriations as needed.

     Traditionally appropriations bills originate in the House of Representatives. Agency hearings are usually held first by the House and later by the Senate. A similar breakdown of subcommittees exists in the Senate Appropriations Committee as does that in the House, with titles published and agency groupings about the same.

              • **Item 1011 (P)**
Y 4.Ap 6/1:CT   • **Item 1011-A (MF)**
COMMITTEE PRINTS. [Irregular]

Y 4.Ap 6/1-10:date   • **Item 1011**
VIEWS AND ESTIMATES ON THE BUDGET PROPOSED FOR FISCAL YEAR (date). [Annual]

              • **Item 1011 (P)**
Y 4.Ap 6/1-11:date   • **Item 1011 (MF)**
COMMITTEE RULES. [Biennial]

     Earlier Y 4.Ap 6/1:R 86/4

COMMITTEE ON APPROPRIATIONS
(Senate)

INFORMATION

Senate Committee on Appropriations
S-128 The Capitol
Washington, D.C. 20510
(202) 224-3471
http://appropriations.senate.gov

              • **Item 1033 (P)**
Y 4.Ap 6/2:nos.   • **Item 1033-A (MF)**
HEARINGS. [Irregular]

     Hearings are published individually by the full committee and the various subcommittees. Each subcommittee has the responsibility of a certain agency or group of related agencies. Titles and general coverage are usually repeated each year and in that sense form continuations. The Library of Congress catalogs each hearing as a monograph rather than as a continuation.

     Hearings for agency appropriations are usually held first by the House of Representatives and later by the Senate. For this reason, the printed volumes for the Senate hearings are much less voluminous than those of the House for comparable hearings.

              • **Item 1033 (P)**
Y 4.Ap 6/2:CT   • **Item 1033-A (MF)**
COMMITTEE PRINTS. [Irregular]

Y 4.Ap 6/2:CT   • **Item 1033**
PUBLICATIONS.

Y 4.Ap 6/2:B 85/5/date   • **Item 1033**
VIEWS OF THE COMMITTEE ON APPROPRIATIONS, UNITED STATES SENATE, ON THE FIRST CONCURRENT RESOLUTION ON THE BUDGET. [Annual]

     Issued as a Committee Print.
     Report covers fiscal year.

SPECIAL COMMITTEE TO INVESTIGATE THE COST OF ARMOR PLANT

Y 4.Ar 5:CT
PUBLICATIONS.

COMMITTEE ON ARMED SERVICES
(House)

INFORMATION

House Committee on Armed Services
2120 Rayburn House Office Building
Washington, D.C. 20515
(202) 225-4151
http://armedservices.house.gov

Y 4.Ar 5/2:nos   • **Item 1012-A (P)**
HEARINGS.   • **Item 1012-B (MF)**
                                 • **Item 1012-C-1**
                                 • **Item 1012-D-1**

Y 4.Ar 5/2:CT   • **Item 1012-A (P)**
COMMITTEE PRINTS. [Irregular]   • **Item 1012-B (MF)**

Y 4.Ar 5/2:Cong./cal.nos.
LEGISLATIVE CALENDAR. [Irregular]

Includes status of bills and resolutions reported by committee; bills enacted into private and public laws; topical index of bills referred to committee (subject and author); executive communications; hearings, investigations, and other matters not directly pertaining to legislation before the committee.

Y 4.Ar 5/2a:Yr./nos.   • **Item 1012-A (P)**
PAPERS, [number] CONGRESS. [Irregular] • **Item 1012-B (MF)**

Consists mainly of hearings. The Papers of each congress are numbered and pages consecutively. Title page, contents, and index are issued separately for each Congress.

Occasionally hearings are printed as separates and not included in the Paper series.

Y 4.Ar 5/2-2:date
NEWS RELEASES AND MISCELLANEOUS PUBLICATIONS. [Irregular]

Y 4.Ar 5/2-12:   • **Item 1012-A (P)**
LAWS.   • **Item 1012-B (MF)**

Y 4.Ar 5/2-13:date   • **Item 1012-A (P)**
REPORT OF THE ACTIVITIES OF THE COMMITTEE • **Item 1012-B (MF)**
ON ARMED SERVICES. [Annual]

Y 4.Ar 5/2-14:date   • **Item 1012-A (P)**
DEFENSE CATALOGING AND STANDARDIZATION • **Item 1012-B (MF)**
ACT OF 1952. [Annual]

Y 4.Ar 5/2-15:date   • **Item 1012-A (P)**
COMMITTEE RULES AND RULES FOR INVESTIGA- • **Item 1012-B (MF)**
TIVE HEARINGS CONDUCTED BY SUBCOMMIT-
TEES OF THE COMMITTEE ON ARMED
SERVICES. [Biennial]

Earlier Y 4.Ar 5/2:R 86/2

Y 4.Ar 5/2-16:   • **Item 1012-A (P)**
REVIEW OF ARMS CONTROL AND DISARMAMENT • **Item 1012-B (MF)**
ACTIVITIES. [Biennial]

Y 4.Ar 5/2-17:   • **Item 1012-A (P)**
LEGISLATIVE CALENDAR.   • **Item 1012-B (MF)**

COMMITTEE ON ARMED SERVICES
(Senate)

INFORMATION

Senate Committee on Armed Services
228 Russell Senate Office Building
Washington, D.C. 20510
(202) 224-3871
http://www.senate.gov/~armed_services

Y 4.Ar 5/3:CT   • **Item 1034-A (P)**
HEARINGS. [Irregular]   • **Item 1034-B (MF)**

Issued as monographs.

Y 4.Ar 5/3:Cong./cal.nos.
LEGISLATIVE CALENDAR. [Irregular]

Includes index by subject and by author; index by report number of all bills and resolutions reported to the Senate; index by conference report number; index of public and private laws by number of veto message; investigations, hearings, and other matters not directly pertaining to legislation before the committee; hearings on nominations referred to committee, subcommittee and special committee appointments and hearings.

ISSN 0364-4146

Y 4.Ar 5/3:Cong.-nos.   • **Item 1034-A (P)**
COMMITTEE PRINTS. [Irregular]   • **Item 1034-B (MF)**

ART AND ANTIQUITIES COMMISSION
(Senate)

CREATION AND AUTHORITY

The Art and Antiquities Commission was created by Senate Resolution 382, of October 1, 1968.

INFORMATION

Senate Commission on Art and Antiquities
Room S-411, Capitol Building
Washington, D.C. 20510
(202) 224-2955

Y 4.Ar 7:CT   • **Item 998**
PUBLICATIONS.

SELECT COMMITTEE ON ASSASSINATIONS
(House)

Y 4.As 7:CT   • **Item 1009**
PUBLICATIONS.

SELECT COMMITTEE ON ASTRONAUTICS AND SPACE EXPLORATION
(House)

Y 4.As 8:CT
PUBLICATIONS.

SPECIAL COMMITTEE ON ATOMIC ENERGY
(Senate)

Y 4.At 7:CT
PUBLICATIONS.

JOINT COMMITTEE ON ATOMIC ENERGY

Y 4.At 7/2:CT   • **Item 999**
HEARINGS. [Irregular]

Issued as monographs.
Hearings are held annually by the Committee for the following two items:

Y 4.At 7/2:At 7/12   • **Item 999**
DEVELOPMENT, GROWTH, AND STATE OF THE
ATOMIC ENERGY INDUSTRY. [Annual]

Held by the full Committee pursuant to section 202 of the Atomic Energy Act of 1954, to receive information on the development, growth and state of the atomic energy industry.

Y 4.At 7/2:L 52   • **Item 999**
AEC AUTHORIZING LEGISLATION, FISCAL YEAR
[date]. 1955–   [Annual]

Held by the Subcommittee on Legislation. Gives background information on each of the projects considered or proposed for authorization, including comprehensive summaries of major projects conducted during the preceding year and new projects proposed for further development.

Y 4.At 7/2:CT
COMMITTEE PRINTS.

Y 4.At 7/2:L 52/2
ATOMIC ENERGY LEGISLATIONS THROUGH
[Congress, Session]. 1957–　[Annual]

Contains a cumulative collection of statutes and material pertaining to atomic energy
legislation for use of the Joint Committee on
Atomic Energy, the Congress, interested
Government agencies, and the public.
Includes table of Atomic Energy Commission appropriations for fiscal years.

Y 4.At 7/2:M 51
CURRENT MEMBERSHIP OF JOINT COMMITTEE
ON ATOMIC ENERGY, MEMBERSHIP, PUB-
LICATIONS, AND OTHER PERTINENT INFOR-
MATION THROUGH [Congress, Session]. [An-
nual]

SELECT COMMITTEE ON INVESTIGATION OF THE ATTORNEY GENERAL
(Senate)

Y 4.At 8:CT
PUBLICATIONS.

SELECT COMMITTEE TO INVESTIGATE THE INCORPORATION OF THE BALTIC STATES INTO THE U.S.S.R.
(House)

Y 4.B 21:CT
PUBLICATIONS.

COMMITTEE ON BANKING, FINANCE AND URBAN AFFAIRS
(House)

Formerly named the Committee on Banking
and Currency.

See Y 4.F 49.20

　　　　　　　　　　　　　• Item 1013-A (P)
Y 4.B 22/1:nos.　　• Item 1013-B (MF)
HEARINGS. [Irregular]
Issued as monographs.

Y 4.B 22/1:Cong./cal.nos.
LEGISLATIVE CALENDAR. [Irregular]

Includes summary of legislation considered
by the committee; member index of bills before
the committee; subject index of bills and resolutions; executive communications referred to committee; President's messages referred to committee; votes in house–bills considered; bills on
which hearings were printed; committee prints;
recapitulation of bills acted upon by the committee.
ISSN 0364-9652

Y 4.B 22/1:CT
COMMITTEE PRINTS.

Y 4.B 22/1:L 52/3
LEGISLATIVE ACTIVITY OF HOUSE COMMITTEE
ON BANKING AND CURRENCY.

　　　　　　　　　　　　　• Item 1013-A(P)
Y 4.B 22/1-10:Cong./nos.　• Item 1013-B (MF)
LEGISLATIVE CALENDAR. [Irregular]

SELECT COMMITTEE ON FAILED NATIONAL BANKS

Y 4.B 22/2:CT
PUBLICATIONS.

COMMITTEE ON BANKING, HOUSING AND URBAN AFFAIRS
(Senate)

INFORMATION

Senate Committee on Banking,
Housing, and Urban Affairs
534 Dirksen Senate Office Building
Washington, D.C. 20510
(202) 224-7391
Fax: (202) 224-5137
http://banking.senate.gov

　　　　　　　　　　　　　• Item 1035-C (P)
Y 4.B 22/3:hrg.-nos.　• Item 1035-D (MF)
HEARINGS. [Irregular]

Issued as monographs.

Y 4.B 22/3:Cong./cal.nos.
LEGISLATIVE CALENDAR. [Irregular]

Includes lists of committee reports, joint committee report (Joint Committee on Defense Production); special reports; index by author and by
subject.
ISSN 0364-4197

　　　　　　　　　　　　　• Item 1035-C (P)
Y 4.B 22/3:CT　　• Item 1035-D (MF)
COMMITTEE PRINTS.

Y 4.B 22/3:Ac 8
SUMMARY OF ACTIVITIES. [Annual]

SPECIAL COMMITTEE TO INVESTIGATE BANKRUPTCY AND RECEIVERSHIP PROCEEDINGS AND ADMINISTRATION OF JUSTICE IN UNITED STATES COURTS
(Senate)

Y 4.B 22/4:CT
PUBLICATIONS.

SPECIAL COMMITTEE APPOINTED UNDER H. RES. 6 CONCERNING VICTOR L. BERGER
(House)

Y 4.B 45:CT
PUBLICATIONS.

SELECT COMMITTEE TO INVESTIGATE THE ESCAPE OF GROVER CLEVELAND BERGDOLL FROM DISCIPLINARY BARRACKS AT GOVERNORS ISLAND, N.Y.
(House)

Y 4.B 45/2:CT
PUBLICATIONS.

JOINT COMMITTEE ON THE ARRANGEMENTS FOR THE COMMEMORATION OF THE BICENTENNIAL

Y 4.B 47:CT
PUBLICATIONS.

JOINT STUDY COMMITTEE ON BUDGET CONTROL

Y 4.B 85:CT
PUBLICATIONS.

COMMITTEE ON THE BUDGET
(Senate)

INFORMATION

Senate Committee on the Budget
Dirksen Senate Office Building
624
Washington, D.C. 20510
(202) 224-0642
http://budget.senate.gov

　　　　　　　　　　　　　• Item 1035-A-1 (P)
Y 4.B 85/2:Cong.-nos.　• Item 1035-A-2 (MF)
COMMITTEE PRINTS. [Irregular]

Y 4.B 85/2:hrg nos.
HEARINGS. [Irregular]
- Item 1035-A-1 (P)
- Item 1035-A-2 (MF)

Y 4.B 85/2:CT
PUBLICATIONS.
- Item 1035-A-1 (P)
- Item 1035-A-2 (MF)

COMMITTEE ON THE BUDGET
(House)

INFORMATION

House Committee on the Budget
Cannon House Office Bldg., Rm. 309
Washington, D.C. 20515
(202) 225-7200
Email:budget@mail.house.gov
http://www.budget.house.gov

Y 4.B 85/3:nos.
HEARINGS.
- Item 1035-B-1 (P)
- Item 1035-B-2 (MF)

Y 4.B 85/3:CT
COMMITTEE PRINTS. [Irregular]
- Item 1035-B-1 (P)
- Item 1035-B-2 (MF)

Y 4.B 85/3:CT
PUBLICATIONS.
- Item 1035-B-2 (P)
- Item 1035-B-2 (MF)

Y 4.B 85/3:Ec 7/11/date
ECONOMIC SUMMARY. 80-1– 1980– [Monthly]
- Item 1035-B

Former title: Monthly Economic Report.

Y 4.B 85/3-10:date
HOUSE RULES OF PROCEDURE.
- Item 1035-B-1 (P)
- Item 1035-B-2 (MF)

Y 4.B 85/3-11:date
VIEWS AND ESTIMATES OF COMMITTEES OF THE HOUSE (TOGETHER WITH SUPPLEMENTAL AND MINORITY VIEWS) ON THE CONGRESSIONAL BUDGET FOR FISCAL YEAR (date). [Annual]
- Item 1035-B-1 (P)
- Item 1035-B-2 (MF)

Y 4.B 85/3-12:date
LEGISLATIVE CALENDAR. [Annual]
- Item 1035-B-1 (P)
- Item 1035-B-2 (MF)

SELECT COMMITTEE ON THE BUDGET
(House)

Y 4.B 86/1:CT
PUBLICATIONS.

COMMITTEE FOR THE CONSIDERATION OF THE NATIONAL BUDGET
(Senate)

Y 4.B 86/2:CT
PUBLICATIONS.

SPECIAL COMMITTEE TO INVESTIGATE CAMPAIGN EXPENDITURES
(House)

Y 4.C 15:CT
PUBLICATIONS.

COMMITTEE ON RELATIONS WITH CANADA
(Senate)

Y 4.C 16:CT
PUBLICATIONS.

SPECIAL COMMITTEE ON THE CENTENNIAL CELEBRATION OF THE LAYING OF THE CORNER STONE OF THE CAPITOL

Y 4.C 17:CT
PUBLICATIONS.

COMMISSION FOR THE EXTENSION OF THE UNITED STATES CAPITOL

Y 4.C 17/2:CT
PUBLICATIONS.

CENSUS COMMITTEE
(House)

Y 4.C 33/1:CT
PUBLICATIONS.

CENSUS COMMITTEE
(Senate)

Y 4.C 33/2:CT
PUBLICATIONS.

SPECIAL COMMITTEE TO INVESTIGATE THE CENTRALIZATION OF HEAVY INDUSTRY IN THE UNITED STATES
(Senate)

Y 4.C 33/3:CT
PUBLICATIONS.

SELECT COMMITTEE TO STUDY CENSURE CHARGES
(Senate)

Y 4.C 33/4:CT
PUBLICATIONS.

CENTENNIAL OF THE ESTABLISHMENT OF THE SEAT OF GOVERNMENT IN WASHINGTON COMMISSION

Y 4.C 333:CT
PUBLICATIONS.

JOINT COMMITTEE ON THE DEDICATION OF CHICKAMAUGA AND CHATTANOOGA NATIONALMILITARY PARK

Y 4.C 43:CT
PUBLICATIONS.

SELECT COMMITTEE ON CHILDREN, YOUTH, AND FAMILIES
(House)

INFORMATION

House Select Committee on Children, Youth and Families
Room 385, House Annex 2
Washington, D.C. 20515
(202) 226-7660

Y 4.C 43/2:CT
HEARINGS. [Irregular]
- Item 1009-B-10 (P)
- Item 1009-C-10 (MF)

Y 4.C 43/2:CT
COMMITTEE PRINTS. [Irregular]
     • Item 1009-B-10 (P)
     • Item 1009-C-10 (MF)

Y 4.C 43/2:CT
PUBLICATIONS.

JOINT SPECIAL COMMITTEE ON CHINESE IMMIGRATION

Y 4.C 44:CT
PUBLICATIONS.
     • Item 1009-C-14 (P) (EL)
     • Item 1009-C-15 (MF)

CIVIL SERVICE COMMITTEE
(House)

Y 4.C 49/1:CT
PUBLICATIONS.

CIVIL SERVICE COMMITTEE
(Senate)

Y 4.C 49/2:CT
PUBLICATIONS.

SELECT COMMITTEE ON THE INVESTIGATION OF ILLEGAL APPOINTMENTS AND DISMISSALS IN THE CIVIL SERVICE
(Senate)

Y 4.C 49/3:CT
PUBLICATIONS.

SPECIAL COMMITTEE TO INVESTIGATE THE ADMINISTRATION AND OPERATION OF THE CIVIL SERVICE LAWS
(Senate)

Y 4.C 49/4:CT
PUBLICATIONS.

COMMITTEE ON CLAIMS
(House)

Y 4.C 52/1:CT
PUBLICATIONS.

COMMITTEE ON CLAIMS
(Senate)

Y 4.C 52/2:CT
PUBLICATIONS.

COMMITTEE ON COAST AND INSULAR SURVEY
(Senate)

Y 4.C 63:CT
PUBLICATIONS.

COMMITTEE ON COINAGE, WEIGHTS AND MEASURES
(House)

Y 4.C 66:CT
PUBLICATIONS.

COMMERCE COMMITTEE
(House)

Y 4.C 73/1:CT
PUBLICATIONS.

COMMITTEE ON COMMERCE
(Senate)

Y 4.C 73/2:CT
HEARINGS. [Irregular]
     • Item 1041

     Issued as monographs.

Y 4.C 73/2:Cong./cal.nos.
LEGISLATIVE CALENDAR. [Irregular]

     Includes list of nominations; reports of committee; miscellaneous reports and documents of committee; standing subcommittees; official papers (executive communications, memorials, petitions, letters, and miscellaneous papers referred to committee); special subcommittees and studies; citations to major laws, bills, and items of interest to committee.
     ISSN 0145-0026

Y 4.C 73/2:CT
COMMITTEE PRINTS.

Y 4.C 73/2:Ac 8
ACTIVITY REPORT OF COMMITTEE ON COMMERCE.

     Issued as a Committee Prints.

SPECIAL COMMITTEE TO INVESTIGATE COMMUNIST PROPAGANDA IN THE UNITED STATES
(House)

Y 4.C 73/3:CT
PUBLICATIONS.

SELECT COMMITTEE TO INVESTIGATE COMMODITY TRANSACTION
(House)

Y 4.C 73/4:CT
PUBLICATIONS.

SELECT COMMITTEE ON COMMUNIST AGGRESSION
(House)

Y 4.C 73/5:CT
PUBLICATIONS.

COMMITTEE ON COMMERCE, SCIENCE, AND TRANSPORTATION
(Senate)

Replaces Commerce Committee (Y 4.C 73/2) and Committee on Aeronautical and Space Sciences (Y 4.Ae 8)

INFORMATION

Senate Committee on Commerce
     Science, and Transportation
Room 508, Dirksen Senate Office Building
Washington, D.C. 20510-6125
(202) 224-5115
Fax: (202) 228-5769
http://commerce.senate.gov

Y 4.C 73/7:hrg.nos
HEARINGS.
     • Item 1041-A (P)
     • Item 1041-B (MF)

Y 4.C 73/7:CT
PUBLICATIONS.

- Item 1041-A (P)
- Item 1041-B (MF)

Y 4.C 73/7:(Cong./cal.nos.)
LEGISLATIVE CALENDAR.

Y 4.C 73/7:nos.
COMMITTEE PRINTS.

- Item 1041-A (P)
- Item 1041-B (MF)

COMMITTEE ON ENERGY AND COMMERCE
(House)

INFORMATION

Committee on Energy and Commerce
2125 Rayburn House Office Bldg.
Washington, D.C. 20515
(202) 225-2927
http://energycommerce.house.gov

Y 4.C 73/8
HEARINGS, PRINTS, AND MISCELLANEOUS PUBLICATIONS.

- Item 1019-A-1 (P)
- Item 1019-B-1 (MF)

Y 4.C 73/8-10
LEGISLATIVE CALENDAR. [Irregular]

- Item 1019-A-1 (P)
- Item 1019-B-1 (MF)

JOINT COMMITTEE ON THE CONDUCT OF THE WAR

Y 4.C 75:CT
PUBLICATIONS.

CONFERENCE COMMITTEES
(House and Senate)

Y 4.C 76/1:CT
PUBLICATIONS.

JOINT SELECT COMMITTEE ON THE IMPORTATION OF CONTRACT LABORERS, CONVICTS, AND PAUPERS

Y 4.C 76/2:CT
PUBLICATIONS.

JOINT COMMITTEE ON THE ORGANIZATION OF CONGRESS

Y 4.C 76/3:CT
PUBLICATIONS.

SELECT COMMITTEE ON CONTRIBUTION INVESTIGATION
(Senate)

Y 4.C 76/4:CT
PUBLICATIONS.

JOINT COMMITTEE ON THE CONSTRUCTION OF THE BUILDING FOR THE MUSEUM OF HISTORY AND TECHNOLOGY FOR SMITHSONIAN INSTITUTION

Y 4.C 76/5
PUBLICATIONS.

SPECIAL COMMITTEE ON THE ORGANIZATION OF CONGRESS
(Senate)

Y 4.C 76/6:CT
PUBLICATIONS.

COMMITTEE ON CONGRESSIONAL OPERATIONS
(Joint)

Y 4.C 76/7:CT
PUBLICATIONS.

- Item 1000-A

SPECIAL COMMITTEE ON OFFICIAL CONDUCT
(Senate)

Y 4.C 76/8:CT
PUBLICATIONS.

SELECT COMMITTEE ON CONGRESSIONAL OPERATIONS
(House)

Y 4.C 76/9:CT
PUBLICATIONS.

- Item 1000-A-1 (P)
- Item 1000-A-2 (MF)

SELECT COMMITTEE TO INVESTIGATE ALLEGED CORRUPT COMBINATIONS OF MEMBERS OF CONGRESS
(House)

Y 4.C 81/1:CT
PUBLICATIONS.

SELECT COMMITTEE TO INVESTIGATE ALLEGED CORRUPTIONS IN GOVERNMENT
(House)

Y 4.C 81/2:CT
PUBLICATIONS.

SELECT COMMITTEE TO INVESTIGATE ALLEGED CREDIT MOBILIER BRIBERY
(House)

Y 4.C 86:CT
PUBLICATIONS.

SPECIAL COMMITTEE TO INVESTIGATE ORGANIZED CRIME IN INTERSTATE COMMERCE
(Senate)

Y 4.C 86/2:CT
PUBLICATIONS.

SELECT COMMITTEE ON CRIME
(House)

Y 4.C 86/3:CT   • Item 1009
HEARINGS.

SELECT COMMITTEE ON CROP INSURANCE
(Senate)

Y 4.C 88:CT
PUBLICATIONS.

COMMITTEE ON CUBA RELATIONS
(Senate)

Y 4.C 89:CT
PUBLICATIONS.

JOINT COMMITTEE ON DEFENSE PRODUCTION

Y 4.D 36:CT   • Item 999-A
HEARINGS.

Y 4.D 36:CT
COMMITTEE PRINTS.

Y 4.D 36:R 29
ANNUAL REPORT OF THE ACTIVITIES OF THE JOINT COMMITTEE ON DEFENSE PRODUCTION . . .WITH MATERIAL ON MOBILIZATION FROM DEPARTMENTS AND AGENCIES. 1st– 1951– [Annual]

Also issued in the Congressional series as either a House or Senate Report.

Y 4.D 36:CT   • Item 999-A
PUBLICATIONS.

Y 4.D 36:P 94   • Item 999-A
DEFENSE PRODUCTION ACT. PROGRESS REPORTS. 1– 1951– [Irregular]

TEMPORARY JOINT COMMITTEE ON DEFICIT REDUCTION

Y 4.D 36/2:CT
PUBLICATIONS.

DEMOCRATIC POLICY COMMITTEE
(1983–   )

Y 4.D 39:CT
GENERAL PUBLICATIONS.

JOINT COMMITTEE TO INVESTIGATE DIRIGIBLE DISASTERS

Y 4.D 62:CT
PUBLICATIONS.

COMMITTEE ON DISTRICT OF COLUMBIA
(House)

INFORMATION

House Committee on the
District of Columbia
1310 Longworth House Office Building
Washington, D.C. 20515
(202) 225-4457

Y 4.D 63/1:nos.   • Item 1014-A (P)
HEARINGS. [Irregular]   • Item 1014-B (MF)

Issued as monographs.

Y 4.D 63/1:Cong./cal.nos.
LEGISLATIVE CALENDAR. [Irregular]

Includes alphabetical index of bills (short title); numerical list of bills showing action taken; bills reported to the House; hearings printed; bills listed according to authors; executive communications; bills referred to subcommittees; Senate bills referred to House.
ISSN 0364-4227

Y 4.D 63/1:CT
COMMITTEE PRINTS.
Y 4.D 63/1:L 52
LEGISLATION RELATING TO DISTRICT OF COLUMBIA, SUMMARY REPORT.

Y 4.D 63/1-10:Cong./ca.no.   • Item 1014-A (P)
LEGISLATIVE CALENDAR. [Irregular]   • Item 1014-B (MF)

Earlier Y 4.D 63/1

Y 4.D 63/1-11:date   • Item 1014-A (P)
COMMITTEE RULES. [Biennial]   • Item 1014-B (MF)

COMMITTEE ON DISTRICT OF COLUMBIA
(Senate)

The Committee on the District of Columbia was superseded in 1977 by the Committee on Governmental Affairs (Y 4.G 74/9).

Y 4.D 63/2:CT   • Item 1036
HEARINGS. [Irregular]

Issued as monographs.

Y 4.D 63/2:Cong./cal.nos.
LEGISLATIVE CALENDAR. [Irregular]

Includes numerical list of House acts referred to Senate committee, studies and investigations; information on printed hearings; bills referred to subcommittees; bills and acts reported to Senate; nominations.
ISSN 0145-0018

JOINT SELECT COMMITTEE TO INVESTIGATE DISTRICT OF COLUMBIA CHARITIES

Y 4.D 63/3:CT
PUBLICATIONS.

SPECIAL COMMITTEE TO INVESTIGATE THE DISTRICT OF COLUMBIA EXCISE BOARD
(Senate)

Y 4.D 63/4:CT
PUBLICATIONS.

JOINT COMMITTEE ON THE FISCAL RELATIONS BETWEEN THE DISTRICT OF COLUMBIA AND THE UNITED STATES

Y 4.D 63/5:CT
PUBLICATIONS.

SELECT COMMITTEE TO INVESTIGATE THE PUBLIC SCHOOL SYSTEM OF THE DISTRICT OF COLUMBIA
(Senate)

Y 4.D 63/6:CT
PUBLICATIONS.

SELECT COMMITTEE TO INVESTIGATE THE FISCAL RELATIONS BETWEEN THE DISTRICT OF COLUMBIA AND THE UNITED STATES
(House)

Y 4.D 63/7:CT
PUBLICATIONS.

JOINT ECONOMIC COMMITTEE

INFORMATION

Joint Economic Committee
SD-GO1 Dirksen Senate Office Building
Washington, D.C. 20510
(202) 224-5171
http://jec.senate.gov/home.htm

• Item 1000-B (P)
• Item 1000-C (MF)
Y 4.Ec 7:CT
HEARINGS.

• Item 1000-B (P)
• Item 1000-C (MF)
Y 4.Ec 7:CT
JOINT COMMITTEE PRINTS. [Irregular]

Y 4.Ec 7:CT • Item 1000-C (MF)
PUBLICATIONS.

Y 4.Ec 7:Ec 7/date • Item 997 (P) (EL)
ECONOMIC INDICATORS. 1948– [Monthly]

PURPOSE:– To supply the need for a convenient source of information for keeping up with current economic conditions.
Prepared by the Council of Economic Advisers.
Presents in chart and tabular form statistics collected by various Government agencies on total output, income, and spending; employment, and wages; production and business activity; prices; currency, credit, and security markets; and Federal Finance.
Indexed by: Public Affairs Information Service.
ISSN 0013-0125

1962 SUPPLEMENT.

Prepared by the Office of Statistical Standards, Bureau of the Budget.
Shows annual data for each series in the same tabular form as current data are published in the monthly Indicators. The explanatory text accompanying each series is intended to meet the need for general information which cannot be repeated every month but which is essential for understanding and interpreting the significance of the current data. The text accompanying each series provides in non-technical language a description of the series, and explanation of how the data are obtained and the series derived, its relation to other series, and its principal uses and limitations. References are also given to primary publications of the series, sources showing more detailed data, and publications which contain more complete and technical explanations.
Previous editions were published in 1953, 1955, 1957, and 1960.

Y 4.Ec 7:40/date
REVIEW OF THE ECONOMY. [Annual]

PURPOSE:– To present an analysis of key economic issues, including an assessment of the system of floating exchange rates, a discussion of the inflation indexing of personal and corporate taxes, and examination of the feasibility of implementing a tax-based incomes policy, and review of tax reduction proposals.

Y 4.Ec 7:N 84.v.nos.&nos.
NOTES FROM THE JOINT ECONOMIC COMMITTEE.

ISSN 0145-1200

• Item 1000-B (P)
• Item 1000-C (MF)
Y 4.Ec 7/10
COMMITTEE PUBLICATIONS AND POLICIES GOVERNING THEIR DISTRIBUTION. [Annual]

Earlier Y 4.Ec 7:P 96

• Item 1000-B (P)
• Item 1000-C (MF)
Y 4.Ec 7/11:date
ANALYSIS OF THE CURRENT SERVICES BUDGET CONTAINED IN THE PRESIDENT'S BUDGET FOR FISCAL YEAR (date). [Annual]

Earlier Y 4.Ec 7:Se 6/5

COMMITTEE ON EDUCATION AND THE WORKFORCE
(House)

Formerly Committee on Education and Labor.

INFORMATION

House Committee on Education and the Workforce
2181 Rayburn House Office Building
Washington, D.C. 20515
(202) 225-4527
http://edworkforce.house.gov

• Item 1015-A (P)
• Item 1015-B (MF)
Y 4.Ed 8/1
HEARINGS. [Irregular]

Issued as monographs.

Y 4.Ed 8/1:Cong./cal.nos.
LEGISLATIVE CALENDAR. [Irregular]

ISSN 0364-4286

• Item 1015-A (P)
• Item 1015-B (MF)
Y 4.Ed 8/1:nos.
COMMITTEE PRINTS.

• Item 1015-A (P)
• Item 1015-B (MF)
Y 4.Ed 8/1-10
LEGISLATIVE CALENDAR. [Irregular]

Y 4.Ed 8/1-11:date • Item 1015-B (MF)
VIEWS AND ESTIMATES OF THE COMMITTEE ON EDUCATION. [Biennial]

Earlier Y 4.Ed 8/1:Ed 8/73

• Item 1015-A (P)
Y 4.Ed 8/1-12:date • Item 1015-B (MF)
COMPILATION OF FEDERAL EDUCATION LAWS. [Biennial]

Earlier Y 4.Ed 8/1:Ed 8/33

COMMITTEE ON EDUCATION
(House)

Y 4.Ed 8/2:CT
PUBLICATIONS.

COMMITTEE ON EDUCATION AND LABOR
(Senate)

Y 4.Ed 8/3:CT
PUBLICATIONS.

SELECT COMMITTEE TO INVESTIGATE EDUCATIONAL AND TRAINING PROGRAM UNDER THE GI BILL
(House)

Y 4.Ed 8/4:CT
PUBLICATIONS.

COMMITTEE ON THE ELECTION OF THE PRESIDENT, VICE-PRESIDENT AND REPRESENTATIVES
(House)

Y 4.EI 2/1:CT
PUBLICATIONS.

COMMITTEE ON ELECTIONS
(House)

Y 4.El 2/2:CT
PUBLICATIONS.

ENERGY AND NATURAL RESOURCES COMMITTEE
(Senate)

Formerly Committee on Interior and Insular Affairs (Senate) (Y 4.In 8/13)

INFORMATION

Committee on Energy and Natural Resources
364 Dirksen Senate Office Building
Washington, D.C. 20510
(202) 224-4971
Fax: (202) 224-6163
Email:committee@energy.senate.gov
http://energy.senate.gov

Y 4.En 2:hrg.nos.   • Item 1040-A (P)
HEARINGS.   • Item 1040-B (MF)

Y 4.En 2:Cong.-nos.   • Item 1040-A (P)
COMMITTEE PRINTS.   • Item 1040-B (MF)

Y 4.En 2:CT   • Item 1040-A (P)
PUBLICATIONS.   • Item 1040-B (MF)

Y 4.En 2:hrg.nos.   • Item 1040-A (P)
HEARINGS.   • Item 1040-B (MF)

Y 4.En 2:P 96/date   • Item 1040
PUBLICATIONS LIST. [Irregular]

Issued as a Committee Print.

AD HOC COMMITTEE ON ENERGY (House)

CREATION AND AUTHORITY

The Ad Hoc Committee on Energy was established by H. Res. 508.

Y 4.En 2/2:CT   • Item 1009
PUBLICATIONS.

COMMITTEE ON ENERGY AND COMMERCE
(House)

Formerly Committee on Interstate and Foreign Commerce (Y 4.In 8/4).

INFORMATION

House Committe on Energy and Commerce
2125 Rayburn House Office Building
Washington, D.C. 20515
(202) 225-2927
http://energycommerce.house.gov

Y 4.En 2/3:nos.   • Item 1019-A (P)
HEARINGS.   • Item 1019-B (MF)

Y 4.En 2/3:nos.   • Item 1019-A (P)
COMMITTEE PRINTS. [Irregular]   • Item 1019-B (MF)

Y 4.En 2/3:CT   • Item 1019-A (P)
PUBLICATIONS.   • Item 1019-B (MF)

Earlier Y 4.In 8/4

Y 4.En 2/3-10:date   • Item 1019-A (P)
LEGISLATIVE CALENDAR. [Irregular]   • Item 1019-B (MF)

Earlier Y 4.En 2/3

Y 4.En 2/3-11:date   • Item 1019-A (P)
RULES. [Biennial]   • Item 1019-B (MF)

Earlier Y 4.En 2/3:R 86

Y 4.En 2/3-12:date   • Item 1019-A (P)
SUBCOMMITTEE ON OVERSIGHT AND INVESTIGA- • Item 1019-B (MF)
TIONS OF THE COMMITTEE ON ENERGY AND
COMMERCE. [Biennial]

Earlier Y 4.En 2/3:R 86/2

SELECT COMMITTEE ON THE ORIGIN, INTRODUCTION AND PREVENTION OF EPIDEMIC DISEASES
(House)

Y 4.Ep 4/1:CT
PUBLICATIONS.

COMMITTEE ON EPIDEMIC DISEASES
(Senate)

Y 4.Ep 4/2:CT
PUBLICATIONS.

SELECT COMMITTEE ON EQUAL EDUCATION OPPORTUNITIES
(Senate)

Y 4.Eq 2:CT
PUBLICATIONS.

SELECT COMMITTEE ON ETHER DISCOVERY
(House)

Y 4.Et 3/1:CT
PUBLICATIONS.

SELECT COMMITTEE ON ETHER DISCOVERY
(Senate)

Y 4.Et 3/2:CT
PUBLICATIONS.

SELECT COMMITTEE ON ETHICS
(House)

The House Select Committee on Ethics was created by H. Res. 383, 95th Congress.

Y 4.Et 3/3:CT   • Item 1009
PUBLICATIONS.

SELECT COMMITTEE ON ETHICS
(Senate)

INFORMATION

Senate Select Committee on Ethics
Hart Senate Office Building, Room 220
Second and Constitution Avenue, N.E.
Washington, D.C. 20510
(202) 224-2981
http://ethics.senate.gov

Y 4.Et 3/4:nos.   • Item 1009-B-4 (P)
HEARINGS.   • Item 1009-C-4 (MF)

Y 4.Et 3/4:CT   • Item 1009-B-4 (P)
PUBLICATIONS.   • Item 1009-C-4 (MF)

Y 4.Et 3/4:Cong.-nos.   • Item 1009-B-4 (P)
COMMITTEE PRINTS.   • Item 1009-C-4 (MF)

SPECIAL COMMITTEE TO INVESTIGATE CHARGES OF EXECUTION WITHOUT A TRIAL IN FRANCE
(Senate)

Y 4.Ex 3:CT
PUBLICATIONS.

COMMITTEE ON THE DISPOSITION OF EXECUTIVE PAPERS
(House)

Y 4.Ex 3/2:CT
PUBLICATIONS.

SELECT COMMITTEE ON THE INVESTIGATION OF EXECUTIVE AGENCIES OF THE GOVERNMENT
(Senate)

Y 4.Ex 3/3:CT
PUBLICATIONS.

SPECIAL COMMITTEE TO INVESTIGATE EXECUTIVE AGENCIES
(House)

Y 4.Ex 3/4:CT
PUBLICATIONS.

COMMITTEE ON EXPENDITURES IN THE DEPARTMENT OF AGRICULTURE
(House)

Y 4.Ex 7/1:CT
PUBLICATIONS.

COMMITTEE ON EXPENDITURES IN THE DEPARTMENT OF COMMERCE AND LABOR
(House)

Y 4.Ex 7/2:CT
PUBLICATIONS.

COMMITTEE ON EXPENDITURES IN THE INTERIOR DEPARTMENT
(House)

Y 4.Ex 7/3:CT
PUBLICATIONS.

COMMITTEE ON EXPENDITURES IN THE DEPARTMENT OF JUSTICE
(House)

Y 4.Ex 7/4:CT
PUBLICATIONS.

COMMITTEE ON EXPENDITURES IN THE NAVY DEPARTMENT
(House)

Y 4.Ex 7/5:CT
PUBLICATIONS.

COMMITTEE ON EXPENDITURES IN THE POST-OFFICE DEPARTMENT
(House)

Y 4.Ex 7/6:CT
PUBLICATIONS.

COMMITTEE ON EXPENDITURES IN PUBLIC BUILDINGS
(House)

Y 4.Ex 7/7:CT
PUBLICATIONS.

COMMITTEE ON EXPENDITURES IN THE STATE DEPARTMENT
(House)

Y 4.Ex 7/8:CT
PUBLICATIONS.

COMMITTEE ON EXPENDITURES IN THE TREASURY DEPARTMENT
(House)

Y 4.Ex 7/9:CT
PUBLICATIONS.

COMMITTEE ON EXPENDITURES IN THE WAR DEPARTMENT
(House)

Y 4.Ex 7/10:CT
PUBLICATIONS.

SELECT COMMITTEE ON EXPENDITURES IN THE WAR DEPARTMENT
(House)

Y 4.Ex 7/11:CT
PUBLICATIONS.

SELECT COMMITTEE INVESTIGATING THE EXPENDITURES IN THE SENATORIAL PRIMARY AND GENERAL ELECTIONS
(Senate)

Y 4.Ex 7/12:CT
PUBLICATIONS.

COMMITTEE ON EXPENDITURES IN THE EXECUTIVE DEPARTMENTS
(House)

Y 4.Ex 7/13:CT
PUBLICATIONS.

COMMITTEE ON EXPENDITURES IN THE EXECUTIVE DEPARTMENTS
(Senate)

Y 4.Ex 7/14:CT
PUBLICATIONS.

SELECT COMMITTEE ON EXPORT CONTROL
(House)

Y 4.Ex 7/15:CT
PUBLICATIONS.

SPECIAL COMMITTEE TO INVESTIGATE FARM LABOR CONDITIONS IN THE WEST
(Senate)

Y 4.F 22:CT
PUBLICATIONS.

JOINT COMMITTEE ON FEDERAL AID IN THE CONSTRUCTION OF POST ROADS

Y 4.F 31:CT
PUBLICATIONS.

JOINT COMMITTEE TO DETERMINE WHAT EMPLOYMENT MAY BE FURNISHED TO FEDERAL PRISONERS

Y 4.F 31/2:CT
PUBLICATIONS.

SPECIAL COMMITTEE ON FEDERAL PENAL AND REFORMATORY INSTITUTIONS
(House)

Y 4.F 31/3:CT
PUBLICATIONS.

SELECT COMMITTEE TO INVESTIGATE THE FEDERAL COMMUNICATIONS COMMISSION
(House)

Y 4.F 31/4:CT
PUBLICATIONS.

COMMITTEE ON FINANCE
(Senate)

INFORMATION

> Senate Committee on Finance
> SD219 Dirksen Senate Office Building
> Wshington, D.C. 20510-6200
> (202) 224-4515
> Fax: (202) 224-5315
> http://finance.senate.gov

Y 4.F 49:hrg.nos.   • Item 1038-A (P)
HEARINGS. [Irregular]   • Item 1038-B (MF)

> Issued as monographs.

Y 4.F 49:Cong.-nos.   • Item 1038-A (P)
COMMITTEE PRINTS.   • Item 1038-B (MF)

Y 4.F 49:Cong./cal.nos.
LEGISLATIVE CALENDAR. [Irregular]

> Includes list of hearings held; bills and reso-
> lutions reported to Senate; bills and resolutions
> enacted into law; index by author and by subject.
> ISSN 0364-4162

Y 4.F 49/2:date
NEWS RELEASES AND MISCELLANEOUS PUBLI-
CATIONS. [Irregular]

COMMITTEE ON FINANCIAL SERVICES
(House)

See also Y4.B/22.

INFORMATION

> House Committee on Financial Services
> 2129 Rayburn House Office Bldg.
> Washington, D.C. 20515
> (202) 225-7502
> http://financialservices.house.gov

Y 4.F 49/20:Serial nos.   • Items 1013-C
HEARINGS.   • Items 1013-D

COMMITTEE ON FISHERIES
(Senate)

Y 4.F 53:CT
PUBLICATIONS.

SELECT COMMITTEE OF FIVE
(House)

Y 4.F 58:CT
PUBLICATIONS.

COMMITTEE ON FLOOD CONTROL
(House)

Y 4.F 65:CT
PUBLICATIONS.

SPECIAL COMMITTEE TO INVESTIGATE FOOD SHORTAGES
(House)

Y 4.F 73:CT
PUBLICATIONS.

SELECT COMMITTEE TO INVESTIGATE THE USE OF CHEMICALS IN FOOD PRODUCTS
(House)

Y 4.F 73/2:CT
PUBLICATIONS.

COMMITTEE ON FOREIGN AFFAIRS
(House)

In March 1975, the name of the Committee on Foreign Affairs was changed to the Committee on International Relations (Y 4.I n 8/16). In March 1979, the Committee reverted to its original name.

INFORMATION

House Committee on Foreign Affairs
2170 Rayburn House Office Building
Washington, D.C. 20515
(202) 225-5021

Y 4.F 76/1:CT   • Item 1017-A (P)
HEARINGS. [Irregular]   • Item 1017-B (MF)

Issued as monographs.
Later Y 4.In 8/16

Y 4.F 76/1:Cong./cal.nos.
LEGISLATIVE CALENDAR. [Irregular]

Includes list of subcommittees; special reports submitted by subcommittees and members of the Committee on Foreign Affairs (in addition to reports on legislation); messages from the President and executive communications (not printed as House documents); memorials and petitions; measures reported but not finally acted upon in House; measures reported and passed by House but not finally acted upon in Senate; resolutions passed; committee publications; bills and resolutions enacted into law; index of bills and resolutions by subject and by sponsor; dates of Members' appointment to the committee.
Later Y 4.In 8/16

Y 4.F 76/1:CT   • Item 1017-A (P)
COMMITTEE PRINTS.   • Item 1017-B (MF)

Y 4.F 76/1:CT
PUBLICATIONS.

Later Y 4.In 8/16

Y 4.F 76/1:Ac 8
SURVEY OF ACTIVITIES OF THE COMMITTEE ON FOREIGN AFFAIRS. 81st Cong.–   1949–
[Annual]

PURPOSE:– To provide Members of Congress, the executive branch, the press, and the public with a record of the work of the House committee charged with the responsibility for legislative matters affecting the foreign relations of the United States.
Report for the first session cover only the one year period. The report issued at the close of the second period. The report issued at the close of the second session covers the two-year period of the Congress.

Y 4.F 76/1:B 85/date   • Item 1017
VIEWS AND ESTIMATES OF THE COMMITTEE ON FOREIGN AFFAIRS ON THE BUDGET. [Annual]

Report submitted to the House Committee on the Budget pursuant to Section 301(c) of the Congressional Budget Act of 1974.
Issued as a Committee Print.
Report covers the fiscal year.

Y 4.F 76/1:In 8/57/date
CHRONOLOGIES OF MAJOR DEVELOPMENTS IN SELECTED AREAS OF INTERNATIONAL RELATIONS. [Monthly] (Committee Print)

Cumulative monthly to annual.
Classed Y 4.In 8/16:In 8/5, beginning April 1975.

Y 4.F 76/1-11:date   • Item 1017-A (P)
                                      • Item 1017-B (MF)
MEETING OF THE CANADA-UNITED STATES INTERPARLIAMENTARY GROUP. [Annual]

Y 4.F 76/1-12:date   • Item 1017-A (P)
                                      • Item 1017-B (MF)
SCIENCE, TECHNOLOGY, AND AMERICAN DIPLOMACY. [Annual]

Y 4.F 76/1-13:   • Item 1017-A (P)
                                      • Item 1017-B (MF)
CONGRESS AND FOREIGN POLICY. [Annual]

Y 4.F 76/1-15:   • Item 1017-A (P)
                                      • Item 1017-B (MF)
COUNTRY REPORTS ON HUMAN RIGHTS PRACTICES. [Annual]

Y 4.F 76/1-16:date   • Item 1017-A (P)
                                      • Item 1017-B (MF)
U.S. ARMS CONTROL AND DISARMAMENT AGENCY, ANNUAL REPORT.

Y 4.F 76/1-17:date   • Item 1017-A (P)
                                      • Item 1017-B (MF)
LEGISLATIVE CALENDAR. [Irregular]

Earlier Y 4.F 76/1

Y 4.F 76/1-18:date   • Item 1017-A (P)
                                      • Item 1017-B (MF)
RULES OF THE COMMITTEE. [Annual]
Y 4.F 76/1-19:date   • Item 1017-A (P)
                                      • Item 1017-B (MF)
LIST OF CONTENTS OF BOUND VOLUMES. [Biennial]

Earlier Y 4.F 76/1:L 69

COMMITTEE ON FOREIGN RELATIONS
(Senate)

INFORMATION

Senate Committee on Foreign Relations
4229 Dirksen Senate Office Building
Washington, D.C. 20510
(202) 224-4651
http:/foreign.senate.gov

Y 4.F 76/2:hrg.nos.   • Item 1039-A (P)
HEARINGS. [Irregular]   • Item 1039-B (MF)

Issued as monographs.

Y 4.F 76/2:Cong./cal.nos.
LEGISLATIVE CALENDAR. [Irregular]

Includes list of treaties; executive communications; nominations; committee publications; other activities of the committee; index by subject.
ISSN 0364-4243

Y 4.F 76/2:CT   • Item 1039-A (P)
COMMITTEE PRINTS.   • Item 1039-B (MF)

Y 4.F 76/2:C 16/2
CANADA-UNITED STATES INTERPARLIAMENTARY GROUP REPORT ON MEETINGS BY SENATE DELEGATION. 1st–

Also published in the Senate Documents series.

Y 4.F 76/2:L 52
LEGISLATIVE HISTORY OF THE COMMITTEE ON FOREIGN RELATIONS. [Annual]

Published by the Committee as a Committee Print. Also issued in the Senate Documents series.
Since enactment of the Legislative Reorganization Act of 1946, as amended, it has been the custom of the Committee on Foreign Relations to publish a report of its activities to the Senate at the conclusion of each Congress.
Items discussed include national security, treaties, Department of State and Foreign Service, financial matters, international organizations and meetings, boundary matters, Senate resolutions, miscellaneous bills, nominations, consultations with the executive branch.
Appendix includes legislative record, roll call votes on foreign policy measures, Committee publications.

Y 4.F 76/2:M 57/8
MEXICO-UNITED STATES INTERPARLIAMENTARY GROUP REPORT OF SENATE DELEGATION. [Irregular]

Issued as a Committee Print.
The purpose of the Mexico-United States Interparliamentary Group is to provide an institutional framework for informal discussion of mutual problems and interests by the legislators of the two countries. The first meeting was held February 6-11, 1961.

Y 4.F 76/2:Na 81a/5
NATO PARLIAMENTARIANS' CONFERENCE, REPORT OF SENATE DELEGATION. 1st–

Issued as a Committee Print.

• Item 1039-A (P)
Y 4.F 76/2-10:date   **• Item 1039-B (MF)**
LEGISLATION ON FOREIGN RELATIONS THROUGH
(date). [Annual]

    Earlier Y 4.F 786/2:L 52

• Item 1039-A (P)
Y 4.F 76/2-11:date   **• Item 1039-B (MF)**
ARMS CONTROL IMPACT STATEMENTS. [Annual]

    Earlier Y 4.F 76/2:Ar 5/20

COMMITTEE ON FOREST RESERVATIONS AND PROTECTION OF GAME
(Senate)

Y 4.F 76/3:CT
PUBLICATIONS.

JOINT COMMITTEE ON FORESTRY

Y 4.F 76/4:CT
PUBLICATIONS.

SELECT COMMITTEE ON FOREIGN AID
(House)

Y 4.F 76/5:CT
PUBLICATIONS.

SPECIAL COMMITTEE TO STUDY FOREIGN AID PROGRAM
(Senate)

Y 4.F 76/6:CT
PUBLICATIONS.

SPECIAL COMMITTEE TO INVESTIGATE THE FUEL SITUATION IN THE MIDDLE WEST
(Senate)

Y 4.F 95:CT
PUBLICATIONS.

SPECIAL COMMITTEE TO INVESTIGATE GASOLINE AND FUEL OIL SHORTAGES
(Senate)

Y 4.G 21:CT
PUBLICATIONS.

INQUIRY COMMISSION ON GOLD AND SILVER
(Senate)

Y 4.G 56:CT
PUBLICATIONS.

SPECIAL COMMITTEE TO INVESTIGATE THE GOVERNMENT HOSPITAL FOR THE INSANE

Y 4.G 74:CT
PUBLICATIONS.

SELECT COMMITTEE ON THE INVESTIGATION OF THE GOVERNMENT PRINTING OFFICE
(Senate)

Y 4.G 74/2:CT
PUBLICATIONS.

SELECT COMMITTEE ON GOVERNMENT ORGANIZATION
(House)

Y 4.G 74/3:CT
PUBLICATIONS.

JOINT COMMITTEE ON GOVERNMENT ORGANIZATION

Y 4.G 74/4:CT
PUBLICATIONS.

SELECT COMMITTEE ON GOVERNMENT ORGANIZATION
(Senate)

Y 4.G 74/5:CT
PUBLICATIONS.

COMMITTEE ON GOVERNMENT OPERATIONS
(Senate)

The Committee on Government Operations was superseded in 1977 by the Committee on Governmental Affairs (Y 4.G 74/9).

Y 4.G 74/6:CT   **• Item 1037**
HEARINGS. [Irregular]

    Issued as monographs.

Y 4.G 74/6:Cong./cal.nos.
LEGISLATIVE CALENDAR. [Irregular]

    Includes list of audit reports and communications from Comptroller of the United States; committee and subcommittee reports and publications; hearings; nominations; negotiated sales of surplus property by General Services Administration and other Federal agencies; public laws, private laws, and resolutions agreed to; reorganization plans.
    ISSN 0364-4251

COMMITTEE ON GOVERNMENT REFORM
(House)

INFORMATION

House Committee on Government Reform
2157 Rayburn House Office Building
Washington, D.C. 20515
(202) 225-5074
http://reform.house.gov

Y 4.G 74/7:CT • Item 1016-A (P)
• Item 1016-B (MF)
HEARINGS. [Irregular]

Y 4.G 74/7:Cong./cal.nos. • Item 353
LEGISLATIVE CALENDAR. [Irregular]

ISSN 0364-4278
Later Y 4.G 74/7-11

Y 4.G 74/7:CT • Item 1016-A (P)
• Item 1016-B (MF)
COMMITTEE PRINTS.

Y 4.G 74/7:Ac 8/3
ACTIVITIES OF HOUSE COMMITTEE ON GOVERNMENT OPERATIONS. [Biennial]
Report issued for each Congress. Reports for the 86th Congress and later have also been issued in the House Report series.
Covers legislation and reorganization plans; studies and investigations; benefits from Committee activities; Committee action on reports of the Comptroller General.

Y 4.G 74/7:P 94
GENERAL REAL AND PERSONAL PROPERTY INVENTORY REPORT (CIVILIAN AND MILITARY) OF THE UNITED STATES GOVERNMENT COVERING ITS PROPERTIES LOCATED IN THE UNITED STATES, IN THE TERRITORIES, AND OVERSEAS, AS OF JUNE 30 [year]. 1st– 1955– [Annual]

PURPOSE:– To present a compilation of assigned values of real and personal property owned or controlled by the Federal Government.
Provides in one volume the necessary information and data on the assets of the U.S. Government which are located throughout the world as of June 30th.

Y 4.G 74/7-10:date • Item 1016-A (P)
• Item 1016-B (MF)
RULES OF THE COMMITTEE ON GOVERNMENT OPERATIONS.

Y 4.G 74/7-11:date • Item 1016-A
• Item 1016-B (MF)
LEGISLATIVE CALENDAR. [Irregular]

Y 4.G 74/7-12:date • Item 1016-A (P)
• Item 1016-B (MF)
INTERIM REPORT OF THE ACTIVITIES. [Irregular]

SELECT COMMITTEE ON GOVERNMENT RESEARCH
(Senate)

Y 4.G 74/8:CT
PUBLICATIONS.

COMMITTEE ON GOVERNMENTAL AFFAIRS
(Senate)

This Committee replaces the Senate Committees on the District of Columbia (Y 4.D 63/2), Government Operations (Y 4. G 74/6), and Post Office and Civil Service (Y 4.P 84/11).

INFORMATION

Senate Committee on Governmental Affairs
340 Dirksen Senate Office Building
Washington, D.C. 20510
(202) 224-4751 (Republican)
(202) 224-2627 (Democrat)
http://www.senate.gov/~gov_affairs/

Y 4.G 74/9:hrg.nos. • Item 1037-B (P)
• Item 1037-C (MF)
HEARINGS.

Y 4.G 74/9:Cong.-nos. • Item 1037-B (P)
• Item 1037-C (MF)
COMMITTEE PRINTS.

Y 4.G 74/9:CT • Item 1037-B (P)
• Item 1037-C (MF)
PUBLICATIONS.

Y 4.G 74/9-10:date • Item 1037-B (P)
• Item 1037-C (MF)
ORGANIZATION OF FEDERAL EXECUTIVE DEPARTMENTS AND AGENCIES. [Annual]

Earlier Y 4.G 74/9:Ex 3

Y 4.G 74/9-11:nos. • Item 1037-B (P)
• Item 1037-C (MF)
PROLIFERATION WATCH. [Bimonthly]

SELECT COMMITTEE ON HAITI AND SANTO DOMINGO
(Senate)

Y 4.H 12:CT
PUBLICATIONS.

SELECT COMMITTEE ON THE HARPERS FERRY INVASION
(Senate)

Y 4.H 23:CT
PUBLICATIONS.

SELECT JOINT COMMITTEE ON THE HARRIMAN GEOGRAPHIC CODE SYSTEM

Y 4.H 23/2:CT
PUBLICATIONS.

SELECT COMMITTEE APPOINTED TO INVESTIGATE THE MEMORIAL OF DAVIS HATCH

Y 4.H 28:CT
PUBLICATIONS.

JOINT COMMITTEE ON HAWAII

Y 4.H 31:CT
PUBLICATIONS.

SELECT COMMITTEE ON HOUSE ROOMS DISTRIBUTION
(House)

Y 4.H 81:CT
PUBLICATIONS.

SPECIAL COMMITTEE TO INVESTIGATE THE MANAGEMENT AND CONTROL OF THE HOUSE RESTAURANT

Y 4.H 81/2:CT
PUBLICATIONS.

COMMITTEE ON HOUSE ADMINISTRATION

INFORMATION

Committee on House Administration
H326 The Capitol
Washington, D.C. 20515
(202) 225-2061
http://www.house.gov/cha

Y 4.H 81/3:nos. • Item 1018-A (P)
• Item 1018-B (MF)
HEARINGS. [Irregular]

Issued as monographs.

Y 4.H 81/3:Cong./cal.nos.
LEGISLATIVE CALENDAR. [Irregular]

Includes list of funds authorized for studies and investigations of Congressional committees; author index.
ISSN 0364-9687

Y 4.H 81/3:CT • Item 1018-A (P)
• Item 1018-B (MF)
COMMITTEE PRINTS.

Y 4.H 81/3:D 63
U.S. HOUSE OF REPRESENTATIVES, DETAILED
STATEMENT OF DISBURSEMENTS. [Semi-
annual]

> One report issued for fiscal year and sec-
ond for period July 1– Dec. 31.

Y 4.H 81/3:2/(Cong./nos.)
STAFF, THE CONGRESSIONAL STAFF JOURNAL.
1975– 1983. [Bimonthly]

> Later Y 4.R 86/2:3

Y 4.H 81/3-10:date • Item 1018-A (P)
 • Item 1018-B (MF)
RULES OF PROCEDURE OF THE COMMITTEE ON
HOUSE ADMINISTRATION. [Annual]

> Earlier Y 4.H 81/3-2

Y 4.H 81/3-11:date • Item 1018-A (P)
 • Item 1018-B (MF)
CALENDAR OF BUSINESS. [Irregular]

> Earlier Y 4.H 81/3

Y 4.H 81/3-12:date
RULES OF PROCEDURE. [Biennial]

JOINT COMMITTEE ON HOUSING

Y 4.H 81/4:CT
PUBLICATIONS

SELECT COMMITTEE PURSUANT TO HOUSE RESOLUTION 1

Y 4.H 81/5:CT
PUBLICATIONS.

SELECT COMMITTEE ON THE HOUSE RESTAURANT
(House)

Y 4.H 81/6:CT • Item 1009
HEARINGS.

COMMITTEE ON HUMAN RESOURCES
(Senate)

> Supersedes the Committee on Labor and Public
Welfare (Y 4. L 11/2). The name was changed to
Committee on Labor and Human Resources (Y 4.
L 11/4) in 1979.

Y 4.H 88:CT • Item 1043
PUBLICATIONS.

SELECT COMMITTEE ON HUNGER
(Senate)

Y 4.H 89:CT • Item 1009-B-11 (P)
 • Item 1009-C-11 (MF)
COMMITTEE PRINTS. [Irregular]

Y 4.H 89 • Item 1009-B-11 (P)
 • Item 1009-C-11 (MF)
PUBLICATIONS. [Irregular]

Y 4.H 89:nos. • Item 1009-B-11 (P)
 • Item 1009-C-11 (MF)
HEARINGS.

Y 4.H 89/10:date • Item 1009-B-11 (P)
 • Item 1009-C-11 (MF)
RULES. [Biennial]

COMMITTEE ON IMMIGRATION AND NATURALIZATION
(House)

Y 4.Im 6/1:CT
PUBLICATIONS.

COMMITTEE ON IMMIGRATION
(Senate)

Y 4.Im 6/2:CT
PUBLICATIONS.

SELECT COMMITTEE ON IMPROPER ACTIVITIES IN LABOR OR MANAGEMENT FIELD
(Senate)

Y 4.Im 7:CT
PUBLICATIONS.

SENATE IMPEACHMENT TRIAL COMMITTEE

Y 4.Im 7/2 • Item 1009-B (P)
 • Item 1009-C (MF)
REPORT OF THE SENATE IMPEACHMENT TRIAL
COMMITTEE.

COMMITTEE ON INDIAN AFFAIRS
(House)

Y 4.In 2/1:CT
PUBLICATIONS.

COMMITTEE ON INDIAN AFFAIRS
(Senate)

Y 4.In 2/2 CT
PUBLICATIONS.

Y 4.In 2/2:L 44
KAPPLER'S COMPILATION OF INDIAN LAWS
AND TREATIES. 1941, reprinted 1977. 5 v.

> This massive collection of laws and trea-
ties dealing with American Indian affairs has
recently been reprinted and placed on sale
after being out of print for many years. It is,
as compiler Charles J. Kappler notes in the
1903 preface to the first volume, "An accurate compilation of the treaties, laws,
Executive Orders, and other matters relating
to Indian affairs, from the organization of the
Government to the present time. . ." Volume 5
carries the compilation as far as June 29,
1938. A collection of Indian-related laws and
treaties from volume 5 to the present is in
progress.

JOINT SPECIAL COMMITTEE ON INDIAN BUREAU

Y 4.In 2/3:CT
PUBLICATIONS.

COMMITTEE ON INDIAN DEPREDATIONS
(Senate)

Y 4.In 2/4:CT
PUBLICATIONS.

SELECT COMMITTEE ON AFFAIRS IN THE INDIAN TERRITORY
(Senate)

Y 4.In 2/5:CT
PUBLICATIONS.

JOINT SPECIAL COMMITTEE ON THE CONDITIONS OF THE INDIAN TRIBES

Y 4.In 2/6:CT
PUBLICATIONS.

COMMITTEE ON INDUSTRIAL ARTS AND EXPOSITIONS
(House)

Y 4.In 2/7:CT
PUBLICATIONS.

COMMITTEE ON INDUSTRIAL EXPOSITIONS
(Senate)

Y 4.In 2/8:CT
PUBLICATIONS.

COMMITTEE ON INDIAN SERVICE INVESTIGATION

Y 4.In 2/9:CT
PUBLICATIONS.

AMERICAN INDIAN POLICY REVIEW COMMISSION

CREATION

The American Indian Policy Review Commission was established by Public Law 93-580.

Y 4.In 2/10:CT
PUBLICATIONS.

SELECT COMMITTEE ON INDIAN AFFAIRS
(Senate)

INFORMATION

Senate Select Committee on Indian Affairs
838 Senate Hart Office Building
Washington, D.C. 20510
(202) 224-2251
http://www.indian.senate.gov/nsindex.html

Y 4.In 2/11:hrg.nos.   • **Item 1009-B-5 (P)**
HEARINGS. [Irregular]   • **Item 1009-C-5 (MF)**

Y 4.In 2/11:Cong.-nos.   • **Item 1009-B-5 (P)**
COMMITTEE PRINTS.   • **Item 1009-C-5 (MF)**

Y 4.In 2/11:CT   • **Item 1009-A (P)**
PUBLICATIONS.   • **Item 1009-C (MF)**

INFORMATION AND FACILITIES COMMISSION
(House)

CREATION AND AUTHORITY

The House Information and Facilities Commission was established by Public Law 93-554.

Y 4.In 3:CT
PUBLICATIONS.

COMMITTEE ON INSULAR AFFAIRS
(House)

Y 4.In 7/1:CT
PUBLICATIONS.

JOINT SELECT COMMITTEE TO INQUIRE INTO AFFAIRS IN THE INSURRECTIONARY STATES

Y 4.In 7/2:CT
PUBLICATIONS.

COMMITTEE ON INTEROCEANIC CANAL
(Senate)

Y 4.In 8/1:CT
PUBLICATIONS.

SELECT COMMITTEE ON INTERNAL REVENUE FRAUDS
(House)

Y 4.In 8/2:CT
PUBLICATIONS.

COMMITTEE ON INTERSTATE AND FOREIGN COMMERCE
(Senate)

Y 4.In 8/3:CT
PUBLICATIONS.

COMMITTEE ON INTERSTATE AND FOREIGN COMMERCE
(House)

CREATION AND AUTHORITY

Name changed to Committee on Energy and Commerce (Y 4.En 2/3).

Y 4.In 8/4:CT   • **Item 1019**
HEARINGS. [Irregular]

Issued as monographs.

Y 4.In 8/4:Cong./cal.nos.
LEGISLATIVE CALENDAR. [Irregular]
Includes list of public hearings held, by full committee and by each subcommittee; reports filed; public laws; executive communications; memorials, petitions, letters and miscellaneous papers; index by subject.

COMMITTEE ON INVALID PENSIONS
(House)

Y 4.In 8/5:CT
PUBLICATIONS.

COMMITTEE ON INVESTIGATION AND ENTRENCHMENT
(Senate)

Y 4.In 8/6:CT
PUBLICATIONS.

SELECT COMMITTEE ON INTERNAL IMPROVEMENTS
(House)

Y 4.In 8/7:CT
PUBLICATIONS.

JOINT COMMITTEE TO INVESTIGATE THE INTERIOR DEPARTMENT AND FORESTRY SERVICE

Y 4.In 8/8:CT
PUBLICATIONS.

JOINT SUBCOMMITTEE ON INTERSTATE COMMERCE

Y 4.In 8/9:CT
PUBLICATIONS.

SELECT COMMITTEE ON THE INVESTIGATION OF THE INTERNAL REVENUE BUREAU
(Senate)

Y 4.In 8/10:CT
PUBLICATIONS.

JOINT COMMITTEE ON INTERNAL REVENUE TAXATION

Y 4.In 8/11:CT   • Item 1002
HEARINGS.

Y 4.In 8/11:CT
PUBLICATIONS.

Y 4.In 8/11:T 19/3
TAX CASES DECIDED WITH OPINIONS BY THE SUPREME COURT. 1943–   [Annual]

Each volume covers a year term of the U.S. Supreme Court. Report prepared by the Committee Staff.

SELECT COMMITTEE TO INVESTIGATE THE INTERSTATE MIGRATION OF DESTITUTE CITIZENS
(House)

Y 4.In 8/12:CT
PUBLICATIONS.

COMMITTEE ON INTERIOR AND INSULAR AFFAIRS
(Senate)

Y 4.In 8/13:CT   • Item 1040
HEARINGS. [Irregular]

Issued as monographs.

Y 4.In 8/13:Cong./cal.nos.
LEGISLATIVE CALENDAR. [Irregular]

Includes Senate and House Reports, public and private laws, in numerical order; special committee actions; calendar of nominations; index by subject and by author.
ISSN 0364-412X

Y 4.In 8/13:CT
COMMITTEE PRINTS.

Y 4.In 8/13:R 24/2
ANNUAL CONFERENCE WITH DIRECTORS OF NATIONAL RECLAMATION ASSOCIATION, MEMORANDUM OF CHAIRMAN TO MEMBERS OF COMMITTEE ON INTERIOR AND INSULAR AFFAIRS. 1st–   1955–   [Annual]

COMMITTEE ON INTERIOR AND INSULAR AFFAIRS
(House)

INFORMATION

House Committee on Interior and
  Insular Affairs
1324 Longworth House Office Building
Washington, D.C. 20515
(202) 225-2761

                                       • Item 1023-A (P)
Y 4.In 8/14:CT   • Item 1023-B (MF)
HEARINGS. [Irregular]

Hearings are numbered consecutively for each Congress.

Y 4.In 8/14:Cong./cal.nos.
LEGISLATIVE CALENDAR. [Irregular]

Includes lists of public and private laws; bills vetoed; executive communications, reports, petitions, and memorials referred to committee; index by author and by subject; index of executive communications.

                                       • Item 1023-A (P)
Y 4.In 8/14:CT   • Item 1023-B (MF)
COMMITTEE PRINTS.

Y 4.In 8/14:Ac 2
ACCOMPLISHMENTS DURING THE CONGRESS. [Biennial]

PURPOSE:– To assemble in one place a ready summary of the legislation the Committee has handled during the previous Congress.
Includes statistical aspects of the Committee's work and discusses briefly the individual bills. The various measures are described under six categories reflecting the principal fields within the jurisdiction of the Committee.
Appendix gives list of hearings and Committee Prints issued.

Y 4.In 8/14:N 88/5   • Item 1023
NUCLEAR REGULATORY LEGISLATION. 95th Congress, 1st session–   1977–   [Annual] (Subcommittee on Energy and the Environment)

Issued as a Committee Print.
Continued: Atomic Energy Legislation (Y 4.At 7/2: L 52/2).

Y 4.In 8/14-2:date
NEWS RELEASES AND MISCELLANEOUS PUBLICATIONS. [Irregular]

                                       • Item 1023-A (P)
Y 4.In 8/14-11:date   • Item 1023-B (MF)
REPORT TO THE COMMITTEE ON THE BUDGET; VIEWS AND ESTIMATES OF THE COMMITTEE ON INTERIOR AND INSULAR AFFAIRS (HOUSE). [Annual]

                                       • Item 1023-A (P)
Y 4.In 8/14-12:date   • Item 1023-B (MF)
LEGISLATIVE CALENDAR. [Irregular]

Earlier Y 4.In 8/14

                                       • Item 1023-A (P)
Y 4.In 8/14-13:date   • Item 1023-B (MF)
RULES FOR THE COMMITTEE ON INTERIOR AND INSULAR AFFAIRS. [Biennial]

COMMITTEE ON INTERNAL SECURITY
(House)

Y 4.In 8/15 • Item 1026
HEARINGS. [Irregular]

Issued as monographs.

COMMITTEE ON INTERNATIONAL RELATIONS
(House)

In March 1975, the name of the Committee on Foreign Affairs was changed to the Committee on International Relations (Y 4.In 8/16). In March 1979, the Committee reverted to its original name.

INFORMATION

Committee on International Relations
2170 Rayburn House Office Bldg.
Washington, D.C. 20515
http://www.house.gov/international_relations

• Item 1017-A-1 (P)
Y 4.In 8/16 • Item 1017-B-1 (MF)
HEARINGS, PRINTS, AND MISCELLANEOUS PUBLICATIONS.

Earlier Y 4.F 76/1

Y 4.In 8/16:In 8/5
CHRONOLOGIES OF MAJOR DEVELOPMENTS IN SELECTED AREAS OF INTERNATIONAL RELATIONS. [Monthly]

Cumulative monthly to annual.
Issued as a Committee Print.
Classed Y 4. F 76/1:I n 8/57, prior to April 1975.

Y 4.In 8/16:Cong./cal.nos.
LEGISLATIVE CALENDAR.

ISSN 0364-572X

• Item 1017-A-6 (P)
Y 4.In 8/16-11 • Item 1017-B-6 (MF)
MEETING OF THE CANADA-UNITED STATES INTERPARLIAMENTARY GROUP. [Annual]

• Item 1017-A-4 (P)
Y 4.In 8/16-12 • Item 1017-B-4 (MF)
SCIENCE, TECHNOLOGY AND AMERICAN DIPLOMACY. [Annual]

• Item 1017-A-3 (P)
Y 4.In 8/16-15 • Item 1017-B-3 (MF)
COUNTRY REPORTS ON HUMAN RIGHTS PRACTICES. [Annual]

• Item 1017-A-5 (P)
Y 4.In 8/16-17 • Item 1017-B-5 (MF)
LEGISLATIVE CALENDAR.

• Item 1017-A-2 (P)
Y 4.In 8/16-18 • Item 1017-B-2 (MF)
RULES OF THE COMMITTEE ON INTERNATIONAL RELATIONS.

SELECT COMMITTEE TO STUDY GOVERNMENT OPERATIONS WITH RESPECT TO INTELLIGENCE ACTIVITIES
(Senate)

Y 4.In 8/17:CT
PUBLICATIONS.

SELECT COMMITTEE ON INTELLIGENCE
(House)

INFORMATION

House Permanent Select Committee on Intelligence
H-405 Capitol Building
Washington, D.C. 20515
(202) 225-4121
http://intelligence.house.gov

• Item 1009-B-6 (P)
Y 4.In 8/18:CT • Item 1009-C-6 (MF)
COMMITTEE PRINTS.

• Item 1009-B-6 (P)
Y 4.In 8/18:CT • Item 1009-C-6 (MF)
HEARINGS.

• Item 1009-B-6 (P)
Y 4.In 8/18:CT • Item 1009-C-6 (MF)
PUBLICATIONS.

• Item 1009-B-6 (P)
Y 4.In 8/18-10:date • Item 1009-C-6 (MF)
RULES OF PROCEDURE FOR THE PERMANENT SELECT COMMITTEE ON INTELLIGENCE. [Biennial]

Earlier Y 4.In 8/18:P 94

SELECT COMMITTEE ON INTELLIGENCE
(Senate)

INFORMATION

Senate Select Committee on Intelligence
SH211 Senate Hart Office Building
Washington, D.C. 20510-6475
(202) 224-1700
http://intelligence.senate.gov

• Item 1009-B-7 (P)
Y 4.In 8/19:Cong.-nos. • Item 1009-C-7 (MF)
COMMITTEE PRINTS.

• Item 1009-B-7 (P)
Y 4.In 8/19:hrg.nos. • Item 1009-C-7 (MF)
HEARINGS.

• Item 1009-B-7 (P)
Y 4.In 8/19:CT • Item 1009-C (MF)
PUBLICATIONS.

SELECT COMMITTEE TO INVESTIGATE COVERT ARMS TRANSACTIONS WITH IRAN

Y 4.In 8/20:hrg.nos. • Item 1009-C (MF)
HEARINGS.

Y 4.In 8/20:CT • Item 1009-C (MF)
RULES OF THE SELECT COMMITTEE TO INVESTIGATE COVERT ARMS TRANSACTIONS WITH IRAN.

COMMITTEE ON IRRIGATION AND RECLAMATION
(Senate)

Y 4.Ir 7/1:CT
PUBLICATIONS.

COMMITTEE ON IRRIGATION AND RECLAMATION
(House)

Y 4.Ir 7/2:CT
PUBLICATIONS.

COMMITTEE ON THE JUDICIARY
(House)

INFORMATION

House Committee on the Judiciary
2138 Rayburn House Office Building
Washington, D.C. 20515
(202) 225-3951
http://www.house.gov/judiciary

• Item 1020-A (P)
Y 4.J 89/1:CT • Item 1020-B (MF)
COMMITTEE PRINTS.

• Item 1020-A (P)
Y 4.J 89/1:nos. • Item 1020-B (MF)
HEARINGS. [Irregular]

Numbered consecutively for each Congress.

Y 4.J 89/1:Cong./cal.nos.
LEGISLATIVE CALENDAR. [Irregular]

Includes list of printed hearings; special reports; tabulations of bills and resolutions referred to committee; bills and resolutions pending before subcommittees, bills and resolutions passed by House and pending in Senate; bills and resolutions enacted into law; bills vetoed by the President; author and topical indexes.
ISSN 0264-4294

Y 4.J 89/1:CT
PUBLICATIONS.

Y 4.J 89/1:D 63/24   • Item 990
DISTRICT OF COLUMBIA CODE. [Irregular]

Contains the laws, general and permanent in their nature, relating to or in force in the District of Columbia (except such laws as are of application in the District of Columbia by reason of being general and permanent laws of the United States in general). Annotated.

The latest edition covers all laws enacted to January 1, 1961 and issued in three volumes. This basic set is kept up-to-date by an annual supplement which covers the period January 3, 1961 to January of the current year.

Y 4.J 89/1:Im 7/4
IMPEACHMENT, SELECTED MATERIALS ON PROCEDURE. 1974. 900 p.

An historical and parliamentary manual of how the impeachment process works in the United States, compiled by the House Judiciary Committee.

Y 4.J 89/1:In 2/9   • Item 1020-A
INDEX TO REPORTS ON PRIVATE AND PUBLIC BILLS AND RESOLUTIONS FAVORABLY REPORTED BY THE COMMITTEE. [Annual]

Earlier Y 4.J 89/1

Y 4.J 89/1:Un 3/3   • Item 991
UNITED STATES CODE. 1926–   [Sexennial]

Contains the general and permanent laws of the United States currently in force.

The 1964 edition is kept up-to-date by annual supplements which over the period January 4, 1965 to January of the current year.

Citation: U.S.C.

                                        • Item 1020-A (P)
Y 4.J 89/1-10:date   • Item 1020-B (MF)
FEDERAL RULES OF APPELLATE PROCEDURE WITH FORMS. [Annual]

                                        • Item 1020-A (P)
Y 4.J 89/1-11:date   • Item 1020-B (MF)
RULES OF CIVIL PROCEDURE FOR THE UNITED STATES DISTRICT COURTS. [Annual]

                                        • Item 1020-A (P)
Y 4.J 89/1-12:date   • Item 1020-B (MF)
RULES OF CRIMINAL PROCEDURE FOR THE UNITED STATES DISTRICT COURTS. [Annual]

                                        • Item 1020-A
Y 4.J 89/1-13:date   • Item 1020-B (MF)
FEDERAL RULES OF EVIDENCE. [Annual]

                                        • Item 1020-A (P)
Y 4.J 89/1-14:date   • Item 1020-B (MF)
INDEX TO REPORTS ON PRIVATE AND PUBLIC BILLS AND RESOLUTIONS FAVORABLY REPORTED BY THE COMMITTEE. [Biennial]

Earlier Y 4.J 89/1:In 2/9

                                        • Item 1020-A (P)
Y 4.J 89/1-15:date   • Item 1020-B (MF)
RULES OF PROCEDURE. [Annual]

Earlier Y 4.J 89/1:R 86/2

                                        • Item 1020-A (P)
Y 4.J 89/1-16:date   • Item 1020-B (MF)
LEGISLATIVE CALENDAR. [Annual]

Earlier Y 4.J 89/1

COMMITTEE ON THE JUDICIARY
(Senate)

INFORMATION

Senate Committee on the Judiciary
224 Dirksen Senate Office Building
Washington, D.C. 20510
(202) 224-7703
Fax: (202) 224-9516
http://judiciary.senate.gov

                                        • Item 1042-A (P)
Y 4.J 89/2:hrg.nos.   • Item 1042-B (MF)
HEARINGS. [Irregular]

Issued as monographs.

Y 4.J 89/2:Cong./cal.nos.
LEGISLATIVE CALENDAR. [Irregular]

Includes list of hearings conducted; bills and resolutions which have been reported; list of executive nominations and action theron; index of executive nominations; legislative index; house bills and resolutions received; numerical index of bills and resolutions.
ISSN 0364-6947

                                        • Item 1042-A (P)
Y 4.J 89/2:CT   • Item 1042-B (MF)
COMMITTEE PRINTS.

Y 4.J 89/2:P 94/22   • Item 1042
COMMITTEE ON THE JUDICIARY PROGRAM. 96th Congress, 1st Session–   1979– [Annual]

Y 4.J 89/2:R 44   • Item 1042
LAYMAN'S GUIDE TO INDIVIDUAL RIGHTS UNDER THE UNITED STATES CONSTITUTION. 1973. 35 p. (Subcommittee on Constitutional Rights)

                                        • 1042-A (P)
Y 4.J 89/2-10   • Item 1042-B (MF)
RULES OF PROCEDURE, COMMITTEE ON THE JUDICIARY.

SPECIAL COMMITTEE INVESTIGATING KANSAS
(House)

Y 4.K 13:CT
PUBLICATIONS.

SELECT COMMITTEE TO CONDUCT THE INVESTIGATION OF FACTS, EVIDENCE AND CIRCUMSTANCES OF THE KATYN FOREST MASSACRE
(House)

Y 4.K 15:CT
PUBLICATIONS.

COMMITTEE ON LABOR
(House)

Y 4.L 11:CT
PUBLICATIONS.

COMMITTEE ON LABOR AND PUBLIC WELFARE
(Senate)

Superseded by the Senate Committee on Human Resources (Y 4.H 88)

                                        • Item 1043-A (P)
Y 4.L 11/2:CT   • Item 1043-B (MF)
HEARINGS. [Irregular]

Issued as monographs.

Y 4.L 11/2:Cong./cal.nos.
LEGISLATIVE CALENDAR. [Irregular]

Includes list of bills and resolutions by number; nominations received by the committee; list of bills and resolutions by subject, and committee action; list of bills and resolutions by author; hearings; bills reported by the committee and enacted into law; bills recommitted; bills passed by the Senate and pending in conference; resolutions reported by the committee and passed by the Senate.
ISSN 0364-4138

JOINT COMMITTEE ON LABOR MANAGEMENT RELATIONS

Y 4.L 11/3:CT
PUBLICATIONS.

COMMITTEE ON HEALTH, EDUCATION, LABOR, AND PENSIONS
(Senate)

The name of the Committee on Human Resources (Y 4. H 88) was changed in 1979 to the Committee on Labor and Human Resources, later changed to present name.

INFORMATION

Senate Committee on Health,
    Education, Labor, and Pensions
428 Dirksen Senate Office Building
Washington, D.C. 20510-6300
(202) 224-5375
http://labor.senate.gov

                                        • Item 1043-A (P)
Y 4.L 11/4:Cong.-nos.   • Item 1043-B (MF)
COMMITTEE PRINTS.

Y 4.L 11/4:hrg.nos.
HEARINGS.

• Item 1043-A (P)
• Item 1043-B (MF)
• Item 1043-A (P)

Y 4.L 11/4:CT
PUBLICATIONS.

• Item 1043-B (MF)

Y 4.L 11/4:C 76
REPORT OF THE SENATE COMMITTEE ON LABOR AND HUMAN RESOURCES PRESENTING ITS VIEWS AND ESTIMATES PURSUANT TO THE CONGRESSIONAL BUDGET ACT, PUBLIC LAW 93-344, TOGETHER WITH THE MINORITY VIEWS TO THE COMMITTEE ON THE BUDGET ON THE BUDGET PROPOSED.

• Item 1043

Issued as a Committee Print.

SPECIAL COMMITTEE ON THE SURVEY OF LAND AND WATER POLICIES OF THE UNITED STATES
(Senate)

Y 4.L 22:CT
PUBLICATIONS.

SELECT COMMITTEE TO STUDY LAW

Y 4.L 41:CT
HEARINGS.

SPECIAL JOINT COMMITTEE ON REVISION OF LAWS

Y 4.L 44/1:CT
PUBLICATIONS.

COMMITTEE ON REVISION OF LAWS
(House)

Y 4.L 44/2:CT
PUBLICATIONS.

JOINT COMMITTEE ON THE LEGISLATIVE BUDGET

Y 4.L 52:CT
PUBLICATIONS.

COMMITTEE ON THE LIBRARY
(House)

Y 4.L 61/1:CT
PUBLICATIONS.

JOINT COMMITTEE ON THE LIBRARY

INFORMATION

Joint Committee on the Library
SR309 Senate Russell Office Building
Washington, D.C. 20515
(202) 224-0291

• Item 1003-A (P)
• Item 1003-B (MF)

Y 4.L 61/2:CT
PUBLICATIONS.

COMMITTEE ON THE LIBRARY
(Senate)

Y 4.L 61/3:CT
PUBLICATIONS.

SELECT COMMITTEE ON THE INVESTIGATION OF CHARGES MADE BY GEORGE L. LILLEY
(House)

Y 4.L 62:CT
PUBLICATIONS.

SELECT COMMITTEE ON LOBBY INVESTIGATION
(House)

Y 4.L 78:CT
PUBLICATIONS.

SPECIAL COMMITTEE TO INVESTIGATE LOBBYING ACTIVITIES
(Senate)

Y 4.L 78/2:CT
PUBLICATIONS.

SELECT COMMITTEE ON LOBBYING ACTIVITIES
(House)

Y 4.L 78/3:CT
PUBLICATIONS.

COMMITTEE TO INVESTIGATE THE ELECTION OF WILLIAM LORIMER
(Senate)

Y 4.L 89:CT
PUBLICATIONS.

CONGRESSIONAL MAILING STANDARDS COMMISSION
(House)

Y 4.M 28:CT
PUBLICATIONS. [Irregular]

COMMITTEE ON MANUFACTURES
(House)

Y 4.M 31/1:CT
PUBLICATIONS.

COMMITTEE ON MANUFACTURES
(Senate)

Y 4.M 31/2:CT
PUBLICATIONS.

SELECT COMMITTEE TO INVESTIGATE CHARGES AGAINST MEMBERS OF CONGRESS
(House)

Y 4.M 51:CT
PUBLICATIONS.

COMMITTEE ON MERCHANT MARINE AND FISHERIES
(House)

Committee was terminated Jan. 4, 1995.

• Item 1021-B (P)
• Item 1021-C (MF)

Y 4.M 53:CT
HEARINGS. [Irregular]

Issued as monographs.

Y 4.M 53:Cong./cal.nos.
LEGISLATIVE CALENDAR. [Irregular]

Includes lists of meetings; open hearings; printed hearings; committee prints and reports issued by committee; public laws; private laws; public laws on legislation of interest not referred to the committee; executive communications, memorials; petitions, author index.
ISSN 0364-4219

• Item 1021-B (P)
• Item 1021-C (MF)

Y 4.M 53:CT
COMMITTEE PRINTS.

Y 4.M 53:L 44/2
COMPILATION OF FEDERAL LAWS RELATING TO CONSERVATION AND DEVELOPMENT OF OUR NATION'S FISH AND WILDLIFE RESOURCES, ENVIRONMENTAL QUALITY, AND OCEANOGRAPHY. 1973. 706 p.

Presented in two major sections; one contains the laws dealing with wildlife conservation, fisheries, and oceanography; the other contains laws dealing with selected aspects of environmental quality.

Y 4.M 53/2:date
NEWS RELEASES AND MISCELLANEOUS PUBLICATIONS. [Irregular]

• Item 1021-B (P)
• Item 1021-C (MF)

Y 4.M 53/11:date
RULES. [Biennial]

Earlier Y 4.M 53:R 86

• Item 1021-B (P)
• Item 1021-C (MF)

Y 4.M 53/12:date
LEGISLATIVE CALENDAR.

SELECT COMMITTEE ON PROCEEDINGS OF THE BOARD OF COMMISSIONERS ON CLAIMS AGAINST MEXICO
(Senate)

Y 4.M 57:CT
PUBLICATIONS.

COMMITTEE ON MILEAGE
(House)

Y 4.M 58:CT
PUBLICATIONS.

COMMITTEE ON MILITARY AFFAIRS
(House)

Y 4.M 59/1:CT
PUBLICATIONS.

COMMITTEE ON MILITARY AFFAIRS
(Senate)

Y 4.M 59/2:CT
PUBLICATIONS.

MILITIA COMMITTEE
(House)

Y 4.M 59/3:CT
PUBLICATIONS.

COMMITTEE ON MINES AND MINING
(House)

Y 4.M 66/1:CT
PUBLICATIONS.

COMMITTEE ON MINES AND MINING
(Senate)

Y 4.M 66/2:CT
PUBLICATIONS.

SELECT COMMITTEE TO INQUIRE INTO ALLEGED FRAUDS IN RECENT ELECTIONS IN MISSISSIPPI
(Senate)

Y 4.M 69/1:CT
PUBLICATIONS.

COMMITTEE ON LEVIES AND IMPROVEMENTS OF THE MISSISSIPPI RIVER
(Senate)

Y 4.M 69/2:CT
PUBLICATIONS.

SELECT COMMITTEE ON MISSING PERSONS IN SOUTHEAST ASIA
(House)

Y 4.M 69/3:CT
PUBLICATIONS.

SPECIAL COMMITTEE INVESTIGATING THE MUNITIONS INDUSTRY
(Senate)

Y 4.M 92:CT
PUBLICATIONS.

JOINT COMMITTEE ON MUSCLE SHOALS

Y 4.M 97:CT
PUBLICATIONS.

SELECT COMMITTEE ON NARCOTICS ABUSE AND CONTROL
(House)

INFORMATION

House Select Committee on Narcotics
 Abuse and Control
H2-234 House Office Building, Annex 2
Washington, D.C. 20515
(202) 225-3040

                     • Item 1009-B-8 (P)
Y 4.N 16:nos.   • Item 1009-C-8 (MF)
HEARINGS.

                     • Item 1009-B-8 (P)
Y 4.N 16:Cong.-nos. • Item 1009-C-8 (MF)
COMMITTEE PRINT.

                     • Item 1009-B (P)
Y 4.N 16:CT   • Item 1009-C (MF)
PUBLICATIONS.

                     • Item 1009-B-8 (P)
Y 4.N 16/10:date • Item 1009-C-8 (MF)
RULES OF THE SELECT COMMITTEE ON NARCOT-
ICS ABUSE AND CONTROL. [Biennial]

COMMITTEE ON THE CONSERVATION OF NATIONAL RESOURCES
(Senate)

Y 4.N 21/1:CT
PUBLICATIONS.

SPECIAL COMMITTEE TO INVESTIGATE THE NATIONAL SECURITY LEAGUE
(House)

Y 4.N 21/2:CT
PUBLICATIONS.

SELECT COMMITTEE TO INVESTIGATE DISABLED SOLDIERS LEAGUE INC.
(House)

Y 4.N 21/3:CT
PUBLICATIONS.

SPECIAL COMMITTEE TO INVESTIGATE THE N.L.R.B.
(House)

Y 4.N 21/4:CT
PUBLICATIONS.

SELECT COMMITTEE INVESTIGATING THE NATIONAL DEFENSE MIGRATION
(House)

Y 4.N 21/5:CT
PUBLICATIONS.

SPECIAL COMMITTEE INVESTIGATING THE NATIONAL DEFENSE PROGRAM
(Senate)

Y 4.N 21/6:CT
PUBLICATIONS.

SELECT COMMITTEE TO CONDUCT THE STUDY AND SURVEY OF THE NATIONAL DEFENSE PROGRAM IN ITS RELATION TO SMALL BUSINESS
(House)

Y 4.N 21/7:CT
PUBLICATIONS.

SELECT COMMITTEE ON NATIONAL WATER RESOURCES
(Senate)

Y 4.N 21/8:CT
PUBLICATIONS.

SPECIAL COMMITTEE ON THE TERMINATION OF THE NATIONAL EMERGENCY
(Senate)

CREATION AND AUTHORITY

     The Special Committee on the Termination of
the National Emergency was established by Senate Resolution 9, 93rd Congress, 1st Session.

Y 4.N 21/9:CT
PUBLICATIONS.

COMMITTEE ON NAVAL AFFAIRS
(House)

Y 4.N 22/1:CT
PUBLICATIONS.

COMMITTEE ON NAVAL AFFAIRS
(Senate)

Y 4.N 22/2:CT
PUBLICATIONS.

JOINT COMMITTEE ON NAVAL AFFAIRS

Y 4.N 22/3:CT
PUBLICATIONS.

JOINT COMMITTEE ON NAVAJO-HOPI INDIAN ADMINISTRATION

Y 4.N 22/4:CT   • Item 1021-A
PUBLICATIONS.

SELECT COMMITTEE ON THE NEW ORLEANS RIOTS
(House)

Y 4.N 42/1:CT
PUBLICATIONS.

SELECT COMMITTEE ON THE ALLEGED NEW YORK ELECTION FRAUDS
(House)

Y 4.N 42/2:CT
PUBLICATIONS.

JOINT SELECT COMMITTEE ON THE NEWBURG, N.Y. MONUMENT AND CENTENNIAL CELEBRATION OF 1883

Y 4.N 42/3:CT
PUBLICATIONS.

SELECT COMMITTEE ON THE NINE FOOT CHANNEL FROM THE GREAT LAKES TO THE GULF
(Senate)

Y 4.N 62:CT
PUBLICATIONS.

JOINT COMMITTEE ON THE INVESTIGATION OF THE NORTHERN PACIFIC RAILROAD LAND GRANTS

Y 4.N 81:CT
PUBLICATIONS.

SELECT COMMITTEE ON NUTRITION AND HUMAN NEEDS
(Senate)

Merged with Senate Committee on Agriculture and Forestry (Y 4.Ag 8/2) to form the Committee on Agriculture, Nutrition and Forestry (Y 4.Ag 8/3)

Y 4.N 95:CT   • Item 1009-B (P)
PUBLICATIONS.   • Item 1009-C (MF)

SELECT COMMITTEE TO INVESTIGATE INDIAN CONTRACTS IN OKLAHOMA

Y 4.Ok 4:CT
PUBLICATIONS.

SELECT COMMITTEE TO INVESTIGATE OLD AGE PENSION PLANS
(House)

Y 4.Ol 1:CT
PUBLICATIONS.

SPECIAL COMMITTEE TO INVESTIGATE THE OLD-AGE PENSION SYSTEM
(Senate)

Y 4.Ol 1/2:CT
PUBLICATIONS.

SELECT COMMITTEE ON HEAVY AND PROJECTILES ORDNANCE
(Senate)

Y 4.Or 2/1:CT
PUBLICATIONS.

SELECT COMMITTEE ON ORDNANCE AND WARSHIPS
(Senate)

Y 4.Or 2/2:CT
PUBLICATIONS.

JOINT SELECT COMMITTEE ON ORDNANCE

Y 4.Or 2/3:CT
PUBLICATIONS.

SELECT COMMITTEE ON THE INVESTIGATION OF ORDNANCE AND AMMUNITION
(House)

Y 4.Or 2/4:CT
PUBLICATIONS.

SELECT COMMITTEE ON INVESTIGATION OF THE ALLEGED OUTRAGES IN THE SOUTHERN STATES
(Senate)

Y 4.Ou 8:CT
PUBLICATIONS.

AD HOC SELECT COMMITTEE ON OUTER CONTINENTAL SHELF
(House)

Y 4.Ou 8/2:CT
PUBLICATIONS. [Irregular]   • Item 1009

COMMITTEE ON THE PACIFIC ISLANDS AND PORTO RICO
(Senate)

Y 4.P 11/1:CT
PUBLICATIONS.

COMMITTEE ON PACIFIC RAILROAD
(Senate)

Y 4.P 11/2:CT
PUBLICATIONS.

COMMITTEE ON PACIFIC RAILROAD
(House)

Y 4.P 11/3:CT
PUBLICATIONS.

JOINT COMMITTEE ON THE PACIFIC COAST NAVAL BASES

Y 4.P 11/4:CT
PUBLICATIONS.

JOINT COMMITTEE TO INVESTIGATE THE GENERAL PARCEL POST

Y 4.P 21:CT
PUBLICATIONS.

PATENTS COMMITTEE
(House)

Y 4.P 27/1:CT
PUBLICATIONS.

PATENTS COMMITTEE
(Senate)

Y 4.P 27/2:CT
PUBLICATIONS.

JOINT COMMITTEE INVESTIGATING THE PEARL HARBOR ATTACK

Y 4.P 31:CT
PUBLICATIONS.

COMMITTEE ON PENSIONS
(House)

Y 4.P 38/1:CT
PUBLICATIONS.

COMMITTEE ON PENSIONS
(Senate)

Y 4.P 38/2:CT
PUBLICATIONS.

SELECT COMMITTEE ON THE PAYMENT OF PENSIONS, BOUNTY, AND BACK PAY

Y 4.P 38/3:CT
PUBLICATIONS.

SPECIAL COMMITTEE INVESTIGATING PETROLEUM RESOURCES
(Senate)

Y 4.P 44:CT
PUBLICATIONS.

COMMITTEE ON THE PHILIPPINES
(Senate)

Y 4.P 53:CT
PUBLICATIONS.

JOINT COMMITTEE TO INVESTIGATE THE ADEQUACY AND USE OF PHOSPHATE RESOURCES OF THE UNITED STATES

Y 4.P 56:CT
PUBLICATIONS.

SPECIAL COMMITTEE TO INVESTIGATE POLITICAL ACTIVITIES, LOBBYING AND CAMPAIGN CONTRIBUTIONS
(Senate)

Y 4.P 75:CT
PUBLICATIONS.

SELECT COMMITTEE ON POPULATION
(House)

Y 4.P 81:Cong./nos
PUBLICATIONS.   • Item 1009

SELECT COMMITTEE ON CURRENT PORNOGRAPHIC MATERIALS
(House)

Y 4.P 82:CT
PUBLICATIONS.

COMMITTEE ON THE POST OFFICE AND POST ROADS
(House)

Y 4.P 84/1:CT
PUBLICATIONS.

COMMITTEE ON THE POST OFFICE AND POST ROADS
(Senate)

Y 4.P 84/2:CT
PUBLICATIONS.

SELECT COMMITTEE ON THE RELATIONS OF THE MEMBERS WITH THE POST OFFICE DEPARTMENTS
(House)

Y 4.P 84/3:CT
PUBLICATIONS.

JOINT COMMITTEE ON THE POSTAGE ON SECOND CLASS MATTER AND THE COMPENSATION FOR TRANSPORTATION OF MAILS

Y 4.P 84/4:CT
PUBLICATIONS.

JOINT COMMISSION ON POSTAL SALARIES

Y 4.P 84/5:CT
PUBLICATIONS.

SELECT COMMITTEE ON POST OFFICE LEASES
(Senate)

Y 4.P 84/6:CT
PUBLICATIONS.

SPECIAL COMMITTEE ON POST-WAR ECONOMIC POLICY AND PLANNING
(Senate)

Y 4.P 84/7:CT
PUBLICATIONS.

SELECT COMMITTEE ON POST-WAR MILITARY POLICY
(House)

Y 4.P 84/8:CT
PUBLICATIONS.

SPECIAL COMMITTEE ON THE POST-WAR ECONOMIC POLICY AND PLANNING
(House)

Y 4.P 84/9:CT
PUBLICATIONS.

COMMITTEE ON POST OFFICE AND CIVIL SERVICE
(House)

INFORMATION

House Committee on the
   Post Office and Civil Service
309 Cannon House Office Building
Washington, D.C. 20515
(202) 225-4054

Y 4.P 84/10:nos.   • Item 1022-B (P)
HEARINGS. [Irregular]   • Item 1022-C (MF)

   Issued as monographs.

Y 4.P 84/10:Cong./cal.nos.
LEGISLATIVE CALENDAR. [Irregular]

   ISSN 0364-4235

Y 4.P 84/10:CT   • Item 1022-B (P)
COMMITTEE PRINTS.   • Item 1022-C (MF)

Y 4.P 84/10:Ac 8
SUMMARY OF ACTIVITIES. 81st–   1950–

Y 4.P 84/10:M 31/5   • Item 1022-A
IMPROVED MANPOWER MANAGEMENT IN FED-
ERAL GOVERNMENT. [Semiannual]

Y 4.P 84/10:R 31/30/date   • Item 1022
BOARD OF ACTUARIES OF THE CIVIL SERVICE
RETIREMENT SYSTEM ANNUAL REPORT.
56th–   1976–   [Annual]

   Issued as a Committee Print.
   Report submitted by the Director of the
Office of Personnel Management pursuant 5
U.S.C. 8347(f).
   1st– 55th Reports, 1921– 75, submitted
by the Civil Service Commission.

Y 4.P 84/10-2:date
NEWS RELEASES AND MISCELLANEOUS PUBLI-
CATIONS. [Irregular]

                                     • Item 1022-B (P)
Y 4.P 84/10-11   • Item 1022-C (MF)
ANNUAL REPORT OF THE FEDERAL LABOR RELA-
TIONS AUTHORITY. [Annual]
                                     • Item 1022-B (P)
Y 4.P 84/10-12:date   • Item 1022-C (MF)
FEDERAL PREVAILING RATE ADVISORY COMMIT-
TEE: ANNUAL REPORT. [Annual]

                                     • Item 1022-B (P)
Y 4.P 84/10-13:date   • Item 1022-C (MF)
LEGISLATIVE CALENDAR. [Annual]

   Earlier Y 4.P 84/10

                                     • Item 1022-B (P)
Y 4.P 84/10-14:date   • Item 1022-C (MF)
RULES OF THE HOUSE COMMITTEE ON POST
OFFICE AND CIVIL SERVICE. [Biennial]

   Earlier Y 4.P 84/10-14:R 86

                                     • Item 1022-B (P)
Y 4.P 84/10-15:date   • Item 1022-C (MF)
CURRENT SALARY SCHEDULES OF FEDERAL
OFFICERS AND EMPLOYEES TOGETHER WITH
A HISTORY OF SALARY AND RETIREMENT
ANNUITY ADJUSTMENTS. [Annual]

   Earlier Y 4.P 84/10:Sa 3/16

COMMITTEE ON POST OFFICE AND CIVIL SERVICE
(Senate)

   The Committee on Post Office and Civil Service was superseded in 1977 by the Committee
on Governmental Affairs (Y 4. G 74/9).

Y 4.P 84/11:CT   • Item 1044
HEARINGS. [Irregular]

   Issued as monographs.

Y 4.P 84/11:Cong./cal.nos.
LEGISLATIVE CALENDAR. [Irregular]

   Includes bills listed by author and by subject;
committee prints, reports, and printed hearings;
executive communications; nominations; private
and public laws.

Y 4.P 84/11:CT
COMMITTEE PRINTS.

Y 4.P 84/11:B 64
BOND OF FEDERAL EMPLOYEES. [Annual]

SPECIAL COMMITTEE TO INVESTIGATE PROPAGANDA OR MONEY ALLEGED TO HAVE BEEN USED BY FOREIGN GOVERNMENTS TO INFLUENCE UNITED STATES SENATORS

Y 4.P 94

SPECIAL COMMITTEE INVESTIGATING PRESIDENTIAL CAMPAIGN EXPENDITURES
(Senate)

Y 4.P 92:CT
PUBLICATIONS.

SPECIAL COMMITTEE ON THE INVESTIGATION OF PRESIDENTIAL AND SENATORIAL CAMPAIGN EXPENDITURES
(Senate)

Y 4.P 92/2:CT
PUBLICATIONS.

SPECIAL COMMITTEE TO INVESTIGATE PRESIDENTIAL, VICE PRESIDENTIAL, AND SENATORIAL CAMPAIGN EXPENDITURES, 1944

Y 4.P 92/3:CT
PUBLICATIONS.

SELECT COMMITTEE ON PRESIDENTIAL CAMPAIGN ACTIVITIES
(Senate)

CREATION AND AUTHORITY

The Select Committee on Presidential Campaign Activities was established by S. Res. 60, 93rd Congress, 1st Session, adopted February 7, 1973.

Y 4.P 92/4:CT • Item 1009-A
PUBLICATIONS.

JOINT COMMITTEE ON PRINTING

INFORMATION

Joint Committee on Printing
346 Russell Senate Office Bldg.
Washington, D.C. 20510
(202) 224-8028
http://jcp.senate.gov

• Item 1004-C (P)
• Item 1004-D (MF)
Y 4.P 93/1:CT
PUBLICATIONS.

Y 4.P 93/1:D 44/date • Item 1004
GOVERNMENT DEPOSITORY LIBRARIES.
[Annual]
Contains text of the Government Depository law plus a list of the Depository Libraries by States.

Y 4.P 93/1:1 • Item 992
CONGRESSIONAL DIRECTORY. 1809–␣␣␣[Annual]

Gives brief biographies of each Member of Congress, terms of service, Committee assignments. Lists Committees, their staffs, and other Capitol officials. Also includes statistical tables on sessions of Congress and election results of recent congressional elections.
Other material includes the officials of the Executive, Judicial, and Legislative Branches of the Government, members of the press galleries, diplomatic representatives of foreign countries, U.S. diplomatic representatives. Maps included for each State showing the congressional districts.

Y 4.P 93/1:1 P
POCKET CONGRESSIONAL DIRECTORY. [Annual]

Y 4.P 93/1:6 • Item 992-A
GOVERNMENT PRINTING & BINDING REGULATIONS.
1–␣␣␣1948–␣␣␣[Annual]

Y 4.P 93/1:7 • Item 1004-B (EL)
GOVERNMENT PAPER SPECIFICATION STANDARDS.
ISSN 0364-1260

Y 4.P 93/1:7/2 • Item 1004
GOVERNMENT PAPER SPECIFICATION STANDARDS.
[Irregular]

PURPOSE:– Issued by the Joint Committee on Printing for the use of Government departments and agencies in the procurement of paper stock for printing.
Part 1 contains detailed standard specifications; part 2 gives the standards to be used in testing; part 3 consists of the definitive color standards for all mimeograph, duplicator, writing, manifold, bond, ledger, and index papers; and part 4 contains Government Printing Office standards for packaging and packing.
Subscription includes basic manual, issued in looseleaf form and punched for 3-ring binder, and supplementary material for an indefinite period.
Latest basic volume: No. 6, May 1, 1967.

Y 4.P 93/1-10:date • Item 1004-E
U.S. GOVERNMENT DEPOSITORY LIBRARIES DIRECTORY. [Annual]. Now Federal Depository Library Directory. See GP 3.36/2.

COMMITTEE ON PRINTING
(House)

Y 4.P 93/2:CT
PUBLICATIONS.

COMMITTEE ON PRINTING
(Senate)

Y 4.P 93/3:CT
PUBLICATIONS.

SELECT COMMITTEE TO INVESTIGATE PUBLIC PRINTING
(Senate)

Y 4.P 93/4:CT
PUBLICATIONS.

COMMITTEE ON PRIVATE LAND CLAIMS
(House)

Y 4.P 93/5:CT
PUBLICATIONS.

COMMITTEE ON PRIVILEGES AND ELECTIONS
(Senate)

Y 4.P 93/6:CT
PUBLICATIONS.

COMMITTEE ON PRIVATE LAND CLAIMS
(Senate)

Y 4.P 93/7:CT
PUBLICATIONS.

SELECT COMMITTEE ON POW/MIA AFFAIRS
(Senate)

Y 4.P 93/8:nos. • Item 1009-B (P)
HEARINGS.
• Item 1009-B-13 (P)
Y 4.P 93/8 • Item 1009-C-13 (MF)
POW/MIA POLICY AND PROCESS.

SPECIAL COMMITTEE TO INVESTIGATE PROPAGANDA OR MONEY ALLEGED TO HAVE BEEN USED BY FOREIGN GOVERNMENTS TO INFLUENCE UNITED STATES SENATORS
(Senate)

Y 4.P 94:CT
PUBLICATIONS.

COMMITTEE ON PUBLIC LANDS
(Senate)

Y 4.P 96/1:CT
PUBLICATIONS.

COMMITTEE ON PUBLIC LANDS
(House)

Y 4.P 96/2:CT
PUBLICATIONS.

SELECT COMMITTEE ON PULP AND PAPER INVESTIGATIONS

Y 4.P 96/3:CT
PUBLICATIONS.

SELECT COMMITTEE ON APPROPRIATIONS FOR THE PREVENTION OF FRAUD IN AND DEPRECIATIONS UPON PUBLIC SERVICE

Y 4.P 96/4:CT
PUBLICATIONS.

COMMITTEE ON PUBLIC EXPENDITURES
(House)

Y 4.P 96/5:CT
PUBLICATIONS.

COMMITTEE ON PUBLIC BUILDINGS AND GROUNDS
(House)

Y 4.P 96/6:CT
PUBLICATIONS.

COMMITTEE ON PUBLIC BUILDINGS AND GROUNDS
(Senate)

Y 4.P 96/7:CT
PUBLICATIONS.

SELECT COMMITTEE ON PUBLIC HEALTH
(House)

Y 4.P 96/8:CT
PUBLICATIONS.

COMMITTEE ON PUBLIC HEALTH AND NATIONAL QUARANTINE
(Senate)

Y 4.P 96/9:CT
PUBLICATIONS.

COMMITTEE ON THE ENVIRONMENT AND PUBLIC WORKS
(Senate)

INFORMATION

> Committee on the
> Environment and Public Works
> Dirksen Senate Office Bldg.
> Washington, D.C. 20510-6175
> (202) 224-8832 (Majority)
> (202) 224-6176 (Minority)
> http://epw.senate.gov

                        • Item 1045-A (P)
Y 4.P 96/10:hrg.nos.   **• Item 1045-B (MF)**
HEARINGS. [Irregular]
    Issued as monographs.

Y 4.P 96/10:Cong./cal.nos.
LEGISLATIVE CALENDAR. [Irregular]
    Includes list of bills considered by committee which have become public law; executive communications; petitions and memorials; index by author and subject; publications of the committee. ISSN 0364-426X

                        • Item 1045-A (P)
Y 4.P 96/10:CT   **• Item 1045-B (MF)**
COMMITTEE PRINTS.

Y 4.P 96/10:L 52
SUMMARY OF LEGISLATIVE ACTIVITIES.

Y 4.P 96/10-2:date
NEWS RELEASES AND MISCELLANEOUS PUBLICATIONS. [Irregular]

COMMITTEE ON PUBLIC WORKS AND TRANSPORTATION
(House)

    Formerly named the Committee on Public Works.

INFORMATION

> House Committee on
> Public Works and Transportation
> 2165 Rayburn House Office Building
> Washington, D.C. 20515
> (202) 225-4472

                    • Item 1024-A (P)
Y 4.P 96/11:Cong.nos.   **• Item 1024-B (MF)**
HEARINGS [and Committee prints]. [Irregular]

    Publications, both hearings and committee prints, are numbered consecutively as issued for each Congress.

                    • Item 1024-A (P)
Y 4.P 96/11:Cong.-nos.   **• Item 1024-B (MF)**
COMMITTEE PRINTS.

                    • Item 1024-A (P)
Y 4.P 96/11-10:date   **• Item 1024-B (MF)**
RULES. [Biennial]

    Earlier Y 4.P 96/11:R 86

                          • Item 1024-A
Y 4.P 96/11-11   **• Item 1024-B (MF)**
LEGISLATIVE CALENDAR.

    Includes status of bills reported to the House; executive communications; petitions and memorials; subject and author index; publications of the committee.
    ISSN 0364-9660

COMMITTEE ON RAILWAYS AND CANALS
(House)

Y 4.R 13:CT
PUBLICATIONS.

COMMITTEE ON RAILROADS
(Senate)

Y 4.R 13/2:CT
PUBLICATIONS.

JOINT COMMITTEE ON RAILROAD RETIREMENT LEGISLATION

Y 4.R 13/3:CT
PUBLICATIONS.

SPECIAL JOINT COMMITTEE ON THE READJUSTMENT OF SERVICE PAY

Y 4.R 22/1:CT
PUBLICATIONS.

SPECIAL COMMITTEE ON THE READJUSTMENT OF SERVICE PAY
(House)

Y 4.R 22/2:CT
PUBLICATIONS.

SELECT COMMITTEE ON THE INVESTIGATION OF REAL ESTATE BONDHOLDERS' REORGANIZATIONS
(House)

Y 4.R 22/3:CT
PUBLICATIONS.

JOINT COMMITTEE ON RECONSTRUCTION

Y 4.R 24/1:CT
PUBLICATIONS.

JOINT COMMISSION ON THE RECLASSIFICATION OF SALARIES

Y 4.R 24/2:CT
PUBLICATIONS.

SELECT COMMITTEE ON RECONSTRUCTION AND PRODUCTION
(Senate)

Y 4.R 24/3:CT
PUBLICATIONS.

JOINT COMMITTEE ON REDUCTION OF FEDERAL EXPENDITURES

Y 4.R 24/4:CT
PUBLICATIONS.

> Y 4.R 24.4:B 85/2/date&nos.
> BUDGET SCOREKEEPING REPORT. [Irregular]
>> Shows status of fiscal year budget.

Y 4.R 24/4:nos.
MONTHLY REPORT ON FEDERAL PERSONNEL AND PAY. 1– 367.   – August 1974.

> Gives statistical data on personnel and pay for the Executive Departments, independent agencies, the Judicial and Legislative Branches, Historical tables give data from 1954 to date.
> Entitled Additional Report of the Joint Committee on Reduction of Federal Expenditures, Pursuant to Sec. 601 of the Revenue Act of 1941, on Federal Personnel and Pay prior to no. 353, June 1973.

SELECT COMMITTEE ON REFORESTATION
(Senate)

Y 4.R 25:CT
PUBLICATIONS.

JOINT COMMITTEE ON THE REORGANIZATION OF THE ADMINISTRATIVE BRANCH OF THE GOVERNMENT

Y 4.R 29:CT
PUBLICATIONS.

SPECIAL COMMITTEE TO STUDY THE REORGANIZATION OF COURTS OF THE UNITED STATES AND REFORM OF JUDICIAL PROCEDURE
(Senate)

Y 4.R 29/2
PUBLICATIONS.

COMMITTEE ON RETRENCHMENT
(Senate)

Y 4.R 31/1:CT
PUBLICATIONS.

JOINT SELECT COMMITTEE ON RETRENCHMENT

Y 4.R 31/2:CT
PUBLICATIONS.

COMMITTEE ON RESOURCES
(House)

Formerly: Committee on Natural Resources.

INFORMATION

Committee on Resources
1324 Longworth House Office Bldg.
Washington, D.C. 20515-6201
(202) 225-2761
http://resourcescommittee.house.gov

	• Item 1023-A (P)
Y 4.R 31/3:CT	• Item 1023-B (MF)

HEARINGS, PRINTS, & MISCELLANEOUS PUBLICATIONS.

	• Item 1023-A (P)
Y 4.R 31/3-11	• Item 1023-B (MF)

REPORT TO THE COMMITTEE ON THE BUDGET VIEWS AND ESTIMATES OF THE COMMITTEE ON NATURAL RESOURCES. [Annual]

	• Item 1023-A (P)
Y 4.R 31/3-12	• Item 1023-B (MF)

LEGISLATIVE CALENDAR.

	• Item 1023-A (P)
Y 4.R 31/3-13	• Item 1032-B (MF)

RULES FOR THE COMMITTEE ON NATURAL RESOURCES. [Biennial]

COMMITTEE ON RIVERS AND HARBORS
(House)

Y 4.R 52:CT
PUBLICATIONS.

COMMITTEE ON ROADS AND CANALS
(Senate)

Y 4.R 53:CT
PUBLICATIONS.

COMMITTEE ON ROADS
(House)

Y 4.R 53/2:CT
PUBLICATIONS.

COMMITTEE ON RULES
(House)

INFORMATION

House Committee on Rules
H312 The Capitol Bldg.
Washington, D.C. 20515-6269
(202) 225-9191
http://www.house.gov/rules

• Item 1025-C (P)
Y 4.R 86/1:CT   • Item 1025-D (MF)
PUBLICATIONS.

• Item 1025-C (P)
Y 4.R 86/1-10:date   • Item 1025-D (MF)
RULES. [Biennial]
Earlier Y 4.R 86/1:R 86/5

• Item 1025-C (P)
Y 4.R 86/1-11:date   • Item 1025-D (MF)
LEGISLATIVE CALENDAR. [Irregular]
Earlier Y 4.R 86/1:CT

• Item 1025-C (P)
Y 4.R 86/1-12:   • Item 1025-D (MF)
RULES ADOPTED BY THE COMMITTEES OF THE
HOUSE OF REPRESENTATIVES.

COMMITTEE ON RULES AND
ADMINISTRATION
(Senate)

INFORMATION

Senate Committee on Rules
and Administration
SR-305 Russell Senate Office Building
Washington, D.C. 20510-6325
(202) 224-6352
Fax: (202) 224-3036
http://rules.senate.gov

• Item 1046-B (P)
Y 4.R 86/2:hrg.nos.   • Item 1046-C (MF)
HEARINGS. [Irregular]
Issued as monographs.

Y 4.R 86/2:Cong./cal.nos.
LEGISLATIVE CALENDAR. [Irregular]

Includes membership of committee and subcommittees, and Joint Committees on Printing
and the Library; numerical list of bills and resolutions referred to the committee with accompanying report numbers; executive calendar, index by
author and by subject; bills and resolutions pending before subcommittees. Appendix lists funds
authorized for inquiries and investigations.
ISSN 0364-4154

• Item 1046-B (P)
Y 4.R 86/2:Cong.-nos.   • Item 1046-C (MF)
COMMITTEE PRINTS.

Y 4.R 86/2:3/(Cong./nos.)   • Item 1046-B
STAFF, THE CONGRESSIONAL STAFF JOURNAL.
1975– 1983. [Bimonthly]
Indexed by Index to U.S. Government Peri-
odicals.
Earlier Y 4.H 81/3:2

JOINT COMMITTEE ON RURAL
CREDITS

Y 4.R 88:CT
PUBLICATIONS.

COMMITTEE ON SCIENCE
(House)

Formerly named the Committee on Science
and Technology; the Committee on Science,
Space and Technology

INFORMATION

House Committee on Science
2320 Rayburn House Office Building
Washington, D.C. 20515
(202) 225-6371
Fax: (202) 226-0113

• Item 1025-A-1 (P)
Y 4.Sci 2:Cong./nos.   • Item 1025-A-2 (MF)
HEARINGS [Papers]. [Irregular]
This series includes committee prints as well
as hearing.
The following hearings are held annually:

ANNUAL REVIEW OF THE NATIONAL SCIENCE
FOUNDATION. [Annual]

Biographical data and photographs of:
NASA astronauts and astronaut candidates,
astronauts and participants in the X-15, X-
20, and Manned Orbiting Laboratory programs, and Soviet-Bloc cosmonauts. Briefly
reviews selection criteria and comparative data
on American and Soviet space flights.

Y 4.Sci 2:Cong./cal.nos.
LEGISLATIVE CALENDAR. [Irregular]

Includes list of other matters referred to the
committee (executive communications, House
documents, petitions and memorials; investigations of subcommittees; index by Public Law number of veto messages, amendments to the National Aeronautics and Space Act of 1958; index
by topic and author, committee publications.)
ISSN 0363-941X

• Item 1025-A-1 (P)
Y 4.Sci 2:CT   • Item 1025-A-2 (MF)
COMMITTEE PRINTS.

Y 4.Sci 2:Ac 8
REPORT OF THE ACTIVITIES OF THE COMMIT-
TEE ON SCIENCE AND ASTRONAUTICS.
1959–   [Annual]

Includes lists of reports and hearings published, review of major subjects under investigations, and review of legislation.

• Item 1025-A-2 (MF)
Y 4.Sci 2-10:date
SUMMARY OF ACTIVITIES. [Annual]
Earlier Y 4.Sci 2:cal.nos.

• Item 1025-A-1 (P)
Y 4.Sci 2/11:date   • Item 1025-A-2 (MF)
LEGISLATIVE CALENDAR. [Irregular]
Earlier Y 4.Sci 2

• Item 1025-A-1 (P)
Y 4.Sci 2/12:date   • Item 1025-A-2 (MF)
RULES.
Earlier Y 4.Sci 2:P 86

COMMISSION ON SECURITY AND
COOPERATION IN EUROPE

CREATION AND AUTHORITY

The Commission on Security and Cooperation in Europe was established by Public Law 94-
304, 1976.

INFORMATION

Commission on Security and Cooperation
in Europe
234 Ford House Office Bldg.
3rd & D Sts., SW
Washington, DC 20525-6460
(202) 225-1901
Fax: (202) 225-4199
E-Mail:csce@mail.house.gov
http://www.csce.gov

• Item 1089-C (P)
Y 4.Se 2:Cong.-nos.   • Item 1089-D (MF)
COMMITTEE PRINTS.

• Item 1089-C (P)
Y 4.Se 2:hrg.nos.   • Item 1089-D (MF)
HEARINGS.

• Item 1089-C (P)
Y 4.Se 2:CT   • Item 1089-D (MF)
REPORTS AND PUBLICATIONS. [Irregular]

• Item 1089-C (P)
Y 4.Se 2/10:date   • Item 1089-D (MF)
ANNUAL REPORT.

• Item 1089-C
Y 4.Se 2/11:v.nos./nos.   • Item 1089-D (MF)
DIGEST.
Previous title: CSCE Digest.

• Item 1089-C (P)
Y 4.Se 2/12:date   • Item 1089-D (MF)
PUBLICATIONS LIST. [Annual]

NATIONAL SECURITY
COMMITTEE
(House)

• Item 1012-A-1 (P)
Y 4.Se 2/1   • Item 1012-B-1 (MF)
HEARINGS, PRINTS, AND MISCELLANEOUS
PUBLICATIONS.

• Item 1012-A-3 (P)
Y 4.Se 2/1 a:nos.   • Item 1012-B-3 (MF)
COMMITTEE ON NATIONAL SECURITY: PAPERS
(numbered).

• Item 1012-A-2 (P)
Y 4.Se 2/1-15   • Item 1012-B-2 (MF)
COMMITTEE RULES AND RULES FOR INVESTIGA-
TIVE HEARINGS CONDUCTED BY SUBCOMMIT-
TEES OF THE COMMITTEE ON ARMED
SERVICES. [Biennial]

• Item 1012-A-4(P)
Y 4.Se 2/1-17:date   • Item 1012-B-4(MF)
LEGISLATIVE CALENDAR.

SELECT AND SPECIAL
COMMITTEES
(House)

Y 4.Se 4/1:CT
PUBLICATIONS.

SELECT AND SPECIAL COMMITTEES
(Senate)

Y 4.Se 4/2:CT
PUBLICATIONS.

COMMITTEE ON SENATE CONTINGENT EXPENSES
(Senate)

Y 4.Se 5:CT
PUBLICATIONS

SELECT COMMITTEE ON SENATORIAL CAMPAIGN EXPENDITURES
(Senate)

Y 4.Se 5/2:CT
PUBLICATIONS.

COMMITTEE TO AUDIT AND CONTROL SENATE CONTINGENT EXPENSES
(Senate)

Y 4.Se 5/3:CT
PUBLICATIONS.

TEMPORARY SELECT COMMITTEE TO STUDY THE SENATE COMMITTEE SYSTEM

Y 4.Se 5/4:CT
PUBLICATIONS.

COMMISSION ON THE OPERATION OF THE SENATE

CREATION AND AUTHORITY

The Commission on the Operation of the Senate was established by S.R. 227 in July 1975. The Commission was abolished March 15, 1977.

Y 4.Se 5/5:CT
PUBLICATIONS.

SELECT COMMITTEE TO INVESTIGATE ALLEGED SHIP SUBSIDY LOBBY
(House)

Y 4.Sh 6:CT
PUBLICATIONS.

SPECIAL COMMITTEE TO INVESTIGATE ALLEGED SHIP PURCHASE LOBBY
(Senate)

Y 4.Sh 6/2:CT
PUBLICATIONS.

SELECT COMMITTEE ON SHIPPING BOARD OPERATIONS
(House)

Y 4.Sh 6/3:CT
PUBLICATIONS.

SELECT COMMITTEE ON THE SHIPPING BOARD EMERGENCY FLEET CORPORATION
(House)

Y 4.Sh 6/4:CT
PUBLICATIONS.

JOINT COMMITTEE ON SHORT TIME RECORD CREDITS

Y 4.Sh 8:CT
PUBLICATIONS.

SELECT COMMITTEE ON SICKNESS AND MORTALITY ON EMIGRANT SHIPS
(Senate)

Y 4.Si 1:CT
PUBLICATIONS.

SPECIAL COMMITTEE ON THE INVESTIGATION OF SILVER
(Senate)

Y 4.Si 3:CT
PUBLICATIONS.

COMMITTEE ON SMALL BUSINESS
(House)

INFORMATION

House Committee on Small Business
2361 Rayburn House Office Building
Washington, D.C. 20515-6315
(202) 225-5821
Fax: (202) 225-3587
E-Mail:smbiz@mail.house.gov
http://www.house.gov/smbiz/

Y 4.Sm 1:hrg.nos.   • Item 1031-A (P)   • Item 1031-B (MF)
HEARINGS. [Irregular]
Issued as monographs.

Y 4.Sm 1:CT   • Item 1031-A (P)   • Item 1031-B (MF)
COMMITTEE PRINTS.

Y 4.Sm 1:10:date   • Item 1031-A (P)   • Item 1031-B (MF)
RULES OF THE COMMITTEE ON SMALL BUSINESS. [Annual]

Y 4.Sm 1:11:date   • Item 1031-A (P)   • Item 1031-B (MF)
LEGISLATIVE CALENDAR. [Annual]
Earlier Y 4.Sm 1

Y 4.Sm 1:12:date
SUMMARY OF SBA PROGRAMS. [Annual]
Earlier Y 4.Sm 1:P 94/16

SELECT COMMITTEE ON SMALL BUSINESS AND ENTREPRENEURSHIP
(Senate)

Formerly Select Committee on Small Business.

INFORMATION

Senate Committee on
Small Business and Entrepreneurship
428A Russell Senate Office Building
Washington, D.C. 20510-6350
(202) 224-5175
Fax: (202) 224-5619
http://www.senate.gov/~sbc/

ANNUAL REPORT.
Issued in Senate Report series.

Y 4.Sm 1/2:hrg.nos.   • Item 1049-J (P)   • Item 1049-K (MF)
HEARINGS. [Irregular]

Y 4.Sm 1/2:prt. nos.   • Item 1049-J (P)   • Item 1049-K (MF)
COMMITTEE PRINTS.

Y 4.Sm 1/2:Cong./cal.nos.   • Item 1049-J
LEGISLATIVE CALENDAR.

SPECIAL COMMITTEE ON SPACE AND ASTRONAUTICS
(Senate)

Y 4.Sp 1:CT
PUBLICATIONS.

SPEAKER'S COMMISSION ON PAGES
(1982)

Y 4.Sp 3:CT   • Item 1009-B
PUBLICATIONS.

SELECT COMMITTEE ON PROFESSIONAL SPORTS
(House)

Y 4.Sp 6:CT
PUBLICATIONS.

COMMITTEE ON STANDARDS, WEIGHTS AND MEASURES
(Senate)

Y 4.St 2:CT
PUBLICATIONS.

SELECT COMMITTEE ON STANDARDS AND CONDUCT
(Senate)

Y 4.St 2/2
PUBLICATIONS.

COMMITTEE ON STANDARDS OF OFFICIAL CONDUCT
(House)

INFORMATION

House Committee on Standards of
    Official Conduct
HT-2 Capitol Building
Washington, D.C. 20515-6328
(202) 225-7103
Fax: (202) 225-7392
http://www.house.gov/ethics

Y 4.St 2/3:CT   • Item 1025-B-1 (P)
                                     • Item 1025-B-2 (MF)
PUBLICATIONS.

Y 4.St 2/3:CT   • Item 1025-B-1 (P)
                                     • Item 1025-B-2 (MF)
COMMITTEE PRINTS.

Y 4.St 2/3:CT   • Item 1025-B-1 (P)
                                     • Item 1025-B-2 (MF)
HEARINGS.

Y 4.St 2/3-10   • Item 1025-B-1 (P)
                                     • Item 1025-B-2 (MF)
CODE OF OFFICIAL CONDUCT. [Annual]

Y 4.St 2/3-11:date   • Item 1025-B-1 (P)
                                     • Item 1025-B-2 (MF)
RULES OF PROCEDURE. [Biennial]
    Earlier Y 4.St 2/3:P 94

SELECT COMMITTEE TO INVESTIGATE THE DISPOSITION OF SURPLUS PROPERTY
(House)

Y 4.Su 7:CT
PUBLICATIONS.

SELECT COMMITTEE ON SURVIVORS BENEFITS
(House)

Y 4.Su 7/2:CT
PUBLICATIONS.

SELECT COMMITTEE ON THE INVESTIGATION OF THE TARIFF COMMISSION
(Senate)

Y 4.T 17:CT
PUBLICATIONS.

JOINT COMMITTEE ON TAX EVASION AND AVOIDANCE

Y 4.T 19:CT
PUBLICATIONS.

SPECIAL COMMITTEE ON THE TAXATION OF GOVERNMENTAL SECURITIES AND SALARIES
(Senate)

Y 4.T 19/2:CT
PUBLICATIONS.

SELECT COMMITTEE TO INVESTIGATE TAX-EXEMPT FOUNDATIONS AND COMPARABLE ORGANIZATIONS
(House)

Y 4.T 19/3:CT
PUBLICATIONS.

JOINT COMMITTEE ON TAXATION

Formerly Joint Committee on Internal Revenue Taxation.

INFORMATION

Joint Committee on Taxation
1015 Longworth House Office Building
Washington, D.C. 20515-6675
(202) 225-3621
Fax: (202) 225-0832
http://www.house.gov/jct

Y 4.T 19/4:CT   • Item 1002-A (P)
                                     • Item 1002-B (MF)
PUBLICATIONS.

Y 4.T 19/4:CT   • Item 1002-A (P)
                                     • Item 1002-B (MF)
COMMITTEE PRINT.

Y 4.T 19/4-10:date   • Item 1002-A (P)
                                     • Item 1002-B (MF)
ESTIMATES OF FEDERAL TAX EXPENDITURES FOR
    FISCAL YEAR. [Annual]

    Earlier Y 4.T 19/4:F 31

SPECIAL COMMITTEE TO INVESTIGATE TAYLOR AND OTHER SYSTEMS OF SHOP MANAGEMENT

Y 4.T 21:CT
PUBLICATIONS.

JOINT COMMITTEE ON CENTENNIAL OF THE TELEGRAPH
(–1944)

Y 4.T 23:CT
PUBLICATIONS.

TEMPORARY NATIONAL ECONOMIC COMMITTEE

Y 4.T 24:CT
PUBLICATIONS.

JOINT COMMITTEE ON THE INVESTIGATION OF THE TENNESSEE VALLEY AUTHORITY

Y 4.T 25:CT
PUBLICATIONS.

COMMITTEE ON TERRITORIES
(House)

Y 4.T 27/1:CT
PUBLICATIONS.

COMMITTEE ON TERRITORIES AND INSULAR AFFAIRS
(Senate)

Y 4.T 27/2:CT
PUBLICATIONS.

COMMITTEE ON THE CAUSES OF REDUCTION OF AMERICAN TONNAGE

Y 4.T 61:CT
PUBLICATIONS.

SELECT COMMITTEE ON TRANSPORTATION ROUTES TO SEABOARD

Y 4.T 68:CT
PUBLICATIONS.

TRANSPORTATION AND INFRASTRUCTURE COMMITTEE
(House)

INFORMATION

Transportation and Infrastructure Committee
2165 Rayburn House Office Bldg.
Washington, D.C. 20515
(202) 225-9446
http://www.house.gov/transportation

Y 4.T 68/2
HEARINGS, PRINTS, AND MISCELLANEOUS PUBLICATIONS.
- Item 1024-A-1 (P)
- Item 1024-B-1 (MF)

Y 4.T 68/2-11
LEGISLATIVE CALENDAR.
- Item 1024-A-2 (P)
- Item 1024-B-2 (MF)

SPECIAL COMMITTEE ON UN-AMERICAN ACTIVITIES
(Senate)

Y 4.Un 1:CT
PUBLICATIONS.

SELECT COMMITTEE ON UN-AMERICAN ACTIVITIES
(House)

Y 4.Un 1/2:CT
PUBLICATIONS.

SELECT COMMITTEE ON UNEMPLOYMENT INSURANCE
(Senate)

Y 4.Un 2:CT
PUBLICATIONS.

SPECIAL COMMITTEE TO INVESTIGATE UNEMPLOYMENT AND RELIEF
(Senate)

Y 4.Un 2/2:CT
PUBLICATIONS.

SPECIAL COMMITTEE ON UNEMPLOYMENT PROBLEMS
(Senate)

Y 4.Un 2/3:CT
PUBLICATIONS.

SELECT COMMITTEE TO ESTABLISH UNIVERSITY OF THE UNITED STATES
(Senate)

Y 4.Un 3/1:CT
PUBLICATIONS.

COMMITTEE TO INVESTIGATE THE UNITED STATES STEEL CORPORATION
(House)

Y 4.Un 3/2:CT
PUBLICATIONS.

COMMITTEE ON VENTILATION AND ACOUSTICS
(House)

Y 4.V 56:CT
PUBLICATIONS.

SELECT COMMITTEE TO INVESTIGATE THE VETERANS BUREAU (Senate)

Y 4.V 64:CT
PUBLICATIONS.

JOINT COMMITTEE ON VETERANS AFFAIRS

Y 4.V 64/2:CT
PUBLICATIONS.

COMMITTEE ON VETERANS' AFFAIRS
(House)

INFORMATION

House Committee on Veterans' Affairs
335 Cannon House Office Building
Washington, D.C. 20515-6335
(202) 225-3527
Fax: (202) 225-5486
http://www.veterans.house.gov

• **Item 1027-A (P)**
• **Item 1027-B (MF)**
Y 4.V 64/3:nos.
COMMITTEE PRINTS.

• **Item 1027-A (P)**
• **Item 1027-B (MF)**
Y 4.V 64/3:hrg.nos.
HEARINGS. [Irregular]

Issued as monographs.
The following hearings are held annually:

Y 4.V 64/3:L 52/8   • **Item 1027**
LEGISLATIVE OBJECTIVES OF VETERANS'
ORGANIZATIONS. [Annual]

• **Item 1027-A (P)**
• **Item 1027-B (MF)**
Y 4.V 64/3:CT
PUBLICATIONS.

Y 4.V 64/3:Cong./cal.nos.
LEGISLATIVE CALENDAR. [Irregular]

• **Item 1027-A (P)**
• **Item 1027-B (MF)**
Y 4.V 64/3-10:date
REPORT TO THE COMMITTEE ON THE BUDGET
FROM THE COMMITTEE ON VETERANS' AFFAIRS.

• **Item 1027-A (P)**
• **Item 1027-B (MF)**
Y 4.V 64/3-11:date
LEGISLATIVE CALENDAR. [Irregular]

Earlier Y 4.V 64/3

• **Item 1027-A (P)**
• **Item 1027-B (MF)**
Y 4.V 64/3-12
RULES OF PROCEDURE. [Annual]

COMMITTEE ON VETERANS' AFFAIRS
(Senate)

INFORMATION

Majority Staff
Senate Committee on Veterans' Affairs
SR-412 Russell Senate Office Building
Washington, D.C. 20510-6375
(202) 224-9126
http://veterans.senate.gov/info.htm

• **Item 1046-A-1 (P)**
• **Item 1046-A-2 (MF)**
Y 4.V 64/4:hrg.nos.
HEARINGS.

Y 4.V 64/4:Cong./cal.nos.   • **Item 998-A**
LEGISLATIVE CALENDAR. [Irregular]

ISSN 0364-8176

• **Item 1046-A-1 (P)**
• **Item 1046-A-2 (MF)**
Y 4.V 64/4:nos.
COMMITTEE PRINTS.

Y 4.V 64/4:Am 3/date
ANNUAL REPORT, AMERICAN BATTLE MONU-
MENTS COMMISSION, FISCAL YEAR (date).

Y 4.V 64/4:M 46/date
ANNUAL REPORT, AUTHORIZED BY 38 U.S.C.
5057, ADMINISTRATOR, VETERANS'
AFFAIRS, ON SHARING MEDICAL FACILI-
TIES, FISCAL YEAR (date). [Annual]

Y 4.V 64/4:M 46/2/date
ANNUAL REPORT AUTHORIZED BY 38 U.S.C.
5057, ADMINISTRATOR, VETERANS'
AFFAIRS, ON EXCHANGE OF MEDICAL
INFORMATION, FISCAL YEAR (date). 1971–
[Annual]

Report submitted by the Veterans' Administration for the fiscal year.

Y 4.V 64/4:M 46/3   • **Item 998-A**
MEDAL OF HONOR RECIPIENTS, 1863– 1973.
1973. 1231 p. il. (Committee Print 15, 93 Congress, 1st Session)
Contains the names and citations of valor
of every American who has been awarded the
Congressional Medal of Honor. The list covers the years from 1863, when the first medal
was awarded, through the Vietnam era to 1973.
Many of the citations render detailed accounts
of the actions which resulted in award of the
Medal of Honor, and they stand as tributes to
the bravery and courage of all our fighting
men throughout our Nation's history.

Y 4.V 64/4:M 46/3   • **Item 998-A**
MEDAL OF HONOR RECIPIENTS, 1863– 1978.
1979. 1113 p.

The Medal of Honor is the highest award
for military valor that can be given to any
individual in the U.S. Since it was first presented in 1863, the medal has amassed a
colorful and inspiring history which has culmi-
nated in the standards applied today for awarding this respected honor. This book provides
historical information about the Medal and
summary of the laws governing its use. In
addition, it records the names and deeds of
the brave individuals who have been awarded
the metal of Honor for their acts of heroism.
Citations of awards are arranged by war, campaign, conflict, or era and contain fascinating
account of patriotism and bravery.

Y 4.V 64/4:M 46/5/date
ANNUAL REPORT ON SHARING MEDICAL RE-
SOURCES.

Report submitted by the Veterans' Administration for the fiscal year.

Y 4.V 64/4:V 64/date
VETERANS ADMINISTRATION ACTIVITIES, SUB-
MITTED BY THE VETERANS ADMINISTRA-
TION. [Monthly]

ISSN 0090-094X

SELECT COMMITTEE TO INVESTIGATE WAGES AND PRICES
(Senate)

Y 4.W 12:CT
PUBLICATIONS.

COMMITTEE ON WAR CLAIMS
(House)

Y 4.W 19:CT
PUBLICATIONS.

SELECT COMMITTEE TO INVESTIGATE THE SEIZURE OF MONTGOMERY WARD AND COMPANY
(House)

Y 4.W 21:CT
PUBLICATIONS.

SPECIAL COMMITTEE TO INVESTIGATE THE WASHINGTON RAILWAY AND ELECTRICAL COMPANY
(Senate)

Y 4.W 27:CT
PUBLICATIONS.

JOINT COMMITTEE ON METROPOLITAN WASHINGTON PROBLEMS

Y 4.W 27/2:CT
PUBLICATIONS.

COMMITTEE ON WATER POWER

Y 4.W 29:CT
PUBLICATIONS.

COMMITTEE ON WAYS AND MEANS
(House)

INFORMATION

House Committee on Ways and Means
1102 Longworth House Office Building
Washington, D.C. 20515-6348
(202) 225-3625
http://waysandmeans.house.gov

Y 4.W 36:hrg.nos.
HEARINGS. [Irregular]
• Item 1028-A (P)
• Item 1028-B (MF)

Y 4.W 36:Cong./cal.nos.   • Item 1028-B (MF)
LEGISLATIVE CALENDAR. [Irregular]

Includes lists of hearings; reports, and other
publications.
ISSN 0364-9644

Y 4.W 36:CT
COMMITTEE PRINTS.
• Item 1028-A (P)
• Item 1028-B-1 (MF)

Y 4.W 36:D 71/2
ANNUAL REPORT OF THE DEPARTMENT OF
TREASURY ON OPERATION AND EFFECT
OF DOMESTIC INTERNATIONAL SALES COR-
PORATION LEGISLATION FOR CALENDAR
YEAR. 1st–   1972–

Y 4.W 36:WMCP 96-1   • Item 1028
MANUAL OF RULES OF THE COMMITTEE ON WAYS
AND MEANS. [Biennial]

Y 4.W 36:2/nos.
QUARTERLY REPORT TO CONGRESS AND THE
EAST-WEST FOREIGN TRADE BOARD ON
TRADE BETWEEN THE UNITED STATES AND THE
NONMARKET ECONOMY COUNTRIES.

Issued as Committee Prints, WMCP (nos.)

Y 4.W 36:3/nos.
QUARTERLY REPORT ON TRADE BETWEEN THE
UNITED STATES AND NONMARKET ECONOMY
COUNTRIES, PURSUANT TO SECTION 411 (c)
OF THE TRADE ACT OF 1974.

Issued as Committee Prints, WMCP (nos.)

Y 4.W 36:10/date
LEGISLATIVE CALENDAR. [Semiannual]
• Item 1028-A (P)
• Item 1028-B (MF)

Y 4.W 36:10-2/date
DESCRIPTION OF THE ADMINISTRATION'S FISCAL
YEAR (date) BUDGET RECOMMENDATIONS UN-
DER THE JURISDICTION OF THE COMMITTEE
ON WAYS AND MEANS. [Annual]

Earlier Y 4.W 36:WMCP

Y 4.W 36:10-3/date/v.nos   • Item 1028-B (MF)
COMPILATION OF THE SOCIAL SECURITY LAWS.
[Annual]
• Item 1028-A (P)

Y 4.W 36:10-4/date
BACKGROUND MATERIAL AND DATA ON PROGRAMS
WITHIN THE JURISDICTION. [Annual]
• Item 1028-A (P)
• Item 1028-B (MF)

Earlier Y 4.W 36:WMCP

Y 4.W 36:10-5/date
MANUAL OF RULES. [Biennial]
• Item 1028-A (P)
• Item 1028-B (MF)

Earlier Y 4.W 36:M 31/2

Y 4.W 36:10-6/date
LEGISLATIVE RECORD. [Biennial]
• Item 1028-A (P)
• Item 1028-B (MF)

Y 4.W 36:10-7/date   • Item 998-F-1 (E)
GREEN BOOK, OVERVIEW OF ENTITLEMENT PRO-
GRAMS. [Annual]

Issued on CD-ROM.

SELECT COMMITTEE ON THE WELFARE AND EDUCATION OF CONGRESSIONAL PAGES
(House)

Y 4.W 45:CT
PUBLICATIONS.

SELECT COMMITTEE ON THE INVESTIGATION OF CHARGES AGAINST BURTON K. WHEELER
(Senate)

Y 4.W 56:CT
PUBLICATIONS.

SELECT COMMITTEE TO CONDUCT AN INVESTIGATION AND STUDY OF THE FINANCIAL POSITION OF THE WHITE COUNTY BRIDGE COMMISSION
(House)

Y 4.W 58:CT
PUBLICATIONS.

SPECIAL COMMITTEE ON WILDLIFE RESOURCES
(Senate)

Y 4.W 64:CT
PUBLICATIONS.

SELECT COMMITTEE ON THE CONSERVATION OF WILDLIFE RESOURCES
(House)

Y 4.W 64/2:CT
PUBLICATIONS.

SELECT COMMITTEE TO INVESTIGATE CERTAIN STATEMENTS MADE BY DOCTOR WILLIAM A. WIRT
(House)

Y 4.W 74:CT
PUBLICATIONS.

SELECT COMMITTEE ON WOMAN SUFFRAGE
(Senate)

Y 4.W 84:CT
PUBLICATIONS.

SPECIAL COMMITTEE TO INVESTIGATE THE PRODUCTION, TRANSPORTATION AND MARKETING OF WOOL
(Senate)

Y 4.W 88:CT
PUBLICATIONS.

COMMITTEE ON WORLD WAR VETERANS LEGISLATION
(House)

Y 4.W 89:CT
PUBLICATIONS.

SELECT AND SPECIAL COMMITTEES (As Appointed)

Y 4.2:
HEARINGS, PRINTS, AND MISCELLANEOUS PUB-
LICATIONS (House).
• Item 1009-B (P)
• Item 1009-C (MF)

Y 4.3:
HEARINGS, PRINTS, AND MISCELLANEOUS PUB-
LICATIONS (Senate).
• Item 1009-B-12 (P)
• Item 1009-C-12 (MF)

MEMORIAL ADDRESSES

Y 7.1 • Item 1005 (MF)
MEMORIAL ADDRESSES. [Irregular]

CONGRESSIONAL BUDGET OFFICE
(1974–   )

CREATION AND AUTHORITY

The Congressional Budget Office was established by the Congressional Budget Act of 1974 (88 Stat. 302; 2 U.S.C. 601), approved July 12, 1974.

INFORMATION

Congressional Budget Office
Ford House Office Bldg.
Washington, D.C. 20515
(202) 226-2600
http://www.cbo.gov

Y 10.1:date • Item 1005-C
ANNUAL REPORT.

Y 10.2:CT • Item 1005-C
GENERAL PUBLICATIONS.

Y 10.2:B 85/8/date • Item 1005-C
ANALYSIS OF THE PRESIDENT'S BUDGETARY PROPOSALS FOR FISCAL YEAR (date). [Annual]

Y 10.8:CT • Item 1005-B
HANDBOOKS, MANUALS, GUIDES.

Y 10.9:nos. • Item 1005-A
BACKGROUND PAPERS. 1–   [Irregular]

Y 10.10:date & report nos.
CONGRESSIONAL BUDGET SCOREKEEPING REPORTS.

ISSN 0363-5813
Earlier Y 10.2:B 85

Y 10.11:nos. • Item 1005-D (MF)
TECHNICAL ANALYSIS PAPERS. 1–   1976– [Irregular]

Y 10.12:CT • Item 1005-E (MF)
BUDGET ISSUE PAPERS. [Irregular]

Y 10.13:date • Item 1005-F (P) (EL)
REPORT TO THE SENATE AND HOUSE COMMITTEES ON THE BUDGET AS REQUIRED BY PUBLIC LAW 93-344. [Annual]

PURPOSE:– To discuss budgetary and policy projections with alternative budgetary strategies for setting long-range goals for the budget and the economy. Includes statistical data.

Y 10.14:date • Item 1005-G (MF)
LIST OF PUBLICATIONS. [Annual]

Consists of a chronological and subject listing of publications issued by the Office on various topics pertaining to budgetary matters.

Y 10.15:CT • Item 1005-H
BIBLIOGRAPHIES AND LISTS OF PUBLICATIONS. [Irregular]

Y 10.16:date • Item 1005-J
BASELINE BUDGET PROJECTIONS, FISCAL YEARS (dates). [Annual]

Issued each year to project new budget authority, outlays, and revenues for the next five fiscal years.

Y 10.17:date • Item 1005-F
ECONOMIC AND BUDGET OUTLOOK, AN UPDATE. [Annual]

Y 10.18:date • Item 1005-E
SEQUESTRATION REPORT FOR FISCAL YEAR (date): A SUMMARY. [Annual]

Y 10.19:date • Item 1005-K
ANALYSIS OF THE PRESIDENT'S BUDGETARY PROPOSALS FOR FISCAL YEAR (date). [Annual]

PURPOSE– To analyze the President's Budget and policy proposals in terms of changes from the Congressional Budget Office's baseline budget projections. Estimates the budgetary impact of the Administration's proposals.
Earlier Y 10.2:B 85/81

Y 10.20:date • Item 1005-E (MF)
RESPONSIBILITIES AND ORGANIZATION. [Biennial]

Y 10.21 • Item 1005-C-1 (E)
ELECTRONIC PRODUCTS. (Misc.)

Y 10.21/2 • Item 1005-C-1 (EL)
MONTHLY BUDGET REVIEW.

Y 10.22 • Item 1005-C-2 (EL)
UNAUTHORIZED APPROPRIATIONS AND EXPIRING AUTHORIZATIONS. [Annual]

COLONIAL DOCUMENTS
(Compilations)

Z 1.1:vol
AMERICAN ARCH

CONTINENTAL CONGRESS PAPERS

Z 2.1:CT
CONSTITUTIONAL OR FEDERAL CONVENTION, 1787.

Z 2.2:vol
DIPLOMATIC CORRESPONDENCE OF AMERICAN REVOLUTION, 1776– 83.

Z 2.3:vol
DIPLOMATIC CORRESPONDENCE OF UNITED STATES, 1783– 89.

Z 2.4:vol
REVOLUTIONARY DIPLOMATIC CORRESPONDENCE, 1775– 85.

Z 2.5:vol
JOURNALS OF CONTINENTAL CONGRESS, 1774– 88.

Z 2.6:vol
JOURNALS OF CONTINENTAL CONGRESS, 1774– 88 (Folwell's reprint).

Z 2.7:vol
JOURNALS OF CONTINENTAL CONGRESS, 1774– 88 (Way & Gideon).

Z 2.8:vol
SECRET JOURNALS OF CONTINENTAL CONGRESS,

DOCUMENTS OF PERIOD OF FIRST 14 CONGRESSES
1789– 1817

Z 3.1:vol
DUFF GREEN'S COMPILATIONS OF AMERICAN STATE PAPERS ON PUBLIC LANDS.

Z 3.2:vol
WAIT'S STATE PAPERS.

Z 3.3:vol
CONGRESSIONAL REGISTER (Lloyd).

Z 3.4:vol
JOURNALS OF SENATE (Gales & Seaton's Reprint).

Z 3.5:vol
JOURNALS OF HOUSE OF REPRESENTATIVES (Gales & Seaton's reprints).

DOCUMENTS OF PERIOD OF FIRST 14 CONGRESSES
1789– 1817
(original prints)

Z 4.1:CT
PUBLICATIONS.

AGENCY CLASS CHRONOLOGY

A 1

| A 1 | 1862- | Agriculture Department |

A 2

| A 2 | 1893-1925 | Accounts and Disbursements Division |

A 3

A 6	1869-1895	[part of] Botany Division
A 3	1895-1901	Agrostology Division
A 19	1901-1942	Plant Industry Bureau
A 77.500	1942-1943	Plant Industry Bureau
	1943-1953	Plant Industry, Soils, and Agricultural Engineering Bureau
	1953-	[Publications Relating to Horticulture]

A 4

A 4	1884-1942	Animal Industry Bureau
A 77.200	1942-1953	Animal Industry Bureau
	1953-	[Publications Relating to the Care of Animals and Poultry]

A 5

A 5	1886	Economic Ornithology and Mammology Division
	1887-1896	Ornithology and Mammology Division
	1896-1905	Biological Survey Division
	1905-1939	Biological Survey Bureau
I 47	1939-1940	Biological Survey Bureau
I 49	1940-	Fish and Wildlife Service

A 6

A 6	1869-1901	Botany Division
A 19	1901-1942	Plant Industry Bureau
A 77.500	1942-1943	Plant Industry Bureau
	1943-1953	Plant Industry, Soils, and Agricultural Engineering Bureau
	1953-	[Publications Relating to Horticulture]

A 7

A 7	1862-1901	Chemistry Division
	1901-1927	Chemistry Bureau
A 47	1927-1938	Chemistry and Soils Bureau
A 70	1938-1942	Agricultural Chemistry and Engineering Bureau
A 77.100	1942-1943	Agricultural Chemistry and Engineering Bureau
	1943-1953	Agricultural and Industrial Chemistry Bureau
A 77	1953-1978	Agricultural Research Service
A 106	1978-1981	Science and Education Administration
A 77	1981-	Agricultural Research Service

A 8

| I 26 | 1877-1880 | Entomological Commission |
| A 8 | 1880-1882 | Entomological Commission |

A 9

A 9	1879-1904	Entomology Division
	1904-1934	Entomology Bureau
A 56	1934-1942	Entomology and Plant Quarantine Bureau
A 77.300	1942-1953	Entomology and Plant Quarantine Bureau
	1953-	[Publications Relating to Plant Quarantine]

A 10

A 10	1888-1915	Experiment Stations Office
	1915-1923	States Relations Office
	1923-1942	Experiment Stations Office
A 77.400	1942-1953	Experiment Stations Office
A 77	1953-1978	Agriculture Research Service
A 106	1978-1981	Science and Education Administration
A 77	1981-	Agriculture Research Service

A 11

| A 11 | 1891-1898 | Fiber Investigations Office |
| A 6 | 1898-1901 | [functions transferred to] Botany Division |

A 12

A 12	1984-1902	Foreign Markets Section
	1902-1903	Foreign Markets Division
A 27	1903-1914	[functions transferred to] Crop Estimates Bureau

A 13

A 13	1880-1901	Forestry Division
	1901-1905	Forestry Bureau
	1905-	Forest Service

A 14

A 14	1862-1901	Gardens and Grounds Division
A 19	1901-1942	Plant Industry Bureau
A 77.500	1942-1943	Plant Industry Bureau
	1943-1953	Plant Industry, Soils, and Agricultural Engineering Bureau
	1953-	[Publications Relating to Horticulture]

A 15

| A 15 | 1890-1896 | Irrigation Inquiry Office |

A 16

| A 16 | 1902-1904 | Labor Employment Board |
| CS 1 | 1904-1978 | [functions transferred to] Civil Service Commission |

A 17

A 17	1862-1962	Library
	1962-1978	National Agricultural Library
A 106.100	1978-1981	Technical Information Systems
A 17	1981-	National Agricultural Library

A 18

| A 18 | 1871-1895 | Microscopy Division |

A 19

A 3	1895-1901	Agrostology Division
A 6	1869-1901	Botany Division
A 14	1862-1901	Gardens and Grounds Division
A 20	1886-1901	Pomology Division
A 23	1898-1901	Seed and Plant Introduction Section
A 24	1868-1901	Seeds Division
A 28	1895-1901	Vegetable Physiology and Pathology Division
A 19	1901-1942	Plant Industry Bureau
A 77.500	1942-1943	Plant Industry Bureau
	1943-1953	Plant Industry, Soils, and Agricultural Engineering Bureau
	1953-	[Publications Relating to Horticulture]

A 20

A 20	1886-1901	Pomology Division
A 19	1901-1942	Plant Industry Bureau
A 77.500	1942-1943	Plant Industry Bureau
	1943-1953	Plant Industry, Soils, and Agricultural Engineering Bureau
	1953-	[Publications Relating to Horticulture]

A 21

A 21	1890-1925	Information Division
	1925-1974	Information Office
	1974-1978	Communications Office
A 107	1978-1987	Governmental and Public Affairs Office
A 21	1987-19xx	Information Office
	19xx-	Communications Office

A 22

A 22	1892-1898	Road Inquiry Office
	1898-1905	Public Road Inquiry Office
	1905-1915	Public Roads Office
	1915-1918	Public Roads and Rural Engineering Office
	1918-1939	Public Roads Bureau
FW 2	1939-1949	Public Roads Administration
GS 3	1949	Public Roads Bureau
C 37	1949-1966	Public Roads Bureau
TD 2.100	1966-1969	Public Roads Bureau
TD 2	1969-	[functions transferred to] Federal Highway Administration

A 23

A 23	1898-1901	Seed and Plant Introduction Section
A 19	1901-1942	Plant Industry Bureau
A 77.500	1942-1943	Plant Industry Bureau
	1943-1953	Plant Industry, Soils, and Agricultural Engineering Bureau
	1953-	[Publications Relating to Horticulture]

A 24

A 24	1868-1901	Seed Division
A 19	1901-1942	Plant Industry Bureau
A 77.500	1942-1943	Plant Industry Bureau
	1943-1953	Plant Industry, Soils, and Agricultural Engineering Bureau
	1953-	[Publications Relating to Horticulture]

A 25

A 25	1899-1891	Silk Section

A 26

A 26	1894-1897	Agricultural Soils Division
	1897-1901	Soils Division
	1901-1927	Soils Bureau
A 47	1927-1938	Chemistry and Soils Bureau
A 70	1938-1942	Agricultural Chemistry and Engineering Bureau
A 77.100	1942-1943	Agricultural Chemistry and Engineering Bureau
	1943-1953	Agricultural and Industrial Chemistry Bureau
A 77	1953-1978	Agricultural Research Service
A 106	1978-1981	Science and Education Administration
A 77	1981-	Agricultural Research Service

A 27

A 27	1863-1903	Statistics Division
	1903-1914	Statistics Bureau
	1914-1921	Crop Estimates Bureau
A 36	1921-1922	Agricultural Economics Bureau
A 77	1953-1978	Agricultural Research Service
A 88	1953-1965	Agricultural Marketing Service
	1965-1972	Consumer and Marketing Service
	1972-	Agricultural Marketing Service

A 28

A 28	1887-1890	Vegetable Pathology Section
	1890-1895	Vegetable Pathology Division
	1895-1901	Vegetable Physiology and Pathology Division
A 19	1901-1942	Plant Industry Bureau
A 77.500	1942-1943	Plant Industry Bureau
	1943-1953	Plant Industry, Soils, and Agricultural Engineering Bureau
	1953-	[Publications Relating to Horticulture]

A 29

A 29	1890-1940	Weather Bureau
C 30	1940-1965	Weather Bureau
C 52	1965-1970	Environmental Science Services Administration
C 55.100	1970-	National Weather Service

A 30

A 30	1896-1916	Appointment Clerk

A 31

A 31	1898-1925	Chief Clerk

A 32

A 32	1907-1914	Food and Drug Inspection Board
A 7	1914-1927	[functions transferred to] Chemistry Bureau
A 33	1914-1955	[functions transferred to] Solicitor of Department of Agriculture

A 33

A 33	1908-1955	Solicitor of Department of Agriculture
	1955-	General Counsel

A 34

A 34	1910-1927	Insecticide and Fungicide Board
A 46	1927-1930	Food, Drug, and Insecticide Administration

A 35

A 35	1912-1928	Federal Horticulture Board
A 48	1928-1932	Plant Quarantine and Control Administration
	1932-1934	Plant Quarantine Bureau
A 56	1934-1942	Entomology and Plant Quarantine Bureau
A 77.300	1942-1953	Entomology and Plant Quarantine Bureau
	1953-	[Publications Relating to Plant Quarantine]

A 36

A 36	1914-1915	Markets Office
	1915-1917	Markets and Rural Organization Office
	1917-1921	Markets Bureau
A 27	1914-1921	Crop Estimates Bureau
A 36	1921-1922	Markets and Crop Estimates Bureau
A 37	1919-1922	Farm Management and Farm Economics Office
A 36	1922-1953	Agricultural Economics Bureau
A 77	1953-1978	Agricultural Research Service
A 106	1978-1981	Science and Education Administration
A 77	1981-	Agricultural Research Service
A 88	1953-1965	Agricultural Marketing Service
	1965-1972	Consumer and Marketing Service
	1972-	Agricultural Marketing Service

A 37

A 37	1915-1919	Farm Management Office
	1919-1922	Farm Management and Farm Economics Office
A 36	1922-1953	Agricultural Economics Bureau
A 77	1953-1978	Agricultural Research Service
A 106	1978-1981	Science and Education Administration
A 77	1981-	Agricultural Research Service
A 88	1953-1965	Agricultural Marketing Service
	1965-1972	Consumer and Marketing Service
	1972-	Agricultural Marketing Service

A 38

A 38	1921-1926	Fixed Nitrogen Research Laboratory

A 39

A 39	1921-1927	Packers and Stockyards Administration
A 4	1927-1942	Animal Industry Bureau
A 77.200	1942-1953	Animal Industry Bureau
	1953-1967	[Publications Relating to the Care of Animals and Poultry]
A 96	1967-1978	Packers and Stockyards Administration
A 88	1953-1965	Agricultural Marketing Service
	1965-1972	Consumer and Marketing Service
	1972-1994	Agricultural Marketing Service
A 113	1994-	The Grain Inspection, Packers & Stockyards Administration

A 40

A 40	1921-1922	Exhibits Office

A 41

A 41	1922-1936	Grain Futures Administration
A 59	1936-1942	Commodity Exchange Administration
A 75.200	1942-1947	Commodity Exchange Administration
A 85	1947-1974	Commodity Exchange Authority
Y 3.C 73/5	1974-	Commodity Futures Trading Commission

A 42

A 42	1923-1942	Home Economics Bureau
A 77.77	1942-1943	Home Economics Bureau
	1943-1953	Human Nutrition and Home Economics Bureau
	1953-1995	[Publications Relating to Home Economics and Human Nutrition]

A 43

A 43	1923-1943	Extension Service
A 80.300	1943-1945	Extension Service
A 43	1945-1953	Extension Service
	1953-1970	Federal Extension Service
	1970-1978	Extension Service
A 106	1978-1981	Science and Education Administration
A 43	1981-	Extension Service

A 44

A 4	1884-1924	[part of] Animal Industry Bureau
A 44	1924-1926	Dairying Bureau
	1926-1942	Dairy Industry Bureau
A 77.600	1942-1953	Dairy Industry Bureau
	1953-	[Publications Relating to Dairy Industry]

A 45

A 45	1926	Agricultural Instruction Office

A 46

A 46	1927-1930	Food, Drug, and Insecticide Administration
	1930-1940	Food and Drug Administration
FS 7	1940-1946	Food and Drug Administration
FS 13.100	1946-1969	Food and Drug Administration
HE 20.1200	1970	Food and Drug Administration
HE 20.4000	1970-	Food and Drug Administration

A 47

A 7	1901-1927	Chemistry Division
A 26	1901-1927	Soils Bureau
A 47	1927-1938	Chemistry and Soils Bureau
A 70	1938-1942	Agricultural Chemistry and Engineering Bureau
A 77.100	1942-1943	Agricultural Chemistry and Engineering Bureau
	1943-1953	Agricultural and Industrial Chemistry Bureau
A 77	1953-1978	Agricultural Research Service
A 106	1978-1981	Science and Education Administration
A 77	1981-	Agricultural Research Service

A 48

A 35	1912-1928	Federal Horticulture Board
A 48	1928-1932	Plant Quarantine and Control Administration
	1932-1934	Plant Quarantine Bureau
A 56	1934-1942	Entomology and Plant Quarantine Bureau
A 77.300	1942-1953	Entomology and Plant Quarantine Bureau
	1953-	[Publications Relating to Plant Quarantine]

A 49

A 49	1925-	Personnel Office

A 50

A 50	1927-1928	Alaska Commission for Department of Agriculture

A 51

A 51	1929-1933	Farmers' Seed Loan Office
FCA 1	1933-1939	Farm Credit Administration
A 72	1939-1942	Farm Credit Administration
A 79.100	1942-1943	Farm Credit Administration [not used]
A 72	1943-1953	Farm Credit Administration
FCA 1	1953-	Farm Credit Administration

A 52

A 52	1931	National Advisory Loan Committee

A 53

A 22	1918-1931	[a division in] Public Roads Bureau
A 53	1931-1938	Agricultural Engineering Bureau
A 70	1938-1942	Agricultural Chemistry and Engineering Bureau
A 77.100	1942-1943	Agricultural Chemistry and Engineering Bureau
A 77	1953-1978	Agricultural Research Service
A 106	1978-1981	Science and Education Administration
A 77	1981-	Agricultural Research Service

A 54

A 54	1918-1933	Crop Production Loan Office
FCA 1	1933-1939	Farm Credit Administration
A 72	1939-1942	Farm Credit Administration
A 79.100	1942-1943	Farm Credit Administration [not used]
A 72	1943-1953	Farm Credit Administration
FCA 1	1953-	Farm Credit Administration

A 55

A 55	1933-1942	Agricultural Adjustment Administration
A 76.400	1942	Agricultural Adjustment Administration
	1942	Agricultural Adjustment Agency
A 79.400	1942-1943	Agricultural Adjustment Agency
A 80.2100	1943-1944	Agricultural Adjustment Agency
A 80.600	1944-1945	Agricultural Adjustment Agency
A 83	1945	Agricultural Adjustment Agency
A 82	1945-1953	Production and Marketing Administration
	1953-1961	Commodity Stabilization Service
	1961-	Agricultural Stabilization and Conservation Service

A 56

A 9	1878-1904	Entomology Division
	1904-1934	Entomology Bureau
A 48	1928-1932	Plant Quarantine and Control Administration
	1932-1934	Plant Quarantine Bureau
A 56	1934-1942	Entomology and Plant Quarantine Bureau
A 77.300	1942-1953	Entomology and Plant Quarantine Bureau
	1953-	[Publications Relating to Plant Quarantine]

A 57

I 30	1933-1935	Soil Erosion Service
A 57	1935-1942	Soil Conservation Service
A 76.200	1942	Soil Conservation Service
A 79.200	1942-1943	Soil Conservation Service
A 80.2000	1943-1944	Soil Conservation Service
A 80.500	1944-1945	Soil Conservation Service
A 57	1945- 1994	Soil Conservation Service
A 57	1994-	Natural Resources Conservation Service

A 58

A 58		Budget and Finance Office

A 59

A 41	1922-1936	Grain Futures Administration
A 59	1936-1942	Commodity Exchange Administration
A 75.200	1942-1947	Commodity Exchange Administration
A 85	1947-1974	Commodity Exchange Authority
Y 3.C 73/5	1974-	Commodity Futures Trading Commission

A 60

A 60	1935-1939	Operations Division
	1939-	Plant and Operations Division

A 61

Y 3.R 31	1935-1937	Resettlement Administration
A 61	1937	Resettlement Administration
	1937-1942	Farm Security Administration
A 80.700	1942-1945	Farm Security Administration
A 61	1945-1946	Farm Security Administration
A 84	1946-	Farmers Home Administration

A 62

A 62	1938-1942	Federal Crop Insurance Corporation
A 76.100	1942	Federal Crop Insurance Corporation
A 79.300	1942-1943	Federal Crop Insurance Corporation
A 80.900	1943-1945	Federal Crop Insurance Corporation
A 80.200	1945-1947	Federal Crop Insurance Corporation
A 62	1947-1995	Federal Crop Insurance Corporation

A 63

A 55	1933-1938	[part of] Agricultural Adjustment Administration
A 63	1938-1942	Sugar Division
A 76.300	1942	Sugar Agency
A 78	1942-1943	Food Distribution Administration
A 80.100	1943-1944	Food Distribution Administration
	1944-1945	Distribution Office
A 80.800	1945	Marketing Services Office
A 81	1945	Marketing Services Office
A 82	1945-1953	Production and Marketing Administration
A 88	1953-1965	Agricultural Marketing Service
	1965-1972	Consumer and Marketing Service
	1972-	Agricultural Marketing Service

A 64

A 36	1930-1938	[a division in] Agricultural Economics Bureau
A 64	1938-1939	Foreign Agricultural Service
A 67	1939-1953	Foreign Agricultural Relations Office
	1953-	Foreign Agricultural Service

A 65

A 55	1933-1937	[a division in] Agricultural Adjustment Administration
A 65	1937-1940	Marketing and Marketing Agreements Division
A 73	1940-1942	Surplus Marketing Administration
A 75	1942	Agricultural Marketing Administration
A 78	1942-1943	Food Distribution Administration
A 80.100	1943-1944	Food Distribution Administration
	1944-1945	Distribution Office
A 80.800	1945	Marketing Services Office
A 81	1945	Marketing Services Office
A 82	1945-1953	Production and Marketing Administration
A 88	1953-1965	Agricultural Marketing Service
	1965-1972	Consumer and Marketing Service
	1972-	Agricultural Marketing Service

A 66

A 66	1939-1942	Agricultural Marketing Service
A 75	1942	Agricultural Marketing Administration
A 78	1942-1943	Food Distribution Administration
A 80.100	1943-1944	Food Distribution Administration
	1944-1945	Distribution Office
A 80.800	1945	Marketing Services Office
A 81	1945	Marketing Services Office
A 82	1945-1953	Production and Marketing Administration
A 88	1953-1965	Agricultural Marketing Service
	1965-1972	Consumer and Marketing Service
	1972-	Agricultural Marketing Service

A 67

A 36	1930-1938	[a division in] Agricultural Economics Bureau
A 64	1938-1939	Foreign Agricultural Service
A 67	1939-1953	Foregin Agricultural Relations Office
	1953-	Foreign Agricultural Service

A 68

Y 3.R 88	1935-1939	Rural Electrification Administration
A 68	1939- 1994	Rural Electrification Administration
	1994-	Rural Utilities Service

A 69

Y 3.F 31/9	1933-1935	Federal Surplus Relief Corporation
A 69	1935-1940	Federal Surplus Commodities Corporation
A 73	1940-1942	Surplus Marketing Administration
A 75	1942	Agricultural Marketing Administration
A 78	1942-1943	Food Distribution Administration
A 80.100	1943-1944	Food Distribution Administration
	1944-1945	Distribution Office
A 80.800	1945	Marketing Services Office
A 81	1945	Marketing Services Office
A 82	1945-1953	Production and Marketing Administration
A 88	1953-1965	Agricultural Marketing Service
	1965-1972	Consumer and Marketing Service
	1972-	Agricultural Marketing Service

A 70

A 47	1927-1938	Chemistry and Soils Bureau
A 53	1931-1938	Agricultural Engineering Bureau
A 70	1938-1942	Agricultural Chemistry and Engineering Bureau
A 77.100	1942-1943	Agricultural Chemistry and Engineering Bureau
	1943-1953	Agricultural and Industrial Chemistry Bureau
A 77	1953-1978	Agricultural Research Service
A 106	1978-1981	Science and Education Administration
A 77	1981-	Agricultural Research Service

A 71

Y 3.C 73	1933-1939	Commodity Credit Corporation
A 71	1939-1943	Commodity Credit Corporation
A 80.400	1943-1945	Commodity Credit Corporation
A 82.300	1945-	Commodity Credit Corporation

A 72

FF 1	1929-1933	Federal Farm Board
FCA 1	1933-1939	Farm Credit Administration
A 72	1939-1942	Farm Credit Administration
A 79.100	1942-1943	Farm Credit Administration [not used]
A 72	1943-1953	Farm Credit Administration
FCA 1	1953-	Farm Credit Administration

A 73

A 65	1937-1940	Marketing and Marketing Agreements Division
A 69	1935-1940	Federal Surplus Commodities Corporation
A 73	1940-1942	Surplus Marketing Administration
A 75	1942	Agricultural Marketing Administration
A 78	1942-1943	Food Distribution Administration
A 80.100	1943-1944	Food Distribution Administration
	1944-1945	Distribution Office
A 80.800	1945	Marketing Services Office
A 81	1945	Marketing Services Office
A 82	1945-1953	Production and Marketing Administration
A 88	1953-1965	Agricultural Marketing Service
	1965-1972	Consumer and Marketing Service
	1972-	Agricultural Marketing Service

A 74

A 74	1941	Agricultural Defense Relations Office
	1941-1943	Agricultural War Relations Office
A 78	1943	[functions transferred to] Food Distribution Administration
A 79	1943	[functions transferred to] Food Production Administration

A 75

A 66	1939-1942	Agricultural Marketing Service
A 73	1940-1942	Surplus Marketing Administration
A 75	1942	Agricultural Marketing Administration
A 78	1942-1943	Food Distribution Administration
A 80.100	1943-1944	Food Distribution Administration
	1944-1945	Distribution Office
A 80.800	1945	Marketing Services Office
A 81	1945	Marketing Services Office
A 82	1945-1953	Production and Marketing Administration
A 88	1953-1965	Agricultural Marketing Service
	1965-1972	Consumer and Marketing Service
	1972-	Agricultural Marketing Service

A 75.100

A 55.63	1933-1942	Consumers' Counsel Office
A 75.100	1942-1943	Consumers' Counsel Division

A 75.200

A 41	1922-1936	Grain Futures Administration
A 59	1936-1942	Commodity Exchange Administration
A 75.200	1942-1947	Commodity Exchange Administration
A 85	1947-1974	Commodity Exchange Authority
Y 3.C 73/5	1974-	Commodity Futures Trading Commission

A 76

A 76	1942	Agricultural Conservation and Adjustment Administration
A 79	1942-1943	Food Production Administration
A 80.200	1943-1944	Food Production Administration
	1944-1945	Production Office

A 76.100

A 62	1938-1942	Federal Crop Insurance Corporation
A 76.100	1942	Federal Crop Insurance Corporation
A 79.300	1942-1943	Federal Crop Insurance Corporation
A 80.900	1943-1945	Federal Crop Insurance Corporation
A 80.200	1945-1947	Federal Crop Insurance Corporation
A 62	1947-	Federal Crop Insurance Corporation

A 76.200

I 30	1933-1935	Soil Erosion Service
A 57	1935-1942	Soil Conservation Service
A 76.200	1942	Soil Conservation Service
A 79.200	1942-1943	Soil Conservation Service
A 80.2000	1943-1944	Soil Conservation Service
A 80.500	1944-1945	Soil Conservation Service
A 57	1945-	Soil Conservation Service

A 76.300

A 55	1933-1938	[part of] Agricultural Adjustment Administration
A 63	1938-1942	Sugar Division
A 76.300	1942	Sugar Agency
A 78	1942-1943	Food Distribution Administration
A 80.100	1943-1944	Food Distribution Administration
	1944-1945	Distribution Office
A 80.800	1945	Marketing Services Office
A 81	1945	Marketing Services Office
A 82	1945-1953	Production and Marketing Administration
A 88	1953-1965	Agricultural Marketing Service
	1965-1972	Consumer and Marketing Service
	1972-	Agricultural Marketing Service

A 76.400

A 55	1933-1942	Agricultural Adjustment Administration
A 76.400	1942	Agricultural Adjustment Administration
	1942	Agricultural Adjustment Agency
A 79.400	1942-1943	Agricultural Adjustment Agency
A 80.2100	1943-1944	Agricultural Adjustment Agency
A 80.600	1944-1945	Agricultural Adjustment Agency
A 83	1945	Agricultural Adjustment Agency
A 82	1945-1953	Production and Marketing Administration
	1953-1961	Commodity Stabilization Service
	1961-	Agricultural Stabilization and Conservation Service

A 77

A 36	1922-1953	Agricultural Economics Bureau
A 77	1942-1953	Agricultural Research Administration
A 77.100	1943-1953	Agricultural and Industrial Chemistry Bureau
A 77.400	1942-1953	Experiment Stations Office
A 77	1953-1978	Agricultural Research Service
A 106	1978-1981	Science and Education Administration
A 77	1981-	Agricultural Research Service

A 77.100

A 47	1927-1938	Chemistry and Soils Bureau
A 53	1931-1938	Agricultural Engineering Bureau
A 70	1938-1942	Agricultural Chemistry and Engineering Bureau
A 77.100	1942-1953	Agricultural Chemistry and Engineering Bureau
A 77	1953-1978	Agricultural Research Service
A 106	1978-1981	Science and Education Administration
A 77	1981-	Agricultural Research Service

A 77.200

A 4	1884-1942	Animal Industry Bureau
A 77.200	1942-1953	Animal Industry Bureau
	1953-	[Publications Relating to the Care of Animals and Poultry]

A 77.300

A 56	1934-1942	Entomology and Plant Quarantine Bureau
A 77.300	1942-1953	Entomology and Plant Quarantine Bureau
	1953-	[Publications Relating to Plant Quarantine]

A 77.400

A 10	1888-1915	Experiment Stations Office
	1915-1923	States Relations Office
	1923-1942	Experiment Stations Office
A 77.400	1942-1953	Experiment Stations Office
A 77	1953-1978	Agriculture Research Service
A 106	1978-1981	Science and Education Administration
A 77	1981-	Agricultural Research Service

A 77.500

A 19	1901-1942	Plant Industry Bureau
A 77.500	1942-1943	Plant Industry Bureau
	1943-1953	Plant Industry, Soils, and Agricultural Engineering Bureau
	1953-	[Publications Relating to Horticulture]

A 77.600

A 4	1884-1942	Animal Industry Bureau
A 44	1924-1926	Dairying Bureau
	1926-1942	Dairy Industry Bureau
A 77.600	1942-1953	Dairy Industry Bureau
	1953-	[Publications Relating to Dairy Research]

A 77.700

A 42	1923-1942	Home Economics Bureau
A 77.700	1942-1943	Home Economics Bureau
	1943-1953	Human Nutrition and Home Economics Bureau
	1953-	[Publications Relating to Home Economics andf Human Nutrition]

A 78

A 75	1942	Agricultural Marketing Administration
A 36.300	1942	Sugar Agency
A 78	1942-1943	Food Distribution Administration
A 80.100	1943-1944	Food Distribution Administration
	1944-1945	Distribution Office
A 80.800	1945	Marketing Services Office
A 81	1945	Marketing Services Office
A 82	1945-1953	Production and Marketing Administration
A 88	1953-1965	Agricultural Marketing Service
	1965-1972	Consumer and Marketing Service
	1972-	Agricultural Marketing Service

A 79

A 76	1942	Agricultural Conservation and Adjustment Administration
A 79	1942-1943	Food Production Administration
A 80.200	1943-1944	Food Production Administration
	1944-1945	Production Office

A 79.100

FCA 1	1933-1939	Farm Credit Administration
A 72	1929-1942	Farm Credit Administration
A 79.100	1942-1943	Farm Credit Administration [not used]
A 72	1943-1953	Farm Credit Administration
FCA 1	1953-	Farm Credit Administration

A 79.200

I 30	1933-1935	Soil Erosion Service
A 57	1935-1942	Soil Conservation Service
A 76.200	1942	Soil Conservation Service
A 79.200	1942-1943	Soil Conservation Service
A 80.2000	1943-1944	Soil Conservation Service
A 80.500	1944-1945	Soil Conservation Service
A 57	1945-	Soil Conservation Service

A 79.300

A 62	1928-1942	Federal Crop Insurance Corporation
A 76.100	1942	Federal Crop Insurance Corporation
A 79.300	1942-1943	Federal Crop Insurance Corporation
A 80.900	1943-1945	Federal Crop Insurance Corporation
A 80.200	1945-1947	Federal Crop Insurance Corporation
A 62	1947-	Federal Crop Insurance Corporation

A 79.400

A 55	1933-1942	Agricultural Adjustment Administration
A 76.400	1942	Agricultural Adjustment Administration
	1942	Agricultural Adjustment Agency
A 79.400	1942-1943	Agricultural Adjustment Agency
A 80.2100	1943-1944	Agricultural Adjustment Agency
A 80.600	1944-1945	Agricultural Adjustment Agency
A 83	1945	Agricultural Adjustment Agency
A 82	1945-1953	Production and Marketing Administration
	1953-1961	Commodity Stabilization Service
	1961-	Agricultural Stabilization and Conservation Service

A 80

A 80	1943	Food Production and Distribution Administration
	1943-1945	War Food Administration

A 80.100

A 75	1942	Agricultural Marketing Administration
A 78	1942-1943	Food Distribution Administration
A 80.100	1943-1944	Food Distribution Administration
	1944-1945	Distribution Office
A 80.800	1945	Marketing Services Office
A 81	1945	Marketing Services Office
A 82	1945-1953	Production and Marketing Administration
A 88	1953-1965	Agricultural Marketing Service
	1965-1972	Consumer and Marketing Service
	1972-	Agricultural Marketing Service

A 80.200

A 76	1942	Agricultural Conservation and Adjustment Administration
A 79	1942-1943	Food Production Administration
A 80.200	1943-1944	Food Production Administration
	1944-1945	Production Office

A 80.300

A 43	1923-1943	Extension Service
A 80.300	1943-1945	Extension Service
A 43	1945-1953	Extension Service
	1953-1970	Federal Extension Service
	1970-1978	Extension Service
A 106	1978-1981	Science and Education Administration
A 43	1981-	Extension Service

A 80.400

Y 3.C 73	1933-1939	Commodity Credit Corporation
A 71	1939-1943	Commodity Credit Corporation
A 80.400	1943-1945	Commodity Credit Corporation
A 82.300	1945-	Commodity Credit Corporation

A 80.500

I 30	1933-1935	Soil Erosion Service
A 57	1935-1942	Soil Conservation Service
A 76.200	1942	Soil Conservation Service
A 79.200	1942-1943	Soil Conservation Service
A 80.2000	1943-1944	Soil Conservation Service
A 80.500	1944-1945	Soil Conservation Service
A 57	1945-	Soil Conservation Service

A 80.600

A 55	1933-1942	Agricultural Adjustment Administration
A 76.400	1942	Agricultural Adjustment Administration
	1942	Agricultural Adjustment Agency
A 79.400	1942-1943	Agricultural Adjustment Agency
A 80.2100	1943-1944	Agricultural Adjustment Agency
A 80.600	1944-1945	Agricultural Adjustment Agency
A 83	1945	Agricultural Adjustment Agency
A 82	1945-1953	Production and Marketing Administration
	1953-1961	Commodity Stabilization Service
	1961-	Agricultural Stabilization and Conservation Service

A 80.700

Y 3.R 31	1935-1937	Resettlement Administration
A 61	1937	Resettlement Administration
	1937-1942	Farm Security Administration
A 80.700	1942-1945	Farm Security Administration
A 61	1945-1946	Farm Security Administration
A 84	1946-	Farmers Home Administration

A 80.800

A 75	1942	Agricultural Marketing Administration
A 76.300	1942	Sugar Agency
A 78	1942-1943	Food Distribution Administration
A 80.100	1943-1944	Food Distribution Administration
	1944-1945	Distribution Office
A 80.800	1945	Marketing Services Office
A 81	1945	Marketing Services Office
A 82	1945-1953	Production and Marketing Administration
A 88	1953-1965	Agricultural Marketing Service
	1965-1972	Consumer and Marketing Service
	1972-	Agricultural Marketing Service

A 80.900

A 62	1938-1942	Federal Crop Insurance Corporation
A 76.100	1942	Federal Crop Insurance Corporation
A 79.300	1942-1943	Federal Crop Insurance Corporation
A 80.900	1943-1945	Federal Crop Insurance Corporation
A 82.200	1945-1947	Federal Crop Insurance Corporation
A 62	1947-	Federal Crop Insurance Corporation

A 80.2000

I 30	1933-1935	Soil Erosion Service
A 57	1935-1942	Soil Conservation Service
A 76.200	1942	Soil Conservation Service
A 79.200	1942-1943	Soil Conservation Service
A 80.2000	1943-1944	Soil Conservation Service
A 80.500	1944-1945	Soil Conservation Service
A 57	1945-	Soil Conservation Service

A 80.2100

A 55	1933-1942	Agricultural Adjustment Administration
A 76.400	1942	Agricultural Adjustment Administration
	1942	Agricultural Adjustment Agency
A 79.400	1942-1943	Agricultural Adjustment Agency
A 80.2100	1943-1944	Agricultural Adjustment Agency
A 80.600	1944-1945	Agricultural Adjustment Agency
A 83	1945	Agricultural Adjustment Agency
A 82	1945-1953	Production and Marketing Administration
	1953-1961	Commodity Stabilization Service
	1961-	Agricultural Stabilization and Conservation Service

A 81

A 75	1942	Agricultural Marketing Administration
A 78	1942-1943	Food Distribution Administration
A 80.100	1943-1944	Food Distribution Administration
	1944-1945	Distribution Office
A 80.800	1945	Marketing Services Office
A 81	1945	Marketing Services Office
A 82	1945-1953	Production and Marketing Administration
A 88	1953-1965	Agricultural Marketing Service
	1965-1972	Consumer and Marketing Service
	1972-	Agricultural Marketing Service

A 82

A 81	1945	Marketing Services Office
A 83	1945	Agricultural Adjustment Agency
A 82	1945-1953	Production and Marketing Administration
	1953-1961	Commodity Stabilization Service
A 88	1953-	Agricultural Marketing Service
A 90	1953-1961	Agricultural Conservation Program Service
A 82	1961-1994	Agricultural Stabilization and Conservation Service

A 82.100

A 82.100	1945-	Field Service Branch

A 82.200

A 62	1938-1942	Federal Crop Insurance Corporation
A 76.100	1942	Federal Crop Insurance Corporation
A 79.300	1942-1943	Federal Crop Insurance Corporation
A 80.900	1943-1945	Federal Crop Insurance Corporation
A 80.200	1945-1947	Federal Crop Insurance Corporation
A 62	1947-	Federal Crop Insurance Corporation

A 82.300

Y 3.C 73	1933-1939	Commodity Credit Corporation
A 71	1939-1943	Commodity Credit Corporation
A 80.400	1943-1945	Commodity Credit Corporation
A 82.300	1945-	Commodity Credit Corporation

A 83

A 55	1933-1942	Agricultural Adjustment Administration
A 76.400	1942	Agricultural Adjustment Administration
	1942	Agricultural Adjustment Agency
A 79.400	1942-1943	Agricultural Adjustment Agency
A 80.2100	1943-1944	Agricultural Adjustment Agency
A 80.600	1944-1945	Agricultural Adjustment Agency
A 83	1945	Agricultural Adjustment Agency
A 82	1945-1953	Production and Marketing Administration
	1953-1961	Commodity Stabilization Service
	1961-	Agricultural Stabilization and Conservation Service

A 84

Y 3.R 31	1935-1937	Resettlement Administration
A 61	1937	Resettlement Administration
	1937-1942	Farm Security Administration
A 80.700	1942-1945	Farm Security Administration
A 61	1945-1946	Farm Security Administration
A 84	1946-	Farmers Home Administration

A 85

A 41	1922-1936	Grain Futures Administration
A 59	1936-1942	Commodity Exchange Administration
A 75.200	1942-1947	Commodity Exchange Administration
A 85	1947-1974	Commodity Exchange Authority
Y 3.C 73/5	1974-	Commodity Futures Trading Commission

A 86

A 86	1948	Food and Feed Conservation Office

A 87

A 87	1947-1949	Administrator of the Research and Marketing Act Office

A 88

A 66	1939-1942	Agricultural Marketing Service
A 75	1942	Agricultural Marketing Administration
A 78	1942-1943	Food Distribution Administration
A 80.100	1943-1944	Food Distribution Administration
	1944-1945	Distribution Office
A 80.800	1945	Marketing Services Office
A 81	1945	Marketing Services Office
A 82	1945-1953	Production and Marketing Administration
A 88	1953-1965	Agricultural Marketing Service
	1965-1972	Consumer and Marketing Service
	1972-	Agricultural Marketing Service

A 89

A 89	1953-1978	Farmer Cooperative Service
A 105	1978-1980	Economics, Statistics, and Cooperatives Service
A 109	1980-	Agricultural Cooperative Service

A 90

A 82.37	1945-1953	Agricultural Conservation Program Branch
A 90	1953-1961	Agricultural Conservation Program Service
A 82	1961-	Agricultural Stabilization and Conservation Service

A 91

A 91	1960-	Administrative Management Office

A 92

A 92	1961-1978	Statistical Reporting Service
A 105	1978-1980	Economics, Statistics, and Cooperatives Service
	1980-1981	Economics and Statistics Service
A 92	1981-1985	Statistical Reporting Service
	1985-	National Agricultural Statistics Service

A 93

A 93	1961-1978	Economic Research Service
A 105	1978-1980	Economics, Statistics, and Cooperatives Service
	1980-1981	Economics and Statistics Service
A 93	1981-	Economic Research Service

A 94

A 94	1961-1978	Cooperative State Research Service
A 106	1978-1981	Science and Education Administration
A 94	1981-1995	Cooperative State Research Service
	1995-	Cooperative State Research, Education and Expansion Service

A 95

A 95	1963-1969	International Agricultural Development Service
A 67	1969	[functions transferred to] Foreign Agricultural Service
A 100	1969-1972	[functions transferred to] Foreign Economic Development Service

A 96

A 39	1921-1927	Packers and Stockyards Administration
A 4	1927-1942	Animal Industry Bureau
A 77.200	1942-1953	Animal Industry Bureau
	1953-1967	[Publications Relating to the Care of Animals and Poultry]
A 96	1967-1978	Packers and Stockyards Administration
A 88	1978-	Agricultural Marketing Service
A 113	1994-	The Grain Inspection, Packers & Stockyards Administration

A 97

A 97	1965-1970	Rural Community Development Service

A 98

A 98	1969-	Food and Nutrition Service

A 99

A 99	1969-1974	Export Marketing Service
A 67	1974-	[functions transferred to] Foreign Agricultural Service

A 100

A 100	1969-1972	Foreign Economic Development Service
A 93	1972-	[functions transferred to] Economic Research Service

A 101

A 101	1971-1972	Animal and Plant Health Service
	1972-	Animal and Plant Health Inspection Service

A 102

A 102	1973-1978	Rural Development Service
A 84	1978-1981	Rural Development Coordination and Planning Office
A 102	1981-1986	Rural Development Policy Office

A 103

A 103	1977-1981	Food Safety and Quality Service
A 110	1981-	Food Safety and Inspection Service

A 104

A 104	1976-1994	Federal Grain Inspection Service
A 113	1994-	The Grain Inspection, Packers & Stockyards Administration

A 105

A 89	1953-1978	Farmer Cooperative Service
A 92	1961-1978	Statistical Reporting Service
A 93	1961-1978	Economic Research Service
A 105	1978-1980	Economics, Statistics, and Cooperatives Service
	1980-1981	Economics and Statistics Service
A 109	1980	[certain functions transferred to Agricultural Cooperative Service]
		[functions returned to reestablished agencies:-
A 92	1981-1985	Statistical Reporting Service
	1985-	National Agricultural Statistics Service
A 93	1981-	Economic Research Service]

A 106

A 43	1970-1978	Extension Service
A 77	1953-1978	Agricultural Research Service
A 94	1961-1978	Cooperative State Research Service
A 106	1978-1981	Science and Education Administration
	1981	[functions transferred to the reestablished agencies:-
A 43	1981-	Extension Service
A 77	1981-	Agricultural Research Service
A 94	1981-	Cooperative State Research Service]

A 106.100

A 17	1862-1962	Library
	1962-1978	National Agricultural Library
A 106.100	1978-1981	Technical Information Systems
A 17	1981-	National Agricultural Library

A 107

A 21	1890-1925	Information Division
	1925-1974	Information Office
	1974-1978	Communications Office
A 107	1978-1987	Governmental and Public Affairs Office
A 21	1987-	Information Office
		Office of Congressional Relations

A 108

A 108	1980-	Transportation Office

A 109

A 89	1953-1978	Farmer Cooperative Service
A 105	1978-1980	Economics, Statistics, and Cooperatives Service
A 109	1980-19xx	Agricultural Cooperative Service
		Rural Business-Cooperative Service

A 110

A 103	1977-1981	Food Safety and Quality Service
A 110	1981-	Food Safety and Inspection Service

A 111

A 111	1981-	Human Nutrition Information Service

A 112

A 112	1994-1996	Consolidated Farm Service Agency
	1996-	Farm Service Agency

A 113

A 104	1976-1994	Federal Grain Inspection Service
A 113	1994-	The Grain Inspection, Packers & Stockyard s Administration

A 114

A 114	199x-	Rural Development

A 115

A 115	199x-	Rural Housing Service

AA 1

AA 1	1971-1994	Action
Y 3.N 21/29	1994-	Corporation for National and Community Service

AA 2

AA 2	1971-	Older Americans Volunteer Programs

AA 3

AA 3	1971-1980	National Student Volunteer Program
	1980-	National Center for Service Learning

AA 4

S 19	1961-1971	Peace Corps
AA 4	1971-1982	Peace Corps
PE 1	1982-	Peace Corps

AC 1

AC 1	1961-1998	Arms Control and Disarmament Agency

AE 1

AE 1	1934-1949	National Archives Establishment
GS 4	1949-1985	National Archives and Records Service
AE 1.100	1985-	National Archives and Records Administration

AE 1.100

AE 1	1934-1949	National Archives Establishment
GS 4	1949-1985	National Archives and Records Service
AE 1.100	1985-	National Archives and Records Administration

AE 2

AE 2	1934-1949	Federal Register Division
GS 4.100	1949-1985	Federal Register Division
AE 2.100	1985-	Federal Register Office

AE 2.100

AE 2	1934-1949	Federal Register Division
GS 4.100	1949-1985	Federal Register Division
AE 2.100	1985-	Federal Register Office

AR 1

AR 1	1890-1907	American Republics Bureau
PA 1	1910-1948	Pan American Union

B 1

B 1		Broadcasting Board of Governors

B 2

B 2	1994-	Intenational Broadcasting Bureau

C 1

C 1	1903-1913	Commerce and Labor Department, Office of Secretary
L 1	1913-	Labor Department, Office of Secretary
C 1	1913-	Commerce Department, Office of Secretary

C 1.56

C 1.56	1969-1979	Minority Business Enterprise Office
	1979-1991	Minority Business Development Agency
C 1.100	1991-	Minority Business Development Agency

C 1.100

C 1.56	1969-1979	Minority Business Enterprise Office
	1979-1991	Minority Business Development Agency
C 1.100	1991-	Minority Business Development Agency

C 1.200

C 1.200		TechnologyAdministration

C 2

C 2	1903-1909	Alaskan Fisheries Division

C 3

I 14	1902-1903	Census Office
C 3	1903-1972	Census Bureau
C 56.200	1972-1975	Census Bureau
C 3	1975-	Census Bureau

C 4

T 11	1816-1834	Survey of the Coast
	1836-1878	Coast Survey
	1878-1903	Coast and Geodetic Survey
C 4	1903-1965	Coast and Geodetic Survey
C 52	1965-1970	Environmental Science Service Administration
C 55.400	1970-1984	National Ocean Survey
	1984-	National Ocean Service

C 5

C 5	1903-1914	Corporations Bureau
FT 1	1914-	Federal Trade Commission

C 6

FC 1	1871-1880	Fish Commission
	1880-1903	Fish and Fisheries Commission
C 6	1903-1939	Fisheries Bureau
I 45	1939-1940	Fisheries Bureau
I 49	1940-	Fish and Wildlife Service

C 7

T 21	1891-1903	Immigration Bureau
C 7	1903-1906	Immigration Bureau
	1906-1913	Immigration and Naturalization Bureau
L 3	1913-1933	Immigration Bureau
L 6	1913-1933	Naturalization Bureau
L 15	1933-1940	Immigration and Naturalization Service
J 21	1940-	Immigration and Naturalization Service

C 8

La 1	1888-1903	Labor Bureau
C 8	1903-1913	Labor Bureau
L 2	1913-	Labor Statistics Bureau

C 9

T 25	1852-1903	Lighthouse Board
C 9	1903-1939	Lighthouses Bureau
T 47	1939-1966	[functions transferred to] Coast Guard

C 10

C 10	1903-1912	Manufacturers Bureau
C 18	1912-1953	Foreign and Domestic Commerce Bureau
C 41	1953-1970	Business and Defense Services Administration
C 42	1953-1961	Foreign Commerce Bureau
C 48	1961-1963	International Business Operation Bureau
C 49	1961-1963	International Programs Bureau
C 42	1963-1972	International Commerce Bureau
C 57.100	1972-1977	International Commerce Bureau
	1977-	Export Development Bureau

C 11

T 30	1884-1903	Navigation Bureau
C 11	1903-1932	Navigation Bureau
C 25	1932-1936	Navigation and Steamboat Inspection Bureau
	1936-1942	Marine Inspection and Navigation Bureau
N 24	1942-1946	[functions transferred to] Coast Guard
T 17	1942-1973	[functions transferred to] Customs Bureau

C 12

T 30	1884-1903	[part of] Navigation Bureau
C 12	1903-1938	Shipping Commissioners

C 13

T 11	1882-1901	[an office in] Coast and Geodetic Survey
T 41	1901-1903	National Bureau of Standards
C 13	1903-1934	Standards Bureau
	1934-1989	National Bureau of Standards
	1989-	National Institute of Standards and Technology

C 14

S 4	1874-1897	Statistics Bureau
	1897-1903	Foreign Commerce Bureau
T 37	1886-1903	Statistics Bureau
C 14	1903-1912	Statistics Bureau
C 18	1912-1953	Foreign and Domestic Commerce Bureau
C 41	1953-1970	Business and Defense Services Administration
C 42	1953-1963	Foreign Commerce Bureau
C 48	1961-1963	International Business Operation Bureau
C 49	1961-1963	International Programs Bureau
C 42	1963-1972	International Commerce Bureau
C 57.100	1972-1977	International Commerce Bureau
	1977-	Export Development Bureau

C 15

T 38	1853-1903	Steamboat Inspection Service
C 15	1903-1932	Steamboat Inspection Service
C 25	1932-1936	Navigation and Steamboat Inspection Bureau
	1936-1942	Marine Inspection and Navigation Bureau
N 24	1942-1946	[functions transferred to] Coast Guard
T 17	1942-1973	[functions transferred to] Customs Bureau

C 16

C 16		Printing and Publications Division

C 17

C 17	1910-1925	Appointments Division

C 18

C 10	1903-1912	Manufacturers Bureau
C 14	1903-1912	Statistics Bureau
C 18	1912-1953	Foreign and Domestic Commerce Bureau
C 41	1953-1970	Business and Defense Services Administration
C 42	1953-1961	Foreign Commerce Bureau
C 48	1961-1963	International Business Operation Bureau
C 49	1961-1963	International Programs Bureau
C 42	1963-1972	International Commerce Bureau
C 57.100	1972-1977	International Commerce Bureau
	1977-	Export Development Bureau

C 19

C 19	1912-1913	Children's Bureau
L 5	1913-1946	Children's Bureau
FS 3.200	1947-1963	Children's Bureau
FS 14.100	1963-1967	Children's Bureau
FS 17.200	1967-1969	Children's Bureau
HE 21.100	1970-1975	Children's Bureau
HE 1.450	1975-1977	Children's Bureau
HE 23.1200	1977-	Children's Bureau

C 20

C 20	1919	Waste Reclamation Service

C 21

I 23	1849-1925	Patent Office
C 21	1925-1975	Patent Office
	1975-	Patent and Trademark Office

C 22

I 28	1910-1925	Mines Bureau
C 22	1925-1934	Mines Bureau
I 28	1934-	Mines Bureau

C 23

C 23	1926-1934	Aeronautics Branch
	1934-1938	Air Commerce Bureau
CA 1	1938-1940	Civil Aeronautics Authority
C 31	1940-1959	Civil Aeronautics Authority

C 24

C 11	1910-1927	[part of] Navigation Bureau
C 24	1927-1932	Radio Division
RC 1	1932-1934	[functions transferred to] Federal Radio Commission

C 25

C 11	1903-1932	Navigation Bureau
C 15	1903-1932	Steamboat Inspection Service
C 25	1932-1936	Navigation and Steamboat Inspection Bureau
	1936-1942	Marine Inspection and Navigation Bureau
N 24	1942-1946	[functions transferred to] Coast Guard
T 17	1942-1973	[functions transferred to] Customs Bureau

C 26

C 26	1931-1934	Federal Employment Stabilization Board
	1934-1939	Federal Employment Stabilization Office
Pr 32.300	1939-1943	National Resources Planning Board

C 27

SB 1	1917-1933	Shipping Board
SB 2	1917-1927	Shipping Board Emergency Fleet Corporation
	1927-1933	Shipping Board Merchant Fleet Corporation
C 27	1933-1936	Shipping Board Bureau
MC 1	1936-1950	United States Maritime Commission
C 39.100	1950-1961	Federal Maritime Board
C 39.200	1950-1981	Maritime Administration
TD 11	1981-	Maritime Administration

C 28

C 28	1933-1935	Business Advisory and Planning Council
	1935-1953	Business Advisory Council

C 29

W 103	1924-1939	Inland Waterways Corporation
C 29	1939-1953	Inland Waterways Corporation

C 30

A 29	1890-1940	Weather Bureau
C 30	1940-1965	Weather Bureau
C 52	1965-1970	Environmental Science Services Administration
C 55.100	1970-	National Weather Service

C 31

C 23	1926-1934	Aeronautics Branch
	1934-1938	Air Commerce Bureau
CA 1	1938-1940	Civil Aeronautics Authority
C 31	1940-1959	Civil Aeronautics Authority

C 31.100

C 31.100	1940-1958	Civil Aeronautics Administration
FAA 1	1958-1967	Federal Aviation Agency
TD 4	1967-	Federal Aviation Administration

C 31.200

C 31.200	1940-1978	Civil Aeronautics Board
CAB 1	1978-1985	Civil Aeronautics Board
		[functions transferred to
P 1	1985-	United States Postal Service
TD 1	1985-	Transportation Department]

C 32

C 32	1940-1963	National Inventors Council

C 33

Y 3.R 24	1932-1939	Reconstruction Finance Corporation
FL 5	1939-1942	Reconstruction Finance Corporation
C 33	1942-1945	Reconstruction Finance Corporation
FL 5	1945-1947	Reconstruction Finance Corporation
Y 3.R 24	1947-1954	Reconstruction Finance Corporation

C 34

C 34	1945	International Trade Operation Office
C 18	1945-1953	[became part of] Foreign and Domestic Commerce Bureau

C 35

Y 3.P 96/6	1945	Publication Board
C 35	1945	Publication Board Office
	1945	Declassification and Technical Service Office
	1945-1953	Technical Services Office
C 41	1953-1970	Business and Defense Services Administration
	1970-1972	Domestic Commerce Bureau
C 57.300	1972-1974	Competitive Assessment and Business Policy Bureau
C 57.500	1974-1980	Domestic Commerce Bureau
C 62	1980-1984	Industrial Economics Bureau
C 61	1984-	[functions transferred to] International Trade Administration

C 36

C 36	1945-1947	Domestic Commerce Office
C 18	1947-1953	[functions transferred to] Foreign and Domestic Commerce Bureau

C 37

A 22	1892-1898	Road Inquiry Office
	1898-1905	Public Road Inquiry Office
	1905-1915	Public Roads Office
	1915-1918	Public Roads and Rural Engineering Office
	1918-1939	Public Roads Bureau
FW 2	1939-1949	Public Roads Administration
GS 3	1949	Public Roads Bureau
C 37	1949-1966	Public Roads Bureau
TD 2.100	1966-1969	Public Roads Bureau
TD 2	1969-	[functions transferred to] Federal Highway Administration

C 38

C 38	1948	Industry Cooperation Office

C 39

C 39		Maritime Administration [not used]

C 39.100

SB 1	1917-1933	Shipping Board
C 27	1933-1936	Shipping Board Bureau
MC 1	1936-1950	United States Maritime Commission
C 39.100	1950-1961	Federal Maritime Board
C 39.200	1961-1981	[functions transferred to] Maritime Administration

C 39.200

SB 1	1917-1933	Shipping Board
C 27	1933-1936	Shipping Board Bureau
MC 1	1936-1950	United States Maritime Commission
C 39.200	1950-1981	Maritime Administration
TD 11	1981-	Maritime Administration

C 40

C 40	1950-1953	National Production Authority
C 41	1953-1970	Business and Defense Services Administration
	1970-1972	Domestic Commerce Bureau
C 57.300	1972-1974	Competitive Assessment and Business Policy Bureau
C 57.500	1974-1980	Domestic Commerce Bureau
C 62	1980-1984	Industrial Economics Bureau
C 61	1984-	[functions transferred to] International Trade Administration

C 41

C 18	1912-1953	Foreign and Domestic Commerce Bureau
C 35	1945-1953	Technical Services Office
C 40	1950-1953	National Production Authority
C 41	1953-1970	Business and Defense Services Administration
	1970-1972	Domestic Commerce Bureau
C 57.300	1972-1974	Competitive Assessment and Business Policy Bureau
C 57.500	1974-1980	Domestic Commerce Bureau
C 62	1980-1984	Industrial Economics Bureau
C 61	1984-	[functions transferred to] International Trade Administration

C 42

C 18	1912-1953	Foreign and Domestic Commerce Bureau
C 42	1953-1961	Foreign Commerce Bureau
C 48	1961-1963	International Business Operation Bureau
C 49	1961-1963	International Programs Bureau
C 42	1963-1972	International Commerce Bureau
C 57.100	1972-1977	International Commerce Bureau
	1977-	Export Development Bureau

C 43

C 43	1953-1972	Business Economics Office
C 56.100	1972-1975	Economic Analysis Bureau
C 59	1975-	Economic Analysis Bureau

C 44

C 44	1955-1961	International Trade Fairs Office
C 48.100	1961-1963	International Trade Fairs Office

C 45

C 45	1956-1958	Area Development Office
C 41	1958-1970	[functions transferred to] Business and Defense Services Administration

C 46

C 46	1961-1965	Area Redevelopment Administration
	1965-	Economic Development Administration

C 47

C 47	1961-1981	United States Travel Service
	1981-1996	United States Travel and Tourism Administration

C 48

C 18	1912-1953	Foreign and Domestic Commerce Bureau
C 42	1953-1961	Foreign Commerce
C 48	1961-1963	International Business Operation Bureau
C 49	1961-1963	International Programs Bureau
C 42	1963-1972	International Commerce Bureau
C 57.100	1972-1977	International Commerce Bureau
	1977-	Export Development Bureau

C 48.100

C 44	1955-1961	International Trade Fairs Office
C 48.100	1961-1963	International Trade Fairs Office

C 48.200

C 48.200	1961-1963	Trade Promotion Office

C 48.300

C 48.300	1963-1970	Commercial Services Office

C 48.400

C 48.400		International Investment Office

C 49

C 18	1912-1953	Foreign and Domestic Commerce Bureau
C 42	1953-1961	Foreign Commerce
C 48	1961-1963	International Business Operation Bureau
C 49	1961-1963	International Programs Bureau
C 42	1963-1972	International Commerce Bureau
C 57.100	1972-1977	International Commerce Bureau
	1977-	Export Development Bureau

C 49.100

C 49.100	1961-1963	Regional Economics Office

C 49.200

C 49.200	1961-1963	Export Control Office

C 49.300

C 49.300	1961-1963	International Economics Programs Office

C 50

C 50	1962-1966	Community Relations Service
J 23	1966-	Community Relations Service

C 51

C 41	1953-1965	[part of] Business and Defense Services Administration
C 51	1965-1970	Clearinghouse for Federal Scientific and Technical Information
	1970-	National Technical Information Service

C 52

C 4	1903-1965	Coast and Geodetic Survey
C 30	1940-1945	Weather Bureau
C 52	1965-1970	Environmental Science Service Administration
C 55	1970-	National Oceanic and Atmospheric Administration
C 55.100	1970-	National Weather Service
C 55.400	1970-1984	National Ocean Survey
	1984-	National Ocean Service

C 53

C 53	1966	Regional Economic Development Office
C 46	1966-	[functions transferred to] Economic Development Administration

C 54

C 54	1968-1974	Foreign Direct Investments Office

C 55

C 52	1965-1970	Environmental Science Service Administration
C 55	1970-	National Oceanic and Atmospheric Administration

C 55.100

A 29	1890-1940	Weather Bureau
C 30	1940-1965	Weather Bureau
C 52	1965-1970	Environmental Science Services Administration
C 55.100	1970-	National Weather Service

C 55.200

C 55.200	1970-19xx	Environmental Data Service
	19xx-	National Environmental Satellite, Data, and Information Service

C 55.280

C 55.280	1970-	National Climatic Center

C 55.290

C 55.290	1970-	National Oceanographic Data Center

C 55.300

C 55.300	1970-	National Marine Fisheries Service

C 55.400

T 11	1816-1834	Survey of the Coast
	1836-1878	Coast Survey
	1878-1903	Coast and Geodetic Survey
C 4	1903-1965	Coast and Geodetic Survey
C 52	1965-1970	Environmental Science Service Administration
C 55.400	1970-1984	National Ocean Survey
	1984-	National Ocean Service

C 55.500

C 55.500	1971-19xx	National Environmental Satellite Service
	19xx-	National Earth Satellite Service

C 55.600

C 55.600	1971-	Environmental Research Laboratories

C 55.690

C 55.690	1972-	National Earthquake Information Center

C 55.700

C 55.700	199x-	Oceanic and Atmospheric Research Office

C 56

C 56	1972-1975	Social and Economic Statistics Administration

C 56.100

C 43	1953-1972	Business Economics Office
C 56.100	1972-1975	Economic Analysis Bureau
C 59	1975-	Economic Analysis Bureau

C 56.200

I 14	1902-1903	Census Office
C 3	1903-1972	Census Bureau
C 56.200	1972-1975	Census Bureau
C 3	1975-	Census Bureau

C 57

C 57	1972-1977	Domestic and International Business Administration
	1977-1980	Industry and Trade Administration
C 61	1980-	International Trade Administration

C 57.100

C 18	1912-1953	Foreign and Domestic Commerce Bureau
C 42	1953-1961	Foreign Commerce Bureau
C 48	1961-1963	International Business Operation Bureau
C 49	1961-1963	International Programs Bureau
C 42	1963-1972	International Commerce Bureau
C 57.100	1972-1977	International Commerce Bureau
	1977-	Export Development Bureau

C 57.200

C 57.200	1972-	Resources and Trade Assistance Bureau

C 57.300

C 18	1912-1953	Foreign and Domestic Commerce Bureau
C 35	1945-1953	Technical Services Office
C 40	1950-1953	National Production Authority
C 41	1953-1970	Business and Defense Services Administration
	1970-1972	Domestic Commerce Bureau
C 57.300	1972-1974	Competitive Assessment and Business Policy Bureau
C 57.500	1974-1980	Domestic Commerce Bureau
C 62	1980-1984	Industrial Economics Bureau
C 61	1984-	[functions transferred to] International Trade Administration

C 57.400

C 57.400	1972-	East-West Trade Bureau

C 57.500

C 18	1912-1953	Foreign and Domestic Commerce Bureau
C 35	1945-1953	Technical Services Office
C 40	1950-1953	National Production Authority
C 41	1953-1970	Business and Defense Services Administration
	1970-1972	Domestic Commerce Bureau
C 57.300	1972-1974	Competitive Assessment and Business Policy Bureau
C 57.500	1974-1980	Domestic Commerce Bureau
C 62	1980-1984	Industrial Economics Bureau
C 61	1984-	[functions transferred to] International Trade Administration

C 58

C 58	1974-1978	National Fire Prevention and Control Administration
	1978-1979	United States Fire Administration
FEM 1.100	1979-	United States Fire Administration

C 59

C 43	1953-1972	Business Economics Office
C 56.100	1972-1975	Economic Analysis Bureau
C 59	1975-	Economic Analysis Bureau

C 60

C 60	1978-	National Telecommunications and Information Administration

C 61

C 57	1972-1977	Domestic and International Business Administration
	1977-1980	Industry and Trade Administration
C 61	1980-	International Trade Administration

C 62

C 18	1912-1953	Foreign and Domestic Commerce Bureau
C 35	1945-1953	Technical Services Office
C 40	1950-1953	National Production Authority
C 41	1953-1970	Business and Defense Services Administration
	1970-1972	Domestic Commerce Bureau
C 57.300	1972-1974	Competitive Assessment and Business Policy Bureau
C 57.500	1974-1980	Domestic Commerce Bureau
C 62	1980-1984	Industrial Economics Bureau
C 61	1984-	[functions transferred to] International Trade Administration

C 63

C 63	1997-19xx	Export Administration Bureau
	20xx-	Industry and Security Bureau

CA 1

C 23	1926-1934	Aeronautics Branch
	1934-1938	Air Commerce Bureau
CA 1	1938-1940	Civil Aeronautics Authority
C 31	1940-1959	Civil Aeronautics Authority

CAB 1

C 31.200	1940-1978	Civil Aeronautics Board
CAB 1	1978-1985	Civil Aeronautics Board
		[functions transferred to
P 1	1985-	United States Postal Service
TD 1	1985-	Transportation Department]

CC 1

RC 1	1927-1934	Federal Radio Commission
CC 1	1934-	Federal Communications Commission

CC 2

CC 2	1934-1937	Broadcast Division
CC 1	1937-	[functions transferred to] Federal Communications Commission

CC 3

CC 3	1934-1937	Telegraph Division
CC 1	1937-	[functions transferred to] Federal Communications Commission

CC 4

CC 4	1934-1937	Telephone Division
CC 1	1937-	[functions transferred to] Federal Communications Commission

CR 1

CR 1	1957-1994	Civil Rights Commission
	1994	United States Civil Rights Commission

CS 1

CS 1	1883-1978	Civil Service Commission
MS 1	1978-	Merit Systems Protection Board
PM 1	1978-	Personal Management Office

CSA 1

PrEx 10	1964-1975	Economic Opportunity Office
CSA 1	1975-1981	Community Services Administration
HE	1981-	Community Services Office

CZ 1

W 79	1912-1945	Canal Zone
M 115	1947-1949	Panama Canal
D 113	1949-1950	Panama Canal
PaC 1	1950-1951	Panama Canal
CZ 1	1950-1979	Panama Canal Zone Company
Y 3.P 19/2	1979-	Panama Canal Commission

D 1

M 1	1947-1949	National Military Establishment
D 1	1949-	Defense Department, Office of Secretary

D 2

W 109.200	1943-1944	Morale Services Division
W 111	1944-1947	Information and Education Division
M 104	1947-1949	Troop Information and Education Division
D 2	1949-1952	Information and Education Division
	1952-1968	Armed Forces Information and Education Office
	1968-1971	Armed Forces Information Service
	1971-1977	Information for the Armed Forces Office
	1977-	American Forces Information Services

D 3

M 5	1947-1949	Munitions Board
D 3	1949-1953	Munitions Board
	1953-	[Publications Relating to Industrial Mobilization and Security]

D 4

M 6	1947-1949	Research and Development Board
D 4	1949-1953	Research and Development Board
	1953-	[Publications Relating to Research and Development]

D 5

M 2	1947-1949	Joint Chiefs of Staff
D 5	1949-	Joint Chiefs of Staff

D 5.100

D 5.100	1960-	Defense Communications Agency

D 5.200

D 5.200	1961-	Defense Intelligence Agency

D 5.300

D 5.300	1972-	Defense Mapping Agency

D 5.400

D 5.400	1977-	National Defense University

D 6

D 6	1949-1962	Public Information Office
	1962-	Public Affairs Office

D 7

D 7	1952-1953	Defense Supply Management Agency
	1953-1977	Defense Supply Agency
	1977-	Defense Logistics Agency

D 8

D 104	1950-1952	[part of] Army Medical Department
D 8	1952-1956	Armed Forces Medical Library
FS 2.200	1956-1969	National Library of Medicine
HE 20.3600	1970-	National Library of Medicine

D 9

D 9	1949-	North Atlantic Treaty Organization

D 10

D 10	1951-1963	Armed Services Technical Information Agency
	1963-1969	Defense Documentation Center for Scientific and Technical Information
	1969-198x	Defense Documentation Center
	198x-	Defense Technical Information Center

D 11

D 11	1949-1959	Armed Services Petroleum Purchasing Agency

D 12

W 70	1908-1916	Militia Affairs Division
	1916-1933	Militia Bureau
	1933-1947	National Guard Bureau
M 114	1947-1949	National Guard Bureau
D 112	1949-1958	National Guard Bureau
D 12	1958-	National Guard Bureau

D 13

Pr 33.800	1950-1951	Federal Civil Defense Administration
FCD 1	1951-1958	Federal Civil Defense Administration
Pr 34.700	1958-1961	Defense and Civilian Mobilization Office
PrEx 4	1961	Civil and Defense Mobilization Office
D 13	1961-1964	Civil Defense Office
D 119	1964-1972	Civil Defense Office
D 14	1972-1971	Defense Civil Preparedness Agency
FEM 1	1979-	Federal Emergency Management Agency

D 14

Pr 33.800	1950-1951	Federal Civil Defense Administration
FCD 1	1951-1958	Federal Civil Defense Administration
Pr 34.700	1958-1961	Defense and Civilian Mobilization Office
PrEx 4	1961	Civil and Defense Mobilization Office
D 13	1961-1964	Civil Defense Office
D 119	1964-1972	Civil Defense Office
D 14	1972-1979	Defense Civil Preparedness Agency
FEM 1	1979-	Federal Emergency Management Agency

D 15

	1942-1946	Manhatten Project
	1946-1959	Armed Forces Special Weapons Project
	1959-1971	Defense Atomic Support Agency
D 15	1971-1995	Defense Nuclear Agency
	1995-1998	Defense Special Weapons Agency
	1998 -	Defense Threat Reduction Agency

D 101

W 1	1789-1947	War Department, Office of Secretary
M 101	1947-1949	Army Department, Office of Secretary
D 101	1949-	Army Department, Office of Secretary

D 102

W 3	1913-1947	Adjutant General's Office
M 108	1947-1949	Adjutant General's Office
D 102	1949-	Adjutant General's Office

D 103

W 7	1802-1947	Engineer Department
M 110	1947-1949	Engineer Department
D 103	1949-	Engineer Corps

D 103.100

W 7.16	1802-1947	Engineer School
M 110.400	1947-1947	Engineer School
D 103.100	1949-	Engineer School

D 103.200

W 33	1841-1947	Northern and Northwestern Lakes Survey
M 110.100	1947-1949	Lake Survey Office
D 103.200	1949-	Lake Survey Office

D 103.300

W 31	1879-1947	Mississippi River Commission
M 110.300	1947-1949	Mississippi River Commission
D 103.300	1949-	Mississippi River Commission

D 104

W 44	1818-1947	Medical Department
M 102	1947-1949	Army Medical Department
D 104	1949-1950	Army Medical Service
	1950-	Army Medical Department

D 105

W 34	1812-1947	Ordnance Department
M 111	1947-1949	Ordnance Department
D 105	1949-1968	Ordnance Corps
	1968-	[Publications Relating to Ordnance]

D 106

W 39	1812-1912	Quartermaster's Department
W 77	1912-1947	Quartermaster Corps
M 112	1947-1949	Quartermaster General of the Army
D 106	1949-	Quartermaster Corps

D 107

W 109.200	1943-1944	Morale Services Division
W 111	1944-1947	Information and Education Division
M 104	1947-1949	Troop Information and Education Division
D 107	1949-1954	Troop Information and Education Division
D 2	1949-1952	Information and Education Division
	1952-1968	Armed Forces Information and Education Office
	1968-1971	Armed Forces Information Service
	1971-1977	Information for the Armed Forces Office
	1977-	American Forces Information Service

D 108

W 10	1849-1864	Judge Advocate General's Office
	1864-1884	Military Justice Office
	1884-1947	Judge Advocate General's Department
M 107	1947-1949	Judge Advocate General's Department
D 108	1949-	Judge Advocate General's Office

D 108.100

D 108.100	1978-	Legal Services Agency

D 109

W 12	1802-1947	Military Academy
M 109	1947-1949	Military Academy
D 109	1949-	Military Academy

D 110

W 28	1881-1947	General Service Schools
M 119	1947-1949	Command and General Staff College
D 110	1949-	Command and General Staff College

D 111

W 42	1869-1947	Signal Office
D 111	1949-1968	Signal Corps
	1968-19xx	[Publications Relating to Communications]
	19xx-	Army Electronics Research and Development Command

D 112

W 70	1908-1916	Militia Affairs Division
	1916-1933	Militia Bureau
	1933-1947	National Guard Bureau
M 114	1947-1949	National Guard Bureau
D 112	1949-1958	National Guard Bureau
D 12	1958-	National Guard Bureau

D 113

W 79	1912-1945	Canal Zone
M 115	1947-1949	Panama Canal
D 113	1949-1950	Panama Canal
PaC 1	1950-1951	Panama Canal
CZ 1	1950-1979	Panama Canal Zone Company
Y 3.P 19/2	1979-	Panama Canal Commission

D 114

W 110	1946-1947	Historical Division
M 103	1947-1949	Historical Division
D 114	1949-1950	Historical Division
	1950-1974	Chief of Military History Office
	1974-	Military History Center

D 115

D 115		Public Information Division [class not used]

D 116

W 91	1918-1946	Chemical War service
	1946-1947	Chemical Corps
D 116	1949-	Chemical Corps

D 117

W 109.300	1944-1947	Chief of Transportation Office
D 117	1949-1968	Transportation Corps
	1968-19xx	[Publications Relating to Transportation]
	19xx-	U.S. Army Air Mobility Research and Development Command

D 118

D 118	1949-	Personnel Operations Office

D 119

Pr 33.800	1950-1951	Federal Civil Defense Administration
FCD 1	1951-1958	Federal Civil Defense Administration
Pr 34.700	1958-1961	Defense and Civilian Mobilization Office
PrEx 4	1961	Civil and Defense Mobilization Office
D 13	1961-1964	Civil Defense Office
D 119	1964-1972	Civil Defense Office
D 14	1972-1979	Defense Civil Preparedness Agency
FEM 1	1979-	Federal Emergency Management Agency

D 120

W 37	1863-1866	Provost Marshall General
D 120	1969-	Provost Marshall General

D 201

N 1	1789-1947	Navy Department, Office of Secretary
M 201	1947-1949	Navy Department, Office of Secretary
D 201	1949-	Navy Department, Office of Secretary

D 202

N 28	1921-1947	Aeronautics Bureau
M 208	1947-1949	Aeronautics Bureau
D 202	1949-1959	Aeronautics Bureau
D 217	1959-1966	Naval Weapons Bureau
D 202	1966-	Naval Air Systems Command

D 203

N 18	1842-1866	Ordnance and Hydrography Bureau
N 6	1866-1947	Hydrographic Office
M 202	1947-1949	Hydrographic Office
D 203	1949-1962	Hydrographic Office
	1962-	Naval Oceanographic Office

D 204

M 204	1947-1949	Industrial Relations Office
D 204	1949-1966	Industrial Relations Office
	1966-	Civilian Manpower Management Office

D 205

N 7	1880-1947	Judge Advocate General
M 214	1947-1949	Judge Advocate General
D 205	1949-	Judge Advocate General

D 206

N 10	1842-1947	Medicine and Surgery Bureau
M 203	1947-1949	Medicine and Surgery Bureau
D 206	1949-	Medicine and Surgery Bureau

D 207

N 27	1915-1947	Naval Operations Office
M 207	1947-1949	Naval Operations Office
D 207	1949-	Naval Operations Office

D 207.100

| **D 207.100** | 1971- | Naval Technical Training Command |

D 207.200

| **D 207.200** | 1972-19xx | Naval Training Command |
| | 19xx- | Naval Education and Training Command |

D 207.300

| **D 207.300** | 1978- | Chief of Naval Reserve |

D 207.400

| **D 207.400** | 199x- | Naval Doctrine Command |

D 208

N 17	1862-1942	Navigation Bureau
	1942-1947	Naval Personnel Bureau
M 206	1947-1949	Naval Personnel Bureau
D 208	1949-1972	Naval Personnel Bureau
	1972-19xx	Naval Training Support Command
	19xx-	Naval Military Personnel Command

D 208.100

N 12	1845-1947	Naval Academy
M 206.100	1947-1949	Naval Academy
D 208.100	1949-	Naval Academy

D 208.200

N 15	1884-1947	Naval War College
M 206.200	1947-1949	Naval War College
D 208.200	1949-	Naval War College

D 209

N 21	1842-1862	Navy Yards and Docks Bureau
	1862-1947	Yards and Docks Bureau
M 205	1947-1949	Yards and Docks Bureau
D 209	1949-1966	Yards and Docks Bureau
	1966-	Naval Facilities Engineering Command

D 210

N 32	1946-1947	Naval Research Office
M 216	1947-1949	Naval Research Office
D 210	1949-	Naval Research Office

D 210.100

| **D 210.100** | | Naval Ocean Research and Development Activity |

D 211

N 4	1862-1940	Construction and Repair Bureau
N 19	1920-1940	Engineering Bureau
N 29	1940-1947	Ships Bureau
M 210	1947-1949	Ships Bureau
D 211	1949-1966	Ships Bureau
	1966-19xx	Naval Ship Systems Command
	19xx-	Naval Sea Systems Command

D 212

N 20	1842-1892	Provisions and Clothing Bureau
	1892-1947	Supplies and Accounts Bureau
M 213	1947-1949	Supplies and Accounts Bureau
D 212	1949-1966	Supplies and Accounts Bureau
	1966-	Naval Supply Systems Command

D 213

N 14	1842-1947	Naval Observatory
M 212	1947-1949	Naval Observatory
D 213	1949-	Naval Observatory

D 214

N 9	1798-1947	Marine Corps
M 209	1947-1949	Marine Corps
D 214	1949-	Marine Corps

D 215

N 18	1842-1866	Ordnance and Hydrography Bureau
	1866-1947	Ordnance Bureau
M 211	1947-1949	Ordnance Bureau
D 215	1949-1959	Ordnance Bureau
D 217	1959-1966	Naval Weapons Bureau
D 215	1966-	Naval Ordnance Systems Command

D 216

| **D 216** | 1949-1970 | Military Sea Transportation Service |
| | 1970- | Military Sealift Command |

D 217

D 202	1949-1959	Aeronautics Bureau
D 215	1949-1959	Ordnance Bureau
D 217	1959-1966	Naval Weapons Bureau
D 202	1966-	Naval Air Systems Command
D 215	1966-	Naval Ordnance Systems Command

D 218

| **D 218** | 1967- | Oceanographer of Navy |

D 219

| **D 219** | 1968- | Electronic Systems Command |

D 220

| **D 220** | 1968- | Naval Weather Service Command |

D 221

| **D 221** | 1980- | Naval Data Automation Command |

D 221

| **D 221** | 199x- | Naval Historical Center |

D 301

W 108	1941-1947	Army Air Force
M 301	1947-1949	Air Force Department, Office of Secretary
D 301	1949-	Air Force Department, Office of Secretary

D 301.45

| **D 301.45** | 1949- | Air Research and Development Command |

D 302

D 302	1949-	Judge Advocate General of Air Force

D 303

M 302	1947-1949	Air Adjutant General's Office
D 303	1949-1958	Air Adjutant General's Office
	1958-	Administrative Services Directorate

D 304

D 304	1949- 19xx	Air Force Medical Service
	19xx-	Surgeon General of the Air Force

D 305

D 305	1954-	Air Force Academy

D 306

D 306	1956-	Inspector General

DM 1

DM1	1951-1953	Defense Materials Procurement Agency

DP 1

Pr 33.1100	1950-1951	Defense Production Administration
DP1	1951-1953	Defense Production Administration
Pr 33.1000	1953	[functions transferred to] Defense Mobilization Office

E 1

ER 1	1975-1977	Energy Research and Development Administration
I 44	1937-1977	Bonneville Power Administration
I 59	1942-1977	Southwestern Power Administration
I 65	1950-1977	Southeastern Power Administration
I 68	1967-1977	Alaska Power Administration
E 1	1977-	Energy Department, Office of Secretary

E 2

FP 1	1930-1977	Federal Power Commission
E 2	1977-	Federal Energy Regulatory Commission

E 3

FE 1	1974-1977	Federal Energy Administration
E 3	1977-	Energy Information Administration

E 4

E 4	1977-	Economic Regulatory Administration

E 5

I 44	1937-1977	Bonneville Power Administration
E 5	1977-	Bonneville Power Administration

E 6

E 6	1977-	Western Area Power Administration

E 7

I 68	1967-1977	Alaska Power Administration
E 1	1977-1993	[part of] Energy Department
E 7	1993-	Alaska Power Administration

E 8

I 65	1950-1977	Southeastern Power Administration
E 1	1977-1995	[part of] Energy Department, Office of Secretary
E 8	1995-	Southeastern Power Administration

E 9

E 9	19xx-	National Renewable Energy Laboratory

EB 1

EB 1	1916-1933	Efficiency Bureau
T 51	1933-1939	[functions transferred to] Budget Bureau

EC 1

EC 1	1916-1946	Employees' Compensation Commission
FS 13.300	1946-1950	Employees' Compensation Bureau
L 26	1950-1972	Employees' Compensation Bureau
L 36.400	1972-1973	Wage Compensation Programs Office
	1973-1975	Workers' Compensation Programs Office

ED 1

I 16	1867-1929	Education Bureau
	1929-1939	Education Office
FS 5	1939-1969	Education Office
HE 5	1970-1972	Education Office
HE 19.100	1972-1979	Education Office
ED 1	1979-	Education Department

ED 1.100

HE 19.300	1972-1979	National Center for Educational Statistics
ED 1.100	1979-	National Center for Education Statistics

ED 1.200

FS 10	1943-1946	Vocational Rehabilitation Office
FS 13.200	1946-1962	Vocational Rehabilitation Office
	1962-1967	Rehabilitation Services Administration
FS 17.100	1967-1969	Rehabilitation Services Administration
HE 17.100	1970-1975	Rehabilitation Services Administration
HE 1.600	1975-1977	Rehabilitation Services Administration
HE 23.4100	1977-1979	Rehabilitation Services Administration
ED 1.200	1979-	Rehabilitation Services Administration

ED 1.300

HE 18	1972-1975	National Institute of Education
HE 19.200	1975-1979	National Institute of Education
ED 1.300	1979-1986	National Institute of Education
	1986-	Educational Research and Improvement Center

ED 1.400

ED 1.400		Elementary and Secondary Education Office

ED 1.500

ED 1.500		Presidential Scholars Commission

EP 1

EP1	1970-	Environmental Protection Agency

EP 2

FS 16	1965-1966	Federal Water Pollution Control Administration
I 67	1966-1970	Federal Water Pollution Control Administration
	1970	Federal Water Quality Administration
EP 2	1970-19xx	Water Quality Office
	19xx- 19xx	Water Programs Operation Office
	19xx-	Water Office

EP 3

HE 20.1400	1970	Solid Waste Management Bureau
EP3	1970-	Solid Waste Management Office

EP 4

HE 20.1300	1970	National Air Pollution Control Administration
EP4	1970-1971	Air Pollution Control Office
	1971-19xx	Air Programs Office
	19xx-	Air Quality Planning and Standards Office

EP 5

EP5	1970-1980	Pesticides Programs Office
	1980-19xx	Pesticides and Toxic Substances Office
	19xx-	Prevention, Pesticides, and Toxic Substances

EP 6

| EP 6 | 1970-19xx | Radiation Programs Office |
| | 19xx- | Radiation Programs and Indoor Air |

EP 7

| EP 7 | 1971- | Technology Transfer |

EP 8

| EP 8 | | Water Regulations and Standards Office |
| | | Wetlands, Oceans, and Watersheds Office |

ER 1

| ER 1 | 1975-1977 | Energy Research and Development Administration |
| E 1 | 1977- | Energy Department, Office of Secretary |

ES 1

| ES 1 | 1950-1953 | Economic Stabilization Agency |

ES 2

| ES 2 | 1950-1953 | Wage Stabilization Board |

ES 3

| ES 3 | 1950-1953 | Price Stabilization Office |

ES 4

| ES 4 | 1950-1953 | Salary Stabilization Board |

ES 5

| ES 5 | 1951-1953 | Rent Stabilization Office |
| Pr 34.200 | 1953-1958 | [functions transferred to] Defense Mobilization Office |

ES 6

| ES 6 | 1952-1953 | National Enforcement Commission |
| J 1 | 1953- | [functions transferred to] Attorney General, Justice Department |

FA 1

| FA 1 | 1910- | Fine Arts Commission |

FAA 1

C 31.100	1940-1958	Civil Aeronautics Administration
FAA 1	1958-1967	Federal Aviation Agency
TD 4	1967-	Federal Aviation Administration

FAA 2

| FAA 2 | 1958-1967 | Systems Research and Development Service |
| TD 4.500 | 1967- | Systems Research and Development Service |

FAA 3

FAA 3	1958-1967	Air Traffic Service
TD 4.300	1967-198x	Air Traffic Service
	198x-	Air Traffic Operations Service

FAA 4

| FAA 4 | 1958-1967 | Facilities Bureau |
| TD 4.700 | 1967- | Airway Facilities Service |

FAA 5

| FAA 5 | 1958-1967 | Flight Standards Bureau |
| TD 4.400 | 1967- | Flight Standards Service |

FAA 6

| FAA 6 | 1958-1967 | National Capital Airports Bureau |

FAA 7

| FAA 7 | 1958-1967 | Aviation Medical Service |
| TD 4.200 | 1967- | Aviation Medical Office |

FAA 8

FAA 8	1958-1967	Airports Service
TD 4.100	1967-19xx	Airports Service
	19xx-	Airport Programs Office

FC 1

FC 1	1871-1880	Fish Commission
	1880-1903	Fish and Fisheries Commission
C 6	1903-1939	Fisheries Bureau
I 45	1939-1940	Fisheries Bureau
I 49	1940-	Fish and Wildlife Service

FCA 1

A 51	1929-1933	Farmers' Seed Loan Office
A 54	1918-1933	Crop Production Loan Office
FF 1	1939-1933	Federal Farm Board
T 48	1916-1933	Federal Farm Loan Bureau
FCA 1	1933-1939	Farm Credit Administration
A 72	1939-1942	Farm Credit Administration
A 79.100	1942-1943	Farm Credit Administration [not used]
A 72	1943-1953	Farm Credit Administration
FCA 1	1953-	Farm Credit Administration

FCD 1

Pr 33.800	1950-1951	Federal Civil Defense Administration
FCD 1	1951-1958	Federal Civil Defense Administration
Pr 34.700	1958-1961	Defense and Civilian Mobilization Office
PrEx 4	1961	Civil and Defense Mobilization Office
D 13	1961-1964	Civil Defense Office
D 119	1964-1972	Civil Defense Office
D 14	1972-1979	Defense Civil Preparedness Agency
FEM 1	1979-	Federal Emergency Management Agency

FE 1

| FE 1 | 1974-1977 | Federal Energy Administration |
| E 3 | 1977- | Energy Information Administration |

FEM 1

D 14	1972-1979	Defense Civil Preparedness Agency
GS 13	1976-1979	Federal Preparedness Agency
HH 12	19xx-1979	Federal Disaster Assistance Administration
FEM 1	1979-	Federal Emergency Management Agency

FEM 1.100

C 58	1974-1978	National Fire Prevention and Control Administration
	1978-1979	United States Fire Administration
FEM 1.100	1979-	United States Fire Administration

FEM 1.200

| HH 10 | 1868-1979 | Federal Insurance Administration |
| FEM 1.200 | 1979- | Federal Insurance Administration |

FF 1

FF 1	1929-1933	Federal Farm Board
FCA 1	1933-1939	Farm Credit Administration
A 72	1939-1942	Farm Credit Administration
A 79.100	1942-1943	Farm Credit Administration [not used]
A 72	1943-1953	Farm Credit Administration
FCA 1	1953-	Farm Credit Administration

FHF 1

| FHL 1 | 1955-1989 | Federal Home Loan Bank Board |
| FHF 1 | 1989- | Federal Housing Finance Board |

FHL 1

Y 3.F 31/3	1932-1939	Federal Home Loan Bank Board
FL 3	1939-1942	Federal Home Loan Bank Board
NHA 3	1942-1947	Federal Home Loan Bank Administration
HH 4	1947-1955	Federal Home Loan Bank Board
FHL 1	1955-1989	Federal Home Loan Bank Board
FHF 1	1989-	Federal Housing Financing Board
T 71	1989-	Thrift Supervisor Office
Y 3.R 31/2	1989-	Resolution Trust Corporation

FIS 1

FIS 1	1939-1950	Federal Interdepartmental Safety Council
L 30	1950-	Federal Safety Council

FL 1

FL 1	1939-1947	Federal Loan Agency
Y 3.R 24	1947-1954	[functions transferred to] Reconstruction Finance Corporation

FL 2

Y 3.F 31/11	1934-1939	Federal Housing Administration
FL 2	1939-1942	Federal Housing Administration
NHA 2	1942-1947	Federal Housing Administration
HH 2	1947-	Federal Housing Administration

FL 3

Y 3.F 31/3	1932-1939	Federal Home Loan Bank Board
FL 3	1939-1942	Federal Home Loan Bank Board
NHA 3	1942-1947	Federal Home Loan Bank Administration
HH 4	1947-1955	Federal Home Loan Bank Board
FHL 1	1955-1989	Federal Home Loan Bank Board
FHF 1	1989-	Federal Housing Financing Board
T 71	1989-	Thrift Supervisor Office
Y 3.R 31/2	1989-	Resolution Trust Corporation

FL 4

Y 3.El 2/2	1933-1939	Electric Home and Farm Authority
FL 4	1939-1942	Electric Home and Farm Authority

FL 5

Y 3.R 24	1932-1939	Reconstruction Finance Corporation
FL 5	1939-1942	Reconstruction Finance Corporation
C 33	1942-1945	Reconstruction Finance Corporation
FL 5	1945-1947	Reconstruction Finance Corporation
Y 3.R 24	1947-1954	Reconstruction Finance Corporation

FM 1

L 19	1938-1947	Conciliation Service
FM 1	1947-	Federal Mediation and Conciliation Service

FMC 1

FMC 1	1961-	Federal Maritime Commission

FO 1

Pr 33.900	1951-1953	Mutual Security Agency
S 1.64	1946-1953	Institute of Inter-American Affairs
FO 1	1953-1955	Foreign Operations Administration
S 17	1955-1961	International Cooperation Administration
S 18	1961-	International Development Agency

FP 1

FP 1	1930-1977	Federal Power Commission
E 2	1977-	Federal Energy Regulatory Commission

FPI 1

FPI 1	1934-1939	Federal Prison Industries, Inc.
J 16.50	1939-	Federal Prison Industries, Inc.

FR 1

FR 1	1913-1935	Federal Reserve Board
	1935-	Federal Reserve System Board of Governors

FS 1

FS 1	1939-1953	Federal Security Agency, Office of Secretary
	1953-1969	Health, Education, and Welfare Department, Office of Secretary
HE 1	1970-1979	Health, Education, and Welfare Department, Office of Secretary
	1979-	Health and Human Services Department

FS 2

T 27	1798-1902	Marine Hospital Service
	1902-1912	Public Health and Marine Hospital Service
	1912-1939	Public Health Service
FS 2	1939-1969	Public Health Service
HE 20	1970-	Public Health Service

FS 2.22

FS 2.22	1939-1969	National Institutes of Health
HE 20.3000	1970-	National Institutes of Health

FS 2.100

C 3	1903-1946	[a division in] Census Bureau
FS 2.100	1946-1969	National Office of Vital Statistics
HE 20.2200	1970-1973	National Center for Health Statistics
HE 20.6200	1973-	National Center for Health Statistics

FS 2.200

D 8	1952-1956	Armed Forces Medical Library
FS 2.200	1956-1969	National Library of Medicine
HE 20.3600	1970-	National Library of Medicine

FS 2.300

FS 2.300	1939-1969	Public Health Service [continued]

FS 3

SS 1	1935-1939	Social Security Board
FS 3	1939-1946	Social Security Board
	1946-1969	Social Security Administration
HE 3	1970-1995	Social Security Administration
SSA 1	1995-	Social Security Administration

FS 3.100

L 7	1918-1939	Employment Service
SS 1	1935-1939	[some functions of] Social Security Board
FS 3.100	1939-1942	Employment Security Bureau
Pr 32.5200	1942-1945	[part of] War Manpower Commission
L 7	1945-1948	Employment Service
FS 3.100	1948-1949	Employment Security Bureau
L 7	1949-1969	Employment Security Bureau
L 33	1969-1975	Unemployment Insurance Service
L 34	1969-1971	Training and Employment Service

FS 3.200

C 19	1912-1913	Children's Bureau
L 5	1913-1946	Children's Bureau
FS 3.200	1947-1963	Children's Bureau
FS 14.100	1963-1967	Children's Bureau
FS 17.200	1967-1969	Children's Bureau
HE 21.100	1970-1975	Children's Bureau
HE 1.450	1975-1977	Children's Bureau
HE 23.1200	1977-	Children's Bureau

FS 3.300

FS 3.300	1948-1969	Federal Credit Union Bureau
HE 3.300	1970	Federal Credit Union Bureau
NCU 1	1970-	National Credit Union Administration

FS 4

Y 3.Em 3	1933-1937	Emergency Conservation Work
Y 3.C 49	1937-1939	Civilian Conservation Corps
FS 4	1939-1943	Civilian Conservation Corps

FS 5

I 16	1867-1929	Education Bureau
	1929-1939	Education Office
FS 5	1939-1969	Education Office
HE 5	1970-1972	Education Office
HE 19.100	1972-1979	Education Office
ED 1	1979-	Education Department

FS 5.100

FS 5.100	1939-1950	Federal Radio Education Committee

FS 5.120

VE 1	1917-1933	Federal Vocational Education Board
I 16.54	1933-1939	Vocational Division
FS 5.120	1939-1945	Vocational Division
	1945-1949	Vocational Education Division

FS 6

Y 3.N 21/14	1935-1939	National Youth Administration
FS 6	1939-1942	National Youth Administration
Pr 32.5250	1942-1944	National Youth Administration

FS 7

A 46	1927-1930	Food, Drug, and Insecticide Administration
	1930-1940	Food and Drug Administration
FS 7	1940-1946	Food and Drug Administration
FS 13.100	1946-1969	Food and Drug Administration
HE 20.1200	1970	Food and Drug Administration
HE 20.4000	1970-	Food and Drug Administration

FS 8

FS 8	1940	Coordinator of Health, Welfare, and Related Defense Activities Office
Pr 32.4500	1941-1943	Defense Health and Welfare Services Office
FS 9	1943-1946	Community War Services Office
FS 12	1943-1946	Physical Fitness Committee

FS 9

FS 8	1940	Coordinator of Health, Welfare, and Related Defense Activities Office
Pr 23.4500	1941-1943	Defense Health and Welfare Services Office
FS 9	1943-1946	Community War Services Office
FS 12	1943-1946	Physical Fitness Committee

FS 10

FS 10	1943-1946	Vocational Rehabilitation Office
FS 13.200	1946-1962	Vocational Rehabilitation Office
	1962-1967	Rehabilitation Services Administration
FS 17.100	1967-1969	Rehabilitation Services Administration
HE 17.100	1970-1975	Rehabilitation Services Administration
HE 1.600	1975-1977	Rehabilitation Services Administration
HE 23.4100	1977-1979	Rehabilitation Services Administration
ED 1.200	1979-	Rehabilitation Services Administration

FS 11

I 1.14	1855-1916	Government Hospital for the Insane
	1916-1939	St. Elizabeth's Hospital
FS 11	1939-1967	St. Elizabeth's Hospital
FS 2.22	1967-1969	[functions transferred to National Institute of Mental Health in] National Institutes of Health

FS 12

FS 8	1940	Coordinator of Health, Welfare, and Related Defense Activities Office
Pr 32.4500	1941-1943	Defense Health and Welfare Services Office
FS 12	1943-1946	Physical Fitness Committee

FS 13

FS 13	1946-1950	Special Services Office

FS 13.100

A 46	1927-1930	Food, Drug, and Insecticide Administration
	1930-1940	Food and Drug Administration
FS 7	1940-1946	Food and Drug Administration
FS 13.100	1946-1969	Food and Drug Administration
HE 20.1200	1970	Food and Drug Administration
HE 20.4000	1970-	Food and Drug Administration

FS 13.130

FS 13.130	1967-1968	Drug Abuse Control Bureau
T 56	1930-1968	Narcotics Bureau
J 24	1968-1973	Narcotics and Dangerous Drugs Bureau
	1973-	Drug Enforcement Administration

FS 13.200

FS 10	1943-1946	Vocational Rehabilitation Office
FS 13.200	1946-1962	Vocational Rehabilitation Office
	1962-1967	Rehabilitation Services Administration
FS 17.100	1967-1969	Rehabilitation Services Administration
HE 17.100	1970-1975	Rehabilitation Services Administration
HE 1.600	1975-1977	Rehabilitation Services Administration
HE 23.4100	1977-1979	Rehabilitation Services Administration
ED 1.200	1979-	Rehabilitation Services Administration

FS 13.300

EC 1	1916-1946	Employees' Compensation Commission
FS 13.300	1946-1950	Employees' Compensation Bureau
L 26	1950-1972	Employees' Compensation Bureau
L 36.400	1972-1973	Wage Compensation Programs Office
	1973-1975	Workers' Compensation Programs Office

FS 14

FS 14	1963-1967	Welfare Administration
FS 17	1967-1969	Social and Rehabilitation Service
HE 17	1970-1977	Social and Rehabilitation Service

FS 14.100

C 19	1912-1913	Children's Bureau
L 5	1913-1946	Children's Bureau
FS 3.200	1947-1963	Children's Bureau
FS 14.100	1963-1967	Children's Bureau
FS 17.200	1967-1969	Children's Bureau
HE 21.100	1970-1975	Children's Bureau
HE 1.450	1975-1977	Children's Bureau
HE 23.1200	1977-	Children's Bureau

FS 14.200

FS 3	1962-1963	[part of] Social Security Administration
FS 14.200	1962-1967	Family Services Bureau
FS 17	1967-1969	[functions transferred to] Social and Rehabilitation Service

FS 15

FS 14.9	1965	Aging Office
FS 15	1965-1967	Aging Administration
FS 17.300	1967-1969	Aging Administration
HE 17.300	1969-1973	Aging Administration
HE 1.200	1973-1977	Aging Administration
HE 23.3000	1977-1991	Aging Administration
HE 1.1000	1991-	Aging Administration

FS 16

FS 16	1965-1966	Federal Water Pollution Control Administration
I 67	1966-1970	Federal Water Pollution Control Administration
	1970	Federal Water Quality Administration
EP 2	1970-19xx	Water Quality Office
	19xx-	Water Programs Operations Office

FS 17

FS 14	1963-1967	Welfare Administration
FS 17	1967-1969	Social and Rehabilitation Service
HE 17	1970-1977	Social and Rehabilitation Service

FS 17.100

FS 10	1943-1946	Vocational Rehabilitation Office
FS 13.200	1946-1962	Vocational Rehabilitation Office
	1962-1967	Rehabilitation Services Administration
FS 17.100	1967-1969	Rehabilitation Services Administration
HE 17.100	1970-1975	Rehabilitation Services Administration
HE 1.600	1975-1977	Rehabilitation Services Administration
HE 23.4100	1977-1979	Rehabilitation Services Administration
ED 1.200	1979-	Rehabilitation Services Administration

FS 17.200

C 19	1912-1913	Children's Bureau
L 5	1913-1946	Children's Bureau
FS 3.200	1947-1963	Children's Bureau
FS 14.100	1963-1967	Children's Bureau
FS 17.200	1967-1969	Children's Bureau
HE 21.100	1970-1975	Children's Bureau
HE 1.450	1975-1977	Children's Bureau
HE 23.1200	1977-	Children's Bureau

FS 17.300

FS 14.9	1965	Aging Office
FS 15	1965-1967	Aging Administration
FS 17.300	1967-1969	Aging Administration
HE 17.300	1969-1973	Aging Administration
HE 1.200	1973-1977	Aging Administration
HE 23.3000	1977-1991	Aging Administration
HE 1.1000	1991-	Aging Administration

FS 17.400

FS 17.400	1967-1969	Assistance Payments Administration
HE 17.400	1970-1977	Assistance Payments Administration
HE 3.400	1977-	Assistance Payments Administration

FS 17.500

FS 2	1939-1967	[part of] Public Health Service
FS 17.500	1967-1969	Medical Services Administration
HE 17.500	1970-1977	Medical Services Administration
HE 22.100	1977-	Medicaid Bureau

FS 17.600

| **FS 17.600** | 1968-1969 | National Center for Social Statistics |
| HE 17.600 | 1970- | National Center for Social Statistics |

FST 1

| **FST 1** | 1865-1890 | Freedman's Savings and Trust Company |

FT 1

| C 5 | 1903-1914 | Corporations Bureau |
| **FT 1** | 1914- | Federal Trade Commission |

FTZ 1

| **FTZ 1** | 1934- | Foreign-Trade Zones Board |

FW 1

| **FW 1** | 1939-1949 | Federal Works Agency |
| GS 1 | 1949- | General Services Administraton |

FW 2

A 22	1892-1898	Road Inquiry Office
	1898-1905	Public Road Inquiry Office
	1905-1915	ublic Roads Office
	1915-1918	Public Roads and Rural Engieering Office
	1918-1939	Public Roads Bureau
FW 2	1939-1949	Public Roads Administration
GS 3	1949	Public Roads Bureau
C 37	1949-1966	Public Roads Bureau
TD 2.100	1966-1969	Public Roads Bureau
TD 2	1969-	[functions transferred to Federal Highway Administration

FW 3

I 40	1937-1939	Housing Authority
FW 3	1939-1942	Housing Authority
NHA 4	1942-1947	Federal Public Housing Admiistration
HH 3	1947-1965	Public Housing Administratin
	1965-1969	Housing Assistance Administation
HH 1	1969-	[functions transferred to Housing and Urban Development Department]

FW 4

| Y 3.W 89/2 | 1935-1939 | Works Progress Administration |
| **FW 4** | 1939-1943 | Works Progress Administration |

FW 5

| Y 3.F 31/4 | 1933-1939 | Federal Emergency Administration of Public Works |
| **FW 5** | 1939-1943 | Public Works Administration |

FW 6

Y 3.P 96/4	1919-1933	Public Buildings Commission
I 28	1933-1939	[functions transferred to] National Park Service
T 58	1933-1939	[a branch in] Procurement Division
FW 6	1939-1949	Public Buildings Administration
GS 6	1949-	Public Buildings Service

FW 7

FW 7	1939-1949	Community Facilities Bureau
GS 1	1949-1950	[Community Facilities Servce in] General Services Administration
HH 5	1950-1965	Community Facilities Administration
	1965-1969	Land and Facilities Development Administration

GA 1

| **GA 1** | 1921- | General Accounting Office |

GA 2

| **GA 2** | 199x- | Personnel Appeals Board |

GB 1

GB 1	1890-1906	Geographic Names Board
	1906-1934	United States Geographic Bord
I 33	1934-	Geographic Names Board

GP 1

| **GP 1** | 1860- | Government Printing Office |

GP 2

| **GP 2** | | Library |

GP 3

I 15	1869-1895	Public Documents Division
GP 3	1895-19xx	Documents Office
	19xx-19xx	Public Documents Division
	19xx-	Superintendent of Documents

GS

GS	1909-1910	General Supply Committee
T 45	1910-1933	General Supply Committee
T 58	1933-1947	Procurement Division
	1947-1949	Federal Supply Bureau
GS 2	1949-1982	Federal Supply Service
	1982-19xx	Personal Property Office
	19xx	Federal Supply and Services Office

GS 1

| FW 1 | 1939-1949 | Federal Works Agency |
| **GS 1** | 1949- | General Services Administraion |

GS 2

GS	1909-1910	General Supply Committee
T 45	1910-1933	General Supply Committee
T 58	1933-1947	Procurement Division
	1947-1949	Federal Supply Bureau
GS 2	1949-1982	Federal Supply Service
	1982-1983	Personal Property Office
	1983-19xx	Federal Supply and Services Office
	19xx-	Federal Supply Service

GS 3

A 22	1892-1898	Road Inquiry Office
	1898-1905	Public Road Inquiry Office
	1905-1915	Public Roads Office
	1915-1918	Public Roads and Rural Engineering Office
	1918-1939	Public Roads Bureau
FW 2	1939-1949	Public Roads Administration
GS 3	1949	Public Roads Bureau
C 37	1949-1966	Public Roads Bureau
TD 2.100	1966-1969	Public Roads Bureau
TD 2	1969-	[functions transferred to] Federal Highway Administration

GS 4

AE 1	1934-1949	National Archives Establishment
GS 4	1949-1985	National Archives and Records Service
AE 1.100	1985-	National Archives and Records Administration

GS 4.100

AE 2	1934-1949	Federal Register Division
GS 4.100	1949-1985	Federal Register Division
AE 2.100	1985-	Federal Register Division

GS 5

Y 3.W19/7:100	1944-1946	Contract Settlement Office
T 67	1946-1949	Contract Settlement Office
GS 5	1949-1952	Contract Settlement Office

GS 6

Y 3.P 96/4	1919-1933	Public Buildings Commission
I 28	1933-1939	[functions transferred to] National Park Service
T 58	1933-1939	[a Branch in] Procurement Division
FW 6	1939-1949	Public Buildings Administration
GS 6	1949-	Public Buildings Service

GS 7

Y 3.R 24	1947-1954	[functions transferred from] Reconstruction Finance Corporation
T 69	1954-1957	Federal Facilities Corporation
GS 7	1957-1961	Federal Facilities Corporation

GS 8

GS 2	1949-19xx	Public Utilities Division of Federal Supply Service
GS 8	1955-1961	Transportation and Public Utilities Service
	1961-1972	Transportation and Communications Service
GS 2	1972-	[functions transferred to] Federal Supply Service
GS 12	1972-	[functions transferred to] Automated Data and Telecommunications Service

GS 9

GS 2	1949-1961	[functions transferred from] Federal Supply Service
GS 6	1949-1961	[functions transferred from] Public Buildings Service
GS 9	1961-1966	Utilization and Disposal Service
GS 10	1966-1973	Property Management and Disposal Service
GS 2	1973-	[functions transferred to] Federal Supply Service
GS 6	1973-	[functions transferred to] Public Buildings Service

GS 10

GS 2	1949-1961	[functions transferred from] Federal Supply Service
GS 6	1949-1961	[functions transferred from] Public Buildings Service
GS 9	1961-1966	Utilization and Disposal Service
GS 10	1966-1973	Property Management and Disposal Service
GS 2	1973-	[functions transferred to] Federal Supply Service
GS 6	1973-	[functions transferred to] Public Buildings Service

GS 11

GS 11	1970-19xx	Consumer Product Information Coordinating Center
	19xx-	Consumer Information Center

GS 12

GS 8	1961-1972	[functions of] Transportation and Communications Service
GS 12	1972-1983	Automated Data and Telecommunications Service
	1983-19xx	Information Resources Management Office
	19xx-	Federal Technology Service

GS 13

GS 13	1976-1979	Federal Preparedness Agency
FEM 1	1979-	Federal Emergency Management Agency

GS 14

GS 14		Joint Financial Management Improvement Program

HE 1

FS 1	1939-1953	Federal Security Agency, Office of Secretary
	1953-1969	Health, Education, and Welfare Department, Office of Secretary
HE 1	1970-1979	Health, Education, and Welfare Department, Office of Secretary
	1979-	Health and Human Services Department, Office of Secretary

HE 1.100

HE 1.100	1971-19xx	Facilities Engineering and Construction Agency
	19xx-	Facilities Engineering and Property Management Office

HE 1.200

FS 14.9	1965	Aging Office
FS 15	1965-1967	Aging Administration
FS 17.300	1967-1969	Aging Administration
HE 17.300	1969-1973	Aging Administration
HE 1.200	1973-1977	Aging Administration
HE 23.3000	1977-1991	Aging Administration
HE 1.1000	1991-	Aging Administration

HE 1.300

HE 17.800	1970-1974	Youth Development and Delinquency Prevention Administration
HE 1.300	1974-1977	Youth Development and Delinquency Prevention Administration
HE 23.1300	1977-	Youth Development Office

HE 1.400

HE 21	1970-1975	Child Development Office
HE 1.400	1975-1977	Child Development Office
HE 23.1000	1977-	Children, Youth and Families Administration

HE 1.450

C 19	1912-1913	Children's Bureau
L 5	1913-1946	Children's Bureau
FS 3.200	1947-1963	Children's Bureau
FS 14.100	1963-1967	Children's Bureau
FS 17.200	1967-1969	Children's Bureau
HE 21.100	1970-1975	Children's Bureau
HE 1.450	1975-1977	Children's Bureau
HE 23.1200	1977-	Children's Bureau

HE 1.460

HE 1.460	1975-1977	Child Development Service Bureau

HE 1.480

HE 1.480	1975-1977	Children's Bureau [continued]

HE 1.500

PrEx 16	1971-1973	Consumer Affairs Office
HE 1.500	1973-	Consumer Affairs Office

HE 1.600

FS 10	1943-1946	Vocational Rehabilitation Office
FS 13.200	1946-1962	Vocational Rehabilitation Office
	1962-1967	Rehabilitation Services Administration
FS 17.100	1967-1969	Rehabilitation Services Administration
HE 17.100	1970-1975	Rehabilitation Services Administration
HE 1.600	1975-1977	Rehabilitation Services Administration
HE 23.4100	1977-1979	Rehabilitation Services Administration
ED 1.200	1979-	Rehabilitation Services Administration

HE 1.700

HE 1.700	1976-1977	Human Development Office
HE 23	1977-	Human Development Services Office

HE 1.800

PrEx 10	1966-1970	[Project Head Start in] Economic Opportunity Office
HE 21.200	1970-1977	Head Start and Child Development Bureau
HE 1.800	1977	Head Start Bureau
HE 23.1100	1977-	Head Start Bureau

HE 1.900

HE 17.700	1970-1977	Community Services Administration
HE 1.900	1977	Public Services Administration
HE 23.2000	1977-	Public Services Administration

HE 1.1000

FS 14.9	1965	Aging Office
FS 15	1965-1967	Aging Administration
FS 17.300	1967-1969	Aging Administration
HE 17.300	1969-1973	Aging Administration
HE 1.200	1973-1977	Aging Administration
HE 23.3000	1977-1991	Aging Administration
HE 1.1000	1991-	Aging Administration

HE 3

SS 1	1935-1939	Social Security Board
FS 3	1939-1946	Social Security Board
	1946-1969	Social Security Administration
HE 3	1970-1995	Social Security Administration
SSA 1	1995-	Social Security Administration

HE 3.300

FS 3.300	1948-1969	Federal Credit Union Bureau
HE 3.300	1970	Federal Credit Union Bureau
NCU 1	1970-	National Credit Union Administration

HE 3.400

FS 17.400	1967-1969	Assistance Payments Administration
HE 17.400	1970-1977	Assistance Payments Administration
HE 3.400	1977-	Assistance Payments Administration

HE 3.500

HE 3.500	1977-1980	Child Support Enforcement Office
HE 24	1980-	Child Support Enforcement Office

HE 5

I 16	1867-1929	Education Bureau
	1929-1939	Education Office
FS 5	1939-1969	Education Office
HE 5	1970-1972	Education Office
HE 19.100	1972-1979	Education Office
ED 1	1979-	Education Department

HE 17

FS 14	1963-1967	Welfare Administration
FS 17	1967-1969	Social and Rehabilitation Service
HE 17	1970-1977	Social and Rehabilitation Service

HE 17.100

FS 10	1943-1946	Vocational Rehabilitation Office
FS 13.200	1946-1962	Vocational Rehabilitation Office
	1962-1967	Rehabilitation Services Administration
FS 17.100	1967-1969	Rehabilitation Services Administration
HE 17.100	1970-1975	Rehabilitation Services Administration
HE 1.600	1975-1977	Rehabilitation Services Administration

HE 23.4100	1977-1979	Rehabilitation Services Administration
ED 1.200	1979-	Rehabilitation Services Administration

HE 17.300

FS 14.9	1965	Aging Office
FS 15	1965-1967	Aging Administration
FS 17.300	1967-1969	Aging Administration
HE 17.300	1969-1973	Aging Administration
HE 1.200	1973-1977	Aging Administration
HE 23.3000	1977-1991	Aging Administration
HE 1.1000	1991-	Aging Administration

HE 17.400

FS 17.400	1967-1969	Assistance Payments Administration
HE 17.400	1970-1977	Assistance Payments Administration
HE 3.400	1977-	Assistance Payments Administration

HE 17.500

FS 2	1939-1967	[part of] Public Health Service
FS 17.500	1967-1969	Medical Services Administration
HE 17.500	1970-1977	Medical Services Administration
HE 22.100	1977-	Medicaid Bureau

HE 17.600

FS 17.600	1968-1969	National Center for Social Statistics
HE 17.600	1970-	National Center for Social Statistics

HE 17.700

HE 17.700	1970-1977	Community Services Administration
HE 1.900	1977	Public Services Administration
HE 23.2000	1977-	Public Services Administration

HE 17.800

HE 17.800	1970-1974	Youth Development and Delinquency Prevention Administration
HE 1.300	1974-1977	Youth Development and Delinquency Prevention Administration
HE 23.1300	1977-	Youth Development Office

HE 18

HE 18	1972-1975	National Institute of Education
HE 19.200	1975-1979	National Institute of Education
ED 1.300	1979-1986	National Institute of Education
	1986-	Educational Research and Improvement Center

HE 19

HE 19	1972-1979	Education Division
ED 1	1979-	[functions transferred to] Department of Education

HE 19.100

I 16	1867-1929	Education Bureau
	1929-1939	Education Office
FS 5	1939-1969	Education Office
HE 5	1970-1972	Education Office
HE 19.100	1972-1979	Education Office
ED 1	1979-	Education Department

HE 19.200

HE 18	1972-1975	National Institute of Education
HE 19.200	1975-1979	National Institute of Education
ED 1.300	1979-1986	National Institute of Education
	1986-	Educational Research and Improvement Center

HE 19.300

HE 19.300	1972-1979	National Center for Educational Statistics
ED 1.100	1979-	National Center for Education Statistics

HE 20

T 27	1798-1902	Marine Hospital Service
	1902-1912	Public Health and Marine Hospital Service
	1912-1939	Public Health Service
FS 2	1939-1969	Public Health Service
HE 20	1970-19xx	Public Health Service
	19xx-	Office of Public Health and Science

HE 20.100

Pr 34.8:Y 8	1956-1963	President's Council on Youth Fitness
Pr 35.8:P 56	1963-1968	President's Council on Physical Fitness
Pr 36.8:P 56	1968-1969	President's Council on Physical Fitness and Sports
Pr 37.8:P 56/2	1970-1978	President's Council on Physical Fitness and Sports
HE 20.100	1978-	President's Council on Physical Fitness and Sports

HE 20.200

HE 20.200		National Center for Health Care Technology

HE 20.300

HE 20.2650	1970-1973	Indian Health Service
HE 20.5300	1973-1983	Indian Health Service
HE 20.9400	1983-1991	Indian Health Service
HE 20.300	1991-	Indian Health Service

HE 20.400

HE 20.8000	1973-1992	Alcohol, Drug Abuse, and Mental Health Administration
	1992-1994	Substance Abuse and Mental Health Services Administration
HE 20.400	1994-	Substance Abuse and Mental Health Services Administration

HE 20.500

HE 20.7900	1983-1995	Toxic Substances and Diseas Registry Agency
HE 20.500	1995-	Toxic Substances and Diseas Registry Agency

HE 20.1000

HE 20.1000	1970	Consumer Protection and Environmental Health Service
	1970	Environmental Health Service

HE 20.1100

HE 20.1100	1970	Environmental Control Administration

HE 20.1200

A 46	1927-1930	Food, Drug, and Insecticide Administration
	1930-1940	Food and Drug Administration
FS 7	1940-1946	Food and Drug Administration
FS 13.100	1946-1969	Food and Drug Administration
HE 20.1200	1970	Food and Drug Administration
HE 20.4000	1970-	Food and Drug Administration

HE 20.1300

HE 20.1300	1970	National Air Pollution Control Administration
EP 4	1970-1971	Air Pollution Control Office
	1971-19xx	Air Programs Office
	19xx-	Air Quality Planning and Standards Office

HE 20.1400

HE 20.1400	1970	Solid Waste Management Bureau
EP 3	1970-	Solid Waste Management Office

HE 20.1500

HE 20.1500	1970	Radiological Health Bureau
HE 20.4100	1970-1983	Radiological Health Bureau
HE 20.4600	1983-	Devices and Radiological Health Center

HE 20.1600

HE 20.1600	1970	Occupational Safety and Health Bureau
L 35	1971-	Occupational Safety and Health Administration

HE 20.1700

HE 20.1700	1970	Water Hygiene Office

HE 20.1800

HE 20.1800	1970-1972	Community Environmental Management Bureau
HE 20.2850	1972-1974	Community Environmental Management Bureau

HE 20.2000

FS 2	1968-1969	[part of] Public Health Service
HE 20.2000	1970-1973	Health Services and Mental Health Administration
HE 20.5000	1973-1982	[functions transferred to] Health Services Administration
HE 20.6000	1973-1982	[functions transferred to] Health Resources Administration
HE 20.7000	1973-	[functions transferred to] Center for Disease Control
HE 20.8000	1973-	[functions transferred to] Alcohol, Drug Abuse, and Mental Health Administration

HE 20.2050

HE 20.2050	1972	Health Maintenance Organization Service

HE 20.2100

HE 20.2100	1970-1973	National Center for Health Services Research and Development
HE 20.6500	1973-19xx	Health Services Research and Evaluation Bureau
	19xx-19xx	National Health Services Research Center
	19xx-	Nation Health Services Research and Health Care Technology Assessment Center

HE 20.2200

C 3	1903-1946	[a division in] Census Bureau
FS 2.100	1946-1969	National Office of Vital Statistics
HE 20.2200	1970-1973	National Center for Health Statistics
HE 20.6200	1973-	National Center for Health Statistics

HE 20.2300

FS 2.60	1951-1969	National Communicable Disease Center
HE 20.2300	1970-1971	National Communicable Disease Center
	1971-1973	Disease Control Center
HE 20.7000	1973-1980	Disease Control Center
	1980-19xx	Disease Control Centers
	19xx-	Centers for Disease Control and Prevention

HE 20.2400

HE 20.2400	1970-1973	National Institute of Mental Health
HE 20.3800	1973	National Institute of Mental Health
HE 20.8100	1973-	National Institute of Mental Health

HE 20.2500

HE 20.2500	1970-1971	Health Facilities Planning and Construction Service
HE 1.100	1971	Facilities Engineering and Construction Agency
HE 20.2500	1971-1973	Health Care Facilities Service
HE 20.6400	1973	Health Care Facilities Service

HE 20.2550

HE 20.2550	1970-1973	Community Health Service
HE 20.5100	1973-19xx	Community Health Services Bureau
	19xx-1983	Health Care Delivery and Assistance Bureau
HE 20.9100	1983-	Health Care Delivery and Assistance Bureau

HE 20.2580

HE 20.2580	1970-1973	Comprehensive Health Planning Service

HE 20.2600

HE 20.2600	1970-1973	Regional Medical Programs Service
HE 20.6300	1973	Regional Medical Programs Service

HE 20.2650

HE 20.2650	1970-1973	Indian Health Service
HE 20.5300	1973-1983	Indian Health Service
HE 20.9400	1983-1991	Indian Health Service
HE 20.300	1991-	Indian Health Service

HE 20.2700

HE 20.2700	1970-1973	Federal Health Program Service
HE 20.5200	1973-1974	Federal Health Program Service

HE 20.2750

HE 20.2750	1970-1973	Maternal and Child Health Service

HE 20.2800

HE 20.2800	1971-1974	National Institute for Occupational Safety and Health
HE 20.7100	1974-	National Institute for Occupational Safety and Health

HE 20.2850

HE 20.1800	1970-1972	Community Environmental Management Bureau
HE 20.2850	1972-1974	Community Environmental Management Bureau

HE 20.2900

HE 20.2900	1972-1973	National Center for Family Planning Service

HE 20.3000

FS 2.22	1939-1969	National Institutes of Health
HE 20.3000	1970-	National Institutes of Health

HE 29.3100

HE 20.3100	1970	Health Professions Education and Manpower Training Bureau
	1970-1973	Health Manpower Education Bureau

HE 20.3150

HE 20.3150	1970-	National Cancer Institute

HE 20.3200

HE 20.3200	1970-1975	National Heart and Lung Institute
	1975-	National Heart, Lung, and Blood Institute

HE 20.3250

HE 20.3250	1970-	National Institute of Allergy and Infectious Diseases

HE 20.3300

HE 20.3300	1970-1973	National Institute of Arthritis and Metabolic Diseases
	1973-1983	National Institute of Arthritis, Metabolism and Digestive Diseases
	1983-1985	National Institute of Arthritis, Diabetes, and Digestive and Kidney Diseases
	1985-	National Institute of Diabetes and Digestive and Kidney Diseases

HE 20.3350

HE 20.3350	1970-	National Institute of Child Health and Human Development

HE 20.3400

HE 20.3400	1970	National Institute of Dental Research
		National Institute of Dental and Craniofacial Research

HE 20.3450

HE 20.3450	1970-	National Institute of General Medical Sciences

HE 20.3500

HE 20.3500	1970-1975	National Institute of Neurological Diseases and Stroke
	1975	National Institute of Neurological and Communicative Disorders and Stroke
		National Institute of Neurological Disorders and Stroke

HE 20.3550

HE 20.3550	1970-	National Institute of Environmental Health Sciences

HE 20.3600

D 8	1952-1956	Armed Forces Medical Library
FS 2.200	1956-1969	National Library of Medicine
HE 20.3600	1970-	National Library of Medicine

HE 20.3650

HE 20.3650	199x-	National Institute on Deafness and Other Communication Disorders

HE 20.3700

HE 20.3700	1970-	John E. Fogarty International Center for Advanced Study in the Health Sciences

HE 20.3750

HE 20.3750	1970-	National Eye Institute

HE 20.3800

HE 20.2400	1970-1973	National Institute of Mental Health
HE 20.3800	1973	National Institute of Mental Health
HE 20.8100	1973-	National Institute of Mental Health

HE 20.3850

HE 20.3850	1976-	National Institute on Aging

HE 20.3900

HE 20.3900	1984-	National Institute of Arthritis and Musculoskeletal and Skin Diseases

HE 20.3950

HE 20.8200	1973-1994	National Institute on Drug Abuse
HE 20.3950	1994-	National Institute on Drug Abuse

HE 20.4000

A 46	1927-1930	Food, Drug, and Insecticide Administration
	1930-1940	Food and Drug Administration
FS 7	1940-1946	Food and Drug Administration
FS 13.100	1946-1969	Food and Drug Administration
HE 20.1200	1970	Food and Drug Administration
HE 20.4000	1970-	Food and Drug Administration

HE 20.4100

HE 20.1500	1970	Radiological Health Bureau
HE 20.4100	1970-1983	Radiological Health Bureau
HE 20.4600	1983-1984	National Center for Devices and Radiological Health
	1984-	Devices and Radiological Health Center

HE 20.4200

HE 20.4200	1971-19xx	Drugs and Biologics Bureau
	19xx-1984	National Drugs and Biologics Center
	1984-1987	Drugs and Biologics Center
HE 20.4700	1987-	Drug Evaluation and Research Center

HE 20.4300

HE 20.4300	1971-1977	Medical Devices and Diagnostic Products Bureau
	1977-1983	Medical Devices Bureau
HE 20.4600	1983-1984	National Devices and Radiological Health Center
	1984-	Devices and Radiological Health Center

HE 20.4400

HE 20.4400	1971-1984	Veterinary Medicine Bureau
	1984-	Center for Veterinary Medicine

HE 20.4500

HE 20.4500	1979-1984	Foods Bureau
	1984-	Food Safety and Applied Nutrition Center

HE 20.4600

HE 20.4100	1970-1983	Radiological Health Bureau
HE 20.4300	1977-1983	Medical Devices Bureau
HE 20.4600	1983-1984	National Center for Devices and Radiological Health
	1984-	Devices and Radiological Health Center

HE 20.4700

HE 20.4200	1971-19xx	Drugs and Biologics Bureau
	19xx-1984	National Drugs and Biologics Center
	1984-1987	Drugs and Biologics Center
HE 20.4700	1987-	Drug Evaluation and Research Center

HE 20.4800

HE 20.4800	1996-	Biologics Evaluation and Research Center

HE 20.5000

HE 20.2000	1970-1973	[part of] Health Services and Mental Health Administration
HE 20.5000	1973-1982	Health Services Administration
HE 20.9000	1982-	Health Resources and Services Administration

HE 20.5100

HE 20.2550	1970-1973	Community Health Service
HE 20.5100	1973-19xx	Community Health Services Bureau
	19xx-1983	Health Care Delivery and Assistance Bureau
HE 20.9100	1983-	Health Care Delivery and Assistance Bureau

HE 20.5200

HE 20.2700	1970-1973	Federal Health Program Service
HE 20.5200	1973-1974	Federal Health Program Service

HE 20.5300

HE 20.2650	1970-1973	Indian Health Service
HE 20.5300	1973-1983	Indian Health Service
HE 20.9400	1983-1991	Indian Health Service
HE 20.300	1991-	Indian Health Service

HE 20.5400

HE 20.5400	1974-	Medical Services Bureau

HE 20.5500

HE 20.5500	1974-1976	Quality Assurance Bureau

HE 20.5600

HE 20.5600	1980-	Health Personnel Development and Service Bureau

HE 20.6000

HE 20.2000	1970-1973	[part of] Health Services and Mental Health Administration
HE 20.6000	1973-1982	Health Resources Administration
HE 20.9000	1982-	Health Resources and Services Administration

HE 20.6100

HE 20.6100	1973-1976	Health Resources Development Bureau
	1976-1978	Health Planning and Resources Development Bureau
	1978-	Health Planning Bureau

HE 20.6200

C 3	1903-1946	[a division in] Census Bureau
FS 2.100	1946-1969	National Office of Vital Statistics
HE 20.2200	1970-1973	National Center for Health Statistics
HE 20.6200	1973-	National Center for Health Statistics

HE 20.6300

HE 20.2600	1970-1973	Regional Medical Programs Service
HE 20.6300	1973	Regional Medical Programs Service

HE 20.6400

HE 20.2500	1970-1971	Health Facilities Planning and Construction Service
HE 1.100	1971	Facilities Engineering and Construction Agency
HE 20.2500	1971-1973	Health Care Facilities Service
HE 20.6400	1973	Health Care Facilities Service

HE 20.6500

HE 20.2100	1970-1973	National Center for Health Services Research and Development
HE 20.6500	1973-19xx	Health Services Research and Evaluation Bureau
	19xx-19xx	National Center for Health Services Research
	1973-1989	National Center for Health Services Research and Health Care Technology Assessment
	1989	Agency for Health Care Policy and Research
		Agency for Healthcare Research and Quality

HE 20.6600

HE 20.6600	1975-19xx	Health Manpower Bureau
	19xx-1983	Health Professions Bureau
HE 20.9300	1983-	Health Professions Bureau

HE 20.6700

HE 20.6700	1978-19xx	Health Facilities Compliance and Conversion Bureau
	19xx-19xx	Health Facilities, Financing, Compliance, and Conversion Bureau
	19xx-	Health Facilities Bureau

HE 20.7000

FS 2.60	1951-1969	National Communicable Disease Center
HE 20.2300	1970-1971	National Communicable Disease Center
	1971-1973	Disease Control Center
HE 20.7000	1973-1980	Disease Control Center
	1980	Disease Control Centers
		Disease Control and Prevention Centers

HE 20.7100

HE 20.2800	1971-1974	National Institute for Occupational Safety and Health
HE 20.7100	1974-	National Institute for Occupational Safety and Health

HE 20.7200

HE 20.7200	1973-1984	Health Education Bureau
HE 20.7600	1984-1991	Health Promotion and Education Center
	1991-	National Center for Chronic Disease Prevention and Health Promotion

HE 20.7300

HE 20.7300	1973-19xx	State Services Bureau
	19xx-19xx	Prevention Services Center
	19xx-	HIV, STD, and TB Prevention Center

HE 20.7400

HE 20.7400	1973-1984	Laboratories Bureau
HE 20.7500	1984	Center for Environmental Health
		National Center for Environmental Health

HE 20.7500

HE 20.7400	1973-1984	Laboratories Bureau
HE 20.7500	1984-	Center for Environmental Health

HE 20.7600

HE 20.7200	1973-1984	Health Education Bureau
HE 20.7600	1984-1991	Health Promotion and Education Center
	1991-	National Center for Chronic Disease Prevention and Health Promotion

HE 20.7700

HE 20.7700	1984-	Professional Development and Training Center

HE 20.7800

HE 20.7800	1984	Center for Infectious Diseases
		National Center for Infectious Diseases

HE 20.7900

HE 20.7900	1983-1995	Toxic Substances and Diseas Registry Agency
HE 20.500	1995-	Toxic Substances and Diseas Registry Agency

HE 20.7950

HE 20.7950	199x-	National Center for Injury Prevention

HE 20.7950

| HE 20.7950 | 199x- | National Center for Injury Prevention and Control |

HE 20.7960

| HE 20.7960 | 199x- | National Immunization Program |

HE 20.8000

HE 20.2000	1970-1973	[part of] Health Services and Mental Health Administration
HE 20.8000	1973-1992	Alcohol, Drug Abuse, and Mental Health Administration
	1992-1994	Substance Abuse and Mental Health Services Administration

HE 20.8100

HE 20.2400	1970-1973	National Institute of Mental Health
HE 20.3800	1973	National Institute of Mental Health
HE 20.8100	1973-	National Institute of Mental Health

HE 20.8200

| HE 20.8200 | 1973-1994 | National Institute on Drug Abuse |
| HE 20.3950 | 1994- | National Institute on Drug Abuse |

HE 20.8300

| HE 20.8300 | 1973- | National Institute on Alcohol Abuse and Alcoholism |

HE 20.9000

HE 20.5000	1973-1982	Health Services Administration
HE 20.6000	1973-1982	Health Resources Administration
HE 20.9000	1982-	Health Resources and Services Administration

HE 20.9100

HE 20.2550	1970-1973	Community Health Service
HE 20.5100	1973-19xx	Community Health Services Bureau
	19xx-1983	Health Care Delivery and Assistance Bureau
HE 20.9100	1983-19xx	Health Care Delivery and Assistance Bureau
	19xx-	Primary Health Care Bureau

HE 20.9200

HE 20.9200	1983-1986	Health Maintenance Organizations and Resources Development Bureau
	1986-19xx	Maternal and Child Health Resources Development Bureau
	19xx-	Maternal and Child Health Bureau

HE 20.9300

HE 20.6600	1975-19xx	Health Manpower Bureau
	19xx-1983	Health Professions Bureau
HE 20.9300	1983-	Health Professions Bureau

HE 20.9400

HE 20.2650	1970-1973	Indian Health Service
HE 20.5300	1973-1983	Indian Health Service
HE 20.9400	1983-1991	Indian Health Service
HE 20.300	1991-	Indian Health Service

HE 20.9500

| HE 20.9500 | 199x-20xx | Health Resources Development Bureau |
| | 20xx- | HIV/AIDS Bureau |

HE 21

HE 21	1970-1975	Child Development Office
HE 1.400	1975-1977	Child Development Office
HE 23.1000	1977-	Children, Youth and Families Administration

HE 21.100

C 19	1912-1913	Children's Bureau
L 5	1913-1946	Children's Bureau
FS 3.200	1947-1963	Children's Bureau
FS 14.100	1963-1967	Children's Bureau

FS 17.200	1967-1969	Children's Bureau
HE 21.100	1970-1975	Children's Bureau
HE 1.450	1975-1977	Children's Bureau
HE 23.1200	1977-	Children's Bureau

HE 21.200

PrEx 10	1966-1970	[Project Head Start in] Economic Opportunity Office
HE 21.200	1970-1977	Head Start and Child Development Bureau
HE 1.800	1977-	Head Start Bureau
HE 23.1100	1977-	Head Start Bureau

HE 22

| HE 22 | 1977- | Health Care Financing Administration |

HE 22.100

FS 2	1939-1967	[part of] Public Health Service
FS 17.500	1967-1969	Medical Services Administration
HE 17.500	1970-1977	Medical Services Administration
HE 22.100	1977-20xx	Medicaid Bureau
	20xx-	Medicaid and State Operations Center

HE 22.200

| HE 22.200 | 1977-20xx | Health Standards and Quality Bureau |
| | 20xx- | Clinical Standards and Quality Office |

HE 22.300

| HE 22.300 | 1979- | Program Policy Bureau |

HE 22.400

| HE 22.400 | 1979-20xx | Program Operations Bureau |
| | 20xx- | Medicare Management Center |

HE 22.500

| HE 22.500 | 1990- | Data Management and Strategy Bureau |

HE 22.600

| HE 22.600 | | Office of Information Services |

HE 23

| HE 1.700 | 1976-1977 | Human Development Office |
| HE 23 | 1977- | Human Development Services Office |

HE 23.100

| HE 23.100 | 1978- | President's Committee on Mental Retardation |

HE 23.1000

HE 21	1970-1975	Child Development Office
HE 1.400	1975-1977	Child Development Office
HE 23.1000	1977-	Children, Youth and Families Administration

HE 23.1100

PrEx 10	1966-1970	[Project Head Start in] Economic Opportunity Office
HE 21.200	1970-1977	Head Start and Child Development Bureau
HE 1.800	1977	Head Start Bureau
HE 23.1100	1977-	Head Start Bureau

HE 23.1200

C 19	1912-1913	Children's Bureau
L 5	1913-1946	Children's Bureau
FS 3.200	1947-1963	Children's Bureau
FS 14.100	1963-1967	Children's Bureau
FS 17.200	1967-1969	Children's Bureau
HE 21.100	1970-1975	Children's Bureau
HE 1.450	1975-1977	Children's Bureau
HE 23.1200	1977-	Children's Bureau

HE 23.1300

HE 17.800	1970-1974	Youth Development and Delinquency Prevention Administration
HE 1.300	1974-1977	Youth Development and Delinquency Prevention Administration
HE 23.1300	1977-	Youth Development Office

HE 23.1400

HE 23.1400	199x-	Child Care Bureau

HE 23.2000

HE 17.700	1970-1977	Community Services Administration
HE 1.900	1977	Public Services Administration
HE 23.2000	1977-	Public Services Administration

HE 23.3000

FS 14.9	1965	Aging Office
FS 15	1965-1967	Aging Administration
FS 17.300	1967-1969	Aging Administration
HE 17.300	1969-1973	Aging Administration
HE 1.200	1973-1977	Aging Administration
HE 23.3000	1977-1991	Aging Administration
HE 1.1000	1991-	Aging Administration

HE 23.3100

HE 23.3100	1977-	National Clearinghouse on Aging

HE 23.4000

HE 23.4000	1977-	Handicapped Individuals Administration

HE 23.4100

FS 10	1943-1946	Vocational Rehabilitation Office
FS 13.200	1946-1962	Vocational Rehabilitation Office
	1962-1967	Rehabilitation Services Administration
FS 17.100	1967-1969	Rehabilitation Services Administration
HE 17.100	1970-1975	Rehabilitation Services Administration
HE 1.600	1975-1977	Rehabilitation Services Administration
HE 23.4100	1977-1979	Rehabilitation Services Administration
ED 1.200	1979-	Rehabilitation Services Administration

HE 23.5000

HE 23.5000	1978-	Native Americans Administration

HE 23.6000

HE 23.6000	198x-	Developmental Disabilities Administration

HE 24

HE 24	1980-	Child Support Enforcement Office

HE 25

HE 25	1986-	Family Support Administration

HH 1

HH 1	1947-1965	Housing and Home Finance Agency
	1965-	Housing and Urban Development Department, Office of Secretary

HH 2

Y 3.F 31/11	1934-1939	Federal Housing Administration
FL 2	1939-1942	Federal Housing Administration
NHA 2	1942-1947	Federal Housing Administration
HH 2	1947-	Federal Housing Administration

HH 3

I 40	1937-1939	Housing Authority
FW 3	1939-1942	Housing Authority
NHA 4	1942-1947	Federal Public Housing Administration
HH 3	1947-1965	Public Housing Administration

HH 1	1965-1969	Housing Assistance Administration
	1969-	[functions transferred to] Housing and Urban Development Department

HH 4

Y 3.F 31/3	1932-1939	Federal Home Loan Bank Board
FL 3	1939-1942	Federal Home Loan Bank Board
NHA 3	1942-1947	Federal Home Loan Bank Administration
HH 4	1947-1955	Federal Home Loan Bank Board
FHL 1	1955-1989	Federal Home Loan Bank Board
FHF 1	1989-	Federal Housing Financing Board
T 71	1989-	Thrift Supervisor Office
Y 3.R 31/2	1989-	Resolution Trust Corporation

HH 5

FW 7	1939-1949	Community Facilities Bureau
GS 1	1949-1950	[Community Facilities Service in] General Services Administration
HH 5	1950-1965	Community Facilities Administration
	1965-1969	Land and Facilities Development Administration

HH 6

Y 3.R 24	1947-1950	[part of] Reconstruction Finance Corporation
HH 6	1950-1968	Federal National Mortgage Association

HH 7

HH 1	1947-1954	[Slum Clearance and Urban Redevelopment Division in] Housing and Home Finance Agency
HH 7	1954-1965	Urban Renewal Administration
	1965-1969	Renewal Assistance Administration

HH 8

HH 8	1969-1974	Urban Management Assistance Administration

HH 9

HH 9	1974-	Community Development Office

HH 10

HH 10	1868-1979	Federal Insurance Administration
FEM 1.200	1979-	Federal Insurance Administration

HH 11

HH 11		New Communities Administration

HH 12

HH 12	19xx-1979	Federal Disaster Assistance Administration
FEM 1	1979-	Federal Emergency Management Agency

HH 13

HH 13	199x-	Multi-Family Housing Office

I 1

I 1	1849-	Interior Department, Office of Secretary

I 2	1790	First Census
I 3	1800	Second Census
I 4	1810	Third Census
I 5	1820	Fourth Census
I 6	1830	Fifth Census
I 7	1840	Sixth Census
I 8	1850	Seventh Census
I 9	1860	Eighth Census
I 10	1870	Ninth Census
I 11	1880	Tenth Census
I 12	1890	Eleventh Census
I 13	1900	Twelfth Census

I 14

I 14	1902-1903	Census Office
C 3	1903-1972	Census Bureau
C 56.200	1972-1975	Census Bureau
C 3	1975-	Census Bureau

I 15

I 15	1869-1895	Public Documents Division
GP 3	1895-19xx	Documents Office
	19xx-	Public Documents Division

I 16

I 16	1867-1929	Education Bureau
	1929-1939	Education Office
FS 5	1939-1969	Education Office
HE 5	1970-1972	Education Office
HE 19.100	1972-1979	Education Office
ED 1	1979-	Education Department

I 17

| I 17 | 1874-1879 | Geographical and Geological Survey of the Rocky Mountain Region (Powell) |
| I 19 | 1879- | Geological Survey |

I 18

I 18	1867-1872	Geological Survey of the Territories
	1872-1879	Geological and Geographical Survey of the Territories
I 19	1879-	Geological Survey

I 19

I 17	1874-1879	Geographical and Geological Survey of the Rocky Mountain Region
I 18	1872-1879	Geological and Geographical Survey of the Territories
I 19	1879-	Geological Survey

I 19.17

I 19.17	1902-1907	Reclamation Service
I 27	1907-1923	Reclamation Service
	1923-1979	Reclamation Bureau
	1979-1981	Water and Power Resources Service
	1981-	Reclamation Bureau

I 19.200

| I 19.200 | 199x- | Biological Resources Division |

I 20

| I 20 | 1839-1947 | Indian Affairs Office |
| | 1947- | Indian Affairs Bureau |

I 21

| I 21 | 1849-1946 | General Land Office |
| I 53 | 1946- | Land Management Bureau |

I 22

| I 22 | 1849-19xx | Library |
| | 19xx- | Natural Resources Library |

I 23

I 23	1849-1925	Patent Office
C 21	1925-1975	Patent Office
	1975-	Patent and Trademark Office

I 24

I 24	1849-1890	Commissioner of Pensions Office
	1890-1930	Pension Bureau
VA 2	1930-1931	Pensions Bureau
VA 1	1931-	[functions transferred to] Veterans Administration

I 25

| I 25 | 1878-1880 | Auditor of Railroad Accounts |
| | 1880-1904 | Railroads Commissioner Office |

I 26

| I 26 | 1877-1880 | Entomological Commission |
| A 8 | 1880-1882 | Entomological Commission |

I 27

I 19.17	1902-1907	Reclamation Service
I 27	1907-1923	Reclamation Service
	1923-1979	Reclamation Bureau
	1979-1981	Water and Power Resources Service
	1981-	Reclamation Bureau

I 28

I 28	1910-1925	Mines Bureau
C 22	1925-1934	Mines Bureau
I 28	1934-1996	Mines Bureau

I 29

| I 29 | 1916- | National Park Service |

I 30

I 30	1933-1935	Soil Erosion Service
A 57	1935-1942	Soil Conservation Service
A 76.200	1942	Soil Conservation Service
A 79.200	1942-1943	Soil Conservation Service
A 80.2000	1943-1944	Soil Conservation Service
A 80.500	1944-1945	Soil Conservation Service
A 57	1945-	Soil Conservation Service

I 31

| I 31 | 1933-1935 | Subsistence Homesteads Division |
| Y 3.R 31 | 1935-1937 | [functions transferred to] Resettlement Administration |

I 32

| I 32 | 1933-1935 | Petroleum Administration Board |

I 33

GB 1	1890-1906	Geographic Names Board
	1906-1934	United States Geographic Board
I 33	1934-	Geographic Names Board

I 34

I 34	1935-1939	National Bituminous Coal Commission
I 46	1939-1943	Bituminous Coal Division
I 51	1943-1947	Solid Fuels Administration for War

I 35

| I 35 | 1934-1950 | Territories and Island Possessions Division |
| | 1950-1971 | Territories Office |

I 36

| I 36 | 1935-1955 | Puerto Rico Reconstruction Administration |
| I 35 | 1955-1971 | [functions transferred to] Territories Office |

I 37

| I 37 | 1935-1939 | Motion Pictures Division |

I 38

I 38	1934-1939	Grazing Control Division
	1939-1946	Grazing Service
I 53	1946-	Land Management Bureau

I 39

I 39	1935-1939	Consumers' Counsel of National Bituminous Coal Commission
I 48.50	1939-1941	Consumers' Counsel Division
Y 3.B 54/2	1941-1943	Bituminous Coal Consumers' Counsel Office

I 40

I 40	1937-1939	Housing Authority
FW 3	1939-1942	Housing Authority
NHA 4	1942-1947	Federal Public Housing Administration
HH 3	1947-1965	Public Housing Administration
	1965-1969	Housing Assistance Administration
HH 1	1969-	[functions transferred to] Housing and Urban Development Department

I 41

I 41	1936-1946	Petroleum Conservation Division [not used]

I 42

I 42		Civilian Conservation Corps [not used]

I 43

I 43	1938-1945	Information Division

I 44

I 44	1937-1977	Bonneville Power Administration
E 5	1977-	Bonneville Power Administration

I 45

FC 1	1871-1880	Fish Commission
	1880-1903	Fish and Fisheries Commission
C 6	1903-1939	Fisheries Bureau
I 45	1939-1940	Fisheries Bureau
I 49	1940-	Fish and Wildlife Service

I 46

I 34	1935-1939	National Bituminous Coal Commission
I 46	1939-1943	Bituminous Coal Division
I 51	1943-1947	Solid Fuels Administration for War

I 47

A 5	1886	Economic Ornithology and Mammology Division
	1887-1896	Ornithology and Mammology Division
	1896-1905	Biological Survey Division
	1905-1939	Biological Survey Bureau
I 47	1939-1940	Biological Survey Bureau
I 49	1940-	Fish and Wildlife Service

I 48

I 48	1941-	Solicitor for Department of the Interior

I 48.50

I 39	1935-1939	Consumers' Counsel of National Bituminous Coal Commission
I 48.50	1939-1941	Consumers' Counsel Division
Y 3.B 54/2	1941-1943	Bituminous Coal Consumers' Counsel Office

I 49

I 45	1939-1940	Fisheries Bureau
I 47	1939-1940	Biological Survey Bureau
I 49	1940-	Fish and Wildlife Service

I 50

I 50	1941-1942	Petroleum Coordinator for National Defense Office
	1942	Petroleum Coordinator for War Office
Y 3.P 44	1942-1946	Petroleum Administration for War

I 51

I 34	1935-1939	National Bituminous Coal Commission
I 46	1939-1943	Bituminous Coal Division
I 51	1943-1947	Solid Fuels Administration for War

I 52

Pr 32.5400	1942-1944	War Relocation Authority
I 52	1944-1946	War Relocation Authority

I 53

I 21	1849-1946	General Land Office
I 38	1939-1946	Grazing Service
I 53	1946-	Land Management Bureau

I 54

I 54	1950-1953	Defense Fisheries Administration

I 55

I 55	1950-1951	Defense Minerals Administration
	1951-1958	Defense Minerals Exploration Administration
	1958-1965	Minerals Exploration Office
I 19	1965-	[functions transferred to] Geological Survey

I 56

I 56	1950-1951	Defense Power Administration
	1951-1953	Defense Electric Power Administration

I 57

I 57	1950-1954	Defense Solid Fuels Administration

I 58

I 58	1950-1954	Petroleum Administration for Defense

I 59

I 59	1943-1977	Southwestern Power Administration
E 1	1977-	Energy Department, Office of Secretary

I 60

I 60	1955-1962	Minerals Mobilization Office
	1962-1971	Minerals and Solid Fuels Office

I 61

I 61	1959-1971	Oil Import Administration
I 64	1971-1974	[functions transferred to] Oil and Gas Office

I 62

I 62	1959-1971	Oil Import Appeals Board

I 63

I 63	1960-1974	Coal Research Office
ER 1	1975-1977	[functions transferred to] Energy Research and Development Administration

I 64

I 64	1946-1974	Oil and Gas Office
FE 1	1974-1977	[functions transferred to] Federal Energy Administration

I 65

I 65	1950-1977	Southeastern Power Administration
E 1	1977-1995	[part of] Energy Department, Office of Secretary
E 8	1995-	Southeastern Power Administration

I 66

I 66	1962-1978	Outdoor Recreation Bureau
I 70	1978-1981	Heritage Conservation and Recreation Service
I 29	1981-	[functions transferred to] National Park Service

I 67

FS 16	1965-1966	Federal Water Pollution Control Administration
I 67	1966-1970	Federal Water Pollution Control Administration
	1970	Federal Water Quality Administration
EP 2	1970-19xx	Water Quality Office
	19xx-	Water Programs Operations Office

I 68

I 68	1967-1977	Alaska Power Administration
E 1	1977-1993	[part of] Energy Department
E 7	1993-	Alaska Power Administration

I 69

I 69	1973-1978	Mining Enforcement and Safety Administration
L 38	1978-	Mine Safety and Health Administration

I 70

I 66	1962-1978	Outdoor Recreation Bureau
I 70	1978-1981	Heritage Conservation and Recreation Service
I 29	1981-	[functions returned to the National Park Service]

I 71

I 71	1977-	Surface Mining Reclamation and Enforcement Office

I 72

I 72	1982-	Minerals Management Service

I 73

I 73	1993-	National Biological Service

IA 1

IA 1	1953-1978	United States Information Agency
ICA 1	1978-1982	International Communication Agency
IA 1	1982-1999	United States Information Agency

IC 1

IC 1	1887-	Interstate Commerce Commission
IC 1 acci	1902-1912	Accident Investigation Division
IC 1 acco	1887-	Accounts Bureau
IC 1 act		Acts to Regulate Comerce
IC 1 air	1934-1938	Air Mail Bureau
IC 1 blo	1908-	Block Signal and Train Control Board
IC 1 def	1950-	Defense Transport Administration
IC 1 eler		Electric Railways
IC 1 exp	1909-	Express Companies
IC 1 gas		Gas Corporations
IC 1 hou		Hours of Service Division
IC 1 loc		Locomotive Inspection Bureau
IC 1 mot	1937-1947	Motor Carriers Bureau
IC 1 pip		Pipe Line Companies
IC 1 rat		Rate Section
IC 1 saf		Safety Bureau
IC 1 sle		Sleeping Car Companies
IC 1 ste		Steam Roads Bureau
IC 1 telg		Telegraph Companies
IC 1 telp		Telephone Division
IC 1 val		Valuation Bureau
IC 1 wat		Carriers by Water Bureau

ICA 1

IA 1	1953-1978	United States Information Agency
ICA 1	1978-1982	International Communication Agency
IA 1	1982-	United States Information Agency

ITC 1

Y 3.T 17/2	1909-1916	Tariff Board
TC 1	1916-1974	Tariff Commission
	1974-1981	International Trade Commission
ITC	1981-	International Trade Commission

J 1

J 1	1789-1870	Office of Attorney General
	1870-	Justice Department, Office of Attorney General

J 1.14

J 1.14	1909-1935	Investigations Bureau
	1935-	Federal Bureau of Investigation

J 2

J 2	1893-1934	Assistance Attorney General for Court of Claims

J 3

J 3	1894-1907	Assistant Attorney General for Indian Depredation Claims

J 4

J 4	1873-	Library

J 5

T 44	1830-1870	Office of Solicitor of Treasury
J 5	1870-1912	Office of Solicitor of Treasury

J 6

J 6	1895-1926	Penitentiary, Fort Levenworth
J 16	1930-	Prisons Bureau

J 7

J 7	1901-1903	Porto Rico, Attorney General

J 8

J 8	1903-1939	National Training School for Boys
J 16	1939-	[transferred to] Prisons Bureau

J 9

J 9	1894-1912	Reform School for Girls of District of Columbia
	1912-1926	National Training School for Girls
J 16	1930-	Prisons Bureau

J 10

J 10	1898-1910	Assistant Attorney General for Spanish Treaty Claims Commission

J 11

J 11	1909-1939	Solicitor General

J 12

J 12	1909-1923	Assistant Attorney General for Customs Matters

J 13

J 13	1910-1926	Penitentiary, McNeil Island
J 16	1930-	Prisons Bureau

J 14

J 14	1910-1926	Penitentiary, Atlanta, Georgia
J 16	1930-	Prisons Bureau

J 15

J 15	1910-1923	Criminal Identification Bureau

J 16

J 16	1930-	Prisons Bureau

J 16.50

FPI 1	1934-1939	Federal Prison Industries, Inc.
J 16.50	1939-	Federal Prison Industries, Inc.

J 16.100

J 16	1974-1991	[Part of] Prisons Bureau
J 16.100	1991-	National Institute of Corrections

J 17

J 17	1930-1933	Prohibition Bureau
J 1.14	1933-1935	[functions transferred to] Investigation Bureau

J 18

J 18	1933-1945	War Risk Litigation Bureau

J 19

Y 3.Al 4	1917-1934	Alien Property Custodian
J 19	1934-1941	Alien Property Bureau
	1941-1942	Alien Property Division
Pr 32.5700	1942-1946	Alien Property Custodian Office
J 22	1946-1966	Alien Property Office

J 20

J 20	1903-1947	Antitrust Division

J 21

T 21	1891-1903	Immigration Bureau
C 7	1903-1906	Immigration Bureau
	1906-1913	Immigration and Naturalization Bureau
L 3	1913-1933	Immigration Bureau
L 6	1913-1933	Naturalization Bureau
L 15	1933-1940	Immigration and Naturalization Service
J 21	1940-	Immigration and Naturalization Service

J 22

Y 3.Al 4	1917-1934	Alien Property Custodian
J 19	1934-1941	Alien Property Bureau
	1941-1942	Alien Property Division
Pr 32.5700	1942-1946	Alien Property Custodian Office
J 22	1946-1966	Alien Property Office

J 23

C 50	1962-1966	Community Relations Service
J 23	1966-	Community Relations Service

J 24

FS 13.130	1967-1968	Drug Abuse Control Bureau
T 56	1930-1968	Narcotics Bureau
J 24	1968-1973	Narcotics and Dangerous Drugs Bureau
	1973-	Drug Enforcement Administration

J 25

J 25	1789-	United States Marshals Service

J 26

J 1	1968-1978	[classed under] Justice Department
J 26	1978-19xx	Law Enforcement Assistnace Administration
	19xx-1991	Justice Assistance, Research, and Statistics Office
	1991-	Justice Assistance Bureau

J 27

J 27		United States Parole Commission

J 28

J 28	1979-	National Institute of Justice

J 29

J 29	1979-	Justice Statistics Bureau

J 30

J 30	19xx-1965	Lands Division
	1965-	Land and Natural Resources Division

J 31

J 31		Executive Office for the United States Attorneys

J 32

J 32	1974-	Juvenile Justice and Delinquency Prevention Office

J 33

J 33	1985-	Attorney Personnel Management Office

J 34

J 34	1992-	Victims of Crime Office

J 35

J 35	199x-	Violence Against Women Office

J 36

J 36		Office of Community Oriiented Policing Services

Ju 1

J 36		Office of Community Oriented Policing Services
Ju 1		Circuit Courts [not used]

Ju 2

Ju 2	19xx-	United States Bankruptcy Court

Ju 3

Ju 3	1855-	Court of Claims

Ju 4

Ju 4		District Courts of the United States

Ju 5

Ju 5	1891-1904	Court of Private Land Claims

Ju 6

Ju 6	1789-	Supreme Court

Ju 7

Ju 7	1909-1929	Court of Customs Appeals
	1929-1982	Court of Customs and Patent Appeals
	1982-	Court of Appeals for the Federal Circuit

Ju 8

Ju 8	1910-1913	Commerce Court

Ju 9

T 20	1890-1926	United States General Appraisers Board
	1926-1930	United States Customs Court
Ju 9	1930-1980	United States Customs Court
	1980-	United States Court of International Trade

Ju 10

Ju 10	1939-	United States Courts Administrative Office

Ju 11

T 61	1936-1942	Processing Tax Board of Review
Y 3.T 19	1924-1942	United States Board of Tax Appeals
Ju 11	1942-	Tax Court of the United States

Ju 12

Ju 12	1942-	Emergency Court of Appeals

Ju 13

Ju 13	1967-	Federal Judicial Center

Ju 14

Ju 14		United States Bankruptcy Court

Ju 15

Ju 15	1988-	U.S. Court of Veterans Appeals

L 1

C 1	1903-1913	Commerce and Labor Department, Office of Secretary
L 1	1913-	Labor Department, Office of Secretary

L 1.39

L 27	1950-1951	Defense Manpower Office
	1951-1953	Defense Manpower Administration
L 1.39	1953-1975	Manpower Administration
L 37	1975-	Employment and Training Administration

L 2

La 1	1888-1903	Labor Bureau
C 8	1903-1913	Labor Bureau
L 2	1913-	Labor Statistics Bureau

L 3

T 21	1891-1903	Immigration Bureau
C 7	1903-1906	Immigration Bureau
	1906-1913	Immigration and Naturalization Bureau
L 3	1913-1933	Immigration Bureau
L 6	1913-1933	Naturalization Bureau
L 15	1933-1940	Immigration and Naturalization Service
J 21	1940-	Immigration and Naturalization Service

L 4

L 4	1913-1948	Publications and Supplies Division

L 5

C 19	1912-1913	Children's Bureau
L 5	1913-1946	Children's Bureau
FS 3.200	1947-1963	Children's Bureau
FS 14.100	1963-1967	Children's Bureau
FS 17.200	1967-1969	Children's Bureau
HE 21.100	1970-1975	Children's Bureau
HE 1.450	1975-1977	Children's Bureau
HE 23.1200	1977-	Children's Bureau

L 6

C 7.10	1903-1913	Naturalization Bureau
L 6	1913-1933	Naturalization Bureau
L 15	1933-1940	Immigration and Naturalization Service
J 21	1940-	Immigration and Naturalization Service

L 7

L 7	1918-1939	Employment Service
FS 3.100	1939-1942	Employment Security Bureau
Pr 32.5200	1942-1945	[part of] War Manpower Commission
L 7	1945-1948	Employment Service
FS 3.100	1948-1949	Employment Security Bureau
L 7	1949-1969	Employment Security Bureau
L 33	1969-1975	Unemployment Insurance Service
L 34	1969-1971	Training and Employment Service
L 1.39	1971-1975	[part of] Manpower Administration
L 37	1975-	Employment and Training Administration

L 8

L 8	1918-1937	Housing Corporation
T 58	1937-1947	[functions transferred to] Procurement Division

L 9

L 9	1918-1919	Information and Education Service

L 10

L 10	1918-1919	National War Labor Board

L 11

L 11	1918-1919	War Labor Policies Board

L 12

L 12	1918-1919	Training Service

L 13

L 13	1920-1971	Women's Bureau
L 36.100	1971-	Women's Bureau

L 14

L 14	1918-1919	Working Conditions Service

L 15

T 21	1891-1903	Immigration Bureau
C 7	1903-1906	Immigration Bureau
	1906-1913	Immigration and Naturalization Bureau
L 3	1913-1933	Immigration Bureau
L 6	1913-1933	Naturalization Bureau
L 15	1933-1940	Immigration and Naturalization Service
J 21	1940-	Immigration and Naturalization Service

L 16

L 16	1934-1948	Labor Standards Division
	1948-1971	Labor Standards Bureau
L 35	1971-	[functions transferred to] Occupational Safety and Health Bureau

L 17

Y 3.N 21/8	1933-1935	[a division in] National Recovery Administration
L 17	1935-1936	Consumers' Division
	1936-1938	Consumers' Project
A 55	1938-1942	[functions transferred to] Agricultural Adjustment Administration

L 18

L 18	1936-1942	Public Contracts Division
L 22	1942-1971	Wage and Hour and Public Contracts Division
L 36.200	1971-	Wage and Hour Division

L 19

L 19	1938-1947	Conciliation Service
FM 1	1947-	Federal Mediation and Conciliation Service

L 20

L 20	1936-1942	Wage and Hour Division
L 22	1942-1971	Wage and Hour and Public Contracts Division
L 36.200	1971-	Wage and Hour Division

L 21

L 21	1913-	Solicitor

L 22

L 18	1936-1942	Public Contracts Division
L 20	1936-1942	Wage and Hour Division
L 22	1942-1971	Wage and Hour and Public Contracts Division
L 36.200	1971-	Wage and Hour Division

L 23

L 16	1934-1942	[Apprenticeship Section in] Labor Standards Division
FS 3.100	1942-	[part of] Employment Security Bureau
Pr 32.5200	1942-1945	[part of] War Manpower Commission
L 23	1945-1948	Apprentice Training Service
	1948-1956	Apprenticeship Bureau
	1956-1976	Apprenticeship and Training Bureau
L 37.100	1975-	Apprenticeship and Training Bureau

L 24

Y 3.W 19/7	1944-1945	[part of] War Mobilization and Reconversion Office
L 24	1945-1947	Retraining and Reemployment Administration

L 25

L 25	1947-1948	Veterans' Reemployment Rights Division
	1948-1964	Veterans' Reemployment Rights Bureau
	1964-	Veterans' Reemployment Rights Office

L 26

EC 1	1916-1946	Employees' Compensation Commission
FS 13.300	1946-1950	Employees' Compensation Bureau
L 26	1950-1972	Employees' Compensation Bureau
L 36.400	1972-1973	Wage Compensation Programs Office
	1973-	Workers' Compensation Programs Office

L 27

L 27	1950-1951	Defense Manpower Office
	1951-1953	Defense Manpower Administration
L 1.39	1953-1975	Manpower Administration
L 37	1975-	Employment and Training Administration

L 28

| **L 28** | 1950- | Employees' Compensation Appeals Board |

L 29

| **L 29** | 1947-1959 | International Labor Affairs Office |
| | 1959- | International Labor Affairs Bureau |

L 30

| FIS 1 | 1939-1950 | Federal Interdepartmental Safety Council |
| **L 30** | 1950- | Federal Safety Council |

L 31

| **L 31** | 1959-1963 | Labor-Management Reports Bureau |

L 32

L 32	1967-1969	Work-Training Programs Bureau
L 34	1969-1971	Training and Employment Service
L 1	1971-1975	[classed under Manpower Administration in] Labor Department
L 37.300	1975-	Employment Service

L 33

SS 1	1935-1939	[part of] Social Security Board
FS 3.100	1939-1949	Employment Security Bureau
L 7	1949-1969	Employment Security Bureau
L 33	1969-1975	Unemployment Insurance Service
L 37.200	1975-	Unemployment Insurance Service

L 34

L 7	1949-1969	Employment Security Bureau
L 32	1967-1969	Work-Training Programs Bureau
L 34	1969-1971	Training and Employment Service
L 1	1971-1975	[classed under Manpower Administration in] Labor Department
L 37.300	1975-	Employment Service

L 35

| **L 35** | 1971- | Occupational Safety and Health Administration |

L 36

| **L 36** | 1971- | Employment Standards Administration |

L 36.100

| L 13 | 1920-1971 | Woman's Bureau |
| **L 36.100** | 1971- | Woman's Bureau |

L 36.200

L 18	1936-1942	Public Contracts Division
L 20	1936-1942	Wage and Hour Division
L 22	1942-1971	Wage and Hour and Public Contracts Division
L 36.200	1971-	Wage and Hour Division

L 36.300

| **L 36.300** | 1971- | Federal Employees' Compensation Office |

L 36.400

EC 1	1916-1946	Employees' Compensation Commission
FS 13.300	1946-1950	Employees' Compensation Bureau
L 26	1950-1972	Employees' Compensation Bureau
L 36.400	1972-1973	Wage Compensation Programs Office
	1973-	Workers' Compensation Programs Office

L 37

L 27	1950-1951	Defense Manpower Office
	1951-1953	Defense Manpower Administration
L 1.39	1953-1975	Manpower Administration
L 37	1975-	Employment and Training Administration

L 37.100

L 16	1934-1942	[Apprenticeship Section in] Labor Standards Division
FS 3.100	1942-	[part of] Employment Security Bureau
Pr 32.5200	1942-1945	[part of] War Manpower Commission
L 23	1945-1948	Apprentice Training Service
	1948-1956	Apprenticeship Bureau
	1956-1975	Apprenticeship and Training Bureau
L 37.100	1975-19xx	Apprenticeship and Training Bureau
	20xx-	Apprenticeship, Training, Employer and Labor Services

L 37.200

SS 1	1935-1939	[part of] Social Security Board
FS 3.100	1939-1949	Employment Security Bureau
L 7	1949-1969	Employment Security Bureau
L 33	1969-1975	Unemployment Insurance Service
L 37.200	1975-19xx	Unemployment Insurance Service
	20xx-	Workforce Security Office

L 37.300

L 7	1918-1939	Employment Service
FS 3.100	1939-1942	Employment Security Bureau
Pr 32.5200	1942-1945	[part of] War Manpower Commission
L 7	1945-1948	Employment Service
FS 3.100	1948-1949	Employment Security Bureau
L 7	1949-1969	Employment Security Bureau
L 34	1969-1971	Training and Employment Service
L 1	1971-1975	[part of] Labor Department
L 37.300	1975-	Employment Service

L 38

| I 69 | 1973-1978 | Mining Enforcement and Safety Administration |
| **L 38** | 1978- | Mine Safety and Health Administration |

L 39

| **L 39** | 199x- | Veterans' Employment and Training Service |

L 40

| **L 40** | 199x- | Pension and Welfare Benefits Administration |

La 1

La 1	1888-1903	Labor Bureau
C 8	1903-1913	Labor Bureau
L 2	1913-	Labor Statistics Bureau

LC 1

| **LC 1** | 1800- | Library of Congress |

LC 1.32

| **LC 1.32** | 1966- | Federal Library Committee |

LC 2

| **LC 2** | 1901-1944 | Bibliography Division |
| | 1944-1981 | General Reference and Bibliography Division |

LC 3

LC 3	1897-	Copyright Office

LC 4

LC 4	1897-	Manuscript Division

LC 5

LC 5	1897-1918	Maps and Charts Division
	1918-1965	Map Division
	1965-	Geography and Map Division

LC 6

LC 6	1907-1944	Periodicals Division
	1944-1956	Serials Division
	1956-19xx	Serial Division
	19xx-	Serial and Government Publications Division Research Services

LC 7

LC 7	1900-1943	Documents Division

LC 8

LC 8	1897-1922	Library Buildings and Grounds Superintendent

LC 9

LC 9	1902-1940	Catalog Division
	1940-	Descriptive Cataloging Division

LC 10

LC 10	1905-1981	Law Library
LC 42	1981-	Law Library

LC 11

LC 11	1905-1921	Prints Division
	1921-1940	Prints and Photographs Division
LC 25	1940-1949	Fine Arts Division
	1949-	Prints and Photographs Division

LC 12

LC 12	1902-1940	Music Division
LC 25	1940-1949	Fine Arts Division
LC 12	1949-	Music Division

LC 13

LC 13	1907-1924	Order Division
	1924-1943	Accession Division

LC 14

LC 14	1929-1971	Legislative Reference Service
	1971-	Congressional Research Service

LC 15

LC 15	1930-1940	Aeronautics Division

LC 16

LC 16	1929-1936	Service for the Blind

LC 17

LC 17	1932-1982	Orientalia Division
	1982-	Asian Division

LC 18

LC 18	1936-	Union Catalog Division

LC 19

LC 19	1931-1938	Books for the Adult Blind
	1938-1941	Project Books for the Adult Blind
	1941-1950	Blind and Physically Handicapped Division
	1950-1967	Blind Division
	1967-1978	Blind and Physically Handicapped Division
	1978-19xx	National Library for the Blind and Physically Handicapped
	19xx-	National Library Services for the Blind and Physically Handicapped

LC 20

LC 20	1937-1939	Semitic Literature Division

LC 21

LC 21	1937-1939	State Law Index

LC 22

LC 22	1934-1940	Cooperative Cataloging and Classification Service

LC 23

LC 23	1938-1944	Rare Book Collections
	1944-1977	Rare Book Division
	1977-	Rare Book and Special Collection Division

LC 24

LC 24	1940-1974	Hispanic Foundation
	1974-	Latin American, Portuguese, and Spanish Division

LC 25

LC 11	1921-1940	Prints and Photographs Division
LC 12	1902-1940	Music Division
LC 25	1940-1949	Fine Arts Division
LC 12	1949-	Music Division
LC 25	1949-	Prints and Photographs Division

LC 26

LC 26	1940-19xx	Subject Cataloging Division
	19xx-	Cataloging Policy and Support Office

LC 27

LC 27	1943-1947	Acquisitions Department

LC 28

LC 28	1940-	Card Division
LC 30	1940-	[transferred to] Processing Department

LC 29

LC 29	1944-	Reference Department

LC 30

LC 30	1940-	Processing Department

LC 31

LC 31	1948-1952	European Affairs Division

LC 32

LC 32	1948-1952	Science and Technology Project

LC 33

LC 33	1952-1960	Science Division
	1960-	Science and Technology Division

LC 34

LC 34	1954-	Stack and Reader Division

LC 35

LC 35	1953-1956	Slavic and East European Division
	1956-1983	Slavic and Central European Division
LC 43	1983-	European Division

LC 36

LC 36	1954-1961	Technical Information Division

LC 37

LC 37	1959-	Decimal Classification Office

LC 38

LC 38	1960-1963	Air Information Division
	1963-1965	Aerospace Information Division
	1965-1973	Aerospace Technology Division

LC 39

LC 39	1976-	American Folklife Center

LC 40

LC 40		Motion Picture, Broadcasting, and Recorded Sound Division

LC 41

LC 41		African and Middle Eastern Division

LC 42

LC 10	1905-1981	Law Library
LC 42	1981-	Law Library

LC 43

LC 35	1953-1956	Slavic and East European Division
	1956-1983	Slavic and Central European Division
LC 43	1983-	European Division

LR 1

Y 3.N 21/10	1933-1934	National Labor Board
Y 3.N 21/13	1934-1935	National Labor Relations Board
LR 1	1935-	National Labor Relations Board

M 1

M 1	1947-1949	National Military Establishment
D 1	1949-	Defense Department, Office of Secretary

M 2

M 2	1947-1949	Joint Chiefs of Staff
D 5	1949-	Joint Chiefs of Staff

M 3

M 3	1947-1948	Army-Navy Explosives Safety Board
	1948-1949	Armed Services Explosives Safety Board

M 4

M 4	1948-1949	Civil Defense Planning Office

M 5

M 5	1947-1949	Munitions Board
D 3	1949-1953	Munitions Board
	1953-	[Publications Relating to Industrial Mobilization and Security]

M 6

Y 3.J 66/2	1946-1947	Joint Research and Development Board
M 6	1947-1949	Research and Development Board
D 4	1949-1953	Research and Development Board
	1953-	[Publications Relating to Research and Development]

M 101

W 1	1789-1947	War Department, Office of Secretary
M 101	1947-1949	Army Department, Office of Secretary
D 101	1949-	Army Department, Office of Secretary

M 102

W 44	1818-1947	Medical Department
M 102	1947-1949	Army Medical Department
D 104	1949-1950	Army Medical Service
	1950-	Army Medical Department

M 103

W 110	1946-1947	Historical Division
M 103	1947-1949	Historical Division
D 114	1949-1950	Historical Division
	1950-1974	Chief of Military History Office
	1974-	Military History Center

M 104

W 109.200	1943-1944	Morale Services Division
W 111	1944-1947	Information and Education Division
M 104	1947-1949	Troop Information and Education Division
D 107	1949-1954	Troop Information and Education Division
D 2	1949-1952	Information and Education Division
	1952-1968	Armed Forces Information and Education Office
	1968-1971	Information for the Armed Forces Office
	1977-	American Forces Information Services

M 105

W 1	1947	[a division in] War Department
M 105	1947-1949	Civil Affairs Division
D 102	1949-	[functions transferred to] Adjutant General's Office
S 1	1949-	[functions transferred to] State Department

M 106

W 100	1918-1947	Military Intelligence Division
M 106	1947-1949	Intelligence Division

M 107

W 10	1849-1864	Judge Advocate General's Office
	1864-1884	Military Justice Office
	1884-1947	Judge Advocate General's Department
M 107	1947-1949	Judge Advocate General's Department
D 108	1949-	Judge Advocate General's Office

M 108

W 3	1813-1947	Adjutant General's Office
M 108	1947-1949	Adjutant General's Office
D 102	1949-	Adjutant General's Office

M 109

W 12	1802-1947	Military Academy
M 109	1947-1949	Military Academy
D 109	1949-	Military Academy

M 110

W 7	1802-1947	Engineer Department
M 110	1947-1949	Engineer Department
D 103	1949-	Engineer Corps

M 110.100

W 33	1841-1947	Northern and Northwestern Lakes Survey
M 110.100	1947-1949	Lake Survey Office
D 103.200	1949-	Lake Survey Office

M 110.200

W 31	1879-1947	Mississippi River Commission
M 110.200	1947-1949	Mississippi River Commission
D 103.300	1949-	Mississippi River Commission

M 110.300

W 7	1933-1947	[part of] Engineer Department
M 110.300	1947-1949	Beach Erosion Board
D 103	1949-	[part of] Engineer Corps

M 110.400

W 7.16	1802-1947	Engineer School
M 110.400	1947-1947	Engineer School
D 103.100	1949-	Engineer School

M 111

W 34	1812-1947	Ordnance Department
M 111	1947-1949	Ordnance Department
D 105	1949-1968	Ordnance Corps
	1968-	[Publications Relating to Ordnance]

M 112

W 77	1912-1947	Quartermaster Corps
M 112	1947-1949	Quartermaster General of the Army
D 106	1949-	Quartermaster Corps

M 113

W 2	1903-1945	General Staff Corps
M 113	1947-1949	General Staff
D 5	1949-	Joint Chiefs of Staff

M 114

W 70	1908-1916	Militia Affairs Division
	1916-1933	Militia Bureau
	1933-1947	National Guard Bureau
M 114	1947-1949	National Guard Bureau
D 112	1949-1958	National Guard Bureau
D 12	1958-	National Guard Bureau

M 115

W 79	1912-1945	Canal Zone
M 115	1947-1949	Panama Canal
D 113	1949-1950	Panama Canal
PaC 1	1950-1951	Panama Canal
CZ 1	1950-1979	Panama Canal Zone Company
Y 3.P 19/2	1979-	Panama Canal Commission

M 116

W 97	1918-1920	Finance Service
	1920-1947	Finance Department
M 116	1947-1949	Finance Department

M 117

W 109.100	1940-1947	Special Services Division
M 117	1947-1949	Special Services Division

M 118

W 107	1941-1946	Public Relations Bureau
	1946-1947	Public Relations Division
M 118	1947-1949	Public Information Division

M 119

W 28	1881-1947	General Service Schools
M 119	1947-1949	Command and General Staff College
D 110	1949-	Command and General Staff College

M 201

N 1	1789-1947	Navy Department, Office of Secretary
M 201	1947-1949	Navy Department, Office of Secretary
D 201	1949-	Navy Department, Office of Secretary

M 202

N 18	1842-1866	Ordnance and Hydrography Bureau
N 6	1866-1947	Hydrographic Office
M 202	1947-1949	Hydrographic Office
D 203	1949-1962	Hydrographic Office
	1962-	Naval Oceanographic Office

M 203

N 10	1842-1947	Medicine and Surgery Bureau
M 203	1947-1949	Medicine and Surgery Bureau
D 206	1949-	Medicine and Surgery Bureau

M 204

M 204	1947-1949	Industrial Relations Office
D 204	1949-1966	Industrial Relations Office
	1966-	Civilian Manpower Management Office

M 205

N 21	1842-1862	Navy Yards and Docks Bureau
	1862-1947	Yards and Docks Bureau
M 205	1947-1949	Yards and Docks Bureau
D 209	1949-1966	Yards and Docks Bureau
	1966-	Naval Facilities Engineering Command

M 206

N 17	1862-1942	Navigation Bureau
	1942-1947	Naval Personnel Bureau
M 206	1947-1949	Naval Personnel Bureau
D 208	1949-1972	Naval Personnel Bureau
	1972-19xx	Naval Training Support Command
	19xx-	Naval Military Personnel Command

M 206.100

N 12	1845-1947	Naval Academy
M 206.100	1947-1949	Naval Academy
D 208.100	1949-	Naval Academy

M 206.200

N 15	1884-1947	Naval War College
M 206.200	1947-1949	Naval War College
D 208.200	1949-	Naval War College

M 207

N 27	1915-1947	Naval Operations Office
M 207	1947-1949	Naval Operations Office
D 207	1949-	Naval Operations Office

M 208

N 28	1921-1947	Aeronautics Bureau
M 208	1947-1949	Aeronautics Bureau
D 202	1949-1959	Aeronautics Bureau
D 217	1959-1966	Naval Weapons Bureau
D 202	1966-	Naval Air Systems Command

M 209

N 9	1798-1947	Marine Corps
M 209	1947-1949	Marine Corps
D 214	1949-	Marine Corps

M 210

N 4	1862-1940	Construction and Repair Bureau
N 19	1920-1940	Engineering Bureau
N 29	1940-1947	Ships Bureau
M 210	1947-1949	Ships Bureau
D 211	1949-1966	Ships Bureau
	1966-19xx	Naval Ship Systems Command
	19xx-	Naval Sea Systems Command

M 211

N 18	1842-1866	Ordnance and Hydrography Bureau
	1866-1947	Ordnance Bureau
M 211	1947-1949	Ordnance Bureau
D 215	1949-1959	Ordnance Bureau
D 217	1959-1966	Naval Weapons Bureau
D 215	1966-	Naval Ordnance Systems Command

M 212

N 14	1842-1947	Naval Observatory
M 212	1947-1949	Naval Observatory
D 213	1949-	Naval Observatory

M 213

N 20	1842-1892	Provisions and Clothing Bureau
	1892-1947	Supplies and Accounts Bureau
M 213	1947-1949	Supplies and Accounts Bureau
D 212	1949-1966	Supplies and Accounts Bureau
	1966-	Naval Supply Systems Command

M 214

N 7	1880-1947	Judge Advocate General
M 214	1947-1949	Judge Advocate General
D 205	1949-	Judge Advocate General

M 215

N 31	1941-1947	Public Relations Office
M 215	1947-1949	Public Relations Office

M 216

N 32	1946-1947	Naval Research Office
M 216	1947-1949	Naval Research Office
D 210	1949-	Naval Research Office

M 301

W 108	1941-1947	Army Air Force
M 301	1947-1949	Air Force Department, Office of Secretary
D 301	1949-	Air Force Department, Office of Secretary

M 302

M 302	1947-1949	Air Adjutant General's Office
D 303	1949-1958	Air Adjutant General's Office
	1958-	Administrative Services Directorate

M 400

M 400		Munitions Board [not used]
M 5	1947-1949	Munitions Board

M 500

M 500		Research and Development Board [not used]
M 6	1947-1949	Research and Development Board

MB 1

RL 1	1920-1926	Railroad Labor Board
MB 1	1926-1934	United States Board of Mediation
NMB 1	1934-	National Mediation Board

MC 1

SB 1	1917-1933	Shipping Board
SB 2	1917-1927	Shipping Board Emergency Fleet Corporation
	1927-1933	Shipping Board Merchant Fleet Corporation
C 27	1933-1936	Shipping Board Bureau
MC 1	1936-1950	United States Maritime Commission
C 39.100	1950-1961	Federal Maritime Board
C 39.200	1950-1981	Maritime Administration
TD 11	1981-	Maritime Administration

MCB 1

MCB 1	1913-1921	United States Board of Mediation and Conciliation

ML 1

ML 1	1938-1942	Maritime Labor Board

MS 1

CS 1	1883-1978	Civil Service Commission
MS 1	1978-	Merit Systems Protection Board

MS 2

MS 2	1978-	Office of the Special Counsel

MuS 1

MuS 1	1976-1981	Museum Services Institute
NF 4	1981-	Museum Services Institute

N 1

N 1	1789-1947	Navy Department, Office of Secretary
M 201	1947-1949	Navy Department, Office of Secretary
D 201	1949-	Navy Department, Office of Secretary

N 2

N 2	1898-1904	Assistant Secretary

N 3

N 3	1886-1888	Admiral of the Navy

N 4

N 4	1842-1862	Construction Equipment and Repair Bureau
N 5	1862-1890	Equipment and Recruiting Bureau
N 4	1862-1940	Construction and Repair Bureau
N 19	1920-1940	Engineering Bureau
N 29	1940-1947	Ships Bureau
M 210	1947-1949	Ships Bureau
D 211	1949-1966	Ships Bureau
	1966-19xx	Naval Ship Systems Command
	19xx-	Naval Sea Systems Command

N 5

N 4	1842-1962	Construction, Equipment and Repair Bureau
N 5	1962-1890	Equipment and Recruiting Bureau
N 17	1890-1942	[functions transferred to] Naviation Bureau
N 5	1890-1910	Equipment Bureau

N 6

N 18	1842-1866	Ordnance and Hydrography Bureau
N 6	1866-1947	Hydrographic Office
M 202	1947-1949	Hydrographic Office
D 203	1949-1962	Hydrographic Office
	1962-	Naval Oceanographic Office

N 7

N 7	1880-1947	Judge Advocate General
M 214	1947-1949	Judge Advocate General
D 205	1949-	Judge Advocate General

N 8

N 8	1908-1947	Solicitor of Navy Department

N 9

N 9	1798-1947	Marine Corps
M 209	1947-1949	Marine Corps
D 214	1949-	Marine Corps

N 10

N 10	1842-1947	Medicine and Surgery Bureau
M 203	1947-1949	Medicine and Surgery Bureau
D 206	1949-	Medicine and Surgery Bureau

N 11

N 11	1849-1947	Nautical Almanac Office
M 212	1947-1949	[functions transferred to] Naval Observatory

N 12

N 12	1845-1947	Naval Academy
M 206.100	1947-1949	Naval Academy
D 208.100	1949-	Naval Academy

N 13

N 13	1882-1947	Naval Intelligence Office

N 14

N 14	1842-1947	Naval Observatory
M 212	1947-1949	Naval Observatory
D 213	1949-	Naval Observatory

N 15

N 15	1884-1947	Naval War College
M 206.200	1947-1949	Naval War College
D 208.200	1949-	Naval War College

N 16

N 16	1895-1915	Library and Naval War Records Office
	1915-1947	Naval Records and Library Office

N 17

N 17	1862-1942	Navigation Bureau
	1942-1947	Naval Personnel Bureau
M 206	1947-1949	Naval Personnel Bureau
D 208	1949-1972	Naval Personnel Bureau
	1972-19xx	Naval Training Support Command
	19xx-	Naval Military Personnel Command

N 18

N 18	1842-1866	Ordance and Hydrography Bureau
N 6	1866-1947	Hydrographic Office
N 18	1842-1947	Ordance and Hydrography Bureau
	1866-1947	Ordnance Bureau
M 211	1947-1949	Ordnance Bureau
D 215	1949-1959	Ordnance Bureau
D 217	1959-1966	Naval Weapons Bureau
D 215	1966-	Naval Ordnance Systems Command

N 19

N 4	1862-1940	Construction and Repair Bureau
N 19	1920-1940	Engineering Bureau
N 29	1940-1947	Ships Bureau
M 210	1947-1949	Ships Bureau
D 211	1949-1966	Ships Bureau
	1966-19xx	Naval Ship Systems Command
	19xx-	Naval Sea Systems Command

N 20

N 20	1842-1892	Provisions and Clothing Bureau
	1892-1947	Supplies and Accounts Bureau
M 213	1947-1949	Supplies and Accounts Bureau
D 212	1949-1966	Supplies and Accounts Bureau
	1966-	Naval Supply Systems Command

N 21

N 21	1842-1862	Navy Yards and Docks Bureau
	1862-1947	Yards and Docks Bureau
M 205	1947-1949	Yards and Docks Bureau
D 209	1949-1966	Yards and Docks Bureau
	1966-	Naval Facilities Engineering Command

N 22

N 22	1912-1916	Naval Radio Service
	1916-1947	Naval Communications Service

N 23

N 23	1914-1918	Naval Militia Affairs Division

N 24

T 24	1878-1915	Life-Saving Service
T 33	1894-1915	Revenue-Cutter Service
T 47	1915-1917	Coast Guard
N 24	1917-1919	Coast Guard
T 47	1919-1941	Coast Guard
N 24	1941-1946	Coast Guard
T 47	1946-1966	Coast Guard
TD 5	1966-	Coast Guard

N 25

N 25	1915-1918	Naval Reserve Force Division

N 26

N 26	1917-1919	Training Camp Activities Commission

N 27

N 27	1915-1947	Naval Operations Office
M 207	1947-1949	Naval Operations Office
D 207	1949-	Naval Operations Office

N 28

N 28	1921-1947	Aeronautics Bureau
M 208	1947-1949	Aeronautics Bureau
D 202	1949-1959	Aeronautics Bureau
D 217	1959-1966	Naval Weapons Bureau
D 202	1966-	Naval Air Systems Command

N 29

N 4	1862-1940	Construction and Repair Bureau
N 19	1920-1940	Engineering Bureau
N 29	1940-1947	Ships Bureau
M 210	1947-1949	Ships Bureau
D 211	1949-1966	Ships Bureau
	1966-19xx	Naval Ship Systems Command
	19xx-	Naval Sea Systems Command

N 30

N 30	1942-1945	Procurement and Material Office

N 31

N 31	1941-1947	Public Relations Office
M 215	1947-1949	Public Relations Office

N 32

N 32	1946-1947	Naval Research Office
M 216	1947-1949	Naval Research Office
D 210	1949-	Naval Research Office

NA 1

NA 1	1863-	National Academy of Science

NA 2

NA 2	1916-	National Research Council

NAS 1

Y 3.N 21/5	1915-1958	National Aeronautics Advisory Committee
NAS 1	1958-	National Aeronautics and Space Administration

NC 1

NC 1	1926-1952	National Capital Park and Planning Commission
NC 2	1952-	National Capital Planning Commission

NC 2

NC 1	1926-1952	National Capital Park and Planning Commission
NC 2	1952-	National Capital Planning Commission

NC 3

NC 3	1952-1966	National Capital Regional Planning Council

NCU 1

FS 3.300	1948-1969	Federal Credit Union Bureau
HE 3.300	1970	Federal Credit Union Bureau
NCU 1	1970-	National Credit Union Administration

NF 1

NF 1	1965-	National Foundation on the Arts and Humanities

NF 2

NF 2	1965-	National Endowment for the Arts

NF 3

NF 3	1965-	National Endowment for the Humanities

NF 4

MuS 1	1976-1981	Museum Services Institute
NF 4	1981-	Museum Services Institute

NH 1

NH 1	1866-1930	National Home for Disabled Volunteer Soldiers
VA 1	1930-	Veterans Administration

NHA 1

NHA 1	1942-1947	National Housing Agency
HH 1	1947-1965	[functions transferred to] Housing and Home Finance Agency

NHA 2

Y 3.F 31/11	1934-1939	Federal Housing Administration
FL 2	1939-1942	Federal Housing Administration
NHA 2	1942-1947	Federal Housing Administration
HH 2	1947-	Federal Housing Administration

NHA 3

Y 3.F 31/3	1932-1939	Federal Home Loan Bank Board
FL 3	1939-1942	Federal Home Loan Bank Board
NHA 3	1942-1947	Federal Home Loan Bank Administration
HH 4	1947-1955	Federal Home Loan Bank Board
FHL 1	1955-1989	Federal Home Loan Bank Board
FHF 1	1989-	Federal Housing Financing Board
T 71	1989-	Thrift Supervisor Office
Y 3.R 31/2	1989-	Resolution Trust Corporation

NHA 4

I 40	1937-1939	Housing Authority
FW 3	1939-1942	Housing Authority
NHA 4	1942-1947	Federal Public Housing Administration
HH 3	1947-1965	Public Housing Administration
	1965-1969	Housing Assistance Administration
HH 1	1969-	[functions transferred to] Housing and Urban Development Department

NMB 1

RL 1	1920-1926	Railroad Labor Board
MB 1	1926-1934	United States Board of Mediation
NMB 1	1934-	National Mediation Board

NMC 1

NMC 1	1936-1940	National Munitions Control Board

NS 1

NS 1	1950-	National Science Foundation

NS 2

NS 2	1958-	Science Information Service Office

NS 3

NS 3		Science Information Council

Ol 1

Ol 1		Old West Regional Action Planning Commission

OP 1

OP 1	1969-	Overseas Private Investment Corporation

P 1

P 1	1792-1970	Post Office Department
	1970-	United States Postal Service

P 2

P 2	1881-1949	First Assistant Postmaster General

P 3

P 3	1879-1949	Second Assistant Postmaster General

P 4

P 4	1836-1949	Third Assistant Postmaster
	1949-	Finance Bureau

P 5

P 5	1892-1970	Fourth Assistant Postmaster General

P 6

P 6	1891-1913	Assistant Attorney General for Post-Office Department
	1913-1952	Solicitor for Post Office Department

P 7

P 7	1815-1904	Dead Letters Division

P 8

P 8	1880-1928	Foreign Mails Division
	1928-1946	International Postal Service Division
	1946-1970	International Postal Transport Division

P 9

P 9	1864-1951	Money Orders Division

P 10

P 10	1869-1946	Railway Mail Service
	1946-1949	Surface Postal Transport Division
	1949	Postal Transportation Service
	1949-1970	Transportation Bureau

P 11

P 11	1885-1936	Topography Division

P 12

P 12	1900-1902	Salaries and Allowances Division

P 13

P 13	1900-1903	Free Delivery Division

P 14

P 14	1905-1916	Post-Office Inspectors Division

P 15

P 15	1904-1949	Purchasing Agent

P 16

P 16	1905-1928	Rural Delivery Division

P 17

P 17	1904-1909	Pneumatic Tube Commission

P 18

P 18	1909-1915	Supplies Division
	1915-1970	Equipment and Supplies Division

P 19

PS 1	1910-1913	Postal Savings System
P 19	1913-1943	Postal Savings System
	1943-1970	Postal Savings Division

P 20

P 20	19xx-1946	Air Mail Service
	1946-1970	Air Postal Transport Division

P 21

P 21	1924-1941	Motor Vehicle Service Division

P 22

P 22	1921-1949	Accounts Bureau

P 23

P 23	1933-1940	Building Operations and Supplies Division

P 24

P 24	1949-1963	Operation Bureau
	1963-1970	Chief Postal Inspector Bureau

P 25

P 25	1954	Controller Bureau

PA 1

AR 1	1890-1907	American Republics Bureau
PA 1	1910-1948	Pan American Union

PaC 1

W 79	1912-1945	Canal Zone
M 115	1947-1949	Panama Canal
D 113	1949-1950	Panama Canal
PaC 1	1950-1951	Panama Canal
CZ 1	1950-1979	Panama Canal Zone Company
Y 3.P 19/2	1979-	Panama Canal Commission

PAS 1

PAS 1		Pan American Sanitary Bureau

PB 1

S 12	1883-1925	State, War and Navy Department Buildings Office
W 38	1867-1925	Public Buildings and Ground Office
PB 1	1925-1933	Public Buildings and Public Parks of the National Capital Office
I 29	1933-	[functions transferred to] National Park Service

PC 1

PC 1	1923-1932	Personnel Classification Board
CS 1	1932-1978	[functions transferred to] Civil Service Commission

PE 1

SE 19	1961-1971	Peace Corps
AA 4	1971-1982	Peace Corps
PE 1	1982-	Peace Corps

PI 1

PI 1	1933-1939	Press Intelligence Division for U.S. Government
Pr 32.200	1939-1942	[functions transferred to] Government Reports Office

PM 1

CS 1	1883-1978	Civil Service Commission
PM 1	1978-	Personnel Management Office

Pr

Pr 1	1789-1797	George Washington
Pr 2	1797-1801	John Adams
Pr 3	1801-1809	Thomas Jefferson
Pr 4	1809-1817	James Madison
Pr 5	1817-1825	James Monroe
Pr 6	1825-1837	John Quincy Adams
Pr 7	1829-1837	Andrew Jackson
Pr 8	1837-1841	Martin Van Buren
Pr 9	1841	William Henry Harrison
Pr 10	1841-1845	John Tyler
Pr 11	1845-1849	James Knox Polk
Pr 12	1849-1850	Zachery Taylor
Pr 13	1850-1853	Millard Fillmore
Pr 14	1853-1857	Franklin Pierce
Pr 15	1857-1861	James Buchanan
Pr 16	1861-1865	Abraham Lincoln
Pr 17	1865-1869	Andrew Johnson
Pr 18	1869-1877	Ulysses Simpson Grant
Pr 19	1877-1881	Rutherford Birchard Hayes
Pr 20	1881	James Abram Garfield
Pr 21	1881-1885	Chester Alan Auther
Pr 22	1885-1889	Grover Cleveland
	1893-1897	Grover Cleveland
Pr 23	1889-1893	Benjamin Harrison
Pr 24		Grover Cleveland [not used, see Pr 22]
Pr 25	1897-1901	William McKinley
Pr 26	1901-1909	Theodore Roosevelt
Pr 27	1909-1913	William Howard Taft
Pr 28	1913-1921	Woodrow Wilson
Pr 29	1921-1923	Warren Gamaliel Harding
Pr 30	1923-1929	Calvin Coolidge
Pr 31	1929-1933	Herbert Hoover

Pr 32

Pr 32	1933-1945	Franklin Delano Roosevelt

Pr 32.100

T 51	1921-1939	Budget Bureau
Pr 32.100	1939-1945	Budget Bureau
Pr 33.100	1945-1953	Budget Bureau
Pr 34.100	1953-1961	Budget Bureau
PrEx 2	1961-1970	Budget Bureau
	1970-	Management and Budget Office

Pr 32.200

Y 3.N 21/9	1933-1939	National Emergency Council
Pr 32.200	1939-1942	Government Reports Office
Pr 32.5000	1942-1945	War Information Office
Pr 33.100	1945-1946	[functions transferred to] Budget Bureau
Pr 33.400	1946-1948	Government Reports Office

Pr 32.300

C 26	1934-1939	Federal Employment Stabilization Board
Y 3.N 21/12	1935-1939	National Resources Committee
Pr 32.300	1939-1943	National Resources Planning Board

Pr 32.400

Pr 34.400	1940-1945	Emergency Management Office

Pr 32.4000

Pr 32.4000	1941-1942	Production Management Office
Pr 32.4800	1942-1945	War Production Board
	1945-1946	Civilian Production Administration
Pr 33.300	1946-1947	Temporary Controls Office

Pr 32.4100

Pr 32.4100	1940-1941	State and Local Cooperation Division
Pr 32.4400	1941-1945	[functions transferred to] Civilian Defense Office

Pr 32.4200

Y 3.C 831:	1940-1941	[a division in] National Defense Council Advisory Commission
Pr 32.4200	1941	Price Administration and Civilian Supply Office
Pr 32.4000	1941-1942	[some functions transferred to] Production Management Office
Pr 32.4200	1941-1946	Price Administration Office
Pr 33.300	1946-1947	Temporary Control Office

Pr 32.4250

Pr 32.4250		Consumer Division

Pr 32.4300

Y3.C 831:100	1940-1941	[an office in] National Defense Council Advisory Commission
Pr 32.4300	1941-1942	Defense Housing Coordination Division
NHA 1	1941-1947	[functions transferred to] National Housing Authority

Pr 32.4400

Pr 32.4000	1941-1945	Civilian Defense Office

Pr 32.4500

FS 8	1940-1941	Coordinator of Health, Welfare, and Related Defense Activities Office
Pr 32.4500	1941-1943	Defense Health and Welfare Services Office
FS 9	1943-1946	Community War Services Office
FS 12	1943-1946	Physical Fitness Committee

Pr 32.4600

Y 3.831:100	1940-1941	[an office in] National Defense Council Advisory Commission
Pr 32.4600	1941-1945	Inter-American Affairs Coordinator's Office
	1945-1946	Inter-American Affairs Office
S 1.64	1946-1953	Institute of Inter-American Affairs
FO 1	1953-1955	Foreign Operations Administration
S 17	1955-1961	International Cooperation Administration
S 18	1961-	International Development Agency

Pr 32.4700

Pr 32.4700	1941-1942	Facts and Figures Office
Pr 32.5000	1942-1945	War Information Office
Pr 33.100	1945-1953	[functions transferred to] Budget Bureau

Pr 32.4800

Pr 32.4000	1941-1942	Production Management Office
Pr 32.4800	1942-1945	War Production Board
	1945-1946	Civilian Production Administration
Pr 33.300	1946-1947	Temporary Controls Office

Pr 32.4900

Y3.C 831:100	1940-1941	[a division in] National Defense Council Advisory Commission
Pr 32.4900	1941-1949	Defense Transportation Office

Pr 32.5000

Pr 32.200	1939-1942	Government Reports Office
Pr 32.5000	1942-1945	War Information Office
Pr 33.100	1945-1946	[functions transferred to] Budget Bureau
S 1	1945-	[functions transferred to] State Department

Pr 32.5100

Pr 32.5100	1942-1945	National War Labor Board
L 1.17	1945-1946	National Wage Stabilization Board

Pr 32.5200

L 7	1918-1939	Employment Service
SS 1	1935-1939	[some functions of] Social Security Board
FS 3.100	1939-1942	Employment Security Bureau
Pr 32.5200	1942-1945	[part of] War Manpower Commission
L 7	1945-1948	Employment Service
FS 3.100	1948-1949	Employment Security Bureau
L 7	1949-1969	Employment Security Bureau
L 33	1969-1975	Unemployment Insurance Service
L 34	1969-1971	Training and Employment Service

Pr 32.5250

Y 3.N 21/14	1935-1939	National Youth Administration
FS 6	1939-1942	National Youth Administration
Pr 32.5250	1942-1944	National Youth Administration

Pr 32.5270

Y 3.Se 4	1940-1942	Selective Service System
Pr 32.5270	1942-1943	Selective Service System
Y 3.Se 4	1943-1947	Selective Service System
	1947-1948	Selective Service Records Office
	1948-	Selective Service System

Pr 32.5300

Pr 32.5300	1942-1946	War Shipping Administration
MC 1	1946-1950	[functions transferred to] U.S. Maritime Commission

Pr 32.5400

Pr 32.5400	1942-1944	War Relocation Authority
I 52	1944-1946	War Relocation Authority

Pr 32.5500

Pr 32.5500	1941-1943	Lend-Lease Administration Office
Pr 32.5800	1943-1945	Foreign Economic Administration

Pr 32.5600

Pr 32.5600	1940-1942	Defense Communications Board
	1942-1947	War Communications Board
CC 1	1947-	[functions transferred to] Federal Communications Commission

Pr 32.5700

Y 3.Al 4	1917-1934	Alien Property Custodian
J 19	1934-1941	Alien Property Bureau
	1941-1941	Alien Property Division
Pr 32.5700	1942-1946	Alien Property Custodian Office
J 22	1946-1966	Alien Property Office

Pr 32.5800

Pr 32.5500	1941-1943	Lend-Lease Administration Office
Y 3.Ec 74/2	1941-1943	Economic Warfare Board
Pr 32.5800	1943-1945	Foreign Economic Administration

Pr 32.5900

Pr 32.5900	1943-1944	War Mobilization Office
Y 3.W19.7:200	1944-1946	War Mobilization and Reconversion Office
Pr 33.300	1946-1947	Temporary Controls Office

Pr 32.6000

Pr 32.6000	1942-1945	Economic Stabilization Office
Y 3.W 19/7	1945-1946	[functions transferred to] War Mobilization and Reconversion Office
Pr 32.6000	1946	Economic Stabilization Office
Y 3.W 19/7	1946	[functions transferred to] War Mobilization and Reconversion Office

Pr 33

Pr 33	1945-1953	Harry S. Truman

Pr 33.9

Pr 33.9	1946-1953	Council of Economic Advisors
Pr 34.9	1953-1961	Council of Economic Advisors
PrEx 6	1961-	Council of Economic Advisors

Pr 33.11

Pr 33.11		Citizens Food Committee

Pr 33.12

Pr 33.12	1950	President's Water Resources Policy Commission

Pr 33.13

Pr 33.13	1950-1951	President's Communications Policy Board

Pr 34.14

Pr 33.14	1950-1951	President's Commission on Migratory Labor

Pr 33.15

Pr 33.15	1951-1952	President's Materials Policy Commission

Pr 33.16

Pr 33.16		President's Airport Commission

Pr 33.17

Pr 33.17	1953	President's Government Contract Compliance Committee
Pr 34.8:C 76/2	1953-1954	President's Government Contract Compliance Committee

Pr 33.18

Pr 33.18	1952-1953	President's Immigration and Naturalization Commission

Pr 33.19

Pr 33.19	1951-1952	President's Health Needs of the National Commission

Pr 33.20

Pr 33.20		President's Management Advisory Committee

Pr 33.22

Pr 33.22	1952-1953	Missouri Basin Survey Commission

Pr 33.100

T 51	1921-1939	Budget Bureau
Pr 32.100	1939-1945	Budget Bureau
Pr 33.100	1945-1953	Budget Bureau
Pr 34.100	1953-1961	Budget Bureau
PrEx 2	1961-1970	Budget Bureau
	1970-	Management and Budget Office

Pr 33.200

FL 5	1945-1946	[War Assets Corporation in] Reconstruction Finance Corporation
Y3.W19/7:200	1945-1946	[some functions of] Surplus Property Administration
Pr 32.200	1946-1947	War Assets Administration
Y 3.W 19/8	1947-1949	War Assets Administration

Pr 33.300

Pr 32.4200	1941-1946	Price Administration Office
Pr 32.4800	1945-1946	Civilian Production Administration
Y 3.W 19/7	1944-1946	War Mobilization and Reconversion Office
Pr 33.300	1946-1947	Temporary Controls Office

Pr 33.400

Y 3.N 21/9	1933-1939	National Emergency Council
Pr 32.200	1939-1942	Government Reports Office
Pr 32.5000	1942-1945	War Information Office
Pr 33.100	1945-1946	[functions transferred to] Budget Bureau
Pr 33.400	1946-1948	Government Reports Office

Pr 33.500

Pr 33.500	1946-1951	Philippine Alien Property Administration

Pr 33.600

Y 3.N 21.17	1947-1949	National Security Council
Pr 33.600	1949-1953	National Security Council
PrEx 3	1961-	National Security Council

Pr 33.650

Y3.N21/17:100	1947-1949	Central Intelligence Agency
Pr 33.650	1949-1953	Central Intelligence Agency
Pr 34.600	1953-1961	Central Intelligence Agency
PrEx 3.10	1961-	Central Intelligence Agency

Pr 33.700

Y 3.N 21/18	1947-1949	National Security Resources Board
Pr 33.700	1949-1953	National Security Resources Board
Pr 34.200	1953-1958	[functions transferred to] Defense Mobilization Office

Pr 33.800

Pr 33.800	1950-1951	Federal Civil Defense Administration
FCD 1	1951-1958	Federal Civil Defense Administration
Pr 34.700	1958-1961	Defense and Civilian Mobilization Office
PrEx 4	1961	Civil and Defense Mobilization Office
D 13	1961-1964	Civil Defense Office
D 119	1964-1972	Civil Defense Office
D 14	1972-1971	Defense Civil Preparedness Agency
FEM 1	1979-	Federal Emergency Management Agency

Pr 33.900

Y 3.Ec 74/3	1948-1951	Economic Cooperation Administration
Pr 33.900	1951-1953	Mutual Security Agency
S 1.64	1946-1953	Institute of Inter-American Affairs
FO 1	1953-1955	Foreign Operations Administration
S 17	1955-1961	International Cooperation Administration
S 18	1961-	International Development Agency

Pr 33.1000

Pr 33.1000	1950-1953	Defense Mobilization Office
Pr 34.200	1953-1958	Defense Mobilization Office
Pr 34.700	1958-1961	Defense and Civilian Mobilization Office
PrEx 4	1961	Civil and Defense Mobilization Office
	1961-1968	Emergency Planning Office
	1968-1973	Emergency Preparedness Office
D 13	1973-1964	Civil Defense Office
GS 13	1973-1979	Federal Preparedness Agency
HH 12	1973-1979	Federal Disaster Assistance Administration
FEM 1	1979-	Federal Emergency Management Agency

Pr 33.1100

Pr 33.1100	1950-1951	Defense Production Administration
DP 1	1951-1953	Defense Production Administration
Pr 33.1000	1953	[functions transferred to] Defense Mobilization Office

Pr 34

Pr 34	1953-1961	Dwight D. Eisenhower

Pr 34.9

Pr 33.9	1946-1953	Council of Economic Advisors
Pr 34.9	1953-1961	Council of Economic Advisors
PrEx 6	1961-	Council of Economic Advisors

Pr 34.11

Pr 34.11		White House Disarmament Staff

Pr 34.100

T 51	1921-1939	Budget Bureau
Pr 32.100	1939-1945	Budget Bureau
Pr 33.100	1945-1953	Budget Bureau
Pr 34.100	1953-1961	Budget Bureau
PrEx 2	1961-1970	Budget Bureau
	1970-	Management and Budget Office

Pr 34.200

Pr 33.1000	1950-1953	Defense Mobilization Office
Pr 34.200	1953-1958	Defense Mobilization Office
Pr 34.700	1958-1961	Defense and Civilian Mobilization Office
PrEx 4	1961	Civil and Defense Mobilization Office
	1961-1968	Emergency Planning Office
	1968-1973	Emergency Preparedness Office
D 13	1973-1964	Civil Defense Office
GS 13	1973-1979	Federal Preparedness Agency
HH 12	1973-1979	Federal Disaster Assistance Administration
FEM 1	1979-	Federal Emergency Management Agency

Pr 34.209

Pr 34.209	1951-1958	Labor Management Manpower Policy Committee

Pr 34.600

Y 3.N 21/17:100	1947-1949	Central Intelligence Agency
Pr 33.650	1949-1953	Central Intelligence Agency
Pr 34.600	1953-1961	Central Intelligence Agency
PrEx 3.10	1961-	Central Intelligence Agency

Pr 34.650

Pr 34.650	1953-1961	Foreign Broadcast Information Service
PrEx 7	1961-	Foreign Broadcast Information Service

Pr 34.700

FCD 1	1951-1958	Federal Civil Defense Administration
Pr 34.200	1953-1958	Defense Mobilization Office
Pr 34.700	1958-1961	Defense and Civilian Mobilization Office
PrEx 4	1961-1973	Civil and Defense Mobilization Office
D 13	1973-1964	Civil Defense Office
GS 13	1973-1979	Federal Preparedness Agency
HH 12	1973-1979	Federal Disaster Assistance Administration
FEM 1	1979-	Federal Emergency Management Agency

Pr 35

Pr 35	1961-1963	John F. Kennedy

Pr 36

Pr 36	1963-1969	Lyndon B. Johnson

Pr 37

Pr 37	1969-1974	Richard M. Nixon

Pr 38

Pr 38	1974-1977	Gerald R. Ford

Pr 39

Pr 39	1977-1981	Jimmy Carter

Pr 40

Pr 40	1981-1989	Ronald Reagan

Pr 41

Pr 41	1989-1993	George H. Bush

Pr 42

Pr 42	1993-2001	William J. Clinton
Pr 43	2001-	George W. Bush

PrEx 1

PrEx 1	1961-	Executive Office of the President

PrEx 1.10

PrEx 1.10	1961-	President's Committee on Employment of the Handicapped

PrEx 2

T 51	1921-1939	Budget Bureau
Pr 32.100	1939-1945	Budget Bureau
Pr 33.100	1945-1953	Budget Bureau
Pr 34.100	1953-1961	Budget Bureau
PrEx 2	1961-1970	Budget Bureau
	1970-	Management and Budget Office

PrEx 3

Y 3.N 21.17	1947-1949	National Security Council
Pr 33.600	1949-1953	National Security Council
PrEx 3	1961-	National Security Council

PrEx 3.10

Y 3.N21/17:100	1947-1949	Central Intelligence Agency
Pr 33.650	1949-1953	Central Intelligence Agency
Pr 34.600	1953-1961	Central Intelligence Agency
PrEx 3.10	1961-	Central Intelligence Agency

PrEx 4

Pr 34.700	1958-1961	Defense and Civilian Mobilization Office
PrEx 4	1961	Civil and Defense Mobilization Office
D 13	1961-1964	Civil Defense Office
PrEx 4	1961-1968	Emergency Planning Office
	1968-1973	Emergency Preparedness Office
D 13	1973-1964	Civil Defense Office
GS 13	1973-1979	Federal Preparedness Agency
HH 12	1973-1979	Federal Disaster Assistance Administration
FEM 1	1979-	Federal Emergency Management Agency

PrEx 5

PrEx 5	1961-1973	National Aeronautics and Space Council

PrEx 6

Pr 33.9	1946-1953	Council of Economic Advisors
Pr 34.9	1953-1961	Council of Economic Advisors
PrEx 6	1961-	Council of Economic Advisors

PrEx 7

Pr 34.650	1953-1961	Foreign Broadcast Information Service
PrEx 7	1961-	Foreign Broadcast Information Service

PrEx 8

PrEx 8	1962-1973	Science and Technology Office
NS 1	1973-1976	[functions transferred to] National Science Foundation
PrEx 23	1976-	Science and Technology Policy Office

PrEx 8.100

PrEx 8.100	1976-	Federal Coordinating Council for Science, Engineering, and Technology

PrEx 9

PrEx 9	1963-1974	Special Representative for Trade Negotiations Office
	1974-	Office of the U.S. Trade Representative

PrEx 10

PrEx 10	1964-1975	Economic Opportunity Office
CSA 1	1975-1981	Community Services Administration
HE	1981-	[functions transferred to] Office of Community Services

PrEx 11

PrEx 11	1964-1965	National Council on the Arts
NF 1	1965-	[functions transferred to] National Foundation on the Arts and Humanities

PrEx 12

PrEx 12	1966-1971	National Council on Marine Resources and Engineering Development

PrEx 13

PrEx 13	1970-1973	National Clearinghouse for Drug Abuse Information
HE 20.8200	1973-	[functions transferred to] National Institute on Drug Abuse

PrEx 14

PrEx 14	1970-	Environmental Quality Council

PrEx 15

PrEx 15	1970-1978	Domestic Council
	1978-1981	Domestic Policy Staff
	1981-	Policy Development Office

PrEx 16		
PrEx 16	1971-1973	Consumer Affairs Office
HE 1.500	1973-	Consumer Affairs Office

PrEx 17		
PrEx 17	1971-1974	Cost of Living Council

PrEx 18		
PrEx 18	1970-1977	Telecommunications Policy Office
C 1.59	1977-	[functions transferred to] Telecommunications Office

PrEx 19		
PrEx 19	1971-1973	Pay Board

PrEx 20		
PrEx 20	1971-1975	Special Action Office for Drug Abuse Prevention

PrEx 21		
PrEx 21	1973-1977	Federal Energy Office

PrEx 22		
PrEx 22	1974-1981	Wage and Price Stability Council

PrEx 23		
PrEx 8	1962-1973	Science and Technology Office
Y 3.F 31/16	1959-1973	Federal Council for Science and Technology
NS 1	1973-1976	[functions transferred to] National Science Foundation
PrEx 23	1976-	Science and Technology Policy Office

PrEx 24		
PrEx 24	1976-1978	Drug Abuse Policy Office

PrEx 25		
PrEx 25	1982-	Regulatory Information Service Center

PrEx 26		
PrEx 26	199x-	National Drug Control Policy Office

PrVp 40		
PrVp 40	1981-1989	George Bush

PrVp 41		
PrVp 41	1989-1993	Dan Quayle

PrVp 42		
PrVp 42	1993-2001	Albert Gore

PrVp 43		
PrVp 43	2001-	Richard Cheney

PS 1		
PS 1	1910-1913	Postal Savings System
P 19	1913-1943	Postal Savings System
	1943-1970	Postal Savings Division

RA 1		
RA 1	1934-	National Railroad Adjustment Board

RA 2		
RA 2		National Railroad Adjustment Board, Second Division [not used]

RA 3		
RA 3	1934-	National Railroad Adjustment Board, Third Division

RB 1		
RB 1	1913-1914	Reserve Bank Organization Committee

RC 1		
RC 1	1927-1934	Federal Radio Commission
CC 1	1934-	Federal Communications Commission

RL 1		
RL 1	1920-1926	Railroad Labor Board
MB 1	1926-1934	United States Board of Mediation
NMB 1	1934-	National Mediation Board

RnB 1		
Y 3.W 19/6	1944-1951	War Contracts Price Adjustment Board
RnB 1	1951-1979	Renegotiation Board

RR 1		
RR 1	1935-	Railroad Retirement Board

S 1		
S 1	1789-	State Department, Office of Secretary

S 2		
S 2		American Republics Bureau [not used]
Ar 1	1890-1907	American Republics Bureau
PA 1	1910-1948	Pan American Union

S 3		
S 3		Arbitrations and Mixed Commission to Settle International Disputes

S 4		
S 4	1874-1897	Statistics Bureau
	1897-1903	Foreign Commerce Bureau
T 37	1886-1903	Statistics Bureau
C 14	1903-1912	Statistics Bureau
C 18	1912-1953	Foreign and Domestic Commerce Bureau
C 41	1953-1970	Business and Defense Services Administration
C 42	1953-1961	Foreign Commerce Bureau

S 5		
S 5		International Congresses, Conferences, and Commissions

S 6		
S 6		International Exhibits and Expositions

S 7		
S 7		Laws of the United States

S 8		
S 8	1874-1921	Rolls and Library Bureau

S 9		
S 9		Treaties

S 10		
W 23	1898-1900	Puerto Rico Department
I 1.40	1900-1909	Puerto Rico
S 10	1909-	Puerto Rico
W 75	1909-1934	Puerto Rico
I 35	1934-1950	[functions transferred to] Territories and Island Possessions Division

S 11

S 11	1903-1912	Trade Relations Bureau

S 12

S 12	1883-1925	State, War and Navy Department Buildings Office
W 28	1867-1925	Public Buildings and Ground Office
PB 1	1925-1933	Public Buildings and Public Parks of the National Capital Office
I 29	1933-	[functions transferred to] National Park Service

S 13

WT 1	1917-1919	War Trade Board
S 13	1919-1924	War Trade Board Section

S 14

S 14	1906-1933	United States Court for China

S 15

S 15	1938-1944	Cultural Relations Division

S 16

S 16	1940-1944	Central Translating Office

S 17

FO 1	1953-1955	Foreign Operations Administration
Y 3.In 8/5	1950-1955	International Development Advisory Board
S 17	1955-1961	International Cooperation Administration
S 18	1961-	International Development Agency

S 18

FO 1	1953-1955	Foreign Operations Administration
Y 3.In 8/5	1950-1955	International Development Advisory Board
S 17	1955-1961	International Cooperation Administration
S 18	1961-	International Development Agency

S 19

S 19	1961-1971	Peace Corps
AA 4	1971-1982	Peace Corps
PE 1	1982-	Peace Corps

S 20

S 20	20xx-	International Information Programs

S 21

S 21	20xx-	Educational and Cultural Affairs Bureau

S 22

S 22	20xx-	Arms Control and International Security

S 22.100

S 22.100	20xx-	Arms Control Bureau

SB 1

SB 1	1917-1933	Shipping Board
SB 2	1917-1927	Shipping Board Emergency Fleet Corporation
	1927-1933	Shipping Board Merchant Fleet Corporation
C 27	1933-1936	Shipping Board Bureau
MC 1	1936-1950	United States Maritime Commission
C 39.100	1950-1961	Federal Maritime Board
C 39.200	1950-1981	Maritime Administration
TD 11	1981-	Maritime Administration

SB 2

SB 1	1917-1933	Shipping Board
SB 2	1917-1927	Shipping Board Emergency Fleet Corporation
	1927-1933	Shipping Board Merchant Fleet Corporation
C 27	1933-1936	Shipping Board Bureau

MC 1	1936-1950	United States Maritime Commission
C 39.100	1950-1961	Federal Maritime Board
C 39.200	1950-	Maritime Administration

SB 3

SB 3	1917-1919	Recruiting Service

SB 4

SB 4	1917-1933	Marine and Dock Industrial Relations Division

SB 5

SB 5	1918-1919	Planning and Statistics Division

SB 6

SB 6	1918-1919	Port and Harbor Facilities Commission

SB 7

SB 7	1916-1933	Shipping Board Research Bureau
C 27.9	1933-1936	Shipping Board Bureau, Research

SB 8

SB 8	1918-1919	Law Bureau

SB 9

SB 9	1917-1920	Operations Bureau

SB 10

SB 10	1918-1920	Finance Bureau

SB 11

SB 11	1918-1933	Constructions Bureau

SBA 1

SBA 1	1953-	Small Business Administration

SDP 1

SDP 1	1951-1953	Small Defense Plants Administration
SBA 1	1953-	[functions transferred to] Small Business Administration

SE 1

SE 1	1934-	Securities and Exchange Commission

SI 1

SI 1	1846-	Smithsonian Institution

SI 2

SI 2	1879-1894	Ethnology Bureau
	1894-	American Ethnology Bureau

SI 3

SI 3	1846-1964	National Museum
	1964-1982	National Museum of History and Technology
	1982-	National Museum of American History

SI 4

SI 4	1889-	American Historical Association

SI 5

SI 5	1896-1948	National Society of the Daughters of the American Revolution

SI 6

SI 6	1921-1937	National Gallery of Art
	1937-1980	National Collection of Fine Arts
	1980-	National Museum of American Art
SI 8	1937-	National Gallery of Art

SI 7

| SI 7 | 1921- | Freer Gallery of Art |

SI 8

| SI 6 | 1921-1937 | National Gallery of Art |
| SI 8 | 1937- | National Gallery of Art |

SI 9

| SI 9 | 1946-1967 | National Air Museum |
| | 1967- | National Air and Space Museum |

SI 10

| SI 10 | 1958-1963 | National Cultural Center |
| | 1963- | John F. Kennedy Center for the Performing Arts |

SI 11

| SI 11 | 1962- | National Portrait Gallery |

SI 12

| SI 12 | 1967- | Woodrow Wilson International Center for Scholars |

SI 13

| SI 13 | 1974- | Hirshhorn Museum and Sculpture Garden |

SI 14

| SI 14 | 1979- | National Museum of African Art |

SS 1

SS 1	1935-1939	Social Security Board
FS 3	1939-1946	Social Security Board
	1946-1969	Social Security Administration
HE 3	1970-1995	Social Security Administration
SSA 1	1995-	Social Security Administration

SSA 1

SS 1	1935-1939	Social Security Board
FS 3	1939-1946	Social Security Board
	1946-1969	Social Security Administration
HE 3	1970-1995	Social Security Administration
SSA 1	1995-	Social Security Administration

T 1

| T 1 | 1789- | Treasury Department, Office of Secretary |

T 1.100

T 1.100	1941-1942	Defense Savings Staff
	1942-1943	War Savings Staff
T 66	1943-1945	War Finance Division
	1945-	Savings Bonds Division

T 2

| T 2 | 1875-1940 | Appointments Division |

T 3

| T 3 | 1817-1921 | Auditor For Treasury Department |
| GA 1 | 1921- | [functions transferred to] General Accounting Office |

T 4

| T 4 | 1817-1921 | Auditor for War Department |
| GA 1 | 1921- | [functions transferred to] General Accounting Office |

T 5

| T 5 | 1817-1921 | Auditor for Interior Department |
| GA 1 | 1921- | [functions transferred to] General Accounting Office |

T 6

| T 6 | 1817-1921 | Auditor for Navy Department |
| GA 1 | 1921- | [functions transferred to] General Accounting Office |

T 7

| T 7 | 1817-1921 | Auditor for State and Other Departments |
| GA 1 | 1921- | [functions transferred to] General Accounting Office |

T 8

| T 8 | 1836-1921 | Auditor For Post Office Department |
| GA 1 | 1921- | [functions transferred to] General Accounting Office |

T 9

T 9	1879-1894	Warrants, Estimates, and Appropriations Divisions
	1894-1940	Bookkeeping and Warrants Division
T 63.100	1940-1973	[functions transferred to] Accounts Bureau

T 10

| T 10 | 1897-1910 | Chief Clerk and Superintendent |

T 11

T 11	1816-1934	Survey of the Coast
	1836-1878	Coast Survey
	1878-1903	Coast and Geodetic Survey
C 4	1903-1965	Coast and Geodetic Survey
C 52	1965-1970	Environmental Science Service Administration
C 55.400	1970-1984	National Ocean Survey
	1984-	National Ocean Service

T 12

| T 12 | 1863- | Comptroller of the Currency |

T 13

T 13	1867-1894	First Comptroller
T 15	1894-1921	Comptroller of the Treasury
GA 1	1921-	[functions transferred to] General Accounting Office

T 14

T 14	1880-1894	Second Comptroller
T 15	1894-1921	Comptroller of the Treasury
GA 1	1921-	[functions transferred to] General Accounting Office

T 15

T 13	1867-1894	First Comptroller
T 14	1880-1894	Second Comptroller
T 16	1849-1894	Customs Commissioner
T 15	1894-1921	Comptroller of the Treasury
GA 1	1921-	[functions transferred to] General Accounting Office

T 16

T 16	1849-1894	Customs Commissioner
T 15	1894-1921	Comptroller of the Treasury
GA 1	1921-	[functions transferred to] General Accounting Office

T 17

T 17	1870-1927	Customs Division
	1927-1973	Customs Bureau
	1973-	Customs Service

T 18

| T 18 | 1862- | Engraving and Printing Bureau |

T 19

| T 19 | 1853-1909 | Examiners Board |

T 20

T 20	1890-1926	United States General Appraisers Board
	1926-1930	United States Customs Court
Ju 9	1930-19xx	United States Customs Court
	19xx-	United States Court of International Trade

T 21

T 21	1891-1903	Immigration Bureau
C 7	1903-1906	Immigration Bureau
	1906-1913	Immigration and Naturalization Bureau
L 3	1913-1933	Immigration Bureau
L 6	1913-1933	Naturalization Bureau
L 15	1933-1940	Immigration and Naturalization Service
J 21	1940-	Immigration and Naturalization Service

T 22

T 22	1862-1953	Internal Revenue Bureau
	1953-	Internal Revenue Service

T 23

T 23	1878-	Library

T 24

T 24	1878-1915	Life-Saving Service
T 33	1894-1915	Revenue-Cutter Service
T 47	1915-1917	Coast Guard
N 24	1917-1919	Coast Guard
T 47	1919-1941	Coast Guard
N 24	1941-1946	Coast Guard
TD 5	1966-	Coast Guard

T 25

T 25	1852-1903	Lighthouse Board
C 9	1903-1939	Lighthouses Bureau
T 47	1939-1966	[functions transferred to] Coast Guard

T 26

T 26	1876-1920	Loans and Currency Division
T 57	1920-1940	Public Debt Service
T 63.200	1940-	Public Debt Bureau

T 27

T 27	1798-1902	Marine Hospital Service
	1902-1912	Public Health and Marine Hospital Service
	1912-1939	Public Health Service
FS 2	1939-1969	Public Health Service
HE 20	1970-	Public Health Service

T 28

T 28	1792-1873	Mint of the United States
	1873-1984	Mint Bureau
	1984-	United States Mint

T 29

T 29	1879-1886	National Board of Health

T 30

T 30	1884-1903	Navigation Bureau
C 11	1903-1932	Navigation Bureau
C 25	1932-1936	Navigation and Steamboat Inspection Bureau
	1936-1942	Marine Inspection and Navigation Bureau
N 24	1942-1946	[functions transferred to] Coast Guard
T 17	1942-1973	[functions transferred to] Customs Bureau

T 31

T 31	1875-1921	Public Moneys Division
T 9	1921-1940	[functions transferred to] Bookkeeping and Warrants Division

T 32

T 32	1870-1920	Register of Treasury
T 57	1920-1940	Public Debt Service
T 63.200	1940-	Public Debt Bureau

T 33

T 24	1878-1915	Life-Saving Service
	1843-1894	Revenue Marine Division
T 33	1894-1915	Revenue-Cutter Service
T 47	1915-1917	Coast Guard
N 24	1917-1919	Coast Guard
T 47	1919-1941	Coast Guard
N 24	1941-1946	Coast Guard
TD 5	1966-	Coast Guard

T 34

T 34	1882-	Secret Service

T 35

T 35	1915-1960	Special Agents Division

T 36

T 36	1875-1927	Printing and Stationery Division

T 37

T 37	1886-1903	Statistics Bureau
C 14	1903-1912	Statistics Bureau
C 18	1912-1953	Foreign and Domestic Commerce Bureau
C 41	1953-1970	Business and Defense Services Administration
C 42	1953-1963	Foreign Commerce Bureau

T 38

T 38	1853-1903	Steamboat Inspection Service
C 15	1903-1932	Steamboat Inspection Service
C 25	1932-1936	Navigation and Steamboat Inspection Bureau
	1936-1942	Marine Inspection and Navigation Bureau
N 24	1942-1946	[functions transferred to] Coast Guard
T 17	1942-1973	[functions transferred to] Customs Bureau

T 39

T 39	1867-1933	Supervising Architect Office
T 58	1933-1939	[Office transferred to Public Buildings Branch in] Procurement Division
FW 6	1939-1949	[Office transferred to] Public Buildings Administration

T 40

T 40	1789-1940	Treasurer of the United States
T 63.300	1940-	Treasurer of the United States

T 41

T 11	1882-1901	[an Office in] Coast and Geodetic Survey
T 41	1901-1903	National Bureau of Standards
C 13	1903-1934	Standards Bureau
	1934-1989	National Bureau of Standards
	1989-	National Institute of Standards and Technology

T 42

T 42	1875-1882	Mercantile Marine and Internal Revenue Division
	1882-1888	Captured Property, Claims, and Lands Division
	1888-1906	Miscellaneous Division

T 43

T 43	1900-1909	Puerto Rico Auditor
W 75.6	1909-1934	Puerto Rico Auditor

T 44

T 44	1830-1870	Solicitor of Treasury Office
J 5	1870-1912	Solicitor of Treasury Office

T 45

GS	1909-1910	General Supply Committee
T 45	1910-1933	General Supply Committee
T 58	1933-1947	Procurement Division
	1947-1949	Federal Supply Bureau
GS 2	1949-1982	Federal Supply Service
	1982-19xx	Personal Property Office
	19xx-	Federal Supply and Services Office

T 46

T 46	1912-1920	Supervising Tea Examiner Office
A 7	1920-1927	[functions transferred to] Chemistry Bureau

T 47

T 24	1878-1915	Life-Saving Service
T 33	1894-1915	Revenue-Cutter Service
T 47	1915-1917	Coast Guard
N 24	1917-1919	Coast Guard
T 47	1919-1941	Coast Guard
N 24	1941-1946	Coast Guard
TD 5	1966-	Coast Guard

T 48

T 48	1916-1933	Federal Farm Loan Bureau
FCA 1	1933-1939	Farm Credit Administration
A 72	1939-1942	Farm Credit Administration
A 79.100	1942-1943	Farm Credit Administration [not used]
A 72	1943-1953	Farm Credit Administration
FCA 1	1953-	Farm Credit Administration

T 49

T 49	1914-1921	War Risk Insurance Bureau
VB 1	1921-1930	Veterans Bureau
VA 3	1930-1931	Veterans Bureau
VA 1	1931-	[functions transferred to] Veterans Administration

T 50

T 50	1919-1935	Government Actuary

T 51

T 51	1921-1932	Budget Bureau
Pr 32.100	1939-1945	Budget Bureau
Pr 33.100	1945-1953	Budget Bureau
Pr 34.100	1953-1961	Budget Bureau
PrEx 2	1961-1970	Budget Bureau
	1970-	Management and Budget Office

T 52

T 52	1922-1927	Supply Bureau
T 55	1927-1935	Supply Division

T 53

T 53	1922-1930	Federal Narcotics Control Board
T 56	1930-1968	Narcotics Bureau
J 24	1968-1973	Narcotics and Dangerous Drugs Bureau
	1973-	Drug Enforcement Administration

T 54

T 54	1930-1933	Industrial Alcohol Bureau
T 22	1933-1953	[functions transferred to] Internal Revenue Bureau

T 55

T 52	1922-1927	Supply Bureau
T 55	1927-1935	Supply Division

T 56

T 53	1922-1930	Federal Narcotics Control Board
T 56	1930-1968	Narcotics Bureau
J 24	1968-1973	Narcotics and Dangerous Drugs Bureau
	1973-	Drug Enforcement Administration

T 57

T 26	1876-1920	Loans and Currency Division
T 32	1870-1920	Register of the Treasury
T 57	1920-1940	Public Debt Service
T 63.200	1940-	Public Debt Bureau

T 58

GS	1909-1910	General Supply Committee
T 45	1910-1933	General Supply Committee

T 58

T 58	1933-1947	Procurement Division
	1947-1949	Federal Supply Bureau
GS 2	1949-1982	Federal Supply Service
	1982-19xx	Personal Property Office
	19xx-	Federal Supply and Services Office

T 59

Y 3.F 31/10	1933-1935	Federal Alcohol Control Administration
T 59	1935-1940	Federal Alcohol Administration
T 22	1940-1953	[functions transferred to] Internal Revenue Bureau

T 60

T 60	1920-1940	Accounts and Deposits Commissioner
T 63.100	1940-1974	Accounts Bureau
	1974-1984	Government Financial Operations Bureau
	1984-	Financial Management Service

T 61

T 61	1936-1942	Processing Tax Board of Review
Ju 11	1942-	Tax Court of the United States

T 62

T 62	1934-1947	Research and Statistics Division
T 68	1947-1953	Technical Staff Office

T 63

T 63	1940-	Fiscal Service

T 63.100

T 60	1920-1940	Accounts and Deposits Commissioner
T 63.100	1940-1974	Accounts Bureau
	1974-1984	Government Financial Operations Bureau
	1984-	Financial Management Service

T 63.200

T 26	1876-1920	Loans and Currency Division
T 32	1870-1920	Register of the Treasury
T 57	1920-1940	Public Debt Service
T 63.200	1940-	Public Debt Bureau

T 63.300

T 40	1789-1940	Treasurer of the United States
T 63.300	1940-	Treasurer of the United States

T 64

T 64	1939-1949	Tax Research Division
	1949-1953	Tax Advisory Staff

T 65

T 65	1940-1947	Foreign Funds Control

T 66

T 1.100	1941-1942	Defense Savings Staff
	1942-1943	War Savings Staff
T 66	1943-1945	War Finance Division
	1945-	Savings Bonds Division

T 67

Y 3.W 19/7:100	1944-1946	Contract Settlement Office
T 67	1946-1949	Contract Settlement Office
GS 5	1949-1952	Contract Settlement Office

T 68

T 62	1934-1947	Research and Statistics Division
T 68	1947-1953	Technical Staff Office

T 69

Y 3.R 24	1947-1954	[functions transferred from] Reconstruction Finance Corporation
T 69	1954-1957	Federal Facilities Corporation
GS 7	1957-1961	Federal Facilities Corporation

T 70

T 70	1972-	Alcohol, Tobacco, and Firearms Bureau

T 71

FHL 1	1955-1989	Federal Home Loan Bank Board
T 71	1989-19xx	Thrift Supervisor Office
	19xx-	Thrift Supervision Office

TC 1

Y 3.T 17/2	1909-1916	Tariff Board
TC 1	1916-1974	Tariff Commission
	1974-1981	International Trade Commission
ITC	1981-	International Trade Commission

TD 1

TD 1	1966-	Transportation Department, Office of Secretary

TD 1.100

TD 1.100	1966-	National Transportation Safety Board

TD 1.200

TD 1.200		Transportation Security Administration

TD 2

TD 2	1966-	Federal Highway Administration

TD 2.100

A 22	1893-1898	Road Inquiry Office
	1898-1905	Public Road Inquiry Office
	1905-1915	Public Roads Office
	1915-1918	Public Roads and Rural Engineering Office
	1918-1939	Public Roads Bureau
FW 2	1939-1949	Public Roads Administration
GS 3	1949	Public Roads Bureau
C 37	1949-1966	Public Roads Bureau
TD 2.100	1966-1969	Public Roads Bureau
TD 2	1969-	[functions transferred to] Federal Highway Administration

TD 2.200

TD 2.200	1966-1970	National Highway Safety Bureau
TD 8	1970-	National Highway Traffic Safety Administration

TD 2.300

TD 2.300	1966-19xx	Motor Carrier Safety Bureau
	19xx-	Federal Motor Carrier Safety Administration

TD 3

TD 3	1966-	Federal Railroad Administration

TD 3.100

TD 3.100	1966-19xx	Railroad Safety Bureau
	19xx-	Railroad Safety Office

TD 4

C 31.100	1940-1958	Civil Aeronautics Administration
FAA 1	1958-1967	Federal Aviation Agency
TD 4	1967-	Federal Aviation Administration

TD 4.100

FAA 8	1958-1967	Airports Service
TD 4.100	1967-19xx	Airports Service
	19xx-	Airport Programs Office

TD 4.150

TD 4.150	20xx	Airport Safety and Standards Office

TD 4.200

FAA 7	1958-1967	Aviation Medical Service
TD 4.200	1967-	Aviation Medicine Office

TD 4.300

FAA 3	1958-1967	Air Traffic Service
TD 4.300	1967-198x	Air Traffic Service
	198x-	Air Traffic Operations Service

TD 4.400

FAA 5	1958-1967	Flight Standards Bureau
TD 4.400	1967-	Flight Standards Service

TD 4.500

FAA 2	1958-1967	Systems Research and Development Service
TD 4.500	1967-	Systems Research and Development Service

TD 4.600

TD 4.600	1967-	Aircraft Development Service

TD 4.700

FAA 4	1958-1967	Facilities Bureau
TD 4.700	1967-	Airway Facilities Service

TD 4.800

TD 4.800	1967-	Civil Aviation Security Service

TD 4.900

TD 4.900	199x-	Aircraft Certification Service

TD 5

T 24	1878-1915	Life-Saving Service
T 33	1894-1915	Revenue-Cutter Service
T 47	1915-1917	Coast Guard
N 24	1917-1919	Coast Guard
T 47	1919-1941	Coast Guard
N 24	1941-1946	Coast Guard
T 47	1946-1966	Coast Guard
TD 5	1966-	Coast Guard

TD 6

Y 3.Sa 2	1954-1966	St. Lawrence Seaway Development Corporation
TD 6	1966-	St. Lawrence Seaway Development Corporation

TD 7

TD 7	1968-19xx	Urban Mass Transportation Administration
	19xx-	Federal Transit Administration

TD 8

TD 2.200	1966-1970	National Highway Safety Bureau
TD 8	1970-	National Highway Traffic Safety Administration

TD 9

TD 9	1975-19xx	Materials Transportation Bureau
	19xx-	Hazardous Materials Transportation Office

TD 10

TD 10	1977-	Research and Special Programs Administration

TD 11

C 39.200	1961-1981	Maritime Administration
TD 11	1981-	Maritime Administration

TD 12

TD 12	1992-	Transportation Statistics Bureau

TD 13

TD 13	199x-	Surface Transportation Board

TDA 1

TDA 1	19xx-	U.S. Trade and Development Agency

VA 1

VA 1	1930-1988	Veterans Administration
	1988-	Veterans Affairs Department

VA 2

I 24	1824-1890	Commissioner of Pensions Office
	1890-1930	Pension Bureau
VA 2	1930-1931	Pensions Bureau
VA 1	1931-	[functions transferred to] Veterans Administration

VA 3

T 49	1914-1921	War Risk Insurance Bureau
VE 1	1917-1921	[Rehabilitation Division in] Federal Board for Vocational Education
VB 1	1921-1930	Veterans Bureau
VA 3	1930-1931	Veterans Bureau
VA 1	1931-	[functions transferred to] Veterans Administration

VB 1

T 49	1914-1921	War Risk Insurance Bureau
VE 1	1917-1921	[Rehabilitation Division in] Federal Board for Vocational Education
VB 1	1921-1930	Veterans Bureau
VA 3	1930-1931	Veterans Bureau
VA 1	1931-	[functions transferred to] Veterans Administration

VE 1

VE 1	1917-1933	Federal Vocational Education Board
I 16.54	1933-1939	Vocational Division
FS 5.120	1939-1945	Vocational Division
	1945-1949	Vocational Education Division

W 1

W 1	1789-1947	War Department, Office of Secretary
M 101	1947-1949	Army Department, Office of Secretary
D 101	1949-	Army Department, Office of Secretary

W 2

W 2	1903-1947	General Staff Corps
M 113	1947-1949	General Staff
D 5	1949-	Joint Chiefs of Staff

W 3

W 3	1913-1947	Adjutant General's Office
M 108	1947-1949	Adjutant General's Office
D 102	1949-	Adjutant General's Office

W 4

W 4	1890-1922	Chickamauga and Chattanooga National Military Park Commission

W 5

W 5	1775-1912	Subsistence Department
W 77	1912-1947	Quartermaster Corps
M 112	1947-1949	Quartermaster General of the Army
D 106	1949-	Quartermaster Corps

W 6

W 6	1898-1900	Customs and Insular Affairs Division
	1900-1902	Insular Affairs Division
	1902-1939	Insular Affairs Bureau
I 35	1934-1950	[functions transferred to] Territories and Island Possessions Division

W 7

W 7	1802-1947	Engineer Department
M 110	1947-1949	Engineer Department
D 103	1949-	Engineer Corps

W 7.16

W 7.16	1802-1947	Engineer School
M 110.400	1947-1949	Engineer School
D 103.100	1949-	Engineer School

W 8

W 8	1869-1884	Geographic Surveys West of 100th Meridian (Wheeler)

W 9

W 9	1874-1947	Inspector General's Department

W 10

W 10	1849-1864	Judge Advocate General's Office
	1864-1884	Military Justice Office
	1884-1947	Judge Advocate General's Department
M 107	1947-1949	Judge Advocate General's Department
D 108	1949-	Judge Advocate General's Department

W 11

W 11	1880-1908	Library

W 12

W 12	1802-1947	Military Academy
M 109	1947-1949	Military Academy
D 109	1949-	Military Academy

W 13

W 13	1858-1965	California Department
	1904-1907	California Department

W 14

W 14	1893-1903	Colorado Department

W 15

W 15	1865-1904	Columbia Department

W 16

W 16	1867-1904	Dakota Department

W 17

W 17	1853-1903	East Department

W 18

W 18	1862-1911	Gulf Department

W 19

W 19	1866-1911	Lakes Department

W 20

W 20	1862-1911	Missouri Department

W 21

W 21	1900-1912	Philippines Division

W 22

W 22	1866-1898	Platte Department

W 23

W 23	1898-1900	Puerto Rico Department
I 1.40	1900-1909	Puerto Rico
S 10	1909	Puerto Rico
W 75	1909-1934	Puerto Rico
I 35	1934-1950	[functions transferred to] Territories and Island Possessions Division

W 24

W 24	1853-1911	Texas Department

W 25

W 25	1898-1902	Cuba Department

W 26

W 26	1892-1903	War Plans Division

W 27

W 27	1874-1909	Military Prison, Fort Leavenworth

W 28

W 28	1881-1947	General Service Schools
M 119	1947-1949	Command and General Staff College
D 110	1949-	Command and General Staff College

W 29

W 29	1867-1916	Coast Artillery School

W 30

W 30	1887-1947	Mounted Service School

W 31

W 31	1879-1947	Mississippi River Commission
M 110.200	1947-1949	Mississippi River Commission
D 103.300	1949-	Mississippi River Commission

W 32

W 32	1884-1902	Missouri River Commission

W 33

W 33	1841-1947	Northern and Northwestern Lakes Survey
M 110.100	1947-1949	Lake Survey Office
D 103.200	1949-	Lake Survey Office

W 34

W 34	1812-1947	Ordnance Department
M 111	1947-1949	Ordnance Department
D 105	1949-1968	Ordnance Corps
	1968-	[Publications Relating to Ordnance]

W 35

W 35	1888-1920	Ordnance and Fortification Board

W 36

W 36	1816-1912	Pay Department
W 77	1912-1947	Quartermaster Corps
M 112	1947-1949	Quartermaster General of the Army
D 106	1949-	Quartermaster Corps

W 37

W 37	1863-1966	Provost Marshall General
D 120	1969-	Provost Marshall General

W 38

W 38	1867-1925	Public Buildings and Ground Office
PB 1	1925-1933	Public Buildings and Public Parks of the National Capital Office
I 29	1933-	[functions transferred to] National Park Service

W 39

W 39	1812-1912	Quartermaster's Department
W 77	1912-1947	Quartermaster Corps
M 112	1947-1949	Quartermaster General of the Army
D 106	1949-	Quartermaster Corps

W 40

W 40	1892-1907	Records and Pension Office

W 41

W 41	1865-1972	Refugees, Freedmen, and Abandoned Lands Bureau

W 42

W 42	1860-1947	Signal Office
D 111	1949-1968	Signal Corps
	1968-19xx	[Publications Relating to Communications]
	19xx-	Army Electronics Research and Development Command

W 43

W 43	1851-1947	District of Columbia Soldiers Home

W 44

W 44	1818-1947	Medical Department
M 102	1947-1949	Army Medical Department
D 104	1949-1950	Army Medical Service
	1950-	Army Medical Department

W 45

W 45	1878-1899	War Records Office

W 46

W 46	1893-1922	Gettysburg National Military Park Commission

W 47

W 47	1899-1900	Cuban Census Office

W 48

W 48	1899-1900	Puerto Rico Census Office

W 49

W 49	1900-1934	Philippine Islands
W 105	1934-1942	U.S. Commissioner to Philippine Islands

W 50

W 50	1893	California Debris Commission

W 51

W 51	1847-1907	Pacific Division

W 52

W 52	1861-1969	Washington Department

W 53

W 53	1901-1941	Coast Artillery Office

W 54

W 54	1899	Vicksburg National Military Park Commission

W 55

W 55	1900-1945	Army War College

W 56

W 56	1900-1914	Luzon Department

W 57

W 57	1898-1900	Pinar Del Rio Department

W 58

W 58	1898-1900	Matanzas and Santa Clara Department

W 59

W 59	1898-1900	Santiago and Puerto Principe Department

W 60

W 60	1900	Western Cuba Department

W 61

W 61	1901-1908	Submarine Defense School

W 62

W 62	1904-1907	Northern Division

W 63

W 63	1894	Shiloah National Military Park Commission

W 64

W 64	1865-1907	Atlantic Division

W 65

W 65	1870-1893	Arizona Department

W 66

W 66	1862-1883	South Department

W 67

W 67	1861-1970	Virginia and North Carolina Department

W 68

W 68	1902-1913	International Waterways Commission

W 69

W 69	1903-1907	Southeastern Division

W 70

W 70	1908-1916	Militia Affairs Division
	1916-1933	Militia Bureau
	1933-1947	National Guard Bureau
M 114	1947-1949	National Guard Bureau
D 112	1949-1958	National Guard Bureau
D 12	1958-	National Guard Bureau

W 71

W 71	1868-1901	Alaska Department

W 72

W 72	1899-1914	Minanao Department

W 73

Y 3.Is 7	1889-1902	Isthmian Canal Commission
W 73	1902-1905	Isthmian Canal Commission

W 74

W 74	1905-1932	Alaska Road Commission
I 35.10/20	1932-1946	Alaska Road Commission

W 75

W 23	1898-1900	Porto Rico Department
I 1.40	1900-1909	Porto Rico
S 10	1909	Porto Rico
W 75	1909-1934	Porto Rico
I 35	1934-1950	[functions transferred to] Territories and Island Possessions Division

W 76

W 76	1911-1920	Western Division
W 99.19	1920-1934	Army Ninth Corps Area

W 77

W 36	1816-1912	Pay Department
W 39	1812-1912	Quartermaster's Department
W 5	1775-1912	Subsistence Department
W 77	1912-1947	Quartermaster Corps
M 112	1947-1949	Quartermaster General of the Army
D 106	1949-	Quartermaster Corps

W 78

W 78	1911-1920	Central Department
W 99.15	1920-1934	Fifth Corps Area
W 99.16	1920-1934	Sixth Corps Area
W 99.17	1920-1934	Seventh Corps Area
W 99.18	1920-1934	Eighth Corps Area

W 79

W 79	1912-1945	Canal Zone
M 115	1947-1949	Panama Canal
D 113	1949-1950	Panama Canal
PaC 1	1950-1951	Panama Canal
CZ 1	1950-1979	Panama Canal Zone Company
Y 3.P 19/2	1979-	Panama Canal Commission

W 80

W 80	1911-1920	Visayas Department
W 99.22	1920-1934	Philippine Department

W 81

W 81	1910-1920	Hawaii Department
W 99.20	1920-1934	Hawaii Department

W 82

W 82	1914-1922	National Board for Promotion of Rifle Practice

W 83

W 83	1913-1920	Southern Department
W 99.18	1920-1934	Army Eighth Corps Area
W 99.19	1920-1934	Army Ninth Corps Area

W 84

W 84	1917-1920	Southeastern Department
W 99.14	1920-1934	Army Fourth Corps Area
W 99.18	1920-1934	Army Eighth Corps Area

W 85

W 85	1917-1919	Training Camp Activities Commission

W 86

W 86	1917-1920	Northeastern Department
W 99.11	1920-1934	Army First Corps Area

W 87

W 87	1918-1941	Air Service
W 109.100	1941-1942	Air Corps
W 108	1942-1947	[functions transferred to] Army Air Force

W 88

W 88	1918-1920	Motor Transport Corps

W 89

W 89	1918-1919	Purchase, Storage, and Traffic Division

W 90

W 90	1918-1919	Tank Corps

W 91

W 91	1918-1946	Chemical War service
	1946-1947	Chemical Corps
D 116	1949-	Chemical Corps

W 92

W 92	1918-1920	Construction Division

W 93

W 93	1919-1922	War Department Claims Board

W 94

W 94	1918-1920	Real Estate Service

W 95

W 95	1914-1920	American Expeditionary Forces

W 96

W 96	1918-1922	Field Artillery Office

W 97

W 97	1918-1920	Finance Service
	1920-1947	Finance Department
M 116	1947-1949	Finance Department

W 98

W 98	1919-1920	Transportation Service

W 99

W 99	1920-1934	Army and Corps Areas and Departments

W 100

W 100	1918-1947	Military Intelligence Division
M 106	1947-1949	Intelligence Division

W 101

W 101	1920-1923	Inland and Coastwise Waterways Service

W 102

W 102	1917-1947	American National Red Cross
Y 3.Am 3/5	1949-1952	American National Red Cross

W 103

W 103	1924-1939	Inland Waterways Corporation
C 29	1939-1953	Inland Waterways Corporation

W 104

W 104	1924-1947	Army Industrial College

W 105

W 49	1900-1934	Philippine Islands
W 105	1934-1942	U.S. Commissioner to Philippine Islands

W 106

W 106	1937-1941	Philippine Island, President

W 107

W 107	1941-1946	Public Relations Bureau
	1946-1947	Public Relations Division
M 118	1947-1949	Public Information Division

W 108

W 108	1941-1947	Army Air Force
M 301	1947-1949	Air Force Department, Office of Secretary
D 301	1949-	Air Force Department, Office of Secretary

W 108.100

W 87	1918-1941	Air Service
W 109.100	1941-1942	Air Corps
W 108	1942-1947	[functions transferred to] Army Air Force

W 109

W 109	1940-1947	Army Service Forces

W 109.100

W 109.100	1940-1947	Special Service Division
M 117	1947-1949	Special Service Division

W 109.200

W 109.200	1943-1944	Morale Services Division
W 111	1944-1947	Information and Education Division
M 104	1947-1949	Troop Information and Education Division
D 2	1949-1952	Armed Forces Information and Education Office
D 107	1949-1954	Troop Information and Education Division

W 109.300

W 109.300	1944-1947	Chief of Transportation Office
D 117	1949-1968	Transportation Corps
	1968-19xx	[Publications Relating to Transportation]
	19xx-	U.S. Army Air Mobility Research and Development Command

W 110

W 110	1946-1947	Historical Division
M 103	1947-1949	Historical Division
D 114	1949-1950	Historical Division
	1950-1974	Chief of Military History Office
	1974-	Military History Center

W 111

W 109.200	1943-1944	Morale Services Division
W 111	1944-1947	Information and Education Division
M 104	1947-1949	Troop Information and Education Division
D 2	1949-1952	Armed Forces Information and Education Office
D 107	1949-1954	Troop Information and Education Division

WT 1

WT 1	1917-1919	War Trade Board
S 13	1919-1924	War Trade Board Section

WT 2

WT 2	1917-1919	Transportation Bureau

WT 3

WT 3	1917-1919	Exports Bureau

WT 4

WT 4	1917-1919	Imports Bureau

WT 5

WT 5	1917-1919	Research Bureau

Y 1

Y 1		[Miscellaneous Publications of Congress]

Y 1.2

Y 1.2	1789-	House of Representatives

Y 1.3

Y 1.3	1789-	Senate

Y 3.Ad 6

Y 3.Ad 6	1964-	Administrative Conference of United States

Y 3.Ac 7

Y 3.Ac 7		National Commission on AIDS

Y 3.Ad 9

Y 3.Ad 9	1936-1937	Advisory Committee on Fiscal Relations Study

Y 3.Ad 9/2

Y 3.Ad 9/2	1937-1939	Advisory Committee on Education

Y 3.Ad 9/3

Y 3.Ad 9/3	1938	Advisory Council on Social Security

Y 3.Ad 9/4

Y 3.Ad 9/4	1946-1953	Advisory Committee on Voluntary Foreign Aid

Y 3.Ad 9/5

Y 3.Ad 9/5	1946-1948	Advisory Commission on Universal Training

Y 3.Ad 9/6

Y 3.Ad 9/6	1953-1957	Advisory Committee on Weather Control

Y 3.Ad 9/7

Y 3.Ad 9/7	1948-1968	Advisory Commission on Information

Y 3.Ad 9/8

Y 3.Ad 9/8	1959-	Advisory Commission on Intergovernmental Relations

Y 3.Ad 9/9

Y 3.Ad 9/9	1961-	Advisory Commission on International Educational and Cultural Affairs

Y 3.Ad 9/10

Y 3.Ad 9/10	1961-1973	Advisory Committee on the Arts

Y 3.Ad 9/11

Y 3.Ad 9/11		Advisory Committee on Federal Pay

Y 3.Ad 9/12

Y 3.Ad 9/12		United States Advisory Commission on Public Diplomacy

Y 3.Ae 8

Y 3.Ae 8	1916-1948	Aeronautics Board
M 5	1948-1949	[functions transferred to] Munitions Board
M 6	1948-1949	[functions transferred to] Research and Development Board

Y 3.Af 8

Y 3.Af 8	1984-	African Development Foundation

Y 3.Ag 8/1

Y 3.Ag 8/1	1913-1916	Commission to Investigate and Study Agricultural Credits in Europe

Y 3.Ag 8/2

Y 3.Ag 8/2	1921-1922	Joint Commission on Agricultural Inquiry

Y 3.Ai 7

Y 3.Ai 7	1917-1919	Aircraft Board

Y 3.Ai 7/2

Y 3.Ai 7/2	1929-1930	Joint Airports Commission

Y 3.Ai 7/3

Y 3.Ai 7/3	1945-1960	Air Coordinating Committee

Y 3.Ai 7/4

Y 3.Ai 7/4	1957-1958	Airways Modernization Board
FAA 1	1958-1967	[functions transferred to] Federal Aviation Agency

Y 3.Ai 7/5

Y 3.Ai 7/5		National Commission on Air Quality

Y 3.Al 1

Y 3.Al 1	1874-1876	First Court of Commissioners of Alabama Claims
	1882-1885	Second Court of Commissioners of Alabama Claims

Y 3.Al 1/2

Y 3.Al 1/2	1978-	National Alcohol Fuels Commission

Y 3.Al 1s

Y 3.Al 1s	1956-1961	Alaska International Rail and Highway Commission

Y 3.Al 1s/2

Y 3.Al 1s/2	1964	Temporary Alaska Claims Commission

Y 3.Al 1s/3

Y 3.Al 1s/3	1964	Federal Reconstruction and Development Planning Commission for Alaska

Y 3.Al 1s/4

Y 3.Al 1s/4	1964-1965	Federal Field Committee for Development Planning in Alaska

Y 3.Al 4

Y 3.Al 4	1917-1934	Alien Property Custodian
J 19	1934-1941	Alien Property Bureau
	1941-1942	Alien Property Division
Pr 32.5700	1942-1946	Alien Property Custodian Office
J 22	1946-1966	Alien Property Office

Y 3.Al 16

Y 3.Al 16		Alcatraz Island, Commission on Disposition of

Y 3.Am 3

Y 3.Am 3	1923-	American Battle Monuments Commission

Y 3.Am 3/2

Y 3.Am 3/2	1926-1931	American Samoan Commission

Y 3.Am 3/3

Y 3.Am 3/3	1919-1923	American Relief Administration

Y 3.Am 3/4

Y 3.Am 3/4	1943-1946	American Commission for Protection and Salvage of Artistic and Historic Monuments in War Areas

Y 3.Am 3/5

W 102	1917-1947	American National Red Cross
Y 3.Am 3/5	1949-1952	American National Red Cross

Y 3.Am 3/6

| Y 3.Am 3/6 | 1966-1973 | American Revolution Bicentennial Commission |
| | 1973-1977 | American Revolution Bicentennial Administration |

Y 3.An 8

| Y 3.An 8 | 1902-1903 | Anthracite Coal Strike Commission |

Y 3.An 8/2

| Y 3.An 8/2 | 1920 | Anthracite Coal Commission |

Y 3.Ap 4

| Y 3.Ap 4 | 1964-1965 | Federal Development Planning Committee for Appalacia |

Y 3.Ap 4/2

| Y 3.Ap 4/2 | 1965- | Appalachian Regional Commission |

Y 3.Ap 4/3

| Y 3.Ap 4/3 | 1972-1973 | Revision of Federal Court Appellate System Commission |

Y 3.Ar 1

| Y 3.Ar 1 | 1921-1925 | Erection of Memorials and Entombment of Bodies in Arlington Memorial Amphitheater Commission |

Y 3.Ar 2

| Y 3.Ar 2 | 1793- | Architect of Capitol |

Y 3.Ar 5

| Y 3.Ar 5 | 1921-1960 | Arlington Memorial Amphitheater Commission |

Y 3.Ar 5/2

| Y 3.Ar 5/2 | 1913-1933 | Arlington Memorial Bridge Commission |
| I 29 | 1933- | [functions transferred to] National Park Service |

Y 3.Ar 5/3

| Y 3.Ar 5/3 | 1939-1948 | Army-Navy Civil Committee on Aircraft Design Criteria |
| | 1948 | Air Force-Navy Civil Committee on Aircraft Design Criteria |

Y 3.Ar 7

| Y 3.Ar 7 | | National Arthritis and Related Musculoskeletal Diseases Commission |

Y 3.At 6

| Y 3.At 6 | 1964-1970 | Atlantic-Pacific Interoceanic Canal Study Commission |

Y 3.At 7

Y 3.At 7	1946-1975	Atomic Energy Commission
ER 1	1975-1977	[functions transferred to] Energy Research and Development Administration
Y 3.N 88	1975-	[functions transferred to] Nuclear Regulatory Commission

Y 3.Av 5

| Y 3.Av 5 | 1970- | Aviation Advisory Commission |

Y 3.Av 5/2

| Y 3.Av 5/2 | 199x- | Aviation Safety Commission |

Y 3.B 22

| Y 3.B 22 | 1970 | Bankruptcy Laws Commission |

Y 3.B 27

| Y 3.B 27 | 1976- | Architectural and Transportation Barriers Compliance Board |

Y 3.B 32

| Y 3.B 32 | 1962-1965 | Battle of New Orleans Sesquicentennial Celebration Commission |

Y 3.B 32/2

| Y 3.B 32/2 | | Battle of Lake Erie Sesquicentennial Celebration Commission |

Y 3.B 45

| Y 3.B 45 | 1894 | Berlin Silver Commission |

Y 3.B 47/2

| Y 3.B 47/2 | 198x- | Bicentennial of the United States Constitution Commission |

Y 3.B 49

| Y 3.B 49 | 198x- | National Bilingual Education Advisory and Coordinating Council |

Y 3.B 54

| Y 3.B 54 | 1919-1920 | Bituminous Coal Commission |

Y 3.B 54/2

I 39	1935-1939	Consumers' Counsel of National Bituminous Coal Commission
I 48.50	1939-1941	Consumers' Counsel Division
Y 3.B 54/2	1941-1943	Bituminous Coal Consumers' Counsel Office

Y 3.B 61

Y 3.B 61	1938-1971	Purchases of Blind-Made Products Committee
Y 3.P 97	1971-1974	Purchase of Products and Services of the Blind and Other Severely Handicapped Committee
Y 3.B 61	1974-199x	Purchase from the Blind and Other Severely Handicapped Committee
Y 3.P 97	199x-	Purchase from People who are Blind or Severely Disabled Committee

Y 3.B 65

| Y 3.B 65 | 1955-1960 | Boston National Historic Sites Commission |

Y 3.B 78

| Y 3.B 78 | 1973- | International Broadcasting Board |

Y 3.B 78/2

| Y 3.B 78/2 | 1990- | Cuba Broadcasting Advisory Board |

Y 3.C 17

| Y 3.C 17 | 1904 | Joint Commission on Plans for Extension and Completion of the Capitol Building |

Y 3.C 17/2

| Y 3.C 17/2 | 1918-1919 | Capital Issues Committee |

Y 3.C 33

| Y 3.C 33 | 1885-1886 | Central and South American Commission |

Y 3.C 33/2

| Y 3.C 33/2 | 1933-1940 | Central Statistical Board |
| Pr 32.100 | 1940-1945 | [functions transferred to] Budget Bureau |

Y 3.C 33/3

| Y 3.C 33/3 | 1935-1942 | Central Housing Committee |
| NHA 1 | 1942-1947 | [functions transferred to] National Housing Agency |

Y 3.C 33/4

| Y 3.C 33/4 | 1935-1939 | Central Statistical Committee |
| Pr 32.100 | 1939-1945 | [functions transferred to] Budget Bureau |

Y 3.C 33/5

| Y 3.C 33/5 | 1937-1938 | Census of Partial Employment, Unemployment and Occupations |

Y 3.C 33/6

| Y 3.C 33/6 | 1941-1945 | Censorship Office |

Y 3.C 42

| Y3.C 42 | 1990 | Chemical Safety Hazard Investigation Board |

Y 3.C 43

| Y 3.C 43 | 1894 | Chicago Strike Commission |

Y 3.C 43/2

| Y 3.C 43/2 | 1971- | National Advisory Council on Child Nutrition |

Y 3.C 43/3

| Y 3.C 43/3 | | U.S. National Commission of the International Year of the Child |

Y 3.C 43/4

| Y 3.C 43/4 | | Interagency Panel on Early Childhood Research and Development |

Y 3.C 43/5

| Y 3.C 43/5 | | National Commission on Children |

Y 3.C 49

Y 3.Em 3	1933-1937	Emergency Conservation Work
Y 3.C 49	1937-1939	Civilian Conservation Corps
FS 4	1939-1943	Civilian Conservation Corps

Y 3.C 49/2

| Y 3.C 49/2 | 1957-1966 | Civil War Centennial Commission |

Y 3.C 49/3

| Y 3.C 49/3 | | [this class not used] |

Y 3.C 49/4

| Y 3.C 49/4 | 1974 | Interagency Committee on Uniform Civil Rights Policies and Practices |

Y 3.C 49/5

| Y 3.C 49/5 | 1977- | Federal Interagency Council on Citizen Participation |

Y 3.C 52

| Y 3.C 52 | 1871-1875 | Claims Commission |

Y 3.C 56

| Y 3.C 56 | 1976-1978 | Interagency Classification Review Committee |

Y 3.C 63

| Y 3.C 63 | 1922-1923 | Coal Commission |

Y 3.C 63/2

| Y 3.C 63/2 | 1967-1981 | Coastal Plains Regional Commission |

Y 3.C 63/3

| Y 3.C 63/3 | 19xx- | Fair Market Value Policy for Federal Coal Leasing Commission |

Y 3.C 66

| Y 3.C 66 | 1965-1975 | Coinage Joint Commission |

Y 3.C 71

| Y 3.C 71 | 1923 | Colorado River Interstate-Government Commission |

Y 3.C 72

| Y 3.C 72 | 1946- | Columbia Basin Inter-Agency Committee |

Y 3.C 73

Y 3.C 73	1933-1939	Commodity Credit Corporation
A 71	1939-1943	Commodity Credit Corporation
A 80.400	1943-1945	Commodity Credit Corporation
A 82.300	1945-	Commodity Credit Corporation

Y 3.C 73/2

| Y 3.C 73/2 | 1942-1945 | United States and Great Britain Combined Raw Material Board |

Y 3.C 73/3

| Y 3.C 73/3 | 1942-1945 | United States, Great Britain, and Canada Combined Production and Resource Board |

Y 3.C 73/4

| Y 3.C 73/4 | 1972 | Interim Compliance Panel |

Y 3.C 73/5

A 41	1922-1936	Grain Futures Administration
A 59	1936-1942	Commodity Exchange Administration
A 75.200	1942-1947	Commodity Exchange Administration
A 85	1947-1974	Commodity Exchange Authority
Y 3.C 73/5	1974-	Commodity Futures Trading Commission

Y 3.C 73/6

| Y 3.C 73/6 | 199x- | Competitiveness Policy Council |

Y 3.C 76

| Y 3.C 76 | 1974- | Construction Industry Collective Bargaining Commission |

Y 3.C 76/2

| Y 3.C 76/2 | 1968- | National Commission on Consumer Finance |

Y 3.C 76/3

| Y 3.C 76/3 | 1972- | Consumer Product Safety Commission |

Y 3.C 76/4

| Y 3.C 76/4 | 199x- | Records of Congress Advisory Committee |

Y 3.C 76/5

| Y 3.C 76/5 | | Conferences in Ocean Shipping Advisory Commission |

Y 3.C 78

| Y 3.C 78 | 1935-1937 | Coordinator for Industrial Cooperation |

Y 3.C 78/2

| Y 3.C 78/2 | 1936-1937 | Cooperative Enterprise in Europe Committee |

<table>
<tr><td colspan="3" align="center">Y 3.C 78/3</td></tr>
</table>

Y 3.C 78/3 | 1941-1942 | Coordinator for Information

Y 3.C 79

Y 3.C 79 | 1974-1979 | National Commission on New Technological Uses of Copyrighted Works

Y 3.C 82

Y 3.C 82 | 1970-1980 | Cost Accounting Standards Board

Y 3.C 83

Y 3.C 83 | 1916-1918 | National Defense Council
Y 3.C 831 | 1940-1941 | National Defense Council

Y 3.C 831

Y 3.C 83 | 1916-1918 | National Defense Council
Y 3.C 831 | 1940-1941 | National Defense Council

Y 3.C 831:100

Y3.C831:100 | 1940-1941 | National Defense Council Advisory Commission
Pr 32.400 | 1941-1945 | [functions transferred to] Emergency Management Office

Y 3.C 86

Y 3.C 86 | 1971- | National Advisory Commission on Criminal Justice Standards and Goals

Y 3.C 86/2

Y 3.C 86/2 | 1984- | National Critical Materials Council

Y 3.C 88

Y 3.C 88 | 1990- | Improvement of the Federal Crop Insurance Program Commission

Y 3.D 36

Y 3.D 36 | 1973- | Defense Manpower Commission

Y 3.D 36/2

Y 3.D 36/2 | 199x- | Defense Base Closure and Realignment Commission

Y 3.D 36/3

Y 3.D 36/3 | 199x- | Defense Nuclear Facilities Safety Board

Y 3.D 37

Y 3.D 37 | | Delaware Valley Tercentenary Commission

Y 3.D 37/2

Y 3.D 37/2 | 1961- | Delaware River Basin Commission

Y 3.D 44

Y 3.D 44 | 1903-1909 | Department Methods Committee

Y 3.D 49

S 17 | 1957-1958 | [part of] International Cooperation Administration
Y 3.D 49 | 1958-1961 | Development Loan Fund
S 18 | 1961- | [functions transferred to] International Development Agency

Y 3.D 63

Y 3.D 63 | 1908-1916 | Commission to Investigate Title of United States to Lands in District of Columbia

Y 3.D 63/2

Y 3.D 63/2 | 1948-1952 | Displaced Persons Commission

Y 3.D 63/3

Y 3.D 63/3 | 199x- | National Council on Disability

Y 3.D 84

Y 3.D 84 | 1976- | National Advisory Council for Drug Abuse Prevention

Y 3.D 84/2

Y 3.D 84/2 | 1987- | National Drug Policy Board

Y 3.Ec 7

Y 3.Ec 7 | 1910-1913 | Economy and Efficiency Commission

Y 3.Ec 7/2

Y 3.Ec 7/2 | 1964-1981 | National Advisory Council on Economic Opportunity

Y 3.Ec 7/3

Y 3.Ec 7/3 | 198x- | National Economic Commission

Y 3.Ec 74

Y 3.Ec 74 | 1934-1936 | Economic Security Committee

Y 3.Ec 74/2

Y 3.Ec 74/2 | 1941 | Economic Defense Board
 | 1941-1943 | Economic Warfare Board
Pr 32.5800 | 1943-1945 | Foreign Economic Administration

Y 3.Ec 74/2:100

Y 3.Ex 7/2 | 1940-1941 | Export Control Administrator Office
Y 3.Ec 74/2 | 1941-1942 | Export Control Office
 | 1942-1943 | Exports Office
Pr 32.5800 | 1943-1945 | [functions transferred to] Foreign Economic Administration

Y 3.Ec 74/3

Y 3.Ec 74/3 | 1948-1951 | Economic Cooperation Administration
Pr 33.900 | 1951-1953 | Mutual Security Agency
FO 1 | 1953-1955 | Foreign Operations Administration
Y 3.In 8/5 | 1950-1955 | International Development Advisory Board
S 17 | 1955-1961 | International Cooperation Administration
S 18 | 1961- | International Development Agency

Y 3.Ed 8

Y 3.Ed 8 | 1964- | Federal Interagency Education Committee

Y 3.Ed 8/2

Y 3.Ed 8/2 | 1965-1982 | National Education of Disadvantaged Children Advisory Council

Y 3.Ed 8/3

Y 3.Ed 8/3 | 1967- | National Advisory Council on Education Professions Development

Y 3.Ed 8/4

Y 3.Ed 8/4 | 1974- | National Advisory Council on Adult Education

Y 3.Ed 8/5

Y 3.Ed 8/5 | 1973- | National Commission on Financing of Postsecondary Education

Y 3.Ed 8/6

Y 3.Ed 8/6 | 1976- | National Advisory Council on Women's Educational Programs

Y 3.Ed 8/7

Y 3.Ed 8/7	1972-	National Advisory Council on Equality of Educational Opportunity

Y 3.Ed 8/8

Y 3.Ed 8/8		National Advisory Council on Continuing Education

Y 3.Ed 8/9

Y 3.Ed 8/9	1990-	Intergovernmental Advisory Council on Education

Y 3.Ei 4

Y 3.Ei 4	1916-1917	Eight Hour Commission

Y 3.El 2

Y 3.El 2	1877	Electoral Commission of 1877

Y 3.El 2/2

Y 3.El 2/2	1933-1939	Electric Home and Farm Authority
FL 4	1939-1942	Electric Home and Farm Authority

Y 3.El 2/3

Y 3.El 2/3	1974-	Federal Election Commission

Y 3.El 2/4

Y 3.El 2/4	1974-	National Commission on Electronic Fund Transfers

Y 3.Em 3

Y 3.Em 3	1933-1937	Emergency Conservation Work
Y 3.C 49	1937-1939	Civilian Conservation Corps
FS 4	1939-1943	Civilian Conservation Corps

Y 3.Em 3/2

Y 3.Em 3/2	1973-	Emergency Loan Guarantee Board

Y 3.Em 7

Y 3.Em 7	1910-1912	Employer's Liability and Workman's Compensation Commission

Y 3.Em 7/2

Y 3.Em 7/2		National Employment and Unemployment Statistics Commission

Y 3.Em 7/3

Y 3.M 31	1975-1978	National Commission for Manpoer Policy
Y 3.Em 7/3	1978-	National Commission for Employment Policy

Y 3.En 2

Y 3.En 2	199x-	United States Enrichment Corporation

Y 3.Eq 2

Y 3.Eq 2	1965-	Equal Employment Opportunity Commission

Y 3.Er 4

Y 3.Er 4	1918	Ericson Memorial Commission

Y 3.Et 3

PM 1	1978-1989	[Part of] Personnel Management Office
Y 3.Et 3	1989-	Government Ethics Office

Y 3.Ex 3

Y 3.Ex 3	1893-1894	Joint Commission on Laws Organizing the Executive Departments

Y 3.Ex 3/2

Y 3.Ex 3/2	1933-1934	Executive Council
Y 3.N 21/9	1934-1939	[functions transferred to] National Emergency Council

Y 3.Ex 3/3

Y 3.Ex 3/3	1967-	Executive Legislative, and Judicial Salaries Commission

Y 3.Ex 7

Y 3.Ex 7	1918-1919	Exports Control Committee

Y 3.Ex 7/2

Y 3.Ex 7/2	1940-1941	Export Control Administrator Office
Y 3.Ec 74/2	1941-1942	Export Control Office
	1942-1943	Exports Office
Pr 32.5800	1943-1945	[functions transferred to] Foreign Economic Administration

Y 3.Ex 7/3

Y 3.Ex 7/3	1945-1968	Export-Import Bank of Washington
	1968-	Export-Import Bank of the United States

Y 3.Ex 8

Y 3.Ex 8	1965-1982	National Extension and Continuing Education Advisory Council
	1982-	National Continuing Education Advisory Council

Y 3.F 22

Y 3.F 22	1937	Farm Tenancy Special Committee

Y 3.F 22/2

Y 3.F 22/2	199x-	Farm Credit System Insurance Corporation

Y 3.F 31

Y 3.F 31	1919-1920	Federal Electric Railways Commission

Y 3.F 31/2

Y 3.F 31/2	1922-1923	Federal Fuel Distributor

Y 3.F 31/3

Y 3.F 31/3	1932-1939	Federal Home Loan Bank Board
FL 3	1939-1942	Federal Home Loan Bank Board
NHA 3	1942-1947	Federal Home Loan Bank Administration
HH 4	1947-1955	Federal Home Loan Bank Board
FHL 1	1955-1989	Federal Home Loan Bank Board
FHF 1	1989-	Federal Housing Financing Board
T 71	1989-	Thrift Supervisor Office
Y 3.R 31/2	1989-	Resolution Trust Corporation

Y 3.F 31/4

Y 3.F 31/4	1933-1939	Federal Emergency Administration of Public Works
FW 5	1939-1943	Public Works Administration

Y 3.F 31/5

Y 3.F 31/5	1933-1938	Federal Emergency Relief Administration

Y 3.F 31/6

Y 3.F 31/6	1933-1936	Federal Coordinator of Transportation

Y 3.F 31/7

Y 3.F 31/7	1933-1934	Federal Civil Works Administration
Y 3.F 31/5	1934-1938	[functions transferred to] Federal Emergency Relief Administration

Y 3.F 31/8

Y 3.F 31/8	1933-	Federal Deposit Insurance Corporation

Y 3.F 31/9

Y 3.F 31/9	1933-1935	Federal Surplus Relief Corporation
A 65	1935-1940	Marketing and Marketing Agreements Division
A 73	1940-1942	Surplus Marketing Administration
A 75	1942	Agricultural Marketing Administration
A 78	1942-1943	Food Distribution Administration
A 80.100	1943-1944	Food Distribution Administration
	1944-1945	Distribution Office
A 80.800	1945	Marketing Services Office
A 81	1945	Marketing Services Office
A 82	1945-1953	Production and Marketing Administration
A 88	1953-1965	Agricultural Marketing Service
	1965-1972	Consumer and Marketing Service
	1972-	Agricultural Marketing Service

Y 3.F 31/10

Y 3.F 31/10	1933-1935	Federal Alcohol Control Administration
T 59	1935-1940	Federal Alcohol Administration
T 22	1940-1953	[functions transferred to] Internal Revenue Bureau

Y 3.F 31/11

Y 3.F 31/11	1934-1939	Federal Housing Administration
FL 2	1939-1942	Federal Housing Administration
NHA 2	1942-1947	Federal Housing Administration
HH 2	1947-	Federal Housing Administration

Y 3.F 31/12

Y 3.F 31/12	1934-1937	Federal Committee on Apprentice Training
L 16	1937-1942	[transferred to Apprenticeship Section in] Labor Standards Division

Y 3.F 31/13

Y 3.F 31/13	1939-1954	Federal Inter-Agency River Basin Committee
Y 3.In 8/8	1954-1956	Interagency Water Resources Committee

Y 3.F 31/13-2

Y 3.F 31/13-2	1977-	Arkansas-White-Red Basins Inter-Agency Committee

Y 3.F 31/14

Y 3.F 31/14	1946-	Federal Inter-Agency Committee on Recreation

Y 3.F 31/15

Y 3.F 31.15	1956-1962	Federal Council on Aging

Y 3.F 31/16

PrEx 8	1962-1973	Science and Technology Office
Y 3.F 31/16	1959-1973	Federal Council for Science and Technology
NS 1	1973-1976	[functions transferred to] National Science Foundation
PrEx 23	1976-	Science and Technology Policy Office

Y 3.F 31/17

Y 3.F 31.17	1959-1970	Federal Radiation Council
EP 1	1970-	[functions transferred to] Environmental Protection Agency

Y 3.F 31/18

Y 3.F 31/18	1964-	Federal Pest Control Committee

Y 3.F 31/19

Y 3.F 31/19	1966-	Federal Committee on Research of Natural Areas

Y 3.F 31/20

Y 3.F 31/20	1962-	Federal Executive Board

Y 3.F 31/21

Y 3.F 31/21	1969-1979	Federal Labor Relations Council
Y 3.F 31/21-3	1979-	Federal Labor Relations Authority

Y 3.F 31/21-2

Y 3.F 31/21-2	1969-	Federal Service Impasses Panel

Y 3.F 31/21-3

Y 3.F 31/21	1969-1979	Federal Labor Relations Council
Y 3.F 31/21-3	1979-	Federal Labor Relations Authority

Y 3.F 31/22

Y 3.F 31/22		Federal Committee on Ecological Reserves

Y 3.F 31/23

Y 3.F 31/23	1979-	Federal Inspector Office, Alaska Natural Gas Transportation System

Y 3.F 31/24

Y 3.F 31/24		Federal Interagency Committee, International Year of Disabled Persons

Y 3.F 31/25

Y 3.F 31/25	1986-	Federal Retirement Thrift Investment Board

Y 3.F 32

Y 3.F 32	199x-	National Financial Institution Reform, Recovery and Enforcement Commission

Y 3.F 49

Y 3.F 49	1979-	Federal Financial Institutions Examination Council

Y 3.F 51

Y 3.F 51	19xx-1973	National Fire Prevention and Control Commission

Y 3.F 73

Y 3.F 73	1917-1920	Food Administration

Y 3.F 76

Y 3.F 76	1934-1935	Special Adviser to the President on Foreign Trade

Y 3.F 76/2

Y 3.F 76/2	1953-1954	Foreign Economic Policy Commission

Y 3.F 76/3

Y 3.W 19/9	1948-1954	War Claims Commission
Y 3.F 76/3	1954-1980	Foreign Claims Settlement Commission
J 1	1980-	[functions transferred to] Justice Department

Y 3.F 76/4

Y 3.F 76/4	1946-	Foreign Scholarships Board

Y 3.F 76/5

Y 3.F 76/5	1972-1974	Commission on the Organization of the Government for the Conduct of Foreign Policy

Y 3.F 77

Y 3.F 77	1885-1886	Fortifications and Other Defense Board

Y 3.F 82

Y 3.F 82	1965-1981	Four Corners Regional Commission

Y 3.F 95

Y 3.F 95	1917-1919	Fuel Administration

Y 3.G 14

Y 3.G 14	1975-	Commission on Review of the National Policy Toward Gambling

Y 3.G 29

Y 3.G 29	1928-1939	George Rogers Clark Sesquicentennial Commission

Y 3.G 57

Y 3.G 57		Commission on Role of Gold in Domestic and International Monetary System

Y 3.G 74

Y 3.G 74	1950-1961	Government Patents Board

Y 3.G 74/2

Y 3.G 74/2	1955-1957	Government Security Commission

Y 3.G 74/3

Y 3.G 74/3	1959-1961	Government Activities Affecting Prices and Costs Committee

Y 3.G 74/4

Y 3.G 74/4	1969-	Government Procurement Commission

Y 3.G 75

Y 3.G 75	1907-1908	Grades and Salaries Committee

Y 3.G 76

Y 3.G 76	1913	Grant Memorial Commission

Y 3.G 79

Y 3.G 79	1936	Great Plains Drought Area Committee
Y 3.G 79/2	1936	Great Plains Committee

Y 3.G 79/2

Y 3.G 79	1936	Great Plains Drought Area Committee
Y 3.G 79/2	1936	Great Plains Committee

Y 3.G 79/3

Y 3.G 79/3	1967-1981	Great Lakes Basin Commission

Y 3.G 81

Y 3.G 81	1884	Board of Officers Considering Relief of Lt. Greely and Party at Lady Franklin Bay

Y 3.G 95

Y 3.G 95	1883-1884	Gun Foundry Board

Y 3.H 18

Y 3.H 18	1954-1958	Alexander Hamilton Bicentennial Commission

Y 3.H 19

HE 19.100	1978-1979	[part of] Education Office
ED 1	1979-1984	[part of] Education Department
Y 3.H 19	1984-	National Council on the Handicapped

Y 3.H 31

Y 3.H 31	1898-1899	Hawaiian Commission

Y 3.H 31/2

Y 3.H 31/2		Native Hawaiians Study Commission

Y 3.H 35/2

Y 3.H 35/2	1881	Heavy Ordnance and Projectile Board

Y 3.H 62

Y 3.H 62	1966-	Advisory Council on Historic Preservation

Y 3.H 62/2

Y 3.H 62/2		United States Capitol Historical Society

Y 3.H 62/3

Y 3.H 62/3	19xx-	U.S. Supreme Court Historical Society

Y 3.H 62/4

Y 3.H 62/4	19xx-	White House Historical Association

Y 3.H 71

Y 3.H 71	1990-	Federal Holiday Commission

Y 3.H 73

Y 3.H 73	1955-	Oliver Wendell Holmes Devise Permanent Committee

Y 3.H 74

Y 3.H 74	19xx-	United States Holocaust Memorial Council

Y 3.H 75

Y 3.H 75	1908	Homes Commission

Y 3.H 75

Y 3.H 75	1991	Interagency Council on the

Y 3.H 81

Y 3.H 81	1905	Commission to Supervise Construction of Building for Offices for House of Representatives

Y 3.H 81/2

Y 3.H 81/2	1947-1951	Housing Expediter Office
ES 1	1951-1953	[functions transferred to] Economic Stabilization Agency

Y 3.H 86

Y 3.H 86		Hudson-Champlain Celebration Commission

Y 3.H 88

Y 3.H 88	1977-	National Commission for the Protection of Human Subjects of Biomedical and Behavioral Research

Y.3.Im 6

Y 3.Im 6	1907-1910	Immigration Commission

Y 3.Im 6/2

Y 3.Im 6/2	1978-	Immigration and Refugee Policy Select Commission

Y 3.In 2

Y 3.In 2	1893	Indian Currency Commission (Great Britain)

Y 3.In 2/2

Y 3.In 2/2	1899-1902	Industrial Commission

Y 3.In 2/3

Y 3.In 2/3	1914-1915	Joint Commission to Investigate Indian Affairs

Y 3.In 2/4

Y 3.In 2/4	1913-1916	Industrial Relations Commission

Y 3.In 2/5

Y 3.In 2/5	1936-1937	Industrial Analysis Committee

Y 3.In 2/6

Y 3.In 2/6	1946-1978	Indian Claims Commission

Y 3.In 2/7

Y 3.In 2/7	1956	Increases Industrial Use of Agricultural Products Commission

Y 3.In 2/8

Y 3.In 2/8	1970-	National Industrial Pollution Control Council

Y 3.In 2/9

Y 3.In 2/9	1968-1974	National Indian Opportunity Council

Y 3.In 2/10

Y 3.In 2/10	1975-	National Advisory Council on Indian Education

Y 3.In 2/11

Y 3.In 2/11	1974-	National Commission for Industrial Peace

Y 3.In 8

Y 3.In 8	1903-1904	International Exchange Commission

Y 3.In 8/2

Y 3.In 8/2	1918-1923	Interdepartmental Social Hygiene Board
T 27	1923-1939	[functions transferred to] Public Health Service

Y 3.In 8/3

Y 3.In 8/3	1935-1939	Interdepartmental Committee to Coordinate Health and Welfare Activities

Y 3.In 8/4

Y 3.In 8/4	1947-1959	Interdepartmental Scientific Research and Development Committee

Y 3.In 8/5

FO 1	1953-1955	Foreign Operations Administration
Y 3.In 8/5	1950-1955	International Development Advisory Board
S 17	1955-1961	International Cooperation Administration
S 18	1961-	International Development Agency

Y 3.In 8/6

Y 3.In 8/6	1948-	Interdepartmental Children and Youth Committee

Y 3.In 8/7

Y 3.In 8/7	1953-1955	Intergovernmental Relations Commission

Y 3.In 8/8

Y 3.F 31/13	1939-1954	Federal Inter-Agency River Basin Committee
Y 3.In 8/8	1954-1956	Interagency Water Resources Committee

Y 3.In 8/9

Y 3.In 8/9	1951-1970	Interdepartmental Narcotics Committee

Y 3.In 8/10

Y 3.In 8/10	1954-	Interdepartmental Committee for the Study of Jurisdiction over Federal Areas within the States

Y 3.In 8/11

Y 3.In 8/11	1954-1956	Interagency Agricultural Surplus Disposal Committee

Y 3.In 8/12

Y 3.In 8/12	1956	Interdepartmental Radiation Preservation of Food Committee

Y 3.In 8/13

Y 3.In 8/13	1954	Interdepartmental Nutrition for National Defense Committee

Y 3.In 8/14

Y 3.In 8/14	1958	Interdepartmental Civilian Compensation Committee

Y 3.In 8/15

Y 3.In 8/15	1958	International Rules of Judicial Procedure Commission

Y 3.In 8/16

Y 3.In 8/16	1960	Interagency Automatic Data Processing Committee

Y 3.In 8/17

Y 3.In 8/17	1959	Interdepartmental Committee to Coordinate Federal Urban Area Assistance Programs

Y 3.In 8/18

Y 3.In 8/18	1960-1970	Interdepartmental Highway Safety Board

Y 3.In 8/19

Y 3.In 8/19	1960	Interdepartmental Federal Tort Claims Committee

Y 3.In 8/20

Y 3.In 8/20	1963	Interagency International Athletics Committee

Y 3.In 8/21

Y 3.In 8/21	1963-1978	Interdepartmental Committee on the Status of Women

Y 3.In 8/22

Y 3.In 8/22	1963-1973	Interagency Export Expansion Committee

Y 3.In 8/23

Y 3.In 8/23	1967-1969	Interagency Mexican American Affairs Committee
Y 3.Sp 2/7	1969-1974	Cabinet Committee on Opportunity for Spanish Speaking Peoples

Y 3.In 8/24

Y 3.In 8/24	1976-	Interstate Potomac River Basin Commission

Y 3.In 8/25

Y 3.In 8/25	1969-	Inter-American Foundation

Y 3.In 8/26

Y 3.In 8/26	1978-	Interagency Intermodal Cargo Committee

Y 3.In 8/27

Y 3.In 8/27		Federal Inspector for the Alaska Natural Gas Transportation System Office

Y 3.In 8/28

Y 3.In 8/28	1911-	International Joint Commission

Y 3.In 8/29

Y 3.In 8/29		Interagency Task Force on Small Business Finance

Y 3.In 8/29-2

Y 3.In 8/29-2		Interparliamentary Union, United States Group

Y 3.In 8/31

Y 3.In 8/31	198x-	Interagency Acid Precipitation Task Force

Y 3.Ir 6

Y 3.Ir 6	1875-1881	Board for Testing Iron, Steel, and Other Metals

Y 3.Is 7

Y 3.Is 7	1889-1902	Isthmian Canal Commission
W 73	1902-1905	Isthmian Canal Commission

Y 3.J 23

Y 3.J 23	1953	Jamestown-Williamsburg-Yorktown Celebration Commission

Y 3.J 27

Y 3.J 27	1975-	Japan-United States Friendship Commission

Y 3.J 66

Y 3.J 66	1946-1979	Joint Publications Research Service
PrEx 7	1979-	[functions transferred to] Foreign Broadcast Information Service

Y 3.J 66/2

Y 3.J 66/2	1946-1947	Joint Research and Development Board
M 6	1947-1949	Research and Development Board
D 4	1949-1953	Research and Development Board
	1953-	[Publications Relating to Research and Development]

Y 3.J 98

Y 3.J 98	1973-	Interdepartmental Council to Coordinate All Federal Juvenile Delinquency Programs

Y 3.L 22

Y 3.L 22	1971-	Interagency Land Acquisition Conference

Y 3.L 44

Y 3.L 44	1897-1899	Commission to Revise and Codify Criminal and Penal Laws
	1899-1906	Commission to Revise and Codify the Laws of the United States

Y 3.L 58

Y 3.L 58	1964-1969	Lewis and Clark Trail Commission

Y 3.L 61

Y 3.L 61	1970-	National Libraries and Information Science Commission

Y 3.L 61/2

Y 3.L 61/2	1972-1974	Federal Interagency Field Librarians Workshop

Y 3.L 63

Y 3.L 63	1957-1960	Lincoln Sesquicentennial Commission

Y 3.L 71

Pr 41.8:L 71	198x-199x	National Literacy Institute
Y 3.L 71	199x-	National Literacy Institute

Y 3.L 95

Y 3.L 95	1975-1977	Lowell Historic Canal District Commission

Y 3.L 95/2

Y 3.L 95/2		Lowell Historic Preservation Commission

Y 3.M 26

Y 3.M 26	1960-	James Madison Memorial Commission

Y 3.M 31

Y 3.M 31	1975-1978	National Manpower Policy Commission
Y 3.Em 7/3	1978-	[functions transferred to] National Commission for Employment Policy

Y 3.M 33

Y 3.M 33	1964-1968	Maritime Advisory Committee

Y 3.M 33/2

Y 3.M 33/2	1970-	Marihuana and Drug Abuse Commission

Y 3.M 33/3

Y 3.M 33/3	1972-	Marine Mammal Commission

Y 3.M 35

Y 3.M 35	1954-1955	John Marshall Bicentennial Commission

Y 3.M 41

Y 3.M 41	1970-	National Materials Policy Commission

Y 3.M 46

Y 3.M 46	1917-1918	Mediation Commission

Y 3.M 46/2

Y 3.M 46/2	1987-	Graduate Medical Education Council

Y 3.M 53

Y 3.M 53	1904-1905	Merchant Marine Commission

Y 3.M 53/2

Y 3.M 53/2	198x-	Merchant Marine and Defense Commission

Y 3.M 56

Y 3.M 56	1975-1982	United States Metric Board

Y 3.M 58

Y 3.M 58	1929-	Migratory Bird Conservation Commission

Y 3.M 58/2

Y 3.M 58/2	1990-	Study of International Migration and Cooperative Economic Development Commission

Y 3.M 59

Y 3.M 59	1860	Commission to Examine the Military Academy

Y 3.M 66

Y 3.M 66	1979-	Federal Mine Safety and Health Review Commission

Y 3.M 66/2

Y 3.M 66/2		Minimum Wage Study Commission

Y 3.M 69

Y 3.M 69	1945-1972	Missouri Basin Inter-Agency Committee
Y 3.M 69/2	1972-1981	Missouri River Basin Commission

Y 3.M 69/2

Y 3.M 69	1945-1972	Missouri Basin Inter-Agency Committee
Y 3.M 69/2	1972-1981	Missouri River Basin Commission

Y 3.M 74

Y 3.M 74	1876	United States Monetary Commission

Y 3.M 74/2

Y 3.M 74/2	1990-	Monitored Retrievable Storage Review Commission

Y 3.M 84

Y 3.M 84	1968-1969	Mortgage Interest Rates Commission

Y 3.M 85

Y 3.M 85	1977	Interagency Motor Vehicle Goals beyond 1980 Task Force

Y 3.M 85/2

Y 3.M 85/2		Motor Carrier Ratemaking Commission

Y 3.M 97

Y 3.M 97	1931	Muscle Shoals Commission

Y 3.N 16

Y 3.N 16	1978-	National Narcotics Intelligence Consumers Committee

Y 3.N 21/1

Y 3.N 21/1	1905	Naturalization Commission

Y 3.N 21/2

Y 3.N 21/2	1908-1912	National Monetary Commission

Y 3.N 21/3

Y 3.N 21/3	1909-1911	National Waterways Commission

Y 3.N 21/4

Y 3.N 21/4	1905-1906	National Coast-Defense Board

Y 3.N 21/5

Y 3.N 21/5	1915-1958	National Aeronautics Advisory Committee
NAS 1	1958-	National Aeronautics and Space Administration

Y 3.N 21/6

Y 3.N 21/6	1911-1976	National Forest Reservation Commission

Y 3.N 21/7

Y 3.N 21/7	1929-1931	National Commission on Law Observance and Enforcement

Y 3.N 21/8

Y 3.N 21/8	1933-1935	National Recovery Administration

Y 3.N 21/9

Y 3.N 21/9	1933-1939	National Emergency Council
Pr 32.200	1939-1942	Government Reports Office
Pr 32.5000	1942-1945	War Information Office
Pr 33.100	1945-1946	[functions transferred to] Budget Bureau
Pr 33.400	1946-1948	Government Reports Office

Y 3.N 21/10

Y 3.N 21/10	1933-1934	National Labor Board
Y 3.N 21/13	1934-1935	National Labor Relations Board
LR 1	1935-	National Labor Relations Board

Y 3.N 21/11

Y 3.N 21/11	1934	National Recovery Review Board

Y 3.N 21/12

Y 3.F 31/4:8	1933-1934	National Planning Board
Y 3.N 21/12	1934-1935	National Resources Board
	1935-1939	National Resources Committee
Pr 32.300	1939-1943	National Resources Planning Board

Y 3.N 21/13

Y 3.N 21/10	1933-1934	National Labor Board
Y 3.N 21/13	1934-1935	National Labor Relations Board
LR 1	1935-	National Labor Relations Board

Y 3.N 21/14

Y 3.N 21/14	1935-1939	National Youth Administration
FS 6	1939-1942	National Youth Administration
Pr 32/5250	1942-1944	National Youth Administration

Y 3.N 21/15

Y 3.N 21/15	1941-1944	National Interregional Highway Committee

Y 3.N 21/16

Y 3.N 21/16	1945-1966	National International Monetary and Financial Problems Advisory Council
	1966-	National International Monetary and Financial Policies Advisory Council

Y 3.N 21/17

Y 3.N 21/17	1947-1949	National Security Council
Pr 33.600	1949-1953	National Security Council
PrEx 3	1961-	National Security Council

Y 3.N 21/17

Y 3.N 21/17	1947-1949	Central Intelligence Agency
Pr 33.650	1949-1953	Central Intelligence Agency
Pr 34.600	1953-1961	Central Intelligence Agency
PrEx 3.10	1961-	Central Intelligence Agency

Y 3.N 21/18

Y 3.N 21/18	1947-1949	National Security Resources Board
Pr 33.700	1949-1953	National Security Resources Board
Pr 34.200	1953-1958	[functions transferred to] Defense Mobilization Office

Y 3.N 21/19

Y 3.N 21-19	1951-1957	National Security Training Commission

Y 3.N 21/20

Y 3.N 21/20	1947-1952	National Capital Sesquicentennial Commission

Y 3.N 21/21

Y 3.N 21/21	1960-1967	National Capital Transportation Agency

Y 3.N 21/22

Y 3.N 21/22	1964	National Food Marketing Commission

Y 3.N 21/23

Y 3.N 21/23	1968-19xx	National Visitors Center Study Commission
	19xx-1975	National Visitor Facilities Advisory Commission

Y 3.N 21/24

Y 3.N 21/24	1968-1973	National Water Commission

Y 3.N 21/25

Y 3.N 21/25	1967-1970	National Product Safety Commission

Y 3.N 21/26

Y 3.N 21/26	1966-1971	National Federal Criminal Laws Reform Commission

Y 3.N 21/27

Y 3.N 21/27	1971-1973	National Business Council for Consumer Affairs

Y 3.N 21/28

Y 3.N 21/27	19xx-	National Academy of Public Administration

Y 3.N 21/29

AA1	1971-1994	ACTION
Y 3.N 21/29	1990-1993	National and Community Service Commission
	1993-19xx	National Service Corporation
	19xx-	National and Community Service Corporation

Y 3.N 27

Y 3.N 27	1920	Near East Relief Commission

Y 3.N 31

Y 3.N 31	1977-1979	National Commission on Neighborhoods

Y 3.N 42

Y 3.N 42	1960	New Jersey Tercentenary Celebration Commission

Y 3.N 42/2

Y 3.N 42/2	1965-1981	New England Regional Commission

Y 3.N 42/3

Y 3.N 42/3	1967-1981	New England River Basins Commission

Y 3.N 51

Y 3.N 51	1889	Nicaragua Canal Commission

Y 3.N 81

Y 3.N 81	1935-1939	Northwest Territory Celebration Commission

Y 3.N 81/2

Y 3.N 81/2	1935-1938	North Carolina Tercentenary Celebration Commission

Y 3.N 81/3

Y 3.N 81/3	1965-	North Atlantic Regional Water Resources Study Coordinating Committee

Y 3.N 81/4

Y 3.N 81/4		Northern Great Plains Resources Program

Y 3.N 81/5

Y 3.N 81/5	1977-	Northwest Federal Regional Council

Y 3.N 81/6

Y 3.N 81/6	1976-1985	Northern Mariana Islands Commission

Y 3.N 81/7

Y 3.N 81/7	198x-	Northwest Indian Fisheries Commission

Y 3.N 88

Y 3.N 88	1975-	Nuclear Regulatory Commission

Y 3.N 88/2

Y 3.N 88/2	1990-	Nuclear Waste Technical Review Board

Y 3.N 95

Y 3.N 95		National Nutrition Monitoring Advisory Council

Y 3.Ob 7

Y 3.Ob 7	1967-1970	Obscenity and Pornography Commission

Y 3.Oc 1

Y 3.Oc 1	1970-	Occupational Safety and Health Review Commission

Y 3.Oc 1/2

Y 3.Oc 1/2		National Occupational Information Coordination Committee

Y 3.Oc 2

Y 3.Oc 2	1971-	National Oceans and Atmosphere Advisory Committee

Y 3.Oi 5

Y 3.Oi 5		Oil Cases, Special Counsel for United States in

Y 3.Or 3

Y 3.Or 3	1947-1949	Organization of the Executive Branch of the Government Commission

Y 3.Or 3/2

Y 3.Or 3/2	1953-1955	Organization of the Executive Branch of the Government Commission

Y 3.Ou 8

Y 3.Ou 8	1958-1962	Outdoor Recreation Resources Review Commission

Y 3.Oz 1

Y 3.Oz 1	1966-1981	Ozarks Regional Commission

Y 3.P 11

Y 3.P 11	1887	Pacific Railway Commission

Y 3.P 11/2

Y 3.P 11/2	1955	Pacific Southwest Inter-Agency Committee

Y 3.P 11/3

Y 3.P 11/3	19xx-1955	Pacific Southwest Federal Interagency Technical Committee

Y 3.P 11/4

Y 3.P 11/4	1967-1981	Pacific Northwest River Basins Commission

Y 3.P 11/5

Y 3.P 11/5	1976-1981	Pacific Northwest Regional Commission

Y 3.P 19

Y 3.P 19	1974-1978	Federal Paperwork Commission

Y 3.P 19/2

W 79	1912-1945	Canal Zone
M 115	1947-1949	Panama Canal
D 113	1949-1950	Panama Canal
PaC 1	1950-1951	Panama Canal
CZ 1	1950-1979	Panama Canal Zone Company
Y 3.P 19/2	1979-	Panama Canal Commission

Y 3.P 27

Y 3.P 27	1902	Commission to Revise Statutes Relating to Patents, Trade, Other Marks and Trade and Commercial Names

Y 3.P 29

Y 3.P 29		Prospective Payment Assessment Commission

Y 3.P 31

Y 3.P 31	1984-	United States Institute of Peace

Y 3.P 38

Y 3.P 38	1972-	Pennsylvania Avenue Development Corporation

Y 3.P 38/2

Y 3.P 38/2	1974-	Pension Benefit Guaranty Corporation

Y 3.P 43

Y 3.P 43	1974-	Federal Working Group on Pest Management

Y 3.P 43/2

Y 3.P 43/2	1973-	Intergovernment Personnel Policy Advisory Council

Y 3.P 44

I 50	1941-1942	Petroleum Coordinator for National Defense Office
	1942	Petroleum Coordinator for War Office
Y 3.P 44	1942-1946	Petroleum Administration for War

Y 3.P 53

Y 3.P 53	1899-1900	Philippine Commission

Y 3.P 53/2

Y 3.P 53/2	1946-1951	Philippine War Damage Commission

Y 3.P 56

Y 3.P 56	198x-	Physician Payment Review Commission

Y 3.P 74

Y 3.P 74	1912-1914	Joint Commission on Government Purchases of Pneumatic Tubes

Y 3.P 74/2

Y 3.P 74/2	1917	Joint Pneumatic Tube Mail Service Commission

Y 3.P 75

Y 3.P 75	1966-	Political Activity of Government Personnel Commission

Y 3.P 81

Y 3.P 81	1970	Population Growth and the American Future Commission

Y 3.P 81/2

Y 3.P 81/2	1974	National Commission for the Observance of World Population Year

Y 3.P 83

Y 3.P 83	1901	Porto Rico Laws Commission

Y 3.P 84/1

Y 3.P 84/1	1898-1901	Commission to Investigate the Postal Service

Y 3.P 84/2

Y 3.P 84/2	1906-1907	Postal Commission

Y 3.P 84/3

Y 3.P 84/3	1920	Joint Postal Service Commission

Y 3.P 84/4

Y 3.P 84/4	1970-	Postal Rate Commission

Y 3.P 84/5

Y 3.P 84/5	1976-1977	Postal Service Commission

Y 3.P 91

Y 3.P 91	1889	Royal (British) Commission Appointed to Inquire to Recent Changes in Relative Values of Precious Metals

Y 3.P 92

Y 3.P 92	1930-1931	President's Emergency Employment Committee
	1931-1932	President's Organization on Unemployment Relief

Y 3.P 92/2

Y 3.P 92/2	1936	President's Crop Insurance Committee

Y 3.P.92/3

Y 3.P 92/3	1936-1937	President's Administrative Management Committee

Y 3.P 92/4

Y 3.P 92/4	1939-1941	President's Civil Service Improvement Committee

Y 3.P 92/5

Y 3.P 92/5	1948-1949	President's Committee on Religious and Moral Welfare and Character Guidance in the Armed Forces
	1949-1951	President's Committee on Religion and Welfare in the Armed Forces

Y 3.P 92/6

Y 3.P 92/6	1990-	Presidential Commission on Catastrophic Nuclear Accidents

Y 3.P 93

Y 3.P 93	1905-1907	Printing Investigation Commission

Y 3.P 93/2

Y 3.P 93/2	1917	Priority in Transportation Commissioner

Y 3.P 93/3

Y 3.P 93/3	1935-1940	Prison Industry Industries Reorganization Administration

Y 3.P 93/4

Y 3.P 93/4	1971-1973	Price Commission

Y 3.P 93/5

Y 3.P 93/5	1974	Privacy Protection Study Commission

Y 3.P 94

Y 3.P 94	1977-1978	National Center for Productivity and Quality of Working Life

Y 3.P 96/1

Y 3.P 96/1	1879-1880	Public Land Commission

Y 3.P 96/2

Y 3.P 96/2	1903-1905	Public Lands Commission

Y 3.P 96/3

Y 3.P 96/3	1917-1919	Public Information Committee

Y 3.P 96/4

Y 3.P 96/4	1919-1933	Public Buildings Commission
I 28	1933-1939	[functions transferred to] National Park Service
T 58	1933-1939	[a branch in] Procurement Division
FW 6	1939-1949	Public Buildings Administration
GS 6	1949-	Public Buildings Service

Y 3.P 96/5

Y 3.P 96/5	1930-1931	Conservation and Administration of the Public Domain Committee

Y 3.P 96/6

Y 3.P 96/6	1945	Publication Board
C 35	1945	Publication Board Office
	1945	Declassification and Technical Service Office
	1945-1953	Technical Services Office
C 41	1953-1970	Business and Defense Services Administration
	1970-1972	Domestic Commerce Bureau
C 57.300	1972-1974	Competitive Assessment and Business Policy Bureau
C 57.500	1974-1980	Domestic Commerce Bureau
C 62	1980-	Industrial Economics Bureau

Y 3.P 96/7

Y 3.P 96/7	1964-1970	Public Land Law Review Commission

Y 3.P 96/9

Y 3.P 96/9		National Commission on Severely Distressed Public Housing

Y 3.P 97

Y 3.B 61	1938-1971	Purchases of Blind-Made Products Committee
Y 3.P 97	1971-1974	Purchase of Products and Services of the Blind and Other Severely Handicapped Committee
Y 3.B 61	1974-199x	Purchase from the Blind and Other Severely Handicapped Committee
Y 3.P 97	199x-	Purchase from People who are Blind or Severely Disabled Committee

Y 3.R 11

Y 3.R 11	1970	Interagency Racial Data Committee

Y 3.R 11/2

Y 3.R 11/2	1980-1982	United States Radiation Policy Council

Y 3.R 13

Y 3.R 13	1910-1911	Railroad Securities Commission

Y 3.R 13/2

Y 3.R 13/2	1918-1939	Railroad Administration

Y 3.R 13/2:10

Y 3.R 13/2:10	1919-1925	Finance Division

Y 3.R 13/2:20

Y 3.R 13/2:20	1918-1920	Operations Division

Y 3.R 13/2:30

Y 3.R 13/2:30	1918-1920	Office of Comptroller

Y 3.R 13/2:40

Y 3.R 13/2:40	1918-1920	Traffic Division

Y 3.R 13/2:50

Y 3.R 13/2:50	1918-1920	Labor Division

Y 3.R 13/2:60

Y 3.R 13/2:60	1918-1933	Law Division

Y 3.R 13/2:70

Y 3.R 13/2:70	1918-1933	Suggestions and Complaints Bureau

Y 3.R 13/2:80

Y 3.R 13/2:80	1919	Public Service Division

Y 3.R 13/2:90

Y 3.R 13/2:90	1920	Liquidation Claims Division

Y 3.R 13/2:100

Y 3.R 13/2:100	1918-1920	Capital Expenditures Division

Y 3.R 13/2:110

Y 3.R 13/2:110	1919-1920	Purchases Division

Y 3.R 13/2:120

Y 3.R 13/2:120		Troop Movement Section

Y 3.R 13/3

Y 3.R 13/3	1970-1972	Railroad Retirement Commission

Y 3.R 13/4

Y 3.R 13/4	1974-1986	United States Railway Association

Y 3.R 24

Y 3.R 24	1932-1939	Reconstruction Finance Corporation
FL 5	1939-1942	Reconstruction Finance Corporation
C 33	1942-1945	Reconstruction Finance Corporation
FL 5	1945-1947	Reconstruction Finance Corporation
Y 3.R 24	1947-1954	Reconstruction Finance Corporation

Y 3.R 24/2

Y 3.R 24/2	1974-1976	National Study Commission on Records and Documents of Federal Officials

Y 3.R 26

Y 3.R 26		Regulatory Council

Y 3.R 26/2

Y 3.R 26/2		Interagency Regulatory Liason Group

Y 3.R 29

Y 3.R 29	1919-1925	Rent Commission of District of Columbia

Y 3.R 29/2

Y 3.R 29/2	1949-1952	Renovation of Executive Mansion Commission

Y 3.R 31

Y 3.R 31	1935-1937	Resettlement Administration
A 61	1937	Resettlement Administration
	1937-1942	Farm Security Administration
A 80.700	1942-1945	Farm Security Administration
A 61	1945-1946	Farm Security Administration
A 84	1946-	Farmers Home Administration

Y 3.R 31/2

Y 3.R 31/2	1990-	Resolution Trust Corporation

Y 3.R 32

Y 3.R 32	1872-1973	Revision of Statutes Commission

Y 3.R 67

Y 3.R 67	1955-1997	Franklin Delano Roosevelt Memorial Commission

Y 3.R 82

Y 3.R 82	1953-1956	Rubber Producing Facilities Disposal Commission
T 69	1956-1957	[functions transferred to] Federal Facilities Corporation

Y 3.R 88

Y 3.R 88	1935-1939	Rural Electrification Administration
A 68	1939-	Rural Electrification Administration

Y 3.R 88/2

Y 3.R 88/2	1954-1963	Rural Development Program Committee
Y 3.R 88/3	1963-1966	Rural Development Committee

Y 3.R 88/3

Y 3.R 88/2	1954-1963	Rural Development Program Committee
Y 3.R 88/3	1963-1966	Rural Development Committee

Y 3.Sa 2

Y 3.Sa 2	1945-1966	St. Lawrence Seaway Development Corporation
TD 6	1966-	St. Lawrence Seaway Development Corporation

Y 3.Sa 2/2

Y 3.Sa 2/2	1962	Saint Augustine Quadricentennial Commission

Y 3.Sa 5

Y 3.Sa 5	1871	Santo Domingo Commission

Y 3.Se 4

Y 3.Se 4	1940-1942	Selective Service System
Pr 32.5270	1942-1943	Selective Service System
Y 3.Se 4	1943-1947	Selective Service System
	1947-1948	Selective Service Records Office
	1948-	Selective Service System

Y 3.Se 5

Y 3.Se 5	198x-	United States Sentencing Commission

Y 3.Se 5/3

Y 3.Se 5/3		National Advisory Committee on Semiconductors

Y 3.Sh 6

Y 3.Sh 6	1946-	Ship Structures Committee

Y 3.Sh 6/2

Y 3.Sh 6/2	1973-	American Shipbuilding Commission

Y 3.Si 2

Y 3.Si 2	1866	Joint Commission to Consider the Present Organization of the Signal Service, Geological Survey, Coast and Geodetic Survey, and Hydrographic Office

Y 3.So 1

Y 3.So 1	1977-	National Commission on Social Security

Y 3.So 8

Y 3.So 8	1967-1973	Souris-Red-Rainy River Basins Commission

Y 3.So 8/2

Y 3.So 8/2	1965-1981	Southwest Border Regional Commission

Y 3.Sp 1

Y 3.Sp 1	198x-	National Commission on Space

Y 3.Sp 2

Y 3.Sp 2	1901-1910	Spanish Treaty Claims Commission

Y 3.Sp 2/7

Y 3.In 8/23	1967-1969	Interagency Mexican American Affairs Committee
Y 3.Sp 2/7	1969-1974	Cabinet Committee on Opportunity for Spanish Speaking Peoples

Y 3.St 8

Y 3.St 8	1972-	Strategy Council on Drug Abuse

Y 3.St 9

Y 3.St 9		National Commission on Student Financial Assistance

Y 3.Su 1

Y 3.Su 1	1950-1973	Subversive Activities Control Board

Y 3.Su 3

Y 3.Su 3	1918-1926	Sugar Equalization Board

Y 3.Su 7

Y 3.Su 7	1919-1936	Surveys and Maps of the Federal Government Board
	1936-1942	Federal Board of Surveys and Maps
Pr 32.100	1942-1945	[functions transferred to] Budget Bureau

Y 3.Su 7/2

Y 3.Su 7/2	1974-1977	National Supplies and Shortages Commission

Y 3.Su 7/3

Y 3.Su 7/3	199x-	National Superconductivity Commission

Y 3.T 17

Y 3.T 17	1882	Tariff Commission

Y 3.T 17/2

Y 3.T 17/2	1909-1916	Tariff Board
TC 1	1916-1974	Tariff Commission
	1974-1981	International Trade Commission
ITC	1981-	International Trade Commission

Y 3.T 19

T 61	1936-1942	Processing Tax Board of Review
Y 3.T 19	1924-1942	United States Board of Tax Appeals
Ju 11	1942-	Tax Court of the United States

Y 3.T 22

Y 3.T 22	1964-1966	National Commission on Technology, Automation, and Economic Progress

Y 3.T 22/2

Y 3.T 22/2	1972-1995	Technology Assessment Office

Y 3.T 25

Y 3.T 25	1933-	Tennessee Valley Authority

Y 3.T 36

Y 3.T 36	1936-1939	Thomas Jefferson Memorial Commission

Y 3.T 55

Y 3.T 55	1912-1914	Commission to Investigate Purchase of American-Grown Tobacco by Foreign Governments

Y 3.T 64

Y 3.T 64	1971-1973	National Tourism Resources Review Committee

Y 3.T 67

Y 3.T 67	1975-1981	East-West Foreign Trade Board

Y 3.T 68

Y 3.T 68	1940-1944	Transportation Investigation and Research Board

Y 3.T 68/2

Y 3.T 68/2	1976-	National Transportation Policy Study Commission

Y 3.T 79

Y 3.T 79	1906	Tuberculosis Committee

Y 3.Un 2

Y 3.Un 2	1976-1980	National Commission on Unemployment Compensation

Y 3.Un 3

Y 3.Un 3	1935-1941	United States Constitution Sesquicentennial Commission

Y 3.Un 3/2

Y 3.Un 3/2	1958-1962	United States Study Commission on Neches, Trinity, Brazos, and San Jacinto River Basins and Intervening Areas

Y 3.Un 3/3

Y 3.Un 3/3	1958	U.S.-FAO Interagency Committee

Y 3.Un 3/4

Y 3.Un 3/4	1958-1963	U.S. Study Commission on the Savannah, Altamaha, Saint Marys, Apalachicola-Chittahoochee and Perdido-Escambia River Basins and Intervening Areas

Y 3.Un 3/5

Y 3.Un 3/5	1964	United States-Puerto Rico Commission on the Status of Puerto Rico

Y 3.Up 6

Y 3.Up 6	1967-1981	Upper Great Lakes Regional Commission

Y 3.V 55

Y 3.V 55	1897	Venezuelan Boundary Commission

Y 3.V 64

Y 3.V 64	1950-1957	Veterans' Education Appeals Board

Y 3.V 85

Y 3.V 85	1968-	National Advisory Council on Vocational Education

Y 3.W 19

Y 3.W 19	1899	War Investigating Commission

Y 3.W 19/2

Y 3.C 83:50	1918	War Industries Board
Y 3.W 19/2	1918	War Industries Board

Y 3.W 19/3

Y 3.W 19/3	1918-1939	War Finance Corporation

Y 3.W 19/4

Y 3.W 19/4	1928-1931	War Claims Arbiter

Y 3.W 19/5

Y 3.W 19/5	1930-1932	War Policies Commission

Y 3.W 19/6

Y 3.W 19/6	1944-1951	War Contracts Price Adjustment Board
GS 1	1951-	[functions transferred to] General Services Administration
RnB 1	1951-	Renegotiation Board

Y 3.W 19/7

Pr 32.5900	1943-1944	War Mobilization Office
Y 3.W 19/7	1944-1946	War Mobilization and Reconversion Office
Pr 33.300	1946-1947	Temporary Controls Office

Y 3.W 19/7:100

Y 3.W 19/7:100	1944-1946	Contract Settlement Office
T 67	1946-1949	Contract Settlement Office
GS 5	1949-1952	Contract Settlement Office

Y 3.W 19/7:200

Pr 32.5908	1944	Surplus War Property Administration
	1944-1945	Surplus Property Board
Y 3.W 19/7:200	1945-1947	Surplus Property Administration
Y 3.W 19/8	1947-1949	War Assets Administration

Y 3.W 19/8

Pr 33.200	1946-1947	War Assets Administration
Y 3.W 19/7:200	1945-1947	Surplus Property Administration
Y 3.W 19/8	1947-1949	War Assets Administration

Y 3.W 19/9

Y 3.W 19/9	1948-1954	War Claims Commission
Y 3.F 76/3	1954-1980	Foreign Claims Settlement Commission
J 1	1980-	[functions transferred to] Justice Department

Y 3.W 19/10

Y 3.W 19/10		Wartime Relocation Commission

Y 3.W 27

Y 3.W 27	1867-1888	Washington Monument Joint Commission

Y 3.W 27/2

Y 3.W 27/2	1924-1932	Washington Bicentennial Celebration Commission

Y 3.W 29

Y 3.W 29	1965-1982	Water Resources Council

Y 3.W 29/2

Y 3.W 29/2	1972	National Water Quality Commission

Y 3.W 52

Y 3.W 52	1965	Select Commission on Western Hemisphere Immigration

Y 3.W 56

Y 3.W 56	1919-1920	Wheat Director

Y 3.W 56:10

Y 3.W 56:10	1919-1920	Grain Corporation

Y 3.W 58

Y 3.W 58	1930	White House Conference on Child Health and Protection

Y 3.W 58/2

Y 3.W 58/2	1954-1955	White House Conference on Education Committee

Y 3.W 58/3

Y 3.W 58/3	1958-1960	White House Conference on Children

Y 3.W 58/3-2

Y 3.W 58/3-2	1970	White House Conference on Children

Y 3.W 58/3-3

Y 3.W 58/3-3	1970-1971	White House Conference on Youth

Y 3.W 58/4

Y 3.W 58/4	1958-1961	White House Conference on Aging

Y 3.W 58/5

Y 3.W 58/5	1962	White House Conference on Narcotic and Drug Abuse

Y 3.W 58/6

Y 3.W 58/6	1962	White House Conference on Conservation

Y 3.W 58/7

Y 3.W 58/7	1962	White House Conference on National Economic Issues

Y 3.W 58/8

Y 3.W 58/8	1963	White House Conference on Export Expansion

Y 3.W 58/9

Y 3.W 58/9	1963	White House Conference on Mental Retardation

Y 3.W 58/10

Y 3.W 58/10	1964-	Committee for Preservation of the White House

Y 3.W 58/11

Y 3.W 58/11	1965	White House Conference on International Cooperation

Y 3.W 58/12

Y 3.W 58/12	1965	White House Conference on Natural Beauty

Y 3.W 58/13

Y 3.W 58/13	1965	White House Conference on Equal Employment Opportunity

Y 3.W 58/14

Y 3.W 58/14	1965	White House Conference on Health

Y 3.W 58/15

Y 3.W 58/15	1966	White House Conference "To Fulfill These Rights"

Y 3.W 58/16

Y 3.W 58/16	1969-1970	White House Conference on Food, Nutrition and Health

Y 3.W 58/17

Y 3.W 58/17	1971	White House Conference on the Industrial World Ahead

Y 3.W 58/18

Y 3.W 58/18	1976	White House Conference on Handicapped Individuals

Y 3.W 58/19

Y 3.W 58/19	1978	White House Conference on Balanced National Growth and Economic Development

Y 3.W 58/20

Y 3.W 58/20	1978	White House Conference on Library and Information Services

Y 3.W 58/21

Y 3.W 58/21		White House Commission on Small Business

Y 3.W 58/22

Y 3.W 58/22	1979	White House Conference on Families

Y 3.W 58/23

Y 3.W 58/23		White House Conference on Indian Education

Y 3.W 74

Y 3.W 74	1904	Inter-Departmental Wireless Telegraphy Board

Y 3.W 74/2

Y 3.W 74/2	1968	National Commission for Review of Federal and State Laws Relating to Wiretapping and Electronic Surveillance

Y 3.W 83

Y 3.W 83	199x-	Wolf Management Committee

Y 3.W 84

Y 3.W 84	1975-1978	National Commission on the Observance of International Women's Year, 1975

Y 3.W 84/2

Y 3.W 84/2	1977-	National Advisory Council on Women's Educational Programs

Y 3.W 84/3

Y 3.W 84/3	198x-	Women, Minorities, and the Handicapped in Science and Technology Task Force

Y 3.W 86

Y 3.W 86	1954	Woodrow Wilson Centennial Celebration Commission

Y 3.W 86/2

Y 3.W 86/2	1961-1966	Woodrow Wilson Memorial Commission

Y 3.W 89

Y 3.W 89	1922-1927	World War Foreign Debt Commission

Y 3.W 89/2

Y 3.W 89/2	1935-1939	Works Progress Administration
FW 4	1939-1943	Works Progress Administration

Y 3.W 89/3

Y 3.W 89/3	1970-	National State Workmen's Compensation Laws Commission

Y 3.Y 8

Y 3.Y 8	1881-1883	Yorktown Centennial Commission

Y 3.Y 8/2

Y 3.Y 8/2	1928-1930	Yorktown Sesquicentennial Commission

		Y 3.2
Y 3.2		Commissions, Committees, and Boards

Y 4

Y 4		Committees of Congress

Y 4.3:T

Y 4.3:T	1998-	Special Committee on the Year 2000 Technology Problem

Y 4.Ac 2

Y 4.Ac 2	1887-1916	House Accounts Committee

Y 4.Ad 6

Y 4.Ad 6	1975-	House Administrative Review Commission

Y 4.Ae 8

| Y 4.Ae 8 | 1958-19xx | Senate Aeronautical and Space Science Committee |
| Y 4.C 73/7 | 19xx- | Senate Commerce, Science, and Transportation Committee |

Y 4.Ag 4

Y 4.Ag 4	1961	Senate Special Aging Committee

Y 4.Ag 4/2

Y 4.Ag 4/2		House Select Aging Committee

Y 4.Ag 8/1

Y 4.Ag 8/1	1900-	House Agriculture Committee

Y 4.Ag 8/2

| Y 4.Ag 8/2 | 1901-19xx | Senate Agriculture and Forestry Committee |
| Y 4.Ag 8/3 | 19xx- | Senate Agriculture, Nutrition, and Forestry Committee |

Y 4.Ag 8/3

Y 4.Ag 8/2	1901-19xx	Senate Agriculture and Forestry Committee
Y 4.N 95	1968-19xx	Senate Select Nutrition and Human Needs Committee
Y 4.Ag 8/3	19xx-	Senate Agriculture, Nutrition, and Forestry Committee

Y 4.Ai 7

Y 4.Ai 7	1925	House Select Committee of Inquiry into Operations of Air Services

Y 4.Ai 7/2

Y 4.Ai 7/2	1933-1935	Senate Special Committee on Investigation of Air Mail and Ocean Mail Contracts

Y 4.Al 1/1

Y 4.Al 1/1	1898	Joint Select Committee on Alcohol in Manufactures and Arts

Y 4.Al 1/2

Y 4.Al 1/2	1890-1926	House Alcohol Liquor Traffic Committee

Y 4.Am 3/1

Y 4.Am 3/1	1870-1887	House American Ship-Building Committee

Y 4.Am 3/2

Y 4.Am 3/2	1911-1912	House Special Committee on Investigation of American Sugar Refining Company

Y 4.Am 3/3

Y 4.Am 3/3	1935-1936	House Special Committee to Investigate American Retail Federation

Y 4.Am 3/4

Y 4.Am 3/4	1939	Senate Special Committee to Investigate Conditions in the American Merchant Marine

Y 4.Am 3/5

Y 4.Am 3/5	1941-1949	Senate Special Committee to Study Problems of American Small Business

Y 4.Ap 6/1

Y 4.Ap 6/1	1880-	House Appropriations Committee

Y 4.Ap 6/2

Y 4.Ap 6/2	1906-	Senate Appropriations Committee

Y 4.Ar 5

Y 4.Ar 5	1915	Special Joint Committee to Investigate the Cost of Armor Plant

Y 4.Ar 5/2

Y 4.Ar 5/2	1947-	House Armed Services Committee

Y 4.Ar 5/3

Y 4.Ar 5/3	1947-	Senate Armed Services Committee

Y 4.Ar 7

Y 4.Ar 7	1968-	Senate Art and Antiquities Commission

Y 4.As 7

Y 4.As 7	1978	House Select Assassinations Committee

Y 4.As 8

Y 4.As 8	1958-1959	House Select Astronautics and Space Exploration Committee

Y 4.At 7

Y 4.At 7	1945-1946	Senate Special Atomic Energy Committee

Y 4.At 7/2

Y 4.At 7/2	1947-	Joint Atomic Energy Committee

Y 4.At 8

Y 4.At 8	1924	Senate Select Committee on Investigation of the Attorney General

Y 4.B 21

| Y 4.B 21 | 1953-1954 | House Select Committee to Investigate the Incorporation of the Baltic States into the U.S.S.R. |
| Y 4.C 73/5 | 1954 | House Select Committee on Communist Aggression |

Y 4.B 22/1

Y 4.B 22/1	-19xx	House Banking and Currency Committee
	19xx-1977	House Banking, Currency, and Housing Committee
	1977-19xx	House Banking, Finance, and Urban Affairs Committee
	19xx-	House Financial Services Committee

Y 4.B 22/2

Y 4.B 22/2	1892-1898	Senate Select Failed National Banks Committee

Y 4.B 22/3

| Y 4.B 22/3 | 1913-19xx | Senate Banking and Currency Committee |
| | 19xx- | Senate Banking, Housing and Urban Affairs Committee |

<table>
<tr><td colspan="3" align="center">Y 4.B 22/4</td></tr>
<tr><td>**Y 4.B 22/4**</td><td>1933-1936</td><td>Senate Special Committee to Investigate Bankruptcy and Receivership Proceedings and Administration of Justice in United States Courts</td></tr>
<tr><td colspan="3" align="center">Y 4.B 45</td></tr>
<tr><td>**Y 4.B 45**</td><td>1919</td><td>House Special Committee Appointed under House Resolution 6 Concerning Victor L. Berger</td></tr>
<tr><td colspan="3" align="center">Y 4.B 45/2</td></tr>
<tr><td>**Y 4.B 45/2**</td><td>1921-1927</td><td>House Select Committee to Investigate the Escape of Grover Cleveland Bergdoll from the Disciplinary Barracks at Governors Island, New York</td></tr>
<tr><td colspan="3" align="center">Y 4.B 47</td></tr>
<tr><td>**Y 4.B 27**</td><td></td><td>Joint Committee on the Arrangements for the Commemoration of the Bicentennial</td></tr>
<tr><td colspan="3" align="center">Y 4.B 85</td></tr>
<tr><td>**Y 4.B 85**</td><td>1971-</td><td>Joint Budget Control Study Committee</td></tr>
<tr><td colspan="3" align="center">Y 4.B 85/2</td></tr>
<tr><td>**Y 4.B 85/2**</td><td></td><td>Senate Budget Committee</td></tr>
<tr><td colspan="3" align="center">Y 4.B 85/3</td></tr>
<tr><td>**Y 4.B 85/3**</td><td></td><td>House Budget Committee</td></tr>
<tr><td colspan="3" align="center">Y 4.B 86/1</td></tr>
<tr><td>**Y 4.B 86/1**</td><td>1919-1920</td><td>House Select Budget Committee</td></tr>
<tr><td colspan="3" align="center">Y 4.B 86/2</td></tr>
<tr><td>**Y 4.B 86/2**</td><td>1919-1920</td><td>Senate Committee for the Consideration of the National Budget</td></tr>
<tr><td colspan="3" align="center">Y 4.C 15</td></tr>
<tr><td>**Y 4.C 15**</td><td>1944-</td><td>House Special Committee to Investigate Campaign Expenditures</td></tr>
<tr><td colspan="3" align="center">Y 4.C 16</td></tr>
<tr><td>**Y 4.C 16**</td><td>1890</td><td>Senate Relations with Canada Committee</td></tr>
<tr><td colspan="3" align="center">Y 4.C 17</td></tr>
<tr><td>**Y 4.C 17**</td><td>1896</td><td>Joint Special Committee on the Centennial Celebration of the Laying of the Corner Stone of the Capitol</td></tr>
<tr><td colspan="3" align="center">Y 4.C 17/2</td></tr>
<tr><td>**Y 4.C 17/2**</td><td>1955</td><td>Extension of the United States Capitol Commission</td></tr>
<tr><td colspan="3" align="center">Y 4.C 33/1</td></tr>
<tr><td>**Y 4.C 33/1**</td><td>1887-1941</td><td>House Census Committee</td></tr>
<tr><td colspan="3" align="center">Y 4.C 33/2</td></tr>
<tr><td>**Y 4.C 33/2**</td><td>1900-1916</td><td>Senate Census Committee</td></tr>
<tr><td colspan="3" align="center">Y 4.C 33/3</td></tr>
<tr><td>**Y 4.C 33/3**</td><td>1944</td><td>Senate Special Committee to Investigate the Centralization of Heavy Industry in the United States</td></tr>
<tr><td colspan="3" align="center">Y 4.C 33/4</td></tr>
<tr><td>**Y 4.C 33/4**</td><td>1954</td><td>Senate Select Committee to Study Censure Charges</td></tr>
</table>

<table>
<tr><td colspan="3" align="center">Y 4.C 333</td></tr>
<tr><td>**Y 4.C 333**</td><td></td><td>Centennial of the Establishment of the Seat of Government in Washington Commission</td></tr>
<tr><td colspan="3" align="center">Y 4.C 43</td></tr>
<tr><td>**Y 4.C 43**</td><td>1896</td><td>Joint Committee on the Dedication of Chickamauga and Chattanooga National Military Park</td></tr>
<tr><td colspan="3" align="center">Y 4.C 43/2</td></tr>
<tr><td>**Y 4.C 43/2**</td><td>1982-</td><td>House Select Committee on Children, Youth, and Families</td></tr>
<tr><td colspan="3" align="center">Y 4.C 44</td></tr>
<tr><td>**Y 4.C 44**</td><td>1877</td><td>Joint Special Chinese Immigration Committee</td></tr>
<tr><td colspan="3" align="center">Y 4.C 49/1</td></tr>
<tr><td>**Y 4.C 49/1**</td><td>1904-1946</td><td>House Civil Service Reform Committee</td></tr>
<tr><td colspan="3" align="center">Y 4.C 49/2</td></tr>
<tr><td>**Y 4.C 49/2**</td><td>1910-1948</td><td>Senate Civil Service and Retrenchment Committee</td></tr>
<tr><td colspan="3" align="center">Y 4.C 49/3</td></tr>
<tr><td>**Y 4.C 49/3**</td><td>1929</td><td>Senate Select Committee on the Investigation of Illegal Appointments and Dismissals in the Civil Service</td></tr>
<tr><td colspan="3" align="center">Y 4.C 49/4</td></tr>
<tr><td>**Y 4.C 49/4**</td><td>1939-1940</td><td>Senate Special Committee to Investigate the Administration and Operation of the Civil Service Laws</td></tr>
<tr><td colspan="3" align="center">Y 4.C 52/1</td></tr>
<tr><td>**Y 4.C 52/1**</td><td>1887-1940</td><td>House Claims Committee</td></tr>
<tr><td colspan="3" align="center">Y 4.C 52/2</td></tr>
<tr><td>**Y 4.C 52/2**</td><td>1887-1941</td><td>Senate Claims Committee</td></tr>
<tr><td colspan="3" align="center">Y 4.C 63</td></tr>
<tr><td>**Y 4.C 63**</td><td>1914</td><td>Senate Coast and Insular Survey Committee</td></tr>
<tr><td colspan="3" align="center">Y 4.C 66</td></tr>
<tr><td>**Y 4.C 66**</td><td>1891-1943</td><td>House Coinage, Weights and Measures Committee</td></tr>
<tr><td colspan="3" align="center">Y 4.C 73/1</td></tr>
<tr><td>**Y 4.C 73/1**</td><td>1819-1892</td><td>House Commerce Committee</td></tr>
<tr><td colspan="3" align="center">Y 4.C 73/2</td></tr>
<tr><td>**Y 4.C 73/2**</td><td>1825-19xx</td><td>Senate Commerce Committee</td></tr>
<tr><td>**Y 4.C 73/7**</td><td>19xx-</td><td>Senate Commerce, Science, and Transportation Committee</td></tr>
<tr><td colspan="3" align="center">Y 4.C 73/3</td></tr>
<tr><td>**Y 4.C 73/3**</td><td>1930-1931</td><td>House Special Committee to Investigate Communist Propaganda in the United States</td></tr>
<tr><td colspan="3" align="center">Y 4.C 73/4</td></tr>
<tr><td>**Y 4.C 73/4**</td><td>1949</td><td>House Select Committee to Investigate Commodity Transaction</td></tr>
<tr><td colspan="3" align="center">Y 4.C 73/5</td></tr>
<tr><td>**Y 4.B 21**</td><td>1953-1954</td><td>House Select Committee to Investigate the Incorporation of the Baltic States into the U.S.S.R.</td></tr>
<tr><td>**Y 4.C 73/5**</td><td>1954</td><td>House Select Communist Aggression Committee</td></tr>
</table>

Y 4.C 73/7

Y 4.Ae 8	1958-19xx	Senate Aeronautical and Space Science Committee
Y 4.C 73/2	1825-19xx	Senate Commerce Committee
Y 4.C 73/7	19xx-	Senate Commerce, Science, and Transportation Committee

Y 4.C 73/8

Y 4.C 78/8	1995-199x	House Committee on Commerce
	199x-	House Energy and Commerce Committee

Y 4.C 75

Y 4.C 75	1884-1885	Joint Committee on the Conduct of the War

Y 4.C 76/1

Y 4.C 76/1	1907-	House and Senate Conference Committees

Y 4.C 76/2

Y 4.C 76/2	1881-1889	Joint Select Committee on the Importation of Contract Laborers, Convicts, and Paupers

Y 4.C 76/3

Y 4.C 76/3	1945-1946	Joint Committee on the Organization of Congress
	1965-1966	Joint Committee on the Organization of Congress

Y 4.C 76/4

Y 4.C 76/4	1956	Senate Select Committee on Contribution Investigation

Y 4.C 76/5

Y 4.C 76/5	1958	Joint Committee on Construction of the Building for the Museum of History and Technology for the Smithsonian Institution

Y 4.C 76/6

Y 4.C 76/6	1966-	Senate Special Committee on the Organization of Congress

Y 4.C 76/7

Y 4.C 76/7	1969-	Joint Congressional Operations Committee

Y 4.C 76/8

Y 4.C 76/8		Senate Special Official Conduct Committee

Y 4.C 76/9

Y 4.C 76/9		House Select Congressional Operations Committee

Y 4.C 81/1

Y 4.C 81/1	1857	House Select Committee to Investigate Alleged Corrupt Combinations of Members of Congress

Y 4.C 81/2

Y 4.C 81/2	1860	House Select Committee to Investigate Alleged Corruptions in Government

Y 4.C 86

Y 4.C 86	1873	House Select Committee to Investigate Alleged Credit Mobilier Bribery

Y 4.C 86/2

Y 4.C 86/2	1950-1951	Senate Special Committee to Investigate Organized Crime in Interstate Commerce

Y 4.C 86/3

Y 4.C 86/3	1969-	House Select Crime Committee

Y 4.C 88

Y 4.C 88	1923	Senate Select Crop Insurance Committee

Y 4.C 89

Y 4.C 89	1900-1902	Senate Cuba Relations Committee

Y 4.D 36

Y 4.D 36	1950-	Joint Defense Production Committee

Y 4.D 36/2

Y 4.D 36/2	198x-	Temporary Joint Deficit Reduction Committee

Y 4.D 39

Y 4.D 39	1983	Democratic Policy Committee

Y 4.D 62

Y 4.D 62	1933	Joint Committee to Investigate Dirigible Disasters

Y 4.D 63/1

Y 4.D 63/1	1913-	House District of Columbia Committee

Y 4.D 63/2

Y 4.D 63/2	1928-1977	Senate District of Columbia Committee
Y 4.G 74/9	1977-	Senate Government Affairs Committee

Y 4.D 63/3

Y 4.D 63/3	1898	Joint Select Committee to Investigate District of Columbia Charities

Y 4.D 63/4

Y 4.D 63/4	1915	Senate Special Committee to Investigate the District of Columbia Excise Board

Y 4.D 63/5

Y 4.D 63/5	1916	Joint Committee on the Fiscal Relations Between the District of Columbia and the United States

Y 4.D 63/6

Y 4.D 63/6	1920	Senate Select Committee to Investigate the Public School System of the District of Columbia

Y 4.D 63/7

Y 4.D 63/7	1931	House Select Committee to Investigate the Fiscal Relations Between the District of Columbia and the United States

Y 4.Ec 7

Y 4.Ec 7	1946-1956	Joint Committee on the Economic Report
	1956-	Joint Economic Committee

Y 4.Ed 8/1

Y 4.Ed 8/1	1867-1883	House Education and Labor Committee
Y 4.Ed 8/2	1883-1947	House Education Committee
Y 4.L 11	1883-1947	House Labor Committee
Y 4.Ed 8/1	1947-199x	House Education and Labor Committee
	199x-	House Education and the Workforce Committee

Y 4.Ed 8/2

Y 4.Ed 8/1	1867-1883	House Education and Labor Committee
Y 4.Ed 8/2	1883-1947	House Education Committee
Y 4.Ed 8/1	1947-	House Education and Labor Committee

Y 4.Ed 8/3

Y 4.Ed 8/3	1885-1946	Senate Education and Labor Committee

Y 4.Ed 8/4

Y 4.Ed 8/4	1951-1952	House Select Committee to Investigate Educational and Training Programs Under the GI Bill

Y 4.El 2/1

Y 4.El 2/1	1906-1935	House Committee on the Election of the President, Vice-President, and Representatives

Y 4.El 2/2

Y 4.El 2/2	1894-1924	House Elections Committee

Y 4.En 2

Y 4.P 96/1	1882-1942	Senate Public Lands Committee
Y 4.In 8/13	1948	Senate Interior and Insular Affairs Committee
Y 4.En 2		Senate Energy and Natural Resources Committee

Y 4.En 2/2

Y 4.En 2/2		House Ad Hoc Energy Committee

Y 4.En 2/3

Y 4.In 8/4	1892-1981	House Interstate and Foreign Commerce Committee
Y 4.En 2/3	1981-	House Energy and Commerce Committee

Y 4.Ep 4/1

Y 4.Ep 4/1	1884-1887	House Select Committee on the Origin, Introduction and Prevention of Epidemic Diseases

Y 4.Ep 4/2

Y 4.Ep 4/2	1884-1887	Senate Epidemic Diseases Committee

Y 4.Eq 2

Y 4.Eq 2	1970-	Senate Select Equal Education Opportunities Committee

Y 4.Et 3/1

Y 4.Et 3/1	1852	House Select Ether Discovery Committee

Y 4.Et 3/2

Y 4.Et 3/2	1853	Senate Select Ether Discovery Committee

Y 4.Et 3/3

Y 4.Et 3/3	1978-	House Select Ethics Committee

Y 4.Et 3/4

Y 4.Et 3/4	1978-	Senate Select Ethics Committee

Y 4.Ex 3

Y 4.Ex 3	1922-1923	Senate Special Committee to Investigate Charges of Execution without a Trial in France

Y 4.Ex 3/2

Y 4.Ex 3/2	1936-1937	House Disposition of Executive Papers Committee

Y 4.Ex 3/3

Y 4.Ex 3/3	1937	Senate Select Committee on the Investigation of Executive Agencies of the Government

Y 4.Ex 3/4

Y 4.Ex 3/4	1943-1946	House Special Committee to Investigate Executive Agencies

Y 4.Ex 7/1

Y 4.Ex 7/1	1907-1916	House Expenditures in the Department of Agriculture Committee

Y 4.Ex 7/2

Y 4.Ex 7/2	1910-1918	House Expenditures in the Department of Commerce and Labor Committee

Y 4.Ex 7/3

Y 4.Ex 7/3	1908-1912	House Expenditures in the Interior Department Committee

Y 4.Ex 7/4

Y 4.Ex 7/4	1874-1913	House Expenditures in the Department of Justice Committee

Y 4.Ex 7/5

Y 4.Ex 7/5	1887-1911	House Expenditures in the Navy Department Committee

Y 4.Ex 7/6

Y 4.Ex 7/6	1908-1921	House Expenditures in the Post-Office Department Committee

Y 4.Ex 7/7

Y 4.Ex 7/7	1908-1918	House Expenditures in Public Buildings Committee

Y 4.Ex 7/8

Y 4.Ex 7/8	1887-1926	House Expenditures in the State Department Committee

Y 4.Ex 7/9

Y 4.Ex 7/9	1911-1915	House Expenditures in the Treasury Department Committee

Y 4.Ex 7/10

Y 4.Ex 7/10	1911-1915	House Expenditures in the War Department Committee

Y 4.Ex 7/11

Y 4.Ex 7/11	1919-1921	House Select Committee on Expenditures in the War Department

Y 4.Ex 7/12

Y 4.Ex 7/12	1927-1928	Senate Select Committee to Investigate the Expenditures in the Senatorial Primary and General Elections

Y 4.Ex 7/13

Y 4.Ex 7/13	1928-1952	House Expenditures in the Executive Departments Committee
Y 4.G 74/7	1952-	House Government Operations Committee

Y 4.Ex 7/14

Y 4.Ex 7/14	1947-1952	Senate Expenditures in the Executive Departments Committee
Y 4.G 74/6	1951-1977	Senate Government Operations Committee
Y 4.G 74/9	1977-	Senate Government Affairs Committee

Y 4.Ex 7/15

Y 4.Ex 7/15	1961-	House Select Export Control Committee

Y 4.F 22

Y 4.F 22	1942	Senate Special Committee to Investigate Farm Labor Conditions in the West

Y 4.F 31

Y 4.F 31	1913-1915	Joint Federal Aid in the Construction of Post Roads Committee

Y 4.F 31/2

Y 4.F 31/2	1923	Joint Committee to Determine What Employment May Be Furnished to Federal Prisoners

Y 4.F 31/3

Y 4.F 31/3	1929	House Special Committee on Federal Penal and Reformatory Institutions

Y 4.F 31/4

Y 4.F 31/4	1943-1944	House Select Committee to Investigate the Federal Communications Commission

Y 4.F 49

Y 4.F 49	1933-	Senate Finance Committee

Y 4.F 53

Y 4.F 53	1912-1917	Senate Fisheries Committee

Y 4.F 58

Y 4.F 58		House Select Committee of Five

Y 4.F 65

Y 4.F 65	1919-1946	House Flood Control Committee

Y 4.F 73

Y 4.F 73	1945	House Special Committee to Investigate Food Shortages

Y 4.F 73/2

Y 4.F 73/2	1950-1952	House Select Committee to Investigate the Use of Chemicals in Food Products

Y 4.F 76/1

Y 4.F 76/1	1789-1975	House Foreign Affairs Committee
Y 4.In 8/16	1975-1979	House International Relations Committee
Y 4.F 76/1	1979-	House Foreign Affairs Committee

Y 4.F 76/2

Y 4.F 76/2	1789-	Senate Foreign Relations Committee

Y 4.F 76/3

Y 4.F 73/3	1912	Senate Forest Reservations and the Protection of Game Committee

Y 4.F 76/4

Y 4.F 76/4	1938-1940	Joint Forestry Committee

Y 4.F 76/5

Y 4.F 76/5	1947-1948	House Select Foreign Aid Committee

Y 4.F 76/6

Y 4.F 76/6	1956-1957	Senate Special Committee to Study Foreign Aid Program

Y 4.F 95

Y 4.F 95	1943	Senate Special Committee to Investigate the Fuel Situation in the Middle West

Y 4.G 21

Y 4.G 21	1941-1943	Senate Special Committee to Investigate Gasoline and Fuel Oil Shortages

Y 4.G 56

Y 4.G 56	1923-1927	Senate Gold and Silver Inquiry Commission

Y 4.G 74

Y 4.G 74	1906-1907	House Special Committee to Investigate the Government Hospital for the Insane

Y 4.G 74/2

Y 4.G 74/2	1888	Senate Select Committee on the Investigation of the Government Printing Office

Y 4.G 74/3

Y 4.G 74/3	1937	House Select Government Organization Committee

Y 4.G 74/4

Y 4.G 74/4	1937	Joint Government Organization Committee

Y 4.G 74/5

Y 4.G 74/5	1937-1940	Senate Select Government Organization Committee

Y 4.G 74/6

Y 4.Ex 7/4	1874-1913	House Expenditures in the Department of Justice Committee
Y 4.G 74/6	1952-1977	Senate Government Operations Committee
Y 4.G 74/9	1977-	Senate Government Affairs Committee

Y 4.G 74/7

Y 4.Ex 7/13	1928-1952	House Expenditures in the Executive Department Committee
Y 4.G 74/7	1952-199x-	House Government Operations Committee
	199x-	House Government Reform Committee

Y 4.G 74/8

Y 4.G 74/8	1963-1964	Senate Select Government Research Committee

Y 4.G 74/9

Y 4.D 63/2	1928-1977	Senate District of Columbia Committee
Y 4.G 74/6	1952-1977	Senate Government Affairs Committee
Y 4.P 84/11	1946-1977	Senate Post Office and Civil Service Committee
Y 4.G 74/9	1977-	Senate Governmental Affairs Committee

Y 4.H 12

Y 4.H 12	1921-1922	Senate Select Haiti and Santo Domingo Committee

Y 4.H 23

Y 4.H 23	1860	Senate Select Harpers Ferry Invasion Committee

Y 4.H 23/2

Y 4.H 23/2	1928	Joint Select Committee on Harriman Geographic Code System

Y 4.H 28

Y 4.H 28	1869	Senate Select Committee Appointed to Investigate the Memorial of Davis Hatch

Y 4.H 31

Y 4.H 31	1937-1938	Joint Hawaii Committee

Y 4.H 81

Y 4.H 81	1908	House Select Committee on House Rooms Distribution

Y 4.H 81/2

Y 4.H 81/2	1934	House Special Committee to Investigate the Management and Control of the House Restaurant

Y 4.H 81/3

Y 4.H 81/3	1947-	House Administration Committee

Y 4.H 81/4

Y 4.H 81/4	1947-1948	Joint Housing Committee

Y 4.H 81/5

Y 4.H 81/5	1967	House Select Committee Pursuant to House Resolution 1 (Adam Clayton Powell Committee)

Y 4.H 81/6

Y 4.H 81/6	1969-	House Select House Restaurant Committee

Y 4.H 88

Y 4.L 11/2	1947-19xx	Senate Labor and Public Welfare Committee
Y 4.H 88	19xx-1979	Senate Human Resource Committee
Y 4.L 11/4	1979-	Senate Labor and Human Resources Committee

Y 4.H 89

Y 4.H 89		Senate Select Committee on Hunger

Y 4.Im 6/1

Y 4.Im 6/1	1892-1946	House Immigration and Naturalization Committee

Y 4.Im 6/2

Y 4.Im 6/2	1906-1946	Senate Immigration Committee

Y 4.Im 7

Y 4.Im 7	1957-1960	Senate Select Committee on Improper Activities in Labor or Management Field

Y 4.Im 7/2

Y 4.Im 7/2	198x-	Senate Impeachment Trial Committee

Y 4.In 2/1

Y 4.In 2/1	1903-1946	House Indian Affairs Committee

Y 4.In 2/2

Y 4.In 2/2	1905-1946	Senate Indian Affairs Committee

Y 4.In 2/3

Y 4.In 2/3	1879	Indian Bureau Joint Special Committee

Y 4.In 2/4

Y 4.In 2/4	1893	Senate Indian Depredations Committee

Y 4.In 2/5

Y 4.In 2/5	1907	Senate Select Committee to Investigate Matters Connected with Affairs in the Indian Territory

Y 4.In 2/6

Y 4.In 2/6	1867	Joint Special Committee on the Conditions of the Indian Tribes

Y 4.In 2/7

Y 4.In 2/7	1906-1926	House Industrial Arts and Expositions Committee

Y 4.In 2/8

Y 4.In 2/8	1910-1912	Senate Industrial Expositions Committee

Y 4.In 2/9

Y 4.In 2/9	1917	House Indian Service Investigation Committee

Y 4.In 2/10

Y 4.In 2/10	1974-	American Indian Policy Review Commission

Y 4.In 2/11

Y 4.In 2/11		Senate Select Indian Affairs Committee

Y 4.In 3

Y 4.In 3	1974	House Information and Facilities Commission

Y 4.In 7/1

Y 4.In 7/1	1902-1946	House Insular Affairs Committee

Y 4.In 7/2

Y 4.In 7/2	1872	Joint Select Committee to Inquire into Conditions of Affairs in the Late Insurrectionary States

Y 4.In 8/1

Y 4.In 8/1	1902-1938	Senate Interoceanic Canal Committee

Y 4.In 8/2

Y 4.In 8/2	1867	House Select Internal Revenue Frauds Committee

Y 4.In 8/3

Y 4.In 8/3	1789-1946	Senate Interstate Commerce Committee
	1946-19xx	Senate Interstate and Foreign Commerce Committee
Y 4.C 73/2	19xx-	[merged into] Senate Commerce Committee

Y 4.In 8/4

Y 4.In 8/4	1892-1981	House Interstate and Foreign Commerce Committee
Y 4.En 2/3	1981-	House Energy and Commerce Committee

Y 4.In 8/5

Y 4.In 8/5	1916-1945	House Invalid Pensions Committee

Y 4.In 8/6

Y 4.In 8/6	1872	Senate Investigation and Retrenchment Committee

Y 4.In 8/7

Y 4.In 8/7	1887	House Select Internal Improvements Committee

Y 4.In 8/8

Y 4.In 8/8	1910	Joint Committee to Investigate the Interior Department and Forestry Service

Y 4.In 8/9

Y 4.In 8/9	1916-1917	Joint Interstate Commerce Subcommittee

Y 4.In 8/10

Y 4.In 8/10	1924-1927	Senate Select Committee on the Investigation of the Internal Revenue Bureau

Y 4.In 8/11

Y 4.In 8/11	1926-19xx	Joint Internal Revenue Taxation Committee
Y 4.T 19/4	19xx-	Joint Taxation Committee

Y 4.In 8/12

Y 4.In 8/12	1940-1941	House Select Committee to Investigate the Interstate Migration of Destitute Citizens

Y 4.In 8/13

Y 4.P 96/1	1882-1942	Senate Public Lands Committee
Y 4.In 8/13	1948-	Senate Interior and Insular Affairs Committee
Y 4.En 2		Senate Energy and Natural Resources Committee

Y 4.IN 8/14

Y 4.In 8/14	1951-	House Interior and Insular Affairs Committee

Y 4.In 8/15

Y 4.Un 1/2	1945-1969	House Un-American Activities Committee
Y 4.In 8/15	1969-	House Internal Security Committee

Y 4.In 8/16

Y 4.F 76/1	1789-1975	House Foreign Affairs Committee
Y 4.In 8/16	1975-1979	House International Relations Committee
Y 4.F 76/1	1979-	House Foreign Affairs Committee

Y 4.In 8/17

Y 4.In 8/17		Senate Select Committee to Study Government Operations with Respect to Intelligence Activities

Y 4.In 8/18

Y 4.In 8/18		House Select Intelligence Committee

Y 4.In 8/19

Y 4.In 8/19		Senate Select Intelligence Committee

Y 4.In 8/20

Y 4.In 8/20	1986-	Select Committee to Investigate Covert Arms Transactions with Iran

Y 4.Ir 7/1

Y 4.Ir 7/1	1890-1946	Senate Irrigation and Reclamation Committee

Y 4.Ir 7/2

Y 4.Ir 7/2	1904-1946	House Irrigation an Reclamation Committee

Y 4.J 89/1

Y 4.J 89/1	1916-	House Judiciary Committee

Y 4.J 89/2

Y 4.J 89/2	1945-	Senate Judiciary Committee

Y 4.K 13

Y 4.K 13	1856	House Special Committee Investigating Kansas

Y 4.K 15

Y 4.K 15	1951-1952	House Select Committee to Conduct the Investigation of Facts, Evidence and Circumstances of the Katyn Forest Massacre

Y 4.L 11

Y 4.Ed 8/1	1967-1883	House Education and Labor Committee
Y 4.Ed 8/2	1883-1947	House Education Committee
Y 4.L 11	1883-1947	House Labor Committee
Y 4.Ed 8/1	1947-	House Education and Labor Committee

Y 4.L 11/2

Y 4.L 11/2	1947-19xx	Senate Labor and Public Welfare Committee
Y 4.H 88	19xx-1979	Senate Human Resources Committee
Y 4.L 11/4	1979-	Senate Labor and Human Resources Committee

Y 4.L 11/3

Y 4.L 11/3	1947	Joint Labor Management Relations committee

Y 4.L 11/4

Y 4.L 11/2	1947-19xx	Senate Labor and Public Welfare Committee
Y 4.H 88	19xx-1979	Senate Human Resources Committee
Y 4.L 11/4	1979-199x	Senate Labor and Human Resources Committee
	199x-	Senate Health, Education, Labor and Pensions Committee

Y 4.L 22

Y 4.L 22	1935	Senate Special Committee on the Survey of Land and Water Policies of the United States

Y 4.L 41

Y 4.L 41	19xx-	Select Committee to Study Law

Y 4.L 44/1

Y 4.L 44/1	1908-1910	Joint Special Committee on the Revision of Laws

Y 4.L 44/2

Y 4.L 44/2	1919-1947	House Revision of Laws Committee

Y 4.L 52

Y 4.L 52	1946-1948	Joint Legislative Budget Committee

Y 4.L 61/1

Y 4.L 61/1	1840-1940	House Library Committee

Y 4.L 61/2

Y 4.L 61/2	1850-1924	Joint Library Committee

Y 4.L 61/3

Y 4.L 61/3	1912-1932	Senate Library Committee

Y 4.L 62

Y 4.L 62	1908	House Select Committee on the Investigation of Charges Made by George L. Lilley

Y 4.L 78

Y 4.L 78	1913	House Select Lobby Investigation Committee

Y 4.L 78/2

Y 4.L 78/2	1935-1938	Senate Special Committee to Investigate Lobbying Activities

Y 4.L 78/3

Y 4.L 78/3	1950	House Select Lobbying Activities Committee

Y 4.L 89

Y 4.L 89	1911-1912	Senate Committee to Investigate the Election of William Lorimer

Y 4.M 28

Y 4.M 28		House Congressional Mailing Standards Commission

Y 4.M 31/1

Y 4.M 31/1	1842-1889	House Manufactures Committee

Y 4.M 31/2

Y 4.M 31/2	1904-1933	Senate Manufactures Committee

Y 4.M 46

Y 4.M 46		Senate Select Committee on Transportation and Sale of Meat Products

Y 4.M 51

Y 4.M 51	1924	House Select Committee to Investigate Alleged Charges Against Members of Congress

Y 4.M 53

Y 4.M 53	1889-1932	House Merchant Marine and Fisheries Committee
	1932-1935	House Merchant Marine, Radio, and Fisheries Committee
	1935-	House Merchant Marine and Fisheries Committee

Y 4.M 57

Y 4.M 57	1854	Senate Select Committee on Proceedings of the Board of Commissioners on Claims against Mexico

Y 4.M 58

Y 4.M 58	1837-1887	House Mileage Committee

Y 4.M 59/1

Y 4.M 59/1	1885-1946	House Military Affairs Committee

Y 4.M 59/2

Y 4.M 59/2	1900-1946	Senate Military Affairs Committee

Y 4.M 59/3

Y 4.M 59/3	1908-1910	House Militia Committee

Y 4.M 66/1

Y 4.M 66/1	1872-1934	House Mines and Mining Committee

Y 4.M 66/2

Y 4.M 66/2	1912-1935	Senate Mines and Mining Committee

Y 4.M 69/1

Y 4.M 69/1	1876-1877	Senate Select Committee to Inquire into Alleged Frauds in Recent Elections in Mississippi

Y 4.M 69/2

Y 4.M 69/2	1906	Senate Levees and Improvements of the Mississippi River Committee

Y 4.M 69/3

Y 4.M 69/3		House Select Committee on Missing Persons in Southeast Asia

Y 4.M 92

Y 4.M 92	1934-1936	Senate Special Committee Investigating the Munitions Industry

Y 4.M 97

Y 4.M 97	1936	Joint Muscle Shoals Committee

Y 4.N 16

Y 4.N 16		House Select Narcotics Abuse and Control Committee

Y 4.N 21/1

Y 4.N 21/1	1911	Senate Conservation of National Resources Committee

Y 4.N 21/2

Y 4.N 21/2	1918-1919	House Special Committee to Investigate the National Security League

Y 4.N 21/3

Y 4.N 21/3	1925	House Select Committee to Investigate the National Disabled Soldiers League Inc.

Y 4.N 21/4

Y 4.N 21/4	1939-1941	House Special Committee to Investigate the National Labor Relations Board

Y 4.N 21/5

Y 4.N 21/5	1941-1942	House Select Committee Investigating National Defense Migration

Y 4.N 21/6

Y 4.N 21/6	1941-1947	Senate Special Committee Investigating the National Defense Program

Y 4.N 21/7

Y 4.N 21/7	1942-1946	House Select Committee to Conduct the Study and Survey of the National Defense Program in its Relation to Small Business

Y 4.N 21/8

Y 4.N 21/8	1951-1961	Senate Select Committee on National Water Resources

Y 4.N 21/9

Y 4.N 21/9	1973-	Senate Special Committee on the Termination of the National Emergency

Y 4.N 22/1

Y 4.N 22/1	1890-1946	House Naval Affairs Committee

Y 4.N 22/2

Y 4.N 22/2	1896-1946	Senate Naval Affairs Committee

Y 4.N 22/3

Y 4.N 22/3	1894	Joint Naval Affairs Committee

Y 4.N 22/4

Y 4.N 22/4	1950	Joint Navajo-Hopi Indian Administration Committee

Y 4.N 42/1

Y 4.N 42/1		House Select New Orleans Riots Committee

Y 4.N 42/2

Y 4.N 42/2	1869	House Select Committee on the Alleged New York Election Frauds

Y 4.N 42/3

Y 4.N 42/3	1888-1889	Joint Select Committee on the Newburg, New York Monument and Centennial Celebration of 1889

Y 4.N 62

Y 4.N 62	1924-1926	Senate Select Committee on the Nine Foot Channel from the Great Lakes to the Gulf

Y 4.N 81

Y 4.N 81	1924-1925	Joint Committee on the Investigation of the Northern Pacific Railroad Land Grants

Y 4.N 95

Y 4.N 95	1968-19xx	Senate Select Nutrition and Human Needs Committee
Y 4.Ag 8/3	19xx-	Senate Agriculture, Nutrition, and Forestry Committee

Y 4.Ok 4

Y 4.Ok 4	1910-1937	House Select Committee to Investigate Indian Contracts in Oklahoma

Y 4.Ol 1

Y 4.Ol 1	1941	House Select Committee to Investigate Old Age Pension Plans

Y 4.Ol 1/2

Y 4.Ol 1/2	1941	Senate Special Committee to Investigate the Old-Age Pension System

Y 4.Or 2/1

Y 4.Or 2/1	1883	Senate Select Committee on Heavy Ordnance and Projectiles

Y 4.Or 2/2

Y 4.Or 2/2	1886	Senate Select Ordnance and Warships Committee

Y 4.Or 2/3

Y 4.Or 2/3		Joint Select Ordnance Committee

Y 4.Or 2/4

Y 4.Or 2/4	1917	House Select Committee on the Investigation of Ordnance and Ammunition

Y 4.Ou 8

Y 4.Ou 8	1871	Senate Select Committee to Investigate the Alleged Outrages in the Southern States

Y 4.Ou 8/2

Y 4.Ou 8/2		House Ad Hoc Select Committee on Outer Continental Shelf

Y 4.P 11/1

Y 4.P 11/1	1900-1917	Senate Pacific Islands and Puerto Rico Committee

Y 4.P 11/2

Y 4.P 11/2	1869	Senate Pacific Railroad Committee

Y 4.P 11/3

Y 4.P 11/3	1856	House Pacific Railroad Committee

Y 4.P 11/4

Y 4.P 11/4	1921	Joint Pacific Coast Naval Bases Committee

Y 4.P 21

Y 4.P 21	1913	Joint Committee to Investigate the General Parcel Post

Y 4.P 27/1

Y 4.P 27/1	1904-1946	House Patents Committee

Y 4.P 27/2

Y 4.P 27/2	1877-1944	Senate Patents Committee

Y 4.P 31

Y 4.P 31	1945-1946	Joint Committee Investigating the Pearl Harbor Attack

Y 4.P 38/1

Y 4.P 38/1	1907-1947	House Pensions Committee

Y 4.P 38/2

Y 4.P 38/2	1908-1941	Senate Pensions Committee

Y 4.P 38/3

Y 4.P 38/3		Select Committee on the Payment of Pensions, Bounty, and Back Pay

Y 4.P 44

Y 4.P 44	1945-1946	Senate Special Committee Investigating Petroleum Resources

Y 4.P 53

Y 4.P 53	1902-1915	Senate Philippines Committee

Y 4.P 56

Y 4.P 56	1939	Joint Committee to Investigate the Adequacy and Use of Phosphate Resources of the United States

Y 4.P 75

Y 4.P 75	1956-1957	Senate Special Committee to Investigate Political Activities, Lobbying and Campaign Contributions

Y 4.P 81

Y 4.P 81		House Select Population Committee

Y 4.P 82

Y 4.P 82	1953	House Select Committee on Current Pornographic Materials

Y 4.P 84/1

Y 4.P 84/1	1887-1946	House Post Office and Post Roads Committee

Y 4.P 84/2

Y 4.P 84/2	1887-1946	Senate Post Office and Post Roads Committee

Y 4.P 84/3

Y 4.P 84/3	1904	House Select Committee on the Relations of the Members with the Post Office Department

Y 4.P 84/4

Y 4.P 84/4	1913-1914	Joint Committee on the Postage on Second Class Mail Matter and the Compensation for Transportation of Mails

Y 4.P 84/5

Y 4.P 84/5	1919-1920	Joint Postal Salaries Commission

Y 4.P 84/6

Y 4.P 84/6	1930-1932	Senate Select Post Office Leases Committee

Y 4.P 84/7

Y 4.P 84/7	1944-1945	Senate Special Post-War Economic Policy and Planning Committee

Y 4.P 84/8

Y 4.P 84/8	1944-1945	House Select Post-War Military Policy Committee

Y 4.P 84/9

Y 4.P 84/9	1944-1945	House Select Post-War Economic Policy and Planning Committee

Y 4.P 84/10

Y 4.P 84/10	1946-	House Post Office and Civil Service Committee

Y 4.P 84/11

Y 4.P 84/11	1946-1977	Senate Post Office and Civil Service Committee
Y 4.G 74/9	1977-	Senate Government Affairs Committee

Y 4.P 92

Y 4.P 92	1928	Senate Special Committee Investigating Presidential Campaign Expenditures

Y 4.P 92/2

Y 4.P 92/2	1933-1934	Senate Special Committee on the Investigation of Presidential and Senatorial Campaign Expenditures

Y 4.P 92/3

Y 4.P 92/3	1944	Senate Special Committee to Investigate Presidential, Vice Presidential, and Senatorial Campaign Expenditures, 1944

Y 4.P 92/4

Y 4.P 92/4	1973	Senate Select Committee on Presidential Campaign Activities

Y 4.P 93/1

Y 4.P 93/1	1809-	Joint Printing Committee

Y 4.P 93/2

Y 4.P 93/2	1887-1946	House Printing Committee

Y 4.P 93/2

Y 4.P 93/2		Senate Select Committee on POW/MIA Affairs

Y 4.P 93/3

Y 4.P 93/3	1886-1946	Senate Printing Committee

Y 4.P 93/4

Y 4.P 93/4	1860	Senate Select Committee to Investigate Public Printing

Y 4.P 93/5

Y 4.P 93/5	1887-1910	House Private Land Claims Committee

Y 4.P 93/6

Y 4.P 93/6	1884-1944	Senate Privileges and Elections Committee

Y 4.P 93/7

Y 4.P 93/7	1957	Senate Private Land Claims Committee

Y 4.P 93/8

Y 4.P 93/8	199x-	Senate Select POW/MIA Affairs Committee

Y 4.P 94

Y 4.P 94	1927-1928	Senate Special Committee to Investigate Propaganda or Money Alleged to Have Been Used by Foreign Governments to Influence United States Senators

Y 4.P 96/1

Y 4.P 96/1	1882-1942	Senate Public Lands Committee
Y 4.In 8/13	1948	Senate Interior and Insular Affairs Committee
Y 4.En 2		Senate Energy and Natural Resources Committee

Y 4.P 96/2

Y 4.P 96/2	1919-1951	House Public Lands Committee

Y 4.P 96/3

Y 4.P 96/3	1908-1909	House Select Pulp and Paper Investigations Committee

Y 4.P 96/4

Y 4.P 96/4	1909	House Select Committee on Appropriations for the Prevention of Fraud in and Depredations upon Public Service

Y 4.P 96/5

Y 4.P 96/5	1967-1887	House Public Expenditures Committee

Y 4.P 96/6

Y 4.P 96/6	1910-1946	House Public Buildings and Grounds Committee

Y 4.P 96/7

Y 4.P 96/7	1912-1946	Senate Public Buildings and Grounds Committee

Y 4.P 96/8

Y 4.P 96/8	1912	House Select Public Health Committee

Y 4.P 96/9

Y 4.P 96/9	1912-1916	Senate Public Health and National Quarantine Committee

Y 4.P 96/10

Y 4.P 96/10	1947-1977	Senate Public Works Committee
	1977-	Senate Environment and Public Works Committee

Y 4.P 96/11

Y 4.P 96/11	1947	House Public Works Committee
	1947-	House Public Works and Transportation Committee

Y 4.R 13/1

Y 4.R 13/1	1887-1920	House Railways and Canals Committee

Y 4.R 13/2

Y 4.R 13/2		Senate Railroads Committee

Y 4.R 13/3

Y 4.R 13/3	1951-1952	Joint Railroad Retirement Legislation Committee

Y 4.R 22/1

Y 4.R 22/1	1920-1922	Special Joint Committee on the Readjustment of Service Pay

Y 4.R 22/2

Y 4.R 22/2	1922	House Special Committee on the Readjustment of Service Pay

Y 4.R 22/3

Y 4.R 22/3	1934-1938	House Select Committee on the Investigation of Real Estate Bondholders' Reorganizations

Y 4.R 24/1

Y 4.R 24/1	1884-1915	Joint Reconstruction Committee

Y 4.R 24/2

Y 4.R 24/2	1919-1920	Joint Reclassification of Salaries Commission

Y 4.R 24/3

Y 4.R 24/3	1921	Senate Select Reconstruction and Production Committee

Y 4.R 24/4

Y 4.R 24/4	1942-1968	Joint Committee on Reduction of Non-Essential Expenditures
	1968-	Joint Committee on Reduction of Federal Expenditures

Y 4.R 25

Y 4.R 25	1925-1924	Senate Select Reforestation Committee

Y 4.R 29

Y 4.R 29	1923-1924	Joint Reorganization of the Administrative Branch of the Government Committee

Y 4.R 29/2

Y 4.R 29/2		Senate Special Committee to Study the Reorganization of Courts of the United States and Reform of Judicial Procedure

Y 4.R 31/1

Y 4.R 31/1	1844	Senate Retrenchment Committee

Y 4.R 31/2

Y 4.R 31/2	1868	Joint Select Retrenchment Committee

Y 4.R 31/3

Y 4.R 31/3	199x-199x 199x-	House Natural Resources Committee House Resources Committee

Y 4.R 52

Y 4.R 52	1887-1946	House Rivers and Harbors Committee

Y 4.R 53

Y 4.R 53		Senate Roads and Canals Committee

Y 4.R 53/2

Y 4.R 53/2	1913-1914	House Roads Committee

Y 4.R 86/1

Y 4.R 86/1	1937-	House Rules Committee

Y 4.R 86/2

Y 4.R 86/2	1859-1947 1947-	Senate Rules Committee Senate Rules and Administration Committee

Y 4.R 88

Y 4.R 88	1915	Joint Rural Credits Committee

Y 4.Sci 2

Y 4.Sci 2	1958-19xx 19xx-1987 1987-19xx 19xx-	House Science and Astronautics Committee House Science and Technology Committee House Science, Space, and Technology Committee Science Committee

Y 4.Se 2

Y 4.Se 2	1976-	Security and Cooperation and Europe Commission

Y 4.Se 2/1

Y 4.Se 2/1	1995-	House Committee on National Security

Y 4.Se 4/1

Y 4.Se 4/1	1887-	House Select and Special Committees

Y 4.Se 4/2

Y 4.Se 4/2	1887-	Senate Select and Special Committees

Y 4.Se 5

Y 4.Se 5		Senate Contingent Expenses Committee

Y 4.Se 5/2

Y 4.Se 5/2	1930-1946	Senate Select Senatorial Campaign Expenditures Committee

Y 4.Se 5/3

Y 4.Se 5/3	1938	Senate Committee to Audit and Control Senate Contingent Expenses

Y 4.Se 5/4

Y 4.Se 5/4		Senate Temporary Select Committee to Study the Senate Committee System

Y 4.Se 5/5

Y 4.Se 5/5	1975-1977	Senate Commission on the Operation of the Senate

Y 4.Sh 6

Y 4.Sh 6	1910-1911	House Select Committee to Investigate Alleged Ship Subsidy Lobby

Y 4.Sh 6/2

Y 4.Sh 6/2	1915	Senate Special Committee to Investigate Alleged Ship Purchase Lobby

Y 4.Sh 6/3

Y 4.Sh 6/3	1920-1921	House Select Shipping Board Operations Committee

Y 4.Sh 6/4

Y 4.Sh 6/4	1924-1925	House Select Committee on the Shipping Board Emergency Fleet Corporation

Y 4.Sh 8

Y 4.Sh 8	1921-1922	Joint Committee on Short Time Record Credits

Y 4.Si 1

Y 4.Si 1	1954	Senate Select Committee on Sickness and Mortality on Emigrant Ships

Y 4.Si 3

Y 4.Si 3	1939-1942	Senate Special Committee on the Investigation of Silver

Y 4.Sm 1

Y 4.Sm 1	1947-	House Small Business Committee

Y 4.Sm 1/2

Y 4.Sm 1/2	1950-199x 199x-	Senate Small Business Committee Senate Small Business and Entrepeneurship Committee

Y 4.Sp 1

Y 4.Sp 1	1958	Senate Special Space and Astronautics Committee

Y 4.Sp 3

Y 4.Sp 4	1982	Speaker's Commission on Pages

Y 4.Sp 6

Y 4.Sp 6		House Select Professional Sports Committee

Y 4.St 2

Y 4.St 2	1921	Senate Standards, Weights and Measures Committee

Y 4.St 2/2

Y 4.St 2/2	1964-	Senate Select Standards and Conduct Committee

Y 4.St 2/3

Y 4.St 2/3	1967-	House Standards of Official Conduct Committee

Y 4.Su 7

Y 4.Su 7	1946-1947	House Select Committee to Investigate the Disposition of Surplus Property

Y 4.Su 7/2

Y 4.Su 7/2	1954-1956	House Select Survivors Benefits Committee

Y 4.T 17

Y 4.T 17	1926-1938	Senate Select Committee on the Investigation of the Tariff Commission

Y 4.T 19

Y 4.T 19	1937	Joint Tax Evasion and Avoidance Committee

Y 4.T 19/2

Y 4.T 19/2	1939-1940	Senate Special Committee on the Taxation of Governmental Securities and Salaries

Y 4.T 19/3

Y 4.T 19/3	1954	House Select Committee to Investigate Tax-Exempt Foundations and Comparable Organizations

Y 4.T 19/4

Y 4.In 8/11	1926-19xx	Joint Internal Revenue Taxation Committee
Y 4.T 19/4	19xx-	Joint Taxation Committee

Y 4.T 21

Y 4.T 21	1912	House Special Committee to Investigate Taylor and Other Systems of Shop Management

Y 4.T 23

Y 4.T 23	19xx-1944	Joint Committee on Centennial of the Telegraph

Y 4.T 24

Y 4.T 24	1938-1941	Senate Temporary National Economic Committee

Y 4.T 25

Y 4.T 25	1939	Joint Committee on the Investigation of the Tennessee Valley Authority

Y 4.T 27/1

Y 4.T 27/1	1904-1946	House Territories Committee

Y 4.T 27/2

Y 4.T 27/2	1888-1946	Senate Territories and Insular Affairs Committee

Y 4.T 61

Y 4.T 61	1870	House Committee on the Causes of the Reduction of American Tonnage

Y 4.T 68

Y 4.T 68	1878-1879	Senate Select Transportation Routes to Seaboard Committee

Y 4.T 68/2

Y 4.T 68/2	1995-	House Committee on Transportation and Infrastructure

Y 4.Un 1

Y 4.Un 1	1934-1935	Senate Special Un-American Activities Committee

Y 4.Un 1/2

Y 4.Un 1/2	1945-1969	House Un-American Activities Committee
Y 4.In 8/15	1969	House Internal Security Committee

Y 4.Un 2

Y 4.Un 2	1931	Senate Select Unemployment Insurance Committee

Y 4.Un 2/2

Y 4.Un 2/2	1938-1939	Senate Special Committee to Investigate Unemployment and Relief

Y 4.Un 2/3

Y 4.Un 2/3	1959-1960	Senate Special Unemployment Problems Committee

Y 4.Un 3/1

Y 4.Un 3/1	1892-1902	Senate Select Committee to Establish University of the United States

Y 4.Un 3/2

Y 4.Un 3/2	1912	House Committee to Investigate the United States Steel Corporation

Y 4.V 56

Y 4.V 56	1865-1887	House Ventilation and Acoustics Committee

Y 4.V 64

Y 4.V 64	1923	Senate Select Committee to Investigate the Veterans Bureau

Y 4.V 64/2

Y 4.V 64/2	1932-1933	Joint Veterans Affairs Committee

Y 4.V 64/3

Y 4.V 64/3	1947-	House Veterans Affairs Committee

Y 4.V 64/4

Y 4.V 64/4		Senate Veterans Affairs Committee

Y 4.W 12

Y 4.W 12	1910	Senate Select Committee to Investigate Wages and Prices

Y 4.W 19

Y 4.W 19	1908-1946	House War Claims Committee

Y 4.W 21

Y 4.W 21	1944	House Select Committee to Investigate the Seizure of Montgomery Ward and Company

Y 4.W 27

Y 4.W 27	1917	Senate Special Committee to Investigate the Washington Railway and Electrical Company

Y 4.W 27/2

Y 4.W 27/2	1957-1960	Joint Metropolitan Washington Problems Committee

Y 4.W 29

Y 4.W 29	1918-1921	House Water Power Committee

Y 4.W 36

Y 4.W 36	1884-	House Ways and Means Committee

Y 4.W 45

Y 4.W 45	1965	House Select Committee on the Welfare and Education of Congressional Pages

Y 4.W 56

Y 4.W 56	1924	Senate Select Committee on the Investigations of Charges Against Burton K. Wheeler

Y 4.W 58

| Y 4.W 58 | 1955-1956 | House Select Committee to Conduct and Investigation and Study of the Financial Position of the White County Bridge Commission |

Y 4.W 64

| Y 4.W 64 | 1931-1937 | Senate Special Wildlife Resources Committee |

Y 4.W 64/2

| Y 4.W 64/2 | 1934-1946 | House Select Committee on the Conservation of Wildlife Resources |

Y 4.W 74

| Y 4.W. 74 | 1934 | House Select Committee to Investigate Certain Statements Made My Doctor William A. Wirt |

Y 4.W 84

| Y 4.W 84 | 1898-1918 | Senate Select Woman Suffrage Committee |

Y 4.W 88

| Y 4.W 88 | 1942-1946 | Senate Special Committee to Investigate the Production, Transportation and Marketing of Wool |

Y 4.W 89

| Y 4.W 89 | 1924-1944 | House World War Veterans Legislation Committee |

Y 5

| Y 5 | 1789- | Contested Elections |

Y 6

| Y 6 | 1789- | Impeachments |

Y 7

| Y 7 | 1789- | Memorial Addresses and Addresses on Acceptance of Statutes |

Y 8

| Y 8 | 1789- | Messages and Documents |

Y 9

| Y 9 | 1789- | Speeches |

Y 10

| Y 10 | 1974- | Congressional Budget Office |

Z 1

| Z1 | | Colonial Documents (Compilations) |

Z 2

| Z2 | 1776-1789 | Continental Congress Papers |

Z 3

| Z3 | 1789-1817 | Documents of Period of First 14 Congresses |

Z 4

| Z4 | 1789-1817 | Documents of Period of First 14 Congresses (original prints) |

AGENCY INDEX

Alaska Department, W 71
Alaska Federal Field Committee for Development
Planning, Y 3.Al 1s/4
Alaska Federal Reconstruction and Development
Planning Commission, Y 3.Al 1s/3
Alaska Fisheries Service, C 6.8
Alaska Game Commission, A 5.10
Alaska, Governor, I 1.5
Alaska International Rail and Highway Commission, Y
3.Al 1s
Alaska Natural Gas Transportation System, Office of the
Federal Inspector, Y 3.F 31/23
Alaska Power Administration, E 7, I 68
Alaska, President's Review Committee for Develop-
ment Planning in, Pr 36.8:Al 1
Alaska Road Commission, W 74
Alaska Water Laboratory, EP 1.22
Alaskan Engineering Commission, Alaskan Railroad, I
1.59
Alaskan Fisheries Division, C 2
Alcohol Abuse and Alcoholism, National Institute, HE
20.8300
Alcohol Administration, Federal, T 59
Alcohol Control Administration, Federal, Y 3.F 31/10
Alcohol, Drug Abuse and Mental Health Administra-
tion, HE 20.8000
Alcohol in Manufactures and Arts, Joint Select
Committee on, Y 4.Al 1/1
Alcohol Fuels Commission, National, Y 3.Al 1
Alcohol Liquor Traffic Committee (House), Y 4.Al 1/2
Alcohol, Tobacco and Firearms, Bureau of, T 70
Alien Property Bureau, J 19
Alien Property Custodian, Y 3.Al 4
Alien Property Custodian Office, Pr 32.5700
Alien Property Division, J 19
Alien Property Office, J 22
Allergy and Infectious Diseases Institute, National, HE
20.3250
All-Volunteer Armed Forces Commission of the
President, Pr 36.8:Ar 5
American Art, National Museum of, SI 6
American Battle Monuments Commission, Y 3.Am 3
American Commission for Protection and Salvage of
Artistic and Historical Monuments in War
Areas, Y 3.Am 3/4
American Ethnology Bureau, SI 2
American Expeditionary Forces, W 95
American Folklife Center, LC 39
American Forces Information Service, D 2
American Historical Association, SI 4
American History, National Museum of, SI 3
American Indian Policy Review Commission, Y 4.In 2/
10
American Merchant Marine, Special Committee to
Investigate, Y 4.Am 3/4
American National Red Cross, W 102, Y 3.Am 3/5
American Relief Administration, Y 3.Am 3/3
American Republic Bureau, AR, S 2
American Retail Federation, Committee on Investiga-
tion (House), Y 4.Am 3/3
American Revolution Bicentennial Administration, Y
3.Am 3/6
American Revolution Bicentennial Commission, Y
3.Am 3/6
American Samoan Commission, Y 3.Am 3/2
American Shipbuilding Commission, Y 3.Sh 6/2
American Shipbuilding Committee (House), Y 4.Am 3/1
American Small Business, Special Committee to Study
Problems of (Senate), Y 4.Am 3/5
American Sugar Refining Company, Special Committee
on Investigation of (House), Y 4.Am 3/2
American Tonnage, Committee on the Causes of
Reduction of, Y 4.T 61
American-Grown Tobacco Purchased by Foreign
Governments, Commission to Investigate, Y
3.T 55
Americans Outdoors, President's Commission on, Pr
40.8:Am 3
Americorps, Y 3.N 21/19:16
Analysis, Bureau of Economic, C 59
Analysis Center, Climate, C 55.191
Analysis Division, EP 1.51/6
Analytical Chemistry Center, C 13.1/8
Animal and Plant Health Inspection Service, A 101
Animal and Plant Health Service, A 101
Animal Health Division, A 77.200
Animal Health Science Research Advisory Board, A
106.40
Animal Industry Bureau, A 4, A 77.200
Animals and Poultry, Publications Relating to the Care
of, A 77.200
Anthracite Coal Commission, Y 3.An 8/2
Anthracite Coal Strike Commission, Y 3.An 8
Antiquities Commission, Y 4.Ar 7
Antitrust Division, J 20

Antitrust Laws and Procedures, National Commission
for the Review of, Pr 39.8:An 8
Appalachian Regional Commission, Y 3.Ap 4/2
Appalachian Regional Commission, President's, Pr
35.8:Ap 4
Appeals Board, Personnel, GA 1.1/2, GA 2
Appeals Court, Ju 2
Appeals Court, Emergency, Ju 12
Appeals for the Federal Circuit, Court of, Ju 7
Appeals, U. S. Circuit Courts, Ju 2
Appellate System, Commission on Revision of the
Federal Court, Y 3.Ap 4/3
Applied Nutrition Center, Food Safety and, HE
20.4500
Appointment Clerk, A 30
Appointments Division, C 17, T 2
Appraisers, General, Board of the United States, T 20
Apprentice Training Committee, Federal, Y 3.F 31/12
Apprenticeship Training, Employer and Labor Services,
L 37.100
Apprenticeship and Training Bureau, L 23, L 37.100
Apprenticeship Bureau, L 23
Apprenticeship Training Service, L 23
Appropriations Committee (House), Y 4.Ap 6/1
Appropriations Committee (Senate), Y 4.Ap 6/2
Appropriations Division, T 9
Aquatic Plant Control Program, D 103.24/13
Arbiter of War Claims, Y 3.W 19/4
Arbitrations and Mixed Commission to Settle
International Disputes, S 3
Arboretum, U.S. National, A 77.26
Archaeologist for Interior Department, I 1.64
Archeological and Historical Data Recovery Program, I
29.59/4
Architect of the Capitol, Y 3.Ar 2
Architect, Supervising, T 39
Architectural and Transportation Barriers Compliance
Board, Y 3.B 27
Archives and Records Administration, National, AE
1.100
Archives and Records Service, National, GS 4
Archives Establishment, National, AE 1
Arctic Construction and Frost Effects Laboratory, D
103.31
Area Development Office, C 45
Area Department, W 65
Argonne National Laboratory, E 1.1/5
Division of Educational Programs, E 1.86
Arizona, Governor, I 1.6
Arkansas-White-Red Basins Inter-Agency Committee,
Y 3.F 31/13-2
Arlington Memorial Amphitheater Commission, Y 3.Ar
5
Arlington Memorial Amphitheater, Commission on
Erection of Memorials and Entombment of
Bodies in, Y 3.Ar 1
Arlington Memorial Bridge Commission, Y 3.Ar 5/2
Armed Forces Information and Education Division, D 2
Armed Forces Information and Education Office, D 2
Armed Forces Information Services, D 2
Armed Forces Institute of Pathology, D 1.16/4, D
101.117/5
Armed Forces Medical Library, D 8
Armed Forces, Office of Information for, D 2
Armed Forces, President's Committee on Equal
Opportunity in, Pr 35.8:Ar 5
Armed Forces Radiobiology Research Institute, D 15
Armed Services Committee (House), Y 4.Ar 5/2
Armed Services Committee (Senate), Y 4.Ar 5/3
Armed Services Explosives Safety Board, M 3
Armed Services Petroleum Purchasing Agency, D 11
Armed Services Technical Information Agency, D 10
Armor Plant, Special Committee to Investigate Cost of,
Y 4.Ar 5
Arms Control and Disarmament Agency, AC
Arms Control and International Security, S22
Arms Control, Bureau of, S 22.102
Arms Transactions with Iran, Select Committee to
Investigate Covert, Y 4.In 8/20
Armstrong Laboratory, D 301.45/27
Army Air Force, W 108
Army Air Mobility Research and Development
Laboratory, D 117.8
Army and Corps Areas and Departments, W 99
Army Cold Regions Research and Engineering
Laboratory, D 103.33
Army Communications Command, D 101.83
Army Department, D 101, M 101
Army Electronics Command, D 111.9
Army Electronics Research and Development Command,
D 111
Army Foreign Science and Technology Center, U.S., D
101.79
Army Industrial College, W 104
Army Institute of Research, Letterman, D 104.29

Army Map Service, D 103.20
Army Materials and Mechanics Research Center, D
101.80
Army Medical Center, Walter Reed, D 104.15
Army Medical Department, D 104
Army Medical Service, D 104
Army Ordnance Center and School, D 105.25
Army Polar Research and Development Center, D
103.37
Army Quartermaster General, D 106, M 112
Army Research Institute for the Behavioral and Social
Sciences, D 101.60/3, D 101.60/6
Army Research Institute for the Behavioral and Social
Sciences, U.S., D 101.1/7
Army Research Laboratory, D 101.1/11
Army Reserve Forces Policy Committee, D 101.1/12
Army Scientific Advisory Panel, D 101.81
Army Training and Evaluation Program, D 101.20/2
Army War College, W 55
Army-Navy Civil Committee on Aircraft Design
Criteria, Y 3.Ar 5/3
Army-Navy Explosives Safety Board, M 3
Arrangements for the Commemoration of the Bicenten-
nial, Joint Commission on, Y 4.B 47
ARS National Research Program, A 77.28
Arsenal, Frankfort, D 105.17
Art and Antiquities Commission, Y 4.Ar 7
Art Gallery–
Freer, SI 7
National, SI 8
Art, National Museum of African, SI 14
Art, National Museum of American, SI 6
Arthritis Advisory Board, National, HE 20.3027/2
Arthritis and Metabolic Diseases Institute, National,
HE 20.330
Arthritis and Musculoskeletal and Skin Diseases,
National Institute, HE 20.3900
Arthritis and Related Musculoskeletal Diseases,
National Commission on, Y 3.Ar 7
Arthritis Interagency Coordinating Committee, HE
20.3032
Arthritis, Metabolism and Digestive Diseases, National
Institute of, HE 20.3300
Arthur, Chester Alan, Pr 21
Arts, Advisory Committee on the, Y 3.Ad 9/10
Arts and Humanities Foundation, National, NF
Arts and Humanities, Presidential Task Force on the, Pr
40.8:Ar 7
Arts Endowment, National, NF 2
Arts, National Council of the, PrEx 11
Arts, President's Advisory Council on, Pr 35.8:Ar 7
Asian Division, LC 17
Assassination of President John F. Kennedy
Commission of the President, Pr 36.8:K 38
Assassinations, Select Committee on (House), Y 4.As 7
Assessment Commission, Prospective Payment, Y 3.P
29
Assessment, National Center for Health Services
Research and Health Care Technology, HE
20.6500
Assessment of Human Health Effects of Great Lakes
Water Quality Committee, Y 3.In 8/28:15
Assessment Program, Climatic Impact, TD 1.38
Assessment Program, National Acid Precipitation, C
55.703
Assistance Bureau, Health Care, HE 20.5100, HE
20.9100
Assistance Payments Administration, FS 17.400, HE
17.400, HE 3.401
Assistance Program, Military, President's Committee to
Study, Pr 34.8:M 59
Association–
American Historical, SI 4
Federal National Mortgage, HH 6
Government National Mortgage, HH 1.1/7
United States Railway, Y 3.R 13/4
White House Historical, Y 3.Y 62/4
Astronautics and Space Exploration, Select Committee
on (House), Y 4.As 8
Astronautics, Committee on Science and (House), Y
4.Sci 2
Atlantic Division, W 64
Atlantic Climate Change Program, C 55.55
Atmosphere, National Advisory Committee on Oceans
and, Y 3.Oc 2
Atmospheric Research Office, C 55.700
Atmospheric Sciences Laboratory, D 111.9/6
Atmospheric Turbulence and Diffusion Laboratory, Air
Resources, C 55.621
Atomic Energy Commission, Y 3.At 7
Atomic Energy Joint Committee, Y 4.At 7/2
Atomic Energy, Special Committee on (Senate), Y 4.At 7
Attorney General–
Assistant for Court of Claims, J 2

Business Advisory and Planning Council, C 28
Business Advisory Council, C 28
Business and Defense Services Administration, C 41
Business Cooperative Service, Rural A 109
Business Council for Consumer Affairs, National, Y 3.N 21/27
Business Development Agency, Minority, C 1.56, C 1.100
Business Development, United States Commission on Minority, Y 3.2:M 66
Business Economics Office, C 43
Business Operations Bureau, International, C 48
Business Policy, Bureau of Competitive Assessment and, C 57.300
Business Taxation Task Force, Pr 37.8:B 96
Business, White House Conference on Small, Y 3.W 58/21

C

Cabinet Advisory Committee on Textiles, President's, Pr 35.8:T 31
Cabinet Committee–
Cable Communications, Pr 37.8:C 11
Opportunity for Spanish Speaking Peoples, Y 3.Sp 2/7
Price Stability, Pr 36.8:P 93
Price Stability for Economic Growth, President's, Pr 34.8:P 93
Small Business, Pr 34.8:Sm 1
Cabinet Task Force on Oil Import Control, Pr 37.8:Oi 5
Cable Communications, Cabinet Committee on, Pr 37.8:C 11
California Debris Commission, W 50
California Department, W 13
Campaign Costs Commission, President's, Pr 35.8:C 15
Campaign Expenditures, Special Committee to Investigate (House), Y 4.C 15
Campus Unrest, President's Commission on, Pr 37.8:C 15
Canada, Committee on Relations with, (Senate), Y 4.C 16
Canal, Lowell Historic, District Commission, Y 3.L 95
Canal Zone, W 79
Canal Zone Government, CZ 1
Cancer Advisory Board, National, HE 20.3027/3
Cancer Biology and Diagnosis Division, HE 20.3151/6
Cancer Cause and Prevention Division, HE 20.3151/3
Cancer Control and Rehabilitation, Division of, HE 20.3151/4
Cancer Epidemiology and Genetics, Division of, HE 20.3196
Cancer, Environmental, and Heart and Lung Diseases, Task Force on, EP 1.82
Cancer Etiology Division, HE 20.3151/3
Cancer Institute, National, HE 20.3150
Cancer, National Black Leadership Initiative on, HE 20.3195
Cancer Prevention and Control Division, HE 20.3151/4
Cancer Program, National, HE 20.3184
Cancer Research Resources and Centers Division, HE 20.3151/2
Cancer Treatment Division, HE 20.3151/5
Cape May Plant Materials Center, A 57.54/2
Capital Airports Bureau, National, FAA 6
Capital Expenditures Division, Y 3.R 13/2:100
Capital Issues Committee, Y 3.C 17/2
Capital Park and Planning Commission, National, NC 1
Capital Planning Commission, National, NC 2
Capital Regional Planning Council, National, NC 3
Capital Sesquicentennial Commission, National, Y 3.N 21/20
Capital Transportation Agency, National, Y 3.N 21/21
Capitol Architect, Y 3.Ar 2
Capitol Building, Joint Commission on Plans for Extension and Completion, Y 3.C 17
Capitol Buildings and Grounds, Superintendent, I 1.7
Capitol Historical Society, United States, Y 3.H 62/2
Capitol, Special Committee on the Centennial Celebration of the Laying of the Corner Stone of, Y 4.C 17
Capitol, United States, Commission for Extension of, Y 4.C 17/2
Captured Property, Claims, and Lands Division, T 42
Card Division, LC 28
Care Bureau, Child, HE 23.1400
Care, Long-term, Division of, HE 20.6001/4
Care of Animals and Poultry, Publications Relating to, A 77.200
Career Advancement, Presidential Task Force on, Pr 36.8:C 18

Career Education, National Advisory Council for, HE 19.116
Cargo, Intermodal, Interagency Committee on, Y 3.In 8/26
Carter, Jimmy, Pr 39
Catalog Division, LC 9
Catalog Division, Union, LC 18
Cataloging and Classification Service, Cooperative, LC 22
Cataloging Division, Descriptive, LC 9
Cataloging Policy and Support Office, LC 26
Catastrophic Nuclear Accidents, Presidential Commission on, Y 3.P 92/6Cause and Prevention, Division of Cancer, HE 20.3151/3
Causes of Reduction of American Tonnage Committee, Y 4.T 61
CCIR, U.S. National Committee of the, S 5.56
Celebration Commission, North Carolina Tercentenary, Y 3.N 81/2
Celebration of the Laying of the Corner Stone of the Capitol, Special Committee on, Y 4.C 17
Cellular and Molecular Basis of Disease Program, HE 20.3466
Censorship Office, Y 3.C 33/6
Censure Charges, Select Committee to Study (Senate), Y 4.C 33/4
Census Bureau, C 3, C 56.200
Census Committee (House), Y 4.C 33/1
Census Committee (Senate), Y 4.C 33/2
Census of Partial Employment, Unemployment and Occupations, Y 3.C 33/5
Census Office, I 14
Census Office of Cuba, W 47
Census Office of Porto Rico, W 48
Centennial of the Telegraph, Joint Committee on, Y 4.T 23
Center–
A, World Data, C 55.220
Aeronautical Chart and Information, D 301.59
Air Force Civil Engineering, D 301.87
Air Force History, D 301.82/7
American Folklife, LC 39
Analytical Chemistry, C 13.1/8
Army Materials and Mechanics Research, D 101.80
Army Ordnance, D 105.25
Army Polar Research and Development, D 103.37
Basic Standards, C 13.1/10
Biologics Evaluation and Research, HE 20.4800
Cape May Plant Materials, A 57.54/2
Chaco, I 29.90
Climate Analysis, C 55.191
Computer Security, D 1.79
Consumer Information, GS 11
Early Development & Learning, National, ED 1.346
Defense Administrative Support, D 7.7/14
Defense Technical Information, D 10
Devices and Radiological Health, HE 20.4600
Devices and Radiological Health, National, HE 20.4600
Disease Control, HE 20.2300, HE 20.7000
Drug Evaluation and Research, HE 20.4700
Drugs and Biologics, HE 20.4200
Educational Research and Improvement, ED 1.300
Educational Resources Information, ED 1.301/2
Educational Statistics, National, HE 19.300
Environmental Health, HE 20.7500
Federal Law Enforcement Training, T 1.60
Food Safety and Applied Nutrition, HE 20.4500
Health Promotion and Education, HE 20.7600
Health Services, National, HE 20.6500
Health Services Research and Health Care Technology Assessment, National, HE 20.6500
HIV, STD, and TB Prevention, HE 20.7301
Hydrographic/Topographic, D 5.317
Hydrologic Engineering, D 103.55
Infectious Diseases, HE 20.7800
Injury Prevention and Control, National, HE 20.7950
International Development, Y 3.T 25:1-17
Laramie Energy Research, ER 1.23
Magnuson Clinical, HE 20.3052
Manhattan Plant Materials, A 57.54/3
Materials Science, C 13.1/9
Medicaid and State Operations, H 22.100
Medicare Management, HE 22.400
Military History, D 114
National Audiovisual, GS 4.17/5
National Computer Security, D 1.79/2
National Foreign Assessment, PrEx 3.10/7
National Geophysical Data, C 55.201/2
National Independent Study, CS 1.92
Naval Air Development, D 201.22, D 202.28

Naval Health Research, D 206.22
Naval Historical, D 221
National Historical Publications and Records, AE 1.114/3
Naval Publications and Form, D 212.1/2
Naval Surface Weapons, D 201.21/6
Naval Weapons, D 201.23
Navy Personnel Research and Development, D 201.1/3
Northwest Fisheries, C 55.326
Northwest Fisheries Science, C 55.331/3
Parklawn Computer, HE 20.4036
Pavements and Soil Trafficability Information Analysis, D 103.24/12
Personnel Management Training, CS 1.65/10
Personnel Research and Development, CS 1.71
Population Research, HE 20.3351/3
Prevention Services, HE 20.7300
Productivity and Quality of Working Life, National, Y 3.P 94
Professional Development and Training, HE 20.7700
Regulatory Information Service, PrEx 25
Research Facilities, C 55.601/4
Research for Mothers and Children, HE 20.3351/2
Scholars, Woodrow Wilson International, SI 12
Service Learning, National, AA 3
Southwest Fisheries, C 55.303/2
Technical Information, TD 1.3/2
U.S. Army Foreign Science and Technology, D 101.79
Veterinary Medicine, HE 20.4400
Walter Reed Army Medical, D 104.15
Warren Grant Magnuson Clinical, HE 20.3052
Centers for Disease Control and Prevention HE 20.7000
Central America, National Bipartisan Commission on, Pr 40.8:B 52
Central and South American Commission, Y 3.C 33
Central Department, W 78
Central European Division, Slavic and, LC 35
Central Housing Committee, Y 3.C 33/3
Central Intelligence Agency, Y 3.N 21/17:100, Pr 33.650, Pr 34.600, PrEx 3
Central States Forest Experiment Station, A 13.68
Central Statistical Board, Y 3.C 33/2
Central Statistical Committee, Y 3.C 33/4
Central Translating Office, S 16
Central, Western, and South Pacific Fisheries Development Program, C 55.329
Centralization of Heavy Industry in United States, Special Committee to Investigate (Senate), Y 4.C 33/3
Certification Service, Aircraft, TD 4.900
Chaco Center, I 29.90
Challenger Accident, Presidential Commission on the Space Shuttle, Pr 40.8:Sp 1
Change Program, Atlantic Climate, C 55.55
Change, White House Conference on Science and Economics Research Related to, Pr 41.8:G 51Character Guidance in the Armed Forces, President's Committee on, Y 3.P 92/5
Charities of the District of Columbia, Joint Select Committee to Investigate, Y 4.D 63/3
Chart and Information Center, Aeronautical, D 301.59
Charts Division, LC 5
Chemical Corps, D 116
Chemical Safety Hazards Investigation Board, Y 3.C42
Chemical Warfare Service, W 91
Chemistry and Engineering, Bureau of Agricultural, A 70, A 77.100
Chemistry and Soils Bureau, A 47
Chemistry Bureau, A 7
Chemistry, Bureau of Industrial, A 77.100
Chemistry, Center for Analytical, C 13.1/8
Chemistry Division, A 7
Chicago Strike Commission, Y 3.C 43
Chickamauga and Chattanooga National Military Park Commission, W 4
Chickamauga and Chattanooga National Military Park, Dedication, Joint Committee on, Y 4.C 43
Chief Clerk, A 31
Chief Clerk and Superintendent, T 10
Chief Clerk and Superintendent of Buildings, I 1.60
Chief of Military History, Office of, D 114
Chief of Naval Reserve, D 207.300
Chief Postal Inspector Bureau, P 24
Chiefs of Staff, Joint, M 2, D 5
Child Abuse and Neglect Information, National Clearinghouse on, HE 23.1216
Child Abuse and Neglect, National Conference on, HE 1.480/5
Child Care Bureau, HE 23.1400
Child Development Office, HE 21, HE 1.400
Child Development Services, Bureau of, HE 1.460

Child Health and Human Development Institute, National, HE 20.3350
Child Health and Protection White House Conference, Y 3.W 58
Child Health and Resources Development Bureau, HE 20.9200
Child Health Service, Maternal and, HE 20.2750
Child Nutrition, National Advisory Council on, Y 3.C 43/2
Child Service Programs Bureau, HE 21.200
Child Support Enforcement Office, HE 3.500
Child, U.S. National Commission on the International Year of, Y 3.C 43/3
Children and Youth Interdepartmental Committee, Y 3.In 8/6
Children, Center for Research for, HE 20.3351/2
Children, National Commission on, Y 3.C 43/5
Children, Youth, and Families, Administration for, HE 23.1000
Children, Youth, and Families, House Select Committee on, Y 4.C 43/2
Children's Bureau, C 19, L 5, FS 3.200, FS 14.100, FS 17.200, HE 21.100, HE 1.450, HE 23.1200
China Court of the United States, S 14
Chinese Immigration, Joint Special Committee on, Y 4.C 44
Chronic Disease Prevention and Health Promotion, National Center for, HE 20.7600
CIA Activities within the United States, Commission on, Pr 38.8:C 33
Circuit Courts, Ju 1
Circuit Courts of Appeals, U. S., Ju 2
Citizen Advisers on Mutual Security Program, President's, Pr 34.8:M 98
Citizen Participation, Federal Interagency Council on, Y 3.C 49/5
Citizens Advisory Committee on Environmental Quality, Pr 37.8:En 8
Citizens' Advisory Committee on Recreation and Natural Beauty, Pr 36.8:R 24
Citizens Food Committee, Pr 33.11
Civil Aeronautics Administration, C 31.100
Civil Aeronautics Authority, CA, C 31
Civil Aeronautics Board, C 31.200, CAB 1
Civil Affairs Division, M 105
Civil and Defense Mobilization Office, PrEx 4
Civil Aviation Security Service, TD 4.800
Civil Committee on Aircraft Design Criteria, Air Force–Navy, Y 3.Ar 5/3
Civil Defense Administration, Federal, FCD, Pr 33.800
Civil Defense Office, D 13, D 119
Civil Defense Planning Office, M 4
Civil Disorders National Advisory Commission, Pr 36.8:C 49
Civil Engineering Center, Air Force, D 301.87
Civil Rights Advisory Council, GA 1.29
Civil Rights Commission, CR
Civil Rights Policies and Practices, Interagency Committee on, Y 3.C 49/4
Civil Service Commission, CS, CS 1
Civil Service Committee (House), Y 4.C 49/1
Civil Service Committee (Senate), Y 4.C 49/2
Civil Service, Committee on Post Office and (House), Y 4.P 84/10
Civil Service, Committee on Post Office and (Senate), Y 4.P 84/11
Civil Service Improvement Committee, President's, Y 3.P 92/4
Civil Service Laws, Special Committee to Investigate Administration and Operation of, Y 4.C 49/4
Civil Service, Select Committee on Investigation of Illegal Appointments in (Senate), Y 4.C 49/3
Civil War Centennial Commission, Y 3.C 49/2
Civil Works Administration, Federal, Y 3.F 31/7
Civilian Compensation Interdepartmental Committee, Y 3.In 8/14
Civilian Conservation Corps, I 42, Y 3.C 49, FS 4
Civilian Conservation Division, I 42
Civilian Defense Office, Pr 32.4400
Civilian Manpower Management Office, D 204
Civilian Production Administration, Pr 32.4800
Civilian Radioactive Waste Management Office, E 1.68/2-7
Claims and Lands Division, T 42
Claims Commission, Y 3.C 52
Claims Commission, Indian, Y 3.In 2/6
Claims Commission, Temporary Alaska, Y 3.Al 1s/2
Claims Committee (House), Y 4.C 52/1
Claims Committee (Senate), Y 4.C 52/2
Claims Court, Ju 3
Claims Court Assistant Attorney General, J 2
Clark, George Rogers, Sesquicentennial Commission, Y 3.G 29
Classification Review Committee, Interagency, Y 3.C 56
Clearinghouse–
    Aging, National, HE 23.3100

Child Abuse and Neglect Information, National, HE 23.1216
Drug Abuse Information, National, PrEx 13
Eisenhower National, ED 1.340
Federal Scientific and Technical Information, C 51
National Air Toxics Information, EP 4.23
Clemency Board, Presidential, Pr 38.8:C 59
Cleveland, Grover, Pr 22
Climate Analysis Center, C 55.191
Climate Change Program, Atlantic, C 55.55
Climate Program, National, C 55.44
Climatic Center, National, C 55.280
Climatic Impact Assessment Program, TD 1.38
Clinical Center, Warren G. Magnuson, HE 20.3052
Clinical Standards and Quality Office, HE 22.200
Clinton, William, Pr 42
Closure and Realignment Commission, Defense Base, Y 3.D 36/2
Clothing Bureau, N 20
Coal Commission, Y 3.C 63
Coal Leasing, Commission on Fair Market Value Policy for Federal, Y 3.C 63/3
Coal, President's Commission on, Pr 39.8:C 63
Coal Research Office, I 63
Coast and Geodetic Survey, C 4, T 11
Coast and Geodetic Survey, and Hydrographic Office, Joint Commission to Consider the Present Organizations of, Y 3.Si 2
Coast and Insular Committee (Senate), Y 4.C 63
Coast Artillery Office, W 53
Coast Artillery School, W 29
Coast Guard, T 47, N 24, TD 5
Coast Survey, T 11
Coastal Engineering Research Center, D 103.42
Coastal Plains Regional Commission, Y 3.C 63/2
Coast-Defense Board, National, Y 3.N 21/4
Codify Criminal and Penal Laws Commission, Y 3.L 44
Codify the Laws of the United States Commission, Y 3.L 44
Coinage Joint Commission, Y 3.C 66
Coinage, Weights and Measures Committee (House), Y 4.C 66
Cold Regions Research and Engineering Laboratory, Army, D 103.33
Collaborative Radiological Health Laboratory, CSU-PHS, HE 20.4119
Collections, Rare Book, LC 23
Collective Bargaining Commission, Construction Industry, Y 3.C 76
College–
    Army Industrial, W 104
    Army War, W 55
    Defense Systems Management, D 1.59/2
    National War, D 5.17
    Naval War, N 15, M 206.200, D 208.200
Colleges and Universities
    National Advisory Committee on, HE 19.140
    Presidents Board of Advisors on Historically Black, ED 1.89/2
    White House Initiative on Historically Black, ED 1.89
Colorado River Basin Project, I 27.71/3
Colorado River Department, W 14
Colorado River Interstate-Government Commission, Y 3.C 71
Columbia Basin Inter-Agency Committee, Y 3.C 72
Columbia Institution for Instruction of Deaf and Dumb, I 1.8
Columbia Railway Company, I 1.9
Columbia River Department, W 15
Combatting Terrorism, Vice Presidents Task Force on, PrVp 40
Combined Production and Resource Board, United States, Great Britain, and Canada, Y 3.C 73/3
Combined Products and Resource Board, United States, Great Britain, and Canada, Y 3.C 73/2
Combined Raw Material Board of the United States and Great Britain, Y 3.C 73/2
Combined Tribal and Bureau Law Enforcement Services, I 20.58
Command–
    Air Mobility Research and Development, U.S. Army, D 117
    Air Research and Development, D 301.45
    Army Communications, D 101.83
    Army Electronics, D 111.9
    Army Electronics Research and Development, D 111
    Electronics Systems, D 219
    Military Sealift, D 216
    Naval Air Systems, D 202
    Naval Doctrine, D 207.400
    Naval Education and Training, D 207.200
    Naval Facilities Engineering, D 209
    Naval Military Personnel, D 208

Naval Ordnance Systems, D 215
Naval Sea Systems, D 211
Naval Ships Systems, D 211
Naval Supply Systems, D 212
Naval Technical Training, D 207.100
Naval Training, D 207.200
Naval Training Support, D 208
Naval Weather Service, D 220
Navy Oceanography, D 222
Command and General Staff College, M 119, D 110
Commemoration of the Bicentennial, Joint Committee on Arrangements for, Y 4.B 47
Commerce and Labor Department, C 1
Commerce Committee (House), Y 4.C 73/1, Y 4.C 73/8
Commerce Committee (Senate), Y 4.C 73/2
Commerce Court, Ju 8
Commerce Department, C 1
Commerce, Science, and Transportation Committee (Senate), Y 4.C 73/7
Commercial Economy Board, Y 3.C 83:10
Commercialization, Synthetic Fuels, Interagency Task Force, Pr 37.8:En /2
Commission–
    Administrative Review (House), Y 4.Ad 6
    Agricultural Inquiry, Y 3.Ag 8/2
    AIDS, National, Y 3.Ac 7
    Air Quality, National, Y 3.Ai 7/5
    Aircraft, Y 3.Ai 7/2
    Airports, President's, Pr 33.16
    Alaska Game, A 5.10
    Alaska International Rail and Highway, Y 3.Al 1s
    Alaska Road, W 74
    All-Volunteer Armed Forces of the President, Pr 36.8:Ar 5
    American Battle Monuments, Y 3.Am 3
    American Indian Policy Review, Y 4.In 2/10
    American Revolution Bicentennial, Y 3.Am 3/6
    American Samoan, Y 3.Am 3/2
    American Shipbuilding, Y 3.Sh 6/2
    Americans Outdoors, President's, Pr 40.8:Am 3
    Anthracite Coal, Y 3.An 8/2
    Anthracite Coal Strike, Y 3.An 8
    Appalachian Region, President's, Pr 35.8:Ap 4
    Appalachian Regional, Y 3.Ap 4/2
    Arlington Memorial Amphitheater, Y 3.Ar 5
    Arlington Memorial Bridge, Y 3.Ar 5/2
    Art and Antiquities, Y 4.Ar 7
    Arthritis and Related Musculoskeletal Diseases, National, Y 3.Ar 7
    Assassination of President John F. Kennedy, President's, Pr 36.8:K 38
    Atomic Energy, Y 3.At 7
    Aviation Advisory, Y 3.Av 5
    Aviation Safety, Y 3.Av 5/2
    Bankruptcy Laws of the United States, Y 3.B 22
    Battle of New Orleans Sesquicentennial Celebration, Y 3.B 32
    Berlin Silver, Y 3.B 45
    Bicentennial of the U.S. Constitution, U.S., Y 3.2:C 73
    Bicentennial of the United States Constitution, Y 3.B 47/2
    Bituminous Coal, Y 3.B 54
    Broadcasting to Cuba, Presidential, Pr 40.8:Br 78
    Budget Concepts of the President, Pr 36.8:B 85
    California Debris, W 50
    Campaign Costs, President's, Pr 35.8:C 15
    Campus Unrest, President's, Pr 37.8:C 15
    Capital Sesquicentennial, National, Y 3.N 21/20
    Catastrophic Nuclear Accidents, Presidential, Y 3.P 92/6
    Causes and Prevention of Violence, National, Pr 36.8:V 81
    Centennial of the Establishment of the Seat of Government in Washington, Y 4.C 333
    Central America, National Bipartisan, Pr 40.8:B 52
    Central and South America, Y 3.C 33
    Chicago Strike, Y 3.C 43
    Chickamauga and Chattanooga National Military Parks, W 4
    Children, National, Y 3.C 43/5
    CIA Activities within the United States, Pr 38.8:C 33
    Civil Disorders, National, Pr 36.8:C 49
    Civil Rights, CR
    Civil Service, CS
    Civil War Centennial, Y 3.C 49/2
    Claims, Y 3.C 52
    Coal, Y 3.C 63
    Coal, President's, Pr 39.8:C 63
    Coastal Plains Region, Y 3.C 63/2
    Coinage, Y 3.C 66
    Colorado River, Interstate-Government, Y 3.C 71
    Commodity Futures Trading, Y 3.C 73/5
    Congressional Mailing Standards, (House), Y 4.M 28

Price, Y 3.P 93/4
Printing Investigation, Y 3.P 93
Priority in Transportation, Y 3.P 93/2
Privacy Protection Study, Y 3.P 93/5
Productivity and Work Quality, National, Pr 37.8:P 94
Productivity, National, Pr 37.8:P 94
Prospective Payment Assessment, Y 3.P 29
Protection and Salvage of Artistic and Historical Monuments in War Areas of America, Y 3.Am 3/4
Protection of Human Subjects of Biomedical and Behavioral Research, National, Y 3.H 88
Public Buildings, Y 3.P 96/4
Public Land, Y 3.P 96/1
Public Land Law Review, Y 3.P 96/7
Public Lands, Y 3.P 96/2
Puerto Rico and United States on Status of Puerto Rico, Y 3.Un 3/5
Railroad Lighter Captains, Pr 35.8:R 13
Railroad Retirement, Y 3.R 13/3
Railroad Securities, Y 3.R 13
Railroads, Presidential, Pr 34.8:R 13
Reclassification of Salaries, Joint, Y 4.R 24/2
Records and Documents of Federal Officials, National Study, Y 3.R 24/2
Reform of Federal Criminal Laws, Y 3.N 21/26
Registration and Voting Participation, President's, Pr 35.8:R 26
Renovation of Executive Mansion, Y 3.R 29/2
Rent of District of Columbia, Y 3.R 29
Review of Antitrust Laws and Procedures, National, Pr 39.8:An 8
Review of Federal and State Laws Relating to Wiretapping and Electronic Surveillance, Y 3.W 74/2
Review of the National Policy Toward Gambling, Y 3.G 14
Revise and Codify Criminal and Penal Laws, Y 3.L 44
Revise and Codify the Laws of the United States, Y 3.L 44
Revise Laws of United States, Y 3.L 44
Revision of Statutes, Y 3.R 32
Revision of the Federal Court Appellate System, Y 3.Ap 4/3
Role of Gold in Domestic and International Monetary Systems, Y 3.G 57
Royal (British) Appointed to Inquire into Recent Changes in Relative Values of Precious Metals, Y 3.P 91
Rubber Producing Facilities Disposal, Y 3.R 82
Rural Poverty, National Advisory, Pr 36.8:R 88
Saint Augustine Quadricentennial, Y 3.Sa 2/2
Santo Domingo, Y 3.Sa 5
Savannah, Altamaha, Saint Marys, Apalachicola-Chattahoochee, and Perdido-Escambia River Basins and Intervening Areas, U.S. Study, Y 3.Un 3/4
School Finance, President's, Pr 37.8:Sch 6
Securities and Exchange, SE
Security and Cooperation in Europe, Y 4.Se 2
Shiloah National Military Park, W 63
Social Security, National, Y 3.So 1, Pr 40.8:So 1
Souris-Red-Rainy River Basins, Y 3.So 8
Southwest Border Regional, Y 3.So 8/2
Space Shuttle Challenger Accident, Presidential, Pr 40.8:Sp 1
Space, National, Y 3.Sp 1
Spanish Treaty Claims, Y 3.Sp 2
State Workmen's Compensation Laws, National, Y 3.W 89/3
Status of Women, President's, Pr 35.8:W 84
Student Financial Assistance, National, Y 3.St 9
Study of Ethical Problems in Medicine and Biomedical and Behavioral Research, President's, Pr 40.8:Et 3
Study of International Migration and Cooperative Economic Development, Y 3.M 58/2
Superconductivity, National, Y 3.Su 7/3
Supervise Construction of Building for Offices for House of Representatives, Y 3.H 81
Supplies and Shortages, National, Y 3.Su 7/2
Tariffs, TC, Y 3.T 17
Temporary Alaska Claims, Y 3.Al 1s/2
Thomas Jefferson Memorial, Y 3.T 36
Technology, Automation, and Economic Progress National, Y 3.T 22
Tobacco, Y 3.T 55
Tourism Resources Review, National, Y 3.T 64
Training Camp Activities, N 26, W 85
Unemployment Compensation, National, Y 3.Un 2
United States Constitution Sesquicentennial, Y 3.Un 3
United States Sentencing, Y 3.Se 5

Universal Training, Y 3.Ad 9/5
Upper Great Lakes Region, Y 3.Up 6
Venezuelan Boundary, Y 3.V 55
Veterans Pensions, President's, Pr 34.8:V 64
Vicksburg National Military Park, W 54
Visitor Facilities, Y 3.N 21/23
War Claims, Y 3.W 19/9
War Investigating, Y 3.W 19
War Manpower, Pr 32.5200
War Policies, Y 3.W 19/5
Wartime Relocation, Y 3.W 19/10
Washington Bicentennial Celebration, Y 3.W 27/2
Washington Monument, Joint, Y 3.W 27
Water Quality, National, Y 3.W 29/2
Water Resources Policy, President's, Pr 33.12
Western Hemisphere Immigration, Select, Y 3.W 52
White House Fellows, President's, Pr 36.8:W 58
White House Fellowships, President's, Pr 40.8:W 58
Woodrow Wilson Centennial Celebration, Y 3.W 86
Woodrow Wilson Memorial, Y 3.W 86/2
World War Foreign Debt, Y 3.W 89
Yorktown Monument or Centennial, Y 3.Y 8
Yorktown Sesquicentennial, Y 3.Y 8/2
Commissioner–
Accounts and Deposits, T 60
Customs, T 16
Priority in Transportation, Y 3.P 93/2
Public Buildings, I 1.51
Railroads, I 25
Commissioners of Shipping, C 12
Commissions, Committees, and Boards, Y 3.2
Commissions, International, S 5
Committee–
Accounts (House), Y 4.Ac 2
Accreditation and Institution Eligibility, Advisory, HE 19.130
Accreditation and Institutional Eligibility, Advisory, ED 1.13
Administration, Rules and (Senate), Y 4.R 86/2
Administrative Management, President's, Y 3.P 92/3
Aeronautical and Space Sciences (Senate), Y 4.Ae 8
Aeronautics, National Advisory, Y 3.N 21/5
Aging, Select, (House), Y 4.Ag 4/2
Aging, Special, (Senate), Y 4.Ag 4
Agricultural Surplus Disposal, Interagency, Y 3.In 8/11
Agriculture, (House), Y 4.Ag 8/1
Agriculture and Forestry (Senate), Y 4.Ag 8/2
Agriculture, Nutrition, and Forestry (Senate), Y 4.Ag 8/3
Air Coordinating, Y 3.Ai 7/3
Air Mail and Ocean Mail Contracts, Investigation of, Special (Senate), Y 4.Ai 7/2
Air Services, Inquiry into Operation of, Select, Y 4.Ai 7
Aircraft Design Criteria, Air Force-Navy Civil, Y 3.Ar 5/3
Alcohol in Manufactures and Arts, Select, Y 4.Al 1/1
Alcohol Liquor Traffic (House), Y 4.Al 1/2
American Ship-Building (House), Y 4.Am 3/1
Appointed to Investigate Memorial of Davis Hatch, Select, Y 4.H 28
Appraise Employment and Unemployment Statistics, President's, Pr 35.8:Em 7/3
Apprentice Training, Federal, Y F 31/12
Appropriations (House), Y 4.Ap 6/1
Appropriations (Senate), Y 4.Ap 6/2
Appropriations for Prevention of Fraud in and Depreciations upon Public Service, Select, Y 4.P 96/4
Arkansas-White-Red Basins Inter-Agency, Y 3.F 31/13-2
Army Reserve Forces Policy, D 101.1/12
Armed Services (House), Y 4.Ar 5/2
Armed Services (Senate), Y 4.Ar 5/3
Army-Navy Civil Aircraft Design Criteria, Y 3.Ar 5/3
Arrangements for the Commemoration of the Bicentennial, Joint, Y 4.B 47
Arthritis Interagency Coordinating, HE 20.3032
Arts, Advisory, Y 3.Ad 9/10
Assassinations, Select, (House), Y 4.As 7
Assessment of Human Health Effects of Great Lakes Water Quality, Y 3.In 8/28:15
Astronautics and Space Exploration, Select House, Y 4.As 8
Atomic Energy, Joint, Y 4.At 7/2
Atomic Energy, Special (Senate), Y 4.At 7
Audit and Control Senate Contingent Expenses (Senate), Y 4.Se 5/3
Automatic Data Processing, Interagency, Y 3.In 8/16

Banking and Currency (House), Y 4.B 22/1
Banking, Housing, and Urban Affairs (Senate), Y 4.B 22/3
Berger, Victor L., Special, Y 4.B 45
Black Higher Education and Black Colleges and Universities, National Advisory, HE 19.140
Budget (House), Y 4.B 85/3
Budget (Senate), Y 4.B 85/2
Budget Control, Joint Study, Y 4.B 85
Budget, Select (House), Y 4.B 86/1
Capital Issues, Y 3.C 17/2
Causes of Reduction of American Tonnage, Y 4.T 61
CCIR, U.S. National, S 5.56
Census (House), Y 4.C 33/1
Census (Senate), Y 4.C 33/2
Centennial Celebration of the Laying of the Corner Stone of the Capitol, Special, Y 4.C 17
Centennial of the Telegraph, Joint, Y 4.T 23
Central Housing, Y 3.C 33/3
Central Statistical, Y 3.C 33/4
Children, Youth, and Families, House Select, Y 4.C 43/2
Chinese Immigration, Joint Special, Y 4.C 44
Citizens Food, Pr 33.11
Civil Service (House), Y 4.C 49/1
Civil Service (Senate), Y 4.C 49/2
Civil Service Improvement, President's, Y 3.P 92/4
Civilian Compensation, Interdepartmental, Y 3.In 8/14
Claims (House), Y 4.C 52/1
Claims (Senate), Y 4.C 52/2
Coast and Insular (Senate), Y 4.C 63
Coinage, Weights and Measures (House), Y 4.C 66
Columbia Basin Inter-Agency, Y 3.C 72
Commerce (House), Y 4.C 73/1, Y 4.C 73/8
Commerce (Senate), Y 4.C 73/2
Committee System, Temporary Select Committee to Study the Senate, Y 4.Se 5/4
Communist Aggression, Select (House), Y 4.C 73/5
Commerce, Science, and Transportation (Senate), Y 4.C 73/7
Conditions of Indian Tribes, Joint Special, Y 4.In 2/6
Conduct and Investigation and Study of Financial Position of White County Bridge Commission, Select (House), Y 4.W 58
Conduct Investigation of Facts, Evidence and Circumstances of Katyn Forest Massacre, Select, Y 4.K 15
Conduct Study and Survey of National Defense Program in its Relation to Small Business, Select (House), Y 4.N 21/7
Conference (House and Senate), Y 4.C 76/1
Congested Production Areas, Pr 32.10
Congressional Operations, Joint, Y 4.C 76/7
Congressional Operations, Select, Y 4.C 76/9
Conservation and Administration of the Public Domain, Y 3.P 96/5
Conservation of National Resources (Senate), Y 4.N 21/1
Consideration of Budget, National (Senate), Y 4.B 86/2
Consumer Interests, President's, Pr 36.8:C 76
Contribution Investigation, Select (Senate), Y 4.C 76/4
Cooperative Enterprise in Europe, Y 3.C 78/2
Coordinate Federal Urban Area Assistance Programs, Interdepartmental, Y 3.In 8/17
Coordinate Health and Welfare Activities, Interdepartmental, Y 3.In 8/3
Corporate Pension Funds and other Private Retirement and Welfare Programs, President's, Pr 35.8:P 38/2
Crime, Select (House), Y 4.C 86/3
Crop Insurance, President's, Y 3.P 92/2
Crop Insurance, Select (Senate), Y 4.C 88
Cuba Relations (Senate), Y 4.C 89
Current Pornographic Materials, Select (House), Y 4.P 82
Dedication of Chickamauga and Chattanooga National Military Park, Joint, Y 4.C 43
Defense Production, Joint, Y 4.D 36
Deficit Reduction, Temporary Joint, Y 4.D 36/2
Democratic Policy, Y 4.D 39
Department Methods, Y 3.D 44
Determine what Employment may be Furnished Federal Prisoners, Joint, Y 4.F 31/2
Development Planning in Alaska, Y 3.Al 1s/4
Development Planning in Alaska, President's Review, Pr 36.8:Al 1
Diabetes Mellitus Coordinating, HE 20.3028
Disposition of Executive Papers (House), Y 4.Ex 3/2
District of Columbia (House), Y 4.D 63/1

District of Columbia (Senate), Y 4.D 63/2
Ecological Reserves, Federal, Y 3.F 31/22
Economic, Joint, Y 4.Ec 7
Economic Impact of Defense and Disarmament, Pr 36.8:Ec 7
Economic Security, Y 3.Ec 74
Education (House), Y 4.Ed 8/2
Education, Advisory, Y 3.Ad 9/2
Education and Labor (House), Y 4.Ed 8/1
Education and Labor (Senate), Y 4.Ed 8/3
Education and the Workforce, Y 4.Ed 8/1
Education beyond High School, President's, Pr 34.8:Ed 3
Education, Federal Interagency, Y 3.Ed 8
Election of President, Vice-President, and Representatives (House), Y 4.El 2/1
Elections (House), Y 4.El 2/2
Employment of People with Disabilities, President's, PrEx 1.10/17
Employment of the Handicapped, President's, PrEx 1.10
Employment of People with Disabilities, President's, PrEx 1.10/16, PrEx 1.10/17-2, PrEx 1.10/19
Employment, President's Emergency, Y 3.P 92
Energy, Ad Hoc, (House), Y 4.En 2/2
Energy and Commerce, Y 4.C 73/8
Energy and Natural Resources (Senate), Y 4.En 2
Energy Materials Coordinating, E 1.52
Engineers and Scientists for Federal Government Programs, President's, Pr 34.8:En 3
Environmental Quality, Citizens Advisory, Pr 37.8:En 8
Epidemic Diseases (Senate), Y 4.Ep 4/2
Equal Education Opportunities, Select (Senate), Y 4.Eq 2
Equal Employment Opportunity, President's, Pr 35.8:Em 7
Equal Opportunity in the Armed Forces, President's, Pr 35.8:Ar 5
Establish University of the United States, Select, Y 4.Un 3/1
Ether Discovery, Select (House), Y 4.Et 3/1
Ether Discovery, Select (Senate), Y 4.Et 3/2
Ethics, Select, (House), Y 4.Et 3/2
Ethics, Select, (Senate), Y 4.Et 3/4
Expenditures in Department of Agriculture (House), Y 4.Ex 7/1
Expenditures in Department of Commerce and Labor (House), Y 4.Ex 7/2
Expenditures in Department of Justice (House), Y 4.Ex 7/4
Expenditures in Interior Department (House), Y 4.Ex 7/3
Expenditures in Navy Department (House), Y 4.Ex 7/5
Expenditures in Post Office Department (House), Y 4.Ex 7/6
Expenditures in Public Buildings (House), Y 4.Ex 7/7
Expenditures in Senatorial Primary and General Elections (Senate), Y 4.Ex 7/12
Expenditures in State Department (House), Y 4.Ex 7/8
Expenditures in the Executive Departments (House), Y 4.Ex 7/13
Expenditures in the Executive Departments (Senate), Y 4.Ex 7/14
Expenditures in Treasury Department (House), Y 4.Ex 7/9
Expenditures in War Department (House), Y 4.Ex 7/9
Expenditures in War Department, Select (House), Y 4.Ex 7/11
Export Control, Select (House), Y 4.Ex 7/15
Export Expansion, Interagency, Y 3.In 8/22
Exports Control, Y 3.Ex 7
Failed National Banks, Select, Y 4.B 22/2
Fair Employment Practice, Pr 32.412
Farm Tenancy, Special, Y 3.F 32/2
Federal Aid in Construction of Post Roads, Joint, Y 4.F 31
Federal Credit Programs, Pr 35.8:C 86
Federal Liberty, LC 1.32/2
Federal Library and Information Center, LC 1.32/4
Federal Office Space, Pr 35.8:Of 2
Federal Pay, Advisory, Y 3.Ad 9/11
Federal Penal and Reformatory Institutions, Special, Y 4.F 31/3
Federal Prevailing Rate Advisory, Y 4.P 84/10-12
Federal Text Claims, Interdepartmental, Y 3.In 8/19
Finance (Senate), Y 4.F 49
Financial Services, Y 4.B 22/1
Fiscal Relations between District of Columbia and United States, Joint, Y 4.D 63/5
Fiscal Relations Study, Y 3.Ad 9

Fisheries (Senate), Y 4.F 53
Flood Control (House), Y 4.F 65
Foreign Affairs (House), Y 4.F 76/1
Foreign Aid, Select (House), Y 4.F 76/5
Foreign Relations (Senate), Y 4.F 76/2
Forest Reservations and Protection of Game (Senate), Y 4.F 76/3
Forestry, Joint, Y 4.F 76/4
General Supply, GS, T 45
Government Activities Affecting Prices and Costs, Y 3.G 74/3
Government Contract Compliance, President's, Pr 33.17
Government Contracts, Pr 34.8:C 76/2
Government Employment Policy, President's, Pr 34.8:Em 7
Government Housing Policies and Programs, President's Advisory, Pr 34.8:H 81
Government Operations (House), Y 4.G 74/7
Government Operations (Senate), Y 4.G 74/6
Government Organization, Joint, Y 4.G 74/4
Government Organization, Select (House), Y 4.G 74/3
Government Organization, Select (Senate), Y 4.G 74/5
Government Reform, Y 4.G 74/7
Government Research, Select (House), Y 4.G 74/8:CT
Governmental Affairs (Senate), Y 4.G 74/9
Grades and Salaries, Y 3.G 75
Great Lakes Basin, Y 3.G 79/3
Great Plains, Y 3.G 79/2
Great Plains Drought Area, Y 3.G 79
Gulf War Veterans' Illnesses, Presidential Advisory, Pr 42.8:Ad 9
Haiti and Santo Domingo (Senate), Y 4.H 12
Handicapped, National Advisory, HE 19.117
Harpers Ferry Invasion, Select (Senate), Y 4.H 23
Harriman Geographic Code System, Select Joint, Y 4.H 23/2
Hawaii, Joint, Y 4.H 31
Health, Education, Labor and Pensions, Y 4.L 11/4
Health Education, President's, Pr 37.8:H 34
Highways Transport, Y 3.C 83:20
House Administration (House), Y 4.H 81/3
House Restaurant, Select (House), Y 4.H 81/6
House Rooms Distribution Select (House), Y 4.H 81
Housing, Joint, Y 4.H 81/4
Human Resources (Senate), Y 4.H 88
Hungarian Refugee Relief, President's Advisory, Pr 34.8:H 89
Hunger (Senate), Select, Y 4.H 89
Immigration and Naturalization (House), Y 4.Im 6/1
Immigration (Senate), Y 4.Im 6/2
Importation of Contract Labor, Convicts, and Paupers, Select (House), Y 4.C 76/2
Improper Activities in Labor Management Field, Select (Senate), Y 4.Im 7
Indian Affairs (House), Y 4.In 2/1
Indian Affairs (Senate), Y 4.In 2/2
Indian Affairs, Select (Senate), Y 4.In 2/11
Indian Depredations, Select (House), Y 4.In 2/4
Indian Service Investigation, Y 4.In 2/9
Industrial Arts and Expositions (House), Y 4.In 2/7
Industrial Expositions (Senate), Y 4.In 2/8
Inquire into Alleged Frauds in Recent Elections in Mississippi, Select, Y 4.M 69/1
Inquire into the Conditions of Affairs in Late Insurrectionary States, Y 4.In 7/2
Insular Affairs, Y 4.In 7/1
Intelligence, Select (House), Y 4.In 8/18
Intelligence, Select (Senate), Y 4.In 8/19
Interagency Classification Review, Y 3.C 56
Interagency Racial Data, Y 3.R 11
Interagency Radiation Research and Policy Coordination, P 1.15
Interior and Insular Affairs (House), Y 4.In 8/14
Interior and Insular Affairs (Senate), Y 4.In 8/13
Intermodal Cargo, Interagency, Y 3.In 8/26
Internal Improvements, Select (House), Y 4.In 8/7
Internal Revenue Frauds, Select (House), Y 4.In 8/2
Internal Revenue Taxation, Joint, Y 4.In 8/11
Internal Security (House), Y 4.In 8/15
International Athletics, Interagency, Y 3.In 8/20
International Relations (House), Y 4.In 8/16
International Rules of Judicial Procedure, Y 3.In 8/15
International Year of Disabled Persons, Federal Interagency, Y 3.F 31/24
Interoceanic Canal (Senate), Y 4.In 8/1
Interregional Highway, National, Y 3.N 21/15
Interstate and Foreign Commerce (House), Y 4.In 8/4

Interstate and Foreign Commerce (Senate), Y 4.In 8/3
Interstate Migration of Destitute Citizens, Select (House), Y 4.In 8/12
Invalid Petitions (House), Y 4.In 8/5
Investigate Administration and Operation of Civil Service Laws, Special, Y 4.C 49/4
Investigate Alleged Charges against Members of Congress, Y 4.M 51
Investigate Alleged Corrupt Combinations of Members of Congress, Select (House), Y 4.C 81/1
Investigate Alleged Corruptions in Government, Select, Y 4.C 81/2
Investigate Alleged Credit Mobilier Bribery, Select (House), Y 4.C 86
Investigate Alleged Ship Purchase Lobby, Special (Senate), Y 4.Sh 6/2
Investigate American Merchant Marine, Special, Y 4.Am 3/4
Investigate Baltic States Incorporation into U.S.S.R., Select (House), Y 4.B 21
Investigate Bankruptcy and Receivership Proceedings in U.S. Courts, Special (Senate), Y 4.C 33/3
Investigate Certain Statements Made by Dr. William A. Wirt, Select, Y 4.W 74
Investigate Charges of Execution without Trial in France, Special, Y 4.Ex 3
Investigate Commodity Transaction, Select (House), Y 4.C 73/4
Investigate Communist Propaganda in United States, Special, Y 4.C 73/3
Investigate Cost of Armor Plant, Special, Y 4.Ar 5
Investigate Covert Arms Transactions with Iran, Select, Y 4.In 8/20
Investigate Dirigible Disasters, Joint, Y 4.D 62
Investigate Disposition of Surplus Property, (House), Y 4.Su 7
Investigate District of Columbia Charities, Joint Select, Y 4.D 63/3
Investigate District of Columbia Excise Board, Special, Y 4.D 63/4
Investigate District of Columbia, Joint Select, Y 4.D 63/3
Investigate Educational and Training Program under GI Bill, Select (House), Y 4.Ed 8/4
Investigate Election of William Lorimer (Senate), Y 4.L 89
Investigate Executive Agencies, Special (House), Y 4.Ex 3/4
Investigate Farm Labor Conditions in the West, Special (Senate), Y 4.F 22
Investigate Federal Communications Commission, Select (House), Y 4.F 31/4
Investigate Fiscal Relations between District of Columbia and U.S., Select, Y 4.D 63/7
Investigate Food Shortages, Special (House), Y 4.F 73
Investigate Fuel Situation in the Middle West, Special (Senate), Y 4.F 95
Investigate Gasoline and Fuel Oil Shortages, Special (Senate), Y 4.G 21
Investigate Indian Contracts in Oklahoma, Y 4.Ok 4
Investigate Interior Department and Forestry Service, Joint, Y 4.In 8/8
Investigate Lobbying Activities, Special (Senate), Y 4.L 78/2
Investigate Management and Control of House Restaurant, Special, Y 4.H 81/2
Investigate Matters Connected with Affairs in Indian Territory, Select (Senate), Y 4.In 2/5
Investigate N.L.R.B., Special (House), Y 4.N 21/4
Investigate National Defense Migration, Select (House), Y 4.N 21/5
Investigate National Defense Program, Special, (Senate), Y 4.N 21/6
Investigate National Disabled Soldiers League, Inc., Select (House), Y 4.N 21/3
Investigate National Security League, Special (House), Y 4.N 21/2
Investigate Old Age Pension Plans, Select (House), Y 4.Ol 1
Investigate Old Age Pension System, Special (Senate), Y 4.Ol 1/2
Investigate Pearl Harbor Attack, Joint, Y 4.P 31
Investigate Petroleum Resources, Special (Senate), Y 4.P 44
Investigate Phosphate Resources in the United States, Joint, Y 4.P 56
Investigate Presidential Campaign Expenditures, Special, Y 4.P 92

Investigate Presidential, Vice Presidential, and Senatorial Campaign Expenditures, 1944, Special, Y 4.P 92/3

Investigate Printing, Public Select, Y 4.P 93/4

Investigate Production, Transportation and Marketing of Wool, Special (Senate), Y 4.W 88

Investigate Propaganda or Money Alleged to have been used by Foreign Governments to Influence United States Senators, Y 4.P 94

Investigate Public School System to District of Columbia (Senate), Y 4.D 63/6

Investigate Seizure of Montgomery Ward & Co., Select (House), Y 4.W 21

Investigate Ship Subsidy Lobby, Alleged, Select, (House), Y 4.Sh 6

Investigate Tax-Exempt Foundations and Comparable Organizations, Select (House), Y 4.T 19/3

Investigate Taylor and other Systems of Shop Management, Special, Y 4.T 21

Investigate the Escape of Grover Cleveland Bergdoll from Disciplinary Barracks at Governors Island, N.Y., Select, (House), Y 4.B 45/2

Investigate Unemployment and Relief, Special, Y 4.Un 2/2

Investigate United States Steel Corporation, Y 4.Un 3/2

Investigate Use of Chemicals in Food Products, Select, Y 4.F 73/2

Investigate Veterans Bureau, Select (Senate), Y 4.V 64

Investigate Wages and Prices, Select, (Senate), Y 4.W 12

Investigate Washington Railway and Electrical Company, Special, Y 4.W 27

Investigating Munitions Industry, Special (Senate), Y 4.M 92

Investigation and Entrenchment (Senate), Y 4.In 8/6

Investigation of Alleged Outrages in Southern States, Select, Y 4.Ou 8

Investigation of American Retail Federation, (House), Y 4.Am 3/3

Investigation of American Sugar Refining Company, Special (House), Y 4.Am 3/2

Investigation of Attorney General, Select, Y 4.At 8

Investigation of Charges against Burton K. Wheeler, Select, Y 4.W 56

Investigation of Charges made by George L. Lilly, Select (House), Y 4.L 62

Investigation of Executive Agencies of Government, Y 4.Ex 3/3

Investigation of Government Hospital for Insane, Special, Y 4.G 74

Investigation of Illegal Appointments in Civil Service (Senate), Select, Y 4.C 49/3

Investigation of Internal Revenue Bureau, Select, Y 4.In 8/10

Investigation of Northern Pacific Railroad Land Grants, Joint, Y 4.N 81

Investigation of Ordnance and Ammunition, Select, Y 4.Or 2/4

Investigation of Presidential and Senatorial Campaign Expenditures, Special, Y 4.P 92/2

Investigation of Real Estate Bondholders' Reorganizations, Select (House), Y 4.R 22/3

Investigation of Silver, Special, Y 4.Si 3

Investigation of Tariff Commission, Select, Y 4.T 17

Irrigation and Reclamation (House), Y 4.Ir 7/2

Irrigation and Reclamation (Senate), Y 4.Ir 7/1

Joint Federal State Action, Pr 34.8:F 31

Judiciary (House), Y 4.J 89/1

Judiciary (Senate), Y 4.J 89/2

Juvenile Delinquency and Youth Crime, President's, Pr 35.8:J 98

Kansas Investigation, Special (House), Y 4.K 13

Kennedy-Johnson Natural Resources Advisory, Pr 35.8:N 21

Labor, Y 3.C 83:30

Labor (House), Y 4.L 11

Labor and Human Resources (Senate), Y 4.L 11/4

Labor and Public Welfare (Senate), Y 4.L 11/2

Labor Management Manpower Policy, Pr 34.209

Labor Management Relations, Joint, Y 4.L 11/3

Labor-Management Policy, President's, Pr 35.8:L 11

Legislative Budge, Joint, Y 4.L 52

Levees and Improvements of Mississippi River (House), Y 4.M 69/2

Library (House), Y 4.L 61/1

Library (Senate), Y 4.L 61/3

Library, Joint, Y 4.L 61/2

Lobby Investigation, Select (House), Y 4.L 78

Lobbying Activities, Select (House), Y 4.L 78/3

Manpower, President's, Pr 36.8:M 31

Manufacturers (House), Y 4.M 31/1

Manufactures (Senate), Y 4.M 31/2

Maritime Advisory, Y 3.M 33

Mediation and Conciliation, President's Advisory, Pr 40.8:M 46

Mental Retardation, President's, Pr 36.8:M 52, Pr 36.8:R 29, HE 23.100

Merchant Marine and Fisheries (House), Y 4.M 53

Mexican American Affairs, Interagency, Y 3.In 8/23

Mileage (House), Y 4.M 58

Military Affairs (Senate), Y 4.M 59/2

Military Affairs (House), Y 4.M 59/1

Militia (House), Y 4.M 59/3

Mines and Mining (House), Y 4.M 66/1

Mines and Mining (Senate), Y 4.M 66/2

Missing Persons in Southeast Asia, Select, (House), Y 4.M 69/3

Missouri Basin, Inter-Agency, Y 3.M 69

Muscle Shoals, Joint, Y 4.M 97

Narcotic and Drug Abuse, President's, Pr 35.8:N 16

Narcotics Abuse and Control, Select, (House), Y 4.N 16

Narcotics Intelligence Consumers, National, Y 3.N 16

Narcotics, Interdepartmental, Y 3.In 8/9

National Advisory Loan, A 52

National Brucellosis, A 1.2:B 83

National Health Resources Advisory, GS 13.9

National Highway Program, President's Advisory, Pr 34.8:H 53

National Highway Safety Advisory, TD 1.13/2

National Land-Use Planning, A 1.39

National Medal of Science, President's, Pr 35.8:M 46

National Resources, Y 3.N 21/12

National Security (House), Y 4.Se 2/1

National War Savings, T 1.26

National Water Resources, Select (Senate), Y 4.N 21/8

Natural Resources, (House), Y 4.R 31/3

Navajo-Hopi Indian Administration, Joint, Y 4.N 22/4

Naval Affairs (House), Y 4.N 22/1

Naval Affairs (Senate), Y 4.N 22/2

Naval Affairs, Joint, Y 4.N 22/3

New Orleans Riots, Select (House), Y 4.N 42/1

New York Election Frauds, Alleged, Select (House), Y 4.N 42/2

Newburg, N.Y., Monument and Centennial Celebration of 1883, Joint Select, Y 4.N 42/3

North Atlantic Regional Water Resources Study Coordinating, Y 3.N 81/3

Nutrition and Human Needs, Select (Senate), Y 4.N 95

Nutrition for National Defense, Interdepartmental, Y 3.In 8/13

Occupational Information Coordinating, National, Y 3.Oc 1/2

Oceans and Atmosphere, National Advisory, Y 3.Oc 2

Official Conduct, Special (Senate), Y 4.C 76/8

Oliver Wendell Holmes Devise Permanent, Y 3.H 73

On Science, Y 4.Sci 2

On Small Business, Y 4.Sm 1/2

Opportunity for Spanish Speaking Peoples, Cabinet, Y 3.Sp 2/7

Ordnance and War-Ships, Select (Senate), Y 4.Or 2/2

Ordnance, Heavy, and Projectiles, Select, (Senate), Y 4.Or 2/1

Ordnance, Joint Select, Y 4.Or 2/3

Organization of Congress, Joint, Y 4.C 76/3

Organization of Congress, Special (Senate), Y 4.C 76/6

Origin, Introduction and Prevention of Epidemic Diseases, Select (House), Y 4.Ep 4/1

Outer Continental Shelf, Ad Hoc Select, (House), Y 4.Ou 8/2

Pacific Coast Naval Bases, Joint, Y 4.P 11/4

Pacific Islands and Porto Rico (Senate), Y 4.P 11/1

Pacific Railroad (House), Y 4.P 11/3

Pacific Railroad (Senate), Y 4.P 11/2

Pacific Southwest Federal Interagency Technical, Y 3.P 11/3

Pacific Southwest, Inter-Agency, Y 3.P 11/2

Patents (House), Y 4.P 27/1

Patents (Senate), Y 4.P 27/2

Payment of Pensions, Bounty, and Back Pay, Select, Y 4.P 38/3

Pensions (House), Y 4.P 38/1

Pensions (Senate), Y 4.P 38/2

Pest Control, Federal, Y 3.F 31/18

Philippines (Senate), Y 4.P 53

Physical Fitness, FS 12

Political Activities, Lobbying and Campaign Contributions, Special, Y 4.P 75

Population and Family Planning, President's, Pr 36.8:P 81

Population, Select, (House), Y 4.P 84/10

Post Office and Civil Service (House), Y 4.P 84/10

Post Office and Civil Service (Senate), Y 4.P 84/11

Post Office and Post Roads (House), Y 4.P 84/1

Post Office and Post Roads (Senate), Y 4.P 84/2

Post War Economic Policy and Planning, Special (House), Y 4.P 84/9

Post War Economic Policy and Planning, Special (Senate), Y 4.P 84/7

Post War Military Policy, Select (House), Y 4.P 84/8

Postage on 2d Class Mail Matter and Compensation for Transportation of Mails, Joint, Y 4.P 84/4

Postal Office Leases, Senate, Y 4.P 84/6

POW/MIA Affairs, Senate Select, Y 4.P 93/8

Preservation of the White House, Y 3.W 58/10

Presidential Campaign Activities, Select, (Senate), Y 4.P 92/4

President's Nuclear Safety Oversight, Pr 40.8:N 88

President's Science Advisory, Pr 34.8:Sci 2

Price Stability, Cabinet, Pr 36.8:P 93

Price Stability for Economic Growth, President's Cabinet, Pr 34.8:P 93

Printing (House), Y 4.P 93/2

Printing (Senate), Y 4.P 93/3

Printing, Joint, Y 4.P 93/1

Private International Law, Secretary of State's, S 1.130

Private Land Claims (House), Y 4.P 93/5

Private Land Claims (Senate), Y 4.P 93/7

Privileges and Elections (Senate), Y 4.P 93/6

Proceedings of Board of Commissioners on Claims against Mexico, Select, Y 4.M 57

Professional Sports, Select (House), Y 4.Sp 6

Public Buildings and Grounds (House), Y 4.P 96/6

Public Buildings and Grounds (Senate), Y 4.P 96/7

Public Expenditures, (House), Y 4.P 96/5

Public Health and National Quarantine (Senate), Y 4.P 96/9

Public Health, Select (House), Y 4.P 96/8

Public Higher Education in District of Columbia, President's, Pr 35.8:Ed 8

Public Information, Y 3.P 96/3

Public Lands (House), Y 4.P 96/2

Public Lands and Surveys (Senate), Y 4.P 96/1

Public Works (House), Y 4.P 96/11

Public Works (Senate), Y 4.P 96/10

Public Works and Transportation (House), Y 4.P 96/11

Pulp and Paper Investigations, Select, Y 4.P 96/3

Purchase from People Who Are Blind or Severely Disabled, Y 3.B6

Purchase from the Blind and Other Severely Handicapped, Y 3.B 61

Purchase of Blind-Made Products, Y 3.B 61

Purchase of Products and Services of the Blind and Other Severely Handicapped, Y 3.P 97

Pursuant to House Resolution 1, Select (House), Y 4.H 81/5

Radiation Preservation of Food, Interdepartmental, Y 3.In 8/12

Radio Education, Federal, FS 5.100

Railroad Retirement Legislation, Joint, Y 4.R 13/3

lroads (Senate), Y 4.R 13/2

Railways and Canals (House), Y 4.R 13

Readjustment of Service Pay, Select, Y 4.R 22

Readjustment of Service Pay, Special Joint (House), Y 4.R 22/2

Reconstruction and Production, Select (Senate), Y 4.R 24/3

Reconstruction, Joint, Y 4.R 24

Records of Congress, Advisory, Y 3.C 76/4

Recreation and Natural Beauty, Pr 36.8:R 24

Recreation, Federal Inter-Agency, Y 3.F 31/14

Reduction of Federal Expenditures, Joint, Y 4.R 24/4

Reforestation, Select (Senate), Y 4.R 25

Relations of Members with Post Office Departments, Select (House), Y 4.P 84/3

Relations with Canada, (Senate), Y 4.C 16

Religion and Welfare in the Armed Forces, President's, Y 3.P 92/5

Religious and Morale Welfare and Character Guidance in the Armed Forces, President's, Y 3.P 92/5
Reorganization of the Administrative Branch of the Government, Joint, Y 4.R 29
Research Natural Areas, Federal, Y 3.F 31/19
Reserve Bank Organization, RB
Resources, Y 4.R 31/3
Retrenchment (Senate), Y 4.R 31/1
Retrenchment, Joint Select, Y 4.R 31/2
Revision of Laws (House), Y 4.L 44/2
Revision of Laws, Special Joint, Y 4.L 44/1
River Basins, Federal Inter-Agency, Y 3.F 31/13
Rivers and Harbors (House), Y 4.R 52
Roads (House), Y 4.R 53/2
Roads and Canals (Senate), Y 4.R 53
Rules and Administration (Senate), Y 4.R 86/2
Rules (House), Y 4.R 86/1
Rural Credits, Joint, Y 4.R 88
Rural Development, Y 3.R 88/3
Rural Development Program, Y 3.R 88/2
Science, Y 4.Sci 2
Science and Astronautics (House), Y 4.Sci 2
Science and Technology (House), Y 4.Sci 2
Science, President's, Pr 35.8:Sci 2
Science, Space, and Technology (House), Y 4.Sci 2
Scientific Research and Development, Interdepartmental, Y 3.In 8/4
Scientists and Engineers, President's, Pr 34.8:Sci 27
Senate Contingent Expenses (Senate), Y 4.Se 5
Senate Impeachment Trial, Y 4.Im 7/2
Senatorial Campaign Expenditures, Select (Senate), Y 4.Se 5/2
Ship Structure, TD 5.63, Y 3.Sh 6
Shipping Board Emergency Fleet Corporation, Select (House), Y 4.Sh 6/4
Shipping Board Operations, Select (House), Y 4.Sh 6/3
Short Times Record Credits, Joint, Y 4.Sh 8
Sickness and Mortality on Emigrant Ships, Select, (Senate), Y 4.Si 1
Small and Minority Business Ownership, Presidential Advisory, Pr 40.8:B 96
Small Business and Entrepeneurship, Y 4.Sm 1/2
Small Business, Cabinet, Pr 34.8:Sm 1
Small Business, Select (House), Y 4.Sm 1
Small Business, Select (Senate), Y 4.Sm 1/2
Small Business of the White House, Pr 35.8:Sm 1
Space and Astronautics, Special (Senate), Y 4.Sp 1
Standards and Conduct, Select (Senate), Y 4.St 2/2
Standards of Official Conduct, Select (Senate), Y 4.St 2/2
Standards of Official Conduct (House), Y 4.St 2/3
Standards, Weights and Measures (Senate), Y 4.St 2
Status of Women, Interdepartmental, Y 3.In 8/21
Study Censure Charges, Select, Y 4.C 33/4
Study Foreign Aid Program, Special (Senate), Y 4.F 76/6
Study Government Operations with Respect to Intelligence Activities, Select (Senate), Y 4.In 8/17
Study Law, Select, Y 4.L 41
Study Military Assistance Program, President's, Pr 34.8:M 59
Study of Jurisdiction over Federal Areas within the States, Interdepartmental, Y 3.In 8/10
Study Problems of American Small Business, Special (Senate), Y 4.Am 3/5
Study the Senate Committee System, Temporary Select, Y 4.Se 5/4

Survey of Land and Water Policies of United States, Special (Senate), Y 4.L 22
Survivors Benefits, Select (House), Y 4.Su 7/2
Tax Evasion and Avoidance, Joint, Y 4.T 19
Taxation, Joint, Y 4.T 19/4
Taxation of Governmental Securities and Salaries, Special (Senate), Y 4.T 19/2
Temporary National Economic, Y 4.T 24
Tennessee Valley Authority, Joint, Y 4.T 25
Termination of the National Emergency, Special, Y 4.N 21/9
Territories (House), Y 4.T 27/1
Territories and Insular Affairs (Senate), Y 4.T 27/2
Textiles, President's Cabinet Advisory, Pr 35.8:T 31
Transfer of Indian Bureau, Joint, Y 4.In 2/3
Transportation and Infrastructure (House), Y 4.T 68/2
Transportation Routes to Seaboard, Select, Y 4.T 68
Tuberculosis, Y 3.T 79
U.S.-FAO Interagency, Y 3.Un 3/3
U.S. Meat Animal Research Center, Advisory, A 77.27

U.S. Trade Relations with East European Countries and the Soviet Union, Pr 36.8:T 67
Un-American Activities, Special (House), Y 4.Un 1/2
Un-American Activities, Special (Senate), Y 4.Un 1
Unemployment Insurance (Senate), Y 4.Un 2
Unemployment Problems, Special (Senate), Y 4.Un 2/3
Uniform Civil Rights Policies and Practices, Interagency, Y 3.C 49/4
Ventilation and Acoustics (House), Y 4.V 56
Veterans Affairs (House), Y 4.V 64/3
Veterans Affairs (Senate), Y 4.V 64/4
Veterans Affairs, Joint, Y 4.V 64/2
Voluntary Foreign Aid, Y 3.Ad 9/4
Voluntary Service National Advisory, VA 1.52
Wage, VA 1.51
War Claims (House), Y 4.W 19
War, Joint, Y 4.C 75
Washington Metropolitan Problems, Joint, Y 4.W 27/2
Water Power (House), Y 4.W 29
Water Resources, Interagency, Y 3.In 8/8
Water Resources Policy, Presidential Advisory, Pr 34.8:W 29
Ways and Means (House), Y 4.W 36
Weather Control, Y 3.Ad 9/6
Welfare and Education of Congressional Pages, Select (House), Y 4.W 45
Wildlife Conservation (House), Y 4.W 64/2
Wildlife Resources, Special (Senate), Y 4.W 64
Wolf Management, Y 3.W 83
Woman Suffrage, Select, (Senate), Y 4.W 84
Woman's, Y 3.C 83:60
World Economic Practices, Pr 34.8:W 89
World War Veterans Legislation (House), Y 4.W 89
Youth Employment, President's, Pr 35.8:Y 8/2

Committees, and Boards, Y 3.2
Committees, Select and Special, (House), Y 4.Se 4/1, Y 4.2
Committees, Select and Special, (Senate), Y 4.Se 4/2, Y 4.3
Commodity Credit Administration, A 80.400
Commodity Credit Corporation, A 71, A 82.300, Y 3.C 73
Commodity Exchange Administration, A 59, A 75.200
Commodity Exchange Authority, A 85
Commodity Futures Trading Commission, Y 3.C 73/5
Commodity Stabilization Service, A 82
Commodity Transaction, Select Committee to Investigate (House), Y 4.C 73/4
Communicable Disease Center, National, HE 20.2300
Communication Agency, International, ICA 1
Communication Office, A 21
Communications Agency, Defense, D 5.100
Communications Command, Army, D 101.83
Communications Commission, Federal, CC
Communication Disorders, National Institute on Deafness and Other, HE 20.3650
Communications Policy Board, President's, Pr 33.13
Communications Policy, President's Task Force on, Pr 36.8:C 76
Communications, Publications Relating to, D 111
Communications Service, Naval, N 22
Communications System, National, PrEx 1.17
Communicative Disorders and Stroke, National Institute of, HE 20.3500
Communist Aggression, Select Committee on (House), Y 4.C 73/5
Communist Propaganda in United States, Special Committee to Investigate, Y 4.C 73/3
Communities Administration, New, HH 11
Community Development Office, HH 9
Community Education Advisory Council, HE 19.132/2
Community Environmental Management Bureau, HE 20.1800, HE 20.2850
Community Facilities Administration, HH 5
Community Facilities Bureau, FW 7
Community Facilities Service, HH 5
Community Health Service, HE 20.2550
Community Health Services, Bureau of, HE 20.5100
Community Relations Service, C 50, J 23
Community Services Administration, HE 17.700, CSA
Community War Services Office, FS 9
Compensation, Federal, President's Panel on, Pr 38.8:C 73
Compensation, National Commission on Unemployment, Y 3.Un 2
Compensation, Advisory Council on Unemployment, Y 3.2:Un 2
Compensation Office, Federal Employees', L 36.300
Compensation, President's Commission on Hostage, Pr 40.8:H 79

Competitive Assessment and Business Policy, Bureau of, C 57.300
Competitiveness Policy Council, Y 3.C 73/6
Competitiveness, President's Commission on Industrial, Pr 40.8:C 73
Competitiveness, President's Council on, Pr 41.8:R 26
Compliance and Conversion Bureau, Health Facilities, HE 20.6700
Compliance Board, Architectural and Transportation Barriers, Y 3.B 27
Compliance Panel, Interim, Y 3.C 73/4
Comprehensive Health Planning Service, HE 20.2580
Comptroller, First, T 13
Comptroller of the Currency, T 12
Comptroller of the Treasury, T 15
Comptroller, Second, T 14
Comptroller's Office, Y 3.R 13/2:30
Computer Center, Parklawn, HE 20.4036
Computer Institute, DoD, D 5.414
Computer Sciences and Technology Institute, C 13.73
Computer Security Center, D 1.79
Computer Security Center, National, D 1.79/2
Computer Systems Laboratory, C 13.77
Conciliation, President's Advisory Committee, Pr 40.8:M 46Conciliation Service, L 19
Conduct of Foreign Policy, Commission on Organization of the Government of, Y 3.F 76/5
Conduct of the War, Joint Committee on, Y 4.C 75
Conduct, Official, Special Committee on (Senate), Y 4.C 76/8
Conference–
    Administrative, of the United States, Pr 35.8:Ad 6, Y 3.Ad 6
    Administrative Procedure, Pr 34.8:Ad 6
    Aging of the White House, Y 3.W 58/4
    Balanced National Growth and Economic Development, White House, Y 3.W 58/19
    Child Abuse and Neglect, National, HE 1.480/5
    Child Health and Protection of the White House, Y 3.W 58
    Children, White House, Y 3.W 58/3, Y 3.W 58/3-2
    Committees (House and Senate), Y 4.C 76/1
    Conservation, White House, Y 3.W 58/6
    Education Committee, White House, Y 3.W 58/2
    Equal Employment Opportunity, White House, Y 3.W 58/13
    Export Expansion, White House, Y 3.W 58/8
    Families, White House, Y 3.W 58/22
    Food, Nutrition, and Health, White House, Y 3.W 58/16
    Handicapped Individuals, White House, Y 3.W 58/18
    Health, White House, Y 3.W 58/14
    Industrial World Ahead, White House, Y 3.W 58/17
    Interagency Land Acquisition, Y 3.L 22
    International Cooperation, White House, Y 3.W 58/11
    Library and Information Services, White House, Y 3.W 58/20
    Mental Retardation, White House, Y 3.W 58/9
    Narcotic and Drug Abuse, White House, Y 3.W 58/5
    National Economic Issues, White House, Y 3.W 58/7
    Natural Beauty, White House, Y 3.W 58/12
    Numerical Ship Hydrodynamics, International, D 211.9/5
    Productivity, White House, Pr 40.8:P 94
    Science and Economics Research Related to Global Change, White House, Pr 41.8:G 51
    Small Business, White House, Y 3.W 58/21
    "To Fulfill These Rights," White House, Y 3.W 58/15
    Women, U.N. Fourth World, Pr 42.8:W 84
    Youth, White House, Y 3.W 58/3-3
Conferences, Congresses, and Commissions, International, S 5
Congested Production Areas Committee, Pr 32.10
Congress, X – Y 1.1
Congress, Advisory Committee on the Records, Y 3.C 76/4
Congress, Joint Committee on Organization of, Y 4.C 76/3
Congress, Library of, LC
Congress, Special Committee on Organization of (Senate), Y 4.C 76/6
Congresses, Conferences, and Commissions, International, S 5
Congressional Agencies, Y 3
Congressional Budget Office, Y 10
Congressional Committees, Y 4
Congressional Mailing Standards Commission, (House), Y 4.M 28

Congressional Operations Joint Committee, Y 4.C 76/7
Congressional Operations, Select Committee on, Y 4.C 76/9
Congressional Research Service, LC 14
Conservation Agency, Natural Resources, A 57
Conservation Bank, Solar Energy and Energy, HH 1.1/3
Conservation Corps, Civilian, Y 3.C 49
Conservation Corps, Youth, I 1.105/3
Conservation Division, Civilian, I 42
Conservation Program, Agricultural, A 55.42–A 55.48
Conservation Program, Emergency, A 82.93
Conservation Program, Habitat, C 55.340
Conservation Program Service, Agricultural, A 90
Conservation, White House Conference on, Y 3.W 58/6
Conservation Work, Emergency, Y 3.Em 3
Consolidated Farm Service Agency, A 112
Constitution, Commission on the Bicentennial of the United States, Y 3.B 47/2
Constitution Sesquicentennial Commission of the United States, Y 3.Un 3
Constitution, U.S. Commission on the Bicentennial
Construction and Frost Effects Laboratory, Arctic, D 103.31
Construction and Repair Bureau, N 4
Construction Bureau, SB 11
Construction Division, W 92
Construction Engineering Research Laboratory, D 103.53
Construction, Equipment and Repair Bureau, N 4
Construction Industry Collective Bargaining Commission, Y 3.C 76
Construction Industry Services Office, L 1.1/2
Construction Office, Y 3.T 25:1-15
Consulting Board, Naval, N 1.28
Consumer Affairs, National Business Council for, Y 3.N 21/27
Consumer Affairs Office, HE 1.500, PrEx 16
Consumer and Food Economics Research Division, A 77.700
Consumer and Marketing Service, A 88
Consumer Bill of Rights and Responsibilities Commission, Y 3.2:C 76/B 49
Consumer Division, Pr 32.4250
Consumer Finance, National Commission on, Y 3.C 76/2
Consumer Information Center, GS 11
Consumer Product Information Coordinating Center, GS 11
Consumer Product Safety Commission, Y 3.C 76/3
Consumer Protection and Environmental Health Service, HE 20.1000
Consumers Committee, National Narcotics Intelligence, Y 3.N 16
Consumers' Counsel Division, A 75.100, I 48.50
Consumers' Counsel of National Bituminous Coal Commission, I 39
Consumers' Counsel Office, L 2.6
Consumers' Division, L 17
Consumers Interests Committee of the President, Pr 36.8:C 76
Consumers' Project, L 17
Continental Shelf, Outer, Ad Hoc Select Committee on, (House), Y 4.Ou 8/2
Continuing Education National Advisory Council, Y 3.Ed 8/8
Continuing Education, National Advisory Council on Extension and, Y 3.Ex 8
Contract Labor, Convicts, and Paupers, Select Committee on Importation of (House), Y 4.C 76/2
Contract Settlement Appeals Board, GS 5
Contract Settlement Office, Y 3.W 19/7:100, T 67, GS 5
Contracts Division, Public, L 18
Contribution Investigation Select Committee (Senate), Y 4.C 76/4
Control and Rehabilitation Division, Cancer, HE 20.3151/4
Control Division, Cancer, HE 20.3151/4
Control, Foreign Funds, T 65
Control, National Center for Injury, HE 20.7950
Control Program, Aquatic Plant, D 103.24/13
Control, Select Committee on Narcotics (House), Y 4.N 16
Controller Bureau, P 25
Controversy Between Certain Air Carriers and Their Employees, Commission to Inquire into, Pr 35.8:Ai 7
Conversion Bureau, Health Facilities, HE 20.6700
Conveyance Commission, Kaho'olawe Island, Y 3.2:K 12
Coolidge, Calvin, Pr 30
Cooling Water Studies Panel, Lake Michigan, EP 1.72
Cooperation Administration, International, S 17
Cooperation in Europe, Commission on ecurity and, Y 4.Se 2

Cooperative Cataloging and Classification Service, LC 22
Cooperative Economic Development, Commission for the Study of International, Y 3.M 58/2
Cooperative Enterprise in Europe Committee, Y 3.C 78/2
Cooperative Extension Work Office, A 43.5
Cooperative State Research Service, A 94
Cooperatives Service, A 105
Coordinating Committee–
    Arthritis Interagency, HE 20.3032
    Diabetes Mellitus, HE 20.3028
    Energy Materials, E 1.52
    National Occupational Information, Y 3.Oc 1/2
Coordinating Council for Science, Engineering, and Technology, Federal, PrEx 8.100
Coordinating Council on Bilingual Education, National, Y 3.B 49
Coordinator–
    Federal Transportation, Y 3.F 31/6
    Health, Welfare, and Related Defense Activities Office, FS 8
    Industrial Cooperation, Y 3.C 78
    Information, Y 3.C 78/3
    Inter-American Affairs Office, Pr 32.4600
    Petroleum for National Defense Office, I 50
    Petroleum for War Office, I 50
Copyright Office, LC 3
Copyrighted Works, National Commission on New Technological Uses of, Y 3.C 79
Corner Stone of the Capitol, Special Committee on the Centennial Celebration of the Laying of, Y 4.C 17
Corporate Pension Funds and other Private Retirement and Welfare Programs Committee, President's, Pr 35.8:P 38/2
Corporation–
    Commodity Credit, Y 3.C 73, A 71, A 80.400, A 82.300
    Deposit Insurance, Federal, Y 3.F 31/8
    Farm Credit System Insurance, Y 3.F 22/2
    Federal Crop Insurance, A 62, A 76.100, A 79.300, A 80.900, A 82.200, A 79.300
    Federal Facilities, T 69
    Federal Surplus Commodities, A 69
    Grain, Y 3.W 56:10
    Housing, L 8
    Inland Waterways, W 103, C 29
    National and Community Service, Y 3.N 21/29
    National Service, Y 3.N21/29
    Overseas Private Investment, OP 1
    Pension Benefit Guaranty, Y 3.P 38/2
    Reconstruction Finance, C 33, FL 5, Y 3.R 24
    Resolution Trust, Y 3.R 31/2
    St. Lawrence Seaway Development, TD 6, Y 3.Sa 2
    Shipping Board Emergency Fleet, SB 2
    Shipping Board Merchant Fleet, SB 2
    Surplus Relief, Federal, Y 3.F 31/9
    United States Enrichment, Y 3.En 2
    War Finance, Y 3.W 19/3
    Western Wheat Quality Laboratory, A 77.39
Corporation Bureau, C 5
Corporation Securities, United States, Task Force on Promoting Increased Foreign Investments in, Pr 35.8:F 76/3
Corporations, United States, Operating Abroad, Task Force for Promoting Increased Foreign Financing of, Pr 35.8:F 76/3
Corps–
    Chemical, D 116
    Civilian Conservation, Y 3.C 49, I 42, FS 4
    Engineers, D 103
    General Staff, W 2
    Marine, N 9, M 209, D 214
    Motor Transport, W 88
    Ordnance, D 105
    Peace, S 19, AA 4, PE 1
    Quartermaster, W 77, D 106
    Signal, D 111
    Tank, W 90
    Transportation, D 117
    Youth Conservation, I 1.105/3
Corrections, National Institute of, J 16.100
Corrupt Combinations of Members of Congress, Alleged, Select Committee to Investigate, (House), Y 4.C 81/1
Corruption in Government, Alleged, Select Committee to Investigate, Y 4.C 81/2
Cost Accounting Standards Board, Y 3.C 82
Cost Control, President's Private Sector Survey on, Pr 40.8:C 82
Cost of Living Council, PrEx 17
Costs Committee, Government Activities Affecting Prices and, Y 3.G 74/3
Council–
    Adult Education, National Advisory, Y 3.Ed 8/4

Aeronautics and Space, National, PrEx 5
Aging, Federal, Y 3.F 31/15
Aging, President's, Pr 35.8:Ag 4
Arts, National, PrEx 11
Arts, President's Advisory, Pr 35.8:Ar 7
Bituminous Coal Consumers, Y 3.B 54/2
Business Advisory, C 28
Business Advisory and Planning, C 28
Career Education, National Advisory, HE 19.116
Child Nutrition, National Advisory, Y 3.C 43/2
Citizen Participation, Federal Interagency, Y 3.C 49/5
Civil Rights, Advisory, GA 1.29
Commerce, National, C 1.9
Community Education Advisory, HE 19.132/2
Competitiveness Policy, Y 3.C 73/6
Consumer Affairs, National Business, Y 3.N 21/27
Continuing Education, National Advisory, Y 3.Ed 8/8
Coordinate all Federal Juvenile Delinquency Programs, Interdepartmental, Y 3.J 98
Cost of Living, PrEx 17
Disability, National, Y 3.D 63/3
Domestic, PrEx 15
Drug Abuse Prevention, National Advisory, Y 3.D 84
Drug Abuse, Strategy, Y 3.St 8
Economic Advisors, Pr 33.9, Pr 34.9, PrEx 6
Economic Opportunity, National Advisory, Y 3.Ec 7/2
Education, Intergovernmental Advisory, Y 3.Ed 8/9
Education of Disadvantaged Children, National, Y 3.Ed 8/2
Education Professions Development, National, Y 3.Ed 8/3
Education Research, National, HE 19.214
Environmental Education, Advisory, HE 5.95
Environmental Quality, PrEx 14
Equal Opportunity, President's, Pr 36.8:Eq 2
Equality of Educational Opportunity, National Advisory, Y 3.Ed 8/7
Executive, Y 3.Ex 3/2
Export, President's, Pr 37.8:Ex 7, Pr 40.8:Ex 7
Extension and Continuing Education, National Advisory, Y 3.Ex 8
Federal Financial Institutions Examination, Y 3.F 49
Federal Fire, GS 1
Federal Labor Relations, Y 3.F 31/21
Federal Regional, Pr 37.8:R 26
Federal Safety, L 30
Financial Aid to Students, Advisory, HE 19.131
Graduate Medical Education, Y 3.M 46/2
Handicapped, National, Y 3.H 19
Health Planning and Development, National, HE 20.6001/5:H 34
Homeless, Interagency, Y 3.H 75
Indian Education, National Advisory, Y 3.In 2/10
Indian Opportunity, National Advisory, Y 3.In 2/10
Integrity and Efficiency, President's, Pr 40.8/3
Interdepartmental Safety, Federal, FIS 1
International Economic Policy, Pr 37.8:In 8/3, Pr 38.8:In 8
International Monetary and Financial Policies, National Advisory, Y 3.N 21/16
International Monetary and Financial Problems, National Advisory, Y 3.N 21/16
International Youth Exchange, President's, Pr 40.8:Y 8
Integrity and Efficiency, President's, Pr 40.8:In 8
Management Improvement, President's, Pr 40.8:M 31
Management Improvement, President's Advisory, Pr 37.8:M 31
Marine Resources and Engineering Development, National, PrEx 12
National Advisory Eye, HE 20.3752:R 31/4
National Critical Materials, Y 3.C 86/2
National Defense, Y 3.C 83, Y 3.C 831
National Defense, Advisory Commission, Y 3.C 831:100
National Emergency, Y 3.N 21/9
National Export Expansion, C 1.42/3
National Industrial Pollution Control, Y 3.In 2/8
National Inventors, C 32
National Professional Standards Review, HE 1.46, HE 20.5010
National Research, NA 2
National Security, Y 3.N 21/17, Pr 33.600, PrEx 3
Northwest Federal Regional, Y 3.N 81/5
Pennsylvania Avenue, President's, Pr 35.8:P 38
Personnel Policy, Intergovernmental, Y 3.P 43/2
Physical Fitness, and Sports, President's, Pr 36.8:P 56, Pr 37.8:P 56/2, HE 20.100

Physical Fitness, President's, Pr 35.8:P 56
President's Crime Prevention, Pr 42.8:C 86
President's Export, Pr 40.8:Ex 7
Radiation, Federal, Y 3.F 31/17
Recreation, Advisory, Pr 35.8:R 24
Regulatory, Y 3.R 26
Science and Technology, Federal, Y 3.F 31/16
Science, Engineering, and Technology, Federal
        Coordinating, PrEx 8.100
Social Security, Y 3.Ad 9/3
Supplemental Centers and Services, National
        Advisory, Pr 36.8:Su 7
Unemployment Compensation, Advisory, Y 3.2:Un
        2
United States Holocaust Memorial, Y 3.H 74
Wage and Price Stability, PrEx 22
Water Resources, Y 3.W 29
Women's Education Programs, National Advisory,
        Y 3.W 84/2
Women's Educational Programs, Advisory, Y 3.Ed
        8/6
Youth Fitness, President's, Pr 34.8:Y 8
Youth Opportunity, President's, Pr 36.8:Y 8, Pr
        37.8:Y 8
Council to the Public Printer, Depository Library, GP
        1.36
Counsel for Consumers' of National Bituminous Coal
        Commission, I 39
Counsel, Office of Consumers', L 2.6
Council on Bilingual Education, National Advisory
        and Coordinating, Y 3.B 49
Court–
    Appeals, Ju 2
    Appeals, Emergency, Ju 12
    Appeals for the Federal Circuit, Ju 7
    Claims, Ju 3
    Commerce, Ju 8
    Commissioners of 1st and 2nd Alabama Claims, Y
        3.Al 1
    Customs, Ju 9
    Customs and Patent Appeals, Ju 7
    Customs Appeals, Ju 7
    Customs of the United States, T 20
    International Trade, United States, Ju 9
    Private Land Claims, Ju 5
    Supreme, Ju 6
    Taxes of the United States, Ju 11
    United States Bankruptcy, Ju 14
Courts–
    Administrative Office, United States, Ju 10
    Circuit, Ju 1
    District, of the United States, Ju 4
Courts of Appeals, U. S. Circuit, Ju 2
Covert Arms Transactions with Iran, Select Committee
        to Investigate, Y 4.In 8/20
Crater Lake National Park, I 1.42
Credit Mobilier Bribery, Alleged, Select Committee to
        Investigate, (House), Y 4.C 86
Credit Programs, Federal, Committee, Pr 35.8:C 86
Credit Union Administration, National, NCU
Credit Union Bureau, Federal, FS 3.300, HE 3.300
Crime in the District of Columbia Commission of the
        President, Pr 36.8:C 86
Crime, Organized, in Interstate Commerce, Special
        Committee to Investigate (Senate), Y 4.C 86/
        2
Crime Prevention Council, President's, Pr 42.8:C 86
Crime, President's Commission on Organized, Pr
        40.8:C 86
Crime, President's Task Force on Victims of, Pr 40.8:V
        66
Crime, Select Committee on (House), Y 4.C 86/3
Criminal and Penal Laws, Commission to Revise and
        Codify, Y 3.L 44
Criminal Identification Bureau, J 15
Criminal Justice Information and Statistics Service,
        National, J 26.10
Criminal Justice Research Utilization Program, J 28
Criminal Justice, National Institute of, J 26.1/3
Criminal Justice Standards and Goals, National
        Advisory Commission on, Y 3.C 86
Critical Materials Council, National, Y 3.C 86/2
Crop Estimates Bureau, A 27, A 36
Crop Insurance Committee, President's, Y 3.P 92/2
Crop Insurance Corporation, Federal, A 62, A 76.100, A
        79.300, A 80.900, A 82.200
Crop Insurance Program, Commission for the
        Improvement of the Federal, Y 3.C 88Crop
        Insurance, Select Committee (Senate), Y 4.C
        88
Crop Production Loan Office, A 54
Crops Research Division, A 77.500
CSU-PHS Collaborative Radiological Health
        Laboratory, HE 20.4119, HE 20.4600
Cuba, Advisory Board for Radio Broadcasting to, Pr
        40.8:R 11

Cuba Broadcasting Advisory Board, Y 3.B 78/2
Cuba, Presidential Commission on Broadcasting to, Pr
        40.8:Br 78, Pr 41.8:Br 78
Cuba Relations Committee (Senate), Y 4.C 89
Cuba, Western, Department, W 60
Cuban Census Office, W 47
Cultural Center, National, SI 10
Cultural Relations Division, S 15
Currency, Committee on Banking and, (House), Y 4.B
        22/1
Currency Comptroller, T 12
Custodian of Alien Property, Y 3.Al 4
Custom Appeals Court, Ju 7
Custom Matters Assistant Attorney General, J 12
Customs and Patent Appeals Court, Ju 7
Customs Bureau, T 17
Customs Commissioner, T 16
Customs Court, Ju 9
Customs Court of the United States, T 20
Customs Division, T 17

D

Dahlgren Laboratory, D 201.21/4
Dairy Industry Bureau, A 44, A 77.600
Dairy Research, Publications Relating to, A 77.600
Dairying Bureau, A 44
Dakota Department, W 16
Dakota, Governor, I 1.10
Dangerous Drugs, Bureau of Narcotics and, J 24
Data, and Information Service, National Environmental
        Satellite,, C 55.200
Data Center A, World, C 55.220
Data Center, National Geophysical, C 55.201/2
Data Management and Strategy Bureau, HE 22.500Data
        Recovery Program, Archeological and
        Historical, I 29.59/4
Daughters of American Revolution National Society, SI
        5
DAWN, Project, J 24.19/2
Dead Letters Division, P 7
Deafness and Other Communication Disorders,
        National Institute on, HE 20.3650
Decimal Classification Office, LC 37
Declassification and Technical Service Office, C 35
Defense Administrative Support Center, D 7.6/14
Defense and Civilian Mobilization Office, Pr 34.700
Defense Acquisition University, D 1.59/3
Defense Base Closure and Realignment Commission, Y
        3.D 36/2
Defense Civil Preparedness Agency, D 14
Defense Commission, Y 3.M 53/2
Defense Communications Agency, D 5.100
Defense Department, D 1
Defense Documentation Center, D 10
Defense Electric Power Administration, I 56
Defense Fisheries Administration, I 54
Defense Health and Welfare Services Office, Pr 32.4500
Defense Housing Coordination Division, Pr 32.4300
Defense Intelligence Agency, D 5.200
Defense Intelligence School, D 5.210
Defense Logistics Agency, D 7
Defense Logistics Agency Publishing System, D 7.41
Defense Management, President's Blue Ribbon
        Commission on, Pr 40.8:D 36
Defense Manpower Administration, L 27
Defense Manpower Commission, Y 3.D 36
Defense Manpower Office, L 27
Defense Mapping Agency, D 5.300
Defense Materials Procurement Agency, DM
Defense Minerals Administration, I 55
Defense Minerals Exploration Administration, I 55
Defense Mobilization Office, Pr 33.1000, Pr 34.200
Defense Nuclear Facilities Safety Board, Y 3.D 36/3
Defense Petroleum Administration, I 58
Defense Power Administration, I 56
Defense Production Administration, Pr 33.1100, DP
Defense Production, Joint Committee on, Y 4.D 36
Defense Property Disposal Service, D 7.6/13
Defense Savings Staff, T 1.100
Defense Solid Fuels Administration, I 57
Defense Supply Agency, D 7
Defense Supply Management Agency, D 7
Defense Systems Management College, D 1.59/2
Defense Technical Information Center, D 10
Defense Threat Reduction Agency, D 15
Defense Transport Administration, IC 1 def
Defense Transportation Office, Pr 32.4900
Defense University, National, D 5.400
Deficit Reduction, Temporary Joint Committee on, Y 4.D
        36/2
Delaware River Basin Commission, Y 3.D 37/2
Delinquency Prevention Administration, Youth
        Development and, HE 1.300, HE 17

Delinquency Prevention, National Institute for, J 26.1/
        2
Delinquency Prevention, Office of Juvenile, J 32
Delivery and Assistance, Bureau of Health Care, HE
        20.5100
Democratic Policy Committee, Y 4.D 39
Demonstration Program, Geothermal Energy, ER 1.31
Dental Research Institute, National, HE 20.3400
Department–
    Acquisitions, LC 27
    Adjutant General, W 3
    Agriculture, A 1
    Air Force, D 301, M 301
    Alaska, W 71
    Arizona, W 65
    Army, M 101, D 101
    California, W 13
    Central, W 78
    Colorado, W 14
    Columbia, W 15
    Commerce, C 1
    Commerce and Labor, C 1
    Cuba, W 25
    Dakota, W 16
    Defense, D 1
    East, W 17
    Education, ED 1
    Energy, E 1
    Engineers, M 110, W 7
    Finance, M 116
    Gulf, W 18
    Hawaii, W 81
    Health and Human Services, HE 1
    Health, Education, and Welfare, FS 1, HE 1
    Housing and Urban Development, HH 1
    Inspector General, W 9
    Interior, I 1
    Judge Advocate General, W 10, M 107, D 108
    Justice, J 1
    Labor, L 1
    Labor Academy, L 1.91
    Lakes, W 19
    Luzon, W 56
    Matanzas and Santa Clara, W 58
    Medical, W 44, M 102
    Mindanao, W 72
    Missouri, W 20
    Navy, N 1, M 201, D 201
    Northeastern, W 86
    Ordnance, W 34, M 111
    Pay, W 36
    Pinor Del Rio, W 57
    Platte, W 22
    Porto Rico, W 23
    Post Office, P 1
    Processing, LC 30
    Quartermaster, W 39
    References, LC 29
    Santiago and Puerto Principe, W 59
    South, W 66
    Southeastern, W 84
    Southern, W 83
    State, S 1
    Subsistence, W 5
    Texas, W 24
    Transportation, TD 1
    Treasury, T 1
    Veterans Affairs, VA 1
    Virginia and North Carolina, W 67
    Visayas, W 80
    War, W 1
    Washington, W 52
    Western Cuba, W 60
Department Methods Committee, Y 3.D 44
Deposit Insurance Corporation, Federal, Y 3.F 31/8
Depository Library Council to the Public Printer, GP
        1.36
Descriptive Cataloging Division, LC 9
Design and Construction, Office of Engineering, Y 3.T
        25:1-15
Developing Institutions, Advisory Council on, ED
        1.16
Development Activity, Naval Ocean Research and, D
        210.100
Development Administration, Energy Research and, ER
        1
Development Advisory Board, International, Y 3.In 8/5
Development Agency, International, S 18
Development and Demonstration Program, Geothermal
        Energy, ER 1.31
Development and Information Technology, Office of
        Software, GS 12.16
Development and Learning, National Center for Early,
        ED 1.346
Development and Training, Center for Professional, HE
        20.7700

Enforcement Task Force Program, Organized Crime Drug, J 1.93
Engineer Agency for Resources Inventories, D 103.50
Engineer Department, W 7, M 110
Engineer School, M 110.400, D 103.100
Engineering and Instrumentation Branch, Biomedical, HE 20.3036/3
Engineering and Property Management Office, Facilities, HE 1.100
Engineering and Technology, Federal Coordinating Council for, PrEx 8.100
Engineering Bureau, N 19
Engineering, Bureau of Agricultural, A 70, A 77.100
Engineering, Bureau of Steam, N 19
Engineering Center, Air Force Civil, D 301.87
Engineering Center, Hydrologic, D 103.55
Engineering Design and Construction Office, Y 3.T 25:1-15
Engineering Development, National Council on Marine Resources and, PrEx 12
Engineering, Office of Rural, A 22
Engineering Program, Value, GS 6.10
Engineering Technical Information System, A 13.84/2
Engineers and Scientists for Federal Government Programs, President's Committee on, Pr 34.8:En 3
Engineers Corps, D 103
Engineers, President's Committee on, Pr 34.8:Sci 27
Engraving and Printing Bureau, T 18
Enrichment Corporation, United States, Y 3.En 2
Entitlement and Tax Reform Bipartisan Commission, Pr 42.8:B 52/F 49
Entombment of Bodies in Arlington Memorial Amphitheater, Commission on Erection of Memorials and, Y 3.Ar 1
Entomological Commission, A 8, I 26
Entomology and Plant Quarantine Bureau, A 56, A 77.300
Entomology and Plant Quarantine, Publications Relating to, A 77.300
Entomology Bureau, A 9
Entomology Division, A 9
Environment, President's Advisory Panel on Timber and the, Pr 37.8:T 48
Environment Research and Development Program, Interagency, EP 1.28/8
Environmental Cancer and Heart and Lung Diseases, Task Force on, EP 1.82
Environmental Control Administration, HE 20.1100
Environmental Control Technology Division, E 1.16
Environmental Data Service, C 55.200
Environmental Education, Advisory Council on, HE 5.95
Environmental Health and Engineering Office, HE 20.5301/2
Environmental Health Center, HE 20.7500
Environmental Health Sciences Institute, National, HE 20.3550
Environmental Health, National Center for, HE 20.7500
Environmental Health Service, HE 20.1000
Environmental Laboratory, Pacific Marine, C 55.601/2
Environmental Management, Bureau of Community, HE 20.2850
Environmental Protection Agency, EP
Environmental Quality Citizens Advisory Committee, Pr 37.8:En 8
Environmental Quality Council, PrEx 14
Environmental Research Laboratories, C 55.600
Environmental Research Laboratory–
    Duluth, EP 1.46/6
    Great Lakes, C 55.620
    Industrial, EP 1.46/5
    Municipal, EP 1.46/7
    Western, EP 1.14
Environmental Satellite, Data, and Information Service, National, C 55.200
Environmental Satellite Service, National, C 55.500
Environmental Science Services Administration, C 52
Epidemic Diseases Committee (Senate), Y 4.Ep 4/2
Epidemic Diseases, Select Committee on Origin, Introduction and Prevention of (House), Y 4.Ep 4/1
Epidemiology and Genetics, Division of Cancer, HE 20.3196
Equal Educational Opportunities, Select Committee on (Senate), Y 4.Eq 2
Equal Employment Opportunity Commission, Y 3.Eq 2
Equal Employment Opportunity Committee, President's, Pr 35.8:Em 7
Equal Employment Opportunity White House Conference, Y 3.W 58/13
Equal Opportunity in the Armed Forces, President's Committee on, Pr 35.8:Ar 5
Equal Opportunity, President's Council on, Pr 36.8:Eq 2

Equality of Educational Opportunity, National Advisory Council on, Y 3.Ed 8/7
Equipment and Recruiting Bureau, N 5
Equipment and Supplies Division, P 18
Equipment Bureau, N 5
Erection of Memorials and Entombment of Bodies in Arlington Memorial Amphitheater Commission, Y 3.Ar 1
Ericsson Memorial Commission, Y 3.Er 4
Escape of Grover Cleveland Bergdoll from Disciplinary Barracks at Governors Island, N.Y., Select Committee to Investigate, (House) Y 4.B 45/2
Establishment–
    National Archives, AE 1
    National Military, M 1
Establishment of the Seat of Government in Washington, Commission on the Centennial of, Y 4.C 333
Estimates and Appropriations Division, T 9
Ether Discovery, Select Committee on (House), Y 4.Et 3/1
Ether Discovery, Select Committee on (Senate), Y 4.Et 3/2
Ethical Problems in Medicine and Biomedical and Behavioral Research, President's Commission for the Study of, Pr 40.8:Et 3
Ethics Law Reform, President's Commission on Federal, Pr 41.8:Et 3
Ethics, Office of Government, Y 3.Et 3
Ethics, Select Committee on (House), Y 4.Et 3/2
Ethics, Select Committee on (Senate), Y 4.Et 3/4
Ethnology Bureau, American, SI 2
Etiology Division, Cancer, HE 20.3151/3
Europe, Commission on Security and Cooperation in, Y 4.Se 2
European Affairs Division, LC 31
European Division, LC 35, LC 43
Evaluation and Research, Center for Biologics, HE 20.4800
Evaluation Program, Army, D 101.20/2
Examination Council, Federal Financial Institutions, Y 3.F 49
Examiners Board, T 19
Excellence for Hispanic Americans, President's Advisory Commission on Educational, ED 1.87
Exchange Commission, Securities and, SE 1
Exchange, President's Commission on Executive, Pr 40.8/2
Execution without Trial in France, Special Committee to Investigate Charges of, Y 4.Ex 3
Executive Agencies of Government, Select Committee on Investigation of, Y 4.Ex 3/3
Executive Agencies, Special Committee to Investigate (House), Y 4.Ex 3/4
Executive Board, Federal, Y 3.F 31/20
Executive Branch of the Government Organization Commission, Y 3.Or 3, Y 3.Or 3/2
Executive Council, Y 3.Ex 3/2
Executive Departments, Joint Commission on Laws Organizing, Y 3.Ex 3
Executive Exchange, President's Commission on, Pr 40.8:Ex 3, Pr 40.8/2
Executive Institute, Treasury, T 1.1/4
Executive, Legislative, and Judicial Salaries Commission, Y 3.Ex 3/3
Executive Office for United States Attorneys, J 31
Executive Office of the President, PrEx 1
Executive Organization, President's Advisory Council on, Pr 37.8:Ex 3
Executive Papers, Committee on Disposition of (House), Y 4.Ex 3/2
Exhibits and Expositions, International, S 6
Exhibits Office, A 40
Expeditionary Forces, American, W 95
Expenditures in Department of Agriculture Committee (House), Y 4.Ex 7/1
Expenditures in Department of Commerce and Labor Committee (House), Y 4.Ex 7/2
Expenditures in Interior Department Committee (House), Y 4.Ex 7/3
Expenditures in Department of Justice Committee (House), Y 4.Ex 7/4
Expenditures in Navy Department Committee (House), Y 4.Ex 7/5
Expenditures in Post Office Department Committee (House), Y 4.Ex 7/6
Expenditures in Public Buildings Committee (House), Y 4.Ex 7/7
Expenditures in Senatorial Primary and General Elections (Senate), Y 4.Ex 7/12
Expenditures in State Department Committee (House), Y 4.Ex 7/8
Expenditures in the Executive Departments, Committee on, (House), Y 4.Ex 7/13

Expenditures in the Executive Departments, Committee on, (Senate), Y 4.Ex 7/14
Expenditures in Treasury Department Committee (House), Y 4.Ex 7/9
Expenditures in War Department Committee (House), Y 4.Ex 7/10
Expenditures in War Department, Select Committee (House), Y 4.Ex 7/11
Experiment Station, Hawaii Agricultural, A 10.9
Experiment Stations Office, A 10, A 77.400
Export Administration, C 61.24
Export Administration Bureau, C 63
Export Control Administrator, Y 3.Ex 7/2
Export Control Office, Y 3.Ec 74/2:100, C 49.200
Export Control, Select Committee on (House), Y 4.Ex 7/15
Export Council, President's, Pr 37.8:Ex 7, Pr 40.8:Ex 7
Export Development Bureau, C 57.100
Export Expansion Council, National, C 1.42/3
Export Expansion, Interagency Committee on, Y 3.In 8/22
Export Expansion, White House Conference, Y 3.W 58/8
Export Marketing Service, A 99
Export-Import Bank of the United States, Y 3.Ex 7/3
Export-Import Bank of Washington, Y 3.Ex 7/3
Exports Bureau, WT 3
Exports Control Committee, Y 3.Ex 1, Y 3.Ex 7
Exports Office, Y 3.Ec 74/2:101
Expositions and Exhibits, International, S 6
Express Companies, IC 1 exp
Extension and Continuing Education, National Advisory Council on, Y 3.Ex 8
Extension Service, A 43, A 80.300
Extension Service, Federal, A 43, A 80.300
Extension Work Office, Cooperative, A 43.5
Eye Council, National Advisory, HE 20.3752:R 31/4
Eye Institute, National, HE 20.3750

F

Facilities Bureau, FAA 4
Facilities Center, Research, C 55.601/4
Facilities Commission, (House), Y 4.In 3
Facilities Corporation, Federal, GS 7, T 69
Facilities Engineering and Construction Agency, HE 1.100
Facilities Engineering and Property Management Office, HE 1.100
Facilities Engineering Command, Naval, D 209
Facilities Safety Board, Defense Nuclear, Y 3.D 36/3
Facilities Service, Airway, TD 4.700
Facilities Service, Community, HH 5
Facts and Figures Office, Pr 32.4700
Fair Employment Practice Committee, Pr 32.412
Fair Market Value Policy for Federal Coal Leasing Commission, Y 3.C 63/3
Families Administration, HE 23.1000
Families, House Select Committee on, Y 4.C 43/2
Families, White House Conference on, Y 3.W 58/22
Family Planning, President's Committee on, Pr 36.8:P 81
Family Planning Service Center, HE 20.2900
Family Services Bureau, FS 14.200
Family Support Administration, HE 25
Famine Early Warning System, S 18.68
FAO-U.S. Interagency Committee, Y 3.Un 3/3
Farm Board, Federal, FF 1
Farm Credit Administration, A 72, A 79.100, FCA
Farm Credit System Insurance Corporation, Y 3.F 22/2
Farm Labor Conditions in the West, Special Committee to Investigate (Senate), Y 4.F 22
Farm Loan Bureau, Federal, T 48
Farm Management and Farm Economics Office, A 37
Farm Management Office, A 37
Farm Resources and Facilities Research Advisory Committee, A 1.103
Farm Security Administration, A 61, A 80.700
Farm Service Agency, A 112
Farm Tenancy Special Committee, Y 3.F 22
Farmer Cooperative Service, A 89
Farmers Home Administration, A 84
Farmers' Seed Loan Office, A 51
Federal Acquisitions Institute, PrEx 2.23
Federal Agency Classification Chiefs Workshop, PM 1.24
Federal Aid in Construction of Post Roads, Joint Committee on, Y 4.F 31
Federal Alcohol Administration, T 59
Federal Alcohol Control Administration, Y 3.F 31/10
Federal and State Laws Relating to Wiretapping and Electronic Surveillance, National Commission for Review of, Y 3.W 74/2
Federal Aviation Administration, TD 4

Federal Aviation Agency, FAA
Federal Board for Vocational Education, VE
Federal Board of Surveys and Maps, Y 3.Su 7
Federal Bureau of Investigation, J 1.14
Federal Bureau of Prisons, J 16
Federal Circuit, Court of Appeals for the, Ju 7
Federal Civil Defense Administration, FCD, Pr 33.800
Federal Civil Works Administration, Y 3.F 31/7
Federal Coal Leasing, Commission on Fair Market Value
    Policy for, Y 3.C 63/3
Federal Committee–
    Apprentice Training, Y 3.F 31/12
    Ecological Reserves, Y 3.F 31/22
    Pest Control, Y 3.F 31/18
    Research Natural Areas, Y 3.F 31/19
Federal Communications Commission, CC
Federal Communications Commission, Select Committee
    to Investigate (House), Y 4.F 31/4
Federal Compensation, President's Panel on, Pr 38.8:C
    73
Federal Coordinating Council for Science, Engineering,
    and Technology, PrEx 8.100
Federal Coordinator of Transportation, Y 3.F 31/6
Federal Council–
    Aging, Y 3.F 31/15
    Science and Technology, Y 3.F 31/16
Federal Court Appellate System, Commission on
    Revision of the, Y 3.Ap 4/3
Federal Credit Programs, Committee, Pr 35.8:C 86
Federal Credit Union Bureau, FS 3.300, HE 3.300
Federal Crop Insurance Corporation, A 62, A 76.100, A
    79.300, A 80.900, A 82.200
Federal Crop Insurance Program, Commission for the
    Improvement, Y 3.C 88Federal Deposit
    Insurance Corporation, Y 3.F 31/8
Federal Disaster Assistance Administration, HH 12
Federal Election Commission, Y 3.El 2/3
Federal Electric Railways Commission, Y 3.F 31
Federal Emergency Administration of Public Works, Y
    3.F 31/4
Federal Emergency Management Agency, FEM 1
Federal Emergency Relief Administration, Y 3.F 31/5
Federal Employees' Compensation Office, L 36.300
Federal Employment Stabilization Board, C 26
Federal Employment Stabilization Office, C 26
Federal Energy Administration, FE 1
Federal Energy Office, PrEx 21
Federal Energy Regulatory Commission, E 2
Federal Equal Opportunity Recruitment Program, PM
    1.42
Federal Ethics Law Reform, President's Commission, Pr
    41.8:Et 3
Federal Executive Board, Y 3.F 31/20
Federal Extension Service, A 43, A 80.300
Federal Facilities Corporation, GS 7, T 69
Federal Farm Board, FF
Federal Farm Loan Bureau, T 48
Federal Field Committee for Development Planning in
    Alaska, Y 3.Al 1s/4
Federal Financial Institutions Examination Council, Y
    3.F 49
Federal Fire Council, GS 1
Federal Fuel Distributor, Y 3.F 31/2
Federal Government Programs, President's Committee
    on Engineers and Scientists for, Pr 34.8:En 3
Federal Grain Inspection Service, A 104
Federal Health Program Service, HE 20.2700, HE
    20.5200
Federal Highway Administration, TD 2
Federal Holiday Commission, Y 3.H 71Federal Home
    Loan Bank Administration, NHA 3
Federal Home Loan Bank Board, Y 3.F 31/3, FL 3, HH
    4, FHL 1
Federal Horticulture Board, A 35
Federal Housing Administration, Y 3.F 31/11, FL 2,
    NHA 2, HH 2
Federal Housing Finance Board, FHF 1
Federal Inspector, Alaska Natural Gas Transportation
    System, Office of the, Y 3.F 31/23
Federal Insurance Administration, HH 10
Federal Insurance and Hazard Mitigation, FEM 1.200
Federal Interagency Committee–
    Education, Y 3.Ed 8
    International Year of Disabled Persons, Y 3.F 31/
    24
    Recreation, Y 3.F 31/14
Federal Interagency Council on Citizen Participation,
    Y 3.C 49/5
Federal Interagency Field Librarians Workshop, Y 3.L
    61/2
Federal Inter-Agency River Basin Committee, I 1.81, Y
    3.F 31/13
Federal Interagency Technical Committee, Pacific
    Southwest, Y 3.P 11/3
Federal Interdepartmental Safety Council, FIS

Federal Judicial Center, Ju 13
Federal Juvenile Delinquency Programs, Interdepart-
    mental Council to Coordinate All, Y 3.J 98
Federal Labor Relations Authority, Y 3.F 31/21-3
Federal Labor Relations Council, Y 3.F 31/21
Federal Law Enforcement Training Center, T 1.60
Federal Library and Information Center Committee, LC
    1.32/4
Federal Library Committee, LC 1.32/2
Federal Loan Agency, FL
Federal Maritime Board, C 39.100
Federal Maritime Commission, FMC
Federal Mediation and Conciliation Service, FM
Federal Mine Safety and Health Review Commission, Y
    3.M 66
Federal Motor Carrier Safety Administration, TD 2.300
Federal Narcotics Control Board, T 53
Federal National Mortgage Association, HH 6
Federal Ocean Program, Pr 39.12
Federal Office Space, Ad Hoc Committee on, Pr 35.8:Of
    2
Federal Officials, National Study Commission on
    Records and Documents of, Y 3.R 24/2
Federal Oil Conservation Board, I 1.67
Federal Paperwork, Commission, Y 3.P 19
Federal Pay, Advisory Committee on, Y 3.Ad 9/11
Federal Penal and Reformatory Institutions Special
    Committee, Y 4.F 31/3
Federal Power Commission, FP
Federal Preparedness Agency, GS 13
Federal Prevailing Rate Advisory Committee, Y 4.P 84/
    10-12
Federal Prison Industries, Inc., FPI
Federal Prisoners, Joint Committee to Determine what
    Employment may be Furnished, Y 4.F 31/2
Federal Procurement Policy Office, PrEx 2.21
Federal Public Housing Administration, NHA 4
Federal Radiation Council, Y 3.F 31/17
Federal Radio Administration, RC
Federal Radio Education Committee, FS 5.100
Federal Railroad Administration, TD 3
Federal Reconstruction and Development Planning
    Commission for Alaska, Y 3.Al 1s/3
Federal Regional Council, Pr 37.8:R 26
Federal Regional Council, Northwest, Y 3.N 81/5
Federal Register Division, AE 2
Federal Register Office, GS 4.100, AE 2.100
Federal Reserve Board, FR 1
Federal Reserve System Board of Governors, FR
Federal Retirement Thrift Investment Board, Y 3.F 31/25
Federal Safety Council, L 30
Federal Scientific and Technical Information,
    Clearinghouse for, C 51
Federal Security Agency, FS 1
Federal Service Impasses Panel, Y 3.F 31/21-2
Federal Service, President's Task Force on Employee-
    Management Relations in, Pr 35.8:Em 7/2
Federal State Action Committee, Joint, Pr 34.8:F 31
Federal Statistics, President's Commission on, Pr
    37.8:St 2
Federal Supply and Services Office, GS 2
Federal Supply Bureau, T 58
Federal Supply Service, GS 2
Federal Surplus Commodities Corporation, A 69
Federal Surplus Relief Corporation, Y 3.F 31/9
Federal Technology Service, GS 12
Federal Text Claims Committee, Interdepartmental, Y
    3.In 8/19
Federal Trade Commission, FT
Federal Transit Administration, TD 7
Federal Urban Areas Assistance Programs, Interdepart-
    mental Committee to Coordinate, Y 3.In 8/17
Federal Water Pollution Control Administration, FS 16,
    I 67
Federal Water Quality Administration, I 67
Federal Working Group on Pest Management, Y 3.P 43
Federal Works Agency, FW
Fellowships, President's Commission on White House,
    Pr 40.8:W 58
Fiber Investigations Office, A 11
Field Artillery Office, W 96
Field Division, Y 3.C 83:80
Field Service Branch, A 82.100
Fillmore, Millard, P 13
Finance and Administration Bureau, P 4
Finance Bureau, SB 10
Finance, Committee on (Senate), Y 4.F 49
Finance, Consumer, National Commission on, Y 3.C 76/
    2
Finance Department, M 116
Finance Division, Y 3.R 13/2:10
Finance, Interagency Task Force on Small Business, Y
    3.In 8/29
Finance Service, W 97
Financial Aid to Students, Advisory Council on, HE
    19.131

Financial Assistance, National Commission on Student,
    Y 3.St 9
Financial Institution Reform, Recovery and Enforce-
    ment, National Commission, Y 3.F 32
Financial Institutions Examination Council, Federal, Y
    3.F 49
Financial Operations, Bureau of Government, T 63.100
Financial Policies, National Advisory Council on
    International, Y 3.N 21/16
Financial Services, Committee on, Y 4.B 22/1, Y 4.F 49/
    20
Financial Services, Task Group on Regulation of, Pr
    40.8:F 49
Financing Administration, Health Care, HE 22
Financing for United States Corporations Operating
    Abroad, Task Force on Promoting Increased
    Foreign, Pr 35.8:F 76/3
Financial Management Service, T 63.100
Financing of Postsecondary Education, National
    Commission on, Y 3.Ed 8/5
Fine Arts Collection, National, SI 6
Fine Arts Commission, FA
Fine Arts Division, LC 25
Fire Academy, National, FEM 1.17/3
Fire Administration, United States, C 58, FEM 1.100
Fire Council, Federal, GS 1
Fire Prevention and Control Administration, National,
    C 58
Fire Prevention and Control, National Commission on,
    Y 3.F 51
Firearms, Bureau of Alcohol, Tobacco and, T 70
First Assistant Postmaster General, P 2
First Comptroller, T 13
Fiscal Relations Study Advisory Committee, Y 3.Ad 9
Fiscal Service, T 63
Fish and Fisheries Commission, FC 1
Fish and Wildlife Service, I 49
Fish Commission, FC
Fisheries Administration, Defense, I 54
Fisheries Bureau, C 6, I 45
Fisheries Center, Northwest, C 55.326
Fisheries Center, Southwest, C 55.303/2
Fisheries Commission, FC 1
Fisheries Commission, Northwest Indian, Y 3.N 81/7
Fisheries Committee (Senate), Y 4.F 53
Fisheries, Committee on Merchant Marine and (House),
    Y 4.M 53
Fisheries Development Program, Central, Western, and
    South Pacific, C 55.329
Fisheries Science Center, Northwest, C 55.331/3
Five Civilized Tribes Commissioner, I 1.11
Fixed Nitrogen Research Laboratory, A 38
Flight Standards Bureau, FAA 5
Flight Standards Service, TD 4.400
Flood Control Committee (House), Y 4.F 65
Fluid Dynamics Laboratory, Geophysical, C 55.601/5
Fogarty, John E., International Center for Advanced
    Study in the Health Sciences, HE 20.3700
Folklife Center, American, LC 39
Food Administration, Y 3.F 73
Food and Drug Administration, A 46, FS 7, FS 13.100,
    HE 20.1200, HE 20.4000
Food and Drug Inspection Board, A 32
Food and Feed Conservation Office, A 86
Food and Fiber National Advisory Commission, Pr
    36.8:F 73
Food and Nutrition Service, A 98
Food Distribution Administration, A 78, A 80.100
Food, Drug, and Insecticide Administration, A 46
Food Marketing National Commission, Y 3.N 21/22
Food, Nutrition, and Health White House Conference,
    Y 3.W 58/16
Food Production Administration, A 79, A 80.200
Food Production and Distribution Administration, A
    80
Food Products, Select Committee to Investigate use of
    Chemicals in, Y 4.F 73/2
Food Safety and Applied Nutrition Center, HE 20.4500
Food Safety and Inspection Service, A 110
Food Safety and Quality Service, A 103
Food Shortages, Special Committee to Investigate
    (House), Y 4.F 73
Foods Bureau, HE 20.4500
Ford, Gerald R., Pr 38
Foreign Affairs Committee (House), Y 4.F 76/1
Foreign Affairs National Academy, President's
    Advisory Panel, Pr 35.8:F 76/2
Foreign Agricultural Relations Office, A 67
Foreign Agricultural Service, A 64, A 67
Foreign Aid Program, Special Committee to Study
    (Senate), Y 4.F 76/6
Foreign Aid, Select Committee on (House), Y 4.F 76/5
Foreign and Domestic Commerce Bureau, C 18
Foreign Assessment Center, National, PrEx 3.10/7
Foreign Broadcast Information Service, Pr 34.650, PrEx
    7

Foreign Claims Settlement Commission, Y 3.F 76/3
Foreign Claims Settlement Commission of the United
    States, J 1.1/6
Foreign Commerce Bureau, S 4
Foreign Commerce, Committee on Interstate and,
    (House), Y 4.In 8/4
Foreign Direct Investments Office, C 54
Foreign Economic Administration, Pr 32.5800
Foreign Economic Development Service, A 100
Foreign Economic Policy Commission, Y 3.F 76/2
Foreign Funds Control, T 65
Foreign Intelligence Advisory Board, President's, Pr
    35.8:F 76
Foreign Investments in United States Corporate
        Securities and Foreign Financing for United
        States Corporations Operating Abroad, Task
        Force on Promoting Increase, Pr 35.8:F 76/3
Foreign Mails Division, P 8
Foreign Markets Division, A 12
Foreign Markets Section, A 12
Foreign Operations Administration, FO 1
Foreign Policy, Commission on Organization of the
        Government for the Conduct of, Y 3.F 76/5
Foreign Relations Committee (Senate), Y 4.F 76/2
Foreign Scholarships Board, Y 3.F 76/4
Foreign Science and Technology Center, U.S. Army, D
    101.79
Foreign Service Institute, S 1.114/3
Foreign Trade Board, East-West, Y 3.T 67
Foreign Trade, Special Adviser to the President on, Y
    3.F 76
Foreign-Trade Zones Board, FTZ
Forest and Range Experiment Station–
    Intermountain, A 13.65
    Northern Rocky Mountains, A 13.30
    Pacific Northwest, A 13.66
    Pacific Southwest, A 13.62
    Rocky Mountains, A 13.69
    Southwestern, A 13.43
Forest Experiment Station–
    Central States, A 13.68
    Lake States, A 13.61
    North Central, A 13.82
    Northeastern, A 13.42
    Northern, A 13.73
    Northwestern, A 13.67
    Southeastern, A 13.63
    Southern, A 13.40
Forest Management Program, A 13.152
Forest Products Laboratory, A 13.27
Forest Reservation Commission, National, Y 3.N 21/6
Forest Reservations and Protection of Game Committee
    (Senate), Y 4.F 76/3
Forest Service, A 13
Forestry Bureau, A 13
Forestry Committee (Senate), Y 4.Ag 8/3
Forestry, Committee on Agriculture and, Y 4.Ag 8/2
Forestry Division, A 13
Forestry, Joint Committee on Agriculture and, Y 4.Ag 8/
    2
Forestry Division, A 13
Forestry, Joint Committee on, Y 4.F 76/4
Form Center, Naval, D 212.1/2
Fort Leavenworth Military Prison, W 27
Fort Leavenworth Penitentiary, J 6
Fortifications and other Defense Board, Y 3.F 77
Fossil and Hydro Power Division, Y 3.T 25:48
Foundation–
    African Development, Y 3.Af 8
    Arts and Humanities, National, NF
    Hispanic, LC 24
    Inter-American, Y 3.In 8/25
    National Science, NS 1
Four Corners Regional Commission, Y 3.F 82
Fourth Assistant Postmaster General, P 5
Frankfort Arsenal, D 105.17
Franklin D. Roosevelt Library, GS 4.9
Franklin Delano Roosevelt Memorial Commission, Y
    3.R 67
Free Delivery Division, P 13
Freedmen's Hospital, I 1.12
Freedman's Savings and Trust Company, FST
Freer Gallery of Art, SI 7
Friendship Commission, Japan-United States, Y 3.J 27
Frost Effects Laboratory, D 103.31
Fuel Administration, Y 3.F 95
Fuel Distributor, Federal, Y 3.F 31/2
Fuel Situation in the Middle West, Special Committee
    to Investigate (Senate), Y 4.F 95
Fuels Commission, National Alcohol, Y 3.Al 1
Fund for Developmental Loan, Y 3.D 49
Fund for the Improvement of Post-Secondary Education,
    ED 1.23/2

G

Gallery, National Portrait, SI 11
Gambling, Commission on Review of the National
    Policy Toward, Y 3.G 14
Gardens and Ground Division, A 14
Garfield, James Abram, Pr 20
Gas and Oil Office, I 64
Gas Corporations, IC 1 gas
Gasoline and Fuel Oil Shortages, Special Committee to
    Investigate (Senate), Y 4.G 21
General Accounting Office, GA
General Counsel, A 33
General Land Office, I 21
General Medical Sciences Institute, National, HE
    20.3450
General Reference and Bibliography Division, LC 2
General Services Administration, GS
General Services Schools, W 28
General Staff, M 113
General Staff Corps, W 2
General Superintendent and Landscape Engineer of
    National Parks, I 1.58
General Supply Committee, GS, T 45
Genetics, Division of Cancer Epidemiology and, HE
    20.3196
Geographic Board, GB
Geographic Names Board, GB 1, I 33
Geographical and Geological Survey of the Rocky
    Mountain Region, (Powell), I 17
Geographical and Geological Survey of the Territories, I
    18
Geographical Surveys West of 100th Meridian
    (Wheeler), W 8
Geography and Map Division, LC 5
Geological Survey, I 19
Geological Survey, Coast and Geodetic Survey, and
        Hydrographic Office, Joint Commission to
        Consider the Present Organizations of, Y
        3.Si 2
Geological Survey of the Territories, I 19
Geophysical Data Center, National, C 55.201/2
Geophysical Fluid Dynamics Laboratory, C 55.601/5
George Rogers Clark Sesquicentennial Commission, Y
    3.G 29
Geothermal Energy Research, Development and
    Demonstration Program, ER 1.31
Gettysburg National Military Park Commission, W 46
Glacier National Park, I 1.52
Global Change, White House Conference on Science
        and Economics Research Related to, Pr
        41.8:G 51Goals beyond 1980, Interagency
        Task Force on Motor Vehicle, Y 3.M 85
Goals, National, Research Staff, Pr 37.8:N 21g
Gold and Silver Inquiry Commission (Senate), Y 4.G 56
Gold in Domestic and International Monetary Systems,
    Commission on the Role of, Y 3.G 57
Gore, Albert, PrVp 42
Government Activities Affecting Prices and Costs
    Committee, Y 3.G 74/3
Government Actuary, T 50
Government, Canal Zone, CZ 1
Government Contracts Committee, Pr 34.8:C 76/2
Government Contract Compliance Committee,
    President's, Pr 33.17
Government Employment Policy Committee,
    President's, Pr 34.8:Em 7
Government Ethics, Office, Y 3.Et 3
Government Financial Operations Bureau, T 63.100
Government Hospital for the Insane, I 1.14
Government Hospital for the Insane, Special Committee
    on Investigation of, Y 4.G 74
Government Housing Policies and Programs,
        President's Advisory Committee on, Pr
        34.8:H 81
Government National Mortgage Association, HH 1.1/7
Government Operations Committee (House), Y 4.G 74/
    7
Government Operations Committee (Senate), Y 4.G 74/
    6
Government Operations with Respect to Intelligence
        Activities, Select Committee to Study,
        (Senate), Y 4.In 8/17
Government Organization for the Conduct of Foreign
        Policy Commission, Y 3.F 76/5
Government Organization, Joint Committee on, Y 4.G
    74/4
Government Organization, Select Committee on
    (Senate), Y 4.G 74/5
Government Organization, Select Committee on
    (House), Y 4.G 74/3
Government Patents Board, Y 3.G 74

Government Printing Office, GP
Government Printing Office, Select Committee on
    Investigation of (Senate), Y 4.G 74/2
Government Procurement, Commission, Y 3.G 74/4
Government Publications Division Research Services,
    Serial and, LC 6
Government Reform, Committee on, Y 4.G 74/7
Government Reports Office, Pr 32.200, Pr 33.400
Government Research, Select Committee on (House), Y
    4.G 74/8
Government Security Commission, Y 3.G 74/2
Governmental Affairs Committee (Senate), Y 4.G 74/9
Governmental and Public Affairs Office, A 107
Government-Industry Special Task Force on Travel, Pr
    36.8:T 69
Grade and Salaries Committee, Y 3.G 75
Graduate Medical Education Council, Y 3.M 46/2
Grain Corporation, Y 3.W 56:10
Grain Futures Administration, A 41
Grain Inspection, Packers and Stockyards Administra-
    tion, A 113
Grain Inspection Service, Federal, A 104
Grant Memorial Commission, Y 3.G 76
Grant Program, Urban Development Action, HH 1.46/5
Grant, Ulysses Simpson, Pr 18
Grazing Control Division, I 38
Grazing Service, I 38
Great Lakes Basin Committee, Y 3.G 79/3
Great Lakes Environmental Research Laboratory, C
    55.620
Great Lakes Pilotage Administration, C 1.47
Great Lakes Pollution, International Reference Group
    on, Y 3.In 8/28:14
Great Lakes Research Advisory Board, Y 3.In 8/28:10
Great Lakes Science Advisory Board, Y 3.In 8/28:12
Great Lakes Water Quality, Committee on the
        Assessment of Human Health Effects of, Y
        3.In 8/28:15
Great Plains Committee, Y 3.G 79/2
Great Plains Drought Area Committee, Y 3.G 79
Great Plains, Northern, Resources Program, Y 3.N 81/4
Grizzly Bear Investigations, Interagency Study Team on
    Yellowstone, I 29.94
Group–
    Great Lakes Pollution from Land Use Activities,
        International Reference, Y 3.In 8/28:14
    Interagency Advisory, CS 1.87
    Interagency Regulatory Liaison, Y 3.R 26
    Interparliamentary Union, United States, Y 3.In 8/
        29-2
    Labor Management Working, LC 3.13
    Regulation of Financial Services, Task, Pr 40.8:F 49
    Regulatory Reform, Domestic Council Review, Pr
        38.8:R 26
    World Hunger Working, Pr 39.8:W 89
Grover Cleveland Bergdoll, Select Committee to
    Investigate the Escape of, Y 4.B 45/2
Guam Agricultural Experiment Station, A 10.22
Gulf Department, W 18
Gulf War Veterans' Illnesses, Presidential Advisory
    Committee on, Pr 42.8:Ad 9
Gun Foundry Board, Y 3.G 95

H

Habitat Conservation Program, C 55.340
Haiti and Santo Domingo Committee (Senate), Y 4.H 12
Halibut Commission, International Pacific, S 5.35
Handicapped, Committee for Purchase from (Senate), Y
    3.B 61
Handicapped, Committee on Purchase of Products and
    Services of, Y 3.P 97
Handicapped Employment Committee of the President,
    PrEx 1.10
Handicapped in Science and Technology Task Force, Y
    3.W 84/3
Handicapped Individuals Administration, HE 23.4000
Handicapped Individuals, White House Conference on,
    Y 3.W 58/18
Handicapped, National Advisory Committee on the, HE
    19.117
Handicapped, National Council on the, Y 3.H 19
Harbors Committee (House), Y 4.R 52
Harding, Warren Gamaliel, Pr 29
Harpers Ferry Invasion, Select Committee (Senate), Y
    4.H 23
Harriman Geographic Code System, Select Joint
    Committee on, Y 4.H 23/2
Harrison, Benjamin, Pr 23
Harrison, William Henry, Pr 9
Harry Diamond Laboratories, D 105.14/5
Hatch, Davis, Select Committee Appointed to
    Investigate Memorial of, Y 4.H 28
Hawaii Agricultural Experiment Station, A 10.9

Hawaii Department, W 81
Hawaii, Governor, I 1.41
Hawaii, Joint Committee on, Y 4.H 31
Hawaiian Commission, Y 3.H 31
Hawaiians Study Commission, Native, Y 3.H 31/2
Hayes, Rutherford Birchard, Pr 19
Hazardous Materials Transportation, Office of, TD 9.3
Head Start and Child Development Bureau, HE 21.100
Head Start and Child Service Programs Bureau, HE
    20.200
Head Start Bureau, HE 1.800, HE 23.1100
Health Administration, Occupational Safety and, L 35
Health, Administration on Mine, L 38
Health and Engineering, Office of Environmental, HE
    20.5301/2
Health and Human Services, Department of, HE 1
Health and Resources Development Bureau, Maternal
    and Child, HE 20.9200
Health and Safety Laboratory, ER 1.27
Health and Science, Office of Public, HE 20
Health and Welfare Activities, Interdepartmental
    Committee to Coordinate, Y 3.In 8/3
Health Board, National, T 29
Health Care Delivery and Assistance Bureau, HE
    20.5100, HE 20.9100
Health Care Facilities Service, HE 20.2500, HE
    20.6400
Health Care Financing Administration, HE 22
Health Care Policy and Research, Agency for , HE
    20.6500
Healthcare, Research and Quality, Agency for, HE
    20.6500
Health, Education, and Welfare Department, FS 1, HE 1
Health Education, Bureau of, HE 20.7200
Health, Education, Labor and Pensions, Committee on,
    Y 4.L 11/4
Health Education, President's Committee on, Pr 37.8:H
    34
Health Effects of Great Lakes Water Quality, Committee
    on the Assessment of Human, Y 3.In 8/28:15
Health Facilities Advisory Commission of the
    President, Pr 36.8:H 34/2
Health Facilities Bureau, HE 20.6700
Health Facilities Compliance and Conversion Bureau,
    HE 20.6700
Health Facilities Planning and Construction Service,
    HE 20.2500
Health Institutes, National, HE 20.3000
Health Laboratory, CSU-PHS Collaborative
    Radiological, HE 20.4119, HE 20.4600
Health Maintenance Organization Service, HE 20.2050
Health Maintenance Organizations and Resources
    Development Bureau, HE 20.9200
Health Manpower Bureau, HE 20.6600
Health Manpower Education Bureau, HE 20.3100
Health Manpower National Advisory Commission, Pr
    36.8:H 34
Health, National Center for Devices and Radiological,
    HE 20.4600
Health, National Center for Environmental, HE 20.7500
Health Needs of the Nation Commission, President's,
    Pr 33.19
Health Planning and Development, National Council
    on, HE 20.6001/5:H 34
Health Planning and Resources Development Bureau,
    HE 20.6100
Health Planning, Bureau of, HE 20.6100
Health Professional Scholarship Program, VA, VA 1.63
Health Professions Bureau, HE 20.6600, HE 20.9300
Health Professions Education and Manpower Training
    Bureau, HE 20.3100
Health Programs Service, Federal, HE 20.2700, HE
    20.5200
Health Promotion and Education Center, HE 20.7600
Health Promotion, National Center for Chronic Disease
    Prevention and, HE 20.7600
Health Research Center, Naval, D 206.22
Health Resources Administration, HE 20.6000
Health Resources Advisory Committee, National, GS
    13.9
Health Resources and Services Administration, HE
    20.9000
Health Resources Development, Bureau of, HE 20.6100,
    HE 20.9500
Health Resources Opportunity Office, HE 20.6001/3
Health Review Commission, Federal Mine, Y 3.M 66
Health Sciences, John E. Fogarty International Center
    for Advanced Study in, HE 20.3700
Health Service–
    Animal and Plant, A 101
    Community, HE 20.2550
    Environmental, HE 20.1000
    Indian, HE 20.2650, HE 20.5300, HE 20.9400
    Maternal and Child, HE 20.2750
    Navajo Area Indian, HE 20.9413
    Public, FS 2, HE 20, T 27

Health Services Administration, HE 20.5000
Health Services and Mental Health Administration, HE
    20.2000
Health Services, National Center for, HE 20.6500
Health Services Research and Development, National
    Center for, HE 20.2100
Health Services Research and Evaluation Bureau, HE
    20.6500
Health Standards and Quality Bureau, HE 22.200
Health Statistics, National Center for, HE 20.2200, HE
    20.6200
Health, Welfare, and Related Defense Activities
    Coordinator's Office, FS 8
Health, White House Conference, Y 3.W 58/14
Heart and Lung Diseases, Task Force on Environmental,
    EP 1.82
Heart and Lung Institute, National, HE 20.3200
Heart Disease, Cancer, and Stroke Commission of the
    President, Pr 36.8:H 35
Heart, Lung, and Blood Institute, National, HE
    20.3200
Heritage Conservation and Recreation Service, I 70
High Commission, International, T 1.23
High School, President's Committee on Education
    beyond, Pr 34.8:Ed 3
Higher Education and Black Colleges and Universities,
    National Advisory Committee, HE 19.140
Higher Education Task Force, Pr 37.8:Ed 8
Highway Administration, Federal, TD 2
Highway Commission, Alaska International Rail and, Y
    3.Al 1s
Highway Program, National, President's Advisory
    Committee on, Pr 34.8:H 53
Highway Safety Advisory Committee, National, TD
    1.13/2
Highway Safety Board, Interdepartmental, Y 3.In 8/18
Highway Safety Bureau, National, TD 2.200
Highway Safety, President's Task Force on, Pr 37.8:H
    53
Highway Traffic Safety Administration, National, TD 8
Highways Transport Committee, Y 3.C 83:20
Hirshhorn Museum and Sculpture Garden, SI 13
Hispanic Americans, President's Advisory Commis-
    sion on Educational Excellence, ED 1.87
Hispanic Foundation, LC 24
Historic Preservation Advisory Council, Y 3.H 62
Historical Association, White House, Y 3.Y 62/4
Historical Center, Naval, D 221
Historical Data Recovery Program, I 29.59/4
Historical Division, W 110, M 103, D 114
Historical Publications and Records Commission,
    National, AE 1.114
Historical Society, United States Capitol, Y 3.H 62/2
Historical Society, U.S. Supreme Court, Y 3.H 62/3
Historically Black Colleges and Universities, White
    House Initiative, ED 1.89
History and Technology, National Museum of, SI 3
History, Center for Air Force, D 301.82/7
History, Center of Military, D 114
History, National Museum of American, SI 3
History, Office of the Chief of Military, D 114
HIV/AIDS Bureau, HE 20.9500
HIV, STD, and TB Prevention, Center for, HE 20.7301
HMO's and Resource Development Bureau, HE
    20.9200
Holiday Commission, Federal, Y 3.H 71Holmes, Oliver
    Wendell, Devise, Permanent Committee for, Y
    3.H 73
Holocaust Memorial Council, United States, Y 3.H 74
Holocaust, President's Commission on, Pr 39.8:H 74
Home Economics and Human Nutrition, Publications
    Relating to, A 77.700
Home Economics Bureau, A 42, A 77.700
Home Loan Bank Administration, Federal, NHA 3
Home Loan Bank Board, Federal, Y 3.F 31/3, FL 3, HH
    4, FHL 1
Homeless Interagency Council, Y 3.H 75
Homes Commission, Y 3.H 75
Hoover, Herbert, Pr 31
Horticulture Board, Federal, A 35
Horticulture, Publications Relating to, A 77.500
Hostage Compensation, President's Commission on, Pr
    40.8:H 79
Hot Springs Reservation, I 1.17
Hot Springs Reservation Commission, I 1.15
Hot Springs Reservation Improvement Office, I 1.16
Hour Division, L 36.200
Hour Division, Wage and, L 36
Hours of Service Division, IC 1 hou
House Administration Committee (House), Y 4.H 81/3
House of Representatives, Y 1.2
House of Representatives, Commission to Supervise
    Construction of Building for Offices for, Y
    3.H 81
House Resolution 1, Select Committee Pursuant to
    (House), Y 4.H 81/5

House Restaurant, Select Committee on (House), Y 4.H
    81/6
House Restaurant, Special Committee to Investigate
    Management and Control of, Y 4.H 81/2
House Rooms Distribution Select Committee (House),
    Y 4.H 81
House Select Committee on Children, Youth, and
    Families, Y 4.C 43/2
Housing Administration, Y 3.F 31/11, FL 2, NHA 2,
    HH 2
Housing Administration, Public, HH 3
Housing Agency, National, NHA
Housing and Home Finance Agency, HH 1
Housing and Urban Affairs, Committee on Banking,
    (Senate), Y 4.B 22/3
Housing and Urban Development Department, HH 1
Housing Assistance Administration, HH 3
Housing Authority, FW 3, I 40
Housing Committee, Central, Y 3.C 33/3
Housing Corporation, L 8
Housing Expediter Office, Y 3.H 81/2
Housing Joint Committee, Y 4.H 81/4
Housing Office, Multi-Family, HH 13
Housing Policies and Programs, President's Advisory
    Committee on Government, Pr 34.8:H 81
Housing, President's Commission on, Pr 40.8:H 81
Housing, Public, Management Improvement Program,
    HH 1.63
Housing Service, Rural, A 115
Howard University, I 1.18
Human Development Office, HE 1.700
Human Development Services, Office of, HE 23
Human Health Effects of Great Lakes Water Quality,
    Committee on the Assessment of, Y 3.In 8/
    28:15
Human Needs, Select Committee on Nutrition and
    (Senate), Y 4.N 95
Human Nutrition and Home Economics Bureau, A
    77.700
Human Nutrition Information Service, A 111
Human Nutrition, Publications Relating to, A 77.700
Human Resources Committee (Senate), Y 4.H 88, Y 4.L
    11/4
Human Resources Laboratory, Air Force, D 301.45/27
Human Rights Year Observance Commission of the
    President, Pr 36.8:H 88
Human Services, Department of Health and, HE 1
Human Subjects of Biomedical and Behavioral
    Research, National Commission for the
    Protection of, Y 3.H 88
Human Systems Division, D 301.45/38-2
Humanities Endowment, National, NF 3
Humanities, National Foundation of the Arts and the,
    NF 1
Humanities, Presidential Task Force on , Pr 40.8:Ar 7
Hungarian Refugee Relief, President's Advisory
    Committee on, Pr 34.8:H 89
Hunger (Senate), Select Committee on, Y 4.H 89
Hunger Working Group, World, Pr 39.8:W 89
Hurricane Research Laboratory, National, C 55.601/3
Hydro Power Division, Y 3.T 25:48
Hydrodynamics, Numerical Ship, International
    Conference, D 211.9/5
Hydrographic Office, N 6, M 202, D 203
Hydrographic Office, Joint Commission to Consider the
    Present Organization of, Y 3.Si 2
Hydrographic/Topographic Center, D 5.317
Hydrography Bureau, N 18
Hydrologic Engineering Center, D 103.55

I

Idaho, Governor, I 1.19
Illnesses, Presidential Advisory Committee on Gulf
    War Veterans', Pr 42.8:Ad 9
Imagery and Mapping Agency, National, D 5.300
Immigrant Policy, Immigration and, Y 3.2:IM 6/AM 3
Immigration and Immigrant Policy, Y 3.2:IM 6/AM 3
Immigration and Naturalization Bureau, C 7
Immigration and Naturalization Commission,
    President's, Pr 33.18
Immigration and Naturalization Committee (House), Y
    4.Im 6/1
Immigration and Naturalization Service, J 21, L 15
Immigration and Refugee Policy, Select Commission on,
    Y 3.Im 6/2
Immigration Bureau, L 3, T 21
Immigration Commission, Y 3.Im 6
Immigration Committee (Senate), Y 4.Im 6/2
Immunization Program, National, HE 20.7960
Impact Assessment Program, Climatic, TD 1.38
Impasses Panel, Federal Service, Y 3.F 31/21-2
Impeachment Trial Committee, Senate, Y 4.Im 7/2
Imports Bureau, WT 4

Improper Activities in Labor Management Field, Select Committee on (Senate), Y 4.Im 7
Improvement Center, Educational, ED 1.300
Improvement of Post-Secondary Education, Fund, ED 1.23/2
Improvement of the Federal Crop Insurance Program Commission, Y 3.C 88
Improvement, President's Council on Management, Pr 40.8:M 31
Improvement Program, Public Housing Management, HH 1.63
Income Maintenance Programs Commission of the President, Pr 36.8:In 2
Increased Industrial use of Agricultural Products Commission, Y 3.In 2/7
Independent Study Center, National, CS 1.92
Indian Affairs Bureau, I 20
Indian Affairs Committee (House), Y 4.In 2/1
Indian Affairs Committee (Senate), Y 4.In 2/2
Indian Affairs, Joint Commission to Investigate, Y 3.In 2/3
Indian Affairs Office, I 20
Indian Affairs, Joint Commission to Investigate, Y 3.In 2/3
Indian Affairs, Select Committee on, (Senate), Y 4.In 2/11
Indian, American, Policy Review Commission, Y 4.In 2/10
Indian Bureau, Joint Committee on Transfer of, Y 4.In 2/3
Indian Claims Commission, Y 3.In 2/6
Indian Currency Commission (Great Britain), Y 3.In 2/1
Indian Depreciation Claims Assistant Attorney General, J 3
Indian Depredations Committee (Senate), Y 4.In 2/4
Indian Education, National Advisory Council on, Y 3.In 2/10
Indian Education, White House Conference on, Y 3.W 58/23
Indian Fisheries Commission, Northwest, Y 3.N 81/7
Indian Health Service, HE 20.300, HE 20.2650, HE 20.5300, HE 20.9400
Indian Health Service, Navajo Area, HE 20.9413
Indian Inspector for Indian Territory, I 1.20
Indian Opportunity National Council, Y 3.In 2/9
Indian Reservation Economies, Presidential Commission on, Pr 40.8:In 2
Indian Service Investigation Committee, Y 4.In 2/9
Indian Territory, Select Committee to Investigate Matters Connected with Affairs in (Senate), Y 4.In 2/5
Indian Tribes, Joint Special Committee on Conditions of, Y 4.In 2/6
Indochina Refugees, Interagency Task Force, Pr 38.8:R 25
Indoor Air, Office of Radiation and, EP6
Industrial Alcohol Bureau, T 54
Industrial Analysis Committee, Y 3.In 2/5
Industrial Arts and Expositions Committee (House), Y 4.In 2/7
Industrial Chemistry Bureau, A 77.100
Industrial Commission, Y 3.In 2/2
Industrial Cooperation Coordinator, Y 3.C 78
Industrial Competitiveness, President's Commission on, Pr 40.8:C 73
Industrial Economics, Bureau of, C 62
Industrial Energy Efficiency Improvement Program, E 1.47
Industrial Environmental Research Laboratory, EP 1.46/5
Industrial Expositions Committee (Senate), Y 4.In 2/8
Industrial Mobilization and Security, Publications Relating to, D 3
Industrial Peace, National Commission for, Y 3.In 2/11
Industrial Pollution Control Council, National, Y 3.In 2/8
Industrial Relations Commission, Y 3.In 2/4
Industrial Relations Office, M 204, D 204
Industrial World Ahead, White House Conference on, Y 3.W 58/17
Industry and Security, Bureau of, C 63
Industry and Trade Administration, C 57
Industry, Bureau of Dairy, A 44
Industry, Bureau of Plant, A 77.500
Industry Cooperation Office, C 38
Industry-Government Special Task Force on Travel, Pr 36.8:T 69
Infectious Diseases Center, HE 20.7800
Infectious Diseases, National Center for, HE 20.7800
Infectious Diseases, National Institute of Allergy and, HE 20.3250
Infectious Diseases Program, HE 20.3263
Information Administration, Energy, E 3
Information Administration, National, C 60
Information Advisory Commission, Y 3.Ad 9/7
Information Agency, Armed Services Technical, D 10

Information Agency of the United States, IA
Information Analysis Center, Pavements and Soil Trafficability, D 103.24/12
Information and Education, Armed Forces Office, D 2
Information and Education Division, W 111
Information and Education Service, L 9
Information and Facilities Commission, (House), Y 4.In 3
Information and Statistics Service, National Criminal Justice, J 26.10
Information Center–
  Aeronautical, D 301.59
  Consumer, GS 11
  Defense Technical , D 10
  Educational Resources, ED 1.301/2
  Federal, LC 1.32/4
  Technical, TD 1.3/2
Information Clearinghouse, National Air Toxics, EP 4.23
Information Committee, Public, Y 3.P 96/3
Information Coordinating Committee, National Occupational, Y 3.Oc 1/2
Information Coordinator, Y 3.C 78/3
Information Division–
  Aerospace, LC 38
  Air, LC 38
  Department of Agriculture, A 21
  Department of Interior, I 43
  Naturalization Service, C 7.11
  Public, D 115
Information, National Clearinghouse on Child Abuse and Neglect, HE 23.1216
Information Office for the Armed Forces, D 2
Information, Office of, A 21
Information Office, Public, D 6, M 118
Information Resources Management Office, GS 12
Information Science, National Commission on Libraries and, Y 3.L 61
Information Service–
  Armed Forces, D 2
  Human Nutrition, A 111
  Foreign Broadcast, PrEx 7
  National Environmental Satellite, C 55.200
Information Service Center, Regulatory, PrEx 25
Information Services, Armed Forces, D 2
Information Services, White House Conference on, Y 3.W 58/20
Information System, Engineering Technical, A 13.84/2
Information Systems, Technical, A 106.100
Information Technology, Office of Software, GS 12.16
Infrastructure Committee (House), Y 4.T 68/2
Inhalation Toxicology Research Institute, E 1.1/6
Initiative on Cancer, National Black Leadership, HE 20.3195
Initiative on Historically Black Colleges and Universities, White House, ED 1.89
Initiatives, President's Task Force on Private Sector, Pr 40.8:P 93
Injury Prevention and Control, National Center for, HE 20.7950
Inland and Coastwise Waterways Service, W 101
Inland Waterways Corporation, C 29, W 103
Insecticide and Fungicide Board, A 34
Inspection, Bureau of Navigation and Steamboat, C 25
Inspection, Grain, Packers and Stockyards Administration, A 113
Inspection Service, Federal Grain, A 104
Inspector, Alaska Natural Gas Transportation System, Office of the Federal, Y 3.F.31/23
Inspector, Bureau of Chief Postal, P 24
Inspector General Office–
  Agricultural Research Service, A 1.1/3
  Air Force, D 306
  Department of Energy, E 1.1/2
  Department of Health and Human Services, HE 1.1/2
  Department of Housing and Urban Development, HH 1.1/2
  DOD, D 1.1/9
  Justice Department, J 1.1/9
  National Archives and Records Administration, AE 1.101/2
Inspector General's Department, W 9
Inspectors Division of the Post Office, P 14
Institute–
  Aging, National, HE 20.3850
  Alcohol Abuse and Alcoholism, National, HE 20.8300
  Allergy and Infectious Diseases, National, HE 20.3250
  Armed Forces Radiobiology Research, D 15
  Arthritis and Metabolic Diseases, National, HE 20.3300
  Arthritis and Musculoskeletal and Skin Diseases, National, HE 20.3900

Arthritis, Metabolism and Digestive Diseases, National, HE 20.3300
Behavioral and Social Sciences, Army Research, D 101.60, D 101.60/3, D 101.60/6
Behavioral and Social Sciences, U.S. Army Research, D 101.1/7
Cancer, National, HE 20.3150
Child Health and Human Development, National, HE 20.3350
Computer Sciences and Technology, C 13.73
Corrections, National, J 16.100
Deafness and Other Communication Disorders, National, HE 20.3650
Dental Research, National, HE 20.3400
Diabetes and Digestive and Kidney Diseases, National, HE 20.3300
DoD Computer, D 5.414
Drug Abuse, National, HE 20.3950
Education, National, HE 18, HE 19.200, ED 1.300
Emergency Management, FEM 1.17/2
Environmental Health Sciences, National, HE 20.3550
Eyes, National, HE 20.3750
Federal Acquisitions, PrEx 2.23
Foreign Service, S 1.114/3
General Medical Sciences, National, HE 20.3450
Heart and Lung, National, HE 20.3200
Justice, National, J 28
Juvenile Justice and Delinquency Prevention, National, J 26.1/2
Law Enforcement and Criminal Justice, National, J 26.1/3
Literacy, National, Y 3.L 71
Lunar and Planetary, NAS 1.67
Management Sciences, CS 1.3/2
Medicaid Management, HE 22.112
Mental Health, National, HE 20.2400, HE 20.3800
Museum Services, MuS 1, NF 4
National Heart, Lung, and Blood, HE 20.3200
National Strategic Studies, D 5.417
Neurological and Communicative Disorders and Stroke, National, HE 20.3500
Neurological Diseases and Stroke, National, HE 20.3500
Occupational Safety and Health, National, HE 20.2800, HE 20.7100
Pathology, Armed Forces, D 1.16/4, D 101.117/5
Research, Letterman Army, D 104.29
Standards and Technology, National, C 13
Telecommunication Sciences, C 60.14
Treasury Executive, T 1.1/4
Tropical Forestry, A 13.64
Water Resources, D 103.57
Institute of Peace, United States, Y 3.P 31
Institute, Inhalation Toxicology Research, E 1.1/6
Institutes of Health, National, FS 2.22, HE 20.3000
Institutional Eligibility, Advisory Committee on, ED 1.13
Institutional Eligibility, Advisory Committee on Accreditation, HE 19.130
Instrumentation Branch, Biomedical, HE 20.3036/3
Insular Affairs Bureau, W 6
Insular Affairs Committee, Y 4.In 7/1
Insular Affairs, Committee on Interior and (House), Y 4.In 8/14
Insular Affairs, Committee on Interior and (Senate), Y 4.In 8/13
Insurance Administration, Federal, HH 10
Insurance and Hazard Mitigation, Federal, FEM 1.200
Insurance Corporation, Farm Credit System, Y 3.F 22/2
Insurrectionary States, Late, Joint Select Committee to Inquire into the Condition of Affairs in, Y 4.In 7/2
Integrity and Efficiency, President's Council on, Pr 40.8:In 8, Pr 40.8/3, Pr 41.8/3
Integrity, Office of Research, HE 20.1/3
Intelligence Activities, Select Committee to Study Government Operations with Respect to, (Senate), Y 4.In 8/17
Intelligence Agency, Central, Pr 33.650, Pr 34.600
Intelligence Agency, Defense, D 5.200
Intelligence Consumers Committee, National Narcotics, Y 3.N 16
Intelligence Division, M 106
Intelligence, Military, Division, W 100
Intelligence Office, Naval, N 13
Intelligence School, Defense, D 5.210
Intelligence, Select Committee on, (House), Y 4.In 8/18
Intelligence, Select Committee on, (Senate), Y 4.In 8/19
Interagency Advisory Group, CS 1.87
Interagency Classification Review Committee, Y 3.C 56
Interagency Committee–
  Agricultural Surplus Disposal, Y 3.In 8/11
  Arkansas-White-Red Basins, Y 3.F 31/13-2
  Automatic Data Processing, Y 3.In 8/16

Education, Federal, Y 3.Ed 8
Export Expansion, Y 3.In 8/22
Intermodal Cargo, Y 3.In 8/26
International Athletics, Y 3.In 8/20
International Year of Disabled Persons, Federal, Y 3.F 31/24
Mexican American Affairs, Y 3.In 8/23
Missouri Basin, Y 3.M 69
Pacific Southwest, Y 3.P 11/2
Uniform Civil Rights Policies and Practices, Y 3.C 49/4
Water Resources, Y 3.In 8/8
Women's Business Enterprise, Pr 40.8:W 84, SBA 1.31
Interagency Coordinating Committee, Arthritis, HE 20.3032
Interagency Council on Citizen Participation, Federal, Y 3.C 49/5
Interagency Council on the Homeless, Y 3.H 75
Interagency Energy-Environment Research and Development Program, EP 2.38/8
Interagency Field Librarian Workshop, Federal, Y 3.L 61/2
Interagency Land Acquisition Conference, Y 3.L 22
Interagency Racial Data Committee, Y 3.R 11
Interagency Radiation Research and Policy Coordination Committee, P 1.15
Interagency Regulatory Liaison Group, Y 3.R 26
Interagency Study Team on Yellowstone Grizzly Bear Investigations, I 29.94
Interagency Task Force–
Acid Precipitation, Y 3.In 8/31
Indochina Refugees, Pr 38.8:R 25
Motor Vehicle Goals Beyond 1980, Y 3.M 85
Product Liability, C 1.66/2
Small Business Finance, Y 3.In 8/29
Synthetic Fuels Commercialization, Pr 37.8:En 2/2
Interagency Technical Committee, Pacific Southwest Federal, Y 3.P 11/3
Inter-American Affairs Office, Pr 32.4600
Inter-American Foundation, Y 3.In 8/25
Interbureau Committee–
Forage, A 1.49
Post-War Programs, A 1.63
Interdepartmental Committee–
Children and Youth, Y 3.In 8/6
Civilian Compensation, Y 3.In 8/14
Coordinate Federal Urban Area Assistance Programs, Y 3.In 8/17
Coordinate Health and Welfare Activities, Y 3.In 8/3
Narcotics, Y 3.In 8/9
Nutrition for National Defense, Y 3.In 8/13
Radiation Preservation of Food, Y 3.In 8/12
Scientific Research and Development, Y 3.In 8/4
Status of Women, Y 3.In 8/21
Study of Jurisdiction over Federal Areas within the States, Y 3.In 8/10
Interdepartmental Council to Coordinate all Federal Juvenile Delinquency Programs, Y 3.J 98
Interdepartmental Federal Text Claims Committee, Y 3.In 8/19
Interdepartmental Highway Safety Board, Y 3.In 8/18
Interdepartmental Safety Council, Federal, FIS
Interdepartmental Social Hygiene Board, Y 3.In 8/2
Intergovernmental Advisory Council on Education, Y 3.Ed 8/9Intergovernmental Relations Advisory Commission, Y 3.Ad 9/8
Intergovernmental Relations Commission, Y 3.In 8/7
Interim Compliance Panel, Y 3.C 73/4
Interior and Insular Affairs Committee (House), Y 4.In 8/14
Interior and Insular Affairs Committee (Senate), Y 4.In 8/13
Interior Department, I 1
Interior Department and Forestry Service, Joint Committee to Investigate, Y 4.In 8/8
Interior Department Auditor, T 5
Interior Department Solicitor, I 48
Intermodal Cargo, Interagency Committee on, Y 3.In 8/26
Intermountain Forest and Range Experiment Station, A 13.65
Internal Improvements Select Committee (House), Y 4.In 8/7
Internal Revenue Bureau, T 22
Internal Revenue Bureau, Select Committee on Investigation of, Y 4.In 8/10
Internal Revenue Division, T 42
Internal Revenue Frauds, Select Committee on (House), Y 4.In 8/2
Internal Revenue Service, T 22
Internal Revenue Taxation, Joint Committee on, Y 4.In 8/11
Internal Security Committee (House), Y 4.In 8/15
International Agricultural Development Service, A 95

International Athletics Interagency Committee, Y 3.In 8/20
International Broadcasting, Board for, Y 3.B 78
International Business Administration, C 57
International Business Operations Bureau, C 48
International Center for Scholars, SI 12
International Commerce Bureau, C 42, C 57.100
International Committee on Status of Women, Y 3.In 8/21
International Communication Agency, ICA 1
International Conference on Numerical Ship Hydrodynamics, D 211.9/5
International Congresses, Conferences, and Commissions, S 5
International Cooperation Administration, S 17
International Cooperation White House Conference, Y 3.W 58/11
International Development Advisory Board, Y 3.In 8/5
International Development Agency, S 18
International Development Center, Y 3.T 25:1-17
International Economic Policy, Council on, Pr 37.8:In 8/3, Pr 38.8:In 8
International Economics Policy and Research Bureau, C 57.26
International Economics Programs Office, C 49.300
International, Educational and Cultural Affairs Advisory Commission, Y 3.Ad 9/9
International Exchange Commission, Y 3.In 8
International High Commission, T 1.23
International Information Programs, S 20
International Joint Commission, Y 3.In 8/28
International Labor Affairs Bureau, L 29
International Labor Affairs Office, L 29
International Law, Private, Secretary of State's Advisory Committee on, S 1.130
International Migration and Cooperative Economic Development, Commission for the Study of, Y 3.M 58/2International Monetary and Financial Policies, National Advisory Council on, Y 3.N 21/16
International Monetary and Financial Problems National Advisory Council, Y 3.N 21/16
International Monetary Systems, Commission on the Role of Gold in, Y 3.G 57
International Pacific Halibut Commission, S 5.35
International Postal Service Division, P 8
International Postal Transport Division, P 8
International Programs Bureau, C 49
International Rail and Highway Commission, Alaska, Y 3.Al 1s
International Reference Group on Great Lakes Pollution from Land Use Activities, Y 3.In 8/28:14
International Relations, Committee on, (House), Y 4.In 8/16
International Rules of Judicial Procedure Commission, Y 3.In 8/15
International Services Bureau, Transportation and, P 10
International Trade Administration, C 61
International Trade Commission, ITC 1
International Trade and Investment Policy, Commission on, Pr 37.8:In 8/2
International Trade Commission, TC 1
International Trade Fairs Office, C 44, C 48.100
International Trade Operations Office, C 34
International Trade, United States Court of, Ju 9
International Waterways Commission, W 68
International Women's Year, National Commission on the Observance of, Y 3.W 84
International Year of Disabled Persons, Federal Interagency Committee, Y 3.F 31/24
International Year of the Child, U.S. National Commission on, Y 3.C 43/3
International Youth Exchange, President's Council for, Pr 40.8:Y 8
Interoceanic Canal Committee (Senate), Y 4.In 8/1
Interparliamentary Union, United States Group, Y 3.In 8/29-2
Interregional Highway Committee, National, Y 3.N 21/15
Interstate and Foreign Commerce Committee (House), Y 4.In 8/4
Interstate and Foreign Commerce Committee (Senate), Y 4.In 8/3
Interstate Commerce Commission, IC
Interstate Commerce Joint Subcommittee, Y 4.In 8/9
Interstate Commission on the Potomac River Basin, Y 3.In 8/24
Interstate Migration of Destitute Citizens, Select Committee on (House), Y 4.In 8/12
Intramural Research Program, Mental Health, HE 20.8136
Invalid Pensions Committee (House), Y 4.In 8/5
Inventors Council, National, C 32
Investigate Covert Arms Transactions with Investment Board, Federal Retirement Thrift, Y 3.F 31/25

Iran, Select Committee to, Y 4.In 8/20
Investigation and Entrenchment Committee (Senate), Y 4.In 8/6
Investigation Bureau, Federal, J 1.14
Investigations, Air Force Office of Special, D 301.88
Investments in United States Corporate Securities and Financing for United States Corporations Operating Abroad, Task Force on Promoting Increased Foreign, Pr 35.8:F 76/3
Iran, Select Committee to Investigate Covert Arms Transactions with, Y 4.In 8/20
Iron, Steel, and other Metals, Board for Testing, Y 3.Ir 6
Irrigation and Reclamation Committee (House), Y 4.Ir 7/2
Irrigation and Reclamation Committee (Senate), Y 4.Ir 7/1
Irrigation Inquiry Office, A 15
Isthmian Canal Commission, W 73, Y 3.Is 7

J

Jackson, Andrew, Pr 7
James Madison Memorial Commission, Y 3.M 26
Jamestown-Williamsburg-Yorktown Celebration Commission, Y 3.J 23
Japan-United States Friendship Commission, Y 3.J 27
Jefferson, Thomas, Pr 3
Jefferson, Thomas, Memorial Commission, Y 3.T 36
Jet Propulsion Laboratory, NAS 1.12/7
John E. Fogarty International Center for Advanced Study of the Health Sciences, HE 20.3700
John F. Kennedy Center for the Performing Arts, SI 10
John Marshall Bicentennial Commission, Y 3.M 35
Johnson, Andrew, Pr 17
Johnson, Lyndon B., Pr 36
Johnson-Kennedy Natural Resources Advisory Committee, Pr 35.8:N 21
Joint Chief's of Staff, M 2, D 5
Joint Commission–
Consider the Present Organizations of the Signal Service, Geological Survey, Coast and Geodetic Survey, and Hydrographic Office, Y 3.Si 2
Government Purchases of Pneumatic Tubes, Y 3.P 74
International, Y 3.In 8/28
Investigate Indian Affairs, Y 3.In 2/3
Pneumatic Tube Mail Service, Y 3.P 74/2
Postal Service, Y 3.P 84/3
Joint Committee–
Arrangements for the Commemoration of the Bicentennial, Y 4.B 47
Centennial of the Telegraph, Y 4.T 23
Deficit Reduction, Temporary, Y 4.D 36/2
Reorganization of the Administrative Branch of the Government, Y 4.R 29
Taxation, Y 4.T 19/4
Joint Federal State Action Committee, Pr 34.8:F 31
Joint Publications Research Service, Y 3.J 66
Joint Research and Development Board, Y 3.J 66/2
Joint Select Committee–
Investigate District of Columbia Charities, Y 4.D 63/3
Retrenchment, Y 4.R 31/2
Joint Special Committee on Chinese Immigration, Y 4.C 44
Joint Study Committee on Budget Control, Y 4.B 85
Judge Advocate General Office–
Air Force, D 302
Army, W 10
Navy, N 7, M 214, D 205
Judge Advocate General's Department, (Army), W 10, M 107, D 108
Judicial Center, Federal, Ju 13
Judicial Discipline & Removal, National Commission, Pr 42.8:D 63
Judicial Salaries Commission, Y 3.Ex 3/3
Judiciary Committee (House), Y 4.J 89/1
Judiciary Committee (Senate), Y 4.J 89/2
Jurisdiction over Federal Areas within the States, Interdepartmental Committee for the Study of, Y 3.In 8/10
Justice and Delinquency Prevention, Office of Juvenile, J 32
Justice Assistance, Bureau of, J 26
Justice Assistance, Research, and Statistics Office, J 26
Justice Department, J 1
Justice Information and Statistics Service, National Criminal, J 26.10
Justice, National Institute of, J 28
Justice Statistics, Bureau of, J 29
Juvenile Delinquency and Youth Crime Committee, President's, Pr 35.8:J 98
Juvenile Delinquency Programs, Federal, Interdepartmental Council to Coordinate, Y 3.J 98

Marine Fisheries Service, National, C 55.300
Marine Hospital Service, T 27
Marine Inspection and Navigation Bureau, C 25
Marine Mammal Commission, Y 3.M 33/3
Marine Pollution Assessment Office, C 55.43
Marine Resources and Engineering Development
    National Council, PrEx 12
Marine Science, Engineering and Resources
    Commission, Pr 36.8:M 33
Maritime Administration, C 39.200, TD 11
Maritime Advisory Committee, Y 3.M 33
Maritime Board, Federal, C 39.100
Maritime Canal Company of Nicaragua, I 1.21
Maritime Commission, Federal, FMC
Maritime Commission of the United States, MC
Maritime Labor Board, ML
Marketing Act, Office of the Administrator of the, A 87
Marketing and Marketing Agreements Division, A 65
Marketing Service, Agricultural, A 66
Marketing Services Office, A 80.800, A 81
Markets Bureau, A 36
Markets Office, A 36
Marshall, John, Bicentennial Commission, Y 3.M 35
Marshals Service, United States, J 25
Mass Transportation Administration, Urban, TD 7
Matanzas and Santa Clara Department, W 58
Materials and Mechanics Research Center, Army, D
    101.80
Materials Center, Cape May Plant, A 57.54/2
Materials Center, Manhattan Plant, A 57.54/3
Materials Council, National Critical, Y 3.C 86/2
Materials Policy Commission, National, Y 3.M 41
Materials Policy Commission, President's, Pr 33.15
Materials Procurement Agency, Defense, DM
Materials Science Center, C 13.1/9
Materials Transportation Bureau, TD 9
Maternal and Child Health and Resources Development
    Bureau, HE 20.9200
Maternal and Child Health Bureau, HE 20.9200
Maternal and Child Health Service, HE 20.2750
McKinley, William, Pr 25
McNeil Island Penitentiary, J 13
Means, Committee on Ways and (House), Y 4.W 36
Measurement Laboratory, National, C 13.1/8, C 13.1/10
Meat Animal Research Center, Advisory Committee for,
    A 77.27
Medal of Science, President's Committee on National,
    Pr 35.8:M 46
Mediation and Conciliation Board of the United States,
    MCB
Mediation and Conciliation, President's Advisory
    Committee, Pr 40.8:M 46
Mediation and Conciliation Service, Federal, FM
Mediation Board, National, NMB
Mediation Board of the United States, MB
Mediation Commission, Y 3.M 46
Medicaid and State Operations, Center for, H 22.100
Medicaid Bureau, HE 22.100
Medicaid Management, Institute for, HE 22.112
Medical Center, Army, Walter Reed, D 104.15
Medical Department of the Army, W 44, M 102, D 104
Medical Devices and Diagnostic Products Bureau, HE
    20.4300
Medical Devices Bureau, HE 20.4300
Medical Education, Council on Graduate, Y 3.M 46/2
Medical Library, Armed Forces, D 8
Medical Programs Service, Regional and, HE 20.2600
Medical Research Service, Veterans Administration, VA
    1.1/4
Medical Section, Y 3.C 83:40
Medical Service, Air Force, D 304
Medical Service, Army, D 104
Medical Services Administration, FS 17.500, HE
    17.500
Medical Services Bureau, HE 20.5400
Medicare Management, Center for, HE 22.400
Medicine and Biomedical and Behavioral Research,
    President's Commission for the Study of
    Ethical Problems in, Pr 40.8:Et 3
Medicine and Surgery Bureau, N 10, M 203, D 206
Medicine, Bureau of Aviation, FAA 7
Medicine, Bureau of Veterinary, HE 20.4400
Medicine, Center for Veterinary, HE 20.4400
Medicine, National Library of, FS 2.200, HE 20.3600
Members of Congress, Select Committee to Investigate
    Alleged Charges Against, Y 4.M 51
Memorial Commission, Woodrow Wilson, Y 3.W 86/2
Memorial Council, United States Holocaust, Y 3.H 74
Mental Health Administration, Health Services and, HE
    20.2000
Mental Health Intramural Research Program, HE
    20.8136
Mental Health, National Institute of, HE 20.2400, HE
    20.3800, HE 20.8100

Mental Health, President's Commission on, Pr 39.8:M
    52
Mental Health Services Administration, HE 20.400, HE
    20.8000
Mental Retardation, President's Committee on, Pr
    36.8:M 52, Pr 36.8:R 29, HE 23.100
Mental Retardation, President's Panel on, Pr 35.8:M
    52
Mental Retardation, White House Conference, Y 3.W
    58/9
Mentally Handicapped Task Force, Pr 37.8:M 52
Mercantile Marine and Internal Revenue Division, T 42
Merchant Marine and Defense Commission, Y 3.M 53/2
Merchant Marine and Fisheries Committee (House), Y
    4.M 53
Merchant Marine Commission, Y 3.M 53
Merchant Marine Safety Office, TD 5.35
Merit Systems Protection Board, MS 1
Mesa Verde National Park, I 1.48
Metabolic Diseases, National Institute of Arthritis and,
    HE 20.3300
Metabolism and Digestive Diseases, National Institute
    of, HE 20.3300
Meteorological Center, National, C 55.190
Metric Board, United States, Y 3.M 56
Mexican American Affairs Interagency Committee, Y
    3.In 8/23
Mexico, Select Committee on Proceedings of Board of
    Commissioners on Claims Against, Y 4.M 57
Microbiology and Infectious Diseases Program, HE
    20.3263
Microscopy Division, A 18
Middle Eastern Division, LC 41
Migration and Cooperative Economic Development,
    Commission for the Study of International, Y
    3.M 58/2
Migratory Bird Conservation Commission, Y 3.M 58
Migratory Labor Commission, President's, Pr 33.15
Mileage Committee (House), Y 4.M 58
Military Academy, W 12, M 109, D 109
Military Academy, Commission to Examine, Y 3.M 59
Military Affairs Committee (House), Y 4.M 59/1
Military Affairs Committee (Senate), Y 4.M 59/2
Military Assistance Program, President's Committee to
    Study, Pr 34.8:M 59
Military Establishment, National, M 1
Military History Center, D 114
Military History Office, D 114
Military History, Office of the Chief of, D 114
Military Intelligence Division, W 100
Military Management Task Force, Pr 40.8:M 59
Military Personnel Command, Naval, D 208
Military Prison, Fort Leavenworth, W 27
Military Sea Transportation Service, D 216
Military Sealift Command, D 216
Militia Affairs Division, Naval, N 23
Militia Committee (House), Y 4.M 59/3
Militia Office, Naval, N 1.26
Mindanao Department, W 72
Mine Inspector for Indian Territory, I 1.20
Mine Inspector for the Territory of New Mexico, I 1.23
Mine Inspector for the Territory of Utah, I 1.33
Mine Safety and Health Administration, L 38
Mine Safety and Health Review Commission, Federal, Y
    3.M 66
Minerals Administration, Defense, I 55
Minerals and Solid Fuels Office, I 60
Minerals Exploration Administration, Defense, I 55
Minerals Exploration Office, I 55
Minerals Management Service, I 72
Minerals Mobilization Office, I 60
Mines and Mining Committee (House), Y 4.M 66/1
Mines and Mining Committee (Senate), Y 4.M 66/2
Mines Bureau, C 22, I 28
Minimum Wage Study Commission, Y 3.M 66/2
Mining Enforcement and Safety Administration, I 69
Mining Reclamation and Enforcement, Office of Surface,
    I 71
Minorities in Science and Technology Task Force, Y
    3.W 84/3
Minority Business Development Agency, C 1.56, C
    1.100
Minority Business Development, United States
    Commission, Y 3.2:M 66
Minority Business Enterprise Office, C 1.56
Minority Business Ownership, Presidential Advisory
    Committee on, Pr 40.8:B 96
Mint Bureau, T 28
Mint, United States, T 28
Miscellaneous Division, T 42
Missile Sites Labor Commission, President's, Pr
    35.8:M 69
Missing Persons in Southeast Asia, Select Committee
    on, (House), Y 4.M 69/3

Mississippi River Commission, W 31, M 110.200, D
    103.300
Mississippi River, Committee on Levees and
    Improvements of (House), Y 4.M 69/2
Mississippi, Select Committee to Inquire into Alleged
    Frauds in Recent Elections in, Y 4.M 69/1
Missouri Basin Inter-Agency Committee, Y 3.M 69
Missouri Basin Survey Commission, Pr 33.22
Missouri Department, W 20
Missouri River Basin Commission, Y 3.M 69/2
Missouri River Commission, W 32
Missouri River Division, D 103.41
Mitigation, Federal Insurance and Hazard, FEM 1.200
Model Cities Task Force, Pr 37.8:M 72
Molecular Basis of Disease Program, HE 20.3466
Monetary and Financial Policies, National Advisory
    Council on International, Y 3.N 21/16
Monetary and Financial Problems, National Advisory
    Council on International, Y 3.N 21/16
Monetary Commission, National, Y 3.N 21/2
Monetary Commission of the United States, Y 3.M 74
Monetary Systems, Commission on the Role of Gold in
    Domestic and International, Y 3.G 57
Money Orders Division, P 9
Monitored Retrievable Storage Review Commission, Y
    3.M 74/2Monroe, James, Pr 5
Monitoring Program, Long Term Resource, I 49.109
Montana, Governor, I 1.22
Monuments, Artistic and Historic, in War Areas,
    American Commission for Protection and
    Salvage, Y 3.Am 3/4
Moral Welfare and Character Guidance in the Armed
    Forces, President's Committee on, Y 3.P 92/
    5
Morale Services Division, W 109.200
Morgantown Energy Technology Center, E 1.74
Mortality on Emigrant Ships, Select Committee on,
    (Senate), Y 4.Si 1
Mortgage Association, Government National, HH 1.1/7
Mortgage Interest Rates Commission, Y 3.M 84
Mothers and Children, Center for Research for, HE
    20.3351/2
Motion Picture, Broadcasting, and Recorded Sound
    Division, LC 40
Motion Pictures Division, I 37
Motor Carrier Ratemaking Commission, Y 3.M 85/2
Motor Carrier Safety Bureau, TD 2.300
Motor Carriers Bureau, IC 1 mot
Motor Transport Corps, W 88
Motor Vehicle Goals beyond 1980, Interagency Task
    Force on, Y 3.M 85
Motor Vehicle Service Administration, P 21
Mount Rainier National Park, I 1.43
Mounted Service School, W 30
Multi-Family Housing Office, HH 13
Municipal Environmental Research Laboratory, EP
    1.46/7, EP 1.46
Munitions Board, M 5, M 400, D 3
Munitions Control Board, National, NMC
Munitions Industry, Special Committee Investigating
    (Senate), Y 4.M 92
Muscle Shoals Commission, Y 3.M 97
Muscle Shoals Joint Committee, Y 4.M 97
Musculoskeletal and Skin Diseases, National Institute,
    HE 20.3900
Musculoskeletal Diseases, National Commission on
    Arthritis and Related, Y 3.Ar 7
Museum–
    Museum of African Art, National, SI 14
    American Art, National, SI 6
    American History, National, SI 3
    Hirshhorn, SI 13
    History and Technology, National, SI 3
    National, SI 3
    National Air, SI 9
    National Air and Space, SI 9
    United States National, SI 3
Museum and Sculpture Garden, Hirshhorn, SI 13
Museum Services Institute, MuS 1, NF 4
Music Committee on People to People Program,
    President's, Pr 35.8:M 97
Music Division, LC 12
Mutual Security Agency, Pr 33.900
Mutual Security Program, President's Citizen Advisers
    on, Pr 34.8:M 98

N

N.L.R.B. Special Committee to Investigate (House), Y
    4.N 21/4
Narcotic and Drug Abuse Advisory Commission,
    President's, Pr 35.8:N 16
Narcotic and Drug Abuse White House Conference, Y
    3.W 58/5

Narcotics Abuse and Control, Select Committee on (House), Y 4.N 16
Narcotics and Dangerous Drugs Bureau, J 24
Narcotics Bureau, T 56
Narcotics Control Board, Federal, T 53
Narcotics Intelligence Consumers Committee, National, Y 3.N 16
Narcotics Interdepartmental Committee, Y 3.In 8/9
National Academy
    Foreign Affairs, President's Advisory Panel on, Pr 35.8:F 76/2
    Public Administration, Y 3.N 21/28
    Science, NA 1
National Acid Precipitation Assessment Program, C 55.703
National Advisory and Coordinating Council on Bilingual Education, Y 3.B 49
National Advisory Commission–
    Civil Disorders, Pr 36.8:C 49
    Criminal Justice Standards and Goals, Y 3.C 86
    Food and Fibers, Pr 36.8:H 34
    Health Manpower, Pr 36.8:H 34
    Rural Poverty, Pr 36.8:R 88

National Advisory Committee–
    Aeronautics, Y 3.N 21/5
    Black Higher Education and Black Colleges and Universities, HE 19.140
    Handicapped, HE 19.117
    Juvenile Justice and Delinquency Prevention, J 26.1/4
    Oceans and Atmosphere, Y 3.Oc 2
    Semiconductors, Y 3.Se 5/3
National Advisory Council–
    Adult Education, Y 3.Ed 8/4
    Black Higher Education and Black Colleges and Universities, ED 1.21
    Career Education, HE 19.116
    Child Nutrition, Y 3.C 43/2
    Continuing Education, Y 3.Ed 8/8
    Drug Abuse Prevention, Y 3.D 84
    Economic Opportunity, Y 3.Ec 7/2
    Education of Disadvantaged Children, Y 3.Ed 8/2
    Education Professions Development, Y 3.Ed 8/3
    Equality of Education Opportunity, Y 3.Ed 8/7
    Extension and Continuing Education, Y 3.Ex 8
    Indian Education, Y 3.In 2/10
    International Monetary and Financial Policies, Y 3.N 21/16
    International Monetary and Financial Problems, Y 3.N 21/16
    Maternal, Infant and Fetal Nutrition, A 98.14/2
    Supplemental Centers and Services, Pr 36.8:Su 7
    Vocational Education, Y 3.V 85
    Women's Education Programs, Y 3.W 84/2
National Advisory Eye Council, HE 20.3752:R 31/4
National Advisory Loan Committee, A 52
National Aeronautics and Space Administration, NAS
National Aeronautics and Space Council, PrEx 5
National Agricultural Advisory Commission, Pr 34.8:N 21a
National Agricultural Library, A 17
National Agricultural Statistics Service, A 92
National Air and Space Museum, SI 9
National Air Museum, SI 9
National Air Pollution Control Administration, HE 20.1300
National Air Toxics Information Clearinghouse, EP 4.23
National and Community Service, Corporation for, Y 3.N 21/29
National and Community Service, Commission on, Y 3.N 21/29
National Arboretum, A 77.26
National Archives and Records Administration, AE 1.100
National Archives and Records Service, GS 4
National Archives Establishment, AE 1
National Alcohol Fuels Commission, Y 3.Al 1
National Arthritis Advisory Board, HE 20.3027/2
National Audiovisual Center, GS 4.17/5
National Bankruptcy Review Commission, Y 3.2:B 22/B 22
National Biological Service, I 73
National Bipartisan Commission on Central America, Pr 40.8:B 52
National Bituminous Coal Commission, I 34
National Black Leadership Initiative on Cancer, HE 20.3195
National Board for Promotion of Rifle Practice, W 82
National Board of Health, T 29
National Brucellosis Committee, A 1.2:B 83
National Bureau of Standards, C 13, T 41
National Business Council for Consumer Affairs, Y 3.N 21/27

National Cancer Advisory Board, HE 20.3027/3
National Cancer Institute, HE 20.3150
National Cancer Program, HE 20.3184/4
National Capital Airports Bureau, FAA 6
National Capital Office Public Buildings and Public Parks, PB
National Capital Park and Planning Commission, NC 2
National Capital Regional Planning Council, NC 3
National Capital Sesquicentennial Commission, Y 3.N 21/20
National Capital Transportation Agency, Y 3.N 21/21
National Center–
    Computer Security, D 1.79/2
    Chronic Disease Prevention and Health Promotion, HE 20.7600
    Devices and Radiological Health, HE 20.4600
    Drugs and Biologics, HE 20.4200
    Early Development and Learning, ED 1.346
    Educational Statistics, HE 19.300, ED 1.100
    Environmental Health, HE 20.7500
    Family Planning Service, HE 20.2900
    Health Services, HE 20.6500
    Health Services Research and Development, HE 20.2100
    Health Services Research and Health Care Technology Assessment, HE 20.6500
    Health Statistics, HE 20.2200, HE 20.6200
    Infectious Diseases, HE 20.7800
    Injury Prevention and Control, HE 20.7950
    Productivity and Quality of Working Life, Y 3.P 94
    Research in Vocational Education, ED 1.33
    Service Learning, AA 3
    Social Statistics, FS 17.600, HE 17.600
National Clearinghouse–
    Aging, HE 23.3100
    Child Abuse and Neglect Information, HE 23.1216
    Drug Abuse Information, PrEx 13
    Eisenhower, ED 1.340
    Poison Control Centers, HE 20.4003/2
National Climate Program, C 55.44
National Climatic Center, C 55.280
National Coast-Defense Board, Y 3.N 21/4
National Collection of Fine Arts, SI 6
National Commission–
    Air Quality, Y 3.Ai 7/5
    AIDS, Y 3.Ac 7
    Arthritis and Related Musculoskeletal Diseases, Y 3.Ar 7
    Causes and Prevention of Violence, Pr 36.8:V 81
    Children, Y 3.C 43/5
    Consumer Finance, Y 3.C 76/2
    Electronic Fund Transfers, Y 3.El 2/4
    Employment and Unemployment Statistics, Y 3.Em 7/2
    Employment Policy, Y 3.Em 7/3
    Financial Institution Reform, Recovery and Enforcement, Y 3.F 32
    Financing of Postsecondary Education, Y 3.Ed 8/5
    Fire Prevention and Control, Y 3.F 51
    Food Marketing, Y 3.N 21/22
    Industrial Peace, Y 3.In 2/11
    International Year of the Child, U.S., Y 3.C 43/3
    Judicial Discipline & Removal, Pr 42.8:D 63
    Law Observance and Enforcement, Y 3.N 21/7
    Libraries and Information Science, Y 3.L 61
    Manpower Policy, Y 3.M 31
    Materials Policy, Y 3.M 41
    Neighborhoods, Y 3.N 31
    New Technological Uses of Copyrighted Works, Y 3.C 79
    Observance of International Women's Year, Y 3.W 84
    Observance of World Population Year, Y 3.P 81/2
    Product Safety, Y 3.N 21/25
    Productivity, Pr 37.8:P 94
    Productivity and Work Quality, Pr 37.8:P 94
    Protection of Human Subjects of Biomedical and Behavioral Research, Y 3.H 88
    Reform of Federal Criminal Laws, Y 3.N 21/26
    Review of Antitrust Laws and Procedures, Pr 39.8:An 8
    Review of Federal and State Laws Relating to Wiretapping and Electronic Surveillance, Y 3.W 74/2
    Severely Distressed Public Housing, Y 3.P 96/9
    Social Security, Y 3.So 1, Pr 40.8:So 1
    Space, Y 3.Sp 1
    State Workmen's Compensation Laws, Y 3.W 89/3
    Student Financial Assistance, Y 3.St 9
    Superconductivity, Y 3.Su 7/3
    Supplies and Shortages, Y 3.Su 7/2
    Technology, Automation, and Economic Progress, Y 3.T 22
    Unemployment Compensation, Y 3.Un 2

    Urban Problems, Pr 36.8:Ur 1
    Water Quality, Y 3.W 29/2
National Committee of the CCIR, U.S., S 5.56
National Committee on Wood Utilization Relief, C 1.15
National Communicable Disease Center, HE 20.2300
National Communications System, PrEx 1.17
National Computer Security Center, D 1.79/2
National Conference on Child Abuse and Neglect, HE 1.480/5
National Conferences on Street and Highway Safety, C 1.21
National Council–
    Arts, PrEx 1
    Commerce, C 1.9
    Disability, Y 3.D 63/3
    Education Research, HE 19.214, ED 1.315
    Handicapped, Y 3.H 19
    Health Planning and Development, HE 20.6001/5:H 34
    Indian Opportunity, Y 3.In 2/9
    Marine Resources and Engineering Development, PrEx 12
National Credit Union Administration, NCU
National Criminal Justice Information and Statistics Service, J 26.10
National Critical Materials Council, Y 3.C 86/2
National Cultural Center, SI 10
National Defense Council, Y 3.C 83, Y 3.C 831
National Defense Migration, Select Committee Investigating (House), Y 4.N 21/5
National Defense, Office of the Petroleum Coordinator for, I 50
National Defense Program in its Relation to Small Business, Select Committee to Conduct Study and Survey of (House), Y 4.N 21/7
National Defense Program, Special Committee Investigating (Senate), Y 4.N 21/6
National Diabetes Advisory Board, HE 20.3027
National Defense University, D 5.400
National Digestive Diseases Advisory Board, HE 20.3027/4
National Disabled Soldiers League, Inc., Select Committee to Investigate (House), Y 4.N 21/3
National Drug Control Policy Office, PrEx 26
National Drug Policy Board, Y 3.D 84/2
National Earth Satellite Service, C 55.500
National Earthquake Information Center, C 55.690
National Economic Commission, Y 3.Ec 7/3
National Economic Issues White House Conference, Y 3.W 58/7
National Emergency Council, Y 3.N 21/9
National Emergency, Special Committee on the Termination of the, Y 4.N 21/9
National Endowment for the Arts, NF 2
National Endowment for the Humanities, NF 3
National Enforcement Commission, ES 6
National Environmental Satellite, Data, and Information Service, C 55.200
National Environmental Satellite Service, C 55.500
National Export Expansion Council, C 1.42/3
National Eye Institute, HE 20.3750
National Fire Academy, FEM 1.17/3
National Fire Prevention and Control Administration, C 58
National Foreign Assessment Center, PrEx 3.10/7
National Forest Reservation Commission, Y 3.N 21/6
National Foundation on the Arts and Humanities, NF 1
National Gallery of Art, SI 8
National Geophysical Data Center, C 55.201/2
National Goals Research Staff, Pr 37.8:N 21g
National Growth and Economic Development, White House Conference on Balanced, Y 3.W 58/19
National Guard Bureau, W 70, M 114, D 112, D 12
National Guard, District of Columbia, D 12.1/2
National Guard, Utah, D 12.1/3
National Health Resources Advisory Committee, GS 13.9
National Heart and Lung Institute, HE 20.3200
National Heart, Lung, and Blood Institute, HE 20.3200
National Highway Program, President's Advisory Committee on, Pr 34.8:H 53
National Highway Safety Advisory Committee, TD 1.13/2
National Highway Safety Bureau, TD 2.200
National Highway Traffic Safety Administration, TD 8
National Historical Publications and Records Commission, AE 1.114, AE 1.114/3
National Home for Disabled Volunteer Soldiers, NH
National Housing Agency, NHA
National Hurricane Research Laboratory, C 55.601/3
National Imagery and Mapping Agency, D 5.300
National Immunization Program, HE 20.7960
National Independent Study Center, CS 1.92

National Industrial Pollution Control Council, Y 3.In 2/8
National Institute–
  Aging, HE 20.3850
  Alcohol Abuse and Alcoholism, HE 20.8300
  Allergy and Infectious Diseases, HE 20.3250
  Arthritis and Metabolic Diseases, HE 20.3300
  Arthritis and Musculoskeletal and Skin Diseases, HE 20.3900
  Arthritis, Metabolism and Digestive Diseases, HE 20.3300
  Child Health and Human Development, HE 20.3350
  Corrections, J 16.100
  Deafness and Other Communication Disorders, HE 20.3650
  Dental Research, HE 20.3400
  Diabetes and Digestive and Kidney Diseases, HE 20.3300
  Drug Abuse, HE 20.3950, HE 20.8200
  Education, HE 18, HE 19.200, ED 1.300
  Environmental Health Sciences, HE 20.3550
  General Medical Sciences, HE 20.3450
  Justice, J 28
  Juvenile Justice and Delinquency Prevention, J 26.1/2
  Law Enforcement and Criminal Justice, J 26.1/3
  Literacy, Pr 41.8:L 71, Y 3.L 71
  Mental Health, HE 20.2400, HE 20.3800, HE 20.8100
  Neurological and Communicative Disorders and Stroke, HE 20.3500
  Neurological Diseases and Stroke, HE 20.3500
  Neurological Disorders and Stroke, HE 20.3500
  Occupational Safety and Health, HE 20.2800, HE 20.7100
  Standards and Technology, C 13
National Institutes of Health, HE 20.2800, HE 20.7100
National Interregional Highway Committee, Y 3.N 21/15
National Inventors Council, C 32
National Juvenile Justice Assessment Centers, J 26.27
National Labor Board, Y 3.N 21/10
National Labor Relations Board, LR, Y 3.N 21/13
National Laboratory, Argonne, E 1.1/5
National Land-Use Planning Committee, A 1.39
National Library of Medicine, FS 2.200, HE 20.3600
National Library Services for the Blind and Physically Handicapped, LC 19
National Marine Fisheries Service, C 55.300
National Measurement Laboratory, C 13.1/8, C 13.1/10
National Medal of Science, President's Committee on, Pr 35.8:M 46
National Mediation Board, NMB
National Meteorological Center, C 55.190
National Military Establishment, M 1
National Monetary Commission, Y 3.N 21/2
National Mortgage Association, Federal, HH 6
National Mortgage Association, Government, HH 1.1/7
National Munitions Control Board, NMC
National Museum, SI 3
  African Art, SI 14
  American Art, SI 6
  American History, SI 3
  History and Technology, SI 3
  United States, SI 13
National Narcotics Intelligence Consumers Committee, Y 3.N 16
National Nutrition Monitoring Advisory Council, Y 3.N 95
National Occupational Information Coordinating Committee, Y 3.Oc 1/2
National Ocean Service, C 55.400
National Ocean Survey, C 55.400
National Oceanic and Atmospheric Administration, C 55
National Oceanographic Data Center, C 55.290, D 203.24
National Oceanographic Instrumentation Center, C 55.70, D 203.32
National Office of Vital Statistics, FS 2.100
National Park Service, I 29
National Policy toward Gambling, Commission on Review of the, Y 3.G 14
National Portrait Gallery, SI 11
National Production Authority, C 40
National Professional Standards Review Council, HE 1.46, HE 20.5010
National Railroad Adjustment Board, RA
National Recovery Administration, Y 3.N 21/8
National Recovery Review Board, Y 3.N 21/11
National Research Council, NA 2
National Research Program, ARS, A 77.28
National Resources Board, Y 3.N 21/12
National Resources Committee, Y 3.N 21/12

National Resources, Committee on Conservation of (Senate), Y 4.N 21/1
National Resources Planning Board, Pr 32.300
National Science Foundation, NS 1
National Security Committee (House), Y 4.Se 2/1
National Security Council, Y 3.N 21/17, Pr 33.600, PrEx 3
National Security League, Special Committee to Investigate (House), Y 4.N 21/2
National Security Resources Board, Pr 33.700, Y 3.N 21/18
National Security Training Commission, Y 3.N 21/19
National Service, Corporation for, Y 3.N 21/29
National Severe Storms Laboratory, C 55.625
National Society of Daughters of American Revolution, SI 5
National Status and Trends Program, C 55.436
National Strategic Studies Institute, D 5.417
National Student Volunteer Program, AA 3
National Study Commission on Records and Documents of Federal Officials, Y 3.R 24/2
National Systematics Laboratory, C 55.341
National Technical Information Service, C 51
National Telecommunications and Information Administration, C 60
National Tourism Resources Review Commission, Y 3.T 64
National Training School for Boys, J 8
National Training School for Girls, J 9
National Transportation Policy Study Commission, Y 3.T 68/2
National Transportation Safety Board, TD 1.100
National Visitor Center Study Commission, Y 3.N 21/23
National Visitor Facilities Advisory Commission, Y 3.N 21/23
National War College, D 5.17
National War Labor Board, L 10, Pr 32.5100
National War Savings Committee, T 1.26
National Water Commission, Y 3.N 21/24
National Water Resources, Select Committee on (Senate), Y 4.N 21/8
National Waterways Commission, Y 3.N 21/3
National Weather Service, C 55.100
National Youth Administration, FS 6, Pr 32.5250, Y 3.N 21/14
Nationwide Urban Runoff Program, EP 1.92
Native Americans Administration, HE 23.5000
Native Hawaiians Study Commission, Y 3.H 31/2
Natural Beauty, President's Task Force on Preservation of, Pr 36.8:N 21
Natural Beauty White House Conference, Y 3.W 58/12
Natural Gas Transportation System, Office of the Federal Inspector, Alaska, Y 3.F 31/23
Natural Resource Development Program, SBA 1.48
Natural Resources Advisory Committee, Kennedy-Johnson, Pr 35.8:N 21
Natural Resources Committee, (House), Y 4.R 31/3
Natural Resources Committee (Senate), Y 4.En 2
Natural Resources Conservation Agency, A 57
Natural Resources Division, J 30
Naturalization Bureau, C 7.10, L 6
Naturalization Commission, Y 3.N 21/1
Naturalization Division, C 7.10
Naturalization Service, Immigration and, J 21
Nautical Almanac Office, N 11
Navajo Area Indian Health Service, Office of Environmental Health and Engineering, HE 20.5301/2, HE 20.9413
Navajo-Hopi Indian Administration Joint Committee, Y 4.N 22/4
Naval Academy, N 12, M 206.100, D 208.100
Naval Aerospace Medical Center, D 206.18
Naval Affairs Committee (House), Y 4.N 22/1
Naval Affairs Committee (Senate), Y 4.N 22/2
Naval Affairs Joint Committee, Y 4.N 22/3
Naval Air Development Center, D 201.22, D 202.28
Naval Air Systems Command, D 202
Naval Communications Service, N 22
Naval Consulting Board, N 1.28
Naval Data Automation Command, D 221
Naval Doctrine Command, D 207.400
Naval Education and Training Command, D 207.200
Naval Facilities Engineering Command, D 209
Naval Health Research Center, D 206.22
Naval Historical Center, D 221
Naval Intelligence Office, N 13
Naval Medical Field Research Laboratory, D 206.19
Naval Medical Neuropsychiatric Research Unit, D 206.21
Naval Military Personnel Command, D 208
Naval Militia Affairs Division, N 23
Naval Militia Office, N 1.26
Naval Observatory, N 14, M 212, D 213

Naval Ocean Research and Development Activity, D 210.100
Naval Oceanographic Office, D 203
Naval Operations Bureau, D 207
Naval Operations Office, N 27, M 207, D 207
Naval Ordnance Systems Command, D 215
Naval Personnel Bureau, N 17, M 206, D 208
Naval Publications and Form Center, D 212.1/2
Naval Radio Service, N 22
Naval Records and Library Office, N 16
Naval Research Office, N 32, M 216, D 210
Naval Reserve, Chief of, D 207.300
Naval Reserve Force Division, N 25
Naval School of Aviation Medicine, D 206.16
Naval Sea Systems Command, D 211
Naval Ship Systems Command, D 211
Naval Submarine Medical Center, D 206.10
Naval Supply Systems Command, D 212
Naval Surface Weapons Center, D 201.21/6
Naval Technical Training Command, D 207.100
Naval Training Command, D 207.200
Naval Training Support Command, D 208
Naval War College, N 15, M 206.200, D 208.200
Naval War Records Office and Library, N 16
Naval Weapons Bureau, D 217
Naval Weapons Center, D 201.23
Naval Weapons Laboratory, D 201.21
Naval Weather Service Command, D 220
Navigation and Steamboat Inspection Bureau, C 25
Navigation Bureau, T 30, C 11
Navigation Bureau, (Navy), N 17
Navy Department, N 1, M 201, D 201
Navy Department Auditor, T 6
Navy Department Solicitor, N 8
Navy Oceanographer, D 218
Navy Oceanography Command, D 222
Navy Personnel Research and Development Center, D 201.1/3
Navy Yards and Docks Bureau, N 21
Near East Relief, Y 3.N 27
Neglect Information, National Clearinghouse on Child Abuse and, HE 23.1216
Neighborhoods, National Commission on, Y 3.N 31
Neurological and Communicative Disorders and Stroke, National Institute of, HE 20.3500
Neurological Disease and Stroke Institute, National, HE 20.3500
eurological Disease and Stroke National Institute of, He 20.3500
New Communities Administration, HH 11
New England Regional Commission, Y 3.N 42/2
New England Regional Office, L 2.71/3
New England River Basins Commission, Y 3.N 42/3
New Jersey Tercentenary Celebration Commission, Y 3.N 42
New Mexico, Governor, I 1.24
New Mexico, Traveling Auditor and Bank Examiner, I 1.42
New Orleans Riots Select Committee (House), Y 4.N 42/1
New Technological Uses of Copyrighted Works, National Commission on, Y 3.C 79
New York Election Frauds, Alleged, Select Committee on (House), Y 4.N 42/2
Newburg, N.Y., Monument and Centennial Celebration of 1883, Joint Select Committee on, Y 4.N 42/3
Nicaragua Canal Commission, Y 3.N 51
NINCDS Research Programs, HE 20.3502
Nine Foot Channel from Great Lakes to the Gulf, Select Committee (Senate), Y 4.N 62
Nixon, Richard M., Pr 37
NOAA Undersea Research Program, C 55.29
North Atlantic Regional Water Resources Study Coordinating Committee, Y 3.N 81/3
North Atlantic Treaty Organization, D 9
North Carolina Tercentenary Celebration Commission, Y 3.N 81/2
North Central Forest Experiment Station, A 13.82
Northeast Corridor Transportation Project, C 1.52
Northeastern Department, W 86
Northeastern Forest Experiment Station, A 13.42, A 13.67
Northern and Northwestern Lakes Survey, W 33
Northern Division, W 62
Northern Forest Experiment Station, A 13.73
Northern Great Plains Resources Program, Y 3.N 81/4
Northern Mariana Islands Commission, Y 3.N 81/6
Northern Pacific Railroad Land Grants, Joint Committee on Investigation of, Y 4.N 81
Northern Rocky Mountain Forest and Range Experiment Station, A 13.30
Northwest Federal Regional Council, Y 3.N 81/5
Northwest Fisheries Center, C 55.326
Northwest Fisheries Science Center, C 55.331/3

Science and Technology, PrEx 8
Science and Technology Policy, PrEx 23
Science Information Service, NS 2
Scientific Research and Development, Pr 32.413
Selective Service Records, Y 3.Se 4
Signal, W 42
Software Development and Information Technology, GS 12.16
Solicitor, L 21
Solid Waste Management, EP 3
Southeastern Regional, L 2.71/8
Special Counsel, MS 2
Special Investigations, Air Force, D 301.88
Special Representative for Trade Negotiations, PrEx 9
Special Services, FS 13
State Technical Services, C 1.53
State, War, and Navy Department Building, S 12
States Relations, A 10
Surface Mining Reclamation and Enforcement, I 71
Technical Services, C 35
Technical Staff, T 68
Technology Assessment, Y 3.T 22/2
Telecommunications, C 1.59
Telecommunications Policy, PrEx 18
Temporary Controls, Pr 33.300
Territories, I 35
Thrift Supervision, T 71
Thrift Supervisor, T 71
Transportation, A 108
Treasurer of the United States, T 63.300
U.S. Trade Representative, PrEx 9
United States Attorneys, Executive, J 31
Veterans Reemployment Rights, L 25
Victims of Crime, J 34
Violence Against Women, J 35
Vocational Rehabilitation, FS 10, FS 13.200
War Information, Pr 32.5000
War Mobilization, Pr 32.5900
War Mobilization and Reconversion, Y 3.W 19/7
War Records, W 45
Water, EP 2
Water Hygiene, HE 20.1700
Water Programs, EP 2
Water Programs Operation, EP 2
Water Quality, EP 2
Water Regulations and Standards, EP 8
Wetlands, Oceans, and Watersheds, EP 8
Workmen's Compensation Program, L 36.400
Youth Development, HE 23.1300
Office Space, Federal, President's Ad Hoc Committee, Pr 35.8:Of 2
Office Space, Presidential, President's Advisory Committee on, Pr 34.8:P 92
Official Conduct, Special Committee on (Senate), Y 4.C 76/8
Ohio River Division Laboratories, D 103.38
Oil and Gas Office, I 64
Oil Import Administration, I 61
Oil Export Appeals Board, I 62
Oil Import Control, Cabinet Task Force on, Pr 37.8:Oi 5
Oil, Office of Gas and, I 64
Oklahoma, Governor, I 1.26
Oklahoma, Select Committee to Investigate Indian Contracts in, Y 4.Ok 4
Old Age Pension Plans, Select Committee to Investigate (House), Y 4.Ol 1
Old-Age Pension System, Special Committee to Investigate (Senate), Y 4.Ol 1/2
Older Americans Volunteer Programs, AA 2
Oliver Wendell Holmes Devise Permanent Committee, Y 3.H 73
Olympic Sports, President's Commission on, Pr 38.8:Ol 9
Operation of the Senate, Commission on, Y 4.Se 5/5
Operation Office, Water Programs, EP 2
Operations Bureau–
    Post Office Department, P 24
    Shipping Board, SB 9
Operations, Bureau of Program, HE 22.400
Operations Division–
    Department of Agriculture, A 60
    Railroad Administration, Y 3.R 13/2:20
Operations, Office of Personnel, D 118
Operations Service, Air Traffic, TD 4.300
Operations, Select Committee on, Y 4.C 76/9
Order Division, LC 13
Ordnance and Ammunition, Select Committee on Investigation of, Y 4.Or 2/4
Ordnance and Fortification Board, W 35
Ordnance and Hydrography Bureau, N 18
Ordnance and War-Ships Select Committee (Senate), Y 4.Or 2/2
Ordnance Bureau, N 18, M 211, D 215
Ordnance Center and School, Army, D 105.25

Ordnance Corps, D 105
Ordnance Department, W 34, M 111
Ordnance, Heavy, and Projectiles, Select Committee on (Senate), Y 4.Or 2/1
Ordnance, Joint Select Committee on, Y 4.Or 2/3
Ordnance, Publications Relating to, D 105
Ordnance Systems Command, Naval, D 215
Organization–
    North Atlantic Treaty, D 9
    Professional Standards Review, HE 22.210
    Unemployment Relief, President's, Y 3.P 92
    War Loan, T 1.27
Organization of the Executive Branch of the Government Commission, Y 3.Or 3, Y 3.Or 3/2
Organization of the Government for the Conduct of Foreign Policy Commission, Y 3.F 76/5
Organization, Office of Rural, A 36
Organizations of the Signal Service, Geological Survey, Coast and Geodetic Survey, and Hydrographic Office, Joint Commission to Consider, Y 3.Si 2
Organized Crime Drug Enforcement Task Force Program, J 1.93
Organized Crime, President's Commission on, Pr 40.8:C 86
Orientalia Division, LC 17
Ornithology and Mammology Division, A 5
Ornithology and Mammology, Division of Economic, A 5
Outdoor Recreation Bureau, I 66
Outdoor Recreation Resources Review Commission, Y 3.Ou 8
Outdoors, President's Commission on Americans, Pr 40.8:Am 3
Outer Continental Shelf, Ad Hoc Select Committee on Investigation of, Y 4.Ou 8
Overseas Private Investment Corporation, OP 1
Oversight Committee, President's Nuclear Safety, Pr 40.8:N 88
Ozarks Regional Commission, Y 3.Oz 1

P

Pacific Coast Naval Bases, Joint Committee, Y 4.P 11/4
Pacific Division, W 51
Pacific Fisheries Development Program, Central, Eastern, and South, C 55.329
Pacific Halibut Commission, International, S 5.35
Pacific Islands and Porto Rico Committee (Senate), Y 4.P 11/1
Pacific Marine Environmental Laboratory, C 55.601/2
Pacific Northwest Forest and Range Experiment Station, A 13.66
Pacific Northwest Regional Commission, Y 3.P 11/5
Pacific Northwest River Basins Commission, Y 3.P 11/4
Pacific Railroad Committee (House), Y 4.P 11/3
Pacific Railroad Committee (Senate), Y 4.P 11/2
Pacific Railway Commission, Y 3.P 11
Pacific Southwest Federal Interagency Technical Committee, Y 3.P 11/3
Pacific Southwest Forest and Range Experiment Station, A 13.62
Pacific Southwest Inter-agency Committee, Y 3.P 11/2
Packers and Stockyards Administration, A 39, A 96, A 113
Pages, Speaker's Commission on, Y 4.Sp 3
Pan American Sanitary Bureau, PAS
Pan American Union, PA
Pan Pacific Conference on Education, Rehabilitation, Reclamation and Recreation, I 1.61
Panama Canal, D 113, M 115, PaC
Panama Canal Commission, Y 3.P 19/2
Panama Canal Zone Company, CZ
Panel–
    Aerospace Safety Advisory, NAS 1.1/7
    Army Scientific Advisory, D 101.81
    Drug Abuse, Ad Hoc, Pr 35.8:D 84
    Federal Compensation, President's , Pr 38.8:C 73
    Federal Service Impasses, Y 3.F 31/21-2
    Interim Compliance, Y 3.C 73/4
    Lake Michigan Cooling Water Studies, EP 1.72
    Mental Retardation, President's, Pr 35.8:M 52
Paperwork, Federal, Commission on, Y 3.P 19
Parcel Post, General, Joint Committee to Investigate, Y 4.P 21
Parklawn Computer Center, HE 20.4036
Parole Commission, United States, J 27
Parole Board, J 1.15
Patent and Trademark Office, C 21
Patent Appeals, Court of Customs and, Ju 7
Patent Office, I 23, C 21

Patent System, President's Commission on, Pr 36.8:P 27
Patents Board, of the Government, Y 3.G 74
Patents Committee (House), Y 4.P 27/1
Patents Committee (Senate), Y 4.P 27/2
Pathology, Armed Forces Institute of, D 1.16/4, D 101.117
Pathology, Division of Vegetable, A 28
Pathology Section, Vegetable, A 28
Pavements and Soil Trafficability Information Analysis Center, D 103.24/12
Pay Board, PrEx 19
Pay Department, W 36
Payment Assessment Commission, Prospective, Y 3.P 29
Payment Review Commission, Physician, Y 3.P 56
Payments Administration, Assistance, HE 3.401
Peace Corps, AA 4, S 19, PE 1
Peace, United States Institute, Y 3.P 31
Pearl Harbor Attack, Joint Committee Investigating, Y 4.P 31
Penal Laws, Commission to Revise and Codify, Y 3.L 44
Penitentiary–
    Atlanta, Georgia, J 14
    Fort Leavenworth, J 6
    McNeil Island, J 13
Pennsylvania Avenue Council, President's, Pr 35.8:P 38
Pennsylvania Avenue Development Corporation, Y 3.P 38
Pennsylvania Avenue, President's Temporary Commission on, Pr 36.8:P 38
Pension and Welfare Benefits Administration, L 40
Pension Benefit Guaranty Corporation, Y 3.P 38/2
Pension Bureau, VA 2
Pension Funds, Corporate, and Other Private Retirement and Welfare Programs, President's Committee on, Pr 35.8:P 38/2
Pension Policy, President's Commission on, Pr 40.8:P 38
Pensions, Bounty, and Back Pay, Select Committee on Payment of, Y 4.P 38/3
Pensions Bureau, I 24
Pensions Committee (House), Y 4.P 38/1
Pensions Committee (Senate), Y 4.P 38/2
Pensions, Veterans, President's Commission on, Pr 34.8:V 64
People to People Program Music Committee, President's, Pr 35.8:M 97
People with Disabilities, President's Committee on Employment, PrEx 1.10/17-2, PrEx 1.10/19
Periodical Division, LC 6
Permanent Committee for the Oliver Wendell Holmes Devise, Y 3.H 73
Perry's Victory Memorial Commission, I 1.62
Personal Property Office, GS 2
Personnel Appeals Board, GA 1.1/2, GA 2
Personnel Bureau, Naval, N 17, D 208
Personnel Classification Board, PC
Personnel Command, Naval Military, D 208
Personnel Interchange Commission of the President, Pr 37.8:P 43
Personnel Management Office, D 118
Personnel Management Office, Attorney, J 33
Personnel Policy, Advisory Council on Intergovernmental, Y 3.P 43/2
Personnel Research and Development Center, CS 1.71
Personnel Research and Development Center, Navy, D 201.1/3
Pest Control Committee, Federal, Y 3.F 31/18
Pest Management, Federal Working Group on, Y 3.P 43
Pesticides and Toxic Substances, Office of, EP 5
Pesticides and Toxic Substances, Office of Prevention, EP 5
Pesticides Programs Office, EP 5
Petroleum Administration Board, I 32
Petroleum Administration for Defense, I 58
Petroleum Administration for War, Y 3.P 44
Petroleum Conservation Division, I 41
Petroleum Coordinator for National Defense Office, I 50
Petroleum Coordinator for War Office, I 50
Petroleum Purchasing Agency, Armed Services, D 11
Petroleum Resources, Special Committee Investigating (Senate), Y 4.P 44
Pharmacy Branch, HE 20.9410
Philippine Alien Property Administration, Pr 33.500
Philippine Commission, Y 3.P 53
Philippine Islands, W 49
Philippine Islands U.S. High Commissioner, W 105
Philippine War Damage Commission, Y 3.P 53/2
Philippines Committee (Senate), Y 4.P 53
Philippines Division, W 21
Phosphate Resources of the United States, Joint Committee to Investigate, Y 4.P 56

Photographs Division, LC 11
Photographs Division, Prints and, LC 25
Physical Fitness and Sports, President's Council on, Pr 36.8:P 56, Pr 37.8:P 56/2, HE 20.100
Physical Fitness Committee, FS 12
Physical Fitness, President's Council on, Pr 35.8:P 56
Physically Handicapped, Division of the Blind and, LC 19
Physically Handicapped, National Library Services for, LC 19
Physically Handicapped Task Force, Pr 37.8:P 56
Physician Payment Review Commission, Y 3.P 56
Pierce, Franklin, Pr 14
Pinar Del Rio Department, W 57
Pipe Line Companies, IC 1 pip
Planetary Institute, NAS 1.67
Planning and Standards Office, Air Quality, EP 4
Planning and Statistics Division, SB 5, Y 3.W 19/2:30
Planning Commission, National Capital, NC 2
Planning Council, Business, C 28
Planning Council, National Capital Regional, NC 3
Planning Office, Aviation Facilities, Pr 34.8:Av 5
Plant and Operations Office, A 60
Plant Health Service, A 101
Plant Industry Bureau, A 19, A 77.500
Plant Industry, Soils, and Agricultural Engineering Bureau, A 77.500
Plant Materials Center, Cape May, A 57.54/2
Plant Materials Center, Manhattan, A 57.54/3
Plant Quarantine and Control Administration, A 48
Plant Quarantine, and Entomology, Bureau, A 56
Plant Quarantine Bureau, A 48
Plant Quarantine, Publications Relating to, A 77.300
Platt National Park, I 1.54
Platte Department, W 22
Pneumatic Tube Commission, P 17
Pneumatic Tube Mail Service Joint Commission, Y 3.P 74/2
Pneumatic Tubes, Joint Commission on Government Purchase of, Y 3.P 74
Polar Research and Development Center, Army, D 103.37
Policies and Programs, Government Housing, President's Advisory Committee on, Pr 34.8:H 81
Policy and Research, Agency for Health Care, HE 20.6500
Policy and Research, Bureau of International Economics, C 57.26
Policy Board, National Drug, Y 3.D 84/2
Policy Bureau, Program, HE 22.300
Policy Coordination Committee, Interagency Radiation, P 1.15
Policy Committee, Army Reserve Forces, D 101.1/12
Policy Committee, Democratic, Y 4.D 39
Policy Council, Competitiveness, Y 3.C 73/6
Policy, Council on International Economic, Pr 37.8:In 8/3
Policy Development Office, PrEx 15
Policy, Immigration and Immigrant, Y 3.2:IM 6/AM 3
Policy, National Commission for Employment, Y 3.Em 7/3
Policy, National Commission for Manpower, Y 3.M 31
Policy, Office of
    Drug Abuse, PrEx 24
    Federal Procurement, PrEx 2.21
    National Drug Control, PrEx 26
    Science and Technology, PrEx 23
Policy, Select Commission on Immigration and Refugee, Y 3.Im 6/2
Political Activities, Lobbying and Campaign Contributions, Special Committee on, Y 4.P 75
Political Activity of Government Personnel Commission, Y 3.P 75
Polk, James Knox, Pr 11
Pollution Assessment Office, Marine, C 55.43
Pollution Control Council, National Industrial, Y 3.In 2/8
Pollution, International Reference Group on Great Lakes, Y 3.In 8/28:14
Polymer Science and Standards Division, C 13.1/7
Pomology Division, A 20
Population and Family Planning, President's Committee on, Pr 36.8:P 81
Population Growth and the American Future, Commission on, Y 3.P 81
Population Research Center, HE 20.3351/3
Population, Select Committee on (House), Y 4.P 81
Pornographic Materials, Current, Select Committee on (House), Y 4.P 82
Port and Harbor Facilities Commission, SB 6
Porto Rico, S 10, W 75
Porto Rico Agricultural Experiment Station, A 10.12
Porto Rico, Attorney General, J 7

Porto Rico Auditor, T 43
Porto Rico Census Office, W 48
Porto Rico Laws Commission, Y 3.P 83
Porto Rico Department, W 23
Portuguese and Spanish Division, LC 24
Post Office and Civil Service Committee (House), Y 4.P 84/10
Post Office and Civil Service Committee (Senate), Y 4.P 84/11
Post Office and Post Roads Committee (House), Y 4.P 84/1
Post Office and Post Roads Committee (Senate), Y 4.P 84/2
Post Office Department, P 1
Post Office Department, Assistant Attorney-General for, P 6
Post Office Department Auditor, T 8
Post Office Department, Select Committee on Relations of Members with (House), Y 4.P 84/3
Post Office Department Solicitor, P 6
Post Office Inspectors Division, P 14
Post Office Leases, Senate Committee, Y 4.P 84/6
Post Office Operations Bureau, P 24
Post War Economic Policy and Planning, Special Committee on (House), Y 4.P 84/9
Post War Economic Policy and Planning, Special Committee on (Senate), Y 4.P 84/7
Post War Military Policy, Select Committee on (House), Y 4.P 84/8
Postage on 2d. Class Mail Matter and Compensation for Transportation of Mails, Joint Committee on, Y 4.P 84/4
Postal Commission, Y 3.P 84/2
Postal Organization Commission of the President, Pr 36.8:P 84
Postal Rate Commission, Y 3.P 84/4
Postal Salaries Joint Commission, Y 3.P 84/5
Postal Savings Division, P 19
Postal Savings System, PS 1, P 19
Postal Service Commission, Y 3.P 84/5
Postal Service Division, International, P 8
Postal Service Joint Commission, Y 3.P 84/3
Postal Service of the United States, P 1
Postal Transport Division, Air, P 20
Postal Transport Division, International, P 8
Postal Transport Division, Surface, P 10
Postal Transportation Service, P 10
Postmaster General, P 1
Postmaster General, First Assistant, P 2
Postmaster General, Fourth Assistant, P 5
Postmaster General, Second Assistant, P 3
Post-Secondary Education, Fund for the Improvement, ED 1.23/2
Postsecondary Education, National Commission on Financing of, Y 3.Ed 8/5
Post-War Programs, Interbureau Committee on, A 1.63
Potomac River Basin, Intestate Commission on, Y 3.In 8/24
Poultry, Publications Relating to Care of, A 77.200
Poverty, Rural, National Advisory Commission on, Pr 36.8:R 88
POW/MIA Affairs, (Senate), Select Committee on, Y 4.P 93/2
Power Administration
    Alaska, E 7
    Defense, I 56
    Southeastern, E 8
    Southwestern, E 1.95/2
Power Commission, Federal, FP
Power, Division of Fossil and Hydro, Y 3.T 25:48
Power Resources Service, I 27
POW/MIA Affairs, Senate Select Committee, Y 4.P 93/8
Precipitation Assessment Program, National Acid, C 55.703
Precipitation, Interagency Task Force on Acid, Y 3.In 8/31
Precious Metals, Royal (British) Commission Appointed to Inquire into Recent Changes in Relative Values of, Y 3.P 91
Preparedness Agency, Federal, GS 13
Present Organizations of the Signal Service, Geological Survey, Coast and Geodetic Survey, and Hydrographic Office, Joint Commission to Consider, Y 3.Si 2
Preservation of Natural Beauty, President's Task Force on, Pr 36.8:N 21
President Executive Office, PrEx 1
President of the Philippine Islands, W 106
President of the United States, Pr
Presidential Advisory Committee
    Gulf War Veterans' Illnesses, Pr 42.8:Ad 9
    Small and Minority Business Ownership, Pr 40.8:B 96
    Water Resources Policy, Pr 34.8:W 29

Presidential and Senatorial Campaign Expenditures, Special Committee on Investigation of, Y 4.P 92/2
Presidential Campaign Activities, Select Committee on, (Senate), Y 4.P 92/4
Presidential Campaign Expenditures, Special Committee Investigating, Y 4.P 92
Presidential Clemency Board, Pr 38.8:C 59
Presidential Commission–
    Broadcasting to Cuba, Pr 40.8:Br 78
    Catastrophic Nuclear Accidents, Y 3.P 92/6
    Drunk Driving, Pr 40.8:D 84
    Indian Reservation Economies, Pr 40.8:In 2
    Space Shuttle Challenger Accident, Pr 40.8:Sp 1
Presidential Office Space, President's Advisory Commission on, Pr 34.8:P 92
Presidential Railroad Commission, Pr 34.8:R 13
Presidential Scholars Commission, Pr 36.8:Sch 6, ED 1.500, Pr 40.8:Sch 6
Presidential Task Force on Career Advancement, Pr 36.8:C 18
Presidential Task Force on the Arts and Humanities, Pr 40.8:Ar 7
Presidential, Vice Presidential, and Senatorial Campaign Expenditures, 1944, Special Committee to Investigate (Senate), Y 4.P 92/3
Presidential Vote for Puerto Rico, Ad Hoc Advisory Group, Pr 37.8:P 96
President's Advisory Board for Cuba Broadcasting, Pr 41.8:Br 78
President's Advisory Commission–
    Educational Excellence for Hispanic Americans, ED 1.87
    Health Facilities, Pr 36.8:H 34/2
    Narcotic and Drug Abuse, Y 3.8:N 16
    Presidential Office Space, Pr 34.8:P 92
President's Advisory Committee–
    Government Housing Policies and Programs, Pr 34.8:H 81
    Hungarian Refugee Relief, Pr 34.8:H 89
    Labor-Management Policy, Pr 35.8:L 11
    Management, Pr 33.20
    Mediation and Conciliation, Pr 40.8:M 46
    National Highway Program, Pr 34.8:H 53
President's Advisory Council–
    Arts, Pr 35.8:Ar 7
    Competitiveness, Pr 41.8:R 26
    Executive Organization, Pr 37.8:Ex 3
    Management Improvement, Pr 37.8:M 31

President's Advisory Panel–
    National Academy of Foreign Affairs, Pr 35.8:F 76/2
    Timber and the Environment, Pr 37.8:T 48
President's Airport Commission, Pr 33.16
President's Appalachian Regional Commission, Pr 35.8:Ap 4
President's Blue Ribbon Commission on Defense Management, Pr 40.8:D 36
President's Board of Advisors on Historically Black Colleges and Universities, ED 1.89/2
President's Cabinet Committee on Price Stability for Economic Growth, Pr 34.8:P 93
President's Cabinet Textile Advisory Committee, Pr 35.8:T 31
President's Citizen Advisers on Mutual Security Program, Pr 34.8:M 98
President's Commission–
    All-Volunteer Armed Forces, Pr 36.8:Ar 5, Pr 37.8:Ar 5, Pr 38.8:Ar 5
    Americans Outdoors, Pr 40.8:Am 3
    Assassination of President John F. Kennedy, Pr 36.8:K 38
    Budget Concepts, Pr 36.8:B 85
    Campaign Costs, Pr 35.8:C 15
    Campus Unrest, Pr 37.8:C 15
    Coal, Pr 39.8:C 63
    Crime in the District of Columbia, Pr 36.8:C 86
    Executive Exchange, Pr 40.8:Ex 3, Pr 40.8/2
    Federal Ethics Law Reform, Pr 41.8:Et 3
    Federal Statistics, Pr 37.8:St 2
    Health Needs of the Nation, Pr 33.19
    Heart Disease, Cancer and Stroke, Pr 36.8:H 35
    Holocaust, Pr 39.8:H 74
    Hostage Compensation, Pr 40.8:H 79
    Housing, Pr 40.8:H 81
    Industrial Competitiveness, Pr 40.8:C 73
    Immigration and Naturalization, Pr 33.18
    Income Maintenance Programs, Pr 36.8:In 2
    Law Enforcement and Administration of Justice, Pr 36.8:L 41
    Mental Health, Pr 39.8:M 52
    Migratory Labor, Pr 33.14
    National Agenda for the Eighties, Pr 39.8:Ag 3
    Observance of Human Rights, Year, Pr 36.8:H 88

Observance of 25th Anniversary of the United
    Nations, Pr 37.8:Un 3
Olympic Sports, Pr 38.8:Ol 9
Organized Crime, Pr 40.8:C 86
Patent System, Pr 36.8:P 27
Pension Policy, Pr 39.8:P 38, Pr 40.8:P 38
Personnel Interchange, Pr 37.8:P 43
Postal Organization, Pr 36.8:P 84
Registration and Voting Participation, Pr 35.8:R
    26
School Finance, Pr 37.8:Sch 6
Status of Women, Pr 35.8:W 84
Study of Ethical Problems in Medicine and
    Biomedical and Behavioral Research, Pr
    40.8:Et 3
Veterans Pensions, Pr 34.8:V 64
White House Fellows, Pr 36.8:W 58
White House Fellowships, Pr 40.8:W 58
World Hunger, Pr 39.8:W 89/3
President's Committee–
Administrative Management, Y 3.P 92/3
Appraise Employment and Unemployment
    Statistics, Pr 35.8:Em 7/3
Civil Service Improvement, Y 3.P 92/4
Consumer Interests, Pr 36.8:C 76
Corporate Pension Funds and Other Private
    Retirement and Welfare Programs, Pr
    35.8:P 38/2
Crop Insurance, Y 3.P 92/2
Education beyond High School, Pr 34.8:Ed 3
Employment of People with Disabilities, PrEx
    1.10/16, PrEx 1.10/17, PrEx 1.10/17-2,
    PrEx 1.10/19
Employment of the Handicapped, PrEx 1.10
Engineers and Scientists for Federal Government
    Programs, Pr 34.8:En 3
Equal Employment Opportunity, Pr 35.8:Em 7
Equal Opportunity in the Armed Forces, Pr 35.8:Ar
    5
Government Contract Compliance, Pr 33.17
Government Employment Policy, Pr 34.8:Em 7
Health Education, Pr 37.8:H 34
Juvenile Delinquency and Youth Crime, Pr 35.8:J
    98
Manpower, Pr 36.8:M 31
Mental Retardation, Pr 36.8:M 52, Pr 36.8:R 29,
    HE 23.100
National Medal of Science, Pr 35.8:M 46
Population and Family Planning, Pr 36.8:P 81
Public Higher Education in District of Columbia,
    Pr 35.8:Ed 8
Religion and Welfare in the Armed Forces, Y 3.P
    92/5
Religious and Moral Welfare and Character
    Guidance in the Armed Forces, Y 3.P 92/
    5
Scientists and Engineers, Pr 34.8:Sci 27
Study Military Assistance Program, Pr 34.8:M 59
Traffic Safety, C 37.7
Youth Employment, Pr 35.8:Y 8/2
President's Communications Policy Board, Pr 33.13
President's Council–
Aging, Pr 35.8:Ag 4
Equal Opportunity, Pr 36.8:Eq 2
Integrity and Efficiency, Pr 40.8:In 8, Pr 40.8/3, Pr
    41.8/3
International Youth Exchange, Pr 40.8:Y 8
Management Improvement, Pr 40.8:M 31
Pennsylvania Avenue, Pr 35.8:P 38
Physical Fitness, Pr 35.8:P 56
Physical Fitness and Sports, Pr 36.8:P 56, Pr
    37.8:P 56/2, HE 20.100
Youth Opportunity, Pr 36.8:Y 8, Pr 37.8:Y 8
President's Counsel on Youth Fitness, Pr 34.8:Y 8
President's Crime Prevention Council, Pr 42.8:C 86
President's Emergency Committee for Employment, Y
    3.P 92
President's Export Council, Pr 37.8:Ex 7, Pr 40.8:Ex 7
President's Foreign Intelligence Advisory Board, Pr
    35.8:F 76
President's Materials Policy Commission, Pr 33.15
President's Missile Sites Labor Commission, Pr
    35.8:M 69
President's Music Committee on People to People
    Program, Pr 35.8:M 97
President's Nuclear Safety Oversight Committee, Pr
    40.8:N 88
President's Organization on Unemployment Relief, Y
    3.P 92
President's Panel–
Federal Compensation, Pr 38.8:C 73
Mental Retardation, Pr 35.8:M 52
President's Private Sector Survey on Cost Control, Pr
    40.8:C 82
President's Reorganization Project, PrEx 1.11

President's Review Committee for Development
    Planning in Alaska, Pr 36.8:Al 1
President's Science Advisory Committee, Pr 34.8:Sci 2
President's Special Committee on U.S. Trade Relations
    with East European Countries and the Soviet
    Union, Pr 36.8:T 67
President's Special Review Board, Pr 40.8:Sp 3
President's Task Force–
Air Pollution, Pr 37.8:Ai 7
Communications Policy, Pr 36.8:C 73
Employee-Management Relations in Federal
    Service, Pr 35.8:Em 7/2
Highway Safety, Pr 37.8:H 53
Manpower Conservation, Pr 35.8:M 31
Preservation of Natural Beauty, Pr 36.8:N 21
Private Sector Initiatives, Pr 40.8:P 93
Victims of Crime, Pr 40.8:V 66
President's Temporary Commission on Pennsylvania
    Avenue, Pr 36.8:P 38
President's Water Resources Policy Commission, Pr
    33.12
Press Intelligence Division for U.S. Government, PI 1
Prevailing Rate Advisory Committee, Federal, Y 4.P
    84/10-12
Prevention and Control Division, Cancer, HE 20.3151/
    4
Prevention and Control, National Center for Injury, HE
    20.7950
Prevention, Centers for Disease Control and, HE
    20.7000
Prevention Council, President's Crime, Pr 42.8:C 86
Prevention, Office of Juvenile Justice and Delinquency,
    J 32
Prevention, Pesticides, and Toxic Substances, Office of,
    EP 5
Prevention Services Center, HE 20.7300
Price Administration and Civilian Supply Office, Pr
    32.4200
Price Administration Office, Pr 32.4200
Price Commission, Y 3.P 93/4
Price Section, Y 3.W 19/2:40
Price Stability Cabinet Committee, Pr 36.8:P 93
Price Stability Council, PrEx 22
Price Stability for Economic Growth, President's
    Cabinet Committee on, Pr 34.8:P 93
Price Stabilization Office, ES 3
Prices and Costs Committee, Government Activities
    Affecting, Y 3.G 74/3
Prices, Select Committee to Investigate, (Senate), Y 4.W
    12
Primary Health Care, Bureau of, HE 20.9110
Printing and Publications Division, C 16
Printing and Stationery Division, T 36
Printing Bureau, Engraving and, T 18
Printing Committee (House), Y 4.P 93/2
Printing Committee (Senate), Y 4.P 93/3
Printing Investigation Commission, Y 3.P 93
Printing, Joint Commission, Y 3.P 93
Printing Office, Government, GP
Printing, Public Select Committee to Investigate, Y 4.P
    93/4
Prints and Photographs Division, LC 11, LC 25
Prints Division, LC 11
Priorities Division, Y 3.W 19/2:10
Priority in Transportation Commissioner, Y 3.P 93/2
Prison Industries, Inc., Federal, FPI
Prison Industries Reorganization Administration, Y
    3.P 93/3
Prisoner Rehabilitation Task Force, Pr 37.8:P 93
Prisons Bureau, J 16
Prisons, Federal Bureau of, J 16
Privacy Protection Study Commission, Y 3.P 93/5
Private International Law, Secretary of State's
    Advisory Committee on, S 1.130
Private Land Claims Committee (House), Y 4.P 93/5
Private Land Claims Committee (Senate), Y 4.P 93/7
Private Land Claims Court, Ju 5
Private Retirement and Welfare Programs, President's
    Committee on, Pr 35.8:P 38/2
Private Sector Initiatives, President's Task Force on, Pr
    40.8:P 93
Private Sector Survey on Cost Control, President's, Pr
    40.8:C 82
Privileges and Elections Committee (Senate), Y 4.P 93/
    6
Processing Department, LC 30
Processing Tax Board of Review, T 61
Procurement and Material Office, N 30
Procurement Division, T 58
Procurement Policy, Office of Federal, PrEx 2.21
Product Liability, Interagency Task Force on, C 1.66/2
Product Safety Commission, Consumer, Y 3.C 76/3
Product Safety National Commission, Y 3.N 21/25
Production Administration, Defense, Pr 33.1100, DP 1
Production and Marketing Administration, A 82

Production and Resource Board, United States, Great
    Britain, and Canada Combined, Y 3.C 73/3
Production Authority, National, C 40
Production Management Office, Pr 32.4000
Production Office, A 80.200
Productivity and Quality of Working Life, National
    Center for, Y 3.P 94
Productivity and Work Quality, National Commission
    on, Pr 37.8:P 94
Productivity, National Commission, Pr 37.8:P 94
Productivity, White House Conference on, Pr 40.8:P 94
Products and Services of the Blind and Other Severely
    Handicapped, Committee on Purchase of, Y
    3.P 97
Professional Development and Training, Center for, HE
    20.7700
Professional Scholarship Program, VA Health, VA 1.63
Professional Sports Select Committee (House), Y 4.Sp 6
Professional Standards Review Council, National, HE
    1.46, HE 20.5010
Professional Standards Review Organization, HE
    22.210
Professions Bureau, Health, HE 20.9300
Program–
Agricultural Conservation, A 55.42
Aquatic Plant Control, D 103.24/13
Archeological and Historical Data Recovery, I
    29.59/4
Army Training and Evaluation, D 101.20/2
ARS National Research, A 77.28
Atlantic Climate Change, C 55.55
Biological Services, I 49.2:B 52
Cellular and Molecular Basis of Disease, HE
    20.3466
Central, Western, and South Pacific Fisheries
    Development, C 55.329
Climatic Impact Assessment, TD 1.38
End-Stage Renal Disease, HE 22.9/2
Emergency Conservation, A 82.93
Federal Ocean, Pr 39.12
Forest Management, A 13.152
Geothermal Energy Research, Development and
    Demonstration, ER 1.31
Habitat Conservation, C 55.340
Industrial Energy Efficiency Improvement, E 1.47
Interagency Energy-Environment Research and
    Development, EP 1.28/8
Long Term Resource Monitoring, I 49.109
Mental Health Intramural Research, HE 20.8136
Microbiology and Infectious Diseases, HE 20.3263
National Acid Precipitation Assessment, C 55.703
National Cancer, HE 20.3184/4
National Climate, C 55.44
National Immunization, HE 20.7960
National Status and Trends, C 55.436
Natural Resource Development, SBA 1.48
NOAA Undersea Research, C 55.29
Northern Great Plains Resources, Y 3.N 81/4
Organized Crime Drug Enforcement Task Force, J
    1.93
Public Housing Management Improvement, HH
    1.63
Refugee Resettlement, HE 3.72
Smoking, Tobacco, and Cancer, HE 20.3184
Urban Development Action Grant, HH 1.46/5
VA Health Professional Scholarship, VA 1.63
Value Engineering, GS 6.10
Weather Research, C 55.626
Women's Educational Equity Act, ED 1.44
Program Operations, Bureau of, HE 22.400
Program Policy Bureau, HE 22.300
Programs Bureau, International, C 49
Programs, National Advisory Council on Women's
    Education, Y 3.W 84/2
Programs Office, Airport, TD 4.100
Programs Operation Office, Water, EP 2
Prohibition Bureau, J 17
Project–
Books for the Adult Blind, LC 19
Colorado River Basin, I 27.71/3
Consumers, L 17
DAWN, J 24.19/2
President's Reorganization, PrEx 1.11
Science and Technology, LC 32
Snake River Birds of Prey Research, I 53.39
Promoting Increased Foreign Investments in United
    States Corporate Securities and Increased
    Foreign Financing for United States
    Corporations Operating
Abroad, Task Force on, Pr 35.8:F 76/3
Promotion of Rifle Practice National Board, W 82
Propaganda or Money Alleged to have been used by
    Foreign Governments to Influence United
    States Senators, Special Committee to
    Investigate, Y 4.P 94
Property Bureau, Alien, J 19

Property Disposal Service, Defense, D 7.6/13
Property Management and Disposal Service, GS 10
Property Management Office, Facilities, HE 1.100
Property, Office of Personal, GS 2
Prospective Payment Assessment Commission, Y 3.P 29
Protection Board, Merit Systems, MS 1
Protection of Human Subjects of Biomedical and Behavioral Research, National Commission for, Y 3.H 88
Protection, Privacy, Study Commission, Y 3.P 93/5
Provisions and Clothing Bureau, N 20
Provost Marshal General, Office of, W 37, D 120
Public Administration, National Academy of, Y 3.N 21/28

Public Affairs Office–
    Department of Agriculture, A 107
    Department of Defense, D 6
Public Buildings Administration, FW 6
Public Buildings and Grounds Committee (House), Y 4.P 96/6
Public Buildings and Grounds Committee (Senate), Y 4.P 96/7
Public Buildings and Grounds Office, W 38
Public Buildings and Public Parks of National Capital Office, PB
Public Buildings Commission, Y 3.P 96/4
Public Buildings Service, GS 6
Public Contracts Division, L 18
Public Debt Bureau, T 63.200
Public Debt Service, T 57
Public Diplomacy, United States Advisory Commission on, Y 3.Ad 9
Public Documents Division, I 15, GP 3
Public Domain, Committee on Conservation and Administration of, Y 3.P 96/5
Public Expenditures, Committee on (House), Y 4.P 96/5
Public Health and Marine Hospital Service, T 27
Public Health and National Quarantine Committee (Senate), Y 4.P 96/9
Public Health and Science, Office of, HE 20
Public Health, Select Committee (House), Y 4.P 96/8
Public Health Service, FS 2, FS 2.300, HE 20, T 27
Public Higher Education in District of Columbia Committee, President's, Pr 35.8:Ed 8
Public Housing Administration, HH 3
Public Housing Administration, Federal, NHA 4
Public Housing Management Improvement Program, HH 1.63
Public Housing, National Commission on Severely Distressed, Y 3.P 96/9
Public Information Committee, Y 3.P 96/3
Public Information Division, M 118, D 115
Public Information Office, D 6
Public Land Commission, Y 3.P 96/1
Public Land Law Review Commission, Y 3.P 96/7
Public Lands and Survey Committee (Senate), Y 4.P 96/1
Public Lands Commission, Y 3.P 96/2
Public Lands Committee (House), Y 4.P 96/2
Public Moneys Division, T 31
Public Printer, Depository Library Council to, GP 1.36
Public Relations Bureau, W 107
Public Relations Office, N 31, M 215
Public Road Inquiries Office, A 22
Public Roads Administration, FW 2
Public Roads and Rural Engineering Office, A 22
Public Roads Bureau, A 22, GS 3, C 37, TD 2.100
Public Roads Office, A 22
Public Service Division, Y 3.R 13/2:80
Public Service, Select Committee on Appropriations for Prevention of Fraud in and Depreciations Upon, Y 4.P 96/4
Public Services Administration, HE 17.700, HE 1.900, HE 23.2000
Public Welfare, Committee on Labor and (Senate), Y 4.L 11/2
Public Works Administration, FW 5
Public Works and Transportation Committee (House), Y 4.P 96/11
Public Works Committee (House), Y 4.P 96/11
Public Works Committee (Senate), Y 4.P 96/10
Public Works Federal Emergency Administration, Y 3.F 31/4
Publication Board, Y 3.P 96/6
Publications and Form Center, Naval, D 212.1/2
Publications and Records Commission, National Historical, AE 1.114, AE 1.114/3
Publications and Supplies Division, L 4
Publications Board Office, C 35
Publications Division Research Services, Serial and Government, LC 6
Publications Relating to–

Care of Animals and Poultry, A 77.200
Communications, D 111
Dairy Research, A 77.600
Entomology and Plant Quarantine, A 77.300
Home Economic and Human Nutrition, A 77.700
Horticulture, A 77.500
Industrial Mobilization and Security, D 3
Ordnance, D 105
Research and Development, D 4
Transportation, D 117
Publications Research Service, Joint, Y 3.J 66
Publicity Bureau, Liberty Loan of 1917, T 1.25
Publishing System, Defense Logistics Agency, D 7.41
Puerto Rico Agricultural Experiment Station, A 77.460
Puerto Rico Commission on Status of Puerto Rico, United States, Y 3.Un 3/5
Puerto Rico, Education Department, I 1.39
Puerto Rico, Interior Department, I 1.40
Puerto Rico Reconstruction Administration, I 36
Pulp and Paper Investigations, Select Committee on, Y 4.P 96/3
Purchase from People Who Are Blind or Severely Disabled, Committee for, Y 3B 6
Purchase from the Blind and Other Severely Handicapped, Committee for, Y 3.B 61
Purchase of American-Grown Tobacco by Foreign Governments, Commission to Investigate, Y 3.T 55
Purchase of Products and Services of the Blind and Other Severely Handicapped Committee, Y 3.P 97
Purchase, Storage, and Traffic Division, W 89
Purchases Division, Y 3.R 13/2:110
Purchasing Agent, P 15

Q

Quality Assurance Bureau, HE 20.5500
Quality Laboratory Corporation, Western Wheat, A 77.39
Quality of Working Life, National Center for Productivity and, Y 3.P 94
Quality Planning and Standards Office, Air, EP 4
Quality Service, Food Safety and, A 103
Quality, Water, National Commission on, Y 3.W 29/2
Quarantine, Bureau of Plant, A 48
Quartermaster Corps, W 77, D 106
Quartermaster General of the Army, M 112, D 106
Quartermaster's Department, W 39
Quayle, Dan, PrVp 41

R

Racial Data Committee, Interagency, Y 3.R 11
Radiation and Indoor Air, Office of, EP 6
Radiation Council, Federal, Y 3.F 31/17
Radiation Office, EP 6
Radiation Preservation of Food, Interdepartment Committee on, Y 3.In 8/12
Radiation Programs Office, EP 6
Radiation Research and Policy Coordination Committee, Interagency, P 1.15
Radio Broadcasting to Cuba Advisory Board, Pr 40.8:R 11
Radio Commission, Federal, RC
Radio Division, C 24
Radio Education Committee, Federal, FS 5.100
Radio Service, Naval, N 22
Radioactive Waste Management Office, Civilian, E 1.68/2-7
Radiobiology Research Institute, Armed Forces, D 15
Radiological Health Bureau, HE 20.1500, HE 20.4100
Radiological Health Center, HE 20.4600
Radiological Health Laboratory, CSU-PHS Collaborative, HE 20.4119, HE 20.4600
Radiological Health Laboratory, Southwestern, EP 1.13
Radiological Health, National Center for, HE 20.4600
Rail and Highway Commission, Alaska International, Y 3.Al 1s
Railroad Accounts, Auditor of, I 25
Railroad Adjustment National Board, RA
Railroad Administration, Y 3.R 13/2
Railroad Administration, Federal, TD 3
Railroad Commission, Presidential, Pr 34.8:R 13
Railroad Labor Board, RL 1
Railroad Lighter Captains Commission, Pr 35.8:R 13
Railroad Retirement Board, RR 1
Railroad Retirement, Commission on, Y 3.R 13/3
Railroad Retirement Legislation Joint Committee, Y 4.R 13/3
Railroad Safety Bureau, TD 3.100
Railroad Safety Office, TD 3.100

Railroad Securities Commission, Y 3.R 13
Railroads Commissioner, I 25
Railroads Committee (Senate), Y 4.R 13/2
Railway Association, United States, Y 3.R 13/4
Railway Mail Service, P 10
Railways and Canals Committee (House), Y 4.R 13
Railways, Electric, IC 1 eler
Rare Book and Special Collections Division, LC 23
Rare Book Collections, LC 23
Rare Book Division, LC 23
Rate Advisory Committee, Federal Prevailing, Y 4.P 84/10-12
Rate Section, IC 1 rat
Ratemaking Commission, Motor Carrier, Y 3.M 85/2
Reactor Research and Development, Division of, E 1.15
Reader Division, Stack and, LC 34
Readjustment of Service Pay, Select Committee on, Y 4.R 22
Readjustment of Service Pay, Special Joint Committee (House), Y 4.R 22/2
Real Estate Bondholders' Reorganizations, Select Committee on Investigation of (House), Y 4.R 22/3
Real Estate Service, W 94
Realignment Commission, Defense Base, Y 3.D 36/2
Reclamation and Enforcement Office, Surface Mining, I 71
Reclamation Bureau, I 27
Reclamation Service, I 19.17, I 27
Reclassification of Salaries, Joint Commission, Y 4.R 24/2
Reconstruction and Production Select Committee, (Senate), Y 4.R 24/3
Reconstruction Finance Corporation, C 33, FL 5, Y 3.R 24
Reconstruction Joint Committee, Y 4.R 24
Reconstruction Research Division, Y 3.C 83:90
Recorded Sound Division, LC 40
Records Administration, National Archives and, AE 1.100
Records and Library Office, Naval, N 16
Records and Pension Office, W 40
Records Commission, National Historical, AE 1.114, AE 1.114/3
Records of Congress, Advisory Committee, Y 3.C 76/4
Records Service, National Archives and, GS 4
Recovery Administration, National, Y 3.N 21/8
Recovery and Enforcement, National Commission on Financial Institution, Y 3.F 32
Recovery Review Board, National, Y 3.N 21/11
Recreation Advisory Council, Pr 35.8:R 24
Recreation and Natural Beauty Citizens' Advisory Committee, Pr 36.8:R 24
Recreation Federal Inter-Agency Committee, Y 3.F 31/14
Recreation Service, I 70
Recruiting Bureau, N 5
Recruiting Publicity Bureau, M 108.75
Recruiting Service, SB 3
Red Basin Inter-agency Committee, Y 3.F 31/13-2
Red Cross, American National, W 102, Y 3.Am 3/5
Reduction of American Tonnage, Committee on the Causes of, Y 4.T 61
Reduction of Federal Expenditures Joint Committee, Y 4.R 24/4
Reed, Walter, Army Medical Center, D 104.15
Reemployment Rights, Bureau of Veterans', L 25
Reemployment Rights Division, Veterans', L 25
Reemployment Rights, Office of Veterans', L 25
Reference and Bibliography Division, General, LC 2
Reference Department, LC 29
Reference Group on Great Lakes Pollution from Land Use Activities, International, Y 3.In 8/28:14
Reforestation, Select Committee (Senate), Y 4.R 25
Reform School for Girls of District of Columbia, J 9
Reform of Federal Criminal Laws, National Commission, Y 3.N 21/26
Reform, Recovery and Enforcement, National Commission on Financial Institution, Y 3.F 32
Refugee Policy, Select Committee on, Y 3.Im 6/2
Refugee Resettlement Program, HE 3.72
Refugees, Freedmen, and Abandoned Lands Bureau, W 41
Refugees, Indochina, Interagency Task Force for, Pr 38.8:R 25
Regional and Medical Programs Service, HE 20.2600
Regional Commission, Pacific Northwest, Y 3.P 11/5
Regional Commission, Southwest Border, Y 3.So 8/2
Regional Council, Federal, Pr 37.8:R 26
Regional Council, Northwest Federal, Y 3.N 81/5
Regional Economic Development Office, C 53
Regional Economics Office, C 49.100
Regional Medical Programs Services, HE 20.6300
Regional Office–

New England, L 2.71/3
Southeastern, L 2.71/8
Register Division, Federal, AE 2
Register of Treasury, T 32
Register Office, Federal, GS 4.100
Registration and Voting Participation Commission,
President's, Pr 35.8:R 26
Registry Agency, Toxic Substances and Disease, HE
20.500, HE 20.7900
Regulation of Financial Services Task Group, Pr 40.8:F
49
Regulations and Standards, Office of Water, EP 8
Regulatory Administration, Economic, E 4
Regulatory Commission–
Federal Energy, E 2
Nuclear, Y 3.N 88
Regulatory Council, Y 3.R 26
Regulatory Information Service Center, PrEx 25
Regulatory Liaison Group, Interagency, Y 3.R 26
Regulatory Reform, Domestic Council Review Group
on, Pr 38.8:R 26
Rehabilitation Act Interagency Coordinating Council,
Annual Report to the President and the
Congress on the Activities of the, J 1.1/5
Rehabilitation Agency, State Vocational, HE 23.4110/2
Rehabilitation Services Administration, FS 17.100, HE
17.100, HE 1.600, HE 23.4100, ED 1.200
Relations, Office for Agricultural War, A 74
Relations with Canada Committee (Senate), Y 4.C 16
Relief Administration of America, Y 3.Am 3/3
Relief for the Near East, Y 3.N 27
Relief, Hungarian Refugee, President's Advisory
Committee on, Pr 34.8:H 89
Religion and Welfare in the Armed Forces Committee,
President's, Y 3.P 92/5
Religious and Moral Welfare and Character Guidance in
the Armed Forces, President's Committee on,
Y 3.P 92/5
Relocation, Commission on Wartime, Y 3.W 19/10
Removal, National Commission on Judicial, Pr 42.8:D
63
Renal Disease Program, End-Stage, HE 22.9/2
Renegotiation Board, RnB
Renewal Assistance Administration, HH 7
Renovation of Executive Mansion Commission, Y 3.R
29/2
Rent Commission of District of Columbia, Y 3.R 29
Rent Stabilization Office, ES 5
Reorganization of the Administrative Branch of the
Government, Joint Committee on, Y 4.R 29
Reorganization Project, President's, PrEx 1.11
Repair Bureau, N 4
Reports Office of the Government, Pr 32.200
Research Advisory Board, Great Lakes, Y 3.In 8/28:10
Research Advisory Committee, Farm Resources and
Facilities, A 1.103
Research, Agency for Health Care Policy and HE
20.6500
Research and Development Activity, Naval Ocean, D
210.100
Research and Development Administration, Energy, ER
Research and Development Board, M 500, M 6, D 4
Research and Development Board, Joint, Y 3.J 66/2
Research and Development Bureau, FAA 2
Research and Development Center, Army Polar, D
103.37
Research and Development Center, Navy Personnel, D
201.1/3
Research and Development Center, Personnel, CS 1.71
Research and Development Command, Army
Electronics, D 111
Research and Development Command, U.S. Army Air
Mobility, D 117
Research and Development, Division of Reactor, E 1.15
Research and Development Laboratory, Air Mobility, D
117.8
Research and Development Office, Region 1, EP 1.1/3
Research and Development Program, Interagency
Energy-Environment, EP 1.28/8
Research and Health Care Technology Assessment,
National Center for Health Services, HE
20.6500
Research and Improvement Center, Educational, ED
1.300
Research and Marketing Act, Office of the Administra-
tor, A 87
Research and Policy Coordination Committee,
Interagency Radiation, P 1.15
Research and Quality, Agency for Healthcare, HE
20.6500
Research and Special Programs Administration, TD 10
Research and Statistics Division, T 62
Research, and Statistics Office, Justice Assistance,, J 26
Research Bureau–
Shipping Board, SB 7

War Trade Board, WT 5
Research, Bureau of International Economics, C 57.26
Research Center–
Army Materials and Mechanics, D 101.80
Biologics, HE 20.4800
Drug, HE 20.4700
Laramie Energy, ER 1.23
Naval Health, D 206.22
Population, HE 20.3351/3
Research Council, National, NA 2
Research, Dairy, Publications Relating to, A 77.600
Research, Development, and Demonstration Program,
Geothermal Energy, ER 1.31
Research Division, Consumer and Food Economics, A
77.700
Research, Education, National Council on, HE 19.214
Research Facilities Center, C 55.601/4
Research for Mothers and Children Center, HE 20.3351/
2
Research Institute–
Armed Forces Radiobiology, D 15
Behavioral and Social Sciences, Army, D 101.60, D
101.60/3, D 101.60/6
Behavioral and Social Sciences, U.S. Army, D
101.1/7
Inhalation Toxicology, E 1.1/6
Research Integrity Office, HE 20.1/3
Research Laboratory–
Army, D 101.1/11
Duluth Environmental, EP 1.46/6
Great Lakes Environmental, C 55.620
Industrial Environmental, EP 1.46/5
Municipal Environmental, EP 1.46/7
National Hurricane, C 55.601/3
Research, Letterman Army Institute of, D 104.29
Research Natural Areas Committee, Federal, Y 3.F 31/19
Research Office–
Aerospace, D 301.69
Information Agency, IA 1.24/3
Naval, N 32, M 216, D 210
Oceanic and Atmospheric, C 55.700
Research Planning Conference, Northwest Shellfish
Sanitation, EP 2.15
Research Program–
ARS National, A 77.28
Mental Health Intramural, HE 20.8136
NINCDS, HE 20.3502
NOAA Undersea, C 55.29
Weather, C 55.626
Research Project, Snake River Birds of Prey, I 53.39
Research Related to Global Change, White House
Conference,, Pr 41.8:G 51
Research Resources and Centers, Division of Cancer,
HE 20.3151/2
Research Service, Congressional, LC 14
Research Service, VA Medical, VA 1.1/4
Research Services, Serial and Government Publications
Division, LC 6
Research Station
Rocky Mountain, A 13.151
Southern, A 13.150
Reservation Economies, Presidential Commission on
Indian, Pr 40.8:In 2
Reserve Bank Organization Committee, RB
Reserve Force Division, Naval, N 25
Reserve Forces Policy Committee, Army, D 101.1/12
Reserves, Ecological, Federal Committee on, Y 3.F 31/
22
Resettlement Administration, A 61, Y 3.R 31
Resettlement Program, Refugee, HE 3.72
Resolution Trust Corporation, Y 3.R 31/2
Resource Board, United States, Great Britain, and
Canada Combined, Y 3.C 73/3
Resource Development Bureau, HMO's and, HE
20.9200
Resource Development Program, Natural, SBA 1.48
Resource Monitoring Program, Long Term, I 49.109
Resources and Services Administration, Health, HE
20.9000
Resources and Trade Assistance Bureau, C 57.200
Resources Board, National, Y 3.N 21/12
Resources Committee, National, Y 3.N 21/12
Resources, Committee on, Y 4.R 31/3
Resources Conservation Agency, Natural, A 57
Resources Development Bureau, Health, HE 20.9500
Resources Development Bureau, Health Maintenance
Organizations and, HE 20.9200
Resources Development Bureau, Maternal and Child,
HE 20.9200
Resources Development, Bureau of Health Planning
and, HE 20.6100
Resources Division, Biological, I 19.200
Resources Information Center, Educational, ED 1.301/2
Resources Laboratory, Air Force Human, D 301.45/27
Resources Management, Office of Information, GS 12

Resources Planning Board, National, Pr 32.300
Resources Program, Northern Great Plains, Y 3.N 81/4
Resources Service, Water and Power, I 27
Retirement and Welfare Programs, Private, President's
Committee on, Pr 35.8:P 38/2
Retirement System, TVA, Y 3.T 25:1-14
Retirement Thrift Investment Board, Federal, Y 3.F 31/
25
Retraining and Re-employment Administration, L 24
Retrenchment Committee (Senate), Y 4.R 31/1
Retrenchment, Joint Select Committee on, Y 4.R 31/2
Retrievable Storage Review Commission, Monitored, Y
3.M 74/2Revenue Cutter Service, T 33
Revenue Marine Division, T 33
Review Board–
Nuclear Waste Technical, Y 3.N 88/2
President's Special, Pr 40.8:Sp 3
Review Commission–
American Indian Policy, Y 4.In 2/10
Federal Mine Safety and Health, Y 3.M 66
Monitored Retrievable Storage, Y 3.M 74/2
National Bankruptcy, Y 3.2:B 22/B 22
Physician Payment, Y 3.P 56
Review Committee, Development Planning in Alaska,
President's, Pr 36.8:Al 1
Review Committee, Interagency Classification, Y 3.C 56
Review Council, National Professional Standards, HE
1.46, HE 20.5010
Review Group on Regulatory Reform, Domestic
Council, Pr 38.8:R 26
Review of Antitrust Laws and Procedures, National
Commission for, Pr 39.8:An 8
Review of Federal and State Laws Relating to
Wiretapping and Electronic Surveillance,
National Commission for, Y 3.W 74/2
Review of the National Policy toward Gambling,
Commission on, Y 3.G 14
Review Organization, Professional Standards, HE
22.210
Revise and Codify Criminal and Penal Laws
Commission, Y 3.L 44
Revise and Codify the Laws of the United States
Commission, Y 3.L 44
Revision of Statutes Commission, Y 3.R 32
Revision of the Federal Court Appellate System,
Commission on, Y 3.Ap 4/3
Revolution Bicentennial Commission, American, Y
3.Am 3/6
Rights, Bureau of Veterans' Reemployment, L 25
Rights Division, Veterans' Reemployment, L 25
Rights, Office of Veterans' Reemployment, L 25
River Basin Committee, Federal Inter-Agency, Y 3.F 31/
13
River Basins Commission, New England, Y 3.N 42/3
Rivers and Canals Committee (Senate), Y 4.R 53
Rivers and Harbors Committee (House), Y 4.R 52
Road Inquiries, Office of Public, A 22
Road Inquiry Office, A 22
Roads and Canals Committee (Senate), Y 4.R 53
Roads Committee (House), Y 4.R 53/2
Roads Bureau, Public, A 22, GS 3, C 37, TD 2.100
Roads, Office of Public, A 22
Rocky Mountain Forest and Range Experiment Station,
A 13.69
Rocky Mountain National Park, I 1.57
Rocky Mountain Research Station, A 13.151
Rolls and Library Bureau, S 8
Roosevelt, Franklin D. Library, GS 4.9
Roosevelt, Franklin Delano, Pr 32
Roosevelt, Franklin Delano, Memorial Commission, Y
3.R 67
Roosevelt, Theodore, Pr 26
Rubber Producing Facilities Disposal Commission, Y
3.R 82
Rules and Administration Committee (Senate), Y 4.R
86/2
Rules Committee (House), Y 4.R 86/1
Rural Business Cooperative Service, A 109
Rural Community Development Service, A 97
Rural Credits, Joint Committee, Y 4.R 88
Rural Delivery Division, P 16
Rural Development, A 114
Rural Development, Committee on, Y 3.R 88/3
Rural Development Program Committee, Y 3.R 88/2
Rural Development Service, A 102
Rural Development Task Force, Pr 37.8:R 88
Rural Electrification Administration, Y 3.R 88, A 68
Rural Engineering Office, A 22
Rural Housing Service, A 115
Rural Organization Office, A 36
Rural Poverty, National Advisory Commission on, Pr
36.8:R 88
Rural Utilities Service, A 68

S

Safety Administration, Mining, L 38
Safety Advisory Panel, Aerospace, NAS 1.1/7
Safety and Applied Nutrition Center, Food, HE 20.4500
Safety and Health Administration, Mine, L 38
Safety and Health Administration, Occupational, L 35
Safety and Health, National Institute of Occupational, HE 20.7100
Safety and Health Review Commission, Federal Mine, Y 3.M 66
Safety Board, Defense Nuclear Facilities, Y 3.D 36/3
Safety Bureau, IC 1 saf
Safety Commission, Aviation, Y 3.Av 5/2
Safety Commission, Consumer Product, Y 3.C 76/3
Select Committee on POW/MIA Affairs, (Senate), Y 4.P 93/8
Safety Council, Federal, L 30
Safety Hazards Investigation Board, Chemical, Y 3. C42
Safety Laboratory, ER 1.27
Safety, Office of Merchant Marine, TD 5.35
Safety Office, Railroad, TD 3.100
Safety Oversight Committee, President's Nuclear, Pr 40.8:N 88
Saint Augustine Quadricentennial Commission, Y 3.Sa 2/2
Saint Elizabeth's Hospital, FS 11
Saint Lawrence Seaway Development Corporation, Y 3.Sa 2, TD 6
Salaries and Allowances Division, P 12
Salaries, Commission on Executive, Legislative, and Judicial, Y 3.Ex 3/3
Salary Stabilization Board, ES 4
Saline Water, Office of, I 1.88
Samoan Commission of America, Y 3.Am 3/2
Santiago and Puerto Principe Department, W 59
Santo Domingo Commission, Y 3.Sa 5
Satellite, Data, and Information Service, National Environmental, C 55.200
Satellite Service, National Earth, C 55.500
Savings Bond Division, T 66
Savings Staff, War, T 1.100
Savings System, Postal, P 19
Scholars Commission, Presidential, ED 1.500, Pr 40.8:Sch 6
Scholars, Woodrow Wilson International Center for, SI 12
Scholarship Program, VA Health Professional, VA 1.63
School, Army Ordnance, D 105.25
School, Defense Intelligence, D 5.210
School Finance, President's Commission on, Pr 37.8:Sch 6
School for Boys, National Training, J 8
School for Girls, National Training, J 9
Science Academy, National, NA 1
Science Advisory Board, Great Lakes, Y 3.In 8/28:12
Science Advisory Committee, President's, Pr 34.8:Sci 2, Pr 35.8:Sci 2
Science and Astronautics Committee (House), Y 4.Sci 2
Science and Economics Research Related to Global Change, White House Conference on, Pr 41.8:G 51
Science and Education Administration, A 106
Science and Standards Division, Polymer, C 13.1/7
Science and Technology Committee (House), Y 4.Sci 2
Science and Technology Division, LC 33
Science and Technology Office, PrEx 8
Science and Technology Policy Office, PrEx 23
Science and Technology, Task Force on Women, Minorities, and the Handicapped in, Y 3.W 84/3
Science and Technology Project, LC 32
Science and Transportation Committee (Senate), Y 4.C 73/7
Science, Center for Materials, C 13.1/9
Science Center, Northwest Fisheries, C 55.331/3
Science, Committee on, Y 4.Sci 2
Science Division, LC 33
Science, Engineering, and Technology, Federal Coordinating Council for, PrEx 8.100
Science Foundation, National, NS 1
Science Information Service Office, NS 2
Science, Office of Public Health and, He 20
Science Policy Task Force, Pr 37.8:Sci 2
Science, President's Committee on the National Medal of, Pr 35.8:M 46
Science, Space, and Technology Committee (House), Y 4.Sci 2
Sciences and Technology, Institute for Computer, C 13.73
Sciences, Army Research Institute for the Behavioral and Social, D 101.60/6

Sciences, Division of Earth, NA 1.1/2
Sciences, U.S. Army Research Institute for the Behavioral and Social, D 101.1/7
Scientific Advisory Panel, Army, D 101.81
Scientific and Technical Information, Clearinghouse for Federal, C 51
Scientific Research and Development Interdepartmental Committee, Y 3.In 8/4
Scientific Research and Development Office, Pr 32.413
Scientists and Engineers, President's Committee on, Pr 34.8:Sci 27
Scientists for Federal Government Programs, President's Committee on, Pr 34.8:En 3
Sculpture Garden, Hirshhorn, SI 13
Sea Systems Command, Naval, D 211
Sea Transportation Service, Military, D 216
Seaboard, Select Committee on Transportation Routes to, Y 4.T 68
Sealift Command, Military, D 216
Seat of Government in Washington, Commission on the Centennial of the Establishment of, Y 4.C 333
Second Assistant Postmaster General, P 3
Second Comptroller, T 14
Secret Service Division, T 34
Secretary of State's Advisory Committee on Private International Law, S 1.130
Section—
    Employment Management, Y 3.W 19/2:20
    Foreign Markets, A 12
    Medical, Y 3.C 83:40
    Price, Y 3.W 19/2:40
    Rates, IC 1 rat
    Seed and Plant Introduction, A 23
    Silk, A 25
    State Councils, Y 3.C 83:70
    Troop Movement, Y 3.R 13/2:120
    Vegetable Pathology, A 28
    War Trade Board, S 13
Securities and Exchange Commission, SE
Security and Cooperation in Europe, Commission on, Y 4.Se 2
Security Center, Computer, D 1.79
Security Center, National Computer, D 1.79/2
Security Commission of the Government, Y 3.G 74/2
Security Committee, National (House), Y 4.Se 2/1
Security Council, National, Y 3.N 21/17, Pr 33.600, PrEx 3
Security Resources Board, National, Pr 33.700, Y 3.N 21/18
Security Service, Civil Aviation, TD 4.800
Security Training Commission, National, Y 3.N 21/19
Seed and Plant Introduction Section, A 23
Seed Division, A 24
Select and Special Committees (House), Y 4.Se 4/1, Y 4.2
Select and Special Committees (Senate), Y 4.Se 4/2, Y 4.3
Select Commission on Immigration and Refugee Policy, Y 3.Im 6/2
Select Committee—
    Aging (House), Y 4.Ag 4/2
    Assassinations (House), Y 4.As 7
    Children, Youth, and Families (House), Y 4.C 43/2
    Congressional Operations, Y 4.C 76/9
    Ethics (House), Y 4.Et 3/2
    Ethics (Senate), Y 4.Et 3/4
    Hunger (Senate), Y 4.H 89
    Indian Affairs (Senate), Y 4.In 2/11
    Intelligence (House), Y 4.In 8/18
    Intelligence (Senate), Y 4.In 8/19
    Investigate Covert Arms Transactions with Iran, Y 4.In 8/20
    Investigate District of Columbia Charities, Joint, Y 4.D 63/3
    Investigate the Escape of Grover Cleveland Bergdoll from Disciplinary Barracks at Governors Island, N.Y., (House), Y 4.B 45/2
    Investigate Wages and Prices (Senate), Y 4.W 12
    Missing Persons in Southeast Asia (House), Y 4.M 69/3
    Narcotics Abuse and Control (House), Y 4.N 16
    Population (House), Y 4.P 81
    Professional Sports (House), Y 4.Sp 6
    Retrenchment, Joint, Y 4.R 31/2

    Sickness and Mortality of Emigrant Ships (Senate), Y 4.Si 1
    Study Government Operations with Respect to Intelligence Activities, (Senate), Y 4.In 8/17
    Study Law, Y 4.L 41
    Study the Senate Committee System, Temporary, Y 4.Se 5/4

Transportation Routes to Seaboard, Y 4.T 68
    Woman Suffrage (Senate), Y 4.W 84
Selective Service Records Office, Y 3.Se 4
Selective Service System, Pr 32.5270, Y 3.Se 4
Selective Service Systems Structure Task Force, Pr 36.8:Se 4
Semiconductors, National Advisory Committee on, Y 3.Se 5/3
Semitic Literature Division, LC 20
Senate, Y 1.3
Senate, Commission on the Operation of, Y 4.Se 5/5
Senate Committee System, Temporary Select Committee to Study, Y 4.Se 5/4
Senate Contingent Expenses Committee (Senate), Y 4.Se 5
Senate Contingent Expenses Committee to Audit and Control (Senate), Y 4.Se 5/3
Senatorial Campaign Expenditures, Select Committee on (Senate), Y 4.Se 5/2
Sentencing Commission, United States, Y 3.Se 5
Sequoia and General Grant National Parks, I 1.29
Serial and Government Publications Division Research Services, LC 6
Serial Division, LC 6
Service—
    Agricultural Conservation Program, A 90
    Agricultural Marketing, A 66, A 88
    Agricultural Research, A 77
    Agricultural Stabilization and Conservation, A 82
    Air, W 87
    Air Mail, P 20
    Air Traffic, FAA 3, TD 4.300
    Air Traffic Operations, TD 4.300
    Aircraft Certification, TD 4.900
    Aircraft Development, TD 4.600
    Airports, FAA 8, TD 4.100
    Airway Facilities, TD 4.700
    Alaskan Fisheries, C 6.8
    American Forces Information, D 2
    Animal and Plant Health, A 101
    Animal and Plant Health Inspection, A 101
    Apprenticeship Training, L 23
    Armed Forces Information, D 2
    Army Map, D 103.20
    Automated Data and Telecommunications, GS 12
    Aviation Medical, FAA 7
    Blind, LC 16
    Chemical Warfare, W 91
    Civil Aviation Security, TD 4.800
    Commodity Stabilization, A 82
    Community Facilities, HH 5
    Community Health, HE 20.2550
    Community Relations, C 50, J 23
    Comprehensive Health Planning, HE 20.2580
    Conciliation, L 19
    Congressional Research, LC 14
    Consumer and Marketing, A 88
    Consumer Protection and Environmental Health, HE 20.1000
    Cooperative Cataloging and Classification, LC 22
    Cooperative Extension Work, A 43.5
    Cooperative State Research, A 94
    Defense Property Disposal, D 7.6/13
    Economic Research, A 93
    Employment, L 7
    Environmental Data, C 55.200
    Environmental Health, HE 20.1000
    Export Marketing, A 99
    Extension, A 43, A 80.300
    Farmer Cooperative, A 89
    Federal Extension, A 43, A 80.300
    Federal Grain Inspection, A 104
    Federal Health Program, HE 20.2700, HE 20.5200
    Federal Mediation and Conciliation, FM
    Federal Supply, GS 2
    Finance, W 97
    Financial Management, T 63.100
    Fiscal, T 63
    Fish and Wildlife, I 49
    Flight Standards, TD 4.400
    Food and Nutrition, A 98
    Food Safety and Quality, A 103
    Foreign Agriculture, A 64, A 67
    Foreign Broadcast Information, Pr 34.650, PrEx 7
    Foreign Economic Development, A 100
    Grazing, I 38
    Health Care Facilities, HE 20.2500, HE 20.6400
    Health Facilities Planning and Construction, HE 20.2500
    Health Maintenance Organization, HE 20.2050
    Heritage Conservation and Recreation, I 70
    Human Nutrition Information, A 111
    Immigration and Naturalization, J 21, L 15
    Impasses Panel, Federal, Y 3.F 31/21-2

Indian Health, HE 20.300, HE 20.2650, HE 20.5300, HE 20.9400
Information and Education, L 9
Inland and Coastwise Waterways, W 101
Internal Revenue, T 22
International Agricultural Development, A 95
Joint Publications Research, Y 3.J 66
Legislative Reference, LC 14
Life-saving, T 24
Marine Hospital, T 27
Maternal and Child Health, HE 20.2750
Minerals Management, I 72
National Agricultural Statistics, A 92
National Archives and Records, GS 4
National Biological, I 73
National Criminal Justice Information and Statistics, J 26.10
National Earth Satellite, C 55.500
National Environmental Satellite, C 55.500
National Environmental Satellite, Data, and Information, C 55.200
National Marine Fisheries, C 55.300
National Ocean, C 55.400
National Parks, I 29
National Technical Information, C 51
National Weather, C 55.100
Navajo Area Indian Health, HE 20.9413
Naval Communications, N 22
Naval Radio, N 22
Postal Transportation, P 10
Property Management and Disposal, GS 10
Public Buildings, GS 6
Public Debt, T 57
Public Health, T 27, FS 2, HE 20
Public Health and Marine Hospital, T 27
Radio, N 22
Railway Mail, P 10
Real Estate, W 94
Reclamation, I 19.17, I 27
Recruiting, SB 3
Regional and Medical Programs, HE 20.2600
Regional Medical Programs, HE 20.6300
Revenue Cutter, T 33
Rural Business Cooperative, A 109
Rural Community Development, A 97
Rural Development, A 102
Rural Housing, A 115
Rural Utilities, A 68
Social and Rehabilitation, FS 17, HE 17
Soil Conservation, A 57, A 76.200, A 79.200, A 80.500, A 80.2000
Soil Erosion, I 30
Statistical Reporting, A 92
Steamboat Inspection, C 15, T 38
Supply, W 109
Systems Research and Development, FAA 2, TD 4.500
Training, L 12
Training and Employment, L 34
Transportation, W 98
Transportation and Communications, GS 8
Transportation and Public Utilities, GS 8
U.S. Employment, L 37.300
Unemployment Insurance, L 33, L 37.200
United States Postal, P 1
United States Marshals, J 25
United States Travel, C 47
Utilization and Disposal, GS 9
VA Medical Research, VA 1.1/4
Veteran's Employment & Training, L 39
Waste Reclamation, C 20
Water and Power Resources, I 27
Working Conditions, L 14
Service Agency, Consolidated Farm, A 112
Service Center, Regulatory Information, PrEx 25
Service Learning, National Center for, AA 3
Service, Office of Declassification and Technical, C 35
Service, Voluntary, National Advisory Committee, VA 1.52
Services Administration, Health, HE 20.9000
Services, Administration of Rehabilitation, HE 23.4100
Services Administration, Public, HE 17.700
Services Administration, Substance Abuse and Mental Health, HE 20.400, HE 20.8000
Services, Armed Forces Information, D 2
Services, Center for Prevention, HE 20.7300
Services, Combined Tribal and Bureau Law Enforcement, I 20.58
Services, Directorate of Administrative, D 303
Services, Human Development, Office of, HE 23
Services, Institute of Museum, MuS 1, NF 4
Services, National Center for Health, HE 20.6500
Services, National Library, for the Blind and Physically Handicapped, LC 19

Services of the Blind and Other Severely Handicapped, Committee on Purchase of, Y 3.P 97
Services, Office of Federal, GS 2
Services, Serial and Government Publications Division Research, LC 6
Severely Distressed Public Housing, National Commission on, Y 3.P 96/9
Severely Handicapped, Committee for Purchase from, Y 3.B 61
Severely Handicapped, Committee on Purchase of Products and Services of, Y 3.P 97
Shellfish Sanitation Research Planning Conference, Northwest, EP 2.15
Shiloah National Military Park Commission, W 63
Ship Hydrodynamics, Numerical, International Conference on, D 211.9/5
Ship Purchase Lobby, Alleged, Special Committee to Investigate (Senate), Y 4.Sh 6/2
Ship Structures Committee, Y 3.Sh 6
Ship Subsidy Lobby, Alleged, Special Committee to Investigate (Senate), Y 4.Sh 6/2
Ship Structure Committee, TD 5.63
Ship Structures Committee, Y 3.Sh 6
Ship Subsidy Lobby, Alleged, Select Committee to Investigate (House), Y 4.Sh 6
Ship Systems Command, Naval, D 211
Shipbuilding Commission, American, Y 3.Sh 6/2
Ship-Building Committee, American, (House), Y 4.Am 3/1
Shipping Board, SB
Shipping Board Bureau, C 27
Shipping Board Emergency Fleet Corporation, SB 2
Shipping Board Emergency Fleet Corporation, Select Committee (House), Y 4.Sh 6/4
Shipping Board Merchant Fleet Corporation, SB 2
Shipping Board Operations, Select Committee (House), Y 4.Sh 6/3
Shipping Commissioners, C 12
Ships Bureau, N 29, M 210, D 211
Short Time Record Credits Joint Committee, Y 4.Sh 8
Shortages, National Commission on Supplies and, Y 3.Su 7/2
Sickness and Mortality on Emigrant Ships, Select Committee on, (Senate), Y 4.Si 1
Signal Corps, D 111
Signal Office, W 42
Signal Service, Geological Survey, Coast and Geodetic Survey, and Hydrographic Office, Joint Commission to Consider the Present Organizations of, Y 3.Si 2
Silk Section, A 25
Silver, Special Committee on the Investigation of, Y 4.Si 3
Skin Diseases, National Institute, HE 20.3900
Slavic and East European Division, LC 35
Sleeping Car Companies, IC 1 sle
Small and Minority Business Ownership, Presidential Advisory Committee on, Pr 40.8:B 96
Small Business Administration, SBA
Small Business and Entrepreneurship, Committee on, Y 4.Sm 1/2
Small Business Committee, Cabinet, Pr 34.8:Sm 1
Small Business Finance, Interagency Task Force on, Y 3.In 8/29
Small Business Prospects Improvement Task Force, Pr 37.8:Sm 1
Small Business, Select Committee on (House), Y 4.Sm 1
Small Business, Select Committee on (Senate), Y 4.Sm 1/2
Small Business, White House Committee on, Pr 35.8:Sm 1
Small Business, White House Conference, Y 3.W 58/21
Small Defense Plants Administration, SDP
Smithsonian Institution, SI 1
Smoking, Tobacco, and Cancer Program, HE 20.3184
Snake River Birds of Prey Research Project, I 53.39
Social and Economic Statistics Administration, C 56
Social and Rehabilitation Service, FS 17, HE 17
Social Hygiene Board, Interdepartmental, Y 3.In 8/2
Social Sciences, Army Research Institute for, D 101.60/3, D 101.60/6
Social Sciences Research Institute, D 101.60
Social Sciences, U.S. Army Research Institute for the, D 101.1/7
Social Security Administration, FS 3, HE 3, SSA 1
Social Security Advisory Board, Y 3.2:AD 9
Social Securiy Advisory Council, Y 3.Ad 9/3
Social Security Board, SS 1, FS 3
Social Security, National Commission on, Y 3.So 1, Pr 40.8:So 1
Social Statistics, National Center for, FS 17.600, HE 17.600
Society, United States Capitol Historical, Y 3.H 62/2
Society, U.S. Supreme Court Historical, Y 3.H 62/3

Software Development and Information Technology Office, GS 12.16
Soil Conservation Service, A 76.200, A 79.200, A 80.2000, A 80.500, A 57
Soil Erosion Service, I 30
Soil Trafficability Information Analysis Center, D 103.24/12
Soils Bureau, A 26
Soils Division, A 26
Soils, Division of Agricultural, A 26
Solar Energy and Energy Conservation Bank, HH 1.1/3
Soldiers Home in District of Columbia, W 43
Solicitor–
  Agriculture Department, A 33
  Interior Department, I 48
  Labor Department, L 21
  Navy Department, N 8
  Post Office Department, P 6
  Treasury, J 5, T 44
Solicitor General, J 11
Solicitor Office, J 21
Solid Fuels Administration, Defense, I 57
Solid Fuels Administration for War, I 51
Solid Fuels, Office of Minerals and, I 60
Solid Waste Management Bureau, HE 20.1400
Solid Waste Management Office of, EP 3
Souris-Red-Rainy River Basins Commission, Y 3.So 8
South, Department of the, W 66
South Pacific Fisheries Development Program, C 55.329
Southeast Asia, Select Committee on Missing Persons in, (House), Y 4.M 69/3
Southeastern Division, W 69, W 84
Southeastern Forest Experiment Station, A 13.63
Southeastern Power Administration, I 65, E 1.95, E 8
Southeastern Regional Office, L 2.71/8
Southern Department, W 83
Southern Forest Experiment Station, A 13.40
Southern Research Station, A 13.150
Southwest Border Regional Commission, Y 3.So 8/2
Southwest Fisheries Center, C 55.303/2
Southwestern Forest and Range Experiment Station, A 13.43
Southwestern Power Administration, I 59, E 1.95/2
Southwestern Radiological Health Laboratory, EP 1.13
Space Administration, National Aeronautics and, NAS 1
Space and Astronautics, Special Committee on (Senate), Y 4.Sp 1
Space and Technology Committee (House), Y 4.Sci 2
Space Council, National Aeronautics and, PrEx 5
Space Museum, National Air and, SI 9
Space, National Commission on, Y 3.Sp 1
Space Sciences, Committee on Aeronautical and, Y 4.Ae 8
Space Shuttle Challenger Accident Presidential Commission, Pr 40.8:Sp 1
Space Task Group, Pr 36.8:Sp 1
Spanish Division, LC 24
Spanish Speaking Peoples, Cabinet Committee on Opportunity for, Y 3.Sp 2/7
Spanish Treaty Claims Commission, Y 3.Sp 2
Spanish Treaty Claims Commission Assistant Attorney General, J 10
Speaker's Commission on Pages, Y 4.Sp 3
Special Action Office for Drug Abuse Prevention, PrEx 20
Special Agents Division, T 35
Special Collections Division, LC 23
Special Committee–
  Aging (Senate), Y 4.Ag 4
  Centennial Celebration of the Laying of the Corner Stone of the Capitol, Y 4.C 17
  Chinese Immigration, Joint, Y 4.C 44
  Official Conduct (Senate), Y 4.C 76/8
  Termination of the National Emergency (Senate), Y 4.N 21/9
  Year 2000 Technology Problem, Y 4.3:T
Special Committees (House), Y 4.Se 4/1
Special Committees (Senate), Y 4.Se 4/2
Special Investigations, Air Force Office of, D 301.88
Special Programs Administration, TD 10
Special Representative for Trade Negotiations Office, PrEx 9
Special Review Board, President's, Pr 40.8:Sp 3
Special Services Division, W 109.100, M 117
Special Services Office, FS 13
Special Task Force on Travel, Industry- Government, Pr 36.8:T 69
Sports, President's Council on, HE 20.100
Sports, Professional, Select Committee on (House), Y 4.Sp 6
Stability, Council on Wage and Price, PrEx 22
Stabilization Office, Federal Employment, C 26
Stack and Reader Division, LC 34

Staff–
Energy Action, HE 20.6001/2
Tax Advisory, T 64
War Savings, T 1.100
Standards and Conduct, Select Committee (Senate), Y 4.St 2/2
Standards and Quality Bureau, Health, HE 22.200
Standards and Technology, National Institute of, C 13
Standards Board, Cost Accounting, Y 3.C 82
Standards Bureau, National, T 41, C 13
Standards, Center for Basic, C 13.1/10
Standards Division, Polymer, C 13.1/7
Standards of Official Conduct Committee (House), Y 4.St 2/3
Standards Office, Air Quality Planning and, EP 4
Standards, Office of Water, EP 8
Standards Review Council, National Professional, HE 1.46, HE 20.5010
Standards, Weights and Measures Committee (Senate), Y 4.St 2
State and Local Cooperation Division, Pr 32.4100
State and Other Departments Auditor, T 7
State Councils Section, Y 3.C 83/70
State Department, S 1
State Federal Action Committee, Joint, Pr 34.8:F 31
State Law Index, LC 21
State Services, Bureau of, HE 20.7300
State Technical Services Office, C 1.53
State Vocational Rehabilitation Agency, HE 23.4110/2
State, War, and Navy Department Building Office, S 12
State Workmen's Compensation Laws, National Commission on, Y 3.W 89/3
States Relations Office, A 10
Station
Rocky Mountain Research, A 13.151
Southern Research, A 13.150
Statistical Board, Central, Y 3.C 33/2
Statistical Committee, Central, Y 3.C 33/4
Statistical Reporting Service, A 92
Statistics and Cooperatives Service, A 105
Statistics Bureau–
Department of Agriculture, A 27
Department of Commerce, C 14
Department of State, S 4
Department of Treasury, T 37
Justice, J 29
Statistics, Bureau of Transportation, TD 12
Statistics Division, A 27
Statistics Office, Justice Assistance, Research, and, J 26
Statistics Service, National Agricultural, A 92
Statistics Service, National Criminal Justice, J 26.10
Status and Trends Program, National, C 55.436
Status of Women, Interdepartmental Committee on the, Y 3.In 8/21
Status of Women, President's Commission on the, Pr 35.8:W 84
Steam Engineering Bureau, N 19
Steam Roads Bureau, IC 1 ste
Steamboat Inspection Bureau, C 25
Steamboat Inspection Service, C 15, T 38
Stockyards Administration, A 113
Storage Review Commission, Monitored Retrievable, Y 3.M 74/2
Strategy Council on Drug Abuse, Y 3.St 8
Strategic Studies, Institute for National, D 5.417
Street and Highway Safety, National Conferences on, C 1.21
Stroke, National Institute of, HE 20.3500
Stroke, National Institute of Neurological Disorders and, HE 20.3500
Structure Committee, Ship, TD 5.63
Student Financial Assistance, National Commission on, Y 3.St 9
Studies, Institute for National Strategic, D 5.417
Studies Panel, Lake Michigan Cooling Water, EP 1.72
Study Center, National Independent, CS 1.92
Study Commission–
National Transportation Policy, Y 3.T 68/2
National Visitor Center, Y 3.N 21/23
Native Hawaiians, Y 3.H 31/2
Privacy Protection, Y 3.P 93/5
Records and Documents of Federal Officials, National, Y 3.R 24/2
Study Committee on Budget Control, Joint, Y 4.B 85
Study Law, Select Committee to, Y 4.L 41
Study of Ethical Problems in Medicine and Biomedical and Behavioral Research, President's Commission for the, Pr 40.8:Et 3
Study of International Migration and Cooperative Economic Development Commission for the, Y 3.M 58/2
Study Team on Yellowstone Grizzly Bear Investigations, Interagency, I 29.94
Study the Senate Committee System, Temporary Select Committee to, Y 4.Se 5

Subject Cataloging Division, LC 26
Submarine Defense School, W 61
Subsistence Department, W 5
Subsistence Homesteads Division, I 31
Substance Abuse and Mental Health Services Administration, HE 20.400, HE 20.8000
Substances and Disease Registry, Agency for Toxic, HE 20.501
Substances, Office of Prevention, Pesticides, and Toxic, EP 5
Subversive Activities Control Board, Y 3.Su 1
Suffrage, Woman, Select Committee on, (Senate), Y 4.W 84
Sugar Agency, A 76.300
Sugar Division, A 63
Sugar Equalization Board, Y 3.Su 3
Suggestions and Complaints Bureau, Y 3.R 13/2:70
Superconductivity, National Commission, Y 3.Su 7/3
Superintendent of Documents, GP 3
Supervising Architect, T 39
Supervising Tea Examiner, T 46
Supplement Labels, Commission on Dietary, Y 3.2:D 56/R 29
Supplemental Centers and Services National Advisory Council, Pr 36.8:Su 7
Supplies and Accounts Bureau, N 20, M 213, D 212
Supplies and Shortages, National Commission on, Y 3.Su 7/2
Supplies Division, P 18
Supply Agency, Defense, D 7
Supply and Services, Office of Federal, GS 2
Supply Bureau, T 52
Supply Bureau, Federal, T 58
Supply Division, T 55
Supply Management Agency, Defense, D 7
Supply Service, Federal, GS 2
Supply Services, W 109
Supply Service, Federal, GS 2
Supply Systems Command, Naval, D 212
Support Administration, Family, HE 25
Support Center, Defense Administrative, D 7.6/14
Supreme Court, Ju 6
Supreme Court Historical Society, Y 3.H 62/3
Surface Mining Reclamation and Enforcement Office, I 71
Surface Postal Transport Division, P 10
Surface Transportation Board, TD 13
Surface Weapons Center, Naval, D 201.21/6
Surgeon General of the Air Force, D 304
Surplus Commodities Corporation, Federal, A 69
Surplus Marketing Administration, A 73
Surplus Property Administration, Y 3.W 19/7:200
Surplus Property Board, Y 3.W 19/7:300
Surplus Property, Select Committee to Investigate Disposition of (House), Y 4.Su 7
Surplus Relief Corporation, Federal, Y 3.F 31/9
Surveillance and Analysis Division, EP 1.51/6
Survey–
Coast and Geodetic, C 4, T 11
Cost Control, President's Private Sector, Pr 40.8:C 82
Geological, I 19
National Ocean, C 55.400
Northern and Northwestern Lakes, W 33
Rocky Mountain Region (Powell), Geographical and Geological, I 17
Territories (Hayden), Geographical and Geological, I 18
Survey, Bureau of Biological, A 5
Surveys and Maps of the Federal Government, Board of, Y 3.Su 7
Survivors Benefits, Select Committee on (House), Y 4.Su 7/2
Synthetic Fuels Commercialization, Interagency Task Force, Pr 37.8:En 2/2
System–
Defense Logistics Agency Publishing, D 7.41
Engineering Technical Information, A 13.84/2
Famine Early Warning, S 18.68
National Communications, PrEx 1.17
Postal Savings, P 19
TVA Retirement, Y 3.T 25:1-14
Systematics Laboratory, National, C 55.341
Systems Command, Naval Sea, D 211
Systems Division, Human, D 301.45/38-2
Systems Laboratory, Computer, C 13.77
Systems Research and Development Service, FAA 2, TD 4.500
Systems, Technical Information, A 106.100

T

Taft, William Howard, Pr 27
Tank Corps, W 90
Tariff Board, Y 3.T 17/2

Tariff Commission, Y 3.T 17, TC
Tariff Commission, Select Committee on Investigation of, Y 4.T 17
Task Force–
Acid Precipitation, Interagency, Y 3.In 8/31
Aging, Pr 37.8:Ag 8
Air Pollution, Pr 37.8:Ai 7
Arts and Humanities, Presidential, Pr 40.8:Ar 7
Business Taxation, Pr 37.8:B 96
Career Advancement, Presidential, Pr 36.8:C 18
Combatting Terrorism, Vice Presidents, PrVp 40
Communications Policy, President's, Pr 36.8:C 73
Economic Growth, Pr 37.8:Ec 7
Employee-Management Relations in Federal Service, President's, Pr 35.8:Em 7/2
Environmental Cancer and Heart and Lung Diseases, EP 1.82
Higher Education, Pr 37.8:Ed 8
Highway Safety, President's, Pr 37.8:H 53
Improving the Prospects of Small Business, Pr 37.8:Sm 1
Indochina Refugees, Interagency, Pr 38.8:R 25
Low-Income Housing, Pr 37.8:H 81
Manpower Conservation, President's, Pr 35.8:M 31
Mentally Handicapped, Pr 37.8:M 52
Military Management, Pr 40.8:M 59
Model Cities, Pr 37.8:M 72
Motor Vehicle Goals beyond 1980, Interagency, Y 3.M 85
Oceanography, Pr 37.8:Oc 2
Oil Import Control, Cabinet, Pr 37.8:Oi 5
Physically Handicapped, Pr 37.8:P 56
Preservation of Natural Beauty, President's, Pr 36.8:N 21
Prisoner Rehabilitation, Pr 37.8:P 93
Private Sector Initiatives, President's, Pr 40.8:P 93
Problems of Aging, Pr 37.8:Ag 4
Product Liability, Interagency, C 1.66/2
Promoting Increased Foreign Investments in United States Corporate Securities and Increased Foreign Financing for United States Corporations Operating Abroad, Pr 35.8:F 76/3
Regulation of Financial Services, Pr 40.8:F 49
Rural Development, Pr 37.8:R 88
Science Policy, Pr 37.8:Sci 2
Small Business Finance, Interagency, Y 3.In 8/29
Structure of Selective Service Systems, Pr 36.8:Se 4
Synthetic Fuels Commercialization, Interagency, Pr 37.8:En 2/2
Travel, Industry-Government Special, Pr 36.8:T 69
Urban Renewal, Pr 37.8:Ur 1
Victims of Crime, President's, Pr 40.8:V 66
Women, Minorities, and the Handicapped in Science and Technology, Y 3.W 84/3
Women's Rights and Responsibilities, Pr 37.8:W 84
Task Force Program, Organized Crime Drug Enforcement, J 1.93
Task Group on Space, Pr 36.8:Sp 1
Tax Advisory Staff, T 64
Tax Appeals Board of the United States, Y 3.T 19
Tax Court of the United States, Y 3.T 19
Tax Evasion and Avoidance, Joint Committee on, Y 4.T 19
Tax Reform Bipartisan Commission, Pr 42.8:B 52/F 49
Tax Research Division, T 64
Taxation, Joint Committee on, Y 4.T 19/4
Taxation of Governmental Securities and Salaries, Special Committee on (Senate), Y 4.T 19/2
Tax-Exempt Foundations and Comparable Organizations, Select Committee to Investigate (House), Y 4.T 19/3
Taylor and other Systems of Shop Management, Special Committee to Investigate, Y 4.T 21
Taylor, Zachary, Pr 12
Tea Examiner Supervisory, T 46
Technical Committee, Pacific Southwest Federal Interagency, Y 3.P 11/3
Technical Information Agency, Armed Services, D 10
Technical Information Center, TD 1.3/2
Technical Information Center, Defense, D 10
Technical Information Division, LC 36
Technical Information Service, National, C 51
Technical Information System, Engineering, A 13.84/2
Technical Information Systems, A 106.100
Technical Review Board, Nuclear Waste, Y 3.N 88/2Technical Services Office, C 35
Technical Staff Office, T 68
Technological Uses of Copyrighted Works, National Commission on New, Y 3.C 79
Technology Administration, C 1.200
Technology Assessment Office, Y 3.T 22/2

Technology, Automation, and Economic Progress
National Commission, Y 3.T 22
Technology Committee (House), Y 4.Sci 2
Technology, Division of Environmental Control, E 1.16
Technology Division, Science and, LC 33
Technology, Federal Coordinating Council for, PrEx
8.100
Technology, Federal Council for Science and, Y 3.F 31/
16
Technology, Institute for Computer, C 13.73
Technology, National Institute of, C 13
Technology, National Museum of, SI 3
Technology Office, Science and, PrEx 8
Technology Office, Software Development and
Information, GS 12.16
Technology Policy Office, PrEx 23
Technology Problem, Special Committee on the Year
2000, Y 4.3:T
Technology, Task Force on Women, Minorities, and the
Handicapped in, Y 3.W 84/3
Technology Transfer, EP 7
Telecommunication Sciences Institute, C 60.14
Telecommunications and Information Administration,
National, C 60
Telecommunications, Office of, C 1.59
Telecommunications Policy Office, PrEx 18
Telecommunications Service, Automated Data and, GS
12
Telegraph Companies, IC 1 telg
Telegraph Division, CC 3
Telegraph, Joint Committee on Centennial of the, Y 4.T
23
Telephone Division, CC 4, IC 1 telp
Temporary Alaska Claims Commission, Y 3.Al 1s/2
Temporary Commission on Pennsylvania Avenue,
President's, Pr 36.8:P 38
Temporary Controls Office, Pr 33.300
Temporary Joint Committee on Deficit Reduction, Y 4.D
36/2
Temporary National Economic Committee, Y 4.T 24
Temporary Select Committee to Study the Senate
Committee System, Y 4.Se 5/4
Tennessee Valley Authority, Y 3.T 25
Tennessee Valley Authority, Joint Committee on the, Y
4.T 25
Tercentenary Celebration Commission, New Jersey, Y
3.N 42
Termination of the National Emergency, Special
Committee on the, Y 4.N 21/9
Territories and Insular Affairs Committee (Senate), Y 4.T
27/2
Territories and Island Possessions Division, I 35
Territories Committee (House), Y 4.T 27/1
Territories, Geological Survey of, I 18
Territories Office, I 35
Terrorism, Vice Presidents Task Force on Combatting,
PrVp 40
Texas Department, W 24
Textiles, President's Cabinet Advisory Committee on,
Pr 35.8:T 31
The Grain Inspection, Packers and Stockyards
Administration, A 113
Thrift Investment Board, Federal Retirement, Y 3.F 31/
25
Thrift Supervision, Office of, T 71
Thrift Supervisor Office, T 71Third Census, I 4
Thomas Jefferson Memorial Commission, Y 3.T 36
Timber and the Environment, President's Advisory
Panel on, Pr 37.8:T 48
"To Fulfill These Rights" White House Conference, Y
3.W 58/15
Tobacco, American-Grown, Purchased by Foreign
Governments, Commission to Investigate, Y
3.T 55
Tobacco and Cancer Program, HE 20.3184
Tobacco and Firearms, Bureau of Alcohol, T 70
Tobacco Commission, Y 3.T 55
Topographic Center, D 5.317
Topography Division, P 11
Tourism Administration, United States, C 47
Tourism Resources Review Commission, National, Y
3.T 64
Toxic Substances and Disease Registry Agency, HE
20.500, HE 20.7900
Toxic Substances, Office of, EP 5
Toxic Substances, Office of Prevention, Pesticides, and,
EP 5
Toxicology Research Institute, Inhalation, E 1.1/6
Toxics Information Clearinghouse, National Air, EP
4.23
Trade Administration, C 57
Trade Administration, International, C 61
Trade Assistance Bureau, C 57.200
Trade Board, East-West Foreign, Y 3.T 67
Trade Commission, Federal, FT

Trade Commission, International, TC 1
Trade Fairs Office, International, C 44, C 48.100
Trade Negotiations Office Special Representative, PrEx
9
Trade Operations Office, International, C 34
Trade Relations Bureau, S 11
Trade Relations of the U.S. with East European
Countries and the Soviet Union Special
Committee of the President, Pr 36.8:T 67
Trade Representative, Office of the U.S., PrEx 9
Trade, United States Court of International, Ju 9
Trademark Office, C 21
Traffic Division, Y 3.R 13/2:40
Traffic Safety Administration, National Highway, TD 8
Traffic Safety, President's Committee on, C 37.7
Training Administration, Employment and, L 37
Training and Employment Service, L 34
Training and Evaluation Program, Army, D 101.20/2
Training, Bureau of Apprenticeship and, L 23, L 37.100
Training Camp Activities Commission, N 26, W 85
Training Center, Federal Law Enforcement, T 1.60
Training, Center for Professional, HE 20.7700
Training Center, Personnel Management, CS 1.65/10
Training Command, Naval, D 207.200
Training School for Boys, National, J 8
Training School for Girls, National, J 9
Training Service, L 12
Training Service, and Veteran's Employment, L 39
Transactions with Iran, Select Committee to Investigate
Covert Arms, Y 4.In 8/20
Transport Administration, Defense, IC 1 def
Transport Committee, Highways, Y 3.C 83:20
Transportation and Communications Service, GS 8
Transportation and Infrastructure Committee (House), Y
4.T 68/2
Transportation and International Services Bureau, P 10
Transportation and Public Utilities Service, GS 8
Transportation Barriers Compliance Board, Y 3.B 27
Transportation Board, Surface, TD 13
Transportation Bureau–
Post Office Department, P 10
War Trade Board, WT 2
Transportation, Bureau of Materials, TD 9
Transportation Committee (House), Y 4.P 96/11
Transportation Committee (Senate), Y 4.C 73/7
Transportation Coordinator, Federal, Y 3.F 31/6
Transportation Corps, D 117
Transportation Department, TD 1
Transportation Investigation and Research Board, Y 3.T
68
Transportation, Office of, A 108
Transportation, Office of Chief, W 109.300
Transportation Policy Study Commission, National, Y
3.T 68/2
Transportation, Priority in, Commission, Y 3.P 93/2
Transportation, Publications Relating to, D 117
Transportation Routes to Seaboard, Select Committee
on, Y 4.T 68
Transportation Safety Board, National, TD 1.100
Transportation Security Administration, TD 1.200
Transportation Service, W 98
Transportation Service, Postal, P 10
Transportation Statistics Bureau, TD 12
Transportation System, Alaska Natural Gas Office of the
Federal Inspector, Y 3.F 31/23
Travel and Tourism Administration, United States, C 47
Travel, Industry-government Special Task Force on, Pr
36.8:T 69
Travel Service, United States, C 47
Treasurer of the United States, T 40, T 63.300
Treasury Comptroller Office, T 15
Treasury Department, T 1
Treasury Executive Institute, T 1.1/4
Treaties, S 9
Treatment, Division of Cancer, HE 20.3151/5
Trends Program, National, C 55.436
Trial Committee, Senate Impeachment, Y 4.Im 7/2
Tribal and Bureau Law Enforcement Services, I 20.58
Troop Information and Education Division, M 104, D
107
Troop Movement Section, Y 3.R 13/2:120
Tropical Forestry, Institute of, A 13.64
Truman, Harry S., Pr 33
Trust Corporation, Resolution, Y 3.R 31/2Tuberculosis
Committee, Y 3.T 79
Twenty-fifth Anniversary of the United Nations,
President's Commission for Observance of,
Pr 37.8:Un 3
TVA Retirement System, Y 3.T 25:1-14
Tyler, John, Pr 10

U

U.N. Fourth World Conference on Women, Pr 42.8:W
84
U.S. Air Mobility Research and Development
Laboratory, D 117.8
U.S. Army Air Mobility Research and Development
Command, D 117
U.S. Army Foreign Science and Technology Center, D
101.79
U.S. Army Research Institute for the Behavioral and
Social Sciences, D 101.1/7
U.S. Circuit Courts of Appeals, Ju 2
U.S. Commission on the Bicentennial of the U.S.
Constitution, Y 3.2:C 73
U.S. Constitution, U.S. Commission on the Bicenten-
nial, Y 3.2:C 73
U.S. Court of Veterans Appeals, Ju 15
U.S. Employment Service, L 37.300
U.S.–FAO Interagency Committee, Y 3.Un 3/3
U.S. High Commissioner to Philippine Islands, W 105
U.S. Meat Animal Research Center, Advisory Committee
for, A 77.27
U.S. National Arboretum, A 77.26
U.S. National Commission on the International Year of
the Child, Y 3.C 43/3
U.S. National Committee of the CCIR, S 5.56
U.S. Trade and Development Agency, TDA 1
U.S. Trade Representative, Office of the, PrEx 9
Un-American Activities, Special Committee on (House),
Y 4.Un 1/2
Un-American Activities, Special Committee on (Senate),
Y 4.Un 1
Undersea Research Program, NOAA, C 55.29
Unemployment and Relief, Special Committee to
Investigate, Y 4.Un 2/2
Unemployment Compensation, Advisory Council, Y
3.2:Un 2
Unemployment Compensation, National Commission
on, Y 3.Un 2
Unemployment Insurance Committee (Senate), Y 4.Un 2
Unemployment Insurance Service, L 33, L 37.200
Unemployment Problems, Special Committee on
(Senate), Y 4.Un 2/3
Unemployment Relief Organization, President's, Y 3.P
92
Unemployment Statistics, National Commission on, Y
3.Em 7/2
Unemployment Statistics, President's Committee to
Appraise, Pr 35.8:Em 7/3
Uniform Civil Rights Policies and Practices,
Interagency Committee on, Y 3.C 49/4
Union Catalog Division, LC 18
Union Pacific Railway, Government Directors, I 1.30
Union, United States Group, Interparliamentary, Y 3.In
8/29-2
United Nations, President's Commission for the
Observance of the Twenty-fifth Anniversary
of, Pr 37.8:Un 3
United States Attorneys, Executive Office for, J 31
United States Bankruptcy Court, Ju 14
United States Bankruptcy Laws, Commission on, Y 3.B
22
United States Board–
Mediation, MB
Mediation and Conciliation, MCB
Tax Appeals, Y 3.T 19
United States Capitol Historical Society, Y 3.H 62/2
United States Commission on Minority Business
Development, Y 3.2:M 66
United States Constitution Bicentennial Commission,
Y 3.B 47/2
United States Constitution Sesquicentennial
Commission, Y 3.Un 3
United States Court for China, S 14
United States Court of International Trade, Ju 9
United States Courts, Administrative Office, Ju 10
United States Customs Court, T 20
United States District Courts, Ju 4
United States Enrichment Corporation, Y 3.En 2
United States Export-Import Bank, Y 3.Ex 7/3
United States Fire Administration, C 58, FEM 1.100
United States Foreign Claims Settlement Commission,
Y 3.F 76/3, J 1.1/6
United States General Appraisers Board, T 20
United States Geographic Board, GB
United States Government Press Intelligence Division,
PI
United States, Great Britain, and Canada Combined
Production and Resource Board, Y 3.C 73/3
United States Group, Interparliamentary Union, Y 3.In
8/29-2
United States Holocaust Memorial Council, Y 3.H 74
United States Information Agency, IA

United States Institute of Peace, Y 3.P 31
United States-Japan Friendship Commission, Y 3.J 27
United States Laws, Commission to Revise, Y 3.L 44
United States Maritime Commission, MC
United States Marshals Service, J 25
United States Metric Board, Y 3.M 56
United States Mint, T 28
United States Monetary Commission, Y 3.M 74
United States National Museum, SI 3
United States, Office of the Treasurer of the, T 63.300
United States Parole Commission, J 27
United States Postal Service, P 1
United States, Puerto Rico Commission on Status of
     Puerto Rico, Y 3.Un 3/5
United States Radiation Policy Council, Y 3.R 11/2
United States Railway Association, Y 3.R 13/4
United States Savings Bonds Division, T 66
United States Sentencing Commission, Y 3.Se 5
United States Steel Corporation Investigation
     Committee, Y 4.Un 3/2
United States Study Commission on Neches, Trinity,
     Brazos, and San Jacinto River Basins and
     Intervening Areas, Y 3.Un 3/2
United States Study Commission on the Savannah,
     Altamaha, Saint Marys, Apalachicola-
     Chattahoochee, and Perdido- Escambia River
     Basins and Intervening Areas, Y 3.Un 3/4
United States Supreme Court Historical Society, Y 3.H
     62/3
United States Tax Court, Ju 11
United States Travel and Tourism Administration, C 47
United States Travel Service, C 47
Universal Training Advisory Commission, Y 3.Ad 9/5
Universities, Black, National Advisory Committee on,
     HE 19.140
Universities, Presidents Board of Advisors on
     Historically Black, ED 1.89/2
Universities, White House Initiative on Historically
     Black, ED 1.89
University, Defense Acquisition, D 1.59/3
University, National Defense, D 5.400
University of the United States, Select Committee to
     Establish, Y 4.Un 3/1
Upper Great Lakes Regional Commission, Y 3.Up 6
Urban Affairs, Committee on Banking, Housing and
     (Senate), Y 4.B 22/3
Urban Development Action Grant Program, HH 1.46/5
Urban Initiatives Anti-crime Program, Interagency, HH
     1.85
Urban Management Assistance Administration, HH 8
Urban Mass Transportation Administration, TD 7
Urban Problems National Commission, Pr 36.8:Ur 1
Urban Renewal Administration, HH 7
Urban Renewal Task Force, Pr 37.8:Ur 1
Uses of Copyrighted Works, National Commission on
     New Technological, Y 3.C 79
Utah Commission, I 1.31
Utah, Governor, I 1.32
Utah National Guard, D 12.1/3
Utilities Service, Rural A 68
Utilization and Disposal Service, GS 9

V

VA Health Professional Scholarship Program, VA 1.63
VA Medical Research Service, VA 1.1/4
Valuation Bureau, IC 1 val
Value Engineering Program, GS 6.10
Van Buren, Martin, Pr 8
Vector-Borne Diseases Division, HE 20.7001/3
Vegetable Pathology Division, A 28
Vegetable Pathology Section, A 28
Vegetable Physiology and Pathology Division, A 28
Venezuelan Boundary Commission, Y 3.V 55
Ventilation and Acoustics Committee (House), Y 4.V 56
Veterans Administration, VA 1
Veterans Affairs Committee (House), Y 4.V 64/3
Veterans Affairs Committee (Senate), Y 4.V 64/4
Veterans Affairs Department, VA 1
Veterans Affairs, Joint Committee on, Y 4.V 64/2
Veterans Bureau, VB 1, VA 3
Veterans Bureau Investigation Select Committee
     (Senate), Y 4.V 64
Veterans' Education Appeals Board, Y 3.V 64
Veterans' Employment & Training Service, L 39
Veterans' Illnesses, Presidential Advisory Committee
     on Gulf War, Pr 42.8:Ad 9
Veterans Pensions, President's Commission on, Pr
     34.8:V 64
Veterans' Reemployment Rights Bureau, L 25

Veterans' Reemployment Rights Division, L 25
Veterans' Reemployment Rights Office, L 25
Veterinary Medicine Bureau, HE 20.4400
Veterinary Medicine Center, HE 20.4400
Vice President of the United States, PrVP
Vice Presidents Task Force on Combatting Terrorism,
     PrVp 40
Vicksburg National Military Park Commission, W 54
Victims of Crime Office, J 34
Victims of Crime, President's Task Force on, Pr 40.8:V
     66
Violence Against Women Office, J 35
Violence, National Commission on the Causes and
     Prevention of, Pr 36.8:V 81
Virgin Islands, I 1.65
Virgin Islands Agricultural Experiment Station, A
     10.26, A 77.490
Virginia and North Carolina Department, W 67
Visayas Department, W 80
Visitor Center, Study Commission on National, Y 3.N
     21/23
Visitor Facilities Advisory Commission, National, Y
     3.N 21/23
VISTA, AA 1.9
Vital Statistics Office, National, FS 2.100
Vocational Rehabilitation Administration, FS 13.200
Vocational Rehabilitation Agency, State, HE 23.4110/2
Vocational Rehabilitation Office, FS 10, FS 13.200
Vocational Division, FS 5.120
Vocational Education, Advisory Council on, Y 3.V 85
Vocational Education Federal Board, VE 1
Voluntary Foreign Aid Advisory Committee, Y 3.Ad 9/
     4
Voluntary Service National Advisory Committee, VA
     1.52
Voting Participation, President's Commission on, Pr
     35.8:R 26

W

Wage and Hour and Public Contracts Division, L 22
Wage and Hour Division, L 20, L 36.200
Wage and Price Stability Council, PrEx 22
Wage Committee, VA 1.51
Wage Stabilization Board, ES 2
Wages and Prices, Select Committee to Investigate
     (Senate), Y 4.W 12
Walter Reed Army Medical Center, D 104.15
War Assets Administration, Pr 33.200, Y 3.W 19/8
War Claims Arbiter, Y 3.W 19/4
War Claims Commission, Y 3.W 19/9
War Claims Committee (House), Y 4.W 19
War College, National, D 5.17
War College, Naval, N 15, D 208.200
War Communication Board, Pr 32.5600
War Contracts Price Adjustment Board, Y 3.W 19/6
War Department, W 1
War Department Auditor, T 4
War Department Claims Board, W 93
War Finance Corporation, Y 3.W 19/3
War Food Administration, A 80
War Industries Board, Y 3.C 83:50, Y 3.W 19/2
War Information Office, Pr 32.5000
War Investigating Commission, Y 3.W 19
War Labor Board, National, L 10, Pr 32.5200
War Mobilization and Reconversion Office, Y 3.W 19/7
War Mobilization Office, Pr 32.5900
War Plans Division, W 26
War Policies Commission, Y 3.W 19/5
War Production Board, Pr 32.4800
War Records Office, W 45
War Relations, Office for Agricultural, A 74
War Relocation Authority, I 52, Pr 32.5400
War Risk Insurance Bureau, T 49
War Risk Litigation Bureau, J 18
War Savings Committee, National, T 1.26
War Savings Staff, T 1.100
War Shipping Administration, Pr 32.5300
War Trade Board, WT
War Trade Board Section, S 13
Ward, Montgomery, & Co., Select Committee to
     Investigate Seizure of (House), Y 4.W 21
Warning System, Famine Early, S 18.68
Warrants, Estimates, and Appropriations Division, T 9
Warren G. Magnuson Clinical Center, HE 20.3052
Wartime Relocation Commission, Y 3.W 19/10
Washington Bicentennial Celebration Commission, Y
     3.W 27/2
Washington, Commission on the Centennial of the
     Establishment of the Seat of Government In,
     Y 4.C 333

Washington Department, W 52
Washington, George, Pr 1
Washington, Governor, I 1.35
Washington Hospital for Foundlings, I 1.34
Washington Metropolitan Problems Joint Committee, Y
     3.W 27/2
Washington Monument Joint Commission, Y 3.W 27
Washington Railway and Electrical Company, Special
     Committee to Investigate, Y 4.W 27
Waste Management Office, Civilian Radioactive, E 1.68/
     2-7
Waste Management, Office of Solid, EP 3
Waste Reclamation Service, C 20
Water and Power Resources Service, I 27
Water Carriers Bureau, IC 1 wat
Water Commission, National, Y 3.N 21/24
Water Hygiene Office, HE 20.1700
Water Laboratory, Alaska, EP 1.22
Water, Office of, EP 2
Water Pollution Control Administration, Federal, FS
     16, I 67
Water Power Committee (House), Y 4.W 29
Water Programs Office, EP 2
Water Programs Operation Office, EP 2
Water Quality Administration, Federal, I 67
Water Quality, Committee on the Assessment of Human
     Health Effects of Great Lakes, Y 3.In 8/28:15
Water Quality, National Commission on, Y 3.W 29/2
Water Quality Office, EP 2
Water Regulations and Standards, Office of, EP 8
Water Resources Council, Y 3.W 29
Water Resources Institute, D 103.57
Water Resources Interagency Committee, Y 3.In 8/8
Water Resources Policy Commission, President's, Pr
     33.12
Water Resources Policy, Presidential Advisory
     Committee on, Pr 34.8:W 29
Water Resources Scientific Information Center, I 1.97
Waterlogging and Salinity in West Pakistan Panel of
     the White House and Department of the
     Interior, Pr 35.8:W 29
Waterways Commission, International, W 68
Waterways Commission, National, Y 3.N 21/3
Waterways Experiment Station, D 103.24
Ways and Means Committee (House), Y 4.W 36
Weapons Bureau, Naval, D 217
Weapons Center, Naval, D 201.23
Weapons Center, Naval Surface, D 201.21/6
Weapons Laboratory, Naval, D 201.21
Weather Bureau, A 29, C 30
Weather Control Advisory Committee, Y 3.Ad 9/6
Weather Research Program, C 55.626
Weather Service Command, Naval, D 220
Weather Service, National, C 55.100
Welfare Administration, FS 14
Welfare and Education of Congressional Pages, Select
     Committee (House), Y 4.W 45
Welfare Benefits Administration, L 40
Welfare Programs, Private, President's Committee on,
     Pr 35.8:P 38/2
Western and South Pacific Fisheries Development
     Program, C 55.329
Western Area Power Administration, E 6
Western Division, W 76
Western Environmental Research Laboratory, EP 1.14
Western Hemisphere Immigration, Select Commission
     on, Y 3.W 52
Western Wheat Quality Laboratory Corporation, A
     77.39
Wetlands, Oceans, and Watersheds, Office of, EP 8
Wheat Director, Y 3.W 56
Wheat Quality Laboratory Corporation, Western, A
     77.39
Wheeler, Burton K., Select Committee on Investigation
     of Charges Against, Y 4.W 56
White County Bridge Commission, Select Committee to
     Conduct and Investigation and Study of
     Finance Position (House), Y 4.W 58
White House Commission on Small Business, Y 3.W 58
White House, Committee for Preservation of, Y 3.W 58/
     10
White House Committee on Small Business, Pr 35.8:Sm
     1
White House Conference–
     Aging, Y 3.W 58/4
     Balanced National Growth and Economic
          Development, Y 3.W 58/19
     Child Health and Protection, Y 3.W 58
     Children, Y 3.W 58/3, Y 3.W 58/3-2
     Conservation, Y 3.W 58/6
     Education Committee, Y 3.W 58/2

Equal Employment Opportunity, Y 3.W 58/13
Export Expansion, Y 3.W 58/8
Families, Y 3.W 58/22
Food, Nutrition, and Health, Y 3.W 58/16
Handicapped Individuals, Y 3.W 58/18
Health, Y 3.W 58/14
Industrial World Ahead, Y 3.W 58/17
International Cooperation, Y 3.W 58/11
Library and Information Services, Y 3.W 58/20
Mental Retardation, Y 3.W 58/9
Narcotic and Drug Abuse, Y 3.W 58/5
National Economic Issues, Y 3.W 58/7
Natural Beauty, Y 3.W 58/12
Productivity, Pr 40.8:P 94
Science and Economics Research Related to Global
    Change, Pr 41.8:G 51
Small Business, Y 3.W 58/21
"To Fulfill These Rights", Y 3.W 58/15
Youth, Y 3.W 58/3-3
White House Department of the Interior Panel on
    Waterlogging and Salinity in West Pakistan,
    Pr 35.8:W 29
White House Disarmament Staff, Pr 34.11
White House Fellows Commission of the President, Pr
    36.8:W 58
White House Fellowships, President's Commission on,
    Pr 40.8:W 58
White House Historical Association, Y 3.Y 62/4
White House Initiative on Historically Black Colleges
    and Universities, ED 1.89
White Oak Laboratory, D 201.21/3
White-Red Basins Inter-Agency Committee, Y 3.F 31/
    13-2
Wildlife Conservation Committee (House), Y 4.W 64/2
Wildlife Resources, Special Committee on (Senate), Y
    4.W 64
Williamsburg-Yorktown-Jamestown Celebration
    Commission, Y 3.J 23
Wilson, Woodrow, Pr 28
Wilson, Woodrow, International Center for Scholars, SI
    12
Wilson, Woodrow, Memorial Commission, Y 3.W 86/2
Wind Cave National Park, I 1.56
Wireless Telegraphy, Inter-Departmental Board on, Y
    3.W 74
Wirt, Dr. William A., Select Committee to Investigate
    Certain Statements made by, Y 4.W 74
Wolf Management Committee, Y 3.W 83
Woman Suffrage, Select Committee on (Senate), Y 4.W
    84
Woman's Committee, Y 3.C 83:60
Women, Minorities, and the Handicapped in Science
    and Technology Task Force, Y 3.W 84/3
Women Office, Violence Against, J 35
Women, U.N. Fourth World Conference, Pr 42.8:W 84
Women's Bureau, L 13, L 36.100
Women's Business Enterprise, Interagency Committee
    on, Pr 40.8:W 84
Women's Education Programs, National Advisory
    Council on, Y 3.W 84/2
Women's Educational Equity Act Program, ED 1.44
Women's Rights and Responsibilities Task Force, Pr
    37.8:W 84
Women's Status Interdepartmental Committee, Y 3.In 8/
    21
Wood Utilization Relief, National Committee on, C 1.15
Woodrow Wilson Centennial Celebration Commission,
    Y 3.W 86
Woodrow Wilson International Center for Scholars, SI
    12
Woodrow Wilson Memorial Commission, Y 3.W 86/2
Wool, Special Committee to Investigate Production,
    Transportation and Marketing of, (Senate), Y
    4.W 88
Workforce Security Office, L 37 200
Work Projects Administration, FW 4
Work Quality, National Commission on Productivity
    and, Pr 37.8:P 94
Working Conditions Service, L 14
Working Group, Labor Management, LC 3.13
Working Group, World Hunger, Pr 39.8:W 89

Workmen's Compensation Laws, National Commission
    on State, Y 3.W 89/3
Workmen's Compensation Program, Office of, L 36.400
Works Agency, Federal, FW 1
Works Progress Administration, Y 3.W 89/2
Workshop, Federal Agency Classification Chiefs, PM
    1.24
Workshop, Federal Interagency Field Librarians, Y 3.L
    61/2
Work-Training Programs Bureau, L 32
World Conference on Women, U.N. Fourth, Pr 42.8:W
    84
World Data Center A, C 55.220
World Economic Practices Committee, Pr 34.8:W 89
World Hunger Working Group, Pr 39.8:W 89
World Population Year, National Commission for the
    Observance of, Y 3.P 81/2
World War Foreign Debt Commission, Y 3.W 89
World War Veterans Legislation Committee (House), Y
    4.W 89
Wyoming, Governor, I 1.36

Y

Yards and Docks Bureau, N 21, M 205, D 209
Yards and Docks, Bureau of Navy, N 21
Year of Disabled Persons, Federal Interagency
    Committee International, Y 3.F 31/24
Year of the Child, International, U.S. National
    Commission on, Y 3.C 43/3
Yellowstone Grizzly Bear Investigations, Interagency
    Study Team on, I 29.94
Yellowstone National Park, I 1.37
Yorktown Monument or Centennial Commission,
    Y 3.Y 8

Yorktown Sesquicentennial Commission, Y 3.Y 8/2
Yorktown-Williamsburg-Jamestown Celebration
    Commission, Y 3.J 23
Yosemite National Park, I 1.38
Youth Administration, National, FS 6, Pr 32.5250, Y
    3.N 21/14
Youth and Families, Administration, HE 23.1000
Youth and Families, House Select Committee on, Y 4.C
    43/2
Youth Conservation Corps, I 1.105/3
Youth Development and Delinquency Prevention
    Administration, HE 17.800, HE 1.300
Youth Development Office, HE 23.1300
Youth Employment Committee of the President, Pr
    35.8:Y 8/2
Youth Exchange, President's Council for International,
    Pr 40.8:Y 8
Youth Fitness, President's Counsel on, Pr 34.8:Y 8
Youth Opportunity Council of the President, Pr 36.8:Y
    8
Youth Opportunity, President's Council on, Pr 37.8:Y
    8
Youth, White House Conference on, Y 3.W 58/3-3

TITLE INDEX

A

A.A.A. Flashes, Facts for Committeemen, A 55.42/11, A 76.410
A.A.A.N.C.R. Agricultural Conservation Program by States, NCR, A 55.43/11
A.A.F. Manuals, W 108.22
A.A.F. Memorandum, W 108.11
A.A.F. Regulations, W 108.6
A.H.D. [Animal Husbandry Divisions] (series), A 77.209
A.I.D. Background Series, S 18.30
A.I.D. Bibliography Series, S 18.21/3
A.I.D. Discussion Papers, S 18.30/2
A.I.D. Memory Documents, S 18.43
A.I.D. Research Abstracts, TN-AAA- (series), S 18.47
A.L.A. Sub-Committee on Federal Publications, LC 2.5
A.L.L. Points Bulletin, ED 1.33/5
A.N.D. [Animal Nutrition Division] (series), A 77.210
A.T. Quarterly, ED 1.79/3
AACS Manuals, D 301.7/5
AAF Bombing Accuracy, Reports, W 108.37
AAM (series), TD 4.210/2
Abbreviated Stock Lists, W 108.9/1
ABM (Acquisition & Business Management) Online, D 201.44
Abortion Surveillance, Annual Summary, HE 20.7011/20
Abrasive Materials in (year), I 28.116
Abridged Index Medicus, HE 20.3612/2
Abridged United States Official Postal Guide, P 1.10/2
Abstract, C 3.37/7
Abstract of Course, N 15.5
Abstract of Internal Revenue Laws In Force, T 22.10
Abstract of Reports of Condition of National Banks, T 12.5
Abstract of Reports of Free and Reduced-Fare Transportation Rendered by Air-mail Carriers, IC 1 air.7
Abstracts, 13th Census, 1910, with Supplements Only for Individual States, C 3.15
Abstracts and Compendium, C 3.28/7
Abstracts from Annual and Technical Reports Submitted by USAMRDC Contractors/Grantees, D 104.23
Abstracts of–
   Active Projects, HE 20.9114, HE 20.9211
   and Indexes for Reports and Testimony, GA 1.16/3-4
   Child Support Techniques (series), HE 24.11
   Completed Research, D 206.21/2
   Current Literature on Venereal Disease, FS 2.11/2
   Declassified Documents, Y 3.At 7:11
   Defense Regulations, GS 4.112
   Earthquake Reports for the United States, MSA-(series), C 55.223, C 55.417, I 19.69
   ESS Staff Reports, A 105.57
   North American Geology, I 19.54
   NSF/RANN Research Reports: Private Sector Productivity, NS 1.13/4
   Personnel Research Reports, D 301.45/27
   Phase I Awards, Small Business Innovation Research, NS 1.46
   Post War Literature, LC 14.16/2
   Recent Published Material on Soil and Water Conservation, A 1.68, A 57.36, A 77.15:41
   Reports and Testimony, GA 1.16/3-3
   Selected Periodical Articles of Military Interest, W 55.8
   "701" Planning Reports, HH 8.9
   Small Business Innovation Research, Phase I and II Projects, HE 20.3047
   Staff Reports, A 93.44/2
   USAPRO Research Publications, D 101.60
Academic Majors Handbook, D 305.6/4
Academic Science/Engineering, Graduate Enrollment and Support, Fall, Detailed Statistical Tables, NS 1.22/4
Academic Science/Engineering, R & D Funds Federal Support Scientists and Engineers Graduate Enrollment and Support, NS 1.22/3-2
Academic Science/Engineering: R & D Funds, Fiscal Year (date), NS 1.22/3
Academic Science/Engineers: Scientist and Engineers, NS 1.22/6
Academic Year Institutes for Secondary School Teachers and Supervisors of Science and Mathematics, NS 1.12
Accelerated Public Works Program, Directory of Approved Projects, C 46.19
Acceptable Methods, Techniques, and Practices: Aircraft Alterations, TD 4.28, TD 4.28/2

Acceptable Methods, Techniques, and Practices: Aircraft Inspection and Repair, FAA 5.15, TD 4.28/2
Accepted Meat and Poultry Equipment, A 101.6/4, A 103.6/3, A 110.12
Access, C 1.57/4, D 102.81
Access: A Technical Circular for the End-User Computing Community, HE 3.4/7
Access America, Y 3.B 27:15
Access, Catalogs and Technical Publications, LC 30.27/7
Access Currents, Y 3.B 27:16
Access EPA, EP 1.8/13
Accessibility Assistance, a Directory of Consultants on Environments for Handicapped People, CSA 1.2:Ac 2
Accession Bulletin, Solid Waste Information Retrieval System, EP 1.18, EP 3.3/2
Accession List–
   Bangladesh, LC 1.30/9
   Ceylon, LC 1.30/7
   Eastern Africa, LC 1.80/8
   Eastern Africa, Annual Serial Supplement, LC 1.30/8-2
   India, LC 1.30/1
   Israel, LC 1.30/4
   Library, FS 1.11
   Middle East, LC 1.30/3
   Nepal, LC 1.30/6
   Pakistan, LC 1.30/2
   Pakistan, Annual Supplement, Cumulative List of Serials, LC 1.30/2-2
   Southeast Asia, LC 1.30/10
Accessions Lists, I 22.8/2
Accessions to Navy Department Library, N 16.8
Accident Analysis, Y 3.F 31/7:9
Accident Analysis (confidential), Y 3.F 31/5:9
Accident and Fire Prevention Bulletin, GS 1.13
Accident and Fire Prevention News, FW 6.10
Accident and Fire Report, VA 1.29
Accident Bulletin, IC 1 acci.3, TD 3.103
Accident Control Reports, I 49.73
Accident Prevention Conference, Publications, C 1.17
Accident Prevention Program, FAA-P-(series), TD 4.32/19
Accident Prevention Series: Bulletins, EC 1.8
Accidents in U.S. Civil Air Carrier and General Aviation Operations, C 31.244/3
Accidents Involving Civil Aircraft; Reports of Investigations of, C 31.213
Accidents of Class 1 Motor Carriers of Passengers, TD 2.310/2
Accidents of Large Motor Carriers of Property, TD 2.310
Accidents Reported by Railroad Companies, Preliminary Summary, IC 1 acci.9
Accomplishments During the Congress, Y 4.In 8/14:Ac 2
Accomplishments for Research, Extension, and Higher Education, A 1.2/12
Account of Receipts and Expenditures, T 32.5
Accountability Memorandum, N 9.13
Accounting Bulletins, IC 1 acco.3
Accounting Circulars, IC 1 mot.17
Accounting Principles Memorandum, GA 1.11/2
Accounting Procedure Memorandum, T 63.110
Accounting Series, GA 1.25
Accounting Series Circulars, IC 1 acco.4
Accounting Series Releases, SE 1.24
Accounting Systems Memorandum, GA 1.11
ACCP (Atlantic Climate Change Program) Newsletter, C 55.55
Accredited Higher Institutions, FS 5.250:50012, HE 5.250:50012
Accredited Postsecondary Institutions and Programs, (year), HE 19.145, ED 1.38
Accuracy of Monthly Mean Flow in Current Releases, I 19.45/2
ACER Technical Memorandum (series), I 27.75
ACDA Annual Report to Congress, AC 1.1
Achievements, PM 1.26
ACIC Technical Reports, D 301.59/2
Acid Precipitation in North America: Annual Data Summary from Acid Deposition System Data Base, EP 1.23/5-4
Acquiescence Ruling (series), HE 3.6/2-2:I
Acquisition Regulation Staff Manual, HE 1.6/8
Acquisition Review Quarterly: Journal of the Defense Acquisition University, D 1.103
Acquisitions and Disposal of CCC Price- Support Inventory, A 82.78
Acquisitions List of Antarctic Cartographic Materials, S 1.120

ACR Research Reports, D 210.15
Acreage, A 105.39
Acreage-Marketing Guides, A 88.26/4
ACS Research Report (series), A 109.10
ACS Service Report, A 109.9
ACSUS Report (Aids Cost and Services Utilization Survey), HE 20.6521
ACT Career Planning Guide Series, L 1.7/9
ACT Manual, C 31.106/3
Actas De La Asamblea Filipina [Spanish Only], W 49.41/5
Action Flyers, AA 1.11/2
Action for the Disadvantaged, HE 20.6021
Action in Docket Cases, Reports, CC 1.33
Action in the United States of America Related to Stratospheric Monitoring, S 1.132
Action News Digest, AA 1.14
Action, Office of the Inspector General, Semiannual Report, AA 1.1/2
Action Pamphlets, AA 1.11
ACTION Program Highlights, AA 1.9/4
Action Transmittals, OCSE-AT- (series), HE 24.14
Action Update, AA 1.15
Actions of Commission, Reports [Broadcast], CC 1.20/2
Actions of Commission, Reports (Telephone and Telegraph), CC 1.20/3
Actions on Motions, Reports, CC 1.32
Activation Analysis: Cockcroft-Walton Generator Nuclear Reactor, LINAC, C 13.46
Active and Announced Price Support Programs Approved by Board of Directors, A 82.310
Active Assignments, GA 1.37
Active Foreign Agricultural Research, A 106.42/2
Active Peacetime Service, T 47.41
Active Solar Installations Survey, E 3.19/3
Active Standardization Projects, Standards, Specifications, Studies and Handbooks, D 7.12
Activities and Programs, PrEx 18.1
Activities at Air Traffic Control Facilities, Fiscal Year, FAA 1.27/2
Activities in the National Capital Region, I 29.65
Activities of Aging Committee, Y 4.Ag 4/2-10
Activities of House Committee on Government Operations, Y 4.G 74/7:Ac 8/3
Activities of the Federal Council for Science and Technology and the Federal Coordinating Council for Science, Engineering and Technology, Report, PrEx 23.9
Activities of the National Institutes of Health in Field of Gerontology, FS 2.22/26
Activities of the NBS Spectrochemical Analysis Section, C 13.46
Activities of the U.S. Geological Survey Water Resources Division, Hawaii, I 19.55/7
Activities of the U.S. Geological Survey, Water Resources Division, Status of Idaho Projects, I 19.55/3
Activities of Water Resources Division, California District, I 19.55
Activities Relating to the Port and Tanker Safety Act, TD 5.34/2
Activities Relating to Title II, Ports and Waterways Safety Act of 1972, Report to Congress, TD 5.34
Activities Report, D 106.18
Activity in Cotton Spinning Industry, C 3.53
Activity of Machinery in Wool Manufactures, C 3.51
Activity Report of Committee on Commerce, Y 4.C 73/2:Ac 8
Activity Report to Congress, NS 1.35
Acts and Public Resolutions, W 49.7/3
Acts and Resolutions of Legislature, I 35.12/5
Acts and Resolutions of the Legislature, W 75.12
Acts and Resolutions Relating Chiefly to Navy, Navy Department, and Marine Corps, Passed at-Session of-Congress, N 1.7
Acts and Resolutions Relating to War Department, W 1.8/3
Acts of Congress, Treaties, and Proclamations Relating to Noncontiguous Territory, W 6.12
ACTS Quarterly, Lewis Research Center, NAS 1.93
Actuarial Notes, FS 3.19, FS 3.19/2, HE 3.19/2
Actuarial Studies, SS 1.34, HE 3.19, SSA 1.25
Ad Hoc Advisory Group on Presidential Vote for Puerto Rico, Pr 37.8:P 96
Ad Hoc Committee for Review of the Special Virus Cancer Program, HE 20.3001/2:V 81/5
ADA and Telecommunications Standards Index, GS 12.10/2
Adahooniligii, Navaho Language Monthly, I 20.37
ADAMHA News, HE 20.8013
ADAMHA Public Advisory Committees, Authority, Structure, Functions, Members, HE 20.8022

ADAMHA Update, HE 20.8013/2
ADAMHA Women's Council Report to the
　Administrator, HE 20.8017
Addenda and Errata Sheets to Federal Specifications, T
　51.7/20
Additions to Columbus Memorial Library, AR 1.7
Address Issued as Press Releases, C 1.18/2
Address List of Agricultural and Mechanical Colleges,
　A 10.20
Address List of Agricultural Experiment Stations, A
　10.19
Address List of (Meat) Inspectors, A 4.11
Address List of State Institutions and Officers in
　Charge of Agricultural Extension Work
　under Smith-Lever Act, A 10.25
Address List, Regional and Subregional Libraries for
　the Blind and Physically Handicapped, LC
　19.17
Address Lists, A 36.198
Addresses–
　Federal Emergency Management Administration
　　FEM 1.15
　Federal Reserve System, FR 1.61
　National Institute on Drug Abuse, HE 20.3962
Addresses, MA SP- (series), C 39.210/2
Addresses S (series), D 6.7/2
Adequacy of Labor Supply in Important Labor Market
　Areas, Pr 32.5217
ADFC Standards for Basic Needs, HE 3.64
Adjudication Instructions, FS 3.32
Adjudications of Attorney General of United States, J
　1.28
Adjustment of College Curriculum to Wartime
　Conditions and Needs, Reports, FS 5.33
Adjustment Orders, Y 3.W 89/2:12
Adjutant General's School, Fort Benjamin Harrison,
　Indiana, Reports and Publications, D 102.25
ADM Bulletins, CC 1.3/2
Administration, C 51.9/6
Administration and Management, TD 1.15/6
Administration and Management, Current Literature, C
　37.15
Administration and Management, Current Literature
　Compiled by Library Staff, TD 1.15/6
Administration Data, Y 3.R 31:22
Administration, DOE/AD (series), E 1.32
Administration in Mental Health, HE 20.8112
Administration of Federal Metal and Nonmetallic Mine
　Safety Act, Annual Report of the Secretary of
　the Interior, I 1.96/2
Administration of Public Health Service: Report to
　Congress, HE 20.1/2
Administration of Public Laws 81-874 and 81-815,
　Annual Report of the Commissioner of
　Education, ED 1.1/2, HE 19.101/2
Administration of Relief Committees, Y 3.P 92:6
Administration of the Federal Metal and Nonmetallic
　Mine Safety Act, I 28.5
Administration of the Marine Mammal Protection Act of
　1972, C 55.327
　Report of the Secretary of the Interior, I 49.84
Administration of the Pesticide Programs, EP 5.19
Administration of the Toxic Substances Control Act, EP
　1.79
Administration on Welfare and Pension Plans
　Disclosure Act, L 1.55
Administrative Areas, Y 3.F 31/11:35
Administrative Conference News, Y 3.Ad 6:9-2
Administrative Decisions, S 3.31/6
Administrative Decisions Under Employer Sanctions
　and Unfair Immigration-Related Employment
　Practices Law of the United States, J 1.103
Administrative Decisions Under Immigration and
　Nationality Laws, J 21.11
Administrative Decisions, Walsh-Healey Public
　Contracts Act, Index-Digest, L 21.2:In 2
Administrative Handbook, Transmittal Sheets, L 1.26
Administrative Instructions [under sections of the
　Plant Quarantine Act], A 77.306/2
Administrative Law Judge and Commission Decisions,
　Y 3.Oc 1:10-2
Administrative Law Judge Decisions, Y 3.F 31/21-3:9-
　3
Administrative Letters, A 55.42/8, A 55.44/8, A 55.46/
　8
Administrative Management Course Program Topics,
　SBA 1.24
Administrative Memorandum, A 77.314
Administrative Notes, GP 3.16/3-2
Administrative Notes Technical Supplement, GP 3.16/
　3-3
Administrative Order DTA (series), IC 1 def.6/4
Administrative Orders, GP 1.16, GS 1.8
Administrative Publications, A 57.10

Administrative Reference Service Reports, N 1.32
Administrative Reports (series)–
　Forest Service, A 13.66/17
　National Marine Fisheries Service, C 55.337
Administrative Review Outline, L 7.45
Administrative Rules and Regulations Under Sections
　of National Housing Act, HH 2.6/2
Administrative Rulings [under House of Service Act],
　IC 1 hou.6
Administrative Series, A 1.61
Administrative Service Series, FS 13.212
Administrative Services, DOE/OAS- (series), E 1.46
Administrative Standards Bulletins, FS 3.111
Administrative Support Manual, P 1.12/10
Administrator's Alert, CS 1.79
Administrator's Annual Financial Report, NCU 1.1/4
Administrator's Decisions, VA 1.8
Administrator's Memorandum, A 77.11
Administrator's Orders, VA 1.7
Admissions Guide, D 305.6/2:Ad 6
Adoptions in (year), HE 17.646
ADP Reports, D 103.53/8
ADP Training Catalog, D 1.45/2
ADTIC Publications, D 301.26/8
Adult Basic and Secondary Level Program Statistics,
　Students and Staff Data, HE 19.319
Adult Basic Education Program Statistics (series), HE
　5.97
Adult Development and Aging Abstracts, HE 20.3359
Adult Development and Aging Research Committee,
　HE 20.3001/2:Ad 9
Adult Education Ideas, FS 5.42
Adult Education in American Education Week, FS
　5.49/2
Adult Education References, FS 5.49
Adult Education Series, I 20.43, C 3.226/3
Advance Automotive Propulsion Systems, E 1.99
Advance BCD, [Business Conditions Digest], C
　56.111/2
Advance Bulletin of Interstate Commerce Acts
　Annotated, IC 1 act.5/3, IC 1 act.5/3-2
Advance Bulletins of New Posters, Pr 32.5027
Advance Copy Proposed Rules and Regulations, NCU
　1.6/a
Advance Data from the Vital and Health Statistics of
　NCHS, HE 20.6209:16, HE 20.6209/3
Advance Data on Peat in (year), I 28.107/2
Advance Monthly Retail Sales Report, C 3.138/4
Advance Release of Statistics on Public Assistance, FS
　3.14/2, FS 14.209, FS 17.10, FS 17.610
Advance Report Immigration Statistics: Fiscal Year, J
　21.20
Advance Report on Engineering Enrollment and
　Degrees, (year), FS 5.254:54004, HE
　5.254:54004
Advance Sheets (series), D 101.102
Advance Sheets from Monthly Summary of the Foreign
　Commerce of the United States, C 18.8
Advance Sheets of 3d Edition of Checklist of United
　States Public Documents, GP 3.14
Advance Sheets of Consular Reports, S 4.5
Advance Statements of Productions of Copper in
　United States (calendar year), I 19.23
Advance Summary of Revenues, Expenses, and Net
　Railway Operating Income, Class 1 Steam
　Railways, IC 1 ste.19/2
Advance, the Journal of the African Development
　Foundation, Y 3.Af 8:9
Advance Training for Workers in the Early and Periodic
　Screening, Diagnosis and Treatment
　Program: Publications, HE 22.111
Advance United States Short Wave Broadcast
　Programs, S 9.13
Advanced Abstracts of Scientific and Technical Papers
　Submitted for Publication and Presentation,
　D 104.23/2
Advanced Education Program in General Dentistry, D
　304.11
Advanced Training for Workers in the Early and
　Periodic Screening, Diagnosis and Treatment
　Program: Publications, HE 22.111
Advanced Waste Treatment Research, I 67.13/3:AWTR
Advancement, NF 2.8/2-19
Advances in Agricultural Technology, AAT (series), A
　106.24, A 77.31
Advances in Education Research, ED 1.317/4
Adventures of Cuthbert (radio scripts), I 29.47
Adverse Action, Law and Regulations, Annotated, CS
　1.41/4:752-1
Adverse Events Following Immunization Surveillance,
　HE 20.7011/36
Advertisement for Airmail Service, P 1.24/3
Advertisement for Temporary Airmail Service, P 1.24/2

Advertisements for Bids, Specifications, etc., for
　Equipment of Public Buildings, T 39.9
Advertisements Inviting Proposals for Carrying Mails
　Airplane or Seaplane, P 1.24
　By States, P 1.5
　(miscellaneous), P 1.8
　Regulation Screen Wagons, P 1.7
　Star Routes (by States), P 1.22
　Steamboat Routes (by States), P 1.23
Advertisements Inviting Proposals for Covered
　Regulation Wagon Mail-Messenger, Transfer,
　and Mail Station Service, P 1.6
Advertising Abroad, C 18.43
Advertising Alert, FT 1.24
Advertising Digest, Y 3.F 31/11:39, FL 2.10
Advertising Media in Certain Foreign Countries, C
　18.44
Advisor, Navy Civilian Manpower Management, D
　204.9
Advisory, PrEx 10.16
Advisory Bulletin, TD 9.13
Advisory Circulars, TD 4.110
Advisory Circulars, AC (series), TD 4.8/5
Advisory Circulates (numbered), TD 4.4/2
Advisory List of National Register of Historic Places, I
　29.76/2
Advisory Memorandums, HE 20.7027
Advisory Memo, HE 20.7816
Advisory Memos, HE 20.2308/2
Advisory Opinion Digests, FT 1.12/2
Advocate, D 108.109
AEC Authorizing Legislation, Fiscal Year [date], Y
　4.At 7/2:L 52
AEC Depository Library Bulletin, Y 3.At 7:47
AEC Licensing Guides, Y 3.At 7:6-4
AEC News Release Index, Y 3.At 7:33-3, Y 3.At 7:44
　N 47
AEC Research and Development Reports, Y 3.At 7:22
AEC-NASA Tech Briefs, NAS 1.29/2
Aerial Crop Control Accidents, C 31.244/2
Aerial Photography Summary Record System, APSRS-
　(series), I 19.77
AERO Reports, D 211.9/3
Aerology Series, N 28.14, N 27.13
Aeromedical Research Unit, Fort Rucker, Ala.;
　USAARU Reports, D 104.21
Aeromedical Review, D 301.26/13-4
Aeronautic Information Bulletins, W 87.12
Aeronautical Bulletins, W 87.21
Aeronautical Bulletins, State Series, C 23.5
Aeronautical Bulletins, State Summaries, W 87.21/3
Aeronautical Chart & Information Bulletin, Europe,
　Africa and Middle East, New Editions of
　Aeronautical Charts Published, D 301.49/3
Aeronautical Chart and Information Center Bulletin, D
　301.59
Aeronautical Chart and Information Center Bulletin
　Digest, New and Revised Editions of
　Aeronautical Charts on Issue as of (date), D
　301.59/5
Aeronautical Chart and Information Squadron Bulletin,
　D 301.59/3
Aeronautical Charts, C 4.9/4, C 4.9/6, C 4.9/13
Aeronautical Communications and Pilot Services
　Handbook 7300.7, Changes, FAA 3.9/2
Aeronautical Dictionary, NAS 1.8:Ae 8
Aeronautical Engineering, A Continuing Bibliography
　with Indexes, NAS 1.21:7037
Aeronautical Engineering Newsletter, TD 5.37
Aeronautical Information List, W 87.13
Aeronautical Information Publication, TD 4.308:Ae 8,
　TD 4.308/2
Aeronautical Research Laboratory, ARL (series), D
　301.69/2
Aeronautical Specifications, N 4.9, N 28.5
Aeronautical Statutes and Related Material, Federal
　Aviation Act of 1958 and Other Provisions
　Relating to Civil Aeronautics, C 31.205:Ae
　8
Aeronautical Supplement to American Nautical
　Almanac, N 11.6/2
Aeronautical World News, C 18.45
Aeronautics and Space Activities, Report to Congress,
　NAS 1.52
Aeronautics Bulletin, C 23.11
Aeronautics Export News, C 18.46
Aeronautics Update, NAS 1.7/3
Aerospace Leaflets, AL- (series), NAS 1.23
Aerospace Maintenance Safety, D 306.8
Aerospace Medicine and Biology, A Continuing
　Bibliography with Indexes, NAS 1.21:7011
Aerospace Power Journal D 301.26/24, D 301.26/24-2,
　D 301.26/24-3
Aerospace Safety, D 301.44

Air Corps Newsletter, W 87.19
Air Corps Technical Reports, W 87.26
Air Defense Artillery, D 101.77
Air Defense Trends, D 101.77
Air Education and Training Command Electronic
    Publishing Library, AETCEPL, 301.116/3
Air Force, D 7.29/2
Air Force Activity Address Code Name/Organization
    to Code, D 301.6/2-2
Air Force Address Directory, D 301.104/9
Air Force Avionics Laboratory Technical Reports,
    AFAL-TR- (series), D 301.45/45-2
Air Force Ballistic Missile Division, Publications, D
    301.68
Air Force Budget, D 301.83
Air Force Bulletins, D 301.3
Air Force Cambridge Research Center: AFCRC
    technical Reports, D 301.45/4
Air Force Civil Engineering Center: AFCEC-TR
    (series), D 301.87
Air Force Command and Control Development
    Division: Technical Notes AFCCDD-TN
    (nos.), D 301.45/24
Air Force Comptroller, D 301.73
Air Force Driver, the Automotive Magazine of the U.S.
    Air Force, D 301.72
Air Force Electronic Publishing Library of Departmen-
    tal Publications and Forms, D 301.116
Air Force Energy Conservation Plan, D 301.89/6-2
Air Force Engineering and Services Quarterly, D
    301.65
Air Force Geophysics Laboratory: Technical Reports, D
    301.45/4
Air Force Handbook (series), D 301.6/8
Air Force Human Resources Laboratory: Annual
    Report, D 301.45/27-5
Air Force Institute of Technology: New Books in
    Library, D 301.45/44
Air Force Issues Book, D 301.1/3
Air Force JAG Law Review, D 302.9
Air Force Journal and Logistics, D 301.91
Air Force Law Review, D 302.9
Air Force Letters, D 301.24
Air Force Logistics Command, Hill Air Force Base,
    Telephone Directory, D 301.104/2
Air Force Manuals, W 108.19
Air Force Medical Logistics Letter, D 304.9
Air Force Missile Test Center: Technical Reports,
    AFMTC TR- (series), D 301.45/23
Air Force News, D 301.122
Air Force News Letter, W 108.7
Air Force Office of Special Investigations, AFOSIP-
    (series), D 301.88
Air Force Pamphlets, AFP- (series), D 301.35
Air Force Procurement Instruction, D 301.6/4
Air Force Public Information Letter, D 301.46
Air Force Register, D 303.7
Air Force Research Resumes, D 301.69/3
Air Force Research Review, D 301.69/6-2
Air Force Reserve Officer Training Corps [textbooks], D
    301.63
Air Force Reserve Pamphlets, AFRESP-(series), D
    301.35/5
Air Force Review, D 302.9
Air Force ROTC Four Year College Scholarship
    Program Application Booklet for High
    School Students Entering College in the
    (year) Fall Term, D 301.95
Air Force Scientific Research Bibliography, D 301.45/
    19-2:700
Air Force Surveys in Geophysics, D 301.45/9
Air Force Systems Command Annual Report, D 301.45/
    38
Air Force Systems Command: Handbooks, Manuals,
    Guides, D 301.45/58
Air Force Systems Command: Publications, D 301.45
Air Force Systems Command: Technical Reports, AFSC-
    TR- (series), D 301.45/21
Air Force Visual Aid Series, D 301.55
Air Force Weapons Laboratory, Research and
    Technology Division, AFWL-TDR, D
    301.45/35
Air Force Writing, Air Force Recurring Publication 10-
    1, D 303.9
Air Force-Navy Aeronautical Design Standards, D
    301.29
Air Force-Navy Aeronautical Standards, D 301.30
Air Freight Loss and Damage Claims, C 31.265
Air Freight Loss and Damage Claims, Annual
    Summaries, C 31.265/3
Air Freight Loss and Damage Claims for the Six Months
    Ended (date), C 31.265/2
Air Mail Schedules, P 20.8
Air Material Command: Technical Reports, D 301.67

Air National Guard Manuals, D 301.23
Air National Guard Register, D 12.9/2
Air Navigation and Air Traffic Control Facility
    Performance and Availability Report,
    Calendar Year, TD 4.710
Air Navigation Development Board Releases, C
    31.142/2
Air Navigation Maps, W 87.22/2
Air Pollution Abstracts, EP 4.11
Air Pollution Aspects of Emission Sources: [various
    subjects], a Bibliography with Abstracts, EP
    1.21/5
Air Pollution Control Office Publications, AP-(series),
    EP 4.9
Air Pollution Control Office Publications APTD-
    (series), EP 4.9/2
Air Pollution Report, Federal Facilities, Air Quality
    Control Regions, EP 4.10
Air Pollution, Sulfur Oxides Pollution Control, Federal
    Research and Development, Planning and
    Programming, FS 2.93/4
Air Pollution Technical Publications of the U.S.
    Environmental Protection Agency, Quarterly
    Bulletin, EP 1.21/8
Air Pollution Training Courses, (year) and University
    Training Programs, Extramural Programs,
    Institute for Air Pollution Training Planning
    and Special Projects, EP 4.13
Air Quality Criteria (series), EP 1.53/2
Air Quality Data, (date) Quarter Statistics, EP 1.53
Air Quality Data from National Air Surveillance
    Networks and Contributing State and Local
    Networks, FS 2.307
Air Research and Development Command: Technical
    Reports, ARDC-TR-, D 301.45/21
Air Reservist, D 301.8
Air Resources Atmospheric Turbulence and Diffusion
    Laboratory: Annual Report, C 55.621
Air Sea Rescue Bulletin, N 24.35, T 47.32
Air Service Bulletin, A.E.F., W 95.21/5
Air Service Information Circular, W 87.11
Air Staff, D 301.25
Air Staff Historical Study (series), D 301.82/6
Air Taxi Operators and Commercial Operators of Small
    Aircraft, TD 4.6:part 135
Air Technical Intelligence Technical Data Digest, M
    301.9
Air Traffic Control Handbook, TD 4.308:Ai 7/3
Air Traffic Control Procedures, FAA 3.9
Air Traffic Patterns for IFR and VFR Aviation, Calendar
    Year, TD 4.19/2
Air Traffic Publications Library, TD 4.78
Air Traffic Survey [maps], C 31.218
Air Training, D 301.38
Air Training Command Historical Monograph (series),
    D 301.38/9
Air Training Command, Miscellaneous Publications, D
    301.38/3
Air Transport Economics in Jet Age, Staff Research
    Reports, C 31.250
Air Transportation Wage Survey, L 2.113/7
Air Travel Consumer Report, TD 1.54
Air University, AFROTC [text books], D 301.26/12
Air University Catalog, D 301.26/16
Air University Compendium of Research Topics, D
    301.26/3-2
Air University Documentary Research Study,
    Publications, D 301.26/3
Air University: Handbooks, Manuals, Guides, D
    301.26/6-8
Air University, Human Resources Research Institute,
    Research Memorandum, D 301.26/7
Air University Library Index to Military Periodicals, D
    301.26/2
Air University Library Master List of Periodicals, D
    301.26/2-2
Air University Publications, D 301.26/6
Air University Review, D 301.26
Air University Review Index, D 301.26:947-87/ind.
Air University, School of Aviation Medicine:
    [publications], D 301.26/13-2
Air War College Studies in National Security, D 301.26
Air War in Indochina (series), D 301.93
Air Waves, Y 3.Ai 7/5:9
Air Weather Service: Bibliography, D 301.42
Air Weather Service Manual, D 301.27
Air Weather Service, Technical Reports, D 301.40
Air Weather Service: Training Guides, D 301.39
Airborne Anomaly Location Maps, Y 3.At 7:31
Airborne Instrumentation Research Project Summary
    Catalog, NAS 1.68
Aircraft Accident and Maintenance Review, D 301.58
Aircraft Accident Reports, TD 1.112

Aircraft Accident Reports, Brief Format, U.S. Civil
    Aviation, NTSB-BA- (series), TD 1.109/13
Aircraft Accident Reports NTSB-AAR-(series), TD
    1.112
Aircraft Accident/Incident Summary Reports, TD 1.112/
    6
Aircraft Alterations, FAA 5.16
Aircraft Certification Directory, TD 4.52/3
Aircraft Certification Service International Strategic
    Plan, TD 4.915
Aircraft Circulars, Y 3.N 21/5:9
Aircraft Emergency Evacuation Reports, C 31.150
Aircraft Emergency Procedures Over Water, T 47.32/2
Aircraft Engine and Propeller Type Certificate Data
    Sheets and Specifications, TD 4.15/2
Aircraft Engine Listing and Propeller Listing, C
    31.120/3
Aircraft Flash, D 301.47
Aircraft in Agriculture, FAA 1.33
Aircraft Instrument Approaches, Fiscal Year, FAA 1.40
Aircraft Instrument Bulletin, Flowmeter Series,
    Flowmeter Bulletins, N 28.19
Aircraft Instrument Bulletins, N 28.10, M 208.9
Aircraft Observer, D 301.38/4
Aircraft Operating Cost and Performance Report, CAB
    1.22, CAB 1.22/2, C 31.259, TD 1.53
Aircraft Plotting Sheets, N 6.30
Aircraft Registration, TD 4.6:part 47
Aircraft Specifications, C 31.120/2, FAA 1.29
Aircraft Type Certificate Data Sheets and Specifications,
    TD 4.15
Aircraft Utilization and Propulsion Reliability Report,
    TD 4.59
Airframe and Equipment Engineering Reports, C 31.156
Airlift, the Journal of the Airlift Operations School, D
    301.56/5
Airline Industry Economic Report, CAB 1.18, C 31.260
Airline Traffic Survey, C 31.225
Airman, Official Journal of the Air Force, D 301.60
Airman's Guide, C 31.127, C 31.136, FAA 1.23
    Pacific Supplement, FAA 1.25/3
Airman's Guide and Flight Information Manual, FAA
    1.25/2
    Pacific Supplement, FAA 1.25
Airman's Information Manual, TD 4.12, TD 4.12/3
Airport Activity Statistics on Certificated Route Air
    Carriers, C 31.251, TD 4.14
Airport Aid Program, TD 4.6:part 152
Airport Bulletins, C 23.7/3
Airport Design Manual, FAA 4.9/3
Airport Design Standards, TD 4.8/4, TD 4.111
Airport/Facility Directory, TD 4.79
Airport Management Series, C 31.137
Airport Obstruction Charts, C 55.411/3
Airport Obstruction Plans, C 4.9/1
Airport Planning, C 31.145
Airports Service, Standards Division Index of Airpower
    Journal, D 301.26/24
Airpower Journal, D 301.26/24-2, D 301.26/24-3
Airpower Journal (Portuguese), D 301.26/24-2
AIRSExecutive PLUS, EP 4.30
Airway Bulletin, C 23.7
Airway Maps, C 23.10
Airways Operating and Training Series Bulletins, C
    31.141
Airworthiness Directive Summary, C 31.145
Airworthiness Standards, Aircraft Engines, TD 4.6:part
    33
Airworthiness Standards, Normal, Utility, and
    Acrobatic Category Airplanes, TD 4.6:part
    23
Airworthiness Standards, Transport Category
    Airplanes, TD 4.6:part 25
Akten Zur Deutschen Auswartigen Politic, S 1.82/2
ALA Catalog, LC 1.9
ALA Portrait Index, LC 1.10
Alaska Agricultural Experiment Station, A 77.440
Alaska Agriculture Statistics, A 92.48
Alaska Airman's Guide, C 31.135, FAA 1.24
Alaska Airman's Guide and Chart Supplement, TD
    4.16/2
Alaska Conveyance News, I 53.37
Alaska Farm Reporter, A 92.45
Alaska Fisheries, C 55.309/2
Alaska Flight Information Manual, C 31.134, FAA 1.21
Alaska Forest Research Center, A 13.73
Alaska Game Commission, Circulars, I 49.12
Alaska Gas Pipeline Update, Y 3.F 31/23:9
Alaska, Governor, Annual Report, I 1.5
Alaska Native Medical Center: Annual Report, HE
    20.5311
Alaska People, I 53.41
Alaska Railroad, Local Passenger Tariffs, I 35.10/7
Alaska Railroad, Press Releases, I 1.82/2

Annual NASA-University Conference on Manual Control, NAS 1.21

Annual National Ability Counts Contest [announcement], PrEx 1.10/6

Annual National Aviation System Planning Review Conference, Summary Report, TD 4.31

Annual Operating Plans, I 27.62

Annual Outlook for Oil and Gas, E 3.11/7-10

Annual Outlook for U.S. Coal, E 3.11/7-8

Annual Outlook for U.S. Electric Power, E 3.50

Annual Peak Discharge at Selected Gaging Stations in Pacific Northwest, I 19.45/3

Annual Pecan Summary, Louisiana Crop Reporting Service, A 88.10/5-2

Annual Performance Plan, A 13.1/4

Annual Performance Report, Minority Business Development Agency, C 1.1/3

Annual Procurement and Financial Assistance Report, E 1.35/4

Annual Procurement Operations Report, E 1.40

Annual Program Plan, J 16.26

Annual Program Plan and Academy Training Schedule, J 16.26

Annual Progress Report, D 104.15/3

Annual Prospects for World Coal Trade, E 3.11/7-9

Annual Prospectus of Winter Use and Facilities [various parks], I 29.69

Annual R.O.P. and Performance Test Summary, A 77.15:44-7

Annual Radiological Environmental Operating Report, Sequoyah Nuclear Plant, Y 3.T 25:57

Annual Register, N 12.5

Annual Register of the United States Naval Academy, D 208.107

Annual Report, A 13.151/7

Annual Report, S 3.25

Annual Report, Federal Emergency Management Agency (by Region), FEM 1.1/2

Annual Report, American Battle Monuments Commission, Fiscal Year (date), Y 4.V 64/4:Am 3

Annual Report and Achievements, Fiscal Year (date), L 38.13

Annual Report and Strategic Investment Plan, D 1.97/2

Annual Report, Authorized by 38 U.S.C. 5057, Administrator, Veterans' Affairs, on Sharing Medical Facilities, Fiscal Year (date), Y 4.V 64/4:M 46

Annual Report by the President to the Congress on the Administration of the Federal Railroad Safety Act of 1970, TD 1.10/7

Annual Report Colorado River Storage Project and Participating Projects for Fiscal Year (date), I 27.71/2

Annual Report Dall Porpoise-Salmon Research, C 55.343

Annual Report, Dependents' Medical Care Program, D 104.16

Annual Report Director of the Bureau of Safety, IC 1 saf.1

Annual Report, Division of Law Enforcement, I 49.1/7

Annual Report, (Fair Debt Collection Practices), FT 1.1/2

Annual Report, Fishery Conservation and Management Act, C 55.330

Annual Report Habitat Conservation Program, C 55.340

Annual Report, Inspector General Department of State and Foreign Service, S 1.1/6

Annual Report, Intramural Research Program Actvities FY, HE 20.8321

Annual Report Manhattan Plant Materials Center, A 57.54/3

Annual Report, Mental Health Intramural Research Program, HE 20.8136

Annual Report, Naval Publications and Form Center, D 212.1/2

Annual Report of Accomplishments Under the Airport Improvement Program, TD 4.61

Annual Report of Administrator, NCU 1.1/3

Annual Report of Army-Air Force Wage Board, D 1.28

Annual Report of Compensatory Education Programs under Title I, Elementary and Secondary Education Act of 1965, FS 5.79

Annual Report of Cooperative Psoroptic Cattle Scabies Eradication Activities, Fiscal Year (date), A 77.233/3

Annual Report of Cooperative State-Federal Sheep Scabies Eradication Activities, Fiscal Year (date), A 77.233/2

Annual Report of Department of Health, Education, and Welfare to the President and the Congress on Federal Activities Related to the Administration of the Rehabilitation Act of 1973, HE 1.609

Annual Report of Department of Treasury on Operation and Effect of Domestic International Sales Corporation Legislation for Calendar Year, Y 4.W 36:D 71/2

Annual Report of Energy Conservation Indicators for (year), E 3.47

Annual Report of Energy Purchased by REA Borrowers, A 68.1/4, A 68.3

Annual Report of Federal Civilian Employment by Geographic Area, CS 1.48

Annual Report of HUD Activities Under the Uniform Relocation Assistance Policies Act of 1970, HH 1.49

Annual Report of Indian Land, I 20.61

Annual Report of Indian Land and Income from Surface, I 20.61/2

Annual Report of Insurance Business Transacted in Canal Zone, CZ 1.9

Annual Report of Intramural Activities, HE 20.3267

Annual Report of Justice System Improvement Act Agencies, J 1.87

Annual Report of Lands under Control of the U.S. Fish and Wildlife Service, I 49.102

Annual Report of Legal Services Program of Office of Economic Opportunity to the American Bar Association, PrEx 10.18

Annual Report of Major Natural Gas Companies, E 3.25/4

Annual Report of National Voluntary Laboratory Accreditation, C 1.71

Annual Report of Operations Under the Airport and Airway Development Act, TD 4.22/2

Annual Report of Operations Under the Federal Airport Act, TD 4.22

Annual Report of Political Committees Supporting Candidates for House of Representatives, Y 1.2/4

Annual Report of Progress on Engineering Research, I 27.54

Annual Report of Radiation Exposures for Doe and Doe Contractor Employees, E 1.42

Annual Report of Research, A 13.27/1

Annual Report of Safety Progress for (year), T 1.41/3

Annual Report of Secretary, Department of Commerce and Labor, C 1.1

Annual Report of Secretary of Health, Education, and Welfare to Congress in Compliance with Public Law 90-148, Air Quality Act of 1967, FS 1.35

Annual Report of Secretary of Transportation of Administration of Natural Gas Pipelines Safety Act of 1968, TD 1.10/4

Annual Report of Sinking Fund and Funded Debt of District of Columbia, for Fiscal Year, T 40.6

Annual Report of Small Arms Target Practice, N 17.15

Annual Report of the Activities of the Effluent Standards and Water Quality Information Advisory Committee, EP 1.1/2

Annual Report of the Activities of the Joint Committee on Defense Production with Material on Mobilization from Departments and Agencies, Y 4.D 36:R 29

Annual Report of the Administration of the Natural Gas Pipeline Safety Act, TD 9.11

Annual Report of the Administrator of General Services, GS 1.1

Annual Report of the Attorney General of the United States, J 1.1

Annual Report of the Board of Trustees of the Federal Old-Age and Survivors Insurance and Disability Insurance Trust Funds, SSA 1.1/4

Annual Report of the Chief Counsel for Advocacy on Implementation of the Regulatory Flexibility Act, SBA 1.1/5

Annual Report of the Chief of Engineers, Army, on Civil Works Activities, Annual Reports, D 103.1

Annual Report of the Chief of Engineers on Civil Works Activities, Extract Reports of the Lower Mississippi Valley Division and Mississippi River Commission, D 103.1/4

Annual Report of the Chief Scientist of the National Park Service, I 29.1/2

Annual Report of the Commissioner of Patents, C 21.1/2

Annual Report of the Comptroller General of the United States, GA 1.1

Annual Report of the Department of Health, Education, and Welfare to Congress on Services Provided to Handicapped Children in Project Head Start, HE 1.409

Annual Report of the Department of Health, Education, and Welfare to the President and the Congress on Federal Activities Related to the Administration of the Rehabilitation Act of 1973, HE 1.609

Annual Report of the Department of Treasury on Operation and Effect of Domestic International Sales Corporation Legislation for Calendar Year, Y 4.W 36:D 71/2

Annual Report of the Deputy Assistant Secretary of Defense (Installations), D 1.1/5

Annual Report of the Director of Locomotive Inspection, IC 1 loc.1

Annual Report of the Farm Credit Administration on the Work of the Cooperative Farm Credit System, FCA 1.1

Annual Report of the Federal Labor Relations Authority, Y 4.P 84/10-11

Annual Report of the Health Insurance Benefits Advisory Council, HE 20.17

Annual Report of the Law Enforcement Assistance Administration, J 1.1/2

Annual Report of the Librarian of Congress, LC 1.1

Annual Report of the National Research Programs, Crop Production, A 106.25, A 106.25/2

Annual Report of the National Digestive Diseases Advisory Board, HE 20.3027/4

Annual Report of the Organized Crime Drug Enforcement Task Force Program, J 1.93

Annual Report of the President on Trade Agreements Program, Pr 41.11

Annual Report of the President of the United States on Trade Agreements Program, Pr 37.10, Pr 40.11

Annual Report of the President on the Trade Agreements Program, Pr 38.13, Pr 39.13, Pr 42.11

Annual Report of the Proceedings of the Judicial Conference of the United States[and] Semiannual Report of the Director of the Administrative Office of the United States Courts, Ju 10.1

Annual Report of the Register of Copyrights, LC 3.1

Annual Report of the Reserve Forces Policy Board, D 1.1/3-2

Annual Report of the Rivers and Trails Conservation Programs, I 29.124

Annual Report of the Secretary of Defense on Reserve Forces, D 1.1/3

Annual Report of the Secretary of Interior Under the Surface Mining Control and Reclamation Act of 1977, I 1.96/5

Annual Report of the Secretary of the Army on Civil Works Activities, D 101.1/13

Annual Report of the Secretary of the Interior Under the Mining and Minerals Policy Act of 1970, I 1.96/3

Annual Report of the Secretary of the Treasury on the State of the Finances, T 1.1

Annual Report of the Secretary of Transportation on Hazardous Materials Control, TD 1.24

Annual Report of the Secretary of Transportation on Hazardous Materials Transportation, TD 9.15

Annual Report of the Southwestern District Branch of Predator & Rodent Control, I 49.61

Annual Report of the Surgical Service, VA 1.1/2

Annual Report of the United States National Committee on Vital and Health Statistics, HE 20.6211

Annual Report of the VISA Office, S 1.1/4

Annual Report of Vegetable Breeding in Southeastern United States, Hawaii, and Puerto Rico, A 77.532

Annual Report of Welfare Programs, HE 17.28

Annual Report, Office of the Deputy Director–Operations, J 24.1/2

Annual Report on Adult Arrestees, J 28.24/5

Annual Report on Activities and Accomplishments Under the Communications Satellite Act of 1962, PrEx 18.9

Annual Report on Activities Conducted to Implement the Runaway Youth Act, HE 23.1309

Annual Report on Alaska Railroad, TD 1.10/8

Annual Report on Alaska's Mineral Resources, I 19.4/4

Annual Report on Carcinogens, HE 20.23/4, HE 20.3562

Annual Report on Cocaine Use Among Arrestees, J 28.15/2-5

Annual Report on Cooperative State-Federal Psoroptic Sheep and Cattle Scabies Eradication Activities, Fiscal Year (date), A 77.233

Annual Report on Government Patent Policy, Y 3.F 31/16:11

Annual Report on Hazardous Materials Transportation, TD 10.1/1

Annual Report on Implementation of Federal Equal Opportunity Recruitment Program, Report to Congress, PM 1.42

Annual Report on In-House Energy Management, E 1.50/2

Annual Report on International Religious Freedom (Bureau for Democracy, Human Rights and Labor), S 1.151

Annual Report on Juvenile Arrestees/Detainees, J 28.24/6

Annual Report on Location of New Federal Offices and Other Facilities, A 1.111

Annual Report on Marijuana Use Among Arrestees, J 28.15/2-6

Annual Report on Methamphetamine Use Among Arrestees, J 28.15/2-7

Annual Report on National Cancer Institute and Environmental Protection Agency Projects, HE 20.3177

Annual Report on Opiate Use Among Arrestees, J 28.15/2-4

Annual Report on Pipeline Safety, TD 10.12

Annual Report on Programming, Y 3.M 69:8

Annual Report on Public Information and Education Countermeasure of Alcohol Safety Action Projects, TD 8.20

Annual Report on School Safety, E 1.1/7

Annual Report on Sharing Medical Resources, Y 4.V 64/4:M 46/5

Annual Report on the Administration of the Natural Gas Pipeline Safety Act, TD 9.11

Annual Report on the Archaeological Programs of the Western Region, I 29.59/3

Annual Report on the Employment of Minorities, Women and Handicapped Individuals in the Federal Government, Y 3.Eq 2:12-5

Annual Report on the Food and Agricultural Sciences, A 1.1/4-2

Annual Report on the HEW/USDA Rural Health Facilities Agreement, A 84.12

Annual Report on the Impact of the Caribbean Basin Economic Recovery Act on U.S. Industries and Consumers, ITC 1.32

Annual Report on the Management Efficiency Pilot Program, VA 1.1/3

Annual Report on the National Housing Goal, HH 1.79

Annual Report on the Status of Equal Employment Opportunity Program, TD 2.17

Annual Report on the Status of U.S. Living Marine Resources, C 55.1/2

Annual Report on the Technical Assistance Training Program in Education, FS 5.214:14046, HE 5.214:14046

Annual Report on Tobacco Statistics, A 88.34/12

Annual Report on Urban Area Traffic Operations Improvement, TD 2.29

Annual Report on U.S. Export Competitiveness as Required by Section 206 of the 1992 Export Enhancement Act, C 1.1/4

Annual Report, Presidents Board of Advisors on Historically Black Colleges and Universities, ED 1.89/2

Annual Report, Surgeon General, United States Army, D 104.1

Annual Report, Title 2, Elementary and Secondary Education Act of 1965, School Library Resources, Textbooks, and Other Instructional Materials, FS 5.220:20108, HE 5.220:20108

Annual Report to Congress, AC 1.1

Annual Report to Congress, Indian Civil Service Retirement Act, PL 96-135, HE 20.9414

Annual Report to Congress on Activities of the Office of the Special Counsel, MS 2.1

Annual Report to Congress on Child Support Enforcement Program, HE 1.53

Annual Report to Congress on Equal Credit Opportunity Act, FR 1.60

Annual Report to Congress on National Industrial Reserve Under Public Law 883, 80th Congress, D 7.21

Annual Report to Congress on Activities of the Office of the Special Counsel, MS 2.1

Annual Report to Congress on Administration of the Marine Protection Research and Sanctuaries Act of 1972, EP 1.69

Annual Report to Congress on the Federal Trade Commission Improvement Act for the Calendar Year, FR 1.57

Annual Report to Congress on the Implementation of the Education of the Handicapped Act, ED 1.32

Annual Report to Congress on the Section 312 Rehabilitation Loan Program, HH 1.87

Annual Report to Membership, PrEx 1.10

Annual Report to Secretary of Transportation on Accident Investigation and Reporting Activities of Federal Highway Administration, TD 2.16

Annual Report to the Administrator, The Office of Exploration, NAS 1.1/5

Annual Report to the Congress, Fiscal Year Executive Summary, D 1.1/7

Annual Report to the Congress Fiscal Year Installations, D 1.1/7-2

Annual Report to the Interstate Commerce Commission, Class I and Class II Motor Carriers of Household Goods, IC 1.39/3

Annual Report to the Interstate Commerce Commission, Class I and Class II Motor Carriers of Property, IC 1.39

Annual Report to the Interstate Commerce Commission, Class I Passenger, IC 1.39/2

Annual Report to the President and Congress of Activities Under the Law Enforcement Assistance Act of 1965, J 1.32

Annual Report to the President and Congress on the State of Energy Conservation Program, E 1.27

Annual Report to the President and the Congress on the Activities of the Rehabilitation Act Interagency Coordinating Council, J 1.1/5

Annual Report to the President and the Congress Submitted by the Secretary of Transportation Under the Emergency Rail Service Act of 1970, TD 1.10/6

Annual Report to the Secretary of Agriculture by the Joint Council on Food and Agricultural Sciences, A 1.1/4

Annual Report to the Secretary of Transportation on the Accident Investigation and Reporting Activities of the Federal Highway Administration in (year), TD 2.16

Annual Report to the Secretary on Accident Investigation and Reporting Activities, TD 8.17

Annual Report, USDA Grain Storage, Handling and Processing Safety Coordinating Subcommittee, A 1.136

Annual Report, Voluntary Home Mortgage Credit Program, HH 1.25

Annual Report, Workforce Profile, FHL 1.1/2

Annual Reports of Assistants to Secretary of Defense, D 1.1/2

Annual Reports of Committees, Councils, Etc., HE 20.5001/2, HE 20.6001/5

Annual Reports of Governor of Alaska on Alaska Game Law, A 5.7

Annual Reports of Political Committees Supporting Candidates for Senate, Y 1.3/5

Annual Reports on Construction of Pension Building, I 1.27

Annual Reports on Operations of Federal Credit Unions, A 72.19

Annual Reports on Salmon Fisheries, C 2.1

Annual Reports on Statistics of Express Companies in the United States, IC 1 exp.1

Annual Reports on Statistics of Railways in United States, IC 1 ste.11

Annual Reports on Street Railroads in District of Columbia, IC 1 eler.5

Annual Reports to Congress (calendar years), C 21.1

Annual Reports to Secretary of Commerce, C 21.1/2

Annual Reports to the Governments of Canada, U.S., Saskatchewan and Montana by the Poplar River Bilateral Monitoring Committee, S 1.147

Annual Research Symposium, EP 1.83

Annual Retail Trade Report, C 3.138/3-2

Annual Review, Airworthiness Civil Air Regulations Meeting, C 31.245

Annual Review of Aircraft Accident Data, U.S. Air Carrier Operations, TD 1.113/5

Annual Review of Aircraft Accident Data, U.S. General Aviation, TD 1.113

Annual Review of Child Abuse and Neglect Research, HE 23.1210/3

Annual Review of U.S. Air Carrier Accidents Occurring in Calendar Year (date), TD 1.113/2

Annual Review of U.S. General Aviation Accidents Occurring in Calendar Year, TD 1.113

Annual Rice Summary, Louisiana Crop Reporting Service, A 88.18/23

Annual School Calendar, I 20.16/6

Annual Statement of Assurance, D 1.101

Annual Statements, Government Life Insurance Fund, VA 1.13

Annual Statistical Digest, FR 1.59

Annual Statistical Report, J 24.1/3

Annual Statistical Report, Fiscal Year (date), D 14.1/2, D 119.1/2

Annual Statistical Report, Rural Electrification Borrowers, A 68.1/2

Annual Statistical Report, Rural Telecommunications Borrowers A 68.1/3

Annual Statistical Report, Rural Telephone Borrowers, A 68.1/3

Annual Statistical Review, Hospital and Medical Services, FS 2.86/6

Annual Statistical Summary, T 34.9

Annual Statistical Summary, Fiscal Year, HE 20.5409

Annual Statistical Supplement, FS 3.3/3

Annual Statistical Supplement to the Social Security Bulletin, SSA 1.22/2

Annual Statistics, NCU 1.9/2

Annual Statistics on Workers Under Social Security, HE 3.40

Annual Summaries, C 3.128/2

Annual Summary of Cost and Quality of Steam-Electric Plant Fuels, FP 1.2:F 95

Annual Summary of Foreign Agricultural Training As of [date], A 67.37

Annual Summary of Investigations in Support of Civil Works Program for Calendar Year, D 103.24/8

Annual Summary of Water Quality Data for Selected Sites in the Pacific Northwest, I 19.46/3

Annual Summary Progress Reports of Population Research Centers and Program Projects, HE 20.3362/4

Annual Survey of Manufactured Products, C 3.24/9-10

Annual Survey of Manufacturers, C 3.24/9, C 3.24/9-2, C 3.24/9-3

Annual Survey of Manufacturers: Annual Volumes, C 56.221/2

Annual Survey of Manufacturers, M (date) (As) (series), C 56.221

Annual Survey of Manufacturers, Miscellaneous Publications, C 3.24/9-4

Annual Survey of Manufactures, Origin of Manufactured Products, C 3.24/9-9

Annual Survey of Manufacturers, Value of Manufacturers' Inventories, C 3.24/9-11

Annual Survey on Certain Stainless Steel and Alloy Tool Steel, ITC 1.25/2

Annual Sweetpotato Summary, Louisiana Crop Reporting Service, A 88.12/24

Annual Technical Report of the Cape May Plant Materials Center, HE 3.67/2

Annual Test Report, Department of Defense Dependents Schools, D 1.1/10

Annual Training Course in Occupational Therapy, W 44.23/8

Annual Training Course in Physiotherapy, W 44.23/7

Annual Training Courses in Dietetics, W 44.23/6

Annual Technical Report of the Cape May Plant Materials Center, A 57.54/2

Annual Typhoon Report, D 220.11

Annual Water Quality Analyses Report for Nevada, I 53.44

Annual Water Quality Data Report, E 1.28/15

Annual Waterfowl Report, Alaska, I 49.55

Annual Work Plan, PrEx 1.10/12

Annual Workshop of the Asthma and Allergic Disease Centers, HE 20.3261

Annuals of Astrophysical Observatory, SI 1.12

Annuals of Congress, X 1

Answer Me This: American Cities Series, I 16.58/1

Answer Me This: Historical Series, I 16.58/5

Answer Me This: Miscellaneous Series, I 16.58/3

Answer Me This: Song Series, I 16.58/4

Antarctic Bibliography, D 202.2:An 8

Antarctic Bibliography, LC 33.9

Antarctic Journal of the United States, NS 1.26

Antarctic Photomap (series), I 19.100/6

Antarctic Regions, C 55.214/50

Antarctic Research Program Maps, I 19.25/8

Antarctic Seismological Bulletin, C 4.36, C 55.414, C 55.610

Antarctic Travelers (series), C 4.56

Antarctical Topographic Series, I 19.100

Anthracite Survey Papers, A 13.42/9

Anthropological Papers (numbered), I 29.77

Antimony, I 28.95

Antimony in (year), I 28.95/2

Antimony Monthly Report, I 28.95

Antirecession Fiscal Assistance to State and Local Governments, T 1.51

Antirecession Payment Summary, T 1.51

Antitrust Laws with Amendments [1890], Y 1.2:An 8

Any Bonds Today, T 66.17

AoA Occasional Papers in Gerontology, HE 23.3111

AOA Reports, HE 1.1016
AOA Update, HE 1.1017
APA, D 101.43/2-2
APH-Correspondence Aid (series), A 77.228
APHIS Facts, A 101.10/3
APHIS Meat and Poultry Inspection Program, Program Issuances for the Period, A 101.6/2-2
APHIS Organizational Directory, A 101.21
APHIS Program Service Directory, A 101.15
APHIS (series), A 101.10
APHIS- (series), A 101.10/2
Apollo Expeditions to the Moon, 1975, NAS 1.21:350
Apollo Over the Moon, a View from Orbit, NAS 1.21:362
Appalachia, Y 3.Ap 4/2:9-2
Appalachian Education Satellite Project Technical Reports, Y 3.Ap 4/2:12
Appalachian Reporter, Y 3.Ap 4/2:11
Apparent Consumption of Industrial Explosives and Blasting Agents in the United States, I 28.112
Appeals (series), Ju 7.9
Appeals Pending Before United States Courts in Customs Cases, T 17.8
Appearances of Soviet Leaders, PrEx 3.10/7-2
Appendix, Budget of the United States Government, Department of Commerce Chapter, C 1.83, C 1.86
Apples, Production by Varieties, with Comparisons, A 88.12/15
Applicable Drawings for Engineer Equipment, W 7.31
Application Development Guide, Talent Search Program, ED 1.8/3
Application Development Guide Upward Bound Program for Program Year (date), ED 1.69/2
Application Document Series, WSDG-AD-(nos.), A 13.87/3
Application for Basic Grants under Library Services for Indian Tribes and Hawaiian Program, ED 1.53/2
Application for Fulbright-Hays Training Grants, ED 1.54
Application for Grants, Formula Grants to Local Educational Agencies, ED 1.410
Application for Grants under Adult Indian Education Programs, ED 1.52
Application for Grants under Fulbright-Hays Foreign Curriculum Consultants, ED 1.59
Application for Grants under Fulbright-Hays Group Projects Abroad, ED 1.62
Application for Grants under Handicapped Children's Early Education Program Demonstration and Auxiliary Activities, ED 1.50/3
Application for Grants under Indian Education Program, ED 1.51
Application for Grants under Post Secondary Education Programs for Handicapped Persons, ED 1.50/2
Application for Grants under Rehabilitation Research, Field Initiated Research, ED 1.70/4
Application for Grants under Strengthening Research Library Resources Program, ED 1.53
Application for Grants under the Cooperative Education Program, ED 1.70/3
Application for Grants under the Endowment Grant Program, ED 1.70/2
Application for Grants under the Secretary's Discretionary Program, ED 1.63
Application for Grants under the Secretary's Discretionary Program for Mathematics, Science, Computer Learning and Critical Foreign Languages, ED 1.64
Application for Grants under Title VI of the Higher Education Act of 1965, as Amended, ED 1.56
Application for Grants under Title VI of the Higher Education Act of 1965, as Amended, ED 1.57
Application for Grants under Upward Bound Program, ED 1.69
Application for New Grants Under Certain Direct Grant Programs, ED 1.214
Application for Seminars Abroad Program, ED 1.59/2
Application Kit Tribal Management Grants, etc., FY [date] Tribal Management Grant Program Announcement, HE 20.317/2
Applications Accepted for Filing by Private Radio Bureau, CC 1.36/9
Applications Accepted for Filing by Safety and Special Radio Services Bureau, CC 1.39/4
Applications and Case Discontinuances for AFDC, HE 3.60/3
Applications and Case Dispositions for Public Assistance, HE 3.16/3, HE 3.60/3, HE 17.613/3

Applications and/or Amendments Thereto Filed with the Civil Aeronautics Board, CAB 1.23, C 31.221
Applications, Cases Approved, and Cases Discontinued for Public Assistance, HE 17.641
Applications for Permits, CC 1.34
Applications, Notices, Orders, T 1.6/2 .
Applications of Modern Technologies to International Development, AID-OST-(series), S 18.42
Applications Pending in Commission for Exemption from Radio Provisions of International Convention for Safety of Life at Sea Convention, London, 1929, Title 3, Pt. 2 of Communications Act of 1934, etc., Reports, CC 1.19
Applications Received, or Acted on, by the Board, FR 1.48
Applied Language and Learning, D 1.105
Applied Mathematics and Mechanics [abstracts], C 41.61
Applied Mathematics Series, C 13.32
Applied Physiology and Bioengineering Study Section, HE 20.3001/2:P 56
Applied Social and Behavioral Sciences Research Initiation Grants, NS 1.10/8
Applied Technology Laboratory, U.S. Army Research and Technology Laboratories, D 117.8/2
Apply Pesticides Correctly, a Guide for Commercial Applicators (series), EP 5.8/2
Appraisal of Potentials for Outdoor Recreational Development [by Area], A 57.57
Appraisal of the Proposed Budget for Food and Agricultural Sciences Report to the President and Congress, A 1.1/4-3
Appraisement Commission, Reports, T 1.21
Apprehension Orders, J 1.14/10
Apprentice Lectures, GP 1.13
Apprentice Series, GP 1.10
Apprentice Training News, Y 3.F 31/12:9
Apprentice Training Series, GP 1.26
Apprenticeship Digest, L 23.12
Apprenticeship Standards, L 16.14
Approach, D 202.13
Approach, Naval Aviation Safety Review, D 202.13
Approach/Mech, D 202.13
Appropriate Technologies for Development (series), PE 1.10
Appropriation Bulletins, N 20.3/2
Appropriation, Digest of, T 63.115
Appropriation Hearings, J 24.21
Approved Codes, Y 3.N 21/8:7
Approved Conference, Rate and Interconference Agreements of Steamship Lines in the Foreign Commerce of the United States, FMC 1.11
Approved Drug Product with Therapeutic Equivalence Evaluations, HE 20.4715
Approved Drug Products with Therapeutic Equivalence Evaluations, HE 20.4210
Approved List, Sanitary Inspected Fish Establishments, C 55.338
Approved Prescription Drug Products with Therapeutic Equivalence Evaluations, HE 20.4210
Approved Recurring Reports Bulletin 12-AY, VA 1.3/4
Approved Task Plans for Category "A" Generic Activities, Y 3.N 88:19
APTI Courses, EP 4.21
APTIC Bulletin, FS 2.93/6
Aquaculture Outlook and Situation, AS-(series), A 105.23/2-2, A 93.42
Aquaculture Outlook, Supplement to Livestock, Dairy, and Poultry Situation and Outlook, A 93.46/3-6
Aquaculture Situation and Outlook Report, A 93.55
Aquatic Environmental Conditions in Chickamuga Reservoir During Operation of Sequoyah Nuclear Plant, Y 3.T 25:54
Aquatic Plant Control Program, Technical Reports, D 103.24/13
Aquatic Sciences and Fisheries Information System: ASFIS Reference Series, C 55.39
AR Today (Acquisition Reform Today), D 1.6/11-3
ARA Case Book, C 46.20
ARA Field Reports, C 46.22
ARA Information Memo, C 46.15
ARA News Roundup, S 1.134/2
ARA Staff Studies, C 46.22/2
Arabian Peninsula, Series 5211, D 5.334
Arbitration Between Republic of Chile and Republic of Peru with Respect to Unfulfilled Provisions of Treaty of Peace of Oct. 20, 1883, S 3.35
Arbitration Series, S 3.39
Arbitrations Under Treaty of Washington, S 3.13

Arbovirus Surveillance, Reference, and Research, HE 20.7811
Arctic Research of the United States, NS 1.51/2
Archaeological Collection Management Project, Archaeological Research Series, I 29.59
Archaeologist for Interior Department Annual Reports, I 1.64
Archeological and Historical Data Recovery Program, I 29.59/4
Archeological Assistance Program, Technical Brief (Series), I 29.59/6
Archeological Assistance Study (series), I 29.59/8
Archeological Collection Management Project ACMP (series), I 29.112
Archeological Completion Report Series, I 29.59/2
Archeological Programs of National Park Service, I 29.2:Ar 2/3
Archeological Reports, A 13.94
Architectural Bulletins, FL 2.20
Archives and Special Collections of the Smithsonian Institution, SI 1.34
Archives II Researcher Bulletin, AE 1.123
Arctic Bibliography, D 1.22
Arctic Bulletin, NS 1.3/3
Arctic Construction and Frost Effects Laboratory, D 103.31
Arctic Regions, C 55.214/49
Arctic Series, W 42.5
ARDC Technical Program Planning Document AF ARPD, D 301.45/49
Area and Country Bibliographic Surveys, D 101.22:550
Area and Industrial Development Aids, C 41.8/2
Area Charts, U.S., D 5.318/6
Area Classification Summary, I 7.51/2
Area Designation Status Reports, C 46.14
Area Development Aid: Area Trend Series, C 41.89
Area Development Aid: Industrial Location Series, C 45.8/3
Area Development Aid: Industry Trend Series, C 45.8/2
Area Development Bulletin, C 46.9
Area Development Memorandum for State Planning and Development Offices, C 45.14
Area Guide Preliminary Series, A 13.36/5
Area Handbook to [Country], D 101.22:550
Area Handbooks, D 101.6
Area Measurement Reports, C 3.208/2
Area Outline Maps, Series 1105, D 5.325,-D 5.325/2
Area Planning, North and South America, D 5.318/5-2
Area Planning, Special Use Airspace, North and South America, D 5.318/5-3
Area Redevelopment Bookshelf of Community Aids, C 46.8/2
Area Redevelopment Manpower Reports, L 7.66/2
Area Redevelopment Technical Leaflets, I 1.93
Area Report MC(P)-S Series, C 3.24/8-4
Area Trend Series, C 45.13
Area Trends in Employment and Unemployment, L 37.13
Area Vocational Education Program Series, FS 5.280, HE 5.280
Area Wage Survey Advance Reports, L 2.107/2
Area Wage Survey Reports, L 2.107
Area Wage Survey Summary (series), L 2.122
  –Baton Rouge, Louisiana, L 2.122/18-3
  –Brunswick, Georgia, L 2.122/10-5
  –Columbus, Mississippi, L 2.122/24-3
  –Eugene-Springfield-Medford-Roseburg- Klamath Falls-Grants Pass, Oregon, L 2.122/37
  –Goldsboro, North Carolina, L 2.122/33-4
  –Greenville-Spartanburg, South Carolina, L 2.122/40-2
  –Norfolk-Virginia Beach-Newport News, Virginia, L 2.122/46-2
  –Oklahoma City, Oklahoma, L 2.122/36-2
  –Providence, Rhode Island, L 2.122/39
  –Southeastern Massachusetts, L 2.122/21-2
  –Tulsa, Oklahoma, L 2.122/36
  –West Virginia, L 2.122/48
  –Yakima-Richland-Kennewick-Pasco-Walla Walla-Pendleton, Washington-Oregon, L 2.122/47
Area Wage Survey (summary): Daytona Beach, Florida, L 2.122/9-5
Area Wage Survey (summary): Selma, Alabama, L 2.122/1-6
Area Wage Survey, Bradenton, Florida, Metropolitan Area, L 2.121/9-5
Area Wage Survey, Cedar Rapids, Iowa (summary), L 2.122/15-3
Area Wage Survey, Danbury, Connecticut, Metropolitan Area, L 2.121/7-2
Area Wage Survey, Duluth Minnesota- Wisconsin (summary), L 2.122/23

Area Wage Survey, Elkhart-Goshen, Indiana, Metropolitan Area, L 2.121/14-4

Area Wage Survey, Gadsden and Anniston, Alabama, L 2.122/1-5

Area Wage Survey, Longview-Marshall, Texas, Metropolitan Area, L 2.121/43-6

Area Wage Survey, Monmouth-Ocean, New Jersey, Metropolitan Area, L 2.121/30-4

Area Wage Survey, Phoenix, Arizona, Metropolitan Area, L 2.121/3

Area Wage Survey, Portland, Oregon- Washington, Metropolitan Area, L 2.121/37

Area Wage Survey, San Angelo, Texas, Metropolitan Area, L 2.121/43-5

Area Wage Survey, South Dakota, L 2.122/41

Area Wage Survey, Tampa-ST. Petersburg- Clearwater, Florida, Metropolitan Area, L 2.121/9-6

Area Wage Survey, Wilmington, Delaware- New Jersey- Maryland, Metropolitan Area, L 2.121/8

Area Wage Survey Summaries by Cities, L 2.113

Area Wage Survey Summaries by States, L 2.113/6

Area Wage Surveys, L 2.3, L 2.121

Areally-Weighted Data, C 55.287/59

Areas Administered by the National Park Service, I 29.66

Areas Eligible for Financial Assistance Designated Under the Public Works and Economic Development Act of 1965, Reports, C 46.25/2

ARED Newsletter, A 93.49

AREI Updates, A 93.47/3

Argentina-Brazil Boundary Arbitration, S 3.20

Argonne Computing Newsletter, E 1.86/5

Argonne National Laboratory, Division of Educational Programs: Annual Report, E 1.86

Argonne National Laboratory: Research and Highlights, E 1.86/4

Argonne News, E 1.86/2

ARI Newsletter, D 101.60/7

Arizona Desert Digest, I 53.54/2

Arizona, Governor, Annual Reports, I 1.6

Arkansas River Water Basin News, D 103.30/2

ARL Regulations, D 101.9/7

ARL Technical Reports, D 301.45/25

ARL-TR (series), D 101.133

ARM Index Rates, FHL 1.34

Armed Forces in Action (series), D 114.9

Armed Forces Information Pamphlets, D 2.7/2

Armed Forces Institute Manuals, D 1.10

Armed Forces Institute of Pathology Annual Research Programs Report, D 101.117/6

Armed Forces Institute of Pathology: Publications, D 1.16/4

Armed Forces Institute Publications, W 1.77

Armed Forces Pest Control Board, Annual Reports, D 104.18/2

Armed Forces Radiobiology Research Institute: Annual Research Report, D 15.1/2

Armed Forces Radiobiology Research Institute: Scientific Reports, D 15.12

Armed Forces Radiobiology Research Institute: Technical Reports, D 15.12/2

Armed Forces Report, Armed Forces Day, C 1.6/3

Armed Forces Song Folio, D 1.14

Armed Forces Staff College Essays on Command Issues, D 5.413/2

Armed Forces Talk, D 2.7

Armed Services Catalog of Medical Material, D 1.9

Armed Services Electro Standards Agency, Lists, D 101.38

Armed Services Medical Procurement Agency; Memorandum Reports, D 1.30

Armed Services Procurement Manual, ASPM-(series), D 1.13/4

Armed Services Procurement Regulation, M 1.8, D 1.13

Armed Services Procurement Regulation, Revision, D 1.13/2

Armed Services Procurement Regulation Supplement, ASPA- (series), D 1.13/2-2

Armed Services Procurement Regulations Supplement, HQ USAF, D 1.13/2-3

Armed Services Research and Development Report on Insect and Rodent Control, D 104.18

Armor, the Magazine of Mobile Warfare, D 101.78/2

Armor-Cavalry, Part 1. Regular Army and Army Reserve, D 114.11:Ar 5

Armour, D 101.78/2

Arms Control, PrEx 7.14/7

Arms, Control and Disarmament, LC 2.10

Arms Control and Disarmament, Studies in Progress or Recently Completed, S 1.117/5

Arms Control Impact Statements, Y 4.F 76/2-11

Arms Control Update, AC 1.17

Armstrong Laboratory, AL/HR-CR, D 301.45/27-11

Armstrong Laboratory Technical Paper, D 301.45/27-4

Armstrong Laboratory Technical Report, D 301.45/27

Army, D 7.29/3

Army Administrator, D 101.86

Army Air Forces in World War II (series), D 301.82

Army Air Forces Library Bulletins, W 108.12

Army Air Forces Radio and Facility Charts, Atlantic and Caribbean Areas, W 108.26

Army Air Forces Radio and Facility Charts, North Pacific Area, W 108.27

Army Air Forces Specifications, W 108.13

Army Air Mobility Research and Development Laboratory, Fort Eustis, Virginia: USAAMRDL Technical Reports, D 117.8/2, D 117.8/4

Army AL&T Bulletin D 101.52/3

Army and Navy Official Gazette, W 1.5

Army Audit Agency Pamphlets, D 101.3/3-2

Army Aviation Digest, D 101.47

Army Ballistic Missile Agency, DC-TR-(series), D 105.15

Army Budget, Fiscal Year, D 101.121

Army Battlefield Environment, D 103.20/7

Army Chaplaincy D 101.114

Army Chemical Journal, D 116.17

Army Club System, Annual Report, D 102.82

Army Coded Card, W 42.6

Army Communicator, D 111.14

Army Conservation Project Posters, W 3.46/7

Army Digest, D 101.12

Army Echoes, D 101.141

Army Electronics Command, Fort Monmouth, N.J.: Research and Development Technical Reports, ECOM (series), D 111.9/4

Army Environmental Sciences, D 103.20/7

Army Extension Courses, W 1.70

Army Extension Courses, Announcements, W 3.51

Army Facilities Energy Plan, D 103.119

Army Families, D 101.123

Army Focus, D 101.1/14

Army Forces Far East, AFFE Pamphlets, D 102.24

Army Health Promotion Program, Fit to Win, D 101.22:600

Army Historian, D 114.2

Army Historical Program, Fiscal Year, D 114.10/2

Army Historical Series, D 114.19

Army Hit Kit of Popular Songs, D 102.10

Army Host, D 102.81

Army History D 114.20

Army Information Digest, W 1.66, M 101.10, D 101.12

Army Institute for Professional Development: Subcourse ISO- (series), D 101.103

Army Intelligence Center and School: SupR (series), D 101.112

Army Issue Paper, D 101.146/4

Army Lawyer, D 108.11

Army Life and United States Recruiting News, M 108.77

Army Lineage Book, D 114.11

Army List and Directory, W 3.10, W 40.6

Army Logistician, D 101.69

Army Map Service Bulletins, W 7.33/4

Army Management Course (series), D 101.94

Army Management Engineering Training Activity: Course Catalog, D 101.94/3

Army Material Command Regulations, D 101.9/2

Army Medical Bulletin, W 44.21/7

Army Medical Equipment and Optical School: Student Handouts (series), D 104.31/3

Army Medical Library Bibliographies, D 104.10

Army Medical Library Catalog, LC 30.13

Army Medical Research Laboratory Reports, D 104.14

Army Meteorological Register, W 44.11

Army Missile Command, Redstone Scientific Information Center, Redstone Arsenal, Alabama, RSIC- (series), D 105.22/3

Army Morale Support Fund, Annual Report, D 102.82/2

Army Morale, Welfare, and Recreation, Fiscal Year Annual Report, D 102.82/2

Army Museum Newsletter, D 114.16

Army National Guard Lineage Series, D 12.20

Army Navy Hit Kit of Popular Songs, M 117.7

Army Nurse, W 44.29

Army Ordnance Center and School, Aberdeen Proving Ground, Maryland: Special Texts, D 105.25

Army Organizational Effectiveness Journal, D 101.91

Army Pay Tables, W 36.10, W 77.7

Army Personnel Bulletin, D 101.39/4

Army Personnel Letter, D 101.39/3

Army, Postal, and Navy Air Service Laws [March 2, 1913], Y 1.2:Ai 7

Army Postal Bulletin, W 3.77

Army Procurement Circulars, D 101.33/2

Army Procurement Procedures, D 101.6/4

Army Procurement Regulations, M 101.11

Army Prosthetics Research Laboratory, Technical Reports, D 104.15/2

Army Quartermaster School Correspondence Subcourse, QM- (series), D 106.22

Army Register, D 102.9

Army Regulations, AR- (series), W 1.6, D 101.9

Army Research and Development, D 101.52/3

Army Research Institute for Behavioral and Social Sciences: Research Reports, D 101.60/2

Army Research Institute for the Behavioral and Social Sciences: Special Reports (series), D 101.60/6

Army Research Institute for the Behavioral Sciences, Study Report, D 101.60/8

Army Research Laboratory, Annual Review, D 101.1/11

Army Research Laboratory Strategic Plan for Fiscal Year, D 101.1/11-2

Army Research Task Summaries, D 101.52/2

Army Reserve Forces Policy Committee, Annual Report, D 101.1/12

Army Reserve Magazine, D 101.43

Army Reservist, D 101.43

Army RD & A Bulletin, D 101.52/3

Army ROTC (pamphlets), D 101.22/31

Army Storage Catalogue, W 34.16/3

Army Talk, W 111.7

Army Technology, D 101.1/16

Army Trainer, D 101.20/3

Army Training and Evaluation Program, ARTEP- (series), D 101.20/2

Army Transportation Engineering Agency: USATEA Reports, D 117.11

Army Transportation Research Command: Interim Reports, D 117.8/3

Army War Casualties, W 107.11

Army-Navy Aeronautical Standards, Index, Y 3.Ae 8:7

Army-Navy Joint Packaging Instructions, N 20.27

Army-Navy War Casualties, Pr 32.5028

Army-Navy-Air Force, List of Products Qualifies Under Military Specifications, D 101.30

ARNG- (series), D 12.12

Arnoldian, D 208.112

ARO-D- (series), D 101.52/7

ARPC Pamphlet (series), , D 301.35/9

Arrearage Tables of Amounts Due and Unpaid, 90 Days or More on Foreign Credits of the United States Government, T 1.45/4

Arrivals and Departures by Selected Ports, Statistics of Foreign Visitor Arrivals and U.S. Citizen Departures Analyzed by U.S. Ports of Entry and Departure, C 47.15/4

Arrowhead, D 101.71

ARS Directory, A 77.15/2

ARS National Research Program, A 77.28

ARS- (series), A 1.107, A 77.15

Arsenal of Democracy Series, Pr 32.408

ARSLOE Informal Report (series), C 55.236

ARS-NC- (series), A 77.15/2

Arson Resource Exchange Bulletin, FEM 1.110/2

Art and Artists in National Parks, I 29.25

Art and Indian Children of the Dakotas (series), I 20.63

Art and Industry, Education in Industrial and Fine Arts in United States, I 16.7

Art in the United States Capitol, Y 1.91-2:H.doc 368

Art Projects Bulletins, T 58.16

Arthritis and Rheumatic Diseases Abstracts, HE 20.3312

Arthritis Interagency Coordinating Committee: Annual Report to the Secretary, Fiscal Year (date), HE 20.3032

Arthritis Program, Annual Report to the Director, HE 20.3321

Arthritis, Rheumatic Diseases, and Related Disorders, HE 20.3320/2

Arthropod-Borne Virus Information Exchange, HE 20.7036

Artifacts, NF 2.14

Artificial Kidney Bibliography, HE 20.3311

Artificial Kidney-Chronic Uremia Advisory Committee, HE 20.3001/2:K 54

Artillery Circulars, W 3.5/1

Artillery Memoranda, W 29.8

Artillery Notes, W 29.7

Artists in Education, NF 2.8/2

Arts Administration Fellows Program, Application Guidelines, NF 2.8/2-24

Arts III Computer Program Functional Specifications (CPFS), TD 4.46

Arts in America, NF 2.8/2-28

Arts in Education, Arts Plus, Application Guidelines for Fiscal Year, NF 2.8/2-37

ArtsReach, Application Guidelines NF 2.15/3

Arts Review, NF 2.13
ASA/NSF/Census Bureau Research Fellow Program, C 3.293
Asbestos in (year), I 28.123
ASC MSRC, Quarterly Journal, D 301.121
ASCS Aerial Photography Status Maps, A 82.84:Ae 8
ASCS Background Information, A 82.82
ASCS Commodity Fact Sheets, A 82.82/2
ASD Technical Note TN (series), D 301.45/26
Aseptic Meningitis Surveillance, Annual Summary, HE 20.7011/26
Ashore, D 207.15/2
Asia and Pacific Rim, Situation and Outlook Series, A 93.29/2-19
Asia Reports, PrEx 7.16
Asian Development Bank Act, Releases, SE 1.25/14
Asphalt Sales, E 3.11/18
Asphalt Sales in (year), I 28.110/2
Asphalt Shipments in (year), I 28.110
Assassination Records Review Board, Reports Y 3.2:AS 7/R 29
Assaults on Federal Officers, J 1.14/7-3
Assembling the Health Planning Structure, HE 20.6114
Assessment Activities, Y 3.T 22/2:2-10
Assessments Completed and Referrals to Manpower Agencies by Welfare Agencies Under Work Incentive Program for AFDC Recipients, HE 17.619
Asset and Liability Trends, T 71.18
Asset and Liability Trends, All Operating Savings and Loan Associations, FHL 1.30
Asset Forfeiture, J 26.29
Assets and Liabilities of All Banks in the United States, FR 1.28
Assets and Liabilities of All Commercial Banks in United States, FR 1.28/4
Assets and Liabilities of All Member Banks, by Districts, FR 1.28/3
Assets, Liabilities, and Capital Accounts, Commercial and Mutual Savings Banks, Y 3.F 31/8:9
Assistance Administration Manual, EP 1.8/2
Associate Degrees and Other Formal Awards Below the Baccalaureate, HE 19.333
Associate Training Programs in the Medical and Biological Sciences at the National Institutes of Health, (Year) Catalog, HE 20.3015
Associated Arms, W 3.50/5
Association of Food and Drug Officials Quarterly Bulletin, HE 20.4003/5
Assumptions for the Annual Energy Outlook, E 3.1/4-3
AsthmaMemo HE 20.3225/2
Astronauts and Cosmonauts, Biographical and Statistical Data, Y 4.Sci 2:95
Astronomical Almanac, D 213.8
Astronomical Journal [abstracts], C 41.73
Astronomical Papers Prepared for Use of American Ephemeris and Nautical Almanac, D 213.9
Astronomical Papers Translated from the Russian, SI 1.12/4
Astronomical Phenomena for the Year [date], D 213.8/3
Astrophysical Observatory, Reports, SI 1.1/a2
ATC Manual, C 31.106/3
ATC Pamphlet, D 301.38/6
Atlanta Helicopter Route Chart, C 55.416/12-8
Atlantian, J 16.13
Atlantic and Gulf Coast of the United States, TD 5.9:2
Atlantic Coast–
    Cape Cod to Sandy Hook, C 55.422:2
    Cape Henry to Key West, C 55.422:4
    Eastport to Cape Cod, C 55.422:1
    Gulf of Mexico, Puerto Rico, and Virgin Islands, C 55.422:5
    Sandy Hook to Cape Henry, C 55.422:3
    United States, TD 5.9:1
Atlantic Coasters' Nautical Almanac, N 11.10
Atlantic Flyway, I 49.24/3
Atlas of American Agriculture Advance Sheets, A 1.30
Atlas of Tumor Pathology, D 1.16
Atlas of Tumor Pathology, 2d Series, D 1.16/3
Atlas of Tumor Pathology, Third Series, D 101.117/4
Atlas to Accompany [War of Rebellion] Official Records of Union and Confederate Armies [or Rebellion Records], W 45.7
Atlases–
    Corps of Engineers, D 103.49/3-2
    National Climatic Center, C 55.287/58
Atlas/State Data Abstract for the United States, D 1.58/4
Atmospheric Programs Bulletin, TD 4.71
Atmospheric Sciences Laboratory: Contractor Reports, ASL-CR (series), D 111.9/6

Atmospheric Sciences Laboratory: Technical Reports, ASL-TR (series), D 111.9/5
Atmospheric Turbidity and Precipitation Chemistry Data for the World, C 55.283
Atoll Research Bulletin, SI 1.25
Atomic Energy [abstracts], C 41.74
Atomic Energy Act of 1946 and Amendments [August 1, 1946], Y 1.2:At 7
Atomic Energy Commission Reports, Opinions of the Atomic Energy Commission with Selected Orders, Y 3.At 7:49
Atomic Energy Commission Research Reports for Sale by Office of Technical Services, C 41.29
Atomic Energy Commission Rules and Regulations, Y 3.At 7:6-2
Atomic Energy in Foreign Countries, Y 3.At 7:13
Atomic Energy Legislations through [Congress, Session], Y 4.At 7/2:L 52/2
Atomic Energy Research in Life and Physical Sciences, Y 3.At 7:48
Atomic Energy: Significant References Covering Various Aspects of Subject, Arranged Topically, LC 14.13
ATRC Manual, D 301.7/7
ATS Fact Book, TD 4.315
ATSDR, CD-ROM Series, HE 20.517, HE 20.7919
Attorney General's Advisory Committee of United States Attorneys Annual Report, J 1.1/8
Attorney General's Annual Report, Federal Law Enforcement and Criminal Justice Assistance Activities, J 1.32/2
Attorney General's Committee on Administrative Procedure, General Publications, J 1.21
Attorney General's Committee on Administrative Procedure, Monographs, J 1.22
Audio Materials, HE 3.22/2
Audiovisual Education Directors in State Departments of Education and in Large City School Systems, FS 5.60
Audiovisual Materials
    Bureau of Alcohol, Tobacco, and Firearms, T 70.12
    Bureau of Reclamation, I 27.7/3-2
    Corps of Engineer, D 103.49/4
    Defense Nuclear Agency, D 15.11
    Department of Education, ED 1.37/2
    Department of Interior, I 1.108
    Department of Labor, L 1.9/4
    Federal Disaster Assistance Administration, HH 12.10
    International Communication Agency, ICA 1.16
    International Development Agency, S 18.60/2
    National Cancer Institute, HE 20.3175/2
    Prisons Bureau, J 16.27
    Public Health Service, HE 20.30/2
Audiovisual Products, CC 1.56
Audiovisual Release Announcements, D 1.70
Audit Discriminant Function Reporting System, T 22.52
Audit Guide Series, A 1.11/4
Audit Journal, TD 1.32
Audit Legal Letter Guidance, PrEx 2.34
Audit of Payments from Special Bank Account to Lockheed Aircraft Corporation for C-5a Aircraft Program, Defense Department, GA 1.13:L 81/2
Audit Standards, Supplemental Series, GA 1.19
Audit Workload Plan, P 1.51
Author, Title, and Subject Index to the Social Security Bulletin, HE 3.3/5
Authorized Construction–Washington, D.C. Area, C 3.215/5
Auto and Traffic Safety, TD 8.36
AUTOFACTS, TD 8.37
Automated Data Processing Plan Update, SSA 1.23
Automated Multiphasic Health Testing Bibliography, HE 20.2710
Automated Reference Materials System (ARMS), VA 1.95/3
Automatic Data Processing Equipment Inventory in the United States Government As of the End of the Fiscal Year, GS 12.10
Automatic Welding [abstracts], C 41.54/6
Automatics, C 41.43
Automatics and Telemechanics Abstracts, C 41.43/2
Automation in the Medical Laboratory Sciences Review Committee, HE 20.3001/2:Au 8
Automobile Credit, FR 1.34/8
Automobile Financing, C 3.69
Automobile Industry, C 41.44
Automobile Installment Credit Developments, FR 1.34/4
Automobile Insurance and Compensation Studies, TD 1.17

Automobile Loans by Major Finance Companies, FR 1.34/6
Automobile Registration Characteristics, FW 2.17
Automobiles, C 3.70
Automotive Foreign Trade Manual, C 18.216
Automotive Fuel Economy Program, Annual Report to Congress, TD 8.26
Automobile Manufacturers Measurements, FMC 1.12
Automotive World News, C 18.49
Autovan, Automatic Global Voice Network, Defense Communications System Directory, D 5.111
AV Bulletin, TD 4.39
Availability of Heavy Fuel Oils by Sulfur Level, E 3.11/8, E 3.11/8-2
Available Bibliographies and Lists, A 17.17:25
Available Information Materials, EP 1.17:58.25
Available Publications of USDA'S Consumer and Marketing Service (except Market News Reports), A 88.40/2:53
Avenue Report, Y 3.P 38:16
Average Annual Wages and Wage Adjustment Index for CETA Prime Sponsors, L 2.44/3
Average Monthly Discharge for 15-year Base Period at Selected Gaging Stations and Change of Storage in Certain Lakes and Reservoirs in Pacific Northwest, I 19.45/3-2
Average Monthly Relief Benefits per Family, Principal City Areas and Remainder of Each State, Y 3.F 31/5:30
Average Monthly Weather Outlook, C 55.109
Average Premiums and Discounts for CCC Settlement Purposes for Offers Received, A 88.11/21
Average Semi-Monthly Retail Meat Prices at New York, Chicago and Kansas City, A 36.179
Average Weight of Measured Cup of Various Foods, A 1.87:41
Average Wholesale Prices and Index Numbers of Individual Commodities, L 2.33
AVFUEL & AVOIL into Plane Contract Listing, D 7.24/2
Aviano Vigileer, D 301.123
Aviation Accident Statistical Summary, Calendar Year, TD 4.413
Aviation Capacity Enhancement Plan, TD 4.77
Aviation Charts, N 6.27
Aviation Circular Letter, D 202.12
Aviation Education (series), TD 4.25, TD 4.70
Aviation Forecasts, Fiscal Years, FAA 1.42
Aviation Medical Education Series, TD 4.209
Aviation Medical Report, AM- (series), TD 4.210
Aviation Medicine, Annotated Bibliography, LC 36.9
Aviation News, FAA 1.41
Aviation Operating Charts, N 6.27/4
Aviation Psychology Program Research Reports, W 108.25
Aviation Series, C 30.65
Aviation Technical Letters, T 47.45
Aviation Technical Orders, T 47.43
Aviation Training Pamphlets, N 17.29
Aviation Weather System Plan, TD 4.62
AVP Bulletin, TD 4.39/2
Awards, Higher Education Act of 1965 (P.L. 89-329) as Amended, Title 3, Strengthening Developing Institutions, HE 5.92/2, HE 19.139
Awards, LEEP Participating Institutions, Program Year, J 1.35/4, J 26.23
Awards, 1st Division (bound edition) Separates Not Classed, RA 1.7
Awards, 1st Division, General Index, RA 1.7/2
Awards, 2nd Division (bound edition), RA 1.8
Awards, 3rd Division (bound edition), RA 1.9
Awards, 4th Division (bound edition), RA 1.10
Aware, C 55.127
AWIC Resource Series, A 17.27/3
AWIC Series, A 17.27

B

B- [Bibliography], S 18.21
B.A.E. News, A 36.16
B.A.E. News, Library Supplements
Babbitt Metal, C 3.71
Background Document for [various products], Noise Emission Regulations, EP 1.6/2
Background Facts on Women Workers in the United States, L 36.114/2
Background for Mutual Security, S 17.35/2
Background Information for Standards of Performance, EP 1.8/5
Background Information on [various subjects], FT 1.27
Background Material and Data on Programs within the Jurisdiction, Y 4.W 36:10-4
Background Notes, S 1.108, S 1.123

Background Notes: Index, S 1.123/2
Background Notes: [Monthly Mailings], S 1.123/3
Background Papers–
   Bureau of Health Manpower, HE 20.6611
   Congressional Budget Office, Y 10.9
   National Employment and Unemployment
      Statistics Commission, Y 3.Em 7/2:9
   Technology Assesment Office, Y 3.T 22/2:12
Background Series, Disarmament Staff, White House, Pr
    34.11/3
Background to Industrial Mobilization, Manual for
    Executive Reservists, C 41.6/7
Backgrounder, E 5.15
Bacteriology and Mycology Study Section, HE
    20.3001/2:B 13
Balance, a Discussion of Conservation Issues, I 66.19
Balance Sheet of Agriculture, A 1.38, A 1.75
Bales of Cotton Delivered in Settlement of Futures on
    New York and New Orleans Cotton
    Exchanges, A 59.10
Ballistic Systems Division, Technical Documentary
    Report BSD-TDR, D 301.45/36
Balloon Bulletins, W 42.28
Balloon Notes, A.E.F., W 95.21/6
Band News from the United States Air Force Band,
    Washington, D.C., D 301.108
Bangladesh, LC 1.30/9
Bang's Disease Work; Statement of Indemnity Claims
    and Averages in Cooperative, A 77.211
Bank Debits, FR 1.14
Bank Debits and Deposit Turnover, FR 1.17
Bank Debits, Deposits, and Deposit Turnover, FR 1.17
Bank Debits to Demand Deposit Accounts (Except
    Interbank and U.S. Government Accounts),
    FR 1.17/2
Bank Operating Statistics, Y 3.F 31/8:19
Bank Rates on Short-Term Business Loans, FR 1.32/5
Banking Institutions Owned and Operated by Negroes,
    Annual Reports, C 1.23
Bankruptcy Laws of the United States, Y 1.2:B 22/2
Banned Products [list], Y 3.C 76/3:9
Banned Toy List, HE 20.4024
BAO Reports, C 55.623
Bar Guides [various areas], TD 5.8/2
Bargaining Calendar, (year), L 2.3/8
Barite in (year), I 28.124
Base Flows As of [date] at Selected Gaging Stations in
    the Columbia River Basin, I 19.2:C 72/2
Base Maps, by States, I 19.27
Baseline Budget Projections, Fiscal Years (dates), Y
    10.16
Basic Data Book, J 16.24
Basic Data on Import Trade and Trade Barriers, C 18.184
Basic Data on the Economy of (country), C 1.50, C
    57.11
Basic Data Relating to the National Institutes of
    Health, HE 20.3002:N 21/4
Basic Data Reports, BD- (series), D 103.211
Basic Data Series Ground-Water Releases (series), I
    19.82
Basic Educational Opportunity Grant Program
    Handbook, HE 19.108/4
Basic Electronics Training (series), D 101.107/11
Basic Field Manual, W 3.63
Basic Life Skills Reports, HE 19.312
Basic Preparatory Programs for Practical Nurses by
    States and Changes in Number of Programs,
    FS 5.133
Basic Radio Propagation Predictions, C 13.31
Basic Research in Behavioral and Social Sciences: U.S.
    Army Research Institute Annual Report, D
    101.1/7-2
Basic Supervision, C 31.155
Basic Tables of Commissioning Allowances, N 28.15
Basic-Data Contributions, I 19.69
Basin Outlook Reports, A 57.46/20
Basin Outlook Reports (Washington), A 57.46/7
Bathroom Accessories (recessed and attachable, all
    clay), C 3.72
Bathymetric Mapping Products (Catalog) 5, United
    States Bathymetric and Fishing Maps, C
    55.418:5
Battlefield Update, I 29.134
BAUER Instructions, D 202.6/3
Bauxite, I 28.80
Bavarian Economics, M 105.20
BCBST, Perceptions II, D 101.22/29-2
BCD Notices, C 41.6/2-5
BCD Technical Papers, C 3.226/2
BDC Official Texts, C 41:BDCOT
BDI-INF (Series), A 77.609
BDSA Bulletins, Information of Interest of Employees,
    C 41.3/2
BDSA Delegations, C 41.6/3

BDSA Emergency Delegations, C 41.6/8
BDSA Export Potential Studies, C 41.107
BDSA Industry Growth Studies, C 41.90/4
BDSA Notices, C 41.6/5
BDSA Orders, C 41.6/4
BDSA Publications, C 41.12:P 96/2
BDSA Regulations, C 41.6/2
BDSA Reporting Delegations, C 41.6/3-2
Beach Utilization Series, A 13.42/19
Beacon (NDPO-Monthly Newsletter), The, J 1.14/25-5
Beacons, Buoys, and Daymarks, T 25.5–T 25.14
Beam, J 16.19
Beam Line, E 1.113
Bean Market News, A 88.65
Bear Biology Association: Conference Series, I 29.94/2
Bear Biology Association: Monograph Series, I 29.94/
    3
Bear Essentials, HE 20.3057, HE 20.3191
Beef Cattle Situation, A 36.90
Beer, T 70.9/4
Behavior and Society, C 51.9/12
Behavioral Risk Factor Surveillance System, HE
    20.7611/3
Behavioral Sciences Research Contract Review
    Committee, HE 20.3001/2:B 39
Belvior Research, Development, and Engineering
    Center: Handbooks, (series), D 101.6/10
Belvoir Research and Development Center: Container
    System Hardware Status Report, D 101.115
BEM [Bureau of Executive Management] Pamphlets, CS
    1.48/2
Bench Comment, a Periodic Guide to Recent Appellate
    Treatment of Practical Procedural Issues, Ju
    13.8/2
Benchnotes USA, D 103.33/13
Beneficiary Studies Notes, FS 3.46
Benefit Series Service, Unemployment Insurance Report,
    L 37.209
Benefits and Costs of the Clean Air Act, The, EP 4.31
Benjamin Franklin Stamp Club, P 1.50
Ben's Guide to U.S. Government for Kids, GP 3.39
BEPQ Series, A 77.308/3
Bering Sea Claims Commission, S 3.7/2
Berlin Arbitration (Northwestern Boundary), S 3.13/3
Beryllium in (year), I 28.138
BES- (series), L 7.71
BESRL Behavior Programs, D 101.67/2
Best Bets for Returning Veterans in Washington, D.C.
    Area, CS 1.43/2
Best Federal Job Opportunities, CS 1.43
Best of ERIC, ED 1.323
Best Opportunities for Federal Employment, CS
    1.28:2280
Better Education for Handicapped Children, Annual
    Report, HE 5.86, HE 5.235:35097
Better Housing, Y 3.F 31/11:9
Better Housing News Flashes Synopsis, Y 3.F 31/
    11:27
Better Marketing, A 55.41
Beyond Relief, Y 3.Af 8:10
BFSA Bulletin, HE 19.138
BHS Programmed Instructions (series), FS 2.6/7
BIA Administrative Reports (series), I 20.65
BIA Education Research Bulletin, I 20.57
Biannual Professional Development Program, ED 1.33/
    2
Biannual Report, J 1/15/1
Bi-annual Statistical Summary, AA 1.12
Bibliographic List–
   Department of State, S 1.92/3
   Department of Transportation, TD 1.15
   Federal Aviation Administration, TD 4.17/3
   Federal Aviation Agency, FAA 1.10/3
Bibliographic Series, D 106.10/3
Bibliographic Series: Current Titles Listing, A 17.18/7
Bibliographical Bulletins, A 1.60
Bibliographical Contributions, A 17.8
Bibliographical Lists, I 19.35
Bibliographical Memoirs, NA 1.6
Bibliographical Series, LC 24.7
Bibliographies–
   Public Documents Division, GP 3.5
   Soil Conservation Service, A 57.27
   United States Institute of Peach, Y 3.P 31:17
Bibliographies and Lists of Publications, A 112.9
Bibliographies and Lists of Publications–
   Aging Administration, HE 1.1011
   Air Force Academy, D 305.12/2
   African and Middle Eastern Division, LC 41.12
   Air Quality Planning and Standards Office, EP
    4.25
   Bureau of Alcohol, Tobacco and Firearms, T 70.13
   Bureau of Foods, HE 20.4509
   Bureau of Economic Analysis, C 59.22

   Bureau of Justice Statistics, J 29.14
   Bureau of Mines, I 28.5/3-2
   Census Bureau, C 3.163/4
   Center for Health Promotion and Education, HE
    20.7610
   Children's Bureau, HE 23.1216
   Defense Technical Information Center, D 10.12
   Drug Evaluation Research Center, HE 20.4709
   Engineer School, D 103.114
   Equal Employment Opportunity Commission, Y
    3.Eq 2:20
   European Division, LC 35.9, LC 43.9
   Federal Emergency Management Agency, FEM 1.24
   Health Care Delivery and Assistance Bureau, HE
    20.9109
   Health Maintenance Organizations and Resource
    Development Bureau, HE 20.9210
   Health Resources and Services Administration, HE
    20.9009
   Human Nutrition Research Branch, A 77.714
   Information Agency, IA 1.27
   Indian Health Service, HE 20.9411
   International Joint Commission, Y 3.In 8/28:13
   Joint Chiefs of Staff, D 5.211/2
   Latin American, Portuguese, and Spanish Division,
    LC 24.7/2
   National Archives and Records Administration,
    AE 1.110
   National Institute of Corrections, J 16.111
   National Institute on Drug Abuse, HE 20.3959
   Office of Child Support Enforcement, HE 24.13
   Office of Juvenile Justice and Delinquency
    Prevention, J 32.11
   Operational Applications Office, D 301.36/10
   President's Council on Physical Fitness and
    Sports, HE 20.112
   Prints and Photographs Division, LC 25.9
   Processing Department, LC 30.27
   Rare Book and Special Collections Division, LC
    23.16
   Relating to Animal Research, A 77.243
   Serial Division, LC 6.9
   Social Security Administration, SSA 1.10
   State Services Bureau, HE 20.7312
   United State Holocaust Memorial Commission, Y
    3.H 74:13
Bibliographies and Literature of Agriculture, A 1.60/3,
    A 105.55, A 106.110/3
Bibliographies and Miscellaneous Lists of Publica-
    tions, L 2.34/2
Bibliographies, Guidance and Student Personnel
    Section, FS 5.16/2
Bibliographies of Technical Reports, Information
    Retrieval Lists, FAA 1.10/2
Bibliographies of the World at War, LC 14.12
Bibliographies, Reference Lists, Etc., J 16.10
Bibliography, D 201.38, S 1.92
Bibliography for Advanced Study, D 207.216
Bibliography for the TVA Program, Y 3.T 25:31 T 25
Bibliography of Aeronautics, FW 4.29, Y 3.N 21/5:7
Bibliography of Agriculture, A 17.18
Bibliography of Documents Issued by GAO on Matters
    Related to ADP, GA 1.16/5
Bibliography of Ethnicity and Ethnic Groups, HE
    20.2417:Et 3
Bibliography of Fire Hazards and Prevention and
    Safety, in Petroleum Industry, C 22.27
Bibliography of Hydrology and Sedimentation of the
    United States and Canada, I 19.13
Bibliography of Lewis Research Center Technical
    Publications Announced in (year), NAS
    1.15/2
Bibliography of Medical Reviews: Cumulations, HE
    20.3610/2
Bibliography of Medical Translations, FS 2.209/3
Bibliography of Motion Pictures and Film Strips, FS
    (series), C 35.11/2, C 41.23
Bibliography of National Environmental Satellite
    Service, C 55.509
Bibliography of North American Geology, I 19.3
Bibliography of Publications for Public Education and
    Membership Training, T 47.50/2
Bibliography of Publications Resulting from
    Extramural Research, HE 20.6509/2
Bibliography of Scientific and Industrial Reports, C
    35.7
Bibliography of Soviet Laser Developments, D 5.211
Bibliography of Soviet Sources on Medicine and
    Public Health in the U.S.S.R., HE
    20.3711:So 8/2
Bibliography of Space Books and Articles from Non-
    aerospace Journals, NAS 1.9/2:Sp 1/957-977
Bibliography of the History of Medicine, HE 20.3615

Bibliography of Translations from Russian Scientific and Technical Literature, LC 1.26

Bibliography of U.S. Army Medical Research and Nutrition Laboratory Reports and Reprints for (year), D 104.17

Bibliography of United States Public Documents, Department Lists, GP 3.10

Bibliography of Weed Investigations, A 77.521

Bibliography on the High Temperature Chemistry and Physics of Gases and Gas- condensed Phase Reactions, C 13.37/3

Bibliography on Poultry Industry, Chickens, Turkeys, Aquatic Fowl, Gamebirds, A 77.411

Bibliography on Smoking and Health, HE 20.11:45

Bibliography on Suicide and Suicide Prevention, HE 20.2417:Su 3

Bibliography on the Climate of [Country] WB/BC- (series), C 52.21

Bibliography on the High Temperature Chemistry and Physics of Gases and Gas- condensed Phase Reactions, C 13.37/3

Bibliography on the High Temperature Chemistry and Physics of Materials in the Condensed State, C 13.37/2

Bibliography on the Urban Crisis, HE 20.2417:Ur 1

Bibliography (series), I 1.84/5, I 22.9/2, I 27.10/5

Bibliography Series (numbered), HE 20.11

Biblio-Profile on Human Communication and Its Disorders, a Capsule State-of-the-art Report and Bibliography, HE 20.3513/2

Bicentennial Bulletin, Y 3.Am 3/6:11

Bicentennial Lecture Series, J 1.34

Bicentennial Series, TD 5.30

Bicentennial Times, Y 3.Am 3/6:10

Bicycling Laws in the United States, TD 8.5/2:3/2

Bid Opening Report, Federal-Aid Highway Construction Contracts, Calendar Year, TD 2.47

Biennial Census of Manufacturers, C 3.24

Biennial HUD Awards for Design Excellence, HH 1.41

Biennial Officer Billet Summary, D 208.24/2

Biennial Officer Billet Summary (Junior Officer Edition), D 208.24

Biennial Report of Depository Libraries, Summary Reports by State, GP 3.33/2

Biennial Report of Depository Libraries, U.S. Summary, GP 3.33

Biennial Report of the National Institutes of Health, HE 20.3001/3

Biennial Report to the Congress, HE 20.3851/2

Biennial Report Under the Great Lakes Water Quality Agreement of 1978, Y 3.In 8/28:11

Biennial Survey of Depository Libraries Results, GP 3.33/4

Biennial Survey of Education in United States, FS 5.23

Bierman, Jessie M., Annual Lectures in Maternal and Child Health, FS 14.110/2

Big Emerging Markets, Outlook and Sourcebook, C 61.45

Billfish Newsletter (Southwest Fisheries Science Center), C 55.346

Bimonthly Grain Update, A 108.12/2

Bimonthly List of Publications and Motion Pictures, A 21.6/5

Bimonthly List of Publications and Visuals, A 107.10

Bimonthly Review of Medicinal Preparation Exports, C 18.50

Bimonthly Review of Toilet Preparations Exports, C 18.51

Bimonthly Summary of Labor Market Developments in Major Areas, L 7.51

Bio Tech Brief, E 6.11

Biochemistry Study Section, HE 20.3001/2:B 52/4

Biofuels Update, E 1.99/5

Biographic Directories, S 1.113

Biographic Register, S 1.69

Biographical Directory of the American Congress, Y 1.92-1:S.doc. 8

Biographical Sketches and Anecdotes of 95 of 120 Principal Chiefs from Indian Tribes of North America, I 20.2:In 2/7

Biological Effects of Electromagnetic Radiation, D 101.52/8

Biological Evaluation (series), A 13.97

Biological Products Memo, A 77.226/2

Biological Products Notices, A 77.226

Biological Reports (series), I 49.89/2

Biological Science Report, I 73.10, I 19.209

Biological Sciences Series, I 53.27

Biological Services Program, I 49.2:B 52

Biological Services Program, I 49.89

Biologics Surveillance, HE 20.7011/37

Biology and Aerospace Medicine, PrEx 7.22/12

Biology and Control of Insect and Related Pests of [various animals], EP 1.94

Biomass Bulletin, E 6.3/2

Biomass Digest, E 6.3/2-2

Biomedical and Behavioral Sciences, PrEx 7.22/13

Biomedical Communications Study Section, HE 20.3001/2:B 52/3

Biomedical Engineering and Instrumentation Branch, Division of Research Branch: Annual Report, HE 20.3036/3

Biomedical Index to PHS-Supported Research, HE 20.3013/2

Biomedical Library Review Committee, HE 20.3001/ 2:B 52/5

Biomedical Research Technology Resources: A Research Resources Directory, HE 20.3037/6

Biomedical Sciences, Applied Studies, E 1.99

Biomedical Sciences, Basic Studies, E 1.99

Biomedical Technology and Engineering, C 51.9/13

Biometrics Monograph Series, VA 1.67

Biometry and Epidemilogy Contract Review Committee, HE 20.3001/2:B 52/6

Biophysics and Biophysical Chemistry A Study Section, HE 20.3001/2:B 52

Biophysics and Biophysical Chemistry B Study Section, HE 20.3001/2:B 52/2

Bioremediation, EP 1.105

Bioren and Duane Edition, S 7.8

Biotechnology Resources, HE 20.3002:B 54/4

Bird Banding Notes, I 49.21

Bird Migration Memorandum, I 49.31

Birth Cohort Linked Birth/Infant Death Data Set, HE 20.6209/4-7

Birth, Still-Birth and Infant Mortality Statistics, Annual Report, C 3.26

Bismuth, I 28.103

Bismuth in (year), I 28.103/2

Bismuth Quarterly Reports, I 28.103

BISNIS Bulletin, C 61.42

BISNIS Search of Partners, C 61.42/2

Bituminous Coal and Lignite Distribution, I 28.33/2, E 3.11/7

Bituminous Coal and Lignite Mine Openings and Closings in Continental United States, (dates), I 28.33/2-2

Bituminous Coal and Lignite Production and Mine Operations, E 3.11/7-3

Bituminous Coal Tables, I 34.21, I 46.13

Bituminous Laboratory United Report, B-(series), I 27.36

Biweekly Cryogenics Awareness Service, C 13.51

Biweekly Review, News and Information of Interest to Field Offices, C 41.13

Bi-Weekly Summary of Peace Corps Trainees and Volunteers, S 19.12

BJA Bulletin, J 28.3/4

BJA Program Plan, J 26.1/5

BJS Data Report, J 29.19

BJS Dicussion Paper, J 29.26

BJS Program Application Kit, Fiscal Year, J 29.22

BJS Statistical Programs, FY, J 29.22

Black Bass and Anglers Division Publications, C 6.17

Black Lung Benefits Act of 1972, Annual Report on the Administration of the Act, L 36.13

Black News Digest, L 1.20/6

Blank Forms, S 1.15, T 1.26/6

Blister Rust Control in California, Cooperative Project of State and Federal Agencies and Private Owners, Annual Reports, A 13.54

Blister Rust News, A 19.21, A 9.15

BLM (Series), L 1.87

BLM-Alaska Frontiers, I 53.41/2

BLM: Alaska Technical Reports, I 53.49

BLM Contract Solicitation, I 53.38

BLM Facts and Figures for Utah, I 53.43

BLM Facts, Oregon and Washington, I 53.43/2

BLM in New Mexico, Oklahoma, Texas and Kansas, I 53.43/5

BLM in Wyoming, I 53.43/3

BLM Monthly Alert I 53.17/2

BLM Newsletter, I 53.21

BLM Westfornet Monthly Alert, I 53.17/2

BLMR Research Studies, L 31.11

Blood Diseases and Resources Advisory Committee, HE 20.3001/2:B 62

Blood Lead, HE 20.7022/5

Blood Lead, Proficiency Testing, HE 20.7412/2

Blowers, Fans, Unit Heaters, and Accessory Equipment, C 3.143

BLS Publications, L 2.3

BLS Reports, L 2.71

BLS Reports on Mass Layoffs in the . . . Quarter, L 2.120/2-14

BLS Staff Papers, L 2.71/5

BLS Update, L 2.131

Blue Books, W 7.30

Blue Eagle, Y 3.N 21/8:19

Blue Eagle letters, Y 3.N 21/8:10

BMCS National Roadside Inspection, TD 2.313/2

BNDD Bulletin, J 24.3

BNDD Personnel Management Series, J 24.16

Board of Actuaries of the Civil Service Retirement System Annual Report, Y 4.P 84/10:R 31/30

Board of Appellate Review, S 1.136

Board of Engineers for Rivers and Harbors, Report of Hearings, D 103.23

Board of Regents, HE 20.3001/2:R 26

Board of Scientific Counselors–

    Division of Cancer Biology and Diagnosis, HE 20.3001/2:Sci 2/4

    Division of Cancer Treatment, HE 20.3001/2:Sci 2/3

    National Eye Institute, HE 20.3001/2:Sci 2/2

    National Institute of Allergy and Infectious Diseases, HE 20.3001/2:Sci 2/7

    National Institute of Arthritis, Metabolism, and Digestive Diseases, HE 20.3001/2:Sci 2/5

    National Institute of Child Health and Human Development, HE 20.3001/2:Sci 2/6

    National Institute of Dental Research, HE 20.3001/2:Sci 2/8

    National Institute of Environmental Health Sciences, HE 20.3001/2:Sci 2/10

    National Institute on Drug Abuse, HE 20.3001/2:Sci 2/9

    Veterans' Appeals Decisions, VA 1.95/2

Boards of Instruction Bulletins, W 37.9

Boat Engineering Newsletter, TD 5.28/2

Boaters Maps (series), D 103.49/2

Boating Safety Circulars, TD 5.4/3

Boating Safety Newsletter, TD 5.28

Boating Statistics, TD 5.11

Bolts, Nuts, and Large Screws of Iron or Steel, ITC 1.17, ITC 1.17/2

Bomb Survey, J 1.14/7-4:B 63

BOMEX [Barbados Oceanographic and Meteorological Experiment] Bulletin, C 55.18

Bond of Federal Employees, Y 4.P 84/11:B 64

Bond Sales for Higher Education, FS 5.252:52004, HE 5.252:52004

Bond Sales for Public School Purposes, HE 19.323

Bond Teller, T 66.24/2

Bond Tips from You U.S. Savings Bond Reporter, T 66.24

Bonds Over America, T 66.11

Bonneville Hydraulic Laboratory, Reports, D 103.27/2

Book News, D 1.26/4

Books and Pamphlets Catalogued, W 34.21

Books for Blind and Physically Handicapped Individuals, LC 19.15/2

Books, Subjects, LC 30.8/3

BOR News, I 66.10

Border Sentinel, J 16.17

Border Sentinel Comment, J 16.17/2

Boron in (year), I 28.125

Borrowers' Bulletin, T 48.5

Boston Helicopter Route Chart, C 55.416/12-7

Botany, Current Literature, A 19.22

Boulder Canyon Project–

    Annual Reports, I 27.21/2

    City Orders, I 27.15

    Final Reports, Bulletins, I 27.21

Boundaries of the United States and the Several States, I 19.3:1212

Boundary and Annexation Survey, Annual Reports, C 56.249

Boundary and Annexation Survey, GE-30 , C 3.260

Bounds Over America, T 66.11

Box Series, C 18.52

Boy Power, L 7.5

Boys and Girls 4-H Club Leader, A 43.5/5

BPR Emergency Readiness Newsletter, C 37.31

BPR Program (series), C 37.32

Braille Book Review, LC 19.9

Braille Book Review, Talking Book Topics, LC 19.23

Braille Books, L 1.92, LC 19.9/2

Braille Publications

    Education Department, ED 1.2/15

    Equal Employment Opportunity Commission, Y 3.Eq 2:21

    Health Care Financing Administration, HE 22.45

    Justice Department, J 1.109/2

    Social Security Administration, SSA 1.2/15

Braille Scores Catalog-Organ, Music and Musicians, LC 19.22

Branch of Fishery Management, Annual Report, I 49.53

Brass Mill Scrap and Metal Consumption and Stocks at Brass and Wire Mills, I 28.79/2
Brazil, LC 1.30/11
Brazil, Annual List of Serials, LC 1.30/11-3
Brazil, Cumulative List of Serials, LC 1.30/11-2
Breakthroughs, E 1.53/5
Breast Cancer Diagnosis Committee, HE 20.3001/2:B 74/2
Breast Cancer Experimental Biology Committee, HE 20.3001/2:B 74
Breast Cancer Treatment Committee, HE 20.3001/2:B 74/3
Breed Distribution of NPIP Participating Flocks by States and Divisions, A 77.15:44-2
Breeding Research and Improvement Activities of Department of Agriculture, Reports, A 1.91
Bretton Woods Agreements Act Releases, SE 1.25/10
Brewers' Code Interpretations, Y 3.F 31/10:8
Brewer's Code Regulations, Y 3.F 31/10:7
Brewers' Dried Grain Production, A 82.59/3
Brewers' Dried Grains Production, A 88.18/6
Brewers' Dried Grains, United States, Production and Stocks in Hands of Producers, A 88.18/6-2
BRH Bulletin, HE 20.4103
BRH Publications Index, HE 20.4120
BRH Technical Information Accession Bulletin, HE 20.4103/2
BRH/DBE (series), HE 20.4114
BRH/DEP (series), HE 20.4110
BRH/DMRE (series), HE 20.4112
BRH/OBD (series), HE 20.4111
Bridges Over Navigable Waters of the U.S., D 103.2:B 76
Brief History of the American Labor Movement, L 2.3:1000
Brief of the Organization and Functions, Secretary of Defense, Deputy Secretary of Defense, Deputy Secretary of Defense, etc., D 1.36
Briefing Book, Alaska Region, A 13.156
Briefly Speaking, A 55.58
Briefs, C 21.10
Briefs in Court of Claims, Cases Prepared or Argued by Tax Division, Department of Justice, J 1.19/8
Briefs (National Center for Early Development & Learning), ED 1.346
Briefs of Accidents Involving–
Aerial Applications Operations, U.S. General Aviation, TD 1.109/4
Air Taxi Operations, U.S. General Aviation, TD 1.109/3
Alcohol As a Cause/Factor, U.S. General Aviation, TD 1.109/9
Amateur Built (homebuilt) Aircraft, U.S. General Aviation, TD 1.109/6
Corporate/Executive Aircraft, U.S. General Aviation, TD 1.109/10
Mid-Air Collisions, U.S. Civil Aviation, TD 1.109/7
Missing Aircraft, U.S. General Aviation, TD 1.109/8
Rotorcraft, U.S. General Aviation, TD 1.109/5
(various) Aircraft, TD 1.109/2
Briefs of Accidents, U.S. Civil Aviation, TD 1.109, C 31.244/6
Briefs of Accidents, U.S. General Aviation , C 31.244/5
Briefs of Aircraft Accidents Involving Turbine Powered Aircraft, U.S. General Aviation, Calendar Year, NTSB-AMM- (series), TD 1.109/14
Briefs of Fatal Accidents Involving Weather As a Cause/Factor, U.S. General Aviation, TD 1.109/12
British Exports of Electrical Apparatus, C 18.53
British-American Agricultural News Service, A 67.22
Broadcasting Radio Stations of the United States, RC 1.9
Broadcasting Stations of the World, PrEx 7.9
Brochures, HE 20.7513
Broiler Chick Report, Louisiana Crop Reporting Service, A 88.15/21
Broiler Chicks Placed, A 88.15/15
Broiler Chicks Placed in 22 States, A 92.9/14
Broiler Hatchery, A 92.46
Broiler Marketing Facts, A 88.15/24
Broiler Marketing Guide, A 88.26/5
Bromine in (year), I 28.126
Brookhaven Highlights, E 1.1/4
Brookhaven National Laboratory: Telephone Directory, E 1.12/2
Broom Corn Brooms: Producers' Shipments, Imports for Consumption, Exports, and Apparent Consumption, ITC 1.23
Brucellosis (Bang's Disease) Work in Cooperation with Various States: Summary of, A 77.212
Brucellosis Surveillance, HE 20.7011/16

BSFA Bulletin, HE 19.138
BUAER Instruction NAVAER, D 202.6/4
BUAER Instructions, D 202.6/3
BUAER Notice, D 202.6/5
BUAER Notice NAVAER, D 202.6/6
BUAER Report, D 202.16
Budget, Y 3.B 78:9
Budget and Finance Circulars, A 1.43
Budget and Legislative Program, Fiscal Year (date), HE 22.30
Budget and Management Circulars, L 1.23
Budget, Board for International Broadcasting, Y 3.B 78:9
Budget Circulars, Pr 32.204/2
Budget Digest, P 1.28
Budget Estimates–
Aircraft and Missile Procurement, D 301.83/2
Coast Guard, TD 5.41
Department of Transportation, TD 1.34/3
Excerpts from the United States Government Budget, HH 1.1/4
Federal Aviation Administration, TD 4.50
Federal Highway Administration, TD 2.52
Federal Railroad Administration, TD 3.18
National Highway Traffic Safety Administration, TD 8.28
Nuclear Regulatory Commission, Y 3.N 88:10-2
United States Department of Agriculture, A 1.93
Urban Mass Transportation Administration, TD 7.16
Budget Explanatory Notes for Committee on Appropriations, A 13.130
Budget Highlights–
Energy Department, E 1.35/2-2
Management and Budget Office, PrEx 2.8/6
Budget in Brief, PrEx 2.8/2, TD 5.62
Budget Issue Papers, Y 10.12
Budget of the U.S. Government: Director's Introduction and Overview Tables, PrEx 2.8/11
Budget of the United States Government, PrEx 2.8
Budget of United States Government, PrEx 2.8/1, Pr 32.107, Pr 33.107, Pr 34.107
Budget of United States Government, District of Columbia, PrEx 2.8/4
Budget Program, Justification of Programs and Estimates for Fiscal Year (date), Submitted to Congress, Y 3.T 25:43
Budget Progress Report, HE 3.87
Budget Revisions, PrEx 2.8/7
Budget Scorekeeping Report, Y 4.R 24/4:B 85/2
Budget Status Report, TD 1.34
Budget System and Concepts of the United States Government, PrEx 2.8/12
Budget-Treasury Regulations, Pr 33.106/2
Buffalo National River Currents, I 29.121
Bug Business, A 13.52/5
Building Abroad, C 18.54
Building and Housing Publications, C 13.25
Building Construction, L 2.6/a 4
Building Construction in Urban Areas in United States, L 2.36
Building for Clean Water, Progress Report on Federal Incentive Grants for Municipal Waste Treatment, Fiscal Year, FS 2.64/6
Building for Clean Water, Report on Federal Incentive Grants for Municipal Waste Treatment, FS 16.9
Building for Clear Water, I 67.15
Building Knowledge About Crime and Justice J 28.36
Building Materials and Structures Report, C 13.29
Building Permit Survey, L 2.12
Building Permits in Principal Cities of U.S., L 2.6/a 4
Building Research, Summary Reports, C 13.40
Building Science Series, C 13.29/2
Building Technology, C 51.9/10
Building with Environmental Protection, Design Case Studies, D 14.16
Buildings with Fallout Protection, Design Case Studies, D 119.14
Bulk Carriers in the World Fleet, C 39.202:B 87, TD 11.20
Bulk Cooling Tanks on Farms Supplying Federal Milk Order Markets, A 82.81/2
Bulletin–
Community Partnerships, J 26.32/2
Department of Education, ED 1.3/2
Department of the Air Force, D 301.59
National Credit Union, NCU 1.3
Bulletin, Biological Service Program News, I 49.81
Bulletin Board, J 16.12
Bulletin Board Placecards, Pr 32.4812/2
Bulletin CBD-S (series), C 41.9/2

Bulletin Digest, New and Revised Editions of Aeronautical Charts on Issue As of (date), D 301.59/5
Bulletin for the Clergy, Y 3.F 73:12
Bulletin of Army Medical Department, D 104.3
Bulletin of Beach Erosion Board, D 103.16
Bulletin of Commerce, C 18.269, C 41.10
Bulletin of Courses, Water Pollution Control Technical Training Program, I 67.17
Bulletin of Engineering Information, N 19.9/2
Bulletin of Hardwood Market Statistics, A 13.79/3
Bulletin of Information, D 211.3
Bulletin of Inventions, C 41.82
Bulletin of Judge Advocate General of Army, D 108.3
Bulletin of Monthly Prices During the War, Y 3.W 19/2:45
Bulletin of Moscow Society of Naturalists, Geological Division, C 41.46/2
Bulletin of Mountain Weather Observatory, A 29.21
Bulletin of Prosthetics Research, VA 1.23/3
Bulletin of Suicidology, FS 2.22/50-6, HE 20.2413
Bulletin of the Global Volcanism Network SI 3.13
Bulletin of the Philosophical Society of Washington, SI 1.10
Bulletin of the School of Medicine, Uniformed Services University of the Health Sciences, D 1.67
Bulletin of Translations from Russian Medical Sciences, FS 2.22/19-2
Bulletin on Economic Crime Enforcement, J 1.3
Bulletin on National Defense Education Act, Public Law 85-864, FS 5.70
Bulletin Reprints, A 89.3/a
Bulletins, T 1.25/3
Bulletins, Agriculture (by States), C 3.14/2, C 3.28/10
Bulletins, Agriculture (Misc.), C 3.28/11
Bulletins (by Principal Industries), C 3.24/4
Bulletins (by States), C 3.24/3
Bulletins, Drainage, C 3.28/13
Bulletins for Retail Merchants, Y 3.F 73:17
Bulletins, Forest Products, C 3.28/16
Bulletins, Income Tax (lettered), T 22.22
Bulletins, Irrigation (by States), C 3.14/8, C 3.28/12
Bulletins, Manufactured (by States), C 3.14/3
Bulletins, Manufacturers (by Industries), C 3.28/15
Bulletins, Manufacturers (by States), C 3.28/14
Bulletins, Mimeographed Series, I 20.3/2
Bulletins, Mines and Quarries (by Industries), C 3.28/18
Bulletins, Mines and Quarries (by States), C 3.28/17
Bulletins, Mines (by States), C 3.14/4
Bulletins [Misc.] (by States), C 3.14/5
Bulletins of Engineering Information, N 29.10
Bulletins of National Archives, GS 4.3
Bulletins of Revenues and Expenses of Steam Roads, IC 1 ste.3
Bulletins on Policy and Procedure, FW 3.9
Bulletins on Topics of Interest to Congress, LC 14.9
Bulletins, OTB- (series), C 1.60/4
Bulletins, Population (by States), C 3.14/1, C 3.28/8
Bulletins, Population (Misc.) [Including Occupations], C 3.28/9
BuMed Circular Letters, N 10.20/2, M 203.9, D 206.13
BuMed Instructions, D 206.6/2
BuMed News Letter, N 10.18, M 203.7
Buoy List, C 9.32, C 9.39
Bureau Finance Manual, C 4.12/3
Bureau for Supplies and Accounts Memoranda, N 20.7/3
Bureau of
Aeronautics Manual, D 202.6/2
Apprenticeship and Training News, L 23.15
Aviation Safety Report, BASR (series), TD 1.114
Census Catalog, C 56.222, C 3.163/3
Census, International Brief, C 3:205/9
Economic Analysis Staff Papers, C 59.14
Economic Analysis Staff Papers, BEA-SP- (series), C 56.113
Economics Staff Reports, FT 1.37
Export Administration Fact Sheets, C 63.24
International Economic Policy and Research: Reports, Studies, Data, C 57.26
Justice Assistance Bulletin, J 26.32
Justice Assistance Publications List, J 26.9/2
Justice Statistics Bulletin, Criminal Victimization, J 29.11/10
Justice Statistics Fiscal Year: At a Glance, J 29.1/2
Justice Statistics Publications Catalog, J 29.14/2
Land Management Office Directory, I 53.45/2
Labor Statistics Catalog of Publications, Bulletins, Reports, Releases, and Periodicals, L 2.34
Land Management 1:100,000-Scale Maps, I 53.11/4

Land Management Maps, Surface and Minerals
    Management Status, Scale 1:100,000, I
    53.11/4-2
Medical Devices Standards Survey, International
    Edition, HE 20.4309
Medical Devices Standards Survey, National
    Edition, HE 20.4309/2
Mines Handbooks (series), I 28.16/3
Mines, Annual Financial Report, I 28.1
Mines Research in (year), I 28.5
Mines Research (year), Summary of Significant
    Results in Mining Metallurgy and
    Energy, I 28.115
Naval Personnel Manual, D 208.6/2
Naval Weapons Directory, Organizational Listing
    and Correspondence Designations, D
    217.25
Personnel Manual, C 4.12/2
Radiological Health Research Grants Program,
    Fiscal Year, (date), HE 20.4116
Reclamation Progress, I 27.56
Reclamation Projects (by States), I 27.55/2
Safety and Service Laws, IC 1 saf.5/2
Safety Pamphlet BOSP (series), C 31.252
Safety Reports, C 31.252/2
Ships, Shop Practice Suggestions, C 41.95
Ships Technical Manual, D 211.7/3
Ships Translations, D 211.14
Sport and Fisheries and Wildlife's In-sight, I
    49.50/2
Steam Roads, IC 1 ste.1
Veterinary Medicine Memo, BVMM- (series), HE
    20.4028
Bureau Practice, FAA 5.10
BUSANDA Notice, Admin, D 212.13
Bush Berries, Indicated Yield and Production, A 92.11/
    13
BuShips Surplus Material List Series, N 29.16
Business America, C 1.58/4, C 61.18
Business America, Michigan, C 61.18/3
Business and Economics, C 51.9/17
Business and Public Administration Notes, FS 5.72
Business Conditions Digest, C 56.111, C 59.9
Business Conditions Digest, Supplements, C 59.9/3
Business Cycle Developments, C 3.226, C 56.111
Business Development Publication, SBA 1.32/2
Business Development Publication (series), SBA 1.32/
    2
Business Economics Series, C 18.275
Business Establishment, Employment and Taxable Pay
    Rolls under Old-Age and Survivors
    Insurance Program, C 18.270
Business Income Tax Returns, T 22.35/2:B 96, T 22/35/
    3:B 96
Business Indexes, FR 1.19
Business Information Service, C 18.182, C 41.8
Business Information Service: Defense Production
    Aids, C 40.7
Business Information Service: General Publications, C
    3.211/3
Business News Reports OBE [release], C 18.281, C
    43.7
Business Press Service, L 1.78/2
Business Service Checklist, C 1.24
Business Situation at Home and Abroad, C 18.54/2
Business Statistics, C 59.11/3
Business Statistics, Biennial Supplement to Survey of
    Current Business, C 56.109/3, C 59.11/3
Business Statistics, Weekly Supplement, C 59.11/2
Business Statistics, Weekly Supplement to Survey of
    Current Business, C 56.109/2
Buyer's Guides, FT 1.8/4
Buyer/Seller Codes Authorized for Reporting to the
    Federal Energy Regulatory Commission, E
    3.35
Buying a Safer Car for Child Passengers, TD 8.66
Buzzard, C 4.45

C

C.A.B. Advance Digest Service, CAB 1.34
C.A.B. Economic Orders and Opinions, CAB 1.31
C.A.B. Initial and Recommended Decisions of
    Administrative Law Judges, CAB 1.38
C.A.B. Notices of Prehearing Conference Hearings, and
    Oral Arguments, CAB 1.36
C.A.B. Notices of Proposed Rulemaking and
    Amendments to All Regulations, CAB 1.37
C.A.B. Prehearing Conference Reports, CAB 1.35
C.A.B. Weekly Calendar of Prehearing Conferences,
    Hearings and Arguments, CAB 1.33
C.A.B. Weekly List of Agreements Filed Under Sec.
    412(a) of the Federal Aviation Act, CAB 1.32

C & G S Technical Manuals, C 4.12/5
C & M S (series), A 88.40/2
C & R Bulletins, N 4.3/2
C.I.A.A. Abstracts, LC 14.16/3
C (series), NAS 1.38
CAA Airworthiness Directive, C 31.147/2
CAA Memo, C 31.154
CAA News Digest, C 31.159
Cabinet Committee on Cable Communications, Pr
    37.8:C 11
Cabinet Task Force on Oil Import Control, Pr 37.8:Oi 5
Cable Television Authorization Actions, Public
    Notices, C 1.45/3
Cable Television Certificate of Compliance Actions, CC
    1.47/3
Cable Television Relay Service, Applications, Reports,
    Public Notices, CC 1.47/2
Cable Television Service Applications, Reports, Public
    Notices, CC 1.47
Cadet Profile, United States Coast Guard Academy, TD
    5.15
Cadmium, I 28.102
Cadmium in (year), I 28.102/2
CADO Reclassification Bulletin, D 301.37
CADO Technical Data Digest, D 301.14
Calcium and Calcium Compounds in (year), I 28.101/4
Calcium-Magnesium Chloride in (year), I 28.101/3
Calendar, FT 1.25, Ju 3.5, Ju 7.7, Y 3.B 47/2:16
Calendar of Events, I 29.37/8, SI 8.11/2
Calendar of Events in Areas Administered by National
    Park Service, I 29.66/2
Calendar of Events in the Library of Congress, LC 1.22/
    2
Calendar of Exhibits and Programs, SI 14.15
Calendar of Federal Regulations, Y 3.R 26:9
Calendar of Interagency Courses, GS 1.26
Calendar of National Meetings, FS 2.315
Calendar of Prehearing Conferences Hearings, and
    Arguments Conferences, C 31.227
Calendar of the Smithsonian Institution, SI 1.35
Calendar of Trade Agreements, S 1.104
Calendar of United States House of Representatives and
    History of Legislation, Y 1.2/2
Calendar or Trade Agreements, S 1.104
Calendars of Business, Y 1.3/3
Calf Crop, Louisiana Crop Reporting Service, A 88.16/
    10-2
Calf Crop Report, A 88.16/10
Calibration and Test Services of the National Bureau of
    Standards, C 13.10:250
Calibration Procedure Change Notice Book, D 217.16/
    2-2
California Desert District Planning Newsletter, I 53.36
California Region, Progress Reports, Progress in (year),
    A 13.1/2
California Rice Stocks and Movement Reports, A
    36.186
Call for Achievement Booklets, Y 3.Am 3/6:12
Call Letters Assigned, CC 2.7
Callback from NASA's Aviation Safety Reporting
    System, NAS 1.89
Camp Life Arithmetic Workbooks, FS 4.10
Campaign Finance Law, Y 3.El 2/3:2-10
Campaign Guide, Y 3.El 2/3:13
Camping Facilities in Areas Administered by National
    Park Service, I 29.71
Campus Board Programs Report (series), ED 1.14
Campus, Navy Education and Training, D 207.209, D
    207.209
Canada-United States Interparliamentary Group Report
    on Meetings by Senate Delegation, Y 4.F 76/
    2:C 16/2
Canadian-American Fisheries Commission, S 5.20
Canadian-American Fisheries Commission, 1893-96, S
    3.26
Canal Record, W 73.8
Cancer Alert Series, L 35.22
Cancer Biology, HE 20.3173/2
Cancer Chemotherapy Abstracts, HE 20.3160/4
Cancer Chemotherapy Reports, HE 20.3160, HE
    20.3160/2, HE 20.3160/3
Cancer Clinical Investigation Review Committee, HE
    20.3001/2:C 16
Cancer Control Advisory Committee, HE 20.3001/2:C
    16/13
Cancer Control and Rehabilitation Advisory
    Committee, HE 20.3001/2:C 16/3
Cancer Control Community Activities Review
    Committee, HE 20.3001/2:C 16/2
Cancer Control Education Review Committee, HE
    20.3001/2:C 16/14

Cancer Control Grant Review Committee, HE 20.3001/
    2:C 16/12
Cancer Control Letter, FS 2.22/3
Cancer Control, Prevention, and Detection Review
    Committee, HE 20.3001/2:C 16/8
Cancer Control Treatment and Rehabilitation Review
    Committee, HE 20.3001/2:C 16/15
Cancer Consortium, HE 20.3199
Cancer Facts, HE 20.3182
Cancer Immunobiology Committee, HE 20.3001/2:C
    16/5
Cancer Immunodiagnosis Committee, HE 20.3001/2:C
    16/6
Cancer Immunotherapy Committee, HE 20.3001/2:C 16/
    4
Cancer Information Clearinghouse, Quarterly
    Accessions List, HE 20.3165/3
Cancer Morbidity Series, FS 2.61
Cancer Progress Report, HE 20.3172/3
Cancer Research Center Review Committee, HE
    20.3001/2:C 16/10
Cancer Research Safety Monograph Series, HE 20.3162/
    2
Cancer Series, FS 2.57
Cancer Services, Facilities and Programs in United
    States, HE 20.2:C 16/5
Cancer Special Program Advisory Committee, HE
    20.3001/2:C 16/9
Cancer Statistics Review, HE 20.3186
Cancer Treatment Advisory Committee, HE 20.3001/
    2:C 16/11
Cancer Treatment Symposia, HE 20.3172/2
Canned and Dried Foods, C 18.72/1
Canned Fishery Products, C 55.309/2
Canned Food Report, C 3.189
Canned Fruits and Vegetables, Production and
    Wholesale Distribution, C 3.168
Canned Poultry, A 88.15/2
CAORF (series), C 39.243
CAORF Technical Reports (series), TD 11.18
CAP Pamphlets, PrEx 10.9/4
Capacity of Elevators, Reporting Grain Stocks, A 36.82
Capacity of Refrigerated Warehouses, A 105.33/3
Capacity of Refrigerated Warehouses in United States,
    A 88.20/3, A 92.21/3
Capacity Utilization in Manufacturing, Quarterly
    Averages, Seasonally Adjusted, FR 1.55
Capacity Utilization: Manufacturing and Materials, FR
    1.55/2
Capital Market Working Papers, SE 1.35
Capital Punishment, J 29.11/3
Carbon Black, E 3.11/10, E 3.11/10-2, I 28.88
Carbon Black in (year), I 28.88/2
Carbon Black Report, I 28.88
Carcinogenesis Abstracts, HE 20.3159
Carcinogenesis Program Scientific Review Committee
    A, HE 20.3001/2:C 17/2
Carcinogenesis Program Scientific Review Committee
    B, HE 20.3001/2:C 17/3
Carcinogenesis Program Scientific Review Committee
    C, HE 20.3001/2:C 17/4
Carcinogenesis Technical Report Series, NCI-CG-TR-
    (series), HE 20.3159/2
Cardiology Advisory Committee, HE 20.3001/2:C 17
Cardiovascular and Pulmonary Study Section, HE
    20.3001/2:C 17/6
Cardiovascular and Renal Study Section, HE 20.3001/
    2:C 17/5
Care of Animals and Stable Management, W 3.50/9
Care of Children Series, L 5.6
Career Connections, T 22.65
Career Guide to Industries, L 2.3/4-3
Career Service Board for Science Reports, FS 1.33
Careers in the United States Department of the Interior, I
    1.73/2:3
Caribbean Basin Initiative Business Bulletins, C 61.35
Caribbean Forester, A 13.64/7
Caring About Kids (series), HE 20.8130
Caring for Children (series), HE 21.210
Carlisle Indian School, I 20.16
Carload Waybill Analyses–
    Distribution of Freight Traffic and Revenue
        Averages by Commodity Groups and
        Rate Territories, IC 1.20
    State by State Distribution of Tonnage by
        Commodity Groups, IC 1.21
    Territorial Distribution, Traffic and Revenue by
        Commodity Groups, IC 1.22
Carload Waybill Statistics–
    Distribution of Freight Traffic and Revenue
        Averages by Commodity Classes, IC
        1.23/8

Mileage Block Distribution, Traffic and Revenue by Commodity Class, Territorial Movement, and Type of Rate, Products of Agriculture, 1 Percent Sample of Terminations in Statement MB-1, IC 1.23/2

Mileage Block Distribution, Traffic and Revenue by Commodity Class, Territorial Movement, and Type of Rate, Animals and Products, 1 Percent Sample of Terminations in Statement MB-2, IC 1.23/3

Mileage Block Distribution, Traffic and Revenue by Commodity Class, Territorial Movement, and Type of Rate, Products of Mines, 1 Percent Sample of Terminations in Statement MB-3, IC 1.23/4

Mileage Block Distribution, Traffic and Revenue by Commodity Class, Territorial Movement, and Type of Rate, Products of Forests, 1 Percent Sample of Terminations in Statement MB-4, IC 1.23/5

Mileage Block Distribution, Traffic and Revenue by Commodity Class, Territorial Movement, and Type of Rate, Manufacturers and Miscellaneous Forwarder Traffic, One Percent Sampling of Terminations Statement MB-5, IC 1.23/6

Quarterly Comparisons, Traffic and Revenue by Commodity Classes, IC 1.23

Statement TD-1, TD 1.22

Territorial Distribution Traffic and Revenue by Commodity Classes, TD 3.14

Traffic and Revenue Progressions by Specified Mileage Blocks for Commodity Groups and Classes, 1 Percent Sample of Carload Terminations in Year Statement MB-6, IC 1.23/7

Carlot Shipments of, from Stations in U.S., A 66.24/2

Car-Lot Shipments of Fruits and Vegetables, by Commodities, States, and Months, A 1.34, A 66.24

Car-Lot Unloads of Certain Fruits and Vegetables, A 66.40

Carlot Unloads of Fruits and Vegetables at Washington, D.C., A 82.46

Carlot Unloads of Fruits and Vegetables by Commodities, A 88.12/5

Carriers by Water, Selected Financial and Operating Data Form Annual Reports, IC 1 wat.10

Carrier Quality Assurance Report, HE 22.415

Carry On, W 44.17

Case Book, Education Beyond High School Practices Underway to Meet the Problems of the Day, FS 5.65

Case History Reports for Industries, Pr 32.5223

Case Information Sheets, Y 3.F 31/21-3:14-11

Case Instruction, Cases, D 208.13

Case Management Information Series, PM 1.41/2

Case Records in Public Assistance, FS 3.23

Case Studies in Environmental Management, HE 20.519

Case Studies in Environmental Medicine, HE 20.7917

Case Studies of IPA's [in various cities], HE 20.24

Casehandling Manual, LR 1.6/2:C 26

Caseload Statistics, HE 1.611

Caseload Statistics of State Vocational Rehabilitation Agencies, FS 17.111, HE 17.111

Caseload Statistics, State Vocational Rehabilitation Agencies, HE 23.4109

Cases, NMB 1.8

Cases Argued and Decided in Supreme Court of United States, Ju 6.8/4

Cases Decided in the Court of Claims of the United States, Ju 3.9

Cases Decided in United States Court of Appeals for the Federal Circuit, Ju 7.5

Cases Decided in United States Court of Appeals for the Federal Circuit: Customs Cases Adjudged in the Court of Appeals for the Federal Circuit, Ju 7.5/2

Cash Income from Farm Marketings, A 36.68

Cassette Books, LC 19.10/3

Cassis Currents Newsletter, C 21.31/12

Casualties and Injuries among Shipyard and Dock Workers, L 16.37

Catalog, D 305.8, D 1.59/2

Catalog and Course Descriptions of the Defense Mapping School, D 5.352

Catalog and Index, U.S. Department of Commerce Publications, C 1.54/2

Catalog and Price List of Stable Isotopes Including Related Materials and Services, Y 3.At 7:35

Catalog and Quick Index to Taxpayer Information Publications, T 22.44/3

Catalog, Department of Health, Education, and Welfare, Publications, HE 1.18/3

Catalog Management Data, D 7.29

Catalog of Activities, FEM 1.17/2-2

Catalog of Adult Education Projects, HE 19.142

Catalog of Audiovisual Materials, HE 20.3002:Au 2

Catalog of Bureau Publications, C 18.22/2

Catalog of Captioned Feature and Special Interest Films and Videos for the Hearing Impaired, ED 1.209/2-3

Catalog of Captioned Films for the Deaf, FS 5.234:34039, HE 5.234:34039, ED 1.209/2

Catalog of Cell Cultures and DNA Samples, HE 20.3464

Catalog of Cell Lines, HE 20.3464

Catalog of Charts and Plans Issued to Vessels of Navy, Portfolios, N 6.5/7

Catalog of Charts of the Great Lakes and Connecting Waters, Also Lake Champlain, New York Canals, Minnesota-Ontario Border Lakes, D 103.208

Catalog of Charts, Sailing Directions and Tide Tables, C 4.18/1

Catalog of Collections, SI 6.5

Catalog of Copyright Entries, Cumulative Series, LC 3.8

Catalog of Copyright Entries, Fourth Series, LC 3.6/6

Catalog of Copyright Entries, Third Series, LC 3.6/5

Catalog of Courses and Training Materials, HE 20.4016/2

Catalog of Courses Fiscal Year, L 1.86

Catalog of Current Joint Publications Research Publications, Y 3.J 66:15

Catalog of DIOR Reports, D 1.33/4

Catalog of Educational Captioned Films/Videos for the Deaf, ED 1.209/2-2

Catalog of Electronic Data Products, HE 20.6209/4-6

Catalog of Federal Assistance Programs, PrEx 10.2:P 94

Catalog of Federal Domestic Assistance, PrEx 2.20

Catalog of Federal Education Assistance Programs, ED 1.29, HE 19.127, C 58.12

Catalog of Federal Grant-In-Aid Programs to State and Local Governments, Y 3.Ad 9/8:20

Catalog of Government Inventions Available for Licensing, C 51.16/2

Catalog of Government Patents, C 51.16

Catalog of Guides to Outdoor Recreation Areas and Facilities, I 66.15:G 94

Catalog of HEW Assistance Providing Financial Support and Service to States, Communities, Organizations, Individuals, HE 1.6/6

Catalog of Information, D 208.109

Catalog of Information on Water Data, I 19.42/5

Catalog of Information on Water Data: Index to Stations in Coastal Areas, I 19.42/6

Catalog of Investment Information and Opportunities, IP, Supplements, S 18.35/2

Catalog of Investment Opportunities Index, Supplements, S 18.35/3

Catalog of Logistics Models, D 1.33/6

Catalog of Maps, Charts, and Related Products, Part 2, Hydrographic Products, D 5.351/2

Catalog of Meteorological Satellite Data: ESSA 9 and NOAA 1 Television Cloud Photography, C 55.219:5.3

Catalog of National Exhibition of Prints, LC 25.8

Catalog of National Historic Landmarks, I 29.120

Catalog of OSRD Reports, LC 29.8

Catalog of Publications, Ju 13.11/2

Catalog of Publications, Audiovisuals, and Software, HE 20.3619/2

Catalog of Publications of the National Center for Health Statistics, HE 20.6216/4

Catalog of Published [State] Maps, I 19.14/6

Catalog of Research Projects, I 1.88/2

Catalog of Seed and Vegetable Stock Available from the Southern Regional Plant Introduction Station [for various plants], A 106.19

Catalog of Seminars, Training Programs and Technical Assistance in Labor Statistics, L 2.114

Catalog of Standard Reference Materials, C 13.10

Catalog of Technical Reports CTR (series), C 41.21/3

Catalog of Title Entries of Books and Other Articles, LC 3.5

Catalog of Topographic and Other Published Maps (by State), I 19.41/6-2

Catalog of Training, I 49.106/7

Catalog of Training Products for the Mining Industry, L 38.11/3

Catalog of United States Census Publications, C 3.163/3

Catalog of U.S. Government Publications (online), GP 3.8/8-9

Catalog, Publications of the Office of Technology Assessment, Y 3.T 22/2:9

Catalog Series, D 203.24:C

Cataloged Serial Holdings, D 5.411/4

Cataloging Handbooks, D 7.6/2

Cataloging Service Bulletin, LC 30.7, LC 30.7/2

Catalogs, LC 1.5

Catalogs and Advertisements of Surplus Equipment for Sale, N 20.14

Catalogs and Lists of American and Foreign Annuals and Periodicals, N 16.7

Catalogs and Technical Publications, LC 30.27/7

Catalogs of Charts, N 14.12

Catalogs of Charts, Coast Pilots and Tide Tables, C 4.5

Catalogs of Ships and Crew's Libraries of the U.S., N 5.6, N 17.19

Catalogs of Training Courses [on various subjects], CS 1.65/9, PM 1.19/4

Catalogue, D 109.8

Catalogue and Index of the Publications of the Hayden, King, Powell, and Wheeler Surveys, I 19.3:222

Catalogue of Accessioned Soviet Publication, C 55.220/2

Catalogue of Articles to be Sold at Auction, P 7.5

Catalogue of Audiovisual Media Programs, Ju 13.9/2

Catalogue of Book and Blanks Furnished by Department of Commerce to Customs Officers, C 1.16

Catalogue of Books and Blanks Used by Officers of Customs at Port of New York, T 36.5/2

Catalogue of Books and Blanks Used in Office of Assistance Treasurer, New York, T 36.5/3

Catalogue of Charts, Coast Pilots, and Tide Tables, T 11.5

Catalogue of Collections, SI 6.5

Catalogue of Copyright Entries, Pt. 1, Books [etc.], LC 3.6/1

Catalogue of Copyright Entries, Pt. 1, Engraving, Cuts and Prints, Chromos and Lithographs, Photographs, Fine Arts, LC 3.6/4

Catalogue of Copyright Entries, Pt. 2, Periodicals, LC 3.6/2

Catalogue of Copyright Entries, Pt. 3, Musical Compositions, LC 3.6/3

Catalogue of Information, D 208.109

Catalogue of Materials and Supplies Required at Arsenals, etc., W 34.16

Catalogue of Photographs and Stereoptican Slides, Y 3.P 96/3:11

Catalogue of Publications of the National Center for Health Statistics, HE 20.6216:C 29

Catalogues, T 23.5

Catalyst, A 13.131, ED 1.2/17, D 101.145

Catalyst for Rural Development, A 21.31

Catfish, A 105.52, A 92.44

Catfish Production, A 92.44/2-2

Cattle and Calves on Feed, Cattle Sold for Slaughter, Selected Markets, MtAn 2-1 (series), A 92.18/6

Cattle and Calves: Weekly Average Price Per 100 Pounds, A 36.18/1

Cattle and Sheep Outlook, Supplement to Livestock, Dairy, and Poultry Situation and Outlook, A 93.46/3-5

Cattle and Sheep, Shipments of Stocker and Feeder Cattle and Sheep into Selected North Central States, A 88.16/18-2

Cattle, Calves, and Vealers: Top Prices and Bulk of Sales, Chicago, A 36.207

Cattle Inventory, A 105.23

Cattle Inventory, Special Report on Number of Cattle and Calves on Farms by Sex and Weight, United States, A 92.18/6-2

Cattle on Feed, A 88.16/6, A 105.23/3

Cattle on Feed, Cattle Sold for Slaughter, Selected Markets, A 92.18/6

Cattle on Feed, Illinois, Iowa, Nebraska, Idaho, and California, A 88.16/7

Cattle, Sheep and Goat Inventory, A 93.18/8

CATV Actions Reports, CC 1.45/2

CATV Requests Filed Pursuant to Sec. 74.1107(a) of the Rules, Public Notice, CC 1.45

Caveat List of United States Registered Bonds, T 26.7

CB (series), ED 1.74/2

CC Information Circulars, FS 3.218

CC Pamphlets, HE 20.13/2

CCB (Common Carrier Bureau) Reports, CC 1.58

CCC Loans on Cotton, A 82.309

CCC Monthly Sales List, A 1.101

CCC Price Support Program Data, A 82.310/3

CCPDS Public Report, HE 20.3180/3

CCPM Pamphlets [commissioned Corps Personnel Manual], HE 20.13

Charts (listed in) Charts and Publications Catalog 1, United States Atlantic and Gulf Coasts, C 55.418/7
Charts (listed in) Charts and Publications Catalog 2, United States Pacific Coast, C 55.418/7
Charts (listed in) Charts and Publications Catalog 3, United States Alaska, C 55.418/7
Charts (listed in) Charts and Publications Catalog 4, United States Great Lakes, C 55.418/7
Charts, Composition of Food Materials, A 10.21
Charts of Great Lakes, W 33.7/2
Check Circulars, J 1.14/15
Check List of Birds of National Parks, I 29.27
Check List of Printed and Processed Publications, A 36.70/2
Check List of Standards for Farm products, A 36.59, A 66.26
Check Payment and Reconciliation Memoranda, CP & R (series), T 63.8
Checklist C (series), GP 3.23
Checklist of Reports and Charts Issued by Agricultural Marketing Service, A 88.33
Checklist of Reports Issued by Economic Research Service and Statistical Reporting Service, A 1.97
Cheddar Cheese Prices, A 92.10/8
Chem Alert, L 35.27
Chemawa American, I 20.42
Chemical and Atmospheric Sciences Program Review, D 301.45/19-8
Chemical and Plastics Division, Technical Report CP (series), D 106.9/5
Chemical and Rubber, C 41.35
Chemical Corps Purchase Description, D 116.10
Chemical Engineering Bulletins, Y 3.T 25:25
Chemical Engineering Reports, Y 3.T 25:19
Chemical, Environmental, and Radiation Carcinogenesis, HE 20.3173/2
Chemical Evaluation and Control Fact Sheets, A 77.239/2
Chemical Information Fact Sheets, EP 5.20
Chemical Industry [abstracts], C 41.53/7
Chemical Safety Data Sheets, EDS-LS-(series), L 16.51/7
Chemical Science and Industry [abstracts], C 41.53/10
Chemical Warfare Field Service Bulletins, W 91.7
Chemical Warfare Laboratories: CWL Special Publications, D 116.13
Chemical Warfare Service Bulletin, W 99.17/12
Chemical-Biological Coordination Center, Reviews, NA 2.7
Chemical/Biological Information-Handling Review Committee, HE 20.3001/2:C 42
Chemicals, C 41.35
Chemicals and Allied Products Entered for Consumption, C 18.55
Chemicals-in-Progress Bulletin, EP 5.15
Chemistry, C 51.9/20, PrEx 7.22/4, E 1.99
Chemistry and Technology of Fuels and Oils [abstracts], C 41.55
Chemistry Laboratory Guidebook, A 110.8/3
Chemotherapy Fact Sheets, HE 20.3164
Cherries, A 105.11/4
Cherry Production, A 92.11/3
Cherry Utilization, A 105.11/3, A 92.11/3-2
Chesapeake Bay Program, EP 1.88
Chesapeake Fisheries, C 55.309/2
Chicago Federal Executive Board Directory, PM 1.31/3
Chicago Helicopter Route Chart, C 55.416/12-5
Chicago Regional Training Center, Course Announcements, PM 1.52
Chicago, World's Columbian Exposition, 1893, S 6.19
Chickens and Eggs, A 92.9/16
Chickens and Eggs, Farm Production, Disposition, Cash Receipts and Gross Income, A 9.9/3
Chickens and Eggs, Farm Production, Disposition, Cash Receipts and Gross Income, Chickens on Farms, Commercial Broilers, by States, A 88.15/18
Chickens and Eggs, Layers and Egg Production, A 88.15/14, A 92.9/13
Chickens and Eggs, Layers and Rate of Lay, First of Each Month, A 88.15/17
Chickens, Number Raised, Preliminary Estimates, A 92.9/7
Chickens Raised, Louisiana Crop Reporting Service, A 88.15/10-2
Chickens Raised on Farms, A 88.15/10
Chief Clerk and Superintendent of Buildings, Annual Report, I 1.60
Chief Counsel: Annual Report, T 22.1/2
Chief Counsel Office Directory, T 22.48/2
Chief Financial Officer's Annual Report– Nuclear Regulatory Commission, Y 3.N 88:60

Small Business Administration, SBA 1.1/6
Chief Financial Officer's Financial Statements, TD 1.1/6
Chief of Naval Air Training, CNAT- (series), D 201.31/3
Chiefs of State and Cabinet Members of Foreign Governments, CR CS- (series), PrEx 3.11/2
Child, L 5.35, FS 3.207
Child Abuse and Neglect Programs, HE 1.480/4, HE 23.1211
Child Abuse and Neglect Reports, HE 1.480/2, HE 23.1212
Child Abuse and Neglect Research: Projects and Publications, HE 1.480/3, HE 23.1210/2
Child Abuse and Neglect (series), HE 1.480, HE 23.1210
Child Care Arrangements of AFDC Recipients Under the Work Incentive Program, HE 17.609
Child Care Bulletin, HE 23.1415
Child Feeding Charts, A 42.7/3
Child Guidance Leaflets, Series on Eating, For Parents, FS 3.211
Child Guidance Leaflets, Series on Eating, for Staff, L 5.51/2
Child Health USA, HE 20.9213
Child Hygiene [letters], T 27.41
Child Labor Bulletins, L 36.203/2
Child Labor Regulations, L 22.6/3
Child Labor Regulations, Orders, L 5.39
Child Labor Series, L 16.27
Child Maltreatment: Reports from the States to the National Child Abuse and Neglect Data System, HE 23.1018
Child Support and Alimony, Current Population Reports, C 3.186/4
Child Support Enforcement Statistics, HE 24.9/2
Child Welfare News Summary, L 5.23
Child Welfare Reports, FS 3.215, L 5.52
Child Welfare Statistics, HE 17.638
Child Welfare Training (series), HE 23.1213
Child-Labor Bulletins, L 22.14
Children, FS 3.207/2, FS 17.209, HE 21.9
Children and Poetry, LC 1.12/2:P 75
Children in Custody, J 29.9/5
Children, Interdisciplinary Journal for Professions Serving Children, FS 14.109
Children Saved by Public Welfare Agencies and Voluntary Child Welfare Agencies and Institutions, HE 17.645
Children Today, HE 1.459, HE 23.1209, HE 23.12
Children with Cancer (series), HE 20.3181
Children's Books, LC 2.11
Children's Year Follow-Up Series, L 5.15
Children's Year Leaflets, L 5.12
Chiliarch, J 16.21
China, 1942, S 1.1/2:C 44
China, International Trade Quarterly Review, ER-CIT (nos.), PrEx 3.10/8
China Reports, PrEx 7.15
China State Council Bulletin, PrEx 7.15/4-2
Chinese and Immigration Circulars, W 49.10/8
Chinese Exclusion Treaties, Laws and Regulations, C 7.5
Chit Chat, an Administrative Letter for Division Employees, A 103.17
CHR Program Update, HE 20.318
Chromite Reports, I 28.84
Chromium, I 28.84
Chromium in (year), I 28.84/2
Chronic Diseases Notes and Report, HE 20.7009/6, HE 20.7617
Chronicle, E 2.25
Chronological List of Official Orders to Commissioned and other Officers, FS 2.28
Chronological Schedule, Institute of Air Pollution Training Courses, EP 4.14/2
Chronologies of Major Developments in Selected Areas of International Relations, Y 4.F 76/1:In 8/57, Y 4.In 8/16:In 8/5
C/HS Pamphlets, PrEx 10.9/4
CHScene, Notes From the Community Health Service, HE 20.2557/2
CIB (Consumer Information Bureau) Annual Report, CC 1.60/1-1
CIB (Consumer Information Bureau) General Publications, CC 1.60/1-2
CID Pamphlet (series), D 101.22/17
Cigar Box Series, C 18.52/2
Cigar Tobacco Adjustment Program, A 55.10
Cigarettes and Cigars, T 70.9/2
Cincinnati, Centennial Exposition, 1897, S 6.17
CIO Information in the News, VA 1.101
CIP Cataloging in Publication, Progress Report, LC 30.16
Circulars, IC 1 blo.4
Circular DC-Nos. Washington Store, GS 2.4/2

Circular Letter, T 1.15
Circular Letter Transmitting Blank Reports, T 12.11/2
Circular Letters–
Corn-Hog Work, A 55.34, A 55.34/2, A 55.34/3
Wheat Work, A 55.35
Circular Letters, IC 1.4/2, J 1.14/5
Circular Letters, C 3.4/2
Circular Letters, 4th Civil Service Region, CS 1.50
Circular Letters (miscellaneous), T 12.11/3
Circular Letters (numbered), T 22.20/1
Circular Letters, Relate to Indian Emergency Conservation Work, I 20.23
Circular Letters [to conservators of national banks], T 12.11/4
Circular Letters to Presidents or Cashiers of National Banks Asking for Report of Conditions of Banks, T 12.11/1
Circular of Information, A 48.11
Circular of Inquiry Concerning Gold and Silver Coinage and Currency of Foreign Countries, Including Production, Import and Export, and Industrial
Consumption of Gold and Silver, T 28.8
Circular Showing Manner of Proceeding to Obtain Title to Land, I 21.12
Circular Statement of United States, T 63.207
Circulars–
International Trade Commission, ITC 1.4
Urban Mass Transportation Administration, TD 7.4
Circulars, EC- (series), D 103.4
Circulars: General Instructions, Consular or Special Instruction, Consular, S 1.4/2
Circulars, Information Circulars, etc., LC 3.4
Circulars of Information, C 3.19, C 13.5
Circulars of Information Relative to Appointment as 1st Lieutenants in Medical Circulars on Cooperative Marketing, FCA 1.4/3
Circulars, Reappraisements of Merchandise by General Appraisers or Reappraisement Circulars, T 20.4/1
Circulars Relating to Plan and Methods of Publication of Official Records of Union and Confederate Armies, W 45.4
Circulars Relating to the War Department, W 3.6
Circulation Statement, T 26.5
Circulation Statement of United States Money, T 63.308
Circulation Statements, T 57.7
Circum-Pacific (CP) Map Series, I 19.91/2
CIRRPC Annual Report, PrEx 1.15
Citation Orders, W 95.15
Citator, Y 3.F 31/21-3:9-4
Citator to Decisions of the Occupational Safety and Health Review Commission, Y 3.Oc 1:10-4
Citizen Action for Affordable Housing, Case Studies, HH 1.97/2
Citizen Airman, D 301.8
Citizen Leaflets, FS 5.67
Citizens Advisory Committee on Environmental Quality, Pr 37.8:En 8
Citizens' Advisory Committee on Environmental Quality: Annual Report, PrEx 14.1/2
Citizen's Guide on How to Use the Freedom of Information Act and the Privacy Act in Requesting Government Documents, Y 1.95-1:H.Rep. 793
Citizenship Day and Constitution Week Bulletins, J 21.14
Citizenship Training Division, L 6.7
Citrus Fruits by States, Production, Use, Value, A 88.12/21
City Documents, C 3.170
City Employment in (year), C 3.140/2
City Government Finances, C 3.191/2-5
City Government Finances in (year), C 56.209, C 3.191/2
City School Circulars, I 16.69
City School Leaflets, I 16.36
Cityscape - A Journal of Policy Development and Research, HH 1.75/2
Civil Aeronautics Authority Reports, CA 1.23
Civil Aeronautics Board Legislative History of Regulations, C 31.206/2:L 52
Civil Aeronautics Bulletins, CA 1.3, C 31.103
Civil Aeronautics Journal, CA 1.17, C 31.7, C 31.118
Civil Aeronautics Manuals [by volume number], C 31.107/2
Civil Aeronautics Manuals (numbered), FAA 1.34
Civil Aeronautics Reports, CAB 1.21, C 31.211
Civil Affairs Activities in Ryukyu Islands, D 102.19/3
Civil Affairs Handbooks, N 27.14
Civil Air Patrol Bulletins, Pr 32.4424
Civil Air Patrol Manuals, CAPM- (series), D 301.7/4
Civil Air Patrol Pamphlet CAPP (series), D 301.35/2
Civil Air Patrol Training Manuals, Pr 32.4412

Compilation of Administrative Policies for National Recreation Areas, National Seashores, National Lakeshores, National Parkways, National Scenic Riverways (Recreational Area Category), I 29.9/4:R 24

Compilation of Federal Laws Relating to Conservation and Development of Our Nation's Fish and Wildlife Resources, Environmental Quality, and Oceanography, Y 4.M 53:L 44/2

Compilation of Contract Research for the Chemical Engineering Branch, Division of Engineering Technology, Y 3.N 88:10-4

Compilation of Contract Research for the Materials Branch, Division of Engineering Safety, Y 3.N 88:10-3

Compilation of Federal Education Laws, Y 4.Ed 8/1-12

Compilation of Hydrologic Data [by area], I 19.58

Compilation of Laws Relating to Mediation, Conciliation, and Arbitration Between Employers and Employees, Laws [on] Disputes Between Carriers and Employers and Subordinate Officials Under Labor Board, Eight-hour Laws, Employers' Liability Laws, Labor and Child Labor Laws, Y 1.2:Em 7/6

Compilation of Meat and Poultry Inspection Issuances, A 110.9

Compilation of Orders, W 99.19/3

Compilation of Public Health Service Regulations, FS 2.52

Compilation of Records of Surface Waters of the United States, I 19.13

Compilation of Supply Circulars and Supply Bulletins, W 89.6/3, W 89.6/4

Compilation of the Social Security Laws, Y 4.W 36:10-3

Compilations and Digest of Orders, Circulars, Regulations, and Decisions, W 7.11/3

Compilations of Acts, W 49.7/4

Compilations of Court Martial Orders, N 1.14

Compilations of Laws, N 1.9

Compiled Rulings of Provost Marshal General, W 37.7

Complete Catalog, Cataloging Distribution Service, LC 30.27/2

Compliance Boards Instructions, Y 3.N 21/8:11

Compliance Guidance Series, HE 20.4608/2

Compliance Manual, L 35.6/3

Compliance Policy Guides, HE 20.4008/5

Compliance Program Guide Manual, HE 20.4008/7

Compliance Testing Reports (series), TD 8.34

Composite List of Eligible Institutions for Guaranteed Loans for College Students, Higher Education Act of 1965, FS 5.83, HE 5.83

Composite List of Eligible Institutions, National Vocation Student Loan Insurance Act of 1965, FS 5.83/2, HE 5.83/2

Comprehensive Clinical and Genetic Services Centers, a National Directory, HE 20.9112/3

Comprehensive Export Control Schedules, Y 3.Ec 74/2:108

Comprehensive Export Schedules, Pr 32.5808, C 34.8, C 18.267, C 42.11/a, C 49.208

Comprehensive Framework Study, Missouri River Basin, Y 3.M 69:9

Comprehensive Health Services Projects, Summary of Project Data, CHSP Reports, HE 20.5115

Comprehensive Plan for the National Capital, NC 2.2:P 69/2

Comprehensive Planning Series, EP 1.45

Comprehensive Studies of Solid Waste Management, Annual Report, EP 1.11

Comptroller Circular Letters, HH 2.8

Comptroller General of the United States, Decisions, Testimonies, Reviews, GA 1.5/2

Comptroller General's Rulings, Y 3.R 31:14

Comptroller General's Special Regulations, GA 1.7

Comptroller of Currency Annual Report, T 12.1

Computer and Biomathematical Sciences Study Section, HE 20.3001/2:C 73

Computer Codes and Mathematical Models, Y 3.N 88:31/0083

Computer Contribution (series), I 19.67

Computer Education, a Catalog of Projects Sponsored by the U.S. Department of Education, ED 1.325

Computer Program Abstracts, NAS 1.44

Computer Research and Technology Divisions: Technical Reports, HE 20.3011

Computer Security Center, CSC-EPL- (series), D 1.79

Computer Services Newsletter, T 22.2/15-2

Computer Systems Laboratory, Annual Report, C 13.77

Computer Training Courses, HE 20.7033

Computerized Geographic Coding Series, C 3.246, C 56.237

Computers, C 51.17

Computers, Control, and Information Theory, C 51.9/8

COMTAC [Communications and Tactical] Publications Index, TD 5.21/5

CONAC Manuals, D 301.7/3

Concepts and Issues, D 214.27

Conceptual Design of 50 MGD Desalination Plants, I 1.87/3

Concerning Workers' Education, Y 3.F 31/4:12

Concorde Monitoring–
Dulles International Airport, TD 4.49
John F. Kennedy International Airport, TD 4.49/2

Concrete and Reinforced Concrete [abstracts], C 41.71/2

Concurrent Receipt of Public Assistance Money Payments and Old-Age, Survivors, and Disability Insurance Cash Benefits by Persons Aged 65 or Over, FS 17.636, HE 17.636

Condensed Classification of Operating Expenses, IC 1 ste.18

Condensed Consolidated Statistical Statements, Class 1 Railways Having Annual Railway Operating Revenues of $10,000,000 or More, IC 1 ste.46

Condensed Reports of Cases in Supreme Court of United States, Ju 6.8/3

Condition of Education, HE 19.314

Condition of Education (separates), ED 1.109/a

Condition of Public School Plants, FS 5.221:21033, HE 5.221:21033

Condition of Weekly Reporting Member Banks in Central Reserve Cities, FR 1.16/2

Condition of Weekly Reporting Member Banks in Leading Cities, FR 1.16

Condition of Weekly Reporting Member Banks in New York and Chicago, FR 1.16/2

Conditions of Major Water System Structures and Facilities, Review of Maintenance, Report of Examination, [various regions and projects], I 27.69

Confectionery Manufacturers' Sales and Distribution, C 41.19, C 57.13

Conference at Quebec, 1944, S 1.1/3:Q 3

Conference Briefs, C 13.62

Conference for Supervisors of Elementary Education in Large Cities, FS 5.58/2

Conference in Matters of Pollution of Navigable Waters, Proceedings, EP 1.16/2

Conference News, S 5.48/3

Conference Notes, D 103.112

Conference of Berlin (Potsdam Conference), 1945, S 1.1/3:P 84

Conference of Model Reporting Area for Blindness, Proceedings, HE 20.3759/2

Conference of Oil Pollution of Navigable Waters, S 5.24

Conference of State and Territorial Health Officers with United States Public Health Service, Transactions, T 27.32, FS 2.34

Conference of State Planning and Development Officers with Federal Officials, Summaries, C 45.11

Conference of State Sanitary Engineers, Report of Proceedings, HE 20.14

Conference on Elementary Education Reports, FS 5.58

Conference on Limitation of Armament, Washington, 1921-22, S 3.29

Conference on Weights and Measures, C 13.7

Conference Proceedings [of] AASHO Committee on Electronics, TD 2.125

Conference Publications, NASA CP- (series), NAS 1.55

Conference Report on Cotton Insect Research and Control, A 77.328

Conference Report Series, FS 2.22/50

Conference Rulings Bulletins, IC 1.8, FT 1.6

Conference (series), E 1.10, S 5.30

Conference Summary Report (series), HE 20.6518

Conferences at Cairo and Teheran, 1943, 1961, S 1.1/3:C 12

Conferences at Malta and Yalta, 1945, S 1.1/3:M 29

Conferences at Washington and Quebec, S 1.1/3:W 27/2

Conferences at Washington, 1941–1942, and Casablanca, S 1.1/3:W 27

Conferences of Educators on Sex Education, T 27.25

Conferences on Inter-American Relations, S 15.5

Confidential Bulletin of Engineering Information, N 19.9/1

Confidential Reports, A 72.24

Congenital Malformations Surveillance, Reports, HE 20.7011/2

Congress and Foreign Policy, Y 4.F 76/1-13

Congress of International Society of Soil Science Publications, A 57.49

Congressional Budget Request, E 1.34

Congressional Budget Request, Federal Energy Regulatory Commission, E 1.34/4

Congressional Budget Request, U.S. Department of Justice, E 1.34/3

Congressional Budget Request, U.S. Department of the Interior, E 1.34/2

Congressional Budget Scorekeeping Reports, Y 10.10

Congressional Directory, Y 4.P 93/1:1

Congressional District Atlas, C 3.62/5, C 56.213/2

Congressional District Data Book, C 3.134/2:C 76, C 56.243/2:C 76

Congressional District Data, CDD- (series), C 3.134/4, C 56.213

Congressional Districts of the United States, C 3.282/4

Congressional Districts of the United States, Summary Tape Files, C 3.282/4

Congressional Globe, X 72–X 180

Congressional Hearings Scheduled, I 20.45/2

Congressional Justification for Estimates, HH 1.105

Congressional Lists; List of Publications Available for Distribution by Members of Congress, A 21.9/3

Congressional Methodology, ED 1.81

Congressional Presentation for Security Assistance Programs, Fiscal Year (date), D 1.85

Congressional Record, X 1.1

Congressional Record (Bound) 1985 and Forward, X

Congressional Record Digest, CS 1.77

Congressional Record, Index and Daily Digest, X 1.1

Congressional Record, Proceedings and Debates, X/a

Congressional Record Proceedings of the House and Senate, Extensions of Remarks, and the Daily Digest, Also the CRI, X 1.1/a

Congressional Record Review, S 18.46

Congressional Research Service Review, LC 14.19

Congressional Sourcebook Series, GA 1.22

Congressional Staff Journal, Y 4.H 81/3:2, Y 4.R 86/2:3

Congressional Watch, Y 3.Ad 9/8:13

Connection, HE 20.8221

Connections, Ju 13.9/3

Connex Newsletter, A 94.21

CONSER Editing Guide, LC 1.6/4-2

CONSER Line, LC 30.22/2

CONSER Tables, (date), LC 30.22

Conservation Agronomy Technical Notes, A 57.63

Conservation Aids, A 57.45

Conservation and Solar Applications, DOE/CS (series), E 1.36

Conservation and Your Community, A 57.75

Conservation Bulletins, I 1.72

Conservation Districts, A 57.2:C 76

Conservation Education Reports, A 57.33

Conservation Folders, A 57.30, A 76.210

Conservation Guide Sheets, A 57.6/4

Conservation Highlights, Digest of the Progress Report of the Soil Conservation Service, A 57.1/2

Conservation in Action, I 49.36

Conservation Information, A 57.44

Conservation Man (radio scripts), I 29.49

Conservation Notes, I 49.36/2

Conservation Papers, FE 1.22

Conservation Planning Memorandum, A 57.53

Conservation Project Support Grant Application and Information, NF 4.10

Conservation Research Reports, A 1.114, A 77.23

Conservation Reserve Program of Soil Bank, Statistical Summaries, A 82.79/2

Conservation Teaching Aids, A 13.72

Conservation Vistas, Regional Conservation Education Newsletter Serving Oregon and Washington, A 13.72/2

Conservation Yearbooks, I 1.95

Conserve-O-Gram, I 29.100

Consolidated Abstracts of Technical Reports, FAA 2.11

Consolidated Abstracts of Technical Reports: General Distribution, FAA 2.11/2

Consolidated Address and Territorial Bulletin, VA Station Addresses, Identification Numbers, and Territorial Jurisdictions, VA 1.69

Consolidated Annual Report for the Office of Community Planning and Development, HE 23.1017

Consolidated Annual Report on State and Territorial Public Health Laboratories, HE 20.7001/2

Consolidated Annual Report to Congress on Community Development Programs, HH 1.46/6

Consolidated Cotton Report, C 3.20/4

Consolidated Development Directory, HH 1.61

Consolidated Federal Funds Report, C 3.266/2

Consolidated Federal Funds Reports, CD-CFFR, C 3.266/3

Consolidated Federal Supply Catalog, D 1.78
Consolidated Financial Report FY, HH 1.1/11
Consolidated Financial Statements of the United States Government, Fiscal Year, T 63.113/3
Consolidated Index of Army Publications and Blank Forms, D 101.22:25-30
Consolidated Index of Opinions and Digests of Opinions of Judge Advocate General, W 10.10
Consolidated List of Debarred, Suspended, and Ineligible Contractors, GS 1.28
Consolidated List of Debarred, Suspended and Ineligible Contractors and Grantees, HH 1.102
Consolidated List of Persons or Firms Currently Debarred for Violations of Various Public Contracts Acts Incorporating Labor Standard Provisions, GA 1.17
Consolidated Listing of Official Gazette Notices Re Patent and Trademark Office Practices and Procedures, Patent Notices, C 21.5/5
Consolidated Management Data List, D 7.29/6
Consolidated Master Cross Reference List, D 7.20
Consolidated of Schedule B Commodity Classifications for Use in Presentation of U.S. Export Statistics, C 3.150:G
Consolidated Publication of Component Lists, D 101.16/3
Consolidated Report of Accessions, D 102.7
Consolidated Review of Current Information, T 23.7/2
Consolidated Subject Index, D 201.37
Consolidated Supply Program, HH 1.90, HH 1.91
Consolidated Translation Survey, Pr 34.610
Constabulary Notes, W 49.32/7
Constitution and Membership, NA 1.7
Constitution of the United States, Analysis and Interpretation, Y 1.92-2:S.doc. 82
Construction Abroad, C 18.59/2
Construction Activity, L 2.22/2
Construction Aids, HH 1.18
Construction and Equipment, PrEx 7.21/3
Construction and Building Materials, Monthly Industry Report, C 40.10
Construction and Building Materials, Statistical Supplements, C 41.30/2
Construction and Related Industry, PrEx 7.22/3-2
Construction Bulletin (series), J 28.3/2
Construction Committees [various cities], Public Sector Bid Calendars by Agencies, L 1.75
Construction Expenditure of State and Local Governments, BC- (series), C 56.223, C 3.215/10
Construction Expenditure of State and Local Governments, GC- (series), C 56.223
Construction Expenditure of State and Local Tax Revenue, C 3.215/10
Construction Industry Series, HE 19.108/2
Construction Industry Stabilization Commission Regulations, ES 2.6/4
Construction Materials, FW 1.16
Construction, Monthly Summary of Current Developments, L 2.22
Construction Problems Relating to Fire Protection, GS 1.14/9
Construction Report: Price Index of New One-family Houses Sold, C 27- (series), C 56.211/2-2
Construction Reports–
 Authorized Construction, Washington, D.C. Area, C 56.211/6
 Building Permits, C 40- (series), C 3.215/7
 Building Permits: C 42- (series), C 3.215/6
 Housing Authorized by Building Permits and Public Contracts, C 3.215/11
 Housing Authorized by Building Permits and Public Contracts, C 40 (series), C 56.211/4
 Housing Completions, C 22 (series), C 3.215/13
 Housing Completions, C 22- (series), C 56.211
 Housing Starts, C 20- (Series), C 56.211/3
 Housing Units Authorized for Demolition in Permit-issuing Places, (year), C 45- (series), C 56.211/8
 New One-family Homes Sold and for Sale, C 25- (series), C 56.211/2
 New Residential Construction in Selected Standard Metropolitan Statistical Areas, C 3.215/15
 Permits Issued for Demolition of Residential Structures in Selected Cities, C 45 (series), C 3.215/12
 Price Index of New One-family Houses Sold, C 27 (series), C 3.215/9-2

Residential Alterations and Repairs, Expenditures on Residential Additions, Alterations, Maintenance and Repairs, and Replacements, C 56.211/7
Value of New Construction Put in Place, C 30- (series), C 56.211/5, C 3.215/3:C 30
Construction Review, C 62.10, C 57.310, C 57.509, C 61.37
Construction Standards, L 35.6/3
Construction Status Report, Nuclear Power Plants, Data for Decisions, Y 3.N 88:16
Construction Trends, I 27.48
Constructive Hints, A 13.33
Consular Regulations, S 1.5
Consular Reports, S 4.10
Consular Reports, Annual Series, C 10.12
Consumer, Y 3.N 21/8:22, L 17.9
Consumer Action Handbook GS 11.9/3
Consumer Advisory Council Report, PrEx 6.10
Consumer Affairs Fact Sheets (series), TD 8.14/3
Consumer Aid Series, TD 8.14/2
Consumer Alert, FT 1.24/2
Consumer Briefing Summary, E 1.29
Consumer Bulletins, FT 1.3/2
Consumer Buying Indicators, C 3.186:P 65
Consumer Buying Practices for Selected Fresh fruits, Canned and Frozen Juices, and Dried Fruits, Related to Family Characteristics, Region and City Size, A 36.173
Consumer Complaint Contact System, Annual Report, Y 3.C 76/3:20
Consumer Credit, FR 1.36
Consumer Credit at Consumer Finance Companies, FR 1.36/7
Consumer Deputy Program (series), Y 3.C 76/3:22
Consumer Education Bibliography, PrEx 16.10:Ed 8
Consumer Energy Atlas, E 1.33/2:10879-01
Consumer Expenditure Survey: Diary Survey, L 2.3/18-2
Consumer Expenditure Survey: Interview Survey, L 2.3/18
Consumer Expenditure Survey: Quarterly Data from the Interview Survey, L 2.3/18-3
Consumer Expenditure Survey Results, L 2.120/2-5
Consumer Fact Sheet, TD 5.60
Consumer Facts, A 21.13/6
Consumer Finance Companies, Loans Outstanding and Volume of Loans Made, FR 1.36/6
Consumer Focus, GS 11.9/3-2
Consumer Goods and Domestic Trade, PrEx 7.21/8
Consumer Goods Research, C 57.118
Consumer Income, C 3.186:P-60
Consumer Information Catalog, GS 11.9
Consumer Information Leaflets, L 1.72
Consumer Information Series–
 Department of Health, Education, and Welfare, HE 1.34/2
 Federal Supply Service, GS 2.16
 General Services Administration, GS 1.1
 National Highway Safety Bureau, TD 2.213
 National Highway Traffic Safety Administration, TD 8.14
 Substance Abuse and Mental Health Services Administration, HE 20.427/2
Consumer Information TV Program Packages, Suggested Scripts, A 21.27
Consumer Installment Credit at Commercial Banks, FR 1.36/2
Consumer Installment Credit Extended and Repaid, FR 1.36/5
Consumer Installment Credits of Industrial Loan Companies, FR 1.36/4
Consumer Installment Loans of Principal Types of Financial Institutions, FR 1.34
Consumer Legislative Monthly Report, HE 1.510
Consumer Loans Made Under Effective State Small Loan Laws, FR 1.36/3
Consumer News, HE 1.509, CC 1.59
Consumer Notes, Y 3.N 21/9:8, A 55.56
Consumer Notice, HH 1.81
Consumer Price Index, a Short Description, L 2.2:P 93/19
Consumer Price Index [by individual cities and commodities], L 2.38/5
Consumer Price Index, Chicago, L 2.38/8-2
Consumer Price Index for All Urban Consumers, L 2.38/9
Consumer Price Index, Mountain-Plain Regions, L 2.38/6
Consumer Price Index News Releases, L 2.38/10
Consumer Price Index, Price Indexes for Selected Items and Groups, L 2.38/4
Consumer Price Index, Washington, D.C. Area, L 2.38/8
Consumer Prices, Pr 32.4258

Consumer Prices: Energy and Food, L 2.38/7
Consumer Product Information, GS 11.9
Consumer Product Safety Review, Y 3.C 76/3:28
Consumer Purchases of Citrus and Other Juices, CPFJ (series), A 93.12
Consumer Purchases of Fruits and Juices, A 88.12/4
Consumer Purchases of Fruits and Juices by Regions and Retail Outlets, A 36.171/2
Consumer Purchases of Selected Fresh Fruits, Canned and Frozen Juices, and Dried Fruits, A 36.171
Consumer Relations Newsletter, HH 1.15/3
Consumer's Resource Handbook, GS 11.9/3
Consumer Spending Update, C 3.276
Consumer Study Outline, A 55.53
Consumer Survey Handbooks, FT 1.8/3
Consumer Update, HE 20.4010/3
Consumers' Advisory Board, General Publications, Y 3.N 21/8:16
Consumers Counsel Division, Consumers' Counsel Series Publications, A 75.11
Consumers' Counsel Division, General Publications, A 55.63
Consumers' Counsel Series, Publications, A 55.49
Consumers' Guide, A 1.67
Consumers' Market Service, A 55.52, A 75.109
Consumers Price Index, L 2.38
Consumers' Price Index for Moderate-income Families (adjusted series), L 2.38/2
Consumers' Resource Handbook, Pr 39.15:C 76, HE 1.508/2
Consumers Service, A 55.72
Consumption of Commercial Fertilizers and Primary Plant Nutrients in United States, A 92.37
Consumption of Explosives, C 22.30
Consumption of Fuel for Production of Electric Energy, FP 1.11/3
Contact, D 301.26/14
Contact Clearing House Service CCHS Summary, FO 1.16
Contact Reports, FS 9.9
Contacts for U.S. Food Products, A 67.40/3
Contaminant Hazard Review, I 19.167
Container Notes, A 80.126
Containers and Packaging, C 18.242, C 40.12, C 41.33, C 57.314, C 57.513
Containerships Under Construction and on Order (including conversions) in United States and Foreign Shipyards Oceangoing Ships of 1,000 Gross Tons and Over, C 39.231
Containerized Cargo Statistics, C 39.233, TD 11.21
Contents and Price List for Microfilm Publications, GS 4.20/2
Contents, Format and Concepts of Federal Budget, Reprint of Selected Pages from Budget of United States Government, PrEx 2.8
Contents of Vaults [of] Treasury Department, T 40.10
Conterminous U.S. AVHRR Biweekly Composites, I 19.120/3
Continental Divide Trail Study Progress Reports, I 66.19/2
Continental Marine and Digest, D 214.23
Continental U.S. Beet Sugar Orders, A 55.17
Continerized Cargo Statistics, C 39.233
Contingency Plans, FE 1.25
Contingent Foreign Liabilities of U.S. Government, T 1.45/3
Continuation Application for Grants under Special Services for Disadvantage Students Program, ED 1.60
Continuation Application for Grants under Talent Search Program, ED 1.55
Continued Increases in Industry Productivity in (year) Reported by BLS, L 1.79/2-3
Continuing Education is Work, Y 3.Ed 8/8:1
Continuing Survey of Food Intake by Individuals, A 111.9/3
Contraceptive Development Contract Review Committee, HE 20.3001/2:C 76
Contraceptive Evaluation Research Contract Review Committee, HE 20.3001/2:C 76/2
Contract Advisory Service Summaries, IC 1.36
Contract and Requisitioned Steamships, SB 2.13
Contract Bulletin, N 20.12, N 20.18
Contract Clearing House Service, Summaries, Pr 33.916
Contract Reports–
 Corps of Engineers, D 103.52
 National Aeronautics and Space Administration, NAS 1.26
 National Telecommunications and Information Administration, C 60.12
 Nuclear Regulatory Commission, Y 3.N 88:25-2
 Waterways Experiment Station, D 103.24/9
Contract Reports and Publications, E 1.99

Contract Research Reports, TD 8.15/2
Contractions Handbook, TD 4.308:C 76
Contractions TD 4.308:C 76
Contractor Fatalities Coal and Metal/Nonmetal Mines, L 38.20/4
Contractor Report (series), ED 1.115
Contractor Reports and Publications
 Arms Control, E 1.99
 Biomass Fuels, E 1.99
 Environmental Sciences, E 1.99
 Fossil-Fueled Power Plants, E 1.99
 Physics, E 1.99
 Power Transmission & Distribution, E 1.99
 Synthetic Fuels, E 1.99
Contractor Research and Development Reports, E 1.28
Contracts for Field Projects & Supporting Research on . . ., E 1.99/2
Contracts for U.S. Food Products, A 67.40/3
Contracts Handbook, TD 4.308:C 76
Contrails, Air Force Cadet Handbook, D 305.16
Contributions from the Center for Northern Studies, I 29.99
Contributions from the Museum of History and Technology, Papers, SI 3.3
Contributions from the U.S. National Herbarium, SI 3.8
Contributions from Thermodynamics Laboratory, Petroleum Experiment Station, Bartlesville, Oklahoma, I 28.105
Contributions from U.S. National Herbarium, A 6.5
Contributions of American Educational History, I 16.15
Contributions to Medical Science, N 10.9
Contributions to Naval History (series), D 207.10/4, D 221.19
Contributions to North American Ethnology, I 17.5
Contributions Toward a Flora of Nevada, A 77.527
Control and Employment of Vessels Trading with United States, SB 5.6
Controller Chart Supplement, TD 4.317
Controller, CR- (series), E 1.35
Controller Patient Census Monographs, VA 1.48/3
Controller's Monthly Financial Report, T 22.67
Controlling Chemical Hazards Series, L 16.25
CONUS Army Installations/Activities by Congressional District, D 101.99
Convection-type Radiators, C 3.75
Convention on International Trade in Endangered Species of Wild Fauna and Flora, Annual Report, I 49.85
Conventional Home Mortgage Rates in Early (month), FHL 1.25/3
Conventional Loans Made in Excess of 80 Percent of Property Appraisal by Federal Savings and Loan Associations, FHL 1.19
Conventional Loans Made to Finance Acquisition and Development of Land, Federal Savings and Loan Associations, FHL 1.22
Conventions, (year): National and International Unions, State Labor Federations, Professional Associations, State Employee Association [list], L 2.103
Conversion Lists, L 2.35
Conversion Tables, C 18.29
Conversion of Neoplasms by Topography and Morphology, HE 20.3197
Conveyer, A 104.10
Cooperage Series, C 18.60
Cooperation in Agriculture, A 17.17:41
Cooperative Area Manpower Planning System, Interagency Cooperative Issuances, L 1.64
Cooperative Bibliographies, LC 2.7
Cooperative Economic Insect Report, A 101.9, A 77.324/3
Cooperative Extension Work in Agriculture and Home Economics, A 10.24
Cooperative Extension Work Office, A 43.5
Cooperative Fishery Unit Report, I 49.66
Cooperative Fishery Units Annual Report, I 49.1/5
Cooperative Forest Fire Prevention Program, A 13.20/4
Cooperative Graduate Fellowship Program for Fiscal Year, Fellowship Awards [and] Program of Summer Fellowships for Graduate Teaching Assistants for Fiscal Year, NS 1.19/2
Cooperative Information Reports, A 105.38/2, A 109.10/2
Cooperative Inter-American Plantation Rubber Development, A 77.519
Cooperative Investigations Reports (series), I 19.83
Cooperative Observer, C 55.118
Cooperative Pest Control Programs, A 77.327
Cooperative Plant Pest Report, A 101.9/2
Cooperative Research and Service Division, Quarterly Reports, A 72.22
Cooperative Research Program: Projects under Contract, FS 5.69

Cooperative Research Reports, A 105.38
Cooperative Savings with Federal Credit Unions, FCA 1.14, FCA 1.14/2
Cooperative Self-Help, Y 3.F 31/5:22
Cooperative State-Federal Bovine Tuberculosis Eradication Program, Statistical Tables, A 101.18
Cooperative State-Federal Brucellosis Eradication Program–
 Brucellosis Bulletin, A 101.18/3
 Charts and Maps, A 77.212/6-2
 Progress Report, A 77.15:91-57
 Statistical Tables, A 101.18/2
 Statistical Tables, Fiscal Year (date), A 77.212/4
Cooperative State-Federal Brucellosis Eradication Programs, A 77.212/6
Cooperative State-Federal Hog Cholera Eradication Program Progress Report, A 77.241
Cooperative State-Federal Sheep and Cattle Scabies, Epidemiology and Related Activities, A 77.233/4
Cooperative State-Federal Sheep and Cattle Scabies Eradication, Progress Report, A 77.233
Cooperative State-Federal Tuberculosis Eradication Program, Statistical Tables, Fiscal Year (date), A 77.212/5
Cooperative State-Federal Tuberculosis Eradication, Progress Report, A 77.15:91-44
Cooperative Studies Reports, C 30.61
Cooperative Studies Technical Papers, C 30.61/2
Cooperative Summary of the Day, C 55.281/2-4
Cooperative Water Resources, Research and Training, I 1.1/4
Cooperative-Creamery Routes, A 72.20
Coordinated Federal Wage System, CS 1.41/4:532-1
Coordination Memorandums, I 66.14
Coordination of Federal Equal Employment Opportunity Programs, Y 3.Eq 2:16
Coordination Service, Digest of Interpretations of Specific Price Schedules and Regulations, Pr 32.4249
Coordinator's Scoreboard, Review of What's New in Placement of the Handicapped, CS 1.75
Copper, C 62.12, C 57.512
Copper in (year), I 28.59/3, I 28.59/4
Copper in the United States, I 28.59/2
Copper Industry, I 28.59/2
Copper Industry, Annual, I 28.59/3
Copper Production, I 28.59/5
Copper Scrap Consumers, I 28.79
Copper Sulfate, I 28.93
Copper, (year) Annual Statistical Supplement, C 57.512/2
Copyright Law Studies, LC 3.9
Coraporter, J 21.18
Core Competencies, GS 14.15
Core Curriculum, PE 1.11
Corn and Wheat Region Bulletins, C 30.7
Corn Circular Letters, Y 3.C 73:9
Corn, Estimated Planted Acreage, Yield, and Production by States, A 66.47
Corn Hog Charts, A 55.14
Corn (Hominy) Grits for Domestic Distribution, A 82.3/4
Corn Meal, A 82.3/8
Corn Meal for Domestic Distribution, A 82.3/3
Corn Meal for Export Distribution, A 82.3/7
Corn-Hog Circular Letters, A 55.34/3
Corporate Author Authority List, C 51.18
Corporate Complex, D 7.6/2-2:5
Corporate Pension Funds, SE 1.25/6
Corporate Securities Offered for Cash, SE 1.25/6
Corporation Income Tax Returns, T 22.35/3:C 81, T 22.35/2:C 81
Corporation Income Tax Returns, Source Book (year), T 22.35/5-2
Corps Connection, TD 2.72
Corps of Engineers Supply Catalogues, W 7.24
Corps of Regular Army, W 44.27
Corpsman, Published for Men and Women of Job Corps, L 1.58/3, PrEx 10.10/2
Correction and Additions to Publications of Officers at Home and Abroad, N 6.6
Correction Series, HE 17.16/2
Correction to USAFE Radio Facility Chart, Weekly Notices to Airmen, M 301.17/2
Correctional Populations in the United States, J 29.17
Correspondence Aids, CA- (series), A 77.18, A 106.23
Correspondence Course, Elements of Surface Weather Observations, Lessons, C 30.26
Correspondence Course Program, Subcourses, D 103.111/2
Correspondence Courses, CS 1.92

Correspondence Courses Offered by Participating Colleges and Universities through the United States Armed Forces Institute, D 1.10/6
Corundum in (year), I 28.159
Cost Analysis of Correctional Standards, [various subjects], J 1.49
Cost and Quality of Fuels, E 3.11/15
Cost and Quality of Fuels for Electric Utility Plants, E 3.11/15-2
Cost and Returns, A 93.9/11
Cost Ascertainment Report, P 4.6
Cost of Clean Air, EP 1.62
Cost of Clean Water , EP 2.14
Cost of Current Series, Electrical Equipment Division, C 18.61
Cost of Flotation, SE 1.26
Cost of Food at Home Estimated for Food Plans at Four Cost Levels, A 98.19/2
Cost of Food at Home Estimated for Food Plans at Three Cost Levels, Southern Region, A 106.39/5
Cost of Living Council News, PrEx 17.7
Cost of Owning and Operating Automobiles and Vans, TD 2.60
Cost of Pipeline and Compressor Station Construction Under Non-Budget Type or Certificate Authorizations As Reported by Pipeline Companies, FP 1.30
Cost of Transporting Freight by Class I and Class II Motor Common Carriers of General Commodities, IC 1 acco 2.F 88, IC 1 acco.13
Cost of Transporting Freight, Class 1 and Class 2 Motor Common Carriers of General Freight, IC 1 acco.13
Cost Reduction Notes, PrEx 2.16
Cost Reduction Reports, D 1.38/2
Cost Reports, FT 1.10
Cost System Outlines, S 17.40
Costa Rica-Nicaragua Boundary Arbitration, S 3.15
Costs and Indexes for Domestic Oil and Gas Field Equipment and Production Operations, E 3.44/2
Costs and Returns, A 93.9/11
Costs of Producing Milk, A 93.53
Cotton, A 67.30:C 82
Cotton and Grain Futures Acts, Commodity Exchange and Warehouse Acts and Other Laws Relating Thereto [August 7, 1916], Y 1.2:C 82
Cotton and Wool Situation, A 93.24/2, A 105.16
Cotton and Wool, Situation and Outlook Yearbook, A 93.24/2-2
Cotton and Wool Update, A 93.24/3
Cotton Circular Letters, Y 3.C 73:10
Cotton Educational Meetings, A 55.39
Cotton Estimated Acreage, Yield, and Production, A 36.114, A 66.41
Cotton Fiber and Processing Test Results, A 88.11/17
Cotton Gin Equipment, A 88.11/19
Cotton Ginned (by States), C 3.20/2
Cotton Ginning Charges, Harvesting Practices, and Selected Marketing Costs, A 93.44/4
Cotton Ginning Reports, C 3.9
Cotton Ginnings, A 92.47
Cotton Ginnings, Report on Cotton Ginnings by Counties, A 20- (series), C 56.239
Cotton Ginnings, Report on Cotton Ginnings by States, A 10- (series), C 56.239/2
Cotton Goods in World Markets, C 18.62
Cotton Grade and Staple Reports, Georgia, A 36.27/1
Cotton Grade and Staple Reports, Texas and Oklahoma, A 36.27/2
Cotton Insect Conditions, A 77.322
Cotton Linters Produced and on Hand at Oil Mills by Type of Cut, by States, Preliminary, C 3.148
Cotton Linters Review, A 82.8
Cotton Literature, Selected References, A 1.50
Cotton Market News, A 88.11/22
Cotton Market Review, A 82.9
Cotton Marketing Quotas Letters, A 55.43/10
Cotton Price Statistics, A 88.11/9, A 82.13
Cotton Price Statistics, Monthly Averages, A 80.128
Cotton Production, A 88.11/5
Cotton Production Adjustments, A 55.23
Cotton Production and Distribution, Year Ending July 31, C 3.3
Cotton Production, CN 1 (series), A 92.20
Cotton Production: Cotton and Cottonseed Production, A 88.11/16
Cotton Production in the United States, Crop of [year], C 3.32
Cotton Quality Crop of (year), A 88.11
Cotton Quality Report for Ginnings, Western Upland Cotton, A 82.68

Arizona, I 53.22/8
Montana, I 53.22/5
Nevada, I 53.22/3
New Mexico, I 53.22/9
Oregon, I 53.22/10
Utah, I 53.22/2
Wyoming, I 53.22/7
Cumberland River Navigation Charts, D 103.66/3
Cumulated Index Medicus, HE 20.3612/3
Cumulated List of New Medical Subject Headings, HE 20.3612/3-2
Cumulative Bulletin, T 22.25
Cumulative Index to Foreign Production and Commercial Reports, C 42.15/3-2
Cumulative Index-Digest, C 31.211/3
Cumulative Index-Digest of Unpublished Decisions, I 1.69/2-3
Cumulative Indexes, NAS 1.9/5
Cumulative List of Malaysia, Singapore and Brunei Serials, LC 1.30/10-2
Cumulative List of Organizations, T 22.2/11
Cumulative List, Organizations Described in Section 170 (c) of the International Revenue Code of 1954, T 22.2:Or 3
Cumulative Listing, FS 2.216/2
Cumulative Price and Status Change Report, GP 3.22/3-4
Cumulative Report of All Specific Risk Investment Guaranties Issued Since the Beginning of the Program through, S 18.26/3
Currency & Banking News Digest, T 22.2/15:7446
Current and Non-current Periodicals in the NIH Library, HE 20.3009/3
Current Articles of Interest Cumulative Index, AC 1.13/2-2
Current Awareness Buildings Energy Technology, DOE/BET, E 1.119
Current Awareness in Health Education, HE 20.7209/2, HE 20.7609
Current Awareness of Translations, EP 1.21/3
Current Bibliographies in Medicine (series), HE 20.3615/2
Current Bibliographies Prepared by the Library, L 1.34/4
Current Bibliography of Epidemiology, HE 20.3617
Current Business Reports, C 3.211/4
    Advance Monthly Retail Sales, CB-(series), C 56.219/6
    Annual Survey of Communication Services, C 3.138/3-6
    Canned Food, Stock, Pack, Shipments, B-1-(series), C 56.219/8
    Green Coffee, Inventories, Imports, Roastings, BG-(series), C 56.219/2
    Monthly Retail Trade, Sales and Accounts Receivable, BR- (series), C 56.219/4
    Monthly Selected Service Receipts, BS-(series), C 56.219/5
    Monthly Wholesale Trade, Sales and Inventories, BW- (series), C 56.219
    Monthly Wholesale Trade, C 3.133
    Retail Trade, C 56.219/4-2
    Service Annual Survey, C 3.138/3-4
    Weekly Retail Sales, CB- (series), C 56.219/7
Current Conservation, I 43.7
Current Construction Reports
    Housing Units Authorized by Building Permits, C 3.215/4:C 40
    New One- Family Houses Sold and for Sale, C 3.215/9
    New Residential Construction in Selected Metropolitan Areas, C 3.215/15
    Special Studies, Expenditures for Nonresidential Improvements and Repairs, C 3.215/8-2
Current Controls Bulletins, Y 3.Ec 74/2:109
Current Developments, A 57.70
Current Developments in Drug Distribution, C 18.212
Current Developments in Electrical Trade, C 18.213
Current Developments in Farm Real Estate Market, A 77.13
Current Developments in Food Distribution, C 18.214
Current Developments Report on European Recovery, S 1.72
Current Diagrams, C 4.28
Current Discharge at Selected Stations in the Pacific Northwest, I 19.45, I 19.47/2
Current Distribution Developments in Hardware and Allied Trades, C 18.215
Current Employment Market for Engineers, Scientists, and Technicians, L 7.63/2
Current Employment Statistics State Operating Manual, L 2.46/4
Current Estimates from the National Health Interview Survey, HE 20.6209/4

Current Events: Power Reactors, Y 3.N 88:12
Current Expenditures Per Pupil in Pubic School Systems, FS 5.222:22000, HE 5.222:22000
Current Export Bulletins, Pr 32.5807, C 34.7, C 18.266, C 42.11, C 49.208/2
Current FAA Telecommunications, Fiscal Year . . ., TD 4.73
Current Facts on Housing, HH 1.10
Current Federal Aid Research Report, Wildlife, I 49.94/2
Current Federal Examination Announcements, PM 1.21
Current Federal Meteorological Research and Development Activities, C 30.75/2
Current Federal Research Reports, Fish, I 49.94
Current Federal Workforce Data, CS 1.72
Current Fisheries Statistics CFS (series), C 55.309/2
Current Fishery Products, Annual Summary, C 55.309/2-4
Current Fishery Statistics, I 49.8/2
Current Housing Market Situation, Report [various localities], HH 2.28/2
Current Housing Reports C 3.215:H 130
Current Housing Reports, C 56.214, C 3.215/14, C 56.214/2
Current Housing Reports: Market Absorption of Apartments, H-130- (series), C 56.230
Current Housing Situation, HH 2.20
Current Industrial Reports, C 3.158, C 56.216
    Manufacturing Profiles, C 3.158/4
    Manufacturing Technology, C 3.158/3 (Multigraphed), C 3.58
Current Information on Occupational Outlook, VA 1.31
Current Information Reports, A 13.91
Current Information Resource Requirements of the Federal Government, PM 1.56
Current Information Statements, A 55.33
Current Information Technology Resources Require-ments of the Federal Government, PrEx 2.12/5
Current Intelligence Bulletin, HE 20.7115
Current Intelligence Bulletins, Summaries, HE 20.7115/2
Current IPA Projects for Improved State and Local Management, CS 1.94
Current Issue Outline (series), C 55.235
Current Laws, Statutes and Executive Orders, EP 1.5:L 44
Current Legal Literature, TD 4.17/4
Current List of Medical Literature, W 44.30, M 102.7, D 104.7, D 8.8, FS 2.208
Current Listing and Topical Index, HE 20.6209/2
Current Listing and Topical Index to the Vital and Health Statistics Series, HE 20.2202:V 83
Current Listing of Aircraft Bonds, T 17.19/2
Current Listings of Carrier's Bonds, T 17.19
Current Literature in Agricultural Engineering, A 70.7
Current Literature on Venereal Disease, FS 2.11/2, HE 20.2311
Current Local Announcements Covering Washington, D.C. Metropolitan Area, CS 1.28:2602-WA
Current Membership of Joint Committee on Atomic Energy, Membership, Publications, and Other Pertinent Information through [congress, Session], Y 4.At 7/2:M 51
Current Mortality Analysis, C 3.152
Current News, D 301.89
Current News Defense Management Edition, D 2.19/5, D 301.89/8, D 301.89/11
Current News, Early Bird Edition, D 2.19
Current News, Special Edition, D 2.19/4
Current News Special Edition, Selected Statements, D 2.19/7, D 301.89/5-2
Current News, Supplemental Clips, D 2.19/3
Current News, Supplemental Special Edition, D 301.89/13
Current News, The Friday Review, D 2.19/8
Current Policy (series), S 1.71/4
Current Policy Digest, S 1.71/4-2
Current Population Reports, C 3.186, C 56.218
Current Population Reports, Household Economic Studies, C 3.186:P-70/2
Current Population Reports, Local Population Estimates, County Population Estimates, C 3.186/20-2
Current Population Research Reports, FS 2.22/61
Current Population Survey, C 3.224/12
Current Procurement News Digest, W 2.14/6
Current Programs and Operations of Housing and Home Finance Agency, Factual Summary for Public Interest Organizations, HH 1.21
Current Projects in Prevention, Control, and Treatment of Crime and Delinquency, FS 2.22/51

Current Projects on Economic and Social Implications of Scientific Research and Development, NS 1.23
Current Publications, Division of Medicine, HE 20.9309/2
Current Publications of the Women's Bureau, L 13.18
Current REA Publications, A 68.3
Current Releases of Non Theatrical Film, C 18.63
Current Report on Marshall Plan, Y 3.Ec 74/3:15
Current Research and Developments in Scientific Documentation, NS 1.15, NS 2.10
Current Research Project Grants, HE 20.3111
Current Retail Trade Reports, C 3.138
Current Review of Soviet Technical Press, C 41.94
Current Reviews of Economic and Social Problems in United Nations, S 1.81
Current Salary Schedules of Federal Officers and Employees Together with a History of Salary and Retirement Annuity Adjustments, Y 4.P 84/10-15
Current Shipping Data, C 25.7
Current Social Security Program Operations, FS 3.43
Current Statement of Loans by Years and Commodities, Y 3.C 73:12
Current Statistics of Relief in Rural and Town Areas, Y 3.W 89/2:25, SS 1.23
Current Trends, SE 1.33
Current Wage Developments, L 2.44
Curriculum Catalog, PM 1.46
Curriculum Guide Series, HE 19.108/3
Curriculum Handbook, D 305.6/3
Customer Assistance Handbook, D 7.6/20
Customer Care Technical Brief, E 6.11/2
Customer Supply Center Catalog, GS 2.23
Customs Administrative Circulars, W 49.10/6
Customs Administrative Orders, W 49.10/10
Customs Bulletin, T 1.11/3
Customs Bulletin and Decisions, T 17.6/3-4
Customs Bulletins (bound volumes), T 1.11/4, T 17.6/3-5
Customs Decisions, W 49.10/5
Customs Information Series, T 17.12
Customs Laboratory Bulletin, T 17.6/4
Customs Laws (general), T 17.6
Customs Marine Circular, W 49.10/9
Customs Performance Reports, T 17.25
Customs Publication (series), T 17.26
Customs Regulations, T 1.9/1
Customs Regulations of the United States, T 17.9
Customs Tariff and Regulations, W 1.7
Customs Today, T 17.16
Customs Trade Quarterly, T 17.16/2
Customs U.S.A., T 17.22
Cut Flowers, Production and Sales, A 88.47
Cutbacks Reported to Production Readjustment Committee, Pr 32.4834
Cutter Radar Project Newsletter, TD 5.38
Cutting Edge, Research & Development for Sustainable Army Installations, D 103.53/11
CWIHP (Cold War International History Project) Bulletin, SI 1.3/2
Cybernetics, Computers, and Automation Technology, PrEx 7.22/5
Cybernotes, J 1.14/23-2
Cyberspokesman, D 301.124
Cystic Fibrosis, HE 20.3320/2-2
CZ/SP (series), C 55.13:CZ/SP

D

DACAS [Drug Abuse Current Awareness System], HE 20.8209
Dahlgren Laboratory: Contract Reports, D 201.21/4
Daily Aerological Cross-Section Pole to Pole along Meridian 75 Degrees W for IGY Period, July 1957-December 1958, C 30.76
Daily Bulletin of Orders Affecting Postal Service, P 10.3
Daily Bulletin of Simultaneous Weather Reports with Synopses Indications, and Facts for Month of, W 42.8/1
Daily Congressional Notification of Grants and Contracts Awarded, NS 1.34
Daily Consular and Trade Reports, C 10.5, C 10.6, C 18.5
Daily Consular Reports, C 14.6
Daily Depository Shipping List, GP 3.16/3
Daily Digest–
    Communications Office, Department of Agriculture, A 21.14
    Federal Communications Commission, CC 1.54
Daily Digest of Reconstruction News, Y 3.C 83:95

Defense Administrative Support Center Handbooks, DASCH- (series), D 7.6/14
Defense Against Chemical Warfare, W 3.50/11
Defense Air Transportation Administrative Orders, C 1.8/2
Defense Atomic Support Agency: Technical Analysis Report DASA (series), D 5.14
Defense Billboard, D 2.9/2
Defense Bulletins, Y 3.C 831:107
Defense Business Innovation Research Program, D 1.73
Defense Cataloging and Standardization Act of 1952, Y 4.Ar 5/2-14
Defense Contract Audit Agency and Strategic Plan, D 1.46/5-2
Defense Contract Audit Agency Bulletin, D 1.46/6
Defense Contract Audit Agency Manual, DCAAM- (series), D 1.46/2
Defense Contract Audit Agency Pamphlets, DCAAP- (series), D 1.46
Defense Communications System Global, Automatic Voice Network Telephone Directory, D 5.111
Defense Environmental Restoration Program: Annual Report to Congress, D 1.97
Defense Food Delegations, A 1.81
Defense Housing Bulletin DH (series), HH 3.3/3
Defense Housing Construction Bulletins, FW 1.11
Defense Housing Financed by Public Funds, Summaries, Pr 32.4307
Defense Indicators, C 56.110, C 59.10, C 3.241
Defense Industry Bulletin, D 1.3/2
Defense Information Bulletins, FS 5.45
Defense Information School: Catalog, D 1.59
Defense Intelligence Agency Regulations (series), D 5.206/2
Defense Intelligence School: Academic Catalog, D 5.210
Defense Issues, D 2.15/4
Defense Logistics Information System (DLIS) Procedures Manual, D 7.6/19
Defense Management Education and Training Catalog, D 1.45
Defense Management Joint Course (series), D 101.94/2
Defense Management Journal, D 1.38/2
Defense Manpower Commission Staff Studies and Supporting Papers, Y 3.D 36:9
Defense Manpower Policy (series), Pr 34.208
Defense Manpower Policy Statement, Pr 33.1010
Defense Mapping Agency Aeronautical Charts and Publications Available from NOAA's National Ocean Service, C 55.418/3
Defense Mapping Agency Catalog of Maps, Charts, and Related Products, D 5.351
Defense Mapping Agency Catalog of Maps, Charts, and Related Products, Semi-Annual Bulletin Digest, Part 2, Hydrographic Products, D 5.351/2-3
Defense Mapping Agency Public Sale Nautical Charts and Publications, C 55.440, D 5.351/2
Defense Mobilization Orders, Pr 33.1006/2, Pr 34.206/2, Pr 34.706/4, PrEx 4.6/3
Defense of Children Series, L 5.41
Defense Procurement Circulars, D 1.13/3
Defense Production Act, Progress Reports, Y 4.D 36:P 94
Defense Production Notes, DP 1.10
Defense Production Record, DP 1.8
Defense Programs, DOE/DP- (series), E 1.15
Defense Property Disposal Service, D 7.6/13
Defense Reutilization and Marketing Service,, D 7.6/13
Defense Savings Staff News, T 1.108
Defense Standardization and Specification Program Policies, Procedures and Instructions, D 7.6/3:4120.3-M
Defense Standardization Program, Directory of Points of Interest, D 7.13/2
Defense Supply Agency Handbooks, DSAH-(series), D 7.6/7
Defense Supply Agency Manuals, DSAM-(series), D 7.6/8
Defense Supply Agency Regulations, DSAR-(series), D 7.6/6
Defense Supply Procurement Regulations, D 7.6/5
Defense Systems Management Review, D 1.53
Defense Trade News, S 1.141
Defense Training Leaflets, FS 5.130
Defense/80, D 2.15/3
Definitions and Abbreviations, TD 4.6:part 4
DEH Digest, D 103.122/3
Delegation of Authority, ES 3.6/11
Delinquency in the United States, J 32.16
Delinquency Prevention Reporter, HE 17.810
Deliveries of Fuel Oil and Kerosene in (date), E 3.40
Demand and Price Situation, A 88.9, A 93.9/2

Demand and Price Situation for Forest Products, A 13.76
Demand Deposits, Currency and Related Items, FR 1.47
Demobilization Circular Letters, Y 3.R 13/2:125
Democracy in Action (radio scripts), I 16.74, FS 5.13/1
   For Labor's Welfare, FS 5.13/4
   Public Health Series, FS 5.13/2
   Roof over America, FS 5.13/5
   Social Security, FS 5.13/3
Demographic Characteristics and Patterns of Drug Use of Clients Admitted to Drug Abuse Treatment Programs in Selected Sites, HE 20.8231, HE 20.8231/2
Demographic Profiles of the Airway Facilities Work Force, TD 4.65
Demographic Reports for Foreign Countries, P 96- (series), C 3.205/5
Demonstrated Reserve Base of Coal in the United States, E 3.11/7-6
Demonstration Notes, Experimental and Demonstration Manpower Programs, L 1.45/2
Demonstration Projects DP (series), TD 2.40
Density of Sea Water (D.W.), C 4.33
Dental Bulletin, W 44.21/12
Dental Care Charges, HE 22.24
Dental Caries Program Advisory Committee, HE 20.3001/2:D 43/2
Dental Caries Research, Fiscal Year (date), HE 20.3409
Dental Internship in U.S. Public Health Service Hospitals, FS 2.89/2
Dental Research in the United States, Canada and Great Britain, Fiscal Year (Date), HE 20.3402:D 43
Dental Research Institutes and Special Programs Advisory Committee, HE 20.3001/2:D 43/4
Dental Services for American Indians and Alaska Natives, HE 20.2659, HE 20.5309
Dental Services for Indians, Annual Reports, Fiscal Year, FS 2.86/3
Denver ARTC Center: Annual Report (Rocky Mountain Region), TD 4.43
Department and Foreign Service Series, S 1.69
Department Bulletins, A 1.3
Department Circulars, T 1.4/2, A 1.14/1, A 1.14/2, C 1.4/2, C 1.4/2
Department Circulars, Public Debt Series, T 1.4/3
Department of Army Chiefs and Executives [organization chart], D 101.36, D 102.23
Department of Army Supply Manual SM (series), D 101.16/2
Department of Commerce List of Currently Essential Activities, Department of Labor List of Currently Critical Occupation, L 7.65
Department of Commerce Trade Tips on the World Market, C 1.32/4
Department of Defense Bibliography of Logistics Studies and Related Documents, D 1.33/3
Department of Defense Cost Reduction Program, Annual Progress Report, D 1.38
Department of Defense Critical Technologies Plan for the Committees on Armed Service, United States Congress, D 1.91
Department of Defense Dictionary of Military and Associated Terms, D 5.12/3
Department of Defense Directives (series), D 1.6/8-2
Department of Defense Exchange Sale of Personal Property Available for Transfer to Federal Agencies, Admin, GS 2.11
Department of Defense Index of Specifications and Standards, D 7.14
Department of Defense Instruction (series), D 1.6/13
Department of Defense List of Excess Personal Property Available for Transfer to Federal Civil Agencies, GS 2.4/3-2
Department of Defense Military Commission Order, D 1.6/18
Department of Defense Program for Research and Development, D 1.81
Department of Defense Telephone Directory, D 1.7/1
Department of Energy Information: Weekly Announcements, E 1.7/2
Department of Everything Else, Highlights of Interior History, I 1.115
Department of Interior in Missouri River Basin Progress Report, I 1.79
Department of Labor Program Reports, L 1.57
Department of Obstetrics and Gynecology, D 1.67/4
Department of State Bulletin, S 1.3
Department of State Newsletter, S 1.118
Department of the Army Annual Financial Report, D 101.1/7
Department of the Army Historical Summary, D 114.15

Department of the Army Prime Contracts ($1 million and over) Placed with Industry, Non-Profit Organizations, Colleges, and Universities, D 101.22:715-4
Department of the Interior Acquisition Regulation, I 1.77/5
Department of Transportation Budget, Excerpts from the President's Budget, TD 1.34/4
Department of Transportation Budget Program: Analysis of Fiscal Year DOT Program by Policy and RD&D Management Objectives, DOT-OST- (series), TD 1.34/2
Department of Transportation National Plan for Navigation, TD 1.19
Department of Veterans Affairs, FY Budget in Brief and Budget Submission, VA 1.83/2
Department of Veterans Affairs Publications Index, VA 1.20
Department Orders, C 1.36
Department Store Credit, FR 1.34/3
Department Store Inventory Price Indexes, L 2.79
Department Store Merchandising Data, FR 1.24/5, FR 1.24/6
Department Store Sales, FR 1.24
Department Store Sales and Stocks, by Major Departments, FR 1.24/4
Department Store Sales, by Cities, FR 1.24/2
Department Store Sales, Preliminary Reports, FR 1.20
Department Store Stocks, FR 1.24/3
Department Store Trade, United States Departmental Sales Indexes, without Seasonal Adjustment, FR 1.24/9
Department Store Trade, United States Departmental Stock Indexes, Without Seasonal Adjustment, FR 1.24/10
Department Store Trade, United States Departmental Stock-Sales Ratios, FR 1.24/11
Department Store Trade, United States Distribution of Sales by Months, FR 1.24/7, FR 1.24/8
Departmental Circulars, Occupational Deferment Series, CS 1.38
Departmental Weekly Reports, HH 1.58
Dependent Children Series, L 5.7
Dependents Schools Manuals, D 1.6/2-2
Depository Invoices, GP 3.16
Depository Library Council Report to the Public Printer, GP 1.35
Depository Library Council to the Public Printer: Addresses, GP 1.36
Deposits of County Banks: Index Numbers of Total, Demand and Time Deposits Selected Groups of States, Specified Periods, A 77.14/3, A 93.9/7
Deposits, Reserves, and Borrowings of Member Banks, FR 1.11/4
Depot and Market Center Operations, D 106.7
Depot Information Bulletin, M 108.7
Depreciation Rate for Carriers by Inland and Coastal Waterways; Sub-Adv, IC 1 wat.13
Depreciation Rates for Equipment of Steam Railroad Companies, IC 1 ste.47
Depreciation Rates for Property of Carriers by Pipe Lines, IC 1 pip.8
Depreciation Rates of Carriers by Water Administrative, IC 1 wat.12
Depreciation Section Series Circulars, IC 1 acco.5
DER (series), FS 2.314/3
Desalting Plants Inventory Reports, I 1.87/4
Deschler's Precedents of the U.S. House of Representatives, X 94-2:H.doc.661
Deschler's Procedure, a Summary of the Modern Precedents and Practices of the U.S. House of Representatives, Y 1.2:D 45
Description of Output Indicators by Function for the Federal Government, L 2.133
Description of Professions Series, Pamphlets, L 7.31
Description of the Administration's Fiscal Year (date) Budget Recommendations under the Jurisdiction of the Committee on Ways and Means, Y 4.W 36:10-2
Description of U.S. Postal Stamp, Historical and Commemorative Issues (Junior Edition), P 4.11
Descriptions of Occupations, L 2.7
Descriptions of [various] Courses, EP 4.14
Descriptive Booklets and Folders on the Individual National Parks, Monuments, etc., I 29.6
Descriptive Report, ED 1.328/11
Design, I 70.22/3, I 29.72/2
Design and Evaluation Methods (series), S 18.52/5
Design, Art, and Architecture in Transportation, TD 1.47
Design Arts, Application Guidelines, Fiscal Year, NF 2.8/2-11

Direct Line to You, HE 3.68/5
Direct Loans Bulletin, ED 1.40/6
Direct Loans Newsletter, ED 1.40/5
Direction, the Navy Public Affairs Magazine, D 201.17
Directions, HE 20.8227
Directive Orders and Opinions, Pr 32.5107
Directives, Publications, and Reports Index, TD 5.21/6
Directorate of Electronic and Material Sciences FY
    Program, D 301.45/19-9
Directorate of Intelligence Publications (numbered),
    PrEx 3.10/7
Directorate of Mathematical and Information Sciences,
    Air Force Office of Scientific Research,
    Research Summaries, D 301.45/19-10
Directorate of Research Analysis, AFOSR/DRA
    (series), D 301.45/19-4
Directories–
    Aging Administration, HE 1.1014
    Agricultural Marketing Service, A 88.69
    Air Force Academy, D 305.20
    Alcohol, Drug Abuse, and Mental Health
        Administration, HE 20.8023
    Bureau of Head Start, HE 23.1113
    Children's Bureau, HE 23.1215
    Commissioner of Customers, T 17.15/2
    Department of Agriculture, A 1.89/3
    Department of Education, ED 1.30/2
    Department of Health and Human Services, HE
        1.28/2
    Department of the Air Force, D 301.104
    Department of the Army, D 101.120
    Department of Transportation, TD 1.9/4
    Department of State, S 1.21/2
    Directories, A 67.49
    Educational Research and Improvement Center, ED
        1.330
    Employment Standards Administration, L 36.15/2
    Executive Office for the United States Attorneys, J
        31.13
    Export Administration Bureau, C 63.10
    Export Development Bureau, C 57.121
    Family Support Administration, HE 25.10
    Federal Emergency Management Agency, FEM
        1.14/2
    Federal Grain Inspection Service, A 104.13
    Environmental Protection Agency, EP 1.102
    Federal Highway Administration, TD 2.68
    Fish and Wildlife Service, I 49.104
    Food and Drug Administration, HE 20.4003/2-2
    General Accounting Office, GA 1.28
    Government Printing Office, GP 3.36
    Grain Inspection, Packers and Stockyards
        Administration, A 113.11
    Health Care Delivery and Assistance Bureau, HE
        20.9112
    Health Care Financing Administration, HE 22.29/2
    Indian Health Service, HE 20.9412, HE 20.310
    Internal Revenue Service, T 22.54
    International Trade Administration, C 61.44
    Justice Department, J 1.89/3
    Latin American, Portuguese, and Spanish Division,
        LC 24.11
    Library of Congress, LC 1.40, LC 1.40/2
    Medicaid Bureau, HE 22.114
    National Bureau of Standards, C 13.69
    National Center for Educational Statistics, ED
        1.130
    National Center for Health Statistics, HE 20.6228
    National Drug Abuse Institute, HE 20.8233
    National Heart, Lung, and Blood Institute, HE
        20.3223
    National Highway Traffic Safety Administration,
        TD 8.35
    National Institute on Deafness and Other
        Communication Disorders, HE 20.3660
    National Institute on Drug Abuse, HE 20.3960
    National Institutes of Health, HE 20.3037/2
    National Library of Medicine, HE 20.3623, HE
        20.3868
    National Literacy Institute, Y 3.L 71:10
    National Oceanic and Atmospheric Administration,
        C 55.48
    National Park Service, I 29.126
    National Science Foundation, NS 1.50
    National Technical Information Service, C 51.19
    Nuclear Regulatory Commission, Y 3.N 88:52
    Pesticides and Toxic Substances Office, EP 5.24
    Rural Development, A 114.10
    Small Business Administration, SBA 1.13/4
    Substance Abuse and Mental Health Services
        Administration, HE 20.410
    Transportation Statistics Bureau, TD 12.10
    United States Holocaust Memorial Commission, Y
        3.H 74:11

    United States Institute of Peace, Y 3.P 31:10
    United States Postal Service, P 1.52
    Urban Mass Transportation Administrtion, TD 7.19
    Veterans Administration, VA 1.62/2
    Victims of Crim Office, J 34.10
    Women's Bureau, L 36.116
Directories of Labor Organizations, L 29.9
Director's Letters, FS 13.214
Director's Memorandum, T 70.17
Director's Newsletter, Chicago District, T 22.55
Directory and Planning Schedule of FSC Class and
    Area Assignments, D 7.13:1
Directory, Aviation Medical Examiners, TD 4.211
Directory, Business Research Advisory Council of the
    Bureau of Labor Statistics, L 2.83
Directory CAP [Community Actions Programs]
    Grantees, PrEx 10.2:C 73-3
Directory, Directors of State Agencies for Surplus
    Property and Regional Representatives,
    Division of Surplus Property Utilization, FS
    1.2:Su 7/2
Directory, Executive Orientation Courses in Automatic
    Data Processing, PrEx 2.12/2
Directory, Extramural Associates, HE 20.3037/5
Directory: Federal, State and Local Government
    Consumer Offices, HE 1.502:St 2
Directory for Reaching Minority Groups, L 23.2:M 66
Directory, Former Grants Associates, HE 20.3037/3
Directory, Local Law Enforcement Organizations
    Participating in Aviation Security, TD 4.809
Directory, Natural Resources Locations, A 106.14/2
Directory, Navy Civil Engineer Corps, D 209.17
Directory of Academic Procurement and Related
    Programs and Courses, GS 1.30
Directory of ADP Training, CS 1.65
Directory of Adult Day Care Centers, HE 22.202:Ad 9
Directory of Air Quality Monitoring Sites Active in
    (year), EP 1.2:Ai 7/5
Directory of Air Service Stations, W 87.9/2
Directory of Airfields, U.S. Army & Navy, C 31.126
Directory of Airports and Seaplane Bases, Airman's
    Guide Supplement, FAA 1.23/2
Directory of Albanian Officials, PrEx 3.10/7-23
Directory of American Agricultural Organizations, A
    37.6
Directory of Animal Disease Diagnostic Laboratories,
    A 101.2:D 63/2, A 101.13
Directory of Associate Members, National Conference
    on Weights and Measures, C 13.66/3
Directory of Automated Criminal Justice Information
    Systems, J 29.8/2
Directory of Awardee Names, E 1.35/2-7
Directory of Awards, BHPR Support, HE 20.9312
Directory of Awards, Directorate for Engineering, NS
    1.50/3
Directory of Awards, NS 1.50/2
Directory of Blood Establishments Registered Under
    Section 510 of the Food, Drug, and Cosmetic
    Act, HE 20.4002:B 62
Directory of Bulgarian Officials, PrEx 3.10/7-12
Directory of Bureau of Animal Industry, A 77.221
Directory of Cement Producers in (year), I 28.29/3
Directory of Chinese Officials and Organizations, PrEx
    3.10/7-13
Directory of Chinese Officials, Provincial Organiza-
    tions, PrEx 3.10/7-9
Directory of Coal Production Ownership, E 3.11/7-5
Directory of Commodities and Services, ES 3.10
Directory of Commodities and Services Exempted or
    Suspended from Price Control, ES 3.10/2
Directory of Community Education Projects, HE
    19.132/3, ED 1.20
Directory of Community High Blood Pressure Control
    Activities, HE 20.3002:B 62/13
Directory of Companies Filing Annual Reports with the
    Securities and Exchange Commission, SE
    1.27
Directory of Companies Producing Phosphate Rock in
    the United States, I 28.119/4
Directory of Companies Producing Salt in the United
    States, I 28.134/2
Directory of Compensation District Offices and Deputy
    Commissioners, L 26.2:D 62
Directory of Computer Softwear Applications, C 51.11/
    5
Directory of Computerized Data Files, C 51.11/2-2
Directory of Computerized Data Files and Related
    Software Available from Federal Agencies, C
    51.11/2
Directory of Computerized Data Files and Related
    Technical Reports, C 1.11/2-2
Directory of Computerized Software, C 51.11/2
Directory of Consumer Offices, HE 1.509/2

Directory of Contacts for International Educational,
    Cultural and Scientific Exchange Programs, S
    1.67/4
Directory of Contract Opportunities, Pr 32.4811
Directory of Cooperating Agencies, A 18.15
Directory of Counselor Educators, FS 5.255:25036, HE
    5.255:25036
Directory of Criminal Justice Information Sources, J
    28.20
Directory of Criminal Justice Information Sources, J
    26.2:In 3, J 28.20
Directory of Czechoslovak Officials, A Reference Aid,
    PrEx 3.10/7-10
Directory of DCAA Offices, D 1.46/4
Directory of DoC Staff Memberships on Outside
    Standards Committees, C 13.69/3
Directory of Employees for the International Trade
    Administration, C 61.32
Directory of Energy Data Collection Forms, E 3.45
Directory of Energy Information Administration Model
    Abstracts, E 3.48
Directory of Environmental Life Scientists, 1974, D
    103.43:1105-2-3
Directory of EPA, State, and Local Environmental
    Activities, EP 1.23/5:600/4-75-001
Directory of ERIC Resource Collection, ED 1.330/2
Directory of Facilities Obligated to Provide
    Uncompensated Services by State and City,
    HE 20.9209
Directory of Federal Agencies and Departments in
    States, Y 3.N 21/9:9
Directory of Federal and State Business Assistance, C
    51.19/2
Directory of Federal and State Departments and
    Agencies, Pr 32.207
Directory of Federal Consumer Offices, HE 1.509/2
Directory of Federal Coordinative Groups for Toxic
    Substances, EP 1.79/2
Directory of Federally Insured Credit Unions, NCU
    1.16
Directory of Federal Laboratory and Technology
    Resources, a Guide to Services, Facilities,
    and Expertise, C 51.19/2-2
Directory of Federal Regional Structure, GS 4.119
Directory of Federal Technology Transfer, PrEx 23.10
Directory of Federal Statistical Data Files, C 51.15
Directory of Field Contacts for the Coordination of the
    Use of Radio Frequencies, CC 1.2/2, CC 1.2/
    10
Directory Former Grants Associates, HE 20.3037/3
Directory of Grants, Awards, and Loans, HE 20.6111,
    HE 20.6612
Directory of Halfway Houses and Community
    Residences for the Mentally Ill, HE 20.8129
Directory of Halfway Houses for the Mentally Ill and
    Alcoholics, HE 20.2402:H 13
Directory of Important Labor Areas, L 7.2:D 62/9
Directory of Indian Service Units, I 20.38
Directory of Information Resources in Agriculture and
    Biology, A 17.2:D 62
Directory of Information Resources in the United States,
    LC 1.31
Directory of Information Systems, TD 1.36
Directory of Institutions for Mentally Disordered
    Offenders, HE 20.2402:Of 2/2
Directory of International Grants and Fellowships in
    the Health Sciences, HE 20.3717
Directory of International Mail, P 1.10/5
Directory of International Trade Union Organizations,
    L 29.9/2
Directory of Iranian Officials, PrEx 3.10/7-22
Directory of Iraqi Officials, PrEx 3.10/7-3
Directory of Japanese Technical Reports, C 51.19/3
Directory of Labor Organizations in [various
    countries], L 2.72/4
Directory of Labor Research Advisory Council to the
    Bureau of Labor Statistics, L 2.83/2
Directory of Law Enforcement and Criminal Justice
    Associations and Research Centers, C
    13.10:480-20
Directory of Library Networks and Cooperative Library
    Organizations, ED 1.129
Directory of Local Employment Security Offices, L
    37.18, L 1.59
Directory of Local Health and Mental Health Units, HE
    20.2015
Directory of Local Health Units, FS 2.77
Directory [of] Market News Broadcasts, A 66.38
Directory of Meat and Poultry Inspection Program
    Establishments, Circuits and Officials, A
    88.16/20
Directory of Medicare Providers and Suppliers of
    Services, HE 3.51/5

Division of Legislative Analysis Highlights, HE 20.3051

Division of Long-Term Care: Annual Report, HE 20.6001/4

Division of Nuclear Power: Monthly Report, T 3.T 25:48-2

Division of Research Grants: Dental Study Section, HE 20.3001/2:D 43/3

Division of Research Service: Annual Report, HE 20.3035

Division of Social Sciences Quarterly Grant List, NS 1.10/5

Division of Stores, Circular Advertisements of Sale, GP 1.8

Division of Telegrams and Reports for Benefit of Commerce and Agriculture, Circular, W 42.21

Division of Water Control Planning: Annual Report, Y 3.T 25:1-12

Division of Water Control Planning: Reports, Y 3.T 25:38

Division Officer's Planning Guide, D 208.6/3-2

Divisional Memorandum, Y 3.F 31/11:28

Divorce Laws as of (date), L 13.6/4, L 36.113/2

Dixie Digest, D 214.23/2

DLAPS Publications, D 7.41

DLMS Handbooks (series), L 1.7/2-2

DLMS Manual (series), L 1.7/2-3

DLSC Line, D 7.33/3

DM&S ADP Plan, VA 1.77/2

DMI Analytic Studies (series), HE 20.6109/2

DMI Health Manpower Information Exchange Reports, HE 20.6109

DMI Reports, HE 20.3114

DMRE (series), FS 2.314

DMS, C 40.6/6

DMS Orders, C 41.6/4-2

DNFSB Site Representatives Weekly Activities Reports, Y 3.D 36/3:11

DNFSB Staff Issue Reports, Y 3.D 36/3:12

Docket of Cases Pending in Court of Claims, General Jurisdiction, Ju 3.12

Docket of Supreme Court, Ju 6.10

Docket Sheet, Ju 6.12

Dockets [Circuit Court of Appeals], FT 1.23

Dockets, Preliminary, C 31.211/2

Doctrine Notes, D 207.416

Document (series), T 22.2/15

Document Catalog, GP 3.6

Document Index, GP 3.7

Document Locator, Cross Reference Index to Government Reports, T 1.46

Document Retrieval Subject Index, A 67.38

Documents and State Papers, S 1.73

Documents Illustrative of the Formation of the Union of the American States, Y 1.69-1:H doc. 398

Documents on Disarmament, AC 1.11/2, S 1.117

Documents on German Policy 1918-45, S 1.82

Documents Retrieval Index, J 28.22

DoD Activity Address Directory (microfiche edition), D 7.6/12

DoD Aeronautical Chart Updating Manual (CHUM), D 5.208

DoD Computer Institute: Course Information, D 5.414/3

DoD Computer Institute: NDU-DODCI Course Catalog, D 5.414/2

DoD Directives System Quarterly Index, D 1.6/8

DoD Directory of Contract Administration Services Components, D 1.6/12

DoD Document Identifiers, D 1.72

DoD Flight Information Publication (Terminal)–

High Altitude Instrument Approach Procedures, D 5.318/2

Low Altitude Approach Procedures, United States Military Aviation Notice, D 5.318/3

DOD Inspector General Semiannual Report to Congress, D 1.1/9

DOD Interchangeability and Substitutability (I&S), Parts I & II, D 7.36

DoD Issuances and Directive

DOD Medical Catalog, D 7.37

DoD Pamphlets, D 2.14

DoDDS Pamphlets (series), D 1.75

DOE Feature, NF- (series), E 1.67/2

DOE Petroleum Demand Watch, E 1.7/3

DOE Information Bridge, E 1.137

DOE Reports Bibliographic Database, E 1.17/2

DOE This Month, E 1.54

DOE Translation List, E 1.13/3

DOE/AF- (series), E 1.80

DOE/BU (series), E 1.122

DOE/CA- (series), E 1.33/2

DOE/CE- (series), E 1.89

DOE/CP (series), E 1.101

DOE/EE (series), E 1.120

DOE/EH (series), E 1.20/3

DOE/EIA/CR- (series), E 3.26/7

DOE/EM (series), E 1.90/3

DOE/EP- (series), E 1.90

DOE/ERA- (series), E 4.10

DOE/ES (series), E 1.102

DOE/FE (series), E 1.84

DOE/FERC- (series), E 2.12

DOE/FM (series), E 1.125

DOE/HR (series), E 1.121

DOE/IA (series), E 1.82

DOE/GC- (series), E 1.71

DOE/MA- (series), E 1.35/2

DOE-NE-STD (Nuclear Safety Policy Standards) (series), E 1.68/5

DOE/NP (series), E 1.68/4

DOE/NS (series), E 1.68/3

DOE/OC, E 1.116

DOE/OR- (series), E 1.104

DOE/PA- (series), E 1.33/3

DOE/PE (Policy and Evaluation) (series), E 1.81

DOE/PO (series), E 1.118

DOE/RG (series), E 4.11

DOE/RL (series), E 1.123

DOE/RW- (series), E 1.68/2

DOE/SA (series), E 1.117

DOE/SR- (series), E 1.77

DOE/US- (series), E 1.94

Doing Business With [Various Countries], C 42.16

Domestic Air Carrier Operation Statistics, CA 1.22, C 31.112

Domestic Air Carriers (trunk lines), Comparative Statement of Balance Sheet Data, C 31.239

Domestic Air Service Instructions, P 1.31/7:31/3

Domestic Airnews, C 23.9

Domestic and International Business News to Use for Trade Association Periodicals, C 1.32/6

Domestic and International Facilitation Program, TD 1.18

Domestic Cannabis Eradication/Suppression Program, J 24.25

Domestic Coinage Executed During (month), T 28.12

Domestic Commerce, C 1.25

Domestic Commerce News Letter, C 18.32/2

Domestic Commerce Series, C 18.28, C 18.271

Domestic Council Review Group on Regulatory Reform, Pr 38.8:R 26

Domestic Dairy Market Review, A 82.38

Domestic Economic Developments, Monthly Business Indicators, C 18.285/2

Domestic Economic Developments, Weekly Business Indicators, C 18.285

Domestic Fixed Satellite Services, CC 1.47/4

Domestic Helicopter Service, Certificated Air-Mail Carriers, C 31.229/4

Domestic Jet Trends, CAB 1.29, C 31.271

Domestic Mail Manual, P 1.12/11

Domestic Oceanborne and Great Lakes Commerce of the United States, C 39.222

Domestic Programs Fact Book, AA 1.9/2

Domestic Public Land Mobile Radio Service [action], Public Notices, CC 1.36/5

Domestic Pumps, Water Systems, and Windmills, Shipments of, C 3.77

Domestic Scheduled Air Line Operation Statistics, C 23.20

Domestic Trade Digest, C 18.283

Domestic Uranium Mining and Milling Industry, (year) Viability Assessment, E 3.46/3

Domestic Violence and Stalking, J 35.21

Domestic Violence Information Series, HE 23.1015

Domestic Violence Monograph Series, HE 23.1015/2

Domestic Water Softening Apparatus, Shipments of, C 3.78

Domestic Waterborne Trade of the United States, C 39.222, TD 11.19

Don't Gamble with Your Health (series), FS 2.50/2

Door Series, C 18.65

Doorway to Legal News, Y 3.At 7:46

DOT Awards to Academic Institutions, TD 10.11/2

DOT Employment Facts, TD 1.46

DOT-FTAMA, TD 7.17/2

DOT News, TD 1.31

DOT Talk, TD 1.25/3

DOT TSC (series), TD 4.32/25

DOT TST- (series), TD 1.20

DOT/OPS (series), TD 1.20/5

DOT-RSPD-DPB (series), TD 1.20/7

DOT-T (series), TD 1.20/10

Dotted Line, TD 1.59

DOT-TSC-OST- (series), TD 1.20/2

DOT-TSC-UMTA- (series), TD 7.17

DOT/UT- (series), TD 7.18

Double-Level Metallization: Annual Report, C 13.58/6

Down of the Farm, Pr 32.4263

Downdraft, I 20.53

DP Pamphlets, FS 2.87

DPDS DEMIL Reference Fiche, D 7.27

DPS Regulations (numbered), C 41.6/2-2

Draft Environmental Impact Statements–

Bureau of Indian Affairs, I 20.56/2

Bureau of Veterinary Medicine, HE 20.4409

Drug Enforcement Administration, J 24.23

Environmental Protection Agency, EP 1.57/4

Federal Energy Regulatory Commission, FERC/DEIS- (series), E 2.11/2

Land Management Bureau, I 53.19

National Oceanic and Atmospheric Administration, C 55.34

National Park Service, I 29.81/2

Soil Conservation Service, A 57.65

Draft Environmental Statements

Forest Service, A 13.92/2

Land Management Bureau, I 53.19

National Park Service, I 29.81/2

Draft Environmental Impact Statements and Related Materials, A 13.92/2

Draft Environmental Studies Plan, I 72.12/8

Draft Environmental Status Report, EP 1.57/6

Draft Information Series, Y 3.Se 4:25

Draft Regulatory Guide, DG-, Y 3.N 88:6-3

Drainage Basin Committee Reports, Y 3.N 21/12:12

Drainage of Agricultural Lands (by States), C 3.37/25

Drawings Accompanying Specifications, I 27.9, I 19.17/7

DRG Annual Report, HE 20.3048

DRG Digital Raster Graphic (series), I 19.128

DRG Newsletter, HE 20.3022

DRG Peer Review Trends, HE 20.3045/2

DRH Bulletin, Radiological Health, HE 20.4612

DRH Radiological Health Bulletin, HE 20.4612

Drill Books, Signal Books and Code Lists, N 17.12/1

Drill Regulations, W 3.16

Drill Regulations, Manuals, and Instructions for Army, W 3.16/1

Driven-In Receipts of Livestock, A 66.28

Driver, Automotive Magazine of the Air Force, D 301.72

Driver Education Evaluation Program (Deep) Study, Report to Congress, TD 8.12/5

Driver License Administration Requirements and Fees, TD 2.61

Driver Licensing Laws Annotated, TD 8.5/3

DRMS World, D 7.6/21

Dropout Rates in the United States, ED 1.329

Drug Abuse Among American School Students, HE 20.8222

Drug Abuse and Drug Abuse Research, HE 20.8220/2

Drug Abuse Prevention Materials for Schools, PrEx 13.2:D 84

Drug Abuse Prevention Monograph Series, HE 20.8228

Drug Abuse Prevention Report, HE 20.8010:33

Drug Abuse Research and Development, Federally Supported Drug Abuse and Tobacco Research and Development, Fiscal Year (date), HE 20.8220

Drug Abuse Services Research Series, HE 20.8235

Drug Abuse Warning Network Series, HE 20.416/3

Drug and Devices, DDNJ- (series), FS 13.108

Drug Dependence, HE 20.2416

Drug Enforcement, J 24.3/2

Drug Formulary, VA 1.73

Drug Index, Formulary, VA 1.73/2

Drug Trafficking in the United States, J 24.29

Drug Use Among American High School Students, HE 20.8219

Drugs and Jail Inmates, J 29.13/3

Dry Cargo Service and Area Report, United States Dry Cargo Shipping Companies by Ships Owned And/or Chartered Type of Service and Area Operated, C 39.213

Dry Casein, Estimated Production and Stocks, United States, A 36.166

Dry Goods Merchants' World News Letter, C 18.66

Dry Land Agriculture Division, Weekly Station Reports, A 77.508

Dry Milk Reports, A 36.180

Dry-Land Agriculture, A 19.35

DSA Poster Series, D 7.19

DSFA Delegations DEL (series), I 57.6/3

DSMC in Review: A Quality Journey, D 1.59/2-3

DSMC Technical Report, D 1.59/2-2

DTA Delegations, IC 1 def.6/3

DTIC Digest, D 10.11

DTIC Review, D 10.11/2

DTICH (series), D 10.7/2

Educational Television Facilities Program: Public Notices, FS 1.24/2

Edwin A. Link Lecture Series, SI 1.21

Eel River Charts, W 7.13/2

EEO Fact Sheet from Office of the Administrator, A 67.41

EEO for State and Local Governments (series), CS 1.76/2

EEO Information on Equal Opportunity for State and Local Governments, PM 1.18/2

EEO Newsletter, A 105.51

EEO Semiannual Report to the Congress, Office of Inspector General, Y 3.Eq 2:1-2

EEO Spotlight, CS 1.76

EEOC Reports, Clearinghouse Service for Business Newsletters and Periodicals, Y 3.Eq 2:7-2

EFC Formula Book, The Expected Family Contribution for Federal Student Aid, ED 1.45/5

EFF HOT Topics, Y 3.L71:18

Effect of Income Tax Law Revision on Electric Taxes and Income, FP 1.23

Effective Programs Monograph, J 26.30/2

Effects on Selected Communities of War Contract Cutbacks and Cancellations [confidential], L 2.20

EG (series), NAS 1.19/4

Egg and Poultry Markets Review, A 82.39

Egg Marketing Facts, A 88.53

Egg Marketing Guide, A 88.26/5

Egg Products, A 105.12/2

Egg Products, Liquid, Frozen, Solids Production, A 92.9/4

Egg Standardization Leaflets, A 36.24

Eggs, Chickens and Turkeys, A 92.9/16, A 105.12/3

EIA Data Index, an Abstract Journal, E 3.27/5

EIA Directory of Electronic Products, E 3.27/7

EIA Personal Computer Products, International Coal Statistics Database, E 3.11/7-11

EIA Publications Directory, E 3.27

EIA Publications, New Releases, E 3.27/4

EIRS Bulletin, D 103.24/19

EIS Directory, HE 20.7025

Eisenhower Consortium Bulletins, A 13.69/11

Elderly News Updates, HH 1.104

Election Case Law, Y 3.El 2/3:12

Election Directory, Y 3.El 2/3:14

Election Law Guidebook, 1974, Summary of Federal and State Laws Regulating Nomination and Election of United States Senators, Revised to January 1, 1974, Y 1.93-2:S.doc. 84

Election Law Updates, Y 3.El 2/3:9-2

Elections, C 3.153

Election Statistics, Y 1.2/10

Elective Course Readings (series), D 5.415/9

Electric and Hybrid Vehicle Program, Annual Report to Congress, E 1.45/2

Electric and Hybrid Vehicle Program, EHV/quarterly Report, E 1.45

Electric Energy and Peak Load Data, E 3.11/17-9

Electric Farming News Exchange of Inter- industry Farm Electric Utilization Council, A 68.19

Electric Home and Farm Authority Publications, Y 3.T 25:9

Electric Light and Power Plants, C 3.38/2

Electric Locomotives (mining and industrial), C 3.81

Electric Plant Cost and Power Production Expenses, E 3.17/4-2

Electric Power Annual, E 3.11/17-10

Electric Power Engineering, E 1.99

Electric Power Monthly, E 3.11/17-8

Electric Power Quarterly, E 3.11/17-11

Electric Power Statistics, FP 1.24, FP 1.27, E 3.18

Electric Sales and Revenue, E 3.22

Electric Trade in the United States, E 3.11/17-12

Electrical and Radio World Trade News, C 18.67

Electrical Commission, 1884, S 5.17

Electrical Communications [abstracts], C 41.66/4

Electrical Goods, C 3.82

Electrical Industrial Trucks and Tractors, C 3.80

Electrical Standards, C 18.30

Electricity [abstracts], C 41.66

Electricity Sales Statistics, Y 3.T 25:13

Electricity Sales Statistics, Distribution of Electricity at TVA Wholesale and Retail Rates, Y 3.T 25:13-2

Electricity Sales Statistics: Rate of Initial Service at TVA Rates and Wholesale Purchases from TVA, Y 3.T 25:13-2

Electro-Economy Supplements, A 68.11

Electromagnetic Meteorology, Current Awareness Service, C 13.54

Electronic Computer Program Library Memorandum, C 37.20

Electronic Equipment Modification, C 31.161

Electronic Forms, D 101.129/4

Electronic Information Products Available by Special Order, GP 3.22/5

Electronic Products–

Aging Administration, HE 1.1018

Agriculture Department, A 1.142

Agricultural Research Service, A 77.40

Air Force Department, D 301.118

Air Quality Planning and Standards Office, EP 4.28

Animal and Plant Health Inspection Service, A 101.32

Appalachian Regional Commission, Y 3.Ap 4/2:16

Armed Forces Information Services, D 2.20

Army Department, D 101.121/2, D 101.129/6

Aviation Medicine Office, TD 4.214

Bonneville Power Administration, E 5.24

Census Bureau, C 3.275

Center for Environmental Health, HE 20.7512

Center for Prevention Services, HE 20.7319

Centers for Disease Control, HE 20.7039/2

Chief of Naval Reserve, D 207.310

Coast Guard, TD 5.67

Commerce Department, C 1.89

Comptroller of the Currency, T 12.19

Congress, Y 1.5

Consolidated Farm Service, A 112.21

Cooperative State Research Service, A 94.22

Defense Department, D 1.95

Defense Logistics Agency, D 7.45

Defense Mapping Agency, D 5.360

Defense Nuclear Facilities Safety Board, Y 3.D 36/3:13

Descriptive Cataloging Division, LC 9.17

Economic Analysis Bureau, C 59.26

Education Department, ED 1.83

Educational Research and Improvement Center, ED 1.334/2

Employment and Training Administration, L 37.25

Energy Department, E 1.111

Environmental Protection Agency, EP 1.104

Executive Office of the President, PrEx 1.21

Export Administration Bureau, C 63.25

Farmer Cooperative Service, A 88.64

Federal Aviation Administration, TD 4.75, TD 4.76

Federal Bureau of Investigation, J 1.14/23

Federal Communications Commission, CC 1.57

Federal Crop Insurance Corporation, A 62.18

Federal Deposit Insurance Corporation, Y 3.F 31/8:32

Federal Emergency Management Agency, FEM 1.27

Federal Highway Administration, TD 2.73

Federal Judicial Center, JU 13.18

Federal Register Office, AE 2.115

Federal Supply and Services Office, GS 2.26

Federal Trade Commission, FT 1.33

Financial Management Service, T 63.130

Fish and Wildlife Service, I 49.108, I 49.113

Food Safety and Inspection Service, A 110.20

Forest Service, A 13.140

General Services Administration, GS 1.35

Geological Survey, I 19.120

Health and Human Services Department, HE 1.60

Health Care Financing Administration, HE 22.44

Housing and Urban Development Department, HH 1.114

Immigration and Naturalization Service, J 21.24

Interior Department, I 1.114

International Development Agency, S 18.65

International Trade Administration, C 61.47

Juvenile Justice and Delinquence Prevention Office, J 32.23

Justice Department, J 1.100

Labor Department, L 1.89

Labor Statistics Bureau, L 2.134

Library of Congress, LC 1.53, LC 1.54

Marine Corps, D 214.34

Military History Center, D 114.21

Military Sealift Command, D 216.11

Mineral Management Service, I 72.19

Multi-Family Housing Office, HH 13.15

National Aeronautics and Space Administration, NAS 1.86

National Agricultural Library, A 17.31

National Agricultural Statistics Service, A 92.51

National Archives and Records Administration, AE 1.127

National Archives and Records Administration, AE 1.127

National Center for Health Statistics, HE 20.6231

National Climatic Center, C 55.281/2-2

National Endowment for the Arts, NF 2.17

National Highway Trafety Setety Administration, TD 8.64

National Institute for Occupational Safety and Health, HE 20.7129

National Institute of Justice, J 28.31

National Institute of Standards and Technology, C 13.79

National Institute on Deafness and Other Communication Disorders, HE 20.3667

National Institutes of Health, HE 20.3064

National Library of Medicine, HE 20.3624/3

National Oceanic and Atmospheric Administration, C 55.54

National Science Foundation, NS 1.60

National Transportation Safety Board, TD 1.132

Naval Data Automation Command, D 221.18

Naval Doctrine Command, D 207.415

Naval Oceanographic Office, D 203.34

Naval Sea Systems Command, D 211.29

Naval Training and Education Command, D 207.217

Navy Department, D 201.40

Nuclear Regulatory Commission, Y 3.N 88:61

Occupational Safety and Health Review Commission, Y 3.OC 1:11

Office of Science and Technology Policy, PrEx 23.12

Office of the President, Pr 42.13

Office of the Vice President, PrVp 42.17

Patent and Trademark Office, C 21.32

Personnel Management Office, PM 1.59

President George H. Bush, Pr 43.13

Prisons Bureau, J 16.33

Processing Department, LC 30.33

Public Documents Division, GP 3.38

Railroad Retirement Board, RR 1.17

Reclamation Bureau, I 27.81

Smithsonian Institution, SI 1.47

Social Security Administration, SSA 1.27

Soil Conservation Service, A 57.76

State Department, S 1.142

Transportation Department, TD 1.56

Transportation Statistics Bureau, TD 12.17

Treasury Department, T 1.66

U.S. Information Agency, IA 1.32/2

United States Postal Service, P 1.59

Veterans Affairs Department, VA 1.95

Vice President Richard Cheney, PrVP 43.17

Violence Against Women Office, J 35.19

Wage and Hour Division, L 36.214

Electronic Products, A 67.50

Electronic Products, Y 3.P 38/2:13

Electronic Research Directorate Technical Memorandum ERD-CRRK-TM (series), D 301.45/12

Electronics and Electrical Engineering, PrEx 7.22/6

Electronics Engineering Information Bulletin, TD 5.3/3

Electronics Engineering Reports, T 47.42

Electronics Information Bulletin, D 201.3/2

Electrotechnology, C 51.9/22, C 51.17/2

Electrotechnology Newsletter, Y 3.T 25:63

Elementary Books , LC 2.6

Elementary Education Circulars, I 16.19

Elementary School Personnel, FS 5.84:El 2, HE 5.84:El 2

Elementary Teacher Education Program, Feasibility Studies, HE 5.87

Elements of Value of Property, Class I Switching and Terminal Companies Used in Common Carrier Service, IC 1 val.11, IC 1 val.12

Elevations and Distances, I 19.2:El 3/2

Elimination of Waste Series, C 1.13

EM Progress, E 1.90/6

EM State Fact Sheets, E 1.90/7

Emergency Bulletins, I 16.52

Emergency Conservation Program, Fiscal Year Statistical Summary, A 112.1/2

Emergency Conservation Program, Fiscal Year Statistical Summary, A 113.1/2

Emergency Conservation Program, Fiscal Year Summary, A 82.93

Emergency Conservation Work Bulletins, L 1.11

Emergency Conservation Work, Project Training Publications, I 29.28

Emergency Fleet News, SB 2.6

Emergency Health Series, HE 20.2013

Emergency Health Services Digest, HE 20.13/2

Emergency Management, FEM 1.16

Emergency Management Institute, Resident Training Programs, FEM 1.17/2

Emergency Management Institute, Schedule of Courses, FEM 1.17/2

Emergency Management of National Economy, D 1.27

Emergency Manual Guides, FS 1.6/4

Emergency Officers, Army List and Directory, W 3.10/2

Emergency Operations Orders, Pr 34.706/6, PrEx 4.6/6

Emergency Parent Education Bulletins, Y 3.F 31/5:16

Enforcement Actions, Significant Actions Resolved, Y 3.N 88:47

Enforcement and Procedure Regulations, ES 3.6/6

Enforcement Report of Postal Inspection Service, Fraud, Obscenity, Extortion, P 1.29/2

Enforcement Story, HE 20.4039/2

Enforcing the ADA, A Status Report from the Department of Justice, J 1.106

Engine and Propeller Specifications, C 31.120/3, FAA 1.29/2

Engineer, D 103.115

Engineer Center Team Minutes, D 103.112/4

Engineer Intelligence Notes, D 103.29

Engineer Historical Studies, D 103.43/2

Engineer Reports, D 103.22

Engineer Research and Development Laboratories Reports, D 103.25

Engineer School Library Bulletin, D 103.107

Engineer School Special Text, ST (series), D 103.109

Engineered Performance Standards for Real Property Maintenance Activities, D 1.6/7

Engineering, C 51.17/4, E 1.99

Engineering and Equipment, PrEx 7.22/7

Engineering and Instrumentation, C 13.22

Engineering Bits and Fax, C 55.116

Engineering Bulletin, EP 1.3/3

Engineering Bulletins–
    Federal Housing Administration, NHA 2.14, HH 2.9
    Fuel Administration, Y 3.F 95:8
    Rural Electrification Administration, Y 3.R 88:18

Engineering Charts, T 47.29

Engineering Command Report, ENCR (series), D 116.14

Engineering Division Publications, A 57.28

Engineering Enrollments and Degrees, FS 5.254:54006, HE 5.254:54006

Engineering for Youth [abstracts], C 41.57

Engineering Handbook Series, P 1.31/2

Engineering Handbooks, EHS- (series), C 55.108/5

Engineering Laboratory Research, Y 3.T 25:35

Engineering Manual, Civil Works Construction, D 103.14

Engineering Manual for Civil Works, W 7.35

Engineering Manual for Emergency Construction, D 103.21

Engineering Manual for Military Construction, D 103.9

Engineering Manual for War Department Construction, W 7.36

Engineering Manual, Military Construction, M 110.13

Engineering Memorandum, A 68.17

Engineering Monographs, I 27.34

Engineering Performance Standards, D 209.14

Engineering Postdoctoral Research Associateship Program, C 13.65/2

Engineering Publications, A 57.12

Engineering Reports, D 111.9/2

Engineering Research Centers: Program Announce-ment, NS 1.47/2

Engineering Technical Information System: EM- (series), A 13.84/2

Engineering Technical Information System: Technical Reports, A 13.84

Engineers Digest, TD 5.17

Engineers Update, D 103.69

English Abstracts of Selected Articles from Soviet Bloc and Mainland China Technical Journals, C 41.84

English Language Proficiency Study (series), ED 1.43

English Teaching Forum, IA 1.17, ICA 1.11, S 21.15

English Teaching Study Units, IA 1.17/3

English-French Glossary, S 1.2:En 3

Enhanced UTCS Software Operator's Manual, Implementation Package (series), TD 2.36

Enjoy Outdoors America Bulletin, I 1.3/3

Enrollment for Masters and Higher Degrees, Fall (year), Final Report, FS 5.254:54019, HE 5.254:54019

Enrollment Information Guide and Plan Comparison Chart, PM 1.8/4, PM 1.8/10
    CSRS/FERS Annuitants, PM 1.8/10
    Federal Civilian Employees, PM 1.8/6
    Federal Civilian Employees in Positions Outside the Continental U.S., PM 1.8/8
    Former Spouses Enrolled in the Federal Employees Health Benefits Program, PM 1.8/7
    Individuals Receiving Compensation from the Office of Workers Compensation Programs, PM 1.8/13
    Open Season, PM 1.8/12
    Retirement Systems Participating in the Federal Employees Health Benefits Program, PM 1.8/4
    U.S. Postal Service Employees, PM 1.8/5

Enrollment Information Guide and Plan Comparison Chart, (Open Season) for Individuals Eligible for Temporary Continuation of Coverage and . . ., PM 1.8/11

Enrollments and Programs in Noncollegiate Postsecondary Schools, HE 19.337/2

Enroute Area Charts (U.S.) Low Altitude, C 55.416/14, C 55.416/15-2

Enroute Change Notice, DoD Flip Enroute VFR Supplement United States, D 5.318/8-2

Enroute High Altitude Charts (Alaska), C 55.416/16-2

Enroute High Altitude Planning Charts (U.S.), C 55.416/17

Enroute High and Low Altitude, U.S., C 55.416/16, D 5.318/4

Enroute IFR Air Traffic Survey, C 31.165, FAA 3.11

Enroute IFR Air Traffic Survey, Peak Day, TD 4.19/3

Enroute IFR Peak Day Charts, Fiscal Year, FAA 3.11/3

Enroute IFR-Supplement, United States, D 5.318/7

Enroute Low Altitude Charts (Alaska), C 55.416/15

Enterovirus Surveillance, HE 20.7011/35

Enterprise, SBA 1.25

Enterprise Statistics, C 3.226, C 56.228

Enterprise Statistics, Preliminary Reports, C 3.230/2

Entomological Control Series, A 77.323

Entomology and Plant Quarantine Bureau, Notices of Quarantine, A 77.317

Entomology Current Literature, A 9.14, A 56.10, A 17.14

Entomology Technical Series, A 56.11

Entrez References, HE 20.3624

Entrez: Document Retrieval System, HE 20.3624

Entrez: Sequences, HE 20.3624

Environment, DOE/EV (series), E 1.16

Environment Midwest, EP 1.28/7

Environment Midwest, Together, EP 1.28/6

Environment News, EP 1.7/4

Environment Series, SI 12.10

Environmental Action PLA Reports (numbered), TD 2.44

Environmental Analysis Records (series) [various areas], I 53.19/3

Environmental and Water Quality Operational Studies, D 103.24/15

Environmental Assessment, DOE/EA (series), E 1.20/2, E 4.9

Environmental Assessment Notebook Series, TD 1.8/2

Environmental Assessment of the Alaskan Continental Shelf, C 55.622/2

Environmental Assessment of the Alaskan Continental Shelf, Principal Investigator's Reports, C 55.622

Environmental Assessment of the Alaskan Continental Shelf [various publications], C 55.622/3

Environmental Assessment (series), I 29.79/5

Environmental Compliance Assessment System (ECAS) Annual Report, D 101.130

Environmental Data Bulletin, C 55.203

Environmental Data Service, C 55.222

Environmental Development Plan, DOE/EDP-(series), E 1.36

Environmental Development Plan, Oil Shale, ER 1.33

Environmental Effects of Dredging, D 103.24/16

Environmental Fact Sheet: Environmental Protection Agency, EP 1.42/2

Environmental Factors on Coastal and Estaurine Waters, Bibliographic Series, I 67.14/2

Environmental Facts, EP 1.42

Environmental Harmony at (various places), D 103.70

Environmental Health Effects Research, 600/1-(series), EP 1.23/4

Environmental Health Factors, Nursing Homes, FS 2.300/2

Environmental Health Perspectives, Experimental Issues, HE 20.3559

Environmental Health Series, FS 2.300, HE 20.1011

Environmental Health Service Series on Community Organization Techniques, HE 20.1811

Environmental History Series, D 103.43/2-2

Environmental Hotline, EP 1.95

Environmental Impact Statements–
    Army Department, D 101.82
    Bureau of Mines, I 28.150
    Coast Guard, TD 5.32
    Consumer Product Safety Commission, Y 3.C 76/3:15
    Corps of Engineers, D 103.62
    Defense Logistics Agency, D 7.35
    Department of Commerce, C 1.68
    Department of Interior, I 1.98
    Department of State, S 1.133
    Department of Transportation, TD 1.41
    Economic Development Administration, C 46.30

Energy Research and Development Administration, ER 1.25

Environmental of Energy, E 1.20
    Federal Aviation Administration, TD 4.48
    Federal Energy Regulatory Commission, , E 2.11/3
    Federal Power Commission, FP 1.33
    Federal Railroad Administration, TD 3.17
    Foreign-Trade Zones Board, FTZ 1.10
    General Services Administration, GS 1.25
    Interstate Commerce Commission, IC 1.32
    Land Management Bureau, I 53.59
    Maritime Administration, C 39.239
    National Institutes of Health, HE 20.3026
    National Marine Fisheries Service, C 55.328
    National Ocean Service, C 55.442
    National Park Service, I 29.79/6
    Pesticides Office, EP 5.14
    Public Buildings Service, GS 6.9
    Rural Electrification Administration, A 68.22
    Urban Mass Transportation Administration, TD 7.15
    Veterans Administration, VA 1.59

Environmental Inventories, C 55.232

Environmental Law Series, EP 1.5/2

Environmental Midwest, EP 1.28/7

Environmental Monitoring, 600/4- (series), EP 1.23/5

Environmental News, EP 1.7/2, EP 1.7/9

Environmental News Summary, EP 1.7/7

Environmental Outlook, EP 1.93

Environmental Overview and Analysis of Mining Effects, I 29.101

Environmental Planning Papers, HH 1.39

Environmental Pollution and Control, C 51.9/5

Environmental Program Administrators, EP 1.77

Environmental Protection Agency Advisory Committees, EP 1.100

Environmental Protection Division Reports, D 106.9/3

Environmental Protection Division, Technical Report EP (series), D 106.9/4

Environmental Protection Newsletter, TD 5.28/3

Environmental Protection Technology, EP 1.23/2

Environmental Quality, PrEx 7.14

Environmental Quality Profile, Pacific Northwest Region, EP 1.87/2

Environmental Quality Profiles (various States), EP 1.87

Environmental Quarterly, E 1.37

Environmental Radiation Data Reports, EP 6.12

Environmental Radioactivity Levels (series), Y 3.T 25:44
    Belefonte Nuclear Plant, Y 3.T 25:52
    Browns Ferry Nuclear Plant, Y 3.T 25:55
    Sequoyah Nuclear Plant, Y 3.T 25:56
    Watts Bar Nuclear Plant, Y 3.T 25:51

Environmental Radon Program, Summaries of Research, E 1.20/4

Environmental Readiness Documents, DOE/ERD (series), E 1.16/2

Environmental Research Brief (series), EP 1.96

Environmental Research in (year), EP 1.46/2

Environmental Research Laboratory, Duluth: Quarterly Report, EP 1.46/6

Environmental Research Papers, D 301.45/39

Environmental Sciences, Aquatic, E 1.99

Environmental Sciences, Atmospheric, E 1.99

Environmental Sciences, Terrestrial, E 1.99

Environmental Statement–
    Agricultural Stabilization and Conservation Service, A 82.85
    Farmers Home Administration, A 84.10

Environmental Statements, A 82.85, A 84.10, I 28.150

Environmental Studies Division, FY (year) Program, EP 1.44

Environmental Technology Partnerships, EP 1.23/10

Environmental Update, D 103.126

Environmental/Resource Assessment and Information, C 55.233

Environmental/Resource Assessment and Information, U.S. Energy/Climate Section, C 55.233/2

Environmental-Social Aspects of Energy Technologies, E 1.99

EnviroVision 2020, D 301.117

EPA Annual Report to Pollution Engineers, EP 1.85

EPA Bulletin, EP 1.3

EPA Citizens' Bulletin, EP 1.3/2

EPA Compendium of Registered Pesticides, EP 5.11, EP 5.11/1-5

EPA Cumulative Bibliography, EP 1.21/7-2

EPA DOC, EP 1.104/2

EPA Intermittent Bulletin, EP 1.3/5

EPA Journal, EP 1.67

EPA Journal Reprint, EP 1.67/a

EPA Log, Weekly Log of Significant Events, EP 1.24

EPA Newsletter, Quality Assurance, EP 1.98
EPA Reports Bibliography Quarterly, EP 1.21/7
EPA Research Program, Annual Report, EP 1.23/6-2
EPA Review of Radiation Protection Activities, EP 6.1/2
EPA Special Reports, EP 1.23/9
EPA Technical Notes, EP 1.7/5
EPA Technology Transfer Capsule Reports, EP 7.11
EPA Update, EP 1.67/2
EPADOC, EP 1.104/2
EPAlert, to Alert You to Important Events, EP 1.7/6
EPA/ORP- (series), EP 6.10/4
EPDA Higher Education Personnel Training Programs, HE 5.258:58025
EPHA Bulletins, NHA 4.3
Ephemeris of Sun, Polaris, and Other Selected Stars, D 213.12
Ephemeris of the Sun, Polaris and Other Selected Stars with Companion Data and Tables for the year [date], I 53.8
Epidemiologic Trends in Drug Abuse, HE 20.3969
Epidemiology, PrEx 7.14/2
Epidemiology and Biometry Advisory Committee, HE 20.3001/2:Ep 4/3
Epidemiology and Disease Control Study Section, HE 20.3001/2:Ep 4/2
Epilepsy Abstracts, FS 2.22/59, HE 20.3509
Epilepsy Bibliography, HE 20.3513:Ep 4
Epoch Discoveries of the Past, Scientific Radio Scripts, I 16.66
EPP (Environmentally Preferable Purchasing) Update, EP 5.28
ePub Illustrated, GP 1.40
Equal Employment Opportunity: Code of Federal Regulations Title 29, Y 3.Eq 2:18-4
Equal Employment Opportunity Commission Decisions, Federal Sector, Y 3.Eq 2:18
Equal Employment Opportunity Federal Register, Y 3.Eq 2:18-6
Equal Employment Opportunity in the Federal Courts, Ju 10.22
Equal Employment Opportunity Management Directives/Bulletins, Y 3.Eq 2:18-5
Equal Employment Opportunity Reports, Y 3.Eq 2:12
Equal Pay [Laws in various States], L 13.6/3
Equine Infectious Anemia, Progress Report and History in the United States, A 77.244
Equine Piroplasmosis Progress Report, A 77.242
Equip Tip, A 13.49/4-2
Equipment Certification and Type Acceptance Actions, Reports, Public Notices, CC 1.48/2
Equipment Development and Test Program, Progress, Plans, Fiscal Year, A 13.49/5
Equipment Development and Test Reports, EDT- (Series), A 13.49/4
Equipment Development Report R.M. (Series), A 13.49/2
Equipment Lists, TD 5.20
Equipment Maintenance Series, Bulletins, CS 1.42
Equipment Manual, W 3.36
Equipment Manuals (series), D 101.107/13
ER- (series), C 55.13/2:ERL, PrEx 3.10/5
ER News, E 1.19/4
ERADCOM Pamphlet (series), D 101.22/8
ERAF (Environmental Reporting Assist File), D 212.16/2
ERDA Critical Review Series, ER 1.14
ERDA Energy Research Abstracts, ER 1.15
ERDA Telephone Directory, ER 1.17
ERDA Translation Lists, ER 1.18
ERIC Annual Report, ED 1.301/2
ERIC Clearinghouse for Social Studies, Social Science Education: Interpretive Studies, HE 18.13
ERIC Database, ED 1.310/6
ERIC Digest, ED 1.331/2
ERIC Products, Bibliography of Information Analysis Publications of ERIC Clearinghouses, HE 5.77/2
ERIC Review, ED 1.331
ERISA Technical Release, L 1.76/2
ERL Program Plan (series), C 55.615
ERL (series), C 55.13:ERL
Erosion and Related Land Use Conditions (by Projects), A 57.24
Erosion Surveys, A 57.24
ERS Field Reports, A 93.37/2
ERS Foreign- (series), A 93.21/2
ERS- (Series), A 93.21, A 105.13
ERS Staff Paper, A 93.44/5
ERS Staff Reports, A 93.44
ERS-NASS Information Directory, A 93.59
ERTS-1, a New Window on Our Planet, I 19.16:929
Erythrocyte Protoporphyrin, HE 20.7022/6

Erythrocyte Protoporphyrin, Proficiency Testing, HE 20.7412/4
ES 2 U.S. Commodity Exports and Imports Related to Output, C 3.229
ES 3 Enterprise Statistics, C 3.230
ESA Directory of Offices, L 36.15
ESC in Review, D 301.106
Escort Interpreter Manual, S 1.40/6
ESCS, A 105.25
ESCS Research Abstracts, A 105.25/2
ESL-TR (series), D 301.65/2
ESN Information Bulletin, D 210.16/2
ESS- (series), A 93.21/4, A 105.56
ESSA Monographs, C 52.13
ESSA News, C 52.7/4
ESSA Operation Data Reports, C 52.22
ESSA Professional Papers, C 52.20
ESSA Research Laboratories Technical Manuals, C 52.8/2
ESSA Technical Memorandums, C 52.15/2
ESSA Technical Reports, C 52.15
ESSA World, C 52.14
Essential Oil Production and Trade, C 18.69
Essential Procedure and Requirements for Naturalization Under General Law (Form C-59), J 21.8
Essential United States Foreign Trade Routes, C 39.202:F 76
Establishing and Operation [Business], C 41.14
Establishments and Products Licensed Under Section 351 of the Public Health Service Act, HE 20.4042
Estate and Gift Tax, T 22.19/3:2
Estimated Amount of Nonfarm Mortgages of $20,000 or Less Recorded, HH 4.8/4
Estimated Defense Expenditures for States, D 1.57/11-2
Estimated Expenditures for States and Selected Areas, D 1.57/11
Estimated Flow of Savings in Savings and Loan Associations, HH 4.8/2
Estimated Grade and Staple Length of Upland Cotton Ginned (by States), A 82.69
Estimated Grade and Staple Length of Upland Cotton Ginned in United States, A 88.11/7
Estimated Home Mortgage Debt and Financing Activity, FHL 1.16
Estimated Mortgage Lending Activity of Savings and Loan Associations, HH 4.8/3
Estimated Numbers of Apple Trees by Varieties and Ages in Commercial and Farm Orchards, A 36.52
Estimated Oil and Gas Reserves, I 72.12/7
Estimated Refrigerator Car Movement of Domestic Fresh Fruits and Vegetables by Regions, A 82.42
Estimated Retail Food Prices by Cities, L 2.37
Estimated Use of Water in the United States, I 19.4/9
Estimated Vessel Operating Expenses, C 39.242, TD 11.32
Estimated Volume of Mail and Special Services and Postal Revenues, P 1.37
Estimated Work Injuries, L 2.77/5
Estimates of Appropriations for Department of Commerce, C 1.5
Estimates of Cotton Crops, A 36.31
Estimates of Federal Tax Expenditures for Fiscal Year, Y 4.T 19/4-10
Estimates of Local Public School System Finances, ED 1.112/3
Estimates of the Population of Puerto Rico and the Outlying Areas, C 3.186/19
Estimates of the Population of the United States, C 3.186:P-25, C 3.186/7
Estimates of the Population of the United States and Components of Change, C 3.186/7-3
Estimates of the Population of the United States, by Age, Sex, and Race, C 3.186/7-2
Estimates of U.S. Biomass Energy Consumption, E 3.58
Estuarine Pollution Study Series, EP 2.19
ET [Employment Training] Handbooks, HE 37.8/2
ET [Entomological Technical] (series), A 77.313
ETA Interchange, L 37.9
Ethics CD, Y 3.Et 3:16
ETL- (series), D 103.20/6
Eurarmy, D 101.42/4
Europe and Latin America Report, Science and Technology, PrEx 7.17/4
Europe, Series 1209, D 5.328
Europe Now, C 61.41
Europe Update, Agriculture and Trade Report, A 93.29/2-21
European and British Commonwealth Series, S 1.74
European Corn Borer, A 9.9
European Financial Notes, C 18.70
European Program, Local Currency Counterpart Funds, Pr 33.911, FO 1.11

European Program, Special Statements, Y 3.Ec 74/3:24
European Recovery Program, Commodity Study, Y 3.Ec 74/3:11
European Recovery Program; Joint Report of United States and United Kingdom Military Governors, M 105.18
European Series, S 1.45
European Transportation Survey, Pr 32.5810
Europe/Latin America Report, PrEx 7.17/4
Evacuation Bulletins, Pr 32.4415
Evaluation and Research Reports ER (series), C 3.223/16
Evaluation Bulletin, HE 20.9122
Evaluation Document Loan Lists, J 1.20/5
Evaluation Methods Series, CS 1.58/2
Evaluation of Employees for Promotion and Internal Placement, CS 1.41/4:335-1
Evaluation of Foreign Fruits and Nuts, A 77.532
Evaluation of Streamflow-data Program in [various States], I 19.59/2
Evaluation of the Urban Homesteading Demonstration Program, HH 1.73
Evaluation of [various States] Water Supply Program, EP 1.61
Evaluation Plan, J 28.25/4
Evaluation Report, Water Resources Appraisal for Hydroelectric Licensing, FP 1.31
Evaluation Reports, S 18.52/4
Evaporated, Condensed, and Dry Milk Report, A 88.14
Evidence Report/Technical Assistance Bulletins, EP 9.17
Evidence Studies, Y 3.N 21/8:23
Exact Location of All Ships in which Shipping Board is Interested, SB 2.10
Examination of the Federal Deposit Insurance Corporation's Financial Statements for the Years Ended ..., GA 1.13/16
Examination of the Inter-American Foundation's Financial Statements, GA 1.13/2
Examination of the Federal Financing Bank's Financial Statements, GA 1.13/4
Examination of the Panama Canal Commission's Financial Statements for the Years Ended, GA 1.13/11
Examination Papers, W 3.18
Examination Papers for Admission, N 12.8/1
Examination Papers [for promotion], N 12.8/2
Examination Staff Procedures Manual for the Hispanic Health and Nutrition Examination Survey, HE 20.6208/2
Examiner's Reports–
    Broadcast Division, CC 1.11
    Telegraph Division, CC 1.11/2
    Telephone Division, CC 1.11/3
Examining Circulars, CS 1.46
Examining Circulars, 4th Civil Service Region, CS 1.46/2
Examining Practices, CS 1.41/4:330-1
Excellence in Surface Coal Mining and Reclamation Awards, I 71.16
Excerpts from Slide Presentations by the Office of Chief of Naval Operations, D 207.14
Excess Personal Property Available for Transfer, Circulars, GS 2.4/3
Excess Property Bulletins, GS 9.3/2
Exchange Lists, LC 7.5
Exchange of Medical Information Program, Annual Report, VA 1.23/4
Excise Taxes, T 22.19/3:4
Executions, J 16.23
Executive Agreement Series, S 9.8
Executive Correspondence Information Bulletin, National Health Service Corps, HE 20.9110/3
Executive Management Bulletin (series), PrEx 2.3/3
Executive/Management Training Handbook, HE 22.8/20
Executive Manpower Management Technical Assistance Papers, EMMTAP, CS 1.85
Executive Orders, Pr 32.5, Pr 33.5
Executive Orders (affecting Resettlement Administration), Y 3.R 31:16
Executive Orders [affecting Works Progress Administration], Y 3.R 31:17
Executive Orders and Proclamations, W 49.35/5
Executive Orders Relating to Panama Canal, W 79.11/8
Executive Reservist, Bulletin from Industrial Mobilization, for Members of National Defense Executive Reserve, C 41.113
Executive Seminar Centers [programs], CS 1.65/3
Executive Summaries, National Highway Safety Bureau Contractors Report, TD 2.212
Executive Summary of HUD Research Project Report (series), HH 1.53

FDA Consumer Memos, HE 20.4010/2
FDA Consumer Special Report, HE 20.4010/4
FDA Current Drug Information, HE 20.4013
FDA Drug and Device Products Approvals, FDA/BD, HE 20.4209
FDA Drug Bulletin, HE 20.4003, HE 20.4003/3
FDA Enforcement Report, HE 20.4039
FDA Federal Register Documents, Chronological Document Listing, 1936–1976, HE 20.4016:C 46
FDA Medical Bulletin, HE 20.4003/3
FDA Medical Device Standards Publication, Technical Reports, FDA-T, HE 20.4310/2
FDA Medical Device Standards Publications, MDS (series), HE 20.4310
FDA Memo for Consumers, CM- (series), FS 13.121
FDA Papers, FS 13.128, HE 20.4010
FDA Posters, FS 13.127
FDA Publications (numbered), HE 20.4015
FDA Publications (series), FS 13.111
FDA Quarterly Activities Report, HE 20.4033
FDA Safety Alerts (on various subjects), HE 20.4616
FDA Technical Bulletins, HE 20.4040
FDA Veterinarian, HE 20.4410
FDA's Life Protection Series, FS 13.129
FDD Field Reports, A 93.37
FDIC Banking Review, Y 3.F 31/8:27
FDIC Consumer News, Y 3.F 31/8:24
FDIC Quarterly Banking Profile, Y 3.F 31/8:29
FDIC Statistics on Banking, Y 3.F 31/8:1-2
FDSN Earthquake Digital Data, I 19.128/2
Feature Picture Pages, T 66.13
Feature Sections of Journals in NWC Library, D 1.26
FEC Index of Communication Costs, Y 3.El 2/3:15-2
FEC Index of Independent Expenditures, Y 3.El 2/3:15-2
FEC Journal of Election Administration, Y 3.El 2/3:10
FEC Reports on Financial Activity, Y 3.El 2/3:15
FED Facts, PM 1.25
FedBizOpps (Federal Business Opportunities), GS 1.41
Fed State Bulletin, T 22.2/15:7208/date
Federal Acquisition Circular, D 1.6/11-2
Federal Acquisition Institute: General Publications, GS 1/6.12
Federal Acquisitions Institute: Publications, PrEx 2.23
Federal Acquisition Regulations, D 1.6/11, GP 3.38/2 GS 1.6/10
Federal Advisory Committees, Annual Report of the President, Pr 37.12, Pr 38.10, Pr 39.10, Pr 40.10, Pr 41.10, Pr 42.10
Federal Agency Classification Chiefs Workshop: Reports, PM 1.24
Federal Aid in Fish and Wildlife Restoration, I 49.29/3
Federal Aid to States, Fiscal Year, T 63.120
Federal Air Surgeons Medical Bulletin, TD 4.215
Federal Aircraft Noise Abatement Plan, Fiscal Year, TD 1.16
Federal Airway Plan, C 31.167
Federal Airways Air Traffic Activity, C 31.158
Federal Airways Manual of Operations, C 31.116/2
Federal Alternative and Fuel Program, Annual Report to Congress, E 1.114/2
Federal and Non-Federal Projects Approved, Y 3.F 31/4:7
Federal and State Commission Jurisdiction and Regulations, Electric, Gas, and Telephone Utilities, FP 1.21
Federal and State Endangered Species Expenditures, I 49.77/6
Federal Archeology Report, I 29.59/5
Federal Art Project, Y 3.W 89/2:40
Federal Assistance for Programs Serving the Handicapped, ED 1.34
Federal Assistance for Projects in Aging, FS 14.12
Federal Audiovisual Activity, AE 1.110/5
Federal Aviation Administration Airworthiness Directives, TD 4.10/4
Federal Aviation Administration Plan for Research, Engineering, and Development, TD 4.64
Federal Aviation Agency Specification, FAA 1.13
Federal Aviation Regulations, TD 4.6
Federal Benefits for Veterans and Dependents, VA 1.34:1
Federal Budget in Brief, PrEx 2.8/2
Federal Budget, Midyear Review, PrEx 2.8/3
Federal Bulletin Board, GP 3.35
Federal Bureau of Prisons Statistical Tables, J 16.23/4
Federal Career Directory, Guide for College Students, CS 1.7/4:C 18
Federal Catalog System, Training Course Catalog, D 7.33/2
Federal Civil Defense Administration Directory, FCD 1.19
Federal Civil Defense Guide, D 119.8/4

Federal Civilian Employment and Wages of Workers Covered by Unemployment Compensation for Federal Employees, L 7.20/4
Federal Civilian Work Force Statistics , PM 1.10/2, PM 1.15, CS 1.55/2
Federal Civilian Work Force Statistics, Occupations of Federal Blue-Collar Workers, PM 1.10:Sm 59-11
Federal Civilian Work Force Statistics, Occupations of Federal White-Collar Workers, PM 1.10:Sm 56-13
Federal Coal Management Report, I 1.96/4
Federal Coal Mine Health Program, Annual Report of the Federal Coal Mine Health and Safety Act, HE 20.2020
Federal Coal Mine Health Program in (year), HE 20.7109
Federal Communication Commission Daily, CC 1.56
Federal Communications Commission Reports, CC 1.12
Federal Communications Commission Reports, Decisions, Reports, Public Notices, and Other Documents of the Federal Communications Commission (2d series), CC 1.12/2a
Federal Communications Commission Reports: Second Series, CC 1.12/2
Federal Communications Reports, CC 1.12
Federal Consumer Focus, GS 11.9/3
Federal Contract Air Service and Travel Directory, GS 8.10
Federal Coordinator for Meteorological Services and Supporting Research, FCM (series), C 55.12
Federal Credit Unions, FCA 1.15
Federal Credit Unions, Quarterly Report on Operations, FCA 1.16
Federal Crop Insurance Corporation, A 82.201
Federal Depository Library Directory, GP 3.36/2
Federal Depository Library Directory (online), GP 3.36/2-2
Federal Design Library (series), NF 2.10
Federal Design Matters, NF 2.9
Federal Digital Cartography Newsletter, I 19.115
Federal Election Commission Record, Y 3.El 2/3:11
Federal Election Commission Record, Index, Y 3.El 2/3:11-2
Federal Elections . . ., Election Results for the U.S. Senate and U.S. House of Representatives, Y 3.El 2/3:16
Federal Emergency Relief Administration Grants, Y 3.F 31/5:32
Federal Emergency Relief Administration Grants Distributed According to Programs and Periods for which Grants were Made, Y 3.F 31/5:33
Federal Employee Facts, CS 1.59
Federal Employee Health Series, HE 20.5410
Federal Employee Substance Abuse Education and Treatment Act of 1986, PM 1.61
Federal Employees Health Benefits, CS 1.41/4:890-1
Federal Employment of Women, CS 1.74
Federal Employment Outlook, CS 1.72/3
Federal Employment Statistics Bulletin, CS 1.55
Federal Energy Guidelines, E 1.8/2
Federal Energy Guidelines (basic volumes), FE 1.8/3
Federal Energy Guidelines, Exceptions and Appeals (basic volumes), FE 1.8/4
Federal Energy Guidelines: FERC Reports, E 2.17
Federal Energy Guidelines, Transmittals, FE 1.8/5
Federal Energy Guidelines: Statutes and Regulations, E 2.18
Federal Energy Regulatory Commission Producer Manual, E 2.12:0030
Federal Energy Management Activities, E 1.89/2
Federal Energy Management Program Annual Reports, FE 1.16
Federal Expenditures by State for Fiscal Year, C 3.266
Federal Facts, CS 1.59
Federal Farm Loan Act with Amendments and Farm Mortgage and Farm Credit Acts, Y 1.2:F 31
Federal Financial Assistance for Projects in Aging, FS 15.13, FS 17.310/2
Federal Financial Management Directory, GA 1.12/2
Federal Financial Management Status Report & Five-Year Plan, PrEx 2.33
Federal Fire Council News Letter, GS 1.14/4
Federal Fire Experience for Fiscal Year (date), GS 1.14/2
Federal Firearms Licensee News, T 70.18
Federal Food, Drug, and Cosmetic Act, Y 1.2:F 31/10
Federal Food, Drug, and Cosmetic Act, as Amended, and General Regulations for its Enforcement, FS 13.105:F 73
Federal Forecast for Engineers, PM 1.23
Federal Fringe Benefit Facts, PM 1.29
Federal Fund-Raising Manual, CS 1.7/5

Federal Funds for Research and Development, Detailed Historical Tables, Fiscal Years, NS 1.18/2
Federal Funds for Research and Development, Federal Obligations for Research by Agency and Detailed Field of Science, Fiscal Years, NS 1.18/3
Federal Funds for Research, Development, and Other Scientific Activities, NS 1.18
Federal Government Receipts from and Payments to (public) Special Analysis 4, PrEx 2.8/a7
Federal Grants and Contracts for Unclassified Research in Life Sciences, NS 1.10
Federal Grants and Contracts for Unclassified Research in Physical Sciences, NS 1.10/2
Federal Guidance for State and Local Civil Defense, D 14.8/5, D 119.8/3
Federal Handbook , GS 2.6/2
Federal Highway Administration Newsletter, TD 2.12/2
Federal Highway Administration Register, TD 2.71
Federal Home Loan Bank Board Digest, FHL 1.14
Federal Home Loan Bank Review, Y 3.F 31/3:9, FL 3.7, NHA 3.8
Federal Hotel/Motel Discount Directory, GS 8.10/2, GS 2.21/2
Federal Housing Administration Annual Report, HH 2.1
Federal Income Tax Guide for Older Americans, Y 4.Ag 4/2-11
Federal Income Tax Information, D 205.9
Federal Income Tax Information [for Persons in Naval Service], N 20.22
Federal Information Locator System, PrEx 2.14/2
Federal Information Processing Standards Publications, C 13.52
Federal Inter-Agency River Basin Committee Publications, I 1.81
Federal IRM Directory, GS 12.19
Federal Item Identification Guides for Supply Cataloging:-
Description Patterns, D 7.6/2:6-2
Indexes, Supplements, D 7.6/2:6-1, D 7.8:1
Reference Drawings, D 7.6/2:6-3
Federal Item Logistics Data Records, D 7.26
Federal Item Name Directory for Supply Cataloging, Handbook, D 7.6/2
Federal Judicial Caseload Statistics JU 10.21
Federal Judicial Workload Statistics, Ju 10.2:W 89, Ju 10.21
Federal Labor Laws, L 22.5/2, L 36.205/2, L 36.205/8
Federal Labor-Management Consultant, PM 1.13, CS 1.80
Federal Labor-Management and Employee Relations Consultant, PM 1.13
Federal Law Enforcement and Criminal Justice Assistance Activities, Annual Report, J 1.32/2
Federal Law Enforcement Training Center: Annual Report, T 1.60
Federal Laws, CC 1.5
Federal Library Committee: Annual Report, LC 1.32/4
Federal Loan Agency News, FL 1.8
Federal Management Circulars (numbered), GS 1.4/3
Federal Management Improvement Conference, Proceedings, PrEx 2.19
Federal Managers' Financial Integrity Act, Secretary's Annual Statement and Report to the President and the Congress, I 1.96/6
Federal Maritime Board and Maritime Administration Releases NR (series), C 39.109
Federal Maritime Board Reports, Decisions, C 39.108
Federal Maritime Commission, FMC 1.10/a2
Federal Maritime Commission, Decisions, Separates, FMC 1.10/a, A 88.17/7
Federal Maritime Commission Speeches, FMC 1.9
Federal Meat and Poultry Inspection, Statistical Summary for (year), A 101.6/3
Federal Meat Inspection, Statistical Summary for (year), A 88.40/2:54
Federal Meteorological Handbooks, C 1.8/4
Federal Milk Order Market Statistics, A 88.14/11, A 1.34/2
Federal Milk Order Market Statistics, Summary, A 82.81
Federal Mine Health Program for (year), HE 20.7109
Federal Mine Safety and Health Review Commission Index, Y 3.M 66:9-2
Federal Motor Carrier Safety Administration, Register, TD 2.314.6/4
Federal Motor Vehicle Fleet Reports, GS 2.18
Federal Motor Vehicle Safety Standards, TD 8.6/4
Federal Motor Vehicle Safety Standards and Regulations, TD 8.6/2
Federal National Mortgage Association News, HH 6.8/2

Federal News Clip Sheet, CS 1.69, PM 1.12
Federal Noise Program Reports, EP 1.73
Federal Noise Research in (various subjects), EP 1.73/3
Federal Occupational Health Memo Series, HE 20.9116
Federal Ocean Program, Annual Report to Congress, Pr 37.11, Pr 38.11, Pr 39.12
Federal Offenders in the United States Courts, Ju 10.11
Federal Offshore Statistics, Leasing, Exploration, Production, Revenue, I 72.10
Federal Oil Conservation Board, I 1.67
Federal Outlays, PrEx 10.24
Federal Parole Decision-Making: Selected Reprints, J 27.9
Federal Personal Data Systems Subject to the Privacy Act of 1974, Annual Report of the President, Pr 38.12, Pr 39.11
Federal Personnel Administration Career Programs, PM 1.41/4:931-1
Federal Personnel Manual: Bulletins, Installments and Letters, PM 1.14/2
Federal Personnel Manual: Supplements, PM 1.14/3
Federal Personnel Manual: Transmittal Sheets, PM 1.14
Federal Plan for Marine Environmental Prediction, Fiscal Year, C 55.16
Federal Plan for Meteorological Services and Supporting Research, Fiscal Year (date), C 55.16/2
Federal Plan for Ocean Pollution Research, Develop-ing, and Monitoring, PrEx 8.109
Federal Plan for Water-Data Acquisition, I 19.74/3
Federal Population and Mortality Schedules (years), in the National Archives and the States, AE 1.115
Federal Power Commission Laws and Hydro- Electric Power Development Laws [June 10, 1920], Y 1.2:F 31/7
Federal Power Commission Reports, Opinions, and Orders, FP 1.20
Federal Power Commission Rules of Practice and Procedure, FP 1.6
Federal Prisons Journal, J 16.30:
Federal Probation, J 16.8, Ju 10.8
Federal Procurement Data System, PrEx 2.24
Federal Procurement Data System, Annual Analysis (series), PrEx 2.24/2
Federal Procurement Data System, Combined Special Analyses, PrEx 2.24/12
Federal Procurement Data System, Contractor Identification File, Alphabetical Listing, PrEx 2.24/14
Federal Procurement Data System, Special Analysis 3, PrEx 2.24/3
Federal Procurement Data System, Special Analysis 8, PrEx 2.24/8
Federal Procurement Data System, Special Analysis 10, PrEx 2.24/10
Federal Procurement Data System, Standard Report, PrEx 2.24/13
Federal Procurement Regulations, GS 1.6/5
Federal Procurement Regulations, FPR Notices, GS 1.6/5-2
Federal Productivity Measurement, PM 1.45
Federal Program in Population Research, Inventory of Population Research Supported by Federal Agencies During Fiscal Year (date), HE 20.3362/2
Federal Property Management Regulations Amend-ments, GS 1.6/8-3
Federal Quality News, PM 1.58
Federal R & D Funding by Budget Function, NS 1.18/4
Federal R&D Project Summaries, E. 142 429-X-24
Federal Radiological Fallout Monitoring Station Directory, D 119.8/3:E 5.11
Federal Radionavigation Plan, D 1.84
Federal Real and Personal Property Inventory Report (Civilian and Military) of the United States Government Covering its Properties Located in the United States, in the Territories, and Overseas, as of June 30 (year), Y 4.G 74/7:P 94
Federal Reclamation Laws, I 27.27:L 44
Federal Reclamation Projects, Water and Land Resource Accomplishments, I 27.55
Federal Recreation Fee Program (year), Including Federal Recreation Visitation Data, a Report to the Congress, I 70.18
Federal Recreation Fee Report, I 29.108
Federal Recreation Fees, I 66.23
Federal Reference Material for State, Economic Development Agencies, C 41.27/2
Federal Regional Council, Pr 37.8:R 26
Federal Register, GS 4.107, AE 2.106

Federal Register: Includes Presidential Proclamations, Executive Orders, Rules, Regulations, and Notices, AE 2.106
Federal Register Proposed Amendments, Y 3.F 31/21-3:9-5
Federal Register Update, GS 4.107/2
Federal Register, What It Is and How to Use It, GS 4.6/2:F 31
Federal Research Natural Areas in, A 13.36/12
Federal Reserve Act, As Amended (compilations), FR 1.13
Federal Reserve Act of 1913 with Amendments and Laws Relating to Banking, Y 1.2:F 31/2
Federal Reserve Board Publications, FR 1.45
Federal Reserve Bulletin, FR 1.3
Federal Reserve Chart Book on Financial and Business Statistics, FR 1.30
Federal Reserve Chart Books, FR 1.25
Federal Reserve Par List, October (year), FR 1.9
Federal Rules and Regulations, Correction Sheets, CC 1.7/3
Federal Rules of Appellate Procedure with Forms, Y 4.J 89/1-10
Federal Rules of Evidence, Y 4.J 89/1-13
Federal Safety News, FIS 1.8
Federal Savings and Loan Insurance Corporation, Financial Statements, FHL 1.2:F 31/2
Federal School Code (Database), ED 1.92/2
Federal School Code List, ED 1.92
Federal Science Program, C 35.9
Federal Scientific and Technical Communication, Progress Report, NS 2.12
Federal Scientific and Technical Workers: Numbers and Characteristics, NS 1.14/3
Federal Scientists and Engineers, NS 1.22/9
Federal Service Impasses Panel Releases, Y 3.F 31/21-3:14-3
Federal Software Exchange Catalog, GS 12.14
Federal Software Exchange Catalog Supplement, GS 12.14/2-2
Federal Specifications, GS 2.8
Federal Specifications Announcements, GS 1.10
Federal Specifications Board, United States Govern-ment Master Specifications, C 13.24
Federal Staffing Digest, PM 1.18/5
Federal Standard Stock Catalog: Sec. 4, Pt. 5, Emergency Federal Specifications, GS 2.8/4
Federal Standards, GS 2.8/3
Federal State Cooperative Snow Surveys and Water Supply Forecasts, A 57.46/9-2
Federal Statistical Directory, PrEx 2.10, C 1.75
Federal Statistics, PrEx 2.10/2
Federal Stock Number Reference Catalog, Numerical Listing of Items Available from General Services Administration, GS 2.10/5
Federal Student Financial Aid Handbook, ED 1.45/4
Federal Student Loan Program Bulletin, ED 1.3/3
Federal Supply Catalog, Department of Defense Section, D 7.9
Federal Supply Catalog for Civil Agencies, Descriptive and Management Data List, D 7.9/2
Federal Supply Catalog: National Supplier Change Index, GS 2.10/7
Federal Supply Circular, GS 2.4
Federal Supply Classification, D 7.6/2:2
Federal Supply Classification Listing of DoD Standardization Documents, D 7.14/2, D 1.76/2
Federal Supply Code for Manufacturers, D 7.6/2:4
Federal Supply Schedule (by groups), GS 2.7/4
Federal Supply Schedule, Checklist and Guide, GS 2.7/3
Federal Supply Schedule Program Guide, GS 2.7/5
Federal Support for Education, ED 1.328/8
Federal Support of Research and Development at Universities and Colleges and Selected Nonprofit Institutions, Fiscal Year, Report to the President and Congress, NS 1.30
Federal Support to Universities, Colleges, and Selected Nonprofit Institutions, Fiscal Year (date), Report to the President and Congress, NS 1.30
Federal Surplus Real Property Public Benefit Discount Program, Parks and Recreation, Report to Congress, I 29.118
Federal Tax Collections, Calendar Year, T 22.7/2
Federal Tax Forms, Includes Non-Calendar Year Products, T 22.51/4
Federal Tax Information for Armed Forces Personnel, D 205.9
Federal Tax Products, GP 3.38/3
Federal Technology Catalog, Summaries of Practical Technology, NTIS Tech Notes Annual Index, C 51.17/11

Federal Telecommunications System Telephone Directory, Y 3.At 7:55-2
Federal Test Method Standards, GS 2.8/7
Federal Textbook on Citizenship, J 21.9
Federal Trade Commission Decisions, FT 1.11/2
Federal Traffic Board, T 51.10
Federal Trainer, an Information Exchange for the Federal Training Community, PM 1.19/3
Federal Trainer, Information Exchange for the Federal Training Community, CS 1.84
Federal Travel Directory, GS 2.21, GS 1.29
Federal Travel Regulations, GS 1.6/8-2
Federal Voting Assistance Program, D 1.80
Federal Water Resources Research Program for Fiscal Year, PrEx 8.9
Federal Women's Program Newsletter, I 28.170
Federal Work and Construction Projects, FW 4.33, Y 3.W 89/2:61
Federal Work Injuries Sustained During Calendar Year, L 26.8
Federal Work Injury Facts, L 26.2:In 5/4
Federal Work Injury Facts, Occupational Distribution, Duration and Direct Cost Factors of Work Injuries to Civilian Federal Employees During Calendar Year, L 26.8/2-2
Federal Work Programs and Public Assistance, FW 4.32
Federal Workforce Outlook, CS 1.72/2
Federal-Aid Airport Program Publications, FAA 8.10
Federal-Aid Highway Relocation Assistance and Payment Statistics, TD 2.28
Federally Coordinated Program of Highway Research and Development, TD 2.42
Federal-State Cooperative Program for Population Estimates, C 3.186:P-26
Federal-State Election Law Survey, Y 3.El 2/3:9
Federal-State Election Law Survey: an Analysis of State Legislation, Federal Legislation and Judicial Decisions, Y 3.El 2/3:2 St 2
Federal-State Market News Reports, Directory of Services Available, A 88.40/2:21
Federal/State Radiation Control Legislation, HE 20.4115
Federal-State-Private Cooperative Snow Surveys–Colorado, Rio Grande, Platte, and Arkansas Drainage Basins, A 57.46/9-2
  Montana, A 57.46/3-2
  Oregon, A 57.46/5-2
  Utah, A 57.46/6-1
FEDLINK Technical Notes, LC 1.32/5
Feds Staff Papers, A 100.10
FEDWARE Magazine, GS 1.39
Fee Licenses Issued for the Month, I 64.12
Feed Grain and Wheat Stabilization Program, A 82.37/3:F 32/2
Feed Grain Situation, A 36.87
Feed Market News, Weekly Summary and Statistics, A 88.18/4
Feed Market Review, A 82.32
Feed Market Summary, A 82.35, A 88.18/3
Feed Outlook and Situation Report, A 93.11/2
Feed, Outlook and Situation Yearbook, A 93.11/2-2
Feed Prospects, A 36.84/2
Feed Situation, A 88.18/12, A 93.11/2, A 105.20/2
Feedback, D 301.45/56
Feldspar, I 28.111/2
Feldspar in (year), I 28.111
Fellowship Program Announcement, J 28.34Felons Sentenced to Probation in State Courts, J 29.11/12
Felony Sentences in the United States, J 29.11/11-2
Felony Laws of the Fifty States and the District of Columbia, J 29.18
Felony Sentences in State Courts, J 29.11/11
FEMA Newsletter, FEM 1.20
FEMA News Releases, FEM 1.28
Females Employed by Class 1 Steams Railways, Number of, IC 1 ste.43
FEMP Focus, E. 1.89/4
FERC News, E 2.9
FERC Statutes and Regulations, Proposed Regulations, E 2.18/3
FERC Statutes and Regulations, Regulations Preambles, E 2.18/2
Fermilab Reports, E 1.92/2
Fermilab Research Program Workbook, E 1.92
Ferret Reports, I 49.90
Ferroalloys in (year), I 28.142
Ferrosilicon, I 28.75, I 28.75/3
Ferrosilicon in (year), I 28.75/2
Ferrosilicon Reports, I 28.75
Ferrous Metals Supply/Demand Data, I 28.169
Fertility of American Women: Current Population Reports, C 3.186/10

Fertility of Population, C 3.186:P-20
Fertilizer Abstracts, Y 3.T 25:36
Fertilizer Situation, A 93.36
Fertilizer Situation for (year), A 82.77
Fertilizer Summary Data, Y 3.T 25:70
Fertilizer Summary Data by States and Geographic
    Areas, Y 3.T 25:29 F 41/7
Fertilizer Supply (year), A 82.77
Fertilizer Trends, Y 3.T 25:29
Fertilizer Trends, Production, Consumption, and Trade,
    Y 3.T 25:66
FES Aid: Sanitation Series, A 43.40
FESA Briefs, D 103.122/2
FESA- (series), D 103.122
Festival of American Folklife, SI 1.43/2
Festival USA, C 47.17
FEWS (Famine Early Warning System) Bulletin, S
    18.68
FEWS (Famine Early Warning System) Special Report,
    S 18.68/2
FFL Newsletter, T 70.18
FGD Newsletter, I 19.115/4
FGD [Flue Gas Desulfurization] Quarterly Report, EP
    1.46/8
FGIS Update, A 104.12/3
FGP Exchange, AA 1.21
FH PAM (series), D 101.22/13
FHA and VA Mortgages Owned and Available for Sale
    by Reconstruction Finance Corporation and
    Federal National Mortgage Association, Y
    3.R 24:14
FHA Home Mortgage Insurance Operations, State,
    County and MSA/PMSA, HH 2.24/8
FHA Homes, Data for States, on Characteristics of FHA
    Operations Under Sec. 203, HH 2.24/4
FHA Honor Awards for Presidential Design, HH 2.25
FHA Low Cost Housing Trends of 1-family Homes
    Insured by FHA, HH 2.26
FHA Manual Admin., HH 2.6/5
FHA Monthly Report of Operations: Home Mortgage
    Programs, HH 2.27/2
FHA Monthly Report of Operations: Project Mortgage
    Insurance Programs, HH 2.27
FHA News Fillers for Use at Any Time, HH 2.18/4
FHA Regulations, HH 2.6
FHA Research and Statistics Release, HH 2.18/3
FHA Special Features for Use at Any Time, HH 2.18/2
FHA Trends, Characteristics of Home Mortgages
    Insured by FHA, HH 2.24
FHFM News Releases, T 71.7/2
FHLB System S & L's Combined Financial Statements:
    Savings and Home Financing Source Book,
    FHL 1.12/2
FHM-NC, A 13.134
FHWA Bulletins, TD 2.3
FHWA Program, HY- (series), TD 2.41
FHWA Research and Development Implementation
    Catalog, TD 2.36/3
FHWA-AD (series), TD 2.30/12
FHWA-CA (series), TD 2.30/9
FHWA-CA-TL- (series), TD 2.30/10
FHWA-CR (series), TD 2.30/18
FHWA/DF (series), TD 2.69
FHWA-FLP, TD 2.30/17
FHWA-JPO, TD 2.30/19
FHWA-MCRT, TD 2.30/20
FHWA-OEP/HEV- (series), TD 2.30/7
FHWA-PD, TD 2.30/16
FHWA-RDDP Reports, TD 2.30/2
FHWA-SA (Series), TD 2.30/13
Fibrinolysis, Thrombolysis, and Blood Clotting
    Bibliography, HE 20.3209
Fibrinolysis, Thrombolysis, and Blood Clotting,
    Bibliography, Annual Compilation, FS 2.22/
    13-6, HE 20.3209
FICE Report, Y 3.Ed 8:9
Fiduciary Income Tax Returns, T 22.35/2:F 44/2
Field and Seed Crops, Farm Production, Farm
    Disposition, Value, by States, A 88.30/4
Field and Seed Crops, Production, Farm Use, Sales,
    Value by States, A 92.19
Field Artillery Journal, D 101.77/2
Field Artillery Notes, W 26.10
Field Charts, M 202.22
Field Circulars, FC- (series), D 101.4/2
Field Crops, Production, Disposition, Value, A 105.9/4
Field Directory, HE 1.17
Field Engineers Bulletins, C 4.31
Field Facility Directory, FAA 1.43
Field Identification Cards, A 13.100
Field Initiated Studies Program, Abstracts of Funded
    Projects, ED 1.337
Field Letter, Information, Legislative, Court Decisions,
    Opinions, L 25.8

Field Letter, National Committee for Conservation of
    Manpower in War Industries, L 1.29
Field Manual and Field Regulations, W 1.33
Field Manuals, W 3.63/2, D 101.20
Field News, Y 3.F 31/11:29
Field Notes, A 13.84/3, Y 3.Eq 2:6-2
Field Office Memorandum, T 60.7
Field Operations Handbook, L 22.18
Field Operations of Bureau of Soils, A 26.5
Field Orders (numbered), T 22.31
Field Organization News Letters, T 1.110
Field Pamphlets, W 42.32
Field Program, A 13.8
Field Releases of Agricultural Marketing Service, A
    88.42
Field Reporter, S 1.42/2
Field Review, I 24.16
Field Seed Stocks, A 92.19/15
Field Seeds, Supply and Disappearance, A 92.19/5
Field Service Modification Work Orders, W 34.33
Field Service Newsletter, C 1.43
Field Studies and Statistics Program, HE 20.3178
Field Surplus Lists, T 58.14
Field Work Series, L 7.10
Field Works, Ideas for Housing and Community
    Development, HH 1.75/3
Fifty American Faces, SI 11.2:Am 3/5
Filler Fact Sheet, L 1.20/4
Film Advertisements, FS 2.36
Film Bulletins, S 1.3/s
Film Calendar, SI 8.11
Film Guides, HE 20.3608/3
Film Reference Guide for Medicine and Allied Sciences,
    HE 20.3608/2
Film Resources on Japan, HE 5.2:J 27
Film Strips of U.S.D.A., Price Lists, A 43.23
Final Bulletins (U.S. Territorial Possessions), C 3.37/
    30
Final Environmental Impact Statements and Related
    Materials, A 13.92
Final Volumes, C 3.31/1
Final Cumulative Finding Aid, House and Senate Bills,
    GP 3.28
Final Environmental Impact Statements–
    Bureau of Indian Affairs, I 20.56
    Bureau of Land Management, I 53.19/2
    Corps of Engineers, D 103.65
    Department of Housing and Urban Development,
        HH 1.55
    Department of Interior, I 1.98
    Department of the Army, D 101.82
    Energy Research and Development Administration,
        ER 1.5
    Environmental Protection Agency, EP 1.57/3
    Federal Energy Administration, FE 1.21
    Forest Service, A 13.92
    Land Management Bureau, I 53.19/2
    Maritime Administration, C 39.239
    National Aeronautics and Space Administration,
        NAS 1.59
    National Oceanic and Atmospheric Administration,
        C 55.34/2
    National Park Service, I 29.81
    Naval Training Support Command, D 208.20
    Navigation Charts, D 103.66
    Occupational Safety and Health Administration, L
        35.21
    Reclamation Bureau, I 27.70
    Soil Conservation Service, A 57.65/2
    Tennessee Valley Authority, Y 3.T 25:45
Final Regulatory Analysis, I 70.14
Final Regulatory Analysis, OSM-RA- (series), I 1.77/4
Final Report of the SEC Government-Business Forum
    on Small Business Capital Formation, SE
    1.35/2
Final Reports, C 3.28/5
Final Reports on Monographs, I 18.5, W 8.5
Final State and Local Data Elements, T 1.64/2
Final TV Broadcast Financial Data, CC 1.43
Final Volumes, C 3.37/5, C 3.940-5
Finance and Supply Circulars, T 47.38
Finance and Supply Memorandum, T 47.39
Finance Circulars, W 97.5
Finance Companies, FR 1.26
Finance Decisions, IC 1.6/a:F
Finance Memorandum, W 97.6
Finance Rate and Other Terms on New and Used Car
    Installment Credit Contracts Purchased from
    Dealers of Major Auto Finance Companies,
    FR 1.34/5
Finance Rate and Other Terms on Selected Categories of
    Consumer Installment Credit Extended by
    Finance Companies, FR 1.34/7

Finance Rates and Other Terms on Selected Types of
    Consumer Installment Credit Extended by
    Major Finance Companies (not seasonally
    adjusted), FR 1.34/9
Finance School Texts, W 97.8/7
Finances of Employee-Retirement Systems of State and
    Local Governments in (year), C 56.209, C
    3.191/2
Finances of Public School Systems, C 3.191/2-6
Financial and Operating Statistics, Class I Railroads, IC
    1 ste.19/4
Financial and Technical Assistance Provided by the
    Department of Agriculture and the
    Department of Housing and Urban
    Development for Nonmetropolitan Planning
    District, Annual Report to Congress, A
    1.113
Financial Assistance by Geographic Area, ED 1.35
Financial Assistance by Geographic Area, Fiscal Year,
    HE 1.57
Financial Assistance for College Students, Undergradu-
    ate and 1st-Professional, FS 5.255:55027,
    HE 5.255:55027
Financial Audit, Environmental and Energy Study
    Conference Financial Statement, GA 1.13/17
Financial Audit, Export-Import Bank's Financial
    Statements, GA 1.13/7
Financial Audit, Federal Home Loan Banks' Financial
    Statements for ..., GA 1.13/13, GA 1.13/13-2
Financial Audit, Federal Savings and Loan Insurance
    Corporation's ... Financial Statements, GA
    1.13/12
Financial Audit, House Recording Studio Revolving
    Fund, GA 1.13/5-2
Financial Audit, House Stationery Revolving Fund
    Statements, GA 1.13/19
Financial Audit, House Restaurant Revolving Fund's
    Financial Statements, GA 1.13/8
Financial Audit, Senate Recording and Photographic
    Studios Revolving Fund, GA 1.13/5
Financial Audit, Senate Restaurants Revolving Fund
    for Fiscal Years, GA 1.13/8-2
Financial Characteristics of U.S. Farms, A 1.75/2
Financial Conditions of [various railroads], Annual
    Report to the President and the Congress, TD
    1.10/6-2
Financial Connection, T 63.128
Financial Data on Housing, Preliminary, C 18.188
Financial Institution Letters (FILS), Y 3.F 31/8:34
Financial Litigation Annual Report, J 1.1/7
Financial Management Capacity Sharing Program, HH
    1.82
Financial Management Manual, P 1.12/9
Financial Management Profile: Department of Health
    and Human Services, GA 1.26
Financial Management Series, SBA 1.32/2
Financial Management Status Report and 5-Year Plan,
    ED 1.1/5
Financial Management Systems Series, C 3.243
Financial Performance Indicators, FCA 1.28
Financial Policy and Procedures Update, D 211.30
Financial Report, HE 22.42
Financial Report, Fiscal Year, Office of Comptroller, D
    201.1/2
Financial Report to the Citizens, T 63.129
Financial Report (year), TD 4.41
Financial Reporting System, Selected Tables, E 3.37/3
Financial Reports, a Newsletter from the Financial
    Investigations Division, T 1.61
Financial Statements, HH 1.59
Financial Statements for Fiscal Year (date), Y 3.T 25:1-2
Financial Statistics for Public Assistance, Calendar
    Year, FS 3.14/3
Financial Statistics of Cities, C 3.142
Financial Statistics of Cities Having a Population of
    Over 100,000, C 3.47/2
Financial Statistics of Cities Having a Population of
    Over 30,000, C 3.47
Financial Statistics of Electric Utilities and Interstate
    Natural Gas Pipeline Companies, E 3.11/2-8
Financial Statistics of Institutions of Higher Education,
    HE 19.316/2-2, ED 1.116
Financial Statistics of Institutions of Higher Education,
    Current Funds, Revenues, and Expenditures,
    HE 19.316/2
Financial Statistics of Institutions of Higher
    Education: Property, HE 19.316
Financial Statistics of Major Investor-Owned Electric
    Utilities, E 3.18/4-2
Financial Statistics of Major U.S. Publicly Owned
    Electric Utilities, E 3.18/4-3
Financial Statistics of Selected Electric Utilities, E
    3.18/4

Foreign Fraud, Unlawful, and Lottery Mail Orders, P 1.12

Foreign Game Leaflets (numbered), I 49.74

Foreign Gold and Exchange Reserves, A 93.34

Foreign Grants and Credits by the United States Government, C 43.11

Foreign Highway News, C 18.77

Foreign Income Tax Returns, T 22.35/2

Foreign Information Series, Pr 32.4226

Foreign Inland Waterway News, Intercoastal Waterways, Rivers, Lakes, Canals, Equipment, C 18.208

Foreign Knit Goods Letter; Special Bulletins, C 18.78

Foreign Labor Interpretation Series, L 7.58

Foreign Labor Trends, L 29.16

Foreign Language Books, LC 19.11/4

Foreign Language Phrase Cards, D 208.6/5

Foreign Lumber Tariff Series, C 8.80

Foreign Market Bulletin, C 18.81

Foreign Market Reports, Accession Listings, C 42.15/3

Foreign Market Reports Service, Listing, C 42.15/2

Foreign Market Surveys, C 41.109

Foreign Markets Bulletins for Raw Materials, C 18.109/2

Foreign Markets for Builders' Hardware, C 18.82

Foreign Markets for Hand Tools, C 18.83

Foreign Markets for Heating and Cooking Appliances, C 18.84

Foreign Markets for Metals and Minerals Circulars, C 18.85/2

Foreign Markets for Scales and Other Weighing Devices, C 18.85

Foreign Meat Inspection, A 1.109/2

Foreign Military Sales Customer Procedures (series), D 7.6/15

Foreign Military Sales, Foreign Military Construction Sales, and Military Assistance Facts, D 1.66

Foreign Minerals Quarterly, I 28.51

Foreign Minerals Survey, I 28.81

Foreign News on Apples, A 36.79

Foreign News on Citrus Fruits, A 36.80

Foreign News on Tobacco, A 36.45

Foreign News on Vegetables, A 36.46

Foreign Newspaper and Gazette Report, LC 29.10

Foreign Noise Research (series), EP 1.73/2

Foreign Oceanborne Trade of United States Containerized Cargo Summary, Selected Trade Routes, C 39.233

Foreign, Overseas and Territorial Air Mail Carriers, C 31.231

Foreign Petroleum Statistics, C 18.86, C 18.86/2

Foreign Plant Quarantines in Service Training Series, A 56.25

Foreign Plants Certified to Export Meat to the United States, A 110.14

Foreign Policy Briefs, S 1.98

Foreign Policy Outlines, S 1.25/3

Foreign Port Series, C 18.34

Foreign Production and Commercial Reports, C 42.15/3

Foreign Publications Accessions List, HH 1.23/4

Foreign Radio Broadcasting Services, C 18.87

Foreign Railway News, C 18.88

Foreign Relations (by countries), S 1.1/2

Foreign Relations of the United States, S 1.1

Foreign Relations of United States, Diplomatic Papers: Conferences, S 1.1/3

Foreign Science Bulletin, LC 38.11

Foreign Service Classification List, S 1.7/2

Foreign Service Institute Bulletin, S 1.114/3-11, S 1.114/4

Foreign Service Institute: Center Paper, S 1.114/3-12

Foreign Service Institute Courses, S 1.114/2

Foreign Service Institute, General Publications, S 1.114/3

Foreign Service Institute, Quarterly Projection of Courses, S 1.114

Foreign Service Institute, Readers, S 1.114/2-2

Foreign Service Institute: Schedule of Courses, S 1.114/3-10

Foreign Service List, S 1.7

Foreign Service Manual, Transmittal Letters, S 1.5/4

Foreign Service News Letter, S 1.109

Foreign Service on Vegetables, A 64.13, A 67.14

Foreign Service Regulations (by chapters), S 1.5/3

Foreign Service Regulations, Memorandum Transmitting Mimeographed Inserts for, S 1.5/2

Foreign Service Reports, A 36.39, A 67.11

Foreign Service Written Examination Registration and Application Form, S 1.137

Foreign Shipping News, C 18.89

Foreign Social Science Bibliographies, C 3.163/5

Foreign Statistical Publications, Accessions List, C 56.238

Foreign Statistics on Apples and Other Deciduous Fruits, A 67.12

Foreign Tariff Notes, C 10.16, C 18.13

Foreign Tariff Series, C 18.12

Foreign Tariffs, C 18.192

Foreign Tax Credit Claimed on Corporation Income Tax Returns, T 22.35/2:F 76

Foreign Technology, C 51.9/32

Foreign Technology Alert-Bibliography (series), C 51.13/3

Foreign Trade Data, C 3.278

Foreign Trade in Farm Machinery and Supplies, A 67.21

Foreign Trade Information on Instrumentation, A 41.92

Foreign Trade Mark Application Service, C 18.90

Foreign Trade Notes, Minerals and Metals, C 18.91/2

Foreign Trade Notes, Minerals and Metals and Petroleum, C 18.91

Foreign Trade Notes, Petroleum, C 18.91/3

Foreign Trade Regulations of (country), C 1.50, C 57.11

Foreign Trade Reports, C 3.164

Foreign Trade [reports by States], S 1.54

Foreign Trade Series, FT 1.9

Foreign Trade Statistics Notes, C 3.167

Foreign Training Letter, to Foreign Agricultural Contacts at Land-Grant Colleges, A 67.31, A 67.31/3

Foreign Training Letters, A 67.31/3

Foreign Transactions of U.S. Government, C 18.278

Foreign Treaties and Conventions (United States not a Signatory), S 9.6

Foreign Versions, Variations, and Diminutives of English Names and Foreign Equivalents of U.S. Military and Civilian Titles, J 21.2:N 15

Foreign Visitor Arrivals by Selected Ports, Calendar Year, C 47.15/6

Foreign Wood Series, A 13.31/2

Foreign Year Trade Notes, C 18.92

Foreign-Language and English Dictionaries in the Physical Sciences and Engineering, Selected Bibliography, 1952–1963, C 13.10:258

Foreign-Owned U.S. Firms, FOF (series), C 3.254

Forensic Science Communications, J 1.14/18-2

Foresight, Civil Preparedness Today, D 14.14

Forest and Windbarrier Planting and Seeding in the United States, Report, A 13.51/2

Forest Atlas, A 13.17

Forest Economic Notes, A 13.42/13

Forest Entomology Briefs, A 9.110

Forest Fire News, A 13.32/4

Forest Fire Statistics, A 13.32/2

Forest Health Highlights, A 13.154

Forest Insect and Disease Conditions, A 13.52/2

Forest Insect and Disease Conditions in the Northern Region, A 13.52/7

Forest Insect and Disease Conditions in the Pacific Northwest, A 13.52/6

Forest Insect and Disease Conditions in the Rocky Mountain Region, A 13.52/13

Forest Insect and Disease Conditions in the Southwest, A 13.52/11

Forest Insect and Disease Conditions, Intermountain Region, A 13.52/12

Forest Insect and Disease Leaflets, A 13.52

Forest Insect and Disease Management (series), A 13.93/3, A 13.106

Forest Insect and Disease Management/Evaluation Reports, A 13.93

Forest Insect and Disease Management/Survey Reports, A 13.93/2

Forest Insect Conditions in Pacific Northwest During (year), A 13.52/6

Forest Insect Conditions in the Northern Region, A 13.52/7

Forest Insect Conditions in the United States, A 13.52/2

Forest Insects and Diseases Group Technical Publications, A 13.93/4

Forest Inspection and Disease Management (series), A 13.93/3

Forest Management Notes, A 13.42/11

Forest Management Papers, A 13.42/12

Forest Management Program Annual Report (National Summary), A 13.152

Forest Pathology Special Releases, A 77.516

Forest Pest Conditions in the North East, A 13.52/9

Forest Pest Conditions Report for the Northeastern Area, A 13.115/2

Forest Pest Leaflets, A 13.52

Forest Pest Management Methods Applications Group: Reports (series), A 13.52/10-3

Forest Pest Observer, A 13.68/11

Forest Planting Leaflets, A 13.9

Forest Planting, Seeding, and Silvical Treatments in the United States, A 13.51/2

Forest Product Notes, A 13.42/18

Forest Product Utilization Technical Reports, A 13.96

Forest Products, C 3.12, C 3.12/7

Forest Products, 1907, C 3.12/1

Forest Products, 1908, C 3.12/2

Forest Products, 1910, C 3.12/4

Forest Products, 1911, C 3.12/5

Forest Products, 1912, C 3.12/6

Forest Products Division Circulars, C 13.92/2

Forest Products Division Paper Circulars, C 18.92/3

Forest Products Industry Notes, Y 3.T 25:28-2

Forest Products Laboratory, Madison, Wisconsin, A 13.27

Forest Products Papers, A 13.67/10

Forest Products Review, C 62.11

Forest Products, Series 1909, C 3.12/3

Forest Research News for the Midsouth, A 13.40/11

Forest Research News for the South, A 13.40/11

Forest Research Notes, A 13.62/7, A 13.66/7

Forest Research Project Reports, A 13.41

Forest Resource Reports, A 13.50

Forest Service Comments on Resolutions Relating to the National Forest System As Adopted, A 13.86

Forest Service Films Available on Loan for Educational Purposes to Schools, Civic Groups, Churches, Television, A 13.55

Forest Service History Line, A 13.98/3

Forest Service Organizational Directory, A 13.36/2-2

Forest Service Translations, A 13.81

Forest Statistics Series (by States), A 13.42/21

Forest Survey Notes, A 13.42/10

Forest Survey Releases–

Central States Forest Experiment Station, A 13.68/9

Intermountain Forest and Range Experiment Station, A 13.65/10

Northeastern Forest Experiment Station, A 13.67/7

Pacific Southwest Forest and Range Experiment Station, A 13.62/8

Progress Reports, A 13.30/5

Rocky Mountain Forest and Range Experiment Station, A 13.69/9

Southeastern Forest Experiment Station, A 13.63/7

Southern Forest Experiment Station, A 13.40/5

Forest Service Report to Congress, A 13.116

Forest Survey Reports, A 13.66/8

Forest Tree Nurseries in the United States, A 13.74

Forest Statistics for Northwest Florida, A 13.80/6

Forest Worker, A 13.19

Forest-Gram South, Dispatch of Current Technical Information for Direct Use by Practicing Forest Resource Manager in the South, A 13.89

Forestry Bulletins, Y 3.T 25:18

Forestry Bulletins, SB-FB/P- (series), A 13.106/2

Forestry Bulletins, SA-FB-U- (series), A 13.106/2-2

Forestry Current Literature, A 13.25

Forestry Incentives Program, from Inception of Program through (date), A 82.92

Forestry Investigation Notes, Y 3.T 25:34

Forestry Laws, A 13.18

Forestry Publications, Y 3.Em 3:7, Y 3.C 49:9, FS 4.7

Forestry Relations Division, Publications, Y 3.T 25:27

Forestry Research Progress in (year) McIntire-Stennis Cooperative Forestry Research Program, A 94.2 F 76/

Forestry Research West, A 13.95, A 13.95/2

Forestry Research: What's New in the West, A 13.95

Forestry Wage Survey (Summary) [various states], L 2.113/8

Formal Docket Decisions, FMC 1.10/2

Form Flow, D 7.41/2

Form of General Balance Sheet Statement, IC 1 ste.13, IC 1 wat.9

Form of General Balance Sheet Statement for Express Companies, IC 1 exp.8

Form of Income and Profit and Loss Statement, IC 1 ste.14

Forms–

Alcohol, Tobacco, and Firearms Bureau, T 70.22

Auditor for Interior Department, TD 5.54

Bureau of Export Development, C 57.120

Bureau of the Census, C 3.272

Coast and Geodetic Survey, TD 11.34

Consolidated Farm Service Agency, A 112.19

Copyright Office, LC 3.Form, LC 3.14

Customs Service, T 17.20

Department of the Treasury, T 1.63/2

Drug Enforcement Administration, J 24.27

Economic Analysis Bureau, C 59.23

Employment Standards Administration, L 36.17

Environmental Protection Agency, EP 1.101

Export Administration Bureau, C 63.13

Farmers Home Administration, A 84.16

G

Gallant American Women (Radio Scripts), FS 5.15

Gallium in (year), I 28.160, I 28.174/2

Galvanized Range Broilers and Tanks for Hot Water Heaters, C 3.86

Galveston Bay Fact Sheet Series, I 49.110

Game Laws, A 1.9

GAO Documents, Catalog of Reports, Decisions and Opinions, Testimonies and Speeches, GA 1.16/4

GAO Document, GA 1.39

GAO Document (series) GA 1.39

GAO. Journal, GA 1.15/2

GAO Manual for Guidance of Federal Agencies, GA 1.6/1

GAO, Office of Public Information, Reports, GA 1.16/3

GAO Online Service, GA 1.34

GAO Policy and Procedures Manual for Guidance of Federal Agencies: Title 6, Pay, Leave, and Allowances, GA 1.6/6

GAO Review, GA 1.15

GAO, Status of Open Recommendations, GA 1.13/18-2

Gap Analysis Program I 19.212

Garden and Home Food Preservation Facts, A 43.29

Garden Facts for Garden Leaders, A 43.29/2

Garment Enforcement Report, L 36.215

Garnet in (year), I 28.161

Garrison Commanders Directory, D 101.120/4

Gas and Meter Inspection, Annual Report, I 1.13

Gas Supplies of Interstate Natural Gas Pipeline Companies, E 3.25/2

Gas Turbine Electric Plant Construction Cost and Annual Production Expenses, E 3.17/2

Gasoline Prices (Preliminary Release), E 3.11/19

Gastroenterology Abstracts and Citations, HE 20.3313

Gateway National Recreation Area Program Guide, I 29.96/3

Gateway Outlook, I 29.96/3

Gazette, LC 1.49

Gazette of the Allied Commission for Austria, D 102.22

Gazetteer Supplements, I 33.8/2

Gazetteers–
Board on Geographic Names, I 33.8
Defense Mapping Agency, D 5.319
Hydrographic Office, N 6.33

GBF/DIME Systems, (GEO nos.), C 3.249

GC Legislative History Files, GA 1.23

GE-10 Geographic Reports, C 3.208

GE-20 Area Measurement Reports, C 3.208/2

GE-40 Census Tract Papers, C 3.227/2

GE-50 United States Maps, C 3.62/4

GE-70 Map Series, C 3.62/8

Gem Stones in (year), I 28.117

GEN, ED 1.76/2

GEN- (series), ED 1.76

General Accounting Office Salary Tables, GA 1.10, GA 1.6/10

General and Miscellaneous, E 1.99

General Aviation Accidents (non-air carrier), Statistical Analysis, C 31.160/2, FAA 1.15

General Aviation Activity and Avionics Survey, TD 4.32/17-2

General Aviation Aircraft Use, FAA 1.39

General Aviation Airworthiness Alerts, TD 4.414

General Aviation Inspection Aids Summary, TD 4.409

General Catalog: MAC NCO Academy West, D 301.80/2

General Catalog of Mariners & Aviators' Charts and Books, N 6.5

General Catalogs of Educational Films, FS 5.10/3

General Catalogue of Homoptera, A 77.20

General Ceiling Price Regulations, ES 3.6/4

General Chart of Northern and Northwestern Lakes [and rivers], W 33.7/1

General Clinical Research Centers Committee, HE 20.3001/2:C 61/2

General Clinical Research Centers: A Research Resources Directory, HE 20.3037/4

General Construction Bulletins, Y 3.R 88:13

General Court-Martial Orders–
Army and Corps Areas and Departments, W 99.11/7, W 99.12/7, W 99.13/7, W 99.14/7, W 99.15/7, W 99.16/7, W 99.17/7, W 99.19/7, W 99.21/7
Department of the Army, W 3.32, W 1.51, M 101.14, D 101.14
Department of the East, W 17.9
Department of the Navy, N 1.14, M 201.9, D 201.9
Hawaii Department, W 81.9
Military Academy, W 12.13, M 109.10

General Crop Report, Louisiana Crop Reporting Service, A 88.24/7

General Crop Reports, A 66.11

General Departmental Circulars, A 1.62

General Description of Foreign-trade Zones, FTZ 1.8

General Displacement Notices, CS 1.49

General Drawings of Snow Removal Equipment, W 7.31/2

General Engine Bulletins, N 28.21

General Foreign Policy Series, S 1.71

General Headquarters, Far East Command, General Publications, D 1.24

General Import, World Area by Commodity Groupings, C 56.210:155

General Imports of Merchandise into United States by Air, Commodity by Country of Origin, C 3.164:231

General Imports of Merchandise into United States by Air, Country of Origin by Commodity, C 3.164:232

General Index to Experiment Station Record, A 10.6/2

General Index to International Law Situations, N 15.7/2

General Indexes to Monthly Consular Reports, S 4.8

General Industry Standards, L 35.6/3

General Information Bulletin, N 4.14

General Information Concerning Patents, C 21.26/2

General Information Concerning Trademarks, C 21.2:T 67, C 21.26

General Information Leaflets–
Department of the Army, D 101.75
National Archives and Records Service, GS 4.22
National Archives and Records Administration, AE 1.113

General Information Letter, MC 1.29

General Information Regarding Dept. of the Interior, I 1.70

General Information Series–
Agricultural Adjustment Administration, A 55.71
Agricultural Adjustment Agency, A 76.408, A 80.614
Federal Communications Commission, CC 1.37/2
Federal Crop Insurance Corporation, A 62.7
Federal Surplus Commodities Corporation, A 69.9

General Information Series, Information from Abroad, N 13.5

General Instructions and Regulations in Relation to Transaction of Business at Mints and Assay Offices with Coinage Laws, T 28.9

General Instructions for Surveys in Philippine Islands, C 4.18/4

General Interpretations, ES 3.6/14

General Land Office, Automated Records Project, Pre-1908 Homestead & Cash Entry Patents, I 53.57

General Legal Bulletin, Foreign Laws Affecting American Business, C 18.95

General Letter, C 11.9

General Letters, FW 4.12

General Letters to State Works Progress Administrators, Y 3.W 89/2:23

General Library Committee Publications, LC 1.32/2

General Maintenance Alert Bulletins, C 31.163/2, FAA 1.31/2

General Maintenance Inspection Aids, C 31.162

General Maintenance Inspection Aids Summary and Supplements, FAA 1.31

General Management Training Center, Calendar of Training Courses, Fiscal Year, CS 1.65/5

General Maximum Price Regulations, Bulletins, Pr 32.4211

General Medicine a Study Section, HE 20.3001/2:M 46/2

General Medicine B Study Section, HE 20.3001/2:M 46/3

General (38) Nautical Charts, D 5.343

General Nautical and International Nautical Charts, D 5.356

General Newspaper Releases, Y 3.W 19/2:5

General Office Orders, GA 1.8

General Operating and Flight Rules, TD 4.6:part 91

General Operating Support Grant Application and Information, NF 4.9

General Orders Embracing Laws Affecting the Army, W 3.8

General Orders in Bankruptcy, Ju 6.9/2

General Overriding Regulations, ES 3.6/9

General Planning, D 5.318/5

General Press Releases, ES 3.7/1

General Procedure, A 62.11

General Progress Bulletins, New Allotments, Y 3.R 88:12

General Publications: National Communications System, PrEx 1.17/2

General Publications Relating to Dairy Research, A 77.602

General Real and Personal Property Inventory Report (Civilian and Military) of the United States Government Covering Its Properties Located in the United States, in the Territories, and Overseas, As of June 30 [year], Y 4.G 74/7:P 94

General Receiver of Customs for Liberia, S 1.24

General Regulations for the Enforcement of the Federal Food, Drug, and Cosmetic Act, FS 13.106/2:1/2

General Relief Operations of Large City Public Welfare Agencies, SS 1.26

General Reports, A 89.11

General Research, GR-(series), I 27.27

General Research Support Program Advisory Committee, HE 20.3001/2:R 31/2

General Revenue Sharing, T 1.53/2

General Revenue Sharing Payments, T 1.53

General Rules and Regulations Prescribed by Board of Supervising Inspectors of Steamboats, T 38.9

General Rules and Regulations Under the Investment Company Act of 1940, As in Effect (date), SE 1.6:R 86/9

General Rules and Regulations Under the Securities Act of 1933, As in Effect (date), SE 1.6:R 86/2

General Rules and Regulations Under the Securities Exchange Act of 1934, As in Effect (date), SE 1.6:R 86/3

General Salary Orders, ES 4.6/3

General Salary Stabilization Regulations GSSR (series), ES 4.6/2

General Schedule of Supplies, GS 1.5/1, T 45.5/1, T 58.8

General Specifications for Building Vessels of Navy, N 29.7, M 210.7

General Specifications for Machinery, N 19.5/2

General Sugar Orders, A 55.19

General Summary of Inventory Status and Movement of Capital and Producers Goods, Plants, Aircraft, and Industry Agent Items, Pr 33.210

General Superintendent and Landscape Engineer of National Parks, Annual Reports, I 1.58

General Supplies Fixed Price Lists, W 77.23/1

General Supplies Lists, W 77.23/2

General Survey of Conditions in Coal Industry, C 22.21

General Survey of Forest Situation, A 13.37

General Technical Reports, A 13.88

General Wage Determinations Issued under the Davis-Bacon and Related Acts, L 36.211

General Wage Regulations, ES 2.6/3

General/Flag Officer Worldwide Roster, D 1.61/8

Generation and Sales Statistics, E 5.14, I 44.8

Generic Letter (series), Y 3.N 88:56

Genetic Bases for Resistance to Avian Diseases, Northeastern States Regional Project, A 94.15

Genetics Study Section, HE 20.3001/2:G 28

Geneva Arbitration (Alabama Claims), S 3.13/1

Geochemistry, C 41.46

Geodesy and Cartography, C 41.46/3

Geodetic Letters, C 4.30

GEO-Drug Enforcement Program Six-month Statistics, J 24.18

GEOnet Names Server, D 5.319/2

Geographic and Global Issues, S 1.119/4

Geographic Area Statistics, C 3.24/9-9

Geographic Base (DIME) file, CUE, [Correction-Update-Extension], C 3.249/2, C 56.255

Geographic Bulletins, S 1.119/2

Geographic Distribution of Federal Funds in (States), CSA 1.10

Geographic Distribution of Radio Sets and Characteristics of Radio Owners in Countries of the World, IA 1.12/2

Geographic Distribution of VA Expenditures, State, County, and Congressional District, VA 1.2/11

Geographic Identification Code Scheme [by regions], C 3.223/13-2

Geographic Mobility, C 3.186

Geographic Names in Coastal Areas (by States), C 4.37

Geographic Names Information System I 19.16/2

Geographic News, C 18.96/3

Geographic Notes, S 1.119/4

Geographic Profile of Employment and Unemployment, L 2.3/12

Geographic Reports, S 1.119

Geographical Mobility, C 3.186/18

Geologic Atlas of the United States, I 19.5/1

Geologic Bulletins, Y 3.T 25:10

Geologic Map Index of (various States), I 19.41/8

Geologic Names of North America Introduced in 1936–1955, I 19.3:1056
Geologic Quadrangle Maps, I 19.38
Geologic Studies in Alaska by the U.S. Geological Survey, I 19.4/8
Geological Map Index of (various States), I 19.86
Geological Quadrangle Maps, I 19.88
Geological Reports, I 27.38
Geological Studies in Alaska by the U.S. Geological Survey, I 19.4/3
Geological Survey Research, I 19.16
GEOnet Names Server, D 5.319/2
Geophysical Abstracts, C 22.32, I 28.25, I 19.43
Geophysical Fluid Dynamics Laboratory: Activities, Plans, C 55.601/5
Geophysical Investigations Maps, I 19.25/2, I 19.87
Geophysical Monitoring for Climatic Change, C 55.618
Geophysical Research Papers, D 301.45/2
Geophysics and Space Data Bulletin, D 301.45/43
Geoscience and Technology Bulletin, LC 38.12
Geosciences, E 1.99
Geothermal Energy, E 1.99
Geothermal Energy Research, Development and Demonstration Program, Annual Report, ER 1.31
Geothermal Energy Update, E 1.66
Geriatric Research, Education, and Clinical Centers, VA 1.92
German Science Bulletin, S 1.91/4
Getting Involved (various subjects) (series), HE 23.1112
Getting to the Corps, Y 3.N 21/29:16-18
GIS Application Note (series), A 13.118
GIST, S 1.128
GIST Index, S 1.128/2
GITI [General Investigation of Tidal Inlets] Reports, D 103.42/7
Glacier National Park, Reports, I 1.52
Glaciological Data Report, C 55.220/6
Glaciological Notes, I 19.60
Glass and Ceramics [abstracts], C 41.68
Glen Echo Park, I 29.98
Global Atmospheric Background Monitoring for Selected Environmental Parameters, C 55.284
Global AUTOVON Telephone Directory, D 5.111
Global Crime, S 1.149
Global Daily Summary, Temperature and Precipitation, C 55.281/2
Global Issues, IA 1.39, S 20.18
Global Market Survey, European Market, C 61.9/2
Global Market Surveys, C 57.109
Global Navigation and Planning Charts, D 5.354
Global Ocean Floor Analysis and Research Data Series, D 203.31
Global Outlook, HH 1.130
Global Trade Talk, T 17.28
Global Volcanism Program, Digital Information Series, SI 1.49
GLOBE Offline, C 55.56
GMENAC Staff Papers, HE 20.6614
GNC - Global Navigation Charts, D 5.324
Goals 2000 A Progress Report, ED 1.85/4
Goals 2000, Community Update, ED 1.85/2
Goddard Space Flight Center, Technical Abstracts, NAS 1.28
Gold and Silver, I 28.61/2
Gold and Silver Exports and Imports: Weekly Statement of, United States, C 3.195
Gold and Silver in (year), I 28.61/3
Gold and Silver Movements: United States, C 3.196
Gold Report [Mine Production], I 28.61
Golden Gate International Exposition, S 6.23
Golf Bulletin, W 99.15/11
Government Depository Libraries, Y 4.P 93/1:D 44
Government Employment, C 56.209/2
Government Employment GE (series), C 3.140/2
Government Ethics Newsgram, Y 3.Et 3:15
Government Finances and Employment at a Glance, C 3.191/3
Government Finances: Public Education Finances, C 3.191/2-10
Government Inventions for Licensing, C 51.9/23
Government Life Insurance Programs for Veterans and Servicemen, VA 1.46
Government National Mortgage Association, GNMA, Annual Report, HH 1.7/7
Government Organization Handbooks, GS 4.109/2
Government Organization Manuals, a Bibliography, LC 1.12/2:G 74
Government Organizations, C 3.171
Government Paper Specification Standards, Y 4.P 93/1:7, Y 4.P 93/1:7/2
Government Printing & Binding Regulations, Y 4.P 93/1:6

Government Reports Announcements, C 51.9/3
Government Reports Announcements and Index, C 51.9/3
Government Reports Annual Index, C 51.9/4
Government Reports Index, C 51.9
Government Reports Index, Quarterly Cumulative, C 51.9/2
Government Reports Topical Announcements, C 51.7/5
Government Salary Tables, T 13.6
Government Vehicle Operators Guide to Service Stations for Gasoline, Oil and Lubrication, D 7.6/7-2
Governmental Finances, C 56.209, C 3.191/2, C 3.191/2-4
Governmental Finances in United States, C 3.191
Government-Supported Research, International Affairs, Research Completed and in Progress, S 1.101/9
Government-Supported Research on Foreign Affairs, Current Project Information, S 1.101/10
GPO Access, GP 1.1/2
GPO Access Training Manual, GP 3.29/2
GPO Bulletin, GP 1.19
GPO Depository Union List of Item Selections, GP 3.32/2
GPO Library Cataloging Transaction Tapes, GP 3.8/4
GPO Locator, GP 3.37
GPO Sales Publications Reference File, GP 3.22/3
GPO Sales Publications Reference File, Update, GP 3.22/3-2
GP-PIA Joint Research Bulletins, GP 1.25
GPT Bulletins, FS 13.215
GR 68 Quarterly Reports on Holdings of Retirement Systems, C 3.242
GR (series), I 27.72
Graduate Education Bulletin, Uniformed Services University of the Health Sciences, D 1.67/2
Graduate Fellowship Announcement, TD 2.64/2
Graduate Fellowship Awards Announced by National Science Foundation, NS 1.19
Graduate School Announcement of Courses, C 13.41
Graduate Student Researchers Program, NAS 1.42/2
Graduate Students and Postdoctorates in Science and Engineering, NS 1.22/11
Grain and Feed Market News, A 88.18/4-2
Grain and Grain Products, C 18.72/4
Grain Crop Quality, (year) Crops, A 88.40/2:44
Grain Division News, A 88.18/27
Grain Inspection Manual, A 88.6/4:G 76
Grain Inspector's Letters, A 36.192
Grain Investigations [publications], A 36.93
Grain Market News and Statistical Report, A 82.71, A 88.18
Grain Market News, Quarterly Summary and Statistics, A 88.18/21
Grain Standardization, A 19.11
Grain Stocks, A 105.20
Grain Transportation Prospect, A 88.68/2
Grain Transportation Report, A 88.68
Grain Transportation Situation, A 108.12
Grand and Petit Juror Service in U.S. District Courts, Ju 10.13
Grand Canyon VFR Aeronautical Chart, TD 4.79/13-6
Grand Canyon VFR Aeronautical Chart, (General Aviation), C 55.416/12-6
Grant Awards, TD 1.39
Grant-in-aid for Fisheries Program Activities, C 55.323
Grants Administration Manual, EP 1.8/2, HE 1.6/7
Grants Administration Manual Circular, HE 1.6/7-2
Grants Administration Report, FS 1.31, HE 1.31
Grants Administration Reports, HE 1.31
Grants and Awards for Fiscal Year (date), NS 1.10/4
Grants Competitions and RFPS: Planned NIE Activities During the Fiscal Year, HE 19.216
Grants Contract Reports, Experimental Technology Incentives Program, GCR-ETIP (series), C 13.57/2
Grants for Training, Construction, Cancer Control, Medical Libraries, HE 20.3013/5
Grants for Training Construction Medical Libraries, HE 20.3013/5
Grants, Juvenile Delinquency Prevention and Control Act, HE 17.21
Grants Policy Directives HE 1.6/7
Grants, Preventive Services, Training, Technical Assistance and Information Services, HE 1.310
Grants to Organizations, Application Forms, NF 2.15/2
Grants to Organizations, Application Guidelines, NF 2.15
Grants to Presenting Organizations, Special Touring Initiatives Application Guidelines, NF 2.8/2-29

Grants-In-Aid and Other Financial Assistance Programs, FS 1.6/6, HE 20.2016
Grants-In-Aid and Other Financial Assistance Programs, Health Services and Mental Health Administration, FS 2.317
Grants-In-Aid Catalogue, I 29.83
Graphic Notes and Supplemental Data, TD 4.12/4
Graphic Pamphlets GP (series), C 3.223/14
Graphic Portfolios, Charts, and Posters, W 1.52
Graphic Training Aids, W 1.53, D 101.21
Graphical Supplement to Monthly Reports, IC 1 ste.33
Graphite in (year), I 28.128/2
Grassroots Development: Journal of the Inter-American Foundation, Y 3.In 8/25:15
Graves Registration Service Bulletins, W 95.16
GrayLit Network, E 1.137/3
Grazing Decisions, I 53.15
GRD Research Notes, D 301.45/16
GRD Research Notes, Geophysics Research Directorate, D 301.45/16
GRD Technical Report, D 301.45/16-3
Great Britain and United States Claims Commission, S 3.8
Great Circle (8) Sailing and Polar Charts, D 5.345
Great Circle Sailing, Polar and Tracking Charts, D 5.356
Great Circle (58) Tracking Charts, D 5.346
Great Lakes, TD 5.9:4, C 55.422:6
Great Lakes Environmental Research Laboratory: Annual Report, C 55.620
Great Lakes Fisheries, C 55.309/2
Great Lakes Intercom, TD 4.26/2
Lake Survey Office, D 103.203
National Ocean Survey, C 55.420
Great Lakes Levels Update, D 103.116/2
Great Lakes Pilotage Administration, C 1.47
Great Lakes Pilotage Regulations and Rules and Orders, C 1.47:R 26
Great Lakes Region Air Traffic Activity, TD 4.19/5
Great Lakes Region Aviation Systems, Ten Year Plan, TD 4.33/4
Great Lakes Research Advisory Board: Annual Report, Y 3.In 8/28:10
Great Lakes Science Advisory Board: Annual Report, Y 3.In 8/28:12, Y 3.In 8/28:16
Great Lakes Water Levels, C 55.420/2
Great Lakes Water Quality Annual Report, Y 3.In 8/28:9
Great Lakes-St. Lawrence Seaway Winter Navigation Board: Annual Report, D 103.1/3
Greatfully Yours, HE 20.3625
Greenhouse Gas Volunteer (Newsletter) E 3.59/3
Green Book, Overview of Entitlement Programs, Y 4.W 36:10-7
Green Coffee Inventories and Roastings, C 3.236
Green Roadsides, TD 2.30/16-2
Gridpoints, NAS 1.97
Grist, I 70.22/2
Grosse Ile Laboratory: Quarterly Report, EP 1.46/4
Ground Accident Abstracts, D 301.53
Ground Archaeology and Ethmography in the Public Interest, I 29.59/5-2
Ground Water Issue, EP 1.43/2
Ground-Water Levels in the United States, I 19.13
Groundwater Recharge Advisory, I 27.80
Group Services Bulletins, Pr 32.4232
Grouped Interest Guides, HE 20.8311/3
Groups with Historically High Incidences of Unemployment, L 36.12
GSA Bulletin FPR, Federal Procurement, GS 1.6/5-3
GSA FIRMR/FAR Regulations, GS 12.15/2
GSA Handbooks (numbered), GS 1.6/9
GSA Interagency Training Center Newsletter, GS 1.26/3
GSA News, GS 1.20
GSA Stockpile Information, GS 1.21
GSA Subcontracting Directory, GS 1.31
GSA Supply Catalog, GS 2.10/6
GSA Supply Catalog Change Bulletin, GS 2.10/6-3
GSA Training Center Catalog and Schedule, GS 1.26, GS 1.26/2-2
GSO Newsline, S 1.144
Guide for Preparation of Proposals and Project Operation, NS 1.20/2
Guide G (series), VA 1.10/4
Guide Leaflets, I 29.12, I 29.12/2
Guide Lines, Y 3.Se 5:17/date
Guide Lines, Guidance and Pupil Personnel Service, FS 5.54
Guide of the U.S. Development of Energy, Board of Contract Appeals and Contract Adjustment Board, E 1.8/4
Guide Specifications for Civil Works, W 7.37

Guide to Computer Program Directories, C 13.10:500-42

Guide to Crop Insurance Protection, A 62.16

Guide to Current Business Data, C 43.12

Guide to Department of Education Programs, ED 1.10/2

Guide to Eligibility of W.P.A. Projects, Y 3.W 89/2:14

Guide to Federal Aviation Administration Publications, TD 4.17/6

Guide to Federal Consumer Services, PrEx 16.8:Se 6

Guide to Federal Estate and Gift Taxation, T 22.19/2:Es 8

Guide to Foreign Trade Statistics, (year), C 56.210/2

Guide to German Records Microfilmed at Alexandria, Va., GS 4.18

Guide to Health Insurance for People with Medicare, HE 22.8/17

Guide to Organized Occupational Curriculums in Higher Education, FS 5.254:54012, HE 5.254:54012

Guide to Processing Personnel Actions, PM 1.14/3-4

Guide to Programs, NS 1.47

Guide to Published Research on Atomic Energy, Y 3.At 7:7

Guide to Record Retention Requirements, GS 4.107/a:R 245

Guide to Russian Scientific Periodical Literature, Y 3.At 7:23

Guide to Selected Legal Sources of Mainland China, LC 1.6/4:C 44

Guide to Subject Indexes for Scientific and Technical Aerospace Reports, NAS 1.9/6

Guide to Substance Abuse Treatment Benefits Under the Federal Employees Health Benefits Program, PM 1.8/9

Guide to the Evaluation of Educational Experiences in the Armed Services, D 1.6/2-3

Guide to the National Archives of the United States, GS 4.6/2:N 21

Guide to the U.S. Department of Energy, Board of Contract Appeals and Contract Adjustment Board, E 1.8/4

Guide to Training Courses, Washington Training Development Services, PM 1.19/4-4

Guidebook, Caribbean Basin Initiative, C 61.8/2

Guideline Manuals, J 27.8/2

Guideline Sentencing Update, Ju 13.8/3

Guideline Technical Report, HE 20.6520/4

Guidelines, Y 3.W 29:8-2

Guidelines for Implementation of Sanitary Requirements in Poultry Establishments, A 88.6/4:P 86/2

Guidelines for the Clinical Evaluation of [various drugs], HE 20.4208/2

Guidelines for [Various Health Professionals and Sub-professional] in Home Health Services, FS 2.6/8

Guidelines: Innovative Collective Bargaining Contract Provisions, J 3.W 29:8-2

Guides to German Records Microfilmed at Alexandria, Virginia, GS 4.18, AE 1.112

Guides to the Microfilmed Records of the German Navy, GS 4.18/2, AE 1.108, AE 1.112/2

Guillain Barre Syndrome Surveillance, HE 20.7011/32

Gulf Coast Shrimp Data, I 49.60

Gulf Fisheries, C 55.309/2

Gulf of Mexico Summary Report/Index, I 72.9/5

Gulf NEWS, D 1.95/5

Gulf War Review, VA 1.104

Gulfstream, C 55.123

Gum Turpentine and Gum Rosin Circular Letters, Y 3.C 73:11

Gypsum, I 28.32

Gypsum in (year), I 28.32/2

Gypsy Moth News, A 13.141

H

H 8-1 Nongovernment Organization Codes for Military Standard Contract Administration Procedures: Name to Code, D 7.6/2:8-1/2

H 8-2 Nongovernment Organization Codes for Military Standard Contract Administration Procedures: Code to Name, D 7.6/2:8-2/2

H.O. Publications, D 5.317

H 6-2 Federal Item Identifications Guides for Supply Cataloging, Part 2, Description Patterns, D 7.6/2:6-2

H 7 Manufacturers Part and Drawing Numbering Systems, D 7.6/2:7

H.T. & S. Office Reports, A 77.523, A 88.39

Habeas & Prison Litigation Case Law Update, Ju 13.8/4

Habitat Conservation Programs of the National Marine Fisheries Service, C 55.340

Habitat Management for [various Animals], A 57.56

Habitat Suitability Index Models (series), I 49.97

Habitat Suitability Information, I 49.97/2

HABS/HAER Review, I 29.74/3

Haiti, American High Commissioner to, S 1.22

Haiti, Annual Reports of Financial Adviser- General Receiver, S 1.23

Haitian Customs Receivership, Annual Reports, S 1.16

Halifax Commission (Fishery Commission), S 3.13/4

Hallmark, D 101.68

Hampton Normal and Agricultural Institute, I 20.17

Handbook AS (series), P 1.31/10

Handbook EL- (series), P 1.31/9

Handbook F (series), P 1.31/14

Handbook for Participation Loans with the Small Business Administration, SBA 1.19:L 78

Handbook for Staff Physicians, HE 20.3044

Handbook for Veterans Administration Contract Representatives, VA 1.10/5:232-68-1/2

Handbook IM (series), P 1.31/15

Handbook of–

  Airline Statistics, C 31.249

  Card Distribution, LC 28.7

  Conservation Practices (by States), A 82.111

  Descriptions of Specialized Fields, Pr 32.5227, L 7.17

  Economic Statistics, PrEx 3.10/7-5, S 1.91/3

  Federal Aid to Communities, C 46.8:C 73

  Hearing Aid Measurement, VA 1.22/3

  Hospital Corps, United States Navy, D 206.6/3:H 79

  International Economic Statistics, PrEx 3.16

  Labor Statistics, L 2.3, L 2.3/5

  Mathematical Functions, C 13.32:55

  Merchant Shipping Statistics, C 39.218

  North American Indians, SI 1.20/2

  Occupational Groups and Series of Classes, PM 1.8/2, SE 1.13/3

  Old-Age and Survivors Insurance Statistics, FS 3.40

  Procedure Memorandum, FS 6.12, Pr 32.5257

  Procedures, Y 3.N 21/14:9

  Procedures Memorandum, FS 6.12

Handbook of Procedures Letters–

  National Youth Administration, Y 3.N 21/14:10

  Works Progress Administration, Y 3.W 89/2:29

  Works Projects Administration, FW 4.9

Handbook, Office of Education, FS 3.211:11002, HE 5.211:11002

Handbook on Programs of Office of Vocational Rehabilitation, FS 13.217

Handbook on Programs of the Department of Health, Education, and Welfare, FS 1.6/5

Handbook on Women Workers, L 36.103

Handbook (series), VA 1.10/5

Handbook for Service Attaches Accredited to the Department of the Air Force, D 301.6/5-2

Handbook T (series), P 1.31/16

Handbooks–

  Action, AA 1.8/2

  Agricultural and Range Conservation Programs, A 55.45/11, A 55.46/11

  Agricultural Conservation Program, A 55.45/12, A 82.37

  Civil Service Commission, CS 1.45

  Defense Civil Preparedness Agency, D 14.8/3

  Defense Supply Agency, D 7.6/7

  Descriptive Cataloging Division, LC 9.15

  Federal Civil Defense Administration, FCD 1.6/4

  National Bureau of Standards, C 13.11

  National Institute of Diabetes and Digestive and Kidney Diseases, HE 20.3358

  Naval Academy, D 208.115

  Office of Civil Defense, D 13.8/3

  Office of Education, HE 5.211:11002

  Plant Safety Branch, FS 2.22/24

  Railroad Safety Office, TD 3.108

  Southern Region, A 55.45/11

  Western Region, A 55.46/11

Handbooks, Manuals, Guides [relating to Entomology and Plant Quarantine], A 77.306/3

Handbooks, DM- (series), P 1.31/11

Handbooks, Manuals, Guides Relating to Industrial Mobilization and Security, D 3.6/3

Handbooks, Manuals, Guides Relating to Research and Development, D 4.10

Handbooks (numbered), C 55.308/2

Handbooks on Programs of Department of Health, Education and Welfare, FS 1.6/5, HE 1.6/5

Handicapped Children's Early Education Program, ED 1.32/4

Handicapped Children's Education Program, Grant Announcements, ED 1.32/3

Handout on Health, HE 20.3916

Handtool Section (FSG 51 and FSG 52 Items), GS 2.10/2-2

Harbor Charts and Charts of Special Localities, W 33.8

Hardware Trade Bulletin, C 18.76

Harmon Memorial Lectures in Military History, D 305.10

Harmonized Tariff Schedule of the U.S. Annotated for Statistical Reporting Purposes, ITC 1.10

Harmonized Tariff Schedule of the United States, ITC 1.10/4

Harness Leather and Skivers, Preliminary Report on, C 3.44

Harriman Alaska Series, SI 1.11

Harry Diamond Laboratories–

  Dimensions, D 105.30

  Special Reports, D 105.14/5

  Washington, D.C., D 105.14/3

Harvard Studies in Marketing Farm Products, A 36.169

Hatcheries and Dealers Participating in the National Poultry Improvement Plan, A 77.15:44-6

Hatchery Production, A 88.15/5, A 105.12/3-2

Hatchery Production, Louisiana Crop Reporting Service, A 88.15/22

Hatchery Reports, A 36.205

Hate Crime: The Violence of Intolerance, CRS Bulletin, J 23.3

Have You Heard, I 16.60/1

Hawaii, Governor, Annual Reports, I 1.41

Hawaii Tax Fund Orders, A 55.28

Hawaiian Volcano Observatory Summary, I 19.29/2

Hazard Analysis Reports [on various subjects], Y 3.C 76/3:17

Hazardous Item Listing, D 7.32

Hazardous Materials Accident Report, NTSB/HZM-(series), TD 1.28

Hazardous Material Control and Management/ Hazardous Materials Information System, D 212.16

Hazardous Materials Information System, D 7.39, D 7.32

Hazardous Materials Information System, Hazardous Item Listing, D 7.6/17

Hazardous Materials Transportation Training Modules TD 10.16

Hazardous Occupations Orders, L 22.26

Hazardous Substances and Public Health, HE 20.516, HE 20.7915

HCFA Common Procedure Coding System, HE 22.37

HCFA Communications Directory, HE 22.14

HCFA Fact Sheet (series), HE 22.40

HCFA Forms Information Catalog, HE 22.32/2

HCFA Health Watch, HE 22.43

HCFA Regional Office Manual–

  General, HE 22.8/8-5

  Medicade, HE 22.8/8-4

  Medicare, HE 22.8/8

  Program Integrity, HE 22.8/8-2

  Standards and Certification Guidelines, HE 22.8/8-3

HCFA Rulings, HE 22.38

HCFA Statistics, HE 22.509

HCFA Telephone Directory, HE 22.14

HCFA's Laws, Regulations, Manuals, HE 22.8/22

HCUP Factbook, HE 20.6514/4

HCUP-3 (Healthcare Cost and Utilization Project) Research Note, HE 20.6514/3

HDS Telephone Directory, HE 23.11

HE Instruction in Agriculture, Programs, Activities, Developments, FS 5.74

Head Start, Child Development Program, Manual of Policies and Instructions, PrEx 10.8:H 34/2

Head Start Newsletter, PrEx 10.12/2, HE 21.209, HE 23.1014

Head Start Program Data, HE 23.1115

Headings and Subheads for Index to Federal Statutes, LC 10.6

Headline Series, FS 3.224, FS 14.117, FS 5.224, HE 5.224

Headquarters' Circulars, N 24.22

Headquarters, Department of the Army Chiefs and Executives, D 202.23

Headquarters European Command, Publications, D 1.23

Headquarters, First United States Army, Deputy Chief of Staff, Information Management, Organization, Mission, and Functions, D 101.1/9

Headquarters Fort George C. Meade Pamphlets (series), D 101.22/10

Headquarters Fort McCoy Regulations, D 101.9/4

Headquarters Intercom, TD 4.5/2

Headquarters Manual, HQM- (series), D 7.6/9

Headquarters Memorandum, W 99.15/9

Headquarters Orders, W 99.13/11
Headquarters Telephone Directory, T 63.126
Heads of Families at 1st Census, C 3.11
Headstart (series), D 1.71
Headwater Herald, A 13.121
Health and Safety, E 1.99
Health and Safety Laboratory: Environmental
    Quarterly, ER 1.27
Health and Safety Statistics, I 28.26
Health and Sanitation Division Newsletters, Pr
    32.4610
Health Aspects of Pesticides, Abstracts Bulletin, HE
    20.4011
Health Bulletins (series), NAS 1.73
Health Care Financing Administration Information
    Systems Development Guide, HE 22.508/2
Health Care Financing Administration Rulings, HE
    22.15
Health Care Financing Administration Rulings on
    Medicare, Medicaid, Professional Standards
    Review and Related Matters, HE 22.15
Health Care Financing Conference Proceedings, HE
    22.19/6
Health Care Financing Extramural Reports (series), HE
    22.19, HE 22.19/9
Health Care Financing, Grants and Contracts Reports,
    HE 22.19
Health Care Financing: Grants for Research and
    Demonstrations, Fiscal Year, HE 22.19/3
Health Care Financing: Issues (series), HE 22.19/8
Health Care Financing Monographs, HE 22.19/7
Health Care Financing Notes, HE 22.19/4
Health Care Financing Program Statistics, HE 22.19/4-
    2
    Analysis of State Medicaid Program Characteris-
        tics, HE 22.19/4-4
    Medicare and Medicaid Data Book, HE 22.19/4-3
Health Care Financing Research and Demonstration
    Series, HE 22.16
Health Care Financing, Research Reports, HE 22.19/2
Health Care Financing Review, HE 22.18, HE 22.512
Health Care Financing Review Annual Supplement, HE
    22.18/2
Health Care Financing Special Report (series), HE
    22.19/10
Health Care Financing Trends, HE 22.20
Health Consequences of Involuntary Smoking, HE
    20.7614
Health Consequences of Smoking, HE 20.7016, HE
    20.25/2
Health Consequences of Smoking, A Public Health
    Service Review, FS 2.309
Health Consequences of Smoking, Report to the
    Surgeon General, HE 20.2019
Health Data Inventory, HE 1.59
Health Economics Series, FS 2.99
Health Economics Studies Information Exchange, FS
    2.76/2
Health Education, I 16.29
Health, Education and Welfare Indicators, FS 1.20
Health, Education and Welfare Trends, FS 1.19, HE 1.19
Health Facilities Construction Program Loan, Loan
    Guarantee and Mortgage Quarterly Status
    Report, HE 20.9013
Health Facilities Series, HE 20.2511
Health Hazard Evaluation Summaries, HE 20.7125
Health Hazards of Smoke, A 13.136
Health Information for International Travel, HE
    20.7009, HE 20.7315, HE 20.7818
Health Information for Travel in [area], HE 20.2:T 69
Health Information Resources in the Federal
    Government, HE 20.37
Health Information Series (numbered), HE 20.10
Health Insurance for the Aged, HE 3.6/4, HE 3.57
Health Insurance Statistics, HE 3.28/5
Health Insurance Statistics, CMS (series), FS 3.28/4,
    HE 3.28/4
Health Insurance Statistics: Current Medicare Survey
    Report, HE 3.28/4
Health Insurance Studies: Contract Research Series, HE
    22.11
Health Leaflets, FS 2.37
Health Maintenance Organizations, HE 20.20
Health Manpower Clearinghouse Series, HE 20.3114/3
Health Manpower Data Series, HE 20.3114/2
Health Manpower Source Book, FS 2.2:M 31, HE
    20:2:M 31, HE 20.3109
Health Manpower Statistics, D 1.62/2
Health Mobilization Series, FS 2.302
Health of the Army, D 104.20
Health Officer, FS 2.15
Health Planning, C 51.9/29
Health Planning Bibliography Series, HE 20.6112/2
Health Planning in Action (series), HE 20.6110/5

Health Planning Information Series, HE 20.6110/2
Health Planning Methods and Technology Series, HE
    20.6110/3
Health Planning Newsletter for Governing Body
    Members, HE 20.6022
Health Professions Education Assistance Program,
    Report to the President and the Congress,
    HE 1.40
Health Resources News, HE 20.6014
Health Resources Opportunity Office: Annual Report,
    HE 20.6001/3
Health Resources Statistics, HE 20.6212
Health Resources Studies, HE 20.6012
Health Sciences Audiovisuals, HE 20.3614/5
Health Sciences Serials, HE 20.3614/3
Health Services and Mental Health Administration
    Public Advisory Committees: Authority,
    Structure, Functions, FS 2.321
Health Services Reports, HE 20.2010/2, HE 20.5009
Health Statistics from the U.S. National Health Survey,
    FS 2.85
Health Statistics Plan, HE 20.16
Health Statistics Report, Fiscal Year (date), HE 20.16/2
Health Technology Assessment Reports (series), HE
    20.6512/7
Health Technology Review, HE 20.6522
Health, United States, HE 20.21, HE 20.6018, HE
    20.6223, HE 20.7042/6
Health United States and Healthy People 2000 Review,
    HE 20.7042, HE 20.7042/3
Health United States and Healthy People 2000 Review
    for Windows, HE 20.7042/2
Health United States and Healthy People 2000 Review,
    Statistical Tables on Lotus Spreadsheets, HE
    20.7042/4
Health Workforce Newslink, HE 20.9315
Healthline, HE 20.3038/2
Healthy People 2000 Review, HE 20.6223/3, HE
    20.7042/5
Healthy People 2000, Statistical Notes, HE 20.6230
Healthy People 2000 Statistics and Surveillance, HE
    20.7040
Healthy That's Me, Parents' Handbooks, HE 21.208/2
Hearing Aid Performance Measurement Data and
    Hearing Aid Selection Procedures, Contract
    Year (date), VA 1.22
Hearing Calendars, CC 1.42
Hearing Process Status Report (White Book), E 2.14/2
Hearings, Y 4.B 22/3
Hearings and Conferences Before Commission on Civil
    Rights, CR 1.8
Hearings in Public Assistance, HE 17.644
Hearings, Prints, and Miscellaneous Publications, Y
    4.2, Y 4.3
Heart and Lung Program Project Committee, HE
    20.3001/2:H 35/2
Heart Health News for Health Departments, FS 2.22/5
Heart Research News, FS 2.22/34
HeartMemo, HE 20.3225
Heat Power Engineering [abstracts], C 41.60
Heating Degree Day Bulletin, C 30.47
Heating Oil Prices and Margins (advance release), E
    3.11/11-2
Heavyweight Motorcycles: Annual Report on Selected
    Economic Indicators, ITC 1.26/2
Heavyweight Motorcycles: Selected Economic
    Indicators, ITC 1.26
HEGIS [Higher Education General Information Survey]
    Ix Requirements and Specifications for
    Surveys of [various subjects], HE 19.309
Helium: Bibliography of Technical and Scientific
    Literature, (year), Including Papers on
    Alpha-Particles, I 28.27
Helium Resources of the United States, I 28.167
Hematology Study Section, HE 20.3001/2:H 37
Hemostasis and Thrombosis, Bibliography, HE
    20.3209/2
Hepatitis Surveillance, Reports, HE 20.7011/6
Herald of Academy of Sciences of Kazakh SSR
    [abstracts], C 41.50/9
Herald of Academy of Sciences of USSR, C 41.50/4
Herald of Communications [abstracts], C 41.59
Herald of Electrical Industry [abstracts], C 41.66/2
Herald of Leningrad University, Mathematics,
    Mechanics, and Astronomy Series [abstracts],
    C 41.50/8
Herald of Leningrad University, Physics and Chemistry
    Series [abstracts], C 41.52/5
Herald of Machine Building [abstracts], C 41.65/4
Herald of Moscow University, Physio- Mathematical
    and Natural Sciences Series [abstracts], C
    41.50/6
Herbicides and Plant Regulators, EP 5.11

Herd Management Area Plan (various locations), I
    53.23/2
Here and There with Home Demonstration Workers, A
    43.5/13
Here's Your Answer, Programs, FE 1.8
HEW Consumer Newsletter, FS 1.34
HEW Fact Sheets, HE 1.213, HE 23.3109
HEW Facts and Figures, HE 1.21
HEW Newsletter, HE 1.27/2
HEW Now, HE 1.27/2
HEW Obligations to Institutions of Higher Education,
    Fiscal Year, FS 1.2:Ed 8/3
HEW Refugee Task Force, Report to the Congress, HE
    1.55
HFORL Memorandum TN (series), D 301.45/7
HFORL Report TR (series), D 301.45/8
HHS News, HE 20.8015
HHS News, Food and Drug Administration, HE
    20.4043
HIA [Hazard Identification and Analysis] Special
    Reports, Y 3.C 76/3:17-2
Hickory Task Force Reports, A 13.63/12
Hidden Killers, S 1.148
High Altitude Instrument Approach Procedures, D
    5.318/2
High Commissioner of Trust Territory of Pacific Islands,
    I 35.16
High Income Tax Returns, T 1.52
High Performance Computing and Communications
    Implementation Plan, PrEx 23.13
High School and Beyond, ED 1.334
High School News Service Report, Basic Fact Edition,
    School Year, D 1.41/2
Higher Education, FS 5.37
Higher Education Act Title 2-b, Library Research and
    Demonstration Program, Abstracts, Fiscal
    Year (date), ED 1.18/8
Higher Education Act, Title II-C, FY Abstracts
    Strengthening Library Resources Program,
    ED 1.18
Higher Education and the Handicapped, Resource
    Directory, ED 1.32/2
Higher Education Basic Student Charges, HE 19.328
Higher Education Circulars, I 16.17
Higher Education Facilities Classification and
    Procedures Manual, FS 5.251:51016, HE
    5.251:51016
Higher Education, Fall Enrollment in Higher
    Education (year), HE 19.325
Higher Education Opportunities for Minorities and
    Women, ED 1.42
Higher Education Personnel Training Programs (year),
    Fellowship Programs, HE 5.92
Higher Education Planning, a Bibliographic
    Handbook, HE 19.208:H 53
Higher Education Planning and Management Data, FS
    5.253:53004, HE 5.253:53004
Higher Education Reports, FS 5.81, HE 5.81
Higher Education Salaries, FS 5.253:53015, HE
    5.253:53015
Higher Education: Students Enrolled for Advanced
    Degrees, Fall (year), HE 19.330
Highlights from Student Drug Use in America, HE
    20.8219/2
Highlights (National Infrastructure Protection Center),
    J 1.14/23-3
Highlights National Oceanographic Data Center, C
    55.291
Highlights of Annual Workshop of Farmer Cooperative
    Service, A 89.16
Highlights of Current Legislation and Activities in
    Mid-Europe, LC 1.27
Highlights of the Department of the Navy Fy...Budget,
    D 201.1/1-2
Highlights of Earth Science and Applications
    Division, NAS 1.1/6
Highlights of Heart Progress, FS 2.22/11
Highlights of Legislation on Aging, FS 1.13/4, FS
    14.912
Highlights of MarAd Port Activities, C 39.223/2
Highlights of the National Youth Gang Survey, J 32.21/
    3
Highlights of Natural Resources Management, I 29.119
Highlights of Progress in Mental Health Research, FS
    2.22/16
Highlights of Progress in Research in Cancer, FS 2.22/
    14
Highlights of Progress in Research on Neurologic
    Disorders, FS 2.22/12
Highlights of Progress in Research on Oral Diseases,
    FS 2.22/23
Highlights of Research Progress in Allergy and
    Infectious Diseases, FS 2.22/17

Index to Tests of Metals at Watertown Arsenal, W 34.14/2

Index to the Published Decisions of the Accounting Officers of the United States, C 1.5

Index to the U.S. Patent Classification, C 21.12/3

Index to Topographic and Other Map Coverage (series), I 19.41/6-3

Index to Treasury Decisions Under Customs and Other Laws, T 1.11/1a

Index to U.S. Army Specifications, W 3.48/2

Index to USGS/DMA 1:50,000-Scale, 15 Minute Quadrangle Mapping, I 19.97/2

Index to Veterans Administration Publications, VA 1.20

Index to World Trade Information Service Reports, C 42.14

Index-Catalogue of Library of Surgeon General's Office, 4th Series, D 104.8

Index-Catalogue of Medical and Veterinary Zoology, A 77.219

Index-Catalogue of Medical and Veterinary Zoology [by Subject], A 77.219/2

Index-Catalogue of Medical and Veterinary Zoology, Special Publications, (numbered), A 77.219/4

Index-Digest of Decisions of the Department of the Interior in Cases Relating to Public Lands, I 1.69/3

Index-Digest of Decisions Under Federal Safety Appliance Acts, IC 1 saf.9

Index-Digest of the Published Decisions of the Comptroller General of the United States, GA 1.5/3

Index-Digest, Published and Important Unpublished Decisions, I 1.69/2

Indexes...Equal Employment Opportunity Commission Decisions, Y 3.Eq 2:18-2

Indexes and Estimates of Domestic Well Drilling Costs, E 3.44

Indexes for Compilations of Records, Briefs, etc., J 1.19/1

Indexes of Average Freight Rates on Railroad Carload Traffic, IC 1.27

Indexes of Change in Straight-Time Average Hourly Earnings for Selected Shipyards, by Type of Construction and Region, L 2.81/2

Indexes of Output Per Man-Hour for the Private Economy, L 2.89/2

Indexes of Output Per Man-Hour, Hourly Compensation, and Unit Labor Costs in the Private Sector of the Economy and the Nonfarm Sector, L 2.2:Ou 8/8

Indexes of Output Per Man-Hour, Selected Industries, L 2.89

Indexes of Prices for Selected Materials, Hydraulic Turbine Industry, L 2.78

Indexes of Production Worker Employment in Manufacturing Industries by Metropolitan Area, L 2.24

Indexes of Rents by Type of Dwelling, L 2.11

Indexes of Retail Prices on Meats in Large Cities, L 2.39/2

Indexes to Advance Sheets of Consular Reports, S 4.6

Indexes to Bureau of Mines Publications, I 28.5/4

Indexes to Papers of President Franklin Delano Roosevelt, PI 1.8

Indexes to Patents (special), I 23.5

Indexes to Specifications, W 77.8/3

Indexes to Yearbooks of Department of Agriculture, A 21.12

Index/Journals of the Continental Congress, GS 4.2:C 76/2

Index/Papers of the Continental Congress, GS 4.2:C 76/3

India, LC 1.30

India, Accessions List, Annual Supplement, Cumulative List of Serials, LC 1.30/1-2

Indian Affairs, Laws and Treaties, I 1.107

Indian Affairs, (year), Progress Report from the Commissioner of Indian Affairs, I 20.1A

Indian and Alaska Native Housing and Community Development Programs, Annual Report to Congress, HH 1.80

Indian Appeals, I 1.69/6

Indian Arts and Crafts Board Publications, I 1.84

Indian Children's Own Writings, I 20.36

Indian Commissioners Board, Annual Reports, I 20.5

Indian Craftsman, I 20.16/5

Indian Education, I 20.26

Indian Forest Management, I 20.61/3

Indian Handicraft Pamphlets, I 20.31

Indian Health Care Improvement Act, Annual Report, HE 20.5301

Indian Health Highlights, HE 20.2:In 25/9

Indian Health Service Directory, HE 20.310/2, HE 20.9412/2

Indian Health Service Regional Differences in Indian Health, HE 20.9422

Indian Health Service Scholarship Program: Applicant Information Instruction Booklet, HE 20.9418

Indian Health Service Scholarship Program Student Handbook, HE 20.9418/2

Indian Health Trends and Services, HE 20.5310

Indian Inspector for Indian Territory, Annual Reports, I 1.20/2

Indian Leader, I 20.39

Indian Life Readers, I 20.33

Indian Reading Series, ED 1.319

Indian Records, I 20.55

Indian School Journal, I 20.41

Indian Schools, (misc. publications), I 20.8

Indian Schools Superintendent, Annual Report, I 20.7

Indian Vital Statistics, FS 2.86/5, HE 20.2660

Indiana [various subjects], I 20.51/2

Indians at Work, I 20.22

Indians of [States or Areas], I 20.51

Indians on Federal Reservations in United States [by areas], FS 2.86

Indians: [various subjects], I 20.51/2

Indicator of the Month (series), ED 1.341

Indicators of School Crime and Safety, ED 1.347

Indicators of Welfare Dependence, HE 1.1/4

Indices of Agricultural Production in [various] Countries, A 67.36, A 93.32

Individual Income Tax Returns, T 22.35/3:In 2, T 22.35/8

Indochina Monographs (series), D 114.18

Indonesia, LC 1.30/5

Indonesia, Cumulative List of Serials, LC 1.30/5-2

Industrial Activities Bulletin, S 18.10

Industrial and Mechanical Engineering, C 51.9/16

Industrial Area Statistical Summaries, L 2.18

Industrial Area Studies, L 2.16

Industrial Banking, Companies, Installment Loans to Consumers, C 18.219

Industrial Classification Code, FS 3.112/2

Industrial Civil Defense Handbooks, C 41.6/12

Industrial Civil Defense Newsletter, C 41.110

Industrial Classification Code, State Operations Bulletins, FS 3.112

Industrial College of the Armed Forces Catalog, D 5.11

Industrial College of the Armed Forces: Perspectives in Defense Management, D 5.16

Industrial College of the Armed Forces: Publications, D 5.13

Industrial Corporation Reports (by industries), FT 1.17

Industrial Development in the TVA Area, Y 3.T 25:30-2

Industrial Development in TVA Area During (date), Y 3.T 25:30 In 27

Industrial Diamonds in (year), I 28.162

Industrial Economics Review, C 62.19

Industrial Education Circulars, I 16.33

Industrial Effluent Standards, EP 1.8/4-4

Industrial Employment Information Bulletin, L 7.8

Industrial Energy Conservation, Fact Sheets, FE 1.27

Industrial Energy Efficiency Improvement Program, Annual Report, E 1.47

Industrial Environmental Research Laboratory: Annual Report, EP 1.46/5

Industrial Environmental Research Laboratory: (year) Research Review, EP 1.46/5-2

Industrial Fact Sheets, C 45.8, C 41.90/3

Industrial Fishery Products, Situation and Outlook CEA-I (series), C 55.309/3, I 49.8/9

Industrial Fishery Products, (year) Annual Summary, C 55.309/2

Industrial Health and Safety Series, L 16.9

Industrial Hygiene News Letters, FS 2.45

Industrial Location Series, C 41.90/2

Industrial Machine Letters, C 18.98

Industrial Marketing Guides, C 41.6/10

Industrial Materials Series: Report M (series), TC 1.27

Industrial Minerals Supply/Demand Data, I 28.169/2

Industrial Mobilization, W 3.50/16

Industrial News, C 46.7/2

Industrial Notes, D 211.10

Industrial Nutrition Service, A 82.66

Industrial Outlook and Economy at Midyear, C 41.42/4

Industrial Personnel Security Review Program, Annual Reports, D 3.12

Industrial Power Engineering [abstracts], C 41.60/4

Industrial Production, FR 1.19/3

Industrial Projects Bulletin, FO 1.18, S 17.18

Industrial Propery Bulletin, C 18.99

Industrial Reference Service, C 18.220, C 34.10

Industrial Reference Service, Business Service, C 18.221

Industrial Reports and Publications, S 18.20

Industrial Safety Subjects, L 16.18

Industrial Safety Summaries, L 16.20

Industrial Security Cartoons, D 3.11/3

Industrial Security Poster PIN (series), D 3.11

Industrial Security Statements, D 3.11/2

Industrial Series–
    Bureau of Foreign and Domestic Commerce, C 18.225
    Children's Bureau, L 5.9
    Office of Domestic Commerce, C 36.7

Industrial Standards, C 18.24

Industrial Survival, for Your Information [Releases], FCD 1.13/9

Industrial Uses of Agricultural Materials, Situation and Outlook Report, A 93.56

Industrial Waste Guide Series, FS 2.71

Industrial Waste Guides, I 67.8/2

Industries and Reciprocal Trade Agreements, Reports on, by Industries, TC 1.15

Industry and Trade Summary, ITC 1.33

Industry and Product Reports, C 3.24/8-2

Industry Circulars, T 70.10

Industry Information, Pr 32.4230

Industry Manpower Surveys, L 7.49, L 34.10

Industry News Letters, Pr 32.4230/2

Industry Pamphlets, L 22.29

Industry Productivity in (year) Reported by BLS, L 2.120/2-9

Industry Profiles, Accession Notices, S 18.36

Industry Releases, C 3.209/2

Industry Report–
    Canned Fruits and Vegetables, Production and Wholesale Distribution, C 18.234
    Chemicals and Allied Products, C 18.235
    Coffee, Tea and Spices, C 18.240
    Construction and Building Materials, C 41.30
    Construction and Construction Materials, C 18.233
    Crude Drugs, Gums, Balsams, and Essential Oils, C 18.236
    Drugs and Pharmaceuticals, C 18.237
    Fats and Oils, C 18.238
    International Iron and Steel, C 41.36
    Leather, C 18.239
    Rubber, C 18.241

Industry Reports, C 41.31
    Domestic Transportation, C 18.232
    Lumber, C 18.230
    Sugar, Molasses and Confectionary, C 18.231

Industry Survey, C 3.231

Industry Survey: Manufacturers' Inventories, Shipments, Incoming Busines [and] Unfilled Orders, C 18.224

Industry Survey, Manufacturers' Sales, Inventories, New and Unfilled Orders, C 43.9

Industry Trade and Technology Review, ITC 1.33/2

Industry Trend Series, C 41.90

Industry Wage Studies Memo, L 2.47/2

[Industry Wage Studies], Series 3, Wage Movements, L 2.47

Industry Wage Survey–
    Banking, L 2.3/22
    Cigarette Manufacturing, L 2.3/26
    Contract Cleaning Services, L 2.3/33
    Department Stores, L 2.3/37
    Hospitals, L 2.3/24
    Industrial Chemicals, L 2.3/31
    Iron and Steel Foundries, L 2.3/32
    Meat Products (year), L 2.3/15
    Men's and Boy's Shirts and Nightwear, L 2.3/35
    Millwork, L 2.3/14
    Nursing and Personal Care Facilities, L 2.3/25
    Petroleum Refining, L 2.3/19
    Pressed or Blown Glassware, L 2.3/29
    Shipbuilding and Repairing, L 2.3/34
    Structural Clay Products, L 2.3/30
    Synthetic Fibers, L 2.3/21
    Textile Mills, L 2.3/23
    Wood Household Furniture, L 2.3/27

Industry Wage Survey Reports, L 2.106

Industry Wage Survey Summaries, L 2.3/3-2

Industry Wage Survey: Temporary Help Survey, L 2.3/38

Inertial Confinement Fusion, ICF Annual Report, E 1.99/7-2

Inertial Confinement Fusion Quarterly Report, E 1.99/7

INF Bulletins, CC 1.3/3

Infant Mortality Series, L 5.5

Infantry, D 102.83

Infantry School Quarterly, D 101.53

Infectious Disease Committee, HE 20.3001/2:In 3

Infectious Disease Research Series, HE 20.3262/2

Inflationary Impact Statements, L 35.20

In-Flight Survey, C 47.15/7

Influenza Immunizations Paid for by Medicare, HE 22.21/4

Influenza-Respiratory Disease Surveillance, Reports, HE 20.2309/10

Info Memo Bulletin, HE 20.3214/2

Infobase, USIA Directives, IA 1.32

InfoLine, HE 20.3214/3

Informal Communications, Pr 32.413/7

Informal Reports, D 203.26/2

Information (series), A 89.15

Information about Postal Savings System, P 19.7/2

Information and Referral Services (series), HE 1.208/2

Information and Technical Assistance Delivered by the Department of Agriculture in Fiscal Year, A 1.1/2

Information and Technology Report, I 73.11, I 19.210

Information Booklets (series), D 101.107/12

Information Brochure for Handling Air Force Constituent Inquiries, D 301.109

Information Bulletins–
   Adjutant General's Department, W 3.82
   Bureau of Air Commerce, C 23.8
   Bureau of Land Management, I 53.9
   Coast Guard, TD 5.3/6
   Defense Civil Prepardness Agency, D 14.13/2
   Department of Energy, E 1.100
   Division of Maternal and Child Health, HE 20.9111
   Environmental Information Division, D 301.38/8
   Federal Civil Defense Administration, FCD 1.13/11
   Field Artillery Office, W 96.5
   General Land Office, I 21.17
   Human Resources Research Center, D 301.36/5
   Library of Congress, LC 1.18
   Metallurgical Advisory Committee on Titanium, D 105.13/2-4
   National Inventors Council, C 32.7
   National Scientific Register, Office of Education, FS 5.47/2
   Office of Civil Defense, D 13.3/2
   Office of Defense and Civilian Mobilization, Pr 34.753/2
   Office of Emergency Preparedness, PrEx 4.3/3
   Office of U.S. High Commissioner for Germany, S 1.85
   Veteran's Administration, VA 1.22/2
   Youth 2000 (series), HE 20.9203/2

Information Circulars–
   Air Service, W 87.10
   Bureau of Mines, C 22.11, I 28.27
   Engineer Department, W 7.15
   Federal National Mortgage Association, FL 5.16
   Field Division, Y 3.C 83:85
   Hydrographic Office, N 6.23
   Inspector General's Department, W 9.8
   National Institute for Occupational Safety and Health, HE 20.7130
   National Youth Administration, Y 3.N 21/14:8
   State Councils Section, Y 3.C 83:75
   War Department Claims Board, W 93.6

Information Collection and Exchange, Manual Series, AA 4.8/3

Information Collection and Exchange (series), PE 1.10

Information Collection and Exchange, Reprint Series, AA 4.12

Information Collection Budget of the United States, PrEx 2.29

Information Concerning Reinstatements, CS 1.23

Information Concerning Removals, Reductions, Suspensions and Furloughs, CS 1.24

Information Concerning Temporary Appointments, CS 1.25

Information Concerning Transfers, CS 1.22

Information Digest, Pr 32.214, Pr 32.5010

Information Directory, Y 21.28/2

Information Exchange, C 3.207/2

Information Exchange Bulletins, FS 6.8

Information File Inserts, A 55.51

Information for Business Executives [and] Firms with Retailing and Wholesale Interests, Y 3.P 93/4:9

Information for Innovators, and Interdisciplinary Information Service, C 51.9/31

Information for United States Businessmen [by country], C 49.11

Information from Abroad (unnumbered), N 13.6

Information from ERDA, ER 1.12/2

Information from ERDA: Reference Information, ER 1.12/3

Information from ERDA, Weekly Announcements, ER 1.12

Information from Health Resource Center, ED 1.22

Information from Plans for Progress, L 1.54/2

Information Governing Distribution of Government Publications and Price Lists, GP 3.18

Information Guidance Series, D 2.17

Information Guide (series), T 22.19/4

Information Intelligency Summary, W 108.32

Information Interchange Service, Y 3.Ad 9/8:14

Information Letters, W 108.21

Information Letters [unrestricted], W 42.41

Information Memorandums–
   Aging Administration, HE 23.3013, HE 1.1013
   Child Support Enforcement Office, HE 24.15
   Head Start Bureau, HE 23.1114
   Health and Human Services, HE 1.47

Information News Letter, L 1.54/3

Information News Service, C 46.13

Information Notes, S 1.84

Information on Education Around the World, FS 5.57/2, FS 5.214:14034, HE 5.214:14034

Information Pamphlets, I 20.34

Information Pamphlets Relating to National Forests, A 13.13

Information Publications DOE/OPA (series), E 1.25

Information, Quarterly Newsletter of the National Institute of Education, HE 19.209

Information Regarding Employment on National Forests, A 13.22

Information Relative to Appointment and Admission of Cadets of Military Academy, W 12.9

Information Releases, A 82.83

Information Report on State Legislation, Y 3.N 88:42

Information Reports, L 38.10

Information Resources Directory, EP 1.12/3

Information Resources Management Handbook (series), GS 12.17

Information Resources Management Newsletter, GS 12.17/3

Information Resources Management Plan (series), TD 4.33/6

Information Respecting the History, Conditions, and Prospects of the Indian Tribes of the United States, Philadelphia, Lippincott, Grambo & Co., I 20.2:In 2

Information Series–
   Bureau of Agricultural Chemistry and Engineering, A 70.11
   Bureau of Agricultural Engineering, A 53.10
   Bureau of Public Roads, A 22.14
   Federal Board of Surveys and Maps, Y 3.Su 7:9
   Federal Crop Insurance Corporation, A 76.108, A 80.907, A 82.207, A 62.9
   National Institute of Education, HE 18.11/2
   Office of Education, HE 19.143

Information Service, P 1.36

Information Service Circulars, HE 3.4

Information Service Letters, Y 3.W 89/2:39, FW 4.15

Information Service Series, FS 13.211

Information Services Fact Sheets, D 301.54

Information Sharing Index, HE 24.12

Information Sheet, S 1.66

Information Sheets (series), D 101.107/8

Information Sources on International Travel, C 47.8

Information Systems Security Products and Services Catalogue, D 1.69/2

Information Systems Strategic Plan, VA 1.86

Information Technology Newsletter, GS 1.37/2

Informational Bulletins, W 108.23

Informational Letters, FS 3.34

Informational Memorandums, FW 2.16

Informations, Region 6, I 49.7/2

Informative Technical Bulletins, Pr 32.4821

InForum, E 1.134

In-House List of Publications, Aeronautical Research Laboratory, D 301.69/4

Initial Analysis and Forecast Charts, C 55.281/2-6

Initial Reports of the Deep Sea Drilling Project, NS 1.38

Initial Sequestration Report for Fiscal Year (date), Y 4.D 36/2

Initiative for Interdisciplinary Artists Inter- Arts, NF 2.8/2-22

Injury Control Research Laboratory: Research Report, ICRL-RR (series), HE 20.1116

Injury Control Update, HE 20.7956

Injury Epidemiology and Control Reprints, HE 20.7009/3

Injury Experience and Related Employment Data for Sand and Gravel Industry, I 28.108/2

Injury Experience in Coal Mining, I 28.27, I 69.9, L 38.10/4

Injury Experience in Metallic Mineral Industries, I 28.27, I 69.9

Injury Experience in Nonmetallic Mining (Except Stone and Coal), L 38.10/5

Injury Experience in Nonmetallic Mining Industries, I 28.27, I 69.9

Injury Experience in Oil and Gas Industry of United States, I 28.108

Injury Experience in Quarrying, I 28.27, I 69.9

Injury Experience in Sand and Gravel Mining, L 38.10/2

Injury Experience in Stone Mining, L 38.10/3

Injury Rates by Industry, L 2.77/2

Injury-Frequency Rates for Selected Manufacturing Industries, L 2.77

Innovations in Election Administration, Y 3.El 2/3:18

Innovations in the Courts: Series on Court Administration, Ju 13.12

Innovations, Mental Health Services, Progress Reports, HE 20.2425

Innovative and Alternative Technology Projects, a Progress Report, EP 2.30

Innovative Finance, TD 2.75/2

Innovative Finance Quarterly, TD 2.75

Innovative Treatment Technologies, EP 1.17/6

Inpatient Utilization of Short-Stay Hospitals by Diagnosis, United States, HE 20.6209/8

Inputs Outlook and Situation, A 93.47

Inquiry, E 1.115

Inquiry Memoranda, C 6.14

Inquiry Reference Service: County Basic Data Sheets, Selected Counties by States, C 18.228

INS Communique, J 21.25

INS Fact Book, J 21.2/11

INS Reporter, J 21.10/2

Insect Life, A 9.7

Insect Pest Survey Bulletins, A 77.310

Insect Pest Survey, Special Supplements, A 77.310/3

Insecticide Decisions, A 1.17

Insecticide Division Publications, A 47.8, A 56.15

Insecticides, Acaricides, Molluscicides, and Antifouling Compounds, EP 5.11/3

Insects in Relation to National Defense, Circulars, A 56.24, A 77.316

Inserts to Postal Laws and Regulations, P 1.11/2

In-Service Training Series, I 29.9/3

Inside Edition, ED 1.87/4

Inside Information, A 107.15, A 21.36

Inside Interior, I 1.75

Inside NIDCD Information Clearinghouse, HE 20.3666

Inside Route Pilot (Atlantic and Gulf Coasts), C 4.6/3

Inside the Greenhouse, EP 1.114

Inside the White House, PrEx 1.12/2

Insights, High Performance Computer and Communications, NAS 1.94

Inspection and Proof Reports, W 34.25

Inspection and Weighing Update, A 104.11

Inspection Guides, Mimeographed, W 9.7

Inspection Handbook, C 31.117

Inspection Manual Bulletins, W 77.15/3

Inspection Manuals, T 54.9

Inspection National News, T 22.2/15:7371

Inspection of Several Branches of National Home for Disabled Volunteer Soldiers, W 9.5

Inspection of State Soldiers and Sailor's Homes, NH 1.5

Inspection Operations Manual Transmittal Notices, HE 20.4008/2

Inspection Service Memorandum, C 23.14

Inspection Standards, Memeographed, W 9.6

Inspector General Audit Reports, TD 1.1/3-2

Inspector General Bulletin, HH 1.93

Inspector General Inspections & Evaluations Reports, TD 1.1/3-3

Inspector General: Master Plan, Y 3.T 25:67

Inspector General Semiannual Reports, Y 3.T 25:1-19

Inspectors of National Cemeteries, Annual Reports, W 39.5

INSS Occasional Paper, Regional Series, D 305.24

Installations: News for and about Basops, D 101.142

Institute, PM 1.54

Institute for Applied Technology, Technical Highlights, Fiscal Year, C 13.1/3

Institute for Basic Standards, Technical Highlights, Fiscal Year, C 13.1/4

Institute for Material Research, Metallurgy Division, Technical Highlights, Fiscal Year, C 13.1/5-2

Institute for Materials Research, Technical Highlights, Fiscal Year, C 13.1/5

Institute for Medicaid Management: Publications, HE 22.112

Institute for National Strategic Studies: General Publications, D 5.417/2

Institute for Telecommunication Sciences: Annual Technical Progress Report, C 60.14

Institute for Water Resources: Research Reports, D 103.57/5

Institute of Inter-American Affairs Publications, S 1.64

Institute of Social Anthropology Publications, SI 1.16

Institute Programs for Advanced Studies, FS 5.84, HE 5.84

Institutes for College and University Faculty, NF 3.14

Institutional Data, FS 5.254:54003, HE 5.254:54003

Institutional Grants for Science, NS 1.10/3

Institutional Meat Purchase Specifications, A 88.17/4, A 103.15

Institutions in United States Giving Instruction in Agriculture, A 10.18

Institutions of Higher Education, Index by State and Congressional District, HE 19.322, ED 1.116/2

Instream Flow Information Papers, I 49.83

Instream Flow Strategies [various States], I 49.83/2

Instruction and Information for Applicants and for Boards of Examiners, CS 1.6

Instruction Books, W 7.19

Instruction Books (series), TD 4.6/2-2

Instruction Bulletins–
  Bureau of Air Commerce, C 23.16
  Southeastern Department, W 84.7

Instruction Circulars, W 42.34/7

Instruction Letters, P 4.5

Instruction Manual
  Classification and Coding Instructions for Divorce Records, HE 20.6208/10
  Classification and Coding Instructions for Fetal Death Records, HE 20.6208/6-2
  Classification and Coding Instructions for Induced Termination of Pregnancy Records, HE 20.6208/8
  Classification and Coding Instructions for Live Birth Records, HE 20.6208/6
  Classification and Coding Instructions for Marriage Records, HE 20.6208/7
  Computer Edits for Mortality Data, HE 20.6208/14
  Computer Edits for Natality Data, HE 20.6208/15
  Data Entry Instructions for the Mortality Medical Indexing, Classification, and Retrieval System (MICAR), HE 20.6208/4-7
  Data Preparation of the Current Sample, HE 20.6208/9
  Demographic Classification and Coding Instructions for Death Records, HE 20.6208/5
  Dental Examiner's Manual for the Hispanic Health and Nutrition Survey, HE 20.6208/2-6
  Dictionary of Valid Terms for the Mortality Medical Indexing, Classification, and Retrieval System (MICAR), HE 20.6208/4-8
  Dietary Interviewer's Manual for the Hispanic Health and Nutrition Examination Survey, HE 20.6208/2-2
  Field Staff Operations for the Hispanic Health and Nutrition Examination Survey, HE 20.6208/2-5
  ICD 9 Acme Decision Tables for Classifying Underlying Causes of Death, HE 20.6208/4-2
  ICDA Eighth Revision of Decision Tables for Classifying Underlying Causes of Death, HE 20.6208/4-5
  Instructions for Classifying Multiple Causes of Death, HE 20.6208/4-3
  Instructions for Classifying the Underlying Cause of Death, HE 20.6208/4-4
  Mobile Examination Center Interviewer's Manual for the Hispanic Health and Nutrition Examination Survey, HE 20.6208/2-4
  NCHS Procedures for Mortality Medical Data System File Preparation and Maintenance, HE 20.6208/4-6
  Nonindexed Terms, Standard Abbreviations, and State Geographic Codes Used in Mortality Data Classification, HE 20.6208/4
  Part 1, Source Records and Control Specifications, HE 20.6209/11
  Part 18, Guidelines for Implementing Field and Query Programs for Registration of Births and Deaths, HE 20.6208/16
  Physician's Examination Manual for the Hispanic Health and Nutrition Examination Survey, HE 20.6208/2-3
  Source Records and Control Specifications, HE 20.6208/11
  Vital Records Geographic Classification, HE 20.6208/3

Instruction Manuals–
  Engineer Department, W 7.20
  War Plans Division, Education and Special Training Committee, W 26.17/5

Instruction Memorandum, D 212.6/2, D 212.11

Instruction Reports, D 103.24/7

Instruction Sheets, W 28.8

Instruction, Special, FR 1.8

Instruction to Candidates, Class of . . ., D 305.8/4

Instructional Cassette Recordings, LC 19.11/3

Instructional Disc Recordings, LC 19.11/3-2

Instructional Equipment Grants Title VI-A, Higher Education Act of 1975, PL 89-329, HE 19.114

Instructional Faculty Salaries for Academic Year, ED 1.131

Instructional Materials . . . for U.S. Army Reserve Schools, D 103.6/8

Instructional Program Notes, VA 1.76

Instructions–
  Bureau of Medicine and Surgery, N 10.5
  Federal Board for Vocational Education, VE 1.9
  Weather Bureau, A 29.12

Instructions and Application for Grants under the Special Needs Program, ED 1.61

Instructions and Application for Grants under the Strengthening Program, ED 1.61/2

Instructions and Data Specifications for Reporting DHHS Obligations to Institutions of Higher Education and Other Nonprofit Organizations, HE 20.3050

Instructions and Information for Applicants and for Boards of Examiners, CS 1.6

Instructions and Regulations, N 25.7

Instructions and Suggestions Relative to Organization, etc., of National Banks, T 12.8

Instructions for Climatological Observers, C 30.4:B

Instructions for Completing Farm Plans (by States), A 80.612

Instructions for Field Work, IC 1 val.6

Instructions for Mailers, P 1.12/5a

Instructions for Preparing Reports, C 3.38/2

Instructions to Applicants, CS 1.9

Instructions to Applicants, Class of, D 305.8/3

Instructions to Bidders and General Specifications, PB 1.5

Instructions to Candidates, D 305.8/4

Instructions to Clerks of Courts Exercising Naturalization Jurisdiction, L 6.10

Instructions to Diplomatic and Consular Officers, S 1.10

Instructions to Examining Surgeons, I 24.13

Instructions to Inspectors of Engineering Materials, N 19.11

Instructions to Lightkeepers, T 25.22, C 9.23

Instructions to Postmasters, PS 1.6, P 19.6

Instructor Set (series), D 12.13

Instructor Training Bulletins, N 17.34

Instructor's Guide for Classes, First Aid Training Courses, N 10.16

Instructor's Guides, IG- (series), D 14.8/4, D 119.8/7

Instructors' Journal, D 301.38/7

Instructor's Training Aids Guide, D 208.9

Instructor's Work Kit, L 7.46

Instrument Approach and Landing Charts, C 4.9/10

Instrument Approach Chart, Radio Beacon, C 4.9/16

Instrument Approach Charts, I.L.S., C 4.9/14

Instrument Approach Procedure Charts, C 55.411

Instrument Approach Procedure Charts [Alaska, Hawaii, U.S. Pacific Islands], C 55.411/2

Instrument Fact Sheet, C 55.71, D 203.32/2

Instrument Flying, D 301.7:51-37

Instrument Manufacture [abstracts], C 41.77/2

Instrument Room [or division] Circulars, A 29.11

Instrumentation, E 1.99

Instrumentation Papers, D 301.45/10

Instruments and Experiment Techniques [abstracts], C 41.77

Insurance and Labor Law Series, C 18.99/2

Insurance Bulletins, T 49.9

Insurance Program Quality, HE 3.28/6-4

Insured Mortgage Portfolio, HH 2.10

Insured Savings and Loan Associations, Average Annual Dividend Rates Paid, FHL 1.21

Insured Unemployed, Personal and Economic Characteristics, L 7.38/2

Insured Unemployment, FS 3.128, L 7.38

Intensity of Relief Maps, Y 3.F 31/5:36

Interaction, AA 1.13

Interactive Courseware, D 301.118/2

Interagency Advisory Committee on Water Data: Summary of Meetings, I 19.74

Interagency Advisory Group: Annual Report, CS 1.87

Interagency Auditor Training Center Bulletin, C 1.61

Interagency Committee on Women's Business Enterprise, Annual Report to Congress, SBA 1.31

Interagency Steering Committee on Radiation Standards, Y 3.N88:10-6

Interagency Directory, Key Contracts for Planning, Scientific and Technical Exchange Programs, Educational Travel, Students, Teachers, Lectures, Research Scholars, Specialists, S 1.67/3

Interagency Energy-Environment Research and Development Program Reports, EP 1.23/8

Interagency Records Administration Conference, Reports of Meetings, GS 4.16

Interagency Reports, I 19.63

Interagency Task Force for Indochina Refugees, Pr 38.8:R 25

Interagency Task Force on Product Liability, C 1.66, C 1.66/2

Interagency Task Force on Synthetic Fuels Commercialization, Pr 37.8:En 2/2

Interagency Technical Committee on Heart, Blood Vessel, Lung, and Blood Diseases; and Blood Resources, HE 20.3001/2:H 35

Interagency Training, Calendar of Courses, PM 1.19/2

Interagency Training Catalog of Courses, PM 1.19

Interagency Training Courses, Calendar, CS 1.65/4

Interagency Training Program (various subjects) (series), GS 1.26/2

Interagency Training Programs, CS 1.65

Interagency Urban Initiatives Anti-crime Program, Report to Congress, HH 1.85

Interagency Working Group on Medical Radiation: Federal Guidance Reports, EP 1.68

Inter-American Affairs Institute, Building a Better Hemisphere Series, Point 4 in Action, S 1.64/3

Inter-American Conference for Maintenance of Peace, 1936, S 5.38

Inter-American Conference on Agriculture, Forestry, and Animal Industry, Washington, Sept. 8-20, 1930, S 5.32

Inter-American Defense Board, S 5.45

Inter-American Development Commission, S 5.43

Inter-American Education Demonstration Centers, FS 5.31

Inter-American Education Demonstration Centers (misc.), FS 5.31

Inter-American Foundation, Y 3.In 8/25

Inter-American Series, S 1.26

Inter-American Technical Aviation Conference, S 5.40

Inter-Arts, Artists' Projects: New Forms, NF 2.8/2-26

Inter-Arts, Presenting Organizations Artist Communities Services to the Arts, Application Guidelines, NF 2.8/2-23

Interbureau Committee on Post-War Programs Publications, A 1.63

Interbureau Forage Committee Publications I.F.C., A 1.49

Interceptor, D 301.70

Interchange, L 1.69

Intercoastal Traffic, SB 7.5/158

Intercom–
  Air Force Department, D 301.101
  Forest Service, A 13.56

Intercontinental Railway Commission, S 5.8

Interdepartmental Trade Agreements Organization, Publications, TC 1.14/2

Interdisciplinary Glossary on Child Abuse and Neglect: Legal, Medical, Social Work Terms, HE 23.1210:G 51

Interdisciplinary Student/teacher Materials in Energy, the Environment, and the Economy, E 1.9

Interdistrict Settlement Fund, FR 1.43

Interest Bearing Debt Outstanding, T 62.8

Interest Rates Charged on Selected Types of Bank Loans, FR 1.32/4

Interest-bearing Debt Outstanding, T 1.29

Intergovernment and Institutional Relations, IR- (series), E 1.33

Intergovernmental Personnel Notes, CS 1.86, PM 1.27

Intergovernmental Perspective, Y 3.Ad 9/8:11

Intergovernmental Solutions Newsletter, GS 1.38

Integrated Postsecondary Education Data System IPEDS, ED 1.334/4

Integrated Resources and Services for [various subjects], C 1.77

Interagency Steering Committee on Radiation Standards, Y 3.N 88:10-6

Interim Administrative Decisions under Immigration and Nationality Laws, J 21.11/2

Interim Decisions, J 1.102/5

Interim Decisions of the Department of Justice, J 21.11/2

Interim Directives, Pr 34.706/2, PrEx 4.612

Interim Federal Specifications, GS 2.8/5

Interim Guide for Environment Assessment, HH 1.6/3:En 8

Interim Issues, VA 1.39

Interim List of Persons or Firms Currently Debarred for Violation of Various Public Contracts Acts Incorporating Labor Standards Provisions, GA 1.17/2

Interim Lists of Periodicals in Collection of Atmospheric Sciences Library and Marine and Earth Sciences Library, C 55.224

Interim Military Specifications, D 1.12/3

Interim Report of the Activities, Y 4.G 74/7-12

Interim Report on European Recovery Programme, Y 3.Ec 74/3:18

Interim Reports, D 103.53/5

Interim Technical Reports, A 13.53

Interior Budget in Brief, Fiscal Year Highlights, I 1.1/6

Interior Department Decisions, Solicitor's Opinions, I 1.69/4

Interior Guard Duty, Lesson Assignment Sheets, W 3.50/7

Interior Museum News, I 1.90

Intermediate Minimum Property Standards for Solar Heating and Domestic Hot Water Systems, HH 1.6/9:So 4

Intermountain Region Organization Directory, A 13.36/2-3

Intermountain Region Yearbooks, A 13.57

Intern Program, IP (series), PM 1.36

Internal Revenue Bulletin, T 22.23

Internal Revenue Bulletin; Bi-Monthly Digest, T 22.24/2

Internal Revenue Bulletin Index-Digest Quarterly System, T 22.25/3, T 22.25/4
   Service 1, Tax Matters Other Than Alcohol, Tobacco, and Firearms, T 22.25/3
   Service 2, Alcohol, Tobacco, and Firearms Taxes, T 22.25/4

Internal Revenue Bulletin Service, Special Bulletins, T 22.23/2

Internal Revenue Collection Districts (multigraphed), T 22.36

Internal Revenue Law in Force, T 22.9

Internal Revenue Manual, T 22.2/15-3

Internal Revenue News, T 22.33

Internal Revenue News Letter, T 22.37

Internal Revenue Regulations and Instructions, T 22.29

International Affairs Series, SI 12.11

International Agreement Reports (series), Y 3.N 88:53

International Agricultural Collaboration Series, A 67.20

International Agricultural Development, A 95.9

International Air Commerce Traffic Pattern, U.S. Flag Carriers, Calendar Year, C 31.153/2

International American Conference, S 5.9
   Buenos Aries, S 5.9/4
   Havana, Cuba, S 5.9/6
   Mexico City, S 5.9/2
   Rio de Janeiro, S 5.9/3
   Santiago, Chile, S 5.9/5

International Animal Feed Symposium Reports, A 67.34

International, Application Guidelines for Fiscal Year, NF 2.8/2-32

International Application Guidelines, International Program: Fellowships and Residencies Partnerships, NF 2.8/2-34

International Application Guidelines, International Program: International Projects Initiative for Organizations Partnerships, NF 2.8/2-35

International Bank for Reconstruction and Development, S 5.51

International Bibliography on Crime and Delinquency, FS 2.22/13-4

International Boundary Commission, U.S.- Mexico, Chamizal Arbitration, S 3.19/3

International Boundary Studies, S 1.119/3

International Broadcasting of All Nations, IA 1.11

International Brief, C 3.205/9

International Bulletin, HH 1.40/6

International Business Publications Checklist, C 42.15:C 41

International (Canadian) Boundary Commissions, S 3.24

International Cancer Research Data Bank Program, HE 20.3170

International Cancer Research Data Bank: Special Listing (series), HE 20.3173

International Chart Series, D 5.344

International Civil Aeronautics Conference, Washington, S 5.28

International Civil Aviation Organization Report of Representatives of United States, S 5.52

International Classification of Diseases, 9th Revision, Clinical Modification, HE 22.41

International Coal Trade, I 28.42

International Code of Signals, United States Edition, D 203.22:102

International Commerce, C 42.8

International Commission for Air Navigation, S 5.42

International Commission for Equitable Distribution of Water of Rio Grande, S 3.19/4

International Commission of Inquiry into Existence of Slavery and Forced Labor in Republic of Liberia, S 5.33

International Comparisons of Hourly Compensation Costs for Production Workers in Manufacturing, L 2.130

International Comparisons of Manufacturing Productivity and Labor Costs Trends, L 2.120/2-6

International Conference Calendar, C 42.24

International Conference for Revision of Convention of 1914 for Safety of Life at Sea, S 5.29

International Conference of American States on Conciliation and Arbitration, S 3.38

International Conference on Maritime Law, S 3.32

International Conference on Numerical Ship Hydrodynamics: Proceedings, D 211.9/5

International Conference on Safety at Sea, Reports, C 1.10

International Conference on Safety of Life at Sea, London, 1929, Reports, C 1.10/2

International Congress Against Alcoholism, S 5.20

International Congress of Military Medicine and Pharmacy, S 5.39

International Congress on Automotive Safety: Proceedings, TD 8.21

International Decade of Ocean Exploration, Progress Reports, C 55.227

International Direct Investment, Global Trends and the U.S. Role, C 61.29

International Economic and Energy Statistical Reveiw, ER-IEESR- (series), PrEx 3.14/2

International Economic Indicators, C 61.14

International Economic Indicators and Competitive Trends, C 57.19, C 57.19/2

International Economic Relations, PrEx 7.21/7

International Economic Report of the President, Pr 37.8:In 8/3/R 29/2

International Economic Review, ITC 1.29

International Economic Review, Special Edition, Chartbook, ITC 1.29/2

International Education and Cultural Exchange, Y 3.Ad 9/9:9

International Energy, E 3.11/20

International Energy Biweekly Statistical Review, ER-IEBSR (series), PrEx 3.14

International Energy Prices, E 3.11/20-2

International Energy Outlook (year) with Projections to (year), E 3.11/20-3

International Energy Statistical Review, ER- IESR (series), PrEx 3.14/2

International Exchange, S 1.67

International Field Year for Great Lakes, IFYGL Bulletins, C 55.21

International Field Year for Great Lakes: News Releases, C 55.21/2

International Field Year for the Great Lakes: Proceedings, IFYGL Symposium, Annual Meetings of the American Geophysical Union, C 55.21/3

International Field Year for the Great Lakes: Technical Manual Series, C 55.21/4

International Finance Discussion Papers, FR 1.62

International Fisheries Commission, S 5.35

International Flight Information Manual, TD 4.309

International Geographic Congress, S 5.5

International Geologic Congress, I 19.34

International Geological Congress, S 5.7

International Geophysical Year World Weather Maps, C 30.22/5

International Halley Watch Newsletter, NAS 1.72

International Health Data Reference Guide, HE 20.6208/13

International Health Planning Method Series, HE 20.22

International Health Planning Reference Series, HE 20.22/2

International Health Planning Series, HE 20.6110/4

International High Commission, T 1.23

International Information and Cultural Affairs Office Publications, S 1.56

International Information and Cultural Series, S 1.67

International Jet Trends, CAB 1.29/2

International Joint Commission on Boundary Waters Between United States and Canada, 1909, S 3.23

International Journal of Government Auditing, GA 1.38

International Judicial Observer, Ju 13.13/2-3

International Knit Goods, News, C 18.101

International Labor Conference, 1st, Washington, 1919, L 1.10

International Labor Studies, L 29.8

International Law Documents, M 206.207

International Law Situations (annual discussions), N 15.7

International Law Studies, D 208.207

International List, Money Order Offices in Foreign Countries, P 9.6

International Map of the World, I 19.21

International Marine Conference, Washington, 1889, S 5.10

International Marketing Events: Country Market Survey, C 61.21/3

International Marketing Events: Export Marketing Guides, C 57.117/3

International Marketing Events Information Series, C 57.117/2

International Marketing Events, Market Research Summary, C 61.21

International Marketing Information Service, C 57.116

International Marketing Information Service: Country Market Survey, C 42.31/2

International Meteorological Observations, W 42.7/1

International Monetary Fund and International Bank for Reconstruction and Development, S 5.46

International Narcotics Control Strategy Report, S 1.146

International News Letter, C 3.217

International Notams, C 31.133, FAA 1.26, TD 4.11

International Notices to Airmen, TD 4.11

International Oil and Gas Exploration and Development, E 3.11/20-6

International Oil and Gas Exploration and Development Activities, E 3.11/20-4

International Organization and Conference Series, S 1.70

International Organization and Conference Series, General, S 1.70/1

International Organization and Conference Series II, Regional, S 1.70/2

International Organization and Conference Series III, United Nations (including commissions), S 1.70/3

International Organization and Conference Series IV, Specialized Agencies, S 1.70/4

International Organization Series, S 1.70/5

International Organizations and Conference Series, S 1.70

International Petroleum Annual, I 28.43/3, E 3.11/5-3

International Petroleum Quarterly, I 28.43/2

International Petroleum Trade, I 28.43

International Petroleum Statistics Report, E 3.11/5-6

International Politics, Selective Monthly Bibliography, S 1.92/4

International Population Reports, C 3.186:P-95

International Population Reports, P-91-(series), C 59.13

International Population Reports Series, C 56.112/2

International Population Statistics Reports, C 56.112

International Population Statistics Reports, P 90-(series), C 59.13/2:90

International Populations Reports, C 3.186:P- 95, C 56.112/2

International Prison Commission, S 5.18/2

International Prison Congress, S 5.18/1

International Programs News, A 13.153

International Radiotelegraph Conference of Madrid, 1932, S 5.26

International Reference Group on Great Lakes Pollution from Land Use Activities: Annual Progress Report, Y 3.In 8/28:14

International Reference Service, C 18.223

International Research Documents, C 3.205/6, C 56.226/2

International Review, HH 1.40/7

International Sanitary Conference, Washington, 1881, S 5.11

International Satellite and Space Probe Summary [and charts], NAS 1.16

International Science and Technology Data Update, NS 1.52

International Science Notes, S 1.22, NS 1.17/2, NS 1.17/3

International Science Reports, NS 1.25

International Shipborne Barge Register, C 39.241, TD 11.24

International Solar-Terrestrial Physics Program, NAS 1.86/3

International Statistical Congress, S 5.5

International Summaries, J 26.17, J 28.16

International Teacher Development Program, Annual Report to Bureau of Educational and Cultural Affairs, Department of State, FS 5.214:14003

International Technical Cooperation Series, HE 3.33

International Telecommunication Union, S 5.50

International Telegraph Conference, Brussels, 1928, S 5.27/2
International Telegraph Conference, Paris, 1925, S 5.27
International Telephone Directory, T 22.48/4
International Trade in Goatskins, C 18.186/2
International Trade in Sheep Skins, C 18.186/3
International Trade Series, C 18.273
International Trade Statistics Series, C 42.9/3
International Training and Advisory Assistance Programs, T 17.29
International Training Programs in Labor Statistics, L 2.128
International Travelers to the U.S., Annual Summary, C 47.15/5
International Veterinary Congress Proceedings, A 4.19
Interoceanic Canal Congress, Paris, 1879, S 5.15
Interpretation, I 29.129
Interpretation Bulletins, ES 2.8
Interpretation of War Statutes, Bulletins, J 1.17
Interpretations, ES 4.6/4
Interpretations, Rulings and Explanations Regarding Laws, Rulings, and Instructions, IC 1 loc.6
Interpretations, Rulings, and Instructions for Inspection and Testing of Locomotives and Tenders and their Appurtenances, IC 1 loc.5
Interpretive Bulletins, L 20.7, L 22.10, L 36.209
Interpretive Prospectus, I 29.79/2
Interpretive Reports, HE 19.211
Interpretive Series, I 29.52
Interstate Appeals Handbook, L 7.48
Interstate Certified Shellfish Shippers List, HE 20.4014
Interstate Commerce Act, Including Text or Related Sections of Other Acts, IC 1 act.5
Interstate Commerce Acts Annotated, IC 1 act.5/2
Interstate Commerce Commission Decisions, IC 1.6/a:F
Interstate Commerce Commission Reports, IC 1.6/1, IC 1.6/10
Interstate Commerce Commission Reports, Decisions of the Interstate Commerce Commission of the United States, IC 1.6
Interstate Commerce Commission Reports, Valuation Reports, IC 1 val.7
Interstate Gas Prices and Financial Data, E 3.11/2-7
Interstate Shellfish Shippers List, HE 20.4014
Interstate System Traveled-Way Study Reports, TD 2.118
Interviewing Aid, L 7.52
Interviewing Guides for Specific Disabilities, L 1.7/7, L 37.8/4
Interviews, S 1.25/5
Interviews with the Past, I 16.61
Intestinal Parasite Surveillance, HE 20.7011/28
Intramural Annual Report, National Institute of Aging, HE 20.3866
Intramural Research, Annual Report–
    National Institute of Allergy and Infectious Diseases, HE 20.3211/3
    National Institute of Neurological and Communica-tive Disorders and Stroke, HE 20.3516/4
Intramural Research Highlights, National Medical Expenditure Survey, HE 20.6517/4
Introduction of Domestic Reindeer into Alaska, I 16.8
Introduction to Federal Supply Catalogs and Related Publications, D 7.33
Introduction to Station Catalogs, N 6.5/10
Introductions to Research in Foreign Law (series), LC 42.15
Inventions Available for Licensing, A 77.35
Inventories, A 6.6
Inventories and Analysis of Federal Population Research, HE 20.3362/2
Inventories and Sales of Fuel Oil and Motor Gasoline, Wholesale Distributions, C 3.263/3
Inventories of Seeds and Plants Imported by Office of Foreign Seed and Plant Introduction, A 19.12
Inventories of Steel Producing Mills, C 3.158:M 33 J
Inventories of World War II, AE 1.19
Inventory and Analysis of NIH Maternal and Child Health Research, HE 20.3363
Inventory Municipal Waste Facilities, EP 2.17
Inventory of Agricultural Research, A 94.14
Inventory of American Intermodal Equipment, C 39.237, TD 11.31
Inventory of Automated Data Processing Equipment in the United States Government for Fiscal Year (date), GS 12.10
Inventory of Automatic Data Processing (ADP) Equipment in Federal Government, PrEx 2.12
Inventory of Automatic Data Processing Equipment in the United States Government, GS 2.15
Inventory of Federal Population Research, Fiscal Year, HE 20.3025

Inventory of Federal Programs that Support Health Manpower Training, HE 20.3114/3
Inventory of Federal Tourism Programs, Federal Agencies, Commissions, Programs Reviewed for Their Participation in the Development of Recreation, Travel, and Tourism in the United States, C 47.2:T 64/3
Inventory of Interstate Carrier Water Supply Systems, EP 1.41
Inventory of Knowledge Series, LC 1.41
Inventory of Nonpurchased Foreign Currencies, T 1.50
Inventory of Nonutility Electric Power Plants in the United States, E 3.29/2
Inventory of Physical Facilities in Institutions of Higher Education, HE 5.92/3, HE 19.310
Inventory of Population Research Supported by Federal Agencies, HE 20.3362/2
Inventory of Power Plants in the United States, E 3.29
Inventory of Recent Publications and Research Studies in the Field of International and Cultural Affairs, S 1.30/4
Inventory of Soil, Water, and Related Resources, A 57.22
Inventory of Unpublished Climatological Tabulations, C 30.64
Inventory of U.S. Greenhouse Gas Emissions and Sinks, EP 1.115
Inventory of Water Resources, Y 3.N 21/12:10
Inventory Report of Jurisdictional Status of Federal Areas within the States, GS 1.15/3
Inventory Report on Real Property Leased to the United States throughout the World, GS 1.15/2
Inventory Report on Real Property Owned by the United States throughout the World, GS 1.15
Investigational Reports, C 6.12, I 45.19
Investigations (series), ITC 1.12
Investigations and News, Y 3.C 42/2:16
Investigations in Fish Control, I 49.70
Investigations of Floods in Hawaii, Progress Reports, I 19.57
Investment Advisers Act of 1940 and General Rules and Regulations thereunder as in Effect (date), SE 1.5:In 8/2
Investment Advisers Act Releases, SE 1.25/9
Investment Guaranties Staff Circular Letters, S 17.43
Investment of Individuals in Savings Accounts, U.S. Savings Bonds and Life Insurance Reserves, FHL 1.13
Investment, Operating and Other Budget Expenditures, Special Analysis D, PrEx 2.8/a8
Investment Opportunities Abroad, Bulletins, C 42.3/2
Investment Opportunity Information, C 42.25
Investment Properties, Y 3.F 31/8:30
Invitation for Bids for Transportation of Enlisted Men of Navy and Marine Corps, N 17.11
Involvement for Community Organizations with Employment of the Mentally Restored, PrEx 1.10/4-3
Iodine in (year), I 28.129
Ionospheric Data, C 55.218
Ionospheric Predictions, C 1.59
IPEDS Integrated Postsecondary Education Data System, Institutional Characteristics, ED 1.23/6
IPS, HH 1.1/8
IPS Wireless File, S 1.58/2
IR (series), C 41.26/2
Ira C. Eaker Distinguished Lecture on National Defense Policy, D 305.10/2
IRAC Gazetteer, C 1.60/5
IRC Bulletin, EP 2.3/3
IRG Bulletin, HE 20.8103/2
IRIG Documents, D 105.23
IRIS, Earth Orientation Bulletin, C 55.437
Irish Free State Tractor Exports, C 18.103
Irish Potatoes, Utilization of Crop with Comparisons, A 92.11/5
IRM Forum, GS 12.17/2
IRMS Directory of Assistance, GS 12.12/3
Iron and Steel Fortnightly, C 18.104
Iron and Steel Fortnightly, Intermediate Issue, C 18.141/2
Iron and Steel in (year), I 28.53/4
Iron and Steel Report, I 28.53/3
Iron and Steel Scrap in (year), I 28.53/2-2
Iron and Steel Scrap Stock Reports, I 28.53
Iron and Steel Slag, I 28.53/5
Iron Ore, I 28.66
Iron Ore in (year), I 28.66/2
Iron Ore Monthly Reports, I 28.66
Iron Oxide Pigments in (year), I 28.163
Irrigation, Agricultural Lands, C 3.37/24
Irrigation and Investigation Schedules, A 10.8

Irrigation Energy Efficiency (series), E 5.13
Irrigation Guides [for areas], A 57.6/3
Irrigation of Agricultural Lands (by States), C 3.940-9
Irrigation Operational and Maintenance Bulletin, I 27.41
Irrigation Photographs, I 27.24
IRS Clip-sheet, T 22.49
IRS Historical Studies, T 22.66
IRS International Telephone Directory, T 22.48
IRS International Spotlight, T 22.2/15:7177
IRS News, T 22.55/2
IRS Phone Book, National Office, T 22.48
IRS Service, T 22.55/2-2
IS (series), I 53.26
ISC Fact Sheets, S 17.24
ISOO (Information Security Oversight Office) Annual Report, AE 1.101/3
Island Lantern, J 16.20
Island of Palmas Arbitration, S 3.18/6
Isotope and Radiation Source Technology, E 1.99
Isotope Developments, Y 3.At 7:27
Isotopes and Radiation Technology, Y 3.At 7:52
Isotopes Branch Circulars, Y 3.At 7:12
ISP Supplemental Course Series, C 3.205/4
ISPO, C 3.205/3
Israel, LC 1.30/4
Issuances of Meat and Poultry Inspection Program, A 101.6/2-2, A 103.9/2, A 110.9
Issue Alert (series), SBA 1.41
Issue Brief, ED 1.322/2
Issue Briefing Papers (series), A 107.16
Issue Bulletin, A 1.141
Issues and Practices, J 28.23
Issues in International Crime, J 28.23/2
Issues in Labor Statistics, L 2.132
Issues of Democracy, IA 1.36, S 20.21
Issues of Merit, MS 1.17
Items of Interest, D 201.27, D 208.3/3
Items of Interest in Seed Control, A 88.63
ITS News, Y 3.N 88:51
ITS Update, TD 1.60
IWR Contract Reports, D 103.57
IWR Proceedings (series), D 103.57/10
IWR User's Manual, D 103.57/11

J

Jackson, C 55.287/20-4
JACS [Journal Article Copy Service] Directory, C 51.11/6
JAG Journal, D 205.7
Jail Inmates, J 29.11/5
Jails in Indian Country, J 29.11/5-3
JANP (series), D 5.8
Japan Productivity Center, United States Operations Mission to Japan, Publications, S 17.44/2
Japan Report, PrEx 7.16
Japan Report, Science and Technology, PrEx 7.16/6
Japan Road Maps, Series L302, D 5.340
Japanese Beetle-European Chafer Control Program, Annual Report, A 77.326
Japanese Economic Statistics Bulletin, D 102.14
Japanese Technical Literature Bulletin, C 1.90
Japanese Trade Studies, TC 1.23
Japanese Trade Studies, Special Industry Analyses, TC 1.23/3
JCH [Job Corps Handbooks], L 1.58
JCH (series), PrEx 10.10
JCS Publications (series), D 5.12
Jefferson's Legacy, LC 1.56
Jet Age Planning, Progress Reports, C 31.168, FAA 1.36
Jet Navigation Charts, D 5.354
Jet Propulsion Laboratory, NAS 1.12/4
Jet Propulsion Laboratory: JPL/HR- (series), NAS 1.12/7
Jet Propulsion Laboratory Publications (numbered), NAS 1.12/7
Jet Propulsion Laboratory: Technical Reports, NAS 1.12/3
JFMIP News, GA 1.12/3, GS 14.7
JNC - Jet Navigation Charts, D 5.323
Job Aids (numbered), D 105.6/4
Job Bank, Frequently Listed Openings, L 37.311
Job Corps Centers, PrEx 10.10/4
Job Corps Handbooks, JCH- (series), L 37.11/3
Job Corps Happenings, L 37.11
Job Corps Happenings, Special Editions, L 37.11/2
Job Corps Staff Newsletter, PrEx 10.10/3
Job Descriptions, L 1.65

Job Family Series, FS 3.124, Pr 32.5212, L 7.34
Job Grading System for Trades and Labor Occupations, Transmittals, CS 1.42/2
Job Grading System for Trades and Labor Organizations, CS 1.41/4:512-1
Job Guide for Young Workers, L 1.7/6
Job Health Hazards Series, L 35.18
Job Patterns for Minorities and Women and Private Industry, Y 3.Eq 2:12-7
Job Patterns for Minorities and Women in Apprenticeship Programs and Referral Unions, Y 3.Eq 2:12-2
Job Patterns for Minorities and Women in State and Local Government, Y 3.Eq 2:12-4
Job Safety and Health, L 35.9/2
Job Sheets, A 57.40/2
Job Specifications, L 7.16
Jobs in New York-Northeastern New Jersey, L 2.71/6-7
Joe Dope Posters, W 34.29/3, W 34.29/4
Johnny Horizon Environmental Program: Action Booklets, I 1.101
Joint Air Forces & Navy Radio Facility Charts, M 301.16
Joint Army and Air Force Bulletins, D 101.3
Joint Army and Air Force Procurement Circulars, D 101.33
Joint Army and Air Force Regulations, M 101.15
Joint Army & Navy Radio Facility Charts, W 108.29
Joint Army-Navy Publications, M 1.79
Joint Army-Navy Specifications, N 20.23, M 213.8
Joint Army-Navy Standards, N 20.28, M 5.7
Joint Chiefs of Staff, D 5.12/2
Joint Circulars, A 1.28
Joint Commission on Hudson's Bay and Puget's Sound, S 3.9
Joint Electronic Library, D 5.21
Joint Federal Travel Regulations, D 1.6/4-2, D 1.6/4-5
Joint Financial Management Improvement Program, Annual Report Fiscal Year (date), GA 1.12
Joint Force Quarterly, D 5.20
Joint Hydrology-Sedimentation Bulletins, Y 3.In 8/8:9, Y 3.W 29:9
Joint Letters, A 55.44/6, A 55.42/6
Joint Military Packaging Training Center Course Outlines, D 1.35
Joint Military-Industry Packaging and Materials Handling Symposium, D 101.51
Joint NCDRH and State Quality Assurance Surveys in Nuclear Medicine, HE 20.4611
Joint Orders, A 1.27
Joint Publications, D 5.12
Joint Series (rehabilitation monographs), VE 1.8
Joint Staff Officer's Guide, D 5.408/2
Joint Stock Land Banks, Progress in Liquidation Including Statements of Condition, A 72.16
Joint Travel Regulations, D 1.6/4
Journal–
  Bureau of Ships, D 211.8
  Coast and Geodetic Survey, C 4.41
  Energy Information Administration, E 3.34/3
  Federal Home Loan Bank Board, FHL 1.27
  House of Representatives, XJH
  National Cancer Institute, FS 2.31, HE 20.3161
  Senate, XJS
  Thrift Supervisor Office, T 71.15
  United States Institute of Peace, Y 3.P 31:15
  U.S. Army Intelligence and Security Command, D 101.85
  War Trade Board, WR 1.5
Journal for Medicaid Management, HE 22.109
Journal Holdings Report, EP 1.31
Journal of Abstracts–
  Electrical Engineering, C 41.66/3
  Mathematics, C 41.61/3
  Mechanics, C 41.65/3
  Metallurgy, C 41.54/9
Journal of Acoustics [abstracts], C 41.48
Journal of Agricultural Economic Research, A 93.26
Journal of Agricultural Research, A 1.23
Journal of Analytical Chemistry [abstracts], C 41.53/6
Journal of Applied Chemistry [abstracts], C 41.53/11
Journal of Executive Proceedings of Senate, Y 1.3/4
Journal of Experimental and Theoretical Physics [abstracts], C 41.52/2
Journal of General Chemistry [abstracts], C 41.53
Journal of Highway Research, Public Roads, C 37.8
Journal of Human Services Abstracts, HE 1.50
Journal of Inorganic Chemistry, C 41.53/4
Journal of Legal Studies, D 305.21/2
Journal of Mycology, A 28.5
Journal of Navy Civilian Manpower Management, D 204.9
Journal of Physical Chemistry [abstracts], C 41.34/5

Journal of Public Inquiry, PR 42.8/4
Journal of Rehabilitation, Research and Development, VA 1.23/3
Journal of Research, Bound Volumes, C 13.22/2
Journal of Research of the U.S. Geological Survey, I 19.61
Journal of Scientific and Applied Photography and Cinematography [abstracts], C 41.69
Journal of Technical Physics [abstracts], C 42.52/6
Journal of the Federal Home Loan Bank Board, FHL 1.27
Journal of the House of Representatives, XJH
Journal of the National Cancer Institute, HE 20.3161
Journal of the Senate, XJS
Journal of Transportation and Statistics, TD 12.18
Journal of United States Artillery, W 29.5
Journals Available in the ERDA Library, ER 1.19
Journals of Continental Congress, Miscellaneous, LC 4.6
Journals of the Continental Congress, LC 4.5
Journals of the Continental Congress, Index, GS 4.2:C 76/2
JPL Facts (various topics), NAS 1.12/9
JPL-SP (series), NAS 1.12/6
JPRS [Joint Publications Research Service], PrEx 7.13
JPRS (DC) L- (series), Y 3.J 66:10
JPRS (NY) L- (series), Y 3.J 66:11
JPRS (NY) Reports, Y 3.J 66:8
JPRS R (series), Y 3.J 66:12
JPRS Report: East Asia, Korea, PrEx 7.16/2-2
JPRS Report: Science and Technology, Europe, PrEx 7.17/6
JPRS Report: Science and Technology, USSR, Life Sciences, PrEx 7.21/14-2
JPRS Report: Soviet Union, World Economy and International Relations, PrEx 7.21/15
JPRS (series), Y 3.J 66:13
JPRS (series) Science & Technology, China: Energy, PrEx 7.15/6-2
JPRS (series) Soviet Union, the Working Class & the Contemporary World, PrEx 7.21/9-2
JPRS (series) USSR Reports, Machine Tools and Metal Working Equipment, PrEx 7.21/3-3
JPRS/DC Reports, Y 3.J 66:9
JS&HQ, L 35.9/3
Judge Advocate General's Department, W 3.65
Judge Advocate Legal Service, D 101.22:27
Judges Information Series, Ju 10.24
Judgments Rendered by Court of Claims, Ju 3.6
Judicial Business of the United States Courts, Ju 10.1/4
Judicial Decisions, SE 1.19
Junior Division News-Letter, L 7.9
Junior-Year Science, Mathematics, and Foreign Language Students, First-Term, FS 5.254:54001, HE 5.254:54001
Juror Utilization in United States District Courts, Ju 10.13
Justice, J 1.101
Justice Assistance News, J 1.59
Justice Expenditure and Employment, J 29.11/2
Justice Expenditure and Employment Extracts, J 29.11/2-2
Justice Expenditure and Employment in the U.S, J 29.11/2-3
Justice Library Review, J 4.7
Justification of Budget and Legislative Program for Office of Management and Budget, HE 22.30/2
Justifications of Appropriation Estimates for Committees on Appropriations, Fiscal Year–
  Department of Education, ED 1.46, ED 1.46/2
  Department of Health and Human Services, HE 1.1/3
  Health Care Financing Administration, HE 22.33
Juvenile Court Statistics, FS 17.213, HE 17.23, J 1.53, J 32.15
Juvenile Delinquency: Facts and Facets, FS 3.222, FS 14.115
Juvenile Delinquency Prevention and Control Act of 19678, Grants, HE 17.811
Juvenile Delinquency Reporter, HE 17.22
Juvenile Justice and Delinquency Prevention, Y 3.C 86:2 J 98
Juvenile Justice Bulletins, J 32.10
Juvenile Justice Conditions of Confinement, J 32.19
Juvenile Justice, Deinstitutionalizing Status Offenders: A Record of Progress, J 32.20/4
Juveniles Taken into Custody, J 32.18

K

Kansas Leaflets, A 62.10

Kappler's Compilation of Indian Laws and Treaties, Y 4.In 2/2:L 44
Keep Well Series, T 27.22
Kennedy Round, Special Reports, C 42.29
Key Audiovisual Personnel in Public Schools and Library Systems in State and Large Cities and In Large Public Colleges and Universities, FS 5.60/2
Key Dates, NAS 1.79
Key Facts, Employment Security Operations, L 7.60
Key Officers of Foreign Service Posts, S 1.40/5
Key Officers of Foreign Service Posts, Guide for Businessmen, S 1.40/2:Of 2
Key to Geophysical Records Documentation, C 55.219/2
Key to Meteorological Records Documentation, C 55.219
Key to Meteorological Records, Environmental Satellite Imagery (series), C 55.219/4
Key to Oceanic and Atmospheric Information Sources, C 55.219/5
Key to Oceanographic Records Documentation, C 55.219/3
KeyNotes, HH 1.121
Keyword Directory, T 17.6/3-3
Keyword Worksheet, T 17.6/3-2
Keywords Index to U.S. Government Technical Reports, C 41.21/5
Kidney Disease and Nephrology Index, HE 20.3318
Kidney, Urology and Hematology, HE 20.3320/2-5
Kindergarten Extensions Series, I 16.18/5
Klamath River Fisheries Assessment Program (series), I 49.107
Knit Fabric Gloves, C 3.129
Knit Wool Gloves and Mittens, C 3.63
Know Your Communist Enemy Series, D 2.13
Knowledge for Survival, You Can Survive Newsletter to State Extension Program Leaders, Rural Defense, A 43.35/2
Korea Road Maps, Series L351, D 5.341
Korean Affairs Report, PrEx 7.16/2
KU (Kidney/Urologic) Notes (series), HE 20.3324
Kyanite and Related Minerals in (year), I 28.131

L

L- (series) Industrial College of the Armed Forces, D 5.10/2
L, ED 1.76/2-4
L.C. Classification, Additions and Changes, LC 1.7/2, LC 26.9/2
L.C. Subject Headings Weekly Lists, LC 26.7/2-2
L.S. Series, C 30.69
LABCERT Bulletin, EP 2.3/4
Labor and Employee Relations Bulletin for SSA Supervisory Personnel, HE 3.68/3
Labor Charts, L 1.9/3
Labor Compliance Manual, Direct Federal and Federal-aid Construction, TD 2.108:L 11
Labor Developments Abroad, L 2.32/2
Labor Digest, L 2.72/3
Labor Education News, L 16.28
Labor Exchange, L 1.92, L 1.93
Labor Force, C 3.186:P-50
Labor Force Bulletin, C 3.156
Labor Force, Gross Changes in the Labor Force, C 3.186:P-59
Labor Force Memorandums, C 3.187
Labor Force, Monthly Report on the Labor Force, C 3.186:P-51, L 1.15
Labor Force, Monthly Reports on, C 3.155
Labor Information Bulletin, L 2.10
Labor Information Circulars, SS 1.14
Labor Law and Practice in (country), L 2.71
Labor Law Series, L 36.10
Labor Laws Affecting Women, Capsule Summary, L 36.111
Labor Laws and Their Administration, L 16.3
Labor Literature, Recent Additions to the Department of Labor Library, L 1.34/5
Labor Management Case Finder, CS 1.41/4:711-2
Labor Management News, Pr 32.4820
Labor Management Relations, CS 1.41/4:711-1
Labor Management Relations Issues in State and Local Governments, CS 1.80/2
Labor Market, FS 3.113/2, Pr 32.5211, L 7.20
Labor Market Developments, FS 3.113
Labor Market Information Area Series: Basic Statements, L 7.22
Labor Market Information Area Series, Current Supplements, FS 3.132, L 7.22/2

Labor Market Information for USES Counseling: Industry Series, Pr 32.5229, L 7.23

Labor Market Information Industry Series: Current Supplements, FS 3.131

Labor Market Information Series [compilations], L 7.23/3

Labor Market Survey (by States), FS 3.134

Labor News, L 2.21

Labor Offices in the United States and Canada, L 16.3

Labor Offices in U.S. and Foreign Countries, L 2.6/a 3

Labor Press Service, L 1.78

Labor Priority Bulletins, Y 3.W 19/2:16

Labor Provisions for Industries (Posters), Y 3.N 21/8:17

Labor Relations Letters, HH 1.117

Labor Relations Today, L 1.66/3

Labor Standards, L 16.11/1

Labor Standards Clearinghouse, L 16.46

Labor Statistics Series, L 2.72

Labor Supply and Demand in Selected Defense Occupations, as Reported by Public Employment Offices, FS 3.116

Labor Supply Available at Public Employment Offices in Selected Defense Occupations, FS 3.117

Labor Surplus Area Zip Code Reference, GS 1.33

Labor Turnover, L 2.42

Labor Turnover in Manufacturing, L 2.42/3

Labor Yearbook, L 1.27

Laboratory Command: Pamphlets, LABCOM-P-(series), D 101.22/24

Laboratory Information Bulletin, HE 20.4003/4

Laboratory Report, SI-, I 27.46

Laboratory Report SI Series, I 27.45

Labor-Management Cooperation Brief, L 1.85

Labor-Management Manpower Policy Committee, Publications, Pr 34.209

Labor-Management Reporting and Disclosures Act, As Amended, Regulations and Interpretative Bulletins, L 1.51/2

LA/C Business Bulletin, C 61.35/2

Lacquers, Sales of, C 3.88

Lake Erie Wastewater Management Study Public Information Fact Sheet, D 103.63/2

Lake Erie Water Quality Newsletter, D 103.63

Lake Mead Water Supply Outlook, I 27.43

Lake Michigan Cooling Water Studies Panel: Reports, EP 1.72

Lake Series, D 103.18

Lake States Aspen Reports, A 13.61/7

Lamb Crop and Wool, A 105.23/7-2

Lamb Crop and Wool Production, Louisiana Crop Reporting Service, A 88.16/19

Lamb Crop Report, A 88.16/11

Lamb Feeding Situation, A 88.16/12

Land, I 53.25

Land and Natural Resources Division Journal, J 30.9

Land and Water Conservation Fund Grants Manual, I 29.107

Land and Water Conservation Fund, Grants- in-Aid Program, Annual Report, I 29.107/2

Land Appeals, I 1.69/5

Land Areas of the National Forest System, A 13.10

Land Between the Lakes [field guides], Y 3.T 25:6-3

Land Decisions, I 21.5

Land Economics Reports, A 36.104

Land Joint Commission, United States and Panama, S 3.30

Land Laws, I 21.7, I 21.8

Land Locomotion Laboratory Reports, D 105.18/2

Land Planning and Housing Bulletins, Y 3.T 25:11

Land Planning Bulletins, HH 2.7

Land Policy Circulars, Y 3.R 31:9, A 61.9, A 36.103

Land Policy Review, A 55.26

Land Protection Plan (series), I 29.111

Land Sale, I 53.32/2

Land Service Bulletin, I 21.16

Land, Today and Tomorrow, I 30.9

Land Use and Land Cover and Associated Maps, I 19.112

Land Use and Soil Conservation, Informational Materials Available to Public, Leaflets (by Regions), A 57.26

Land Use Decisions and Rangeland Program Summary, I 53.23/2

Land Use Notes, A 1.128

Land Use Planning Publications, Y 3.R 31:23, A 61.8

Land Use Projects, A 36.108

Land-Grant Colleges and Universities, Preliminary Report for Year Ended June 30, FS 5.250:50025, HE 5.250:50025

Landmarks at Risk, I 29.117/3

Landsat 2, World Standard Catalog, NAS 1.48/3

Landsat 3, World Standard Catalog, NAS 1.48/4

Landsat Data Users Notes, I 19.78, C 55.45

Landsat: Non-U.S. Standard Catalog, NAS 1.48/2

Landsat: U.S. Standard Catalog, NAS 1.48

LandView II, Mapping of Selected EPA-Regulated Sites, TIGER/Line and Census of Population and Housing, EP 1.104/4

Landview IV/The Federal Geographic Data, C 3.301

Langley Research Center, Langley Field, VA., Releases, NAS 1.7/2

[Language Guides] PT-(series), D 202.6/8

Language Usage Series, I 16.75, FS 5.12

Lantern Slide Series, A 43.5/8

Laramie Energy Center: Annual Report, ER 1.23

Laramie Energy Technology Center: Annual Report, E 1.1/3

Large Space Structures and Systems in the Space Station ERA, A Bibliography with Indexes, NAS 1.21:7085

Large-Print Scores and Books, LC 19.11/3-3

Laser Induced Damage in Optical Materials, C 13.10/4

Last Salute, Civil and Military Funerals, D 101.2:F 96

Latest Consumer Price Index (Tables for U.S. and 6 Cities in Midwest), L 2.38/8-4

Latest Editions, Airport Obstruction Charts, C 55.411/3-2

Latest Editions of U.S. Air Force Aeronautical Charts, C 55.418/3

Latin America Report, PrEx 7.19

Latin American Circulars, C 18.106

Latin American Financial Notes, C 18.107

Latin American Public Utilities Survey, Y 3.Ec 74/2:7

Latin American Series, LC 1.16, L 2.6/a 7

Latin American Series, Monthly Labor Review, L 2.6/a 7

Latin American Trade Review, C 61.38

Latin American Transportation Survey, Y 3.Ec 74/2:8

Laundry and Dry Cleaning Wage Survey Summaries by Cities, L 2.113/2

Law Accession List (of) Library, FS 3.7

Law Bulletin, RR 1.8, TD 5.3/5

Law Enforcement Legal Update, T 70.5/2

Law Enforcement Manual, I 49.6/4

Law Enforcement Officers Killed and Assaulted, Uniform Crime Report, J 1.14/7-6

Law Enforcement Report, P 1.29/2

Law Enforcement Standards Program, LESP- RPT-(series), J 1.41

Law Enforcement Standards Program, NILECJ-STD-(series), J 1.41/2, J 26.20

Law, Higher Education, and Substance Abuse Prevention, A Biannual Newsletter, ED 1.2/16

Law in Action, PrEx 10.17

Law Library Reporter, I 1.74

Law of the Sea, PrEx 7.14/3

Laws, A 112.5

Laws–

Advisory Council on Historic Preservation, Y 3.H 62:5

Committee on Armed Services, Y 4.Ar 5/2-12

Comptroller of the Currency, T 12.24

Economic Development Administration, C 46.5

Interior Department, I 1.109

International Trade Commission, ITC 1.5

Maritime Administration, TD 11.6

Mine Safety and Health Administration, L 38.5

Violence Against Women Office, J 35.5

Laws Administered by Governor of Virgin Islands, I 35.13/5

Laws (Administered by the Bureau), I 53.5

Laws Affecting Corps Engineers, W 7.6/1

Laws and Executive Orders Relating to Compensation, Pension, Emergency Officers' Retirement, etc., VA 1.14

Laws and Regulations, HE 3.5/2

Laws and Regulations Enforced or Administered by the United States Customs Service, T 17.6/2

Laws and Regulations for Protection of Commercial Fisheries of Alaska, I 45.11

Laws and Regulations Relating to Lighthouse Establishment, C 9.16

Laws and Regulations Relating to National Parks, Reservations, etc., I 1.47

Laws Applicable to Immigration and Nationality, J 21.5

Laws Authorizing Issuance of Medals and Commemorative Coins, Y 1.2:M 46

Laws, Compilations and Digests, T 1.7

Laws, Executive Orders, Rules and Regulations, CS 1.41/4:990-1

Laws (general), I 20.9/1

Laws Governing Granting of Army and Navy Pensions, VA 2.5/2

Laws Governing Granting of Army and Navy Pensions and Bounty Land, I 24.14

Laws Governing Steamboat Inspection, C 25.5

Laws Governing Steamboat Inspection Service, T 28.5/1, C 15.5

Laws (Miscellaneous), T 22.32

Laws Relating Chiefly to Navy, Navy Department, and Marine Corps, M 201.10

Laws Relating to–

Agriculture [February 18, 1922], Y 1.2:Ag 8/5

Civil Defense, Pr 34.755

Civil Service Retirement, Y 1.2:R 31/2

Civil Service Salary Classification, Civil Service Preference, Etc., Y 1.2:Sa 3/2

Coast and Geodetic Survey, T 11.8, C 4.8

Coinage, T 26.6/2, T 28.10

Commercial Air Service and Miscellaneous Air Laws [May 10, 1916], Y 1.2:Ai 7

Construction of Bridges over Navigable Waters, W 7.6/2

Department of the Interior, I 1.44

Espionage, Sabotage, etc., Y 1.2:Es 6

Federal Aid and Construction of Roads, Y 1.2:R 53

Federal Corrupt Practices and Political Activities, Federal Corrupt Practices Act, Hatch Political Activities Act, Miscellaneous Related Acts and Regulations, Y 1.2:F 31/8

Forestry, Game Conservation, Flood Control and Related Subjects, Y 1.2:F 76/4

Interstate Commerce and Transportation, Y 1.2:In 8/3

Loans and Currency, T 26.6/1

National Park Service, T 29.46:L 44

Navy, N 7.7, M 214.8

Securities Commission, Exchanges and Holding Companies [May 27, 1933], Y 1.2:Se 2

Shipping and Merchant Marine [September 7, 1916], Y 1.2:Sh 6

Social Security and Unemployment Compensation [August 14, 1935], Y 1.2:So 1

Veterans, Y 1.2:V 64

Vocational Education and Agricultural Extension Work [May 8, 1914], Y 1.2:V 85/2

Laws Relative to Light House Establishment, C 9.15

Laws, Rules, and Instructions for Inspection and Testing of Locomotives Other Than Steam, IC 1 loc.8

Laws, Rules and Regulations, CS 1.7

Laws, Rules and Regulations (special), CS 1.7/2

Laws, Rulings, and Instructions for Inspection and Testing of Locomotives and Tenders and Their Appurtenances, IC 1 loc.5

Laws (special), I 20.9/2

Layers and Egg Production, A 105.12/7

Layers, Potential Lays and Rate of Lay First Month, A 92.9/12

Layman's Guide to Individual Rights Under the United States Constitution, Y 4.J 89/2:R 44

LBL News Magazine, E 1.53/2

LBL Research Review, E 1.53/2

LC Acquisition Trends, LC 30.17/2

LC Cataloging Newsline, LC 1.55

LC Folk Archive Finding Aid (numbered), LC 39.13/2

LC Folk Archive Reference Aids, LCCEP LC Science Tracer Bulletin, TB (series), LC 33.10

LCC [Life Cycle Costing], D 1.6/6

LCCEP Annual Report, D 301.107

LCFARA- (series), LC 39.13

LEAA [activities], J 1.1/2-2

LEAA Grants and Contracts, J 1.33

LEAA Grants and Contracts: Dissemination Document, J 1.33/2

LEAA News Releases, J 1.33/4

LEAA Newsletter, J 1.33/3, J 26.12

Lead in (year), I 28.87/2

Lead Industry, I 28.87

Lead Mine Production, I 28.60

Lead Post, HH 1.122

Lead Production, I 28.87, I 28.87/3

Lead Report, I 28.87

Lead Scrap Consumers Reports, I 28.67

Leader's Digest, T 22.59

Leader's Guide, Special Bulletin Series in Support of Annual National Civil Defense Week, FCD 1.7/3

Leading Edge, D 301.125

Leaflets, A 1.35, D 14.12, D 119.13, GP 3.13, L 36.110, FEM 1.11

Leaflets Accompanying Exhibit of Coast and Geodetic Survey at Pan-American Exposition, Buffalo, N.Y. 1901, T 11.18

Leaflets Accompanying Exhibit of Coast and Geodetic Survey at World's Fair, Chicago, Illinois, 1893, T 11.20

Leaflets for Action, A 80.708

Lineal List of Commissioned and Warrant Officers of the Marine Corps Reserves, D 214.11/2

Lineman, A 68.15

Linens and Laces, C 18.113

Link, A 68.15

Link, Enlisted Personnel Distribution Bulletin, D 208.19

Linkages, Y 3.L 71:21

Linking Employment Problems to Economic Status, L 2.3/28

Liquid Fossil Fuel Technology, DOE/BETC/QPR-(series), E 1.97

Liquid, Frozen, and Dried Egg Production, A 88.15

Liquefied Natural Gas, Literature Survey, C 13.37/6

Liquefied Petroleum Gas Sales, E 3.11/13

Liquor Laws [August 8, 1890], Y 1.2:L 66

List and Order Blank for Forms and Publications, FP 1.26

List and Station of Commission Officers, T 33.10

List and Stations of Naval Inspectors of Engineering Material, N 19.6

List of Acceptable Interstate Carrier Equipment Having Sanitation Significances, FS 2.78

List of Acquisitions of Municipal Reference Service, C 3.198

List of Addresses of Navy Recruiting Stations, N 17.13, N 17.21

List of American and Foreign Ships Owned under Requisition of Chartered to Shipping Board, SB 2.11

List of Atomic Energy Commission Documents Available for Sale, Y 3.At 7:15

List of Audiovisual Materials Produced by the United States Government (series), GS 4.17/5-2, AE 1.110/2

List of Available Farmers Bulletins and Leaflets, A 21.9/9

List of Available Publications, A 107.12:11

List of Available Publications for Distribution, A 13.64/9

List of Available Publications of the United States Department of Agriculture, A 21.9/8:11

List of Available Surplus Property Located in District of Columbia, T 58.23

List of Available USDA Publications for Sale from GPO, A 43.51

List of Aviation Medical Examiners, FAA 7.8

List of Awards, W 77.14

List of Awards Showing Contractors and Prices Contained in General Schedule of Supplies, T 45.6

List of Awards Showing Contractors and Prices for Material and Supplies Contained in General Schedule, Fiscal Year, GS 1.6

List of Basic Materials and Alternates, DP 1.9

List of Bituminous Coal Producers who have Accepted Bituminous Coal Code Promulgated June 21, 1972, I 34.17, I 46.9

List of Books Available for Ship and Station Libraries, Navy, N 17.26

List of Books, Pamphlets, and Maps Received, New Series, S 8.7

List of Books, Received, W 104.8

List of Books Received, Old Series, S 8.6

List of Bulletins and Circulars Issued by Department of Agriculture for Distribution, A 21.5

(List of) Bulletins of Bureau of Plant Industry, A 19.8

List of Bureau of Mines Publications and Articles, I 28.5

List of Cadets Admitted (cumulative), W 12.7

List of CFR Sections Affected, GS 4.108/3, AE 2.106/2-2

List of Changes of Stations, Etc., T 27.13

List of Chemical Compounds Authorized for Use Under USDA Meat, Poultry, Rabbit and Egg Inspection Programs, A 103.13

List of Chemical Compounds Authorized for Use Under USDA Poultry, Meat, Rabbit and Egg Products Inspection Programs, A 88.6:C 42, A 101.6:C 42

List of Classes in 1950 Revision of Classified List of United States Government Publications by Departments and Bureaus, GP 3.24

List of Code Number Producers of Bituminous Coal, I 34.22

List of Collection Districts, T 22.6

List of Committee Hearings, Committee Prints and Publications of the United States Senate, Y 1.3/10

List of Contents of Bound Volumes, Y 4.F 76/1-19

List of Corporate Names of Common Carriers, IC 1.15

List of Current Studies, BR (series), S 1.101/6

List of Department of Defense Purchasing Offices, D 1.77

List of Distillery Warehouses, T 22.21

List of Duplicates Offered as Exchanges, A 17.5

List of Electric Power Suppliers with Annual Operating Revenues of $2,500,000 or More Classified As Public Utilities Under Federal Power Act, FP 1.28

List of Export Licenses Approved, C 1.44

List of Extension Publications of State Agricultural Colleges Received by Office of Experiment Stations Library, A 43.5/9

List of FAA Publications, FAA 1.10

List of Fishery Cooperatives in the United States, C 55.338/2

List of Foreign Consular Officers in United States, S 1.12

List of Forms, Records, Laws, and Regulations Pertaining to Internal Revenue Service, T 22.39

List of Fully Processed Oceanography Cruise, D 203.24/5

List of GAO Publications, GA 1.16:P 96, GA 1.16/2

List of Geological Survey Geologic and Water-Supply Reports and Maps for (various States), I 19.41/7

List of Health Information Leaflets and Pamphlets of the Public Health Service, FS 2.24:In 3

List of Illinois River Terminals, Docks, Mooring Locations, and Warehouses, D 103.58

List of Inspection Points Under the Grain Standards Act, A 88.2:G 76/6

List of Intercepted Plant Pests, A 77.308/2, A 101.10/2:82-5

List of International and Foreign Scientific and Technical Meetings, NS 1.8

List of Items for Selection by Depository Libraries, GP 3.32

List of Journals Indexed in AGRICOLA, A 17.18/5

List of Journals Indexed in Index Medicus, HE 20.3612/4

List of Laboratories Approved to Receive Soil, A 101.34

List of Legal Investment for Trust Funds in D.C., DC 21.9

List of Lights and Fog Signals, D 203.22

List of Lights and Other Marine Aids, T 47.52, TD 5.9

List of Local Boards of the Selective Service System, Y 3.Se 4:24

List of Manufacturers and Jobbers of Fruit and Vegetable Containers, A 36.60

List of Masters, Mates, [etc.] of Merchant Steam, Motor, and Sail Vessels, Licensed during Calendar Year, T 38.7

List of Material Acceptable for Use on Systems of REA Electrification Borrowers and List of Materials Accepted on a Trial Basis, A 68.6/2

List of Materials Acceptable for Use on Telephone Systems of REA Borrowers, A 68.6/5

List of Member Banks by Districts, RB 1.5

List of Members of Bureau of Mines, I 28.12

List of Merchant Vessels, T 37.11, T 30.5

List of Mississippi River Terminals, Docks, Mooring Locations, and Warehouses, D 103.58/2

List of National Archives Microfilm Publications, GS 4.17/2

List of National Bank Examiners, T 12.10

List of Newspapers Designated to Publish Advertisements of War Department, W 1.9

List of OAR Research Efforts, D 301.69/7

List of Officers of Merchant Steam, Motor and Sail Vessels Licensed During (calendar year), C 15.7

List of Official International Conferences and Meetings, S 5.49

List of Official Publications of Government Distributed for Library of Congress through Smithsonian Institution, SI 1.5

List of OTC Margin Stocks, FR 1.46/4

List of Participating Institutions, Fiscal Year (date), J 1.43

List of Parties Excluded from Federal Procurement or Nonprocurement Programs, GS 1.28

List of Pensioners, I 24.6

List of Periodicals in NWC Library, D 1.26/2

List of Plants Operating Under USDA and Egg Grading and Egg Products Inspection Programs, A 103.10

List of Plants Operating Under USDA Poultry and Egg Inspection and Grading Programs, A 88.15/23

List of Proprietary Substance and Nonfood Compounds, A 110.9/2

List of Proprietary Substances and Nonfood Compounds Authorized for Use under USDA Inspection and Grading Programs, A 110.15

List of Publications–
Aeronautical Research Laboratory, D 301.69/4
Agricultural Education, A 10.14
Agricultural Marketing Service, A 66.32
Air Training Command, Human Resources Research Center, D 301.36
Army Engineer Waterways Experiment Station Available for Purchase, D 103.24/6
Bureau of Agricultural Chemistry and Engineering, A 70.10
Bureau of Agricultural Economics, A 36.70
Bureau of Agricultural Engineering, A 53.11
Bureau of Biological Survey, A 5.13
Bureau of Fisheries, C 6.6
Bureau of Foreign and Domestic Commerce, C 18.22/1, C 18.22/3
Bureau of Labor Statistics, L 2.5
Bureau of Mines (miscellaneous), I 28.5/3
Bureau of Plant Industry, A 19.10
Bureau of Soils, A 26.6/1
Bureau of Statistics, C 14.11
Bureau of the Census, C 3.13, C 3.163/2
Civil Aeronautics Administration, C 31.162
Civil Aeronautics Board, C 31.255
Cold Regions Research and Engineering Laboratory, D 103.33/6
Commodity Exchange Authority, A 85.13
Congressional Budget Office, Y 10.14
Department of Commerce and Labor, C 16.5
Division of Public Documents, GP 3.22
Farm Credit Administration, A 72.21, FCA 1.20
Farmer Cooperative Service, A 89.15:4
Federal Trade Commission, FT 1.22
Food and Nutrition of Man, A 10.15
Forest Products Laboratory, A 13.27/7, A 13.27/8
Forest Service, A 13.11, A 13.11/2
Irrigation and Drainage, A 10.16
National Bureau of Standards, C 13.37
North Central Forest Experiment Station, A 13.82/9
Office of Communications, A 21.10
Office of Education, I 16.14
Office of Experiment Stations, A 77.409
Public Health Service, FS 2.24/2
Rocky Mountain Forest and Range Experiment Station, A 13.69/10
Surplus Marketing Administration, A 73.10
Waterways Experiment Station, D 103.24/6
Weather Bureau, A 29.31/2

List of Publications and Patents, with Abstracts, A 77.17/2

List of Publications, Annotated, A 13.82/9

List of Publications Available for Distribution by Members of Congress, A 21.9/8:1

List of Publications, LP (Series), C 13.37

List of Publications on [subject], A 13.27/7

List of Radio Broadcast Stations, CC 1.10

List of Radio Broadcast Stations, Alphabetically by Call Letters, CC 1.21

List of Radio Broadcast Stations by Frequency, CC 1.22

List of Radio Broadcast Stations by State and City, CC 1.23

List of Radio Broadcast Stations, by Zone and State, CC 2.12

List of Radio Stations of United States, C 11.7/6

List of Recent Accessions and Foreign Patent Translations of the Scientific Library, C 21.17/2

List of Record Groups in National Archives and Federal Records Centers, GS 4.19

List of Reports and Publications Relating to Vital Statistics, C 3.137

List of Reports Received in Library, C 13.33/3

List of Rural Delivery County Maps, P 11.7

List of Serials Indexed for Online Users, HE 20.3618/2

List of Small Companies for Research and Development Work, SBA 1.16

List of Smithsonian Publications Available, SI 1.17

List of State and Local Trade Associations (by States), C 18.200

List of State Designated Agencies, Officials and Working Contracts, L 1.53/3

List of State Extension Entomologists and Extension Agriculturists, A 43.32

List of Station Publications Received by Office of Experiment Stations, A 10.17

List of Stocks Registered on National Securities Exchange and of Redeemable Securities of Certain Investment Companies, As of June 30, FR 1.46

List of Subject Headings, Additions, Corrections, and Supplements, LC 9.6/3

[List of Subject Headings] (Advance Prints), LC 9.6/2

List of Subjects (by date), C 3.13

List of Technical Studies, HH 2.23/2

M

Mail Room Companion, P 1.47/2

Mailing List, W 30.8

Mailing List of Consular Service of United States, S 1.19

Main Line Natural Gas Sales to Industrial Users, E 3.11/14

Mainland Cane Sugar Orders, A 55.67

Mainstreaming Preschoolers (series), HE 23.1110

Maintenance, D 301.84

Maintenance Handbook, MS- (series), P 1.31/6

Maintenance Operations Division Instructions, C 31.106/4, FAA 1.6/3

Maintenance, Preventive Maintenance, Rebuilding and Alterations, TD 4.6:part 43

Major Activities in Programs of National Aeronautics and Space Administration, NAS 1.1/2

Major Activities in the Atomic Energy Programs, Y 3.At 7:2 P 94/2

Major BLS Programs, L 2.87

Major Collective Bargaining Settlements in Private Industry, L 2.45/2

Major Data Processing and Telecommunication Acquisition Plans of Federal Executive Agencies, PrEx 2.12/3

Major Information Technology Systems, Acquisition Plans of Federal Executive Agencies, PrEx 2.27

Major Legislation of the Congress, LC 14.18

Major Matters Before the Commission, CC 1.2:M 43

Major Matters Before the Federal Communications Commission, CC 1.50

Major Metropolitan Market Areas, C 47.15/3

Major News Releases and Speeches, A 107.18

Major Nondeposit Funds of Commercial Banks, FR 1.39/4

Major Policy Initiatives, PrEx 2.8/10

Major Programs, Bureau of Labor Statistics, L 2.125

Major Programs of the U.S. Department of Housing and Urban Development, Fact Sheets, HH 1.43/2

Major Shippers Report, C 61.53

Major Work Stoppages, L 2.45/3

Making of American Scenery, I 29.10

Maktaba Afrikana Series, LC 2.12, LC 41.11

Malaria Folders, FS 2.41

Malaria Surveillance, Annual Report, HE 20.2309/13

Malaria Surveillance, Annual Summary, HE 20.7011/8

Malleable Iron Castings, C 3.89

Malmstrom Air Force Base Pamphlet (series), D 301.35/7

Mammalian Mutant Cell Lines Committee, HE 20.3001/2:M 31

Mammography Matters, HE 20.4619

Management, PM 1.11/2

Management, A Continuing Bibliography with Indexes, NAS 1.21:7500

Management Aids, SBA 1.32

Management Aids for Small Manufacturers, SBA 1.10

Management Analysis Series, CS 1.65/7, PM 1.49

Management and Productivity Improvement Report, VA 1.89

Management Bulletins–
    Bureau of the Budget, Pr 32.108, Pr 33.108, Pr 34.108, PrEx 2.3/2
    Department of Agriculture, A 1.3/2
    Forest Service, A 13.105/2

Management Data List–
    Air Force, D 7.29/2
    Army, D 7.29/3
    Marine Corps, D 7.29/5
    Navy, D 7.29/4

Management Data Series, P 1.46

Management Design and Development Technical Bulletins, HH 1.96

Management Experience Notes, FW 3.10

Management Highlights Releases, I 1.92

Management Improvement, A 1.74

Management Improvement Program, Plowback, Improvements Reports, D 101.63

Management Improvement Series, Administrative, T 1.42

Management Information on ERL's Scientific and Technical Publications, C 52.21/5

Management Instruction (series), P 1.53

Management Notes, Pr 33.114

Management of the United States Government, Fiscal Year (date), PrEx 2.8/9

Management Plan & Environmental Assessment, I 53.59/2

Management Plans (series), C 55.32/6

Management Procedure Notices, L 22.24

Management Reports, GS 1.23

Management Research Summary (series), SBA 1.12/2

Management Sciences Institute, Philadelphia Region: Bulletins, CS 1.3/2

Management Series, I 70.11/3, I 29.106

Management Service Notices, FAA 1.19

Management Statistics for United States Courts, Ju 10.14

Manager's Calendar, HE 3.81

Managing Clinical Costs, VA 1.84

Managing Federal Information Resources, PrEx 2.25

Managing the Nation's Public Lands, I 53.12/2

Managing Your Woodland, How to Do It Guides, A 13.36/3

Manchurian Soy Bean Trade, C 18.197

Mandrid, Columbian Historical Exposition, 1892-1893, S 6.7

Maneuver Memorandum, W 99.17/19

Manganese, I 28.54

Manganese in (year), I 28.54/2

Manila Custom-House General Orders, W 49.10/7

Manned Space Flight Resources Summary, Budget Estimates, NAS 1.54

Manned Undersea Science and Technology Fiscal Year Reports, C 55.29

Manpower, L 1.39/9

Manpower Administration Notice, L 1.22/4

Manpower Administration Orders, L 1.22/3

Manpower and Automation Research, L 1.39/5

Manpower Daily Reporter, L 1.39/7

Manpower Development and Training, Projects Approved, FS 5.76

Manpower Development Program Highlights, L 7.66

Manpower Development Research Program, Report, D 1.50

Manpower Evaluation Reports, L 1.39/2

Manpower Program Evaluation, L 1.45

Manpower Report of the President and Report on Manpower Requirements, Resources, Utilization, and Training by the U.S. Department of Labor, L 1.42/2

Manpower Reports–
    Bureau of Labor Statistics, L 2.57
    Manpower Administration, L 1.39

Manpower Requirements Report, D 1.52

Manpower Research Bulletins, L 1.39/6

Manpower Research Projects, Sponsored by the Manpower Administration through (date), L 1.39/6

Manpower Research Report, D 1.50/2

Manpower Review, Pr 32.5209

Manpower Technical Exchange, L 1.39/10

Manpower Training Facts, L 1.40/2

Manpower Utilization-Job Security in Longshore Industry [by port], L 1.50

Manpower/Automation Research Monographs, L 1.39/3

Manpower/Automation Research Notices, L 1.39/4

Manprint, D 101.3/6-2

Manprint Bulletin, D 101.3/6

Manual Amendment Circulars, W 36.7/2

Manual for Army Cooks, W 5.5

Manual for Courts-Martial–
    Air Force Supplement, D 1.15/3
    Army Supplement, D 1.15/2
    Navy Supplement, D 1.15/4
    United States, D 1.15

Manual for Medical Department, W 44.9

Manual for Medical Department, Navy (separates), N 10.5/1a

Manual for Pay Department, W 36.7/1

Manual for Quartermaster Corps, W 7.16/1

Manual for Radiosonde Code (WBAN), C 30.6/2:R 11

Manual for Review and Comment, HE 20.2588/2

Manual for Subsistence Department, W 5.6

Manual for Synoptic Code (WBAN), C 30.6/2:Sy 7/2

Manual for Upper Wind Code (SBAN), C 30.6/2:W 72

Manual for Use of Inspectors of Ordnance, W 34.7/3

Manual of Acceptable Practices, HH 1.6/9

Manual of Barometry, C 30.6/2:B 26

Manual of Bureau of Navigation, N 17.24/1

Manual of Bureau of Ships (by chapters), N 29.13

Manual of Classification, C 21.12

Manual of Engineering Instructions, N 19.8/1

Manual of Engineering Instructions (by chapters), N 29.11

Manual of Engineering Instructions, Individual Chapters, N 19.8/2

Manual of Examinations, C 1.8

Manual of Finance and Statistics Memorandum, FS 6.17

Manual of Finance and Statistics Memorandum of National Youth Administration, Pr 32.5258

Manual of Foreign Lumber Tariffs, C 18.114/2

Manual of Information–
    Isthmian Canal Commission, W 73.11
    Philippine Islands Civil Service Bureau, W 49.5/6

Manual of Instructions, J 1.14/6

Manual of Instructions for Survey of Mineral Lands in United States, I 21.11/4

Manual of Instructions for Survey of Public Lands of United States, I 53.7

Manual of Laws Affecting Federal Credit Unions, NCU 1.8/2

Manual of Laws Affecting Federally Insured State Credit Unions, NCU 1.8:St 2/2

Manual of Marine Meteorological Observations, C 30.4:M

Manual of Meat Inspection Procedures of the Department of Agriculture, A 88.6/4:M 46

Manual of Medical Department, Navy, D 206.8, D 206.8/2

Manual of Navy Enlisted Manpower and Personnel Classifications and Occupational Standards Section II Navy Enlisted Classifications, D 208.6/3-4

Manual of Operations, C 23.6/5, CA 1.14, C 31.116

Manual of Patent Examining Procedures, C 21.15

Manual of Policies and Procedure for Military Specifications, D 3.6/2

Manual of Regulations, I 28.11

Manual of Regulations and Instructions Relating to the Disclosure of Federal Campaign Funds for Candidates for the Office of President or Vice President of the United States and Political Committees Supporting Such Candidates, GA 1.14:C 15

Manual of Regulations and Procedures for Radio Frequency Management, PrEx 18.8:R 11

Manual of Rules, Y 4.W 36:10-5

Manual of Rules of the Committee on Ways and Means, Y 4.W 36:WMCP 96-1

Manual of Rules Regulations, Transmittal Letters, FW 4.30

Manual of Surface Observations, C 30.4

Manual of Surveying Instructions (general), I 21.11/1

Manual of the Bureau of Reclamation, I 27.20

Manual of Winds-Aloft Observations, C 30.4O

Manual on Fund-raising Within the Federal Services for Voluntary Health and Welfare Agencies, CS 1.7/5

Manual on Uniform Control Devices for Streets and Highways, TD 2.8:T 67

Manual on Uniform Traffic Control Devices for Streets and Highways: Official Rulings on Requests for Interpretations, Changes, and Experimentations, TD 2.8/2

Manual Series, D 203.24:M

Manual Transmittal Letter, L 7.44

Manuals–
    Air Force Systems Command, D 301.45/14
    Air National Guard, D 301.23
    Air Weather Service, D 301.27
    Armed Forces Institute, D 1.10
    Bureau of Naval Personnel, D 208.6/2
    Bureau of Ships, D 211.7
    Civil Aeronautics Administration, C 31.107
    Civil Aeronautics Authority, CA 1.10
    Civil Air Patrol, D 301.7/4
    Defense Contract Audit Agency, D 1.46/2
    Defense Logistics Service Center, D 7.6/10
    Defense Supply Agency, D 7.6/3, D 7.6/8
    Department of Health, Education, and Welfare, FS 1.6/2
    Department of the Air Force, D 301.7
    Federal Civil Defense Administration, FCD 1.6/6
    Federal Security Agency, FS 1.6/2
    Fleet Marine Force, D 214.9/4
    General Reference and Bibliography Division, LC 2.8
    Marine Corps, D 214.9
    Military Air Transportation Service, D 301.7/6
    National Guard Bureau, D 112.7
    Ordnance Corps, D 105.6/2
    Quartermaster Corps, D 106.6/2
    Quartermaster's Department, W 39.9/2
    ROTC, D 101.48
    Volunteer Probation Programs, FS 17.8/2, HE 17.8/2

Manuals, AFM- (series), D 301.7

Manuals, AFSCM- (series), D 301.45/14

Manuals and Handbooks (miscellaneous), I 53.7/2

Manuals, DIAM- (series), D 5.208/3

Manuals, EM- (series), D 103.6/3

Manuals for Volunteer Probation Programs, HE 17.8/2

Manuals (general), T 22.28

Manuals, M- (series), VA 1.18

Manuals (numbered), VA 1.10/2

Manuals of General Reference and Bibliography Division, LC 2.8

Manuals (series), D 101.107/9

Materials and Components in Fossil Energy Applications, E 1.23
Materials and Components in Fossil Energy Applications, and ERDA Newsletter, ER 1.13
Materials Digest, Pr 32.4247
Materials in the U.S. Economy, I 28.2:M 66/6
Materials Laboratories Report, I 27.31
Materials Science & Engineering Research, Research Programs and Publications, D 210.17/4
Materials Science and Metallurgy, PrEx 7.22/10
Materials Sciences, C 51.9/7
Materials Survey, I 28.97
Materials Survey Reports, C 40.17
Materials Surveys, C 41.38
Maternal and Child Health Information, HE 20.2761
Maternal and Child Health Services, FS 17.213
Maternal and Child Health Technical Information Series, HE 20.9111/2
Maternal and Child Welfare Bulletins, L 5.34
Mathematical Analysis Groups Reports, I 27.39
Mathematical Sciences, C 13.22
Mathematical Sciences Postdoctoral Research Fellowships, NS 1.45
Mathematical Tables, C 13.30
Mathematics Symposium [abstracts], C 41.61/6
MATS Flyer, D 301.56
MATS Manuals, D 301.7/6
MATS Regulations, D 301.6/3
Maturity Distribution of Euro-Dollar Deposits in Foreign Branches of U.S. Banks, FR 1.54
Maturity Distribution of Outstanding Negotiable Time Certificates of Deposit, FR 1.54/2
Maumee River Basin, Y 3.G 79/3:10
Maximum Price Regulations, Pr 32.4210
Maximum Rent Regulations, Pr 32.4214
Maximum Travel Per Diem Allowances for Foreign Areas, S 1.76/3-2
MC Reports, D 201.20
MCD Series, EP 2.28
MCH Research Series, HE 20.5114
MCH Statistical Series, HE 20.5113
MCHS Statistics Series, HE 20.2760
MCI- (series), D 214.25
McNair Papers (series), D 5.416
MCP- (series), D 304.10
MCRP (Marine Corp Reference Publication) Series, D 214.9/8
MDTA Experimental and Demonstration Findings, L 1.56
Measles Surveillance, Reports, HE 20.2309/4, HE 20.7011
Measurement of Vessels, T 17.9/2
Measurement Systems Operation Procedure, D 217.16/4-2
Measurement Techniques [abstracts], C 41.75
Measurement Users Bulletin, C 13.10/2
Measuring and Dispensing Pumps, Gasoline, Oil, etc. Shipments of, C 3.90
Meat and Dairy Monthly Imports, A 67.18:FDLMT
Meat and Poultry Inspection Directory, A 101.15, A 103.9, A 110.11
Meat and Poultry Inspection Manual, A 101.8:M 46/2, A 110.8/2, A 110.8/2, A 103.8/3
Meat and Poultry Inspection Manual and Compilation of Meat and Poultry Inspection Issuances, A 101.8:M 46/2
Meat and Poultry Inspection Program, Program Issuances, A 88.17/8
Meat and Poultry Inspection Regulations, A 110.6/2, A 103.6/4, A 110.6/2-2
Meat and Poultry Inspection, Report of the Secretary of Agriculture, A 1.109, A 110.11/2
Meat Animals, Farm Production, Disposition, and Income by States, A 88.17/3
Meat Animals, Production, Disposition, and Income, A 105.23/6
Meat Cooking Charts, A 42.7/4
Meat Graded by Bureau of Agricultural Economics, A 36.190
Meat Inspection Branch, Summary of Activities, A 77.201/2
Meat Inspection Directory, A 4.10
Meat Inspection Division Memorandums, A 78.16
Meat Inspection Division Regulations, A 77.206:M 46
Meat Inspection Rulings, A 4.12
Meat Meal and Tankage Production, Semiannual Report, A 92.17/2
Meat Scraps and Tankage Production, A 88.17/2
Meats, Livestock, Fats and Oils, C 18.72/5
MECAP News, Y 3.C 76/3:27
MECH, D 202.19
Mechanical Analyses of Data for Soil Types [by County], A 57.39

Mechanical Stokers, C 3.91
Mechanization of Construction [abstracts], C 41.47/2
Mechanization of Labor and Heavy Work, C 41.65/5
Mechanized Information Services Catalog, C 13.46:814
Medal of Honor Recipients, Y 4.V 64/4:M 46/3
Media Arts: Film/Radio/Television, NF 2.8/2-10
Media Feature Service, T 22.46/2
Media Resource Catalog from the National Audiovisual Center, AE 1.110/4
Medicaid Action Transmittals, HE 22.28
Medicaid and Other Medical Care Financed from Public Assistance Funds, HE 17.620, HE 17.621
Medicaid Data, HE 22.110
Medicaid, Fiscal Year, NCSS Report B-5, FS 17.620
Medicaid Managed Care Enrollment Report, HE 22.13/2
Medicaid Management Reports, HE 22.109/2, HE 22.410, HE 22.410/2
Medicaid Medicare Exchange, HE 22.409
Medicaid Services State by State, HE 22.12/2
Medicaid Statistics, HE 22.13
Medicaid Statistics, Program and Financial Statistics, HE 22.115
Medical and Health Related Sciences Thesaurus, HE 20.3023
Medical and Hospital Lists, W 77.23/8
Medical and Surgical History of War of Rebellion, 1861-65, W 44.10
Medical Assistance Financed under Assistance Titles of Social Security Act, NCSS Report B-1, FS 17.616
Medical Assistance Financed under Public Assistance Titles of Social Security Act, FS 17.2:M 46/2, HE 17.2:M 46/2
Medical Assistance for the Aged, Fact Sheet, FS 14.218
Medical Assistance (Medicaid) Financed Under Title XIX of Social Security Act, HE 17.616
Medical Bulletin–
  Department of the Army, D 101.42/3
  Veteran's Administration, VA 1.9, VA 1.23/3
Medical Care in Public Assistance, Guides and Recommended Standards, FS 14.208/2
Medical Catalog of Audiovisual Materials Produced by the United States Government, GS 4.17/6
Medical Circulars, Y 3.Se 4:8
Medical Circulars of Selective Service Bureau, Pr 32.5281
Medical Department Equipment List, D 104.9
Medical Department of the Army in World War II, D 104.11
Medical Department Supply Catalogues, W 44.26
Medical Department, United States Army in Vietnam, D 104.11/2
Medical Devices and Diagnostic Products Standards Survey–
  International Edition, HE 20.4035
  National Edition, HE 20.4035/2
Medical Devices Application Program, Annual Report, HE 20.3210
Medical Devices Bulletin, HE 20.4612/2
Medical Information Resources Management Office: Newsletter, VA 1.56/4
Medical Internship in U.S. Public Health Service Hospitals, FS 2.89
Medical Monographs, HE 20.8223
Medical Museum of Armed Forces Institute of Pathology Publications, D 1.16/2
Medical News Letter, D 206.7
Medical Newsletter, FAA 7.11
Medical Research and Development Board, Research Progress Report, D 104.12, D 104.12/2
Medical Research Committee Publications, Pr 32.413/9
Medical Research in Veterans Administration, Annual Report, VA 1.43
Medical Research Laboratory Report, N 10.22
Medical Research Program, Synopsis, VA 1.43/4
Medical Research Service Advisory Groups, VA 1.91
Medical Science Publications, D 104.13
Medical Service Digest, D 304.8
Medical Statistics Bulletins, Y 3.Se 4:15
Medical Statistics, Navy, Statistical Report of the Surgeon General, Navy, Occurrence of Diseases and Injuries in the Navy for Fiscal Year (date), D 206.11
Medical Subject Headings–, FS 2.212
  Annotated Alphabetical List, HE 20.3602:H 34, HE 20.3612/3-4
  Supplement to Index Medicus, HE 20.3612/3-8
  Supplementary Chemical Records, HE 20.3612/3-7
  Tree Annotations, HE 20.3612/3-6
  Tree Structures, HE 20.3602:H 34/2, HE 20.3612/3-5
Medical Subject Headings, HE 20.3612/3-9
Medical Supply Catalog, FS 2.79, HE 1.64

Medical Technicians Bulletin, Supplement to U.S. Armed Forces Medical Journal, D 1.11/2
Medical Transmittal Memorandums, Y 3.Se 4:16
Medical War Manual, W 44.18
Medicare and Medicaid Program Manual, Transmittals and Program Memos, HE 22.8/23
Medicare Annual Report, HE 22.21
Medicare Carriers Manual–
  Claims Process, HE 22.8/7
  Fiscal Administration, HE 22.8/7-2
  Part 4, Professional Relations, HE 22.8/7-4
  Program Administration, HE 22.8/7-3
Medicare Carrier Quality Assurance Handbook, HE 22.8/7-5
Medicare Christian Science Sanatorium Hospital Manual Supplement, HE 22.8/2-2
Medicare Coverage Issues Manual, HE 22.8/14
Medicare Directory of Prevailing Charges, HE 22.29
Medicare Health Maintenance Organization/ Competitive Medical Plan Manual, HE 22.8/21
Medicare Home Health Agency Manual, HE 22.8/5
Medicare Hospice Benefits, HE 22.21/5
Medicare Hospice Manual, HE 22.8/18
Medicare Hospital Information Report, HE 22.34
Medicare Hospital Manual, HE 22.8/2
Medicare Hospital Mortality Information: Vol. 1, Alabama - California, HE 22.34
Medicare Hospital Mortality Information: Vol. 2, Colorado - Illinois, HE 22.34
Medicare Hospital Mortality Information: Vol. 3, Indiana - Maryland, HE 22.34
Medicare Hospital Mortality Information: Vol. 4, Massachusetts - Nevada, HE 22.34
Medicare Hospital Mortality Information; Vol. 5, New Hampshire - Ohio, HE 22.34
Medicare Hospital Mortality Information: Vol. 6, Oklahoma - Tennessee, HE 22.34
Medicare Hospital Mortality Information; Vol. 7, Texas - Guam, HE 22.34
Medicare Intermediary Letters, HE 22.8/6-5
Medicare Intermediary Manual, Part 2, Audits-Reimbursement Program Administration, HE 22.8/6-2
Medicare Intermediary Manual, Part 3, Claims Process, HE 22.8/6
Medicare, Medicaid, State Operations Manual, Provider Certification, HE 22.8/12
Medicare Newsletter, FS 3.53
Medicare Outpatient Physical Therapy Provider Manual, HE 22.8/9
Medicare, Outpatient Physical Therapy and Comprehensive Outpatient Rehabilitation Facility Manual, HE 22.8/9
Medicare Part A Intermediary Manual, Part 1, Fiscal Administration, HE 22.8/6-3
Medicare Part A Intermediary Manual, Part 4, Audit Procedures, HE 22.8/6-4
Medicare Peer Review Organizational Manual, HE 22.8/15
Medicare Program Statistics, HE 22.21/2
Medicare Program Statistics, Medicare Utilization, HE 22.21/2-2
Medicare Prospective Payment and the American Health Care System, Y 3.P 29:3
Medicare Provider Reimbursement Manual, HE 22.8/4
Medicare Renal Dialysis Facility Manual, HE 22.8/13
Medicare Rural Health Clinic Manual, HE 22.8/19
Medicare Skilled Nursing Facility Manual, HE 22.8/3
Medicare Unique Physician Identification Number Directory, HE 22.414, HE 22.414/2
Medicare/Medicaid Directory of Medical Facilities, HE 22.213
Medicare/Medicaid Nursing Home Information (State), HE 22.35
Medicare/Medicaid Sanction, Reinstatement Report, HE 22.36
Medicinal Chemistry A Study Section, HE 20.3001/2:M 46/5
Medicinal Chemistry B Study Section, HE 20.3001/2:M 46/6
Medicine and Biology, C 51.9/24
Medicine for the Layman (series), HE 20.3031
Medico-Military Review for Medical Department, Army, W 44.22
MedPAC Report to Congress, Y 3.M 46/3:1
MEDTEP Update, HE 20.6517/5
Meeting Leaders Guide, W 3.84/2, M 108.79/2
Meeting of the Canada-United States Interparliamentary Group, Y 4.F 76/1-11, Y 4.In 8/16:11
Megamarketplace East, Directory of Women Business Owners, C 1.37/2
Melbourne, International Exhibition, 1880, S 6.8/1
Melbourne International Exhibition, 1888, S 6.8/2

Member Bank Call Report, FR 1.11
Member Bank Earnings, FR 1.11/3
Member Bank Income, FR 1.11/3
Member Bank Loans, FR 1.11/2
Members of Advisory Councils, Study Sections, and
    Committees of National Institutes of Health,
    FS 2.22/22
Members of the Federal Home Loan Bank System, FHL
    1.31
MEMCPM Regulations, D 1.65/2
Memo, HE 20.3915
Memo AG (series), D 101.32/2
Memo for Small Business, Y 3.Ec 74/3:19-2
Memo for Small Business MSA/SBM (series), Pr 33.914
Memo to Mailers, P 1.47
Memoirs, NA 1.5
Memoranda, W 87.16
Memoranda for Information of Officers Pay Corps, etc., N
    20.7/1
Memoranda (numbered), T 40.7
Memorandum, A 1.41, A 48.6, A 60.7
Memorandum (series), HE 20.9115
Memorandum for Aviators, D 5.316, D 203.11
Memorandum for Chiefs of Bureaus and Offices, A 49.7
Memorandum for Information, S 1.62
Memorandum for Japanese Government, M 105.23, D
    102.14
Memorandum [Inquiry], I 45.12, I 49.11
Memorandum on Exchange Charges, FR 1.9/2
Memorandum on Women's Alcohol, Drug Abuse, and
    Mental Health Issues, HE 20.8019
Memorandum, Opinions and Orders, Initial Decisions,
    Etc., CC 1.12/a 8
Memorandum Opinions of Judge Advocate General of
    the Army, D 108.8
Memorandum Regarding Personnel and Policy
    Changes, I 29.3/2
Memorandum Report BRL-MR, D 105.10
Memorandum Reports, D 206.10/2, TD 8.23/2
Memorandum Series, HE 20.7026
Memorandum to All Administrators of Emergency
    Educational Programs, I 16.53
Memorandum to All Nurses in the Public Health
    Service, HE 20.36
Memorandum to Aviators, N 6.31
Memorandum to Editors [wholesale prices selected
    fruits and vegetables], L 1.20/5
Memorandum to Heads of Department of Agriculture
    Agencies, A 1.79
Memorandum to Sate Procurement Officers, T 58.17
Memorandum to State Directors, Y 3.Se 4:21
Memorandum Transmitting Mimeographed Inserts for
    Foreign Service Regulations, S 1.5/2
Memorandums, L 29.11, NAS 1.10
Memorial Address, Y 7.1
Men's Youth's and Boy's Clothing Cut, C 3.92
Mental Defectives and Epileptics in State Institutions,
    C 3.60
Mental Health Demographic Profile System, MHDPS
    Working Papers, HE 20.8133
Mental Health Digest, HE 20.8009
Mental Health Directory, HE 20.410/2, HE 20.8123
Mental Health Directory of State and National
    Agencies Administering Public Mental
    Health and Related Programs, FS 2.22/49
Mental Health Emergencies Alert, HE 20.8113/2
Mental Health in Deafness, HE 20.8127
Mental Health Manpower, Current Statistical and
    Activities Reports, FS 2.54/3
Mental Health Matters, HE 20.8124
Mental Health Monographs, FS 2.22/31
Mental Health Program Reports, FS 2.22/50-4, HE
    20.2419, HE 20.8117
Mental Health Research Findings (year), FS 2.22:M 52/
    44
Mental Health Research Grant Awards, Fiscal Year, HE
    20.2423
Mental Health Resources in the Greater Washington
    Area, HE 20.8119
Mental Health Series, FS 2.53
Mental Health Service System Reports, HE 20.8110/2
Mental Health Service System Reports and Statistical
    Notes Publication Listing, HE 20.8113/5
Mental Health Statistics: Current Facility Reports, HE
    17.117
Mental Health Statistics, Current Report Series, FS
    2.115, FS 2.53/2
Mental Health Statistics Series, HE 20.8110
Mental Health Training Grant Awards, FS 2.22/7-4
Mental Health, United States, HE 20.8137
Mental Patients in State Hospitals, C 3.59
Mental Retardation Abstracts, FS 2.22/52, HE 17.113

Mental Retardation Activities of the Department of
    Health, Education, and Welfare, FS 1.23/5,
    HE 1.23/5
Mental Retardation and Development Disabilities
    Abstracts, HE 1.49
Mental Retardation and the Law, a Report on Status of
    Current Court Cases, HE 23.110
Mental Retardation and the Law, a Report on the Status
    of Current Court Cases, HE 1.51
Mental Retardation Grants, Fiscal Year, HE 1.23/3
Mental Retardation Reports, FS 1.23/4, HE 1.23/4
Mental Retardation Research Committee, HE 20.3001/
    2:M 52
Mental Retardation Source Book, HE 1.23/6
MEPCOM Regulations, D 1.6/9
MEPCOM- (series), D 1.65
MEPS, Chartbook, HE 20.6517/7
MEPS Highlights, HE 20.6517/6
MEPS (Medical Expenditure Panel Survey) Research
    Findings, HE 20.6517/9
Merchandise Line Sales, BC-MLS (series), C 3.202/19
Merchant Fleet in Service on Great Lakes, C 27.9/5
Merchant Fleet News, SB 2.16
Merchant Fleets of the World, C 39.212
Merchant Fleets of the World, Sea-Going Steam and
    Motor Ships of 1,000 Gross Tons and Over,
    TD 11.14
Merchant Marine Bulletin, C 25.12
Merchant Marine Council, Proceedings, TD 5.13
Merchant Marine Data Sheet, C 39.238
Merchant Marine Examination Questions, TD 5.57, TD
    5.57/2
Merchant Marine Statistics, C 11.10, C 25.10, T 17.10
Merchant Mariner, Devoted to Men of American
    Merchant Marine, SB 3.5
Merchant Ships Built in United States and Other
    Countries in Employment Report of United
    States Flag Merchant Seagoing Vessels 1,000
    Tons and Over, C 39.211
Merchant Vessels of United States, TD 5.12/2, T 17.11/2
Merchant Vessels of United States: Monthly
    Supplement to, T 17.11
Merchantable Potato Stocks, with Comparisons, A
    88.12/9
Mercury, D 101.128
Mercury, I 28.55
Mercury in (year), I 28.55/2
Mercury Reports, I 28.55
Merger Decisions, Y 3.F 31/8:1-3
Merit System Methods, FS 1.25
Meritorious Suggestions Digest, C 1.29
MESA Information Report, I 69.9
MESA Reports, C 55.617
MESA Safety Reviews: Coal-Mine Fatalities, I 69.10
MESA Safety Reviews: Coal-Mine Injuries and
    Worktime, I 69.10/2
MESA Safety Reviews: Injuries at Sand and Gravel
    Plants, I 69.10/3
MESA, the Magazine of Mining Health and Safety, I
    69.11
Mesa Verde National Park, Annual Reports, I 1.48
Message from the Presidents's Committee on Mental
    Retardation, Pr 36.8:M 52/M56
Metabolism Study Section, HE 20.3001/2:M 56/2
Metal Industry Indicators, I 19.129, I 28.173
Metallography and Heat Treatment of Metals [abstracts],
    C 41.54/7
Metallurgical Advisory Committee on Titanium
    Information Bulletins, D 105.13/2-4
Metallurgist [abstracts], C 41.54/3
Metal/Nonmetal, Surface and Underground Fatalities, L
    38.19/4
Metal/Nonmetal-Surface Fatalities, L 38.19/3
Metal/Nonmetal-Underground Fatalities, L 38.19/2
Metals Laboratory Unit Report, I 27.35
Meteorological Chart of–
    Great Lakes, A 29.13, A 29.13/2
    Indian Ocean, A 29.27
    North Atlantic Ocean, A 29.23
    North Pacific Ocean, A 29.24
    South Atlantic Ocean, A 29.25
    South Pacific Ocean, A 29.26
Meteorological Record, W 42.24
Meteorological Summaries, C 30.16
Meteorological Summary, Washington, D.C., C 30.10
Meteorology and Hydrology [abstracts], C 41.78
Meteorology Data Report, C 55.220/5
Method of Transportation Code, Exports, C 3.140:N
Methodological Series, HE 20.422
Methodology Papers: U.S. National Income and
    Product Accounts, BEA-MP- (series), C
    59.19
Methodology Report, HE 20.6517/8
Methodology Report, ED 1.328/9

Methods for Determination of Radioactive Substances
    in Water and Fluvial Sediments, I 19.15/5
Methods for the Collection and Analysis of Aquatic
    Biological and Microbiological Samples, I
    19.15/5
Methods Handbook, P 1.31/7
Methods of Urban Impact Analysis (series), HH 1.76
Methyl BromideAlternatives, A 77.517
Mexican Boundary Commission, S 3.19/2
Mexican Boundary Survey, S 3.19/1
Mexico-United States Interparliamentary Group Report
    of Senate Delegation, Y 4.F 76/2:M 57/8
MI Magazine, D 101.84
Mica in (year), I 28.130
Microbial Chemistry Study Section, HE 20.3001/2:M
    58
Microbiology and Infectious Diseases Program, Annual
    Report, HE 20.3263
Microcard Availability Lists, Y 3.At 7:30
Microcomputer Training Catalog, The DOL Academy, L
    1.86/2
Microcomputers in Transportation (various titles), TD
    1.52
Microfilm Lists, GS 4.17/4
Microgravity News, NAS 1.92
Midcentury White House Conference on Children and
    Youth, Progress Bulletins, FS 3.217
Mid-continent Memo, I 66.19/3
Middle Atlantic Fisheries, C 55.309/2
Middle Atlantic Regional Office Publications, L 2.92
Middle East and North Africa, Situation and Outlook
    Report, A 93.29/2-6
Middle East [United Arab Republic], LC 1.30/3
Mid-East Briefing Graphic, Series 1211s, D 5.329
Mid-East Briefing Maps, Series 1308, D 5.330
Mideast Directions (series), LC 41.10
Mid-Session Review of the Budget, PrEx 2.31
Midwest Region Annual Science Report, I 29.113
Midwest Region: Research/Resources Management
    Reports, I 29.105/2
Midwest Regional Member Relations Conference
    Sponsored by American Institute of
    Cooperation and Farmer Cooperative Service,
    A 89.17
Midwestern Cities, A 88.12/31:2
Midyear Financial & Statistical Report, NCU 1.9/3-2
Mid-Year Statistics, NCU 1.9/3
Migrant Health Projects, Summary of Project Data, HE
    20.5116
Migration and Settlement on Pacific Coast, Reports, A
    36.131
Migration of Birds, I 49.4:16
Migratory Labor Notes, L 16.43/2
Migratory Sheep Ranches, A 93.9/11
Mileage Block Progressions, IC 1.23/7:MB-6
Mileage Conservation Letter, Pr 32.4266
Mileage Distribution of Carloads for Each Commodity
    Class by Type of Car, IC 1.23/16:TC-1
Milestones Along Recovery Highway, Y 3.N 21/8:18
Militarily Critical Technologies, D 10.13
Military Affairs, PrEx 7.21/4
Military Air Traffic Activity Report, TD 4.19/4
Military and Civil Aircraft and Aircraft Engine
    Production, Monthly Production Report, C
    31.130
Military Assistance Program Address Directory, D 7.6/
    4:M 59/6
Military Aviation Notices, D 301.9/2
    Corrections, D 301.48/2
    Corrections to Enroute-Low Altitude- Alaska, D
        301.13/4
    Corrections to Supplementary Flight Information
        Document, Pacific and Far East, D
        301.50/2
    Corrections to Supplementary Flight Information,
        Europe, Africa and Middle East, D
        301.49/2
    North Atlantic and East Canada, D 301.11/2
    Pacific, D 301.12/2
    West Canada and Alaska, D 301.13/2
Military Career Guide, Employment and Training
    Opportunities in the Military, D 1.6/14
Military Careers: A Guide to Military Occupations and
    Selected Military Career Paths, D 1.6/15
Military Chaplains' Review, D 101.73, D 101.22:165,
    D 101.114
Military Child Care Project (series), D 1.63
Military Commands and Posts, etc., W 3.20
Military Compensation Background Papers, D 1.54
Military Discipline, Courtesies, and Customs of
    Service, W 3.50/12
Military Family, D 1.63/2
Military Fields, United States, Instrument Approach
    Procedure Charts, C 55.418/4

Military Forces in Transition, D 1.74
Military Geology (series), D 103.40
Military Government, Austria, Report of United States
  Commissioner, W 1.74, M 105.10
Military Government of Ryukyu Islands: Ryukyu
  Statistical Bulletin, D 102.19
Military Government Regulations, W 1.72/4
Military Government Weekly Field Reports, W 1.81
Military Government Weekly Information Bulletins, W
  1.72/5, M 101.16, M 105.8
Military History Section: Japanese Operational
  Monograph Series, D 1.24/2
Military Hydrology Bulletins, D 103.32
Military Intelligence, D 101.93
Military Law–
  Courts-Martial, W 3.50/13
  Law of Military Offenses, W 3.50/14
  Lesson Assignment Sheets, W 3.50/3
Military Law Review, D 101.22:27-100
Military Laws of United States (Army), D 108.5/2
Military Manpower Statistics, D 1.61
Military Media Review, D 101.92
Military Negotiation Regulations, D 1.8
Military Notes on Training and Instruction, W 26.16/5
Military Operations of Civil War, Guide-Index to
  Official Records of Union and Confederate
  Armies, GS 4.21
Military Personnel Update, D 1.104/3
Military Police Journal, D 101.84/2
Military Prime Contract Awards by State, D 1.57/6-2
Military Publications: Index of AMC Publications and
  Blank Forms, D 101.22/3:310.1
Military Renegotiation Regulations Under Renegotia-
  tion Act of 1948, RnB 1.6/4
Military Reservations, W 1.32
Military Review, D 110.7
Military Sanitation and First Aid, W 3.50/4
Military Sea Transportation Service Magazine, D 216.8
Military Sealift Command, D 216.8
Military Specifications, D 1.12, GS 2.8/3-2
Military Specifications, Temporary, D 1.12/2
Military Standard (designs), D 202.11
Military Standard MIL-STD (Navy) Series, D 201.13
Military Standard MIL-STD Series, D 7.10
Military Standard Requisitioning and Issue Procedure,
  D 7.6/4:M 59
Military Standards, D 3.7
Military Standards (preliminary), D 7.10/2
Military Traffic Management Bulletins, D 101.3/2
Military Traffic Management Command Publications, D
  101.129/3
Military Women in the Department of Defense, D 1.90
Military-Civilian Occupational Source Book, D 1.51
Militia Bureau Regulations (general), W 70.7
Milk Distributors, Sales and Costs, A 93.13/2
Milk Distributors, Sales and Costs MDSC (series), A
  88.14/9
Milk, Farm Production, Disposition, and Income, A
  88.14/8
Milk Inspector Letters, A 44.8
Milk Plant Letters, A 4.17, A 44.7
Milk Production, A 105.17
Milk Production and Dairy Products, Annual
  Statistical Summary, A 92.10/6
Milk Production, Disposition, and Income, A 92.10/2,
  A 105.17/5
Milk Production on Farms and Statistics of Dairy Plant
  Products, A 88.14/7
Milk Sugar, A 36.165
Mill Margins Report, Cotton Cloth and Yarn Values,
  Cotton Prices and Mill Margins for
  Unfinished Carded Cotton Cloth and Yarn,
  Revised Estimates, A 88.11/10-2
Mill Margins Report [new Series], A 88.11/10-3
Milling Division Circulars, Y 3.F 73:15
MILSTRIP, D 1.87
MILSTRIP, Military Standard Requisitioning and Issue
  Procedures, D 7.6/17
MILSTRIP Routing and Identifier and Distribution
  Codes, D 1.87/2
MILSTRIP Routing Identifier Codes, D 7.6/16
Mind over Matter, HE 20.3965/3
Mindflights, D 305.22/2
Mimeographed Circulars, A 47.9
Mine Emergency Operations Telephone Book, L 38.21
Mine Injuries and Worktime, L 38.16
Mine Inspector for Indian Territory, Annual Reports,
  1894-1907, I 1.20
Mine Inspector for Territory of Alaska, Annual Reports,
  I 28.9
Mine Inspector for the Territory of New Mexico, Annual
  Reports, 1895-1912, I 1.23
Mine Inspector for the Territory of Utah, Annual
  Reports, 1893-95, I 1.33

Mine Production of Copper, I 28.59
Mine Production of Gold, I 28.61
Mine Production of Lead, I 28.60
Mine Production of Silver, Monthly Reports, I 28.62
Mine Production of Zinc, Monthly Reports, I 28.57
Mine Safety and Health, L 38.9
Mineral Commodities Summaries, I 28.148
Mineral Commodity Profiles, I 28.37/3
Mineral Commodity Summaries, I 19.165
Mineral Deposits Reports, I 19.36
Mineral Facts and Problems, I 28.3, I 28.3/2
Mineral Frontiers on Indian Lands, I 20.61/4
Mineral In . . ., I 28.156/3
Mineral Industries, C 3.940-12
Mineral Industry Health Programs, Technical Progress
  Reports, I 28.26/2
Mineral Industry Surveys, I 19.160, I 19.161
  Aluminum, I 19.130
  Antimony, I 19.131
  Bauxite and Alumina, I 19.132
  Bismuth, I 19.133
  Cement, I 19.134
  Chromium, I 19.135
  Cobalt, I 19.136
  Copper, I 19.137
  Crushed Stone and Sand, I 19.138
  Directory of Principal Construction Sand and
    Gravel Producers in the . . ., Annual
    Advanced Summary Supplement, I
    19.138/3
  Fluorspar, I 19.139
  Gypsum, I 19.140
  Iron and Steel Scrap, I 19.141
  Iron Ore, I 19.142
  Lead, I 19.143
  Lime, I 19.144
  Magnesium, I 19.145
  Manganese, I 19.158
  Manufactured Abrasives, I 19.146
  Marketable Phosphate Rock, I 19.147
  Mineral Industry of (Country) Minerals, I 19.163
  Mineral Industry of [State] Minerals, I 19.162
  Molybdenum, I 19.159
  Nickel, I 19.148
  Precious Metals, I 19.149
  Silicon, I 19.150
  Soda Ash and Sodium Sulfate, I 19.151
  Sulfur, I 19.152
  Tin, I 19.153
  Titanium, I 19.154
  Tungsten, I 19.155
  Vanadium, I 19.156
  Zinc, I 19.157
Mineral Investigations, Field Studies Maps, I 19.39
Mineral Investigations Resource Maps, I 19.90
Mineral Investigations Series, I 28.13
Mineral Issues, I 28.156/2
Mineral Issues, an Analytical Series, I 28.156
Mineral Market Reports, I 28.28
Mineral Market Reports, I.S.P. (series), I 28.53/2
Mineral Orders MO (series), DM 1.6/3
Mineral Perspectives, I 28.37/2
Mineral Products of the United States, I 19.7
Mineral Resources Newsletter, I 19.115/3
Mineral Resources of the United States, I 19.8
Mineral Resources West of Rocky Mountains, T 28.6
Mineral Revenues, the Report on Receipts from Federal
  and Indian Leases, I 72.13
Mineral Trade Notes, I 28.39
Minerals and Materials, a Monthly Survey, I 28.149
Minerals and Materials Information, I 28.37/7, I 19.120/
  4
Minerals in the U.S. Economy, I 28.2:M 66/6
Minerals Management Quad (maps), I 53.11/6
Minerals Today, I 28.149/2
Minerals Yearbook, C 22.8/2, I 28.37, I 28.37/a
Miners Circulars, I 28.6
Mini Conference Report (series), Y 3.W 58/4:10
Miniature Portraits, Wildlife at National Parks, I 29.51
Minimum Construction Requirements for New
  Dwellings, FL 2.11
Minimum Enroute IFR Altitudes Over Particular
  Routes and Intersections, TD 4.3/6
Minimum Enroute IFR Altitudes Over Particular
  Routes and Intersections, TD 4.316
Minimum Property Requirements for Properties of One
  or Two Living Units Located in the [various
  States], HH 2.17
Minimum Property Standards, HH 2.17/3
Minimum Property Standards for 1 and 2 Living Units,
  HH 2.17/4

Minimum Wage and Maximum Hours Under the Fair
  Labor Standards Act, L 36.9
Mining and Manufacturing Industries in the American
  Republics, TC 1.21
Mining Journal [abstracts], C 41.54/4
Mining Research Contract Review, I 28.154
Mining Research Review, I 28.153
Mink, A 105.48
Mink Production, Pelts Produced in (year), A 92.18/11
Minor Nonmetals in (year), Annual Advance Summary, I
  28.121
Minorities and Women in Public Elementary and
  Secondary Schools, Y 3.Eq 2:12-3
Minorities and Women in State and Local Government,
  Y 3.Eq 2:12-4
Minorities and Women in Undergraduate Education,
  Geographic Distributions for Academic Year,
  HE 20.9314
Minority and Female Motor Carrier Listings, IC 1.38
Minority Biomedical Research Support Program, HE
  20.3037/7
Minority Business Enterprise in HUD Programs,
  Annual Report, HH 1.60
Minority Business Today, C 1.79
Minority Programs of the National Heart, Lung, and
  Blood Institute, HE 20.3224
Mint Set of Commemorative Stamps, P 1.26/4, P 1.54
Mint Set of Definitive Stamps, P 1.54/2
Minute Man, T 66.7
Minutes, Annual Meeting, PrEx 1.10:M 66
Minutes of, C 40.16
Minutes of Annual Meeting, GS 1.14/3
Minutes of Meeting–
  Arkansas-White-Red Basins Inter-Agency
    Committee, Y 3.F 31/13-2:2 M 66
  National Institute of Neurological and Communica-
    tive Disorders and Stroke, HE 20.3519
Minutes of the Annual Meeting of the Treasury Safety
  Council, T 1.41/2
Minutes of U.S. Sentencing Commission Meetings, Y
  3.Se 5:16
MIP [Meat Inspection Program] Guidelines, A 88.17/6
Misbranding Regulations, Y 3.F 31/10:10
Misbranding Rulings, Y 3.F 31/10:11
Miscellaneous, A 1.5/2
Miscellaneous Circulars, A 1.5/1
Miscellaneous Correspondence of Navy Department
  Concerning Schley's Court of Inquiry, N
  1.21/2
Miscellaneous Extension Publications, A 43.5/18
Miscellaneous Field Studies Maps, I 19.113
Miscellaneous Geologic Investigations Maps, I 19.91
Miscellaneous Papers, A 13.62/9, D 103.15/2, D
  103.24/4, D 103.31/2, D 103.38/2, D
  103.42/2, D 103.57/6, D 103.210
Miscellaneous Processed Documents, AE 1.13
Miscellaneous Publications, A 13.30/11, A 13.61/9, A
  13.65/9, A 13.68/8, A 13.73/10, A 57.13, D
  14.10, D 103.42/8, D 119.11, FCA 1.13
Miscellaneous Publications of Congress, Y 1
Miscellaneous Series, D 103.11, EP 1.23/6
Miscellaneous Special Reports, A 1.7
Miscellaneous Unclassified Publications of Both
  House and Senate, Y 1.1
Missile Purchase Description, D 105.21
Mission, Y 3.Eq 2:15
Mission Reports, NAS 1.45
Mission Status Bulletins, NAS 1.12/8
Mississippi Flyway, I 49.24/6
Mississippi River, D 103.66/6
Mississippi River Fisheries, C 55.309/2
Mississippi River System of the United States, TD 5.9:5
Mississippi Weekly Weather-Crops Bulletins, A 88.49
Missouri Basin Inter-Agency Committee Publications, I
  1.78
Missouri Basin Survey Commission, Reports and
  Publications, Pr 33.22
Missouri River, D 103.66
Missouri River Basin Investigations Project Reports, I
  20.52
Missouri River Division: M.R.D. Sediment Series, D
  103.41
Missouri River Main Stream Reservoir Regulation
  Studies, D 103.41/3
Missouri-Mississippi River Summary and Forecasts, C
  55.110/3
MISTRIP, Defense Program for Redistribution of Assets
  (DEPRA) Procedures, D 1.87/3
Mixed Claims Commission, United States and Germany,
  S 3.31
Mixed Claims Commissions, United States and Mexico,
  S 3.34/1
MMPA Bulletin, C 55.313/2
MMS Today, I 72.17

MMSLD Letter, D 7.42
MMWR CDC Surveillance Summaries, HE 20.7009/2
MMWR, Morbidity and Morality Weekly Report, HE 20.7039/3
MMWR Recommendations and Reports, HE 20.7009/2-2
MMWR Reports on AIDS, HE 20.7009/5
MMWR Surveillance Summaries from the Center for Infectious Diseases, HE 20.7009/2-3
Mobility Forum, D 301.56/7
Mobility of the Population of the United States, C 3.186:P-20
Mobilization Regulations, W 1.29
Mobilization Training Program, W 1.37
Model Cities Management Series, Bulletins, HH 1.42
Model Documentation Reports, E 3.26/6
Model Programs, Title III, Elementary and Secondary Education Act, HE 18.12
Model State Regulations [on various subjects] As Adopted by the National Conference on Weights and Measures, C 13.55/3
Model Town Home Selector, Y 3.F 31/11:33
Model Weights and Measures Ordinance (year), Provisions As Adopted by the National Conference on Weights and Measures, C 13.55
Modern Foreign Language Fellowship Program, National Defense Education Act, Title 6 and NDEA Related Awards under Fullbright-Hays Act, FS 5.255:55034, HE 5.255:55034
Modern World at Work, FS 6.11
Modernization Credit Plan, Bulletins, Y 3.F 31/11:12
Modification Instructions, D 217.16/6
Modification Work Orders–
    Civil Aeronautics Administration, C 31.116/3
    Department of the Army, W 1.56, D 101.29
Modular Individualized Learning for Electronics Training, D 207.109
Module, D 301.26/17-4
Module (series)–
    Centers for Disease Control, HE 20.7030
    Department of the Air Force, D 301.26/7-4
Mohair Production and Income, A 36.200
Mohair Production and Value, A 92.29/4
Mohair Production and Value of Sales, A 88.35/4
Molasses Market News, A 88.23
Molasses Market News Annual Summary, A 88.40/2:2
Molasses Market News, Market Summary, A 88.23/2
Molasses Market News, Market Summary (year), A 88.51
Molecular Biology Study Section, HE 20.3001/2:M 73/2
Molecular Control Working Group, HE 20.3001/2:M 73
Molybdenum, I 28.58/3
Molybdenum Reports, I 28.58
Molybdenum Reports [new series], I 28.58/2
Monday Morning Highlights, J 16.29
Monetary Conferences, S 5.13
Money Income and Poverty Status of Families and Persons in the United States, C 3.186/11
Money Income of Households, Families, and Persons in the United States, C 3.186/2
Money Payments to Recipients of Special Types of Public Assistance, HE 17.627
Money Payments to Recipients of Special Types of Public Assistance, NCSS Report D-4, FS 17.627, HE 17.627
Money Stock Measures and Components of Money Stock Measures and Related Items, FR 1.47
Mongolia Report, PrEx 7.16/3
Monitor, E 2.19
Monitoring and Air Quality Trends Report, EP 1.59
Montana Pilot Bulletin, TD 4.66
Monograph (series)–
    Bureau of Mines, C 22.24
    Childrens Bureau, C 19.5
    Environmental Science Services Administration, C 52.13
    Industrial College of the Armed Forces, D 5.10
    International Labor Affairs Bureau, L 29.13
    Joint Chiefs of Staff, D 5.9/4
    Law Enforcement Assistance Administration, J 26.15/2
    National Bureau of Standards, C 13.44
    National Cancer Institute, FS 2.22/18
    National Commission for Employment Policy, Y 3.Em 7/3:11
    National Institute of Neurological Diseases and Stroke, FS 2.22/55
    Naval Military Personnel Command, D 208.23
    Naval Support Force, D 201.15/3
    Office of Aerospace Research, D 301.69/10

Vocation Division, FS 5.128
Monograph Series on American Military Participation in World War, W 26.15/6
Monographs, J 26.30, L 37.14/2
Monographs and Data for Health Resources Planning Series, HE 20.6110
Monographs on Career Education (series), ED 1.15, HE 19.111/2
Monographs on Evaluation in Education, HE 19.111
Monographs on Social Economics, La 1.6
Montana, Governor, Annual Report, 1878-89, I 1.22
Montana Pilot Bulletin, TD 4.66
Month-End Summary of Domestic Trade Services Rendered by Field Offices, C 41.37
Month in Review GA 1.16/3
Monthly Accession List of Library, Legal Reference Section, SS 1.22
Monthly Alert, A 13.123
Monthly and Annual Earnings of Train and Engine Service Employees, RL 1.9
Monthly and Seasonal Weather Outlook, C 55.109
Monthly Averages of Temperature and Precipitation for State Climatic Divisions, C 55.286/2
Monthly Benefit Statistics–, HE 3.28/6
    Calendar Year Benefit Data, FS 3.28/6-2
    Fiscal Year Benefit Data, FS 3.28/6-3
Monthly Benefit Statistics
    Old-age, Survivors, Disability, and Health Insurance, Summary Benefit Data, HE 3.28/6
    Railroad Retirement and Unemployment Insurance Programs, RR 1.13
Monthly Benefit Statistics, Summary Program Data, Calendar Year (date), HE 3.28/6-2
Monthly Bibliography of Medical Reviews, HE 20.3610
Monthly Bulletin of Hawaiian Volcano Observatory, I 19.28
Monthly Bulletin of Lake Levels for the Great Lakes, D 103.116
Monthly Bulletin of Social Statistics, L 5.32
Monthly Catalog Index, GP 3.8/2
Monthly Catalog of United States Government Publications, GP 3.8, GP 3.8/7, GP 3.8/8
Monthly Catalog of United States Government Publications, Periodical Supplement, GP 3.8/8-8
Monthly Cement Statement, C 22.29, I 28.29
Monthly Checklist of State Publications, LC 30.9
Monthly Climatic Data for the World, C 55.211
Monthly Coal Distribution Report, C 22.23
Monthly Coal Market Summary, C 22.22
Monthly Coke Report, C 22.15, I 28.30
Monthly Commodity State of Surplus, W 77.20
Monthly Comment of Aviation Trends, C 31.152
Monthly Commodity Futures Statistics on Futures Trading in Commodities Regulated under the Commodity Exchange Act, A 85.15/2
Monthly Comparative Sales of Confectionery and Competitive Chocolate Products, C 3.135
Monthly Comparative Sales on Confectionery, C 18.72/11
Monthly Comparisons of Peak Demands and Energy Load, E 3.11/17-5
Monthly Consular Reports, C 14.8
Monthly Copper Reports, I 28.59/2
Monthly Corrections Affecting Portfolio Chart List and Index-Catalog of Nautical Charts and Publications, D 203.22/2
Monthly Cotton Linters Review, A 88.11/3
Monthly Crop Reporter, A 27.6/2, A 36.10
Monthly Crop Synopsis, A 27.7
Monthly Deliveries of Sugar by States, A 82.72/2
Monthly Department Store Sales in Selected Areas, C 3.211/5
Monthly Digest to Members of Congress, L 2.66
Monthly Domestic Dairy Markets Review, A 88.13
Monthly Egg and Poultry Markets Review, A 88.13/3
Monthly Electric Utility Sales and Revenue Report with State Distributions, E 3.11/17-14
Monthly Energy Indicators, FE 1.14
Monthly Energy Review, E 3.9, FE 1.17
Monthly Energy Review Database, E 3.9/2
Monthly Expenditures for Family Relief, L 5.28
Monthly Highway Construction Contracts Awarded by State and Federal Agencies and Toll Authorities, TD 2.51
Monthly Hotline Report, EP 1.111
Monthly Index of Russian Accessions, LC 30.10
Monthly Information Bulletins, N 13.10
Monthly Japanese Foreign Trade Statistics, D 102.11/4
Monthly Labor Review, L 2.6

Monthly Labor Review, Statistical Supplements, L 2.6/2
Monthly Letter, C 18.21
Monthly Letters, A 9.12
Monthly Lime Report, Mineral Market Report LM (series), I 28.28/2
Monthly List of GAO Reports, GA 1.16/3
Monthly List of Military Information, W 26.7
Monthly List of Officers Absent on Leave in Excess of Time, W 3.15
Monthly List of Outside Publications and Addresses, I 49.18/4
Monthly List of Publications–
    Department of Agriculture, A 21.6/1
    Division of Printing and Publications, C 16.6
    Public Health Service, T 27.18
Monthly List of Publications for Foreign Distribution, A 21.6/2
Monthly List of State Publications, LC 7.6
Monthly Listing of Awards for Construction Grants for Wastewater Treatment Works, EP 1.56
Monthly Loan Data Report, Y 3.T 25:13-3
Monthly Management Report, TD 4.53
Monthly Mean Discharge at Selected Gaging Stations and Change of Storage in Certain Lakes and Reservoirs in Columbia River Basin, I 19.47
Monthly Memorandum for Cooperating Agencies, L 5.30
Monthly Meterological Summary, A 29.30
Monthly Motor Fuel Reported by States, TD 2.46/2
Monthly Motor Gasoline Reported by States, TD 2.46
Monthly Motor Truck Production Report, C 41.39
Monthly Normals of Temperature, Precipitation, and Heating and Cooling Degree Days, C 55.286
Monthly OEDP Status Report, C 46.21
Monthly Petroleum Product Price Report, E 3.24, FE 1.9/5
Monthly Petroleum Statistics Report, E 3.12, FE 1.9/4
Monthly Political Report, S 1.20
Monthly Political Reports, Confidential, Changes in Foreign Service, S 1.14
Monthly Power Plant Report, E 3.11/17-13
Monthly Product Announcement, C 3.163/7
Monthly Progress Report, C 51.10
Monthly Receipts from Sale of Principal Farm Products by Sates, A 36.81/2
Monthly Record, Administration of Packers and Stockyards Act, A 39.5, A 4.28
Monthly Release [of] Federal Civilian Manpower Statistics, CS 1.55/2
Monthly Relief Bulletin, L 5.29
Monthly Report, C 55.331/2
Monthly Report for Public Advisory Board, Pr 33.910
Monthly Report of Activities–
    National Ocean Survey, C 55.401/2
    Training and Employment Service, L 7.11
Monthly Report of Condition for U.S. Agencies, Branches and Domestic Banking Subsidiaries of Foreign Banks, FR 1.16/3
Monthly Report of Farmers Home Administration, A 84.7
Monthly Report of Federal Employment, CS 1.32/2
Monthly Report of Reagents Evaluation, HE 20.7032, HE 20.7810
Monthly Report of the Military Governor for German (U.S.), M 105.7
Monthly Report on Adverse Reactions to Drugs and Therapeutic Devices, FS 13.123
Monthly Report on European and Far East Programs, FO 1.10
Monthly Report on Federal Personnel and Pay, Y 4.R 24/4
Monthly Report on Foreign Direct Investment Activity in the United States, C 61.25/3
Monthly Report on Housing, HH 1.13
Monthly Report on Labor Force, Employment, Unemployment, Hours and Earnings, L 2.84
Monthly Report on Loans and Discounts, FCA 1.12
Monthly Report on Selected Congressional Activities, NS 1.28/3
Monthly Report on Selected Steel Industry Data, ITC 1.27
Monthly Report Prepared by Technical Staff, Fuel Committee, Allied Control Authority, W 1.83, M 105.15
Monthly Reports of Department of Health, W 79.12/5
Monthly Reports of Organizations and Operations of Federal Credit Unions, A 72.14
Monthly Reports on Labor Force, C 3.155
Monthly Retail Sales, C 3.138/3-3
Monthly Retail Trade Report, C 3.138/3
Monthly Review, J 21.10, RR 1.7/2
Monthly Safety Bulletin, Y 3.Em 3:10, Y 3.C 49:7
Monthly Selected Services Receipts, C 3.239

Monthly Selected Services Receipts, Revised [compilations], C 3.239/2

Monthly Series on Mass Layoffs, L 1.94

Monthly Slab Zinc Reports, I 28.56

Monthly State, Regional and National Heating Degree Days Weighted by Population, C 55.287/60-2

Monthly State, Regional and National Cooling Degree Days Weighted by Population, C 55.287/60-3

Monthly Statement of Coal-Mine Fatalities in United States, I 28.10/1

Monthly Statement of Paper Currency of Each Denomination Outstanding, T 40.8

Monthly Statement of Public Debt of the United States, T 1.5/3

Monthly Statement of Receipts and Outlays of the United States Government, T 1.5/2

Monthly Statement of the Public Department of the United States, T 63.215

Monthly Station List of Officers, W 36.8

Monthly Statistical Release–
  Beer, T 70.9/4
  Cigarettes and Cigars, T 70.9/2
  Distilled Spirits, T 70.9/3
  Wines, T 70.9/5

Monthly Summary of Commerce and Finance, T 37.8, C 14.14

Monthly Summary of Commerce of Cuba, W 6.9

Monthly Summary of Commerce of Porto Rico, W 6.7

Monthly Summary of Commodity Future Statistics, A 85.15

Monthly Summary of Export Credit Guarantee Program Activity, A 67.47

Monthly Summary of Export Credit Guarantee Program Activity, Commodity Credit Corporation, A 67.18:ECG

Monthly Summary of Fishery Trade, Landings, Receipts, Processing, and Storage, I 49.34

Monthly Summary of Foreign Commerce of United States, C 18.7

Monthly Summary of Statistics of Operations, L 22.21

Monthly Summary of Work, FT 1.15

Monthly Summary Solar Radiation Data, C 55.289

Monthly Summary, The Gulf Stream, D 203.28, D 203.29

Monthly Supplement to Commerce Reports, C 18.5/3

Monthly Supplement to Merchant Vessels of United States, T 17.11

Monthly Thrift Data, T 71.21

Monthly Tin Reports, I 28.96

Monthly Trade Report, China, C 18.154

Monthly Trade Report, Japan, C 18.155

Monthly Trade Review of France, C 18.189

Monthly Trade Update, C 61.46

Monthly Traffic Fatality Report, TD 8.38

Monthly Translations List and Current Contents, EP 1.21/2

Monthly Treasury Statement of Receipts and Outlays of the United States Government, T 63.113/2

Monthly Vital Statistics Bulletins, C 3.127

Monthly Vital Statistics Report, HE 20.6009, HE 20.6217

Monthly Vital Statistics Report from the National Center for Health Statistics, Advance Report of Final Natality Statistics, HE 20.6217/2

Monthly Weather Review, C 55.11

Monthly Weather Review, Signal Office, W 42.20

Monthly Wholesale Trade Report: Sales and Inventories, C 3.133, C 3.133/2

Monthly Workload Trend Report, HE 3.28/7

Monthly Workload Trend Report, Quarterly Summary, HE 3.28/7-2

Morale Items, W 2.11

Morbidity and Mortality Weekly Report, HE 20.7009

Morbidity Weekly Report, Injury Prevention Reprints, HE 20.7009/4

More Important Insect Records, A 77.310/2

Morgantown Energy Technology Center, E 1.74

Mortality Index, FS 2.107

Mortality Statistics, C 3.3, C 3.40

Mortgage Interest Rates on Conventional Loans, Largest Insured Savings and Loan Associations, FHL 1.24

Mortgage Lending Activity of Savings and Loan Associations, FHL 1.7/3

Mortgage Recording Letter, FHL 1.9, HH 4.9

MOSAIC, NS 1.29

Motion Picture Films, I 28.35

Motion Picture Guides, FS 2.211/2

Motion Picture Theaters Throughout the World, C 18.116/2

Motion Pictures Abroad, C 18.115, C 41.16

Motion Pictures and Filmstrips, LC 30.8/4

Motion Pictures Distributed by Photographic Section, I 43.9

Motion Pictures Educational [and] Industrial, C 18.116

Motion Pictures of Department of Agriculture, A 43.24

Motion-Picture Films, C 22.26/1

Motive Power and Car Equipment of Class I Railroads in the United States, IC 1 ste.36

Motor and Vehicles Fixed Price Lists, W 77.23/9

Motor and Vehicles Lists, W 77.23/10

Motor Carrier, IC 1 mot.8/a:M

Motor Carrier Accident Investigation Reports, TD 2.309

Motor Carrier Cases, IC 1 mot.8

Motor Carrier, Finance, IC 1 mot.8/a 2

Motor Carrier Freight Commodity Statistics Class 1 Common and Contract Carriers of Property, IC 1 mot.22

Motor Carrier Investigation Reports, IC 1 mot.18

Motor Carriers of Passengers, Class 1 Accident Data, IC 1 mot.21/2

Motor Carriers of Property, Accident Data, IC 1 mot.21

Motor Carriers, Special Circulars, IC 1 mot.15

Motor Freight Transportation and Warehousing Survey, C 3.138/3-5

Motor Gasoline Watch, E 3.13/6

Motor Transport, Technical Service Bulletins, W 77.31

Motor Vehicle Report, Pr 33.112

Motor Vehicle Safety Defect Recall Campaigns, TD 8.9

Motor Vehicle Safety Defect Recall Campaigns Reported to the Department of Transportation by Domestic and Foreign Vehicle Manufacturers, TD 2.209

Motorboat Safety, T 47.49

Motorists Guides, I 29.24

Mount Rainier National Park, Annual Reports, I 1.43

Mountain Views, A 13.120

Mourning Dove, Breeding Population Status, I 49.106/5

Mourning Dove Newsletter, I 49.50

Mourning Dove Status Report, I 49.15/3

Movements of Vessels, N 17.8

Movements of Vessels [fiscal year], N 1.28

Moving and Storage Wage Survey Summaries by Cities, L 2.113/5

Moving and Storage Wage Survey Summary (series), L 2.123

Moving and Storage Wage Surveys, Summaries by State, L 2.113/5-2

MPI [Meat and Poultry Inspection] Guidelines (series), A 103.8/2

MPR Revisions, HH 2.17/2

MRBC Basic Bulletin, Y 3.M 69/2:3

MSA, C 4.42

MSA Country Series, Pr 33.919

MSHA Instruction Guide Series, L 38.17/3

MSHA Policy Memorandum (series), L 38.17

MSHA Program Information Bulletin (series), L 38.17/2

MSHA Program Policy Letter (Series), L 38.17/2-2

MSS, C 4.43

MTMC Expediter, D 101.66/3

MTMC Pamphlets, D 101.22/6

Multidisciplinary Accident Investigations, TD 8.11, TD 8.11/2

Multifactor Productivity Measures, L 2.120/2-10

Multiple Award Federal Supply Schedule, GS 2.7/6

Multiple Risk Intervention Trial, Public Annual Report, HE 20.3213

Multiplier, S 17.33, S 18.32

Multipurpose Arthritis Centers Personnel Directory, HE 20.3322

Mumps Surveillance, HE 20.7011/34

Municipal and Cooperative Distributors of TVA Power, (date) Operations, Y 3.T 25:1-3

Municipal Environmental Research Laboratory: Quarterly Report, EP 1.46/7

Municipal Environmental Research Laboratory: Report of Progress, EP 1.46/7-2

Municipal Government Wage Surveys, L 2.105

Municipal Water Facilities, FS 2.84/3

Munitions Board Manuals, D 3.8

Museum Assessment Program, Grant Application and Information, NF 4.11

Museum Manuscript Register Series, D 214.17

Museum of Natural History, Annual Report, SI 3.1/2

Museums, Application Guidelines FY (year), NF 2.8/2-7

Mushrooms, A 92.11/10-5, A 105.24/6

Music and Musicians (series), LC 19.19

Music and Phonorecords, LC 30.8/6

Music Circulars, LC 19.14

Music Ensembles Chamber Music/New Music/Jazz Ensembles/Choruses/Orchestras/Composer in Residence/Consortium Commissioning, NF 2.8/2-14

Music Fellowships: Composers, Jazz, Solo Recitalists, Applications Guidelines, NF 2.8/2-8

Music Presenters and Festivals Jazz Management and Special Projects, NF 2.8/2-9

Music Professional Training Career Development Organizations, Music Recording Services to Composers, Centers for New Music Resources Special Projects, Music, Application Guidelines, NF 2.8/2-5

Musical Mainstream, LC 19.12

Musketry Bulletins, W 95.3/2

Mutual Security Program, Summary Presentation, S 17.35

Mycoses Surveillance, Reports, HE 20.7011/3

N

N.L.R.B. Election Reports, LR 1.16

N.L.R.B. Statistical Summary Covering the Three Month Period, LR 1.15/3

N.O.I. Publications (confidential), N 13.9

NAEP Newsletter, HE 19.209/2, ED 1.316

NAEP . . . Technical Report, ED 1.335/3

NAEP Trends in Academic Progress, ED 1.335/4

NAEPFacts, ED 1.335

NA-FB/M (series), A 13.106/3

NA-FB/P (series), A 13.106

NAFTA Review, PrEx 9.12

NAFTA Situation and Outlook Series A 93.29/2-20

NA-GR (series), A 13.106/3-2

NAMC-AEL (series), D 217.21

Name and Address of Air Service Officers, W 87.9

Name Authorities, Cumulative Edition, LC 30.21

Name Authorities, Cumulative Microform Edition, LC 30.21

Names of Counties Declared to be Modified Accredited Bang's Disease-Free Areas, A 4.33

NAPAP Newsletter, Y 3.In 8/31:15

NAPCA Abstracts-Bulletins, EP 4.11

NARA Bulletin (series), AE 1.103

NARIC, Disability Research Resources, ED 1.79

NARIC Quarterly, ED 1.79/2

Narcotic and Dangerous Drug Section Monographs (series), J 1.90

Narcotics Intelligence Estimate (year), J 24.22

Narratives, C 3.940-8

NASA Activities, NAS 1.46

NASA Aeronautics Research and Technology, Annual Report, NAS 1.19/2

NASA Annual Procurement Report, NAS 1.30

NASA BITS [Brief Ideas, Thoughts, Suggestions], NAS 1.36

NASA Budget Estimates, NAS 1.85

NASA Earth Resources Survey Program, C 51.9/11

NASA Educational Briefs for the Classroom (series), NAS 1.69

NASA Excellence Award for Quality and Productivity, NAS 1.78

NASA Facts, NAS 1.20

NASA Historical Reports, NAS 1.31

NASA History: News and Notes, NAS 1.96

NASA Information Summaries, NAS 1.90

NASA Information Systems Newsletter, NAS 1.90/2

NASA Magazine, NAS 1.87

NASA Mishap and Injury Data, NAS 1.57

NASA NP (series), NAS 1.83

NASA Patent Abstracts Bibliography, NAS 1.21:7039

NASA Patents, NAS 1.71

NASA PED (series), NAS 1.84

NASA Picture Sets, NAS 1.43/2

NASA Posters, NAS 1.43

NASA Procurement Regulation Directive, NAS 1.6/3

NASA Procurement Regulation (NHB 5100.2), NAS 1.6/2

NASA Reference Publications, RP- (series), NAS 1.61

NASA Report to Educators, NAS 1.49

NASA Republications, NAS 1.13

NASA Scientific and Technical Publications, NAS 1.21:7063

NASA SP (series), NAS 1.21

NASA STD (Series), NAS 1.82

NASA STI Directory, NAS 1.24/4

NASA Tech Briefs, NAS 1.29, NAS 1.29/3, NAS 1.29/3-2

NASA Technical Reports (bound volumes), NAS 1.12/2

NASA Thesaurus Supplement, NAS 1.21:7064

NASA-Industry Program Plans Conference, NAS 1.17

NASA'S University Program, Quarterly Report of Active Grants and Research Contracts, NAS 1.42

Nashville, Tennessee, Centennial Exposition, 1897, S 6.15

Natick Laboratories, Natick, Mass., Technical Reports, D 106.21

Nation to Nation, J 1.105

National Acid Precipitation Assessment Program, Report to Congress, Y 3.In 8/31:1-2, C 55.703

National Action Plan on Breast Cancer Fact Sheets (series), HE 20.38/2

National Advisory Board Council for Grazing Districts, Proceedings of Annual Meetings, I 53.16

National Advisory Child Health and Human Development Council, HE 20.3001/2:C 43

National Advisory Committee for Juvenile Justice and Delinquency Prevention: Annual Report, J 1.48/2, J 26.1/4

National Advisory Committee on Black Higher Education and Black Colleges and Universities: Annual Report, HE 19.140, ED 1.21

National Advisory Committee on the Handicapped: Annual Report, HE 19.117

National Advisory Council for Career Education: Publications, HE 19.116

National Advisory Council on Maternal, Infant and Fetal Nutrition: Biennial Report, A 98.14/2

National Advisory Council on Economic Opportunity, Annual Report, PrEx 10.22

National Advisory Council on Vocational Education Annual Report, HE 5.85

National Advisory Dental Research Council, HE 20.3001/2:D 43

National Advisory Dental Research Council, Summary Minutes, HE 20.3416

National Advisory Environmental Health Sciences Council, HE 20.3001/2:En 8

National Advisory Eye Council, HE 20.3001/2:Ey 3

National Advisory Eye Council: Annual Report on Vision Research Projects, HE 20.3752:R 31/4

National Advisory General Medical Sciences Council, HE 20.3001/2:M 46

National Advisory Neurological and Communicative Disorders and Stroke Council, HE 20.3001/2:N 39/5

National Agricultural Lands Study: Interim Reports, A 1,30/2

National Agricultural Library ... Annual Report, A 17.1

National Air Monitoring Program: Air Quality and Emission Trends, Annual Report, EP 1.47

National Air Quality and Emissions Trends Report, EP 4.22/2

National Air Pollutant Emission Estimates, EP 4.24

National Air Toxics Information Clearinghouse: Newsletter, EP 4.23

National Airport Plan, Fiscal Years [dates], TD 4.109

National Airport System Plan, TD 4.33/3

National Airspace System Documentation Facility Catalog, TD 4.42

National Airspace System Plan, TD 4.2/10

National Airway System Annual Report, TD 4.57/3

National Ambulatory Medical Care Survey, HE 20.6209/4-5

National Applied Mathematics Laboratoties, Projects and Publications, Quarterly Report, C 13.43

National Apprenticeship and Training Standards for [various occupations], L 37.106/2

National Arboretum Contributions, A 77.526

National Arboretum Leaflets, A 77.526/2

National Archives Accessions, GS 4.8

National Archives and Records Administration Strategic Plan for a Challenging Federal Environment, AE 1.125

National Archives and Records Administration Telephone Directory, AE 1.122

National Archives, Calendar of Events, AE 1.129

National Archives Facsimiles, AE 1.21

National Archives Inventory Series, GS 4.10/2

National Archives Microfilm Publications Pamphlet, AE 1.119

National Archives Microfilm Publications: Pamphlets Accompanying Microcopy, GS 4.20

National Archives Reference Information Papers, GS 4.15

National Archives Update, AE 1.118

National Arthritis Advisory Board: Annual Report, HE 20.3027/2

National Arthritis, Metabolism, and Digestive Diseases Advisory Council, HE 20.3001/2:Ar 7/2

National Assessment of Education Progress: Reports, HE 19.312

National Assessment of Educational Progress Publications (numbered), ED 1.118/2

National Assessment of Educational Progress [reports] (unnumbered), HE 19.312/2

National Association of Women Business Owners, Membership Roster, C 1.85

National Atlas, I 19.111

National Atlas of the United States, I 19.2:N 21 a, I 19.111

National Atmospheric Sciences Program, PrEx 8.110

National Aviation Facilities Experimental Center, Atlantic City, New Jersey: Report NA-(series), TD 4.32

National Aviation System Plan, TD 4.33

National Aviation System-Policy Summary, TD 4.33/2

National Basic Intelligence Factbook, PrEx 3.10:N 21

National Biennial RCRA Hazardous Waste Report, EP 1.104/3

National Blood Resource Program Advisory Committee, HE 20.3001/2:B 62/2

National Brucellosis Committee, A 1.2:B 83

National Bulletin, A 82.37:N 21

National Bureau of Standards Certificate of Calibration, C 13.45

National Bureau of Standards Interagency Reports, C 13.58

National Calendar of Events, I 29.57

National Campaign News, I 1.110/3

National Cancer Advisory Board: Annual Report, HE 20.3027/3

National Cancer Institute Budget Estimate, HE 20.3190

National Cancer Institute Fact Book, HE 20.3174

National Cancer Institute Monographs, FS 2.22/18

National Cancer Institute Smoking and Health Program, HE 20.3171

National Cancer Program Publications Series, HE 20.3168/3

National Cancer Program, Report of the Director, HE 20.3168/4

National Cancer Program: Report of the National Cancer Advisory Board, HE 20.3168

National Cancer Program: Report of the President's Cancer Panel, HE 20.3168/5

National Cancer Program Review for Communicators, HE 20.3168/6

National Cancer Program, Strategic Plan Series, HE 20.3168/2

National Carpentry Apprenticeship and Training Standards, L 23.2:C 22

National Cartographic Information Center: Newsletter, I 19.71

National Cemetary System, VA-NCS-IS-(series), VA 1.53

National Center for Education Statistics, Education Policy Issues: Statistical Perspectives, ED 1.336

National Center for Education Statistics, Technical/Methodology Report, ED 1.328/10

National Center for Health Statistics, Series 21, CD-ROM, HE 20.6209/12

National Center for Research in Vocational Education: Publications, ED 1.33

National Citizens Committee Bulletin, C 60.3/2

National Citizens Conference on Rehabilitation of the Disabled and Disadvantaged [publications], HE 17.20

National Civil Defense Day (or Week) Publications, Pr 34.762

National Civil Defense Week Publications, FCD 1.23

National Clearinghouse for Alcohol Information: Grouped Interest Guides, HE 20.8311/3

National Clearinghouse for Mental Health Information Abstracts, HE 20.2429

National Clearinghouse for Poison Control Centers, Bulletin, HE 20.4003/2

National Clearinghouse on Child Abuse and Neglect Information Catalog, HE 23.1216/2

National Climate Program: Annual Report, C 55.44

National Climatic Center Publications, C 55.281

National Climatic Data Center Periodical Publications, C 55.287/63

National Commission for the Review of Anti-Trust Laws and Procedures, Pr 39.8:An 8

National Commission for United Nations Educational, Scientific and Cultural Organization Publications, S 5.48, S 5.48/9, S 5.48/10

National Commission News, S 5.48/2

National Commission on Productivity and Work Quality: Publications, Pr 37.8:P 94

National Committee on Wood Utilization, C 1.14

National Communicable Disease Center Foodborne Outbreaks, Annual Summary, FS 2.60/18

National Communicable Disease Center Hepatitis Surveillance, Reports, FS 2.60/13

National Communicable Disease Center, Neurotropic Viral Diseases Surveillance: Annual Encephalitis Summary, FS 2.60/14:En 1

National Communicable Disease Center Neurotropic Viral Diseases Surveillance, Annual Poliomyelitis Summary, FS 2.60/14:P 75

National Communicable Disease Center Neurotropic Viral Diseases Surveillance [reports], FS 2.60/14

National Communicable Disease Center Rubella Surveillance [Reports], FS 2.60/16

National Communicable Disease Center Salmonella Surveillance, Annual Summary, FS 2.60/12-2

National Communicable Disease Center Salmonella Surveillance, Reports, FS 2.60/12

National Communicable Disease Center Shigella Surveillance, Reports, Atlanta, Georgia, FS 2.60/16

National Communicable Disease Center Zoonoses Surveillance, Annual Summary, Psittacosis, FS 2.60/15:P 95

National Communicable Disease Center Zoonoses Surveillance [reports], FS 2.60/15

National Communications System Annual Report, PrEx 1.17

National Compensation Survey Bulletins, Summaries, and Supplemental Tables for National, L 2.121/57

National Compensation Survey Divisions, L 2.121/56

National Computer Security Center, NCSC- WA-(series), D 1.79/2

National Conference of Prevention and Control of Juvenile Delinquency, J 1.24

National Conference on Child Abuse and Neglect: Proceedings, HE 1.480/5

National Conference on Merchant Marine, SB 1.14

National Conference on Public Health Training, Report to the Surgeon General, FS 2.2:T 68/6, HE 20.2:T 68/6

National Conference on Radiation Control, HE 20.4118

National Conference on Radiation Control Proceedings, HE 20.4118

National Conference on Wheat Utilization Research, Proceedings, A 77.15:74

National Conference Veterans' Employment Representatives, FS 3.123

National Conferences on Street and Highway Safety, C 1.21

National Consumer Buying Alert, Pr 39.14

National Cooperative Observer Newsletter, C 55.118/6

National Corrections Reporting Program, J 29.11/13

National Council of Commerce, Proceedings of Annual Meetings, C 1.9/1

National Council on Education Research: Annual Report, HE 19.214, ED 1.315

National Council on Health Planning and Development, HE 20.6001/5:H 34

National Credit Union Administration Rules and Regulations, NCU 1.6:R 86

National Credit Union Share Insurance Fund: Annual Report, NCU 1.18

National Crime Survey Reports, J 29.9

National Criminal Justice: Document Retrieval Index, J 1.42

National Criminal Justice Information and Statistics Service, J 1.37

National Criminal Justice Information and Statistics Service: [reports], J 26.10

National Criminal Justice Information and Statistics Service, Statistics Center Report, J 1.37/2

National Criminal Justice Reference Service Document Data Base, J 28.31/2

National Criminal Justice Reference Service: Document Retrieval Index, J 26.26

National Criminal Justice Reference Service: Miscellaneous Publications Series, J 1.42/3

National Criminal Justice Thesaurus, J 28.28

National Death Index Announcements (numbered), HE 20.6224

National Defense and Direct Student Loan Program, Directory of Designated Low- Income Schools for Teacher Cancellation Benefits, ED 1.40/2

National Defense and Neutrality, Proclamations, Executive Orders, etc., Pr 32.213

National Defense Bulletins, LC 14.11

National Defense Executive Reserve, Annual Report to the President, FEM 1.10

National Defense Graduate Fellowships, Graduate Programs, FS 5.255:55017, HE 5.255:55017

National Labor Relations Board, Publications, Lists of, LR 1.13

National Lakeshores [Information Circulars], I 29.6/3

National Land Cover Dataset, I 19.168

National Land-use Planning Committee Publications, A 1.39

National Leadership Grants, Grant, Application & Guidelines, NF 4.11/2

National Level Bibliographic Record (series), LC 30.23

National Library of Medicine Audiovisuals Catalog, HE 20.3609/4

National Library of Medicine Catalog, LC 30.13, HE 20.3609/3-2

National Library of Medicine Current Catalog: Annual Cumulation, HE 20.3609/3

National Library of Medicine Current Catalog, Cumulative Listing, HE 20.3609/2

National Library of Medicine Current Catalog (Monthly Listings), FS 2.216, HE 20.3609

National Library of Medicine Fact Sheets, HE 20.3621

National Library of Medicine News, HE 20.3619

National Library of Medicine News: NLM Publications, HE 20.3619/2

National Library of Medicine Newsline HE 20.3619

National Library of Medicine Staff Directory, HE 20.3619/3

National Library Service Bulletin, I 16.31/5

National Listing of Medicare Providers Furnishing Kidney Dialysis and Transplant Services, HE 22.510

National Listing of Medicare Providers Furnishing Kidney Dialysis & Transplant Services, HE 22.216

National Listing of Providers Furnishing Kidney Dialysis and Transplant Services, HE 22.25

National Listing of Renal Providers Furnishing Kidney Dialysis and Transplant Services, HE 22.510/2

National Longitudinal Surveys, Discussion Paper, L 2.71/5-2

National Mapping Program (series), I 19.80

National Marine Pollution Program, PrEx 8.109

National Maritime SAR Review, TD 5.24

National Measurement Laboratory, News Features, C 13.70/2

National Medical Audiovisual Center Catalog, HE 20.3608/4

National Medical Care Utilization and Expenditure Survey, Preliminary Data Reports (series), HE 22.26

National Medical Care Utilization and Expenditure Survey Series A, Methodological Report, HE 22.26/2

National Medical Care Utilization and Expenditure Survey, Series B, HE 22.26/3

National Medical Care Utilization and Expenditure Survey, Series C, HE 22.26/4

National Medical Expenditure Survey Methods, HE 20.6517/3

National Medical Expenditure Survey, Research Findings (Series), HE 20.6517

National Medical Libraries Assistance Advisory Board, HE 20.3001/2:M 46/8

National Mental Health Program Progress Reports, FS 2.65

National Meterological Center Publications, C 55.190

National Military Command System Information Processing System 360 Formatted File System , D 5.109

National Military Establishment Standards, M 5.8

National Money Laundering Strategy, T 1.67/2

National Monuments and National Military Parks: Information Circulars, I 29.21

National Motor Vehicle Safety Advisory Council Summary Report, TD 1.13

National Negro Health News, T 27.30, FS 2.19

National Nosocomial Infections Study, Reports, HE 20.7011/10

National Ocean Survey Abstracts, C 55.413/2

National Ocean Survey Catalog of Aeronautical Charts and Related Publications, C 55.418/2

National Oceanographic Data Center, List of Fully Processed Oceanographic Cruise, D 203.24/5

National Oceanographic Data Center Publications, D 203.24, D 203.24/3

National Oceanographic Fleet Operating Schedules, D 218.11, D 203.33

National Oceanographic Instrumentation Center Publications, C 55.72

National Oceanography Data Center: Annual Report, C 55.291/2

National Painting and Decorating Apprenticeship and Training Standards Adopted by the National Joint Painting and Decorating Apprenticeship and Training Committee, L 23.2:P 16

National Park Conferences, I 29.5

National Park Location Maps, I 29.53

National Park Series, I 19.106

National Park Service Annual Science Report, I 29.1/3

National Park Service Bulletin, I 29.3/2

National Park Service Governor's Books [by State], I 29.75

National Park Service Guide to the Historic Places of the American Revolution, I 29.9/2:Am 3

National Park Service Handbooks (numbered), I 29.9/5

National Park Service History Series, I 29.58/2

National Park Statistical Abstract, I 29.114

National Park System and Related Areas, Index, I 29.103

National Parks and Landmarks, I 29.66

National Parks: Camping Guide, I 29.71

National Parks Program [Radio Broadcasts], I 29.17

National Parks, USA [poster series], I 29.20/2

National Patterns of Science and Technology Resources, NS 1.22/2

National Peace Essay Contest Brochures Available, Y 3.P 31:3

National Performance Audit Program, Ambient Air Audits of Analytical Proficiency, EP 1.23/5-2

National Petroleum Reserve in Alaska Task Force Study Reports, I 1.106

National Photovoltaics Program Review, E 1.108

National Physical Demands Information Series, L 7.26

National Plan for American Forestry, A 13.26

National Plan for Civil Defense and Defense Mobilization, PrEx 4.6/7

[National Plan for Civil Defense] NP-nos., D 13.8/4

National Plan for Emergency Preparedness, PrEx 4.6/8

National Plan of Integrated Airport Systems, TD 4.63

National Planning Board Circular Letters, Y 3.F 31/4:8

National Plant Materials Centers: Annual Technical Reports, A 57.54

National Poison Prevention Week, Y 3.C 76/3:12

National Policy on Career Education, Reports, Y 3.V 85:9

National Portrait Gallery Calendar of Events, SI 11.15

National Portrait Gallery Permanent Collection Illustrated Checklist, SI 11.2:P 42

National Postsecondary Student Aid Study, ED 1.333

National Potato Breeding Report, A 77.36

National Potato Germplasm Evaluation and Enhancement Report, A 77.36

National Potato Utilization Conference Report, A 77.15:74

National Poultry Improvement Plan Reports, A 106.22

National Preservation Report, LC 1.36

National Preserves (series), I 29.97

National Priorities List Sites, EP 1.107

National Prisoner Statistics, J 16.23

National Prisoner Statistics Bulletin, J 1.33/5

National Professional Standards Review Council: Annual Report, HE 1.46, HE 20.5010

National Program for Acquisitions and Cataloging: Progress Reports, LC 30.15

National Recreation Areas I 29.39

National Reference List of Water Quality Stations, Water Year (date), I 19.53/3

National Referral Center for Science and Technology Publications, LC 1.31

National Register of Historic Places, I 29.76, I 70.2:H 62/2, I 70.17

National Register of Historic Places Bulletins, I 29.76/3

National Register of Microform Masters, LC 30.8/8

National Reporting System for Family Planning Services: Annual Report, HE 20.6219

National Research and Teaching Conference in Agricultural Cooperation, A 89.18

National Research Council, Circulars, NA 2.4

National Research Initiative Competitive Grants Program, A 94.24

National Resources Conference Conducted by Industrial College of Armed Forces, D 5.9

National Rivers [information circulars], I 29.6/4

National Roster of Minority Professional Consulting Services, C 1.57/3

National SARE/ACE Report to Congress, A 94.19

National Scenic Trails Information Circulars, I 29.6/5

National Science and Technology Council: General Publications, PrEx 23.14

National Science Board, NS 1.28

National Science Foundation, Directory of NSF-Supported Teacher Enhancement Projects, NS 1.44/2

National Science Foundation Quarterly Report to the Congress, NS 1.35

National Screw Thread Commission, C 13.23

National Sea Grant Program Annual Retreat Report, C 55.38/2

National Seashore, I 29.6/2

National Security Affairs Issue Papers, D 5.409/2

National Security Affairs Monographs, D 5.409

National Security Agency Publications, D 1.25

National Security Essay Series, D 5.413

National Security Management, D 5.9/3, D 5.410

National Security Management Programs Instructor's Guide (Series), D 5.410/2

National Security Seminar: Presentation, D 5.9

National Security Seminar Presentation Outlines and Reading List, D 5.9/2

National Service News, Y 3.N 21/29:16-15

National Severe Storms Laboratory, Annual Report, Fiscal Year (date), C 55.625

National Shellfish Register of Classified Growing Waters, C 55.441

National Shellfish Sanitation Workshop, Proceedings, HE 20.4032

National Shipbuilding Research Program (various subjects) (series), C 39.245

National Shipping Authority: Safety Bulletin, C 39.209

National Space Science Data Center: Newsletter, NAS 1.37/2

National Space Science Data Center, NSSDC- (series), NAS 1.37

National Standard Reference Data Series, C 13.48

National Status and Trends Program for Marine Environmental Quality, C 55.436/2

National Status and Trends Program for Marine Environmental Quality, FY Program Description, C 55.436/3

National Status and Trends Program, Water Quality Cruise Data Reports (series), C 55.436, C 55.436/4

National Status on Control of Garbage- feeding, A 101.20

National Stay-in-School Campaign May- September 1958 [release], L 1.36

National Summary of Business Conditions, FR 1.19/2

National Summary of State Medicaid Managed Care Programs, HE 22.116

National Summary of State Medicaid Managed Care Programs, Program Descriptions, HE 22.12/3

National Survey of Community Solid Waste Practices, HE 20.1409

National Survey of Compensation Paid Scientists and Engineers Engaged in Research and Development Activities, E 1.34

National Survey of Fishing, Hunting, and Wildlife-Associated Recreation, I 49.98/4

National Survey of Old-Age and Survivors Insurance Beneficiaries: Highlight Reports, FS 3.48

National Survey of Professional, Administrative, Technical, and Clerical Pay, L 2.3, L 2.2/10, L 2.3/13

National Survey of Professional, Administrative, Technical, and Clerical Pay: Private Service Industries, L 2.3/13-2

National Survey of White-Collar Pay, L 2.43/3

National Survey Results on Drug Use from the Monitoring the Future Study, HE 20.3968

National Systematics Laboratory Report for Calendar Year (date), C 55.341

National Telephone Directory, E 1.12/3

National Tick Surveillance Program, A 77.237/2

National Timber Bridge Initiative Fiscal Year, A 13.113/2

National Toxicology Program, Annual Plan, Fiscal Year, HE 20.3551/2

National Toxicology Program, Annual Plan, Fiscal Year (date), HE 20.23/2

National Toxicology Program, Review of Current DHEW Research Related to Toxicology, Fiscal Year (date), HE 20.23

National Toxicology Program, Review of Current DHHS, DOE, and EPA Research Related to Toxicology, HE 20.23

National Toxicology Program, Technical Report series, HE 20.3564

National Toxicology Program, Toxicity Report series, HE 20.3564/2

National Trade Data Bank, C 1.88

National Trade Estimate, Report on Foreign Trade Barriers, PrEx 1.14, PrEx 9.10

National Traffic Safety Newsletter, TD 8.18
National Trails Directory Series, I 29.123
National Transportation Report, TD 1.26
National Transportation Safety Board Decisions, TD 1.122
National Transportation Statistics, Annual Report, TD 10.9, TD 12.1/2
National Trends in Electric Energy Resource Use, E 3.11/17
National Truck Characteristic Report, TD 2.55
National Undersea Research Program Technical Report, C 55.29/3
National Union Catalog, LC 30.8
National Union Catalog of Manuscript Collections, LC 9.8
National Union Catalog: Register of Addition Locations, LC 30.8/7
National Update, J 29.24
National Uranium Resource Evaluation: Annual Activity Report, E 1.51
National Urban Mass Transportation Statistics, TD 7.11/2
National Urban Recreation Study (series), I 66.24
National VISTA News, AA 1.9/6, Y 3.N 21/29:17-15
National Voluntary Laboratory Accreditation: Annual Report, C 1.71
National War College: Publications, D 5.17
National War College Strategic Studies (series), D 5.415
National War Savings Committee, T 1.26
National Water Conditions, I 19.42
National Water Quality Inventory, Report to Congress, EP 2.17/2
National Water Quality Laboratory Newsletter, I 19.125
National Water Summary, I 19.13/3
National Weather Bulletin, A 29.7
National Weights and Measures Law, (year), C 13.55/2
National Wetlands Inventory, I 49.6/7, I 49.6/7-2
National Wetlands Inventory (maps) by States, I 49.6/7
National Wildlife Coordinating Group: Handbooks, Manuals, Guides, A 13.99/8
National Wildlife Refuges, I 49.44/2
National Wildlife Refuges Planning Update, I 49.44/3
National Woman's Liberty Loan Committee, T 1.27/11-19
National Zip Code and Post Office Directory, P 1.10/8
National Zip Code Directory, P 1.10/8
National Zoological Park: Annual Report, SI 1.1/2
National Zoological Park, Reports, SI 1.1/a4
National-Bank Act As Amended, T 12.6
Nationwide Food Consumption Survey (year), Reports, A 111.9
Nationwide Food Consumption Survey (year), Preliminary Reports, A 111.9/2
Nationwide Outdoor Recreation Plan, I 70.20
Nationwide Personal Transportation Study: Reports, TD 2.31
Native American, HE 1.710
Native American Arts (series), I 1.84/4
Native American Monograph, HE 20.3162/4
Native Sulfur, I 28.63
NATO Parliamentarians' Conference, Report of Senate Delegation, Y 4.F 76/2:Na 81a/5
NATO Review, S 1.135
NATO Supply Code for Manufacturers, D 7.6/2-2:4-3
Natural Charts and Other Publications Recently Issued, C 4.5/2
Natural Disaster Survey Reports, C 55.20
Natural Gas, I 28.98, E 3.11, E 1.99
Natural Gas Annual, E 3.11/2-2, E 3.11/2-10
Natural Gas Deliveries and Curtailments to End-use Customers and Potential Needs for Additional Alternate Fuels, E 3.11/2-5
Natural Gas in (year), I 28.98/4
Natural Gas . . . Issues and Trends, E 3.11/2-11
Natural Gas Liquids, I 28.47, E 3.11/2
Natural Gas Processing Plants in United States, I 28.98/3
Natural Gas Production and Consumption, I 28.98/6
Natural Gas Star Partner Update, EP 6.15
Natural Gas Weekly Market Update, E 1.133
Natural Gasoline, I 28.47
Natural Graphite in (year), I 28.128
Natural History Handbook Series, I 29.62
Natural History Theme Studies, I 29.62/2
Natural Inquirer, A Research and Science Journal, The, A 13.155
Natural Resource Development Program Annual Report, SBA 1.48
Natural Resources, C 51.9/25
Natural Resources, A Selection of Bibliographies, D 103.50:3
Natural Resources of [state], I 1.91

Natural Resources Reports, I 29.89
Natural Resources Section Preliminary Studies, W 1.80/2
Natural Resources Section Reports, W 1.80
Natural Resources Section Weekly Summary, D 102.12
Natural-Gas Production and Consumption, E 3.38
Natural Resource Year in Review I 29.1/4
Naturalist Program, Arcadia National Park, I 29.60
Naturalist Program, Great Smokey Mountains National Park, I 29.60/2
Naturalist Program, Mount Rainier National Park, I 29.60/3
Naturalist Program, Shenandoah National Park, I 29.60/4
Naturality Laws [August 31, 1935], Y 1.2:N 39
Naturalization Laws and Regulations, C 7.10/5, L 6.5
Naturalization Laws [May 9, 1918], Y 1.2:N 21/3
Nature Notes, Clip Sheets, I 29.22
Nature to Be Commanded, I 19.16:950
Nautical Almanac for the Year [date], D 213.11
Nautical Chart Catalogs, C 55.418
Nautical Charts and Publications, C 55.440
Nautical Charts and Publications, Region 1, United States and Canada, C 55.440:1
Nautical Monographs, N 6.10
Nautical Monographs (Maury), N 14.11
NAVAER Publications Index [Restricted], N 28.17
Navaho Historical Series, I 20.40
Navair (series), D 222.9
Navajo Area Indian Health Service, Office of Environmental Health and Engineering: Annual Report, HE 20.5301/2, HE 20.9413
Navajo Historical Series, I 20.40
Navajo Nation & Regional Areas Resource Directory, HE 20.310/3
Navajo Yearbook of Planning in Action, I 20.44
Naval Aerospace Medical Institute, D 206.18
Naval Air Development Center, Johnsville, PA., Aeronautical Electronic and Electrical Laboratory, Report NADC-EL (series), D 202.14
Naval Air Development Center Reports NADA (series), D 202.23
Naval Aviation News, D 202.9, D 202.9/2, D 207.7, D 207.7/2
Naval Aviation News, Restricted, N 27.16, M 207.7/2, D 207.7/2, D 202.9/2
Naval Aviation System Plan, TD 4.33
Naval Aviation Training Series, N 28.11
Naval Documents of the American Revolution, D 207.12
Naval Engineering Experiment Station, Annapolis. Md., D 211.15
Naval Engineering Memorandum, T 47.46
Naval Expenditures, D 212.8
Naval Firepower, N 18.12
Naval History Bibliographies (series), D 221.17
Naval Law Review, D 205.7
Naval Material Inspection Districts under Inspectors of Naval Material, N 19.6/2
Naval Medical Bulletin, D 206.3
Naval Medical Research Institute: Lecture and Review Series, D 206.14
Naval Medical Research Institute Reports, D 206.9
Naval Military Personnel Manual, D 208.6/2
Naval Militia Circular Letters, N 23.6
Naval Oceanographic Newsletter, D 203.28
Naval Ordnance Bulletins, N 18.11
Naval Ordnance Laboratory, Corona, Calif.: Reports, D 215.13
Naval Ordnance Papers, N 18.8
Naval Petroleum and Oil Shale Reserves, Annual Report of Operations, E 1.84/2
Naval Professional Papers, N 17.5
Naval Research Laboratory, Annual Report, D 210.17/2
Naval Research Laboratory, Fact Book, D 210.17/3
Naval Research Laboratory Quarterly on Nuclear Science and Technology, Progress Reports, D 210.21
Naval Research Laboratory Reports, N 32.7, M 216.7
Naval Research Laboratory, Review, D 210.17/2
Naval Research Logistics Quarterly, D 201.12
Naval Research Reviews, D 210.11
Naval Research Task Summary, D 210.20
Naval Reserve Circular Letters, N 17.28
Naval Reserve Circular Letters and Instructions, N 25.5
Naval Reserve Regulations, N 25.7/2
Naval Reservist News, D 207.309
Naval Reservist, News of Interest to the Naval Reservist, D 208.10
Naval Surface Weapons Center, NSWC-AP-(series), D 201.21/6
Naval Ship Research and Development Center Reports, D 211.9

Naval Ship Systems Command Technical News, D 211.8
Naval Stores, A 105.49
Naval Stores Report, A 88.29, A 88.29/2
Naval Support Force Antarctica, D 201.15/3
Naval Support Force, Antarctica, Publications, D 201.15/2
Naval Surface Warfare Center Dahlgren Division, Technical Digest, D 201.21/8
Naval Surface Weapons Center, Technical Reports, D 201.21/5
Naval Torpedo Station, Keyport, Washington: Publications, D 211.23
Naval Training Bulletin, D 208.7
Naval War College Review, D 208.209
Naval Warfare Publications, D 207.9
NavComp Notice, D 201.6/5
NavCompt Instruction Nos, D 201.6/4
NavFac Technical Training Center: NTTC Courses, D 209.16
NAVFAC-P- (series), D 209.17/2
NAVFACENGCOM Documentation Index, D 209.17/2-2
Navigation and Vessel Inspection Circulars, N 24.27, T 47.34
Navigation and Vessel Inspection Circulars (numbered), TD 5.4/2
Navigation Charts, D 5.534
    Alleghaney and Monongahela Rivers, D 103.66/4
    Corps of Engineers, D 103.66
    Missouri River, D 103.66
    Numbered Rivers, D 103.66/3
    Ohio River, D 103.66/2
Navigation Conditions for (name), D 103.66/7
Navigation Dictionary, D 203.22:220
Navigation Laws, T 30.6, C 11.6
Navigation Laws of U.S., C 25.5/2
Navigator, D 5.359, D 301.38/4
NavMed VD [leaflets], N 10.19
NavNews, a Navy News Service, D 201.24
NavOrd Reports, D 215.7
NavSea Journal, D 211.24
NavWeps Reports, D 217.18
Navy, D 7.29/4
Navy and Marine Corps List and Directory, N 1.24
Navy Chaplain, D 207.19/2
Navy Chaplains Bulletin, D 208.3/2, D 207.19
Navy Chaplains Newsletter, D 208.3/2
Navy Civil Engineer, D 209.13
Navy Comptroller Manual, D 201.6/2
Navy Comptroller Manual, Advance Changes, D 201.6/3
Navy Current Procurement Directives, NCPD (series), D 201.6/13
Navy Department Specifications, D 212.9
Navy Department Specifications and Federal Specifications, Monthly Bulletin, N 20.20
Navy Editor Service, D 201.26
Navy Electronics Lab., San Diego, Calif., Publications (misc.), D 211.11/2
Navy Electronics Laboratory Reports, D 211.11
Navy Expenditures, N 20.21
Navy Family Lifeline, D 201.25
Navy Guide for Retired Personnel and Their Families, D 208.26
Navy Life, Reading and Writing for Success in the Navy, D 208.11/3
Navy Lifeline, Naval Safety Journal, D 207.15
Navy Management Review, D 201.14
Navy Medical and Dental Materiel Bulletin, D 206.3/2
Navy Military Personnel Statistics, D 208.25
Navy Procurement Directives, D 201.6/10
Navy Property Redistribution and Disposal Regulations, D 201.6/9
Navy Recruiter, D 208.16
Navy Register, N 1.10
Navy Regulations, N 1.11/1, D 201.11
Navy Regulations, Proposed Changes, N 1.11/3
Navy Scientific and Technical Information Program, Newsletter, D 210.26
Navy Shipping Guide, N 20.17
Navy Shipping Guide, Changes, N 20.17/2
Navy Supply Corps Newsletter, D 212.14
Navy Surplus by Auction Catalogs, N 20.14/2
Navy Surplus Supplies; Catalog, N 20.14/3
Navy Training Courses, N 17.25, D 208.11
Navy Training Text Materials, D 208.11/2, D 207.208/4
Navy Transportation Schedules, N 17.10
Navy V-12 Bulletins, N 17.36
Navy War Maps, N 17.35
Navy Wifeline, D 201.25
(Navy Yard) Examination Orders, N 1.25
Navy Yard Orders, N 1.15
Nazi-Soviet Relations, 1939–41, Documents from the German Foreign Office, S 1.2:N 23

NBL Certified Reference Materials Catalog, E 1.98:
NBLIC (National Black Leadership Initiative on Cancer) News, HE 20.3195
NBS Consumer Information Series, C 13.53
NBS Handbook, Specifications, Tolerances, and Other Technical Requirements for Weighing and Measuring Devices, C 13.11/2
NBS Publications Newsletter, C 13.36/5
NBS Reactor: Summary of Activities, C 13.46/2
NBS Serial Holdings, C 13.58/5
NBS Standard, C 13.42
NBS Standard Reference Materials [announcements], C 13.48/2
NBS Standard Reference Materials Price List, C 13.48/4-2
NBS Time and Frequency Broadcast Services, C 13.60
NBS Update, C 13.36/7
NC News, A 13.82/9-2
NCADI Publications Catalog, HE 20.419, HE 20.8012/2
NCBE Forum, ED 1.71/3
NCBE, Program Information Guide Series, ED 1.8/4
NCBI Newsletter, HE 20.3624/2
NCEL Contract Report, D 209.12/4
NCEL Techdata, D 201.27
NCES Announcements, ED 1.128
NCES Bulletins, ED 1.126
NCG [Nuclear Catering Group] Technical Reports, D 103.54
NCH Statistics Series, HE 20.5113
NCHCT Fact Sheet, HE 20.28
NCHCT Monograph Series, HE 20.26
NCHS Atlas CD-ROM, HE 20.6209/12
NCHS Catalog of University Presentations, HE 20.6225
NCHS CD-ROM Series (23), HE 20.6209/10
NCHS Health Interview Statistics, Publications from the National Health Interview Survey, Advance Data Reports, HE 20.6216/5
NCHS Publications on [various subjects], HE 20.6220
NCHSR Health Care for the Aging, HE 20.6514/2
NCHSR Program Solicitation (series), HE 20.6512/9
NCHSR Program Solicitation, Grants for Health Services Dissertation Research, HE 20.6512/8-2
NCHSR Program Solicitation, Individual and Institutional, HE 20.6512/8
NCHSR Research Activities, HE 20.6512/5
NCHSR Research Digest Series, HE 20.6511
NCHSR Research Management (series), HE 20.6512/4
NCHSR Research Proceedings Series, HE 20.6512/3
NCHSR Research Report Series, HE 20.6512
NCHSR Research Summary Series, HE 20.6512/2
NCI Fact Book, HE 20.3174
NCI Grant Supported Literature Index, HE 20.3179
NCI Grants Awarded, by Principal Investigator, HE 20.3176/2
NCI Grants Awarded, Fiscal Year (date), HE 20.3176
NCI Investigational Drugs, Chemical Information, HE 20.3180/2
NCI Investigational Drugs, Pharmaceutical Data, HE 20.3180
NCI Monographs, HE 20.3162, HE 20.3162/3
NCIC Newsletter, J 1.14/19
NCIC 2000 Newsletter, J 1.107
NCJRS Abstracts Database, J 28.31/2-2
NCJRS Document Loan Program, Document Lists, J 1.20/4
NCO Call, D 101.118/3
NCO Journal, D 101.127
NCSC-TG (series), D 1.79/4
NCSS (National Cooperative Soil Survey) Newsletter, A 57.78
NCSS Report, H-, HE 17.640
NCUA Digest, NCU 1.13
NCUA Investment Report, NCU 1.22
NCUA Letter to Credit Unions, NCU 1.19
NCUA News, NCU 1.20
NCUA Quarterly, NCU 1.3/2
NCUA Report, NCU 1.12
NCUA Review, NCU 1.15
NCWM Publications, C 13.10/3-3
NDATUS Instruction Manual, HE 20.8021
NDC Report, D 103.130
NDC Research Abstracts, D 5.411/2
NDE of Stainless Steel and On-Line Leak Monitoring of LWRS, Annual Report, Y 3.N 88:25-5, Y 3.N 88:25-9
NDEA Counseling and Guidance Institutes, FS 5.255:25015, HE 5.255:25015
NDPO-Fact Sheet, J 1.14/25-4
NDPO-Information Bulletins, J 1.14/25-3
Nealon Report, The, HE 20.3152/15
NE Regional Reports, L 2.71/3

NE Regional Staff Letter, A 77.29, A 106.38
NE/NA-INF, A 13.110/15
Near and Middle Eastern Series, S 1.86
Near East and Africa Reports, PrEx 7.20
Near East and South Asia Report, PrEx 7.20
Near East and South Asian Series, S 1.86/2
Near Eastern Series, S 1.31
Nebraska Weekly Weather and Crop Report, A 36.208
NECTP [Northeast Corridor Transportation Project] , TD 3.13
Needs and Offers List, GP 3.31
Neglected or Delinquent Children Living in State Operated or Supported Institutions, HE 19.335
Negro Economics Division, L 1.8
Negro Extension News, A 43.7/2
Negro Notes, S 1.83
Negro Population: March (year), C 3.186:P-20
Negro Statistics Bulletin, C 3.131
Negroes in the United States, C 3.3
NEH Exhibitions Today, NF 3.24
NEH Fellowships University Teachers, College Teachers, and Independent Scholars Anniversary and Commemorative Initiatives, NF 3.13/4
NEH News, NF 3.7
NEH Teacher-Scholar Program for Elementary and Secondary School Teachers, Guidelines and Application Instructions, NF 3.18
NEH Travel to Collections, Small Grants for Research Travel to Libraries, Archives, Museums, and Other Repositories, NF 3.19
Neighborhood Health Centers, Summary of Project Data, HE 20.5115
Neighborhood Networks Fact Sheet, HH 13.16/5
Neighborhood Networks News, HH 13.16
Neighborhood Networks News Brief, HH 1.127
Neighborhood Networks Newsline, HH 1.127/2
Neighborhood Youth Corps Publications, L 1.49
NE-INF- (series), A 13.42/25
NEISS Data Highlights, Y 3.C 76/3:7-3
NEISS [National Electronic Injury Surveillance System] News, Product Safety, HE 20.4026, Y 3.C 76/3:7-2
NEPA/BRAC, D 103.128
Nepal, LC 1.30/6
NEPH Newsletters, L 16.44
NESDIS (series), C 55.13:NESDIS
NESS (series), C 55.13:NESS, C 55.13/2:NESS
NET (Net Electronic Titles), GP 3.40
Net Migration of the Population, by Age, Sex and Color, A 93.35
Net Spendable Earnings, L 2.75, LC 30.24
Network, SBA 1.38, T 22.2/15:7375
Network News, HE 20.9117
Network of Knowledge, Directory of Criminal Justice Information Sources, J 28.20
Network Planning Papers (series), LC 1.37
Networked Audiovisuals, VA 1.81
Neurological Diseases and Stroke Science Information Program Advisory Committee, HE 20.3001/2:N 39/6
Neurological Disorders Program-Project Review A Committee, HE 20.3001/2:N 39/3
Neurological Disorders Program-Project Review B Committee, HE 20.3001/2:N 39/4
Neurology A Study Section, HE 20.3001/2:N 39
Neurology B Study Section, HE 20.3001/2:N 39/2
Neuropsychiatric Research Unit, San Diego, California, Abstracts of Completed Research, D 206.21/2
Neurotropic Viral Diseases Surveillance, HE 20.7011/5
Nevada Annual Data Summary Water Year, A 57.46/4-2
Nevada Progress Report, I 53.43/4
Nevada Today, Developments in Business, Technology and International Trade, C 1.65
Newport Papers, D 208.212
New Application for Grants under Research in Education of the Handicapped, ED 1.50
New at the Energy Library, E 1.13/5
New Beneficiary Survey (series), HE 3.78
New Books–
    Documents Office, GP 3.17/6
    National Defense University, D 5.411/3
New Braille Musician, LC 19.12/2
New Counterfeits (numbered), T 34.7
New Counterfeits Circular Letters, T 34.4/2
New Crop Varieties, A 43.33/2
New Developments in Employee and Labor Relations, PM 1.62
New Developments in Highways, TD 2.22
New Digest, ED 1.71
New Dimensions in Higher Education, FS 5.250, HE 5.250
New Dimensions in Mental Health, HE 20.8122

New Dimensions in Mental Health, Report from the Director (series), HE 20.8122/2
New Domestic Public Land Mobile Radio Service Applications Accepted for Filing During Past Week, CC 1.36
New Drug Evaluation Statistical Report, HE 20.4211
New Dwelling Units Authorized by Local Building Permits, L 2.51/5
New England Economy, Employment, Etc., Releases, L 2.49/4
New England Fisheries, C 55.309/2
New England Highway Weather Bulletin, A 29.32
New ERA, J 16.11
New Federal Credit Union Charters, Quarterly Report of Organization, FS 3.307
New Focus, ED 1.49/2
New for Consumers, Highlights of New Federal Consumer Publications, GS 11.9/2
New from North Central Publications, A 13.89/2
New Grants and Awards, HE 20.3034
New Health and Hospital Projects Authorized for Construction under Controlled Materials Plan, FS 2.73/2
New Housing Units Authorized by Local Building Permits and New Dwelling Units Authorized in Local Building Permits, C 3.215/4
New Information from the Office of Educational Research and Improvement, ED 1.303/3
New Item Introductory Schedule, GS 2.22
New Jersey Unemployment Rate ..., L 2.71/6-8
New Jersey Unemployment Rate, L 2.71/6-4
New Medical Science for the 21st Century, HE 20.3459
New Mexico Annual Data Summary, A 57.46/18-2
New Mexico, Governor, Annual Reports, 1878-1912, I 1.24
New Mexico, Traveling Auditor and Bank Examiner, Annual Reports, I 1.24/2
New Mexico Water Supply Outlook and Federal-State-Private Cooperative Snow Surveys, A 57.46/18
New Nuclear Data, Annual Cumulations, Y 3.At 7:16-3
New Orders for Pulverizers, for Pulverized Fuel Installations, C 3.103
New Orleans Jazz Study Newsletter, I 29.131
New Passenger Automobile Rationing Regulations, Orders, Pr 32.4208
New Perspectives, CR 1.12
New Plant Introductions (annual lists), A 19.15
New Private Mortgage Insurance Activity, HH 1.99/8
New Product Ideas, Process Improvements, and Cost-Saving Techniques, Relating to [various subjects], NASA/SBA FA- (series), NAS 1.56
New Products Annual Directory, C 61.10/2
New Products from the U.S. Government, GP 3.17/6
New Publication Lists (numbered), I 49.18/2
New Publications–
    Bureau of Mines, C 22.7/3
    Denver Office, I 49.66/3
    Fish and Wildlife Service, I 49.66/2
    Forest Service, A 13.69/10
    Geological Survey, I 19.14/4
    Mine Safety and Health Administration, L 38.11/2
    National Bureau of Standards, C 13.15
    Office of Communications, A 21.6/3
New Publications Available, A 13.42/23
New Publications from NBS, C 13.36/2
New Publications from the National Institute of Mental Health, HE 20.8113/6
New Publications in Wages and Industrial Relations, L 2.74/2
New Publications of the Geological Survey, I 19.14/4
New Publications Rocky Mountain Research Station, A 13.151/2-2
New Reports, A 93.18/3-2
New Reports by Geological Survey About Water in the Pacific Northwest, I 19.14/5
New Research and Development Reports Available to Industry, C 42.21/4
New Serial Titles, LC 1.23/3
New Ship Construction, TD 11.15
New Ship Construction, Oceangoing Ships of 1,000 Gross Tons and Over in United States and Foreign Shipyards, C 39.212/3
New Ship Deliveries, Calendar Year, C 39.212/2
New Ship Techniques and Development of Research Services Division, Annual Report, D 301.45/11
New Uses for Cotton Series, C 18.117
New Way of Saving (series), GS 12.11
New York City, New York's World's Fair, 1939-40, S 6.24
New York City's Unemployment Rate ..., L 2.71/6-10

NIH Library Translations Index, FS 2.22:T 68/2
NIH Peer Review Notes, HE 20.3045
NIH Program Evaluation Reports, HE 20.3039
NIH Public Advisory Groups: Authority, Structure, Functions, HE 20.3018
NIH Publications List, HE 20.3009
NIH Quarterly Publications List, FS 2.22/13-9
NIH Record, FS 2.22/2, HE 20.3007/3
NIH Statistical Reference Book of International Activities, HE 20.3760
NIH Training Center Catalog and Calendar, HE 20.3060
NIJ Guide, J 28.8/3
NIJ Reports, A Bimonthly Journal of the National Institute of Justice, J 28.14
NIJ Reports/SNI (reprints), J 28.14/a
NIJ Research Forum, J 28.35
NIJ Research Review, The, J 28.24/10
NILECJ Evaluation Series, J 1.46/2
NILECJ-guides, J 1.41/3
NIMA Aeronautical Charts and Publications, TD 4.84
NIMA Nautical Charts, Public Sale Region 1, United States and Canada, 4.82:1
NIMA Nautical Charts, Public Sale Region 2, Central and South America and Antarctica, 4.82:2
NIMA Nautical Charts, Public Sale Region 3, Western Europe, Iceland, Greenland, and the Arctic, 4.82:3
NIMA Nautical Charts, Public Sale Region 4, Scandinavia, Baltic and Russia, 4.82:4
NIMA Nautical Charts, Public Sale Region 5, Western Africa and the Mediterranean, 4.82:5
NIMA Nautical Charts, Public Sale Region 6, Indian Ocean, 4.82.6
NIMA Nautical Charts, Public Sale Region 7, Australia, Indonesia, and New Zealand, 4.82:7
NIMA Nautical Charts, Public Sale Region 8, Oceania, 4.82:8
NIMA Nautical Charts, Public Sale Region 9, East Asia, 4.82:9
NIMH Analyses Series, FS 2.22/27
NIMH Library Acquisition List, HE 20.8113/4
NIMH Report to Physicians (series), HE 20.8111
NINBD Monographs, FS 2.22/55
NINCDS Amyotrophic Lateral Sclerosis Research Program, HE 20.3502:Am 9/2
NINCDS Cerebral Palsy Research Program, HE 20.3502:C 33/3
NINCDS Epilepsy Research Program, HE 20.3502:Ep 4/2
NINCDS Hearing, Speech, and Language Research Program, HE 20.3502:H 35/3
NINCDS Huntington's Disease Research Program, HE 20.3502:H 92/2
NINCDS Index to Research Grants and Awards, HE 20.3516
NINCDS Multiple Sclerosis Research Program, HE 20.3502:M 91
NINCDS Neuromuscular Disorders Research Program, HE 20.3502:N 39/3
NINCDS Parkinson's Disease Research Program, HE 20.3502:P 22
NINCDS Research Program, Stroke, HE 20.3512/2
NINCDS Spinal Cord Injury Research Program, HE 20.3502:Sp 4/2
NINCDS Stroke Research Program, HE 20.3502:St 8
NINDS Bibliography Series, HE 20.3513/3
NINDS Index to Research Grants and Contracts, HE 20.3516
NINDS Monographs, HE 20.3510
NINDS Research Profiles, HE 20.3512
1990 Census Profile, C 3.223/7-5
1990 Housing Highlights, C 3.224/3-8
1990 Planning Conference Series, C 3.271
1950 Census of Population and Housing Announcements, C 3.950-4/3
1953 Sample Census of Agriculture, C 3.31/6
1954 Census of Agriculture, Farms, Farm Characteristics, Farm Products, Preliminary Reports, Series AC 54-1, C 3.31/7
1997 Economic Censuses, C 3.277/2
NIOSH Alert, HE 20.7123
NIOSH Certified Equipment List, HE 20.7124
NIOSH Health and Safety Guides for [various businesses], HE 20.7108/2
NIOSH Health Hazard Evaluation Report, HE 20.7125/2
NIOSH Projects for (Fiscal Year), HE 20.7127
NIOSH Publications Catalog, HE 20.7114/2
NIOSH Research and Demonstration Grants, HE 20.7126
NIOSH Research Reports, HE 20.7111
NIOSH Schedule of Courses, HE 20.7128

NIOSH Surveillance Reports, HE 20.7111/3
NIOSH Technical Reports, HE 20.7111/2
NIOSH Worker Bulletin (series), HE 20.7117/2
NIST Conference Calendar, C 13.10/3-2
NIST Handbook, Specifications, Tolerances, and Other Technical Requirements for Weighing and Measuring Devices, C 13.11/2
NIST Serial Holdings, C 13.58/5
NIST Update, C 13.36/7
NIST-GCR Grantee/Contractor Report (Series), C 13.57/2
Nitrogen in (year), I 28.132
NLM Catalog Supplement, HE 20.3609/3-3
NLM LOCATORplus, HE 20.3626
NLM Name and Series Authorities, HE 20.3609/5
NLM Technical Bulletin, HE 20.3603/2
NLS News, National Longitudinal Surveys, L 2.135
NMC: Monthly Performance Summary, C 55.196
NMC Monthly Performance Summary, C 55.196
NMFS Northwest Region, Organization and Activities, Fiscal Year, C 55.301/2
NMFS (series), C 55.13:NMFS, C 55.13/2:NMFS
NMRC (series), C 39.244, TD 11.17
NMSS Licensee Newsletter, Y 3.N 88:57
NOAA, C 55.14
NOAA Annual Operating Plan, C 55.1/3
NOAA Atlas NESDIS, C 55.242
NOAA Atlases, C 55.22
NOAA Circular (series), C 55.4
NOAA Coastal Ocean Program, Decisions Analysis Series, C 55.49/3
NOAA Coastal Ocean Program, Project News Update, C 55.49/4
NOAA Coastal Ocean Program, Regional Synthesis Series, C 55.49/2
NOAA Computer Programs and Problems, C 55.13/3
NOAA Data Reports C 55.36
NOAA Data Report, MESA- (series), C 55.36
NOAA Data Reports, OMPA- (series), C 55.36
NOAA Dumpsite Evaluation Reports, C 55.35
NOAA Estuary-of-the-Month, Seminar Series, C 55.49
NOAA Handbooks, C 55.8/2
NOAA Manuals (numbered), C 55.8/3
NOAA National Status and Trends Program and Quality Assurance Program for Marine Environmental Measurements, C 55.434
NOAA Organization Directory (series), C 55.48/2
NOAA Paleoclimate Publications Series Report (series), C 55.241
NOAA Photoessays, C 55.19
NOAA Professional Papers, C 55.25
NOAA Program Plans, C 55.15
NOAA Publications Announcements, C 55.17
NOAA Report, C 55.53
NOAA Scientific and Technical Publications Announcements, C 55.228/2
NOAA Special Reports, NOS OMA- (series), C 55.13/6
NOAA Technical Memorandums, C 55.13/2
NOAA Technical Reports, C 55.13
NOAA Western Region Computer Programs and Problems (series), C 55.13/3
Nobel Prize Laureates, HE 20.3463
NODC Environmental Information Summaries, C 55.299
NODC Quarterly Accessions, Computer Produced Indexes, American Meteorological Society Meteorological and Geoastrophysical Abstracts, D 203.24/6
Noise Diagnostics for Safety Assessment, Standards, and Regulation, E 1.28/10
Noise Emission Standards for Construction Equipment, Background Document for [various items], EP 1.6/3
Noise Facts Digest, EP 1.30
Noise Standards, Aircraft Type and Airworthiness Certification, TD 4.6:part 36
Nominate a Small Business Person or Advocate of the Year, SBA 1.43
Non Compulsory Radio Fixes, TD 4.311
Non-Appropriated Employees, CS 1.41/4:532-2
Noncitrus Fruits and Nuts, Annual Summary, A 105.11
Noncitrus Fruits and Nuts, Midyear Supplement, A 92.11/2-3
Nonconventional Technical Information Systems in Current Use, NS 2.8
Nonfarm Housing Characteristics, 1950 Housing Census Report H-B (series), C 3.950/3
Nonfarm Housing Starts, C 56.211/3
Nonfarm Mortgage Investments of Life Insurance Companies, FHL 1.18
Nonfarm Real Estate Foreclosure Report, FHL 1.8
Nonfarm Real Estate Foreclosures, Y 3.F 31/3:10, FL 3.8, NHA 3.9
Nonferrous Metals, C 41.54
Nonferrous Metals Supply, Demand Data, I 28.169/3

Nonferrous Scrap Dealers Reports, I 28.65
Nongovernment Organization Codes for Military Standard Contract Administration Procedures, D 7.6/2:8
Nonpartisan Review, NC 3.11
Nonpublic Schools in Large Cities, HE 5.93/11
Nonresidential Buildings Energy Consumption Survey, E 3.43/2
Nonresidential Buildings Energy Consumption Survey: Commercial Buildings Survey, E 3.43/2-2
Nonrubber Footwear, ITC 1.21, ITC 1.21/2
NORDA Reports, D 210.109
North America and Oceania Outlook and Situation Report, A 93.29/2-16
North American Fauna (series), I 49.30
North Atlantic Coast Fisheries Arbitration, S 3.18/3
North Atlantic Route Chart, C 55.416/8
North Atlantic Route Chart, TD 4.79/9
North Central Region, A 106.39/3
North Central Regional Medical Education Center: Newsletter, VA 1.56/2
North Central Regional Membership Relations Conference, A 89.17/2
North Central Regional Office Publications, L 2.94
North Central States Regional Poultry Breeding Project, Annual Report, A 77.236
North Central Volume, HE 20.6202:N 93 NC
North Dakota Leaflets, A 62.12
North Eastern Regional Office Publications, L 2.93
North Pacific Oceanic Route Chart, C 55.416/9
North Pacific Oceanic Route Chart, C 55.416/9-2
North Pacific Route Chart Composite, TD 4.79/10
North Pacific Route Chart Northeast Area, TD 4.70/10-1
Northeast Corridor Improvement Project Annaul Report, TD 3.13/3
Northeast Corridor Transportation Project, C 1.52
Northeast Employment Cost Index, L 2.117/2
Northeast Region, A 106.39/2
Northeast Region Outdoor Memo, I 66.21
Northeast, Population and Per Capita Income Estimates for Counties and Incorporated Places, C 3.186/27
Northeast Volume, HE 20.6202:N 93 NE
Northeastern Area, NA-FR- (series), A 13.102
Northeastern Area State and Private Forestry [publications], A 13.52/8
Northeastern Boundary Arbitration, S 3.10/1
Northeastern Forest Pest Reporter, A 13.52/3
Northeastern General Technical Reports, A 13.42/28
Northeastern Information Series, NE-INF-, A 13.106/4
Northeastern Pest Reporter, A 13.42/22
Northeastern Radiological Health Laboratory, BRH/ NERHL- (series), HE 20.4109
Northeastern Research Notes, A 13.42/20, A 13.42/27, A 13.42/29
Northeastern Resource Bulletins, A 13.42/26
Northeastern States Regional Poultry Breeding Project, Annual Report, A 77.234
Northwest and Alaska Fisheries Center, Quarterly Report, C 55.331/2
Northwest Fisheries Center: Publications, C 55.326
Northwest Fisheries Science Center, Quarterly Report, C 55.331/3
Northwest Indian Fisheries Commission, I 20.1/3
Northwest Shellfish Sanitation Research Planning Conference, Proceedings, EP 2.15
Northwestern Boundary Commission, 1957-61, S 3.10/2
NOS Oceanographic Circulatory Survey Reports, C 55.429
NOS Publications (numbered), C 55.419
NOS (series), C 55.13:NOS, C 55.13/2:NOS
NOS Technical Manuals, C 55.408/2
Not for Women Only, D 7.30
Notes, D 214.30
Notes and Decisions on Application of Decimal Classification, LC 22.7, LC 26.8
Notes and Suggestions, Y 3.N 21/9:7
Notes for Louisiana Purchase Exposition, St Louis, Mo., 1904, LC 1.8
Notes for Medical Catalogers, HE 20.3611
Notes from Foreign News Bureau, Y 3.C 83:67
Notes from the Joint Economic Committee, Y 4.Ec 7:N 84
Notes: National Conservation Training Center, I 49.106/7-2
Notes on Construction of Ordnance, W 34.8
Notes on Forest Trees Suitable for Planting in the U.S., A 13.7

Notes on Graduate Studies and Research in Home Economics and Home Economics Education, A 1.53

Notes on Hydrologic Activities, Bulletins, Y 3.F 31/13:3, Y 3.In 8/8:7

Notes on Labor Abroad, L 2.32

Notes on Patent Matters, C 21.19

Notes on Recent Operations, W 95.13

Notes on Sedimentation Activities, I 19.74/2, Y 3.W 29:10

Notes to Agents on [subject] (series), A 43.39

Noteworthy Maps, LC 5.5

Notice, D 301.32

Notice and Posting System, PM 1.14/4

Notice Mariners–
    Bureau of Lighthouses, C 9.20, C 9.26, C 9.38
    Coast and Geodetic Survey, C 4.11
    Defense Mapping Agency, D 5.315
    Hydrographic Office, N 6.11, M 202.8, D 203.8
    Manilla Suboffice, S 4.18/2
    Naval Oceanographic Office, D 203.8

Notice of Judgment under Caustic Poison Act, A 46.9

Notice of Judgment under Food and Drug Act, A 46.6

Notice of Judgment under Insecticide Act, A 46.7

Notice of Judgment under Regulations of Naval Stores, A 46.8

Notice of Purchases (of miscellaneous materials, etc.), N 20.9

Notice of Purchases (of miscellaneous materials, etc., for western States), N 20.10

Notice of Quarantine, A 48.5

Notice to Aviators, D 203.7

Notice to Mariners, Affecting Lighthouses and other Navigational Aids, T 47.19

Notice to Mariners, Affecting Lights, Buoys, and Other Aids to Navigation, N 24.12

Notice to Mariners, Great Lakes, C 9.41, T 47.20, N 24.13, T 6.12

Notice to Mariners, North American- Caribbean Edition, N 6.11/5, M 202.10, D 203.10

Notice to Mariners on Great Lakes, Special, N 6.13

Notice to Mariners Relating to Great Lakes and Tributary Waters West of Montreal, D 203.9, TD 5.10

Notice to Mariners, Restricted, N 6.11/2, M 202.8/2, D 203.8/2

Notice to Trade [various commodities], C 57.315

Notices, T 22.63

Notices (numbered), TD 4.47

Notices (series), P 1.55

Notices, Activities of Licensed Establishments Supervised by Virus-Serum Control Division, A 4.31, A 77.217

Notices of Determinations by Jurisdictional Agencies Under the Natural Gas Policy Act of 1978, E 2.22

Notices of Insecticide Act Judgement, A 1.18

Notices of Judgement, Food and Drug Act, A 1.16

Notices of Judgement Under Federal Insecticide, Fungicide, and Rodenticide Act, A 77.325, A 82.56

Notices of Judgement Under Insecticide Act, A 82.34

Notices of Judgment, Food and Drug Act, A 1.16, A 32.6

Notices of Judgment Summarizing Judicial Review of Orders under Sec. 701 (F) of Federal Food, Drug and Cosmetic Act, FS 7.17, FS 13.116

Notices of Judgment under–
    Caustic Poison Act, FS 7.9, FS 13.112
    Federal Food, Drug, and Cosmetic Act: Cosmetics, A 46.21, FS 7.13, FS 13.113
    Federal Food, Drug, and Cosmetic Act: Drugs and Devices, A 46.22, FS 7.12
    Federal Food, Drug, and Cosmetic Act: Foods, A 46.20, FS 7.10
    Federal Hazardous Substances Labeling Act, FS 13.112/2

Notices of Judgment Under the Federal Insecticide, Fungicide, and Rodenticide Act, EP 1.70

Notices of Quarantine, A 77.317

Notices to Airmen, TD 4.12/2

Noticias De La Semana, a News Summary for Hispanos, L 1.20/7

Notifications, HCRS Information Exchange (series), I 70.25

NPA Delegations, C 40.6/3

NPA Notices, C 40.9

NPA Orders, C 40.6/4

NPA Organization Statements, C 40.6/7

NPA Production Series, Quarterly Indexes of Shipments for Products of Metalworking Industries, C 40.15

NPA Regulations, C 40.6/2

NPA Regulatory Material and Forms, Digest, C 40.6/8

NPDP (National Practitioner Data Bank) News, HE 20.9316

NPRDC-TR- (series), D 201.34

NPS Strategic Planning, National Park Scan, I 29.132

NRA News, Y 3.N 21/8:9

NRAC Technical Reports, PrEx 4.18

NRC Committee on Aviation Psychology Publications, NA 2.9

NRC Information Notice, Y 3.N 88:56-2

NRC Public Document Room Collection, Y 3.N 88:62

NRC Regulatory Agenda, Y 3.N 88:45

NRC Switchboard, SL (series), LC 33.11

NRC-TLD Direct Radiation Monitoring Network, Y 3.N 88:43

NREVSS Monthly Report, HE 20.7011/39

NRI Annual Report, A 94.18/2

NRI Research Highlights, A 94.18

NRL Memorandum Report (series), D 210.8/2

NRL [Naval Research Laboratory] Bibliographies, D 210.13

NRL Reports, D 210.8

NRL Reprints, D 210.9

NRVSS Monthly Report, HE 20.7011/39

NSA Orders (National Shipping Authority), C 39.206/2

NSF Bulletin, NS 1.3

NSF Directions, NS 1.54

NSF Visiting Professorships for Women, NS 1.48

NSHCIC Bulletins, HH 1.77

NSSB (National Skill Standards Board) Annual Report, L 1.1/5

NSSB, Skills Today L 1.94

NSWC MP (series), D 201.21/7

NTIA Reports, C 60.10

NTIS Digest, C 51.11/7

NTIS Information Services, C 51.11:In 3

NTIS Information Services, General Catalogs, C 51.11/4

NTIS Monthly Marketing, C 51.7/6

NTIS Products and Services Catalog, C 51.11/8

NTIS Published Search Mini Catalog, C 51.13/2-2

NTIS Searchers, C 51.13

NTIS Tech Express, C 51.21

NTP Technical Bulletin, HE 20.23/3

NTPSC Special Reports, Y 3.T 68/2:9

NTSB News Digest, TD 1.131

NTSB Safety Recommendation (series), TD 1.129

NTSB-AAS [National Transportation Safety Board, Aspects of Aviation Safety] (series), TD 1.121

NTSB-PAM- (series), TD 1.123

NTSB/RP (series), TD 1.130

NU Reports, J 28.15/2

NUC Books, LC 30.26

Nuclear Data Tables, Y 3.At 7:16-4

Nuclear Development and Proliferation, PrEx 7.14/4

Nuclear Energy, E 1.68

Nuclear Fuels, E 1.99

Nuclear Industry, Y 3.At 7:56

Nuclear Notes for Industry, Y 3.At 7:31

Nuclear Power Plant Construction Activity, E 3.17/6

Nuclear Power Plants, E 1.99

Nuclear Reactor Technology, E 1.99

Nuclear Regulatory Commission Issuances, Y 3.N 88:11-2

Nuclear Regulatory Commission Issuances: Opinions and Decisions of the Nuclear Regulatory Commission with Selected Orders, Y 3.N 88:11

Nuclear Regulatory Legislation, Y 4.In 8/14:N 88/5

Nuclear Safety, Y 3.N 88:9, E 1.93

Nuclear Safety Index, Y 3.N 88:9-2

Nuclear Science Abstracts, ER 1.10

Nuclear Theory Reference Book, Y 3.At 7:53

Nuclear Waste, Quarterly Report on DOE'S Nuclear Waste Program, GA 1.13/9

Number and Percentage of Farms Electrified with Central Station Service, A 68.20

Number of Employees at Middle of Month, IC 1 ste.25/2

Number of Farms by States, A 88.21/2

Number of Females Employed by Class 1 Steams Railways, IC 1 ste.43

Number of Foreclosures [and rate of foreclosure] by FSLIC Insured Savings and Loan Associations, FHL 1.26

Number of New Dwelling Units and Permit Valuation of Building Construction Authorized by Class of Construction in Mountain and Pacific Division by Civil Division and State, L 2.51, L 2.51/2, L 2.51/3

Number of New Permanent Nonfarm Dwelling Units Started by Urban or Rural Location, Public or Private Ownership, and Type of Structure Cumulative Year-to L 2.51/4

Number of Recipients and Amounts of Payments Under Medicaid and Other Medical Programs Financed from Public Assistance Funds, HE 17.617/3

Numbered River, D 103.66/3

Numbers of Farms Participating in 1934 AAA Voluntary Control Programs (by States), A 55.55

Numeric List of Educational Institutions, ED 1.65

Numeric List of Lenders, ED 1.67

Numeric List of Product Class Codes, Commodity Transportation Survey, C 3.163/4-2

Numerical and Functional Index of Command Forms, D 301.45/14-2:0-9

Numerical Index for Station Catalogs, N 6.5/8

Numerical Index of AFSC Publications, D 301.45/14-2:0-2

Numerical Index of Departmental Forms, D 301.6:0-9

Numerical Index of Specialty Training Standards, D 301.6:0-8

Numerical Index of Standard and Recurring Air Force Publications, D 301.6:0-2

Numerical Index of Standard and Recurring Air Force Publications Available to NATO Security Assistance Customers, D 301.6:0-22

Numerical Index of Standard and Recurring Air Force Publications Available to Security Assistance Customers, D 301.6:0-20

Numerical Index of Technical Publications, M 301.13, D 301.17

Numerical Index Supplement to Bibliography of Technical Reports, C 35.7/3

Numerical List Covering Army Air Forces and Army-Navy Aeronautical Standard Parts, W 108.15

Numerical List of Treaty Series, Executive Agreement Series and Treaties and other International Acts Series, S 9.11/3

Numerical List of U.S. Air Force and Air Force-navy Aeronautical Standard Drawings, D 301.16

Numerical List, U.S. Air Force and Army- Navy Aeronautical Standard Drawings, M 301.12

Numerical Lists and Schedule of Volumes of Reports and Documents of Congress, GP 3.7/2

Numerical Tables and Schedule of Volumes (for Document Index), GP 3.15

Numerical Weather Prediction Activities, National Meteorological Center, C 55.115

NUREG- (series), Y 3.N 88:10

NUREG/CP (series), Y 3.N 88:27

NUREG/GR, Y 3.N 88:58

Nurse Planning Information Series, HE 20.6613

Nurse Training Act of 1975, Report to Congress, HE 20.6615

Nursery Products, Production and Sales, A 88.48

Nurses in Public Health, HE 20.3110

Nursing Clinical Conferences Presented by the Nursing Department of Clinical Center, HE 20.3021

[Nursing Education] Leaflets, FS 2.46

Nutmeg Guidon, J 16.15

Nutrition and Food Conservation Series, A 1.65

Nutrition Charts, A 42.7

Nutrition Education Series Pamphlets, FS 5.34

Nutrition News Letters, A 82.48

Nutrition Program News, A 77.710, A 106.20, A 106.111

Nutrition Study Section, HE 20.3001/2:N 95

Nutrition Surveillance, Annual Summary, HE 20.7011/24

Nutrition Surveys [by country], FS 2.22/57

NWC Administrative Publications (series), D 201.21/6-2

NWC Technical Publications, D 201.23

NWCG Handbooks, A 13.99

NWHC Technical Report (National Wildlife Health Center), I 19.211

NWL Administrative Reports, D 201.21/2

NWL Reports, D 217.17

NWL Technical Report, D 201.21, D 215.14

NWRC Research Update A 101.29

NWS-TDL-CP- (series), C 55.13/4

O

O & NAV Instructions, D 207.8

O.P.O. Publications, A 60.8

O.W.I. Reports, Pr 32.5020

OA Manual, HH 1.6/2

Office of Research [reports], IA 1.24/3
Office of Revenue Sharing: Annual Report, T 1.1/2
Office of Saline Water, I 1.82/3
Office of Science and Technology Annual Report, HE 20.4618
Office of Science Monograph Series, HE 20.8232
Office of Selective Service Records Regulations, Y 3.Se 4:19
Office of Solid Wastes Information Series, SW- (series), FS 2.305
Office of Technical Services Reports Suitable for Commercial Publications, Bulletins, C 35.10
Office of Technology and Forecast: Publications, C 21.24
Office of Technology Assessment and Forecast: Publications, C 1.62
Office of Women's Health-General Publications, HE 20.41/2
Office of the Chief Administrative Hearing Officer (OCAHO) Cases, J 1.102, J 21.23
Office of the Chief Administrative Hearing Officer (OCAHO) Files, J 1.102/2
Office of the Chief Administrative Hearing Officer Subpoenas, J 1.102/4
Office of the Chief Scientist: Annual Report, I 29.1/2
Office of the Directory, Annual Report, HE 20.3189
Office of the Inspector General: Annual Report, E 1.1/2
Office of the Inspector General: Semiannual Report, EP 1.1/5
Office of the Inspector General: Semiannual Report to the Congress, CSA 1.1/2
Office of the Secretary, DOE/S- (series), E 1.60
Office of the Secretary Petitions for Reconsideration of Actions in Rule Making Proceedings Filed, Public Notices, CC 1.38/2
Office of U.S. High Commissioner for German Publications, S 1.91
Office of United States Economic Coordinator for Cento Affairs, Non-Government Central Treaty Organization, S 5.54
Office of United States High Commissioner for Austria, General Publications, S 1.89/4
Office of Water Environmental and Program Information Systems Compendium, EP 2.29/2
Office of Water Operating Guidance and Accountability System, EP 2.29
Office of Water Research and Technology: Annual Report, I 1.1/5
Office Orders, W 34.31
Office Review, Y 3.W 19/1:17
Office Workers, Salaries, Hours of Work, Supplementary Benefits (by cities), L 2.43
Officer Correspondence Courses (series), D 207.208/5
Officer Directory, D 103.71
Officer Personnel Newsletter, D 208.21
Officer Specialty (series), D 101.88
Officer Text (series), D 207.208/6
Officers' Call, M 101.33, D 101.17, D 101.118
Officers in the Marine Corps Reserve, D 214.11/3
Officers of Army in or Near District of Columbia, W 3.81
Officers of Army, Stations of Troops, and List of Garrisoned Towns, W 21.7/2
Officers of Army, Their Families and Families of Deceased Officers, Residing in or Near District of Columbia, W 1.11
Officers of Navy and Marine Corps in District of Columbia, N 1.20
Officers on Active Duty in the Marine Corps, D 214.11
Offices of Processed Products Standardization and Inspection Branch, A 88.43
Official Army and Air Force Register, M 101.19, M 108.8
Official Army National Guard Register, D 12.9
Official Army Register of Volunteer Force of U.S. Army, 1861-65, W 3.12
Official Bulletin–
   Committee on Public Information, Y 3.P 93/3:3
   Federal Radio Commission, RC 1.5
Official Bulletins, I 29.37/5
Official Bulletins, National Trophy Matches, D 101.61
Official Circulars, I 16.9
Official Circulars, V.D., T 27.23
Official Classification of . . . Watering Points, FS 2.75
Official Gazette–
   Adjutant General's Office, D 102.16
   Allied High Commission for Germany, S 1.88
   Control Council for Germany, W 1.73, M 105.9
   Patent and Trademark Office, C 21.5
   Patent Office, I 23.8
   Philippine Islands, W 49.16
Official Gazette [Japanese] English Edition, D 102.16
Official Gazette of Allied High Commission for Germany, S 1.88

Official Gazette of U.S. Patent Office, Trademarks, C 21.5/4
Official Grain Standards of the United States, A 88.6/2:G 761
Official Hours and Holidays to Be Observed by Federal Reserve Offices During Year (date), FR 1.50
Official Journal of the Plant Variety Protection Office, A 88.52
Official List of Commissioned and Other Officers of U.S. Public Health and Marine Hospital Service, T 27.5
Official List of Officers of Officers Reserve Corps, Army, W 3.44
Official List of Rural Free Delivery Offices, P 13.6
Official List of Section 13(f) Securities, SE 1.34
Official National Guard Register, D 112.8
Official Opening and Closing Hours of Board of Governors and Federal Reserve Banks, also Holiday During Month, FR 1.50
Official Opinions, P 6.5
Official Opinions of Attorney-General, W 49.23/5
Official Opinions of the Attorneys General of the United States, J 1.5
Official Parcel Post Zone Keys–
   Hawaii, P 1.25/4
   Puerto Rico, P 1.25/3
   United States, P 1.25/1
   Virgin Islands, P 1.25/2
Official Postal Maps, P 11.8
Official Record, Department of Agriculture, A 1.33
Official Records of Union and Confederal Navies in War of Rebellion, N 16.6
Official Register–
   Life-Saving Service, T 24.5
   National Guard Bureau, D 112.8
Official Register of Officers and Cadets, W 12.5, M 109.11, D 109.7
Official Register of Officers Volunteers in Service of United States, W 3.21
Official Register of the United States, C 3.10, CS 1.31
Official Register (or Blue Book) Biennial, I 1.25
Official Reports of the Supreme Court, Preliminary Prints, Ju 6.8/a
Official Road Maps for Allied Forces Europe, Series M305, D 5.342
Official Roster of Officers and Employees, W 49.5/5
Official Statement of United States Food Administration, Y 3.F 73:19
Official Statement of Wheat Director, Y 3.W 56:5
Official Summary of Security Transactions and Holdings, SE 1.9
Official Table of Distances, W 36.9
Official United States Standards for Beans, A 113.10/3
Official United States Standards for Grain, A 104.6/2, A 113.10
Official United States Standards for Peas & Lentils, A 113.10/4
Official United States Standards for Rice, A 113.10/2
Officials of Department of Agriculture, A 1.89/2
Offshore Scientific and Technical Publications, I 72.14, I 72.14/2
Offshore Stats, I 72.18
OFPP Pamphlets, PrEx 2.22
OGC Adviser, GA 1.24
Ogden Service Center Telephone Users Guide, T 22.48/5
OH (series), HE 20.2810
OHA Law Journal, HE 3.66/3, SSA 1.5/3
OHA Law Reporter, HE 3.66
OHA Newsletter, HE 3.66/2
OHA Telephone Directory, HE 3.51/6
OHD, Grants Administration Manual, TN-(series), HE 1.709
Ohio River, D 103.66/2
Ohio River Charts, W 7.13/3
Ohio River Flood Plain Charts, W 7.13/4
Ohio River Summary and Forecasts, C 55.110
OHM Newsletter, TD 9.12
OHRO Digest, HE 20.6019
OIG Highlights, I 1.1/7-2
OIG Communique, HH 1.109
OIG News, A 1.80/3
Oil and Gas Field Code Master List, E 3.34/2
Oil and Gas Investigation Charts, I 19.25/5, I 19.92
Oil and Gas Investigations Maps, I 19.25/4, I 19.93
Oil and Hazardous Material Program Series, EP 2.11
Oil Burners, C 3.93
Oil Contract Bulletin, D 11.3
Oil Crops Outlook and Situation Report, A 93.23/2
Oil Crops, Situation and Outlook Yearbook, A 93.23/2-2
Oil Import Totals, I 64.11

Oil Lands Leasing Act of 1920 with Amendments and Other Laws Relating to Mineral Lands [March 2, 1919], Y 1.2:Oi 5
Oil Market Simulation Model, E 3.55
Oil Pollution Abstracts, EP 1.25/2
Oil Pollution Research Newsletter, EP 1.25
Oil Shales and Tar Sands, E 1.99
OILA Memorandum Monthly Service of Office of International Labor Affairs, L 1.21
Oilseeds and Oilseed Products, A 67.30:Oi 5
OIR Reports, S 1.57
OIT Technical Reports, E 1.140
OJJDP Annual Report on Missing Children, J 32.17
OJJDP Discretionary Program Announcement, J 32.22
OJJDP Fact Sheet (series), J 32.21
OJJDP Fiscal Year, Program Plan, J 32.10/2
OJJDP News @ a Glance, J 32.25
OJJDP Report & Research Report, J 32.20/3
OJJDP Summary & Program Summary, J 32.20/2
OJJDP Summary & Research Summary, J 32.20
OJJDP Youth in Action Fact Sheet, J 32.21/2
OKARNG- (series), D 12.12/2
Oklahoma, Governor, Annual Reports, 1891-1907, I 1.26
Old-Age and Survivors Insurance, Regulations, FS 3.6/2
Old-Age Insurance Operating Statistics Review, SS 1.33
Older Americans in Action, AA 2.9
Omaha, Trans-Mississippi and International Exposition, 1898, S 6.16
OMAT-O-GRAM, for Staff Members of Office of Manpower, Automation, and Training, L 1.41
OMB Submission, VA 1.83
OMBE Outlook, News from the Office of Minority Business Enterprise, C 1.57/2
Omega Plotting Charts, D 5.356
Omega Plotting (31) Charts Series 7500, D 5.347
Omega Plotting (112) Charts Series 7600, D 5.347/2
Omega Tables, D 5.317
Omnibus Solicitation for the Small Business Innovative Research, HE 20.28
Omnibus Solicitation of the Public Health Service for Small Business Innovation Research (SBIR) Grant Applications, HE 20.3047/2
On Call Positions in Spot Cotton Based on New York Cotton Futures Reported by Merchants in Special Account Status, Y 3.C 73/5:11
On Guard, Bureau of Motor Carrier Safety Bulletin, TD 2.303
On Guard Series, Y 3.F 73:11
On-Highway Diesel Prices, E 3.13/8
On Scene, National Maritime SAR [Search and Rescue] Review, TD 5.24
On The Beat: Community Oriented Policing Services J 1.107
On the Job Training Program, JP Series, D 301.38/5
On the Record, AE 1.116
ONC - Operational Navigation Charts, D 5.322
Oncology Overview, NCI/ICRDB, HE 20.3173/3
ONDCP Brief, PrEx 1.3/3
ONDCP Bulletin, PrEx 1.3/2
1A Circular (series), D 101.4/4
1A Pamphlets (series), D 101.22/9-2
O-NET (Online Database), L 1.96
One Hundred Companies Receiving the Largest Dollar Volume of Prime Contract Awards, D 1.57
One Hundred Years of Federal Forestry, A 1.75:402
102 Monitor, Environmental Impact Statements, PrEx 14.10, EP 1.76
Onion Stocks, A 88.12/25
Online Literature Searching and Databases, EP 1.21/10
ONO [Office of Naval Research] Reports, D 210.15
ONR Report ARC (series), D 210.15
ONR Reports, DR- (series), D 210.15
ONR Symposium Reports, D 210.5
ONR Technical Report RLT (series), D 210.8/3-2
OOE, C 55.13
OPA Bulletins for Schools and Colleges, Pr 32.4224
OPA Chart Book Releases, Pr 32.4250
OPA Economic Data Series, Pr 33.307
OPA Food Guide for Retailers, Pr 32.4241
OPA Information Leaflets for Schools and Colleges, Pr 32.4240
OPA Manual News Letters, Pr 32.4248
OPA Trade Bulletins, Pr 32.4244
OPE Reports, HE 20.4034
OPEC Direct Investment in the United States, C 61.25
Open Season for Game, A 5.9
Open Window, the Newsletter of the National Library of Education, ED 1.345
Open-File Reports, I 19.76, I 28.155
Opening Doors, HE 20.9120
Opening Fall Enrollment in Higher Education, FS 5.254:54043, HE 5.254:54023

Opening Indian Reservations, I 21.14

Open-Market Money Rates and Bond Prices, FR 1.44

Opera-Musical Theater, Application Guidelines, NF 2.8/2-12

Operating Bank Offices Insured by the Federal Deposit Insurance Corporation, as of [date], Y 3.F 31/8:18

Operating Data from Monthly Reports of Large Telegraph Cable, and Radiotelegraph Carriers, CC 1.13

Operating Data from Monthly Reports of Telephone Carriers Filing Annual and Monthly Reports, CC 1.14

Operating Experience, Bulletin Information Report, Y 3.N 88:13

Operating Instruction for Merchant Marine Examination Questions Books, Navigation General Book 3, TD 5.57/2

Operating Manual for Qualification Standards for General Schedule Positions, PM 1.8/14

Operating Manual Update, PM 1.14/3-2

Operating Procedure Memorandum, Y 3.W 89/2:30, FW 4.8

Operating Reactors Licensing Actions Summary, Y 3.N 88:35

Operating Revenues and Operating Expenses by Class of Service, Class 1 Steam Railways in United States, IC 1 ste.32

Operating Revenues and Operating Expenses Class 1 Steam Railway in United States, IC 1 ste.19

Operating Revenues and Operating Expenses of Class I Railroads in the United States, IC 1 ste.19/3

Operating Revenues and Operating Expenses of Large Steam Roads with Annual Operating Revenues Above $25,000,000, IC 1 ste.20

Operating Statistics of Class 1 Steam Roads, Freight and Passenger Service, IC 1 ste.21

Operating Statistics of Large Railroads, Selected Items, IC 1 ste.22

Operating Units Status Report, Licensed Operations Reactors Data for Decisions, Y 3.N 88:15

Operating Year Guidance, EP 1.8/11

Operation and Effect of the Domestic International Sales Corporation Legislation, T 1.54

Operation and Effect of the International Boycott Provisions of the Internal Revenue Code, T 1.56

Operation and Effect of the Possessions Corporation System of Taxation, T 1.55

Operation Breakthrough, Site Planner's Report (series), HH 1.48

Operation Division Circulars, A 1.45

Operation Golden Eagle, Directory of Federal Recreation Areas Changing Entrance, Admission and User Fees, I 66.16

Operation of the Colorado River Basin, Projected Operations, Annual Report, I 27.71

Operation Papers, CS 1.71/8

Operation Studies, D 106.19

Operational Applications Laboratory, Air Force Cambridge Research Center, OAL- TM, D 301.45/37

Operational Navigation Charts, D 5.354

Operations and Enforcement Office: Annual Report, TD 9.14

Operations Instructions (series), J 21.6/2-2

Operations, Instructions, Regulations, and Interpretations, J 21.6/2

Operations Letters, Pr 32.4418

Operations of National Weather Service, C 55.111

Operations of Office of Private Resources, S 18.1/2

Operations of the Bureau of Commercial Fisheries Under the Saltonstall-Kennedy Act, I 49.48

Operations of the Employment Security Program, FS 3.3/a3

Operations of the Trade Agreements Program, TC 1.14/3, ITC 1.24

Operations of the Weather Bureau, C 30.83

Operations Report, S 18.16

Operators Letters, HH 2.21

OPICNews, OP 1.10

Opinion Digest, SBA 1.47

Opinion Papers, LC 1.50

Opinions, Ju 3.7, Ju 6.6, Ju 12.7, L 28.8

Opinions and Orders, TD 1.126

Opinions and Decisions, S 3.34/6

Opinions of Attorney General, J 1.5

Opinions of Judge Advocate General, Army, W 10.9

Opinions of Supreme Court, Ju 6.8/1b

Opinions of the Office of Legal Counsel, J 1.5/4

Opinions of the Solicitor of the Department of the Interior Relating to Indian Affairs, I 1.69/9

Opinions United States Tax Court Reports, Ju 11.7/a

Opium and Narcotic Laws [February 9, 1909], Y 1.2:Op 3

OPM, the Year in Review, PM 1.1

Opportunities Abroad for Educators, ED 1.19, IA 1.29

Opportunities Abroad for Teachers (series), HE 5.99/2, ED 1.19

Opportunities for Teachers Abroad, HE 19.112

Opportunities for Teachers of French Language and Literature, FS 5.64/3

Opportunities for Teachers of Spanish and Portuguese, FS 5.64/4

Opportunity, PrEx 10.27

Opportunity II, CSA 1.11

OPS Guides, ES 3.6/7

OPS Trade Aid TA (series), ES 3.6/15

OPS Trade Bulletins, ES 3.9

OPS Trade Guide TP (series), ES 3.6/13

Optics and Spectroscopy [abstracts], C 41.63

Oral Argument [before a panel of the Review Board], CC 1.42/4

Oral Biology and Medicine Study Section, HE 20.3001/2:Or 1

ORD Annual Report, EP 1.1/6

ORD Engineering Highlights, EP 1.110

ORD Publications Announcement, EP 1.21/6-2

ORD Publications Summary, EP 1.21/6

ORD Science Highlights, EP 1.110/2

Order of Battle of United States Land Forces, D 114.10

Order of Duties, etc., W 44.6/5

Order Point Bulletin, T 22.2/15:7141

Order Series, A 55.36

Orderly Liquidation of Stock of Agricultural Commodities Held by the Commodity Credit Corporation, A 1.102

Orders:-
  Bureau of Indian Affairs, I 20.20
  Civil Aeronautics Board, C 31.207
  Consumer Product Safety Commission, Y 3.C 76/3:6-2
  Department of the Interior, I 1.63
  Federal Energy Regulatory Commission, E 2.10
  Federal Power Commission, FP 1.19
  Federal Railroad Administration, TD 3.8/2
  Interstate Commerce Commission, IC 1.9
  Publications Relating to the Care of Animals and Poultry, A 77.218
  United States Postal Service, P 1.19

Orders and Regulations, D 103.6/2

Orders As to Procedure, Ju 3.10/2

Orders, Notices, Rulings and Decisions Issued by Hearing Examiners and by the Commission in Formal Docketed Proceedings before the Federal Maritime Commission, FMC 1.10/a2

Orders, Series 1930, P 1.19/2

Orders to Officers, U.S.N., N 17.9

Ordnance Bulletins, W 99.17/16

Ordnance Circular Letters, N 18.9

Ordnance Corps Manuals, D 105.6/2

Ordnance Corps Pamphlets, D 105.9

Ordnance Department Circulars, W 34.4/3, W 34.4/4

Ordnance Department Orders, D 105.8

Ordnance Department Safety Bulletin, D 105.7

Ordnance Equipment Charts, W 34.39

Ordnance Field Service Bulletins, W 34.26, W 34.32

Ordnance Field Service Technical Bulletins, W 34.36

Ordnance Fiscal Bulletin, W 34.30

Ordnance Instructions for Navy, N 18.5

Ordnance Magazine, W 34.29

Ordnance Manual, W 34.7/1

Ordnance Materials Research Offices, Watertown Arsenal, Omro Publications, D 105.13/3

Ordnance Memoranda, W 34.10

Ordnance Notes, W 34.11

Ordnance Orders, W 34.9

Ordnance Pamphlets, OP- (series), D 215.9

Ordnance Publications for Supply Index, W 34.23/3

Ordnance Recruiting Bulletins, W 34.22

Ordnance Recruiting Posters, W 34.29/2

Ordnance Storage and Shipment Charts, W 34.38

Ordnance Supply Manual, W 34.7/2

Ordnance Technical Library Bulletins, W 34.21/3

Ordnance Technical Notes, W 34.27

Oregon and Washington Planned Land Sales, I 53.32

Oregon Annual Data Summary, Water Year, A 57.46/5-3

Organ Site Carcinogenesis Skin, HE 20.3173/2

Organic Chemistry: Air Pollution Studies Characterization of Chemical Structures; Synthesis of Research Materials, C 13.46

Organization and Fact Book, HE 20.3319

Organization and Policy Manual Letters, CS 1.7/3

Organization and Staffing for Full Time Local Health Services, FS 2.80

Organization Charts, Y 3.R 31:20

Organization Directory-
  Adjutant General's Department, W 3.42
  Civilian Production Administration, Pr 32.4830

Organization Directory, U.S. Department of Agriculture, A 60.10

Organization of Army, W 3.50/17

Organization of Federal Executive Departments and Agencies, Y 4.G 74/9-10

Organization Orders, VA 1.17

Organization Regulations, C 31.206/6

Organizational Directory of Key Officials, PM 1.31/2

Organizations Designated Under E.O. 10450, Consolidated List (SCS Form 385), CS 1.63

Organizations Visual Arts, Application Guidelines, NF 2.8/2-15

Organized Reserves Bulletin, W 99.17/17

Organized Reserves Circular, W 99.16/12

Organized Reserves Memorandum, W 99.18/8

Oriental Studies, SI 7.7

Orientation Material, Tribal Operations, Administrative, I 20.49

ORO- (series), HE 20.4113

ORP Contract Reports, EP 6.10/9

ORP/CSD (series), EP 6.10/3

ORP/SID (series), EP 6.10/2

ORRC Study Reports, Y 3.Ou 8:10

OSAHRE Reports: Decisions of the Occupational Safety and Health Review Commission, Y 3.Oc 1:10

OSAP Cultural Competence Series, HE 20.8018/5

OSAP Prevention Monograph (series), HE 20.8018/2

OSAP Put on the Brakes Bulletin, HE 20.8018/4

OSAP Technical Report (Series), HE 20.8018/3

OSC Update, J 21.5/3

OSERS News in Print, ED 1.213, ED 1.85/3

OSFA Program Book, ED 1.29/2

OSHA Documents and Files, L 35.26

OSHA National Training Institute Catalog of Courses, L 35.25/2

OSHA Safety and Health Standards Digests, L 35.6/4

OSHA Standards and Regulations, L 35.6/3

OSPAM- (series), D 105.27

OSRD [reports], Pr 32.413/3

OST-NDER Bulletin, TD 1.43

OST/TST Reports, TD 1.20/3

OSWER Training Course Catalog, EP 1.103

OT Contractor Reports, C 1.60/7

OT- (series), A 108.11

OT Series, L 38.20/6

OT Special Publication (series), C 1.60/2

OT Technical Memorandums, C 1.60/8

OTES (series), C 55.13

Other Carriers [12-month comparisons], C 31.247/2

Other Carriers [quarterly comparisons], C 31.247

Other Regulations and Procedures, C 35.6/3

Other Synthetic and Natural Fuels, E 1.99

OTS Briefs, C 41.102

OTS Technology Guide Circulars, C 35.12

OTT Times, E 1.128

Ottawa National Forest, A 13.28/a

Our Library Presents, ITC 1.9/2

Our Merchant Fleet, MC 1.28

Our Nation's Children, FS 3.212, L 5.49

Our Nation's Highways: Selected Facts and Figures, TD 2.23/6

Our Own Spanish-American Citizens and the Southwest Which They Colonized, I 29.40

Our Public Lands, I 53.12

Our Rivers, I 27.25

Our War, W 3.80

Our Wonder World, I 16.56/3

Outbreaks of Disease Caused by Milk and Milk Products as Reported by Health Authorities as having Occurred in U.S., T 27.42

Outdoor Recreation Action, I 66.17

Outdoor Recreation Grants-In-Aid Manual, I 66.8

Outdoor Recreation Research, I 66.18

Outdoors in the Santa Monica Mountains National Recreation Area, I 29.6/7, I 29.135

Outer Continental Shelf Environmental Assessment Program Final Reports of Principal Investigators, C 55.433

Outer Continental Shelf Environmental Studies Advisory Committee: Publications, I 1.99/2

Outer Continental Shelf Oil and Gas Information Program, Summary Reports (various regions), I 72.9

Outer Continental Shelf Oil and Gas Leasing and Production Program Annual Report, I 72.12/3-2

Outer Continental Shelf Research Management Advisory Board: Annual Report, I 1.99

Outer Continental Shelf Standard, GSS-OCS (series), I 19.73
Outer Continental Shelf Statistical Summary, I 72.12/3-3
Outline Maps, A 36.37
Outline of Agricultural Conservation Program, A 55.44/12
Outlines, LR 1.11
Outlook, ED 1.409, J 16.14, HE 20.3766
Outlook and Situation Reports (various areas), A 93.29/2
Outlook and Situation, Summary, A 93.29/2-17
Outlook and Year-End Economic Review, C 1.41
Outlook Charts, A 36.50
Outlook for Agricultural Exports, A 1.80/2
Outlook for Timber in the United States, A 13.50:20/2
Outlook for U.S. Agricultural Exports, A 93.43
Outpatient Psychiatric Clincis, Community Service Activities, FS 2.22/38-3
Outpatient Psychiatric Clincis, Special Statistical Series Reports, FS 2.22/40
Output of Refineries in United States, I 28.19
Outreach, D 214.31, SBA 1.46
OVC Bulletin, J 34.3
OVC Fact Sheets, J 34.4
OVC's Legal Series Bulletin, J 34.3/3
Over Change Claim Circulars, Y 3.R 13/2:35
Overlap, Measurement Agreement through Process Evaluation, C 13.56
Overseas Business Reports, C 1.50, C 57.11, C 61.12
Overseas Common Carrier Section 214 Applications for Filing, CC 1.36/4
Overseas Employment Opportunities for Educators, D 1.68
Overseas Export Promotion Calendar, C 57.117, C 61.19
Overseas Outlook, LC 19.13/3
Overseas Television Developments, IA 1.16
Overseas Trade Promotion Calendar, C 57.12
Over-the-Counter Brokers and Dealers Registered with Securities & Exchange Commission, SE 1.15
Overview of Endowment Programs, NF 3.15
OWCP Annual Report, L 36.401
Oxygen [abstracts], C 41.50

P

P- (series), ED 1.45/3
P.A.D. Districts Supply/Demand, E 3.11/6-2, E 3.11/6-3, E 3.11/6-4, I 28.18/6, I 28.18/7,
P. and S. Docket, Monthly Report of Action Stockyards Act, A 88.16/5
P. and S. Docket, Monthly Report of Action Taken on Cases Arising Under Packers and Stockyards Act, A 82.14
P.B.A. Circulars, A 49.4
P.C. Producer-Consumer Series, A 55.65
P.D.C. Manuals, CS 1.40
P.P.C. (series), A 77.308/4
P.S. Payroll Savings Bulletin, T 66.16
PACAF [Pacific Air Forces] Basic Bibliographies, D 301.62
Pacesetter, C 1.94
Pacesetters in Innovation, FS 5.220:20103, HE 5.220:20103
Pacific Airman's Guide and Chart Supplement, TD 4.16
Pacific and Arctic Coasts, Alaska, Cape Spencer to Beaufort Sea, C 55.422/9
Pacific Basin Consortium for Hazardous Waste Research Newsletter, E 1.110
Pacific Coast, Alaska, Dixon Entrance to Cape Spencer, C 55.422:8
Pacific Coast and Pacific Islands, TD 5.9:3
Pacific Coast, California, Oregon, Washington, and Hawaii, C 55.422:7
Pacific Coast Salmon Park, C 6.11
Pacific Coast States Fisheries, C 55.309/2
Pacific Coaster's Nautical Almanac, N 11.8
Pacific Flyway, I 49.24/5
Pacific Halibut Fishery Regulations, S 5.35:5
Pacific Marine Environmental Laboratory: Annual Report, C 55.601/2
Pacific Northwest and Alaska Bioenergy Program Yearbook, E 5.12
Pacific Northwest Research Station: Miscellaneous Publications, A 13.129
Pacific Rim Agriculture and Trade Reports: Situation and Outlook Series, A 92.29/2-19
Pacific Summary/Index, I 72.9/7
PACAF [Pacific Air Forces] Basic Bibliographies, D 301.62
Pacesetters in Innovation, FS 5.220:20103, HE 5.220:20103
Pacific Airman's Guide and Chart Supplement, TD 4.16

Pacific and Arctic Coasts, Alaska, Cape Spencer to Beaufort Sea, C 55.422:9
Pacific Coast, Alaska, Dixon Entrance to Cape Spencer, C 55.422:8
Pacific Coast and Pacific Islands, TD 5.9:3
Pacific Coast, California, Oregon, Washington, and Hawaii, C 55.422:7
Pacific Coast Salmon Park, C 6.11
Pacific Coast States Fisheries, C 55.309/2
Pacific Coaster's Nautical Almanac, N 11.8
Pacific Flyway, I 49.24/5
Pacific Halibut Fishery Regulations, S 5.35:5
Pacific Marine Environmental Laboratory: Annual Report, C 55.601/2
Pacific Northwest and Alaska Bioenergy Program Yearbook, E 5.12
Pacific Northwest Environmental Research Laboratory: Quarterly Progress Report, EP 1.19
Pacific Northwest Monthly Precipitation and Temperature, C 55.114
Pacific Northwest Monthly Streamflow Summary, I 19.46/4
Pacific Northwest Water Laboratory: Quarterly Progress Report, EP 2.22
Pacific Northwest Water Resources Summary, I 19.46
Pacific Outer Continental Shelf Studies Program Statistical Reports, I 72.12/3-4
Personnel Research Highlights, PM 1.57
Pacific Region, C 55.118/5, C 55.119
Pacific Salmon Pack, I 49.23
Pacific Waterfowl Flyway Report, I 49.55/2
Package X, Informational Copies of Federal Tax Forms, T 22.2/12
Packaged Fishery Products, C 55.309/2
Packaged Literature Searches (series), C 55.229/3
Packaging Requirements Code, D 7.20:726C
Packers and Stockyards Resume, A 88.16/5-2, A 96.9
Packers and Stockyards Statistical Report, A 113.15
Paid Shipments, Y 3.Ec 74/3:13, Pr 33.909
Paid Shipments (by country), Special Statements, Y 3.Ec 74/3:13-2
Paid Shipments, European and Far East Program, FO 1.9
Paint, Varnish, Lacquer, and Fillers, C 3.94
Pakistan, LC 1.30/2
Pakistan, Index [cumulations], LC 1.30/2-3
Paleoclimate Data Record, C 55.240
Pamphlet EP (series), D 103.43
Pamphlets–
   Civil Service Commission, CS 1.48
   Community Services Administration, CSA 1.9
   Department of the Air Force, D 301.35/3
   Electronic Products (Department of the Army), D 101.22
   Federal Employees' Compensation Office, L 36.309
   Merit Systems Protection Board, MS 1.9
   National Guard Bureau, D 12.8
   Naval Supply Systems Command, D 211.12
   Oceanographer of the Navy, D 218.9
   PAM– (series), NAS 1.75
   Personnel Management Office, PM 1.10
   Veterans Administration, VA 1.19
   Women's Bureau, L 36.112
   Worker's Compensation Programs Office, L 36.409
Pan American Club News, FS 5.35, FS 5.26/a 2
Pan American Financial Conference, 2d, Washington, 1920, T 1.22/2
Pan American Financial Conference, Washington, D.C., May 24, 1915, T 1.22
Pan American Scientific Congress, 3d Lima, Peru, 1924-25, S 5.14/3
Pan American Child Congress, 6th Lima, S 5.34
Panama Canal Company, Annual Report, CZ 1.1
Panama Canal Review, CZ 1.8, Y 3.P 19/2:10
Panama Canal Spillway, CZ 1.11, Y 3.P 19/2:9
Pan-American Congress of Highways, 1st, Buenos Aires, S 5.23
Pan-American Congress on Highways, 2d, Rio de Janerio, S 5.23/2
Pan-American Medical Congress, Washington, 1893, S 5.16
Pan-American Scientific Congress, 2d, Washington, D.C., S 5.14/2
Pan-American Scientific Congress, Santiago, Chile, S 5.14
Pan-American Series, I 16.68
P&SA (series), A 96.10
Panel of International Law, S 1.130/2:L 41
Pan-Pacific Educational Conference, 1st Honolulu, August 1921, S 5.21/2, S 5.22
Pan-Pacific Scientific Conference, 1st Honolulu, 1920, S 5.21/1
Paper Currency of Each Denomination Outstanding, Monthly Statements, T 63.307

Paperboard, C 3.95
Papers Approved for Publication or Presentation, FS 2.22/9
Papers in Education Finance, HE 19.144
Papers in Re, C 31.212, J 1.13
Papers in Re in Circuit Courts, J 1.76
Papers in Re in Court of Appeals, J 1.77
Papers in Re in Court of Claims, J 1.80
Papers in Re in Court of Customs and Patent Appeals, J 1.79
Papers in Re in District Courts, J 1.75
Papers in Re in Patent Office (Interferences), J 1.81
Papers in Re in State Courts of Appeal, J 1.83
Papers in Re in State Supreme Courts, J 1.82
Papers in Re in Supreme Court, J 1.78
Papers in Re, Indexes, J 1.13/3s
Papers in Re Indian Claims Commission, J 1.85
Papers in Re (miscellaneous), J 1.84
Papers in Re [proceedings of inquiry, general investigations, etc.], IC 1.13/2
Papers in Re World War Risk Insurance, J 1.13/2
Papers, [number] Congress, Y 4.Ar 5/2:a
Paper No. DPR (series), E 2.23/2
Papers of American Historical Association, SI 4.5
Papers on the National Health Guidelines, HE 20.6020
Papers Relating to Foreign Relations of the United States, S 1.1
Parachute Jumping, TD 4.6:part 105
Parameters, Journal of the U.S. Army War College, D 101.72
Parent Education Letters, I 16.48
Parent Education Messenger, A 43.14
Parents and Beginning Readers (series), HE 5.91
Paris Air Show News Fillers, C 42.27/2
Paris Air Show Newsletter, C 42.27
Paris, Universal Exposition
   1867, S 6.9
   1878, S 6.10
   1889, S 6.11
   1900, S 6.12
Park Areas and Employment Opportunities for Summer, I 29.110
Park Practice Grist, I 29.72
Park Science, Resource Management Bulletin, I 29.3/4
Park Service Bulletins, I 29.3
Parkinson's Disease and Related Disorders, Citations from the Literature, HE 20.3511
Parkinson's Disease and Related Disorders: Cumulative Bibliography, HE 20.3511/3
Parkinson's Disease and Related Disorders, International Directory of Scientists, HE 20.3511/2
Parklawn Computer Center: Annual Report, HE 20.4036
Parklawn Computer Center: Computer Training Courses, HE 20.4036/2
Parklawn Computer Center Technical News, HE 20.31
Parklawn Training Center, Quarterly Calendar, HE 20.32/2
Parklawn Training Center: Training Catalog, HE 20.32
Parks, I 29.85
Parole in the United States, J 29.12/2
Parole Series, HE 17.16
Participation in Adult Education, ED 1.123
Participation Loan Transactions, FHL 1.17
Participation of American and Foreign-Flag Vessels in Shipments under United States Foreign Relief Programs, C 3.164:976
Participation of Principal National Flags in United States Oceanborne Foreign Trade, C 39.221
Particle Accelerators, E 1.99
Partner Update, E 1.120/2
Partners in Prevention Update, HE 20.3182/4
Partnership for Health News, FS 2.319, HE 20.2559
Parts Manufacturer Approvals, TD 4.2/11
Parts Specification Management for Reliability, D 4.9
Passenger Traffic Statements (other than commutation) of Class 1 Steam Railways in the United States Separated Between Coach Traffic and Parlor and Sleeping Car Traffic, IC 1 ste.40
Passenger Traffic Statistics (other than commutation) of Class I Steam Railways in the United States Separated Between Coach Traffic and Parlor and Sleeping Car Traffic, IC 1 ste.39
Passenger Train Performance of Class I Railroads in the United States, IC 1 ste.37
Passenger Travel between United States and Foreign Countries [annual summary reports], J 21.13
Passengers Denied Confirmed Space, C 31.268, CAB 1.9
Passport Control Acts [February 1, 1917], Y 1.2:P 26
Passport Office [newsletter], S 1.27/3
Passport Series, S 1.27

Patent Abstract Section, C 21.5/a 8
Patent Abstract Series, C 1.33
Patent and Trademark Office Notices, C 21.5/4-2
Patent Attorneys and Agents Available to Represent
Inventors Before the United States Patent
Office, C 21.9/2
Patent Calendar, Ju 7.7/2
Patent Laws, C 21.7
Patent Office News Letter, C 21.13
Patent Profiles, C 21.25
Patent Public Advisory Committee Annual Report, C
21.1/4
Patentee/Assignee Index, C 21.27
Patents, C 21.23
Patents and Trademarks, ASSIGN, C 21.31/13
Patents Assign, U.S. Patents Assignments Recorded at
the USPTO, C 21.31/4
Patents Assist, Full Text of Patent Search Tools, C
21.31/5
Patents BIB, C 21.31/2
Patents BIB and Patents SNAP, C 21.31/16
Patents Class, Current Classifications of US Patents, C
21.31/3
Patents Snap, Concordance of U.S. Patent Application
Serial Numbers to U.S. Patent Numbers, C
21.31/6
Pathologist; News Letter for Extension Workers
Interested in Plant Disease Control, A 43.20
Pathology A Study Section, HE 20.3001/2:P 27
Pathology B Study Section, HE 20.3001/2:P 27/2
Patient Movement Data, State and Mental Hospitals, FS
2.22/46
Patients in Hospitals for Mental Disease, C 3.59/2
Patients in Mental Institutions, FS 2.59
Patrols with Park Rangers, I 29.42
Patterns of Global Terrorism, S 1.138
Patterns for Progress in Aging, HE 1.211
Patterns for Progress in Aging Case Studies, FS 1.13/3,
FS 14.9/5
Patterns of Foreign Travel in the U.S., C 47.18
Patterns of Industrial Growth (series), C 41.90/5
Pavements and Soil Trafficability Information Analysis
Center, PSTIAC Reports, D 103.24/12
Pay and Supply Instructions, Circulars, N 24.26, T
47.8/2
Pay Structure of the Federal Civil Service, PM 1.10/2-4
Pay Structure on the Federal Civil Service, CS 1.48:33
Pay Tables for Use of Pay Officers, N 20.5
Payload Flight Assignments NASA Mixed Fleet, NAS
1.81
PBGC [Pension Benefit Guaranty Corporation] Fact
Sheets, L 1.51/5
PCMR Newsbreak, HE 23.109
PD News, Special Editions, T 63.213
Peace and War, United States Foreign Policy, S 1.2:P
31/8
Peace Conference, Paris, 1919, S 3.28
Peace Corps in [various countries], AA 1.17
Peace Corps News, S 19.9
Peace Corps Opportunity Newsletter of Special Interest
to Professional and Technical People, S
19.13
Peace Corps Program and Training Journal Manual
Series, AA 4.8/2
Peace Corps Program Directory, S 19.16
Peace Corps Programs and Training Journal, AA 4.10/2
Peace Corps Times, AA 4.10/2, PE 1.9
Peace Corps Volunteer, S 19.11/2
Peace Corps Volunteer, Quarterly Statistical Summary, S
19.11
Peace Essay Contest, Y 3.P 31:4
Peace Watch, Y 3.P 31:15-2
Peaceworks (series), Y 3.P 31:19
Peanut Letters, A 55.38
Peanut Market News, A 88.10
Peanut Millers List, A 92.14/3
Peanut Processors List, A 88.10/6, A 92.14/4
Peanut Reports, A 82.10
Peanut Shellers and Crushers List, A 88.10/3
Peanuts, Stocks and Processing, A 88.10/2, A 88.10/2-
2, A 105.29
Peat, I 28.107/2
Peat Producers in United States, I 28.107
Pecan Report, Louisiana Crop Reporting Service, A
88.10/5
Pedestrian Laws in the United States, October 1974,
TD 8.5/2:3/3
Pell Grant Formula, ED 1.45/2
Pell Grant Payment Schedule, ED 1.45/3-2
Pennsylvania Anthracite, I 28.49/2
Pennsylvania Anthracite Distribution, E 3.11/3-3
Pennsylvania Anthracite Weekly, E 3.11/3

Pension Building, Annual Reports on Construction of,
1883-87, I 1.27
Pension Cases, Decisions, I 1.55
Pension Decisions, I 24.8
Pension Insurance Data Book:PBGC Single-Employer
Program, Y 3.P 38/2:12
Pension Laws [June 25, 1918], Y 1.2:P 38/2
People Land and Water, I 1.116
Percent Changes in Gross Average Hourly Earnings
Over Selected Periods, L 2.63/2, L 2.63/3
Percent Changes in Gross Hourly and Weekly Earnings
over Selected Periods, L 2.63
Performance, PM 1.32
Performance Guides (series)-
Army Department, D 101.107/3-2
Forest Service, A 13.65/12-2
Performance Evaluation Summary Analysis-
Mycology, HE 20.7037
Bacteriology, HE 20.7037/2
Parasitology, HE 20.7037/3
Performance Monitoring System: Summary of Lock
Statistics, D 103.57/12
Performance Plan, Fiscal Year...and Revised Final Fiscal
Year...Performance Plan, SSA 1.2:P41
Performance Profiles of Major Energy Producers, E 3.37
Performance, Story of the Handicapped, PrEx 1.10/3
Performing Arts, LC 1.46
Periodic Inspection Reports, D 103.310
Periodic Reports of Agricultural Economics, Economic
Research Service, Statistical Reporting
Service, A 1.99
Periodic Supplement, Selected United States
Government Publications, GP 3.17/3
Periodicals and Serials Received in the Library of the
National Bureau of Standards, C 13.10
Periodicals Currently Received in NIH Library, FS
2.22/13-3
Periodicals Supplement, GP 3.8/5
Periodontal Diseases Advisory Committee, HE
20.3001/2:P 41
Periscope, J 16.16
Perlite in (year), I 28.133
Permanent Court of International Justice, S 1.29
Permanent International Association of Road Congress,
S 5.31
Permanent Mass Layoffs and Plant Closings, L 2.3/36
Permit Valuation and Number of New Dwelling Units
Provided in Housekeeping and Dwellings
Authorized in Metropolitan Area of
Washington, D.C. by Type of Dwelling and
Source of Funds, L 2.51/7
Permuted Medical Subject Headings, HE 20.3612/3-3
Personal Computer-Annual Energy Outlook, E 3.1/5
Personal Finance Companies, Installment Loans to
Consumers, C 18.222
Personal Panorama, C 4.46
Personal Weather Estimated from Estate Tax Returns
Filed during Calendar Year, T 22.35/2:W 37
Personnel, W 3.43
Personnel Advisory Series, CS 1.82
Personnel and Personnel Practices in Public
Institutions for Delinquent Children, FS 2.13
Personnel Appeals Board, Annual Report, GA 1.1/2
Personnel Bibliography Series, CS 1.61/3, PM 1.22/2
Personnel Bulletins-
Indian Affairs Bureau, I 20.28
Interior Department, I 1.73
Government Printing Office, GP 1.20
Labor Department, L 1.3/2
Personnel Office, Department of Agriculture, A
49.3/2
Personnel Circular Letters, VA 1.4/2
Personnel Circulars, A 1.44, A 49.4/2
Personnel Development for Vocational Education, HE
19.124
Personnel Handbook, Series P-1, Position Description
and Salary Schedules, Transmittal Letters, P
1.31
Personnel Handbooks, P 1.31/5
Personnel Instructions, L 1.25
Personnel Law: Civilian Personnel and Military
Personnel, GA 1.5/13
Personnel Literature, CS 1.62, PM 1.16
Personnel Management Publications, I 1.73/2
Personnel Management Reform, Progress in State and
Local Governments, PM 1.11/3
Personnel Management Series, CS 1.54, PM 1.28
Personnel Management Training Center: Course
Catalog, CS 1.65/10
Personnel Management Training Division I, PM 1.28/2
Personnel Management Training Units, L 1.38
Personnel Measurement Research and Development
Center, CS 1.71
Personnel Methods Series, CS 1.58

Personnel Needs and Training for Biomedical and
Behavioral Research, HE 20.3036/2
Personnel of Naval Shores Establishment, D 204.8
Personnel Records and Files, CS 1.41/4:293-31
Personnel Research and Development Center: Technical
Memorandum, CS 1.71/4
Personnel Research Reports, CS 1.71/7, PM 1.43
Personnel Research Series, A 49.9
Personnel Section Bulletins, T 47.15
Personnel Statistics Reports, CS 1.33
Persons Furnishing Cars to or on Behalf of Carriers by
Railroad or Express Companies, Summary of
Quarterly Reports, IC 1.18
Persons of Spanish Origin in the United States,
Advance Report, C 3.186/14
Perspective, D 208.22
Perspectives, CR 1.12, D 104.28
Perspectives in Defense Management, D 5.16
Perspectives in Reading Research, ED 1.317/3
Perspectives on Crime and Justice, Lecture Series, J
28.24/3-2
Perspectives on Education Policy Research, ED 1.336/
2
Perspectives on Medicaid and Medicare Management,
HE 22.411
Perspectives on Policing (series), J 28.27
Pest Alert (NA-TP series), A 13.52/10-4
Pesticide Data Program, A 88.60
Pesticide Registration Eligibility Decisions (REDs),
EP 5.27
Pesticide Registration Standards, EP 5.17
Pesticide Review (year), A 82.76
Pesticide Station for (year), A 82.76
Pesticides Abstracts, EP 5.9
Pesticides and Toxic Substances Monitoring Report,
EP 5.16
Pesticides Documentation Bulletin, A 17.20
Pesticides Monitoring Journal, Pr 37.8:En 8/P 43,
PrEx 14.9, Y 3.F 31/18:9
Pesticides Study Series, EP 2.25
PETC Review, E 1.112
Petitions, Y 3.Sp 2:5
Petitions for Certiorari and Briefs on Merits and in
Opposition for U.S. in Supreme Court of U.S.,
J 1.19/6
Petitions for Patent Waiver, NAS 1.18/3
Petroleum, E 1.99
Petroleum Economy [abstracts], C 41.55/3
Petroleum Forecast, I 28.41
Petroleum Imports Reporting System, Weekly Situation
Report, FE 1.9/2
Petroleum Market Shares, FE 1.12
Petroleum Market Shares, Report on Sales of Refined
Petroleum Products, E 3.13
Petroleum Market Shares, Report on Sales of Retail
Gasoline, E 3.13/2
Petroleum Market Shares, [reports on various subjects],
FE 1.12/2, E 3.13/3
Petroleum Marketing, E 3.13/4-2
Petroleum Marketing Monthly, E 3.13/4
Petroleum Products, Secondary Inventories and Storage
Capacity, C 3.213
Petroleum Products Survey, PPS- (series), I 28.18/3
Petroleum Refineries in the United States and Puerto
Rico, I 28.17/2, E 3.11/5-4
Petroleum Refinery Statistics, I 28.17, I 28.18
Petroleum Situation Report, FE 1.9
Petroleum Statement, I 28.18/2, I 28.18/4, E 3.11/5, E
3.11/5-2
Petroleum Statistics, I 22.9, I 22.9/2
Petroleum Supply Annual, E 3.11/5-5
Petroleum Supply Monthly, E 3.11/5
Petroleum Worker [abstracts], C 41.55/2
PHA Grants Administration Manual, HE 20.8/2
PHA Honor Awards for Design Excellence, HH 3.10
PHA Low-Rent Housing Bulletins, HH 3.3/4
Pharmacology and Biorelated Chemistry Program:
Biennial Report, HE 20.3461/3
Pharmacology Research Associate Program, HE
20.3461/2
Pharmacology Study Section, HE 20.3001/2:P 49
Pharmacology-Toxicology Program, HE 20.3461
Pharmacology-Toxicology Program Committee, HE
20.3001/2:P 49/2
Pharmacy Newsletter, HE 20.3054
Pharmacy Residences in Public Health Service
Hospitals, FS 2.89/3
Philadelphia, International Exhibition, S 6.13
Philadelphia, Sesquicentennial International
Exposition, S 6.22
Philatelic Dedicatory Lecture Series, SI 3.12
Philatelic Releases, P 1.29/3
Philippine Agricultural Review, W 49.21/7
Philippine Copra Market, C 18.199

Philippine Craftsman, W 49.6/5
Philippine Farmer, W 49.21/10
Philippine Health Service, Monthly Bulletin, W 49.15/6
Philippine Insurgent Records, W 6.10
Philippine Islands Census, 1903; Bulletins, C 3.8/2
Philippine Islands Census, 1903; Reports, C 3.8/1
Philippine Journal of Agriculture, W 49.55/5
Philippine Journal of Science, W 49.31/5
Philippine Tariffs, W 6.11
Phosphate Crop Year, I 28.119/2
Phosphate Rock, I 28.119/3
Phosphate Rock in (year), I 28.119
Photo Series, A 1.100/2
Photoelastic Group Reports, I 27.33
Photogrammetric Instructions, C 4.48
Photographs of A-Bomb Test, Operation Doorstep, Yucca Flat, Nevada, March 17, 1953, FCD 1.11/2
Photographs of Scenes in National Parks (by name of park), I 29.32
Photographs of Scenes of National Parks, etc., I 29.29
PHPC (Public Housing Primary Care Program) Bulletin, HE 20.9121
PHS Dental Notes, HE 20.8/4
PHS Grants Administration Manual, HE 20.8/2
PHS Grants Policy Memorandum, HE 1.6/7-3, HE 20.8/3
PHS Public Advisory Groups, Authority, Structures, Functions, HE 20.2:Ad 9/2
PHS Rehabilitation Guide Series, FS 2.6/2, FS 2.6/6
Physical Education Series, I 16.40
Physical Fitness Research Digest, HE 20.110, Pr 37.8:P 56/2 R 31/2
Physical Fitness/Sports Medicine Bibliography, HE 20.111
Physical Land Surveys, A 76.212, A 80.2012, A 80.510
Physical Sciences, C 51.17/9
Physical Sciences Research Papers, D 301.45/40
Physician Requirements for [various subjects] (series), HE 20.6024
Physicians Memorandum, HE 20.36/2
Physician's Pocket Reference to International List of Causes of Death, C 3.54
Physics, C 51.9/27
Physics and Mathematics, PrEx 7.22/11
Physics of Metals and Metallography [abstracts], C 41.54/2
Physics Research, E 1.99
Physiological Chemistry, Study Section, HE 20.3001/2:P 56/3
Physiology Study Section, HE 20.3001/2:P 56/2
PIC Highlights, HE 1.62
Picture of Subsidized Households, HH 1.124
Picture Sheets, A 56.20, A 77.320
Picture Story, A 1.100
Picture Story (series), A 21.26
Pig Crop Report, A 88.16/3
Pig Crop Report, Louisiana Crop Reporting Service, A 88.16/3-2
PI-H (series), ES 3.11
Pilot Chart of–
   Central American Waters, N 6.24, M 202.15, D 203.15
   Greenland and Barnets Seas, N 6.15/4
   Indian Ocean, N 6.17, M 202.16, D 203.16
   North Atlantic Ocean, N 6.15, M 202.17, D 203.17
   North Pacific Ocean, N 6.16, M 202.19, D 203.19
   South Atlantic Ocean, N 6.20, M 202.18, D 203.18
   South Pacific Ocean, N 6.12, M 202.20, D 203.20
   Upper Air, North Atlantic Ocean, N 6.28
   Upper Air, North Pacific Ocean, N 6.29
Pilot Chart of Indian Ocean, D 203.16
Pilot Chart of North Atlantic Ocean, D 203.17
Pilot Chart of North Pacific Ocean, D 203.19
Pilot Chart of South Atlantic Ocean, D 203.18
Pilot Chart of South Pacific Ocean, D 203.20
Pilot Charts of Central American Waters, D 203.15
Pilot Cities Program, J 1.46/2
Pilot Rules, T 38.8, C 15.8
Pilot Rules for Certain Inland Waters of Atlantic and Pacific Coasts of Gulf of Mexico, C 25.9
Pilot Rules for Rivers whose Waters Flow into Gulf of Mexico and Their Tributaries and Red River of the North, C 25.8
Pilot Schools, TD 4.6:part 141
Piloting and Ocean Navigation Pamphlets, N 24.23
Pipe Line Carriers, Annual Guide Prices and Indices, IC 1 pip.9
Pipeline, D 301.91
Pipeline Accident Reports, TD 1.118
Pipeline Accident Reports: Brief Format, NTSB-PAB-(series), TD 1.118/3

Pipeline Accident Reports, NTSB-PAR-(series), TD 1.118
Pipeline Accident/Incident Summary Reports, TD 1.118/4
Pitman-Robertson Quarterly, I 49.29
PK-M (series), ES 3.6/12
Placement Activities, Pr 32.5218
Places where Civil Service Examinations are Held, CS 1.28:2300
Plain Talk About [various subjects], HE 20.8128
Plan of Work for Cooperative Hydrology Investigations, I 53.47
Planners and Project Managers Annual Report, D 1.1/11
Planners and Project Managers Program, D 103.132
Planning and Development Reports, CA 1.11
Planning, Current Literature, FW 1.15, C 37.12
Planning Division, Instruction and Procedure, GP 1.23/3
Planning Division Process and Procedures, D 301.61
Planning for Housing Security (series), HH 1.6/11
Planning Status Reports, FP 1.29
Planning Survey Memorandum, A 22.12, FW 2.9
Planning Your Career, Vocational Guidance Series, I 16.67
Plans for Progress Publications, L 1.54
Plans of Public Buildings, T 39.6/2
Plans Office Technical Reports, NAS 1.39
Plant and Equipment Expenditures of U.S. Business, SE 1.25/6
Plant and Installation Data, PrEx 7.15/3
Plant and Operations Circulars, A 60.4/3
Plant Disease Bulletins, A 19.18
Plant Disease, Decay, Etc., Control Activities of Department of Agriculture, Reports, A 1.90
Plant Disease Posters, A 77.517
Plant Disease Reporter, A 77.511, A 106.21
Plant Disease Reporter Supplements, A 77.512
Plant Disease Survey Special Publications, A 77.520
Plant Immigrants, A 19.16
Plant Inventory, A 77.515, A 106.11
Plant Laboratory [abstracts], C 41.58
Plant Materials Annual Progress Reports, A 57.55
Plant Materials Centers Annual Reports, A 57.54
Plant Pest Control Cooperative Programs, Western Region, Fiscal Year (date), A 77.327/2
Plant Pest News, A 101.23
Plant Quarantine, A 77.217/2
Plant Quarantine Decisions, A 35.6
Plant Quarantine Import Requirements of (country), A 77.339
Plant Quarantine Import Requirements of [various countries], A 101.11
Plant Quarantine Memorandum, A 77.314/2
Plant Regulatory Announcements, A 77.308/5
Plant Requirements, S 18.22
Plant Requirements Reports (series), FO 1.28, S 17.28
Plant Safety Branch Handbooks, FS 2.22/24
Plant Science Literature, Selected References, A 19.22/2, A 17.11
Plant Tours for International Visitors to the United States, C 47.2:P 69
Plant Variety Protection Database, A 88.53/2
Planting Intentions, A 36.38
Plants Under USDA Continuous Inspection, Processed Fruits and Vegetables and Related Products, A 88.43/2
Plastec Reports, D 4.11
Plasted Notes, D 4.11/2
Plastic Paints, Cold Water Paints, and Calcimines, C 3.96
Plastics Technical Evaluation Center: Plastic Reports, D 4.11, D 4.11/2
Platforms of the Democratic Party and the Republican Party, Y 1.2:P 69
Platinum Group Metals, I 28.77
Platinum Group Metals in (year), I 28.77/2
Platinum Metals Reports, I 28.77/1
Platt National Park, Annual Reports, I 1.54
Plays and Pageants, Y 3.W 27/2:12
Pleasantdale Folks; 2d Series, FS 3.18
Pleasure and Business Visitors to U.S. by Port of Entry and Mode of Travel, C 47.15/2
PLCO News, HE 20.3194
Plentiful Foods, A 88.37/3
Plowback, I 29.73
Plumbing Brass, C 3.97
Plumbing Supplies Reports, C 18.118
PM Circular, P 1.12/6-2
PM (series), L 1.58/2
PMA Procedure Check List, A 82.63
PMG [Poultry Marketing Guides] (series), A 88.26/5
PMS Blue Book, HE 20.4001/2
PNERL Working Papers, EP 1.37/2

P-90 International Population Statistics Reports, C 3.205
Pocket Congressional Directory, Y 4.P 93/1:1 P
Pocket Data Book, C 56.243/3
Pocket Data Book, USA (year), C 3.134/3
Pocket Guides to [country], W 109.119, W 109.215, D 2.8, D 101.22:360-400
Pocket Manuals PM (series), FCD 1.6/8, Pr 34.761/5, PrEx 4.12/6, D 13.8/2
POCS Events, I 72.12/6
POCS Reference Papers (series), I 1.98/2, I 53.29
POCS Technical Paper, I 1.98/3, I 53.29/2
Point to Point Microwave Radio Service, CC 1.36/8
Point Value Charts, Pr 32.4245
Poison Control Statistics, HE 20.4019
Poisonous Snakes of the World, D 206.6/3:Sn 1
Pole Attachment Filings, CC 1.47/5
Pole Series, C 18.119
Policies and Trends in Municipal Waste Treatment (series), EP 1.26
Policy and Programs Series, L 35.17
Policy Briefs, Action Guides for Legislators and Government Executives, J 28.8/2
Policy Information Notice (series), HE 20.9118
Policy Letters, D 7.46
Policy Letters (series), PrEx 2.26
Policy Research Studies, S 1.101/8
Policy Studies (series), D 103.57/8
Poliomyelitis Surveillance Summary, HE 20.7011/31
Political Activity and Political Assessments of Federal Office-Holders and Employees, CS 1.34
Political Activity of Government Personnel Commission, Y 3.P 75
Political and Sociological Affairs, PrEx 7.21/5
Political, Sociological and Military Affairs, PrEx 7.15/4, PrEx 7.17/2
Pollutant Identification Research Highlights, EP 1.37/3
Polluting Incidents in and Around U.S. Waters, TD 5.51
Pollution-Caused Fish Kills, FS 2.94, I 67.9
Pollution Prevention Handbook, I 1.77/3
Pollution Prevention News, EP 5.26
Polymer Dividers Imprinted with (SuDocs) Classification Number System to Convert Microfiche House and Senate Reports and Documents into the Congressional Serial Set, Y 1.1/9
Polymer Science and Standards Division, Annual Report, C 13.1/7
POMS Program Operations Manual System, SSA 1.8/2
Popcorn Acreage for Harvest, A 92.11/7
Popcorn Production, A 88.12/14
Poppies and Porticos, a HCRS Heritage Newsletter, I 70.21
Popular Bulletins, W 49.21/8
Popular Publications for Farmer, Suburbanite, Homemaker, Consumer, A 21.9/8:5, A 107.12:5
Popular Study Series; Histories, I 29.45
Population, 2d Series, C 3.940-13/2
Population, 3d Series (by States), C 3.940-37
Population, 4th Series (by States), C 3.940-37/2
Population and Housing (by States), C 3.940-38
Population and Reproduction Research Abstracts, HE 20.3360
Population Bulletins, 1st Series (by States), C 3.37/8
Population Bulletins, 2d Series (by States), C 3.37/9
Population Bulletins, Families, C 3.37/10
Population Characteristics, C 3.186:P-20
Population [Congested Areas], C 3.160
Population Division Working Paper Series, C 3.223/26
Population Estimates and Projection, C 3.186:P-25, C 3.223/27
Population, Outlying Possessions, C 3.940-39
Population Paper Listings (PPL series), C 3.223/25
Population Profile of the United States, Current Population Reports, C 3.186/8
Population Research Committee, HE 20.3001/2:P 81
Population Research Reports, HE 20.3362
Population Research Study Section, HE 20.3001/2:P 81/2
Population Sciences, Index of Biomedical Research , HE 20.3362/5
Population Sciences, Inventory of Private Agency Population Research, HE 20.3362/2-2
Population, Special Reports, C 3.161
Population Trends, C 3.288
Population Trends and Environmental Policy, I 22.10
Populations, 1st Series (by States), C 3.940-13
Population-Weighted Data, C 55.287/60
Porcelain Enameled Flat Ware, C 3.98
Porcelain Plumbing Fixtures (all clay), C 3.99
Port Allocations of [various commodities], A 82.86
Port and Terminal Facilities, W 7.34

Program Memorandum State Survey Agencies, HE 22.28/4

Program Notes, A 88.55, HE 20.6512/6

Program of Water Resources Division, Texas District, and Summary of District Activities, Fiscal Year, I 19.55/2

Program of University Research Report Reprinted, TD 1.20/6-2

Program Operations Manual System, HE 3.6/5

Program Plan by Program Areas for Fiscal Year, HE 20.7121

Program Plan, Fiscal Year (date), J 26.24

Program Plan of the National Institute for Occupational Safety and Health, HE 20.7127

Program Regulation Guides [issued by various departments], HE 1.47/3

Program Report of the United States Travel Service, C 47.1

Program Reports [various subjects], NS 1.37

Program Research and Development Announcements, ER 1.30

Program Results Inventory, J 1.51

Program Solicitation (series), NS 1.33

Program Solicitation, Small Business Innovation Research Program, A 94.16

Program Summary Report, Y 3.N 88:26

Program Year, I 1.105/3

Programme of Competition for Selection of Architect for Building for Department, T 39.10

Programmed Instruction (series), D 101.107/10

Programmed Instruction Workbooks (series), L 38.18

Programmed Lesson (series), D 101.47/7

Programmed Text, USAAVNA PT- (series), D 101.47/5

Programmed Texts, D 103.109/2

Programmer's Manual (series), D 101.107/7

Programs and Plans, Environmental Research Laboratories, C 55.615/2

Programs and Schedules, Services of Supply Staff Course, W 28.11/3

Programs by States, A 55.42/9

Programs for College Teachers of Science, Mathematics, and Engineering, NS 1.12

Programs for the Handicapped, A 1.23/4

Programs (numbered), Y 3.W 27/2:9

Programs of HUD, HH 1.100

Programs, (year), Guide to Programmed Instructional Materials Available to Educators by (date), FS 5.234:34015, HE 5.234:34015

Progress, Y 3.T 25:65

Progress Against Cancer, Report by National Advisory Cancer Council, HE 20.3024, HE 20.3163

Progress Against Cancer (series), HE 20.3169

Progress Analysis, Pr 33.214

Progress Bulletins, General, A 68.8

Progress Check Book (series), D 101.107/15

Progress During. . .Strong-Motion Earthquake in California and Elsewhere, C 4.25/3

Progress in Aging, Y 4.Ag 4/2:Ag 4/5

Progress in American Education, HE 5.210:10064

Progress in Candy Research, Reports, A 77.109

Progress in Fishery Research, I 49.96

Progress in Management Improvement, T 1.43

Progress in Radiation Protection, HE 20.4117

Progress in Rural Development Program, Annual Reports, A 1.85

Progress in Soil and Water Conservation Research, Quarterly Reports, A 77.528

Progress in the Prevention and Control of Air Pollution in (year), Report to Congress, EP 4.16

Progress Maps, FW 2.12

Progress, Missouri River Basin, I 1.80

Progress Notes, D 104.15/5

Progress of Chemistry [abstracts], C 41.53/3

Progress of Education in the U.S. of America, HE 19.133, ED 1.41

Progress of Mathematical Sciences [abstracts], C 41.61/4

Progress of Physical Sciences [abstracts], C 41.52

Progress of Public Education in the United States of America, FS 5.210:10005, HE 5.210:10005

Progress of Public Education in United States of America, FS 5.62

Progress Report–
  Air Service, Engineering Division, W 87.14
  Department of Commerce, C 1.32
  Federal Civil Defense Administration, FCD 1.1/2
  Forest Taxation Inquiry, A 13.21
  Hill-Burton Program, FS 2.96
  National Institute of Health, FS 2.22/10
  National Mental Health Program, FS 2.65
  Northern Rocky Mountain Forest and Range Experiment Station, A 13.30/6

President's Medical Programs for Heart Disease, Cancer, and Stroke, and Related Diseases, FS 2.313

School Facilities Survey, FS 5.46

War Assets Administration, Pr 33.215

Progress Report, Annual Varietal and Environmental Study of Fiber and Spinning Properties of Cottons, A 77.530

Progress Report, Interim Statistical Report, Pr 34.751

Progress Report on Alzheimer's Disease, HE 20.3869

Progress Report on Pesticides and Related Activities, A 1.2:P 43/3

Progress Report on Staff Development, FS 14.220

Progress Report on Staff Development for Fiscal Year, NCSS Report E-3, FS 17.630, HE 17.630

Progress Report to Congress by War Assets Administration, Pr 33.211, Y 3.W 19/8:11

Progress Report to the President, Pr 42.8/3

Progress Report to the Secretary of Education from the President's Advisory Commission on Educational Excellence for Hispanic Americans, ED 1.87

Progress Report USAISC, D 101.1/15

Progress, U.S. Army, D 101.50

Progress–American Women, Y 3.In 8/21:7-2

Progressive Fish Culturist, I 49.35

Project, Y 3.F 31/5:13

Project Analysis Series, Pr 32.5411, I 52.10

Project Connection: Best Strategy (series), HE 20.8221/2

Project DAWN [Drug Abuse Warning Network], Annual Report, J 24.19/2

Project Head Start, HE 1.36

Project Head Start (series), PrEx 10.12, HE 21.212, HE 1.469

Project Independence, FE 1.18

Project Label, Alphabetical Listings by Controlled Generic Drug Ingredients, J 24.24/2

Project Label, Alphabetical Listings by Drug Labeler of Discontinued Products, J 24.24/3

Project Label, Alphabetical Listings by Drug Labeler, J 24.24

Project Label, Alphabetical Listings by Drug Product, J 24.24/4

Project Management Series, PM 1.41

Project Match Monograph, HE 20.8323

Project on the Status and Education of Women, Field Evaluation Draft, ED 1.42/2

Project Phoenix Reports, C 55.623

Project Planning Reports, I 27.44

Project Register, I 67.16

Project Register, Projects Approved Under Sec. 8 of Federal Water Pollution Control Act (Pub. Law 660, 84th Cong.), As Amended and Sec. 3, of Public Works Acceleration Act (Pub. Law 658, 87th Cong.), EP 2.13

Project Register, Waste Water Treatment Construction Grants, EP 1.9/2, EP 1.56/2

Project Reports, N 10.21

Project Skywater, Annual Report, I 27.57

Project Skywater, CRADP DAT Inventory, I 27.57/3

Project Skywater Data Inventory SCPP Season, I 27.57/2

Project Stormfury, Annual Report, D 220.9

Project Summaries, NS 1.39/2

Project Summaries (by subject), A 61.12

Project Summaries FY (year), Center for Building Technology, C 13.59

Project Summary (series), EP 1.89/2

Project Training Series, I 1.71

Projections: Number of Returns to be Filed, T 22.2/13

Projections of Educational Statistics, HE 19.320, ED 1.120

Projections of the Number of Households and Families, C 3.186/15

Projections of the Population of Voting Age, for States, C 3.186/26

Projections, Number of Returns to be Filed, T 22.2/13

Projects and Experiments, LC 19.13/4

Projects, by Field of Activity and County, S 18.29

Projects in Progress, ED 1.33/2-2

Projects Initiated under Title VII, National Defense Education Act, FS 5.234:34013, FS 5.234:34021, HE 5.234:34013, HE 5.234:34021

Projects Operated by Work Projects Administration, Accomplishments on (by States), FW 4.31

Projects Recommended for Deauthorization, Annual Report, D 103.1/4, D 103.22/2

Proliferation Watch, Y 4.G 74/9-11

Prologue, AE 1.111

Prologue, Journal of the National Archives, GS 4.23

Pro-Mimeographs, T 22.30

PROMIS [prosecutor's Management Information System] Research Project Publications, J 1.52

Pro-Monographs, T 54.7

Propane Watch, E 3.13/7

Property, Emergency Procurement and Funds, W 3.50/6

Property Regulations (numbered), VB 1.14

Proposals, P 1.13

Proposals, Advertisements, General Information, etc., N 1.17

Proposals and Specifications, T 18.5

Proposals (and specifications for supplies) for Indian Service, I 20.14

Proposals and Specifications for Supplies, Schedules, P 1.13/2

Proposals for Construction of Public Buildings; Specifications and Proposals for Repairs, etc. at Public Buildings, T 39.7

Proposals for Indian Service, I 20.14

Proposals for [Supplies to Accompany Circular Proposals], W 73.10/2

Proposals Received and Contracts Awarded for Supplies for Indian Service, I 20.11

Proposed Effluent Guidelines, EP 1.8/4-3

Proposed Federal Specifications, Preliminary, GS 2.8/6

Proposed Foreign Aid Program Fiscal Year, Summary Presentation to Congress, S 18.28/a

Proposed Foreign Aid Program, Summary Presentation to Congress, S 18.28

Proposed Mental Retardation Programs, HE 1.23

Proposed Multi-Year Operating Plan, Statistics of Income Division, T 22.2/3, T 22.2/10

Proposed Streamflow Data Program for [State], I 19.59

Proposed Trade Practice Rules, FT 1.16/2

Prosecution of Felony Arrest, J 29.9/4

Prosecutions and Seizures Under the Federal Seed Act, A 88.30/7

Prosecutions Under Act to Regulate Commerce, IC 1 act.6

Prosecutors in State Courts, J 29.11/15

Prospective Plantings, A 105.9/3

Prospective Strawberry Acreage, Louisiana Crop Reporting Service, A 88.12/27

Prospects for Foreign Trade in [various commodities], A 67.30

Protecting Human Subjects, E 1.144

Protection Report (series), A 13.105/4

Protection Services Division [Reports], Pr 32.4427

Protective Construction Series, Pr 32.4409

Protective Structures, Shelter Design Series, D 13.15

Protocall, HE 20.3192, HE 20.3198

Provider Studies Research Note, HE 20.6514

Provisional Estimates of the Population of Counties, C 3.186/20

PS (series), PM 1.48

PS, the Preventive Maintenance Monthly, D 101.87

PSI Highlights, PrEx 1.13

Psittacosis, Annual Summary, HE 20.7011/7

Psoroptic Sheep Scabies Outbreaks in (State), A 77.240

Psychological Warfare School Special Texts, D 101.44

Psychopharmacology Abstracts, HE 20.8109/2

Psychopharmacology Bulletin, HE 20.8109

PTO Pulse, C 21.33

PTSD (Post-Traumatic Stress Disorder) Clinical Quarterly, VA 1.94/2

PTSD Research Quarterly, VA 1.94

Public Acts and Resolutions Relating to Post Office Department and Postal Service, P 1.20

Public Administration Bulletin [for Vietnam], S 18.38

Public Administration Practices and Perspectives, Digest of Current Materials, S 18.24

Public Advisories, IC 1.31

Public Advisory Board, Reports, Y 3.Ec 74/3:7

Public Advisory Committees: Authority, Structure, Functions, HE 20.4022

Public Advisory Committees: Authority, Structure, Functions, Members, HE 20.1000

Public Affairs Abstracts (new series), LC 14.14

[Public Affairs] Booklet PA-B (series), FCD 1.17/2

Public Affairs Bulletin, LC 14.9

Public Affairs Flyer PA-F (series), FCD 1.17

Public Affairs PA (series), FCD 1.13

Public and Indian Housing FY . . . Program Fungins Plan, HH 1.80/2

Public Assistance, FS 3.3/a2, FS 2.13/3

Public Assistance, Annual Statistical Data, FS 14.212, FS 17.13, FS 17.615, HE 17.615

Public Assistance Bureau, Applications: Old- Age Assistance, Aid to Dependent Children, Aid to the Blind [and] General Assistance, FS 3.17

Public Assistance, Costs of State and Local Administration, Services, and Training, FS 17.633, HE 17.633

Public Assistance, Quarterly Review of Statistics for U.S., SS 1.13

Public Assistance Recipients and Cash Payments, HE 3.61

Public Assistance Recipients in Standard Metropolitan Statistical Areas, HE 3.61/2

Public Assistance Reports, HE 17.19

Public Assistance Statistics, HE 3.60, HE 17.610

Public Assistance, Statistics for U.S., SS 1.25/a.1

Public Assistance: Vendor Payments for Medical Care by Type of Service, Fiscal Year Ended (date), HE 17.617

Public Booklet PB (series), Pr 34.764, D 13.11

Public Buildings Act of 1926, with Amendments, Condemnation Laws with Amendments, Public Works and Construction Laws [May 7, 1926], Y 1.2:P 96/3

Public Circulars, T 1.33

Public Construction, GS 1.7

Public Debt and Cash in Treasury, T 9.9

Public Documents Highlights, GP 3.27

Public Documents Highlights, Microfiche Cumulation, GP 3.27/2

Public Elementary and Secondary Education in the United States, ED 1.112/2

Public Elementary and Secondary Education Statistics: School Year, ED 1.328/12

Public Employment in (year), C 3.140/2, C 3.140/2-4

Public Employment Program, Annual Report to Congress, L 1.68

Public Health Bibliography Series, FS 2.21

Public Health Broadcasts, T 27.35

Public Health Bulletins, T 27.12, FS 2.3

Public Health Conference on Records and Statistics, National Meeting Announcement, HE 20.6214/2

Public Health Conference on Records and Statistics, Proceedings, FS 2.122

Public Health Engineering Abstracts, T 27.28, FS 2.13

Public Health Monograph Series, HE 20.2018

Public Health Monographs, FS 2.62

Public Health Personnel in Local Health Units, FS 2.80

Public Health Reports, HE 20.30, HE 20.6011

Public Health Service Bibliography Series, HE 20.11

Public Health Service Film Catalog, FS 2.36/2

Public Health Service Grants and Awards, HE 20.3013

Public Health Service International Postdoctorate Research Fellowships Awards for Study in the United States, HE 20.3709

Public Health Service Posters, HE 20.26/2

Public Health Service Support of Cardiovascular Research, Training and Community Programs, FS 2.22/11-2

Public Health Service Water Pollution Surveillance System, FS 2.84/2

Public Health Service Prospective Payment Activity, HE 20.6516

Public Health Technical Monographs, FS 2.62

Public Hearings, Y 3.Se 5:14

Public Hearings (various cities), Y 3.Al 1:9

Public Housing, FW 3.7, NHA 4.8

Public Housing Management Improvement Program: Technical Memorandums, HH 1.63

Public Humanities Projects, Guidelines and Application Instructions, NF 3.8/2-9

Public Information [releases], TC 1.29

Public Information (series), P 1.36/2

Public Information Communicator (series), FS 14.16

Public Information Series, S 1.71/5

Public Land Statistics, I 53.1/2

Public Law 480, Agricultural Export Activities, Annual Report of the President, Pr 37.13

Public Law 85-742, Safety and Health Administration, Annual Report, L 16.48

Public Laws, S 7.5/3

Public Laws and Resolutions, W 49.7/1

Public Laws with Amendments, W 49.7/2

Public Libraries in the United States, ED 1.134

Public Library Data, ED 1.334/3

Public Mail Series, PMS- (series), NAS 1.74

Public Management Sources, PrEx 2.9

Public Merchandise Warehousing, C 3.102

Public Moneys Depositaries) Circulars, W 3.25

Public Notice, LMNOD-SP- (series), D 103.117

Public Notices, CC 1.37, TC 1.28

Public Notices [concerning irrigation projects], I 27.40

Public Notices (concerning irrigation projects of reclamation service), I 1.49

Public Notices: Petitions for Rule Making Field, CC 1.38

Public Notices: Safety and Special Radio Services, Report, CC 1.39

Public Papers of the Presidents of the United States, AE 2.114, GS 4.113

Public Programs, NF 3.26

Public Relations, HH 1.12

Public Report of the Vice President's Task Force on Combatting Terrorism, PrVp 40.2:T 27

Public Resolutions, GS 4.110/2, S 7.5/2

Public Roads, Journal of Highway Research, TD 2.19

Public Roads Round-Up, C 37.29

Public Safety Newsletter, Y 3.At 7:58

Public Sale Catalog: Aeronautical Charts and Publications, D 5.351/3-2

Public Sale Catalog: Topographical Maps and Publications, D 5.319/3, D 5.351/3

Public School Finance Programs, HE 19.126

Public Sector Labor Relations Information Exchange: Calendar of Events, L 1.66/2

Public Sector Labor Relations Information Exchange [publications], L 1.66

Public Service Office, Series S-, S 1.106/2

Public Sewage Treatment Plant Construction, FS 2.56/2

Public Support for Coastal Zone Management Programs Implementation of the Coastal Zone Management Act of 1972, C 55.32/5

Public Use Data Tape Documentation–

Chest X-Ray, Pulmonary Diffusion, and Tuberculin TeST Results Ages 25-74, HE 20.6226/5-2

Detail Natality, HE 20.6226/2

Divorce Data, Detail, HE 20.6226/4

Fetal Deaths Detail Records, HE 20.6226/11

Interviewer's Manual National Interview Survey, HE 20.6226/8

Medical Coding Manual and Short Index, HE 20.6226/9

Medical History, Ages 12-74 Years, HE 20.6226/5

Mortality Cause-of-Death Summary Data, HE 20.6226/6

Mortality Local Area Summary, HE 20.6226/7

Natality Local Area Summary, HE 20.6226/3

Natality State Summary, HE 20.6226

National Health Interview Survey, HE 20.6226/10

Public Use Files Catalog HE 22.616

Public Use Microdata Files, C 3.285

Public Use of National Parks, Statistical Report, I 29.63

Public Use, Tabulation of Visitors to Areas Administrated by National Park Service, I 29.63

Public Welfare Personnel, Annual Statistical Data, HE 17.629

Public Works Administration of Federal Works Agency, Reports Showing Status of Funds and Analyses of Expenditures, T 63.108

Public Works Digest, D 103.122/3

Public Works of Art Project, I 1.30

Publication Announcement and Order Form, Annual Survey of Manufacturers, C 3.24/9-5

Publication Announcements, NAS 1.9

Publication Catalogue and Order Form, HE 20.3183/3

Publication Note Series, HE 20.6216/3

Publication Notice; PN- (series), C 4.49

Publications–

Accident Prevetion Conference, C 1.17

Agricultural Adjustment Agency–
East Central Region, A 76.441, A 79.441, A 80.2141

North Central Region, A 76.451, A 79.451, A 80.2151

Northeast Region, A 76.461, A 79.461, A 80.2161

Southern Region, A 76.471, A 79.471, A 80.2171

Western Region, A 76.481, A 79.481, A 80.2181

Air Force Ballistic Missile Division, D 301.68

Air Force Cambridge Research Laboratories, D 301.45/23-3

Air Force Missile Test Center, D 301.45/23-1

Air Force Office of Scientific Research, D 301.45/19-2

Air Pollution Control Office, EP 4.9

Air University, D 301.26/6

Air University, Documentary Research Study, D 301.26/3

Air University, School of Aviation Medicine, D 301.26/3-2

Ajutant General's School, D 102.25

American Folklife Center, LC 39.9

Anthropology (series), I 29.92

Archeology, I 29.59

Armed Forces Institute of Pathology, D 1.16/4

Army Audit Agency, D 101.62

Army Language School, D 101.64

Army Map Service, D 103.20

Army Scientific Advisory Panel, D 101.81

Available for Free Distribution, I 27.10

Available for Purchase, U.S. Army Engineer Waterways Experiment Station and Other Corps of Engineers Agencies, D 103.39

Available for Sale, I 27.10/2

Available from Northern Prairie Science Center, I 49.18/9

Bureau of Community Health Services, HE 20.5110:P 96

Bureau of Education, I 16.14/2

Bureau of Entomology Available for Free Distribution, A 9.13

Bureau of Home Economics, A 42.5

Bureau of Labor Statistics, L 2.71

Bureau of Mines, C 22.7/1, I 28.5/8

Bureau of Public Roads, A 22.5

Bureau of Sport Fisheries and Wildlife, I 49.18/6

Bureau of the Census, C 3.163

Central States Forest Experiment Station, A 13.68/12-2

Checklists, LC 1.15

Children's Bureau, FS 3.209, FS 14.111, FS 17.210, HE 21.110

Coast and Geodetic Survey, C 4.19/2

Communicable Disease Center, FS 2.60/2

Congress of International Society of Soil Science, A 57.49

Corn-Hog Board of Review, A 55.30

Department of Agriculture Available for Distribution, A 21.6/4

Department of Commerce, C 1.2:P 96

Department of Labor, L 1.34/6

Department of State, Quarterly List, S 1.30

Directorate of Weather; Special Series, W 108.17

Environmental Data Service, C 55.228

Federal Fire Council, GS 1.14/5

Federal National Mortgage Association, FL 5.17

Federal Reserve Board, FR 1.45

Federal-Aid Airport Program, FAA 8.10

Food and Drug Administration, FS 13.111

Foreign Countries, Annotated Accession List, C 3.199

Goddard Space Flight Center, NAS 1.34

Great Lakes Pilotage Administration, C 1.47

Headquarters European Command, D 1.23

Historical Division, D 101.42/2

Home Owners' Loan Corporation, FL 3.9

Howard University, FS 5.41

Human Research Unit, D 101.46

Inter-American Education Demonstration Centers, FS 5.31

Internation Reference Service, C 34.11

Issued, A 77.16/2

Issued Since 1897, LC 1.12

Lake States Forest Experiment Station [list], A 13.61/12

Land Economics Division, Water Utilization Section, A 36.149

List, Y 4.Ag 4:P 96, Y 4.En 2:P 96

Maritime Administration, W 39.227:P 96

Microanalytical Division, A 46.17, FS 7.16

Museum Behavior, SI 1.39

Mutual Security Mission to China, FO 1.27

National Air Pollution Control Administration, FS 2.93/3

National Applied Mathematics Laboratories, C 13.43

National Archives and Records Service, GS 4.17

National Bureau of Standards, C 13.10:305

National Center for Education Statistics, HE 19.317:P 96

National Center for Health Statistics, HE 20.7042/7

National Climatic Center, C 55.281

National Committee on Wood Utilization, C 1.14

National Conference on Air Pollution, FS 2.98

National Conference on Water Pollution, FS 2.64/3

National Conferences on Street and Highway Safety, C 1.21

National Earthquake Information Center, C 55.691

National Export Expansion Council, C 1.42/3

National Geodetic Survey, C 55.413/3

National Historical Publications Commission, GS 4.14

National Institute of Mental Health, HE 20.8113/3

National Meterological Center, C 55.190

National Ocean Survey, C 55.419

National Oceanographic Data Center, D 203.24, D 203.24/2, C 55.292

National Security Agency, D 1.25

National Wage Stabilization Board, L 1.17
Naval Observatory, D 213.10
Naval Oceanographic Office, D 203.22
Naval Propellant Plant, D 215.12, D 217.15
Naval Support Force, Antarctica, D 201.15/2
Naval Torpedo Station, D 211.23
Navy Electronics Laboratory, D 211.11/2
Newly Available, A 13.62/11-3
Nutrition and Food Conservation Branch, A
80.123
Office of Aerospace Research, D 301.69/5
Office of Air Programs, EP 4.9
Office of Education, FS 5.9, FS 5.10, FS
5.211:11000, HE 5.211:11000
Office of Technology Assessment and Forecast, C
1.62
Office of Technology and Forecast, C 21.24
Office, Chief of Military History, D 114.10
Ordnance Materials Research Offices, D 105.13/3
Pacific Northwest Forest and Range Experiment
Station, A 13.66/15
Panama Railroad Company, D 113.9
Patents, A 77.17/3, A 77.17/4, A 77.17/5
Patents of Division of Insecticide Investigations,
List of, A 77.318
Plant and Operations Office, A 60.8
Potomac River Naval Command, D 201.12
President's Conference on Fire Prevention, FW 6.9
President's Highway Safety Conference, FW 2.18
President's Organization of Unemployment Relief,
C 1.15
Production Economics Research Branch, A 77.16
Public Health and Marine-Hospital Service, T
27.16
Recruiting Publicity Bureau, D 102.75
Research and Analysis Branch, Y 3.C 78/3:7, W
2.13
Rocky Mountain Forest and Range Experiment
Station, A 13.69/10-2
Russian Scientific Translation Program, FS 2.22/19
Sale, L 2.34/3
School of Aviation Medicine, Index, Fiscal Year, D
301.26/13-3
Scientific Research and Development Office, Pr
32.413
Scientific Translation Program, FS 2.214
Slavage Archeology, SI 1.22
Southern Forest Experiment Station, A 13.40/8-3
Special Representative in Europe, FO 1.23/2
Staff and Cooperators, Intermountain Forest and
Range Experiment Station, A 13.65/14
Supreme Allied Commander in Europe, D 9.8
Supreme Commander for Allied Powers, D 102.11
Tariff Commission, TC 1.34
Task Force on Prescription Drugs, FS 1.32, HE 1.32
Technology Transfer Seminar, EP 7.10
U.S. Antarctic Projects Officer, D 1.32
U.S. Army Foreign Science and Technology Center,
D 101.79
U.S. Army Headquarters in Europe, D 101.42
United States Court of Military Appeals, D 1.19/2
United States Postal Service, P 1.57
Upper Mississippi Valley Region, A 57.18
Weather Bureau, C 30.17/2
Weather Bureau Available for Distribution, A 29.31
Weather Research Center, W 108.16
World War I, D 114.8
[year], A 13.69/10-2
Publications, A Quarterly Guide, EP 1.21/7-3
Publications and Final Reports on Contracts and
Grants, C 55.13/2-2
Publications and Reports of Cryogenic Interest Noted
List, C 13.51
Publications Announcements, GP 3.21
Publications Bulletin, D 101.139
Publications by Staff and Cooperators, Intermountain
Forest and Range Experiment Station, A
13.65/14
Publications Catalog of the U.S. Department of
Commerce, C 1.54/2-2
Publications Catalog, U.S. Department of Health and
Human Services, HE 3.38/5
Publications for Instruction, etc. of Naval Militia, N
1.27/7
Publications for Sale, I 27.10/2
Publications in Anthropology, I 29.92
Publications in Archeology, I 29.59
Publications in Museum Behavior, SI 1.39
Publications in Print, LC 1.12/2-3
Publications in Salvage Archeology, SI 1.22
Publications List—
National Institute on Deafness and Other
Communication Disorders, HE 20.3659/
2

National Science Foundation, NS 1.13/6
Senate Committee on Energy and Natural
Resources, Y 4.En 2:P 96
Senate Special Committee on Aging, Y 4.Ag 4:P 96
Publications List for Health Professionals, HE
20.3183/2
Publications List for the Public and Patients, HE
20.3183
Publications Newly Available, A 13.62/11-3
Publications of the National Science Foundation, NS
1.13/5
Publications Received, A 93.18
Publications Reference File on Microfiche, GP 3.22/3
Publications Relating to Dairy Industry, A 44.11
Publications, Second Series, M 212.10
Publications Series, S 18.62
Publications Stocked by the Marine Corps, D 214.28
Publications (unnumbered), C 55.220/4
Publicity Bureau, T 1.27/21-29
Publicity Bureau, Liberty Loan of 1917, T 1.25
Published Ordinances, Firearms, T 70.5:F 51
Published Search Bibliographies, C 51.13/2
PubMed, HE 20.3627
PubScience, E 1.137/2
Puerto Rico Administrative Rulings, A 55.18/3
Puerto Rico Censuses, Announcements, C 3.219
Puerto Rico, Education Department Annual Reports, I
1.39
Puerto Rico, Interior Department Annual Reports, I
1.40
Puerto Rico Orders, A 63.8
Puerto Rico Special Commissioner (Carroll), T 1.17
Puerto Rico Sugar Orders, A 55.18
Puerto Rico Tax Fund Orders, A 55.18/2
Puget Sound Notes, EP 1.97
Pullet Chick Replacements for Broiler Hatchery Supply
Flocks, A 88.15/19
Pullet Chicks for Broiler Hatchery Supply Flocks, Pou
2-7 (series), A 92.90
Pulp and Paper Industry Reports, C 18.229
Pulp, Paper and Board, C 57.313, C 57.511
Pulp, Paper and Board Industry Report, C 40.11
Pulpwood Prices in the Southeast, A 13.79/2
Pulpwood Production in the Lake States, A 13.80/5-2
Pulpwood Production in the North-Central Region by
County, A 13.80/5
Pulpwood Production in the Northeast, A 13.80/3
Pulse, VA 1.51
Pulse Check, PrEx 26.10
Pulverizers, for Pulverized Fuel Installations, New
Order for, C 3.103
Pumice and Pumicite in (year), I 28.122
Pumice and Volcanic Cinder in (year), I 28.122
Pupil Mobility in Public Elementary and Secondary
Schools During the (date) School Year, HE
5.93/6
Purchase and Sales Reports, A 82.61/2
Purchase and Storage Notices, W 77.19, W 89.8
Purchase Circulars, GP 1.21
Purchase Descriptions, P 1.33
Purchase Report, A 82.44
Purchase Reports, A 82.60
Purchasing Office Circulars, I 1.66
PWA Bulletins, Y 3.F 31/4:24
PWA Circulars, Y 3.F 31/4:23
Pyroxylin-Coated Textiles, C 3.104

Q

Q & A (series), C 46.16
QMC Historical Studies, D 106.8
QMC Historical Studies, Series II, D 106.8/2
QMC Pamphlets, D 106.13
QMFCIAF Reports, D 106.16
QMG Circulars, M 112.4
QMS- (series), D 101.6/9
Quads, Report on Energy Activities, A 13.98/2
Qualification Standards Handbook, D 106.8
Qualification Standards for Postal Field Service, CS
1.45
Qualification Standards for Wage Board Positions, CS
1.45
Qualification Standards for White Collar Positions
Under the General Schedule, CS 1.45:X-118,
PM 1.8/3:X-118
Qualified Areas Under Public Works and Economic
Development Act of 1965, Public Law 89-
136, Reports, C 46.25
Qualified Products Lists—
Department of Defense, D 1.17
Department of the Air Force, D 301.22

Qualifying Facilities Report, E 2.12/3
Quality and Prices of Cotton Linters Produced in
United States, A 66.37
Quality and Reliability Assurance Handbooks, D 7.6/
11
Quality Assurance, QA Reporter, D 7.23
Quality Control and Reliability Technical Reports, D
7.15
Quality Control Digests, C 31.166, FAA 5.11
Quality Control Notes, Pr 32.4835
Quality Control Reports, Pr 32.4833
Quality Evaluation Program Manual, D 7.6/4-3
Quality of Cotton Classed Under Smith- Doxey Act,
United States, A 88.11/23
Quality of Cotton in Carry-Over, A 88.11/14
Quality of Grain Crops Based on Inspected Receipts at
Representative Markets, A 36.206
Quality of Surface Waters of the United States, I 19.13
Quality Publications, NPC 200 (series), NAS 1.22
Quarantine Laws and Regulations, T 27.9
Quarterly Awards Listing Grants Assistance Programs,
EP 1.35
Quarterly Benefit Statistics Report, RR 1.16
Quarterly Bibliography of Major Tropical Diseases, HE
20.3614/4
Quarterly Bulletin for Part 2, Hydrographic Products,
D 5.351/2-2
Quarterly Bulletin, Intelligence Continuing Education
Program, D 5.212
Quarterly Calendar of Environmental Meetings, EP
1.39
Quarterly Canned Foods Stocks Reports, C 3.136
Quarterly Cargo Review, C 31.264
Quarterly Check List, USAF/USN Flight Information
Publications, Planning, D 301.52/2
Quarterly Circular Information Bulletin, D 103.42/11
Quarterly Coke Report, E 3.11/9
Quarterly Compilation of Periodical Literature
Reflecting the Use of Records in the National
Archives, AE 1.126, AE 1.128
Quarterly Cumulative Report of Technical Assistance, C
46.23
Quarterly Debt Management Report, HE 20.9311
Quarterly Digest of Unpublished Decisions of the
Comptroller General of the United States:
Personnel Law, Civilian Personnel, GA 1.5/
5, GA 1.5/10, GA 1.5/11
Quarterly Economic and Financial Review: Federal
Republic of Germany and Western Sectors of
Berlin, S 1.91/2
Quarterly Financial Report for Manufacturing, Mining,
and Trade Corporations, FT 1.18, C 3.267
Quarterly Financial Report, United States Manufactur-
ing Corporations, FT 1.18
Quarterly Financial Report, United States Retail and
Wholesale Corporations, FT 1.20
Quarterly Flax Market Review, A 36.115
Quarterly Freight Loss and Damage Claims, Class 1,
Line-Haul Railroads, IC 1 acco.12
Quarterly Freight Loss and Damage Claims Reported by
Common and Contract Motor Carriers of
Property, IC 1 acco.11
Quarterly Graduate Bulletin, D 5.210/2
Quarterly Gypsum Reports, C 22.33, I 28.32
Quarterly Index of Technical Documentary Reports, D
301.45/15
Quarterly Index to Periodical Literature, Eastern and
Southern Africa, LC 1.30/8-4
Quarterly Intelligence Trends, J 24.18/4
Quarterly Interim Financial Report, Certificated Route
Air Carriers and Supplemental Air Carries,
CAB 1.14
Quarterly Interim Financial Report, Certified Route Air
Carriers and Supplemental Air Carriers, C
31.240/3
Quarterly Journal of Current Acquisitions, LC 2.17
Quarterly Journal of Library of Congress, LC 1.17
Quarterly Journal, Comptroller of the Currency, T 12.18
Quarterly Listing of Interim Issuances, D 7.6/
7:5025.1:pt. 2
Quarterly Natural Gas Reports, I 28.98
Quarterly Nonimmigrant Statistics, J 21.2/10-2
Quarterly Operating Data of 63 Telephone Carriers, CC
1.14
Quarterly Operating Data of 70 Telephone Carriers, CC
1.14
Quarterly Operating Data of Telegraph Carriers, CC 1.13
Quarterly Progress Report, D 103.33/10
Quarterly Progress Report, Nationwide Urban Runoff
Program, EP 1.92
Quarterly Progress Report on Fission Product
Behavior in LWRs, E 1.28/2

Regional Contract Charts, A 55.7/2, A 55.7/3, A 55.7/4

Regional Cotton Variety Tests, A 106.28

Regional Data on Compensation Show Wages, Salaries and Benefits Costs in the Northeast, L 2.71/6-6

Regional Differences in Indian Health, HE 20.319

Regional Distribution and Types of Stores where Consumers Buy Selected Fresh Fruits, Canned and Frozen Juices, and Dried Fruits, A 36.172

Regional Economic Information System (REIS), C 59.24

Regional Handbooks, A 57.22

Regional Information Series, A 55.42/5, A 55.44/5, A 55.46/5

Regional Information Series Leaflets, A 55.43/6, A 55.45/5

Regional Labor Statistics Bulletin, L 2.71/7

Regional Office Directory, Professional and Administrative Personnel, FS 1.17/2

Regional Profiles, S 18.54

Regional Reports, L 2.71/2

Regional Reports, Middle Atlantic Region, L 2.71/6

Regional Reports (numbered), L 2.71/3

Regional Reports (series), L 2.71/4

Regional Research Bulletins, N.Y. and New England, Y 3.W 89/2:60

Regional Review, Region 1, I 29.36

Regional Studies Plan, Fiscal Year, Atlantic OCS Region, I 72.12/15

Regional Tide and Tidal Current Tables, C 55.425/3

Registar, C 3.126, FS 2.111

Register, Y 3.Se 4:27

Register, Department of Justice and the Courts of the United States, J 1.7

Register, Department of State, S 1.6

Register of Civil Engineer Corps Commissioned and Warrant Officers of United States Navy and Naval Reserve on Active Duty, D 209.9

Register of Commissioned and Warrant Officers–

    Coast Guard Reserve, T 47.10/2

    Marine Corps Reserve, N 9.20

    Naval Militia, N 1.27/6

    Naval Reserve, N 17.38

    Naval Reserve Force, N 25.6

    Navy and Marine Corps and Reserve Officers on Activie Duty, D 208.12

    United States Naval Reserve, D 208.12/2

    United States Navy and Marine Corps, M 206.10

Register of Debates, X 43 –X 71

Register of Employees, P 1.14

Register of Military Personnel in the Washington, D.C. Area, TD 5.19/3

Register of Money Order Post Offices in United States, P 9.5

Register of Naval Militia, N 23.5

Register of Office of Attorney General, J 1.12

Register of Officers and Cadets, TD 5.19

Register of Officers and Graduates (triennial), W 12.12

Register of Officers and Vessels, T 33.6

Register of Projects Approved Under Manpower Development and Training Act, L 1.53

Register of Reporting Employers, L 1.81

Register of Reporting Labor Organizations, L 1.84

Register of Reporting Surety Companies, L 1.82

Register of Reserve Officers, TD 5.19/2

Register of Retired Commissioned and Warrant Officers, Regular and Reserve, of the United States Navy and Marine Corps, D 208.12/3

Register of the Department of the Interior, I 1.28

Register of U.S. Commissioners, J 1.18

Register of Visitors, S 1.52

Register of Voluntary Agencies, S 18.12

Register of War Department, W 1.10

Register Planned Emergency Producers, D 7.11/2

Registered Bona Fide and Legitimate Farmers' Cooperative Organizations under Bituminous Coal Act of 1937, I 46.15

Registered Distributors under Bituminous Coal Act of 1973 [lists], I 46.14

Registered Group-Joint Apprenticeship Programs in Construction Industry (by trades), L 23.9

Registers of Papers in the Manuscript Division of the Library of Congress, LC 4.10

Registrant Facts, J 24.17

Registrants Processing Manual, Y 3.Se 4:10-2 R 26

Registration, Employment and Unemployment, U.S. Zone, Statistical Report, W 1.72/3

Registration Record, Securities Act of 1933, SE 1.13/1

Registration Record, Securities Act of 1933, Indexes, SE 1.13/2

Registry of Toxic Effects of Chemical Substances, HE 20.7112/3

Registry of Toxic Effects of Chemical Substances (cumulative) Supplement, HE 20.7112/5

Registry of Toxic Effects of Chemical Substances, Permuted Molecular Formula, Index, HE 20.7112/4

Regulations (numbered), Pr 32.4406

Regulations, AFSCR (series), D 301.45/14-2

Regulations, Alcohol Tax Unit, T 22.17/2

Regulations and Interpretations, L 22.9

Regulations and Interpretive Bulletins, L 1.7/4

Regulations and Policy Statements, C 31.224/2

Regulations and Procedure, VB 1.10/3, VB 1.10/4

Regulations and Programme of Instruction, W 29.6

Regulations, ER- (series), D 103.6/4

Regulations: Export Administration Bureau, C 63.23

Regulations for Clerks of Courts Who Take Passport Applications, S 1.18

Regulations for Government of Ordenance Department (general), W 34.12/1

Regulations for Government of Public Health and Marine Hospital Service, T 27.8

Regulations for Government of United States Army General Hospital, W 44.15

Regulations for Military Academy (general), W 12.6/1

Regulations for Quartermaster's Department (general), W 39.9/1

Regulations for Revenue-Cutter Service (general), T 33.7

Regulations for Sale of Lake Survey Charts, W 33.5

Regulations for the Administration and Enforcement of the Radiation Control for Health and Safety Act of 1968, HE 20.4606/2

Regulations for Subsistence Department, W 5.7

Regulations for United States Corps of Cadets Prescribed by Commandant of Cadets, M 109.6/2

Regulations Governing Admission of Candidates into Naval Academy As Midshipmen and Sample Examination Questions, D 208.108

Regulations Governing Meat Inspection of the U.S. Department of Agriculture, A 88.6/3:188

Regulations Governing Uniform, N 1.18/1

Regulations Governing Uniform and Equipment of Officers and Enlisted Men, N 9.8

Regulations Governing Uniforms, T 27.7

Regulations No. 4, Old-Age and Survivors Insurance, FS 3.6/2

Regulations of Administrator, C 31.140, FAA 1.6/4

Regulations of Department of Agriculture, A 1.19

Regulations of General Services Administration, GS 1.6/4

Regulations of Indian Office (general), I 20.13/1

Regulations of the Civil Aeronautics Board, C 31.206/7, CAB 1.16

Regulations of the Office of the Secretary, TD 1.6/2

Regulations, Plant, A 35.8

Regulations (pt. nos. of Title 26 of the Code of Federal Regulations), T 70.6/2

Regulations (pt. nos. of Title 27 Code of Federal Regulations), T 22.17/4, T 70.6/3

Regulations, Rules, Instructions, A 112.6

Regulations, Rules and Instructions–

    Census Bureau, C 3.6

    Center for Professional Development and Training, HE 20.7709

    Comptroller of the Currency, T 12.25

    Court of Customs Appeals, Ju 7.8/2

    Customs Division, T 17.5

    Department of Education, ED 1.47

    Department of Transportation, TD 1.6

    Federal Emergency Management Agency, FEM 1.6

    Food and Nutrition Service, A 98.18

    Grain Inspection, Packers and Stockyards Administration, A 113.12

    International Trade Commission, ITC 1.6

    National Center for Devices and Radiological Health, HE 20.4606

    National Defense University, D 5.406

    Naval Research Office, D 210.6

    Office of Information Resources Management, GS 12.15

    Office of Thrift Supervisor, T 71.6

    Office of Water Programs, EP 2.6

    Research and Special Programs Administration, TD 10.6

    Rules, Instructions, J 36.6

    United States Parole Commission, J 27.6

Regulations S-X Under the Securities Act of 1933, SE 1.6:F 49

Regulations Series 5, T 22.15

Regulations (special), T 17.5

Regulations, Title 29, Code of Federal Regulations, L 36.206/2

Regulations Under Fair Labor Standards Act, L 22.22

Regulations Under Federal Power Act, FP 1.7:P 87/2

Regulations Under the Natural Gas Act, August 1, 1967, FP 1.7:G 21/3

Regulations Under the Persihable Agricultural Commdoties Act 1930, and Perishable Agricultural Commodities Act, A 88.6:P 41

Regulatory Alert, NCU 1.6/2

Regulatory Announcements, I 49.24

Regulatory and Technical Reports (Abstract Index Journal), Y 3.N 88:21-3

Regulatory Calendar, E 2.16

Regulatory Guide List, Y 3.N 88:6-4

Regulatory Guides, Y 3.N 88:6-2

Regulatory Impact Analysis (series), EP 6.14/2

Regulatory Information Service Center: General Publications, GS 1.6.11

Regulatory Licensing Status Summary Reports, Y 3.N 88:44

Regulatory Licensing, Status Summary Report, Systematic Evaluation Program, Y 3.N 88:29

Regulatory Procedures Manual, HE 20.4008/6

Regulatory Program of the United States Government, PrEx 2.30

Regulatory Reporter, Y 3.R 26/2:9

Rehab Brief, ED 1.48

Rehabilitation Leaflets, VE 1.7

Rehabilitation R and D Progress Reports, VA 1.23/3-2

Rehabilitation Record, FS 13.216, FS 17.109, HE 17.109

Rehabilitation Service Administration, Quarterly Indicies, HE 17.120

Rehabilitation Service Series, FS 13.207, FS 17.110/3, HE 17.110/3

Rehabilitation Standards Memorandum, FS 13.209

Reintroduction and Management of Wolves in Yellowstone National Park and the Central Idaho Wilderness Area, Y 3.W 83

Reinvention Express, PrVp 42.16

Reinvention Roundtable, Helping Federal Workers Create a Government that Works Better and Cost Less, PrVp 42.15

Related Publications, Y 3.Eq 2:18-3

Related Training Letters, FS 6.9

Relative Cost of Shipbuilding, TD 11.15/2

Relative Cost of Shipbuilding in Various Coastal Districts of the United States, Report to Congress, C 39.216/2

Relative Importance of Components in the Consumer Price Indexes, L 2.3/9

Relay Broadcast Stations, CC 1.31

Release for Publication (series), FP 1.25/2

Release (of action taken) Prior to January 22, 1936, Reports, CC 4.8

Releases, ITC 1.7

Releases, Air Research and Development Command, D 301.45/3

Releases CGS (series), C 3.209

Releases, Corporate Reorganization, SE 1.25/1

Releases, Holding Company Act of 1935, SE 1.25/2

Releases, Investment Company Act of 1940, SE 1.25/3

Releases Pertaining to Personnel, C 13.36/3

Releases Relating to Orders, ES 3.7/3

Releases, Securities Act of 1933, SE 1.25/4

Releases, Securities Exchange Act of 1934, SE 1.25/5

Releases, Trust Indenture Act of 1939, SE 1.25/7

Reliability Abstracts and Technical Reviews, NAS 1.35

Reliability and Quality Assurance Publications, NAS 1.22/3

Reliability Publications, NPC 250 (series), NAS 1.22/2

Relief in Rural and Town Areas, SS 1.25/a 2

Relief in Urban Areas, SS 1.10, SS 1.25/a 3

Relief Notices, Y 3.F 31/5:23

Religious Press Bulletin, Y 3.F 73:13

Relocation from Urban Renewal Project Areas, HH 7.14

REMR Bulletin: News from the Repair, Evaluation, Maintenance and Rehabilitation Research Program, D 103.72

Renal Disease and Hypertension, Proceedings, Annual Conference, HE 20.5412

Renegotiation Board Regulations, RnB 1.6/2

Renegotiation Board Rulings, RnB 1.6/5

Renegotiation Staff Bulletins, RnB 1.6/3

Renewable Energy: Issues and Trends, E 3.19/2-2

Renewable Resources Remote Sensing Research Program Report, NAS 1.70

Renewing Government, HH 1.1/10

Report AAF (series), TD 4.709

Report and Recommendations of Fact-Finding Boards, L 1.16

Report and Studies in the History of Art, SI 8.9

Report by the Advisory Board for Cuba Broadcasting, Y 3.B 78/2:1

Report by the FCCSET Committee on Life Sciences and Health, PrEx 8.111/2

Report on Foreign Currencies Held by the U.S. Government Fiscal Year and Transition Quarter, T 63.118/2

Report on Forestry, A 13.5

Report on Funding Levels and Allocations of Funds, TD 7.20

Report on Hawaii, C 8.6

Report on Hides, Skins and Leather, C 3.45

Report on High Speed Ground Transportation Act of 1965, TD 1.10

Report on Inadvertent Releases of Restricted Data...that Occured before October 17, 1998, E 1.143

Report on Incidence of Anthrax in Animals in United States, A 77.225

Report on Indian Health, FS 2.86/2

Report on Internal Audit Activities of the Internal Revenue Service, T 22.53

Report on National Growth, PrEx 15.9

Report on National Growth and Development, PrEx 15.9

Report on OPM, GAO'S Annual Report on Activities of OPM, Fiscal Year, GA 1.13/15

Report on Plan Preparation on State and Local Public Works, FW 7.7

Report on Principal Bills Introduced into Congress Affecting Education Either Directly or Indirectly, FS 5.66

Report on Progress in (year) of the Status of Women, Y 3.In 8/21:1

Report on Progress of Works Program, Y 3.W 89/2:32

Report on Quality Changes for (year) Model Passenger Cars, L 1.79/2, L 2.120/2-7

Report on Salmon Fisheries of Alaska, T 35.6

Report on Scientific Research Projects Conducted During Fiscal Year, Y 3.T 25:32

Report on Status of Multiple Use and Joint Development, TD 2.121

Report on Survey of U.S. Shipbuilding and Repair Facilities, TD 11.25

Report on the American Workforce, L 1.90/2

Report on the Financial Condition and Performance of the Farm Credit System, FCA 1.1/2

Report on the Implementation to Title 1 and Title 2 of the Speedy Trial Act of 1974, Ju 10.16

Report on the International Technical Conference on Experimental Safety Vehicles, TD 8.16

Report on the Militia of U.S., W 3.35

Report on the Significant Actions of the Office of Personnel Management, MS 1.16

Report on the National Defense Education Act, HE 5.210:10004

Report on Trade Conditions, C 10.11

Report on Traffic Accidents and Injuries for (year), TD 8.32

Report on Underwriting Practices, Y 3.F 31/8:35

Report on U.S. Export Controls to the President and the Congress, C 57.30

Report on U.S. Government Research and Studies in the Field of Arms Control and Disarmament Matters, AC 1.14

Report on USDA Human Nutrition Research and Education Activities, A Report to Congress, A 1.1/5

Report on Vessels Trading with United States, SB 5.5

Report on Volume of Water Borne Foreign Commerce of U.S. by Ports of Origin and Destination (fiscal year), C 27.9/10, MC 1.17

Report on Washington Conference of Mayors and Other Local Government Executives on National Security, FCD 1.18

Report on Washington Conference on National Women's Advisory Committee on FCDA, FCD 1.18/2

Report R- (series), Office of Chief Engineer, CC 1.46

Report, SE- (series), C 55.220/5

Report Series, HE 20.8010, HE 20.8215

Report TES (series), TD 1.35

Report to Army, M 104.8, D 107.7

Report to Congress, IA 1.1

Report to Congress and East-West Foreign Trade Board on Trade Between United States and Nonmarket Economy Countries, TC 1.38

Report to Congress by the Secretary of the Interior and the Secretary of Agriculture on Administration of the Wild Free-roaming Horses and Burro Act, I 1.100

Report to Congress Concerning the Demonstration of Fare-Free Mass Transportation, TD 7.13

Report to Congress, Endangered and Threatened Species Recovery Program, I 49.77/3

Report to Congress, Office of Federal Procurement Policy, PrEx 2.21

Report to Congress on Abnormal Occurrences, Y 3.N 88:20

Report to Congress on Administration of Ocean Dumping Activities, D 103.68

Report to Congress on Conrail Performance, Y 3.R 13/4:9

Report to Congress on Economic Cooperation Administration, Y 3.Ec 74/3:8

Report to Congress on Foreign Assistance Program, S 18.1

Report to Congress on Foreign Surplus Disposal, S 1.47

Report to Congress on Implementation of Public Law 94-142, HE 19.117/2, ED 1.32

Report to Congress on Lend-lease Operations, S 1.43

Report to Congress on Ocean Dumping and Other Man-Induced Changes to Ocean Ecosystems, C 55.31

Report to Congress on Ocean Pollution, Monitoring and Research, C 55.31/3, C 55.439

Report to Congress on Ocean Pollution, Overfishing, and Offshore Development, C 55.31/2

Report to Congress on Operations of UNRRA Under Act of March 28, 1944, S 1.44

Report to Congress on the Administration of the Highway Safety Act of 1966, TD 1.10/3

Report to Congress on the Administration of the National Traffic Vehcile Safety Act of 1966, TD 1.10/2

Report to Congress on the Ballistic Missile Defense Organization, D 1.1/6

Report to Congress on the Economic Impact of Energy Actions As Required by Public Law 93-275, Section 18 (d), E 1.59, FE 1.15/2

Report to Congress on the Emergency Homeowner's Relief Act, HH 1.64

Report to Congress on Title 20 of the Social Security Act, HE 23.2009

Report to Congress on United States Foreign Relief Program, S 1.63

Report to Congress on Voting Practices in the United Nations, S 1.1/8

Report to Employees FY, Washington, D.C. Post Office, P 1.1/2

Report to Field Staff, L 23.14

Report to Insured Banks, Y 3.F 31/8:17

Report to the Administrator by the NASA Aerospace Safety Advisory Panel, NAS 1.58

Report to the Advisory Child Health and Human Development Council, HE 20.3362/7

Report to the Attorney General (series), J 1.96

Report to the Committee on the Budget from the Committee on Veterans' Affairs, Y 4.V 64/3-10

Report to the Committee on the Budget; Views and Estimates of the Committee on Interior and Insular Affairs (House), Y 4.In 8/14-11

Report to the Committee on the Budget; Views and Estimates of the Committee on Natural Resources, Y 4.R 31/3-11

Report to the Congress, D 201.1

Report to the Congress and the Trade Policy Committee on Trade Between the U.S. and the Nonmarket Economy Countries, ITC 1.13

Report to the Congress on Coastal Zone Management, C 55.32

Report to the Congress on the Status of the Public Ports of the United States, TD 11.30

Report to the Congress on the Strategic Defense Initiative, D 1.1/6

Report to the Federal Land Bank Associations for Year Ended June 30 (date), FCA 1.23

Report to the National Farm Loan Associations, FCA 1.23

Report to the President and Congress on the Drug Abuse, Prevention, and Treatment Functions, HE 1.58

Report to the President and Congress on the Status of Health Personnel in the United States, HE 20.9310

Report to the President and Congress on the Status of Health Professions Personnel in the United States, HE 20.6619

Report to the President and the Congress on the Effectiveness of the Rail Passenger Services Act, IC 1.34

Report to the President by Director of Defense Mobilization, Pr 33.1008

Report to the President by Director of Office of Defense Mobilization, Pr 34.201

Report to the Public, T 34.1/2

Report to the Secretary, Federal Manager's Financial Integrity Act, TD 1.1/7

Report to the Senate and House Committees on the Budget As Required by Public Law 93-344, Y 10.13

Report to the U.S. Congress and the U.S. Secretary of Energy from the Nuclear Waste Technical Review Board, Y 3.N 88/2:1

Report to the United States Congress on Federal Activities on Alcohol Abuse and Alcoholism, HE 20.8316

Report UCDP (series), TD 2.43

Reported Anthropod-Borne Encephalidites in Horces and Other Equidae, A 77.230/2

Reported Incidence of Infectious Equine Encephalomy-elitis and Related Encephalitides in the United States, Calendar Year (date), A 77.230

Reported Incidence of Rabies in United States, A 77.232

Reported Tuberculosis Data, HE 20.7017

Reporter, D 302.11

Reports (series), A 93.18/3

Reports and Analysis Handbook Series, L 7.36

Reports and Guidelines from White House Conference on Aging (series), FS 1.13/2

Reports and Orders Recommended by Joint Boards, IC 1 mot.19

Reports and Publications, Y 3.B 49, Y 4.Se 2

Reports and Statistical Tables on Fur-Seal Investigations in Alaska, T 35.7

Reports and Testimony, GA 1.16/3

Reports Bulletin, HE 17.29

Reports, CCL- (series), D 105.16

Reports, Consolidated Pamphlets, Ju 11.7/a2

Reports Control Symbol Darcom Manufacturing Technology, RCS DRCMT-(series), D 101.110

Reports FAA-ASP (series), TD 4.32/14

Reports FHWA-HO (series), TD 2.30/6

Reports FHWA-TD (series), TD 2.30/4

Reports for Consultation on Air Quality Control Regions, FS 2.93/5

Reports FRA/TTC- (series), TD 3.15/7

Reports from USDA's Economic Research Service, A 93.18/3

Reports, HM- (series), I 27.39/3

Reports Issued by Agricultural Marketing Service, A 66.19

Reports, NADC-CS- (series), D 201.22

Reports of Academy of Sciences of USSR, C 41.50

Reports of Action Taken, CC 3.8

Reports of Activities During Year, A 13.13/2

Reports of Agents and Superintendents in Charge of Indians, I 20.15

Reports of Applications Received, CC 2.8, CC 3.7, CC 4.7

Reports of Applications Received in Radio Broadcast Stations, CC 1.26

Reports of Applications Received in Telegraph Section, CC 1.27, CC 1.28

Reports of Bankruptcy Matters, J 1.9

Reports of Cases Adjudged in the Court of Customs and Patent Appeals, Ju 7.5

Reports of Committee on Tidal Hydraulics, D 103.28

Reports of Construction Permits Retired to Closed Files, etc., CC 1.29

Reports of Division of Research , C 31.131

Reports of Emergency Boards, NMB 1.7

Reports of Industries, L 20.12

Reports of Investigations, I 28.23

Reports of Investigations of Accidents Involving Civil Aircraft, C 31.213

Reports of Military Operations during Rebellion, 1860-65, W 45.9

Reports of President to Congress Showing Status of Funds and Operations under Emergency Relief Appropriation Acts, T 63.114

Reports of Project on Research in Agricultural and Industrial Development in Tennessee Valley Region, Y 3.T 25:26

Reports of Special Agent for Purchase and Distribution of Seeds, A 24.5

Reports of Special Agents and Commissions, I 20.6

Reports of Subversive Activities Control Board, Y 3.Su 1:8-2

Reports of Technical Study Groups on Soviet Agriculture, A 1.94

Reports of the Advisory Committee to the Administrator on Standards for the Administration of Juvenile Justice, J 1.48

Reports of the Chaco Center, I 29.90

Reports of the National Juvenile Justice Assessment Centers (series), J 26.27

Reports of the Proceedings of the Judicial Conference of the United States [and] Annual Report of the Director of the Administrative Office of the U.S. Courts, Ju 10.1/2

Reports of the Surgeon General, HE 20.7615

Reports of the Tax Court, Ju 11.7

Reports of Trade Conditions, C 1.7

Reports of United States Trade Missions, C 42.19, C 48.9

Reports [on agenda], L 1.10/5

Reports on Airline Service, Fares Traffic, Load Factors and Market Shares, CAB 1.27

Reports on Apprentice Selection Programs, L 23.11

Reports on Bankruptcy Matters, J 1.9

Reports on Case Handling Developments of the Office of the General Counsel, Y 3.F 31/21-3:12

Reports on Condition of Banks in U.S., T 1.6

Reports on Foreign Markets for Agricultural Products, A 36.8

Reports on Geneva Tariff Concessions, C 18.223/2

Reports on Hatchery Sales in California, A 36.194

Reports on Investigations and Inquiries, TC 1.39

Reports on Investigations of Individual Accidents, IC 1 acci.5

Reports [on Projects], C 13.38

Reports on Reproduction and Population Research (series), FS 2.22/13-7

Reports on Trade Conditions, C 1.7

Reports, OTR- (series), C 1.60/3

Reports Prepared for Foreign Service of United States, Listings, C 42.22

Reports, Register of Approved Recurring Reports, D 101.22/3:335-1

Reports, RE-TR- (series), D 105.22

Reports, RG-TR- (series), D 105.22/2-2

Reports, RT-TR- (series), D 105.22/2

Reports Showing Financial Status of Funds Provided in Emergency Relief Appropriation Acts, T 60.11

Reports Showing Status of Funds and Analyses of Expenditures, Emergency Appropriation Acts, T 60.13

Reports Showing Status of Funds and Analyses of Expenditures, Public Works Administration Federal Works Agency, T 60.14

Reports Showing Status of Funds Provided in Emergency Relief Appropriation Acts, T 60.12

Reports, Table of Proceedings Reported, Y 3.T 19:8

Reports to Aid Nation's Defense Effort, A 13.27/13

Reports to Congress on Audits, Reviews, and Examinations, GA 1.13

Reports to Congress on Lend-Lease Operations, Pr 32.402:L 54, Pr 32.5507

Reports to Congress on United States Participation in Operations of UNRRA under Act of March 28, 1944, Pr 32.5812

Reports, UMTA-PA- (series), TD 7.11

Representative Construction Cost of Hill- Burton Hospitals and Related Health Facilities, FS 2.74/6, HE 20.2510

Representative Construction Costs of Hospitals and Related Health Facilities, HE 1.109

Reprint and Circular Series, NA 2.5

Reprint of Hydrographic Information, N 6.19

Reprint Series, Y 3.Se 5:15

Reprints from Bulletin 556, Mineral Facts and Problems, I 28.3/b, I 28.3/c

Reprints from Marketing Activities, A 82.17/1

Reprints from Public Health Reports, T 27.6/a

Reprints from the Occupational Outlook Handbook, Bulletins, L 2.3/4 a

Reprints of Articles Published Concerning NIH Consensus Development Conferences, HE 20.3030/2

Reprints, R- (series), D 103.42/4

Reproducible Federal Tax Forms for Use in Libraries, T 22.57

Request for Grant Applications (series), HE 20.3220

Request for Hearings in Public Assistance, Fiscal Year (date), HE 3.60/2

Request for New or Modified Broadcast Call Signs, CC 1.44

Request for Proposal, NIE-R- (series), ED 1.324

Request for Proposal (series), ED 1.72

Request for Proposals, J 16.28

Request for Research Grant Applications (series), HE 20.3864

Requirement for Individual Water-Supply and Sewage- Disposal Systems (by States), NHA 2.17, HH 2.11

Requirement Forms, T 45.7

Research Abstracts, A 93.39, J 28.24/4, Y 3.N 21/5:14

Research Accomplished, A 13.40/8-4

Research Achievement Sheet, A 77.7

Research and Activities Under Saltonstall- Kennedy Act, Annual Report of Secretary of Interior, I 1.1/2

Research and Demonstrations Brief [Bring Research into Effective Focus], HE 17.18

Research and Demonstrations in Health Care Financing, HE 22.16/2

Research and Development Abstracts of USAEC, RDA (series), Y 3.At 7:51

Research and Development Contracts, Fiscal Year Funds, HE 20.3013/4

Research and Development Division Reports, D 212.12

Research and Development Findings, L 1.56

Research and Development in Industry, NS 1.22:In 2

Research and Development Progress, C 39.202:R 31

Research and Development Progress Reports, I 1.88

Research and Development Projects, C 13.2:R 31/4

Research and Development: Public Awareness/ participation Support Plan, Fiscal Year (date), EP 1.90

Research and Development Report, E 5.10/2, ED 1.328/ 6

Research and Development Reports, C 21.18, ER 1.11

Research and Development Series, HE 19.218

Research and Development Technical Reports, D 211.13/2

Research and Development Yearbook, E 5.10

Research and Discovery, Advances in Behavioral and Social Science Research, HE 20.3036/4

Research and Evaluation Plan, J 28.25/5

Research and Evaluation Report Series, L 37.22/2

Research and Special Studies Progress Report, D 301.26/15

Research and Statistics Legislative Notes, FS 3.28/3

Research and Statistics Letters, FS 3.28

Research and Statistics Notes, HE 3.28/2, HE 22.17

Research and Technology, Annual Report, NAS 1.65

Research and Technology, Annual Report of the Langley Research Center, NAS 1.65/3

Research and Technology Fiscal Year (date) Annual Report of the Goddard Space Flight Center, NAS 1.65/2

Research and Technology Program, HH 1.88

Research and Technology Program Digest, Flash Index, NAS 1.41

Research and Technology Program, Fiscal Year (date), HH 1.88

Research and Technology Transporter, TD 2.70

Research and Technology Work on Explosives, Explosions, and Flames, T 28.27

Research and Training Grants and Awards of Public Health Service, FS 2.22/8

Research and Training Opportunities Abroad (year), Educational Programs in Foreign Language and Area Studies, HE 5.99

Research Announcement, NAS 1.53/3

Research Areas, E 1.106

Research at Southeastern Forest Experiment Station, A 13.63/3

Research Attainment Report, Fiscal Year, A 13.82/11

Research Awards Index, HE 20.3013/2

Research Briefs, FS 17.18

Research Bulletins, J 28.19

Research Bulletins–

Air Training Command, Human Resources Research Center, D 301.36/3

Federal Emergency Relief Administration, Y 3.F 31/ 5:28

Works Progress Administration, Y 3.W 89/2:13

Research Demonstration and Evaluation Studies, HE 23.1010

Research, Demonstration, and Evaluation Stuides, HE 1.402:R 31

Research Division Maps, C 27.9/13

Research Division Reports–

Bureau of Apprenticeship and Training, L 23.19

National Endowment for the Arts, NF 2.12

Research Divison, Quarterly Progress Report, D 103.33/9

Research Documentation List, C 3.232

Research Documents, C 56.248

Research, Evaluation, and Demonstration Projects, L 37.22

Research Facilities Center: Annual Report, C 55.601/4

Research for Progress in Education, Annual Report, HE 5.212:12051

Research Grants, Data Book, HE 20.3516/2

Research Grants, Environmental Engineering and Food Protection, FS 2.300/3

Research Grants Index, HE 20.3013/2

Research Grants Index, Fiscal Year, FS 2.22/7-2

Research Grants, Training Awards, Summary Tables, HE 20.3516/3

Research Highlights, EP 1.81

Research Highlights of the NMC Development Division, C 55.197

Research Highlights in Aging, FS 2.22/25

Research Highlights, National Institutes of Health, FS 2.22/28

Research in Action (series), J 28.15/2-2, J 28.24/3-2

Research in Brief, ED 1.322

Research in Brief (series), J 28.24

Research in Education, FS 5.77, HE 5.77, HE 18.10

Research in Forest Products, A 13.27/11

Research in Progress, Calendar Year, D 101.52/5

Metallurgy and Materials Sciences, Mechanics and Aeronautics, Chemistry and Biological Sciences, D 101.52/5-5

Physics, Electronics, Mathematics, Geosciences, D 101.52/5-4

Research in the Teaching of Science, FS 5.229:29000, HE 5.229:29000

Research Information Abstracts, A 106.37/2

Research Information Digest, Recent Publications of Southeastern Forest Experiment Station, A 13.63/13

Research Information Letter, A 106.37

Research Institute for the Behavioral and Social Sciences: Technical Papers, D 101.60

Research Issues, HE 20.8214

Research Library Abstracts; Domestic, Y 3.W 89/2:20

Research Library, Recent Acquisitions, FR 1.29, FR 1.29/2

Research Memorandum–

Air University, Human Resources Report Institute, D 301.26/7

National Labor Relations Board, LR 1.10

Social Security Administration, SS 1.28, FS 1.28

Research Monograph Series, HE 20.3965, HE 20.8216

Research Monographs, Y 3.W 89/2:17, FW 4.35

Research News, Y 3.N 88:54

Research News (press releases), HE 20.3407

Research Notes–

Forest Service, A 13.79

National Center for Health Services Research, HE 20.6514

Research Objectives, D 301.69/3

Research on Bird Repellents, Progress Reports, I 49.47/ 2

Research on U.S. International Trade, C 42.32

Research Opportunities at the Census Bureau, C 3.293

Research Opportunities for Women Scientists and Engineers, NS 1.48/2

Research Papers–

Forest Service, A 13.78

Thrift Supervisor Office, T 71.16

Research Papers, Separates from the Journal of Research, C 13.22

Research Participation for Teachers of Science and Mathematics, NS 1.12/3

Research Plan, J 28.25/3

Research Preview, J 28.24/7

Research Product (series), D 101.60/5

Research Profiles, FS 2.22/43

Research Program Plan, J 28.25/3

Research Programs in Aging, FS 2.22/25-2

Research Progress and Plans of the Weather Bureau, C 30.75

Research Progress in (year), a Report of the Agricultural Research Service, A 77.1

Research Progress (year), A 13.66/1

Research Project Summaries, National Institute of Mental Health, FS 2.22/16-2

Research Projects–

Department of State, S 1.96

Federal Emergency Management Agency, FEM 1.22

Research Publications of the National Biological Service, I 73.9

Research Relating to Children, FS 17.211

Research Relating to Children, Bulletins, HE 19.120

Research Relating to Children, Inventory of Studies in Progress, FS 3.220

Research Relating to Special Groups of Children, FS 3.220/2, FS 14.114/2

Research Report, A 13.43/8

Research Report AFPTRC-TN (series), D 301.36/6

Research Reports–

Air Force Academy, D 305.14

Air Training Command, Human Resources Research Center, D 301.36/6

Air University, D 301.26/13

Arms Control and Disarmament Agency, AC 1.15

Army Ballistic Missile Agency, D 105.15

Bureau of Federal Credit Unions, FS 3.309

Children's Bureau, FS 17.214

Cold Regions Research and Engineering Laboratory, D 103.33/3

Department of the Air Force, D 301.26/7-2

Economics, Statistics, and Cooperatives Service, A 105.31
Farm Security Administration, A 61.15
Forest Products Laboratory, A 13.27/14
Injury Control Report Laboratory, FS 2.316
Lake Survey Office, D 103.209
National Cancer Institute, FS 2.22/32
National Commission for Employment Policy, Y 3.Em 7/3:10/nos
National Environmental Research Center, EP 1.21/9
National Institue of Justice, J 28.24/3
National Institute of Mental Health, HE 20.2420/4, HE 20.8114/2
Naval Research Laboratory, D 210.22
Naval School of Aviation Medicine, D 206.16
Office of Information for the Armed Forces, D 2.12
Packers and Stockyards Administration, A 96.10
Publications Relating to Horticulture, A 77.522
Smithsonian Institution, SI 1.37
Social Security Administration, FS 3.49, HE 3.49
Southwestern Forest and Range Experiment Station, A 13.43/8
Walter Reed Army Institute of Research, D 104.15
Waterways Experiment Station, D 103.24/5
Research Report from the NICHD, HE 20.3364/2
Research Reports, National Environmental Research Center, Las Vegas [list], EP 1.21/9
Research Reports Supported by Office of Water Resources Research Under the Water Resources Research Act of 1964 Received During the Period (date), I 1.97/2
Research Resources Reporter, HE 20.3013/6
Research Resources Reports (separates), HE 20.3013/6 a
Research Review–
　　Air Training Command, Human Resources Research Center, D 301.36/4
　　Department of the Air Force, D 301.69/6-2
　　Economic Development Administration, C 46.26
　　Office of Aerospace Research, D 301.69/6
Research Results Utilization, Research Project Control System, Status Summary Report, Y 3.N 88:36
Research Series, C 1.93, J 1.44
Research Studies–
　　Defense Civil Preparedness Agency, D 14.17
　　Department of State, S 1.101/12
Research Summary (series), E 1.107, EP 1.89, SBA 1.20/3
Research Study (series), NCU 1.21
Research Summary (Series), SBA 1.20/3
Research Surveys, D 110.11
Research Technical Library Biweekly Accession List, PrEx 4.15
Research to Improve Health Services for Mothers and Children, HE 20.5114/2
Research Update, C 13.78, HE 20.3222
Research Updates in Kidney and Urologic Health, HE 20.3324/2
Research Utilization Series, FS 2.22/41
Research Working Papers (series), FHL 1.35
Research (year), Annotated List of Research and Demonstration Grants, HE 17.15
Research-Reference Accessions, Y 3.R 31:29, A 61.15, A 36.110
Research/Resources Management Reports, I 29.105
Reserve Component Programs, D 1.1/3-2
Reserve Fleet Safety Review, C 39.219
Reserve Manpower Statistics, D 1.61/7
Reserve Marine, D 214.10
Reserve Officers Training Corps Bulletin, W 99.17/18
Reserve Positions of Major Reserve City Banks, FR 1.15/2
Reserve Training Publications Index, TD 5.21
Resettlement Recap, FS 14.15
Resident, Extension, and Other Enrollments in Institutions of Higher Education, FS 5.254:54000, HE 5.254:54000
Resident Leader, HH 1.113/2
Resident Research Associateships, Postdoctoral, Tenable and National Bureau of Standards, C 13.47
Residential Buildings Energy Consumption Survey, E 3.43/5
Residential Electric Bills in Major Cities, E 3.11/17-2
Residential Energy Consumption Survey, E 3.43, E 3.43/4
Residential Energy Consumption Survey: Housing Characteristics, E 3.43/3
Residential Program Highlights, FEM 1.17
Residential Solar Program Reports, HH 1.74
Residents of Farms & Rural Areas, C 3.186/25
Resolutions, ES 2.6/5

Resource and Potential Reclamation Evaluation Reports, I 53.31
Resource Applications, E 1.30
Resource Bulletins, A 13.80
Resource Conservation and Development Plans, A 57.62
Resource Conservation Development Plan, A 57.65
Resource Decisions in the National Forests of the Eastern Region, A 13.90
Resource Directory, HE 20.3660/2
Resource Exchange Bulletin, FEM 1.110
Resource Guide for Health Science Students: Occupational and Environmental Health, HE 20.7108:H 34/2
Resource Inventory Notes, I 53.24
Resource Management, D 101.89
Resource Management Monographs, D 1.44
Resource Management Quarterly Information Summary, C 55.9/3
Resource Papers in Administrative Law, Y 3.Ad 6:11
Resource Publications, I 49.66
Resource Reports, A 13.80/2
Resource Reports (series), C 55.317
Resource Status Reports, I 49.67
Resources Analysis Memos, HE 20.3014/2
Resources and Staffing, HE 20.4102:R 31
Resources Atlas Project: Thailand, Atlas, D 103.49
Resources Evaluation Newsletter, A 13.69/14
Resources for Biomedical Research and Education, Reports, HE 20.3014
Resources for Change, a Guide to Projects, HE 19.9:R 31
Resources for Freedom, Research to the President by President's Materials Policy Commission, Pr 33.15
Resources for Medical Research and Education, Reports, HE 20.3014
Resources for Medical Research, Reports, FS 2.22/33
Resources in Education, ED 1.11, HE 19.210
Resources in Women's Educational Equality, ED 1.17/2, HE 19.128:W 84/2
Resources Management Plan Annual Update, I 53.50
Resources (series), HE 20.8218
Response, Report on Actions for a Better Environment, A 21.30
Responsibilities and Organization, Y 10.20
Results of Observations made at C. & G. Survey Magnetic Observatories, C 4.16
Results of Regional Cotton Variety Tests by Cooperating Agricultural Experiment Stations, A 77.15:34
Results of Services Conference, C 61.56
Results under the Small Business Innovation Development Act of 1982, SBA 1.1/4
Resume of U.S. Civil Air Carrier and General Aviation Aircraft Accidents, Calendar Year, C 31.244
Retail Bulletins, Y 3.N 21/8:12
Retail Food Price Index, L 2.39
Retail Food Price Index, Washington, D.C., Area, L 2.39/3
Retail Furniture Report, FR 1.41
Retail Gasoline Prices, E 3.13/9
Retail Installment Credit and Funiture and Household Appliance Stores, FR 1.34/2
Retail Prices, L 2.6/a 2
Retail Prices and Indexes of Fuels and Electricity, L 2.40
Retail Prices and Indexes of Fuels and Utilities, L 2.40
Retail Prices on Food, L 2.3
Retail Sales, Independent Stores, Summary for States, C 3.138
Retail Stores Section Flyers, Y 3.F 73:16
Retail Trade Bulletins, C 3.202/2
Retail Trade (by States), C 3.940-10
Retail Trade Report–
　　East North Central, C 3.176
　　East South Central, C 3.177
　　Middle Atlantic Region, C 3.174
　　Mountain Region, C 3.180
　　New England, C 3.173
　　Pacific Region, C 3.181
　　South Atlantic Region, C 3.175
　　United States Summary, C 3.138/2
　　West North Central, C 3.178
　　West South Central, C 3.179
Retail, Wholesale, Service Trades, Subject Bulletin, RWS (series), C 3.202/9
Retailers' Bulletins, Pr 32.4221
Retiree Newsletter, TD 5.45
Retirement, CS 1.41/4:831-1
Retirement and Survivors Insurance Semiannual Analysis, HE 3.57/2
Retirement Circulars, CS 1.29

Retirement Reports, Fiscal Yr., C.S. Retirement Act, Panama Canal Annuity Act, CS 1.29/2
Return on Investment Case Study, D 103.53/8
Reusable News, EP 1.17/5
Revenue and Traffic Carriers by Water, IC 1 wat.11
Revenue and Traffic of Class A and B Water Carriers, IC 1 wat.11
Revenue Commission, Reports (general), T 1.18/1
Revenue Commission, Special Reports (numbered), T 1.18/2
Revenue Procedures, T 22.19/6
Revenue Programs for the Public Schools in the United States, FS 5.222:22013, HE 5.222:22013
Revenue Sharing Quarterly Payment, T 1.53/3
Revenue, Special Commissioner, Annual Reports, T 1.19
Revenue Traffic Statistics of Class I Railroads in the United States, IC 1 ste.24
Revenues and Classes of Post Offices, P 4.13
Revenues and Expenditures for Public and Elementary and Secondary Education, ED 1.119
Revenues and Income of Privately Owned Class a & B Electric Utilities in the U.S., FP 1.11/5
Revenues, and Office of Revenue Sharing Newsletter, T 1.49
Revenues, Expenses, and Statistics of Class 1 Motor Carriers of Passengers, IC 1 mot.11
Revenues, Expenses, and Statistics of Class 1 Motor Carriers of States, IC 1 ste.24
Revenues, Expenses, and Statistics of Freight Forwarders, IC 1.19
Revenues, Expenses, Other Income, and Statistics of Class 1 Motor Carriers of Passengers, IC 1 mot.12
Revenues, Expenses, Other Income, and Statistics of Large Motor Carriers of Property, IC 1 mot.13
Review of Alcohol as a Cause Factor, TD 1.129
Review of Arms Control and Disarmament Activities, Y 4.Ar 5/2-16
Review of Budget, Pr 34.107/3
Review of Bureau of Mines Coal Program, I 28.17, I 28.27
Review of Bureau of Mines Energy Program, I 28.27
Review of Current DHHS, DOE, and EPA Research Related to Toxicology, HE 20.3563
Review of Current Information in Treasury Library, T 23.7
Review of Current Periodicals, New Series, SE 1.23
Review of Foreign Developments, Prepared for Internal Circulation, FR 1.49
Review of Month, L 2.59
Review of Mutual Cooperation in Public Administration, S 17.46
Review of Operations–
　　Information Agency, IA 1.1/2
　　Social Security Administration, FS 3.15
Review of Power Planning in Pacific Northwest, Calendar Year, Y 3.P 11/4:9
Review of Selected U.S. Government Research and Development Reports, OTR-(series), C 13.49
Review of Some Recent Magazine Articles Relating to Housing, I 40.9
Review of Soviet Ground Forces, D 5.209
Review of Standards of Performance for New Stationary Sources, EP 4.19
Review of the Air Force Materials Research and Development Program, D 301.45
Review of the Economy, Y 4.Ec 7:Ec 7/40
Review of the Month, Pr 33.212
Review of the World's Commerce, S 4.12, C 14.15
Review of U.S. Patents Relating to Insecticides and Fungicides, A 7.9
Review of U.S. Patents Relating to Pest Control, A 47.7
Review of United States Oceanborne Foreign Trade, C 39.202:Oc 2
Review of United States Patents Related to Pest Control, A 77.311
Review of USTTA International Markets, and Summary of Cooperative Advertising Opportunities, C 47.20
Review of War Surgery and Medicine, W 44.16
Review of Waste Package Verification Test, Y 3.N 88:25-3
Review of World's Commerce, C 10.9
Review, Statistical Review of Ordnance Accident Experiment, W 34.42
Reviewing and Acting on Medical Certificates, CS 1.41/4:339-31
Reviews and Lectures, D 211.13/3
Reviews of Data on Research and Development, NS 1.11
Reviews of Data on Science Resources, NS 1.11/2
Reviews of New Reports, HE 20.6229

Reviews of New Reports from the Centers for Disease Control and Prevention/National Center for Health Statistics, HE 20.6216/6
Revised Customs Regulations, T 1.9/2
Revised Guide to the Law and Legal Literature of Mexico, L 1.36:38
Revised Monthly Retail Sales in Inventories, C 3.138/3-3
Revised Statutes, S 7.10
Revision of Rules (all classes), C 15.9/3
RFC Mortgage Company, Circulars, Y 3.R 24:9
RFC Small Business Activities, FL 5.15
RFC Surplus Property News, FL 5.12
Rh Hemolytic Disease Surveillance, HE 20.7011/19
Rhenium in (year), I 28.145
Rheumatoid Arthritis, Handout on Health, HE 20.3916
Rice Administration Orders, A 55.20
Rice Annual Market Summary, A 88.40/2:18
Rice Market News, A 88.18/9
Rice Market News Supplement, Rough Rice Receipts, A 88.18/20
Rice Market Review, A 82.33
Rice Production, Louisiana Crop Reporting Service, A 88.18/26
Rice Situation, A 88.18/18, A 93.11/3, A 105.20/4
Rice, Situation and Outlook Report, A 93.11/3
Rice Stocks, A 92.43
Rice, Stocks, and Movement, California Mills, A 82.49, A 88.18/10
Rice, Stocks and Movement, Southern Mills, A 82.50
Rice Stocks, Rough and Milled, A 105.42
Rice Yearbook, A 93.11/4
Rickettsial Disease Surveillance, HE 20.7011/27
RIF [Reading Is Fundamental] Newsletter, SI 1.36
Right to Read, ED 1.12, HE 19.125
RIIES Bibliographic Studies, SI 1.40
RIIES Occasional Papers, SI 1.40/2
RIIES Research Notes, SI 1.40/3
Rings of Saturn, NAS 1.22:343
Rio de Janeiro, International Exposition of Centenary of Independence of Brazil, 1922-23, S 6.20
Risk Analysis of Farm Credit System Operations and Economic Outlook, FCA 1.23/2-2
River Basins of the United States, I 19.56
River Currents, TD 5.27
River Forecasts Provided by the National Weather Service, C 55.117/2, C 55.285
River Mile Index, Y 3.P 11/4:10
River Summary and Forecast, [Lower Mississippi Region], C 55.110/7
River Summary and Forecast, New Orleans, Louisiana, C 55.110/2-2
River Summary and Forecasts [Memphis, Tenn. area], C 55.110/2
River Temperature at Selected Stations in the Pacific Northwest, I 19.46/2-2, I 19.46/2-3
RM-TT- (series), A 13.69/15
RMP Bulletin, I 72.3/2
RMRScience, A 13.151/6
Road & Rec, D 301.72/2
Road to the United States Census 2000, C 3.296
Roads Circular, I 20.24
Rockwell International, Rocky Flats Plant, E 1.12/4
Rocky Mountain National Park, Annual Reports, I I 1.57
Rocky Mountain Regional Aviation System Plan, TD 4.33/5
Rocky Mountain Research Station Directory, A 13.151/4-2
Rocky Mountain Research Station: Bibliographies and Lists of Publications, A 13.151/2
Rocky Mountain Research Station: General Publications, A 13.151
Rocky Mountain Research Station: Handbooks, Manuals, Guides, A 13.151/4
Rocky Mountain Research Station: Maps, A 13.151/3
ROD Annual Report, EP 1.1/7
Rodenticides and Mammal, Bird and Fish Toxicants, EP 5.11/4
Rodman Process Laboratory, Watertown Arsenal, Reports, D 105.13
RO/EERL Series, EP 6.10
Roll of Honor, W 39.7
Roll of Honor, Supplemental Statement of Disposition of Bodies of Deceased Union Soldiers and Prisoners of War Removed to National Cemeteries in Southern and Western United States, W 39.8
Rolla Research Center Annual Progress Report FY, I 28.154/2
Roosevelt Library, Annual Report of Archivest of United States, GS 4.9
Rosenwal (Lessing J.) Collection Catalog, LC 1.2:R 72/3

Roster and Directory of Troops in Hawaiian Department, W 81.5
Roster and Station of Officers of Signal Corps, W 42.9
Roster of Attorneys and Agents Registered to Practice before the U.S. Patent Office, C 21.9
Roster of Commissioned Officers and Employees, A 29.28
Roster of Disqualified Attorneys, I 24.12
Roster of Examining Surgeons, I 24.10
Roster of Field Officers, I 21.15
Roster of General Officers of General Staff, Volunteers, W 3.27
Roster of Members of PHS Public Advisory Groups, Councils, Committees, Boards, Panels, Study Sections, HE 20.2:Ad 9/3
Roster of Officers, Adjutant-General's Department, W 3.34
Roster of Officers and Troops, W 12.8
Roster of Officers of Indian Service, I 20.10
Roster of Organizaed Militia of United States, by Divisions, Brigades, Regiments, Companies, and other Organizations, with their Stations, W 70.5
Roster of Prepaid Dental Care Plans, FS 2.2:D 54/7
Roster of Subsistence Department, W 5.8
Roster Showing Stations and Duties of Officers, W 39.12, W 77.6
ROTC Manuals, D 101.48
Rotorcraft External-Load Operations, TD 4.6:part 133
Rough and Milled Rice Stocks, A 88.18/17
Rough List of More Important Additions, W 11.7
Rounds of the Teaching Staff, VA 1.61
Route Charts, C 4.9/9, C 4.9/17
Route Information Series, W 87.21/2
Routes to Indian Agencies and Schools, I 20.19
RPI (series), D 101.43/2
RRB Actuarial Studies, RR 1.14
RRB Quarterly Review, RR 1.7/3
RRB-SSA Financial Interchange: Calculations for Fiscal Year with Respect to OASI, DI, and HI Trust Funds, RR 1.15
RSC (series), D 101.104
RSI Quality Appraisal Awards and Disallowances Monthly Statistical Summary, HE 3.28/9
RSI Quality Appraisal Postadjudicative Monthly Statistical Summary, HE 3.28/8
RSIM (series), A 77.529
RSVP Exchange, AA 1.9/11-2
RTC Review, T 71.20, Y 3.R 31/2:17
RTD Technology Briefs, D 301.45/34
RTP-TR- (series), J 24.14
Rubber, Annual Report, C 1.28
Rubber Laboratory, Mare Island Naval Shipyard, Vallejo, California, Reports, D 211.16
Rubber News Letter, C 18.140/2
Rubber Products Trade News, C 18.201
Rubber Series, L 16.19
Rubella Surveillance, [reports], HE 20.7011/12
Rug and Floor Covering Material Notes, C 18.122
Rules, Ju 3.10
Rules Adopted by the Committees of the House of Representatives, Y 4.R 86/1-12
Rules and Procedures Manual, J 27.8/2
Rules and Regulations and Statements of Procedure, LR 1.6:R 86
Rules and Regulations for Federal Savings and Loan System, with Amendments to [date], FHL 1.6:Sa 9
Rules and Regulations for Foreign Vessels Operating in the Navigable Waters of the United States, TD 5.6:V 63/7
Rules and Regulations for Government and Discipline of United States Penitentiaries, J 1.16
Rules and Regulations Governing Paroling of Prisoners from Penitentiaries, State Institutions, J 1.15/5
Rules and Regulations Governing Paroling of Prisoners from U.S. Penitentiaries [etc.] (special), J 1.15/6
Rules and Regulations (miscellaneous), FP 1.7
Rules and Regulations of Bureau of Imports, WT 4.5
Rules and Regulations of National Parks, I 1.47/2
Rules and Regulations of Service, IC 1.12/1
Rules and Regulations, Title 10, Code of Federal Regulations, Chapter 1, Y 3.N 88:6
Rules for Inspection of Safety Appliances, IC 1 saf.6
Rules for the Committee on Interior and Insular Affairs, Y 4.In 8/14-13
Rules Governing Monthly Reports of Railway Accidents, IC 1 acci.6
Rules of Civil Procedure for District Courts in U.S., Ju 6.9/3

Rules of Civil Procedure for the United States District Courts, Y 4.J 89/1-11
Rules of Courts (by States), Ju 10.7
Rules of Criminal Procedure for the United States District Courts, Y 4.J 89/1-12
Rules of Flight, FAA 1.6/9
Rules of Practice–
   Board of Tax Appeals, Y 3.T 19:7
   Bureau of Domestic Commerce, C 41.6/11
   Federal Power Commission, FP 1.8
   Federal Trade Commission, FT 1.7
   General Land Office, I 21.9
   Patent and Trademark Office, C 21.8
   Patent Office, I 23.12
   Shipping Board, SB 1.7
Rules of Practice and Procedure, FP 1.6, TC 1.8
Rules of Practice and Rules Relating to Investigations and Code of Behavior Governing Exparte Communications Between Persons Outside the Commission and Decisional Employees, SE 1.6:R 86/4
Rules of Practice in Patent Cases, C 21.14:P 27
Rules of Practice under Title 4, Regulations and Orders, CA 1.14
Rules of Procedure, Y 4.Ag 4/2, Y 4.Ag 4/2-12, Y 4.St 2/3-11
Rules of Procedure, Committee on the Judiciary, Y 4.J 89/2-10
Rules of Procedure for the Permanent Select Committee on Intelligence, Y 4.In 8/18-10
Rules of Procedure of the Committee on House Administration, Y 4.H 81/3-10
Rules of the Committee on Government Operations, Y 4.G 74/7-10
Rules of the Committee on International Relations, Y 4.In 8/16:18
Rules of the Committee on Small Business, Y 4.Sm 1-10
Rules of the Select Committee on Narcotics Abuse and Control, Y 4.N 16/10
Rules of United States Court of Customs and Patent Appeals, Ju 7.8
Rules Pertaining to Aircraft Accidents, Incidents, Overdue Aircraft, and Safety Investigations, TD 1.106/2
Rules, Regulations, Instructions, A 94.6
Rules, Rulings and Instructions, A 55.69
Rulings and Interpretations, L 22.11
Rulings on Requests for Review of the Assistant Secretary of Labor for Labor- management Relations Pursuant to Executive Order 11491, As Amended, L 1.51/6
Rum: Annual Report on Selected Economic Indicators, ITC 1.31
Rum War at Sea, T 47.2:R 86
Runaways and Otherwise Homeless Youth Fiscal Year, Annual Report on the Runaway Youth Act, HE 23.1309/2
Rural Areas Development Newsletter, A 21.25/3
Rural Child Welfare Series, L 5.11
Rural Conditions and Trends, A 93.41/3
Rural Development Goals, Pr 37.14
Rural Development Goals, Annual Report of the Secretary of Agriculture to the Congress, A 1.85/2
Rural Development Perspectives, A 93.41/2, A 105.40/2
Rural Development Program News, A 21.25
Rural Development Research Reports, A 93.41, A 105.40
Rural Electrification News, A 68.9
Rural Housing (New Jersey), A 84.17
Rural Information Center Publication Series, A 17.29
Rural Life Studies, A 36.136
Rural Lines, A 68.18
Rural Manpower Developments, L 1.63
Rural Opportunities, PrEx 10.14
Rural Rehabilitation, Y 3.F 31/5:11
Rural Resource Leaflets, A 21.25/2
Rural School Circulars, I 16.42
Rural School Leaflets, I 16.35
Rural Telephone Bank Publications, A 1.116
Russian Economic Notes, C 18.123
Russian Scientific Translation Program Publications, FS 2.22/19
Russian Series, S 1.17

S

S.O.C. [Synthetic Organic Chemicals], TC 1.25/3, TC 1.25/4
S.R. [Sugar Requirements and Quotas] (series), A 82.6/2

Safe Work Guide, OSHA, L 35.11
Safe Work Guides, SWG LS- (series), L 16.51/2
Safe Work Practices Series, L 35.11/2
Safeguard Our Nation's Youth on the Job, L 15.51/5
Safety and Fire Protection Bulletins, Y 3.At 7:3
Safety and Health Requirments, L 16.23
Safety and Special Actions, Reports, Public Notices, CC 1.39/2
Safety and Special Radio Services Bulletins, CC 1.39/3
Safety Appliances Act [text], IC 1 saf.5
Safety Bulletins–
　Bureau of Employees' Compensation, FS 13.307, L 26.7
　Civil Aeronautics Board, C 31.214
　Civil Conservation Corps, FS 4.8
　Employees Compensation Commission, EC 1.9
　Federal Emergency Relief Administration, Y 3.F 31/ 5:24
　Government Printing Office, GP 1.24
　National Shipping Authority, C 39.209
　National Youth Administration, FS 6.16
　Works Progress Administration, Y 3.W 89/2:11
　Works Projects Administration, FW 4.20
Safety Bus Checks, TD 2.302:B 96
Safety Competition, National Crushed Stone Association, I 28.26/4
Safety Competition, National Lime Association, I 28.26/3
Safety Competition, National Sand and Gravel, I 28.26/ 3
Safety Competitions, National Limestone Institute, I 28.26/7
Safety Conference Guides, I 1.77/3
Safety Department Bulletins, Y 3.F 31/7:10
Safety Digest, W 34.37, D 101.22/3:385
Safety Division Bulletins, Y 3.Em 3:8
Safety Effectiveness Evaluation, NTSB-SEE-(series), TD 1.125
Safety Evaluation Series, TD 2.62
Safety, Fire Prevention, and Occupational Health Management, by Objectives Review, D 301.99
Safety in Industry, L 16.3
Safety in Mineral Industries, I 28.113
Safety Investigation Regulations, SIR (series), C 31.206/4
Safety Management Information, EP 1.7/3
Safety Management Series, L 35.19
Safety Manuals, I 69.8/2, L 38.8/2
Safety Musketeers, I 16.63
Safety News, Y 3.C 76/3:11-4
Safety News Letter, Y 3.F 31/5:17
Safety News Letter, Current Information in the Federal Safety Field, L 30.8
Safety, Occupational Health and Fire Protection Bulletin, VA 1.22:13-1
Safety Pamphlets, GP 1.18
Safety Post Cards, I 29.54

Safety Posters–
　Department of the Navy, N 1.31/2
　Federal Public Housing Authority, NHA 4.9
Safety Recommendations, TD 1.106/3
Safety Related Recall Campaigns for Motor Vehicles and Motor Vehicle Equipment, Including Tires, TD 8.9/2
Safety Reports, NTSB-SR (series), TD 1.106/4
Safety Research Programs Sponsored by Office of Nuclear Regulatory Research, Y 3.N 88:48
Safety Review, D 204.7
Safety Section Circulars, Y 3.R 13/2:26
Safety Series, Bulletins, IC 1 mot.10
Safety Standards, L 35.9
Safety Studies, C 31.223
Safety Studies, NTSB/SS (series), TD 1.27
Safetyline, D 207.15/2
SA-FR (series), A 13.102/2
Sagamore Army Materials Research Conference Proceedings (series), D 101.122
Sailing Dates of Steamships from the Principal Ports of the United States to Ports in Foreign Countries, C 15.19, C 18.10
Sailing Directions, D 5.317
　Coast and Geodetic Survey, C 4.18/3
　Naval Oceanographic Office, D 203.22
Saint Elizabeth's Hospital, Sun Dial, I 1.14/5
Saint Lawrence Survey [reports], C 1.22
Saint Louis, Louisiana Purchase Exposition, S 6.18
Saint Marys Falls Canal, Michigan, Statistical Report of Lake Commerce Passing through Canals at Sault Ste. Marie, Michigan and Ontario, W 7.26, M 110.16, D 103.17
Salable [and total] Receipts of Livestock at Public Markets, in Order of Volume, A 88.16/15

Salad Dressing, Mayonnaise and Related Products, C 57.316, C 57.514
Salaries and Fringe Benefits, HE 19.332
Salaries of State Public Health Workers, FS 2.82
Salary Procedural Regulations, ES 4.6/5
Salary Tables, Executive Branch of the Government, CS 1.73, PM 1.9
Sales by Producers of Natural Gas to Interstate Pipe-Line Companies, FP 1.21
Sales Finance Companies–
　Bureau of the Census, C 3.151
　Federal Reserve System Board of Governors, FR 1.26
Sales of Capital Assets Reported on Individual Income Tax Returns, T 22.35/2:C 17
Sales of Condemned Ordnance and Stores, W 34.15
Sales of Electric Energy to Ultimate Consumers, FP 1.11/6
Sales of Firm Electric Power for Resale, by Private Electric Utilities, by Federal Projects, by Municipals, FP 1.21
Sales of Fuel Oil and Kerosene in (year), I 28.45/5
Sales of Lacquers, C 3.88
Sales of New One-Family Homes, C 3.215/9
Sales Product Catalog (online), GP 3.22/7
Sales, Profits, and Dividends of Large Corporations, FR 1.40
Sales Reports, A 82.61
Sales, Revenue, and Income for Electric Utilities, E 3.11/2-6
Sales, Revenue, and Income of Electric Utilities, E 3.11/ 2-8
Sales Tax Rulings, T 22.26
Sales Tax Rulings, Cumulative Bulletin, T 22.27
Saline Water Conservation Program, Reports and Publications, I 1.83
Saline Water Conversion Demonstration Plant, I 1.87/2
Saline Water Conversion Report for (year), I 1.1/3
Saline Water Research and Development Progress Reports, I 1.88
Salmonella Surveillance, Annual Summary, HE 20.7011/15
Salmonella Surveillance, Reports, HE 20.2309
Salt in (year), I 28.134
Salvage News Letters, Pr 32.4823
SAMHSA News, HE 20.8026
Sand and Gravel in (year), I 28.146, I 28.146/2
Sandhill Crane Harvest and Hunter Activity in the Central Flyway During the Hunting Season, I 49.106/4
Sandia Technology, E 1.20/5
Sanitary Climatology Circulars, A 29.15
Sanitation Handbook of Consumer Protection Programs, A 88.6/4:Sa 5
Sanitation Series, A 43.40
Santiago, Chile, International Exhibition, 1875, S 6.5
Santa Monica Mountains and Seashore, I 29.6/7
SAR Statistics, TD 5.50
Satcom Quarterly, NAS 1.12/7:410-33
Satellite Activities of NOAA, C 55.510
Satellite Applications Information Notes, C 55.37
Satellite Situation Report, NAS 1.40
Saval Ranch Research and Evaluation Project, Progress Report, I 53.40
Savings and Home Financing Chart Book, FHL 1.11/2
Savings and Home Financing, Source Book, FHL 1.11, T 71.17
Savings and Loan Activity in (Month), FHL 1.15/2
Savings and Mortgage Financing Data, HH 4.10
Savings and Mortgage Lending Activity, Selected Balance Sheet Items, F.S.L.I.C. Insured Savings and Loan Associations, FHL 1.20/2
Savings Letter, T 1.26/8, T 1.27/36
Savings, Mortgage Financing and Housing Data, FHL 1.10
[Savings Program] Posters, W 109.211/2
Savings System, T 1.27/31-39
SBA Economic Review, SBA 1.27
SBA News, SBA 1.7/2
SBIC Digest, the Equity Financing Arm of SBA, SBA 1.30
SBIC Industry Reports, SBA 1.29
SB/TA (series), C 52.21/2
Scales and Weighing Memorandums, A 96.11
Scanner, HE 23.3010
SCC [Ship Structure Committee], Y 3.Sh 6:6/SSC
Schedule A. Statistical Classification on Commodities Imported into the United States with Rates of Duty and Tariff Paragraphs, C 3.150:A
Schedule Arrival Performance in the Top 200 Markets by Carrier, C 31.261, CAB 1.19
Schedule B. Statistical Classification of Domestic and Foreign Commodities Exported from the United States, C 3.150:B

Schedule C. Code Classification of Countries, C 3.150:C
Schedule, Changes, C 3.150/2
Schedule D. Code Classification of U.S. Customs Districts and Ports, C 3.150:D
Schedule G. Consolidation of Schedule B Commodity Classifications for Use in Presentation of U.S. Export Statistics, C 3.150:G
Schedule H. Statistical Classification and Code Numbers of Shipments of Merchandise to Alaska from United States, C 3.150:H
Schedule J. Code Classification of Flag of Vessel, C 3.150:J
Schedule K. Code Classification of Foreign Ports by Geographic Trade Area and Country, C 3.150:K
Schedule L. Statistical Classification of Foreign Merchandise Reports in In-transit Trade of United States, C 3.150:L
Schedule N. Method of Transportation Code, Exports, C 3.150:N
Schedule of Annual and Period Indices for Carriers by Pipeline, IC 1 acco.10
Schedule of Blind-made Products, Y 3.B 61:8
Schedule of Courses, S 1.2:C 83/2
Schedule of Examinations for 4th-class Postmasters (by States), CS 1.27
Schedule of International Conferences, S 1.70/6
Schedule of Lists for Permissible Mine Equipment, I 28.8
Schedule of Mail Routes, P 10.12/16
Schedule of Mail Trains, P 10.12
Schedule of NIH Conferences, HE 20.3040
Schedule of Sailings of Steam Vessels Registered Under Laws of United States and Intended to Load General Cargo at Ports in United States for Foreign Destinations, IC 1 rat.8
Schedule of Sales, Y 3.W 19/8:8
Schedule of Sales Offerings, Pr 33.213
Schedule of Steamers Appointed to Convey Mails to Foreign Countries, P 8.5
Schedule of Training and Services for Fiscal Year, J 16.109
Schedule of Volumes (for document index), GP 3.11
Schedule P. Commodity Classification for Reporting Shipments from Puerto Rico to U.S., C 3.150:P
Schedule Q. Commodity Classification for Compiling Statistics on Shipments from U.S., C 3.150:Q
Schedule R. Code Classification and Definitions of Foreign Trade Areas, C 3.150:R
Schedule S. Statistical Classification of Domestic and Foreign Merchandise Exported from U.S., C 3.150:S
Schedule T. Statistical Classification of Imports into U.S. Arranged in Shipping Commodity GROUPS., C 3.150:T
Schedule W. Statistical Classification of U.S. Waterborne Exports and Imports, C 3.150:W
Schedule X. Statistical Classification of Domestic and Foreign Merchandise Exported from United States by Air Arranged in Shipping Commodity Groups, C 3.150:X
Schedule Y. Statistical Classification of Imports into United States Arranged in Shipping Commodity Groups, C 3.150:Y
Scheduled International Operations, International Trunks, C 31.262
Schedules, SE 1.10
Schedules of Basic Rates (by name of park or monument), I 29.33
Schedules of Payments to Holders of Cotton Options and Participation Trust Certificates by Congressional District of States, A 55.57
Schedules of Railway Post Offices, P 10.5
Scheley Court of Inquiry Proceedings, N 1.21/1
Scheme of City Distribution, P 1.18
Schemes for Separation of Mail by States, P 1.21
Schemes of City Distribution, P 10.9
Schemes of States (for use of publishers in distribution 2d class mail), P 10.10
Schemes of States (from certain standpoints), P 10.8
Schemes of States (general), P 10.6
Schizophrenia Bulletin, HE 20.2414, HE 20.8115
Scholarship Program, Applicant Information Bulletin, HE 20.6023
Scholarship Program, Applicant Information Instruction Booklet, HE 20.317
Scholarships and Fellowship Information, FS 5.63
School Children and the War Series, Leaflets, FS 5.32
School Desegregation in [various localities], CR 1.14
School District Data Book, ED 1.334/6
School Enrollment: October (year), C 3.186:P-20

School Enrollment, Social and Economic Characteristics of Students, C 3.186/12
School Facilities Service (lists & references), FS 5.10/2
School Garden Army Leaflets (general), I 16.28/6
School Health Studies, I 16.38
School Home-Garden Circulars, I 16.16
School Life, I 16.26, FS 5.7
School Lunch Series, A 73.13, A 75.18
School of Advanced Airpower Studies, D 301.26/6-9
School of Aerospace Medicine: Technical Documentary Report SAM-TDR (series), D 301.26/13-6
School of Aviation Medicine: General Publications, D 301.26/13-5
School of Instruction, T 33.11
School of Military Packaging Technology Booklets, SMPT-BKLT- (series), D 105.31
School Sanitation Leaflets, I 16.24
Schools and Safety Staffing Survey, ED 1.332
Schools at War, War Savings News Bulletins for Teachers, T 66.9
SCID-TR- (series), J 24.14
Science Activities in Energy, E 1.38/3
Science and Engineering Doctorates, NS 1.44
Science and Life [abstracts], C 41.67
Science and Technology, PrEx 7.15/6, PrEx 7.18/2
Science and Technology Agriculture Reporter (STAR), S 18.64
Science and Technology, Annual Report to Congress, NS 1.40
Science and Technology Fellowship Program, C 1.86
Science and Technology in Japan, Reports, M 105.24, D 102.13
Science and Technology in Review, E 1.28/18
Science and Technology News Features, C 1.32/2
Science and Technology Policy, PrEx 7.22/14
Science and Technology Review, E 1.53
Science Course Improvement Projects, NS 1.24
Science Education Origin, D 210.18
Science Findings, A 13.66/19
Science Indicators, NS 1.28/2
Science Information News, NS 1.17
Science Monographs, HE 20.8131/2
Science of Fingerprints, Classification and Uses, J 1.14/2:F 49
Science Reports (series), HE 20.8131
Science Resources Studies Highlights, NS 1.31
Science Study Aids, A 1.104
Science, Technology, and American Diplomacy, Y 4.F 76/1-12, Y 4.In 8/16:12
Science Writer Seminar Series, HE 20.3859
Scientific Activities in Universities and Colleges, NS 1.22:C 83/3
Scientific Affairs, PrEx 7.17/3
Scientific Aids to Learning Committee, Publications, NA 2.6
Scientific and Engineering Research Facilities at Universities and Colleges, NS 1.53
Scientific and Technical Aerospace Reports, NAS 1.9/4
Scientific and Technical Assessments Reports, EP 1.23/7
Scientific and Technical Personnel in the Federal Government, NS 1.22:G 74
Scientific and Technical Publications of ESSA Research Laboratories, C 52.21/4, C 52.21/4-2
Scientific Bulletin, D 210.3/3
Scientific Directory and Annual Bibliography, HE 20.3017
Scientific Information Activities of Federal Agencies, NS 1.16
Scientific Information Report, Pr 34.609
Scientific Inquiry Memoranda, C 6.15
Scientific Inventory Management Series, GS 2.6/4
Scientific Manpower Bulletins, NS 1.3/2
Scientific Manpower Series, FS 5.47
Scientific Manpower, Significant Developments, Views and Statistics, NS 1.14
Scientific Monograph Series, I 29.80
Scientific Monographs, D 201.16/3
Scientific Personnel Bulletin, D 210.7
Scientific Reports of Higher Schools–
    Chemistry and Chemical Technology, C 41.53/9
    Electro-Mechancis and Automation, C 41.65/7
    Machine Construction and Instruments Manufacture, C 41.65/8
    Metallurgy, C 41.54/4
Scientific Research Institutes of the USSR, LC 38.10
Scientific Translation Program Publications, FS 2.214
Sci-Tech Information, C 13.74
SCP Exchange, Y 3.N 21/29:15
SCS Aids, A 57.40
SCS Flood Reports, A 57.40/3
SCS National Engineering Handbook, A 57.6/2:En 3

SCS-CI- [Conservation Aids] (series), A 57.45
SD Developments, S 18.67
SD-TR (series), D 301.45/21-2
SE Asia Briefing Map, Series 5213, D 5.335
Sea Clipper, D 208.8
Sea Grant Annual Report, C 55.38
Sea Newsmakers, A 106.41
Sea Water Conversion, Solar Research Station (series), I 1.87
Seabee Items of Interest, N 21.13
Seafaring Guide, and Directory of Labor- Management Affiliations, C 39.206/3:Se 1
Seafaring Wage Rates, Atlantic, Gulf and Pacific Districts, C 39.202:W 12
Seafood Dealers of the Southwest Region, C 55.337/2
Sealed Bid/Invitation for Bids, D 7.34
Sealed Bids (series), D 7.34
Sealed Source and Device Newsletter (SS&D), Y 3.N 21/29:18-1
Sealift, Magazine of the Military Sealift Command, D 216.8
Seamen's Act As Amended and Other Laws Relating to Seamen [March 4, 1915], Y 1.2:Se 1/2
SEAN Bulletin, SI 3.13
Search, Administrative Research Bulletins, ARB- (series), VA 1.47
Search for Health (series), HE 20.3038
Search Tips Series, A 17.25
Season Tobacco Market News Reports Type 12, A 36.188
Seasonally Adjusted Capacity and Traffic–
    Scheduled Domestic Operations, Domestic Trunks, C 31.262/3
    Scheduled International Operations, International Trunks, C 31.262
    Scheduled Operations: System, Domestic, and International Trunks Plus Local Service Carrier, CAB 1.20
    Scheduled Operations, System Trunks, C 31.262/2
Seasonally Adjusted Capacity and Traffic Scheduled Operations–
    Local Service Carriers, C 31.262/4
    System Trunks and Regional Carriers, C 31.262/5
Seaword, Developments in American Flag Shipping, C 39.236
SEC Docket, SE 1.29
SEC Monthly Statistical Review, SE 1.20
SEC Special Studies, SE 1.38
Second Army Pamphlets (series), D 101.22/9
Second Army, 2A Circulars (series), D 101.4/3
Second Supplement on Aging, Version 2, HE 20.6232
Secondary Aluminum, I 28.71/3
Secondary Education, FS 5.53
Secondary Market Prices and Yields and Interest Rates for Home Loans, HH 1.99/3
Secondary School Circulars, I 16.22
Secondary School Personnel, FS 5.84:Se 2, HE 5.84:Se 2
Second-Order Leveling, List of Standard Elevations, C 4.39
Secretaries of State, Portraits and Biographical Sketches, S 1.69:162
Secretary of State Press Conferences, S 1.25/4
Secretary of State's Advisory Committee on Private International Law: Publications, S 1.130
Secretary's Annual Report to Congress, Posture Statement, Outlook and Program Review, E 1.60:0010
Secretary's Community Health Promotion Awards, HE 20.7612
Secretary's Instruction, L 1.22
Secretary's Letter, FS 1.30
Secretary's Notice, L 1.22/5
Secretary's Orders, L 1.22/2
Secretary's Semiannual Management Report to the Congress, S 1.1/9
Secretary's Semiannual Management Report, U.S. Department of Labor, L 1.1/3
Secretary's Semiannual Report to the Congress, HH 1.1/6, TD 1.1/4
Secretary's Task Force on Competition in the U.S. Domestic Airline Industry, TD 1.57
Section 106 Update, Y 3.H 62:9
Sectional Aeronautical Charts, C 55.416/10
Sectional Aeronautical Charts, TD 4.79/11
Sector Notebook Project, EP 1.113
Securities Act of 1933, As Amended to (date), SE 1.5:Se 2/3
Securities Exchange Act of 1934, As Amended to (date), SE 1.5:Se 4
Securities Traded on Exchanges Under the Securities Exchange Act, SE 1.16
Security Awareness Bulletin, D 1.3/3

Security Pamphlets, Y 3.At 7:18
Security Procedures, GP 1.23/2
Security Program, TD 1.33
Sedimentation Bulletins, Y 3.F 31/13:8, Y 3.In 8/8:8
Sedimentation Studies, A 57.14
Seed and Plant Introduction and Distribution, A 19.6
Seed Crops, A 88.30
Seed Crops Annual Summary, A 88.30/3, A 105.18
Seed Crops, Certified Seed Potato Report, A 88.30/6, A 92.19/6
Seed Crops Forecasts, A 92.19/2
Seed Crops Stock Reports, A 92.19/3
Seed Crops, Vegetable Seed Report, A 92.19/7
Seed Reporter, A 36.6
Seer Monograph, HE 20.3162/5
SEIDB Publications Bulletin, E 1.87
Seismological Reports, C 4.25
Seizures and Arrests, T 70.9/6
Select Lists, GS 4.17/5
Selected Abstracts of Completed Research Studies, Fiscal Year (date), SBA 1.18/4
Selected Abstracts of Planning Reports, HH 8.9
Selected Agricultural Activities of Public Employment Offices, L 7.59
Selected Audiovisual Records, Photographs of (various subjects), GS 4.17/7
Selected Bibliography of Range Management Literature, A 13.30/9
Selected Bibliography of Regional Medical Programs, HE 20.2612
Selected Compensation and Pension Data by State of Residence, VA 1.88
Selected Court Case Abstracts, Y 3.El 2/3:19
Selected Current Acquisitions, Lists, D 102.28/3
Selected Data on . . ., NS 1.55
Selected Data on Federal Support to Universities and Colleges, Fiscal Year, NS 1.30/2-2
Selected Decision of Comptroller General Applicable to Naval Service, N 20.7/4
Selected Documents, S 1.131
Selected DOE Headquarters Publications, E 1.13/4
Selected Economic Indicators, D 1.43
Selected Elements of Value of Property Used in Common Carrier Service, Before and After Recorded Depreciation and Amortization, Class I Line Haul Railways, Including Their Lessors and Proprietary Companies, IC 1 val.10
Selected English Teaching Materials Catalogue, IA 1.17/2
Selected Financial and Operating Data from Annual Reports, CC 1.30
Selected Findings, J 29.28
Selected Income and Balance-Sheet Items of Class I Railroads in the United States, IC 1 ste.34
Selected Industrial Films SIF (series), C 41.23/3
Selected Interest and Exchange Rates for Major Countries and the U.S., FR 1.32/3
Selected Interest Rates and Bond Prices, FR 1.32/6, FR 1.32/7
Selected Library Acquisitions–
    Department of Transportation, TD 1.15/3
    Small Business Administration, SBA 1.21
Selected List of Additions to Research Library, FR 1.22/2
Selected List of American Agricultural Books in Print and Current Agricultural Periodicals, A 17.17:1
Selected List of Articles in Current Periodicals of Interest to Ordnance Department, W 34.21/2
Selected List of Audiovisuals, FS 2.211/3
Selected List of Postsecondary Education Opportunities for Minorities and Women, ED 1.42
Selected List of Publications Added to the Library, W 34.21/4
Selected List of Recent Additions to the Library, L 1.19
Selected List of References on Old-Age Security, Y 3.F 31/5:20
Selected List of Technical Reports in Dentistry, HE 20.3412
Selected Manpower Statistics, D 1.61/4
Selected Medical Care Statistics, D 1.62
Selected Metropolitan Areas, L 2.3
Selected Multifamily Status Reports, Mortgage Insurance Programs by Name and Location of Each Project, HH 1.50
Selected Papers from Bureau of Radiological Health Seminar Program (numbered), HE 20.1109
Selected Papers in School Finance, ED 1.310/5
Selected Papers in the Hydrologic Sciences, I 19.13/2
Selected Periodical Literature, Lists, D 102.28/5
Selected Publications of the United States International Trade Commission, ITC 1.9/3
Selected Readings and Documents on Postwar American Defense Policy, D 305.12/2:D 36

Selected Reference Series, HE 20.8215/2
Selected References, FS 5.43, FS 5.220:20002A, HE 5.220:20002A
Selected References for Labor Attaches, List of Readily Available Materials, L 1.34/2
Selected References on Aging, FS 1.18/2, FS 14.9/4, FS 15.12/2
Selected References on Environmental Quality As It Relates to Health, HE 20.3616
Selected References on Housing, Y 3.C 33/3:8
Selected References on [various subjects], LC 33.9/2
Selected Rehabilitation Abstracts, FS 13.210
Selected Reports of Cases before Veterans' Education Appeals Board, Y 3.V 64:7
Selected Revenues, Expenses, Other Income, and Statistics of Class II Carriers of Property, IC 1 mot.13/2
Selected Safety Road Checks Motor Carriers of Property, TD 2.311
Selected Speeches and News Releases, A 1.134, A 21.24/2
Selected State Department Publications, S 1.30/3-2
Selected Statistical Data by Sex, S 18.56
Selected Statistics for Class 3 Motor Carriers of Property, IC 1 mot.14/2
Selected Summaries of Water Research, I 67.12
Selected Technical Publications, HE 20.4023
Selected Technical Reports, Information Retrieval Bulletin, TD 4.17/2
Selected Topic Digests, J 1.42/2
Selected United States Government Publications, GP 3.17, GP 3.17/2
Selected United States Marketing Terms and Definitions, English [foreign Language], C 41.93
Selected Urban Storm Water Runoff Abstracts, EP 2.10:11024
Selected Water Resources Abstracts, I 1.94/2
Selected Worldwide Weather Broadcasts, C 55.119
Selected-Current Acquisitions, TC 1.34/2
Selection of Patients for X-Ray Examinations (series), HE 20.4617
Selective Notification of Information, J 28.14
Selective Notification of Information SNI, J 26.19
Selective Service, Y 3.Se 4:9, Pr 32.5279, Y 3.Se 4:20
Selective Service Act As Amended [May 18, 1917], Y 1.2:Se 4
Selective Service College Qualification Test, Bulletin of Information, Y 3.Se 4:22
Selective Service Manual, Pr 32./5280
Selective Service Memorandums to All Navy Contractors, N 1.30
Selective Service News, Y 3.Se 4:20
Selective Service Regulations, Y 3.Se 4:6, Y 3.Se 4:7
Selenium, I 28.104
Selenium and Tellurium in (year), I 28.104/2
Selenium Report, I 28.104
Self-Employment Claims and Payment by Agencies, VA 1.35
Self-Evaluation Instrument (series), HE 20.7116
Self-Guiding Nature Trail Leaflets, Glacier National Park, I 29.61
Self-Guiding Nature Trail Leaflets, Mount Rainier National Park, I 29.61/2
Self-Instructional Texts (series), D 101.107/6
Selling in Army and Air Force Careers, W 3.84, M 108.79
Self-Study Course 3010-G, Environmental Health Sciences (series), HE 20.7021/11
Self-Study Course 3010-G, Environmental Health Sciences Manuals (series), HE 20.7021/11-2
Self-Study Course 3014-G, Waterborne Disease Control Manuals, HE 20.7021/4-2
Selling in (country), C 1.50, C 57.11
Selling to Navy Prime Contractors, D 201.2:Se 4/2
Semiannual Checklist, Bureau of International Commerce International Business Publications, C 42.15:C 41
Semiannual Consolidated Report of Balances of Foreign Currencies Acquired Without Payment of Dollars As of December 31 (year), T 63.117
Semi-Annual Checklist of the EEOC Orders, Y 3.Eq 2:19
Semiannual Interest Rate Bulletins, T 66.3/2
Semi-annual List of Reports Prepared for or by the Office of Toxic Substances, EP 1.65
Semiannual Procurement Report, NAS 1.30
Semiannual Report, Y 3.Se 4:1
Semiannual Report, Implementation of Helsinki Accord, S 1.129
Semi-Annual Report of Schools for Freedmen, W 41.5
Semiannual Report of the Inspector General, L 1.74, VA 1.55

Semiannual Report of the Inspector General to Congress, C 1.1/2
Semi-annual Report of the Inspector General, U.S. Small Business Administration, SBA 1.1/3
Semi-Annual Report of the Secretary of Commerce on the United States Travel Service, C 47.1
Semiannual Report, Office of Inspector General, A 1.1/3
Semiannual Report on Operations Under Mutual Defense Assistance Control Act of 1951, FO 1.1/2
Semiannual Report on Strategic Special Nuclear Material Inventory Differences, E 1.15/2
Semiannual Report to Congress on the Effectiveness of the Civil Aviation Security Program, TD 4.810
Semiannual Report to the Congress (Office of the Inspector General), T 1.1/5
Semiannual Reports to Congress on Audit Follow-Up, ED 1.1/4, ED 1.26/2
Semiannual Reports, NAS 1.1
Semiannual Reports on Operations under Mutual Defense Assistance Act, S 17.1/2
Semiannual Reports under Mutual Defense Assistance Control Act, Pr 33.901/2
Semi-Monthly Honey Reports, A 36.105, A 88.19
Semimonthly Means of Sea Surface Temperature, C 55.193
Semi-Monthly Military Government Report for U.S. Occupied Area of Germany, M 105.21
Semi-Monthly News Letter, Federal Threatre Project, Y 3.W 89/2:33
Semi-monthly Report on Employment Situation, L 2.53
Seminar of Manpower Policy and Program, L 1.39/8
Seminar on Industrial Issues (various topics), C 62.18
Semper Fidelis, D 214.35
Senate Budget Scorekeeping Report, Y 1.3/7
Senate Concurrent Resolutions, Y 1.1/4
Senate Executive Reports and Documents, Y 1.Cong.
Senate History (series), Y 1.3/8
Senate Printed Amendments, Y 1.4/5
Senate Procedure, Precedents and Practice, Y 1.93-1:S.doc. 21
Senate Treaty Documents, Y 1.1/4
Sending Gift Packages to Various Countries, C 49.9
Senior Executive Service, Forum Series, L 1.95
Senior Executive Service Newsletter, L 1.46/2
Sensory Biology of Sharks, Skates, and Rays, D 210.2
Separate Sheets of Selected Thematic and General Reference Maps from the National Atlas of the United States of America, I 19.111a
Sequestration Report for Fiscal Year (date): A Summary, Y 10.18
Sequoia and General Grant National Parks, Annual Reports, I 1.29
Sergeants' Business, D 101.118/3
Serial Holdings, HE 20.7019:Se 6
Serial Publications Indexed to Bibliography of Agriculture, A 17.17:75
Serial Titles Newly Received, LC 1.23
Serials Currently Received by the National Agricultural Library, A 17.18/2:Se 6
Serie De Estudios De Paises, Y 3.In 8/25:17
Series 1, Evaluation of Foreign Fruits and Nuts, A 77.533
Series Available and Estimating Methods, BLS Current Employment Statistics Program, L 2.124/2
Series Available and Estimating Methods, BLS National Payroll Employment Program, L 2.124
Series Data Handbook, HH 2.24/6
Series HC Reports, C 3.950-4/2
Series H/HH Savings Bonds, T 63.209/8-4
Series ISP, CENTS [Census Tabulation System], C 56.226
Series of Educational Illustrations (Charts), A 43.5/10, A 43.22
Series of Educational Illustrations for Schools (posters), A 45.5
Series on Religion Nationalism and Intolerance, Y 3.P 31:18
Series PC Reports, C 3.950-4
Series W- (numbered), VA 1.57
Serologic Tests for Syphilis, FS 2.60/7:Sy 7/2, HE 20.2308:Sy 7/2
SERVE - General Publications, ED 1.348/3
SERVE - Special Report, A, ED 1.348/2
Service and Regulatory Announcements-
  Agricultural Marketing Administration, A 75.16
  Agricultural Marketing Service, A 66.27, A 88.6/3
  Agricultural Research Service, A 77.6/2
  Agricultural Stabilization and Conservation Service, A 82.23
Service and Regulatory
  Alaska Game Commission, A 5.10/5

  Bureau of Agricultural Economics, A 36.5
  Bureau of Animal Industry, A 4.13, A 77.208
  Bureau of Biological Survey, A 5.6
  Bureau of Chemistry, A 7.6
  Bureau of Dairy Industry, A 44.5
  Bureau of Entomology and Plant Quarantine, A 56.14
  Bureau of Plant Industry, A 19.13
  Bureau of Plant Quarantine, A 48.7
  Bureau of Soils, A 26.7
  Caustic Poison, A 46.13, FS 13.110
  Civil Service Commission, CS 1.5
  Federal Horticulture Board, A 35.9
  Food and Drug, A 46.12
  Food Distruction Administration, A 80.118
  Food, Drug, and Cosmetic, A 46.19, FS 7.8, FS 13.115
  Import Milk, A 46.11, FS 13.114
  Insecticide and Fungicide, A 46.15
  Insecticide and Fungicide Board, A 34.6
  List of Intercepted Plant Pests, A 77.308/2
  Naval Stores, A 46.18
  Publications Relating to Entomology and Plant Quarantine, A 77.308
  Publications Relating to the Care of Animals and Poultry, A 77.208
  SRA-C&MS- (series), A 88.6/3
  Tea, A 46.14, FS 7.14
Service Bulletin, I 19.26
Service Bulletins of Defense Training in Vocational Schools, FS 5.24
Service Coordinators Chronicle, HH 1.125
Service Directory, A 13.8/2
Service Establishments (by States), C 3.940-11
Service Letters, VA 1.32
Service Reports-
  Energy Information Administration, E 3.26/5
  Farmer Cooperative Service, A 89.12
Service Series Posters, W 3.46/3
Service Series Special Posters, W 3.46/4
Service Survey, I 49.22
Service Trade Bulletins, Pr 32.4222
Service Trade Reports, C 3.185
Service, USDA's Report to Consumers, A 21.29, A 107.11
Servicemen's Group Life Insurance Program, Annual Report, VA 1.46/2
Services Research Branch Notes, HE 20.8216/4
Services Research Monograph Series, HE 20.8216/2-2
Services Research Monograph Series, National Polydrug Collaborative Project, Treatment Manuals, HE 20.8216/2
Services Research Reports, HE 20.8216/3
Services to AFDC Families, Annual Report to Congress, HE 17.709
Serving Many, A 82.27
SES Bulletins, D 101.140
Session Laws of Pamphlet Laws (State Department edition), S 7.6:C & S
Session Laws, or Pamphlet Laws (Little, Brown and Company edition), S 7.13:C & S
Settlement Opportunities on Reclamation Projects, I 27.49
Seventh Circuit Digest, Ju 2.9
Seventy-Fifth USA Maneuver Area Command, Annual Report and Historical Supplement, D 101.1/8
Seville, Spain, Ibero-American Exposition, October 12, 1928, S 6.21
Sewage and Water Works Construction, I 67.11
Sewage Facilities Construction, (year), EP 2.20
Sewage Treatment Works Contract Awards, FS 2.56/3
Sex Roles: a Research Bibliography, HE 20.8113:Se 9
Sexually Transmitted Disease Statistics, HE 20.7309
Sexually Transmitted Disease Surveillance, HE 20.7309/2
Sexually Transmitted Diseases, Abstracts and Bibliographies, HE 20.7311
SFA Update, C 55.344
Sharing, HE 1.56
Sharing Our World Through Talented Hands, ED 1.344
Sharing Promising Practices PE 1.13.SH 2
Shawnee Quarterly, the Shawnee National Forest Schedule of Projects, A 13.138
Shawnee Sportsman's Maps (series), A 13.28/3
Sheep, A 92.18/9
Sheep and Goats, A 105.23/8
Sheep and Lamb on Feed, A 88.16/13, A 105.47
Sheep and Lamb Situation, A 36.91
Sheep and Lambs: Weekly Average Price per 100 Pounds, A 36.183
Sheets of National Atlas of United States-
  Agricultural Research Service, A 77.19
  Bureau of the Census, C 3.62/3
  Census of Agriculture, C 3.31/10
  Coast and Geodetic Survey, C 4.9/21

Forest Service, A 13.28/2
Geological Survey, I 19.5/3
Interstate Commerce Commission, IC 1.30
Tennessee Valley Authority, Y 3.T 25:7-2
Weather Bureau, C 30.22/4
Shellfish Market Review, Current Economic Analysis S, C 55.309/4
Shellfish Situation and Outlook, CEA-S (series), C 55.309/4, I 49.8/8
Shenandoah National Park Chips, I 29.67
Sherman Pamphlets, I 20.30
Shift Colors, the Newsletter for Navy Retirees, D 208.12/3-2
Shigella Surveillance, Reports, HE 20.7011/18
Ship Construction Manuals, N 24.37, T 47.37
Ship Operations Report, National Ocean Survey, C 55.423
Ship Structure Committee, TD 5.63
Shipbuilders Bulletin, SB 2.9
Shipbuilding and Conversion Program, D 207.13
Shipbuilding Progress Report for Month Ending, C 39.216
Shipment of Liquefied Petroleum Gases and Methane in (year), I 28.98/5
Shipment Under the United States Foreign Aid Programs Made on Army- or Navy- Operated Vessels (American flag) by Port of Lading by Country of Destination, C 3.164:976
Shipments of Asphalt, I 28.110
Shipments of Domestic Pumps, Water Systems, and Windmills, C 3.77
Shipments of Domestic Water Softening Apparatus, C 3.78
Shipments of Measuring and Dispensing Pumps, Gasoline, Oil, etc., C 3.90
Shipments of Stocker and Feeder Cattle and Sheep, A 88.16/18
Shipping Coordinating Committee, S 1.130/2:Sh 6
Shipping Point Inspection Circulars, A 36.201
Shipping Weight and Dollar Value of Merchandise Laden on and Unladen from Vessels at United States Ports During the In-transit Movement of the Merchandise from One Foreign Country to Another, C 3.164:981
Ships Registered Under Liberian, Panamanian, and Honduran Flags Deemed by the Navy Department to Be Under Effective U.S. Control, C 39.228
Shipyard Bulletin, SB 2.8
Shipyards, L 16.47/3
Shock and Vibration Bulletin, D 4.12, D 210.27/2
Shock and Vibration Digest, D 4.12/2, D 210.27
Shock and Vibration Monographs, D 1.42, D 210.27/3
Shooting News, W 82.5
Shorn Wool Production, A 88.35/2
Short-term Energy Outlook, E 3.31
Shrimp Landings, C 55.309/2
Sickle Cell Disease Advisory Committee, HE 20.3001/2:Si 1
Side Runs of Paper Trade, C 18.124
SIGCAT CD-ROM Compendium, GP 3.22/6
Signal Communication for All Arms and Services, W 3.50/8
Signal Corps Bulletin, W 42.3
Signal Corps Library Record, W 42.39
Signal Corps Memorandum, W 42.26
Signal Corps Technical Information Letters, W 42.40
Signal School Pamphlets, W 42.34/6
Signal Service Notes, W 42.14
Significant Arrearages Due the United States Government and Unpaid 90 Days or More by Official Foreign Obligors, T 1.45/5
Significant Cases, Federal Employee and Labor-Management Relations, PM 1.63
Significant Features of Fiscal Federalism, Y 3.Ad 9/8:18
Significant Incidents of Political Violence Against Americans, S 1.138/2
Significant NASA Inventions Available for Licensing in Foreign Countries, NAS 1.21:7038
Significant Provisions of State Unemployment Compensation Laws, SS 1.19, L 33.10
Significant Provisions of State Unemployment Insurance Laws, L 37.210
Silicon, I 28.75
Silicon in (year), I 28.75/2
Silicon Report, I 28.106
Silk and Rayon and Other Synthetic Textile Fibers, C 18.125
Silver [Mine Production], I 28.62
Silver Lining, T 71.22, Y 3.R 31/2:16
Silvical Leaflets, A 13.12
Silvical Series, A 13.66/11
Simplified Practice Recommendations, C 13.12

Simplifying Federal Aid to States and Communities, Annual Report to the President of an Interagency Program, PrEx 2.18
Singing Sands Almanac, I 29.6/3-2
Single Award Federal Supply Schedule, GS 2.7/7
SIPP Data News, C 3.274
SIPRE Reports, D 103.26
Sisal, Hemp, Jute and Miscellaneous Fibers, C 18.126
SITE , EP 1.89/4
SITE Technology Demonstration Summary, EP 1.89/4-3
SITE Demonstration Bulletin, EP 1.89/4-2
Sixth Quadrennial Review of Military Compensation, D 1.89
Sky Diagrams, N 11.11
SL [Statistical Lists] (series), I 49.42
Slab Zinc Reports, I 28.56
Slag-Iron and Steel in (year), I 28.53/5
Slim Selected Library in Microfiche, J 26.28
Slip Laws (public), GS 4.110, AE 2.110
Slip Laws: Public Laws, S 7.5:C.S.
Slip Opinions, Ju 6.8/b, Ju 15.9
Slope Maps, I 19.109
SMA Memo, HE 20.4614
Small Area Data Notes, C 56.217, C 3.238
Small Business Administration and Investment Act, Y 1.3:Sm 1
Small Business Administration and Investment Act, with Amendments [1953], Y 1.2:Sm 1
Small Business Administration Publications, Classification of Management Publications, SBA 1.18/3
Small Business Administration Publications [lists], SBA 1.18
Small Business Advocate, SBA 1.51
Small Business Aids, C 18.268
Small Business Aids (series), C 40.7/2
Small Business Bibliographies, SBA 1.3
Small Business Circular FOA/SBC (series), FP 1.13
Small Business Circular MSA/CBC (series), Pr 33.913
Small Business Circulars, Y 3.Ec 74/3:19
Small Business Economic Indicators, SBA 1.1/2-2
Small Business Innovation Research for Fiscal Year, C 1.82
Small Business Innovation Research Program Solicitation, TD 10.13
Small Business Innovation Research (SBIR) Program, D 1.48/3
Small Business Investment Companies Licensed by Small Business Administration, SBA 1.23
Small Business Investment Companies Licensed by the Small Business Administration As of (date), SBA 1.2:In 8
Small Business Lending in the United States, SBA 1.52
Small Business Management Series, SBA 1.12
Small Business Memo FOA/SBM (series), FO 1.14
Small Business Memo, ICA/SBM Series, S 17.14
Small Business Ombudsman Update, EP 1.117
Small Business Performance, by Claimant Program, D 1.48/2
Small Business Profiles, SBA 1.50
Small Business Report, D 7.18
Small Business Report to Congress for Fiscal Year, E 1.39/2
Small Business Research Series, SBA 1.20
Small Business Specialists, D 1.6/17
Small Business Subcontracting Directory, SBA 1.2/2, SBA 1.2/10
Small Business Weekly Summary, Trade Opportunities and Information for American Suppliers, FO 1.17
Small Claims Decisions, FMC 1.10/3
Small Farm Digest, A 94.23
Small Farm Family Newsletter, A 1.125
Small Grains, Annual Summary and Crop Winter Wheat and Rye Seedings, A 105.20/6, A 92.42
Small Industry Series, Cottage Industries Bulletins, S 17.37
Small Marketers Aids, SBA 1.14
Small-Area Data Activities, C 3.238
Small-Area Statistics, C 56.217/2
Small-Area Statistics Papers, C 3.238/2
Smaller War Plants Corporation Program and Progress Reports, Pr 32.4825
Small-scale Appropriate Energy Technology Grants Program, E 1.76
SMART Update, HE 20.4049
Smithsonian Annals of Flight, SI 9.9
Smithsonian Contributions to–
  Anthropology, SI 1.33
  Astrophysics, SI 1.12/2
  Botany, SI 1.29
  Earth Sciences, SI 1.26
  Knowledge, SI 1.6
  Paleobiology, SI 1.30

  the Marine Sciences, SI 1.41
  Zoology, SI 1.27
Smithsonian Folklife Studies, SI 1.43
Smithsonian Institution Information Systems Innovations, SI 1.32
Smithsonian Institution Press, Annual Reports, SI 1.1/a6
Smithsonian Institution Press, New Titles, SI 1.17/4
Smithsonian International Exchange Service Annual Report, SI 1.1/a3
Smithsonian Journal of History, SI 1.23
Smithsonian Miscellaneous Collection, SI 1.7
Smithsonian Opportunities for Research and Study in History, Art, Science, SI 1.44
Smithsonian Physical Tables, SI 1.7:120
Smithsonian Studies in Air and Space, SI 1.42
Smithsonian Studies in History and Technology, SI 1.28
Smithsonian Torch, SI 1.24
Smithsonian (Web Magazine), S 1.10
Smithsonian Year (date) Annual Report of the Smithsonian Institution, SI 1.
Smithsonian Year (date), Statement by the Secretary, SI 1.1/4
Smoking and Health Bulletin, HE 20.7610/2, HE 20.7613/2
Smoking and Health, a National Status Report, HE 20.7613
Smoking and Health Bibliographical Bulletin, FS 2.24/4
Smoking and Health Bulletin, HE 20.7012, HE 20.7211
Smoking and Tobacco Control Monographs, HE 20.3184/2
Smutty Wheat Reports, A 36.56, A 66.30
Snake River Birds of Prey Research Project, Annual Report, I 53.39
Smokey's Campaign Catalog, A 13.111/2
Snow and Ice Bulletin, A 29.16
Snow Survey and Soil Moisture Measurements, Basic Data Summary for Western United States, Including Columbia River Drainage in Canada, A 57.46/17
Snow Survey Phase of Project Skywater, Colorado, Annual Report, A 57.56/16
Snow Surveys and Water Supply Outlook for Alaska, A 57.46/13
Snow Surveys for Alaska, A 57.46/13
So–You Want to Be a [Occupation], PrEx 10.20
Socioeconomic Environmental Studies, EP 1.23/3
Social and Economic Characteristics of U.S. School Districts, HE 19.336
Social and Rehabilitation Record, HE 17.27
Social and Rehabilitation Service Reports Bulletins, HE 17.29
Social and Rehabilitation Service Research and Demonstration Projects, FS 17.15
Social Hygiene Monthly, T 27.21
Social Problems, Y 3.W 89/2:57, FW 4.19
Social Research Reports, A 61.10
Social Security Acquiescence Ruling (series), SSA 1.6/2
Social Security Administration Baltimore Directory, HE 3.58/2
Social Security Administration Publications Catalog, HE 3.38/3
Social Security Agreements (various countries) SSA 1.29
Social Security Beneficiaries by State and County, HE 3.73/2
Social Security Beneficiaries by Zip Code Area, HE 3.73
Social Security Beneficiaries in Metropolitan Areas, HE 3.73/3
Social Security Bulletin, HE 3.3
Social Security Bulletin, Statistical Supplement, HE 3.3/3
Social Security Bulletins, SSA 1.22
Social Security, Facts and Figures, SSA 1.19/2
Social Security Handbook, HE 3.6/8, SSA 1.8/3
Social Security Handbooks, HE 3.6/3:So 1/3
Social Security Information, HE 3.52
Social Security Information Items, HE 3.82
Social Security Programs in the United States, SSA 1.24/2
Social Security Programs Throughout the World, HE 3.49:31, HE 3.49/3, SSA 1.24
Social Security Rulings, Cumulative Bulletins, HE 3.44/2
Social Security Rulings on Federal Old-age, Survivors, Disability, and Health Insurance, HE 3.44
Social Security Student Gazette, HE 3.59
Social Security Today, SSA 1.28
Social Security Yearbook, FS 3.3/2
Social Seminar Discussion Guides, HE 20.2408/2

Special Announcements (series), HE 20.8318/2
Special Announcements Concerning Research Reports from Department of Commerce OTS, C 41.28/2
Special Appointed Committees, PrEx 1.19
Special Bibliographical Series, D 114.14
Special Bibliographies, HE 20.8211/2, D 102.28, D 301.26/11
Special Bibliography, Artillery and Guided Missile School Library, D 101.49
Special Bibliography (series), TD 8.13/2, D 305.12
Special Bulletin Addressed to Victory Speakers, Pr 32.5017/2
Special Bulletins–
    Bureau of Foreign and Domestic Commerce, Textile Division, C 18.127
    Civil Service Commission, CS 1.47
    Employees' Compensation Commission, EC 1.3/2
    Manufacturers Division, C 3.7
    United States Administration of Ryukyu Islands, D 102.19/2
Special Cement Bulletins, C 18.128
Special Census, 1923, High Point, N.C.; Virgin Islands 1917, C 3.23
Special Census of (city or area), C 3.186:P-28
Special Censuses, Summaries, C 3.186:P-29
Special Circulars, IC 1 rat.5
Special Civil Air Regulations, C 31.206/3
Special Committees and Commissions, Pr 43.8
Special Consular Reports, S 4.9, C 14.10, C 10.7, C 18.9
Special Court-Martial Orders, W 99.16/11, D 101.31
Special Current Business Reports: Monthly Department Store Sales in Selected Areas, BD- (series), C 56.219/3
Special Education Personnel in State Education Departments, FS 5.235:35051
Special Enrollment Examination, T 22.2/14
Special Express Company Circulars, IC 1 exp.4
Special Features Service, Y 3.P 96/3:8
Special Foreign Currency Science Information Program, List of Translations in Process for Fiscal Year, Coordinated and Administered by the National Science Foundation, C 51.12
Special Foreign Trade Reports, C 3.164/2
Special Hazard Review, HE 20.7113
Special History Studies (series), I 29.88/5
Special Industrial Relations Reports, L 2.58
Special Information Bulletins, FS 2.73
Special International Exhibitions, Annual Report, IA 1.22
Special Investigation Reports, TD 1.112/2
Special Issue, Consular Reports, S 4.13
Special Labor Force Reports, L 2.98
Special List (series), AE 1.115
Special Market Study Releases, SE 1.28
Special Memorandum Series, I 49.43
Special Meteorological Summaries, C 30.10/2
Special Monographs, Y 3.Se 4:17
Special Needs Offenders, Bulletin, Ju 13.17
Special News Letter, A 88.41
Special Notice (series), C 55.416/18
Special Notice Concerning Basic Agreements Teleprocessing Services Program (TSP) Industrial Group 737, Industrial Class 7374, GS 12.13
Special Notice to Mariners, D 203.8/3, TD 5.56
Special Notices, C 55.416/8
Special Notices, Supplement to Radio Facility Charts and In-flight Data, Europe, D 301.9/3
Special Notices to Airmen, CA 1.7/2, C 31.10, C 31.110
Special Occupational Hazard Review with Control Recommendations, HE 20.7113
Special Orders, A 1.13, IC 1.10, LC 1.6/3
Special Picture Pages, T 1.112
Special Press Feature, S 1.77/2
Special Promotion [releases] SP (series), FCD 1.7/2
Special Promotion Series from Office of Civil and Defense Mobilization, Battle Creek, Michigan, Bulletins, Pr 34.757/3
Special Publication, C 3.268
Special Publications, NTIA-SP- (series), C 60.9
Special Publications, SP- (series), D 203.22/3
Special Reference Briefs, A 17.24
Special Regulations, W 1.18
Special Releases [of Foreign Broadcast Intelligence Service], W 100.9
Special Report, Fresh Views of Employment of the Mentally Handicapped, PrEx 1.10/4-2
Special Report on Aging, HE 20.3862
Special Report Series, A 89.20
Special Report Series Circulars, IC 1.4/4
Special Report to the U.S. Congress on Alcohol and Health, HE 20.8313
Special Reports–
    Air Force Systems Command, D 301.45/42

    Bureau of Labor, C 8.5
    Bureau of the Census, C 3.5
    Central Housing Committee, Y 3.C 33/3:9
    Coastal Engineering Research Center, D 103.42/6
    Cold Regions Research and Engineering Laboratory, D 103.33/2
    Construction Engineering Research Laboratory, D 103.53/4
    Earth Sciences Division, D 106.17/2
    Executive Office of the President, PrEx 1.10/14
    Farm Credit Administration, FCA 1.21, A 72.9
    Farmer Cooperative Service, A 89.20
    Harry Diamond Laboratories, D 105.14/5
    Justice Statistics Bureau, J 29.13
    National Archives, AE 1.18
    Naval Submarine Medical Center, D 206.10/3
    Porto Rico, Labor Bureau, W 75.14/4
    Publications Relating to Home Economics and Human Relations, A 77.711
    Soil Conservation Service, A 57.72
    Soil Conservation Service, Office of Research, Sedimentation Section, A 76.215, A 80.2013
Special Reports (1948 Consuption Surveys), A 77.711
Special Reports to Congress and East-West Foreign Trade Board, TC 1.38/2
Special Resource Study (series), I 29.58/4
Special Resources for Research (series), LC 30.31
Special River Bulletins, A 29.19
Special Rules, WT 2.6
Special Scientific Report: Fisheries, C 55.312
Special Series–
    Bureau of Foreign and Domestic Commerce, Paper Division, C 18.146
    Military Intelligence Division, W 100.7
    Office of Education, FS 5.41
Special Series Reports of Division of Research, C 31.131/2
Special Service Digest, W 109.108
Special Services Memorandums, A 82.109
Special Statistical Reports on United States Water-borne Commerce, C 3.203
Special Studies, C 3.186:P-23, D 102.29, S 18.52/3
Special Studies, Current Population Reports, C 3.186:P-23
Special Studies Papers, FR 1.58
Special Studies Series, D 114.17
Special Study, NTSB-HSS (series), TD 1.126
Special Study Report, NTSB-HSS- (series), TD 1.120
Special Supplements to Survey of Current Business, C 56.109/4
Special Supplements to the Survey of Current Business, C 59.11/4
Special Tariff Permission, CA 1.16
Special Tariff Permission Under Section 224.1 of Economic Regulations, C 31.210
Special Tariffs, W 79.13/6
Special Text, M 114.8
Special Text (series), D 101.107/14, D 101.111/2
Special Text of Judge Advocate General's School, D 108.9
Special Texts, D 105.25
Special VD Education Circulars, FS 2.38
Special Warfare, D 101.124
Specialized Bibliography Series, HE 20.3614/6
Specials, T 22.18
Species Range Maps (series), A 13.107
Specifications–
    Agriculture Department, A 1.25
    General Services Administration, GS 1.9
    Geological Survey, I 19.17/6
    Interior Department, I 1.46
    Naval Facilities Engineering Command, D 209.11
    Reclamation Bureau, I 27.8
    State Department, S 1.32
    United States Postal Service, P 1.16, P 1.32
Specifications and Code Numbers for Individual Commodities, L 2.61/3
Specifications and Drawings of Patents, C 21.11
Specifications and Drawings of Patents Relating to Electricity, I 23.17
Specifications and Proposals for Supplies, T 58.7
Specifications Bulletins, D 301.19
Specifications for Public Buildings, T 39.6
Specifications for Retail Prices, L 2.65
Specifications for Supplies, SI 1.9
Specifications, International Aircraft Standards, C 13.9
Specifications, Proposals, and Advertisements, GP 1.7
Spectrum Series, HE 20.3417
Speeches and Remarks, FMC 1.9/3
SPEEDE/ExPRESS Newsletter, ED 1.133
SPI State Personal Income, C 59.25
Spinoff, Annual Report, NAS 1.1/4
Spokefish Monthly, C 55.50

Sponsored Reports Series, HE 19.311
Sponsored Research Programs, J 28.24/2
Sport Fishery Abstracts, I 49.40/2
Sport Fishery and Wildlife Research, I 49.1/6
Spot Announcements, L 22.28
Spot Cotton Quotations, Designated Markets, A 82.73, A 88.11/4
Spot News from Field, Y 3.F 31/11:22
Spot the Danger, User's Guide to [various products] Safety Series, Y 3.C 76/3:8-3
Spotlight, PM 1.18
Spotlight on Affirmative Employment Programs, PM 1.18/4
Spotlight on Organization and Supervision in Large High Schools, FS 5.50
Spring and Early-Summer Potatoes, A 88.26/4
Spring Potatoes, A 88.26/4
Spring Vegetables and Melons, A 88.26/4
Spring Vegetables, Spring Melons, Spring Potatoes, A 88.26/4
Squadron Bulletin, D 301.59/3
SRB Research Report, A 92.49
SRE Special Publication, FO 1.23
SRS (series), A 92.34
SRS Data Brief, NS 1.11/3
SSA Administrative Directives System Transmittal Notice, HE 3.68
SSA Baltimore Telephone Directory, SSA 1.9/2
SSA Management Newsletter for Supervisors and Management Personnel, HE 3.68/2
SSA Program Circulars–
    Disability, HE 3.4/4
    General Series, HE 3.4/2
    Public Information, HE 3.4/3
    Retirement and Survivors Insurance, HE 3.4/5
    Supplemental Security Income, HE 3.4/6
SSA Publications on CD-ROM, SSA 1.8/4
SSA Training Data Review Technician, Basic Training Course, HE 3.69/3
SSA Training (series): Technical CORE Curriculum, HE 3.69/2
SSA Workload Analysis Report, HE 3.79
SSA's Accountability Report for FY..., SSA 1.1/2
SSA's Accountability Report for FY...Summary, SSA 1.1/3
SSC, Y 3.Sh 6:SSC
SSI Recipients by State and County, HE 3.71, SSA 1.17
SSIG and SG. (Series), ED 1.76/2-3
Staff Accounting Bulletins, SE 1.31
Staff Development Series, FS 14.208/4
Staff Discussion Paper (series), E 2.23
Staff Economic Studies, FR 1.51
Staff Information Circulars, GS 4.12
Staff Information Papers, GS 4.12
Staff Instructions, A 68.21
Staff Manual Guide, HE 20.4008/4
Staff Memo from U.S. Secretary of Labor, L 1.33
Staff Memorandums, SS 1.29
Staff Papers, C 45.10
Staff Papers, Background Papers and Major Testimony, Y 3.Ec 7/3
Staff Papers, BIE-SP- (series), C 62.15
Staff Papers, FJC-SP- (series), Ju 13.10/2
Staff Practice and Procedure Digest, Y 3.N 88:23
Staff Publications, A 13.62/11
Staff Report Electric Power Supply and Demand for the Contiguous United States, E 1.126
Staff Report, FPC/OCE (series), FP 1.7/4
Staff Report of Monthly Report Cost and Quality of Fuels for Electric Utility Plants, E 2.13
Staff Report on Monthly Report of Cost and Quality of Fuels for Steam-Electric Plant, FP 1.32
Staff Reports, C 1.48
Staff Research Studies, TC 1.37
Staff Research Study (series), ITC 1.22
Staff, the Congressional Staff Journal, Y 4.R 86/2:3
Staff Training in Extramural Programs, HE 20.3053
Staffing Analysis Report, T 22.56
Stages and Discharges, Mississippi River and its Outlets and Tributaries, W 31.5, M 110.207, D 103.309
Stages and Discharges of Mississippi River and Tributaries and Other Watersheds in the New Orleans District, D 103.45/4
Stages and Discharges of Mississippi River and Tributaries in the Memphis District, D 103.45/2
Stages and Discharges of Mississippi River and Tributaries in the St. Louis District, D 103.45/3
Stages and Discharges of Mississippi River and Tributaries in the Vicksburg District, D 103.45

Stages of the Missouri River, W 32.6
Standard and Optional Forms Facsimile Handbook, GS 4.6/3, GS 12.18
Standard Broadcast Applications Ready and Available for Processing Pursuant to Sec. 1.354 (c) of Commission's Rules, Lists, CC 1.26/2
Standard Designs, I 27.6
Standard Distribution List, TD 5.61
Standard Field Tables, I 53.10
Standard Forms Catalog, GS 2.10/4
Standard Industrial Classification Manual, PrEx 2.6/2:In 27
Standard Instrument Approach Procedures, FAA 5.13, TD 4.60
Standard Instrument Departure (SID) Charts, Eastern U.S., C 55.416/5
Standard Instrument Departure (SID) Charts, Western United States, C 55.416/6
Standard Nomenclature Lists, W 34.22
Standard Nomenclature Lists, Obsolete General Supplies, W 32.23/4
Standard Number Series, N 4.7
Standard Occupational Classification Manual, PrEX 2.6/3
Standard Posters, A 13.20/2
Standard Reference Materials, C 13.10:260, C 13.48/4
Standard Reference Materials Price List, C 13.48/4-3
Standard School Lectures, Civilian Protection, Pr 32.4411
Standard Specification, I 27.11
Standard Specifications–
    Bureau of Yards and Docks, N 21.10
    Engineer Department, W 7.18
Standard Specifications for Construction of Airports, TD 4.24
Standard Terminal Arrival (STAR) Charts, C 55.416/3
Standardization [abstracts], C 41.72
Standardization and Data Management Newsletter, D 1.88
Standardization Directories, D 7.13
Standardization of Petroleum Specifications Committee, Bulletins, I 28.15
Standardization of Work Measurement, D 7.6/4-2
Standardized Government Civilian Allowance Regulations, Allowance Circulars, S 1.76
Standardized Government Post Differential Regulations, Differential Circulars, S 1.76/2
Standardized Regulations (Government Civilians, Foreign Areas), S 1.76/3
Standards and Labeling Policy Book, A 110.18
Standards Development Status Summary Report, Y 3.N 88:32
Standards, FAA-STD (series), TD 4.24/2
Standards for Fruits and Vegetables, A 104.6/3
Standards for Specifying Construction of Airports, TD 4.24
Standards Laboratory Cross-Check Procedure, Department of Navy, BUWEPS-BUSHIPS Calibration Program, D 217.16
Standards Laboratory Instrument Calibration Procedure, Department of Navy, BUWEPS-BUSHIPS Calibration Program, D 217.16/2
Standards Laboratory Instrument Calibration Technique, D 217.16/7
Standards Laboratory Measurements System Operation Procedure, Department of Navy, BUWEPS-BUSHIPS Calibration Program, D 217.16/3
Standards Support and Environmental Impact Statements, EP 1.57/5
Standards Yearbooks, C 13.10
STAR, Scientific and Technical Aerospace Reports, NAS 1.9/4
Stars in Service, T 66.14
Starting and Managing Series, SBA 1.15
Starting Out Series, SBA 1.35
STAT-USA, C 1.91
Stat-USA: The Newsletter, C 1.91/2
State Administered Federal Engineer Funds, HE 19.122
State Agricultural and Marketing Officers, A 36.55
State Agricultural Departments and Marketing Agencies, with Names of Officials, A 66.45
State Air Pollution Implementation Plan Progress Report, EP 1.52
State Air Programs, Digest, Fiscal Year (date), EP 1.33
State and Federal Marketing Activities and Other Economic Work, A 36.21
State and Local Government Collective Bargaining Settlements, L 2.45/4
State and Local Government Employment and Payrolls, L 2.41/4
State and Local Government Functional Profile Series, Y 3.Eq 2:14
State and Local Government Quarterly Employment Survey, C 3.140

State and Local Government Special Studies, C 3.145, C 56.231
State and Local Grant Awards, EP 1.35/2
State and Local Personnel Systems, Annual Statistical Report, CS 1.95
State and Local Programs on Smoking and Health, HE 20.25/4
State and Metropolitan Area Data Book, C 3.134/5
State and Metropolitan Area Data Book, A Statistical Supplement, C 3.134/5-2
State and Metropolitan Area Employment and Unemployment, L 2.111/5
State and Metropolitan Area Unemployment, L 2.111/5
State and National Reports, Y 3.N 21/9:10
State and Private Forestry:–
    Forestry Bulletins, A 13.110/10
    Forestry Reports, A 13.110/9
    General Publications, A 13.110/2
    General Reports, A 13.110/12
    Handbooks, Manuals, Guides, A 13.110/8
    Miscellaneous Reports, A 13.110/11
    Technical Publications, A 13.110/13
    Technical Reports, A 13.110/14
State and Regional Unemployment, L 2.120/2
State Assistance Programs for SSI Recipients, SSA 1.17/2
State Bulletins, C 3.31/2
State Bulletins, 2d Series (Statistics by counties), C 3.31/3
State Buy-in Manual, HE 22.8/11
State Carlot Shipments of Fruits and Vegetables, by Commodities, Counties, and Billing Stations, A 88.12/10
State Chartered Credit Unions, Annual Report, NCU 1.1/2
State Child-Labor Standards (by States), L 16.21
State Climatologist, C 55.281/3
State Clinical and Environmental Laboratory Legislation, HE 20.7028
State Coastal Zone Management Activities, C 55.32/3
State Committee Letters, A 55.43/9, A 55.46/6
State Compendiums, C 3.28/19
State Conference Report from (State), Y 3.W 58/4:9
State, County and Municipal Survey, L 2.13
State, County and Selected City Employment and Unemployment, L 2.111
State, County and Selected City Employment and Unemployment, BLS/PWEDA/MR-(series), L 2.111/2
State, County and Selected City Employment and Unemployment, BLS/PWEDA/SP-(series), L 2.111/4
State Court Prosecutors in Large Districts, J 29.11/16
State Data Center Exchange, C 3.238/8
State Data Profiles, Calendar Year (date), Selected Ascs Program Activity and Other Agricultural Data, A 82.90
State Department, International Law (texts, precedents and discussions published by the State Department), S 7.14
State Distribution of Defense Contract Awards, Pr 32.4013
State Distribution of Public Employment in (year), C 3.140/2
State Documents, C 3.162
State Education Agency Operations, Revenues, Expenditures, and Employees, ED 1.108/3
State Educational Records and Reports Series, HE 19.308/2
State Energy Data Reports, E 3.42
State Energy Data System, E 3.42/5
State Energy Overview, E 3.42/2
State Energy Price and Expenditure Data System, E 3.42/4
State Energy Price and Expenditure Report, E 3.42/3
State Exchange Service Item Series, FS 13.213
State Expenditures for Public Assistance Programs, HE 17.2:St 2/2
State Export Series, C 57.29, C 61.30
State Export Series, (State) Exports, C 61.30
State Export-Origin Series: Exports from [State], C 42.28
State - Federal Judicial Observer, Ju 13.13/2
State Forest Tax Law Digest, A 13.21/2
State Government Finances, C 3.191/2-3
State Government Tax Collections, C 3.191/2-8
State Health Profile, HE 20.7043/1—51
State Higher Education Profiles, ED 1.116/3
State Labor Legislation in (year), L 2.6/1:L 524
State Law Digest, Reports, LC 14.8
State Law for Soil Conservation, A 13.60
State Law Index, LC 14.5
State Laws and Published Ordinances, T 70.14

State Laws and Regulations Prohibiting Employment of Minors in Hazardous Occupations, L 22.6/2
State Legislation of 1941: Summaries of Laws Currently Received in Library of Congress, LC 14.10
State Legislation on Smoking and Health, HE 20.7210, HE 20.25/3
State Legislative Fact Sheet, TD 8.65
State Legislative Summary, Children and Youth Issues, HE 24.16
State Letters, FS 3.31
State List of Post Offices, P 1.10/3
State Map Series–
    Panimetric, I 19.102
    Planimetric, I 19.105
    Planimetric, Topographic and Shaded Relief, I 19.102
    Shaded Relief, I 19.104
    Topographic, I 19.103
State Maps, I 19.21/3
State Maximums and Other Methods of Limiting Money Payments to Recipients of Special Types of Public Assistance, HE 17.626
State Medicaid Manual, HE 22.26, HE 22.8/10
State Member Banks of the Federal Reserve System, FR 1.11/5
State Mineral Profiles, I 28.37/4
State Municipal Project Priority Lists, Grants Assistance Programs, EP 1.56/3
State of Fair Housing, Report to the Congress, HH 1.1/9
State of Federal Facilities, The, EP 1.116
State of Small Business, a Report to the President, SBA 1.1/2
State of the Public Range in Wyoming, I 53.56
State of the Rocky Mountain Region, I 29.125
State Office Memorandum, A 55.46/10
State Officers Analyzer Sheets, C 46.12
State Park Statistics, I 29.68
State Planning Activities Progress Reports, Y 3.N 21/12:9
State Population and Household Estimates with Age, Sex, and Components of Change, C 3.186/21
State Postal Maps, P 1.39/2
State Priority Lists for Construction Grants for Wastewater Treatment Works, Fiscal Year (date), EP 1.56/4
State Prisoners: Admissions and Releases, J 16.23/2
State Programs, NF 1.8/2-17
State Programs for Public School Support, FS 5.222:22023, HE 5.222:22023
State Publications Issued in Cooperation with Agricultural Marketing Service, A 88.42/2
State Publications Issued in Cooperation with Federal Extension Service, A 43.37
State Quarterly Economic Developments, C 59.16/1, C 59.16/52
State Radiation Control Legislation, HE 20.1112
State Regulatory Commissions and Fuel Tax Divisions, IC 1.3/2-2
State Rehabilitation Facilities Specialist Exchange, HE 17.122
State Renewable Energy News, E 1.141
State Reports Issued in Cooperation with Statistical Reporting Service, A 92.36
State Resources and Services for Alcohol and Drug Abuse Problems, HE 20.8319
State Safety Digest, L 16.29
State Safety Program Work Sheets, L 16.39
State Salary Ranges, Selected Classes [of positions] in Employment Security, Public Welfare, Public Health, Mental Health, Vocational Rehabilitation, Civil Defense, Emergency Planning, CS 1.81, FS 1.22, HE 1.22, GS 1.8
State Sentencing of Convicted Felons, J 29.11/11-3
State Solid Waste Planning Grants, Agencies, and Progress, Report of Activities, EP 3.10
State Statistical and Economic Abstract Series, C 1.87
State Summary of War Casualties, N 1.34
State Summary Series, A 55.40
State Supervisors of Pupil Transportation, Directory, FS 5.2:T 68/2
State Tables Fiscal Year (date), Medicaid: Recipients, Payments and Services, HE 22.12
State Tax Collections in (year), C 56.209, C 3.191/2
State Technical Services Newsletters, C 1.53
State Traffic Safety Information, TD 8.62
State Trends, HH 2.24/2
State Unemployment, L 2.111/5-2
State Vocational Rehabilitation Agency: Fact Sheet Booklets, HE 17.119/2, HE 1.610
State Vocational Rehabilitation Agency Program and Financial Plan, HE 23.4110
State Vocational Rehabilitation Agency: Program Data, HE 23.4110/2

State Workers' Compensation: Administration Profiles, L 36.16, L 36.411

State Workers' Compensation Laws, L 36.412

State Workmen's Compensation Laws, Comparison of Major Provisions with Recommended Standards, L 16.3:212

State-EPA Agreements, Annual Report, EP 1.86

State-Local Businessmen's Organizations, C 18.200/2

Statement (various topics), HE 20.3182/8

Statement of a Proper Military Policy for the United States, W 26.8

Statement of Active Loans and Financial Guarantees, Y 3.Ex 7/3 , Y 3.Ex 7/3:12

Statement of Balances, Appropriations, and Disbursements, T 9.7

Statement of Condition of Federal Land Banks, Joint Stock Land Banks, etc., FCA 1.7

Statement of Expenditures, A 76.409

Statement of Federal Financial Accounting Concepts, PrEX 2.35

Statement of Federal Financial Accounting Standards, PrEX 2.35

Statement of Financial Condition, HH 2.22

Statement of Foreign Commerce and Immigration, T 37.5

Statement of Foreign Currencies Purchased with Dollars, T 63.118/3

Statement of Indemnity Claims and Averages in Cooperative Bang's Disease Work, A 4.29

Statement of Indemnity Claims and Averages in Cooperative Tuberculosis Eradication, A 4.30

Statement of Loans and Commodities Owned, A 71.7, A 82.307

Statement of Operations, Y 3.F 31/8:1

Statement of Postal Receipts at 50 Industrial Offices, P 4.8

Statement of Postal Receipts at 50 Selected Offices, P 4.9

Statement of Public Debt of United States, T 63.112

Statement of Recruiting for Line of Army at General Recruiting Stations and Their Auxiliaries, W 3.17/2

Statement of Taxes, Dividends, Salaries and Wages, Class a and Class B Privately Owned Electric Utilities in U.S., FP 1.22

Statement of Treasury, Daily, T 9.8

Statement of United States Currency and Coin, T 63.188, T 63.308

Statement of Voluntary Credit Restraint Committee, FR 1.35

Statement Showing Amount of National Bank Notes Outstanding [ect], T 12.9

Statement Showing Rank Duties and Address of Officers of Corps of Engineers, W 7.7

Statements, S 1.25/6

Statements by Presidents of the United States on International Cooperation in Space, Y 1.92-1:S.doc. 40

Statements of Condition of Joint Stock Land Banks, FCA 1.7/2

Statements of Conditions of Federal Land Banks, etc., T 48.6

Statements of Expenditures, A 55.62

Statements of Facts, and Briefs, J 10.5/1

Statements of Loans and Commodities Owned, A 80.407

States Activities Report, C 55.438

States and Small Business: Programs and Activities, SBA 1.34

States and Their Indian Citizens, I 20.2:St 2/3

States and Urban Strategies (various States) (series), HH 1.89

State-Wide Highway Planning Surveys, A 22.13

Statewide Highway Planning Surveys; News Bulletins, FW 2.10

Statewide Transportation Planning and Management Series, TD 2.57

Station and Program Notes, W 100.8

Station Directory, N 12.9

Station List, W 24.8

Station Meterological Summary, C 30.10

Station Notes, A 13.42/15, A 13.68/10

Station Papers, A 13.30/8, A 13.42/16, A 13.61/8, A 13.63/9, A 13.67/8, A 13.69/7, A 13.73/8

Stationary Source Enforcement Series, EP 1.8/7

Station-List of Officers of Medical Department, W 44.13

Stations of Army, W 3.30, W 40.5

Statistic Report of Marine Commerce of Duluth-Superior Harbor, Minn. and Wis., D 103.13

Statistical Abstract of the United States, C 3.134, C 3.134/7, C 56.243

Statistical Analysis of Carrier's Monthly Hours of Service Reports, IC 1 hou.9

Statistical Analysis of the World's Merchant Fleet, TD 11.12

Statistical Analysis of World's Merchant Fleets Showing Age, Size, Speed, and Draft by Frequency Groupings, As of (date), C 39.224

Statistical Analysis Report, ED 1.120/2, ED 1.328/5

Statistical Brief from the Bureau of the Census (series), C 3.205/8

Statistical Briefs (series), VA 1.74

Statistical Briefs from Around the World, C 3.205/2

Statistical Bulletins–
Bureau of Fisheries, C 6.5, I 45.8, I 49.8
Department of Agriculture, A 1.34
Farm Credit Administration, FCA 1.3/2
Fish Commission, FC 1.5
Military Government of Ryukyu Islands, D 102.19
Office of Civil Defense, Pr 32.4425
Philippine Islands, Commerce and Industry Bureau, W 49.52/5
Rural Electrification Administration, A 68.13
Securities and Exchange Commission, SE 1.20
Work Projects Administration, FW 4.13
Works Progress Administration, Y 3.W 89/2:58

Statistical Cards, L 5.25

Statistical Circulars, I 16.39, FS 5.39

Statistical Classification and Code Numbers of Shipments of Merchandise to Alaska from United States, C 3.150:H

Statistical Classification of Domestic and Foreign Commodities Exported from the United States, C 3.150:B

Statistical Classification of Domestic and Foreign Merchandise Exported from U.S., C 3.150:S

Statistical Classification of Foreign Merchandise Reports in In-Transit Trade of United States, C 3.150:L

Statistical Classification of Imports into U.S. Arranged in Shipping Commodity Groups, C 3.150:T

Statistical Classification of Imports into United States Arranged in Shipping Commodity Groups, C 3.150:Y

Statistical Classification of U.S. Waterborne Exports and Imports, C 3.150:W

Statistical Classification on Commodities Imported into the United States with Rates of Duty and Tariff Paragraphs, C 3.150:A

Statistical Compendium, I 28.37/6

Statistical Compendium on Alcohol and Health, HE 20.8317

Statistical Digests, C 55.316, I 49.32

Statistical Evaluation Reports, PrEx 2.13

Statistical Handbook of Civil Aviation, C 31.144

Statistical Letter, FS 2.11/3

Statistical Materials, Y 3.N 21/8:24

Statistical Notes–
National Clearinghouse on Aging, HE 23.3112
National Institute of Mental Health, HE 20.3812
Rehabilitation Services Administration, HE 17.114

Statistical Notes for Health Planners, HE 20.6218

Statistical Policy Working Papers, C 1.70, PrEx 2.28

Statistical Profile, Redevelopment Area Series, C 1.45

Statistical Profile Series SP, C 3.228

Statistical Profiles, Rural Redevelopment Areas, SP (Series), C 1.45/2

Statistical Programs of the United States Government, PrEx 2.10/3

Statistical Publications, A 55.60

Statistical Reference Book of International Activities, HE 20.3712

Statistical Report, J 1.1/10, J 1.55, J 16.23/5, J 31.10

Statistical Report, Annual Tabulations of Model Reporting Area for Blindness Statistics, FS 2.22/37-2

Statistical Report, Fiscal Year (date), J 16.2:P 93/3

Statistical Report, Great Lake Pilotage, C 1.47:St 2

Statistical Report, Great Lakes Pilotage, C 1.47:St 2

Statistical Report of Commerce Passing through Canals at Sault Ste. Marie, Mich. and Ontario, Salt Water Ship Movements for Season of (year), D 103.17/2

Statistical Report of Marine Commerce of Duluth-Superior Harbor, Minn. and Wis., D 103.13

Statistical Report on Social Services, Form FS-2069, Quarter Ended (date), FS 17.12, FS 17.628

Statistical Reporter, C 1.69, PrEx 2.11

Statistical Reports, FT 1.28

Statistical Reports on Older Americans, HE 23.3112/2

Statistical Series–
Annual Data, Data from the Drug Abuse Warning Network (DAWN), HE 20.416
Children's Bureau, FS 3.214, FS 14.113, FS 17.213
Federal Power Commission, FP 1.21

National Institute on Drug Abuse, HE 20.8212, HE 20.8212/2, HE 20.8212/3, HE 20.8212/5, HE 20.8212/6

Securities and Exchange Commission, SE 1.25/6

Social and Rehabilitation Service, HE 17.23

Statistical Series, Annual Data, Data from the Drug Abuse Warning Network (DAWN), Series I, HE 20.8212/11

Statistical Series Annual Data, Data from the Drug Abuse Warning Network (DAWN) Series I, HE 20.8212/11

Statistical Series Circulars, IC 1.4/3

Statistical Series, Quarterly Report, HE 20.8212

Statistical Series, Quarterly Report, Series D, HE 20.8212/2

Statistical Series, Reports, I 66.12

Statistical Series, Series A, HE 20.8212/5

Statistical Series, Series B, HE 20.8212/8

Statistical Series, Series C, HE 20.8212/9

Statistical Series, Series E, HE 20.8212/3

Statistical Series, Series F, HE 20.8212/6

Statistical Series, Series G, HE 20.8212/7

Statistical Series, Series H, HE 20.8212/10

Statistical Study of U.S. Civil Aircraft, C 31.160, FAA 1.32/2

Statistical Summaries [various commodity programs], A 82.37/3

Statistical Summary, A 88.28

Statistical Summary and Analysis of Foreign Visitor Arrivals, U.S. Citizen and Non-U.S. Citizen Departures, C 47.15

Statistical Summary for Fish and Wildlife Restoration, I 49.29/4

Statistical Summary of Aid to Dependent Children of Unemployed Parents, FS 3.39/3

Statistical Summary of Municipal Water Facilities, FS 2.84

Statistical Summary of the Physical Research Program as of June 30 (year), Y 3.At 7:2 P 56/2

Statistical Summary, Railroad Retirement Board Operations, RR 1.11

Statistical Summary, Rural Areas Development and Area Redevelopment, Quarterly Progress Report, A 43.38

Statistical Supplement of Monthly Domestic Dairy Markets Review, A 88.13/2

Statistical Supplement to Monthly Egg and Poultry Market Review, A 88.13/4

Statistical Tables for the Federal Judiciary, Ju 10.21/2

Statistical Tables Showing Progress of Eradication of Brucellosis and Tuberculosis in Livestock in United States and Territories for Fiscal Year, A 77.212/3

Statistical Yearbook, HH 1.38

Statistical Yearbook of the Immigration and Naturalization Service, J 21.2:St 2, J 21.2/2, J 21.2/10

Statistical Yearbook of the Quartermaster Corps, D 106.12

Statistics and Agriculture, A 36.134

Statistics Bulletins, HH 1.11

Statistics Concerning Indian Education, Fiscal Year, I 20.46

Statistics for Industry Groups and Industries, C 3.24/9-7

Statistics for (year) on Blindness in the Model Reporting Area, HE 20.3759

Statistics in Brief, ED 1.328/4

Statistics of American Listed Corporations, SE 1.17/3

Statistics of Bituminous Coal Loaded for Shipment on Railroads and Waterways As Reported by Operators, I 28.34

Statistics of Capital Movements Between U.S. and Foreign Countries, T 62.9

Statistics of Class 1 Motor Carriers, IC 1 mot.14

Statistics of Class A Telephone Carriers Reporting Annually to the Commission, As of December 31 (year) and for Year Then Ended, CC 1.14/2

Statistics of Communications Common Carriers, CC 1.35

Statistics, Distributors of TVA Power Fiscal Years, Y 3.T 25:1-18

Statistics of Diseases and Injuries in Navy, N 10.15, M 203.10

Statistics of Education in the United States, FS 5.220:20032, HE 5.220:20032

Statistics of Electric Utilities in the United States, Calasses A and B Publicly Owned Companies, FP 1.21

Statistics of Farmer Cooperatives, A 89.19

Statistics of Income, T 22.35, T 22.35/2

Statistics of Income, Corporation Income Tax Returns, T 22.35/5

Statistics of Income, Corporation Income Tax Returns Documentation Guides, T 22.35/7

Statistics of Income, Final Volumes, T 22.35/2

Statistics of Income, Partnership Returns, T 22.35/6
Statistics of Income, Preliminary Reports, T 22.35/3
Statistics of Interstate Natural Gas Pipeline Companies, E 3.25
Statistics of Land-Grant Colleges and Universities, FS 5.250:50002, HE 5.250:5002
Statistics of Local Public School Systems–
　Fall (year), HE 5.93/8
　Finance, (year), HE 19.318/2
　Pupils and Staff, HE 19.318/4
Statistics of Navy Medicine, D 206.15
Statistics of Nonpublic Elementary and Secondary Schools, (year), HE 5.93/9
Statistics of Nonpublic Elementary Schools, FS 5.220:20064
Statistics of Principal Domestic and International Telegraph Carriers Reporting to the Commission As of December 31 (year) and for Year Then Ended, CC 1.41
Statistics of Privately Owned Electric Utilities in the United States, E 3.18/2
Statistics of Public Elementary and Secondary Day Schools, HE 19.326
Statistics of Public Library Systems Serving Populations of 35,000–49,999, FS 5.215:15035, HE 5.215:15035
Statistics of Public Library Systems Serving Populations of 50,000–99,999, FS 5.215:15034, HE 5.215:15034
Statistics of Public Library Systems Serving Populations of 100,000 or more, FS 5.215:15033, HE 5.215:15033
Statistics of Public Libraries, ED 1.122/2
Statistics of Public School Libraries, FS 5.215:51049, HE 5.215:15049
Statistics of Public School Systems in Twenty Largest U.S. Cities, ED 1.112/4
Statistics of Public Schools, Advance Report, Fall, HE 19.318
Statistics of Publicly Owned Electric Utilities in the United States, E 3.18/3
Statistics of State School Systems, HE 19.318/3
Statistics of the Communications Industry in the United States, CC 1.35
Statistics of Trends in Education, HE 19.302:St 2/2
Statistics on Banking, Y 3.F 31/8:1-2
Statistics on Manpower, Supplement to Manpower Report of the President, L 1.42/2-2
Statistics on Pupil Transportation, FS 5.220:20022, HE 5.220:20022
Statistics Research Analysis Microfiles Catalog, HE 3.38/4
Statistics Technical Reports, J 1.40
Status, a Monthly Chartbook of Social and Economic Trends, C 3.251
Status and Progress Reports, Releases, A 61.19
Status of Active Foreign Credits of the United States Government: Foreign Credits by United States Government Agencies, T 1.45/2
Status of CAA Releases, Manuals, and Regulations, C 31.151
Status of Children, HE 23.1009
Status of Civil Air Regulations and Civil Aeronautics Manuals, FAA 1.18
Status of Compliance, Public School districts, 17 Southern and Border States, Reports, FS 5.80, HE 5.80
Status of Federal Aviation Regulations, New, TD 4.13
Status of Handicapped Children in Head Start Programs, HE 23.1012
Status of Open Recommendations Improving Operations of Federal Departments and Agencies, GA 1.13/18
Status of Perkins Loan Default, ED 1.40/4
Status of Slum-Clearance and Low-Rent Housing Projects, I 40.7
Status of Strategic Petroleum Reserve Activities as of (date), GA 1.13/3
Status of the Department of Energy's Implementation of Nuclear Waste Policy Act, GA 1.13/10
Status of the Nation's Local Public Transportation, Conditions and Performance, Report to Congress, TD 7.18
Status of Vessel Construction and Reconditioning under Merchant Marine Acts of 1920 and 1938, SB 7.5:1105, C 27.9/8
Status of Waterfowl & Fall Flight Forecast, I 49.100/3
Status Report, Y 3.F 31/15:10
Status Report of the Energy-Related Inventions Program, C 13.72
Status Report of the Operation and Maintenance of Sanitation Facilities Serving American Indians and Alaska Natives, HE 20.9416

Status Report of the U.S. Treasury-Owned Gold, T 63.131
Status Report on Water and Power Resources Service Programs Within (various States), I 27.74
Status Report, Voluntary and Non-Profit Agency Technical Crop Ration Contracts with International Cooperation Administration, S 17.41/2
Status Report: Workable Program for Community Improvement, HH 1.47
Statutes and Court Decisions, FT 1.13
Statutes and Decisions Pertaining to the Federal Trade Commission, FT 1.13/2
Statutes at Large, S 7.9
Statutory Debt Limitation As of, T 63.208
Steam Generator Group Project, Y 3.N 88:25-10
Steam Generator Tube Integrity Program, Y 3.N 88:17
Steam Railways in Hands of Receivers and Trustees, and Changes in List of Companies Affected by Receiver Ship of Trusteeship, IC 1 ste.45
Steamboat Inspector's Manual, T 38.6, C 15.6
Steamboat-Inspection Service Bulletin, C 15.10
Steam-Electric Plant Construction Cost and Annual Production Expenses, E 3.17
Steamship Department Bulletins, Y 3.F 73:24
STECS Data Link, HE 3.86
Steel, C 41.51
Steel Barrels and Drums, C 3.106
Steel Boilers, C 3.107
Steel Import Data, C 41.114
Steel Import Data, Shipments from Exporting Countries in Calendar Year, C 57.209
Steel Office Furniture, Shelving, and Lockers, and Fireproof Safes, C 3.108
STI Bulletin, NAS 1.76
Stipulations, FT 1.11/3
Sti-Recon Bulletin and Tech Info News, NAS 1.76
Stock Catalog Identification List, GS 2.10/6:pt 2
Stock Lists, W 108.107, W 108.9
Stock of Hops, A 88.44
Stock on Hand at Refineries, I 28.21
Stockholders' Report, A 13.114
Stockpile Information, GS 10.7/2
Stockpile Report to the Congress, FEM 1.12, GS 1.22
Stocks of Coal and Days' Supply, FP 1.11/4
Stocks of Evaporated and Condensed Milk Held by Wholesale Grocers, A 88.14/5
Stocks of Feed Grains, A 36.174
Stocks of Flaxseed, Stocks of Soybeans, A 88.18/13
Stocks of Grain in All Positions, A 88.18/14
Stocks of Grain in Deliverable Positions for Chicago Board of Trade, Futures Contracts in Exchange-Approved and Federally Licensed Warehouses, as Reported by Those Warehouses, A 85.14, Y 3.C 73/5:10
Stocks of Hops, A 88.44, A 92.30
Stocks of Leaf Tobacco, C 3.3
Stocks of Leaf Tobacco Owned by Dealers and Manufacturers, A 80.124
Stocks of Soybeans in All Positions, A 92.15/5
Stocks of Wheat and Rye, A 36.174/2
Stocks on Hand at Refineries, I 28.20
Stolen Money-Order Forms, P 4.7
Stone in (year), I 28.118
Stoppage Circulars, W 36.6, W 97.7, W 77.5, W 2.10
Storage Capacity of Elevators Reporting Commercial Grain Stocks, A 88.18/15
Storage Catalogue, W 34.16/2
Storage Dams, I 27.51
Storage in Major Power Reservoirs in the Columbia River Basin, I 19.47/2
Storage-Gage Precipitation Data for Western United States, C 55.225
Store Stock Catalog, General Services Administration, Zone Price Lists, Zone 1, GS 2.10
Stores Stock Catalog, GS 2.10/2
Stores Stock Catalog, Price Lists, GS 2.10/3
Stories of American Industry, C 1.20
Storm Bulletin, A 29.17
Storm Data, C 55.212
Stove Rationing Industry Letters, Pr 32.4237
STP Newsletter (series), C 55.220/9
Strategic Air Command, Grissom Air Force Base Telephone Directory, D 301.104/6
Strategic Air Command, Vandenberg Air Force Base Telephone Directory, D 301.104/7
Strategic Air Command, Wurtsmith Air Force Base, Telephone Directory, D 301.104/5
Strategic and Critical Materials Report to the Congress (semiannual), D 1.94
Strategic Bombing Survey Publications, W 1.71
Strategic Forum, D 5.417
Strategic Petroleum Reserve, E 1.30

Strategic Petroleum Reserve Quarterly Report, E 1.90/2
Strategic Studies Institute, Conference Report, D 101.146/2
Strategic Studies Institute, General Publications, D 101.146
Strategic Studies Institute, Special Report, D 101.146/7
Strategy Conference Series, D 101.146/6
Stratigraphic Notes, I 19.3/6
Street Directory of Principal Cities of United States, P 7.6
Strengthening Developing Institutions, Title 3 of the Higher Education Act of 1965, Annual Report, HE 19.139/2
Strikes in, L 2.69
Strikes in the United States, L 2.3:651
Strong-Motion Program Report, I 19.4/6
Strontium in (year), I 28.166
Structural Clay Products (common brick, face brick, vitrified paving brick, hollow building tile), C 3.109
Structural Engineering Bulletin, HH 1.95
Structural Engineering Series, TD 2.48
Structural Research Laboratory Report, I 27.29
Student Conference on United States Affairs, D 109.9
Student Guide, Five Federal Financial Aid Programs, ED 1.8/2
Student Handbook (series)–
　Corps of Engineers, D 103.120/2
　Department of Defense, D 1.67/3
　Department of the Army, D 101.47/3, D 101.47/4
Student Information Sheets (series), D 101.112/2
Student Manual, SM- (series), D 14.8/2
Student Manuals, SM- (series), D 119.8/8
Student Package (series), D 101.47/8
Student Pamphlet (series), D 103.120/3
Student Performance Guides (series), D 101.107/3
Student Reference Book (series), D 101.47/6
Student Reference Sheets, SR- (series), FS 13.122
Student Report (series), D 301.26/7-3
Student Texts, ST- (series), D 5.352/2
Student Work Sheets, Department of Labor Safety Training Programs, SWS-LS-(series), L 16.51
Student Workout (series), D 103.120
Students Enrolled for Advanced Degrees, HE 19.330
Studies from Interagency Data Linkages (series), HE 3.62
Studies in Administrative Law and Procedure, Y 3.Ad 6:10
Studies in American Folklife, LC 39.11
Studies in Asymmetry, D 101.146/8
Studies in Communist Affairs, D 301.85
Studies in Comparative Education, FS 5.59
Studies in Comparative Education, Bibliography, Publications, FS 5.214, HE 5.214
Studies in Comparative Education, Education in [country], FS 5.212, HE 5.212
Studies in Cultural Resource Management, A 13.101/2
Studies in Delinquency, HE 17.16/4
Studies in Income Distribution (series), HE 3.67/2
Studies in Intelligence, PrEX 3.19
Studies in Medical Care Administration, FS 2.311
Studies in Military Engineering (series), D 103.43/4
Studies in Plains Anthropology and History, I 20.50
Studies of Small Business Finance, Y 3.In 8/29:9
Studies in Social Change, HE 20.8132
Studies in the Economics of Production, C 1.81
Studies in Workmen's Compensation and Radiation Injury, Y 3.At 7:2 R 11/28
Studies (numbered), Y 3.Ai 7/5:10
Studies of Automatic Technology, L 2.76
Studies of Family Clothing Supplies, Preliminary Reports, A 77.712
Studies on Administrative Management in Government of U.S., Y 3.P 92/3:7
Studies on Household Sewage Disposal System, FS 2.56
Study Grants for College Teachers, NF 3.25
Study Guides, E 1.8/3
Study Kits, C 30.78
Study of Air Traffic Control, Reports, C 31.123
Study of Consumer Purchases, A 42.8
Study of Methods Used in Measurement and Analysis of Sediment Loads in Streams, Reports, Y 3.F 31/13:9, Y 3.In 8/8:10
Study of MSPB Appeals Decisions for FY (year), MS 1.15
Study of the International Travel Market [various countries], C 47.19
Study of WIC Participant and Program Characteristics, A 98.17
Stumpage Prices for Sawtimber Sold from National Forests, by Selected Species and Region, A 13.58/2
Sub Marinus, C 55.40/2

Subcommittee on Oversight and Investigations of the Committee on Energy and Commerce, Y 4.En 2/3-12

Subcontracting Directory, D 1.16/16

Subfile of the Registry of Toxic Effects of Chemical Substances, HE 20.7112/2

Subfiles of the NIOSH Toxic Substances List, HE 20.7112/2

Subject Area Bibliographies, HE 20.8311/2

Subject Bibliographies, GP 3.22/2

Subject Bibliographies from Highway Safety Literature, SB- (series), TD 8.13/3

Subject Catalog, Cumulative List of Works Represented by Library of Congress Printed Cards, LC 30.11

Subject Cataloging Manual, Shelf Listing, LC 26.8/5

Subject Cataloging Manual: Subject Headings, LC 26.8/4

Subject Catalogues, W 11.5

Subject Headings, LC 9.6/1

Subject Headings Used in the Dictionary Catalogs of the Library of Congress, LC 26.7

Subject Index of Current Research Grants and Contracts Administered by the National Heart, Lung, and Blood Institute, HE 20.3212

Subject List of Farmers' Bulletins (Front Space), A 21.9/6

Subject Matter Index with Cross-Reference Table, Y 3.F 31/21:11

Subject Matter Indexes to Decisions of the Federal Labor Relations Authority, Y 3.F 31/21-3:10-3

Subject Offerings and Enrollments, Grades 9–12, Nonpublic Secondary Schools, FS 5.224:24012, HE 5.224:24012

Subject Reports, C 3.286

Subject-Matter Index and Table of Cases, Y 3.F 31/21-2:9

Sub-Saharan Africa Report, PrEx 7.20/2

Sub-Saharan Africa, Situation and Outlook Report, A 93.29/2-13

Subsidy for United States Certificated Air Carriers, C 31.257

Subsistence and Environmental Health, E 1.90/5

Substitute Chemical Program, Initial Scientific and Minieconomic Review of [various chemicals], EP 5.13

Sugar and Sweetener, Outlook and Situation, A 105.53/2, A 93.31/3

Sugar and Sweetener Report, A 1.115

Sugar and Sweetener Situation, A 93.31/2

Sugar and Sweetener, Situation and Outlook Report, A 93.31/3

Sugar and Sweetener, Situation and Outlook Yearbook, A 93.31/3-2

Sugar Beet Sugar Orders, A 55.66

Sugar Confectionery, Nuts, C 18.72/6

Sugar Determination, A 55.37, A 63.7, A 76.307, A 80.117, A 80.817, A 81.16, A 82.19

Sugar Information Series, Publications, A 63.9

Sugar Market News, A 88.54

Sugar Market Statistics, A 92.41, A 105.53

Sugar Reports, A 82.47

Sugar Requirements and Quoats S.R. (series), A 82.6/2

Sugar Situation, A 88.36

Sugarcane Variety Tests in Florida, Harvest Season, A 106.27

Suggested Co-op Electrification Adviser Training Outline, A 68.16

Suggested Safe Practices for Longshoremen, L 16.51/3-2

Suggested Safety Practices for Shipyard Workers, L 16.51/3

Suggested Two-year Post-High School Curriculums, HE 19.118

Suicide Surveillance Summary, HE 20.7611

Sulfur, I 28.63

Sulfur in (year), I 28.63/2

Sulfur in (year), Advance Summary, I 28.63/3

Sulfur Oxides Control Technology Series, EP 7.12

Sulphuric Acid, Production, Stocks, etc. Reported by Fertilizer Manufacturers, C 3.110

Summaries, FCA 1.18

Summaries of Federal Milk Marketing Orders, A 88.2:M 59/28

Summaries of Foreign Government Environmental Reports, EP 1.21/4

Summaries of FY (date) Research in Nuclear Physics, E 1.19/3

Summaries of Projects Completed in Fiscal Year, NS 1.39

Summaries of Research, Naval Dental Research Institute, D 206.1/2

Summaries of Research Reported on During Calendar Year (date), D 206.17

Summaries of Studies in Agricultural Education Supplements, FS 5.281:81002, HE 5.281:81002

Summaries of Tariff Information, TC 1.26

Summaries of Trade and Tariff Information, TC 1.26/2

Summary, A 82.37:Su 6/4

Summary and Analysis of International Travel to the U.S., C 47.15

Summary and Review of International Meteorological Observations for Month of, W 42.7/2

Summary Characteristics for Governmental Units and Standard Metropolitan Statistical Areas (series), C 3.223/23:

Summary Data from the Employment Situation News Release, L 2.53/2-2

Summary Data from the Producer Price Index News Release, L 2.61/10-2

Summary Information Report, Y 3.N 88:41

Summary Minutes of Meeting, S 5.48/12

Summary of Accident Investigation Reports, IC 1 accu.7

Summary of Accidents Investigated by the Federal Railroad Administration in Fiscal Year, TD 3.111

Summary of Accidents Investigated by the Federal Railroad Administration in the Fiscal Year (dates), TD 3.110/2

Summary of Accidents Reported by All Line-Haul and Switching and Terminal Railroad Companies, TD 3.9

Summary of Accidents Reported by Steam Railways, IC 1 ste.31

Summary of Accounts and Deposits in All Commercial and Mutual Savings Banks, Y 3.F 31/8:22

Summary of Accounts and Deposits in All Commercial Banks [by districts], Y 3.F 31/8:20 CT

Summary of Accounts and Deposits in All Mutual Savings Banks, Y 3.F 31/8:21

Summary of Activities–
  Animal and Plant Health Inspection Service, A 101.27
  House Post Office and Civil Service Committee, Y 4.P 84/10:Ac 8
  House Science and Technology Committee, Y 4.Sci 2-10
  Senate Banking, Houseing, and Urban Affairs Committee, Y 4.B 22/3:Ac 8

Summary of Activities, in Fiscal [year], CC 1.1/2

Summary of Activities, Meat Inspection Division, A 88.40/2:20

Summary of Agricultural Reports, FS 3.126

Summary of Air Carrier Statistics, C 31.240/2

Summary of Air Information, W 95.11

Summary of Airworthiness Directives, TD 4.10/2

Summary of Airworthiness Directives for Large Aircraft, TD 4.10/3

Summary of Airworthiness Directives for Small Aircraft, FAA 1.28/2

Summary of Assets and Liabilities, T 12.14

Summary of Awards, NS 1.10/7

Summary of Bang's Disease Control Program Conducted by Bureau of Animal Industry in Cooperation with Various States, A 4.23

Summary of Bang's Disease Work in Cooperation with Various States, A 4.21

Summary of Biostatistics, C 3.165

Summary of Bovine Brucellosis Eradication Activities in Cooperation with States, A 77.212/2

Summary of Bovine Tuberculosis Eradication in Cooperation with Various States, Statement of Indemnity and Averages in Cooperative Bovine Brucellosis Work, A 77.216/2

Summary of Brucellosis (Bang's Disease) Control Program Conducted by Bureau of Animal Industry in Cooperation with Various States, A 77.213

Summary of Brucellosis Eradication Activities in Cooperation with Various States Under Cull and Dry Cow Testing Program, A 77.212/7

Summary of Brucellosis Eradication Activiteis in Cooperation with the Various States Under the Market Cattle Testing Program, A 77.212/8

Summary of Carlot Shipments, A 82.45

Summary of Cases Relatingo Farmers' Cooperative Associations, A 72.18

Summary of Chart Corrections, D 5.315/2

Summary of Circular, A 67.19/9

Summary of Cold Storage Stocks, A 36.191

Summary of Comerce of Dominican Republic, W 6.13/5

Summary of Cooperative Cases, A 89.9

Summary of Cooperative Cases, Legal Series, A 89.9/2

Summary of Cotton Fiber and Processing Test Results, Crop of (year), A 88.11/17-2

Summary of CPI News Releases, L 2.38/10

Summary of Emergency Relief Statistics, Y 3.F 31/5:34

Summary of Equity Security Transactions and Ownership of Directors, Officers, and Principal Stockholders of Member State Banks As Reported Pursuant to Section 16(a) of the Securities Exchange Act of 1934, FR 1.31/2

Summary of Federal ADP Activities for Fiscal Year (date), GS 12.9

Summary of Federal Hunting Regulations for (year), I 49.24/2

Summary of Financial Statements and Sales Statistics, Distributors of TVA Power, Y 3.T 25:1-16

Summary of Foods in the United States, I 19.13

Summary of Foreign Government Environmental Reports, EP 1.21/4

Summary of Governmental Finances in (year), C 56.209, C 3.191/2

Summary of Grants and Contracts Active on June 30, (year), HE 20.6510

Summary of Grants and Contracts Administered by the National Center for Health Services Research and Development, HE 20.2116

Summary of Health Information for International Travel, HE 20.7315/2, HE 20.781812

Summary of Hourly Observations, W 95.10

Summary of Intelligence, W 95.12

Summary of Legislative Activities, Y 4.P 96/10:L 52

Summary of Loan Activity and Operating Results through (date) Issued by CCC, A 82.83/2

Summary of Major Provisions of Convention and of Law Relating to Factory Inspection (by States), L 16.32

Summary of Manufacturing Earnings Series, L 2.90

Summary of Meeting Depositry Library Council to the Printer, GP 3.30/2

Summary of Mining and Petroleum Laws of the World, I 28.27

Summary of Monthly Reports of Large Telephone Companies, IC 1 telp.6

Summary of Mortality from Automobile Accidents, C 3.39

Summary of Mortgage Insurance Operations and Contract Authority, HH 2.24/5

Summary of Motor Carrier Accidents, IC 1 mot.21/3

Summary of Motor Vehicle Accident Fatalities, C 3.128/3

Summary of Natural Hazard Deaths in the United States, C 55.134

Summary of Offerings and Enrollments in Public and Secondary Schools, HE 19.334

Summary of Operations, Labor-Management Reporting and Disclosure Act, L 1.51

Summary of Operations of Production Credit Associations, A 72.25

Summary of Operations, Office of General Counsel, LR 1.1/2

Summary of Orders, ES 3.6/10

Summary of Passport Office Accomplishments, S 1.1/5

Summary of Passport Statistics, S 1.27/2

Summary of Policies, Reports, and Other Publications, Y 3.F 31/5:14

Summary of Prescribed Unit Costs and Hourly Rate for Return on Investment and Tax Allowance, C 31.272, CAB 1.10

Summary of Press Comments, A 55.27

Summary of Progress, SS 1.16

Summary of Regional Cold Storage Holdings, A 88.20/2

Summary of Report, A 93.50

Summary of Reports Received by Committee on Medical Research, Pr 32.413/10

Summary of Research Projects Monthly Reports, A 57.34

Summary of Safety Management Audits, TD 2.66

Summary of Sanitation Inspection of International Cruise Ships, HE 20.7511

Summary of Savings Accounts by Geographic Area, FSLIC-Insured Savings and Loan Associations, FHL 1.29

Summary of SBA Programs, Y 4.Sm 1/12

Summary of Small Business Financing by SBIC's, SBA 1.28

Summary of State Government Finances in (year), C 56.209, C 3.191/2

Summary of State Labor Laws for Women, L 13.14/2

Summary of State Unemployment Compensation Laws, SS 1.19/2

Summary of Supplemental Type Certificates, TD 4.36

Summary of Supplemental Type Certificates and Approved Replacement Parts, FAA 1.14, FAA 5.12

Survey of Current Business, C 3.33/1, C 56.109, C 59.11, C 59.11/1

Survey of Current Business, Weekly Supplements, C 3.34

Survey of Federal Libraries, HE 19.311:L 61

Survey of Federally-Funded Marine Mammal Research and Studies, Y 3.M 33/3:9-2

Survey of Food and Nutrition Research in United States, NA 2.8

Survey of Foreign Fisheries, Oceanographic, and Atmospheric Literature, C- (series), C 55.325/3

Survey of Foreign Fisheries, Translated Tables of Contents, and New Translations, C 55.325/4

Survey of Graduate Students and Postdoctorates in Science Engineer, NS 1.56

Survey of Labor Law Administration, L 16.11

Survey of Minority-Owned Business Enterprises, MB (series), C 56.250, C 3.258, C 56.260

Survey of Mortgage Lending Activity, HH 1.99, HH 1.99/2, HH 1.99/2-3

Survey of Mortgage Lending Activity State Estimates, HH 1.99/2-2

Survey of Mortgage-Related Security Holdings of Major Institutions, HH 1.99/4-2

Survey of Negro World War II Veterans and Vacancy and Occupancy of Dwelling Units Available to Negroes [in city areas], L 2.31

Survey of Nuclear Power Plant Construction Costs, E 3.17/5

Survey of Pension Fund Investment in Mortgage Instruments, HH 1.99/4

Survey of Procurement Statistics, D 201.6/14

Survey of Real Estate Trends, Y 3.F 31/8:28

Survey of State Legislation Relating to Higher Education, FS 5.250:50008, HE 5.250:50008

Survey of State Prison Inmates, J 29.25

Survey of U.S. Uranium Exploration Activity, E 3.46

Survey of United States Uranium Marketing Activity, E 3.46/2

Survey of World War II Veterans and Dwelling Unit Vacancy and Occupancy [in city areas], L 2.30

Survey of World War II Veterans and Dwelling Unit Vacancy and Occupancy (in Specified Areas), C 3.194

Survey Report (series), ED 1.328

Survey with Safety, C 4.51

Surveys of Agricultural Labor Conditions, A 61.11

Surveys of Science Resources Series, NS 1.22

Surveys of Wage and Wage Rates in Agriculture, Reports, A 36.156

Survival Plant Recognition Cards, D 210.14/5

Survivial Series, For Your Information [releases], FCD 1.13/10

Sweetpotato Report, Louisiana Crop Reporting Service, A 88.12/4-2

Symbols of American Libraries, LC 1.45, LC 30.32

Symposia Series for Undersea Research, NOAA'S Undersea Research Program, C 55.29/2

Symposium on Naval Hydrodynamics, D 210.19

Syncrisis, the Dynamics of Health, HE 1.42

Synergist, AA 3.9

Synopsis of the Annual Energy Review and Outlook, E 3.1/3

Synopsis of U.S. Government Proposed Procurement and Contract Awards, C 18.284

Synoptical Series, 1869, T 1.14

Synthetic Liquid Fuels Abstracts, I 28.86

Synthetic Organic Chemicals, United States Production and Sales, TC 1.33, ITC 1.14

Synthetic Organic Chemicals, United States Production and Sales, Preliminaries, TC 1.33/2

System Package Program, NS-SPP- (series), TD 4.30

System Requirements, GS 14.17

Systems Engineering Group, Research and Technology Division, Air Force Systems Command, Wright-Patterson Air Force Base, Ohio, Technical Documentary Report No. SEG TDR, D 301.45/48

Systems Information Newsletter, HE 3.68/4

Systems Maintenance Division Instructions, FAA 1.6/7

Systems Technology Information Update, HE 3.80

T

T.B. Folders, FS 2.42

T.I.D.C. Projects on German Industrial Economic Disarmament, Pr 32.5813

T.I.S.C.A. [Technical Information System for Carrier Aviation] Technical Information Indexes: Naval Carrier Aviation Abstract Bulletin with Cross Reference Index, D 202.22

Table of All Primitive Roots for Primes Less Than 5000, D 210.8:7070

Table of Allowances, M 301.20, D 101.23

Table of Cases Cited in Opinions, IC 1.6/3

Table of Cases Decided, LR 1.8/9-2

Table of Cases in Both ICC Reports and Ic Reports, IC 1.6/5

Table of Cases on Formal Docket of ICC Not Disposed of in Printed Reports, IC 1.6/8

Table of Commodities in the Decisions, IC 1.6/7

Table of Decisions and Reports, SE 1.21

Table of Defendants Before Interstate Commerce Commission, IC 1.6/4

Table of Distances Between Ports, D 203.22:151

Table of Investment Yields for United States Savings Bonds of Series E. Official Use, T 66.23

Table of Redemption Values for United States Savings Bonds, Series A to E, Inclusive, T 63.209/2

Table Olives, A 67.18:FOL

Tables and Formulas for Use of Surveyors and Engineers on Public Land Surveys, I 21.11/3

Tables Computed for the American Ephemeris and Nautical Almanac, N 11.9

Tables from American Practical Navigator (Bowditch), D 203.22:9

Tables of Allowances, W 1.28, M 101.29, D 101.23

Tables of Bankruptcy Statistics, Ju 10.9

Tables of Basic Allowances, W 1.27

Tables of Cases and Opinions, IC 1.6/2

Tables of Equipment, W 1.26

Tables of Laws Affected, GS 4.111/2

Tables of Organization, W 1.25, W 70.12

Tables of Organization and Equipment, W 1.44, M 101.21, D 101.19

Tables of Organization and Equipment, Department of the Air Force, M 301.7

Tables of Redemption Values for United States Savings Bonds–

    Series A-E, T 63.209

    Series E, T 63.209/6

    Series EE, T 63.209/7

    Series J, T 63.209/3

Tables of Redemption Values for $50 Series EE and $25 Series E Savings Bond, T 63.209/5-2

Tables of Redemption Values for United States Series E Savings Bonds and Savings Notes, T 63.210/2

Tables of Redemption Values for United States Savings Notes, T 63.210

Tables of Redemption Values of $25 Series E Savings Bonds Series, T 63.209/5

Tables on Hatchery and Flock Participation in the National Poultry Improvement Plan, A 77.15:44-3

Tables on Hatchery and Flock Participation in the National Turkey Improvement Plan, A 77.15:44-4

Tables (Statistical), A 13.45

Tables to Convert [Foreign Moneys, Weights and Measures into U.S. Standards], C 1.11

Tabulated Results of Discharge Measurements, W 31.6

Tabulation of Air Navigation Radio Aids, C 23.18, CA 1.9, C 31.8, C 31.108

Tabulation of Project Note Sales for Low- income Housing, HH 1.71/2

Tabulation of Statistics Pertaining to Block Signals and Telegraph and Telephone for Transmission of Train Orders, IC 1 blo.5

Tabulations of Statistics Pertaining to Signals, Interlocking, Automatic, Train Control, Telegraph and Telephone for Transmission of Train Orders, and Spring Switches As Used on Railroads of United States, IC 1 saf.10

TAC Attack, D 301.94

Tactical Pilotage Charts, D 5.354

Tactical Plan, T 63.125

Take Pride in America, Awards Program, I 1.110

Take Pride in America, National Awards Ceremony, I 1.110/2

Talc, I 28.136

Talc, Soapstone and Pyrophyllite in (year), I 28.136

Talking Book Topics, LC 19.10

Talking Books Adult, LC 19.10/2

Tall Fescue, Oregon, A 92.19/13

Tall Fescue, Southern States, A 92.19/12

Talon, D 101.144

Tankers in the World Fleet, TD 11.29

TA/OST- (series), S 18.42/2

TAPES Newsletter, D 101.137

Tar, Nicotine, and Carbon Dioxide of the Smoke of...Varieties of Domestic Cigarettes for the Year, FT 1.36

Target, Pr 33.217

Tariff Circulars–

    Federal Communications Commission, CC 1.16

    Maritime Commission, MC 1.21

    Shipping Board, SB 1.8

    War Department, W 1.13

    Rate Section, Interstate Commerce Commission, IC 1 rat.4

Tariff Correction Circular, C 18.147

Tariff Information Series, TC 1.5

Tariff Information Surveys, TC 1.6

Tariff Item, C 18.205

Tariff Schedules of the United States, TC 1.35/3

Tariff Schedules of the United States, Annotated, TC 1.35/2, ITC 1.10

Tariff Series, C 10.10

Tariffs–

    Bureau of Customs, T 17.7

    Canal Zone, W 79.6

Task Force on–

    Aging, Pr 37.8:Ag 8

    Air Pollution, Pr 37.8:Ai 7

    Business Taxation, Pr 37.8:B 96

    Economic Growth, Pr 37.8:Ec 7

    Environmental Cancer and Heart and Lung Diseases: Annual Report to Congress, EP 1.82

    Higher Education, Pr 37.8:Ed 8

    Highway Safety, Pr 37.8:H 53

    Improving and Prospects of Small Business, Pr 37.8:Sm 1

    Low-Income Housing, Pr 37.8:H 81

    Mentally Handicapped, Pr 37.8:M 52

    Model Cities, Pr 37.8:M 72

    Oceanography, Pr 37.8:Oc 2

    Physically Handicapped, Pr 37.8:P 56

    Prescription Drugs, HE 1.32

    Problems of Aging, Pr 37.8:Ag 4/Ct

    Rural Development, Pr 37.8:R 88

    Science Policy, Pr 37.8:Sci 2

    Urban Renewal, Pr 37.8:Ur 1

    Women's Rights and Responsibilities, Pr 37.8:W 84

Tax Capacity of the States, Y 3.Ad 9/8:19

Tax Cases Decided with Opinions by the Supreme Court, Y 4.In 8/11:T 19/3

Tax Court Memoranda, Ju 11.7/2

Tax Delinquency of Rural Real Estate, A 36.78

Tax Guide for Small Business, T 22.19/2:Sm 1, T 22.19/2-3

Tax Guide for U.S. Citizens Abroad, T 22.19/2:C 49

Tax Information, IRS Publications (numbered), T 22.44/2

Tax Policy and Administration ... Annual Report on GAO'S Tax-Related Work, GA 1.13/6

Tax Policy Research Studies, T 1.44

Tax Practitioner Reproducible Kit, T 22.51/2

Tax Practitioner Update, T 22.51/3

Taxfax, T 22.64

Taylor Model Basin Report, D 211.9/2

TB Notes, HE 20.7013/2

TBT News, C 13.70

TC in the Current National Emergency, Historical Report No., D 117.9, D 117.9/2

TDA Update, TDA 1.15

TDC Employee News Bulletin, C 1.49

TDL-CP- (series), C 55.13/5

Teacher Exchange Opportunities Abroad, Teaching, Summer Seminars under International Educational Exchange Program of Department of States [announcements], FS 5.64/2

Teacher Exchange Opporunities under International Educational Exchange Program, FS 5.64, FS 5.214:14047, HE 5.214:14047

Teachers' Leaflets, I 16.20

Teaching Aids for Developing International Understanding, FS 5.52

Teaching Opportunities, Directory of Placement Information, FS 5.226:2600, HE 5.226:2600

Teamwork, Y 3.T 25:22

TEC Lessons (series), D 101.6/7

TechBeat, J 28.37

Tech Data Sheet (series), D 201.27

Tech Notes, C 51.17, C 51.17/12

Tech Notes: Energy, C 51.17/3

Tech Transfer Highlights, E 1.86/10

Tech Trends, EP 1.106

Technical Activities, Center for Analytical Chemistry, C 13.58/2

Technical Activities, Center for Chemical Physics, C 13.58/9
Technical Activities, Office of Standard Reference Data, C 13.58/3
Technical Activities, Surface Science Division, C 13.71
Technical Advisory Services, Health Office, For Your Information, TAS (series), FCD 1.13/2
Technical Aids, L 1.49/2
Technical Aids for Small Business, Annuals, SBA 1.11/2
Technical Aids for Small Manufacturers, SBA 1.11
Technical Alfalfa Conference, Proceedings, A 77.15:74
Technical Analysis Papers–
  Congressional Budget Office, Y 10.11
  Department of Health, Education, and Welfare, HE 1.52
Technical Analysis Report DASA (series), D 5.14
Technical Appendix from Vital Statistics of the United States, HE 20.6210/a
Technical Appendixes to the Report and Recommendations to the Secretary, U.S. Department of Health and Human Services, Y 3.P 29:1-2
Technical Assistance Aid, L 1.48
Technical Assistance Aids, L 31.8
Technical Assistance Bulletins, I 66.22, HE 20.415/2
Technical Assistance Guide (series), J 1.8/4
Technical Assistance Guides, L 37.308/2
Technical Assistance Publication Series, HE 20.415, HE 20.8025
Technical Assistance Reminders, L 31.8/2
Technical Brief, A 13.82/10
Technical Bulletin, D 203.32/3
Technical Bulletin of Committee on Tidal Hydraulics, D 103.28/2
Technical Circulars, HH 2.12
Technical Committee Executive Summary (series), Y 3.W 58/4:11
Technical Committee Reports, Y 3.W 58/4:12
Technical Data Digest, W 108.18
Technical Development Notes, C 31.12, C 31.125
Technical Development Reports, CA 1.20, C 31.11, C 31.119, FAA 2.8
Technical Digest–
  Bureau of Yards and Docks, M 205.8
  International Cooperation Administration, S 17.45
  Naval Facilities Engineering Command, D 209.8
Technical Digest Feature, S 18.18
Technical Digest Service, C 41.24
Technical Disclosure Bulletin, D 210.3/2
Technical Division Report, TAS (series), C 41.26
Technical Division Reports, C 35.13
Technical Documentary Report–
  APL-TDR, D 301.45/51
  FDL-TDR, D 301.45/46
  ML-TDR, D 301.45/47
  SEG-TDR, D 301.45/48
Technical Documentary Reports–
  AAL-TDR- (series), D 301.45/30-2
  AEDC-TDR- (series), D 301.45/33-2
  AFSWC-TDR- (series), D 301.45/20-3
  AL-TDR- (series), D 301.45/45
  AMRL-TDR- (series), D 301.45/32
  ASD-TDR- (series), D 301.45/26-3
  ESD-TDR- (series), D 301.45/28-2
  RADC-TDR- (series), D 301.57/3
  RTD-TDR- (series), D 301.45/34-2
  SAM-TDR- (series), D 301.26/13-6:1056
  WADC-TDR- (series), D 301.45/5
Technical Equipment Reports, A 13.49/3
Technical Fact Sheets, Y 3.C 76/3:11-2
Technical Handbook for Facilities Engineering and Construction Manuals, HE 1.108/2
Technical Highlights Mining Research, I 28.151/2
Technical Highlights of the National Bureau of Standards, C 13.1
Technical Information Bulletins, FS 2.2/3, FS 3.52/2, HE 3.52/2
Technical Information Center: Bulletins, TD 1.3/2
Technical Information Circulars, Y 3.N 21/14:11, FS 6.14
Technical Information Handbooks, FTC-TIH-, D 301.45/31-4
Technical Information Indexes: Naval Carrier Aviation Abstract Bulletin with Cross Reference Index, D 202.22
Technical Information Memorandum (series), D 1.83
Technical Information Notes, I 40.11, FW 3.11
Technical Information on Building Materials for Use in Design of Low-cost Housing, C 13.27
Technical Information Pamphlets, D 103.53/6
Technical Information Paper, AE 1.126
Technical Information Release, T 22.42/2
Technical Inquiry Service, S 18.23

Technical Instruction Book Manuscript, TD 4.32/13
Technical Letter, A 57.35
Technical Library Bibliographic Series, D 106.10
Technical Literature Research Series, N 29.17
Technical Manuals, D 214.9/3
Technical Manuscripts, D 103.53/2
Technical Memoranda for Municipal, Industrial and Domestic Water Supplies, Pollution Abatement, Public Health, FS 2.301
Technical Memorandum–
  Beach Erosion Board, D 103.19
  Defense Civil Preparedness Agency, D 119.8/5
  Defense Communications Agency, D 5.110
  Energy Information Adeministration, E 3.26,
  National Aeronautics and Space Administration, NAS 1.15
  National Bureau of Standards, Applied Mathematics Division, C 13.39
  National Telecommunications and Information Administration, C 60.11
  Reclamation Bureau, I 27.31/2
  Technology Assessment Office, Y 3.T 22/2:11
Technical Memorandum–To United States Study Commission, Southeast River Basins, A 57.50
Technical Monographs, Y 3.T 25:16
Technical News Bulletin, C 13.13
Technical News from Department of Commerce, National Bureau of Standards, C 13.36/6
Technical Notes–
  Air Force Department–
    Aeronautical Systems Division, D 301.45/26
    Air Proving Ground Center, D 301.45/50
    Alaskan Air Command, Arctic Aeromedical Laboratory, D 301.66
    Arnold Engineering Development Center, D 301.45/33-3
    Atmospheric Analysis Laboratory, D 301.45/30 3
    Cambridge Research Center, D 301.45/4-2
    Command and Control Development Division, D 301.45/24
    Electronics Research Directorate, D 301.45/12-2
    Geophysics Research Directorate, D 301.45/16-2
    Meteorological Development Laboratory, D 301.45/17-2
    Office of Scientific Research, D 301.45/18
    Rome Air Development Center, D 301.57/2
    Special Weapons Center, D 301.45/20-2
    Wright Air Development Center, D 301.45/13
  Ballistics Research Laboratories, D 105.10/3
  Census Bureau, C 56.215, C 3.212/2
  Coast Artillery Target Practice, W 3.37
  Environmental Protection Agency, EP 1.7/5
  Forest Service–
    Forest Products Laboratory, A 13.27/9
    Lake States Forest Experiment Station, A 13.61/10
    Northeastern Forest Experiment Station, A 13.67/9, A 13.42/7
    Northern Forest Experiment Station, A 13.73/9
    Southeastern Forest Experiment Station, A 13.63/8
    WSDG-TN- (nos), A 13.27/9, A 13.87/4
  Labor Department, L 1.79/3
  National Aeronautics and Space Administration, NAS 1.14
  National Bureau of Standards, C 13.46
  Naval Air Systems Command, N 28.6, M 208.10, D 202.7
  Picatinny Arsenal, D 105.12/2, D 105.12/4
  Weather Bureau, C 30.82
Technical Orders, D 202.8
Technical Papers, C 1.73, I 53.30
Technical Papers, AFHRL-TP- (series), D 301.45/27-4
Technical Personnel Pamphlets, D 12.8/2
Technical Plan for the Great Lakes Environmental Research Laboratory, C 55.620/2
Technical Preservation Services Reading Lists, I 70.15/2
Technical Problems Affecting National Defense, C 32.8
Technical Procedures Bulletins, C 55.128
Technical Progress Bulletin, C 13.58/11
Technical Progress Reports, I 28.26/6
Technical Publication Announcements, C 13.58/10
Technical Publications, A 57.15, TD 5.43
Technical Publications (series), I 19.14/7
Technical Publications Announcements with Indexes, NAS 1.9/3
Technical Publications for Air Force Technical Libraries, Book Lists, D 301.20
Technical Publications NAVDOCKS TP, D 209.10

Technical Publications, SA-TP (series), A 13.40/12
Technical Reference (series), I 53.35
Technical References, TR-LS- (series), L 16.51/6
Technical Report, ED 1.328/7, VA 1.45
Technical Report (numbered), L 37.309
Technical Report (series), E 3.26/3
Technical Report, AFAPL-TR, D 301.45/51-2
Technical Report AFML-TR, D 301.45/47-2
Technical Report Analysis Condensation Evaluation (Trace), D 301.45/27-3
Technical Report, APGC-TR, D 301.45/50-2
Technical Report, BRL TR (series), D 105.10/3-2
Technical Report DNFSB/TECH- (series), Y 3.D 36/3:9
Technical Report Index, Maritime Administration Research and Development, C 39.227:T 22
Technical Report Memorandum AFHRL (TT)-TRM, D 301.45/27-2
Technical Report NGF (series), D 215.10
Technical Report Series, FEM 1.115
Technical Report Series: Research Customer Service Group, C 55.287/62
Technical Report Summaries, D 301.45/19-6
Technical Reports–
  Animal and Plant Health Inspection Service, A 101.30
  Energy Information Administration, E 3.26/3
  Environmental Protection Agency, EP 1.78
  Federal Energy Administration, FE 1.20
  National Institute on Drug Abuse, HE 20.8236
  National Park Service, J 29.15, I 29.109
Technical Reports, AEDC-TR, D 301.45/33
Technical Reports, AFFDL-TR, D 301.45/46-2
Technical Reports, AFHRL-TR- (series), D 301.45/27
Technical Reports, AFMDC-TR–N(series), D 301.45/17
Technical Reports, AFOSR-TR-, D 301.45/19
Technical Reports, AFSWC-TR, D 301.45/20
Technical Reports, AFWAL-TR- (series), D 301.45/57
Technical Reports, AMD-TR- (series), D 301.45/52
Technical Reports, AMRA CR- (series), D 105.26
Technical Reports, ASD-TR- (series), D 301.45/26-2
Technical Reports, DNA-TR- (series), D 15.13
Technical Reports, DTIC/TR- (series), D 7.15/2
Technical Reports, ESD-TR- (series), D 301.45/28
Technical Reports, FRL-TR- (series), D 105.12/3
Technical Reports from the Study of the Sustaining Effects of Compensatory Education on Basic Skills, HE 19.137
Technical Reports, FTC-TR- (series), D 301.45/31
Technical Reports, MA-RD- (series), C 39.246, TD 11.23
Technical Reports, Naval Research Office London, D 210.16
Technical Reports, NAVTRADEVCEN-(series), D 210.14
Technical Reports News Letters, C 41.21/2
Technical Reports, NSWC/WOL/TR- (series), D 201.21/3
Technical Reports Published in (year), D 117.8/2-2
Technical Reports, R- (series), NAS 1.12
Technical Reports, RT- (series), D 105.14
Technical Reports, SAM-TR- (series), D 301.26/13-6:1057
Technical Reports, TR- (series), D 103.25/2, E 3.57
Technical Reprints, NAS 1.27
Technical Research Reports Published by Air Force Personnel and Training Center Air Research and Development Command, D 301.26/10
Technical Section Bulletins, W 95.21/7
Technical Series, A 9.8
Technical Series Bulletins, S 18.50
Technical Series Reports, C 55.33
Technical Services, C 35.8
Technical Services and Research, OSM/TM-(series), I 71.3/2
Technical Services Office General Publications, C 41.22
Technical Services Research, OSM-TR-(series), I 71.3
Technical Specification Improvement Program Highlights, Y 3.N 88:31/0110
Technical Standard Order Authorizations, TD 4.6:part 37
Technical Standards Orders, C 31.143, FAA 1.38
Technical Standards Register, C 31.143/2
Technical Standards Training Guides, HH 2.6/7
Technical Studies Reports, EP 2.26, HH 2.23
Technical Tables, A 57.21
Technical Terms of the Meat Industry, A 88.17/6:6
Technical Working Paper Series, C 3.223/27
Technology and Development Program, A 13.137
Technology Fact Sheet, E 1.90/10
Technology Transfer Today, Gaining the Competitive Edge, D 201.42
Technology Transfer Update, I 28.151/3
Technical Translations, NAS 1.13/2, NAS 1.77

Titrimetry, Gravimetry, Flame Photometry, Spectro Photometry, and Gas Evolution, C 13.46

TM-DPSC– (series), D 7.6/18

To Farm Journal Editors, A 55.22

To Mayor of Each City with Local Airline Service, C 31.256

To the First Americans, Annual Report of the Indian Health Program, FS 2.867/4, HE 20.2014/2, HE 20.5312

Tobacco Crop Summary, A 88.34/9

Tobacco Letters, A 55.31

Tobacco Market News Summary, A 88.34/10

Tobacco Market Review, A 88.34/5-8

Tobacco Market Reviews, A 36.189

Tobacco Markets and Conditions Abroad, C 18.152

Tobacco Reports, C 3.18/1, C 3.18/2

Tobacco Situation, A 36.94, A 88.34/2, A 93.25, A 105.32

Tobacco, Situation and Outlook Report, A 93.25

Tobacco, Situation and Outlook Yearbook, A 93.25/2

Tobacco Stocks Reports, A 82.11, A 88.34

Tobacco Tax Guide, T 22.19/5

Today's Health Problems, Series for Teachers, FS 2.97

Tomorrow's Work, FS 6.10

Tons of Revenue Freight Originated and Tons Terminated by States and by Commodity Class, IC 1.23/15:SS-7

Tons of Revenue Freight Originated and Tons Terminated in Carloads by Classes of Commodities and by Geographic Areas, Class 1 Steam Railways, IC 1 ste.42

TOP Bulletin, C 61.13

Top Five Contractors Receiving the Largest Dollar Volume of Prime Contract Awards in Each State, D 1.57/2-2

Topical Briefs: Fish and Wildlife Resources and Electric Power Generation, I 49.78

Topical Indexes to Decisions and Opinions of the Department of the Interior, I 1.69/2-2

Topical Report Review Status, Y 3.N 88:34

Topics, OP 1.9

Topographic Atlas of the United States, I 19.10

Topographic Instructions, I 19.15/4

Topographic Map of the United States, I 19.12

Topographic Mapping, Status and Progress of Operations, I 19.95

Topographic Maps, I 19.40

Topographic Maps Circulars, I 19.11

Topographic Quadrangle Maps of Alluvial Valley of Lower Mississippi River, D 103.308

Topographical Maps, 7.5 Minute Series, I 19.81

Topographical Quadrangle Maps, I 19.81

Topographical Quadrangle Maps, 15' Series, I 19.81/2

Topographically Speaking, I 19.116

Torch, Safety Magazine of AETC, D 301.44/3

Tornado Circulars, W 42.16

Total Commercial Production of All Vegetables and Melons for Fresh Market and Processing, A 92.11/10-3

Total for 41 Cities, A 88.12/31:5

Total Livestock Slaughter, Meat and Lard Production, A 88.16/16

Total Obligations Incurred for Emergency Relief from All Public Funds by State and Local Relief Administration in Continental United States, Y 3.F 31/5:35

Total Potato Stocks, Pot 1-2 (series), A 92.11/11

Total Values of Imports and Exports, T 37.7, C 14.12, C 18.6

Tourist and Recreation Potential [by areas], I 66.13

Toward Interagency Coordination, Federal Research and Development on Adolescence, HE 23.1013

Toward Interagency Coordination: Federal Research and Development on Early Childhood, HE 23.1013/2

Toward New Horizons, Pr 32.5023

Towards Improved Health and Safety for America's Coal Miners, Annual Report of the Secretary of the Interior, I 1.96

Tower University: Education Service Plan, D 101.93/2

Townsite Plats, I 27.12

Toxic Chemical Release Inventory, EP 5.22

Toxic Chemical Release Inventory Reporting Form R and Instructions, EP 5.22/3

Toxic Release Inventory, EP 5.22/2

Toxic Substance List, HE 20.7112

Toxic Substances Control Act, Report to Congress for Fiscal Year (date), EP 1.79

Toxicity Bibliography, HE 20.3613

Toxicological Profile, HE 20.7918

Toxicological Profiles, HE 20.518

Toxicology Research Projects Directory, HE 1.48

Toxicology Study Section, HE 20.3001/2:T 66

Toxics Integration Information Series, EP 1.79/2, EP 5.18

Toxics Integration Policy Series, EP 1.79/3

Toxics-Release Inventory: A National Prospective, EP 5.18/2

Toxics-Release Inventory: Executive Summary, EP 5.18/2-2

TOX-TIPS, Toxicology Testing in Progress, HE 20.3620

TQM Quarterly, D 7.40

TR- (series), EP 2.18

Tracking Offenders, J 29.11/9

Trade Agreement Digest, TC 1.24

Trade Agreements (by countries), TC 1.14

Trade and Employment, C 3.269

Trade and Industry Publications, L 23.16

Trade Center Announcements, C 1.51

Trade Data (series), C 57.17

Trade in Cotton Futures, A 82.30

Trade in Grain Futures, A 82.29

Trade in Wool Top Futures, A 59.12, A 75.210

Trade Information Bulletins, C 18.25

Trade Leads, A 67.40/2

Trade List Catalog, C 42.10/2

Trade Lists, C 57.22

Trade of the United States with, C 18.204

Trade Opportunity Program, TOP Bulletin, C 57.27

Trade Policies and Market Opportunities for U.S. Farm Exports, Annual Report, A 67.40/5

Trade Policy Agenda and Annual Report of the President of the Agreements Program, PrEx 9.11

Trade Practice Rules, FT 1.16

Trade Promotion Series, C 18.27

Trade Relations Bulletin, C 34.9

Trade Review of Canada, C 18.157

Trade World Illinois, C 61.39/3

Trade World Michigan, C 61.39

Trade World New York, C 61.39/5

Trade World, Ohio C 61.39/6

Trademark Examining Procedure Directives, C 21.15/2

Trademark Laws, C 21.7/4

Trademark Public Advisory Committee Annual Report, C 21.1/3

Trademark Rules of Practice of the Patent Office, with Forms and Statutes, C 21.14:T 67/2

Trademark Supplement, C 21.5/a 3

Trademarks Assign, U.S. Trademarks Assignments Recorded at the USPTO, C 21.31/9

Trademarks Assist, C 21.31/10

Trademarks BIB, C 21.31/18

Trademarks Pending, Bibliographic Information from Pending US Trademarks, C 21.31/8

Trademarks Registered, C 21.31/14

Trademarks Registered, Bibliographic Information from Registered US Trademarks, C 21.31/7

Tradewinds, C 61.27, C 61.36

TraDiv Letters, N 17.33

TRADOC Historical Monograph Series, D 101.108

TRADOC Historical Study Series, D 101.108/2

TRADOC Pamphlet (series), D 101.22/22

Traffic and Revenue by Commodity Classes, IC 1.23:QC-1

Traffic Circulars, MC 1.21

Traffic, Decisions, IC 1.6/a

Traffic in Opium and Other Dangerous Drugs, J 24.9

Traffic Information Letters, T 58.12

Traffic Laws Commentary, TD 8.5/2

Traffic Report of the St. Lawrence Seaway, TD 6.9

Traffic Safety Data ASCII and SAS Versions, TD 1.56/3

Traffic Safety Digest, TD 8.40

Traffic Safety Evaluation Research Review, TD 8.18/2

Traffic Safety Newsletter, TD 8.18

Traffic Service Letters, GS 2.9

Traffic Speed Trends, TD 2.115

Traffic Techs, TD 8.63

Traffic Volume Trends, FW 2.11, FW 2.14, GS 3.7, C 37.9, TD 2.50

Train and Yard Service of Class I Railroads in the United States, IC 1 ste.38/2

Train of Thought, TD 3.18

Trainees and Fellows Supported by the National Institute of Dental Research and Trained During Fiscal Year, HE 20.3402:T 68, HE 20.3410

Trainers of Teachers, Other Education Personnel and Undergraduates, FS 5.84:T 22, HE 5.84:T 22

Training Analysis and Development, Information Bulletin, D 301.38/2

Training and Development Services, PM 1.19/4-2

Training and Education Bulletin TEB (series), FCD 1.9

Training and Employment Report of the Secretary of Labor, L 37.23

Training and Manpower Development Activities Supported by the Administration on Aging Under Title IV-A of the Older Americans Act of 1965, As Amended, Descriptions of Funded Projects, HE 23.3002:T 68/2

Training Branch Newsletter, C 3.273

Training Bulletin, School Series, FCD 1.9/3

Training Bulletin, Training Officer Series, FCD 1.9/2

Training Bulletins–
Army and Corps Areas and Departments, Seventh Corps Area, W 99.77/11
Federal Works Agency, FW 1.11

Training Circulars–
Army and Corps Areas and Departments
Second Corps Area, W 99.12/8
Seventh Corps Area, W 99.17/8
Department of the Army, M 101.22, D 101.24
Department of the East, W 17.8
National Guard Bureau, W 70.11
War Department, W 1.36
War Plans Division, W 26.11

Training Course Calendar, J 1.91

Training Device Developments, D 210.14/4

Training Facts, Reports, L 1.40

Training Films, FO 1.29, S 17.29/1

Training Guide, Insect Control Series, FS 2.60/7, HE 20.2308

Training Guides, VA 1.38

Training Health Professionals, HE 20.6618

Training Manual–
Agency for International Development, S 18.8/2
Department of Health, Education, and Welfare, FS 1.10, HE 1.10
Department of War, W 1.23
Federal Security Agency, FS 1.10
International Cooperation Administration, S 17.6/4
United States Army, W 3.39/3

Training Manuals, HE 1.10, S 18.8/2

Training Material, S 18.17

Training Memorandum, W 99.11/8, W 99.13/8, W 99.14/8, W 99.15/8, W 99.16/8, W 99.18/10, W 99.19/11, W 99.20/7

Training Memorandums, W 1.34

Training Opportunities, Course Curriculum Catalog, S 1.139

Training Pamphlets, W 42.31

Training Papers, C 55.121

Training Program, I 71.15

Training Publications, N 29.14

Training Publications, Recessions, W 1.21/3

Training Regulations, W 1.21

Training Support Developments, D 210.14/4

Training Text (series), A 13.36/4

Training Texts, A 13.85

Training Tips and Trends, T 22.62

Training within Industry Abstracts, British Engineering Bulletins, Pr 32.4822, Pr 32.5215

Training within Industry Bulletin Series, Pr 32.5208/2

Training within Industry, Bulletins, Pr 32.4011

Training within Industry, Examples, Pr 32.4012, Pr 32.4808

Training within the Industry; Bulletin, Pr 32.4816, Pr 32.5208

Transactions and Proceedings Series, I 29.91

Transactions of Naval Militia Association of United States, N 1.27/5

Transactions of Research Conferences in Pulmonary Diseases, VA 1.40/2

Transactions of Research Conferences on Cooperative Chemotherapy Studies in Psychiatry and Research Approaches to Mental Illness, VA 1.41

Trans-Atlantic, from Office of Labor Advisors, ESC Labor News Letter, Y 3.Ec 74/3:31

Trans-Atlantic, from Office of Labor Advisors, MSA Labor News Letter, Pr 33.915

Transcript CONTU Meetings (numbered), Y 3.C 79:9

Transcripts of Proceedings, Meeting of Depository Council to the Public Printer, GP 3.30

Transfer Circulars, CS 1.37

Transients, Y 3.F 31/5:27

Transition, a Magazine for Former ACTION Volunteers, AA 1.10

Transition Assistance Program Military Civilian One Good Job Deserves Another Participant Manual, L 39.8/2

Transition Series, GA 1.33

Translated Polish Patents, C 41.85/2

Translated Swiss Patents, C 41.85

Translated Tables of Contents of Current Foreign Fisheries, Oceanographic, and Atmospheric Publications, C 55.325

U.S. Agricultural Trade Update, A 93.17/7-5
U.S. Air Force Academy Bulletin, D 305.8/2
U.S. Air Force and U.S. Navy Flight Planning
Document, D 301.52
U.S. Air Force Fine Arts Series, D 301.76/4
U.S. Air Force Plan for Defense Research Sciences, D
301.45/19-5
U.S. Air Force Policy Letter Digest, D 301.120
U.S. Air Force Public Affairs Staff Directory, D 301.104/
4
U.S. Air Force Radio Facility Charts, Atlantic and
Caribbean Area, M 301.15
U.S. Air Force Radio Facility Charts, North Pacific
Area, M 301.14
U.S. Air Force Standards, D 301.31
U.S. Air Service in World War I, D 301.82/2
U.S. Airborne Exports and General Imports, Shipping
Weight and Value, C 3.164/986
U.S. Alcohol Epidemiologic Data Reference Manual, HE
20.8308/3
U.S. Antarctic Projects Officer, Bulletin, D 1.32/2
U.S. Antarctic Projects Officer, Publications, D 1.32
U.S. Area Handbook for (country), D 101.22:550
U.S. Arms Control and Disarmament Agency, Annual
Report, Y 4.F 76/1-16
U.S. Army and Air Force Recruiting Service Letter, M
208.76
U.S. Army and Navy Directory of Airfields, C 31.125
U.S. Army Audit Agency Bulletins, D 101.3/3
U.S. Army Ballistic Missile Agency, DG- TR-(series), D
105.15/2
U.S. Army Campaigns of World War II, D 114.7/5
U.S. Army Educational Manuals, W 3.47
U.S. Army Electronic Proving Ground, USAEPG-SIG
(series), D 111.12
U.S. Army Engineer District, Los Angeles: Reports
(numbered), D 103.59
U.S. Army Engineer School: Student Handout, D
103.120/2
U.S. Army Engineer School: Student Workbook, D
103.120
U.S. Army Equipment Index of Modification Work
Orders, D 101.22:750-10
U.S. Army in Action Series, D 114.7/4
U.S. Army Materiel Command, Annual Historical
Review, D 101.1/4-2
U.S. Army Medical Doctrine, Publications, D 104.36
U.S. Army Military Personnel Center: Pamphlets
(series), D 101.22/16
U.S. Army Mobility R & D Laboratory: USAAMRDL
CR- (series), D 117.8/6
U.S. Army Natick Laboratories, Food Division, Natick,
Mass. Technical Report FD-, D 106.20
U.S. Army Pocket Recruiting Guide, D 101.6/11
U.S. Army Recruiting and Reenlisting Journal, D 118.9
U.S. Army Recruiting Command Pamphlets, USAREC
PAM- (series), D 101.22/7
U.S. Army Research and Development Program Guide,
D 101.52/4
U.S. Army Specifications, W 3.48/1, W 1.49, M 101.26,
D 101.28
U.S. Army Training Manuals, W 3.39
U.S. Army Training Manuals Numbered, W 3.39/1
U.S. Atmospheric Nuclear Weapons Tests, Nuclear Test
Personnel Review, D 15.10
U.S. Auto Industry, ITC 1.16/4
U.S. Automobile Industry, C 1.84
U.S. Automobile Industry: Monthly Report on Selected
Economic Indicators, ITC 1.16/3
U.S. Automotive Trade Statistics, Series A: Motor
Vehicles, ITC 1.16
U.S. Automotive Trade Statistics, Series B, Passenger
Automobiles, ITC 1.16/2
U.S. Average, A 106.39
U.S. Book Exchange Service, S 18.27
U.S. Bureau of Mines, Minerals and Materials
Information, I 28.37/7
U.S. Census of Housing–
City Blocks, Series HC (3), C 3.224/6
Components of Inventory Change, Final Report HC
(4) series, C 3.224/6
Special Reports for Local Housing Authorities,
series HC (S 1), C 3.224/8
State and Small Areas, Final Report HC (1) (series),
C 3.224/3
U.S. Census of Population: Number of Inhabitants, C
3.223/5
U.S. Census of Wholesale Trade Industry Series, C
3.256/3-2
U.S. Central Station Nuclear Electric Generating Units,
Significant Milestones, E 1.41
U.S. Civil Aviation Briefs of Accidents, C 31.244/6

U.S. Coast Guard Civilian Workforce Report, TD 5.65
U.S. Coast Guard Historical Monograph Program, TD
5.29
U.S. Coast Pilots–
Alaska, C 4.7/2, C 4.7/3, C 4.7/7
Atlantic Coast, C 4.6/1
Gulf Coast, Puerto Rico, and Virgin Islands, C 4.6,
C 4.6/4
Hawaiian Islands, C 4.7/4, C 4.7/5
Inside Route Pilot, C 4.6/3
Pacific Coast, California, Oregon, Washington, and
Hawaii, C 4.7/1
Philippine Islands, C 4.18/5
Wartime Information to Mariners, C 4.7/6
West Indies, C 4.6/2
U.S. Commodity Exports and Imports As Related to
Output, C 56.232
U.S. Constitution, a National Historic Landmark Theme
Study, I 29.117
U.S. Cotton Quality Report for Ginnings, A 80.134, A
80.824
U.S. . . . . Crop Quality, A 104.12/2-4
U.S. Crude Oil and Natural Gas Reserves, (year) Annual
Report, E 3.34
U.S. Crude Oil, Natural Gas, and Natural Gas Liquids
Reserves, E 3.34
U.S. Customs Guide for Private Flyers, T 17.23
U.S.D.A, A 1.57
U.S.D.A. Administrative Information, A 1.57
U.S.D.A. Summary of Registered Agricultural Pesticide
Chemical Uses, A 77.302:P 43/4
U.S. Dairy Forage Research Center, A 77.37
U.S. Department of Agriculture Budget Summary, A
1.138
U.S. Decennial Life Tables, HE 20.6215
U.S. Department of Commerce Periodicals to Aid
Business Men, C 1.54
U.S. Department of Labor, Accountability Report, L
1.1/4
U.S. Department of Labor Program Highlights, Fact
Sheet (Series), L 1.88
U.S. Department of State Dispatch, S 1.3/5
U.S. Department of State Indexes of Living Costs
Abroad, S 1.76/4
U.S. Department of State Indexes of Living Costs
Abroad and Living Quarters Allowances, L
2.101
U.S. Department of State Indexes of Living Costs
Abroad and Quarters Allowances, April, L
2.101/2
U.S. Department of Transportation FY...Procurement
Forecast, TD 1.62
U.S. Direct Investment Abroad, Operations of U.S.
Parent Companies and Their Foreign
Affiliates, Preliminary Estimates, C 59.20/2
U.S. Divisional and Station Climatic and Normals, C
55.281/2-3
U.S. Divisional and Station Climatic Data and Normals,
C 55.281/2-3
U.S. Energy Industry Financial Developments, E 3.56
U.S. Export and Import Trade in Leaf and Manufactured
Tobacco, C 18.152/2
U.S. Export Corn Quality, A 104.12
U.S. Export Sales, A 67.40
U.S. Export Sales, Outstanding Export Sales
(Unshipped Balances) on . . ., A 67.48
U.S. Export, Schedule B, Commodity by Country, C
3.164:446
U.S. Export Soybean Quality, A 104.12/2
U.S. Export Wheat Quality, A 104.12/2-2
U.S. Exports and Imports by Air, C 3.164:785
U.S. Exports and Imports by Harmonized Commodity, C
3.164:947
U.S. Exports and Imports Transshipped Via Canadian
Ports, TD 11.28
U.S. Exports and Imports, Working-Day and Seasonal
Adjustment Factors and Months for Cyclical
Dominance (MCD), C 3.235
U.S. Exports by Air, Country by Commodity, C
3.164:790
U.S. Exports, Commodity by Country, C 56.210:410, C
3.164:410
U.S. Exports, Commodity, Country, and Method of
Transportation, C 3.164:750
U.S. Exports, Country by Commodity Grouping, C
1.64:420
U.S. Exports, Country by Commodity Groupings, C
3.164:420
U.S. Exports, Geographic Area, Country, Schedule B
Commodity Groupings, and Method of
Transportation, C 3.164:455
U.S. Exports, Harmonized Schedule B Commodity by
Country, FT-447, C 3.164:447

U.S. Exports of Domestic Merchandise, SIC- based
Products and Area, C 3.164:610
U.S. Exports of Petroleum and Petroleum Products of
Domestic Origin, Commodity by Customs
District, C 3.164:527
U.S. Exports of Reported Agricultural Commodities for
(dates), Marketing Years, A 67.40/4
U.S. Exports of Merchandise, C 3.278/3
U.S. Exports of Textiles and Apparel Products, C 61.50
U.S. Exports, Schedule B Commodity Groupings,
Geographic Area, Country, and Method of
Transportaion, C 3.164:450
U.S. Exports, World Area by Schedule E Commodity
Groupings, C 3.164:455
U.S. Exports-Commodity by Country, C 3.164:410
U.S. Foreign Affairs on CD-ROM, S 1.142/2
U.S. Foreign Agriculatral Trade Statistical Report, A
93.17/3
U.S. Foreign Policy Agenda, IA 1.38, S 20.17
U.S. Foreign Trade (by Commodities), C 18.211
U.S. Foreign Trade in Pulp and Paper, C 18.198
U.S. Foreign Trade [reports], C 56.210
U.S. Foreign Trade Highlights, C 61.28/2
U.S. Foreign Trade: Schedules, C 56.210/3
U.S. Foreign Waterborne Transportation Statistics
Quarterly, TD 11.35
U.S. Forest Planting Report, A 13.109
U.S. Forest Products Annual Market Review and
Prospects, A 13.79/4
U.S. General Aviation Accident Prevention Bulletin, C
31.203/2
U.S. General Aviation Briefs of Accidents, C 31.244/5
U.S. General Imports–
Commodity, Country and Method of Transporation,
C 3.164:350
Geographic Area, Country, Schedule A Commodity
Groupings, and Method of
Transporation, C 3.164:155
Schedule A Commodity Groupings by World Area,
C 56.210:FT 150
Schedule A Commodity Groupings, Geographic
Area, Country, and Method of
Transportation, C 3.164:150
Various Products, C 56.210:30
World Area and Country of Origin by Schedule A
Commodity Groupings, C 3.164:155
U.S. General Imports and Imports for Consumption,
Schedule A Commodity and Country, C
3.164:135
U.S. Geological Survey, Fiscal Year Yearbook, I 19.1/2
U.S. Global Trade Outlook, C 61.34/2
U.S. Global Trade Outlook 1995-2000 Toward the 21st
Century, C 61.34/3
U.S. Government Books, GP 3.17/5
U.S. Government Campaign to Promote Production,
Sharing, and Proper Use of Food, Pr 32.5019
U.S. Government Depository Libraries Directory, Y 4.P
93/1-10
U.S. Government Environmental Datafiles & Software,
C 51.20
U.S. Government Films for Public Educational Use, FS
5.234:34006, HE 5.234:34006
U.S. Government Printing Office Style Manual, GP
1.23/4:St 9
U.S. Government Program to Promote Production,
Sharing and Proper Use of Food, Pr 32.5019/
2
U.S. Government Purchasing and Sales Directory
Guide for Selling or Buying in the
Government Market, SBA 1.13/3
U.S. Government Purchasing Directory, SBA 1.13
U.S. Government Research, C 41.21, C 51.9/3
U.S. Government Salary Tables, Post-Office Dept, P
1.15
U.S. Government Securities Yields and Prices, FR 1.46/
2
U.S. Government Security Yields and Prices (Yields in
per cent per annum), FR 1.46/3
U.S. Government Specifications Directory, SBA 1.13
U.S. Government Working Group on Electronic
Commerce, C 1.1/7
U.S. Government's Preferred Products List, D 1.69
U.S. Grain Export Quality Report, Wheat, Corn,
Soybeans, A 104.12/2-3
U.S. Great Lakes Ports, Statistics for Overseas and
Canadian Waterborne Commerce, TD 6.10
U.S. Gulf Coast VFR Aeronautical Chart, C 55.416/12
U.S. Gulf Coast VFR Aeronautical Chart, TD 4.79/13
U.S. Highways, TD 2.65
U.S. House of Representatives, Detailed Statement of
Disbursements, Y 4.H 81/3:D 63
U.S. Housing Market Conditions, HH 1.120
U.S. Import and Export Price Indexes, L 2.60/3

U.S. Import for Consumption, USUSA Commodity by Country of Origin, C 56.210:146
U.S. Imports and Exports of Natural Gas, E 3.25/3
U.S. Imports for Consumption and General Imports, SIC-Based Products and Area, C 3.164:210
U.S. Imports for Consumption & General Imports, Tariff Schedules Annotated by Country, C 3.150/6
U.S. Imports for Consumption and General Imports-TSUSA Commodity by Country: (year), C 3.164:246
U.S. Imports for Consumption and General Improts, Tariff Schedules Annotated by Country, C 3.150/6
U.S. Imports for Consumption, Harmonized TSUSA Commodity by Country of Origin, FT 247, C 3.164:247
U.S. Imports of Fruits and Vegetables under Plant Quarantine Regulations, A 93.44/3
U.S. Imports of Merchandise, C 3.278/2
U.S. Imports of Merchandise for Consumption, C 3.164:125
U.S. Imports of Textile and Apparel Products, C 61.52
U.S. Imports of Textiles and Apparel under the Multifiber Arrangement, Statistical Report, ITC 1.30
U.S. Imports–General and Consumption, Schedule a Commodity and Country, C 3.164:135
U.S. Imprints on Sub-Saharan Africa, LC 41.12/2
U.S. Industrial Outlook, C 57.18, C 61.34
U.S. Industrial Outlook for 200 Industries with Projections for (year), C 62.17
U.S. Industrial Outlook, (year), with Projections to (year), C 57.309
U.S. Industry and Trade Outlook, C 61.48
U.S. International Air Freight Traffic, C 31.265/4
U.S. International Air Passenger and Freight Statistics, Calendar Year, TD 1.40/4
U.S. International Air Travel Statistics, TD 1.40
U.S. International Air Travel Statistics, Calendar Year, TD 1.40/3
U.S. International Air Travel Statistics, Fiscal Year, TD 1.40/2
U.S. Lumber Exports, C 57.24
U.S. Lumber Imports, C 57.24/2
U.S. MAB Bulletin, S 1.145
U.S. Maps, C 56.242/2
U.S. Marshals Service Fact Sheets, J 25.15
U.S. Merchandise Trade: Exports and General Imports by County, C 3.164:927
U.S. Merchandise Trade: Exports, General Imports, and Imports for Consumption, C 61.40
U.S. Merchandise Trade Position at Midyear, C 61.40
U.S. Merchandise Trade: Seasonally Adjusted Exports, Imports, and Trade Balance, FT-900, C 3.164:900
U.S. Merchandise Trade; Selected Highlights, FT-920, C 3.164:920
U.S. Merchant Marine Data Sheet, TD 11.10
U.S. National Arboretum: Annual Report, A 77.26
U.S. National Arboretum Contribution, A 77.38
U.S. National Arboretum Elite Plant, A 77.38/2
U.S. National Commission for UNESCO, S 5.48/7
U.S. National Commission for UNESCO Memos, S 5.48/14
U.S. National Commission for UNESCO Newsletter, S 5.48/5
U.S. National Committee of the CCIR [Comite Consultatif International des Radiocommunication]: Publications, S 5.56
U.S. Naval Control of Shipping Report, D 201.30
U.S. Naval Oceanographic Office Chart Correction List, D 203.21/2
U.S. Naval Ordnance Test Station, Inyokern, Technical Memorandums, D 215.11
U.S. Naval Propellant Plant Publications, D 215.12
U.S. Naval Radiological Defense Laboratory, Research and Development Report USNRDL (series), D 211.13
U.S. Navy Civil Engineer Corps Bulletin, N 21.14, M 205.7, D 209.7
U.S. Navy in the Modern World Series, D 221.16
U.S. Navy Marine Climatic Atlas of the World, D 202.2:At 6
U.S. Navy Medicine, D 206.7
U.S. Navy Regulations, D 201.11
U.S. Navy Travel Instructions, Instruction Memoranda, N 20.13/3
U.S. NRC Facilities License Application Record, Y 3.N 88
U.S. Nuclear Plants Cost Per KW Report, Office of Nuclear Power, Y 3.T 25:63, Y 3.T 25:68
U.S. Nuclear Regulatory Commission Regulations [List], Y 3.N 88:21
U.S. Oceanborne Foreign Trade Forecast, TD 11.13/2

U.S. Oceanborne Foreign Trade Routes, TD 11.13
U.S. Official Postal Guide, P 1.10
U.S. Participation in the United Nations, Report by the President to Congress, S 1.70
U.S. Patent Applications, C 21.31/17
U.S. Per Diem Rates (CONUS), GS 1.36
U.S. Planting Seed Trade, A 67.18/3
U.S. Production, Imports and Import/Production Ratios for Cotton, Wool and Man- made Textiles and Apparel, C 61.26
U.S. Production of Fish Fillets and Steaks, Annual Summary, C 55.309/2-6
U.S. Real Property Sales List, GS 1.15/5
U.S. Rice Distribution Patterns, A 93.51
U.S. Savings Bond Comprehensive Savings Bond Value Tables (Series EE, I Bond, Series E and Savings Notes), T 63.210/3
U.S. Scientists and Engineers, NS 1.22/7
U.S. Seed Exports, A 67.18:FFVS
U.S. Senate Telephone Directory, Y 1.3/10
U.S. Society & Values, IA 1.35, S 20.19
U.S. Standards for Fruits and Vegetables, A 66.16
U.S. Statutes Concerning the Registration of Trademarks, C 21.7/2
U.S. Statutes Concerning the Registration of Prints and Labels, C 21.7/3
U.S. Supreme Court, Government Briefs in Cases Argued, Indexes, J 1.19/4
U.S. Supreme Court, Government Briefs in Cases Argued by Solicitor General, Indexes, J 1.19/3
U.S.T.S. [poster series], C 47.10/2
U.S. Terminal Procedures, C 55.411
U.S. Terminal Procedures, TD 4.80
U.S. Textile and Apparel Category System, C 61.54
U.S. Timber Production, Trade, Consumption, and Price Statistics, A 13.113
U.S. Trade Performance in (year) and Outlook, C 61.28
U.S. Trade Shifts in Selected Commodity Areas, ITC 1.15
U.S. Trade Status with Communist Countries, C 57.28, C 57.413, C 61.22
U.S. Trade with Puerto Rico and U.S. Possessions, FT-895, C 3.164:895
U.S. Travel Bureau, I 29.37
U.S. Treasury Savings Stamp News, T 66.22
U.S. Trust Territory of the Pacific, Series 9203, D 5.339
U.S. v. Salvador Arbitration Tribunal, S 3.14
U.S. Warehouse Act Licensed Warehouses, A 112.22
U.S. Waterborne Exports and General Imports, C 3.164:985
U.S. Water Borne Intercoastal Traffic by Ports of Origin and Destination and Principal Commodities, SB 7.5/317, C 27.9/9, MC 1.9
U.S. Waterborne Foreign Trade, Summary Report, C 3.164:985
U.S. Waterborne Foreign Trade, Trade Area by U.S. Coastal District, C 3.164:600
U.S. Wheat Quality, A 104.12/2-5
U.S. Working Women: a Databook, L 2.3:1977
UDAG Grants Total for Large and Small Communities, HH 1.99/5-2
UDAG Grants Total ... for ... Smaller Communities, HH 1.99/5
UI Data Summary, L 37.214
Ukranian Mathematics Journal [abstracts], C 41.61/7
Ultraviolet Radiation and Skin Cancer Working Group, HE 20.3001/2:R 11/2
UMTA Newsnotes, TD 7.14
UMTA Transcript, TD 7.14
Unaccommodated Passengers, by Carrier and Market, C 31.268/2
Unauthorized Appropriations and Expiring Authorizations, Y 10.22
Unclassified DOD Issuances on CD-ROM, D 1.95/3
Uncle Sam Says, T 66.19
Undergraduate Engineering Curricular Accredited by Engineer's Council for Professional Development, FS 5.61
Underground Natural Gas Storage in the United States, (date) Heating Year, E 3.11/2-9
Underground Stocks of Lp-Gases, I 28.98/2
Underground Storage of Natural Gas by Interstate Pipeline Companies, E 3.11/2-4
Undersea Warfare, D 207.18/2
Undersea Warfare Committee Publications, NA 2.10
Undersecretary's Report to the Field, Newsletter for Department of Labor Field Representatives, L 1.37
Understanding Taxes, Teacher's Guide, T 22.19/2-2
Understanding the Atom Series, Y 3.At 7:54
Understanding the Earth, I 19.1/2
Underware and Allied Products, C 3.113

Unemployed-Parent Segment of Aid to Families with Dependent Children, FS 14.210, FS 17.11, FS 17.611
Unemployment Allowance Claims and Payment Data by Agencies, VA 1.36
Unemployment Bulletins (by States), C 3.37/16
Unemployment Compensation Circulars, SS 1.12
Unemployment Compensation Interpretation Service, Benefit Series, SS 1.32, FS 3.108
Unemployment Compensation Interpretation Service, Federal Service, Federal Series, SS 1.20
Unemployment Compensation Interpretation Service, State Series, SS 1.21, FS 3.109
Unemployment Compensation Laws, SS 1.7
Unemployment Compensation Program Letters, FS 34.29
Unemployment in Major Areas, L 7.64
Unemployment in States, L 2.111/5-2
Unemployment in States and Local Areas, L 2.41/9
Unemployment Insurance Claims, L 1.62, L 37.12/2
Unemployment Insurance Claims Weekly Report, L 37.12/2-2
Unemployment Insurance Occasional Papers, L 37.20, L 37.213/2
Unemployment Insurance Program Letters, L 7.50
Unemployment Insurance Quality Appraisal Results, L 37.213
Unemployment Insurance Quality Control, Annual Report, L 37.20/3
Unemployment Insurance Review, L 7.18/3
Unemployment Insurance Statistics, L 1.62/2, L 37.12
Unemployment Insurance Tax Rates by Industry, L 7.70, L 33.11
Unemployment Insurance, Technical Staff Papers, L 37.20/2
Unemployment Insurance Weekly Claims Reports, L 37.12/2, L 37.12/2-2
Unemployment Rate by Race and Hispanic Origin in Major Metropolitan Areas, L 2.111/6
Unemployment Rates for States and Local Governments, BLS/PWEDA/QR- (series), L 2.111/3
UNESCO Conference Newsletter, S 5.48/4
UNESCO Facts, S 5.48/8
UNESCO World Review Weekly Radio News from United Nations Educational, Scientific, and Cultural Organization, Paris, France, S 5.48/6
Unfinished Cotton Cloth Prices, Cotton Prices, and Mill Margins, A 82.51, A 88.11/6
Uniform Circulars, T 47.40
Uniform Crime Reporting, J 1.14/7-2
Uniform Crime Reports Bomb Summary, J 1.14/7-7
Uniform Crime Reports for the United States, J 1.14/7
Uniform Facility Data Set (UFDS): Data, HE 20.423
Uniform Parole Reports, J 29.12
Uniform System of Accounts and Reports for Certificated Route Air Carriers in Accordance with Sec. 407 of the Federal Aviation Act, C 31.206/5
Uniform System of Accounts for–
    Carriers by Inland and Coastal Waterways, IC 1 wat.14
    Electric Railways, IC 1 eler.9
    Express Companies, IC 1 exp.9
    Gas Corporations and Electric Corporations in the District of Columbia, IC 1 gas.5
    Pipe Lines, IC 1 pip.5, IC 1 pip.6
    Steam Railways, IC 1 ste.44
    Telegraph and Cable Companies, IC 1 telg.5
    Telephone Companies, IC 1 telp.5
Uniform System of Accounts Prescribed for Natural Gas Companies, FP 1.7/2
Uniform System of Accounts Prescribed for Public Utilities and Licenses, FP 1.7/3
Union Catalog, Selected List of Unlocated Research Books, LC 18.7
Union Conventions, National and International Unions, State Organizations, L 2.85
Union Conventions, (year) National and International Unions, State Organizations, L 1.85
Union Membership in, L 2.120/2-12
Union Pacific Railway, Government Directors, Annual Reports, 1864-1898, I 1.30
Union Recognition in the Federal Government, Statistical Summary, PM 1.47
Union Series, L 13.13
Union Wage Scale Studies, L 2.29
Union Wage Studies Manual of Procedures, L 2.55
Union Wages and Benefits, L 2.3/6
Union Wages and Hours, L 2.3
Unit Costs (selected expense accounts) of Class 1 Steam Roads, IC 1 ste.23
United Nations Conference on Food and Agriculture, S 5.41

United Nations Conference on International Organization, S 5.44

United Nations Educational, Scientific and Cultural Organization News [releases], S 5.48/13

United States Active Civil Aircraft by State and County, C 31.132/2, FAA 1.35

United States Advisory Commission on Information, Semiannual Report to Congress, S 1.93

United States Air Force Academy Assembly, Proceedings, D 305.11

United States Air Force Academy Journal of Professional Military Ethics, D 305.21

United States Air Force and Navy Supplementary Flight Information Document, Pacific and Far East, D 301.50

United States Air Force and Navy Supplementary Flight Information, Europe, Africa, and Middle East, D 301.49

United States Air Force and United States Navy Radio Facility Charts, Central Pacific-Far East, D 301.12

United States Air Force, Commands and Agencies Basic Information, D 301.26/23

United States Air Force Fact Sheets, D 301.128

United States Air Force General Histories (series), D 301.82/3

United States Air Force History, a Guide to Documentary Sources, D 301.6/5:H 62

United States Air Force History Program, Summary of Activities, D 301.1/2

United States Air Force in Southeast Asia (series), D 301.86/2

United States Air Force Jag Law Review, D 302.9

United States Air Force Medical Service Digest, D 304.8

United States Air Force, Navy, Royal Canadian Air Force and Royal Canadian Navy, Navy Radio Facility Charts and In-Flight Data, Alaska, Canada and North Atlantic, D 301.13/3

United States Air Force, Navy, Royal Canadian Air Force, and Royal Canadian Navy Supplementary Flight Information, North American Area (excluding Mexico and Caribbean area), D 301.48

United States Air Force, Navy, Royal Canadian Air Force and Royal Canadian Supplementary Flight Information, North American Area (excluding Mexico and Caribbean area), D 301.48

United States Air Force Radio Facility Charts, Caribbean and South American Area, D 301.10

United States Air Force Radio Facility Charts, Europe, Africa, Middle East, D 301.9

United States Air Force Reference Series, D 301.82/5

United States Air Force Special Studies, D 301.82/4

United States Air Force Statistical Digest, D 301.112

United States Air Force, United States Navy and Royal Canadian Air Force Radio Facility Charts, West Canada and Alaska, D 301.13

United States Air Force, United States Navy Radio Facility Charts, North Atlantic Area, D 301.11

United States Airborne Exports of Domestic and Foreign Merchandise, Commodity (Schedule X) by Country of Destination, C 3.164:780

United States Airborne Exports of Domestic and Foreign Merchandise, Country of Destination by Commodity, C 3.164:790

United States Airborne Foreign Trade, Customs District by Continent, C 3.164:986

United States, Airborne General Imports of Merchandise, Commodity by Country of Origin, C 3.164:380

United States Airborne General Imports of Merchandise, Country of Origin by Commodity, C 3.164:390

United States and Canada Cattle, A 92.18/6-3

United States and Canadian Great Lakes Fleets, C 39.214

United States and Chilean Claims Commission, 1892-94, S 3.21/2

United States and Chilean Claims Commission, 1900-01, S 3.21/3

United States and Mexican Claims Commission, 1869-76, S 3.12

United States and United National Report Series, S 1.49

United States Antarctic Programs, Annual Report, D 201.15

United States Arctic Research Plan, NS 1.51

United States Armed Forces Medical Journal, D 1.11

United States Army in Vietnam (series), D 114.7/3

United States Army in World War, M 103.9

United States Army in World War II, D 114.7

United States Army in World War II: Master Index, Reader's Guide, D 114.7/2

United States Army Installations and Major Activities in Continental U.S., D 101.22:210-1

United States Army Medical Research Institute of Infectious Disease: Annual Progress Report, D 104.27

United States Army Occupational Handbook, D 101.40

United States Army Research and Development Series, D 101.52

United States Army Training Publications, W 3.39/2

United States Attorney's Bulletins, J 31.12

United States: Base Maps, I 19.123

United States Census of Agriculture, 1950: Announcements, C 3.950-9/6

United States Census of Agriculture, 1950: V. 2 General Report (separates), C 3.950-9/5

United States Censuses of Population and Housing: Geographic Identification Code Scheme, Phc (2) (series), C 3.223/13

United States Chiefs of Mission, S 1.69:147

United States Civil Administration of Ryukyu Islands; Special Bulletins, D 102.19/2

United States Civil Aircraft Register, TD 4.18/2

United States Coast Guard Academy, New London, Connecticut: Bulletin of Information, TD 5.16/2

United States Coast Guard Annotated Bibliography, TD 5.21/3

United States Coast Pilot, Atlantic Coast, T 11.6

United States Coast Pilot, Pacific Coast, Alaska, pt. 1, Dixon Entrance to Yakutat Bay, T 11.7/2

United States Coast Pilots, C 55.422

United States Code, Y 1.2/5, Y 1.2/5-2, Y 4.J 89/1:Un 3/3

United States Congressional Serial Set Catalog: Numerical Lists and Schedule of Volumes, GP 3.34

United States Congressional Serial Set Supplement, GP 3.8/6

United States Consumption of Rubber, C 40.14, C 41.31

United States Contributions to International Organizations, S 1.70, S 1.70/9

United States Cotton Quality Report for Ginnings, A 82.28

United States Court Directory, Ju 10.17

United States Court of International Trade Reports, Ju 9.5/2

United States Court of Military Appeals, D 1.19/2

United States Court of Military Appeals and the Judge Advocates General of the Armed Forces and the General Counsel of the Department of the Treasury,

United States Court of Military Appeals, Pubs, D 1.19/2

United States Courts, Pictorial Summary, Ju 10.12

United States Courts: Selected Reports, Ju 10.1/2

United States Customs Court Reports, Ju 9.5

United States Department of Commerce News, C 1.32/8

United States District Courts Sentences Imposed Chart, Ju 10.18

United States Earthquakes, C 55.417/2, I 19.65/2

United States Employment Service Test Research Reports, L 7.69

United States Exports and Imports of Gold and Silver, Total United States Trade in Gold and Silver and United States Trade in Gold and Silver with Latin American Republics and Canada, C 3.164:859

United States Exports by Air of Domestic and Foreign Merchandise Commodity by Country of Destination, C 3.164:731

United States Exports by Air of Domestic and Foreign Merchandise Country of Destination by Commodity, C 3.164:732

United States Exports of Aluminum, C 41.112/2, C 57.10

United States Exports of Domestic and Foreign Merchandise–
Commodity by Country of Destination, C 3.164:410
Country of Destination by Subgroup, C 3.164:420
To Canada (Including Lend-Lease Exports), C 3.157/4
Under Lend-Lease Program, Calendar Year, C 3.164:405
Under Lend-Lease Program, Commodity by Country of Destination, C 3.164:415
Under Lend-Lease Program, Country of Destination by Commodity, C 3.164:421, C 3.164:425

Under United Nations Relief and Rehabilitation Program, Country of Destination by Commodity, C 3.164:426

Under United Nations Relief and Rehabilitation Program, Commodity by Country of Destination, C 3.164:416

United States Exports of Domestic Merchandise (Including Lend-Lease Exports), C 3.164:400

United States Exports of Domestic Merchandise to Latin American Republics, C 3.157

United States Exports of Foreign Merchandise to Latin American Republics, C 3.157/2

United States Exports of Petroleum and Petroleum Products of Domestic Origin, Commodity by Country of Destination, C 3.164:526

United States Exports Under United Nations Relief and Rehabilitation Program, C 3.164:960

United States Fisheries Systems and Social Sciences: a Bibliography of Work and Directory of Researchers, C 55.332:So 1

United States Flag Containerships and United States Flag Ships with Partial Capacities for Containers And/or Vehicles, C 39.232

United States Food Leaflets, A 1.26

United States Foreign Policy, S 1.71

United States Foreign Trade, C 3.164:930, C 3.164:950

United States Foreign Trade in Photographic Goods, C 41.108

United States Foreign Trade Statistical Publications, C 3.166

United States Foreign Trade Statistics, C 18.185

United States Foreign Trade Statistics Publications, C 3.166

United States Foreign Trade, Trade by Air, C 3.164:971

United States Foreign Trade, Trade by Customs District, C 3.164:970

United States Foreign Trade, Trade with E.C.A. Countries, C 3.164:951

United States Foreign Trade, Trade with U.S.S.R. and Other Eastern Europe, C 3.164:954

United States Foreign Trade, Waterborne Trade by Trade Area, C 3.164:973

United States Foreign Trade, Waterborne Trade by United States Ports, C 3.164:972

United States Foreign Trade–Bunker Oil and Coal Laden in the United States on Vessels, C 3.164:810

United States General Imports and Imports for Consumption from Canada and Mexico, Exluding Strategic, Military and Critical Materials, Country by Commodity Totals, C 3.164:121

United States General Imports from Canada, Excluding Strategic and Critical Materials and Military Equipment, C 3.157/5

United States General Imports from Latin American Republics, C 3.157/3

United States General Imports of Cotton Manufacturers, C 3.164/2-2

United States General Imports of Cotton Manufacturers: Country of Origin by Geneva Agreement Category, C 56.210:130, C 3.164:130

United States General Imports of Cotton Manufacturers; TQ-2190, C 3.164/2-8

United States General Imports of Merchandise, Commodity by Country of Origin, C 3.164:10

United States General Imports of Textile Manufactures, Except Cotton and Wool, Grouping by Country of Origin and Schedule a Commodity by Country of Origin TQ-2501, C 3.164/2-7

United States General Imports of Wool Manufacture Except Floor Coverings, Quantity Totals in Terms of Equivalent Square Yards in Country of Origin by Commodity Grouping Arrangement, TQ-2203, C 3.164/2-6

United States General Imports of Wool Manufacture Except for Floor Coverings, Country of Origin by Wool Grouping, TQ-2202, C 3.164/2-5

United States Geological Survey Yearbook, I 19.1

United States Gold and Silver Movements in (Month), C 56.210:2402, C 3.164:2402

United States Government Annual Report, T 63.101/2

United States Government, Annual Report, Appendix, T 1.1/3

United States Government Flight Information Publication: Pacific Chart Supplement, C 55.427

United States Government Interdepartmental Standards, T 51.11/7

United States Government Manual, GS 4.109, AE 2.108/2

United States Government Organization Manual, GS 4.109

United States Immigration Laws, General Information, J 21.5/2

United States Immunization Survey, HE 20.2314, HE 20.7313

United States Import Duties, TC 1.10:Im 7/4, TC 1.35

United States Import Duties Annotated, C 3.150/4

United States Import Duties Annotated, Public Bulletins, C 3.150/5

United States Imports for Immediate Consumption, Entries into Bonded Manufacturing Warehouse for Manufacture and Exports, Entries into Bonded Storage Warehouse and Withdrawals from Bonded Storage Warehouse for Consumption of Petroleum and Its Products, C 3.164:576

United States Imports of Aluminum, C 57.10/2

United States Imports of Merchandise for Consumption: Commodity by Country of Origin, C 3.164:110

United States Imports of Merchandise for Consumption; Country of Origin by Subgroup, C 3.164:120

United States Individual Retirement Bonds, Tables of Redemption Values for All Denomination Bonds, T 63.209/8

United States LPPSD [Low Pollution Power Systems Development] Technical Information Exchange Documents, ER 1.16

United States LPPSD Technical Information Exchange Documents, EP 1.50

United States Lumber Exports, C 41.101

United States Lumber Imports, C 41.101/2

United States Maps, C 56.242, C 3.62/10

United States Merchant Marine, Brief History, C 39.202:M 53/2

United States Meterological Yearbook, A 29.45, C 30.25

United States Military Posture for Fy (date), D 5.19

United States Mineral Resources, I 19.16:820

United States Mission to the United Nations Press Releases, S 5.55

United States National Arboretum, A 1.68:309

United States Naval Academy, Superintendent's Statement to Board of Visitors, D 208.110

United States Naval Aviation, D 202.2:Av 5/2, D 202.2:Av 5/2/910-70

United States Naval Medical Bulletin, N 10.11

United States Navy and the Vietnam Conflict (series), D 207.10/3

United States Oceanborne Foreign Trade Routes, C 39.240

United States Operations Mission to the Philippines, Publications, S 18.31

United States Operations Mission to Vietnam, Publications, S 18.31/2

United States Participation in the United Nations, S 1.70/8

United States Policy Toward USSR and International Communism, Monthly Digest of Pertinent Data Appearing in Department of State Publications, S 1.97

United States Quarterly Book List, LC 1.20

United States Renal Data System, Annual Data Report, HE 20.3325

United States Reports, Cases Adjudged in Supreme Court at October Term, Ju 6.8

United States Retirement Plan Bonds, Tables of Redemption Values for All Denomination Bonds, T 63.209/8-2

United States Savings Bonds Issued and Redeemed Through (date), T 63.7

United States Section, Reports of Meetings, T 1.23/7

United States Senate, a Historical Bibliography, Y 1.3:Se 5/11

United States Series of Topographic Maps, I 19.98

United States, Series 8205 and 8206, D 5.337

United States Special Operations Forces, Posture Statement, D 1.98

United States Standard Facilities Flight Check Manual, FAA 5.9

United States Standard Flight Inspection Manual, C 31.163/3

United States Standards, A 36.35/2

United States Standards for Fruits and Vegetables, A 36.35, A 75.19, A 80.121, A 80.822

United States Standards for Grades of [commodity], A 88.6/2

United States Standards for Grades of [fruits, vegetables, etc.], A 82.20

United States Standards for [various foods], A 103.6/2

United States Statutes at Large, GS 4.111, AE 2.111

United States Topographic/Bathymetric Maps, I 19.101

United States Trade with Puerto Rico and with United States Possessions, C 56.210:800, C 3.164:800

United States Trade with the Territories and Possessions, C 3.164:980

United States Treaties and Other International Agreements, S 9.12

United States Treaty Developments, S 9.11

United States Treaty Developments, Transmittal Sheets, S 9.11/2

United States v. Chile, Alsop Claims, S 3.21/4

United States v. Chile, Arbitration of Case of Brig. Macedonian, S 3.21/1

United States Waterborne Foreign Commerce, a Review of [year], C 3.211/2

United States Waterborne Foreign Commerce, Great Lakes Area [year], C 3.211/2

United States Winter Wheat and Rye Reports, A 36.74

United States 1:1,000,000-Scale Maps, I 19.107

United States 1:1,000,000-Scale Series, Intermediate Scale Maps, I 19.110

United States-United Nations Information Series, S 1.50

Universities and Their Relationships with the National Oceanic and Atmospheric Administration, C 55.40

University Centers of Foreign Affairs Research, Selective Directory, S 1.2:Un 3

University of Maryland College Park 2x4 Loop Test Facility, Y 3.N 88:25-7

University Research: Summary of Awards, Program of University Research, TD 1.45

University Transportation Center Project Abstracts, TD 10.14

University-Federal Agency Conference on Career Development, Conference Reports, CS 1.70

Unloads of Tomatoes in 66 Cities by States of Origin, A 36.187

Unpublished Comptroller General Decisions, With Index, D 301.100

Unreported Opinions, Reparation [indexes], IC 1.7/2

Unreported Opinions, IC 1.7/1, IC 1.7/3:A

Unreported Opinions, Indexes, IC 1.7/4

Unresolved Safety Issues Summary, Aqua Book, Y 3.N 88:30

UNTA Abstract, TD 7.10/2

Update–

Department of Housing and Urban Development, HH 1.68

Department of the Interior, I 1.112

Electronics Manufacturing Productivity Facility, D 201.36

IRS International, T 22.2/15:7177

National Cancer Institute, HE 20.3182/2

National Commission on the Observance of International Women's Year, Y 3.W 84:11

National Endowment for the Humanities, NF 3.23

Update, Forest Health Technology, Enterprise Team Update, A 13.110/17

Update from State, S 1.118/2

Update on ACTION, AA 1.9/5

Upland Cotton Program, A 82.37/3:C 82/81

Upper Atmosphere Geophysics, Reports UAG-(series), C 52.16/2, C 55.220

Upper Atmospheric Programs Bulletin, NAS 1.63

Upper Mississippi Valley Region, Publications, A 57.18

URA Demonstration Grant Summaries, HH 7.18

URA Honor Awards Program in Urban Renewal Design, HH 7.16

Uranium Enrichment Annual Report, E 1.36/2

Uranium in (year), I 28.147

Uranium Industry, E 3.46/5

Uranium Purchases Report, E 3.46/5-2

Urban Atlas, Tract Data for Standard Metropolitan Statistical Areas, C 3.62/7, C 56.242/4

Urban Business Profile, C 46.27

Urban Consortium Information Bulletins, HH 1.3/3

Urban Development Action Grant Program, HH 1.46/5

Urban Development Action Grants, HH 1.110

Urban Ecology Series, I 29.78

Urban Employment Survey: Reports (numbered), L 2.97

Urban Mass Transportation Abstracts, TD 7.10/3

Urban Mortgage Finance Reading Lists, NHA 2.16

Urban Planning Assistance Program, Project Directory, HH 1.26, HH 7.8/3

Urban Planning Bulletins, HH 7.3/4

Urban Renewal Bulletins, HH 1.19

Urban Renewal Demonstration Grant Program, Project Directory, HH 7.2:G 76

Urban Renewal Handbook, HH 1.6/6

Urban Renewal Handbooks, HH 1.6/6:RHA 7200.0

Urban Renewal Manual, Policies and Requirements for Local Public Agencies, HH 7.9

Urban Renewal Notes, HH 7.12

Urban Renewal Project Characteristics, HH 7.8

Urban Renewal Project Directory, HH 7.8/2

Urban Renewal Service Bulletins, HH 7.7/3

Urban Studies, CR 1.11

Urban Studies Division Bulletins, NHA 1.7

Urban Technology, C 51.9/14

Urban Transportation and Planning, TD 1.15/5

Urban Transportation and Planning, Current Literature Compiled by Library Staff, TD 1.15/5

USA Counties, A Statistical Abstract Supplement, C 3.134/6

USA Statistics in Brief, C 3.134/2:St 2, C 3.134/2-2

USA Trade World Nevada, C 61.39/2

USA Trade World, Ohio, C 61.39/6

USA Trade World, Pennsylvania & Delaware, C 61.39/4

USAADASCH PAM (series), D 101.22/14

USAAMRDL CR- (series), D 117.8/6

USAAPGISA Pamphlets (series), D 105.9/3

USAARMC Pamphlets (series), D 101.22/20

USAAVNC PAM- (series), D 101.22/11

USAAVSCOM TM (series), D 101.131

USAAVSCOM TR (series), D 101.132

USAEHA Pamphlet, D 105.33

USAF Extension Course Catalog, D 301.26/4

USAF Fighter Weapons Review, D 301.102

USAF Formal Schools, D 301.6:50-5

USAF Historical Aircraft Photopaks, D 301.76/2

USAF Medical Logistics Directory, D 304.9/2

USAF Military Aviation Notices, Amending SFID, Caribbean and South America, D 301.51/2

USAF Southeast Asia Monograph Series, D 301.86

USAF Statistical Digest, D 301.83/3

USAF Warrior Studies, D 301.96

USAFAC Pamphlet (series), D 101.22/21

USAFA-TR- (series), D 305.15

USAFI Catalog, D 1.10/4

USAFI Information Letter, D 1.10/2

USAFI Supply Notice, D 1.10/3

USAID Highlights, S 18.61

USAMark: Facsimile Images of Registered United States Trademarks, C 21.31/11

USAPAT, Facsimile Images of United States Patents, C 21.31

USAPRO Technical Research Notes, D 101.60

USAPRO Technical Research Reports, D 101.60/2

USAR Training Bulletin, D 103.113

USAREC Regulations, D 101.9/5

USAREC Research Memorandums (numbered), D 101.106/2

USAREC Research Notes (series), D 101.106

USARTL-TN, Technical Notes, D 117.8/4

USASSC Field Circulars, D 101.4/2

USCC Pamphlet, D 109.15

USC/FAR Consolidated Plan for Foreign Affairs Research, PrEx 3.12

USDA Consumer Expenditure Survey Reports, A 77.22

USDA Food Deliveries, A 82.43

USDA Meat Porduction Reports, A 82.54

USDA Meat Production Reports, A 88.17

USDA/Aid News Digest, A 1.108

USDA-C&MS Visual Aids (series), A 88.6/5

USDA Photo Feature (series), A 1.137/2

Use Book, A 13.14/1

Use Book Sections, A 13.14/2

Use of Materials Bulletins, HH 2.14

Useful Information for Newly Commissioned Officers, D 207.215

Useful Trees of United States, A 13.46

User Manual Series, HE 23.1210/4

USERDA Translation Lists, ER 1.18

User-Oriented Materials for UTPS [Urban Transportation Planning System], TD 2.54

Uses of Research Sponsored by the Administration on Aging, Case Studies, HE 23.3012

Uses of State Administered Federal Education Funds, HE 19.122

Uses Test Research Reports (series), L 37.312

USGS Research on Energy Resources, Program and Abstracts, I 19.4/5

USGS Research on Mineral Resources, Program and Abstracts, I 19.4/7

USGS/NGIC Geomagnetic Observatory Data, I 19.120/2

USGS-TD- (series), I 19.64

USIA Correspondent, IA 1.20

USIA INFO BASE (Quick Reference Guide), IA 1.32

USIA Feature, Special, S 1.100

USIA Private Sector Committees Annual Report, IA 1.28
USIA Strategic Information Resources Management (IRM) Plan, Fiscal Year, IA 1.33
USIA Telephone Directory, IA 1.26
USIA Video Library Catalog, IA 1.30
USIA World, IA 1.25, IA 1.34
USICA World, ICA 1.13, ICA 1.13/2
USIS Feature, IA 1.9
USL Reports, D 211.21
USMA Library Bulletin, D 109.10
USPS Stamp Posters, P 1.26/3
USPTO Today, C 21.33/2, C 21.33/2-2
USRL Research Reports, D 210.22
USSR and Adjacent Areas, D 5.333
USSR and Eastern European Scientific Abstracts, Geophysics, Astronomy, and Space, Y 3.J 66:14
USSR Grain Situation and Outlook, A 67.18:SG
USSR Report International Affairs, PrEx 7.21/7-2
USSR Report: National Economy, PrEx 7.21/2-2
USSR Reports (General), PrEx 7.21
USSR Reports (Scientific and Technical), PrEx 7.22
USSR, Situation and Outlook Report, A 93.29/2-8
USSR-Administrative Areas, Series 5103, D 5.332
Usual Weekly Earnings of Wage and Salary Workers, L 2.126
Utah, Annual Data Summary, A 57.46/6-3
Utah Commission, Annual Reports, I 1.31
Utah, Governor, Annual Reports, I 1.32
Utah National Guard, Annual Report, D 12.1/3
Utah Water Supply Outlook, A 57.46/6
Utilities Demonstration Series, HH 1.66
Utilization of American Cotton Studies, A 36.64
Utilization of Short-Stay Hospitals United States, Annual Summary, HE 20.6209/7
Utilization Posters, Y 3.R 88:14
Utilization Report (series), A 13.105/3
Utilization Research Reports, A 1.88

V

V.D. War Letters, FS 2.44
VA ADP and Telecommunications Plan, VA 1.77
VA Benefits in Brief, VA 1.14
VA Catalog, VA 1.30
VA Catalogs (numbered), VA 1.20/4
VA Fact Sheets, IS- (series), VA 1.34
VA Health Professional Scholarship Program: Publications, VA 1.63
VA Health Services Research & Development Service Progress Reports, VA 1.1/7
VA Medical Center, Allen Park, Michigan: Newsletter, VA 1.56/5
VA Medical Center, Phoenix, Arizona: Newsletter, VA 1.56/3
VA Medical Research Conference Abstracts, VA 1.43/2
VA Medical Research Service, Annual Report, VA 1.1/4
VA Monographs, VA 1.48
VA Statistical Summary, VA 1.27
VA-DMA-IS (series), VA 1.53
Valuation Dockets, IC 1 vol.7/a
Valuation Orders, IC 1 vol.5
Valuation Reports, IC 1 vol.7, IC 1 vol.9
Valuation Reports (separates), IC 1 vol.9/a
Value Engineering Information Letters, C 39.220
Value Engineering Program: Annual Report, GS 6.10
Value of Exports, Including Reexports, by Grand Visions and Principal Countries, C 18.6/2
Value of New Construction Put in Place, C 3.215/3
Value of Prime Contracts Awarded by Federal Agencies in Areas of Substantial Labor Surplus, C 46.10
Value of Product Shipments, C 3.24/9-6
Value Series, C 42.14/2
Values of German Exports of Electrical Appraratus and Equipment, C 18.158
Vanadium, I 28.78
Vanadium in (year), I 28.78/2
Vandium Reports, I 28.78
Vanguard, VA 1.93
VCR and Film Catalog, IA 1.27/2
VD Education Circulars, FS 2.39
VD Fact Sheet, HE 20.7018
VD Folderes, FS 2.32
VD Statistical Letter, HE 20.7018/2, HE 20.7309
Vegetable Report, Louisiana Crop Reporting Service, A 88.12/26
Vegetable Seed Stocks, A 92.19/6
Vegetable Seeds, A 92.19/17
Vegetable Situation, A 88.12/8, A 93.12/1, A 105.24

Vegetable, Situation and Outlook, A 93.12/2
Vegetable Situation and Outlook Yearbook, A 93.12/2-3
Vegetables, A 105.24/2-2
Vegetables for the Hot, Humid Tropics (series), A 106.26
Vegetables, Fresh Market [and] Processing, A 92.11
Vegetables, Fresh Market, Annual Summary, Acreage, Production, etc., A 92.11/10-2
Vegetables, Preliminary Acreage, Yield, Production and Value, A 92.11/10-6
Vegetables, Processing, A 92.11/14
Vegetables, Processing, Annual Summary, Acreage Productions, etc., A 92.11/10
Vegetables, (year) Annual Summary, A 105.24/2
Vegetable-Seed Stocks, A 88.30/5
Vendor Payments for Medical Care Under Public Assistance, by Program and Type of Service, Fiscal Year (date), HE 17.617/4
Veneer and Plywood Series, C 18.159
Veneral Disease Bulletins, T 27.20, FS 2.11
Veneral Disease Information, T 27.26, FS 2.9
Venezulean Mixed Claims Commissions, Caracas 1902 and 1903, S 3.17
Verification Case Studies, ED 1.70
Vermiculite in (year), I 28.137
Vessel Entrances and Clearances: Calendar Year (date), C 56.210:975, C 3.174:975
Vessel Inventory Report, C 39.221, TD 11.11
Vessel Inventory Report, United States Flag Dry Cargo and Tanker Fleets, 1,000 Gross Tons and Over, C 39.217
Vessel Safety Review, TD 5.12/3
Vessels Receiving Benefits of Construction Loans under Merchant Marine Act of 1928, SB 7.8
Vesting Orders, Pr 33.507
Veteran Preference , CS 1.30
Veterans Administration Activities, Submitted by the Veterans Administration, Y 4.V 64/4:V 64
Veterans Administration Instructions, VA 1.15
Veterans Administration Medical Center, Tucson, Arizona, Formulary, VA 1.73/5
Veterans Administration Summary of Medical Programs, VA 1.43/5
Veterans Assistance Information, Printed and Processed, Y 3.Se 4:18
Veterans Education Newsletter, VA 1.49
Veterans' Emergency Housing Program: Community Action Bulletin, NHA 1.14
Veterans Emergency Housing Program: Community Action Report to Mayor's Emergency Housing Committee, NHA 1.12, Y 3.H 81/2:8
Veterans Employment News, L 7.29
Veterans Employment Service Handbooks, L 7.30
Veterans' Reemployment Rights Handbooks, L 25.6/2:V 64
Veterinary Biological Products, Licensees and Permittees, A 101.2/10
Veterinary Biologics Division Notices, A 77.226/3
Veterinary Biologics Notices, A 101.14
Veterinary Bulletins, W 44.21/9
VFR Helicopter Chart of Los Angeles, C 55.416/12-2
VFR-Supplement, United States, D 5.318/8
VFR/IFR Planning Chart, C 55.416/7
VHA Employee Newsletter, VA 1.100
Victimization, Fear of Crime and Altered Behavior (series), HH 1.70
Victims of Trafficking and Violence Protection Act: 2000, Trafficking in Persons Report, S 1.152
Victory, Pr 32.5021
Victory Crops Series Pamphlets, FS 5.29
Victory Fleet, MC 1.24
Victory; Office Weekly Bulletins, Pr 32.5008
Victory Speaker; An Arsenal of Information for Speakers, Pr 32.5017
Vienna, International Exhibition, 1873, S 6.14
Viet-Nam Information Notes, S 1.38
Vietnam Report, PrEx 7.16/5
Vietnam Studies (series), D 101.74
Viewpoints, a Selection from the Pictorial Collections of the Library of Congress, LC 25.2:V 67
Views and Estimates of Committees of the House (together with Supplemental and Minority Views) on the Congressional Budget for Fiscal Year (date), Y 4.B 85/3-11
Views and Estimates of the Committee on Education, Y 4.Ed 8/1-11
Views and Estimates of the Committee on Foreign Affairs on the Budget, Y 4.F 76/1:B 85
Views and Estimates on the Budget Proposed for Fiscal Year (date), Y 4.Ap 6/1-10

Views of the Committee on Appropriations, United States Senate, on the First Concurrent Resolution on the Budget, Y 4.Ap 6/2:B 85/5
Viking Picture Sets, NAS 1.43/5
Violence Against Women Act News, J 35.20
Viral Tumorigenesis Report, HE 20.3167
Virginia Crops and Livestock, A 88.31
Virology Study Section, HE 20.3001/2:V 81
Virus Cancer Program Advisory Committee, HE 20.3001/2:V 81/4
Virus Cancer Program Scientific Review Committee A, HE 20.3001/2:V 81/2
Virus Cancer Program Scientific Review Committee B, HE 20.3001/2:V 81/3
Visa Bulletin, S 1.3/4
Visa Requirements of Foreign Governments, S 1.2:V 82/2
Vision (Newsletter of SERVE), The, ED 1.348
Vision Research Program Committee, HE 20.3001/2:V 82/3
Visiting Expert Series, S 1.87
Visiting Fellowship Program Reports, J 26.11
Visitor Accommodations Furnished by Concessioners in Areas Administered by National Park Service, I 29.70
Visitor Services Training Series, I 29.9/3-2
Visitors–Report to Nurses' Station Before Entering Room, HE 20.7029
VISTA, PrEx 10.13
    Currents, AA 1.9/3
    Directories, Y 3.N 21/29:17-16 CT
    Fact Book, AA 1.9, PrEx 10.21
    Forms, Y 3.N 21/19:17-4
    Manuals, PrEx 10.8/2
    News Flash, Y 3.N 21/29:17-3
    Pamphlets, PrEx 10.13/3
    Source, Y 3.N 21/29:16-16
    Voice, PrEx 10.13/2
Visual Artists Fellowships, NF 2.8/2-13
Visual Arts Grants to Organizations, NF 2.8/2-15
Visual Sciences a Study Section, HE 20.3001/2:V 82
Visual Sciences B Study Section, HE 20.3001/2:V 82/2
Vital and Health Statistics, HE 20.6209
Vital Statistics Bulletin, FS 2.110
Vital Statistics of Latin America, C 18.160
Vital Statistics of the United States, HE 20.6210, C 3.139
Vital Statistics, Special Reports, C 3.67
Vital Statistics, Special Reports (abstracts), C 3.67/2
Vitreous-China Plumbing Fixtures, C 3.114
V-line, Bulletin of Information, PrEx 10.13/4
VOA, Voice of America, Broadcast Schedule for Languages Other than English, IA 1.6/4
VOA, Voice of America, English Broadcast Guide, IA 1.6/3
Vocational and Technical Education Abstracts, C 41.62
Vocational Division Leaflets, FS 5.129
Vocational Division [miscellaneous] Circulars, FS 5.127
Vocational Education Information (series), HE 19.121
Vocational Education Letters, I 16.23
Vocational Education; Schools for Careers, an Analysis of Occupational Courses Offered by Secondary and Postsecondary Schools, HE 19.321
Vocational Education Study Publications, HE 19.219
Vocational Educator, ED 1.33/3
Vocational Instructional Materials Available from Federal Agencies, ED 1.17/3
Vocational Instructional Materials for Marketing and Distributive Education, ED 1.17/3
Vocational Rehabilitation Administration Research and Demonstration Projects, FS 13.202:R 31/2
Vocational Rehabilitation Series Bulletins, FS 5.28, FS 10.7
Vocational Rehabilitation Series, Opportunity Monographs, VE 1.6
Vocational Summary, Circulars of Information, VE 1.5
Vocational Training Activities of Public Employment Offices, FS 3.119
Voice of America Forum Lectures–
    Mass Communication Series, IA 1.19
    Music Series, IA 1.19/3
    Space Science Series, IA 1.19/2
    University Series, IA 1.19/4
Voice of Z39, News About Library, Information Science, and Publishing Standards, C 13.163
Volcano Letter, I 19.29
Volpe Transportation Journal, TD 8.27/2
Volume and Composition of Individuals' Savings– Federal Reserve System Board of Governors, FR 1.53

Securities and Exchange Commission, SE 1.25/6
Volume Review Exercise (series), D 301.26/17-5
Voluntary Business Energy Conservation Program, Progress Reports, E 1.39
Voluntary Foreign Relief Programs, Activities of Registered American Voluntary Agencies, S 18.19
Voluntary Industrial Energy Conservation, C 57.25, E 1.22
Voluntary Reporting of Greenhouse Gases Annual Report, E 3.59/2
Voluntary Service National Advisory Committee: Report of Annual Meeting, VA 1.52
Volunteer, S 19.19
Volunteer Manpower Booklet, VM (series), FCD 1.10
Volunteer Opportunities, A 13.112
Volunteers, Bulletin for Those Who Direct Their Activities, Pr 32.4264
Volunteers in the National Forests (series), A 13.112/2
Volunteers Who Produce Books, Braille, Tape, Large Type, LC 19.21
Voting and Registration in the Election of (name), C 3.186/3-2
Voting and Registration in the Election of November (date), C 3.186/3
Voting Information Bulletins, D 2.3/2
Voting Information News, D 1.96
Voucher Examination Memorandum, T 60.8, T 63.111
VR-ISC (series), FS 13.204

W

W.I.B. Price Bulletins, Y 3.W 19/2:47
Wabash River Charts, W 7.13/5
WADC Technical Notes, D 301.45/13
Wage Chronologies, L 2.3
Wage Chronology Series, L 2.6/a 10
Wage Chronology Series 4, L 2.64
Wage Committee: Annual Report of Activities, VA 1.51
Wage Developments in Manufacturing, Summary Release, L 2.44/2
Wage Developments in the New England Region, L 2.49/5
Wage Operations Manual of Procedures, L 2.54
Wage Payment (by States), L 16.24
Wage Rates in Selected Farm Activities, L 7.55/2-2
Wage Series Reports, RL 1.8
Wage Stabilization Bulletin, L 22.17
Wage Stabilization Committee Releases, WSC (series), ES 2.7/2
Wage Stabilization, General Orders and Interpretations, Pr 32.5112
Wage Statistics of Class 1 Railroads in the United States, IC 1 ste.25
Wage Structure, Series 2, L 2.27
Wage Survey Summaries, L 2.3/3-3
Wage Trends for Occupational Groups in Metropolitan Areas, Summary Release, L 2.86/2
Wage-Hour News Letter, L 22.27/2
WAIS, GP 3.36
Wall Charts, L 2.70/3
Walnut Production, A 92.11/2-4
Walsh-Healey Public Contracts Act, Decisions, L 22.23
Walsh-Healey Public Contracts Act Minimum Wage Determination (for various industries), L 22.19
Walter Reed Army Institute of Research, Research Reports WRAIR (series), D 104.15
Walter Reed Army Medical Center, Army Prosthetics Research Laboratory, Technical Reports, D 104.15/2
Want Lists (lettered), LC 6.5
Want Lists (unlettered and unnumbered), LC 6.6
Wanted Flyer Apprehension Orders, J 1.14/14
Wanted Flyers, J 1.14/13
War Background Studies, SI 1.14
War Bonds in Action, T 66.12
War Changes in Industry Series, Reports, TC 1.18
War Circulars, A 72.23
War Contract Terminations and Settlements, Report to Congress, Y 3.W 19/7:107, T 67.7
War Department Catalogs, W 1.67, W 89.7
War Housing Technical Bulletins, NHA 4.10
War Information Series, Y 3.P 96/3:7
War, Literature, and the Arts, D 305.22/3
War Loan Organization, T 1.27
War Minerals Reports, I 28.99
War Notes, Information from Abroad, N 13.7
War of Rebellion, Compilation of Official Records of Union and Conferate Armies [or Rebellion Records], W 45.5

War of the American Revolution, D 114.2:Am 3
War on Hunger, Monthly New Report, S 18.34
War Production Drive, Progress Report, Pr 32.4815
War Profits Studies, Pr 32.4227, Pr 33.312
War Records, Monographs, A 1.69
War Records Project, Reports, A 36.150
War Reports for Loggers and Mill Men, W 107.9
War Saver, T 1.26/7
War Series, Information from Abroad, N 13.8
War Trade Board Journal, S 13.5
War Trade Board Pamphlets, WT 1.6
Warehouses Licensed under United States Warehouse Act, A 36.182, A 88.56, A 82.98
Warm Air Furnaces, Winter Air-conditioning Systems, and Accessory Equipment, C 3.144
Warren Grant Magnuson Clinical Center: Annual Brochure, HE 20.3052/2
Wartime Information to Mariners Supplementing U.S. Coast Pilots, C 4.7/6
Wartime Report Release Lists, Y 3.N 21/5:12
Wartime Reports, Y 3.N 21/5:11
Washington Annual Data Summary Water Year, A 57.46/7-2
Washington Aqueduct, Annual Reports, I 1.45
Washington Arbitration (American-British Mixed Claims Commission), S 3.13/2
Washington, D.C. Unloads of Fresh Fruits and Vegetables, A 88.12/17
Washington, Governor, Annual Reports, 1878-90, I 1.35
Washington Helicopter Route Chart, C 55.416/12-4
Washington Hospital for Foundlings, Annual Reports, I 1.34
Washington Office Telephone Directory, I 53.45
Wastewater Management Reports, D 103.60
Wastewater Treatment Construction Grants Data Base, Public Law 92-500 Project Records, Grants Assistance Programs, New Projects Funded During (Month), EP 1.56
Water and Related Land Resources [by area], A 1.105
Water and Sewer Bond Sales in United States, FS 2.56/4, I 67.10
Water and Sewer Facilities Grant Program, HUD Information Series, HH 1.17
Water Bank Program, from Inception of Program through (date), A 82.94
Water Borne Commerce of United States Including Foreign Intercoastal and Coastwise Traffic and Commerce of U.S. Noncontiguous Territory, SB 7.5/295
Water Borne Foreign and Domestic Commerce of U.S., C 27.9/11, MC 1.20
Water Borne Foreign Commerce of United States, SB 7.5/216, SB 7.7
Water Borne Passenger Traffic of U.S., SB 7.5/157, C 27.9/12
Water Conservation Report WC (series), I 27.53
Water Data Coordination Directory, I 19.118
Water Facilities Area Plans (by States), A 36.148
Water Fact Sheets (series), I 19.114
Water Information Series Reports, I 19.53/4
Water Levels in Observation Wells in Santa Barbara County, California, I 19.49
Water Operation and Maintenance Bulletin, I 27.41
Water Management and Conservation Program, I 27.78
Water Operations Technical Support: WOTS, D 103.24/15
Water Pollution Control, Federal Costs, Report to Congress, I 67.1/2
Water Pollution Control Research and Training Grants, FS 2.64/7, I 67.13
Water Pollution Control Research Series, EP 1.16, EP 2.10
Water Pollution Publications, FS 2.64
Water Quality in Galveston Bay, I 49.110
Water Quality Management Accomplishments, Compendiums, EP 1.75
Water Quality Management Bulletin, EP 1.71
Water Quality Management Five Year Strategy FY-Baseline, EP 1.91
Water Quality Management Guidance, EP 1.8/8
Water Quality Records of [States], I 19.53/2
Water Quality Standards Criteria Digest, Compilation of Federal/State Criteria on [various subjects], EP 1.29/2
Water Quality Standards Summary [for various States] (series), EP 1.29
Water Reactor Safety Research, Buff Book I, Y 3.N 88:18
Water Research Capsule Report (series), I 1.103
Water Resources Activities in Illinois, I 19.55/5
Water Resources Bulletins, I 19.3/3
Water Resources Data, I 19.15/6
Water Resources Data for [State], I 19.53/2

Water Resources Development by Army Corps of Engineers in [State], D 103.35
Water Resources Development by Corps of Engineers by Area, D 103.35
Water Resources Development in [State], D 103.35–D 103.35/53
Water Resources Development in Delaware in (year), D 103.35/8
Water Resources Development in District of Columbia, D 103.35/51
Water Resources Development in Idaho, D 103.35/12
Water Resources Development in Illinois, D 103.35/13
Water Resources Development in Indiana, D 103.35/14
Water Resources Development in Iowa, D 103.35/15
Water Resources Development in Kentucky, D 103.35/17
Water Resources Development in Massachusetts, D 103.35/21
Water Resources Development in Maryland, D 103.35/20
Water Resources Development in Michigan, D 103.35/22
Water Resources Development in Minnesota, D 103.35/23
Water Resources Development in Missouri, D 103.35/25
Water Resources Development in Nevada, D 103.35/28
Water Resources Development in New Jersey (year), D 103.35/30
Water Resources Development in New Mexico, D 103.35/31
Water Resources Development in New York, D 103.35/32
Water Resources Development in North Carolina, D 103.35/33
Water Resources Development in North Dakota, D 103.35/34
Water Resources Development in Ohio, D 103.35/35
Water Resources Development in South Carolina, D 103.35/40
Water Resources Development in Virginia, D 103.35/46
Water Resources Development in West Virginia, D 103.35/48
Water Resources Development in Wisconsin, D 103.35/49
Water Resources Divisions Bulletin of Training, I 19.3/4
Water Resources Investigations, I 19.42/4-2
Water Resources Investigations (numbered), I 19.42/4
Water Resources Investigations Folders, I 19.42/4
Water Resources Investigations in [States], I 19.42/3
Water Resources Reports, WR- (series), Y 3.T 25:59
Water Resources Research Catalog, I 1.94
Water Resources Research Program of the U.S. Geological Survey, I 19.42/4-3
Water Resources Review, I 19.42
Water Resources Review, Annual Summary, Water Year, I 19.42/2
Water Resources Scientific Information Center, WRSIC- (series), I 1.97
Water Resources Teaching Guide (series), I 27.76
Water Resources/Water Quality, Y 3.T 25:59-2
Water Reuse, OWRT/RU-, I 1.97/3
Water Safety Program Catalog, D 103.124
Water Specturm, D 103.48
Water Supply and Pollution Control, FS 2.64/2
Water Supply and Waste Disposal Series, TD 2.32
Water Supply Bulletins, I 19.3/5
Water Supply Forecasts, C 30.58
Water Supply Outlook, Federal-State-Private Cooperative Snow Surveys [Colorado], A 57.46/15
Water Supply Outlook for Northeastern United States, C 55.113/2
Water Supply Outlook for Western United States, Water Year, C 55.113
Water Supply Outlook Reports, A 57.46
Water Supply Papers, I 19.13
Water Temperatures, Coast and Geodetic Survey Tide Stations, C 4.34
Waterborne Commerce of the United States, D 103.1/2
Water-Borne Foreign and Noncontiguous Commerce and Passenger Traffic of United States, MC 1.23
Waterborne Passenger Traffic of U.S., MC 1.15
Waterfowl Monitoring Investigations, Y 3.T 25:27-2
Waterfowl Status Report, I 49.15/3, I 49.100/2
Waterfowl 2000, I 49.100/4
Waterfowl, Population Status, I 49.100/3
Watermark, FEM 1.23
Water-Related Disease Outbreaks Surveillance, HE 20.7011/33
Water-Resources Bulletins, I 19.3/3
Watershed Work Plan [by Area], A 57.59

Watertown Arsenal Laboratory, Report WAL (series), D 105.13/2

Watertown Arsenal Laboratory: Technical Report (series), D 105.13/2-2

Watertown Arsenal: Technical Report Ward, TR (series), D 105.13/2-3

Waterways Experiment Station Capabilities, D 103.24/ 10

Wave Propagation Group Reports, Pr 32.413/6

We the Americans (series), C 56.234

"We the People" Calendar, Y 3.H 62/2:9

Weapon Systems, D 101.95

Wearing Apparel in World Markets, C 18.161

Weather Bureau Engineering Handbooks EHB-(series), C 30.6/5

Weather Bureau Forecasters Handbooks, C 30.6/4

Weather Bureau Marine Services Charts, C 30.22/6

Weather Bureau Observing Handbooks, C 30.6/6

Weather Bureau Training Papers, C 30.48

Weather, Crops, and Markets, A 36.11

Weather Maps–
  Signal Office, W 42.23
  Weather Bureau, C 30.12

Weather Modification Activity Reports, C 55.27/2

Weather Modification, Annual Report, NS 1.21

Weather Modification Reporting Program, C 55.27/3

Weather Modification, Summary Report, C 55.27

Weather Outlook, A 29.38, C 30.13

Weather Service Bulletin, W 108.35

Weather Service for Merchant Shipping, C 30.79

Weather Service Observing Handbooks, C 55.108/2

Weather-Crop Bulletin, W 42.27

Weed & Seed In-Sites, J 1.110

Week in the United States, S 1.79

Week of the War, Pr 32.5014

Weekly Abstracts: NASA Earth Resources Survey Program, C 51.9/11

Weekly Accession List (of) Library, SS 1.17, FS 3.8

Weekly Accident Bulletins, C 3.128

Weekly Advertising Digest, Y 3.F 31/11:30

Weekly Anthracite and Beehive Coke Reports, I 28.49

Weekly Anthracite Report, WAR Series, I 28.49/2

Weekly Averages of Member Bank Reserves, Reserve Bank Credit and Related Items and Statement of Condition of the Federal Reserve Bank, FR 1.15

Weekly Bulletin on Raw Materials, Y 3.W 19/2:35

Weekly Bulletins, Y 3.F 73:5

Weekly Business Survey of 33 Cities, C 3.66

Weekly Business Survey of Key Cities, C 1.19

Weekly Census Report of U.S. Marine and Contract Hospitals, T 26.36

Weekly Climate Bulletin, C 55.129/2

Weekly Coal Report, I 28.33, E 3.11/4

Weekly Compilation of Presidential Documents, GS 4.114, AE 2.109

Weekly Condition Report of Large Commercial Banks in New York and Chicago, FR 1.16

Weekly Consular and Trade Reports, C 10.14

Weekly Corn and Wheat Region Bulletin, A 29.43

Weekly Cotton Linters Review, A 88.11/3

Weekly Cotton Market Review, A 88.11/2

Weekly Cotton Region Bulletins, A 29.39

Weekly Cotton Service Bulletins, C 18.162

Weekly Crude Oil Stock Reports, I 28.46

Weekly Earnings of Wage and Salary Workers, L 2.126

Weekly Electric Output, United States, FP 1.11/7

Weekly European Citrus Fruit Market Cable, A 36.67

Weekly Feed Review, A 88.18/4

Weekly Fruit Exports, C 18.72/13

Weekly Government Abstracts, WGA-(series), C 51.9/ 5–C 51.9/30

Weekly Health Index, C 3.41

Weekly Information Report, Y 3.N 88:37, Y 3.N 88:50, Y 3.N 88:55

Weekly Labor News Digest, L 1.28, L 2.50

Weekly List of Selected U.S. Government Publications, GP 3.17

Weekly Molasses Market Reports, A 82.62

Weekly News Letter [to Crop Correspondents], A 1.22

Weekly News Series, A 43.27

Weekly News Summary, HH 1.15/2

Weekly Newspaper Service, L 1.77

Weekly Notices to Airmen, C 23.15, CA 1.7, C 31.9, C 31.109

Weekly Oil Update, E 3.32/2

Weekly Peanut Reports, A 36.106, A 88.10

Weekly Periodical Index, D 103.108

Weekly Petroleum Statistics Reports, FE 1.9/3

Weekly Petroleum Status Report, E 1.63, E 3.32

Weekly Population Report, J 16.32

Weekly Poultry Slaughter Report, A 88.15/7

Weekly Report [Cotton], A 85.12

Weekly Report of Certificated Stock in Licensed Warehouses, A 88.11/24

Weekly Report of Vessels under Jurisdiction of Shipping Board, SB 2.12

Weekly Report on Japan, D 102.13

Weekly Report on Production of Bituminous Coal, Etc, I 19.30

Weekly Reports of Office of Western Irrigation Agriculture, A 19.25

Weekly Retail Sales Report, C 3.138/5

Weekly Review, RR 1.7, Y 3.W 19/2:6

Weekly Review of Periodicals, FR 1.22

Weekly Review of Recent Developments, L 2.56

Weekly Rice Market Review, A 88.18/9

Weekly Roundup of World Production and Trade, WR (series), A 67.42

Weekly Roundups, Economic Letter, S 1.80

Weekly Runoff Report, Pacific Northwest Water Resources, I 19.46/2

Weekly Statement of Bonds Held in Trust for National Banks, T 40.9

Weekly Statement of Gold and Silver Exports and Imports, United States, C 3.195

Weekly Station Reports of Office of Dry Land Agriculture Investigations, A 19.24

Weekly Statistical News, Y 3.W 19/2:36

Weekly Statistical Reports, Y 3.F 31/11:24

Weekly Summary, A 21.6/6

Weekly Summary: AAA Press Releases, A 55.64

Weekly Summary of Banking and Credit Measures, FR 1.52

Weekly Summary of Export Opportunities for Small Business, Pr 33.917

Weekly Summary of F.O.B. Prices of Fresh Fruits and Vegetables in Representative Shipping Districts, A 88.12/2, A 82.53

Weekly Summary of Federal Legislation Relating to National Resources Committee, Activities Bulletins, Y 3.N 21/12:15

Weekly Summary of Fruit and Vegetable Carlot Shipments, A 88.12

Weekly Summary of Health Information for International Travel, HE 20.7023

Weekly Summary of N.L.R.B. Cases, LR 1.15/2

Weekly Summary of NLRB Cases, LR 1.5/2

Weekly Summary of Orders and Regulations, C 31.208

Weekly Summary of Wholesale Prices of Fresh Fruits and Vegetables at New York City and Chicago, A 88.12/3

Weekly Summary of Wholesale Prices of Fruits and Vegetables at New York City and Chicago, A 82.52

Weekly Summary (Press Division), A 107.17

Weekly Tobacco Market News Summary, A 88.34/7

Weekly Trading Data on New York Exchanges, SE 1.25/6

Weekly Weather and Crop Bulletin, C 55.209

Weekly Weather and Crop Bulletin, National Summary, C 30.11, C 55.209

Weekly Weather Chronicle, W 42.18

Weight Distribution of Carloads for Each Commodity Class by Type of Car, IC 1.23/16:TC-2

Weights and Measures Directory, C 13.66

Weights and Measures Today, C 13.66/2

Welcoming America's Newest Commonwealth: Reports, Y 3.N 81/6:9

Welding Practice [abstracts], C 41.54/8

Welfare in Review, HE 17.9

Welfare Research Researchs, FS 14.14

Welfare Work Series, Y 3.C 83:35

WEPS, E 3.11/20-5

West Coast of North and South America (including the Hawaiian Islands), C 4.15/5

West Europe Report, PrEx 7.18

West North Central, Population and Per Capita Income Estimates for Counties and Incorporated Places, C 3.186/27-3

West, Population and Per Capita Income Estimates for Counties and Incorporated Places, C 3.186/ 27-2

West Side VA Medical Center Formulary, VA 1.78

Western Cities, A 88.12/31:4

Western Environmental Research Laboratory: Annual Report, EP 1.14/2

Western Environmental Research Laboratory: Monthly Activities Report, EP 1.14

Western Europe Reports, PrEx 7.18

Western European Series, S 1.118

Western Europe, Situation and Outlook Report, A 93.29/2-9

Western Hemisphere, Outlook and Situation Report, A 93.29/2-18

Western Hemisphere, Situation and Outlook Series, A 93.29/2-20

Western Range, A 13.29

Western Range and Livestock Report, A 92.18/10

Western Region, C 55.118

Western Regional Newsletter, J 21.17

Western Space and Missile Center: Regulations, WSMCR- (series), D 301.6/7

Western States Regional Turkey Breeding Project, Annual Report, A 77.235

Western Training Center, Catalogs and Schedule of Courses, D 13.16

Western U.S. Water Plan, (year) Progress Report, I 27.61

Western United States, Dates of Latest Prints, Instrument Approach Procedure Charts and Airport Obstruction Plans, C 4.9/20

Western Volume, HE 20.6202:N 93 W

Western Water Policy Review Advisory Commission, Y 3.W 52/2

Westfornet Monthly Alert, A 13.108

Wetlands Inventories, I 49.64

What Price America, I 43.8

What Social Security Means to Industries, SS 1.18

What the Soldier Thinks, Monthly Digest of War Department Studies on Attitudes of American Troops, W 1.65

What You Have to Know about SSI, HE 3.90

What We Are Doing About Agricultural Surpluses, A 82.80

What We Defend (Radio Scripts), I 29.48

What's Doing in Your Town, Y 3.F 31/11:23

What's Happening in the Personnel Field, D 217.13

What's New in Research, A 13.62/13

What's New, Tips for Supervisors from Oaas, L 1.43

What's Noteworthy on ... (series), ED 1.9/2

Wheat and Rye Summary, Crop Year, A 88.18/16

Wheat and Wheat-Flour Stocks Held by Mills, C 3.115

Wheat Flour, A 82.3/10

Wheat Flour for Domestic Distribution, A 82.3/6

Wheat Flour for Export Distribution, A 82.3/9

Wheat Ground and Wheat-Milling Products, C 3.116

Wheat Ground and Wheat-Milling Products, by States, C 3.117

Wheat Ground and Wheat-Milling Products, Merchant and Other Mills, C 3.118

Wheat Outlook and Situation Report, A 93.11

Wheat, Outlook and Situation Yearbook, A 93.11/2-3

Wheat Pasture Report, A 92.33

Wheat Production Adjustment, A 43.5/16

Wheat, Rice, Feed Grains, Dry Peas, Dry Beans, Seeds, Hops, A 67.30:W 56

Wheat Situation, A 88.18/8, A 93.11, A 105.20/3

Wheat Situation and Outlook Yearbook, A 93.11/2-3

When You Get Social Security Disability Benefits, What You Need to Know, SSA 1.21

When You Get Social Security Retirement or Survivors Benefits, What You Need to Know, SSA 1.20

Where to Write for Birth and Death Records, FS 2.102:B 53/3

Where to Write for Birth and Death Records of U.S. Citizens Who Were Born or Died Outside of the United States and Birth Certifications for Alien Children Adopted by U.S. Citizens, FS 2.102:B 53/7

Where to Write for Divorce Records, FS 2.102:D 64

Where to Write for Marriage Record, FS 2.102:M 34

Where to Write for Vital Records, HE 20.6210/2

Which Jobs for Young Workers, L 5.45

White House Conference Happenings, Y 3.W 58:6

White House Fellowships, Pr 40.12, Pr 41.12, Pr 42.12

White House Initiative on Historically Black Colleges and Universities, Newsletter, ED 1.89

White House Report to Students, PrEx 1.12

White Oak Laboratory: Technical Reports, NSWC/ WOL/TR- (series), D 201.21/3

White Pine Blister Control, Annual Report, A 13.59

White River Charts, W 7.13/6

White-Collar Salaries, L 2.43/2

Wholesale Bulletins, Pr 32.4223

Wholesale Code Regulations, Y 3.F 31/10:15

Wholesale (Preliminary Market) Price Index, L 2.61/5

Wholesale Price Index (1947-49=100), Indexes for Groups, Subgroups, and Project Classes of Commodities, L 2.61/2

Wholesale Price Index (1947-49=100), Prices and Price Relatives for Individual Commodities, 1951- 53, L 2.61/6, L 2.61/6-2

Wholesale Price Index, Major Specification Changes 1947-53, L 2.61/7

Wholesale Price Index, Preliminary Estimate, L 2.61/9

Wholesale Price Index Series 1947-48 100: Economic Sector Indexes, L 2.61/8

Wholesale Price Indexes, Advance Summary, L 2.61/10

Wholesale Prices 1922–1966, L 2.8

Wholesale Prices and Price Indexes, L 2.61

Pastics, C 18.173
Plastic Paints, C 18.172
Prepared Medicines, C 18.174
Synthetic Aromatics, C 18.175
Toilet Preparations, C 18.176
Veterinary Preparations, C 18.177
Wood, Furniture, Floor, Metal and Automobile
    Polishes, C 18.178
World Trade Information Series, C 41.13, C 49.8
World Trade Notes on Chemicals and Allied Products,
    C 18.179
World Trade Series, C 42.9/2
World War and 1939 European War, A 36.119
World War I (1917–19) Publications, D 114.8
World War II, Dispatch, D 1.100
World War II Fact Sheet, D 201.39
World War II History of Department of Commerce, C
    1.27
World War II Honor List of Dead and Missing (by
    States), W 107.13
World Weather Records, SI 1.7
World Wheat Prospects, A 36.44
World Wide Motion Picture Developments, C 18.180
World Wise Schools Presents Destinations, PE 1.13
World Wood Situation, A 36.36
World's Poultry Congress and Exposition, A 1.48
World's Wool Digest, C 18.181
Worldwide Communist Propaganda Activities, IA 1.8/2
Worldwide Distribution of Radio Receiver Sets, IA
    1.12
Worldwide Geographic Location Codes, GS 1.34
Worldwide Manpower Distribution by Geographical
    Area, D 1.61/3
Worldwide Marine Weather Broadcasts, C 55.119
Worldwide Public Affairs Offices Directory, D 101.120/
    2
Worldwide Reports, PrEx 7.14
Worldwide U.S. Active Duty Military Personnel
    Casualties, D 1.61/6
Wounded Americans Series, T 66.10
WPA Week in National Defense, FW 4.37
Wright Aeronautical Serial Reports, D 301.45/22
Writers' Publications, FW 4.28
Writings of George Washington, Y 3.W 27/2:13
WS Reports, HE 19.129
WSDG Technical Papers, WSDG-TP- (series), A 13.87/
    2
WSUN (series), E 1.88
Wyoming BLM Wildlife Technical Bulletins, I 53.34
Wyoming Land Use Decisions (series), I 53.23

Y

Yard Service Performance of Class I Railroads in the
    United States, IC 1ste.38
Year in Review at Goddard Space Flight Center, NAS
    1.1/3
Year in Review Carderock Division, D 211.28
Year of Progress, Annual Summary, A 95.1
Yearbook of Agriculture, A 1.10
Yearbook of Enlisted Training, N 17.30
Yearbook, Park and Recreation Progress, I 29.44
Yellow Book, C 13.67
Yellowstone Center for Resources, I 29.138/2
Yellowstone Grizzly Bear Investigations, Annual
    Report of the Interagency Study Team, I 29.94
Yellowstone National Park, Annual Reports, 1898-90,
    I 1.37
Yellowstone Wolf Project Annual Report, I 29.138
Yosemite National Park, Annual Reports, I 1.38
You and Your USA series, D 2.11
You Can Survive, Rural Defense Fact Sheets, A 43.35
You-in (series), HE 20.3116
Younger Scholars, NF 3.8/2-6
Your Changing Forest, News on the Black Hills
    National Forest Plan Revision, A 13.128
Your Defense Budget, D 1.1/4
Your Federal Budget, Pr 34.107/4
Your Federal Income Tax, T 22.44
Your Guide to Federal Waterfowl Production Areas, I
    49.6/3
Your Medicare Handbook, HE 22.8/16
Your Navy, from the Viewpoint of the Nation's Finest
    Artists, D 201.9
Your New Social Security, Fact Sheets, FS 3.25
Your Social Security, HE 3.89
Your Social Security Rights and Responsibilities,
    Disability Benefits, HE 3.88
Your Social Security Rights & Responsibilities,
    Retirement & Survivors Benefits, HE 3.88/2,
    HE 3.93

Youth Advisory Board Newsletter, EP 1.27
Youth Employment Tables TS (series), L 16.41
Youth Fatal Crash and Alcohol Facts, TD 8.39
Youth in Action Bulletin, J 32.21/2-2
Youth Indicators, Trends in the Well-Being of American
    Youth, ED 1.327
Youth Program Models and Innovations, L 37.19
Youth Reporter, HE 1.311
Youth Reports, HE 21.109

Z

Zinc, I 28.69/2
Zinc Industry, I 28.69
Zinc Industry in (year), I 28.69/2
Zinc Mine Production, I 28.57
Zinc Oxide, I 28.90
Zinc Reports, I 28.69
Zinc Scrap, I 28.68
Zinc Scrap Consumers Reports, I 28.68
Zip Code Business Patterns, C 3.294
ZIP Code Business Patterns C 3.298
ZIP Code Directories [by States], P 1.10/7
ZIP + 4, State Directories, P 1.10/9
Zirconium and Halfnium in (year), I 28.83/2
Zirconium Reports, I 28.83

KEYWORD IN TITLE INDEX

A

A-Bomb

Photographs of **A-Bomb** Test, Operation Doorstep, Yucca Flat, Nevada, March 17, 1953, FCD 1.11/2

A.A.A.

A.A.A. Flashes, Facts for Committeemen, A 55.42/11, A 76.410

A.A.A.N.C.R.

A.A.A.N.C.R. Agricultural Conservation Program by States, NCR, A 55.43/11

A.A.F.

A.A.F. Manuals, W 108.22

A.A.F. Memorandum, W 108.11

A.A.F. Regulations, W 108.6

A.E.F.

Balloon Notes **A.E.F.**, W 95.21/6

A.H.D.

A.H.D. [Animal Husbandry Divisions] (series), A 77.209

A.I.D.

A.I.D. Background Series, S 18.30

A.I.D. Bibliography Series, S 18.21/3

A.I.D. Discussion Papers, S 18.30/2

A.I.D. Memory Documents, S 18.43

A.I.D. Research Abstracts, TN-AAAN (series), S 18.47

A.L.A.

A.L.A. Sub-Committee on Federal Publications, LC 2.5

A.L.L.

A.L.L. Points Bulletin, ED 1.33/5

A.N.D.

A.N.D. Animal Nutrition Division (series), A 77.210

A.T.

A.T. Quarterly, ED 1.79/3

AAA

Weekly Summary: **AAA** Press Releases, A 55.64

AACS

AACS Manuals, D 301.7/5

AAF

AAF Bombing Accuracy, Reports, W 108.37

Index of Specifications Approved for **AAF** Procurement, W 108.13/3

Report **AAF** (series), TD 4.709

AAL

Technical Documentary Report **AAL**-TDR- (series), D 301.45/30-2

AAM

AAM (series), TD 4.210/2

AASHO

Conference Proceedings [of] **AASHO** Committee on Electronics, TD 2.125

AAT

Advances in Agricultural Technology, **AAT** (series), A 106.24, A 77.31

AB

Findings of (year) **AB** [Aid to the Blind] Study, HE 17.639/4

Abatement

Federal Aircraft Noise **Abatement** Plan, Fiscal Year, TD 1.16

Technical Memoranda for Municipal, Industrial and Domestic Water Supplies, Pollution **Abatement**, Public Health, FS 2.301

Abbreviated

Abbreviated Stock Lists, W 108.9/1

Abbreviations

Definitions and **Abbreviations**, TD 4.6:part 1

Instructions for Classifying the Underlying Cause of Death: Nonindexed Terms, Standard **Abbreviations**, and State Geographic Codes Used in Mortality Data Classification, HE 20.6208/4

Aberdeen Proving Ground

Army Ordnance Center and School **Aberdeen Proving Ground** Maryland: Special Texts, D 105.25

Ability

Annual National **Ability** Counts Contest [announcement], PrEx 1.10/6

ABM

ABM (Acquisition & Business Management) Online, D 201.44

Abnormal

Report to Congress on **Abnormal** Occurrences, Y 3.N 88:20

Abortion

Abortion Surveillance, Annual Summary, HE 20.7011/20

Abrasive

Abrasive Materials in (year), I 28.116

Abrasives

Manufactured **Abrasives**, I 28.171

Abridged

Abridged Index Medicus, HE 20.3612/2

Abridged United States Official Postal Guide, P 1.10/2

Abroad

Advertising **Abroad**, C 18.43

Application for Grants under Fulbright-Hays Group Projects **Abroad**, ED 1.62

Application for Seminars **Abroad** Program, ED 1.59/2

Building **Abroad**, C 18.54

Business Situation at Home and **Abroad**, C 18.54/2

Competitive Position of United States Farm Products **Abroad**, A 67.28

Construction **Abroad**, C 18.59/2

Correction and Additions to Publications of Officers at Home and **Abroad**, N 6.6

Fur Bearing Animals **Abroad**, News Jottings from Field for American Breeders, Bulletins, C 18.93

Home and **Abroad** with Bureau of Foreign and Domestic Commerce, C 18.191

Information from **Abroad** (unnumbered), N 13.6

Labor Developments **Abroad**, L 2.32/2

Marketing U.S. Tourism **Abroad**, C 47.20, C 61.49

Motion Pictures **Abroad**, C 18.115, C 41.16

Notes on Labor **Abroad**, L 2.32

Opportunities **Abroad** for Educators, ED 1.19, IA 1.29

Opportunities **Abroad** for Teachers (series), HE 5.99/2, ED 1.19

Opportunities for Teachers **Abroad**, HE 19.112

Quarterly Summary of Future Construction **Abroad**, C 57.113

Recent Educational Policy and Legislative Developments **Abroad** (series), HE 5.94

Research and Training Opportunities **Abroad** (year), Educational Programs in Foreign Language and Area Studies, HE 5.99

Tax Guide for U.S. Citizens **Abroad**, T 22.19/2:C 49

Teacher Exchange Opportunities **Abroad**, Teaching, Summer Seminars under International Educational Exchange Program of Department of States [announcements], FS 5.64/2

Tobacco Markets and Conditions **Abroad**, C 18.152

U.S. Department of State Indexes of Living Costs **Abroad** and Living Quarters Allowances, L 2.101

U.S. Department of State Indexes of Living Costs **Abroad** and Quarters Allowances, April, L 2.101/2

U.S. Department of State Indexes of Living Costs **Abroad**, S 1.76/4

U.S. Direct Investment **Abroad**, Operations of U.S. Parent Companies and Their Foreign Affiliates, Preliminary Estimates, C 59.20/2

War Notes, Information from **Abroad**, N 13.7

War Series, Information from **Abroad**, N 13.8

Absence

Leaves of **Absence** Granted Officers, N 17.14

Absent

Monthly List of Officers **Absent** on Leave in Excess of Time, W 3.15

Absorption

Current Housing Reports: Market **Absorption** of Apartments, H-130 (series), C 56.230

Abstract

Disability Statistics **Abstract**, ED 1.215/4

Patent **Abstract** Section, C 21.5/a 8

Patent **Abstract** Series, C 1.33

Preliminary **Abstract** of Statistics of Railway Statistics, IC 1.14

Regulatory and Technical Reports (**Abstract** Index Journal), Y 3.N 88:21-3

State Statistical and Economic **Abstract** Series, C 1.87

Statistical **Abstract** of the United States, C 3.134, C 3.134/7, C 56.243

Supplements to Statistical **Abstract** of United States, C 3.134/2

Supplements to the Statistical **Abstract** of the United States, C 56.243/2

T.I.S.C.A. [Technical Information System for Carrier Aviation] Technical Information Indexes: Naval Carrier Aviation **Abstract** Bulletin with Cross Reference Index, D 202.22

Technical Information Indexes: Naval Carrier Aviation **Abstract** Bulletin with Cross Reference Index, D 202.22

UNTA **Abstract**, TD 7.10/2

USA Counties, a Statistical **Abstract** Supplement, C 3.134/6

Abstracts

Abstracts of and Indexes For Reports and Testimony, Fiscal Year, GA 1.16/3-4

Abstracts of Phase I Awards, Small Business Innovation Research, NS 1.46

Abstracts of Reports and Testimony, GA 1.16/3-3

Directory of Energy Information Administration Model **Abstracts**, E 3.48

NASA Patent **Abstracts** Bibliography, NAS 1.21:7039

NCJRS **Abstracts** Database, J 28.31/2-2

Oil Pollution **Abstracts**, EP 1.25/2

Optics and Spectroscopy [**abstracts**], C 41.63

Pesticides **Abstracts**, EP 5.9

Population and Reproduction Research **Abstracts**, HE 20.3360

Postwar **Abstracts**, LC 14.16

Psychopharmacology **Abstracts**, HE 20.8109/2

Public Affairs **Abstracts** (new series), LC 14.14

Public Health Engineering **Abstracts**, T 27.28, FS 2.13

Reliability **Abstracts** and Technical Reviews, NAS 1.35

Research **Abstracts**, A 93.39, J 28.24/4, Y 3.N 21/5:14

Research and Development **Abstracts** of USAEC, RDA (series), Y 3.At 7:51

Research Information **Abstracts**, A 106.37/2

Research Library **Abstracts**; Domestic, Y 3.W 89/2:20

Selected **Abstracts** of Completed Research Studies, Fiscal Year (date), SBA 1.18/4

Selected **Abstracts** of Planning Reports, HH 8.9

Selected Rehabilitation **Abstracts**, FS 13.210

Selected Urban Storm Water Runoff **Abstracts**, EP 2.10:11024

Selected Water Resources **Abstracts**, I 1.94/2

Sexually Transmitted Diseases, **Abstracts** and Bibliographies, HE 20.7311

Solid Waste Management Monthly **Abstracts** Bulletin, EP 1.17/3

Sport Fishery **Abstracts**, I 49.40/2

Synthetic Liquid Fuels **Abstracts**, I 28.86

Thermoelectricty **Abstracts**, D 210.23

Training within Industry **Abstracts**, British Engineering Bulletins, Pr 32.4822, Pr 32.5215

University Transportation Center Project **Abstracts**, TD 10.14

Urban Mass Transportation **Abstracts**, TD 7.10/3

USGS Research on Energy Resources, Program and **Abstracts**, I 19.4/5

USGS Research on Mineral Resources, Program and **Abstracts**, I 19.4/7

USSR and Eastern European Scientific **Abstracts**, Geophysics, Astronomy, and Space, Y 3.J 66:14

VA Medical Research Conference **Abstracts**, VA 1.43/2

Vital Statistics, Special Reports (**abstracts**), C 3.67/2

Vocational and Technical Education **Abstracts**, C 41.62

Weekly **Abstracts**: NASA Earth Resources Survey Program, C 51.9/11

Weekly Government **Abstracts**, WGA-(series), C 51.9/5C 51.9/30

Wildlife **Abstracts**, I 49.17/2

Abuse

Alcohol, Drug **Abuse**, Mental Health, Research Grant Awards, Fiscal Year, HE 20.8118

Annual Review of Child **Abuse** and Neglect Research, HE 23.1210/3

Child **Abuse** and Neglect (series), HE 1.480, HE 23.1210

Child **Abuse** and Neglect Programs, HE 1.480/4, HE 23.1211

Child **Abuse** and Neglect Reports, HE 1.480/2, HE 23.1212

Child **Abuse** and Neglect Research: Projects and Publications, HE 1.480/3, HE 23.1210/2

Community Drug **Abuse** Prevention Program Series, J 24.13

CSAP Substance **Abuse** Resource Guide, HE 20.409/2

DACAS [Drug **Abuse** Current Awareness System], HE 20.8209

Demographic Characteristics and Patterns of Drug Use of Clients Admitted to Drug **Abuse** Treatment Programs in Selected States, Trend Data, HE 20.8231/2

Drug **Abuse** Among American School Students, HE 20.8222

Drug **Abuse** Prevention Materials for Schools, PrEx 13.2:D 84

Drug **Abuse** Prevention Monograph Series, HE 20.8228

Drug **Abuse** Prevention Report, HE 20.8010:33

Drug **Abuse** Research and Development, Federally Supported Drug **Abuse** and Tobacco Research and Development, Fiscal Year (date), HE 20.8220

Drug **Abuse** Services Research Series, HE 20.8235

National Clearinghouse on Child **Abuse** and Neglect Information Catalog, HE 23.1216/2

National Directory of Drug **Abuse** and Alcoholism Treatment and Prevention Programs, HE 20.8320, HE 20.410/3

National Household Survey on Drug **Abuse**: Main Findings, HE 20.417/3

Posters Alcohol, Drug **Abuse**, and Mental Health Administration, HE 20.8014

Prevention Activities of the Alcohol, Drug **Abuse**, and Mental Health Administration, HE 20.8018

Proceedings Annual Alcoholism Conference of the National Institute on Alcohol **Abuse** and Alcoholism, HE 20.2430/2

Report to the United States Congress on Federal Activities on Alcohol **Abuse** and Alcoholism, HE 20.8316

Rules of the Select Committee on Narcotics **Abuse** and Control, Y 4.N 16/10

Statistical Series Annual Data, Data from the Drug **Abuse** Warning Network (DAWN) Series I, HE 20.8212/11

Statistical Series National Institute on Drug **Abuse**, HE 20.8212, HE 20.8212/2, HE 20.8212/3, HE 20.8212/5, HE 20.8212/6

Statistical Series Securities and Exchange Commission, SE Statistical Series, Annual Data, Data from the Drug **Abuse** Warning Network (DAWN), Series I, HE 20.8212/11

Summary Proceedings of ADAMHA Annual Conference of the State and Territorial Alcohol, Drug **Abuse**, and Mental Health Authorities, HE 20.8011

Tune in, Drug **Abuse** News, PrEx 13.11

Academic

Academic Year Institutes for Secondary School Teachers and Supervisors of Science and Mathematics, NS 1.12

Directory of **Academic** Procurement and Related Programs and Courses, GS 1.30

DOT Awards to **Academic** Institutions, TD 10.11/2

Instructional Faculty Salaries for **Academic** Year, ED 1.131

Minorities and Women in Undergraduate Education, Geographic Distributions for **Academic** Year, HE 20.9314

NAEP Trends in **Academic** Progress, ED 1.335/4

The Fund for the Improvement of Postsecondary Education (FIPSE), Special Focus Competition: College-School Partnerships to Improve Learning of Essential **Academic** Subjects, Kindergarten through College, ED 1.23/9

Academic Catalog

Defense Intelligence School: **Academic** Catalog, D 5.210

Academy

Annapolis, the United States Naval **Academy** Catalog, D 208.109

Annual Program Plan and **Academy** Training Schedule, J 16.26

Annual Register of the United States Naval **Academy**, D 208.107

Cadet Profile, United States Coast Guard **Academy**, TD 5.15

Coast Guard **Academy**, Catalogue of Courses, TD 5.16

Course of Instruction at Merchant Marine **Academy**, C 39.225

FBI National **Academy** Associates Newsletter, J 1.14/20

Formulary, USAF **Academy** Hospital, D 305.17

General Catalog: MAC NCO **Academy** West, D 301.80/2

Herald of **Academy** of Sciences of Kazakh SSR [abstracts], C 41.50/9

Herald of **Academy** of Sciences of USSR, C 41.50/4

Information Relative to Appointment and Admission of Cadets of Military **Academy**, W 12.9

Microcomputer Training Catalog, The DOL **Academy**, L 1.86/2

News of **Academy** of Sciences of Armenian SSR, Phsyco-Mathematical, Natural and Technical Sciences Series, C 41.50/7

News of **Academy** of Sciences of Estonia SSR, Technical and Physiomathematical Sciences, C 41.50/5

News of **Academy** of Sciences of USSR; Department of Chemical Science, C 41.53/2

News of **Academy** of Sciences of USSR; Department of Technical Services, C 41.50/3

News of **Academy** of Sciences of USSR; Geography Series, C 41.46/4

News of **Academy** of Sciences of USSR; Geology Series, C 41.52/7

News of **Academy** of Sciences of USSR; Mathematics Series, C 41.61/5

News of **Academy** of Sciences of USSR; Physics Series, C 41.52/3

Proceedings Air Force **Academy** Assembly, D 305.11

Regulations for Military **Academy** (general), W 12.6/1

Regulations Governing Admission of Candidates into Naval **Academy** As Midshipmen and Sample Examination Questions, D 208.108

Report of Board of Visitors to Naval **Academy**, M 206.101, D 208.101

Reports of **Academy** of Sciences of USSR, C 41.50

Research Reports Air Force **Academy**, D 305.14

U.S. Air Force **Academy** Bulletin, D 305.8/2

United States Air Force **Academy** Assembly, Proceedings, D 305.11

United States Air Force **Academy** Journal of Professional Military Ethics, D 305.21

United States Coast Guard **Academy**, New London, Connecticut: Bulletin of Information, TD 5.16/2

United States Naval **Academy**, Superintendent's Statement to Board of Visitors, D 208.110

Acaricides

Insecticides, **Acaricides**, Molluscicides, and Antifouling Compounds, EP 5.11/3

Accelerated

Accelerated Public Works Program, Directory of Approved Projects, C 46.19

Community Facilities Administration News about New **Accelerated** Public Works Program, HH 5.7/2

Accelerators

Particle **Accelerators**, E 1.99

Acceptable

Acceptable Methods, Techniques, and Practices: Aircraft Alterations, TD 4.28, TD 4.28/2

List of **Acceptable** Interstate Carrier Equipment Having Sanitation Significances, FS 2.78

List of Material **Acceptable** for Use on Systems of REA Electrification Borrowers and List of Materials Accepted on a Trial Basis, A 68.6/2

List of Materials **Acceptable** for Use on Telephone Systems of REA Borrowers, A 68.6/5

Manual of **Acceptable** Practices, HH 1.6/9

Acceptance

Equipment Certification and Type **Acceptance** Actions, Reports, Public Notices, CC 1.48/2

Acceptances

Commercial and Industrial Loans to U.S. Addressess Excluding Bankers **Acceptances** and Commercial Paper, by Industry, FR 1.39/2

Accepted

Accepted Meat and Poultry Equipment, A 101.6/4, A 103.6/3, A 110.12

FM Broadcast Applications **Accepted** for Filing and Notification of Cut-off Date, CC 1.26/3

List of Bituminous Coal Producers who have **Accepted** Bituminous Coal Code Promulgated June 21, 1972, I 34.17, I 46.9

List of Material Acceptable for Use on Systems of REA Electrification Borrowers and List of Materials **Accepted** on a Trial Basis, A 68.6/2

TV Broadcast Applications **Accepted** for Filing and Notification of Cut-off Date, CC 1.26/5

Access

Access, C 1.57/4, EP 1.8/13

Access: A Technical Circular for the End-User Computing Community, HE 3.4/7

Access America, Y 3.B 27:15

Access, Catalogs and Technical Publications, LC 30.27/7

Access Currents, Y 3.B 27:16

Access EPA, EP 1.8/13

Data **Access** Descriptions Miscellaneous Series, C 56.212/6

Data **Access** Descriptions Policy and Administration Series, C 3.240/4

Data **Access** Descriptions; Automated Address Coding Guide and Data Retrieval Series, ACC (nos.), C 3.240/2

Data **Access** Descriptions; Census Geography Series, CG (nos), C 3.240/6, C 56.212/5

Data **Access** Descriptions; Census Tabulations Available on Computer Tape Series CT (nos), C 3.240/3, C 56.212/3

Data **Access** Descriptions; Collection, Evaluation and Processing Series, CEP (nos), C 3.240/5, C 56.212

Data **Access** Descriptions; Economic Censuses Printed Reports Series, C 56.212/4

Data **Access** Descriptions; Matching Studies Series, MS (nos.), C 3.240

Data **Access** Descriptions; Miscellaneous Series, C 56.212/6

Data **Access** Descriptions; Policy and Administration Series, C 3.240/4

Data **Access** Descriptions; [miscellaneous], C 3.240/7

Easy **Access**, J 32.24

GPO **Access**, GP 1.1/2

GPO **Access** Training Manual, GP 3.29/2

IMS **Access**, NF 4.15

Accessibility

Accessibility Assistance, a Directory of Consultants on Environments for Handicapped People, CSA 1.2:Ac 2

Accession

Accession Bulletin, Solid Waste Information Retrieval System, EP 1.18, EP 3.3/2

Accession List: Bangladesh, LC 1.30/9

Accession List: Ceylon, LC 1.30/7

Accession List: Eastern Africa, LC 1.80/8

Accession List: India, LC 1.30/1

Accession List: Israel, LC 1.30/4

Accession List: Library, FS 1.11

Accession List: Middle East, LC 1.30/3

Accession List: Nepal, LC 1.30/6

Accession List: Pakistan, LC 1.30/2

Accession List: Southeast Asia, LC 1.30/10

BRH Technical Information **Accession** Bulletin, HE 20.4103/2

Foreign Market Reports, **Accession** Listings, C 42.15/3

Industry Profiles, **Accession** Notices, S 18.36

Law **Accession** List (of) Library, FS 3.7

Monthly **Accession** List of Library, Legal Reference Section, SS 1.22

Publications Foreign Countries, Annotated **Accession** List, C 3.199

Report of **Accession**, M 105.16, M 108.9

Research Technical Library Biweekly **Accession** List, PrEx 4.15

Weekly **Accession** List (of) Library, SS 1.17, FS 3.8

Accessioned

Catalogue of **Accessioned** Soviet Publication, C 55.220/2

Oceanography Catalogue of **Accessioned** Soviet Publications, C 55.220/2

World Data Center A Oceanography Catalogue of **Accessioned** Soviet Publications, C 55.220/2

World Data Center A Oceanography, Catalog of **Accessioned** Publications, C 55.220/2-2
World Data Center A Oceanography, Data of **Accessioned** Soviet Publications, C 55.220/2

Accessions
Accessions Lists, I 22.8/2
Accessions to Navy Department Library, N 16.8
Cancer Information Clearinghouse, Quarterly **Accessions** List, HE 20.3165/3
Consolidated Report of **Accessions**, D 102.7
East European **Accessions** List, LC 30.12
Foreign Publications **Accessions** List, HH 1.23/4
Foreign Statistical Publications, **Accessions** List, C 56.238
From the ACIR Library: **Accessions** List, Y 3.Ad 9/8:12
India, **Accessions** List, Annual Supplement, Cumulative List of Serials, LC 1.30/1-2
Library **Accessions**, Y 3.F 31/5:38, Y 3.W 89/2:41, FW 4.11, FW 1.11
Library **Accessions** of the Bureau of Reclamation, I 27.10/4
List of Recent **Accessions** and Foreign Patent Translations of the Scientific Library, C 21.17/2
Monthly Index of Russian **Accessions**, LC 30.10
Research-Reference **Accessions**, Y 3.R 31:29, A 61.15, A 36.110
Southern Asia, Publications in Western Languages, Quarterly **Accessions** List, LC 17.7
World Data Center A Glaciology (Snow and Ice): New **Accessions** List, C 55.220/8

Accessories
Bathroom **Accessories** (recessed and atachable all clay), C 3.72

Accessory
Warm-Air Furnaces, Winter Air-conditioning Systems, and **Accessory** Equipment, C 3.144

Accessory Equipment
Blowers Fans Unit Heaters and **Accessory** **Equipment**, C 3.143

Accident
Accident Analysis, Y 3.F 31/7:9
Accident Analysis (confidential), Y 3.F 31/5:9
Accident and Fire Prevention Bulletin, GS 1.13
Accident and Fire Prevention News, FW 6.10
Accident and Fire Report, VA 1.29
Accident Bulletin, IC 1 acci.3, TD 3.103
Accident Control Reports, I 49.73
Accident Prevention Bulletin, U.S. General Aviation, C 31.203/2, C 1.17
Accident Prevention Conference, Publications, C 1.17
Accident Prevention Program, FAA-PN (series), TD 4.32/19
Accident Prevention Series: Bulletins, EC 1.8
Aircraft **Accident** and Maintenance Review, D 301.58
Aircraft **Accident** Reports, TD 1.112
Aircraft **Accident** Reports NTSB-AAR (series), TD 1.112
Aircraft **Accident** Reports, Brief Format, U.S. Civil Aviation, NTSB-BA (series), TD 1.109/13
Analysis and Summary of **Accident** Investigations, TD 2.312/3
Analysis of **Accident** Reports Involving Fire, TD 2.312/2
Analysis of Aircraft **Accident** Data, U.S. Air Carrier Operations, TD 1.113/5
Analysis of Aircraft **Accident** Data, U.S. General Aviation, TD 1.113/3
Annual Report to Secretary of Transportation on **Accident** Investigation and Reporting Activities of Federal Highway Administration, TD 2.16
Annual Report to the Secretary of Transportation on the **Accident** Investigation and Reporting Activities of the Federal Highway Administration in (year), TD 2.16
Annual Report to the Secretary on **Accident** Investigation and Reporting Activities, TD 8.17
Annual Review of Aircraft **Accident** Data, U.S. Air Carrier Operations, TD 1.113/5
Annual Review of Aircraft **Accident** Data, U.S. General Aviation, TD 1.113
Aviation **Accident** Statistical Summary Calendar Year, TD 4.413

Employee Benefits Survey Sickness and **Accident** Coding Manual, L 2.46/6
Fatal **Accident** Reporting System Annual Report, TD 8.27
Fatal Facts: **Accident** Report, L 35.11/3
Ground **Accident** Abstracts, D 301.53
Hazardous Materials **Accident** Report, NTSB/HZM-(series), TD 1.28
Highway **Accident** Reports, TD 1.117
Highway **Accident** Reports, Brief Format, TD 1.117/2
Highway **Accident**/Incident Summary Reports, TD 1.117/3
Marine **Accident** Reports, TD 1.116, TD 5.49
Marine **Accident** Reports, Brief Format, TD 1.116/3
Marine **Accident**/Incident Summary Reports (series), TD 1.116/4
Motor Carrier **Accident** Investigation Reports, TD 2.309
Motor Carriers of Passengers, Class 1 **Accident** Data, IC 1 mot.21/2
Motor Carriers of Property, **Accident** Data, IC 1 mot.21
Multidisciplinary **Accident** Investigations, TD 8.11, TD 8.11/2
Preliminary Analysis of Aircraft **Accident** Data, U.S. Civil Aviation, TD 1.113/6
Publications **Accident** Prevention Conference, C 1.17
Rail-Highway-Grade Crossing **Accident**/Incidents Bulletin, TD 3.109
Railroad **Accident** Investigation Reports, TD 3.10, TD 3.110
Railroad **Accident** Investigation Reports: Compilations, TD 3.110/4
Railroad **Accident** Reports, Brief Format, TD 1.112/5
Railroad **Accident** Reports, TD 1.112/3
Railroad **Accident**/Incident Summary Reports, TD 1.112/7
Railroad Employee **Accident** Investigation Reports, TD 3.110/3
Railroad-Highway **Accident** Reports, TD 1.112/4
Review, Statistical Review of Ordnance **Accident** Experiment, W 34.42
Summary of **Accident** Investigation Reports, IC 1 accu.7
Summary of Motor Vehicle **Accident** Fatalities, C 3.128/3
Tri-level **Accident** Investigation Summaries, TD 8.19
U.S. General Aviation **Accident** Prevention Bulletin, C 31.203/2
Weekly **Accident** Bulletins, C 3.128

Accidents
Accidents in U.S. Civil Air Carrier and General Aviation Operations, C 31.244/3
Accidents Involving Civil Aircraft; Reports of Investigations of, C 31.213
Accidents of Class 1 Motor Carriers of Passengers, TD 2.310/2
Accidents of Large Motor Carriers of Property, TD 2.310
Accidents Reported by Railroad Companies, Preliminary Summary, IC 1 acci.9
Aerial Crop Control **Accidents**, C 31.244/2
Analysis of **Accidents** Involving Air Taxi Operations, U.S. General Aviation, TD 1.113/4
Analysis of Defective Vehicle **Accidents** of Motor Carriers, IC 1 mot.20
Analysis of Motor Carrier **Accidents** Involving Vehicle Defects of Mechanical Failure, TD 2.312
Annual Review of U.S. Air Carrier **Accidents** Occurring in Calendar Year (date), TD 1.113/2
Annual Review of U.S. General Aviation **Accidents** Occurring in Calendar Year, TD 1.113
Briefs of **Accidents** Involving (various) Aircraft, TD 1.109/2
Briefs of **Accidents** Involving Aerial Applications Operations U.S. General Aviation, TD 1.109/4
Briefs of **Accidents** Involving Air Taxi Operations U.S. General Aviation, TD 1.109/3
Briefs of **Accidents** Involving Alcohol As a Cause-Factor U.S. General Aviation, TD 1.109/9
Briefs of **Accidents** Involving Amateur Built (homebuilt) Aircraft U.S. General Aviation, TD 1.109/6

Briefs of **Accidents** Involving Corporate-Executive Aircraft U.S. General Aviation, TD 1.109/10
Briefs of **Accidents** Involving Mid-Air Collisions U.S. Civil Aviation, TD 1.109/7
Briefs of **Accidents** Involving Missing Aircraft U.S. General Aviation, TD 1.109/8
Briefs of **Accidents** Involving Rotocraft U.S. General Aviation, TD 1.109/5
Briefs of **Accidents** U.S. Civil Aviation, TD 1.109 C 31.244/6
Briefs of **Accidents** U.S. General Aviation , C 31.244/5
Briefs of Aircraft **Accidents** Involving Turbine Powered Aircraft U.S. General Aviation Calendar Year NTSB-AMM (series), TD 1.109/14
Fatal **Accidents** Involving Drowning at Coal and Metal/Nonmetal Mines, L 38.19/3-2
Fatal and Injury **Accidents** Rates on Federal-aid and Other Highway Systems, TD 2.20
General Aviation **Accidents** (non-air carrier), Statistical Analysis, C 31.160/2, FAA 1.15
How to Use Injury Statistics to Prevent Occupational **Accidents**, L 16.42
Listing of Aircraft **Accidents**/incidents by Make and Model, U.S. Civil Aviation, TD 1.109/15
Precursors to Potential Severe Core Damage **Accidents**, Y 3.N 88:25-6
Rail-Highway Grade-Crossing **Accidents**, IC 1 acci.8
Recreational Boating in United States, Report of **Accidents**, Numbering and Related Activies, T 47.54
Report on Traffic **Accidents** and Injuries for (year), TD 8.32
Reports of Investigations of **Accidents** Involving Civil Aircraft, C 31.213
Reports on Investigations of Individual **Accidents**, IC 1 acci.5
Resume of U.S. Civil Air Carrier and General Aviation Aircraft **Accidents**, Calendar Year, C 31.244
Rules Governing Monthly Reports of Railway **Accidents**, IC 1 acci.6
Rules Pertaining to Aircraft **Accidents**, Incidents, Overdue Aircraft, and Safety Investigations, TD 1.106/2
Summary of **Accidents** Investigated by the Federal Railroad Administration in Fiscal Year, TD 3.111
Summary of **Accidents** Investigated by the Federal Railroad Administration in the Fiscal Year (dates), TD 3.110/2
Summary of **Accidents** Reported by All Line-Haul and Switching and Terminal Railroad Companies, TD 3.9
Summary of **Accidents** Reported by Steam Railways, IC 1 ste.31
Summary of Mortality from Automobile **Accidents**, C 3.39
Summary of Motor Carrier **Accidents**, IC 1 mot.21/3
Summary Reports of **Accidents**, U.S. Civil Aviation, C 31.244/4
U.S. Civil Aviation Briefs of **Accidents**, C 31.244/6
U.S. General Aviation Briefs of **Accidents**, C 31.244/5

Accommodations
Visitor **Accommodations** Furnished by Concessioners in Areas Administered by National Park Service, I 29.70

Accompanying
Drawings **Accompanying** Specifications, I 27.9, I 19.17/7

Accomplishment
Food and Drug Administration, Summary of Significant **Accomplishment** and Activities, HE 20.4046

Accomplishments
Accomplishments During the Congress, Y 4.In 8/14:Ac 2
Annual **Accomplishments** Report, Affirmative Action Program for Minorities and Women, C 13.68
Annual Report of **Accomplishments** Under the Airport Improvement Program, TD 4.61
Federal Reclamation Projects, Water and Land Resource **Accomplishments**, I 27.55

Fiscal Year Priorities and Fiscal Year **Accomplish-ments** For Research, Extension, and Higher Education, A Report to the Secretary of Agriculture, A 1.2/13

Projects Operated by Work Projects Administration, **Accomplishments** on (by States), FW 4.31

Recent Research **Accomplishments** of the Air Force Office of Scientific Research, D 301.45/19-7

Summary of Passport Office **Accomplishments**, S 1.1/5

Water Quality Management **Accomplishments**, Compendiums, EP 1.75

Accord
Semiannual Report, Implementation of Helsinki **Accord**, S 1.129

Account
Account of Receipts and Expenditures, T 32.5
Counterpart Funds and AID Foreign Currency **Account**, S 18.14

Accountability
Annual **Accountability** Report, E 1.1/6
Accountability Memorandum, N 9.13
FCA **Accountability** Report, FCA 1.1/4
Office of Water Operating Guidance and **Accountability** System, EP 2.29
SSA's **Accountability** Report for FY...Summary, SSA 1.1/3
SSA's **Accountability** Report for FY..., SSA 1.1/2
U.S. Department of Labor, **Accountability** Report, L 1.1/4

Accounting
Accounting Bulletins, IC 1 acco.3
Accounting Circulars, IC 1 mot.17
Accounting Principles Memorandum, GA 1.11/2
Accounting Procedure Memorandum, T 63.110
Accounting Series, GA 1.25
Accounting Series Circulars, IC 1 acco.4
Accounting Series Releases, SE 1.24
Accounting Systems Memorandum, GA 1.11
DFAS: The DOD **Accounting** Firm, D 1.104
General **Accounting** Office Salary Tables, GA 1.10, GA 1.6/10
Index to the Published Decisions of the **Accounting** Officers of the United States, GA 1.5
National Economic **Accounting** Training Program, C 59.21
Preliminary Reports of Income **Accounting** of Railways in United States, IC 1 ste.6
Staff **Accounting** Bulletins, SE 1.31
Statement of Federal Financial **Accounting** Concepts, PrEX 2.35/2
Statement of Federal Financial **Accounting** Standards, PrEX 2.35
Telegraph **Accounting** Circulars, CC 1.17
Telephone **Accounting** Circulars, CC 1.18
Telephone Directory General **Accounting** Office, GA 1.27
Treasury Department-General **Accounting** Office Joint Regulations, T 1.38

Accounts
Bureau for Supplies and **Accounts** Memoranda, N 20.7/3
Classification of **Accounts**, W 79.13/5
Classification of Income and Profit and Loss **Accounts**, IC 1 wat.8
Classification of Income, Profit & Loss, and General Balance Sheet **Accounts**, IC 1 ste.15
Counterpart Funds and FOA Foreign Currency **Accounts**, FO 1.11/3
Counterpart Funds and ICA Foreign Currency **Accounts**, S 17.11/3
Current Business Reports; Monthly Retail Trade, Sales and **Accounts** Receivable, BR (series), C 56.219/4
Functions and Organization of Bureau of Supplies and **Accounts**, Control Record, N 20.25
Methodology Papers: U.S. National Income and Product **Accounts**, BEA-MP- (series), C 59.19
Receipts and Disbursements of Government Consolidated into Bureau of **Accounts**, Fiscal Service in Treasury Department by President's Reorganization Plan no. 3, T 9.11
National Income and Product **Accounts** of the United States, C 59.11/5

Report of Calls, Assets, Liabilities, Capital, **Accounts**, Commercial and Mutual Savings Banks (unnumbered), Y 3.F 31/8:9-2
Summary of **Accounts** and Deposits in All Commercial and Mutual Savings Banks, Y 3.F 31/8:22
Summary of **Accounts** and Deposits in All Commercial Banks [by districts], Y 3.F 31/8:20 CT
Summary of **Accounts** and Deposits in All Mutual Savings Banks, Y 3.F 31/8:21
Summary of Savings **Accounts** by Geographic Area, FSLIC-Insured Savings and Loan Associations, FHL 1.29
Uniform System of **Accounts** and Reports for Certificated Route Air Carriers in Accordance with Sec. 407 of the Federal Aviation Act, C 31.206/5
Uniform System of **Accounts** for Carriers by Inland and Coastal Waterways, IC 1 wat.14
Uniform System of **Accounts** for Electric Railways, IC 1 eler.9
Uniform System of **Accounts** for Express Companies, IC 1 exp.9
Uniform System of **Accounts** for Gas Corporations and Electric Corporations in the District of Columbia, IC 1 gas.5
Uniform System of **Accounts** for Pipe Lines, IC 1 pip.5, IC 1 pip.6
Uniform System of **Accounts** for Steam Railways, IC 1 ste.44
Uniform System of **Accounts** for Telegraph and Cable Companies, IC 1 telg.5
Uniform System of **Accounts** for Telephone Companies, IC 1 telp.5
Uniform System of **Accounts** Prescribed for Natural Gas Companies, FP 1.7/2
Uniform System of **Accounts** Prescribed for Public Utilities and Licenses, FP 1.7/3
Unit Costs (selected expense **accounts**) of Class 1 Steam Roads, IC 1 ste.23

Accounts Receivable
Manufacturers Sales and Collections on **Accounts** Receivable, C 18.195

ACCP
ACCP (Atlantic Climate Change Program) Newsletter, C 55.55

Accreditation
Annual Report of National Voluntary Laboratory **Accreditation**, C 1.71

Accredited
Accredited Higher Institutions, FS 5.250:50012, HE 5.250:50012
Accredited Postsecondary Institutions and Programs, (year), HE 19.145, ED 1.38
Undergraduate Engineering Curricular **Accredited** by Engineer's Council for Professional Development, FS 5.61

Accuracy
AAF Bombing **Accuracy**, Reports, W 108.37
Accuracy of Monthly Mean Flow in Current Releases, I 19.45/2
Precision and **Accuracy** Assessments for State and Local Air Monitoring Networks, EP 1.23/5-3

ACER
ACER Technical Memorandum (series), I 27.75

Acetate
Cellulose Plastic Products (Nitro-Cellulose and Cellulose **Acetate** Sheets, Rods and Tubes), C 3.73

Achievement
Call for **Achievement** Booklets, Y 3.Am 3/6:12
Research **Achievement** Sheet, A 77.7

Achievements
Achievements, PM 1.26
Annual Report and **Achievements**, Fiscal Year (date), L 38.13
Climate Analysis Center, Annual **Achievements**, C 55.191/2
DIS (Defense Investigative Service) **Achievements**, D 1.1/8

ACIC
ACIC Technical Reports, D 301.59/2

Acid
Acid Precipitation in North America: Annual Data Summary from Acid Deposition System Data Base, EP 1.23/5-4
End Uses of Sulfur and Sulfuric **Acid** in (year), I 28.63/4

National **Acid** Precipitation Assessment Program, Report to Congress, Y 3.In 8/31:1-2, C 55.703
Sulphuric **Acid**, Production, Stocks, etc. Reported by Fertilizer Manufacturers, C 3.110

Acid Deposition
Acid Precipitation in North America: Annual Data Summary from **Acid Deposition** System Data Base, EP 1.23/5-4

ACIR
From the **ACIR** Library: Accessions List, Y 3.Ad 9/8:12
From the **ACIR** Library: Periodical Index, Y 3.Ad 9/8:12-2

Acme
Instruction Manual: ICD 9 **Acme** Decision Tables for Classifying Underlying Causes of Death, HE 20.6208/4-2

Acoustics
Journal of **Acoustics** [abstracts], C 41.48

Acquired
Semiannual Consolidated Report of Balances of Foreign Currencies **Acquired** Without Payment of Dollars As of December 31 (year), T 63.117

Acquiescence
Social Security **Acquiescence** Ruling (series), SSA 1.6/2

Acquisition
ABM (**Acquisition** & Business Management) Online, D 201.44
Acquisition Regulation Staff Manual, HE 1.6/8
Acquisition Review Quarterly: Journal of the Defense Acquisition University, D 1.103
AR Today (**Acquisition** Reform Today), D 1.6/11-3
Conventional Loans Made to Finance **Acquisition** and Development of Land, Federal Savings and Loan Associations, FHL 1.22
Defense **Acquisition** Circulars, D 1.13/3
Defense **Acquisition** Deskbook, D 1.95/2
Defense **Acquisition** Management Data System Code Translations, D 1.57/10
Federal **Acquisition** Circular, D 1.6/11-2
Federal **Acquisition** Institute: General Publications, GS 1/6.12
Federal **Acquisition** Regulation, GS 1.6/10, GP 3.38/2
Federal **Acquisition** Regulations, D 1.6/11
Federal Plan for Water-Data **Acquisition**, I 19.74/3
LC **Acquisition** Trends, LC 30.17/2
Library **Acquisition** Lists, I 27.47
Long Range **Acquisition** Estimates, D 201.35
Major Data Processing and Telecommunication **Acquisition** Plans of Federal Executive Agencies, PrEx 2.12/3
Major Information Technology Systems, **Acquisition** Plans of Federal Executive Agencies, PrEx 2.27
NIMH Library **Acquisition** List, HE 20.8113/4

Acquisitions
Acquisitions and Disposal of CCC Price-Support Inventory, A 82.78
Acquisitions List of Antarctic Cartographic Materials, S 1.120
F.T.C. Statistical Report on Mergers and **Acquisitions**, FT 1.2:M 54/3
Federal **Acquisitions** Institute: Publications, PrEx 2.23
Foreign **Acquisitions** Program Newsletter, LC 30.17
HUD Library Recent **Acquisitions**, HH 1.23/5
Library of Congress **Acquisitions**: Geography and Map Division, LC 5.6
Library of Congress **Acquisitions**: Manuscript Division, LC 4.9
Library of Congress **Acquisitions**: Rare Book and Special Collections Division, LC 23.9
Library of Congress **Acquisitions**: Various Divisions, LC 1.39
Library of the Department of State, New **Acquisitions**, S 1.30/5
Library Reference List, Selected List of Current **Acquisitions**, C 1.31
List of **Acquisitions** of Municipal Reference Service, C 3.198
Lists of Selected Current **Acquisitions**, D 102.28/3
National Program for **Acquisitions** and Cataloging: Progress Reports, LC 30.15
Research Library, Recent **Acquisitions**, FR 1.29, FR 1.29/2
Selected Current **Acquisitions**, Lists, D 102.28/3

Selected Library **Acquisitions** Department of
Transportation, TD 1.15/3
Selected Library **Acquisitions** Small Business
Administration, SBA 1.21
Selected-Current **Acquisitions**, TC 1.34/2
ACR
ACR Research Reports, D 210.15
Acreage
Acreage, A 105.39
Acreage-Marketing Guides, A 88.26/4
Corn, Estimated Planted **Acreage**, Yield, and
Production by States, A 66.47
Cotton Estimated **Acreage**, Yield, and Production,
A 36.114, A 66.41
Crop Production, **Acreage**, A 92.24/4-2
Louisiana Soybeans for Beans, **Acreage**, Yield and
Production, A 88.18/25
Popcorn **Acreage** for Harvest, A 92.11/7
Prospective Strawberry **Acreage**, Louisiana Crop
Reporting Service, A 88.12/27
Soil and Water Conservation Districts, Status of
Organization, by States, Approximate
Acreage, and Farms in Organized
Districts, A 57.32
Soybeans Harvested for Beans by Countries,
Acreage, Yield, Production, A 88.18/19
Vegetables, Fresh Market, Annual Summary,
Acreage, Production, etc., A 92.11/10-2
Vegetables, Preliminary **Acreage**, Yield,
Production and Value, A 92.11/10-6
Vegetables, Processing, Annual Summary, **Acreage**
Productions, etc., A 92.11/10
Acrobatic
Airworthiness Standards, Normal, Utility, and
Acrobatic Category Airplanes, TD
4.6:part 23
ACS
ACS Research Report (series), A 109.10
ACS Service Report, A 109.9
ACSUS
ACSUS Report , HE 20.6521
ACT
ACT Career Planning Guide Series, L 1.7/9
ACT Manual, C 31.106/3
Act
Benefits and Costs of the Clean **Air** Act, The, EP
4.31
Federal Managers' Financial Integrity **Act,**
Secretary's Annual Statement and Report
to the President and the Congress, I
1.96/6
P. and S. Docket, Monthly Report of Action
Stockyards **Act**, A 88.16/5
P. and S. Docket, Monthly Report of Action Taken
on Cases Arising Under Packers and
Stockyards **Act**, A 82.14
Privacy **Act** Issuances Compilation, AE 2.106/4
Privacy **Act** Issuances, GS 4.107/a:P 939/2
Project Register, Projects Approved Under Sec. 8
of Federal Water Pollution Control **Act**
(Pub. Law 660, 84th Cong.), As
Amended and Sec. 3, of Public Works
Projects Initiated under Title VII, National Defense
Education **Act**, FS 5.234:34013, FS
5.234:34021, HE 5.234:34013, HE
5.234:34021
Prosecutions and Seizures Under the Federal Seed
Act, A 88.30/7
Prosecutions Under **Act** to Regulate Commerce, IC
1 act.6
Public Buildings **Act** of 1926, with Amendments,
Condemnation Laws with Amendments,
Public Works and Construction Laws
[May 7, 1926], Y 1.2:P 96/3
Public Support for Coastal Zone Management
Programs Implementation of the Coastal
Zone Management **Act** of 1972, C 55.32/
5
Qualified Areas Under Public Works and Economic
Development **Act** of 1965, Public Law
89-136, Reports, C 46.25
Quality of Cotton Classed Under Smith-Doxey **Act**,
United States, A 88.11/23
Quarterly Report on Trade Between the United
States and Nonmarket Economy
Countries, Pursuant to Section 411 (c) of
the Trade **Act** of 1974, Y 4.W 36:3
Rail Passenger Service **Act**, Report to Congress, TD
1.10/5
Railroad Retirement and Unemployment Insurance
Act, As Amended [August 29, 1935], Y
1.2:R 13

Reconstruction Finance Corporation **Act** with
Amendments and Small Business
Administration **Act** with Amendments
Including Related Acts on Small
Business, Y 1.2:R 24/2
Records and Briefs in Cases Arising Under
Agricultural Adjustment **Act**, Bankhead
Act, and Kerr-Smith Tobacco **Act**, J 1.19/
7
Register of Projects Approved Under Manpower
Development and Training **Act**, L 1.53
Registered Bona Fide and Legitimate Farmers'
Cooperative Organizations under
Bituminous Coal **Act** of 1937, I 46.15
Registered Distributors under Bituminous Coal
Act of 1973 [lists], I 46.14
Registration Record, Securities **Act** of 1933,
Indexes, SE 1.13/2
Registration Record, Securities **Act** of 1933, SE
1.13/1
Regulations for the Administration and
Enforcement of the Radiation Control for
Health and Safety **Act** of 1968, HE
20.4606/2
Regulations S-X Under the Securities **Act** of 1933,
SE 1.6:F 49
Regulations Under Fair Labor Standards **Act**, L
22.22
Regulations Under Federal Power **Act**, FP 1.7:P
87/2
Regulations Under the Natural Gas **Act**, August 1,
1967, FP 1.7:G 21/3
Regulations Under the Perishable Agricultural
Commodoties **Act** 1930, and Perishable
Agricultural Commodities **Act**, A 88.6:P
41
Releases, Holding Company **Act** of 1935, SE 1.25/2
Releases, Investment Company **Act** of 1940, SE
1.25/3
Releases, Securities **Act** of 1933, SE 1.25/4
Releases, Securities Exchange **Act** of 1934, SE
1.25/5
Releases, Trust Indenture **Act** of 1939, SE 1.25/7
Report of Activities under Research and Marketing
Act, A 77.8
Report of the Attorney General to the Congress of
the United States on the Administration
of the Foreign Agents Registration **Act**
of 1938, As Amended, J 1.30
Report of the Attorney General, Pursuant to
Section 252(i) of the Energy Policy and
Conservation **Act**, J 1.27/2
Report of the National Defense Education **Act**, FS
5.210:10004
Report of the Senate Committee on Labor and
Human Resources Presenting its View
and Estimates Pursuant to the
Congressional Budget **Act**, Y 4.L 11/4:C
76
Report of the U.S. Department of Justice Pursuant to
Section 8 of the Federal Coal Leasing
Amendments **Act** of 1975, J 1.27/3
Report on Activities Under Highway Safety **Act**,
TD 8.12/2
Report on Activities Under the National Traffic and
Motor Vehicle Safety **Act**, TD 8.12
Report on High Speed Ground Transportation **Act**
of 1965, TD 1.10
Report on the Implementation to Title 1 and Title 2
of the Speedy Trial **Act** of 1974, Ju 10.16
Report on the National Defense Education **Act**, HE
5.210:10004
Report to Congress by the Secretary of the Interior
and the Secretary of Agriculture on
Administration of the Wild Free-roaming
Horses and Burro **Act**, I 1.100
Report to Congress on Operations of UNRRA
Under **Act** of March 28, 1944, S 1.44
Report to Congress on the Administration of the
Highway Safety **Act** of 1966, TD 1.10/3
Report to Congress on the Administration of the
National Traffic Vehicle Safety **Act** of
1966, TD 1.10/2
Report to Congress on the Emergency
Homeowner's Relief **Act**, HH 1.64
Report to Congress on Title 20 of the Social
Security **Act**, HE 23.2009
Report to the President and the Congress on the
Effectiveness of the Rail Passenger
Services **Act**, IC 1.34
Reports to Congress on United States Participation
in Operations of UNRRA under **Act** of
March 28, 1944, Pr 32.5812

Research and Activities Under Saltonstall-
Kennedy **Act**, Annual Report of
Secretary of Interior, I 1.1/2
Research Reports Supported by Office of Water
Resources Research Under the Water
Resources Research **Act** of 1964
Received During the Period (date), I
1.97/2
Results under the Small Business Innovation
Development **Act** of 1982, SBA 1.1/4
Retirement Reports, Fiscal Yr., C.S. Retirement **Act**,
Panama Canal Annuity **Act**, CS 1.29/2
Runaways and Otherwise Homeless Youth Fiscal
Year, Annual Report on the Runaway
Youth **Act**, HE 23.1309/2
Safety Appliances **Act** [text], IC 1 saf.5
Seamen's **Act** As Amended and Other Laws
Relating to Seamen [March 4, 1915], Y
1.2:Se 1/2
Section 16(a) of the Securities Exchange **Act** of
1934, FR 1.31/2
Securities **Act** of 1933, As Amended to (date), SE
1.5:Se 2/3
Securities Exchange **Act** of 1934, As Amended to
(date), SE 1.5:Se 2
Securities Traded on Exchanges Under the
Securities Exchange **Act**, SE 1.16
Selective Service **Act** As Amended [May 18, 1917],
Y 1.2:Se 4
Semiannual Report on Operations Under Mutual
Defense Assistance Control **Act** of 1951,
FO 1.1/2
Semiannual Reports on Operations under Mutual
Defense Assistance **Act**, S 17.1/2
Semiannual Reports under Mutual Defense
Assistance Control **Act**, Pr 33.901/2
Small Business Administration and Investment **Act**,
with Amendments [1953], Y 1.2:Sm 1
Small Business Administration and Investment **Act**,
Y 1.3:Sm 1
Soldiers' and Sailors' Civil Relief **Act** of 1940 and
Amendments, Y 1.2:So 4/7, Y 1.2:So 4/2
Special and Administrative Provisions of the Tariff
Act of 1930, As Amended, As in Effect
on [date], TC 1.10/2
Status of the Department of Energy's Implementa-
tion of Nuclear Waste Policy **Act**, GA
1.13/10
Strengthening Developing Institutions, Title 3 of
the Higher Education **Act** of 1965,
Annual Report, HE 19.139/2
Summary of Operations, Labor-Management
Reporting and Disclosure **Act**, L 1.51
Surplus Property **Act** of 1944, and Amendments, Y
1.2:Su 7
Title 1, Elementary and Secondary Education **Act** of
1965, States Report, FS 5.79, HE 5.79
Title 1 of Elementary and Secondary Education **Act**
of 1965; Annual Report, FS
5.237:37013, HE 5.237:37013
Title II, Elementary and Secondary Education **Act**
of 1965, School Library Resources,
Textbooks and Other Instructional
Materials, Annual Report, HE 5.79/2
Toxic Substances Control **Act**, Report to Congress
for Fiscal Year (date), EP 1.79
Training and Manpower Development Activities
Supported by the Administration on
Aging Under Title IV-A of the Older
Americans **Act** of 1965, As Amended,
Descriptions of Funded Projects, HE
23.3002:T 68/2
TSCA [Toxic Substances Control **Act**] Chemical
Assessment Series, EP 5.15/2
TSCA [Toxic Substances Control **Act**] Chemicals-
in-progress Bulletin, EP 5.15
Uniform System of Accounts and Reports for
Certificated Route Air Carriers in
Accordance with Sec. 407 of the Federal
Aviation **Act**, C 31.206/5
Vessels Receiving Benefits of Construction Loans
under Merchant Marine **Act** of 1928, SB
7.8
Violence Against Women **Act** News, J 35.20
Walsh-Healey Public Contracts **Act** Minimum
Wage Determination (for various
industries), L 22.19
Walsh-Healey Public Contracts **Act**, Decisions, L
22.23
Warehouses Licensed under United States
Warehouse **Act**, A 36.182, A 88.56, A
82.98

Report to Congress on Administration of Ocean Dumping **Activities**, D 103.68

Report to the United States Congress on Federal **Activities** on Alcohol Abuse and Alcoholism, HE 20.8316

Reports of **Activities** During Year, A 13.13/2

Reports of Subversive **Activities** Control Board, Y 3.Su 1:8-2

Reprints from Marketing **Activities**, A 82.17/1

Research and **Activities** Under Saltonstall-Kennedy Act, Annual Report of Secretary of Interior, I 1.1/2

Review of Arms Control and Disarmament **Activities**, Y 4.Ar 5/2-16

RFC Small Business **Activities**, FL 5.15

Satellite **Activities** of NOAA, C 55.510

Science **Activities** in Energy, E 1.38/3

Scientific **Activities** in Universities and Colleges, NS 1.22:C 83/3

Scientific Information **Activities** of Federal Agencies, NS 1.16

Selected Agricultural **Activities** of Public Employment Offices, L 7.59

Small-Area Data **Activities**, C 3.238

South Korea Interim Government **Activities**, M 105.13

Southwestern Radiological Health Laboratory: Monthly **Activities** Report, EP 1.13

Special Analysis of Federal **Activities** in Public Works and Other Construction in Budget, PrEx 2.8/a2

State and Federal Marketing **Activities** and Other Economic Work, A 36.21

State Coastal Zone Management **Activities**, C 55.32/3

State Planning **Activities** Progress Reports, Y 3.N 21/12:9

State Solid Waste Planning Grants, Agencies, and Progress, Report of **Activities**, EP 3.10

States **Activities** Report, C 55.438

States and Small Business: Programs and **Activities**, SBA 1.34

Statistical Reference Book of International **Activities**, HE 20.3712

Status of Strategic Petroleum Reserve **Activities** as of (date), GA 1.13/3

Summary of **Activities** Animal and Plant Health Inspection Service, A 101.27

Summary of **Activities** House Post Office and Civil Service Committee, Y 4.P 84/10:Ac 8

Summary of **Activities** House Science and Technology Committee, Y 4.Sci 2-10

Summary of **Activities** Senate Banking, Housing, and Urban Affairs Committee, Y 4.B 22/3:Ac 8

Summary of **Activities**, in Fiscal [year], CC 1.1/2

Summary of **Activities**, Meat Inspection Division, A 88.40/2:20

Summary of Bovine Brucellosis Eradication **Activities** in Cooperation with States, A 77.212/2

Summary of Brucellosis Eradication **Activities** in Cooperation with Various States Under Cull and Dry Cow Testing Program, A 77.212/7

Summary of Bucellosis Eradication **Activities** in Cooperation with the Various States Under the Market Cattle Testing Program, A 77.212/8

Summary of Federal ADP **Activities** for Fiscal Year (date), GS 12.9

Summary of Legislative **Activities**, Y 4.P 96/10:L 52

Summation of Non-Military **Activities** in Japan, W 1.75, M 105.11

Summation of United States Army Military Government **Activities** in Korea, W 1.76

Summation of United States Army Military Government **Activities** in Ryukyu Islands, W 1.78, M 105.12

Survey of **Activities** of the Committee on Foreign Affairs, Y 4.F 76/1:Ac 8

Technical **Activities**, Center for Analytical Chemistry, C 13.58/2

Technical **Activities**, Center for Chemical Physics, C 13.58/9

Technical **Activities**, Office of Standard Reference Data, C 13.58/3

Technical **Activities**, Surface Science Division, C 13.71

Training and Manpower Development **Activities** Supported by the Administration on Aging Under Title IV-A of the Older Americans Act of 1965, As Amended, Descriptions of Funded Projects, HE 23.3002:T 68/2

Tribal **Activities** Bulletin, HE 20.9403/2

United States Air Force History Program, Summary of **Activities**, D 301.1/2

United States Army Installations and Major **Activities** in Continental U.S., D 101.22:210-1

Veterans Administration **Activities**, Submitted by the Veterans Administration, Y 4.V 64/4:V 64

Vocational Training **Activities** of Public Employment Offices, FS 3.119

Voluntary Foreign Relief Programs, **Activities** of Registered American Voluntary Agencies, S 18.19

Volunteers, Bulletin for Those Who Direct Their **Activities**, Pr 32.4264

Wage Committee: Annual Report of **Activities**, VA 1.51

Wage Rates in Selected Farm **Activities**, L 7.55/2-2

Water Resources **Activities** in Illinois, I 19.55/5

Weekly Summary of Federal Legislation Relating to National Resources Committee, **Activities** Bulletins, Y 3.N 21/12:15

Western Environmental Research Laboratory: Monthly **Activities** Report, EP 1.14

Worldwide Communist Propaganda **Activities**, IA 1.8/2

Activity

IITF **Activity** Reports, PrEx 23.11

Monthly Summary of Export Credit Guarantee Program **Activity**, A 67.47

Monthly Summary of Export Credit Guarantee Program **Activity**, Commodity Credit Corporation, A 67.18:ECG

Political **Activity** and Political Assessments of Federal Office-Holders and Employees, CS 1.34

Political **Activity** of Government Personnel Commission, Y 3.P 75

Procurement Regulatory **Activity** Report, PrEx 2.24/15

Product/**Activity** Status Bulletin, C 3.238/6

Program **Activity** Reports, Public Law 85-864, FS 5.71

Projects, by Field of **Activity** and County, S 18.29

Public Health Service Prospective Payment **Activity**, HE 20.6516

Report of IPA Grant **Activity**, GS 1.94

Savings and Loan **Activity** in (Month), FHL 1.15/2

Savings and Mortgage Lending **Activity**, Selected Balance Sheet Items, F.S.L.I.C. Insured Savings and Loan Associations, FHL 1.20/2

Solar Collector Manufacturing **Activity** and Applications in the Residential Sector, E 3.19

Solar Collector Manufacturing **Activity**, E 3.19/2

State Data Profiles, Calendar Year (date), Selected Ascs Program **Activity** and Other Agricultural Data, A 82.90

Summary of Loan **Activity** and Operating Results through (date) Issued by CCC, A 82.83/2

Survey of Compounds which have Been Tested for Carcinogenic **Activity**, HE 20.3187

Survey of Mortgage Lending **Activity** State Estimates, HH 1.99/2-2

Survey of Mortgage Lending **Activity**, HH 1.99, HH 1.99/2, HH 1.99/2-3

Survey of U.S. Uranium Exploration **Activity**, E 3.46

Survey of United States Uranium Marketing **Activity**, E 3.46/2

Thrift Institution **Activity** in (month), FHL 1.33

Title Survey of Compounds which Have Been Tested for Carcinogenic **Activity**, HE 20.3187

Weather Modification **Activity** Reports, C 55.27/2

Acts

Emergency Relief Appropriation **Acts**, Reports of President to Congress Showing Status of Funds and Operations Under, T 63.114

Passport Control **Acts** [February 1, 1917], Y 1.2:P 26

Public **Acts** and Resolutions Relating to Post Office Department and Postal Service, P 1.20

Reports of President to Congress Showing Status of Funds and Operations under Emergency Relief Appropriation **Acts**, T 63.114

Reports Showing Financial Status of Funds Provided in Emergency Relief Appropriation **Acts**, T 60.11

Reports Showing Status of Funds and Analyses of Expenditures, Emergency Appropriation **Acts**, T 60.13

Reports Showing Status of Funds Provided in Emergency Relief Appropriation **Acts**, T 60.12

Status of Vessel Construction and Reconditioning under Merchant Marine **Acts** of 1920 and 1938, SB 7.5:1105, C 27.9/8

Treaties and Other International **Acts** of U.S., S 9.5/1

Treaties and Other International **Acts** Series, S 9.10

Actual

Wholesale Prices of Lumber, Based on **Actual** Sales Made F.O.B. Each Market, A 13.15, A 13.17

Actuarial

Actuarial Notes, FS 3.19, FS 3.19/2, HE 3.19/2

Actuarial Studies, SS 1.34, HE 3.19, SSA 1.25/2

RRB **Actuarial** Studies, RR 1.14

Actuaries

Board of **Actuaries** of the Civil Service Retirement System Annual Report, Y 4.P 84/10:R 31/30

Ad Hoc

Ad Hoc Advisory Group on Presidential Vote for Puerto Rico, Pr 37.8:P 96

Ad Hoc Committee for Review of the Special Virus Cancer Program, HE 20.3001/2:V 81/5

ADA

ADA and Telecommunications Standards Index, GS 12.10/2

Enforcing the **ADA**, A Status Report from the Department of Justice, J 1.106

Adahooniligii

Adahooniligii, Navaho Language Monthly, I 20.37

ADAMHA

ADAMHA News, HE 20.8013

HRA, HSA, CDS, **ADAMHA** Public Advisory Committees, HE 20.6013

Summary Proceedings of **ADAMHA** Annual Conference of the State and Territorial Alcohol, Drug Abuse, and Mental Health Authorities, HE 20.8011

ADC

Animal Damage Control, **ADC**- (series), I 49.101

Addenda

Addenda and Errata Sheets to Federal Specifications, T 51.7/20

Addiction

Directory of Narcotic **Addiction** Treatment Agencies in the United States, HE 20.2402:N 16/3

Additions

Additions to Columbus Memorial Library, AR 1.7

Classification of Expenditures for **Additions** and Betterments, IC 1 ste.12

Construction Reports; Residential Alterations and Repairs, Expenditures on Residential **Additions**, Alterations, Maintenance and Repairs, and Replacements, C 56.211/7

Correction and **Additions** to Publications of Officers at Home and Abroad, N 6.6

Decimal Classification, **Additions**, Notes and Decisions, LC 37.8

Dewey Decimal Classification, **Additions**, Notes and Decisions, LC 37.8

Expenditures for **Additions**, Alterations, Maintenance and Repairs, and Replacements on One-Housing-Unit Owner-Occupied Properities, C 3.215/8:Pt-2

Expenditures on Residential **Additions**, Alterations, Maintenance and Repairs, and Replacements, C 3.215/8:Pt 1

L.C. Classification, **Additions** and Changes, LC 1.7/2, LC 26.9/2

Labor Literature, Recent **Additions** to the Department of Labor Library, L 1.34/5

List of Subject Headings, **Additions**, Corrections, and Supplements, LC 9.6/3

Recent Library **Additions**, I 27.10/4

Rough List of More Important **Additions**, W 11.7

Selected List of **Additions** to Research Library, FR 1.22/2

Selected List of Recent **Additions** to the Library, L 1.19

Advisory Councils
    Members of **Advisory Councils**, Study Sections,
        and Committees of National Institutes of
        Health, FS 2.22/22
Advisory Group
    Ad Hoc **Advisory Group** on Presidential Vote for
        Puerto Rico, Pr 37.8:P 96
Advisory Memo
    Advisory Memo, HE 20.7816
Advisory Panel
    Report of the **Advisory Panel** on Alzheimer's
        Disease, HE 20.8024
Advocate
    Advocate, D 108.109
    Nominate a Small Business Person or **Advocate** of
        the Year, SBA 1.43
    Small Business **Advocate**, SBA 1.51
    Special Text of Judge **Advocate** General's School, D
        108.9
Advocates
    United States Court of Military Appeals and the
        Judge **Advocates** General of the Armed
        Forces and the General Counsel of the
        Department of the Treasury,
AEC
    AEC Authorizing Legislation, Fiscal Year [date],
        Y 4.At 7/2:L 52
    AEC Depository Library Bulletin, Y 3.At 7;47
    AEC Licensing Guides, Y 3.At 7:6-4
    AEC News Release Index, Y 3.At 7:33-3, Y 3.At
        7:44 N 47
    AEC Research and Development Reports, Y 3.At
        7:22
AEC-NASA
    AEC-NASA Tech Briefs, NAS 1.29/2
AEDC
    Technical Documentary Report **AEDC**-TDR-
        (series), D 301.45/33-2
    Technical Reports, **AEDC**-TR, D 301.45/33
Aerial
    Aerial Crop Control Accidents, C 31.244/2
    Aerial Photography Summary Record System,
        APSRS (series), I 19.77
    Briefs of Accidents Involving **Aerial** Applications
        Operations U.S. General Aviation, TD
        1.109/4
    Extent of **Aerial** Photography by Agriculture
        Department, Completed, in Progress and
        Approved, A 1.51
Aerial Photography
    ASCS **Aerial Photography** Status Maps, A
        82.84:Ae 8
    Index to National **Aerial Photography**, I 19.97/4
AERO
    AERO Reports, D 211.9/3
Aero
    AFAPL-TR Air Force **Aero** Propulsion Laboratory,
        D 301.45/51-2
Aerological
    Daily **Aerological** Cross-Section Pole to Pole
        along Meridian 75 Degrees W for IGY
        Period, July 1957-December 1958, C
        30.76
Aerology
    Aerology Series, N 28.14, N 27.13
Aeromedical
    Aeromedical Research Unit, Fort Rucker, Ala.;
        USAARU Reports, D 104.21
    Aeromedical Review, D 301.26/13-4
    Alaskan Air Command, Arctic **Aeromedical**
        Laboratory: Technical Notes, D 301.66
    Technical Notes Department of the Air Force
        Alaskan Air Command, Arctic
        Aeromedical Laboratory, D 301.66
Aeronautic
    Aeronautic Information Bulletins, W 87.12
Aeronautical
    Aeronautical Bulletins, W 87.21
    Aeronautical Bulletins, State Series, C 23.5
    Aeronautical Bulletins, State Summaries, W 87.21/
        3
    Aeronautical Chart and Information Bulletin,
        Europe, Africa and Middle East, Grand
        Canyon VFR **Aeronautical** Chart,
        (general aviation), C 55.416/12-6
    New Editions of **Aeronautical** Charts Published,
        D 301.49/3
    Aeronautical Chart and Information Center
        Bulletin, D 301.59
    Aeronautical Chart and Information Center
        Bulletin Digest, New and Revised
        Editions of Aeronautical Charts on Issue
        as of (date), D 301.59/5

Aeronautical Chart and Information Squadron
    Bulletin, D 301.59/3
Aeronautical Charts, C 4.9/4, C 4.9/6, C 4.9/13
Aeronautical Communications and Pilot Services
    Handbook 7300.7, Changes, FAA 3.9/2
Aeronautical Dictionary, NAS 1.8:Ae 8
Aeronautical Engineering Newsletter, TD 5.37
Aeronautical Information List, W 87.13
Aeronautical Information Publication, TD
    4.308:Ae 8
Aeronautical Research Laboratory, ARL (series), D
    301.69/2
Aeronautical Specifications, N 4.9, N 28.5
Aeronautical Statutes and Related Material,
    Federal Aviation Act of 1958 and Other
    Provisions Relating to Civil
    Aeronautics, C 31.205:Ae 8
Aeronautical Supplement to American Nautical
    Almanac, N 11.6/2
Aeronautical World News, C 18.45
Air Force-Navy **Aeronautical** Design Standards, D
    301.29
Air Force-Navy **Aeronautical** Standards, D 301.30
Alphabetical List Covering Army Air Forces and
    Army-Navy **Aeronautical** Standard
    Parts, W 108.15/2, M 301.11
Alphabetical List, U.S. Air Force and Air Force-
    Navy **Aeronautical** Standard Drawings,
    D 301.15
Army-Navy **Aeronautical** Standards Index, Y 3.Ae
    8:7
Bulletin Digest New and Revised Editions of
    Aeronautical Charts on Issue As of
    (date), D 301.59/5
In-House List of Publications, **Aeronautical**
    Research Laboratory, D 301.69/4
Index of U.S. Air Force, Air Force-Navy
    Aeronautical and Military (MS)
    Standards (sheet form), D 301.16/2
Latest Editions of U.S. Air Force **Aeronautical**
    Charts, C 55.418/3
NIMA **Aeronautical** Charts and Publications, TD
    4.84
Numerical List Covering Army Air Forces and
    Army-Navy **Aeronautical** Standard
    Parts, W 108.15
Numerical List of U.S. Air Force and Air Force-
    Navy **Aeronautical** Standard Drawings,
    D 301.16
Numerical List, U.S. Air Force and Army-Navy
    Aeronautical Standard Drawings, M
    301.12
Public Sale Catalog: **Aeronautical** Charts and
    Publications, D 5.351/3-2
Regional **Aeronautical** Charts, C 23.10/4, C 4.9/5
Sectional **Aeronautical** Charts, C 55.416/10
Technical Notes Department of the Air Force
    Aeronautical Systems Division, D
    301.45/26
U.S. Gulf Coast VFR **Aeronautical** Chart, C
    55.416/12
World **Aeronautical** Charts, C 4.9/8, C 55.416/13
Wright **Aeronautical** Serial Reports, D 301.45/22
Aeronautical Chart
    DoD **Aeronautical Chart** Updating Manual
        (CHUM), D 5.208
Aeronautical Charts
    Dates of Latest Editions, **Aeronautical Charts**, C
        55.409
    Defense Mapping Agency **Aeronautical Charts**
        and Publications Available from
        NOAA's National Ocean Service, C
        55.418/3
Aeronautical Engineering
    News of Institutes of Higher Learning; **Aeronauti-
        cal Engineering**, C 41.56/2
Aeronautics
    Aeronautics and Space Activities, Report to
        Congress, NAS 1.52
    Aeronautics Bulletin, C 23.11
    Aeronautics Export News, C 18.46
    Aeronautics Update, NAS 1.7/3
    Applications and/or Amendments Thereto Filed
        with the Civil **Aeronautics** Board, CAB
        1.23, C 31.221
    Bibliography of **Aeronautics**, FW 4.29 Y 3.N 21/
        5:7
    Bureau of **Aeronautics** Manual, D 202.6/2
    Civil **Aeronautics** Authority Reports, CA 1.23
    Civil **Aeronautics** Board Legislative History of
        Regulations, C 31.206/2:L 52
    Civil **Aeronautics** Bulletins, CA 1.3, C 31.103

Civil **Aeronautics** Journal, CA 1.17, C 31.7, C
    31.118
Civil **Aeronautics** Manuals (numbered), FAA 1.34
Civil **Aeronautics** Manuals [by volume number], C
    31.107/2
Civil **Aeronautics** Reports, CAB 1.21, C 31.211
Contract Reports National **Aeronautics** and Space
    Administration, NAS 1.26
International Civil **Aeronautics** Conference,
    Washington, S 5.28
Major Activities in Programs of National
    Aeronautics and Space Administration,
    NAS 1.1/2
NASA **Aeronautics** Research and Technology,
    Annual Report, NAS 1.19/2
Orders Civil **Aeronautics** Board, C 31.207
Regulations of the Civil **Aeronautics** Board, C
    31.206/7, CAB 1.16
Research in Progress, Calendar Year Metallurgy
    and Materials Sciences, Mechanics and
    Aeronautics, Chemistry and Biological
    Sciences, D 101.52/5-5
Safety Bulletins Civil **Aeronautics** Board, C
    31.214
Speaking of Space & **Aeronautics**, NAS 1.32
Status of Civil Air Regulations and Civil
    Aeronautics Manuals, FAA 1.18
Technical Memorandum National **Aeronautics** and
    Space Administration, NAS 1.15
Technical Notes National **Aeronautics** and Space
    Administration, NAS 1.14
Aerospace
    Aerospace Leaflets, AL (series), NAS 1.23
    Aerospace Maintenance Safety, D 306.8
    Aerospace Medicine and Biology, A Continuing
        Bibliography with Indexes, NAS
        1.21:7011
    Aerospace Power Journal D 301.26/24, D 301.26/
        24-2, D 301.26/24-3
    Aerospace Safety, D 301.44
    Aerospace Safety Advisory Panel, Annual Report,
        NAS 1.1/7
    Aerospace Technology Innovation, NAS 1.95
    Biology and **Aerospace** Medicine, PrEx 7.22/12
    Guide to Subject Indexes for Scientific and
        Technical **Aerospace** Reports, NAS 1.9/6
    Naval **Aerospace** Medical Institute, D 206.18
    Publications Office of **Aerospace** Research, D
        301.69/5
    Report to the Administrator by the NASA
        Aerospace Safety Advisory Panel, NAS
        1.58
    Research Review, Office of **Aerospace** Research, D
        301.69/6
    School of **Aerospace** Medicine: Technical
        Documentary Report SAM-TDR (series),
        D 301.26/13-6
    Scientific and Technical **Aerospace** Reports, NAS
        1.9/4
    Space Benefits: Secondary Application of
        Aerospace Technology in Other Sectors
        of the Economy, NAS 1.66
    STAR, Scientific and Technical **Aerospace** Reports,
        NAS 1.9/4
AETCEPL
    Air Education and Training Command Electronic
        Publishing Library, **AETCEPL**,
        301.116/3
AF
    AF Press Clips, S 1.134
    AF Regulations, M 301.6
    AF Technical Reports, Wright Air Development
        Center, D 301.45/6
AFAC
    AFAC (series), D 301.6/2-3
AFAL-TR
    Air Force Avionics Laboratory Technical Reports,
        AFAL-TR-(series), D 301.45/45-2
AFAPL
    Technical Report, **AFAPL**-TR, D 301.45/51-2
AFAPL-TR
    AFAPL-TR Air Force Aero Propulsion Laboratory,
        D 301.45/51-2
AFB
    F.E. Warren **AFB**, FEWP- (series), D 301.35/6
AFCCDD-TN
    Air Force Command and Control Development
        Division: Technical Notes **AFCCDD-TN**
        (nos.), D 301.45/24
AFCEC-TR
    Air Force Civil Engineering Center: **AFCEC-TR**
        (series), D 301.87

AFCRC

AFCRC Technical Notes TN (series), D 301.45/4-2

AFCRC Technical Reports, D 301.45/4

Air Force Cambridge Research Center: **AFCRC** Technical Reports, D 301.45/4

AFCRL

AFCRL (series), D 301.45/4-3

AFDC

AFDC and Related Income Maintenance Studies, HE 3.67

AFDC Standards for Basic Needs, HE 3.64

AFDC Update, News of the Alternative Fuels Data Center, E 1.114

Applications and Case Discontinuances for **AFDC**, HE 3.60/3

Assessments Completed and Referrals to Manpower Agencies by Welfare Agencies Under Work Incentive Program for **AFDC** Recipients, HE 17.619

Child Care Arrangements of **AFDC** Recipients Under the Work Incentive Program, HE 17.609

How They Do It, Illustrations of Practice in Administration of **AFDC** (series), HE 17.408/2

OAA and **AFDC**, Cost Standards for Basic Needs and Percent of Such Standards Met for Specified Types of Cases, FS 17.625, HE 17.625

Preliminary Report of Findings, (year) **AFDC** Study, HE 17.639

Report of Findings, **AFDC** Study, HE 17.639/3

Services to **AFDC** Families, Annual Report to Congress, HE 17.709

AFDC Update, News of the Alternative Fuels Data Center, E 1.114

Affairs

Civil **Affairs** Activities in Ryukyu Islands, D 102.19/3

Civil **Affairs** Handbooks, N 27.14

Consumer **Affairs** Fact Sheets (series), TD 8.14/3

Directory of Veterans Organizations and State Departments of Veterans **Affairs**, VA 1.62

Economic **Affairs**, PrEx 7.15/2, PrEx 7.21/2

Economic and Industrial **Affairs**, PrEx 7.17

FCDA Public **Affairs** Newsletter, FCD 1.15

Foreign **Affairs** Background Summary, S 1.53

Foreign **Affairs** Highlights, S 1.75

Foreign **Affairs** Manual Circulars, S 1.5/6-2

Foreign **Affairs** Notes, S 1.126/3

Foreign **Affairs** Research Papers Available, S 1.126

Foreign **Affairs** Research Special Papers Available, S 1.126/2

Foreign **Affairs** Research, a Directory of Government Resources, S 1.2:F 76a/4

Government-Supported Research on Foreign **Affairs**, Current Project Information, S 1.101/10

Government-Supported Research, International **Affairs**, Research Completed and in Progress, S 1.101/9

Indian **Affairs**, (year), Progress Report from the Commissioner of Indian **Affairs**, I 20.1

Indian **Affairs**, (year), Progress Report from the Commissioner of Indian **Affairs**, I 20.1

Indian **Affairs**, Laws and Treaties, I 1.107

Indian **Affairs**, Laws and Treaties, I 1.107

Institute of Inter-American **Affairs** Publications, S 1.64

International **Affairs** Series, SI 12.11

International Teacher Development Program, Annual Report to Bureau of Educational and Cultural **Affairs**, Department of State, FS 5.214:14003

Korean **Affairs** Report, PrEx 7.16/2

Military **Affairs**, PrEx 7.21/4

Orders Bureau of Indian **Affairs**, I 20.20

Personnel Bulletins Indian **Affairs** Bureau, I 20.28

Political and Sociological **Affairs**, PrEx 7.21/5

Political, Sociological and Military **Affairs**, PrEx 7.15/4, PrEx 7.17/2

Proceedings National Security **Affairs** Conference, D 5.412

Public **Affairs** Abstracts (new series), LC 14.14

Public **Affairs** Bulletin, LC 14.9

Public **Affairs** Flyer PA-F (series), FCD 1.17

Public **Affairs** PA (series), FCD 1.13

Report to the Committee on the Budget from the Committee on Veterans' **Affairs**, Y 4.V 64/3-10

Report to the Committee on the Budget; Views and Estimates of the Committee on Interior and Insular **Affairs** (House), Y 4.In 8/14-11

Rules for the Committee on Interior and Insular **Affairs**, Y 4.In 8/14-13

Scientific **Affairs**, PrEx 7.17/3

Some Recent Books on Public **Affairs** Available for Circulation in the Book Forms, LC 1.25

Soviet Union, Political **Affairs**, PrEx 7.21/5-2

Student Conference on United States **Affairs**, D 109.9

Studies in Communist **Affairs**, D 301.85

Summary of Activities Senate Banking, Housing, and Urban **Affairs** Committee, Y 4.B 22/3:Ac 8

Survey of Activities of the Committee on Foreign **Affairs**, Y 4.F 76/1:Ac 8

U.S. Air Force Public **Affairs** Staff Directory, D 301.104/4

University Centers of Foreign **Affairs** Research, Selective Directory, S 1.2:Un 3

USC/FAR Consolidated Plan for Foreign **Affairs** Research, PrEx 3.12

USSR Report International **Affairs**, PrEx 7.21/7-2

Views and Estimates of the Committee on Foreign **Affairs** on the Budget, Y 4.F 76/1:B 85

World **Affairs**, S 1.59/5

Worldwide Public **Affairs** Offices Directory, D 101.120/2

[Public **Affairs**] Booklet PA-B (series), FCD 1.17/2

AFFDL

Technical Reports, **AFFDL**-TR, D 301.45/46-2

AFFE

Army Forces Far East **AFFE** Pamphlets, D 102.24

Affected

Steam Railways in Hands of Receivers and Trustees, and Changes in List of Companies **Affected** by Receiver Ship of Trusteeship, IC 1 ste.45

Tables of Laws **Affected**, GS 4.111/2

Affecting

Daily Bulletin of Orders **Affecting** Postal Service, P 10.3

Summary of Watershed Conditions **Affecting** Water Supply of the Lower Colorado River, I 27.43

Affiliates

U.S. Direct Investment Abroad, Operations of U.S. Parent Companies and Their Foreign **Affiliates**, Preliminary Estimates, C 59.20/2

Affiliations

Maritime Labor, Management **Affiliations** Guide, TD 11.8/2

Seafaring Guide, and Directory of Labor-Management **Affiliations**, C 39.206/3:Se 1

Affirmative

Annual **Affirmative** Employment Accomplishment and Activities in Fiscal . . ., HE 20.4048

Spotlight on **Affirmative** Employment Programs, PM 1.18/4

Affirmative Action

Annual Accomplishments Report, **Affirmative Action** Program for Minorities and Women, C 13.68

Disabled Veterans, **Affirmative Action** Plan, P 1.56

Affordable

Affordable Housing Demonstration, Case Studies, HH 1.97

Citizen Action for **Affordable** Housing, Case Studies, HH 1.97/2

AFGL

Daily Magnetograms for ... from the **AFGL** Network, D 301.45/4-4

AFHRL

Technical Papers, **AFHRL**-TP- (series), D 301.45/27-4

Technical Report Memorandum **AFHRL** (TT)-TRM, D 301.45/27-2

Technical Reports, **AFHRL**-TR- (series), D 301.45/27

AFHRL-TP

AFHRL-TP (series), D 301.45/27-4

AFI-TP

AFI-TP (series), D 217.11

AFMDC

Technical Reports, **AFMDC**-TRN(series), D 301.45/17

AFML

Technical Report **AFML**-TR, D 301.45/47-2

AFMTC

Air Force Missile Test Center: Technical Reports, **AFMTC** TR (series), D 301.45/23

AFMTCP

AFMTCP-[Air Force Missile Test Center, D 301.45/23-1

AFOS

AFOS Handbook (series), C 55.108/6

AFOSIP

Air Force Office of Special Investigations, **AFOSIP** (series), D 301.88

AFOSR

Technical Reports, **AFOSR**-TR-, D 301.45/19

AFOSR/DRA

Directorate of Research Analysis, **AFOSR/DRA** (series), D 301.45/19-4

AFPS

AFPS News, D 2.21

AFPTRC-TN

Development Report **AFPTRC-TN** (series), D 301.36/7

Development Report **AFPTRC-TN** (series), D 301.36/7

Research Report **AFPTRC-TN** (series), D 301.36/6

AFR

AFR Regulations, D 301.6

AFRESP

Air Force Reserve Pamphlets, **AFRESP**- (series), D 301.35/5

Africa

Accession List: Eastern **Africa**, LC 1.80/8

Aeronautical Chart and Information Bulletin, Europe, **Africa** and Middle East, New Editions of Aeronautical Charts Published, D 301.49/3

Africa, Series 2201, D 5.331

Agricultural Situation: **Africa** and the Middle East, A 93.29/2-2

Agricultural Situation: **Africa** and the Middle East, A 93.29/2-2

Eastern **Africa**, LC 1.30/8

Eastern **Africa**, Annual Publishers Directory, LC 1.30/8-3

Eastern **Africa**, Annual Serial Supplement, LC 1.30/8-2

Flight Information Publication: Enroute High Altitude, Europe, **Africa**, Middle East, D 301.9/4

Flight Information Publication: Terminal Low Altitude, **Africa** and Southwest Asia, D 301.13/6

French-Speaking Central **Africa**, a Guide to Official Publications in American Libraries, LC 2.8:Af 8/3

History of **Africa**, Australia, New Zealand, Etc., LC 26.9:DT-DX

Military Aviation Notices; Corrections to Supplementary Flight Information, Europe, **Africa** and Middle East, D 301.49/2

Nautical Charts and Publications, Region 5, Western **Africa** and the Mediterranean, C 55.440:5

Near East and **Africa** Reports, PrEx 7.20

NIMA Nautical Charts, Public Sale Region 5, Western **Africa** and the Mediterranean, TD 4.82:5

Radio Facility Charts, Europe, **Africa**, Middle East, M 301.17

Quarterly Index to Periodical Literature, Eastern and Southern **Africa**, LC 1.30/8-4

South **Africa**, Serials Supplement, LC 1.30/10-4

Soviet Union, People of Asia and **Africa**, PrEx 7.21/7-3

Sub-Saharan **Africa** Report, PrEx 7.20/2

Sub-Saharan **Africa**, Situation and Outlook Report, A 93.29/2-13

Terminal Low Altitude, **Africa** and Southwest Asia, D 301.13/6

Tide Tables Europe and East Coast of **Africa**, C 4.15/7

Tide Tables, High and Low Water Predictions Europe and West Coast of **Africa**, Including the Mediterranean Sea, C 55.421/3

U.S. Imprints on Sub-Saharan **Africa**, LC 41.12/2

United States Air Force and Navy Supplementary Flight Information, Europe, **Africa**, and Middle East, D 301.49

United States Air Force Radio Facility Charts, Europe, **Africa**, Middle East, D 301.9

Agents
- Charter Report, Government-Owned Dry-Cargo Vessels, Operated by Bareboat Charters and/or **Agents** of Maritime Administration, C 39.215
- Newsletter to Sales **Agents**, GP 3.25
- Notes to **Agents** on [subject] (series), A 43.39
- Patent Attorneys and **Agents** Available to Represent Inventors Before the United States Patent Office, C 21.9/2
- Report of the Attorney General to the Congress of the United States on the Administration of the Foreign **Agents** Registration Act of 1938, As Amended, J 1.30
- Reports of **Agents** and Superintendents in Charge of Indians, I 20.15
- Reports of Special **Agents** and Commissions, I 20.6
- Roster of Attorneys and **Agents** Registered to Practice before the U.S. Patent Office, C 21.9
- Special **Agents** Series, C 10.13, C 18.11

AGERS
- **AGERS** (series), A 93.21/3

Ages
- Estimated Numbers of Apple Trees by Varieties and **Ages** in Commercial and Farm Orchards, A 36.52

Aggregate
- **Aggregate** Reserves and Member Bank Deposits, FR 1.15/3, HE 1.210

Aging
- Activities of **Aging** Committee, Y 4.Ag 4/2-10
- Adult Development and **Aging** Abstracts, HE 20.3359
- Adult Development and **Aging** Research Committee, HE 20.3001/2:Ad 9
- **Aging**, FS 1.13, FS 14.9, FS 15.10, FS 17.309, HE 17.309, HE 23.3110, HE 1.1015
- **Aging**, GAO Activities in Fiscal Year, GA 1.13/14
- **Aging** Review Committee, HE 20.3001/2:Ag 4/2
- **Aging** Trends, HE 20.6233
- Fact Sheets **Aging** Administration, HE 1.213
- Facts on **Aging**, FS 13.5, FS 14.9/3
- Federal Assistance for Projects in **Aging**, FS 14.12
- Federal Financial Assistance for Projects in **Aging**, FS 15.13, FS 17.310/2
- Highlights of Legislation on **Aging**, FS 1.13/4, FS 14.912
- Intramural Annual Report, National Institute of **Aging**, HE 20.3866
- NCHSR Health Care for the **Aging**, HE 20.6514/2
- 1990 Census of Population and Housing Special Tabulation on **Aging**, C 3.281/2
- 1990 Census of Population and Housing, Special Tabulation on **Aging**, Federal Region 1, Connecticut-Maine-Massachusetts-New Hampshire-Rhode Island-Vermont, Cd 90-AOA1, C 3.218/2:CD 90-AOA
- Patterns for Progress in **Aging** Case Studies, FS 1.13/3, FS 14.9/5
- Patterns for Progress in **Aging**, HE 1.211
- Posters National Institute on **Aging**, HE 20.3867
- Progress in **Aging**, Y 4.Ag 4/2:Ag 4/5
- Publications List Senate Special Committee on **Aging**, Y 4.Ag 4:P 96
- Reports and Guidelines from White House Conference on **Aging** (series), FS 1.13/2
- Research Highlights in **Aging**, FS 2.22/25
- Research Programs in **Aging**, FS 2.22/25-2
- Second Supplement on **Aging**, HE 20.6232
- Selected References on **Aging**, FS 1.18/2, FS 14.9/4, FS 15.12/2
- Special Report on **Aging**, HE 20.3862
- Statistical Notes National Clearinghouse on **Aging**, HE 23.3112
- Task Force on **Aging**, Pr 37.8:Ag 8
- Task Force on Problems of **Aging**, Pr 37.8:Ag 4/Ct
- Training and Manpower Development Activities Supported by the Administration on **Aging** Under Title IV-A of the Older Americans Act of 1965, As Amended, Descriptions of Funded Projects, HE 23.3002:T 68/2
- Uses of Research Sponsored by the Administration on **Aging**, Case Studies, HE 23.3012

AGPO
- **AGPO**, GP 1.14

Agreement
- Annual Report on the HEW/USDA Rural Health Facilities **Agreement**, A 84.12
- Executive **Agreement** Series, S 9.8
- International **Agreement** Reports (series), Y 3.N 88:53

Marketing **Agreement** Series, A 55.9, A 65.9, A 73.7
- Master **Agreement**, J 25.13
- Overlap, Measurement **Agreement** through Process Evaluation, C 13.56
- Trade **Agreement** Digest, TC 1.24
- United States General Imports of Cotton Manufacturers: Country of Origin by Geneva **Agreement** Category, C 56.210:130, C 3.164:130

Agreements
- **Agreements**, Y 3.R 13/2:6
- **Agreements** Filed with CAB Under 412(a) During Week Ending, C 31.228
- Annual Report of the President of the United States on Trade **Agreements** Program, Pr 37.10, Pr 40.11
- Annual Report of the President on the Trade **Agreements** Program, Pr 38.13, Pr 39.13, Pr 42.11
- Bretton Woods **Agreements** Act Releases, SE 1.25/10
- Calendar for Hearings Concerning Trade **Agreements**, S 1.103
- Calendar of Trade **Agreements**, S 1.104
- Collective Bargaining **Agreements** Received by Bureau of Labor Statistics, L 2.45
- Imports Under Reciprocal Trade **Agreements**, by Countries, TC 1.13
- Industries and Reciprocal Trade **Agreements**, Reports on, by Industries, TC 1.15
- Lists of Commercial Treaties and Conventions, and **Agreements** Affected by Exchange of Notes or Declarations in Force Between United States and Other Countries, S 9.9
- Marketing and Marketing **Agreements** Division, Marketing Section Publications, A 55.59
- Operations of the Trade **Agreements** Program, TC 1.14/3, ITC 1.24
- Special Notice Concerning Basic **Agreements** Teleprocessing Services Program (TSP) Industrial Group 737, Industrial Class 7374, GS 12.13
- State-EPA **Agreements**, Annual Report, EP 1.86
- Trade **Agreements** (by countries), TC 1.14
- Trade Policy Agenda and Annual Report of the President of the **Agreements** Program, PrEx 9.11
- Treaties and **Agreements**, I 20.18
- Treaties and Other International **Agreements** of United States, S 9.12/2
- United States Treaties and Other International **Agreements**, S 9.12
- Woodland Management Plan, **Agreements** and Farm Codes, A 57.37

AGRI
- **AGRI**-TOPICS (series), A 17.18/6

AGRICOLA
- List of Journals Indexed in **AGRICOLA**, A 17.18/5

Agricultural
- A.A.A.N.C.R. **Agricultural** Conservation Program by States, NCR, A 55.43/11
- Active Foreign **Agricultural** Research, A 106.42/2
- Address List of **Agricultural** and Mechanical Colleges, A 10.20
- Address List of **Agricultural** Experiment Stations, A 10.19
- Address List of State Institutions and Officers in Charge of **Agricultural** Extension Work under Smith-Lever Act, A 10.25
- Advances in **Agricultural** Technology, AAT (series), A 106.24, A 77.31
- **Agricultural** and Chemical Development, (date) Annual Report, Y 3.T 25:1-5, A 82.100
- **Agricultural** and Credit Outlook, FCA 1.24
- **Agricultural** Census Analyses: Changes in Land in Farms by Size of Farm, A 36.137/1
- **Agricultural** Census Analyses: Changes in Number of Farms by Size of Farm, A 36.137/2
- **Agricultural** Conservation Practices (by States), A 80.608
- **Agricultural** Conservation Program (by States), A 55.44/14, A 80.613, A 82.110, A 82.112, A 90.8
- **Agricultural** Conservation Program (by States), A 82.112, A 1.107
- **Agricultural** Conservation Program Service Publications, A 82.37/2
- **Agricultural** Conservation Program, Statistical Summary, A 90.10

Agricultural Conservation Program, Summary, A 90.10/2
- **Agricultural** Cooperation, A 36.12, FF 1.7
- **Agricultural** Development, IADS News Digest, A 95.10/2
- **Agricultural** Economic Reports, A 88.52, A 93.28, A 1.107
- **Agricultural** Economic Reports and Services, A 36.58
- **Agricultural** Economics Bibliographies, A 36.13
- **Agricultural** Economics Branch Reports, Y 3.T 25:29-2, A 88.27, A 93.26
- **Agricultural** Economics Literature, A 36.20, A 17.10
- **Agricultural** Economics Research, A 36.167, A 88.27, A 93.26, A 105.21
- **Agricultural** Economics Research, A 105.21
- **Agricultural** Engineering Publications, Y 3.T 25:23, A 93.9/8
- **Agricultural** Engineering, Current Literature, A 53.9
- **Agricultural** Export Assistance Update Quarterly Report, A 67.46
- **Agricultural** Exports, A 93.43
- **Agricultural** Finance Outlook, A 105.19/3
- **Agricultural** Finance Review, A 36.111, A 93.9/10, A 105.35, A 77.14
- **Agricultural** Finance Statistics, AFS (series), A 93.9/10-2
- **Agricultural** Finance, and Income Situation and Outlook Report, A 93.9/8
- **Agricultural** Handbooks, A 1.76
- **Agricultural** History Series, A 36.133
- **Agricultural** Implements and Farm Equipment, Monthly Export and Import Bulletin, C 18.47
- **Agricultural** Information Bulletins, A 1.75
- **Agricultural** Labor Situation, A 1.56
- **Agricultural** Land Values and Markets, Outlook and Situation Report, A 93.29/2-4
- **Agricultural** Legislation in the Congress, Y 4.Ag 8/1:L 52
- **Agricultural** Libraries Information Notes, A 106.109
- **Agricultural** Library Notes, A 17.9
- **Agricultural** Loans by States, A 36.132
- **Agricultural** Marketing, A 88.26/3
- **Agricultural** Opportunities, C 7.11/5
- **Agricultural** Outlook, A 92.10/2
- **Agricultural** Outlook Chartbook, A 1.98
- **Agricultural** Outlook Charts, A 88.8/3, A 88.8/2
- **Agricultural** Outlook Digest, A 93.10, A 88.9/3
- **Agricultural** Outlooks (individual), A 36.83
- **Agricultural** Prices, A 36.163, A 88.9/5, A 92.16, A 105.26
- **Agricultural** Prices, Annual Summary, A 92.16/2, A 105.26/2
- **Agricultural** Prices, Louisiana Crop Reporting Service, A 88.9/4
- **Agricultural** Prices, Semiannual Summaries, A 92.16/2
- **Agricultural** Programs, A 43.49/2
- **Agricultural** Relations Division Publications, Y 3.T 25:29, A 77.12
- **Agricultural** Research, A 106.9
- **Agricultural** Research and Marketing Act Publications, A 1.72
- **Agricultural** Research Results, A 106.13
- **Agricultural** Research Results, ARR (series), A 106.12, A 77.32
- **Agricultural** Resources, Cropland, Water, and Conservation, A 93.47/2
- **Agricultural** Review and Manuals, A 106.12, A 77.30
- **Agricultural** Science Review, A 94.11
- **Agricultural** Section, Circular Letters, Y 3.R 13/2:45
- **Agricultural** Situation, A 36.15, A 88.8, A 92.23, A 105.10
- **Agricultural** Situation in Relation to Banking, A 36.129
- **Agricultural** Situation Supplements (various areas), A 93.29/2-2
- **Agricultural** Situation, Special Edition for Crop and Price Reports, A 36.15/2
- **Agricultural** Situation: Africa and the Middle East, A 93.29/2-2
- **Agricultural** Statistics, A 1.47, A 1.47/2
- **Agricultural** Statistics Board Catalog, A 92.35/2
- **Agricultural** Supply and Demand Estimates, A 1.110
- **Agricultural** Technology Circulars, A 19.20

Agricultural Trade Development and Assistance Act of 1954 and Amendments, Y 1.2:Ag 8/6

Agricultural Trade Highlights, A 67.45, A 67.18:ATH

Agricultural Trade Policy, ATP (series), A 67.39

Agricultural, Pastoral, and Forest Industries in American Republics, TC 1.19

Agricultural, Pastoral, and Forest Industries in American Republics, TC 1.19

Agricultural-Food Policy Review, A 93.16/2, A 105.50

Agronomy, Weed Science, Soil Conservation, **Agricultural** Programs, A 106.36

Alaska **Agricultural** Experiment Station, A 77.440

Annual Report on the Food and **Agricultural** Sciences, A 1.1/4-2

Annual Summary of Foreign **Agricultural** Training as of [date], A 67.37

Appraisal of the Proposed Budget for Food and **Agricultural** Sciences Report to the President and Congress, A 1.1/4-3

British-American **Agricultural** News Service, A 67.22

Census of Distribution; Distribution of **Agricultural** Commodities, C 3.37/34

Checklist of Reports and Charts Issued by **Agricultural** Marketing Service, A 88.33

Crops Research: Results of Regional Cotton Variety Tests by Cooperating **Agricultural** Experiment Stations, A 77.15:34

Current Literature in **Agricultural** Engineering, A 70.7

Digest of Decisions of Secretary of Agriculture under Perishable **Agricultural** Commodities Act, A 82.55

Digest of Decisions Secretary of Agriculture under Perishable **Agricultural** Commodities Act, A 82.55

Directory of American **Agricultural** Organizations, A 37.6

Drainage of **Agricultural** Lands (by States), C 3.37/25

Farm Relief and **Agricultural** Adjustment Acts [June 15, 1929], Y 1.2:F 22

FAS Letter to **Agricultural** Attaches and Officers, A 67.31/2

Field Releases of **Agricultural** Marketing Service, A 88.42

Food and **Agricultural** Export Directory, A 67.26:201

Foreign Agricultural Bulletins, A 67.3

Foreign **Agricultural** Circulars, A 67

Foreign **Agricultural** Economic Reports, A 93.27, A 105.22

Foreign **Agricultural** Service, Miscellaneous, A 67.26

Foreign **Agricultural** Situation, Maps and Charts, A 67.24

Foreign **Agricultural** Trade, A 67.19

Foreign **Agricultural** Trade Digest of United States, A 67.19/8

Foreign **Agricultural** Trade of the United States, A 93.17/7, A 105.14

Foreign **Agricultural** Trade of the United States Digest, A 93.17/2

Foreign **Agricultural** Trade of the United States, Fiscal Year, A 93.17/6

Foreign **Agricultural** Trade of the United States, Fiscal Year Supplement, A 93.17/7-2

Foreign **Agricultural** Trade of the United States, Statistical Report, A 93.17

Foreign **Agricultural** Trade of the United States, Trade by Commodities, A 93.17/8

Foreign **Agricultural** Trade of the United States, Trade by Countries, A 93.17/4

Foreign Agricultural Trade of the United States, Trade in **Agricultural** Products with Individual Countries by Calendar Year, A 67.19/6

Foreign **Agricultural** Trade of the United States; Imports of Fruits and Vegetables under Quarantine by Countries of Origin and Ports of Entry, A 67.19/7, A 93.17/5

Foreign **Agricultural** Trade Statistical Report, A 105.14/2

Foreign Training Letter, to Foreign **Agricultural** Contacts at Land-Grant Colleges, A 67.31, A 67.31/3

Funds for Research at State **Agricultural** Experimental Stations, A 94.10

Hampton Normal and **Agricultural** Institute, I 20.17

Indices of **Agricultural** Production in [various] Countries, A 67.36, A 93.32

Industrial Uses of **Agricultural** Materials, Situation and Outlook Report, A 93.56

International **Agricultural** Collaboration Series, A 67.20

International **Agricultural** Development, A 95.9

Inventory of **Agricultural** Research, A 94.14

Irrigation of **Agricultural** Lands (by States), C 3.940-9

Irrigation, **Agricultural** Lands, C 3.37/24

Journal of **Agricultural** Economic Research, A 93.26

Journal of **Agricultural** Research, A 1.23

Laws relating to Vocational Education and **Agricultural** Extension Work, Y 1.2:V 85/2

List of Extension Publications of State **Agricultural** Colleges Received by Office of Experiment Stations Library, A 43.5/9

Meat Graded by Bureau of **Agricultural** Economics, A 36.190

Observational Study of **Agricultural** Aspects of Arkansas River Multiple-purpose Project, Annual Report, A 57.60

Office of Inspector General, **Agricultural** Research Service: Annual Report, A 1.1/3

Orderly Liquidation of Stock of **Agricultural** Commodities Held by the Commodity Credit Corporation, A 1.102

Outline of **Agricultural** Conservation Program, A 55.44/12

Outlook for **Agricultural** Exports, A 1.80/2

Outlook for U.S. **Agricultural** Exports, A 93.43

Periodic Reports of **Agricultural** Economics, Economic Research Service, Statistical Reporting Service, A 1.99

Philippine **Agricultural** Review, W 49.21/7

Public Law 480, **Agricultural** Export Activities, Annual Report of the President, Pr 37.13

Publications **Agricultural** Adjustment Agency East Central Region, A 76.441, A 79.441, A 80.2141

Publications **Agricultural** Adjustment Agency North Central Region, A 76.451, A 79.451, A 80.2151

Publications **Agricultural** Adjustment Agency Northeast Region, A 76.461, A 79.461, A 80.2161

Publications **Agricultural** Adjustment Agency Southern Region, A 76.471, A 79.471, A 80.2171

Publications **Agricultural** Adjustment Agency Western Region, A 76.481, A 79.481, A 80.2181

Radio Talks Bureau of **Agricultural** Economics, A 13.144

Records and Briefs in Cases Arising Under **Agricultural** Adjustment Act, Bankhead Act, and Kerr-Smith Tobacco Act, J 1.19/7

Recruiting Bulletins **Agricultural** Marketing Service, A 88.3/2

Regulations Under the Perishable **Agricultural** Commodoties Act 1930, and Perishable **Agricultural** Commodities Act, A 88.6:P 41

Report of **Agricultural** Aviation Research Conferences, A 77.2:Av 5

Report of United States Government to the Food and **Agricultural** Organization of the United Nations, A 67.35

Report of Virgin Islands **Agricultural** Research and Extension Program, A 77.491

Report on **Agricultural** Experiment Stations, A 10.1/2

Reports Issued by **Agricultural** Marketing Service, A 66.19

Reports of Project on Research in **Agricultural** and Industrial Development in Tennessee Valley Region, Y 3.T 25:26

Reports on Foreign Markets for **Agricultural** Products, A 36.8

Research Progress in (year), a Report of the **Agricultural** Research Service, A 77.1

Results of Regional Cotton Variety Tests by Cooperating **Agricultural** Experiment Stations, A 77.15:34

Selected **Agricultural** Activities of Public Employment Offices, L 7.59

Selected List of American **Agricultural** Books in Print and Current **Agricultural** Periodicals, A 17.17:1

Serials Currently Received by the National **Agricultural** Library, A 17.18/2:Se 6

Service and Regulatory Announcements **Agricultural** Marketing Service, A 66.27, A 75.16, A 88.6/3

Service and Regulatory Announcements **Agricultural** Research Service, A 77.6/2

Service and Regulatory Announcements **Agricultural** Stabilization and Conservation Service, A 82.23

Service and Regulatory Announcements Bureau of **Agricultural** Economics, A 36.5

Sheets of National Atlas of United States **Agricultural** Research Service, A 77.19

Southern Region **Agricultural** Conservation, A 55.45/8

State **Agricultural** and Marketing Officers, A 36.55

State **Agricultural** Departments and Marketing Agencies, with Names of Officials, A 66.45

State Data Profiles, Calendar Year (date), Selected Ascs Program Activity and Other **Agricultural** Data, A 82.90

State Publications Issued in Cooperation with **Agricultural** Marketing Service, A 88.42/2

Summaries of Studies in **Agricultural** Education Supplements, FS 5.281:81002, HE 5.281:81002

Summary of **Agricultural** Reports, FS 3.126

Surveys of **Agricultural** Labor Conditions, A 61.11

U.S. **Agricultural** Exports, A 67.32

U.S. **Agricultural** Imports, Fact Sheet, A 67.32/2, A 93.30, A 93.30/2

U.S. **Agricultural** Real Estate Trends, FCA 1.24/2

U.S. **Agricultural** Trade Update, A 93.17/7-5

U.S. Exports of Reported **Agricultural** Commodities for (dates), Marketing Years, A 67.40/4

U.S.D.A. Summary of Registered **Agricultural** Pesticide Chemical Uses, A 77.302:P 43/4

What We Are Doing About **Agricultural** Surpluses, A 82.80

World **Agricultural** Outlook and Situation, A 93.29/2

World **Agricultural** Production and Trade, Statistical Report, A 67.8/3

World **Agricultural** Production, A 67.18:WAP

World **Agricultural** Situation Supplements: Africa and the Middle East, A 93.29/2-2

World **Agricultural** Situation, A 67.27, A 93.29, A 93.29/2, A 105.10/3, A 105.10/3-2

World **Agricultural** Supply and Demand Estimates, A 1.110, A 93.29/3

World Economic Conditions in Relation to **Agricultural** Trade, A 93.34/2, A 105.22/2

World Indices of **Agricultural** and Food Production, A 1.34/3

World Monetary Conditions in Relation to **Agricultural** Trade, A 93.34/2

World Survey of **Agricultural** Machinery and Equipment, C 41.91

Agricultural Sciences
Annual Report to the Secretary of Agriculture by the Joint Council on Food and **Agricultural Sciences**, A 1.1/4

Agriculture
1953 Sample Census of Agriculture, C 3.31/6

Agriculture, PrEx 7.15, PrEx 7.21

Agriculture (by States), C 3.37/11

Agriculture (Miscellaneous Reports), C 3.37/15

Agriculture and Food, C 51.9/19

Agriculture and the Environment, A 1.127

Agriculture Census of 1945, Special Reports, C 3.31/5

Agriculture Chartbook, A 1.76/2

Agriculture Decisions, A 1.58

Agriculture Economics Extension, A 43.5/17

Agriculture Fact Sheets, AFS (series), A 1.121, A 21.35, A 107.14

Agriculture Financial Review, A 93.9/10

Agriculture Handbooks, A 1.76

Agriculture in Defense, A 21.13/9, A 17.16

Agriculture in National Defense, A 1.83

Agriculture in the Americas, A 67.15 1

Agriculture in the Classroom, Notes, A 1.135

Agriculture Information Bulletins, A 1.75

Agriculture Information Posters, A 106.18
Agriculture Information Series, A 1.64
Agriculture Monographs, A 1.78
Agriculture Outlook, A 105.27
Agriculture Statistics, A 1.47
Agriculture Technology for Developing Countries, Technical Series Papers, S 18.45
Agriculture War Information Series, A 1.59
Agriculture, 1st Series (by States), C 3.940-14, C 3.37/12
Agriculture, 2d Series (by States), C 3.940-15, C 3.37/13
Agriculture, 3d Series (by States), C 3.940-16, C 3.37/14
Agriculture-Economics Reports, A 93.39
Aircraft in Agriculture, FAA 1.33
Alaska Agriculture Statistics, A 92.48
Announcements, Census of Agriculture, C 3.31/8
Atlas of American Agriculture Advance Sheets, A 1.30
Balance Sheet of Agriculture, A 1.38 A 1.75
Bibliographies and Literature of Agriculture, A 1.60/3 A 106.110/3
Bibliographies and Literature of Agriculture, A 105.55
Bibliography of Agriculture, A 17.18
Breeding Research and Improvement Activities of Department of Agriculture Reports, A 1.91
Bulletins, Agriculture (by States), C 3.14/2, C 3.28/10, C 3.28/11
Carload Waybill Statistics, Mileage Block Distribution, Traffic and Revenue by Commodity Class, Territorial Movement, and Type of Rate, Products of Agriculture, 1 Percent Sample of Terminations in Statement MB-1, IC 1.23/2
Census of Agriculture, A 92.53
Census of Agriculture, C 3.31, C 3.31/4
Census of Agriculture; Area Reports, C 56.227
Census of Agriculture; Final Volumes, A 92.53/57
Census of Agriculture; Final Volumes other than Area Reports and Special Reports, C 56.227/3
Census of Agriculture; General Publications, C 56.227/5
Census of Agriculture; General Reports, C 3.31/9
Census of Agriculture; Preliminary and/or Advance Reports, C 56.227/4
Census of Agriculture; Special Reports, C 56.227/2
Census of Agriculture, Vol 1, Geographic Area Series, A 92.53/56
Census of Agriculture, Vol 2, Subject Series, A 92.54
Commodity Exchange Act, As Amended, Regulations of the Secretary of Agriculture Thereunder, Orders of the Commodity Exchange Commission Pursuant to Sec. 4a and 5a(4), A 85.6:C 73
Cooperation in Agriculture, A 17.17:41
Cooperative Extension Work in Agriculture and Home Economics, A 10.24
Digest of Decisions of Secretary of Agriculture under Perishable Agricultural Commodities Act, A 82.55
Directory of Information Resources in Agriculture and Biology, A 17.2:D 62
Directory of Small-Scale Agriculture, A 94.17
Directory of State Departments of Agriculture, A 88.40/2:17, A 88.59
Dry Land Agriculture Division, Weekly Station Reports, A 77.508
Dry-Land Agriculture, A 19.35
Economic and Agriculture Censuses, C 3.277
Educational and Training Opportunities in sustainable Agriculture, A 17.32
Europe Update, Agriculture and Trade Report, A 93.29/2-21
Expenditures of Department of Agriculture, A 2.5
Extent of Aerial Photography by Agriculture Department, Completed, in Progress and Approved, A 1.51
Facts about U.S. Agriculture, A 1.38/2
Financial and Technical Assistance Provided by the Department of Agriculture and the Department of Housing and Urban Development for Nonmetropolitan Planning District, Annual Report to Congress, A 1.113
Food and Agriculture Competitively Awarded Research and Education Grants, A 106.42

Foreign Agriculture, A 67.1/2
Foreign Agriculture Reports, A 67.16
Foreign Agriculture, A Review of Foreign Farm Policy, Production, and Trade, A 67.7
Foreign Agriculture, Including Foreign Crops and Markets, A 67.7
Foreign Agriculture, Review of Foreign Farm Policy, Production and Trade, A 36.88, A 64.7, A 67.7
HE Instruction in Agriculture, Programs, Activities, Developments, FS 5.74
Indexes to Yearbooks of Department of Agriculture, A 21.12
Information and Technical Assistance Delivered by the Department of Agriculture in Fiscal Year, A 1.1/2
Institutions in United States Giving Instruction in Agriculture, A 10.18
Inter-American Conference on Agriculture, Forestry, and Animal Industry, Washington, Sept. 8-20, 1930, S 5.32
Laws relating to Agriculture, Y 1.2:Ag 8/5
List of Available Publications of the United States Department of Agriculture, A 21.9/8:11
List of Bulletins and Circulars Issued by Department of Agriculture for Distribution, A 21.5
List of Workers in Subjects Pertaining to Agriculture, A 10.23
Management Bulletins: Department of Agriculture, A 1.3/2
Manual of Meat Inspection Procedures of the Department of Agriculture, A 88.6/4:M 46
Meat and Poultry Inspection, Report of the Secretary of Agriculture, A 1.109, A 110.11/2
Memorandum to Heads of Department of Agriculture Agencies, A 1.79
Motion Pictures of Department of Agriculture, A 43.24
News Releases and Miscellaneous Publications; Committee on Agriculture, (House), Y 4.Ag 8/1-2
News Releases and Miscellaneous Publications; Committee on Agriculture, Nutrition, and Forestry, (Senate), Y 4.Ag 8/3-2
Official Record, Department of Agriculture, A 1.33
Officials of Department of Agriculture, A 1.89/2
Organization Directory, U.S. Department of Agriculture, A 60.10
Pacific Rim Agriculture and Trade Reports: Situation and Outlook Series, A 92.29/2-19
Personnel Bulletins Personnel Office, Department of Agriculture, A 49.3/2
Philippine Journal of Agriculture, W 49.55/5
Plant Disease, Decay, Etc., Control Activities of Department of Agriculture, Reports, A 1.90
Press Notices Department of Agriculture, A 1.31
Price List of Publications of Department of Agriculture for Sale by Superintendent of Documents, A 21.8
Products of Agriculture, IC 1.23/10:SS-2
Program Aids Department of Agriculture, A 1.68
Publications Department of Agriculture Available for Distribution, A 21.6/4
Radio Service Agriculture in Defense, A 21.13/9
Regulations Governing Meat Inspection of the U.S. Department of Agriculture, A 88.6/3:188
Regulations of Department of Agriculture, A 1.19
Report of the Secretary of Agriculture, A 1.1
Report to Congress by the Secretary of the Interior and the Secretary of Agriculture on Administration of the Wild Free-roaming Horses and Burro Act, I 1.100
Reports of Technical Study Groups on Soviet Agriculture, A 1.94
Rural Development Goals, Annual Report of the Secretary of Agriculture to the Congress, A 1.85/2
Science and Technology Agriculture Reporter (STAR), S 18.64
Serial Publications Indexed to Bibliography of Agriculture, A 17.17:75
Sheets of National Atlas of United States Census of Agriculture, C 3.31/10
Specifications Agriculture Department, A 1.25
Statistical Bulletins Department of Agriculture, A 1.34
Statistics and Agriculture, A 36.134

Surveys of Wage and Wage Rates in Agriculture, Reports, A 36.156
Telephone Directory Agriculture Department, Alphabetical Listing, A 1.89/4
U.S. Department of Agriculture Budget Summary, A 1.138
United Nations Conference on Food and Agriculture, S 5.41
United States Census of Agriculture, 1950: Announcements, C 3.950-9/6
United States Census of Agriculture, 1950: V. 2 General Report (separates), C 3.950-9/5
Weekly Reports of Office of Western Irrigation Agriculture, A 19.25
Weekly Station Reports of Office of Dry Land Agriculture Investigations, A 19.24
Yearbook of Agriculture, A 1.10
Agriculture Outlook
 Agriculture Outlook, Conference Proceedings, A 1.144
Agriculture Department
 Agriculture Department Graduate School Publications, A 1.42
Agriculturists
 List of State Extension Entomologists and Extension Agriculturists, A 43.32
Agristars
 Agristars Annual Report, A 1.132
Agronomy
 Agronomy Technical Notes, A 57.67
 Agronomy, Current Literature, A 19.23
 Agronomy, Weed Science, Soil Conservation, Agricultural Programs, A 106.36
 Conservation Agronomy Technical Notes, A 57.63
Agrotechnology
 Life Sciences: Agrotechnology and Food Resources, PrEx 7.22/3
AHB
 American Housing Brief (AHB) from the American Housing Survey, C 3.215/20
AHCPR
 AHCPR Grant Announcement, HE 20.6519/2
 AHCPR Long-Term Care Studies (series), HE 20.6519
 AHCPR National Medical Expenditure Survey Data Summary, HE 20.6517/2
 AHCPR Research Activities HE 20.6512/5
AHRQ
 AHRQ Publications Catalog, HE 20.6509/3
 AHRQ Research Activities HE 20.6512/5
 AHRQ Research Report Series, HE 20.6512
AHS
 AHS Pamphlets, D 101.22/19
AIC
 AIC (Series), A 17.28
AID
 AID Background Series, S 18.30
 Aid for Analyzing Markets (by States), C 18.38
 Aid Highlights, S 18.61
 AID Procurement Information Bulletin, S 18.3/2
 AID Project Impact Evaluation Reports, S 18.52
 AID Reports, LC 38.9
 AID Small Business Circular, S 18.4/2
 AID Small Business Memo, Trade Information for American Suppliers, S 18.9
 Aid to Familes with Dependent Children, HE 3.65, HE 17.625
 AID-Financed Awards, S 18.11
 Airport Aid Program, TD 4.6:part 152
 Characteristics of Families Receiving Aid to Dependent Children, FS 3.39
 Characteristics of State Plans for Aid to Families with Dependent Children Under the Social Security Act Title IV-A, HE 3.65/2
 Consumer Aid Series, TD 8.14/2
 Counselor's Handbook, a Federal Student Aid Reference, ED 1.45
 Counterpart Funds and AID Foreign Currency Account, S 18.14
 Current Federal Aid Research Report, Wildlife, I 49.94/2
 EFC Formula Book, The Expected Family Contribution for Federal Student Aid, ED 1.45/5
 Employment Hours and Earnings on Student Aid Projects of NYA, Y 3.W 89/2:27
 Federal Aid in Fish and Wildlife Restoration, I 49.29/3
 Federal Aid to States, Fiscal Year, T 63.120
 Federal Student Financial Aid Handbook, ED 1.45/4

Federal-**Aid** Airport Program Publications, FAA 8.10
Federal-**Aid** Highway Relocation Assistance and Payment Statistics, TD 2.28
FES **Aid**: Sanitation Series, A 43.40
Findings of (year) AB [**Aid** to the Blind] Study, HE 17.639/4
Foreign **Aid** by the U.S. Government, C 18.279
Handbook of Federal **Aid** to Communities, C 46.8:C 73
Hospital and Mental Facilities Construction Program under Title 6 of Public Health Service Act, Semiannual Analysis of Projects Approved for Federal **Aid**, FS 2.74/2
Interviewing **Aid**, L 7.52
Laws relating to Federal **Aid** and Construction of Roads, Y 1.2:R 53
LC Folk Archive Finding **Aid**, LC 39.13/2
National Postsecondary Student **Aid** Study (NPSAS), ED 1.333
OPS Trade **Aid** TA (series), ES 3.6/15
Price Trends for Federal-**Aid** Highway Construction, C 37.22, TD 2.49
Price Trends for Federal-**aid**-highway Construction, TD 2.49
Proposed Foreign **Aid** Program Fiscal Year, Summary Presentation to Congress, S 18.28/a
Proposed Foreign **Aid** Program, Summary Presentation to Congress, S 18.28
Public Assistance Bureau, Applications: Old- Age Assistance, **Aid** to Dependent Children, **Aid** to the Blind [and] General Assistance, FS 3.17
Publications Federal-**Aid** Airport Program, FAA 8.10
Report of Classified Program of Exports and Value by American Agencies Voluntarily Registered with Advisory Committee on Voluntary Foreign **Aid**, S 1.99/2
Reports to **Aid** Nation's Defense Effort, A 13.27/13
Shipment Under the United States Foreign **Aid** Programs Made on Army- or Navy- Operated Vessels (American flag) by Port of Lading by Country of Destination, C 3.164:976
Simplifying Federal **Aid** to States and Communities, Annual Report to the President of an Interagency Program, PrEx 2.18
Special Analysis of Federal **Aid** to State and Local Governments in Budget, PrEx 2.8/a3
Statistical Summary of **Aid** to Dependent Children of Unemployed Parents, FS 3.39/3
Student Guide, Five Federal Financial **Aid** Programs, ED 1.8/2
Summary Statement of Income and Expenditures of Voluntary Relief Agencies Registered with Advisory Committee on Voluntary Foreign **Aid**, S 1.99/3
Technical Assistance **Aid**, L 1.48
U.S. Department of Commerce Periodicals to **Aid** Business Men, C 1.54
Unemployed-Parent Segment of **Aid** to Families with Dependent Children, FS 14.210, FS 17.11, FS 17.611
USDA/**Aid** News Digest, A 1.108

AID-OST
AID-OST (series), S 18.42
Applications of Modern Technologies to International Development, **AID-OST** (series), S 18.42

Aided
Program Facts on Federally **Aided** Public Assistance Income Maintenance Programs, HE 17.614

AIDS
AIDS Bibliography, HE 20.3615/3
AIDS Bulletin (series), J 28.3/3
Aids to Navigation, C 9.29
Aids to Navigation Bulletin, TD 5.3/2
CDC, HIV/ **AIDS** Prevention, HE 20.7038/3
CDC NCHSTP Daily News Update (**AIDS** Daily Summaries), HE 20.7318
Coastal Engineering Technical **Aids** (numbered), D 103.42/12
Conservation **Aids**, A 57.45
Construction **Aids**, HH 1.18
Correspondence **Aids**, CA (series), A 77.18, A 106.23
Educational **Aids**, A 89.14, I 49.54
Facts about **AIDS**, HE 20.7038

General Aviation Inspection **Aids** Summary, TD 4.409
General Maintenance Inspection **Aids**, C 31.162
General Maintenance Inspection **Aids** Summary and Supplements, FAA 1.31
HIV/**AIDS** Prevention Newsletter, HE 20.7038/2
HIV/**AIDS** Surveillance, HE 20.7011/38
Job **Aids** (numbered), D 105.6/4
Local List of Lights and Other Marine **Aids**, Pacific, T 47.25/2
MMWR Reports on **AIDS**, HE 20.7009/5
Program **Aids** Defense Savings Staff, T 1.109
Program **Aids** Department of Agriculture, A 1.68
Radio **Aids** to Navigation, Great Lakes, United States and Canada, T 47.26/2
Reference **Aids**, PrEx 3.11
Science Study **Aids**, A 1.104
Scientific **Aids** to Learning Committee, Publications, NA 2.6
SCS **Aids**, A 57.40
SCS-CI- [Conservation **Aids**] (series), A 57.45
Small Business **Aids** (series), C 40.7/2
Small Business **Aids**, C 18.268
Small Marketers **Aids**, SBA 1.14
Tabulation of Air Navigation Radio **Aids**, C 23.18, CA 1.9, C 31.8, C 31.108
Teaching **Aids** for Developing International Understanding, FS 5.52
Technical **Aids** for Small Business, Annuals, SBA 1.11/2
Technical **Aids** for Small Manufacturers, SBA 1.11
Technical **Aids**, L 1.49/2
Technical Assistance **Aids**, L 31.8
USDA-C&MS Visual **Aids** (series), A 88.6/5

Air
Air Almanac, D 213.7
Air Bulletin, S 1.59
Air Carrier Traffic Statistics Monthly, TD 10.9/3
Air Chief (Clearinghouse for Inventory and Emission Factors), EP 1.109
Air Commerce Bulletin, C 23.12, CAB 1.8
Air Commerce Manuals, C 23.6/4
Air Commerce Traffic Patterns, C 3.153, FAA 4.11
Air Commerce Traffic Patterns (scheduled carriers), Fiscal Year, FAA 8.9
Air Service Bulletin, A.E.F., W 95.21/5
Air Service Information Circular, W 87.11
Air Staff, D 301.25
Air Technical Intelligence Technical Data Digest, M 301.9
Air Traffic Publications Library, TD 4.78
Air Transportation Wage Survey, L 2.113/7
Air Travel Consumer Report, TD 1.54
Air University, AFROTC [text books], D 301.26/12
All Certificated **Air** Cargo Carriers, C 31.232
American **Air** Almanac, M 212.7
Annual Review, Airworthiness Civil **Air** Regulations Meeting, C 31.245
Civil **Air** Regulations, C 31.209
Civil **Air** Regulations (compilations), C 23.6/2, C 23.6/3
Civil **Air** Regulations Draft Release, C 31.209/2
Cost of Clean **Air**, EP 1.62
Daily Upper **Air** Bulletin, D 210.10
Directory of **Air** Service Stations, W 87.9/2
En Route **Air** Traffic Control, TD 4.308:En 1
FAA **Air** Traffic Activity, TD 4.19
Federal **Air** Surgeons Medical Bulletin, TD 4.215
Federal Contract **Air** Service and Travel Directory, GS 8.10
Foreign **Air** News Digest, C 31.216
General Imports of Merchandise into United States by **Air**, Commodity by Country of Origin, C 3.164:231
General Imports of Merchandise into United States by **Air**, Country of Origin by Commodity, C 3.164:232
Index of U.S. Air Force, **Air** Force-Navy Aeronautical and Military (MS) Standards (sheet form), D 301.16/2
International **Air** Commerce Traffic Pattern, U.S. Flag Carriers, Calendar Year, C 31.153/2
Laws relating to Commercial **Air** Service and Miscellaneous **Air** Laws, Y 1.2:Ai 7
Monitoring and **Air** Quality Trends Report, EP 1.59
National **Air** Pollutant Emission Estimates, EP 4.24
National **Air** Quality and Emissions Trends Report, EP 4.22/2
National **Air** Toxics Information Clearinghouse: Newsletter, EP 4.23

National Performance Audit Program, Ambient **Air** Audits of Analytical Proficiency, EP 1.23/5-2
Naval **Air** Development Center Reports NADA (series), D 202.23
Organic Chemistry: **Air** Pollution Studies Characterization of Chemical Structures; Synthesis of Research Materials, C 13.46
Paris **Air** Show News Fillers, C 42.27/2
Paris **Air** Show Newsletter, C 42.27
Pilot Chart of Upper **Air**, North Atlantic Ocean, N 6.28
Pilot Chart of Upper **Air**, North Pacific Ocean, N 6.29
Precision and Accuracy Assessments for State and Local **Air** Monitoring Networks, EP 1.23/5-3
Profiles of Scheduled **Air** Carrier Airport Operations by Equipment Type, Top 100 U.S. Airports, TD 4.44/4
Profiles of Scheduled **Air** Carrier Airport Operations, Top 100 U.S. Airports, TD 4.44
Profiles of Scheduled **Air** Carrier Operations by Stage Length, TD 4.44/3
Profiles of Scheduled **Air** Carrier Passenger Traffic, Top 100 U.S. Airports, TD 4.44/2
Progress in the Prevention and Control of **Air** Pollution in (year), Report to Congress, EP 4.16
Progress Report **Air** Service, Engineering Division, W 87.14
Publications **Air** Pollution Control Office, EP 4.9
Publications **Air** University, D 301.26/6
Publications **Air** University, Documentary Research Study, D 301.26/3
Publications **Air** University, School of Aviation Medicine, D 301.26/3-2
Publications National **Air** Pollution Control Administration, FS 2.93/3
Publications National Conference on **Air** Pollution, FS 2.98
Publications Office of **Air** Programs, EP 4.9
Quarterly Interim Financial Report, Certificated Route **Air** Carriers and Supplemental **Air** Carriers, CAB 1.14
Quarterly Interim Financial Report, Certified Route **Air** Carriers and Supplemental **Air** Carriers, C 31.240/3
Quarterly Report of **Air** Carrier Operating Factors, C 31.240
Recapitulation by Carrier Groups, Certified **Air** Carriers, C 31.233
Recurrent Report of Financial Data: Domestic **Air** Mail Trunk Carriers, Quarters [comparisons], C 31.234
Recurrent Report of Mileage and Traffic Data All Certificated **Air** Cargo Carriers, C 31.232
Recurrent Report of Mileage and Traffic Data Domestic **Air** Mail Carriers, C 31.230
Recurrent Report of Mileage and Traffic Data Foreign, Overseas and Territorial **Air** Mail Carriers, C 31.231
Regional **Air** Cargo Workshop, C 31.258
Releases, **Air** Research and Development Command, D 301.45/3
Reports for Consultation on **Air** Quality Control Regions, FS 2.93/5
Research Bulletins **Air** Training Command, Human Resources Research Center, D 301.36/3
Research Memorandum **Air** University, Human Resources Report Institute, D 301.26/7
Research Reports **Air** Training Command, Human Resources Research Center, D 301.36/6
Research Reports **Air** University, D 301.26/13
Research Review, **Air** Training Command, Human Resources Research Center, D 301.36/4
Resume of U.S. Civil **Air** Carrier and General Aviation Aircraft Accidents, Calendar Year, C 31.244
Schedule X. Statistical Classification of Domestic and Foreign Merchandise Exported from United States by **Air** Arranged in Shipping Commodity Groups, C 3.150:X
Smithsonian Studies in **Air** and Space, SI 1.42
Soil, Water, **Air** Sciences Directory, A 106.14/2
Soil, Water, **Air** Sciences Research Annual Report, A 106.14
Special **Air** Traffic Rules and Airport Traffic Patterns, TD 4.6:part 93
Special Civil **Air** Regulations, C 31.206/3
State **Air** Pollution Implementation Plan Progress Report, EP 1.52

Index of U.S. Air Force, **Air Force**-Navy Aeronautical and Military (MS) Standards (sheet form), D 301.16/2

Joint Army and **Air Force** Bulletins, D 101.3

Joint Army and **Air Force** Procurement Circulars, D 101.33

Joint Army and **Air Force** Regulations, M 101.15

Latest Editions of U.S. **Air Force** Aeronautical Charts, C 55.418/3

Numerical Index of Standard and Recurring **Air Force** Publications Available to NATO Security Assistance Customers, D 301.6:0-22

Numerical List of U.S. **Air Force** and **Air Force**-Navy Aeronautical Standard Drawings, D 301.16

Numerical List, U.S. **Air Force** and Army-Navy Aeronautical Standard Drawings, M 301.12

Official Army and **Air Force** Register, M 101.19, M 108.8

Operational Applications Laboratory, **Air Force** Cambridge Research Center, OAL- TM, D 301.45/37

Pamphlets Department of the **Air Force**, D 301.35/3

Posters **Air Force** Department, M 301.76/5

Proceedings **Air Force** Academy Assembly, D 305.11

Publications **Air Force** Ballistic Missile Division, D 301.68

Publications **Air Force** Cambridge Research Laboratories, D 301.45/23-3

Publications **Air Force** Missile Test Center, D 301.45/23-1

Publications **Air Force** Office of Scientific Research, D 301.45/19-2

Qualified Products Lists Department of the **Air Force**, D 301.22

Recent Research Accomplishments of the **Air Force** Office of Scientific Research, D 301.45/19-7

Research Reports **Air Force** Academy, D 305.14

Research Reports Department of the **Air Force**, D 301.26/7-2

Research Review, Department of the **Air Force**, D 301.69/6-2

Review of the **Air Force** Materials Research and Development Program, D 301.45

Selling in Army and **Air Force** Careers, W 3.84, M 108.79

Special Reports **Air Force** Systems Command, D 301.45/42

Strategic Air Command, Grissom **Air Force** Base Telephone Directory, D 301.104/6

Strategic Air Command, Vandenberg **Air Force** Base Telephone Directory, D 301.104/7

Strategic Air Command, Wurtsmith **Air Force** Base, Telephone Directory, D 301.104/5

Systems Engineering Group, Research and Technology Division, **Air Force** Systems Command, Wright-Patterson Air Force Base, Ohio, Technical Documentary Report No. SEG TDR, D 301.45/48

Tables of Organization and Equipment, Department of the **Air Force**, M 301.7

Technical Notes Department of the **Air Force** Aeronautical Systems Division, D 301.45/26

Technical Notes Department of the **Air Force** Air Proving Ground Center, D 301.45/50

Technical Notes Department of the **Air Force** Alaskan Air Command, Arctic Aeromedical Laboratory, D 301.66

Technical Notes Department of the **Air Force** Arnold Engineering Development Center, D 301.45/33-3

Technical Notes Department of the **Air Force** Atmospheric Analysis Laboratory, D 301.45/30 3

Technical Notes Department of the **Air Force** Cambridge Research Center, D 301.45/4-2

Technical Notes Department of the **Air Force** Command and Control Development Division, D 301.45/24

Technical Notes Department of the **Air Force** Electronics Research Directorate, D 301.45/12-2

Technical Notes Department of the **Air Force** Geophysics Research Directorate, D 301.45/16-2

Technical Notes Department of the **Air Force** Meteorological Development Laboratory, D 301.45/17-2

Technical Notes Department of the **Air Force** Office of Scientific Research, D 301.45/18

Technical Notes Department of the **Air Force** Rome Air Development Center, D 301.57/2

Technical Notes Department of the **Air Force** Special Weapons Center, D 301.45/20-2

Technical Notes Department of the **Air Force** Wright Air Development Center, D 301.45/13

Technical Publications for **Air Force** Technical Libraries, Book Lists, D 301.20

Technical Research Reports Published by **Air Force** Personnel and Training Center Air Research and Development Command, D 301.26/10

U.S. **Air Force** Academy Bulletin, D 305.8/2

U.S. **Air Force** and U.S. Navy Flight Planning Document, D 301.52

U.S. **Air Force** Fine Arts Series, D 301.76/4

U.S. **Air Force** Plan for Defense Research Sciences, D 301.45/19-5

U.S. **Air Force** Policy Letter Digest, D 301.120

U.S. **Air Force** Public Affairs Staff Directory, D 301.104/4

U.S. **Air Force** Radio Facility Charts, Atlantic and Caribbean Area, M 301.15

U.S. **Air Force** Radio Facility Charts, North Pacific Area, M 301.14

U.S. **Air Force** Standards, D 301.31

U.S. Army and **Air Force** Recruiting Service Letter, M 208.76

United States **Air Force** Academy Assembly, Proceedings, D 305.11

United States **Air Force** Academy Journal of Professional Military Ethics, D 305.21

United States **Air Force** and Navy Supplementary Flight Information Document, Pacific and Far East, D 301.50

United States **Air Force** and Navy Supplementary Flight Information, Europe, Africa, and Middle East, D 301.49

United States **Air Force** and United States Navy Radio Facility Charts, Central Pacific-Far East, D 301.12

United States **Air Force** Fact Sheets, D 301.128

United States **Air Force** General Histories (series), D 301.82/3

United States **Air Force** History Program, Summary of Activities, D 301.1/2

United States **Air Force** History, a Guide to Documentary Sources, D 301.6/5:H 62

United States **Air Force** in Southeast Asia (series), D 301.86/2

United States **Air Force** Jag Law Review, D 302.9

United States **Air Force** Medical Service Digest, D 304.8

United States **Air Force** Radio Facility Charts, Caribbean and South American Area, D 301.10

United States **Air Force** Radio Facility Charts, Europe, Africa, Middle East, D 301.9

United States **Air Force** Reference Series, D 301.82/5

United States **Air Force** Special Studies, D 301.82/4

United States **Air Force**, Commands and Agencies Basic Information, D 301.26/23

United States **Air Force**, Navy, Royal Canadian **Air Force** and Royal Canadian Navy, Navy Radio Facility Charts and In- Flight Data, Alaska, Canada and North Atlantic, D 301.13/3

United States **Air Force**, Navy, Royal Canadian **Air Force** and Royal Canadian Supplementary Flight Information, North American Area (excluding Mexico and Caribbean area), D 301.48

United States **Air Force**, Navy, Royal Canadian **Air Force**, and Royal Canadian Navy Supplementary Flight Information, North American Area (excluding Mexico and Caribbean area), D 301.48

United States **Air Force**, United States Navy and Royal Canadian **Air Force** Radio Facility Charts, West Canada and Alaska, D 301.13

United States **Air Force**, United States Navy Radio Facility Charts, North Atlantic Area, D 301.11

Air Force Band

Band News from the United States **Air Force Band**, Washington, D.C., D 301.108

Air Force Base

Systems Engineering Group, Research and Technology Division, Air Force Systems Command, Wright-Patterson **Air Force Base**, Ohio, Technical Documentary Report No. SEG TDR, D 301.45/48

Air Forces

Alphabetical List Covering Army **Air Forces** and Army-Navy Aeronautical Standard Parts, W 108.15/2, M 301.11

Army **Air Forces** in World War II (series), D 301.82

Army **Air Forces** Library Bulletins, W 108.12

Army **Air Forces** Radio and Facility Charts Atlantic and Caribbean Areas, W 108.26

Army **Air Forces** Radio and Facility Charts North Pacific Area, W 108.27

Army **Air Forces** Specifications, W 108.13

Joint **Air Forces** & Navy Radio Facility Charts, M 301.16

Numerical List Covering Army **Air Forces** and Army-Navy Aeronautical Standard Parts, W 108.15

PACAF [Pacific **Air Forces**] Basic Bibliographies, D 301.62

Air Freight

Air Freight Loss and Damage Claims, C 31.265

Air Freight Loss and Damage Claims for the Six Months Ended (date), C 31.265/2

Air Freight Loss and Damage Claims, Annual Summaries, C 31.265/3

Annual Economic Report of **Air Freight** Forwarders, C 31.270

Air Line

Domestic Scheduled **Air Line** Operation Statistics, C 23.20

Air Mail

Air Mail Schedules, P 20.8

Foreign **Air Mail** Service, P 8.6

Foreign, Overseas and Territorial **Air Mail** Carriers, C 31.231

Air Material

Air Material Command: Technical Reports, D 301.67

Air Mobility

Army **Air Mobility** Research and Development Laboratory Fort Eustis Virginia: USAAMRDL Technical Reports, D 117.8/2 D 117.8/4

Air National Guard

Air National Guard Manuals, D 301.23

Air National Guard Register, D 12.9/2

Air Navigation

Air Navigation and Air Traffic Control Facility Performance and Availability Report, Calendar Year, TD 4.710

Air Navigation Development Board Releases, C 31.142/2

Air Navigation Maps, W 87.22/2

FAA Plan for **Air Navigation** and Air Traffic Control Systems, FAA 1.37

Air Passenger

U.S. International **Air Passenger** and Freight Statistics, Calendar Year, TD 1.40/4

Air Patrol

Civil **Air Patrol** Bulletins, Pr 32.4424

Civil **Air Patrol** Manuals, CAPM (series), D 301.7/4

Civil **Air Patrol** Pamphlet CAPP (series), D 301.35/2

Civil **Air Patrol** Training Manuals, Pr 32.4412

Air Pollution

Air Pollution Abstracts, EP 4.11

Air Pollution Aspects of Emission Sources: [various subjects], a Bibliography with Abstracts, EP 1.21/5

Air **Pollution** Control Office Publications APTD (series), EP 4.9/2

Air Pollution Control Office Publications, AP (series), EP 4.9

Air Pollution Report, Federal Facilities, Air Quality Control Regions, EP 4.10

Air Pollution Technical Publications of the U.S. Environmental Protection Agency, Quarterly Bulletin, EP 1.21/8

Air Pollution Training Courses, (year) and University Training Programs, Extramural Programs, Institute for **Air Pollution** Training Planning and Special Projects, EP 4.13

Air Pollution, Sulfur Oxides Pollution Control, Federal Research and Development, Planning and Programming, FS 2.93/4

Air Pollution, Sulfur Oxides Pollution Control, Federal Research and Development, Planning and Programming, FS 2.93/4

Chronological Schedule, Institute of **Air Pollution** Training Courses, EP 4.14/2

Compendium of State **Air Pollution** Control Agencies, 1972, EP 1.2:St 2/972

Digest of State **Air Pollution** Laws, FS 2.93

Air Quality
Air Pollution Report, Federal Facilities, **Air Quality** Control Regions, EP 4.10
Air Quality Criteria (series), EP 1.53/2
Air Quality Data from National Air Surveillance Networks and Contributing State and Local Networks, FS 2.307
Air Quality Data, (date) Quarter Statistics, EP 1.53
Annual Report of Secretary of Health, Education, and Welfare to Congress in Compliance with Public Law 90-148, **Air Quality** Act of 1967, FS 1.35
Directory of **Air Quality** Monitoring Sites Active in (year), EP 1.2:Ai 7/5

Air Research
Air Research and Development Command: Technical Reports, ARDC-TR , D 301.45/21

Air Reservist
Air Reservist, D 301.8

Air Resources
Air Resources Atmospheric Turbulence and Diffusion Laboratory: Annual Report, C 55.621

AIRS
AIRS Executive+, EP 4.27
AIRS Executive Plus, EP 4.30

Air Sea
Air Sea Rescue Bulletin, N 24.35, T 47.32

Air Service
Army Postal and Navy **Air Service** Laws [March 2 1913], Y 1.2:Ai 7
Changes in **Air Service** Information Circular, W 87.11/3
Domestic **Air Service** Instructions, P 1.31/7:31/3
Laws relating to Commercial **Air Service** and Miscellaneous Air Laws, Y 1.2:Ai 7

Air Staff
Air Staff Historical Study (series), D 301.82/6

Air Surveillance
Air Quality Data from National **Air Surveillance** Networks and Contributing State and Local Networks, FS 2.307

Air Taxi
Air Taxi Operators and Commerical Operators of Small Aircraft, TD 4.6:part 135
Analysis of Accidents Involving **Air Taxi** Operations, U.S. General Aviation, TD 1.113/4
Briefs of Accidents Involving **Air Taxi** Operations U.S. General Aviation, TD 1.109/3

Air Traffic
Air Traffic Patterns for IFR and VFR Aviation, Calendar Year, TD 4.19/2
Air Traffic Survey [maps], C 31.218
ANC Procedures for Control of **Air Traffic**, C 31.106/2
Enroute IFR **Air Traffic** Survey, C 31.165, FAA 3.11
Enroute IFR **Air Traffic** Survey, Peak Day, TD 4.19/3
Federal Airways **Air Traffic** Activity, C 31.158
Great Lakes Region **Air Traffic** Activity, TD 4.19/5
Military **Air Traffic** Activity Report, TD 4.19/4

Air Traffic Control
Activities at **Air Traffic Control** Facilities, Fiscal Year, FAA 1.27/2
Air Traffic Control Handbook, TD 4.308:Ai 7/3
Air Traffic Control Procedures, FAA 3.9
FAA Plan for Air Navigation and **Air Traffic Control** Systems, FAA 1.37
Marine **Air Traffic Control** Detachment Handbook, PCN nos, D 214.9/7

Air Training
Air Training, D 301.38
Air Training Command, Miscellaneous Publications, D 301.38/3

Air Transport
Air Transport Economics in Jet Age, Staff Research Reports, C 31.250

Air Transportation
Defense **Air Transportation** Administrative Orders, C 1.8/2

Air Travel
Certification and Operations; **Air Travel** and Clubs Using Large Airplanes, TD 4.6:part 123

Air University
Air University Catalog, D 301.26/16

Air University Compendium of Research Topics, D 301.26/3-2
Air University Documentary Research Study, Publications, D 301.26/3
Air University Library Index to Military Periodicals, D 301.26/2
Air University Library Master List of Periodicals, D 301.26/2-2
Air University Publications, D 301.26/6
Air University Review, D 301.26
Air University, AFROTC [text books], D 301.26/12
Air University, Human Resources Research Institute, Research Memorandum, D 301.26/7
Air University, Human Resources Research Institute, Research Memorandum, D 301.26/7
Air University, School of Aviation Medicine: [publications], D 301.26/13-2
Air University: Handbooks, Manuals, Guides, D 301.26/6-8
Extension Course Institute, **Air University**: Career Development Course, D 301.26/17-2

Air War
Air War in Indochina (series), D 301.93

Air Waves
Air Waves, Y 3.Ai 7/5:9

Air Weather Service
Air Weather Service Manual, D 301.27
Air Weather Service, Technical Reports, D 301.40
Air Weather Service: Bibliography, D 301.42
Air Weather Service: Training Guides, D 301.39

Air-conditioning
Warm-Air Furnaces, Winter **Air-conditioning** Systems, and Accessory Equipment, C 3.144

Air-Cured
Dark **Air-Cured** Tobacco Market Review, A 88.34/3
Fire-Cured and Dark **Air-Cured** Tobacco Market Review, A 88.34/8

Air-Mail
Domestic Helicopter Service, Certificated **Air-Mail** Carriers, C 31.229/4

Air-mail Carriers
Abstract of Reports of Free and Reduced-Fare Transportation Rendered by **Air-mail Carriers**, IC 1 air.7

Airborne
Airborne Anomaly Location Maps, Y 3.At 7:31
Airborne Instrumentation Research Project Summary Catalog, NAS 1.68
U.S. **Airborne** Exports and General Imports, Shipping Weight and Value, C 3.164:986
United States **Airborne** Exports of Domestic and Foreign Merchandise, Commodity (Schedule X) by Country of Destination, C 3.164:780
United States **Airborne** Exports of Domestic and Foreign Merchandise, Country of Destination by Commodity, C 3.164:790
United States **Airborne** Foreign Trade, Customs District by Continent, C 3.164:986
United States **Airborne** General Imports of Merchandise, Country of Origin by Commodity, C 3.164:390

Aircraft
Acceptable Methods, Techniques, and Practices: **Aircraft** Alterations, TD 4.28, TD 4.28/2
Acceptable Methods, Techniques, and Practices: **Aircraft** Inspection and Repair, FAA 5.15, TD 4.28/2
Air Taxi Operators and Commerical Operators of Small **Aircraft**, TD 4.6:part 135
Aircraft Accident and Maintenance Review, D 301.58
Aircraft Accident Reports, TD 1.112
Aircraft Accident Reports NTSB-AAR (series), TD 1.112
Aircraft Accident Reports, Brief Format, U.S. Civil Aviation, NTSB-BA (series), TD 1.109/13
Aircraft Alterations, FAA 5.16
Aircraft Certification Directory, TD 4.52/3
Aircraft Certification Service International Strategic Plan, TD 4.915
Aircraft Circulars, Y 3.N 21/5:9
Aircraft Emergency Evacuation Reports, C 31.150
Aircraft Emergency Procedures Over Water, T 47.32/2
Aircraft Engine and Propeller Type Certificate Data Sheets and Specifications, TD 4.15/2

Aircraft Engine Listing and Propeller Listing, C 31.120/3
Aircraft Flash, D 301.47
Aircraft in Agriculture, FAA 1.33
Aircraft Instrument Approaches, Fiscal Year, FAA 1.40
Aircraft Instrument Bulletin, Flowmeter Series, Flowmeter Bulletins, N 28.19
Aircraft Instrument Bulletins, N 28.10, M 208.9
Aircraft Observer, D 301.38/4
Aircraft Operating Cost and Performance Report, CAB 1.22, CAB 1.22/2, C 31.259
Aircraft Plotting Sheets, N 6.30
Aircraft Registration, TD 4.6:part 47
Aircraft Specifications, C 31.120/2, FAA 1.29
Aircraft Type Certificate Data Sheets and Specifications, TD 4.15
Aircraft Utilization and Propulsion Reliability Report, TD 4.59
Airworthiness Standards, **Aircraft** Engines, TD 4.6:part 33
Analysis of **Aircraft** Accident Data, U.S. Air Carrier Operations, TD 1.113/5
Analysis of **Aircraft** Accident Data, U.S. General Aviation, TD 1.113/3
Annual Review of **Aircraft** Accident Data, U.S. Air Carrier Operations, TD 1.113/5
Annual Review of **Aircraft** Accident Data, U.S. General Aviation, TD 1.113
Audit of Payments from Special Bank Account to Lockheed **Aircraft** Corporation for C-5a Aircraft Program Defense Department, GA 1.13:L 81/2
Briefs of Accidents Involving (various) **Aircraft**, TD 1.109/2
Briefs of Accidents Involving Amateur Built (homebuilt) **Aircraft** U.S. General Aviation, TD 1.109/6
Briefs of Accidents Involving Corporate-Executive **Aircraft** U.S. General Aviation, TD 1.109/10
Briefs of Accidents Involving Missing **Aircraft** U.S. General Aviation, TD 1.109/8
Briefs of **Aircraft** Accidents Involving Turbine Powered **Aircraft** U.S. General Aviation Calendar Year NTSB-AMM (series), TD 1.109/14
Budget Estimates; **Aircraft** and Missile Procurement, D 301.83/2
Census of U.S. Civil **Aircraft** As of December 31, (year), TD 4.18
Certification and Operations; Air Carriers and Commercial Operators of Large **Aircraft**, TD 4.6:part 121
Certification and Operations; Land Airports Serving CAB-Certificated Scheduled Air Carriers Operating Large **Aircraft**, TD 4.6:part 139
Civil **Aircraft** by States and by Counties with States, C 31.132
Current Listing of **Aircraft** Bonds, T 17.19/2
Encyclopedia of U.S. Air Force **Aircraft** and Missile Systems, D 301.90
FAA **Aircraft** Program Data Feedback, TD 4.410
Federal **Aircraft** Noise Abatement Plan, Fiscal Year, TD 1.16
General Aviation **Aircraft** Use, FAA 1.39
General Summary of Inventory Status and Movement of Capital and Producers Goods, Plants, **Aircraft**, and Industry Agent Items, Pr 33.210
Index and User Guide Vol. 1, Airworthiness Directives Small **Aircraft**, TD 4.10/5
Index and User Guide Vol. 2, Airworthiness Directives Large **Aircraft**, TD 4.10/5-2
Listing of **Aircraft** Accidents/incidents by Make and Model, U.S. Civil Aviation, TD 1.109/15
Local Service Air Carrier, Selected Flight Load Data by City Pair, by Frequency Grouping, by **Aircraft** Type, C 31.253/2
Military and Civil Aircraft and **Aircraft** Engine Production, Monthly Production Report, C 31.130
Noise Standards, **Aircraft** Type and Airworthiness Certification, TD 4.6:part 36
Preliminary Analysis of **Aircraft** Accident Data, U.S. Civil Aviation, TD 1.113/6
Reports of Investigations of Accidents Involving Civil **Aircraft**, C 31.213
Resume of U.S. Civil Air Carrier and General Aviation **Aircraft** Accidents, Calendar Year, C 31.244

Rules Pertaining to **Aircraft** Accidents, Incidents, Overdue **Aircraft**, and Safety Investigations, TD 1.106/2

Specifications, International **Aircraft** Standards, C 13.9

Statistical Study of U.S. Civil **Aircraft**, C 31.160, FAA 1.32/2

Summary of Airworthiness Directives for Large **Aircraft**, TD 4.10/3

Summary of Airworthiness Directives for Small **Aircraft**, FAA 1.28/2

United States Active Civil **Aircraft** by State and County, C 31.132/2, FAA 1.35

United States Civil **Aircraft** Register, TD 4.18/2

USAF Historical **Aircraft** Photopaks, D 301.76/2

Airfields

Directory of **Airfields**, U.S. Army & Navy, C 31.126

U.S. Army and Navy Directory of **Airfields**, C 31.125

Airframe

Airframe and Equipment Engineering Reports, C 31.156

Airlift

Airlift, the Journal of the Airlift Operations School, D 301.56/5

Airline

Airline Industry Economic Report, CAB 1.18, C 31.260

Airline Traffic Survey, C 31.225

Handbook of **Airline** Statistics, C 31.249

Reports on **Airline** Service, Fares Traffic, Load Factors and Market Shares, CAB 1.27

To Mayor of Each City with Local **Airline** Service, C 31.256

Secretary's Task Force on Competition in the U.S. Domestic **Airline** Industry, TD 1.57

Airmail

Advertisement for **Airmail** Service, P 1.24/3

Advertisement for Temporary **Airmail** Service, P 1.24/2

Recurrent Report of Mileage and Traffic Data Domestic Helicopter Service, Certificated **Airmail** Carriers, C 31.229/4

Airman

Airman, Official Journal of the Air Force, D 301.60

Citizen **Airman**, D 301.8

Life of Soldier and **Airman**, D 102.77

Soldier, Sailor, **Airman**, Marine (SAM), D 1.55

Airman's

Airman's Guide, C 31.127, C 31.136, FAA 1.23

Airman's Guide and Flight Information Manual, FAA 1.25/2

Airman's Guide and Flight Information Manual; Pacific Supplement, FAA 1.25

Airman's Guide; Pacific Supplement, FAA 1.25/3

Airman's Information Manual, TD 4.12, TD 4.12/3

Alaska **Airman's** Guide, C 31.135, FAA 1.24

Alaska **Airman's** Guide and Chart Supplement, TD 4.16/2

Pacific **Airman's** Guide and Chart Supplement, TD 4.16

Airmen

Certification; **Airmen** other than Flight Crewmembers, TD 4.6:part 65

International Notices to **Airmen**, TD 4.11

Notices to **Airmen**, TD 4.12/2

Special Notices to **Airmen**, CA 1.7/2, C 31.10, C 31.110

Weekly Notices to **Airmen**, C 23.15, CA 1.7, C 31.9, C 31.109

Airnews

Domestic **Airnews**, C 23.9

Airplane

Advertisements Inviting Proposals for Carrying Mails by **Airplane** or Seaplane, P 1.24

Airplanes

Airworthiness Standards, Normal, Utility, and Acrobatic Category **Airplanes**, TD 4.6:part 23

Airworthiness Standards, Transport Category **Airplanes**, TD 4.6:part 25

Certification and Operations; Air Travel and Clubs Using Large **Airplanes**, TD 4.6:part 123

Airport

Airport Activity Statistics on Certificated Route Air Carriers, C 31.251, TD 4.14

Airport Aid Program, TD 4.6:part 152

Airport Bulletins, C 23.7/3

Airport Design Manual, FAA 4.9/3

Airport Design Standards, TD 4.8/4, TD 4.111

Airport/Facility Directory, TD 4.79

Airport Management Series, C 31.137

Airport Obstruction Charts, C 55.411/3

Airport Obstruction Plans, C 4.9/11

Airport Planning, C 31.145

Annual Report of Accomplishments Under the **Airport** Improvement Program, TD 4.61

Annual Report of Operations Under the **Airport** and Airway Development Act, TD 4.22/2

Annual Report of Operations Under the Federal **Airport** Act, TD 4.22

Climatography of the United States; **Airport** Climatological Summary, C 55.286/3

Concorde Monitoring; Dulles International **Airport**, TD 4.49

Concorde Monitoring; John F. Kennedy International **Airport**, TD 4.49/2

Eastern United States, Dates of Latest Prints, Instrument Approach Procedure Charts and **Airport** Obstruction Plans (OP), C 4.9/19

Federal-Aid **Airport** Program Publications, FAA 8.10

Flight Information Publication: **Airport**/Facility Directory, C 55.416/2

Latest Editions, **Airport** Obstruction Charts, C 55.411/3-2

National **Airport** Plan, Fiscal Years [dates], TD 4.109

National Plan of Integrated **Airport** Systems, TD 4.63

Profiles of Scheduled Air Carrier **Airport** Operations by Equipment Type, Top 100 U.S. Airports, TD 4.44/4

Profiles of Scheduled Air Carrier **Airport** Operations, Top 100 U.S. Airports, TD 4.44

Publications Federal-Aid **Airport** Program, FAA 8.10

Report of President's **Airport** Commission, Pr 33.16

Special Air Traffic Rules and **Airport** Traffic Patterns, TD 4.6:part 93

Western United States, Dates of Latest Prints, Instrument Approach Procedure Charts and **Airport** Obstruction Plans, C 4.9/20

Airports

Airports Service, Standards Division Index of Advisory Circulars, TD 4.110

Certification and Operations; Land **Airports** Serving CAB-Certificated Scheduled Air Carriers Operating Large Aircraft, TD 4.6:part 139

Directory of **Airports** and Seaplane Bases, Airman's Guide Supplement, FAA 1.23/2

Profiles of Scheduled Air Carrier Airport Operations by Equipment Type, Top 100 U.S. **Airports**, TD 4.44/4

Profiles of Scheduled Air Carrier Airport Operations, Top 100 U.S. **Airports**, TD 4.44

Profiles of Scheduled Air Carrier Passenger Traffic, Top 100 U.S. **Airports**, TD 4.44/2

Standard Specifications for Construction of **Airports**, TD 4.24

Standards for Specifying Construction of **Airports**, TD 4.24

Airpower

Airpower Journal (Hispanoamericana), D 201.26/24-3

Airpower Journal (Portuguese), D 301.26/24-2

School of Advanced **Airpower** Studies, D 301.26/6-9

AIRS

AIRS Executive+, EP 4.27

AIRSExecutive

AIRSExecutive PLUS, EP 4.30

Airspace

Area Planning Special Use **Airspace** North America and South America, D 5.318/5-3

Airway

Airway Bulletin, C 23.7

Airway Maps, C 23.10

Annual Report of Operations Under the Airport and **Airway** Development Act, TD 4.22/2

Demographic Profiles of the **Airway** Facilities Work Force, TD 4.65

Federal **Airway** Plan, C 31.167

National **Airway** System Annual Report, TD 4.57/3

Airways

Airways Operating and Training Series Bulletins, C 31.141

Federal **Airways** Air Traffic Activity, C 31.158

Federal **Airways** Manual of Operations, C 31.116/2

Office of Federal **Airways** Maintenance Engineering Division Newsletter, C 31.149

Airworthiness

Airworthiness Directive Summary, C 31.145

Airworthiness Standards, Aircraft Engines, TD 4.6:part 33

Airworthiness Standards, Normal, Utility, and Acrobatic Category Airplanes, TD 4.6:part 23

Airworthiness Standards, Transport Category Airplanes, TD 4.6:part 25

Annual Review, **Airworthiness** Civil Air Regulations Meeting, C 31.245

CAA **Airworthiness** Directive, C 31.147/2

FAA **Airworthiness** Directive, TD 4.10

Federal Aviation Administration **Airworthiness** Directives, TD 4.10/4

General Aviation **Airworthiness** Alerts, TD 4.414

Index and User Guide Vol. 1, **Airworthiness** Directives Small Aircraft, TD 4.10/5

Index and User Guide Vol. 2, **Airworthiness** Directives Large Aircraft, TD 4.10/5-2

Noise Standards, Aircraft Type and **Airworthiness** Certification, TD 4.6:part 36

Summary of **Airworthiness** Directives for Large Aircraft, TD 4.10/3

Summary of **Airworthiness** Directives for Small Aircraft, FAA 1.28/2

Summary of **Airworthiness** Directives, TD 4.10/2

Tentative **Airworthiness** Standards, TD 4.411

Akten

Akten Zur Deutschen Auswartigen Politic, S 1.82/2

AL

Aerospace Leaflets, **AL** (series), NAS 1.23

Technical Documentary Report **AL**-TDR- (series), D 301.45/45

ALA

ALA Catalog, LC 1.9

ALA Portrait Index, LC 1.10

Alabama

Fish Monitoring Investigations, Browns Ferry Nuclear Plant, Wheeler Reservoir, **Alabama**, Y 3.T 25:37

Geneva Arbitration (**Alabama** Claims), S 3.13/1

Medicare Hospital Mortality Information: Vol. 1, **Alabama** - California, HE 22.34

Alaska

Alaska 1:250,000-Scale Series (maps), I 19.99

Alaska Agricultural Experiment Station, A 77.440

Alaska Agriculture Statistics, A 92.48

Alaska Airman's Guide, C 31.135, FAA 1.24

Alaska Airman's Guide and Chart Supplement, TD 4.16/2

Alaska Conveyance News, I 53.37

Alaska Farm Reporter, A 92.45

Alaska Fisheries, C 55.309/2

Alaska Flight Information Manual, C 31.134, FAA 1.21

Alaska Forest Research Center, A 13.73

Alaska Game Commission, Circulars, I 49.12

Alaska Gas Pipeline Update, Y 3.F 31/23:9

Alaska Native Medical Center: Annual Report, HE 20.5311

Alaska Railroad Records, I 1.59/5

Alaska Railroad, Local Passenger Tariffs, I 35.10/7

Alaska Railroad, Press Releases, I 1.82/2

Alaska Reconnaissance Topographic Series, I 19.41

Alaska Region Leaflets, A 13.103/2

Alaska Region Reports, A 13.103

Alaska Region-Ten Year Plan, TD 4.56

Alaska Resources Development Studies, I 68.9

Alaska Road Commission, I 35.10/21

Alaska Snow Survey, Annual Data Summary, A 57.46/13-3

Alaska Summary Report, I 72.9/3-2

Alaska Summary/Index, I 72.9/6

Alaska Technical Report, I 53.28

Alaska Terminal Charts, C 55.416/4

Alaska Water Laboratory Quarterly Research Reports, EP 1.22/2

Alaska Water Laboratory, College, Alaska: Reports, EP 1.22

Alaska, Governor, Annual Report, I 1.5

Annual Report on **Alaska** Railroad, TD 1.10/8

Annual Reports of Governor of **Alaska** on **Alaska** Game Law, A 5.7

Annual Waterfowl Report **Alaska**, I 49.55

BLM-**Alaska** Frontiers, 1.53.41/2

BLM: **Alaska** Technical Reports, I 53.49

Briefing Book, **Alaska** Region, A 13.156
Census of Housing: Detailed Housing Characteristics for American Indian and **Alaska** Native Areas, C 3.224/3-5
Census of Housing: General Housing Characteristics for American Indian and **Alaska** Native Areas, C 3.224/3-2
Census of Nurses Employed for Public Health Work in United States, in Territories of **Alaska** and Hawaii, and in Puerto Rico and Virgin Islands, FS 2.81
Census of Population: General Population Characteristics for American Indian and **Alaska** Native Areas, C 3.223/6-2
Census of Population: Social and Economic Characteristics for American Indian and **Alaska** Native Areas, C 3.223/7-2
Certificated Air Carrier Financial Data; Territorial Intra-**Alaska** and Other **Alaska** [quarterly comparisons], C 31.243
Certificated Air Carrier Financial Data; Territorial Intra-**Alaska** and Other Than **Alaska** [12-month comparisons], C 31.243/2
Climatological Data; **Alaska** Section, A 29.33, C 30.21
CRREL in **Alaska**, Annual Report (year), D 103.33/8
Dictionary of **Alaska** Place Names, I 19.16:567
Fisheries of the United States and **Alaska**, a Preliminary Review, I 49.28
Geologic Studies in **Alaska** by the U.S. Geological Survey, I 19.4/8
Geological Studies in **Alaska** by the U.S. Geological Survey, I 19.4/3
Harriman **Alaska** Series, SI 1.11
IFR Enroute High Altitude Charts (**Alaska**), TD 4.49/17-2
IFR Enroute Low Altitude (**Alaska**), TD 4.79/16
Indian and **Alaska** Native Housing and Community Development Programs, Annual Report to Congress, HH 1.80
Instrument Approach Procedure Charts [**Alaska**, Hawaii, U.S. Pacific Islands], C 55.411/2
Laws and Regulations for Protection of Commercial Fisheries of **Alaska**, I 45.11
Lexicon of Geologic Names of the United States, Including **Alaska**, I 19.3:896
Manuscript Reports Issued by Biological Laboratory, Auke Bay, **Alaska**, I 49.57
Military Aviation Notices; Corrections to Enroute-Low Altitude-**Alaska**, D 301.13/4
Military Aviation Notices; West Canada and **Alaska**, D 301.13/2
Mine Inspector for Territory of **Alaska**, Annual Reports, I 28.9
Pacific and Arctic Coasts, **Alaska**, Cape Spencer to Beaufort Sea, C 55.422:9
Pacific Coast, **Alaska**, Dixon Entrance to Cape Spencer, C 55.422:8
Pacific Northwest and **Alaska** Bioenergy Program Yearbook, E 5.12
Press Releases **Alaska** Railroad, I 1.82/2
Report on Salmon Fisheries of **Alaska**, T 35.6
Reports and Statistical Tables on Fur-Seal Investigations in **Alaska**, T 35.7
Schedule H. Statistical Classification and Code Numbers of Shipments of Merchandise to **Alaska** from United States, C 3.150:H
Service and Regulatory Announcements **Alaska** Game Commission, A 5.10/5
Snow Surveys and Water Supply Outlook for **Alaska**, A 57.46/13
Snow Surveys for **Alaska**, A 57.46/13
Statistical Classification and Code Numbers of Shipments of Merchandise to **Alaska** from United States, C 3.150:H
Status Report of the Operation and Maintenance of Sanitation Facilities Serving American Indians and **Alaska** Natives, HE 20.9416
Supplement **Alaska**, TD 4.79/2
Supplemental Tidal Predictions, Anchorage, Nikishka, Seldovia, and Valdez, **Alaska**, C 55.432
U.S. Coast Pilots **Alaska**, C 4.7/2, C 4.7/3, C 4.7/7
United States Air Force, Navy, Royal Canadian Air Force and Royal Canadian Navy, Navy Radio Facility Charts and In-Flight Data, **Alaska**, Canada and North Atlantic, D 301.13/3

United States Air Force, United States Navy and Royal Canadian Air Force Radio Facility Charts, West Canada and **Alaska**, D 301.13
United States Coast Pilot, Pacific Coast, **Alaska**, pt. 1, Dixon Entrance to Yakutat Bay, T 11.7/2
Alaska Natives
Dental Services for American Indians and **Alaska Natives**, HE 20.2659, HE 20.5309
Alaska Snow
Alaska Snow Surveys and Federal-State Private Cooperative Surveys, A 57.46/13
Alaska's
Annual Report on **Alaska's** Mineral Resources, I 19.4/4
Alaskan
Alaskan Air Command, Arctic Aeromedical Laboratory: Technical Notes, D 301.66
Alaskan Boundary Tribunal, 1903, S 3.16/2
Alaskan Engineering Commission, Alaska Railroad Record, I 1.59/5
Alaskan-Canadian Boundary Commission, 1892n95, S 3.16/1
Environmental Assessment of the **Alaskan** Continental Shelf, C 55.622/2
Environmental Assessment of the **Alaskan** Continental Shelf [various publications], C 55.622/3
Environmental Assessment of the **Alaskan** Continental Shelf, Principal Investigator's Reports, C 55.622
Technical Notes Department of the Air Force **Alaskan** Air Command, Arctic Aeromedical Laboratory, D 301.66
Albanian
Directory of **Albanian** Officials, PrEx 3.10/7-23
Album
Treasury of Stamps **Album**, School Year (date), P 1.49
Albuquerque
Daily Weather and River Bulletin [Albuquerque, New Mexico Area], C 55.110/4
Alcohol
Alcohol and Health Notes, HE 20.8309/2
Alcohol and Tobacco Newsletter, T 70.18/2
Alcohol and Tobacco Summary Statistics, Distilled Spirits, Wine, Beer, Tobacco, Enforcement Taxes, Fiscal Year, T 70.9
Alcohol and Tobacco, Summary Statistics, T 22.43
Alcohol and You, HSMHA Employee Health Program on Alcoholism, HE 20.2711
Alcohol Fuels Programs Technical Review, E 1.80/2
Alcohol Health and Research World, HE 20.2430, HE 20.3813, HE 20.8309
Alcohol Research and Health HE 22.616
Alcohol, Drug Abuse, Mental Health Research Grant Awards, HE 20.8016, HE 20.8118
Alcohol, Tobacco and Firearms Cumulative Bulletin, T 70.7/2
Alcohol, Tobacco, and Firearms, T 70.7
Annual Report on Public Information and Education Countermeasure of **Alcohol** Safety Action Projects, TD 8.20
Briefs of Accidents Involving **Alcohol** As a Cause-Factor U.S. General Aviation, TD 1.109/9
Memorandum on Women's **Alcohol**, Drug Abuse, and Mental Health Issues, HE 20.8019
Posters **Alcohol**, Drug Abuse, and Mental Health Administration, HE 20.8014
Prevention Activities of the **Alcohol**, Drug Abuse, and Mental Health Administration, HE 20.8018
Proceedings Annual Alcoholism Conference of the National Institute on **Alcohol** Abuse and Alcoholism, HE 20.2430/2
Regulations, **Alcohol** Tax Unit, T 22.17/2
Report to the United States Congress on Federal Activities on **Alcohol** Abuse and Alcoholism, HE 20.8316
Review of **Alcohol** as a Cause Factor, TD 1.129
Special Report to the U.S. Congress on **Alcohol** and Health, HE 20.8313
State Resources and Services for **Alcohol** and Drug Abuse Problems, HE 20.8319
Statistical Compendium on **Alcohol** and Health, HE 20.8317
Summary Proceedings of ADAMHA Annual Conference of the State and Territorial **Alcohol**, Drug Abuse, and Mental Health Authorities, HE 20.8011

U.S. **Alcohol** Epidemologic Data Reference Manual, HE 20.8308/3
Youth Fatal Crash and **Alcohol** Facts, TD 8.39
Alcohol Abuse
Announcement, National Institute on **Alcohol Abuse** and Alcoholism, HE 20.8318
Alcoholics
Directory of Halfway Houses for the Mentally Ill and **Alcoholics**, HE 20.2402:H 13
Alcoholism
Alcohol and You, HSMHA Employee Health Program on **Alcoholism**, HE 20.2711
Announcement, National Institute on Alcohol Abuse and **Alcoholism**, HE 20.8318
Annual **Alcoholism** Conference of the National Institute on Alcohol Abuse and **Alcoholism**, Proceedings, HE 20.8314
International Congress Against **Alcoholism**, S 5.20
National Directory of Drug Abuse and **Alcoholism** Treatment and Prevention Programs, HE 20.8320, HE 20.410/3
Proceedings Annual **Alcoholism** Conference of the National Institute on Alcohol Abuse and **Alcoholism**, HE 20.2430/2
Report to the United States Congress on Federal Activities on Alcohol Abuse and **Alcoholism**, HE 20.8316
Alert
Administrator's **Alert**, CS 1.79
Advertising **Alert**, FT 1.24
Alert (series), D 2.16
Alert, Administrative News Highlights for Supervisors, A 1.129/2
Alert Bulletin, L 35.24/2
Alert Sheets, Y 3.C 76/3:11-3
Cancer **Alert** Series, L 35.22
Chem **Alert**, L 35.27
Civil Defense **Alert**, FCD 1.8
Consumer **Alert**, FT 1.24/2
EP**Alert**, to **Alert** You to Important Events, EP 1.7/6
FCC Actions **Alert**, CC 1.49
Food Marketing **Alert**, A 88.37/3
Foreign Technology **Alert**: Bibliography (series), C 51.13/3
General Maintenance **Alert** Bulletins, C 31.163/2, FAA 1.31/2
Issue **Alert** (series), SBA 1.41
Mental Health Emergencies **Alert**, HE 20.8113/2
Monthly **Alert**, A 13.123
National Consumer Buying **Alert**, Pr 39.14
NIOSH **Alert**, HE 20.7123
Pest **Alert** (NA-TP series), A 13.52/10-4
Westfornet Monthly **Alert**, A 13.108
Alerts
FDA Safety **Alerts** (on various subjects), HE 20.4616
General Aviation Airworthiness **Alerts**, TD 4.414
OCC **Alerts**, T 12.21
Alexandria, Virginia
Guides to German Records Microfilmed at **Alexandria, Virginia**, GS 4.18
Alfalfa
Alfalfa, A 92.19/14
Alfalfa Improvement Conferences, Reports, A 19.30
Alfalfa Meal Production, A 82.59/2, A 88.18/5
Alfalfa Seed, A 105.18/5
Report of **Alfalfa** Improvement Conference, A 77.531
Technical **Alfalfa** Conference, Proceedings, A 77.15:74
Alien
Where to Write for Birth and Death Records of U.S. Citizens Who Were Born or Died Outside of the United States and Birth Certifications for **Alien** Children Adopted by U.S. Citizens, FS 2.102:B 53/7
Aliens
Annual Indicators of Immigration into the United States of **Aliens** in Professional and Related Occupations, J 21.15
Alimony
Child Support and **Alimony**, Current Population Reports, C 3.186/4
ALJ
ALJ Decisions, Y 3.OC 1:10-5
All
All Participants Memoranda, HH 1.23/8, HH 1.37/4

All Hands
All Hands, Bureau of Naval Personnel Career
Publications, D 208.3
All Hands, Bureau of Naval Personnel Information
Bulletin, D 207.17
All Points
All Points Bulletin, the Army Financial
Management Newsletter, D 101.96
All-Cargo
Trends in Scheduled **All-Cargo** Service, C 31.264/
2
All-Risk
All-Risk Update, A 62.13
All-Union
News of **All-Union** Geographical Society, C 41.46/
6
All-volunteer
President's Commission on **All-volunteer** Armed
Forces, Pr 37.8:Ar 5
Alleghaney
Alleghaney and Monongahela Rivers, D 103.66/4
Navigation Charts; **Alleghaney** and Monongahela
Rivers, D 103.66/4
Allen Park
VA Medical Center, **Allen Park**, Michigan:
Newsletter, VA 1.56/5
Allergic
Allergic Diseases Research (series), HE 20.3262
Annual Workshop of the Asthma and **Allergic**
Disease Centers, HE 20.3261
Allergy
Allergy and Immunology Study Section, HE
20.3001/2:Al 5
Highlights of Research Progress in **Allergy** and
Infectious Diseases, FS 2.22/17
Intramural Research, Annual Report: National
Institute of **Allergy** and Infectious
Diseases, HE 20.3211/3
Allied
Allied High Commission, Germany, Publications,
Non-govt, S 5.53
Chemicals and **Allied** Products Entered for
Consumption, C 18.55
Gazette of the **Allied** Commission for Austria, D
102.22
Industry Report, Chemicals and **Allied** Products, C
18.235
Lumber Manufacturing, Wood Using and **Allied**
Associations, A 13.77
Official Gazette **Allied** High Commission for
Germany, S 1.88
Official Gazette of **Allied** High Commission for
Germany, S 1.88
Publications Supreme **Allied** Commander in
Europe, D 9.8
Publications Supreme Commander for **Allied**
Powers, D 102.11
Recent Articles on Petroleum and **Allied**
Substances, I 28.22
Report of United States High Commissioner,
Statistical Annex, U.S. Element, **Allied**
Commission for Austria, S 1.89/2
Report of United States High Commissioner, U.S.
Element, **Allied** Commission for Austria,
S 1.89
Supreme Commander for **Allied** Powers,
Publications, D 102.11
Supreme Commander for **Allied** Powers: Japanese
Economic Statistics Bulletin, D 102.18
Supreme Commander for **Allied** Powers: Natural
Resources Section Reports, D 102.20
Textiles and **Allied** Products, C 18.150
Underware and **Allied** Products, C 3.113
World Trade Notes on Chemicals and **Allied**
Products, C 18.179
Allied Forces
Official Road Maps for **Allied Forces** Europe, Series
M305, D 5.342
Allied Trades
Current Distribution Developments in Hardware
and **Allied Trades**, C 18.215
Allocation
Alphabetical Listing, Register or Planned
Mobilization Producers, Manufacturers
of War Material Registered Under
Production **Allocation** Program, D 7.11
Commercial Resource **Allocation** Guides [for
various countries], C 1.64/2
Allocations
Port **Allocations** of [various commodities], A 82.86
Allotments
Allotments, Authorizations, and Paid Shipments,
Data, FO 1.9/2

Procurement Authorization and **Allotments**,
European and Far East Programs, FO 1.8
Procurement Authorization and **Allotments**, Pr
33.908
Report on Funding Levels and **Allocations** of
Funds, TD 7.20
Allowance
Allowance of Articles under Cognizance of Bureau
of Construction and Repair for Vessels of
the Navy, N 4.5
Experimental Housing **Allowance** Program, Annual
Report, HH 1.54
Readjustment **Allowance** Activities, VA 1.24
Standardized Government Civilian **Allowance**
Regulations, **Allowance** Circulars, S
1.76
Summary of Prescribed Unit Costs and Hourly Rate
for Return on Investment and Tax
Allowance, C 31.272, CAB 1.10
Supply Table of Medical Department, Navy, with
Allowance for Ships, N 10.8
Unemployment **Allowance** Claims and Payment
Data by Agencies, VA 1.36
Allowances
Allowances for Vessels of the Navy, N 5.5
Basic Tables of Commissioning **Allowances**, N
28.15
GAO Policy and Procedures Manual for Guidance
of Federal Agencies: Title 6, Pay, Leave,
and **Allowances**, GA 1.6/6
Maximum Travel Per Diem **Allowances** for Foreign
Areas, S 1.76/3-2
Tables of **Allowances**, W 1.28, M 101.29, D 101.23
Tables of Basic **Allowances**, W 1.27
U.S. Department of State Indexes of Living Costs
Abroad and Living Quarters **Allow-
ances**, L 2.101
U.S. Department of State Indexes of Living Costs
Abroad and Quarters **Allowances**, April,
L 2.101/2
Alloy
Alloy Development for Irradiation Performance, E
1.64
Aluminum **Alloy** Ingot, Monthly Reports, I 28.71
Annual Survey on Certain Stainless Steel and
Alloy Tool Steel, ITC 1.25/2
Quarterly Survey on Certain Stainless Steel and
Alloy Tool Steel, ITC 1.25
Alluvial
Index of Topographic Quadrangle Maps of **Alluvial**
Valley of Lower Mississippi River, D
103.308/2
Map of **Alluvial** Valley of Mississippi River,
Quadrangles, W 31.9
Topographic Quadrangle Maps of **Alluvial** Valley of
Lower Mississippi River, D 103.308
Almanac
Aeronautical Supplement to American Nautical
Almanac, N 11.6/2
Air **Almanac**, D 213.7
Almanac for Computers, D 213.14
American Air **Almanac**, M 212.7
American Ephemeris and Nautical **Almanac** for the
Year [date], N 11.5, M 212.8, D 213.8
American Nautical **Almanac**, N 11.6, M 212.9
Astronomical **Almanac**, D 213.8
Nautical **Almanac** for the Year [date], D 213.11
NIH **Almanac**, HE 20.3016
NIH **Almanac** Update, HE 20.3182/5
Pacific Coaster's Nautical **Almanac**, N 11.8
Singing Sands **Almanac**, I 29.6/3-2
Tables Computed for the American Ephemeris and
Nautical **Almanac**, N 11.9
Almond
Almond Production, A 92.11/2-5
Alotments
General Progress Bulletins, New **Alotments**, Y 3.R
88:12
Alpha-Particles
Helium: Bibliography of Technical and Scientific
Literature, (year), Including Papers on
Alpha-Particles, I 28.27
Alphabetic
Alphabetic List of Lenders, ED 1.66
Alphabetical
Alphabetical Index to Horizontal Control Data, C
55.430/2
Alphabetical List Covering Army Air Forces and
Army-Navy Aeronautical Standard Parts,
W 108.15/2, M 301.11
Alphabetical List of CMIC Directives, D 116.9
Alphabetical List of DoD Prime Contractors, D
1.57/3-3

Alphabetical List of Educational Institutions, ED
1.68
Alphabetical List of Employees, GP 1.5
Alphabetical List of Projects and Alphabetical
List of Owners Projects Licensed,
Exempted, and Applications Pending, E
2.26
Alphabetical List, U.S. Air Force and Air Force-
Navy Aeronautical Standard Drawings,
D 301.15
Alphabetical Listing of (year) Presidential
Campaign Receipts, GA 1.20
Alphabetical Listing of Completed War Supply
Contracts (compilations), Pr 32.4842/3
Alphabetical Listing of Major War Supply
Contracts, Pr 32.4842
Alphabetical Listing, Register or Planned
Mobilization Producers, Manufacturers
of War Material Registered Under
Production Allocation Program, D 7.11
Alphabetical Summary of Prime Contract Awards
Over $25,000, D 1.57/3-4
Census of Population and Housing: **Alphabetical**
Index of Industries and Occupations, C
3.223/22:90-R3
Federal Procurement Data System, Contractor
Identification File, **Alphabetical**
Listing, PrEx 2.24/14
Medical Subject Headings; Annotated **Alphabeti-
cal** List, HE 20.3602:H 34, HE 20.3612/
3-4
Project Label, **Alphabetical** Listings by
Controlled Generic Drug Ingredients, J
24.24/2
Project Label, **Alphabetical** Listings by Drug
Labeler of Discontinued Products, J
24.24/3
Project Label, **Alphabetical** Listings by Drug
Labeler, J 24.24
Project Label, **Alphabetical** Listings by Drug
Product, J 24.24/4
Telephone Directory Agriculture Department,
Alphabetical Listing, A 1.89/4
Thesaurus of ERIC Descriptors **Alphabetical**
Display, ED 1.310/3-2
Alphabetically
List of Radio Broadcast Stations, **Alphabetically**
by Call Letters, CC 1.21
Alsop
United States v. Chile, **Alsop** Claims, S 3.21/4
Alterations
Acceptable Methods, Techniques, and Practices:
Aircraft **Alterations**, TD 4.28, TD 4.28/2
Aircraft **Alterations**, FAA 5.16
Construction Reports; Residential **Alterations** and
Repairs, Expenditures on Residential
Additions, **Alterations**, Maintenance
and Repairs, and Replacements, C
56.211/7
Expenditures for Additions, **Alterations**,
Maintenance and Repairs, and
Replacements on One-Housing-Unit
Owner-Occupied Properities, C 3.215/
8:Pt-2
Expenditures on Residential Additions,
Alterations, Maintenance and Repairs,
and Replacements, C 3.215/8:Pt 1
Maintenance, Preventive Maintenance, Rebuilding
and **Alterations**, TD 4.6:part 43
Radio Broadcast Stations in United States,
Containing **Alterations** and Corrections,
CC 1.24
Altered
Victimization, Fear of Crime and **Altered** Behavior
(series), HH 1.70
Alternate
Alternate Fuels, E 2.20
Alternates
List of Basic Materials and **Alternates**, DP 1.9
Alternative
AFDC Update, News of the **Alternative** Fuels Data
Center, E 1.114
Alternative Dispute Resolution Series, D 103.57/
13
Alternative Fuel News, E 1.114/4
Alternative Fuels in Trucking, E 1.114/3
Economic Impact Analysis of **Alternative**
Pollution Control Technologies (series),
EP 1.8/10
Federal **Alternative** and Fuel Program, Annual
Report to Congress, E 1.114/2
Innovative and **Alternative** Technology Projects, a
Progress Report, EP 2.30

Altitude
Data Report: High **Altitude** Meteorological Data, C 55.280
Enroute High and Low **Altitude**, U.S., D 5.318/4
Flight Information Publication: Enroute High **Altitude** and Low **Altitude**, U.S., D 5.318/4
Flight Information Publication: Enroute High **Altitude**, Europe, Africa, Middle East, D 301.9/4
Flight Information Publication: Enroute Intermediate **Altitude**, United States, D 301.13/5
Flight Information Publication: Enroute-High **Altitude**, United States, Northeast [and Southeast], D 301.43/3, D 301.43/3-2
Flight Information Publication: Low **Altitude** Instrument Approach Procedures, D 5.318
Flight Information Publication: Terminal High **Altitude**, Pacific and Southeast Asia, D 301.12/4
Flight Information Publication: Terminal Low **Altitude**, Africa and Southwest Asia, D 301.13/6
Flight Information Publication: Terminal Low **Altitude**, Pacific and Southeast Asia, D 301.12/3
High **Altitude** Instrument Approach Procedures, D 5.318/2
IFR **Altitude** Usage Peak Day, FAA 3.11/2
IFR Enroute High **Altitude** Charts (Alaska), TD 4.49/17-2
IFR Enroute High **Altitude** (U.S.), TD 4.79/17
IFR Enroute Low **Altitude** (Alaska), TD 4.79/16
IFR Enroute Low **Altitude** (U.S.), TD 4.79/15
IFR Enroute Low **Altitude** Planning Chart, TD 4.79/16-3
Low **Altitude** Approach Procedures, United States Military Aviation Notice, D 5.318/3
Low **Altitude** Instrument Approach Procedures, D 5.318
Military Aviation Notices; Corrections to Enroute-Low **Altitude**-Alaska, D 301.13/4
Terminal High **Altitude**, Pacific and Southeast Asia, D 301.12/4
Terminal Low **Altitude**, Africa and Southwest Asia, D 301.13/6
Altitudes
Dictionary of **Altitudes** in the United States, I 19.3:274
Minimum Enroute IFR **Altitudes** Over Particular Routes and Intersections, TD 4.316
Alumina
Mineral Industry Surveys, Bauxite and **Alumina**, I 19.132
Aluminum
Aluminum, I 28.85
Aluminum Alloy Ingot, Monthly Reports, I 28.71
Aluminum and Bauxite in (year), I 28.80/2
Aluminum Imports and Exports, C 41.112, C 57.14
Aluminum Metal Supply and Shipments of Products to Consumers, C 41.112/4
Aluminum Scrap and Secondary Ingot, I 28.71/2
Aluminum Scrap and Secondary Ingot, Secondary Aluminum Monthly Report, I 28.71/3
Mineral Industry Surveys, **Aluminum**, I 19.130
Primary **Aluminum**, Monthly Report, I 28.85
Secondary **Aluminum**, I 28.71/3
United States Exports of **Aluminum**, C 41.112/2, C 57.10
United States Imports of **Aluminum**, C 57.10/2
Alzheimer's
Progress Report on **Alzheimer's** Disease, HE 20.3869
Report of the Advisory Panel on **Alzheimer's** Disease, HE 20.8024
AM
AM Broadcast Applications Accepted for Filing and Notification of Cut-off Date, CC 1.26/4
AM-FM Broadcast Financial Data, CC 1.43/2
Educational **AM** and FM Radio and Education Television Stations, FS 5.234:34016, HE 5.234:34016
Amateur Built
Briefs of Accidents Involving **Amateur Built** (homebuilt) Aircraft U.S. General Aviation, TD 1.109/6
Ambient
Ambient Water Quality Criteria for [various chemicals], EP 1.29/3

Ambient
National Performance Audit Program, **Ambient** Air Audits of Analytical Proficiency, EP 1.23/5-2
Ambulatory
Ambulatory Care, HE 20.6209:5
Development and Management of **Ambulatory** Care Programs, HE 20.9109/2
National **Ambulatory** Medical Care Survey, HE 20.6209/4-5
AMC
AMC CD-ROM Publications, D 101.129/5
AMC Circulars (series), D 101.4/5
AMC Laboratories and Research, Development and Engineering Centers, Technical Accomplishments, D 101.1/4
Military Publications: Index of **AMC** Publications and Blank Forms, D 101.22/3:310.1
AMCCOM
AMCCOM Handbooks, D 101.6/8
Annual Historical Review, Armament, Munitions and Chemical Command, (**AMCCOM**)-(series), D 101.1/5
AMCCOMP
AMCCOMP- (series), D 101.22/12
AMD
Technical Reports, **AMD**-TR- (series), D 301.45/52
AMEDD
AMEDD Spectrum, D 104.26
Annual Historical Report, **AMEDD** Activities for the Calendar Year, D 104.30
Amended
Amended Type Certificate Data Sheets and Specifications, TD 4.15/10
Railroad Retirement and Unemployment Insurance Act, As **Amended** [August 29, 1935], Y 1.2:R 13
Seamen's Act As **Amended** and Other Laws Relating to Seamen [March 4, 1915], Y 1.2:Se 1/2
Securities Act of 1933, As **Amended** to (date), SE 1.5:Se 2/3
Securities Exchange Act of 1934, As **Amended** to (date), SE 1.5:Se 2
Selective Service Act As **Amended** [May 18, 1917], Y 1.2:Se 4
Special and Administrative Provisions of the Tariff Act of 1930, As **Amended**, As in Effect on [date], TC 1.10/2
Amendment
Amendment to Rules and Regulations Under Sections of National Housing Act, HH 2.6/3
Manual **Amendment** Circulars, W 36.7/2
Amendments
Amendments to 1911 Edition of Use Book and National Forest Manual, A 13.14
Amendments to Regulations, Public Health Service, T 27.8/2
Amendments to Social Security Laws, SSI, HE 3.25/2
Amendments to Use Book and National Forest Manual, A 13.14/5
C.A.B. Notices of Proposed Rulemaking and **Amendments** to All Regulations, CAB 1.37
Detailed Summary of Housing **Amendments**, HH 1.5/2
Federal Register Proposed **Amendments**, Y 3.F 31/21-3:9-5
Federal Reserve Act of 1913 with **Amendments** and Laws Relating to Banking, Y 1.2:F 31/2
Hospital Survey and Construction Act with **Amendments** [August 13, 1946], Y 1.2:H 79
Public Buildings Act of 1926, with **Amendments**, Condemnation Laws with **Amendments**, Public Works and Construction Laws [May 7, 1926], Y 1.2:P 96/3
Public Laws with **Amendments**, W 49.7/2
Reconstruction Finance Corporation Act with **Amendments** and Small Business Administration Act with **Amendments** Including Related Acts on Small Business, Y 1.2:R 24/2
Report of the U.S. Department of Justice Pursuant to Section 8 of the Federal Coal Leasing **Amendments** Act of 1975, J 1.27/3
Rules and Regulations for Federal Savings and Loan System, with **Amendments** to [date], FHL 1.6:Sa 9
Senate Printed **Amendments**, Y 1.4/5

Small Business Administration and Investment Act, with **Amendments** [1953], Y 1.2:Sm 1
Surplus Property Act of 1944, and **Amendments**, Y 1.2:Su 7
Amepnka
Amepnka, This Is a Russian Edition of America, S 1.55
America
Amepnka, This Is a Russian Edition of **America**, S 1.55
America Illustrated, IA 1.14, ICA 1.10
America the Beautiful (posters), A 57.8/2
America 2000, ED 1.85
America's Commitment: Federal Programs Benefiting Women and New Initiatives as Follow-up to the U.N. Fourth World Conference on Women, Pr 42.8:W 84
Area Planning North **America** and South **America**, D 5.318/5-2
Area Planning Special Use Airspace North **America** and South **America**, D 5.318/5-3
Arts in **America**, NF 2.8/2-28
Biographical Sketches and Ancedotes of 95 of 120 Principal Chiefs from Indian Tribes of North **America**, I 20.2:In 2/27
Bonds Over **America**, T 66.11
Business **America**, C 1.58/4, C 61.18
Business **America**, Michigan, C 61.18/3
Commerce **America**, C 1.58/2
Commerce **America** [by State], C 1.58/3
East Coast of North **America** and South **America** (including Greenland), C 4.15/4
Export **America**, C 61.18/2
Facts about **America** Series, Pr 32.5408
Geologic Names of North **America** Introduced in 1936-1955, I 19.3:1056
Index to Geologic Names of North **America**, I 19.3:1056
Latin **America** Report, PrEx 7.19
Maps for **America**, I 19.2:M 32/12
North **America** and Oceania Outlook and Situation Report, A 93.29/2-16
Separate Sheets of Selected Thematic and General Reference Maps from the National Atlas of the United States of **America**, I 19.111a
Take Pride in **America**, Awards Program, I 1.110
Take Pride in **America**, National Awards Ceremony, I 1.110/2
Tide Tables East Coast of North and South **America**, C 4.15/4
Tide Tables West Coast of North and South **America**, C 4.15/5
Tide Tables, High and Low Water Predictions East Coast of North and South **America** Including Greenland, C 55.421/2
Tide Tables, High and Low Water Predictions West Coast of North and South **America** Including Hawaiian Islands, C 55.421
Tung Oil Monthly, Production in **America**, Foreign Trade, etc., C 18.209
Voice of **America** Forum Lectures Mass Communication Series, IA 1.19
Voice of **America** Forum Lectures Music Series, IA 1.19/3
Voice of **America** Forum Lectures Space Science Series, IA 1.19/2
Voice of **America** Forum Lectures University Series, IA 1.19/4
West Coast of North and South **America** (including the Hawaiian Islands), C 4.15/5
What Price **America**, I 43.8
Working Together for Rural **America**, A 13.125
America's
America's Families and Living Arrangements, C 186.17-2
America's Hour of Destiny, Radio Series, I 29.30, I 29.30/2
National Forests, **America's** Great Outdoors, A 13.122
Report on **America's** National Scenic, National Historic, and National Recreation Trails (fiscal year), I 29.130
Telling **America's** Story to the World, IA 1.7
Towards Improved Health and Safety for **America's** Coal Miners, Annual Report of the Secretary of the Interior, I 1.96
Welcoming **America's** Newest Commonwealth: Reports, Y 3.N 81/6:9

General Aviation Accidents (non-air carrier), Statistical **Analysis**, C 31.160/2, FAA 1.15

Global Ocean Floor **Analysis** and Research Data Series, D 203.31

Hazard **Analysis** Reports [on various subjects], Y 3.C 76/3:17

HIA [Hazard Identification and **Analysis**] Special Reports, Y 3.C 76/3:17-2

Historical **Analysis** Series, D 114.19/2

Historical Comparison of Budget Receipts and Expenditures by Function, Special **Analysis** G, PrEx 2.8/a10

Homestudy Course; Community Health **Analysis** (series), HE 20.7021/8

Homestudy Course; Community Health **Analysis**-I Manuals, HE 20.7021/8-2

Homestudy Course; Community Health **Analysis**-II, HE 20.7021/8-3

Hospital and Mental Facilities Construction Program under Title 6 of Public Health Service Act, Semiannual **Analysis** of Projects Approved for Federal Aid, FS 2.74/2

Index **Analysis** of Federal Statutes, LC 10.5

Inventories and **Analysis** of Federal Population Research, HE 20.3362/2

Inventory and **Analysis** of NIH Maternal and Child Health Research, HE 20.3363

Mathematical **Analysis** Groups Reports, I 27.39

Methods for the Collection and **Analysis** of Aquatic Biological and Microbiological Samples, I 19.15/5

Methods of Urban Impact **Analysis** (series), HH 1.76

Pavements and Soil Trafficability Information **Analysis** Center, PSTIAC Reports, D 103.24/12

Performance Evaluation Summary **Analysis** Bacteriology, HE 20.7037/2

Performance Evaluation Summary **Analysis** Mycology, HE 20.7037

Performance Evaluation Summary **Analysis** Parasitology, HE 20.7037/3

Preliminary **Analysis** of Aircraft Accident Data, U.S. Civil Aviation, TD 1.113/6

Product **Analysis** Service, Pr 33.920

Proficiency Testing Summary **Analysis**, Parasitology, HE 20.7022/3-4

Proficiency Testing Summary **Analysis**, Public Health Immunology, HE 20.7022/3-3

Proficiency Testing Summary **Analysis**: General Immunology, HE 20.7022/3, HE 20.7412

Program **Analysis** (series), FS 1.29, HE 1.29

Progress **Analysis**, Pr 33.214

Project **Analysis** Series, Pr 32.5411, I 52.10

Publications Research and **Analysis** Branch, Y 3.C 78/3:7, W 2.13

Radio Chemical **Analysis**, Nuclear Instrumentation, Radiation Techniques, Nuclear Chemistry, Radioisotope Techniques, C 13.46

Recent Products of Applied **Analysis**, E 3.27/3

Regulatory Impact **Analysis** (series), EP 6.14/2

Reports and **Analysis** Handbook Series, L 7.36

Resources **Analysis** Memos, HE 20.3014/2

Retirement and Survivors Insurance Semiannual **Analysis**, HE 3.57/2

Shellfish Market Review, Current Economic **Analysis** S, C 55.309/4

Special **Analysis** of Federal Activities in Public Works and Other Construction in Budget, PrEx 2.8/a2

Special **Analysis** of Federal Aid to State and Local Governments in Budget, PrEx 2.8/a3

Special **Analysis** of Federal Credit Programs in Budget, PrEx 2.8/a5

Special **Analysis** of Federal Research and Development Programs in Budget, PrEx 2.8/a4

Special **Analysis** of Principal Federal Statistical Programs in Budget, PrEx 2.8/a6

Special **Analysis**, United States Budget, Fiscal Year, PrEx 2.8/5

SSA Workload **Analysis** Report, HE 3.79

Staffing **Analysis** Report, T 22.56

Statistical **Analysis** of Carrier's Monthly Hours of Service Reports, IC 1 hou.9

Statistical **Analysis** of the World's Merchant Fleet, TD 11.12

Statistical **Analysis** of World's Merchant Fleets Showing Age, Size, Speed, and Statistical **Analysis** Report, ED 1.328/5

Draft by Frequency Groupings, As of (date), C 39.224

Statistical Summary and **Analysis** of Foreign Visitor Arrivals, U.S. Citizen and Non-U.S. Citizen Departures, C 47.15

Statistics Research **Analysis** Microfiles Catalog, HE 3.38/4

Study of Methods Used in Measurement and **Analysis** of Sediment Loads in Streams, Reports, Y 3.F 31/13:9, Y 3.In 8/8:10

Summary and **Analysis** of International Travel to the U.S., C 47.15

Surveillance and **Analysis** Division, Region 8, Denver Colo., Technical Support Branch: SA/TSB-1- (series), EP 1.51/3

Surveillance and **Analysis** Division, Region 8: Technical Investigations Branch, SA/TIB-(series), EP 1.51/4

Surveillance and **Analysis** Division, Region 9, San Francisco, California: Technical Reports, EP 1.51

Surveillance and **Analysis** Division, Region 10: Working Papers, EP 1.51/6

Technical **Analysis** Papers Congressional Budget Office, Y 10.11

Technical **Analysis** Papers Department of Health, Education, and Welfare, HE 1.52

Technical **Analysis** Report DASA (series), D 5.14

Technical Notes Department of the Air Force Atmospheric **Analysis** Laboratory, D 301.45/30 3

Technical Report **Analysis** Condensation Evaluation (Trace), D 301.45/27-3

Terrain **Analysis** (series), D 5.321

Training **Analysis** and Development, Information Bulletin, D 301.38/2

TSCA Economic **Analysis** Series, EP 5.15/3

Vocational Education; Schools for Careers, an **Analysis** of Occupational Courses Offered by Secondary and Postsecondary Schools, HE 19.321

World Tobacco **Analysis** (Quarterly), A 67.25

Analysis of the President's Budgetary Proposals for Fiscal Year (date), Y 10.2 B 85/8

Analytic

Analytic Reports, FS 5.254:54007, HE 5.254:54007

Analytic Series: A, HE 20.424

Library Statistics of Colleges and Universities; **Analytic** Report, FS 5.215:15031, HE 5.215:15031

Library Statistics of Colleges and Universities; Fall (year), Part C, **Analytic** Report, HE 5.92/7

Analytical

Air Carrier **Analytical** Charts and Summaries, Including Supplemental Air Carrier Statistics, C 31.241/2

Analytical Notes, FS 3.47

Analytical Reference Service Reports (numbered), EP 2.16

Analytical Reference Service Studies, FS 2.300/5, HE 20.1113, HE 20.1709

Journal of **Analytical** Chemistry [abstracts], C 41.53/6

Mineral Issues, an **Analytical** Series, I 28.156

Manufacturing: **Analytical** Report Series, C 3.24/9-12

National Performance Audit Program, Ambient Air Audits of **Analytical** Proficiency, EP 1.23/5-2

Technical Activities, Center for **Analytical** Chemistry, C 13.58/2

Analyzer

State Officers **Analyzer** Sheets, C 46.12

Analyzing

Aid for **Analyzing** Markets (by States), C 18.38

Digest of State Pesticide Use and Application Laws, Guide for **Analyzing** Pesticide Legislation, EP 5.8:P 43

ANC

ANC Bulletins, Y 3.Ae 8:8

ANC Bulletins and Documents, D 3.9

ANC Documents, M 5.9

ANC Procedures for Control of Air Traffic, C 31.106/2

ANC [publications], Y 3.Ar 5/3:7

Anchorage

Supplemental Tidal Predictions, **Anchorage**, Nikishka, Seldovia, and Valdez, Alaska, C 55.432

Andrews

Economic Resource Impact Statement **Andrews** Air Force Base, D 301.105/7

KEY>Androgenic

Androgenic and Myogenic Endocrine Bioassay Data, FS 2.22/48

Anemia

Anemia Dispensary Service, W 75.5

Equine Infectious **Anemia**, Progress Report and History in the United States, A 77.244

ANG

ANG- (series), D 12.11

Anglers

Anglers' Guide to the United States Atlantic Coast, C 55.308:An 4

Anglers' Guide to the United States Pacific Coast, C 55.308:An 4/2

Black Bass and **Anglers** Division Publications, C 6.17

Anglo

Anglo-American Caribbean Commission Publications, S 5.47

Animal

A.H.D. [**Animal** Husbandry Divisions](series), A 77.209

A.N.D. **Animal** Nutrition Division (series), A 77.210

Animal and Vegetable Fats and Oils, C 3.56

Animal Care Matters, A 101.24

Animal Damage Control, ADC- (series), I 49.101

Animal Damage Control Program, A 101.28

Animal Health Science Research Advisory Board, A 106.40

Animal Husbandry Division, A 77.209

Animal Husbandry Division Mimeographs, A 4.26

Animal Morbidity Report, A 101.12, A 101.12/2, A 77.229

Animal Morbidity Report, Calendar Year (date), A 77.229/2, A 101.12/2

Animal Resources Advisory Committee, HE 20.3001/2:An 5

Animal Welfare Enforcement Fiscal Year, A 101.22/2

Animal Welfare Information Center Newsletter, A 17.27/2

Animal Welfare Legislation: Bills and Public Laws, A 17.26

Animal Welfare: List of Licensed Dealers, A 101.26

Biology and Control of Insect and Related Pests of [various **animals**], EP 1.94

Directory of **Animal** Disease Diagnostic Laboratories, A 101.2:D 63/2, A 101.13

Extension **Animal** Husbandman, A 77.214

Factory Consumption of **Animal** and Vegetable Fats and Oils by Classes of Products, C 3.154

Factory Consumption of **Animal** and Vegetable Fats and Oils by Classes of Products, C 3.154

Foreign **Animal** Diseases Report, A 101.17

Inter-American Conference on Agriculture, Forestry, and **Animal** Industry, Washington, Sept. 8-20, 1930, S 5.32

International **Animal** Feed Symposium Reports, A 67.34

Maps [Concerning **Animal** Industry], A 77.238

Service and Regulatory Announcements Bureau of **Animal** Industry, A 4.13, A 77.208

Summary of Activities **Animal** and Plant Health Inspection Service, A 101.27

Summary of Bang's Disease Control Program Conducted by Bureau of **Animal** Industry in Cooperation with Various States, A 4.23

Summary of Brucellosis (Bang's Disease) Control Program Conducted by Bureau of **Animal** Industry in Cooperation with Various States, A 77.213

Animal Industry

Directory of Bureau of **Animal Industry**, A 77.221

Animals

Animals and Products, IC 1.23/11:SS-3

Animals Imported for Breeding Purposes, etc., A 4.15

Animals Slaughtered under Federal Meat Inspection in Districts Represented by Cities, A 36.199

Care of **Animals** and Stable Management, W 3.50/9

Carload Waybill Statistics, Mileage Block Distribution, Traffic and Revenue by Commodity Class, Territorial Movement, and Type of Rate, **Animals** and Products, 1 Percent Sample of Terminations in Statement MB-2, IC 1.23/3

Farm Production and Income from Meat **Animals**, A 66.34

Fur Bearing **Animals** Abroad, News Jottings from Field for American Breeders, Bulletins, C 18.93

Habitat Management for [various **Animals**], A 57.56

Meat **Animals**, Farm Production, Disposition, and Income by States, A 88.17/3

Meat **Animals**, Production, Disposition, and Income, A 105.23/6

Orders Publications Relating to the Care of **Animals** and Poultry, A 77.218

Report on Incidence of Anthrax in **Animals** in United States, A 77.225

Service and Regulatory Announcements Publications Relating to the Care of **Animals** and Poultry, A 77.208

ANN

ANN, ED 1.76/2-2

Annals

Annals of Astrophysical Observatory, SI 1.12

Annals of Congess, X 1 - X 42

Annals of the Smithsonian Institution, SI 1.48

Smithsonian **Annals** of Flight, SI 9.9

Annapolis

Annapolis Field Office, Middle Atlantic Region 3, Philadelphia, Pa.: Technical Reports, EP 1.51/2

Annapolis, the United States Naval Academy Catalog, D 208.109

Naval Engineering Experiment Station, **Annapolis**, Maryland, D 211.15

Annex

Report of United States High Commissioner, Statistical **Annex**, U.S. Element, Allied Commission for Austria, S 1.89/2

Annexation

Boundary and **Annexation** Survey Annual Reports, C 56.249

Boundary and **Annexation** Survey GE-30 , C 3.260

Anniston

Area Wage Survey, Gadsden and **Anniston**, Alabama, L 2.122/1-5

Anniversary

President's Commission for Observance of 25th **Anniversary** of the United Nations, Pr 37.8:Un 3

Annotated

Annotated Bibliography of CDA Curriculum Materials, HE 23.111/2

Annotated Bibliography of Technical Films [by subject], S 17.29/2

Annotated Index of Registered Fungicides and Nematicides, Their Uses in the United States, A 77.302:F 96

Annotated Manual of Statutes and Regulations of the Federal Home Loan Bank Board, FHL 1.6/2:St 2

Census Bureau Methodological Research, (year), **Annotated** List of Papers and Reports, C 56.222/3:M 56

Digest **Annotated** and Digested Opinions, U.S. Court of Military Appeals, D 1.19/3

Driver Licensing Laws **Annotated**, TD 8.5/3

Medical Subject Headings; **Annotated** Alphabetical List, HE 20.3602:H 34, HE 20.3612/3-4

Publications Foreign Countries, **Annotated** Accession List, C 3.199

Research (year), **Annotated** List of Research and Demonstration Grants, HE 17.15

Tariff Schedules of the United States, **Annotated**, TC 1.35/2, ITC 1.10

U.S. Imports for Consumption & General Imports, Tariff Schedules **Annotated** by Country, C 3.150/6

U.S. Imports for Consumption and General Imports, Tariff Schedules **Annotated** by Country, C 3.150/6

United States Coast Guard **Annotated** Bibliography, TD 5.21/3

United States Import Duties **Annotated**, C 3.150/4

United States Import Duties **Annotated**, Public Bulletins, C 3.150/5

Annotation

Annotation, the Newsletter of the National Historical Publications and Records Commission, GS 4.14/2

Annotations

Clearinghouse on Health Indexes: Cumulated **Annotations**, HE 20.6216/2

Medical Subject Headings; Tree **Annotations**, HE 20.3612/3-6

Announced

Active and **Announced** Price Support Programs Approved by Board of Directors, A 82.310

Graduate Fellowship Awards **Announced** by National Science Foundation, NS 1.19

Announcement

AHCPR Grant **Announcement**, HE 20.6519/2

Announcement (Press Releases), HE 20.8107

Announcement from the Copyright Office, ML (series), LC 3.12

Announcement of Opportunities for Participation, NAS 1.53

Announcement of Water-Resources Reports Released for Public Inspection, I 19.48

Announcement, National Institute on Alcohol Abuse and Alcoholism, HE 20.8318

Graduate Fellowship **Announcement**, TD 2.64/2

Graduate School **Announcement** of Courses, C 13.41

Monthly Product **Announcement**, C 3.163/7

OJJDP Discretionary Program **Announcement**, J 32.22

ORD Publications **Announcement**, EP 1.21/6-2

Program **Announcement**, Graduate Research Fellowship Program, J 28.25

Program **Announcement**, Visiting Fellowship Program, J 28.25/2

Public Health Conference on Records and Statistics, National Meeting **Announcement**, HE 20.6214/2

Publication **Announcement** and Order Form, Annual Survey of Manufacturers, C 3.24/9-5

Research **Announcement**, NAS 1.53/3

Title **Announcement** Bulletin, D 10.9

Announcements

1950 Census of Population and Housing **Announcements**, C 3.950-4/3

Announcements, D 203.24/4, P 1.38

Announcements (of Sales), A 82.74

Announcements of Examinations, I 20.25

Announcements of Examinations, 4th District, CS 1.26/3

Announcements of Examinations, Field and Local, CS 1.26/4

Announcements of Summary Conferences for College Teachers, NS 1.12/2

Announcements [of examinations for appointment of officers in Public Health Service], FS 2.91

Announcements [of examinations], PM 1.21/2

Announcements [of reports published], L 2.74

Announcements, Census of Agriculture, C 3.31/8

Announcements, Census of Manufacturers, C 3.24/10

CDC Course **Announcements**, HE 20.7034

Census of Construction Industries; **Announcements** and Order Forms, C 3.245/2

Census of Population; Housing: **Announcements**, C 3.223/3

Clean Water, **Announcements** [for radio and television], FS 2.64/5

Clearinghouse **Announcements** in Science and Technology, C 51.7/5

Current Federal Examination **Announcements**, PM 1.21

Current Local **Announcements** Covering Washington, D.C. Metropolitan Area, CS 1.28:2602-WA

Data **Announcements** (series), C 55.239

Department of Energy Information: Weekly **Announcements**, E 1.7/2

Export Sales Promotions **Announcements**, C 42.23/2

Fast **Announcements**, C 51.7/2

Federal Specifications **Announcements**, GS 1.10

Government Reports **Announcements**, C 51.9/3

Government Reports **Announcements** and Index, C 51.9/3

Government Reports Topical **Announcements**, C 51.7/5

Handicapped Children's Education Program, Grant **Announcements**, ED 1.32/3

Information from ERDA, Weekly **Announcements**, ER 1.12

NOAA Publications **Announcements**, C 55.17

NOAA Scientific and Technical Publications **Announcements**, C 55.228/2

OERI **Announcements** (series), ED 1.75

Plant Regulatory **Announcements**, A 77.308/5

Pre-Solicitation **Announcements**, Small Business Innovation Programs, SBA 1.37

Program Research and Development **Announcements**, ER 1.30

Publication **Announcements**, NAS 1.9

Publications **Announcements**, GP 3.21

Puerto Rico Censuses, **Announcements**, C 3.219

Recruitment **Announcements**, D 103.34

Regulatory **Announcements**, I 49.24

Service and Regulatory **Announcements** Agricultural Marketing Administration, A 75.16

Service and Regulatory **Announcements** Agricultural Marketing Service, A 66.27, A 88.6/3

Service and Regulatory **Announcements** Agricultural Research Service, A 77.6/2

Service and Regulatory **Announcements** Agricultural Stabilization and Conservation Service, A 82.23

Service and Regulatory **Announcements** Alaska Game Commission, A 5.10/5

Service and Regulatory **Announcements** Bureau of Agricultural Economics, A 36.5

Service and Regulatory **Announcements** Bureau of Animal Industry, A 4.13, A 77.208

Service and Regulatory **Announcements** Bureau of Biological Survey, A 5.6

Service and Regulatory **Announcements** Bureau of Chemistry, A 7.6

Service and Regulatory **Announcements** Bureau of Dairy Industry, A 44.5

Service and Regulatory **Announcements** Bureau of Entomology and Plant Quarantine, A 56.14

Service and Regulatory **Announcements** Bureau of Plant Industry, A 19.13

Service and Regulatory **Announcements** Bureau of Plant Quarantine, A 48.7

Service and Regulatory **Announcements** Bureau of Soils, A 26.7

Service and Regulatory **Announcements** Caustic Poison, A 46.13, FS 13.110

Service and Regulatory **Announcements** Civil Service Commission, CS 1.5

Service and Regulatory **Announcements** Federal Horticulture Board, A 35.9

Service and Regulatory **Announcements** Food and Drug, A 46.12

Service and Regulatory **Announcements** Food, Drug, and Cosmetic, A 46.19, FS 7.8, FS 13.115

Service and Regulatory **Announcements** Import Milk, A 46.11, FS 13.114

Service and Regulatory **Announcements** Insecticide and Fungicide Board, A 34.6

Service and Regulatory **Announcements** Insecticide and Fungicide, A 46.15

Service and Regulatory **Announcements** List of Intercepted Plant Pests, A 77.308/2

Service and Regulatory **Announcements** Naval Stores, A 46.18

Service and Regulatory **Announcements** Publications Relating to Entomology and Plant Quarantine, A 77.308

Service and Regulatory **Announcements** Publications Relating to the Care of Animals and Poultry, A 77.208

Service and Regulatory **Announcements** SRA-C&MS- (series), A 88.6/3

Service and Regulatory **Announcements** Tea, A 46.14, FS 7.14

Service and Regulatory **Announcements**, Office of Distribution, A 80.118

Special **Announcements** (series), HE 20.8318/2

Special **Announcements** Concerning Research Reports from Department of Commerce OTS, C 41.28/2

Special **Announcements**, C 51.7/3

Spot **Announcements**, L 22.28

Teacher Exchange Opportunities Abroad, Teaching, Summer Seminars under International Educational Exchange Program of Department of States [**announcements**], FS 5.64/2

Technical Publication **Announcements**, C 13.58/10

Technical Publications **Announcements** with Indexes, NAS 1.9/3
Trade Center **Announcements**, C 1.51
United States Census of Agriculture, 1950: **Announcements**, C 3.950-9/6
Annual
Annual Accountability Report, E 1.1/6
Annual Area Report, Advance Summary, I 28.94
Annual Benchmark Report for Retail Trade, C 138/3-8
Annual Benchmark Report for Wholesale Trade, C 3.133/5
Annual Cancer Statistics Review, HE 20.3186
Annual Department of Defense Bibliography of Logistics Studies and Related Documents, D 1.33/3-2
Annual Education Report, Bureau of Indian Affairs, I 20.46
Annual Medicare Program Statistics, HE 22.21/3
Annual Outlook for U.S. Electric Power, E 3.50
Annual Performance Plan, A 13.1/4
Annual Program Plan and Academy Training Schedule, J 16.26
Annual Report (Fair Debt Collection Practices), FT 1.1/2
Annual Statistical Report, Rural Telecommunications Borrowers A 68.1/3
Combined **Annual** and Revised Monthly Wholesale Trade, C 3.133/4
Directory of Principal U.S. Gemstone Producers **Annual** Advance Summary, I 28.117
Division of Cancer Epidemiology and Genetics, **Annual** Research Directory, HE 20.3188/2
Division of Clinical Sciences, **Annual** Research Directory, HE 20.3151/9
FCA **Annual** Performance Plan, FCA 1.1/3
Federal Managers' Financial Integrity Act, Secretary's **Annual** Statement and Report to the President and the Congress, I 1.96/6
Mineral Industry Surveys, Directory of Principal Construction Sand and Gravel Producers in the . . ., **Annual** Advanced Summary Supplement, I 19.138/3
Office of Inspector General FY, **Annual** Plan, A 1.1/6
Office of Management and Systems **Annual** Perfomance Report, HE 20.4001/3
Personal Computer-**Annual** Energy Outlook, E 3.1/5
Petroleum Supply **Annual**, E 3.11/5-5
Plant Materials **Annual** Progress Reports, A 57.55
Primate Zoonoses Surveillance, Reports, **Annual** Summary, HE 20.7011/9
Proceedings **Annual** Alcoholism Conference of the National Institute on Alcohol Abuse and Alcoholism, HE 20.2430/2
Proceedings **Annual** Clinical Spinal Cord Injury Conference, VA 1.42
Proceedings **Annual** Conference of Mental Health Career Development Program, FS 2.22/45
Proceedings **Annual** Conference of Model Reporting Area for Blindness Statistics, FS 2.22/37
Proceedings **Annual** Conference of the Surgeon General, Public Health Service, and Chief, Children's Bureau, with State and Territorial Health Officers, FS 2.83
Proceedings **Annual** Conference on Model Reporting Area for Mental Hospital Statistics, FS 2.22/44
Proceedings **Annual** Conference, Surgeon General, Public Health Service, with State and Territorial Mental Health Authorities, FS 2.83/3
Proceedings **Annual** Statistical Engineering Symposium, D 116.12
Proceedings **Annual** Western International Forest Disease Work Conference, A 13.69/13
Processed Fishery Statistics, **Annual** Summary, C 55.309/2-9
Production Credit Associations, **Annual** Summary of Operations, FCA 1.22
Public Assistance, **Annual** Statistical Data, FS 14.212, FS 17.13, FS 17.615, HE 17.615
Recordkeeping Requirements for Firms Selected to Participate in the **Annual** Survey of Occupational Injuries and Illnesses, L 2.129
Renal Disease and Hypertension, Proceedings, **Annual** Conference, HE 20.5412

Report of Proceedings of Regular **Annual** Meeting of Judicial Conference of the United States, Ju 10.10
Resources Management Plan **Annual** Update, I 53.50
Rice **Annual** Market Summary, A 88.40/2:18
Schedule of **Annual** and Period Indices for Carriers by Pipeline, IC 1 acco.10
Steam-Electric Plant Construction Cost and **Annual** Production Expenses, E 3.17
Summary Proceedings of ADAMHA **Annual** Conference of the State and Territorial Alcohol, Drug Abuse, and Mental Health Authorities, HE 20.8011
Thermal-Electric Plant Construction Cost and **Annual** Production Expenses, E 3.17/4
United States Army Medical Research Institute of Infectious Disease: **Annual** Progress Report, D 104.27
Utilization of Short-Stay Hospitals United States, **Annual** Summary, HE 20.6209/7
Voluntary Service National Advisory Committee: Report of **Annual** Meeting, VA 1.52
Warren Grant Magnuson Clinical Center: **Annual** Brochure, HE 20.3052/2
World Crude Oil Production **Annual** (year), I 28.18/5
Year of Progress, **Annual** Summary, A 95.1
Annual Data
Alaska Snow Survey, **Annual Data** Summary, A 57.46/13-3
Oregon **Annual Data** Summary, Water Year, A 57.46/5-3
Utah, **Annual Data** Summary, A 57.46/6-3
Washington **Annual Data** Summary Water Year, A 57.46/7-2
Annual Report
Annual Report: Division of Law Enforcement, I 49.1/7
Annual Report: Intramural Research Program Actvities FY, HE 20.8321
Annual Report of Major Natural Gas Companies, E 3.25/4
Annual Report of the Board of Trustees of the Federal Old-Age and Survivors Insurance and Disability Insurance Trust Funds, SSA 1.1/4
Annual Report on Cocaine Use Among Arrestees, J 28.15/2-5
Annual Report on International Religious Freedom (Bureau for Democracy, Human Rights and Labor), S 1.151
Annual Report on Marijuana Use Among Arrestees, J 28.15/2-6
Annual Report on Methamphetamine Use Among Arrestees, J 28.15/2-7
Annual Report on Opiate Use Among Arrestees, J 28.15/2-4
Annual Report on School Safety, E 1.1/7
Annual Report of the President on Trade Agreements Program, Pr 42.11
Annual Report on Carcinogens, HE 20.3562
Annual Report: Presidents Board of Advisors on Historically Black Colleges and Universities, ED 1.89/2
Agency for Toxic Substances and Disease Registry **Annual Report**, HE 20.501/2
Chief Financial Officer **Annual Report**, SBA 1.1/6
Consolidated **Annual Report** for the Office of Community Planning and Development, HE 23.1017
Environmental Compliance Assessment System (ECAS) **Annual Report**, D 101.130
ERIC (Educational Resources Information Center) **Annual Report**, ED 1.301/2
Federal Advisory Committee **Annual Report** of the President, Pr 42.10
FOIA **Annual Report** (Freedom of Information Act), J 1.1/11
Forest Management Program **Annual Report** (National Summary), A 13.152
Government National Mortgage Association, GNMA, **Annual Report**, HH 1.1/7
Inertial Confinement Fusion, ICF **Annual Report**, E 1.99/7-2
National Transportation Statistics, **Annual Report**, TD 12.1/2
Natural Resource Development Program **Annual Report**, SBA 1.48
Observational Study of Agricultural Aspects of Arkansas River Multiple-purpose Project, **Annual Report**, A 57.60

OJJDP **Annual Report** on Missing Children, J 32.17
Office of Administrative Procedure, **Annual Report**, J 1.29
Office of Construction Industry Services: **Annual Report**, L 1.1/2
Office of Engineering Design and Construction: **Annual Report**, Y 3.T 25:1-15
Office of Health and Environmental Science: **Annual Report**, Y 3.T 25:1-10
Office of Inspector General, Agricultural Research Service: **Annual Report**, A 1.1/3
Office of Inspector General: **Annual Report**, HE 1.1/2
Office of Juvenile Justice and Delinquency Prevention: **Annual Report**, J 1.47
Office of Marine Pollution Assessment: **Annual Report**, C 55.43
Office of Operations and Enforcement: **Annual Report**, TD 10.11
Office of Pesticide Programs **Annual Report**, EP 5.1
Office of Research and Development, Region 1: **Annual Report**, EP 1.1/3
Office of Revenue Sharing: **Annual Report**, T 1.1/2
Office of the Chief Scientist: **Annual Report**, I 29.1/2
Office of the Inspector General: **Annual Report**, E 1.1/2
Office of Water Research and Technology: **Annual Report**, I 1.1/5
Operation of the Colorado River Basin, Projected Operations, **Annual Report**, I 27.71
Operations and Enforcement Office: **Annual Report**, TD 9.14
ORD **Annual Report**, EP 1.1/6
Outer Continental Shelf Oil and Gas Leasing and Production Program **Annual Report**, I 72.12/3-2
Outer Continental Shelf Research Management Advisory Board: **Annual Report**, I 1.99
Pacific Marine Environmental Laboratory: **Annual Report**, C 55.601/2
Panama Canal Company, **Annual Report**, CZ 1.1
Parklawn Computer Center: **Annual Report**, HE 20.4036
Polymer Science and Standards Division, **Annual Report**, C 13.1/7
Power **Annual Report**, Y 3.T 25:1-7
Presidential Advisory Committee on Small and Minority Business Ownership, **Annual Report**, PrEx 1.15
President's Committee on Employment of People with Disabilities **Annual Report**, PrEx 1.10/16-2
President's Committee on Employment of the Handicapped, **Annual Report** to Membership, .PrEx 1.10/13
Productivity, **Annual Report**, Pr 37.8:P 94/R 29
Recreation Boating Safety R & D, **Annual Report**, TD 5.28/4
Region 4: **Annual Report**, I 49.1/4
Report Coordinating Group **Annual Report** to the Securities and Exchange Commission, SE 1.32
Report on OPM, GAO'S **Annual Report** on Activities of OPM, Fiscal Year, GA 1.13/15
Research and Technology, **Annual Report** of the Langley Research Center, NAS 1.65/3
Research and Technology Fiscal Year (date) **Annual Report** of the Goddard Space Flight Center, NAS 1.65/2
Research Facilities Center: **Annual Report**, C 55.601/4
Research for Progress in Education, **Annual Report**, HE 5.212:12051
Superfund Emergency Response Actions, A Summary of Federally-Funded Removals, **Annual Report**, EP 1.89/5
Task Force on Environmental Cancer and Heart and Lung Diseases: **Annual Report** to Congress, EP 1.82
Tax Policy and Administration ... **Annual Report** on GAO'S Tax-Related Work, GA 1.13/6
United States Antarctic Programs, **Annual Report**, D 201.15
United States Government **Annual Report**, T 63.101/2
United States Government, **Annual Report**, Appendix, T 1.1/3
Uranium Enrichment **Annual Report**, E 1.36/2

USIA Private Sector Committees **Annual Report**, IA 1.28

VA Medical Research Service, **Annual Report**, VA 1.1/4

Value Engineering Program: **Annual Report**, GS 6.10

Western Environmental Research Laboratory: **Annual Report**, EP 1.14/2

Western States Regional Turkey Breeding Project, **Annual Report**, A 77.235

White Pine Blister Control, **Annual Report**, A 13.59

Wildlife Research Center, Denver, Colorado: **Annual Report**, I 49.47/5

Women's Advisory Council: **Annual Report**, GA 1.30

Women's Educational Equity Act Program, **Annual Report**, ED 1.44

Work Incentive Program: **Annual Report** to Congress, L 1.71

World Strength of the Communist Party Organizations, **Annual Report**, S 1.111

Yellowstone Grizzly Bear Investigations, **Annual Report** of the Interagency Study Team, I 29.94

Annual Reports

Directory of Companies Filing **Annual Reports** with the Securities and Exchange Commission, SE 1.27

Oklahoma, Governor, **Annual Reports**, 1891-1907, I 1.26

Pension Building, **Annual Reports** on Construction of, 1883-87, I 1.27

Plant Materials Centers **Annual Reports**, A 57.54

Platt National Park, **Annual Reports**, I 1.54

Revenue, Special Commissioner, **Annual Reports**, T 1.19

Union Pacific Railway, Government Directors, **Annual Reports**, 1864-1898, I 1.30

Utah Commission, **Annual Reports**, I 1.31

Utah, Governor, **Annual Reports**, I 1.32

Washington Aqueduct, **Annual Reports**, I 1.45

Washington, Governor, **Annual Reports**, 1878-90, I 1.35

Washington Hospital for Foundlings, **Annual Reports**, I 1.34

Wind Cave National Park, **Annual Reports**, I 1.56

Yellowstone National Park, **Annual Reports**, 1898-90, I 1.37

Yosemite National Park, **Annual Reports**, I 1.38

Annually

Statistics of Class a Telephone Carriers Reporting **Annually** to the Commission, As of December 31 (year) and for Year Then Ended, CC 1.14/2

Annuals

Technical Aids for Small Business, **Annuals**, SBA 1.11/2

Annuitants

Enrollment Information Guide and Plan Comparison Chart CSRS/FERS **Annuitants**, PM 1.8/10

Anomaly

Airborne **Anomaly** Location Maps, Y 3.At 7:31

Answer

Answer Me This: American Cities Series, I 16.58/1

Answer Me This: Historical Series, I 16.58/5

Answer Me This: Miscellaneous Series, I 16.58/3

Answer Me This: Song Series, I 16.58/4

Here's Your **Answer**, Programs, FE 1.8

Question and **Answer** Handbooks, I 28.48, I 28.48/2

Questions & **Answer** Service, C 35.14

Questions from **Answer** Me This, Radio Program, I 16.58/2

Answers

Questions and Answers About..., HE 20.3917

Questions and **Answers** on Controlled Materials Plan, Q & A (series), C 40.13

Questions and **Answers** on Rent Control, ES 5.7/2

Questions and **Answers**, QA-IND- (series), L 22.30

Questions and **Answers**, S 1.107

Antarctic

Acquisitions List of **Antarctic** Cartographic Materials, S 1.120

Antarctic Bibliography, D 202.2:An 8, LC 33.9

Antarctic Journal of the United States, NS 1.26

Antarctic Photomap (series), I 19.100/6

Antarctic Regions, C 55.214/50

Antarctic Research Program Maps, I 19.25/8

Antarctic Seismological Bulletin, C 4.36, C 55.414, C 55.610

Antarctic Travers (series), C 4.56

Climatological Data; **Antarctic** Stations, C 30.21/3

Publications U.S. **Antarctic** Projects Officer, D 1.32

U.S. **Antarctic** Projects Officer, Bulletin, D 1.32/2

U.S. **Antarctic** Projects Officer, Publications, D 1.32

United States **Antarctic** Programs, Annual Report, D 201.15

Antarctica

Nautical Charts and Publications, Region 2, Central and South America and **Antarctica**, C 55.440:2

Naval Support Force **Antarctica**, D 201.15/3

Naval Support Force, **Antarctica**, Publications, D 201.15/2

NIMA Nautical Charts, Public Sale Region 2, Central and South America and **Antarctica**, TD 4.82:2

Publications Naval Support Force, **Antarctica**, D 201.15/2

Antarctical

Antarctical Topographic Series, I 19.100

Anthracite

Anthracite Survey Papers, A 13.42/9

Coal, Pennsylvania **Anthracite**, E 3.11/3-2

Coal, Pennsylvania **Anthracite** in (year), I 28.50/4

Distribution of Pennsylvania **Anthracite** for Coal Year (date), I 28.50/3

Pennsylvania **Anthracite** Distribution, E 3.11/3-3

Pennsylvania **Anthracite** Weekly, E 3.11/3

Pennsylvania **Anthracite**, I 28.49/2

Preliminary Estimates of Production of Pennsylvania **Anthracite** and Beehive Coke, I 28.50

Weekly **Anthracite** and Beehive Coke Reports, I 28.49

Weekly **Anthracite** Report, WAR Series, I 28.49/2

Anthrax

Report on Incidence of **Anthrax** in Animals in United States, A 77.225

Anthropod-Borne

Reported **Anthropod-Borne** Encephalidites in Horses and Other Equidae, A 77.230/2

Anthropological

Anthropological Papers (numbered), I 29.77

Anthropology

Institute of Social **Anthropology** Publications, SI 1.16

Publications **Anthropology** (series), I 29.92

Publications in **Anthropology**, I 29.92

Smithsonian Contributions to **Anthropology**, SI 1.33

Studies in Plains **Anthropology** and History, I 20.50

anti-rebate

Decision Under Elkins [**anti-rebate**] Act, IC 1 act.8

Antidumping

Countervailing Duty and **Antidumping** Case Reference List, T 17.18

Antifouling

Insecticides, Acaricides, Molluscicides, and **Antifouling** Compounds, EP 5.11/3

Antimony

Antimony, I 28.95

Antimony in (year), I 28.95/2

Antimony Monthly Report, I 28.95

Mineral Industry Surveys, **Antimony**, I 19.131

Antirecession

Antirecession Fiscal Assistance to State and Local Governments, T 1.51

Antitrust

Antitrust Laws with Amendments [1890], Y 1.2:An 8

Any

Any Bonds Today, T 66.17

AoA

AoA Occasional Papers in Gerontology, HE 23.3111

AOA Update, HE 1.1017

APA

APA, D 101.43/2-2

Apartments

Current Housing Reports: Market Absorption of **Apartments**, H-130 (series), C 56.230

APGC

Technical Report, **APGC**-TR, D 301.45/50-2

APH

APH-Correspondence Aid (series), A 77.228

APHIS

APHIS (series), A 101.10, A 101.10/2

APHIS Facts, A 101.10/3

APHIS Meat and Poultry Inspection Program, Program Issuances for the Period, A 101.6/2-2

APHIS Organizational Directory, A 101.21

APHIS Program Service Directory, A 101.15

APL

Technical Documentary Report **APL**-TDR, D 301.45/51

Apollo

Apollo Expeditions to the Moon, 1975, NAS 1.21:350

Apollo Over the Moon, a View from Orbit, NAS 1.21:362

Appalachia

Appalachia, Y 3.Ap 4/2:9-2

Appalachian

Appalachian Education Satellite Project Technical Reports, Y 3.Ap 4/2:12

Appalachian Reporter, Y 3.Ap 4/2:11

Apparatus

British Exports of Electrical **Apparatus**, C 18.53

Shipments of Domestic Water Softening **Apparatus**, C 3.78

Apparel

Facts for **Apparel** Trade, Pr 32.4262

Textile and **Apparel** Trade Balance Report, C 61.51

U.S. Exports of Textiles and **Apparel** Products, C 61.50

U.S. Imports of Textile and **Apparel** Products, C 61.52

U.S. Imports of Textiles and **Apparel** under the Multifiber Arrangement, Statistical Report, ITC 1.30

U.S. Production, Imports and Import/Production Ratios for Cotton, Wool and Man-made Textiles and **Apparel**, C 61.26

U.S. Textile and **Apparel** Category System, C 61.54

Wearing **Apparel** in World Markets, C 18.161

Apparent

Apparent Consumption of Industrial Explosives and Blasting Agents in the United States, I 28.112

Appeal

Papers in Re in State Courts of **Appeal**, J 1.83

Proceedings Contract Settlement **Appeal** Board, FS 5.7/a

Appeal Board

Decisions of **Appeal Board**, GS 5.7, T 67.8/2

Appeals

Appeals (series), Ju 7.9

Appeals Pending Before United States Courts in Customs Cases, T 17.8

Board of Veterans' **Appeals** Decisions, VA 1.95/2

Courts-Martial Reports, Holdings and Decisions of Judge Advocates General, Boards of Review, and United States Court of Military **Appeals**, D 1.29

Decisions of Land **Appeals**, I 1.69/5

Decisions Office of Administrative Law Judges and Office of Administrative **Appeals**, L 1.5/2

Decisions on Contract **Appeals**, I 1.69/7

Decisions on Indian **Appeals**, I 1.69/6

Digest and Decisions of the Employees' Compensation **Appeals** Board, L 28.9

Digest Annotated and Digested Opinions, U.S. Court of Military **Appeals**, D 1.19/3

Digest of Decisions of Armed Services Board of Contract **Appeals**, D 1.21

Digest of Decisions of Corps of Engineers Board of Contract **Appeals**, D 103.36

Federal Energy Guidelines, Exceptions and **Appeals** (basic volumes), FE 1.8/4

Guide of the U.S. Development of Energy, Board of Contract **Appeals** and Contract Adjustment Board, E 1.8/4

Guide to the U.S. Department of Energy, Board of Contract **Appeals** and Contract Adjustment Board, E 1.8/4

Indian **Appeals**, I 1.69/6

Interstate **Appeals** Handbook, L 7.48

Land **Appeals**, I 1.69/5

Office of Hearings and **Appeals** Handbook, HE 3.6/7

Papers in Re in Court of **Appeals**, J 1.77

Papers in Re in Court of Customs and Patent **Appeals**, J 1.79

Publications United States Court of Military **Appeals**, D 1.19/2

Regulations, Rules and Instructions Court of Customs **Appeals**, Ju 7.8/2

Reports of Cases Adjudged in the Court of Customs
and Patent **Appeals**, Ju 7.5
Rules of Practice Board of Tax **Appeals**, Y 3.T 19:7
Rules of United States Court of Customs and Patent
Appeals, Ju 7.8
Selected Reports of Cases before Veterans'
Education **Appeals** Board, Y 3.V 64:7
Study of MSPB **Appeals** Decisions for FY (year),
MS 1.15
United States Court of Military **Appeals** and the
Judge Advocates General of the Armed
Forces and the General Counsel of the
Department of the Treasury,
United States Court of Military **Appeals**, D 1.19/2
Appeals Board
Decisions of Employees' Compensation **Appeals
Board**, L 28.9
Appellate
Bench Comment, a Periodic Guide to Recent
Appellate Treatment of Practical
Procedural Issues, Ju 13.8/2
Board of **Appellate** Review, S 1.136
Federal Rules of **Appellate** Procedure with Forms,
Y 4.J 89/1-10
Appendix
Summary Report of the Commissioner, Bureau of
Reclamation [and] Statistical **Appendix**, I
27.1/2
Technical **Appendix** from Vital Statistics of the
United States, HE 20.6210/a
United States Government, Annual Report,
Appendix, T 1.1/3
Appendixes
Technical **Appendixes** to the Report and
Recommendations to the Secretary, U.S.
Department of Health and Human
Services, Y 3.P 29:1-2
Apple
Estimated Numbers of **Apple** Trees by Varieties and
Ages in Commercial and Farm Orchards,
A 36.52
Apples
Apples, Production by Varieties, with Compari-
sons, A 88.12/15
Commercial **Apples**, Production by Varieties, with
Comparisons, A 92.11/9
Foreign News on **Apples**, A 36.79
Foreign Statistics on **Apples** and Other Deciduous
Fruits, A 67.12
Appliance
Decisions Under Safety **Appliance** Acts
[compilations], IC 1 saf.8
Decisions Under Safety **Appliance** Acts
[individual cases], IC 1 saf.7
Index-Digest of Decisions Under Federal Safety
Appliance Acts, IC 1 saf.9
Retail Installment Credit and Furniture and
Household **Appliance** Stores, FR 1.34/2
Appliances
Foreign Markets for Heating and Cooking
Appliances, C 18.84
Market for Selected U.S. Household and
Commercial Gas **Appliances** in [various
countries], C 41.106
Rules for Inspection of Safety **Appliances**, IC 1 saf.6
Safety **Appliances** Act [text], IC 1 saf.5
Applicable
Applicable Drawings for Engineer Equipment, W
7.31
Selected Decision of Comptroller General
Applicable to Naval Service, N 20.7/4
Applicant
Indian Health Service Scholarship Program:
Applicant Information Instruction
Booklet, HE 20.9418
Scholarship Program, **Applicant** Information
Bulletin, HE 20.6023
Tests and Other **Applicant** Appraisal Procedures,
CS 1.41/4:271-2
Applicants
Instruction and Information for **Applicants** and for
Boards of Examiners, CS 1.6
Instructions and Information for **Applicants** and for
Boards of Examiners, CS 1.6
Instructions to **Applicants**, CS 1.9
Reasons for Disposition of **Applicants** Other Than
by Approval, HE 17.643
Application
Air Force ROTC Four Year College Scholarship
Program **Application** Booklet for High
School Students Entering College in the
(year) Fall Term, D 301.95

Application Development Guide Upward Bound
Program for Program Year (date), ED
1.69/2
Application Development Guide, Talent Search
Program, ED 1.8/3
Application Document Series, WSDG-AD (nos.),
A 13.87/3
Application for Basic Grants under Library
Services for Indian Tribes and Hawaiian
Program, ED 1.53/2
Application for Fulbright-Hays Training Grants,
ED 1.54
Application for Grants under Adult Indian
Education Programs, ED 1.52
Application for Grants, Formula Grants to Local
Educational Agencies, ED 1.410
Application for Grants under Fulbright-Hays
Foreign Curriculum Consultants, ED
1.59
Application for Grants under Fulbright-Hays
Group Projects Abroad, ED 1.62
Application for Grants under Handicapped
Children's Early Education Program
Demonstration and Auxiliary Activities,
ED 1.50/3
Application for Grants under Indian Education
Program, ED 1.51
Application for Grants under Post Secondary
Education Programs for Handicapped
Persons, ED 1.50/2
Application for Grants under Rehabilitation
Research, Field Initiated Research, ED
1.70/4
Application for Grants under Strengthening
Research Library Resources Program, ED
1.53
Application for Grants under the Cooperative
Education Program, ED 1.70/3
Application for Grants under the Endowment
Grant Program, ED 1.70/2
Application for Grants under the Secretary's
Discretionary Program, ED 1.63
Application for Grants under the Secretary's
Discretionary Program for Mathematics,
Science, Computer Learning and Critical
Foreign Languages, ED 1.64
Application for Grants under Title VI of the Higher
Education Act of 1965, as Amended, ED
1.56, ED 1.57
Application for Grants under Upward Bound
Program, ED 1.69
Application for Seminars Abroad Program, ED
1.59/2
Application Kit Tribal Management Grants, etc.,
FY [date] Tribal Management Grant
Program Announcement, HE 20.317/2
BJS Program **Application** Kit, Fiscal Year, J 29.22
Challenge Grants **Application** Guidelines, NF 2.8/
2-3
Challenge Grants Program Guidelines and
Application Materials, NF 3.8/2-4
Conservation Project Support Grant **Application**
and Information, NF 4.10
Continuation **Application** for Grants under Special
Services for Disadvantage Students
Program, ED 1.60
Continuation **Application** for Grants under Talent
Search Program, ED 1.55
Digest of State Pesticide Use and **Application**
Laws, Guide for Analyzing Pesticide
Legislation, EP 5.8:P 43
Facilities License **Application** Record, Y 3.N
88:33
FIPSE, Drug Prevention Programs in Higher
Education, Information and **Application**
Procedures, ED 1.23/7, ED 1.23/8
Foreign Service Written Examination Registration
and **Application** Form, S 1.137
Foreign Trade Mark **Application** Service, C 18.90
General Operating Support Grant **Application** and
Information, NF 4.9
GIS **Application** Note (series), A 13.118
Grants to Presenting Organizations, Special
Touring Initiatives **Application**
Guidelines, NF 2.8/2-29
Instructions and **Application** for Grants under the
Special Needs Program, ED 1.61
Instructions and **Application** for Grants under the
Strengthening Program, ED 1.61/2
Inter-Arts, Presenting Organizations Artist
Communities Services to the Arts,
Application Guidelines, NF 2.8/2-23

International, **Application** Guidelines for Fiscal
Year, NF 2.8/2-32
Local Arts Agencies Program, **Application**
Guidelines, NF 2.8/2-31
Local Programs, **Application** Guidelines, NF 2.8/
2-21
Medical Devices **Application** Program, Annual
Report, HE 20.3210
NEH Teacher-Scholar Program for Elementary and
Secondary School Teachers, Guidelines
and **Application** Instructions, NF 3.18
New **Application** for Grants under Research in
Education of the Handicapped, ED 1.50
Notes and Decisions on **Application** of Decimal
Classification, LC 22.7, LC 26.8
Opera-Musical Theater, **Application** Guidelines,
NF 2.8/2-12
Organizations Visual Arts, **Application**
Guidelines, NF 2.8/2-15
Patents Snap, Concordance of U.S. Patent
Application Serial Numbers to U.S.
Patent Numbers, C 21.31/6
Presenters and Festivals Jazz Management, Jazz
Special Projects, Music, **Application**
Guidelines, NF 2.8/2-9
Preservation Programs Guidelines and **Applica-
tion** Instructions, NF 3.8/2-3
Program **Application** Reports, HE 17.25/2
Public Humanities Projects, Guidelines and
Application Instructions, NF 3.8/2-9
Space Benefits: Secondary **Application** of
Aerospace Technology in Other Sectors
of the Economy, NAS 1.66
Summer Seminars for College Teachers, Guidelines
and **Application** Forms for Directors, NF
3.13/2
Summer Seminars for College Teachers Guidelines
and **Application** Form for Participants,
NF 3.13/2-2
Summer Seminars for Secondary School Teachers
Guidelines and **Application** Form for
Directors, NF 3.13/3-3
Summer Stipends, Guidelines and **Application**
Forms, NF 3.8/2
Theater **Application** Guidelines, NF 2.8/2-6
U.S. NRC Facilities License **Application** Record, Y
3.N 88
Application Guidelines
Arts Administration Fellows Program, **Application
Guidelines**, NF 2.8/2-24
International **Application Guidelines**, Interna-
tional Program: Fellowships and
Residencies Partnerships, NF 2.8/2-34
International **Application Guidelines**, Interna-
tional Program: International Projects
Initiative For Organizations Partner-
ships, NF 2.8/2-35
Application
FIPSE, **Application** For Grants Under the
Comprehensive Program,, ED 1.23/2
Applications
Alphabetical List of Projects and Alphabetical List
of Owners Projects Licensed, Exempted,
and **Applications** Pending, E 2.26
AM Broadcast **Applications** Accepted for Filing
and Notification of Cut-off Date, CC
1.26/4
Applications Accepted for Filing by Private Radio
Bureau, CC 1.36/9
Applications Accepted for Filing by Safety and
Special Radio Services Bureau, CC 1.39/
4
Applications and Case Discontinuances for AFDC,
HE 3.60/3
Applications and Case Dispositions for Public
Assistance, HE 3.60/3, HE 17.613/3
Applications and/or Amendments Thereto Filed
with the Civil Aeronautics Board, CAB
1.23, C 31.221
Applications for Permits, CC 1.34
Applications, Notices, Orders, T 1.6/2
Applications of Modern Technologies to
International Development, AID-OST
(series), S 18.42
Applications Pending in Commission for
Exemption from Radio Provisions of
International Convention for Safety of
Life at Sea Convention, London, 1929,
Title 3, Pt. 2 of Communications Act of
1934, etc., Reports, CC 1.19
Applications Received, or Acted on, by the Board,
FR 1.48

Applications, Cases Approved, and Cases Discontinued for Public Assistance, HE 17.641

Briefs of Accidents Involving Aerial **Applications** Operations U.S. General Aviation, TD 1.109/4

Cable Television Relay Service, **Applications**, Reports, Public Notices, CC 1.47/2

Cable Television Service **Applications**, Reports, Public Notices, CC 1.47

Clinical **Applications** and Prevention Advisory Committee, HE 20.3001/2:C 61

Conservation and Solar **Applications**, DOE/CS (series), E 1.36

Directory of Computer Softwear **Applications**, C 51.11/5

Earth Resources Satellite Data **Applications** Series, NAS 1.64

Fixed Public Service **Applications** Received for Filing During Past Week, Public Notices, CC 1.40

FM and TV Translator **Applications** Ready and Available for Processing and Notification of Cut-off Date, CC 1.26/6

FM Broadcast **Applications** Accepted for Filing and Notification of Cut-off Date, CC 1.26/3

Forest Pest Management Methods **Applications** Group: Reports (series), A 13.52/10-3

Materials and Components in Fossil Energy **Applications**, E 1.23

Materials and Components in Fossil Energy **Applications**, and ERDA Newsletter, ER 1.13

New Domestic Public Land Mobile Radio Service **Applications** Accepted for Filing During Past Week, CC 1.36

Operational **Applications** Laboratory, Air Force Cambridge Research Center, OAL- TM, D 301.45/37

Overseas Common Carrier Section 214 **Applications** for Filing, CC 1.36/4

Public Assistance Bureau, **Applications**: Old- Age Assistance, Aid to Dependent Children, Aid to the Blind [and] General Assistance, FS 3.17

Quarterly Report of **Applications** in Process, S 18.26/2

Regulations for Clerks of Courts Who Take Passport **Applications**, S 1.18

Report on **Applications** for Orders Authorizing or Approving the Interception of Wire or Oral Communications, Ju 10.19

Reports of **Applications** Received in Radio Broadcast Stations, CC 1.26

Reports of **Applications** Received in Telegraph Section, CC 1.27, CC 1.28

Reports of **Applications** Received, CC 2.8, CC 3.7, CC 4.7

Request for Grant **Applications** (series), HE 20.3220

Request for Research Grant **Applications** (series), HE 20.3864

Resource **Applications**, E 1.30

Satellite **Applications** Information Notes, C 55.37

Solar Collector Manufacturing Activity and **Applications** in the Residential Sector, E 3.19

Space Science and **Applications** Program, NAS 1.33

Standard Broadcast **Applications** Ready and Available for Processing Pursuant to Sec. 1.354 (c) of Commission's Rules, Lists, CC 1.26/2

Summer Seminars for Secondary School Teachers Guidelines and **Applications** Form for Participants, NF 3.13/3-2

Technology **Applications** Report, D 1.91/2

Technology **Applications** (series), E 1.72

Theory of Probability and Its **Applications**, C 41.61/8

TV Broadcast **Applications** Accepted for Filing and Notification of Cut-off Date, CC 1.26/5

U.S. Patient **Applications**, C 21.31/17

Applicators

Apply Pesticides Correctly, a Guide for Commercial **Applicators** (series), EP 5.8/2

Applied

Applied Mathematics and Mechanics [abstracts], C 41.61

Applied Mathematics Series, C 13.32

Applied Physiology and Bioengineering Study Section, HE 20.3001/2:P 56

Applied Social and Behavioral Sciences Research Initiation Grants, NS 1.10/8

Applied Technology Laboratory, U.S. Army Research and Technology Laboratories, D 117.8/2

Institute for **Applied** Technology, Technical Highlights, Fiscal Year, C 13.1/3

Journal of **Applied** Chemistry [abstracts], C 41.53/11

Journal of Scientific and **Applied** Photography and Cinematography [abstracts], C 41.69

Publications National **Applied** Mathematics Laboratories, C 13.43

Recent Products of **Applied** Analysis, E 3.27/3

Technical Memorandum National Bureau of Standards, **Applied** Mathematics Division, C 13.39

Applied Research

Forum for **Applied Research** and Public Policy, Y 3.T 25:61

Apply

Apply Pesticides Correctly, a Guide for Commercial Applicators (series), EP 5.8/2

Applying

Change Sheets **Applying** to Organization Directory, W 3.42/2

Appointment

Circulars of Information Relative to **Appointment** as 1st Lieutenants in Medical Circulars on Cooperative Marketing, FCA 1.4/3

Appointment

Information Relative to **Appointment** and Admission of Cadets of Military Academy, W 12.9

Appointments

Information Concerning Temporary **Appointments**, CS 1.25

Appraisal

Appraisal of Potentials for Outdoor Recreational Development [by Area], A 57.57

Appraisal of the Proposed Budget for Food and Agricultural Sciences Report to the President and Congress, A 1.1/4-3

Conventional Loans Made in Excess of 80 Percent of Property **Appraisal** by Federal Savings and Loan Associations, FHL 1.19

Evaluation Report, Water Resources **Appraisal** for Hydroelectric Licensing, FP 1.31

RSI Quality **Appraisal** Awards and Disallowances Monthly Statistical Summary, HE 3.28/9

RSI Quality **Appraisal** Postadjudicative Monthly Statistical Summary, HE 3.28/8

Tests and Other Applicant **Appraisal** Procedures, CS 1.41/4:271-2

Unemployment Insurance Quality **Appraisal** Results, L 37.213

Appraisement

Appraisement Commission, Reports, T 1.21

Appraisers

Circulars, Reappraisements of Merchandise by General **Appraisers** or Reappraisement Circulars, T 20.4/1

Index to Reappraisements Made by Board of General **Appraisers**, T 20.4/2

Report of Conference of Local **Appraisers** Held at New York, T 20.5

Values of German Exports of Electrical **Apparatus** and Equipment, C 18.158

Apprehension

Apprehension Orders, J 1.14/10

Wanted Flyer **Apprehension** Orders, J 1.14/14

Apprehensions

Surrenders and **Apprehensions** Reported of Men Charged with Desertion from Army, W 3.38

Apprentice

Apprentice Lectures, GP 1.13

Apprentice Series, GP 1.10

Apprentice Training News, Y 3.F 31/12:9

Apprentice Training Series, GP 1.26

Reports on **Apprentice** Selection Programs, L 23.11

Apprenticeship

Apprenticeship Digest, L 23.12

Apprenticeship Standards, L 16.14

Bureau of **Apprenticeship** and Training News, L 23.15

Job Patterns for Minorities and Women in **Apprenticeship** Programs and Referral Unions, Y 3.Eq 2:12-2

Registered Group-Joint **Apprenticeship** Programs in Construction Industry (by trades), L 23.9

Research Division Reports Bureau of **Apprenticeship** and Training, L 23.19

Telephone Directory, Bureau of **Apprenticeship** and Training, L 37.109

Approach

Approach, D 202.13

Approach, Naval Aviation Safety Review, D 202.13

Eastern United States, Dates of Latest Prints, Instrument **Approach** Procedure Charts and Airport Obstruction Plans (OP), C 4.9/19

Flight Information Publication: Low Altitude Instrument **Approach** Procedures, D 5.318

High Altitude Instrument **Approach** Procedures, D 5.318/2

Index of Standard Instrument **Approach** Procedures, TD 4.312

Instrument **Approach** and Landing Charts, C 4.9/10

Instrument **Approach** Chart, Radio Beacon, C 4.9/16

Instrument **Approach** Charts, I.L.S., C 4.9/14

Instrument **Approach** Procedure Charts, C 55.411

Instrument **Approach** Procedure Charts [Alaska, Hawaii, U.S. Pacific Islands], C 55.411/2

Low Altitude **Approach** Procedures, United States Military Aviation Notice, D 5.318/3

Low Altitude Instrument **Approach** Procedures, D 5.318

Military Fields, United States, Instrument **Approach** Procedure Charts, C 55.418/4

Standard Instrument **Approach** Procedures, FAA 5.13, TD 4.60

Western United States, Dates of Latest Prints, Instrument **Approach** Procedure Charts and Airport Obstruction Plans, C 4.9/20

Approach Procedures

DoD Flight Information Publication (Terminal) Low Altitude **Approach Procedures**, United States Military Aviation Notice, D 5.318/3

Approach/Mech

Approach/Mech, D 202.13

Approaches

Aircraft Instrument **Approaches**, Fiscal Year, FAA 1.40

Transactions of Research Conferences on Cooperative chemotherapy Studies in Psychiatry and Research **Approaches** to Mental Illness, VA 1.41

Appropriate

Appropriate Technologies for Development (series), PE 1.10

Small-scale **Appropriate** Energy Technology Grants Program, E 1.76

Appropriation

Appropriation Bulletins, N 20.3/2

Appropriation Hearings, J 24.21

Appropriation, Digest of, T 63.115

Digest of **Appropriation**, T 63.115

Emergency Relief **Appropriation** Acts, Reports of President to Congress Showing Status of Funds and Operations Under, T 63.114

Justifications of Appropriation Estimates for Committees on **Appropriations**, Fiscal Year, HE 1.1/3, ED 1.46

Justifications of **Appropriation** Estimates for Committees on Appropriations: Department of Education, ED 1.46, ED 1.46/2

Justifications of **Appropriation** Estimates for Committees on Appropriations: Department of Health and Human Services, HE 1.1/3

Justifications of **Appropriation** Estimates for Committees on Appropriations: Health Care Financing Administration, HE 22.33

Reports of President to Congress Showing Status of Funds and Operations under Emergency Relief **Appropriation** Acts, T 63.114

Reports Showing Financial Status of Funds Provided in Emergency Relief **Appropriation** Acts, T 60.11

Reports Showing Status of Funds and Analyses of Expenditures, Emergency **Appropriation** Acts, T 60.13

Arctic

Alaskan Air Command, **Arctic** Aeromedical Laboratory: Technical Notes, D 301.66

Arctic Bibliography, D 1.22

Arctic Bulletin, NS 1.3/3

Arctic Constrction and Frost Effects Laboratory, D 103.31

Arctic Regions, C 55.214/49

Arctic Research of the United States, NS 1.51/2

Arctic Series, W 42.5

Nautical Charts and Publications, Region 3, Western Europe, Iceland, Greenland, and the **Arctic**, C 55.440:3

NIMA Nautical Charts, Public Sale Region 3, Western Europe, Iceland, Greenland, and the **Arctic**, TD 4.82:3

Pacific and **Arctic** Coasts, Alaska, Cape Spencer to Beaufort Sea, C 55.422:9

Technical Notes Department of the Air Force Alaskan Air Command, **Arctic** Aeromedical Laboratory, D 301.66

United States **Arctic** Research Plan, NS 1.51

ARDC

ARDC Technical Program Planning Document AF ARPD, D 301.45/49

ARDC-TR

Air Research and Development Command: Technical Reports, **ARDC-TR**, D 301.45/21

Area

Area and Country Bibliographic Surveys, D 101.22:550

Area and Industrial Development Aids, C 41.8/2

Area Charts U.S., D 5.318/6

Area Classification Summary, I 7.51/2

Area Designation Status Reports, C 46.14

Area Development Aid: **Area** Trend Series, C 41.89

Area Development Aid: Industrial Location Series, C 45.8/3

Area Development Aid: Industry Trend Series, C 45.8/2

Area Development Bulletin, C 46.9

Area Development Memorandum for State Planning and Development Offices, C 45.14

Area Guide Preliminary Series, A 13.36/5

Area Handbook to [Country], D 101.22:550

Area Handbooks, D 101.6

Area Measurement Reports, C 3.208/2

Area Outline Maps Series 1105, D 5.325-D 5.325/2

Area Planning North America and South America, D 5.318/5-2

Area Planning Special Use Airspace North America and South America, D 5.318/5-3

Area Redevelopment Bookshelf of Community Aids, C 46.8/2

Area Redevelopment Manpower Reports, L 7.66/2

Area Redevelopment Technical Leaflets, L 1.93

Area Report MC(P)-S Series, C 3.24/8-4

Area Trend Series, C 45.13

Area Trends in Employment and Unemployment, L 37.13

Area Vocational Education Program Series, FS 5.280 HE 5.280

Area Wage Survey Advance Reports, L 2.107/2

Area Wage Survey Reports, L 2.107

Area Wage Survey Summaries by Cities, L 2.113

Area Wage Survey Summaries by States, L 2.113/6

Area Wage Surveys, L 2.3

Census of Agriculture; **Area** Reports, C 56.227

Census of Construction Industries; **Area** Statistics, C 56.254/4

Census of Manufactures; **Area** Series, C 56.244/7

Census of Mineral Industries; **Area** Series, C 56.236/4

Census of Mineral Industries; Subject, Industry, and **Area** Statistics, C 56.236/6

Census of Retail Trade; Geographic **Area** Statistics, C 3.255/2

Census of Retail Trade; Geographic **Area** Statistics, Advance Reports, C 3.255/2-2

Census of Retail Trade; Preliminary **Area** Reports, C 56.251/7

Census of Selected Service Industries; **Area** Statistics Series, C 56.253/3

Census of Selected Service Industries; Preliminary **Area** Series, C 56.253/2

Census of Service Industries; Geographic **Area** Series, C 3.257/2

Census of Service Industries; Geographic **Area** Series, Advance Reports, C 3.257/2-2

Census of the Americas, Population Census, Urban **Area** Data, C 3.211

Census of Wholesale Trade; Geographic **Area** Series, C 3.256/2

Census of Wholesale Trade; Geographic **Area** Series, Advance Reports, C 3.256/2-2

Census of Wholesale Trade; Preliminary **Area** Series, C 56.252/2

CETA **Area** Employment and Unemployment, L 2.110

CETA **Area** Employment and Unemployment, BLS/CETA/MR (series), L 2.110/2

CETA **Area** Employment and Unemployment, Special Reports, BLS/CETA/SP (series), L 2.110/3

Code Classification of Foreign Ports by Geographic Trade **Area** and Country, C 3.150:K

Compilation of Administrative Policies for National Parks and National Monuments of Scientific Significance (Natural **Area** Category), I 29.9/4:N 21

Compilation of Administrative Policies for National Recreation Areas, National Seashores, National Lakeshores, National Parkways, National Scenic Riverways (Recreational **Area** Category), I 29.9/4:R 24

Conference of Model Reporting **Area** for Blindness, Proceedings, HE 20.3759/2

Danger **Area** Charts, C 4.9/15

Dry Cargo Service and **Area** Report, United States Dry Cargo Shipping Companies by Ships Owned and/or Chartered Type of Service and Area Operated, C 39.213

Flight Information Publication: **Area** Charts, U.S., D 5.318/6

GE-20 **Area** Measurement Reports, C 3.208/2

Geographic **Area** Statistics, C 3.24/9-9

Local **Area** Personal Income, C 59.18

Prime Contract Awards in Labor Surplus **Area**, D 1.57/7

Proceedings Annual Conference of Model Reporting **Area** for Blindness Statistics, FS 2.22/37

Proceedings Annual Conference on Model Reporting **Area** for Mental Hospital Statistics, FS 2.22/44

Program Development Handbooks for State and **Area** Agencies on [various subjects], HE 23.3009

Public Use Data Tape Documentation Mortality Local **Area** Summary, HE 20.6226/7

Public Use Data Tape Documentation Natality Local **Area** Summary, HE 20.6226/3

Recent Publications of Range Research, Arid South **Area**, A 77.17/6

Recreational Demonstration **Area** (by area), I 29.39

Research and Training Opportunities Abroad (year), Educational Programs in Foreign Language and **Area** Studies, HE 5.99

Schedule K. Code Classification of Foreign Ports by Geographic Trade **Area** and Country, C 3.150:K

Semi-Monthly Military Government Report for U.S. Occupied **Area** of Germany, M 105.21

Seventy-Fifth USA Maneuver **Area** Command, Annual Report and Historical Supplement, D 101.1/8

Small **Area** Data Notes, C 56.217, C 3.238

Social Security Beneficiaries by Zip Code **Area**, HE 3.73

State and Metropolitan **Area** Data Book, C 3.134/5

State and Metropolitan **Area** Employment and Unemployment, L 2.111/5

State and Metropolitan **Area** Unemployment, L 2.111/5

Statistical Profile, Redevelopment **Area** Series, C 1.45

Statistical Report, Annual Tabulations of Model Reporting **Area** for Blindness Statistics, FS 2.22/37-2

Statistical Summary, Rural Areas Development and **Area** Redevelopment, Quarterly Progress Report, A 43.38

Statistics for (year) on Blindness in the Model Reporting **Area**, HE 20.3759

Subject **Area** Bibliographies, HE 20.8311/2

Summary of Savings Accounts by Geographic **Area**, FSLIC-Insured Savings and Loan Associations, FHL 1.29

Summary of War Supply and Facility Contracts by State and Industrial **Area**, Pr 32.4828

Telephone Listing, Washington **Area**, T 63.202/10

Terminal **Area** Charts (VFR), C 55.416/11

Training Bulletins Army and Corps Areas and Departments, Seventh Corps **Area**, W 99.77/11

Training Circulars Army and Corps Areas and Departments, Second Corps **Area**, W 99.12/8

Training Circulars Army and Corps Areas and Departments, Seventh Corps **Area**, W 99.17/8

Transmittals (NOAA Washington **Area** Personnel Locator), C 55.47

U.S. Air Force Radio Facility Charts, Atlantic and Caribbean **Area**, M 301.15

U.S. Air Force Radio Facility Charts, North Pacific **Area**, M 301.14

U.S. **Area** Handbook for (country), D 101.22:550

U.S. Exports of Domestic Merchandise, SIC- based Products and **Area**, C 3.164:610

U.S. Exports, Geographic **Area**, Country, Schedule B Commodity Groupings, and Method of Transportation, C 3.164:455

U.S. Exports, Schedule B Commodity Groupings, Geographic **Area**, Country, and Method of Transportaion, C 3.164:450

U.S. Exports, World **Area** by Schedule E Commodity Groupings, C 3.164:455

U.S. General Imports Geographic **Area**, Country, Schedule A Commodity Groupings, and Method of Transporation, C 3.164:155

U.S. General Imports Schedule A Commodity Groupings by World **Area**, C 56.210:FT 150

U.S. General Imports Schedule A Commodity Groupings, Geographic **Area**, Country, and Method of Transportation, C 3.164:150

U.S. General Imports World **Area** and Country of Origin by Schedule A Commodity Groupings, C 3.164:155

U.S. Imports for Consumption and General Imports, SIC-Based Products and **Area**, C 3.164:210

U.S. Waterborne Foreign Trade, Trade **Area** by U.S. Coastal District, C 3.164:600

United States Air Force Radio Facility Charts, Caribbean and South American **Area**, D 301.10

United States Air Force, Navy, Royal Canadian Air Force and Royal Canadian Supplementary Flight Information, North American **Area** (excluding Mexico and Caribbean area), D 301.48

United States Air Force, Navy, Royal Canadian Air Force, and Royal Canadian Navy Supplementary Flight Information, North American **Area** (excluding Mexico and Caribbean area), D 301.48

United States Air Force, United States Navy Radio Facility Charts, North Atlantic **Area**, D 301.11

United States Foreign Trade, Waterborne Trade by Trade **Area**, C 3.164:973

United States Waterborne Foreign Commerce, Great Lakes **Area** [year], C 3.211/2

Water Facilities **Area** Plans (by States), A 36.148

Water Resources Development by Corps of Engineers by **Area**, D 103.35

Watershed Work Plan [by **Area**], A 57.59

Worldwide Manpower Distribution by Geographical **Area**, D 1.61/3

Area Charts

Enroute **Area** Charts (U.S.) Low Altitude, C 55.416/14, C 55.416/15-2

Area Report

Annual **Area Report**, Advance Summary, I 28.94

Areally-Weighted

Areally-Weighted Data, C 55.287/59

Areas

Administrative **Areas**, Y 3.F 31/11:35

Areas Administered by the National Park Service, I 29.66

Areas Eligible for Financial Assistance Designated Under the Public Works and Economic Development Act of 1965 Reports, C 46.25/2

Catalog of Guides to Outdoor Recreation **Areas** and Facilities, I 66.15:G 94

Census of Retail Trade; Major Retail Centers in Standard Metropolitan Statistical **Areas**, RC (series), C 56.251/5

Changes in Different Types of Public and Private Relief in Urban **Areas**, L 5.33

News Releases and Miscellaneous Publications; Committee on **Armed Services**, (House), Y 4.Ar 5/2-2

Armenian

News of Academy of Sciences of **Armenian** SSR, Phsyco-Mathematical, Natural and Technical Sciences Series, C 41.50/7

Armies

Military Operations of Civil War, Guide-Index to Official Records of Union and Confederate **Armies**, GS 4.21

War of Rebellion, Compilation of Official Records of Union and Confederate **Armies** [or Rebellion Records], W 45.5

Armor

Armor the Magazine of Mobile Warfare, D 101.78/2

U.S.A. **Armor** School Subcourses, D 101.78

Armor-Cavalry

Armor-**Cavalry** Part 1. Regular Army and Army Reserve, D 114.11:Ar 5

Armour

Armour, D 101.78/2

Arms

Annual Report of Small **Arms** Target Practice, N 17.15

Associated **Arms**, W 3.50/5

Automated Reference Materials System (**ARMS**), VA 1.95/3

Report on U.S. Government Research and Studies in the Field of **Arms** Control and Disarmament Matters, AC 1.14

Research Reports **Arms** Control and Disarmament Agency, AC 1.15

Review of **Arms** Control and Disarmament Activities, Y 4.Ar 5/2-16

Signal Communication for All **Arms** and Services, W 3.50/8

U.S. **Arms** Control and Disarmament Agency, Annual Report, Y 4.F 76/1-16

World Military Expenditures and **Arms** Transfer, S 22.116

Arms Control

Arms Control and Disarmament, LC 2.10

Arms Control and Disarmament Studies in Progress or Recently Completed, S 1.117/5

Army

All Points Bulletin, the **Army** Financial Management Newsletter, D 101.96

Alphabetical List Covering **Army** Air Forces and **Army**-Navy Aeronautical Standard Parts, W 108.15/2, M 301.11

Annual Report of **Army**-Air Force Wage Board, D 1.28

Annual Report of the Chief of Engineers, **Army**, on Civil Works Activities, Annual Reports, D 103.1

Annual Report, Surgeon General, United States **Army**, D 104.1

Armor-Cavalry Part 1. Regular **Army** and **Army** Reserve, D 114.11:Ar 5

Army, D 7.29/3

Army Administrator, D 101.86

Army Air Forces in World War II (series), D 301.82

Army Air Forces Library Bulletins, W 108.12

Army Air Forces Radio and Facility Charts Atlantic and Caribbean Areas, W 108.26

Army Air Forces Radio and Facility Charts North Pacific Area, W 108.27

Army Air Forces Specifications, W 108.13

Army Air Mobility Research and Development Laboratory Fort Eustis Virginia: USAAMRDL Technical Reports, D 117.8/2 D 117.8/4

Army AL&T Bulletin D 101.52/3

Army and Navy Official Gazette, W 1.5

Army Audit Agency Pamphlets, D 101.3/3-2

Army Aviation Digest, D 101.47

Army Ballistic Missile Agency DC-TR (series), D 105.15

Army Budget, Fiscal Year, D 101.121

Army Chaplaincy D 101.114

Army Chemical Journal, D 116.17

Army Club System Annual Report, D 102.82

Army Coded Card, W 42.6

Army Communicator, D 111.14

Army Conservation Project Posters, W 3.46/7

Army Digest, D 101.12

Army Echoes, D 101.141

Army Electronics Command Fort Monmouth N.J.: Research and Development Technical Reports ECOM (series), D 111.9/4

Army Environmental Sciences, D 103.20/7

Army Extension Courses, W 1.70

Army Extension Courses Announcements, W 3.51

Army Facilities Energy Plan, D 103.119

Army Families, D 101.123

Army Forces Far East AFFE Pamphlets, D 102.24

Army Health Promotion Program, Fit to Win, D 101.22:600

Army Historian, D 114.2

Army Historical Program Fiscal Year, D 114.10/2

Army Historical Series, D 114.19

Army History D 114.20

Army Hit Kit of Popular Songs, D 102.10

Army Host, D 102.81

Army Information Digest, W 1.66 M 101.10 D 101.12

Army Institute for Professional Development: Subcourse ISO (series), D 101.103

Army Intelligence Center and School: SupR (series), D 101.112

Army Issue Paper, D 101.146/4

Army Lawyer, D 108.11

Army Life and United States Recruiting News, M 108.77

Army Lineage Book, D 114.11

Army List and Directory, W 3.10 W 40.6

Army Logistician, D 101.69

Army Management Course (series), D 101.94

Army Management Engineering Training Activity: Course Catalog, D 101.94/3

Army Map Sevice Bulletins, W 7.33/4

Army Material Command Regulations, D 101.9/2

Army Medical Bulletin, W 44.21/7

Army Medical Library Bibliographies, D 104.10

Army Medical Library Catalog, LC 30.13

Army Medical Research Laboratory Reports, D 104.14

Army Meteorological Register, W 44.11

Army Missile Command Redstone Scientific Information Center Redstone Arsenal Alabama RSIC (series), D 105.22/3

Army Morale Support Fund Annual Report, D 102.82/2

Army Morale Welfare and Recreation Fiscal Year Annual Report, D 102.82/2

Army Museum Newsletter, D 114.16

Army National Guard Lineage Series, D 12.20

Army Navy Hit Kit of Popular Songs, M 117.7

Army Nurse, W 44.29

Army Ordnance Center and School Aberdeen Proving Ground Maryland: Special Texts, D 105.25

Army Organizational Effectiveness Journal, D 101.91

Army Pay Tables, W 36.10 W 77.7

Army Personnel Bulletin, D 101.39/4

Army Personnel Letter, D 101.39/3

Army Postal and Navy Air Service Laws [March 2 1913], Y 1.2:Ai 7

Army Postal Bulletin, W 3.77

Army Procurement Circulars, D 101.33/2

Army Procurement Procedures, D 101.6/4

Army Procurement Regulations, M 101.11

Army Prosthetics Research Laboratory Technical Reports, D 104.15/2

Army Quartermaster School Correspondence Subcourse QM (series), D 106.22

Army RD&A Bulletin, D 101.52/3

Army Register, D 102.9

Army Regulations AR (series), W 1.6 D 101.9

Army Research and Development, D 101.52/3

Army Research Institute for Behavioral and Social Sciences: Research Reports, D 101.60/2

Army Research Institute for the Behavioral and Social Sciences: Special Reports (series), D 101.60/6

Army Research Institute for the Behavioral Sciences, Study Report, D 101.60/8

Army Research Laboratory Strategic Plan for Fiscal Year, D 101.1/11-2

Army Research Task Summaries, D 101.52/2

Army Reserve Magazine, D 101.43

Army Reservist, D 101.43

Army ROTC (pamphlets), D 101.22/3

Army Storage Catalogue, W 34.16/3

Army Talk, W 111.7

Army Trainer, D 101.20/3

Army Training and Evaluation Program ARTEP (series), D 101.20/2

Army Transportation Engineering Agency: USATEA Reports, D 117.11

Army Transportation Research Command: Interim Reports, D 117.8/3

Army War Casualties, W 107.11

Army-Navy Aeronautical Standards Index, Y 3.Ae 8:7

Army-Navy Joint Packaging Instructions, N 20.27

Army-Navy War Casualties, Pr 32.5028

Army-Navy-Air Force List of Products Qualified Under Military Specifications, D 101.30

Atlas to Accompany [War of Rebellion] Official Records of Union **Army** and Confederate **Army** [or Rebellion Records], W 45.7

Bibliography of U.S. **Army** Medical Research and Nutrition Laboratory Reports and Reprints for (year), D 104.17

Bulletin of **Army** Medical Department, D 104.3

Bulletin of Judge Advocate General of **Army**, D 108.3

Center for **Army** Lessons Learned (series), D 101.22/25

Changes in **Army** Regulations, W 1.6/2

Circulars Relating to Plan and Methods of Publication of Official Records of Union **Army** and Confederate **Army**, W 45.4

Circulars Relating to Plan and Methods of Publication of Official Records of Union **Army** and Confederate **Army**, W 45.4

Classification of Periodicals, **Army** Medical Library, W 44.24

Compendium of General Orders Amending **Army** Regulations, W 3.13

CONUS **Army** Installations/Activities by Congressional District, D 101.99

Corps of Regular **Army**, W 44.27

Department of **Army** Chiefs and Executives [organization chart], D 101.36, D 102.23

Department of **Army** Supply Manual SM (series), D 101.16/2

Department of the **Army** Annual Financial Report, D 101.1/7

Department of the **Army** Historical Summary, D 114.15

Department of the **Army** Prime Contracts ($1 million and over) Placed with Industry, Non-Profit Organizations, Colleges, and Universities, D 101.22:715-4

Digest of Opinions of Judge-Advocate-General, **Army**, W 10.8

Directory of Airfields, U.S. **Army** & Navy, C 31.126

Drill Regulations, Manuals, and Instructions for **Army**, W 3.16/1

Employment Bulletin, Current Openings, G-11 and Above, at **Army** Material Command Activities Throughout the United States, D 101.3/5

Extracts from Reports by Regular and Military Officers on Joint **Army** and Militia Coast-Defense Exercises, W 2.7

First **Army** Pamphlets (series), D 101.22/9-2

First **Army**, 1a Regulations, D 101.9/6

Four Minute Men, **Army** Bulletins, Y 3.P 96/3:6

General Court-Martial Orders: **Army** and Corps Areas and Departments, W 99.11/7, W 99.12/7, W 99.13/7, W 99.14/7, W 99.15/7, W 99.16/7, W 99.17/7, W 99.19/7, W 99.21/7

General Court-Martial Orders: Department of the **Army**, W 3.32, W 1.51, M 101.14, D 101.14

General Orders Embracing Laws Affecting the **Army**, W 3.8

Headquarters, Department of the **Army** Chiefs and Executives, D 202.23

Headquarters, First United States **Army**, Deputy Chief of Staff, Information Management, Organization, Mission, and Functions, D 101.1/9

Health of the **Army**, D 104.20

Historical Review, U.S. **Army** Belvoir Research and Development Center, D 101.98

Historical Review, U.S. **Army** Mobility Equipment Research and Development Command, D 101.98

Index of Specifications and Standards used by Department of **Army**, Military Index, V. 2, D 101.34

Index of United States Army, Joint **Army**-Navy, and Federal Specifications and Standards, M 101.23

Index of United States Army, Joint **Army**-Navy, and Federal Specifications and Standards, M 101.23

Index to U.S. **Army** Specifications, W 3.48/2

Joint **Army** & Navy Radio Facility Charts, W 108.29

Joint **Army** and Air Force Bulletins, D 101.3

Joint **Army** and Air Force Procurement Circulars, D 101.33

Joint **Army** and Air Force Regulations, M 101.15

Joint **Army**-Navy Publications, W 1.79

Joint **Army**-Navy Specifications, N 20.23, M 213.8

Joint **Army**-Navy Standards, N 20.28, M 5.7

Laws Governing Granting of **Army** and Navy Pensions, VA 2.5/2

Laws Governing Granting of **Army** and Navy Pensions and Bounty Land, I 24.14

Letterman **Army** Institute of Research: Institute Reports, D 104.29

List of Unclassified Reports Received from Department of **Army**, Signal Corps, C 13.33/4

Manual for **Army** Cooks, W 5.5

Medical Department of the **Army** in World War II, D 104.11

Medical Department, United States **Army** in Vietnam, D 104.11/2

Medico-Military Review for Medical Department, **Army**, W 44.22

Memorandum Opinions of Judge Advocate General of the **Army**, D 108.8

Military Laws of United States (**Army**), D 108.5/2

Newsletter of the U.S. **Army** Medical Department, D 104.24

Numerical List Covering **Army** Air Forces and **Army**-Navy Aeronautical Standard Parts, W 108.15

Numerical List Covering **Army** Air Forces and **Army**-Navy Aeronautical Standard Parts, W 108.15

Numerical List, U.S. Air Force and **Army**-Navy Aeronautical Standard Drawings, M 301.12

Officers of **Army** in or Near District of Columbia, W 3.81

Officers of **Army** in or Near **District of Columbia**, W 3.81

Officers of **Army**, Their Families and Families of Deceased Officers, Residing in or Near District of Columbia, W 1.11

Army and Air Force Register, M 101.19, M 108.8

Official **Army** National Guard Register, D 12.9

Official **Army** Register of Volunteer Force of U.S. **Army**, 1861-65, W 3.12

Official List of Officers of Officers Reserve Corps, **Army**, W 3.44

Opinions of Judge Advocate General, **Army**, W 10.9

Organization of **Army**, W 3.50/17

Parameters, Journal of the U.S. **Army** War College, D 101.72

Performance Guides (series) **Army** Department, D 101.107/3-2

Posters **Army** Medical Department, D 104.34

Progress, U.S. **Army**, D 101.50

Publications **Army** Audit Agency, D 101.62

Publications **Army** Language School, D 101.64

Publications **Army** Map Service, D 103.20

Publications **Army** Scientific Advisory Panel, D 101.81

Publications Available for Purchase, U.S. **Army** Engineer Waterways Experiment Station and Other Corps of Engineers Agencies, D 103.39

Publications U.S. **Army** Foreign Science and Technology Center, D 101.79

Publications U.S. **Army** Headquarters in Europe, D 101.42

Recruiting Bulletins **Army** and Corps Areas and Departments, Seventh Corps Area, W 99.17/10

Recruiting for Line of **Army**, W 3.17/1

Regulations for Government of United States **Army** General Hospital, W 44.15

Report of the Chief of Staff of the United States **Army**, D 101.1/2

Report to **Army**, M 104.8, D 107.7

Research Reports **Army** Ballistic Missile Agency, D 105.15

Research Reports Walter Reed **Army** Institute of Research, D 104.15

Sagamore **Army** Materials Research Conference Proceedings (series), D 101.122

School Garden **Army** Leaflets (general), I 16.28/6

Second **Army** Pamphlets (series), D 101.22/9

Second **Army**, 2A Circulars (series), D 101.4/3

Selling in **Army** and Air Force Careers, W 3.84, M 108.79

Shipment Under the United States Foreign Aid Programs Made on **Army**- or Navy-Operated Vessels (American flag) by Port of Lading by Country of Destination, C 3.164:976

Statement of Recruiting for Line of **Army** at General Recruiting Stations and Their Auxiliaries, W 3.17/2

Stations of **Army**, W 3.30, W 40.5

Student Handbook (series) Department of the **Army**, D 101.47/3, D 101.47/4

Summation of United States **Army** Military Government Activities in Korea, W 1.76

Summation of United States **Army** Military Government Activities in Ryukyu Islands, W 1.78, M 105.12

Surrenders and Apprehensions Reported of Men Charged with Desertion from **Army**, W 3.38

Telephone Directory **Army** Department, (by area), D 101.97

The U.S. **Army** Campaigns of World War II, D 114.7/5

Tips, **Army** Personnel Magazine, D 102.80

Training Bulletins **Army** and Corps Areas and Departments, Seventh Corps Area, W 99.77/11

Training Circulars **Army** and Corps Areas and Departments, Second Corps Area, W 99.12/8

Training Circulars **Army** and Corps Areas and Departments, Seventh Corps Area, W 99.17/8

Training Circulars Department of the **Army**, M 101.22, D 101.24

Training Manual United States **Army**, W 3.39/3

U.S. **Army** and Air Force Recruiting Service Letter, M 208.76

U.S. **Army** and Navy Directory of Airfields, C 31.125

U.S. **Army** Audit Agency Bulletins, D 101.3/3

U.S. **Army** Ballistic Missile Agency, DG- TR-(series), D 105.15/2

U.S. **Army** Educational Manuals, W 3.47

U.S. **Army** Electronic Proving Ground, USAEPG-SIG (series), D 111.12

U.S. **Army** Engineer District, Los Angeles: Reports (numbered), D 103.59

U.S. **Army** Equipment Index of Modification Work Orders, D 101.22:750-10

U.S. **Army** in Action Series, D 114.7/4

U.S. **Army** Materiel Command, Annual Historical Review, D 101.1/4-2

U.S. **Army** Medical Doctrine, Publications, D 104.36

U.S. **Army** Military Personnel Center: Pamphlets (series), D 101.22/16

U.S. **Army** Mobility R & D Laboratory: USAAMRDL CR- (series), D 117.8/6

U.S. **Army** Natick Laboratories, Food Division, Natick, Mass. Technical Report FD-, D 106.20

U.S. **Army** Pocket Recruiting Guide, D 101.6/11

U.S. **Army** Recruiting and Reenlisting Journal, D 118.9

U.S. **Army** Recruiting Command Pamphlets, USAREC PAM- (series), D 101.22/7

U.S. **Army** Research and Development Program Guide, D 101.52/4

U.S. **Army** Specifications, W 3.48/1, W 1.49, M 101.26, D 101.28

U.S. **Army** Training Manuals Numbered, W 3.39/1

U.S. **Army** Training Manuals, W 3.39

United States **Army** in Vietnam (series), D 114.7/3

United States **Army** in World War II, D 114.7

United States **Army** in World War II: Master Index, Reader's Guide, D 114.7/2

United States **Army** in World War, M 103.9

United States **Army** Installations and Major Activities in Continental U.S., D 101.22:210-1

United States **Army** Medical Research Institute of Infectious Disease: Annual Progress Report, D 104.27

United States **Army** Occupational Handbook, D 101.40

United States **Army** Research and Development Series, D 101.52

United States **Army** Training Publications, W 3.39/2

Walter Reed **Army** Institute of Research, Research Reports WRAIR (series), D 104.15

Walter Reed **Army** Medical Center, **Army** Prosthetics Research Laboratory, Technical Reports, D 104.15/2

Water Resources Development by **Army** Corps of Engineers in [State], D 103.35

Army Publications

Consolidated Index of **Army Publications** and Blank Forms, D 101.22:25-30

Army Research Institute

Basic Research in Behavioral and Social Sciences: U.S. **Army Research Institute** Annual Report, D 101.1/7-2

ARNG

ARNG (series), D 12.12

Arnold

Technical Notes Department of the Air Force **Arnold** Engineering Development Center, D 301.45/33-3

Arnoldian

Arnoldian, D 208.112

ARO-D

ARO-D (series), D 101.52/7

Aromatics

World Trade in Synthetic **Aromatics**, C 18.175

Around

Statistical Briefs from **Around** the World, C 3.205/2

ARPC

ARPC Pamphlet (series), , D 301.35/9

ARR

Agricultural Research Results, **ARR** (series), A 106.12, A 77.32

Arranged

Schedule T. Statistical Classification of Imports into U.S. **Arranged** in Shipping Commodity GROUPS., C 3.150:T

Arrangement

Classed Subject **Arrangement**, LC 1.23/5

U.S. Imports of Textiles and Apparel under the Multifiber **Arrangement**, Statistical Report, ITC 1.30

United States General Imports of Wool Manufacture Except Floor Coverings, Quantity Totals in Terms of Equivalent Square Yards in Country of Origin by Commodity Grouping **Arrangement**, TQ-2203, C 3.164/2-6

Arrangements

Child Care **Arrangements** of AFDC Recipients Under the Work Incentive Program, HE 17.609

Marital Status and Living **Arrangements**, C 3.186/6

Arrearage Tables

Arrearage Tables of Amounts Due and Unpaid 90 Days or More on Foreign Credits of the United States Government, T 1.45/4

Arrearages

Significant **Arrearages** Due the United States Government and Unpaid 90 Days or More by Official Foreign Obligors, T 1.45/5

Arrest

Prosecution of Felony **Arrest**, J 29.9/4

Arrestees

Annual Report on Adult **Arrestees**, J 28.24/5

Annual Report on Cocaine Use Among **Arrestees**, J 28.15/2-5

Annual Report on Juvenile **Arrestees**/Detainees, J 28.24/6

Annual Report on Marijuana Use Among **Arrestees**, J 28.15/2-6

Annual Report on Methamphetamine Use Among **Arrestees**, J 28.15/2-7

Annual Report on Opiate Use Among **Arrestees**, J 28.15/2-4

Arrests

Seizures and **Arrests**, T 70.9/6

Arrival

Fresh Fruit and Vegetable **Arrival** Totals, A 88.12/31-4

Fruit and Vegetable Market News, Weekly **Arrival** Summary, A 88.12/18

Schedule **Arrival** Performance in the Top 200 Markets by Carrier, C 31.261, CAB 1.19

Standard Terminal **Arrival**(STAR) Charts, C 55.416/3

Arrivals

Arrivals and Departures by Selected Ports Statistics of Foreign Visitor **Arrivals** and U.S. Citizen Departures Analyzed by U.S. Ports of Entry and Departure, C 47.15/4

Arrivals and Departures by Selected Ports
Statistics of Foreign Visitor Arrivals and
U.S. Citizen Departures Analyzed by
U.S. Ports of Entry and Departure, C
47.15/4
Foreign Visitor **Arrivals** by Selected Ports,
Calendar Year, C 47.15/6
Statistical Summary and Analysis of Foreign Visitor
Arrivals, U.S. Citizen and Non-U.S.
Citizen Departures, C 47.15

Arrowhead
Arrowhead, D 101.71

ARS
ARS (series), A 1.107 A 77.15
ARS Directory, A 77.15/2
ARS National Research Program NRP (series), A
77.28

ARS-NC
ARS-NC (series), A 77.15/2

Arsenal
Army Missile Command Redstone Scientific
Information Center Redstone **Arsenal**
Alabama RSIC (series), D 105.22/3
Arsenal of Democracy Series, Pr 32.408
Frankford **Arsenal**: Technical Memorandums, D
105.17/3
Frankford **Arsenal**: Technical Reports, D 105.17/4
Index to Tests of Metals at Watertown **Arsenal**, W
34.14/2
Ordnance Materials Research Offices, Watertown
Arsenal, Omro Publications, D 105.13/3
Rodman Process Laboratory, Watertown **Arsenal**,
Reports, D 105.13
Technical Notes Picatinny **Arsenal**, D 105.12/2, D
105.12/4
Test of Metals at Watertown **Arsenal**, W 34.14
Victory Speaker; An **Arsenal** of Information for
Speakers, Pr 32.5017
Watertown **Arsenal** Laboratory, Report WAL
(series), D 105.13/2
Watertown **Arsenal** Laboratory: Technical Report
(series), D 105.13/2-2
Watertown **Arsenal**: Technical Report Ward, TR
(series), D 105.13/2-3

Arsenals
Catalogue of Materials and Supplies Required at
Arsenals, etc., W 34.16

ARSLOE
ARSLOE Informal Report (series), C 55.236

Arson
Arson Resource Exchange Bulletin, FEM 1.110/2

Art
American **Art** in the Barbizon Mood, SI 6.2:B 23
Art and Artists in National Parks, I 29.25
Art and Indian Children of the Dakotas (series), I
20.63
Art and Industry Education in Industrial Arts and
Fine Arts in United States, I 16.7
Art in the United States Capitol, Y 1.91-2:H.doc
368
Art Projects Bulletins, T 58.16
Design, **Art**, and Architecture in Transportation,
TD 1.47
Federal **Art** Project, Y 3.W 89/2:40
Posters National Gallery of **Art**, SI 8.10
Public Works of **Art** Project, T 1.30
Report and Studies in the History of **Art**, SI 8.9
Smithsonian Opportunities for Research and Study
in History, **Art**, Science, SI 1.44

ARTC
Denver **ARTC** Center: Annual Report (Rocky
Mountain Region), TD 4.43

ARTEP
Army Training and Evaluation Program **ARTEP**
(series), D 101.20/2

Arthritis
Arthritis and Rheumatic Diseases Abstracts, HE
20.3312
Arthritis Interagency Coordinating Committee:
Annual Report to the Secretary Fiscal
Year (date), HE 20.3032
Arthritis Program Annual Report to the Director,
HE 20.3321
Arthritis, Rheumatic Diseases, and Related
Disorders, HE 20.3320/2
Highlights of Research Progress in **Arthritis** and
Metabolic Diseases, FS 2.22/21
Multipurpose **Arthritis** Centers Personnel
Directory, HE 20.3322

Arthropod
Arthropod-Borne Virus Information Exchange, HE
20.7036

Artic
Climatological Data; **Artic** Stations, C 30.21/2

Article
JACS [Journal **Article** Copy Service] Directory, C
51.11/6

Articles
Abstracts of Selected Periodical **Articles** of
Military Interest, W 55.8
Allowance of **Articles** under Cognizance of Bureau
of Construction and Repair for Vessels of
the Navy, N 4.5
Catalog of Title Entries of Books and Other
Articles, LC 3.5
Catalogue of **Articles** to be Sold at Auction, P 7.5
Current **Articles** of Interest Cumulative Index, AC
1.13/2-2
English Abstracts of Selected **Articles** from Soviet
Bloc and Mainland China Technical
Journals, C 41.84
Recent **Articles** on Petroleum and Allied
Substances, I 28.22
Reprints of **Articles** Published Concerning NIH
Consensus Development Conferences,
HE 20.3030/2
Review of Some Recent Magazine **Articles** Relating
to Housing, I 40.9
Selected List of **Articles** in Current Periodicals of
Interest to Ordnance Department, W
34.21/2
Transportation of Dangerous **Articles** and
Magnetized Materials, TD 4.6:part 103

Artifacts
Artifacts, NF 2.14
Facts and **Artifacts**, I 29.23

Artificial
Annual Contractors' Conference on **Artificial**
Kidney Program, Proceedings, HE
20.3314
Artificial Kidney Bibliography, HE 20.3311
Artificial Kidney-Chronic Uremia Advisory
Committee, HE 20.3001/2:K 54

Artillery
Air Defense **Artillery**, D 101.77
Artillery Circulars, W 3.5/1
Artillery Memoranda, W 29.8
Artillery Notes, W 29.7
Coast **Artillery** Memoranda, W 3.14, W 53.6
Field **Artillery** Notes, W 26.10
Journal of United States **Artillery**, W 29.5
Special Bibliography, **Artillery** and Guided
Missile School Library, D 101.49
Technical Notes Coast **Artillery** Target Practice, W
3.37

Artist
Inter-Arts, Presenting Organizations **Artist**
Communities Services to the Arts,
Application Guidelines, NF 2.8/2-23

Artists
Art and **Artists** in National Parks, I 29.25
Artists in Education, NF 2.8/2
Initiative for Interdisciplinary **Artists** Inter-Arts,
NF 2.8/2-22
Inter-Arts, **Artists**' Projects: New Forms, NF 2.8/2-
26
Visual **Artists** Fellowships, NF 2.8/2-13
Your Navy, from the Viewpoint of the Nation's
Finest **Artists**, D 201.9

Arts
Arts Administration Fellows Program, Application
Guideline For Fiscal Year, NF 2.8/2-24
Arts Administration Fellows Program, Application
Guidelines, NF 2.8/2-24
Arts in America, NF 2.8/2-28
Arts in Education, Arts Plus, Application
Guidelines For Fiscal Year, NF 2.8/2-37
Arts Review, NF 2.13
Catalogue of Copyright Entries, Pt. 1, Engraving,
Cuts and Prints, Chromos and
Lithographs, Photographs, Fine **Arts**,
LC 3.6/4
Catalogue of Copyright Entries, Pt. 1, Engraving,
Cuts and Prints, Chromos and
Lithographs, Photographs, Fine **Arts**,
LC 3.6/4
Exploring Visual **Arts** and Crafts Careers, HE
19.108:Ex 7/4
Fact Sheets: Sources of Indian and Eskimo **Arts** and
Crafts, I 1.84/3
Indian **Arts** and Crafts Board Publications, I 1.84
Inter-Arts, Presenting Organizations **Artist**
Communities Services to the **Arts**,
Application Guidelines, NF 2.8/2-23

Local **Arts** Agencies Program, Application
Guidelines, NF 2.8/2-31
Native American **Arts** (series), I 1.84/4
Organizations Visual **Arts**, Application
Guidelines, NF 2.8/2-15
Performing **Arts**, LC 1.46
Research Division Reports National Endowment
for the **Arts**, NF 2.12
U.S. Air Force Fine **Arts** Series, D 301.76/4
Visual **Arts** Grants to Organizations, NF 2.8/2-15
War, Literature, and the **Arts**, D 305.22/3

Arts III
Arts III Computer Program Functional Specifications (CPFS), TD 4.46

ArtsReach
ArtsReach, Application Guidelines NF 2.15/3

AS
Handbook **AS** (series), P 1.31/10

ASA
ASA/NSF/Census Bureau Research Fellow
Program, C 3.293

Asamblea
Actas De La **Asamblea** Filipina [Spanish Only], W
49.41/5

Asbestos
Asbestos in (year), I 28.123

ASC MSRC
ASC MSRC, Quarterly Journal, D 301.121

Ascertainment
Cost **Ascertainment** Report, P 4.6

ASCII
Traffic Safety Data **ASCII** and SAS Versions, TD
1.56/3

ASCS
ASCS Aerial Photography Status Maps, A
82.84:Ae 8
ASCS Background Information, A 82.82
ASCS Commodity Fact Sheets, A 82.82/2
State Data Profiles, Calendar Year (date), Selected
Ascs Program Activity and Other
Agricultural Data, A 82.90

ASD
ASD Technical Note TN (series), D 301.45/26
Technical Documentary Report **ASD**-TDR- (series),
D 301.45/26-3
Technical Reports, **ASD**-TR- (series), D 301.45/26-
2

Aseptic
Aseptic Meningitis Surveillance Annual Summary,
HE 20.7011/26

ASFIS
Aquatic Sciences and Fisheries Information System:
ASFIS Reference Series, C 55.39

Ash
Soda **Ash** and Sodium Sulfate: U.S. Production,
Trade and Consumption, I 28.135/2

Ashore
Ashore, D 207.15/2

Asia
Accession List: Southeast **Asia**, LC 1.30/10
Asia and Pacific Rim, Situation and Outlook
Series, A 93.29/2-19
Asia Reports, PrEx 7.16
Eastern **Asia**, Series 5305, D 5.336
Flight Information Publication: Terminal High
Altitude, Pacific and Southeast **Asia**, D
301.12/4
Flight Information Publication: Terminal Low
Altitude, Africa and Southwest **Asia**, D
301.13/6
Flight Information Publication: Terminal Low
Altitude, Pacific and Southeast **Asia**, D
301.12/3
Nautical Charts and Publications, Region 9, East
Asia, C 55.440:9
Near East and South **Asia** Report, PrEx 7.20
Quarterly Trade Report, Southeastern **Asia**, C
18.156
SE **Asia** Briefing Map, Series 5213, D 5.335
South and East **Asia** Report, PrEx 7.16/4
South **Asia** Outlook and Situation Report, A
93.29/2-15
South **Asia**, LC 1.30/10-3
Southeast **Asia** Report, PrEx 7.16/4
Southeast **Asia**, Burma, Thailand, and Laos, LC
1.30/10-5
Southeast **Asia**, LC 1.30/10
Southern **Asia**, Publications in Western
Languages, Quarterly Accessions List,
LC 17.7
Soviet Union, People of **Asia** and Africa, PrEx
7.21/7-3

Terminal High Altitude, Pacific and Southeast
Asia, D 301.12/4
Terminal Low Altitude, Africa and Southwest Asia,
D 301.13/6
United States Air Force in Southeast Asia (series),
D 301.86/2
USAF Southeast Asia Monograph Series, D 301.86

Asian
Asian Development Bank Act Releases, SE 1.25/14
East Asian and Pacific Series, S 1.38
Near East and South Asian Series, S 1.86/2
Posters Asian Division, LC 17.10

ASPA
Armed Services Procurement Regulation
Supplement ASPA (series), D 1.13/2-2

Aspects
Environmental-Social Aspects of Energy
Technologies, E 1.99
NTSB-AAS [National Transportation Safety Board,
Aspects of Aviation Safety] (series), TD
1.121

Aspen
Lake States Aspen Reports, A 13.61/7

Asphalt
Asphalt Sales, E 3.11/18
Asphalt Sales in (year), I 28.110/2
Asphalt Shipments in (year), I 28.110
Shipments of Asphalt, I 28.110

ASPM
Armed Services Procurement Manual ASPM
(series), D 1.13/4

Assassination
Assassination Records Review Board, Reports Y
3.2: AS 7/R 29

Assaulted
Law Enforcement Officers Killed and Assaulted,
Uniform Crime Report, J 1.14/7-6

Assaults
Analysis of Assaults on Federal Officers, J 1.14/7-3
Assaults on Federal Officers, J 1.14/7-3

Assay
General Instructions and Regulations in Relation
to Transaction of Business at Mints and
Assay Offices with Coinage Laws, T 28.9

Assembling
Assembling the Health Planning Structure, HE
20.6114

Assembly
Proceedings Air Force Academy Assembly, D
305.11
Proceedings Assembly of State Librarians, LC
30.14
Report of the United States Delegation to the
World Health Assembly, HE 20.19
United States Air Force Academy Assembly,
Proceedings, D 305.11

Assessment
Assessment Activities, Y 3.T 22/2:2-10
Climate Impact Assessment, Foreign Countries, C
55.233
Climate Impact Assessment, Foreign Countries
Annual Summary, C 55.233/3
Climatic Impact Assessment Program; Newsletter,
TD 1.38/2
Climatic Impact Assessment Program; Technical
Abstract Report, TD 1.38
Committee on the Assessment of Human Health
Effects of Great Lakes Water Quality:
Annual Report, Y 3.In 8/28:15
Environmental Assessment (series), I 29.79/5
Environmental Assessment Notebook Series, TD
1.8/2
Environmental Assessment of the Alaskan
Continental Shelf, C 55.622/2
Environmental Assessment of the Alaskan
Continental Shelf [various publications],
C 55.622/3
Environmental Assessment of the Alaskan
Continental Shelf, Principal
Investigator's Reports, C 55.622
Environmental Assessment, DOE/EA (series), E
1.20/2, E 4.9
Environmental Compliance Assessment System
(ECAS) Annual Report, D 101.130
Environmental/Resource Assessment and
Information, C 55.233, C 55.233/2
Exploratory Research and Problem Assessment:
Abstracts of NSF Research Results, NS
1.13/2
Five Year Medical Facility Construction Needs
Assessment, VA 1.68
Foreign Energy Supply Assessment Program
Series, E 3.30

Health Technology Assessment Reports (series),
HE 20.6512/7
Interim Guide for Environment Assessment, HH
1.6/3:En 8
Klamath River Fisheries Assessment Program
(series), I 49.107
Management Plan & Environmental Assessment, I
53.59/2
Marine Environmental Assessment, Gulf of Mexico,
Annual Summary, C 55.237
Museum Assessment Program, Grant Application
and Information, NF 4.11
National Acid Precipitation Assessment Program,
Report to Congress, C 55.703
National Foreign Assessment Center Publications
(numbered), PrEx 3.10/7
Noise Diagnostics for Safety Assessment,
Standards, and Regulation, E 1.28/10
Office of Technology Assessment and Forecast:
Publications, C 1.62
Outer Continental Shelf Environmental
Assessment Program Final Reports of
Principal Investigators, C 55.433
Publications Office of Technology Assessment and
Forecast, C 1.62
Radiological Impact Assessment, Browns Ferry
Nuclear Plant, Y 3.T 25:53
Reports of the National Juvenile Justice
Assessment Centers (series), J 26.27
Supplemental Reports to the Second National
Water Assessment, Y 3.W 29:13
Technical Memorandum Technology Assessment
Office, Y 3.T 22/2:11
Technology Assessment and Forecast, Report, C
21.24:T 22
Technology Assessment Program, NIJ Standard, J
28.15
TSCA [Toxic Substances Control Act] Chemical
Assessment Series, EP 5.15/2

Assessments
Assessments Completed and Referrals to
Manpower Agencies by Welfare
Agencies Under Work Incentive Program
for AFDC Recipients, HE 17.619
Market Assessments for [various countries], C
57.412
Political Activity and Political Assessments of
Federal Office-Holders and Employees,
CS 1.34
Precision and Accuracy Assessments for State and
Local Air Monitoring Networks, EP
1.23/5-3
Scientific and Technical Assessments Reports, EP
1.23/7

Asset
Asset and Liability Trends, T 71.18
Asset and Liability Trends All Operating Savings
and Loan Associations, FHL 1.30
Asset Forfeiture, J 26.29
Real Estate Asset Inventoryy, Y 3.F 31/8:31, Y 3.R
31/2:15

Assets
All Banks in the United States and Other Areas,
Principal Assets and Liabilities by
States, FR 1.28/2
Assets and Liabilities of All Banks in the United
States, FR 1.28
Assets and Liabilities of All Commercial Banks in
United States, FR 1.28/4
Assets and Liabilities of All Member Banks by
Districts, FR 1.28/3
Assets Liabilities and Capital Accounts
Commercial Banks and Mutual Savings
Banks, Y 3.F 31/8:9
MISTRIP, Defense Program for Redistribution of
Assets (DEPRA) Procedures, D 1.87/3
Progress Report to Congress by War Assets
Administration, Pr 33.211, Y 3.W 19/
8:11
Progress Report War Assets Administration, Pr
33.215
Report of Calls, Assets, Liabilities, Capital,
Accounts, Commercial and Mutual
Savings Banks (unnumbered), Y 3.F 31/
8:9-2
Sales of Capital Assets Reported on Individual
Income Tax Returns, T 22.35/2:C 17
Summary of Assets and Liabilities, T 12.14
Summary Report, Assets and Liabilities of Member
Banks, FR 1.11
Trust Assets of Financial Institutions, Y 3.F 31/
8:23

Assign
Patents and Trademarks, ASSIGN, C 21.31/13
Patents Assign, U.S. Patents Assignments
Recorded at the USPTO, C 21.31/4
Trademarks Assign, U.S. Trademarks Assignments
Recorded at the USPTO, C 21.31/9

Assigned
Call Letters Assigned, CC 2.7

Assignee
Patentee/Assignee Index, C 21.27

Assignment
Employment under the Executive Assignment
Systems, CS 1.41/4:305-1
Extension Course of Medical Field Service School;
Lesson Assignment Sheets, W 3.71
Military Law; Lesson Assignment Sheets, W 3.50/
3

Assignments
Directory and Planning Schedule of FSC Class and
Area Assignments, D 7.13:1
Patents Assign, U.S. Patents Assignments
Recorded at the USPTO, C 21.31/4
Payload Flight Assignments NASA Mixed Fleet,
NAS 1.81
Trademarks Assign, U.S. Trademarks Assignments
Recorded at the USPTO, C 21.31/9

Assist
ERAF (Environmental Reporting Assist File), D
212.16/2
Patents Assist, Full Text of Patent Search Tools, C
21.31/5
Trademarks Assist, C 21.31/10

Assistance
Advance Release of Statistics on Public
Assistance, FS 3.14/2, FS 14.209, FS
17.10, FS 17.610
Agricultural Export Assistance Update Quarterly
Report, A 67.46
Agricultural Trade Development and Assistance
Act of 1954 and Amendments, Y 1.2:Ag
8/6
Annual Report of HUD Activities Under the
Uniform Relocation Assistance Policies
Act of 1970, HH 1.49
Antirecession Fiscal Assistance to State and Local
Governments, T 1.51
Applications and Case Dispositions for Public
Assistance, HE 3.60/3, HE 17.613/3
Applications, Cases Approved, and Cases
Discontinued for Public Assistance, HE
17.641
Archeological Assistance Study (series), I 29.59/8
Areas Eligible for Financial Assistance Designated
Under the Public Works and Economic
Development Act of 1965 Reports, C
46.25/2
Assistance Administration Manual, EP 1.8/2
Attorney General's Annual Report Federal Law
Enforcement and Criminal Justice
Assistance Activities, J 1.32/2
Bureau of Justice Assistance Bulletin, J 26.32
Bureau of Justice Assistance Publications List, J
26.9/2
Catalog of Federal Assistance Programs, PrEx
10.2:P 94
Catalog of Federal Domestic Assistance, PrEx 2.20
Catalog of Federal Education Assistance Programs,
ED 1.29, HE 19.127, C 58.12
Catalog of HEW Assistance Providing Financial
Support and Service to States,
Communities, Organizations,
Individuals, HE 1.6/6
Catalog of HEW Assistance Providing Financial
Support and Service to States,
Communities, Organizations,
Individuals, HE 1.6/6
Catalog of Seminars, Training Programs and
Technical Assistance in Labor Statistics,
L 2.114
Catalogue of Books and Blanks Used in Office of
Assistance Treasurer, New York, T 36.5/
3
CETA Technical Assistance Documents, L 37.8/2
Coastal Zone Management Technical Assistance
Documents, C 55.32/2
Community Assistance Series, HH 10.10
Comparative Statistics of General Assistance
Operations of Public Agencies in
Selected Large Cities, FS 3.16

Concurrent Receipt of Public **Assistance** Money Payments and Old-Age, Survivors, and Disability Insurance Cash Benefits by Persons Aged 65 or Over, FS 17.636, HE 17.636

Concurrent Receipt of Public **Assistance** Money Payments and Old-Age, Survivors, and Disability Insurance Cash Benefits by Persons Aged 65 or Over, FS 17.636, HE 17.636

Customer **Assistance** Handbook, D 7.6/20

Disposition of Public **Assistance** Cases Involving Question of Fraud, HE 3.63

Executive Manpower Management Technical **Assistance** Papers, EMMTAP, CS 1.85

Expenditures for Public **Assistance** Payments and for Administrative Costs, by Program and Source of Funds, HE 17.632

Expenditures for Public **Assistance** Programs, HE 3.69

Fair Hearings in Public **Assistance**, HE 17.644

Federal **Assistance** for Programs Serving the Handicapped, ED 1.34

Federal **Assistance** for Projects in Aging, FS 14.12

Federal Financial **Assistance** for Projects in Aging, FS 15.13, FS 17.310/2

Federal Law Enforcement and Criminal Justice **Assistance** Activities, Annual Report, J 1.32/2

Federal Voting **Assistance** Program, D 1.80

Federal Work Programs and Public **Assistance**, FW 4.32

Federal-Aid Highway Relocation **Assistance** and Payment Statistics, TD 2.28

Financial and Technical **Assistance** Provided by the Department of Agriculture and the Department of Housing and Urban Development for Nonmetropolitan Planning District, Annual Report to Congress, A 1.113

Financial **Assistance** by Geographic Area, ED 1.35

Financial **Assistance** by Geographic Area, Fiscal Year, HE 1.57

Financial **Assistance** for College Students, Undergraduate and First-Professional, FS 5.255:55027, HE 5.255:55027

Financial Statistics for Public **Assistance**, Calendar Year, FS 3.14/3

Focus on Federal Employee Health **Assistance** Programs, PM 1.55

Foreign Military Sales, Foreign Military Construction Sales, and Military **Assistance** Facts, D 1.66

Grants, Preventive Services, Training, Technical **Assistance** and Information Services, HE 1.310

Grants-In-Aid and Other Financial **Assistance** Programs, FS 1.6/6, HE 20.2016

Grants-In-Aid and Other Financial **Assistance** Programs, Health Services and Mental Health Administration, FS 2.317

Health Professions Education **Assistance** Program, Report to the President and the Congress, HE 1.40

Hearings in Public **Assistance**, HE 17.644

Illustrations from State Public **Assistance** Agencies, Current Practices in Staff Training, FS 3.20

Impact on Public Assistance Caseloads of (a) Training Programs under Manpower Development and Training Act and Read Redevelopment Act, and (b) Public **Assistance** Work and Training Programs, FS 14.219, FS 17.409, FS 17.635

Implementation of Section 620(s) of the Foreign **Assistance** Act of 1961, as Amended, A Report to Congress, S 18.1/3

Information and Technical **Assistance** Delivered by the Department of Agriculture in Fiscal Year, A 1.1/2

International Training and Advisory **Assistance** Programs, T 17.29

IRMS Directory of **Assistance**, GS 12.12/3

Justice **Assistance** News, J 1.59

Legal Opinions of the Office of General Counsel of the Law Enforcement **Assistance** Administration, J 1.5/3

Medicaid and Other Medical Care Financed from Public **Assistance** Funds, HE 17.620, HE 17.621

Medical **Assistance** (Medicaid) Financed Under Title XIX of Social Security Act, HE 17.616

Medical Assistance Financed under **Assistance** Titles of Social Security Act, FS 17.616

Medical Assistance Financed under Public **Assistance** Titles of Social Security Act, FS 17.2:M 46/2, HE 17.2:M 46/2

Medical **Assistance** for the Aged, Fact Sheet, FS 14.218

Medical Care in Public **Assistance**, Guides and Recommended Standards, FS 14.208/2

Military **Assistance** Program Address Directory, D 7.6/4:M 59/6

Money Payments to Recipients of Special Types of Public **Assistance**, FS 17.627, HE 17.627

Program Facts on Federally Aided Public **Assistance** Income Maintenance Programs, HE 17.614

Public **Assistance** Bureau, Applications: Old- Age Assistance, Aid to Dependent Children, Aid to the Blind [and] General **Assistance**, FS 3.17

Public Assistance Bureau, Applications: Old- Age **Assistance**, Aid to Dependent Children, Aid to the Blind [and] General Assistance, FS 3.17

Public **Assistance** Recipients and Cash Payments, HE 3.61

Public **Assistance** Recipients in Standard Metropolitan Statistical Areas, HE 3.61/ 2

Public **Assistance** Reports, HE 17.19

Public **Assistance** Statistics, HE 3.60, HE 17.610

Public **Assistance**, Annual Statistical Data, FS 14.212, FS 17.13, FS 17.615, HE 17.615

Public **Assistance**, Costs of State and Local Administration, Services, and Training, FS 17.633, HE 17.633

Public **Assistance**, FS 3.3/a2, FS 2.13/3

Public **Assistance**, Quarterly Review of Statistics for U.S., SS 1.13

Public **Assistance**, Statistics for U.S., SS 1.25/a 1

Public **Assistance**: Vendor Payments for Medical Care by Type of Service, Fiscal Year Ended (date), HE 17.617

Quarterly Awards Listing Grants **Assistance** Programs, EP 1.35

Quarterly Cumulative Report of Technical **Assistance**, C 46.23

Quarterly Public **Assistance** Statistics, HE 3.60/4, HE 25.15

Reasons for Discontinuing Money Payments to Public **Assistance** Cases, HE 17.613/2

Reasons for Opening and Closing Public **Assistance** Cases, FS 3.45, FS 14.214, FS 17.411, FS 17.613

Reasons for Opening Public **Assistance** Cases, HE 17.613

Recipients and Amounts of Medical Vendor Payments Under Public **Assistance** Programs, HE 17.617/2

Recipients of Public **Assistance** Money Payments and Amounts of Such Payments, by Program, State, and County, HE 17.627/2

Report of Urban Planning **Assistance** Program, HH 7.11

Report on Disposition of Public **Assistance** Cases Involving Questions of Fraud, Fiscal Year, HE 17.642

Report to Congress on Foreign **Assistance** Program, S 18.1

Request for Hearings in Public **Assistance**, Fiscal Year (date), HE 3.60/2

Semiannual Report on Operations Under Mutual Defense **Assistance** Control Act of 1951, FO 1.1/2

Semiannual Reports on Operations under Mutual Defense **Assistance** Act, S 17.1/2

Semiannual Reports under Mutual Defense **Assistance** Control Act, Pr 33.901/2

Source of Funds Expended for Public **Assistance** Payments and for Cost of Administration, Services, and Training, HE 17.634

Source of Funds Expended for Public **Assistance** Payments, FS 14.215, FS 17.631, HE 17.631, HE 17.19/2

State **Assistance** Programs for SSI Recipients, SSA 1.17/2

State Expenditures for Public **Assistance** Programs, HE 17.2:St 2/2

State Maximums and Other Methods of Limiting Money Payments to Recipients of Special Types of Public **Assistance**, HE 17.626

State Municipal Project Priority Lists, Grants **Assistance** Programs, EP 1.56/3

Technical **Assistance** Aid, L 1.48

Technical **Assistance** Aids, L 31.8

Technical **Assistance** Bulletins, I 66.22, HE 20.415/2

Technical **Assistance** Guide (series), J 1.8/4

Technical **Assistance** Guides, L 37.308/2

Technical **Assistance** Publication Series, HE 20.8025

Technical **Assistance** Reminders, L 31.8/2

Transition **Assistance** Program Military Civilian One Good Job Deserves Another Participant Manual, L 39.8/2

Trend Report: Graphic Presentation of Public **Assistance** and Related Data, HE 17.612

Urban Planning **Assistance** Program, Project Directory, HH 1.26, HH 7.8/3

Vendor Payments for Medical Care Under Public **Assistance**, by Program and Type of Service, Fiscal Year (date), HE 17.617/4

Veterans **Assistance** Information, Printed and Processed, Y 3.Se 4:18

Wastewater Treatment Construction Grants Data Base, Public Law 92-500 Project Records, Grants **Assistance** Programs, New Projects Funded During (Month), EP 1.56

Assistant

Rulings on Requests for Review of the **Assistant** Secretary of Labor for Labor- Management Relations Pursuant to Executive Order 11491, As Amended, L 1.51/6

Supplemental Digest and Index of Published Decisions of the **Assistant** Secretary of Labor for Labor-Management Relations Pursuant to Executive Order 11491, Y 3.F 31/21-3:10

Assistants

Cooperative Graduate Fellowship Program for Fiscal Year, Fellowship Awards [and] Program of Summer Fellowships for Graduate Teaching **Assistants** for Fiscal Year, NS 1.19/2

Associate

Associate Degrees and Other Formal Awards Below the Baccalaureate, HE 19.333

Associate Training Programs in the Medical Sciences and Biological Sciences at the National Institutes of Health (Year) Catalog, HE 20.3015

Pharmacology Research **Associate** Program, HE 20.3461/2

Associated

Associated Arms, W 3.50/5

Dictionary of Military and **Associated** Terms, D 5.12:1

Associates

FBI National Academy **Associates** Newsletter, J 1.14/20

Associateship

Engineering Postdoctoral Research **Associateship** Program, C 13.65/2

Associateships

Postdoctoral Research **Associateships**, C 13.65

Resident Research **Associateships**, Postdoctoral, Tenable and National Bureau of Standards, C 13.47

Association

Association of Food and Drug Officials Quarterly Bulletin, HE 20.4003/5

Conventions, (year): National and International Unions, State Labor Federations, Professional Associations, State Employee **Association** [list], L 2.103

Cow Testing **Association** Letter, A 44.6

Federal National Mortgage **Association** News, HH 6.8/2

FHA and VA Mortgages Owned and Available for Sale by Reconstruction Finance Corporation and Federal National Mortgage **Association**, Y 3.R 24:14

Government National Mortgage **Association**, GNMA, Annual Report, HH 1.1/7

Papers of American Historical **Association**, SI 4.5

Permanent International **Association** of Road Congress, S 5.31

Proceedings Medical **Association** of Isthmian Canal Zone, W 79.12/6

Publications Federal National Mortgage **Association**, FL 5.17

Safety Competition, National Crushed Stone **Association**, I 28.26/4

Safety Competition, National Lime **Association**, I 28.26/3

Transactions of Naval Militia **Association** of United States, N 1.27/5

Associations

Analysis and Summary of Conditions and Performances of the Farm Credit Banks and **Associations**, FCA 1.23/2

Conventional Loans Made in Excess of 80 Percent of Property Appraisal by Federal Savings and Loan **Associations**, FHL 1.19

Conventional Loans Made to Finance Acquisition and Development of Land, Federal Savings and Loan **Associations**, FHL 1.22

Conventions, (year): National and International Unions, State Labor Federations, Professional **Associations**, State Employee Association [list], L 2.103

Directory of Law Enforcement and Criminal Justice **Associations** and Research Centers, C 13.10:480-20

Estimated Flow of Savings in Savings and Loan **Associations**, HH 4.8/2

Estimated Mortgage Lending Activity of Savings and Loan **Associations**, HH 4.8/3

Flow of Savings in Savings and Loan **Associations**, FHL 1.7/2

FSLIC Insured Savings and Loan **Associations**, Savings and Mortgage Activity, Selected Balance Sheet Items, FHL 1.20/2

List of State and Local Trade **Associations** (by States), C 18.200

Loans and Discounts of Farm Credit Banks and **Associations**, Annual Report, FCA 1.12/2

Number of Foreclosures [and rate of foreclosure] by FSLIC Insured Savings and Loan **Associations**, FHL 1.26

Production Credit **Associations**, Annual Summary of Operations, FCA 1.22

Production Credit **Associations**, Summary of Operations, A 72.25

Report to the Federal Land Bank **Associations** for Year Ended June 30 (date), FCA 1.23

Report to the National Farm Loan **Associations**, FCA 1.23

Savings and Mortgage Lending Activity, Selected Balance Sheet Items, F.S.L.I.C. Insured Savings and Loan **Associations**, FHL 1.20/2

Summary of Cases Relating to Farmers' Cooperative **Associations**, A 72.18

Summary of Operations of Production Credit **Associations**, A 72.25

Summary of Savings Accounts by Geographic Area, FSLIC-Insured Savings and Loan **Associations**, FHL 1.29

Assumptions

Assumptions for the Annual Energy Outlook, E 3.1/4-3

Program and Financial Plan, Basic **Assumptions** and Guidelines, HE 1.610/2

Assurance

Annual Statement of **Assurance**, D 1.101

Carrier Quality **Assurance** Report, HE 22.415

HUD Scorecard, Quality **Assurance** Program, HH 1.83

Joint NCDRH and State Quality **Assurance** Surveys in Nuclear Medicine, HE 20.4611

Program Memorandum Quality **Assurance**, HE 22.28/3

Quality and Reliability **Assurance** Handbooks, D 7.6/11

Quality **Assurance**, QA Reporter, D 7.23

Radiological Health Quality **Assurance** Series, HE 20.4108/2

Reliability and Quality **Assurance** Publications, NAS 1.22/3

Asthma

Annual Workshop of the **Asthma** and Allergic Disease Centers, HE 20.3261

AsthmaMemo

AsthmaMemo HE 20.3225/2

Astronautics

Report of the Activities of the Committee on Science and **Astronautics**, Y 4.Sci 2:Ac 8

Astronauts

Astronauts and Cosmonauts Biographical and Statistical Data, Y 4.Sci 2:95

Astronomical

Astronomical Almanac, D 213.8

Astronomical Journal [abstracts], C 41.73

Astronomical Papers Prepared for Use of American Ephemeris and Nautical Almanac, D 213.9

Astronomical Papers Translated from the Russian, SI 1.12/4

Astronomical Phenomena for the Year [date], D 213.8/3

Astronomy

Herald of Leningrad University, Mathematics, Mechanics, and **Astronomy** Series [abstracts], C 41.50/8

Soviet-Bloc Research in Geophysics, **Astronomy** and Space, Y 3.J 66:14

USSR and Eastern European Scientific Abstracts, Geophysics, **Astronomy**, and Space, Y 3.J 66:14

Astrophysical

Annals of **Astrophysical** Observatory, SI 1.12

Annuals of **Astrophysical** Observatory, SI 1.12

Astrophysical Observatory Reports, SI 1.1/a2

Astrophysics

Smithsonian Contributions to **Astrophysics**, SI 1.12/2

Asymmetry

Studies in **Asymmetry**, D 101.146/8

ATC

ATC Manual, C 31.106/3

ATC Pamphlet, D 301.38/6

Atlanta

Atlanta Helicopter Route Chart, C 55.416/12-8

Atlantian

Atlantian, J 16.13

Atlantic

ACCP (**Atlantic** Climate Change Program) Newsletter, C 55.55

Anglers' Guide to the United States **Atlantic** Coast, C 55.308:An 4

Army Air Forces Radio and Facility Charts **Atlantic** and Caribbean Areas, W 108.26

Atlantic Coasters' Nautical Almanac, N 11.10

Atlantic Flyway, I 49.24/3

Collected Reprints; **Atlantic** Oceanographic and Meteorological Laboratories, C 55.612

Hydrologic Bulletin, Hourly and Daily Precipitation; North **Atlantic** District, C 30.30

Ice Supplement to North **Atlantic** Pilot Chart, N 6.15/2

Inside Route Pilot (**Atlantic** and Gulf Coasts), C 4.6/3

Light List, **Atlantic** and Gulf Coasts of United States, N 24.30, T 47.35

Light List, **Atlantic** Coast of U.S. Intercoastal Waterway, Hampton Roads to Rio Grande Including Inside Waters, N 24.17, T 47.28

Light List, **Atlantic** Coast of United States, Southern Part, N 24.16, T 47.24

Light List: Vol. 2, **Atlantic** Coast, Toms River, New Jersey to Little River, South Carolina, TD 5.9:v 2

Lights and Fog Signals, **Atlantic** and Gulf Coasts, T 25.16

Marine Calendar, **Atlantic**, A 29.41

Marine Recreational Fishery Statistics Survey, **Atlantic** and Gulf Coasts, C 55.309/2-3

Middle **Atlantic** Fisheries, C 55.309/2

Middle **Atlantic** Regional Office Publications, L 2.92

Military Aviation Notices; North **Atlantic** and East Canada, D 301.11/2

Pilot Chart of North **Atlantic** Ocean, D 203.17, N 6.15, M 202.17, D 203.17

Pilot Chart of South **Atlantic** Ocean, D 203.18, N 6.20, M 202.18, D 203.18

Pilot Chart of Upper Air, North **Atlantic** Ocean, N 6.28

Pilot Rules for Certain Inland Waters of **Atlantic** and Pacific Coasts of Gulf of Mexico, C 25.9

Regional Reports, Middle **Atlantic** Region, L 2.71/6

Regional Studies Plan, Fiscal Year, **Atlantic** OCS Region, I 72.12/15

Retail Trade Report Middle **Atlantic** Region, C 3.174

Retail Trade Report South **Atlantic** Region, C 3.175

Seafaring Wage Rates, **Atlantic**, Gulf and Pacific Districts, C 39.202:W 12

South **Atlantic** Fisheries, C 55.309/2

Tide Current Tables, **Atlantic** Coast of North America, C 55.425

Tide Tables **Atlantic** Coast of (Calendar Year), T 11.13, C 4.13

Tide Tables **Atlantic** Ocean, C 4.15/3

U.S. Air Force Radio Facility Charts, **Atlantic** and Caribbean Area, M 301.15

U.S. Coast Pilots **Atlantic** Coast, C 4.6/1

United States Air Force, Navy, Royal Canadian Air Force and Royal Canadian Navy, Navy Radio Facility Charts and In- Flight Data, Alaska, Canada and North **Atlantic**, D 301.13/3

United States Air Force, United States Navy Radio Facility Charts, North **Atlantic** Area, D 301.11

United States Coast Pilot, **Atlantic** Coast, T 11.6

Atlantic Coast

Atlantic Coast and Gulf Coast of the United States, TD 5.9:2

Atlantic Coast; Cape Cod to Sandy Hook, C 55.422:2

Atlantic Coast; Cape Henry to Key West, C 55.422:4

Atlantic Coast; Eastport to Cape Cod, C 55.422:1

Atlantic Coast; Gulf of Mexico Puerto Rico and Virgin Islands, C 55.422:5

Atlantic Coast; Sandy Hook to Cape Henry, C 55.422:3

Atlantic Coast; United States, TD 5.9:1

Lumber Shipments from Pacific Coast to **Atlantic** Coast, SB 7.5/162

North **Atlantic Coast** Fisheries Arbitration, S 3.18/3

Atlantic Ocean

Meterological Chart of the North **Atlantic Ocean**, A 29.23

Meterological Chart of the South **Atlantic Ocean**, A 29.25

Tropical Cyclones of the North **Atlantic Ocean**, C 55.202:C 99/871-977

Atlas

Atlas of American Agriculture Advance Sheets, A 1.30

Atlas of Tumor Pathology, D 1.16

Atlas of Tumor Pathology 2d Series, D 1.16/3

Atlas of Tumor Pathology, Third Series, D 101.117/4

Atlas to Accompany [War of Rebellion] Official Records of Union Army and Confederate Army [or Rebellion Records], W 45.7

Atlas/State Data Abstract for the United States, D 1.58/4

Climate Prediction Center **Atlas**, C 55.136

Congressional District **Atlas**, C 3.62/5, C 56.213/2

Congressional District **Atlas**, C 3.282/5

Consumer Energy **Atlas**, E 1.33/2:10879-01

Data **Atlas**, C 55.411/4

Forest **Atlas**, A 13.17

Geologic **Atlas** of the United States, I 19.5/1

National **Atlas**, I 19.111

National **Atlas** of the United States, I 19.2:N 21 a, I 19.111

NCHS **Atlas** CD-ROM, HE 20.6209/12

Oceanographic **Atlas** of the International Indian Ocean Expedition, NS 1.2:In 2/4

Resources **Atlas** Project: Thailand, **Atlas**, D 103.49

Separate Sheets of Selected Thematic and General Reference Maps from the National **Atlas** of the United States of America, I 19.111a

Sheets of National **Atlas** of United States Agricultural Research Service, A 77.19

Sheets of National **Atlas** of United States Bureau of the Census, C 3.62/3

Sheets of National **Atlas** of United States Census of Agriculture, C 3.31/10

Sheets of National **Atlas** of United States Coast and Geodetic Survey, C 4.9/21

Sheets of National **Atlas** of United States Forest Service, A 13.28/2

Sheets of National **Atlas** of United States Geological Survey, I 19.5/3

Sheets of National **Atlas** of United States Interstate Commerce Commission, IC 1.30

Sheets of National **Atlas** of United States Tennessee Valley Authority, Y 3.T 25:7-2

Sheets of National **Atlas** of United States Weather Bureau, C 30.22/4

Topographic **Atlas** of the United States, I 19.10

U.S. Navy Marine Climatic **Atlas** of the World, D 202.2:At 6

Urban **Atlas**, Tract Data for Standard Metropolitan
Statistical Areas, C 3.62/7, C 56.242/4
World Ocean **Atlas**, C 55.297
Atlases
Atlases; Corps of Engineers, D 103.49/3-2
Atlases; National Climatic Center, C 55.287/58
Historical Climatology Series, **Atlases**, C 55.287/58
Hydrologic Investigation **Atlases** (maps), I 19.89
IFYGL **Atlases**, C 55.21/5
Maps and **Atlases**: Agricultural Stabilization and
Conservation Service, A 82.91
Maps and **Atlases**: Central Intelligence Agency,
PrEx 3.10/4
Maps and **Atlases**: Department of State, S 1.33/2
Maps and **Atlases**: Environmental Data Service, C
55.231
Maps and **Atlases**: Environmental Protection
Agency, EP 1.99
Maps and **Atlases**: Library of Congress, Processing
Department, LC 30.8/5
Maps and **Atlases**: National Science Foundation,
NS 1.41
Maps and **Atlases**: Veterans Administration, VA
1.70
Maps, Charts, and **Atlases**, D 5.353
NOAA **Atlases**, C 55.22
Atmosphere
Upper **Atmosphere** Geophysics, Reports UAG-
(series), C 52.16/2, C 55.220
World Data Center A Upper **Atmosphere**
Geophysics, Report UAG- (series), C
55.220
Atmospheric
Air Resources **Atmospheric** Turbulence and
Diffusion Laboratory: Annual Report, C
55.621
Atmospheric Sciences Laboratory: Contractor
Reports ASL-CR (series), D 111.9/6
Atmospheric Sciences Laboratory: Technical
Reports ASL-TR (series), D 111.9/5
Atmospheric Turbidity and Precipitation
Chemistry Data for the World, C 55.283
Collected Reprints; **Atmospheric** Physics and
Chemistry Laboratory, C 55.612/3
Environmental Sciences, **Atmospheric**, E 1.99
Global **Atmospheric** Background Monitoring for
Selected Environmental Parameters, C
55.284
Interim Lists of Periodicals in Collection of
Atmospheric Sciences Library and
Marine and Earth Sciences Library, C
55.224
Key to Oceanic and **Atmospheric** Information
Sources, C 55.219/5
Professional Papers National Oceanic and
Atmospheric Administration, C 55.25
Received or Planned Current Fisheries, Oceano-
graphic, and **Atmospheric** Translations,
A- (series), C 55.325/2
Survey of Foreign Fisheries, Oceanographic, and
Atmospheric Literature, C- (series), C
55.325/3
Technical Notes Department of the Air Force
Atmospheric Analysis Laboratory, D
301.45/30 3
Translated Tables of Contents of Current Foreign
Fisheries, Oceanographic, and
Atmospheric Publications, C 55.325
U.S. **Atmospheric** Nuclear Weapons Tests, Nuclear
Test Personnel Review, D 15.10
Universities and Their Relationships with the
National Oceanic and **Atmospheric**
Administration, C 55.40
Upper **Atmospheric** Programs Bulletin, NAS 1.63
Atoll
Atoll Research Bulletin, SI 1.25
Atom
Understanding the **Atom** Series, Y 3.At 7:54
World of the **Atom** Series Booklets, Y 3.At 7:54-2
Atomic
Atomic Energy Act of 1946 and Amendments
[August 1 1946], Y 1.2:At 7
Atomic Energy Commission Reports Opinions of
the Atomic Energy Commssion with
Selected Orders, Y 3.At 7:49
Atomic Energy Commission Research Reports for
Sale by Office of Technical Services, C
41.29
Atomic Energy Commission Rules and Regula-
tions, Y 3.At 7:6-2
Atomic Energy in Foreign Countries, Y 3.At 7:13

Atomic Energy Legislations through [Congress
Session], Y 4.At 7/2:L 52/2
Atomic Energy Research in Life Sciences and
Physical Sciences, Y 3.At 7:48
Atomic Energy [abstracts], C 41.74
Atomic Energy: Significant References Covering
Various Aspects of Subject Arranged
Topically, LC 14.13
Defense **Atomic** Support Agency: Technical
Analysis Report DASA (series), D 5.14
Legislative Histories of **Atomic** Energy Acts, Y
3.At 7:5-2
List of **Atomic** Energy Commission Documents
Available for Sale, Y 3.At 7:15
Major Activities in the **Atomic** Energy Programs,
Y 3.At 7:2 P 94/2
Work Injuries in **Atomic** Energy, L 2.71
Atomic Energy
Current Membership of Joint Committee on **Atomic**
Energy, Membership, Publications, and
Other Pertinent Information through
[Congress, Session], Y 4.At 7/2:M 51
Development, Growth, and State of the **Atomic**
Energy Industry, Y 4.At 7/2:At 7/12
Guide to Published Research on **Atomic Energy**, Y
3.At 7:7
ATP
Agricultural Trade Policy, **ATP**- (series), A 67.39
ATRC
ATRC Manual, D 301.7/7
ATS
ATS Fact Book, TD 4.315
ATSDR
ATSDR, CD-ROM Series, HE 20.517, HE 20.7919
Attaches
FAS Letter to Agricultural **Attaches** and Officers, A
67.31/2
Handbook for Service **Attaches** Accredited to the
Department of the Air Force, D 301.6/5-2
Selected References for Labor **Attaches**, List of
Readily Available Materials, L 1.34/2
Attachment
Pole **Attachment** Filings, CC 1.47/5
Attack
Impact of Air **Attack** in World War II, Selected Data
for Civil Defense Planning, FCD 1.12
TAC **Attack**, D 301.94
Attainment
Educational **Attainment**, C 3.186:P-20
Educational **Attainment** in the United States, C
3.186/23
Research **Attainment** Report, Fiscal Year, A 13.82/
11
Attitudes
Changing Public **Attitudes** on Governments and
Taxes, Y 3.Ad 9/8:17
What the Soldier Thinks, Monthly Digest of War
Department Studies on **Attitudes** of
American Troops, W 1.65
Attorney
Posters Office of **Attorney** Personnel Management, J
33.9
Report of the United States **Attorney** for the
District of Columbia, J 1.1/4
Attorney General
Adjudications of **Attorney General** of United
States, J 1.28
Annual Evaluation Report on Drugs and Crime: A
Report to the President, the **Attorney**
General, and the Congress, J 28.29
Annual Report of the **Attorney General** of the
United States, J 1.1
Digest of Official Opinions of **Attorney General**, J
1.6
Identical Bidding in Public Procurement Report of
Attorney General Under Executive
Order 10936, J 1.31
Opinions of **Attorney General**, J 1.5
Register of Office of **Attorney General**, J 1.12
Report of the **Attorney General** on Competition in
the Synthetic Rubber Industry, J 1.26
Report of the **Attorney General** Pursuant to
Section 2 of the Joint Resolution of July
28, 1955, Consenting to an Interstate
Compact to Conserve Oil and Gas, J 1.27
Report of the **Attorney General** to the Congress of
the United States on the Administration
of the Foreign Agents Registration Act
of 1938, As Amended, J 1.30
Report of the **Attorney General**, Pursuant to
Section 252(i) of the Energy Policy and
Conservation Act, J 1.27/2

Report of the Office of the United States **Attorney**
General for the Southern District of
Texas, Year in Review, J 1.1/12
Report of the U.S. **Attorney General** for the District
of (area) to the **Attorney General**, J 31.9
Report to the **Attorney General** (series), J 1.96
Attorney General's
Attorney General's Annual Report Federal Law
Enforcement and Criminal Justice
Assistance Activities, J 1.32/2
Attorney General's Committee on Administrative
Procedure General Publications, J 1.21
Attorney General's Committee on Administrative
Procedure Monographs, J 1.22
The **Attorney General's** Advisory Committee of
United States Attorneys Annual Report,
J 1.1/8
Attorney-General
Official Opinions of **Attorney-General**, W 49.23/5
Attorney's
United States **Attorney's** Bulletins, J 31.12
Attorneys
List of U.S. Judges, **Attorneys** and Marshalls, J 1.11
Patent **Attorneys** and Agents Available to
Represent Inventors Before the United
States Patent Office, C 21.9/2
Roster of **Attorneys** and Agents Registered to
Practice before the U.S. Patent Office, C
21.9
Roster of Disqualified **Attorneys**, I 24.12
The Attorney General's Advisory Committee of
United States **Attorneys** Annual Report,
J 1.1/8
Attorneys General
Official Opinions of the **Attorneys General** of the
United States, J 1.5
Attractions
Traveler's Guides to Special **Attractions**, C 47.12/
2
Auction
Catalogue of Articles to be Sold at **Auction**, P 7.5
Navy Surplus by **Auction** Catalogs, N 20.14/2
Audio
Audio Materials, HE 3.22/2
Audiovisual
Audiovisual Education Directors in State
Departments of Education and in Large
City School Systems, FS 5.60
Audiovisual
Audiovisual Materials
Audiovisual Materials; Bureau of Alcohol Tobacco
and Firearms, T 70.12
Audiovisual Materials; Bureau of Reclamation, I
27.7/3-2
Audiovisual Materials; Corps of Engineer, D
103.49/4
Audiovisual Materials; Defense Nuclear Agency, D
15.11
Audiovisual Materials; Department of Education,
ED 1.37/2
Audiovisual Materials; Department of Interior, I
1.108
Audiovisual Materials; Department of Labor, L 1.9/
4
Audiovisual Materials; Federal Disaster
Assistance Administration, HH 12.10
Audiovisual Materials; International Communica-
tion Agency, ICA 1.16
Audiovisual Materials; International Development
Agency, S 18.60/2
Audiovisual Materials; National Cancer Institute,
HE 20.3175/2
Audiovisual Materials; Prisons Bureau, J 16.27
Audiovisual Materials; Public Health Service, HE
20.30/2
Audiovisual Products, CC 1.56
Audiovisual Release Announcements, D 1.70
Catalog of **Audiovisual** Materials, HE 20.3002:Au
2
Catalogue of **Audiovisual** Media Programs, Ju 13.9/
2
Directory of U.S. Government **Audiovisual**
Personnel, GS 4.24
Directory of U.S. Government **Audiovisual**
Personnel, GS 4.24
Federal **Audiovisual** Activity, AE 1.110/5
Key **Audiovisual** Personnel in Public Schools and
Library Systems in State and Large
Cities and In Large Public Colleges and
Universities, FS 5.60/2
List of **Audiovisual** Materials Produced by the
United States Government (series), GS
4.17/5-2

Medical Catalog of **Audiovisual** Materials Produced by the United States Government, GS 4.17/6

Quarterly Update, a Comprehensive Listing of New **Audiovisual** Materials and Services Offered by the Audiovisual Center, GS 4.17/5-3, AE 1.109

Quarterly Update, a Comprehensive Listing of New Audiovisual Materials and Services Offered by the **Audiovisual** Center, GS 4.17/5-3, AE 1.109

Reference List of **Audiovisual** Materials Produced by the United States Government, GS 4.2:Au 2

Selected **Audiovisual** Records, Photographs of (various subjects), GS 4.17/7

Audiovisuals

Catalog of Publications, **Audiovisuals**, and Software, HE 20.3619/2

Health Sciences **Audiovisuals**, HE 20.3614/5

Networked **Audiovisuals**, VA 1.81

Selected List of **Audiovisuals**, FS 2.211/3

Audit

Annual **Audit** Plan, HH 1.1/5

Army **Audit** Agency Pamphlets, D 101.3/3-2

Audit Discriminant Function Reporting System, T 22.52

Audit Guide Series, A 1.11/4

Audit Journal, TD 1.32

Audit Legal Letter Guidance, PrEx 2.34

Audit of Payments from Special Bank Account to Lockheed Aircraft Corporation for C-5a Aircraft Program Defense Department, GA 1.13:L 81/2

Audit Standards Supplemental Series, GA 1.19

Defense Contract **Audit** Agency Bulletin, D 1.46/6

Defense Contract **Audit** Agency Manual, DCAAM (series), D 1.46/2

Defense Contract **Audit** Agency Pamphlets, DCAAP (series), D 1.46

Financial **Audit**, Environmental and Energy Study Conference Financial Statement, GA 1.13/17

Financial **Audit**, Export-Import Bank's Financial Statements, GA 1.13/7

Financial **Audit**, Federal Home Loan Banks' Financial Statements for ..., GA 1.13/13, GA 1.13/13-2

Financial **Audit**, Federal Savings and Loan Insurance Corporation's ... Financial Statements, GA 1.13/12

Financial **Audit**, House Recording Studio Revolving Fund, GA 1.13/5-2

Financial **Audit**, House Restaurant Revolving Fund's Financial Statements, GA 1.13/8

Financial **Audit**, House Stationery Revolving Fund Statements, GA 1.13/19

Financial **Audit**, Senate Recording and Photographic Studios Revolving Fund, GA 1.13/5

Financial **Audit**, Senate Restaurants Revolving Fund for Fiscal Years, GA 1.13/8-2

Footnote, Journal of the HEW **Audit** Agency, HE 1.37

Inspector General **Audit** Reports, TD 1.1/3-2

Medicare Part A Intermediary Manual, Part 4, **Audit** Procedures, HE 22.8/6-4

National Performance **Audit** Program, Ambient Air Audits of Analytical Proficiency, EP 1.23/5-2

Office of Inspector General, **Audit** and Inspection Plan, C 1.1/2-2

Publications Army **Audit** Agency, D 101.62

Report on Activities Defense Contract **Audit** Agency, D 1.46/5

Report on Internal **Audit** Activities of the Internal Revenue Service, T 22.53

Semiannual Reports to Congress on **Audit** Follow-up, ED 1.1/4

U.S. Army **Audit** Agency Bulletins, D 101.3/3

Audit Follow-up

Semiannual Reports to Congress on **Audit Follow-up**, ED 1.26/2

Audit Plan

Annual **Audit Plan** FY, Office of Inspector General, L 1.74/2

Auditing

International Journal of Government **Auditing**, GA 1.38

Auditor

Interagency **Auditor** Training Center Bulletin, C 1.61

New Mexico, Traveling **Auditor** and Bank Examiner, Annual Reports, I 1.24/2

Audits

Medicare Intermediary Manual, Part 2, **Audits**-Reimbursement Program Administration, HE 22.8/6-2

Reports to Congress on **Audits**, Reviews, and Examinations, GA 1.13

Summary of Safety Management **Audits**, TD 2.66

August 1921

Pan-Pacific Educational Conference, 1st Honolulu, **August 1921**, S 5.21/2, S 5.22

Auke Bay, Alaska

Manuscript Reports Issued by Biological Laboratory, **Auke Bay, Alaska**, I 49.57

Australia

History of Africa, **Australia**, New Zealand, Etc., LC 26.9:DT-DX

Nautical Charts and Publications, Region 7, **Australia**, Indonesia, and New Zealand, C 55.440:7

NIMA Nautical Charts, Public Sale Region 7, **Australia**, Indonesia, and New Zealand, TD 4.82:7

Austria

Gazette of the Allied Commission for **Austria**, D 102.22

Military Government, **Austria**, Report of United States Commissioner, W 1.74, M 105.10

Military Government, **Austria**, Report of United States Commissioner, W 1.74, M 105.10

Office of United States High Commissioner for **Austria**, General Publications, S 1.89/4

Report of **Austria**, Office of U.S. High Commissioner for **Austria**, S 1.89/3

Report of United States High Commissioner, Statistical Annex, U.S. Element, Allied Commission for **Austria**, S 1.89/2

Report of United States High Commissioner, U.S. Element, Allied Commission for **Austria**, S 1.89

Report on **Austria**, Office of U.S. High Commissioner for Austria, S 1.89/3

Report on Austria, Office of U.S. High Commissioner for **Austria**, S 1.89/3

Tripartite Claims Commission (U.S., **Austria**, and Hungary), S 3.37

Auswartigen

Akten Zur Deutschen **Auswartigen** Politic, S 1.82/2

Author

Corporate **Author** Authority List, C 51.18

Library of Congress **Author** Catalog, Annual Cumulation, LC 30.8/2

Author Index

Author Index Title Index and Subject Index to the Social Security Bulletin, HE 3.3/5

Authorities

Directory of State and Territorial Health **Authorities**, FS 2.77/2

Directory of State, Territorial, and Regional Health **Authorities**, HE 20.2015/2

Local **Authorities** Participating in HAA Low-Rent Programs, HH 3.9

Local **Authorities** Participating in Low-Rent Housing Programs, HH 1.51

Monthly Highway Construction Contracts Awarded by State and Federal Agencies and Toll **Authorities**, TD 2.51

NLM Name and Series **Authorities**, HE 20.3609/5

Proceedings Annual Conference, Surgeon General, Public Health Service, with State and Territorial Mental Health **Authorities**, FS 2.83/3

Summary Proceedings of ADAMHA Annual Conference of the State and Territorial Alcohol, Drug Abuse, and Mental Health **Authorities**, HE 20.8011

U.S. Census of Housing Special Reports for Local Housing **Authorities**, series HC (S 1), C 3.224/8

Authority

Classified Index of Dispositions of ULP [Unfair Labor Practices] Charges by the General Counsel of the Federal Labor Relations **Authority**, Y 3.F 31/21-3:11

Classified Index of Dispositions of ULP [Unfair Labor Practices] Charges by the General Counsel of the Federal Labor Relations **Authority**, Y 3.F 31/21-3:11

Companies Holding Certificates of **Authority** from Secretary of Treasury As Acceptable Securities on Federal Bonds, T 1.24, T 63.116

Corporate Author **Authority** List, C 51.18

Delegation of **Authority**, ES 3.6/11

Health Services and Mental Health Administration Public Advisory Committees: **Authority**, Structure, Functions, FS 2.321

Housing **Authority** Project Note Offerings on (date), HH 1.71

Index of EPA Legal **Authority** Statutes and Legislative History, Executive Orders, Regulations, EP 1.5/4

NIH Public Advisory Groups: **Authority**, Structure, Functions, HE 20.3018

PHS Public Advisory Groups, **Authority**, Structures, Functions, HE 20.2:Ad 9/2

Posters Tennessee Valley **Authority**, Y 3.T 25:49

Prime Contract Awards by Statutory **Authority**, Number of Actions, and Net Value by Department, D 1.57/3-2

Public Advisory Committees: **Authority**, Structure, Functions, HE 20.4022

Public Advisory Committees: **Authority**, Structure, Functions, Members, HE 20.1000

Recruiting **Authority** Circulars, CS 1.53

Safety Bulletins National Shipping **Authority**, C 39.209

Safety Posters Federal Public Housing **Authority**, NHA 4.9

Sheets of National Atlas of United States Tennessee Valley **Authority**, Y 3.T 25:7-2

Subject Matter Indexes to Decisions of the Federal Labor Relations **Authority**, Y 3.F 31/21-3:10-3

Summary of Mortgage Insurance Operations and Contract **Authority**, HH 2.24/5

Authorization

Cable Television **Authorization** Actions, Public Notices, CC 1.45/3

Authorization

Procurement **Authorization** and Allotments, European and Far East Programs, FO 1.8

Procurement **Authorization** and Allotments, Pr 33.908

Report of Secretary of Defense to the Congress on the Budget, **Authorization** Request, and Defense Programs, D 1.1

Authorizations

Allotments, **Authorizations**, and Paid Shipments, Data, FO 1.9/2

Cost of Pipeline and Compressor Station Construction Under Non-Budget Type or Certificate **Authorizations** As Reported by Pipeline Companies, FP 1.30

Unauthorized Appropriations and Expiring **Authorizations**, Y 10.22

Authorized

Authorized Construction—Washington D.C. Area, C 3.215/5

Companies **Authorized** under Act of August 13, 1894 to be Accepted as Sureties on Federal Bonds, T 2.5

Construction Reports; **Authorized** Construction, Washington, D.C. Area, C 56.211/4, C 56.211/6

Construction Reports; Housing **Authorized** by Building Permits and Public Contracts, C 40 (series)

Construction Reports; Housing Units **Authorized** for Demolition in Permit-issuing Places, (year), C 45 (series), C 56.211/8

Construction Reports; Housing Units **Authorized** for Demolition in Permit-issuing Places, (year), C 45 (series), C 56.211/8

Export Licenses Approved and Reexports **Authorized**, C 57.410, C 61.20

Facilities Expansions **Authorized** Listed by Major Types of Products, Pr 32.4843

Housing **Authorized** by Building Permits and Public Contracts, C 3.215/4

List of Chemical Compounds **Authorized** for Use Under USDA Meat, Poultry, Rabbit and Egg Inspection Programs, A 103.13

List of Chemical Compounds **Authorized** for Use Under USDA Poultry, Meat, Rabbit and Egg Products Inspection Programs, A 88.6:C 42, A 101.6:C 42

Auto
  Auto and Traffic Safety, TD 8.36
  Finance Rate and Other Terms on New Car and Used
      Car Installment Credit Contracts
      Purchased from Dealers of Major Auto
      Finance Companies, FR 1.34/5
  U.S. Auto Industry, ITC 1.16/4
Autofacts
  Autofacts, TD 8.37
Automated
  Automated Multiphasic Health Testing
      Bibliography, HE 20.2710
  Automated Reference Materials System (ARMS),
      VA 1.95/3
  Data Access Descriptions; Automated Address
      Coding Guide and Data Retrieval Series,
      ACC (nos.), C 3.240/2
  Directory of Automated Criminal Justice
      Information Systems, J 29.8/2
  Telephone Directory Automated Data and
      Telecommunications Service, Region 1,
      GS 12.12/2:1
Automated Data Processing
  Bibliography of Documents Issued by GAO on
      Matters Related to ADP (Automated
      Data Processing), GA 1.16/5
  Inventory of Automated Data Processing
      Equipment in the United States
      Government for Fiscal Year (date), GS
      12.10
Automated Records
  General Land Office, Automated Records Project,
      Pre-1908 Homestead & Cash Entry
      Patents, I 53.57
Automatic
  Automatic Data Processing Equipment Inventory
      in the United States Government As of
      the End of the Fiscal Year, GS 12.10
  Automatic Welding [abstracts], C 41.54/6
  Defense Communications System Global,
      Automatic Voice Network Telephone
      Directory, D 5.111
  Directory, Executive Orientation Courses in
      Automatic Data Processing, PrEx 2.12/
      2
  Inventory of Automatic Data Processing (ADP)
      Equipment in Federal Government, GS
      2.15, PrEx 2.12
  Studies of Automatic Technology, L 2.76
  Tabulations of Statistics Pertaining to Signals,
      Interlocking, Automatic, Train Control,
      Telegraph and Telephone for Transmis-
      sion of Train Orders, and Spring
      Switches As Used on Railroads of
      United States, IC 1 saf.10
Automatics
  Automatics, C 41.43
  Automatics and Telemechanics Abstracts, C 41.43/
      2
Automation
  Automation in the Medical Laboratory Sciences
      Review Committee, HE 20.3001/2:Au 8
  Center for Information Management and Automa-
      tion: Calendar for Fiscal Year, PM 1.51
  Cybernetics, Computers, and Automation
      Technology, PrEx 7.22/5
  Manpower and Automation Research, L 1.39/5
  Manpower/Automation Research Monographs, L
      1.39/3
  Manpower/Automation Research Notices, L 1.39/
      4
  OMAT-O-GRAM, for Staff Members of Office of
      Manpower, Automation, and Training, L
      1.41
  Scientific Reports of Higher Schools Electro-
      Mechanics and Automation, C 41.65/7
Automobile
  Automobile Credit, FR 1.34/8
  Automobile Financing, C 3.69
  Automobile Industry, C 41.44
  Automobile Installment Credit Developments, FR
      1.34/4
  Automobile Insurance and Compensation Studies,
      TD 1.17
  Automobile Loans by Major Finance Companies,
      FR 1.34/6
  Automobile Manufacturers Measurements, FMC
      1.12
  Automobile Registration Characteristics, FW 2.17
  New Passenger Automobile Rationing
      Regulations, Orders, Pr 32.4208

Summary of Mortality from Automobile Accidents,
      C 3.39
  U.S. Automobile Industry, C 1.84
  U.S. Automobile Industry: Monthly Report on
      Selected Economic Indicators, ITC 1.16/
      3
  World Trade in Wood, Furniture, Floor, Metal and
      Automobile Polishes, C 18.178
Automobiles
  Automobiles, C 3.70
  Cost of Owning and Operating Automobiles and
      Vans, TD 2.60
  U.S. Automotive Trade Statistics, Series B,
      Passenger Automobiles, ITC 1.16/2
Automotive
  Advance Automotive Propulsion Systems, E 1.99
  Air Force Driver, the Automotive Magazine of the
      U.S. Air Force, D 301.72
  Automotive Foreign Trade Manual, C 18.216
  Automotive Fuel Economy Program, Annual
      Report to Congress, TD 8.26
  Automotive World News, C 18.49
  Driver, Automotive Magazine of the Air Force, D
      301.72
  U.S. Automotive Trade Statistics, Series A: Motor
      Vehicles, ITC 1.16
  U.S. Automotive Trade Statistics, Series B,
      Passenger Automobiles, ITC 1.16/2
AUTOVON
  Global AUTOVON Telephone Directory, D 5.111
Auxiliaries
  Statement of Recruiting for Line of Army at General
      Recruiting Stations and Their
      Auxiliaries, W 3.17/2
Auxiliary
  Classification of Revenues and Expenses of
      Sleeping Car Operations, of Auxiliary
      Operations and of Other Properties for
      Sleeping Car Companies, IC 1 sle.5
  Classification of Revenues and Expenses of
      Sleeping Car Operations, of Auxiliary
      Operations and of Other Properties for
      Sleeping Car Companies, IC 1 sle.5
  Coast Guard Auxiliary Bibliography of
      Publications, TD 5.21/2
AV
  AV Bulletin, TD 4.39
Availabilities
  Foreign Currency Availabilities and Uses, Special
      Analysis E, PrEx 2.8/a9
  World Food Needs and Availabilities, A 93.48
Availability
  Air Navigation and Air Traffic Control Facility
      Performance and Availability Report,
      Calendar Year, TD 4.710
  Availability of Heavy Fuel Oils by Sulfur Level, E
      3.11/8 E 3.11/8-2
  Microcard Availability Lists, Y 3.At 7:30
  Price and Availability List of U.S. Geological
      Survey Publications, I 19.41/9
  Production and Availability of Construction
      Materials, Pr 32.4827
Available
  Available Bibliographies and Lists, A 17.17:25
  Available Information Materials, EP 1.17:58.25
  Available Publications of USDA'S Consumer and
      Marketing Service (except Market News
      Reports), A 88.40/2:53
  Civil Defense Publications Available from
      Superintendent of Documents, FCD 1.21
  Data Access Descriptions; Census Tabulations
      Available on Computer Tape Series CT
      (nos), C 3.240/3, C 56.212/3
  Energy Library, Journals Available, E 1.13/2
  Excess Personal Property Available for Transfer,
      Circulars, GS 2.4/3
  Federal Stock Number Reference Catalog, Numerical
      Listing of Items Available from General
      Services Administration, GS 2.10/5
  FHA and VA Mortgages Owned and Available for
      Sale by Reconstruction Finance
      Corporation and Federal National
      Mortgage Association, Y 3.R 24:14
  FM and TV Translator Applications Ready and
      Available for Processing and
      Notification of Cut-off Date, CC 1.26/6
  Foreign Affairs Research Papers Available, S 1.126
  Foreign Affairs Research Special Papers Available,
      S 1.126/2
  Foreign Area Research Documentation Center:
      Papers Available, S 1.126

Forest Service Films Available on Loan for
      Educational Purposes to Schools, Civic
      Groups, Churches, Television, A 13.55
  Journals Available in the ERDA Library, ER 1.19
  Labor Supply Available at Public Employment
      Offices in Selected Defense Occupations,
      FS 3.117
  List of Atomic Energy Commission Documents
      Available for Sale, Y 3.At 7:15
  List of Available Farmers Bulletins and Leaflets, A
      21.9/9
  List of Available Publications, A 107.12:11
  List of Available Publications for Distribution, A
      13.64/9
  List of Available Publications of the United States
      Department of Agriculture, A 21.9/8:11
  List of Available Surplus Property Located in
      District of Columbia, T 58.23
  List of Books Available for Ship and Station
      Libraries, Navy, N 17.26
  List of Publications Available for Distribution by
      Members of Congress, A 21.9/8:1
  List of Smithsonian Publications Available, SI
      1.17
  Listing of Land in Urban Renewal Project Areas
      Available for Private Redevelopment,
      HH 7.15
  New Research and Development Reports Available
      to Industry, C 42.21/4
  Publications Weather Bureau Available for
      Distribution, A 29.31
  Selected References for Labor Attaches, List of
      Readily Available Materials, L 1.34/2
  Series Available and Estimating Methods, BLS
      Current Employment Statistics Program,
      L 2.124/2
  Series Available and Estimating Methods, BLS
      National Payroll Employment Program,
      L 2.124
  Solid Waste Management, Available Information
      Materials, EP 1.17:58.25
  Some Recent Books on Public Affairs Available for
      Circulation in the Book Forms, LC 1.25
  Standard Broadcast Applications Ready and
      Available for Processing Pursuant to
      Sec. 1.354 (c) of Commission's Rules,
      Lists, CC 1.26/2
  Title List of Documents Made Publicly Available,
      Y 3.N 88:21-2
  Tuberculosis Beds in Hospitals and Sanatoria,
      Index of Beds Available, FS 2.69
Avenue
  Avenue Report, Y 3.P 38:16
Average
  Average Annual Wages and Wage Adjustment
      Index for CETA Prime Sponsors, L 2.44/3
  Average Monthly Discharge for 15-year Base
      Period at Selected Gaging Stations and
      Change of Storage in Certain Lakes and
      Reservoirs in Pacific Northwest, I 19.45/
      3-2
  Average Monthly Relief Benefits per Family
      Principal City Areas and Remainder of
      Each State, Y 3.F 31/5:30
  Average Monthly Weather Outlook, C 55.109
  Average Premiums and Discounts for CCC
      Settlement Purposes for Offers Received,
      A 88.11/21
  Average Semi-Monthly Retail Meat Prices at New
      York Chicago and Kansas City, A 36.179
  Average Weight of Measured Cup of Various Foods,
      A 1.87:41
  Average Wholesale Prices and Index Numbers of
      Individual Commodities, L 2.33
  Cattle and Calves: Weekly Average Price Per 100
      Pounds, A 36.18/1
  Coach Traffic, Revenue, Yield and Average On-
      flight Trip Length by Fare Category for
      the 48-state Operations of the Domestic
      Trunks, C 31.269
  CPI Detailed Report, Consumer Price Index, U.S.
      City Average and Selected Areas, L 2.38/
      3
  Crop Values, Season Average Prices Received by
      Farmers and Value of Production, A
      92.24/3
  Historical Climatology Series 6-1: Statewide
      Average Climatic History, C 55.287/61
  Hogs: Weekly Average Price per 100 Pounds, A
      36.204

Index of Straight-time **Average** Hourly Earnings for Hydraulic Turbine Operations, L 2.78/2

Indexes of **Average** Freight Rates on Railroad Carload Traffic, IC 1.27

Indexes of Change in Straight-Time **Average** Hourly Earnings for Selected Shipyards, by Type of Construction and Region, L 2.81/2

Percent Changes in Gross **Average** Hourly Earnings Over Selected Periods, L 2.63/2, L 2.63/3

Sheep and Lambs: Weekly **Average** Price per 100 Pounds, A 36.183

Trunk Carriers, Coach Class, Traffic, Revenue, Yield, Enplanements and **Average** On-flight Trip Length by Fare Category, CAB 1.24

U.S. **Average**, A 106.39

Averages

Bang's Disease Work; Statement of Indemnity Claims and **Averages** in Cooperative, A 77.211

Capacity Utilization in Manufacturing, Quarterly **Averages**, Seasonally Adjusted, FR 1.55

Carload Waybill Analyses, Distribution of Freight Traffic and Revenue **Averages** by Commodity Groups and Rate Territories, IC 1.20

Carload Waybill Statistics, Distribution of Freight Traffic and Revenue **Averages** by Commodity Classes, IC 1.23/8

Climatography of the United States; Monthly **Averages** of Temperature and Precipitation for State Climatic Division, C 55.286/2

Comparative Statement of Operating **Averages**, Class I Steam Railways in United States, IC 1 ste.27

Cotton Price Statistics, Monthly **Averages**, A 80.128

Decennial Census of United States, Climate: Monthly **Averages** for State Climatic Divisions, C 30.71/7:85

Distribution of Freight Traffic and Revenue **Averages** by Commodity Classes, IC 1.23/8:MS-1

Monthly **Averages** of Temperature and Precipitation for State Climatic Divisions, C 55.286/2

Statement of Indemnity Claims and **Averages** in Cooperative Bang's Disease Work, A 4.29

Statement of Indemnity Claims and **Averages** in Cooperative Tuberculosis Eradication, A 4.30

Summary of Bovine Tuberculosis Eradication in Cooperation with Various States, Statement of Indemnity and **Averages** in Cooperative Bovine Brucellosis Work, A 77.216/2

Tuberculosis Eradication: Statement of Indemnity Claims and **Averages** in Cooperative, A 77.214

Weekly **Averages** of Member Bank Reserves, Reserve Bank Credit and Related Items and Statement of Condition of the Federal Reserve Bank, FR 1.15

AVFUEL

AVFUEL & AVOIL into Plane Contract Listing, D 7.24/2

AVHRR

Conterminous U.S. **AVHRR** Biweekly Composites, I 19.120/3

Avian

Genetic Bases for Resistance to **Avian** Diseases, Northeastern States Regional Project, A 94.15

Aviano

Aviano Vigileer, D 301.123

Aviation

Accident Prevention Bulletin, U.S. General **Aviation**, C 31.203/2, C 1.17

Accidents in U.S. Civil Air Carrier and General **Aviation** Operations, C 31.244/3

Aeronautical Statutes and Related Material, Federal **Aviation** Act of 1958 and Other Provisions Relating to Civil Aeronautics, C 31.205:Ae 8

Air University, School of **Aviation** Medicine: [publications], D 301.26/13-2

Aircraft Accident Reports, Brief Format, U.S. Civil **Aviation**, NTSB-BA (series), TD 1.109/13

Analysis of Accidents Involving Air Taxi Operations, U.S. General **Aviation**, TD 1.113/4

Analysis of Aircraft Accident Data, U.S. General **Aviation**, TD 1.113/3

Annual International **Aviation** Research and Development Symposium, Report of Proceedings, FAA 2.9

Annual National **Aviation** System Planning Review Conference, Summary Report, TD 4.31

Annual Review of U.S. General **Aviation** Accidents Occurring in Calendar Year, TD 1.113

Approach, Naval **Aviation** Safety Review, D 202.13

Army **Aviation** Digest, D 101.47

Aviation Accident Statistical Summary Calendar Year, TD 4.413

Aviation Capacity Enhancement Plan, TD 4.77

Aviation Charts, N 6.27

Aviation Circular Letter, D 202.12

Aviation Education (series), TD 4.25

Aviation Forecasts Fiscal Years, FAA 1.42

Aviation Medical Education Series, TD 4.209

Aviation Medical Report AM (series), TD 4.210

Aviation Medicine Anotated Bibliography, LC 36.9

Aviation News, FAA 1.41

Aviation Operating Charts, N 6.27/4

Aviation Psychology Program Research Reports, W 108.25

Aviation Series, C 30.65

Aviation Technical Letters, T 47.45

Aviation Technical Orders, T 47.43

Aviation Training Pamphlets, N 17.29

Aviation Weather System Plan, TD 4.62

Briefs of Accidents Involving Aerial Applications Operations U.S. General **Aviation**, TD 1.109/4

Briefs of Accidents Involving Air Taxi Operations U.S. General **Aviation**, TD 1.109/3

Briefs of Accidents Involving Alcohol As a Cause-Factor U.S. General **Aviation**, TD 1.109/9

Briefs of Accidents Involving Amateur Built (homebuilt) Aircraft U.S. General **Aviation**, TD 1.109/6

Briefs of Accidents Involving Corporate-Executive Aircraft U.S. General **Aviation**, TD 1.109/10

Briefs of Accidents Involving Mid-Air Collisions U.S. Civil **Aviation**, TD 1.109/7

Briefs of Accidents Involving Missing Aircraft U.S. General **Aviation**, TD 1.109/8

Briefs of Accidents Involving Rotorcraft U.S. General **Aviation**, TD 1.109/5

Briefs of Accidents U.S. Civil **Aviation**, TD 1.109 C 31.244/6

Briefs of Accidents U.S. General **Aviation** , C 31.244/5

Briefs of Aircraft Accidents Involving Turbine Powered Aircraft U.S. General **Aviation** Calendar Year NTSB-AMM (series), TD 1.109/14

Briefs of Fatal Accidents Involving Weather As a Cause-Factor U.S. General **Aviation**, TD 1.109/12

Bureau of **Aviation** Safety Report, BASR (series), TD 1.114

C.A.B. Weekly List of Agreements Filed Under Sec. 412(a) of the Federal **Aviation** Act, CAB 1.32

Callback from NASA's **Aviation** Safety Reporting System, NAS 1.89

Civil **Aviation** [abstracts], C 41.56

Directory, **Aviation** Medical Examiners, TD 4.211

Directory, Local Law Enforcement Organizations Participating in **Aviation** Security, TD 4.809

FAA **Aviation** Forecasts, TD 4.57/2

FAA **Aviation** Medical Research Reports, FAA 7.10

FAA **Aviation** News, FAA 1.41/2, TD 4.9

FAA **Aviation** Safety Journal, TD 4.68

FAA General **Aviation** News, TD 4.9

FAA Statistical Handbook of Civil **Aviation**, TD 4.20

Federal **Aviation** Administration Airworthiness Directives, TD 4.10/4

Federal **Aviation** Administration Plan for Research, Engineering, and Development, TD 4.64

Federal **Aviation** Agency Specification, FAA 1.13

Federal **Aviation** Regulations, TD 4.6

Fly-By, Official Employee Publication of Federal **Aviation** Agency, FAA 1.11

General **Aviation** Accidents (non-air carrier), Statistical Analysis, C 31.160/2, FAA 1.15

General **Aviation** Activity and Avionics Survey, TD 4.32/17-2

General **Aviation** Aircraft Use, FAA 1.39

General **Aviation** Airworthiness Alerts, TD 4.414

General **Aviation** Inspection Aids Summary, TD 4.409

Grand Canyon VFR Aeronautical Chart, (general **aviation**), C 55.416/12-6

Great Lakes Region **Aviation** Systems, Ten Year Plan, TD 4.33/4

Guide to Federal **Aviation** Administration Publications, TD 4.17/6

Index of **Aviation** Charts, N 6.27/2

Inter-American Technical **Aviation** Conference, S 5.40

International Civil **Aviation** Organization Report of Representatives of United States, S 5.52

List of **Aviation** Medical Examiners, FAA 7.8

Listing of Aircraft Accidents/incidents by Make and Model, U.S. Civil **Aviation**, TD 1.109/15

Low Altitude Approach Procedures, United States Military **Aviation** Notice, D 5.318/3

Military **Aviation** Notices, D 301.9/2

Military **Aviation** Notices; Corrections, D 301.48/2

Military **Aviation** Notices; Corrections to Enroute-Low Altitude-Alaska, D 301.13/4

Military **Aviation** Notices; Corrections to Supplementary Flight Information Document, Pacific and Far East, D 301.50/2

Military **Aviation** Notices; Corrections to Supplementary Flight Information, Europe, Africa and Middle East, D 301.49/2

Military **Aviation** Notices; North Atlantic and East Canada, D 301.11/2

Military **Aviation** Notices; Pacific, D 301.12/2

Military **Aviation** Notices; West Canada and Alaska, D 301.13/2

Monthly Comment of **Aviation** Trends, C 31.152

Naval **Aviation** News, Restricted, N 27.16, M 207.7/2, D 207.7/2, D 202.9/2

Naval **Aviation** System Plan, TD 4.33

Naval **Aviation** Training Schools, N 28.11

News Features from Federal **Aviation** Agency, FAA 1.7/4

NRC Committee on **Aviation** Psychology Publications, NA 2.9

NTSB-AAS [National Transportation Safety Board, Aspects of **Aviation** Safety] (series), TD 1.121

Office of **Aviation** Medicine Encyclopedia of Medical Program Data, TD 4.213

Office of **Aviation** Policy and Plans: Report FAA-AV- (series), TD 4.32/4

Preliminary Analysis of Aircraft Accident Data, U.S. Civil **Aviation**, TD 1.113/6

Publications Air University, School of **Aviation** Medicine, D 301.26/3-2

Publications School of **Aviation** Medicine, Index, Fiscal Year, D 301.26/13-3

Report of Agricultural **Aviation** Research Conferences, A 77.2:Av 5

Research Reports Naval School of **Aviation** Medicine, D 206.16

Resume of U.S. Civil Air Carrier and General **Aviation** Aircraft Accidents, Calendar Year, C 31.244

Rocky Mountain Regional **Aviation** System Plan, TD 4.33/5

School of **Aviation** Medicine: General Publications, D 301.26/13-5

Semiannual Report to Congress on the Effectiveness of the Civil **Aviation** Security Program, TD 4.810

Soviet Union **Aviation** and Cosmonautics, PrEx 7.21/10-2

Statistical Handbook of Civil **Aviation**, C 31.144

Status of Federal **Aviation** Regulations, New, TD 4.13

Summary Reports of Accidents, U.S. Civil **Aviation**, C 31.244/4

Background Papers; Congressional Budget Office, Y 10.9

Background Papers; National Employment and Unemployment Statistics Commission, Y 3.Em 7/2:9

Background Series Disarmament Staff White House, Pr 34.11/3

Background to Industrial Mobilization Manual for Executive Reservists, C 41.6/7

CSS **Background** Information, A 82.82

Food for Freedom Program, **Background** Information Series, A 21.17

Foreign Affairs **Background** Summary, S 1.53

Global Atmospheric **Background** Monitoring for Selected Environmental Parameters, C 55.284

Military Compensation **Background** Papers, D 1.54

Noise Emission Standards for Construction Equipment, **Background** Document for {various items}, EP 1.6/3

Staff Papers, **Background** Papers and Major Testimony, Y 3.Ec 7/3

Two Centuries of Tariffs, the **Background** and Emergence of the U.S. International Trade Commission, TC 1.2:T 17/20

War **Background** Studies, SI 1.14

Background Paper
Background Paper, Y 3.T 22/2:12

Backgrounder
Backgrounder, E 5.15

Bacon
Davis-**Bacon** Wage Determinations, L 36.211/2

Bacteriology
Bacteriology and Mycology Study Section, HE 20.3001/2:B 13

Performance Evaluation Summary Analysis **Bacteriology**, HE 20.7037/2

Balance
Annual Energy **Balance**, E 3.1/a

Savings and Mortgage Lending Activity, Selected **Balance** Sheet Items, F.S.L.I.C. Insured Savings and Loan Associations, FHL 1.20/2

Textile and Apparel Trade **Balance** Report, C 61.51

Balance Sheet
All Operating Savings and Loan Associations, Selected **Balance Sheet** Data, FHL 1.20

Balance Sheet of Agriculture, A 1.38 A 1.75

Classification of Income, Profit & Loss, and General **Balance Sheet** Accounts, IC 1 ste.15

Comparative Statement of **Balance Sheet** Data of Domestic Air Carriers, C 31.239

Form of General **Balance Sheet** Statement, IC 1 ste.13, IC 1 wat.9

Form of General **Balance Sheet** Statement for Express Companies, IC 1 exp.8

FSLIC Insured Savings and Loan Associations, Savings and Mortgage Activity, Selected **Balance Sheet** Items, FHL 1.20/2

Selected Income and **Balance-Sheet** Items of Class I Railroads in the United States, IC 1 ste.34

Balances
Combined Statement of Receipts, Expenditures, and **Balances** of United States, T 63.113

Semiannual Consolidated Report of **Balances** of Foreign Currencies Acquired Without Payment of Dollars As of December 31 (year), T 63.117

Statement of **Balances**, Appropriations, and Disbursements, T 9.7

Balboa
Tide Tables **Balboa** and Cristobal, Canal Zone, M 115.7, D 113.7

Bales
Bales of Cotton Delivered in Settlement of Futures on New York and New Orleans Cotton Exchanges, A 59.10

Ballistic
Air Force **Ballistic** Missile Division, Publications, D 301.68

Army **Ballistic** Missile Agency DC-TR (series), D 105.15

Ballistic Systems Division Technical Documentary Report BSD-TDR, D 301.45/36

Publications Air Force **Ballistic** Missile Division, D 301.68

Report to Congress on the **Ballistic** Missile Defense Organization, D 1.1/6

Research Reports Army **Ballistic** Missile Agency, D 105.15

U.S. Army **Ballistic** Missile Agency, DG- TR- (series), D 105.15/2

Ballistics
Technical Notes **Ballistics** Research Laboratories, D 105.10/3

Balloon
Balloon Bulletins, W 42.28
Balloon Notes A.E.F., W 95.21/6

Balloons
Type Certificate Data Sheets and Specifications, Rotorcraft, Gliders, and **Balloons**, TD 4.15/6

Balsams
Industry Report, Crude Drugs, Gums, **Balsams**, and Essential Oils, C 18.236

Baltic
Nautical Charts and Publications, Region 4, Scandinavia, **Baltic**, and the Former Soviet Union, C 55.440:4

NIMA Nautical Charts, Public Sale Region 4, Scandinavia, **Baltic** and Russia, TD 4.82:4

Baltics
Newly Independent States and the **Baltics**, Situation and Outlook Series A 93.29/2-7

Baltimore
Social Security Administration **Baltimore** Directory, HE 3.58/2

SSA **Baltimore** Telephone Directory, SSA 1.9/2

Tide Calendar **Baltimore** and Cape Henry, N 6.22/2

Tide, Moon and Sun Calendar, **Baltimore**, Md., D 203.12

Band
Band News from the United States Air Force Band, Washington, D.C., D 301.108

Banding
Bird **Banding** Notes, I 49.21

Bang's
Statement of Indemnity Claims and Averages in Cooperative **Bang's** Disease Work, A 4.29

Summary of **Bang's** Disease Control Program Conducted by Bureau of Animal Industry in Cooperation with Various States, A 4.23

Summary of **Bang's** Disease Work in Cooperation with Various States, A 4.21

Summary of Brucellosis (**Bang's** Disease) Control Program Conducted by Bureau of Animal Industry in Cooperation with Various States, A 77.213

Bang's Disease
Bang's Disease Work; Statement of Indemnity Claims and Averages in Cooperative, A 77.211

Brucellosis (**Bang's Disease**) Work in Cooperation with Various States: Summary of, A 77.212

Bangladesh
Accession List: **Bangladesh**, LC 1.30/9
Bangladesh, LC 1.30/9

Bank
Aggregate Reserves and Member **Bank** Deposits, FR 1.15/3, HE 1.210

Annotated Manual of Statutes and Regulations of the Federal Home Loan **Bank** Board, FHL 1.6/2:St 2

Asian Development **Bank** Act Releases, SE 1.25/14

Bank Operating Statistics, Y 3.F 31/8:19

Bank Rates on Short-Term Business Loans, FR 1.32/5

Changes in State **Bank** Membership, Announce-ments, FR 1.33

Combined Financial Statements of Members of the Federal Home Loan **Bank** System, FHL 1.12

Conservation Reserve Program of Soil **Bank**, Statistical Summaries, A 82.79/2

Digest of National **Bank** Decisions, T 12.7

Distribution of **Bank** Deposits by Counties and Standard Metropolitan Areas, FR 1.11/6

Factors Affecting **Bank** Reserves and Condition Statement of F.R. Banks, FR 1.15

Federal Home Loan **Bank** Board Digest, FHL 1.14

Federal Home Loan **Bank** Review, Y 3.F 31/3:9, FL 3.7, NHA 3.8

International **Bank** for Reconstruction and Development, S 5.51

Job **Bank**, Frequently Listed Openings, L 37.311

Journal of the Federal Home Loan **Bank** Board, FHL 1.27

List of National **Bank** Examiners, T 12.10

Member **Bank** Call Report, FR 1.11

Member **Bank** Earnings, FR 1.11/3

Member **Bank** Income, FR 1.11/3

Member **Bank** Loans, FR 1.11/2

Members of the Federal Home Loan **Bank** System, FHL 1.31

National-**Bank** Act As Amended, T 12.6

New Mexico, Traveling Auditor and **Bank** Examiner, Annual Reports, I 1.24/2

Operating **Bank** Offices Insured by the Federal Deposit Insurance Corporation, as of {date}, Y 3.F 31/8:18

Press Releases Federal Home Loan **Bank** Board, FHL 1.7

Report of the Federal Home Loan **Bank** Board, FHL 1.1

Report to the Federal Land **Bank** Associations for Year Ended June 30 (date), FCA 1.23

Rural Telephone **Bank** Publications, A 1.116

Soil **Bank** Handbooks, A 82.6/3

Soil **Bank** Summaries, A 82.79

Statement Showing Amount of National **Bank** Notes Outstanding {ect}, T 12.9

Water **Bank** Program, from Inception of Program through (date), A 82.94

Weekly Averages of Member **Bank** Reserves, Reserve **Bank** Credit and Related Items and Statement of Condition of the Federal Reserve **Bank**, FR 1.15

Bank Debits
Bank Debits, FR 1.14
Bank Debits and Deposit Turnover, FR 1.17
Bank Debits Deposits and Deposit Turnover, FR 1.17
Bank Debits to Demand Deposit Accounts (Except Interbank and U.S. Government Accounts), FR 1.17/2

Bank's
Financial Audit, Export-Import **Bank's** Financial Statements, GA 1.13/7

Bankers
Commercial and Industrial Loans to U.S. Addressess Excluding **Bankers** Acceptances and Commercial Paper, by Industry, FR 1.39/2

Bankhead
Records and Briefs in Cases Arising Under Agricultural Adjustment Act, **Bankhead** Act, and Kerr-Smith Tobacco Act, J 1.19/7

Banking
Agricultural Situation in Relation to **Banking**, A 36.129

Banking Institutions Owned and Operated by Negroes Annual Reports, C 1.23

Currency & **Banking** News Digest, T 22.2/15:7446

FDIC **Banking** Review, Y 3.F 31/8:27

FDIC Quarterly **Banking** Profile, Y 3.F 31/8:29

FDIC Statistics on **Banking**, Y 3.F 31/8:1-2

Federal Reserve Act of 1913 with Amendments and Laws Relating to **Banking**, Y 1.2:F 31/2

Historical Statistics on **Banking**, Y 3.F 31/8:26

Industrial **Banking**, Companies, Installment Loans to Consumers, C 18.219

Industry Wage Survey: **Banking**, L 2.3/22

Legislative Activity of House Committee on **Banking** and Currency, Y 4.B 22/1:L 52/3

Monthly Report of Condition for U.S. Agencies, Branches and Domestic **Banking** Subsidiaries of Foreign Banks, FR 1.16/3

Occupational Earnings in **Banking**, Selected Metropolitan Areas Summary, L 2.86/4

Statistics on **Banking**, Y 3.F 31/8:1-2

Summary of Activities Senate **Banking**, Housing, and Urban Affairs Committee, Y 4.B 22/3:Ac 8

The National **Banking** Review, T 12.16

Weekly Summary of **Banking** and Credit Measures, FR 1.52

Bankruptcy
Bankruptcy Laws of the United States, Y 1.2:B 22/2

General Orders in **Bankruptcy**, Ju 6.9/2

Reports of **Bankruptcy** Matters, J 1.9

Reports on **Bankruptcy** Matters, J 1.9

Tables of **Bankruptcy** Statistics, Ju 10.9

Banks
Abstract of Reports of Condition of National **Banks**, T 12.5

All **Banks** in the United States and Other Areas, Principal Assets and Liabilities by States, FR 1.28/2

Analysis and Summary of Conditions and Performances of the Farm Credit **Banks** and Associations, FCA 1.23/2

Assets and Liabilities of All **Banks** in the United States, FR 1.28

Assets and Liabilities of All Commercial **Banks** in United States, FR 1.28/4

Assets and Liabilities of All Member **Banks** by Districts, FR 1.28/3

Assets Liabilities and Capital Accounts Commercial **Banks** and Mutual Savings **Banks**, Y 3.F 31/8:9

Changes Among Operating **Banks** and Branches, Y 3.F 31/8:25

Changes in State Member **Banks**, FR 1.33

Changes in Status of **Banks** and Branches During Month, Name and Location of Banks and Branches, FR 1.33/2

Circular Letters to Presidents or Cashiers of National **Banks** Asking for Report of Conditions of **Banks**, T 12.11/1

Circular Letters {to conservators of national **banks**}, T 12.11/4

Condition of Weekly Reporting Member **Banks** in Central Reserve Cities, FR 1.16/2

Condition of Weekly Reporting Member **Banks** in Leading Cities, FR 1.16

Condition of Weekly Reporting Member **Banks** in New York and Chicago, FR 1.16/2

Consumer Installment Credit at Commercial **Banks**, FR 1.36/2

Databook: Operating **Banks** and Branches, Summary of Deposits, Y 3.F 31/8:22

Deposits of County **Banks**: Index Numbers of Total, Demand and Time Deposits Selected Groups of States, Specified Periods, A 77.14/3, A 93.9/7

Deposits, Reserves, and Borrowings of Member **Banks**, FR 1.11/4

Digest of Decisions of Relating to National **Banks**, T 12.7/2

District Reserve Electors for Member **Banks** in District, RB 1.6

Duties and Liabilities of Directors of National and Member **Banks** of Federal Reserve System, T 12.12

Earnings, Expenses and Dividends of Active **Banks** in District of Columbia, Abstract, T 12.15

Factors Affecting Bank Reserves and Condition Statement of F.R. **Banks**, FR 1.15

Farm-Mortgage Lending Experience of 19 Life Insurance Companies, Federal Land **Banks**, and Farmers Home Administration, A 93.9/5

Instructions and Suggestions Relative to Organization, etc., of National **Banks**, T 12.8

Joint Stock Land **Banks**, Progress in Liquidation Including Statements of Condition, A 72.16

List of Member **Banks** by Districts, RB 1.5

Loan Commitments at Selected Large Commercial **Banks**, FR 1.39/3

Loans and Discounts of Farm Credit **Banks** and Associations, Annual Report, FCA 1.12/2

Major Nondeposit Funds of Commercial **Banks**, FR 1.39/4

Maturity Distribution of Euro-Dollar Deposits in Foreign Branches of U.S. **Banks**, FR 1.54

Monthly Report of Condition for U.S. Agencies, Branches and Domestic Banking Subsidiaries of Foreign **Banks**, FR 1.16/3

Official Opening and Closing Hours of Board of Governors and Federal Reserve **Banks**, also Holiday During Month, FR 1.50

Report of Calls, Assets, Liabilities, Capital, Accounts, Commercial and Mutual Savings **Banks** (unnumbered), Y 3.F 31/8:9-2

Report to Insured **Banks**, Y 3.F 31/8:17

Reports on Condition of **Banks** in U.S., T 1.6

Reserve Positions of Major Reserve City **Banks**, FR 1.15/2

State Member **Banks** of the Federal Reserve System, FR 1.11/5

Statement of Condition of Federal Land **Banks**, Joint Stock Land **Banks**, etc., FCA 1.7

Statements of Condition of Joint Stock Land **Banks**, FCA 1.7/2

Statements of Conditions of Federal Land **Banks**, etc., T 48.6

Summary of Accounts and Deposits in All Commercial and Mutual Savings **Banks**, Y 3.F 31/8:22

Summary of Accounts and Deposits in All Commercial **Banks** {by districts}, Y 3.F 31/8:20 CT

Summary of Accounts and Deposits in All Mutual Savings **Banks**, Y 3.F 31/8:21

Summary of Equity Security Transactions and Ownership of Directors, Officers, and Principal Stockholders of Member State **Banks** As Reported Pursuant to

Summary Report, Assets and Liabilities of Member **Banks**, FR 1.11

Weekly Condition Report of Large Commercial **Banks** in New York and Chicago, FR 1.16

Weekly Statement of Bonds Held in Trust for National **Banks**, T 40.9

Banned
Banned Products {list}, Y 3.C 76/3:9
Banned Toy List, HE 20.4024

BAO
BAO Reports, C 55.623

Bar
Annual Report of Legal Services Program of Office of Economic Opportunity to the American **Bar** Association, PrEx 10.18
Bar Guides {various areas}, TD 5.8/2

Barbados
BOMEX {**Barbados** Oceanographic and Meteorological Experiment} Bulletin, C 55.18

Barbizon
American Art in the **Barbizon** Mood, SI 6.2:B 23

Bareboat
Charter Report, Government-Owned Dry-Cargo Vessels, Operated by **Bareboat** Charters and/or Agents of Maritime Administration, C 39.215

Bargaining
Bargaining Calendar (year), L 2.3/8
Collective **Bargaining** Agreements Received by Bureau of Labor Statistics, L 2.45
Collective **Bargaining** Summaries, L 2.108
Major Collective **Bargaining** Settlements in Private Industry, L 2.45/2
State and Local Government Collective **Bargaining** Settlements, L 2.45/4

Barite
Barite in (year), I 28.124

Barnets
Pilot Chart of Greenland and **Barnets** Seas, N 6.15/4

Barometry
Manual of **Barometry**, C 30.6/2:B 26

Barracks
Price List of Subsistence Stores in Washington **Barracks**, D.C., W 77.9

Barrels
Reconditioned Steel **Barrels** and Drums Report, C 3.218
Steel **Barrels** and Drums, C 3.106

Barriers
Basic Data on Import Trade and Trade **Barriers**, C 18.184

Bartlesville, Oklahoma
Contributions from Thermodynamics Laboratory, Petroleum Experiment Station, **Bartlesville, Oklahoma**, I 28.105

Base
Base Flows As of {date} at Selected Gaging Stations in the Columbia River Basin, I 19.2:C 72/2
Base Maps by States, I 19.27
Data Bases and Data **Base** Systems, a Bibliography with Indexes, NAS 1.21:7048
Economic **Base** for Power Markets, I 44.9
Geographic **Base** (DIME) File, CUE, {Correction-Update-Extension}, C 3.249/2, C 56.255
Historical **Base** Maps (series), I 29.79/4
Strategic Air Command, Grissom Air Force **Base** Telephone Directory, D 301.104/6
Strategic Air Command, Vandenberg Air Force **Base** Telephone Directory, D 301.104/7
Strategic Air Command, Wurtsmith Air Force **Base**, Telephone Directory, D 301.104/5

Wastewater Treatment Construction Grants Data **Base**, Public Law 92-500 Project Records, Grants Assistance Programs, New Projects Funded During (Month), EP 1.56

Based
Wholesale Prices of Lumber, **Based** on Actual Sales Made F.O.B. Each Market, A 13.15, A 13.17

Baseline
Baseline Budget Projections Fiscal Years (dates), Y 10.16

Bases
Data **Bases** and Data Base Systems, a Bibliography with Indexes, NAS 1.21:7048
Genetic **Bases** for Resistance to Avian Diseases, Northeastern States Regional Project, A 94.15

Basic
Adult **Basic** and Secondary Level Program Statistics, Students and Staff Data, HE 19.319
Adult **Basic** Education Program Statistics (series), HE 5.97
AFDC Standards for **Basic** Needs, HE 3.64
Basic Educational Opportunity Grant Program Handbook, HE 19.108/4
Basic Electronics Training (series), D 101.107/11
Basic Field Manual, W 3.63
Basic Life Skills Reports, HE 19.312
Basic Preparatory Programs for Practical Nurses by States and Changes in Number of Programs, FS 5.133
Basic Radio Propagation Predictions, C 13.31
Basic Supervision, C 31.155
Basic Tables of Commissioning Allowances, N 28.15
College Costs, **Basic** Student Charges 2-year and 4-year Institutions, ED 1.121/3
College Costs, **Basic** Student Charges, 2-year Institutions, ED 1.121/2
College Costs, **Basic** Student Charges, 4-year Institutions, ED 1.121
Dictionary of Basic Military Terms: a Soviet View, D 301.79:9
High School News Service Report, **Basic** Fact Edition, School Year, D 1.41/2
Higher Education **Basic** Student Charges, HE 19.328
Homestudy Courses; **Basic** Mathematics, HE 20.7021/5
Institute for **Basic** Standards, Technical Highlights, Fiscal Year, C 13.1/4
List of **Basic** Materials and Alternates, DP 1.9
MRBC **Basic** Bulletin, Y 3.M 69/2:3
Program and Financial Plan, **Basic** Assumptions and Guidelines, HE 1.610/2
Receipts and Classes of Post Offices, with **Basic** Salaries of Postmasters, P 24.7, P 25.8
Schedules of **Basic** Rates (by name of park or monument), I 29.33
Snow Survey and Soil Moisture Measurements, **Basic** Data Summary for Western United States, Including Columbia River Drainage in Canada, A 57.46/17
Special Notice Concerning **Basic** Agreements Teleprocessing Services Program (TSP) Industrial Group 737, Industrial Class 7374, GS 12.13
SSA Training Data Review Technician, **Basic** Training Course, HE 3.69/3
Tables of **Basic** Allowances, W 1.27
Technical Reports from the Study of the Sustaining Effects of Compensatory Education on **Basic** Skills, HE 19.137
United States Air Force, Commands and Agencies **Basic** Information, D 301.26/23

Basic Data
Basic Data Book, J 16.24
Basic Data on Import Trade and Trade Barriers, C 18.184
Basic Data on the Economy of (country), C 1.50 C 57.11
Basic Data Relating to the National Institutes of Health, HE 20.3002:N 21/4
Basic Data Reports BD (series), D 103.211
Basic Data Series Ground-Water Releases (series), I 19.82

Basic Grants
Application for **Basic Grants** under Library Services for Indian Tribes and Hawaiian Program, ED 1.53/2

Basic Needs
OAA and AFDC, Cost Standards for **Basic Needs** and Percent of Such Standards Met for Specified Types of Cases, FS 17.625, HE 17.625

Basic Research
Basic Research in Behavioral and Social Sciences: U.S. Army Research Institute Annual Report, D 101.1/7-2

Basic-Data
Basic-Data Contributions, I 19.69

Basin
Basin Outlook Reports, A 57.46/20
Basin Outlook Reports (Washington), A 57.46/7
Colorado River **Basin** Project, Annual Report, I 27.71/3
Columbia **Basin** Joint Investigations {Reports on Problems}, I 27.23
Comprehensive Framework Study, Missouri River **Basin**, Y 3.M 69:9
Daily Totals of Precipitation in Muskingum River **Basin**, A 80.2010
Department of Interior in Missouri River **Basin** Progress Report, I 1.79
Drainage **Basin** Committee Reports, Y 3.N 21/12:12
Maumee River **Basin**, Y 3.G 79/3:10
Missouri **Basin** Inter-Agency Committee Publications, I 1.78
Missouri **Basin** Survey Commission, Reports and Publications, Pr 33.22
Missouri River **Basin** Investigations Project Reports, I 20.52
Monthly Mean Discharge at Selected Gaging Stations and Change of Storage in Certain Lakes and Reservoirs in Columbia River **Basin**, I 19.47
Operation of the Colorado River **Basin**, Projected Operations, Annual Report, I 27.71
Pacific **Basin** Consortium for Hazardous Waste Research Newsletter, A 1.110
Precipitation in Muskingum River **Basin**, A 57.21/2
Precipitation in Tennessee River **Basin**, Y 3.T 25:14
Progress, Missouri River **Basin**, I 1.80
Storage in Major Power Reservoirs in the Columbia River **Basin**, I 19.47/2
Taylor Model **Basin** Report, D 211.9/2

Basins
River **Basins** of the United States, I 19.56
Technical Memorandum To United States Study Commission, Southeast River **Basins**, A 57.50

Basops
Installations: News for and about **Basops**, D 101.142

BASR
Bureau of Aviation Safety Report, **BASR** (series), TD 1.114

Bass
Black **Bass** and Anglers Division Publications, C 6.17
Emergency Striped **Bass** Research Study, I 49.103

Bathroom
Bathroom Accessories (recessed and atachable all clay), C 3.72

Bathymetric
Bathymetric Mapping Products (Catalog) 5, United States Bathymetric and Fishing Maps, C 55.418:5
United States Topographic/**Bathymetric** Maps, I 19.101

Baton Rouge
Area Wage Survey Summary **Baton Rouge**, Louisiana, L 2.122/18-3

Battle
Annual Report, American **Battle** Monuments Commission, Fiscal Year (date), Y 4.V 64/4:Am 3

Battle
Order of **Battle** of United States Land Forces, D 114.10

Battle Command
CTC Trends, **Battle Command** Training Program, D 101.22/29

Battle Creek
Special Promotion Series from Office of Civil and Defense Mobilization, **Battle Creek**, Michigan, Bulletins, Pr 34.757/3

Battlefield
Battlefield Update, I 29.134

Bauer
Bauer Instructions, D 202.6/3

Bauxite
Aluminum and **Bauxite** in (year), I 28.80/2
Bauxite, I 28.80
Mineral Industry Surveys, **Bauxite** and Alumina, I 19.132

Bavarian
Bavarian Economics, M 105.20

BC-MLS
Merchandise Line Sales, **BC-MLS** (series), C 3.202/19

BCBST
BCBST, Perceptions II, D 101.22/29-2

BCD
Advance **BCD**, {Business Conditions Digest}, C 56.111/2
BCD Notices, C 41.6/2-5
BCD Technical Papers, C 3.226/2

BD
Basic Data Reports **BD** (series), D 103.211
Special Current Business Reports: Monthly Department Store Sales in Selected Areas, **BD**- (series), C 56.219/3

BDC
BDC Official Texts, C 41:BDCOT

BDI-INF
BDI-INF (Series), A 77.609

BDSA
BDSA Bulletins Information of Interest of Employees, C 41.3/2
BDSA Delegations, C 41.6/3
BDSA Emergency Delegations, C 41.6/8
BDSA Export Potential Studies, C 41.107
BDSA Industry Growth Studies, C 41.90/4
BDSA Notices, C 41.6/5
BDSA Orders, C 41.6/4
BDSA Publications, C 41.12:P 96/2
BDSA Regulations, C 41.6/2
BDSA Reporting Delegations, C 41.6/3-2

BEA
OBERS, **BEA** Regional Projections, C 59.17

BEA-SP
Bureau of Economic Analysis Staff Papers, **BEA-SP** (series), C 56.113

Beach
Beach Utilization Series, A 13.42/19
Technical Memorandum **Beach** Erosion Board, D 103.19

Beach Erosion
Bulletin of **Beach Erosion** Board, D 103.16

Beacon
Instrument Approach Chart, Radio **Beacon**, C 4.9/16
Beacon (NDPO-Monthly Newsletter), The, J 1.14/25-5
Radio **Beacon** System (maps), T 47.22

Beacons
Beacons Buoys and Daymarks, T 25.5-T 25.14

Beam
Beam, J 16.19
Beam Line, E 1.113

Bean
Bean Market News, A 88.65
Foreign **Bean** Market Information, C 18.72/10
Report of Dry **Bean** Research Conference, A 77.15:74
World Dry **Bean** Prospects, A 36.47

Beans
Louisiana Soybeans for **Beans**, Acreage, Yield and Production, A 88.18/25
Official United States Standards for Beans, A 113.10/3
Soybeans Harvested for **Beans** by Counties, A 92.15/3
Soybeans Harvested for **Beans** by Countries, Acreage, Yield, Production, A 88.18/19
Wheat, Rice, Feed Grains, Dry Peas, Dry **Beans**, Seeds, Hops, A 67.30:W 56

Bear
Bear Biology Association: Conference Series, I 29.94/2
Bear Biology Association: Monograph Series, I 29.94/3
Bear Essentials, HE 20.3057, HE 20.3191
Yellowstone Grizzly **Bear** Investigations, Annual Report of the Interagency Study Team, I 29.94

Beaufort Sea
Pacific and Arctic Coasts, Alaska, Cape Spencer to **Beaufort Sea**, C 55.422:9

Beautiful
America the **Beautiful** (posters), A 57.8/2

Beauty
Highway **Beauty** Awards Competition, TD 2.14

Beds
Tuberculosis **Beds** in Hospitals and Sanatoria, Index of Beds Available, FS 2.69

Beef
Beef Cattle Situation, A 36.90

Beehive
Preliminary Estimates of Production of Coal and **Beehive** Coke, I 28.31
Preliminary Estimates of Production of Pennsylvania Anthracite and **Beehive** Coke, I 28.50
Weekly Anthracite and **Beehive** Coke Reports, I 28.49

Beer
Alcohol and Tobacco Summary Statistics, Distilled Spirits, Wine, **Beer**, Tobacco, Enforcement Taxes, Fiscal Year, T 70.9
Beer, T 70.9/4
Monthly Statistical Release; **Beer**, T 70.9/4

Beet
Continental U.S. **Beet** Sugar Orders, A 55.17
Sugar **Beet** Sugar Orders, A 55.66

Beetle
Japanese **Beetle**-European Chafer Control Program, Annual Report, A 77.326

Beginning
Parents and **Beginning** Readers (series), HE 5.91

Behavior
Behavior and Society, C 51.9/12
BESRL **Behavior** Programs, D 101.67/2
Publications in Museum **Behavior**, SI 1.39
Publications Museum **Behavior**, SI 1.39
Quarterly Progress Report on Fission Product **Behavior** in LWRs, E 1.28/2
Rules of Practice and Rules Relating to Investigations and Code of **Behavior** Governing Exparte Communications Between Persons Outside the Commission and Decisional Employees, SE 1.6:R 86/4
Victimization, Fear of Crime and Altered **Behavior** (series), HH 1.70

Behavioral
Applied Social and **Behavioral** Sciences Research Initiation Grants, NS 1.10/8
Army Research Institute for **Behavioral** and Social Sciences: Research Reports, D 101.60/2
Army Research Institute for the **Behavioral** and Social Sciences: Special Reports (series), D 101.60/6
Army Research Institute for the **Behavioral** Sciences, Study Report, D 101.60/8
Basic Research in **Behavioral** and Social Sciences: U.S. Army Research Institute Annual Report, D 101.1/7-2
Behavioral Risk Factor Surveillance System, HE 20.7611/3
Behavioral Sciences Research Contract Review Committee, HE 20.3001/2:B 39
Biomedical and **Behavioral** Sciences, PrEx 7.22/13
Developmental **Behavioral** Sciences Study Section, HE 20.3001/2:B 39/2
Life Sciences: Biomedical and **Behavioral** Sciences, PrEx 7.22
Personnel Needs and Training for Biomedical and **Behavioral** Research, HE 20.3036/2
Program in Biomedical and **Behavioral** Nutrition Research and Training, Fiscal Year, HE 20.3036
Research and Discovery, Advances in **Behavioral** and Social Science Research, HE 20.3036/4
Research Institute for the **Behavioral** and Social Sciences: Technical Papers, D 101.60

Behavioral Sciences
Newsletter for Research in Mental Health and **Behavioral Sciences**, VA 1.22:15-5

Belefonte
Environmental Radioactivity Levels **Belefonte** Nuclear Plant, Y 3.T 25:52

Belvoir
Belvoir Research, Development, and Engineering Center: Handbooks, (series), D 101.6/10
Belvoir Research and Development Center: Container System Hardware Status Report, D 101.115
Historical Review, U.S. Army **Belvoir** Research and Development Center, D 101.98

BEM
BEM {Bureau of Executive Management} Pamphlets, CS 1.48/2

Ben's
Ben's Guide to U.S. Government for Kids, GP 3.39

Bench
  Bench Comment, a Periodic Guide to Recent
    Appellate Treatment of Practical
    Procedural Issues, Ju 13.8/2
  Tidal **Bench** Marks, C 4.32
Bench Marks
  Index Maps, Tidal **Bench Marks**, C 4.32/2
Benchmark
  Annual **Benchmark** Report for Wholesale Trade, C
    3.133/5
Benchnotes
  Benchnotes USA, D 103.33/13
Beneficiaries
  Characteristics of Social Security Disability
    Insurance **Beneficiaries**, HE 3.91
  Program and Demographic Characteristics of
    Supplemental Security Income
    Beneficiaries, HE 3.71/2
  OASDI **Beneficiaries** by State and County, SSA
    1.17/4
  Social Security **Beneficiaries** by State and County,
    HE 3.73/2
  Social Security **Beneficiaries** by Zip Code Area,
    HE 3.73
  Social Security **Beneficiaries** in Metropolitan
    Areas, HE 3.73/3
Beneficiary
  Beneficiary Studies Notes, FS 3.46
Benefit
  Benefit Series Service Unemployment Insurance
    Report, L 37.209
  Fact Sheets (Pension **Benefit** Guaranty
    Corporation), Y 3.P 38/2:14
  Federal Fringe **Benefit** Facts, PM 1.29
  Monthly **Benefit** Statistics, Summary Program
    Data, Calendar Year (date), HE 3.28/6-2
  Monthly **Benefit** Statistics; Calendar Year **Benefit**
    Data, FS 3.28/6-2
  Monthly Benefit Statistics; Fiscal Year **Benefit**
    Data, FS 3.28/6-3
  Monthly Benefit Statistics; Old-age, Survivors,
    Disability, and Health Insurance,
    Summary **Benefit** Data, HE 3.28/6
  Monthly **Benefit** Statistics; Railroad Retirement
    and Unemployment Blood Pressure
  National High **Blood Pressure** Education Program,
    HE 20.3214
  PBGC {Pension **Benefit** Guaranty Corporation}
    Fact Sheets, L 1.51/5
  Quarterly **Benefit** Statistics Report, RR 1.16
  Unemployment Compensation Interpretation
    Service, **Benefit** Series, SS 1.32, FS
    3.108
Benefiting
  America's Commitment: Federal Programs
    Benefiting Women and New Initiatives
    as Follow-up to the U.N. Fourth World
    Conference on Women, Pr 42.8:W 84
Benefits
  Annual Report of the Health Insurance **Benefits**
    Advisory Council, HE 20.17
  Average Monthly Relief **Benefits** per Family
    Principal City Areas and Remainder of
    Each State, Y 3.F 31/5:30
  Benefits and Costs of the Clean Air Act, The, EP
    4.31
  Black Lung **Benefits** Act of 1972 Annual Report
    on the Administration of the Act, L
    36.13
  Concurrent Receipt of Public Assistance Money
    Payments and Old-Age, Survivors, and
    Disability Insurance Cash **Benefits** by
    Persons Aged 65 or Over, FS 17.636, HE
    17.636
  Concurrent Receipt of Public Assistance Money
    Payments and Old-Age, Survivors, and
    Disability Insurance Cash **Benefits** by
    Persons Aged 65 or Over, FS 17.636, HE
    17.636
  Employee **Benefits** in Medium and Large Firms, L
    2.3/10
  Employee **Benefits** in Medium and Large Private
    Establishments L 2.3/10
  Employee **Benefits** in State and Local Govern-
    ments, L 2.3/10-2
  Employee **Benefits** Survey Defined Benefit
    Pension Coding Manual, L 2.46/7
  Employee **Benefits** Survey Defined Contribution
    Coding Manual, L 2.46/8
  Employee **Benefits** Survey Health Coding Manual,
    L 2.46/5

  Employee **Benefits** Survey Sickness and Accident
    Coding Manual, L 2.46/6
  Enrollment Information Guide and Plan
    Comparison Chart Former Spouses
    Enrolled in the Federal Employees
    Health **Benefits** Program, PM 1.8/7
  Federal **Benefits** for Veterans and Dependents, VA
    1.34:1
  Federal Employees Health **Benefits**, CS 1.41/
    4:890-1
  Guide to Substance Abuse Treatment **Benefits**
    Under the Federal Employees **Health**
    Benefits Program, PM 1.8/9
  Guide to Substance Abuse Treatment Benefits
    Under the Federal Employees Health
    Benefits Program, PM 1.8/9
  Medicare Hospice **Benefits**, HE 22.21/5
  Occupational Compensation Survey: Pay and
    Benefits, L 2.121, L 2.122
  Office Workers, Salaries, Hours of Work,
    Supplementary **Benefits** (by cities), L
    2.43
  Regional Data on Compensation Show Wages,
    Salaries and **Benefits** Costs in the
    Northeast, L 2.71/6-6
  Report, Civil Service Requirement, Federal
    Employees' Group Life Insurance,
    Federal Employees Health **Benefits**,
    Retired Federal Employees Health
    Benefits, Fiscal Year (date), CS 1.29/3
  Salaries and Fringe **Benefits**, HE 19.332
  Space **Benefits**: Secondary Application of
    Aerospace Technology in Other Sectors
    of the Economy, NAS 1.66
  Union Wages and **Benefits**, L 2.3/6
  VA **Benefits** in Brief, VA 1.14
  Vessels Receiving **Benefits** of Construction Loans
    under Merchant Marine Act of 1928, SB
    7.8
  Your Social Security Rights & Responsibilities,
    Retirement & Survivors **Benefits**, HE
    3.88/2, HE 3.93
  Your Social Security Rights and Responsibilities,
    Disability **Benefits**, HE 3.88
Benjamin Franklin
  Benjamin Franklin Stamp Club, P 1.50
Benzenoid
  Imports of **Benzenoid** Chemicals and Products, TC
    1.36, ITC 1.19
BEPQ
  BEPQ Series, A 77.308/3
Bering
  Bering Sea Claims Commission, S 3.7/2
  Berlin Arbitration (Northwestern Boundary), S
    3.13/3
  Conference of **Berlin** (Potsdam Conference), 1945, S
    1.1/3:P 84
  Quarterly Economic and Financial Review: Federal
    Republic of Germany and Western
    Sectors of **Berlin**, S 1.91/2
Berries
  Bush **Berries**, Indicated Yield and Production, A
    92.11/13
Beryllium
  Beryllium in (year), I 28.138
BES
  BES- (series), L 7.71
BESRL
  BESRL Behavior Programs, D 101.67/2
Best
  Best Bets for Returning Veterans in Washington
    D.C. Area, CS 1.43/2
  Best Federal Job Opportunities, CS 1.43
  Best of ERIC, ED 1.323
  Best Opportunities for Federal Employment, CS
    1.28:2280
  Project Connection: **Best** Strategy (series), HE
    20.8221/2
Bets
  Best **Bets** for Returning Veterans in Washington
    D.C. Area, CS 1.43/2
Better
  Better Education for Handicapped Children
    Annual Report, HE 5.86 HE
    5.235:35097
  Better Housing, Y 3.F 31/11:9
  Better Housing News Flashes Synopsis, Y 3.F 31/
    11:27
  Better Marketing, A 55.41
  Local Chairman of **Better** Housing Program
    Committee, Y 3.F 31/11:11
  Response, Report on Actions for a **Better**
    Environment, A 21.30

Betterments
  Classification of Expenditures for Additions and
    Betterments, IC 1 ste.12
Beyond
  Beyond Relief, Y 3.Af 8:10
BFSA
  BFSA Bulletin, HE 19.138
BHPR
  Directory of Awards, **BHPR** Support, HE 20.9312
BHS
  BHS Programmed Instructions (series), FS 2.6/7
BIA
  BIA Administrative Reports (series), I 20.65
  BIA Education Research Bulletin, I 20.57
Biannual
  Biannual Professional Development Program, ED
    1.33/2
BIB
  Patents **BIB**, C 21.31/2
  Patents **BIB** and Patents SNAP, C 21.31/16
  Trademarks **BIB**, C 21.31/18
Biblio-Profile
  Biblio-Profile on Human Communication and Its
    Disorders a Capsule State-of-the-art
    Report and Bibliography, HE 20.3513/2
Bibliographic
  Area and Country **Bibliographic** Surveys, D
    101.22:550
  Bibliographic List; Department of State, S 1.92/3
  Bibliographic List; Department of Transportation,
    TD 1.15
  Bibliographic List; Federal Aviation Administra-
    tion, TD 4.17/3
  Bibliographic List; Federal Aviation Agency, FAA
    1.10/3
  Bibliographic Series, D 106.10/3
  Environmental Factors on Coastal and Estaurine
    Waters, **Bibliographic** Series, I 67.14/2
  Higher Education Planning, a **Bibliographic**
    Handbook, HE 19.208:H 53
  Hispanic Foundation **Bibliographic** Series, LC
    24.7
  Quick **Bibliographic** Series, A 17.18/4
  RIIES **Bibliographic** Studies, SI 1.40
  Technical Library **Bibliographic** Series, D 106.10
  Trademarks Pending, **Bibliographic** Information
    from Pending US Trademarks, C 21.31/8
  Trademarks Registered, **Bibliographic** Information
    from Registered US Trademarks, C 21.31/
    7
Bibliographical
  Bibliographical Bulletins, A 1.60
  Bibliographical Contributions, A 17.8
  Bibliographical Lists, I 19.35
  Bibliographical Memoirs, NA 1.6
  Bibliographical Series, LC 24.7
  Smoking and Health **Bibliographical** Bulletin, FS
    2.24/4
  Special **Bibliographical** Series, D 114.14
Bibliographies
  Agricultural Economics **Bibliographies**, A 36.13
  Army Medical Library **Bibliographies**, D 104.10
  Available **Bibliographies** and Lists, A 17.17:25
  Bibliographies and Literature of Agriculture, A
    1.60/3 A 106.110/3
  Bibliographies and Literature of Agriculture, A
    105.55
  Bibliographies Guidance and Student Personnel
    Section, FS 5.16/2
  Bibliographies of Technical Reports Information
    Retrieval Lists, FAA 1.10/2
  Bibliographies of the World at War, LC 14.12
  Bibliographies Reference Lists Etc, J 16.10
  Cooperative **Bibliographies**, LC 2.7
  Current **Bibliographies** in Medicine (series), HE
    20.3615/2
  Current **Bibliographies** Prepared by the Library, L
    1.34/4
  Foreign Social Science **Bibliographies**, C 3.163/5
  Marine Corps Historical **Bibliographies**, D 214.15
  Natural Resources, A Selection of **Bibliographies**,
    D 103.50:3
  NRL {Naval Research Laboratory} **Bibliogra-
    phies**, D 210.13
  PACAF {Pacific Air Forces} Basic **Bibliographies**,
    D 301.62
  Published Search **Bibliographies**, C 51.13/2
  Sexually Transmitted Diseases, Abstracts and
    Bibliographies, HE 20.7311
  Small Business **Bibliographies**, SBA 1.3
  Soil Conservation **Bibliographies**, A 57.27/2
  Special **Bibliographies**, HE 20.8211/2, D 102.28,
    D 301.26/11

Subject Area **Bibliographies**, HE 20.8311/2
Subject **Bibliographies** from Highway Safety
  Literature, SB- (series), TD 8.13/3
Subject **Bibliographies**, GP 3.22/2
Bibliography
  A.I.D. **Bibliography** Series, S 18.21/3
  Aerospace Medicine and Biology, A Continuing
    Bibliography with Indexes, NAS
    1.21:7011
  Air Force Scientific Research **Bibliography**, D
    301.45/19-2:700
  Annotated **Bibliography** of CDA Curriculum
    Materials, HE 23.111/2
  Annotated **Bibliography** of Technical Films {by
    subject}, S 17.29/2
  Arctic **Bibliography**, D 1.22
  Bibliography, D 201.38
  Bibliography, S 1.92
  Bibliography (series), I 1.84/5 I 22.9/2 I 27.10/5
  Bibliography for Advanced Study, D 207.216
  Bibliography for the TVA Program, Y 3.T 25:31 T
    25
  Bibliography of Aeronautics, FW 4.29 Y 3.N 21/
    5:7
  Bibliography of Agriculture, A 17.18
  Bibliography of Documents Issued by GAO on
    Matters Related to ADP (Automated
    Data Processing), GA 1.16/5
  Bibliography of Ethnicity and Ethnic Groups, HE
    20.2417:Et 3
  Bibliography of Fire Hazards and Prevention and
    Safety in Petroleum Industry, C 22.27
  Bibliography of Hydrology and Sedimentation of
    the United States and Canada, I 19.13
  Bibliography of Lewis Research Center Technical
    Publications Announced in (year), NAS
    1.15/2
  Bibliography of Medical Reviews: Cumulations,
    HE 20.3610/2
  Bibliography of Medical Translations, FS 2.209/3
  Bibliography of Motion Pictures and Film Strips
    FS (series), C 35.11/2 C 41.23
  Bibliography of National Environmental Satellite
    Service, C 55.509
  Bibliography of North American Geology, I 19.3
  Bibliography of Publications for Public Education
    and Membership Training, T 47.50/2
  Bibliography of Publications Resulting from
    Extramural Research, HE 20.6509/2
  Bibliography of Scientific and Industrial Reports,
    C 35.7
  Bibliography of Soviet Laser Developments, D
    5.211
  Bibliography of Soviet Sources on Medicine and
    Public Health in the U.S.S.R., HE
    20.3711:So 8/2
  Bibliography of Space Books and Articles from
    Non-aerospace Journals, NAS 1.9/2:Sp
    1/957-977
  Bibliography of the History of Medicine, HE
    20.3615
  Bibliography of Translations from Russian
    Scientific and Technical Literature, LC
    1.26
  Bibliography of U.S. Army Medical Research and
    Nutrition Laboratory Reports and
    Reprints for (year), D 104.17
  Bibliography of United States Public Documents
    Department Lists, GP 3.10
  Bibliography of Weed Investigations, A 77.521
  Bibliography on Poultry Industry Chickens
    Turkeys Aquatic Fowl Gamebirds, A
    77.411
  Bibliography on Smoking and Health, HE
    20.11:45
  Bibliography on Suicide and Suicide Prevention,
    HE 20.2417:Su 3
  Bibliography on the Climate of {Country} WB/BC
    (series), C 52.21
  Bibliography on the High Temperature Chemistry
    and Physics of Gases and Gas-
    condensed Phase Reactions, C 13.37/3
  Bibliography on the High Temperature Chemistry
    and Physics of Materials in the
    Condensed State, C 13.37/2
  Bibliography on the Urban Crisis, HE 20.2417:Ur
    1
  Bibliography Series (numbered), HE 20.11
  Cerebrovascular **Bibliography**, HE 20.3513/4
  CLVD (Current Literature on Venereal Disease)
    Abstracts and **Bibliography**, HE
    20.7311
  Consumer Education **Bibliography**, PrEx 16.10:Ed
    8

Current **Bibliography** of Epidemiology, HE
  20.3617
Data Bases and Data Base Systems, a **Bibliography**
  with Indexes, NAS 1.21:7048
Earth Resources, A Continuing **Bibliography** with
  Indexes, NAS 1.21:7041
Energy, Continuing **Bibliography** with Indexes,
  NAS 1.21:7043
EPA Reports **Bibliography** Quarterly, EP 1.21/7
Epilepsy **Bibliography**, HE 20.3513:Ep 4
ERIC Products, **Bibliography** of Information
  Analysis Publications of ERIC
  Clearinghouses, HE 5.77/2
Fibrinolysis, Thrombolysis, and Blood Clotting,
  Bibliography, FS 2.22/13-6, HE
  20.3209
Food **Bibliography**, GA 1.16/6
Foreign Technology Alert: **Bibliography** (series),
  C 51.13/3
Foreign-Language and English Dictionaries in the
  Physical Sciences and Engineering,
  Selected **Bibliography**, 1952-1963, C
  13.10:258
Government Organization Manuals, a **Bibliogra-
  phy**, LC 1.12/2:G 74
Health Planning **Bibliography** Series, HE
  20.6112/2
Helium: **Bibliography** of Technical and Scientific
  Literature, (year), Including Papers on
  Alpha-Particles, I 28.27
Hemostasis and Thrombosis, **Bibliography**, HE
  20.3209/2
Historical **Bibliography** (series), D 110.12
HUD User **Bibliography** Series, HH 1.23/7
Human Services, **Bibliography** Series, HE 1.18/4
Immunization Abstracts and **Bibliography**, HE
  20.7311/2
Index Medicus, Including **Bibliography** of Medical
  Reviews, HE 20.3612
Manuals of General Reference and **Bibliography**
  Division, LC 2.8
Monthly **Bibliography** of Medical Reviews, HE
  20.3610
NHSQIC Annual **Bibliography**, HE 22.212
NINDS **Bibliography** Series, HE 20.3513/3
Numerical Index Supplement to **Bibliography** of
  Technical Reports, C 35.7/3
Parkinson's Disease and Related Disorders:
  Cumulative **Bibliography**, HE 20.3511/
  3
Personnel **Bibliography** Series, CS 1.61/3, PM
  1.22/2
Physical Fitness/Sports Medicine **Bibliography**,
  HE 20.111
Price List, Selective **Bibliography** of Government
  Research Reports and Translations, C
  41.21/3
Public Health **Bibliography** Series, FS 2.21
Public Health Service **Bibliography** Series, HE
  20.11
Quarterly **Bibliography** of Major Tropical
  Diseases, HE 20.3614/4
Scientific Directory and Annual **Bibliography**, HE
  20.3017
Selected **Bibliography** of Range Management
  Literature, A 13.30/9
Selected **Bibliography** of Regional Medical
  Programs, HE 20.2612
Serial Publications Indexed to **Bibliography** of
  Agriculture, A 17.17:75
Sex Roles: a Research **Bibliography**, HE
  20.8113:Se 9
Solar **Bibliography** (series), HH 1.23/6
Soviet **Bibliography**, S 1.92/2
Special **Bibliography** (series), TD 8.13/2, D 305.12
Special **Bibliography**, Artillery and Guided
  Missile School Library, D 101.49
Specialized **Bibliography** Series, HE 20.3614/6
Studies in Comparative Education, **Bibliography**,
  Publications, FS 5.214, HE 5.214
Technology for Large Space Systems, a **Bibliogra-
  phy** with Indexes, NAS 1.21:7046
Toxicity **Bibliography**, HE 20.3613
United States Coast Guard Annotated **Bibliogra-
  phy**, TD 5.21/3
United States Fisheries Systems and Social
  Sciences: a **Bibliography** of Work and
  Directory of Researchers, C 55.332:So 1
United States Senate, a Historical **Bibliography**, Y
  1.3:Se 5/11
Woman and Mental Health: a **Bibliography**, HE
  20.8113:W 84
Bicentennial
  Bicentennial Bulletin, Y 3.Am 3/6:11

Bicentennial Lecture Series, J 1.34
Bicentennial Series, TD 5.30
Bicentennial Times, Y 3.Am 3/6:10
History of George Washington **Bicentennial**
  Celebration, Y 3.W 27/2:14
Posters **Bicentennial** of the United States
  Constitution Commission, Y 3.B 47/
  2:12
Bicycling
  Bicycling Laws in the United States, TD 8.5/2:3/2
Bid
  Construction Committees {various cities}, Public
    Sector **Bid** Calendars by Agencies, L
    1.75
  Food Purchase Reports & Invitations to **Bid**, A
    88.67
  Sealed **Bid/Invitation** for **Bids**, D 7.34
Bid Opening
  Bid Opening Report Federal-Aid Highway
    Construction Contracts Calendar Year,
    TD 2.47
Bidders
  Instructions to **Bidders** and General Specifications,
    PB 1.5
Bidding
  Identical **Bidding** in Public Procurement Report of
    Attorney General Under Executive Order
    10936, J 1.31
Bids
  Advertisements for **Bids**, Specifications, etc., for
    Equipment of Public Buildings, T 39.9
  Sealed **Bids** (series), D 7.34
BIE
  Staff Papers, **BIE**-SP- (series), C 62.15
Biennial
  Biennial Report to the Congress, HE 20.3851/2
  Biennial Report to the President of the United
    States, I 49.1/8
  Biennial Survey of Depository Libraries Results,
    GP 3.33/4
  Proceedings **Biennial** Conference of State and
    Territorial Dental Directors with Public
    Health Service and Children's Bureau,
    FS 2.83/2
Bierman
  Bierman Jessie M. Annual Lectures in Maternal
    Health and Child Health, FS 14.110/2
Bilingual Education
  Focus Occasional Papers in **Bilingual Education**,
    ED 1.49/2-2
Billfish
  Billfish Newsletter (Southwest Fisheries Science
    Center), C 55.346
Billet
  Biennial Officer **Billet** Summary (Junior Officer
    Edition), D 208.24
Billing
  State Carlot Shipments of Fruits and Vegetables, by
    Commodities, Counties, and **Billing**
    Stations, A 88.12/10
Bills
  All Electric Homes in the United States, Annual
    Bills, January 1, (year), FP 1.10
  All Electric Homes, Annual **Bills**, E 3.16
  Digest of Public General **Bills** and Related
    Resolutions, with Index, LC 14.6
  Final Cumulative Finding Aid, House and Senate
    Bills, GP 3.28
  Index to Reports on Private and Public **Bills** and
    Resolutions Favorably Reported by the
    Committee, Y 4.J 89/1:In 2/9, Y 4.J 89/1-
    14
  Market Prices and Yields of Outstanding Bonds,
    Notes, and **Bills** of U.S., T 62.7
  Report on Principal **Bills** Introduced in
    Congress Affecting Education Either
    Directly or Indirectly, FS 5.66
  Residential Electric **Bills** in Major Cities, E 3.11/
    17-2
  Typical Commercial and Industrial Electric **Bills**,
    FP 1.16/4
  Typical Electric **Bills** (by States), FP 1.16/2
  Typical Electric **Bills**, E 3.22
  Typical Electric **Bills**, Typical Net Monthly **Bills** of
    January (year), for Residential
    Commercial and Industrial Services, FP
    1.10
  Typical Residential Electric **Bills**, FP 1.16/3
Binding
  Government Printing and **Binding** Regulations, Y
    4.P 93/1:6
Bio Tech
  Bio Tech Brief, E 6.11

Bioassay
Androgenic and Myogenic Endocrine **Bioassay** Data, FS 2.22/48.

Biochemistry
Biochemistry Study Section, HE 20.3001/2:B 52/4

Bioenergy
Pacific Northwest and Alaska **Bioenergy** Program Yearbook, E 5.12

Bioengineering
Applied Physiology and **Bioengineering** Study Section, HE 20.3001/2:P 56

Biofuels
Biofuels Update, E 1.99/5

Biographic
Biographic Directories, S 1.113
Biographic Register, S 1.69

Biographical
Astronauts and Cosmonauts **Biographical** and Statistical Data, Y 4.Sci 2:95
Biographical Directory of the American Congress, Y 1.92-1:S.doc. 8
Biographical Sketches and Ancedotes of 95 of 120 Principal Chiefs from Indian Tribes of North America, I 20.2:In 2/27
Secretaries of State, Portraits and **Biographical** Sketches, S 1.69:162

Biographies
Famous Indians, a Collection of Short **Biographies**, I 20.2:In 2/26

Biological
Associate Training Programs in the Medical Sciences and **Biological** Sciences at the National Institutes of Health (Year) Catalog, HE 20.3015
Biological Effects of Electromagnetic Radiation, D 101.52/8
Biological Evaluation (series), A 13.97
Biological Products Memo, A 77.226/2
Biological Products Notices, A 77.226
Biological Reports (series), I 49.89/2
Biological Science Report, I 73.10, I 19.209
Biological Sciences Series, I 53.27
Biological Services Program, I 49.2:B 52 I 49.89
Chemical-**Biological** Coordination Center, Reviews, NA 2.7
Chemical-**Biological** Information-Handling Review Committee, HE 20.3001/2:C 42

Biological
Crisp **Biological** Research Information, HE 20.3013/2-4
Manuscript Reports Issued by **Biological** Laboratory, Auke Bay, Alaska, I 49.57
Methods for the Collection and Analysis of Aquatic **Biological** and Microbiological Samples, I 19.15/5
Report of the Division of **Biological** Effects, HE 20.4114/2
Research in Progress, Calendar Year Metallurgy and Materials Sciences, Mechanics and Aeronautics, Chemistry and **Biological** Sciences, D 101.52/5-5
Service and Regulatory Announcements Bureau of **Biological** Survey, A 5.6
Veterinary **Biological** Products, Licensees and Permittees, A 101.2/10

Biologics
Biologics Surveillance, HE 20.7011/37
Veterinary **Biologics** Division Notices, A 77.226/3
Veterinary **Biologics** Notices, A 101.14

Biology
Aerospace Medicine and **Biology**, A Continuing Bibliography with Indexes, NAS 1.21:7011
Bear **Biology** Association: Conference Series, I 29.94/2
Bear **Biology** Association: Monograph Series, I 29.94/3
Biology and Aerospace Medicine, PrEx 7.22/12
Biology and Control of Insect and Related Pests of {various animals}, EP 1.94
Breast Cancer Experimental **Biology** Committee, HE 20.3001/2:B 74
Cancer **Biology**, HE 20.3173/2
Cell **Biology** Study Section, HE 20.3001/2:C 33
Directory of Information Resources in Agriculture and **Biology**, A 17.2:D 62
Medicine and **Biology**, C 51.9/24
Molecular **Biology** Study Section, HE 20.3001/2:M 73/2
Oceanic **Biology** Program Abstract Book, D 210:28

Oral **Biology** and Medicine Study Section, HE 20.3001/2:Or 1
Recent Reviews, Cancer Virology and **Biology**, Supplement to the Cancergrams, HE 20.3173/2-4
Sensory **Biology** of Sharks, Skates, and Rays, D 210.2

Biomass
Biomass Bulletin, E 6.3/2
Biomass Digest, E 6.3/2-2
Estimates of U.S. **Biomass** Energy Consumption, E 3.58

Biomathematical
Computer and **Biomathematical** Sciences Study Section, HE 20.3001/2:C 73

Biomedical
Biomedical and Behavioral Sciences, PrEx 7.22/13
Biomedical Communications Study Section, HE 20.3001/2:B 52/3
Biomedical Engineering and Instrumentation Branch, Division of Research Branch: Annual Report, HE 20.3036/3
Biomedical Index to PHS-Supported Research, HE 20.3013/2
Biomedical Library Review Committee, HE 20.3001/2:B 52/5
Biomedical Sciences Applied Studies, E 1.99
Biomedical Sciences Basic Studies, E 1.99
Biomedical Technology and Engineering, C 51.9/13
Life Sciences: **Biomedical** and Behavioral Sciences, PrEx 7.22
Minority **Biomedical** Research Support Program, HE 20.3037/7
Personnel Needs and Training for **Biomedical** and Behavioral Research, HE 20.3036/2
Population Sciences, Index of **Biomedical** Research, HE 20.3362/5
Program in **Biomedical** and Behavioral Nutrition Research and Training, Fiscal Year, HE 20.3036
Resources for **Biomedical** Research and Education, Reports, HE 20.3014

Biometrics
Biometrics Monograph Series, VA 1.67

Biometry
Biometry and Epidemilogy Contract Review Committee, HE 20.3001/2:B 52/6
Epidemiology and **Biometry** Advisory Committee, HE 20.3001/2:Ep 4/3

Biophysical
Biophysics and **Biophysical** Chemistry A Study Section, HE 20.3001/2:B 52
Biophysics and **Biophysical** Chemistry B Study Section, HE 20.3001/2:B 52/2

Biophysics
Biophysics and Biophysical Chemistry A Study Section, HE 20.3001/2:B 52
Biophysics and Biophysical Chemistry B Study Section, HE 20.3001/2:B 52/2

Biorelated
Pharmacology and **Biorelated** Chemistry Program: Biennial Report, HE 20.3461/3

Bioremediation
Bioremediation, EP 1.105

Bioren
Bioren and Duane Edition, S 7.8

Biostatistics
Summary of **Biostatistics**, C 3.165

Biotechnology
Biotechnology Resources, HE 20.3002:B 52/4

Bird
Bird Banding Notes, I 49.21
Bird Migration Memorandum, I 49.31
Research on **Bird** Repellents, Progress Reports, I 49.47/2
Rodenticides and Mammal, **Bird** and Fish Toxicants, EP 5.11/4
Check List of **Birds** of National Parks, I 29.27
Check List of **Birds** of National Parks, I 29.27
Directory of Officers and Organizations Concerned with Protection of **Birds** and Game, A 5.8
Migration of **Birds**, I 49.4:16

Birds of Prey
Snake River **Birds of Prey** Research Project, Annual Report, I 53.39

Birth
Birth Cohort Linked Birth/Infant Death Data Set, HE 20.6209/4-7
Birth Still-**Birth** and Infant Mortality Statistics Annual Report, C 3.26

Instruction Manual: Classification and Coding Instructions for Live **Birth** Records, HE 20.6208/6
Where to Write for **Birth** and Death Records of U.S. Citizens Who Were Born or Died Outside of the United States and **Birth** Certifications for Alien Children Adopted by U.S. Citizens, FS 2.102:B 53/7
Where to Write for **Birth** and Death Records, FS 2.102:B 53/3

Births
Instruction Manual Part 18, Guidelines For Implementing Field and Query Programs For Registration of **Births** and Deaths, HE 20.6208/16

Bismuth
Bismuth, I 28.103
Bismuth in (year), I 28.103/2
Bismuth Quarterly Reports, I 28.103
Mineral Industry Surveys, **Bismuth**, I 19.133

BISNIS
BISNIS Bulletin, C 61.42
BISNIS Search of Partners, C 61.42/2

Bits
Engineering **Bits** and Fax, C 55.116

Bituminous
Bituminous Coal and Lignite Distribution, I 28.33/2 E 3.11/7
Bituminous Coal and Lignite Mine Openings and Closings in Continental United States (dates), I 28.33/2-2
Bituminous Coal and Lignite Production and Mine Operations, E 3.11/7-3
Bituminous Coal Tables, I 34.21 I 46.13
Bituminous Laboratory Unit Report B (series), I 27.36
Coal **Bituminous** and Lignite in (year), I 28.42/3
Coal, **Bituminous** and Lignite, E 3.11/7-2
List of Bituminous Coal Producers who have Accepted **Bituminous** Coal Code Promulgated June 21, 1972, I 34.17, I 46.9
List of Bituminous Coal Producers who have Accepted **Bituminous** Coal Code Promulgated June 21, 1972, I 34.17, I 46.9
List of Code Number Producers of **Bituminous** Coal, I 34.22
Preliminary Estimates of Production of **Bituminous** Coal, I 34.15, I 46.11
Preliminary Estimates on Production of **Bituminous** Coal and Lignite, I 28.64
Price Schedules National **Bituminous** Coal Commission, I 34.19
Registered Bona Fide and Legitimate Farmers' Cooperative Organizations under **Bituminous** Coal Act of 1937, I 46.15
Registered Distributors under **Bituminous** Coal Act of 1973 {lists}, I 46.14
Statistics of **Bituminous** Coal Loaded for Shipment on Railroads and Waterways As Reported by Operators, I 28.34
Weekly Report on Production of **Bituminous** Coal, Etc, I 19.30

Biweekly
Research Technical Library **Biweekly** Accession List, PrEx 4.15

Biweekly Review
Biweekly Review, News and Information of Interest to Field Offices, C 41.13

BJA
BJA Bulletin, J 28.3/4
BJA Program Plan, J 26.1/5

BJS
BJS Data Report, J 29.19
BJS Dicussion Paper, J 29.26
BJS Program Application Kit, Fiscal Year, J 29.22

BKLT
School of Military Packaging Technology Booklets, SMPT-**BKLT**- (series), D 105.31

Black
Black News Digest, L 1.20/6
NBLIC (National **Black** Leadership Initiative on Cancer) News, HE 20.3195

Black Bass
Black Bass and Anglers Division Publications, C 6.17

Black Colleges
Faculty Graduate Study Program for Historically **Black Colleges** and Universities, NF 3.8/2-7

Historically **Black Colleges** and Universities, Faculty Projects, Summer College Humanities Programs for High School Juniors, NF 3.8/2-8

White House Initiative on Historically **Black Colleges** and Universities, Newsletter, ED 1.89

Black Hills
Your Changing Forest, News on the **Black Hills** National Forest Plan Revision, A 13.128

Black Lung
Black Lung Benefits Act of 1972 Annual Report on the Administration of the Act, L 36.13

Blank
Circular Letter Transmitting **Blank** Reports, T 12.11/2

Consolidated Index of Army Publications and **Blank** Forms, D 101.22:25-30

Military Publications: Index of AMC Publications and **Blank** Forms, D 101.22/3:310.1

Blank Forms
Blank Forms, S 1.15 T 1.26/6

Blanks
Catalogue of Book and **Blanks** Furnished by Department of Commerce to Customs Officers, C 1.16

Catalogue of Books and **Blanks** Used by Officers of Customs at Port of New York, T 36.5/2

Catalogue of Books and **Blanks** Used in Office of Assistance Treasurer, New York, T 36.5/3

Blasting Agents
Apparent Consumption of Industrial Explosives and **Blasting Agents** in the United States, I 28.112

Blind
Address List, Regional and Subregional Libraries for the **Blind** and Physically Handicapped, LC 19.17

Books for **Blind** and Physically Handicapped Individuals, LC 19.15/2

CD **Blind**, National Library Service for the **Blind** and Physically Handicapped, LC 19.24

Findings of (year) AB {Aid to the **Blind**} Study, HE 17.639/4

Library Resources for the **Blind** and Physically Handicapped, LC 19.16

Posters National Library for the **Blind** and Physically Handicapped, LC 19.18

Public Assistance Bureau, Applications: Old- Age Assistance, Aid to Dependent Children, Aid to the **Blind** {and} General Assistance, FS 3.17

Supplemental Security Income Program for the Aged, **Blind**, and Disabled, HE 3.77

Blind-made
Schedule of **Blind-made** Products, Y 3.B 61:8

Blindness
Annual Conference of Model Reporting Area for **Blindness** Statistics, Proceedings, FS 2.22/37

Conference of Model Reporting Area for **Blindness**, Proceedings, HE 20.3759/2

Proceedings Annual Conference of Model Reporting Area for **Blindness** Statistics, FS 2.22/37

Statistical Report, Annual Tabulations of Model Reporting Area for **Blindness** Statistics, FS 2.22/37-2

Statistics for (year) on **Blindness** in the Model Reporting Area, HE 20.3759

Blister
White Pine **Blister** Control, Annual Report, A 13.59

Blister Rust
Blister Rust Control in California Cooperative Project of State and Federal Agencies and Private Owners Annual Reports, A 13.54

Blister Rust News, A 19.21 A 9.15

BLM
BLM (Series), L 1.87
BLM-Alaska Frontiers, 153.41/2
BLM Contract Solicitation, I 53.38
BLM Facts and Figures for Utah, I 53.43
BLM Facts, Oregon and Washington, I 53.43/2
BLM in New Mexico, Oklahoma, Texas and Kansas, I 53.43/5
BLM in Wyoming, I 53.43/3
BLM Monthly Alert I 53.17/2
BLM Newsletter, I 53.21
BLM Westfornet Monthly Alert, I 53.17/2

BLM: Alaska Technical Reports, I 53.49
Wyoming **BLM** Wildlife Technical Bulletins, I 53.34

BLMR
BLMR Research Studies, L 31.11

Bloc
Soviet **Bloc** International Geophysical Year Information, C 41.40

Block
Carload Waybill Statistics, Mileage **Block** Distribution, Traffic and Revenue by Commodity Class, Territorial Movement, and Type of Rate, Products of Agriculture, 1 Percent Sample of Terminations in Statement MB-1, IC 1.23/2

Carload Waybill Statistics, Mileage **Block** Distribution, Traffic and Revenue by Commodity Class, Territorial Movement, and Type of Rate, Animals and Products, 1 Percent Sample of Terminations in Statement MB-2, IC 1.23/3

Carload Waybill Statistics, Mileage **Block** Distribution, Traffic and Revenue by Commodity Class, Territorial Movement, and Type of Rate, Products of Mines, 1 Percent Sample of Terminations in Statement MB-3, IC 1.23/4

Carload Waybill Statistics, Mileage **Block** Distribution, Traffic and Revenue by Commodity Class, Territorial Movement, and Type of Rate, Products of Forests, 1 Percent Sample of Terminations in Statement MB-4, IC 1.23/5

Carload Waybill Statistics, Mileage **Block** Distribution, Traffic and Revenue by Commodity Class, Territorial Movement, and Type of Rate, Manufacturers and Miscellaneous Forwarder Traffic, One Percent Sampling MB-5, IC 1.23/6

Carload Waybill Statistics, Mileage **Block** Distribution, Traffic and Revenue by Commodity Class, Territorial Movement, and Type of Rate, Products of Agriculture, 1 Percent Sample of Terminations in Statement MB-1, IC 1.23/2

Carload Waybill Statistics, Mileage **Block** Distribution, Traffic and Revenue by Commodity Class, Territorial Movement, and Type of Rate, Animals and Products, 1 Percent Sample of Terminations in Statement MB-2, IC 1.23/3

Carload Waybill Statistics, Mileage **Block** Distribution, Traffic and Revenue by Commodity Class, Territorial Movement, and Type of Rate, Products of Mines, 1 Percent Sample of Terminations in Statement MB-3, IC 1.23/4

Carload Waybill Statistics, Mileage **Block** Distribution, Traffic and Revenue by Commodity Class, Territorial Movement, and Type of Rate, Products of Forests, 1 Percent Sample of Terminations in Statement MB-4, IC 1.23/5

Carload Waybill Statistics, Mileage **Block** Distribution, Traffic and Revenue by Commodity Class, Territorial Movement, and Type of Rate, Manufacturers and Miscellaneous Forwarder Traffic, One Percent Sampling MB-5, IC 1.23/6

Census of Housing; **Block** Statistics, C 3.224/5

Census of Population and Housing **Block** Statistics, C 3.282/3

Community Development **Block** Grant Program Annual Reports, HH 1.46/3

County **Block** Maps, C 3.62/9

Mileage **Block** Progressions, IC 1.23/7:MB-6

Tabulation of Statistics Pertaining to **Block** Signals and Telegraph and Telephone for Transmission of Train Orders, IC 1 blo.5

Blocks
Carload Waybill Statistics, Traffic and Revenue Progressions by Specified Mileage **Blocks** for Commodity Groups and Classes, 1 Percent Sample of Carload Terminations in Year Statement MB-6, IC 1.23/7

U.S. Census of Housing City **Blocks**, Series HC (3), C 3.224/6

Blood
Analysis of Current Pulmonary Research Programs Supported by the National Heart, Lung, and **Blood** Institute, HE 20.3202:P 96/2

Blood Diseases and Resources Advisory Committee, HE 20.3001/2:B 62

Blood Lead, HE 20.7022/5

Blood Lead Proficiency Testing, HE 20.7412/2

Directory of **Blood** Establishments Registered Under Section 510 of the Food, Drug, and Cosmetic Act, HE 20.4002:B 62

Fibrinolysis, Thrombolysis, and **Blood** Clotting, Bibliography, FS 2.22/13-6, HE 20.3209

Index of Federally Supported Programs in Heart, Blood Vessel, Lung, and **Blood** Disorders, HE 20.3013/2-3

Interagency Technical Committee on Heart, Blood Vessel, Lung, and **Blood** Diseases; and **Blood** Resources, HE 20.3001/2:H 35

Subject Index of Current Research Grants and Contracts Administered by the National Heart, Lung, and **Blood** Institute, HE 20.3212

Blood Pressure
Directory of Community High **Blood Pressure** Control Activities, HE 20.3002:B 62/13

Blood Vessel
Index of Federally Supported Programs in Heart, **Blood Vessel**, Lung, and Blood Disorders, HE 20.3013/2-3

Blowers
Blowers Fans Unit Heaters and Accessory Equipment, C 3.143

Blown
Industry Wage Survey: Pressed or **Blown** Glassware, L 2.3/29

BLS
BLS Publications, L 2.3
BLS Reports, L 2.71
BLS Reports on Mass Layoffs in the . . . Quarter, L 2.120/2-14
BLS Staff Papers, L 2.71/5
BLS Update, L 2.131
Industry Productivity in (year) Reported by **BLS**, L 2.120/2-9
Major **BLS** Programs, L 2.87
News, **BLS** Reports on Survey of Occupational Injuries and Illnesses in ..., L 2.120/2-11
Series Available and Estimating Methods, **BLS** Current Employment Statistics Program, L 2.124/2
Series Available and Estimating Methods, **BLS** National Payroll Employment Program, L 2.124
Unemployment Rates for States and Local Governments, **BLS**/PWEDA/QR-(series), L 2.111/3

BLS/CETA/MR
CETA Area Employment and Unemployment, **BLS/CETA/MR** (series), L 2.110/2

BLS/CETA/SP
CETA Area Employment and Unemployment, Special Reports, **BLS/CETA/SP** (series), L 2.110/3

BLS/PWEDA/MR
State, County and Selected City Employment and Unemployment, **BLS/PWEDA/MR**-(series), L 2.111/2

BLS/PWEDA/SP
State, County and Selected City Employment and Unemployment, **BLS/PWEDA/SP**-(series), L 2.111/4

Blue
PMS **Blue** Book, HE 20.4001/2
Red, White, and **Blue** Series, Y 3.P 96/3:6

Blue Book
Official Register (or **Blue Book**) Biennial, I 1.25

Blue Books
Blue Books, W 7.30

Blue Eagle
Blue Eagle, Y 3.N 21/8:19
Blue Eagle Letters, Y 3.N 21/8:10

Blue-Collar
Federal Civilian Work Force Statistics, Occupations of Federal **Blue-Collar** Workers, PM 1.10:Sm 59-11

Occupations of Federal White-Collar and **Blue-Collar** Workers, PM 1.10/2-2

Bluegrass
Commercial Tobacco-Livestock Farms, **Bluegrass** Area, Kentucky and Penny-Royal Grass Area, Kentucky-Tennessee, A 93.9/11

Blueprint
   Soldier Shows, **Blueprint** Specials, W 109.114
Bluetongue
   Incidence of **Bluetongue** Reported in Sheep During Calendar Year, A 77.231
BMCS
   BMCS National Roadside Inspection, TD 2.313/2
BNDD
   BNDD Bulletin, J 24.3
   BNDD Personnel Management Series, J 24.16
Board
   Active and Announced Price Support Programs Approved by **Board** of Directors, A 82.310
   Agricultural Statistics **Board** Catalog, A 92.35/2
   Board of Actuaries of the Civil Service Retirement System Annual Report, Y 4.P 84/10:R 31/30
   Board of Appellate Review, S 1.136
   Board of Engineers for Rivers and Harbors Report of Hearings, D 103.23
   Board of Regents, HE 20.3001/2:R 26
   Board of Scientific Counselors, HE 20.3001/2:Sci 2
   Campus **Board** Programs Report (series), ED 1.14
   Chicago Federal Executive **Board** Directory, PM 1.31/3
   Classified Index of Decisions of Regional Directors of National Labor Relations **Board** in Representation Proceedings, LR 1.8/6-2
   Classified Index of Dispositions of ULP {Unfair Labor Practices} Charges by the General Counsel of the National Labor Relations **Board**, LR 1.8/8
   Classified Index of the National Labor Relations **Board** Decisions and Related Court Decisions, LR 1.8/6
   Crop Reporting **Board** Catalog, A 92.35/2
   Inter-American Defense **Board**, S 5.45
   Official Opening and Closing Dates of **Board** of Governors and Federal Reserve Banks, also Holiday During Month, FR 1.50
   Oral Argument {before a panel of the Review **Board**}, CC 1.42/4
   Orders Civil Aeronautics **Board**, C 31.207
   Outer Continental Shelf Research Management Advisory **Board**: Annual Report, I 1.99
   Pamphlets Merit Systems Protection **Board**, MS 1.9
   Posters Merit Systems Protection **Board**, MS 2.9
   Posters Office of the Special Counsel, Merit Systems Protection **Board**, MS 1.12
   Presidential Clemency **Board**: Publications, Pr 38.8:C 59
   President's Advisory **Board** for Cuba Broadcasting, Pr 41.8:Br 78
   Press Releases Federal Home Loan Bank **Board**, FHL 1.7
   Proceedings **Board** of Managers, NH 1.6
   Proceedings **Board** of Supervising Inspectors, T 38.10
   Proceedings Contract Settlement Appeal **Board**, FS 5.7/a
   Proceedings Interdepartmental **Board** on Simplified Office Procedure, Executive Committee Meeting, T 51.11/5
   Public Advisory **Board**, Reports, Y 3.Ec 74/3:7
   Publications Corn-Hog **Board** of Review, A 55.30
   Publications Federal Reserve **Board**, FR 1.45
   Publications National Wage Stabilization **Board**, L 1.17
   Pulp, Paper and **Board** Industry Report, C 40.11
   Pulp, Paper and **Board**, C 57.313, C 57.511
   Qualification Standards for Wage **Board** Positions, CS 1.45
   Quarterly Progress Reports by Surplus Property **Board** to Congress, Y 3.W 19/7:207
   Quarterly Report to Congress and the East- West Foreign Trade **Board** on Trade Between the United States and the Nonmarket Economy Countries, Y 4.W 36:2
   Regulations of the Civil Aeronautics **Board**, C 31.206/7, CAB 1.16
   Renegotiation **Board** Regulations, RnB 1.6/2
   Renegotiation **Board** Rulings, RnB 1.6/5
   Report by the Advisory **Board** for Cuba Broadcasting, Y 3.B 78/2:1
   Report of **Board** of Visitors to Naval Academy, M 206.101, D 208.101
   Report of **Board** of Visitors, D 305.9
   Report of Career Service **Board** for Science, HE 1.33

Report of the Federal Home Loan Bank **Board**, FHL 1.1
Report of the Secretary and Financial Report of the Executive Committee of the **Board** of Regents, SI 1.1/a
Report to Congress and East-West Foreign Trade **Board** on Trade Between United States and Nonmarket Economy Countries, TC 1.38
Report to the U.S. Congress and the U.S. Secretary of Energy from the Nuclear Waste Technical Review **Board**, Y 3.N 88/2:1
Reports of Subversive Activities Control **Board**, Y 3.Su 1:8-2
Research Memorandum National Labor Relations **Board**, LR 1.10
Rules of Practice **Board** of Tax Appeals, Y 3.T 19:7
Rules of Practice Shipping **Board**, SB 1.7
Safety Bulletins Civil Aeronautics **Board**, C 31.214
Sales Finance Companies Federal Reserve System **Board** of Governors, FR 1.26
Selected Reports of Cases before Veterans' Education Appeals **Board**, Y 3.V 64:7
Service and Regulatory Announcements Federal Horticulture **Board**, A 35.9
Service and Regulatory Announcements Insecticide and Fungicide **Board**, A 34.6
Special Reports to Congress and East-West Foreign Trade **Board**, TC 1.38/2
Statistical Summary, Railroad Retirement **Board** Operations, RR 1.11
Stocks of Grain in Deliverable Positions for Chicago **Board** of Trade, Futures Contracts in Exchange-Approved and Federally Licensed Warehouses, as Reported by Those Warehouses, A 85.14, Y 3.C 73/5:10
Superintendent's Statement to **Board** of Visitors, D 208.110
Tariff Circulars Shipping **Board**, SB 1.8
Technical Memorandum Beach Erosion **Board**, D 103.19
Telephone Directory National Transportation Safety **Board**, TD 1.124
Transmittal Memo {for} Local **Board** Memorandums, Y 3.Se 4:13
United States Naval Academy, Superintendent's Statement to **Board** of Visitors, D 208.110
Volume and Composition of Individuals' Savings Federal Reserve System **Board** of Governors, FR 1.53
War Trade **Board** Journal, S 13.5
War Trade **Board** Pamphlets, WT 1.6
Weekly Report of Vessels under Jurisdiction of Shipping **Board**, SB 2.12
Youth Advisory **Board** Newsletter, EP 1.27
Boards
   Boards of Instruction Bulletins, W 37.9
   Compliance **Boards** Instructions, Y 3.N 21/8:11
   Instruction and Information for Applicants and for **Boards** of Examiners, CS 1.6
   Report and Recommendations of Fact-Finding **Boards**, L 1.16
   Reports and Orders Recommended by Joint **Boards**, IC 1 mot.19
   Reports of Emergency **Boards**, NMB 1.7
   Roster of Members of PHS Public Advisory Groups, Councils, Committees, **Boards**, Panels, Study Sections, HE 20.2:Ad 9/3
Boat
   Boat Engineering Newsletter, TD 5.28/2
Boaters
   Boaters Maps (series), D 103.49/2
Boating
   Boating Safety Circulars, TD 5.4/3
   Boating Safety Newsletter, TD 5.28
   Boating Statistics, TD 5.11
   Recreation **Boating** Safety R & D, Annual Report, TD 5.28/4
   Recreational **Boating** Guide, TD 5.8:B 63
   Recreational **Boating** in United States, Report of Accidents, Numbering and Related Activies, T 47.54
Bodies
   Radionuclide Migration around Uranium Ore **Bodies** Analogue of Radioactive Waste Repositories, Y 3.N 88:25-11

Roll of Honor, Supplemental Statement of Disposition of **Bodies** of Deceased Union Soldiers and Prisoners of War Removed to National Cemeteries in Southern and Western United States, W 39.8
Body
   Health Planning Newsletter for Governing **Body** Members, HE 20.6022
Boilers
   Steel **Boilers**, C 3.107
Bolivia
   Commission of Inquiry and Conciliation, **Bolivia** and Paraguay, Report of Chairman, S 3.40
Bolts
   Bolts Nuts and Large Screws of Iron or Steel, ITC 1.17 ITC 1.17/2
Bomb
   Bomb Survey, J 1.14/7-4:B 63
   FBI **Bomb** Data Program, General Information Bulletins, J 1.14/8-2
   Uniform Crime Reports **Bomb** Summary, J 1.14/7-7
Bombing
   AAF **Bombing** Accuracy, Reports, W 108.37
   Strategic **Bombing** Survey Publications, W 1.71
BOMEX
   BOMEX {Barbados Oceanographic and Meteorological Experiment} Bulletin, C 55.18
Bona Fide
   Registered **Bona Fide** and Legitimate Farmers' Cooperative Organizations under Bituminous Coal Act of 1937, I 46.15
Bond
   Bond of Federal Employees, Y 4.P 84/11:B 64
   Bond Sales for Higher Education, FS 5.252:52004 HE 5.252:52004
   Bond Sales for Public School Purposes, HE 19.323
   Bond Teller, T 66.24/2
   Bond Tips from Your U.S. Savings Bond Reporter, T 66.24
   Open-Market Money Rates and **Bond** Prices, FR 1.44
   Selected Interest Rates and **Bond** Prices, FR 1.32/6, FR 1.32/7
   Tables of Redemption Values for $50 Series EE and $25 Series E Savings **Bond**, T 63.209/5-2
   Water and Sewer **Bond** Sales in United States, FS 2.56/4, I 67.10
Bonded
   United States Imports for Immediate Consumption, Entries into **Bonded** Manufacturing Warehouse for Manufacture and Exports, Entries into **Bonded** Storage Warehouse and Withdrawals from Bonded Storage Warehouse for Consumption of Petroleum and Its Products
BondPro
   BondPro, U.S. Savings Bond Pricing System, T 63.217
Bonds
   Any **Bonds** Today, T 66.17
   Bonds Over America, T 66.11
   Caveat List of United States Registered **Bonds**, T 26.7
   Companies Authorized under Act of August 13, 1894 to be Accepted as Sureties on Federal **Bonds**, T 2.5
   Companies Holding Certificates of Authority from Secretary of Treasury As Acceptable Securities on Federal **Bonds**, T 1.24, T 63.116
   Current Listing of Aircraft **Bonds**, T 17.19/2
   Current Listings of Carrier's **Bonds**, T 17.19
   Market Prices and Investment Values of Outstanding **Bonds** and Notes, T 50.5
   Market Prices and Yields of Outstanding **Bonds**, Notes, and Bills of U.S., T 62.7
   Series H/HH Savings **Bonds**, T 63.209/8-4
   Table of Investment Yields for United States Savings **Bonds** of Series E. Official Use, T 66.23
   Tables of Redemption Values for United States Savings **Bonds** Series A-E, T 63.209, T 63.209/2
   Tables of Redemption Values for United States Savings **Bonds** Series EE, T 63.209/7
   Tables of Redemption Values for United States Savings **Bonds** Series J, T 63.209/3
   Tables of Redemption Values of $25 Series E Savings **Bonds** Series, T 63.209/5

Briefs of Accidents Involving Corporate-Executive Aircraft U.S. General Aviation, TD 1.109/10

Briefs of Accidents Involving Mid-Air Collisions U.S. Civil Aviation, TD 1.109/7

Briefs of Accidents Involving Missing Aircraft U.S. General Aviation, TD 1.109/8

Briefs of Accidents Involving Rotocraft U.S. General Aviation, TD 1.109/5

Briefs of Accidents U.S. Civil Aviation, TD 1.109 C 31.244/6

Briefs of Accidents U.S. General Aviation , C 31.244/5

Briefs of Aircraft Accidents Involving Turbine Powered Aircraft U.S. General Aviation Calendar Year NTSB-AMM (series), TD 1.109/14

Briefs of Fatal Accidents Involving Weather As a Cause-Factor U.S. General Aviation, TD 1.109/12

Conference **Briefs**, C 13.62

Disarmament **Briefs**, S 1.117/4

Economic **Briefs**, FHL 1.28

Educational **Briefs** for the Middle and Secondary Level Classroom, NAS 1.19/3

Energy **Briefs** for Editors/News Directors, E 1.67

Export **Briefs**, A 67.40/2

Food & Nutrition Research **Briefs**, A 17.30

Foreign Policy **Briefs**, S 1.98

Forest Entomology **Briefs**, A 9.110

HUD International **Briefs**, HH 1.40/2

In Supreme Court of U.S., **Briefs**, Petitions, and Motions of Wm. Marshall Bullett, Solicitor General, J 1.19/2

Indexes for Compilations of Records, **Briefs**, etc., J 1.19/1

Occupational **Briefs**, W 1.63, M 101.28

Occupational Outlook **Briefs** {Excerpts from Occupational Outlook Handbook}, L 2.3/a 2

OTS **Briefs**, C 41.102

Petitions for Certiorari and **Briefs** on Merits and in Opposition for U.S. in Supreme Court of U.S., J 1.19/6

Policy **Briefs**, Action Guides for Legislators and Government Executives, J 28.8/2

Preservation **Briefs**, I 29.84, I 70.12

Records and **Briefs** in Cases Arising Under Agricultural Adjustment Act, Bankhead Act, and Kerr-Smith Tobacco Act, J 1.19/7

Records and **Briefs** in Circuit Courts of Appeals and Court of Appeals, District of Columbia, J 1.19/5

Records and **Briefs** in U.S. Cases Decided by Supreme Court of United States, J 1.19

Research **Briefs**, FS 17.18

RTD Technology **Briefs**, D 301.45/34

Special Reference **Briefs**, A 17.24

Statements of Facts, and **Briefs**, J 10.5/1

Statistical **Briefs** (series), VA 1.74

Statistical **Briefs** from Around the World, C 3.205/2

Statistics in **Brief**, ED 1.328/4

Topical **Briefs**: Fish and Wildlife Resources and Electric Power Generation, I 49.78

U.S. Civil Aviation **Briefs** of Accidents, C 31.244/6

U.S. General Aviation **Briefs** of Accidents, C 31.244/5

U.S. Supreme Court, Government **Briefs** in Cases Argued by Solicitor General, Indexes, J 1.19/3

U.S. Supreme Court, Government **Briefs** in Cases Argued, Indexes, J 1.19/4

Brig.

United States v. Chile, Arbitration of Case of **Brig.** Macedonian, S 3.21/1

Brigades

Roster of Organized Militia of United States, by Divisions, **Brigades**, Regiments, Companies, and other Organizations, with their Stations, W 70.5

Briquets

Fuel-**Briquets** and Packaged-Fuel Producers, Annual, I 28.109

British

American and **British** Claims Arbitration, S 3.33

British Exports of Electrical Apparatus, C 18.53

British-American Agricultural News Service, A 67.22

European and **British** Commonwealth Series, S 1.74

Training within Industry Abstracts, **British** Engineering Bulletins, Pr 32.4822, Pr 32.5215

Washington Arbitration (American-**British** Mixed Claims Commission), S 3.13/2

British Columbia

Lights and Fog Signals, Pacific Coast and **British** Columbia, T 25.18

BRL

Technical Report, **BRL** TR (series), D 105.10/3-2

Broadcast

Actions of Commission, Reports {**Broadcast**}, CC 1.20/2

Advance United States Short Wave **Broadcast** Programs, S 9.13

AM **Broadcast** Applications Accepted for Filing and Notification of Cut-off Date, CC 1.26/4

AM-FM **Broadcast** Financial Data, CC 1.43/2

Crop and Market News Radio **Broadcast** Schedules, A 36.26

Final TV **Broadcast** Financial Data, CC 1.43

FM **Broadcast** Applications Accepted for Filing and Notification of Cut-off Date, CC 1.26/3

List of Radio **Broadcast** Stations, CC 1.10

List of Radio **Broadcast** Stations by Frequency, CC 1.22

List of Radio **Broadcast** Stations by State and City, CC 1.23

List of Radio **Broadcast** Stations, Alphabetically by Call Letters, CC 1.21

List of Radio **Broadcast** Stations, by Zone and State, CC 2.12

NBS Time and Frequency **Broadcast** Services, C 13.60

Radio **Broadcast** Stations in United States, Containing Alterations and Corrections, CC 1.24

Relay **Broadcast** Stations, CC 1.31

Reports of Applications Received in Radio **Broadcast** Stations, CC 1.26

Request for New or Modified **Broadcast** Call Signs, CC 1.44

Special Releases {of Foreign **Broadcast** Intelligence Service}, W 100.9

Standard **Broadcast** Applications Ready and Available for Processing Pursuant to Sec. 1.354 (c) of Commission's Rules, Lists, CC 1.26/2

TV **Broadcast** Applications Accepted for Filing and Notification of Cut-off Date, CC 1.26/5

Broadcasters

Farm **Broadcasters** Letters, A 21.34, A 107.13/2

Broadcasting

Broadcasting Radio Stations of the United States, RC 1.9

Broadcasting Stations of the World, PrEx 7.9

Budget Board for International **Broadcasting**, Y 3.B 78:9

Foreign Radio **Broadcasting** Services, C 18.87

Income Tax Brevities for Use by Radio **Broadcasting** Stations, T 22.38

International **Broadcasting** of All Nations, IA 1.11

Report by the Advisory Board for Cuba **Broadcasting**, Y 3.B 78/2:1

Broadcasts

Daily Report, Foreign Radio **Broadcasts**, PrEx 7.10

Directory of Weather **Broadcasts**, C 30.73

Directory {of} Market News **Broadcasts**, A 66.38

President's Advisory Board for Cuba **Broadcast**-ing, Pr 41.8:Br 78

Public Health **Broadcasts**, T 27.35

Selected Worldwide Weather **Broadcasts**, C 55.119

VOA, Voice of America, **Broadcast** Schedule For Languages Other Than English, IA 1.6/4

VOA, Voice of America, English **Broadcast** Guide, IA 1.6/3

Worldwide Marine Weather **Broadcasts**, C 55.119

Brochure

Quarterly Statistical **Brochure**, HE 20.8212/4

Warren Grant Magnuson Clinical Center: Annual **Brochure**, HE 20.3052/2

Brochures

Brochures, HE 20.7513

National Peace Essay Contest **Brochures** Available, Y 3.P 31:3

Broiler

Broiler Chick Report Louisiana Crop Reporting Service, A 88.15/21

Broiler Chicks Placed, A 88.15/15

Broiler Chicks Placed in 22 States, A 92.9/14

Broiler Hatchery, A 92.46

Broiler Marketing Facts, A 88.15/24

Broiler Marketing Guide, A 88.26/5

Commercial **Broiler** Farms, Maine, Delmarva, and Georgia, A 93.9/11

Commercial **Broiler** Production, A 88.15/13

Pullet Chick Replacements for **Broiler** Hatchery Supply Flocks, A 88.15/19

Pullet Chicks for **Broiler** Hatchery Supply Flocks, Pou 2-7 (series), A 92.90

Broilers

Chickens and Eggs, Farm Production, Disposition, Cash Receipts and Gross Income, Chickens on Farms, Commercial **Broilers**, by States, A 88.15/18

Commercial **Broilers** Production in 22 States, A 92.9/10

Galvanized Range **Broilers** and Tanks for Hot Water Heaters, C 3.86

Brokers

Over-the-Counter **Brokers** and Dealers Registered with Securities & Exchange Commission, SE 1.15

Bromide

Methyl **Bromide** Alternatives, A 77.517

Bromine

Bromine in (year), I 28.126

Brooke Army Medical Center

Surgical Research Unit, **Brooke Army Medical Center**, Fort Sam Houston, Texas: Annual Research Progress Report, D 104.22

Brookhaven

Brookhaven Highlights, E 1.1/4

Brookhaven National Laboratory: Telephone Directory, E 1.12/2

Broom Corn

Broom Corn Brooms: Producers' Shipments Imports for Consumption Exports and Apparent Consumption, ITC 1.23

Brooms

Broom Corn **Brooms**: Producers' Shipments Imports for Consumption Exports and Apparent Consumption, ITC 1.23

Browns Ferry

Environmental Radioactivity Levels **Browns Ferry** Nuclear Plant, Y 3.T 25:55

Fish Monitoring Investigations, **Browns Ferry** Nuclear Plant, Wheeler Reservoir, Alabama, Y 3.T 25:37

Radiological Impact Assessment, **Browns Ferry** Nuclear Plant, Y 3.T 25:53

Brucellosis

Brucellosis (Bang's Disease) Work in Cooperation with Various States: Summary of, A 77.212

Brucellosis Surveillance, HE 20.7011/16

Cooperative State-Federal **Brucellosis** Eradication Program; **Brucellosis** Bulletin, A 101.18/3

Cooperative State-Federal **Brucellosis** Eradication Program; Charts and Maps, A 77.212/6-2

Cooperative State-Federal **Brucellosis** Eradication Program; Progress Report, A 77.15:91-57

Cooperative State-Federal **Brucellosis** Eradication Program; Statistical Tables, A 101.18/2

Cooperative State-Federal **Brucellosis** Eradication Program; Statistical Tables, Fiscal Year (date), A 77.212/4

Cooperative State-Federal **Brucellosis** Eradication Programs, A 77.212/6

National **Brucellosis** Committee, A 1.2:B 83

Proceedings National **Brucellosis** Committee and Progress Report of the Cooperative State-Federal **Brucellosis** Eradication Program, A 77.202:B 83/16

Statistical Tables Showing Progress of Eradication of **Brucellosis** and Tuberculosis in Livestock in United States and Territories for Fiscal Year, A 77.212/3

Summary of Bovine **Brucellosis** Eradication Activities in Cooperation with States, A 77.212/2

Summary of Bovine Tuberculosis Eradication in Cooperation with Various States, Statement of Indemnity and Averages in Cooperative Bovine **Brucellosis** Work, A 77.216/2

Summary of **Brucellosis** (Bang's Disease) Control Program Conducted by Bureau of Animal Industry in Cooperation with Various States, A 77.213

Summary of **Brucellosis** Eradication Activities in Cooperation with Various States Under Cull and Dry Cow Testing Program, A 77.212/7

Summary of **Brucellosis** Eradication Activities in Cooperation with the Various States Under the Market Cattle Testing Program, A 77.212/8

Brunei
Cumulative List of Malaysia, Singapore and **Brunei** Serials, LC 1.30/10-2

Brunswick
Area Wage Survey Summary **Brunswick**, Georgia, L 2.122/10-5

BSD-TDR
Ballistic Systems Division Technical Documentary Report **BSD-TDR**, D 301.45/36

BSFA
BSFA Bulletin, HE 19.138

BUAER
BUAER Instruction NAVAER, D 202.6/4
BUAER Instructions, D 202.6/3
BUAER Notice, D 202.6/5
BUAER Notice NAVAER, D 202.6/6
BUAER Report, D 202.16

Budget
Air Force **Budget**, D 301.83
Analysis of the Current Services **Budget** Contained in the President's Budget for Fiscal Year (date), Y 4.Ec 7-11
Appraisal of the Proposed **Budget** for Food and Agricultural Sciences Report to the President and Congress, A 1.1/4-3
Army **Budget**, Fiscal Year, D 101.121
Baseline **Budget** Projections Fiscal Years (dates), Y 10.16
Budget, Y 3.B 78:9
Budget and Finance Circulars, A 1.43
Budget and Management Circulars, L 1.23
Budget Board for International Broadcasting, Y 3.B 78:9
Budget Circulars, Pr 32.204/2
Budget Digest, P 1.28
Budget Estimates Excerpts from the United States Government **Budget**, HH 1.1/4
Budget Estimates; Aircraft and Missile Procurement, D 301.83/2
Budget Estimates; Coast Guard, TD 5.41
Budget Estimates; Department of Transportation, TD 1.34/3
Budget Estimates; Federal Aviation Administration, TD 4.50
Budget Estimates; Federal Highway Administration, TD 2.52
Budget Estimates; Federal Railroad Administration, TD 3.18
Budget Estimates; National Highway Traffic Safety Administration, TD 8.28
Budget Estimates; United States Department of Agriculture, A 1.93
Budget Estimates; Urban Mass Transporation Administration, TD 7.16
Budget Explanatory Notes for Committee on Appropriations, A 13.130
Budget Highlights, PrEx 2.8/6
Budget in Brief, PrEx 2.8/2, TD 5.62
Budget Issue Papers, Y 10.12
Budget of the United States Government, PrEx 2.8
Budget of the U.S. Government: Director's Introduction and Overview Tables, PrEx 2.8/11
Budget of United States Government, Pr 32.107 Pr 33.107 Pr 34.107, PrEx 2.8/1
Budget of United States Government District of Columbia, PrEx 2.8/4
Budget Program Justification of Programs and Estimates for Fiscal Year (date) Submitted to Congress, Y 3.T 25:43
Budget Revisions, PrEx 2.8/7
Budget Scorekeeping Report, Y 4.R 24/4:B 85/2
Budget Status Report, TD 1.34
Budget-Treasury Regulations, Pr 33.106/2
Commerce **Budget** in Brief, Fiscal Year, C 1.39
Congressional **Budget** Request, E 1.34
Congressional **Budget** Request, Federal Energy Regulatory Commission, E 1.34/4
Congressional **Budget** Request, U.S. Department of Justice, E 1.34/3

Congressional **Budget** Request, U.S. Department of the Interior, E 1.34/2
Congressional **Budget** Scorekeeping Reports, Y 10.10
Contents, Format and Concepts of Federal **Budget**, Reprint of Selected Pages from **Budget** of United States Government, PrEx 2.8
Cost of Pipeline and Compressor Station Construction Under Non-**Budget** Type or Certificate Authorizations As Reported by Pipeline Companies, FP 1.30
Department of Transportation **Budget** Program: Analysis of Fiscal Year DOT Program by Policy and RD&D Management Objectives, DOT-OST (series), TD 1.34/2
Department of Transportation **Budget**, Excerpts from the President's **Budget**, TD 1.34/4
Department of Veterans Affairs, FY **Budget** in Brief and Budget Submission, VA 1.83/2
Description of the Administration's Fiscal Year (date) **Budget** Recommendations under the Jurisdiction of the Committee on Ways and Means, Y 4.W 36:10-2
Economic and **Budget** Outlook, an Update, Y 10.17
Federal **Budget** in Brief, PrEx 2.8/2
Federal **Budget**, Midyear Review, PrEx 2.8/3
Federal R & D Funding by **Budget** Function, NS 1.18/4
FY **Budget** Highlights Federal Drug Control Programs, PrEx 26.1/4
Highlights of the Department of the Navy FY...**Budget**, D 201.1/1-2
Historical Comparison of **Budget** Receipts and Expenditures by Function, Special Analysis G, PrEx 2.8/a10
Information Collection **Budget** of the United States, PrEx 2.29
Interior **Budget** in Brief, Fiscal Year Highlights, I 1.1/6
Investment, Operating and Other **Budget** Expenditures, Special Analysis D, PrEx 2.8/a8
Justification of **Budget** and Legislative Program for Office of Management and Budget, HE 22.30/2
Management Bulletins: Bureau of the **Budget**, Pr 32.108, Pr 33.108, Pr 34.108, PrEx 2.3/2
Manned Space Flight Resources Summary, **Budget** Estimates, NAS 1.54
Mid-Session Review of the **Budget**, PrEx 2.31
NASA **Budget** Estimates, NAS 1.85
National Cancer Institute **Budget** Estimate, HE 20.3190
Office of Human Development Services **Budget** Request, HE 23.13
Posters Office of Management and **Budget**, PrEx 2.32
Report of Secretary of Defense to the Congress on the **Budget**, Authorization Request, and Defense Programs, D 1.1
Report of the Senate Committee on Labor and Human Resources Presenting its View and Estimates Pursuant to the Congressional **Budget** Act, Y 4.L 11/4:C 76
Report to the Committee on the **Budget** from the Committee on Veterans' Affairs, Y 4.V 64/3-10
Report to the Committee on the **Budget**; Views and Estimates of the Committee on Interior and Insular Affairs (House), Y 4.In 8/14-11
Report to the Committee on the **Budget** Views and Estimates of the Committee on Natural Resources, Y 4.R 31/3-11
Report to the Senate and House Committees on the **Budget** As Required by Public Law 93-344, Y 10.13
Review of **Budget**, Pr 34.107/3
Senate **Budget** Scorekeeping Report, Y 1.3/7
Special Analyses, **Budget** of United States Fiscal Year, PrEx 2.8/5
Special Analysis of Federal Activities in Public Works and Other Construction in **Budget**, PrEx 2.8/a2
Special Analysis of Federal Aid to State and Local Governments in **Budget**, PrEx 2.8/a3
Special Analysis of Federal Credit Programs in **Budget**, PrEx 2.8/a5

Special Analysis of Federal Research and Development Programs in **Budget**, PrEx 2.8/a4
Special Analysis of Principal Federal Statistical Programs in **Budget**, PrEx 2.8/a6
Special Analysis, United States **Budget**, Fiscal Year, PrEx 2.8/5
Summary of the **Budget**, EP 1.1/4
Technical Analysis Papers Congressional **Budget** Office, Y 10.11
U.S. Department of Agriculture **Budget** Summary, A 1.138
Views and Estimates of Committees of the House (together with Supplemental and Minority Views) on the Congressional **Budget** for Fiscal Year (date), Y 4.B 85/3-11
Views and Estimates of the Committee on Foreign Affairs on the **Budget**, Y 4.F 76/1:B 85
Views and Estimates on the **Budget** Proposed for Fiscal Year (date), Y 4.Ap 6/1-10
Views of the Committee on Appropriations, United States Senate, on the First Concurrent Resolution on the **Budget**, Y 4.Ap 6/2:B 85/5
Your Defense **Budget**, D 1.1/4
Your Federal **Budget**, Pr 34.107/4

Budget Estimates
Budget Estimates Excerpts from the United States Government Budget, HH 1.1/4
Budget Estimates Nuclear Regulatory Commission, Y 3.N 88:10-2

Budget System
Budget System and Concepts of the United States Government, PrEx 2.8/12

Budgetary
Analysis of the President's **Budgetary** Proposals for Fiscal Year (date), Y 10.2 B 85/8
Quarterly Report of **Budgetary** Operations, C 1.30

Buenos Aires
Pan-American Congress of Highways, 1st, **Buenos Aires**, S 5.23
International American Conference: **Buenos Aries**, S 5.9/4

Buff
Water Reactor Safety Research, **Buff** Book I, Y 3.N 88:18

Bug
Bug Business, A 13.52/5

Builder
Machine **Builder** {abstracts}, C 41.65

Builders
Foreign Markets for **Builders**' Hardware, C 18.82

Building
Annual Reports on Construction of Pension **Building**, I 1.27
Building Abroad, C 18.54
Building and Housing Publications, C 13.25
Building Construction, L 2.6/a 4
Building Construction in Urban Areas in United States, L 2.36
Building for Clean Water Progress Report on Federal Incentive Grants for Municipal Waste Treatment Fiscal Year, FS 2.64/6
Building for Clean Water Report on Federal Incentive Grants for Municiapl Waste Treatment, FS 16.9
Building for Clear Water, I 67.15
Building Knowledge About Crime and Justice J 28.36
Building Permit Survey, L 2.12
Building Research Summary Reports, C 13.40
Building Science Series, C 13.29/2
Building Technology, C 51.9/10
Building with Environmental Protection Design Case Studies, D 14.16
Center for **Building** Technology, Project Summaries, C 13.59
General Specifications for **Building** Vessels of Navy, N 29.7, M 210.7
Herald of Machine **Building** {abstracts}, C 41.65/4
HUD **Building** Technology Reports, HH 1.72
Pension **Building**, Annual Reports on Construction of, 1883-87, I 1.27
Programme of Competition for Selection of Architect for **Building** for Department, T 39.10
Project Summaries FY (year), Center for **Building** Technology, C 13.59
Structural Clay Products (common brick, face brick, vitrified paving brick, hollow **building** tile), C 3.109

Building Materials
Building Materials and Structures Report, C 13.29
Construction and Building Materials, Monthly Industry Report, C 40.10
Construction and Building Materials, Statistical Supplements, C 41.30/2
Industry Report, Construction and Building Materials, C 41.30
Technical Information on Building Materials for Use in Design of Low-cost Housing, C 13.27
Wholesale Prices of Building Materials, C 13.14

Building Permits
Building Permits in Principal Cities of U.S., L 2.6/a 4
Construction Reports; Building Permits, C 40 (series), C 3.215/7
Construction Reports; Building Permits: C 42 (series), C 3.215/6
Construction Reports; Housing Authorized by Building Permits and Public Contracts, C 3.215/11
Current Construction Reports, Housing Units Authorized by Building Permits, C 3.215/4:C 40
Housing Authorized by Building Permits and Public Contracts, C 3.215/4
New Dwelling Units Authorized by Local Building Permits, L 2.51/5

Buildings
Advertisements for Bids, Specifications, etc., for Equipment of Public Buildings, T 39.9
Buildings with Fallout Protection Design Case Studies, D 119.14
Chief Clerk and Superintendent of Buildings, Annual Report, I 1.60
Commercial Buildings Characteristics, E 3.43/2
Commercial Buildings Energy Consumption Survey (DBECS), E 3.43/2-4
Commissioner of Public Buildings, Annual Reports, I 1.51
Current Awareness Buildings Energy Technology, DOE/BET, E 1.119
Expenditures for Plant and Equipment, Book Value of Fixed Assets, Rental Payments for Buildings and Equipment, Depreciation and Retirements, C 3.24/9-8
Farms of Nonwhite Farm Operators, Number of Farms, Land in Farm, Cropland Harvested, and Value of Land and Buildings, by Tenure, Censuses of 1945 and 1940 (by States), C 3.193
Historic American Buildings Survey, I 29.74
Nonresidential Buildings Energy Consumption Survey (NBECS) (Diskettes), E 3.43/2-3
Plans of Public Buildings, T 39.6/2
Proposals for Construction of Public Buildings; Specifications and Proposals for Repairs, etc. at Public Buildings, T 39.7
Public Buildings Act of 1926, with Amendments, Condemnation Laws with Amendments, Public Works and Construction Laws {May 7, 1926}, Y 1.2:P 96/3
Residential Buildings Energy Consumption Survey. (Diskettes), E 3.43/5
Specifications for Public Buildings, T 39.6

Built
Merchant Ships Built in United States and Other Countries in Employment Report of United States Flag Merchant Seagoing Vessels 1,000 Tons and Over, C 39.211

Bulgarian
Directory of Bulgarian Officials, PrEx 3.10/7-12

Bulk
Bulk Cooling Tanks on Farms Supplying Federal Milk Order Markets, A 82.81/2
Cattle, Calves, and Vealers: Top Prices and Bulk of Sales, Chicago, A 36.207

Bulk Carriers
Bulk Carriers in the World Fleet, C 39.202:B 87 TD 11.20

Bulletin
Alert Bulletin, L 35.24/2
Biomass Bulletin, E 6.3/2
BJA Bulletin, J 28.3/4
Bulletin Department of Education, ED 1.3/2
Bulletin Department of the Air Force, D 301.59
Bulletin National Credit Union, NCU 1.3
Bulletin of Hardwood Market Statistics, A 13.79/3
Bulletin of the Global Volcanism Network SI 3.13
Bureau of Justice Assistance Bulletin, J 26.32
Child Care Bulletin, HE 23.1415
Climate Variations Bulletin, C 55.287/61

Commandant's Bulletin, TD 5.3/9
Customs Bulletin and Decisions, T 17.6/3-4
Daily Bulletin of Orders Affecting Postal Service, P 10.3
Daily Bulletin of Simultaneous Weather Reports with Synopses Indications, and Facts for Month of, W 42.8/1
Department of State Bulletin, S 1.3
Direct Loans Bulletin, ED 1.40/6
Eastern Europe Business Bulletin, C 61.43
Employee Relations Bulletin, D 101.136
Endangered Special Bulletin I 49.77
EPA Intermittent Bulletin, EP 1.3/5
Evaluation Bulletin, HE 20.9122
FDA Medical Bulletin, HE 20.4003/3
Federal Air Surgeons Medical Bulletin, TD 4.215
FEWS (Famine Early Warning System) Bulletin, S 18.68
Hate Crime: The Violence of Intolerance, CRS Bulletin, J 23.3
HTIS Bulletin, D 7.32/3
National Bulletin, A 82.37:N 21
Navy Medical and Dental Materiel Bulletin, D 206.3/2
OERI Bulletin ED 1.303/2
Official Bulletin Committee on Public Information, Y 3.P 93/3:3
Official Bulletin Federal Radio Commission, RC 1.5
Oil Contract Bulletin, D 11.3
On Guard, Bureau of Motor Carrier Safety Bulletin, TD 2.303
Operating Experience, Bulletin Information Report, Y 3.N 88:13
Order Point Bulletin, T 22.2/15:7141
Ordnance Department Safety Bulletin, D 105.7
Ordnance Fiscal Bulletin, W 34.30
Organized Reserves Bulletin, W 99.17/17
P.S. Payroll Savings Bulletin, T 66.16
Park Science, Resource Management Bulletin, I 29.3/4
Philippine Health Service, Monthly Bulletin, W 49.15/6
PHPC (Public Housing Primary Care Program) Bulletin, HE 20.9121
Port Safety Bulletin, TD 5.3/4
Postal Bulletin, P 1.3
Postal Inspection Service Bulletin, P 1.3/2
Postal Service Institute Bulletin, P 1.44
Power Engineering Bulletin, C 41.60/3
Preprints from Bulletin 585, Mineral Facts and Problems, I 28.3/c
Product/Activity Status Bulletin, C 3.238/6
Program Integrity Bulletin, HH 1.3/5
Psychopharmacology Bulletin, HE 20.8109
Public Administration Bulletin {for Vietnam}, S 18.38
Public Affairs Bulletin, LC 14.9
Publications Bulletin, D 101.139
Quarterly Bulletin for Part 2, Hydrographic Products, D 5.351/2-2
Quarterly Bulletin, Intelligence Continuing Education Program, D 5.212
Quarterly Circular Information Bulletin, D 103.42/11
Quarterly Graduate Bulletin, D 5.210/2
Quarterly Seismology Bulletin MSP (series), C 4.25/4
Quarterly Statistical Bulletin, Electric Program, A 68.13/2
Quarterly Statistical Bulletin, Telephone Program, A 68.13/3
Quartermaster Food and Container Institute for Armed Forces: Library Bulletin, D 106.3/2
Quartermaster Professional Bulletin, D 106.3/4
Radio Compass Bulletin, N 19.10
Rail-Highway-Grade Crossing Accident/Incidents Bulletin, TD 3.109
Recombinant DNA Technical Bulletin, HE 20.3460, HE 20.3264
Recruitment Bulletin, VA 1.3/3
Regional Labor Statistics Bulletin, L 2.71/7
Religious Press Bulletin, Y 3.F 73:13
REMR Bulletin: News from the Repair, Evaluation, Maintenance and Rehabilitation Research Program, D 103.72
Reports Bulletin, HE 17.29
Reprints from Bulletin 556, Mineral Facts and Problems, I 28.3/b, I 28.3/c
Reserve Officers Training Corps Bulletin, W 99.17/18
Resource Exchange Bulletin, FEM 1.110
Retail, Wholesale, Service Trades, Subject Bulletin, RWS (series), C 3.202/9

Safety, Occupational Health and Fire Protection Bulletin, VA 1.22:13-1
Sales Tax Rulings, Cumulative Bulletin, T 22.27
Schizophrenia Bulletin, HE 20.2414, HE 20.8115
Scholarship Program, Applicant Information Bulletin, HE 20.6023
Scientific Bulletin, D 210.3/3
Scientific Personnel Bulletin, D 210.7
SEAN Bulletin, SI 3.13
SEIDB Publications Bulletin, E 1.87
Selected Technical Reports, Information Retrieval Bulletin, TD 4.17/2
Selective Service College Qualification Test, Bulletin of Information, Y 3.Se 4:22
Service Bulletin, I 19.26
Shipbuilders Bulletin, SB 2.9
Shipyard Bulletin, SB 2.8
Signal Corps Bulletin, W 42.3
Smoking and Health Bibliographical Bulletin, FS 2.24/4
Smoking and Health Bulletin, HE 20.7012, HE 20.7211, HE 20.7610/2, HE 20.7613/2
Snow and Ice Bulletin, A 29.16
Social Security Bulletin, HE 3.3
Social Security Bulletin, Statistical Supplement, HE 3.3/3
SOI Bulletin, T 22.35/4
Solar Bulletin, E 1.58
Solid Waste Management Monthly Abstracts Bulletin, EP 1.17/3
Solid Waste Management Training Bulletin of Courses, EP 3.12
Special Bulletin Addressed to Victory Speakers, Pr 32.5017/2
Special Needs Offenders, Bulletin, Ju 13.17
Squadron Bulletin, D 301.59/3
Steamboat-Inspection Service Bulletin, C 15.10
STI Bulletin, NAS 1.76
Sti-Recon Bulletin and Tech Info News, NAS 1.76
Storm Bulletin, A 29.17
Structural Engineering Bulletin, HH 1.95
Supplements to Veneral Disease Information Bulletin, FS 2.10
Supreme Commander for Allied Powers: Japanese Economic Statistics Bulletin, D 102.18
T.I.S.C.A. {Technical Information System for Carrier Aviation} Technical Information Indexes: Naval Carrier Aviation Abstract Bulletin with Cross Reference Index, D 202.22
TDC Employee News Bulletin, C 1.49
Technical Bulletin of Committee on Tidal Hydraulics, D 103.28/2
Technical Bulletin, D 203.32/3
Technical Disclosure Bulletin, D 210.3/2
Technical Information Indexes: Naval Carrier Aviation Abstract Bulletin with Cross Reference Index, D 202.22
Technical News Bulletin, C 13.13
Telecommunications Bulletin, TD 5.3/8
Third Branch, a Bulletin of the Federal Courts, Ju 10.3/2
TIB {Technical Information Bulletin} (series), HE 3.52/2
Time and Frequency Bulletin, C 13.3/4
Title Announcement Bulletin, D 10.9
TOP Bulletin, C 61.13
Trade Opportunity Program, TOP Bulletin, C 57.27
Trade Relations Bulletin, C 34.9
Training Analysis and Development, Information Bulletin, D 301.38/2
Training and Education Bulletin TEB (series), FCD 1.9
Training Bulletin, School Series, FCD 1.9/3
Training Bulletin, Training Officer Series, FCD 1.9/2
Training within Industry Bulletin Series, Pr 32.5208/2
Training within the Industry; Bulletin, Pr 32.4816, Pr 32.5208
Translog, Defense Transportation System Bulletin, D 101.66/2-2
Transportation Safety Regulatory Bulletin, E 1.135
Travel USA Bulletin, I 29.55
Treasury Bulletin, T 1.3, T 63.103/2
Treasury Safety Council Safety Bulletin, Administrative, T 1.41
Treaty Information Bulletin, S 9.7
Tribal Activities Bulletin, HE 20.9403/2
Tribal Child Care Bulletin, HE 23.1415/2
Truss Connector Bulletin, HH 1.94
TSCA {Toxic Substances Control Act} Chemicals-in-progress Bulletin, EP 5.15
208 Bulletin, EP 1.71
U.S. Air Force Academy Bulletin, D 305.8/2

U.S. Antarctic Projects Officer, **Bulletin**, D 1.32/2
U.S. General Aviation Accident Prevention
    Bulletin, C 31.203/2
U.S. Navy Civil Engineer Corps **Bulletin**, N 21.14,
    M 205.7, D 209.7
United States Coast Guard Academy, New London,
    Connecticut: **Bulletin** of Information, TD
    5.16/2
United States Naval Medical **Bulletin**, N 10.11
Upper Atmospheric Programs **Bulletin**, NAS 1.63
USAR Training **Bulletin**, D 103.113
USMA Library **Bulletin**, D 109.10
V-line, **Bulletin** of Information, PrEx 10.13/4
Veterans' Emergency Housing Program:
    Community Action **Bulletin**, NHA 1.14
Visa **Bulletin**, S 1.3/4
Vital Statistics **Bulletin**, FS 2.110
Volunteers, **Bulletin** for Those Who Direct Their
    Activities, Pr 32.4264
Wage Stabilization **Bulletin**, L 22.17
Water Operation and Maintenance **Bulletin**, I 27.41
Water Quality Management **Bulletin**, EP 1.71
Water Resources Divisions **Bulletin** of Training, I
    19.3/4
Weather Service **Bulletin**, W 108.35
Weather-Crop **Bulletin**, W 42.27
Weekly **Bulletin** on Raw Materials, Y 3.W 19/2:35
Weekly Climate **Bulletin**, C 55.129/2
Weekly Corn and Wheat Region **Bulletin**, A 29.43
Weekly Weather and Crop **Bulletin**, National
    Summary, C 30.11, C 55.209
Winter Energy Data **Bulletin**, E 3.28
Wireless **Bulletin**, S 1.58
Youth in Action **Bulletin**, J 32.21/2-2
Bulletin Board
    The Federal **Bulletin Board**, GP 3.35
Bulletins
    Bulletins (by States), C 3.24/3
    Bulletins, Drainage, C 3.28/13
    Civilian Personnel **Bulletins** (CPBs), D 101.138
    Consumer **Bulletins**, FT 1.3/2
    Crop Insurance Manager's **Bulletins**, A 112.20
    Crop Insurance Research and Development
        Bulletins, A 112.17, A 62.17
    Current Intelligence **Bulletins**, Summaries, HE
        20.7115/2
    Economic **Bulletins**, D 101.143
    Equal Employment Opportunity Management
        Directives/**Bulletins**, Y 3.Eq 2:18-5
    FCA **Bulletins**, FCA 1.3
    Information **Bulletins**: Adjutant General's
        Department, W 3.82
    Information **Bulletins**: Bureau of Air Commerce, C
        23.8
    Information **Bulletins**: Bureau of Land Manage-
        ment, I 53.9
    Information **Bulletins**: Coast Guard, TD 5.3/6
    Information **Bulletins**: Defense Civil Prepardness
        Agency, D 14.13/2
    Information **Bulletins**: Department of Energy, E
        1.100
    Information **Bulletins**: Division of Maternal and
        Child Health, HE 20.9111
    Information **Bulletins**: Environmental Information
        Division, D 301.38/8
    Information **Bulletins**: Federal Civil Defense
        Administration, FCD 1.13/11
    Information **Bulletins**: Field Artillery Office, W
        96.5
    Information **Bulletins**: General Land Office, I 21.17
    Information **Bulletins**: Human Resources Research
        Center, D 301.36/5
    Information **Bulletins**: Library of Congress, LC
        1.18
    Information **Bulletins**: Metallurgical Advisory
        Committee on Titanium, D 105.13/2-4
    Information **Bulletins**: National Inventors Council,
        C 32.7
    Information **Bulletins**: National Scientific Register,
        Office of Education, FS 5.47/2
    Information **Bulletins**: Office of Civil Defense, D
        13.3/2
    Information **Bulletins**: Office of Defense and
        Civilian Mobilization, Pr 34.753/2
    Information **Bulletins**: Office of Emergency
        Preparedness, PrEx 4.3/3
    Information **Bulletins**: Office of U.S. High
        Commissioner for Germany, S 1.85
    Information **Bulletins**: Veteran's Administration,
        VA 1.22/2
    Information **Bulletins**: Youth 2000 (series), HE
        20.9203/2
    OCC **Bulletins**, T 12.20
    Occupational **Bulletins**, Y 3.Se 4:12

Official **Bulletins**, I 29.37/5
Official **Bulletins**, National Trophy Matches, D
    101.61
OPA **Bulletins** for Schools and Colleges, Pr
    32.4224
OPA Trade **Bulletins**, ES 3.9, Pr 32.4244
Ordnance **Bulletins**, W 99.17/16
Ordnance Field Service **Bulletins**, W 34.26, W
    34.32
Ordnance Field Service Technical **Bulletins**, W
    34.36
Ordnance Recruiting **Bulletins**, W 34.22
Ordnance Technical Library **Bulletins**, W 34.21/3
Park Service **Bulletins**, I 29.3
Personnel **Bulletins** Government Printing Office,
    GP 1.20
Personnel **Bulletins** Indian Affairs Bureau, I 20.28
Personnel **Bulletins** Interior Department, I 1.73
Personnel **Bulletins** Labor Department, L 1.3/2
Personnel **Bulletins** Personnel Office, Department
    of Agriculture, A 49.3/2
Personnel Section **Bulletins**, T 47.15
PHA Low-Rent Housing **Bulletins**, HH 3.3/4
Philippine Islands Census, 1903; **Bulletins**, C 3.8/
    2
Plant Disease **Bulletins**, A 19.18
Popular **Bulletins**, W 49.21/8
Population **Bulletins**, 1st Series (by States), C
    3.37/8
Population **Bulletins**, 2d Series (by States), C 3.37/
    9
Population **Bulletins**, Families, C 3.37/10
Power O. and M. **Bulletins**, I 27.45
Price Fixing **Bulletins**, Y 3.W 19/2:46
Priorities **Bulletins**, Y 3.Ec 74/3:30, Pr 33.912
Prisoners of War **Bulletins**, W 102.6
Procurement Division **Bulletins**, T 58.15
Procurement Information **Bulletins**, FO 1.3
Progress **Bulletins**, General, A 68.8
Public Health **Bulletins**, T 27.12, FS 2.3
PWA **Bulletins**, Y 3.F 31/4:24
Radar **Bulletins**, N 27.15
Radio Service **Bulletins**, CC 1.3/2, CC 1.25
REA **Bulletins**, A 68.3
Recreation **Bulletins**, FS 8.8, Pr 32.4509, FS 9.7
Recruiting **Bulletins** Agricultural Marketing
    Service, A 88.3/2
Recruiting **Bulletins** Army and Corps Areas and
    Departments, Seventh Corps Area, W
    99.17/10
Recruiting **Bulletins** Civil Service Commission, CS
    1.51
Reemployment **Bulletins**, Pr 32.5282
Regional **Bulletins**, A 57.16
Regional Research **Bulletins**, N.Y. and New
    England, Y 3.W 89/2:60
Regulations and Interpretive **Bulletins**, L 1.7/4
Renegotiation Staff **Bulletins**, RnB 1.6/3
Reprints from the Occupational Outlook
    Handbook, **Bulletins**, L 2.3/4 a
Research **Bulletins** Air Training Command, Human
    Resources Research Center, D 301.36/3
Research **Bulletins** Federal Emergency Relief
    Administration, Y 3.F 31/5:28
Research **Bulletins** Works Progress Administra-
    tion, Y 3.W 89/2:13
Research **Bulletins**, J 28.19
Research Relating to Children, **Bulletins**, HE
    19.120
Resource **Bulletins**, A 13.80
Retail **Bulletins**, Y 3.N 21/8:12
Retail Trade **Bulletins**, C 3.202/2
Retailers' **Bulletins**, Pr 32.4221
Safety and Fire Protection **Bulletins**, Y 3.At 7:3
Safety and Special Radio Services **Bulletins**, CC
    1.39/3
Safety **Bulletins** Bureau of Employees' Compensa-
    tion, FS 13.307, FS 13.3/2
Safety **Bulletins** Civil Aeronautics Board, C 31.214
Safety **Bulletins** Civil Conservation Corps, FS 4.8
Safety **Bulletins** Employees' Compensation
    Commission, EC 1.9
Safety **Bulletins** Federal Emergency Relief
    Administration, Y 3.F 31/5:24
Safety **Bulletins** Government Printing Office, GP
    1.24
Safety **Bulletins** National Shipping Authority, C
    39.209
Safety **Bulletins** National Youth Administration,
    FS 6.16
Safety **Bulletins** Works Progress Administration, Y
    3.W 89/2:11
Safety **Bulletins** Works Projects Administration,
    FW 4.20

Safety Department **Bulletins**, Y 3.F 31/7:10
Safety Division **Bulletins**, Y 3.Em 3:8
Safety Series, **Bulletins**, IC 1 mot.10
Schools at War, War Savings News **Bulletins** for
    Teachers, T 66.9
Scientific Manpower **Bulletins**, NS 1.3/2
Search, Administrative Research **Bulletins**, ARB-
    (series), VA 1.47
Sedimentation **Bulletins**, Y 3.F 31/13:8, Y 3.In 8/
    8:8
Semiannual Interest Rate **Bulletins**, T 66.3/2
Service **Bulletins** of Defense Training in Vocational
    Schools, FS 5.24
Service Trade **Bulletins**, Pr 32.4222
SES **Bulletins**, D 101.140
Shock and Vibration **Bulletins**, D 4.12
Small Industry Series, Cottage Industries **Bulletins**,
    S 17.37
Social and Rehabilitation Service Reports
    Bulletins, HE 17.29
Social Security Rulings, Cumulative **Bulletins**, HE
    3.44/2
Speakers' **Bulletins**, Y 3.F 73:8
Speaking Division **Bulletins**, Y 3.P 96/3:10
Special **Bulletins** Bureau of Foreign and Domestic
    Commerce, Textile Division, C 18.127
Special **Bulletins** Civil Service Commission, CS
    1.47
Special **Bulletins** Employees' Compensation
    Commission, EC 1.3/2
Special **Bulletins** Manufacturers Division, C 3.7
Special **Bulletins** United States Administration of
    Ryukyu Islands, D 102.19/2
Special Cement **Bulletins**, C 18.128
Special Information **Bulletins**, FS 2.73
Special Promotion Series from Office of Civil and
    Defense Mobilization, Battle Creek,
    Michigan, **Bulletins**, Pr 34.757/3
Special River **Bulletins**, A 29.19
Specifications **Bulletins**, D 301.19
Staff Accounting **Bulletins**, SE 1.31
Standardization of Petroleum Specifications
    Committee, **Bulletins**, I 28.15
State and Private Forestry: Forestry **Bulletins**, A
    13.110/10
State **Bulletins**, 2d Series (Statistics by counties),
    C 3.31/3
State **Bulletins**, C 3.31/2
Statewide Highway Planning Surveys; News
    Bulletins, FW 2.10
Statistical **Bulletins** Bureau of Fisheries, C 6.5, I
    45.8, I 49.8
Statistical **Bulletins** Department of Agriculture, A
    1.34
Statistical **Bulletins** Farm Credit Administration,
    FCA 1.3/2
Statistical **Bulletins** Fish Commission, FC 1.5
Statistical **Bulletins** Military Government of
    Ryukyu Islands, D 102.19
Statistical **Bulletins** Office of Civil Defense, Pr
    32.4425
Statistical Bulletins Philippine Islands, Commerce
    and Industry Bureau, W 49.52/5
Statistical **Bulletins** Rural Electrification
    Administration, A 68.13
Statistical **Bulletins** Securities and Exchange
    Commission, SE 1.20
Statistical **Bulletins** Work Projects Administra-
    tion, FW 4.13
Statistical **Bulletins** Works Progress Administra-
    tion, Y 3.W 89/2:58
Statistics **Bulletins**, HH 1.11
Steamship Department **Bulletins**, Y 3.F 73:24
Subject List of Farmers' **Bulletins** (Front Space), A
    21.9/6
Summer Training Camp **Bulletins**, W 99.19/10
Supervisor's **Bulletins** (occasional), L 1.24
Supplements {to} **Bulletins**, T 29.3/2
Supply **Bulletins**, W 89.5, W 1.61, M 101.27, D
    101.15
Surplus Materials **Bulletins**, M 1.27
Surplus Property **Bulletins**, PrEx 4.3/5
Technical Assistance **Bulletins**, I 66.22, HE
    20.415/2
Crop Insurance Research and Development
    Bulletins, A 112.17
Technical Information **Bulletins**, FS 2.2/3, FS 3.52/
    2, HE 3.52/2
Technical Information Center: **Bulletins**, TD 1.3/2
Technical Procedures **Bulletins**, C 55.128
Technical Section **Bulletins**, W 95.21/7
Technical Series **Bulletins**, S 18.50
Tennis **Bulletins**, W 99.15/10, W 99.18/9

Title 1 Fall Program, Modernize for Winter, Special Field **Bulletins**, Y 3.F 31/11:34
Trade Information **Bulletins**, C 18.25
Training **Bulletins** Army and Corps Areas and Departments, Seventh Corps Area, W 99.77/11
Training **Bulletins** Federal Works Agency, FW 1.11
Training within Industry Abstracts, British Engineering **Bulletins**, Pr 32.4822, Pr 32.5215
Training within Industry, **Bulletins**, Pr 32.4011
Transportation **Bulletins**, Pr 32.4416
Transportation Committee **Bulletins**, Pr 32.4235
Tree Preservation **Bulletins**, I 29.26
U.S. Army Audit Agency **Bulletins**, D 101.3/3
Unemployment **Bulletins** (by States), C 3.37/16
United States Attorney's **Bulletins**, J 31.12
United States Civil Administration of Ryukyu Islands; Special **Bulletins**, D 102.19/2
United States Import Duties Annotated, Public **Bulletins**, C 3.150/5
Urban Consortium Information **Bulletins**, HH 1.3/3
Urban Planning **Bulletins**, HH 7.3/4
Urban Renewal **Bulletins**, HH 1.19
Urban Renewal Service **Bulletins**, HH 7.7/3
Urban Studies Division **Bulletins**, NHA 1.7
Use of Materials **Bulletins**, HH 2.14
Veneral Disease **Bulletins**, T 27.20, FS 2.11
Veterinary **Bulletins**, W 44.21/9
Victory; Office Weekly **Bulletins**, Pr 32.5008
Vocational Rehabilitation Series **Bulletins**, FS .5.28, FS 10.7
Voting Information **Bulletins**, D 2.3/2
W.I.B. Price **Bulletins**, Y 3.W 19/2:47
War Housing Technical **Bulletins**, NHA 4.10
Water Resources **Bulletins**, I 19.3/3
Water Supply **Bulletins**, I 19.3/5
Water-Resources **Bulletins**, I 19.3/3
Weekly Accident **Bulletins**, C 3.128
Weekly **Bulletins**, Y 3.F 73:5
Weekly Cotton Region **Bulletins**, A 29.39
Weekly Cotton Service **Bulletins**, C 18.162
Weekly Summary of Federal Legislation Relating to National Resources Committee, Activities **Bulletins**, Y 3.N 21/12:15
Wholesale **Bulletins**, Pr 32.4223
Wildlife Research **Bulletins**, I 49.19
Wyoming BLM Wildlife Technical **Bulletins**, I 53.34

Bullett
In Supreme Court of U.S., Briefs, Petitions, and Motions of Wm. Marshall **Bullett**, Solicitor General, J 1.19/2

BuMed
BuMed Circular Letters, N 10.20/2, M 203.9, D 206.13
BuMed Instructions, D 206.6/2
BuMed News Letter, N 10.18, M 203.7

Bunker
United States Foreign Trade **Bunker** Oil and Coal Laden in the United States on Vessels, C 3.164:810

Buoy
Buoy List, C 9.32, C 9.39
Data **Buoy** Technical Bulletin, C 55.30
NOAA Environmental Buoy Data, C 55.297
Proceedings National Data **Buoy** Systems Scientific Advisory Meetings, TD 5.23

Buoys
Beacons **Buoys** and Daymarks, T 25.5-T 25.14
Light List, Lights, **Buoys**, and Day Marks, Mississippi and Ohio Rivers, C 9.29/2
Lights, **Buoys** and Day Marks, C 9.5, C 9.17, C 9.19, C 9.27, C 9.28
Notice to Mariners, Affecting Lights, **Buoys**, and Other Aids to Navigation, N 24.12

Bureau
Bureau of Economics Staff Reports, FT 1.37
Bureau of Export Administration Fact Sheets, C 63.24
Bureau of Justice Assistance Bulletin, J 26.32
Bureau of Justice Assistance Publications List, J 26.9/2
Bureau of Justice Statistics Fiscal Year: At a Glance, J 29.1/2
Bureau of Labor Statistics Surveys, L 2.136
Official Register National Guard **Bureau**, D 112.8
On Guard, **Bureau** of Motor Carrier Safety Bulletin, TD 2.303
Operations of the **Bureau** of Commercial Fisheries Under the Saltonstall-Kennedy Act, I 49.48
Operations of the Weather **Bureau**, C 30.83
Orders **Bureau** of Indian Affairs, I 20.20

Pamphlets National Guard **Bureau**, D 12.8
Pamphlets Women's **Bureau**, L 36.112
Periodicals and Serials Received in the Library of the National **Bureau** of Standards, C 13.10
Personnel Bulletins Indian Affairs **Bureau**, I 20.28
Posters **Bureau** of Medicine and Surgery, D 206.23
Posters Census **Bureau**, C 3.270
Posters Children's **Bureau**, HE 23.1214
Posters Federal **Bureau** of Investigation, J 1.14/21
Posters Head Start **Bureau**, HE 21.213
Posters National Guard **Bureau**, D 12.14
President Research Associateships, Post- Doctoral, Tenable at National **Bureau** of Standards, C 13.47
Press Notices **Bureau** of Foreign and Domestic Commerce, C 18.31
Press Notices National **Bureau** of Standards, C 13.18
Private Radio **Bureau**, CC 1.36/10
Proceedings Annual Conference of the Surgeon General, Public Health Service, and Chief, Children's **Bureau**, with State and Territorial Health Officers, FS 2.83
Proceedings Biennial Conference of State and Territorial Dental Directors with Public Health Service and Children's **Bureau**, FS 2.83/2
Public Assistance **Bureau**, Applications: Old-Age Assistance, Aid to Dependent Children, Aid to the Blind {and} General Assistance, FS 3.17
Publications **Bureau** of Community Health Services, HE 20.5110:P 96
Publications **Bureau** of Education, I 16.14/2
Publications **Bureau** of Entomology Available for Free Distribution, A 9.13
Publications **Bureau** of Home Economics, A 42.5
Publications **Bureau** of Labor Statistics, L 2.71
Publications **Bureau** of Mines, A 22.7/1, I 28.5/8
Publications **Bureau** of Public Roads, A 22.5
Publications **Bureau** of Sport Fisheries and Wildlife, I 49.18/6
Publications **Bureau** of the Census, C 3.163
Publications Children's **Bureau**, FS 3.209, FS 14.111, FS 17.210, HE 21.110
Publications National **Bureau** of Standards, C 13.10:305
Publications Recruiting Publicity **Bureau**, D 102.75
Publications Weather **Bureau** Available for Distribution, A 29.31
Publications Weather **Bureau**, C 30.17/2
Publicity **Bureau**, Liberty Loan of 1917, T 1.25
Publicity **Bureau**, T 1.27/21-29
Radio Talks **Bureau** of Agricultural Economics, A 13.144
Radio Talks **Bureau** of Foreign and Domestic Commerce, C 18.40
REC-OCE Reclamation **Bureau**-Office of Chief Engineer (series), I 27.60
Receipts and Disbursements of Government Consolidated into Bureau of Accounts, Fiscal Service in Treasury Department by President's Reorganization Plan no. 3, T 9.11
Recruiting Publicity **Bureau** Posters, D 102.78
Recruiting Publicity **Bureau** Publications, D 102.75
Regulations, Rules and Instructions Census **Bureau**, C 3.6
Report of **Bureau** of Commercial Fisheries for Calendar Year (date), I 49.1/2
Research Division Reports **Bureau** of Apprenticeship and Training, L 23.19
Research Progress and Plans of the Weather **Bureau**, C 30.75
Research Reports **Bureau** of Federal Credit Unions, FS 3.309
Research Reports Children's **Bureau**, FS 17.214
Resident Research Associateships, Postdoctoral, Tenable and National **Bureau** of Standards, C 13.47
Review of **Bureau** of Mines Coal Program, I 28.17, I 28.27
Review of **Bureau** of Mines Energy Program, I 28.27
Rules and Regulations of **Bureau** of Imports, WT 4.5
Rules of Practice **Bureau** of Domestic Commerce, C 41.6/11
Safety Bulletins **Bureau** of Employees' Compensation, FS 13.307, L 26.7

Sales Finance Companies **Bureau** of the Census, C 3.151
Selected Papers from **Bureau** of Radiological Health Seminar Program (numbered), HE 20.1109
Semiannual Checklist, **Bureau** of International Commerce International Business Publications, C 42.15:C 41
Service and Regulatory Announcements **Bureau** of Agricultural Economics, A 36.5
Service and Regulatory Announcements **Bureau** of Animal Industry, A 4.13, A 77.208
Service and Regulatory Announcements **Bureau** of Biological Survey, A 5.6
Service and Regulatory Announcements **Bureau** of Chemistry, A 7.6
Service and Regulatory Announcements **Bureau** of Dairy Industry, A 44.5
Service and Regulatory Announcements **Bureau** of Entomology and Plant Quarantine, A 56.14
Service and Regulatory Announcements **Bureau** of Plant Industry, A 19.13
Service and Regulatory Announcements **Bureau** of Plant Quarantine, A 48.7
Service and Regulatory Announcements **Bureau** of Soils, A 26.7
Sheets of National Atlas of United States **Bureau** of the Census, C 3.62/3
Sheets of National Atlas of United States Weather **Bureau**, C 30.22/4
Special Bulletins **Bureau** of Foreign and Domestic Commerce, Textile Division, C 18.127
Special Reports **Bureau** of Labor, C 8.5
Special Reports **Bureau** of the Census, C 3.5
Special Reports Justice Statistics **Bureau**, J 29.13
Special Reports Porto Rico, Labor **Bureau**, W 75.14/4
Special Series **Bureau** of Foreign and Domestic Commerce, Paper Division, C 18.146
Specifications Reclamation **Bureau**, I 27.8
Standard Specifications **Bureau** of Yards and Docks, N 21.10
Statistical Brief from the **Bureau** of the Census (series), C 3.205/8
Statistical Bulletins **Bureau** of Fisheries, C 6.5, I 45.8, I 49.8
Statistical Bulletins Philippine Islands, Commerce and Industry **Bureau**, W 49.52/5
Statistical Series Children's **Bureau**, FS 3.214, FS 14.113, FS 17.213
Summary of Bang's Disease Control Program Conducted by **Bureau** of Animal Industry in Cooperation with Various States, A 4.23
Summary of Brucellosis (Bang's Disease) Control Program Conducted by **Bureau** of Animal Industry in Cooperation with Various States, A 77.213
Summary Report of the Commissioner, **Bureau** of Reclamation {and} Statistical Appendix, I 27.1/2
Tariffs **Bureau** of Customs, T 17.7
Technical Digest **Bureau** of Yards and Docks, M 205.8
Technical Highlights of the National **Bureau** of Standards, C 13.1
Technical Memorandum National **Bureau** of Standards, Applied Mathematics Division, C 13.39
Technical Memorandum Reclamation **Bureau**, I 27.31/2
Technical News from Department of Commerce, National **Bureau** of Standards, C 13.36/6
Technical Notes **Bureau** of the Census, C 56.215, C 3.212/2
Technical Notes National **Bureau** of Standards, C 13.46
Technical Notes Weather **Bureau**, C 30.82
Technology News from the **Bureau** of Mines, I 28.152
Telephone Directory, **Bureau** of Apprenticeship and Training, L 37.109
Telephone Directory Engraving and Printing **Bureau**, T 18.6
Telephone Directory Reclamation **Bureau**, I 27.77
Training Circulars National Guard **Bureau**, W 70.11
Transportation Series **Bureau** of Foreign and Domestic Commerce, C 18.274
U.S. Travel **Bureau**, I 29.37
Weather **Bureau** Engineering Handbooks EHB-(series), C 30.6/5
Weather **Bureau** Forecasters Handbooks, C 30.6/4

Cancergrams
   Recent Reviews, Cancer Diagnosis and Therapy,
      Supplement to the **Cancergrams**, HE
      20.3173/2-3
   Recent Reviews, Cancer Virology and Biology,
      Supplement to the **Cancergrams**, HE
      20.3173/2-4
Candidates
   Annual Report of Political Committees Supporting
      Candidates for House of Representa-
      tives, Y 1.2/4
   Annual Reports of Political Committees
      Supporting **Candidates** for Senate, Y
      1.3/5
   If Elected. . . Unsuccessful **Candidates** for the
      Presidency, SI 11.2:P 92/2
   Instructions to **Candidates**, D 305.8/4
   Manual of Regulations and Instructions Relating to
      the Disclosure of Federal Campaign
      Funds for Candidates for the Office of
      President or Vice President of the U.S.
      and . . . **Candidates**, GA 1.14:C 15
   Regulations Governing Admission of **Candidates**
      into Naval Academy As Midshipmen and
      Sample Examination Questions, D
      208.108
Candy
   Progress in **Candy** Research, Reports, A 77.109
Cane
   Proceedings Technical Session on **Cane** Sugar
      Refining Research, A 106.27/2
Cane Sugar
   Mainland **Cane Sugar** Orders, A 55.67
Cannabis
   Domestic **Cannabis** Eradication/Suppression
      Program, J 24.25
Canned
   Canned and Dried Foods, C 18.72/1
   Canned Fishery Products, C 55.309/2
   Canned Food Report, C 3.189
   Canned Fruits and Vegetables, Production and
      Wholesale Distribution, C 3.168
   Canned Poultry, A 88.15/2
   Consumer Buying Practices for Selected Fresh
      Fruits, **Canned** and Frozen Juices, and
      Dried Fruits, Related to Family
      Characteristics, Region and City Size, A
      36.173
   Consumer Purchases of Selected Fresh Fruits,
      Canned and Frozen Juices, and Dried
      Fruits, A 36.171
   Industry Report, **Canned** Fruits and Vegetables,
      Production and Wholesale Distribution,
      C 18.234
   Quarterly **Canned** Foods Stocks Reports, C 3.136
   Regional Distribution and Types of Stores where
      Consumers Buy Selected Fresh Fruits,
      Canned and Frozen Juices, and Dried
      Fruits, A 36.172
Canned Food
   Current Business Reports; **Canned Food**, Stock,
      Pack, Shipments, B-1 (series), C 56.219/
      8
Canning
   Poultry Slaughtered Under Federal Inspection and
      Poultry Used in **Canning** and Processed
      Foods, A 88.15/9-2
CAORF
   CAORF (series), C 39.243
   CAORF Technical Reports (series), TD 11.18
CAP
   CAP Pamphlets, PrEx 10.9/4
   Directory **CAP** {Community Actions Programs}
      Grantees, PrEx 10.2:C 73-3
Capabilities
   Waterways Experiment Station **Capabilities**, D
      103.24/10
Capacities
   United States Flag Containerships and United
      States Flag Ships with Partial
      Capacities for Containers And/or
      Vehicles, C 39.232
Capacity
   Aviation **Capacity** Enhancement Plan, TD 4.77
   Capacity of Elevators, Reporting Grain Stocks, A
      36.82
   Capacity of Refrigerated Warehouses, A 105.33/3
   Capacity of Refrigerated Warehouses in United
      States, A 88.20/3, A 92.21/3
   Capacity Utilization in Manufacturing, Quarterly
      Averages, Seasonally Adjusted, FR 1.55
   Capacity Utilization: Manufacturing and
      Materials, FR 1.55/2

Financial Management **Capacity** Sharing Program,
   HH 1.82
Petroleum Products, Secondary Inventories and
   Storage **Capacity**, C 3.213
Power Production, Generating **Capacity**, E 3.11/
   17-7
Preliminary Power Production, Fuel Consumption
   and Installed **Capacity** Data, E 3.11/17-
   6
Preliminary Power Production, Fuel Consumption,
   and Installed **Capacity** Data for (year), E
   3.11/17-4
Production of Electric Energy and **Capacity** of
   Generating Plants, FP 1.21
Seasonally Adjusted **Capacity** and Traffic
   Scheduled Domestic Operations,
   Domestic Trunks, C 31.262/3
Seasonally Adjusted **Capacity** and Traffic
   Scheduled International Operations,
   International Trunks, C 31.262
Seasonally Adjusted **Capacity** and Traffic
   Scheduled Operations Local Service
   Carriers, C 31.262/4
Seasonally Adjusted **Capacity** and Traffic
   Scheduled Operations System Trunks
   and Regional Carriers, C 31.262/5
Seasonally Adjusted **Capacity** and Traffic
   Scheduled Operations, System Trunks, C
   31.262/2
Seasonally Adjusted **Capacity** and Traffic
   Scheduled Operations: System,
   Domestic, and International Trunks Plus
   Local Service Carrier, CAB 1.20
Storage **Capacity** of Elevators Reporting
   Commercial Grain Stocks, A 88.18/15
Survey of **Capacity** of Refrigerated Storage
   Warehouses in United States, A 82.58
Tax **Capacity** of the States, Y 3.Ad 9/8:19
Cape Cod
   Atlantic Coast; **Cape Cod** to Sandy Hook, C
      55.422:2
   Atlantic Coast; Eastport to **Cape Cod**, C 55.422:1
Cape Henry
   Atlantic Coast; **Cape Henry** to Key West, C
      55.422:4
   Atlantic Coast; Sandy Hook to **Cape Henry**, C
      55.422:3
   Tide Calendar Baltimore and **Cape Henry**, N 6.22/2
Cape May
   Annual Technical Report of the **Cape May** Plant
      Materials Center, HE 3.67/2
Cape Spencer
   Pacific and Arctic Coasts, Alaska, **Cape Spencer** to
      Beaufort Sea, C 55.422:9
   Pacific Coast, Alaska, Dixon Entrance to **Cape
      Spencer**, C 55.422:8
Capita
   West North Central, Population and Per **Capita**
      Income Estimates for Counties and
      Incorporated Places, C 3.186/27-3
   West, Population and Per **Capita** Income Estimates
      for Counties and Incorporated Places, C
      3.186/27-2
Capital
   Activities in the National **Capital** Region, I 29.65
   Capital Market Working Papers, SE 1.35
   Comprehensive Plan for the National **Capital**, NC
      2.2:P 69/2
   Final Report of the SEC Government-Business
      Forum on Small Business **Capital**
      Formation, SE 1.35/2
   General Summary of Inventory Status and
      Movement of **Capital** and Producers
      Goods, Plants, Aircraft, and Industry
      Agent Items, Pr 33.210
   Report of Calls, Assets, Liabilities, **Capital**,
      Accounts, Commercial and Mutual
      Savings Banks (unnumbered), Y 3.F 31/
      8:9-2
   Sales of **Capital** Assets Reported on Individual
      Income Tax Returns, T 22.35/2:C 17
   Statistics of **Capital** Movements Between U.S. and
      Foreign Countries, T 62.9
   Working **Capital** Funds, D 1.58/3
   Working **Capital** of U.S. Corporations, SE 1.25/6
Capital Accounts
   Assets Liabilities and **Capital Accounts**
      Commercial Banks and Mutual Savings
      Banks, Y 3.F 31/8:9
Capital Expenditures
   Annual **Capital Expenditures**, C 3.289
Capital Punishment
   Capital Punishment, J 29.11/3

Capitalization
   Preliminary Statement of **Capitalization** and
      Income, Class I Steam Railways in
      United States, IC 1 ste.28
Capitol
   Art in the United States **Capitol**, Y 1.91-2:H.doc
      368
CAPM
   Civil Air Patrol Manuals, **CAPM** (series), D 301.7/
      4
CAPP
   Civil Air Patrol Pamphlet **CAPP** (series), D
      301.35/2
Capsule
   EPA Technology Transfer **Capsule** Reports, EP
      7.11
   Water Research **Capsule** Report (series), I 1.103
Capsules
   NIDA **Capsules** (Series), HE 20.8234, HE
      20.3967/2
Captioned
   Catalog of **Captioned** Films for the Deaf, FS
      5.234:34039, HE 5.234:34039, ED
      1.209/2
   Catalog of Educational **Captioned** Films/Videos for
      the Deaf, ED 1.209/2-2
   Catalog of **Captioned** Feature and Special Interest
      Films and Videos for the Hearing
      Impaired, ED 1.209/2-3
Car
   Buying a Safer **Car** for Child Passengers, TD 8.66
   Classification of Revenues and Expenses of
      Sleeping **Car** Operations, of Auxiliary
      Operations and of Other Properties for
      Sleeping **Car** Companies, IC 1 sle.5
   Estimated Refrigerator **Car** Movement of Domestic
      Fresh Fruits and Vegetables by Regions,
      A 82.42
   Finance Rate and Other Terms on New **Car** and
      Used **Car** Installment Credit Contracts
      Purchased from Dealers of Major Auto
      Finance Companies, FR 1.34/5
   Mileage Distribution of Carloads for Each
      Commodity Class by Type of **Car**, IC
      1.23/16:TC-1
   Motive Power and **Car** Equipment of Class I
      Railroads in the United States, IC 1
      ste.36
   Passenger Traffic Statements (other than
      commutation) of Class 1 Steam Railways
      in United States Separated Between
      Coach Traffic and Parlor and Sleeping
      Car Traffic, IC 1 ste.40
   Passenger Traffic Statistics (other than commuta-
      tion) of Class I Steam Railways in the
      United States Separated Between Coach
      Traffic and Parlor and Sleeping **Car**
      Traffic, IC 1 ste.39
   Territorial Distribution of Carloads for Each
      Commodity Class by Type of **Car**, IC
      1.23/19:TC-3
   Weight Distribution of Carloads for Each
      Commodity Class by Type of **Car**, IC
      1.23/16:TC-2
Car-Lot
   Car-Lot Shipments of Fruits and Vegetables, by
      Commodities, States, and Months, A
      1.34, A 66.24
   Car-Lot Unloads of Certain Fruits and Vegetables,
      A 66.40
Car-Miles
   Classification of Train-Miles, Locomotive-Miles
      and **Car-Miles**, IC 1 ste.11
Caracas
   Venezuelan Mixed Claims Commissions, **Caracas**
      1902 and 1903, S 3.17
Carbon Black
   Carbon Black, E 3.11/10, E 3.11/10-2, I 28.88
   Carbon Black in (year), I 28.88/2
   Carbon Black Report, I 28.88
Carbon Dioxide
   Tar, Nicotine, and **Carbon Dioxide** of the Smoke of...
      Varieties of Domestic Cigarettes for the
      Year, FT 1.36
Carbonate
   Sodium **Carbonate** in (year), I 28.135/3
Carcinogenesis
   Carcinogenesis Abstracts, HE 20.3159
   Carcinogenesis Program Scientific Review
      Committee A, HE 20.3001/2:C 17/2
   Carcinogenesis Program Scientific Review
      Committee B, HE 20.3001/2:C 17/3
   Carcinogenesis Program Scientific Review
      Committee C, HE 20.3001/2:C 17/4

Depreciation Rate for **Carriers** by Inland and Coastal Waterways, IC 1 wat.13

Depreciation Rates for Property of **Carriers** by Pipe Lines, IC 1 pip.8

Depreciation Rates of **Carriers** by Water Administration, IC 1 wat.12

Foreign, Overseas and Territorial Air Mail **Carriers**, C 31.231

Fuel Consumption and Cost, Certificated Route and Supplemental Air **Carriers**, Domestic and International Operations, IC 31.267

Fuel Cost and Consumption, Certified Route and Supplemental Air **Carriers**, Domestic and International Operations, Twelve Months Ended (date), C 31.267/2

List of Corporate Names of Common **Carriers**, IC 1.15

List of U.S. Air **Carriers**, CAB 1.26

List of U.S. **Carriers**, C 31.254

Local Service Air **Carriers'** Unit Costs, C 31.253

Medicare **Carriers** Manual; Claims Process, HE 22.8/7

Medicare **Carriers** Manual; Fiscal Administration, HE 22.8/7-2

Medicare **Carriers** Manual; Program Administration, HE 22.8/7-3

Motor Carrier Freight Commodity Statistics Class 1 Common and Contract **Carriers** of Property, IC 1 mot.22

Motor **Carriers** of Passengers, Class 1 Accident Data, IC 1 mot.21/2

Motor **Carriers** of Property, Accident Data, IC 1 mot.21

Motor **Carriers**, Special Circulars, IC 1 mot.15

Operating Data from Monthly Reports of Large Telegraph Cable, and Radiotelegraph **Carriers**, CC 1.13

Operating Data from Monthly Reports of Telephone **Carriers** Filing Annual and Monthly Reports, CC 1.14

Other **Carriers** {12-month comparisons}, C 31.247/2

Other **Carriers** {quarterly comparisons}, C 31.247

Persons Furnishing Cars to or on Behalf of **Carriers** by Railroad or Express Companies, Summary of Quarterly Reports, IC 1.18

Productivity and Cost of Employment: Local Service **Carriers**, Calendar Year, C 31.263

Quarterly Freight Loss and Damage Claims Reported by Common and Contract Motor **Carriers** of Property, IC 1 acco.11

Quarterly Interim Financial Report, Certificated Route Air **Carriers** and Supplemental Air **Carriers**, CAB 1.14

Quarterly Interim Financial Report, Certified Route Air **Carriers** and Supplemental Air **Carriers**, C 31.240/3

Quarterly Operating Data of 63 Telephone **Carriers**, CC 1.14

Quarterly Operating Data of 70 Telephone **Carriers**, CC 1.14

Quarterly Operating Data of Telegraph **Carriers**, CC 1.13

Recapitulation by Carrier Groups, Certified Air **Carriers**, C 31.233

Recurrent Report of Financial Data: Domestic Air Mail Trunk **Carriers**, Quarters {comparisons}, C 31.234

Recurrent Report of Mileage and Traffic Data All Certificated Air Cargo **Carriers**, C 31.232

Recurrent Report of Mileage and Traffic Data Domestic Air Mail **Carriers**, C 31.230

Recurrent Report of Mileage and Traffic Data Domestic Helicopter Service, Certificated Airmail **Carriers**, C 31.229/4

Recurrent Report of Mileage and Traffic Data Domestic Local Service **Carriers**, C 31.229

Recurrent Report of Mileage and Traffic Data Foreign, Overseas and Territorial Air Mail **Carriers**, C 31.231

Revenue and Traffic **Carriers** by Water, IC 1 wat.11

Revenue and Traffic of Class A and B Water **Carriers**, IC 1 wat.11

Revenues, Expenses, and Statistics of Class 1 Motor **Carriers** of Passengers, IC 1 mot.11

Revenues, Expenses, and Statistics of Class 1 Motor **Carriers** of States, IC 1 ste.24

Revenues, Expenses, Other Income, and Statistics of Class 1 Motor **Carriers** of Passengers, IC 1 mot.12

Revenues, Expenses, Other Income, and Statistics of Large Motor **Carriers** of Property, IC 1 mot.13

Schedule of Annual and Period Indices for **Carriers** by Pipeline, IC 1 acco.10

Seasonally Adjusted Capacity and Traffic Scheduled Operations Local Service **Carriers**, C 31.262/4

Seasonally Adjusted Capacity and Traffic Scheduled Operations System Trunks and Regional **Carriers**, C 31.262/5

Selected Revenues, Expenses, Other Income, and Statistics of Class II **Carriers** of Property, IC 1 mot.13/2

Selected Safety Road Checks Motor **Carriers** of Property, TD 2.311

Selected Statistics for Class 3 Motor **Carriers** of Property, IC 1 mot.14/2

Statistics of Class 1 Motor **Carriers**, IC 1 mot.14

Statistics of Class a Telephone **Carriers** Reporting Annually to the Commission, As of December 31 (year) and for Year Then Ended, CC 1.14/2

Statistics of Communications Common **Carriers**, CC 1.35

Statistics of Principal Domestic and International Telegraph **Carriers** Reporting to the Commission As of December 31 (year) and for Year Then Ended, CC 1.41

Subsidy for United States Certificated Air **Carriers**, C 31.257

Trunk **Carriers**, Coach Class, Traffic, Revenue, Yield, Enplanements and Average On-flight Trip Length by Fare Category, CAB 1.24

Uniform System of Accounts and Reports for Certificated Route Air **Carriers** in Accordance with Sec. 407 of the Federal Aviation Act, C 31.206/5

Uniform System of Accounts for **Carriers** by Inland and Coastal Waterways, IC 1 wat.14

Carroll
    Puerto Rico Special Commissioner (**Carroll**), T 1.17

Carry
    Carry On, W 44.17

Carry Over
    Production and **Carry Over** of Fruit and Vegetable Containers, A 36.61
    Quality of Cotton in **Carry-Over**, A 88.11/14

Carrying
    Advertisements Inviting Proposals for **Carrying** Mails (miscellaneous), P 1.8
    Advertisements Inviting Proposals for **Carrying** Mails by Airplane or Seaplane, P 1.24
    Advertisements Inviting Proposals for **Carrying** Mails by Regulation Screen Wagons, P 1.7
    Advertisements Inviting Proposals for **Carrying** Mails by Star Routes (by States), P 1.22
    Advertisements Inviting Proposals for **Carrying** Mails By States, P 1.5
    Advertisements Inviting Proposals for **Carrying** Mails by Steamboat Routes (by States), P 1.23

Cars
    Fuel and Power for Locomotives and Rail Motor **Cars** of Class I Steam Railways in United States, IC 1 ste.30
    Persons Furnishing **Cars** to or on Behalf of Carriers by Railroad or Express Companies, Summary of Quarterly Reports, IC 1.18
    Recent Purchases of **Cars**, Houses and Other Durables and Expectations to Buy During the Month Ahead: Survey Data Through, C 3.186:P-65
    Report on Quality Changes for (year) Model Passenger **Cars**, L 1.79/2, L 2.120/2-7

Cartographic
    Acquisitions List of Antarctic **Cartographic** Materials, S 1.120
    National **Cartographic** Information Center: Newsletter, I 19.71

Cartography
    Federal Digital **Cartography** Newsletter, I 19.115
    Geodesy and **Cartography**, C 41.46/3

Cartoons
    Industrial Security **Cartoons**, D 3.11/3

Casablanca
    Conferences at Washington, 1941-1942, and **Casablanca**, S 1.1/3:W 27

Case
    Applications and **Case** Discontinuances for AFDC, HE 3.60/3
    Applications and **Case** Dispositions for Public Assistance, HE 3.60/3, HE 17.613/3
    ARA **Case** Book, C 46.20
    Case Book, Education Beyond High School Practices Underway to Meet the Problems of the Day, FS 5.65
    Case History Reports for Industries, Pr 32.5223
    Case Information Sheets, Y 3.F 31/21-3:14-11
    Case Instruction, Cases, D 208.13
    Case Management Information Series, PM 1.41/2
    Case Records in Public Assistance, FS 3.23
    Case Studies in Environmental Medicine, HE 20.7917
    Case Studies in Environmental Management, HE 20.519
    Case Studies of IPA's **in various cities**, HE 20.24
    Community Development: **Case** Studies, S 18.17/2
    Countervailing Duty and Antidumping **Case** Reference List, T 17.18
    FLRA Report on **Case** Decisions and FSIP Releases, Y 3.F 31/21-3:9, Y 3.F 31/21:10
    Freedom of Information **Case** List, J 1.56
    Habeas & Prison Litigation **Case Law** Update, Ju 13.8/4
    Labor Management **Case** Finder, CS 1.41/4:711-2
    Legal Guide and **Case** Digest, Veterans' Reemployment Rights Under the Universal Military Training and Service Act, As Amended, and Related Acts, L 25.6/2:L 52
    Patterns for Progress in Aging **Case** Studies, FS 1.13/3, FS 14.9/5
    Preservation **Case** Studies, I 29.104, I 70.12/2
    Quarterly Report on **Case** Developments, LR 1.15/4
    Report of **Case** Decisions, Y 3.F 31/21-3:9
    Reports on **Case** Handling Developments of the Office of the General Counsel, Y 3.F 31/21-3:12
    Return on Investment **Case** Study, D 103.53/8
    United States v. Chile, Arbitration of **Case** of Brig. Macedonian, S 3.21/1
    Uses of Research Sponsored by the Administration on Aging, **Case** Studies, HE 23.3012

Case Studies
    Community Stabilization **Case Studies**, HH 1.67
    FDA Compilation of **Case Studies** of Drug Recalls, HE 20.4027

Case Study
    Design **Case Study** (series), FEM 1.18

Casehandling
    Casehandling Manual, LR 1.6/2:C 26

Casein
    Dry **Casein**, Estimated Production and Stocks, United States, A 36.166

Caseload
    Caseload Statistics, HE 1.611
    Caseload Statistics of State Vocational Rehabilitation Agencies, FS 17.111, HE 17.111, HE 23.4109

Caseloads
    Impact on Public Assistance **Caseloads** of (a) Training Programs under Manpower Development and Training Act and Read Redevelopment Act, and (b) Public Assistance Work and Training Programs, FS 14.219, FS 17.409, FS 17.635

Cases
    Cases, NMB 1.8
    Cases Argued and Decided in Supreme Court of United States, Ju 6.8/4
    Cases Decided in the Court of Claims of the United States, Ju 3.9
    Commission Instructions in Docket **Cases**, CC 1.33/2
    Condensed Reports of **Cases** in Supreme Court of United States, Ju 6.8/3
    Decisions of the Commissioner of Patents and of United States Courts in Patent and Trademark **Cases**, C 21.6
    Digests and Tables of **Cases**, Decisions of the Federal Labor Relations Authority, Y 3.F 31/21-3:9-3
    Digests and Tables of **Cases**, Decisions of the Federal Labor Relations Authority, Y 3.F 31/21-3:9-2, Y 3.F 31/21-3:9-3
    Disposition of Public Assistance **Cases** Involving Question of Fraud, HE 3.63
    Extraterritorial **Cases**, S 14.5

Census of Nurses Employed for Public Health Work in United States, in Territories of Alaska and Hawaii, and in Puerto Rico and Virgin Islands, FS 2.81

Census of Nurses Employed for Public Health Work in United States, in Territories of Alaska and Hawaii, and in Puerto Rico and Virgin Islands, FS 2.81

Census of Population, C 3.223/12

Census of Population; Advance Estimates of Social Economic, and Housing Characteristics, Supplementary Reports, PHC A2 (series), C 3.223/21-2

Census of Population; Advance Reports, C 3.223/4

Census of Population and Housing, Advance Reports, PHC, C 3.223/19

Census of Population and Housing: Alphabetical Index of Industries and Occupations, C 3.223/22:90-R3

Census of Population and Housing Announcements, C 3.950-4/3

Census of Population and Housing Block Statistics, C 3.282/3

Census of Population and Housing: Classified Index of Industries and Occupations, C 3.223/22:90-R4

Census of Population and Housing: Finders Guide to **Census** Tract Reports, C 3.223/11-2

Census of Population and Housing: Geographic Identification Code Scheme, C 3.223/22:90-R5

Census of Population and Housing Guide Part B, Glossary, C 3.223/22:90-R1

Census of Population and Housing: History, C 3.223/22:90-R2

Census of Population and Housing, Preliminary Reports, C 3.223/18

Census of Population and Housing, Public Law 94-171 DATA, C 3.281

Census of Population and Housing: Reference Reports, C 3.223/22:90-R

Census of Population and Housing Tabulation and Publication Program for Puerto Rico, C 3.223/24

Census of Population and Housing: Users Guide, C 3.223/22-2

Census of Population; Characteristics of the Population, C 3.223/9

Census of Population; Congressional Districts, C 3.223/20

Census of Population; Detailed Characteristics, C 3.223/8

Census of Population; Final Volumes (other than by States), C 3.223/10

Census of Population; General Population Characteristics, C 3.223/6

Census of Population: General Population Characteristics for American Indian and Alaska Native Areas, C 3.223/6-2

Census of Population; General Publications, C 3.223

Census of Population: General Population Characteristics for Metropolitan Statistical Areas, C 3.223/6-3

Census of Population: General Population Characteristics for Urbanized Areas, C 3.223/6-4

Census of Population; General Social and Economic Characteristics, C 3.223/7

Census of Population; Housing: Announcements, C 3.223/3

Census of Population; Housing: Evaluation and Research Program, C 56.223/16

Census of Population; Preliminary Reports, C 3.223/2

Census of Population; Reference Reports, C 3.223/22

Census of Population: Social and Economic Characteristics for American Indian and Alaska Native Areas, C 3.223/7-2

Census of Population: Social and Economic Characteristics for Metropolitan Statistical Areas, C 3.223/7-3

Census of Population: Social and Economic Characteristics for Urbanized Areas, C 3.223/7-4

Census of Population; Subject Reports, C 56.223/10

Census of Population; Supplementary Reports, C 3.223/21

Census of Population; Supplementary Reports PC (S1) (series), C 56.223/12

Census Product Update, C162/7-2

Census of Religious Bodies, C 3.35

Census of Retail Trade Nonemployer Statistics Series, C 3.255/7

Census of Retail Trade: Area Statistics (series), C 56.251/2

Census of Retail Trade: Final Volumes, C 56.251/6, C 3.255/6

Census of Retail Trade: General Publications, C 3.255, C 56.251

Census of Retail Trade: Geographic Area Series, C 225/8-2

Census of Retail Trade: Geographic Area Statistics, C 3.255/2

Census of Retail Trade: Geographic Area Statistics, Advance Reports, C 3.255/2-2

Census of Retail Trade: Industry Series, C 3.225/3-3

Census of Retail Trade: Geographic Area - Summary, C 257/6-2

Census of Retail Trade: Major Retail Centers in Standard Metropolitan Statistical Areas, RC (series), C 56.251/5

Census of Retail Trade: Major Retail Centers Statistics, C 3.255/5

Census of Retail Trade; Preliminary Area Reports, C 56.251/7

Census of Retail Trade; Preliminary Report Industry Series, C 3.255/3-2

Census of Retail Trade; Retail Merchandise Lines Service, C 56.251/4, C 3.255/4

Census of Retail Trade; Subject Reports, C 56.251/3, C 3.255/3

Census of Selected Service Industries; Area Statistics Series, C 56.253/3

Census of Selected Service Industries; Final Volumes, C 56.253/5

Census of Selected Service Industries; General Publications, C 56.253

Census of Selected Service Industries; Preliminary Area Series, C 56.253/2

Census of Selected Service Industries; Subject Reports, C 56.253/4

Census of Service Industries Industry Series, C 3.257/3-4

Census of Service Industries Nonemployer Statistics Series, C 3.257/5

Census of Service Industries; Final Reports, C 3.257/4

Census of Service Industries; General Publications, C 3.257

Census of Service Industries; Geographic Area Series, C 3.257/2, C 257/6-2

Census of Service Industries; Geographic Area Series, Advance Reports, C 3.257/2-2

Census of Service Industries; Preliminary Report Industry Series, C 3.257/3-3

Census of Service Industries; Subject Series, C 3.257/3

Census of Service Industries - Summary, C 257/6

Census of The Americas, Population **Census**, Urban Area Data, C 3.211

Census of Transportation, Communications, and Utilities, C 3.292

Census of Transportation; Final Reports, C 3.233/5, C 56.246/2

Census of Transportation; General Publications, C 56.246

Census of Transportation; Publication Program, C 3.233/4-2

Census of Transportation; {Volumes}, C 56.246/3

Census of U.S. Civil Aircraft As of December 31, (year), TD 4.18

Census of War Commodities, C 3.27

Census of Wholesale Trade-

Census of Wholesale Trade; Area Statistics (series), C 56.252/3

Census of Wholesale Trade; Final Reports, C 3.256/4

Census of Wholesale Trade; Final Volumes, C 56.252/5

Census of Wholesale Trade: Geographic Area Series, C 256/7-2

Census of Wholesale Trade: Geographic Area - Summary, C 256/7

Census of Wholesale Trade; General Publications, C 56.252, C 3.256

Census of Wholesale Trade; Geographic Area Series, C 3.256/2

Census of Wholesale Trade; Geographic Area Series, Advance Reports, C 3.256/2-2

Census of Wholesale Trade; Industry Series, C 3.256/6

Census of Wholesale Trade; Preliminary Area Series, C 56.252/2

Census of Wholesale Trade; Preliminary Report Industry Series, C 3.256/3-2

Census of Wholesale Trade; Subject Series, C 3.256/3, C 56.252/4

Census of Wholesale Trade; Wholesale Commodity Line Sales, C 3.256/5

Census Portraits, C 56.258

Census Publications, C 3.163

Census Publications, List of Publications Issued, C 3.163/2

Census Reports (Final Volumes) 13th Census, 1910, C 3.16

Census Supervisor, C 3.206

Census Survey of Business, C 3.120/2

Census Telephone Listing of Bureau Activities Admin, C 3.220

Census Tract Manual, C 3.6/2:C 33

Census Tract Memos, C 3.227, C 56.235/2

Census Tract Papers, GE-40 (series), C 56.235

Census Update, Supplement to Data User News, C 3.238/3

Census Use Studies, C 56.220, C 3.244

Census Use Study Reports, C 3.244

Census User's Guide, C 3.6/2:C 33/2

Census Users Bulletins, C 56.212/2

Census/Equal Employment Opportunity (EEO) Special File, C 3.283

Censuses of Population and Housing: **Census** County Division Boundary Description, Phc (3) series, C 3.223/15

Censuses of Population and Housing: **Census** Tract Reports, C 3.223/11

Committee on 1950 **Census** of the Americas, C 3.188

Company Statistics Bulletins, **Census** of Business, Manufactures and Mineral Industries, C 3.222

Company Statistics Series (Economic **Census**), C 3.277/3

Controller Patient **Census** Monographs, VA 1.48/3

Data Access Descriptions; **Census** Geography Series, CG (nos), C 3.240/6, C 56.212/5

Data Access Descriptions; **Census** Tabulations Available on Computer Tape Series CT (nos), C 3.240/3, C 56.212/3

Decadal **Census** of Weather Stations by States, C 30.66/3

Decennial **Census** of United States Climate, C 55.221/2

Decennial **Census** of United States, Climate: Climate Summary of United States, Supplement 1951-60, Climatography of United States, No. 86 (series), C 30.71/8

Decennial **Census** of United States, Climate: Daily Normals of Temperature and Heating Degree Days, C 30.71/7:84

Decennial **Census** of United States, Climate: Heating Degree Day Normals, C 30.71/7:83

Decennial **Census** of United States, Climate: Monthly Averages for State Climatic Divisions, C 30.71/7:85

Decennial **Census** of United States, Climate: Monthly Normals of Temperature, Precipitation, and Heating Degree Days, C 30.71/4

Decennial **Census** of United States, Climate: Summary of Hourly Observations, C 30.71/5:82

Detailed Characteristics (by States), 1950 Population **Census** Report PC (series), C 3.950-7/4

Extended Care **Census** Reports, VA 1.50

Fluoridation **Census**, FS 2.304, HE 20.3112, HE 20.7317

GE-40 **Census** Tract Papers, C 3.227/2

Heads of Families at 1st **Census**, C 3.11

Housing **Census** Separate Reports and Bulletins, C 3.950-8/4

1990 **Census** of Population and Housing, Special Tabulation on Aging, Federal Region 1, Connecticut-Maine-Massachusetts-New Hampshire-Rhode Island-Vermont, Cd 90-AOA1, C 3.218/2:CD 90-AOA

1990 **Census** Profile, C 3.223/7-5

Nonfarm Housing Characteristics, 1950 Housing **Census** Report H-B (series), C 3.950/3

Philippine Islands **Census**, 1903; Bulletins, C 3.8/2

Philippine Islands **Census**, 1903; Reports, C 3.8/1

Posters **Census** Bureau, C 3.270

Press Summaries, 13th **Census**, 1910, C 3.17

Publications Bureau of the **Census**, C 3.163

World Data **Center** A Upper Atmosphere Geophysics, Report UAG- (series), C 55.220

Year in Review at Goddard Space Flight **Center**, NAS 1.1/3

Centers
330-Funded Community Health **Centers** Directory, HE 20.9112/2

Inter-American Education Demonstration **Centers**, FS 5.31

Multipurpose Arthritis **Centers** Personnel Directory, HE 20.3322

Plant Materials **Centers** Annual Reports, A 57.54

Primate Research **Centers** Advisory Committee, HE 20.3001/2:P 93

Publications Inter-American Education Demonstration **Centers**, FS 5.31

Reports of the National Juvenile Justice Assessment **Centers** (series), J 26.27

University **Centers** of Foreign Affairs Research, Selective Directory, S 1.2:Un 3

Cento Affairs
Office of United States Economic Coordinator for **Cento Affairs**, Non-Government Central Treaty Organization, S 5.54

Central
Central Business District Statistics Bulletin CBD (series), C 3.202/13

Central Executive Council, Reports of Meetings, T 1.23/6

Central Flyway, I 49.24/4

Central Liquidity Facility: Annual Report, NCU 1.17

Central Office Bulletin, HE 3.3/6

Central Radio Propagation Laboratory Ionospheric Predictions, C 13.31/3

Central Radio Propagation Laboratory Reports, C 13.33

Central Region, C 55.118/3

Central States Forest Experiment Station, A 13.68

Central Valley Project Studies {Reports on Problems}, I 27.26

Central Valley Project, Annual Report, I 27.26/2

Central, Western, and South Pacific Fisheries Development Program Report for Calendar Year, C 55.329

Condition of Weekly Reporting Member Banks in **Central** Reserve Cities, FR 1.16/2

East **Central** Communique, ED 1.71/2

East **Central** Regional Office Publications, L 2.91

Focus on **Central** and Eastern Europe, S 1.140

Nautical Charts and Publications, Region 2, **Central** and South America and Antarctica, C 55.440:2

NIMA Nautical Charts, Public Sale Region 2, **Central** and South America and Antarctica, TD 4.82:2

Pilot Chart of **Central** American Waters, N 6.24, M 202.15, D 203.15

Pilot Charts of **Central** American Waters, D 203.15

Publications **Central** States Forest Experiment Station, A 13.68/12-2

Quarterly Report of **Central** Propagation Laboratory, C 13.33/2

Reintroduction and Management of Wolves in Yellowstone National Park and the **Central** Idaho Wilderness Area, Y 3.W 83

Retail Trade Report East North **Central**, C 3.176

Retail Trade Report East South **Central**, C 3.177

Retail Trade Report West North **Central**, C 3.178

Retail Trade Report West South **Central**, C 3.179

Sandhill Crane Harvest and Hunter Activity in the **Central** Flyway During the Hunting Season, I 49.106/4

Soil Organic Matter Levels in the **Central** Great Plains, A 77.15/3

Special Reports **Central** Housing Committee, Y 3.C 33/3:9

Telephone Directory **Central** Office and Regions, GS 12.12

Telephone Directory Geological Survey, **Central** Region, I 19.84/2

Tide Tables **Central** and Western Pacific Ocean and Indian Ocean, C 4.15/6

Tide Tables, High and Low Water Predictions **Central** and Western Pacific Ocean and Indian Ocean, C 55.421/4

U.S. **Central** Station Nuclear Electric Generating Units, Significant Milestones, E 1.41

United States Air Force and United States Navy Radio Facility Charts, **Central** Pacific-Far East, D 301.12

West North **Central**, Population and Per Capita Income Estimates for Counties and Incorporated Places, C 3.186/27-3

Central Africa
French-Speaking **Central Africa**, a Guide to Official Publications in American Libraries, LC 2.8:Af 8/3

Central American
Central American Peace Conference, Washington, 1907, S 5.12

Central Area
Cottonseed Review, South **Central Area**, A 82.65

Central Pacific
Central Pacific, Western Pacific, and South Pacific Fisheries Development Program Report for Calendar Year, C 55.329

Central Station
Number and Percentage of Farms Electrified with **Central Station** Service, A 68.20

CENTS
Series ISP, **CENTS** {Census Tabulation System}, C 56.226

Centuries
Two **Centuries** of Tariffs, the Background and Emergence of the U.S. International Trade Commission, TC 1.2:T 17/20

Century 21
Century 21 U.S. Science Exhibit Releases, C 1.32/3

CEPPO
CEPPO Alerts, EP 9.16

Ceramics
Glass and **Ceramics** {abstracts}, C 41.68

CERC
CERC Bulletin and Summary Report of Research, Fiscal Year (date), D 103.42/3

CERCLIS
CERCLIS (Comprehensive Environmental Response Compensation, and Liability Information System), EP 1.104/5

CERCular
CERCular, D 103.42/11

Cerebral Palsy
NINCDS **Cerebral Palsy** Research Program, HE 20.3502:C 33/3

Cerebrovascular
Cerebrovascular Bibliography, HE 20.3513/4

Ceremony
Take Pride in America, National Awards **Ceremony**, I 1.110/2

CERL
CERL Abstracts, Information Exchange Bulletin, D 103.73

CERL Reports, Information Exchange Bulletin, D 103.74

Certain
Car-Lot Unloads of **Certain** Fruits and Vegetables, A 66.40

Preliminary Study of **Certain** Financial Laws and Institutions (by country), T 1.37

Certificate
Aircraft Engine and Propeller Type **Certificate** Data Sheets and Specifications, TD 4.15/2

Aircraft Type **Certificate** Data Sheets and Specifications, TD 4.15

Cable Television **Certificate** of Compliance Actions, CC 1.47/3

Certificate Authorizations As Reported by Pipeline Companies, FP 1.30

Certificate of Analyses of Standard Samples, C 13.17

Cost of Pipeline and Compressor Station Construction Under Non-Budget Type or **Certificate** Authorizations As Reported by Pipeline Companies, FP 1.30

Type **Certificate** Data Sheets and Specifications, Rotorcraft, Gliders, and Balloons, TD 4.15/6

Certificated
All **Certificated** Air Cargo Carriers, C 31.232

Certificated Air Carrier Financial Data; Domestic Helicopter Service {12-month comparisons}, C 31.242/2

Certificated Air Carrier Financial Data; Domestic Helicopter Service {quarterly comparisons}, C 31.242

Certificated Air Carrier Financial Data; Domestic Local Service 12-month Comparisons, C 31.235/2

Certificated Air Carrier Financial Data; Domestic Local Service {quarterly comparisons}, C 31.235

Certificated Air Carrier Financial Data; Foreign or Overseas {12-month comparisons}, C 31.236/2

Certificated Air Carrier Financial Data; Foreign or Overseas {quarterly comparisons}, C 31.236

Certificated Air Carrier Financial Data; Recapitulation by Carrier Groups {12-month comparisons}, C 31.238/2

Certificated Air Carrier Financial Data; Recapitulation by Carrier Groups {quarterly comparisons}, C 31.238

Certificated Air Carrier Financial Data; Territorial Intra-Alaska and Other Alaska {quarterly comparisons}, C 31.243

Certificated Air Carrier Financial Data; Territorial Intra-Alaska and Other Than Alaska {12-month comparisons}, C 31.243/2

Certificated Air Carrier Financial Data; Territorial Intra-Alaska and Other Than Alaska {12-month comparisons}, C 31.243/2

Certification and Operations; Land Airports Serving CAB-**Certificated** Scheduled Air Carriers Operating Large Aircraft, TD 4.6:part 139

Certification and Operations; Land Airports Serving CAB-**Certificated** Scheduled Air Carriers Operating Large Aircraft, TD 4.6:part 139

Recurrent Report of Mileage and Traffic Data All **Certificated** Air Cargo Carriers, C 31.232

Recurrent Report of Mileage and Traffic Data Domestic Helicopter Service, **Certificated** Airmail Carriers, C 31.229/4

Subsidy for United States **Certificated** Air Carriers, C 31.257

Weekly Report of **Certificated** Stock in Licensed Warehouses, A 88.11/24

Certificated Route
Airport Activity Statistics on **Certificated Route** Air Carriers, C 31.251, TD 4.14

Fuel Consumption and Cost, **Certificated Route** and Supplemental Air Carriers, Domestic and International Operations, C 31.267

Quarterly Interim Financial Report, **Certificated Route** Air Carriers and Supplemental Air Carriers, CAB 1.14

Uniform System of Accounts and Reports for **Certificated Route** Air Carriers in Accordance with Sec. 407 of the Federal Aviation Act, C 31.206/5

Certificates
Companies Holding **Certificates** of Authority from Secretary of Treasury As Acceptable Securities on Federal Bonds, T 1.24, T 63.116

Maturity Distribution of Outstanding Negotiable Time **Certificates** of Deposit, FR 1.54/2

Reviewing and Acting on Medical **Certificates**, CS 1.41/4:339-31

Schedules of Payments to Holders of Cotton Options and Participation Trust **Certificates** by Congressional District of States, A 55.57

Summary of Supplemental Type **Certificates** and Approved Replacement Parts, FAA 1.14, FAA 5.12

Summary of Supplemental Type **Certificates**, TD 4.36

Certification
Aircraft **Certification** Directory, TD 4.52/3

Aircraft Certification Service International Strategic Plan, TD 4.915

Certification and Operations; Air Carriers and Commercial Operators of Large Aircraft, TD 4.6:part 121

Certification and Operations; Air Travel and Clubs Using Large Airplanes, TD 4.6:part 123

Certification and Operations; Land Airports Serving CAB-Certificated Scheduled Air Carriers Operating Large Aircraft, TD 4.6:part 139

Certification and Operations; Land Airports Serving CAB-Certificated Scheduled Air Carriers Operating Large Aircraft, TD 4.6:part 139

Certification and Operations; Scheduled Air Carriers with Helicopters, TD 4.6:part 127

Certification Procedures for Products and Parts, TD 4.6:part 21

Certification; Airmen other than Flight
 Crewmembers, TD 4.6:part 65
Certification; Flight Crewmembers other than
 Pilots, TD 4.6:part 63
Certification; Pilots and Flight Instructors, TD
 4.6:part 61
Directory of Federal Government **Certification**
 and Related Programs (Special Publication 739), C
 13.10:739
Equipment **Certification** and Type Acceptance
 Actions, Reports, Public Notices, CC
 1.48/2
HCFA Regional Office Manual; Standards and
 Certification Guidelines, HE 22.8/8-3
Medicare, Medicaid, State Operations Manual,
 Provider **Certification**, HE 22.8/12
Noise Standards, Aircraft Type and Airworthiness
 Certification, TD 4.6:part 36
Certifications
 Where to Write for Birth and Death Records of U.S.
  Citizens Who Were Born or Died
  Outside of the United States and Birth
  Certifications for Alien Children
  Adopted by U.S. Citizens, FS 2.102:B
  53/7
Certified Shippers of Fresh and Frozen Oyster,
 Clams, and Mussles, FS 2.16
Foreign Plants **Certified** to Export Meat to the
 United States, A 110.14
Fuel Cost and Consumption, **Certified** Route and
 Supplemental Air Carriers, Domestic and
 International Operations, Twelve
 Months Ended (date), C 31.267/2
NBL **Certified** Reference Materials Catalog, E
 1.98:
NIOSH **Certified** Equipment List, HE 20.7124
Quarterly Interim Financial Report, **Certified**
 Route Air Carriers and Supplemental Air
 Carriers, C 31.240/3
Recapitulation by Carrier Groups, **Certified** Air
 Carriers, C 31.233
Seed Crops, **Certified** Seed Potato Report, A
 88.30/6, A 92.19/6
Certified
 Foreign Countries and Plants **Certified** to Export
  Meat and Poultry to the United States, A
  110.14/2
Certiorari
 Petitions for **Certiorari** and Briefs on Merits and in
  Opposition for U.S. in Supreme Court of
  U.S., J 1.19/6
Cesium
 Cesium and Rubidium in (year), I 28.139
CETA
 Average Annual Wages and Wage Adjustment
  Index for **CETA** Prime Sponsors, L 2.44/
  3
 CETA Area Employment and Unemployment, L
  2.110
 CETA Area Employment and Unemployment, BLS/
  CETA/MR (series), L 2.110/2
 CETA Area Employment and Unemployment,
  Special Reports, BLS/CETA/SP (series),
  L 2.110/3
 CETA Program Models (series), L 37.8/6
 CETA Technical Assistance Documents, L 37.8/2
 CETA Technical Documents (series), L 37.8/3
Ceylon
 Accession List: **Ceylon**, LC 1.30/7
 Ceylon, LC 1.30/7
CFA
 CFA Design Awards Program, HH 5.10
CFF
 Factfinder for the Nation, **CFF**, C 3.252
CFR
 CFR Index and Finding Aids, AE 2.106/3-2
 List of **CFR** Sections Affected, GS 4.108/3
CFS
 Current Fisheries Statistics **CFS** (series), C 55.309/
  2
CFSA
 CFSA Commodity Fact Sheet, A 112.15
CFSTI
 CFSTI News, C 51.7/4
CFTC
 CFTC Staff Interpretative Letters, Y 3.C 73/5:12
CG-B
 Report **CG-B**- (series), TD 5.11/2
CG-D
 Report, **CG-D** (series), TD 5.33
 Office of Research and Development: Reports **CG-
  D**- (series), TD 5.25/2
CG-WEP
 Report **CG-WEP**- (series), TD 5.36

CGS
 Releases **CGS** (series), C 3.209
CH-S
 1990 Housing Highlights (series **CH-S**), C 3.224/
  3-8
Chaco
 Reports of the **Chaco** Center, I 29.90
Chafer
 Japanese Beetle-European **Chafer** Control
  Program, Annual Report, A 77.326
Chairman
 Local **Chairman** of Better Housing Program
  Committee, Y 3.F 31/11:11
Challange
 HUD **Challange**, HH 1.36
 HUD **Challange** Reprints, HH 1.36/a
 Challenge, ED 1.77
 Challenge Cost-Share Program Report, A 13.124/2,
  I 53.55
 Challenge Grants Application Guidelines, NF 2.8/
  2-3
 Challenge Grants Program Guidelines and
  Application Materials, NF 3.8/2-4
 Challenge Network Membership Directory, ED
  1.30/3
 Challenge-Response {papers}, HH 1.62
 Fisheries, Wildlife, and TES Species **Challenge**
  Cost-Share Program Report for the
  Intermountain Region, A 13.124
 Literacy: Meeting the **Challenge** (series), ED 1.27
Challenge III
 Challenge III Grants, NF 2.8/2-10
 Challenge III Grants, Application Guidelines, NF
  2.8/2-20
Chamber Music
 Music Ensembles **Chamber Music**/New Music/
  Jazz Ensembles/Choruses/Orchestras/
  Composer in Residence/Consortium
  Commissioning, NF 2.8/2-14
 The Library of Congress Presents a Season of
  Chamber Music, LC 12.9
Chamizal
 International Boundary Commission, U.S.-Mexico,
  Chamizal Arbitration, S 3.19/3
Champlain
 Catalog of Charts of the Great Lakes and
  Connecting Waters, Also Lake
  Champlain, New York Canals,
  Minnesota-Ontario Border Lakes, D
  103.208
 Catalog of Charts of the Great Lakes and
  Connecting Waters, Also Lake
  Champlain, New York Canals,
  Minnesota-Ontario Border Lakes, D
  103.208
CHAMPUS
 CHAMPUS Chartbook of Statistics, D 1.82
 Civilian Health and Medical Program of Uniformed
  Service {fact Sheets}, **CHAMPUS**, D
  2.18
Change
 ACCP (Atlantic Climate **Change** Program)
  Newsletter, C 55.55
 Calibration Procedure **Change** Notice Book, D
  217.16/2-2
 Change Sheets Applying to Organization
  Directory, W 3.42/2
 Classification **Change** Notices, NAS 1.25
 Cumulative Price and Status **Change** Report, GP
  3.22/3-4
 Enroute **Change** Notice, DoD Flip Enroute VFR
  Supplement United States, D 5.318/8-2
 Federal Supply Catalog: National Supplier **Change**
  Index, GS 2.10/7
 Geophysical Monitoring for Climatic **Change**, C
  55.618
 GSA Supply Catalog **Change** Bulletin, GS 2.10/6-
  3
 Indexes of **Change** in Straight-Time Average
  Hourly Earnings for Selected Shipyards,
  by Type of Construction and Region, L
  2.81/2
 Monthly Mean Discharge at Selected Gaging
  Stations and **Change** of Storage in
  Certain Lakes and Reservoirs in
  Columbia River Basin, I 19.47
 Over **Change** Claim Circulars, Y 3.R 13/2:35
 Resources for **Change**, a Guide to Projects, HE
  19.9:R 31
 State Population and Household Estimates with
  Age, Sex, and Components of **Change**, C
  3.186/21
 Studies in Social **Change**, HE 20.8132

U.S. Census of Housing Components of Inventory
 Change, Final Report HC (4) series, C
 3.224/6
Changes
 Changes
  Schedule, **Changes**, C 3.150/2
 Changes in Air Service Information Circular, W
  87.11/3
 Changes in Army Regulations, W 1.6/2
 Changes in Commercial and Industrial Loans by
  Industry, FR 1.39
 Changes in Cost of Living, L 2.6/a 5
 Changes in Different Types of Public and Private
  Relief in Urban Areas, L 5.33
 Changes in Drill Books, N 17.12/2
 Changes in Drill Regulations, W 42.13/2
 Changes in Engineer Regulations, W 7.11/4
 Changes in Equipment Manuals, W 3.36/2
 Changes in List of Commodities Included in
  Wholesale Price Index, L 2.61/4
 Changes in Manual for Medical Department
  (numbered), W 44.9/2
 Changes in Manual for Medical Department, Navy,
  N 10.5/2
 Changes in Manual of Bureau of Navigation, N
  17.24/2
 Changes in Manual of Engineering Instructions, N
  19.8/3
 Changes in Manuals, W 77.15/2
 Changes in Marine Corps Pamphlets, N 9.12
 Changes in Military Laws of United States, W 1.8/
  4
 Changes in Navy Regulations, N 1.11/2
 Changes in Regulations, N 17.16/2
 Changes in Regulations (compilations), W 70.7/3
 Changes in Regulations (general), W 70.7/2
 Changes in Regulations and Instructions
  (numbered), W 2.6/2, W 26.9/2
 Changes in Signal Corps Manuals (numbered), W
  42.22/3
 Changes in State Bank Membership, Announce-
  ments, FR 1.33
 Changes in State Member Banks, FR 1.33
 Changes in Status of Banks and Branches During
  Month, Name and Location of Banks and
  Branches, FR 1.33/2
 Changes in Training Regulations, W 1.21/2
 Changes in Uniform Regulations, N 1.18/2
 Changes to Rules, Regulations and Instructions,
  W 77.10/2
 Changes {in} Circulars, W 77.4/2
 Changes {in} Hospital Drill Regulations, W 44.8/
  2
 Changes {to}. Supply Circulars and Supply
  Bulletins, W 89.6/2
 L.C. Classification, Additions and **Changes**, LC
  1.7/2, LC 26.9/2
 Labor Force, Gross **Changes** in the Labor Force, C
  3.186:P-59
 List of **Changes** of Stations, Etc., T 27.13
 Manual on Uniform Traffic Control Devices for
  Streets and Highways: Official Rulings
  on Requests for Interpretations,
  Changes, and Experimentations, TD 2.8/
  2
 Percent **Changes** in Gross Average Hourly
  Earnings Over Selected Periods, L 2.63/
  2, L 2.63/3
 Percent **Changes** in Gross Hourly and Weekly
  Earnings over Selected Periods, L 2.63
 Record of **Changes** in Memberships of National
  Home for Disabled Volunteer Soldiers,
  NH 1.6
 Report on Quality **Changes** for (year) Model
  Passenger Cars, L 1.79/2, L 2.120/2-7
 Report to Congress on Ocean Dumping and Other
  Man-Induced **Changes** to Ocean
  Ecosystems, C 55.31
 Steam Railways in Hands of Receivers and Trustees,
  and **Changes** in List of Companies
  Affected by Receiver Ship of Trusteeship,
  IC 1 ste.45
 War **Changes** in Industry Series, Reports, TC 1.18
 Wholesale Price Index, Major Specification
  Changes 1947-53, L 2.61/7
Changing
 Changing Public Attitudes on Governments and
  Taxes, Y 3.Ad 9/8:17
 For Commanders, This **Changing** World, D 2.15
 Your **Changing** Forest, News on the Black Hills
  National Forest Plan Revision, A 13.128
Channel
 Committee on **Channel** Stabilization: Technical
  Reports, D 103.64

United States Government Flight Information Publication: Pacific **Chart** Supplement, C 55.427

VFR Helicopter **Chart** of Los Angeles, C 55.416/12-2

VFR/IFR Planning **Chart**, C 55.416/7

Washington Helicopter Route **Chart**, C 55.416/12-4

Chart Book

Federal Reserve **Chart Book** on Financial and Business Statistics, FR 1.30

Federal Reserve **Chart Books**, FR 1.25

Chartbook

Agricultural Outlook **Chartbook**, A 1.98

Agriculture **Chartbook**, A 1.76/2

CHAMPUS **Chartbook** of Statistics, D 1.82

Chartbook on Prices, Wages, and Productivity, L 2.102/2

International Economic Review, Special Edition, **Chartbook**, ITC 1.29/2

MEPS, (Medical Expenditure Panel Survey), **Chartbook**, HE 20.6517/7

Status, a Monthly **Chartbook** of Social and Economic Trends, C 3.251

Chartbooks

Chartbooks, HE 20.6017

Charter

Charter Report, Government-Owned Dry-Cargo Vessels, Operated by Bareboat Charters and/or Agents of Maritime Administration, C 39.215

Chartered

Dry Cargo Service and Area Report, United States Dry Cargo Shipping Companies by Ships Owned and/or **Chartered** Type of Service and Area Operated, C 39.213

Chartered

List of American and Foreign Ships Owned under Requisition of **Chartered** to Shipping Board, SB 2.11

State **Chartered** Credit Unions, Annual Report, NCU 1.1/2

Charters

Charter Report, Government-Owned Dry-Cargo Vessels, Operated by Bareboat **Charters** and/or Agents of Maritime Administration, C 39.215

New Federal Credit Union **Charters**, Quarterly Report of Organization, FS 3.307

Charts

Aeronautical **Charts**, C 4.9/4, C 4.9/6, C 4.9/13

Agricultural Outlook **Charts**, A 88.8/3, A 88.8/2

Air Carrier Analytical **Charts** and Summaries, Including Supplemental Air Carrier Statistics, C 31.241/2

Area **Charts** U.S., D 5.318/6

Army Air Forces Radio and Facility **Charts** Atlantic and Caribbean Areas, W 108.26

Army Air Forces Radio and Facility **Charts** North Pacific Area, W 108.27

Bulletin Digest New and Revised Editions of Aeronautical **Charts** on Issue As of (date), D 301.59/5

Catalog of **Charts** and Plans Issued to Vessels of Navy, Portfolios, N 6.5/7

Catalog of **Charts** of the Great Lakes and Connecting Waters, Also Lake Champlain, New York Canals, Minnesota-Ontario Border Lakes, D 103.208

Catalog of **Charts** of the Great Lakes and Connecting Waters, Also Lake Champlain, New York Canals, Minnesota-Ontario Border Lakes, D 103.208

alog of **Charts**, Sailing Directions and Tide Tables, C 4.18/1

Catalog of Maps, **Charts**, and Related Products, Part 2, Hydrographic Products, D 5.351/2

Catalogs of **Charts**, N 14.12

Catalogs of **Charts**, Coast Pilots and Tide Tables, C 4.5

Catalogue of **Charts**, Coast Pilots, and Tide Tables, T 11.5

Charts, FCA 1.8/2, I 53.11/2, A 13.44, A 57.24

Charts and Posters, D 202.15

Charts of Great Lakes, W 33.7/2

Charts, Composition of Food Materials, A 10.21

Checklist of Reports and **Charts** Issued by Agricultural Marketing Service, A 88.33

Child Feeding **Charts**, A 42.7/3

Climatic **Charts** for U.S., A 29.44

Clothing Selection **Charts**, A 42.7/5

Coast **Charts** of Great Lakes, W 33.7/3

Coastal Warning Facilities **Charts**, C 30.22/3

Commodity Credit Corporation **Charts**, A 82.311

Corn Hog **Charts**, A 55.14

Defense Mapping Agency Catalog of Maps, **Charts**, and Related Products, D 5.351

Defense Mapping Agency Catalog of Maps, **Charts**, and Related Products, Semi-Annual Bulletin Digest, Part 2, Hydrographic Products, D 5.351/2-3

Defense Mapping Agency Public Sale Nautical **Charts** and Publications, C 55.440

Display Plotting **Charts**, D 5.349, D 5.349/2, D 5.349/3, D 5.349/4

Eastern United States, Dates of Latest Prints, Instrument Approach Procedure **Charts** and Airport Obstruction Plans (OP), C 4.9/19

Engineering **Charts**, T 47.29

Enroute High Altitude **Charts** (Alaska), C 55.416/16-2

Enroute IFR Peak Day **Charts**, Fiscal Year, FAA 3.11/3

Explanations and Sailing Directions to Accompany Wind and Current **Charts**, N 14.9

FAA Aeronautical **Charts** and Related Products, TD 4.81

FAA Aeronautical **Charts** and Related Products Price List, TD 4.81/2

Foreign Agricultural Situation, Maps and **Charts**, A 67.24

General (38) Nautical **Charts**, D 5.343

General Catalog of Mariners & Aviators' **Charts** and Books, N 6.5

Global Navigation and Planning **Charts**, D 5.354

GNC- Global Navigation **Charts**, D 5.324

Graphic Portfolios, **Charts**, and Posters, W 1.52

Great Circle (8) Sailing and Polar **Charts**, D 5.345

Great Circle (58) Tracking **Charts**, D 5.346

Habor Charts and **Charts** of Special Localities, W 33.8

Harbor **Charts** and Charts of Special Localities, W 33.8

Household Refrigeration **Charts**, A 42.7/2

How to Inspect **Charts**, HTIC LS (series), L 16./3

IFR Area **Charts** (U.S.), TD 4.79/16-2

IFR Enroute High Altitude **Charts** (Alaska), TD 4.49/17-2

Index of Aviation **Charts**, N 6.27/2

Index to H.O. **Charts** on Issue, N 6.5/9

Instrument Approach and Landing **Charts**, C 4.9/10

Instrument Approach **Charts**, I.L.S., C 4.9/14

Instrument Approach Procedure **Charts**, C 55.411

Instrument Approach Procedure **Charts** {Alaska, Hawaii, U.S. Pacific Islands}, C 55.411/2

JNC- Jet Navigation **Charts**, D 5.323

Joint Air Forces & Navy Radio Facility **Charts**, M 301.16

Joint Army & Navy Radio Facility **Charts**, W 108.29

Labor **Charts**, L 1.9/3

Latest Editions of U.S. Air Force Aeronautical **Charts**, C 55.418/3

Latest Editions, Airport Obstruction **Charts**, C 55.411/3-2

Legal **Charts**, L 5.21

Location Sheets of Maps and **Charts**, W 31.7/2

Loran A (19) Plotting **Charts** Series 7300, D 5.348

Loran C Plotting **Charts** Series 7800, D 5.348/2

Lunar **Charts**, NAS 1.43/3

Lunar **Charts** and Mosaics Series, D 301.49/4

Maps and **Charts**: Bureau of Federal Credit Unions, FS 3.308

Maps and **Charts**: Civil Rights Commission, CR 1.13

Maps and **Charts**: Coast and Geodetic Survey, C 4.9, C 4.9/2

Maps and **Charts**: Coastal and Engineering Research Center, D 103.42/8

Maps and **Charts**: Economic Development Administration, C 46.17

Maps and **Charts**: Federal Aviation Agency, FAA 1.16

Maps and **Charts**: National Highway Traffic Safety Commission, TD 8.31

Maps and **Charts**: National Weather Service, C 55.122

Maps and **Charts**: Naval Oceanographic Office, D 203.21

Maps and **Charts**: Public Health Service, FS 2.72

Maps and **Charts**: Weather Bureau, C 30.22, C 30.22/2

Maps and **Charts**: Western Area Power Administration, E 6.10

Maps, **Charts**, and Atlases, D 5.353

Maps, **Charts**, Posters, A 82.84, C 13.64, ER 1.21

Marine Weather Services **Charts**, C 55.112

Meat Cooking **Charts**, A 42.7/4

Monthly Corrections Affecting Portfolio Chart List and Index-Catalog of Nautical **Charts** and Publications, D 203.22/2

Natural **Charts** and Other Publications Recently Issued, C 4.5/2

Nautical **Charts** and Publications, C 55.440

Navigation **Charts**; Alleghaney and Monongahela Rivers, D 103.66/4

Navigation **Charts**; Missouri River, D 103.66

Navigation **Charts**; Numbered Rivers, D 103.66/3

Navigation **Charts**; Ohio River, D 103.66/2

NIMA Aeronautical **Charts** and Publications, TD 4.84

NIMA Nautical **Charts**, Public Sale 1, United States and Canada, TD 4.82:1

NIMA Nautical **Charts**, Public Sale Region 2, Central and South America and Antarctica, TD 4.82:2

NIMA Nautical **Charts**, Public Sale Region 3, Western Europe, Iceland, Greenland, and the Arctic, TD 4.82:3

NIMA Nautical **Charts**, Public Sale Region 4, Scandinavia, Baltic and Russia, TD 4.82:4

NIMA Nautical **Charts**, Public Sale Region 5, Western Africa and the Mediterranean, TD 4.82:5

NIMA Nautical **Charts**, Public Sale Region 6, Indian Ocean, TD 4.82:6

NIMA Nautical **Charts**, Public Sale Region 7, Australia, Indonesia, and New Zealand, TD 4.82:7

NIMA Nautical **Charts**, Public Sale Region 8, Oceania, TD 4.82:8

NIMA Nautical **Charts**, Public Sale Region 9, East Asia, TD 4.82:9

Occupational Safety **Charts**, L 16.8/2:Oc 1

Ohio River **Charts**, W 7.13/3

Ohio River Flood Plain **Charts**, W 7.13/4

Oil and Gas Investigation **Charts**, I 19.25/5, I 19.92

Omega Plotting (31) **Charts** Series 7500, D 5.347

Omega Plotting (112) **Charts** Series 7600, D 5.347/2

Omega Plotting **Charts**, D 5.356

ONC - Operational Navigation **Charts**, D 5.322

Operational Navigation **Charts**, D 5.354

Ordnance Equipment **Charts**, W 34.39

Ordnance Storage and Shipment **Charts**, W 34.38

Organization **Charts**, Y 3.R 31:20

Outlook **Charts**, A 36.50

Pilot **Charts** of Central American Waters, D 203.15

Point Value **Charts**, Pr 32.4245

Posters and **Charts**, HE 3.22, HE 20.5118, LR 1.12

Poultry Cooking **Charts**, A 42.7/6

Price Support Program, **Charts** and Tables, Selected Activities, A 82.310/2

Public Sale Catalog: Aeronautical **Charts** and Publications, D 5.351/3-2

Radio **Charts**, C 4.9/3

Radio Communication **Charts**, N 22.5

Radio Facility **Charts** and Supplementary Information, United States, LF/MF Edition, D 301.43

Radio Facility **Charts** United States, VOR edition, D 301.43/2

Radio Facility **Charts**, C 4.9/12

Radio Facility **Charts**, Caribbean and South American Area, M 301.19

Radio Facility **Charts**, Europe, Africa, Middle East, M 301.17

Radio Service Housekeepers' **Charts**, A 21.13/8

Recreational **Charts** (series), C 55.418/5

Regional Aeronautical **Charts**, C 23.10/4, C 4.9/5

Regional Contract **Charts**, A 55.7/2, A 55.7/3, A 55.7/4

Regulations for Sale of Lake Survey **Charts**, W 33.5

Route **Charts**, C 4.9/9, C 4.9/17

Sectional Aeronautical **Charts**, C 55.416/10

Sectional Aeronautical **Charts**, TD 4.79/11

Series of Educational Illustrations (**Charts**), A 43.5/10, A 43.22

Special Notices, Supplement to Radio Facility **Charts** and In-flight Data, Europe, D 301.9/3

Standard Instrument Departure (SID) **Charts**, Eastern U.S., C 55.416/5

Standard Instrument Departure (SID) **Charts**, Western United States, C 55.416/6
Standard Terminal Arrival (STAR) **Charts**, C 55.416/3
Supplement to Pilot **Charts**, N 6.26
Tactical Pilotage **Charts**, D 5.354
Terminal Area **Charts** (VFR), C 55.416/11
Terminal Area **Charts** (VFR), TD 4.79/12
Tidal Current **Charts**, C 55.424
U.S. Air Force Radio Facility **Charts**, Atlantic and Caribbean Area, M 301.15
U.S. Air Force Radio Facility **Charts**, North Pacific Area, M 301.14
United States Air Force and United States Navy Radio Facility **Charts**, Central Pacific-Far East, D 301.12
United States Air Force Radio Facility **Charts**, Caribbean and South American Area, D 301.10
United States Air Force Radio Facility **Charts**, Europe, Africa, Middle East, D 301.9
United States Air Force, Navy, Royal Canadian Air Force and Royal Canadian Navy, Navy Radio Facility **Charts** and In- Flight Data, Alaska, Canada and North Atlantic, D 301.13/3
United States Air Force, United States Navy and Royal Canadian Air Force Radio Facility **Charts**, West Canada and Alaska, D 301.13
United States Air Force, United States Navy Radio Facility **Charts**, North Atlantic Area, D 301.11
Wabash River **Charts**, W 7.13/5
Wall **Charts**, L 2.70/3
Weather Bureau Marine Services **Charts**, C 30.22/6
Western United States, Dates of Latest Prints, Instrument Approach Procedure **Charts** and Airport Obstruction Plans, C 4.9/20
White River **Charts**, W 7.13/6
Wind and Current **Charts**, Series A, Tract **Charts**, N 14.10/1
World Aeronautical **Charts**, C 4.9/8, C 55.416/13
World Aeronautical **Charts**, TD 4.79/14
Chats
Housekeepers' **Chats**, A 21.13/8
Check
Check Circulars, J 1.14/15
Check List of Birds of National Parks, I 29.27
Check List of Printed and Processed Publications, A 36.70/2
Check List of Standards for Farm Products, A 36.59, A 66.26
Check Payment and Reconciliation Memoranda, CP & R (series), T 63.8
PMA Procedure **Check** List, A 82.63
Practical **Check** Lists, W 9.8/2
Progress **Check** Book (series), D 101.107/15
Pulse **Check**, PrEx 26.10
United States Standard Facilities Flight **Check** Manual, FAA 5.9
Check List
Quarterly **Check List**, USAF/USN Flight Information Publications, Planning, D 301.52/2
Checklist
Advance Sheets of 3d Edition of **Checklist** of United States Public Documents, GP 3.14
Business Service **Checklist**, C 1.24
Checklist C (series), GP 3.23
Checklist of Reports and Charts Issued by Agricultural Marketing Service, A 88.33
Checklist of Reports Issued by Economic Research Service and Statistical Reporting Service, A 1.97
Federal Supply Schedule, **Checklist** and Guide, GS 2.7/3
Monthly **Checklist** of State Publications, LC 30.9
Radio Markets **Checklist** of Circulars, C 18.120/3
Semi-Annual **Checklist** of the EEOC Orders, Y 3.Eq 2:19
Semiannual **Checklist**, Bureau of International Commerce International Business Publications, C 42.15:C 41
Checklists
Preliminary **Checklists**, AE 1.15
Publications **Checklists**, LC 1.15
Checks
Safety Bus **Checks**, TD 2.302:B 96
Selected Safety Road **Checks** Motor Carriers of Property, TD 2.311
Cheddar Cheese
Cheddar Cheese Prices, A 92.10/8

Cheese
Cheddar **Cheese** Prices, A 92.10/8
Creamery Butter and American **Cheese** Production Estimates, A 36.196
Household Purchases of Butter, **Cheese**, Nonfat Dry Milk Solids and Margarine, A 88.14/6
Chem
Chem Alert, L 35.27
Chemawa
Chemawa American, I 20.42
Chemical
Agricultural and **Chemical** Development, (date) Annual Report, Y 3.T 25:1-5, A 82.100
Agricultural **Chemical** Usage, Vegetables, Summary, A 92.50
Analysis of Miscellaneous **Chemical** Imports through New York, TC 1.17
Annual Historical Review, Armament, Munitions and **Chemical** Command, (AMCCOM)-(series), D 101.1/5
Army **Chemical** Journal, D 116.17
Chemical and Plastics Division, Technical Report CP (series), D 106.9/5
Chemical and Rubber, C 41.35
Chemical Engineering Bulletins, Y 3.T 25:25
Chemical Engineering Reports, Y 3.T 25:19
Chemical Evaluation and Control Fact Sheets, A 77.239/2
Chemical Industry {abstracts}, C 41.53/7
Chemical Information Fact Sheets, EP 5.20
Chemical Safety Data Sheets, EDS-LS- (series), L 16.51/7
Chemical Science and Industry {abstracts}, C 41.53/10
Chemical Warfare Field Service Bulletins, W 91.7
Chemical Warfare Laboratories: CWL Special Publications, D 116.13
Chemical Warfare Service Bulletin, W 99.17/12
Chemical, Environmental, and Radiation Carcinogenesis, HE 20.3173/2
Chemical-Biological Coordination Center, Reviews, NA 2.7
Chemical-Biological Information-Handling Review Committee, HE 20.3001/2:C 42
Controlling **Chemical** Hazards Series, L 16.25
List of **Chemical** Compounds Authorized for Use Under USDA Meat, Poultry, Rabbit and Egg Inspection Programs, A 103.13
List of **Chemical** Compounds Authorized for Use Under USDA Poultry, Meat, Rabbit and Egg Products Inspection Programs, A 88.6:C 42, A 101.6:C 42
Medical Subject Headings; Supplementary **Chemical** Records, HE 20.3612/3-7
NCI Investigational Drugs, **Chemical** Information, HE 20.3180/2
News of Academy of Sciences of USSR; Department of **Chemical** Science, C 41.53/2
Organic Chemistry: Air Pollution Studies Characterization of **Chemical** Structures; Synthesis of Research Materials, C 13.46
Radio **Chemical** Analysis, Nuclear Instrumentation, Radiation Techniques, Nuclear Chemistry, Radioisotope Techniques, C 13.46
Registry of Toxic Effects of **Chemical** Substances (cumulative) Supplement, HE 20.7112/5
Registry of Toxic Effects of **Chemical** Substances, HE 20.7112/3
Registry of Toxic Effects of **Chemical** Substances, Permuted Molecular Formula, Index, HE 20.7112/4
Scientific Reports of Higher Schools Chemistry and **Chemical** Technology, C 41.53/9
Subfile of the Registry of Toxic Effects of **Chemical** Substances, HE 20.7112/2
Substitute **Chemical** Program, Initial Scientific and Minieconomic Review of {various chemicals}, EP 5.13
Technical Activities, Center for **Chemical** Physics, C 13.58/9
Toxic **Chemical** Release Inventory, EP 5.22
Toxic **Chemical** Release Inventory Reporting Form R and Instructions, EP 5.22/3
TSCA {Toxic Substances Control Act} **Chemical** Assessment Series, EP 5.15/2
U.S.D.A. Summary of Registered Agricultural Pesticide **Chemical** Uses, A 77.302:P 43/4
Chemical Corps
Chemical Corps Purchase Description, D 116.10
Index of **Chemical Corps** Drawings, D 116.11
Index of **Chemical Corps** Specifications, D 116.8

Chemical Warfare
Defense Against **Chemical Warfare**, W 3.50/11
Chemical-Biological
Chemical-Biological Information-Handling Review Committee, HE 20.3001/2:C 42
Chemicals
Chemicals, C 41.35
Chemicals and Allied Products Entered for Consumption, C 18.55
Chemicals-in-Progress Bulletin, EP 5.15
Coke and Coal **Chemicals**, I 28.30, E 3.11/9
Coke and Coal **Chemicals** in (year), I 28.30/4
Coke and Coal **Chemicals**, Annual, I 28.30/4
Facts for Industry Series 6-2 and 6-10, Organic **Chemicals** and Plastic Materials, TC 1.25/2
Imports of Benzenoid **Chemicals** and Products, TC 1.36, ITC 1.19
Industry Report, **Chemicals** and Allied Products, C 18.235
Industry Wage Survey: Industrial **Chemicals**, L 2.3/31
Preliminary Report on Production on Specified Synthetic Organic **Chemicals** in United States; Facts for Industry Series, TC 1.25
Preliminary Report on U.S. Production of Selected Synthetic Organic **Chemicals**, ITC 1.14/2
S.O.C. {Synthetic Organic **Chemicals**}, TC 1.25/3, TC 1.25/4
Substitute Chemical Program, Initial Scientific and Minieconomic Review of {various **chemicals**}, EP 5.13
Synthetic Organic **Chemicals**, United States Production and Sales, TC 1.33, TC 1.33/2, ITC 1.14
TSCA Status Report for Existing **Chemicals**, EP 5.15/4
World Trade Notes on **Chemicals** and Allied Products, C 18.179
Chemicals-in-progress
TSCA {Toxic Substances Control Act} **Chemicals-in-progress** Bulletin, EP 5.15
Chemistry
Atmospheric Turbidity and Precipitation **Chemistry** Data for the World, C 55.283
Bibliography on the High Temperature **Chemistry** and Physics of Gases and Gas-condensed Phase Reactions, C 13.37/3
Bibliography on the High Temperature **Chemistry** and Physics of Materials in the Condensed State, C 13.37/2
Biophysics and Biophysical **Chemistry** A Study Section, HE 20.3001/2:B 52
Biophysics and Biophysical **Chemistry** B Study Section, HE 20.3001/2:B 52/2
Chemistry, C 51.9/20, PrEx 7.22/4, E 1.99
Chemistry and Technology of Fuels and Oils {abstracts}, C 41.55
Chemistry, C 51.9/20, PrEx 7.22/4, E 1.99
Coke and Chemistry {abstracts}, C 41.64
Collected Reprints; Atmospheric Physics and **Chemistry** Laboratory, C 55.612/3
Herald of Leningrad University, Physics and **Chemistry** Series {abstracts}, C 41.52/5
Journal of Analytical **Chemistry** {abstracts}, C 41.53/6
Journal of Applied **Chemistry** {abstracts}, C 41.53/11
Journal of General **Chemistry** {abstracts}, C 41.53
Journal of Inorganic **Chemistry**, C 41.53/4
Journal of Physical **Chemistry** {abstracts}, C 41.34/5
Medicinal **Chemistry** A Study Section, HE 20.3001/2:M 46/5
Medicinal **Chemistry** B Study Section, HE 20.3001/2:M 46/6
Microbial **Chemistry** Study Section, HE 20.3001/2:M 58
News of Institutes of Higher Learning; Chemistry, and **Chemistry** Technology, C 41.53/8
News of Institutes of Higher Learning; Chemistry, and **Chemistry** Technology, C 41.53/8
Organic **Chemistry**: Air Pollution Studies Characterization of Chemical Structures; Synthesis of Research Materials, C 13.46
Pharmacology and Biorelated **Chemistry** Program: Biennial Report, HE 20.3461/3
Physiological **Chemistry**, Study Section, HE 20.3001/2:P 56/3
Progress of **Chemistry** {abstracts}, C 41.53/3

CID
CID Pamphlet (series), D 101.22/17
CID
District Director's Responsibility and Authority
for **CID** Activity, T 22.60
Cigar
Cigar Tobacco Adjustment Program, A 55.10
Cigar Box
Cigar Box Series, C 18.52/2
Cigarette
Industry Wage Survey: **Cigarette** Manufacturing, L
2.3/26
Cigarettes
Cigarettes and Cigars, T 70.9/2
Monthly Statistical Release; **Cigarettes** and
Cigars, T 70.9/2
Tar, Nicotine, and Carbon Dioxide of the Smoke of....
Varieties of Domestic **Cigarettes** for the
Year, FT 1.36
Cigars
Cigarettes and **Cigars**, T 70.9/2
Monthly Statistical Release; Cigarettes and
Cigars, T 70.9/2
Cincinnati
Cincinnati, Centennial Exposition, 1897, S 6.17
News of Environmental Research in **Cincinnati**, EP
1.49
Cinder
Pumice and Volcanic **Cinder** in (year), I 28.122
Cinematography
Journal of Scientific and Applied Photography and
Cinematography {abstracts}, C 41.69
CIO
CIO Information in the News, VA 1.101
CIP
CIP Cataloging in Publication, Progress Report,
LC 30.16
Circle
Full **Circle**, E 1.90/4
Great **Circle** (8) Sailing and Polar Charts, D 5.345
Great **Circle** (58) Tracking Charts, D 5.346
Circuit
DC **Circuit** Update, Ju 2.10
Papers in Re in **Circuit** Courts, J 1.76
Records and Briefs in **Circuit** Courts of Appeals
and Court of Appeals, District of
Columbia, J 1.19/5
Seventh **Circuit** Digest, Ju 2.9
Circuits
Directory of Meat and Poultry Inspection Program
Establishments, **Circuits** and Officials, A
88.16/20
Working Reference of Livestock Regulatory
Establishments, **Circuits** and Officials, A
88.16/20
Circum-Pacific
Circum-Pacific (CP) Map Series, I 19.91/2
Circular
1A **Circular** (series), D 101.4/4
OES **Circular** Letters, A 77.410
Ordnance **Circular** Letters, N 18.9
Organized Reserves **Circular**, W 99.16/12
Personnel **Circular** Letters, VA 1.4/2
PM **Circular**, P 1.12/6-2
Proposals for {Supplies to Accompany **Circular**
Proposals}, W 73.10/2
Quarterly **Circular** Information Bulletin, D 103.42/
11
Reprint and **Circular** Series, NA 2.5
Roads **Circular**, I 20.24
Small Business **Circular** FOA/SBC (series), FP
1.13
Small Business **Circular** MSA/CBC (series), Pr
33.913
Summary of **Circular**, A 67.19/9
Tariff Correction **Circular**, C 18.147
Circulars
(Public Moneys Depositaries) **Circulars**, W 3.25
AMC **Circulars** (series), D 101.4/5
Information **Circulars**: Air Service, W 87.10
Information **Circulars**: Bureau of Mines, C 22.11, I
28.27
Information **Circulars**: Engineer Department, W
7.15
Information **Circulars**: Federal National Mortgage
Association, FL 5.16
Information **Circulars**: Field Division, Y 3.C
83:85
Information **Circulars**: Hydrographic Office, N
6.23
Information **Circulars**: Inspector General's
Department, W 9.8
Information **Circulars**: National Youth
Administration, Y 3.N 21/14:8

Information **Circulars**: State Councils Section, Y
3.C 83:75
Information **Circulars**: War Department Claims
Board, W 93.6
Miners **Circulars**, I 28.6
OEP Economic Stabilization **Circulars**, PrEx 4.4/3
Official **Circulars**, I 16.9
Official **Circulars**, V.D., T 27.23
Operation Division **Circulars**, A 1.45
Ordnance Department **Circulars**, W 34.4/3, W
34.4/4
OTS Technology Guide **Circulars**, C 35.12
Over Change Claim **Circulars**, Y 3.R 13/2:35
P.B.A. **Circulars**, A 49.4
Pay and Supply Instructions, **Circulars**, N 24.26, T
47.8/2
Personnel **Circulars**, A 1.44, A 49.4/2
Plant and Operations **Circulars**, A 60.4/3
Procurement **Circulars** Printed and Processed, W
1.31
Procurement **Circulars**, W 1.24/5
Procurement Legal Service **Circulars**, D 101.33/3
Products List **Circulars**, SBA 1.4/2
Public **Circulars**, T 1.33
Purchase **Circulars**, GP 1.21
Purchasing Office **Circulars**, I 1.66
PWA **Circulars**, Y 3.F 31/4:23
QMG **Circulars**, M 112.4
Radio **Circulars**, C 30.23
Radio Markets Checklist of **Circulars**, C 18.120/3
Reappraisement **Circulars**, Ju 9.4
Recruiting Authority **Circulars**, CS 1.53
Recruiting **Circulars**, 4th Civil Service District,
CS 1.35
Recruiting **Circulars**, 4th Civil Service Region, CS
1.35/2
Reference **Circulars**, LC 6.4/3, LC 19.4/2
Retirement **Circulars**, CS 1.29
RFC Mortgage Company, **Circulars**, Y 3.R 24:9
Rural School **Circulars**, I 16.42
Safety Section **Circulars**, Y 3.R 13/2:26
Sanitary Climatology **Circulars**, A 29.15
School Home-Garden **Circulars**, I 16.16
Second Army, 2A **Circulars** (series), D 101.4/3
Secondary School **Circulars**, I 16.22
Shipping Point Inspection **Circulars**, A 36.201
Small Business **Circulars**, Y 3.Ec 74/3:19
Special **Circulars**, IC 1 rat.5
Special Express Company **Circulars**, IC 1 exp.4
Special Report Series **Circulars**, IC 1.4/4
Special VD Education **Circulars**, FS 2.38
SSA Program **Circulars** Disability, HE 3.4/4
SSA Program **Circulars** General Series, HE 3.4/2
SSA Program **Circulars** Public Information, HE
3.4/3
SSA Program **Circulars** Retirement and Survivors
Insurance, HE 3.4/5
SSA Program **Circulars** Supplemental Security
Income, HE 3.4/6
Staff Information **Circulars**, GS 4.12
Standardized Government Civilian Allowance
Regulations, Allowance **Circulars**, S
1.76
Standardized Government Post Differential
Regulations, Differential **Circulars**, S
1.76/2
Statistical **Circulars**, I 16.39, FS 5.39
Statistical Series **Circulars**, IC 1.4/3
Stoppage **Circulars**, W 36.6, W 97.7, W 77.5, W
2.10
Supply **Circulars**, W 89.6/1
Tariff **Circulars** Federal Communications
Commission, CC 1.16
Tariff **Circulars** Maritime Commission, MC 1.21
Tariff **Circulars** Rate Section, Interstate Commerce
Commission, IC 1 rat.4
Tariff **Circulars** Shipping Board, SB 1.8
Tariff **Circulars** War Department, W 1.13
Technical **Circulars**, HH 2.12
Technical Information **Circulars**, Y 3.N 21/14:11,
FS 6.14
Telegraph Accounting **Circulars**, CC 1.17, CC 1.18
Topographic Maps **Circulars**, I 19.11
Tornado **Circulars**, W 42.16
Traffic **Circulars**, MC 1.21
Training **Circulars** Army and Corps Areas and
Departments, Second Corps Area, W
99.12/8
Training **Circulars** Army and Corps Areas and
Departments, Seventh Corps Area, W
99.17/8
Training **Circulars** Department of the Army, M
101.22, D 101.24
Training **Circulars** Department of the East, W 17.8

Training **Circulars** National Guard Bureau, W
70.11
Training **Circulars** War Department, W 1.36
Training **Circulars** War Plans Division, W 26.11
Transfer **Circulars**, CS 1.37
Unemployment Compensation **Circulars**, SS 1.12
Uniform **Circulars**, T 47.40
USASSC Field **Circulars**, D 101.4/2
VD Education **Circulars**, FS 2.39
Vocational Division {miscellaneous} **Circulars**, FS
5.127
Vocational Summary, **Circulars** of Information, VE
1.5
War **Circulars**, A 72.23
Wildlife **Circulars**, I 49.16
Circulation
Circulation Statement, T 26.5
Circulation Statement of United States Money, T
63.308
Circulation Statements, T 57.7
Review of Foreign Developments, Prepared for
Internal **Circulation**, FR 1.49
Some Recent Books on Public Affairs Available for
Circulation in the Book Forms, LC 1.25
Circulatory
NOS Oceanographic **Circulatory** Survey Reports,
C 55.429
CIRRPC
CIRRPC Annual Report, PrEx 1.15
Citation
Citation Orders, W 95.15
Citations
Gastroenterology Abstracts and **Citations**, HE
20.3313
How to Find U.S. Statutes and U.S. Code
Citations, GS 4.102:St 2
Parkinson's Disease and Related Disorders,
Citations from the Literature, HE
20.3511
Citator
Citator, Y 3.F 31/21-3:9-4
Citator to Decisions of the Occupational Safety
and Health Review Commission, Y 3.Oc
1:10-4
Cited
Table of Cases **Cited** in Opinions, IC 1.6/3
Cities
Answer Me This: American **Cities** Series, I 16.58/1
Building Permits in Principal **Cities** of U.S., L 2.6/
a 4
Comparative Statistics of General Assistance
Operations of Public Agencies in
Selected Large **Cities**, FS 3.16
Condition of Weekly Reporting Member Banks in
Central Reserve **Cities**, FR 1.16/2
Condition of Weekly Reporting Member Banks in
Leading **Cities**, FR 1.16
Conference for Supervisors of Elementary
Education in Large **Cities**, FS 5.58/2
Construction Committees {various cities}, Public
Sector Bid Calendars by Agencies, L
1.75
Construction Reports; Permits Issued for
Demolition of Residential Structures in
Selected **Cities**, C 45 (series), C 3.215/12
Consumer Price Index {by individual cities and
commodities}, L 2.38/5
Eating and Drinking Places and Motels Wage
Survey Summaries by **Cities**, L 2.113/4
Estimated Retail Food Prices by **Cities**, L 2.37
Farmers' Bulletins of Interest to Persons Residing
in **Cities** or Towns, A 21.9/2
Financial Statistics of **Cities**, C 3.142
Financial Statistics of **Cities** Having a Population
of Over 30,000, C 3.47
Financial Statistics of **Cities** Having a Population
of Over 100,000, C 3.47/2
Fresh Fruit and Vegetable Unload Totals for 41
Cities, Calendar Year (date), A 88.40/2:7
Fresh Fruit and Vegetable Unloads in Eastern
Cities, A 88.40/2:3
Fresh Fruit and Vegetable Unloads in Midwestern
Cities, A 88.40/2:5
Fresh Fruit and Vegetable Unloads in Southern
Cities, A 88.40/2:6
Fresh Fruit and Vegetable Unloads in Western
Cities, A 88.40/2:4
Income Tax Returns: Number of Individual by
States, Counties, **Cities**, and Towns, T
22.40
Indexes of Retail Prices on Meats in Large **Cities**, L
2.39/2

Classification of Important Labor Market Areas, L 7.19

Classification of Imports and Exports, C 18.18/2

Classification of Income and Profit and Loss Accounts, IC 1 wat.8

Classification of Income, Profit & Loss, and General Balance Sheet Accounts, IC 1 ste.15

Classification of Investment in Road Equipment, IC 1 ste.16

Classification of Labor Market Areas According to Relative Adequacy of Labor Supply, L 7.19/2

Classification of Operating Expenses, IC 1 ste.7, IC 1 wat.5

Classification of Operating Expenses of Electric Railways, IC 1 eler.7

Classification of Operating Expenses of Express Companies, IC 1 exp.6, IC 1 exp.7

Classification of Operating Revenues, IC 1 ste.9, IC 1 wat.6

Classification of Operating Revenues and Operating Expenses, IC 1 ste.17

Classification of Operating Revenues of Electric Railways, IC 1 eler.8

Classification of Operating Revenues of Express Companies, IC 1 exp.7

Classification of Patents, C 21.5/a 1

Classification of Periodicals, Army Medical Library, W 44.24

Classification of Revenues and Expenses by Outside Operations, IC 1 ste.10

Classification of Train-Miles, Locomotive-Miles and Car-Miles, IC 1 ste.11

Classification Outline for Decisions of the NLRB and Related Court Decisions, LR 1.8/7

Classification Outline Scheme of Classes, LC 9.5

Classification Rulings and Decisions: Index Harmonized Tariff Schedules of the United States of America, T 17.6/3-6

Classification Schedules, C 14.17, C 18.18

Code **Classification** and Definitions of Foreign Trade Areas, C 3.150:R

Code **Classification** of Countries, C 3.150:C

Code **Classification** of Flag of Vessel, C 3.150:J

Code **Classification** of Foreign Ports by Geographic Trade Area and Country, C 3.150:K

Code **Classification** of U.S. Customs Districts and Ports, C 3.150:D

Commodity **Classification** for Compiling Statistics on Shipments from U.S., C 3.140:Q

Commodity **Classification** for Reporting Shipments from Puerto Rico to U.S., C 3.150:P

Condensed **Classification** of Operating Expenses, IC 1 ste.18

Decimal **Classification**, Additions, Notes and Decisions, LC 37.8

Dewey Decimal **Classification**, Additions, Notes and Decisions, LC 37.8

Digest of Significant **Classification** Decisions and Opinions, PM 1.40

Federal Agency **Classification** Chiefs Workshop: Reports, PM 1.24

Federal Supply **Classification**, D 7.6/2:2

Federal Supply **Classification** Listing of DoD Standardization Documents, D 7.14/2

Foreign Service **Classification** List, S 1.7/2

Freight **Classification** Data File, D 7.28

Higher Education Facilities **Classification** and Procedures Manual, FS 5.251:51016, HE 5.251:51016

Index to **Classification**, C 21.12/2

Index to the U.S. Patent **Classification**, C 21.12/3

Industrial **Classification** Code, FS 3.112/2

Industrial **Classification** Code, State Operations Bulletins, FS 3.112

Instruction Manual: **Classification** and Coding Instructions for Divorce Records, HE 20.6208/10

Instruction Manual: **Classification** and Coding Instructions for Fetal Death Records, HE 20.6208/6-2

Instruction Manual: **Classification** and Coding Instructions for Induced Termination of Pregnancy Records, HE 20.6208/8

Instruction Manual: **Classification** and Coding Instructions for Live Birth Records, HE 20.6208/6

Instruction Manual: **Classification** and Coding Instructions for Marriage Records, HE 20.6208/7

International **Classification** of Diseases, 9th Revision, Clinical Modification, HE 22.41

L.C. **Classification**, Additions and Changes, LC 1.7/2, LC 26.9/2

Laws relating to Civil Service Salary **Classification**, Civil Service Preference, Etc., Y 1.2:Sa 3/2

Library of Congress **Classification** Schedules, LC 26.9

Manual of **Classification**, C 21.12

Notes and Decisions on Application of Decimal **Classification**, LC 22.7, LC 26.8

Official **Classification** of . . . Watering Points, FS 2.75

Position **Classification** and Pay in State and Territorial Public Health Laboratories, HE 20.7413

Position **Classification** Plans for {various cities or districts}, CS 1.39/3

Position **Classification** Standards for Positions Subject to the Classification Act of 1949, CS 1.39, PM 1.30

Prime Contract Awards by Service Category and Federal Supply **Classification**, D 1.57/4

Schedule A. Statistical **Classification** on Commodities Imported into the United States with Rates of Duty and Tariff Paragraphs, C 3.150:A

Schedule B. Statistical **Classification** of Domestic and Foreign Commodities Exported from the United States, C 3.150:B

Schedule C. Code **Classification** of Countries, C 3.150:C

Schedule D. Code **Classification** of U.S. Customs Districts and Ports, C 3.150:D

Schedule H. Statistical **Classification** and Code Numbers of Shipments of Merchandise to Alaska from United States, C 3.150:H

Schedule J. Code **Classification** of Flag of Vessel, C 3.150:J

Schedule K. Code **Classification** of Foreign Ports by Geographic Trade Area and Country, C 3.150:K

Schedule L. Statistical **Classification** of Foreign Merchandise Reports in In-transit Trade of United States, C 3.150:L

Schedule P. Commodity **Classification** for Reporting Shipments from Puerto Rico to U.S., C 3.150:P

Schedule Q. Commodity **Classification** for Compiling Statistics on Shipments from U.S., C 3.150:Q

Schedule R. Code **Classification** and Definitions of Foreign Trade Areas, C 3.150:R

Schedule S. Statistical **Classification** of Domestic and Foreign Merchandise Exported from U.S., C 3.150:S

Schedule T. Statistical **Classification** of Imports into U.S. Arranged in Shipping Commodity GROUPS., C 3.150:T

Schedule W. Statistical **Classification** of U.S. Waterborne Exports and Imports, C 3.150:W

Schedule X. Statistical **Classification** of Domestic and Foreign Merchandise Exported from United States by Air Arranged in Shipping Commodity Groups, C 3.150:X

Schedule Y. Statistical **Classification** of Imports into United States Arranged in Shipping Commodity Groups, C 3.150:Y

Science of Fingerprints, **Classification** and Uses, J 1.14/2:F 49

Small Business Administration Publications, **Classification** of Management Publications, SBA 1.18/3

Standard Industrial **Classification** Manual, PrEx 2.6/2:In 27

Statistical **Classification** and Code Numbers of Shipments of Merchandise to Alaska from United States, C 3.150:H

Statistical **Classification** of Domestic and Foreign Commodities Exported from the United States, C 3.150:B

Statistical **Classification** of Domestic and Foreign Merchandise Exported from U.S., C 3.150:S

Statistical **Classification** of Foreign Merchandise Reports in In-Transit Trade of United States, C 3.150:L

Statistical **Classification** of Imports into U.S. Arranged in Shipping Commodity Groups, C 3.150:T

Statistical **Classification** of Imports into United States Arranged in Shipping Commodity Groups, C 3.150:Y

Statistical **Classification** of U.S. Waterborne Exports and Imports, C 3.150:W

Statistical **Classification** on Commodities Imported into the United States with Rates of Duty and Tariff Paragraphs, C 3.150:A

Classifications

Consolidated of Schedule B Commodity **Classifications** for Use in Presentation of U.S. Export Statistics, C 3.150:G

Schedule G. Consolidation of Schedule B Commodity **Classifications** for Use in Presentation of U.S. Export Statistics, C 3.150:G

Patents Class, Current **Classifications** of US Patents, C 21.31/3

Classified

Census of Population and Housing: **Classified** Index of Industries and Occupations, C 3.223/22:90-R4

Classified Index of Dispositions of ULP {Unfair Labor Practices} Charges by the General Counsel of the Federal Labor Relations Authority, Y 3.F 31/21-3:11

Classified Index of Dispositions of ULP {Unfair Labor Practices} Charges by the General Counsel of the National Labor Relations Board, LR 1.8/8

Classified Index of the National Labor Relations Board Decisions and Related Court Decisions, LR 1.8/6

Classified List of Publications, A 26.6/2

Inactive or Discontinued Items from the 1950 Revision of the **Classified** List, GP 3.24/2

List of Classes in 1950 Revision of **Classified** List of United States Government Publications by Departments and Bureaus, GP 3.24

List of Electric Power Suppliers with Annual Operating Revenues of $2,500,000 or More **Classified** As Public Utilities Under Federal Power Act, FP 1.28

National Shellfish Register of **Classified** Growing Waters, C 55.441

Report of **Classified** Program of Exports and Value by American Agencies Voluntarily Registered with Advisory Committee on Voluntary Foreign Aid, S 1.99/2

Classified List

Inactive or Discontinued Items from the 1950 Revision of the **Classified List**, GP 3.24

Classifying

Instructions for **Classifying** Multiple Causes of Death, HE 20.6208/4-3

Instructions for **Classifying** the Underlying Cause of Death, HE 20.6208/4-4

Instructions for **Classifying** the Underlying Cause of Death: Mobile Examination Center Interviewer's Manual for the Hispanic Health and Nutrition Examination Survey, HE 20.6208/2-4

Instructions for **Classifying** the Underlying Cause of Death: Nonindexed Terms, Standard Abbreviations, and State Geographic Codes Used in Mortality Data Classification, HE 20.6208/4

Instructions for **Classifying** the Underlying Cause of Death: Physician's Examination Manual for the Hispanic Health and Nutrition Examination Survey, HE 20.6208/2-3

Instructions for **Classifying** the Underlying Cause of Death: Source Records and Control Specifications, HE 20.6208/11

Instructions for **Classifying** the Underlying Cause of Death: Vital Records Geographic Classification, HE 20.6208/3

Classroom

AG in the **Classroom** Notes, A 1.135

Agriculture in the **Classroom**, Notes, A 1.135

Civil Defense Education Project, **Classroom** Practices, FS 5.45/3

Educational Briefs for the Middle and Secondary Level **Classroom**, NAS 1.19/3

Clay

Bathroom Accessories (recessed and atachable all **clay**), C 3.72

Clay Products of United States, I 19.18

Industry Wage Survey: Structural **Clay** Products, L 2.3/30

Structural **Clay** Products (common brick, face brick, vitrified paving brick, hollow building tile), C 3.109

Clays

Clays in (year), I 28.140

Clean

Benefits and Costs of the **Clean** Air Act, The, EP 4.31

Building for **Clean** Water Report on Federal Incentive Grants for Municiapl Waste Treatment, FS 16.9

Clean

Clean Coal Today, E 1.84/4

Clean Coal Technology Compendium (Tropical Reports), E 1.84/5

Clean Coal Technology Demonstration Program, Program Update, E 1.84/6

Clean Coal Technology Demonstration Program, Project Fact Sheets, E 1.84/7

Clean Grain Notes for Cooperators in **Clean** Grain Program, A 43.30

Clean Water, Announcements {for radio and television}, FS 2.64/5

Clean Water, Report to Congress (year), EP 1.43

Clean Water SRF Program Information for the State of..., EP 2.33

Cost of **Clean** Air, EP 1.62

Cost of **Clean** Water , EP 2.14

Working for **Clean** Water, EP 1.8/12

Clean Water

Building for **Clean Water** Progress Report on Federal Incentive Grants for Municipal Waste Treatment Fiscal Year, FS 2.64/6

Cleaning

Industry Wage Survey: Contract **Cleaning** Services, L 2.3/33

Laundry and Dry **Cleaning** Wage Survey Summaries by Cities, L 2.113/2

Clear

Building for **Clear** Water, I 67.15

Clearances

Verific Vessel Entrances and **Clearances**: Calendar Year (date), C 56.210:975, C 3.174:975

Clearing House

Contract **Clearing House** Service, Summaries, Pr 33.916

Clearinghouse

Air Chief (**Clearinghouse** for Inventory and Emission Factors), EP 1,109

Cancer Information **Clearinghouse**, Quarterly Accessions List, HE 20.3165/3

Clearinghouse Announcements in Science and Technology, C 51.7/5

Clearinghouse Exchange of Publications of State Departments of Education, FS 5.10/5

Clearinghouse of Studies on Higher Education, Reporter, FS 5.250:50004, HE 5.250:50004

Clearinghouse on Health Indexes, HE 20.6216/2-2

Clearinghouse on Health Indexes: Cumulated Annotations, HE 20.6216/2

Clearinghouse Publications, CR 1.10

Clearinghouse Publications: Urban Series, CR 1.11/2

Contact **Clearinghouse** Service CCHS Summary, FO 1.16

Diabetes Dateline, the National Diabetes Information Clearinghouse Bulletin, HE 20.3310/3

Digestive Diseases **Clearinghouse** Fact Sheets, HE 20.3323

EEOC Reports, **Clearinghouse** Service for Business Newsletters and Periodicals, Y 3.Eq 2:7-2

Energy Efficiency and Renewable Energy, **Clearinghouse**, E 1.99/13

ERIC **Clearinghouse** for Social Studies, Social Science Education: Interpretive Studies, HE 18.13

Health Manpower **Clearinghouse** Series, HE 20.3114/3

HUD **Clearinghouse** Service, HCS (series), HH 1.35

Hypoglycemia, National Diabetes Information **Clearinghouse**, HE 20.3323/2

Inside NIDCD Information **Clearinghouse**, HE 20.3666

Labor Standards **Clearinghouse**, L 16.46

National Air Toxics Information **Clearinghouse**: Newsletter, EP 4.23

National **Clearinghouse** on Child Abuse and Neglect Information Catalog, HE 23.1216/2

Statistical Notes National **Clearinghouse** on Aging, HE 23.3112

Clearinghouses

ERIC Products, Bibliography of Information Analysis Publications of ERIC **Clearinghouses**, HE 5.77/2

Clearwater

Area Wage Survey, Tampa-St. Petersburg-**Clearwater**, Florida, Metropolitan Area, L 2.121/9-6

Cleft

Cleft Palate Team Directory, HE 20.3402:C 58/2

Clemency

Presidential **Clemency** Board: Publications, Pr 38.8:C 59

Clergy

Bulletin for the **Clergy**, Y 3.F 73:12

Clerical

Clerical Workshop Series, VA 1.28

Clerk

Chief **Clerk** and Superintendent of Buildings, Annual Report, I 1.60

Clerks

Regulations for **Clerks** of Courts Who Take Passport Applications, S 1.18

Clerks of Courts

Instructions to **Clerks of Courts** Exercising Naturalization Jurisdiction, L 6.10

Cleveland

Sun and Moon Tables for **Cleveland**, Ohio, D 203.14/2

Clients

Demographic Characteristics and Patterns of Drug Use of **Clients** Admitted to Drug Abuse Treatment Programs in Selected States, Trend Data, HE 20.8231/2

Climate

ACCP (Atlantic **Climate** Change Program) Newsletter, C 55.55

Bibliography on the **Climate** of {Country} WB/BC (series), C 52.21

Climate and Health, A 29.8

Climate Bulletin, C 55.129/2

Climate Diagnostic Bulletin, C 55.194

Climate Impact Assessment, Foreign Countries, C 55.233

Climate Impact Assessment, Foreign Countries Annual Summary, C 55.233/3

Climate Prediction Center Atlas, C 55.136

Climate Review, Metropolitan Washington, C 55.129

Climate Variations Bulletin, C 55.287/61

Climatography of the United States; **Climate** of the United States, C 55.221

Decennial Census of United States **Climate**, C 55.221/2

Decennial Census of United States, **Climate**: **Climate** Summary of United States, Supplement 1951-60, Climatography of United States, No. 86 (series), C 30.71/8

Decennial Census of United States, **Climate**: Daily Normals of Temperature and Heating Degree Days, C 30.71/7:84

Decennial Census of United States, **Climate**: Heating Degree Day Normals, C 30.71/7:83

Decennial Census of United States, **Climate**: Monthly Averages for State Climatic Divisions, C 30.71/7:85

Decennial Census of United States, **Climate**: Monthly Normals of Temperature, Precipitation, and Heating Degree Days, C 30.71/4

Decennial Census of United States, **Climate**: Summary of Hourly Observations, C 30.71/5:82

National **Climate** Program: Annual Report, C 55.44

Weekly **Climate** Bulletin, C 55.129/2

Climates

Climates of the States, C 30.71/3:60

Climatic

Atlases; National **Climatic** Center, C 55.287/58

Climatic Charts for U.S., A 29.44

Climatic Data Base, Y 3.T 25:50

Climatic Guides, C 30.67

Climatic Impact Assessment Program; Newsletter, TD 1.38/2

Climatic Impact Assessment Program; Technical Abstract Report, TD 1.38

Climatic Maps of United States, C 52.11

Climatic Summaries of Resort Areas, C 30.71/6:21

Climatic Summary of the United States, Supplement, C 30.3/2

Climatography of the United States; Monthly Averages of Temperature and Precipitation for State **Climatic** Division, C 55.286/2

Geophysical Monitoring for **Climatic** Change, C 55.618

Historical Climatology Series 6-1: Statewide Average **Climatic** History, C 55.287/61

Mariners Worldwide **Climatic** Guide to Tropical Storms at Sea, D 220.8:St 7

Monthly Averages of Temperature and Precipitation for State **Climatic** Divisions, C 55.286/2

Monthly **Climatic** Data for the World, C 55.211

National **Climatic** Data Center Periodical Publications, C 55.287/63

Publications National **Climatic** Center, C 55.281

U.S. Divisional and Station **Climatic** Data and Normals, C 55.281/2-3

U.S. Navy Marine **Climatic** Atlas of the World, D 202.2:At 6

Climatography

Climatography of the United States; Airport Climatological Summary, C 55.286/3

Climatography of the United States; Climate of the United States, C 55.221

Climatography of the United States; Monthly Normals of Temperature, Precipitation, and Heating and Cooling Degree Days, C 55.286

Climatography of the United States; No. 60, C 55.286/5

Climatography of the United States; No. 84, C 55.286/8

Decennial Census of United States, Climate: Climate Summary of United States, Supplement 1951-60, **Climatography** of United States, No. 86 (series), C 30.71/8

Climatological

Climatography of the United States; Airport **Climatological** Summary, C 55.286/3

Climatological Data, A 29.29, A 29.29/2

Climatological Data, National Summary, C 55.214

Climatological Data; Alaska Section, A 29.33, C 30.21

Climatological Data; Antarctic Stations, C 30.21/3

Climatological Data; Artic Stations, C 30.21/2

Climatological Data; Hawaii Section, A 29.34, C 30.19

Climatological Data; Pacific, C 30.19/2

Climatological Data; Porto Rico Section, A 29.35

Climatological Data; United States, C 30.18-C 30.18/38, C 55.214/2-C 55.214/47

Climatological Data; West Indies and Caribbean Service, A 29.36, C 30.20

Climatological Substation Summaries, C 30.71

Climatological Summary, San Juan, Puerto Rico, C 30.45

Instructions for **Climatological** Observers, C 30.4:B

Local **Climatological** Data, C 55.217

Local **Climatological** Data, Annual Summaries, C 55.287

Local **Climatological** Data, Dulles International Airport, C 55.287/3

Local **Climatological** Data, National Airport, C 55.287/2

Local **Climatological** Data, (various states), C 55.286/6-54

Local **Climatological** Data, Washington, D.C., Dulles International Airport, C 55.217/2

Local **Climatological** Summary with Comparative Data, C 30.10/3

Marine **Climatological** Summaries, C 55.282

Climatologist

State **Climatologist**, C 55.281/3

Climatology

Historical **Climatology** Series 6-1: Statewide Average Climatic History, C 55.287/61

Historical **Climatology** Series, Atlases, C 55.287/58

Sanitary **Climatology** Circulars, A 29.15

Clinic

Medicare Rural Health **Clinic** Manual, HE 22.8/19

Clinical

Cancer **Clinical** Investigation Review Committee, HE 20.3001/2:C 16

Clinical Applications and Prevention Advisory Committee, HE 20.3001/2:C 61

Clinical Bulletins, VA 1.11

Clinical Center, Current **Clinical** Studies and Patient Referral Procedures, HE 20.3010

Clinical Center: Medical Staff Directory, HE 20.3002:M 46/4

Code of Regulations of U.S. of America, AE 2.8
Code Series, Y 3.F 31/10:9
Cumulative List, Organizations Described in
Section 170 (c) of the International
Revenue Code of 1954, T 22.2:Or 3
Drill Books, Signal Books and Code Lists, N
17.12/1
Equal Employment Opportunity, Code of Federal
Regulations Title 29, Y 3.Eq 2:18-4
Federal Supply Code for Manufacturers, D 7.6/2:4
Geographic Identification Code Scheme {by
regions}, C 3.223/13-2
How to Find U.S. Statutes and U.S. Code Citations,
GS 4.102:St 2
Industrial Classification Code, FS 3.112/2
Industrial Classification Code, State Operations
Bulletins, FS 3.112
List of Bituminous Coal Producers who have
Accepted Bituminous Coal Code
Promulgated June 21, 1972, I 34.17, I
46.9
Manual for Radiosonde Code (WBAN), C 30.6/2:R
1 1
Manual for Synoptic Code (WBAN), C 30.6/2:Sy
7/2
Manual for Upper Wind Code (SBAN), C 30.6/2:W
72
Method of Transportation Code, Exports, C
3.140:N
National Health Related Items Code Directory, HE
20.4030
NATO Supply Code for Manufacturers, D 7.6/2-
2:4-3/date
Nongovernment Organization Codes for Military
Standard Contract Administration
Procedures: Code to Name, D 7.6/2:8-2/
2
Nongovernment Organization Codes for Military
Standard Contract Administration
Procedures: Name to Code, D 7.6/2:8-1/
2
Oil and Gas Field Code Master List, E 3.34/2
Operation and Effect of the International Boycott
Provisions of the Internal Revenue
Code, T 1.56
Packaging Requirements Code, D 7.20:726C
Regulations (pt. nos. of Title 26 of the Code of
Federal Regulations), T 70.6/2
Regulations (pt. nos. of Title 27 Code of Federal
Regulations), T 22.17/4, T 70.6/3
Regulations, Title 29, Code of Federal Regulations,
L 36.206/2
Rules and Regulations, Title 10, Code of Federal
Regulations, Chapter 1, Y 3.N 88:6
Rules of Practice and Rules Relating to Investiga-
tions and Code of Behavior Governing
Exparte Communications Between
Persons Outside the Commission and
Decisional Employees, SE 1.6:R 86/4
Schedule C. Code Classification of Countries, C
3.150:C
Schedule D. Code Classification of U.S. Customs
Districts and Ports, C 3.150:D
Schedule H. Statistical Classification and Code
Numbers of Shipments of Merchandise to
Alaska from United States, C 3.150:H
Schedule J. Code Classification of Flag of Vessel, C
3.150:J
Schedule K. Code Classification of Foreign Ports
by Geographic Trade Area and Country,
C 3.150:K
Schedule N. Method of Transportation Code,
Exports, C 3.150:N
Schedule R. Code Classification and Definitions of
Foreign Trade Areas, C 3.150:R
Specifications and Code Numbers for Individual
Commodities, L 2.61/3
Statistical Classification and Code Numbers of
Shipments of Merchandise to Alaska from
United States, C 3.150:H
United States Censuses of Population and
Housing: Geographic Identification
Code Scheme, Phc (2) (series), C 3.223/
13
United States Code, Y 1.2/5, Y 4.J 89/1:Un 3/3
Wholesale Code Regulations, Y 3.F 31/10:15
ZIP Code Directories {by States}, P 1.10/7
Code Number
List of Code Number Producers of Bituminous
Coal, I 34.22

Code to Name
H 8-2 Nongovernment Organization Codes for
Military Standard Contract Administra-
tion Procedures: Code to Name, D 7.6/
2:8-2/2
Coded
Army Coded Card, W 42.6
Codes
Approved Codes, Y 3.N 21/8:7
Buyer-Seller Codes Authorized for Reporting to
the Federal Energy Regulatory
Commission, E 3.35
Codes of Fair Competition, Y 3.N 21/8
Comparisons of State Safety Codes with A S A, L
16.7/2
Instructions for Classifying the Underlying Cause
of Death: Nonindexed Terms, Standard
Abbreviations, and State Geographic
Codes Used in Mortality Data
Classification, HE 20.6208/4
MILSTRIP Routing and Identifier and Distribution
Codes, D 1.87/2
MILSTRIP Routing Identifier Codes, D 7.6/16
Nongovernment Organization Codes for Military
Standard Contract Administration
Procedures: Code to Name, D 7.6/2:8-2/
2
Nongovernment Organization Codes for Military
Standard Contract Administration
Procedures: Name to Code, D 7.6/2:8-1/
2
Nongovernment Organization Codes for Military
Standard Contract Administration
Procedures, D 7.6/2:8
Woodland Management Plan, Agreements and Farm
Codes, A 57.37
Worldwide Geographic Location Codes, GS 1.34
Codification
Codification of Presidential Proclamations and
Executive Orders, GS 4.113/3
Coding
Computerized Geographic Coding Series, C 3.246,
C 56.237
Data Access Descriptions; Automated Address
Coding Guide and Data Retrieval Series,
ACC (nos.), C 3.240/2
Employee Benefits Survey Defined Benefit Pension
Coding Manual, L 2.46/7
Employee Benefits Survey Defined Contribution
Coding Manual, L 2.46/8
Employee Benefits Survey Health Coding Manual,
L 2.46/5
Employee Benefits Survey Sickness and Accident
Coding Manual, L 2.46/6
HCFA Common Procedure Coding System, HE
22.37
Instruction Manual: Classification and Coding
Instructions for Divorce Records, HE
20.6208/10
Instruction Manual: Classification and Coding
Instructions for Fetal Death Records, HE
20.6208/6-2
Instruction Manual: Classification and Coding
Instructions for Induced Termination of
Pregnancy Records, HE 20.6208/8
Instruction Manual: Classification and Coding
Instructions for Live Birth Records, HE
20.6208/6
Instruction Manual: Classification and Coding
Instructions for Marriage Records, HE
20.6208/7
Instruction Manual: Demographic Classification
and Coding Instructions for Death
Records, HE 20.6208/5
Public Use Data Tape Documentation Medical
Coding Manual and Short Index, HE
20.6226/9
Coffee
Coffee Inventories and Roastings, C 3.169
Current Business Reports; Green Coffee,
Inventories, Imports, Roastings, BG
(series), C 56.219/2
Green Coffee Inventories and Roastings, C 3.236
Industry Report, Coffee, Tea and Spices, C 18.240
Cognitive
Questionnaire Design in the Cognitive Research
Laboratory, HE 20.6209:6
Coin
Statement of United States Currency and Coin, T
63.188, T 63.308
Coinage
Domestic Coinage Executed During (month), T
28.12

General Instructions and Regulations in Relation
to Transaction of Business at Mints and
Assay Offices with Coinage Laws, T
28.9
Laws relating to Coinage, T 26.6/2, T 28.10
World Coinage Report, T 28.14
Coins
Laws Authorizing Issuance of Medals and
Commemorative Coins, Y 1.2:M 46
Coke
Coke and Byproducts Tables, I 28.36
Coke and Chemistry {abstracts}, C 41.64
Coke and Coal Chemicals, I 28.30, E 3.11/9
Coke and Coal Chemicals in (year), I 28.30/4
Coke Distribution, E 3.11/16
Coke Distribution, Annual, I 28.30/3
Coke Producers, E 3.11/16-2
Coke Producers in the United States in (year), I
28.30/2
Monthly Coke Report, C 22.15, I 28.30
Preliminary Estimates of Production of Coal and
Beehive Coke, I 28.31
Preliminary Estimates of Production of Pennsylva-
nia Anthracite and Beehive Coke, I
28.50
Quarterly Coke Report, E 3.11/9
Coke
Weekly Anthracite and Beehive Coke Reports, I
28.49
COL
COL- (series), ED 1.40/3
Cold
Cold Regions Research and Engineering
Laboratory R & D Notes, D 103.33/11
Cold Regions Science and Engineering, D 103.33/
7
Cold Regions Technical Digest (series), D 103.33/
13, D 103.33/14
Cold Storage, A 105.33
Cold Storage Holdings by States, A 36.197
Cold Storage Holdings of Fishery Products, I 49.8/
4
Cold Storage Reports, A 82.15, A 88.20
Cold Storage Stocks of Frozen Fruits and
Vegetables by Container Size, A 82.36
Cold Wave Bulletin, A 29.9
CWIHP (Cold War International History Project)
Bulletin, SI 1.3/2
Plastic Paints, Cold Water Paints, and Calcimines,
C 3.96
Regional Cold Storage Holdings, A 105.33/2
Research Reports Cold Regions Research and
Engineering Laboratory, D 103.33/3
Special Reports Cold Regions Research and
Engineering Laboratory, D 103.33/2
Summary of Cold Storage Stocks, A 36.191
Summary of Regional Cold Storage Holdings, A
88.20/2
Collaboration
International Agricultural Collaboration Series, A
67.20
Collaborative
Services Research Monograph Series, National
Polydrug Collaborative Project,
Treatment Manuals, HE 20.8216/2
Colleague
Dear Colleague (letter), HE 20.7035
Collected
Collected Reprints, C 52.23, C 55.334, C 55.428
Collected Reprints ESSA Institute for Oceanogra-
phy, C 52.23
Collected Reprints; Atlantic Oceanographic and
Meteorological Laboratories, C 55.612
Collected Reprints; Atmospheric Physics and
Chemistry Laboratory, C 55.612/3
Collected Reprints; Wave Propagation Laboratory,
C 55.612/2
Imported Merchandise Entered for Consumption in
United States, and Duties Collected
Thereon During the Quarter Ending, C
18.17
Collected Reprints
Collected Reprints National Marine Fisheries
Service, C 55.334
Collected Reprints National Ocean Survey, C
55.428
Collection
Collection of Circulars, etc., Issued by Office of
Internal Revenue, T 22.5
Collection of Legal Opinions, EP 1.63
Collection of Ordnance Reports and other
Important Papers Relating to Ordnance
Department, W 34.17

Columbia River
Base Flows As of {date} at Selected Gaging Stations in the **Columbia River** Basin, I 19.2:C 72/2
Storage in Major Power Reservoirs in the **Columbia River** Basin, I 19.47/2
Columbia River Basin
Monthly Mean Discharge at Selected Gaging Stations and Change of Storage in Certain Lakes and Reservoirs in **Columbia** River Basin, I 19.47
Columbian
Chicago, World's **Columbian** Exposition, 1893, S 6.19
Mandrid, **Columbian** Historical Exposition, S 6.7
Columbium
Columbium and Tantalum in (year), I 28.141
Columbus
Additions to **Columbus** Memorial Library, AR 1.7
Area Wage Survey Summary **Columbus**, Mississippi, L 2.122/24-3
Columns
Final **Columns**, C 3.31/1
Combat
Combat Connected Naval Casualties, World War II, by States, N 1.34/2
Combat Crew, D 301.81
Combat Orders, W 28.9
Combat Narratives, D 207.20
CTC Trends, **Combat** Maneuver Training Center (CMTC), D 101.22/26
Fixed Gunnery and **Combat** Tactics Series, N 27.12
The **Combat** Edge, D 301.44/2
Combatting
Public Report of the Vice President's Task Force on **Combatting** Terrorism, PrVp 40.2:T 27
Combined
Combined Annual and Revised Monthly Retail Trade, C 3.138/3-7
Combined Annual and Revised Monthly Wholesale Trade, C 3.133/4
Combined Compilation of Meat and Poultry Inspection Issuances, A 110.9/2, A 110.15:10
Combined Employment and Unemployment Releases, L 1.20/2
Combined Federal/State Disclosure Directory, Y 3.El 2/3:14-2
Combined Financial Statements of Members of the Federal Home Loan Bank System, FHL 1.12
Combined Lineal List of Officers on Active Duty in the Marine Corps, D 214.11
Combined Meat and Poultry Inspection Issuances for (year), A 110.9/2
Combined Production and Resources Board, United States, Great Britain, and Canada, Y 3.C 73/3
Combined Statement of Receipts, Expenditures, and Balances of United States, T 63.113
Combined Summary of Orders, ES 3.6/10-2
Combined Tribal and Bureau Law Enforcement Services: Annual Report, I 20.58
Farm Telephone and Electricity **Combined** Report, A 88.45/2
FHLB System S & L's **Combined** Financial Statements: Savings and Home Financing Source Book, FHL 1.12/2
Combustion
Coal, Quarterly Reports; Power and **Combustion**, ER 1.28, E 1.31/2
Coming
Work with Children **Coming** before the Courts, FS 3.223, FS 14.116
Comite
U.S. National Committee of the CCIR {**Comite** Consultatif International des Radiocommunication}: Publications, S 5.56
Command
Air Force **Command** and Control Development Division: Technical Notes AFCCDD-TN (nos.), D 301.45/24
Air Force Systems **Command** Annual Report, D 301.45/38
Armed Forces Staff College Essays on **Command** Issues, D 5.413/2
Army Material **Command** Regulations, D 101.9/2
Army Missile **Command** Redstone Scientific Information Center Redstone Arsenal Alabama RSIC (series), D 105.22/3
Army Transportation Research **Command**: Interim Reports, D 117.8/3
Command, D 2.15/3

Command Historical Report, D 206.1/3
Command Information Package, D 101.118/5
Command Employment Bulletin, Current Openings, G-11 and Above, at Army Material **Command** Activities Throughout the United States, D 101.3/5
Engineering **Command** Report, ENCR (series), D 116.14
General Headquarters, Far East **Command**, General Publications, D 1.24
Headquarters European **Command**, Publications, D 1.23
Military Sealift **Command**, D 216.8
Numerical and Functional Index of **Command** Forms, D 301.45/14-2:0-9
Pamphlets Naval Supply Systems **Command**, D 211.12
Posters Military Sealift **Command**, D 216.10
Potomac River Naval **Command** Publications, D 201.12
Publications Headquarters European **Command**, D 1.23
Publications Potomac River Naval **Command**, D 201.12
Releases, Air Research and Development **Command**, D 301.45/3
Research Bulletins Air Training **Command**, Human Resources Research Center, D 301.36/3
Research Reports Air Training **Command**, Human Resources Research Center, D 301.36/6
Research Review, Air Training **Command**, Human Resources Research Center, D 301.36/4
Sealift, Magazine of the Military Sealift **Command**, D 216.8
Seventy-Fifth USA Maneuver Area **Command**, Annual Report and Historical Supplement, D 101.1/8
Special Reports Air Force Systems **Command**, D 301.45/42
Specifications Naval Facilities Engineering **Command**, D 209.11
Strategic Air **Command**, Grissom Air Force Base Telephone Directory, D 301.104/6
Strategic Air **Command**, Vandenberg Air Force Base Telephone Directory, D 301.104/7
Strategic Air **Command**, Wurtsmith Air Force Base, Telephone Directory, D 301.104/5
Supply and Maintenance **Command** Regulations, D 101.9/3
Supply and Maintenance **Command**, SMC Pamphlets, D 101.22/5
Systems Engineering Group, Research and Technology Division, Air Force Systems **Command**, Wright-Patterson Air Force Base, Ohio, Technical Documentary Report No. SEG TDR, D 301.45/48
Technical Digest Naval Facilities Engineering **Command**, D 209.8
Technical Notes Department of the Air Force Alaskan Air **Command**, Arctic Aeromedical Laboratory, D 301.66
Technical Notes Department of the Air Force **Command** and Control Development Division, D 301.45/24
Technical Notes Naval Air Systems **Command**, N 28.6, M 208.10, D 202.7
Technical Research Reports Published by Air Force Personnel and Training Center Air Research and Development **Command**, D 301.26/10
Transportation Research and Development **Command**: Research Technical Memorandums, D 117.8
U.S. Army Materiel **Command**, Annual Historical Review, D 101.1/4-2
U.S. Army Recruiting **Command** Pamphlets, USAREC PAM- (series), D 101.22/7
Commandant
Commandant of the Marine Corps FY Posture Statement, D 214.1
Regulations for United States Corps of Cadets Prescribed by **Commandant** of Cadets, M 109.6/2
Commandant's
Commandant's Bulletin, TD 5.3/9
Commandant's International Technical Series, TD 5.48
Commanded
Nature to Be **Commanded**, I 19.16:950
Commander
Publications Supreme Allied **Commander** in Europe, D 9.8

Publications Supreme **Commander** for Allied Powers, D 102.11
Supreme **Commander** for Allied Powers, Publications, D 102.11
Supreme **Commander** for Allied Powers: Japanese Economic Statistics Bulletin, D 102.18
Supreme **Commander** for Allied Powers: Natural Resources Section Reports, D 102.20
Commanders
Commanders Call Support Materials, D 101.22:360
Commanders Digest, D 2.15/2
Commanders Digest Indexes, D 2.15/2-2
For **Commanders**, This Changing World, D 2.15
Commands
Military **Commands** and Posts, etc., W 3.20
United States Air Force, **Commands** and Agencies Basic Information, D 301.26/23
Commemorative
Commemorative Stamp Posters, P 1.26/2
Laws Authorizing Issuance of Medals and **Commemorative** Coins, Y 1.2:M 46
Marines in World War II **Commemorative** Series, D 214.14/4
Mint Set of **Commemorative** Stamps, P 1.26/4, P 1.54
NEH Fellowships University Teachers, College Teachers, and Independent Scholars Anniversary and **Commemorative** Initiatives, NF 3.13/4
Description of U.S. Postal Stamp, Historical and **Commemorative** Issues (Junior Edition), P 4.11
Comment
Bench **Comment**, a Periodic Guide to Recent Appellate Treatment of Practical Procedural Issues, Ju 13.8/2
Manual for Review and **Comment**, HE 20.2588/2
Monthly **Comment** of Aviation Trends, C 31.152
News, Reviews, and **Comment**, Y 3.N 88:49
Commentary
Traffic Laws **Commentary**, TD 8.5/2
Comments
Comments on Economic and Housing Situation, HH 2.19
Comments on the Office of Inspector General's Semiannual Report to the Congress, Y 3.L 52:1/2
Forest Service **Comments** on Resolutions Relating to the National Forest System As Adopted, A 13.86
Summary of Press **Comments**, A 55.27
Commerce
Activity Report of Committee on **Commerce**, Y 4.C 73/2:Ac 8
Advance Bulletin of Interstate **Commerce** Acts Annotated, IC 1 act.5/3, IC 1 act.5/3-2
Advance Sheets from Monthly Summary of the Foreign **Commerce** of the Unted States, C 18.8
Air **Commerce** Bulletin, C 23.12, CAB 1.8
Air **Commerce** Manuals, C 23.6/4
Air **Commerce** Traffic Patterns, C 3.153, FAA 4.11
Air **Commerce** Traffic Patterns (scheduled carriers), Fiscal Year, FAA 8.9
Annual Report of Secretary, Department of **Commerce** and Labor, C 1.1
Approved Conference Rate and Interconference Agreements of Steamship Lines in the Foreign **Commerce** of the United States, FMC 1.11
Bulletin of **Commerce**, C 18.269 C 41.10
Catalog and Index, U.S. Department of **Commerce** Publications, C 1.54/2
Catalogue of Book and Blanks Furnished by Department of **Commerce** to Customs Officers, C 1.16
Commerce America, C 1.58/2
Commerce America {by State}, C 1.58/3
Commerce Budget in Brief, Fiscal Year, C 1.39
Commerce Business Daily, C 1.76, C 57.20
Commerce in Firearms in the United States T 70.24
Commerce in {year}, Annual Report of the Secretary of **Commerce**, C 1.1
Commerce Library Bulletin, C 1.67
Commerce Log, C 1.38
Commerce News Digest, C 1.40
Commerce News, Recent **Commerce** Publications, C 1.24/2
Commerce Publications Catalog and Index, C 1.54/2
Commerce Publications Update, C 1.24/3
Commerce Reports, C 18.5/1
Commerce Today, C 1.58

Commercial Tobacco-Livestock Farms, Bluegrass Area, Kentucky and Penny-Royal Grass Area, Kentucky-Tennessee, A 93.9/11

Commercial Vegetables TC (series), A 88.12/6

Commercial Wheat Farms, Plains and Pacific Northwest, A 93.9/11

Consumer Installment Credit at Commercial Banks, FR 1.36/2

Consumption of Commercial Fertilizers and Primary Plant Nutrients in United States, A 92.37

Country Commercial Guides, S 1.40/7

Country Commercial Program for {various countries}, C 1.64

Cumulative Index to Foreign Production and Commercial Reports, C 42.15/3-2

Economic Control and Commercial Policy in American Republics, TC 1.20

Estimated Numbers of Apple Trees by Varieties and Ages in Commercial and Farm Orchards, A 36.52

Foreign Production and Commercial Reports, C 42.15/3

Household and Commercial Pottery Industry in {various countries}, C 41.100

Index to Foreign Production and Commercial Reports, Cumulative Indexes, C 42.15/3-3

Laws and Regulations for Protection of Commercial Fisheries of Alaska, I 45.11

Laws Relating to Commercial Air Service and Miscellaneous Air Laws, Y 1.2:Ai 7

Lists of Commercial Treaties and Conventions, and Agreements Affected by Exchange of Notes or Declarations in Force Between United States and Other Countries, S 9.9

Loan Commitments at Selected Large Commercial Banks, FR 1.39/3

Major Nondeposit Funds of Commercial Banks, FR 1.39/4

Market for Selected U.S. Household and Commercial Gas Appliances in {various countries}, C 41.106

Occupational Radiation Exposure at Commercial Nuclear Power Reactors and Other Facilities, Y 3.N 88:10-5

Office of Technical Services Reports Suitable for Commercial Publications, Bulletins, C 35.10

Operations of the Bureau of Commercial Fisheries Under the Saltonstall-Kennedy Act, I 49.48

Report of Bureau of Commercial Fisheries for Calendar Year (date), I 49.1/2

Report of Calls, Assets, Liabilities, Capital, Accounts, Commercial and Mutual Savings Banks (unnumbered), Y 3.F 31/8:9-2

Storage Capacity of Elevators Reporting Commercial Grain Stocks, A 88.18/15

Summary of Accounts and Deposits in All Commercial and Mutual Savings Banks, Y 3.F 31/8:22

Summary of Accounts and Deposits in All Commercial Banks {by districts}, Y 3.F 31/8:20 CT

Total Commercial Production of All Vegetables and Melons for Fresh Market and Processing, A 92.11/10-3

Typical Commercial and Industrial Electric Bills, FP 1.16/4

Typical Electric Bills, Typical Net Monthly Bills of January (year), for Residential Commercial and Industrial Services, FP 1.10

Weekly Condition Report of Large Commercial Banks in New York and Chicago, FR 1.16

World List of Future International Meeting: Pt. 2, Social, Cultural, Commercial, Humanistic, LC 2.9/2

Commission

Actions of Commission, Reports (Telephone and Telegraph), CC 1.20/3

Actions of Commission, Reports {Broadcast}, CC 1.20/2

Administrative Law Judge and Commission Decisions, Y 3.Oc 1:10-2

Civil Service Commission Offices, CS 1.28:2301

Commission Appointed to Examine French Spoilation Claims Presented Under Treaty with France of July 4, 1831, S 3.5

Commission Decisions, Y 3.Oc 1:10-6

Commission Instructions in Docket Cases, CC 1.33/2

Commission Letters, CS 1.67

Commission Meeting Agenda, CC 1.52

Commission of Inquiry and Conciliation, Bolivia and Paraguay, Report of Chairman, S 3.40

Commission on CIA Activities Within the United States: Report, Pr 38.8:C 33

Commission on Extraterritorial Jurisdiction in China, S 3.36

Commission on International Trade and Investment Policy, Pr 37.8:In 8/2

Commission to Arbitrate Claims of Venezuela Steam Transportation Company of New York against Venezuela, S 3.11

Commission to Revise the Laws of the United States: Publications, J 1.10

Commission, FMC 1.10/a2

Construction Industry Stabilization Commission Regulations, ES 2.6/4

Federal Communication Commission Daily, CC 1.56

Federal Communications Commission Reports: Second Series, CC 1.12/2

Inter-American Development Commission, S 5.43

National Commission News, S 5.48/2

Official Bulletin Federal Radio Commission, RC 1.5

Official Gazette of Allied High Commission for Germany, S 1.88

Orders Consumer Product Safety Commission, Y 3.C 76/3:6-2

Orders Federal Energy Regulatory Commission, E 2.10

Orders Federal Power Commission, FP 1.19

Orders Interstate Commerce Commission, IC 1.9

Orders, Notices, Rulings and Decisions Issued by Hearing Examiners and by the Commission in Formal Docketed Proceedings before the Federal Maritime Commission

OSAHRE Reports: Decisions of the Occupational Safety and Health Review Commission, Y 3.Oc 1:10

Pamphlets Civil Service Commission, CS 1.48

Papers in Re Indian Claims Commission, J 1.85

Political Activity of Government Personnel Commission, Y 3.P 75

Posters Bicentennial of the United States Constitution Commission, Y 3.B 47/2:12

Posters Civil Service Commission, CS 1.89

Posters Federal Holiday Commission, Y 3.H 71:12

Posters Federal Trade Commission, FT 1.31

President's Commission for Observance of 25th Anniversary of the United Nations, Pr 37.8:Un 3

President's Commission on All-volunteer Armed Forces, Pr 37.8:Ar 5

President's Commission on Campus Unrest, Pr 37.8:C 15

President's Commission on Coal, Pr 39.8:C 63

President's Commission on Federal Statistics, Pr 37.8:St 2

President's Commission on Holocaust, Pr 39.8:H 74

President's Commission on Mental Health, Pr 39.8:M 52

President's Commission on National Agenda for the Eighties, Pr 39.8:Ag 3

President's Commission on Olympic Sports, Pr 38.8:Ol 9

President's Commission on Pension Policy, Pr 39.8:P 38

President's Commission on Personnel Interchange, Pr 37.8:P 43

President's Commission on School Finance, Pr 37.8:Sch 6

Press Releases Securities and Exchange Commission, SE 1.25/8

Price Schedules National Bituminous Coal Commission, I 34.19

Progress Report to the Secretary of Education from the President's Advisory Commission on Educational Excellence for Hispanic Americans, ED 1.87

Publications National Historical Publications Commission, GS 4.14

Publications Tariff Commission, TC 1.34

Quarterly Review of Commission Proceedings, NC 2.11

Recruiting Bulletins Civil Service Commission, CS 1.51

Regulations, Rules and Instructions International Trade Commission, ITC 1.6

Regulations, Rules and Instructions United States Parole Commission, J 27.6

Report Coordinating Group Annual Report to the Securities and Exchange Commission, SE 1.32

Report of Federal Trade Commission on Rates of Return (after taxes) for Identical Companies in Selected Manufacturing Industries, FT 1.21

Report of Interagency Substances Data Commission, EP 1.79/4

Report of President's Airport Commission, Pr 33.16

Report of United States High Commissioner, Statistical Annex, U.S. Element, Allied Commission for Austria, S 1.89/2

Report of United States High Commissioner, U.S. Element, Allied Commission for Austria, S 1.89

Resources for Freedom, Research to the President by President's Materials Policy Commission, Pr 33.15

Revenue Commission, Reports (general), T 1.18/1

Revenue Commission, Special Reports (numbered), T 1.18/2

Rules of Practice and Rules Relating to Investigations and Code of Behavior Governing Exparte Communications Between Persons Outside the Commission and Decisional Employees, SE 1.6:R 86/4

Rules of Practice Federal Power Commission, FP 1.8

Rules of Practice Federal Trade Commission, FT 1.7

Safety Bulletins Employees Compensation Commission, EC 1.9

Selected Publications of the United States International Trade Commission, ITC 1.9/3

Service and Regulatory Announcements Alaska Game Commission, A 5.10/5

Service and Regulatory Announcements Civil Service Commission, CS 1.5

Sheets of National Atlas of United States Interstate Commerce Commission, IC 1.30

Spanish-American Peace Commission, S 3.22

Special Bulletins Civil Service Commission, CS 1.47

Special Bulletins Employees' Compensation Commission, EC 1.3/2

Statistical Bulletins Fish Commission, FC 1.5

Statistical Bulletins Securities and Exchange Commission, SE 1.20

Statistical Series Federal Power Commission, FP 1.21

Statistical Series Securities and Exchange Commission, SE Statistical Series, Annual Data, Data from the Drug Abuse Warning Network (DAWN), Series I, HE 20.8212/11

Statistics of Class a Telephone Carriers Reporting Annually to the Commission, As of December 31 (year) and for Year Then Ended, CC 1.14/2

Statistics of Principal Domestic and International Telegraph Carriers Reporting to the Commission As of December 31 (year) and for Year Then Ended, CC 1.41

Statutes and Decisions Pertaining to the Federal Trade Commission, FT 1.13/2

Supplement to Index to Commission Decisions, SE 1.11/2

Table of Defendants Before Interstate Commerce Commission, IC 1.6/4

Tariff Circulars Federal Communications Commission, CC 1.16

Tariff Circulars Maritime Commission, MC 1.21

Tariff Circulars Rate Section, Interstate Commerce Commission, IC 1 rat.4

Technical Memorandum To United States Study Commission, Southeast River Basins, A 57.50

Telephone Directory Civil Rights Commission, CR 1.16

Telephone Directory Federal Communications Commission, CC 1.53

Telephone Directory Federal Energy Regulatory Commission, E 2.12/2

Telephone Directory Interstate Commerce Commission, IC 1.37

Telephone Directory Nuclear Regulatory Commission, Y 3.N 88

Treasury Cattle **Commission**, Reports, T 1.20

Tripartite Claims **Commission** (U.S., Austria, and Hungary), S 3.37

Two Centuries of Tariffs, the Background and Emergence of the U.S. International Trade **Commission**, TC 1.2:T 17/20

U.S. National **Commission** for UNESCO Memos, S 5.48/14

U.S. National **Commission** for UNESCO Newsletter, S 5.48/5

U.S. National **Commission** for UNESCO, S 5.48/7

U.S. Nuclear Regulatory **Commission** Regulations {List}, Y 3.N 88:21

United States Advisory **Commission** on Information, Semiannual Report to Congress, S 1.93

United States and Chilean Claims **Commission**, 1892-94, S 3.21/2

United States and Chilean Claims **Commission**, 1900-01, S 3.21/3

United States and Mexican Claims **Commission**, 1869-76, S 3.12

Update National **Commission** on the Observance of Update from State, S 1.118/2

Utah **Commission**, Annual Reports, I 1.31

Volume and Composition of Individuals' Savings Securities and Exchange **Commission**, SE 1.25/6

Washington Arbitration (American-British Mixed Claims **Commission**), S 3.13/2

Working Papers National Transportation Policy Study **Commission**, Y 3.T 68/2:10

Commission Officers

List and Station of **Commission Officers**, T 33.10

Commission's

Standard Broadcast Applications Ready and Available for Processing Pursuant to Sec. 1.354 (c) of **Commission's** Rules, Lists, CC 1.26/2

Commissional

Presidential **Commissional** on World Hunger, Pr 39.8:W 89/3

Commissioned

CCPM Pamphlets {**Commissioned** Corps Personnel Manual}, HE 20.13

Chronological List of Official Orders to **Commissioned** and Other Officers, FS 2.28

Commissioned Corps Bulletin, HE 20.3/2

Commissioned Corps Personnel Manual, HE 20.13/3

Lineal List of **Commissioned** and Warrant Officers of the Marine Corps Reserves, D 214.11/2

Official List of **Commissioned** and Other Officers of U.S. Public Health and Marine Hospital Service, T 27.5

Register of Civil Engineer Corps **Commissioned** and Warrant Officers of United States Navy and Naval Reserve on Active Duty, D 209.9

Register of **Commissioned** and Warrant Officers Coast Guard Reserve, T 47.10/2

Register of **Commissioned** and Warrant Officers Marine Corps Reserve, N 9.20

Register of **Commissioned** and Warrant Officers Naval Militia, N 1.27/6

Register of **Commissioned** and Warrant Officers Naval Reserve Force, N 25.6

Register of **Commissioned** and Warrant Officers Naval Reserve, N 17.38

Register of **Commissioned** and Warrant Officers Navy and Marine Corps and Reserve Officers on Active Duty, D 208.12

Register of **Commissioned** and Warrant Officers United States Naval Reserve, D 208.12/2

Register of **Commissioned** and Warrant Officers United States Navy and Marine Corps, M 206.10

Register of Retired **Commissioned** and Warrant Officers, Regular and Reserve, of the United States Navy and Marine Corps, D 208.12/3

Roster of **Commissioned** Officers and Employees, A 29.28

Useful Information for Newly **Commissioned** Officers, D 207.215

Commissioner

American High **Commissioner** to Haiti, S 1.22

Commissioner, Y 3.J 27:7

Commissioner of Public Buildings, Annual Reports, I 1.51

Cuba and Puerto Rico Special **Commissioner**, T 1.16

High **Commissioner** of Trust Territory of Pacific Islands, I 35.16

Historical Monographs of Office of U.S. High **Commissioner** for Germany, S 1.95

Indian Affairs, (year), Progress Report from the **Commissioner** of Indian Affairs, I 20.1

Military Government, Austria, Report of United States **Commissioner**, W 1.74, M 105.10

Preliminary Report of **Commissioner** of Internal Revenue, T 22.7

Puerto Rico Special **Commissioner** (Carroll), T 1.17

Quarterly Report on Germany, Office of U.S. High **Commissioner** for Germany, S 1.90

Report of Austria, Office of U.S. High **Commissioner** for Austria, S 1.89/3

Report of United States High **Commissioner**, Statistical Annex, U.S. Element, Allied Commission for Austria, S 1.89/2

Report of United States High **Commissioner**, U.S. Element, Allied Commission for Austria, S 1.89

Report on Austria, Office of U.S. High **Commissioner** for Austria, S 1.89/3

Revenue, Special **Commissioner**, Annual Reports, T 1.19

Summary Report of the **Commissioner**, Bureau of Reclamation {and} Statistical Appendix, I 27.1/2

Commissioner's

Commissioner's Letters, FW 4.39

Commissioner's Report on the Education Professions, HE 19.124

Commissioners

Register of U.S. **Commissioners**, J 1.18

Commissioning

Basic Tables of **Commissioning** Allowances, N 28.15

Commissions

Reports of Special Agents and **Commissions**, I 20.6

Special Committees and **Commissions**, Pr 43.8

State Regulatory **Commissions** and Fuel Tax Divisions, IC 1.3/2-2

Venezuelan Mixed Claims **Commissions**, Caracas 1902 and 1903, S 3.17

Commitment

America's **Commitment**: Federal Programs Benefiting Women and New Initiatives as Follow-up to the U.N. Fourth World Conference on Women, Pr 42.8:W 84

Commitment, HE 20.6015

Commitments

Commitments of Large Traders in Cotton Futures, A 85.9

Commitments of Traders in Commodity Futures, Y 3.C 73/5:9/2

Commitments of Traders in Commodity Futures with Market Concentration Ratios, Y 3.C 73/5:9

Commitments of Traders in Commodity Futures, Cotton, Frozen Concentrated Orange Juice, Potatoes, A 85.9

Commitments of Traders in Commodity Futures, Cotton, Wool, Potatoes, A 85.9

Commitments of Traders in Wheat, Corn, Oats, Rye, Soybeans, Soybean Oil, Soybean Meal, Shell Eggs, A 85.9/2

Commitments of Traders in Wool and Wool Top Futures, New York Cotton Exchange, A 85.9/3

Loan **Commitments** at Selected Large Commercial Banks, FR 1.39/3

Committee

A Report by the FCCSET **Committee** on Life Sciences and Health, PrEx 8.111/2

Activities of House **Committee** on Government Operations, Y 4.G 74/7:Ac 8/3

Activity Report of **Committee** on Commerce, Y 4.C 73/2:Ac 8

Adult Development and Aging Research **Committee**, HE 20.3001/2:Ad 9

Budget Explanatory Notes for **Committee** on Appropriations, A 13.130

Committee Publications and Policies Governing their Distribution, Y 4.Ec 7-10

Federal Advisory **Committee** Annual Report of the President, Pr 42.10

Interagency **Committee** on Women's Business Enterprise, Annual Report to Congress, Pr 40.8:W 84, SBA 1.31

Interbureau Forage **Committee** Publications I.F.C., A 1.49

List of Committee Hearings, **Committee** Prints and Publications of the United States Senate, Y 1.3/10

Official Bulletin **Committee** on Public Information, Y 3.P 93/3:3

Outer Continental Shelf Environmental Studies Advisory **Committee**: Publications, I 1.99/2

Periodontal Diseases Advisory **Committee**, HE 20.3001/2:P 41

Pharmacology-Toxicology Program **Committee**, HE 20.3001/2:P 49/2

Population Research **Committee**, HE 20.3001/2:P 81

President's **Committee** on Employment of the Handicapped, Annual Report to Membership, .PrEx 1.10/13

President's **Committee** on Employment of the Handicapped: People with Disabilities in Our Nation's Job Training Partnership Act Programs, PrEx 1.10/15

President's **Committee** on Employment of the Handicapped: Press Releases, PrEx 1.10/4

President's **Committee** on Health Education, Pr 37.8:H 34

Presidential Advisory **Committee** on Small and Minority Business Ownership, Annual Report, PrEx 1.16

Primate Research Centers Advisory **Committee**, HE 20.3001/2:P 93

Proceedings Interdepartmental Board on Simplified Office Procedure, Executive **Committee** Meeting, T 51.11/5

Proceedings National Brucellosis **Committee** and Progress Report of the Cooperative State-Federal Brucellosis Eradication Program, A 77.202:B 83/16

Program Guide President's **Committee** on Employment of the Handicapped, PrEx 1.10/7

Publications List Senate **Committee** on Energy and Natural Resources, Y 4.En 2:P 96

Publications List Senate Special **Committee** on Aging, Y 4.Ag 4:P 96

Publications National **Committee** on Wood Utilization, C 1.14

Report of Classified Program of Exports and Value by American Agencies Voluntarily Registered with Advisory **Committee** on Voluntary Foreign Aid, S 1.99/2

Report of the Activities of the **Committee** on Armed Services, Y 4.Ar 5/2-13

Report of the Activities of the **Committee** on Science and Astronautics, Y 4.Sci 2:Ac 8

Report of the FCCSET **Committee** on Education and Human Resources, PrEx 8.111

Report of the Interdepartment Radio Advisory **Committee**, C 60.15

Report of the Secretary and Financial Report of the Executive **Committee** of the Board of Regents, SI 1.1/a

Report of the Senate **Committee** on Labor and Human Resources Presenting its View and Estimates Pursuant to the Congressional Budget Act, Y 4.L 11/4:C 76

Report of the Senate Impeachment Trial **Committee**, Y 4.Im 7/2

Report on Washington Conference on National Women's Advisory **Committee** on FCDA, FCD 1.18/2

Report to the **Committee** on the Budget from the Committee on Veterans' Affairs, Y 4.V 64/3-10

Report to the **Committee** on the Budget; Views and Estimates of the **Committee** on Interior and Insular Affairs (House), Y 4.In 8/14-11

Report to the **Committee** on the Budget Views and Estimates of the **Committee** on Natural Resources, Y 4.R 31/3-11

Report to the Congress and the Trade Policy **Committee** on Trade Between the U.S. and the Nonmarket Economy Countries, ITC 1.13

Reports of **Committee** on Tidal Hydraulics, D 103.28

Reports of the Advisory **Committee** to the Administrator on Standards for the Administration of Juvenile Justice, J 1.48

Rules for the **Committee** on Interior and Insular Affairs, Y 4.In 8/14-13

Rules of Procedure, **Committee** on the Judiciary, Y 4.J 89/2-10

Rules of Procedure for the Permanent Select **Committee** on Intelligence, Y 4.In 8/18-10

Rules of Procedure of the **Committee** on House Administration, Y 4.H 81/3-10

Rules of the **Committee** on Government Operations, Y 4.G 74/7-10

Rules of the **Committee** on Small Business, Y 4.Sm 1-10

Rules of the Select **Committee** on Narcotics Abuse and Control, Y 4.N 16/10

SCC {Ship Structure **Committee**}, Y 3.Sh 6:6/SSC

Scientific Aids to Learning **Committee**, Publications, NA 2.6

Secretary of State's Advisory **Committee** on Private International Law: Publications, S 1.130

Shipping Coordinating **Committee**, S 1.130/2:Sh 6

Sickle Cell Disease Advisory **Committee**, HE 20.3001/2:Si 1

Special Reports Central Housing **Committee**, Y 3.C 33/3:9

Standardization of Petroleum Specifications **Committee**, Bulletins, I 28.15

State **Committee** Letters, A 55.43/9, A 55.46/6

Statement of Voluntary Credit Restraint **Committee**, FR 1.35

Subcommittee on Oversight and Investigations of the **Committee** on Energy and Commerce, Y 4.En 2/3-12

Summary of Activities House Post Office and Civil Service **Committee**, Y 4.P 84/10:Ac 8

Summary of Activities House Science and Technology **Committee**, Y 4.Sci 2-10

Summary of Activities Senate Banking, Housing, and Urban Affairs **Committee**, Y 4.B 22/3:Ac 8

Summary of Reports Received by **Committee** on Medical Research, Pr 32.413/10

Summary Progress Report, Tropical Deterioriation **Committee**, Pr 32.413/11

Summary Statement of Income and Expenditures of Voluntary Relief Agencies Registered with Advisory **Committee** on Voluntary Foreign Aid, S 1.99/3

Summary Technical Report of National Defense Research **Committee**, Pr 32.413/12

Survey of Activities of the **Committee** on Foreign Affairs, Y 4.F 76/1:Ac 8

Technical Bulletin of **Committee** on Tidal Hydraulics, D 103.28/2

Technical **Committee** Executive Summary (series), Y 3.W 58/4:11

Technical **Committee** Reports, Y 3.W 58/4:12

Therapeutic Evaluations **Committee**, HE 20.3001/2:T 34

Third National Cancer Survey Utilization Advisory **Committee**, HE 20.3001/2:C 16/7

Transplantation and Immunology **Committee**, HE 20.3001/2:T 68

Transportation **Committee** Bulletins, Pr 32.4235

Transportation **Committee** News, Pr 32.4261

U.S. National **Committee** of the CCIR {Comite Consultatif International des Radiocommunication}: Publications, S 5.56

Undersea Warfare **Committee** Publications, NA 2.10

Veterans Emergency Housing Program: Community Action Report to Mayor's Emergency Housing **Committee**, NHA 1.12, Y 3.H 81/2:8

Views and Estimates of the **Committee** on Education, Y 4.Ed 8/1-11

Views and Estimates of the **Committee** on Foreign Affairs on the Budget, Y 4.F 76/1:B 85

Views of the **Committee** on Appropriations, United States Senate, on the First Concurrent Resolution on the Budget, Y 4.Ap 6/2:B 85/5

Virus Cancer Program Advisory **Committee**, HE 20.3001/2:V 81/4

Virus Cancer Program Scientific Review **Committee** A, HE 20.3001/2:V 81/2

Vision Research Program **Committee**, HE 20.3001/2:V 82/3

Voluntary Service National Advisory **Committee**: Report of Annual Meeting, VA 1.52

Wage **Committee**: Annual Report of Activities, VA 1.51

Wage Stabilization **Committee** Releases, WSC (series), ES 2.7/2

Weekly Summary of Federal Legislation Relating to National Resources **Committee**, Activities Bulletins, Y 3.N 21/12:15

Woman's Liberty Loan **Committee** (miscellaneous publications), T 1.25/5

Committee Rules

Committee Rules and Rules for Investigative Hearings Conducted by Subcommittees of the Committee on Armed Services, Y 4.Ar 5/2-15

Committeeman's

Committeeman's Practice Handbooks (by States), A 82.107

Committeemen

A.A.A. Flashes, Facts for **Committeemen**, A 55.42/11, A 76.410

Committeemen's Letters, A 55.32, A 55.42/7, A 55.43/7, A 55.44/7, A 5.45/7, A 55.46/7

Facts for Northeast **Committeemen**, A 55.14/13

Production-Conservation Program, **Committeemen's** Handbooks, A 80.2158

Committees

Administration of Relief **Committees**, Y 3.P 92:6

Annual Report of Political **Committees** Supporting Candidates for House of Representatives, Y 1.2/4

Public Advisory **Committees**: Authority, Structure, Functions, HE 20.4022

Public Advisory **Committees**: Authority, Structure, Functions, Members, HE 20.1000

Report to the Senate and House **Committees** on the Budget As Required by Public Law 93-344, Y 10.13

Roster of Members of PHS Public Advisory Groups, Councils, **Committees**, Boards, Panels, Study Sections, HE 20.2:Ad 9/3

Rules Adopted by the **Committees** of the House of Representatives, Y 4.R 86/1-12

Special **Committees** and Commissions, Pr 43.8

USIA Private Sector **Committees** Annual Report, IA 1.28

Views and Estimates of **Committees** of the House (together with Supplemental and Minority Views) on the Congressional Budget for Fiscal Year (date), Y 4.B 85/3-11

Commodities

All **Commodities**, IC 1.23/9:SS-1

Average Wholesale Prices and Index Numbers of Individual **Commodities**, L 2.33

Car-Lot Shipments of Fruits and Vegetables, by **Commodities**, States, and Months, A 1.34, A 66.24

Carlot Unloads of Fruits and Vegetables by **Commodities**, A 88.12/5

Census of Business; 1939, Retail Trade, Commodity Sales (by **Commodities**), C 3.940-24

Census of Distribution; Distribution of Agricultural **Commodities**, C 3.37/34

Census of War **Commodities**, C 3.27

Changes in List of **Commodities** Included in Wholesale Price Index, L 2.61/4

Commodities Schedule A. Statistical Classification on **Commodities** Imported into the United States with Rates of Duty and Tariff Paragraphs, C 3.150:A

Commodities Schedule B. Statistical Classification of Domestic and Foreign **Commodities** Exported from the United States, C 3.150:Bc

Commodities and Services Manual, L 2.46/2

Commodities Included in (various) Products Group for Revised Wholesale Price Index, L 2.61/3

Consumer Price Index {by individual cities and **commodities**}, L 2.38/5

Current Statement of Loans by Years and **Commodities**, Y 3.C 73:12

Digest of Decisions of Secretary of Agriculture under Perishable Agricultural **Commodities** Act, A 82.55

Digest of Decisions Secretary of Agriculture under Perishable Agricultural **Commodities** Act, A 82.55

Directory of **Commodities** and Services, ES 3.10

Directory of **Commodities** and Services Exempted or Suspended from Price Control, ES 3.10/2

Foreign Agricultural Trade of the United States, Trade by **Commodities**, A 93.17/8

Freight Revenue and Wholesale Value at Destination of **Commodities** Transported by by Class I Line-haul Railroads, IC 1.29

Fresh Fruit and Vegetable Shipments by States, **Commodities**, Counties, Stations, Calendar Year (date), A 88.12/31:6, A 88.40/2:12

Fresh Fruit and Vegetable Shipments, by **Commodities**, States, Months, Calendar Year (date), A 88.12/31:7, A 88.40/2:14

Imports and Exports of **Commodities** by U.S. Coastal Districts and Foreign Trade Regulations, SB 7.5/275, C 27.9/4, MC 1.11

Index Numbers of Wholesale Prices by Groups and Subgroups of **Commodities**, L 2.49/3

Mineral **Commodities** Summaries, I 28.148

Monthly Commodity Futures Statistics on Futures Trading in **Commodities** Regulated under the Commodity Exchange Act, A 85.15/2

Orderly Liquidation of Stock of Agricultural **Commodities** Held by the Commodity Credit Corporation, A 1.102

Specifications and Code Numbers for Individual **Commodities**, L 2.61/3

State Carlot Shipments of Fruits and Vegetables, by **Commodities**, Counties, and Billing Stations, A 88.12/10

Statement of Loans and **Commodities** Owned, A 71.7, A 80.407, A 82.307

Statistical Classification of Domestic and Foreign **Commodities** Exported from the United States, C 3.150:B

Statistical Classification on **Commodities** Imported into the United States with Rates of Duty and Tariff Paragraphs, C 3.150:A

Table of **Commodities** in the Decisions, IC 1.6/7

Tons of Revenue Freight Originated and Tons Terminated in Carloads by Classes of **Commodities** and by Geographic Areas, Class 1 Steam Railways, IC 1 ste.42

U.S. Exports of Reported Agricultural **Commodities** for (dates), Marketing Years, A 67.40/4

U.S. Foreign Trade (by **Commodities**), C 18.211

U.S. Water Borne Intercoastal Traffic by Ports of Origin and Destination and Principal **Commodities**, SB 7.5/317, C 27.9/9, MC 1.9

Wholesale Price Index (1947-49=100), Indexes for Groups, Subgroups, and Project Classes of **Commodities**, L 2.61/2

Wholesale Price Index (1947-49=100), Prices and Price Relatives for Individual **Commodities**, 1951-53, L 2.61/6, L 2.61/6-2

Commodity

ASCS **Commodity** Fact Sheets, A 82.82/2

Carload Waybill Analyses, Distribution of Freight Traffic and Revenue Averages by **Commodity** Groups and Rate Territories, IC 1.20

Carload Waybill Analyses, State by State Distribution of Tonnage by **Commodity** Groups, IC 1.21

Carload Waybill Analyses, Territorial Distribution, Traffic and Revenue by **Commodity** Groups, IC 1.22

Carload Waybill Statistics, Distribution of Freight Traffic and Revenue Averages by **Commodity** Classes, IC 1.23/8

Carload Waybill Statistics, Quarterly Comparisons, Traffic and Revenue by **Commodity** Classes, IC 1.23

Carload Waybill Statistics, Territorial Distribution Traffic and Revenue by **Commodity** Classes, TD 3.14

Carload Waybill Statistics,..., Traffic and Revenue by **Commodity** Class, Territorial Movement, and Type of Rate, Products of Mines, 1 Percent Sample of Terminations in Statement MB-3, IC 1.23/4

Carload Waybill Statistics,..., Traffic and Revenue by **Commodity** Class, Territorial Movement, and Type of Rate, Products of Agriculture, 1 Percent Sample of Terminations in Statement MB-1, IC 1.23/2

United States Exports of Domestic and Foreign
Merchandise Under Lend-Lease
Program, Country of Destination by
Commodity, C 3.164:421, C 3.164:425
United States Exports of Domestic and Foreign
Merchandise Under United Nations
Relief and Rehabilitation Program,
Country of Destination by **Commodity**,
C 3.164:426
United States Exports of Domestic and Foreign
Merchandise Under United Nations
Relief and Rehabilitation Program,
Commodity by Country of Destination,
C 3.164:416
United States Exports of Petroleum and Petroleum
Products of Domestic Origin,
Commodity by Country of Destination,
C 3.164:526
United States General Imports and Imports for
Consumption from Canada and Mexico,
Exluding Strategic, Military and Critical
Materials, Country by **Commodity**
Totals, C 3.164:121
United States General Imports of Merchandise,
Commodity by Country of Origin, C
3.164:10
United States General Imports of Textile
Manufactures, Except Cotton and Wool,
Grouping by Country of Origin and
Schedule a **Commodity** by Country of
Origin, TQ-2501, C 3.164/2-7
United States General Imports of Wool Manufacture
Except Floor Coverings, Quantity Totals
in Terms of Equivalent Square Yards in
Country of Origin by **Commodity**
Grouping Arrangement, TQ-2203, C
3.164/2-6
United States Imports of Merchandise for
Consumption: **Commodity** by Country
of Origin, C 3.164:110
United States Standards for Grades of {**commod-
ity**}, A 88.6/2
United States, Airborne General Imports of
Merchandise, **Commodity** by Country of
Origin, C 3.164:380
Weight Distribution of Carloads for Each
Commodity Class by Type of Car, IC
1.23/16:TC-2
Commodore
Commodore, D 211.25
Common
CCB (**Common** Carrier Bureau) Reports, CC 1.58
COBOL {**Common** Business Oriented Language},
D 1.31
Common Carrier Actions, Reports, Public Notices,
CC 1.36/2
Common Carrier Public Mobile Services
Information, CC 1.36/6
Common Ground Archaelogy and Ethnography in
the Public Interest, I 29.59/5-2
Cost of Transporting Freight, Class 1 and Class 2
Motor **Common** Carriers of General
Freight, IC 1 acco.13
Elements of Value of Property, Class I Switching
and Terminal Companies Used in
Common Carrier Service, IC 1 val.11, IC
1 val.12
HCFA **Common** Procedure Coding System, HE
22.37
List of Corporate Names of **Common** Carriers, IC
1.15
Motor Carrier Freight Commodity Statistics Class 1
Common and Contract Carriers of
Property, IC 1 mot.22
Overseas **Common** Carrier Section 214
Applications for Filing, CC 1.36/4
Quarterly Freight Loss and Damage Claims
Reported by **Common** and Contract
Motor Carriers of Property, IC 1 acco.11
Selected Elements of Value of Property Used in
Common Carrier Service, Before and
After Recorded Depreciation and
Amortization, Class I Line Haul
Railways, Including Their Lessors and
Proprietary Companies, IC 1 val.10
Statistics of Communications **Common** Carriers,
CC 1.35
Structural Clay Products (**common** brick, face
brick, vitrified paving brick, hollow
building tile), C 3.109
Commonwealth
European and British **Commonwealth** Series, S
1.74

Welcoming America's Newest **Commonwealth**:
Reports, Y 3.N 81/6:9
Communicable
Communicable Disease Summary, FS 2.117
Homestudy Course; **Communicable** Disease
Control, HE 20.7710
Homestudy Courses; **Communicable** Disease
Control, HE 20.7021/2
Publications **Communicable** Disease Center, FS
2.60/2
Communication
Biblio-Profile on Human **Communication** and Its
Disorders a Capsule State-of-the-Art
Report and Bibliography, HE 20.3513/2
Communication, C 51.9/28
Communication Circular Letters, N 27.6
Communication Division Bulletin, N 27.7
Current Business Reports: Annual Survey of
Communication Services, C 3.138/3-6
Directory of Resources for Cultural and Educa-
tional Exchanges and International
Communication, ICA 1.12
FEC Index of **Communication** Costs, Y 3.El 2/
3:15-2
Federal **Communication** Commission Daily, CC
1.56
Federal Scientific and Technical **Communication**,
Progress Report, NS 2.12
Foreign **Communication** News, C 18.74
Press Notices Office of **Communication**, A 21.7
Radio **Communication** Charts, N 22.5
Radio **Communication** Laws and Regulations, C
11.7/5
Radio **Communication** Pamphlets, W 42.29
Signal **Communication** for All Arms and Services,
W 3.50/8
Voice of America Forum Lectures Mass **Communi-
cation** Series, IA 1.19
Communications
Aeronautical **Communications** and Pilot Services
Handbook 7300.7, Changes, FAA 3.9/2
Annual Report on Activities and Accomplishments
Under the **Communications** Satellite
Act of 1962, PrEx 18.9
Applications Pending in Commission for
Exemption from Radio Provisions of
International Convention for Safety of
Life at Sea Convention, London, 1929,
Title 3, Pt. 2 of **Communications** Act of
1934, etc., Reports, CC 1.19
Autovan Automatic Global Voice Network Defense
Communications System Directory, D
5.111
Biomedical **Communications** Study Section, HE
20.3001/2:B 52/3
Cabinet Committee on Cable **Communications**, Pr
37.8:C 11
Census of Transportation, **Communications**, and
Utilities, C 3.292
Communications Handbooks, C 55.108/4
Communications Procedures, ATM-2-B, FAA 3.9/
4
COMTAC {**Communications** and Tactial}
Publications Index, TD 5.21/5
Daily Digest **Communications** Office, Department
of Agriculture, A 21.14
Daily Digest Federal **Communications**
Commission, CC 1.54
Defense **Communications** System Global,
Automatic Voice Network Telephone
Directory, D 5.111
Electrical **Communications** {abstracts}, C 41.66/4
Federal **Communications** Commission Reports, CC
1.12
Federal **Communications** Commission Reports,
Decisions, Reports, Public Notices, and
Other Documents of the Federal
Communications Commission (2d series),
CC 1.12/2a
Federal **Communications** Commission Reports:
Second Series, CC 1.12/2
Forensic Science **Communications**, J 1.14/18-2
HCFA **Communications** Directory, HE 22.14
Herald of **Communications** {abstracts}, C 41.59
High Performance Computing and **Communica-
tions** Implementation Plan, PrEx 23.13
Informal **Communications**, Pr 32.413/7
Insights, High Performance Computer and
Communications, NAS 1.94
Major Matters Before the Federal **Communications**
Commission, CC 1.50

Market for U.S. Microwave, Forward Scatter, and
Other Radio **Communications**
Equipment and Radar in {various
countries}, C 41.105
Report on Applications for Orders Authorizing or
Approving the Interception of Wire or
Oral **Communications**, Ju 10.19
Rules of Practice and Rules Relating to Investiga-
tions and Code of Behavior Governing
Exparte **Communications** Between
Persons Outside the Commission and
Decisional Employees, SE 1.6:R 86/4
Statistics of **Communications** Common Carriers,
CC 1.35
Statistics of the **Communications** Industry in the
United States, CC 1.35
Tariff Circulars Federal **Communications**
Commission, CC 1.16
Technical Memorandum Defense **Communications**
Agency, D 5.110
Telephone Directory Federal **Communications**
Commission, CC 1.53
Telephone Directory International **Communica-
tions** Agency, ICA 1.15
Wire **Communications** Pamphlets, W 42.30
Communicative
Communicative Disorders Review Committee, HE
20.3001/2:C 73/3
Communicative Sciences Study Section, HE
20.3001/2:C 73/2
Intramural Research, Annual Report: National
Institute of Neurological and
Communicative Disorders and Stroke,
HE 20.3516/4
Report of the Panel on Pain to the National
Advisory Neurological and **Communi-
cative** Disorders and Stroke Council, HE
20.3517
Communicator
Army **Communicator**, D 111.14
Communicator, Y 3.G 79/3:9
Public Information **Communicator** (series), FS
14.16
Communicators
National Cancer Program Review for **Communica-
tors**, HE 20.3168/6
Communique
Council **Communique**, Y 3.H 75:15
East Central **Communique**, ED 1.71/2
INS **Communique**, J 21.25
OE **Communique**, D 101.91
OIG **Communique**, HH 1.109
WI **Communique**, Issues of the Special
Supplemental Food Program for Women,
Infants, and Children, A 98.14
Communism
Problems of **Communism**, IA 1.8
United States Policy Toward USSR and
International **Communism**, Monthly
Digest of Pertinent Data Appearing in
Department of State Publications, S 1.97
Communist
Know Your **Communist** Enemy Series, D 2.13
Studies in **Communist** Affairs, D 301.85
Trends in **Communist** Media, PrEx 7.12
U.S. Trade Status with **Communist** Countries, C
57.28, C 57.413, C 61.22
World Strength of the **Communist** Party
Organizations, Annual Report, S 1.111
Worldwide **Communist** Propaganda Activities, IA
1.8/2
Communities
Communities in Action, PrEx 10.9, PrEx 10.9/2
Handbook of Federal Aid to **Communities**, C
46.8:C 73
Inter-Arts, Presenting Organizations Artist
Communities Services to the Arts,
Application Guidelines, NF 2.8/2-23
Simplifying Federal Aid to States and **Communi-
ties**, Annual Report to the President of
an Interagency Program, PrEx 2.18
UDAG Grants Total ... for ... Smaller **Communities**,
HH 1.99/5
UDAG Grants Total for Large and Small
Communities, HH 1.99/5-2
Community
American **Community** Survey, C 3.297
Area Redelvelopment Bookshelf of **Community**
Aids, C 46.8/2
Cancer Control **Community** Activities Review
Committee, HE 20.3001/2:C 16/2
CHScene, Notes from the **Community** Health
Service, HE 20.2557/2
Community Action (series), PrEx 10.9/3

Factors Affecting Bank Reserves and **Condition**
Statement of F.R. Banks, FR 1.15
Findings from the **Condition** of Education, ED
1.109/2-2
Joint Stock Land Banks, Progress in Liquidation
Including Statements of **Condition**, A
72.16
Monthly Report of **Condition** for U.S. Agencies,
Branches and Domestic Banking
Subsidiaries of Foreign Banks, FR 1.16/3
Reports on **Condition** of Banks in U.S., T 1.6
Report on the Financial **Condition** and Performance
of the Farm Credit System, FCA 1.1/2
Statement of **Condition** of Federal Land Banks,
Joint Stock Land Banks, etc., FCA 1.7
Statement of Financial **Condition**, HH 2.22
Statements of **Condition** of Joint Stock Land Banks,
FCA 1.7/2
Summary Report of Bureau's Financial **Condition**
and Operations for Fiscal Year, I 27.1/3
Weekly Averages of Member Bank Reserves,
Reserve Bank Credit and Related Items
and Statement of **Condition** of the
Federal Reserve Bank, FR 1.15
Weekly **Condition** Report of Large Commercial
Banks in New York and Chicago, FR
1.16
Conditions
Analysis and Summary of **Conditions** and
Performances of the Farm Credit Banks
and Associations, FCA 1.23/2
Business **Conditions** Digest, C 56.111, C 59.9, C
59.9/3
Circular Letters to Presidents or Cashiers of
National Banks Asking for Report of
Conditions of Banks, T 12.11/1
Compensation and Working **Conditions**, L 2.44, L
2.44/4
Cotton Insect **Conditions**, A 77.322
Erosion and Related Land Use **Conditions** (by
Projects), A 57.24
Farm Labor Market **Conditions**, FS 3.120
Financial **Conditions** of {various railroads},
Annual Report to the President and the
Congress, TD 1.10/6-2
Forest Insect and Disease **Conditions**, A 13.52/2
Forest Insect and Disease **Conditions** in the
Northern Region, A 13.52/7
Forest Insect and Disease **Conditions** in the Pacific
Northwest, A 13.52/6
Forest Insect and Disease **Conditions** in the
Southwest, A 13.52/11
Forest Insect and Disease **Conditions**, Intermoun-
tain Region, A 13.52/12
Forest Insect **Conditions** in Pacific Northwest
During (year), A 13.52/6
st Insect **Conditions** in the Northern Region, A
13.52/7
Forest Insect **Conditions** in the United States, A
13.52/2
Forest Pest **Conditions** in the North East, A 13.52/
9
General Survey of **Conditions** in Coal Industry, C
22.21
Information Respecting the History, **Conditions**,
and Prospects of the Indian Tribes of the
United States, Philadelphia, Lippincott,
Grambo & Co, I 20.2:In 2
Juvenile Justice **Conditions** of Confinement, J 32.19
National Water **Conditions**, I 19.42
Profile of Labor **Conditions** (various countries), L
29.14
Report of Financial **Conditions** and Operations, As
of {date}, A 82.308
Report on Trade **Conditions**, C 1.7, C 10.11
Rural **Conditions** and Trends, A 93.41/3
Statements of **Conditions** of Federal Land Banks,
etc., T 48.6
Status of the Nation's Local Public Transportation,
Conditions and Performance, Report to
Congress, TD 7.18
Surveys of Agricultural Labor **Conditions**, A 61.11
Terms, **Conditions** and Limitations, with Form
Proposal, C 7.9
Tobacco Markets and **Conditions** Abroad, C 18.152
U.S. Housing Market **Conditions**, HH 1.120
Wind Erosion **Conditions**, Great Plains, Summary
of Local Estimates, A 57.47
World Economic **Conditions** in Relation to
Agricultural Trade, A 93.34/2, A 105.22/
2
World Monetary **Conditions** in Relation to
Agricultural Trade, A 93.34/2

Confectionary
Industry Reports Sugar, Molasses and
Confectionary, C 18.231
Confectionery Manufacturers' Sales and
Distribution, C 41.19, C 57.13
Monthly Comparative Sales of **Confectionery**, C
18.72/11
Monthly Comparative Sales of **Confectionery** and
Competitive Chocolate Products, C
3.135
Sugar **Confectionery**, Nuts, C 18.72/6
Confederal
Official Records of Union and **Confederal** Navies
in War of Rebellion, N 16.6
Confederate
Military Operations of Civil War, Guide-Index to
Official Records of Union and
Confederate Armies, GS 4.21
War of Rebellion, Compilation of Official Records of
Union and **Confederate** Armies {or
Rebellion Records}, W 45.5
Confederate Army
Atlas to Accompany {War of Rebellion} Official
Records of Union Army and **Confeder-
ate Army** {or Rebellion Records}, W
45.7
Circulars Relating to Plan and Methods of
Publication of Official Records of Union
Army and **Confederate Army**, W 45.4
Conference
Accident Prevention **Conference**, Publications, C
1.17
Administrative **Conference** News, Y 3.Ad 6:9-2
Agriculture Outlook, **Conference** Proceedings, A
1.144
America's Commitment: Federal Programs
Benefiting Women and New Initiatives
as Follow-up to the U.N. Fourth World
Conference on Women, Pr 42.8:W 84
C.A.B. Prehearing **Conference** Reports, CAB 1.35
Central American Peace **Conference**, Washington,
1907, S 5.12
Conference (series), E 1.10, S 5.30
Conference at Quebec, 1944, S 1.1/3:Q 3
Conference Briefs, C 13.62
Conference for Supervisors of Elementary
Education in Large Cities, FS 5.58/2
Conference in Matters of Pollution of Navigable
Waters, Proceedings, EP 1.16/2
Conference News, S 5.48/3
Conference Notes, D 103.112
Conference of Berlin (Potsdam **Conference**), 1945,
S 1.1/3:P 84
Conference of Model Reporting Area for
Blindness, Proceedings, HE 20.3759/2
Conference of Oil Pollution of Navigable Waters,
S 5.24
Conference of State and Territorial Health Officers
with United States Public Health
Service, Transactions, T 27.32, FS 2.34
Conference of State Planning and Development
Officers with Federal Officials,
Summaries, C 45.11
Conference of State Sanitary Engineers, Report of
Proceedings, HE 20.14
Conference on Elementary Education Reports, FS
5.58
Conference on Limitation of Armament,
Washington, 1921n22, S 3.29
Conference on Weights and Measures, C 13.7
Conference Proceedings {of} AASHO Committee
on Electronics, TD 2.125
Conference Publications, NASA CP (series), NAS
1.55
Conference Report on Cotton Insect Research and
Control, A 77.328
Conference Report Series, FS 2.22/50
Conference Rulings Bulletins, IC 1.8, FT 1.6
Conference Summary Report (series), HE 20.6518
Directory of Associate Members, National
Conference on Weights and Measures, C
13.66/3
FAA Forecast **Conference** Proceedings, TD 4.55
Financial Audit, Environmental and Energy Study
Conference Financial Statement, GA
1.13/17
Inter-American **Conference** for Maintenance of
Peace, 1936, S 5.38
Inter-American **Conference** on Agriculture,
Forestry, and Animal Industry,
Washington, Sept. 8-20, 1930, S 5.32
Inter-American Technical Aviation **Conference**, S
5.40

International American **Conference**: Buenos Aries,
S 5.9/4
International American **Conference**: Havana, Cuba,
S 5.9/6
International American **Conference**: Mexico City, S
5.9/2
International American **Conference**; Rio de Janeiro,
S 5.9/3
International American **Conference**; Santiago,
Chile, S 5.9/5
International **Conference** Calendar, C 42.24
International **Conference** of American States on
Conciliation and Arbitration, S 3.38
International **Conference** on Maritime Law, S 3.32
International Organization and **Conference** Series,
S 1.70
Mini **Conference** Report (series), Y 3.W 58/4:10
1990 Planning **Conference** Series, C 3.271
NIST **Conference** Calendar, C 13.10/3-2
Pan American Financial **Conference**, 2d,
Washington, 1920, T 1.22/2
Pan American Financial **Conference**, Washington,
D.C., May 24, 1915, T 1.22
Pan-Pacific Educational **Conference**, 1st
Honolulu, August 1921, S 5.21/2, S 5.22
Pan-Pacific Scientific **Conference**, 1st Honolulu,
1920, S 5.21/1
Peace **Conference**, Paris, 1919, S 3.28
President's **Conference** on Industrial Safety News
Letter, L 16.30
Proceedings Annual Alcoholism **Conference** of the
National Institute on Alcohol Abuse
and Alcoholism, HE 20.2430/2
Proceedings Annual Clinical Spinal Cord Injury
Conference, VA 1.42
Proceedings Annual **Conference** of Mental Health
Career Development Program, FS 2.22/45
Proceedings Annual **Conference** of Model
Reporting Area for Blindness Statistics,
FS 2.22/37
Proceedings Annual **Conference** of the Surgeon
General, Public Health Service, and
Chief, Children's Bureau, with State and
Territorial Health Officers, FS 2.83
Proceedings Annual **Conference** on Model
Reporting Area for Mental Hospital
Statistics, FS 2.22/44
Proceedings Annual **Conference**, Surgeon General,
Public Health Service, with State and
Territorial Mental Health Authorities, FS
2.83/3
Proceedings Annual Western International Forest
Disease Work **Conference**, A 13.69/13
Proceedings Biennial **Conference** of State and
Territorial Dental Directors with Public
Health Service and Children's Bureau,
FS 2.83/2
Proceedings **Conference** in Matters of Pollution
and Navigable Waters, EP 1.16/2
Proceedings **Conference** of State Sanitary
Engineers, FS 2.83/4
Proceedings International **Conference** on
Numerical Ship Hydrodynamics, D
211.9/5
Proceedings Interstate **Conference** on Labor
Statistics, L 2.80
Proceedings National Security Affairs **Conference**,
D 5.412
Proceedings Northwest Shellfish Sanitation
Research Planning **Conference**, EP 2.15
Proceedings Public Health **Conference** on Records
and Statistics, FS 2.122, HE 20.2214,
HE 20.6214
Proceedings Southern Pasture and Forage Crop
Improvement **Conference**, A 106.29
Public Health **Conference** on Records and
Statistics, National Meeting Announce-
ment, HE 20.6214/2
Public Health **Conference** on Records and
Statistics, Proceedings, FS 2.122
Publications Accident Prevention **Conference**, C
1.17
Publications National **Conference** on Air
Pollution, FS 2.98
Publications National **Conference** on Water
Pollution, FS 2.64/3
Publications President's **Conference** on Fire
Prevention, FW 6.9
Publications President's Highway Safety
Conference, FW 2.18
Recommendations and Reports of the Administra-
tive **Conference** of the United States, Y
3.Ad 6:9

Renal Disease and Hypertension, Proceedings, Annual **Conference**, HE 20.5412

Report from the White House **Conference** on Families, Y 3.W 58/22:9

Report of Alfalfa Improvement **Conference**, A 77.531

Report of **Conference** of Local Appraisers Held at New York, T 20.5

Report of Dry Bean Research **Conference**, A 77.15:74

Report of Proceedings of Regular Annual Meeting of Judicial **Conference** of the United States, Ju 10.10

Report of Proceedings of Special Session of Judicial **Conference** of the United States, Ju 10.10/2

Report of the National **Conference** on Weights and Measures, C 13.10, C 13.10/3

Report on Dry Bean Research **Conference**, A 77.15:74

Report on the International Technical **Conference** on Experimental Safety Vehicles, TD 8.16

Report on Washington **Conference** of Mayors and Other Local Government Executives on National Security, FCD 1.18

Report on Washington **Conference** on National Women's Advisory Committee on FCDA, FCD 1.18/2

Reports and Guidelines from White House **Conference** on Aging (series), FS 1.13/2

Reports of the Proceedings of the Judicial **Conference** of the United States {and} Annual Report of the Director of the Administrative Office of the U.S. Courts, Ju 10.1/2

Safety **Conference** Guides, I 1.77/3

Sagamore Army Materials Research **Conference** Proceedings (series), D 101.122

State **Conference** Report from (State), Y 3.W 58/4:9

Student **Conference** on United States Affairs, D 109.9

Summary Proceedings of ADAMHA Annual **Conference** of the State and Territorial Alcohol, Drug Abuse, and Mental Health Authorities, HE 20.8011

Technical Alfalfa **Conference**, Proceedings, A 77.15:74

UNESCO **Conference** Newsletter, S 5.48/4

United Nations **Conference** on Food and Agriculture, S 5.41

United Nations **Conference** on International Organization, S 5.44

University-Federal Agency **Conference** on Career Development, **Conference** Reports, CS 1.70

VA Medical Research **Conference** Abstracts, VA 1.43/2

White House **Conference** Happenings, Y 3.W 58:6

World Power **Conference**, S 5.36

Conferences

C.A.B. Weekly Calendar of Prehearing **Conferences**, Hearings and Arguments, CAB 1.33

Calendar of Prehearing **Conferences** Hearings, and Arguments **Conferences**, C 31.227

Conferences at Cairo and Tehran, 1943, 1961, S 1.1/3:C 12

Conferences at Malta and Yalta, 1945, S 1.1/3:M 29

Conferences at Washington and Quebec, S 1.1/3:W 27/2

Conferences at Washington, 1941-1942, and Casablanca, S 1.1/3:W 27

Conferences of Educators on Sex Education, T 27.25

Conferences on Inter-American Relations, S 15.5

Foreign Relations of United States, Diplomatic Papers: **Conferences**, S 1.1/3

Hearings and **Conferences** before Commission on Civil Rights, CR 1.8

List of Official International **Conferences** and Meetings, S 5.49

Proceedings Standards Laboratory **Conferences**, C 13.10

Publications National **Conferences** on Street and Highway Safety, C 1.21

Report of Agricultural Aviation Research **Conferences**, A 77.2:Av 5

Reprints of Articles Published Concerning NIH Consensus Development **Conferences**, HE 20.3030/2

Schedule of International **Conferences**, S 1.70/6

Schedule of NIH **Conferences**, HE 20.3040

Secretary of State Press **Conferences**, S 1.25/4

Transactions of Research **Conferences** in Pulmonary Diseases, VA 1.40/2

Transactions of Research **Conferences** on Cooperative Chemotherapy Studies in Psychiatry and Research Approaches to Mental Illness, VA 1.41

Conferred

Earned Degrees **Conferred**, FS 4.254:54013, HE 5.92/5, HE 5.254:54013, HE 19.329

Summary Report of Bachelor's and Higher Degrees **Conferred** During (school year), FS 5.254:54010, HE 5.254:54010

Confidential

Confidential Bulletin of Engineering Information, N 19.9/1

Confidential Reports, A 72.24

Family Security **Confidential** Bulletins, FS 8.9

Confinement

Inertial **Confinement** Fusion, ICF Annual Report, E 1.99/7-2

Inertial **Confinement** Fusion Quarterly Report, E 1.99/7

Juvenile Justice Conditions of **Confinement**, J 32.19

Conflict

United States Navy and the Vietnam **Conflict** (series), D 207.10/3

Congenital

Congenital Malformations Surveillance, Reports, HE 20.7011/2

Congess

Annals of **Congess**, X 1 - X 42

Congested

Population {**Congested** Areas}, C 3.160

Congress

Accomplishments During the **Congress**, Y 4.In 8/14:Ac 2

Activity Report to **Congress**, NS 1.35

Acts of **Congress**, Treaties, and Proclamations Relating to Noncontiguous Territory, W 6.12

Annals of **Congress**, X 1

Biennial Report to the **Congress**, HE 20.3851/2

Biographical Directory of the American **Congress**, Y 1.92-1:S.doc. 8

Bulletins on Topics of Interest to **Congress**, LC 14.9

Congress and Foreign Policy, Y 4.F 76/1-13

Congress of International Society of Soil Science Publications, A 57.49

Congressional Lists; List of Publications Available for Distribution by Members of **Congress**, A 21.9/3

Consolidated Annual Report to **Congress** on Community Development Programs, HH 1.46/6

Cultural Presentations USA, (year), Report to **Congress** and the Public, S 1.67

Digest, Inspector General Report to the **Congress**, VA 1.55/2

Emergency Relief Appropriation Acts, Reports of President to **Congress** Showing Status of Funds and Operations Under, T 63.114

End-Stage Renal Disease Program, Annual Report to **Congress**, HE 22.9/2

Energy Information Reported to **Congress** As Required by Public Law 93-319, FE 1.15

Energy Information, Report to **Congress**, E 3.15

Federal Managers' Financial Integrity Act, Secretary's Annual Statement and Report to the President and the **Congress**, I 1.96/6

Federal Ocean Program, Annual Report to **Congress**, Pr 37.11, Pr 38.11, Pr 39.12

Federal Recreation Fee Program (year), Including Federal Recreation Visitation Data, a Report to the **Congress**, I 70.18

Federal Support of Research and Development at Universities and Colleges and Selected Nonprofit Institutions, Fiscal Year, Report to the President and **Congress**, NS 1.30

Federal Support to Universities, Colleges, and Selected Nonprofit Institutions, Fiscal Year (date), Report to the President and **Congress**, NS 1.30

Financial Conditions of {various railroads}, Annual Report to the President and the **Congress**, TD 1.10/6-2

Food and Drug Administration and the **Congress**, HE 20.4038

Index/Journals of the Continental **Congress**, GS 4.2:C 76/2

Index/Papers of the Continental **Congress**, GS 4.2:C 76/3

Indian and Alaska Native Housing and Community Development Programs, Annual Report to **Congress**, HH 1.80

International **Congress** Against Alcoholism, S 5.20

Journals of Continental **Congress**, Miscellaneous, LC 4.6

Journals of the Continental **Congress**, LC 4.5

Journals of the Continental **Congress**, Index, GS 4.2:C 76/2

Letters of Delegates to **Congress**, LC 1.34

List of Publications Available for Distribution by Members of **Congress**, A 21.9/8:1

Major Legislation of the **Congress**, LC 14.18

Mary Pickford Theater in the Library of **Congress**, LC 40.10

Miscellaneous Publications of **Congress**, Y 1

Monthly Digest to Members of **Congress**, L 2.66

Numerical Lists and Schedule of Volumes of Reports and Documents of **Congress**, GP 3.7/2

Office of Inspector General, Semiannual Report to **Congress** Department of Education, ED 1.26

Office of Inspector General, Semiannual Report to **Congress** Department of Transportation, TD 1.1/3

Office of Inspector General, Semiannual Report to **Congress** General Services Administration, GS 1.1/3

Office of Inspector General: Report to the **Congress**, HH 1.1/2

Office of the Inspector General: Semiannual Report to the **Congress**, CSA 1.1/2

Pan American Child **Congress**, 6th Lima, S 5.34

Pan American Scientific **Congress**, 3d Lima, Peru, 1924-25, S 5.14/3

Pan-American **Congress** of Highways, 1st, Buenos Aires, S 5.23

Pan-American **Congress** on Highways, 2d, Rio de Janerio, S 5.23/2

Pan-American Medical **Congress**, Washington, 1893, S 5.16

Pan-American Scientific **Congress**, 2d, Washington, D.C., S 5.14/2

Pan-American Scientific **Congress**, Santiago, Chile, S 5.14

Papers, {number} **Congress**, Y 4.Ar 5/2:a

Permanent International Association of Road **Congress**, S 5.31

Progress in the Prevention and Control of Air Pollution in (year), Report to **Congress**, EP 4.16

Progress Report to **Congress** by War Assets Administration, Pr 33.211, Y 3.W 19/8:11

Proposed Foreign Aid Program Fiscal Year, Summary Presentation to **Congress**, S 18.28/a

Proposed Foreign Aid Program, Summary Presentation to **Congress**, S 18.28

Public Employment Program, Annual Report to **Congress**, L 1.68

Publications **Congress** of International Society of Soil Science, A 57.49

Quarterly Journal of Library of **Congress**, LC 1.17

Quarterly Progress Reports by Surplus Property Board to **Congress**, Y 3.W 19/7:207

Quarterly Report to **Congress** and the East-West Foreign Trade Board on Trade Between the United States and the Nonmarket Economy Countries, Y 4.W 36:2

Rail Passenger Service Act, Report to **Congress**, TD 1.10/5

Refugee Resettlement Program, Report to **Congress**, HE 3.72, HE 25.16

Registers of Papers in the Manuscript Division of the Library of **Congress**, LC 4.10

Relative Cost of Shipbuilding in Various Coastal Districts of the United States, Report to **Congress**, C 39.216/2

Report of Secretary of Defense to the **Congress** on the Budget, Authorization Request, and Defense Programs, D 1.1

Report of Secretary of Labor to **Congress** on Research and Training Activities, L 1.42

Report of Secretary to President and **Congress** on Mineral Exploration Program, I 1.85

Health **Consequences** of Smoking, Report to the Surgeon General, HE 20.2019

CONSER
CONSER Editing Guide, LC 1.6/4-2
CONSER Line, LC 30.22/2
CONSER Tables, (date), LC 30.22

Conservation
A.A.A.N.C.R. Agricultural **Conservation** Program by States, NCR, A 55.43/11
Abstracts of Recent Published Material on Soil and Water **Conservation**, A 1.68, A 57.36, A 77.15:41
Agricultural **Conservation** Practices (by States), A 80.608
Agricultural **Conservation** Program (by States), A 55.44/14, A 80.613, A 82.110, A 82.112, A 90.8
Agricultural **Conservation** Program (by States), A 82.112, A 1.107
Agricultural **Conservation** Program Service Publications, A 82.37/2
Agricultural **Conservation** Program, Statistical Summary, A 90.10
Agricultural **Conservation** Program, Summary, A 90.10/2
Agricultural Resources, Cropland, Water, and **Conservation**, A 93.47/2
Agronomy, Weed Science, Soil **Conservation**, Agricultural Programs, A 106.36
Air Force Energy **Conservation** Plan, D 301.89/6-2
Annual Report Habitat **Conservation** Program, C 55.340
Annual Report of Energy **Conservation** Indicators for (year), E 3.47
Annual Report of the Rivers and Trails **Conservation** Programs, I 29.124
Annual Report to the President and Congress on the State of Energy **Conservation** Program, E 1.27
Annual Report, Fishery **Conservation** and Management Act, C 55.330
Army **Conservation** Project Posters, W 3.46/7
Balance a Discussion of **Conservation** Issues, I 66.19
Circular Letters, Relate to Indian Emergency **Conservation** Work, I 20.23
Conservation Agronomy Technical Notes, A 57.63
Conservation Aids, A 57.45
Conservation and Solar Applications, DOE/CS (series), E 1.36
Conservation and Your Community, A 57.75
Conservation Bulletins, I 1.72
Conservation Districts, A 57.2:C 76
Conservation Education Reports, A 57.33
Conservation Folders, A 57.30, A 76.210
Conservation Guide Sheets, A 57.6/4
Conservation Highlights, Digest of the Progress Report of the Soil Conservation Service, A 57.1/2
Conservation Highlights, Digest of the Progress Report of the Soil **Conservation** Service, A 57.1/2
Conservation in Action, I 49.36
Conservation Information, A 57.44
Conservation Man (radio scripts), I 29.49
Conservation Notes, I 49.36/2
Conservation Papers, FE 1.22
Conservation Planning Memorandum, A 57.53
Conservation Project Support Grant Application and Information, NF 4.10
Conservation Research Reports, A 1.114, A 77.23
Conservation Reserve Program of Soil Bank, Statistical Summaries, A 82.79/2
Conservation Teaching Aids, A 13.72
Conservation Vistas, Regional **Conservation** Education Newsletter Serving Oregon and Washington, A 13.72/2
Conservation Yearbooks, I 1.95
Current **Conservation**, I 43.7
Emergency **Conservation** Program, Fiscal Year Statistical Summary, A 112.1/2, A 113.1/2
Emergency **Conservation** Program, Fiscal Year Summary, A 82.93
Emergency **Conservation** Work Bulletins, L 1.11
Emergency **Conservation** Work, Project Training Publications, I 29.28
Energy **Conservation** Fact Sheets, TD 1.30
Energy **Conservation** Indicators, Annual Report, E 3.47
Energy **Conservation**, Consumption and Utilization, E 1.99

Exploration and **Conservation** of Natural Resources, C 41.45
Federal Oil **Conservation** Board, I 1.67
Field Letter, National Committee for **Conservation** of Manpower in War Industries, L 1.29
Fishery **Conservation** and Management Act, Annual Report, C 55.330
Food **Conservation** Notes, Y 3.F 73:25
Fuel **Conservation** Circulars, Y 3.R 13/2:28
Habitat **Conservation** Programs of the National Marine Fisheries Service, C 55.340
Handbook of **Conservation** Practices (by States), A 82.111
Industrial Energy **Conservation**, Fact Sheets, FE 1.27
Land and Water **Conservation** Fund Grants Manual, I 29.107
Land and Water **Conservation** Fund, Grants-in-Aid Program, Annual Report, I 29.107/2
Land Use and Soil **Conservation**, Informational Materials Available to Public, Leaflets (by Regions), A 57.26
Laws relating to Forestry, Game **Conservation**, Flood Control and Related Subjects, Y 1.2:F 76/4
Mileage **Conservation** Letter, Pr 32.4266
Nutrition and Food **Conservation** Series, A 1.65
Outline of Agricultural **Conservation** Program, A 55.44/12
Posters Soil **Conservation** Service, A 57.71
Procedure for Making Soil **Conservation** Surveys, Outlines, A 57.17
Production-**Conservation** Program, Committeemen's Handbooks, A 80.2158
Progress in Soil and Water **Conservation** Research, Quarterly Reports, A 77.528
Publications Nutrition and Food **Conservation** Branch, A 80.123
Quarterly Tracking System, Energy Using and **Conservation** Equipment in Homes, E 3.23
Report of Forest Service Training Activities, Civilian **Conservation** Corps, A 13.71
Report of the Attorney General, Pursuant to Section 252(i) of the Energy Policy and **Conservation** Act, J 1.27/2
Resource **Conservation** and Development Plans, A 57.62
Resource **Conservation** Development Plan, A 57.65
Safety Bulletins Civil **Conservation** Corps, FS 4.8
Saline Water **Conservation** Program, Reports and Publications, I 1.83
SCS-CI- {**Conservation** Aids} (series), A 57.45
Service and Regulatory Announcements Agricultural Stabilization and **Conservation** Service, A 82.23
Soil and Water **Conservation** District Resources Inventories (series), A 57.38/2
Soil and Water **Conservation** Districts, Status of Organization, by States, Approximate Acreage, and Farms in Organized Districts, A 57.32
Soil and Water **Conservation** News, A 57.9/2
Soil and Water **Conservation** Research Needs Executive Summary, A 57.73
Soil **Conservation** Bibliographies, A 57.27/2
Soil **Conservation** Districts, A 76.214, A 80.2009, A 80.508
Soil **Conservation** Literature, Selected Current References, A 57.20, A 17.15
Soil **Conservation** Service, A 57.1/3
Soil **Conservation**, A 80.2007, A 80.507, A 57.9
Soil **Conservation**; Official Organ, A 76.208, A 79.207
Southern Region Agricultural **Conservation**, A 55.45/8
Special Reports Soil **Conservation** Service, A 57.72
Special Reports Soil **Conservation** Service, Office of Research, Sedimentation Section, A 76.215, A 80.2013
State Law for Soil **Conservation**, A 13.60
Voluntary Business Energy **Conservation** Program, Progress Reports, E 1.39
Voluntary Industrial Energy **Conservation**, C 57.25, E 1.22
Water **Conservation** Report WC (series), I 27.53
Water Management and **Conservation** Program, I 27.78
Wildlife **Conservation** and Restoration Notes, A 43.5/20

Conservationists
Celebrated **Conservationists** in Our National Parks, I 29.31
Conservators
Circular Letters {to **conservators** of national banks}, T 12.11/4
Conserve
Report of the Attorney General Pursuant to Section 2 of the Joint Resolution of July 28, 1955, Consenting to an Interstate Compact to **Conserve** Oil and Gas, J 1.27
Conserve-O-Gram
Conserve-O-Gram, I 29.100
Consolidated
Consolidated Abstracts of Technical Reports, FAA 2.11
Consolidated Abstracts of Technical Reports: General Distribution, FAA 2.11/2
Consolidated Address and Territorial Bulletin, VA Station Addresses, Identification Numbers, and Territorial Jurisdictions, VA 1.69
Consolidated Annual Report for the Office of Community Planning and Development, HE 23.1017
Consolidated Annual Report on State and Territorial Public Health Laboratories, HE 20.7001/2
Consolidated Annual Report to Congress on Community Development Programs, HH 1.46/6
Consolidated Cotton Report, C 3.20/4
Consolidated Development Directory, HH 1.61
Consolidated Federal Funds Report, C 3.266/2
Consolidated Federal Supply Catalog, D 1.78
Consolidated Financial Report, HH 1.1/11
Consolidated Financial Statements of the United States Government, Fiscal Year, T 63.113/3
Consolidated Index of Army Publications and Blank Forms, D 101.22:25-30
Consolidated Index of Opinions and Digests of Opinions of Judge Advocate General, W 10.10
Consolidated List of Debarred, Suspended, and Ineligible Contractors, GS 1.28
Consolidated List of Persons or Firms Currently Debarred for Violations of Various Public Contracts Acts Incorporating Labor Standard Provisions, GA 1.17
Consolidated Listing of Official Gazette Notices Re Patent and Trademark Office Practices and Procedures, Patent Notices, C 21.5/5
Consolidated Management Data List, D 7.29/6
Consolidated Master Cross Reference List, D 7.20
Consolidated of Schedule B Commodity Classifications for Use in Presentation of U.S. Export Statistics, C 3.150:G
Consolidated Publication of Component Lists, D 101.16/3
Consolidated Report of Accessions, D 102.7
Consolidated Review of Current Information, T 23.7/2
Consolidated Subject Index, D 201.37
Consolidated Supply Program, HH 1.90
Consolidated Translation Survey, Pr 34.610
Organizations Designated Under E.O. 10450, **Consolidated** List (SCS Form 385), CS 1.63
Receipts and Disbursements of Government **Consolidated** into Bureau of Accounts, Fiscal Service in Treasury Department by President's Reorganization Plan no. 3, T 9.11
Reports, **Consolidated** Pamphlets, Ju 11.7/a2
Semiannual **Consolidated** Report of Balances of Foreign Currencies Acquired Without Payment of Dollars As of December 31 (year), T 63.117
USC/FAR **Consolidated** Plan for Foreign Affairs Research, PrEx 3.12
Consolidation
Consolidation
Schedule G. **Consolidation** of Schedule B Commodity Classifications for Use in Presentation of U.S. Export Statistics, C 3.150:G
Consortia
FIPSE European Community/United States of America Joint **Consortia** for Cooperation in Higher Education, ED 1.23/10

Consortium
Eisenhower **Consortium** Bulletins, A 13.69/11
Pacific Basin **Consortium** for Hazardous Waste
Research Newsletter, E 1.110
Urban **Consortium** Information Bulletins, HH 1.3/
3
Constabulary
Constabulary Notes, W 49.32/7
Constants
Tidal Harmonic **Constants**, C 4.35
Constitution
Constitution and Membership, NA 1.7
Constitution of the United States, Analysis and
Interpretation, Y 1.92-2:S.doc. 82
Layman's Guide to Individual Rights Under the
United States **Constitution**, Y 4.J 89/2:R
44
Posters Bicentennial of the United States
Constitution Commission, Y 3.B 47/
2:12
U.S. **Constitution**, a National Historic Landmark
Theme Study, I 29.117
Constitution Week
Citizenship Day and **Constitution Week** Bulletins,
J 21.14
Constitutional
Analysis of **Constitutional** Provisions Affecting
Public Welfare in States, Y 3.W 89/2:36
Construction
Allowance of Articles under Cognizance of Bureau
of **Construction** and Repair for Vessels of
the Navy, N 4.5
Annual Historical Summary; Defense **Construction**
Supply Center, D 7.1/9
Annual Reports on **Construction** of Pension
Building, I 1.27
Arctic **Construction** and Frost Effects Laboratory,
D 103.31
Authorized **Construction**—Washington D.C. Area,
C 3.215/5
Bid Opening Report Federal-Aid Highway
Construction Contracts Calendar Year,
TD 2.47
Building **Construction**, L 2.6/a 4
Building **Construction** in Urban Areas in United
States, L 2.36
Census of Business; 1939, **Construction** (by
States), C 3.940-28
Census of **Construction** Industries: Final Reports,
C 3.245/3
Census of **Construction** Industries: Final Reports,
Bound Volumes, C 3.245/6
Census of **Construction** Industries: Final Reports,
Special Reports, C 3.245/5
Census of **Construction** Industries; Advance
Industry Reports, C 3.245
Census of **Construction** Industries; Announce-
ments and Order Forms, C 3.245/2
Census of **Construction** Industries; Area Statistics,
C 56.254/4
Census of **Construction** Industries; Bound
Volumes, C 56.254/6
Census of **Construction** Industries; Final Reports,
C 56.254/3
Census of **Construction** Industries; General
Publications, C 56.254
Census of **Construction** Industries; Preliminary
Reports, C 56.254/2
Census of **Construction** Industries; Special
Reports, C 56.254/5
Census of **Construction** Industries, Subject Series,
C 3.245/8
Census of Distribution; **Construction** Industry,
State Series, C 3.37/21
Construction Abroad, C 18.59/2
Construction Activity, L 2.22/2
Construction Aids, HH 1.18
Construction and Building Materials, Monthly
Industry Report, C 40.10
Construction and Building Materials, Statistical
Supplements, C 41.30/2
Construction and Equipment, PrEx 7.21/3
Construction and Related Industry, PrEx 7.22/3-2
Construction Bulletin (series), J 28.3/2
Construction Committees {various cities}, Public
Sector Bid Calendars by Agencies, L
1.75
Construction Expenditure of State and Local
Governments, BC (series), C 56.223, C
3.215/10
Construction Expenditure of State and Local
Governments, GC (series), C 56.223
Construction Expenditure of State and Local Tax
Revenue, C 3.215/10

Construction Industry Series, HE 19.108/2
Construction Industry Stabilization Commission
Regulations, ES 2.6/4
Construction Materials, FW 1.16
Construction Problems Relating to Fire
Protection, GS 1.14/9
Construction Report: Price Index of New One-
Family Houses Sold, C 27 (series), C
56.211/2-2
Construction Reports; Authorized **Construction**,
Washington, D.C. Area, C 56.211/6
Construction Reports; Building Permits, C 40
(series), C 3.215/7
Construction Reports; Building Permits: C 42
(series), C 3.215/6
Construction Reports; Housing Authorized by
Building Permits and Public Contracts,
C 3.215/11
Construction Reports; Housing Completions, C 22
(series), C 3.215/13, C 56.211
Construction Reports; Housing Starts, C 20
(Series), C 56.211/3
Construction Reports; Housing Units Authorized
for Demolition in Permit-issuing Places,
(year), C 45 (series), C 56.211/8
Construction Reports; New One-family Homes
Sold and for Sale, C 25 (series), C
56.211/2
Construction Reports; New Residential
Construction in Selected Standard
Metropolitan Statistical Areas (SMSA),
C 3.215/15
Construction Reports; Permits Issued for
Demolition of Residential Structures in
Selected Cities, C 45 (series), C 3.215/12
Construction Reports; Price Index of New One-
family Houses Sold, C 27 (series), C
3.215/9-2
Construction Reports; Residential Alterations and
Repairs, Expenditures on Residential
Additions, Alterations, Maintenance and
Repairs, and Replacements, C 56.211/7
Construction Reports; Value of New **Construction**
Put in Place, C 30 (series), C 56.211/5
Construction Review, C 62.10, C 57.310, C 57.509
Construction Standards, L 35.6/3
Construction Status Report, Nuclear Power Plants,
Data for Decisions, Y 3.N 88:16
Construction Trends, I 27.48
Construction, Monthly Summary of Current
Developments, L 2.22
Containerships Under **Construction** and on Order
(including conversions) in United States
and Foreign Shipyards Oceangoing
Ships of 1,000 Gross Tons and Over, C
39.231
Cost of Pipeline and Compressor Station
Construction Under Non-Budget Type
or Certificate Authorizations As
Reported by Pipeline Companies, FP
1.30
Current **Construction** Reports, Housing Units
Authorized by Building Permits, C
3.215/4:C 40
Current **Construction** Reports, New One-Family
Houses Sold and for Sale, C 3.215/9
Current **Construction** Reports: New Residential
Construction in Selected Metropolitan
Areas, C21-, C 3.215/15
Current **Construction** Reports, Special Studies,
Expenditures for Nonresidential
Improvements and Repairs, C 3.215/8-2
Defense Housing **Construction** Bulletins, FW 1.11
Engineering Manual for Emergency **Construction**,
D 103.21
Engineering Manual for Military **Construction**, D
103.9
Engineering Manual for War Department
Construction, W 7.36
Engineering Manual, Civil Works **Construction**, D
103.14
Engineering Manual, Military **Construction**, M
110.13
Federal Work and **Construction** Projects, FW 4.33,
Y 3.W 89/2:61
Five Year Medical Facility **Construction** Needs
Assessment, VA 1.68
Foreign Military Sales, Foreign Military
Construction Sales, and Military
Assistance Facts, D 1.66
Gas Turbine Electric Plant **Construction** Cost and
Annual Production Expenses, E 3.17/2
General **Construction** Bulletins, Y 3.R 88:13

Grants for Training **Construction** Medical
Libraries, HE 20.3013/5
Grants for Training, **Construction**, Cancer Control,
Medical Libraries, HE 20.3013/5
Health Facilities **Construction** Program Loan,
Loan Guarantee and Mortgage Quarterly
Status Report, HE 20.9013
Highway **Construction** Contracts Awarded by
State Highway Departments, C 37.25
Highway **Construction** Contracts Awarded by
State Highway Departments, Tables, FW
2.19
Hospital and Mental Facilities **Construction**
Program under Title 6 of Public Health
Service Act, Semiannual Analysis of
Projects Approved for Federal Aid, FS
2.74/2
Hospital **Construction** and Activation, Summary,
VA 1.33
Hospital Survey and **Construction** Act with
Amendments {August 13, 1946}, Y
1.2:H 79
Housing and **Construction** Reports (series), C
3.215
Housing Legal Digest, Decisions, Opinions,
Legislations Relating to Housing
Construction and Finance, Y 3.C 33/
3:10
Hydraulic and Engineering **Construction**, C 41.47
Hydro Electric Plant **Construction** Cost and
Annual Production Expenses, E 3.17/3
Indexes of Change in Straight-Time Average Hourly
Earnings for Selected Shipyards, by Type
of **Construction** and Region, L 2.81/2
Industry Report, **Construction** and Building
Materials, C 41.30
Industry Report, Construction and **Construction**
Materials, C 18.233
Labor Compliance Manual, Direct Federal and
Federal-aid **Construction**, TD 2.108:L
11
Laws Relating to **Construction** of Bridges over
Navigable Waters, W 7.6/2
Laws Relating to Federal Aid and **Construction** of
Roads, Y 1.2:R 53
Library Programs, Public Library **Construction**:
An Overview and Analysis, ED 1.18/7
Mechanization of **Construction** {abstracts}, C
41.47/2
Mineral Industry Surveys, Directory of Principal
Construction Sand and Gravel
Producers in the . . ., Annual Advanced
Summary Supplement, I 19.138/3
Minimum **Construction** Requirements for New
Dwellings, FL 2.11
Monthly Highway **Construction** Contracts
Awarded by State and Federal Agencies
and Toll Authorities, TD 2.51
Monthly Listing of Awards for **Construction**
Grants for Wastewater Treatment Works,
EP 1.56
New Health and Hospital Projects Authorized for
Construction under Controlled
Materials Plan, FS 2.73/2
New Ship **Construction**, TD 11.15
Noise Emission Standards for **Construction**
Equipment, Background Document for
{various items}, EP 1.6/3
Notes on **Construction** of Ordnance, W 34.8
Occupational Safety and Health **Construction**
Standards and Interpretations, L 35.6/3-
3
Office of **Construction** Industry Services: Annual
Report, L 1.1/2
Office of Engineering Design and **Construction**:
Annual Report, Y 3.T 25:1-15
Pension Building, Annual Reports on **Construc-
tion** of, 1883-87, I 1.27
Price Trends for Federal-Aid Highway **Construc-
tion**, C 37.22, TD 2.49
Price Trends for Federal-Aid Highway **Construc-
tion** TD 2.30/16-3
Production and Availability of **Construction**
Materials, Pr 32.4827
Project Register, Waste Water Treatment
Construction Grants, EP 1.9/2, EP 1.56/
2
Proposals for **Construction** of Public Buildings;
Specifications and Proposals for Repairs,
etc. at Public Buildings, T 39.7
Protective **Construction** Series, Pr 32.4409

Public Buildings Act of 1926, with Amendments, Condemnation Laws with Amendments, Public Works and **Construction** Laws {May 7, 1926}, Y 1.2:P 96/3

Public **Construction**, GS 1.7

Public Sewage Treatment Plant **Construction**, FS 2.56/2

Quarterly Summary of Future **Construction** Abroad, C 57.113

Railroad **Construction** Indices, IC 1 acco.8

Registered Group-Joint Apprenticeship Programs in **Construction** Industry (by trades), L 23.9

Reports of **Construction** Permits Retired to Closed Files, etc., CC 1.29

Representative **Construction** Cost of Hill- Burton Hospitals and Related Health Facilities, FS 2.74/6, HE 20.2510

Representative **Construction** Costs of Hospitals and Related Health Facilities, HE 1.109

Scientific Reports of Higher Schools Machine **Construction** and Instruments Manufacture, C 41.65/8

Sewage and Water Works **Construction**, I 67.11

Sewage Facilities **Construction**, (year), EP 2.20

Ship **Construction** Manuals, N 24.37, T 47.37

Special Analysis of Federal Activities in Public Works and Other **Construction** in Budget, PrEx 2.8/a2

Special Reports **Construction** Engineering Research Laboratory, D 103.53/4

Standard Specifications for **Construction** of Airports, TD 4.24

Standards for Specifying **Construction** of Airports, TD 4.24

State Priority Lists for **Construction** Grants for Wastewater Treatment Works, Fiscal Year (date), EP 1.56/4

Status of Vessel **Construction** and Reconditioning under Merchant Marine Acts of 1920 and 1938, SB 7.5:1105, C 27.9/8

Steam-Electric Plant **Construction** Cost and Annual Production Expenses, E 3.17

Survey of Nuclear Power Plant **Construction** Costs, E 3.17/5

Technical Handbook for Facilities Engineering and **Construction** Manuals, HE 1.108/2

Telecommunications Engineering and **Construction** Manual, A 68.6/4

Telephone Engineering and **Construction** Manual, A 68.6/4

Thermal-Electric Plant **Construction** Cost and Annual Production Expenses, E 3.17/4

Value of New **Construction** Put in Place, C 3.215/3

Vessels Receiving Benefits of **Construction** Loans under Merchant Marine Act of 1928, SB 7.8

Wastewater Treatment **Construction** Grants Data Base, Public Law 92-500 Project Records, Grants Assistance Programs, New Projects Funded During (Month), EP 1.56

Work Injuries, Contract **Construction**, L 2.77/3

Constructions

Prices of Cotton Cloth and Raw Cotton, and Mill Margins for Certain **Constructions** of Unfinished Cloth, A 88.11/10

Constructive

Constructive Hints, A 13.33

Consular

Advance Sheets of **Consular** Reports, S 4.5

Circulars: General Instructions, **Consular** or Special Instruction, **Consular**, S 1.4/2

Consular Regulations, S 1.5

Consular Reports, S 4.10

Consular Reports, Annual Series, C 10.12

Daily **Consular** and Trade Reports, C 10.5, C 10.6, C 18.5

Daily **Consular** Reports, C 14.6

Digest of Circular Instruction to **Consular** Officers, S 1.4/3

Foreign **Consular** Offices in the U.S., S 1.34, S 1.69, S 1.68/2

General Indexes to Monthly **Consular** Reports, S 4.8

Index to Daily **Consular** Reports, C 14.7

Index to Monthly **Consular** Reports, C 14.9

Indexes to Advance Sheets of **Consular** Reports, S 4.6

Instructions to Diplomatic and **Consular** Officers, S 1.10

List of Foreign **Consular** Officers in United States, S 1.12

Monthly **Consular** Reports, C 14.8

Special **Consular** Reports, S 4.9, C 14.10, C 10.7, C 18.9

Special Issue, **Consular** Reports, S 4.13

Weekly **Consular** and Trade Reports, C 10.14

Consular Service

Mailing List of **Consular Service** of United States, S 1.19

Consultant

Federal Labor-Management **Consultant**, PM 1.13, CS 1.80

Consultants

Accessibility Assistance, a Directory of **Consultants** on Environments for Handicapped People, CSA 1.2:Ac 2

Consultatif

U.S. National Committee of the CCIR {Comite **Consultatif** International des Radiocommunication}: Publications, S 5.56

Consultation

Reports for **Consultation** on Air Quality Control Regions, FS 2.93/5

Consumed

Report of Cotton **Consumed**, on Hand, Imported and Exported and Active Spindles, C 3.21

Consumer

Air Travel **Consumer** Report, TD 1.54

Available Publications of USDA'S **Consumer** and Marketing Service (except Market News Reports), A 88.40/2:53

CIB (**Consumer** Information Bureau) Annual Report, CC 1.60/1-1

CIB (**Consumer** Information Bureau) General Publications, CC 1.60/1-2

Consumer, Y 3.N 21/8:22, L 17.9

Consumer Action Handbook, GS 11.9/3

Consumer Advisory **Council** Report, PrEx 6.10

Consumer Affairs Fact Sheets (series), TD 8.14/3

Consumer Aid Series, TD 8.14/2

Consumer Alert, FT 1.24/2

Consumer Briefing Summary, E 1.29

Consumer Bulletins, FT 1.3/2

Consumer Buying Indicators, C 3.186:P 65

Consumer Complaint Contact System, Annual Report, Y 3.C 76/3:20

Consumer Credit, FR 1.36

Consumer Credit at **Consumer** Finance Companies, FR 1.36/7

Consumer Deputy Program (series), Y 3.C 76/3:22

Consumer Education Bibliography, PrEx 16.10:Ed 8

Consumer Energy Atlas, E 1.33/2:10879-01

Consumer Expenditure Survey: Quarterly Data from the Interview Survey, L 2.3/18-3

Consumer Expenditure Survey Results, L 2.120/2-5

Consumer Expenditure Survey: Diary Survey, L 2.3/18-2

Consumer Expenditure Survey: Interview Survey, L 2.3/18

Consumer Fact Sheet, TD 5.60

Consumer Facts, A 21.13/6

Consumer Finance Companies, Loans Outstanding and Volume of Loans Made, FR 1.36/6

Consumer Focus, GS 11.9/3-2

Consumer Goods and Domestic Trade, PrEx 7.21/8

Consumer Goods Research, C 57.118

Consumer Income, C 3.186:P-60

Consumer Information Catalog, GS 11.9

Consumer Information Leaflets, L 1.72

Consumer Information Series, GS 1.1, GS 2.16, HE 1.34/2, TD 2.213, TD 8.14, HE 20.427/2

Consumer Information TV Program Packages, Suggested Scripts, A 21.27

Consumer Installment Credit at Commercial Banks, FR 1.36/2

Consumer Installment Credit Extended and Repaid, FR 1.36/5

Consumer Installment Credits of Industrial Loan Companies, FR 1.36/4

Consumer Installment Loans of Principal Types of Financial Institutions, FR 1.34

Consumer Legislative Monthly Report, HE 1.510

Consumer Loans Made Under Effective State Small Loan Laws, FR 1.36/3

Consumer News, HE 1.509, CC 1.59

Consumer Notes, Y 3.N 21/9:8, A 55.56

Consumer Notice, HH 1.81

Consumer Price Index, Chicago, L 2.38/8-2

Consumer Product Information, GS 11.9

Consumer Product Safety Review, Y 3.C 76/3:28

Consumer Purchases of Citrus and Other Juices, CPFJ (series), A 93.12

Consumer Purchases of Fruits and Juices, A 88.12/4

Consumer Purchases of Fruits and Juices by Regions and Retail Outlets, A 36.171/2

Consumer Purchases of Selected Fresh Fruits, Canned and Frozen Juices, and Dried Fruits, A 36.171

Consumer Relations Newsletter, HH 1.15/3

Consumer Study Outline, A 55.53

Consumer Survey Handbooks, FT 1.8/3

Consumer Update, HE 20.4010/3

CQ, **Consumer** Quarterly, HE 20.4010/5

Directory of **Consumer** Offices, HE 1.509/2

Directory of Federal **Consumer** Offices, HE 1.509/2

Directory of State, County, and City Government **Consumer** Offices, HE 1.502:St 2, PrEx 16.2:St 2/2

Directory: Federal, State and Local Government **Consumer** Offices, HE 1.502:St 2

Education Research **Consumer** Guide, ED 1.308/2

Energy **Consumer**, E 1.29/2

Facts for **Consumer** Durables Trade, Pr 32.4267

FDA **Consumer**, HE 20.4010

FDA **Consumer** Memos, HE 20.4010/2

FDA **Consumer** Special Report, HE 20.4010/4

FDIC **Consumer** News, Y 3.F 31/8:24

Federal **Consumer** Focus, GS 11.9/3

Finance Rate and Other Terms on Selected Categories of **Consumer** Installment Credit Extended by Finance Companies, FR 1.34/7

Finance Rates and Other Terms on Selected Types of **Consumer** Installment Credit Extended by Major Finance Companies (not seasonally adjusted), FR 1.34/9

Guide to Federal **Consumer** Services, PrEx 16.8:Se 6

HEW **Consumer** Newsletter, FS 1.34

Latest **Consumer** Price Index (Tables for U.S. and 6 Cities in Midwest), L 2.38/8-4

National **Consumer** Buying Alert, Pr 39.14

NBS **Consumer** Information Series, C 13.53

New for Consumers, Highlights of New Federal **Consumer** Publications, GS 11.9/2

Orders **Consumer** Product Safety Commission, Y 3.C 76/3:6-2

P.C. Producer-**Consumer** Series, A 55.65

Popular Publications for Farmer, Suburbanite, Homemaker, **Consumer**, A 21.9/8:5, A 107.12:5

Radio Service **Consumer** Facts, A 21.13/6

Relative Importance of Components in the **Consumer** Price Indexes, L 2.3/9

Sanitation Handbook of **Consumer** Protection Programs, A 88.6/4:Sa 5

Study of **Consumer** Purchases, A 42.8

USDA **Consumer** Expenditure Survey Reports, A 77.22

Women/**Consumer** Calendar of Events, EP 1.84

Consumer Price Index

Consumer **Price Index** {by individual cities and commodities}, L 2.38/5

Consumer Price Index, a Short Description, L 2.2:P 93/19

Consumer Price Index, Mountain Region and Plain Region, L 2.38/6

Consumer Price Index, Price Indexes for Selected Items and Groups, L 2.38/4

Consumer Price Index, Washington, D.C. Area, L 2.38/8

CPI Detailed Report, **Consumer Price Index**, U.S. City Average and Selected Areas, L 2.38/3

Latest **Consumer Price Index** (Tables for U.S. and 6 Cities in Midwest), L 2.38/8-4

News, **Consumer Price Index**, L 2.38/3-2

Consumer Prices

Consumer Prices, Pr 32.4258

Consumer Prices: Energy and Food, L 2.38/7

Consumers

Aluminum Metal Supply and Shipments of Products to **Consumers**, C 41.112/4

Annual Report on the Impact of the Caribbean Basin Economic Recovery Act on U.S. Industries and **Consumers**, ITC 1.32

Coal **Consumers'** Digest, I 39.8, I 48.58, Y 3.B 54/2:7

Consumers Counsel Division, **Consumers'** Counsel Series Publications, A 75.11

Consumers Service, A 55.72

Consumers' Advisory Board, General Publications, Y 3.N 21/8:16

United States Army Installations and Major
Activities in **Continental** U.S., D
101.22:210-1
Continental Congress
Index/Journals of the **Continental Congress**, GS
4.2:C 76/2
Index/Papers of the **Continental Congress**, GS
4.2:C 76/3
Journals of **Continental Congress**, Miscellaneous,
LC 4.6
Journals of the **Continental Congress**, LC 4.5
Journals of the **Continental Congress**, Index, GS
4.2:C 76/2
Continental Divide
Continental Divide Trail Study Progress Reports, I
66.19/2
Continental Shelf
Environmental Assessment of the Alaskan
Continental Shelf, C 55.622/2
Environmental Assessment of the Alaskan
Continental Shelf {various publica-
tions}, C 55.622/2
Environmental Assessment of the Alaskan
Continental Shelf, Principal
Investigator's Reports, C 55.622
Continerized
Continerized Cargo Statistics, C 39.233
Contingency
Contingency Plans, FE 1.25
Contingent
Contingent Foreign Liabilities of U.S. Govern-
ment, T 1.45/3
Continuation
Continuation Application for Grants under Special
Services for Disadvantage Students
Program, ED 1.60
Continuation Application for Grants under Talent
Search Program, ED 1.55
Continued
Continued Increases in Industry Productivity in
(year) Reported by BLS, L 1.79/2-3
Continuing
Community Service and **Continuing** Education,
Title 1, Higher Education Act of 1965,
FS 5.78
Continuing Education is Work, Y 3.Ed 8/8:1
Continuing Survey of Food Intake by Individuals,
A 111.9/3
Energy, **Continuing** Bibliography with Indexes,
NAS 1.21:7043
Quarterly Bulletin, Intelligence **Continuing**
Education Program, D 5.212
Continuous
Plants Under USDA **Continuous** Inspection,
Processed Fruits and Vegetables and
Related Products, A 88.43/2
Contraceptive
Contraceptive Development Contract Review
Committee, HE 20.3001/2:C 76
Contraceptive Evaluation Research Contract
Review Committee, HE 20.3001/2:C 76/
2
Contract
Annual Historical Summary; Defense **Contract**
Administration Services {by region}, D
7.1/4
AVFUEL & AVOIL into Plane **Contract** Listing, D
7.24/2
Behavioral Sciences Research **Contract** Review
Committee, HE 20.3001/2:B 39
Biometry and Epidemilogy **Contract** Review
Committee, HE 20.3001/2:B 52/6
BLM **Contract** Solicitation, I 53.38
Consolidated List of Persons or Firms Currently
Debarred for Violations of Various Public
Contracts Acts Incorporating Labor
Standard Provisions, GA 1.17
Contraceptive Development **Contract** Review
Committee, HE 20.3001/2:C 76
Contraceptive Evaluation Research **Contract**
Review Committee, HE 20.3001/2:C 76/
2
Contract Advisory Service Summaries, IC 1.36
Contract and Requisitioned Steamships, SB 2.13
Contract Bulletin, N 20.12, N 20.18
Contract Clearing House Service, Summaries, Pr
33.916
Contract Reports, NAS 1.26, C 60.12, D 103.24/9,
D 103.52, E 1.99, Y 3.N 88:25-2
Contract Reports Corps of Engineers, D 103.52
Contract Reports National Aeronautics and Space
Administration, NAS 1.26
Contract Reports National Telecommunications
and Information Administration, C 60.12

Contract Reports Nuclear Regulatory Commission,
Y 3.N 88:25-2
Contract Reports Waterways Experiment Station,
D 103.24/9
Contract Research Reports, TD 8.15/2
Cooperative Research Program: Projects under
Contract, FS 5.69
Dahlgren Laboratory: **Contract** Reports, D 201.21/
4
Defense **Contract** Audit Agency and Strategic
Plan, D 1.46/5-2
Defense **Contract** Audit Agency Bulletin, D 1.46/6
Defense **Contract** Audit Agency Manual, DCAAM
(series), D 1.46/2
Defense **Contract** Audit Agency Pamphlets,
DCAAP (series), D 1.46
Digest of Decisions of Armed Services Board of
Contract Appeals, D 1.21
Digest of Decisions of Corps of Engineers Board of
Contract Appeals, D 103.36
Directory of **Contract** Opportunities, Pr 32.4811
DoD Directory of **Contract** Administration
Services Components, D 1.6/12
Educational and Nonprofit Institutions Receiving
Prime **Contract** Awards for Research,
Development, Test and Evaluation, D
1.57/8
Extramural Grant and **Contract** Awards by
Principal Investigator/Contractor, HE
20.3176/3
Extramural Grant and **Contract** Awards by State,
City Institution and Number, HE
20.3176/4
Federal **Contract** Air Service and Travel Directory,
GS 8.10
Forecast **Contract** Opportunities, S 1.150
Forecast of **Contract** Opportunities, Fiscal Year,
HH 1.116
Grants **Contract** Reports, Experimental Technology
Incentives Program, GCR-ETIP (series),
C 13.57/2
Guide of the U.S. Development of Energy, Board of
Contract Appeals and **Contract**
Adjustment Board, E 1.8/4
Guidelines: Innovative Collective Bargaining
Contract Provisions, FM 1.9
Handbook for Veterans Administration **Contract**
Representatives, VA 1.10/5:232-68-1/2
Health Insurance Studies: **Contract** Research
Series, HE 22.11
Industry Wage Survey: **Contract** Cleaning
Services, L 2.3/33
Mining Research **Contract** Review, I 28.154
Motor Carrier Freight Commodity Statistics Class 1
Common and **Contract** Carriers of
Property, IC 1 mot.22
NCEL **Contract** Report, D 209.12/4
Nongovernment Organization Codes for Military
Standard **Contract** Administration
Procedures: Code to Name, D 7.6/2:8-2/
2
Nongovernment Organization Codes for Military
Standard **Contract** Administration
Procedures: Name to Code, D 7.6/2:8-1/
2
Nongovernment Organization Codes for Military
Standard **Contract** Administration
Procedures, D 7.6/2:8
Oil **Contract** Bulletin, D 11.3
One Hundred Companies Receiving the Largest
Dollar Volume of Prime **Contract**
Awards, D 1.57
ORP **Contract** Reports, EP 6.10/9
Prime **Contract** Awards by Region and State, D
1.57/5
Prime **Contract** Awards by Service Category and
Federal Supply Classification, D 1.57/4
Prime **Contract** Awards by State, D 1.57/6
Prime **Contract** Awards by Statutory Authority,
Number of Actions, and Net Value by
Department, D 1.57/3-2
Prime **Contract** Awards in Labor Surplus Area, D
1.57/7
Prime **Contract** Awards, D 1.57/3
Prime **Contract** Awards, Size Distribution, D 1.57/
3-5
Proceedings **Contract** Settlement Appeal Board, FS
5.7/a
Quarterly Freight Loss and Damage Claims
Reported by Common and **Contract**
Motor Carriers of Property, IC 1 acco.11
Regional **Contract** Charts, A 55.7/2, A 55.7/3, A
55.7/4

Report on Activities Defense **Contract** Audit
Agency, D 1.46/5
Sewage Treatment Works **Contract** Awards, FS
2.56/3
Solicitation of the Public Health Service and the
Health Care Financing Administration
for Small Business Innovation Research
Contract Proposals, HE 22.31
Solicitation of the Public Health Service for Small
Business Research (SBIR) **Contract**
Proposals, HE 20.28/2
State Distribution of Defense **Contract** Awards, Pr
32.4013
Summary of Mortgage Insurance Operations and
Contract Authority, HH 2.24/5
Synopsis of U.S. Government Proposed
Procurement and **Contract** Awards, C
18.284
Term **Contract**, TC- (series), GS 2.12
Top Five Contractors Receiving the Largest Dollar
Volume of Prime **Contract** Awards in
Each State, D 1.57/2-2
Trends in Utilization of Indian Health Service and
Contract Hospitals, HE 20.9417
War **Contract** Terminations and Settlements, Report
to Congress, Y 3.W 19/7:107, T 67.7
Weekly Census Report of U.S. Marine and **Contract**
Hospitals, T 26.36
Work Injuries, **Contract** Construction, L 2.77/3
Contract Appeals
Decisions on **Contract Appeals**, I 1.69/7
Contracting
Forecast **Contracting** and Subcontracting
Opportunities, E 1.122/2
Lessons Learned in **Contracting** RPMA, D
103.121
Postal **Contracting** Manual, P 1.12/6
Contractions
Contractions, TD 4.308:C 76
Contractions Handbook, TD 4.308:C 76
Contractor
Annual Report of Radiation Exposures for DOE
and DOE **Contractor** Employees, E 1.42
Atmospheric Sciences Laboratory: **Contractor**
Reports ASL-CR (series), D 111.9/6
Contractor Fatalities Coal and Metal/Nonmetal
Mines, L 38.20/4
Contractor Report (series), ED 1.115
Contractor Research and Development Reports, E
1.28
Farm Labor **Contractor** Registration Act, Public
Registry, National Listing of Contractors
and Employees Registered, L 36.14
Federal Procurement Data System, **Contractor**
Identification File, Alphabetical Listing,
PrEx 2.24/14
Licensee **Contractor** and Vendor Inspection Status
Report, Y 3.N 88:24
NIST-GCR Grantee/ **Contractor** Report, C 13.57/2
OT **Contractor** Reports, C 1.60/7
Contractors
Abstracts from Annual and Technical Reports
Submitted by USAMRDC **Contractors**/
Grantees, D 104.23
Alphabetical List of DoD Prime **Contractors**, D
1.57/3-3
Annual **Contractors'** Conference on Artificial
Kidney Program, Proceedings, HE
20.3314
Consolidated List of Debarred, Suspended, and
Ineligible **Contractors**, GS 1.28
Devices and Technology Branch **Contractors**
Meeting, Summary and Abstracts, HE
20.3219
Farm Labor Contractor Registration Act, Public
Registry, National Listing of
Contractors and Employees Registered,
L 36.14
Five-hundred **Contractors** Receiving the Largest
Dollar Volume of Prime Contracts for
RDT&E, D 1.57/2
List of Awards Showing **Contractors** and Prices
Contained in General Schedule of
Supplies, T 45.6
List of Awards Showing **Contractors** and Prices
for Material and Supplies Contained in
General Schedule, GS 1.6
Selective Service Memorandums to All Navy
Contractors, N 1.30
Selling to Navy Prime **Contractors**, D 201.2:Se 4/
2
Top Five **Contractors** Receiving the Largest Dollar
Volume of Prime Contract Awards in
Each State, D 1.57/2-2

Contracts
Administrative Decisions, Walsh-Healey Public
   Contracts Act, Index-Digest, L 21.2:In 2
Alphabetical Listing of Completed War Supply
   Contracts (compilations), Pr 32.4842/3
Alphabetical Listing of Major War Supply
   Contracts, Pr 32.4842
Bid Opening Report Federal-Aid Highway
   Construction **Contracts** Calendar Year,
   TD 2.47
Construction Reports; Housing Authorized by
   Building Permits and Public **Contracts**,
   C 3.215/11
Construction Reports; Housing Authorized by
   Building Permits and Public **Contracts**,
   C 40 (series), C 56.211/4
Contracts for Field Projects & Supporting
   Research on . . ., E 1.99/2
Contracts for U.S. Food Products, A 67.40/3
Contracts Handbook, TD 4.308:C 76
Daily Congressional Notification of Grants and
   Contracts Awarded, NS 1.34
Decisions under Walsh-Healey Public **Contracts**
   Act, L 22.12
Department of the Army Prime **Contracts** ($1
   million and over) Placed with Industry,
   Non-Profit Organizations, Colleges, and
   Universities, D 101.22:715-4
Energy Data **Contracts** Finder, E 3.39
Federal Grants and **Contracts** for Unclassified
   Research in Life Sciences, NS 1.10
Federal Grants and **Contracts** for Unclassified
   Research in Physical Sciences, NS 1.10/
   2
Finance Rate and Other Terms on New Car and Used
   Car Installment Credit **Contracts**
   Purchased from Dealers of Major Auto
   Finance Companies, FR 1.34/5
Five-hundred Contractors Receiving the Largest
   Dollar Volume of Prime **Contracts** for
   RDT&E, D 1.57/2
Futures Trading and Open **Contracts** in Butter,
   Eggs and Potatoes, A 85.11/4
Futures Trading and Open **Contracts** in Cotton and
   Cottonseed Oil, A 85.11/5
Futures Trading and Open **Contracts** in Frozen
   Concentrated Orange Juice, A 85.11/8
Futures Trading and Open **Contracts** in Potatoes,
   A 85.11/3
Futures Trading and Open **Contracts** in Potatoes
   and Rice, A 85.11
Futures Trading and Open **Contracts** in Soybean
   Meal and Cottonseed Meal, A 85.11/6
Futures Trading and Open **Contracts** in Wheat,
   Corn, Oats, Rye, Soybeans and Products,
   A 85.11/7
Futures Trading and Open **Contracts** in {Wheat,
   Corn, Oats, etc.} on Chicago Board of
   Trade, A 88.11/18
Health Care Financing, Grants and **Contracts**
   Reports, HE 22.19
Highway Construction **Contracts** Awarded by
   State Highway Departments, C 37.25
Highway Construction **Contracts** Awarded by
   State Highway Departments, Tables, FW
   2.19
Housing Authorized by Building Permits and
   Public **Contracts**, C 3.215/4
ICA **Contracts** Notice, S 7.26/2
Interagency Directory, Key Contacts for Planning,
   Scientific and Technical Exchange
   Programs, Educational Travel, Students,
   Teachers, Lecturers, Research Scholars,
   Specialists, S 1.67/3
Interim List of Persons or Firms Currently Debarred
   for Violation of Various Public
   Contracts Acts Incorporating Labor
   Standards Provisions, GA 1.17/2
LEAA Grants and **Contracts**, J 1.33
LEAA Grants and **Contracts**: Dissemination
   Document, J 1.33/2
List of State Designated Agencies, Officials and
   Working **Contracts**, C 1.53/3
Listing of Major War Supply **Contracts** by State
   and County, Pr 32.4841
Monthly Highway Construction **Contracts**
   Awarded by State and Federal Agencies
   and Toll Authorities, TD 2.51
National Defense Program, **Contracts** and
   Expenditures as Reported in Press
   Releases: Tabulations, Pr 32.212
NINDS Index to Research Grants and **Contracts**,
   HE 20.3516

Procurement and **Contracts** Management, DOE/
   PR- (series), E 1.49
Proposals Received and **Contracts** Awarded for
   Supplies for Indian Service, I 20.11
Publications and Final Reports on **Contracts** and
   Grants, C 55.13/2-2
Research and Development **Contracts**, Fiscal Year
   Funds, HE 20.3013/4
Status Report, Voluntary and Non-Profit Agency
   Technical Crop Ration **Contracts** with
   International Cooperation Administra-
   tion, S 17.41/2
Stocks of Grain in Deliverable Positions for
   Chicago Board of Trade, Futures
   Contracts in Exchange-Approved and
   Federally Licensed Warehouses, as
   Reported by Those Warehouses, A 85.14,
   Y 3.C 73/5:10
Subject Index of Current Research Grants and
   Contracts Administered by the National
   Heart, Lung, and Blood Institute, HE
   20.3212
Summary of Grants and **Contracts** Active on June
   30, (year), HE 20.6510
Summary of Grants and **Contracts** Administered by
   the National Center for Health Services
   Research and Development, HE 20.2116
Summary of War Supply and Facility **Contracts** by
   State and Industrial Area, Pr 32.4828
Value of Prime **Contracts** Awarded by Federal
   Agencies in Areas of Substantial Labor
   Surplus, C 46.10
Walsh-Healey Public **Contracts** Act Minimum
   Wage Determination (for various
   industries), L 22.19
Walsh-Healey Public **Contracts** Act, Decisions, L
   22.23
Contrails
   Contrails, Air Force Cadet Handbook, D 305.16
Contribution
   Computer **Contribution** (series), I 19.67
   Distribution of Rail Revenue **Contribution** by
      Commodity Groups, IC 1 acco.9
   EFC Formula Book, The Expected Family
      Contribution for Federal Student Aid,
      ED 1.45/5
Contributions
   Basic-Data **Contributions**, I 19.69
   Bibliographical **Contributions**, A 17.8
   Contributions from the Center for Northern
      Studies, I 29.99
   Contributions from the Museum of History and
      Technology, Papers, SI 3.3
   Contributions from the U.S. National Herbarium, SI
      3.8
   Contributions from Thermodynamics Laboratory,
      Petroleum Experiment Station,
      Bartlesville, Oklahoma, I 28.105
   Contributions from U.S. National Herbarium, A 6.5
   Contributions of American Educational History, I
      16.15
   Contributions to Medical Science, N 10.9
   Contributions to Naval History (series), D 207.10/
      4
   Contributions to North American Ethnology, I
      17.5
   Contributions Toward a Flora of Nevada, A 77.527
   Family **Contributions** to War and Post-War Morale,
      FS 5.38
   Smithsonian **Contributions** to Anthropology, SI
      1.33
   Smithsonian **Contributions** to Astrophysics, SI
      1.12/2
   Smithsonian **Contributions** to Botany, SI 1.29
   Smithsonian **Contributions** to Earth Sciences, SI
      1.26
   Smithsonian **Contributions** to Knowledge, SI 1.6
   Smithsonian **Contributions** to Paleobiology, SI
      1.30
   Smithsonian **Contributions** to the Marine Sciences,
      SI 1.41
   Smithsonian **Contributions** to Zoology, SI 1.27
   United States **Contributions** to International
      Organizations, S 1.70, S 1.70/9
Control
   Accident **Control** Reports, I 49.73
   Administration of the Toxic Substances **Control**
      Act, EP 1.79
   Air Force Command and **Control** Development
      Division: Technical Notes AFCCDD-TN
      (nos.), D 301.45/24
   Air Navigation and Air Traffic **Control** Facility
      Performance and Availability Report,
      Calendar Year, TD 4.710

Air Pollution, Sulfur Oxides Pollution **Control**,
   Federal Research and Development,
   Planning and Programming, FS 2.93/4
Animal Damage **Control** Program, A 101.28
Annual Conference on Advanced Pollution
   Control for the Metal Finishing
   Industry, EP 1.80
Annual Conference Report on Cotton-Insect
   Research and **Control**, A 106.28/2
Annual NASA-University Conference on Manual
   Control, NAS 1.21
Annual Report of the Secretary of Transportation on
   Hazardous Materials **Control**, TD 1.24
Aquatic Plant **Control** Program Technical Reports,
   D 103.24/13
Biology and **Control** of Insect and Related Pests of
   {various animals}, EP 1.94
Blister Rust **Control** in California Cooperative
   Project of State and Federal Agencies
   and Private Owners Annual Reports, A
   13.54
Bulletin of Courses Water Pollution **Control**
   Technical Training Program, I 67.17
Cabinet Task Force on Oil Import **Control**, Pr
   37.8:Oi 5
Cancer **Control** Advisory Committee, HE 20.3001/
   2:C 16/13
Cancer **Control** and Rehabilitation Advisory
   Committee, HE 20.3001/2:C 16/3
Cancer **Control** Community Activities Review
   Committee, HE 20.3001/2:C 16/2
Cancer **Control** Education Review Committee, HE
   20.3001/2:C 16/14
Cancer **Control** Grant Review Committee, HE
   20.3001/2:C 16/12
Cancer **Control** Letter, FS 2.22/3
Cancer **Control** Treatment and Rehabilitation
   Review Committee, HE 20.3001/2:C 16/
   15
Cancer **Control**, Prevention, and Detection Review
   Committee, HE 20.3001/2:C 16/8
Chemical Evaluation and **Control** Fact Sheets, A
   77.239/2
Compendium of State Air Pollution **Control**
   Agencies, 1972, EP 1.2:St 2/972
Comprehensive Export **Control** Schedules, Y 3.Ec
   74/2:108
Computers, **Control**, and Information Theory, C
   51.9/8
Conference Report on Cotton Insect Research and
   Control, A 77.328
Control and Employment of Vessels Trading with
   United States, SB 5.6
Cooperative Pest **Control** Programs, A 77.327
Current Projects in Prevention, **Control**, and
   Treatment of Crime and Delinquency, FS
   2.22/51
DCAS Manufacturing Cost **Control** Digest, D 7.22
Diabetes Control Program Update, HE 20.7314
Disease **Control** Services Activities, A 77.212/9
EC {Entomological **Control**} (series), A 77.323
Economic **Control** and Commercial Policy in
   American Republics, TC 1.20
Economic Impact Analysis of Alternative Pollution
   Control Technologies (series), EP 1.8/
   10
En Route Air Traffic **Control**, TD 4.308:En 1
Entomological **Control** Series, A 77.323
Environmental Pollution and **Control**, C 51.9/5
Epidemiology and Disease **Control** Study Section,
   HE 20.3001/2:Ep 4/2
Export **Control**, C 1.26
Export **Control** Bulletin, C 57.409/2
Export **Control** Regulations, C 42.11/3, C 57.409
Export **Control** Schedules (numbered), Y 3.Ec 74/
   2:107
Export **Control**, Quarterly Reports, C 1.26
Extension Pathologist; News Letter for Extension
   Workers Interested in Plant Disease
   Control, A 43.20
FAA Plan for Air Navigation and Air Traffic
   Control Systems, FAA 1.37
Federal/State Radiation **Control** Legislation, HE
   20.4115
Fire **Control** Notes, A 13.32
Fireword, a Bulletin From the National Fire
   Prevention and **Control** Administration,
   C 58.10
For Your Information; Operations **Control**
   Services, FCD 1.13/4
Functions and Organization of Bureau of Supplies
   and Accounts, **Control** Record, N 20.25
FY Budget Highlights Federal Drug **Control**
   Programs, PrEx 26.1/4

Grants for Training, Construction, Cancer **Control**, Medical Libraries, HE 20.3013/5

Grants, Juvenile Delinquency Prevention and **Control** Act, HE 17.21

Homestudy Course; Vectorborne Disease **Control** (series), HE 20.7021/7-2

Homestudy Courses; Communicable Disease **Control**, HE 20.7021/2

Homestudy Courses; Foodborne Disease **Control**, HE 20.7021/6

Homestudy Courses; Vectorborne Disease **Control**, HE 20.7021/7

Homestudy Courses; Waterborne Disease **Control**, HE 20.7021/4

Horizontal **Control** Data, C 55.430

Immediate Water Pollution **Control** Needs, I 67.13/5

Injury **Control** Research Laboratory: Research Report, ICRL-RR (series), HE 20.1116

Injury Epidemiology and **Control** Reprints, HE 20.7009/3

Instructions for Classifying the Underlying Cause of Death: Source Records and **Control** Specifications, HE 20.6208/11

International Narcotics **Control** Strategy Report, S 1.146

Items of Interest in Seed **Control**, A 88.63

Japanese Beetle-European Chafer **Control** Program, Annual Report, A 77.326

Juvenile Delinquency Prevention and **Control** Act of 1968, Grants, HE 17.811

Laws Relating to Forestry, Game Conservation, Flood **Control** and Related Subjects, Y 1.2:F 76/4

Manual on Uniform **Control** Devices for Streets and Highways, TD 2.8:T 67

Manual on Uniform Traffic **Control** Devices for Streets and Highways: Official Rulings on Requests for Interpretations, Changes, and Experimentations, TD 2.8/2

Marine Air Traffic **Control** Detachment Handbook, PCN nos, D 214.9/7

Molecular **Control** Working Group, HE 20.3001/2:M 73

National Drug **Control** Policy, PrEx 26.1/2

Notices, Activities of Licensed Establishments Supervised by Virus-Serum **Control** Division, A 4.31, A 77.217

Numbers of Farms Participating in 1934 AAA Voluntary **Control** Programs (by States), A 55.55

Official Gazette **Control** Council for Germany, W 1.73, M 105.9

Passport **Control** Acts {February 1, 1917}, Y 1.2:P 26

Pathologist; News Letter for Extension Workers Interested in Plant Disease **Control**, A 43.20

Plant Disease, Decay, Etc., **Control** Activities of Department of Agriculture, Reports, A 1.90

Plant Pest **Control** Cooperative Programs, Western Region, Fiscal Year (date), A 77.327/2

Poison **Control** Statistics, HE 20.4019

Price **Control** Fact Sheets, Pr 32.4268

Price **Control** Reports, Pr 32.4234

Progress in the Prevention and **Control** of Air Pollution in (year), Report to Congress, EP 4.16

Project Register, Projects Approved Under Sec. 8 of Federal Water Pollution **Control** Act (Pub. Law 660, 84th Cong.), As Amended and Sec. 3, of Public Works

Publications Air Pollution **Control** Office, EP 4.9

Publications National Air Pollution **Control** Administration, FS 2.93/3

Quality **Control** and Reliability Technical Reports, D 7.15

Quality **Control** Digests, C 31.166, FAA 5.11

Quality **Control** Notes, Pr 32.4835

Quality **Control** Reports, Pr 32.4833

Quarterly Report of Progress at Fish **Control** Laboratory, La Crosse, Wisconsin, Southeastern Fish **Control** Laboratory, Warm Springs, Georgia, and Hammond Bay Biological Station, Millersburg, Michigan, I 49.75

Questions and Answers on Rent **Control**, ES 5.7/2

Regulations for the Administration and Enforcement of the Radiation **Control** for Health and Safety Act of 1968, HE 20.4606/2

Report on U.S. Government Research and Studies in the Field of Arms **Control** and Disarmament Matters, AC 1.14

Reports **Control** Symbol Darcom Manufacturing Technology, RCS DRCMT-(series), D 101.110

Reports for Consultation on Air Quality **Control** Regions, FS 2.93/5

Reports of Subversive Activities **Control** Board, Y 3.Su 1:8-2

Research Reports Arms **Control** and Disarmament Agency, AC 1.15

Research Reports Injury **Control** Report Laboratory, FS 2.316

Research Results Utilization, Research Project **Control** System, Status Summary Report, Y 3.N 88:36

Review of Arms **Control** and Disarmament Activities, Y 4.Ar 5/2-16

Review of U.S. Patents Relating to Pest **Control**, A 47.7

Review of United States Patents Related to Pest **Control**, A 77.311

Rules of the Select Committee on Narcotics Abuse and **Control**, Y 4.N 16/10

Self-Study Course 3014-G, Waterborne Disease **Control** Manuals, HE 20.7021/4-2

Semiannual Report on Operations Under Mutual Defense Assistance **Control** Act of 1951, FO 1.1/2

Semiannual Reports under Mutual Defense Assistance **Control** Act, Pr 33.901/2

Ships Registered Under Liberian, Panamanian, and Honduran Flags Deemed by the Navy Department to Be Under Effective U.S. **Control**, C 39.228

Smoking and Tobacco **Control** Monographs, HE 20.3184/2

Special Occupational Hazard Review with **Control** Recommendations, HE 20.7113

State Radiation **Control** Legislation, HE 20.1112

Study of Air Traffic **Control**, Reports, C 31.123

Sulfur Oxides **Control** Technology Series, EP 7.12

Summary of Bang's Disease **Control** Program Conducted by Bureau of Animal Industry in Cooperation with Various States, A 4.23

Summary of Brucellosis (Bang's Disease) **Control** Program Conducted by Bureau of Animal Industry in Cooperation with Various States, A 77.213

Summary of U.S. Export **Control** Regulations, C 42.6:Ex 7/2

Tabulations of Statistics Pertaining to Signals, Interlocking, Automatic, Train **Control**, Telegraph and Telephone for Transmission of Train Orders, and Spring Switches As Used on Railroads of United States, IC 1 saf.10

Technical Notes Department of the Air Force Command and **Control** Development Division, D 301.45/24

Terminal Air Traffic **Control**, TD 4.308:T 27

Toxic Substances **Control** Act, Report to Congress for Fiscal Year (date), EP 1.79

Training Guide, Insect **Control** Series, FS 2.60/7, HE 20.2308

TSCA {Toxic Substances **Control** Act} Chemical Assessment Series, EP 5.15/2

TSCA {Toxic Substances **Control** Act} Chemicals-in-progress Bulletin, EP 5.15

Tuberculosis **Control** Issues, FS 2.7/a 2

Unemployment Insurance Quality **Control**, Annual Report, L 37.20/3

U.S. Arms **Control** and Disarmament Agency, Annual Report, Y 4.F 76/1-16

U.S. Naval **Control** of Shipping Report, D 201.30

Water Pollution **Control** Research and Training Grants, FS 2.64/7, I 67.13

Water Pollution **Control** Research Series, EP 1.16, EP 2.10

Water Pollution **Control**, Federal Costs, Report to Congress, I 67.1/2

Water Supply and Pollution **Control**, FS 2.64/2

White Pine Blister **Control**, Annual Report, A 13.59

Controlled

New Health and Hospital Projects Authorized for Construction under **Controlled** Materials Plan, FS 2.73/2

Project Label, Alphabetical Listings by **Controlled** Generic Drug Ingredients, J 24.24/2

Questions and Answers on **Controlled** Materials Plan, Q & A (series), C 40.13

Controller

Controller Chart Supplement, TD 4.317

Controller Patient Census Monographs, VA 1.48/3

Controller, CR (series), E 1.35

Controller's

Controller's Monthly Financial Report, T 22.67

Controlling

Controlling Chemical Hazards Series, L 16.25

Controls

Current **Controls** Bulletins, Y 3.Ec 74/2:109

Price Trends and **Controls** in Latin America, Fortnightly Review, Pr 32.4246

Report on U.S. Export **Controls** to the President and the Congress, C 57.30

CONTU

Transcript **CONTU** Meetings (numbered), Y 3.C 79:9

CONUS

CONUS Army Installations/Activities by Congressional District, D 101.99

Convection-type

Convection-type Radiators, C 3.75

Convention

Convention on International Trade in Endangered Species of Wild Fauna and Flora, Annual Report, I 49.85

U.S. Per Diem Rates (**CONUS**), GS 1.36

Summary of Major Provisions of **Convention** and of Law Relating to Factory Inspection (by States), L 16.32

Conventional

Conventional Home Mortgage Rates in Early (month), FHL 1.25/3

Conventional Loans Made in Excess of 80 Percent of Property Appraisal by Federal Savings and Loan Associations, FHL 1.19

Mortgage Interest Rates on **Conventional** Loans, Largest Insured Savings and Loan Associations, FHL 1.24

Rates & Terms on **Conventional** Home Mortgages Annual Summary, FHF 1.15

Conventions

American **Conventions**, C 18.272

Foreign Treaties and **Conventions** (United States not a Signatory), S 9.6

Lists of Commercial Treaties and **Conventions**, and Agreements Affected by Exchange of Notes or Declarations in Force Between United States and Other Countries, S 9.9

Postal Treaties and **Conventions**, P 1.9, S 9.5/3

Union **Conventions**, (year), National and International Unions, State Organizations, L 1.85

Union **Conventions**, National and International Unions, State Organizations, L 2.85

Conversion

Coal **Conversion** Systems Technical Data Book, E 1.56

Conversion Lists, L 2.35

Conversion of Neoplasms by Topography and Morphology, HE 20.3197

Conversion Tables, C 18.29

Direct Energy **Conversion**, E 1.99

Direct Energy Conversion Literature Abstracts, D 210.23

Ocean Thermal Energy **Conversion**, Report to Congress, Fiscal Year, C 55.42

Saline Water **Conversion** Demonstration Plant, I 1.87/2

Saline Water **Conversion** Report for (year), I 1.1/3

Sea Water **Conversion**, Solar Research Station (series), I 1.87

Shipbuilding and **Conversion** Program, D 207.13

Convert

Tables to **Convert** {Foreign Moneys, Weights and Measures into U.S. Standards}, C 1.11

Conveyance

Alaska **Conveyance** News, I 53.37

Conveyer

Conveyer, A 104.10

Cooking

Foreign Markets for Heating and **Cooking** Appliances, C 18.84

Cooking

Meat **Cooking** Charts, A 42.7/4

Poultry **Cooking** Charts, A 42.7/6

Cooks

Manual for Army **Cooks**, W 5.5

Cooled

High-Temperature Gas-**Cooled** Reactor Safety Studies, E 1.28/7

High-Temperature Gas-**Cooled** Reactor Safety
Studies for the Division of Reactor Safety
Research Quarterly Progress Report, E
1.28/7

Cooling
Bulk **Cooling** Tanks on Farms Supplying Federal
Milk Order Markets, A 82.81/2
Lake Michigan **Cooling** Water Studies Panel:
Reports, EP 1.72
Monthly Normals of Temperature, Precipitation, and
Heating and **Cooling** Degree Days, C
55.286
Monthly State, Regional and National **Cooling**
Degree Days Weighted by Population, C
55.287/60-3

Cooperage
Cooperage Series, C 18.60

Cooperating
Crops Research: Results of Regional Cotton Variety
Tests by **Cooperating** Agricultural
Experiment Stations, A 77.15:34
Directory of **Cooperating** Agencies, A 18.15
Monthly Memorandum for **Cooperating** Agencies,
L 5.30
Results of Regional Cotton Variety Tests by
Cooperating Agricultural Experiment
Stations, A 77.15:34

Cooperation
Agricultural **Cooperation**, A 36.12, FF 1.7
Cooperation in Agriculture, A 17.17:41
Digest Security and **Cooperation** in Europe
Commission, Y 4.Se 2/11:13/3
Economic **Cooperation** Series, S 1.65
FIPSE European Community/United States of
America Joint Consortia for **Cooperation**
in Higher Education, ED 1.23/10
Midwest Regional Member Relations Conference
Sponsored by American Institute of
Cooperation and Farmer Cooperative
Service, A 89.17
Newsletter of Community Development in
Technical **Cooperation**, S 17.31
Newsletter on Community Development in
Technical **Cooperation**, FO 1.31
Report to Congress on Economic **Cooperation**
Administration, Y 3.Ec 74/3:8
Review of Mutual **Cooperation** in Public
Administration, S 17.46
Statements by Presidents of the United States on
International **Cooperation** in Space, Y
1.92-1:S.doc. 40
Status Report, Voluntary and Non-Profit Agency
Technical Crop Ration Contracts with
International **Cooperation** Administra-
tion, S 17.41/2
Technical Digest International **Cooperation**
Administration, S 17.45
Training Manual International **Cooperation**
Administration, S 17.6/4

Cooperative
Alaska Snow Surveys and Federal-State Private
Cooperative Surveys, A 57.46/13
Annual Report of **Cooperative** Psoroptic Cattle
Scabies Eradication Activities, Fiscal
Year (date), A 77.233/3
Annual Report of **Cooperative** State-Federal Sheep
Scabies Eradication Activities, Fiscal
Year (date), A 77.233/2
Annual Report on **Cooperative** State-Federal
Psoroptic Sheep and Cattle Scabies
Eradication Activities, Fiscal Year
(date), A 77.233
Bang's Disease Work; Statement of Indemnity
Claims and Averages in **Cooperative**, A
77.211
CMC (**Cooperative** Monitoring Center) Monitor
Newsletter E 1.139
Colorado Water Supply Outlook and Federal-State-
Private **Cooperative** Snow Survey, A
57.46/19
Commercial Fisheries {Economics **Cooperative**
Marketing Leaflets}, I 49.41
Cooperative Area Manpower Planning System,
Interagency Cooperative Issuances, L
1.64
Cooperative Bibliographies, LC 2.7
Cooperative Creamery Routes, A 72.20
Cooperative Economic Insect Report, A 101.9, A
77.324/3
Cooperative Extension Work in Agriculture and
Home Economics, A 10.24
Cooperative Extension Work Office, A 43.5
Cooperative Fishery Unit Report, I 49.66

Cooperative Fishery Units Annual Report, I 49.1/5
Cooperative Forest Fire Prevention Program, A
13.20/4
Cooperative Graduate Fellowship Program for
Fiscal Year, Fellowship Awards {and}
Program of Summer Fellowships for
Graduate Teaching Assistants for Fiscal
Year, NS 1.19/2
Cooperative Information Reports, A 105.38/2, A
109.10/2
Cooperative Inter-American Plantation Rubber
Development, A 77.519
Cooperative Investigations Reports (series), I
19.83
Cooperative Observer, C 55.118
Cooperative Pest Control Programs, A 77.327
Cooperative Plant Pest Report, A 101.9/2
Cooperative Research and Service Division,
Quarterly Reports, A 72.22
Cooperative Research Program: Projects under
Contract, FS 5.69
Cooperative Research Reports, A 105.38
Cooperative Savings with Federal Credit Unions,
FCA 1.14, FCA 1.14/2
Cooperative Self-Help, Y 3.F 31/5:22
Cooperative State-Federal Bovine Tuberculosis
Eradication Program, Statistical Tables,
A 101.18
Cooperative State-Federal Brucellosis Eradication
Program; Brucellosis Bulletin, A
101.18/3
Cooperative State-Federal Brucellosis Eradication
Program; Charts and Maps, A 77.212/6-2
Cooperative State-Federal Brucellosis Eradication
Program; Progress Report, A 77.15:91-
57
Cooperative State-Federal Brucellosis Eradication
Program; Statistical Tables, A 101.18/2
Cooperative State-Federal Brucellosis Eradication
Program; Statistical Tables, Fiscal Year
(date), A 77.212/4
Cooperative State-Federal Brucellosis Eradication
Programs, A 77.212/6
Cooperative State-Federal Hog Cholera
Eradication Program Progress Report, A
77.241
Cooperative State-Federal Sheep and Cattle
Scabies Eradication, Progress Report, A
77.233
Cooperative State-Federal Sheep and Cattle
Scabies, Epidemiology and Related
Activities, A 77.233/4
Cooperative State-Federal Tuberculosis
Eradication Program, Statistical Tables,
Fiscal Year (date), A 77.212/5
Cooperative State-Federal Tuberculosis
Eradication, Progress Report, A
77.15:91-44
Cooperative Studies Reports, C 30.61
Cooperative Studies Technical Papers, C 30.61/2
Cooperative Summary of the Day, C 55.281/2-4
Cooperative Water Resources, Research and
Training, I 1.1/4
Farmer **Cooperative** Films, A 89.15:2
Farmer **Cooperative** Statistics, A 109.11/2
Farmer's **Cooperative** Income Tax Returns, T 22.35/
2:F 22
Federal State **Cooperative** Snow Surveys and Water
Supply Forecasts, A 57.46/9-2
Federal-State **Cooperative** Program for Population
Estimates, C 3.186:P-26
Federal-State-Private **Cooperative** Snow Surveys:
Colorado, Rio Grande, Platte, and
Arkansas Drainage Basins, A 57.46/9-2
Federal-State-Private **Cooperative** Snow Surveys:
Montana, A 57.46/3-2
Federal-State-Private **Cooperative** Snow Surveys:
Oregon, A 57.46/5-2
Federal-State-Private **Cooperative** Snow Surveys:
Utah, A 57.46/6-1
Forestry Research Progress in (year) McIntire-
Stennis **Cooperative** Forestry Research
Program, A 94.2 F 76/
Highlights of Annual Workshop of Farmer
Cooperative Service, A 89.16
Library of Congress Catalogs: Chinese **Coopera-
tive** Catalog, LC 30.18
Midwest Regional Member Relations Conference
Sponsored by American Institute of
Cooperation and Farmer **Cooperative**
Service, A 89.17
Municipal and **Cooperative** Distributors of TVA
Power, (date) Operations, Y 3.T 25:1-3

News of the **Cooperative** Health Statistics System,
HE 20.6213
Plan of Work for **Cooperative** Hydrology
Investigations, I 53.47
Plant Pest Control **Cooperative** Programs, Western
Region, Fiscal Year (date), A 77.327/2
Proceedings National Brucellosis Committee and
Progress Report of the **Cooperative**
State-Federal Brucellosis Eradication
Program, A 77.202:B 83/16
Registered Bona Fide and Legitimate Farmers'
Cooperative Organizations under
Bituminous Coal Act of 1937, I 46.15
Report of **Cooperative** Cattle Fever Tick
Eradication Activities, Fiscal Year
(date), A 77.237
Report of **Cooperative** Research to Improve the
Nation's Schools, FS 5.82
Report on **Cooperative** Research to Improve the
Nation's Schools, HE 5.82
Review of USTTA International Markets, and
Summary of **Cooperative** Advertising
Opportunities, C 47.20
Service Reports Farmer **Cooperative** Service, A
89.12, A 89.20
Statement of Indemnity Claims and Averages in
Cooperative Bang's Disease Work, A
4.29
Statement of Indemnity Claims and Averages in
Cooperative Tuberculosis Eradication,
A 4.30
Summary of Bovine Tuberculosis Eradication in
Cooperation with Various States,
Statement of Indemnity and Averages in
Cooperative Bovine Brucellosis Work,
A 77.216/2
Summary of Cases Relating to Farmers' **Coopera-
tive** Associations, A 72.18
Summary of **Cooperative** Cases, A 89.9
Summary of **Cooperative** Cases, Legal Series, A
89.9/2
Transactions of Research Conferences on
Cooperative Chemotherapy Studies in
Psychiatry and Research Approaches to
Mental Illness, VA 1.41
Tuberculosis Eradication: Statement of Indemnity
Claims and Averages in **Cooperative**, A
77.214
Water Supply Outlook, Federal-State-Private
Cooperative Snow Surveys {Colorado},
A 57.46/15

Cooperative Education
Application for Grants under the **Cooperative
Education** Program, ED 1.70/3

Cooperative Library
Directory of Library Networks and **Cooperative
Library** Organizations, ED 1.129

Cooperatives
Farm **Cooperatives** (by States), FCA 1.19
Farmer **Cooperatives**, FCA 1.19, A 1.76, A 89.8, A
105.19, A 109.11
List of Fishery **Cooperatives** in the United States,
C 55.338/2
News for Farmer **Cooperatives**, FCA 1.10
Research Reports Economics, Statistics, and
Cooperatives Service, A 105.31

Cooperatives
Statistics of Farmer **Cooperatives**, A 89.19

Cooperators
Clean Grain Notes for **Cooperators** in Clean Grain
Program, A 43.30
Publications by Staff and **Cooperators**,
Intermountain Forest and Range
Experiment Station, A 13.65/14
Publications Staff and **Cooperators**, Intermountain
Forest and Range Experiment Station, A
13.65/14

Coordinated
Coordinated Federal Wage System, CS 1.41/4:532-
1
Federally **Coordinated** Program of Highway
Research and Development, TD 2.42
Index, **Coordinated** Purchase Descriptions, D
106.14
Report of **Coordinated** Meeting of Federal
Agencies (by States), Y 3.N 21/9:11

Coordinating
Diabetes Mellitus **Coordinating** Committee,
Annual Report to the Director, National
Institutes of Health, Fiscal Year (date),
HE 20.3028
Diabetes Mellitus **Coordinating** Committee:
Annual Report, HE 20.3317

Digestive Diseases **Coordinating** Committee, HE 20.3001/2:D 56

Energy Materials **Coordinating** Committee: Annual Technical Report, E 1.52

Report **Coordinating** Group Annual Report to the Securities and Exchange Commission, SE 1.32

Shipping **Coordinating** Committee, S 1.130/2:Sh 6

Coordination

Chemical-Biological **Coordination** Center, Reviews, NA 2.7

Coordination Memorandums, I 66.14

Coordination of Federal Equal Employment Opportunity Programs, Y 3.Eq 2:16

Coordination Service, Digest of Interpretations of Specific Price Schedules and Regulations, Pr 32.4249

Implementation Plan Review for {Various States} As Required by the Energy Supply and Environmental **Coordination** Act, EP 1.58

News from the Center {for the **Coordination** of Foreign Manuscript Copying}, LC 1.33

Toward Interagency **Coordination**, Federal Research and Development on Adolescence, HE 23.1013

Toward Interagency **Coordination**: Federal Research and Development on Early Childhood, HE 23.1013/2

Water Data **Coordination** Directory, I 19.118

Coordinative

Directory of Federal **Coordinative** Groups for Toxic Substances, EP 1.79/2

Coordinator

Federal **Coordinator** for Meterological Services and Supporting Research, FCM (series), C 55.12

Coordinators

Coordinator's Scoreboard, Review of What's New in Placement of the Handicapped, CS 1.75

Service **Coordinators** Chronicle, HH 1.125

Copies

Package X, Informational **Copies** of Federal Tax Forms, T 22.2/12

Copper

Advance Statements of Productions of **Copper** in United States (calendar year), I 19.23

Copper, C 62.12, C 57.512

Copper in (year), I 28.59/3, I 28.59/4

Copper in the United States, I 28.59/2

Copper Industry, I 28.59/2

Copper Industry, Annual, I 28.59/3

Copper Production, I 28.59/5

Copper Scrap Consumers, I 28.79

Copper Sulfate, I 28.93

Copper, (year) Annual Statistical Supplement, C 57.512/2

Mine Production of **Copper**, I 28.59

Mineral Industry Surveys, **Copper**, I 19.137

Monthly **Copper** Reports, I 28.59/2

Refined Metal and **Copper** Scrap Operations at Brass and Wire Mills, Brass Mill Report, I 28.79/2

Copra

Philippine **Copra** Market, C 18.199

Copy

JACS {Journal Article **Copy** Service} Directory, C 51.11/6

Copying

News from the Center {for the Coordination of Foreign Manuscript **Copying**}, LC 1.33

Copyright

Announcement from the **Copyright** Office, ML (series), LC 3.12

Catalog of **Copyright** Entries, Cumulative Series, LC 3.8

Catalog of **Copyright** Entries, Fourth Series, LC 3.6/6

Catalog of **Copyright** Entries, Third Series, LC 3.6/5

Catalogue of **Copyright** Entries, Pt. 1, Books **etc.**, LC 3.6/1

Catalogue of **Copyright** Entries, Pt. 2, Periodicals, LC 3.6/2

Catalogue of **Copyright** Entries, Pt. 3, Musical Compositions, LC 3.6/3

Compendium of **Copyright** Office Practices, LC 3.11

Copyright Law Studies, LC 3.9

Decisions of the United States Courts Involving **Copyright**, LC 3.3

Decisions of the United States Courts Involving **Copyright** and Literary Property, 1789-1909, Bulletins, LC 3.3/2

Copyrights

Annual Report of the Register of **Copyrights**, LC 3.1

Coraporter

Coraporter, J 21.18

Core

Core Curriculum, PE 1.11

Precursors to Potential Severe **Core** Damage Accidents, Y 3.N 88:25-6

CORE

CORE Competencies, GS 14.15

SSA Training (series): Technical **CORE** Curriculum, HE 3.69/2

Corn

Broom **Corn** Brooms: Producers' Shipments Imports for Consumption Exports and Apparent Consumption, ITC 1.23

Commercial **Corn** Belt Farms, A 93.9/11

Commitments of Traders in Wheat, **Corn**, Oats, Rye, Soybeans, Soybean Oil, Soybean Meal, Shell Eggs, A 85.9/2

Corn (Hominy) Grits for Domestic Distribution, A 82.3/4

Corn and Wheat Region Bulletins, C 30.7

Corn Circular Letters, Y 3.C 73:9

Corn Hog Charts, A 55.14

Corn, Estimated Planted Acreage, Yield, and Production by States, A 66.47

European **Corn** Borer, A 9.9

Futures Trading and Open Contracts in Wheat, **Corn**, Oats, Rye, Soybeans and Products, A 85.11/7

Futures Trading and Open Contracts in {Wheat, **Corn**, Oats, etc.} on Chicago Board of Trade, A 88.11/18

Publications **Corn**-Hog Board of Review, A 55.30

U.S. Export **Corn** Quality, A 104.12

U.S. Grain Export Quality Report, Wheat, **Corn**, Soybeans, A 104.12/2-3

Weekly **Corn** and Wheat Region Bulletin, A 29.43

With the **Corn** Borer, A 1.37

Corn Meal

Corn Meal, A 82.3/8

Corn Meal for Domestic Distribution, A 82.3/3

Corn Meal for Export Distribution, A 82.3/7

Export **Corn Meal** Bulletin, A 82.3/2

Corn-Hog

Circular Letters; **Corn-Hog** Work, A 55.34, A 55.34/2, A 55.34/3

Corn-Hog

Commodity Information Series; **Corn-Hog** Leaflets, A 55.25/7

Corn-Hog Circular Letters, A 55.34/3

Corona

Naval Ordnance Laboratory, **Corona**, California: Reports, D 215.13

Corporate

Briefs of Accidents Involving **Corporate**-Executive Aircraft U.S. General Aviation, TD 1.109/10

Corporate Author Authority List, C 51.18

Corporate Complex, D 7.6/2-2:5

Corporate Pension Funds, SE 1.25/6

Corporate Securities Offered for Cash, SE 1.25/6

List of **Corporate** Names of Common Carriers, IC 1.15

Releases, **Corporate** Reorganization, SE 1.25/1

Corporation

Americorps Leaders Program, A Service Leadership Development Program of the **Corporation** for National Service, Y 3.N 21/29:16-17

Annual Report of Department of Treasury on Operation and Effect of Domestic International Sales **Corporation** Legislation for Calendar Year, Y 4.W 36:D 71/2

Commodity Credit **Corporation** Charts, A 82.311

Corporation Income Tax Returns, T 22.35/3:C 81, T 22.35/2:C 81

Corporation Income Tax Returns, Source Book (year), T 22.35/5-2

Federal Crop Insurance **Corporation**, A 82.201

Federal Savings and Loan Insurance **Corporation**, Financial Statements, FHL 1.2:F 31/2

FHA and VA Mortgages Owned and Available for Sale by Reconstruction Finance **Corporation** and Federal National Mortgage Association, Y 3.R 24:14

Foreign Tax Credit Claimed on **Corporation** Income Tax Returns, T 22.35/2:F 76

Home Owners' Loan **Corporation** Publications, FL 3.9, Y 3.F 31/3:8

Industrial **Corporation** Reports (by industries), FT 1.17}

Monthly Summary of Export Credit Guarantee Program Activity, Commodity Credit **Corporation**, A 67.18:ECG

Operation and Effect of the Domestic International Sales **Corporation** Legislation, T 1.54

Operation and Effect of the Possessions **Corporation** System of Taxation, T 1.55

PBGC {Pension Benefit Guaranty **Corporation**} Fact Sheets, L 1.51/5

Press Notices Grain **Corporation**, Y 3.W 56:15

Publications Home Owners' Loan **Corporation**, FL 3.9

Reconstruction Finance **Corporation** Act with Amendments and Small Business Administration Act with Amendments Including Related Acts on Small Business, Y 1.2:R 24/2

Report of the President of the Commodity Credit **Corporation**, A 82.301

Smaller War Plants **Corporation** Program and Progress Reports, Pr 32.4825

Statistics of Income, **Corporation** Income Tax Returns Documentation Guides, T 22.35/7

Statistics of Income, **Corporation** Income Tax Returns, T 22.35/5

Corporations

American Listed **Corporations**, Survey of: Quarterly Sales Data, SE 1.22

Census of American Listed **Corporations**, Reports, SE 1.17

Quarterly Financial Report for Manufacturing, Mining, and Trade **Corporations**, FT 1.18, C 3.267

Quarterly Financial Report, United States Manufacturing **Corporations**, FT 1.18

Quarterly Financial Report, United States Retail and Wholesale **Corporations**, FT 1.20

Sales, Profits, and Dividends of Large **Corporations**, FR 1.40

Statistics of American Listed **Corporations**, SE 1.17/3

Survey of American Listed **Corporations**, General Publications, SE 1.17/2

Survey of American Listed **Corporations**, Reported Information on Selected Defense Industries, SE 1.18/2

Survey of American Listed **Corporations**, Reports, SE 1.18/3

Survey of American Listed **Corporations**, SE 1.18

Survey of American Listed **Corporations**: Quarterly Sales Data, SE 1.22

Uniform System of Accounts for Gas **Corporations** and Electric **Corporations** in the District of Columbia, IC 1 gas.5

Working Capital of U.S. **Corporations**, SE 1.25/6

Corps

CCPM Pamphlets {Commissioned **Corps** Personnel Manual}, HE 20.13

Commissioned **Corps** Bulletin, HE 20.3/2

Commissioned **Corps** Personnel Manual, HE 20.13/3

Corps Connection, TD 2.72

Corps of Engineers Supply Catalogues, W 7.24

Corps of Regular Army, W 44.27

Four the **Corps**, D 214.26/2

Getting to the **Corps**, Y 3.N 21/29:16-18

Hospital **Corps** Quarterly, M 203.3/2

Ordnance **Corps** Manuals, D 105.6/2

Ordnance **Corps** Pamphlets, D 105.9

Publications Available for Purchase, U.S. Army Engineer Waterways Experiment Station and Other **Corps** of Engineers Agencies, D 103.39

Quartermaster **Corps** Manual, D 106.6/2

Recruiting Bulletins Army and **Corps** Areas and Departments, Seventh **Corps** Area, W 99.17/10

Register of Civil Engineer **Corps** Commissioned and Warrant Officers of United States Navy and Naval Reserve on Active Duty, D 209.9

Regulations for United States **Corps** of Cadets Prescribed by Commandant of Cadets, M 109.6/2

Report of Forest Service Training Activities, Civilian Conservation **Corps**, A 13.71

Reserve Officers Training **Corps** Bulletin, W 99.17/18

Council

Activities of the Federal **Council** for Science and Technology and the Federal Coordinating **Council** for Science, Engineering and Technology, Report, PrEx 23.9

Central Executive **Council**, Reports of Meetings, T 1.23/6

Community **Council** Circulars, Y 3.C 83:5

Community Education Advisory **Council**: Reports, HE 19.132/2

Council Communique, Y 3.H 75:15

Council Memorandum, C 55.336

Council on Graduate Medical Education (General Publications), HE 20.9019

Council Ring, I 29.38

Depository Library **Council** Report to the Public Printer, GP 1.35

Depository Library **Council** to the Public Printer: Addresses, GP 1.36

Federal Fire **Council** News Letter, GS 1.14/4

National Science and Technology **Council**: General Publications, PrEx 23.14

Occasional Papers **Council** of Scholars (series), LC 1.42

Official Gazette Control **Council** for Germany, W 1.73, M 105.9

Posters President's **Council** on Physical Fitness and Sports, HE 20.113

Posters United States Holocaust Memorial **Council**, Y 3.H 74:9

President's Advisory **Council** on Executive Organization, Pr 37.8:Ex 3

President's Advisory **Council** on Management Improvement, Pr 37.8:M 31

President's **Council** on Competitiveness, Pr 41.8:R 26

President's **Council** on Integrity and Efficiency: Reports, Pr 41.8/3

President's **Council** on Physical Fitness and Sports, Pr 37.8:P 56/2

President's **Council** on Youth Opportunity, Pr 37.8:Y 8

President's Export **Council**: Publications, Pr 37.8:Ex 7

Proceedings Joint Meeting with its Advisory **Council**, Y 3.Ou 8:9

Proceedings Merchant Marine **Council**, N 24.32, T 47.31

Progress Against Cancer, Report by National Advisory Cancer **Council**, HE 20.3024, HE 20.3163

Publications Federal Fire **Council**, GS 1.14/5

Publications National Export Expansion **Council**, C 1.42/3

Report of Advisory **Council** on Social Security Financing, HE 3.41

Report of National Advisory **Council** on Economic Opprotunity, PrEx 10.22

Report of the Panel on Pain to the National Advisory Neurological and Communicative Disorders and Stroke **Council**, HE 20.3517

Report to the Advisory Child Health and Human Development **Council**, HE 20.3362/7

Summary of Meeting Depository Library **Council** to the Printer, GP 3.30/2

Transcripts of Proceedings, Meeting of Depository **Council** to the Public Printer, GP 3.30

Treasury Safety **Council** Safety Bulletin, Administrative, T 1.41

Undergraduate Engineering Curricular Accredited by Engineer's **Council** for Professional Development, FS 5.61

Women's Advisory **Council**: Annual Report, GA 1.30

Councils

Roster of Members of PHS Public Advisory Groups, **Councils**, Committees, Boards, Panels, Study Sections, HE 20.2:Ad 9/3

Counsel

Chief **Counsel** Office Directory, T 22.48/2

Chief **Counsel**: Annual Report, T 22.1/2

Classified Index of Dispositions of ULP {Unfair Labor Practices} Charges by the General **Counsel** of the Federal Labor Relations Authority, Y 3.F 31/21-3:11

Classified Index of Dispositions of ULP {Unfair Labor Practices} Charges by the General **Counsel** of the National Labor Relations Board, LR 1.8/8

Consumers **Counsel** Division, Consumers' **Counsel** Series Publications, A 75.11

Consumers' **Counsel** Division, General Publications, A 55.63

Consumers' **Counsel** Series, Publications, A 55.49

Digest and Index of Opinions of **Counsel**, Informal Rulings of Federal Reserve Board and Matter Relating Thereto, from Federal Reserve Bulletin, FR 1.10

Opinions of the Office of Legal **Counsel**, J 1.5/4

Posters Office of the Special **Counsel**, Merit Systems Protection Board, MS 1.12

Reports on Case Handling Developments of the Office of the General **Counsel**, Y 3.F 31/21-3:12

Summary of Operations, Office of General **Counsel**, LR 1.1/2

Counseling

Counseling Guides, GS 1.6/6-2

Directory, State Department of Education Personnel for Guidance, **Counseling**, and Testing, FS 5.255:25037:A, HE 5.255:25037:A

Employee **Counseling** Service Program Memo, HE 20.9113/2

Employee **Counseling** Service Program, Annual Report, HE 20.9113/3

Labor Market Information for USES **Counseling**: Industry Series, Pr 32.5229, L 7.23

Recruiting and Career **Counseling** Journal, D 118.9

Counselor

Directory of **Counselor** Educators, FS 5.255:25036, HE 5.255:25036

Counselor's

Counselor's Handbook, a Federal Student Aid Reference, ED 1.45

Counterfeits

New **Counterfeits** (numbered), T 34.7

New **Counterfeits** Circular Letters, T 34.4/2

Countermeasure

Countermeasure, D 101.125

Counterpart

Counterpart Funds and AID Foreign Currency Account, S 18.14

Counterpart Funds and FOA Foreign Currency Accounts, FO 1.11/3

Counterpart Funds and ICA Foreign Currency Accounts, S 17.11/3

European Program, Local Currency **Counterpart** Funds, Pr 33.911, FO 1.11

Far East Program, Local Currency **Counterpart** Funds, Pr 33.911/2, FO 1.11/2

Local Currency **Counterpart** Funds, Y 4.Ec 74/3:12

Countervailing

Countervailing Duty and Antidumping Case Reference List, T 17.18

Counties

Civil Aircraft by States and by **Counties** with States, C 31.132

Cotton Ginnings, Report on Cotton Ginnings by **Counties**, A 20 (series), C 56.239

Distribution of Bank Deposits by **Counties** and Standard Metropolitan Areas, FR 1.11/6

Fresh Fruit and Vegetable Shipments by States, Commodities, **Counties**, Stations, Calendar Year (date), A 88.12/31:6, A 88.40/2:12

Income Tax Returns: Number of Individual by States, **Counties**, Cities, and Towns, T 22.40

Inquiry Reference Service: County Basic Data Sheets, Selected **Counties** by States, C 18.228

Provisional Estimates of the Population of **Counties**, C 3.186/20

Recovery Guides, Participating **Counties**, Y 3.Ec 74/3:16

Report on Cotton Ginnings by **Counties**, C 3.20/3

South, Population and Per Capita Income Estimates for **Counties** and Incorporated Places, C 3.186/27-5

Soybeans Harvested for Beans by **Counties**, A 92.15/3

State Bulletins, 2d Series (Statistics by **counties**), C 3.31/3

State Carlot Shipments of Fruits and Vegetables, by Commodities, **Counties**, and Billing Stations, A 88.12/10

USA **Counties**, A Statistical Abstract Supplement, C 3.134/6

West North Central, Population and Per Capita Income Estimates for **Counties** and Incorporated Places, C 3.186/27-3

West, Population and Per Capita Income Estimates for **Counties** and Incorporated Places, C 3.186/27-2

Countries

Agriculture Technology for Developing **Countries**, Technical Series Papers, S 18.45

Circular of Inquiry Concerning Gold and Silver Coinage and Currency of Foreign **Countries**, Including Production, Import and Export, and Industrial Consumption of Gold and Silver, T 28.8

Climate Impact Assessment, Foreign **Countries**, C 55.233

Climate Impact Assessment, Foreign **Countries** Annual Summary, C 55.233/3

Code Classification of **Countries**, C 3.150:C

Commercial Regulations of Foreign **Countries**, S 1.9

Countries

Schedule C. Code Classification of **Countries**, C 3.150:C

Foreign Agricultural Trade of the United States, Trade by **Countries**, A 93.17/4

Foreign Agricultural Trade of the United States, Trade in Agricultural Products with Individual **Countries** by Calendar Year, A 67.19/6

Foreign Agricultural Trade of the United States; Imports of Fruits and Vegetables under Quarantine by **Countries** of Origin and Ports of Entry, A 67.19/7, A 93.17/5

Foreign **Countries** and Plants Certified to Export Meat and Poultry to the United States, A 110.14/2

Geographic Distribution of Radio Sets and Characteristics of Radio Owners in **Countries** of the World, IA 1.12/2

Household and Commercial Pottery Industry in {various countries}, C 41.100

Imports Under Reciprocal Trade Agreements, by **Countries**, TC 1.13

Indices of Agricultural Production in {various} **Countries**, A 67.36, A 93.32

Labor Offices in U.S. and Foreign **Countries**, L 2.6/a 3

Lists of Commercial Treaties and Conventions, and Agreements Affected by Exchange of Notes or Declarations in Force Between United States and Other **Countries**, S 9.9

Merchant Ships Built in United States and Other **Countries** in Employment Report of United States Flag Merchant Seagoing Vessels 1,000 Tons and Over, A 39.211

Passenger Travel between United States and Foreign **Countries** {annual summary reports}, J 21.13

Publications Foreign **Countries**, Annotated Accession List, C 3.199

Quarterly Report on Trade Between the United States and Nonmarket Economy **Countries**, Pursuant to Section 411 (c) of the Trade Act of 1974, Y 4.W 36:3

Quarterly Report to Congress and the East- West Foreign Trade Board on Trade Between the United States and the Nonmarket Economy **Countries**, Y 4.W 36:2

Report of Japan's Export Shipments and Import Receipts Stated by Areas and **Countries** of Destination and Origin, with Value Expressed in United States Dollars, D 102.11/3

Report of Passenger Travel between the United States and Foreign **Countries**, J 21.13/2

Report to Congress and East-West Foreign Trade Board on Trade Between United States and Nonmarket Economy **Countries**, TC 1.38

Report to the Congress and the Trade Policy Committee on Trade Between the U.S. and the Nonmarket Economy **Countries**, ITC 1.13

Sailing Dates of Steamships from the Principal Ports of the United States to Ports in Foreign **Countries**, C 15.19, C 18.10

Schedule of Steamers Appointed to Convey Mails to Foreign **Countries**, P 8.5

Selected Interest and Exchange Rates for Major **Countries** and the U.S., FR 1.32/3

Sending Gift Packages to Various **Countries**, C 49.9

Significant NASA Inventions Available for Licensing in Foreign **Countries**, NAS 1.21:7038

Soybeans Harvested for Beans by **Countries**, Acreage, Yield, Production, A 88.18/19

Statistics of Capital Movements Between U.S. and Foreign **Countries**, T 62.9

Steel Import Data, Shipments from Exporting **Countries** in Calendar Year, C 57.209

Study of the International Travel Market {various **countries**}, C 47.19

Trade Agreements (by **countries**), TC 1.14

U.S. Trade Status with Communist **Countries**, C 57.28, C 57.413, C 61.22

United States Foreign Trade, Trade with E.C.A. **Countries**, C 3.164:951

Value of Exports, Including Reexports, by Grand Visions and Principal **Countries**, C 18.6/2

Working Document Services (various **countries**), S 18.51

World Population: Recent Demographic Estimates for the **Countries** and Regions of the World, C 3.205/3

Country

Area and **Country** Bibliographic Surveys, D 101.22:550

Code Classification of Foreign Ports by Geographic Trade Area and **Country**, C 3.150:K

Country Commercial Guides, S 1.40/7

Country Commercial Program for {various countries}, C 1.64

Country Demographic Profiles for Foreign **Country** Series, ISP 30 (series), C 56.218/2

Country Focus Series, Y 3.In 8/25:16

Country Law Studies, D 1.40

Country Market Sectoral Surveys, C 57.119

Country Market Survey, CMS- (series), C 61.9, C 57.112

Country Profiles, S 18.53

Country Reports on Human Rights Practices, Y 4.F 76/1-15, Y 4.In 8/16:15

Country Reports on the World Refugee Situation, A Report to Congress, S 1.1/7

Country Report Series, HH 1.32

Country Series, S 17.25

Country-by-Commodity Series, C 49.12, C 42.14

FOA **Country** Series, FO 1.25

FY Projects, by **Country** and Field of Activity, S 18.29

General Imports of Merchandise into United States by Air, Commodity by **Country** of Origin, C 3.164:231

General Imports of Merchandise into United States by Air, **Country** of Origin by Commodity, C 3.164:232

MSA **Country** Series, Pr 33.919

Schedule K. Code Classification of Foreign Ports by Geographic Trade Area and **Country**, C 3.150:K

Shipment Under the United States Foreign Aid Programs Made on Army- or Navy-Operated Vessels (American flag) by Port of Lading by **Country** of Destination, C 3.164:976

Shipping Weight and Dollar Value of Merchandise Laden on and Unladen from Vessels at United States Ports During the In-transit Movement of the Merchandise from One Foreign **Country** to Another, C 3.164:981

Sources of Milk for Federal Order Markets by State & **County**, A 88.14/11-3

Studies in Comparative Education, Education in {**country**}, FS 5.212, HE 5.212

U.S. Export, Schedule B, Commodity by **Country**, C 3.164:446

U.S. Exports by Air, **Country** by Commodity, C 3.164:790

U.S. Exports, Commodity by **Country**, C 56.210:410, C 3.164:410

U.S. Exports, Commodity, **Country**, and Method of Transportation, C 3.164:750

U.S. Exports, **Country** by Commodity Grouping, C 1.64:420

U.S. Exports, Geographic Area, **Country**, Schedule B Commodity Groupings, and Method of Transportation, C 3.164:455

U.S. Exports, Harmonized Schedule B Commodity by **Country**, FT-447, C 3.164:447

U.S. Exports, Schedule B Commodity Groupings, Geographic Area, **Country**, and Method of Transportaion, C 3.164:450

U.S. Exports-Commodity by **Country**, C 3.164:410

U.S. General Imports and Imports for Consumption, Schedule A Commodity and **Country**, C 3.164:135

U.S. General Imports Commodity, **Country** and Method of Transporation, C 3.164:350

U.S. General Imports Geographic Area, **Country**, Schedule A Commodity Groupings, and Method of Transporation, C 3.164:155

U.S. General Imports Schedule A Commodity Groupings, Geographic Area, **Country**, and Method of Transportation, C 3.164:150

U.S. General Imports World Area and **Country** of Origin by Schedule A Commodity Groupings, C 3.164:155

U.S. Import for Consumption, USUSA Commodity by **Country** of Origin, C 56.210:146

U.S. Imports for Consumption & General Imports, Tariff Schedules Annotated by **Country**, C 3.150/6

U.S. Imports for Consumption and General Imports-TSUSA Commodity by **Country**: (year), C 3.164:246

U.S. Imports, General and Consumption, Schedule a Commodity and **Country**, C 3.164:135

United States Airborne Exports of Domestic and Foreign Merchandise, Commodity (Schedule X) by **Country** of Destination, C 3.164:780

United States Airborne Exports of Domestic and Foreign Merchandise, **Country** of Destination by Commodity, C 3.164:790

United States Airborne General Imports of Merchandise, **Country** of Origin by Commodity, C 3.164:390

United States Exports by Air of Domestic and Foreign Merchandise Commodity by **Country** of Destination, C 3.164:731

United States Exports by Air of Domestic and Foreign Merchandise **Country** of Destination by Commodity, C 3.164:732

United States Exports of Domestic and Foreign Merchandise Commodity by **Country** of Destination, C 3.164:410

United States Exports of Domestic and Foreign Merchandise **Country** of Destination by Subgroup, C 3.164:420

United States Exports of Domestic and Foreign Merchandise Under Lend-Lease Program, Commodity by **Country** of Destination, C 3.164:415

United States Exports of Domestic and Foreign Merchandise Under Lend-Lease Program, **Country** of Destination by Commodity, C 3.164:421, C 3.164:425

United States Exports of Domestic and Foreign Merchandise Under United Nations Relief and Rehabilitation Program, **Country** of Destination by Commodity, C 3.164:426

United States Exports of Domestic and Foreign Merchandise Under United Nations Relief and Rehabilitation Program, Commodity by **Country** of Destination, C 3.164:416

United States Exports of Petroleum and Petroleum Products of Domestic Origin, Commodity by **Country** of Destination, C 3.164:526

United States General Imports and Imports for Consumption from Canada and Mexico, Exluding Strategic, Military and Critical Materials, **Country** by Commodity Totals, C 3.164:121

United States General Imports of Cotton Manufacturers: **Country** of Origin by Geneva Agreement Category, C 56.210:130, C 3.164:130

United States General Imports of Merchandise, Commodity by **Country** of Origin, C 3.164:10

United States General Imports of Textile Manufactures, Except Cotton and Wool, Grouping by **Country** of Origin and Schedule a Commodity by **Country** of Origin, TQ-2501, C 3.164/2-7

United States General Imports of Wool Manufacture Except Floor Coverings, Quantity Totals in Terms of Equivalent Square Yards in **Country** of Origin by Commodity Grouping Arrangement, TQ-2203, C 3.164/2-6

United States General Imports of Wool Manufacture Except for Floor Coverings, **Country** of Origin by Wool Grouping, TQ- 2202, C 3.164/2-5

United States Imports of Merchandise for Consumption: Commodity by **Country** of Origin, C 3.164:110

United States Imports of Merchandise for Consumption; **Country** of Origin by Subgroup, C 3.164:120

United States, Airborne General Imports of Merchandise, Commodity by **Country** of Origin, C 3.164:380

Country Reports

County

Census of Distribution; **County** Series, Preliminary (by States), C 3.37/20

Censuses of Population and Housing: Census **County** Division Boundary Description, Phc (3) series, C 3.223/15

County and City Data Book, C 3.134/2:C 83/2, C 3.134/2-1, C 56.243/2:C 83

County Block Maps, C 3.62/9

County Business Patterns, (year), C 3.204, C 3.204/2, C 3.204/4

County Business Patterns, (year), CBP (series), C 56.233

County Business Patterns, United States, C 3.204/3

County Business Patterns, (various states), C 204/5

County Committee Memorandum, A 5.46/9

County Finances, C 3.192

County Government Employment, C 3.140/2-5

County Government Finances, C 3.191/2-7

County List of Post Offices, P 1.10/6

County Map Series, I 19.108

County Office Procedure, A 55.46/13

County Planning Series, A 36.120

County Subdivision Maps, C 3.62/6

County-to-County Migration File, C 3.284

Current Population Reports, Local Population Estimates, **County** Population Estimates, C 3.186/20-2

Deposits of **County** Banks: Index Numbers of Total, Demand and Time Deposits Selected Groups of States, Specified Periods, A 77.14/3, A 93.9/7

Inquiry Reference Service: **County** Basic Data Sheets, Selected Counties by States, C 18.228

List of Rural Delivery **County** Maps, P 11.7

Projects, by Field of Activity and **County**, S 18.29

Pulpwood Production in the North-Central Region by **County**, A 13.80/5

Recipients of Public Assistance Money Payments and Amounts of Such Payments, by Program, State, and **County**, HE 17.627/2

Social Security Beneficiaries by State and **County**, HE 3.73/2

Sources of Milk for Federal Order Markets, by State and **County**, A 88.40

State, **County** and Municipal Survey, L 2.13

State, **County** and Selected City Employment and Unemployment, BLS/PWEDA/MR- (series), L 2.111/2

State, **County** and Selected City Employment and Unemployment, BLS/PWEDA/SP- (series), L 2.111/4

State, **County** and Selected City Employment and Unemployment, L 2.111

Supplemental Security Income, State and **County** Data, HE 3.71

United States Active Civil Aircraft by State and **County**, C 31.132/2, FAA 1.35

Courier

Courier, the National Park Service Newsletter, I 29.96

Course

Abstract of **Course**, N 15.5

Administrative Management **Course** Program Topics, SBA 1.24

Catalog and **Course** Descriptions of the Defense Mapping School, D 5.352

CDC **Course** Announcements, HE 20.7034

Correspondence **Course** Program, Subcourses, D 103.111/2

Correspondence **Course**, Elements of Surface Weather Observations, Lessons, C 30.26

Course (series), D 301.26/17-3

Course Management Plan and Program of Instruction (series), D 101.107/4

New Federal **Credit Union** Charters, Quarterly Report of Organization, FS 3.307

Credit Union
Annual Reports on Operations of Federal **Credit Unions**, A 72.19
Cooperative Savings with Federal **Credit Unions**, FCA 1.14, FCA 1.14/2
Credit Unions, Installment Loans to Consumers, C 18.226
Federal **Credit Unions**, FCA 1.15
Federal **Credit Unions**, Quarterly Report on Operations, FCA 1.16
Manual of Laws Affecting Federal **Credit Unions**, NCU 1.8/2
Manual of Laws Affecting Federally Insured State **Credit Unions**, NCU 1.8:St 2/2
Monthly Reports of Organizations and Operations of Federal **Credit Unions**, A 72.14
NCUA Letter to **Credit Unions**, NCU 1.19

Credits
Consumer Installment **Credits** of Industrial Loan Companies, FR 1.36/4
Foreign **Credits** by United States Government, C 43.11/2
Foreign **Credits** by United States Government, Status of Active Foreign **Credits** of United States Government and of International Organizations, T 1.45
Foreign Grants and **Credits** by the United States Government, C 43.11
Illuminating Glassware Manufactures, Sales and **Credits**, C 3.146
Status of Active Foreign **Credits** of the United States Government: Foreign Credits by United States Government Agencies, T 1.45/2

Creeks
Flood Hazard Studies {various rivers, **creeks**, and areas}, A 57.64/3

Crew
Combat **Crew**, D 301.81

Crew's
Catalogs of Ships and **Crew's** Libraries of the U.S., N 5.6, N 17.19

Crewmembers
Certification; Airmen other than Flight **Crewmembers**, TD 4.6:part 65
Certification; Flight **Crewmembers** other than Pilots, TD 4.6:part 63

Crime
Annual Evaluation Report on Drugs and **Crime**: A Report to the President, the Attorney General, and the Congress, J 28.29
Building Knowledge About **Crime** and Justice J 28.36
Crime and Delinquency Abstracts, FS 2.22/13-4, HE 20l.2420
Crime and Delinquency Topics: Monograph Series, HE 20.8114, HE 20.8114/3
Crime Data Brief, J 29.27
Crime File (series), J 28.26
Crime Gun Trade Reports, T 70.25
Crime Laboratory Digest, J 1.14/18
Crime, Kidnapping, and Prison Laws {June 21, 1902}, Y 1.2:C 86
Crime in the Nation, Household, J 29.11/8
Crime in the United States, J 1.14/7-8
Current Projects in Prevention, Control, and Treatment of **Crime** and Delinquency, FS 2.22/51
FBI Uniform **Crime** Reports {on various subjects}, J 1.14/7-4
FBI Uniform **Crime** Reports: Law Enforcement Officers Killed, J 1.14/7-5
Global **Crime**, S 1.149
Hate **Crime**: The Violence of Intolerance, CRS Bulletin, J 23.3
Indicators of School **Crime** and Safety, ED 1.347
International Bibliography on **Crime** and Delinquency, FS 2.22/13-4
Issues in International **Crime**, J 28.23/2
Law Enforcement Officers Killed and Assaulted, Uniform **Crime** Report, J 1.14/7-6
National **Crime** Survey Reports, J 29.9
Perspectives on **Crime** and Justice, Lecture Series, J 28.24/3-2
Teenage Victims, A National **Crime** Survey Report, J 29.23
Uniform **Crime** Reporting, J 1.14/7-2
Uniform **Crime** Reports Bomb Summary, J 1.14/7-7
Uniform **Crime** Reports for the United States, J 1.14/7

Victimization, Fear of **Crime** and Altered Behavior (series), HH 1.70

Criminal
Bureau of Justice Statistics Bulletin, **Criminal** Victimization, J 29.11/10
Criminal Justice Agencies, J 1.39
Criminal Justice Information Policy (series), J 29.9/8
Criminal Justice Monograph Series, J 1.37/3
Criminal Justice Perspectives (series), J 26.14
Criminal Justice Research, J 28.17
Criminal Justice Research Series, J 1.37/4
Criminal Justice Research Solicitations, J 1.37/5, J 26.18
Criminal Justice Research Utilization Program (series), J 28.13
Criminal Victimization in the United States, J 1.42/3
Criminal Victimization in the United States: Trends, J 29.9/2-2
Directory of **Criminal** Justice Information Sources, J 26.2:In 3, J 28.20
Directory of Law Enforcement and **Criminal** Justice Associations and Research Centers, C 13.10:480-20
Federal Law Enforcement and **Criminal** Justice Assistance Activities, Annual Report, J 1.32/2
National **Criminal** Justice Reference Service Document Data Base, J 28.31/2
Network of Knowledge, Directory of **Criminal** Justice Information Sources, J 28.20
Privacy and Security of **Criminal** History Information (series), J 29.10
Rape and Its Victims: a Report for Citizens, Health Facilities, and **Criminal** Justice Agencies, J 1.8/3:R 18
Rules of **Criminal** Procedure for the United States District Courts, Y 4.J 89/1-12
Sourcebook of **Criminal** Justice Statistics, J 1.42/3, J 29.9/6, J 29.9/6-2
Truth in **Criminal** Justice Series, J 1.95

Criminal Justice
Attorney General's Annual Report Federal Law Enforcement and **Criminal Justice** Assistance Activities, J 1.32/2
CJIS, Newsletter for the **Criminal Justice** Community, J 1.14/24
Criminal Justice Information Exchange Directory, J 28.20/2
Criminal Justice Information Policy (series), J 29.9/8
Directory of Automated **Criminal Justice** Information Systems, J 29.8/2

Criminals
Trials of War **Criminals** Before Nuremberg Military Tribunals, D 102.8

Criminology
Recent Publications of **Criminology** and Penology, J 16.9

Crimson Clover
Crimson Clover, A 92.19/9

Crippled
Crippled Children's Program, FS 17.213

Crisis
Bibliography on the Urban **Crisis**, HE 20.2417:Ur 1

Crisp
Crisp Biological Research Information, HE 20.3013/2-4

Cristobal
Tide Tables Balboa and **Cristobal**, Canal Zone, M 115.7, D 113.7
Tide, Moon and Sunrise Tables, Panama, and **Cristobal**, Colon, W 79.8

Criteria
Air Quality **Criteria** (series), EP 1.53/2
Ambient Water Quality **Criteria** for {various chemicals}, EP 1.29/3
Criteria for a Recommended Standard, Occupational Exposure to {various subjects}, HE 20.7110
Criteria for Use in Planning New Facilities, CR (series), P 24.6/3
Water Quality Standards **Criteria** Digest, Compilation of Federal/State **Criteria** on {various subjects}, EP 1.29/2

Critical
Critical Project Status Report, E 2.14
Department of Commerce List of Currently Essential Activities, Department of Labor List of Currently **Critical** Occupation, L 7.65

Department of Defense **Critical** Technologies Plan for the Committees on Armed Service, United States Congress, D 1.91
ERDA **Critical** Review Series, ER 1.14
Militarily **Critical** Technologies, D 10.13
Strategic and **Critical** Materials Report to the Congress (semiannual), D 1.94

Critical Path
Critical Path, C 55.132

Crop
Aerial **Crop** Control Accidents, C 31.244/2
Agricultural Situation, Special Edition for **Crop** and Price Reports, A 36.15/2
Calf **Crop** Report, A 88.16/10
Calf **Crop**, Louisiana Crop Reporting Service, A 88.16/10-2
Cotton Production in the United States, **Crop** of {year}, C 3.32
Cotton Quality **Crop** of (year), A 88.11
Cotton Region Weather **Crop** Bulletin, A 29.20
Cotton, Truck, and Forage **Crop** Disease Circulars, A 19.17
CR {**Crop** Research} (series), A 77.534
Crop and Market News Radio Broadcast Schedules, A 36.26
Crop Circulars, A 27.5
Crop Insurance Manager's Bulletins, A 112.20
Crop Insurance Research and Development Bulletins, A 112.17, A 62.17
Crop Insurance Update, A 62.13
Crop Production, A 88.24, A 105.9
Crop Production Research, A 77.33
Crop Production, Acreage, A 92.24/4-2
Crop Production, Annual Summary, A 92.24/4, A 105.9/2
Crop Production, Prospective Plantings, A 88.24/4, A 88.30/2
Crop Production, Winter Wheat and Rye, A 88.18/11
Crop Production: Quarterly Grain Stocks in Farms, Revised Estimates, A 88.18/22
Crop Report as of . . . Various Crops, A 88.24/2
Crop Report, by Federal Reserve District, FR 1.37
Crop Reporter, A 27.6
Crop Reporting Board Catalog, A 92.35/2
Crop Reporting Board, (year) Issuance Dates and Contents, A 92.35:C 88
Crop Reporting Procedure, A 36.92, A 66.22
Crop Reports to be Issued by **Crop** Reporting Board, A 66.29
Crop Values, A 88.24/5
Crop Values, Season Average Prices Received by Farmers and Value of Production, A 92.24/3
Employment on Farms of **Crop** Reporters, A 36.69
Federal **Crop** Insurance Corporation, A 82.201
Forage Crop Gazette, News Letter for Staff Workers, Division of Forage **Crop**s and Diseases, A 77.509
Foreign **Crop** and Livestock Reports, A 27.11
Fruit and Nut **Crop** Prospects, A 66.39
Fruit **Crop** Prospects, A 36.32
General Crop Report, Louisiana **Crop** Reporting Service, A 88.24/7
General **Crop** Reports, A 66.11
Grain Crop Quality, (year) **Crop**s, A 88.40/2:44
Guide to **Crop** Insurance Protection, A 62.16
Hatchery Production, Louisiana **Crop** Reporting Service, A 88.15/22
Honey Report, Louisiana **Crop** Reporting Service, A 88.19/2-2
Lamb **Crop** and Wool, A 105.23/7-2
Lamb Crop and Wool Production, Louisiana **Crop** Reporting Service, A 88.16/19
Lamb **Crop** Report, A 88.16/11
Livestock Slaughter, Louisiana **Crop** Reporting Service, A 88.16/2-2
Loans Made, United States and Territories, by **Crop** Years, from Date of Organization (1933) through June 30 (year), A 82.311
Louisiana Annual Crop Summary, Louisiana **Crop** Reporting Service, A 88.24/6
Louisiana Annual Vegetable Summary, Louisiana **Crop** Reporting Service, A 88.12/23
Louisiana Weekly Weather and **Crop** Bulletin, A 88.49/2
Markets and Crop Estimates Bureau, Foreign **Crop** and Livestock Reports, A 36.19
Monthly **Crop** Reporter, A 27.6/2, A 36.10
Monthly **Crop** Synopsis, A 27.7
Nebraska Weekly Weather and **Crop** Report, A 36.208

New **Crop** Varieties, A 43.33/2

Pecan Report, Louisiana **Crop** Reporting Service, A 88.10/5

Phosphate **Crop** Year, I 28.119/2

Pig **Crop** Report, A 88.16/3

Pig **Crop** Report, Louisiana **Crop** Reporting Service, A 88.16/3-2

Potash in **Crop** Year (date), I 28.120/2

Potato and Sweet Potato **Crop** Prospects, A 36.34

Proceedings Southern Pasture and Forage **Crop** Improvement Conference, A 106.29

Prospective Strawberry Acreage, Louisiana **Crop** Reporting Service, A 88.12/27

Rice Production, Louisiana **Crop** Reporting Service, A 88.18/26

Small Grains, Annual Summary and **Crop** Winter Wheat and Rye Seedings, A 105.20/6, A 92.42

Soybeans and Flaxseed Summary, **Crop** Year, A 88.18/13-2

Status Report, Voluntary and Non-Profit Agency Technical **Crop** Ration Contracts with International Cooperation Administration, S 17.41/2

Summary of Cotton Fiber and Processing Test Results, **Crop** of (year), A 88.11/17-2

Sweetpotato Report, Louisiana **Crop** Reporting Service, A 88.12/4-2

Tobacco **Crop** Summary, A 88.34/9

Truck **Crop** Estimate Reports, A 36.101, A 66.17

Truck **Crop** Farms, Adjustments on (by States), A 36.135

Turkeys Raised, Louisiana **Crop** Reporting Service, A 88.15/11-2

U.S. . . . . **Crop** Quality, A 104.12/2-4

Vegetable Report, Louisiana **Crop** Reporting Service, A 88.12/26

Weather-**Crop** Bulletin, W 42.27

Weekly News Letter {to **Crop** Correspondents}, A 1.22

Weekly Weather and **Crop** Bulletin, C 55.209

Weekly Weather and **Crop** Bulletin, National Summary, C 30.11, C 55.209

Wheat and Rye Summary, **Crop** Year, A 88.18/16

Winter Wheat Report, Louisiana **Crop** Reporting Service, A 88.18/24

World **Crop** Production, A 67.18:WCP

Crop Production

Annual Report of the National Research Programs, **Crop Production**, A 106.25, A 106.25/2

Cropland

Agricultural Resources, **Cropland**, Water, and Conservation, A 93.47/2

Cropland Use and Supply, Outlook and Situation Report, A 93.29/2-14

Farms of Nonwhite Farm Operators, Number of Farms, Land in Farm, **Cropland** Harvested, and Value of Land and Buildings, by Tenure, Censuses of 1945 and 1940 (by States), C 3.193

Crops

Crop Report as of . . . Various **Crops**, A 88.24/2

Crops and Markets, A 1.52, A 88.24/3

Crops Research: Results of Regional Cotton Variety Tests by Cooperating Agricultural Experiment Stations, A 77.15:34

Estimates of Cotton **Crops**, A 36.31

Field and Seed **Crops**, Farm Production, Farm Disposition, Value, by States, A 88.30/4

Field and Seed **Crops**, Production, Farm Use, Sales, Value by States, A 92.19

Field **Crops**, Production, Disposition, Value, A 105.9/4

Floriculture **Crops**, A 105.30

Floriculture **Crops**, Production Area and Sales, A 92.32

Forage **Crop** Gazette, News Letter for Staff Workers, Division of Forage **Crops** and Diseases, A 77.509

Foreign Agriculture, Including Foreign **Crops** and Markets, A 67.7

Foreign **Crops** and Markets, A 67.8

Fruit and Vegetable **Crops** and Diseases Division, Semi-monthly News Letters, A 77.510

Marketing Order Actions, a Summary of Actions Under Marketing Orders for Fruit, Vegetables, and Speciality **Crops**, A 88.12/33

Mississippi Weekly Weather-**Crops** Bulletins, A 88.49

Oil **Crops** Outlook and Situation Report, A 93.23/2

Oil **Crops**, Situation and Outlook Yearbook, A 93.23/2-2

Quality of Grain **Crops** Based on Inspected Receipts at Representative Markets, A 36.206

Seed **Crops** Annual Summary, A 88.30/3, A 105.18

Seed **Crops** Forecasts, A 92.19/2

Seed **Crops** Stock Reports, A 92.19/3

Seed **Crops**, A 88.30

Seed **Crops**, Certified Seed Potato Report, A 88.30/6, A 92.19/6

Seed **Crops**, Vegetable Seed Report, A 92.19/7

Trends in Forage **Crops** Varieties, A 43.33

Victory **Crops** Series Pamphlets, FS 5.29

Virginia **Crops** and Livestock, A 88.31

Weather, **Crops**, and Markets, A 36.11

{Truck **Crops**} TD-Series, A 88.16/6-2

Cross Reference

Consolidated Master **Cross Reference** List, D 7.20

Master **Cross Reference** List, Marine Corps, D 7.20/3

Cross-Check

Cross-Check Procedure, D 217.16/8

Standards Laboratory **Cross-Check** Procedure, Department of Navy, BUWEPS-BUSHIPS Calibration Program, D 217.16

Cross-Reference

Cross-Reference Index of Current FHWA Directives, TD 2.67

Subject Matter Index with **Cross-Reference** Table, Y 3.F 31/21:11

Cross-Section

Daily Aerological **Cross-Section** Pole to Pole along Meridian 75 Degrees W for IGY Period, July 1957-December 1958, C 30.76

Crossing

Rail-Highway Grade-**Crossing** Accidents, IC 1 acci.8

Rail-Highway-Grade **Crossing** Accident/Incidents Bulletin, TD 3.109

CRREL

CRREL in Alaska, Annual Report (year), D 103.33/8

CRREL Monographs, D 103.33/7

CRREL Reports, D 103.33/12

CRS

CRS Media Relations, Newspapers, Magazines, Radio, Television, C 50.7/2

CRS Media Relations, Newspapers, Magazines, Radio, Television, Informational Monitoring Service, J 23.7

CRS Studies in the Public Domain (series), LC 14.20

Hate Crime: The Violence of Intolerance, **CRS** Bulletin, J 23.3

Crude

Crude Petroleum and Petroleum Products, I 28.18/4

Crude Petroleum Reports by Refineries, I 32.9, I 28.45

U.S. **Crude** Oil, Natural Gas, and Natural Gas Liquids Reserves (Diskettes), E 3.34

U.S. **Crude** Oil and Natural Gas Reserves, (year) Annual Report, E 3.34

Weekly **Crude** Oil Stock Reports, I 28.46

World **Crude** Oil Production Annual (year), I 28.18/5

Crude Drugs

Industry Report, **Crude** Drugs, Gums, Balsams, and Essential Oils, C 18.236

Crude-oil

Crude-oil and Product Pipelines, E 3.11/12

Crude-oil and Refined-products Pipeline Mileage in the United States, I 28.45/2

Forecast of Motor-Fuel Demand and Required **Crude-Oil** Production by States, Monthly Forecast, I 28.41

Cruise

List of Fully Processed Oceanography **Cruise**, D 203.24/5

National Status and Trends Program, Water Quality **Cruise** Data Reports (series), C 55.436, C 55.436/4

Summary of Sanitation Inspection of International **Cruise** Ships, HE 20.7511

Crush

Soybean **Crush** Products, Preliminary Report, C 3.121

Crushed

Cotton Seed **Crushed** and Linters Obtained, C 3.22

Cottonseed Received, **Crushed** and on Hand; Cotton Linters Produced; and Linters on Hand at Oil Mills, Preliminary Reports, C 3.149

Cottonseed Received, **Crushed**, and on Hand, Etc, Preliminary Report, C 3.25

Crushed Stone and Sand and Gravel in the Quarter of, I 28.118/4

Crushed Stone in (year), I 28.118/2-2

Directory of Principal **Crushed** Stone Producers in the United States in (year), I 28.118/2

Mineral Industry Surveys, **Crushed Stone** and Sand, I 19.138

Safety Competition, National **Crushed** Stone Association, I 28.26/4

Crushers

List, Peanut Millers (shellers and **crushers**), A 92.14/3

List, Peanut Shellers and **Crushers**, A 88.10/3

Peanut Shellers and **Crushers** List, A 88.10/3

Cryogenic

Cryogenic Materials Data Handbook, C 13.6/3

Cryogenic Materials Data Handbook, Yearly Summary Reports, D 301.45/41

Publications and Reports of **Cryogenic** Interest Noted List, C 13.51

Cryogenics

Biweekly **Cryogenics** Awareness Service, C 13.51

Crystallography

Crystallography {abstracts}, C 41.79

Crystals

Quartz **Crystals** in (year), I 28.164

CSA

CSA Guidance (series), CSA 1.8/3

CSAP

CSAP Cultural Competence Series, HE 20.420

CSAP Healthy Delivery, HE 20.8028

CSAP Prevention Monograph, HE 20.426

CSAP Special Reports, HE 20.8027

CSAP, Substance Abuse Resource Code, Violence, HE 20.409/2

CSAP Substance Abuse Resource Guide, HE 20.409/2

CSAP Technical Report, HE 20.415/3

CSC-EPL-

Computer Security Center, **CSC-EPL-** (series), D 1.79

CSC-STD

CSC-STD (series), D 1.79/3

CSL

CSL Bulletin, C 13.76

CSREES

CSREES - Update, A 94.20

CSRS

CSRS (series), A 94.10

CSRS and FERS Handbook for Personnel and Payroll, PM 1.14/3-3

CSRS Research Information Letter, A 94.13

CSRS/FERS

Enrollment Information Guide and Plan Comparison Chart **CSRS/FERS** Annuitants, PM 1.8/10

CSS

CSS Background Information, A 82.82

CSU-PHS

CSU-PHS {Colorado State University-Public Health Service} Collaborative Radiological Health Laboratory: Annual Report, HE 20.4119, HE 20.4613

CTC

CTC Quarterly Bulletin, D 101.22/30

CTC Trends, Battle Command Training Program, D 101.22/29

CTC Trends, Combat Maneuver Training Center (CMTC), D 101.22/26

CTC Trends, Joint Readiness Training Center, D 101.22/28

CTC Trends, NTC, D 101.22/27

Cuba

Cuba and Puerto Rico Special Commissioner, T 1.16

Cuba, Handbook of Trade Statistics, PrEx 3.20

Cuba, Post Department, Annual Reports, P 1.17

Directory of Officials of the Republic of **Cuba**, PrEx 3.10/7-18

Monthly Summary of Commerce of **Cuba**, W 6.9

President's Advisory Board for **Cuba** Broadcasting, Pr 41.8:Br 78

Report by the Advisory Board for **Cuba** Broadcasting, Y 3.B 78/2:1

CUE

Geographic Base (DIME) File, **CUE**, {Correction-Update-Extension}, C 3.249/2, C 56.255

Cull
  Summary of Brucellosis Eradication Activities in Cooperation with Various States Under **Cull** and Dry Cow Testing Program, A 77.212/7
Cultivation
  Cultivation of Neglected Tropical Fruits with Promise (series), A 106.26/2
Cultural
  CSAP **Cultural** Competence Series, HE 20.420
  Cultural Landscape Publication, I 29.86/4
  Cultural Post, NF 2.11
  Cultural Presentation Programs of the Department of State, S 1.67
  Cultural Presentations USA, (year), Report to Congress and the Public, S 1.67
  Cultural Properties Programs, Year-end Report, I 70.19
  Cultural Resource Management Studies, I 29.86, I 70.11, I 70.11/2
  Cultural Resource Series (Utah), I 53.22/2
  Cultural Resources Information Series, I 53.22/11
  Cultural Resources Management Bulletin, I 29.86/2
  Cultural Resources Overview (series), A 13.101
  Cultural Resources Publications (series), I 53.22/4
  Cultural Resources Reports, I 29.86/3
  Cultural Resources Series, I 53.22
  Cultural Resources Series (Nevada), I 53.22/3
  Cultural Resources Series Arizona, I 53.22/8
  Cultural Resources Series Montana, I 53.22/5
  Cultural Resources Series New Mexico, I 53.22/9
  Cultural Resources Series Oregon, I 53.22/10
  Cultural Resources Series Utah, I 53.22/2
  Cultural Resources Series Wyoming, I 53.22/7
  Directory of Contacts for International Educational, **Cultural** and Scientific Exchange Programs, S 1.67/4
  Directory of Resources for **Cultural** and Educational Exchanges and International Communication, ICA 1.12
  External Information and **Cultural** Relations Programs: {various countries}, IA 1.23
  International Education and **Cultural** Exchange, Y 3.Ad 9/9:9
  International Information and **Cultural** Affairs Office Publications, S 1.56
  International Information and **Cultural** Series, S 1.67
  International Teacher Development Program, Annual Report to Bureau of Educational and **Cultural** Affairs, Department of State, FS 5.214:14003
  OSAP **Cultural** Competence Series, HE 20.8018/5
  Southwest **Cultural** Resources Center: Professional Papers, I 29.116
  Studies in **Cultural** Resource Management, A 13.101/2
  UNESCO World Review Weekly Radio News from United Nations Educational, Scientific, and **Cultural** Organization, Paris, France, S 5.48/6
  United Nations Educational, Scientific and **Cultural** Organization News {releases}, S 5.48/13
  World List of Future International Meeting: Pt. 2, Social, **Cultural**, Commercial, Humanistic, LC 2.9/2
Cultures
  Catalog of Cell **Cultures** and DNA Samples, HE 20.3464
Culturist
  Progressive Fish **Culturist**, I 49.35
Cumulated
  Clearinghouse on Health Indexes: **Cumulated** Annotations, HE 20.6216/2
  Cumulated Index Medicus, HE 20.3612/3
  Cumulated List of New Medical Subject Headings, HE 20.3612/3-2
Cumulation
  Public Documents Highlights, Microfiche **Cumulation**, GP 3.27/2
Cumulations
  Highway Safety Literature Annual **Cumulations**, TD 8.10/3
Cumulative
  Cumulative Bulletin, T 22.25
  Cumulative Index to Foreign Production and Commercial Reports, C 42.15/3-2
  Cumulative Index-Digest, C 31.211/3

Cumulative Index-Digest of Unpublished Decisions, I 1.69/2-3
Cumulative Indexes, NAS 1.9/5
Cumulative List of Malaysia, Singapore and Brunei Serials, LC 1.30/10-2
Cumulative List, Organizations Described in Section 170 (c) of the International Revenue Code of 1954, T 22.2:Or 3
Cumulative Listing, FS 2.216/2
Cumulative Price and Status Change Report, GP 3.22/3-4
Cumulative Report of All Specific Risk Investment Guaranties Issued Since the Beginning of the Program through, S 18.26/3
Decennial **Cumulative** Index, GP 3.8/3
EPA **Cumulative** Bibliography, EP 1.21/7-2
Final **Cumulative** Finding Aid, House and Senate Bills, GP 3.28
Government Reports Index, Quarterly **Cumulative**, C 51.9/2
Index of Board Decisions, **Cumulative** Supplements, LR 1.8/4
Index to Foreign Production and Commercial Reports, **Cumulative** Indexes, C 42.15/3-3
India, Accessions List, Annual Supplement, **Cumulative** List of Serials, LC 1.30/1-2
Indonesia, **Cumulative** List of Serials, LC 1.30/5-2
Parkinson's Disease and Related Disorders: **Cumulative** Bibliography, HE 20.3511/3
Quarterly **Cumulative** Report of Technical Assistance, C 46.23
Sales Tax Rulings, **Cumulative** Bulletin, T 22.27
Social Security Rulings, **Cumulative** Bulletins, HE 3.44/2
Subject Catalog, **Cumulative** List of Works Represented by Library of Congress Printed Cards, LC 30.11
Supplement to LC Subject Headings, Quarterly **Cumulative** Supplement, LC 26.7
Cup
  Average Weight of Measured **Cup** of Various Foods, A 1.87:41
Curiors
  Firearms, **Curiors** and Relics List, T 70.15
Curios
  Firearms, and Ammunition **Curios** and Relics List, T 70.15
Currencies
  Inventory of Nonpurchased Foreign **Currencies**, T 1.50
  Report on Foreign **Currencies** Held by the U.S. Government Fiscal Year and Transition Quarter, T 63.118/2
  Semiannual Consolidated Report of Balances of Foreign **Currencies** Acquired Without Payment of Dollars As of December 31 (year), T 63.117
  Statement of Foreign **Currencies** Purchased with Dollars, T 63.118/3
Currency
  Circular of Inquiry Concerning Gold and Silver Coinage and **Currency** of Foreign Countries, Including Production, Import and Export, and Industrial Consumption of Gold and Silver, T 28.8
  Counterpart Funds and AID Foreign **Currency** Account, S 18.14
  Counterpart Funds and FOA Foreign **Currency** Accounts, FO 1.11/3
  Counterpart Funds and ICA Foreign **Currency** Accounts, S 17.11/3
  Currency & Banking News Digest, T 22.2/15:7446
  Demand Deposits, **Currency** and Related Items, FR 1.47
  European Program, Local Currency Counterpart Funds, Pr 33.911, FO 1.11
  Far East Program, Local **Currency** Counterpart Funds, Pr 33.911/2, FO 1.11/2
  Foreign **Currency** Availabilities and Uses, Special Analysis E, PrEx 2.8/a9
  Laws relating to Loans and **Currency**, T 26.6/1
  Legislative Activity of House Committee on Banking and **Currency**, Y 4.B 22/1:L 52/3
  Local **Currency** Counterpart Funds, Y 4.Ec 74/3:12
  Monthly Statement of Paper **Currency** of Each Denomination Outstanding, T 40.8
  Paper **Currency** of Each Denomination Outstanding, Monthly Statements, T 63.307

Quarterly Journal, Comptroller of the **Currency**, T 12.18
Special Foreign **Currency** Science Information Program, List of Translations in Process for Fiscal Year, Coordinated and Administered by the National Science Foundation, C 51.12
Statement of United States **Currency** and Coin, T 63.188, T 63.308
Current
  Abstracts of **Current** Literature on Venereal Disease, FS 2.11/2
  Analysis of the **Current** Services Budget Contained in the President's Budget for Fiscal Year (date), Y 4.Ec 7-11
  Business Statistics, Biennial Supplement to Survey of **Current** Business, C 56.109/3
  Business Statistics, Weekly Supplement to Survey of **Current** Business, C 56.109/2
  Catalog of **Current** Joint Publications Research Publications, Y 3.J 66:15
  Clinical Center, **Current** Clinical Studies and Patient Referral Procedures, HE 20.3010
  Consolidated Review of **Current** Information, T 23.7/2
  Construction, Monthly Summary of **Current** Developments, L 2.22
  Cost of **Current** Series, Electrical Equipment Division, C 18.61
  Current and Non-current Periodicals in the NIH Library, HE 20.3009/3
  Current Awareness in Health Education, HE 20.7209/2, HE 20.7609
  Current Awareness of Translations, EP 1.21/3
  Current Bibliographies in Medicine (series), HE 20.3615/2
  Current Bibliographies Prepared by the Library, L 1.34/4
  Current Bibliography of Epidemiology, HE 20.3617
  Current Business Reports, C 3.211/4
  Current Business Reports Service Annual Survey, C 3.138/3-4
  Current Business Reports; Advance Monthly Retail Sales, CB (series), C 56.219/6
  Current Business Reports: Annual Survey of Communication Services, C 3.138/3-6
  Current Business Reports; Canned Food, Stock, Pack, Shipments, B-1 (series), C 56.219/8
  Current Business Reports; Green Coffee, Inventories, Imports, Roastings, BG (series), C 56.219/2
  Current Business Reports; Monthly Retail Trade, Sales and Accounts Receivable, BR (series), C 56.219/4
  Current Business Reports; Monthly Selected Service Receipts, BS (series), C 56.219/5
  Current Business Reports; Monthly Wholesale Trade, Sales and Inventories, BW (series), C 56.219
  Current Business Reports; Retail Trade, C 56.219/4-2
  Current Business Reports; Weekly Retail Sales, CB (series), C 56.219/7
  Current Conservation, I 43.7
  Current Construction Reports, Housing Units Authorized by Building Permits, C 3.215/4:C 40
  Current Construction Reports, New One-Family Houses Sold and for Sale, C 3.215/9
  Current Construction Reports, Special Studies, Expenditures for Nonresidential Improvements and **Repairs**, C 3.215/8-2
  Current Controls Bulletins, Y 3.Ec 74/2:109
  Current Developments, A 57.70
  Current Developments in Drug Distribution, C 18.212
  Current Developments in Electrical Trade, C 18.213
  Current Developments in Farm Real Estate Market, A 77.13
  Current Developments in Food Distribution, C 18.214
  Current Developments Report on European Recovery, S 1.72
  Current Diagrams, C 4.28
  Current Discharge at Selected Stations in the Pacific Northwest, I 19.45, I 19.47/2
  Current Distribution Developments in Hardware and Allied Trades, C 18.215

Current Employment Market for Engineers, Scientists, and Technicians, L 7.63/2

Current Employment Statistics State Operating Manual, L 2.46/4

Current Estimates from the National Health Interview Survey, HE 20.6209/4

Current Events: Power Reactors, Y 3.N 88:12

Current Expenditures Per Pupil in Pubic School Systems, FS 5.222:22000, HE 5.222:22000

Current Export Bulletins, Pr 32.5807, C 34.7, C 18.266, C 42.11, C 49.208/2

Current Facts on Housing, HH 1.10

Current Federal Aid Research Report, Wildlife, I 49.94/2

Current Federal Examination Announcements, PM 1.21

Current Federal Meteorological Research and Development Activities, C 30.75/2

Current Federal Research Reports, Fish, I 49.94

Current Federal Workforce Data, CS 1.72

Current Fisheries Statistics CFS (series), C 55.309/2

Current Fishery Products, Annual Summary, C 55.309/2-4

Current Fishery Statistics, I 49.8/2

Current Housing Market Situation, Report {various localities}, HH 2.28/2

Current Housing Reports C 3.215:H 130

Current Housing Reports, C 56.214, C 3.215/14, C 56.214/2

Current Housing Reports: Market Absorption of Apartments, H-130 (series), C 56.230

Current Housing Situation, HH 2.20

Current Industrial Reports, C 3.158, C 56.216

Current Industrial Reports (Multigraphed), C 3.58

Current Industrial Reports: Manufacturing Technology, C 3.158/3

Current Information on Occupational Outlook, VA 1.31

Current Information Reports, A 13.91

Current Information Resource Requirements of the Federal Government, PM 1.56

Current Information Statements, A 55.33

Current Information Technology Resources Requirements of the Federal Government, PrEx 2.12/5

Current Intelligence Bulletin, HE 20.7115

Current Intelligence Bulletins, Summaries, HE 20.7115/2

Current IPA Projects for Improved State and Local Management, CS 1.94

Current Issue Outline (series), C 55.235

Current Laws, Statutes and Executive Orders, EP 1.5:L 44

Current Legal Literature, TD 4.17/4

Current List of Medical Literature, W 44.30, M 102.9, D 104.7, D 8.8, FS 2.208

Current Listing and Topical Index, HE 20.6209/2

Current Listing and Topical Index to the Vital and Health Statistics Series, HE 20.2202:V 83

Current Listing of Aircraft Bonds, T 17.19/2

Current Listings of Carrier's Bonds, T 17.19

Current Literature in Agricultural Engineering, A 70.7

Current Literature on Venereal Disease, FS 2.11/2, HE 20.2311

Current Local Announcements Covering Washington, D.C. Metropolitan Area, CS 1.28:2602-WA

Current Membership of Joint Committee on Atomic Energy, Membership, Publications, and Other Pertinent Information through {Congress, Session}, Y 4.At 7/2:M 51

Current Mortality Analysis, C 3.152

Current News, D 301.89

Current News Defense Management Edition, D 2.19/5, D 301.89/8, D 301.89/11

Current News Special Edition, Selected Statements, D 2.19/7, D 301.89/5-2

Current News, Early Bird Edition, D 2.19

Current News, Special Edition, D 2.19/4

Current News, Supplemental Clips, D 2.19/3

Current News, Supplemental Special Edition, D 301.89/13

Current News, The Friday Review, D 2.19/8

Current Policy (series), S 1.71/4

Current Policy Digest, S 1.71/4-2

Current Population Reports, C 3.186, C 56.218

Current Population Reports, Household Economic Studies, C 3.186:P-70/2

Current Population Reports, Local Population Estimates, County Population Estimates, C 3.186/20-2

Current Population Research Reports, FS 2.22/61

Current Population Survey, C 3.224/12

Current Procurement News Digest, W 2.14/6

Current Programs and Operations of Housing and Home Finance Agency, Factual Summary for Public Interest Organizations, HH 1.21

Current Projects in Prevention, Control, and Treatment of Crime and Delinquency, FS 2.22/51

Current Projects on Economic and Social Implications of Scientific Research and Development, NS 1.23

Current Publications of the Women's Bureau, L 13.18

Current REA Publications, A 68.3

Current Releases of Non-Theatrical Film, C 18.63

Current Report on Marshall Plan, Y 3.Ec 74/3:15

Current Research and Developments in Scientific Documentation, NS 1.15, NS 2.10

Current Research Project Grants, HE 20.3111

Current Retail Trade Reports, C 3.138

Current Review of Soviet Technical Press, C 41.94

Current Reviews of Economic and Social Problems in United Nations, S 1.81

Current Salary Schedules of Federal Officers and Employees Together with a History of Salary and Retirement Annuity Adjustments, Y 4.P 84/10-15

Current Shipping Data, C 25.7

Current Social Security Program Operations, FS 3.43

Current Statement of Loans by Years and Commodities, Y 3.C 73:12

Current Statistics of Relief in Rural and Town Areas, Y 3.W 89/2:25, SS 1.23

Current Trends, SE 1.33

Current Wage Developments, L 2.44

DACAS {Drug Abuse **Current** Awareness System}, HE 20.8209

Employment Bulletin, **Current** Openings, G-11 and Above, at Army Material Command Activities Throughout the United States, D 101.3/5

Entomology **Current** Literature, A 9.14, A 56.10, A 17.14

Exempt Organizations **Current** Developments, T 22.50

Explanations and Sailing Directions to Accompany Wind and **Current** Charts, N 14.9

Facts from FDA, **Current** and Useful Information from Food and Drug Administration, HE 20.4029

FDA **Current** Drug Information, HE 20.4013

Financial Statistics of Institutions of Higher Education, **Current** Funds, Revenues, and Expenditures, HE 19.316/2

Forest-Gram South, Dispatch of **Current** Technical Information for Direct Use by Practicing Forest Resource Manager in the South, A 13.89

Forestry **Current** Literature, A 13.25

Government-Supported Research on Foreign Affairs, **Current** Project Information, S 1.101/10

Guide to **Current** Business Data, C 43.12

Health Insurance Statistics: **Current** Medicare Survey Report, HE 3.28/4

Highlights of **Current** Legislation and Activities in Mid-europe, LC 1.27

Highways, **Current** Literature, A 22.10, FW 2.8, C 37.10

Illustrations from State Public Assistance Agencies, **Current** Practices in Staff Training, FS 3.20

Index of **Current** Regulations of Federal Maritime Board, Maritime Administration, National Shipping Authority, C 39.106/2, C 39.206/4, TD 11.22

Index of **Current** Water Resources Activities in Ohio, I 19.55/6

Instruction Manual: Data Preparation of the **Current** Sample, HE 20.6208/9

Letters Relative to **Current** Developments in Medical Science and Medical Military Information, FS 2.40

Mental Health Manpower, **Current** Statistical and Activities Reports, FS 2.54/3

Mental Health Statistics, **Current** Report Series, FS 2.115, FS 2.53/2

Mental Health Statistics: **Current** Facility Reports, HE 17.117

Mental Retardation and the Law, a Report on Status of **Current** Court Cases, HE 23.110

Mental Retardation and the Law, a Report on the Status of **Current** Court Cases, HE 1.51

Monthly Translations List and **Current** Contents, EP 1.21/2

Navy **Current** Procurement Directives, NCPD (series), D 201.6/13

OAR Quarterly Index of **Current** Research Results, D 301.69/8

Patents Class, **Current** Classifications of US Patents, C 21.31/3

Planning, **Current** Literature, FW 1.15, C 37.12

Population Profile of the United States, **Current** Population Reports, C 3.186/8

Public Administration Practices and Perspectives, Digest of **Current** Materials, S 18.24

Quarterly Journal of **Current** Acquisitions, LC 2.17

Recap, Reclamation's **Current** Awareness Program, I 27.52

Received or Planned **Current** Fisheries, Oceanographic, and Atmospheric Translations, A- (series), C 55.325/2

Regional Tide and Tidal **Current** Tables, C 55.425/3

Report on **Current** Hydraulic Laboratory Research in U.S., C 13.26

Review of **Current** DHHS, DOE, and EPA Research Related to Toxicology, HE 20.3563

Review of **Current** Information in Treasury Library, T 23.7

Review of **Current** Periodicals, New Series, SE 1.23

Safety News Letter, **Current** Information in the Federal Safety Field, L 30.8

Selected **Current** Acquisitions, Lists, D 102.28/3

Selected List of American Agricultural Books in Print and **Current** Agricultural Periodicals, A 17.17:1

Selected List of Articles in **Current** Periodicals of Interest to Ordnance Department, W 34.21/2

Selected-**Current** Acquisitions, TC 1.34/2

Series Available and Estimating Methods, BLS **Current** Employment Statistics Program, L 2.124/2

Shellfish Market Review, **Current** Economic Analysis S, C 55.309/4

Soil Conservation Literature, Selected **Current** References, A 57.20, A 17.15

Special **Current** Business Reports: Monthly Department Store Sales in Selected Areas, BD- (series), C 56.219/3

Special Studies, **Current** Population Reports, C 3.186:P-23

Special Supplements to the Survey of **Current** Business, C 59.11/4

Subject Index of **Current** Research Grants and Contracts Administered by the National Heart, Lung, and Blood Institute, HE 20.3212

Supplement (special) to Survey of **Current** Business, C 59.11/4

Survey of **Current** Business, C 3.33/1, C 56.109, C 59.11, C 59.11/1

Survey of **Current** Business, Weekly Supplements, C 3.34

TC in the **Current** National Emergency, Historical Report No., D 117.9, D 117.9/2

Tidal **Current** Charts, C 55.424

Tidal **Current** Tables, C 4.22, C 4.23, C 55.425

Tide **Current** Tables, Atlantic Coast of North America, C 55.425

Translated Tables of Contents of **Current** Foreign Fisheries, Oceanographic, and Atmospheric Publications, C 55.325

Transportation, **Current** Literature Compiled by Library Staff, TD 1.15/4

Urban Transportation and Planning, **Current** Literature Compiled by Library Staff, TD 1.15/5

Wind and **Current** Charts, Series A, Tract Charts, N 14.10/1

Currently

Interim List of Persons or Firms **Currently** Debarred for Violation of Various Public Contracts Acts Incorporating Labor Standards Provisions, GA 1.17/2

Newspapers **Currently** Received, LC 6.7

Periodicals **Currently** Received in NIH Library, FS 2.22/13-3

Serials **Currently** Received by the National Agricultural Library, A 17.18/2:Se 6

Currents
  Access **Currents**, Y 3.B 27:16
  Cassis **Currents** Newsletter, C 21.31/12
  River **Currents**, TD 5.27
  VISTA **Currents**, AA 1.9/3

Curricular
  Undergraduate Engineering **Curricular** Accredited by Engineer's Council for Professional Development, FS 5.61

Curriculum
  Adjustment of College **Curriculum** to Wartime Conditions and Needs, Reports, FS 5.33
  Annotated Bibliography of CDA **Curriculum** Materials, HE 23.111/2
  Application for Grants under Fulbright-Hays Foreign **Curriculum** Consultants, ED 1.59
  College **Curriculum** Support Project, Updates, C 3.163/9
  Core **Curriculum**, PE 1.11
  Course Offering, Enrollments, and **Curriculum**, Practices in Public Secondary Schools, HE 19.334/2
  Curriculum Catalog, PM 1.46
  Curriculum Guide Series, HE 19.108/3
  Curriculum Handbook, D 305.6/3
  ENC, Eisenhower National Clearinghouse, A Collection of **Curriculum** Standards and Framework, ED 1.340/3
  SSA Training (series): Technical CORE **Curriculum**, HE 3.69/2
  Training Opportunities, Course **Curriculum** Catalog, S 1.139

Curriculums
  Directory of Secondary Schools with Occupational **Curriculums**, Public and Nonpublic, HE 5.96
  Guide to Organized Occupational **Curriculums** in Higher Education, FS 5.254:54012, HE 5.254:54012
  Suggested Two-year Post-High School **Curriculums**, HE 19.118

Custody
  Children in **Custody**, J 29.9/5
  Civilian Personnel Liberated from Japanese **Custody**, W 107.12
  Juveniles Taken into **Custody**, J 32.18

Customer
  Customer Assistance Handbook, D 7.6/20
  Customer Care Technical Brief, E 6.1/2, E 6.11/2
  Customer Supply Center Catalog, GS 2.23
  Foreign Military Sales **Customer** Procedures (series), D 7.6/15

Custom-House
  Manila **Custom-House** General Orders, W 49.10/7

Customs
  Appeals Pending Before United States Courts in **Customs** Cases, T 17.8
  Catalogue of Book and Blanks Furnished by Department of Commerce to **Customs** Officers, C 1.16
  Catalogue of Books and Blanks Used by Officers of **Customs** at Port of New York, T 36.5/2
  Code Classification of U.S. **Customs** Districts and Ports, C 3.150:D
  Customs
  Schedule D. Code Classification of U.S. **Customs** Districts and Ports, C 3.150:D
  Customs Administrative Circulars, W 49.10/6
  Customs Administrative Orders, W 49.10/10
  Customs Bulletin, T 1.11/3
  Customs Bulletin and Decisions, T 17.6/3-4
  Customs Bulletins (bound volume), T 1.11/4
  Customs Decisions, W 49.10/5
  Customs Information Series, T 17.12
  Customs Laboratory Bulletin, T 17.6/4
  Customs Laws (general), T 17.6
  Customs Marine Circular, W 49.10/9
  Customs Performance Reports, T 17.25
  Customs Publication (series), T 17.26
  Customs Regulations, T 1.9/1
  Customs Regulations of the United States, T 17.9
  Customs Tariff and Regulations, W 1.7
  Customs Today, T 17.16
  Customs Trade Quarterly, T 17.16/2
  Customs U.S.A., T 17.22
  General Receiver of **Customs** for Liberia, S 1.24
  Haitian **Customs** Receivership, Annual Reports, S 1.16

Index to Treasury Decisions Under **Customs** and Other Laws, T 1.11/1a

Liberia, General Receiver of **Customs** for, S 1.24

Military Discipline, Courtesies, and **Customs** of Service, W 3.50/12

Papers in Re in Court of **Customs** and Patent Appeals, J 1.79

Posters **Customs** Service, T 17.21

Reappraisement Decisions, for Review by U.S. **Customs** Court As Published in Weekly Treasury Decisions, T 1.11/2a

Regulations, Rules and Instructions Court of **Customs** Appeals, Ju 7.8/2

Regulations, Rules and Instructions **Customs** Division, T 17.5

Reports of Cases Adjudged in the Court of **Customs** and Patent Appeals, Ju 7.5

Revised **Customs** Regulations, T 1.9/2

Rules of United States Court of **Customs** and Patent Appeals, Ju 7.8

Tariffs Bureau of **Customs**, T 17.7

Telephone Directory **Customs** Service, T 17.15

U.S. **Customs** Guide for Private Flyers, T 17.23

U.S. Exports of Petroleum and Petroleum Products of Domestic Origin, Commodity by **Customs** District, C 3.164:527

United States Airborne Foreign Trade, **Customs** District by Continent, C 3.164:986

United States **Customs** Court Reports, Ju 9.5

United States Foreign Trade, Trade by **Customs** District, C 3.164:970

Cut
  Cotton Linters Produced and on Hand at Oil Mills by Type of **Cut**, by States, Preliminary, C 3.148
  Cut Flowers, Production and Sales, A 88.47
  Work Clothing (garments **cut**), C 3.64

Cut-off
  FM Broadcast Applications Accepted for Filing and Notification of **Cut-off** Date, CC 1.26/3
  TV Broadcast Applications Accepted for Filing and Notification of **Cut-off** Date, CC 1.26/5

Cut-off Date
  AM Broadcast Applications Accepted for Filing and Notification of **Cut-off Date**, CC 1.26/4
  FM and TV Translator Applications Ready and Available for Processing and Notification of **Cut-off Date**, CC 1.26/6

Cutbacks
  Cutbacks Reported to Production Readjustment Committee, Pr 32.4834

Cuthbert
  Adventures of **Cuthbert** (radio scripts), I 29.47

Cuts
  Catalogue of Copyright Entries, Pt. 1, Engraving, **Cuts** and Prints, Chromos and Lithographs, Photographs, Fine Arts, LC 3.6/4

Cutter
  Cutter Radar Project Newsletter, TD 5.38
  Historical Register, U.S. Revenue **Cutter** Service Officers, TD 5.19/4
  Regulations for Revenue-**Cutter** Service (general), T 33.7

Cutting Edge
  Cutting Edge, Research & Development for Sustainable Army Installations, D 103.53/11

CWIHP
  CWIHP, (Cold War International History Project) Bulletin, SI 1.3/2

Cybernetics
  Cybernetics, Computers, and Automation Technology, PrEx 7.22/5

Cybernotes
  Cybernotes, J 1.14/23-2

Cyberspokesman
  Cyberspokesman, D 301.124

Cycle
  Business **Cycle** Developments, C 3.226, C 56.111
  World Nuclear Fuel **Cycle** Requirements, E 3.46/4

Cyclical
  U.S. Exports and Imports, Working-Day and Seasonal Adjustment Factors and Months for **Cyclical** Dominance (MCD), C 3.235

Cyclones
  Tropical **Cyclones** of the North Atlantic Ocean, C 55.202:C 99/871-977

Cystic
  Cystic Fibrosis, HE 20.3320/2-2

CZ/SP
  CZ/SP (series), C 55.13:CZ/SP

Czechoslovak
  Directory of **Czechoslovak** Officials, A Reference Aid, PrEx 3.10/7-10

D

DACAS
  DACAS {Drug Abuse Current Awareness System}, HE 20.8209

Daguerreotypes
  Facing the Light, Historic American Portrait **Daguerreotypes**, SI 11.2:L 62

Dahlgren
  Dahlgren Laboratory: Contract Reports, D 201.21/4
  Naval Surface Warfare Center **Dahlgren** Division, Technical Digest, D 201.21/8

Daily
  CDC NCHSTP **Daily** News Update (AIDS Daily Summaries), HE 20.7318
  Congressional Record, Index and **Daily** Digest, X 1.1
  Daily Bulletin of Orders Affecting Postal Service, P 10.3
  Daily Bulletin of Simultaneous Weather Reports with Synopses Indications, and Facts for Month of, W 42.8/1
  Daily Depository Shipping List, GP 3.16/3
  Daily Digest Communications Office, Department of Agriculture, A 21.14
  Daily Digest Federal Communications Commission, CC 1.54
  Daily Digest of Reconstruction News, Y 3.C 83:95
  Daily Index of REA News, Y 3.R 88:15
  Daily Indexes and Spot Market Prices, L 2.60/2
  Daily Magnetograms for ... from the AFGL Network, D 301.45/4-4
  Daily Mississippi River Stage and Forecast Bulletin, C 30.54
  Daily Missouri-Mississippi River Bulletin, C 30.54
  Daily Ohio River Bulletin, C 30.54/17, C 55.110
  Daily Operations Highlights, TD 5.31
  Daily Press Digest, FS 3.26
  Daily Series, Synoptic Weather Maps, C 55.213/2
  Daily Shipping Bulletins, N 22.6, SB 1.12
  Daily Spot Cotton Quotations, A 88.11/4
  Daily Spot Market Price Indexes and Prices, Weekly Summary, L 2.60
  Daily Statement of the Treasury, T 1.5
  Daily Temperature, Degree Day and Precipitation Normals, C 30.62
  Daily Totals of Precipitation in Muskingum River Basin, A 80.2010
  Daily Treasury Statement, T 63.113/2-2
  Daily Weather and River Bulletin {New Orleans, La. Area}, C 55.110/5
  Daily Weather Bulletin, C 30.43
  Daily Weather Maps, C 55.195
  Daily Weather Maps, Weekly Series, C 55.213
  Federal Communication Commission **Daily**, CC 1.56
  Manpower **Daily** Reporter, L 1.39/7

Dairy
  Commercial **Dairy** Farms, Northeast and Midwest, A 93.9/11
  Dairy and Poultry Market Statistics Annual Summaries, A 1.34, A 36.54, A 66.35
  Dairy Cattle and **Dairy** and Poultry Products, A 67.30:D 14
  Dairy Herd Improvement Letter, A 77.608, A 106.34
  Dairy Industry Bureau, A 77.600
  Dairy Library List, A 44.9
  Dairy Market Statistics, Annual Summary, A 88.14/13
  Dairy Monthly Imports, A 67.18:FDMI
  Dairy Outlook, A 36.71
  Dairy Outlook and Situation Report, A 93.13
  Dairy Plants Surveyed and Approved for USDA Grading Service, A 88.14/12, A 103.12
  Dairy Production, A 88.14/2
  Dairy Products, A 105.17/3
  Dairy Products, Annual Summary (year), A 105.17/4
  Dairy Short Course, A 21.13/2
  Dairy Situation, A 88.14/4, A 93.13, A 105.17/2

Dairy, Livestock, and Poultry: U.S. Trade and
Prospects, A 67.18:FDLP
Dairy, Situation and Outlook Yearbook, A 93.13/2-2
Domestic Dairy Market Review, A 82.38
Economic Indicators of the Farm Sector, Cost of
Production: Livestock and Dairy, A
93.45/2-2
General Publications Relating to Dairy Research,
A 77.602
Livestock, Dairy and Poultry Situation and
Outlook, A 93.46/3
Meat and Dairy Monthly Imports, A 67.18:FDLMT
Milk Production and Dairy Products, Annual
Statistical Summary, A 92.10/6
Milk Production on Farms and Statistics of Dairy
Plant Products, A 88.14/7
Monthly Domestic Dairy Markets Review, A 88.13
Production of Manufactured Dairy Products, A
88.14/10
Publications Relating to Dairy Industry, A 44.11
Radio Service Dairy Short Course, A 21.13/2
Service and Regulatory Announcements Bureau of
Dairy Industry, A 44.5
Statistical Supplement of Monthly Domestic Dairy
Markets Review, A 88.13/4
U.S. Dairy Forage Research Center, A 77.37
World Dairy and Poultry News Section, C 18.72/8
World Dairy Prospects, A 36.41

Dakota
Dakota, Governor, Annual Reports, 1878-1912, I
1.10

Dakotas
Art and Indian Children of the Dakotas (series), I
20.63

Dall Porpoise
Annual Report Dall Porpoise-Salmon Research, C
55.343

Dam
Report on Flows and Diversions at Imperial Dam
and All Actions Affecting Coordination
Thereof, I 27.42

Damage
Air Freight Loss and Damage Claims, C 31.265
Air Freight Loss and Damage Claims, Annual
Summaries, C 31.265/3
Air Freight Loss and Damage Claims for the Six
Months Ended (date), C 31.265/2
Animal Damage Control, ADC- (series), I 49.101
Animal Damage Control Program, A 101.28
Damage Analysis and Fundamental Studies, E 1.65
Floods in {location}; How to Avoid Damage, D
103.47/2
Precursors to Potential Severe Core Damage
Accidents, Y 3.N 88:25-6
Quarterly Freight Loss and Damage Claims
Reported by Common and Contract
Motor Carriers of Property, IC 1 acco.11
Quarterly Freight Loss and Damage Claims, Class
1, Line-Haul Railroads, IC 1 acco.12

Damaged
Damaged and Threatened National Historic
Landmarks, I 29.117/2, I 29.117/4

Dams
Storage Dams, I 27.51

Danbury
Area Wage Survey, Danbury, Connecticut,
Metropolitan Area, L 2.121/7-2

Dance
Dance, NF 2.8/2-4
Exploring Dance Careers, HE 19.108:Ex 7

Danger
Danger Area Charts, C 4.9/15
Spot the Danger, User's Guide to {various
products} Safety Series, Y 3.C 76/3:8-3

Dangerous
Traffic in Opium and Other Dangerous Drugs, J
24.9
Transportation of Dangerous Articles and
Magnetized Materials, TD 4.6:part 103

DANTES
DANTES External Degree Catalog, D 1.33/7
DANTES Independent Study Catalog, D 1.33/7-2

Darcom
DARCOM Pamphlets, D 101.22/3
Reports Control Symbol Darcom Manufacturing
Technology, RCS DRCMT-(series), D
101.110

Dark
Fire-Cured and Dark Air-Cured Tobacco Market
Review, A 88.34/8

Dark Air-Cured
Dark Air-Cured Tobacco Market Review, A 88.34/3

DASA
Defense Atomic Support Agency: Technical
Analysis Report DASA (series), D 5.14
Technical Analysis Report DASA (series), D 5.14

DASCH
Defense Administrative Support Center
Handbooks, DASCH (series), D 7.6/14

Dash One
Dash One, a Guide to Cadet Training and DASIAC
Special Reports, D 5.14/2

DASIAC
Dash One, a Guide to Cadet Training and DASIAC
Special Reports, D 5.14/2
DASIAC Special Reports, D 5.14/2

DAT
Project Skywater, CRADP DAT Inventory, I 27.57/
3

Data
Acid Precipitation in North America: Annual Data
Summary from Acid Deposition System
Data Base, EP 1.23/5-4
AFDC Update, News of the Alternative Fuels Data
Center, E 1.114
AHCPR National Medical Expenditure Survey
Data Summary, HE 20.6517/2
Amended Type Certificate Data Sheets and
Specifications, TD 4.15/10
Atlas/State Data Abstract for the United States, D
1.58/4
Background Material and Data on Programs within
the Jurisdiction, Y 4.W 36:10-4
BJS Data Report, J 29.19
Catalog Management Data, D 7.29
Catalog of Electronic Data Products, HE 20.6209/
4-6
Climatological Data, A 29.29, A 29.29/2
Climatological Data; Alaska Section, A 29.33, C
30.21
Climatological Data; Antarctic Stations, C 30.21/3
Climatological Data; Artic Stations, C 30.21/2
Climatological Data; Hawaii Section, A 29.34, C
30.19
Climatological Data; Pacific, C 30.19/2
Climatological Data; Porto Rico Section, A 29.35
Climatological Data; United States, C 30.18-C
30.18/38, C 55.214/2-C 55.214/47
Climatological Data; West Indies and Caribbean
Service, A 29.36, C 30.20
County and City Data Book, C 3.134/2:C 83/2, C
3.134/2-1, C 56.243/2:C 83
Crime Data Brief, J 29.27
Current Federal Workforce Data, CS 1.72
Data Access Descriptions Miscellaneous Series, C
56.212/6
Data Access Descriptions Policy and Administra-
tion Series, C 3.240/4
Data Announcements (series), C 55.239
Data Atlas, C 55.411/4
Data Catalog, Satellite and Rocket Experiments,
NSSDA (nos), NAS 1.37
Data Developments, C 3.238/7
Data Environmental Impact Statements, A 57.65
Data Environmental Statements, I 27.70/2
Data Finders, C 3.162/6
Data Integrity and Run to Run Balancing, T 22.58
Data on Female Veterans, VA 1.2/12
Data on Licensed Pharmacists (place), HE 20.6221
Data on Licensed Pharmacists Series by State, HE
20.6621
Data on Vietnam Era Veterans, VA 1.2/2, VA 1.2/10
Data Report, I 49.59
Data Report (series), EP 1.51/5
Data Report: High Altitude Meteorological Data,
C 55.280
Data Report, Meteorological Rocket Network
Firings, C 52.16
Data Reports, C 55.324
Data Reports (numbered), TD 4.34
Data User News, C 3.238, C 3.238/a, C 56.217
Data Users Guide, I 19.80/3
Defense Acquisition Management Data System
Code Translations, D 1.57/10
Demographic Characteristics and Patterns of Drug
Use of Clients Admitted to Drug Abuse
Treatment Programs in Selected States,
Trend Data, HE 20.8231/2
Department Store Merchandising Data, FR 1.24/5,
FR 1.24/6
Digital Data Digest, D 103.20/8
Digital Data Series, I 19.121
Earnings and Employment Data for Wage and
Salary Workers Covered under Social
Security by State and County, HE 3.95

EIA Data Index, an Abstract Journal, E 3.27/5
Federal Personal Data Systems Subject to the
Privacy Act of 1974, Annual Report of
the President, Pr 38.12, Pr 39.11
Federal Procurement Data System, PrEx 2.24
Federal Procurement Data System, Annual
Analysis (series), PrEx 2.24/2
Federal Procurement Data System, Combined
Special Analyses, PrEx 2.24/12
Federal Procurement Data System, Contractor
Identification File, Alphabetical Listing,
PrEx 2.24/14
Federal Procurement Data System, Special Analysis
3, PrEx 2.24/3
Federal Procurement Data System, Special Analysis
8, PrEx 2.24/8
Federal Procurement Data System, Special Analysis
10, PrEx 2.24/10
Federal Procurement Data System, Standard Report,
PrEx 2.24/13
Final State and Local Data Elements, T 1.64/2
Focus (Joint Center for Integrated Product Data
Environment), D 215.15
Freight Classification Data File, D 7.28
Geophysics and Space Data Bulletin, D 301.45/43
Home Mortgage Disclosure Act Data (State), FR
1.63
Index and User Guide to Type Certificate Data
Sheets and Specifications, TD 4.15/9
Instruction Manual: Data Preparation of the
Current Sample, HE 20.6208/9
Instruction Manual Part 2d, NCHS Procedures for
Mortality Medical Data System File
Preparation and Maintenance, HE
20.6208/4-6
Instruction Manual Part 2g, Data Entry
Instructions for the Mortality Medical
Indexing, Classification, and Retrieval
System (MICAR), HE 20.6208/4-7
Instructions and Data Specifications for Reporting
DHHS Obligations to Institutions of
Higher Education and Other Nonprofit
Organizations, HE 20.3050
Instructions for Classifying the Underlying Cause
of Death: Nonindexed Terms, Standard
Abbreviations, and State Geographic
Codes Used in Mortality Data
Classification, HE 20.6208/4
Interagency Advisory Committee on Water Data:
Summary of Meetings, I 19.74
Integrated Postsecondary Education Data System
IPEDS, ED 1.334/4
International Science and Technology Data Update,
NS 1.52
Mechanical Analyses of Data for Soil Types {by
County}, A 57.39
National Climatic Data Center Periodical
Publications, C 55.287/63
National Economic Social & Environmental Data
Bank (NESEDB), C 1.88/2
National Trade Data Bank, C 1.88
NEISS Data Highlights, Y 3.C 76/3:7-3
NOAA Data Reports C 55.36
NPDP (National Practitioner Data Bank) News,
HE 20.9316
Oceanographic Data Exchange, NS 1.32
Oceanography Semiannual Report of Oceano-
graphic Data Exchange, C 55.220/3
OPA Economic Data Series, Pr 33.307
Operating Data from Monthly Reports of Large
Telegraph Cable, and Radiotelegraph
Carriers, CC 1.13
Operating Data from Monthly Reports of Telephone
Carriers Filing Annual and Monthly
Reports, CC 1.14
Operating Units Status Report, Licensed
Operations Reactors Data for Decisions,
Y 3.N 88:15
Oregon Annual Data Summary, Water Year, A
57.46/5-3
Paleoclimate Data Record, C 55.240
Patient Movement Data, State and Mental
Hospitals, FS 2.22/46
Pension Insurance Data Book: PBGC Single-
Employer Program, Y 3.P 38/2:12
Pesticide Data Program, A 88.60
Plant and Installation Data, PrEx 7.15/3
Pocket Data Book, C 56.243/3
Pocket Data Book, USA (year), C 3.134/3
Population-Weighted Data, C 55.287/60

Postsecondary Education Fall Enrollment in Higher Education (year): Institutional **Data**, HE 19.325/2

Precipitation **Data** from Storage-Gage Stations, C 30.59/44

Preliminary Analysis of Aircraft Accident **Data**, U.S. Civil Aviation, TD 1.113/6

Preliminary **Data** on Unemployment Insurance, L 7.43

Preliminary **Data** Summary, D 103.42/13

Preliminary Power Production, Fuel Consumption and Installed Capacity **Data**, E 3.11/17-6

Preliminary Power Production, Fuel Consumption, and Installed Capacity **Data** for (year), E 3.11/17-4

Preliminary Report and Forecast of Solar Geophysical **Data**, C 55.627

Proceedings National **Data** Buoy Systems Scientific Advisory Meetings, TD 5.23

Program **Data**, HE 1.610/3

Project Skywater **Data** Inventory SCPP Season, I 27.57/2

Proposed Streamflow **Data** Program for {State}, I 19.59

Public Assistance, Annual Statistical **Data**, FS 14.212, FS 17.13, FS 17.615, HE 17.615

Public Library **Data**, ED 1.334/3

Public Use **Data** Tape Documentation Chest X-Ray, Pulmonary Diffusion, and Tuberculin Test Results Ages 25-74, HE 20.6226/5-2

Public Use **Data** Tape Documentation Detail Natality, HE 20.6226/2

Public Use **Data** Tape Documentation Divorce **Data**, Detail, HE 20.6226/4

Public Use **Data** Tape Documentation Fetal Deaths Detail Records, HE 20.6226/11

Public Use **Data** Tape Documentation Interviewer's Manual National Interview Survey, HE 20.6226/8

Public Use **Data** Tape Documentation Medical Coding Manual and Short Index, HE 20.6226/9

Public Use **Data** Tape Documentation Medical History, Ages 12-74 Years, HE 20.6226/5

Public Use **Data** Tape Documentation Mortality Cause-of-Death Summary **Data**, HE 20.6226/6

Public Use **Data** Tape Documentation Mortality Local Area Summary, HE 20.6226/7

Public Use **Data** Tape Documentation Natality Local Area Summary, HE 20.6226/3

Public Use **Data** Tape Documentation Natality State Summary, HE 20.6226

Public Use **Data** Tape Documentation National Health Interview Survey, HE 20.6226/10

Public Welfare Personnel, Annual Statistical **Data**, HE 17.629

Publications Environmental **Data** Service, C 55.228

Publications National Oceanographic **Data** Center, D 203.24, D 203.24/2, C 55.292

Quarterly Operating **Data** of 70 Telephone Carriers, CC 1.14

Quarterly Operating **Data** of Telegraph Carriers, CC 1.13

Radiological **Data** and Reports, EP 6.9

Radiological Health **Data** and Reports, HE 20.1110

Radiological Health **Data**, Monthly Report, FS 2.90

Recent Purchases of Cars, Houses and Other Durables and Expectations to Buy During the Month Ahead: Survey **Data** Through, C 3.186:P-65

Recurrent Report of Financial **Data**: Domestic Air Mail Trunk Carriers, Quarters {comparisons}, C 31.234

Recurrent Report of Mileage and Traffic **Data** All Certificated Air Cargo Carriers, C 31.232

Recurrent Report of Mileage and Traffic **Data** Domestic Air Mail Carriers, C 31.230

Recurrent Report of Mileage and Traffic **Data** Domestic Helicopter Service, Certificated Airmail Carriers, C 31.229/4

Recurrent Report of Mileage and Traffic **Data** Domestic Local Service Carriers, C 31.229

Recurrent Report of Mileage and Traffic **Data** Foreign, Overseas and Territorial Air Mail Carriers, C 31.231

Reference **Data** Report, C 13.48/3

Regional **Data** on Compensation Show Wages, Salaries and Benefits Costs in the Northeast, L 2.71/6-6

Report of Interagency Substances **Data** Commission, EP 1.79/4

Reported Tuberculosis **Data**, HE 20.7017

Research Grants, **Data** Book, HE 20.3516/2

Reviews of **Data** on Research and Development, NS 1.11

Reviews of **Data** on Science Resources, NS 1.11/2

Savings and Mortgage Financing **Data**, HH 4.10

Savings, Mortgage Financing and Housing **Data**, FHL 1.10

Selected Compensation and Pension **Data** by State of Residence, VA 1.88

Selected **Data** on Federal Support to Universities and Colleges, Fiscal Year, NS 1.30/2-2

Selected Financial and Operating **Data** from Annual Reports, CC 1.30

Selected Statistical **Data** by Sex, S 18.56

Series **Data** Handbook, HH 2.24/6

SIPP **Data** News, C 3.274

Small Area **Data** Notes, C 56.217, C 3.238

Small-Area **Data** Activities, C 3.238

Snow Survey and Soil Moisture Measurements, Basic **Data** Summary for Western United States, Including Columbia River Drainage in Canada, A 57.46/17

Solar-Geophysical **Data** {reports}, C 55.215

Solar-Geophysical **Data**, IER-FB- (series), C 52.18, C 55.215

Sources of Morbidity **Data**, FS 2.76

Special Notices, Supplement to Radio Facility Charts and In-flight **Data**, Europe, D 301.9/3

SRS **Data** Brief, NS 1.11/3

SSA Training **Data** Review Technician, Basic Training Course, HE 3.69/3

Standardization and **Data** Management Newsletter, D 1.88

State and Metropolitan Area **Data** Book, C 3.134/5

State **Data** Center Exchange, C 3.238/8

State **Data** Profiles, Calendar Year (date), Selected Ascs Program Activity and Other Agricultural **Data**, A 82.90

State **Data** Profiles, Calendar Year (date), Selected Ascs Program Activity and Other Agricultural **Data**, A 82.90

State Energy **Data** Reports, E 3.42

State Energy **Data** System, E 3.42/5

State Energy Price and Expenditure **Data** System, E 3.42/4

State Vocational Rehabilitation Agency: Program **Data**, HE 23.4110/2

Statistical Series Annual **Data**, **Data** from the Drug Abuse Warning Network (DAWN) Series I, HE 20.8212/11

Statistical Series Securities and Exchange Commission, SE Statistical Series, Annual **Data**, **Data** from the Drug Abuse Warning Network (DAWN), Series I, HE 20.8212/11

STECS **Data** Link, HE 3.86

Steel Import **Data**, C 41.114

Steel Import **Data**, Shipments from Exporting Countries in Calendar Year, C 57.209

Storage-Gage Precipitation **Data** for Western United States, C 55.225

Storm **Data**, C 55.212

Studies from Interagency **Data** Linkages (series), HE 3.62

Summary **Data** from the Employment Situation News Release, L 2.53/2-2

Summary **Data** from the Producer Price Index News Release, L 2.61/10-2

Summary Statistics Project **Data**, I 27.1/4-2

Summary Statistics, Water, Land and Related **Data**, I 27.1/4

Supplement to Producer Prices and Price Indexes **Data** for (year), L 2.61/11

Supplemental Security Income, State and County **Data**, HE 3.71

Survey of American Listed Corporations: Quarterly Sales **Data**, SE 1.22

Tech **Data** Sheet (series), D 201.27

Technical Activities, Office of Standard Reference **Data**, C 13.58/3

Technical **Data** Digest, W 108.18

Telephone Companies, Selected Financial and Operating **Data** from Annual Reports, IC 1 telp.7

Telephone Contacts for **Data** Users, C 3.238/5

Telephone Directory Automated **Data** and Telecommunications Service, Region 1, GS 12.12/2:1

Trade **Data** (series), C 57.17

Treatment Episode **Data** Set (TEDS), HE 20.423/2

Trend **Data**, VA 1.71

Trend Report: Graphic Presentation of Public Assistance and Related **Data**, HE 17.612

Type Certificate **Data** Sheets and Specifications, Rotorcraft, Gliders, and Balloons, TD 4.15/6

U.S. Alcohol Epidemiologic **Data** Reference Manual, HE 20.8308/3

U.S. Divisional and Station Climatic **Data** and Normals, C 55.281/2-3

U.S. Merchant Marine **Data** Sheet, TD 11.10

UI **Data** Summary, L 37.214

Unemployment Allowance Claims and Payment **Data** by Agencies, VA 1.36

Uniform Facility **Data** Set (UFDS): Data, HE 20.423

United States Air Force, Navy, Royal Canadian Air Force and Royal Canadian Navy, Navy Radio Facility Charts and In- Flight **Data**, Alaska, Canada and North Atlantic, D 301.13/3

United States Policy Toward USSR and International Communism, Monthly Digest of Pertinent **Data** Appearing in Department of State Publications, S 1.97

United States Renal **Data** System, Annual **Data** Report, HE 20.3325

Urban Atlas, Tract **Data** for Standard Metropolitan Statistical Areas, C 3.62/7, C 56.242/4

Utah, Annual **Data** Summary, A 57.46/6-3

Washington Annual **Data** Summary Water Year, A 57.46/7-2

Water **Data** Coordination Directory, I 19.118

Water Resources **Data** for {State}, I 19.53/2

Water Resources **Data**, I 19.15/6

Weekly Trading **Data** on New York Exchanges, SE 1.25/6

Winter Energy **Data** Bulletin, E 3.28

World **Data** Center-A for Marine Geology and Geophysics Report, C 55.220/10

World **Data** Center A Glaciology (Snow and Ice), Glaciological **Data** Report, GD- (nos), C 55.220/6

World **Data** Center A Glaciology (Snow and Ice): New Accessions List, C 55.220/8

World **Data** Center A Meteorology **Data** Report, C 55.220/5

World **Data** Center A Meteorology: Publications (unnumbered), C 55.220/7

World **Data** Center A Oceanography Catalogue of Accessioned Soviet Publications, C 55.220/2

World **Data** Center A Oceanography, Catalog of Accessioned Publications, C 55.220/2-2

World **Data** Center A, Oceanography, Catalogue of **Data**, C 55.220/3

World **Data** Center A Oceanography, Catalogue of **Data**, WDCA-OC- (series), C 55.220/2-3

World **Data** Center A Oceanography, **Data** of Accessioned Soviet Publications, C 55.220/2

World **Data** Center A Oceanography, **Data** of Accessioned Soviet Publications, C 55.220/2

World **Data** Center A Oceanography, Semiannual Report of Oceanography **Data** Exchange, C 55.220/3

World **Data** Center A Publications (unnumbered), C 55.220/4, C 55.220/5-2

World **Data** Center A Upper Atmosphere Geophysics, Report UAG- (series), C 55.220

World Military Expenditures and Related **Data**, AC 1.16

World Power **Data**, FP 1.2:W 89

Data Base

Climatic **Data Base**, Y 3.T 25:50

Energy Information **Data Base** Energy Categories, E 1.55/3

Energy Information **Data Base**: Subject Categories, E 1.55/2

Energy Information **Data Base**: Subject Thesaurus, E 1.55

National Criminal Justice Reference Service Document **Data Base**, J 28.31/2

Wastewater Treatment Construction Grants **Data Base**, Public Law 92-500 Project Records, Grants Assistance Programs, New Projects Funded During (Month), EP 1.56

Data Files
Directory of Computerized **Data Files**, C 51.11/2-2
Directory of Computerized **Data Files** and Related Software Available from Federal Agencies, C 51.11/2
Directory of Computerized **Data Files** and Related Technical Reports, C 1.11/2-2
Directory of Federal Statistical **Data Files**, C 51.15

Data Processing
Automatic **Data Processing** Equipment Inventory in the United States Government As of the End of the Fiscal Year, GS 12.10
Automated **Data Processing** Plan Update, SSA 1.23
Bibliography of Documents Issued by GAO on Matters Related to ADP (Automated **Data Processing**), GA 1.16/5
Directory, Executive Orientation Courses in Automatic **Data Processing**, PrEx 2.12/2
Fiscal Year Plan, Automated **Data Processing** Update, HE 3.84
Inventory of Automatic **Data Processing** (ADP) Equipment in Federal Government, PrEx 2.12
Inventory of Automatic **Data Processing** Equipment in the United States Government, GS 2.15
Inventory of Automated **Data Processing** Equipment in the United States Government for Fiscal Year (date), GS 12.10
Major **Data Processing** and Telecommunication Acquisition Plans of Federal Executive Agencies, PrEx 2.12/3

Database
EIA Personal Computer Products, International Coal Statistics **Database**, E 3.11/7-11
Monthly Energy Review **Database**, E 3.9/2

Databases
Databases and Browseable Lists of the Regulatory Plan and the Unified Agenda of Federal Regulatory and Deregulatory Actions, GS 1.6/11-2
Online Literature Searching and **Databases**, EP 1.21/10

Databook
Databook: Operating Banks and Branches, Summary of Deposits, Y 3.F 31/8:22
U.S. Working Women: a **Databook**, L 2.3:1977

Datafiles
Directory of U.S. Government **Datafiles** for Mainframes & Microcomputers, C 51.19/4
U.S. Government Environmental **Datafiles** & Software, C 51.20

Date
TV Broadcast Applications Accepted for Filing and Notification of Cut-off **Date**, CC 1.26/5

Dated
Dated Periodical Schedules, GP 1.22
Dated Publications, GP 1.12

Dateline
Diabetes **Dateline**, the National Diabetes Information Clearinghouse Bulletin, HE 20.3310/3

Dates
Crop Reporting Board, (year) Issuance **Dates** and Contents, A 92.35:C 88
Dates of Latest Editions, Aeronautical Charts, C 55.409
Dates of Latest Editions, Nautical Charts and Miscellaneous Maps, C 55.409/2
Dates of Latest Prints, Instrument Flight Charts, C 4.9/18
Dates of Retirement of Officers of Corps of Engineers, W 7.17
Imported **Dates** Packed and Shipped, C 3.130
Sailing **Dates** of Steamships from the Principal Ports of the United States to Ports in Foreign Countries, C 15.19, C 18.10
Western United States, **Dates** of Latest Prints, Instrument Approach Procedure Charts and Airport Obstruction Plans, C 4.9/20

Datos
Datos Sobre el Cancer (Cancer Facts), HE 20.3182/6-2
Datos Sobre Tipos de Cancer (series), HE 20.3182/6

DAUList
DAUList (series), C 3.247, C 56.241

David W. Taylor
David W. Taylor Model Basin Report R (series), D 211.9/2

Davis-Bacon
Davis-Bacon Wage Determinations, L 36.211/2
General Wage Determinations Issued under the **Davis-Bacon** and Related Acts, L 36.211

DAWN
DAWN {Drug Abuse Warning Network} Quarterly Report, J 24.19
Project **DAWN** {Drug Abuse Warning Network}, Annual Report, J 24.19/2
Statistical Series Securities and Exchange Commission, SE Statistical Series, Annual Data, Data from the Drug Abuse Warning Network (**DAWN**), Series I, HE 20.8212/11

Day
Armed Forces Report, Armed Forces **Day**, C 1.6/3
Case Book, Education Beyond High School Practices Underway to Meet the Problems of the **Day**, FS 5.65
Citizenship **Day** and Constitution Week Bulletins, J 21.14
Cooperative Summary of the **Day**, C 55.281/2-4
Daily Temperature, Degree **Day** and Precipitation Normals, C 30.62
Enroute IFR Air Traffic Survey, Peak **Day**, TD 4.19/3
Enroute IFR Peak **Day** Charts, Fiscal Year, FAA 3.11/3
Speakers' Guide for Service Spokesmen, Power for Peace, Armed Forces **Day**, D 1.6/3
Statistics of Public Elementary and Secondary **Day** Schools, HE 19.326

Day Care
Day Care USA {publications}, HE 1.410
Directory of Adult **Day Care** Centers, HE 22.202:Ad 9

Day Schools
Fall {year} Enrollment, Teachers, and School-Housing in Full-Time Public Elementary and Secondary **Day Schools**, FS 5.220:20007, HE 5.220:20007

Day-Night
Directory of Outpatient Psychiatric Clinics, Psychiatric **Day-Night** Services and Other Mental Health Resources in the United States and Territories, FS 2.22/38-4

Daylighter
Daylighter, D 217.24

Daymarks
Beacons Buoys and **Daymarks**, T 25.5-T 25.14

Days
Monthly Normals of Temperature, Precipitation, and Heating and Cooling Degree **Days**, C 55.286
Monthly State, Regional and National Cooling Degree **Days** Weighted by Population, C 55.287/60-2, C 55.287/60-3

Days'
Stocks of Coal and **Days'** Supply, FP 1.11/4

Daytona Beach
Area Wage Survey (summary): **Daytona Beach**, Florida, A 2.122/9-5

DBECS
Commercial Buildings Energy Consumption Survey (**DBECS**), E 3.43/2-4

DBPH
DBPH News, LC 19.13
DBPH Update, LC 19.13/2

DC
Circular **DC**-Nos. Washington Store, GS 2.4/2
DC Circuit Update, Ju 2.10

DCA
DCA Circulars, D 5.104

DCAA
DCAA Bulletin, D 1.46/3
DCAA Regulations (series), D 1.6/10
Directory of **DCAA** Offices, D 1.46/4
Index of **DCAA** Numbered Publications and Memorandums, D 1.33/5

DCAAM
Defense Contract Audit Agency Manual, **DCAAM** (series), D 1.46/2

DCAAP
Defense Contract Audit Agency Pamphlets, **DCAAP** (series), D 1.46

DCAS
DCAS Manufacturing Cost Control Digest, D 7.22

DCEG
DCEG (Division of Cancer Epidemiology and Genetics) Linkage, HE 20.3196

DCSC
DCSC Communicator, D 7.43/2
DCSC Fiscal Year Procurement Estimates Catalog, D 7.17

DCT
DCT Bulletin, HE 20.3153/3

DC-TR
Army Ballistic Missile Agency **DC-TR** (series), D 105.15

DDNJ
Drug and Devices, **DDNJ** (series), FS 13.108

DEA
DEA Drug Enforcement Statistics Report, J 24.18/2
DEA Personnel Management Series, J 24.16
DEA World, J 24.20

Dead
World War II Honor List of **Dead** and Missing (by States), W 107.13

Deaf
Catalog of Captioned Films for the **Deaf**, FS 5.234:34039, HE 5.234:34039, ED 1.209/2
Catalog of Educational Captioned Films/Videos for the **Deaf**, ED 1.209/2-2

Deafness
Mental Health in **Deafness**, HE 20.8127

Dealers
Animal Welfare: List of Licensed **Dealers**, A 101.26
Finance Rate and Other Terms on New Car and Used Car Installment Credit Contracts Purchased from **Dealers** of Major Auto Finance Companies, FR 1.34/5
Hatcheries and **Dealers** Participating in the National Poultry Improvement Plan, A 77.15:44-6
Nonferrous Scrap **Dealers** Reports, I 28.65
Over-the-Counter Brokers and **Dealers** Registered with Securities & Exchange Commission, SE 1.15
Seafood **Dealers** of the Southwest Region, C 55.337/2
Stocks of Leaf Tobacco Owned by **Dealers** and Manufacturers, A 80.124

Dear
Dear Colleague (letter), HE 20.7035

Death
Birth Cohort Linked Birth/Infant **Death** Data Set, HE 20.6209/4-7
Facts of Life and **Death**, Selected Statistics on Nation's Health and People, FS 2.102:H 34
Instruction Manual: Classification and Coding Instructions for Fetal **Death** Records, HE 20.6208/6-2
Instruction Manual: Demographic Classification and Coding Instructions for **Death** Records, HE 20.6208/5
Instruction Manual: ICD 9 Acme Decision Tables for Classifying Underlying Causes of **Death**, HE 20.6208/4-2
Instruction Manual: ICDA Eighth Revision of Decision Tables for Classifying Underlying Causes of **Death**, HE 20.6208/4-5
Instructions for Classifying Multiple Causes of **Death**, HE 20.6208/4-3
Instructions for Classifying the Underlying Cause of **Death**, HE 20.6208/4-4
Instructions for Classifying the Underlying Cause of **Death**: Mobile Examination Center Interviewer's Manual for the Hispanic Health and Nutrition Examination Survey, HE 20.6208/2-4
Instructions for Classifying the Underlying Cause of **Death**: Nonindexed Terms, Standard Abbreviations, and State Geographic Codes Used in Mortality Data Classification, HE 20.6208/4
Instructions for Classifying the Underlying Cause of **Death**: Physician's Examination Manual for the Hispanic Health and Nutrition Examination Survey, HE 20.6208/2-3
Instructions for Classifying the Underlying Cause of **Death**: Source Records and Control Specifications, HE 20.6208/11
Instructions for Classifying the Underlying Cause of **Death**: Vital Records Geographic Classification, HE 20.6208/3

National **Death** Index Announcements (numbered), HE 20.6224

Physician's Pocket Reference to International List of Causes of **Death**, C 3.54

Where to Write for Birth and **Death** Records of U.S. Citizens Who Were Born or Died Outside of the United States and Birth Certifications for Alien Children Adopted by U.S. Citizens, FS 2.102:B 53/7

Where to Write for Birth and **Death** Records, FS 2.102:B 53/3

Deaths
Instruction Manual Part 18, Guidelines For Implementing Field and Query Programs For Registration of Births and **Deaths**, HE 20.6208/16

Newly Reported Tuberculosis Cases and Tuberculosis **Deaths**, United States and Territories, FS 2.42/2

Public Use Data Tape Documentation Fetal **Deaths** Detail Records, HE 20.6226/11

Summary of Natural Hazard **Deaths** in the United States, C 55.134

Deauthorization
Projects Recommended for **Deauthorization**, Annual Report, D 103.1/4, D 103.22/2

DEAWorld
DEAWorld, J 24.20

Debarred
Consolidated List of **Debarred**, Suspended, and Ineligible Contractors, GS 1.28

Consolidated List of Persons or Firms Currently **Debarred** for Violations of Various Public Contracts Acts Incorporating Labor Standard Provisions, GA 1.17

Interim List of Persons or Firms Currently **Debarred** for Violation of Various Public Contracts Acts Incorporating Labor Standards Provisions, GA 1.17/2

Debates
Congressional Record, Proceedings and **Debates**, X/a

Register of **Debates**, X 43 X 71

Debits
Bank **Debits**, FR 1.14

Bank **Debits** and Deposit Turnover, FR 1.17

Bank **Debits** Deposits and Deposit Turnover, FR 1.17

Bank **Debits** to Demand Deposit Accounts (Except Interbank and U.S. Government Accounts), FR 1.17/2

Debits, Demand Deposits, and Turnover at 233 Individual Centers, FR 1.17/3

Debt
Annual Report (Fair **Debt** Collection Practices), FT 1.1/2

Annual Report of Sinking Fund and Funded **Debt** of District of Columbia, for Fiscal Year, T 40.6

Estimated Home Mortgage **Debt** and Financing Activity, FHL 1.16

Farm Mortgage **Debt**, A 93.9/12

Farm Real Estate **Debt**, RED (series), A 93.9/9

Interest Bearing **Debt** Outstanding, T 62.8

Monthly Statement of Public **Debt** of the United States, T 1.5/3

Public **Debt** and Cash in Treasury, T 9.9

Quarterly **Debt** Management Report, HE 20.9311

Statement of Public **Debt** of United States, T 63.112

Statutory **Debt** Limitation As of, T 63.208

Decadal
Decadal Census of Weather Stations by States, C 30.66/3

Decade
Decade of the Brain, LC 1.54/3

Decay
Plant Disease, **Decay**, Etc., Control Activities of Department of Agriculture, Reports, A 1.90

Deceased
Officers of Army, Their Families and Families of **Deceased** Officers, Residing in or Near District of Columbia, W 1.11

Roll of Honor, Supplemental Statement of Disposition of Bodies of **Deceased** Union Soldiers and Prisoners of War Removed to National Cemeteries in Southern and Western United States, W 39.8

Decennial
Decennial Census of United States Climate, C 55.221/2

Decennial Census of United States, Climate: Climate Summary of United States, Supplement 1951-60, Climatography of United States, No. 86 (series), C 30.71/8

Decennial Census of United States, Climate: Daily Normals of Temperature and Heating Degree Days, C 30.71/7:84

Decennial Census of United States, Climate: Heating Degree Day Normals, C 30.71/7:83

Decennial Census of United States, Climate: Monthly Averages for State Climatic Divisions, C 30.71/7:85

Decennial Census of United States, Climate: Monthly Normals of Temperature, Precipitation, and Heating Degree Days, C 30.71/4

Decennial Census of United States, Climate: Summary of Hourly Observations, C 30.71/5:82

Decennial Cumulative Index, GP 3.8/3

Decennial Index to Bulletins, C 13.3/2

Profiles in School Support, **Decennial** Overview, FS 5.222:22022, HE 5.222:22022

U.S. **Decennial** Life Tables, HE 20.6215

Decided
Cases Argued and **Decided** in Supreme Court of United States, Ju 6.8/4

Cases **Decided** in the Court of Claims of the United States, Ju 3.9

Supplement to Table of Cases **Decided**, LR 1.8/9

Table of Cases **Decided**, LR 1.8/9-2

Deciduous
Foreign Statistics on Apples and Other **Deciduous** Fruits, A 67.12

Fruit Flashes, Foreign News on Fruits by Cable and Radio: **Deciduous** {fruits}, A 67.10

Decimal
Decimal Classification, Additions, Notes and Decisions, LC 37.8

Dewey **Decimal** Classification, Additions, Notes and Decisions, LC 37.8

Notes and Decisions on Application of **Decimal** Classification, LC 22.7, LC 26.8

Decision
Decision Leaflets, C 21.5/a 2

Decision List, FE 1.11

Decision Series, EP 1.74

Decision Under Elkins {anti-rebate} Act, IC 1 act.8

Instruction Manual: ICD 9 Acme **Decision** Tables for Classifying Underlying Causes of Death, HE 20.6208/4-2

Selected **Decision** of Comptroller General Applicable to Naval Service, N 20.7/4

Decision-Making
Federal Parole **Decision-Making**: Selected Reprints, J 27.9

Decisional
Rules of Practice and Rules Relating to Investigations and Code of Behavior Governing Exparte Communications Between Persons Outside the Commission and **Decisional** Employees, SE 1.6:R 86/4

Decisions
Administrative **Decisions**, S 3.31/6

Administrative **Decisions** Under Employer Sanctions and Unfair Immigration-Related Employment Practices Law of the United States, J 1.103

Administrative **Decisions** Under Immigration and Nationality Laws, J 21.11

Administrative **Decisions**, Walsh-Healey Public Contracts Act, Index-Digest, L 21.2:In 2

Administrative Law Judge and Commission **Decisions**, Y 3.Oc 1:10-2

Administrative Law Judge **Decisions**, Y 3.F 31/21-3:9-3

Administrator's **Decisions**, VA 1.8

Agriculture **Decisions**, A 1.58

ALJ **Decisions**, Y 3.OC 1:10-5

Board of Veterans' Appeals **Decisions**, VA 1.95/2

C.A.B. Initial and Recommended **Decisions** of Administrative Law Judges, CAB 1.38

Citator to **Decisions** of the Occupational Safety and Health Review Commission, Y 3.Oc 1:10-4

Classification Outline for **Decisions** of the NLRB and Related Court **Decisions**, LR 1.8/7

Classification Rulings and **Decisions**: Index Harmonized Tariff Schedules of the United States of America, T 17.6/3-6

Classified Index of the National Labor Relations Board Decisions and Related Court **Decisions**, LR 1.8/6

Commission **Decisions**, Y 3.Oc 1:10-6

Compilations and Digest of Orders, Circulars, Regulations, and **Decisions**, W 7.11/3

Construction Status Report, Nuclear Power Plants, Data for **Decisions**, Y 3.N 88:16

Court **Decisions**, FT 1.13, L 6.6

Court **Decisions** of Interest to Labor, L 2.6/a 8

Court **Decisions** Relating to the National Labor Relations Act, LR 1.14

Courts-Martial Reports, Holdings and **Decisions** of Judge Advocates General, Boards of Review, and United States Court of Military Appeals, D 1.29

Cumulative Index-Digest of Unpublished **Decisions**, I 1.69/2-3

Customs Bulletin and **Decisions**, T 17.6/3-4

Customs **Decisions**, W 49.10/5

Decimal Classification, Additions, Notes and **Decisions**, LC 37.8

Decisions and Interpretations of the Federal Labor Relations Council, Y 3.F 31/21:9

Decisions and Orders, Y 3.Oc 1:9

Decisions and Orders Alcohol, Tobacco and Firearms Bureau, T 70.16

Decisions and Orders Occupational Safety and Health Review Commission Center, Y 3.Oc 1:9

Decisions and Orders of the National Labor Relations Board, LR 1.8

Decisions and Reports on Rulings of the Assistant Secretary of Labor for Labor-Management Relations Pursuant to Executive Order 11491, L 1.51/4, Y 3.F 31/21-3:10-2

Decisions by Department of Interior, I 1.69

Decisions Department of Commerce, C 1.6

Decisions Department of Labor, L 1.5

Decisions General Accounting Office, GA 1.5/a-2

Decisions Geographic Names Board, I 33.5, I 33.6

Decisions of Administrator, VA 1.8/3

Decisions of Commissioner of Patents, I 23.10

Decisions of Geographic Names in the United States, I 33.5/2

Decisions of Secretary **of Labor** in Matter of Determination of Prevailing Minimum Wage in Industries, L 1.12

Decisions of the Administrator and Decisions of the General Counsel, EP 1.66

Decisions of the Commissioner of Patents and of United States Courts in Patent and Trademark Cases, C 21.6

Decisions of the Department of the Interior, I 1.69, I 1.69/a

Decisions of the Federal Labor Relations Authority, Y 3.F 31/21-3:10-4

Decisions of the Interstate Commerce Commission of the United States, IC 1.6

Decisions of the Maritime Commission, Federal Maritime Board, and Maritime Administration, FMC 1.10

Decisions of the Maritime Subsidy Board, C 39.226

Decisions of U.S. Merit Systems Protection Board, MS 1.10

Decisions Office of Administrative Law Judges and Office of Administrative Appeals, L 1.5/2

Decisions on Indian Appeals, I 1.69/6

Decisions on Tort and Irrigation Claims, I 1.69/8

Decisions Under Hours of Service Act {compilations}, IC 1 hou.8

Decisions Under Hours of Service Act {individual cases}, IC 1 hou.7

Decisions Under Locomotive Inspection Act {individual cases}, IC 1 loc.7

Decisions under Walsh-Healey Public Contracts Act, L 22.12

Decisions Veterans Administration, VA 1.8/2

Decisions, Solicitor's Opinions, I 1.69/4

Decisions/Rulings, T 17.6/3

Decisions; Reports {of action taken}, CC 1.20

Digest & Index of **Decisions** of NLRB, LR 1.8/2

Digest and **Decisions** of the Employees' Compensation Appeals Board, L 28.9

Digest and Index of Published **Decisions** of the Assistant Secretary of Labor for Labor-Management Relations Pursuant to Executive Order 11491, As Amended, L 1.51/3

Digest of **Decisions** Federal Trade Commission, FT 1.12

Digest of **Decisions** National Labor Relations Board, Annual Supplements, LR 1.8/3

Digest of **Decisions** National Labor Relations Board, BW-(series), LR 1.8/5-2

Digest of **Decisions** National Labor Relations Board, CS-(series), LR 1.8/5

Digest of **Decisions** of Relating to National Banks, T 12.7/2

Digest of **Decisions** Post Office Inspectors Division, P 14.5

Digest of **Decisions** Relating to National Banks, T 12.7/2

Digest of **Decisions** Secretary of Agriculture under Perishable Agricultural Commodities Act, A 82.55

Digest of Grazing **Decisions**, I 53.15

Digest of Laws, **Decisions** and Rulings, I 24.9

Digest of Unpublished **Decisions** of the Comptroller General of the United States on General Government Matters, Appropriations and Miscellaneous, GA 1.5/12

Digest of {and} **Decisions**, I 21.6

Digests and Indexes of Treasury **Decisions**, T 1.12

Digests and Tables of Cases, **Decisions** of the Federal Labor Relations Authority, Y 3.F 31/21-3:9-2, Y 3.F 31/21-3:9-3

Digests of **Decisions** and Regulations, T 22.8/2

Economic **Decisions**, C 31.211

Equal Employment Opportunity Commission **Decisions**, Federal Sector, Y 3.Eq 2:18

Federal Communications Commission Reports, **Decisions**, Reports, Public Notices, and Other Documents of the Federal Communications Commission (2d series), CC 1.12/2a

Federal Maritime Board Reports, **Decisions**, C 39.108

Federal Maritime Commission, **Decisions**, Separates, FMC 1.10/a, A 88.17/7

Federal Trade Commission **Decisions**, FT 1.11/2

Federal-State Election Law Survey: an Analysis of State Legislation, Federal Legislation and Judicial **Decisions**, Y 3.El 2/3:2 St 2

Field Letter, Information, Legislative, Court **Decisions**, Opinions, L 25.8

Finance **Decisions**, IC 1.6/a:F

FLRA Report on Case **Decisions** and FSIP Releases, Y 3.F 31/21-3:9, Y 3.F 31/21:10

Food Inspection **Decisions**, A 7.5, A 32.5, A 1.15

GAO Documents, Catalog of Reports, **Decisions** and Opinions, Testimonies and Speeches, GA 1.16/4

Housing Legal Digest, **Decisions**, Opinions, Legislations Relating to Housing Construction and Finance, Y 3.C 33/3:10

Index of **Decisions**, Federal Service Impasses Panel, PM 1.65

Index Digest of **Decisions**, RL 1.6/3

Index Digest, **Decisions** and Opinions of Department of Interior, I 1.69/2

Index of Board **Decisions**, Cumulative Supplements, LR 1.8/4

Index to Commission **Decisions**, SE 1.11/2

Index to **Decisions**, Y 3.Oc 1:10-3

Index to the Published **Decisions** of the Accounting Officers of the United States, GA 1.5

Index to Treasury **Decisions** Under Customs and Other Laws, T 1.11/1a

Index-Digest of **Decisions** of the Department of the Interior in Cases Relating to Public Lands, I 1.69/3

Index-Digest of **Decisions** Under Federal Safety Appliance Acts, IC 1 saf.9

Index-Digest of the Published **Decisions** of the Comptroller General of the United States, GA 1.5/3

Index-Digest, Published and Important Unpublished **Decisions**, I 1.69/2

Insecticide **Decisions**, A 1.17

Interim Administrative **Decisions** under Immigration and Nationality Laws, J 21.11/2

Interim **Decisions**, J 1.102/5

Interim **Decisions** of the Department of Justice, J 21.11/2

Judicial **Decisions**, SE 1.19

Memorandum, Opinions and Orders, Initial **Decisions**, Etc., CC 1.12/a 8

Notes and **Decisions** on Application of Decimal Classification, LC 22.7, LC 26.8

Operating Units Status Report, Licensed Operations Reactors Data for **Decisions**, Y 3.N 88:15

Opinions and **Decisions**, S 3.34/6

Orders, Notices, Rulings and **Decisions** Issued by Hearing Examiners and by the Commission in Formal Docketed Proceedings before the Federal Maritime

OSAHRE Reports: **Decisions** of the Occupational Safety and Health Review Commission, Y 3.Oc 1:10

Pension **Decisions**, I 24.8

Plant Quarantine **Decisions**, A 35.6

Postal **Decisions** of United States and Other Courts Affecting Post Office Department and Postal Service, P 14.5

Quarterly Digest of Unpublished **Decisions** of the Comptroller General of the United States: Personnel Law, Civilian Personnel, GA 1.5/5, GA 1.5/10, GA 1.5/11

Reappraisement **Decisions**, for Review by U.S. Customs Court As Published in Weekly Treasury **Decisions**, T 1.11/2a

Report of Case **Decisions**, Y 3.F 31/21-3:9

Resource **Decisions** in the National Forests of the Eastern Region, A 13.90

Statutes and Court **Decisions**, FT 1.13

Statutes and **Decisions** Pertaining to the Federal Trade Commission, FT 1.13/2

Study of MSPB Appeals **Decisions** for FY (year), MS 1.15

Subject Matter Indexes to **Decisions** of the Federal Labor Relations Authority, Y 3.F 31/21-3:10-3

Supplement to Index to Commission **Decisions**, SE 1.11/2

Supplemental Digest and Index of Published **Decisions** of the Assistant Secretary of Labor for Labor-Management Relations Pursuant to Executive Order 11491, Y 3.F 31/21-3:10

Table of Commodities in the **Decisions**, IC 1.6/7

Table of **Decisions** and Reports, SE 1.21

Topical Indexes to **Decisions** and Opinions of the Department of the Interior, I 1.69/2-2

Traffic, **Decisions**, IC 1.6/a

Treasury **Decisions** Under Internal Revenue Laws, T 22.8

Treasury **Decisions**, T 1.11/1, T 1.11/2

Unpublished Comptroller General **Decisions**, With Index, D 301.100

Walsh-Healey Public Contracts Act, **Decisions**, L 22.23

Wyoming Land Use **Decisions** (series), I 53.23

Deck
Comparison **Deck** Numbers, FS 2.119

Declarations
Declarations, A 4.20

Declared
Declared Excess Personal Property Listing, D 7.34/2

Exports **Declared** for United States, S 4.11

Declassified
Abstracts of **Declassified** Documents, Y 3.At 7:11

Declinations
Magnetic **Declinations**, C 4.24

Decline
Home Mortgage Interest Rates Continue to **Decline** in Early (Month), FHL 1.25/2

Dedicatory
Philatelic **Dedicatory** Lecture Series, SI 3.12

DEEP
Driver Education Evaluation Program (**DEEP**) Study, Report to Congress, TD 8.12/5

Deep
Initial Reports of the **Deep** Sea Drilling Project, NS 1.38

Default
Status of Perkins Loan **Default**, ED 1.40/4

Defect
Motor Vehicle Safety **Defect** Recall Campaigns, TD 8.9

Motor Vehicle Safety **Defect** Recall Campaigns Reported to the Department of Transportation by Domestic and Foreign Vehicle Manufacturers, TD 2.209

Defective
Analysis of **Defective** Vehicle Accidents of Motor Carriers, IC 1 mot.20

Defectives
Mental **Defectives** and Epileptics in State Institutions, C 3.60

Defects
Analysis of Motor Carrier Accidents Involving Vehicle **Defects** of Mechanical Failure, TD 2.312

Defend
What We **Defend** (Radio Scripts), I 29.48

Defendants
Pretrial Release of Felony **Defendants**, J 29.11/14

Table of **Defendants** Before Interstate Commerce Commission, IC 1.6/4

Defense
Abstracts of **Defense** Regulations, GS 4.112

Agriculture in **Defense**, A 21.13/9, A 17.16

Agriculture in National **Defense**, A 1.83

Air **Defense** Artillery, D 101.77

Air **Defense** Trends, D 101.77

Annual Historical Summary; **Defense** Construction Supply Center, D 7.1/9

Annual Historical Summary; **Defense** Contract Administration Services {by region}, D 7.1/4

Annual Historical Summary; **Defense** Depots, D 7.1/7

Annual Historical Summary; **Defense** Documentation Center, D 7.1/10

Annual Historical Summary; **Defense** Fuel Supply Center, D 7.1/6

Annual Historical Summary; **Defense** General Supply Center, D 7.1/8

Annual Historical Summary; **Defense** Industrial Plant Equipment Center, D 7.1/3

Annual Management Report of the **Defense** Supply Agency, D 7.1/13

Annual Report of the Activities of the Joint Committee on **Defense** Production with Material on Mobilization from Departments and Agencies, Y 4.D 36:R 29

Annual Report of the Secretary of **Defense** on Reserve Forces, D 1.1/3

Annual Reports of Assistants to Secretary of **Defense**, D 1.1/2

Brief of the Organization and Functions Secretary of **Defense** Deputy Secretary of Defense etc., D 1.36

Bulletin on National **Defense** Education Act, Public Law 85-864, FS 5.70

Business Information Service: **Defense** Production Aids, C 40.7

Civil and **Defense** Mobilization Directory, Pr 34.708/2, PrEx 4.8/2

Civil **Defense** Alert, FCD 1.8

Civil **Defense** Education Project, Classroom Practices, FS 5.45/3

Civil **Defense** Education Project, Information Sheets, FS 5.45/2

Civil **Defense** Planning Advisory Bulletins, Pr 33.707

Civil **Defense** Publications Available from Superintendent of Documents, FCD 1.21

Civil **Defense** Technical Bulletins, Pr 34.753, PrEx 4.3/2

Current News **Defense** Management Edition, D 2.19/5, D 301.89/8, D 301.89/11

Defense Acquisition Deskbook, D 1.95/2

Defense Acquisition Management Data System Code Translations, D 1.57/10

Defense Acquisition University Catalog, D 1.59/3

Defense Billboard, D 2.9/2

Defense Bulletins, Y 3.C 831:107

Defense Cataloging and Standardization Act of 1952, Y 4.Ar 5/2-14

Defense Communications System Global, Automatic Voice Network Telephone Directory, D 5.111

Defense Environmental Restoration Program: Annual Report to Congress, D 1.97

Defense Food Delegations, A 1.81

Defense Housing Financed by Public Funds, Summaries, Pr 32.4307

Defense Indicators, C 56.110, C 59.10, C 3.241

Defense Industry Bulletin, D 1.3/2

Defense Information Bulletins, FS 5.45

Defense Information School: Catalog, D 1.59

Defense Information School: Academic Catalog, D 5.206/2

Defense Intelligence Agency Regulations (series), D 5.206/2

Defense Intelligence School: Academic Catalog, D 5.210

Defense Issues, D 2.15/4

Defense Logistics Information System (DLIS) Procedures Manual, D 7.6/19

Defense Management Education and Training Catalog, D 1.45

Defense Management Joint Course (series), D 101.94/2

Defense Management Journal, D 1.38/2

Defense Manpower Commission Staff Studies and Supporting Papers, Y 3.D 36:9

Defense Manpower Policy (series), Pr 34.208

Defense Manpower Policy Statement, Pr 33.1010

Defense Mapping Agency Catalog of Maps, Charts, and Related Products, D 5.351

Defense Mapping Agency Catalog of Maps, Charts, and Related Products, Semi-Annual Bulletin Digest, Part 2, Hydrographic Products, D 5.351/2-3

Defense Mapping Agency Public Sale Nautical Charts and Publications, C 55.440

Defense Mobilization Orders, Pr 33.1006/2, Pr 34.206/2, Pr 34.706/4, PrEx 4.6/3

Defense Procurement Circulars, D 1.13/3

Defense Production Act, Progress Reports, Y 4.D 36:P 94

Defense Production Notes, DP 1.10

Defense Production Record, DP 1.8

Defense Programs, DOE/DP- (series), E 1.15

Defense Property Disposal Service, D 7.6/13

Defense Reutilization and Marketing Service,, D 7.6/13

Defense Savings Staff News, T 1.108

Defense Standardization and Specification Program Policies, Procedures and Instructions, D 7.6/3:4120.3-M

Defense Standardization Program, Directory of Points of Interest, D 7.13/2

Defense Supply Agency Handbooks, DSAH- (series), D 7.6/7

Defense Supply Agency Manuals, DSAM-(series), D 7.6/8

Defense Supply Agency Regulations, DSAR- (series), D 7.6/6

Defense Supply Procurement Regulations, D 7.6/5

Defense Systems Management Review, D 1.53

Defense Trade News, S 1.141

Defense Training Leaflets, FS 5.130

Defense/80, D 2.15/3

Department of **Defense** Military Commission Order, D 1.6/18

Detailed Listing of Real Property Owned by the United States and Used by the Department of **Defense** for Military Functions Throughout the World, GS 1.15/4-2

Directory of USSR Ministry of **Defense** and Armed Forces Officials, PrEx 3.10/7-11

DIS (**Defense** Investigative Service) Achievements, D 1.1/8

DISA (**Defense** Information Systems Agency, D 5.112

Education and National **Defense** Series Pamphlets, FS 5.22

Estimated **Defense** Expenditures for States, D 1.57/11-2

Executive Reservist, Bulletin from Industrial Mobilization, for Members of National **Defense** Executive Reserve, C 41.113

Extracts from Reports by Regular and Military Officers on Joint Army and Militia Coast-**Defense** Exercises, W 2.7

Farm **Defense** Program, A 74.7

Federal Civil **Defense** Administration Directory, FCD 1.19

Federal Civil **Defense** Guide, D 119.8/4

Federal Guidance for State and Local Civil **Defense**, D 14.8/5, D 119.8/3

Federal Supply Catalog, Department of **Defense** Section, D 7.9

Friday Review of **Defense** Literature, D 1.33/2

Impact of Air Attack in World War II, Selected Data for Civil **Defense** Planning, FCD 1.12

Index to Federal Civil **Defense** Administration Publications, FCD 1.21/2

Industrial Civil **Defense** Handbooks, C 41.6/12

Industrial Civil **Defense** Newsletter, C 41.110

Industrial College of the Armed Forces: Perspectives in **Defense** Management, D 5.16

Insects in Relation to National **Defense**, Circulars, A 56.24, A 77.316

Inter-American **Defense** Board, S 5.45

Knowledge for Survival, You Can Survive! Newsletter to State Extension Program Leaders, Rural **Defense**, A 43.35/2

MISTRIP, **Defense** Program for Redistribution of Assets (DEPRA) Procedures, D 1.87/3

Modern Foreign Language Fellowship Program, National **Defense** Education Act, Title 6 and NDEA Related Awards under Fullbright-Hays Act, FS 5.255:55034, HE 5.255:55034

National **Defense** Bulletins, LC 14.11

National **Defense** Graduate Fellowships, Graduate Programs, FS 5.255:55017, HE 5.255:55017

New Books: National **Defense** University, D 5.411/3

Newsletter, by, for, and about Women in Civil **Defense**, FCD 1.24

Perspectives in **Defense** Management, D 5.16

Posters **Defense** Intelligence Agency, D 5.213

Program Aids **Defense** Savings Staff, T 1.109

Program Guide Federal Civil **Defense** Administration, FCD 1.6/7

Progress Report Federal Civil **Defense** Administration, FCD 1.1/2

Projects Initiated under Title VII, National **Defense** Education Act, FS 5.234:34013, FS 5.234:34021, HE 5.234:34013, HE 5.234:34021

Qualified Products Lists Department of **Defense**, D 1.17

Radio Service Agriculture in **Defense**, A 21.13/9

Radio-TV **Defense** Dialog, D 2.19/2

Real and Personal Property of the Department of **Defense**, As of June 30, D 1.2:P 94/8

Regulations, Rules and Instructions National **Defense** University, D 5.406

Report of Secretary of **Defense** to the Congress on the Budget, Authorization Request, and Defense Programs, D 1.1

Report of Secretary of Defense to the Congress on the Budget, Authorization Request, and **Defense** Programs, D 1.1

Report of the National **Defense** Education Act, FS 5.210:10004, HE 5.210:10004

Report on Activities **Defense** Contract Audit Agency, D 1.46/5

Report to Congress on the Ballistic Missile **Defense** Organization, D 1.1/6

Report to the Congress on the Strategic **Defense** Initiative, D 1.1/6

Report to the President by Director of **Defense** Mobilization, Pr 33.1008

Report to the President by Director of Office of **Defense** Mobilization, Pr 34.201

Reports to Aid Nation's **Defense** Effort, A 13.27/13

Research Studies **Defense** Civil Preparedness Agency, D 14.17

Selected Readings and Documents on Postwar American **Defense** Policy, D 305.12/2:D 36

Semiannual Report on Operations Under Mutual **Defense** Assistance Control Act of 1951, FO 1.1/2

Semiannual Reports on Operations under Mutual **Defense** Assistance Act, S 17.1/2

Semiannual Reports under Mutual **Defense** Assistance Control Act, Pr 33.901/2

Service Bulletins of **Defense** Training in Vocational Schools, FS 5.24

Special Promotion Series from Office of Civil and **Defense** Mobilization, Battle Creek, Michigan, Bulletins, Pr 34.757/3

State Distribution of **Defense** Contract Awards, Pr 32.4013

State Salary Ranges, Selected Classes {of positions} in Employment Security, Public Welfare, Public Health, Mental Health, Vocational Rehabilitation, Civil **Defense**, Emergency Planning, CS 1.81, FS 1.22, HE 1.22, GS 1.8

Statistical Bulletins Office of Civil **Defense**, Pr 32.4425

Student Handbook (series) Department of **Defense**, D 1.67/3

Summary Technical Report of National **Defense** Research Committee, Pr 32.413/12

Survey of American Listed Corporations, Reported Information on Selected **Defense** Industries, SE 1.18/2

Technical Memorandum **Defense** Civil Preparedness Agency, D 119.8/5

Technical Memorandum **Defense** Communications Agency, D 5.110

Technical Problems Affecting National **Defense**, C 32.8

Telephone Directory General Services Administration and **Defense** Materials Procurement Agency, GS 1.11

This Week in **Defense**, Pr 32.215

Translog, **Defense** Transportation System Bulletin, D 101.66/2-2

U.S. Air Force Plan for **Defense** Research Sciences, D 301.45/19-5

U.S. Naval Radiological **Defense** Laboratory, Research and Development Report USNRDL (series), D 211.13

WPA Week in National **Defense**, FW 4.37

You Can Survive, Rural **Defense** Fact Sheets, A 43.35

Your **Defense** Budget, D 1.1/4

Defense Communications
Autovan Automatic Global Voice Network **Defense Communications** System Directory, D 5.111

Defense Department
Audit of Payments from Special Bank Account to Lockheed Aircraft Corporation for C-5a Aircraft Program **Defense Department**, GA 1.13:L 81/2

Deferment
Departmental Circulars, Occupational **Deferment** Series, CS 1.38

Defined Benefit
Employee Benefits Survey **Defined Benefit** Pension Coding Manual, L 2.46/7

Definitions
Classification **Definitions**, C 21.3/2

Code Classification and **Definitions** of Foreign Trade Areas, C 3.150:R

Definitions and Abbreviations, TD 4.6:part 1

Schedule R. Code Classification and **Definitions** of Foreign Trade Areas, C 3.150:R

Selected United States Marketing Terms and **Definitions**, English {foreign Language}, C 41.93

Definitive
Mint Set of **Definitive** Stamps, P 1.54/2

Degree
DANTES External **Degree** Catalog, D 1.33/7

Degree Day
Daily Temperature, **Degree Day** and Precipitation Normals, C 30.62

Heating **Degree Day** Bulletin, C 30.47

Degree Days
Climatography of the United States; Monthly Normals of Temperature, Precipitation, and Heating and Cooling **Degree Days**, C 55.286

Decennial Census of United States, Climate: Monthly Normals of Temperature, Precipitation, and Heating **Degree Days**, C 30.71/4

Monthly Normals of Temperature, Precipitation, and Heating and Cooling **Degree Days**, C 55.286

Monthly State, Regional and National Cooling **Degree Days** Weighted by Population, C 55.287/60-3

Monthly State, Regional and National Heating **Degree Days** Weighted by Population, C 55.287/60-2

Degrees
Advance Report on Engineering Enrollment and **Degrees**, (year), FS 5.254:54004, HE 5.254:54004

Associate **Degrees** and Other Formal Awards Below the Baccalaureate, HE 19.333

Earned **Degrees** Conferred, FS 4.254:54013, HE 5.92/5, HE 5.254:54013, HE 19.329

Engineering Enrollments and **Degrees**, FS 5.254:54006, HE 5.254:54006

Enrollment for Masters and Higher **Degrees**, Fall (year), Final Report, FS 5.254:54019, HE 5.254:54019

Higher Education: Students Enrolled for Advanced **Degrees**, Fall (year), HE 19.330

Home Economics in Institutions Granting Bachelor's or Higher **Degrees**, FS 5.283:83008, HE 5.283:83008

Students Enrolled for Advanced **Degrees**, HE 19.330

Summary Report of Bachelor's and Higher **Degrees** Conferred During (school year), FS 5.254:54010, HE 5.254:54010

Summary Report on Survey of Students Enrolled for Advanced **Degrees**: Fall (year), FS 5.254:54009, HE 5.254:54009

Trends in Bachelors and Higher **Degrees**, ED 1.132/2

DEH
DEH Digest, D 103.122/3

Deinstitutionalizing
Juvenile Justice, **Deinstitutionalizing** Status Offenders: A Record of Progress, J 32.20/4

DEL
DSFA Delegations **DEL** (series), I 57.6/3

Delaware
USA Trade World, Pennsylvania & **Delaware**, C 61.39/4
Water Resources Development in **Delaware** in (year), D 103.35/8

Delegates
Family Planning Grantees, **Delegates**, and Clinics Directory, HE 20.33

Delegation
Canada-United States Interparliamentary Group Report on Meetings by Senate **Delegation**, Y 4.F 76/2:C 16/2
Delegation of Authority, ES 3.6/11
Mexico-United States Interparliamentary Group Report of Senate **Delegation**, Y 4.F 76/2:M 57/8
Report of American **Delegation**, S 3.29/1
Report of the United States **Delegation** to the World Health Assembly, HE 20.19

Delegations
BDSA **Delegations**, C 41.6/3
BDSA Emergency **Delegations**, C 41.6/8
BDSA Reporting **Delegations**, C 41.6/3-2
DSFA **Delegations DEL** (series), I 57.6/3
DTA **Delegations**, IC 1 def.6/3
NPA **Delegations**, C 40.6/3

Delinquency
Analysis and Evaluation, Federal Juvenile **Delinquency** Programs, J 26.25
Crime and **Delinquency** Abstracts, FS 2.22/13-4, HE 20I.2420
Crime and **Delinquency** Topics: Monograph Series, HE 20.8114, HE 20.8114/3
Current Projects in Prevention, Control, and Treatment of Crime and **Delinquency**, FS 2.22/51
Grants, Juvenile **Delinquency** Prevention and Control Act, HE 17.21
International Bibliography on Crime and **Delinquency**, FS 2.22/13-4
Juvenile **Delinquency** Prevention and Control Act of 1968, Grants, HE 17.811
Juvenile **Delinquency** Reporter, HE 17.22
Juvenile **Delinquency**: Facts and Facets, FS 3.222, FS 14.115
Juvenile Justice and **Delinquency** Prevention, Y 3.C 86:2 J 98
News Notes on Juvenile **Delinquency**, FS 3.219
Office of Juvenile Justice and **Delinquency** Prevention: Annual Report, J 1.47
Report to Congress, Title V Incentive Grants for Local **Delinquency** Prevention Programs, J 32.10/3
Studies in **Delinquency**, HE 17.16/4
Tax **Delinquency** of Rural Real Estate, A 36.78

Delinquent
Directory of Public Training Schools Serving **Delinquent** Children, FS 14.102:T 68
Neglected or **Delinquent** Living in State Operated or Supported Institutions, HE 19.335
Personnel and Personnel Practices in Public Institutions for **Delinquent** Children, FS 2.13

Deliverable
Stocks of Grain in **Deliverable** Positions for Chicago Board of Trade, Futures Contracts in Exchange-Approved and Federally Licensed Warehouses, as Reported by Those Warehouses, A 85.14, Y 3.C 73/5:10

Delivered
Information and Technical Assistance **Delivered** by the Department of Agriculture in Fiscal Year, A 1.1/2

Deliveries
Deliveries of Fuel Oil and Kerosene in (date), E 3.40

Monthly **Deliveries** of Sugar by States, A 82.72/2
New Ship **Deliveries**, Calendar Year, C 39.212/2
USDA Food **Deliveries**, A 82.43

Delivery
CSAP Healthy **Delivery**, HE 20.8028

Delmarva
Commercial Broiler Farms, **Maine**, Delmarva, and Georgia, A 93.9/11

Demand
Agricultural Supply and **Demand** Estimates, A 1.110
Demand and Price Situation for Forest Products, A 13.76
Demand and Price Situation, A 88.9, A 93.9/2
Demand Deposits, Currency and Related Items, FR 1.47
Deposits of County Banks: Index Numbers of Total, **Demand** and Time Deposits Selected Groups of States, Specified Periods, A 77.14/3, A 93.9/7
DOE Petroleum **Demand** Watch, E 1.7/3
Forecast of Motor-Fuel **Demand** and Required Crude-Oil Production by States, Monthly Forecast, I 28.41
Nonferrous Metals Supply, **Demand** Data, I 28.169/3
P.A.D. Districts Supply/**Demand**, E 3.11/6-2, E 3.11/6-3, E 3.11/6-4, I 28.18/6, I 28.18/7,
Supply, **Demand**, and Stocks of All Oils by P.A.D. Districts, I 28.18/7
World Agricultural Supply and **Demand** Estimates, A 1.110, A 93.29/3

Demand Deposit
Bank Debits to **Demand Deposit** Accounts (Except Interbank and U.S. Government Accounts), FR 1.17/2
Debits, **Demand Deposits**, and Turnover at 233 Individual Centers, FR 1.17/3
Demand Deposits, Currency and Related Items, FR 1.47
Staff Report Electric Power Supply and **Demand** for the Contiguous United States, E 1.126

Demands
Monthly Comparisons of Peak **Demands** and Energy Load, E 3.11/17-5

Demobilization
Demobilization Circular Letters, Y 3.R 13/2:125

Democracy
Annual Report on Inernational Religious Freedom (Bureau for **Democracy**, Human Rights and Labor), S. 1.151
Arsenal of **Democracy** Series, Pr 32.408
Democracy in Action, I 16.74, FS 5.13/1
Democracy in Action; For Labor's Welfare, FS 5.13/4
Democracy in Action; Public Health Series, FS 5.13/2
Democracy in Action; Roof over America, FS 5.13/5
Democracy in Action; Social Security, FS 5.13/3
Invasion Intervention, "Intervasion": A Concise History of the U.S. Army in Operation Uphold **Democracy**, D 110.13
Issues of **Democracy**, IA 1.36, S 20.21

Democratic
Platforms of the **Democratic** Party and the Republican Party, Y 1.2:P 69

Demographic
Country **Demographic** Profiles for Foreign Country Series, ISP 30 (series), C 56.218/2
Demographic Characteristics and Patterns of Drug Use of Clients Admitted to Drug Abuse Treatment Programs in Selected Sites, HE 20.8231, HE 20.8231/2
Demographic Profiles of the Airway Facilities Work Force, TD 4.65
Demographic Reports for Foreign Countries, P 96- (series), C 3.205/5
Instruction Manual: **Demographic** Classification and Coding Instructions for Death Records, HE 20.6208/5
Mental Health **Demographic** Profile System, MHDPS Working Papers, HE 20.8133
Program and **Demographic** Characteristics of Supplemental Security Income Beneficiaries, HE 3.71/2
World Population: Recent **Demographic** Estimates for the Countries and Regions of the World, C 3.205/3

Demolition
Construction Reports; Housing Units Authorized for **Demolition** in Permit-issuing Places, (year), C 45 (series) C 56.211/8
Construction Reports; Permits Issued for **Demolition** of Residential Structures in Selected Cities, C 45 (series), C 3.215/12

Demonstrated
Demonstrated Reserve Base of Coal in the United States, E 3.11/7-6

Demonstration
Coal, Quarterly Reports; **Demonstration** Plants, ER 1.28/3, E 1.31/4
Demonstration Notes, Experimental and Demonstration Manpower Programs, L 1.45/2
Demonstration Notes, Experimental and **Demonstration** Manpower Programs, L 1.45/2
Demonstration Projects DP (series), TD 2.40
Directory of Research, Development and **Demonstration** Projects, TD 7.9
Evaluation of the Urban Homesteading **Demonstration** Program, HH 1.73
Geothermal Energy Research, Development and **Demonstration** Program, Annual Report, ER 1.31
Facility-Based HIV/AIDS Education **Demonstration** Project FY, VA 1.97
Health Care Financing Research and **Demonstration** Series, HE 22.16
Here and There with Home **Demonstration** Workers, A 43.5/13
Higher Education Act Title 2-b, Library Research and **Demonstration** Program, Abstracts, Fiscal Year (date), HE 19.135
Home **Demonstration** Review, A 43.5/14
Inter-American Education **Demonstration** Centers, FS 5.31
MDTA Experimental and **Demonstration** Findings, L 1.56
Publications Inter-American Education **Demonstration** Centers, FS 5.31
Quarterly Report, **Demonstration** Projects Program, TD 2.40/2
Recreational **Demonstration** Area (by area), I 29.39
Report to Congress Concerning the **Demonstration** of Fare-Free Mass Transportation, TD 7.13
Research (year), Annotated List of Research and **Demonstration** Grants, HE 17.15
Research **Demonstration** and Evaluation Studies, HE 23.1010
Research, **Demonstration**, and Evaluation Studies, HE 1.402:R 31
Research, Evaluation, and **Demonstration** Projects, L 37.22
Saline Water Conversion **Demonstration** Plant, I 1.87/2
SITE (Superfund Innovative Technology Evaluation) **Demonstration** Bulletin, EP 1.89/4-2
SITE Technology **Demonstration** Summary, EP 1.89/4-3
Social and Rehabilitation Service Research and **Demonstration** Projects, FS 17.15
URA **Demonstration** Grant Summaries, HH 7.18
Urban Renewal **Demonstration** Grant Program, Project Directory, HH 7.2:G 76
Utilities **Demonstration** Series, HH 1.66
Vocational Rehabilitation Administration Research and **Demonstration** Projects, FS 13.202:R 31/2

Demonstrations
Health Care Financing: Grants for Research and **Demonstrations**, Fiscal Year, HE 22.19/3
Office of Research and **Demonstrations** Publications Catalog, HE 22.22/2
Research and **Demonstrations** Brief {Bring Research into Effective Focus}, HE 17.18
Research and **Demonstrations** in Health Care Financing, HE 22.16/2

Denied
Passengers **Denied** Confirmed Space, C 31.268, CAB 1.9

Denomination
Monthly Statement of Paper Currency of Each **Denomination** Outstanding, T 40.8
Paper Currency of Each **Denomination** Outstanding, Monthly Statements, T 63.307

Technical Notes **Department** of the Air Force Air Proving Ground Center, D 301.45/50

Technical Notes **Department** of the Air Force Alaskan Air Command, Arctic Aeromedical Laboratory, D 301.66

Technical Notes **Department** of the Air Force Arnold Engineering Development Center, D 301.45/33-3

Technical Notes **Department** of the Air Force Atmospheric Analysis Laboratory, D 301.45/30 3

Technical Notes **Department** of the Air Force Cambridge Research Center, D 301.45/4-2

Technical Notes **Department** of the Air Force Command and Control Development Division, D 301.45/24

Technical Notes **Department** of the Air Force Electronics Research Directorate, D 301.45/12-2

Technical Notes **Department** of the Air Force Geophysics Research Directorate, D 301.45/16-2

Technical Notes **Department** of the Air Force Meteorological Development Laboratory, D 301.45/17-2

Technical Notes **Department** of the Air Force Office of Scientific Research, D 301.45/18

Technical Notes **Department** of the Air Force Rome Air Development Center, D 301.57/2

Technical Notes **Department** of the Air Force Special Weapons Center, D 301.45/20-2

Technical Notes **Department** of the Air Force Wright Air Development Center, D 301.45/13

Telephone Directory Agriculture **Department**, Alphabetical Listing, A 1.89/4

Telephone Directory Army **Department**, (by area), D 101.97

Telephone Directory Education **Department**, ED 1.24

Telephone Directory Energy **Department**, E 1.12

Telephone Directory Housing and Urban Development **Department**, HH 1.92

Telephone Directory Justice **Department**, J 1.89

Telephone Directory Labor **Department**, L 1.67

Topical Indexes to Decisions and Opinions of the **Department** of the Interior, I 1.69/2-2

Training Circulars **Department** of the Army, M 101.22, D 101.24

Training Circulars **Department** of the East, W 17.8

Training Circulars War **Department**, W 1.36

Training Manual **Department** of Health, Education, and Welfare, FS 1.10, HE 1.10

Training Manual **Department** of War, W 1.23

Transportation Series Engineer **Department**, W 7.23, M 110.17

Treasury **Department**-General Accounting Office Joint Regulations, T 1.38

U.S. **Department** of Agriculture Budget Summary, A 1.138

U.S. **Department** of Commerce Periodicals to Aid Business Men, C 1.54

U.S. **Department** of Labor, Accountability Report, L 1.1/4

U.S. **Department** of Labor Program Highlights, Fact Sheet (Series), L 1.88

U.S. **Department** of State Dispatch, S 1.3/5

U.S. **Department** of State Indexes of Living Costs Abroad and Living Quarters Allowances, L 2.101

U.S. **Department** of State Indexes of Living Costs Abroad and Quarters Allowances, April, L 2.101/2

U.S. **Department** of State Indexes of Living Costs Abroad, S 1.76/4

U.S. **Department** of Transportation FY...Procurement Forecast, TD 1.62

Undersecretary's Report to the Field, Newsletter for **Department** of Labor Field Representatives, L 1.37

United States Court of Military Appeals and the Judge Advocates General of the Armed Forces and the General Counsel of the **Department** of the Treasury,

United States **Department** of Commerce News, C 1.32/8

United States Policy Toward USSR and International Communism, Monthly Digest of Pertinent Data Appearing in **Department** of State Publications, S 1.97

Update **Department** of Housing and Urban Development, HH 1.68

Update **Department** of the Interior, I 1.112

War **Department** Catalogs, W 1.67, W 89/1

What the Soldier Thinks, Monthly Digest of War **Department** Studies on Attitudes of American Troops, W 1.65

Working Papers **Department** of Education, ED 1.80

World War II History of **Department** of Commerce, C 1.27

Department of Defense

Annual **Department of Defense** Bibliography of Logistics Studies and Related Documents, D 1.33/3-2

Department of Education

Office of Inspector General, Semiannual Report to Congress **Department of Education**, ED 1.26

Department of Labor

Occupational Safety Aid, **Department of Labor** Safety Training Programs, OSA-OSHA-~(series), L 35.10

Department of State

Cultural Presentation Programs of the **Department of State**, S 1.67

Department of Transportation

Office of Inspector General, Semiannual Report to Congress **Department of Transportation**, TD 1.1/3

Department Store

Department Store Inventory Price Indexes, L 2.79

Department Store Merchandising Data, FR 1.24/5, FR 1.24/6

Department Store Sales, FR 1.24

Department Store Sales and Stocks, by Major Departments, FR 1.24/4

Department Store Sales, by Cities, FR 1.24/2

Department Store Sales, Preliminary Reports, FR 1.20

Department Store Stocks, FR 1.24/3

Department Store Trade, United States Departmental Sales Indexes, without Seasonal Adjustment, FR 1.24/9, FR 1.24/10

Department Store Trade, United States Departmental Stock-Sales Ratios, FR 1.24/11

Department Store Trade, United States Distribution of Sales by Months, FR 1.24/7, FR 1.24/8

Monthly **Department Store** Sales in Selected Areas, C 3.211/5

Departmental

Department Store Trade, United States **Departmental** Sales Indexes, without Seasonal Adjustment, FR 1.24/9, FR 1.24/10

Department Store Trade, United States **Departmental** Stock-Sales Ratios, FR 1.24/11

Departmental Circulars, Occupational Deferment Series, CS 1.38

Departmental Weekly Reports, HH 1.58

Numerical Index of **Departmental** Forms, D 301.6:0-9

Departments

Organization of Federal Executive **Departments** and Agencies, Y 4.G 74/9-10

Recruiting Bulletins Army and Corps Areas and **Departments**, Seventh Corps Area, W 99.17/10

Special Education Personnel in State Education **Departments**, FS 5.235:35051

State Agricultural **Departments** and Marketing Agencies, with Names of Officials, A 66.45

Status of Open Recommendations Improving Operations of Federal **Departments** and Agencies, GA 1.13/18

Training Bulletins Army and Corps Areas and **Departments**, Seventh Corps Area, W 99.77/11

Training Circulars Army and Corps Areas and **Departments**, Second Corps Area, W 99.12/8

Training Circulars Army and Corps Areas and **Departments**, Seventh Corps Area, W 99.17/8

Departure

Standard Instrument **Departure** (SID) Charts, Eastern U.S., C 55.416/5

Standard Instrument **Departure** (SID) Charts, Western United States, C 55.416/6

Departures

Arrivals and **Departures** by Selected Ports Statistics of Foreign Visitor Arrivals and U.S. Citizen **Departures** Analyzed by U.S. Ports of Entry and Departure, C 47.15/4

Arrivals and **Departures** by Selected Ports Statistics of Foreign Visitor Arrivals and U.S. Citizen Departures Analyzed by U.S. Ports of Entry and **Departure**, C 47.15/4

Forecast of Citizen **Departures** to Europe, S 1.121

Statistical Summary and Analysis of Foreign Visitor Arrivals, U.S. Citizen and Non-U.S. Citizen **Departures**, C 47.15

Dependence

Drug **Dependence**, HE 20.2416

Problems of Drug **Dependence**, HE 20.8216/5

Dependent

Characteristics of Families Receiving Aid to **Dependent** Children, FS 3.39

Characteristics of State Plans for Aid to Families with **Dependent** Children Under the Social Security Act Title IV-A, HE 3.65/2

Dependent Children Series, L 5.7

Public Assistance Bureau, Applications: Old-Age Assistance, Aid to **Dependent** Children, Aid to the Blind {and} General Assistance, FS 3.17

Statistical Summary of Aid to **Dependent** Children of Unemployed Parents, FS 3.39/3

Unemployed-Parent Segment of Aid to Families with **Dependent** Children, FS 14.210, FS 17.11, FS 17.611

Dependent Children

Aid to Familes with **Dependent Children**, HE 3.65, HE 17.625

Dependents

Annual Report, **Dependents'** Medical Care Program, D 104.16

Dependents Schools Manuals, D 1.6/2-2

Federal Benefits for Veterans and **Dependents**, VA 1.34:1

Deposit

Bank Debits and **Deposit** Turnover, FR 1.17

Bank Debits to Demand **Deposit** Accounts (Except Interbank and U.S. Government Accounts), FR 1.17/2

Maturity Distribution of Outstanding Negotiable Time Certificates of **Deposit**, FR 1.54/2

Operating Bank Offices Insured by the Federal **Deposit** Insurance Corporation, as of {date}, Y 3.F 31/8:18

Deposit Insurance

Examination of the Federal **Deposit Insurance** Corporation's Financial Statements for the Years Ended ..., GA 1.13/16

Depositaries

(Public Moneys **Depositaries**) Circulars, W 3.25

Depository

AEC **Depository** Library Bulletin, Y 3.At 7:47

Biennial Survey of **Depository** Libraries Results, GP 3.33/4

Daily **Depository** Shipping List, GP 3.16/3

Depository Invoices, GP 3.16

Depository Library Council Report to the Public Printer, GP 1.35

Depository Library Council to the Public Printer: Addresses, GP 1.36

Federal **Depository** Library Directory, GP 3.36/2

Federal **Depository** Library Directory (online), GP 3.36/2-2

Government **Depository** Libraries, Y 4.P 93/1:D 44

GPO **Depository** Union List of Item Selections, GP 3.32/2

Proceedings of the Annual Federal **Depository** Library Conference, . . . Regional Federal Depository Seminar, GP 3.30/3

Summary of Meeting **Depository** Library Council to the Printer, GP 3.30/2

Transcripts of Proceedings, Meeting of **Depository** Council to the Public Printer, GP 3.30

U.S. Government **Depository** Libraries Directory, Y 4.P 93/1-10

Depository Libraries

Biennial Report of **Depository Libraries** Summary Reports by State, GP 3.33/2

Biennial Report of **Depository** Libraries U.S. Summary, GP 3.33

Deposits

Aggregate Reserves and Member Bank **Deposits**, FR 1.15/3, HE 1.210

Bank Debits **Deposits** and Deposit Turnover, FR 1.17

Databook: Operating Banks and Branches, Summary of **Deposits**, Y 3.F 31/8:22

Demand **Deposits**, Currency and Related Items, FR 1.47

United States Exports of Petroleum and Petroleum Products of Domestic Origin, Commodity by Country of **Destination**, C 3.164:526

Destinations
Schedule of Sailings of Steam Vessels Registered Under Laws of United States and Intended to Load General Cargo at Ports in United States for Foreign **Destinations**, IC 1 rat.8
World Wise Schools Presents **Destinations**, PE 1.13

Destiny
America's Hour of **Destiny**, Radio Series, I 29.30, I 29.30/2

Desulfurization
FGD {Flue Gas **Desulfurization**} Quarterly Report, EP 1.46/8

DET
RA-**DET**, Y 3.At 7:19

Detachment
Marine Air Traffic Control **Detachment** Handbook, PCN nos, D 214.9/7

Detail
Public Use Data Tape Documentation **Detail** Natality, HE 20.6226/2
Public Use Data Tape Documentation Divorce Data, **Detail**, HE 20.6226/4
Public Use Data Tape Documentation Fetal Deaths **Detail** Records, HE 20.6226/11

Detailed
Census of Housing: **Detailed** Housing Characteristics, C 3.224/3:90-CH-2
Census of Population; **Detailed** Characteristics, C 3.223/8
CPI **Detailed** Report, Consumer Price Index, U.S. City Average and Selected Areas, L 2.38/3
Detailed Diagnoses and Procedures for Patients Discharged from Short-Stay Hospitals, United States, HE 20.6209/9
Detailed Diagnoses and Surgical Procedures for Patients Discharged from Short-Stay Hospitals, HE 20.6222
Detailed Listing of Real Property Owned by the United States and Used by Civil Agencies Throughout the World, GS 1.15/4
Detailed Listing of Real Property Owned by the United States and Used by the Department of Defense for Military Functions Throughout the World, GS 1.15/4-2
Detailed Mock-Up Information, W 108.20
Detailed Summary of Housing Amendments, HH 1.5/2
Federal Funds for Research and Development, **Detailed** Historical Tables, Fiscal Years, NS 1.18/2
Federal Funds for Research and Development, Federal Obligations for Research by Agency and **Detailed** Field of Science, Fiscal Years, NS 1.18/3
U.S. House of Representatives, **Detailed** Statement of Disbursements, Y 4.H 81/3:D 63

Detainees
Annual Report on Juvenile Arrestees/**Detainees**, J 28.24/6

Detection
Cancer Control, Prevention, and **Detection** Review Committee, HE 20.3001/2:C 16/8
Tumor Virus **Detection** Working Group, HE 20.3001/2:T 83

Detentions
Commercial Import **Detentions**, HE 20.4017
Report of Import **Detentions**, FS 13.120

Deterioriation
Summary Progress Report, Tropical **Deterioriation** Committee, Pr 32.413/11

Determination
Determination of Injury (series), TC 1.31/2
Determination of No Injury or Likelihood Thereof, TC 1.31
Methods for **Determination** of Radioactive Substances in Water and Fluvial Sediments, I 19.15/5
Preliminary **Determination** of Epicenters, C 55.412, I 19.66/2
Preliminary **Determination** of Epicenters, Monthly Listing, C 55.690, I 19.66
Sugar **Determination**, A 55.37, A 63.7, A 76.307, A 80.117, A 80.817, A 81.16, A 82.19

Walsh-Healey Public Contracts Act Minimum Wage **Determination** (for various industries), L 22.19

Determinations
Determinations of the National Mediation Board, NMB 1.9
General Wage **Determinations** Issued under the Davis-Bacon and Related Acts, L 36.211
Notices of **Determinations** by Jurisdictional Agencies Under the Natural Gas Policy Act of 1978, E 2.22

Determining
Determining Suitability for Federal Employment, CS 1.41/4

Detox
Solar **Detox** Update, E 1.99/5-2

Deutschen
Akten Zur **Deutschen** Auswartigen PolitIc, S 1.82/2

Developed
Hydroelectric Power Resources of the United States, **Developed** and Undeveloped, FP 1.123

Developing
Federal Plan for Ocean Pollution Research, **Developing**, and Monitoring, PrEx 8.109
Strengthening **Developing** Institutions, Title 3 of the Higher Education Act of 1965, Annual Report, HE 19.139/2
Teaching Aids for **Developing** International Understanding, FS 5.52

Developing Countries
Agriculture Technology for **Developing Countries**, Technical Series Papers, S 18.45

Developing Institutions
Awards Higher Education Act of 1965 (P.L. 89-329) as Amended Title 3 Strengthening **Developing Institutions**, HE 5.92/2 HE 19.139

Development
Adult **Development** and Aging Abstracts, HE 20.3359
Adult **Development** and Aging Research Committee, HE 20.3001/2:Ad 9
Advance, the Journal of the African **Development** Foundation, Y 3.Af 8:9
AEC Research and **Development** Reports, Y 3.At 7:22
Agricultural and Chemical **Development**, (date) Annual Report, Y 3.T 25:1-5, A 82.100
Agricultural **Development**, IADS News Digest, A 95.10/2
Agricultural Trade **Development** and Assistance Act of 1954 and Amendments, Y 1.2:Ag 8/6
Air Force Command and Control **Development** Division: Technical Notes AFCCDD-TN (nos.), D 301.45/24
Air Navigation **Development** Board Releases, C 31.142/2
Air Pollution, Sulfur Oxides Pollution Control, Federal Research and **Development**, Planning and Programming, FS 2.93/4
Air Pollution, Sulfur Oxides Pollution Control, Federal Research and **Development**, Planning and Programming, FS 2.93/4
Air Research and **Development** Command: Technical Reports, ARDC-TR , D 301.45/21
Alaska Resources **Development** Studies, I 68.9
Alloy **Development** for Irradiation Performance, E 1.64
AMC Laboratories and Research, **Development** and Engineering Centers, Technical Accomplishments, D 101.1/4
Americorps Leaders Program, A Service Leadership **Development** Program of the Corporation for National Service, Y 3.N 21/29:16-17
Annual International Aviation Research and **Development** Symposium, Report of Proceedings, FAA 2.9
Annual Report of Operations Under the Airport and Airway **Development** Act, TD 4.22/2
Application **Development** Guide Upward Bound Program for Program Year (date), ED 1.69/2
Application **Development** Guide, Talent Search Program, ED 1.8/3
Applications of Modern Technologies to International **Development**, AID-OST (series), S 18.42
Appraisal of Potentials for Outdoor Recreational **Development** {by Area}, A 57.57

Appropriate Technologies for **Development** (series), PE 1.10
Area and Industrial **Development** Aids, C 41.8/2
Area **Development** Aid: Area Trend Series, C 41.89
Area **Development** Aid: Industrial Location Series, C 45.8/3
Area **Development** Aid: Industry Trend Series, C 45.8/2
Area **Development** Bulletin, C 46.9
Area **Development** Memorandum for State Planning and Development Offices, C 45.14
Areas Eligible for Financial Assistance Designated Under the Public Works and Economic **Development** Act of 1965 Reports, C 46.25/2
Army Air Mobility Research and **Development** Laboratory Fort Eustis Virginia: USAAMRDL Technical Reports, D 117.8/2 D 117.8/4
Army Electronics Command Fort Monmouth N.J.: Research and **Development** Technical Reports ECOM (series), D 111.9/4
Army Institute for Professional **Development**: Subcourse ISO (series), D 101.103
Army Research and **Development**, D 101.52/3
Asian **Development** Bank Act Releases, SE 1.25/14
Belvior Research, **Development**, and Engineering Center: Handbooks, (series), D 101.6/10
Biannual Professional **Development** Program, ED 1.33/2
Business **Development** Publication (series), SBA 1.32/2
Catalyst for Rural **Development**, A 21.31
Center for Vocational and Technical Education, Ohio State University: Research and **Development** Series, HE 18.11
Central Pacific, Western Pacific, and South Pacific Fisheries **Development** Program Report for Calendar Year, C 55.329
Cityscape - A Journal of Policy **Development** and Research, HH 1.75/2
Commercial Fisheries {Market **Development** Lists}, I 49.33
Community **Development**, HH 1.46/2
Community **Development** Block Grant Program Annual Reports, HH 1.46/3
Community **Development** Bulletins, S 17.36
Community **Development** Evaluation Series, HH 1.46
Community **Development** Review, S 18.25
Community **Development** Series, C 41.97
Community **Development**: Case Studies, S 18.17/2
Community Planning and **Development** Evaluation: Evaluation Series, HH 1.46/4
Community Planning and **Development**, Program Guides, HH 1.6/10
Compilation of Federal Laws Relating to Conservation and **Development** of Our Nation's Fish and Wildlife Resources, Environmental Quality, and Oceanography, Y 4.M 53:L 44/2
Conference of State Planning and **Development** Officers with Federal Officials, Summaries, C 45.11
Consolidated Annual Report for the Office of Community Planning and **Development**, HE 23.1017
Consolidated Annual Report to Congress on Community **Development** Programs, HH 1.46/6
Consolidated **Development** Directory, HH 1.61
Contraceptive **Development** Contract Review Committee, HE 20.3001/2:C 76
Contractor Research and **Development** Reports, E 1.28
Conventional Loans Made to Finance Acquisition and **Development** of Land, Federal Savings and Loan Associations, FHL 1.22
Cooperative Inter-American Plantation Rubber **Development**, A 77.519
Crop Insurance Research and **Development** Bulletins, A 112.17, A 62.17
Current Federal Meteorological Research and **Development** Activities, C 30.75/2
Current Projects on Economic and Social Implications of Scientific Research and **Development**, NS 1.23
Department of Defense Program for Research and **Development**, D 1.81

Development and Management of Ambulatory Care Programs, HE 20.9109/2
Development Concept (series), I 29.79/3
Development Digest, S 18.33
Development Disabilities Abstracts, HE 1.49
Development Document for Effluent Limitations Guidelines and New Source Performance Standards for {various industries}, EP 1.8/3
Development Letter, C 46.9/4
Development of Multiple Use Facilities on Highway Right of Way, TD 2.121/2
Development of Qualification Standards, CS 1.41/4:271-1
Development Report AFPTRC-TN (series), D 301.36/7
Development Studies Program Occasional Papers, S 18.59
Development USA, C 46.9/5
Directory of Research, **Development** and Demonstration Projects, TD 7.9
Drug Abuse Research and **Development**, Federally Supported Drug Abuse and Tobacco Research and **Development**, Fiscal Year (date), HE 20.8220
EARI **Development** Research Series, Reports, D 103.50
Economic **Development**, C 46.92/
Economic **Development** Research Reports, C 46.29
Economic **Development** U.S.A., C 46.9/3
Educational and Nonprofit Institutions Receiving Prime Contract Awards for Research, **Development**, Test and Evaluation, D 1.57/8
Employee **Development** Guides, L 1.7/3
Employee Training and Career **Development** Catalog, HE 22.39
Engineer Research and **Development** Laboratories Reports, D 103.25
Environmental **Development** Plan, DOE/EDP (series), E 1.36
Environmental **Development** Plan, Oil Shale, ER 1.33
Equipment **Development** and Test Program, Progress, Plans, Fiscal Year, A 13.49/5
Equipment **Development** and Test Reports, EDT (Series), A 13.49/4
Equipment **Development** Report R.M. (Series), A 13.49/2
Expenditures for Staff **Development** and Training Activities, HE 17.630
Extension Course Institute, Air University: Career **Development** Course, D 301.26/17-2
Extension Service Update, Community and Rural **Development** (CRD), A 43.49/3
Federal Aviation Administration Plan for Research, Engineering, and **Development**, TD 4.64
Federal Funds for Research and **Development**, Detailed Historical Tables, Fiscal Years, NS 1.18/2
Federal Funds for Research and **Development**, Federal Obligations for Research by Agency and Detailed Field of Science, Fiscal Years, NS 1.18/3
Federal Funds for Research, **Development**, and Other Scientific Activities, NS 1.18
Federal Power Commission Laws and Hydro-Electric Power **Development** Laws {June 10, 1920}, Y 1.2:F 31/7
Federal Reference Material for State, Economic **Development** Agencies, C 41.27/2
Federal Support of Research and **Development** at Universities and Colleges and Selected Nonprofit Institutions, Fiscal Year, Report to the President and Congress, NS 1.30
Federally Coordinated Program of Highway Research and **Development**, TD 2.42
FHWA Research and **Development** Implementation Catalog, TD 2.36/3
Field Works, Ideas for Housing and Community **Development**, HH 1.75/3
Financial and Technical Assistance Provided by the Department of Agriculture and the Department of Housing and Urban **Development** for Nonmetropolitan Planning District, Annual Report to Congress, A 1.113
Firms in the 8(a) Business **Development** Program, SBA 1.36
Fishery Market **Development** Series, C 55.320
Fishery Marketing **Development** Series, I 49.49/2

Foreign Economic **Development** Report, A 93.38
Foreign Economic **Development** Service Annual Summary, A 100.1/2
Geothermal Energy Research, **Development** and Demonstration Program, Annual Report, ER 1.31
Guide of the U.S. **Development** of Energy, Board of Contract Appeals and Contract Adjustment Board, E 1.8/4
Handbooks, Manuals, Guides Relating to Research and **Development**, D 4.10
Head Start, Child **Development** Program, Manual of Policies and Instructions, PrEx 10.8:H 34/2
Health Care Financing Administration Information Systems **Development** Guide, HE 22.508/2
Highway Joint **Development** and Multiple Use, TD 2.56
Highway Research and **Development** News, Plant Ecology and Esthetics, Progress and Implementation, TD 2.113/2
Highway Research and **Development** Studies using Federal-Aid Research and Planning Funds, TD 2.113
Historical Review, U.S. Army Belvoir Research and **Development** Center, D 101.98
Historical Review, U.S. Army Mobility Equipment Research and **Development** Command, D 101.98
Housing and Urban **Development** Notes, HH 1.30
Housing and Urban **Development** Trends, HH 1.14
How Federal Agencies Develop Management Talent, Management Staff **Development** Series Reports, CS 1.56
Human **Development** News, HE 23.10
Human Embryology and **Development** Study Section, HE 20.3001/2:Em 1
Ideas, 4 H and Youth **Development**, A 43.36
Impact on Public Assistance Caseloads of (a) Training Programs under Manpower **Development** and Training Act and Read Redevelopment Act, and (b) Public Assistance Work and Training Programs, FS 14.219, FS 17.409, FS 17.635
Indian and Alaska Native Housing and Community **Development** Programs, Annual Report to Congress, HH 1.80
Industrial **Development** in the TVA Area, Y 3.T 25:30-2
Industrial **Development** in TVA Area During (date), Y 3.T 25:30 In 27
Inter-American **Development** Commission, S 5.43
International Agricultural **Development**, A 95.9
International Bank for Reconstruction and **Development**, S 5.51
International Oil and Gas Exploration and **Development**, E 3.11/20-6
International Teacher **Development** Program, Annual Report to Bureau of Educational and Cultural Affairs, Department of State, FS 5.214:14003
Inventory of Federal Tourism Programs, Federal Agencies Commissions, Programs Reviewed for Their Participation in the **Development** of Recreation, Travel, and Tourism in the United States, C 47.2:T 64/3
Journal of Rehabilitation, Research and **Development**, VA 1.23/3
Management Design and **Development** Technical Bulletins, HH 1.96
Manpower **Development** and Training, Projects Approved, FS 5.76
Manpower **Development** Program Highlights, L 7.66
Manpower **Development** Research Program, Report, D 1.50
Medical Research and **Development** Board, Research Progress Report, D 104.12, D 104.12/2
Mental Retardation and **Development** Disabilities Abstracts, HE 1.49
Natural Resource **Development** Program Annual Report, SBA 1.48
Naval Air **Development** Center Reports NADA (series), D 202.23
Naval Ship Research and **Development** Center Reports, D 211.9
New Research and **Development** Reports Available to Industry, C 42.21/4

New Ship Techniques and **Development** of Research Services Division, Annual Report, D 301.45/11
Newsletter of Community **Development** in Technical Cooperation, FO 1.31, S 17.31
Newsletter, Research and **Development** in Health Care, VA 1.66
Nuclear **Development** and Proliferation, PrEx 7.14/4
Office of Research and **Development**, Region 1: Annual Report, EP 1.1/3
Office of Research and **Development**: Reports CG-D- (series), TD 5.25/2
Personnel **Development** for Vocational Education, HE 19.124
Personnel Measurement Research and **Development** Center, CS 1.71
Personnel Research and **Development** Center: Technical Memorandum, CS 1.71/4
Planning and **Development** Reports, CA 1.11
Posters Housing and Urban **Development** Department, HH 1.98
Posters International **Development** Agency, S 18.60
Proceedings Annual Conference of Mental Health Career **Development** Program, FS 2.22/45
Procurement Regulations Agency for International **Development**, S 18.6/2
Productivity and Technological **Development** Division Publications, L 2.19
Program **Development** Handbooks for State and Area Agencies on {various subjects}, HE 23.3009
Program Research and **Development** Announcements, ER 1.30
Progress in Rural **Development** Program, Annual Reports, A 1.85
Progress Report on Staff **Development** for Fiscal Year, NCSS Report E-3, FS 17.630, HE 17.630
Progress Report on Staff **Development**, FS 14.220
Publications Scientific Research and **Development** Office, Pr 32.413
Qualified Areas Under Public Works and Economic **Development** Act of 1965, Public Law 89-136, Reports, C 46.25
Quarterly Review, 503 and 504 Economic **Development** Loan Programs, SBA 1.27/2
Register of Projects Approved Under Manpower **Development** and Training Act, L 1.53
Regulations, Rules and Instructions Center for Professional **Development** and Training, HE 20.7709
Releases, Air Research and **Development** Command, D 301.45/3
Report on National Growth and **Development**, PrEx 15.9
Report on Status of Multiple Use and Joint **Development**, TD 2.121
Report to Congress on Ocean Pollution, Overfishing, and Offshore **Development**, C 55.31/2
Report to the Advisory Child Health and Human **Development** Council, HE 20.3362/7
Reports of Project on Research in Agricultural and Industrial **Development** in Tennessee Valley Region, Y 3.T 25:26
Reprints of Articles Published Concerning NIH Consensus **Development** Conferences, HE 20.3030/2
Research and **Development** Abstracts of USAEC, RDA (series), Y 3.At 7:51
Research and **Development** Contracts, Fiscal Year Funds, HE 20.3013/4
Research and **Development** Division Reports, D 212.12
Research and **Development** Findings, L 1.56
Research and **Development** in Industry, NS 1.22:In 2
Research and **Development** Progress Reports, I 1.88
Research and **Development** Progress, C 39.202:R 31
Research and **Development** Projects, C 13.2:R 31/4
Research and **Development** Reports, C 21.18, E 5.10/2, ER 1.11
Research and **Development** Series, HE 19.218
Research and **Development** Technical Reports, D 211.13/2
Research and **Development** Yearbook, E 5.10
Research and **Development**: Public Awareness/participation Support Plan, Fiscal Year (date), EP 1.90

Research Review, Economic **Development**
Administration, C 46.26
Resource Conservation and **Development** Plans, A
57.62
Resource Conservation **Development** Plan, A 57.65
Results under the Small Business Innovation
Development Act of 1982, SBA 1.1/4
Review of Selected U.S. Government Research and
Development Reports, OTR-(series), C
13.49
Review of the Air Force Materials Research and
Development Program, D 301.45
Reviews of Data on Research and **Development**, NS
1.11
Rural Areas **Development** Newsletter, A 21.25/3
Rural **Development** Goals, Annual Report of the
Secretary of Agriculture to the Congress,
A 1.85/2
Rural **Development** Goals, Pr 37.14
Rural **Development** Perspectives, A 93.41/2, A
105.40/2
Rural **Development** Program News, A 21.25
Rural **Development** Research Reports, A 93.41, A
105.40
Saline Water Research and **Development** Progress
Reports, I 1.88
Solar Energy Research and **Development** Report, E
1.38, ER 1.32
Special Analysis of Federal Research and
Development Programs in Budget, PrEx
2.8/a4
Staff **Development** Series, FS 14.208/4
Standards **Development** Status Summary Report, Y
3.N 88:32
Statistical Summary, Rural Areas **Development** and
Area Redevelopment, Quarterly Progress
Report, A 43.38
Summary of Grants and Contracts Administered by
the National Center for Health Services
Research and **Development**, HE 20.2116
Summary Report of Utilization Research and
Development, Fiscal Year (date), A
77.2:Ut 3
Task Force on Rural **Development**, Pr 37.8:R 88
Technical **Development** Notes, C 31.12, C 31.125
Technical **Development** Reports, CA 1.20, C 31.11,
C 31.119, FAA 2.8
Technical Notes Department of the Air Force
Arnold Engineering **Development**
Center, D 301.45/33-3
Technical Notes Department of the Air Force
Command and Control **Development**
Division, D 301.45/24
Technical Notes Department of the Air Force
Meteorological **Development**
Laboratory, D 301.45/17-2
Technical Notes Department of the Air Force Rome
Air **Development** Center, D 301.57/2
Technical Notes Department of the Air Force
Wright Air **Development** Center, D
301.45/13
Technical Report Index, Maritime Administration
Research and **Development**, C 39.227:T
22
Technical Research Reports Published by Air Force
Personnel and Training Center Air
Research and **Development** Command, D
301.26/10
Technology and **Development** Program, A 13.137
Telecommunication Policy, Research and
Development, PrEx 7.14/5
Telephone Directory Housing and Urban
Development Department, HH 1.92
Toward Interagency Coordination, Federal Research
and **Development** on Adolescence, HE
23.1013
Toward Interagency Coordination: Federal
Research and **Development** on Early
Childhood, HE 23.1013/2
Training Analysis and **Development**, Information
Bulletin, D 301.38/2
Training and **Development** Services, PM 1.19/4-2
Training and Manpower **Development** Activities
Supported by the Administration on
Aging Under Title IV-A of the Older
Americans Act of 1965, As Amended,
Descriptions of Funded Projects, HE
23.3002:T 68/2
Training Manual Agency for International
Development, S 18.8/2
Transportation Research and **Development**
Command: Research Technical
Memorandums, D 117.8

U.S. Army Research and **Development** Program
Guide, D 101.52/4
U.S. Naval Radiological Defense Laboratory,
Research and **Development** Report
USNRDL (series), D 211.13
Undergraduate Engineering Curricular Accredited
by Engineer's Council for Professional
Development, FS 5.61
United States Army Research and **Development**
Series, D 101.52
United States LPPSD {Low Pollution Power
Systems **Development**} Technical
Information Exchange Documents, ER
1.16
University-Federal Agency Conference on Career
Development, Conference Reports, CS
1.70
Update Department of Housing and Urban
Development, HH 1.68
Urban **Development** Action Grant Program, HH
1.46/5
Urban **Development** Action Grants, HH 1.110
Water Resources **Development** by Army Corps of
Engineers in {State}, D 103.35
Water Resources **Development** by Corps of
Engineers by Area, D 103.35
Water Resources **Development** in Delaware in
(year), D 103.35/8
Water Resources **Development** in District of
Columbia, D 103.35/51
Water Resources **Development** in Idaho, D 103.35/
12
Water Resources **Development** in Illinois, D
103.35/13
Water Resources **Development** in Indiana, D
103.35/14
Water Resources **Development** in Iowa, D 103.35/
15
Water Resources **Development** in Kentucky, D
103.35/17
Water Resources **Development** in Maryland, D
103.35/20
Water Resources **Development** in Massachusetts, D
103.35/21
Water Resources **Development** in Michigan, D
103.35/22
Water Resources **Development** in Minnesota, D
103.35/23
Water Resources **Development** in Missouri, D
103.35/25
Water Resources **Development** in Nevada, D
103.35/28
Water Resources **Development** in New Jersey (year),
D 103.35/30
Water Resources **Development** in New Mexico, D
103.35/31
Water Resources **Development** in New York, D
103.35/32
Water Resources **Development** in North Carolina, D
103.35/33
Water Resources **Development** in North Dakota, D
103.35/34
Water Resources **Development** in Ohio, D 103.35/
35
Water Resources **Development** in South Carolina, D
103.35/40
Water Resources **Development** in Virginia, D
103.35/46
Water Resources **Development** in West Virginia, D
103.35/48
Water Resources **Development** in Wisconsin, D
103.35/49
Water Resources **Development** in {State}, D
103.35D 103.35/53
Women in **Development** (series), S 18.55
Development Center
Belvoir Research and **Development** Center:
Container System Hardware Status
Report, D 101.115
Developmental
Developmental Behavioral Sciences Study Section,
HE 20.3001/2:B 39/2
Developments
Bibliography of Soviet Laser **Developments**, D
5.211
Bimonthly Summary of Labor Market **Developments**
in Major Areas, L 7.51
Business Cycle **Developments**, C 3.226, C 56.111
Chronologies of Major **Developments** in Selected
Areas of International Relations, Y 4.F
76/1:In 8/57, Y 4.In 8/16:In 8/5
Construction, Monthly Summary of Current
Developments, L 2.22

Current **Developments**, A 57.70
Current **Developments** in Drug Distribution, C
18.212
Current **Developments** in Electrical Trade, C 18.213
Current **Developments** in Farm Real Estate Market,
A 77.13
Current **Developments** in Food Distribution, C
18.214
Current **Developments** Report on European
Recovery, S 1.72
Current Distribution **Developments** in Hardware
and Allied Trades, C 18.215
Current Research and **Developments** in Scientific
Documentation, NS 1.15, NS 2.10
Current Wage **Developments**, L 2.44
Data **Developments**, C 3.238/7
Developments in Labor Productivity, L 2.73
Exempt Organizations Current **Developments**, T
22.50
Farm Labor **Developments**, L 7.55, L 1.63
Farm Real Estate Market **Developments**, A 93.9/4,
A 105.19/2
Farm Real Estate Taxes, Recent Trends and
Developments, A 93.9/6
Fur Trade **Developments**, C 18.94
HE Instruction in Agriculture, Programs,
Activities, **Developments**, FS 5.74
Nevada Today, **Developments** in Business,
Technology and International Trade, C
1.65
New **Developments** in Employee and Labor
Relations, PM 1.62
New **Developments** in Highways, TD 2.22
Overseas Television **Developments**, IA 1.16
Quarterly Report on Case **Developments**, LR 1.15/4
Recent **Developments** in Foreign Trade of American
Republics, TC 1.22
Recent Educational Policy and Legislative
Developments Abroad (series), HE 5.94
Report of **Developments** on Eradication of Vesicular
Exanthema, A 77.224
Reports on Case Handling **Developments** of the
Office of the General Counsel, Y 3.F 31/
21-3:12
Review of Foreign **Developments**, Prepared for
Internal Circulation, FR 1.49
Rural Manpower **Developments**, L 1.63
Scientific Manpower, Significant **Developments**,
Views and Statistics, NS 1.14
SD **Developments**, S 18.67
Seaword, **Developments** in American Flag
Shipping, C 39.236
State Quarterly Economic **Developments**, C 59.16/
1, C 59.16/52
Summary of Technological **Developments** Affecting
War Production, L 2.17
Training Device **Developments**, D 210.14/4
Training Support **Developments**, D 210.14/4
U.S. Energy Industry Financial **Developments**, E
3.56
United States Treaty **Developments**, S 9.11
United States Treaty **Developments**, Transmittal
Sheets, S 9.11/2
Wage **Developments** in Manufacturing, Summary
Release, L 2.44/2
Wage **Developments** in the New England Region, L
2.49/5
Weekly Review of Recent **Developments**, L 2.56
World Wide Motion Picture **Developments**, C
18.180
Device
FDA Drug and **Device** Products Approvals, FDA/
BD, HE 20.4209
FDA Medical **Device** Standards Publication,
Technical Reports, FDA-T, HE 20.4310/2
FDA Medical **Device** Standards Publications, MDS
(series), HE 20.4310
Sealed Source and **Device** Newsletter (SS&D), Y
3.N 21/29:18-1
Training **Device** Developments, D 210.14/4
Devices
Bureau of Medical **Devices** Standards Survey,
International Edition, HE 20.4309
Bureau of Medical **Devices** Standards Survey,
National Edition, HE 20.4309/2
Center for **Devices** and Radiological Health
Publications Index, HE 20.4609/2
Devices and Technology Branch Contractors
Meeting, Summary and Abstracts, HE
20.3219
Drug and **Devices**, DDNJ (series), FS 13.108
Foreign Markets for Scales and Other Weighing
Devices, C 18.85

Manual on Uniform Control **Devices** for Streets and
Highways, TD 2.8:T 67
Manual on Uniform Traffic Control **Devices** for
Streets and Highways: Official Rulings
on Requests for Interpretations, Changes,
and Experimentations, TD 2.8/2
Medical **Devices** and Diagnostic Products
Standards Survey; International Edition,
HE 20.4035
Medical **Devices** and Diagnostic Products
Standards Survey; National Edition, HE
20.4035/2
Medical **Devices** Application Program, Annual
Report, HE 20.3210
Medical **Devices** Bulletin, HE 20.4612/2
Monthly Report on Adverse Reactions to Drugs
and Therapeutic **Devices**, FS 13.123
NIST Handbook, Specifications, Tolerances, and
Other Technical Requirements for
Weighing and Measuring **Devices**, C
13.11/2
Notices of Judgement under Federal Food, Drug,
and Cosmetic Act: Drugs and **Devices**, A
46.22, FS 7.12
Regulations, Rules and Instructions National
Center for **Devices** and Radiological
Health, HE 20.4606
Superconducting **Devices** and Materials, C 13.37/5
Superconducting **Devices**, C 13.75/5
Superconducting **Devices**, Literature Survey, C
13.37/5
Dewey
Dewey Decimal Classification, Additions, Notes
and Decisions, LC 37.8
DFAS
DFAS: The DOD Accounting Firm, D 1.104
DFO
DFO {Defense Food Orders}, A 82.64
DFSC
DFSC Chronicle, D 7.31
DG
Draft Regulatory Guide, DG-, Y 3.N 88:6-3
DG(series), D 103.6/6
U.S. Army Ballistic Missile Agency, **DG**- TR-
(series), D 105.15/2
DHEW
DHEW Obligations to Institutions of Higher
Learning, HE 1.2:ED 8/3
DHEW Obligations to {various institutions}, HE
1.41
DHHS
Instructions and Data Specifications for Reporting
DHHS Obligations to Institutions of
Higher Education and Other Nonprofit
Organizations, HE 20.3050
DHIA
DHIA Cow Performance Index List, Registered
Progeny of DHIA Sires, A 77.15:44
DHIA Sire Summary List, A 77.15:44
DI
RRB-SSA Financial Interchange: Calculations for
Fiscal Year with Respect to OASI, **DI**,
and HI Trust Funds, RR 1.15
DIA
FAA News **DIA** (series), FAA 1.7/3
Diabetes
Diabetes Control Program Update, HE 20.7314
Diabetes Dateline, the National **Diabetes**
Information Clearinghouse Bulletin, HE
20.3310/3
Diabetes Literature Index, HE 20.3310
Diabetes Literature Index, Annual Index Issue, HE
20.3310/2
Diabetes Mellitus, HE 20.3320/2-4
Diabetes Mellitus Coordinating Committee,
Annual Report to the Director, National
Institutes of Health, Fiscal Year (date),
HE 20.3028
Hypoglycemia, National **Diabetes** Information
Clearinghouse, HE 20.3323/2
National **Diabetes** Advisory Board: Annual
Report, HE 20.3027
National **Diabetes** Advisory Board: Publications,
HE 20.3029
National **Diabetes** Information Clearinghouse HE
20.3323/2
Prevent **Diabetes** Problems HE 20.3326
Diagnoses
Detailed **Diagnoses** and Procedures for Patients
Discharged from Short-Stay Hospitals,
United States, HE 20.6209/9
Detailed **Diagnoses** and Surgical Procedures for
Patients Discharged from Short-Stay
Hospitals, HE 20.6222

Diagnosis
Advance Training for Workers in the Early and
Periodic Screening, **Diagnosis** and
Treatment Program: Publications, HE
22.111
Advanced Training for Workers in the Early and
Periodic Screening, **Diagnosis** and
Treatment Program: Publications, HE
22.111
Breast Cancer **Diagnosis** Committee, HE 20.3001/
2:B 74/2
Diagnosis and Therapy, HE 20.3173/2
Division of Cancer Biology and **Diagnosis**:
Annual Report, HE 20.3151/6
Inpatient Utilization of Short-Stay Hospitals by
Diagnosis, United States, HE 20.6209/8
Recent Reviews, Cancer **Diagnosis** and Therapy,
Supplement to the Cancergrams, HE
20.3173/2-3
Diagnostic
Climate **Diagnostic** Bulletin, C 55.194
Diagnostic Radiology Committee, HE 20.3001/2:R
11/3
Directory of Animal Disease **Diagnostic**
Laboratories, A 101.2:D 63/2, A 101.13
Medical Devices and **Diagnostic** Products
Standards Survey; International Edition,
HE 20.4035
Medical Devices and **Diagnostic** Products
Standards Survey; National Edition, HE
20.4035/2
Diagnostics
Diagnostics Report of the National Hurricane
Center, C 55.131
Noise **Diagnostics** for Safety Assessment,
Standards, and Regulation, E 1.28/10
Diagram
Diagram Booklets (series), D 101.101
Diagrams
Current **Diagrams**, C 4.28
Sky **Diagrams**, N 11.11
Dial
Saint Elizabeth's Hospital, Sun **Dial**, I 1.14/5
Dialog
Dialog for the Service Education Officer, D 1.10/5
Radio-TV Defense **Dialog**, D 2.19/2
Dialysis
Medicare Renal **Dialysis** Facility Manual, HE 22.8/
13
National Listing of Medicare Providers Furnishing
Kidney **Dialysis** and Transplant
Services, HE 22.510
National Listing of Renal Providers Furnishing
Kidney **Dialysis** and Transplant
Services, HE 22.510/2
Diamond
Harry **Diamond** Laboratories, Washington, D.C., D
105.14/3
Harry **Diamond** Laboratories: Special Reports, D
105.14/5
Diamonds
Industrial **Diamonds** in (year), I 28.162
Diary
Consumer Expenditure Survey: **Diary** Survey, L
2.3/18-2
Diatomite
Diatomite in (year), I 28.127
Dictionaries
Dictionaries, Glossaries, etc., NAS 1.8

Foreign-Language and English **Dictionaries** in the
Physical Sciences and Engineering,
Selected Bibliography, 1952-1963, C
13.10:258
Dictionary
Aeronautical **Dictionary**, NAS 1.8:Ae 8
Color Universal Language and **Dictionary** of
Names, C 13.10:440
Department of Defense **Dictionary** of Military and
Associated Terms, D 5.12/3
Dictionary of American-Naval Fight Ships, D
207.10
Dictionary of Basic Military Terms: a Soviet View,
D 301.79:9
Dictionary of Military and Associated Terms, D
5.12:1
Instruction Manual Part 2h, **Dictionary** of Valid
Terms for the Mortality Medical Indexing,
Classification, and Retrieval System
(MICAR), HE 20.6208/4-8
Navigation **Dictionary**, D 203.22:220
Subject Headings Used in the **Dictionary** Catalogs
of the Library of Congress, LC 26.7

Supplement to State Court Model Statistical
Dictionary, J 29.9/3
Did
Why **Did** It Happen, A 13.47
DIDA
DIDA Notes, HE 20.8217/4
DIDS
DIDS Procedures Manual, D 7.6/19
Died
Where to Write for Birth and Death Records of U.S.
Citizens Who Were Born or **Died**
Outside of the United States and Birth
Certifications for Alien Children
Adopted by U.S. Citizens, FS 2.102:B
53/7
Diesel
On-Highway **Diesel** Prices, E 3.13/8
Diet
Food and **Diet** Charts, A 10.7
Dietary
Instruction Manual: **Dietary** Interviewer's Manual
for the Hispanic Health and Nutrition
Examination Survey, HE 20.6208/2-2
Dietetic
Dietetic Internship, Public Health Service
Hospital, Staten Island, N.Y., FS 2.89/4
Dietetics
Annual Training Courses in **Dietetics**, W 44.23/6
Differences
Semiannual Report on Strategic Special Nuclear
Material Inventory **Differences**, E 1.15/2
Different
Changes in **Different** Types of Public and Private
Relief in Urban Areas, L 5.33
Rain and Dry Winds, Computed for **Different**
Geographical Districts, W 42.12
Differential
Standardized Government Post **Differential**
Regulations, **Differential** Circulars, S
1.76/2
Diffusion
Air Resources Atmospheric Turbulence and
Diffusion Laboratory: Annual Report, C
55.621
Increase & **Diffusion**, SI 1.46
Public Use Data Tape Documentation Chest X-Ray,
Pulmonary **Diffusion**, and Tuberculin
Test Results Ages 25-74, HE 20.6226/5-
2
Digest
Annual **Digest** of State and Federal Labor
Legislation, L 16.3
Biomass **Digest**, E 6.3/2-2
Civil Rights **Digest**, CS 1.12
Compilations and Digest of Orders, Circulars,
Regulations, and Decisions, W 7.11/3
Congressional Record, Index and Daily **Digest**, X
1.1
Conservation Highlights, **Digest** of the Progress
Report of the Soil Conservation Service,
A 57.1/2
Current Policy **Digest**, S 1.71/4-2
Daily **Digest** Communications Office, Department of
Agriculture, A 21.14
Daily **Digest** Federal Communications Commission,
CC 1.54
Daily **Digest** of Reconstruction News, Y 3.C 83:95
Digest & Index of Decisions of NLRB, LR 1.8/2
Digest and Decisions of the Employees'
Compensation Appeals Board, L 28.9
Digest Economic Opportunity Office, PrEx 10.25
Digest for Official Use Only, W 109.210
Digest for Reporters, A 93.23/2
Digest Merit Systems Protection Board, MS 1.11
Digest of Appropriation, T 63.115
Digest of Decisions Federal Trade Commission, FT
1.12
Digest of Decisions National Labor Relations
Board, Annual Supplements, LR 1.8/3
Digest of Decisions National Labor Relations
Board, BW-(series), LR 1.8/5-2
Digest of Decisions National Labor Relations
Board, CS-(series), LR 1.8/5
Digest of Decisions Post Office Inspectors
Division, P 14.5
Digest of Decisions Relating to National Banks, T
12.7/2
Digest of Decisions Secretary of Agriculture under
Perishable Agricultural Commodities
Act, A 82.55
Digest of Educational Statistics, ED 1.326, HE
19.315
Digest of Functions of Federal Agencies, Pr
32.5022

Digest of Geodetic Publications, C 4.21
Digest of Grazing Decisions, I 53.15
Digest of Health and Insurance Plans, L 2.99/2
Digest of Income Tax Rulings, T 22.24, T 22.25/2
Digest of International Law, S 7.12
Digest of Laws, Decisions and Rulings, I 24.9
Digest of Opinions, J 5.5
Digest of Policies, Reports, and Other Publications, Y 3.W 89/2:10
Digest of Prepaid Dental Care Plans, HE 20.2:D 54/7
Digest of Procedure Manual Materials, Y 3.R 31:15
Digest of Procedures, FW 4.10
Digest of Rulings, FR 1.12
>Digest of Rulings (OASI) Transmittal Sheets, FS 3.24/2
Digest of Rulings (Old-Age and Survivors Insurance), FS 3.24
Digest of Science and Engineering Presentations, C 4.55
Digest of Selected Federal Retirement Systems, CS 1.29/4
Digest of Selected Health and Insurance Plans, L 2.99/2
Digest of State Laws Relating to Taxation and Revenue, C 3.50
Digest of State Program Plans, EP 2.21
Digest of Trade Hints for Paint and Varnish Merchants, C 18.194
Digest of United States Practice in International Law, S 7.12/3
Digest of War Department Directives and Index of General Orders, Bulletins, and Numbered Circulars, W 1.41
Digest of {and} Decisions, I 21.6
Digest Rulings, FR 1.12
Digest Security and Cooperation in Europe Commission, Y 4.Se 2/11:13/3
Digest, Disarmament Information Summary, Pr 34.11/2
Digest, Inspector General Report to the Congress, VA 1.55/2
Digital Data **Digest**, D 103.20/8
DTIC **Digest**, D 10.11
Early Childhood **Digest**, ED 1.343/2
ERIC **Digest**, ED 1.331/2
Housing Index-**Digest**, Y 3.C 33/3:7
Housing Legal **Digest**, Decisions, Opinions, Legislations Relating to Housing Construction and Finance, Y 3.C 33/3:10
Information **Digest**, Pr 32.214, Pr 32.5010
New **Digest**, ED 1.71
OHRO **Digest**, HE 20.6019
Physical Fitness Research **Digest**, HE 20.110, Pr 37.8:P 56/2 R 31/2
PPL **Digest**, E 1.103
Press **Digest**, Y 3.F 31/11:20, Y 3.F 31/11:38, FL 2.9, NHA 2.9
Program and Resource **Digest**, J 1.86
Public Administration Practices and Perspectives, **Digest** of Current Materials, S 18.24
Quarterly **Digest** of Unpublished Decisions of the Comptroller General of the United States: Personnel Law, Civilian Personnel, GA 1.5/5, GA 1.5/10, GA 1.5/11
Research and Technology Program **Digest**, Flash Index, NAS 1.41
Research Information **Digest**, Recent Publications of Southeastern Forest Experiment Station, A 13.63/13
Safety **Digest**, W 34.37, D 101.22/3:385
SBIC **Digest**, the Equity Financing Arm of SBA, SBA 1.30
Seventh Circuit **Digest**, Ju 2.9
Shock and Vibration **Digest**, D 4.12/2, D 210.27
Small Farm **Digest**, A 94.23
Special Service **Digest**, W 109.108
Staff Practice and Procedure **Digest**, Y 3.N 88:23
State Air Programs, **Digest**, Fiscal Year (date), EP 1.33
State Forest Tax Law **Digest**, A 13.21/2
State Law **Digest**, Reports, LC 14.8
State Safety **Digest**, L 16.29
Supplemental **Digest** and Index of Published Decisions of the Assistant Secretary of Labor for Labor-Management Relations Pursuant to Executive Order 11491, Y 3.F 31/21-3:10
Technical Data **Digest**, W 108.18
Technical **Digest** Bureau of Yards and Docks, M 205.8

Technical **Digest** Feature, S 18.18
Technical **Digest** International Cooperation Administration, S 17.45
Technical **Digest** Naval Facilities Engineering Command, D 209.8
Technical **Digest** Service, C 41.24
Trade Agreement **Digest**, TC 1.24
Traffic Safety **Digest**, TD 8.40
U.S. Air Force Policy Letter **Digest**, D 301.120
United States Air Force Medical Service **Digest**, D 304.8
United States Policy Toward USSR and International Communism, Monthly **Digest** of Pertinent Data Appearing in Department of State Publications, S 1.97
USDA/Aid News **Digest**, A 1.108
Water Quality Standards Criteria **Digest**, Compilation of Federal/State Criteria on {various subjects}, EP 1.29/2
Weekly Advertising **Digest**, Y 3.F 31/11:30
Weekly Labor News **Digest**, L 1.28, L 2.50
What the Soldier Thinks, Monthly **Digest** of War Department Studies on Attitudes of American Troops, W 1.65
World Lumber **Digest**, C 18.163
World's Wool **Digest**, C 18.181
Digestive
  Digestive Diseases, HE 20.3320/2-3
  Digestive Diseases Clearinghouse Fact Sheets, HE 20.3323
  Digestive Diseases Coordinating Committee, HE 20.3001/2:D 56
Digestive Diseases
  Annual Report of the National **Digestive Diseases** Advisory Board, HE 20.3027/4
Digests
  Consolidated Index of Opinions and **Digests** of Opinions of Judge Advocate General, W 10.10
  Digests, S 7.12
  Digests and Indexes of Treasury Decisions, T 1.12
  Digests for Retailers, Pr 32.4218
  Digests of Decisions and Regulations, T 22.8/2
  Digests of Legal Opinions, VB 1.13
  Digests of United States Reports, Ju 6.8/2
  OSHA Safety and Health Standards **Digests**, L 35.6/4
  Quality Control **Digests**, C 31.166, FAA 5.11
  Selected Topic **Digests**, J 1.42/2
  Statistical **Digests**, C 55.316, I 49.32
Digital
  American Memory **Digital** Collections, LC 1.54/3
  Digital Data Digest, D 103.20/8
  Digital Data Series, I 19.121
  Digital Orthophotoquads DOQ For, I 19.124
  Digital Raster Graphics (DRG) for [State], I 19.128
  DRG **Digital** Raster Graphic (series), I 19.128
  Federal **Digital** Cartography Newsletter, I 19.115
  Global Volcanism Program, **Digital** Information Series, SI 1.49
  Index to **Digital** Line Graphs, I 19.97/5
  Index to Land Use and Land Cover Maps and **Digital** Data, I 19.97/3
  Periodic Report from the National **Digital** Library Program, L 37.215
DIME
  Geographic Base (**DIME**) File, CUE, {Correction-Update-Extension}, C 3.249/2, C 56.255
Dimension
  Dimension Stone in (year), I 28.118/3-2
  Directory of Principal **Dimension** Stone Producers in the United States, I 28.118/3
Dimensions
  Dimensions, NBS, C 13.13
  Harry Diamond Laboratories: **Dimensions**, D 105.30
  New **Dimensions** in Higher Education, FS 5.250, HE 5.250
  New **Dimensions** in Mental Health, HE 20.8122
  New **Dimensions** in Mental Health, Report from the Director (series), HE 20.8122/2
Diminutives
  Foreign Versions, Variations, and **Diminutives** of English Names and Foreign Equivalents of U.S. Military and Civilian Titles, J 21.2:N 15
Dingell
  Dingell-Johnson Quarterly, I 49.29/2
DIOR
  Catalog of **DIOR** Reports, D 1.33/4
Diplomacy
  Science, Technology, and American **Diplomacy**, Y 4.F 76/1-12, Y 4.In 8/16:12

Diplomatic
  Diplomatic List, S 1.8
  Diplomatic Security Training Resources, etc. Fiscal Year, S 1.139/2
  Employees of **Diplomatic** Missions, S 1.8/2
  Foreign Relations of United States, **Diplomatic** Papers: Conferences, S 1.1/3
  Instructions to **Diplomatic** and Consular Officers, S 1.10
Diptheria
  Diptheria Surveillance, Reports, HE 20.2309/14
Direct
  Direct Line to You, HE 3.68/5
  Direct Loans Bulletin, ED 1.40/6
  Direct Loans Newsletter, ED 1.40/5
  Foreign **Direct** Investment in the United States, C 61.25/2
  Foreign **Direct** Investment in the United States, Establishment Data For Manufacturing, C 59.20/3
  Monthly Report on Foreign **Direct** Investment Activity in the United States, C 61.25/3
  OPEC **Direct** Investment in the United States, C 61.25
  Profiles of Foreign **Direct** Investment in U.S. Energy, E 3.52
  U.S. **Direct** Investment Abroad, Operations of U.S. Parent Companies and Their Foreign Affiliates, Preliminary Estimates, C 59.20/2
Direct Cost
  Federal Work Injury Facts, Occupational Distribution, Duration and **Direct Cost** Factors of Work Injuries to Civilian Federal Employees During Calendar Year, L 26.8/2-2
Direct Deposit
  Direct Deposit Marketing, T 63.127
Direction
  Direction, the Navy Public Affairs Magazine, D 201.17
Directions
  Catalog of Charts, Sailing **Directions** and Tide Tables, C 4.18/1
  Directions, HE 20.8227
  Explanations and Sailing **Directions** to Accompany Wind and Current Charts, N 14.9
  FJC **Directions**, a Publication of the Federal Judicial Center, Ju 13.13
  Mideast **Directions** (series), LC 41.10
  NSF **Directions**, NS 1.54
  Sailing **Directions** Coast and Geodetic Survey, C 4.18/3
  Sailing **Directions** Naval Oceanographic Office, D 203.22
  Sailing **Directions**, D 5.317
Directive
  Airworthiness **Directive** Summary, C 31.145
  CAA Airworthiness **Directive**, C 31.147/2
  Directive Orders and Opinions, Pr 32.5107
  FAA Airworthiness **Directive**, TD 4.10
Directives
  Alphabetical List of CMIC **Directives**, D 116.9
  Department of Defense **Directives** (series), D 1.6/8-2
  Directives, Publications, and Reports Index, TD 5.21/6
  Equal Employment Opportunity Management **Directives**/Bulletins, Y 3.Eq 2:18-5
  Federal Aviation Administration Airworthiness **Directives**, TD 4.10/4
  Index and User Guide Vol. 1, Airworthiness **Directives** Small Aircraft, TD 4.10/5
  Index and User Guide Vol. 2, Airworthiness **Directives** Large Aircraft, TD 4.10/5-2
  Interim **Directives**, Pr 34.706/2, PrEx 4.612
  Navy Current Procurement **Directives**, NCPD (series), D 201.6/13
  Navy Procurement **Directives**, D 201.6/10
  SSA Administrative **Directives** System Transmittal Notice, HE 3.68
  Summary of Airworthiness **Directives** for Large Aircraft, TD 4.10/3
  Summary of Airworthiness **Directives** for Small Aircraft, FAA 1.28/2
  Summary of Airworthiness **Directives**, TD 4.10/2
  Trademark Examining Procedure **Directives**, C 21.15/2
Director
  Official Statement of Wheat **Director**, Y 3.W 56:5
  Problems of Mobilization and Reconversion, Reports to the President, Senate, and House of Representatives by **Director** of War Mobilization and Reconversion, Y 3.W 19/7:8

Report to the President by **Director** of Defense Mobilization, Pr 33.1008

Report to the President by **Director** of Office of Defense Mobilization, Pr 34.201

Reports of the Proceedings of the Judicial Conference of the United States {and} Annual Report of the **Director** of the Administrative Office of the U.S. Courts, Ju 10.1/2

The **Director**, T 1.27/37

Director General

News Letter from **Director General** of Foreign Service, S 1.68

Director's

Budget of the U.S. Government: **Director's** Introduction and Overview Tables, PrEx 2.8/11

Director's Letters, FS 13.214

Director's Memorandum, T 70.17

Director's Newsletter, Chicago District, T 22.55

Directorate

Directorate of Electronic and Material Sciences FY Program, D 301.45/19-9

Directorate of Intelligence Publications (numbered), PrEx 3.10/7

Directorate of Mathematical and Information Sciences, Air Force Office of Scientific Research, Research Summaries, D 301.45/19-10

Directory of Awards, **Directorate** for Engineering, NS 1.50/3

Electronic Research **Directorate** Technical Memorandum ERD-CRRK-TM (series), D 301.45/12

GRD Research Notes, Geophysics Research **Directorate**, D 301.45/16

Publications **Directorate** of Weather; Special Series, W 108.17

Technical Notes Department of the Air Force Electronics Research **Directorate**, D 301.45/12-2

Technical Notes Department of the Air Force Geophysics Research **Directorate**, D 301.45/16-2

Directories

Directories [Aging Administration], HE 1.1014

Directories [Agriculture Department], A 1.89/3

Directories [Agricultural Marketing Service], A 88.69

Directories [Air Force Academy], D 305.20

Directories [Air Force Department], D 301.104

Directories [Alcohol, Drug Abuse, and Mental Health Administration], HE 20.8023

Directories [Army Department], D 101.120

Directories [Children's Bureau], HE 23.1215

Directories [Customs Commissioner], T 17.15/2

Directories [Education Department], ED 1.30/2

Directories [Educational Research and Improvement Center], ED 1.330

Directories [Environmental Protection Agency], EP 1.102

Directories [Export Administration Bureau], C 63.10

Directories [Export Development Bureau], C 57.121

Directories [Family Support Adminsitration], HE 25.10

Directories [Federal Emergency Management Agency], FEM 1.14/2

Directories [Federal Grain Instpection Service], A 104.13

Directories [Federal Highway Administration], TD 2.68

Directories [Fish and Wildlife Service], I 49.104

Directories [General Accounting Office], GA 1.28

Directories [Government Printing Office], GP 3.36

Directories [Grain Inspection, Packers and Stockyards Administration], A 113.11

Directories [Head Start Bureau], HE 23.1113

Directories [Health and Human Services Department], HE 1.28/2

Directories [Health Care Delivery and Assistance Bureau], HE 20.9112

Directories [Health Care Financing Administration], HE 22.29/2

Directories [Indian Health Service], HE 20.9412, HE 20.310

Directories [Internal Revenue Service], T 22.54

Directories [International Trade Administration], C 61.44

Directories [Justice Department], J 1.89/3

Directories [Latin American, Portuguese, and Spanish Division], LC 24.11

Directories [Library of Congress], LC 1.40, LC 1.40/2

Directories [Medicaid Bureau], HE 22.114

Directories [National Bureau of Standards], C 13.69

Directories [National Center for Educational Statistics], ED 1.130

Directories [National Center for Health Statistics], HE 20.6228

Directories [National Drug Abuse Institute], HE 20.8233

Directories [National Heart, Lung, and Blood Institute], HE 20.3223

Directories [National Highway Traffic Safety Administration], TD 8.35

Directories [National Institute on Aging], HE 20.3868

Directories [National Institute on Deafness and Other Communication Disorders], HE 20.3660

Directories [National Institute on Drug Abuse], HE 20.3960

Directories [National Institutes of Health], HE 20.3037/2

Directories [National Library of Medicine], HE 20.3623

Directories [National Literacy Institute], Y 3.L 71:10

Directories [National Oceanic and Atmospheric Administration], C 55.48

Directories [National Park Service], I 29.126

Directories [National Science Foundation], NS 1.50

Directories [National Technical Information Service], C 51.19

Directories [Nuclear Regulatory Commission], Y 3.N 88:52

Directories [Pesticides and Toxic Substances Office], EP 5.24

Directories [Rural Development], A 114.10

Directories [Small Business Administration], SBA 1.13/4

Directories [State Department], S 1.21/2

Directories [Substance Abuse and Mental Health Services Administration], HE 20.410

Directories [Transportation Department], TD 1.9/4

Directories [Transportation Statistics Bureau], TD 12.10

Directories [United States Holocaust Memorial Council], Y 3.H 74:11

Directories [United States Institute of Peace], Y 3.P 31:10

Directories [United States Postal Service], P 1.52

Directories [Urban Mass Transportation Administration], TD 7.19

Directories [Veterans Administration], VA 1.62/2

Directories [Women's Bureau], L 36.116

Directories [Victims of Crim Office], J 34.10

Directories of Labor Organizations, L 29.9

FTS **Directories** {for various areas}, GS 12.12/2

Guide to Computer Program **Directories**, C 13.10:500-42

Postal Zone **Directories**, P 1.35

Social Service Resource **Directories**, J 16.7

Standardization **Directories**, D 7.13

ZIP + 4, State **Directories**, P 1.10/9

ZIP Code **Directories** {by States}, P 1.10/7

Directors

Classified Index of Decisions of Regional **Directors** of National Labor Relations Board in Representation Proceedings, LR 1.8/6-2

Compensation of Officers, **Directors**, Etc., Class 1 Railroads, Line-Haul and Switching and Terminal Companies, IC 1.26

Memorandum to State **Directors**, Y 3.Se 4:21

Proceedings Biennial Conference of State and Territorial Dental **Directors** with Public Health Service and Children's Bureau, FS 2.83/2

Summary of Equity Security Transactions and Ownership of **Directors**, Officers, and Principal Stockholders of Member State Banks As Reported Pursuant to

Summer Seminars for College Teachers, Guidelines and Application Forms for **Directors**, NF 3.13/2

Summer Seminars For **Directors**, For College Teachers, For School Teachers, Guidelines and Application Form for Participants, NF 3.13/3-5

Summer Seminars for Secondary School Teachers Guidelines and Application Form for **Directors**, NF 3.13/3-3

Union Pacific Railway, Government **Directors**, Annual Reports, 1864-1898, I 1.30

Directory

Air Force Address **Directory**, D 301.104/9

Aircraft Certification **Directory**, TD 4.52/3

APHIS Organizational **Directory**, A 101.21

APHIS Program Service **Directory**, A 101.15

Bureau of Naval Weapons **Directory**, Organizational Listing and Correspondence Designations, D 217.25

Change Sheets Applying to Organization **Directory**, W 3.42/2

Chicago Federal Executive Board **Directory**, PM 1.31/3

Chief Counsel Office **Directory**, T 22.48/2

Civil and Defense Mobilization **Directory**, Pr 34.708/2, PrEx 4.8/2

Civil Rights **Directory**, CR 1.10:15

Cleft Palate Team **Directory**, HE 20.3402:C 58/2

Clinical Center: Medical Staff **Directory**, HE 20.3002:M 46/4

Commercial News USA, New Products Annual **Directory**, C 61.10/2

Congressional **Directory**, Y 4.P 93/1:1

Consolidated Development **Directory**, HH 1.61

CPSC Telephone **Directory**, Y 3.C 76/3:23

Credit Union **Directory**, NCU 1.16

Criminal Justice Information Exchange **Directory**, J 28.20/2

Directory CAP {Community Actions Programs} Grantees, PrEx 10.2:C 73-3

Directory for Reaching Minority Groups, L 23.2:M 66

Directory Former Grants Associates, HE 20.3037/3

Directory of ADP Training, CS 1.65

Directory of Adult Day Care Centers, HE 22.202:Ad 9

Directory of Air Quality Monitoring Sites Active in (year), EP 1.2:Ai 7/5

Directory of Air Service Stations, W 87.9/2

Directory of Airfields, U.S. Army & Navy, C 31.126

Directory of Airports and Seaplane Bases, Airman's Guide Supplement, FAA 1.23/2

Directory of American Agricultural Organizations, A 37.6

Directory of Animal Disease Diagnostic Laboratories, A 101.2:D 63/2, A 101.13

Directory of Associate Members, National Conference on Weights and Measures, C 13.66/3

Directory of Automated Criminal Justice Information Systems, J 29.8/2

Directory of Awardee Names, E 1.35/2-7

Directory of Awards, NS 1.50/2

Directory of Awards, BHPR Support, HE 20.9312

Directory of Awards, Directorate for Engineering, NS 1.50/3

Directory of Blood Establishments Registered Under Section 510 of the Food, Drug, and Cosmetic Act, HE 20.4002:B 62

Directory of Bulgarian Officials, PrEx 3.10/7-12

Directory of Bureau of Animal Industry, A 77.221

Directory of Cement Producers in (year), I 28.29/3

Directory of Chinese Officials and Organizations, PrEx 3.10/7-13

Directory of Chinese Officials, Provincial Organizations, PrEx 3.10/7-5

Directory of Coal Production Owership, E 3.11/7-5

Directory of Commodities and Services, ES 3.10

Directory of Commodities and Services Exempted or Suspended from Price Control, ES 3.10/2

Directory of Community Education Projects, HE 19.132/3, ED 1.20

Directory of Community High Blood Pressure Control Activities, HE 20.3002:B 62/13

Directory of Companies Filing Annual Reports with the Securities and Exchange Commission, SE 1.27

Directory of Companies Producing Salt in the United States, I 28.134/2

Directory of Compensation District Offices and Deputy Commissioners, L 26.2:D 62

Directory of Computer Softwear Applications, C 51.11/5

Directory of Computerized Data Files, C 51.11/2-2

Directory of Computerized Data Files and Related Software Available from Federal Agencies, C 51.11/2

Directory of Computerized Data Files and Related Technical Reports, C 1.11/2-2

Directory of Computerized Software, C 51.11/2

Directory of Consumer Offices, HE 1.509/2

Directory of Contacts for International Educational, Cultural and Scientific Exchange Programs, S 1.67/4

Directory of Contract Opportunities, Pr 32.4811

Directory of Cooperating Agencies, A 18.15

Directory of Counselor Educators, FS 5.255:25036, HE 5.255:25036

Directory of Criminal Justice Information Sources, J 26.2:In 3, J 28.20

Directory of Czechoslovak Officials, A Reference Aid, PrEx 3.10/7-10

Directory of DCAA Offices, D 1.46/4

Directory of DoC Staff Memberships on Outside Standards Committees, C 13.69/3

Directory of Employees for the International Trade Administration, C 61.32

Directory of Energy Data Collection Forms, E 3.45

Directory of Energy Information Administration Model Abstracts, E 3.48

Directory of Environmental Life Scientists, 1974, D 103.43:1105-2-3

Directory of EPA, State, and Local Environmental Activities, EP 1.23/5:600/4-75-001

Directory of Facilities Obligated to Provide Uncompensated Services by State and City, HE 20.9209

Directory of Federal Agencies and Departments in States, Y 3.N 21/9:9

Directory of Federal and State Business Assistance, C 51.19/2

Directory of Federal and State Departments and Agencies, Pr 32.207

Directory of Federal Consumer Offices, HE 1.509/2

Directory of Federal Coordinative Groups for Toxic Substances, EP 1.79/2

Directory of Federal Government Certification and Related Programs (Special Publication 739), C 13.10:739

Directory of Federal Laboratory and Technology Resources, a Guide to Services, Facilities, and Expertise, C 51.19/2-2

Directory of Federal Regional Structure, GS 4.119

Directory of Federal Statistical Data Files, C 51.15

Directory of Federal Technology Transfer, PrEx 23.10

Directory of Grants, Awards, and Loans, HE 20.6111, HE 20.6612

Directory of Halfway Houses and Community Residences for the Mentally Ill, HE 20.8129

Directory of Halfway Houses for the Mentally Ill and Alcoholics, HE 20.2402:H 13

Directory of Important Labor Areas, L 7.2:D 62/9

Directory of Indian Service Units, I 20.38

Directory of Information Resources in Agriculture and Biology, A 17.2:D 62

Directory of Information Resources in the United States, LC 1.31

Directory of Information Systems, TD 1.36

Directory of Institutions for Mentally Disordered Offenders, HE 20.2402:Of 2/2

Directory of International Mail, P 1.10/5

Directory of International Trade Union Organizations, L 29.9/2

Directory of Iranian Officials, PrEx 3.10/7-22

Directory of Iraqi Officials, PrEx 3.10/7-3

Directory of Japanese Technical Reports, C 51.19/3

Directory of Labor Organizations in {various countries}, L 2.72/4

Directory of Labor Research Advisory Council to the Bureau of Labor Statistics, L 2.83/2

Directory of Law Enforcement and Criminal Justice Associations and Research Centers, C 13.10:480-20

Directory of Library Networks and Cooperative Library Organizations, ED 1.129

Directory of Local Employment Security Offices, L 37.18, L 1.59

Directory of Local Health and Mental Health Units, HE 20.2015

Directory of Local Health Units, FS 2.77

Directory of Meat and Poultry Inspection Program Establishments, Circuits and Officials, A 88.16/20

Directory of Medicare Providers and Suppliers of Services, HE 3.51/5

Directory of Multifamily Project Mortgage Insurance Programs by Project Status, HH 1.50

Directory of Narcotic Addiction Treatment Agencies in the United States, HE 20.2402:N 16/3

Directory of National and International Labor Unions in the United States, L 2.3

Directory of National Unions and Employees Associations, L 2.2:Un 33/9

Directory of Nursing Home Facilities, HE 20.6202:N 93

Directory of NVLAP Accredited Laboratories, C 13.58/7

Directory of Officers and Organizations Concerned with Protection of Birds and Game, A 5.8

Directory of Officials of the Democratic People's Republic of Korea, PrEx 3.10/7-6

Directory of Officials of the Republic of Cuba, PrEx 3.10/7-18

Directory of Officials of Vietnam, A Reference Aid, PrEx 3.10/7-25

Directory of On-going Research in Smoking and Health, HE 20.25, HE 20.7015

Directory of Outpatient Psychiatric Clinics, Psychiatric Day-Night Services and Other Mental Health Resources in the United States and Territories, FS 2.22/38-4

Directory of Personnel Responsible for Radiological Health Programs, HE 20.4122

Directory of Post Offices, P 1.10/4

Directory of Postsecondary Institutions, ED 1.111/4

Directory of Postsecondary Schools with Occupational Programs, HE 19.337

Directory of Principal Crushed Stone Producers in the United States in (year), I 28.118/2

Directory of Principal Dimension Stone Producers in the United States, I 28.118/3

Directory of Principal U.S. Gemstone Producers (Annual Advance Summary), I 28.117

Directory of Private Programs for Minority Business Enterprise, C 1.56

Directory of Programs Preparing Registered Nurses for Expanded Roles, HE 20.6610

Directory of Providers of Services of Extended Care Facilities, HE 3.51/3

Directory of Providers of Services of Home Health Services, HE 3.51

Directory of Providers of Services of Hospitals, HE 3.51/2

Directory of Providers of Services of Independent Laboratories, HE 3.51/4

Directory of Public and Secondary Schools in Selected District, Enrollment and Staff by Racial/Ethnic Group, HE 1.38

Directory of Public Training Schools Serving Delinquent Children, FS 14.102:T 68

Directory of Refrigerated Warehouses in the United States, A 92.34:1

Directory of Representative Work Education Programs, HE 5.2:W 89/2

Directory of Research Natural Areas on Federal Lands of United States of America, Y 3.F 31/19:9

Directory of Research, Development and Demonstration Projects, TD 7.9

Directory of Resources for Cultural and Educational Exchanges and International Communication, ICA 1.12

Directory of Romanian Officials, A Reference Aid, PrEx 3.10/7-24

Directory of Secondary Schools with Occupational Curriculums, Public and Nonpublic, HE 5.96

Directory of Services, ED 1.30/4

Directory of Small-Scale Agriculture, A 94.17

Directory of Soviet Officials, National Organizations, PrEx 3.10/7-4

Directory of Soviet Officials: Republic Organizations, A Reference Aid, PrEx 3.10/7-14

Directory of Soviet Officials: Science and Education, PrEx 3.10/7-16

Directory of Standards Laboratories in the United States, C 13.2:St 2/2

Directory of State and Territorial Health Authorities, FS 2.77/2

Directory of State Departments of Agriculture, A 88.40/2:17, A 88.59

Directory of State Mental Health Personnel and Regional Offices of Department of Health, Education, and Welfare, FS 2.22:M 52/40

Directory of State Merit Systems, FS 1.2:M 54

Directory of State Officials, HE 20.4037/2

Directory of State, County, and City Government Consumer Offices, PrEx 16.2:St 2/2

Directory of State, Territorial, and Regional Health Authorities, HE 20.2015/2

Directory of STD Clinics, HE 20.7316

Directory of Suppliers of Services: Independent Laboratories, FS 3.51/4

Directory of Teachers Giving Courses in Rural Sociology and Rural Life, A 36.57

Directory of Telecommunications Management, Annual Report, PrEx 4.17

Directory of the Labor Research Advisory Council to the Bureau of Labor Statistics, L 2.109

Directory of the Republic of Nicaragua, PrEx 3.10/7-19

Directory of U.S. Government Audiovisual Personnel, GS 4.24

Directory of U.S. Government Datafiles for Mainframes & Microcomputers, C 51.19/4

Directory of U.S. Institutions of Higher Education, Fall (year), FS 5.250:50052, HE 5.250:50052

Directory of United States Poison Control Centers and Services, HE 20.4003/2-2

Directory of United States Probation Officers, Ju 10.15

Directory of United States Standardization Activities, C 13.10:288, C 13.10:417

Directory of Urban Public Transportation Service, TD 7.19/2

Directory of USSR Foreign Trade Organization and Officials, PrEx 3.10/7-7

Directory of USSR Ministry of Defense and Armed Forces Officials, PrEx 3.10/7-11

Directory of USSR Ministry of Foreign Affairs Officials, PrEx 3.10/7-17

Directory of Veterans Administration Facilities, VA 1.62/2-2

Directory of Veterans Organizations and State Departments of Veterans Affairs, VA 1.62

Directory of Voting Members (National Information Standards Organization), C 13.69/2

Directory of Wage Chronologies, L 2.64/2

Directory of Weather Broadcasts, C 30.73

Directory of Women Business Owners, Megamarketplace East/West, C 1.37/3

Directory of World Federation of Trade Unions, L 29.9/3

Directory of World Seismograph Stations, C 55.220/5:25

Directory of Yugoslav Officials, PrEx 3.10/7-8

Directory {of} Market News Broadcasts, A 66.38

Directory, Aviation Medical Examiners, TD 4.211

Directory, Business Research Advisory Council of the Bureau of Labor Statistics, L 2.83

Directory, Directors of State Agencies for Surplus Property and Regional Representatives, Division of Surplus Property Utilization, FS 1.2:Su 7/2

Directory, Executive Orientation Courses in Automatic Data Processing, PrEx 2.12/2

Directory, Local Law Enforcement Organizations Participating in Aviation Security, TD 4.809

Directory, Poison Control Centers, HE 20.2:P 75/2, HE 20.4002:P 75

Directory, State Department of Education Personnel for Guidance, Counseling, and Testing, FS 5.255:25037:A, HE 5.255:25037:A

Directory, State Officials Charged with Enforcement of Food, Drug, Cosmetic, and Feed Laws, FS 13.102:St 2

Directory, United States, Territories, and Canada, HE 20.6213/2

Directory: Federal, State and Local Government Consumer Offices, HE 1.502:St 2

Directory: State, County, and City Government Consumer Offices, HE 1.502:St 2

Division of Cancer Epidemiology and Genetics, Annual Research Directory, HE 20.3188/2

Division of Clinical Sciences, Annual Research Directory, HE 20.3151/9

DoD Directory of Contract Administration Services Components, D 1.6/12

Eastern Africa, Annual Publishers Directory, LC 1.30/8-3

EDA Directory of Approved Projects, C 46.19/2

Energy Information in the Federal Government, a Directory of Energy Sources Identified by the Interagency Task Force on Energy Information, FE 1.24

Energy Information Referral Directory, E 3.33

ERDA Telephone Directory, ER 1.17

ESA Directory of Offices, L 36.15

FAA Directory, TD 4.52

Federal Career **Directory**, Guide for College Students, CS 1.7/4:C 18

Federal Civil Defense Administration **Directory**, FCD 1.19

Federal Contract Air Service and Travel **Directory**, GS 8.10

Federal Financial Management **Directory**, GA 1.12/2

Federal Hotel/Motel Discount **Directory**, GS 8.10/2, GS 2.21/2

Federal Item Name **Directory** for Supply Cataloging, Handbook, D 7.6/2

Federal Radiological Fallout Monitoring Station **Directory**, D 119.8/3:E 5.11

Federal Statistical **Directory**, PrEx 2.10, C 1.75

Federal Telecommunications System Telephone **Directory**, Y 3.At 7:55-2

Federal Travel **Directory**, GS 2.21, GS 1.29

Federal-State Market News Reports, **Directory** of Services Available, A 88.40/2:21

Field **Directory**, HE 1.17

Field Facility **Directory**, FAA 1.43

Flight Information Publication: Airport/Facility **Directory**, C 55.416/2

Food and Agricultural Export **Directory**, A 67.26:201

Food and Drug Administration Location **Directory**, HE 20.4037

Foreign Affairs Research, a **Directory** of Government Resources, S 1.2:F 76a/4

Forest Service Organizational **Directory**, A 13.36/2-2

Garrison Commanders **Directory**, D 101.120/4

HCFA Communications **Directory**, HE 22.14

(HCFA) Medicare Unique Physician Identification Number (**Directory**), HE 22.414/2

HCFA Telephone **Directory**, HE 22.14

HDS Telephone **Directory**, HE 23.11

Higher Education and the Handicapped, Resource **Directory**, ED 1.32/2

Indian Health Service **Directory**, HE 20.9412/2

Interagency Directory, Key Contacts for Planning, Scientific and Technical Exchange Programs, Educational Travel, Students, Teachers, Lecturers, Research Scholars, Specialists, S 1.67/3

Intermountain Region Organization **Directory**, A 13.36/2-3

Keyword **Directory**, T 17.6/3-3

Meat and Poultry Inspection **Directory**, A 101.15, A 103.9, A 110.11

Meat Inspection **Directory**, A 4.10

Medicare **Directory** of Prevailing Charges, HE 22.29

Medicare Unique Physician Identification Number **Directory**, HE 22.414

Mental Health **Directory** of State and National Agencies Administering Public Mental Health and Related Programs, FS 2.22/49

Military Assistance Program Address **Directory**, D 7.6/4:M 59/6

Mineral Industry Surveys, **Directory** of Principal Construction Sand and Gravel Producers in the . . ., Annual Advanced Summary Supplement, I 19.138/3

NASA STI **Directory**, NAS 1.24/4

National Archives and Records Administration Telephone **Directory**, AE 1.122

National **Directory** of Drug Abuse and Alcoholism Treatment and Prevention Programs, HE 20.410/3

National **Directory** of Farmers Markets, A 88.69/2

National Zip Code and Post Office **Directory**, P 1.10/8

National Zip Code **Directory**, P 1.10/8

Navajo Nation & Regional Areas Resource **Directory**, HE 20.310/3

Navy and Marine Corps List and **Directory**, N 1.24

Network of Knowledge, **Directory** of Criminal Justice Information Sources, J 28.20

New Products Annual **Directory**, C 61.10/2

OCDM Telephone **Directory**, PrEx 4.8

OERI **Directory** of Computer Tapes, ED 1.24/2

Office and Project **Directory**, I 27.28

Office of Administration and Resources Management, Research Triangle Park, N.C.: Telephone **Directory**, EP 1.12/2

Officer **Directory**, D 103.71

OHA Telephone **Directory**, HE 3.51/6

Operation Golden Eagle, **Directory** of Federal Recreation Areas Changing Entrance, Admission and User Fees, I 66.16

Organization **Directory** Adjutant General's Department, W 3.42

Organization **Directory** Civilian Production Administration, Pr 32.4830

Organization **Directory** U.S. Department of Agriculture, A 60.10

Organizational **Directory** of Key Officials, PM 1.31/2

Parkinson's Disease and Related Disorders, International **Directory** of Scientists, HE 20.3511/2

Peace Corps Program **Directory**, S 19.16

Pocket Congressional **Directory**, Y 4.P 93/1:1 P

Procurement Equipment **Directory** D (series), D 7.13/2

Production Equipment **Directory** D (series), D 7.13/3

Regional Office **Directory**, Professional and Administrative Personnel, FS 1.17/2

Resource **Directory**, HE 20.3660/2

Rocky Mountain Research Station **Directory**, A 13.151/4-2

Roster and **Directory** of Troops in Hawaiian Department, W 81.5

Scientific **Directory** and Annual Bibliography, HE 20.3017

Seafaring Guide, and **Directory** of Labor-Management Affiliations, C 39.206/3:Se 1

Service **Directory**, A 13.8/2

Small Business Subcontracting **Directory**, SBA 1.2/2, SBA 1.2/10

Social Security Administration Baltimore **Directory**, HE 3.58/2

Soil, Water, Air Sciences **Directory**, A 106.14/2

Southern Research Station **Directory** of Research Scientists, A 13.150/4

State Supervisors of Pupil Transportation, **Directory**, FS 5.2:T 68/2

Station **Directory**, N 12.9

Strategic Air Command, Grissom Air Force Base Telephone **Directory**, D 301.104/6

Strategic Air Command, Vandenberg Air Force Base Telephone **Directory**, D 301.104/7

Strategic Air Command, Wurtsmith Air Force Base, Telephone **Directory**, D 301.104/5

Street **Directory** of Principal Cities of United States, P 7.6

Teaching Opportunities, **Directory** of Placement Information, FS 5.226:2600, HE 5.226:2600

Telephone and Service **Directory**, HE 20.3037

Telephone **Directory** Agriculture Department, Alphabetical Listing, A 1.89/4

Telephone **Directory** Army Department, (by area), D 101.97

Telephone **Directory** Automated Data and Telecommunications Service, Region 1, GS 12.12/2:1

Telephone **Directory**, Bureau of Apprenticeship and Training, L 37.109

Telephone **Directory** Central Office and Regions, GS 12.12

Telephone **Directory** Civil Rights Commission, CR 1.16

Telephone **Directory** Customs Service, T 17.15

Telephone **Directory** Education Department, ED 1.24

Telephone **Directory** Energy Department, E 1.12

Telephone **Directory** Engraving and Printing Bureau, T 18.6

Telephone **Directory**: Executive Office of the President, PrEx 1.22

Telephone **Directory** Federal Aviation Administration, TD 4.52/2

Telephone **Directory** Federal Communications Commission, CC 1.53

Telephone **Directory** Federal Energy Regulatory Commission, E 2.12/2

Telephone **Directory**: Federal Trade Commission, FT 1.35

Telephone **Directory** General Accounting Office, GA 1.27

Telephone **Directory** General Services Administration and Defense Materials Procurement Agency, GS 1.11

Telephone **Directory** Geological Survey, Central Region, I 19.84/2

Telephone **Directory** Geological Survey, I 19.84

Telephone **Directory** Goddard Space Flight Center, Greenbelt, Md, NAS 1.24/2

Telephone **Directory** Government Printing Office, GP 1.39

Telephone **Directory** House of Representatives, Y 1.2/7

Telephone **Directory** Housing and Urban Development Department, HH 1.92

Telephone **Directory** Internal Revenue Service, Salt Lake City District, T 22.48/3

Telephone **Directory** International Communications Agency, ICA 1.15

Telephone **Directory** Interstate Commerce Commission, IC 1.37

Telephone **Directory** Jet Propulsion Laboratory, NASA, NAS 1.12/7-2

Telephone **Directory** Justice Department, J 1.89

Telephone **Directory** Kennedy Space Center, NAS 1.24/3

Telephone **Directory** Labor Department, L 1.67

Telephone **Directory** NASA, Headquarters, Washington, D.C., NAS 1.24

Telephone **Directory** National Transportation Safety Board, TD 1.124

Telephone **Directory** Nuclear Regulatory Commission, Y 3.N 88

Telephone **Directory** Office of Personnel Management, PM 1.31

Telephone **Directory** Reclamation Bureau, I 27.77

Telephone **Directory** Republic 7500, Executive 6300, District 0525, GS 6.7

Telephone **Directory** Rockwell International, Rocky Flats Plant, E 1.12/4

Telephone **Directory** Salt Lake City District, T 22.48/3

Telephone **Directory** Selective Service System, Y 3.Se 4:26

Telephone **Directory** United States Courts Administrative Office, Ju 10.20

Telephone **Directory** Veterans Administration, VA 1.60

330-Funded Community Health Centers **Directory**, HE 20.9112/2

Toxicology Research Projects **Directory**, HE 1.48

U.S. Air Force Public Affairs Staff **Directory**, D 301.104/4

U.S. Army and Navy **Directory** of Airfields, C 31.125

U.S. Government Depository Libraries **Directory**, Y 4.P 93/1-10

U.S. Government Purchasing and Sales **Directory** Guide for Selling or Buying in the Government Market, SBA 1.13/3

U.S. Government Purchasing **Directory**, SBA 1.13

U.S. Government Specifications **Directory**, SBA 1.13

U.S. Senate Telephone **Directory**, Y 1.3/10

United States Court **Directory**, Ju 10.17

United States Fisheries Systems and Social Sciences: a Bibliography of Work and **Directory** of Researchers, C 55.332:So 1

University Centers of Foreign Affairs Research, Selective **Directory**, S 1.2:Un 3

Urban Planning Assistance Program, Project **Directory**, HH 1.26, HH 7.8/3

Urban Renewal Demonstration Grant Program, Project **Directory**, HH 7.2:G 76

Urban Renewal Project **Directory**, HH 7.8/2

USAF Medical Logistics **Directory**, D 304.9/2

USIA Telephone **Directory**, IA 1.26

Washington Office Telephone **Directory**, I 53.45

Water Data Coordination **Directory**, I 19.118

Weights and Measures **Directory**, C 13.66

World Trade **Directory** Reports, C 18.280

Worldwide Public Affairs Offices **Directory**, D 101.120/2

DIS

DIS (Defense Investigative Service) Achievements, D 1.1/8

DISA

DISA (Defense Information Systems Agency), D 5.112

Disabilities

Development **Disabilities** Abstracts, HE 1.49

Interviewing Guides for Specific **Disabilities**, L 1.7/7, L 37.8/4

Mental Retardation and Development **Disabilities** Abstracts, HE 1.49

President's Committee on Employment of the Handicapped: People with **Disabilities** in Our Nation's Job Training Partnership Act Programs, PrEx 1.10/15

Disability

Annual Report of the Board of Trustees of the Federal Old-Age and Survivors Insurance and **Disability** Insurance Trust Funds, SSA 1.1/4

Characteristics of Social Security **Disability** Insurance Beneficiaries, HE 3.91

Concurrent Receipt of Public Assistance Money Payments and Old-Age, Survivors, and **Disability** Insurance Cash Benefits by Persons Aged 65 or Over, FS 17.636, HE 17.636

Disability Forum Report, ED 1.215/3

Disability Network News, PrEx 1.10/20, PrEx 1.10/20-2

Disability Notes SSA 1.31

Disability Statistics Abstract, ED 1.84/2, ED 1.215/4

Disability Statistics Report, ED 1.215/2

Disability Statistics Report (series), ED 1.84

Disability Studies Notes, FS 3.54

Monthly Benefit Statistics; Old-age, Survivors, **Disability**, and Health Insurance, Summary Benefit Data, HE 3.28/6

NARIC, **Disability** Research Resources, ED 1.79

National **Disability** Policy: A Progress Report, Y 3.D 63/3:1-2

Social Security Rulings on Federal Old-age, Survivors, **Disability**, and Health Insurance, HE 3.44

SSA Program Circulars **Disability**, HE 3.4/4

When You Get Social Security **Disability** Benefits, What You Need to Know, SSA 1.21

Your Social Security Rights and Responsibilities, **Disability** Benefits, HE 3.88

Disabled

Disabled USA, PrEx 1.10/3-2

Disabled Veterans, Affirmative Action Plan, P 1.56

Employment of **Disabled** and Vietnam Era Veterans in Federal Government, CS 1.93

From the Social Security Survey of the **Disabled**, Reports, HE 3.54/2

Inspection of Several Branches of National Home for **Disabled** Volunteer Soldiers, W 9.5

Record of Changes in Memberships of National Home for **Disabled** Volunteer Soldiers, NH 1.6

Supplemental Security Income Program for the Aged, Blind, and **Disabled**, HE 3.77

Disadvantage

Continuation Application for Grants under Special Services for **Disadvantage** Students Program, ED 1.60

Action for the **Disadvantaged**, HE 20.6021

DISAM

DISAM Catalog, D 1.45/3

Disallowances

RSI Quality Appraisal Awards and **Disallowances** Monthly Statistical Summary, HE 3.28/9

Disappearance

Field Seeds, Supply and **Disappearance**, A 92.19/5

Disarmament

Arms Control and **Disarmament**, LC 2.10

Arms Control and **Disarmament** Studies in Progress or Recently Completed, S 1.117/5

Digest, **Disarmament** Information Summary, Pr 34.11/2

Disarmament Briefs, S 1.117/4

Disarmament Document Series, S 1.117/3, AC 1.11

Disarmament Series, S 1.117/2

Documents on **Disarmament**, AC 1.11/2, S 1.117

Report on U.S. Government Research and Studies in the Field of Arms Control and **Disarmament** Matters, AC 1.14

Research Reports Arms Control and **Disarmament** Agency, AC 1.15

Review of Arms Control and **Disarmament** Activities, Y 4.Ar 5/2-16

T.I.D.C. Projects on German Industrial Economic **Disarmament**, Pr 32.5813

U.S. Arms Control and **Disarmament** Agency, Annual Report, Y 4.F 76/1-16

Disaster

Disaster Information, FEM 1.9, HH 12.9

Disaster Preparedness Report, C 55.127

Disaster Response and Recovery, FEM 1.211

Natural **Disaster** Survey Reports, C 55.20

Disbursements

Receipts and **Disbursements** of Government Consolidated into Bureau of Accounts, Fiscal Service in Treasury Department by President's Reorganization Plan no. 3, T 9.11

Statement of Balances, Appropriations, and **Disbursements**, T 9.7

U.S. House of Representatives, Detailed Statement of **Disbursements**, Y 4.H 81/3:D 63

Disc

Instructional **Disc** Recordings, LC 19.11/3-2

Discharge

Annual Peak **Discharge** at Selected Gaging Stations in Pacific Northwest, I 19.45/3

Average Monthly **Discharge** for 15-year Base Period at Selected Gaging Stations and Change of Storage in Certain Lakes and Reservoirs in Pacific Northwest, I 19.45/3-2

Current **Discharge** at Selected Stations in the Pacific Northwest, I 19.45, I 19.47/2

Monthly Mean **Discharge** at Selected Gaging Stations and Change of Storage in Certain Lakes and Reservoirs in Columbia River Basin, I 19.47

National Hospital **Discharge** Survey: Annual Summary, HE 20.6209/7

National Hospital **Discharge** Survey, HE 20.6209/7-2

Tabulated Results of **Discharge** Measurements, W 31.6

Discharged

Detailed Diagnoses and Surgical Procedures for Patients **Discharged** from Short-Stay Hospitals, HE 20.6222

Discharges

Annual Maximum, Minimum, and Mean **Discharges** of Mississippi River and Its Outlets and Tributaries, D 103.309/2

Stages and **Discharges** of Mississippi River and Tributaries and Other Watersheds in the New Orleans District, D 103.45/4

Stages and **Discharges** of Mississippi River and Tributaries in the Memphis District, D 103.45/2

Stages and **Discharges** of Mississippi River and Tributaries in the St. Louis District, D 103.45/3

Stages and **Discharges** of Mississippi River and Tributaries in the Vicksburg District, D 103.45

Stages and **Discharges**, Mississippi River and its Outlets and Tributaries, W 31.5, M 110.207, D 103.309

Disciplinary

Quarterly Report **Disciplinary** and Related Actions, T 22.2/15:5528

Discipline

Military **Discipline**, Courtesies, and Customs of Service, W 3.50/12

Rules and Regulations for Government and **Discipline** of United States Penitentiaries, J 1.16

Disclosure

Administration on Welfare and Pension Plans **Disclosure** Act, L 1.55

Combined Federal/State **Disclosure** Directory, Y 3.El 2/3:14-2

HMDA **Disclosure** Reports, FR 1.63/55

Home Mortgage **Disclosure** Act Data (State), FR 1.63

Manual of Regulations and Instructions Relating to the **Disclosure** of Federal Campaign Funds for Candidates for the Office of President or Vice President of the United States and . . . Candidates, GA 1.14:C 15

Summary of Operations, Labor-Management Reporting and **Disclosure** Act, L 1.51

Technical **Disclosure** Bulletin, D 210.3/2

Discontinuances

Applications and Case **Discontinuances** for AFDC, HE 3.60/3

Discontinued

Applications, Cases Approved, and Cases **Discontinued** for Public Assistance, HE 17.641

Inactive or **Discontinued** Items from the 1950 Revision of the Classified List, GP 3.24, GP 3.24/2

Project Label, Alphabetical Listings by Drug Labeler of **Discontinued** Products, J 24.24/3

Discontinuing

Reasons for **Discontinuing** Money Payments to Public Assistance Cases, HE 17.613/2

Discount

Federal Hotel/Motel **Discount** Directory, GS 8.10/2, GS 2.21/2

Discounts

Average Premiums and **Discounts** for CCC Settlement Purposes for Offers Received, A 88.11/21

Monthly Report on Loans and **Discounts**, FCA 1.12

Quarterly Report on Loans and **Discounts**, A 71.12

Discoveries

Epoch **Discoveries** of the Past, Scientific Radio Scripts, I 16.66

Discovery

Discovery: Faculty Publications and Presentations, Fiscal Year (date), D 305.18

Discretionary

OJJDP **Discretionary** Program Announcement, J 32.22

Discriminant

Audit **Discriminant** Function Reporting System, T 22.52

Discriminaton

Age **Discriminaton** in Employment Act of 1967, Reports Covering Activities Under the Act During (year), L 36.11

Discussion

A.I.D. **Discussion** Papers, S 18.30/2

BJS **Discussion** Paper, J 29.26

Community **Discussion** Papers, A 55.50

Discussion, A 43.9

Discussion Group Topics, A 1.46

Discussion Guide, Tape-Recorded Department of State Briefings, S 1.40/4

Discussion Guides {to films}, S 1.40/4-2

Discussion Paper Series, T 1.47

Discussion Papers, S 18.52/2

Discussion Series, A 1.66, A 43.10, A 43.11, A 43.12, A 43.13

Discussion Statements, A 55.29

Discussion {leaflets}, A 36.146

Economic **Discussion** Papers, L 29.15

Social Seminar **Discussion** Guides, HE 20.2408/2

Staff **Discussion** Paper (series), E 2.23

Discussions

State Department, International Law (texts, precedents and **discussions** published by the State Department), S 7.14

Disease

Abstracts of Current Literature on Venereal **Disease**, FS 2.11/2

Agency for Toxic Substances and **Disease** Biennial Report, HE 20.7901

Agency for Toxic Substances and **Disease** Registry Annual Report, HE 20.7901/2, HE 20.501/2

Annual Workshop of the Asthma and Allergic **Disease** Centers, HE 20.3261

Bang's **Disease** Work; Statement of Indemnity Claims and Averages in Cooperative, A 77.211

Chronic **Disease** Notes & Reports, HE 20.7617

CLVD (Current Literature on Venereal **Disease**) Abstracts and Bibliography, HE 20.7311

Communicable **Disease** Summary, FS 2.117

Cotton, Truck, and Forage Crop **Disease** Circulars, A 19.17

Current Literature on Venereal **Disease**, FS 2.11/2, HE 20.2311

Directory of Animal **Disease** Diagnostic Laboratories, A 101.2:D 63/2, A 101.13

Disease Control Services Activities, A 77.212/9

End-Stage Renal **Disease** Medical Information System Facility Reports, HE 22.9

End-Stage Renal **Disease** Program Medical Information System, Facility Survey Tables (year), HE 22.9/3

End-Stage Renal **Disease** Program, Annual Report to Congress, HE 22.9/2

Epidemiology and **Disease** Control Study Section, HE 20.3001/2:Ep 4/2

Extension Pathologist; News Letter for Extension Workers Interested in Plant **Disease** Control, A 43.20

Fish **Disease** Leaflets, I 49.28/3

Foodborne and Waterborne **Disease** Outbreaks, Annual Summary, HE 20.7011/13

Forest Insect and **Disease** Conditions, A 13.52/2

Forest Insect and **Disease** Conditions in the Northern Region, A 13.52/7

Forest Insect and **Disease** Conditions in the Pacific Northwest, A 13.52/6

Forest Insect and **Disease** Conditions in the Rocky Mountain Region, A 13.52/13

Forest Insect and **Disease** Conditions in the Southwest, A 13.52/11

Forest Insect and **Disease** Conditions, Intermountain Region, A 13.52/12

Forest Insect and **Disease** Leaflets, A 13.52

Forest Insect and **Disease** Management (series), A 13.93/3, A 13.106

Forest Insect and **Disease** Management/Evaluation Reports, A 13.93

Forest Insect and **Disease** Management/Survey Reports, A 13.93/2

Forest Inspection and **Disease** Management (series), A 13.93/3

Homestudy Course; Communicable **Disease** Control, HE 20.7710

Homestudy Course; Vectorborne **Disease** Control (series), HE 20.7021/7-2

Homestudy Courses; Communicable **Disease** Control, HE 20.7021/2

Homestudy Courses; Foodborne **Disease** Control, HE 20.7021/6

Homestudy Courses; Vectorborne **Disease** Control, HE 20.7021/7

Homestudy Courses; Waterborne **Disease** Control, HE 20.7021/4

Infectious **Disease** Committee, HE 20.3001/2:In 3

Infectious **Disease** Research Series, HE 20.3262/2

Influenza-Respiratory **Disease** Surveillance, Reports, HE 20.2309/10

Kidney **Disease** and Nephrology Index, HE 20.3318

National Center for Chronic **Disease** Prevention and Health Promotion (NCCDPHP), HE 20.7039, HE 20.7616

National Institutes of Health **Disease** Prevention Report, HE 20.3058

NINCDS Huntington's **Disease** Research Program, HE 20.3502:H 92/2

NINCDS Parkinson's **Disease** Research Program, HE 20.3502:P 22

Outbreaks of **Disease** Caused by Milk and Milk Products as Reported by Health Authorities as having Occurred in U.S., T 27.42

Parkinson's **Disease** and Related Disorders, Citations from the Literature, HE 20.3511

Parkinson's **Disease** and Related Disorders, International Directory of Scientists, HE 20.3511/2

Parkinson's **Disease** and Related Disorders: Cumulative Bibliography, HE 20.3511/3

Pathologist; News Letter for Extension Workers Interested in Plant **Disease** Control, A 43.20

Patients in Hospitals for Mental **Disease**, C 3.59/2

Plant **Disease** Bulletins, A 19.18

Plant **Disease** Posters, A 77.517

Plant **Disease** Reporter Supplements, A 77.512

Plant **Disease** Reporter, A 77.511, A 106.21

Plant **Disease** Survey Special Publications, A 77.520

Plant **Disease**, Decay, Etc., Control Activities of Department of Agriculture, Reports, A 1.90

Proceedings Annual Western International Forest **Disease** Work Conference, A 13.69/13

Publications Communicable **Disease** Center, FS 2.60/2

Report of the Advisory Panel on Alzheimer's **Disease**, HE 20.8024

Renal **Disease** and Hypertension, Proceedings, Annual Conference, HE 20.5412

Rh Hemolytic **Disease** Surveillance, HE 20.7011/19

Rickettsial **Disease** Surveillance, HE 20.7011/27

Self-Study Course 3014-G, Waterborne **Disease** Control Manuals, HE 20.7021/4-2

Sexually Transmitted **Disease** Statistics, HE 20.7309

Sexually Transmitted **Disease** Surveillance, HE 20.7309/2

Sickle Cell **Disease** Advisory Committee, HE 20.3001/2:Si 1

Southeastern Forest Insect and **Disease** Newsletters, A 13.63/14

Statement of Indemnity Claims and Averages in Cooperative Bang's **Disease** Work, A 4.29

Summary of Bang's **Disease** Control Program Conducted by Bureau of Animal Industry in Cooperation with Various States, A 4.23

Summary of Bang's **Disease** Work in Cooperation with Various States, A 4.21

Summary of Brucellosis (Bang's **Disease**) Control Program Conducted by Bureau of Animal Industry in Cooperation with Various States, A 77.213

Supplements to Veneral **Disease** Information Bulletin, FS 2.10

Tropical **Disease** Reports, Pr 32.413/2

United States Army Medical Research Institute of Infectious **Disease**: Annual Progress Report, D 104.27

Veneral **Disease** Bulletins, T 27.20, FS 2.11

Veneral **Disease** Reports, T 27.26, FS 2.9

Water-Related **Disease** Outbreaks Surveillance, HE 20.7011/33

Diseases

Allergic **Diseases** Research (series), HE 20.3262

Arthritis and Rheumatic **Diseases** Abstracts, HE 20.3312

Blood **Diseases** and Resources Advisory Committee, HE 20.3001/2:B 62

Chronic **Diseases** Notes and Report, HE 20.7009/6

Digestive **Diseases**, HE 20.3320/2-3

Digestive **Diseases** Clearinghouse Fact Sheets, HE 20.3323

Digestive **Diseases** Coordinating Committee, HE 20.3001/2:D 56

Emerging Infectious **Diseases**, HE 20.7009/7, HE 20.7817

Forage Crop Gazette, News Letter for Staff Workers, Division of Forage Crops and **Diseases**, A 77.509

Foreign Animal **Diseases** Report, A 101.17

Forest Insects and **Diseases** Group Technical Publications, A 13.93/4

Fruit and Vegetable Crops and **Diseases** Division, Semi-monthly News Letters, A 77.510

Genetic Bases for Resistance to Avian **Diseases**, Northeastern States Regional Project, A 94.15

Highlights of Progress in Research on Oral **Diseases**, FS 2.22/23

Highlights of Research Progress in Allergy and Infectious **Diseases**, FS 2.22/17

Highlights of Research Progress in Arthritis and Metabolic **Diseases**, FS 2.22/21

ICD.9.CM International Classification of **Diseases**, HE 22.41/2

Interagency Technical Committee on Heart, Blood Vessel, Lung, and Blood **Diseases**; and Blood Resources, HE 20.3001/2:H 35

International Classification of **Diseases**, 9th Revision, Clinical Modification, HE 22.41

Medical Statistics, Navy, Statistical Report of the Surgeon General, Navy, Occurrence of **Diseases** and Injuries in the Navy for Fiscal Year (date), D 206.11

Microbiology and Infectious **Diseases** Program, Annual Report, HE 20.3263

MMWR Surveillance Summaries from the Center for Infectious **Diseases**, HE 20.7009/2-3

National Kidney and Urologic **Diseases** Information Clearinghouse Factsheet HE 20.3323/3

Neurological **Diseases** and Stroke Science Information Program Advisory Committee, HE 20.3001/2:N 39/6

Neurotropic Viral **Diseases** Surveillance, HE 20.7011/5

NIAMDD Research Advances (on various **diseases**), HE 20.3320

Periodontal **Diseases** Advisory Committee, HE 20.3001/2:P 41

Poultry **Diseases** Activities Report, A 77.15:91-54

Progress Report President's Medical Programs for Heart Disease, Cancer, and Stroke and Related **Diseases**, FS 2.313

Quarterly Bibliography of Major Tropical **Diseases**, HE 20.3614/4

Sexually Transmitted **Diseases**, Abstracts and Bibliographies, HE 20.7311

Statistics of **Diseases** and Injuries in Navy, N 10.15, M 203.10

Task Force on Environmental Cancer and Heart and Lung **Diseases**: Annual Report to Congress, EP 1.82

Transactions of Research Conferences in Pulmonary **Diseases**, VA 1.40/2

Disinfectants

Disinfectants, EP 5.11/5

Disk

HRCD, Human Resources Compact **Disk**, PM 1.59/2

Diskette

Diskette Series, HE 20.6209/4-4

Diskettes

Natural Gas Annual (**Diskettes**), E 3.11/2-2

Nonresidential Buildings Energy Consumption Survey (NBECS) (**Diskettes**), E 3.43/2-3

Residential Buildings Energy Consumption Survey. (**Diskettes**), E 3.43/5

Disorders

Arthritis, Rheumatic Diseases, and Related **Disorders**, HE 20.3320/2

Biblio-Profile on Human Communication and Its **Disorders** a Capsule State-of-the-art Report and Bibliography, HE 20.3513/2

Communicative **Disorders** Review Committee, HE 20.3001/2:C 73/3

Highlights of Progress in Research on Neurologic **Disorders**, FS 2.22/12

Index of Federally Supported Programs in Heart, Blood Vessel, Lung, and Blood **Disorders**, HE 20.3013/2-3

Neurological **Disorders** Program-Project Review B Committee, HE 20.3001/2:N 39/4

NINCDS Neuromuscular **Disorders** Research Program, HE 20.3502:N 39/3

Report of the Panel on Pain to the National Advisory Neurological and Communicative **Disorders** and Stroke Council, HE 20.3517

Dispatch

Forest-Gram South, **Dispatch** of Current Technical Information for Direct Use by Practicing Forest Resource Manager in the South, A 13.89

U.S. Department of State **Dispatch**, S 1.3/5

Dispensary

Anemia **Dispensary** Service, W 75.5

Dispensing

Measuring and **Dispensing** Pumps, Gasoline, Oil, etc. Shipments of, C 3.90

Shipments of Measuring and **Dispensing** Pumps, Gasoline, Oil, etc., C 3.90

Displacement

General **Displacement** Notices, CS 1.49

Display

Display Plotting Charts, D 5.349, D 5.349/2, D 5.349/3, D 5.349/4

Display Posters, Y 3.F 73:26

Thesaurus of ERIC Descriptors Alphabetical **Display**, ED 1.310/3-2

Thesaurus of ERIC Descriptors Rotated **Display**, ED 1.310/3-4

Disposal

Acquisitions and **Disposal** of CCC Price-Support Inventory, A 82.78

Defense Property **Disposal** Service, D 7.6/13

Navy Property Redistribution and **Disposal** Regulations, D 201.6/9

Offerings and Sales of Office of Personal Property **Disposal**, Y 3.W 19/8:12

Report to Congress on Foreign Surplus **Disposal**, S 1.47

Requirement for Individual Water-Supply and Sewage-**Disposal** Systems (by States), NHA 2.17, HH 2.11

Studies on Household Sewage **Disposal** System, FS 2.56

Water Supply and Waste **Disposal** Series, TD 2.32

Disposed

Surplus Property **Disposed** of to Public Health and Educational Institutions, FS 1.15

Disposition

Chickens and Eggs, Farm Production, **Disposition**, Cash Receipts and Gross Income, Chickens on Farms, Commercial Broilers, by States, A 88.15/18

Chickens and Eggs, Farm Production, **Disposition**, Cash Receipts and Gross Income, A 9.9/3

Disposition of Federal Records, GS 4.6/2

Disposition of Public Assistance Cases Involving Question of Fraud, HE 3.63

Farm Production, **Disposition**, Cash Receipts and Gross Income, Turkeys, A 88.15/16, A 105.35/2

Field and Seed Crops, Farm Production, Farm **Disposition**, Value, by States, A 88.30/4

Field Crops, Production, **Disposition**, Value, A 105.9/4

Meat Animals, Farm Production, **Disposition**, and Income by States, A 88.17/3

Meat Animals, Production, **Disposition**, and Income, A 105.23/6

Milk Production, **Disposition**, and Income, A 92.10/2, A 105.17/5

Milk, Farm Production, **Disposition**, and Income, A 88.14/8

Poultry Production, **Disposition** and Income, A 105.12/6

Poultry Production, **Disposition** and Income, Final Estimates, A 1.34/5

Production, Farm **Disposition**, and Value of Principal Fruits and Tree Nuts, A 88.12/16

Reasons for **Disposition** of Applicants Other Than by Approval, HE 17.643

Receipts and **Disposition** of Livestock at 66 Public Markets, A 82.41

Receipts and **Disposition** of Livestock at Public Markets, A 88.16

Receipts and **Disposition** of Livestock at Public Stockyards, A 36.203

Report on **Disposition** of Public Assistance Cases Involving Questions of Fraud, Fiscal Year, HE 17.642

Roll of Honor, Supplemental Statement of **Disposition** of Bodies of Deceased Union Soldiers and Prisoners of War Removed to National Cemeteries in Southern and Western United States, W 39.8

Dispositions

Applications and Case **Dispositions** for Public Assistance, HE 3.60/3, HE 17.613/3

Classified Index of **Dispositions** of ULP {Unfair Labor Practices} Charges by the General Counsel of the Federal Labor Relations Authority, Y 3.F 31/21-3:11

Classified Index of **Dispositions** of ULP {Unfair Labor Practices} Charges by the General Counsel of the National Labor Relations Board, LR 1.8/8

Dispute

Alternative **Dispute** Resolution Series, D 103.57/13

Disputes

Compilation . . . , Laws {on} **Disputes** Between Carriers and Employers and Subordinate Officials Under Labor Board, Eight-hour Laws, Employers' Liability Laws, Labor and Child Labor Laws, Y 1.2:Em 7/6

Disqualified

Roster of **Disqualified** Attorneys, I 24.12

Disseminating

FIPSE, **Disseminating** Proven Reforms, ED 1.23/11

Dissemination

Dissemination of Research Results {on Poultry and Egg Marketing Subjects}, A 82.75, A 88.15/8

Dissertations

American Doctoral **Dissertations** on the Arab Worlds, LC 1.12/2:Ar 1

Dissertations and Theses Relating to Personnel Administration, CS 1.61/2

Distance

Distance Circulars, W 36.5

Distances

Distances Between Ports, D 203.22:151

Elevations and **Distances**, I 19.2:El 3/2

Official Table of **Distances**, W 36.9

Table of **Distances** Between Ports, D 203.22:151

Distillate

Distillate Oil Burners, C 3.76

Distillate Watch, E 3.13/5

Distilled

Alcohol and Tobacco Summary Statistics, **Distilled** Spirits, Wine, Beer, Tobacco, Enforcement Taxes, Fiscal Year, T 70.9

Distilled Spirits, T 70.9/3

Distilled Spirits

Monthly Statistical Release; **Distilled Spirits**, T 70.9/3

Distillers

Distillers' Dried Grain Production, A 88.18/7, A 82.59/4

Distillers' Dried Grains, United States, Production by Kinds by Months, A 88.18/7-2

Distinguished

President's Awards for **Distinguished** Federal Civilian Service, CS 1.64

Distinquished Design Awards, D 103.67

Distributed

Federal Emergency Relief Administration Grants **Distributed** According to Programs and Periods for which Grants were Made, Y 3.F 31/5:33

Motion Pictures **Distributed** by Photographic Section, I 43.9

Distribution

Bituminous Coal and Lignite **Distribution**, I 28.33/2 E 3.11/7

Breed **Distribution** of NPIP Participating Flocks by States and Divisions, A 77.15:44-2

Canned Fruits and Vegetables, Production and Wholesale **Distribution**, C 3.168

Carload . . ., Mileage Block **Distribution**, Traffic and Revenue by Commodity Class, Territorial Movement, and Type of Rate, Products of Agriculture, 1 Percent Sample of Terminations in Statement MB-1, IC 1.23/2

Carload . . ., Mileage Block **Distribution**, Traffic and Revenue by Commodity Class, Territorial Movement, and Type of Rate, Animals and Products, 1 Percent Sample of Terminations in Statement MB-2, IC 1.23/3

Carload . . ., Mileage Block **Distribution**, Traffic and Revenue by Commodity Class, Territorial Movement, and Type of Rate, Products of Mines, 1 Percent Sample of Terminations in Statement MB-3, IC 1.283/4

Carload . . ., Mileage Block Distribution, Traffic and Revenue by Commodity Class, Territorial Movement, and Type of Rate, Products of Forests, 1 Percent Sample of Terminations in Statement MB-4, IC 1.23/5

Carload . . ., Mileage Block **Distribution**, Traffic and Revenue by Commodity Class, Territorial Movement, and Type of Rate, Manufacturers and Miscellaneous Forwarder Traffic Terminations Statement MB-5, IC 1.23/6

Carload Waybill Analyses, **Distribution** of Freight Traffic and Revenue Averages by Commodity Groups and Rate Territories, IC 1.20

Carload Waybill Analyses, State by State **Distribution** of Tonnage by Commodity Groups, IC 1.21

Carload Waybill Analyses, Territorial **Distribution**, Traffic and Revenue by Commodity Groups, IC 1.22

Carload Waybill Statistics, **Distribution** of Freight Traffic and Revenue Averages by Commodity Classes, IC 1.23/8

Carload Waybill Statistics, Territorial **Distribution** Traffic and Revenue by Commodity Classes, TD 3.14

Census of **Distribution** Industry Statistics, C 3.245/6

Census of **Distribution**; (By Place Names) Preliminary, C 3.37/17

Census of **Distribution**; Construction Industry, State Series, C 3.37/21

Census of **Distribution**; County Series, Preliminary (by States), C 3.37/20

Census of **Distribution**; **Distribution** of Agricultural Commodities, C 3.37/34

Census of **Distribution**; Hotels, Preliminary Report, C 3.37/36

Census of **Distribution**; Merchandising Series, C 3.37/18

Census of **Distribution**; Preliminary Reports, States Summary Series (by States), C 3.37/19

Census of **Distribution**; Retail **Distribution** (by States), C 3.37/22

Census of **Distribution**; Retail **Distribution** Trade Series, C 3.37/39

Census of **Distribution**; Retail **Distribution**, Special Series, C 3.37/40

Census of **Distribution**; Small City and Rural Trade Series, C 3.37/38

Census of **Distribution**; Wholesale **Distribution**, Special Series, C 3.37/37

Census of **Distribution**; Wholesale **Distribution**, Trade Series, C 3.37/35

Census of **Distribution**; Wholesale Trade Bulletins, State Series, C 3.37/23

Coal **Distribution** Companies in the United States, E 3.11/7-4

Coke **Distribution**, E 3.11/16

Coke **Distribution**, Annual, I 28.30/3

Committee Publications and Policies Governing their **Distribution**, Y 4.Ec 7-10

Commodity Purchases for Domestic **Distribution**, A 82.87

Commodity Purchases for Export **Distribution**, A 82.87/2

Complete Catalog, Cataloging **Distribution** Service, LC 30.27/2

Confectionery Manufacturers' Sales and **Distribution**, C 41.19, C 57.13

Consolidated Abstracts of Technical Reports: General **Distribution**, FAA 2.11/2

Corn (Hominy) Grits for Domestic **Distribution**, A 82.3/4

Corn Meal for Domestic **Distribution**, A 82.3/3

Corn Meal for Export **Distribution**, A 82.3/7

Cotton Production and **Distribution**, Year Ending July 31, C 3.3

Current Developments in Drug **Distribution**, C 18.212

Current Developments in Food **Distribution**, C 18.214

Current **Distribution** Developments in Hardware and Allied Trades, C 18.215

Department Store Trade, United States **Distribution** of Sales by Months, FR 1.24/7, FR 1.24/8

Distribution Cost Studies, C 18.33

Distribution Data Guide, C 41.11

Distribution of Bank Deposits by Counties and Standard Metropolitan Areas, FR 1.11/6

Distribution of Coal Shipments, I 28.24

Distribution of Freight Traffic and Revenue Averages by Commodity Classes, IC 1.23/8:MS-1

Distribution of Pennsylvania Anthracite for Coal Year (date), I 28.50/3

Distribution of Personnel by State and by Selected Locations, D 1.61/5

Distribution of Petroleum Products by Petroleum Administration Districts, IC 1.24

Distribution of Rail Revenue Contribution by Commodity Groups, IC 1 acco.9

Distribution of Sales (Rotoprint), C 3.57

Distribution Orders, ES 3.6/3

Distribution Regulations, ES 3.6/8

Electricity Sales Statistics, **Distribution** of Electricity at TVA Wholesale and Retail Rates, Y 3.T 25:13-2

Farmers' Bulletins (Available for **Distribution**), A 21.9/1

Federal Work Injury Facts, Occupational **Distribution**, Duration and Direct Cost Factors of Work Injuries to Civilian Federal Employees During Calendar Year, L 26.8/2-2

Fish **Distribution** Reports, I 49.69

Geographic **Distribution** of Federal Funds in (States), CSA 1.10

Geographic **Distribution** of Radio Sets and Characteristics of Radio Owners in Countries of the World, IA 1.12/2

Geographic **Distribution** of VA Expenditures, State, County, and Congressional District, VA 1.2/11

Handbook of Card **Distribution**, LC 28.7

Industry Report, Canned Fruits and Vegetables, Production and Wholesale **Distribution**, C 18.234

Information Governing **Distribution** of Government Publications and Price Lists, GP 3.18

MARC **Distribution** Services, LC 30.28

Maturity **Distribution** of Euro-Dollar Deposits in Foreign Branches of U.S. Banks, FR 1.54

Maturity **Distribution** of Outstanding Negotiable Time Certificates of Deposit, FR 1.54/2

Mileage **Distribution** of Carloads for Each Commodity Class by Type of Car, IC 1.23/16:TC-1

MILSTRIP Routing and Identifier and **Distribution** Codes, D 1.87/2

Monthly Coal **Distribution** Report, C 22.23

Monthly List of Publications for Foreign **Distribution**, A 21.6/2

Pennsylvania Anthracite **Distribution**, E 3.11/3-3

Primary Sugar **Distribution** for Week, A 82.72

Prime Contract Awards, Size **Distribution**, D 1.57/3-5

Publications Available for Free **Distribution**, I 27.10

Publications Bureau of Entomology Available for Free **Distribution**, A 9.13

Publications Weather Bureau Available for **Distribution**, A 29.31

Receipts for State Administered Highways, Official **Distribution**, C 37.19

Regional **Distribution** and Types of Stores where Consumers Buy Selected Fresh Fruits, Canned and Frozen Juices, and Dried Fruits, A 36.172

Reports of Special Agent for Purchase and **Distribution** of Seeds, A 24.5

Scheme of City **Distribution**, P 1.18, P 10.9

Schemes of States (for use of publishers in **Distribution** 2d class mail), P 10.10

Seed and Plant Introduction and **Distribution**, A 19.6

Service and Regulatory Announcements, Office of **Distribution**, A 80.118

Solid Fuels **Distribution** Reports, I 28.74

State **Distribution** of Defense Contract Awards, Pr 32.4013

State **Distribution** of Public Employment in (year), C 3.140/2

Studies in Income **Distribution** (series), HE 3.67/2

Supply and **Distribution** of Cotton in United States, C 3.36

Territorial **Distribution** of Carloads for Each Commodity Class by Type of Car, IC 1.23/19:TC-3

Territorial **Distribution**, Traffic and Revenue by Commodity Classes, IC 1.23/18:TD-1

Time **Distribution** Summary, L 7.42

Turkeys in NTIP Flocks and Their **Distribution** by States and Varieties, A 77.15:44-11

U.S. Rice **Distribution** Patterns, A 93.51

Weight **Distribution** of Carloads for Each Commodity Class by Type of Car, IC 1.23/16:TC-2

Wheat Flour for Domestic **Distribution**, A 82.3/6

Wheat Flour for Export **Distribution**, A 82.3/9

Worldwide **Distribution** of Radio Receiver Sets, IA 1.12

Worldwide Manpower **Distribution** by Geographical Area, D 1.61/3

Distributions

Monthly Electric Utility Sales and Revenue Report with State **Distributions**, E 3.11/17-14

Distributive

Vocational Instructional Materials for Marketing and **Distributive** Education, ED 1.17/3

Distributors

Milk **Distributors**, Sales and Costs, A 88.14/9, A 93.13/2

Municipal and Cooperative **Distributors** of TVA Power, (date) Operations, Y 3.T 25:1-3

Registered **Distributors** under Bituminous Coal Act of 1973 {lists}, I 46.14

Statistics, **Distributors** of TVA Power Fiscal Years, Y 3.T 25:1-18

Summary of Financial Statements and Sales Statistics, **Distributors** of TVA **Power**, Y 3.T 25:1-16

District

California Desert **District** Planning Newsletter, I 53.36

Central Business **District** Statistics Bulletin CBD (series), C 3.202/13

Congressional **District** Atlas, C 3.62/5, C 56.213/2

Congressional **District** Data Book, C 3.134/2:C 76, C 56.243/2:C 76

Congressional **District** Data, CDD (series), C 3.134/4, C 56.213

CONUS Army Installations/Activities by Congressional **District**, D 101.99

Crop Report, by Federal Reserve **District**, FR 1.37

District Director's Responsibility and Authority for CID Activity, T 22.60

District Office Releases, C 18.64

District Pamphlets, D 103.43/3

District Reserve Electors for Member Banks in District, RB 1.6

Map of **District** Infected with Splenetic Fever, A 4.6

Papers in Re in **District** Courts, J 1.75

Program of Water Resources Division, Texas **District**, and Summary of District Activities, Fiscal Year, I 19.55/2

Program of Water Resources Division, Texas District, and Summary of **District** Activities, Fiscal Year, I 19.55/2

Recruiting Circulars, 4th Civil Service **District**, CS 1.35

Report of the U.S. Attorney General for the **District** of (area) to the Attorney General, J 31.9

Report of the United States Attorney for the **District** of Columbia, J 1.1/4

Rules of Civil Procedure for **District** Courts in U.S., Ju 6.9/3

Rules of Civil Procedure for the United States **District** Courts, Y 4.J 89/1-11

Rules of Criminal Procedure for the United States **District** Courts, Y 4.J 89/1-12

Schedules of Payments to Holders of Cotton Options and Participation Trust Certificates by Congressional **District** of States, A 55.57

Soil and Water Conservation **District** Resources Inventories (series), A 57.38/2

Telephone Directory Internal Revenue Service, Salt Lake City **District**, T 22.48/3

Telephone Directory Republic 7500, Executive 6300, **District** 0525, GS 6.7

Telephone Directory Salt Lake City **District**, T 22.48/3

U.S. Army Engineer **District**, Los Angeles: Reports (numbered), D 103.59

U.S. Exports of Petroleum and Petroleum Products of Domestic Origin, Commodity by Customs **District**, C 3.164:527

U.S. Waterborne Foreign Trade, Trade Area by U.S. Coastal **District**, C 3.164:600

United States Airborne Foreign Trade, Customs **District** by Continent, C 3.164:986

United States **District** Courts Sentences Imposed Chart, Ju 10.18

United States Foreign Trade, Trade by Customs **District**, C 3.164:970

District Courts

Grand and Petit Juror Service in U.S. **District Courts**, Ju 10.13

Juror Utilization in United States **District Courts**, Ju 10.13

District of Columbia

Annual Report of Sinking Fund and Funded Debt of **District of Columbia**, for Fiscal Year, T 40.6

Annual Reports on Street Railroads in **District of Columbia**, IC 1 eler.5

Budget of United States Government **District of Columbia**, PrEx 2.8/4

District of Columbia Code, Y 4.J 89/1:D 63/24

District of Columbia National Guard: Annual Report, D 12.1/2

Earnings, Expenses and Dividends of Active Banks in **District of Columbia**, Abstract, T 12.15

Officers of Army, Their Families and Families of Deceased Officers, Residing in or Near **District of Columbia**, W 1.11

Officers of Navy and Marine Corps in **District of Columbia**, N 1.20

Records and Briefs in Circuit Courts of Appeals and Court of Appeals, **District of Columbia**, J 1.19/5

Uniform System of Accounts for Gas Corporations and Electric Corporations in the **District of Columbia**, IC 1 gas.5

Water Resources Development in **District of Columbia**, D 103.35/51

District V

District V Petroleum Statement, E 3.11/6, I 28.45/3

Districts

Census of Population; Congressional **Districts**, C 3.223/20

Code Classification of U.S. Customs **Districts** and Ports, C 3.150:D

Conservation **Districts**, A 57.2:C 76

Districts

Schedule D. Code Classification of U.S. Customs **Districts** and Ports, C 3.150:D

P.A.D. **Districts** Supply/Demand, E 3.11/6-2, E 3.11/6-3, E 3.11/6-4, I 28.18/6, I 28.18/7,

Rain and Dry Winds, Computed for Different Geographical **Districts**, W 42.12

Relative Cost of Shipbuilding in Various Coastal **Districts** of the United States, Report to Congress, C 39.216/2

Seafaring Wage Rates, Atlantic, Gulf and Pacific **Districts**, C 39.202:W 12

Social and Economic Characteristics of U.S. School **Districts**, HE 19.336

Soil and Water Conservation **Districts**, Status of Organization, by States, Approximate Acreage, and Farms in Organized Districts, A 57.32

Soil Conservation **Districts**, A 76.214, A 80.2009, A 80.508

Status of Compliance, Public School **districts**, 17 Southern and Border States, Reports, FS 5.80, HE 5.80

Supply, Demand, and Stocks of All Oils by P.A.D. **Districts**, I 28.18/7

Weekly Summary of F.O.B. Prices of Fresh Fruits and Vegetables in Representative Shipping **Districts**, A 88.12/2, A 82.53

Ditty

Ports of the World, **Ditty** Box Guide Book Series, N 17.22

Diversions

Report on Flows and **Diversions** at Imperial Dam and All Actions Affecting Coordination Thereof, I 27.42

Divide

Continental **Divide** Trail Study Progress Reports, I 66.19/2

Dividends

Dividends from Wood Research, A 13.27/7-2

Earnings, Expenses and **Dividends** of Active Banks in District of Columbia, Abstract, T 12.15

Sales, Profits, and **Dividends** of Large Corporations, FR 1.40

Statement of Taxes, **Dividends**, Salaries and Wages, Class a and Class B Privately Owned Electric Utilities in U.S., FP 1.22

Division

Civil **Division**, J 1.92

Civil **Division** Telephone Directory, J 1.89/2

Division Memorandums, GP 3.20

Division of Cancer Biology and Diagnosis: Annual Report, HE 20.3151/6

Division of Cancer Cause and Prevention: Annual Report, HE 20.3151/3

Division of Cancer Control and Rehabilitation: Annual Report, HE 20.3151/4

Division of Cancer Research Resources and Centers: Annual Report, HE 20.3151/2

Division of Clinical Sciences, Annual Research Directory, HE 20.315/9

Livestock & Seed **Division**, A 88.61

Operation **Division** Circulars, A 1.45

Personnel Management Training **Division** I, PM 1.28/2

Planning **Division** Process and Procedures, D 301.61

Planning **Division**, Instruction and Procedure, GP 1.23/3

Polymer Science and Standards **Division**, Annual Report, C 13.1/7

Population **Division** Working Paper Series, C 3.223/26

Posters Asian **Division**, LC 17.10

Posters Wage and Hour **Division**, L 36.210

Price Lists **Division** of Public Documents, GP 3.9

Procurement **Division** Bulletins, T 58.15

Productivity and Technological Development **Division** Publications, L 2.19

Program and Services, Report of Educational Materials Laboratory, **Division** of International Studies and Services, FS 5.214:14031, HE 5.214:14031

Program of Water Resources **Division**, Texas District, and Summary of District Activities, Fiscal Year, I 19.55/2

Progress Report Air Service, Engineering **Division**, W 87.14

Proposed Multi-Year Operating Plan, Statistics of Income **Division**, T 22.2/3, T 22.2/10

Protection Services **Division** {Reports}, Pr 32.4427

Publications Air Force Ballistic Missile **Division**, D 301.68

Publications Historical **Division**, D 101.42/2

Publications Land Economics **Division**, Water Utilization Section, A 36.149

Publications Microanalytical **Division**, A 46.17, FS 7.16

Publications Patents of **Division** of Insecticide Investigations, List of, A 77.318

Radiation and Organisms **Division**, Reports, SI 1.1/a5

Registers of Papers in the Manuscript **Division** of the Library of Congress, LC 4.10

Regulations, Rules and Instructions Customs **Division**, T 17.5

Report of the **Division** of Biological Effects, HE 20.4114/2

Report of the **Division** of Cancer Treatment, NCI, HE 20.3172

Reports of **Division** of Research, C 31.131

Research and Development **Division** Reports, D 212.12

Research **Division** Maps, C 27.9/13

Research **Divison**, Quarterly Progress Report, D 103.33/9

Research **Division** Reports Bureau of Apprenticeship and Training, L 23.19

Research **Division** Reports National Endowment for the Arts, NF 2.12

Safety **Division** Bulletins, Y 3.Em 3:8

Space Systems **Division**: Technical Documentary Report TDR (series), D 301.71

Speaking **Division** Bulletins, Y 3.P 96/3:10

Special Bulletins Bureau of Foreign and Domestic Commerce, Textile **Division**, C 18.127

Special Bulletins Manufacturers **Division**, C 3.7

Special Reports Earth Sciences **Division**, D 106.17/2

Special Series Bureau of Foreign and Domestic Commerce, Paper **Division**, C 18.146

Special Series Military Intelligence **Division**, W 100.7

Special Series Reports of **Division** of Research, C 31.131/2

Summary of Activities, Meat Inspection **Division**, A 88.40/2:20

Surveillance and Analysis **Division**, Region 8, Denver Colo., Technical Support Branch: SA/TSB-1- (series), EP 1.51/3

Surveillance and Analysis **Division**, Region 8: Technical Investigations Branch, SA/TIB-(series), EP 1.51/4

Surveillance and Analysis **Division**, Region 9, San Francisco, California: Technical Reports, EP 1.51

Surveillance and Analysis **Division**, Region 10: Working Papers, EP 1.51/6

Systems Engineering Group, Research and Technology **Division**, Air Force Systems Command, Wright-Patterson Air Force Base, Ohio, Technical Documentary Report No. SEG TDR, D 301.45/48

Systems Maintenance **Division** Instructions, FAA 1.6/7

Technical Activities, Surface Science **Division**, C 13.71

Technical **Division** Report, TAS (series), C 41.26

Technical **Division** Reports, C 35.13

Technical Memorandum National Bureau of Standards, Applied Mathematics **Division**, C 13.39

Technical Notes Department of the Air Force Aeronautical Systems **Division**, D 301.45/26

Technical Notes Department of the Air Force Command and Control Development **Division**, D 301.45/24

10th Mountain **Division** (LI) and Fort Drum: Pamphlets (series), D 101.22/23

Training Circulars War Plans **Division**, W 26.11

U.S. Army Natick Laboratories, Food **Division**, Natick, Mass. Technical Report FD-, D 106.20

Urban Studies **Division** Bulletins, NHA 1.7

Veterinary Biologics **Division** Notices, A 77.226/3

Vocational **Division** Leaflets, FS 5.129

Vocational **Division** {miscellaneous} Circulars, FS 5.127

Weekly Summary (Press **Division**), A 107.17

Divisional

Divisional Memorandum, Y 3.F 31/11:28

Divisions

Roster of Organizaed Militia of United States, by **Divisions**, Brigades, Regiments, Companies, and other Organizations, with their Stations, W 70.5

State Regulatory Commissions and Fuel Tax **Divisions**, IC 1.3/2-2

U.S. **Divisional** and Station Climatic Data and Normals, C 55.281/2-3

Water Resources **Divisions** Bulletin of Training, I 19.3/4

Divorce

Instruction Manual: Classification and Coding Instructions for **Divorce** Records, HE 20.6208/10

Marriage and **Divorce**, Annual Reports, C 3.46

Public Use Data Tape Documentation **Divorce** Data, Detail, HE 20.6226/4

Where to Write for **Divorce** Records, FS 2.102:D 64

Divorce Laws

Divorce Laws as of (date), L 13.6/4, L 36.113/2

Dixie

Dixie Digest, D 214.23/2

Dixon

United States Coast Pilot, Pacific Coast, Alaska, pt. 1, **Dixon** Entrance to Yakutat Bay, T 11.7/2

Dixon Entrance

Pacific Coast, Alaska, **Dixon Entrance** to Cape Spencer, C 55.422:8

DLAPS

DLAPS Publications, D 7.41

DLIS

Defense Logistics Information System (**DLIS**) Procedures Manual, D 7.6/19

DLMS

DLMS Handbooks (series), L 1.7/2-2

DLMS Manual (series), L 1.7/2-3

DLSC

DLSC Line, D 7.33/3

DM

Handbooks, **DM**- (series), P 1.31/11

DM&S

DM&S ADP Plan, VA 1.77/2

DMA

VA-**DMA**-IS (series), VA 1.53

DMI

DMI Analytic Studies (series), HE 20.6109/2

DMI Health Manpower Information Exchange Reports, HE 20.6109

DMI Reports, HE 20.3114

DMRE

DMRE (series), FS 2.314

DMS

DMS, C 40.6/6

DMS Orders, C 41.6/4-2

DNA

Catalog of Cell Cultures and **DNA** Samples, HE 20.3464

Recombinant **DNA** Advisory Committee, Minutes of Meeting, HE 20.3043/2

Recombinant **DNA** Research (series), HE 20.3043

Recombinant **DNA** Technical Bulletin, HE 20.3460, HE 20.3264

Technical Reports, **DNA**-TR- (series), D 15.13

DNFSB

DNFSB Site Representatives Weekly Activities Reports, Y 3.D 36/3:11

DNFSB Staff Issue Reports, Y 3.D 36/3:12

Recommendations of the **DNFSB**, Y 3.D 36/3:10

Technical Report **DNFSB/TECH**- (series), Y 3.D 36/3:9

DoC

Directory of **DoC** Staff Memberships on Outside Standards Committees, C 13.69/3

Dock

Casualities and Injuries among Shipyard and **Dock** Workers, L 16.37

Docket

Commission Instructions in **Docket** Cases, CC 1.33/2

Docket of Cases Pending in Court of Claims, General Jurisdiction, Ju 3.12

Docket Sheet, Ju 6.12

Formal **Docket** Decisions, FMC 1.10/2

P. and S. **Docket**, Monthly Report of Action Stockyards Act, A 88.16/5

P. and S. **Docket**, Monthly Report of Action Taken on Cases Arising Under Packers and Stockyards Act, A 82.14

SEC **Docket**, SE 1.29

Table of Cases on Formal **Docket** of ICC Not Disposed of in Printed Reports, IC 1.6/8

Docket Cases

Action in **Docket Cases**, Reports, CC 1.33

Dockets

Dockets {Circuit Court of Appeals}, FT 1.23

Dockets, Preliminary, C 31.211/2

Postal Rate Hearings **Dockets**, Y 3.P 84/4:9

Preliminary **Dockets**, C 31.211/2

Valuation **Dockets**, IC 1 val.7/a

Docks

Index of Bureau of Yards and **Docks** Publications, D 209.15

Standard Specifications Bureau of Yards and **Docks**, N 21.10

Technical Digest Bureau of Yards and **Docks**, M 205.8

Doctoral

American **Doctoral** Dissertations on the Arab Worlds, LC 1.12/2:Ar 1

Energy-Related **Doctoral** Scientists and Engineers in the United States, E 1.21

Doctorates

Science and Engineering **Doctorates**, NS 1.44

Doctrine

Doctrine Notes, D 207.416

Marine Corps **Doctrine** Manuals, D 214.9/9

U.S. Army Medical **Doctrine**, Publications, D 104.36

Document

Application **Document** Series, WSDG-AD-(nos.), A 13.87/3

Document (series), T 22.2/15

Document Catalog, GP 3.6

Document Index, GP 3.7

Document Locator, Cross Reference Index to Government Reports, T 1.46

ENTREZ: **Document** Retrieval System, HE 20.3624

NRC Public **Document** Room Collection, Y 3.N 88:62

Supplementary Flight Information **Document**, Caribbean and South America, D 301.51

U.S. Air Force and U.S. Navy Flight Planning **Document**, D 301.52

United States Air Force and Navy Supplementary Flight Information **Document**, Pacific and Far East, D 301.50

Working **Document** Services (various countries), S 18.51

Document Retrieval

Document Retrieval Subject Index, A 67.38

Documentary

Ballistic Systems Division Technical **Documentary** Report BSD-TDR, D 301.45/36

Publications Air University, **Documentary** Research Study, D 301.26/3

Quarterly Index of Technical **Documentary** Reports, D 301.45/15

School of Aerospace Medicine: Technical **Documentary** Report SAM-TDR (series), D 301.26/13-6

Space Systems Division: Technical **Documentary** Report TDR (series), D 301.71

Systems Engineering Group, Research and Technology Division, Air Force Systems Command, Wright-Patterson Air Force Base, Ohio, Technical **Documentary** Report No. SEG TDR, D 301.45/48

Technical **Documentary** Report AAL-TDR-(series), D 301.45/30-2

Technical **Documentary** Report AEDC-TDR-(series), D 301.45/33-2

Technical **Documentary** Report AFSWC-TDR-(series), D 301.45/20-3

Technical **Documentary** Report AL-TDR-(series), D 301.45/45

Technical **Documentary** Report AMRL-TDR-(series), D 301.45/32

Technical **Documentary** Report APL-TDR, D 301.45/51

Technical **Documentary** Report ASD-TDR-(series), D 301.45/26-3

Technical **Documentary** Report ESD-TDR-(series), D 301.45/28-2

Technical **Documentary** Report FDL-TDR, D 301.45/46

Technical **Documentary** Report ML-TDR, D 301.45/47

Technical **Documentary** Report RADC-TDR-(series), D 301.57/3

Technical **Documentary** Report RTD-TDR-(series), D 301.45/34-2

Technical **Documentary** Report SAM-TDR-(series), D 301.26/13-6:1056

Technical **Documentary** Report SEG-TDR, D 301.45/48

Technical **Documentary** Report WADC-TDR-(series), D 301.45/5

United States Air Force History, a Guide to **Documentary** Sources, D 301.6/5:H 62

Documentation
Annual Historical Summary; Defense **Documentation** Center, D 7.1/10
Foreign Area Research **Documentation** Center: Papers Available, S 1.126
Key to Geophysical Records **Documentation**, C 55.219/2
Key to Meteorological Records **Documentation**, C 55.219
Key to Oceanographic Records **Documentation**, C 55.219/3
Model **Documentation** Reports, E 3.26/6
Public Use Data Tape **Documentation** Chest X-Ray, Pulmonary Diffusion, and Tuberculin Test Results Ages 25-74, HE 20.6226/5-2
Public Use Data Tape **Documentation** Detail Natality, HE 20.6226/2
Public Use Data Tape **Documentation** Divorce Data, Detail, HE 20.6226/4
Public Use Data Tape **Documentation** Fetal Deaths Detail Records, HE 20.6226/11
Public Use Data Tape **Documentation** Interviewer's Manual National Interview Survey, HE 20.6226/8
Public Use Data Tape **Documentation** Medical Coding Manual and Short Index, HE 20.6226/9
Public Use Data Tape **Documentation** Medical History, Ages 12-74 Years, HE 20.6226/5
Public Use Data Tape **Documentation** Mortality Cause-of-Death Summary Data, HE 20.6226/6
Public Use Data Tape **Documentation** Mortality Local Area Summary, HE 20.6226/7
Public Use Data Tape **Documentation** Natality Local Area Summary, HE 20.6226/3
Public Use Data Tape **Documentation** Natality State Summary, HE 20.6226
Public Use Data Tape **Documentation** National Health Interview Survey, HE 20.6226/10
Research **Documentation** List, C 3.232
Statistics of Income, Corporation Income Tax Returns **Documentation** Guides, T 22.35/7
Documents
Documents and State Papers, S 1.73
New Books: **Documents** Office, GP 3.17/6
OSHA **Documents** and Files, L 35.26
Posters Superintendent of **Documents**, GP 3.21/2
Price List of Publications of Department of Agriculture for Sale by Superintendent of **Documents**, A 21.8
Price Lists Division of Public **Documents**, GP 3.9
Program Approval **Documents**, Executive Summaries, ER 1.22
Public **Documents** Highlights, GP 3.27
Public **Documents** Highlights, Microfiche Cumulation, GP 3.27/2
Research **Documents**, C 56.248
Selected **Documents**, S 1.131
Selected Readings and **Documents** on Postwar American Defense Policy, D 305.12/2:D 36
Senate Executive Reports and **Documents**, Y 1.Cong.
State **Documents**, C 3.162
Title List of **Documents** Made Publicly Available, Y 3.N 88:21-2
United States LPPSD Technical Information Exchange **Documents**, EP 1.50
United States LPPSD {Low Pollution Power Systems Development} Technical Information Exchange **Documents**, ER 1.16
Weekly Compilation of Presidential **Documents**, GS 4.114, AE 2.109
DoD
Alphabetical List of **DoD** Prime Contractors, D 1.57/3-3
DoD Activity Address Directory (microfiche edition), D 7.6/12
DoD Aeronautical Chart Updating Manual (CHUM), D 5.208
DoD Computer Institute: Course Information, D 5.414/3
DoD Computer Institute: NDU-DODCI Course Catalog, D 5.414/2
DoD Directory of Contract Administration Services Components, D 1.6/12
DoD Document Identifiers, D 1.72

DoD Flight Information Publication (Terminal) High Altitude Instrument Approach Procedures, D 5.318/2
DoD Flight Information Publication (Terminal) Low Altitude Approach Procedures, United States Military Aviation Notice, D 5.318/3
DoD Interchangeability and Substitutability (I&S), Parts I & II, D 7.36
DoD Issuances and Directive, D 1.95/4
DoD Medical Catalog, D 7.37
DoD Pamphlets, D 2.14
Enroute Change Notice, **DoD** Flip Enroute VFR Supplement United States, D 5.318/8-2
Federal Supply Classification Listing of **DoD** Standardization Documents, D 7.14/2
Unclassified **DOD** Issuances on CD-ROM, D 1.95/3
DoDDS
DoDDS Pamphlets (series), D 1.75
DOE
Annual Report of Radiation Exposures for **DOE** and **DOE** Contractor Employees, E 1.42
DOE Feature, NF- (series), E 1.67/2
DOE Information Bridge, E 1.137
DOE Reports Bibliographic Database, E 1.17/2
DOE This Month, E 1.54
DOE Translation List, E 1.13/3
Review of Current DHHS, **DOE**, and EPA Research Related to Toxicology, HE 20.3563
Selected **DOE** Headquarters Publications, E 1.13/4
Translation Series, **DOE**-TR-, E 1.43
DOE/AD
Administration, **DOE/AD** (series), E 1.32
DOE/AF
DOE/AF- (series), E 1.80
DOE/CA
DOE/CA- (series), E 1.33/2
DOE/CE
DOE/CE- (series), E 1.89
DOE/CP
DOE/CP (series), E 1.101
DOE/DP
Defense Programs, **DOE/DP**- (series), E 1.15
DOE/EA
Environmental Assessment, **DOE/EA** (series), E 1.20/2, E 4.9
DOE/EDP
Environmental Development Plan, **DOE/EDP** (series), E 1.36
DOE/EH
DOE/EH (series), E 1.20/3
DOE/EIA/CR
DOE/EIA/CR- (series), E 3.26/7
DOE/EP
DOE/EP- (series), E 1.90
DOE/ERA
DOE/ERA- (series), E 4.10
DOE/ERD
Environmental Readiness Documents, **DOE/ERD** (series), E 1.16/2
DOE/ES
DOE/ES (series), E 1.102
DOE/EV
Environment, **DOE/EV** (series), E 1.16
DOE/FE
DOE/FE (series), E 1.84
DOE/FERC
DOE/FERC- (series), E 2.12
DOE/GC
DOE/GC- (series), E 1.71
DOE/IA
DOE/IA (series), E 1.82
DOE/IG
Office of Inspector General, **DOE/IG**- (series), E 1.48
DOE/MA
DOE/MA- (series), E 1.35/2
DOE/NS
DOE/NS (series), E 1.68/3
DOE/OASN
Administrative Services, **DOE/OASN** (series), E 1.46
DOE/OC
DOE/OC, E 1.116
DOE/OPA
Information Publications **DOE/OPA** (series), E 1.25
DOE/OR
DOE/OR- (series), E 1.104
DOE/PA
DOE/PA- (series), E 1.33/3

DOE/PE
DOE/PE (Policy and Evaluation) (series), E 1.81
DOE/PR
Procurement and Contracts Management, **DOE/PR**- (series), E 1.49
DOE/RG
DOE/RG (series), E 4.11
DOE/RW
DOE/RW- (series), E 1.68/2
DOE/S
Office of the Secretary, **DOE/S**- (series), E 1.60
DOE/SR
DOE/SR- (series), E 1.77
DOE/US
DOE/US- (series), E 1.94
DOL
Microcomputer Training Catalog, The **DOL** Academy, L 1.86/2
Domestic
Domestic Violence and Stalking, J 35.21
National **Domestic** Preparedness Office - General Publications, J 1.14/25-2
Secretary's Task Force on Competition in the U.S. **Domestic** Airline Industry, TD 1.57
Doors
Opening **Doors**, HE 20.9120
Preservation Tech Notes, **Doors**, I 29.84/3-10
DOQ
Digital Orthophotoquads **DOQ** For, I 19.124
DOT
DOT Talk, TD 1.25/3
DOT-FTAMA
DOT-FTAMA, TD 7.17/2
DOT-T
DOT-T (series), TD 1.20/10
Dotted
Dotted Line, TD 1.59
Dove
Mourning **Dove**, Breeding Population Status, I 49.106/5
Draft
Draft Regulatory Guide, DG-, Y 3.N 88:6-3
Draw
Quick **Draw**, HE 1.65
DRG
Digital Raster Graphics (**DRG**) for [State], I 19.128
DRG Digital Raster Graphic (series), I 19.128
Drowning
Fatal Accidents Involving **Drowning** at Coal and Metal/Nonmetal Mines, L 38.19/3-2
Drug
Community **Drug** Alert Bulletin, HE 20.3971
Demographic Characteristics and Patterns of **Drug** Use of Clients Admitted to **Drug** Abuse Treatment Programs in Selected States, Trend Data, HE 20.8231/2
Drug Abuse Services Research Series, HE 20.8235
Drug Abuse Warning Network Series, HE 20.416/3
Drug Trafficking in the United States, J 24.29
Epidemiologic Trends in **Drug** Abuse, HE 20.3969
National Directory of **Drug** Abuse and Alcoholism Treatment and Prevention Programs, HE 20.410/3
National **Drug** Control Policy, PrEx 26.1/2
National **Drug** Intelligence Center (NDIC): General Publications, J 1.112
National Household Survey on **Drug** Abuse: Main Findings, HE 20.417/3
National Household Survey on **Drug** Abuse: Preliminary Results..., HE 20.417/4
National Household Survey on **Drug** Abuse: Race/ Ethnicity, . . ., HE 20.417
National Household Survey on **Drug** Abuse: Summary of Findings, HE 20.417/5
New **Drug** Evaluation Statistical Report, HE 20.4211
Office of **Drug** Evaluation Annual Report, HE 20 4618/2
Statistical Series, Annual Data, Data from the **Drug** Abuse Warning Network , HE 20.416
Therapy Manuals for **Drug** Addiction, HE 20.3958/2
Drugs
Annual Evaluation Report on **Drugs** and Crime: A Report to the President, the Attorney General, and the Congress, J 28.29
Drugs and Jail Inmates, J 29.13/3
DSMC
DSMC in Review: A Quality Journey, D 1.59/2-3
DSMC Technical Report, D 1.59/2-2
DTIC
DTIC Digest, D 10.11
DTIC Review, D 10.11/2

Duck
    Trends in **Duck** Breeding Populations, I 49.106/2
Ducks
    Preliminary Estimates of Age and Sex Composi-
        tions of **Ducks** and Geese Harvested in
        the Hunting Season in Comparison with
        Prior Years, I 49.106/3
DWRC
    DWRC Research Report, A 101.29/2
    DWRC Research Update, A 101.29

E

E.C.A.
    United States Foreign Trade, Trade with **E.C.A.**
        Countries, C 3.164:951
E.D.
    E.D. Tabs (series), ED 1.328/3
E.O.
    Organizations Designated Under **E.O.** 10450,
        Consolidated List (SCS Form 385), CS
        1.63
Eagle
    Blue **Eagle**, Y 3.N 21/8:19
    Blue **Eagle** Letters, Y 3.N 21/8:10
    Eagle, J 16.18
    Eagle and the Shield, S 1.69:161
    Operation Golden **Eagle**, Directory of Federal
        Recreation Areas Changing Entrance,
        Admission and User Fees, I 66.16
EARI
    EARI Development Research Series, Reports, D
        103.50
Early
    Cotton Varieties Planted in **Early** Producing
        Section of Texas, (year), A 88.11/11
    Early Childhood Digest, ED 1.343/2
    Early Childhood Update, ED 1.343
    FEWS (Famine **Early** Warning System) Bulletin, S
        18.68
    FEWS (Famine **Early** Warning System) Special
        Report, S 18.68/2
    Handicapped Children's **Early** Education Program,
        ED 1.32/4
    Toward Interagency Coordination: Federal
        Research and Development on **Early**
        Childhood, HE 23.1013/2
Early Bird
    Current News, **Early Bird** Edition, D 2.19
Early Education
    Application for Grants under Handicapped
        Children's **Early Education** Program
        Demonstration and Auxiliary Activities,
        ED 1.50/3
Early-Summer
    Spring and **Early-Summer** Potatoes, A 88.26/4
Earned
    Earned Degrees Conferred, FS 4.254:54013, HE
        5.92/5, HE 5.254:54013, HE 19.329
Earnings
    Earnings and Employment Data for Wage and
        Salary Workers Covered under Social
        Security by State and County, HE 3.95,
        SSA 1.17/3
    Earnings of Workers and Their Families, L 2.118
    Earnings, Expenses and Dividends of Active
        Banks in District of Columbia, Abstract,
        T 12.15
    Employment and **Earnings** and Monthly Report on
        Labor Force, L 2.41/2
    Employment and **Earnings** Characteristics of
        Families, L 2.118/2
    Employment and **Earnings** in the Mountain Plains
        Region, L 2.41/8
    Employment and **Earnings** Statistics for States and
        Areas, L 2.3
    Employment Hours and **Earnings** on Student Aid
        Projects of NYA, Y 3.W 89/2:27
    Employment, Hours and **Earnings**, L 2.20/3, L
        2.41/3
    Hours and **Earnings** Industry Reports, L 2.41
    Index of Straight-time Average Hourly **Earnings** for
        Hydraulic Turbine Operations, L 2.78/2
    Indexes of Change in Straight-Time Average Hourly
        Earnings for Selected Shipyards, by
        Type of Construction and Region, L
        2.81/2
    Member Bank **Earnings**, FR 1.11/3
    Monthly and Annual **Earnings** of Train and Engine
        Service Employees, RL 1.9

Monthly Report on Labor Force, Employment,
    Unemployment, Hours and **Earnings**, L
    2.84
Net Spendable **Earnings**, L 2.75, LC 30.24
Occupational **Earnings** and Wage Trends in
    Metropolitan Areas, Summary, L 2.86
Occupational **Earnings** in All Metropolitan Areas,
    L 2.86/5
Occupational **Earnings** in Banking, Selected
    Metropolitan Areas Summary, L 2.86/4
Occupational **Earnings** in Major Labor Market
    Summary Release, L 2.86
Occupational **Earnings** in Selected Areas,
    Summary, L 2.86/3
Percent Changes in Gross Average Hourly
    Earnings Over Selected Periods, L 2.63/
    2, L 2.63/3
Percent Changes in Gross Hourly and Weekly
    Earnings over Selected Periods, L 2.63
Real **Earnings**, L 2.115
Summary of Manufacturing **Earnings** Series, L 2.90
Supplement to Employment and **Earnings**, L 2.41/
    2-2
Usual Weekly **Earnings** of Wage and Salary
    Workers, L 2.126
Weekly **Earnings** of Wage and Salary Workers, L
    2.126
Earth
    Annual **Earth** Resources Program Review, NAS
        1.47
    Division of Earth Sciences: Annual Report, NA
        1.1/2
    Earth Laboratory Report, EM (series), I 27.37
    Earth Laboratory Section, Denver: **Earth**
        Laboratory Report (EM) Series, I 27.37
    Earth Notes, EP 1.108
    Earth Resources Satellite Data Applications
        Series, NAS 1.64
    Earth Resources Technology Satellite: Standard
        Catalog, NAS 1.488
    Earth Resources, A Continuing Bibliography with
        Indexes, NAS 1.21:7041
    Earth Sciences, PrEx 7.22/8
    Earth Sciences Division: Special Report S (series),
        D 106.17/2
    Earth Sciences Division: Technical Report ES
        (series), D 106.17
    Earth System Monitor, C 55.52
    Highlights of **Earth** Science and Applications
        Division, NAS 1.1/6
    Interim Lists of Periodicals in Collection of
        Atmospheric Sciences Library and
        Marine and **Earth** Sciences Library, C
        55.224
    IRIS, **Earth** Orientation Bulletin, C 55.437
    Smithsonian Contributions to **Earth** Sciences, SI
        1.26
    Special Reports **Earth** Sciences Division, D
        106.17/2
    Understanding the **Earth**, I 19.1/2
    Weekly Abstracts: NASA **Earth** Resources Survey
        Program, C 51.9/11
    World Data Center A for Solid **Earth** Geophysics
        Report, SE Series, C 55.220/5
Earthquake
    Abstracts of **Earthquake** Reports for the United
        States, MSAN (series), C 55.223, C
        55.417, I 19.69
    Earthquake Data Reports, EDR (series), C 55.426
    Earthquake Hazards Reduction Series, FEM 1.25
    Earthquake History of the United States, C
        55.202:Ea 7
    Earthquake Information Bulletin, I 19.65, C
        55.410, C 55.611
    National **Earthquake** Information Center
        {publications}, C 55.691
    Progress During. . .Strong-Motion **Earthquake** in
        California and Elsewhere, C 4.25/3
    Publications National **Earthquake** Information
        Center, C 55.691
Earthquakes
    Earthquakes and Volcanoes, I 19.65
    Earthquakes in the United States, I 19.4/2
    FDSN **Earthquake** Digital Data, I 19.128/2
    United States **Earthquakes**, C 55.417/2, I 19.65/2
East
    East Central Communique, ED 1.71/2
    East North Central, Population and Per Capita
        Income Estimates for Counties and
        Incorporated Places, C 3.186/27-4
    General Headquarters, Far **East** Command, General
        Publications, D 1.24

Monthly Report on European and Far **East**
    Programs, FO 1.10
Problems of the Far **East**, PrEx 7.21/12
Quarterly Report to Congress and the **East**-West
    Foreign Trade Board on Trade Between
    the United States and the Nonmarket
    Economy Countries, Y 4.W 36:2
Retail Trade Report **East** North Central, C 3.176
Retail Trade Report **East** South Central, C 3.177
South and **East** Asia Report, PrEx 7.16/4
Special Reports to Congress and **East**-West
    Foreign Trade Board, TC 1.38/2
Tide Tables **East** Coast of North and South America,
    C 4.15/4
Tide Tables Europe and **East** Coast of Africa, C
    4.15/7
Tide Tables, High and Low Water Predictions **East**
    Coast of North and South America
    Including Greenland, C 55.421/2
Training Circulars Department of the **East**, W 17.8
East Asia
    East Asia, Korea: Kulloja, PrEx 7.16/2
    East Asia, Vietnam: TAP CHI CONG SAN, PrEx
        7.16/4-2
    JPRS Report: **East Asia**, Korea, PrEx 7.16/2-2
    Nautical Charts and Publications, Region 9, **East
        Asia**, C 55.440:9
    NIMA Nautical Charts, Public Sale Region 9, **East
        Asia**, TD 4.82:9
East Asian
    East Asian and Pacific Series, S 1.38
East Canada
    Military Aviation Notices; North Atlantic and
        East Canada, D 301.11/2
East Central
    East Central Regional Office Publications, L 2.91
    Publications Agricultural Adjustment Agency
        East Central Region, A 76.441, A
        79.441, A 80.2141
East Coast
    East Coast of North America and South America
        (including Greenland), C 4.15/4
East European
    East European Accessions List, LC 30.12
East-West
    East-West Foreign Trade Board Report, Y 3.T 67:1
    East-West Trade Policy Staff Papers, C 61.17
    Report to Congress and **East-West** Foreign Trade
        Board on Trade Between United States
        and Nonmarket Economy Countries, TC
        1.38
Eastern
    Eastern Europe Business Bulletin, C 61.43
    Eastern Travel Today, I 29.37/9
    Eastern United States, Dates of Latest Prints,
        Instrument Approach Procedure Charts
        and Airport Obstruction Plans (OP), C
        4.9/19
    Quarterly Index to Periodical Literature, **Eastern**
        and Southern Africa, LC 1.30/8-4
    Resource Decisions in the National Forests of the
        Eastern Region, A 13.90
    Standard Instrument Departure (SID) Charts,
        Eastern U.S., C 55.416/5
    United States Foreign Trade, Trade with U.S.S.R.
        and Other **Eastern** Europe, C 3.164:954
    USSR and **Eastern** European Scientific Abstracts,
        Geophysics, Astronomy, and Space, Y 3.J
        66:14
Eastern Africa
    Accession List: **Eastern Africa**, LC 1.80/8
    Eastern Africa, LC 1.30/8
    Eastern Africa, Annual Publishers Directory, LC
        1.30/8-3
    Eastern Africa, Annual Serial Supplement, LC
        1.30/8-2
Eastern Asia
    Eastern Asia, Series 5305, D 5.336
Eastern Cities
    Fresh Fruit and Vegetable Unloads in **Eastern
        Cities**, A 88.40/2:3
Eastern Europe
    Eastern Europe Reports, PrEx 7.17
    Eastern Europe, Situation and Outlook Report, A
        93.29/2-10
    Focus on Central and **Eastern Europe**, S 1.140
Eastern European
    Eastern European Series, S 1.35
Eastern Region
    Eastern Region, C 55.118/4

Eastport
   Atlantic Coast; **Eastport** to Cape Cod, C 55.422:1
Easy
   Easy Access, J 32.24
Eating
   Child Guidance Leaflets, Series on **Eating**, for
      Parents, FS 3.211
   Child Guidance Leaflets, Series on **Eating**, for Staff,
      L 5.51/2
   Eating and Drinking Places and Motels Wage
      Survey Summaries by Cities, L 2.113/4
EC
   EC Bulletin, TD 4.38
   EC {Entomological Control} (series), A 77.323
ECAS
   Environmental Compliance Assessment System
      ECAS Annual Report, D 101.130
ECI
   ECI Clip Sheet, D 301.26/9
   ECI Letter, D 301.26/5
Echoes
   Army **Echoes**, D 101.141
ECOL
   ECOL Tech Paper, A 13.66/18
Ecological
   Coast **Ecological** Inventory, I 49.6/5
   Ecological Monitoring Program at the Waste
      Isolation Pilot Plant, Annual Report, E
      1.28/16
   Ecological Research Series, EP 2.32
   Ecological Research, 600/3 (series), EP 1.23
   Ecological Services Bulletins, I 29.3/3
   Florida Coastal **Ecological** Inventory Characteriza-
      tion, I 49.6/6
Ecology
   Highway Research and Development News, Plant
      Ecology and Esthetics, Progress and
      Implementation, TD 2.113/2

   Urban **Ecology** Series, I 29.78
ECOM
   Army Electronics Command Fort Monmouth N.J.:
      Research and Development Technical
      Reports **ECOM** (series), D 111.9/4
Economic
   Agricultural **Economic** Reports, A 88.52, A 93.28,
      A 1.107
   Agricultural **Economic** Reports and Services, A
      36.58
   Airline Industry **Economic** Report, CAB 1.18, C
      31.260
   Analysis of **Economic** Groups of Domestic Exports
      from and Imports into U.S., C 18.6/3
   Annual **Economic** Report of Air Freight
      Forwarders, C 31.270
   Annual Report of Legal Services Program of Office
      of **Economic** Opportunity to the
      American Bar Association, PrEx 10.18
   Annual Report on the Impact of the Caribbean
      Basin **Economic** Recovery Act on U.S.
      Industries and Consumers, ITC 1.32
   Areas Eligible for Financial Assistance Designated
      Under the Public Works and **Economic**
      Development Act of 1965 Reports, C
      46.25/2
   Bureau of **Economic** Analysis Staff Papers, C 59.14
   Bureau of **Economic** Analysis Staff Papers, BEA-
      SP (series), C 56.113
   Bureau of International **Economic** Policy and
      Research: Reports, Studies, Data, C
      57.26
   C.A.B. **Economic** Orders and Opinions, CAB 1.31
   Census of Population; Advance Estimates of Social
      Economic, and Housing Characteristics,
      Supplementary Reports, PHC A2
      (series), C 3.223/21-2
   Census of Population; General Social and
      Economic Characteristics, C 3.223/7
   Census of Population: Social and **Economic**
      Characteristics for American Indian and
      Alaska Native Areas, C 3.223/7-2
   Census of Population: Social and **Economic**
      Characteristics for Metropolitan
      Statistical Areas, C 3.223/7-3
   Census of Population: Social and **Economic**
      Characteristics for Urbanized Areas, C
      3.223/7-4
   Checklist of Reports Issued by **Economic** Research
      Service and Statistical Reporting
      Service, A 1.97

Clinical Handbook on **Economic** Poisons,
   Emergency Information for Treating
   Poisoning, EP 5.8:P 75
Comments on **Economic** and Housing Situation,
   HH 2.19
Commerce Works! A Summary of the **Economic**
   Accomplishments of the Department, C
   1.1/5
Company Statistics Series (Economic Census), C
   3.277/3
Cooperative **Economic** Insect Report, A 101.9, A
   77.324/3
Current Population Reports, Household **Economic**
   Studies, C 3.186:P-70/2
Current Projects on **Economic** and Social
   Implications of Scientific Research and
   Development, NS 1.23
Current Reviews of **Economic** and Social Problems
   in United Nations, S 1.81
Designated Redevelopment Areas Under the Public
   Works and **Economic** Development Act
   of 1965, C 46.25/3
Digest **Economic** Opportunity Office, PrEx 10.25
Domestic **Economic** Developments, Monthly
   Business Indicators, C 18.285/2
Domestic **Economic** Developments, Weekly
   Business Indicators, C 18.285
Economic Affairs, PrEx 7.15/2, PrEx 7.21/2
Economic Analysis of Pretreatment Standards
   Series, EP 1.8/4-2
Economic Analysis of Proposed Effluent
   Guidelines, EP 1.8/4
Economic and Agriculture Censuses, C 3.277
Economic and Budget Outlook, an Update, Y
   10.17
Economic and Energy Indicators, PrEx 3.14/2
Economic and Industrial Affairs, PrEx 7.17
Economic and Social Analysis Workshop:
   Proceedings, D 103.57/10
Economic Base for Power Markets, I 44.9
Economic Briefs, FHL 1.28
Economic Bulletins, Y 3.C 73/5:3-2, D 101.143
Economic Censuses of Outlying Areas, C 56.259
Economic Censuses of Outlying Areas, OAC
   (Series), C 3.253/2
Economic Censuses: Reference Series, C 3.253
Economic Characteristics of Households in the
   United States, C 3.186:P-70/2
Economic Circulars, C 6.7
Economic Control and Commercial Policy in
   American Republics, TC 1.20
Economic Cooperation Series, S 1.65
Economic Decisions, C 31.211
Economic Development, C 46.92/
Economic Development Research Reports, C 46.29
Economic Development U.S.A., C 46.9/3
Economic Discussion Papers, L 29.15
Economic Edge, Y 3 T 25:72
Economic Forces in United States in Facts and
   Figures, FO 1.30, S 17.8
Economic Foreign Policy Series, S 1.71/3
Economic Growth Trends {by region}, S 18.37
Economic Impact Analysis of Alternative
   Pollution Control Technologies (series),
   EP 1.8/10
Economic Impact Tinker Air Force Base, FY, D
   301.105/11
Economic Indicators, Y 4.Ec 7:Ec 7
Economic Indicators of the Farm Sector, A 93.45
Economic Indicators of the Farm Sector, Cost of
   Production: Livestock and Dairy, A
   93.45/2-2
Economic Indicators Weekly Review, ER-EI
   (series), PrEx 3.13
Economic Library Lists, A 36.113
Economic Notes, A 13.61/11
Economic Papers, I 28.38
Economic Perspectives, IA 1.37, S 20.16
Economic Publications, A 57.29
Economic Report, E-(series), C 41.42
Economic Report of the President, Pr 37.9, Pr 38.9,
   Pr 39.9, Pr 40.9, Pr 41.9, Pr 42.9, Pr 43.9
Economic Report to the Secretary of Commerce, C
   43.10
Economic Resource Impact Statement, D 301.105/
   10
Economic Resource Impact Statement 305th Air
   Refueling Wing, Grissom Air Force Base,
   Indiana, D 301.105/8
Economic Resource Impact Statement Andrews Air
   Force Base, D 301.105/7

Economic Resource Impact Statement George Air
   Force Base, California, D 301.105/4
Economic Resource Impact Statement Grand Forks
   Air Force Base, D 301.105/2
Economic Resource Impact Statement Holloman
   AFB, New Mexico, D 301.105/6
Economic Resource Impact Statement K. I. Sawyer
   AFB, D 301.105
Economic Resource Impact Statement Kelly Air
   Force Base, D 301.105/3
Economic Resource Impact Statement Luke Air
   Force Base, New Mexico, D 301.105/5
Economic Resources Impact Statements, D 103.105
Economic Series Arms Control and Disarmament
   Agency, AC 1.10
Economic Series Bureau of Foreign and Domestic
   Commerce, C 18.206
Economic Stabilization Program, Bi-weekly
   Summary, PrEx 17.9/2
Economic Summary, Y 4.B 85/3:Ec 7/11
Economic Trends and Their Implications for the
   United States, C 42.30
Economic Working Papers, T 12.22
Farm **Economic** Series, A 21.13/4
Federal Reference Material for State, **Economic**
   Development Agencies, C 41.27/2
Fish Meal and Oil Market Review, Current
   Economic Analysis I, C 55.309/3
Foreign Agricultural **Economic** Reports, A 93.27,
   A 105.22
Foreign **Economic** Collection and Industrial
   Espionage, Y 3.C 83/2:1-2
Foreign **Economic** Development Report, A 93.38
Foreign **Economic** Development Service Annual
   Summary, A 100.1/2
Foreign **Economic** Reports, C 3.264, C 59.12
Foreign **Economic** Trends and Their Implications
   for the United States, C 57.111, C 61.11
Forest **Economic** Notes, A 13.42/13
Handbook of **Economic** Statistics, S 1.91/3
History of the **Economic** Censuses, C 3.253/3
Household Economic Studies, **Economic**
   Characteristics of Households in the
   United States, C 3.186:P-70
Household Economic Studies, **Economic**
   Characteristics of Households in the
   United States, C 3.186:P-70
Independent **Economic** Analysis Board (IEAB)
   Documents, Y 3.N 81/8:15
International **Economic** Review, ITC 1.29
International **Economic** Review, Special Edition,
   Chartbook, ITC 1.29/2
Japanese **Economic** Statistics Bulletin, D 102.14
Journal of Agricultural **Economic** Research, A
   93.26
National **Economic** Accounting Training Program,
   C 59.21
National **Economic** Social & Environmental Data
   Bank (NESEDB), C 1.88/2
Notes from the Joint **Economic** Committee, Y 4.Ec
   7:N 84
OEP **Economic** Stabilization Circulars, PrEx 4.4/3
Office of United States **Economic** Coordinator for
   Cento Affairs, Non-Government Central
   Treaty Organization, S 5.54
OPA **Economic** Data Series, Pr 33.307
Outlook and Year-End **Economic** Review, C 1.41
Periodic Reports of Agricultural Economics,
   Economic Research Service, Statistical
   Reporting Service, A 1.99
Postwar **Economic** Studies, FR 1.27
Prices, Escalation, and **Economic** Stability, L
   2.100
Regional **Economic** Information System (REIS), C
   59.24
Risk Analysis of Farm Credit System Operations
   and **Economic** Outlook, FCA 1.23/2-2
Qualified Areas Under Public Works and
   Economic Development Act of 1965,
   Public Law 89-136, Reports, C 46.25
Quarterly **Economic** and Financial Review: Federal
   Republic of Germany and Western
   Sectors of Berlin, S 1.91/2
Quarterly Review, 503 and 504 **Economic**
   Development Loan Programs, SBA 1.27/
   2
Report of Formal **Economic** Proceedings, C 31.219
Report of National Advisory Council on **Economic**
   Opprotunity, PrEx 10.22
Report to Congress on **Economic** Cooperation
   Administration, Y 3.Ec 74/3:8

International **Education** and Cultural Exchange, Y 3.Ad 9/9:9

Inventory of Physical Facilities in Institutions of Higher **Education**, HE 5.92/3, HE 19.310

IPEDS Integrated Postsecondary **Education** Data System, Institutional Characteristics, ED 1.23/6

Labor **Education** News, L 16.28

Library **Education** Directory, FS 5.215:1546, HE 5.215:15046

Listing of **Education** in Archeological Programs, I 29.59/7

March of **Education**, FS 5.19

March of **Education**, News Letter for School Officers, I 16.26/3

Minorities and Women in Undergraduate **Education**, Geographic Distributions for Academic Year, HE 20.9314

Model Programs, Title III, Elementary and Secondary **Education** Act, HE 18.12

Modern Foreign Language Fellowship Program, National Defense **Education** Act, Title 6 and NDEA Related Awards under Fullbright-Hays Act, FS 5.255:55034, HE 5.255:55034

Monographs on Career **Education** (series), ED 1.15, HE 19.111/2

Monographs on Evaluation in **Education**, HE 19.111

National Advisory Council for Career **Education**: Publications, HE 19.116

National Advisory Council on Vocational **Education** Annual Report, HE 5.85

National Center For Education Statistics, **Education** Policy Issues: Statistical Perspectives, ED 1.336

National Directory of **Education** Programs in Gerontology, HE 1.214

National **Education** Goals Report, ED 1.1/3

National High Blood Pressure **Education** Program, HE 20.3214

National Household **Education** Survey, ED 1.334/5

National Policy on Career **Education**, Reports, Y 3.V 85:9

New Application for Grants under Research in **Education** of the Handicapped, ED 1.50

New Dimensions in Higher **Education**, FS 5.250, HE 5.250

News of Institutes of Higher Learning; Ministry of Higher **Education**, Physics, C 41.52/4

News of Institutes of Higher Learning; Ministry of Higher **Education**, USSR, Mathematics, C 41.61/2

NIE Papers in **Education** and Work, HE 19.212

North Central Regional Medical **Education** Center: Newsletter, VA 1.56/2

Notes on Graduate Studies and Research in Home Economics and Home Economics **Education**, A 1.53

Nutrition **Education** Series Pamphlets, FS 5.34

Occupational **Education** Enrollments and Programs in Noncollegiate Postsecondary Schools, HE 19.337/2

Occupational Home Economics **Education** Series, HE 19.134

Open Window, the Newsletter of the National Library of **Education**, ED 1.345

Opening Fall Enrollment in Higher **Education**, FS 5.254:54043, HE 5.254:54023

Papers in **Education** Finance, HE 19.144

Parent **Education** Letters, I 16.48

Parent **Education** Messenger, A 43.14

Participation in Adult **Education**, ED 1.123

Personnel Development for Vocational **Education**, HE 19.124

Perspectives on **Education** Policy Research, ED 1.336/2

Physical **Education** Series, I 16.40

Postsecondary **Education** Fall Enrollment in Higher **Education** (year): Institutional Data, HE 19.325/2

President's Committee on Health **Education**, Pr 37.8:H 34

Press Releases Department of **Education**, ED 1.25

Priorities for Research, Extension and Higher **Education**, A 1.2/10

Product Safety **Education** Unit (series), Y 3.C 76/3:19

Professional Opportunities for Women in Research and **Education**, NS 1.61

Progress in American **Education**, HE 5.210:10064

Progress of **Education** in the U.S. of America, HE 19.133, ED 1.41

Progress of Public **Education** in the United States of America, FS 5.62, FS 5.210:10005, HE 5.210:10005

Progress Report to the Secretary of **Education** from the President's Advisory Commission on Educational Excellence for Hispanic Americans, ED 1.87

Project on the Status and **Education** of Women, Field Evaluation Draft, ED 1.42/2

Projects Initiated under Title VII, National Defense **Education** Act, FS 5.234:34013, FS 5.234:34021, HE 5.234:34013, HE 5.234:34021

Public Elementary and Secondary **Education** in the United States, ED 1.112/2

Public Elementary and Secondary **Education** Statistics: School Year, ED 1.328/12

Publications Bureau of **Education**, I 16.14/2

Publications Inter-American **Education** Demonstration Centers, FS 5.31

Publications National Center for **Education** Statistics, HE 19.317:P 96

Publications Office of **Education**, FS 5.9, FS 5.10, FS 5.211:11000, HE 5.211:11000

Puerto Rico, **Education** Department Annual Reports, I 1.39

Quarterly Bulletin, Intelligence Continuing **Education** Program, D 5.212

Regulations, Rules and Instructions Department of **Education**, ED 1.47

Report of the FCCSET Committee on **Education** and Human Resources, PrEx 8.111

Report of the National Defense **Education** Act, FS 5.210:10004

Report on Principal Bills Introduced into Congress Affecting **Education** Either Directly or Indirectly, FS 5.66

Report on the National Defense **Education** Act, HE 5.210:10004

Report on USDA Human Nutrition Research and **Education** Activities, A Report to Congress, A 1.1/5

Research for Progress in **Education**, Annual Report, HE 5.212:12051

Research in **Education**, FS 5.77, HE 5.77, HE 18.10

Resident, Extension, and Other Enrollments in Institutions of Higher **Education**, FS 5.254:54000, HE 5.254:54000

Resources for Biomedical Research and **Education**, Reports, HE 20.3014

Resources for Medical Research and **Education**, Reports, HE 20.3014

Resources in **Education**, ED 1.11, HE 19.210

Revenues and Expenditures for Public and Elementary and Secondary **Education**, ED 1.119

Science **Education** Origin, D 210.18

Secondary **Education**, FS 5.53

Selected List of Postsecondary **Education** Opportunities for Minorities and Women, ED 1.42

Selected Reports of Cases before Veterans' **Education** Appeals Board, Y 3.V 64:7

Southwestern Monuments, Museum and **Education** Series, Letters, I 29.15/3

Special **Education** Personnel in State Education Departments, FS 5.235:35051

Special Education Personnel in State **Education** Departments, FS 5.235:35051

Special Series Office of **Education**, FS 5.41

Special VD **Education** Circulars, FS 2.38

State **Education** Agency Operations, Revenues, Expenditures, and Employees, ED 1.108/3

State Higher **Education** Profiles, ED 1.116/3

Statistics Concerning Indian **Education**, Fiscal Year, I 20.46

Statistics of **Education** in the United States, FS 5.220:20032, HE 5.220:20032

Statistics of Trends in **Education**, HE 19.302:St 2/2

Strengthening Developing Institutions, Title 3 of the Higher **Education** Act of 1965, Annual Report, HE 19.139/2

Studies in Comparative **Education**, Bibliography, Publications, FS 5.214, HE 5.214

Studies in Comparative **Education**, **Education** in {country}, FS 5.212, HE 5.212

Studies in Comparative **Education**, FS 5.59

Summaries of Studies in Agricultural **Education** Supplements, FS 5.281:81002, HE 5.281:81002

Summary Report, Faculty and Other Professional Staff in Institutions of Higher **Education**, FS 5.253:53014, HE 5.253:53014

Survey of State Legislation Relating to Higher **Education**, FS 5.250:50008, HE 5.250:50008

Task Force on Higher **Education**, Pr 37.8:Ed 8

Technical Analysis Papers Department of Health, **Education**, and Welfare, HE 1.52

Technical Reports from the Study of the Sustaining Effects of Compensatory **Education** on Basic Skills, HE 19.137

Telephone Directory **Education** Department, ED 1.24

The Fund for the Improvement of Postsecondary **Education** (FIPSE), Special Focus Competition: College-School Partnerships to Improve Learning of Essential Academic Subjects, Kindergarten through College, ED 1.23/9

Title I, Elementary and Secondary **Education** Act of 1965, States Report, FS 5.79, FS 5.237:37013, HE 5.237:37013, HE 5.79

Title II, Elementary and Secondary **Education** Act of 1965, School Library Resources, Textbooks and Other Instructional Materials, Annual Report, HE 5.79/2

Tower University: **Education** Service Plan, D 101.93/2

Trainers of Teachers, Other **Education** Personnel and Undergraduates, FS 5.84:T 22, HE 5.84:T 22

Training and **Education** Bulletin TEB (series), FCD 1.9

Training Manual Department of Health, **Education**, and Welfare, FS 1.10, HE 1.10

Trends in **Education**, ED 1.132

Uses of State Administered Federal **Education** Funds, HE 19.122

VD **Education** Circulars, FS 2.39

Veterans **Education** Newsletter, VA 1.49

Views and Estimates of the Committee on **Education**, Y 4.Ed 8/1-11

Vocational and Technical **Education** Abstracts, C 41.62

Vocational **Education** Information (series), HE 19.121

Vocational **Education** Letters, I 16.23

Vocational **Education** Study Publications, HE 19.219

Vocational **Education**; Schools for Careers, an Analysis of Occupational Courses Offered by Secondary and Postsecondary Schools, HE 19.321

Vocational Instructional Materials for Marketing and Distributive **Education**, ED 1.17/3

Working Papers Department of **Education**, ED 1.80

Education's

American **Education's** Annual Guide to OE Programs, HE 5.211:11015

Educational

Alphabetical List of **Educational** Institutions, ED 1.68

Application for Grants, Formula Grants to Local **Educational** Agencies, ED 1.410

Argonne National Laboratory Division of **Educational** Programs: Annual Report, E 1.86

Basic **Educational** Opportunity Grant Program Handbook, HE 19.108/4

Catalog of **Educational** Captioned Films/Videos for the Deaf, ED 1.209/2-2

Contributions of American **Educational** History, I 16.15

Cotton **Educational** Meetings, A 55.39

Digest of **Educational** Statistics, ED 1.326, HE 19.315

Directory of Contacts for International **Educational**, Cultural and Scientific Exchange Programs, S 1.67/4

Directory of Resources for Cultural and **Educational** Exchanges and International Communication, ICA 1.12

Educational Aids, A 89.14, I 49.54

Educational AM and FM Radio and Education Television Stations, FS 5.234:34016, HE 5.234:34016

Educational and Nonprofit Institutions Receiving Prime Contract Awards for Research, Development, Test and Evaluation, D 1.57/8

Educational and Training Opportunities in Sustainable Agriculture, A 17.32

Educational Attainment, C 3.186:P-20

Educational Attainment in the United States, C 3.186/23

Educational Briefs for the Middle and Secondary Level Classroom, NAS 1.19/3

Educational Directory, FS 5.25

Educational Extension Division, I 16.31

Educational Horizons, NAS 1.49/2

Educational Leaflets, I 29.11

Educational Manuals, W 1.55

Educational Materials Laboratory Report, FS 5.214:14031, HE 5.214:14031

Educational Pamphlets (series), C 55.431

Educational Program, EP- (series), NAS 1.19

Educational Programs and Resources, SI 14.16

Educational Programs at Fort Benjamin Harrison, D 101.93/3

Educational Publications, FS 2.20

Educational Series Bureau of Marine Inspection and Navigation, C 25.16

Educational Series Coast Guard, N 24.28, T 47.36

Educational Series Federal Board of Surveys and Maps, Y 3.Su 7:8

Educational Services Brochure and Schedule of Courses, D 101.93

Educational Statistics, ED 1.328/13

Educational Television Facilities Program: Program Bulletins, FS 1.24

Educational Television Facilities Program: Public Notices, FS 1.24/2

ERIC (**Educational** Resources Information Center) Annual Report, ED 1.301/2

FCS **Educational** Circulars, A 89.4/2

Food and Nutrition Information and **Educational** Materials Center Catalog, A 17.18/3

Forest Service Films Available on Loan for **Educational** Purposes to Schools, Civic Groups, Churches, Television, A 13.55

General Catalogs of **Educational** Films, FS 5.10/3

Human Genetics Informational and **Educational** Materials, HE 20.5117

Interagency Directory, Key Contacts for Planning, Scientific and Technical Exchange Programs, **Educational** Travel, Students, Teachers, Lecturers, Research Scholars, Specialists, S 1.67/3

International Teacher Development Program, Annual Report to Bureau of **Educational** and Cultural Affairs, Department of State, FS 5.214:14003

Memorandum to All Administrators of Emergency **Educational** Programs, I 16.53

Motion Pictures **Educational** {and} Industrial, C 18.116

Numeric List of **Educational** Institutions, ED 1.65

Pan-Pacific **Educational** Conference, 1st Honolulu, August 1921, S 5.21/2, S 5.22

Program and Services, Report of **Educational** Materials Laboratory, Division of International Studies and Services, FS 5.214:14031, HE 5.214:14031

Progress Report to the Secretary of Education from the President's Advisory Commission on **Educational** Excellence for Hispanic Americans, ED 1.87

Projections of **Educational** Statistics, HE 19.320, ED 1.120

Recent **Educational** Policy and Legislative Developments Abroad (series), HE 5.94

Research and Training Opportunities Abroad (year), **Educational** Programs in Foreign Language and Area Studies, HE 5.99

Resources in Women's **Educational** Equality, ED 1.17/2, HE 19.128:W 84/2

Series of **Educational** Illustrations (Charts), A 43.5/10, A 43.22

Series of **Educational** Illustrations for Schools (posters), A 45.5

Solar **Educational** Programs and Courses, E 1.85

State **Educational** Records and Reports Series, HE 19.308/2

Surplus Property Disposed of to Public Health and **Educational** Institutions, FS 1.15

Teacher Exchange Opportunities Abroad, Teaching, Summer Seminars under International **Educational** Exchange Program of Department of States {announcements}, FS 5.64/2

Teacher Exchange Opporunities under International **Educational** Exchange Program, FS 5.64, FS 5.214:14047, HE 5.214:14047

Title VII-New **Educational** Media News and Reports, FS 5.234:34002, HE 5.234:34002

U.S. Army **Educational** Manuals, W 3.47

U.S. Government Films for Public **Educational** Use, FS 5.234:34006, HE 5.234:34006

UNESCO World Review Weekly Radio News from United Nations **Educational**, Scientific, and Cultural Organization, Paris, France, S 5.48/6

United Nations **Educational**, Scientific and Cultural Organization News {releases}, S 5.48/13

Women's **Educational** Equity Act Program, Annual Report, ED 1.44

Women's **Educational** Equity Act, HE 19.136

Educator

Food Safety **Educator**, A 110.19

Vocational **Educator**, ED 1.33/3

Educators

Conferences of **Educators** on Sex Education, T 27.25

Directory of Counselor **Educators**, FS 5.255:25036, HE 5.255:25036

Implementing Title IX and Attaining Sex Equity; A Workshop for Elementary-Secondary **Educators**, HE 19.141, HE 19.141/2

Opportunities Abroad for **Educators**, ED 1.19, IA 1.29

Overseas Employment Opportunities for **Educators**, D 1.68

Programs, (year), Guide to Programmed Instructional Materials Available to **Educators** by (date), FS 5.234:34015, HE 5.234:34015

Eel

Eel River Charts, W 7.13/2

EEO

Census/Equal Employment Opportunity (**EEO**) Special File, C 3.283

EEO Fact Sheet from Office of the Administrator, A 67.41

EEO for State and Local Governments (series), CS 1.76/2

EEO Information on Equal Opportunity for State and Local Governments, PM 1.18/2

EEO Newsletter, A 105.51

EEO Spotlight, CS 1.76

EEOC

EEOC Reports, Clearinghouse Service for Business Newsletters and Periodicals, Y 3.Eq 2:7-2

Semi-Annual Checklist of the **EEOC** Orders, Y 3.Eq 2:19

EFC

EFC Formula Book, The Expected Family Contribution for Federal Student Aid, ED 1.45/5

EFF

EFF HOT Topics, Y 3.L 71:18

Effect

Annual Report of Department of Treasury on Operation and **Effect** of Domestic International Sales Corporation Legislation for Calendar Year, Y 4.W 36:D 71/2

Operation and **Effect** of the Domestic International Sales Corporation Legislation, T 1.54

Operation and **Effect** of the International Boycott Provisions of the Internal Revenue Code, T 1.56

Operation and **Effect** of the Possessions Corporation System of Taxation, T 1.55

Special and Administrative Provisions of the Tariff Act of 1930, As Amended, As in **Effect** on {date}, TC 1.10/2

Effective

Consumer Loans Made Under **Effective** State Small Loan Laws, FR 1.36/3

Effective Programs Monograph, J 26.30/2

Effectiveness

Army Organizational **Effectiveness** Journal, D 101.91

Report to the President and the Congress on the **Effectiveness** of the Rail Passenger Services Act, IC 1.34

Safety **Effectiveness** Evaluation, NTSB-SEE-(series), TD 1.125

Semiannual Report to Congress on the **Effectiveness** of the Civil Aviation Security Program, TD 4.810

Effects

Committee on the Assessment of Human Health **Effects** of Great Lakes Water Quality: Annual Report, Y 3.In 8/28:15

Environmental **Effects** of Dredging, D 103.24/16

Environmental Health **Effects** Research, 600/1 (series), EP 1.23/4

Environmental Overview and Analysis of Mining **Effects**, I 29.101

Registry of Toxic **Effects** of Chemical Substances (cumulative) Supplement, HE 20.7112/5

Registry of Toxic **Effects** of Chemical Substances, HE 20.7112/3

Registry of Toxic **Effects** of Chemical Substances, Permuted Molecular Formula, Index, HE 20.7112/4

Report of the Division of Biological **Effects**, HE 20.4114/2

Subfile of the Registry of Toxic **Effects** of Chemical Substances, HE 20.7112/2

Technical Reports from the Study of the Sustaining **Effects** of Compensatory Education on Basic Skills, HE 19.137

Efficiency

A Report of the Secretary of Transportation Pursuant to the Intermodal Surface Transportation **Efficiency** Act of 1991, TD 1.1/5

Annual Report on the Management **Efficiency** Pilot Program, VA 1.1/3

Energy **Efficiency** and Renewable Energy, Clearinghouse, E 1.99/13

Energy **Efficiency** Research, ER 1.29

Industrial Energy **Efficiency** Improvement Program, Annual Report, E 1.47

Manufacturing Energy Consumption Survey: Changes in Energy **Efficiency**, E 3.54/2

President's Council on Integrity and **Efficiency**: Reports, Pr 41.8/3

Effluent

Annual Report of the Activities of the **Effluent** Standards and Water Quality Information Advisory Committee, EP 1.1/2

Development Document for **Effluent** Limitations Guidelines and New Source Performance Standards for {various industries}, EP 1.8/3

Economic Analysis of Proposed **Effluent** Guidelines, EP 1.8/4

Industrial **Effluent** Standards, EP 1.8/4-4

Proposed **Effluent** Guidelines, EP 1.8/4-3

Effort

Reports to Aid Nation's Defense **Effort**, A 13.27/13

EG

EG, NAS 1.19/4

Egg

Chickens and **Eggs**, Layers and **Egg** Production, A 88.15/14, A 92.9/13

Commercial **Egg** Movement Report, A 88.15/20

Dissemination of Research Results {on Poultry and **Egg** Marketing Subjects}, A 82.75, A 88.15/8

Egg and Poultry Markets Review, A 82.39

Egg Marketing Facts, A 88.53

Egg Marketing Guide, A 88.26/5

Egg Products, A 105.12/2

Egg Products, Liquid, Frozen, Solids Production, A 92.9/4

Egg Standardization Leaflets, A 36.24

Monthly **Egg** and Poultry Markets Review, A 88.13/3

Poultry and **Egg** Outlook, A 36.72

Poultry and **Egg** Production Reports, A 36.102

Poultry and **Egg** Production, A 66.43

Poultry and **Egg** Situation, A 88.15/3, A 93.20, A 105.12/4

Report of **Egg** Production Tests, United States and Canada, A 77.15:44-78

Statistical Supplement to Monthly **Egg** and Poultry Market Review, A 88.13/4

Eggs

Chickens and **Eggs**, A 92.9/16

Chickens and **Eggs**, Farm Production, Disposition, Cash Receipts and Gross Income, A 9.9/3

Chickens and **Eggs**, Farm Production, Disposition, Cash Receipts and Gross Income, Chickens on Farms, Commercial Broilers, by States, A 88.15/18

Chickens and **Eggs**, Farm Production, Disposition, Cash Receipts and Gross Income, A 9.9/3

Chickens and **Eggs**, Layers and Rate of Lay, First of Each Month, A 88.15/17

Commitments of Traders in Wheat, Corn, Oats, Rye, Soybeans, Soybean Oil, Soybean Meal, Shell **Eggs**, A 85.9/2

Eggs, Chickens and Turkeys, A 92.9/16, A 105.12/3

Futures Trading and Open Contracts in Butter, **Eggs** and Potatoes, A 85.11/4

EHB

Weather Bureau Engineering Handbooks **EHB**- (series), C 30.6/5

EIA

EIA Data Index, an Abstract Journal, E 3.27/5

EIA Personal Computer Products, International Coal Statistics Database, E 3.11/7-11

EIA Publications Directory, E 3.27

EIA Publications, New Releases, E 3.27/4

Eight-hour

Compilation . . . Between Employers and Employees, Laws {on} Disputes Between Carriers and Employers and Subordinate Officials Under Labor Board, **Eight-hour** Laws, . . ., Labor and Child Labor Laws, Y 1.2:Em 7/6

Eighties

President's Commission on National Agenda for the **Eighties**, Pr 39.8:Ag 3

EIRS

EIRS Bulletin, D 103.24/19

EIS

EIS Directory, HE 20.7025

EIS/EA

OCS **EIS/EA** (Series), I 72.12/11

Eisenhower

Eisenhower Consortium Bulletins, A 13.69/11

ENC, **Eisenhower** National Clearinghouse, A Collection of Curriculum Standards and Framework, ED 1.340/3

EL

Handbook **EL**- (series), P 1.31/9

El Viajero

Traveler/**El Viajero**, Quarterly Newsletter for Migrant and Seasonal Farm Workers, PrEx 10.19

Elderly

Elderly News Updates, HH 1.104

Elected

If **Elected**. . . Unsuccessful Candidates for the Presidency, SI 11.2:P 92/2

Election

Election Case Law, Y 3.El 2/3:12

Election Law Guidebook, 1974, Summary of Federal and State Laws Regulating Nomination and **Election** of U.S. Senators, Revised to January 1, 1974, Y 1.93-2:S.doc. 84

Election Law Updates, Y 3.El 2/3:9-2

Election Statistics, Y 1.2/10

FEC Journal of **Election** Administration, Y 3.El 2/3:10

Federal **Election** Commission Record, Y 3.El 2/3:11

Federal **Election** Commission Record, Index, Y 3.El 2/3:11-2

Federal-State **Election** Law Survey, Y 3.El 2/3:9

Federal-State **Election** Law Survey: an Analysis of State Legislation, Federal Legislation and Judicial Decisions, Y 3.El 2/3:2 St 2

Innovations in **Election** Administration, Y 3.El 2/3:18

Voting and Registration in the **Election** of (name), C 3.186/3-2

Voting and Registration in the **Election** of November (date), C 3.186/3

Elections

Elections, C 3.153

Federal **Elections** . . ., Election Results for the U.S. Senate and U.S. House of Representatives, Y 3.El 2/3:16

Elective

Elective Course Readings (series), D 5.415/9

Electives

Clinical **Electives** for Medical and Dental Students at the National Institutes of Health, Catalog, HE 20.3042

Electric

All **Electric** Homes in the United States, Annual Bills, January 1, (year), FP 1.10

All **Electric** Homes, Annual Bills, E 3.16

Annual Outlook for U.S. **Electric** Power, E 3.50

Annual Summary of Cost and Quality of Steam-**Electric** Plant Fuels, FP 1.2:F 95

Consumption of Fuel for Production of **Electric** Energy, FP 1.11/3

Cost and Quality of Fuels for **Electric** Utility Plants, E 3.11/15-2

Electric and Hybrid Vehicle Program, Annual Report to Congress, E 1.45/2

Electric Energy and Peak Load Data, E 3.11/17-9

Electric Farming News Exchange of Inter-industry Farm **Electric** Utilization Council, A 68.19

Electric Home and Farm Authority Publications, Y 3.T 25:9 CT

Electric Light and Power Plants, C 3.38/2

Electric Locomotives (mining and industrial), C 3.81

Electric Power Annual, E 3.11/17-10

Electric Power Engineering, E 1.99

Electric Power Monthly, E 3.11/17-8

Electric Power Statistics, FP 1.24, FP 1.27, E 3.18

Electric Sales and Revenue, E 3.22

Electric Trade in the United States, E 3.11/17-12

Federal and State Commission Jurisdiction and Regulations, **Electric**, Gas, and Telephone Utilities, FP 1.21

Federal Power Commission Laws and Hydro-**Electric** Power Development Laws {June 10, 1920}, Y 1.2:F 31/7

Financial Statistics of Major Investor-Owned **Electric** Utilities, E 3.18/4-2

Financial Statistics of Major U.S. Publicly Owned **Electric** Utilities, E 3.18/4-3

Financial Statistics of Selected Investor-Owned **Electric** Utilities, E 3.18/4-2

Financial Statistics of Selected Publicly Owned **Electric** Utilities, E 3.18/4-3

Gas Turbine **Electric** Plant Construction Cost and Annual Production Expenses, E 3.17/2

Historical Plant Cost and Annual Production Expenses for Selected **Electric** Plants, E 3.17/4-2

Hydro **Electric** Plant Construction Cost and Annual Production Expenses, E 3.17/3

Hydro**electric** Power Resources of the United States, Developed and Undeveloped, FP 1.123

Inventory of Nonutility **Electric** Power Plants in the United States, E 3.29/2

Market for Selected U.S. **Electric** Housewares in {various countries}, C 41.103

Monthly **Electric** Utility Sales and Revenue Report with State Distributions, E 3.11/17-14

Production and Utilization of **Electric** Energy in United States, FP 1.11/2

Production of **Electric** Energy and Capacity of Generating Plants, FP 1.21

Quarterly Statistical Bulletin, **Electric** Program, A 68.13/2

Residential **Electric** Bills in Major Cities, E 3.11/17-2

Revenues and Income of Privately Owned Class A & B **Electric** Utilities in the U.S., FP 1.11/5

Sales of **Electric** Energy to Ultimate Consumers, FP 1.11/6

Sales of Firm **Electric** Power for Resale, by Private **Electric** Utilities, by Federal Projects, by Municipals, FP 1.21

Sales, Revenue, and Income for **Electric** Utilities, E 3.11/2-6

Sales, Revenue, and Income of **Electric** Utilities, E 3.11/2-8

Staff Report **Electric** Power Supply and Demand for the Contiguous United States, E 1.126

Staff Report of Monthly Report Cost and Quality of Fuels for **Electric** Utility Plants, E 2.13

Statement of Taxes, Dividends, Salaries and Wages, Class a and Class B Privately Owned **Electric** Utilities in U.S., FP 1.22

Statistics of **Electric** Utilities in the United States, Classes A and B Publicly Owned Companies, FP 1.21

Statistics of Privately Owned **Electric** Utilities in the United States, E 3.18/2

Statistics of Publicly Owned **Electric** Utilities in the United States, E 3.18/3

Steam-**Electric** Plant Construction Cost and Annual Production Expenses, E 3.17

Thermal-**Electric** Plant Construction Cost and Annual Production Expenses, E 3.17/4

Topical Briefs: Fish and Wildlife Resources and **Electric** Power Generation, I 49.78

Typical Commercial and Industrial **Electric** Bills, FP 1.16/4

Typical **Electric** Bills (by States), FP 1.16/2

Typical **Electric** Bills, E 3.22

Typical **Electric** Bills, Typical Net Monthly Bills of January (year), for Residential Commercial and Industrial Services, FP 1.10

Typical Residential **Electric** Bills, FP 1.16/3U.S.A., Pr 32.5025

U.S. Central Station Nuclear **Electric** Generating Units, Significant Milestones, E 1.41

Uniform System of Accounts for **Electric** Railways, IC 1 eler.9

Uniform System of Accounts for Gas Corporations and **Electric** Corporations in the District of Columbia, IC 1 gas.5

Weekly **Electric** Output, United States, FP 1.11/7

Electric Railways

Classification of Expenditures for Roads and Equipment of **Electric Railways**, IC 1 eler.6

Classification of Operating Expenses of **Electric Railways**, IC 1 eler.7

Classification of Operating Revenues of **Electric Railways**, IC 1 eler.8

Electric Utilities

Financial Statistics of **Electric Utilities** and Interstate Natural Gas Pipeline Companies, E 3.11/2-8

Financial Statistics of Selected **Electric Utilities**, E 3.18/4

Electrical

British Exports of **Electrical** Apparatus, C 18.53

Census of **Electrical** Industries, C 3.38

Cost of Current Series, **Electrical** Equipment Division, C 18.61

Current Developments in **Electrical** Trade, C 18.213

Electrical and Radio World Trade News, C 18.67

Electrical Commission, 1884, S 5.17

Electrical Communications {abstracts}, C 41.66/4

Electrical Goods, C 3.82

Electrical Industrial Trucks and Tractors, C 3.80

Electrical Standards, C 18.30

Electronics and **Electrical** Engineering, PrEx 7.22/6

Herald of **Electrical** Industry {abstracts}, C 41.66/2

Trends in **Electrical** Goods Trade, C 3.172

Values of German Exports of **Electrical** Apparatus and Equipment, C 18.158

Electrical Engineering

Journal of Abstracts, **Electrical Engineering**, C 41.66/3

Electricity

Electricity Sales Statistics, Y 3.T 25:13

Electricity Sales Statistics, Distribution of Electricity at TVA Wholesale and Retail Rates, Y 3.T 25:13-2

Electricity Sales Statistics: Rate of Initial Service at TVA Rates and Wholesale Purchases from TVA, Y 3.T 25:13-2

Farm **Electricity** Report, A 88.46

Farm Telephone and **Electricity** Combined Report, A 88.45/2

Production of **Electricity** for Public Use in the U.S., I 19.32, I 19.33

Production of **Electricity** for Public Use in U.S., FP 1.11

Retail Prices and Indexes of Fuels and **Electricity**, L 2.40

Specifications and Drawings of Patents Relating to **Electricity**, I 23.17

Electrification

Annual Statistical Report, Rural **Electrification** Borrowers, A 68.1/2

Report of the Administrator of the Rural **Electrification** Administration, A 68.1

Rural **Electrification** News, A 68.9
Statistical Bulletins Rural **Electrification** Administration, A 68.13
Suggested Co-op **Electrification** Adviser Training Outline, A 68.16

Electrified
Number and Percentage of Farms **Electrified** with Central Station Service, A 68.20

Electro
Armed Services **Electro** Standards Agency Lists, D 101.38
Electro-Economy Supplements, A 68.11
Scientific Reports of Higher Schools **Electro**-Mechanics and Automation, C 41.65/7

Electromagnetic
Biological Effects of **Electromagnetic** Radiation, D 101.52/8
Electromagnetic Meteorology, Current Awareness Service, C 13.54

Electromechanics
News of Institutes of Higher Learning; **Electromechanics**, C 41.65/6

Electronic
Catalog of **Electronic** Data Products, HE 20.6209/4-6
Directorate of **Electronic** and Material Sciences FY Program, D 301.45/19-9
Electronic Computer Program Library Memorandum, C 37.20
Electronic Equipment Modification, C 31.161
Electronic Information Products Available by Special Order, GP 3.22/5
Electronic Products [Aging Administration], HE 1.1018
Electronic Products [Agricultural Research Service], A 77.40
Electronic Products [Agriculture Department], A 1.142
Electronic Products [Air Force Department], D 301.118
Electronic Products [Air Quality Planning and Standards Office], EP 4.28
Electronic Products [Animal and Plant Health Inspection Service], A 101.32
Electronic Products [Appalachian Regional Commission], Y 3.Ap 4/2:16
Electronic Products [Armed Forces Information Services], D 2.20
Electronic Products [Army Department], D 101.129/6, D 101.121/1
Electronic Products [Aviation Medicine Office], TD 4.214
Electronic Products [Bonneville Power Administration], E 5.24
Electronic Products [Census Bureau], C 3.275
Electronic Products [Center for Environmental Health], HE 20.7512
Electronic Products [Center for Prevention Services], HE 20.7319
Electronic Products [Chief of Naval Reserve], D 207.310
Electronic Products [Coast Guard], TD 5.67
Electronic Products [Commerce Department], C 1.89
Electronic Products [Comptroller of the Currency], T 12.19
Electronic Products [Consolidated Farm Service], A 112.21
Electronic Products [Cooperative State Research Service], A 94.22
Electronic Products [Defense Department], D 1.95
Electronic Products [Defense Logistics Agency], D 7.45
Electronic Products [Defense Mapping Agency], D 5.360
Electronic Products [Defense Nuclear Facilities Safety Board], Y 3.D 36/3:13
Electronic Products [Descriptive Cataloging Division], LC 9.17
Electronic Products [Economic Analysis Bureau], C 59.26
Electronic Products [Education Department], ED 1.83
Electronic Products [Energy Department], E 1.111
Electronic Products [Environmental Protection Agency], EP 1.104
Electronic Products [Executive Office of the President], PrEx 1.21
Electronic Products [Export Administration Bureau], C 63.25
Electronic Products [Farmer Cooperative Service], A 88.64

Electronic Products [Federal Aviation Administration], TD 4.75, TD 4.76
Electronic Products [Federal Bureau of Investigation], J 1.14/23
Electronic Products [Federal Communications Commission], CC 1.57
Electronic Products [Federal Crop Insurance Corporation], A 62.18
Electronic Products [Federal Deposit Insurance Corporation], Y 3.F 31/8:32
Electronic Products [Federal Emergency Management Agency], FEM 1.27
Electronic Products [Federal Highway Administration], TD 2.73
Electronic Products [Federal Register Office], AE 2.115
Electronic Products [Federal Supply and Services Office], GS 2.26
Electronic Products [Federal Trade Commission], FT 1.33
Electronic Products [Financial Management Service], T 63.130
Electronic Products [Fish and Wildlife Service], I 49.113
Electronic Products [Food Safety and Inspection Service], A 110.20
Electronic Products [Forest Service], A 13.140
Electronic Products [General Services Agency], GS 1.35
Electronic Products [Geological Survey], I 19.120
Electronic Products [Health and Human Services Department], HE 1.60
Electronic Products [Health Care Financing Administration], HE 22.44
Electronic Products [Housing and Urban Development Department], HH 1.114
Electronic Products [Immigration and Naturalization Service], J 21.24
Electronic Products [Interior Department], I 1.114
Electronic Products [International Development Agency], S 18.65
Electronic Products [International Trade Administration], C 61.47
Electronic Products [Justice Department], J 1.100
Electronic Products [Juvenile Justice and Delinquence Prevention Office], J 32.23
Electronic Products [Library of Congress], LC 1.53, LC 1.54
Electronic Products [Marine Corps], D 214.32
Electronic Products [Medicine and Surgery Bureau], D 206.24
Electronic Products [Military History Center], D 114.21
Electronic Products [Military Sealift Command], D 216.11
Electronic Products [Minerals Management Service], I 72.19
Electronic Products [Multi-Family Housing Office], HH 13.15
Electronic Products [National Aeronautics and Space Admnistration], NAS 1.86
Electronic Products [National Agricultural Library], A 17.31
Electronic Products [National Agricultural Statistics Service], A 92.51
Electronic Products [National Archives and Records Administration], AE 1.127
Electronic Products [National Cancer Institute], HE 20.3193
Electronic Products [National Center for Health Statistics], HE 20.6231
Electronic Products [National Endowment for the Arts], NF 2.17
Electronic Products [National Institute for Occupational Safety and Health], HE 20.7129
Electronic Products [National Institute of Standards and Technology], C 13.79
Electronic Products [National Institute on Deafness and Other Communication Disorders], HE 20.3667
Electronic Products [National Institutes of Health], HE 20.3064
Electronic Products [National Library of Medicine], HE 20.3624/3
Electronic Products [National Science Foundation], NS 1.60
Electronic Products [National Transportation Safety Board], TD 1.132

Electronic Products [Naval Doctrine Command], D 207.415
Electronic Products [Naval Sea Systems Command], D 211.29
Electronic Products [Naval Training and Education Command], D 207.217
Electronic Products [Nuclear Regulatory Commission], Y 3.N 88:61
Electronic Products [Occupational Safety and Health Review Commission], Y 3.OC 1:11
Electronic Products [Patent and Trademark Office], C 21.32
Electronic Products [Prisons Bureau], J 16.33
Electronic Products [Processing Department], LC 30.33
Electronic Products [Public Documents Division], GP 3.38
Electronic Products [Railroad Retirement Board], RR 1.17
Electronic Products [Reclamation Bureau], I 27.81
Electronic Products [Science and Technology Policy Office], PrEx 23.12
Electronic Products [Smithsonian Institution], SI 1.47
Electronic Products [Social Security Administration], SSA 1.27
Electronic Products [Soil Conservation Service], A 57.76
Electronic Products [State Department], S 1.142
Electronic Products [Transportation Department], TD 1.56
Electronic Products [Transportation Statistics Bureau], TD 12.17
Electronic Products [Treasury Department], T 1.66
Electronic Products [United States Congress], Y 1.5
Electronic Products [United States Information Agency], IA 1.32/2
Electronic Products [United States Postal Service], P 1.59
Electronic Products [Veterans Affairs Department], VA 1.95
Electronic Products [Vice President Office], PrVp 42.17
Electronic Products [Violence Against Women Office], J 35.19
Electronic Products [Wage and Hour Division], L 36.214
Electronic Research Directorate Technical Memorandum ERD-CRRK-TM (series), D 301.45/12
NET (New **Electronic** Titles), GP 3.40
U.S. Army **Electronic** Proving Ground, USAEPG-SIG (series), D 111.12
U.S. Government Working Group on **Electronic** Commerce, C 1.1/7

Electronic Publishing
Air Education and Training Command **Electronic Publishing** Library, AETCEPL, 301.116/3
Air Force **Electronic Publishing** Library of Departmental Publications and Forms, D 301.116

Electronics
Army **Electronics** Command Fort Monmouth N.J.: Research and Development Technical Reports ECOM (series), D 111.9/4
Basic **Electronics** Training (series), D 101.107/11
Conference Proceedings {of} AASHO Committee on **Electronics**, TD 2.125
Electronics and Electrical Engineering, PrEx 7.22/6
Electronics Engineering Information Bulletin, TD 5.3/3
Electronics Engineering Reports, T 47.42
Electronics Information Bulletin, D 201.3/2
FLITE {Federal Legal Information Through **Electronics**} Newsletter, D 302.10
Joint **Electronic** Library, D 5.21
Modular Individualized Learning for **Electronics** Training, D 207.109
National **Electronic** Catalog, P 1.58
Navy **Electronics** Laboratory Reports, D 211.11
Navy **Electronics** Laboratory, San Diego, California, Publications (misc.), D 211.11/2
Publications Navy **Electronics** Laboratory, D 211.11/2
Radio Engineering and **Electronics** {abstracts}, C 41.49/2

Research in Progress, Calendar Year Physics, **Electronics**, Mathematics, Geosciences, D 101.52/5-4

Technical Notes Department of the Air Force **Electronics** Research Directorate, D 301.45/12-2

Update (**Electronics** Manufacturing Productivity Facility), D 201.36

Electrotechnology

Electrotechnology Newsletter, Y 3.T 25:63

Electrotechnology, C 51.9/22, C 51.17/2

Element

Report of United States High Commissioner, Statistical Annex, U.S. **Element**, Allied Commission for Austria, S 1.89/2

Report of United States High Commissioner, U.S. **Element**, Allied Commission for Austria, S 1.89

Elementary

Annual Report of Compensatory Education Programs under Title I, **Elementary** and Secondary Education Act of 1965, FS 5.79

Annual Report, Title 2, **Elementary** and Secondary Education Act of 1965, School Library Resources, Textbooks, and Other Instructional Materials, FS 5.220:20108, HE 5.220:20108

Conference on **Elementary** Education Reports, FS 5.58

Elementary Books, LC 2.6

Elementary Education Circulars, I 16.19

Elementary School Personnel, FS 5.84:El 2, HE 5.84:El 2

Elementary Teacher Education Program, Feasibility Studies, HE 5.87

Expenditures and Revenues for Public **Elementary** and Secondary Education, HE 19.313

Fall {year} Enrollment, Teachers, and School-Housing in Full-Time Public **Elementary** and Secondary Day Schools, FS 5.220:20007, HE 5.220:20007

Implementing Title IX and Attaining Sex Equity; A Workshop for **Elementary**-Secondary Educators, HE 19.141/2

Minorities and Women in Public **Elementary** and Secondary Schools, Y 3.Eq 2:12-3

Model Programs, Title III, **Elementary** and Secondary Education Act, HE 18.12

NEH Teacher-Scholar Program for **Elementary** and Secondary School Teachers, Guidelines and Application Instructions, NF 3.18

Public **Elementary** and Secondary Education in the United States, ED 1.112/2

Public **Elementary** and Secondary Education Statistics: School Year, ED 1.328/12

Pupil Mobility in Public **Elementary** and Secondary Schools During the (date) School Year, HE 5.93/6

Revenues and Expenditures for Public and **Elementary** and Secondary Education, ED 1.119

Statistics of Nonpublic **Elementary** and Secondary Schools, (year), HE 5.93/9

Statistics of Nonpublic **Elementary** Schools, FS 5.220:20064

Statistics of Public **Elementary** and Secondary Day Schools, HE 19.326

Title 1 of **Elementary** and Secondary Education Act of 1965; Annual Report, FS 5.79, FS 5.237:37013, HE 5.79, HE 5.237:37013

Title II, **Elementary** and Secondary Education Act of 1965, School Library Resources, Textbooks and Other Instructional Materials, Annual Report, HE 5.79/2

Elementary Education

Conference for Supervisors of **Elementary** Education in Large Cities, FS 5.58/2

Elements

Correspondence Course, **Elements** of Surface Weather Observations, Lessons, C 30.26

Elements of Value of Property, Class I Switching and Terminal Companies Used in Common Carrier Service, IC 1 val.11, IC 1 val.12

Final State and Local Data **Elements**, T 1.64/2

Hospital **Elements**, Planning and Equipment for 50- and 200-Bed General Hospitals, FS 2.12/2

Rare **Elements** and Thorium in (year), I 28.144

Selected **Elements** of Value of Property Used in Common Carrier Service, Before and After Recorded Depreciation and Amortization, Class I Line Haul Railways, Including Their Lessors and Proprietary Companies, IC 1 val.10

Elevations

Elevations and Distances, I 19.2:El 3/2

Second-Order Leveling, List of Standard **Elevations**, C 4.39

Elevators

Capacity of **Elevators**, Reporting Grain Stocks, A 36.82

Storage Capacity of **Elevators** Reporting Commercial Grain Stocks, A 88.18/15

Eligibility

Guide to **Eligibility** of W.P.A. Projects, Y 3.W 89/2:14

Eligible

Areas **Eligible** for Financial Assistance Designated Under the Public Works and Economic Development Act of 1965 Reports, C 46.25/2

Composite List of **Eligible** Institutions for Guaranteed Loans for College Students, Higher Education Act of 1965, FS 5.83, HE 5.83

Composite List of **Eligible** Institutions, National Vocation Student Loan Insurance Act of 1965, FS 5.83/2, HE 5.83/2

Elimination

Elimination of Waste Series, C 1.13

Elite

U.S. National Arboretum **Elite** Plant, A 77.38/2

Elkhart

Area Wage Survey, **Elkhart**-Goshen, Indiana, Metropolitan Area, L 2.121/14-4

EM

EM Progress, E 1.90/6

EM State Fact Sheets, E 1.90/7

Embassy

American **Embassy**, Rome: Quarterly Statistical Bulletin, S 1.115

Embracing

General Orders **Embracing** Laws Affecting the Army, W 3.8

Embrittlement

Long-Term **Embrittlement** of Cast Duplex Stainless Steels in LWR Systems, Y 3.N 88:25-5

Embryology

Human **Embryology** and Development Study Section, HE 20.3001/2:Em 1

Emergence

Two Centuries of Tariffs, the Background and **Emergence** of the U.S. International Trade Commission, TC 1.2:T 17/20

Emergencies

Mental Health **Emergencies** Alert, HE 20.8113/2

Emergency

Aircraft **Emergency** Evacuation Reports, C 31.150

Aircraft **Emergency** Procedures Over Water, T 47.32/2

Annual **Emergency** Room Data Series, HE 20.416/2

Annual Report to the President and the Congress Submitted by the Secretary of Transportation Under the **Emergency** Rail Service Act of 1970, TD 1.10/6

Annual Report, Federal **Emergency** Management Agency (by Region), FEM 1.1/2

BDSA **Emergency** Delegations, C 41.6/8

BPR **Emergency** Readiness Newsletter, C 37.31

Circular Letters, Relate to Indian **Emergency** Conservation Work, I 20.23

Clinical Handbook on Economic Poisons, **Emergency** Information for Treating Poisoning, EP 5.8:P 75

Emergency Bulletins, I 16.52

Emergency Conservation Program, Fiscal Year Statistical Summary, A 112.1/2, A 113.1/2

Emergency Conservation Program, Fiscal Year Summary, A 82.93

Emergency Conservation Work Bulletins, L 1.11

Emergency Conservation Work, Project Training Publications, I 29.28

Emergency Fleet News, SB 2.6

Emergency Health Series, HE 20.2013

Emergency Health Services Digest, HE 20.13/2

Emergency Management, FEM 1.16

Emergency Management Institute, Resident Training Programs, FEM 1.17/2

Emergency Management Institute, Schedule of Courses, FEM 1.17/2

Emergency Management of National Economy, D 1.27

Emergency Manual Guides, FS 1.6/4

Emergency Officers, Army List and Directory, W 3.10/2

Emergency Operations Orders, Pr 34.706/6, PrEx 4.6/6

Emergency Parent Education Bulletins, Y 3.F 31/5:16

Emergency Relief Appropriation Acts, Reports of President to Congress Showing Status of Funds and Operations Under, T 63.114

Emergency Relief Appropriation Acts, Reports Showing Status of Funds, T 63.107

Emergency Relief Bulletins, Y 3.R 24:8

Emergency Striped Bass Research Study, I 49.103

Emergency Tariff Laws of 1921 and Reciprocal Trade Agreement Act of 1934, with all Amendments {May, 1934}, Y 1.2:T 17/2

EMS {**Emergency** Medical Services} Resource Exchange Bulletin, FEM 1.110/3

EMSC (**Emergency** Medical Services for Children) News, HE 20.9212

Engineering Manual for **Emergency** Construction, D 103.21

Famine **Emergency** Committee Publications, A 1.70

Federal **Emergency** Relief Administration Grants, Y 3.F 31/5:32

Federal **Emergency** Relief Administration Grants Distributed According to Programs and Periods for which Grants were Made, Y 3.F 31/5:33

Federal Standard Stock Catalog: Sec. 4, Pt. 5, **Emergency** Federal Specifications, GS 2.8/4

Memorandum to All Administrators of **Emergency** Educational Programs, I 16.53

Mine **Emergency** Operations Telephone Book, L 38.21

Occupant **Emergency** Plan Handbook for the Frances Perkins Building, L 1.1/2-2:2-8

Posters Federal **Emergency** Management Agency, FEM 1.21

Property, **Emergency** Procurement and Funds, W 3.50/6

Register Planned **Emergency** Producers, D 7.11/2

Regulations, Rules and Instructions Federal **Emergency** Management Agency, FEM 1.6

Report to Congress on the **Emergency** Homeowner's Relief Act, HH 1.64

Reports of **Emergency** Boards, NMB 1.7

Reports of President to Congress Showing Status of Funds and Operations under **Emergency** Relief Appropriation Acts, T 63.114

Reports Showing Financial Status of Funds Provided in **Emergency** Relief Appropriation Acts, T 60.11

Reports Showing Status of Funds and Analyses of Expenditures, **Emergency** Appropriation Acts, T 60.13

Reports Showing Status of Funds Provided in **Emergency** Relief Appropriation Acts, T 60.12

Research Bulletins Federal **Emergency** Relief Administration, Y 3.F 31/5:28

Research Projects Federal **Emergency** Management Agency, FEM 1.22

Safety Bulletins Federal **Emergency** Relief Administration, Y 3.F 31/5:24

State Salary Ranges, Selected Classes {of positions} in Employment Security, Public Welfare, Public Health, Mental Health, Vocational Rehabilitation, Civil Defense, **Emergency** Planning, CS 1.81, FS 1.22, HE 1.22, GS 1.8

Summary of **Emergency** Relief Statistics, Y 3.F 31/5:34

Superfund **Emergency** Response Actions, A Summary of Federally-Funded Removals, Annual Report, EP 1.89/5

TC in the Current National **Emergency**, Historical Report No., D 117.9, D 117.9/2

Total Obligations Incurred for **Emergency** Relief from All Public Funds by State and Local Relief Administration in Continental United States, Y 3.F 31/5:35

Veterans **Emergency** Housing Program: Community Action Report to Mayor's **Emergency** Housing Committee, NHA 1.12, Y 3.H 81/2:8

Veterans' **Emergency** Housing Program: Community Action Bulletin, NHA 1.14

Emerging

Big **Emerging** Markets, Outlook and Sourcebook, C 61.45

Emerging Infectious Diseases, HE 20.7009/7, HE 20.7817

Emerging Technology Bulletin, EP 1.3/4

EMIC

EMIC Information Circulars, L 5.46

Preliminary Monthly Statistical Report on **EMIC** Program, L 5.50, FS 3.208

Emission

Air Chief (Clearinghouse for Inventory and **Emission** Factors), EP 1.109

Air Pollution Aspects of **Emission** Sources: {various subjects}, a Bibliography with Abstracts, EP 1.21/5

Background Document for {various products} Noise **Emission** Regulations, EP 1.6/2

National Air Pollutant **Emission** Estimates, EP 4.24

Noise **Emission** Standards for Construction Equipment, Background Document for {various items}, EP 1.6/3

Emissions

Emissions of Greenhouse Gases in the United States, E 3.59

Inventory of U.S. Greenhouse Gas **Emissions** and Sinks, EP 1.115

National Air Quality and **Emissions** Trends Report, EP 4.22/2

National **Emissions** Report, EP 1.64

EMMTAP

Executive Manpower Management Technical Assistance Papers, **EMMTAP**, CS 1.85

Employed

Census of Nurses **Employed** for Public Health Work in United States, in Territories of Alaska and Hawaii, and in Puerto Rico and Virgin Islands, FS 2.81

Females **Employed** by Class 1 Steams Railways, Number of, IC 1 ste.43

Number of Females **Employed** by Class 1 Steam Railways, IC 1 ste.43

Employee

Alcohol and You, HSMHA **Employee** Health Program on Alcoholism, HE 20.2711

Conventions, (year): National and International Unions, State Labor Federations, Professional Associations, State **Employee** Association {list}, L 2.103

Employee and Labor Relations, P 1.12/7

Employee Benefits in Medium and Large Firms, L 2.3/10

Employee Benefits in Medium and Large Private Establishments L 2.3/10

Employee Benefits in State and Local Governments, L 2.3/10-2

Employee Benefits Survey Defined Benefit Pension Coding Manual, L 2.46/7

Employee Benefits Survey Defined Contribution Coding Manual, L 2.46/8

Employee Benefits Survey Health Coding Manual, L 2.46/5

Employee Benefits Survey Sickness and Accident Coding Manual, L 2.46/6

Employee Bulletin, C 21.21

Employee Counseling Service Program Memo, HE 20.9113/2

Employee Counseling Service Program, Annual Report, HE 20.9113/3

Employee Development Guides, L 1.7/3

Employee Publications, FS 3.42

Employee Relations Bulletin, D 101.136

Employee Retirement Income Security Act, Report to Congress, L 1.76, L 40.15

Employee Survival Bulletin, C 1.34

Employee Training and Career Development Catalog, HE 22.39

Employee Training in the Federal Service, PM 1.19/4-3

Employee Training in the Federal Service, Fiscal Year (date), CS 1.48:T-7

Employer Costs for **Employee** Compensation, L 2.120/2-113, L 2.120/2-16

Federal **Employee** Facts, CS 1.59

Federal **Employee** Health Series, HE 20.5410

Federal **Employee** Substance Abuse Education and Treatment Act of 1986, PM 1.61

Finances of **Employee**-Retirement Systems of State and Local Governments in (year), C 56.209, C 3.191/2

Fly-By, Official **Employee** Publication of Federal Aviation Agency, FAA 1.11

Focus on Federal **Employee** Health Assistance Programs, PM 1.55

Holdings of Selected Public **Employee** Retirement Systems, GR (series), C 56.224, C 3.242

New Developments in **Employee** and Labor Relations, PM 1.62

Railroad **Employee** Accident Investigation Reports, TD 3.110/3

Railroad **Employee** Fatalities Investigated by the Federal Railroad Administration in (year), TD 3.110/5

Significant Cases, Federal **Employee** and Labor-Management Relations, PM 1.63

TDC **Employee** News Bulletin, C 1.49

VHA **Employee** Newsletter, VA 1.100

Employees

Alphabetical List of **Employees**, GP 1.5

Annual Report of Radiation Exposures for DOE and DOE Contractor **Employees**, E 1.42

BDSA Bulletins Information of Interest of **Employees**, C 41.3/2

Bond of Federal **Employees**, Y 4.P 84/11:B 64

Census Bulletin, Official Information for Census **Employees**, C 3.3/3

Chit Chat, an Administrative Letter for Division **Employees**, A 103.17

Compilation . . ., and Arbitration Between Employers and **Employees**, Laws {on} Disputes Between Carriers and Employers . . ., Eight-hour

Laws, Employers' Liability Laws, Labor and Child Labor Laws, Y 1.2:Em 7/6

Compilation of Laws Relating to Mediation, Conciliation, and Arbitration Between Employers and **Employees**, Laws {on} Disputes Between Carriers and Employers and Subordinate Officials. . ., Y 1.2:Em 7/6

Current Salary Schedules of Federal Officers and **Employees** Together with a History of Salary and Retirement Annuity Adjustments, Y 4.P 84/10-15

Directory of **Employees** for the International Trade Administration, C 61.32

Directory of National Unions and **Employees** Associations, L 2.2:Un 33/9

Employees Booklets, RR 1.9

Employees Compensation Commission, FS 13.300

Employees in Private and Government Shipyards by Region, L 2.81

Employees of Diplomatic Missions, S 1.8/2

Employees' Health Service Folders, FS 2.49

Employment and Wages of Workers Covered by State Unemployment Insurance Laws and Unemployment Compensation for Federal **Employees**, by Industry and State, L 7.20/3, L 1.61

Employment and Wages, a Quarterly Summary of Workers Covered by State Unemployment Insurance Laws and Unemployment Compensation for Federal **Employees**, L 2.104

Employment under Works Program, Exclusive of Administrative **Employees**, Y 3.W 89/2:15

Enrollment Information Guide and Plan Comparison Chart Retirement Systems Participating in the Federal **Employees** Health Benefits Program, PM 1.8/4

Enrollment Information Guide and Plan Comparison Chart U.S. Postal Service **Employees**, PM 1.8/5 .

Evaluation of **Employees** for Promotion and Internal Placement, CS 1.41/4:335-1

Farm Labor Contractor Registration Act, Public Registry, National Listing of Contractors and **Employees** Registered, L 36.14

Federal Civilian Employment and Wages of Workers Covered by Unemployment Compensation for Federal **Employees**, L 7.20/4

Federal **Employees** Health Benefits, CS 1.41/4:890-1

Federal Work Injury Facts, Occupational Distribution, Duration and Direct Cost Factors of Work Injuries to Civilian Federal **Employees** During Calendar Year, L 26.8/2-2

Monthly and Annual Earnings of Train and Engine Service **Employees**, RL 1.9

Non-Appropriated **Employees**, CS 1.41/4:532-2

Number of **Employees** at Middle of Month, IC 1 ste.25/2

Occupational Health Services for Civilian **Employees**, CS 1.41/4:792-1

Official Roster of Officers and **Employees**, W 49.5/5

Political Activity and Political Assessments of Federal Office-Holders and **Employees**, CS 1.34

Postal Life, the Magazine for Postal **Employees**, P 1.43

Register of **Employees**, P 1.14

Report to **Employees** FY, Washington, D.C. Post Office, P 1.1/2

Report, Civil Service Requirement, Federal **Employees'** Group Life Insurance, Federal **Employees** Health Benefits, Retired Federal **Employees** Health Benefits, Fiscal Year (date), CS 1.29/3

Roster of Commissioned Officers and **Employees**, A 29.28

Rules of Practice and Rules Relating to Investigations and Code of Behavior Governing Exparte Communications Between Persons Outside the Commission and Decisional **Employees**, SE 1.6:R 86/4

Safety Bulletins **Employees** Compensation Commission, EC 1.9

Special Bulletins **Employees'** Compensation Commission, EC 1.3/2

State Education Agency Operations, Revenues, Expenditures, and **Employees**, ED 1.108/3

Employees'

Digest and Decisions of the **Employees'** Compensation Appeals Board, L 28.9

Pamphlets Federal **Employees'** Compensation Office, L 36.309

Safety Bulletins Bureau of **Employees'** Compensation, FS 13.307, L 26.7

Employer

Administrative Decisions Under Employer Sanctions and Unfair Immigration-Related Employment Practices Law of the United States, J 1.103

Employer Costs for Employee Compensation, L 2.120/2-113, L 2.120/2-16

Employer Guide (series), PrEx 1.10/11

Employers

Compilation . . .Between **Employers** and Employees, Laws {on} Disputes Between Carriers and **Employers** and Subordinate Officials Under Labor Board, Eight-hour

Laws, **Employers'** Liability Laws, . . ., Y 1.2:Em 7/6

Compilation of Laws Relating to Mediation, Conciliation, and Arbitration Between **Employers** and Employees, Laws {on} Disputes Between Carriers and **Employers** and Subordinate Officials. . ., Y 1.2:Em 7/6

Employers' Estimates of Labor Needs in Selected Defense Industries, FS 3.121

Register of Reporting **Employers**, L 1.81

Employment

Age Discriminaton in **Employment** Act of 1967, Reports Covering Activities Under the Act During (year), L 36.11

Analysis of Production, Wages and **Employment** in Manufacturing Industries, Y 3.C 78:7

Annual Affirmative **Employment** Accomplishment and Activities in Fiscal . . ., HE 20.4048

Annual Report of Federal Civilian **Employment** by Geographic Area, CS 1.48

Annual Report on the **Employment** of Minorities, Women and Handicapped Individuals in the Federal Government, Y 3.Eq 2:12-5

Annual Report on the Status of Equal **Employment** Opportunity Program, TD 2.17

Area Trends in **Employment** and Unemployment, L 37.13

Best Opportunities for Federal **Employment**, CS 1.28:2280

Business Establishment, **Employment** and Taxable Pay Rolls under Old-Age and Survivors Insurance Program, C 18.270

Census/Equal **Employment** Opportunity (EEO) Special File, C 3.283

CETA Area **Employment** and Unemployment, L 2.110

CETA Area **Employment** and Unemployment, BLS/CETA/MR (series), L 2.110/2

CETA Area **Employment** and Unemployment, Special Reports, BLS/CETA/SP (series), L 2.110/3

Chart Book on Government Finances and **Employment**: (year), C 56.209, C 3.191/2

City **Employment** in (year), C 3.140/2

Civil **Employment** and Payrolls in Executive Branch of U.S. Government, CS 1.32

Combined **Employment** and Unemployment Releases, L 1.20/2

Control and **Employment** of Vessels Trading with United States, SB 5.6

County Government **Employment**, C 3.140/2-5

Current **Employment** Market for Engineers, Scientists, and Technicians, L 7.63/2

Current **Employment** Statistics State Operating Manual, L 2.46/4

Directory of Local **Employment** Security Offices, L 37.18, L 1.59

DOT **Employment** Facts, TD 1.46

Earnings and **Employment** Data for Wage and Salary Workers Covered under Social Security by State and County, HE 3.95, SSA 1.17/3

Employment and Earnings L 2.41/2

Employment and Earnings and Monthly Report on Labor Force, L 2.41/2

Employment and Earnings Characteristics of Families, L 2.118/2

Employment and Earnings in the Mountain Plains Region, L 2.41/8

Employment and Earnings Statistics for States and Areas, L 2.3

Employment and Pay Rolls, Emergency Work Relief Program, Y 3.F 31/5:31

Employment and Payrolls, L 2.9

Employment and Population Changes, Special Economic Reports, C 56.240

Employment and Training Report of the President, L 1.42/2

Employment and Trends as of . . ., PM 1.15

Employment and Unemployment in States and Local Areas, L 2.41/9, L 2.41/10

Employment and Wage Supplement, Farm Labor Market Developments, L 7.55/2

Employment and Wages of Workers Covered by State Unemployment Compensation Laws: Estimated, FS 3.122

Employment and Wages of Workers Covered by State Unemployment Insurance Laws and Unemployment Compensation for Federal Employees, by Industry and State, L 7.20/3, L 1.61

Employment and Wages, a Quarterly Summary of Workers Covered by State Unemployment Insurance Laws and Unemployment Compensation for Federal Employees, L 2.104

Employment and Wages, Annual Average, L 2.104/2

Employment Bulletin, Current Openings, G-11 and Above, at Army Material Command Activities Throughout the United States, D 101.3/5

Employment by Geographic Area, PM 1.10/3

Employment Cost Index, L 2.117

Employment Data on Title 38 Physicians, Dentists, and Nurses, VA 1.75

Employment Fact Book, J 1.57

Employment Hours and Earnings on Projects Operated by WPA, Y 3.W 89/2:26

Employment Hours and Earnings on Student Aid Projects of NYA, Y 3.W 89/2:27

Employment in Nonagricultural Establishments, FR 1.42

Employment in Nuclear Energy Activities, a Highlights Report, E 1.33:0049

Employment in Perspective: Minority Workers, L 2.41/11-2

Employment in Perspective: Women in the Labor Force, L 2.41/11

Employment in the Mountain States, L 2.41/6

Employment in the Plains States, L 2.41/7

Employment of Disabled and Vietnam Era Veterans in Federal Government, CS 1.93

Employment Office Manual Series (lettered), L 7.15

Employment Office Training Programs, Pr 32.5220

Employment on Farms of Crop Reporters, A 36.69

Employment Opportunities, D 202.17, D 215.8

Employment Outlook for {various occupations}, L 13.2

Employment Plans and Suggestions Committee, Y 3.P 92:7

Employment Profiles for Selected Low-Income Areas, PHC (3) (series), C 3.223/17

Employment Report of United States Flag Merchant Fleet, Oceangoing Vessels 1,000 Gross Tons and Over, C 39.208

Employment Reports, L 2.82

Employment Security Activities, L 7.40

Employment Security Exchange Series, L 7.56

Employment Security Memorandum, FS 3.110

Employment Security Research and Reporting Exchange Series, L 7.56/2

Employment Security Research Exchange, L 7.56/3

Employment Service Manual, Pr 32.5221

Employment Service News, L 7.14, FS 3.107

Employment Service Review, L 7.18, FS 3.130

Employment Service Statistics, L 7.18/2-2, L 1.60

Employment Service Technical Reports, L 1.70

Employment Services for Veterans, Annual Report, L 7.30/2

Employment Situation, L 2.53/2

Employment Tax, T 22.19/3:3

Employment under the Executive Assignment Systems, CS 1.41/4:305-1

Employment under Works Program, Exclusive of Administrative Employees, Y 3.W 89/2:15

Employment, Hours and Earnings, L 1.20/3, L 2.41/3

Equal **Employment** Opportunity, Code of Federal Regulations Title 29, Y 3.Eq 2:18-4

Equal **Employment** Opportunity Commission Decisions, Federal Sector, Y 3.Eq 2:18

Equal **Employment** Opportunity Federal Register, Y 3.Eq 2:18-6

Equal **Employment** Opportunity in the Federal Courts, Ju 10.22

Equal **Employment** Opportunity Management Directives/Bulletins, Y 3.Eq 2:18-5

Equal **Employment** Opportunity Reports, Y 3.Eq 2:12

ET {Employment Training} Handbooks, L 37.8/2

Fair **Employment** Practice Committee {publications}, Pr 32.412

Farmer's Tax Guide, Income and Self **Employment** Taxes, T 22.19/2:F 22

Federal Civilian **Employment** and Wages of Workers Covered by Unemployment Compensation for Federal Employees, L 7.20/4

Federal **Employment** of Women, CS 1.74

Federal **Employment** Outlook, CS 1.72/3

Federal **Employment** Statistics Bulletin, CS 1.55

Geographic Profile of **Employment** and Unemployment, L 2.3/12

Government **Employment**, C 56.209/2

Government **Employment** GE (series), C 3.140/2

Government Finances and **Employment** at a Glance, C 3.191/3

Indexes of Production Worker **Employment** in Manufacturing Industries by Metropolitan Area, L 2.24

Industrial **Employment** Information Bulletin, L 7.8

Information Regarding **Employment** on National Forests, A 13.22

Injury Experience and Related **Employment** Data for Sand and Gravel Industry, I 28.108/2

Justice Expenditure and **Employment**, J 29.11/2

Justice Expenditure and **Employment** Extracts, J 29.11/2-2

Justice Expenditure and **Employment** in the U.S, J 29.11/2-3

Key Facts, **Employment** Security Operations, L 7.60

Local Government **Employment** in Major County Areas, C 3.140/2-6

Maritime Manpower Report: Sea Faring, Longshore, and Shipyard **Employment** as of (date), C 39.202:Se 1/2, C 39.235

Merchant Ships Built in United States and Other Countries in **Employment** Report of United States Flag Merchant Seagoing Vessels 1,000 Tons and Over, C 39.211

Monthly Report of Federal **Employment**, CS 1.32/2

Monthly Report on Labor Force, **Employment**, Unemployment, Hours and Earnings, L 2.84

New England Economy, **Employment**, Etc., Releases, L 2.49/4

News, **Employment** and Average Annual Pay for Large Companies L 2.120/2-17

News, **Employment** and Wages in Foreign-Owned Businesses in the United States, L 2.41/12

News Regional and State **Employment** and Unemployment, L 2.111/7

Newsletter, Tips and Trends in **Employment** of the Mentally Handicapped, PrEx 1.10/5

News, Metropolitan Areas Employment and Unemployment L 2.111/5

Northeast **Employment** Cost Index, L 2.117/2

Occupational **Employment** in Manufacturing Industries, L 2.3/16

Occupational **Employment** in Selected Nonmanufacturing Industries, L 2.3/16-2

Operations of the **Employment** Security Program, FS 3.3/a3

Overseas **Employment** Opportunities for Educators, D 1.68

Park Areas and **Employment** Opportunities for Summer, I 29.110

Preliminary Report of Railroad **Employment**, Class 1 Line-haul Railroads, IC 1 ste.25/3

President's Committee on **Employment** of the Handicapped, Annual Report to Membership, .PrEx 1.10/13

President's Committee on **Employment** of the Handicapped: People with Disabilities in Our Nation's Job Training Partnership Act Programs, PrEx 1.10/15

President's Committee on **Employment** of the Handicapped: Press Releases, PrEx 1.10/4

Production, Prices **Employment**, and Trade in Northwest Forest Industries, A 13.66/13

Productivity and Cost of **Employment**: Local Service Carriers, Calendar Year, C 31.263

Productivity and Cost of **Employment**: System Trunks, Calendar Year, C 31.263/2

Program Guide President's Committee on **Employment** of the Handicapped, PrEx 1.10/7

Public **Employment** in (year), C 3.140/2, C 3.140/2-4

Public **Employment** Program, Annual Report to Congress, L 1.68

Quarterly Report on **Employment** of American Merchant Vessels, SB 7.5/300, C 27.9/7

Quarterly Report on **Employment** of American Steam and Motor Merchant Vessels, MC 1.8

Registration, **Employment** and Unemployment, U.S. Zone, Statistical Report, W 1.72/3

Report of Railroad **Employment**, Class 1 Line-Haul Railroads, IC 1 ste.25/3-2

Selected Agricultural Activities of Public **Employment** Offices, L 7.59

Semi-monthly Report on **Employment** Situation, L 2.53

Series Available and Estimating Methods, BLS Current **Employment** Statistics Program, L 2.124/2

Series Available and Estimating Methods, BLS National Payroll **Employment** Program, L 2.124

Special Report, Fresh Views of **Employment** of the Mentally Handicapped, PrEx 1.10/4-2

Spotlight on Affirmative **Employment** Programs, PM 1.18/4

State and Local Government **Employment** and Payrolls, L 2.41/4

State and Local Government Quarterly **Employment** Survey, C 3.140

State and Metropolitan Area **Employment** and Unemployment, L 2.111/5

State Distribution of Public **Employment** in (year), C 3.140/2

State Laws and Regulations Prohibiting **Employment** of Minors in Hazardous Occupations, L 22.6/2

Value **Engineering** Information Letters, C 39.220

Value **Engineering** Program: Annual Report, GS 6.10

Weather Bureau **Engineering** Handbooks EHB-(series), C 30.6/5

Women and Minorities in Science and **Engineering**, NS 1.49

Engineers

Annual Report of the Chief of **Engineers**, Army, on Civil Works Activities, Annual Reports, D 103.1

Atlases; Corps of **Engineers**, D 103.49/3-2

Board of **Engineers** for Rivers and Harbors Report of Hearings, D 103.23

Coast Guard **Engineers** Digest, TD 5.17

Conference of State Sanitary **Engineers**, Report of Proceedings, HE 20.14

Corps of **Engineers** Supply Catalogues, W 7.24

Current Employment Market for **Engineers**, Scientists, and Technicians, L 7.63/2

Energy-Related Doctoral Scientists and **Engineers** in the United States, E 1.21

Engineers Digest, TD 5.17

Engineers Update, D 103.69

EPA Annual Report to Pollution **Engineers**, EP 1.85

Federal Forecast for **Engineers**, PM 1.23

Federal Scientists and **Engineers**, NS 1.22/9

Field **Engineers** Bulletins, C 4.31

Immigrant Scientists and **Engineers**, NS 1.22/5

Index of Specifications Used by Corps of **Engineers**, M 110.9, D 103.12

Proceedings Conference of State Sanitary **Engineers**, FS 2.83/4

Publications Available for Purchase, U.S. Army Engineer Waterways Experiment Station and Other Corps of **Engineers** Agencies, D 103.39

Research Opportunities for Women Scientists and **Engineers**, NS 1.48/2

Statement Showing Rank Duties and Address of Officers of Corps of **Engineers**, W 7.7

Student Handbook (series) Corps of **Engineers**, D 103.120/2

Tables and Formulas for Use of Surveyors and **Engineers** on Public Land Surveys, I 21.11/3

Transportation Series Corps of **Engineers**, D 103.10

U.S. Scientists and **Engineers**, NS 1.22/7

Water Resources Development by Army Corps of **Engineers** in {State}, D 103.35

Water Resources Development by Corps of **Engineers** by Area, D 103.35

Working Papers Corps of **Engineers**, D 103.57/9

Engines

Airworthiness Standards, Aircraft **Engines**, TD 4.6:part 33

English

English Abstracts of Selected Articles from Soviet Bloc and Mainland China Technical Journals, C 41.84

English Language Proficiency Study (series), ED 1.43

English Teaching Forum, IA 1.17, ICA 1.11, S 21.15

English Teaching Study Units, IA 1.17/3

English-French Glossary, S 1.2:En 3

Foreign Versions, Variations, and Diminutives of **English** Names and Foreign Equivalents of U.S. Military and Civilian Titles, J 21.2:N 15

Foreign-Language and **English** Dictionaries in the Physical Sciences and Engineering, Selected Bibliography, 1952-1963, C 13.10:258

Library Programs, Library Services for Individuals with Limited **English** Proficiency, ED 1.18/8

Official Gazette {Japanese} **English** Edition, D 102.16

Selected **English** Teaching Materials Catalogue, IA 1.17/2

Selected United States Marketing Terms and Definitions, **English** {foreign Language}, C 41.93

VOA, Voice of America, **English** Broadcast Guide, IA 1.6/3

Engraving

Catalogue of Copyright Entries, Pt. 1, **Engraving**, Cuts and Prints, Chromos and Lithographs, Photographs, Fine Arts, LC 3.6/4

Telephone Directory **Engraving** and Printing Bureau, T 18.6

Enhanced

Enhanced UTCS Software Operator's Manual, Implementation Package (series), TD 2.36

Enhancement

Aviation Capacity **Enhancement** Plan, TD 4.77

National Potato Germplasm Evaluation and **Enhancement** Report, A 77.36

National Science Foundation, Directory of NSF-Supported Teacher **Enhancement** Projects, NS 1.44/2

Enlisted

Hi-line, Newsletter for **Enlisted** Personnel, TD 5.40

Manual of Navy **Enlisted** Manpower and Personnel Classifications and Occupational Standards Section II Navy Enlisted Classifications, D 208.6/3-4

Regulations Governing Uniform and Equipment of Officers and **Enlisted** Men, N 9.8

Yearbook of **Enlisted** Training, N 17.30

Enplanements

Trunk Carriers, Coach Class, Traffic, Revenue, Yield, **Enplanements** and Average On-flight Trip Length by Fare Category, CAB 1.24

Trunkline Carrier Domestic Passenger **Enplanements**, C 31.266/2

Enrichment

Uranium **Enrichment** Annual Report, E 1.36/2

Enrolled

All **Enrolled** Bills of the 103rd Congress from the Beginning of the 1st Session, 1994, Y 1.6

Higher Education: Students **Enrolled** for Advanced Degrees, Fall (year), HE 19.330

Students **Enrolled** for Advanced Degrees, HE 19.330

Summary Report on Survey of Students **Enrolled** for Advanced Degrees: Fall (year), FS 5.254:54009, HE 5.254:54009

Enrollment

Advance Report on Engineering **Enrollment** and Degrees, (year), FS 5.254:54004, HE 5.254:54004

Directory of Public and Secondary Schools in Selected District, **Enrollment** and Staff by Racial/Ethnic Group, HE 1.38

Enrollment for Masters and Higher Degrees, Fall (year), Final Report, FS 5.254:54019, HE 5.254:54019

Enrollment Information Guide and Plan Comparison Chart, PM 1.8/4, PM 1.8/11

Enrollment Information Guide and Plan Comparison Chart CSRS/FERS Annuitants, PM 1.8/10

Enrollment Information Guide and Plan Comparison Chart Federal Civilian Employees in Positions Outside the Continental U.S., PM 1.8/8

Enrollment Information Guide and Plan Comparison Chart Former Spouses Enrolled in the Federal Employees Health Benefits Program, PM 1.8/7

Enrollment Information Guide and Plan Comparison Chart Individuals Receiving Compensation from the Office of Workers Compensation Programs, PM 1.8/13

Enrollment Information Guide and Plan Comparison Chart Open Season, PM 1.8/12

Enrollment Information Guide and Plan Comparison Chart Retirement Systems Participating in the Federal Employees Health Benefits Program, PM 1.8/4

Enrollment Information Guide and Plan Comparison Chart U.S. Postal Service Employees, PM 1.8/5

Fall **Enrollment** Colleges and Universities, ED 1.124

Fall **Enrollment** in Higher Education (year), HE 19.325

Fall **Enrollment** in Higher Education (Year): Institutional Data, HE 19.325/2

Fall {year} **Enrollment**, Teachers, and School-Housing in Full-Time Public Elementary and Secondary Day Schools, FS 5.220:20007, HE 5.220:20007

Higher Education, Fall **Enrollment** in Higher Education (year), HE 19.325

Opening Fall **Enrollment** in Higher Education, FS 5.254:54043, HE 5.254:54023

Postsecondary Education Fall **Enrollment** in Higher Education (year): Institutional Data, HE 19.325/2

Preprimary **Enrollment**, ED 1.112/5

Preprimary **Enrollment**, **October** (year), HE 19.327

School **Enrollment**, Social and Economic Characteristics of Students, C 3.186/12

School **Enrollment**: October (year), C 3.186:P-20

Special **Enrollment** Examination, T 22.2/14

Enrollments

Course Offering, **Enrollments**, and Curriculum, Practices in Public Secondary Schools, HE 19.334/2

Engineering **Enrollments** and Degrees, FS 5.254:54006, HE 5.254:54006

Enrollments and Programs in Noncollegiate Postsecondary Schools, HE 19.337/2

Occupational Education **Enrollments** and Programs in Noncollegiate Postsecondary Schools, HE 19.337/2

Resident, Extension, and Other **Enrollments** in Institutions of Higher Education, FS 5.254:54000, HE 5.254:54000

Subject Offerings and **Enrollments**, Grades 912, Nonpublic Secondary Schools, FS 5.224:24012, HE 5.224:24012

Summary of Offerings and **Enrollments** in Public and Secondary Schools, HE 19.334

Enroute

Enroute Area Charts (U.S.) Low Altitude, C 55.416/14, C 55.416/15-2

Enroute Change Notice, DoD Flip Enroute VFR Supplement United States, D 5.318/8-2

Enroute Change Notice, DoD Flip **Enroute** VFR Supplement United States, D 5.318/8-2

Enroute High Altitude Charts (Alaska), C 55.416/16-2

Enroute High Altitude Planning Charts (U.S.), C 55.416/17

Enroute High and Low Altitude, U.S., D 5.318/4

Enroute IFR Air Traffic Survey, C 31.165, FAA 3.11

Enroute IFR Air Traffic Survey, Peak Day, TD 4.19/3

Enroute IFR Peak Day Charts, Fiscal Year, FAA 3.11/3

Enroute IFR-Supplement, United States, D 5.318/7

Enroute Low Altitude Charts (Alaska), C 55.416/15

Flight Information Publication: **Enroute** High Altitude and Low Altitude, U.S., D 5.318/4

Flight Information Publication: **Enroute** High Altitude, Europe, Africa, Middle East, D 301.9/4

Flight Information Publication: **Enroute** Intermediate Altitude, United States, D 301.13/5

Flight Information Publication: **Enroute**-High Altitude, United States, Northeast {and Southeast}, D 301.43/3, D 301.43/3-2

IFR **Enroute** Low Altitude (U.S.), C 55.416/14

Military Aviation Notices; Corrections to **Enroute**-Low Altitude-Alaska, D 301.13/4

Minimum **Enroute** IFR Altitudes Over Particular Routes and Intersections, TD 4.316

Ensembles

Music **Ensembles** Chamber Music/New Music/Jazz Ensembles/Choruses/Orchestras/Composer in Residence/Consortium Commissioning, NF 2.8/2-14

Enterovirus

Enterovirus Surveillance, HE 20.7011/35

Enterprise

Directory of Private Programs for Minority Business **Enterprise**, C 1.56

Research Reports, National **Environmental**
Research Center, Las Vegas {list}, EP
1.21/9
Resource Guide for Health Science Students:
Occupational and **Environmental**
Health, HE 20.7108:H 34/2
Selected References on **Environmental** Quality As
It Relates to Health, HE 20.3616
Self-Study Course 3010-G, **Environmental** Health
Sciences (series), HE 20.7021/11
Socioeconomic **Environmental** Studies, EP 1.23/3
Southeast **Environmental** Research Laboratory:
Quarterly Summary, EP 1.60
Standards Support and **Environmental** Impact
Statements, EP 1.57/5
State Clinical and **Environmental** Laboratory
Legislation, HE 20.7028
Subsistence and **Environmental** Health, E 1.90/5
Summary of Foreign Government **Environmental**
Reports, EP 1.21/4
Task Force on **Environmental** Cancer and Heart and
Lung Diseases: Annual Report to
Congress, EP 1.82
Technical Notes **Environmental** Protection
Agency, EP 1.7/5
Technical Plan for the Great Lakes **Environmental**
Research Laboratory, C 55.620/2
Technical Reports **Environmental** Protection
Agency, EP 1.78
U.S. Government **Environmental** Datafiles &
Software, C 51.20
Western **Environmental** Research Laboratory:
Annual Report, EP 1.14/2
Western **Environmental** Research Laboratory:
Monthly Activities Report, EP 1.14
Working Papers **Environmental** Protection
Agency, Pacific Northwest Environmen-
tal Research Laboratory, EP 1.37/2
Environmental Planning
Division of **Environmental Planning**: Annual
Report, Y 3.T 25:1-13
Environmentally
EPP (**Environmentally** Preferable Purchasing)
Update, EP 5.28
Environments
Accessibility Assistance, a Directory of
Consultants on **Environments** for
Handicapped People, CSA 1.2:Ac 2
EnviroVision
EnviroVision 2020, D 301.117
EP
Pamphlet **EP** (series), D 103.43
EPA
Access **EPA**, EP 1.8/13
Directory of **EPA**, State, and Local Environmental
Activities, EP 1.23/5:600/4-75-001
EPA Annual Report to Pollution Engineers, EP
1.85
EPA Bulletin, EP 1.3
EPA Citizens' Bulletin, EP 1.3/2
EPA Compendium of Registered Pesticides, EP
5.11/1-5
EPA Cumulative Bibliography, EP 1.21/7-2
EPA Intermittent Bulletin, EP 1.3/5
EPA Journal, EP 1.67
EPA Journal Reprint, EP 1.67/a
EPA Log, Weekly Log of Significant Events, EP
1.24
EPA Newsletter, Quality Assurance, EP 1.98
EPA Publications Bibliograpy, EP 1.2/7
EPA Reports Bibliography Quarterly, EP 1.21/7
EPA Review of Radiation Protection Activities, EP
6.1/2
EPA Special Reports, EP 1.23/9
EPA Technical Notes, EP 1.7/5
EPA Technology Transfer Capsule Reports, EP 7.11
EPA Update, EP 1.67/2
Index of **EPA** Legal Authority Statutes and
Legislative History, Executive Orders,
Regulations, EP 1.5/4
Review of Current DHHS, DOE, and **EPA** Research
Related to Toxicology, HE 20.3563
State-**EPA** Agreements, Annual Report, EP 1.86
EPA/ORP
EPA/ORP (series), EP 6.10/4
EPAlert
EPAlert, to Alert You to Important Events, EP 1.7/
6
EPA-Regulated

LandView II, Mapping of Selected **EPA-Regulated**
Sites, TIGER/Line and Census of
Population and Housing, EP 1.104/4
EPDA
EPDA Higher Education Personnel Training
Programs, HE 5.258:58025
EPADOC
EPADOC, EP 1.104/2
EPHA
EPHA Bulletins, NHA 4.3
Ephemeris
American **Ephemeris** and Nautical Almanac for the
Year {date}, N 11.5, M 212.8, D 213.8
Astronomical Papers Prepared for Use of American
Ephemeris and Nautical Almanac, D
213.9
Ephemeris of Sun, Polaris, and Other Selected
Stars, D 213.12
Ephemeris of the Sun, Polaris and Other Selected
Stars with Companion Data and Tables
for the year {date}, I 53.8
Improved Lunar **Ephemeris**, D 213.8/2
Tables Computed for the American **Ephemeris** and
Nautical Almanac, N 11.9
Epicenters
Preliminary Determination of **Epicenters**, C 55.412,
C 55.690, I 19.66, I 19.66/2
Epidemiologic
Epidemiologic Trends in Drug Abuse, HE 20.3969
U.S. Alcohol **Epidemiologic** Data Reference
Manual, HE 20.8308/3
Epidemiology
Biometry and **Epidemiology** Contract Review
Committee, HE 20.3001/2:B 52/6
Cooperative State-Federal Sheep and Cattle
Scabies, **Epidemiology** and Related
Activities, A 77.233/4
Current Bibliography of **Epidemiology**, HE
20.3617
DCEG (Division of Cancer **Epidemiology** and
Genetics) Linkage, HE 20.3196
Division of Cancer **Epidemiology** and Genetics,
Annual Research Directory, HE 20.3188/
2
Epidemiology, PrEx 7.14/2
Epidemiology and Biometry Advisory Committee,
HE 20.3001/2:Ep 4/3
Epidemiology and Disease Control Study Section,
HE 20.3001/2:Ep 4/2
Homestudy Courses; Principles of **Epidemiology**,
HE 20.7021/3
Epilepsy
Epilepsy Abstracts, FS 2.22/59, HE 20.3509
Epilepsy Bibliography, HE 20.3513:Ep 4
NINCDS **Epilepsy** Research Program, HE
20.3502:Ep 4/2
Epileptics
Mental Defectives and **Epileptics** in State
Institutions, C 3.60
Episode
Treatment **Episode** Data Set (TEDS), HE 20.423/2
Epoch
Epoch Discoveries of the Past, Scientific Radio
Scripts, I 16.66
EPP
EPP (Environmentally Preferable Purchasing)
Update, EP 5.28
ePub
ePub Illustrated, GP 1.40
Equal
Annual Report on Implementation of Federal **Equal**
Opportunity Recruitment Program,
Report to Congress, PM 1.42
Annual Report on the Status of **Equal** Employment
Opportunity Program, TD 2.17
Annual Report to Congress on **Equal** Credit
Opportunity Act, FR 1.60
Census/**Equal** Employment Opportunity (EEO)
Special File, C 3.283
Coordination of Federal **Equal** Employment
Opportunity Programs, Y 3.Eq 2:16
EEO Information on **Equal** Opportunity for State
and Local Governments, PM 1.18/2
Equal Employment Opportunity, Code of Federal
Regulations Title 29, Y 3.Eq 2:18-4
Equal Employment Opportunity Commission
Decisions, Federal Sector, Y 3.Eq 2:18
Equal Employment Opportunity Federal Register,
Y 3.Eq 2:18-6

Equal Employment Opportunity in the Federal
Courts, Ju 10.22
Equal Employment Opportunity Management
Directives/Bulletins, Y 3.Eq 2:18-5
Equal Employment Opportunity Reports, Y 3.Eq
2:12
Equal Pay {Laws in various States}, L 13.6/3
Equality
Resources in Women's Educational **Equality**, ED
1.17/2, HE 19.128:W 84/2
Equidae
Reported Anthropod-Borne Encephalidites in
Horses and Other **Equidae**, A 77.230/2
Equine
Equine Infectious Anemia, Progress Report and
History in the United States, A 77.244
Equine Piroplasmosis Progress Report, A 77.242
Reported Incidence of Infectious **Equine**
Encephalomyelitis and Related
Encephalitides in the United States,
Calendar Year (date), A 77.230
Equip
Equip Tip, A 13.49/4-2
Equipment
Accepted Meat and Poultry **Equipment**, A 101.6/4,
A 103.6/3, A 110.12
Advertisements for Bids, Specifications, etc., for
Equipment of Public Buildings, T 39.9
Agricultural Implements and Farm **Equipment**,
Monthly Export and Import Bulletin, C
18.47
Air Conditioning Systems and **Equipment**, C 3.68
Airframe and **Equipment** Engineering Reports, C
31.156
Annual Historical Summary; Defense Industrial
Plant **Equipment** Center, D 7.1/3
Applicable Drawings for Engineer **Equipment**, W
7.31
Automatic Data Processing **Equipment** Inventory
in the United States Government As of
the End of the Fiscal Year, GS 12.10
Blowers Fans Unit Heaters and Accessory
Equipment, C 3.143
Catalogs and Advertisements of Surplus
Equipment for Sale, N 20.14
Changes in **Equipment** Manuals, W 3.36/2
Classification of Expenditures for Real Property
and **Equipment**, IC 1 wat.7
Classification of Expenditures for Real Property
and **Equipment** of Express Companies,
IC 1 exp.5
Classification of Expenditures for Road and
Equipment, IC 1 ste.8
Classification of Expenditures for Roads and
Equipment of Electric Railways, IC 1
eler.6
Classification of Investment in Road **Equipment**, IC
1 ste.16
Construction and **Equipment**, PrEx 7.21/3
Cost of Current Series, Electrical **Equipment**
Division, C 18.61
Costs and Indexes for Domestic Oil and Gas Field
Equipment and Production Operations,
E 3.44/2
Cotton Gin **Equipment**, A 88.11/19
Electronic **Equipment** Modification, C 31.161
Energy Related Laboratory **Equipment** Catalog, E
1.19/2
Engineering and **Equipment**, PrEx 7.22/7
Equipment Certification and Type Acceptance
Actions, Reports, Public Notices, CC
1.48/2
Equipment Development and Test Program,
Progress, Plans, Fiscal Year, A 13.49/5
Equipment Development and Test Reports, EDT
(Series), A 13.49/4
Equipment Development Report R.M. (Series), A
13.49/2
Equipment Lists, TD 5.20
Equipment Maintenance Series, Bulletins, CS 1.42
Equipment Manual, W 3.36
Equipment Manuals (series), D 101.107/13
Expenditures for Plant and **Equipment**, Book Value
of Fixed Assets, Rental Payments for
Buildings and Equipment, Depreciation
and Retirements, C 3.24/9-8
Facilities and **Equipment** Fact Sheet, A 77.239

Fire Extinguishing **Equipment**, Report of Shipments, C 3.84

Food Service **Equipment** Catalog, D 7.38

Foreign Inland Waterway News, Intercoastal Waterways, Rivers, Lakes, Canals, **Equipment**, C 18.208

General Drawings of Snow Removal **Equipment**, W 7.31/2

Historical Review, U.S. Army Mobility **Equipment** Research and Development Command, D 101.98

Hospital Elements, Planning and **Equipment** for 50- and 200-Bed General Hospitals, FS 2.12/2

Instructional **Equipment** Grants Title VI-A, Higher Education Act of 1975, PL 89-329, HE 19.114

Inventory of American Intermodal **Equipment**, C 39.237, TD 11.31

Machine Tools and Metal Working **Equipment**, PrEx 7.22/3-3

Manufacture and Sale of Farm **Equipment**, C 3.55

Market for U.S. Microwave, Forward Scatter, and Other Radio Communications **Equipment** and Radar in {various countries}, C 41.105

Market for U.S. Telecommunications **Equipment** in {various countries}, C 41.104

Medical Department **Equipment** List, D 104.9

Motive Power and Car **Equipment** of Class I Railroads in the United States, IC 1 ste.36

NIOSH Certified **Equipment** List, HE 20.7124

Noise Emission Standards for Construction **Equipment**, Background Document for {various items}, EP 1.6/3

Office **Equipment** Guide, D 201.6/7

Office **Equipment** Handbook, D 201.6/6

Office **Equipment** News, D 201.6/8

Ordnance **Equipment** Charts, W 34.39

Plant and **Equipment** Expenditures of U.S. Business, SE 1.25/6

Procurement **Equipment** Directory D (series), D 7.13/2

Production **Equipment** Directory D (series), D 7.13/3

Profiles of Scheduled Air Carrier Airport Operations by **Equipment** Type, Top 100 U.S. Airports, TD 4.44/4

Quarterly Tracking System, Energy Using and Conservation **Equipment** in Homes, E 3.23

Regulations Governing Uniform and **Equipment** of Officers and Enlisted Men, N 9.8

Safety Related Recall Campaigns for Motor Vehicles and Motor Vehicle **Equipment**, Including Tires, TD 8.9/2

Schedule of Lists for Permissible Mine **Equipment**, I 28.8

Tables of **Equipment**, W 1.26

Tables of Organization and **Equipment**, Department of the Air Force, M 301.7

Tables of Organization and **Equipment**, W 1.44, M 101.21, D 101.19

Technical **Equipment** Reports, A 13.49/3

U.S. Army **Equipment** Index of Modification Work Orders, D 101.22:750-10

Values of German Exports of Electrical Apparatus and **Equipment**, C 18.158

Warm-Air Furnaces, Winter Air-conditioning Systems, and Accessory **Equipment**, C 3.144

World Survey of Agricultural Machinery and **Equipment**, C 41.91

Equity

Implementing Title IX and Attaining Sex **Equity**; A Workshop for Elementary-Secondary Educators, HE 19.141/2

Implementing Title IX and Attaining Sex **Equity**; A Workshop Package for Postsecondary Educators, HE 19.141

SBIC Digest, the **Equity** Financing Arm of SBA, SBA 1.30

Summary of **Equity** Security Transactions and Ownership of Directors, Officers, and Principal Stockholders of Member State Banks As Reported Pursuant to

Women's Educational **Equity** Act Program, Annual Report, ED 1.44

Women's Educational **Equity** Act, HE 19.136

Equivalent

United States General Imports of Wool Manufacture Except Floor Coverings, Quantity Totals in Terms of **Equivalent** Square Yards in Country of Origin by Commodity Grouping Arrangement, TQ-2203, C 3.164/2-6

Equivalents

Foreign Versions, Variations, and Diminutives of English Names and Foreign **Equivalents** of U.S. Military and Civilian Titles, J 21.2:N 15

ER

ER (series), C 55.13/2:ERL, PrEx 3.10/5

ER News, E 1.19/4

Regulations, **ER**- (series), D 103.6/4

ER-CIT

China, International Trade Quarterly Review, **ER-CIT** (nos.), PrEx 3.10/8

Era

Large Space Structures and Systems in the Space Station **Era**, A Bibliography with Indexes, NAS 1.21:7085

New **ERA**, J 16.11

Reclamation **Era**, I 27.5

ERADCOM

ERADCOM Pamphlet (series), D 101.22/8

Eradication

Annual Report of Cooperative Psoroptic Cattle Scabies **Eradication** Activities, Fiscal Year (date), A 77.233/3

Annual Report of Cooperative State-Federal Sheep Scabies **Eradication** Activities, Fiscal Year (date), A 77.233/2

Annual Report on Cooperative State-Federal Psoroptic Sheep and Cattle Scabies **Eradication** Activities, Fiscal Year (date), A 77.233

Cooperative State-Federal Bovine Tuberculosis **Eradication** Program, Statistical Tables, A 101.18

Cooperative State-Federal Brucellosis **Eradication** Program; Brucellosis Bulletin, A 101.18/3

Cooperative State-Federal Brucellosis **Eradication** Program; Charts and Maps, A 77.212/6-2

Cooperative State-Federal Brucellosis **Eradication** Program; Progress Report, A 77.15:91-57

Cooperative State-Federal Brucellosis **Eradication** Program; Statistical Tables, A 101.18/2

Cooperative State-Federal Brucellosis **Eradication** Program; Statistical Tables, Fiscal Year (date), A 77.212/4

Cooperative State-Federal Brucellosis **Eradication** Programs, A 77.212/6

Cooperative State-Federal Hog Cholera **Eradication** Program Progress Report, A 77.241

Cooperative State-Federal Sheep and Cattle Scabies **Eradication**, Progress Report, A 77.233

Cooperative State-Federal Tuberculosis **Eradication** Program, Statistical Tables, Fiscal Year (date), A 77.212/5

Cooperative State-Federal Tuberculosis **Eradication**, Progress Report, A 77.15:91-44

Proceedings National Brucellosis Committee and Progress Report of the Cooperative State-Federal Brucellosis **Eradication** Program, A 77.202:B 83/16

Report of Cooperative Cattle Fever Tick **Eradication** Activities, Fiscal Year (date), A 77.237

Report of Developments on **Eradication** of Vesicular Exanthema, A 77.224

Statement of Indemnity Claims and Averages in Cooperative Tuberculosis **Eradication**, A 4.30

Statistical Tables Showing Progress of **Eradication** of Brucellosis and Tuberculosis in Livestock in United States and Territories for Fiscal Year, A 77.212/3

Summary of Bovine Brucellosis **Eradication** Activities in Cooperation with States, A 77.212/2

Summary of Bovine Tuberculosis **Eradication** in Cooperation with Various States, Statement of Indemnity and Averages in Cooperative Bovine Brucellosis Work, A 77.216/2

Summary of Brucellosis **Eradication** Activities in Cooperation with Various States Under Cull and Dry Cow Testing Program, A 77.212/7

Summary of Bucellosis **Eradication** Activities in Cooperation with the Various States Under the Market Cattle Testing Program, A 77.212/8

Summary of Tuberculosis **Eradication** in Cooperation with Various States, A 77.216

Tuberculosis **Eradication**: Statement of Indemnity Claims and Averages in Cooperative, A 77.214

Eradication/Suppression

Domestic Cannabis **Eradication/Suppression** Program, J 24.25

ERAF

ERAF [Environmental Reporting Assist File], D 212.16/2

ERC

REC-**ERC** (series), I 27.60

ERD-CRRK-TM

Electronic Research Directorate Technical Memorandum **ERD-CRRK-TM** (series), D 301.45/12

ERDA

ERDA Critical Review Series, ER 1.14

ERDA Energy Research Abstracts, ER 1.15

ERDA Telephone Directory, ER 1.17

ERDA Translation Lists, ER 1.18

Information from **ERDA**, ER 1.12/2

Information from **ERDA**, Weekly Announcements, ER 1.12

Information from **ERDA**: Reference Information, ER 1.12/3

Journals Available in the **ERDA** Library, ER 1.19

Materials and Components in Fossil Energy Applications, and **ERDA** Newsletter, ER 1.13

ERIC

Best of **ERIC**, ED 1.323

ERIC Annual Report, ED 1.301/2

ERIC Clearinghouse for Social Studies, Social Science Education: Interpretive Studies, HE 18.13

ERIC Database, ED 1.310/6

ERIC Digest, ED 1.331/2

ERIC Products, Bibliography of Information Analysis Publications of **ERIC** Clearinghouses, HE 5.77/2

ERIC Review, ED 1.331

Thesaurus of **ERIC** Descriptors Alphabetical Display, ED 1.310/3-2

Thesaurus of **ERIC** Descriptors Rotated Display, ED 1.310/3-4

Thesaurus of **ERIC** Descriptors, ED 1.310/3

ERISA

ERISA Technical Release, L 1.76/2

ERL

ERL (series), C 55.13:ERL

ERL Program Plan (series), C 55.615

ERL's

Management Information on **ERL's** Scientific and Technical Publications, C 52.21/5

Erosion

Bulletin of Beach **Erosion** Board, D 103.16

Erosion and Related Land Use Conditions (by Projects), A 57.24

Erosion Surveys, A 57.24

Technical Memorandum Beach **Erosion** Board, D 103.19

Wind **Erosion** Conditions, Great Plains, Summary of Local Estimates, A 57.47

Errata

Addenda and **Errata** Sheets to Federal Specifications, T 51.7/20

ERS

ERS (Series), A 93.21, A 105.13

ERS Field Reports, A 93.37/2

ERS Foreign (series), A 93.21/2

ERS Staff Paper, A 93.44/5

ERS Staff Reports, A 93.44

Erts-1
ERTS-1, a New Window on Our Planet, I 19.16:929
Erythrocyte
Erythrocyte Protoporphyrin, HE 20.7022/6
Erythrocyte Protoporphyrin, Proficiency Testing, HE 20.7412/4
ES
ES 2 U.S. Commodity Exports and Imports Related to Output, C 3.229
ES 3 Enterprise Statistics, C 3.230
ESA
ESA Directory of Offices, L 36.15
ESC
ESC in Review, D 301.106
Trans-Atlantic, from Office of Labor Advisors, **ESC** Labor News Letter, Y 3.Ec 74/3:31
Escalation
Prices, **Escalation**, and Economic Stability, L 2.100
Escort
Escort Interpreter Manual, S 1.40/6
ESCS
ESCS, A 105.25
ESCS Research Abstracts, A 105.25/2
ESD
Technical Documentary Report **ESD**-TDR- (series), D 301.45/28-2
ESD
Technical Reports, **ESD**-TR- (series), D 301.45/28
Eskimo
Fact Sheets: Sources of Indian and **Eskimo** Arts and Crafts, I 1.84/3
ESL-TR
ESL-TR (series), D 301.65/2
ESN
ESN Information Bulletin, D 210.16/2
Espionage
Foreign Economic Collection and Industrial **Espionage**, Y 3.C 83/2:1-2
ESS
Abstracts of **ESS** Staff Reports, A 105.57
ESS (series), A 93.21/4, A 105.56
ESSA
Catalog of Meteorological Satellite Data: **ESSA** 9 and NOAA 1 Television Cloud Photography, C 55.219:5.3
Collected Reprints **ESSA** Institute for Oceanography, C 52.23
ESSA Monographs, C 52.13
ESSA News, C 52.7/4
ESSA Operation Data Reports, C 52.22
ESSA Professional Papers, C 52.20
ESSA Research Laboratories Technical Manuals, C 52.8/2
ESSA Technical Memorandums, C 52.15/2
ESSA Technical Reports, C 52.15
ESSA World, C 52.14
Scientific and Technical Publications of **ESSA** Research Laboratories, C 52.21/4, C 52.21/4-2
Essay
National Peace **Essay** Contest Brochures Available, Y 3.P 31:3
National Security **Essay** Series, D 5.413
Peace **Essay** Contest, Y 3.P 31:4
Essential
Department of Commerce List of Currently **Essential** Activities, Department of Labor List of Currently Critical Occupation, L 7.65
Essential Oil Production and Trade, C 18.69
Essential Procedure and Requirements for Naturalization Under General Law (Form C-59), J 21.8
Essential United States Foreign Trade Routes, C 39.202:F 76
Industry Report, Crude Drugs, Gums, Balsams, and **Essential** Oils, C 18.236
Establishing
Establishing and Operation {Business}, C 41.14
Establishment
Business **Establishment**, Employment and Taxable Pay Rolls under Old-Age and Survivors Insurance Program, C 18.270
Civilian Personnel of Naval Shore **Establishment**, M 204.8
Personnel of Naval Shores **Establishment**, D 204.8
Establishments
Approved List Sanitary Inspected Fish **Establishments**, C 55.338

Directory of Blood **Establishments** Registered Under Section 510 of the Food, Drug, and Cosmetic Act, HE 20.4002:B 62
Directory of Meat and Poultry Inspection Program **Establishments**, Circuits and Officials, A 88.16/20
Employment in Nonagricultural **Establishments**, FR 1.42
Establishments and Products Licensed Under Section 351 of the Public Health Service Act, HE 20.4042
Guidelines for Implementation of Sanitary Requirements in Poultry **Establishments**, A 88.6/4:P 86/2
Notices, Activities of Licensed **Establishments** Supervised by Virus-Serum Control Division, A 4.31, A 77.217
Service **Establishments** (by States), C 3.940-11
Working Reference of Livestock Regulatory **Establishments**, A 77.221/2
Working Reference of Livestock Regulatory **Establishments**, Circuits and Officials, A 88.16/20
Estate
Estate and Gift Tax, T 22.19/3:2
Guide to Federal **Estate** and Gift Taxation, T 22.19/2:Es 8
Personal Weather Estimated from **Estate** Tax Returns Filed during Calendar Year, T 22.35/2:W 37
Estaurine
Environmental Factors on Coastal and **Estaurine** Waters, Bibliographic Series, I 67.14/2
Esthetics
Highway Research and Development News, Plant Ecology and **Esthetics**, Progress and Implementation, TD 2.113/2
Estimate
Analysis Report, **Estimate** of the (year) Cost of Oil Imports into the United States, E 3.26/4
Truck Crop **Estimate** Reports, A 36.101, A 66.17
Wholesale Price Index, Preliminary **Estimate**, L 2.61/9
Estimated
Corn, **Estimated** Planted Acreage, Yield, and Production by States, A 66.47
Cost of Food at Home **Estimated** for Food Plans at Four Cost Levels, A 98.19/2
Cost of Food at Home **Estimated** for Food Plans at Three Cost Levels, Southern Region, A 106.39/5
Cotton **Estimated** Acreage, Yield, and Production, A 36.114, A 66.41
Dry Casein, **Estimated** Production and Stocks, United States, A 36.166
Employment and Wages of Workers Covered by State Unemployment Compensation Laws: **Estimated**, FS 3.122
Estimated Amount of Nonfarm Mortgages of $20,000 or Less Recorded, HH 4.8/4
Estimated Defense Expenditures for States, D 1.57/11-2
Estimated Expenditures for States and Selected Areas, D 1.57/11
Estimated Flow of Savings in Savings and Loan Associations, HH 4.8/2
Estimated Grade and Staple Length of Upland Cotton Ginned (by States), A 82.69
Estimated Grade and Staple Length of Upland Cotton Ginned in United States, A 88.11/7
Estimated Home Mortgage Debt and Financing Activity, FHL 1.16
Estimated Mortgage Lending Activity of Savings and Loan Associations, HH 4.8/3
Estimated Numbers of Apple Trees by Varieties and Ages in Commercial and Farm Orchards, A 36.52
Estimated Oil and Gas Reserves, I 72.12/7
Estimated Refrigerator Car Movement of Domestic Fresh Fruits and Vegetables by Regions, A 82.42
Estimated Retail Food Prices by Cities, L 2.37
Estimated Vessel Operating Expenses, C 39.242
Estimated Volume of Mail and Special Services and Postal Revenues, P 1.37

Estimated Work Injuries, L 2.77/5
Estimates
Agricultural Supply and Demand **Estimates**, A 1.110
Budget **Estimates**; Aircraft and Missile Procurement, D 301.83/2
Budget **Estimates**; Coast Guard, TD 5.41
Budget **Estimates**; Department of Transportation, TD 1.34/3
Budget **Estimates**; Federal Aviation Administration, TD 4.50
Budget **Estimates**; Federal Highway Administration, TD 2.52
Budget **Estimates**; Federal Railroad Administration, TD 3.18
Budget **Estimates**; National Highway Traffic Safety Administration, TD 8.28
Budget **Estimates**; United States Department of Agriculture, A 1.93
Budget **Estimates**; Urban Mass Transporation Administration, TD 7.16
Budget Program Justification of Programs and **Estimates** for Fiscal Year (date) Submitted to Congress, Y 3.T 25:43
Census of Population; Advance **Estimates** of Social Economic, and Housing Characteristics, Supplementary Reports, PHC A2 (series), C 3.223/21-2
Chickens, Number Raised, Preliminary **Estimates**, A 92.9/7
Congressional Justification for **Estimates**, HH 1.105
Creamery Butter and American Cheese Production **Estimates**, A 36.196
Crop Production: Quarterly Grain Stocks in Farms, Revised **Estimates**, A 88.18/22
Current **Estimates** from the National Health Interview Survey, HE 20.6209/4
Employers' **Estimates** of Labor Needs in Selected Defense Industries, FS 3.121
Estimates of Appropriations for Department of Commerce, C 1.5
Estimates of Cotton Crops, A 36.31
Estimates of Federal Tax Expenditures for Fiscal Year, Y 4.T 19/4-10
Estimates of Local Public School System Finances, ED 1.112/3
Estimates of the Population of Puerto Rico and the Outlying Areas, C 3.186/19
Estimates of the Population of the United States, C 3.186:P-25
Estimates of U.S. Biomass Energy Consumption, E 3.58
Federal-State Cooperative Program for Population **Estimates**, C 3.186:P-26
Indexes and **Estimates** of Domestic Well Drilling Costs, E 3.44
Justifications of Appropriation **Estimates** for Committees on Appropriations, Fiscal Year, HE 1.1/3, ED 1.46
Justifications of Appropriation **Estimates** for Committees on Appropriations: Department of Education, ED 1.46, ED 1.46/2
Justifications of Appropriation **Estimates** for Committees on Appropriations: Department of Health and Human Services, HE 1.1/3
Justifications of Appropriation **Estimates** for Committees on Appropriations: Health Care Financing Administration, HE 22.33
Long Range Acquisition **Estimates**, D 201.35
Manned Space Flight Resources Summary, Budget **Estimates**, NAS 1.54
Markets and Crop **Estimates** Bureau, Foreign Crop and Livestock Reports, A 36.19
Mill Margins Report, Cotton Cloth and Yarn Values, Cotton Prices and Mill Margins for Unfinished Carded Cotton Cloth and Yarn, Revised **Estimates**, A 88.11/10-2
NASA Budget **Estimates**, NAS 1.85
Population **Estimates** and Projection, C 3.186:P-25

HIV/AIDS **Evaluation** Monograph Series, HE 20.9515

Manpower **Evaluation** Reports, L 1.39/2

Manpower Program **Evaluation**, L 1.45

Monographs on **Evaluation** in Education, HE 19.111

Monthly Report of Reagents **Evaluation**, HE 20.7032, HE 20.7810

National **Evaluation** Program, J 1.46, J 26.21, J 28.11, J 28.21

National Experimental and **Evaluation** Program Projects, (Reports), TD 2.53

National Potato Germplasm **Evaluation** and Enhancement Report, A 77.36

New Drug **Evaluation** Statistical Report, HE 20.4211

NIH Program **Evaluation** Reports, HE 20.3039

NILECJ **Evaluation** Series, J 1.46/2

NIOSH Health Hazard **Evaluation** Report, HE 20.7125/2

NOAA Dumpsite **Evaluation** Reports, C 55.35

OEG Report; Operations **Evaluation** Group, N 27.19

Overlap, Measurement Agreement through Process **Evaluation**, C 13.56

Performance **Evaluation** Summary Analysis Bacteriology, HE 20.7037/2

Performance **Evaluation** Summary Analysis Mycology, HE 20.7037

Performance **Evaluation** Summary Analysis Parasitology, HE 20.7037/3

Plastics Technical **Evaluation** Center: Plastic Reports, D 4.11, D 4.11/2

Project on the Status and Education of Women, Field **Evaluation** Draft, ED 1.42/2

Quality **Evaluation** Program Manual, D 7.6/4-3

Reagents **Evaluation** Program, HE 20.7809, HE 20.7810/2

Regulatory Licensing, Status Summary Report, Systematic **Evaluation** Program, Y 3.N 88:29

REMR Bulletin: News from the Repair, **Evaluation**, Maintenance and Rehabilitation Research Program, D 103.72

Research and **Evaluation** Report Series, L 37.22/2

Research Demonstration and **Evaluation** Studies, HE 23.1010

Research, Demonstration, and **Evaluation** Studies, HE 1.402:R 31

Research, **Evaluation**, and Demonstration Projects, L 37.22

Resource and Potential Reclamation **Evaluation** Reports, I 53.31

Resources **Evaluation** Newsletter, A 13.69/14

Safety Effectiveness **Evaluation**, NTSB-SEE-(series), TD 1.125

Safety **Evaluation** Series, TD 2.62

Saval Ranch Research and **Evaluation** Project, Progress Report, I 53.40

Series 1, **Evaluation** of Foreign Fruits and Nuts, A 77.533

SITE (Superfund Innovative Technology **Evaluation**) Demonstration Bulletin, EP 1.89/4-2

SITE (Superfund Innovative Technology **Evaluation**), EP 1.89/4

Statistical **Evaluation** Reports, PrEx 2.13

Technical Report Analysis Condensation **Evaluation** (Trace), D 301.45/27-3

Test and **Evaluation** Reports, D 210.25

Traffic Safety **Evaluation** Research Review, TD 8.18/2

World Integrated Nuclear **Evaluation** System, E 3.51/2

Evaluation

Research and **Evaluation** Plan, J 28.25/5

Evaluations

Approved Prescription Drug Products with Therapeutic Equivalence **Evaluations**, HE 20.4210

Inspector General Inspections & **Evaluations** Reports, TD 1.1/3-3

Therapeutic **Evaluations** Committee, HE 20.3001/ 2:T 34

Evaporated

Evaporated, Condensed, and Dry Milk Report, A 88.14

Stocks of **Evaporated** and Condensed Milk Held by Wholesale Grocers, A 88.14/5

Events

Adverse **Events** Following Immunization Surveillance, HE 20.7011/36

Calendar of **Events**, I 29.37/8

Calendar of **Events** in Areas Administered by National Park Service, I 29.66/2

Calendar of **Events** in the Library of Congress, LC 1.22/2

Current **Events**: Power Reactors, Y 3.N 88:12

EPA Log, Weekly Log of Significant **Events**, EP 1.24

EPAlert, to Alert You to Important **Events**, EP 1.7/ 6

FCC Calendar of **Events** for the Week of (date), CC 1.42/2

National Calendar of **Events**, I 29.57

POCS **Events**, I 72.12/6

Power Reactor **Events**, Y 3.N 88:12-2

Public Sector Labor Relations Information Exchange: Calendar of **Events**, L 1.66/2

Solar **Events** Calendar and Call for Papers, E 1.91

Women/Consumer Calendar of **Events**, EP 1.84

Evidence

Evidence Report/Technology Assessment, HE 20.6524

Evidence Studies, Y 3.N 21/8:23

Federal Rules of **Evidence**, Y 4.J 89/1-13

Evolution

Titrimetry, Gravimetry, Flame Photometry, Spectro Photometry, and Gas **Evolution**, C 13.46

Exact

Exact Location of All Ships in which Shipping Board is Interested, SB 2.10

Exam-O-Grams

IFR and VFR Pilot **Exam-O-Grams**, TD 4.54

Examination

Conditions of Major Water System Structures and Facilities, Review of Maintenance, Report of **Examination**, {various regions and projects}, I 27.69

Current Federal **Examination** Announcements, PM 1.21

Examination of the Federal Deposit Insurance Corporation's Financial Statements for the Years Ended ..., GA 1.13/16

Examination of the Federal Financing Bank's Financial Statements, GA 1.13/4

Examination of the Inter-American Foundation's Financial Statements, GA 1.13/2

Examination of the Panama Canal Commission's Financial Statements for the Years Ended ..., GA 1.13/11

Examination Papers, W 3.18

Examination Papers for Admission, N 12.8/1

Examination Papers {for promotion}, N 12.8/2

Examination Staff Procedures Manual for the Hispanic Health and Nutrition **Examination** Survey, HE 20.6208/2

Foreign Service Written **Examination** Registration and Application Form, S 1.137

Instruction Manual: Dietary Interviewer's Manual for the Hispanic Health and Nutrition **Examination** Survey, HE 20.6208/2-2

Instructions for Classifying the Underlying Cause of Death: Physician's **Examination** Manual for the Hispanic Health and Nutrition **Examination** Survey, HE 20.6208/2-3

Instructions for Classifying the Underlying Cause of Death: Physician's Examination Manual for the Hispanic Health and Nutrition **Examination** Survey, HE 20.6208/2-3

Merchant Marine **Examination** Questions, TD 5.57

National Health and Nutrition **Examination** Survey, HE 20.6209/4-8

(Navy Yard) **Examination** Orders, N 1.25

News of the Hispanic Health and Nutrition **Examination** Survey, HE 20.6213/3

Operating Instruction for Merchant Marine **Examination** Questions Books, Navigation General Book 3, TD 5.57/2

Regulations Governing Admission of Candidates into Naval Academy As Midshipmen and Sample **Examination** Questions, D 208.108

Special Enrollment **Examination**, T 22.2/14

Voucher **Examination** Memorandum, T 60.8, T 63.111

Examinations

Announcements of **Examinations**, I 20.25

Announcements of **Examinations**, 4th District, CS 1.26/3

Announcements of **Examinations**, Field and Local, CS 1.26/4

Announcements {of **examinations** for appointment of officers in Public Health Service}, FS 2.91

Announcements {of **examinations**}, PM 1.21/2

Manual of **Examinations**, CS 1.8

Places where Civil Service **Examinations** are Held, CS 1.28:2300

Reports to Congress on Audits, Reviews, and **Examinations**, GA 1.13

Schedule of **Examinations** for 4th-class Postmasters (by States), CS 1.27

Selection of Patients for X-Ray **Examinations** (series), HE 20.4617

Examiner

New Mexico, Traveling Auditor and Bank **Examiner**, Annual Reports, I 1.24/2

Examiner's

Examiner's Reports: Broadcast Division, CC 1.11

Examiner's Reports: Telegraph Division, CC 1.11/ 2

Examiner's Reports: Telephone Divison, CC 1.11/ 3

Instruction Manual: Dental **Examiner's** Manual for the Hispanic Health and Nutrition Survey, HE 20.6208/2-6

Examiners

Instruction and Information for Applicants and for Boards of **Examiners**, CS 1.6

Instructions and Information for Applicants and for Boards of **Examiners**, CS 1.6

Orders, Notices, Rulings and Decisions Issued by Hearing **Examiners** and by the Commission in Formal Docketed Proceedings before the Federal Maritime

Examining

Examining Circulars, CS 1.46

Examining Circulars, 4th Civil Service Region, CS 1.46/2

Examining Practices, CS 1.41/4:330-1

Instructions to **Examining** Surgeons, I 24.13

Manual of Patent **Examining** Procedures, C 21.15

Roster of **Examining** Surgeons, I 24.10

Trademark **Examining** Procedure Directives, C 21.15/2

Examples

Training within Industry, **Examples**, Pr 32.4012, Pr 32.4808

Exanthema

Report of Developments on Eradication of Vesicular **Exanthema**, A 77.224

Excavation

Hydraulic and **Excavation** Tables, I 27.16

Excellence

Biennial HUD Awards for Design **Excellence**, HH 1.41

Excellence in Surface Coal Mining and Reclamation Awards, I 71.16

NASA **Excellence** Award for Quality and Productivity, NAS 1.78

PHA Honor Awards for Design **Excellence**, HH 3.10

Progress Report to the Secretary of Education from the President's Advisory Commission on Educational **Excellence** for Hispanic Americans, ED 1.87

Exceptional

Education of **Exceptional** Children and Youth: Special Education Personnel in State Education Departments, FS 5.235:35003, HE 5.235:35003

Exceptions

Federal Energy Guidelines, **Exceptions** and Appeals (basic volumes), FE 1.8/4

Excerpts

Budget Estimates **Excerpts** from the United States Government Budget, HH 1.1/4

Excerpts from Slide Presentations by the Office of Chief of Naval Operations, D 207.14

Excess

Department of Defense List of **Excess** Personal Property Available for Transfer to Federal Civil Agencies, GS 2.4/3-2

Excess Personal Property Available for Transfer, Circulars, GS 2.4/3

Excess Property Bulletins, GS 9.3/2

Monthly List of Officers Absent on Leave in **Excess** of Time, W 3.15

Exchange

Clearinghouse **Exchange** of Publications of State Departments of Education, FS 5.10/5

Commitments of Traders in Wool and Wool Top Futures, New York Cotton **Exchange**, A 85.9/3

Revenues, **Expenses**, and Statistics of Class 1
Motor Carriers of States, IC 1 ste.24
Revenues, **Expenses**, and Statistics of Freight
Forwarders, IC 1.19
Revenues, **Expenses**, Other Income, and Statistics of
Class 1 Motor Carriers of Passengers, IC
1 mot.12
Revenues, **Expenses**, Other Income, and Statistics of
Large Motor Carriers of Property, IC 1
mot.13
Selected Revenues, **Expenses**, Other Income, and
Statistics of Class II Carriers of Property,
IC 1 mot.13/2
Steam-Electric Plant Construction Cost and
Annual Production **Expenses**, E 3.17
Thermal-Electric Plant Construction Cost and
Annual Production **Expenses**, E 3.17/4
Experience
Experience the Willamette National Forest, A
13.119
Farm-Mortgage Lending **Experience** of 19 Life
Insurance Companies, Federal Land
Banks, and Farmers Home Administra-
tion, A 93.9/5
FDA Clinical **Experience** Abstracts, HE 20.4009
Federal Fire **Experience** for Fiscal Year (date), GS
1.14/2
Injury **Experience** and Related Employment Data
for Sand and Gravel Industry, I 28.108/2
Injury **Experience** in Coal Mining, I 28.27, I 69.9
Injury **Experience** in Metallic Mineral Industries, I
28.27, I 69.9
Injury **Experience** in Nonmetallic Mining
Industries, I 28.27, I 69.9
Injury **Experience** in Oil and Gas Industry of
United States, I 28.108
Injury **Experience** in Quarrying, I 28.27, I 69.9
Injury **Experience** in Stone Mining, L 38.10/3
Management **Experience** Notes, FW 3.10
Operating **Experience**, Bulletin Information Report,
Y 3.N 88:13
Work and Wage **Experience** Studies, Reports, L
2.28
Experiment
Address List of Agricultural **Experiment** Stations,
A 10.19
Alaska Agricultural **Experiment** Station, A 77.440
BOMEX {Barbados Oceanographic and
Meteorological **Experiment**} Bulletin, C
55.18
Central States Forest **Experiment** Station, A 13.68
Contributions from Thermodynamics Laboratory,
Petroleum **Experiment** Station,
Bartlesville, Oklahoma, I 28.105
Crops Research: Results of Regional Cotton Variety
Tests by Cooperating Agricultural
Experiment Stations, A 77.15:34
General Index to **Experiment** Station Record, A
10.6/2
Naval Engineering **Experiment** Station,
Annapolis, Maryland, D 211.15
Occasional Papers Forest Service Northeastern
Forest **Experiment** Station, A 13.42/8, A
13.42/8-2
Occasional Papers Forest Service Southern Forest
Experiment Station, A 13.40/6
Progress Report Northern Rocky Mountain Forest
and Range **Experiment** Station, A 13.30/
6
Publications Available for Purchase, U.S. Army
Engineer Waterways **Experiment** Station
and Other Corps of Engineers Agencies,
D 103.39
Publications by Staff and Cooperators, Intermoun-
tain Forest and Range **Experiment**
Station, A 13.65/14
Publications Central States Forest **Experiment**
Station, A 13.68/12-2
Publications Lake States Forest **Experiment**
Station {list}, A 13.61/12
Publications Pacific Northwest Forest and Range
Experiment Station, A 13.66/15
Publications Rocky Mountain Forest and Range
Experiment Station, A 13.69/10-2
Publications Southern Forest **Experiment** Station,
A 13.40/8-3
Publications Staff and Cooperators, Intermountain
Forest and Range **Experiment** Station, A
13.65/14
Recent Publications of the Pacific Northwest
Forest and Range **Experiment** Station, A
13.66/14

Report on Agricultural **Experiment** Stations, A
10.1/2
Research at Southeastern Forest **Experiment**
Station, A 13.63/3
Research Information Digest, Recent Publications
of Southeastern Forest **Experiment**
Station, A 13.63/13
Research Reports Southwestern Forest and Range
Experiment Station, A 13.43/8
Research Reports Waterways **Experiment** Station,
D 103.24/5
Results of Regional Cotton Variety Tests by
Cooperating Agricultural **Experiment**
Stations, A 77.15:34
Review, Statistical Review of Ordnance Accident
Experiment, W 34.42
Technical Notes Forest Service Lake States Forest
Experiment Station, A 13.61/10
Technical Notes Forest Service Northeastern Forest
Experiment Station, A 13.67/9, A 13.42/
7
Technical Notes Forest Service Northern Forest
Experiment Station, A 13.73/9
Technical Notes Forest Service Southeastern Forest
Experiment Station, A 13.63/8
Waterways **Experiment** Station Capabilities, D
103.24/10
Work of Reclamation Project **Experiment** Farm, A
19.14
Experiment Station
Contract Reports Waterways **Experiment Station**,
D 103.24/9
Experiment Station Hydraulics Bulletin, W 31.10
Experiment Station Letters, A 94.12
Experiment Station Office, A 77.400
Experiment Station Record, A 10.6, A 57.19, A
77.408
Experiment Station Work, A 1.9, A 10.11
Experimental
Breast Cancer **Experimental** Biology Committee,
HE 20.3001/2:B 74
Demonstration Notes, **Experimental** and
Demonstration Manpower Programs, L
1.45/2
Environmental Health Perspectives, **Experimental**
Issues, HE 20.3559
Experimental Actions, Reports, Public Notices,
CC 1.37/3
Experimental Housing Allowance Program,
Annual Report, HH 1.54
Experimental Projects (series), TD 2.40/4
Experimental Psychology Study Section, HE
20.3001/2:P 95
Experimental Safety Vehicle Program and Vehicle
Safety Research, Progress Report, TD
8.16/2
Experimental Technology Incentives Program,
Program Area Description, C 13.57
Experimental Therapeutics Study Section, HE
20.3001/2:T 34/2
Funds for Research at State Agricultural
Experimental Stations, A 94.10
Grants Contract Reports, **Experimental**
Technology Incentives Program, GCR-
ETIP (series), C 13.57/2
Journal of **Experimental** and Theoretical Physics
{abstracts}, C 41.52/2
MDTA **Experimental** and Demonstration Findings,
L 1.56
National **Experimental** and Evaluation Program
Projects, (Reports), TD 2.53
Report on the International Technical Conference
on **Experimental** Safety Vehicles, TD
8.16
Experimentations
Manual on Uniform Traffic Control Devices for
Streets and Highways: Official Rulings
on Requests for Interpretations, Changes,
and **Experimentations**, TD 2.8/2
Experiments
Data Catalog, Satellite and Rocket **Experiments**,
NSSDA (nos), NAS 1.37
Projects and **Experiments**, LC 19.13/4
Expert
Visiting **Expert** Series, S 1.87
Explanations
Explanations and Sailing Directions to
Accompany Wind and Current Charts, N
14.9
Interpretations, Rulings and **Explanations**
Regarding Laws, Rulings, and
Instructions, IC 1 loc.6

Explanatory
Budget **Explanatory** Notes for Committee on
Appropriations, A 13.130
Explanatory Bulletin, L 22.10/2, Pr 32.4219
Exploration
Annual Report to the Administrator, The Office of
Exploration, NAS 1.1/5
Exploration and Conservation of Natural
Resources, C 41.45
Federal Offshore Statistics, Leasing, **Exploration**,
Production, Revenue, I 72.10
International Oil and Gas **Exploration** and
Development, E 3.11/20-6
International Oil and Gas **Exploration** and
Development Activities, E 3.11/20-4
Report of Secretary to President and Congress on
Mineral **Exploration** Program, I 1.85
Survey of U.S. Uranium **Exploration** Activity, E
3.46
Explorations
Explorations and Field-work of Smithsonian
Institution, SI 1.13
Explorations and Surveys for Railroad from
Mississippi River to Pacific Ocean, W
7.14
Exploratory
Exploratory Research and Problem Assessment:
Abstracts of NSF Research Results, NS
1.13/2
Explore
Explore (series), D 103.118
Exploring
Exploring Careers, L 2.3:2001
Exploring Careers in the Humanities, HE
19.108:Ex 7/8
Exploring Careers, a Student Guidebook, HE
19.108
Exploring Dance Careers, HE 19.108:Ex 7
Exploring Music Careers, HE 19.108:Ex 7/10
Exploring Theater and Media Careers, HE
19.108:Ex 7/6
Exploring Visual Arts and Crafts Careers, HE
19.108:Ex 7/4
Exploring Writing Careers, HE 19.108:Ex 7/2
Explosions
Explosions and Explosives, E 1.99
Research and Technology Work on Explosives,
Explosions, and Flames, T 28.27
Explosives
Apparent Consumption of Industrial **Explosives**
and Blasting Agents in the United
States, I 28.112
Consumption of **Explosives**, C 22.30
Explosions and **Explosives**, E 1.99
Explosives, I 28.112
Explosives Circulars, I 19.20
Explosives Incidents, Annual Report, T 70.11
Explosives Safety, D 211.26
Research and Technology Work on **Explosives**,
Explosions, and Flames, T 28.27
World Trade in **Explosives**, C 18.169
Exponent
Exponent, I 29.87
Export
Aeronautics **Export** News, C 18.46
Agricultural **Export** Assistance Update Quarterly
Report, A 67.46
Agricultural Implements and Farm Equipment,
Monthly **Export** and Import Bulletin, C
18.47
BDSA **Export** Potential Studies, C 41.107
Bureau of **Export** Administration Fact Sheets, C
63.24
Circular of Inquiry Concerning Gold and Silver
Coinage and Currency of Foreign
Countries, Including Production, Import
and **Export**, and Industrial Consumption
of Gold and Silver, T 28.8
Commodity Purchases for **Export** Distribution, A
82.87/2
Comprehensive **Export** Control Schedules, Y 3.Ec
74/2:108
Comprehensive **Export** Schedules, Pr 32.5808, C
34.8, C 18.267, C 42.11/a, C 49.208
Consolidated of Schedule B Commodity
Classifications for Use in Presentation of
U.S. **Export** Statistics, C 3.150:G
Corn Meal for **Export** Distribution, A 82.3/7
Current **Export** Bulletins, Pr 32.5807, C 34.7, C
18.266, C 42.11, C 49.208/2
Export Administration Annual Report, C 61.24
Export Administration Bulletin, C 57.409, C
61.23/2

FAA Historical Fact Book, a Chronology, 1926-1971, TD 4.2:H 62/926-71
FAA Intercom, TD 4.5/2
FAA National Supply Catalog, FAA 1.17
FAA News DIA (series), FAA 1.7/3
FAA Plan for Air Navigation and Air Traffic Control Systems, FAA 1.37
FAA Publications, TD 4.17
FAA Statistical Handbook of Civil Aviation, TD 4.20
FAA Training Programs, Annual Report, TD 4.40
FAA World, TD 4.9/2
Standards, FAA-STD (series), TD 4.24/2
FAA DS
    Report FAA DS- (series), TD 4.611
FAA-AAP
    Report FAA-AAP (series), TD 4.112/2
FAA-AEE
    Report FAA-AEE (series), TD 4.509/2
FAA-AEM
    Report FAA-AEM (series), TD 4.32/16
FAA-AEQ
    Report FAA-AEQ (series), TD 5.409/2
FAA-AP
    Report FAA-AP (series), TD 4.32/15
FAA-APO
    FAA-APO (series), TD 4.57
FAA-ASF
    FAA-ASF (series), TD 4.32/18
FAA-ASP
    Reports FAA-ASP (series), TD 4.32/14
FAA-AVP
    Report FAA-AVP- (series), TD 4.32/11
FAA-C
    Report FAA-C (series), TD 4.32/12
FAA-E
    Report FAA-E (series), TD 4.32/9
FAA-ED
    Report FAA-ED (series), TD 4.32/7
FAA-EE
    FAA-EE (series), TD 4.32/8
.FAA-EQ
    Report FAA-EQ (series), TD 4.32/8
FAA-ER
    Report FAA-ER (series), TD 4.32/13
FAA-MA
    Report FAA-MA- (series), TD 4.32/17
FAA-NO
    Office of Noise Abatement: Report FAA-NO (series), TD 4.32/2
FAA-P
    FAA-P, TD 4.32/26
FAA-PM
    FAA-PM (series), TD 4.32/20
FAA-PN
    Accident Prevention Program, FAA-PN (series), TD 4.32/19
FAA-QS
    Report FAA-QS (series), TD 4.32/10
FAA-RD
    Report, FAA-RD, TD 4.509
FAA-S
    FAA-S- (series), TD 4.32/22
FAA-T
    FAA-T (series), TD 4.32/21
FAA/AT
    FAA/AT- (series), TD 4.32/23
FAA/CT
    FAA/CT- (series), TD 4.32/24
FAAviation
    FAAviation News, TD 4.9
Fabric
    Knit Fabric Gloves, C 3.129
Fabricated
    Fabricated Steel Plate, C 3.83
Fabrication
    Fabrication Instructions, D 217.16/5
Fabrics
    Flammable Fabrics Report, Y 3.C 76/3:18
    Flammable Fabrics, Annual Report, HE 20.4020
    Report of Finishers of Cotton Fabrics, FR 1.18
Face
    Structural Clay Products (common brick, face brick, vitrified paving brick, hollow building tile), C 3.109
Faceplate
    Faceplate, D 211.22, D 211.22/2
Faces
    Fifty American Faces, SI 11.2:Am 3/5
Facets
    Juvenile Delinquency: Facts and Facets, FS 3.222, FS 14.115

Facilitation
    Domestic and International Facilitation Program, TD 1.18
Facilities
    Activities at Air Traffic Control Facilities, Fiscal Year, FAA 1.27/2
    Air Pollution Report, Federal Facilities, Air Quality Control Regions, EP 4.10
    Annual Prospectus of Winter Use and Facilities {various parks}, I 29.69
    Annual Report on Location of New Federal Offices and Other Facilities, A 1.111
    Annual Report on the HEW/USDA Rural Health Facilities Agreement, A 84.12
    Annual Report, Authorized by 38 U.S.C. 5057, Administrator, Veterans' Affairs, on Sharing Medical Facilities, Fiscal Year (date), Y 4.V 64/4:M 46
    Army Facilities Energy Plan, D 103.119
    Camping Facilities in Areas Administered by National Park Service, I 29.71
    Cancer Services, Facilities and Programs in United States, HE 20.2:C 16/5
    Catalog of Guides to Outdoor Recreation Areas and Facilities, I 66.15:G 94
    Coastal Warning Facilities Charts, C 30.22/3
    Community Facilities Administration News about New Accelerated Public Works Program, HH 5.7/2
    Conditions of Major Water System Structures and Facilities, Review of Maintenance, Report of Examination, {various regions and projects}, I 27.69
    Criteria for Use in Planning New Facilities, CR (series), P 24.6/3
    Development of Multiple Use Facilities on Highway Right of Way, TD 2.121/2
    Directory of Facilities Obligated to Provide Uncompensated Services by State and City, HE 20.9209
    Directory of Nursing Home Facilities, HE 20.6202:N 93
    Educational Television Facilities Program: Program Bulletins, FS 1.24
    Educational Television Facilities Program: Public Notices, FS 1.24/2
    Extended Care Facilities, FS 3.51/3
    Facilities, J 16.31
    Facilities and Equipment Fact Sheet, A 77.239
    Facilities Engineering and Housing Annual Summary of Operations, D 101.1/10
    Facilities Expansions Authorized Listed by Major Types of Products, Pr 32.4843
    Facilities Handbooks, P 1.31/3
    Facilities License Application Record, Y 3.N 88:33
    Farm Resources and Facilities Research Advisory Committee Report, A 1.103
    Health Facilities Series, HE 20.2511
    Higher Education Facilities Classification and Procedures Manual, FS 5.251:51016, HE 5.251:51016
    Hill-Burton Health Facilities Series, HE 20.6010, HE 20.6113
    Hospital and Medical Facilities Series under Hill-Burton Program, FS 2.74/3
    Hospital and Medical Facilities Series, Facilities for the Mentally Retarded, FS 2.74/5
    Hospital and Medical Facilities Series, Health Professions Education, FS 2.74/4
    Hospital and Mental Facilities Construction Program under Title 6 of Public Health Service Act, Semiannual Analysis of Projects Approved for Federal Aid, FS 2.74/2
    Industry Wage Survey: Nursing and Personal Care Facilities, L 2.3/25
    Inventory Municipal Waste Facilities, EP 2.17
    Inventory of Physical Facilities in Institutions of Higher Education, HE 5.92/3, HE 19.310
    Medicare/Medicaid Directory of Medical Facilities, HE 22.213
    Municipal Water Facilities, FS 2.84/3
    Port and Terminal Facilities, W 7.34
    Progress Report School Facilities Survey, FS 5.46
    Qualifying Facilities Report, E 2.12/3
    Rape and Its Victims: a Report for Citizens, Health Facilities, and Criminal Justice Agencies, J 1.8/3:R 18
    Report on Survey of U.S. Shipbuilding and Repair Facilities, TD 11.25

Representative Construction Cost of Hill-Burton Hospitals and Related Health Facilities, FS 2.74/6, HE 20.2510
Representative Construction Costs of Hospitals and Related Health Facilities, HE 1.109
Research Facilities Center: Annual Report, C 55.601/4
School Facilities Service (lists & references), FS 5.10/2
Scientific and Engineering Research Facilities at Universities and Colleges, NS 1.53
Sewage Facilities Construction, (year), EP 2.20
Specifications Naval Facilities Engineering Command, D 209.11
State of Federal Facilities, The, EP 1.116
State Rehabilitation Facilities Specialist Exchange, HE 17.122
Statistical Summary of Municipal Water Facilities, FS 2.84
Status Report of the Operation and Maintenance of Sanitation Facilities Serving American Indians and Alaska Natives, HE 20.9416
Technical Digest Naval Facilities Engineering Command, D 209.8
Technical Handbook for Facilities Engineering and Construction Manuals, HE 1.108/2
U.S. NRC Facilities License Application Record, Y 3.N 88
United States Standard Facilities Flight Check Manual, FAA 5.9
Water and Sewer Facilities Grant Program, HUD Information Series, HH 1.17
Water Facilities Area Plans (by States), A 36.148
Facility
    Air Navigation and Air Traffic Control Facility Performance and Availability Report, Calendar Year, TD 4.710
    Airport/Facility Directory, TD 4.79
    Central Liquidity Facility: Annual Report, NCU 1.17
    Correction to USAFE Radio Facility Chart, Weekly Notices to Airmen, M 301.17/2
    End-Stage Renal Disease Medical Information System Facility Reports, HE 22.9
    End-Stage Renal Disease Program Medical Information System, Facility Survey Tables (year), HE 22.9/3
    Facility Performance Report, Calendar Year, TD 4.710/2
    Facility Security Program Bulletins, Pr 32.4420
    Field Facility Directory, FAA 1.43
    Five Year Medical Facility Construction Needs Assessment, VA 1.68
    Flight Information Publication: Airport/Facility Directory, C 55.416/2
    Joint Air Forces & Navy Radio Facility Charts, M 301.16
    Joint Army & Navy Radio Facility Charts, W 108.29
    Medicare Renal Dialysis Facility Manual, HE 22.8/13
    Medicare Skilled Nursing Facility Manual, HE 22.8/3
    Mental Health Statistics: Current Facility Reports, HE 17.117
    Radio Facility Charts and Supplementary Information, United States, LF/MF Edition, D 301.43
    Radio Facility Charts United States, VOR edition, D 301.43/2
    Radio Facility Charts, C 4.9/12
    Radio Facility Charts, Caribbean and South American Area, M 301.19
    Radio Facility Charts, Europe, Africa, Middle East, M 301.17
    Special Notices, Supplement to Radio Facility Charts and In-flight Data, Europe, D 301.9/3
    Summary of War Supply and Facility Contracts by State and Industrial Area, Pr 32.4828
    U.S. Air Force Radio Facility Charts, Atlantic and Caribbean Area, M 301.15
    U.S. Air Force Radio Facility Charts, North Pacific Area, M 301.14
    Uniform Facility Data Set (UFDS): Data, HE 20.423
    United States Air Force and United States Navy Radio Facility Charts, Central Pacific-Far East, D 301.12
    United States Air Force Radio Facility Charts, Caribbean and South American Area, D 301.10
    United States Air Force Radio Facility Charts, Europe, Africa, Middle East, D 301.9

United States Air Force, Navy, Royal Canadian Air Force and Royal Canadian Navy, Navy Radio **Facility** Charts and In- Flight Data, Alaska, Canada and North Atlantic, D 301.13/3

United States Air Force, United States Navy and Royal Canadian Air Force Radio **Facility** Charts, West Canada and Alaska, D 301.13

United States Air Force, United States Navy Radio **Facility** Charts, North Atlantic Area, D 301.11

University of Maryland College Park 2x4 Loop Test **Facility**, Y 3.N 88:25-7

Update (Electronics Manufacturing Productivity **Facility**), D 201.36

Facility-Based

Facility-Based HIV/AIDS Education Demonstration Project FY, VA 1.97

Facing

Facing the Light, Historic American Portrait Daguerreotypes, SI 11.2:L 62

Facsimile

Standard and Optional Forms **Facsimile** Handbook, GS 4.6/3, GS 12.18

USAPAT, **Facsimile** Images of United States Patents, C 21.31

Facsimiles

Facsimiles, GS 4.11, GS 4.11/2, LC 1.28

USAMark: **Facsimile** Images of Registered United States Trademarks, C 21.31/11

Fact

Fact Sheets and technical Assistance Bulletins, EP 9.17

Fact Sheets of Public-Private Partnerships for Child Care, He 20.1402

Findings of **Fact** and Recommendations of Reference, L 21.14

Fact Book

Domestic Programs **Fact Book**, AA 1.9/2

Employment **Fact Book**, J 1.57

INS **Fact Book**, J 21.2/11

Organization and **Fact Book**, HE 20.3319

VISTA **Fact Book**, AA 1.9, PrEx 10.21

Fact Sheet

Consumer **Fact Sheet**, TD 5.60

Education **Fact Sheet**, FS 5.56/2

Galveston Bay **Fact Sheet** Series, I 49.110

EEO **Fact Sheet** from Office of the Administrator, A 67.41

HCFA **Fact Sheet** (series), HE 22.40

Instrument **Fact Sheet**, C 55.71, D 203.32/2

National Kidney and Urologic Diseases Information Clearinghouse **Fact Sheet** HE 20.3323/3

OJJDP **Fact Sheet** (series), J 32.21

OJJDP Youth in Action **Fact Sheet**, J 32.21/2

State Vocational Rehabilitation Agency: **Fact Sheet** Booklets, HE 17.119/2, HE 1.610

U.S. Agricultural Imports, **Fact Sheet**, A 67.32/2, A 93.30, A 93.30/2

U.S. Department of Labor Program Highlights, **Fact Sheet** (Series), L 1.88

VD **Fact Sheet**, HE 20.7018

Fact Sheets

Agriculture **Fact Sheets**, AFS (series), A 1.121, A 21.35, A 107.14

Bureau of Export Administration **Fact Sheets**, C 63.24

Chemical Evaluation and Control **Fact Sheets**, A 77.239/2

Chemotherapy **Fact Sheets**, HE 20.3164

Consumer Affairs **Fact Sheets** (series), TD 8.14/3

Digestive Diseases Clearinghouse **Fact Sheets**, HE 20.3323

EM State **Fact Sheets**, E 1.90/7

Energy Conservation **Fact Sheets**, TD 1.30

Fact Sheets [Action], AA 1.22

Fact Sheets [Aging Administration], HE 1.213

Fact Sheets [Agricultural Stabilization and Conservation Service], A 82.40

Fact Sheets [Agriculture Department], A 1.71

Fact Sheets [Animal and Plant Health Inspection Service], A 101.31

Fact Sheets [Armed Forces Information Service], D 2.10

Fact Sheets [Commodity Credit Corporation], A 71.10

Fact Sheets [Consumer Product Safety Commission], Y 3.C 76/3:11

Fact Sheets [Defense Mapping Agency], D 5.361

Fact Sheets [Defense Nuclear Agency], D 15.9

Fact Sheets [Employment and Training Administration], L 37.21

Fact Sheets [Environmental Protection Agency], EP 4.27

Fact Sheets [Financial Management Service], T 63.123

Fact Sheets [Food and Drug Administration], FS 13.130

Fact Sheets [Food Distribution Service], A 80.131

Fact Sheets [Foreign Operations Administration], FO 1.24

Fact Sheets [Housing and Urban Development Department], HH 1.43/2

Fact Sheets [Information Services], D 301.54

Fact Sheets [Justice Assistance Bureau], J 26.33

Fact Sheets [National Cancer Institute], HE 20.3182

Fact Sheets [National Center for Early Development and Learning], ED 1.346/2

Fact Sheets [National Center for Health Care Technology], HE 20.210

Fact Sheets [National Heart, Lung, and Blood Institute], HE 20.3218

Fact Sheets [National Institute of Neurological and Communicative Disorders and Stroke], HE 20.3520

Fact Sheets [Navy Department], D 201.39

Fact Sheets of Fossil Energy Project, E 1.90/9

Fact Sheets [Office of Education], FS 5.56

Fact Sheets [Office of Information for the Armed Forces], D 2.10

Fact Sheets [Public Health Service], HE 20.38

Fact Sheets [Pension Benefit Guaranty Corporation], Y 3.P 38/2:14

Fact Sheets [Social Security Administration], FS 3.21

Fact Sheets [Toxic Substances and Disease Registry Agency], HE 20.7916

Fact Sheets [Transportation Department], TD 1.37

Fact Sheets [Treasury Department], T 1.62

Fact Sheets [Wage and Hour Division], L 36.213

National Action Plan on Breast Cancer **Fact Sheets** (series), HE 20.38/2

NHSC **Fact Sheets**, HE 20.9110/5

OVC **Fact Sheets**, J 34.4

PBGC {Pension Benefit Guaranty Corporation} **Fact Sheets**, L 1.51/5

Price Control **Fact Sheets**, Pr 32.4268

Project **Fact Sheets**, E 1.90/8

Technical **Fact Sheets**, Y 3.C 76/3:11-2

VA **Fact Sheets**, IS- (series), VA 1.34

United States Air Force **Fact Sheets**, D 301.128

Water **Fact Sheets** (series), I 19.114

You Can Survive, Rural Defense **Fact Sheets**, A 43.35

Your New Social Security, **Fact Sheets**, FS 3.25

Fact-Finding

Report and Recommendations of **Fact-Finding** Boards, L 1.16

Factbook

HCUP **Factbook**, HE 20.6514/4

World **Factbook**, PrEx 3.15

Factfinder

American **Factfinder**, C 3.300

Factfinder for the Nation, CFF, C 3.252

Factor

Briefs of Accidents Involving Alcohol As a Cause-**Factor** U.S. General Aviation, TD 1.109/9

Briefs of Fatal Accidents Involving Weather As a Cause-**Factor** U.S. General Aviation, TD 1.109/12

Review of Alcohol as a Cause **Factor**, TD 1.129

Factors

Air Chief (Clearinghouse for Inventory and Emission **Factors**), EP 1.109

Environmental **Factors** on Coastal and Estaurine Waters, Bibliographic Series, I 67.14/2

Environmental Health **Factors**, Nursing Homes, FS 2.300/2

Factors Affecting Bank Reserves and Condition Statement of F.R. Banks, FR 1.15

Quarterly Report of Air Carrier Operating **Factors**, C 31.240

Reports on Airline Service, Fares Traffic, Load **Factors** and Market Shares, CAB 1.27

Trends in Selected Economic and Real Estate **Factors** in United States, NHA 2.15

Trends in Selected Economic **Factors**, United States, HH 2.16

U.S. Exports and Imports, Working-Day and Seasonal Adjustment **Factors** and Months for Cyclical Dominance (MCD), C 3.235

Factory

Factory Consumption of Animal and Vegetable Fats and Oils by Classes of Products, C 3.154

Factory Labor Turnover, L 2.42/2

Summary of Major Provisions of Convention and of Law Relating to **Factory** Inspection (by States), L 16.32

Facts

A.A.A. Flashes, **Facts** for Committeemen, A 55.42/11, A 76.410

APHIS **Facts**, A 101.10/3

Consumer **Facts**, A 21.13/6

Current **Facts** on Housing, HH 1.10

Economic Forces in United States in **Facts** and Figures, FO 1.30, S 17.8

ED **Facts**, ED 1.9

Egg Marketing **Facts**, A 88.53

Environmental **Facts**, EP 1.42

Facts (series), LC 19.15

Facts About, SBA 1.49/2

Facts about (various subjects) (series), A 1.131

Facts about AIDS, HE 20.7038

Facts about U.S. Agriculture, A 1.38/2

Facts and Services from the U.S. Department of Labor, L 1.31

Facts for Business, FT 1.32/2, FT 1.32/3

Facts for Consumers (series), FT 1.32

Facts on Working Women, L 36.114/3

Fast **Facts** & Figures About Social Security, HE 3.94

Fatal **Facts**: Accident Report, L 35.11/3

Federal Work Injury **Facts**, Occupational Distribution, Duration and Direct Cost Factors of Work Injuries to Civilian Federal Employees During Calendar Year, L 26.8/2-2

Focus on the **Facts**, SBA 1.49

Food **Facts** of Interest to the Trade, Pr 32.4260

Important **Facts** About the Pacific Northwest Region, A 13.117

JPL **Facts** (various topics), NAS 1.12/9

Mineral **Facts** and Problems, I 28.3

NAEP**Facts**, ED 1.335

Postal **Facts**, P 1.60

Preliminary Report on Production on Specified Synthetic Organic Chemicals in United States; **Facts** for Industry Series, TC 1.25

Preprints from Bulletin 585, Mineral **Facts** and Problems, I 28.3/c

Program **Facts** on Federally Aided Public Assistance Income Maintenance Programs, HE 17.614

Radio Service Consumer **Facts**, A 21.13/6

Registrant **Facts**, J 24.17

Reprints from Bulletin 556, Mineral **Facts** and Problems, I 28.3/b, I 28.3/c

Statements of **Facts**, and Briefs, J 10.5/1

Training **Facts**, Reports, L 1.40

Turkey Marketing **Facts**, A 88.15/25

UNESCO **Facts**, S 5.48/8

Youth Fatal Crash and Alcohol **Facts**, TD 8.39

Factsheets

Factsheets, E 1.57

Factual

Current Programs and Operations of Housing and Home Finance Agency, **Factual** Summary for Public Interest Organizations, HH 1.21

Faculty

Discovery: **Faculty** Publications and Presentations, Fiscal Year (date), D 305.18

Faculty and Other Professional Staff in Institutions of Higher Education, FS 5.253:53000, HE 5.253:53000

Faculty and Student Programs, E 1.86/6

Faculty Graduate Study Program for Historically Black Colleges and Universities, NF 3.8/2-7

Faculty Salaries in Land-Grant Colleges and State Universities, FS 5.253:53023, HE 5.253:53023

Historically Black Colleges and Universities, **Faculty** Projects, Summer College Humanities Programs for High School Juniors, NF 3.8/2-8

Institutes for College and University **Faculty**, NF 3.14

Instructional **Faculty** Salaries for Academic Year, ED 1.131

Summary Report, **Faculty** and Other Professional Staff in Institutions of Higher Education, FS 5.253:53014, HE 5.253:53014

Farm Labor Report, A 36.140

Farm Labor Reports Varying Title, A 66.10

Farm Management Reports, A 36.118

Farm Mobilization Fact Sheets, A 21.21

Farm Mortgage Debt, A 93.9/12

Farm Numbers, A 92.24/5

Farm Paper Letter, A 107.13, A 107.13/3

Farm Population, C 3.201

Farm Population and Rural Life Activities, A 36.23

Farm Population of the United States, C 3.186:P-27

Farm Population, Annual Estimates by States, Major Geographical Division, and Regions, A 88.21

Farm Power News, Y 3.R 88:16

Farm Production and Income from Meat Animals, A 66.34

Farm Production Expenditures for (year), A 92.40

Farm Production, Disposition, Cash Receipts and Gross Income, Turkeys, A 88.15/16, A 105.35/2

Farm Products Prices, A 36.184

Farm Real Estate Debt, RED (series), A 93.9/9

Farm Real Estate Market Developments, A 93.9/4, A 105.19/2

Farm Real Estate Taxes, A 36.63

Farm Real Estate Taxes, Recent Trends and Developments, A 93.9/6

Farm Relief and Agricultural Adjustment Acts {June 15, 1929}, Y 1.2:F 22

Farm Resources and Facilities Research Advisory Committee Report, A 1.103

Farm Returns, Summary of Reports of Farm Operators, A 36.124

Farm Telephone and Electricity Combined Report, A 88.45/2

Farm Telephones, A 88.45

Farm Unit Plats, I 27.13

Farm Value, Gross Income, and Cash Income from Farm Production, A 36.125

Farm Vehicle Activity Memorandums, Pr 32.4910

Farm Wage Rates and Related Data, A 36.77, A 66.10

Farm Woodlands of States (Charts) (by States), A 13.34

Farm-Management Office-Circulars, A 1.21

Farm-Mortgage Lending Experience of 19 Life Insurance Companies, Federal Land Banks, and Farmers Home Administration, A 93.9/5

Farm-Mortgage Recordings (by States), A 36.109

Farm-Retail Price Spreads, A 36.138

Farms of Nonwhite Farm Operators, Number of Farms, Land in Farm, Cropland Harvested, and Value of Land and Buildings, by Tenure, Censuses of 1945 and 1940 (by States), C 3.193

Farms of Nonwhite Farm Operators, Number of Farms, Land in Farm, Cropland Harvested, and Value of Land and Buildings, by Tenure, Censuses of 1945 and 1940 (by States), C 3.193

Federal Farm Loan Act with Amendments and Farm Mortgage and Farm Credit Acts, Y 1.2:F 31

Federal Farm Loan Act with Amendments and Farm Mortgage and Farm Credit Acts, Y 1.2:F 31

Field and Seed Crops, Farm Production, Farm Disposition, Value, by States, A 88.30/4

Field and Seed Crops, Production, Farm Use, Sales, Value by States, A 92.19

Foreign Agriculture, A Review of Foreign Farm Policy, Production, and Trade, A 67.7

Foreign Agriculture, Review of Foreign Farm Policy, Production and Trade, A 36.88, A 64.7, A 67.7

Foreign Trade in Farm Machinery and Supplies, A 67.21

FPL {Farm Paper Letter}, A 21.32

Harvard Studies in Marketing Farm Products, A 36.169

Hired Farm Work Force of {year}, A 1.75, A 88.40, A 93.21, A 93.28, A 1.107

Instructions for Completing Farm Plans (by States), A 80.612

Lists of Maps, Townsite, and Farm Unit Plots, I 27.7/2

Manufacture and Sale of Farm Equipment, C 3.55

Maps, Townsite, and Farm Unit Plots, Lists of, I 27.7/2

Meat Animals, Farm Production, Disposition, and Income by States, A 88.17/3

Milk, Farm Production, Disposition, and Income, A 88.14/8

Monthly Receipts from Sale of Principal Farm Products by States, A 36.81/2

National Farm Data Program, A 21.16

National Farm Safety Week: Annual Report, Y 3.T 25:1-8

National Farm Safety Week: Bulletins, Y 3.T 25:3-2

National Farm Safety Week: Circulars, Y 3.T 25:4-2

Production Practices, 1943 Farm Program, A 79.458

Production, Farm Disposition, and Value of Principal Fruits and Tree Nuts, A 88.12/16

Radio Service Farm Flashes, A 21.13/7

Receipts from Sale of Principal Farm Products by States, A 36.81/1

Report on the Financial Condition and Performance of the Farm Credit System, FCA 1.1/2

Report to the National Farm Loan Associations, FCA 1.23

Research Reports Farm Security Administration, A 61.15

Residents of Farms & Rural Areas, C 3.186/25

Risk Analysis of Farm Credit System Operations and Economic Outlook, FCA 1.23/2-2

Small Farm Digest, A 94.23

Small Farm Family Newsletter, A 1.125

Special Reports Farm Credit Administration, FCA 1.21, A 72.9

Statistical Bulletins Farm Credit Administration, FCA 1.3/2

To Farm Journal Editors, A 55.22

Trade Policies and Market Opportunities for U.S. Farm Exports, Annual Report, A 67.40/5

Traveler/El Viajero, Quarterly Newsletter for Migrant and Seasonal Farm Workers, PrEx 10.19

Wage Rates in Selected Farm Activities, L 7.55/2-2

Woodland Management Plan, Agreements and Farm Codes, A 57.37

Work of Reclamation Project Experiment Farm, A 19.14

Farmer

Farmer and the War, A 36.145

Farmer Co-ops, A 72.17

Farmer Cooperative Films, A 89.15:2

Farmer Cooperative Statistics, A 109.11/2

Farmer Cooperatives, FCA 1.19, A 1.76, A 89.8, A 105.19, A 109.11

Highlights of Annual Workshop of Farmer Cooperative Service, A 89.16

Midwest Regional Member Relations Conference Sponsored by American Institute of Cooperation and Farmer Cooperative Service, A 89.17

News for Farmer Cooperatives, FCA 1.10

Philippine Farmer, W 49.21/10

Popular Publications for Farmer, Suburbanite, Homemaker, Consumer, A 21.9/8:5, A 107.12:5

Service Reports Farmer Cooperative Service, A 89.12, A 89.20

Statistics of Farmer Cooperatives, A 89.19

Farmer's

Farmer's Cooperative Income Tax Returns, T 22.35/2:F 22

Farmer's Tax Guide, Income and Self Employment Taxes, T 22.19/2:F 22

Farmers

Crop Values, Season Average Prices Received by Farmers and Value of Production, A 92.24/3

Farm-Mortgage Lending Experience of 19 Life Insurance Companies, Federal Land Banks, and Farmers Home Administration, A 93.9/5

Farmers Home Administration Features, A 84.9

Farmers Weekly Cotton Price Quotations, A 82.67

Farmers' Bulletins, A 1.9, W 49.21/5

Farmers' Bulletins (Available for Distribution), A 21.9/1

Farmers' Bulletins (Complete List), A 21.9/3

Farmers' Bulletins (Indexes), A 21.9/5

Farmers' Bulletins (Subject List), A 21.9/4, A 21.9/7

Farmers' Bulletins of Interest to Persons Residing in Cities or Towns, A 21.9/2

Farmers' Institute Lectures, A 10.13

Farmers' Newsletter, A 93.40, A 105.10/2

National Directory of Farmers Markets, A 88.69/2

Posters Farmers Home Administration, A 84.15

Prices Paid by Farmers, A 36.75

Prices Received by Farmers for Manufacturing Grade Milk in Minnesota and Wisconsin, A 92.16/3

Registered Bona Fide and Legitimate Farmers' Cooperative Organizations under Bituminous Coal Act of 1937, I 46.15

Subject List of Farmers' Bulletins (Front Space), A 21.9/6

Summary of Cases Relating to Farmers' Cooperative Associations, A 72.18

Farming

Electric Farming News Exchange of Inter-industry Farm Electric Utilization Council, A 68.19

Farming Out Bulletin, Y 3.C 831:111, Pr 32.4007

Farmlands

Important Farmlands, A 57.69

Farmline

Farmline, A 93.33/2, A 105.10/4

Farms

Agricultural Census Analyses: Changes in Land in Farms by Size of Farm, A 36.137/1

Agricultural Census Analyses: Changes in Number of Farms by Size of Farm, A 36.137/2

Bulk Cooling Tanks on Farms Supplying Federal Milk Order Markets, A 82.81/2

Cattle Inventory, Special Report on Number of Cattle and Calves on Farms by Sex and Weight, United States, A 92.18/6-2

Chickens and Eggs, Farm Production, Disposition, Cash Receipts and Gross Income, Chickens on Farms, Commercial Broilers, by States, A 88.15/18

Chickens Raised on Farms, A 88.15/10

Commercial Broiler Farms, Maine, Delmarva, and Georgia, A 93.9/11

Commercial Corn Belt Farms, A 93.9/11

Commercial Dairy Farms, Northeast and Midwest, A 93.9/11

Commercial Tobacco Farms, Coastal Plain, North Carolina, A 93.9/11

Commercial Tobacco-Livestock Farms, Bluegrass Area, Kentucky and Penny-Royal Grass Area, Kentucky-Tennessee, A 93.9/11

Commercial Wheat Farms, Plains and Pacific Northwest, A 93.9/11

Crop Production: Quarterly Grain Stocks in Farms, Revised Estimates, A 88.18/22

Employment on Farms of Crop Reporters, A 36.69

Farms of Nonwhite Farm Operators, Number of Farms, Land in Farm, Cropland Harvested, and Value of Land and Buildings, by Tenure, Censuses of 1945 and 1940 (by States), C 3.193

Financial Characteristics of U.S. Farms, A 1.75/2

Milk Production on Farms and Statistics of Dairy Plant Products, A 88.14/7

Number and Percentage of Farms Electrified with Central Station Service, A 68.20

Number of Farms by States, A 88.21/2

Numbers of Farms Participating in 1934 AAA Voluntary Control Programs (by States), A 55.55

Soil and Water Conservation Districts, Status of Organization, by States, Approximate Acreage, and Farms in Organized Districts, A 57.32

Truck Crop Farms, Adjustments on (by States), A 36.135

Turkey Breeder Hens on Farms, A 88.15/12

Turkeys Raised on Farms, A 88.15/11

FAS

FAS Letter to Agricultural Attaches and Officers, A 67.31/2

FAS Report, Status of U.S. Sugar Import Quotas, A 67.42/2

Fashion

Fashion Industry Series, HE 5.288

Fast

Fast Announcements, C 51.7/2

Fast Facts & Figures About Social Security, HE 3.94, SSA 1.26

Fatal

Briefs of Fatal Accidents Involving Weather As a Cause-Factor U.S. General Aviation, TD 1.109/12

Fatal Accident Reporting System Annual Report, TD 8.27

Fatal Accidents Involving Drowning at Coal and Metal/Nonmetal Mines, L 38.19/3-2

Fatal and Injury Accidents Rates on Federal-aid and Other Highway Systems, TD 2.20

Fatal Facts: Accident Report, L 35.11/3

Youth **Fatal** Crash and Alcohol Facts, TD 8.39

Fatalgrams

Fatalgrams (series), L 38.15

Fatalities

Coal **Fatalities**, L 38.20/3-3

Coal Mine **Fatalities**, I 28.10/2

Coal, Surface and Underground **Fatalities**, L 38.20/5

Contractor **Fatalities** Coal and Metal/Nonmetal Mines, L 38.20/4

Fatalities in Small Underground Coal Mines, L 38.20

Firefighter **Fatalities**, FEM 1.116

MESA Safety Reviews: Coal-Mine **Fatalities**, I 69.10

Metal/Nonmetal, Surface and Underground **Fatalities**, L 38.19/4

Metal/Nonmetal-Surface **Fatalities**, L 38.19/3

Metal/Nonmetal-Underground **Fatalities**, L 38.19/2

Monthly Statement of Coal-Mine **Fatalities** in United States, I 28.10/1

Power Haulage **Fatalities**, Coal and Metal/Nonmetal Mines, L 38.19

Railroad Employee **Fatalities** Investigated by the Federal Railroad Administration in (year), TD 3.110/5

Summary of Motor Vehicle Accident **Fatalities**, C 3.128/3

Fatality

Monthly Traffic **Fatality** Report, TD 8.38

Fathom

Fathom, Surface Ship and Submarine Safety Review, D 202.20, D 201.32

Fats

Animal and Vegetable **Fats** and Oils, C 3.56

Factory Consumption of Animal and Vegetable **Fats** and Oils by Classes of Products, C 3.154

Fats and Oils Situation, A 88.32, A 93.23, A 105.28

Fats and Oils Subjected to Supphonation, C 3.124

Industry Report, **Fats** and Oils, C 18.238

Meats, Livestock, **Fats** and Oils, C 18.72/5

Production, Consumption, and Stocks of **Fats** and Oils, C 3.123

FATUS

FATUS, A 93.17/7

Fauna

Convention on International Trade in Endangered Species of Wild **Fauna** and Flora, Annual Report, I 49.85

Fauna Series, I 29.13

North American **Fauna** (series), I 49.30

Tennessee Valley Streams, Their Fish, Bottom **Fauna**, and Aquatic Habitat {by areas}, Y 3.T 25:41

Fax

Engineering Bits and **Fax**, C 55.116

FB

FB Pamphlet (series), D 103.109/3

FBI

FBI Bomb Data Program, General Information Bulletins, J 1.14/8-2

FBI Law Enforcement Bulletin, J 1.14/8

FBI National Academy Associates Newsletter, J 1.14/20

FBI Uniform Crime Reports {on various subjects}, J 1.14/7-4

FBI Uniform Crime Reports: Law Enforcement Officers Killed, J 1.14/7-5

FBIS

FBIS Publications Reports, PrEx 7.10/3

FCA

FCA Accountability Report, FCA 1.1/4

FCA Annual Performance Plan, FCA 1.1/3

FCA Bulletins, FCA 1.3

FCA Newsline, FCA 1.26

FCA Research Journal, FCA 1.25

FCA Strategic Plan FY..., FCA 1.1/5

FCC

FCC Actions Alert, CC 1.49

FCC Calendar of Events for the Week of (date), CC 1.42/2

FCC Filings, CC 1.51

FCC Record, CC 1.12/3

FCCSET

A Report by the **FCCSET** Committee on Life Sciences and Health, PrEx 8.111/2

Report of the **FCCSET** Committee on Education and Human Resources, PrEx 8.111

FCDA

FCDA Public Affairs Newsletter, FCD 1.15

Report on Washington Conference on National Women's Advisory Committee on **FCDA**, FCD 1.18/2

FCI

FCI Information Series, A 76.108

FCIM

FCIM Focus, D 215.15

FCS

FCS Bulletins, A 89.3

FCS Circulars, A 89.4

FCS Educational Circulars, A 89.4/2

FCS Information (series), A 89.15

FCS Research Reports, A 89.19

FD

U.S. Army Natick Laboratories, Food Division, Natick, Mass. Technical Report **FD**-, D 106.20

FDA

Facts from **FDA**, Current and Useful Information from Food and Drug Administration, HE 20.4029

FDA Almanac, HE 20.4047

FDA By-lines, HE 20.4041

FDA Clinical Experience Abstracts, HE 20.4009

FDA Compilation of Case Studies of Drug Recalls, HE 20.4027

FDA Consumer, HE 20.4010

FDA Consumer Memos, HE 20.4010/2

FDA Consumer Special Report, HE 20.4010/4

FDA Current Drug Information, HE 20.4013

FDA Drug and Device Products Approvals, FDA/BD, HE 20.4209

FDA Drug Bulletin, HE 20.4003, HE 20.4003/3

FDA Enforcement Report, HE 20.4039

FDA Federal Register Documents, Chronological Document Listing, 1936-1976, HE 20.4016:C 46

FDA Medical Bulletin, HE 20.4003/3

FDA Medical Device Standards Publication, Technical Reports, FDA-T, HE 20.4310/2

FDA Medical Device Standards Publications, MDS (series), HE 20.4310

FDA Memo for Consumers, CM (series), FS 13.121

FDA Papers, FS 13.128, HE 20.4010

FDA Posters, FS 13.127

FDA Publications (numbered), HE 20.4015

FDA Publications (series), FS 13.111

FDA Quarterly Activities Report, HE 20.4033

FDA Safety Alerts (on various subjects), HE 20.4616

FDA Technical Bulletins, HE 20.4040

FDA Veterinarian, HE 20.4410

FDA's

FDA's Life Protection Series, FS 13.129

FDD

FDD Field Reports, A 93.37

FDIC

FDIC Consumer News, Y 3.F 31/8:24

FDL

Technical Documentary Report **FDL**-TDR, D 301.45/46

FDSN

FDSN Earthquake Digital Data, I 19.128/2

Fear

Victimization, **Fear** of Crime and Altered Behavior (series), HH 1.70

Feasibility

Elementary Teacher Education Program, **Feasibility** Studies, HE 5.87

Feature

Catalog of Captioned **Feature** and Special Interest Films and Videos for the Hearing Impaired, ED 1.209/2-3

CD News **Feature** Page, D 1.34

Feature Picture Pages, T 66.13

Feature Sections of Journals in NWC Library, D 1.26

Media **Feature** Service, T 22.46/2

News **Feature** Page, PrEx 4.7/4

News, **Feature**, A 1.133/3

NIAA Information and **Feature** Service, HE 20.8312

Press **Feature**, S 1.77

Special Press **Feature**, S 1.77/2

Technical Digest **Feature**, S 18.18

USDA Photo **Feature** (series), A 1.137/2

USIA **Feature**, Special, S 1.100

USIS **Feature**, IA 1.9

Woman's Page **Feature**, Y 3.F 31/11:25

Features

Farmers Home Administration **Features**, A 84.9

News and **Features** from NIH, Portfolio Series, HE 20.3007/2

News **Features**, FCD 1.16

News **Features** from Federal Aviation Agency, FAA 1.7/4

Science and Technology News **Features**, C 1.32/2

Significant **Features** of Fiscal Federalism, Y 3.Ad 9/8:18

Special **Features** Service, Y 3.P 96/3:8

Summary Statistics, Finances and Physical **Features**, I 27.1/4-3

FEC

FEC Index of Communication Costs, Y 3.El 2/3:15-2

FEC Index of Independent Expenditures, Y 3.El 2/3:15-2

FEC Journal of Election Administration, Y 3.El 2/3:10

FEC Reports on Financial Activity, Y 3.El 2/3:15

FED

FED Facts, PM 1.25

FED State Bulletin, T 22.2/15:7208

FedBizOpps

FedBizOpps (Federal Business Opportunities), GS 1.41

Federal

Air Pollution, Sulfur Oxides Pollution Control, **Federal** Research and Development, Planning and Programming, FS 2.93/4

America's Commitment: **Federal** Programs Benefiting Women and New Initiatives as Follow-up to the U.N. Fourth World Conference on Women, Pr 42.8:W 84

Analysis of Assaults on **Federal** Officers, J 1.14/7-3

Annual Report of the **Federal** Labor Relations Authority, Y 4.P 84/10-11

Catalog of **Federal** Grant-In-Aid Programs to State and Local Governments, Y 3.Ad 9/8:20

Chicago **Federal** Executive Board Directory, PM 1.31/3

Compendium of **Federal** Justice Statistics, J 29.20

Contents, Format and Concepts of **Federal** Budget, Reprint of Selected Pages from Budget of United States Government, PrEx 2.8

Current **Federal** Aid Research Report, Wildlife, I 49.94/2

Current **Federal** Examination Announcements, PM 1.21

Current **Federal** Meteorological Research and Development Activities, C 30.75/2

Current **Federal** Research Reports, Fish, I 49.94

Current **Federal** Workforce Data, CS 1.72

Current Salary Schedules of **Federal** Officers and Employees Together with a History of Salary and Retirement Annuity Adjustments, Y 4.P 84/10-15

Determining Suitability for **Federal** Employment, CS 1.41/4

Digest of Functions of **Federal** Agencies, Pr 32.5022

Digest of Selected **Federal** Retirement Systems, CS 1.29/4

Directory of **Federal** Government Certification andRelated Programs (Special Publication 739), C 13.10:739

Directory of **Federal** Laboratory and Technology Resources, a Guide to Services, Facilities, and Expertise, C 51.19/2-2

Directory of Research Natural Areas on **Federal** Lands of United States of America, Y 3.F 31/19:9

EFC Formula Book, The Expected Family Contribution for **Federal** Student Aid, ED 1.45/5

Enrollment Information Guide and Plan Comparison Chart **Federal** Civilian Employees in Positions Outside the Continental U.S., PM 1.8/8

Equal Employment Opportunity, Code of **Federal** Regulations Title 29, Y 3.Eq 2:18-4

Equal Employment Opportunity **Federal** Register, Y 3.Eq 2:18-6

Estimates of **Federal** Tax Expenditures for Fiscal Year, Y 4.T 19/4-10

Examination of the **Federal** Deposit Insurance Corporation's Financial Statements for the Years Ended ..., GA 1.13/16

Examination of the **Federal** Financing Bank's Financial Statements, GA 1.13/4

FedBizOpps (Federal Business Opportunities), GS 1.41

Federal Acquisition Institute: General Publications, GS 1/6.12

Federal Acquisition Regulation, GP 3.38/2

Federal Air Surgeons Medical Bulletin, TD 4.215

Federal and Non-Federal Projects Approved, Y 3.F 31/4:7

Federal Archeology Report, I 29.59/5

Federal Advisory Committee Annual Report of the President, Pr 42.10

Federal and State Endangered Species Expenditures, I 49.77/6

Federal Audiovisual Activity, AE 1.110/5

Federal Aviation Administration Plan for Research, Engineering, and Development, TD 4.64

Federal Communication Commission Daily, CC 1.56

Federal Communications Commission Reports: Second Series, CC 1.12/2

Federal Depository Library Directory, GP 3.36/2

Federal Depository Library Directory (online), GP 3.36/2-2

Federal Digital Cartography Newsletter, I 19.115

Federal Elections . . ., Election Results for the U.S. Senate and U.S. House of Representatives, Y 3.El 2/3:16

Federal Firearms Licensee News, T 70.18

Federal Handbook , GS 2.6/2

Federal Income Tax Guide for Older Americans, Y 4.Ag 4/2-11

Federal Information Locator System, PrEx 2.14/2

Federal Information Processing Standards Publications, C 13.52

Federal IRM Directory, GS 12.19

Federal Item Identifications Guides for Supply Cataloging, Part 2, Description Patterns, D 7.6/2:6-2

Federal Judicial Caseload Statistics JU 10.21

Federal Justice Statistics, ED 1.328/13

Federal Laws, CC 1.5

Federal Managers' Financial Integrity Act, Secretary's Annual Statement and Report to the President and the Congress, I 1.96/6

Federal Motor Carrier Safety Administration, Register, TD 2.314.6/4

Federal Plan for Water-Data Acquisition, I 19.74/3

Federal Population and Mortality Schedules (years), in the National Archives and the States, AE 1.115

Federal Prisons Journal, J 16.30

Federal Procurement Data System, Contractor Identification File, Alphabetical Listing, PrEx 2.24/14

Federal Quality News, PM 1.58

Federal R & D Funding by Budget Function, NS 1.18/4

Federal Radionavigation Plan, D 1.84

Federal R & D Project Summaries, E 1.142 429-X-24

Federal Register Proposed Amendments, Y 3.F 31/21-3:9-5

Federal Rules of Appellate Procedure with Forms, Y 4.J 89/1-10

Federal Rules of Evidence, Y 4.J 89/1-13

Federal School Code (Database), ED 1.92/2

Federal School Code List, ED 1.92

Federal Scientific and Technical Workers: Numbers and Characteristics, NS 1.14/3

Federal Scientists and Engineers, NS 1.22/9

Federal Service Impasses Panel Releases, Y 3.F 31/21-3:14-3

Federal Tax Products, GP 3.38/3

Focus on Federal Employee Health Assistance Programs, PM 1.55

FY Budget Highlights Federal Drug Control Programs, PrEx 26.1/4

Index of Decisions, Federal Service Impasses Panel, PM 1.65

Landview IV/The Federal Geographic Data, C 3.301

Occupations of Federal White-Collar and Blue-Collar Workers, PM 1.10/2-2

Office of Federal Airways Maintenance Engineering Division Newsletter, C 31.149

Official Bulletin Federal Radio Commission, RC 1.5

One Hundred Years of Federal Forestry, A 1.75:402

Operating Bank Offices Insured by the Federal Deposit Insurance Corporation, as of {date}, Y 3.F 31/8:18

Operation Golden Eagle, Directory of Federal Recreation Areas Changing Entrance, Admission and User Fees, I 66.16

Orders Federal Energy Regulatory Commission, E 2.10

Orders Federal Power Commission, FP 1.19

Orders Federal Railroad Administration, TD 3.8/2

Orders, Notices, Rulings and Decisions Issued by Hearing Examiners and by the Commission in Formal Docketed Proceedings before the Federal Maritime

Organization of Federal Executive Departments and Agencies, Y 4.G 74/9-10

Package X, Informational Copies of Federal Tax Forms, T 22.2/12

Pamphlets Federal Employees' Compensation Office, L 36.309

Pay Structure of the Federal Civil Service, PM 1.10/2-4

Pay Structure on the Federal Civil Service, CS 1.48:33

Political Activity and Political Assessments of Federal Office-Holders and Employees, CS 1.34

Posters Federal Bureau of Investigation, J 1.14/21

Posters Federal Emergency Management Agency, FEM 1.21

Posters Federal Highway Administration, TD 2.59/2

Posters Federal Holiday Commission, Y 3.H 71:12

Posters, Federal, Maps, CC 1.8

Posters Federal Trade Commission, FT 1.31

Poultry Slaughtered Under Federal Inspection and Poultry Used in Canning and Processed Foods, A 88.15/9-2

President's Awards for Distinguished Federal Civilian Service, CS 1.64

President's Commission on Federal Statistics, Pr 37.8:St 2

President's Panel on Federal Compensation, Pr 38.8:C 73

Press Releases Federal Home Loan Bank Board, FHL 1.7

Price Lists Federal Prison Industries, Inc., FPI 1.7

Price Trends for Federal-Aid Highway Construction, C 37.22, TD 2.49

Price Trends for Federal-aid-highway Construction, TD 2.49

Prices and Yields of Public Marketable Securities Issued by United States Government and by Federal Agencies, T 68.7

Prime Contract Awards by Service Category and Federal Supply Classification, D 1.57/4

Prisoners in State and Federal Institutions on (date), J 29.9/7

Prisoners in State and Federal Institutions, J 16.23

Proceedings National Brucellosis Committee and Progress Report of the Cooperative State-Federal Brucellosis Eradication Program, A 77.202:B 83/16

Program Guide Federal Civil Defense Administration, FCD 1.6/7

Progress Report Federal Civil Defense Administration, FCD 1.1/2

Project Register, Projects Approved Under Sec. 8 of Federal Water Pollution Control Act (Pub. Law 660, 84th Cong.), As Amended and Sec. 3, of Public Works

Proposed Federal Specifications, Preliminary, GS 2.8/6

Prosecutions and Seizures Under the Federal Seed Act, A 88.30/7

Publications Federal Fire Council, GS 1.14/5

Publications Federal National Mortgage Association, FL 5.17

Publications Federal-Aid Airport Program, FAA 8.10

Public Works Administration of Federal Works Agency, Reports Showing Status of Funds and Analyses of Expenditures, T 63.108

Quarterly Economic and Financial Review: Federal Republic of Germany and Western Sectors of Berlin, S 1.91/2

Quarterly Summary of Federal, State, and Local Tax Revenue, C 3.145/6

Railroad Employee Fatalities Investigated by the Federal Railroad Administration in (year), TD 3.110/5

Regulations (pt. nos. of Title 26 of the Code of Federal Regulations), T 70.6/2

Regulations (pt. nos. of Title 27 Code of Federal Regulations), T 22.17/4, T 70.6/3

Regulations Under Federal Power Act, FP 1.7:P 87/2

Regulations, Rules and Instructions Federal Emergency Management Agency, FEM 1.6

Regulations, Title 29, Code of Federal Regulations, L 36.206/2

Reinvention Roundtable, Helping Federal Workers Create A Government That Works Better and Cost Less, Prvp 42.15

Report of Coordinated Meeting of Federal Agencies (by States), Y 3.N 21/9:11

Report of Federal Trade Commission on Rates of Return (after taxes) for Identical Companies in Selected Manufacturing Industries, FT 1.21

Report of the Federal Home Loan Bank Board, FHL 1.1

Report of the U.S. Department of Justice Pursuant to Section 8 of the Federal Coal Leasing Amendments Act of 1975, J 1.27/3

Report to Congress, Office of Federal Procurement Policy, PrEx 2.21

Report to the Federal Land Bank Associations for Year Ended June 30 (date), FCA 1.23

Report to the United States Congress on Federal Activities on Alcohol Abuse and Alcoholism, HE 20.8316

Report, Civil Service Requirement, Federal Employees' Group Life Insurance, Federal Employees Health Benefits, Retired Federal Employees Health Benefits, Fiscal Year (date), CS 1.29/3

Reports Showing Status of Funds and Analyses of Expenditures, Public Works Administration Federal Works Agency, T 60.14

Reproducible Federal Tax Forms for Use in Libraries, T 22.57

Research Bulletins Federal Emergency Relief Administration, Y 3.F 31/5:28

Research Projects Federal Emergency Management Agency, FEM 1.22

Research Reports Bureau of Federal Credit Unions, FS 3.309

Rules and Regulations for Federal Savings and Loan System, with Amendments to {date}, FHL 1.6:Sa 9

Rules and Regulations, Title 10, Code of Federal Regulations, Chapter 1, Y 3.N 88:6

Rules of Practice Federal Power Commission, FP 1.8

Rules of Practice Federal Trade Commission, FT 1.7

Safety Bulletins Federal Emergency Relief Administration, Y 3.F 31/5:24

Safety News Letter, Current Information in the Federal Safety Field, L 30.8

Safety Posters Federal Public Housing Authority, NHA 4.9

Sales of Firm Electric Power for Resale, by Private Electric Utilities, by Federal Projects, by Municipals, FP 1.21

Scientific Information Activities of Federal Agencies, NS 1.16

Semi-Monthly News Letter, Federal Theatre Project, Y 3.W 89/2:33

Service and Regulatory Announcements Federal Horticulture Board, A 35.9

Significant Cases, Federal Employee and Labor-Management Relations, PM 1.63

Significant of Federal Financial Accounting Concepts, PrEX 2.35/2

Significant of Federal Financial Accounting Standards, PrEX 2.35

Simplifying Federal Aid to States and Communities, Annual Report to the President of an Interagency Program, PrEx 2.18

Single Award Federal Supply Schedule, GS 2.7/7

Social Security Rulings on Federal Old-age, Survivors, Disability, and Health Insurance, HE 3.44

Sources of Milk for Federal Order Markets, by State and County, A 88.40, A 88.14/11-3

Special Analysis of Federal Activities in Public Works and Other Construction in Budget, PrEx 2.8/a2

Special Analysis of Federal Aid to State and Local Governments in Budget, PrEx 2.8/a3

Special Analysis of Federal Credit Programs in Budget, PrEx 2.8/a5

Special Analysis of Federal Research and Development Programs in Budget, PrEx 2.8/a4

Special Analysis of Principal Federal Statistical Programs in Budget, PrEx 2.8/a6

State Administered Federal Engineer Funds, HE 19.122

State and Federal Marketing Activities and Other Economic Work, A 36.21

State - Federal Judicial Observer, Ju 13.13/2

State of Federal Facilities, The, EP 1.116

State Publications Issued in Cooperation with **Federal** Extension Service, A 43.37

Statement of Condition of **Federal** Land Banks, Joint Stock Land Banks, etc., FCA 1.7

Statements of Conditions of **Federal** Land Banks, etc., T 48.6

Statistical Series **Federal** Power Commission, FP 1.21

Statistical Tables for the **Federal** Judiciary, Ju 10.21/2

Status of **Federal** Aviation Regulations, New, TD 4.13

Status of Open Recommendations Improving Operations of **Federal** Departments and Agencies, GA 1.13/18

Statutes and Decisions Pertaining to the **Federal** Trade Commission, FT 1.13/2

Student Guide, Five **Federal** Financial Aid Programs, ED 1.8/2

Subject Matter Indexes to Decisions of the **Federal** Labor Relations Authority, Y 3.F 31/21-3:10-3

Summaries of **Federal** Milk Marketing Orders, A 88.2:M 59/28

Summary of Accidents Investigated by the **Federal** Railroad Administration in Fiscal Year, TD 3.111

Summary of Accidents Investigated by the **Federal** Railroad Administration in the Fiscal Year (dates), TD 3.110/2

Summary of **Federal** ADP Activities for Fiscal Year (date), GS 12.9

Summary of **Federal** Hunting Regulations for (year), I 49.24/2

Survey of **Federal** Libraries, HE 19.311:L 61

Tariff Circulars **Federal** Communications Commission, CC 1.16

Technical Reports **Federal** Energy Administration, FE 1.20

Telephone Directory **Federal** Aviation Administration, TD 4.52/2

Telephone Directory **Federal** Communications Commission, CC 1.53

Telephone Directory **Federal** Energy Regulatory Commission, E 2.12/2

Third Branch, a Bulletin of the **Federal** Courts, Ju 10.3/2

Toward Interagency Coordination, **Federal** Research and Development on Adolescence, HE 23.1013

Toward Interagency Coordination: **Federal** Research and Development on Early Childhood, HE 23.1013/2

Training Bulletins **Federal** Works Agency, FW 1.11

Training Manual **Federal** Security Agency, FS 1.10

Unemployment Compensation Interpretation Service, **Federal** Service, **Federal** Series, SS 1.20

Uniform System of Accounts and Reports for Certificated Route Air Carriers in Accordance with Sec. 407 of the **Federal** Aviation Act, C 31.206/5

University-**Federal** Agency Conference on Career Development, Conference Reports, CS 1.70

Uses of State Administered **Federal** Education Funds, HE 19.122

Value of Prime Contracts Awarded by **Federal** Agencies in Areas of Substantial Labor Surplus, C 46.10

Vocational Instructional Materials Available from **Federal** Agencies, ED 1.17/3

Water Pollution Control, **Federal** Costs, Report to Congress, I 67.1/2

Water Quality Standards Criteria Digest, Compilation of **Federal**/State Criteria on {various subjects}, EP 1.29/2

Water Supply Outlook, **Federal**-State-Private Cooperative Snow Surveys {Colorado}, A 57.46/15

Weekly Summary of **Federal** Legislation Relating to National Resources Committee, Activities Bulletins, Y 3.N 21/12:15

Your **Federal** Budget, Pr 34.107/4

Your **Federal** Income Tax, T 22.44

Your Guide to **Federal** Waterfowl Production Areas, I 49.6/3

Federal -Aid

Price Trends for **Federal-Aid** Highway Construction TD 2.30/16-3

Federal Government

Annual Report on the Employment of Minorities, Women and Handicapped Individuals in the **Federal Government**, Y 3.Eq 2:12-5

Current Information Resource Requirements of the **Federal Government**, PM 1.56

Description of Output Indicators by Function for the **Federal Government**, L 2.133

Productivity Statistics for **Federal Government** Functions, Fiscal Year, L 2.119/2

Real Property Owned by the **Federal Government** in {various States}, EP 4.15

Scientific and Technical Personnel in the **Federal Government**, NS 1.22:G 74

Union Recognition in the **Federal Government**, Statistical Summary, PM 1.47

Federal Reserve

Digest and Index of Opinions of Counsel, Informal Rulings of Federal Reserve Board and Matter Relating Thereto, from **Federal Reserve** Bulletin, FR 1.10

Official Hours and Holidays to Be Observed by **Federal Reserve** Offices During Year (date), FR 1.50

Official Opening and Closing Hours of Board of Governors and **Federal Reserve** Banks, also Holiday During Month, FR 1.50

Publications **Federal Reserve** Board, FR 1.45

Sales Finance Companies **Federal Reserve** System Board of Governors, FR 1.26

State Member Banks of the **Federal Reserve** System, FR 1.11/5

Volume and Composition of Individuals' Savings **Federal Reserve** System Board of Governors, FR 1.53

Weekly Averages of Member Bank Reserves, Reserve Bank Credit and Related Items and Statement of Condition of the **Federal Reserve** Bank, FR 1.15

Federal-Aid

Bid Opening Report **Federal-Aid** Highway Construction Contracts Calendar Year, TD 2.47

Federalism

Significant Features of Fiscal **Federalism**, Y 3.Ad 9/8:18

Federally

Program Facts on **Federally** Aided Public Assistance Income Maintenance Programs, HE 17.614

Stocks of Grain in Deliverable Positions for Chicago Board of Trade, Futures Contracts in Exchange-Approved and **Federally** Licensed Warehouses, as Reported by Those Warehouses, A 85.14, Y 3.C 73/5:10

Federally-Funded

Superfund Emergency Response Actions, A Summary of **Federally-Funded** Removals, Annual Report, EP 1.89/5

Survey of **Federally-Funded** Marine Mammal Research and Studies, Y 3.M 33/3:9-2

Federation

Directory of World **Federation** of Trade Unions, L 29.9/3

Federations

Conventions, (year): National and International Unions, State Labor **Federations**, Professional Associations, State Employee Association {list}, L 2.103

FEDLINK

FEDLINK Technical Notes, LC 1.32/5

Feds

Feds Staff Papers, A 100.10

FEDWARE

FEDWARE Magazine, GS 1.39

Fee

Federal Recreation **Fee** Program (year), Including Federal Recreation Visitation Data, a Report to the Congress, I 70.18

Federal Recreation **Fee** Report, I 29.108

Fee Licenses Issued for the Month, I 64.12

Feed

Cattle and Calves on Feed, Cattle Sold for Slaughter, Selected Markets, A 92.18/6

Feed

Cattle on **Feed**, A 88.16/6, A 105.23/3

Cattle on **Feed**, Cattle Sold for Slaughter, Selected Markets, A 92.18/6

Cattle on **Feed**, Illinois, Iowa, Nebraska, Idaho, and California, A 88.16/7

Directory, State Officials Charged with Enforcement of Food, Drug, Cosmetic, and **Feed** Laws, FS 13.102:St 2

Feed Grain and Wheat Stabilization Program, A 82.37/3:F 32/2

Feed Grain Situation, A 36.87

Feed Market News, Weekly Summary and Statistics, A 88.18/4

Feed Market Review, A 82.32

Feed Market Summary, A 82.35, A 88.18/3

Feed Outlook and Situation Report, A 93.11/2

Feed Prospects, A 36.84/2

Feed Situation, A 88.18/12, A 93.11/2, A 105.20/2

Feed, Outlook and Situation Yearbook, A 93.11/2-2

Grain and **Feed** Market News, A 88.18/4-2

International Animal **Feed** Symposium Reports, A 67.34

Sheep and Lamb on **Feed**, A 88.16/13, A 105.47

Stocks of **Feed** Grains, A 36.174

Weekly **Feed** Review, A 88.18/4

Wheat, Rice, **Feed** Grains, Dry Peas, Dry Beans, Seeds, Hops, A 67.30:W 56

World **Feed** Grain Prospects, A 36.84/1

Feedback

FAA Aircraft Program Data **Feedback**, TD 4.410

Feedback, D 301.45/56

Feeder

Cattle and Sheep, Shipments of Stocker and **Feeder** Cattle and Sheep into Selected North Central States, A 88.16/18-2

Shipments of Stocker and **Feeder** Cattle and Sheep, A 88.16/18

Feeding

Child **Feeding** Charts, A 42.7/3

Fees

Driver License Administration Requirements and **Fees**, TD 2.61

Federal Recreation **Fees**, I 66.23

Highway Taxes and **Fees**: How They are Collected and Distributed, TD 2.64

Operation Golden Eagle, Directory of Federal Recreation Areas Changing Entrance, Admission and User **Fees**, I 66.16

Feldspar

Feldspar, I 28.111/2

Feldspar in (year), I 28.111

Fellows

Arts Administration **Fellows** Program, Application Guideline For Fiscal Year, NF 2.8/2-24

ASA/NSF/Census Bureau Research **Fellows** Program, C 3.293

Trainees and **Fellows** Supported by the National Institute of Dental Research and Trained During Fiscal Year, HE 20.3402:T 68, HE 20.3410

Fellowship

Cooperative Graduate **Fellowship** Program for Fiscal Year, **Fellowship** Awards {and} Program of Summer Fellowships for Graduate Teaching Assistants for Fiscal Year, NS 1.19/2

Fellowship Program Announcement, J 28.34

Graduate **Fellowship** Announcement, TD 2.64/2

Graduate **Fellowship** Awards Announced by National Science Foundation, NS 1.19

International Application Guidelines, International Program: **Fellowships** and Residencies Partnerships, NF 2.8/2-34

Literacy Leader **Fellowship** Program Reports, Y 3.L 71:16

Literature **Fellowship** Application Guidelines, NF 2.16

Modern Foreign Language **Fellowship** Program, National Defense Education Act, Title 6 and NDEA Related Awards under Fullbright-Hays Act, FS 5.255:55034, HE 5.255:55034

Program Announcement, Graduate Research **Fellowship** Program, J 28.25

Program Announcement, Visiting **Fellowship** Program, J 28.25/2

Scholarships and **Fellowship** Information, FS 5.63

Science and Technology **Fellowship** Program, C 1.86

Summer Research **Fellowship** Program at the National Institutes of Health, HE 20.3015/2

Visiting **Fellowship** Program Reports, J 26.11

Fellowships

Mathematical Sciences Postdoctoral Research **Fellowships**, NS 1.45

Music **Fellowships**: Composers, Jazz, Solo
Recitalists, Applications Guidelines, NF
2.8/2-8
National Defense Graduate **Fellowships**, Graduate
Programs, FS 5.255:55017, HE
5.255:55017
NEH **Fellowships** University Teachers, College
Teachers, and Independent Scholars
Anniversary and Commemorative
Initiatives, NF 3.13/4
Public Health Service International Postdoctorate
Research **Fellowships** Awards for Study
in the United States, HE 20.3709
Visual Artists **Fellowships**, NF 2.8/2-13
White House **Fellowships**, Pr 40.12, Pr 42.12
Felons
Felons Sentenced to Probation in State Courts, J
29.11/12
State Sentencing of Convicted **Felons**, J 29.11/11-3
Felony Laws of the Fifty States and the District of
Columbia, J 29.18
Felony Sentences in State Courts, J 29.11/11
Felony Sentences in the United States, J 29.11/11-2
Pretrial Release of **Felony** Defendants, J 29.11/14
Prosecution of **Felony** Arrest, J 29.9/4
FEMA
FEMA Newsletter, FEM 1.20
FEMA News Releases, FEM 1.28
FEMP
FEMP Focus, E 1.89/4
Female
Data on **Female** Veterans, VA 1.2/12
Minority and **Female** Motor Carrier Listings, IC
1.38
Females
Females Employed by Class 1 Steams Railways,
Number of, IC 1 ste.43
Number of **Females** Employed by Class 1 Steam
Railways, IC 1 ste.43
Number of **Females** Employed by Class I Steam
Railways, IC 1 ste.43
FERC
Federal Energy Guidelines: **FERC** Reports, E 2.17
FERC News, E 2.9
FERC Statutes and Regulations, Proposed
Regulations, E 2.18/3
FERC Statutes and Regulations, Regulations
Preambles, E 2.18/2
Fermilab
Fermilab Reports, E 1.92/2
Fermilab Research Program Workbook, E 1.92
Ferret
Ferret Reports, I 49.90
Ferroalloys
Ferroalloys in (year), I 28.142
Ferrosilicon
Ferrosilicon, I 28.75, I 28.75/3
Ferrosilicon in (year), I 28.75/2
Ferrosilicon Reports, I 28.75
Ferrous
Ferrous Metals Supply/Demand Data, I 28.169
FERS
CSRS and **FERS** Handbook for Personnel and
Payroll, PM 1.14/3-3
Fertilizer
Fertilizer Abstracts, Y 3.T 25:36
Fertilizer Situation, A 93.36
Fertilizer Situation for (year), A 82.77
Fertilizer Summary Data by States and Geographic
Areas, Y 3.T 25:29 F 41/7
Fertilizer Supply (year), A 82.77
Fertilizer Trends, Y 3.T 25:29
Fertilizer Trends, Production, Consumption, and
Trade, Y 3.T 25:66
Sulphuric Acid, Production, Stocks, etc. Reported
by **Fertilizer** Manufacturers, C 3.110
Superphosphates, Production, etc., Reported by
Fertilizer Manufacturers, C 3.111
Fertilizers
Commercial **Fertilizers**, A 105.41, A 105.41/2
Commercial **Fertilizers**, Consumption by Class for
Year Ended (date), A 92.37/3
Consumption of Commercial **Fertilizers** and Primary
Plant Nutrients in United States, A
92.37
FES
FES Aid: Sanitation Series, A 43.40
FESA
FESA Briefs, D 103.122/2
FESA- (series), D 103.122
Fescue
Tall **Fescue**, Oregon, A 92.19/13
Tall **Fescue**, Southern States, A 92.19/12

Festival
Festival of American Folklife, SI 1.43/2
Festival USA, C 47:17
Festivals
Presenters and **Festivals** Jazz Management, Jazz
Special Projects, Music, Application
Guidelines, NF 2.8/2-9
Fetal
Instruction Manual: Classification and Coding
Instructions for **Fetal** Death Records, HE
20.6208/6-2
National Advisory Council on Maternal, Infant and
Fetal Nutrition: Biennial Report, A
98.14/2
Public Use Data Tape Documentation **Fetal** Deaths
Detail Records, HE 20.6226/11
Fever
Map of District Infected with Splenetic **Fever**, A 4.6
Report of Cooperative Cattle **Fever** Tick
Eradication Activities, Fiscal Year
(date), A 77.237
FEWP
F.E. Warren AFB, **FEWP**- (series), D 301.35/6
FEWS
FEWS (Famine Early Warning System) Bulletin, S
18.68
FEWS (Famine Early Warning System) Special
Report, S 18.68/2
FGD
FGD {Flue Gas Desulfurization} Quarterly Report,
EP 1.46/8
FGIS
FGIS Update, A 104.12/3
FGP
FGP Exchange, AA 1.21
FH PAM
FH PAM (series), D 101.22/13
FHA
Characteristics of **FHA** Single-Family Mortgages,
HH 2.24/7
FHA and VA Mortgages Owned and Available for
Sale by Reconstruction Finance
Corporation and Federal National
Mortgage Association, Y 3.R 24:14
FHA
FHA Home Mortgage Insurance Operations, State,
County and MSA/PMSA, HH 2.24/8
FHA Homes, Data for States, on Characteristics of
FHA Operations Under Sec. 203, HH
2.24/4
FHA Honor Awards for Presidential Design, HH
2.25
FHA Low Cost Housing Trends of One-family
Homes Insured by **FHA**, HH 2.26
FHA Manual, HH 2.6/5
FHA Monthly Report of Operations: Home
Mortgage Programs, HH 2.27/2
FHA Monthly Report of Operations: Project
Mortgage Insurance Programs, HH 2.27
FHA News Fillers for Use at Any Time, HH 2.18/4
FHA Regulations, HH 2.6
FHA Research and Statistics Release, HH 2.18/3
FHA Special Features for Use at Any Time, HH
2.18/2
FHA Trends, Characteristics of Home Mortgages
Insured by **FHA**, HH 2.24
FHFM
FHFM News Releases, T 71.7/2
FHLB
FHLB System S & L's Combined Financial
Statements: Savings and Home
Financing Source Book, FHL 1.12/2
FHM-NC
FHM-NC, A 13.134
FHWA
Cross-Reference Index of Current **FHWA** Directives,
TD 2.67
FHWA Bulletins, TD 2.3
FHWA Program, HY (series), TD 2.41
FHWA Research and Development Implementation
Catalog, TD 2.36/3
FHWA-CR
FHWA-CR, TD 2.30/18
FHWA DP-PC
Report **FHWA DP-PC** (series), TD 2.40/3
FHWA-AD
FHWA-AD (series), TD 2.30/12
FHWA-CA
FHWA-CA (series), TD 2.30/9
FHWA-CA-TL
FHWA-CA-TL (series), TD 2.30/10
FHWA/DF
FHWA/DF (series), TD 2.69

FHWA-FLP
FHWA-FLP, TD 2.30/17
FHWA/HI
Report **FHWA/HI**, TD 2.30/15
FHWA-HO
Reports **FHWA-HO** (series), TD 2.30/6
FHWA-JPO
FHWA-JPO, TD 2.30/19
FHWA/MC
Report **FHWA/MC**, TD 2.30/14
FHWA-MCRT
FHWA-MCRT, TD 2.30/20
FHWA-OEP/HEV
FHWA-OEP/HEV (series), TD 2.30/7
FHWA-PD
FHWA-PD, TD 2.30/16
FHWA/PL
Report **FHWA/PL** (series), TD 2.30/5
FHWA-RDDP
FHWA-RDDP Reports, TD 2.30/2
FHWA-RT
Report **FHWA-RT** (Series), TD 2.30/11
FHWA-SA
FHWA-SA (Series), TD 2.30/13
FHWA-TD
Reports **FHWA-TD** (series), TD 2.30/4
FHWA-TO
Report **FHWA-TO**- (series), TD 2.30/8
Fiber
Cotton **Fiber** and Processing Test Results, A 88.11/
17
Progress Report, Annual Varietal and Environmen-
tal Study of **Fiber** and Spinning
Properties of Cottons, A 77.530
Rayon and Other Synthetic Textile **Fiber** Imports, C
18.121
Summary of Cotton **Fiber** and Processing Test
Results, Crop of (year), A 88.11/17-2
Fibers
Commercial Stocks of Wool and Related **Fibers**,
Tops, Moils, Waste Clips and Rags in
U.S., C 3.52/3
Industry Wage Survey: Synthetic **Fibers**, L 2.3/21
Silk and Rayon and Other Synthetic Textile **Fibers**,
C 18.125
Sisal, Hemp, Jute and Miscellaneous **Fibers**, C
18.126
Fibrinolysis
Fibrinolysis, Thrombolysis, and Blood Clotting,
Bibliography, FS 2.22/13-6, HE 20.3209
Fibrosis
Cystic **Fibrosis**, HE 20.3320/2-2
FICE
FICE Report, Y 3.Ed 8:9
Fiduciary
Fiduciary Income Tax Returns, T 22.35/2:F 44/2
Field
ARA **Field** Reports, C 46.22
Basic **Field** Manual, W 3.63
Chemical Warfare **Field** Service Bulletins, W 91.7
Contracts for **Field** Projects & Supporting Research
on . . ., E 1.99/2
Costs and Indexes for Domestic Oil and Gas **Field**
Equipment and Production Operations,
E 3.44/2
EDA **Field** Reports, C 46.22
ERS **Field** Reports, A 93.37/2
FDD **Field** Reports, A 93.37
Federal Funds for Research and Development,
Federal Obligations for Research by
Agency and Detailed **Field** of Science,
Fiscal Years, NS 1.18/3
Field and Seed Crops, Farm Production, Farm
Disposition, Value, by States, A 88.30/4
Field and Seed Crops, Production, Farm Use, Sales,
Value by States, A 92.19
Field Artillery Notes, W 26.10
Field Charts, M 202.22
Field Circulars, FC- (series), D 101.4/2
Field Crops, Production, Disposition, Value, A
105.9/4
Field Directory, HE 1.17
Field Engineers Bulletins, C 4.31
Field Facility Directory, FAA 1.43
Field Identification Cards, A 13.100
Field Initiated Studies Program, Abstracts of
Funded Projects, ED 1.337
Field Letter, Information, Legislative, Court
Decisions, Opinions, L 25.8
Field Letter, National Committee for Conservation
of Manpower in War Industries, L 1.29
Field Manual and **Field** Regulations, W 1.33
Field Manuals, W 3.63/2, D 101.20

Cooperative Forest **Fire** Prevention Program, A 13.20/4

Federal **Fire** Council News Letter, GS 1.14/4

Federal **Fire** Experience for Fiscal Year (date), GS 1.14/2

Fire Control Notes, A 13.32

Fire Extinguishing Equipment, Report of Shipments, C 3.84

Fire Facts, Y 3.T 25:20

Fire Fighting Bulletins, I 38.7

Fire Handbook, Region 7, A 13.24

Fire in the United States, C 58.13, FEM 1.117

Fire Loss to Government Property, GS 1.14/2

Fire Management Notes, A 13.32

Fire Management Today A 13.32

Fire Research Publications, C 13.58/4

Fire Safety Activities, GS 1.14/8

Fire Safety Activities {list} Administrative, GS 1.14/8

Fire Safety Focus Sheets, Y 3.C 76/3:24

Fire Technology Abstracts, C 58.11, FEM 1.109

Fireword, a Bulletin From the National **Fire** Prevention and Control Administration, C 58.10

Forest **Fire** News, A 13.32/4

Forest **Fire** Statistics, A 13.32/2

Profile on **Fire** in the United States, FEM 1.117/2

Publications Federal **Fire** Council, GS 1.14/5

Publications President's Conference on **Fire** Prevention, FW 6.9

Safety and **Fire** Protection Bulletins, Y 3.At 7:3

Safety, **Fire** Prevention, and Occupational Health Management, by Objectives Review, D 301.99

Safety, Occupational Health and **Fire** Protection Bulletin, VA 1.22:13-1

Fire-Cured

Fire-Cured and Dark Air-Cured Tobacco Market Review, A 88.34/8

Fire-Cured Tobacco Market Review, A 88.34/4

Firearms

Alcohol, Tobacco and **Firearms** Cumulative Bulletin, T 70.7/2

Alcohol, Tobacco, and **Firearms**, T 70.7

Commerce in **Firearms** in the United States T 70.24

Federal **Firearms** Licensee News, T 70.18

Firearms, and Ammunition Curios and Relics List, T 70.15

Firearms, Curiors and Relics List, T 70.15

Published Ordinances, **Firearms**, T 70.5:F 51

Firefighter

Firefighter, Fatalities, FEM 1.116

Firepower

Firepower, W 34.40

Naval **Firepower**, N 18.12

Fireproof

Steel Office Furniture, Shelving, and Lockers, and **Fireproof** Safes, C 3.108

Fireview

Fireview, C 13.61

Fireword

Fireword, a Bulletin From the National **Fire** Prevention and Control Administration, C 58.10

Firing

Firing Tables, W 34.34, D 101.58

Firm

Sales of **Firm** Electric Power for Resale, by Private Electric Utilities, by Federal Projects, by Municipals, FP 1.21

FIRMR

GSA **FIRMR**/FAR Regulations, GS 12.15/2

Firms

Consolidated List of Persons or **Firms** Currently Debarred for Violations of Various Public Contracts Acts Incorporating Labor Standard Provisions, GA 1.17

Employee Benefits in Medium and Large **Firms**, L 2.3/10

Firms in the 8(a) Business Development Program, SBA 1.36

Foreign-Owned U.S. **Firms**, FOF (series), C 3.254

Information for Business Executives {and} **Firms** with Retailing and Wholesale Interests, Y 3.P 93/4:9

Interim List of Persons or **Firms** Currently Debarred for Violation of Various Public Contracts Acts Incorporating Labor Standards Provisions, GA 1.17/2

Procurement from Small and Other Business **Firms**, D 1.48

Recordkeeping Requirements for **Firms** Selected to Participate in the Annual Survey of Occupational Injuries and Illnesses, L 2.129

Sources for Information on American **Firms** for International Buyers, C 42.2:Am 3

First

First Army Pamphlets (series), D 101.22/9-2

First Army, 1a Regulations, D 101.9/6

First Line, Newsletter for Federal Supervisors and Midmanagers, PM 1.17, CS 1.91

To the **First** Americans, Annual Report of the Indian Health Program, FS 2.867/4, HE 20.2014/2, HE 20.5312

Views of the Committee on Appropriations, United States Senate, on the **First** Concurrent Resolution on the Budget, Y 4.Ap 6/2:B 85/5

First Aid

Instructor's Guide for Classes, **First Aid** Training Courses, N 10.16

Military Sanitation and **First Aid**, W 3.50/4

First Class

First Class Post Offices with Named Stations and Branches, P 24.8

FirstGov

Firstgov, GS 1.40

First-Professional

Financial Assistance for College Students, Undergraduate and **First-Professional**, FS 5.255:55027, HE 5.255:55027

First-Term

Junior-Year Science, Mathematics, and Foreign Language Students, **First-Term**, FS 5.254:54001, HE 5.254:54001

FISAP

FISAP Workshop, ED 1.82

Fiscal

Aging, GAO Activities in **Fiscal** Year, GA 1.13/14

Fiscal Handbook, Series F, P 1.31/12

Fiscal Letters, FS 3.27

Fiscal Year ... Air Force Technical Objective Document, D 301.45/27-10

Fiscal Year ... OSHA Training Institute Schedule of Courses and Registration Requirements, L 35.25

Fiscal Year Plan, Automated Data Processing Update, HE 3.84

Fiscal Year {report}, CS 1.71/5

Interior Budget in Brief, **Fiscal** Year Highlights, I 1.1/6

Medicare Carriers Manual; **Fiscal** Administration, HE 22.8/7-2

Medicare Part A Intermediary Manual, Part 1, **Fiscal** Administration, HE 22.8/6-3

OJJDP **Fiscal** Year, Program Plan, J 32.10/2

Ordnance **Fiscal** Bulletin, W 34.30

Plant Pest Control Cooperative Programs, Western Region, **Fiscal** Year (date), A 77.327/2

Significant Features of **Fiscal** Federalism, Y 3.Ad 9/8:18

Fiscal Year

Army Budget, **Fiscal Year**, D 101.121

Catalog of Courses **Fiscal Year**, L 1.86

U.S. Geological Survey, **Fiscal Year** Yearbook, I 19.1/2

Fish

Annual **Fish** Passage Report, North Pacific Divisions, D 103.27

Approved List Sanitary Inspected **Fish** Establishments, C 55.338

Compilation of Federal Laws Relating to Conservation and Development of Our Nation's **Fish** and Wildlife Resources, Environmental Quality, and Oceanography, Y 4.M 53:L 44/2

Current Federal Research Reports, **Fish**, I 49.94

Federal Aid in **Fish** and Wildlife Restoration, I 49.29/3

Fish and Wildlife Annual Project Summary, E 5.11

Fish and Wildlife Habitat Management Leaflets, A 57.56/2

Fish and Wildlife Leaflets, I 49.13/5

Fish and Wildlife News, I 49.88

Fish and Wildlife Report, I 49.56

Fish and Wildlife Research (series), I 49.99

Fish and Wildlife Service Publications, Printed and Duplicated Material, I 49.18/3

Fish and Wildlife Technical Reports (series), I 49.100

Fish Disease Leaflets, I 49.28/3

Fish Distribution Reports, I 49.69

Fish Health Bulletin, I 49.79/2

Fish Health News, I 49.79

Fish Inventory Data, Y 3.T 25:40

Fish Kills Caused by Pollution in (year), EP 2.24

Fish Meal and Oil, C 55.309/2

Fish Meal and Oil Market Review, Current Economic Analysis I, C 55.309/3

Fish Monitoring Investigations, Browns Ferry Nuclear Plant, Wheeler Reservoir, Alabama, Y 3.T 25:37

Fish Monitoring Investigations: Sequoyah Nuclear Plant, Chickamauga Reservoir, Tennessee, Y 3.T 25:37-3

Fish Protein Concentrate, Reports, I 49.58

Fish Stick Report, C 55.309/2

Fish Sticks, **Fish** Portions, and Breaded Shrimp (CFS series), C 55.309/2

Fish-Passage Research Program Progress Reports, I 49.63

Food **Fish** Situation and Outlook, Annual Review Issue, I 49.8/7

Food **Fish**, Market Review and Outlook, C 55.309/5

Food **Fish**, Situation and Outlooks, I 49.8/6

Frozen **Fish** Report, I 49.8/3

Frozen **Fish** Report (preliminary), C 55.309

Important **Fish** and Wildlife Habitats of (various States), I 49.91

Investigations in **Fish** Control, I 49.70

National **Fish** Hatchery Leaflets {various locations}, I 49.86

Pollution-Caused **Fish** Kills, FS 2.94, I 67.9

Progressive **Fish** Culturist, I 49.35

Quarterly Report of Progress at **Fish** Control Laboratory, La Crosse, Wisconsin, Southeastern **Fish** Control Laboratory, Warm Springs, Georgia, and Hammond Bay Biological Station, Millersburg, Michigan, I 49.75

Rodenticides and Mammal, Bird and **Fish** Toxicants, EP 5.11/4

Statistical Bulletins **Fish** Commission, FC 1.5

Statistical Summary for **Fish** and Wildlife Restoration, I 49.29/4

Tennessee Valley Streams, Their **Fish**, Bottom Fauna, and Aquatic Habitat {by areas}, Y 3.T 25:41

Topical Briefs: **Fish** and Wildlife Resources and Electric Power Generation, I 49.78

U.S. Production of **Fish** Fillets and Steaks, Annual Summary, C 55.309/2-6

Wildlife, **Fish**, Rare Plant, Partnership Update, A 13.133

Fisheries

Alaska **Fisheries**, C 55.309/2

American-Canadian **Fisheries** Conference, 1918, S 3.27

Annual Reports on Salmon **Fisheries**, C 2.1

Aquatic Sciences and **Fisheries** Information System: ASFIS Reference Series, C 55.39

Billfish Newsletter (Southwest **Fisheries** Science Center), C 55.346

Bureau of Sport and **Fisheries** and Wildlife's In-sight, I 49.50/2

Canadian-American **Fisheries** Commission, S 5.20

Canadian-American **Fisheries** Commission, 1893-96, S 3.26

Census of Commercial **Fisheries**, Preliminary Reports, C 3.234/2

Census of Commercial **Fisheries**: Final Volumes, C 3.234

Central Pacific, Western Pacific, and South Pacific **Fisheries** Development Program Report for Calendar Year, C 55.329

Central, Western, and South Pacific **Fisheries** Development Program Report for Calendar Year, C 55.329

Chesapeake **Fisheries**, C 55.309/2

Chesapeake **Fisheries**, C 55.309/2

Collected Reprints National Marine **Fisheries** Service, C 55.334

Commercial **Fisheries** Abstracts, I 49.40

Commercial **Fisheries** Review, I 49.10

Commercial **Fisheries** Technology Leaflets, I 49.46

Commercial **Fisheries** {Economics Cooperative Marketing Leaflets}, I 49.41

Commercial **Fisheries** {Education Leaflets}, I 49.37

Commercial **Fisheries** {Market Development Lists}, I 49.33

Current **Fisheries** Statistics CFS (series), C 55.309/2

Fisheries, I 49.15/2

Fisheries and Fishing Industries, FC 1.6

Farm **Flashes**, A 21.13/7
Fruit **Flashes**, Foreign News on Fruits by Cable
and Radio: Citrus {fruits}, A 67.9
Fruit **Flashes**, Foreign News on Fruits by Cable
and Radio: Deciduous {fruits}, A 67.10
Radio Service Farm **Flashes**, A 21.13/7
Flat Ware
Porcelain Enameled **Flat Ware**, C 3.98
Flax
Flax Market Review, A 66.25
Quarterly **Flax** Market Review, A 36.115
Flaxseed
Soybeans and **Flaxseed** Summary, Crop Year, A
88.18/13-2
Stocks of **Flaxseed**, Stocks of Soybeans, A 88.18/13
World **Flaxseed** Prospects, A 36.42
FLC
FLC {Federal Library Committee} Newsletter, LC
1.32
Fleet
Bulk Carriers in the World **Fleet**, C 39.202:B 87 TD
11.20
Emergency **Fleet** News, SB 2.6
Employment Report of United States Flag Merchant
Fleet, Oceangoing Vessels 1,000 Gross
Tons and Over, C 39.208
Federal Motor Vehicle **Fleet** Reports, GS 2.18
Fleet Marine Force Manuals, FMFM (series), D
214.9/4
Fleet Marine Force Reference Publications, FMFRP
(series), D 214.9/6
Merchant **Fleet** in Service on Great Lakes, C 27.9/5
Merchant **Fleet** News, SB 2.16
Our Merchant **Fleet**, MC 1.28
Payload Flight Assignments NASA Mixed **Fleet**,
NAS 1.81
Reserve **Fleet** Safety Review, C 39.219
Statistical Analysis of the World's Merchant **Fleet**,
TD 11.12
Tankers in the World **Fleet**, TD 11.29
Victory **Fleet**, MC 1.24
Fleets
Merchant **Fleets** of the World, C 39.212
Merchant **Fleets** of the World, Sea-Going Steam and
Motor Ships of 1,000 Gross Tons and
Over, TD 11.14
Ocean Going Merchant **Fleets** of Principal Maritime
Nations, SB 7.5/100, SB 7.5/1100, C
27.9/6, MC 1.16
Statistical Analysis of World's Merchant **Fleets**
Showing Age, Size, Speed, and Draft by
Frequency Groupings, As of (date), C
39.224
United States and Canadian Great Lakes **Fleets**, C
39.214
Vessel Inventory Report, United States Flag Dry
Cargo and Tanker **Fleets**, 1,000 Gross
Tons and Over, C 39.217
FLICC
FLICC Newsletter, LC 1.32
Fliers
Fliers, A 36.128
Flight
Airman's Guide and **Flight** Information Manual,
FAA 1.25/2
Airman's Guide and **Flight** Information Manual;
Pacific Supplement, FAA 1.25
Alaska **Flight** Information Manual, C 31.134, FAA
1.21
Certification; Airmen other than **Flight**
Crewmembers, TD 4.6:part 65
Certification; **Flight** Crewmembers other than
Pilots, TD 4.6:part 63
Certification; Pilots and **Flight** Instructors, TD
4.6:part 61
DoD **Flight** Information Publication (Terminal)
High Altitude Instrument Approach
Procedures, D 5.318/2
DoD **Flight** Information Publication (Terminal)
Low Altitude Approach Procedures,
United States Military Aviation Notice,
D 5.318/3
Flight Case Planning Chart, C 55.416/7-2
Flight Engineering Reports, C 31.114
Flight Information Bulletins, C 31.121
Flight Information Manual, C 31.128, FAA 1.20,
FAA 3.13/2
Flight Information Manual, Pacific Supplement,
FAA 1.25/4
Flight Information Publication: Airport/Facility
Directory, C 55.416/2
Flight Information Publication: Area Charts, U.S.,
D 5.318/6

Flight Information Publication: Enroute High
Altitude and Low Altitude, U.S., D
5.318/4
Flight Information Publication: Enroute High
Altitude, Europe, Africa, Middle East, D
301.9/4
Flight Information Publication: Enroute
Intermediate Altitude, United States, D
301.13/5
Flight Information Publication: Enroute-High
Altitude, United States, Northeast {and
Southeast}, D 301.43/3, D 301.43/3-2
Flight Information Publication: Flight Preparation
Training Series, N 27.9
Flight Information Publication: Low Altitude
Instrument Approach Procedures, D
5.318
Flight Information Publication: Terminal High
Altitude, Pacific and Southeast Asia, D
301.12/4
Flight Information Publication: Terminal Low
Altitude, Africa and Southwest Asia, D
301.13/6
Flight Information Publication: Terminal Low
Altitude, Pacific and Southeast Asia, D
301.12/3
Flight Safety Bulletins, TD 5.3/7, D 202.10
Flight Services Handbook, TD 4.308:F 64
Flight Standards Information Manual, TD 4.8/3
Flight Standards Service Directory, TD 4.415
Flight Surgeon Topics, W 44.25
General Operating and **Flight** Rules, TD 4.6:part 91
Goddard Space **Flight** Center, Technical Abstracts,
NAS 1.28
International **Flight** Information Manual, TD 4.309
Manned Space **Flight** Resources Summary, Budget
Estimates, NAS 1.54
Military Aviation Notices; Corrections to
Supplementary **Flight** Information
Document, Pacific and Far East, D
301.50/2
Military Aviation Notices; Corrections to
Supplementary **Flight** Information,
Europe, Africa and Middle East, D
301.49/2
National **Flight** Data Digest, TD 4.314
Payload **Flight** Assignments NASA Mixed Fleet,
NAS 1.81
Publications Goddard Space **Flight** Center, NAS
1.34
Quarterly Check List, USAF/USN **Flight**
Information Publications, Planning, D
301.52/2
Research and Technology Fiscal Year (date) Annual
Report of the Goddard Space **Flight**
Center, NAS 1.65/2
Rules of **Flight**, FAA 1.6/9
Smithsonian Annals of **Flight**, SI 9.9
Status of Waterfowl & Fall **Flight** Forecast, I
49.100/3
Supplementary **Flight** Information Document,
Caribbean and South America, D 301.51
Telephone Directory Goddard Space **Flight** Center,
Greenbelt, Md, NAS 1.24/2
U.S. Air Force and U.S. Navy **Flight** Planning
Document, D 301.52
United States Air Force and Navy Supplementary
Flight Information Document, Pacific and
Far East, D 301.50
United States Air Force and Navy Supplementary
Flight Information, Europe, Africa, and
Middle East, D 301.49
United States Air Force, Navy, Royal Canadian Air
Force and Royal Canadian Supplemen-
tary **Flight** Information, North American
Area (excluding Mexico and Caribbean
area), D 301.48
United States Government **Flight** Information
Publication: Pacific Chart Supplement, C
55.427
United States Standard Facilities **Flight** Check
Manual, FAA 5.9
United States Standard **Flight** Inspection Manual,
C 31.163/3
Year in Review at Goddard Space **Flight** Center,
NAS 1.1/3
Flight Charts
Dates of Latest Prints, Instrument **Flight Charts**, C
4.9/18
Flip
Enroute Change Notice, DoD **Flip** Enroute VFR
Supplement United States, D 5.318/8-2

FLITE
FLITE {Federal Legal Information Through
Electronics} Newsletter, D 302.10
Flock
Tables on Hatchery and **Flock** Participation in the
National Poultry Improvement Plan, A
77.15:44-3
Flock
Tables on Hatchery and **Flock** Participation in the
National Turkey Improvement Plan, A
77.15:44-4
Flocks
Breed Distribution of NPIP Participating **Flocks**
by States and Divisions, A 77.15:44-2
Pullet Chick Replacements for Broiler Hatchery
Supply **Flocks**, A 88.15/19
Pullet Chicks for Broiler Hatchery Supply **Flocks**,
Pou 2-7 (series), A 92.90
Turkeys in NTIP **Flocks** and Their Distribution by
States and Varieties, A 77.15:44-11
Flood
Flood Hazard Analyses, A 57.64/2
Flood Hazard Series, A 57.64/3
Flood Hazard Studies {various rivers, creeks, and
areas}, A 57.64/3
Flood Insurance Rate Maps, HH 10.9/2
Flood Insurance Studies, FEM 1.209
Flood Insurance Studies (by State), HH 10.9
Flood Insurance Studies (various areas), FEM
1.209
Flood Plain Information (series), D 103.47
Flood Plain Management Study, A 57.64/4
Flood Plain Report {various locations}, A 57.64
Flood Report, Y 3.T 25:46
Flood-Prone Areas of {various cities}, I 19.70
Ohio River **Flood** Plain Charts, W 7.13/4
SCS **Flood** Reports, A 57.40/3
Floods
Floods in {location}; How to Avoid Damage, D
103.47/2
Floor
Floor and Wall Tile (except quarry tile), C 3.85
Global Ocean **Floor** Analysis and Research Data
Series, D 203.31
Rug and **Floor** Covering Material Notes, C 18.122
World Trade in Wood, Furniture, **Floor**, Metal and
Automobile Polishes, C 18.178
Flora
Contributions Toward a **Flora** of Nevada, A 77.527
Convention on International Trade in Endangered
Species of Wild Fauna and **Flora**,
Annual Report, I 49.85
Floriculture
Floriculture Crops, A 105.30
Floriculture Crops, Production Area and Sales, A
92.32
Florida
Florida Coastal Ecological Inventory Characteriza-
tion, I 49.6/6
Florida Coastal Ecological Inventory Characteriza-
tion, I 49.6/6
Marketing Margins for **Florida** Oranges in Ten
Major Cities, A 36.175
Sugarcane Variety Tests in **Florida**, Harvest Season,
A 106.27
Flotation
Cost of **Flotation**, SE 1.26
Flour
Export Wheat **Flour** Bulletin, A 82.3/5
Wheat and Wheat-**Flour** Stocks Held by Mills, C
3.115
Wheat **Flour** for Domestic Distribution, A 82.3/6
Wheat **Flour** for Export Distribution, A 82.3/9
Wheat **Flour**, A 82.3/10
Flow
Estimated **Flow** of Savings in Savings and Loan
Associations, HH 4.8/2
Form **Flow**, D 7.41/2
Flow of Funds, Seasonally Adjusted and
Unadjusted, FR 1.56
Flow of Funds, Unadjusted, FR 1.56/2
Flow of Savings in Savings and Loan Associations,
FHL 1.7/2
Instream **Flow** Information Papers, I 49.83
Instream **Flow** Strategies {various States}, I 49.83/2
Pilot Rules for Rivers whose Waters **Flow** into Gulf
of Mexico and Their Tributaries and Red
River of the North, C 25.8
Flow Charts
Flow Charts, Y 3.R 31:18
Flowers
Cut **Flowers**, Production and Sales, A 88.47
Flowers and Foliage Plants, Production and Sales,
A 92.32

Flowmeter
  Aircraft Instrument Bulletin, **Flowmeter** Series, Flowmeter Bulletins, N 28.19
Flows
  Base **Flows** As of {date} at Selected Gaging Stations in the Columbia River Basin, I 19.2:C 72/2
  Report on **Flows** and Diversions at Imperial Dam and All Actions Affecting Coordination Thereof, I 27.42
FLRA
  FLRA Bulletin, Y 3F:31/21-3:15
  FLRA News, Y 3F31/21-3:14-14
  FLRA Report on Case Decisions and FSIP Releases, Y 3.F 31/21-3:9, Y 3.F 31/21:10
Flue
  FGD {**Flue** Gas Desulfurization} Quarterly Report, EP 1.46/8
Flue-Cured
  Flue-Cured, A 88.34/6
  Flue-Cured Tobacco Letters, A 55.68
Fluid
  Fluid Milk and Cream Report, A 88.14/3
  Fluid Milk and Cream Report, Da 1-3 (series), A 92.10/3
  Fluid Milk Prices in City Markets, A 36.152
  Geophysical **Fluid** Dynamics Laboratory: Activities, Plans, C 55.601/5
Fluoridated
  Fluoridated Drinking Water, HE 20.7022/4
  Fluoridated Drinking Water, Proficiency Testing, HE 20.7412/3
Fluoridation
  Annual **Fluoridation** Census Report, HE 20.2:F 67/8
  Fluoridation Census, FS 2.304, HE 20.3112, HE 20.7317
  Homestudy Course; Water **Fluoridation**, HE 20.7021/9-2
  Homestudy Course; Water **Fluoridation** Test Exercise, HE 20.7021/9-3
  Homestudy Courses; Water **Fluoridation**, HE 20.7021/9
Fluorspar
  Fluorspar, I 28.70, I 28.70/2
  Fluorspar Reports, I 28.70, I 28.70/2
  Mineral Industry Surveys, **Fluorspar**, I 19.139
Fluvial
  Methods for Determination of Radioactive Substances in Water and **Fluvial** Sediments, I 19.15/5
Fly-By
  Fly-By, Official Employee Publication of Federal Aviation Agency, FAA 1.11
Flyer
  MAC **Flyer**, D 301.56
  Public Affairs **Flyer** PA-F (series), FCD 1.17
  Wanted **Flyer** Apprehension Orders, J 1.14/14
Flyers
  Action **Flyers**, AA 1.11/2
  Retail Stores Section **Flyers**, Y 3.F 73:16
  U.S. Customs Guide for Private **Flyers**, T 17.23
  Wanted **Flyers**, J 1.14/13
Flying
  Instrument **Flying**, D 301.7:51-37
Flyway
  Atlantic **Flyway**, I 49.24/3
  Central **Flyway**, I 49.24/4
  Mississippi **Flyway**, I 49.24/6
  Pacific **Flyway**, I 49.24/5
  Pacific Waterfowl **Flyway** Report, I 49.55/2
  Sandhill Crane Harvest and Hunter Activity in the Central **Flyway** During the Hunting Season, I 49.106/4
FM
  AM-**FM** Broadcast Financial Data, CC 1.43/2
  Educational AM and **FM** Radio and Education Television Stations, FS 5.234:34016, HE 5.234:34016
  FM and TV Translator Applications Ready and Available for Processing and Notification of Cut-off Date, CC 1.26/6
  FM Broadcast Applications Accepted for Filing and Notification of Cut-off Date, CC 1.26/3
FMFRP
  Fleet Marine Force Reference Publications, **FMFRP** (series), D 214.9/6
FMRs
  Income Limits and Section 8 Fair Market Rents (**FMRs**), HH 1.126
FNS
  FNS (series), A 98.9

FNS (FS) Handbooks, A 98.8/2
FOA
  Counterpart Funds and **FOA** Foreign Currency Accounts, FO 1.11/3
FOA
  FOA Country Series, FO 1.25
  FOA Fact Sheets, FO 1.24
  FOA Financed Awards, FO 1.26
  Small Business Circular **FOA**/SBC (series), FP 1.13
  Small Business Memo **FOA**/SMB (series), FO 1.14
Focal Points
  Focal Points, HE 20.7212
Focus
  Army **Focus**, D 101.1/14
  Country **Focus** Series, Y 3.In 8/25:16
  ENC **Focus**, ED 1.340/2
  FCIM **Focus**, D 215.15
  Federal Consumer **Focus**, GS 11.9/3
  Fire Safety **Focus** Sheets, Y 3.C 76/3:24
  Focus, ED 1.49, TD 2.30/13-2
  Focus, (Joint Center for Integrated Product Data Environment), D 215.15
  Focus Occasional Papers in Bilingual Education, ED 1.49/2-2
  Focus on Central and Eastern Europe, S 1.140
  Focus on Federal Employee Health Assistance Programs, PM 1.55
  Focus on Follow Through, HE 5.88
  Focus on Great Lakes Water Quality, Y 3.In 8/28:17
  Focus on Health Maintenance Organizations, HE 20.20/2
  Focus on NAEP, ED 1.335/2
  Focus on Special Education Legal Practices, ED 1.212
  Focus on the Facts, SBA 1.49
  Focus, Recruiting, TD 5.39
  Highway **Focus**, TD 2.34
  Hispanic **Focus** (series), LC 24.10
  New **Focus**, ED 1.49/2
  Program **Focus**, J 28.30
Fogarty
  Fogarty International Center Proceedings, HE 20.3710
  Fogarty International Center Series on Preventive Medicine, HE 20.3713
  Fogarty International Center Series on the Teaching of Preventative Medicine, HE 20.3714
FOIA
  FOIA Annual Report (Freedom of Information Act), J 1.1/11
  FOIA {Freedom of Information Act} Update, J 1.58
  FOIA Post, J 1.58/1
Folder
  Folder Suggestions, A 43.31
Folderes
  VD **Folderes**, FS 2.32
Folders
  Conservation **Folders**, A 57.30, A 76.210
  Descriptive Booklets and **Folders** on the Individual National Parks, Monuments, etc, I 29.6
  Employees' Health Service **Folders**, FS 2.49
  Folders, FS 2.25, HE 21.111
  Folders, Grain Standards, A 36.53
  Systems Technology Information Update, HE 3.80T.B. **Folders**, FS 2.42
  Travel **Folders**, USTS (series), C 47.16
Foliage
  Flowers and **Foliage** Plants, Production and Sales, A 92.32
Folios
  Soldier Shows, **Folios**, W 109.116
Folk
  Folk Recordings, Selected from the Archive of **Folk** Song, LC 40.2:F 71
  LC **Folk** Archive Finding Aid (numbered), LC 39.13/2
  LC **Folk** Archive Reference Aids, LCCEP LC Science Tracer Bulletin, TB (series), LC 33.10
Folk Music
  American Folk **Music** and Folklore Recordings, a Selected List, LC 39.12
  Folk and Traditional Arts, Application Guidelines For Fiscal Years, NF 2.8/2-36
  Folk Music of United States, LC 12.7
Folk Song
  Folk Recordings, Selected from the Archive of **Folk** Song, LC 40.2:F 71
Folklife
  Festival of American **Folklife**, SI 1.43/2
  Folklife Center News, LC 39.10
  Publications American **Folklife** Center, LC 39.9

Smithsonian **Folklife** Studies, SI 1.43
  Studies in American **Folklife**, LC 39.11
Folklore
  American Folk Music and **Folklore** Recordings, a Selected List, LC 39.12
Folks
  Pleasantdale **Folks**; 2d Series, FS 3.18
Follow Through
  Focus on **Follow Through**, HE 5.88
Follow-Up
  America's Commitment: Federal Programs Benefiting Women and New Initiatives as **Follow-up** to the U.N. Fourth World Conference on Women, Pr 42.8:W 84
  Children's Year **Follow-Up** Series, L 5.15
  Semiannual Reports to Congress on Audit **Follow-up**, ED 1.1/4
Food
  Agricultural-**Food** Policy Review, A 93.16/2, A 105.50
  Agriculture and **Food**, C 51.9/19
  AMS **Food** Purchases, A 88.57
  Annual Report on the **Food** and Agricultural Sciences, A 1.1/4-2
  Annual Report to the Secretary of Agriculture by the Joint Council on **Food** and Agricultural Sciences, A 1.1/4
  Appraisal of the Proposed Budget for **Food** and Agricultural Sciences Report to the President and Congress, A 1.1/4-3
  Association of **Food** and Drug Officials Quarterly Bulletin, HE 20.4003/5
  Canned **Food** Report, C 3.189
  Characteristics of **Food** Stamp Households, A 98.21
  Characteristics of **Food** Stamp Households Advance Report, A 98.21/2
  Charts, Composition of **Food** Materials, A 10.21
  Consumer Prices: Energy and **Food**, L 2.38/7
  Contracts for U.S. **Food** Products, A 67.40/3
  Cost of **Food** at Home Estimated for **Food** Plans at Four Cost Levels, A 98.19/2
  Cost of **Food** at Home Estimated for **Food** Plans at Three Cost Levels, Southern Region, A 106.39/5
  Current Business Reports; Canned **Food**, Stock, Pack, Shipments, B-1 (series), C 56.219/8
  Current Developments in **Food** Distribution, C 18.214
  Defense **Food** Delegations, A 1.81
  DFO {Defense **Food** Orders}, A 82.64
  Directory, State Officials Charged with Enforcement of **Food**, Drug, Cosmetic, and Feed Laws, FS 13.102:St 2
  Estimated Retail **Food** Prices by Cities, L 2.37
  Federal **Food**, Drug, and Cosmetic Act, Y 1.2:F 31/10
  Federal **Food**, Drug, and Cosmetic Act, as Amended, and General Regulations for its Enforcement, FS 13.105:F 73
  Food and Agricultural Export Directory, A 67.26:201
  Food and Agriculture Competitively Awarded Research and Education Grants, A 106.42
  Food and Diet Charts, A 10.7
  Food and Drug Administration and the Congress, HE 20.4038
  Food and Drug Administration Location Directory, HE 20.4037
  Food and Drug Circulars, FS 7.4
  Food and Drug Review, A 7.8, FS 7.7, FS 13.107
  Food and Drug Technical Bulletins, FS 13.103/2
  Food and Grocery Bulletins, Y 3.N 21/8:15
  Food and Home Notes, A 21.33, A 107.9
  Food and Nutrition, A 98.11
  Food and Nutrition Information and Educational Materials Center Catalog, A 17.18/3
  Food and Nutrition Newsletter of the **Food** and Nutrition Service, A 98.11/2
  Food and Nutrition Research Briefs, A 77.518
  Food Assistance and Nutrition Research Program, A 93.61
  Food Assistance and Nutrition Research Report, A 93.60
  Food & Nutrition Research Briefs, A 17.30
  Food Bibliography, GA 1.16/6
  Food Conservation Notes, Y 3.F 73:25
  Food Cost Review, A 1.107/2
  Food Exports and Imports, C 18.218
  Food Facts of Interest to the Trade, Pr 32.4260
  Food Fights for Freedom Round-Up, A 21.19
  Food Fish Situation and Outlook, Annual Review Issue, I 49.8/7

Food Fish, Market Review and Outlook, C 55.309/5

Food Fish, Situation and Outlooks, I 49.8/6

Food for Consumers, A 103.16

Food for Freedom Program, Background Information Series, A 21.17

Food for Peace Bulletin, PrEx 1.9

Food for Peace, Annual Report on Public Law 480, A 1.119, A 67.44

Food for Peace, Monthly Newsletter About Activities Under PL 480, PrEx 1.9/2

Food Information Series, A 21.18

Food Inspection Decisions, A 7.5, A 32.5, A 1.15

Food Marketing Alert, A 88.37/3

Food News for Consumers, A 110.10

Food News Notes for Public Libraries, Y 3.F 73:9

Food Production Memorandum, A 79.7, A 80.208

Food Products, A 19.5

Food Purchase Reports & Invitations to Bid, A 88.67

Food Safety Educator, A 110.19

Food Selection and Meal Planning Charts, A 10.21/2

Food Service Equipment Catalog, D 7.38

Food Stamp Series, A 73.11

Food Stuffs Around the World, C 18.72

Food Supply Reports, A 82.16

Food Surveys, A 36.7

Food Thrift Series, A 1.24

Food Trade Letters, A 71.9, A 80.125, A 80.410

FSIS Food Safety Review, A 110.17

FSQS Food Purchase, Annual Summary, A 103.11/2

FSQS Food Purchases, A 103.11/4

Garden and Home Food Preservation Facts, A 43.29

General Regulations for the Enforcement of the Federal Food, Drug, and Cosmetic Act, FS 13.106/2:1/2

HHS News, Food and Drug Administration, HE 20.4043

Household Food Consumption Survey (year), Reports, A 1.86

National Food Review, A 105.15, A 93.16/3

National Food Situation, A 88.37, A 93.16

Nationwide Food Consumption Survey (year), Preliminary Reports, A 111.9/2

Nationwide Food Consumption Survey (year), Reports, A 111.9

Notice of Judgment under Food and Drug Act, A 46.6

Notices of Judgement under Federal Food, Drug, and Cosmetic Act: Drugs and Devices, A 46.22, FS 7.12

Notices of Judgement under Federal Food, Drug, and Cosmetic Act: Foods, A 46.20, FS 7.10

Notices of Judgement, Food and Drug Act, A 32.6, A 1.16

Nutrition and Food Conservation Series, A 1.65

Official Statement of United States Food Administration, Y 3.F 73:19

OPA Food Guide for Retailers, Pr 32.4241

Posters Food and Nutrition Service, A 98.16

Posters Food Safety and Inspection Service, A 103.18

Publications Food and Drug Administration, FS 13.111

Publications Nutrition and Food Conservation Branch, A 80.123

Quartermaster Food and Container Institute for Armed Forces: Library Bulletin, D 106.3/2

Regulations, Rules and Instructions Food and Nutrition Service, A 98.18

Report of United States Government to the Food and Agricultural Organization of the United Nations, A 67.35

Research Grants, Environmental Engineering and Food Protection, FS 2.300/3

Retail Food Price Index, L 2.39

Retail Food Price Index, Washington, D.C., Area, L 2.39/3

Retail Prices on Food, L 2.3

Service and Regulatory Announcements Food and Drug, A 46.12

Service and Regulatory Announcements Food, Drug, and Cosmetic, A 46.19, FS 7.8, FS 13.115

Survey of Food and Nutrition Research in United States, NA 2.8

U.S. Army Natick Laboratories, Food Division, Natick, Mass. Technical Report FD-, D 106.20

U.S. Government Campaign to Promote Production, Sharing, and Proper Use of Food, Pr 32.5019

U.S. Government Program to Promote Production, Sharing and Proper Use of Food, Pr 32.5019/2

United Nations Conference on Food and Agriculture, S 5.41

United States Food Leaflets, A 1.26

USDA Food Deliveries, A 82.43

WI Communique, Issues of the Special Supplemental Food Program for Women, Infants, and Children, A 98.14

World Food Needs and Availabilities, A 93.48

World Indices of Agricultural and Food Production, A 1.34/3

Food Intake

Continuing Survey of Food Intake by Individuals, A 111.9/3

Food Safety

Center for Food Safety and Applied Nutrition Technical Plan, HE 20.4515

Food Service

Food Service Information Bulletin, D 214.22

Foodborne

Foodborne and Waterborne Disease Outbreaks, Annual Summary, HE 20.7011/13

Foodborne

Homestudy Courses; Foodborne Disease Control, HE 20.7021/6

Foods

Average Weight of Measured Cup of Various Foods, A 1.87:41

Canned and Dried Foods, C 18.72/1

Commodity Foods, A 98.19

Facts on Surplus Foods, A 69.8

Foods, FNJ (series), FS 13.109

Notices of Judgement under Federal Food, Drug, and Cosmetic Act: Foods, A 46.20, FS 7.10

Plentiful Foods, A 88.37/3

Poultry Slaughtered Under Federal Inspection and Poultry Used in Canning and Processed Foods, A 88.15/9-2

Poultry Used in Canning and Other Processed Foods, A 88.15/9

Quarterly Canned Foods Stocks Reports, C 3.136

Summary of Foods in the United States, I 19.13

Supplies of Important Foods in Retail Stores, L 2.67

United States Standards for {various foods}, A 103.6/2

Foodstuffs

Foodstuffs around the World, C 18.203

Footlight

Footlight, SI 10.9

Footnote

Footnote, Journal of the HEW Audit Agency, HE 1.37

Footnotes

Footnotes, HH 1.65

Footwear

Footwear and Leather Series Reports, D 106.9

Footwear Industry Revitalization Program, Annual Progress Report, C 1.72

Nonrubber Footwear, ITC 1.21, ITC 1.21/2

For

Survival Series, For Your Information {releases}, FCD 1.13/10

Technical Advisory Services, Health Office, For Your Information, TAS (series), FCD 1.13/2

For Sale

Construction Reports; New One-family Homes Sold and for Sale, C 25 (series), C 56.211/2

Forage

Cotton, Truck, and Forage Crop Disease Circulars, A 19.17

Forage Crop Gazette, News Letter for Staff Workers, Division of Forage Crops and Diseases, A 77.509

4-H Forage, A 43.15

Interbureau Forage Committee Publications I.F.C., A 1.49

Proceedings Southern Pasture and Forage Crop Improvement Conference, A 106.29

Trends in Forage Crops Varieties, A 43.33

U.S. Dairy Forage Research Center, A 77.37

Force

Employment and Earnings and Monthly Report on Labor Force, L 2.41/2

Employment in Perspective: Women in the Labor Force, L 2.41/11

Fleet Marine Force Manuals, FMFM (series), D 214.9/4

Priorities in Force, Pr 32.4814

Priorities Orders in Force, Pr 31.410

Publications Naval Support Force, Antarctica, D 201.15/2

Register of Commissioned and Warrant Officers Naval Reserve Force, N 25.6

Secretary's Task Force on Competition in the U.S. Domestic Airline Industry, TD 1.57

Special Labor Force Reports, L 2.98

Summary, Special Labor Force Reports, L 2.98/2

Treaties in Force, S 9.14

Forced Labor

International Commission of Inquiry into Existence of Slavery and Forced Labor in Republic of Liberia, S 5.33

Forces

American Forces in Action Series, W 110.7, M 103.8

Annual Report of the Secretary of Defense on Reserve Forces, D 1.1/3

Economic Forces in United States in Facts and Figures, FO 1.30, S 17.8

Order of Battle of United States Land Forces, D 114.10

Review of Soviet Ground Forces, D 5.209

United States Special Operations Forces, Posture Statement, D 1.98

Forecast

Daily Mississippi River Stage and Forecast Bulletin, C 30.54

FAA Forecast Conference Proceedings, TD 4.55

Federal Forecast for Engineers, PM 1.23

Forecast Contract Opportunities, S 1.150

Forecast Contracting and Subcontracting Opportunities, E 1.122/2

Forecast Division Circulars, A 29.37

Forecast of Citizen Departures to Europe, S 1.121

Forecast of Contract Opportunities, Fiscal Year, HH 1.116

Forecast of Motor-Fuel Demand and Required Crude-Oil Production by States, Monthly Forecast, I 28.41

Forecast Tracks and Probabilities for Hurricanes (by name), C 55.126

Initial Analysis and Forecast Charts, C 55.281/2-6

Office of Technology and Forecast: Publications, C 21.24

Office of Technology Assessment and Forecast: Publications, C 1.62

Petroleum Forecast, I 28.41

Preliminary Report and Forecast of Solar Geophysical Data, C 55.627

Publications Office of Technology and Forecast, C 21.24

Publications Office of Technology Assessment and Forecast, C 1.62

River Summary and Forecast, New Orleans, Louisiana, C 55.110/2-2

River Summary and Forecast, {Lower Mississippi Region}, C 55.110/7

Status of Waterfowl & Fall Flight Forecast, I 49.100/3

Technology Assessment and Forecast, Report, C 21.24:T 22

Transportation Forecast, TD 1.14

U.S. Oceanborne Foreign Trade Forecast, TD 11.13/2

Forecasters

Forecasters Handbooks, C 55.108/3

Weather Bureau Forecasters Handbooks, C 30.6/4

Forecasting

DUF: Drug Use Forecasting, J 28.15/2-3

Forecasting Guide, C 30.6/3

Program for Regional Observing and Forecasting Services, C 55.626/2

Terminal Forecasting Reference Manual (by Terminals), C 30.52

Forecasts

Aviation Forecasts Fiscal Years, FAA 1.42

Comparison of Annual Energy Outlook, Forecasts with Other Forecasts, Supplement to the Annual Energy Outlook, E 3.1/4-2

Energy Forecasts for (year), E 3.53

FAA Aviation Forecasts, TD 4.57/2

Federal State Cooperative Snow Surveys and Water Supply Forecasts, A 57.46/9-2

Missouri-Mississippi River Summary and Forecasts, C 55.110/3

Ohio River Summary and Forecasts, C 55.110

Radio Propagation Forecasts, C 13.31/2

River Forecasts Provided by the National Weather Service, C 55.117/2, C 55.285

River Summary and **Forecasts** {Memphis, Tenn. area}, C 55.110/2
Seed Crops **Forecasts**, A 92.19/2
Water Supply **Forecasts**, C 30.58
Foreclosure
Nonfarm Real Estate **Foreclosure** Report, FHL 1.8
Number of Foreclosures {and rate of **foreclosure**} by FSLIC Insured Savings and Loan Associations, FHL 1.26
Real Estate **Foreclosure** Report, FHL 1.8/2
Foreclosures
Number of **Foreclosures** {and rate of foreclosure} by FSLIC Insured Savings and Loan Associations, FHL 1.26
Foreign
Active **Foreign** Agricultural Research, A 106.42/2
Advance Sheets from Monthly Summary of the **Foreign** Commerce of the Unted States, C 18.8
Advertising Media in Certain **Foreign** Countries, C 18.44
American Flag Services in **Foreign** Trade and with U.S. Possessions, MC 1.12
American Flag Services in **Foreign** Trade with U.S., C 27.9/1
American **Foreign** Policy, Current Documents, S 1.71/2
Annual **Foreign** Policy Report to Congress, C 61.11/2
Annual Summary of **Foreign** Agricultural Training as of {date}, A 67.37
Application for Grants under Fulbright-Hays **Foreign** Curriculum Consultants, ED 1.59
Application for Grants under the Secretary's Discretionary Program for Mathematics, Science, Computer Learning and Critical **Foreign** Languages, ED 1.64
Approved Conference Rate and Interconference Agreements of Steamship Lines in the **Foreign** Commerce of the United States, FMC 1.11
Arrearage Tables of Amounts Due and Unpaid 90 Days or More on **Foreign** Credits of the United States Government, T 1.45/4
Arrivals and Departures by Selected Ports Statistics of **Foreign** Visitor Arrivals and U.S. Citizen Departures Analyzed by U.S. Ports of Entry and Departure, C 47.15/4
Atomic Energy in **Foreign** Countries, Y 3.At 7:13
Automotive **Foreign** Trade Manual, C 18.216
Catalogs and Lists of American and **Foreign** Annuals and Periodicals, N 16.7
Certificated Air Carrier Financial Data; **Foreign** or Overseas {12-month comparisons}, C 31.236/2
Certificated Air Carrier Financial Data; **Foreign** or Overseas {quarterly comparisons}, C 31.236
Chiefs of State and Cabinet Members of **Foreign** Governments, CR CS- (series), PrEx 3.11/2
Circular of Inquiry Concerning Gold and Silver Coinage and Currency of **Foreign** Countries, Including Production, Import and Export, and Industrial Consumption of Gold and Silver, T 28.8
Climate Impact Assessment, **Foreign** Countries, C 55.233
Climate Impact Assessment, **Foreign** Countries Annual Summary, C 55.233/3
Coal Notices for **Foreign** Ports, N 5.8, N 20.11
Code Classification and Definitions of **Foreign** Trade Areas, C 3.150:R
Code Classification of **Foreign** Ports by Geographic Trade Area and Country, C 3.150:K
Commercial Regulations of **Foreign** Countries, S 1.9
Comparative Statement of **Foreign** Commerce of U.S. Ports by States, SB 7.6/298, C 27.9/2, MC 1.10
Comparative Statement of **Foreign** Commerce of United States Ports Handling Cargo Tonnage of 100,000 Long Tons and Over, SB 7.5/296
Comparative Summary of Water Borne **Foreign** Commerce, SB 7.5/399, C 27.9/3, MC 1.19
Congress and **Foreign** Policy, Y 4.F 76/1-13

Containerships Under Construction and on Order (including conversions) in United States and **Foreign** Shipyards Oceangoing Ships of 1,000 Gross Tons and Over, C 39.231
Contingent **Foreign** Liabilities of U.S. Government, T 1.45/3
Counterpart Funds and AID **Foreign** Currency Account, S 18.14
Counterpart Funds and FOA **Foreign** Currency Accounts, FO 1.11/3
Counterpart Funds and ICA **Foreign** Currency Accounts, S 17.11/3
Country Demographic Profiles for **Foreign** Country Series, ISP 30 (series), C 56.218/2
Cumulative Index to **Foreign** Production and Commercial Reports, C 42.15/3-2
Demographic Reports for **Foreign** Countries, P 96- (series), C 3.205/5
Directory of USSR **Foreign** Trade Organization and Officials, PrEx 3.10/7-7
Directory of USSR Ministry of **Foreign** Affairs Officials, PrEx 3.10/7-17
East-West **Foreign** Trade Board Report, Y 3.T 67:1
Economic **Foreign** Policy Series, S 1.71/3
Educational Programs in **Foreign** Language and Area Studies (series), HE 5.99
ERS **Foreign** (series), A 93.21/2
Essential United States **Foreign** Trade Routes, C 39.202:F 76
Evaluation of **Foreign** Fruits and Nuts, A 77.532
Foreign Acquisitions Program Newsletter, LC 30.17
Foreign Affairs Background Summary, S 1.53
Foreign Affairs Highlights, S 1.75
Foreign Affairs Manual Circulars, S 1.5/6-2
Foreign Affairs Notes, S 1.126/3
Foreign Affairs Research Papers Available, S 1.126
Foreign Affairs Research Special Papers Available, S 1.126/2
Foreign Affairs Research, a Directory of Government Resources, S 1.2:F 76a/4
Foreign Agricultural Bulletins, A 67.3
Foreign Agricultural Circulars, A 67
Foreign Agricultural Economic Reports, A 93.27, A 105.22
Foreign Agricultural Service, Miscellaneous, A 67.26
Foreign Agricultural Situation, Maps and Charts, A 67.24
Foreign Agricultural Trade, A 67.19
Foreign Agricultural Trade Digest of United States, A 67.19/8
Foreign Agricultural Trade of the United States, A 93.17/7, A 105.14
Foreign Agricultural Trade of the United States Digest, A 93.17/2
Foreign Agricultural Trade of the United States, Fiscal Year, A 93.17/6
Foreign Agricultural Trade of the United States, Fiscal Year Supplement, A 93.17/7-2
Foreign Agricultural Trade of the United States, Statistical Report, A 93.17
Foreign Agricultural Trade of the United States, Trade by Commodities, A 93.17/8
Foreign Agricultural Trade of the United States, Trade by Countries, A 93.17/4
Foreign Agricultural Trade of the United States, Trade in Agricultural Products with Individual Countries by Calendar Year, A 67.19/6
Foreign Agricultural Trade of the United States; Imports of Fruits and Vegetables under Quarantine by Countries of Origin and Ports of Entry, A 67.19/7, A 93.17/5
Foreign Agricultural Trade Statistical Report, A 105.14/2
Foreign Agriculture, A 67.1/2
Foreign Agriculture Reports, A 67.16
Foreign Agriculture, A Review of **Foreign** Farm Policy, Production, and Trade, A 67.7
Foreign Agriculture, Including **Foreign** Crops and Markets, A 67.7
Foreign Agriculture, Review of **Foreign** Farm Policy, Production and Trade, A 36.88, A 64.7, A 67.7
Foreign Aid by the U.S. Government, C 18.279
Foreign Air Mail Service, P 8.6
Foreign Air News Digest, C 31.216
Foreign Animal Diseases Report, A 101.17
Foreign Area Research Documentation Center: Papers Available, S 1.126
Foreign Bean Market Information, C 18.72/10

Foreign Buyer Program Export Interest Directory (series), C 61.19/2
Foreign Claims Settlement Commission of the United States: Annual Report, J 1.1/6
Foreign Commerce and Navigation of United States, C 3.159
Foreign Commerce Weekly, C 42.8
Foreign Commerce Yearbooks, C 18.26/2, C 42.12
Foreign Communication News, C 18.74
Foreign Consular Offices in the U.S., S 1.34, S 1.69, S 1.68/2
Foreign Countries and Plants Certified to Export Meat and Poultry to the United States, A 110.14/2
Foreign Credits by United States Government, C 43.11/2
Foreign Credits by United States Government, Status of Active **Foreign** Credits of United States Government and of International Organizations, T 1.45
Foreign Crop and Livestock Reports, A 27.11
Foreign Crops and Markets, A 67.8
Foreign Currency Availabilities and Uses, Special Analysis E, PrEx 2.8/a9
Foreign Direct Investment in the United States, C 61.25/2
Foreign Direct Investment in the United States, Establishment Data For Manufacturing, C 59.20/3
Foreign Economic Collection and Industrial Espionage, Y 3.C 83/2:1-2
Foreign Economic Development Report, A 93.38
Foreign Economic Development Service Annual Summary, A 100.1/2
Foreign Economic Reports, C 3.264, C 59.12
Foreign Economic Trends and Their Implications for the United States, C 57.111, C 61.11
Foreign Education Circulars, I 16.50
Foreign Education Leaflets, I 16.41
Foreign Energy Supply Assessment Program Series, E 3.30
Foreign Exchange Rates, FR 1.32/2
Foreign Exchange Rates for Week, FR 1.32
Foreign Fishery Leaflets, C 55.314/2
Foreign Flag Merchant Ships Owned by U.S. Parent Companies, TD 11.16
Foreign Fraud, Unlawful, and Lottery Mail Orders, P 1.12
Foreign Game Leaflets (numbered), I 49.74
Foreign Gold and Exchange Reserves, A 93.34
Foreign Grants and Credits by the United States Government, C 43.11
Foreign Highway News, C 18.77
Foreign Income Tax Returns, T 22.35/2
Foreign Information Series, Pr 32.4226
Foreign Inland Waterway News, Intercoastal Waterways, Rivers, Lakes, Canals, Equipment, C 18.208
Foreign Knit Goods Letter; Special Bulletins, C 18.78
Foreign Labor Interpretation Series, L 7.58
Foreign Labor Trends, L 29.16
Foreign Language Books, LC 19.11/4
Foreign Language Phrase Cards, D 208.6/5
Foreign Lumber Tariff Series, C 8.80
Foreign Market Bulletin, C 18.81
Foreign Market Reports Service, Listing, C 42.15/2
Foreign Market Reports, Accession Listings, C 42.15/3
Foreign Market Surveys, C 41.109
Foreign Markets Bulletins for Raw Materials, C 18.109/2
Foreign Markets for Builders' Hardware, C 18.82
Foreign Markets for Hand Tools, C 18.83
Foreign Markets for Heating and Cooking Appliances, C 18.84
Foreign Markets for Metals and Minerals Circulars, C 18.85/2
Foreign Markets for Scales and Other Weighing Devices, C 18.85
Foreign Meat Inspection, A 1.109/2
Foreign Military Sales Customer Procedures (series), D 7.6/15
Foreign Military Sales, **Foreign** Military Construction Sales, and Military Assistance Facts, D 1.66
Foreign Minerals Quarterly, I 28.51
Foreign Minerals Survey, I 28.81
Foreign News on Apples, A 36.79
Foreign News on Citrus Fruits, A 36.80
Foreign News on Tobacco, A 36.45
Foreign News on Vegetables, A 36.46
Foreign Newspaper and Gazette Report, LC 29.10

Foreign Noise Research (series), EP 1.73/2

Foreign Oceanborne Trade of United States Containerized Cargo Summary, Selected Trade Routes, C 39.233

Foreign Petroleum Statistics, C 18.86, C 18.86/2

Foreign Plant Quarantines in Service Training Series, A 56.25

Foreign Plants Certified to Export Meat to the United States, A 110.14

Foreign Policy Briefs, S 1.98

Foreign Policy Outlines, S 1.25/3

Foreign Port Series, C 18.34

Foreign Production and Commercial Reports, C 42.15/3

Foreign Publications Accessions List, HH 1.23/4

Foreign Radio Broadcasting Services, C 18.87

Foreign Railway News, C 18.88

Foreign Relations (by countries), S 1.1/2

Foreign Relations of the United States, S 1.1

Foreign Relations of United States, Diplomatic Papers: Conferences, S 1.1/3

Foreign Science Bulletin, LC 38.11

Foreign Shipping News, C 18.89

Foreign Social Science Bibliographies, C 3.163/5

Foreign Statistical Publications, Accessions List, C 56.238

Foreign Statistics on Apples and Other Deciduous Fruits, A 67.12

Foreign Tariff Notes, C 10.16, C 18.13

Foreign Tariff Series, C 18.12

Foreign Tariffs, C 18.192

Foreign Tax Credit Claimed on Corporation Income Tax Returns, T 22.35/2:F 76

Foreign Technology, C 51.9/32

Foreign Technology Alert: Bibliography (series), C 51.13/3

Foreign Trade Data, C 3.278

Foreign Trade in Farm Machinery and Supplies, A 67.21

Foreign Trade Information on Instrumentation, C 41.92

Foreign Trade Mark Application Service, C 18.90

Foreign Trade Notes, Minerals and Metals, C 18.91/2

Foreign Trade Notes, Minerals and Metals and Petroleum, C 18.91

Foreign Trade Notes, Petroleum, C 18.91/3

Foreign Trade Regulations of (country), C 1.50, C 57.11

Foreign Trade Reports, C 3.164

Foreign Trade Series, FT 1.9

Foreign Trade Statistics Notes, C 3.167

Foreign Trade {reports by States}, S 1.54

Foreign Training Letter, to Foreign Agricultural Contacts at Land-Grant Colleges, A 67.31, A 67.31/3

Foreign Training Letters, A 67.31/3

Foreign Transactions of U.S. Government, C 18.278

Foreign Treaties and Conventions (United States not a Signatory), S 9.6

Foreign Versions, Variations, and Diminutives of English Names and Foreign Equivalents of U.S. Military and Civilian Titles, J 21.2:N 15

Foreign Visitor Arrivals by Selected Ports, Calendar Year, C 47.15/6

Foreign Wood Series, A 13.31/2

Foreign Year Trade Notes, C 18.92

Foreign, Overseas and Territorial Air Mail Carriers, C 31.231

Fruit Flashes, Foreign News on Fruits by Cable and Radio: Citrus {fruits}, A 67.9

Fruit Flashes, Foreign News on Fruits by Cable and Radio: Deciduous {fruits}, A 67.10

General Description of Foreign-trade Zones, FTZ 1.8

General Foreign Policy Series, S 1.71

General Legal Bulletin, Foreign Laws Affecting American Business, C 18.95

Government-Supported Research on Foreign Affairs, Current Project Information, S 1.101/10

Home and Abroad with Bureau of Foreign and Domestic Commerce, C 18.191

Implementation of Section 620(s) of the Foreign Assistance Act of 1961, as Amended, A Report to Congress, S 18.1/3

Imports and Exports of Commodities by U.S. Coastal Districts and Foreign Trade Regulations, SB 7.5/275, C 27.9/4, MC 1.11

Index to Foreign Market Reports, C 57.110, C 61.16

Index to Foreign Production and Commercial Reports, Cumulative Indexes, C 42.15/3-3

Industrial Series: Bureau of Foreign and Domestic Commerce, C 18.225

International List, Money Order Offices in Foreign Countries, P 9.6

Introductions to Research in Foreign Law (series), LC 42.15

Inventory of Nonpurchased Foreign Currencies, T 1.50

Junior-Year Science, Mathematics, and Foreign Language Students, First-Term, FS 5.254:54001, HE 5.254:54001

Manual of Foreign Lumber Tariffs, C 18.114/2

Markets and Crop Estimates Bureau, Foreign Crop and Livestock Reports, A 36.19

Maturity Distribution of Euro-Dollar Deposits in Foreign Branches of U.S. Banks, FR 1.54

Maximum Travel Per Diem Allowances for Foreign Areas, S 1.76/3-2

Modern Foreign Language Fellowship Program, National Defense Education Act, Title 6 and NDEA Related Awards under Fullbright-Hays Act, FS 5.255:55034, HE 5.255:55034

Monthly Japanese Foreign Trade Statistics, D 102.11/4

Monthly List of Publications for Foreign Distribution, A 21.6/2

Monthly Report of Condition for U.S. Agencies, Branches and Domestic Banking Subsidiaries of Foreign Banks, FR 1.16/3

Monthly Report on Foreign Direct Investment Activity in the United States, C 61.25/3

Monthly Summary of Foreign Commerce of United States, C 18.7

Motor Vehicle Safety Defect Recall Campaigns Reported to the Department of Transportation by Domestic and Foreign Vehicle Manufacturers, TD 2.209

National Foreign Assessment Center Publications (numbered), PrEx 3.10/7

National Trade Estimate, Report on Foreign Trade Barriers, PrEx 1.14, PrEx 9.10

Nazi-Soviet Relations, 1939-41, Documents from the German Foreign Office, S 1.2:N 23

News from the Center {for the Coordination of Foreign Manuscript Copying}, LC 1.33

Notes from Foreign News Bureau, Y 3.C 83:67

Oceangoing Foreign Flag Merchant Type Ships of 1,000 Gross Tons and Over Owned by the United States Parent Companies, C 39.230

Papers Relating to Foreign Relations of the United States, S 1.1

Participation of American and Foreign-Flag Vessels in Shipments under United States Foreign Relief Programs, C 3.164:976

Participation of Principal National Flags in United States Oceanborne Foreign Trade, C 39.221

Passenger Travel between United States and Foreign Countries {annual summary reports}, J 21.13

Patterns of Foreign Travel in the U.S., C 47.18

Peace and War, United States Foreign Policy, S 1.2:P 31/8

Press Notices Bureau of Foreign and Domestic Commerce, C 18.31

Profiles of Foreign Direct Investment in U.S. Energy, E 3.52

Proposed Foreign Aid Program Fiscal Year, Summary Presentation to Congress, S 18.28/a

Proposed Foreign Aid Program, Summary Presentation to Congress, S 18.28

Prospects for Foreign Trade in {various commodities}, A 67.30

Publications Foreign Countries, Annotated Accession List, C 3.199

Publications U.S. Army Foreign Science and Technology Center, D 101.79

Quarterly Report to Congress and the East-West Foreign Trade Board on Trade Between the United States and the Nonmarket Economy Countries, Y 4.W 36:2

Quarterly Summary of Foreign Commerce of the United States, C 3.147

Radio Talks Bureau of Foreign and Domestic Commerce, C 18.40

Recent Developments in Foreign Trade of American Republics, TC 1.22

Recurrent Report of Mileage and Traffic Data Foreign, Overseas and Territorial Air Mail Carriers, C 31.231

Report of Classified Program of Exports and Value by American Agencies Voluntarily Registered with Advisory Committee on Voluntary Foreign Aid, S 1.99/2

Report of Passenger Travel between the United States and Foreign Countires, J 21.13/2

Report of the Attorney General to the Congress of the United States on the Administration of the Foreign Agents Registration Act of 1938, As Amended, J 1.30

Report on Foreign Currencies Held by the U.S. Government Fiscal Year and Transition Quarter, T 63.118/2

Report on Volume of Water Borne Foreign Commerce of U.S. by Ports of Origin and Destination (fiscal year), C 27.9/10, MC 1.17

Report to Congress and East-West Foreign Trade Board on Trade Between United States and Nonmarket Economy Countries, TC 1.38

Report to Congress on Foreign Assistance Program, S 18.1

Report to Congress on Foreign Surplus Disposal, S 1.47

Report to Congress on United States Foreign Relief Program, S 1.63

Reports on Foreign Markets for Agricultural Products, A 36.8

Research and Training Opportunities Abroad (year), Educational Programs in Foreign Language and Area Studies, HE 5.99

Review of Foreign Developments, Prepared for Internal Circulation, FR 1.49

Review of United States Oceanborne Foreign Trade, C 39.202:Oc 2

Rules and Regulations for Foreign Vessels Operating in the Navigable Waters of the United States, TD 5.6:V 63/7

Sailing Dates of Steamships from the Principal Ports of the United States to Ports in Foreign Countries, C 15.19, C 18.10

Schedule K. Code Classification of Foreign Ports by Geographic Trade Area and Country, C 3.150:K

Schedule L. Statistical Classification of Foreign Merchandise Reports in In-transit Trade of United States, C 3.150:L

Schedule of Sailings of Steam Vessels Registered Under Laws of United States and Intended to Load General Cargo at Ports in United States for Foreign Destinations, IC 1 rat.8

Schedule of Steamers Appointed to Convey Mails to Foreign Countries, P 8.5

Schedule R. Code Classification and Definitions of Foreign Trade Areas, C 3.150:R

Schedule S. Statistical Classification of Domestic and Foreign Merchandise Exported from U.S., C 3.150:S

Schedule X. Statistical Classification of Domestic and Foreign Merchandise Exported from United States by Air Arranged in Shipping Commodity Groups, C 3.150:X

Semiannual Consolidated Report of Balances of Foreign Currencies Acquired Without Payment of Dollars As of December 31 (year), T 63.117

Series 1, Evaluation of Foreign Fruits and Nuts, A 77.533

Shipment Under the United States Foreign Aid Programs Made on Army- or Navy-Operated Vessels (American flag) by Port of Lading by Country of Destination, C 3.164:976

Shipping Weight and Dollar Value of Merchandise Laden on and Unladen from Vessels at United States Ports During the In-transit Movement of the Merchandise from One Foreign Country to Another, C 3.164:981

Significant Arrearages Due the United States Government and Unpaid 90 Days or More by Official Foreign Obligors, T 1.45/5

Significant NASA Inventions Available for Licensing in Foreign Countries, NAS 1.21:7038

Soviet Union, **Foreign** Military History Journal, PrEx 7.21/4-3

Soviet Union, **Foreign** Military Review, PrEx 7.21/2-3, PrEx 7.21/4-2

Special Bulletins Bureau of **Foreign** and Domestic Commerce, Textile Division, C 18.127

Special **Foreign** Currency Science Information Program, List of Translations in Process for Fiscal Year, Coordinated and Administered by the National Science Foundation, C 51.12

Special **Foreign** Trade Reports, C 3.164/2

Special Releases {of **Foreign** Broadcast Intelligence Service}, W 100.9

Special Reports to Congress and East-West **Foreign** Trade Board, TC 1.38/2

Special Series Bureau of **Foreign** and Domestic Commerce, Paper Division, C 18.146

Standardized Regulations (Government Civilians, **Foreign** Areas), S 1.76/3

Statement of **Foreign** Commerce and Immigration, T 37.5

Statement of **Foreign** Currencies Purchased with Dollars, T 63.118/3

Statistical Classification of Domestic and **Foreign** Commodities Exported from the United States, C 3.150:B

Statistical Classification of Domestic and **Foreign** Merchandise Exported from U.S., C 3.150:S

Statistical Classification of **Foreign** Merchandise Reports in In-Transit Trade of United States, C 3.150:L

Statistical Summary and Analysis of **Foreign** Visitor Arrivals, U.S. Citizen and Non-U.S. Citizen Departures, C 47.15

Statistics of Capital Movements Between U.S. and **Foreign** Countries, T 62.9

Status of Active **Foreign** Credits of the United States Government: **Foreign** Credits by United States Government Agencies, T 1.45/2

Summaries of **Foreign** Government Environmental Reports, EP 1.21/4

Summary Statement of Income and Expenditures of Voluntary Relief Agencies Registered with Advisory Committee on Voluntary **Foreign** Aid, S 1.99/3

Survey of Activities of the Committee on **Foreign** Affairs, Y 4.F 76/1:Ac 8

Survey of **Foreign** Fisheries, Oceanographic, and Atmospheric Literature, C- (series), C 55.325/3

Survey of **Foreign** Fisheries, Translated Tables of Contents, and New Translations, C 55.325/4

Tables to Convert {**Foreign** Moneys, Weights and Measures into U.S. Standards}, C 1.11

Translated Tables of Contents of Current **Foreign** Fisheries, Oceanographic, and Atmospheric Publications, C 55.325

Translations of {**Foreign**} Patents, C 21.22

Transportation Series Bureau of **Foreign** and Domestic Commerce, C 18.274

Trends in U.S. **Foreign** Trade, C 18.190, C 57.23

Tung Oil Monthly, Production in America, **Foreign** Trade, etc., C 18.209

U.S. Direct Investment Abroad, Operations of U.S. Parent Companies and Their **Foreign** Affiliates, Preliminary Estimates, C 59.20/2

U.S. **Foreign** Affairs on CD-ROM, S 1.142/2

U.S. **Foreign** Agriculutral Trade Statistical Report, A 93.17/3

U.S. **Foreign** Policy Agenda, IA 1.38, S 20.17

U.S. **Foreign** Trade (by Commodities), C 18.211

U.S. **Foreign** Trade Highlights, C 61.28/2

U.S. **Foreign** Trade in Pulp and Paper, C 18.198

U.S. **Foreign** Trade {reports}, C 56.210

U.S. **Foreign** Trade: Schedules, C 56.210/3

U.S. **Foreign** Waterborne Transportation Statistics Quarterly, TD 11.35

U.S. Oceanborne **Foreign** Trade Forecast, TD 11.13/2

U.S. Oceanborne **Foreign** Trade Routes, TD 11.13

U.S. Waterborne **Foreign** Trade, Summary Report, C 3.164:985

U.S. Waterborne **Foreign** Trade, Trade Area by U.S. Coastal District, C 3.164:600

United States Airborne Exports of Domestic and **Foreign** Merchandise, Commodity (Schedule X) by Country of Destination, C 3.164:780

United States Airborne Exports of Domestic and **Foreign** Merchandise, Country of Destination by Commodity, C 3.164:790

United States Airborne **Foreign** Trade, Customs District by Continent, C 3.164:986

United States Exports by Air of Domestic and **Foreign** Merchandise Commodity by Country of Destination, C 3.164:731, C 3.164:732

United States Exports of Domestic and **Foreign** Merchandise Commodity by Country of Destination, C 3.164:410

United States Exports of Domestic and **Foreign** Merchandise Country of Destination by Subgroup, C 3.164:420

United States Exports of Domestic and **Foreign** Merchandise To Canada (Including Lend-Lease Exports), C 3.157/4

United States Exports of Domestic and **Foreign** Merchandise Under Lend-Lease Program, Calendar Year, C 3.164:405

United States Exports of Domestic and **Foreign** Merchandise Under Lend-Lease Program, Commodity by Country of Destination, C 3.164:415

United States Exports of Domestic and **Foreign** Merchandise Under Lend-Lease Program, Country of Destination by Commodity, C 3.164:421, C 3.164:425

United States Exports of Domestic and **Foreign** Merchandise Under United Nations Relief and Rehabilitation Program, Country of Destination by Commodity, C 3.164:426

United States Exports of Domestic and **Foreign** Merchandise Under United Nations Relief and Rehabilitation Program, Commodity by Country of Destination, C 3.164:416

United States Exports of **Foreign** Merchandise to Latin American Republics, C 3.157/2

United States **Foreign** Policy, S 1.71

United States **Foreign** Trade Bunker Oil and Coal Laden in the United States on Vessels, C 3.164:810

United States **Foreign** Trade in Photographic Goods, C 41.108

United States **Foreign** Trade Statistics Publications, C 3.166

United States **Foreign** Trade Statistics, C 18.185

United States **Foreign** Trade, C 3.164:930, C 3.164:950

United States **Foreign** Trade, Trade by Air, C 3.164:971

United States **Foreign** Trade, Trade by Customs District, C 3.164:970

United States **Foreign** Trade, Trade with E.C.A. Countries, C 3.164:951

United States **Foreign** Trade, Trade with U.S.S.R. and Other Eastern Europe, C 3.164:954

United States **Foreign** Trade, Waterborne Trade by Trade Area, C 3.164:973

United States **Foreign** Trade, Waterborne Trade by United States Ports, C 3.164:972

United States Oceanborne **Foreign** Trade Routes, C 39.240

United States Waterborne **Foreign** Commerce, a Review of {year}, C 3.211/2

United States Waterborne **Foreign** Commerce, Great Lakes Area {year}, C 3.211/2

University Centers of **Foreign** Affairs Research, Selective Directory, S 1.2:Un 3

USC/FAR Consolidated Plan for **Foreign** Affairs Research, PrEx 3.12

Views and Estimates of the Committee on **Foreign** Affairs on the Budget, Y 4.F 76/1:B 85

Visa Requirements of **Foreign** Governments, S 1.2:V 82/2

Voluntary **Foreign** Relief Programs, Activities of Registered American Voluntary Agencies, S 18.19

Water Borne Commerce of United States Including **Foreign** Intercoastal and Coastwise Traffic and Commerce of U.S. Noncontiguous Territory, SB 7.5/295

Water Borne **Foreign** and Domestic Commerce of U.S., C 27.9/11, MC 1.20

Water Borne **Foreign** Commerce of United States, SB 7.5/216, SB 7.7

Water-Borne **Foreign** and Noncontiguous Commerce and Passenger Traffic of United States, MC 1.23

Wood Products: International Trade and **Foreign** Markets, A 67.18:WP

World Survey of **Foreign** Railways, C 18.166

Foreign Service

American **Foreign** Service, S 1.13

Annual Report, Inspector General Department of State and **Foreign** Service, S 1.1/6

Commercial News for the **Foreign** Service, C 57.114

Foreign Service Classification List, S 1.7/2

Foreign Service Institute Bulletin, S 1.114/4

Foreign Service Institute Courses, S 1.114/2

Foreign Service Institute, General Publications, S 1.114/3

Foreign Service Institute, Quarterly Projection of Courses, S 1.114

Foreign Service Institute, Readers, S 1.114/2-2

Foreign Service List, S 1.7

Foreign Service Manual, Transmittal Letters, S 1.5/4

Foreign Service News Letter, S 1.109

Foreign Service on Vegetables, A 64.13, A 67.14

Foreign Service Regulations (by chapters), S 1.5/3

Foreign Service Regulations, Memorandum Transmitting Mimeographed Inserts for, S 1.5/2

Foreign Service Reports, A 36.39, A 67.11

Foreign Service Written Examination Registration and Application Form, S 1.137

Key Officers of **Foreign** Service Posts, S 1.40/5

Key Officers of **Foreign** Service Posts, Guide for Businessmen, S 1.40/2:Of 2

Memorandum Transmitting Mimeographed Inserts for **Foreign** Service Regulations, S 1.5/2

News Letter from Director General of **Foreign** Service, S 1.68

Reports Prepared for **Foreign** Service of United States, Listings, C 42.22

Foreign-Language

Foreign-Language and English Dictionaries in the Physical Sciences and Engineering, Selected Bibliography, 1952-1963, C 13.10:258

Foreign-Owned

News, Employment and Wages in **Foreign-Owned** Businesses in the United States, L 2.41/12

Foreign-Owned U.S. Firms, FOF (series), C 3.254

Forensic

Forensic Science Communications, J 1.14/18-2

Foresight

Foresight, Civil Preparedness Today, D 14.14

Forest

Agricultural, Pastoral, and **Forest** Industries in American Republics, TC 1.19

Alaska **Forest** Research Center, A 13.73

Amendments to 1911 Edition of Use Book and National **Forest** Manual, A 13.14

Amendments to Use Book and National **Forest** Manual, A 13.14/5

Bulletins, **Forest** Products, C 3.28/16

Central States **Forest** Experiment Station, A 13.68

Cooperative **Forest** Fire Prevention Program, A 13.20/4

Demand and Price Situation for **Forest** Products, A 13.76

Forest and Windbarrier Planting and Seeding in the United States, Report, A 13.51/2

Forest Atlas, A 13.17

Forest Economic Notes, A 13.42/13

Forest Entomology Briefs, A 9.110

Forest Fire News, A 13.32/4

Forest Fire Statistics, A 13.32/2

Forest Health Highlights, A 13.154

Forest Insect and Disease Conditions, A 13.52/2

Forest Insect and Disease Conditions in the Northern Region, A 13.52/7

Forest Insect and Disease Conditions in the Pacific Northwest, A 13.52/6

Forest Insect and Disease Conditions in the Rocky Mountain Region, A 13.52/13

Forest Insect and Disease Conditions in the Southwest, A 13.52/11

Forest Insect and Disease Conditions, Intermountain Region, A 13.52/12

Forest Insect and Disease Leaflets, A 13.52

Forest Insect and Disease Management (series), A 13.93/3, A 13.106

Forest Insect and Disease Management/Evaluation Reports, A 13.93

Forest Insect and Disease Management/Survey Reports, A 13.93/2

Forest Insect Conditions in Pacific Northwest During (year), A 13.52/6

Forest Insect Conditions in the Northern Region, A 13.52/7

Forest Insect Conditions in the United States, A 13.52/2

Forest Insects and Diseases Group Technical Publications, A 13.93/4

Forest Inspection and Disease Management (series), A 13.93/3

Forest Management Notes, A 13.42/11

Forest Management Papers, A 13.42/12

Forest Management Program Annual Report (National Summary), A 13.152

Forest Pathology Special Releases, A 77.516

Forest Pest Conditions in the North East, A 13.52/9

Forest Pest Leaflets, A 13.52

Forest Pest Management Methods Applications Group: Reports (series), A 13.52/10-3

Forest Pest Observer, A 13.68/11

Forest Planting Leaflets, A 13.9

Forest Planting, Seeding, and Silvical Treatments in the United States, A 13.51/2

Forest Product Notes, A 13.42/18

Forest Product Utilization Technical Reports, A 13.96

Forest Products, C 3.12, C 3.12/7

Forest Products Division Circulars, C 13.92/2

Forest Products Division Paper Circulars, C 18.92/3

Forest Products Industry Notes, Y 3.T 25:28-2

Forest Products Laboratory, Madison, Wisconsin, A 13.27

Forest Products Papers, A 13.67/10

Forest Products Review, C 62.11

Forest Products, 1907, C 3.12/1

Forest Products, 1908, C 3.12/2

Forest Products, 1909, C 3.12/3

Forest Products, 1910, C 3.12/4

Forest Products, 1911, C 3.12/5

Forest Products, 1912, C 3.12/6

Forest Research News for the Midsouth, A 13.40/11

Forest Research News for the South, A 13.40/11

Forest Research Notes, A 13.62/7, A 13.66/7

Forest Research Project Reports, A 13.41

Forest Resource Reports, A 13.50

Forest Statistics Series (by States), A 13.42/21

Forest Survey Notes, A 13.42/10

Forest Survey Releases: Central States Forest Experiment Station, A 13.68/9

Forest Survey Releases: Intermountain Forest and Range Experiment Station, A 13.65/10

Forest Survey Releases: Northeastern Forest Experiment Station, A 13.67/7

Forest Survey Releases: Pacific Southwest Forest and Range Experiment Station, A 13.62/8

Forest Survey Releases: Progress Reports, A 13.30/5

Forest Survey Releases: Rocky Moutain Forest and Range Experiment Station, A 13.69/9

Forest Survey Releases: Southeastern Forest Experiment Station, A 13.63/7

Forest Survey Releases: Southern Forest Experiment Station, A 13.40/5

Forest Survey Reports, A 13.66/8

Forest Tree Nurseries in the United States, A 13.74

Forest Worker, A 13.19

Forest-Gram South, Dispatch of Current Technical Information for Direct Use by Practicing Forest Resource Manager in the South, A 13.89

General Survey of Forest Situation, A 13.37

Indian Forest Management, I 20.61/3

National Forest Annual Reports (various regions), A 13.114/4

National Forest Manual, A 13.14/3

National Forest Manual, Sections, A 13.14/4

National Forest System Areas, A 13.10

Northeastern Forest Pest Reporter, A 13.52/3

Notes on Forest Trees Suitable for Planting in the U.S., A 13.7

Occasional Papers Forest Service Northeastern Forest Experiment Station, A 13.42/8, A 13.42/8-2

Occasional Papers Forest Service Southern Forest Experiment Station, A 13.40/6

Ottawa National Forest, A 13.28/a

Proceedings Annual Western International Forest Disease Work Conference, A 13.69/13

Production, Prices Employment, and Trade in Northwest Forest Industries, A 13.66/13

Products of Forest, IC 1.23/13:SS-5

Progress Report Forest Taxation Inquiry, A 13.21

Progress Report Northern Rocky Mountain Forest and Range Experiment Station, A 13.30/6

Publications by Staff and Cooperators, Intermountain Forest and Range Experiment Station, A 13.65/14

Publications Central States Forest Experiment Station, A 13.68/12-2

Publications Lake States Forest Experiment Station {list}, A 13.61/12

Publications Pacific Northwest Forest and Range Experiment Station, A 13.66/15

Publications Rocky Mountain Forest and Range Experiment Station, A 13.69/10-2

Publications Southern Forest Experiment Station, A 13.40/8-3

Publications Staff and Cooperators, Intermountain Forest and Range Experiment Station, A 13.65/14

Recent Publications of the Pacific Northwest Forest and Range Experiment Station, A 13.66/14

Report of Forest and Windbarrier Planting in the United States, A 13.75

Research at Southeastern Forest Experiment Station, A 13.63/3

Research in Forest Products, A 13.27/11

Research Information Digest, Recent Publications of Southeastern Forest Experiment Station, A 13.63/13

Research Reports Forest Products Laboratory, A 13.27/14

Research Reports Southwestern Forest and Range Experiment Station, A 13.43/8

Shawnee Quarterly, the Shawnee National Forest Schedule of Projects, A 13.138

Southeastern Forest Insect and Disease Newsletters, A 13.63/14

Southern Forest Insect Reporter, A 13.40/9

Southern Forest Pest Reporter, A 13.52/4

Southern Forest Research, A 13.40/10

State Forest Tax Law Digest, A 13.21/2

Technical Notes Forest Service Forest Products Laboratory, A 13.27/9

Technical Notes Forest Service Lake States Forest Experiment Station, A 13.61/10

Technical Notes Forest Service Northeastern Forest Experiment Station, A 13.67/9, A 13.42/7

Technical Notes Forest Service Northern Forest Experiment Station, A 13.73/9

Technical Notes Forest Service Southeastern Forest Experiment Station, A 13.63/8

Tropical Forest Notes, A 13.64/8

Update, Forest Health Technology, Enterprise Team Update, A 13.110/17

U.S. Forest Planting Report, A 13.109

U.S. Forest Products Annual Market Review and Prospects, A 13.79/4

Your Changing Forest, News on the Black Hills National Forest Plan Revision, A 13.128

Forest Service

Administrative Reports Forest Service, A 13.66/17

Forest Service Comments on Resolutions Relating to the National Forest System As Adopted, A 13.86

Forest Service Films Available on Loan for Educational Purposes to Schools, Civic Groups, Churches, Television, A 13.55

Forest Service History Line, A 13.98/3

Forest Service Organizational Directory, A 13.36/2-2

Forest Service Translations, A 13.81

Occasional Papers Forest Service Institute of Tropical Forestry, A 13.64/10

Occasional Papers Forest Service Northeastern Forest Experiment Station, A 13.42/8, A 13.42/8-2

Occasional Papers Forest Service Southern Forest Experiment Station, A 13.40/6

Performance Guides (series) Forest Service, A 13.65/12-2

Report of Forest Service Training Activities, Civilian Conservation Corps, A 13.71

Report of the Chief of the Forest Service, A 13.1

Report of the Forest Service, Fiscal Year (date), A 13.1/3

Research Notes Forest Service, A 13.79

Research Papers Forest Service, A 13.78

Sheets of National Atlas of United States Forest Service, A 13.28/2

Technical Notes Forest Service Forest Products Laboratory, A 13.27/9

Technical Notes Forest Service Lake States Forest Experiment Station, A 13.61/10

Technical Notes Forest Service Northeastern Forest Experiment Station, A 13.67/9, A 13.42/7

Technical Notes Forest Service Northern Forest Experiment Station, A 13.73/9

Technical Notes Forest Service Southeastern Forest Experiment Station, A 13.63/8

Technical Notes Forest Service WSDG-TN- (nos), A 13.27/9, A 13.87/4

Forest-Gram

Forest-Gram South, Dispatch of Current Technical Information for Direct Use by Practicing Forest Resource Manager in the South, A 13.89

Forester

Caribbean Forester, A 13.64/7

Extension Forester, A 43.5/11, A 43.17

Foresters

Random Forestry Notes for Extension Foresters, A 43.28

Forestry

Division of Forestry Development, Annual Report, Y 3.T 25:1-4

Forestry Bulletins, Y 3.T 25:18

Forestry Bulletins, SA-FB-U (series), A 13.106/2-2

Forestry Bulletins, SB-FB/P (series), A 13.106/2

Forestry Current Literature, A 13.25

Forestry Incentives Program, from Inception of Program through (date), A 82.92

Forestry Investigation Notes, Y 3.T 25:34

Forestry Laws, A 13.18

Forestry Publications, Y 3.Em 3:7, Y 3.C 49:9, FS 4.7

Forestry Relations Division, Publications, Y 3.T 25:27

Forestry Research Progress in (year) McIntire-Stennis Cooperative Forestry Research Program, A 94.2 F 76/

Forestry Research West, A 13.95/2

Forestry Research: What's New in the West, A 13.95

Inter-American Conference on Agriculture, Forestry, and Animal Industry, Washington, Sept. 8-20, 1930, S 5.32

National Plan for American Forestry, A 13.26

News Releases and Miscellaneous Publications; Committee on Agriculture, Nutrition, and Forestry, (Senate), Y 4.Ag 8/3-2

Northeastern Area State and Private Forestry {publications}, A 13.52/8

Occasional Forestry Papers, I 29.41

Occasional Papers Forest Service Institute of Tropical Forestry, A 13.64/10

One Hundred Years of Federal Forestry, A 1.75:402

Random Forestry Notes for Extension Foresters, A 43.28

Report on Forestry, A 13.5

Southern Forestry Notes, A 13.40/7

State and Private Forestry: Forestry Bulletins, A 13.110/10

State and Private Forestry: Forestry Reports, A 13.110/9

State and Private Forestry: General Publications, A 13.110/2

State and Private Forestry: General Reports, A 13.110/12

State and Private Forestry: Handbooks, Manuals, Guides, A 13.110/8

State and Private Forestry: Miscellaneous Reports, A 13.110/11

State and Private Forestry: Technical Publications, A 13.110/13

State and Private Forestry: Technical Reports, A 13.110/14

Forests

Annual Fire Report for National Forests, Calendar Year (date), A 13.32/3

Carload Waybill Statistics, . . ., and Type of Rate, Products of Forests, 1 Percent Sample of Terminations in Statement MB-4, IC 1.23/5

Information Pamphlets Relating to National Forests, A 13.13

Information Regarding Employment on National Forests, A 13.22

National Forests, America's Great Outdoors, A 13.122

National Forests, Reports of Activities During Year, A 13.13/2

Recreation Guide to Grand Mesa, Uncompahgre and Gunnison National **Forests**, A 13.36/2-7

Resource Decisions in the National **Forests** of the Eastern Region, A 13.90

Stumpage Prices for Sawtimber Sold from National **Forests**, by Selected Species and Region, A 13.58/2

ers in the National **Forests** (series), A 13.112/2

Forfeiture
Asset **Forfeiture**, J 26.29

Form
Form Flow, D 7.41/2
Form of General Balance Sheet Statement, IC 1 ste.13, IC 1 wat.9
Form of General Balance Sheet Statement for Express Companies, IC 1 exp.8
Form of Income and Profit and Loss Statement, IC 1 ste.14
Publication Catalogue and Order **Form**, HE 20.3183/3
Region Index of Publications, Forms and **Form** Letters, D 7.16/2
Statistical Report on Social Services, **Form** FS-2069, Quarter Ended (date), FS 17.12, FS 17.628
Summer Seminars for College Teachers Guidelines and Application **Form** for Participants, NF 3.13/2-2
Summer Seminars for Secondary School Teachers Guidelines and Application **Form** for Directors, NF 3.13/3-3
Summer Seminars for Secondary School Teachers Guidelines and Applications **Form** for Participants, NF 3.13/3-2
Terms, Conditions and Limitations, with **Form** Proposal, C 7.9

Formal
Formal Docket Decisions, FMC 1.10/2
Report of **Formal** Economic Proceedings, C 31.219
Table of Cases on **Formal** Docket of ICC Not Disposed of in Printed Reports, IC 1.6/8
USAF **Formal** Schools, D 301.6:50-5

Format
Contents, **Format** and Concepts of Federal Budget, Reprint of Selected Pages from Budget of United States Government, PrEx 2.8

Former
Nautical Charts and Publications, Region 4, Scandinavia, Baltic, and the **Former** Soviet Union, C 55.440:4
Soviet Union As Reported by **Former** Soviet Citizens, Reports, S 1.102
Transition, a Magazine for **Former** ACTION Volunteers, AA 1.10

Former Spouses
Enrollment Information Guide and Plan Comparison Chart **Former Spouses** Enrolled in the **Federal Employees** Health Benefits Program, PM 1.8/7

Forms
Blank **Forms**, S 1.15 T 1.26/6
Census of Construction Industries; Announcements and Order **Forms**, C 3.245/2
Consolidated Index of Army Publications and Blank **Forms**, D 101.22:25-30
Federal Rules of Appellate Procedure with **Forms**, Y 4.J 89/1-10
Federal Tax **Forms**, Includes Non-calendar Year Products, T 22.51/4
Forms [Alcohol, Tobacco, and Firearms Bureau], T 70.22
Forms [Auditor for Interior Department], TD 5.54
Forms [Census Bureau], C 3.272
Forms [Coast and Geodetic Survey], TD 11.34
Forms [Consolidated Farm Agency], A 112.19
Forms [Copyright Office], LC 3.Form, LC 3.14
Forms [Customs Service], T 17.20
Forms [Drug Enforcement Administration], J 24.27
Forms [Economic Analysis Bureau], C 59.23
Forms [Employment Standards Administration], L 36.17
Forms [Environmental Protection Agency], EP 1.101
Forms [Export Administration Bureau], C 63.13
Forms [Federal Communications Commission], CC 1.55/2
Forms [Federal Energy Regulatory Commission], E 2.24
Forms [Federal Retirement Thrift Investment Board], Y 3.F 31/25:13
Forms [Food and Drug Administration], HE 20.4044

Forms [General Supply Administraton], GS 1.13
Forms [Health Care Financing Administration], HE 22.32
Forms [Indian Health Service], HE 20.9420, HE 20.313
Forms [Internal Revenue Service], T 22.51
Forms [Justice Department], J 1.98
Forms [Labor Department], L 1.83
Forms [Labor Relations Board], LR 1.17
Forms [Labor Statistics Bureau], L 2.127
Forms [Library of Congress], LC 1.48
Forms [National Agricultural Statistics Service], A 92.52
Forms [National Cancer Institute], HE 20.3138, HE 20.3185
Forms [National Center for Health Services Research and Health Care Technology Assessment], HE 20.6515
Forms [National Institute of Mental Health], HE 20.8138
Forms [Occupational Safety and Health Administration], L 35.28
Forms [Pension Benefit Guaranty Corporation], Y 3.P 38/2:11
Forms [Personnel Management Office], PM 1.53
Forms [Security and Exchange Commission], SE 1.37
Forms [Small Business Administration], SBA 1.40
Forms [Social Security Administration], HE 3.96], SSA 1.13
Forms [Treasury Department], T 1.63/2
Forms [United States Institute of Peace], Y 3.P 31:13
Forms [Veterans Affairs Department], VA 1.85
Forms [Wage and Hour Division], L 36.212
Forms [Youth Development Bureau], HE 23.1016
Forms and Publications, List and Order Blank, FP 1.26
Forms Catalog, T 1.63
HCFA **Forms** Information Catalog, HE 22.32/2
Index of Standard **Forms**, A 13.23
Military Publications: Index of AMC Publications and Blank **Forms**, D 101.22/3:310.1
NPA Regulatory Material and **Forms**, Digest, C 40.6/8
Numerical and Functional Index of Command **Forms**, D 301.45/14-2:0-9
Package X, Informational Copies of Federal Tax **Forms**, T 22.2/12
Region Index of Publications, **Forms** and Form Letters, D 7.16/2
Reproducible Federal Tax **Forms** for Use in Libraries, T 22.57
Requirement **Forms**, T 45.7
Some Recent Books on Public Affairs Available for Circulation in the Book **Forms**, LC 1.25
Standard and Optional **Forms** Facsimile Handbook, GS 4.6/3, GS 12.18
Standard **Forms** Catalog, GS 2.10/4
Stolen Money-Order **Forms**, P 4.7
Summer Seminars for College Teachers, Guidelines and Application **Forms** for Directors, NF 3.13/2
Summer Stipends, Guidelines and Application **Forms**, NF 3.8/2
Trademark Rules of Practice of the Patent Office, with **Forms** and Statutes, C 21.14:T 67/2
Working Papers, Publication Order **Forms**, C 56.229/2

Formula
EFC **Formula** Book, The Expected Family Contribution for Federal Student Aid, ED 1.45/5
Registry of Toxic Effects of Chemical Substances, Permuted Molecular **Formula**, Index, HE 20.7112/4

Formulary
Drug **Formulary**, VA 1.73
Formulary, VA 1.73/3
Formulary, USAF Academy Hospital, D 305.17
Formulary, VA Medical Center Sepulveda, Georgia, VA 1.73/6
Formulary, West Side Medical Center, Chicago, Illinois, VA 1.73/4
Veterans Administration Medical Center, Tucson, Arizona, **Formulary**, VA 1.73/5
West Side VA Medical Center **Formulary**, VA 1.78

Formulas
Tables and **Formulas** for Use of Surveyors and Engineers on Public Land Surveys, I 21.11/3

Fort Belvoir
Courses, Engineer School, **Fort Belvoir**, Virginia, D 103.111

Fort Benjamin Harrison
Educational Programs at **Fort Benjamin Harrison**, D 101.93/3

Fort Drum
10th Mountain Division (LI) and **Fort Drum**: Pamphlets (series), D 101.22/23

Fort George C. Meade
Headquarters **Fort George** C. Meade Pamphlets (series), D 101.22/10

Fort Jackson
Fort Jackson Pamphlets (series), D 101.22/18

Fort Lee
Fort Lee Pamphlets (series), D 101.22/15

Fort McCoy
Headquarters **Fort McCoy** Regulations, D 101.9/4

Fort Rucker
Aeromedical Research Unit, **Fort Rucker**, Ala.; USAARU Reports, D 104.21

Fort Sam Houston
Surgical Research Unit, Brooke Army Medical Center, **Fort Sam Houston**, Texas: Annual Research Progress Report, D 104.22

Fortitudine
Fortitudine, Newsletter of Marine Corps Historical Program, D 214.20

Fortnighttly
Price Trends and Controls in Latin America, **Fortnighttly** Review, Pr 32.4246

Forum
Civil Rights **Forum**, J 1.104
Disability **Forum** Report, ED 1.215/3
Energy **Forum**, E 1.69
English Teaching **Forum**, IA 1.17, ICA 1.11
Forum, HE 22.10
Forum for Applied Research and Public Policy, Y 3.T 25:61
Mobility **Forum**, D 301.56/7
NIJ Research **Forum**, J 28.35
Voice of America **Forum** Lectures Mass Communication Series, IA 1.19
Voice of America **Forum** Lectures Music Series, IA 1.19/3
Voice of America **Forum** Lectures Space Science Series, IA 1.19/2
Voice of America **Forum** Lectures University Series, IA 1.19/4

Forward
Forward Plan for Health, HE 20.18
Market for U.S. Microwave, **Forward** Scatter, and Other Radio Communications Equipment and Radar in {various countries}, C 41.105

Forwarder
Carload Waybill Statistics, . . . , Territorial Movement, and Type of Rate, Manufacturers and Miscellaneous **Forwarder** Traffic, One Percent Sampling of Terminations Statement MB-5, IC 1.23/6
Manufactures and Miscellaneous and **Forwarder** Traffic, IC 1.23/14:SS-6
Annual Economic Report of Air Freight **Forwarders**, C 31.270
Revenues, Expenses, and Statistics of Freight **Forwarders**, IC 1.19

Fossil
Division of **Fossil** and Hydro Power, Monthly Report, Y 3.T 25:48
Fact Sheets of **Fossil** Energy Project, E 1.90/9
Fossil and Hydro Power Monthly Report, Y 3.T 25:62
Fossil Fuel Utilization, E 1.36:0046
Index of Generic Names of **Fossil** Plants, I 19.3:1013
Materials and Components in **Fossil** Energy Applications, E 1.23
Materials and Components in **Fossil** Energy Applications, and ERDA Newsletter, ER 1.13

Foster
Foster Family Services Selected Reading List, HE 1.452:F 81/4

Foundation
Graduate Fellowship Awards Announced by National Science **Foundation**, NS 1.19
Grassroots Development: Journal of the Inter-American **Foundation**, Y 3.In 8/25:15
Hispanic **Foundation** Bibliographic Series, LC 24.7
Publications List National Science **Foundation**, NS 1.13/6
Publications of the National Science **Foundation**, NS 1.13/5

Automotive **Fuel** Economy Program, Annual Report to Congress, TD 8.26

Availability of Heavy **Fuel** Oils by Sulfur Level, E 3.11/8 & 3.11/8-2

Consumption of **Fuel** for Production of Electric Energy, FP 1.11/3

Deliveries of **Fuel** Oil and Kerosene in (date), E 3.40

Federal Alternative and **Fuel** Program, Annual Report to Congress, E 1.114/2

Forecast of Motor-**Fuel** Demand and Required Crude-Oil Production by States, Monthly Forecast, I 28.41

Fossil **Fuel** Utilization, E 1.36:0046

Fuel and Power for Locomotives and Rail Motor Cars of Class I Steam Railways in United States, IC 1 ste.30

Fuel Conservation Circulars, Y 3.R 13/2:28

Fuel Consumption and Cost, Certificated Route and Supplemental Air Carriers, Domestic and International Operations, C 31.267

Fuel Cost and Consumption, CAB 1.15

Fuel Cost and Consumption, Certified Route and Supplemental Air Carriers, Domestic and International Operations, Twelve Months Ended (date), C 31.267/2

Fuel Cost and Consumption, Twelve Months Ended December 31, (year), CAB 1.15/2

Fuel Economy Guide, E 1.8/5

Fuel Economy News, E 1.79, TD 8.33

Fuel Oil and Kerosene Sales, E 3.11/11-3, E 3.11/11-4

Fuel Oil Industry Letters, Pr 32.4228

Fuel Oil Sales, E 3.11/11

Fuel Oils by Sulfur Content, I 28.45/4

Fuel Performance Annual Report, Y 3.N 88:25-4

Fuel-Briquets and Packaged-**Fuel** Producers, Annual, I 28.109

Manufacturing Energy Consumption Survey: **Fuel** Switching, E 3.54/3

Monthly Motor **Fuel** Reported by States, TD 2.46/2

Monthly Report Prepared by Technical Staff, **Fuel** Committee, Allied Control Authority, W 1.83, M 105.15

New Orders for Pulverizers, for Pulverized **Fuel** Installations, C 3.103

Preliminary Power Production, **Fuel** Consumption and Installed Capacity Data, E 3.11/17-4, E 3.11/17-6

Pulverizers, for Pulverized **Fuel** Installations, New Order for, C 3.103

Reactor and **Fuel** Processing Technology, Y 3.At 7:36

Reactor **Fuel** Processing, Y 3.At 7:37

Sales of **Fuel** Oil and Kerosene in (year), I 28.45/5

State Regulatory Commissions and **Fuel** Tax Divisions, IC 1.3/2-2

World Nuclear **Fuel** Cycle Requirements, E 3.46/4

Fuels

AFDC Update, News of the Alternative **Fuels** Data Center, E 1.114

Alcohol **Fuels** Programs Technical Review, E 1.80/2

Alternate **Fuels**, E 2.20

Alternative **Fuels** in Trucking, E 1.114/3

Annual Summary of Cost and Quality of Steam-Electric Plant **Fuels**, FP 1.2:F 95

Chemistry and Technology of **Fuels** and Oils {abstracts}, C 41.55

Cost and Quality of **Fuels**, E 3.11/15

Cost and Quality of **Fuels** for Electric Utility Plants, E 3.11/15-2

Fuels and Energy Data, I 28.27

Retail Prices and Indexes of **Fuels** and Utilities, L 2.40

Solid **Fuels** Distribution Reports, I 28.74

Solid **Fuels** Orders SFO (series), I 57.6/2

Staff Report of Monthly Report Cost and Quality of **Fuels** for Electric Utility Plants, E 2.13

Staff Report on Monthly Report of Cost and Quality of **Fuels** for Steam-Electric Plant, FP 1.32

Synthetic Liquid **Fuels** Abstracts, I 28.86

Winter **Fuels** Report, E 3.32/3

Fugitives

Fugitives Wanted by Police, J 1.14/8

Fulbright-Hays

Application for **Fulbright-Hays** Training Grants, ED 1.54

Application for Grants under **Fulbright-Hays** Foreign Curriculum Consultants, ED 1.59

Application for Grants under **Fulbright-Hays** Group Projects Abroad, ED 1.62

Full

Full Circle, E 1.90/4

Patents Assist, **Full** Text of Patent Search Tools, C 21.31/5

Full-Resolution

Magellan **Full-Resolution** Radar Mosaics, NAS 1.86/2

Full-Time

Fall {year} Enrollment, Teachers, and School-Housing in **Full-Time** Public Elementary and Secondary Day Schools, FS 5.220:20007, HE 5.220:20007

Organization and Staffing for **Full-Time** Local Health Services, FS 2.80

Fullbright-Hays

Modern Foreign Language Fellowship Program, National Defense Education Act, Title 6 and NDEA Related Awards under **Fullbright-Hays** Act, FS 5.255:55034, HE 5.255:55034

Fully

Fully Involved, FEM 1.111

Fully Involved {special issues}, FEM 1.111/2

Function

Description of Output Indicators by **Function** for the Federal Government, L 2.133

Historical Comparison of Budget Receipts and Expenditures by **Function**, Special Analysis G, PrEx 2.8/a10

Functional

Numerical and **Functional** Index of Command Forms, D 301.45/14-2:0-9

State and Local Government **Functional** Profile Series, Y 3.Eq 2:14

Functions

Brief of the Organization and **Functions** Secretary of Defense Deputy Secretary of Defense etc., D 1.36

Detailed Listing of Real Property Owned by the United States and Used by the Department of Defense for Military **Functions** Throughout the World, GS 1.15/4-2

Digest of **Functions** of Federal Agencies, Pr 32.5022

Functions and Organization of Bureau of Supplies and Accounts, Control Record, N 20.25

Handbook of Mathematical **Functions**, C 13.32:55

Headquarters, First United States Army, Deputy Chief of Staff, Information Management, Organization, Mission, and **Functions**, D 101.1/9

Health Services and Mental Health Administration Public Advisory Committees: Authority, Structure, **Functions**, FS 2.321

NIH Public Advisory Groups: Authority, Structure, **Functions**, HE 20.3018

PHS Public Advisory Groups, Authority, Structures, **Functions**, HE 20.2:Ad 9/2

Productivity Statistics for Federal Government **Functions**, Fiscal Year, L 2.119/2

Public Advisory Committees: Authority, Structure, **Functions**, HE 20.4022

Public Advisory Committees: Authority, Structure, **Functions**, Members, HE 20.1000

Report to the President and Congress on the Drug Abuse, Prevention, and Treatment **Functions**, HE 1.58

Fund

Annual Report of Sinking **Fund** and Funded Debt of District of Columbia, for Fiscal Year, T 40.6

Annual Statements, Government Life Insurance **Fund**, VA 1.13

Army Morale Support **Fund** Annual Report, D 102.82/2

Fund for the Improvement of Postsecondary Education: Publications (series), HE 19.9

Hawaii Tax **Fund** Orders, A 55.28

Puerto Rico Tax **Fund** Orders, A 55.18/2

Survey of Pension **Fund** Investment in Mortgage Instruments, HH 1.99/4

The **Fund** for the Improvement of Postsecondary Education (FIPSE), Special Focus Competition: College-School Partnerships to Improve Learning of Essential Academic Subjects, Kindergarten through College, ED 1.23/9

Fundamental

Fundamental Nuclear Energy Research, Y 3.At 7:48

Reading is **Fundamental**, Inc., Book Supplier Profile, SI 1.36/2

RIF {Reading Is **Fundamental**} Newsletter, SI 1.36

Funded

Annual Report of Sinking Fund and **Funded** Debt of District of Columbia, for Fiscal Year, T 40.6

EXPRO, Listing of Extramural Projects to Be **Funded** in Fiscal Year, EP 1.32

Funded Indebtedness of District of Columbia, T 40.5

330-**Funded** Community Health Centers Directory, HE 20.9112/2

Superfund Emergency Response Actions, A Summary of Federally- **Funded** Removals, Annual Report, EP 1.89/5

Training and Manpower Development Activities Supported by the Administration on Aging Under Title IV-A of the Older Americans Act of 1965, As Amended, Descriptions of **Funded** Projects, HE 23.3002:T 68/2

Wastewater Treatment Construction Grants Data Base, Public Law 92-500 Project Records, Grants Assistance Programs, New Projects **Funded** During (Month), EP 1.56

Funding

Federal R & D **Funding** by Budget Function, NS 1.18/4

Funding Opportunities at NIE, FY (year), ED 1.321

Funding Opportunities at NIE, Grants Competitions and Requests for Proposals in Fiscal Year, HE 19.216/2

Referral Guidelines for **Funding** Components of PHS, HE 20.3008/4

Report on **Funding** Levels and Allocations of Funds, TD 7.20

Fund-Raising

Federal **Fund-Raising** Manual, CS 1.7/5

Manual on **Fund-raising** Within the Federal Services for Voluntary Health and Welfare Agencies, CS 1.7/5

Funds

Consolidated Federal **Funds** Report, C 3.266/2

Corporate Pension **Funds**, SE 1.25/6

Counterpart **Funds** and AID Foreign Currency Account, S 18.14

Counterpart **Funds** and FOA Foreign Currency Accounts, FO 1.11/3

Counterpart **Funds** and ICA Foreign Currency Accounts, S 17.11/3

Emergency Relief Appropriation Acts, Reports of President to Congress Showing Status of **Funds** and Operations Under, T 63.114

Emergency Relief Appropriation Acts, Reports Showing Status of **Funds**, T 63.107

Emergency Relief Appropriation Acts, Reports Showing Status of **Funds** and Analyses to Expenditures, T 63.109

European Program, Local Currency Counterpart **Funds**, Pr 33.911, FO 1.11

Expenditures for Public Assistance Payments and for Administrative Costs, by Program and Source of **Funds**, HE 17.632

Far East Program, Local Currency Counterpart **Funds**, Pr 33.911/2, FO 1.11/2

Federal **Funds** for Research and Development, Detailed Historical Tables, Fiscal Years, NS 1.18/2

Federal **Funds** for Research and Development, Federal Obligations for Research by Agency and Detailed Field of Science, Fiscal Years, NS 1.18/3

Federal **Funds** for Research, Development, and Other Scientific Activities, NS 1.18

Financial Statistics of Institutions of Higher Education, Current **Funds**, Revenues, and Expenditures, HE 19.316/2

Flow of **Funds**, Seasonally Adjusted and Unadjusted, FR 1.56

Flow of **Funds**, Unadjusted, FR 1.56/2

Funds for Research at State Agricultural Experimental Stations, A 94.10

Geographic Distribution of Federal **Funds** in (States), CSA 1.10

Highway Research and Development Studies using Federal-Aid Research and Planning **Funds**, TD 2.113

Major Nondeposit **Funds** of Commercial Banks, FR 1.39/4

Manual of Regulations and Instructions Relating to the Disclosure of Federal Campaign **Funds** for Candidates for the Office of President or Vice President of the United States and . . . Candidates, GA 1.14:C 15

Medicaid and Other Medical Care Financed from Public Assistance **Funds**, HE 17.620, HE 17.621

Property, Emergency Procurement and **Funds**, W 3.50/6

Public Works Administration of Federal Works Agency, Reports Showing Status of **Funds** and Analyses of Expenditures, T 63.108

Report on Funding Levels and Allocations of **Funds**, TD 7.20

Reports of President to Congress Showing Status of **Funds** and Operations under Emergency Relief Appropriation Acts, T 63.114

Reports Showing Financial Status of **Funds** Provided in Emergency Relief Appropriation Acts, T 60.11

Reports Showing Status of **Funds** and Analyses of Expenditures, Emergency Appropriation Acts, T 60.13

Reports Showing Status of **Funds** and Analyses of Expenditures, Public Works Administration Federal Works Agency, T 60.14

Reports Showing Status of **Funds** Provided in Emergency Relief Appropriation Acts, T 60.12

Research and Development Contracts, Fiscal Year **Funds**, HE 20.3013/4

RRB-SSA Financial Interchange: Calculations for Fiscal Year with Respect to OASI, DI, and HI Trust **Funds**, RR 1.15

Source of **Funds** Expended for Public Assistance Payments and for Cost of Administration, Services, and Training, HE 17.634

Source of **Funds** Expended for Public Assistance Payments, FS 14.215, FS 17.631, HE 17.631, HE 17.19/2

State Administered Federal Engineer **Funds**, HE 19.122

Total Obligations Incurred for Emergency Relief from All Public **Funds** by State and Local Relief Administration in Continental United States, Y 3.F 31/ 5:35

Uses of State Administered Federal Education **Funds**, HE 19.122

Working Capital **Funds**, D 1.58/3

Fungicide

Notices of Judgement Under Federal Insecticide, **Fungicide**, and Rodenticide Act, A 77.325, A 82.56

Notices of Judgement Under the Federal Insecticide, **Fungicide**, and Rodenticide Act, EP 1.70

Service and Regulatory Announcements Insecticide and **Fungicide** Board, A 34.6, A 46.15

Fungicides

Annotated Index of Registered **Fungicides** and Nematicides, Their Uses in the United States, A 77.302:F 96

Fungicides and Nematicides, EP 5.11/2

Review of U.S. Patents Relating to Insecticides and **Fungicides**, A 7.9

Fur

Fur Bearing Animals Abroad, News Jottings from Field for American Breeders, Bulletins, C 18.93

Fur Seal Arbitration, Paris, S 3.7/1, S 3.7/1a

Fur Trade Developments, C 18.94

Reports and Statistical Tables on **Fur**-Seal Investigations in Alaska, T 35.7

Furloughs

Information Concerning Removals, Reductions, Suspensions and **Furloughs**, CS 1.24

Furnaces

Warm-Air **Furnaces**, Winter Air-conditioning Systems, and Accessory Equipment, C 3.144

Furnished

Catalogue of Book and Blanks **Furnished** by Department of Commerce to Customs Officers, C 1.16

Visitor Accommodations **Furnished** by Concessioners in Areas Administered by National Park Service, I 29.70

Furnishing

Historic **Furnishing** Study (series), I 29.88/2

Furnishings

Historic **Furnishings** Report, HFC, I 29.88/2-2

Furniture

Industry Wage Survey: Wood Household **Furniture**, L 2.3/27

Retail **Furniture** Report, FR 1.41

Retail Installment Credit and **Furniture** and Household Appliance Stores, FR 1.34/2

Steel Office **Furniture**, Shelving, and Lockers, and Fireproof Safes, C 3.108

World Trade in Wood, **Furniture**, Floor, Metal and Automobile Polishes, C 18.178

Fusion

Fusion Energy, E 1.99

Fusion Fuels, E 1.99

Inertial Confinement **Fusion**, ICF Annual Report, E 1.99/7-2

Inertial Confinement **Fusion** Quarterly Report, E 1.99/7

Future

Future Drive, E. 1.86/8

National Survey Results on Drug Use from the Monitoring the **Future** Study, HE 20.3968

Quarterly Summary of **Future** Construction Abroad, C 57.113

World List of **Future** International Meeting: Pt. 2, Social, Cultural, Commercial, Humanistic, LC 2.9/2

World List of **Future** International Meetings 19591969, LC 2.9

Futures

Bales of Cotton Delivered in Settlement of **Futures** on New York and New Orleans Cotton Exchanges, A 59.10

Commitments of Large Traders in Cotton **Futures**, A 85.9

Commitments of Traders in Commodity **Futures**, Y 3.C 73/5:9/2

Commitments of Traders in Commodity **Futures** with Market Concentration Ratios, Y 3.C 73/5:9

Commitments of Traders in Commodity **Futures**, Cotton, Frozen Concentrated Orange Juice, Potatoes, A 85.9

Commitments of Traders in Commodity **Futures**, Cotton, Wool, Potatoes, A 85.9

Commitments of Traders in Wool and Wool Top **Futures**, New York Cotton Exchange, A 85.9/3

Cotton and Grain **Futures** Acts, Commodity Exchange and Warehouse Acts and Other Laws Relating Thereto {August 7, 1916}, Y 1.2:C 82

Futures For the Class of . . ., D 1.41/2

Futures Trading and Open Contracts in Butter, Eggs and Potatoes, A 85.11/4

Futures Trading and Open Contracts in Cotton and Cottonseed Oil, A 85.11/5

Futures Trading and Open Contracts in Frozen Concentrated Orange Juice, A 85.11/8

Futures Trading and Open Contracts in Potatoes, A 85.11/3

Futures Trading and Open Contracts in Potatoes and Rice, A 85.11

Futures Trading and Open Contracts in Soybean Meal and Cottonseed Meal, A 85.11/6

Futures Trading and Open Contracts in Wheat, Corn, Oats, Rye, Soybeans and Products, A 85.11/7

Futures Trading and Open Contracts in {Wheat, Corn, Oats, etc.} on Chicago Board of Trade, A 88.11/18

Futures Trading in Cotton, Wool and Wool Tops, A 85.11/2

Monthly Commodity Futures Statistics on **Futures** Trading in Commodities Regulated under the Commodity Exchange Act, A 85.15/2

Monthly Summary of Commodity **Futures** Statistics, A 85.15

On Call Positions in Spot Cotton Based on New York Cotton **Futures** Reported by Merchants in Special Account Status, Y 3.C 73/5:11

Recreation **Futures** for Colorado, I 53.48

Stocks of Grain in Deliverable Positions for Chicago Board of Trade, **Futures** Contracts in Exchange-Approved and Federally Licensed Warehouses, as Reported by Those Warehouses, A 85.14, Y 3.C 73/5:10

Trade in Cotton **Futures**, A 82.30

Trade in Grain **Futures**, A 82.29

Trade in Wool Top **Futures**, A 59.12, A 75.210

FVUS

Fresh Fruit and Vegetable Unloads, **FVUS** (series), A 88.12/31

FWP

FWP Newsletter, I 28.170

FY

FY Budget, Summary, HH 1.1/4-2

FY Projects, by Country and Field of Activity, S 18.29

Summaries of **FY** (date) Research in Nuclear Physics, E 1.19/3

FYI/FMHA

FYI/FMHA, A 84.11

G

Gadsden

Area Wage Survey, **Gadsden** and Anniston, Alabama, L 2.122/1-5

Gaging

Annual Peak Discharge at Selected **Gaging** Stations in Pacific Northwest, I 19.45/3

Monthly Mean Discharge at Selected **Gaging** Stations and Change of Storage in Certain Lakes and Reservoirs in Columbia River Basin, I 19.47

Gaging Stations

Average Monthly Discharge for 15-year Base Period at Selected **Gaging Stations** and Change of Storage in Certain Lakes and Reservoirs in Pacific Northwest, I 19.45/ 3-2

Base Flows As of {date} at Selected **Gaging Stations** in the Columbia River Basin, I 19.2:C 72/2

Gallant

Gallant American Women, FS 5.15

Gallery

National Portrait **Gallery** Calendar of Events, SI 11.15

Posters National **Gallery** of Art, SI 8.10

Gallium

Gallium in . . ., I 28.174/2

Gallium in (year), I 28.160

Galvanized

Galvanized Range Broilers and Tanks for Hot Water Heaters, C 3.86

Galveston Bay

Galveston Bay Fact Sheet Series, I 49.110

Gamble

Don't **Gamble** with Your Health (series), FS 2.50/ 2

Game

Alaska **Game** Commission, Circulars, I 49.12

Annual Reports of Governor of Alaska on Alaska **Game** Law, A 5.7

Directory of Officers and Organizations Concerned with Protection of Birds and **Game**, A 5.8

Foreign **Game** Leaflets (numbered), I 49.74

Game Laws, A 1.9

Open Season for **Game**, A 5.9

Service and Regulatory Announcements Alaska **Game** Commission, A 5.10/5

Gamebirds

Bibliography on Poultry Industry Chickens Turkeys Aquatic Fowl **Gamebirds**, A 77.411

Gang

Highlights of the National Youth **Gang** Survey, J 32.21/3

GAO

Aging, **GAO** Activities in Fiscal Year, GA 1.13/14

Bibliography of Documents Issued by **GAO** on Matters Related to ADP (Automated Data Processing), GA 1.16/5

GAO Documents, Catalog of Reports, Decisions and Opinions, Testimonies and Speeches, GA 1.16/4

GAO Document, GA 1.39

GAO Document (series) GA 1.39

GAO Journal, GA 1.15/2

GAO Manual for Guidance of Federal Agencies, GA 1.6/1

GAO Policy and Procedures Manual for Guidance of Federal Agencies: Title 6, Pay, Leave, and Allowances, GA 1.6/6

GAO Review, GA 1.15

GAO, Office of Public Information, Reports, GA 1.16/3

General Accounting Office Salary Tables, GA 1.10, GA 1.6/10

General and Miscellaneous, E 1.99

General Aviation Accidents (non-air carrier), Statistical Analysis, C 31.160/2, FAA 1.15

General Aviation Activity and Avionics Survey, TD 4.32/17-2

General Aviation Aircraft Use, FAA 1.39

General Aviation Airworthiness Alerts, TD 4.414

General Aviation Inspection Aids Summary, TD 4.409

General Catalog of Mariners & Aviators' Charts and Books, N 6.5

General Catalog: MAC NCO Academy West, D 301.80/2

General Catalogs of Educational Films, FS 5.10/3

General Catalogue of Homoptera, A 77.20

General Ceiling Price Regulations, ES 3.6/4

General Chart of Northern and Northwestern Lakes {and rivers}, W 33.7/1

General Clinical Research Centers Committee, HE 20.3001/2:C 61/2

General Construction Bulletins, Y 3.R 88:13

General Court-Martial Orders: Army and Corps Areas and Departments, W 99.11/7, W 99.12/7, W 99.13/7, W 99.14/7, W 99.15/7, W 99.16/7, W 99.17/7, W 99.19/7, W 99.21/7

General Court-Martial Orders: Department of the Army, W 3.32, W 1.51, M 101.14, D 101.14

General Court-Martial Orders: Department of the East, W 17.9

General Court-Martial Orders: Department of the Navy, N 1.14, M 201.9, D 201.9

General Court-Martial Orders: Hawaii Department, W 81.9

General Court-Martial Orders: Military Academy, W 12.13, M 109.10

General Crop Report, Louisiana Crop Reporting Service, A 88.24/7

General Crop Reports, A 66.11

General Departmental Circulars, A 1.62

General Description of Foreign-trade Zones, FTZ 1.8

General Displacement Notices, CS 1.49

General Drawings of Snow Removal Equipment, W 7.31/2

General Engine Bulletins, N 28.21

General Foreign Policy Series, S 1.71

General Headquarters, Far East Command, **General** Publications, D 1.24

General Import, World Area by Commodity Groupings, C 56.210:155

General Imports of Merchandise into United States by Air, Commodity by Country of Origin, C 3.164:231

General Imports of Merchandise into United States by Air, Country of Origin by Commodity, C 3.164:232

General Index to Experiment Station Record, A 10.6/2

General Index to International Law Situations, N 15.7/2

General Indexes to Monthly Consular Reports, S 4.8

General Industry Standards, L 35.6/3

General Information Bulletin, N 4.14

General Information Concerning Trademarks, C 21.2:T 67, C 21.26

General Information Leaflets: Department of the Army, D 101.75

General Information Leaflets: National Archives and Records Service, GS 4.22

General Information Letter, MC 1.29

General Information Regarding Department of the Interior, I 1.70

General Information Series, Information from Abroad, N 13.5

General Information Series: Agricultural Adjustment Administration, A 55.71

General Information Series: Agricultural Adjustment Agency, A 76.408, A 80.614

General Information Series: Federal Communications Commission, CC 1.37/2

General Information Series: Federal Crop Insurance Corporation, A 62.7

General Information Series: Federal Surplus Commodities Corporation, A 69.9

General Instructions and Regulations in Relation to Transaction of Business at Mints and Assay Offices with Coinage Laws, T 28.9

General Instructions for Surveys in Philippine Islands, C 4.18/4

General Interpretations, ES 3.6/14

General Land Office, Automated Records Project, Pre-1908 Homestead & Cash Entry Patents, I 53.57

General Legal Bulletin, Foreign Laws Affecting American Business, C 18.95

General Letter, C 11.9

General Letters, FW 4.12

General Letters to State Works Progress Administrators, Y 3.W 89/2:23

General Library Committee Publications, LC 1.32/2

General Maintenance Alert Bulletins, C 31.163/2, FAA 1.31/2

General Maintenance Inspection Aids, C 31.162

General Maintenance Inspection Aids Summary and Supplements, FAA 1.31

General Management Plan, I 29.79/3

General Management Training Center, Calendar of Training Courses, Fiscal Year, CS 1.65/5

General Maximum Price Regulations, Bulletins, Pr 32.4211

General Medicine A Study Section, HE 20.3001/2:M 46/2

General Medicine B Study Section, HE 20.3001/2:M 46/3

General Nautical and International Nautical Charts, D 5.356

General Newspaper Releases, Y 3.W 19/2:5

General Office Orders, GA 1.8

General Operating and Flight Rules, TD 4.6:part 91

General Operating Support Grant Application and Information, NF 4.9

General Orders Embracing Laws Affecting the Army, W 3.8

General Orders in Bankruptcy, Ju 6.9/2

General Overriding Regulations, ES 3.6/9

General Planning, D 5.318/5

General Press Releases, ES 3.7/1

General Procedure, A 62.11

General Progress Bulletins, New Alotments, Y 3.R 88:12

General Publications Relating to Dairy Research, A 77.602

General Real and Personal Property Inventory Report (Civilian and Military) of the U.S. Government Covering Its Properties Located in the U.S., in the Territories, and Overseas, As of June 30 {year}, Y 4.G 74/7:P 94

General Receiver of Customs for Liberia, S 1.24

General Regulations for the Enforcement of the Federal Food, Drug, and Cosmetic Act, FS 13.106/2:1/2

General Relief Operations of Large City Public Welfare Agencies, SS 1.26

General Reports, A 89.11

General Research Support Program Advisory Committee, HE 20.3001/2:R 31/2

General Research, GR- (series), I 27.27

General Revenue Sharing, T 1.53/2

General Revenue Sharing Payments, T 1.53

General Rules and Regulations Prescribed by Board of Supervising Inspectors of Steamboats, T 38.9

General Rules and Regulations Under the Investment Company Act of 1940, as in Effect (date), SE 1.6:R 86/9

General Rules and Regulations Under the Securities Act of 1933, as in Effect (date), SE 1.6:R 86/2

General Rules and Regulations Under the Securities Exchange Act of 1934, as in Effect (date), SE 1.6:R 86/3

General Salary Orders, ES 4.6/3

General Salary Stabilization Regulations GSSR (series), ES 4.6/2

General Schedule of Supplies, GS 1.5/1, T 45.5/1, T 58.8

General Specifications for Building Vessels of Navy, N 29.7, M 210.7

General Specifications for Machinery, N 19.5/2

General Sugar Orders, A 55.19

General Summary of Inventory Status and Movement of Capital and Producers Goods, Plants, Aircraft, and Industry Agent Items, Pr 33.210

General Superintendent and Landscape Engineer of National Parks, Annual Reports, I 1.58

General Supplies Fixed Price Lists, W 77.23/1

General Supplies Lists, W 77.23/2

General Survey of Conditions in Coal Industry, C 22.21

General Survey of Forest Situation, A 13.37

General Technical Reports, A 13.88

General Wage Determinations Issued under the Davis-Bacon and Related Acts, L 36.211

General Wage Regulations, ES 2.6/3

General/Flag Officer Worldwide Roster, D 1.61/8

GITI {General Investigation of Tidal Inlets} Reports, D 103.42/7

HCFA Regional Office Manual; **General**, HE 22.8/8-5

Hospital Elements, Planning and Equipment for 50- and 200-Bed **General** Hospitals, FS 2.12/2

Inspector **General** Semiannual Reports, Y 3.T 25:1-19

Inspector **General**: Master Plan, Y 3.T 25:67

Journal of **General** Chemistry {abstracts}, C 41.53

Next **General** Weather Radar (series), C 1.80

Operating Instruction for Merchant Marine Examination Questions Books, Navigation **General** Book 3, TD 5.57/2

Papers in Re {proceedings of inquiry, **general** investigations, etc.}, IC 1.13/2

Posters **General** Service Administration, GS 1.32

Posters National Institute of **General** Medical Sciences, HE 20.3467

Preliminary **General** Statistics, C 3.24/8-3

Proceedings Annual Conference of the Surgeon **General**, Public Health Service, and Chief, Children's Bureau, with State and Territorial Health Officers, FS 2.83

Proceedings Annual Conference, Surgeon **General**, Public Health Service, with State and Territorial Mental Health Authorities, FS 2.83/3

Proficiency Testing Summary Analysis: **General** Immunology, HE 20.7022/3, HE 20.7412

Progress Bulletins, **General**, A 68.8

Proposals, Advertisements, **General** Information, etc., N 1.17

Qualification Standards for White Collar Positions Under the **General** Schedule, CS 1.45:X-118, PM 1.8/3:X-118

Quarterly Digest of Unpublished Decisions of the Comptroller **General** of the United States: Personnel Law, Civilian Personnel, GA 1.5/5, GA 1.5/10, GA 1.5/11

Quarterly Report of the **General** Sales Manager, A 1.117, A 67.43

Register of Office of Attorney **General**, J 1.12

Regulations for Government of United States Army **General** Hospital, W 44.15

Regulations of **General** Services Administration, GS 1.6/4

Report of the Attorney **General** on Competition in the Synthetic Rubber Industry, J 1.26

Report of the Attorney **General** Pursuant to Section 2 of the Joint Resolution of July 28, 1955, Consenting to an Interstate Compact to Conserve Oil and Gas, J 1.27

Report of the Attorney **General** to the Congress of the United States on the Administration of the Foreign Agents Registration Act of 1938, As Amended, J 1.30

Report of the Attorney **General**, Pursuant to Section 252(i) of the Energy Policy and Conservation Act, J 1.27/2

Report of the U.S. Attorney **General** for the District of (area) to the Attorney **General**, J 31.9

Report to the Attorney **General** (series), J 1.96

Reports of the Surgeon **General**, HE 20.7615

Reports on Case Handling Developments of the Office of the **General** Counsel, Y 3.F 31/21-3:12

Resume of U.S. Civil Air Carrier and **General** Aviation Aircraft Accidents, Calendar Year, C 31.244

Roster of **General** Officers of **General** Staff, Volunteers, W 3.27

Rules of Practice **General** Land Office, I 21.9

Schedule of Sailings of Steam Vessels Registered Under Laws of United States and Intended to Load **General** Cargo at Ports in United States for Foreign Destinations, IC 1 rat.8

School of Aviation Medicine: **General** Publications, D 301.26/13-5

Selected Decision of Comptroller **General** Applicable to Naval Service, N 20.7/4

Semi-annual Report of the Inspector **General**, U.S. Small Business Administration, SBA 1.1/3

Semiannual Report of the Inspector **General** to Congress, C 1.1/2

Semiannual Report of the Inspector **General**, L 1.74, VA 1.55

Semiannual Report, Office of Inspector **General**, A 1.1/3

Separate Sheets of Selected Thematic and **General** Reference Maps from the National Atlas of the United States of America, I 19.111a

Sequoia and **General** Grant National Parks, Annual Reports, I 1.29

Specifications **General** Services Administration, GS 1.9

SSA Program Circulars **General** Series, HE 3.4/2

Standard Nomenclature Lists, Obsolete **General** Supplies, W 32.23/4

State and Private Forestry: **General** Publications, A 13.110/2

State and Private Forestry: **General** Reports, A 13.110/12

Statement of Recruiting for Line of Army at **General** Recruiting Stations and Their Auxiliaries, W 3.17/2

Store Stock Catalog, **General** Services Administration, Zone Price Lists, Zone 1, GS 2.10

Summary of Operations, Office of **General** Counsel, LR 1.1/2

Supplement to **General** Rules and Regulations, C 15.9/2

Survey of American Listed Corporations, **General** Publications, SE 1.17/2

Technical Services Office **General** Publications, C 41.22

Telephone Directory **General** Accounting Office, GA 1.27

Telephone Directory **General** Services Administration and Defense Materials Procurement Agency, GS 1.11

Treasury Department-**General** Accounting Office Joint Regulations, T 1.38

U.S. Airborne Exports and **General** Imports, Shipping Weight and Value, C 3.164:986

U.S. **General** Aviation Accident Prevention Bulletin, C 31.203/2

U.S. **General** Aviation Briefs of Accidents, C 31.244/5

U.S. **General** Imports and Imports for Consumption, Schedule A Commodity and Country, C 3.164:135

U.S. **General** Imports Commodity, Country and Method of Transportation, C 3.164:350

U.S. **General** Imports Geographic Area, Country, Schedule A Commodity Groupings, and Method of Transportation, C 3.164:155

U.S. **General** Imports Schedule A Commodity Groupings by World Area, C 56.210:FT 150

U.S. **General** Imports Schedule A Commodity Groupings, Geographic Area, Country, and Method of Transportation, C 3.164:150

U.S. **General** Imports Various Products, C 56.210/4

U.S. **General** Imports World Area and Country of Origin by Schedule A Commodity Groupings, C 3.164:155

U.S. Imports for Consumption & **General** Imports, Tariff Schedules Annotated by Country, C 3.150/6

U.S. Imports for Consumption and **General** Imports, SIC-Based Products and Area, C 3.164:210

U.S. Imports for Consumption and **General** Imports, Tariff Schedules Annotated by Country, C 3.150/6

U.S. Imports for Consumption and **General** Imports-TSUSA Commodity by Country: (year), C 3.164:246

U.S. Imports, **General** and Consumption, Schedule a Commodity and Country, C 3.164:135

U.S. Supreme Court, Government Briefs in Cases Argued by Solicitor **General**, Indexes, J 1.19/3

U.S. Waterborne Exports and **General** Imports, C 3.164:985

United States Air Force **General** Histories (series), D 301.82/3

United States Airborne **General** Imports of Merchandise, Country of Origin by Commodity, C 3.164:390

United States Census of Agriculture, 1950: V. 2 **General** Report (separates), C 3.950-9/5

United States Court of Military Appeals and the Judge Advocates **General** of the Armed Forces and the **General** Counsel of the Department of the Treasury,

United States **General** Imports and Imports for Consumption from Canada and Mexico, Exluding Strategic, Military and Critical Materials, Country by Commodity Totals, C 3.164:121

United States **General** Imports from Canada, Excluding Strategic and Critical Materials and Military Equipment, C 3.157/5

United States **General** Imports from Latin American Republics, C 3.157/3

United States **General** Imports of Cotton Manufacturers, C 3.164/2-2

United States **General** Imports of Cotton Manufacturers: Country of Origin by Geneva Agreement Category, C 56.210:130, C 3.164:130

United States **General** Imports of Cotton Manufacturers; TQ-2190, C 3.164/2-8

United States **General** Imports of Merchandise, Commodity by Country of Origin, C 3.164:10

United States **General** Imports of Textile Manufactures, Except Cotton and Wool, Grouping by Country of Origin and Schedule a Commodity by Country of Origin, TQ-2501, C 3.164/2-7

United States **General** Imports of Wool Manufacture Except Floor Coverings, Quantity Totals in Terms of Equivalent Square Yards in Country of Origin by Commodity Grouping Arrangement, TQ-2203, C 3.164/2-6

United States **General** Imports of Wool Manufacture Except for Floor Coverings, Country of Origin by Wool Grouping, TQ- 2202, C 3.164/2-5

United States Immigration Laws, **General** Information, J 21.5/2

United States, Airborne **General** Imports of Merchandise, Commodity by Country of Origin, C 3.164:380

Unpublished Comptroller **General** Decisions, With Index, D 301.100

Wage Stabilization, **General** Orders and Interpretations, Pr 32.5112

General Aviation

Accident Prevention Bulletin, U.S. **General Aviation**, C 31.203/2, C 1.17

Accidents in U.S. Civil Air Carrier and **General Aviation** Operations, C 31.244/3

Analysis of Accidents Involving Air Taxi Operations, U.S. **General Aviation**, TD 1.113/4

Analysis of Aircraft Accident Data, U.S. **General Aviation**, TD 1.113/3

Annual Review of Aircraft Accident Data, U.S. **General Aviation**, TD 1.113

Annual Review of U.S. **General Aviation** Accidents Occurring in Calendar Year, TD 1.113

Briefs of Accidents Involving Aerial Applications Operations U.S. **General Aviation**, TD 1.109/4

Briefs of Accidents Involving Air Taxi Operations U.S. **General Aviation**, TD 1.109/3

Briefs of Accidents Involving Alcohol As a Cause-Factor U.S. **General Aviation**, TD 1.109/9

Briefs of Accidents Involving Amateur Built (homebuilt) Aircraft U.S. **General Aviation**, TD 1.109/6

Briefs of Accidents Involving Corporate-Executive Aircraft U.S. **General Aviation**, TD 1.109/10

Briefs of Accidents Involving Missing Aircraft U.S. **General Aviation**, TD 1.109/8

Briefs of Accidents Involving Rotocraft U.S. **General Aviation**, TD 1.109/5

Briefs of Accidents U.S. **General Aviation** , C 31.244/5

Briefs of Fatal Accidents Involving Weather As a Cause-Factor U.S. **General Aviation**, TD 1.109/12

General Imports

U.S. Merchandise Trade: Exports, **General Imports**, and Imports for Consumption, C 3.164:925

General Orders

Digest of War Department Directives and Index of **General Orders**, Bulletins, and Numbered Circulars, W 1.41

General Publications

Office of United States High Commissioner for Austria, **General Publications**, S 1.89/4

General Services

Annual Report of the Administrator of **General Services**, GS 1.1

Federal Stock Number Reference Catalog, Numerical Listing of Items Available from **General Services** Administration, GS 2.10/5

General Services Administration

Office of Inspector General, Semiannual Report to Congress **General Services Administration**, GS 1.1/3

General's

Publications Adjutant **General's** School, D 102.25

Roster of Officers, Adjutant-**General's** Department, W 3.34

Special Text of Judge Advocate **General's** School, D 108.9

Generating

Power Production, **Generating** Capacity, E 3.11/17-7

Production of Electric Energy and Capacity of **Generating** Plants, FP 1.21

U.S. Central Station Nuclear Electric **Generating** Units, Significant Milestones, E 1.41

Generation

Generation and Sales Statistics, I 44.8

Topical Briefs: Fish and Wildlife Resources and Electric Power **Generation**, I 49.78

Generator

Cockcroft-Walton **Generator** Nuclear Reactor, C 13.46

Steam **Generator** Group Project, Y 3.N 88:25-10

Steam **Generator** Tube Integrity Program, Y 3.N 88:17

Generic

Approved Task Plans for Category "A" **Generic** Activities, Y 3.N 88:19

Generic Letter (series), Y 3.N 88:56

Project Label, Alphabetical Listings by Controlled **Generic** Drug Ingredients, J 24.24/2

Generic Names

Index of **Generic Names** of Fossil Plants, I 19.3:1013

Genetic

Genetic Bases for Resistance to Avian Diseases, Northeastern States Regional Project, A 94.15

Genetics

DCEG (Division of Cancer Epidemiology and **Genetics**) Linkage, HE 20.3196

Division of Cancer Epidemiology and **Genetics**, Annual Research Directory, HE 20.3188/2

Genetics Study Section, HE 20.3001/2:G 28

Human **Genetics** Informational and Educational Materials, HE 20.5117

Geneva

Geneva Arbitration (Alabama Claims), S 3.13/1

Reports on **Geneva** Tariff Concessions, C 18.223/2

United States General Imports of Cotton Manufacturers: Country of Origin by **Geneva** Agreement Category, C 56.210:130, C 3.164:130

Genome

Human **Genome** News, E 1.99/3

Human **Genome** Project Progress Report, Fiscal Years, HE 20.3063

GEO

GEO-Drug Enforcement Program Six-month Statistics, J 24.18

Geochemistry

Geochemistry, C 41.46

Geodesy

Geodesy and Cartography, C 41.46/3

Geodetic

Coast and **Geodetic** Survey C & GS Update, C 55.51

Digest of **Geodetic** Publications, C 4.21

Geodetic Letters, C 4.30

Publications Coast and **Geodetic** Survey, C 4.19/2

Publications National **Geodetic** Survey, C 55.413/3

Sailing Directions Coast and **Geodetic** Survey, C 4.18/3

Sheets of National Atlas of United States Coast and **Geodetic** Survey, C 4.9/21

Water Temperatures, Coast and **Geodetic** Survey Tide Stations, C 4.34

Geographic

Census of Population and Housing: **Geographic** Identification Code Scheme, C 3.223/22:90-R5

Census of Retail Trade; **Geographic** Area Statistics, C 3.255/2

Census of Retail Trade; **Geographic** Area Statistics, Advance Reports, C 3.255/2-2

Census of Service Industries; **Geographic** Area Series, C 3.257/2

Census of Service Industries; **Geographic** Area Series, Advance Reports, C 3.257/2-2

Census of Wholesale Trade; **Geographic** Area Series, C 3.256/2

Census of Wholesale Trade; **Geographic** Area Series, Advance Reports, C 3.256/2-2

Code Classification of Foreign Ports by **Geographic** Trade Area and Country, C 3.150:K

Computerized **Geographic** Coding Series, C 3.246, C 56.237

Decisions **Geographic** Names Board, I 33.5, I 33.6

Employment by **Geographic** Area, PM 1.10/3

GE-10 **Geographic** Reports, C 3.208

Geographic and Global Issues, S 1.119/4

Geographic Area Statistics, C 3.24/9-9

Geographic Base (DIME) File, CUE, {Correction-Update-Extension}, C 3.249/2, C 56.255

Geographic Bulletins, S 1.119/2

Geographic Distribution of Federal Funds in (States), CSA 1.10

Geographic Distribution of Radio Sets and Characteristics of Radio Owners in Countries of the World, IA 1.12/2

Geographic Distribution of VA Expenditures, State, County, and Congressional District, VA 1.2/11

Geographic Identification Code Scheme {by regions}, C 3.223/13-2

Geographic Mobility, C 3.186

Geographic Names in Coastal Areas (by States), C 4.37

Geographic Names Information System I 19.16/2

Geographic News, C 18.96/2

Geographic Notes, S 1.119/4

Geographic Profile of Employment and Unemployment, L 2.3/12

Geographic Reports, S 1.119

Instructions for Classifying the Underlying Cause of Death: Nonindexed Terms, Standard Abbreviations, and State **Geographic** Codes Used in Mortality Data Classification, HE 20.6208/4

Instructions for Classifying the Underlying Cause of Death: Vital Records **Geographic** Classification, HE 20.6208/3

International **Geographic** Congress, S 5.5

Landview IV/The Federal **Geographic** Data, C 3.301

Minorities and Women in Undergraduate Education, **Geographic** Distributions for Academic Year, HE 20.9314

Schedule K. Code Classification of Foreign Ports by **Geographic** Trade Area and Country, C 3.150:K

Summary of Savings Accounts by **Geographic** Area, FSLIC-Insured Savings and Loan Associations, FHL 1.29

Tons of Revenue Freight Originated and Tons Terminated in Carloads by Classes of Commodities and by **Geographic** Areas, Class 1 Steam Railways, IC 1 ste.42

U.S. Exports, **Geographic** Area, Country, Schedule B Commodity Groupings, and Method of Transportation, C 3.164:455

U.S. Exports, Schedule B Commodity Groupings, **Geographic** Area, Country, and Method of Transportaion, C 3.164:450

U.S. General Imports **Geographic** Area, Country, Schedule A Commodity Groupings, and Method of Transporation, C 3.164:155

U.S. General Imports Schedule A Commodity Groupings, **Geographic** Area, Country, and Method of Transportation, C 3.164:150

United States Censuses of Population and Housing: **Geographic** Identification Code Scheme, Phc (2) (series), C 3.223/13

Worldwide **Geographic** Location Codes, GS 1.34

Geographic Area

Annual Report of Federal Civilian Employment by **Geographic Area**, CS 1.48

Geographical

Facts for Marketers: Standard Metropolitan Statistical Areas in { } Regional **Geographical** Division, C 41.2:M 34/3

Farm Population, Annual Estimates by States, Major **Geographical** Division, and Regions, A 88.21

Geographical Mobility, C 3.186/18

News of All-Union **Geographical** Society, C 41.46/6

Rain and Dry Winds, Computed for Different **Geographical** Districts, W 42.12

Worldwide Manpower Distribution by **Geographical** Area, D 1.61/3

Geography

News of Academy of Sciences of USSR; **Geography** Series, C 41.46/4

Geologic

Geologic Atlas of the United States, I 19.5/1

Geologic Bulletins, Y 3.T 25:10

Geologic Map Index of (various States), I 19.41/8

Geologic Names of North America Introduced in 1936-1955, I 19.3:1056

Geologic Quadrangle Maps, I 19.38

Geologic Studies in Alaska by the U.S. Geological Survey, I 19.4/8

Index to **Geologic** Mapping in United States (by State) Maps, I 19.37

Index to **Geologic** Mapping of the United States, I 19.86

Index to **Geologic** Names of North America, I 19.3:1056

International **Geologic** Congress, I 19.34

Miscellaneous **Geologic** Investigations Maps, I 19.91

Geological

Bulletin of Moscow Society of Naturalists, **Geological** Division, C 41.46/2

Geological Quadrangle Maps, I 19.88

Geological Reports, I 27.38

Geological Studies in Alaska by the U.S. Geological Survey, I 19.4/3

Geological Survey Research, I 19.16

International **Geological** Congress, S 5.7

New Publications of the **Geological** Survey, I 19.14/4

Price and Availability List of U.S. **Geological** Survey Publications, I 19.41/9

Professional Papers **Geological** Survey, I 19.16

Sheets of National Atlas of United States **Geological** Survey, I 19.5/3

Specifications **Geological** Survey, I 19.17/6

Telephone Directory **Geological** Survey, Central Region, I 19.84/2

Telephone Directory **Geological** Survey, I 19.84

United States **Geological** Survey Yearbook, I 19.1

Water Resources Research Program of the U.S. **Geological** Survey, I 19.42/4-3

Geological Survey

Index to River Surveys Made by the **Geological Survey** and Other Agencies, I 19.13:995

Journal of Research of the U.S. **Geological Survey**, I 19.61

New Reports by **Geological Survey** About Water in the Pacific Northwest, I 19.14/5

U.S. **Geological Survey**, Fiscal Year Yearbook, I 19.1/2

Geology

Abstracts of North American **Geology**, I 19.54

Bibliography of North American **Geology**, I 19.3

Military **Geology** (series), D 103.40

News of Academy of Sciences of USSR; **Geology** Series, C 41.52/7

World Data Center-A for Marine **Geology** and Geophysics Report, C 55.220/10

Geomagnetic

USGS/NGIC **Geomagnetic** Observatory Data, I 19.120/2

GEOnet

GEOnet Names Server, D 5.319/2

Geophysical

Geophysical Abstracts, C 22.32, I 28.25, I 19.43

Geophysical Fluid Dynamics Laboratory: Activities, Plans, C 55.601/5

Geophysical Investigations Maps, I 19.25/2, I 19.87

Geophysical Monitoring for Climatic Change, C 55.618

Geophysical Research Papers, D 301.45/2

International Field Year for the Great Lakes: Proceedings, IFYGL Symposium, Annual Meetings of the American **Geophysical** Union, C 55.21/3

Key to **Geophysical** Records Documentation, C 55.219/2

Preliminary Report and Forecast of Solar **Geophysical** Data, C 55.627

Solar-**Geophysical** Data {reports}, C 55.215

Solar-**Geophysical** Data, IER-FB- (series), C 52.18, C 55.215

Soviet Bloc International **Geophysical** Year Information, C 41.40

Geophysics

Air Force Surveys in **Geophysics**, D 301.45/9

Geophysics and Space Data Bulletin, D 301.45/43

GRD Research Notes, **Geophysics** Research Directorate, D 301.45/16

Soviet-Bloc Research in **Geophysics**, Astronomy and Space, Y 3.J 66:14

Technical Notes Department of the Air Force **Geophysics** Research Directorate, D 301.45/16-2

Upper Atmosphere **Geophysics**, Reports UAG- (series), C 52.16/2, C 55.220

USSR and Eastern European Scientific Abstracts, **Geophysics**, Astronomy, and Space, Y 3.J 66:14

World Data Center-A for Marine Geology and **Geophysics** Report, C 55.220/10

World Data Center A for Solid Earth **Geophysics** Report, SE Series, C 55.220/5

World Data Center A Upper Atmosphere **Geophysics**, Report UAG- (series), C 55.220

George

Economic Resource Impact Statement **George** Air Force Base, California, D 301.105/4

Georgia

Commercial Broiler Farms, Maine, Delmarva, and **Georgia**, A 93.9/11

Cotton Grade and Staple Reports, **Georgia**, A 36.27/1

Tide Calendar Savannah, **Georgia**, N 6.22/3, M 202.14, D 203.14

Geoscience

Geoscience and Technology Bulletin, LC 38.12

Geosciences

Geosciences, E 1.99

Research in Progress, Calendar Year Physics, Electronics, Mathematics, **Geosciences**, D 101.52/5-4

Geothermal

Geothermal Energy, E 1.99

Geothermal Energy Research, Development and Demonstration Program, Annual Report, ER 1.31

Geothermal Energy Update, E 1.66

Geriatric

Geriatric Research, Education, and Clinical Centers, VA 1.92

German

German Science Bulletin, S 1.91/4

Guide to **German** Records Microfilmed at Alexandria, Va., GS 4.18

Guides to **German** Records Microfilmed at Alexandria, Virginia, GS 4.18

Guides to the Microfilmed Records of the **German** Navy, GS 4.18/2

Nazi-Soviet Relations, 1939-41, Documents from the **German** Foreign Office, S 1.2:N 23

Office of U.S. High Commissioner for **German** Publications, S 1.91

T.I.D.C. Projects on **German** Industrial Economic Disarmament, Pr 32.5813

Values of **German** Exports of Electrical Appraratus and Equipment, C 18.158

German Policy

Documents on **German Policy** 1918-45, S 1.82

Germany

Allied High Commission, **Germany**, Publications, Non-govt, S 5.53

Historical Monographs of Office of U.S. High Commissioner for **Germany**, S 1.95

Mixed Claims Commission, United States and **Germany**, S 3.31

Monthly Report of the Military Governor for **Germany** (U.S.), M 105.7

News of **Germany**, W 1.72/8

Official Gazette Allied High Commission for **Germany**, S 1.88

Official Gazette Control Council for **Germany**, W 1.73, M 105.9

Official Gazette of Allied High Commission for **Germany**, S 1.88

Quarterly Economic and Financial Review: Federal Republic of **Germany** and Western Sectors of Berlin, S 1.91/2

Quarterly Report on **Germany**, Office of U.S. High Commissioner for Germany, S 1.90

Semi-Monthly Military Government Report for U.S. Occupied Area of **Germany**, M 105.21

Germplasm

National Potato **Germplasm** Evaluation and Enhancement Report, A 77.36

Gerontology

Activities of the National Institutes of Health in Field of **Gerontology**, FS 2.22/26

AoA Occasional Papers in **Gerontology**, HE 23.3111

National Directory of Education Programs in **Gerontology**, HE 1.214

Getting

Getting Involved (various subjects) (series), HE 23.1112

Getting to the Corps, Y 3.N 21/29:16-18

Gift

Estate and **Gift** Tax, T 22.19/3:2

Guide to Federal Estate and **Gift** Taxation, T 22.19/2:Es 8

Sending **Gift** Packages to Various Countries, C 49.9

Gin

Cotton **Gin** Equipment, A 88.11/19

Ginned

Cotton **Ginned** (by States), C 3.20/2

Estimated Grade and Staple Length of Upland Cotton **Ginned** (by States), A 82.69

Estimated Grade and Staple Length of Upland Cotton **Ginned** in United States, A 88.11/7

Ginning

Charges for **Ginning** Cotton, Costs of Selected Services Incident to Marketing, and Related Information, Season, A 88.11/12

Cotton **Ginning** Reports, C 3.9

Ginning Cotton

Changes for **Ginning Cotton**, Costs of Selected Services Incident to Marketing, and Related Information, Season, A 88.11/12

Ginnings

Cotton **Ginnings**, A 92.47

Cotton **Ginnings**, Report on Cotton **Ginnings** by Counties, A 20 (series), C 56.239

Cotton **Ginnings**, Report on Cotton **Ginnings** by States, A 10 (series), C 56.239/2

Cotton Quality Report for **Ginnings**, Western Upland Cotton, A 82.68

Cotton Quality Reports for **Ginnings**, A 82.70

Report on Cotton **Ginnings** by Counties, C 3.20/3

Report on Cotton **Ginnings** by States (Preliminary), C 3.20

Report on Cotton **Ginnings**, C 3.32

U.S. Cotton Quality Report for **Ginnings**, A 80.134, A 80.824

United States Cotton Quality Report for **Ginnings**, A 82.28

Girls

Boys and **Girls** 4-H Club Leader, A 43.5/5

GIS

GIS Application Note (series), A 13.118

GIST

GIST, S 1.128

GIST Index, S 1.128/2

GITI

GITI {General Investigation of Tidal Inlets} Reports, D 103.42/7

Glacier

Glacier National Park, Reports, I 1.52

Self-Guiding Nature Trail Leaflets, **Glacier** National Park, I 29.61

Glaciological

Glaciological Data Report, C 55.220/6

Glaciological Notes, I 19.60

World Data Center A Glaciology (Snow and Ice), **Glaciological** Data Report, GD- (nos), C 55.220/6

Glaciology

World Data Center A **Glaciology** (Snow and Ice), Glaciological Data Report, GD- (nos), C 55.220/6

World Data Center A **Glaciology** (Snow and Ice): New Accessions List, C 55.220/8

Glance

Bureau of Justice Statistics Fiscal Year: At a **Glance**, J 29.1/2

Government Finances and Employment at a **Glance**, C 3.191/3

Technology at a **Glance**, C 13.75

Glass

Glass and Ceramics {abstracts}, C 41.68

Glassware

Illuminating **Glassware** Manufactures, Sales and Credits, C 3.146

Glassware

Industry Wage Survey: Pressed or Blown **Glassware**, L 2.3/29

Glen Echo Park

Glen Echo Park, I 29.98

Gliders

Type Certificate Data Sheets and Specifications, Rotorcraft, **Gliders**, and Balloons, TD 4.15/6

Global

Bulletin of the **Global** Volcanism Network SI 3.13

Geographic and **Global** Issues, S 1.119/4

Global Atmospheric Background Monitoring for Selected Environmental Parameters, C 55.284

Global AUTOVON Telephone Directory, D 5.111

Global Crime, S 1.149

Global Issues, IA 1.39, S 20.18

Global Market Survey, European Market, C 61.9/2

Global Market Surveys, C 57.109

Global Navigation and Planning Charts, D 5.354

Global Ocean Floor Analysis and Research Data Series, D 203.31

Global Outlook, HH 1.130

Global Trade Talk, T 17.28

Global Volcanism Program, Digital Information Series, SI 1.49

GNC- **Global** Navigation Charts, D 5.324

Patterns of **Global** Terrorism, S 1.138

U.S. **Global** Trade Outlook, C 61.34/2

U.S. **Global** Trade Outlook 1995-2000 Toward the 21st Century, C 61.34/3

Globe

Congressional **Globe**, X 72-X 180

GLOBE Offline, C 55.56

Glossaries

Dictionaries, **Glossaries**, etc., NAS 1.8

Glossary

Census of Population and Housing Guide Part B, **Glossary**, C 3.223/22:90-R1

English-French **Glossary**, S 1.2:En 3

Wildland Planning **Glossary**, A 13.88:PSW-13

Gloves

Knit Fabric **Gloves**, C 3.129

Knit Wool **Gloves** and Mittens, C 3.63

GMENAC

GMENAC Staff Papers, HE 20.6614

GNC

GNC- Global Navigation Charts, D 5.324

GNMA

Government National Mortgage Association, **GNMA**, Annual Report, HH 1.1/7

Goals

Goals 2000, Community Update, ED 1.85/2

Goals 2000 A Progress Report, ED 1.85/4

National Education **Goals** Report, ED 1.1/3, ED 1.1/3-2

Rural Development **Goals**, Annual Report of the Secretary of Agriculture to the Congress, A 1.85/2

Rural Development **Goals**, Pr 37.14

Goat

Cattle, Sheep and **Goat** Inventory, A 93.18/8

Goats

Sheep and **Goats**, A 105.23/8

Goddard

Goddard Space Flight Center, Technical Abstracts, NAS 1.28

Publications **Goddard** Space Flight Center, NAS 1.34

Research and Technology Fiscal Year (date) Annual Report of the **Goddard** Space Flight Center, NAS 1.65/2

Telephone Directory **Goddard** Space Flight Center, Greenbelt, Md, NAS 1.24/2

Year in Review at **Goddard** Space Flight Center, NAS 1.1/3

Gold

Circular of Inquiry Concerning **Gold** and Silver Coinage and Currency of Foreign Countries, Including Production, Import and Export, and Industrial Consumption of **Gold** and Silver, T 28.8

Foreign **Gold** and Exchange Reserves, A 93.34

Gold and Silver, I 28.61/2

Gold and Silver Exports and Imports: Weekly Statement of, United States, C 3.195

Gold and Silver in (year), I 28.61/3

Gold and Silver Movements: United States, C 3.196

Gold Report {Mine Production}, I 28.61

Mine Production of **Gold**, I 28.61

Summary of U.S. Exports and Imports of **Gold** and Silver, Calendar Year, C 3.196/3

Summary of U.S. Exports and Imports of **Gold** and Silver, Fiscal Year, C 3.196/2

Status Report of the U.S. Treasury-Owned **Gold**, T 63.131

United States Exports and Imports of Gold and Silver, Total United States Trade in **Gold** and Silver and United States Trade in **Gold** and Silver with Latin American Republics and Canada, C 3.164:859

United States **Gold** and Silver Movements in (Month), C 56.210:2402, C 3.164:2402

Weekly Statement of **Gold** and Silver Exports and Imports, United States, C 3.195

Golden

Operation **Golden** Eagle, Directory of Federal Recreation Areas Changing Entrance, Admission and User Fees, I 66.16

Golden Gate

Golden Gate International Exposition, S 6.23

Goldsboro

Area Wage Survey Summary **Goldsboro**, North Carolina, L 2.122/33-4

Golf

Golf Bulletin, W 99.15/11

Good

Report of the **Good** Neighbor Enviornmental Board to the President and Congress of the United States, EP 1.1/9

Transition Assistance Program Military Civilian One **Good** Job Deserves Another Participant Manual, L 39.8/2

Goods

Consumer **Goods** and Domestic Trade, PrEx 7.21/8

Consumer **Goods** Research, C 57.118

Cotton **Goods** in World Markets, C 18.62

Electrical **Goods**, C 3.82

Foreign Knit **Goods** Letter; Special Bulletins, C 18.78

General Summary of Inventory Status and Movement of Capital and Producers **Goods**, Plants, Aircraft, and Industry Agent Items, Pr 33.210

News to Use, Wartime Facts about **Goods** You Sell, Pr 32.4819

Trends in Dry **Goods** Trade, C 3.197

Trends in Electrical **Goods** Trade, C 3.172

United States Foreign Trade in Photographic **Goods**, C 41.108

Goshen

Area Wage Survey, Elkhart-**Goshen**, Indiana, Metropolitan Area, L 2.121/14-4

Governing

Health Planning Newsletter for **Governing** Body Members, HE 20.6022

Rules and Regulations **Governing** Paroling of Prisoners from Penitentiaries, State Institutions, J 1.15/5

Rules and Regulations **Governing** Paroling of Prisoners from U.S. Penitentiaries {etc.} (special), J 1.15/6

Rules **Governing** Monthly Reports of Railway Accidents, IC 1 acci.6

Rules of Practice and Rules Relating to Investigations and Code of Behavior **Governing** Exparte Communications Between Persons Outside the Commission and Decisional Employees, SE 1.6:R 86/4

Treaty, Laws and Rules **Governing** Admission of Chinese, L 3.7, L 15.12

Government

Ben's Guide to U.S. **Government** for Kids, GP 3.39

Activities of House Committee on **Government** Operations, Y 4.G 74/7:Ac 8/3

Budget of the U.S. **Government**: Director's Introduction and Overview Tables, PrEx 2.8/11

Catalog of **Government** Inventions Available for Licensing, C 51.16/2

Catalog of **Government** Patents, C 51.16

Catalog of U.S. **Government** Publications (online), GP 3.8/8-9

Chart Book on **Government** Finances and Employment: (year), C 56.209, C 3.191/2

Citizen's Guide on How to Use the Freedom of Information Act and the Privacy Act in Requesting **Government** Documents, Y 1.95-1:H.Rep. 793

City **Government** Finances in (year), C 56.209, C 3.191/2

Compendium of State **Government** Finances in (year), C 56.209, C 3.191/2

Contingent Foreign Liabilities of U.S. **Government**, T 1.45/3

County **Government** Employment, C 3.140/2-5

County **Government** Finances, C 3.191/2-7

Current Information Resource Requirements of the Federal **Government**, PM 1.56

Description of Output Indicators by Function for the Federal **Government**, L 2.133

Digest of Unpublished Decisions of the Comptroller General of the United States on General **Government** Matters, Appropriations and Miscellaneous, GA 1.5/12

Directory: Federal, State and Local **Government** Consumer Offices, HE 1.502:St 2

Directory of State, County, and City **Government** Consumer Offices, PrEx 16.2:St 2/2

Directory of U.S. **Government** Datafiles for Mainframes & Microcomputers, C 51.19/4

Document Locator, Cross Reference Index to **Government** Reports, T 1.46

Employees in Private and **Government** Shipyards by Region, L 2.81

Employment of Disabled and Vietnam Era Veterans in Federal **Government**, CS 1.93

Energy Information in the Federal **Government**, a Directory of Energy Sources Identified by the Interagency Task Force on Energy Information, FE 1.24

Energy Management in the Federal **Government**, E 1.50

Federal **Government** Receipts from and Payments to (public) Special Analysis 4, PrEx 2.8/a7

Federal Real Property and Personal Property Inventory Report of the United States **Government** Covering its Properties Located in the U.S., in the Territories, and Overseas, as of June 30 (year), Y 4.G 74/7:P 94

Federal Specifications Board, United States **Government** Master Specifications, C 13.24

Final Report of the SEC **Government**-Business Forum on Small Business Capital Formation, SE 1.35/2

Financial Statistics of State and Local **Government**, C 3.49, C 3.49/2

Fire Loss to **Government** Property, GS 1.14/2

Foreign Affairs Research, a Directory of **Government** Resources, S 1.2:F 76a/4

Foreign Aid by the U.S. **Government**, C 18.279

Foreign Credits by United States **Government**, C 43.11/2

Foreign Credits by United States Government, Status of Active Foreign Credits of United States **Government** and of International Organizations, T 1.45

Foreign Grants and Credits by the United States **Government**, C 43.11

Foreign Transactions of U.S. **Government**, C 18.278

General Real and Personal Property Inventory Report (Civilian and Military) of the U.S. **Government** Covering Its Properties Located in the U.S., in the Territories, and Overseas, As of June 30 {year}, Y 4.G 74/7:P 94

Government Depository Libraries, Y 4.P 93/1:D 44

Government Employment, C 56.209/2

Government Employment GE (series), C 3.140/2

Government Ethics Newsgram, Y 3.Et 3:15

Government Finances and Employment at a Glance, C 3.191/3

Government Inventions for Licensing, C 51.9/23

Government Life Insurance Programs for Veterans and Servicemen, VA 1.46

Government National Mortgage Association, GNMA, Annual Report, HH 1.1/7

Government Organization Handbooks, GS 4.109/2

Government Organization Manuals, a Bibliography, LC 1.12/2:G 74

Government Organizations, C 3.171

Government Paper Specification Standards, Y 4.P 93/1:7, Y 4.P 93/1:7/2

Government Printing and Binding Regulations, Y 4.P 93/1:6

Government Reports Announcements, C 51.9/3

Government Reports Announcements and Index, C 51.9/3

Government Reports Annual Index, C 51.9/4

Government Reports Index, C 51.9

Government Reports Index, Quarterly Cumulative, C 51.9/2

Government Reports Topical Announcements, C 51.7/5

Government Salary Tables, T 13.6

Government Vehicle Operators Guide to Service Stations for Gasoline, Oil and Lubrication, D 7.6/7-2

Improved Manpower Management in Federal **Government**, Y 4.P 84/10:M 31/5

Index of Activities of Federal **Government**, T 51.7/21

Information Governing Distribution of **Government** Publications and Price Lists, GP 3.18

International Journal of **Government** Auditing, GA 1.38

Keywords Index to U.S. **Government** Technical Reports, C 41.21/5

Local **Government** Employment in Major County Areas, C 3.140/2-6

Local **Government** Finances in Major County Areas, C 3.191/2-9

Management of the United States **Government**, Fiscal Year (date), PrEx 2.8/9

Marketing Moves, the Marketing Bulletin from the U.S. **Government** Printing Office, GP 1.38

Medical Catalog of Audiovisual Materials Produced by the United States **Government**, GS 4.17/6

Memorandum for Japanese **Government**, M 105.23, D 102.14

Military **Government** of Ryukyu Islands: Ryukyu Statistical Bulletin, D 102.19

Military **Government** Regulations, W 1.72/4

Military **Government** Weekly Field Reports, W 1.81

Military **Government** Weekly Information Bulletins, W 1.72/5, M 101.16, M 105.8

Military **Government**, Austria, Report of United States Commissioner, W 1.74, M 105.10

Minorities and Women in State and Local **Government**, Y 3.Eq 2:12-4

Monthly Catalog of United States **Government** Publications, GP 3.8

Monthly Catalog of United States **Government** Publications, Periodical Supplement, GP 3.8/8-8

Monthly Statement of Receipts and Outlays of the United States **Government**, T 1.5/2

Municipal **Government** Wage Surveys, L 2.105

Periodic Supplement, Selected United States **Government** Publications, GP 3.17/3

Personnel Bulletins **Government** Printing Office, GP 1.20

Policy Briefs, Action Guides for Legislators and **Government** Executives, J 28.8/2

Political Activity of **Government** Personnel Commission, Y 3.P 75

Price List, Selective Bibliography of **Government** Research Reports and Translations, C 41.21/3

Price Lists of **Government** Publications, GP 3.19

Prices and Yields of Public Marketable Securities Issued by United States **Government** and by Federal Agencies, T 68.7

Productivity Statistics for Federal **Government** Functions, Fiscal Year, L 2.119/2

Quarterly Report, **Government** Sponsored and **Government** Supported Research, Social Sciences and Interdisciplinary Areas, NS 1.9

Real Property Owned by the Federal **Government** in {various States}, EP 4.15

Receipts and Disbursements of **Government** Consolidated into Bureau of Accounts, Fiscal Service in Treasury Department by President's Reorganization Plan no. 3, T 9.11

Reference List of Audiovisual Materials Produced by the United States **Government**, GS 4.2:Au 2

Regulations for **Government** of Ordnance Department (general), W 34.12/1

Regulations for **Government** of Public Health and Marine Hospital Service, T 27.8

Regulations for **Government** of United States Army General Hospital, W 44.15

Regulatory Program of the United States **Government**, PrEx 2.30

Report of United States **Government** to the Food and Agricultural Organization of the United Nations, A 67.35

Report on Foreign Currencies Held by the U.S. **Government** Fiscal Year and Transition Quarter, T 63.118/2

Report on U.S. **Government** Research and Studies in the Field of Arms Control and Disarmament Matters, AC 1.14

Report on Washington Conference of Mayors and Other Local **Government** Executives on National Security, FCD 1.18

Renewing **Government**, HH 1.1/10

Review of Selected U.S. **Government** Research and Development Reports, OTR-(series), C 13.49

Rules and Regulations for **Government** and Discipline of United States Penitentiaries, J 1.16

Rules of the Committee on **Government** Operations, Y 4.G 74/7-10

Safety Bulletins **Government** Printing Office, GP 1.24

Salary Tables, Executive Branch of the **Government**, CS 1.73, PM 1.9

Scientific and Technical Personnel in the Federal **Government**, NS 1.22:G 74

Selected United States **Government** Publications, GP 3.17, GP 3.17/2

Semi-Monthly Military **Government** Report for U.S. Occupied Area of Germany, M 105.21

Significant Arrearages Due the United States **Government** and Unpaid 90 Days or More by Official Foreign Obligors, T 1.45/5

South Korea Interim **Government** Activities, M 105.13

Standardized **Government** Civilian Allowance Regulations, Allowance Circulars, S 1.76

Standardized **Government** Post Differential Regulations, Differential Circulars, S 1.76/2

Standardized Regulations (**Government** Civilians, Foreign Areas), S 1.76/3

State and Local **Government** Collective Bargaining Settlements, L 2.45/4

State and Local **Government** Employment and Payrolls, L 2.41/4

State and Local **Government** Functional Profile Series, Y 3.Eq 2:14

State and Local **Government** Quarterly Employment Survey, C 3.140

State and Local **Government** Special Studies, C 3.145, C 56.231

State **Government** Finances, C 3.191/2-3

State **Government** Tax Collections, C 3.191/2-8

Statistical Bulletins Military **Government** of Ryukyu Islands, D 102.19

Statistical Programs of the United States **Government**, PrEx 2.10/3

Status of Active Foreign Credits of the United States **Government**: Foreign Credits by United States **Government** Agencies, T 1.45/2

Studies on Administrative Management in **Government** of U.S., Y 3.P 92/3:7

Summary of Foreign **Government** Environmental Reports, EP 1.21/4

Summary of State **Government** Finances in (year), C 56.209, C 3.191/2

Summation of United States Army Military **Government** Activities in Korea, W 1.76

Summation of United States Army Military **Government** Activities in Ryukyu Islands, W 1.78, M 105.12

Surplus **Government** Property Special Listings, FL 5.13, Pr 33.209

Surplus **Government** Property Special Offerings, Y 3.W 19/8:9

Synopsis of U.S. **Government** Proposed Procurement and Contract Awards, C 18.284

Telephone Directory **Government** Printing Office, GP 1.39

U.S. **Government** Books, GP 3.17/5

U.S. **Government** Campaign to Promote Production, Sharing, and Proper Use of Food, Pr 32.5019

U.S. **Government** Depository Libraries Directory, Y 4.P 93/1-10

U.S. **Government** Environmental Datafiles & Software, C 51.20

U.S. **Government** Films for Public Educational Use, FS 5.234:34006, HE 5.234:34006

U.S. **Government** Printing Office Style Manual, GP 1.23/4:St 9

U.S. **Government** Program to Promote Production, Sharing and Proper Use of Food, Pr 32.5019/2

U.S. **Government** Purchasing and Sales Directory Guide for Selling or Buying in the **Government** Market, SBA 1.13/3

U.S. **Government** Purchasing Directory, SBA 1.13

U.S. **Government** Research, C 41.21, C 51.9/3

U.S. **Government** Salary Tables, Post-Office Dept, P 1.15

U.S. **Government** Securities Yields and Prices, FR 1.46/2

U.S. **Government** Security Yields and Prices (Yields in per cent per annum), FR 1.46/3

U.S. **Government** Specifications Directory, SBA 1.13

U.S. **Government** Working Group on Electronic Commerce, C 1.1/7

U.S. Supreme Court, **Government** Briefs in Cases Argued by Solicitor General, Indexes, J 1.19/3

U.S. Supreme Court, **Government** Briefs in Cases Argued, Indexes, J 1.19/4

Union Pacific Railway, **Government** Directors, Annual Reports, 1864-1898, I 1.30

Union Recognition in the Federal **Government**, Statistical Summary, PM 1.47

United States **Government** Annual Report, T 63.101/2

United States **Government** Flight Information Publication: Pacific Chart Supplement, C 55.427

United States **Government** Interdepartmental Standards, T 51.11/7

United States **Government** Manual, GS 4.109, AE 2.108/2

United States **Government** Organization Manual, GS 4.109

United States **Government**, Annual Report, Appendix, T 1.1/3

Weekly **Government** Abstracts, WGA-(series), C 51.9/5C 51.9/30

Weekly List of Selected U.S. **Government** Publications, GP 3.17

Government's

U.S. **Government's** Preferred Products List, D 1.69

Government-Owned

Charter Report, **Government-Owned** Dry-Cargo Vessels, Operated by Bareboat Charters and/or Agents of Maritime Administration, C 39.215

Government-Supported

Government-Supported Research on Foreign Affairs, Current Project Information, S 1.101/10

Government-Supported Research, International Affairs, Research Completed and in Progress, S 1.101/9

Governmental

Governmental Finances, C 3.191/2, C 56.209

Governmental Finances in United States, C 3.191

Summary Characteristics for **Governmental** Units and Standard Metropolitan Statistical Areas (series), C 3.223/23:

Summary of **Governmental** Finances in (year), C 56.209, C 3.191/2

Governments

Census of **Governments**, C 3.145/4, C 56.247/2

Census of **Governments**; Advance Release CGA (series), C 3.145/2

Census of **Governments**; Announcements, C 3.145/3

Census of **Governments**; Preliminary Reports, C 56.247

Changing Public Attitudes on **Governments** and Taxes, Y 3.Ad 9/8:17

Chiefs of State and Cabinet Members of Foreign **Governments**, CR CS- (series), PrEx 3.11/2

Construction Expenditure of State and Local **Governments**, BC (series), C 56.223, C 3.215/10

Construction Expenditure of State and Local **Governments**, GC (series), C 56.223

EEO for State and Local **Governments** (series), CS 1.76/2

EEO Information on Equal Opportunity for State and Local **Governments**, PM 1.18/2

Employee Benefits in State and Local **Governments**, L 2.3/10-2

Finances of Employee-Retirement Systems of State and Local **Governments** in (year), C 56.209, C 3.191/2

Financial Statistics of State **Governments**, C 3.29

Personnel Management Reform, Progress in State and Local **Governments**, PM 1.11/3

Problem-solving Technology for State and Local **Governments**, C 51.9/30

Special Analysis of Federal Aid to State and Local **Governments** in Budget, PrEx 2.8/a3

Unemployment Rates for States and Local **Governments**, BLS/PWEDA/QR- (series), L 2.111/3

Visa Requirements of Foreign **Governments**, S 1.2:V 82/2

Governor

Alaska, **Governor**, Annual Report, I 1.5

Hawaii, **Governor**, Annual Reports, I 1.41

Idaho, **Governor**, Annual Reports, 1878 90, I 1.19

Montana, **Governor**, Annual Report, 1878 89, I 1.22

Monthly Report of the Military **Governor** for Germany (U.S.), M 105.7

New Mexico, **Governor**, Annual Reports, 1878n1912, I 1.24

Oklahoma, **Governor**, Annual Reports, 1891-1907, I 1.26

Utah, **Governor**, Annual Reports, I 1.32

Washington, **Governor**, Annual Reports, 1878-90, I 1.35

Governors

European Recovery Program; Joint Report of United States and United Kingdom Military **Governors**, M 105.18

Sales Finance Companies Federal Reserve System Board of **Governors**, FR 1.26

Volume and Composition of Individuals' Savings Federal Reserve System Board of **Governors**, FR 1.53

GP-PIA

GP-PIA Joint Research Bulletins, GP 1.25

GPO

Exhausted **GPO** Sales Publications Reference File, GP 3.22/3-3

GPO Access Training Manual, GP 3.29/2

GPO Bulletin, GP 1.19

GPO Depository Union List of Item Selections, GP 3.32/2

GPO Library Cataloging Transaction Tapes, GP 3.8/4

GPO Locator, GP 3.37

GPO Sales Publications Reference File, GP 3.22/3

GPO Sales Publications Reference File, Update, GP 3.22/3-2

List of Available USDA Publications for Sale from **GPO**, A 43.51

Lists USDA Publications for Sale by **GPO** Showing Date of Issue or Revision, GPO Stock Number, and Price, A 43.51

GPT

GPT Bulletins, FS 13.215

GR

GR 68 Quarterly Reports on Holdings of Retirement Systems, C 3.242

GR (series), I 27.72

Grade

Cotton **Grade** and Staple Reports, Georgia, A 36.27/1

Cotton **Grade** and Staple Reports, Texas and Oklahoma, A 36.27/2

Estimated **Grade** and Staple Length of Upland Cotton Ginned (by States), A 82.69

Estimated **Grade** and Staple Length of Upland Cotton Ginned in United States, A 88.11/7

Prices Received by Farmers for Manufacturing **Grade** Milk in Minnesota and Wisconsin, A 92.16/3

Rail-Highway **Grade**-Crossing Accidents, IC 1 acci.8

Rail-Highway-**Grade** Crossing Accident/Incidents Bulletin, TD 3.109

Graded

Meat **Graded** by Bureau of Agricultural Economics, A 36.190

Grades

Subject Offerings and Enrollments, **Grades** 912, Nonpublic Secondary Schools, FS 5.224:24012, HE 5.224:24012

United States Standards for **Grades** of {commodity}, A 88.6/2

United States Standards for **Grades** of {fruits, vegetables, etc.}, A 82.20

Grading

Job **Grading** System for Trades and Labor Occupations, CS 1.41/4:512-1, CS 1.42/2

Grading Service

Dairy Plants Surveyed and Approved for USDA **Grading Service**, A 88.14/12, A 103.12

Graduate

Cooperative **Graduate** Fellowship Program for Fiscal Year, Fellowship Awards {and} Program of Summer Fellowships for **Graduate** Teaching Assistants for Fiscal Year, NS 1.19/2

Council on **Graduate** Medical Education (General Publications), HE 20.9019

Faculty **Graduate** Study Program for Historically Black Colleges and Universities, NF 3.8/2-7

Graduate Education Bulletin, Uniformed Services University of the Health Sciences, D 1.67/2

Graduate Fellowship Announcement, TD 2.64/2

Graduate Fellowship Awards Announced by National Science Foundation, NS 1.19

Graduate Student Researchers Program, NAS 1.42/2

Graduate Students and Postdoctorates in Science and Engineering, NS 1.22/11

National Defense **Graduate** Fellowships, Graduate Programs, FS 5.255:55017, HE 5.255:55017

National Defense Graduate Fellowships, **Graduate** Programs, FS 5.255:55017, HE 5.255:55017

Notes on **Graduate** Studies and Research in Home Economics and Home Economics Education, A 1.53

Program Announcement, **Graduate** Research Fellowship Program, J 28.25

Quarterly **Graduate** Bulletin, D 5.210/2

Graduate School

Agriculture Department **Graduate School** Publications, A 1.42

Graduate School Announcement of Courses, C 13.41

Survey of **Graduate** Students and Postdoctorates in Science Engineer, NS 1.56

Graduates

Characteristics of Recent Science and Engineering **Graduates**, NS 1.22/8

Register of Officers and **Graduates** (triennial), W 12.12

Survey of College **Graduates**, ED 1.127

Grain

Bimonthly **Grain** Update, A 108.12/2

Brewers' Dried **Grain** Production, A 82.59/3

Capacity of Elevators, Reporting **Grain** Stocks, A 36.82

Clean Grain Notes for Cooperators in Clean **Grain** Program, A 43.30

Commercial **Grain** Stocks, A 88.18/2-2

Commercial **Grain** Stocks Reports, A 80.827, A 81.19, A 82.31, A 88.18/2

Commercial **Grain** Stocks {Revised Figures for Calendar Year}, A 88.18/2-2, A 82.31/2

Cotton and **Grain** Futures Acts, Commodity Exchange and Warehouse Acts and Other Laws Relating Thereto {August 7, 1916}, Y 1.2:C 82

Crop Production: Quarterly **Grain** Stocks in Farms, Revised Estimates, A 88.18/22

Distillers' Dried **Grain** Production, A 88.18/7, A 82.59/4

Feed **Grain** and Wheat Stabilization Program, A 82.37/3:F 32/2

Feed **Grain** Situation, A 36.87

Folders, **Grain** Standards, A 36.53

Grain and Feed Market News, A 88.18/4-2

Grain and **Grain** Products, C 18.72/4

Grain Crop Quality, (year) Crops, A 88.40/2:44

Grain Division News, A 88.18/27

Grain Inspection Manual, A 88.6/4:G 76

Grain Inspector's Letters, A 36.192

Grain Investigations {publications}, A 36.93

Grain Market News and Statistical Report, A 82.71, A 88.18

Grain Market News, Quarterly Summary and Statistics, A 88.18/21

Grain Standardization, A 19.11

Grain Stocks, A 105.20

Grain Transportation Prospect, A 88.68/2

Grain Transportation Report, A 88.68

Grain Transportation Situation, A 108.12

Grain, World Markets and Trade, A 67.18:FG

Official **Grain** Standards of the United States, A 88.6/2:G 761

Official United States Standards for **Grain**, A 104.6/2, A 113.10

Press Notices **Grain** Corporation, Y 3.W 56:15

Quality of **Grain** Crops Based on Inspected Receipts at Representative Markets, A 36.206

Stocks of **Grain** in All Positions, A 88.18/14

Stocks of **Grain** in Deliverable Positions for Chicago Board of Trade, Futures Contracts in Exchange-Approved and Federally Licensed Warehouses, as Reported by Those Warehouses, A 85.14, Y 3.C 73/5:10

Storage Capacity of Elevators Reporting Commercial **Grain** Stocks, A 88.18/15

Trade in **Grain** Futures, A 82.29

U.S. **Grain** Export Quality Report, Wheat, Corn, Soybeans, A 104.12/2-3

USSR **Grain** Situation and Outlook, A 67.18:SG

World Feed **Grain** Prospects, A 36.84/1

World **Grain** Situation and Outlook, A 67.18:FG

Grains

Brewers' Dried **Grains** Production, A 88.18/6

Brewers' Dried **Grains** United States Production and Stocks in Hands of Producers, A 88.18/6-2

Distillers' Dried **Grains**, United States, Production by Kinds by Months, A 88.18/7-2

Small **Grains**, Annual Summary and Crop Winter Wheat and Rye Seedings, A 105.20/6, A 92.42

Stocks of Feed **Grains**, A 36.174

Wheat, Rice, Feed **Grains**, Dry Peas, Dry Beans, Seeds, Hops, A 67.30:W 56

Grambo

Information Respecting the History, Conditions, and Prospects of the Indian Tribes of the United States, Philadelphia, Lippincott, **Grambo** & Co, I 20.2:In 2

Grand

Grand and Petit Juror Service in U.S. District Courts, Ju 10.13

Grand Canyon VFR Aeronautical Chart, TD 4.79/13-6

Grand Canyon

Grand Canyon VFR Aeronautical Chart, (general aviation), C 55.416/12-6

Grand Forks

Economic Resource Impact Statement **Grand Forks** Air Force Base, D 301.105/2

Grand Mesa

Recreation Guide to **Grand Mesa**, Uncompahgre and Gunnison National Forests, A 13.36/2-7

Grand Visions

Value of Exports, Including Reexports, by **Grand Visions** and Principal Countries, C 18.6/2

Grant

AHCPR **Grant** Announcement, HE 20.6519/2

Alcohol, Drug Abuse, Mental Health Research **Grant** Awards, HE 20.8016, HE 20.8118

Basic Educational Opportunity **Grant** Program Handbook, HE 19.108/4

Cancer Control **Grant** Review Committee, HE 20.3001/2:C 16/12

Community Development Block **Grant** Program Annual Reports, HH 1.46/3

Division of Social Sciences Quarterly **Grant** List, NS 1.10/5

Extramural **Grant** and Contract Awards by Principal Investigator/Contractor, HE 20.3176/3

Extramural **Grant** and Contract Awards by State, City Institution and Number, HE 20.3176/4

Grant Awards, TD 1.39

Handicapped Children's Education Program, **Grant** Announcements, ED 1.32/3

Research **Grant** Publications and Reports, I 67.13/2

Mental Health Research **Grant** Awards, Fiscal Year, HE 20.2423

Mental Health Training **Grant** Awards, FS 2.22/7-4

Museum Assessment Program, **Grant** Application and Information, NF 4.11

National Research Initiative Competitive **Grant** Program, A 94.24

National Sea **Grant** Program Annual Retreat Report, C 55.38/2

NCI **Grant** Supported Literature Index, HE 20.3179

Pell **Grant** Formula, ED 1.45/2

Pell **Grant** Payment Schedule, ED 1.45/3-2

Report of IPA **Grant** Activity, GS 1.94

Request for **Grant** Applications (series), HE 20.3220

Request for Research **Grant** Applications (series), HE 20.3864

Sea **Grant** Annual Report, C 55.38

Sequoia and General **Grant** National Parks, Annual Reports, I 1.29

State and Local **Grant** Awards, EP 1.35/2

URA Demonstration **Grant** Summaries, HH 7.18

Urban Development Action **Grant** Program, HH 1.46/5

Urban Renewal Demonstration **Grant** Program, Project Directory, HH 7.2:G 76

Water and Sewer Facilities **Grant** Program, HUD Information Series, HH 1.17

Grant-In-Aid

Catalog of Federal **Grant-In-Aid** Programs to State and Local Governments, Y 3.Ad 9/8:20

Grant-in-aid for Fisheries Program Activities, C 55.323

Grantee

NIST-GCR **Grantee**/Contractor Report, C 13.57/2

Grantees

Abstracts from Annual and Technical Reports Submitted by USAMRDC Contractors/**Grantees**, D 104.23

Directory CAP {Community Actions Programs} **Grantees**, PrEx 10.2:C 73-3

Educational and Cultural Exchange Program Fiscal Year, American **Grantees**, S 1.67/2

Family Planning **Grantees** and Clinics, Directory, HE 20.5119/3

Family Planning **Grantees**, Delegates, and Clinics Directory, HE 20.33

Grants

Application for **Grants**, Formula Grants to Local Educational Agencies, ED 1.410

Application for **Grants** under Adult Indian Education Programs, ED 1.52

Application for New **Grants** Under Certain Direct Grant Programs, ED 1.214

Application for **Grants** under Fulbright-Hays Foreign Curriculum Consultants, ED 1.59

Application for **Grants** under Fulbright-Hays Group Projects Abroad, ED 1.62

Application for **Grants** under Handicapped Children's Early Education Program Demonstration and Auxiliary Activities, ED 1.50/3

Application for **Grants** under Indian Education Program, ED 1.51

Application for **Grants** under Post Secondary Education Programs for Handicapped Persons, ED 1.50/2

Application for **Grants** under Rehabilitation Research, Field Initiated Research, ED 1.70/4

Application for **Grants** under Strengthening Research Library Resources Program, ED 1.53

Application for **Grants** under the Cooperative Education Program, ED 1.70/3

Application for **Grants** under the Endowment Grant Program, ED 1.70/2

Application for **Grants** under the Secretary's Discretionary Program, ED 1.63

Application for **Grants** under the Secretary's Discretionary Program for Mathematics, Science, Computer Learning and Critical Foreign Languages, ED 1.64

Application for **Grants** under Title VI of the Higher Education Act of 1965, as Amended, ED 1.56, ED 1.57

Application for **Grants** under Upward Bound Program, ED 1.69

Application Kit Tribal Management **Grants**, etc., FY [date] Tribal Management Grant Program Announcement, HE 20.317/2

Building for Clean Water Progress Report on Federal Incentive **Grants** for Municipal Waste Treatment Fiscal Year, FS 2.64/6

Building for Clean Water Report on Federal Incentive **Grants** for Municiapl Waste Treatment, FS 16.9

Bureau of Radiological Health Research **Grants** Program, Fiscal Year, (date), HE 20.4116

Challenge **Grants** Application Guidelines, NF 2.8/2-3

Challenge **Grants** Program Guidelines and Application Materials, NF 3.8/2-4

Continuation Application for **Grants** under Special Services for Disadvantage Students Program, ED 1.60

Continuation Application for **Grants** under Talent Search Program, ED 1.55

Current Research Project **Grants**, HE 20.3111

Directory Former **Grants** Associates, HE 20.3037/3

Directory of **Grants**, Awards, and Loans, HE 20.6111, HE 20.6612

DRG {Division of Research **Grants**} Newsletter, HE 20.3022

Federal Emergency Relief Administration **Grants**, Y 3.F 31/5:32

Federal Emergency Relief Administration **Grants** Distributed According to Programs and Periods for which **Grants** were Made, Y 3.F 31/5:33

Federal **Grants** and Contracts for Unclassified Research in Life Sciences, NS 1.10

Federal **Grants** and Contracts for Unclassified Research in Physical Sciences, NS 1.10/2

FIPSE, Application For **Grants** Under the Comprehensive Program,, ED 1.23/2

Food and Agriculture Competitively Awarded Research and Education **Grants**, A 106.42

Foreign **Grants** and Credits by the United States Government, C 43.11

Funding Opportunities at NIE, **Grants** Competitions and Requests for Proposals in Fiscal Year, HE 19.216/2

Grants Administration Manual, EP 1.8/2, HE 1.6/7

Grants Administration Manual Circular, HE 1.6/7-2

Grants Administration Report, FS 1.31, HE 1.31

Grants and Awards for Fiscal Year (date), NS 1.10/4

Grants Competitions and RFPS: Planned NIE Activities During the Fiscal Year, HE 19.216

Grants Contract Reports, Experimental Technology Incentives Program, GCR-ETIP (series), C 13.57/2

Grants for Training Construction Medical Libraries, HE 20.3013/5

Grants for Training, Construction, Cancer Control, Medical Libraries, HE 20.3013/5

Grants Policy Directives HE 1.6/7

Grants to Organizations, Application Forms, NF 2.15/2

Grants to Organizations, Application Guidelines, NF 2.15

Grants to Presenting Organizations, Special Touring Initiatives Application Guidelines, NF 2.8/2-29

Grants, Juvenile Delinquency Prevention and Control Act, HE 17.21

Grants, Preventive Services, Training, Technical Assistance and Information Services, HE 1.310

Health Care Financing, **Grants** and Contracts Reports, HE 22.19

Health Care Financing: **Grants** for Research and Demonstrations, Fiscal Year, HE 22.19/3

Institutional **Grants** for Science, NS 1.10/3

Instructional Equipment **Grants** Title VI-A, Higher Education Act of 1975, PL 89-329, HE 19.114

Instructions and Application for **Grants** under the Special Needs Program, ED 1.61

Instructions and Application for **Grants** under the Strengthening Program, ED 1.61/2

Juvenile Delinquency Prevention and Control Act of 1968, **Grants**, HE 17.811

Mental Retardation **Grants**, Fiscal Year, HE 1.23/3

Monthly Listing of Awards for Construction **Grants** for Wastewater Treatment Works, EP 1.56

National Leadership **Grants**, Grant Application & Guidelines, NF 4.11/2

NCHSR Program Solicitation, **Grants** for Health Services Dissertation Research, HE 20.6512/8-2

NCI **Grants** Awarded, by Principal Investigator, HE 20.3176/2

NCI **Grants** Awarded, Fiscal Year (date), HE 20.3176

NEH Travel to Collections, Small **Grants** for Research Travel to Libraries, Archives, Museums, and Other Repositories, NF 3.19

New Application for **Grants** under Research in Education of the Handicapped, ED 1.50

New **Grants** and Awards, HE 20.3034

NIGMS Research **Grants**, HE 20.3465, HE 20.3465/2

NINCDS Index to Research **Grants** and Awards, HE 20.3516

NINDS Index to Research **Grants** and Contracts, HE 20.3516

OHD, **Grants** Administration Manual, TN-(series), HE 1.709

PHA **Grants** Administration Manual, HE 20.8/2

PHS **Grants** Policy Memorandum, HE 1.6/7-3, HE 20.8/3

Project Register, Waste Water Treatment Construction **Grants**, EP 1.9/2, EP 1.56/2

Public Health Service **Grants** and Awards, HE 20.3013

Publications and Final Reports on Contracts and **Grants**, C 55.13/2-2

Quarterly Awards Listing **Grants** Assistance Programs, EP 1.35

Research (year), Annotated List of Research and Demonstration **Grants**, HE 17.15

Research and Training **Grants** and Awards of Public Health Service, FS 2.22/8

Research **Grants** Index, Fiscal Year, FS 2.22/7-2

Research **Grants** Index, HE 20.3013/2

Research **Grants**, Data Book, HE 20.3516/2

Research **Grants**, Environmental Engineering and Food Protection, FS 2.300/3

Research **Grants**, Training Awards, Summary Tables, HE 20.3516/3

Small-scale Appropriate Energy Technology **Grants** Program, E 1.76

State Municipal Project Priority Lists, **Grants** Assistance Programs, EP 1.56/3

State Priority Lists for Construction **Grants** for Wastewater Treatment Works, Fiscal Year (date), EP 1.56/4

State Solid Waste Planning **Grants**, Agencies, and Progress, Report of Activities, EP 3.10

Study **Grants** For College Teachers, NF 3.25

Subject Index of Current Research **Grants** and Contracts Administered by the National Heart, Lung, and Blood Institute, HE 20.3212

Summary of **Grants** and Contracts Active on June 30, (year), HE 20.6510

Summary of **Grants** and Contracts Administered by the National Center for Health Services Research and Development, HE 20.2116

UDAG **Grants** Total for Large and Small Communities, HH 1.99/5, HH 1.99/5-2

Urban Development Action **Grants**, HH 1.110

Visual Arts **Grants** to Organizations, NF 2.8/2-15

Wastewater Treatment Construction **Grants** Data Base, Public Law 92-500 Project Records, Grants Assistance Programs, New Projects Funded During (Month), EP 1.56

Water Pollution Control Research and Training **Grants**, FS 2.64/7, I 67.13

Grants Pass

Area Wage Survey Summary Eugene-Springfield-Medford-Roseburg-Klamath Falls-**Grants Pass**, Oregon, L 2.122/37

Grants-In-Aid

Grants-In-Aid and Other Financial Assistance Programs, FS 1.6/6, HE 20.2016

Grants-In-Aid and Other Financial Assistance Programs, Health Services and Mental Health Administration, FS 2.317

Grants-In-Aid Catalogue, I 29.83

Land and Water Conservation Fund, **Grants-in-Aid** Program, Annual Report, I 29.107/2

Outdoor Recreation **Grants-In-Aid** Manual, I 66.8

Graphic

DRG Digital Raster **Graphic** (series), I 19.128

Graphic Notes and Supplemental Data, TD 4.12/4

Graphic Pamphlets GP (series), C 3.223/14

Graphic Portfolios, Charts, and Posters, W 1.52

Graphic Training Aids, W 1.53, D 101.21

Trend Report: **Graphic** Presentation of Public Assistance and Related Data, HE 17.612

Graphical

Graphical Supplement to Monthly Reports, IC 1 ste.33

Graphite

Graphite in (year), I 28.128/2

Natural **Graphite** in (year), I 28.128

Grassroots

Grassroots Development: Journal of the Inter-American Foundation, Y 3.In 8/25:15

Gravel

Crushed Stone and Sand and **Gravel** in the Quarter of, I 28.118/4

Injury Experience and Related Employment Data for Sand and **Gravel** Industry, I 28.108/2

MESA Safety Reviews: Injuries at Sand and **Gravel** Plants, I 69.10/3

Mineral Industry Surveys, Directory of Principal Construction Sand and **Gravel** Producers in the . . ., Annual Advanced Summary Supplement, I 19.138/3

Safety Competition, National Sand and **Gravel**, I 28.26/3

Sand and **Gravel** in (year), I 28.146

Sand and **Gravel** (Construction) in . . ., I 28.146/2

Graves

Graves Registration Service Bulletins, W 95.16

Gravimetry

Titrimetry, **Gravimetry**, Flame Photometry, Spectro Photometry, and Gas Evolution, C 13.46

Gray Cloth

Comparisons of International **Gray Cloth** Prices, C 18.59/1

GrayLit

GrayLit Network, E 1.137/3

Grazing

Annual **Grazing** Statistical Report, A 13.83

Digest of **Grazing** Decisions, I 53.15

Grazing Decisions, I 53.15

GRD

GRD Research Notes, Geophysics Research Directorate, D 301.45/16

GRD Technical Report, D 301.45/16-3

Great Britain

Combined Production and Resources Board, United States, **Great Britain**, and Canada, Y 3.C 73/3

Dental Research in the United States, Canada and **Great Britain**, Fiscal Year (Date), HE 20.3402:D 43

Great Britain and United States Claims Commission, S 3.8

Great Circle

Great Circle (8) Sailing and Polar Charts, D 5.345

Great Circle (58) Tracking Charts, D 5.346

Great Lakes

Biennial Report Under the **Great Lakes** Water Quality Agreement of 1978, Y 3.In 8/28:11

Catalog of Charts of the **Great Lakes** and Connecting Waters, Also Lake Champlain, New York Canals, Minnesota-Ontario Border Lakes, D 103.208

Charts of **Great Lakes**, W 33.7/2

Coast Charts of **Great Lakes**, W 33.7/3

Committee on the Assessment of Human Health Effects of **Great Lakes** Water Quality: Annual Report, Y 3.In 8/28:15

Domestic Oceanborne and **Great Lakes** Commerce of the United States, C 39.222

Focus on **Great Lakes** Water Quality, Y 3.In 8/28:17

Great Lakes, TD 5.9:4, C 55.422:6

Great Lakes Environmental Research Laboratory: Annual Report, C 55.620

Great Lakes Fisheries, C 55.309/2

Great Lakes Intercom, TD 4.26/2

Great Lakes Levels Update, D 103.116/2

Great Lakes Pilot; Lake Survey Office, D 103.203

Great Lakes Pilot; National Ocean Survey, C 55.420

Great Lakes Pilotage Administration, C 1.47

Great Lakes Pilotage Regulations and Rules and Orders, C 1.47:R 26

Great Lakes Region Air Traffic Activity, TD 4.19/5

Great Lakes Region Aviation Systems, Ten Year Plan, TD 4.33/4

Great Lakes Research Advisory Board: Annual Report, Y 3.In 8/28:10

Great Lakes Science Advisory Board: Annual Report, Y 3.In 8/28:12, Y 3.In 8/28:16

Great Lakes Water Levels, C 55.420/2

Great Lakes Water Quality Annual Report, Y 3.In 8/28:9

Great Lakes-Saint Lawrence Seaway Winter Navigation Board: Annual Report, D 103.1/3

International Field Year for the **Great Lakes**: Proceedings, IFYGL Symposium, Annual Meetings of the American Geophysical Union, C 55.21/3

Merchant Fleet in Service on **Great Lakes**, C 27.9/5

Meterological Chart of the **Great Lakes**, A 29.13, A 29.13/2

Monthly Bulletin of Lake Levels for the **Great Lakes**, D 103.116

Notice to Mariners on **Great Lakes**, Special, N 6.13

Notice to Mariners Relating to **Great Lakes** and Tributary Waters West of Montreal, D 203.9, TD 5.10

Notice to Mariners, **Great Lakes**, C 9.41, T 47.20, N 24.13, T 6.12

Publications **Great Lakes** Pilotage Administration, C 1.47

Radio Aids to Navigation, **Great Lakes**, United States and Canada, T 47.26/2

Statistical Report, **Great Lakes** Pilotage, C 1.47:St 2

Technical Plan for the **Great Lakes** Environmental Research Laboratory, C 55.620/2

U.S. **Great Lakes** Ports, Statistics for Overseas and Canadian Waterborne Commerce, TD 6.10

United States and Canadian **Great Lakes** Fleets, C 39.214

United States Waterborne Foreign Commerce, **Great Lakes** Area {year}, C 3.211/2

Great Plains

Soil Organic Matter Levels in the Central **Great Plains**, A 77.15/3

Wind Erosion Conditions, **Great Plains**, Summary of Local Estimates, A 57.47

Great Smokey Mountains

Naturalist Program, **Great** Smokey Mountains National Park, I 29.60/2

Greater

Mental Health Resources in the **Greater** Washington Area, HE 20.8119

Greatfully

Greatfully Yours, HE 20.3625

Green

Current Business Reports; **Green** Coffee, Inventories, Imports, Roastings, BG (series), C 56.219/2

Green Coffee Inventories and Roastings, C 3.236

Green Roadsides, TD 2.30/16-2

Green Book

Green Book, Overview of Entitlement Programs, Y 4.W 36:10-7

Greenbelt

Telephone Directory Goddard Space Flight Center, **Greenbelt**, Md, NAS 1.24/2

Greenhouse

Emissions of **Greenhouse** Gases in the United States, E 3.59

Greenhouse Gas Volunteer (Newsletter), E 3.59/3

Inside the **Greenhouse**, EP 1.114

Inventory of U.S. **Greenhouse** Gas Emissions and Sinks, EP 1.115

Voluntary Reporting of **Greenhouse** Gases Annual Report, E 3.59/2

Greenland

East Coast of North America and South America (including **Greenland**), C 4.15/4

Nautical Charts and Publications, Region 3, Western Europe, Iceland, **Greenland**, and the Arctic, C 55.440:3

NIMA Nautical Charts, Public Sale Region 3, Western Europe, Iceland, **Greenland**, and the Arctic, TD 4.82:3

Pilot Chart of **Greenland** and Barnets Seas, N 6.15/4

Tide Tables, High and Low Water Predictions East Coast of North and South America Including **Greenland**, C 55.421/2

Greenville
 Area Wage Survey Summary **Greenville**-Spartanburg, South Carolina, L 2.122/40-2

Gridpoints
 Gridpoints, NAS 1.97

Grievances
 Quarterly Report on Private **Grievances** and Redresses, E 1.73, FE 1.26

Grissom
 Economic Resource Impact Statement 305th Air Refueling Wing, **Grissom** Air Force Base, Indiana, D 301.105/8
 Strategic Air Command, **Grissom** Air Force Base Telephone Directory, D 301.104/6

Grist
 Grist, I 70.22/2
 Index to Design, **Grist**, Trends, I 70.22/4
 Park Practice **Grist**, I 29.72

Grits
 Corn (Hominy) **Grits** for Domestic Distribution, A 82.3/4

Grizzly
 Yellowstone **Grizzly** Bear Investigations, Annual Report of the Interagency Study Team, I 29.94

Grocers
 Stocks of Evaporated and Condensed Milk Held by Wholesale **Grocers**, A 88.14/5

Grocery
 Food and **Grocery** Bulletins, Y 3.N 21/8:15
 Trends in **Grocery** Trade, C 3.183

Gross
 Farm Production, Disposition, Cash Receipts and **Gross** Income, Turkeys, A 88.15/16, A 105.35/2
 Percent Changes in **Gross** Average Hourly Earnings Over Selected Periods, L 2.63/2, L 2.63/3
 Percent Changes in **Gross** Hourly and Weekly Earnings over Selected Periods, L 2.63

Gross Income
 Chickens and Eggs, Farm Production, Disposition, Cash Receipts and **Gross Income**, Chickens on Farms, Commercial Broilers, by States, A 88.15/18
 Chickens and Eggs, Farm Production, Disposition, Cash Receipts and **Gross Income**, A 9.9/3
 Farm Value, **Gross Income**, and Cash Income from Farm Production, A 36.125

Ground
 Ground Accident Abstracts, D 301.53
 Ground Archaeology and Ethmography in the Public Interest, I 29.59/5-2
 Ground Water Issue, EP 1.43/2
 Report on High Speed **Ground** Transportation Act of 1965, TD 1.10
 Review of Soviet **Ground** Forces, D 5.209
 Technical Notes Department of the Air Force Air Proving **Ground** Center, D 301.45/50
 U.S. Army Electronic Proving **Ground**, USAEPG-SIG (series), D 111.12
 Wheat **Ground** and Wheat-Milling Products, by States, C 3.117
 Wheat **Ground** and Wheat-Milling Products, C 3.116
 Wheat **Ground** and Wheat-Milling Products, Merchant and Other Mills, C 3.118

Ground-Water
 Basic Data Series **Ground-Water** Releases (series), I 19.82
 Ground-Water Levels in the United States, I 19.13

Grounds
 Historic Structure and **Grounds** Report (series), I 29.88/4

Groundwater
 Groundwater Recharge Advisory, I 27.80

Group
 Commodities Included in (various) Products **Group** for Revised Wholesale Price Index, L 2.61/3
 Group Services Bulletins, Pr 32.4232
 Interagency Advisory **Group**: Annual Report, CS 1.87
 Meeting of the Canada-United States Interparliamentary **Group**, Y 4.In 8/16:11
 Photoelastic **Group** Reports, I 27.33
 Platinum **Group** Metals in (year), I 28.77/2
 Platinum **Group** Metals, I 28.77

Registered **Group**-Joint Apprenticeship Programs in Construction Industry (by trades), L 23.9
Report Coordinating **Group** Annual Report to the Securities and Exchange Commission, SE 1.32
Report, Civil Service Requirement, Federal Employees' **Group** Life Insurance, Federal Employees Health Benefits, Retired Federal Employees Health Benefits, Fiscal Year (date), CS 1.29/3
Servicemen's **Group** Life Insurance Program, Annual Report, VA 1.46/2
Solid Tumor Virus Working **Group**, HE 20.3001/2:T 83/2
Special Notice Concerning Basic Agreements Teleprocessing Services Program (TSP) Industrial **Group** 737, Industrial Class 7374, GS 12.13
Steam Generator **Group** Project, Y 3.N 88:25-10
Systems Engineering **Group**, Research and Technology Division, Air Force Systems Command, Wright-Patterson Air Force Base, Ohio, Technical Documentary Report No. SEG TDR, D 301.45/48
Tumor Virus Detection Working **Group**, HE 20.3001/2:T 83
Ultraviolet Radiation and Skin Cancer Working **Group**, HE 20.3001/2:R 11/2
Wave Propagation **Group** Reports, Pr 32.413/6
World Hunger Working **Group**, Pr 39.8:W 89

Group Projects
 Application for Grants under Fulbright-Hays **Group Projects** Abroad, ED 1.62

Grouped
 Grouped Interest Guides, HE 20.8311/3

Grouping
 U.S. Exports, Country by Commodity **Grouping**, C 1.64:420
 United States General Imports of Textile Manufactures, Except Cotton and Wool, **Grouping** by Country of Origin and Schedule a Commodity by Country of Origin, TQ-2501, C 3.164/2-7
 United States General Imports of Wool Manufacture Except Floor Coverings, Quantity Totals in Terms of Equivalent Square Yards in Country of Origin by Commodity **Grouping** Arrangement, TQ-2203, C 3.164/2-6
 United States General Imports of Wool Manufacture Except for Floor Coverings, Country of Origin by Wool **Grouping**, TQ- 2202, C 3.164/2-5

Groupings
 General Import, World Area by Commodity **Groupings**, C 56.210:155
 Statistical Analysis of World's Merchant Fleets Showing Age, Size, Speed, and Draft by Frequency **Groupings**, As of (date), C 39.224
 U.S. Exports, Country by Commodity **Groupings**, C 3.164:420
 U.S. Exports, Geographic Area, Country, Schedule B Commodity **Groupings**, and Method of Transportation, C 3.164:455
 U.S. Exports, Schedule B Commodity **Groupings**, Geographic Area, Country, and Method of Transportaion, C 3.164:450
 U.S. Exports, World Area by Schedule E Commodity **Groupings**, C 3.164:455
 U.S. General Imports Geographic Area, Country, Schedule A Commodity **Groupings**, and Method of Transporation, C 3.164:155
 U.S. General Imports Schedule A Commodity **Groupings**, Geographic Area, Country, and Method of Transportation, C 3.164:150
 U.S. General Imports World Area and Country of Origin by Schedule A Commodity **Groupings**, C 3.164:155

Groups
 Consumer Price Index, Price Indexes for Selected Items and **Groups**, L 2.38/4
 Forest Service Films Available on Loan for Educational Purposes to Schools, Civic **Groups**, Churches, Television, A 13.55
 Groups with Historically High Incidences of Unemployment, L 36.12
 Index Numbers of Wholesale Prices by **Groups** and Subgroups of Commodities, L 2.49/3
 PHS Public Advisory **Groups**, Authority, Structures, Functions, HE 20.2:Ad 9/2

Potatoes and Sweetpotatoes, Estimates by States and Seasonal **Groups**, A 88.12/19
Recapitulation by Carrier **Groups**, Certified Air Carriers, C 31.233
Reports of Technical Study **Groups** on Soviet Agriculture, A 1.94
Research Relating to Special **Groups** of Children, FS 3.220/2, FS 14.114/2
Roster of Members of PHS Public Advisory **Groups**, Councils, Committees, Boards, Panels, Study Sections, HE 20.2:Ad 9/3
Schedule T. Statistical Classification of Imports into U.S. Arranged in Shipping Commodity **GROUPS**., C 3.150:T
Schedule X. Statistical Classification of Domestic and Foreign Merchandise Exported from United States by Air Arranged in Shipping Commodity **Groups**, C 3.150:X
Schedule Y. Statistical Classification of Imports into United States Arranged in Shipping Commodity **Groups**, C 3.150:Y
Statistical Classification of Imports into U.S. Arranged in Shipping Commodity **Groups**, C 3.150:T, C 3.150:Y
Statistics for Industry **Groups** and Industries, C 3.24/9-7
Wage Trends for Occupational **Groups** in Metropolitan Areas, Summary Release, L 2.86/2
Wholesale Price Index (1947-49=100), Indexes for **Groups**, Subgroups, and Project Classes of Commodities, L 2.61/2

Growing
 National Shellfish Register of Classified **Growing** Waters, C 55.441

Growth
 BDSA Industry **Growth** Studies, C 41.90/4
 Economic **Growth** Trends {by region}, S 18.37
 Patterns of Industrial **Growth** (series), C 41.90/5
 Report on National **Growth** and Development, PrEx 15.9
 Task Force on Economic **Growth**, Pr 37.8:Ec 7

GS
 Coast and Geodetic Survey C & **GS** Update, C 55.51

GSA
 GSA Bulletin FPR, Federal Procurement, Gs 1.6/5-3
 GSA FIRMR/FAR Regulations, GS 12.15/2
 GSA Handbooks (numbered), GS 1.6/9
 GSA Interagency Training Center Newsletter, GS 1.26/3
 GSA News, GS 1.20
 GSA Stockpile Information, GS 1.21
 GSA Subcontracting Directory, GS 1.31
 GSA Supply Catalog, GS 2.10/6
 GSA Supply Catalog Change Bulletin, GS 2.10/6-3
 GSA Training Center Catalog and Schedule, GS 1.26, GS 1.26/2-2

GSO
 GSO Newsline, S 1.144

GSS-OCS
 Outer Continental Shelf Standard. **GSS-OCS** (series), I 19.73

GSSR
 General Salary Stabilization Regulations **GSSR** (series), ES 4.6/2

Guam
 Medicare Hospital Mortality Information; Vol. 7, Texas - **Guam**, HE 22.34

Guarantee
 Monthly Summary of Export Credit **Guarantee** Program Activity, A 67.47, A 67.18:ECG

Guaranteed
 Composite List of Eligible Institutions for **Guaranteed** Loans for College Students, Higher Education Act of 1965, FS 5.83, HE 5.83

Guarantees
 Statement of Active Loans and Financial **Guarantees**, Y 3.Ex 7/3:12

Guaranties
 Cumulative Report of All Specific Risk Investment **Guaranties** Issued Since the Beginning of the Program through, S 18.26/3
 Quarterly Report of All Investment **Guaranties** Issued, S 18.26

Guaranty
 PBGC {Pension Benefit **Guaranty** Corporation} Fact Sheets, L 1.51/5

Guard
  Interior **Guard** Duty, Lesson Assignment Sheets, W 3.50/7
  Posters National **Guard** Bureau, D 12.14
  Wolverine **Guard**, D 102.84
Guatemalan
  Honduran-**Guatemalan** Boundary Commission, 1918, S 3.25
Guidance
  Audit Legal Letter **Guidance**, PrEx 2.34
  Bibliographies **Guidance** and Student Personnel Section, FS 5.16/2
  Child **Guidance** Leaflets, Series on Eating, for Parents, FS 3.211
  Child **Guidance** Leaflets, Series on Eating, for Staff, L 5.51/2
  CSA **Guidance** (series), CSA 1.8/3
  Directory, State Department of Education Personnel for **Guidance**, Counseling, and Testing, FS 5.255:25037:A, HE 5.255:25037:A
  Federal **Guidance** for State and Local Civil Defense, D 14.8/5, D 119.8/3
  GAO Manual for **Guidance** of Federal Agencies, GA 1.6/1
  Guide Lines, **Guidance** and Pupil Personnel Service, FS 5.54
  Information **Guidance** Series, D 2.17
  Office of Water Operating **Guidance** and Accountability System, EP 2.29
  Operating Year **Guidance**, EP 1.8/11
  Planning Your Career, Vocational **Guidance** Series, I 16.67
  Water Quality Management **Guidance**, EP 1.8/8
Guide
  Abridged United States Official Postal **Guide**, P 1.10/2
  ACT Career Planning **Guide** Series, L 1.7/9
  Admissions **Guide**, D 305.6/2:Ad 6
  Airman's **Guide**, C 31.127, C 31.136, FAA 1.23
  Airman's **Guide** and Flight Information Manual, FAA 1.25/2
  Airman's **Guide** and Flight Information Manual: Pacific Supplement, FAA 1.25
  Airman's **Guide**; Pacific Supplement, FAA 1.25/3
  Anglers' **Guide** to the United States Atlantic Coast, C 55.308:An 4
  Anglers' **Guide** to the United States Pacific Coast, C 55.308:An 4/2
  Bench Comment, a Periodic **Guide** to Recent Appellate Treatment of Practical Procedural Issues, Ju 13.8/2
  Census of Population and Housing: Finders **Guide** to Census Tract Reports, C 3.223/11-2
  Census of Population and Housing **Guide** Part B, Glossary, C 3.223/22:90-R1
  Census of Population and Housing: Users **Guide**, C 3.223/22-2
  Citizen's **Guide** on How to Use the Freedom of Information Act and the Privacy Act in Requesting Government Documents, Y 1.95-1:H.Rep. 793
  Compliance Program **Guide** Manual, HE 20.4008/7
  Conservation **Guide** Sheets, A 57.6/4
  Consumers' **Guide**, A 1.67
  CSAP Substance Abuse Resource **Guide**, HE 20.409/2
  Curriculum **Guide** Series, HE 19.108/3
  Education Research Consumer **Guide**, ED 1.308/2
  Enrollment Information **Guide** and Plan Comparison Chart, PM 1.8/11
  Federal Income Tax **Guide** for Older Americans, Y 4.Ag 4/2-11
  Guide G (series), VA 1.10/4
  Guide Leaflets, I 29.12, I 29.12/2
  Guide Lines, Guidance and Pupil Personnel Service, FS 5.54
  Guide to Crop Insurance Protection, A 62.16
  Guide to Department of Education Programs, ED 1.10/2
  Guide to German Records Microfilmed at Alexandria, Va., GS 4.18
  Guide to Health Insurance for People with Medicare, HE 22.8/17
  Guide to Programs, NS 1.47
  Guide to Processing Personnel Actions, PM 1.14/3-4
  Guide to Substance Abuse Treatment Benefits Under the Federal Employees Health Benefits Program, PM 1.8/9
  Information **Guide** (series), T 22.19/4
  Interim **Guide** for Environment Assessment, HH 1.6/3:En 8

Military Careers: A **Guide** to Military Occupations and Selected Military Career Paths, D 1.6/15
Navy **Guide** for Retired Personnel and Their Families, D 208.26
Occupational **Guide** Series: Job Descriptions, L 7.32, FS 3.133
Occupational **Guide** Series: Labor Market Information, L 7.32/2, FS 3.133/2
OPA Food **Guide** for Retailers, Pr 32.4241
OPS Trade **Guide** TP (series), ES 3.6/13
OTS Technology **Guide** Circulars, C 35.12
Pacific Airman's **Guide** and Chart Supplement, TD 4.16
PHS Rehabilitation **Guide** Series, FS 2.6/2, FS 2.6/6
Ports of the World, Ditty Box **Guide** Book Series, N 17.22
Practical **Guide** Series, HE 20.3108/2
Professional **Guide**-PG (series), D 13.8/6
Program **Guide** Environmental Protection Agency, EP 1.8/9
Program **Guide** Federal Civil Defense Administration, FCD 1.6/7
Program **Guide** President's Committee on Employment of the Handicapped, PrEx 1.10/7
Program **Guide** Veterans Administration, VA 1.10/3
Program Information **Guide** Series, ED 1.8/4
Programs, (year), **Guide** to Programmed Instructional Materials Available to Educators by (date), FS 5.234:34015, HE 5.234:34015
Publications, A Quarterly **Guide**, EP 1.21/7-3
Quick Reference **Guide** for Clinicians, HE 20.6520/2
Radio War **Guide**, Pr 32.5009
Reading **Guide** to Cancer-Virology Literature, FS 2.22/56
Recreation **Guide**, A 13.36/2-6
Recreation **Guide** to Grand Mesa, Uncompahgre and Gunnison National Forests, A 13.36/2-7
Recreational Boating **Guide**, TD 5.8:B 63
Regulatory **Guide** List, Y 3.N 88:6-4
Resource **Guide** for Health Science Students: Occupational and Environmental Health, HE 20.7108:H 34/2
Resources for Change, a **Guide** to Projects, HE 19.9:R 31
Revised **Guide** to the Law and Legal Literature of Mexico, L 1.36:38
Safe Work **Guide**, OSHA, L 35.11
Seafaring **Guide**, and Directory of Labor-Management Affiliations, C 39.206/3:Se 1
Someone Who Cares, A **Guide** to Hiring an In-Home Caregiver, HE 1.1009
Speakers **Guide** for Service Spokesmen, D 6.8
Speakers' **Guide** for Service Spokesmen, Power for Peace, Armed Forces Day, D 1.6/3
Spot the Danger, User's **Guide** to {various products} Safety Series, Y 3.C 76/3:8-3
Student **Guide**, Five Federal Financial Aid Programs, ED 1.8/2
Supervisor's **Guide** Series, L 1.24/2
Tax **Guide** for Small Business, T 22.19/2:Sm 1, T 22.19/2-3
Tax **Guide** for U.S. Citizens Abroad, T 22.19/2:C 49
Technical Assistance **Guide** (series), J 1.8/4
Tobacco Tax **Guide**, T 22.19/5
Training **Guide**, Insect Control Series, FS 2.60/7, HE 20.2308
Turkey Marketing **Guide**, A 88.26/5
U.S. Army Pocket Recruiting **Guide**, D 101.6/11
U.S. Army Research and Development Program **Guide**, D 101.52/4
U.S. Customs **Guide** for Private Flyers, T 17.23
U.S. Government Purchasing and Sales Directory **Guide** for Selling or Buying in the Government Market, SBA 1.13/3
U.S. Official Postal **Guide**, P 1.10
Understanding Taxes, Teacher's **Guide**, T 22.19/2-2
United States Air Force History, a **Guide** to Documentary Sources, D 301.6/5:H 62
United States Army in World War II: Master Index, Reader's **Guide**, D 114.7/2
USIA INFO BASE (Quick Reference **Guide**), IA 1.32
Water Resources Teaching **Guide** (series), I 27.76
World Holidays Listed, **Guide** to Business Travel, C 42.8/a:H 717/2

Your **Guide** to Federal Waterfowl Production Areas, I 49.6/3
Guidebook
  Election Law **Guidebook**, 1974, Summary of Federal and State Laws Regulating Nomination and Election of United States Senators, Revised to January 1, 1974, Y 1.93-2:S.doc. 84
  Exploring Careers, a Student **Guidebook**, HE 19.108
  Guidebook, Caribbean Basin Initiative, C 61.8/2
Guided
  Special Bibliography, Artillery and **Guided** Missile School Library, D 101.49
Guideline
  Clinical Practice **Guideline**, HE 20.6520
  Guideline Manuals, J 27.8/2
  Guideline Sentencing Update, Ju 13.8/3
  Guideline Technical Report, HE 20.6520/4
  OAQPS **Guideline** Series, EP 1.8/6
  OCZM **Guideline** Papers, C 55.32/4
Guidelines
  Challenge Grants Application **Guidelines**, NF 2.8/2-3
  Challenge Grants Program **Guidelines** and Application Materials, NF 3.8/2-4
  Clinical Practice **Guidelines**, HE 20.6520/3
  Development Document for Effluent Limitations **Guidelines** and New Source Performance Standards for {various industries}, EP 1.8/3
  Economic Analysis of Proposed Effluent **Guidelines**, EP 1.8/4
  Grants to Presenting Organizations, Special Touring Initiatives Application **Guidelines**, NF 2.8/2-29
  Guidelines, Y 3.Se 5:17, Y 3.W 29:8-2
  Guidelines for Implementation of Sanitary Requirements in Poultry Establishments, A 88.6/4:P 86/2
  Guidelines for the Clinical Evaluation of {various drugs}, HE 20.4208/2
  Guidelines for {Various Health Professionals and Sub-professional} in Home Health Services, FS 2.6/8
  Guidelines: Innovative Collective Bargaining Contract Provisions, FM 1.9
  International, Application **Guidelines** for Fiscal Year, NF 2.8/2-32
  Local Arts Agencies Program, Application **Guidelines**, NF 2.8/2-31
  Local Programs, Application **Guidelines**, NF 2.8/2-21
  MIP {Meat Inspection Program} **Guidelines**, A 88.17/6
  NEH Teacher-Scholar Program for Elementary and Secondary School Teachers, **Guidelines** and Application Instructions, NF 3.18
  OEH **Guidelines**, HE 20.2658/2
  Opera-Musical Theater, Application **Guidelines**, NF 2.8/2-12
  Organizations Visual Arts, Application **Guidelines**, NF 2.8/2-15
  Papers on the National Health **Guidelines**, HE 20.6020
  Presenters and Festivals Jazz Management, Jazz Special Projects, Music, Application **Guidelines**, NF 2.8/2-9
  Preservation Programs **Guidelines** and Application Instructions, NF 3.8/2-3
  Procedures and **Guidelines** for Impeachment Trials in the U.S. Senate, Y 1.93-2:S.doc 102
  Program and Financial Plan, Basic Assumptions and **Guidelines**, HE 1.610/2
  Proposed Effluent **Guidelines**, EP 1.8/4-3
  Public Humanities Projects, **Guidelines** and Application Instructions, NF 3.8/2-9
  Referral **Guidelines** for Funding Components of PHS, HE 20.3008/4
  Reports and **Guidelines** from White House Conference on Aging (series), FS 1.13/2
  Summer Seminars for College Teachers **Guidelines** and Application Form for Participants, NF 3.13/2-2
  Summer Seminars for College Teachers, **Guidelines** and Application Forms for Directors, NF 3.13/2
  Summer Seminars for Secondary School Teachers **Guidelines** and Application Form for Directors, NF 3.13/3-3
  Summer Seminars for Secondary School Teachers **Guidelines** and Applications Form for Participants, NF 3.13/3-2

Summer Stipends, **Guidelines** and Application Forms, NF 3.8/2

Theater Application **Guidelines**, NF 2.8/2-6

Guides

Acreage-Marketing **Guides**, A 88.26/4

AEC Licensing **Guides**, Y 3.At 7:6-4

Climatic **Guides**, C 30.67

Commercial Resource Allocation **Guides** {for various countries}, C 1.64/2

Compliance Policy **Guides**, HE 20.4008/5

Country Commercial **Guides**, S 1.40/7

NIOSH Health and Safety **Guides** for {various businesses}, HE 20.7108/2

Occupational **Guides**, L 1.7/5

OPS **Guides**, ES 3.6/7

Performance **Guides** (series) Army Department, D 101.107/3-2

Performance **Guides** (series) Forest Service, A 13.65/12-2

PMG {Poultry Marketing **Guides**} (series), A 88.26/5

Pocket **Guides** to {country}, W 109.119, W 109.215, D 2.8, D 101.22:360-400

Policy Briefs, Action **Guides** for Legislators and Government Executives, J 28.8/2

Port **Guides**, D 208.6/4

Program Regulation **Guides** {issued by various departments}, HE 1.47/3

Recovery **Guides**, Participating Counties, Y 3.Ec 74/3:16

Reference **Guides** (Series), LC 1.6/5

Reference **Guides**, FS 2.22/4

Regulatory **Guides**, Y 3.N 88:6-2

Safe Work **Guides**, SWG LS- (series), L 16.51/2

Safety Conference **Guides**, I 1.77/3

Social Seminar Discussion **Guides**, HE 20.2408/2

State and Private Forestry: Handbooks, Manuals, **Guides**, A 13.110/8

Statistics of Income, Corporation Income Tax Returns Documentation **Guides**, T 22.35/7

Student Performance **Guides** (series), D 101.107/3

Study **Guides**, E 1.8/3

Technical Assistance **Guides**, L 37.308/2

Technical Standards Training **Guides**, HH 2.6/7

Tire Rationing **Guides**, Pr 32.4220

Training **Guides**, VA 1.38

Traveler's **Guides** to Special Attractions, C 47.12/2

Workable Program for Community Improvement, Program **Guides**, HH 1.6/4

Workshop **Guides**, Y 3.W 84:10

Guidon

Nutmeg **Guidon**, J 16.15

Guillain Barre

Guillain Barre Syndrome Surveillance, HE 20.7011/32

Gulf

Gulf Fisheries, C 55.309/2

Gulf NEWS, D 1.95/5

Hydrologic Bulletin, Hourly and Daily Precipitation; Lower Mississippi-West **Gulf** District, C 30.35

Inside Route Pilot (Atlantic and **Gulf** Coasts), C 4.6/3

Marine Recreational Fishery Statistics Survey, Atlantic and **Gulf** Coasts, C 55.309/2-3

Seafaring Wage Rates, Atlantic, **Gulf** and Pacific Districts, C 39.202:W 12

U.S. **Gulf** Coast VFR Aeronautical Chart, TD 4.79/13

Gulf Coast

Atlantic Coast and **Gulf Coast** of the United States, TD 5.9:2

Gulf Coast Shrimp Data, I 49.60

U.S. Coast Pilots **Gulf Coast**, Puerto Rico, and Virgin Islands, C 4.6, C 4.6/4

U.S. **Gulf Coast** VFR Aeronautical Chart, C 55.416/12

Gulf of Mexico

Atlantic Coast; **Gulf of Mexico** Puerto Rico and Virgin Islands, C 55.422:5

Gulf of Mexico Summary Report/Index, I 72.9/5

Marine Environmental Assessment, **Gulf** of Mexico, Annual Summary, C 55.237

Pilot Rules for Certain Inland Waters of Atlantic and Pacific Coasts of **Gulf of Mexico**, C 25.9

Pilot Rules for Rivers whose Waters Flow into **Gulf of Mexico** and Their Directory, HH 7.8/2

Gulf Stream

Monthly Summary, The **Gulf Stream**, D 203.28, D 203.29

Gulf War

Gulf War Review, VA 1.104

Gulfstream

Gulfstream, C 55.123

Gum

Gum Turpentine and **Gum** Rosin Circular Letters, Y 3.C 73:11

Gums

Industry Report, Crude Drugs, **Gums**, Balsams, and Essential Oils, C 18.236

Gun

Crime **Gun** Trade Reports, T 70.25

Gunnery

Fixed **Gunnery** and Combat Tactics Series, N 27.12

Report of **Gunnery** Exercises, T 47.16

Gunnison

Recreation Guide to Grand Mesa, Uncompahgre and **Gunnison** National Forests, A 13.36/2-7

Gynecology

Department of Obstetrics and **Gynecology**, D 1.67/4

Gypsum

Gypsum, I 28.32

Gypsum in (year), I 28.32/2

Mineral Industry Surveys, **Gypsum**, I 19.140

Quarterly **Gypsum** Reports, C 22.33, I 28.32

Gypsy Moth

Gypsy Moth News, A 13.141

H

H.O.

H.O. Publications, D 5.317

Index to **H.O.** Charts on Issue, N 6.5/9

Supplementary Notices to Mariners, Correction Sheets for **H.O.** Publications, N 6.11/4

H.T. & S.

H.T. & S. Office Reports, A 77.523, A 88.39

Habeas

Habeas & Prison Litigation Case Law Update, Ju 13.8/4

Habitat

Annual Report **Habitat** Conservation Program, C 55.340

Fish & Wildlife **Habitat** Management Leaflets, A 57.56/2

Habitat Conservation Programs of the National Marine Fisheries Service, C 55.340

Habitat Management for {various Animals}, A 57.56

Habitat Suitability Index Models (series), I 49.97

Habitat Suitability Information, I 49.97/2

Tennessee Valley Streams, Their Fish, Bottom Fauna, and Aquatic **Habitat** {by areas}, Y 3.T 25:41

Habitats

Important Fish and Wildlife **Habitats** of (various States), I 49.91

Habor

Habor Charts and Charts of Special Localities, W 33.8

Haiti

American High Commissioner to **Haiti**, S 1.22

Haiti, Annual Reports of Financial Adviser-General Receiver, S 1.23

Haitian

Haitian Customs Receivership, Annual Reports, S 1.16

Halfnium

Zirconium and **Halfnium** in (year), I 28.83/2

Halfway Houses

Directory of **Halfway Houses** and Community Residences for the Mentally Ill, HE 20.8129

Directory of **Halfway Houses** for the Mentally Ill and Alcoholics, HE 20.2402:H 13

Halibut

Pacific **Halibut** Fishery Regulations, S 5.35:5

Halifax

Halifax Commission (Fishery Commission), S 3.13/4

Halley

International **Halley** Watch Newsletter, NAS 1.72

Hallmark

Hallmark, D 101.68

Hampton

Hampton Normal and Agricultural Institute, I 20.17

Hampton Roads

Tide Calendar **Hampton Roads** (Sewalls Point), Virginia, M 202.13, D 203.13

Hand

Cottonseed Products Manufactured and on **Hand** at Oil Mills by States, C 3.125

Cottonseed Received, Crushed and on **Hand**; Cotton Linters Produced; and Linters on **Hand** at Oil Mills, Preliminary Reports, C 3.149

Cottonseed Received, Crushed, and on **Hand**, Etc, Preliminary Report, C 3.25

Foreign Markets for **Hand** Tools, C 18.83

Report of Cotton Consumed, on **Hand**, Imported and Exported and Active Spindles, C 3.21

Stock on **Hand** at Refineries, I 28.21

Stocks on **Hand** at Refineries, I 28.20

Handbook

AFOS **Handbook** (series), C 55.108/6

Air Force **Handbook** (series), D 301.6/8

Consumer Action **Handbook** GS 11.9/3

Consumer's Resource **Handbook**, GS 11.9/3

Curriculum **Handbook**, D 305.6/3

Customer Assistance **Handbook**, D 7.6/20

Fire **Handbook**, Region 7, A 13.24

Franchise Opportunities **Handbook**, C 1.108/2

Handbook AS (series), P 1.31/10

Handbook EL- (series), P 1.31/9

Handbook F (series), P 1.31/14

Handbook IM (series), P 1.31/15

Handbook of Hearing Aid Measurement, VA 1.22/3

Handbook of International Economic Statistics, PrEx 3.16

Indian Health Service Scholarship Program Student **Handbook**, HE 20.9418/2

Marine Air Traffic Control Detachment **Handbook**, PCN nos, D 214.9/7

NBS **Handbook**, Specifications, Tolerances, and Other Technical Requirements for Weighing and Measuring Devices, C 13.11/2

NIAAA Treatment **Handbook** Series, HE 20.8308/2

NIST **Handbook**, Specifications, Tolerances, and Other Technical Requirements for Weighing and Measuring Devices, C 13.11/2

Occupant Emergency Plan **Handbook** for the Frances Perkins Building, L 1.1/2-2:2-8

Occupational Outlook **Handbook**, L 2.3/4-4

Office of Hearings and Appeals **Handbook**, HE 3.6/7

Personnel **Handbook**, Series P-1, Position Description and Salary Schedules, Transmittal Letters, P 1.31

Poultry Inspectors **Handbook**, A 88.6/4:P 86

Reports and Analysis **Handbook** Series, L 7.36

Reprints from the Occupational Outlook **Handbook**, Bulletins, L 2.3/4 a

Sanitation **Handbook** of Consumer Protection Programs, A 88.6/4:Sa 5

SCS National Engineering **Handbook**, A 57.6/2:En 3

Series Data **Handbook**, HH 2.24/6

Social Security **Handbook**, HE 3.6/8

Soldiers' **Handbook**, W 3.29

Standard and Optional Forms Facsimile **Handbook**, GS 4.6/3, GS 12.18

Statistical **Handbook** of Civil Aviation, C 31.144

Student **Handbook** (series) Corps of Engineers, D 103.120/2

Student **Handbook** (series) Department of Defense, D 1.67/3

Student **Handbook** (series) Department of the Army, D 101.47/3, D 101.47/4

Technical **Handbook** for Facilities Engineering and Construction Manuals, HE 1.108/2

U.S. Area **Handbook** for (country), D 101.22:550

United States Army Occupational **Handbook**, D 101.40

Urban Renewal **Handbook**, HH 1.6/6

Your Medicare **Handbook**, HE 22.8/16

Handbooks

Consumer Survey **Handbooks**, FT 1.8/3

Handbooks on Programs of Department of Health, Education and Welfare, FS 1.6/5, HE 1.6/5

Handbooks, DM- (series), P 1.31/11

Handbooks: Action, AA 1.8/2

Handbooks: Agricultural and Range Conservation Programs, A 55.45/11, A 55.46/11

Handbooks: Agricultural Conservation Program, A 55.45/12, A 82.37

Handbooks: Civil Service Commission, CS 1.45

Haul
 Selected Elements of Value of Property Used in
 Common Carrier Service, Before and After
 Recorded Depreciation and Amortiza-
 tion, Class I Line **Haul** Railways,
 Including Their Lessors and Proprietary
 Companies, IC 1 val.10

Haulage
 Power **Haulage** Fatalities, Coal and Metal/
 Nonmetal Mines, L 38.19

Hauling
 Refuse **Hauling** Wage Survey Summaries by Cities,
 L 2.113/3

Havana, Cuba
 International American Conference: **Havana, Cuba**,
 S 5.9/6

Have
 Have You Heard, I 16.60/1

Hawaii
 Activities of the U.S. Geological Survey Water
 Resources Division, **Hawaii**, I 19.55/7
 Annual Report of Vegetable Breeding in
 Southeastern United States, **Hawaii**, and
 Puerto Rico, A 77.532
 Census of Nurses Employed for Public Health
 Work in United States, in Territories of
 Alaska and **Hawaii**, and in Puerto Rico
 and Virgin Islands, FS 2.81
 Climatological Data; **Hawaii** Section, A 29.34, C
 30.19
 General Court-Martial Orders: **Hawaii** Department,
 W 81.9
 Hawaii Tax Fund Orders, A 55.28
 Hawaii, Governor, Annual Reports, I 1.41
 Instrument Approach Procedure Charts {Alaska,
 Hawaii, U.S. Pacific Islands}, C 55.411/
 2
 Official Parcel Post Zone Keys **Hawaii**, P 1.25/4
 Pacific Coast, California, Oregon, Washington, and
 Hawaii, C 55.422:7
 Report on **Hawaii**, C 8.6
 U.S. Coast Pilots Pacific Coast, California, Oregon,
 Washington, and **Hawaii**, C 4.7/1

Hawaiian
 Application for Basic Grants under Library
 Services for Indian Tribes and **Hawaiian**
 Program, ED 1.53/2
 Hawaiian Volcano Observatory Summary, I 19.29/2
 Library Programs, Library Services for Indian
 Tribes and **Hawaiian** Natives Program,
 ED 1.18/3
 Library Programs, Library Services for Indian
 Tribes and **Hawaiian** Natives Program,
 Review of Program Activities, ED 1.18/
 3-2
 Monthly Bulletin of **Hawaiian** Volcano
 Observatory, I 19.28
 Roster and Directory of Troops in **Hawaiian**
 Department, W 81.5

Hawaiian Islands
 Tide Tables, High and Low Water Predictions West
 Coast of North and South America
 Including **Hawaiian Islands**, C 55.421
 U.S. Coast Pilots **Hawaiian Islands**, C 4.7/4, C
 4.7/5
 West Coast of North and South America (including
 the **Hawaiian Islands**), C 4.15/5

Hayden
 Catalogue and Index of the Publications of the
 Hayden, King, Powell, and Wheeler
 Survyes, I 19.3:222

Hays
 Modern Foreign Language Fellowship Program,
 National Defense Education Act, Title 6
 and NDEA Related Awards under
 Fullbright-**Hays** Act, FS 5.255:55034,
 HE 5.255:55034

Hazard
 Contaminant **Hazard** Review, I 19.167
 Flood **Hazard** Analyses, A 57.64/2
 Flood **Hazard** Series, A 57.64/3
 Flood **Hazard** Studies {various rivers, creeks, and
 areas}, A 57.64/3
 Hazard Analysis Reports {on various subjects}, Y
 3.C 76/3:17
 HIA {**Hazard** Identification and Analysis} Special
 Reports, Y 3.C 76/3:17-2
 NIOSH Health **Hazard** Evaluation Report, HE
 20.7125/2
 Special **Hazard** Review, HE 20.7113
 Special Occupational **Hazard** Review with Control
 Recommendations, HE 20.7113
 Summary of Natural **Hazard** Deaths in the United
 States, C 55.134

Hazardous
 Annual Report of the Secretary of Transportation on
 Hazardous Materials Transportation, TD
 9.15
 Hazardous Item Listing, D 7.6/17
 Hazardous Item Listing, D 7.32
 Hazardous Material Control and Management/
 Hazardous Materials Information System,
 D 212.16
 Hazardous Materials Accident Report, NTSB/
 HZM- (series), TD 1.28
 Hazardous Materials Information System, D 7.32
 Hazardous Materials Information System,
 Hazardous Materials Transportation Training
 Modules TD 10.16
 Hazardous Occupations Orders, L 22.26
 Hazardous Substances and Public Health, HE
 20.516, HE 20.7915
 National Biennial RCRA **Hazardous** Waste Report,
 EP 1.104/3
 National Center for Chronic Disease Prevention
 and **Health** Promotion (NCCDPHP), HE
 20.7039, HE 20.7616
 Notices of Judgement under Federal **Hazardous**
 Substances Labeling Act, FS 13.112/2
 Oil and **Hazardous** Material Program Series, EP
 2.11
 Pacific Basin Consortium for **Hazardous** Waste
 Research Newsletter, E 1.110
 State Laws and Regulations Prohibiting
 Employment of Minors in **Hazardous**
 Occupations, L 22.6/2

Hazardous Materials
 Annual Report of the Secretary of Transportation on
 Hazardous Materials Control, TD 1.24

Hazards
 Bibliography of Fire **Hazards** and Prevention and
 Safety in Petroleum Industry, C 22.27
 Controlling Chemical **Hazards** Series, L 16.25
 Earthquake **Hazards** Reduction Series, FEM 1.25
 Health **Hazards** of Smoke, A 13.136
 Job Health **Hazards** Series, L 35.18
 Occupational **Hazards** to Young Workers Reports,
 L 16.40
 Occupational **Hazards** to Young Workers, L 16.3
 Occupational Safety and Health **Hazards** (series),
 HE 20.7117

HC
 Series **HC** Reports, C 3.950-4/2
 U.S. Census of Housing City Blocks, Series **HC** (3),
 C 3.224/6
 U.S. Census of Housing Components of Inventory
 Change, Final Report **HC** (4) series, C
 3.224/6
 U.S. Census of Housing Special Reports for Local
 Housing Authorities, series **HC** (S 1), C
 3.224/8
 U.S. Census of Housing State and Small Areas,
 Final Report **HC** (1) (series), C 3.224/3

HCFA
 HCFA Common Procedure Coding System, HE
 22.37
 HCFA Communications Directory, HE 22.14
 HCFA Fact Sheet (series), HE 22.40
 HCFA Forms Information Catalog, HE 22.32/2
 HCFA Health Watch, HE 22.43
 (**HCFA**) Medicare Unique Physician Identification
 Number (Directory), HE 22.414/2
 HCFA Regional Office Manual; General, HE 22.8/
 8-5
 HCFA Regional Office Manual; Medicade, HE
 22.8/8-4
 HCFA Regional Office Manual; Medicare, HE 22.8/
 8
 HCFA Regional Office Manual; Program Integrity,
 HE 22.8/8-2
 HCFA Regional Office Manual; Standards and
 Certification Guidelines, HE 22.8/8-3
 HCFA Rulings, HE 22.38
 HCFA Telephone Directory, HE 22.14

HCFA's
 HCFA's Laws, Regulations, Manuals, HE 22.8/22

HCRS
 Notifications, **HCRS** Information Exchange
 (series), I 70.25
 Poppies and Porticos, a **HCRS** Heritage
 Newsletter, I 70.21

HCUP
 HCUP Factbook, HE 20.6514/4

HCUP-3
 HCUP-3 (Healthcare Cost and Utilization Project)
 Research Note, HE 20.6514/3

HDS
 HDS Telephone Directory, HE 23.11

HE
 HE Instruction in Agriculture, Programs,
 Activities, Developments, FS 5.74

Head Start
 Annual Report of the Department of Health,
 Education, and Welfare to Congress on
 Services Provided to Handicapped
 Children in Project **Head Start**, HE
 1.409
 Head Start Newsletter, PrEx 10.12/2, HE 21.209,
 HE 23.1014
 Head Start Program Data, HE 23.1115
 Head Start, Child Development Program, Manual
 of Policies and Instructions, PrEx
 10.8:H 34/2
 Posters **Head Start** Bureau, HE 21.213
 Project **Head Start** (series), PrEx 10.12, HE
 21.212, HE 1.469
 Project **Head Start**, HE 1.36
 Status of Handicapped Children in **Head Start**
 Programs, HE 23.1012

Headings
 Cumulated List of New Medical Subject **Headings**,
 HE 20.3612/3-2
 Headings and Subheads for Index to Federal
 Statutes, LC 10.6
 Medical Subject **Headings**; Annotated Alphabeti-
 cal List, HE 20.3602:H 34, HE 20.3612/
 3-4
 Medical Subject **Headings**; Supplementary
 Chemical Records, HE 20.3612/3-7
 Medical Subject **Headings**; Tree Annotations, HE
 20.3612/3-6
 Medical Subject **Headings**; Tree Structures, HE
 20.3602:H 34/2, HE 20.3612/3-5
 Permuted Medical Subject **Headings**, HE 20.3612/
 3-3
 Subject Cataloging Manual: Subject **Headings**, LC
 26.8/4
 Subject **Headings** Used in the Dictionary Catalogs
 of the Library of Congress, LC 26.7
 Subject **Headings**, LC 9.6/1
 Supplement to LC Subject **Headings**, Quarterly
 Cumulative Supplement, LC 26.7

Headline
 Headline Series, FS 3.224, FS 14.117, FS 5.224, HE
 5.224

Headquarters
 General **Headquarters**, Far East Command, General
 Publications, D 1.24
 Headquarters European Command, Publications,
 D 1.23
 Headquarters Fort George C. Meade Pamphlets
 (series), D 101.22/10
 Headquarters Fort McCoy Regulations, D 101.9/4
 Headquarters Intercom, TD 4.5/2
 Headquarters Manual, HQM (series), D 7.6/9
 Headquarters Memorandum, W 99.15/9
 Headquarters Orders, W 99.13/11
 Headquarters Telephone Directory, T 63.126
 Headquarters' Circulars, N 24.22
 Headquarters, Department of the Army Chiefs and
 Executives, D 202.23
 Headquarters, First United States Army, Deputy
 Chief of Staff, Information Management,
 Organization, Mission, and Functions, D
 101.1/9
 Publications **Headquarters** European Command, D
 1.23
 Publications U.S. Army **Headquarters** in Europe,
 D 101.42
 Selected DOE **Headquarters** Publications, E 1.13/
 4
 Telephone Directory NASA, **Headquarters**,
 Washington, D.C., NAS 1.24

Heads
 Heads of Families at 1st Census, C 3.11

 Memorandum to **Heads** of Department of
 Agriculture Agencies, A 1.79

Headstart
 Headstart (series), D 1.71

Headwater
 Headwater Herald, A 13.121

Healey
 Walsh-**Healey** Public Contracts Act Minimum
 Wage Determination (for various
 industries), L 22.19
 Walsh-**Healey** Public Contracts Act, Decisions, L
 22.23

Health
 A Report by the FCCSET Committee on Life
 Sciences and **Health**, PrEx 8.111/2

Activities of the National Institutes of **Health** in Field of Gerontology, FS 2.22/26
Administration in Mental **Health**, HE 20.8112
Advance Data from the Vital and **Health** Statistics of NCHS, HE 20.6209/3
Alcohol and **Health** Notes, HE 20.8309/2
Alcohol and You, HSMHA Employee **Health** Program on Alcoholism, HE 20.2711
Alcohol **Health** and Research World, HE 20.2430, HE 20.3813, HE 20.8309
Alcohol Research and **Health** HE 20.8309
Alcohol, Drug Abuse, Mental **Health**, Research Grant Awards, Fiscal Year, HE 20.8118
Amendments to Regulations, Public **Health** Service, T 27.8/2
Animal **Health** Science Research Advisory Board, A 106.40
Annual Report of the United States National Committee on Vital and **Health** Statistics, HE 20.6211
Annual Report on the HEW/USDA Rural **Health** Facilities Agreement, A 84.12
Annual Report, Mental **Health** Intramural Research Program, HE 20.8136
Army **Health** Promotion Program, Fit to Win, D 101.22:600
Assembling the **Health** Planning Structure, HE 20.6114
Associate Training Programs in the Medical Sciences and Biological Sciences at the National Institutes of **Health** (Year) Catalog, HE 20.3015
Automated Multiphasic **Health** Testing Bibliography, HE 20.2710
Basic Data Relating to the National Institutes of **Health**, HE 20.3002:N 21/4
Bibliography of Soviet Sources on Medicine and Public **Health** in the U.S.S.R., HE 20.3711:So 8/2
Bibliography on Smoking and **Health**, HE 20.11:45
Bierman Jessie M. Annual Lectures in Maternal **Health** and Child **Health**, FS 14.110/2
Bulletin of the School of Medicine, Uniformed Services University of the **Health** Sciences, D 1.67
Bureau of Radiological **Health** Research Grants Program, Fiscal Year, (date), HE 20.4116
Catalog of Publications of the National Center for **Health** Statistics, HE 20.6216/4
Catalog, Department of **Health**, Education, and Welfare, Publications, HE 1.18/3
CDC Veterinary Public **Health** Notes, HE 20.7010
Census of Nurses Employed for Public **Health** Work in United States, in Territories of Alaska and Hawaii, and in Puerto Rico and Virgin Islands, FS 2.81
Center for Devices and Radiological **Health** Publications Index, HE 20.4609/2
Child **Health** USA, HE 20.9213
CHScene, Notes from the Community **Health** Service, HE 20.2557/2
Citator to Decisions of the Occupational Safety and **Health** Review Commission, Y 3.Oc 1:10-4
Civilian **Health** and Medical Program of Uniformed Service {fact Sheets}, CHAMPUS, D 2.18
Civilian Medical Division **Health** Messages, W 1.54
Clearinghouse on **Health** Indexes, HE 20.6216/2-2
Clearinghouse on **Health** Indexes: Cumulated Annotations, HE 20.6216/2
Climate and **Health**, A 29.8
Clinical Electives for Medical and Dental Students at the National Institutes of **Health**, Catalog, HE 20.3042
Committee on the Assessment of Human **Health** Effects of Great Lakes Water Quality: Annual Report, Y 3.In 8/28:15
Community **Health** Scene, HE 20.5112, HE 20.5109
Community **Health** Series, FS 2.35
Compilation of Public **Health** Service Regulations, FS 2.52
Comprehensive **Health** Services Projects, Summary of Project Data, CHSP Reports, HE 20.5115
Conference of State and Territorial **Health** Officers with United States Public **Health** Service, Transactions, T 27.32, FS 2.34

CSU-PHS {Colorado State University-Public **Health** Service} Collaborative Radiological **Health** Laboratory: Annual Report, HE 20.4119, HE 20.4613
Current Awareness in **Health** Education, HE 20.7209/2, HE 20.7609
Current Estimates from the National **Health** Interview Survey, HE 20.6209/4
Current Listing and Topical Index to the Vital and **Health** Statistics Series, HE 20.2202:V 83
Diabetes Mellitus Coordinating Committee, Annual Report to the Director, National Institutes of **Health**, Fiscal Year (date), HE 20.3028
Digest of **Health** and Insurance Plans, L 2.99/2
Digest of Selected **Health** and Insurance Plans, L 2.99/2
Directory of Local **Health** and Mental **Health** Units, HE 20.2015
Directory of Local **Health** Units, FS 2.77
Directory of On-going Research in Smoking and **Health**, HE 20.25, HE 20.7015
Directory of Outpatient Psychiatric Clinics, Psychiatric Day-Night Services and Other Mental **Health** Resources in the United States and Territories, FS 2.22/38-4
Directory of Personnel Responsible for Radiological **Health** Programs, HE 20.4122
Directory of Providers of Services of Home **Health** Services, HE 3.51
Directory of State and Territorial **Health** Authorities, FS 2.77/2
Directory of State Mental **Health** Personnel and Regional Offices of Department of Health, Education, and Welfare, FS 2.22:M 52/40
Directory of State, Territorial, and Regional **Health** Authorities, HE 20.2015/2
Division of **Health** and Safety, Annual Report, Y 3.T 25:1-9
DMI **Health** Manpower Information Exchange Reports, HE 20.6109
Don't Gamble with Your **Health** (series), FS 2.50/2
DRH Bulletin, Radiological **Health**, HE 20.4612
DRH Radiological **Health** Bulletin, HE 20.4612
Emergency **Health** Series, HE 20.2013
Emergency **Health** Services Digest, HE 20.13/2
Employee Benefits Survey **Health** Coding Manual, L 2.46/5
Employees' **Health** Service Folders, FS 2.49
Enrollment Information Guide and Plan Comparison Chart Former Spouses Enrolled in the Federal Employees **Health** Benefits Program, PM 1.8/7
Enrollment Information Guide and Plan Comparison Chart Retirement Systems Participating in the Federal Employees **Health** Benefits Program, PM 1.8/4
Environmental **Health** Effects Research, 600/1 (series), EP 1.23/4
Environmental **Health** Factors, Nursing Homes, FS 2.300/2
Environmental **Health** Perspectives, Experimental Issues, HE 20.3559
Environmental **Health** Series, FS 2.300, HE 20.1011
Environmental **Health** Service Series on Community Organization Techniques, HE 20.1811
Establishments and Products Licensed Under Section 351 of the Public **Health** Service Act, HE 20.4042
Facts of Life and Death, Selected Statistics on Nation's **Health** and People, FS 2.102:H 34
Federal Coal Mine **Health** Program in (year), HE 20.7109
Federal Coal Mine **Health** Program, Annual Report of the Federal Coal Mine **Health** and Safety Act, HE 20.2020
Federal Employee **Health** Series, HE 20.5410
Federal Employees **Health** Benefits, CS 1.41/4:890-1
Federal Mine **Health** Program for (year), HE 20.7109
Federal Mine Safety and **Health** Review Commission Index, Y 3.M 66:9-2
Federal Occupational **Health** Memo Series, HE 20.9116
Fish **Health** Bulletin, I 49.79/2
Fish **Health** News, I 49.79

Focus on Federal Employee **Health** Assistance Programs, PM 1.55
Focus on **Health** Maintenance Organizations, HE 20.20/2
Forward Plan for **Health**, HE 20.18
Forest **Health** Highlights, A 13.154
Graduate Education Bulletin, Uniformed Services University of the **Health** Sciences, D 1.67/2
Grants-In-Aid and Other Financial Assistance Programs, **Health** Services and Mental **Health** Administration, FS 2.317
Guidelines for {Various **Health** Professionals and Sub-professional} in Home **Health** Services, FS 2.6/8
Handbooks on Programs of Department of **Health**, Education and Welfare, FS 1.6/5, HE 1.6/5
Hazardous Substances and Public **Health**, HE 20.7915
HCFA **Health** Watch, HE 22.43
Health and Safety, E 1.99
Health and Safety Laboratory: Environmental Quarterly, ER 1.27
Health and Safety Statistics, I 28.26
Health and Sanitation Division Newsletters, Pr 32.4610
Health Aspects of Pesticides, Abstracts Bulletin, HE 20.4011
Health Care Financing Administration Information Systems Development Guide, HE 22.508/2
Health Care Financing Administration Rulings, HE 22.15
Health Care Financing Administration Rulings on Medicare, Medicaid, Professional Standards Review and Related Matters, HE 22.15
Health Care Financing Conference Proceedings, HE 22.19/6
Health Care Financing Extramural Reports (series), HE 22.19, HE 22.19/9
Health Care Financing, Grants and Contracts Reports, HE 22.19
Health Care Financing: Grants for Research and Demonstrations, Fiscal Year, HE 22.19/3
Health Care Financing: Issues (series), HE 22.19/8
Health Care Financing Monographs, HE 22.19/7
Health Care Financing Notes, HE 22.19/4
Health Care Financing Program Statistics, HE 22.19/4-2
Health Care Financing Research and Demonstration Series, HE 22.16
Health Care Financing, Research Reports, HE 22.19/2
Health Care Financing Review, HE 22.18, HE 22.512
Health Care Financing Review Annual Supplement, HE 22.18/2
Health Care Financing Special Report (series), HE 22.19/10
Health Care Financing Trends, HE 22.20
Health Consequences of Involuntary Smoking, HE 20.7614
Health Consequences of Smoking, HE 20.7016, HE 20.25/2
Health Consequences of Smoking, A Public **Health** Service Review, FS 2.309
Health Consequences of Smoking, Report to the Surgeon General, HE 20.2019
Health Data Inventory, HE 1.59
Health Economics Series, FS 2.99
Health Economics Studies Information Exchange, FS 2.76/2
Health Education, I 16.29
Health Facilities Construction Program Loan, Loan Guarantee and Mortgage Quarterly Status Report, HE 20.9013
Health Facilities Series, HE 20.2511
Health Hazard Evaluation Summaries, HE 20.7125
Health Hazards of Smoke, A 13.136
Health Information for International Travel, HE 20.7009, HE 20.7818
Health Information for Travel in {area}, HE 20.2:T 69
Health Information Resources in the Federal Government, HE 20.37
Health Information Series (numbered), HE 20.10
Health Leaflets, FS 2.37
Health Maintenance Organizations, HE 20.20
Health Manpower Clearinghouse Series, HE 20.3114/3
Health Manpower Data Series, HE 20.3114/2

Occupational Safety and **Health** Regulations, L
35.6/2
Occupational Safety and **Health** Statistics of the
Federal Government, L 35.13
Office of **Health** and Environmental Science:
Annual Report, Y 3.T 25:1-10
Office of Women's **Health** - General Publications,
HE 20.41/2
Omnibus Solicitation of the Public **Health** Service
for Small Business Innovation Research
(SBIR) Grant Applications, HE 20.3047/
2
Organization and Staffing for Full Time Local
Health Services, FS 2.80
OSAHRE Reports: Decisions of the Occupational
Safety and **Health** Review Commission,
Y 3.Oc 1:10
OSHA Safety and **Health** Standards Digests, L
35.6/4
Outbreaks of Disease Caused by Milk and Milk
Products as Reported by **Health**
Authorities as having Occurred in U.S.,
T 27.42
Papers on the National **Health** Guidelines, HE
20.6020
Partnership for **Health** News, FS 2.319, HE
20.2559
Pharmacy Residences in Public **Health** Service
Hospitals, FS 2.89/3
Philippine **Health** Service, Monthly Bulletin, W
49.15/6
Portraits in Community **Health**, FS 2.35/2
Position Classification and Pay in State and
Territorial Public **Health**
Health Laboratories, HE 20.7413
Posters **Health** Care Financing Administration, HE
22.27
Posters **Health** Resources and Services Administra-
tion, HE 20.9012
Posters Mine Safety and **Health** Administration, L
38.14/2
Preamble Compilation, Radiological **Health**, HE
20.4006/2
President's Commission on Mental **Health**, Pr
39.8:M 52
President's Committee on **Health** Education, Pr
37.8:H 34
President's Report on Occupational Safety and
Health, Pr 38.2:Oc 1
Prevention Activities of the Alcohol, Drug Abuse,
and Mental **Health** Administration, HE
20.8018
Proceedings Annual Conference of Mental **Health**
Career Development Program, FS 2.22/45
Proceedings Annual Conference of the Surgeon
General, Public **Health** Service, and
Chief, Children's Bureau, with State and
Territorial **Health** Officers, FS 2.83
Proceedings Annual Conference, Surgeon General,
Public **Health** Service, with State and
Territorial Mental **Health** Authorities, FS
2.83/3
Proceedings Biennial Conference of State and
Territorial Dental Directors with Public
Health Service and Children's Bureau,
FS 2.83/2
Proceedings Public **Health** Conference on Records
and Statistics, FS 2.122, HE 20.2214,
HE 20.6214
Proficiency Testing Summary Analysis, Public
Health Immunology, HE 20.7022/3-3
Program Memorandum **Health** Maintenance
Organization/Competitive Medical Plan,
HE 22.28/2
Program Plan of the National Institute for
Occupational Safety and **Health**, HE
20.7127
Progress Report National Institute of **Health**, FS
2.22/10
Progress Report National Mental **Health** Program,
FS 2.65
Public **Health** Bibliography Series, FS 2.21
Public **Health** Broadcasts, T 27.35
Public **Health** Bulletins, T 27.12, FS 2.3
Public **Health** Conference on Records and
Statistics, National Meeting Announce-
ment, HE 20.6214/2
Public **Health** Conference on Records and
Statistics, Proceedings, FS 2.122
Public **Health** Engineering Abstracts, T 27.28, FS
2.13
Public **Health** Monograph Series, HE 20.2018
Public **Health** Monographs, FS 2.62

Public **Health** Personnel in Local **Health** Units, FS
2.80
Public **Health** Reports, HE 20.30, HE 20.6011
Public **Health** Service Bibliography Series, HE
20.11
Public **Health** Service Film Catalog, FS 2.36/2
Public **Health** Service Grants and Awards, HE
20.3013
Public **Health** Service International Postdoctorate
Research Fellowships Awards for Study
in the United States, HE 20.3709
Public **Health** Service Posters, FS 2.26/2
Public **Health** Service Prospective Payment
Activity, HE 20.6516
Public **Health** Service Support of Cardiovascular
Research, Training and Community
Programs, FS 2.22/11-2
Public **Health** Service Water Pollution Surveil-
lance System, FS 2.84/2
Public **Health** Technical Monographs, FS 2.62
Public Law 85-742, Safety and **Health** Administra-
tion, Annual Report, L 16.48
Public Use Data Tape Documentation National
Health Interview Survey, HE 20.6226/
10
Publications Bureau of Community **Health**
Services, HE 20.5110:P 96
Publications List for **Health** Professionals, HE
20.3183/2
Publications National Institute of Mental **Health**,
HE 20.8113/3
Publications Public **Health** and Marine-Hospital
Service, T 27.16
Radiological **Health** Data and Reports, HE
20.1110
Radiological **Health** Data, Monthly Report, FS
2.90
Radiological **Health** Quality Assurance Series, HE
20.4108/2
Radiological **Health** Training Resources Catalog,
HE 20.4610
Rape and Its Victims: a Report for Citizens, **Health**
Facilities, and Criminal Justice Agencies,
J 1.8/3:R 18
Regional Differences in Indian **Health**, HE 20.319
Regulations for Government of Public **Health** and
Marine Hospital Service, T 27.8
Regulations for the Administration and
Enforcement of the Radiation Control for
Health and Safety Act of 1968, HE
20.4606/2
Regulations, Rules and Instructions National
Center for Devices and Radiological
Health, HE 20.4606
Report of State and Local Radiological **Health**
Programs, HE 20.4121
Report of the United States Delegation to the
World **Health** Assembly, HE 20.19
Report on Indian **Health**, FS 2.86/2
Report to the Advisory Child **Health** and Human
Development Council, HE 20.3362/7
Report to the President and Congress on the Status
of **Health** Personnel in the United States,
HE 20.9310
Report to the President and Congress on the Status
of **Health** Professions Personnel in the
United States, HE 20.6619
Report, Civil Service Requirement, Federal
Employees' Group Life Insurance,
Federal Employees **Health** Benefits,
Retired Federal Employees **Health**
Benefits, Fiscal Year (date), CS 1.29/3
Representative Construction Cost of Hill- Burton
Hospitals and Related **Health** Facilities,
FS 2.74/6, HE 20.2510
Representative Construction Costs of Hospitals
and Related **Health** Facilities, HE 1.109
Reprints from Public **Health** Reports, T 27.6/a
Research and Demonstrations in **Health** Care
Financing, HE 22.16/2
Research and Training Grants and Awards of Public
Health Service, FS 2.22/8
Research Highlights, National Institutes of **Health**,
FS 2.22/28
Research Notes National Center for **Health** Services
Research, HE 20.6514
Research Project Summaries, National Institute of
Mental **Health**, FS 2.22/16-2
Research Reports National Institute of Mental
Health, HE 20.2420/4, HE 20.8114/2
Research to Improve **Health** Services for Mothers
and Children, HE 20.5114/2

Resource Guide for **Health** Science Students:
Occupational and Environmental
Health, HE 20.7108:H 34/2
Rheumatoid Arthritis, Handout on **Health**, HE
20.3916
Safety and **Health** Requirments, L 16.23
Safety, Fire Prevention, and Occupational **Health**
Management, by Objectives Review, D
301.99
Safety, Occupational **Health** and Fire Protection
Bulletin, VA 1.22:13-1
Salaries of State Public **Health** Workers, FS 2.82
School **Health** Studies, I 16.38
Search for **Health** (series), HE 20.3038
Secretary's Community **Health** Promotion Awards,
HE 20.7612
Selected Papers from Bureau of Radiological **Health**
Seminar Program (numbered), HE
20.1109
Selected References on Environmental Quality As
It Relates to **Health**, HE 20.3616
Self-Study Course 3010-G, Environmental **Health**
Sciences (series), HE 20.7021/11
Smoking and **Health** Bibliographical Bulletin, FS
2.24/4
Smoking and **Health** Bulletin, HE 20.7012, HE
20.7211, HE 20.7610/2, HE 20.7613/2
Smoking and **Health**, a National Status Report, HE
20.7613
Solicitation of the Public **Health** Service and the
Health Care Financing Administration
for Small Business Innovation Research
Contract Proposals, HE 22.31
Solicitation of the Public **Health** Service for Small
Business Research (SBIR) Contract
Proposals, HE 20.28/2
Southwestern Radiological **Health** Laboratory:
Monthly Activities Report, EP 1.13
Special Report to the U.S. Congress on Alcohol
and **Health**, HE 20.8313
State and Local Programs on Smoking and **Health**,
HE 20.25/4
State **Health** Profile, HE 20.7043/1—51
State Legislation on Smoking and **Health**, HE
20.7210, HE 20.25/3
State Salary Ranges, Selected Classes (of
positions) in Employment Security,
Public Welfare, Public **Health**, Mental
Health, Vocational Rehabilitation, Civil
Defense, Emergency Planning, CS 1.81,
FS 1.22, HE 1.22, GS 1.8
Statistical Compendium on Alcohol and **Health**,
HE 20.8317
Statistical Notes for **Health** Planners, HE 20.6218
Statistical Notes National Institute of Mental
Health, HE 20.3812
Subsistence and Environmental **Health**, E 1.90/5
Summary of Activities Animal and Plant **Health**
Inspection Service, A 101.27
Summary of Grants and Contracts Administered by
the National Center for **Health** Services
Research and Development, HE 20.2116
Summary of **Health** Information for International
Travel, HE 20.7315/2, HE 20.781812
Summary of **Health** Information for International
Travel, HE 20.7818/2
Summary Proceedings of ADAMHA Annual
Conference of the State and Territorial
Alcohol, Drug Abuse, and Mental
Health Authorities, HE 20.8011
Summer Research Fellowship Program at the
National Institutes of **Health**, HE
20.3015/2
Surplus Property Disposed of to Public **Health** and
Educational Institutions, FS 1.15
Syncrisis, the Dynamics of **Health**, HE 1.42
Technical Advisory Services, **Health** Office, For
Your Information, TAS (series), FCD
1.13/2
Technical Analysis Papers Department of **Health**,
Education, and Welfare, HE 1.52
Technical Appendixes to the Report and
Recommendations to the Secretary, U.S.
Department of **Health** and Human
Services, Y 3.P 29:1-2
Technical Memoranda for Municipal, Industrial and
Domestic Water Supplies, Pollution
Abatement, Public **Health**, FS 2.301
Teenage **Health** Teaching Modules (series), HE
20.7024
The Recruiter: A Newsletter For the **Health**
Professional Recruiter, HE 20.9017

Herald of Leningrad University, Physics and
Chemistry Series {abstracts}, C 41.52/5
Herald of Machine Building {abstracts}, C 41.65/4
Herald of Moscow University, Physio-
Mathematical and Natural Sciences
Series {abstracts}, C 41.50/6

Herbarium
Contributions from the U.S. National **Herbarium**,
SI 3.8
Contributions from U.S. National **Herbarium**, A
6.5

Herbicides
Herbicides and Plant Regulators, EP 5.11

Herd
Herd Management Area Plan (various locations), I
53.23/2

Here
Here and There with Home Demonstration Workers,
A 43.5/13

Here's
Here's Your Answer, Programs, FE 1.8

Heritage
National **Heritage** Corridor Journal, I 29.122
Poppies and Porticos, a HCRS **Heritage**
Newsletter, I 70.21

Heroes
American **Heroes**, T 66.15

HEW
Annual Report of Department of **Health, Education,
and Welfare** to the President and the
Congress on Federal Activities Related
to the Administration of the Rehabilita-
tion Act of 1973, HE 1.609
Annual Report of Secretary of **Health, Education,
and Welfare** to Congress in Compliance
with Public Law 90-148, Air Quality
Act of 1967, FS 1.35
Annual Report of the Department of **Health,
Education, and Welfare** to Congress on
Services Provided to Handicapped
Children in Project Head Start, HE 1.409
Annual Report on the **HEW**/USDA Rural Health
Facilities Agreement, A 84.12
Catalog of **HEW** Assistance Providing Financial
Support and Service to States,
Communities, Organizations,
Individuals, HE 1.6/6
Catalog, Department of **Health, Education, and
Welfare**, Publications, HE 1.18/3
Footnote, Journal of the **HEW** Audit Agency, HE
1.37
HEW Consumer Newsletter, FS 1.34
HEW Fact Sheets, HE 1.213, HE 23.3109
HEW Facts and Figures, HE 1.21
HEW Newsletter, HE 1.27/2
HEW Now, HE 1.27/2
HEW Obligations to Institutions of Higher
Education, Fiscal Year, FS 1.2:Ed 8/3
HEW Refugee Task Force, Report to the Congress,
HE 1.55

HFORL
HFORL Memorandum TN (series), D 301.45/7
HFORL Report TR (series), D 301.45/8

HHS
HHS News, HE 20.8015
HHS News, Food and Drug Administration, HE
20.4043

HI
RRB-SSA Financial Interchange: Calculations for
Fiscal Year with Respect to OASI, DI,
and **HI** Trust Funds, RR 1.15

HIA
HIA {Hazard Identification and Analysis} Special
Reports, Y 3.C 76/3:17-2

Hickory
Hickory Task Force Reports, A 13.63/12

Hidden
Hidden Killers, S 1.148

Hides
Report on **Hides**, Skins and Leather, C 3.45

High
American **High** Commissioner to Haiti, S 1.22
Bibliography on the **High** Temperature Chemistry
and Physics of Gases and Gas-
condensed Phase Reactions, C 13.37/3
Bibliography on the **High** Temperature Chemistry
and Physics of Materials in the
Condensed State, C 13.37/2
Data Report: **High** Altitude Meteorological Data, C
55.280
DoD Flight Information Publication (Terminal)
High Altitude Instrument Approach
Procedures, D 5.318/2

Enroute **High** and Low Altitude, U.S., D 5.318/4
Enroute **High** Altitude Charts (Alaska), C 55.416/
16-2
Enroute **High** Altitude Planning Charts (U.S.), C
55.416/17
Flight Information Publication: Enroute **High**
Altitude and Low Altitude, U.S., D
5.318/4
Flight Information Publication: Enroute **High**
Altitude, Europe, Africa, Middle East, D
301.9/4
Flight Information Publication: Enroute-**High**
Altitude, United States, Northeast {and
Southeast}, D 301.43/3, D 301.43/3-2
Flight Information Publication: Terminal **High**
Altitude, Pacific and Southeast Asia, D
301.12/4
Haiti, American **High** Commissioner to, S 1.22
High Altitude Instrument Approach Procedures, D
5.318/2
High Commissioner of Trust Territory of Pacific
Islands, I 35.16
High Income Tax Returns, T 1.52
High Performance Computing and Communications
Implementation Plan, PrEx 23.13
High-Temperature Gas-Cooled Reactor Safety
Studies for the Division of Reactor Safety
Research Quarterly Progress Report, E
1.28/7
High-Temperature Gas-Cooled Reactor Safety
Studies, E 1.28/7
Historical Monographs of Office of U.S. **High**
Commissioner for Germany, S 1.95
HPC (**High** Performance Computing) Moderniza-
tion Plan, D 1.106
IFR Enroute **High** Altitude Charts (Alaska), TD
4.49/17-2
IFR Enroute **High** Altitude (U.S.), TD 4.79/17
Insights, **High** Performance Computer and
Communications, NAS 1.94
International **High** Commission, T 1.23
Office of U.S. **High** Commissioner for German
Publications, S 1.91
Office of United States **High** Commissioner for
Austria, General Publications, S 1.89/4
Official Gazette of Allied **High** Commission for
Germany, S 1.88
Quarterly Report on Germany, Office of U.S. **High**
Commissioner for Germany, S 1.90
Report of Austria, Office of U.S. **High** Commissioner
for Austria, S 1.89/3
Report of United States **High** Commissioner,
Statistical Annex, U.S. Element, Allied
Commission for Austria, S 1.89/2
Report of United States **High** Commissioner, U.S.
Element, Allied Commission for Austria,
S 1.89
Report on Austria, Office of U.S. **High** Commis-
sioner for Austria, S 1.89/3
Report on **High** Speed Ground Transportation Act
of 1965, TD 1.10
Terminal **High** Altitude, Pacific and Southeast Asia,
D 301.12/4
Tide Tables **High** and Low Water Prediction, C
55.421
Tide Tables, **High** and Low Water Predictions
Central and Western Pacific Ocean and
Indian Ocean, C 55.421/4
Tide Tables, **High** and Low Water Predictions East
Coast of North and South America
Including Greenland, C 55.421/2
Tide Tables, **High** and Low Water Predictions
Europe and West Coast of Africa,
Including the Mediterranean Sea, C
55.421/3
Tide Tables, **High** and Low Water Predictions West
Coast of North and South America
Including Hawaiian Islands, C 55.421

High Blood Pressure
Directory of Community **High Blood Pressure**
Control Activities, HE 20.3002:B 62/13
National **High Blood Pressure** Education Program,
HE 20.3214

High Point
Special Census, 1923, **High Point**, N.C.; Virgin
Islands 1917, C 3.23

High School
Air Force ROTC Four Year College Scholarship
Program Application Booklet for **High
School** Students Entering College in the
(year) Fall Term, D 301.95

Case Book, Education Beyond **High School**
Practices Underway to Meet the
Problems of the Day, FS 5.65
Drug Use Among American **High School** Students,
HE 20.8219
High School and Beyond, ED 1.334
High School News Service Report, Basic Fact
Edition, School Year, D 1.41/2
Historically Black Colleges and Universities,
Faculty Projects, Summer College
Humanities Programs for **High School**
Juniors, NF 3.8/2-8
Spotlight on Organization and Supervision in
Large **High Schools**, FS 5.50
Suggested Two-year Post-**High School** Curricu-
lums, HE 19.118

Higher
Enrollment for Masters and **Higher** Degrees, Fall
(year), Final Report, FS 5.254:54019, HE
5.254:54019
Inventory of Physical Facilities in Institutions of
Higher Education, HE 5.92/3, HE
19.310
Opening Fall Enrollment in **Higher** Education, FS
5.254:54043, HE 5.254:54023
Postsecondary Education, Fall Enrollment in
Higher Education (year): Institutional
Data, HE 19.325/2
Priorities for Research, Extension and **Higher**
Education, A 1.2/10
Resident, Extension, and Other Enrollments in
Institutions of **Higher** Education, FS
5.254:54000, HE 5.254:54000
Scientific Reports of **Higher** Schools Chemistry and
Chemical Technology, C 41.53/9
Scientific Reports of **Higher** Schools Electro-
Mechanics and Automation, C 41.65/7
Scientific Reports of **Higher** Schools Machine
Construction and Instruments
Manufacture, C 41.65/8
Scientific Reports of **Higher** Schools Metallurgy, C
41.54/4
State **Higher** Education Profiles, ED 1.116/3
Strengthening Developing Institutions, Title 3 of
the **Higher** Education Act of 1965,
Annual Report, HE 19.139/2
Summary Report of Bachelor's and **Higher** Degrees
Conferred During (school year), FS
5.254:54010, HE 5.254:54010
Summary Report, Faculty and Other Professional
Staff in Institutions of **Higher** Education,
FS 5.253:53014, HE 5.253:53014
Survey of State Legislation Relating to **Higher**
Education, FS 5.250:50008, HE
5.250:50008
Task Force on **Higher** Education, Pr 37.8:Ed 8
Trends in Bachelors and **Higher** Degrees, ED
1.132/2

Higher Degrees
Home Economics in Institutions Granting
Bachelor's or **Higher Degrees**, FS
5.283:83008, HE 5.283:83008

Higher Education
Annual Conference on **Higher Education**, General
Information Survey (HEGIS), HE 19.331
Application for Grants under Title VI of the **Higher
Education** Act of 1965, as Amended, ED
1.56, ED 1.57
Awards **Higher Education** Act of 1965 (P.L. 89-
329) as Amended Title 3 Strengthening
Developing Institutions, HE 5.92/2 HE
19.139
Bond Sales for **Higher Education**, FS 5.252:52004
HE 5.252:52004
Clearinghouse of Studies on **Higher Education**,
Reporter, FS 5.250:50004, HE
5.250:50004
Community Service and Continuing Education,
Title 1, **Higher Education** Act of 1965,
FS 5.78
Composite List of Eligible Institutions for
Guaranteed Loans for College Students,
Higher Education Act of 1965, FS 5.83,
HE 5.83
Directory of U.S. Institutions of **Higher Education**,
Fall (year), FS 5.250:50052, HE
5.250:50052
EPDA **Higher Education** Personnel Training
Programs, HE 5.258:58025
Faculty and Other Professional Staff in Institutions
of **Higher Education**, FS 5.253:53000,
HE 5.253:53000

Fall Enrollment in **Higher Education** (year), HE 19.325

Fall Enrollment in **Higher Education** (Year): Institutional Data, HE 19.325/2

Financial Statistics of Institutions of **Higher Education**, HE 19.316/2-2, ED 1.116

Financial Statistics of Institutions of **Higher Education**, Current Funds, Revenues, and Expenditures, HE 19.316/2

Financial Statistics of Institutions of **Higher Education**: Property, HE 19.316

FIPSE, Drug Prevention Programs in **Higher Education**, Information and Application Procedures, ED 1.23/7, ED 1.23/8

FIPSE European Community/United States of America Joint Consortia for Cooperation in **Higher Education**, ED 1.23/10

Fiscal Year Priorities and Fiscal Year Accomplishments For Research, Extension, and **Higher Education**, A Report to the Secretary of Agriculture, A 1.2/13

Guide to Organized Occupational Curriculums in **Higher Education**, FS 5.254:54012, HE 5.254:54012

HEGIS {**Higher** Education General Information Survey} Ix Requirements and Specifications for Surveys of {various subjects}, HE 19.309

HEW Obligations to Institutions of **Higher Education**, Fiscal Year, FS 1.2:Ed 8/3

Higher Education, FS 5.37

Higher Education Act Title 2-b, Library Research and Demonstration Program, Abstracts, Fiscal Year (date), HE 19.135

Higher Education Act, Title II-C, FY Abstracts Strengthening Library Resources Program, ED 1.18

Higher Education and the Handicapped, Resource Directory, ED 1.32/2

Higher Education Basic Student Charges, HE 19.328

Higher Education Circulars, I 16.17

Higher Education Facilities Classification and Procedures Manual, FS 5.251:51016, HE 5.251:51016

Higher Education Opportunities for Minorities and Women, ED 1.42

Higher Education Personnel Training Programs (year), Fellowship Programs, HE 5.92

Higher Education Planning and Management Data, FS 5.253:53004, HE 5.253:53004

Higher Education Planning, a Bibliographic Handbook, HE 19.208:H 53

Higher Education Reports, FS 5.81, HE 5.81

Higher Education Salaries, FS 5.253:53015, HE 5.253:53015

Higher Education, Fall Enrollment in **Higher Education** (year), HE 19.325

Higher Education: Students Enrolled for Advanced Degrees, Fall (year), HE 19.330

Index of Institutions of **Higher Education** by State and Congressional District, HE 5.92/4

Institutions of **Higher Education**, Index by State and Congressional District, HE 19.322, ED 1.116/2

Instructional Equipment Grants Title VI-A, **Higher Education** Act of 1975, PL 89-329, HE 19.114

Instructions and Data Specifications for Reporting DHHS Obligations to Institutions of **Higher Education** and Other Nonprofit Organizations, HE 20.3050

Law, **Higher Education**, and Substance Abuse Prevention, A Biannual Newsletter, ED 1.2/16

New Dimensions in **Higher Education**, FS 5.250, HE 5.250

News of Institutes of Higher Learning; Ministry of **Higher Education**, Physics, C 41.52/4

News of Institutes of Higher Learning; Ministry of **Higher Education**, USSR, Mathematics, C 41.61/2

Higher Institutions
Accredited **Higher Institutions**, FS 5.250:50012, HE 5.250:50012

Higher Learning
DHEW Obligations to Institutions of **Higher Learning**, HE 1.2:ED 8/3

News of Institutes of **Higher Learning**; Aeronautical Engineering, C 41.56/2

News of Institutes of Higher Learning; Chemistry, and Chemistry Technology, C 41.53/8

News of Institutes of **Higher** Learning; Electromechanics, C 41.65/6

News of Institutes of **Higher Learning**; Ministry of Higher Education, Physics, C 41.52/4

News of Institutes of **Higher Learning**; Ministry of Higher Education, USSR, Mathematics, C 41.61/2

News of Institutes of **Higher** Learning; Petroleum and Gas, C 41.55/4

Highlights
ACTION Program **Highlights**, AA 1.9/4

Agricultural Trade **Highlights**, A 67.45

Aid **Highlights**, S 18.61

Argonne National Laboratory: Research and **Highlights**, E 1.86/4

Agricultural Trade **Highlights**, A 67.18:ATH

Brookhaven **Highlights**, E 1.1/4

Budget **Highlights**, PrEx 2.8/6

Center for Radiation Research, Technical **Highlights**, Fiscal Year, C 13.1/2

Coastal Pollution Research **Highlights**, EP 1.37

Conservation **Highlights**, Digest of the Progress Report of the Soil Conservation Service, A 57.1/2

Employment in Nuclear Energy Activities, a **Highlights** Report, E 1.33:0049

Foreign Affairs **Highlights**, S 1.75

FY Budget **Highlights** Federal Drug Control Programs, PrEx 26.1/4

Highlights (year) Safety Standards Activity, L 16.52

Highlights from Student Drug Use in America, HE 20.8219/2

Highlights National Oceanographic Data Center, C 55.291

Highlights of Annual Workshop of Farmer Cooperative Service, A 89.16

Highlights of Current Legislation and Activities in Mid-europe, LC 1.27

Highlights of Heart Progress, FS 2.22/11

Highlights of Legislation on Aging, FS 1.13/4, FS 14.912

Highlights of MarAd Port Activities, C 39.223/2

Highlights (National Infrastructure Protection Center), J 1.14/23-3

Highlights of Natural Resources Management, I 29.119

Highlights of Progress in Mental Health Research, FS 2.22/16

Highlights of Progress in Research in Cancer, FS 2.22/14

Highlights of Progress in Research on Neurologic Disorders, FS 2.22/12

Highlights of Progress in Research on Oral Diseases, FS 2.22/23

Highlights of Research Progress in Allergy and Infectious Diseases, FS 2.22/17

Highlights of Research Progress in Arthritis and Metabolic Diseases, FS 2.22/21

Highlights of Research Progress in General Medical Sciences, FS 2.22/20

Highlights of the Department of the Navy FY...Budget, D 201.1/1/-2

Highlights of the National Youth Gang Survey, J 32.21/3

Highlights of U.S. Exports and Import Trade, C 3.164:990

Highlights of VA Medical Research, VA 1.43/3

Indian Health **Highlights**, HE 20.2:In 25/9

Institute for Applied Technology, Technical **Highlights**, Fiscal Year, C 13.1/3

Institute for Basic Standards, Technical **Highlights**, Fiscal Year, C 13.1/4

Institute for Material Research, Metallurgy Division, Technical **Highlights**, Fiscal Year, C 13.1/5-2

Institute for Materials Research, Technical **Highlights**, Fiscal Year, C 13.1/5

Interior Budget in Brief, Fiscal Year **Highlights**, I 1.1/6

Management **Highlights** Releases, I 1.92

Manpower Development Program **Highlights**, L 7.66

MEPS (Medical Expenditure Panel Survey) **Highlights**, HE 20.6517/6

Monday Morning **Highlights**, J 16.29

New for Consumers, **Highlights** of New Federal Consumer Publications, GS 11.9/2

NICHD Research **Highlights** and Topics of Interest, HE 20.3364

1990 Housing **Highlights**, C 3.224/3-8

OIG **Highlights**, I 1.1/7-2

ORD Engineering **Highlights**, EP 1.110

ORD Science **Highlights**, EP 1.110/2

Personnel Research **Highlights**, PM 1.57

PIC **Highlights**, HE 1.62

Pollutant Identification Research **Highlights**, EP 1.37/3

Program **Highlights**, HE 20.3033

PSI **Highlights**, PrEx 1.13

Public Documents **Highlights**, GP 3.27

Public Documents **Highlights**, Microfiche Cumulation, GP 3.27/2

Recruiting **Highlights**, PM 1.18/4

Research **Highlights** in Aging, FS 2.22/25

Research **Highlights**, EP 1.81

Research **Highlights**, National Institutes of Health, FS 2.22/28

Residential Program **Highlights**, FEM 1.17

Science Resources Studies **Highlights**, NS 1.31

Southwest Fisheries Center: Research **Highlights**, Monthly Report, C 55.331

Technical **Highlights** Mining Research, I 28.151/2

Technical **Highlights** of the National Bureau of Standards, C 13.1

Technical Specification Improvement Program **Highlights**, Y 3.N 88:31/0110

Test **Highlights**, D 301.45/33-4

U.S. Department of Labor Program **Highlights**, Fact Sheet (Series), L 1.88

U.S. Foreign Trade **Highlights**, C 61.28/2

U.S. Merchandise Trade; Selected **Highlights**, FT-920, C 3.164:920

USAID **Highlights**, S 18.61

Highway •
Annual **Highway** Awards Competition, TD 2.14/2

Annual Report to Secretary of Transportation on Accident Investigation and Reporting Activities of Federal **Highway** Administration, TD 2.16

Bid Opening Report Federal-Aid **Highway** Construction Contracts Calendar Year, TD 2.47

Development of Multiple Use Facilities on **Highway** Right of Way, TD 2.121/2

Executive Summaries, National **Highway** Safety Bureau Contractors Report, TD 2.212

Fatal and Injury Accidents Rates on Federal-aid and Other **Highway** Systems, TD 2.20

Federal **Highway** Administration Newsletter, TD 2.12/2

Federal-Aid **Highway** Relocation Assistance and Payment Statistics, TD 2.28

Federally Coordinated Program of **Highway** Research and Development, TD 2.42

Foreign **Highway** News, C 18.77

Highway Accident Reports, TD 1.117

Highway Accident Reports, Brief Format, TD 1.117/2

Highway Accident/Incident Summary Reports, TD 1.117/3

Highway and Its Environment, Annual Awards Competition, TD 2.14

Highway and Traffic Safety, TD 8.12/3

Highway and Urban Mass Transportation, TD 2.18

Highway Beauty Awards Competition, TD 2.14

Highway Construction Contracts Awarded by State **Highway** Departments, C 37.25

Highway Construction Contracts Awarded by State **Highway** Departments, Tables, FW 2.19

Highway Finance, C 37.18

Highway Focus, TD 2.34

Highway Information Quarterly, TD 2.23/4

Highway Information Update, TD 2.23/5

Highway Joint Development and Multiple Use, TD 2.56

Highway Planning Notes, TD 2.13

Highway Planning Technical Reports, TD 2.25

Highway Progress, TD 2.21

Highway Progress (year) Annual Report of the Bureau of Public Roads, C 37.1

Highway Research and Development News, Plant Ecology and Esthetics, Progress and Implementation, TD 2.113/2

Highway Research and Development Studies using Federal-Aid Research and Planning Funds, TD 2.113

Highway Research Newsletter, C 37.24

Highway Safety Literature Annual Cumulations, TD 8.10/3

Highway Safety Literature, Supplements, TD 8.10/4

Highway Safety Program Manual, TD 8.8/3

Highway Safety Program Standards, TD 2.38, TD 8.8/4

Highway Safety Stewardship Report, TD 2.58

Highway Statistics, TD 2.23
Highway Statistics Summary, TD 2.23/2
Highway Taxes and Fees: How They are Collected and Distributed, TD 2.64
Highway Traffic Noise in the United States: Problem and Response, TD 2.23/7
Highway Transportation, TD 2.18
Highway Transportation Surveys, A 22.8
Highway Trust Fund, Financial Statement, TD 2.23/3
Journal of Highway Research, Public Roads, C 37.8
Milestones Along Recovery Highway, Y 3.N 21/8:18
Monthly Highway Construction Contracts Awarded by State and Federal Agencies and Toll Authorities, TD 2.51
New England Highway Weather Bulletin, A 29.32
On-Highway Diesel Prices, E 3.13/8
Posters Federal Highway Administration, TD 2.59/2
Price Trends for Federal-Aid Highway Construction, C 37.22, TD 2.49
Price Trends for Federal-Aid Highway Construction TD 2.30/16-3
Price Trends for Federal-aid-highway Construction, TD 2.49
Public Roads, Journal of Highway Research, TD 2.19
Publications National Conferences on Street and Highway Safety, C 1.21
Publications President's Highway Safety Conference, FW 2.18
R & D Highway & Safety Transportation System Studies, TD 2.24
Rail-Highway Grade-Crossing Accidents, IC 1 acci.8
Rail-Highway-Grade Crossing Accident/Incidents Bulletin, TD 3.109
Railroad-Highway Accident Reports, TD 1.112/4
Report on Activities Under Highway Safety Act, TD 8.12/2
Report to Congress on the Administration of the Highway Safety Act of 1966, TD 1.10/3
State-Wide Highway Planning Surveys, A 22.13
Statewide Highway Planning Surveys; News Bulletins, FW 2.10
Subject Bibliographies from Highway Safety Literature, SB- (series), TD 8.13/3
Task Force on Highway Safety, Pr 37.8:H 53
Highways
Highways Transport Committee Circulars, Y 3.C 83:24
Highways, Current Literature, A 22.10, FW 2.8, C 37.10
Manual on Uniform Control Devices for Streets and Highways, TD 2.8:T 67
Manual on Uniform Traffic Control Devices for Streets and Highways: Official Rulings on Requests for Interpretations, Changes, and Experimentations, TD 2.8/2
New Developments in Highways, TD 2.22
Our Nation's Highways: Selected Facts and Figures, TD 2.23/6
Pan-American Congress of Highways, 1st, Buenos Aires, S 5.23
Pan-American Congress on Highways, 2d, Rio de Janerio, S 5.23/2
Railways Freight and Passenger Traffic Handled on Highways, Class 1 Steam Railways, IC 1 ste.41
Receipts for State Administered Highways, Official Distribution, C 37.19
U.S. Highways, TD 2.65
Hi-Line
Hi-Line, Newsletters for Enlisted Personnel, TD 5.40
Hi-lites
Range Research Hi-lites, A 13.30/10History
NASA History: News and Notes, NAS 1.96
Hill
Progress Report Hill-Burton Program, FS 2.96
Representative Construction Cost of Hill- Burton Hospitals and Related Health Facilities, FS 2.74/6, HE 20.2510
Hill Air Force Base
Air Force Logistics Command, Hill Air Force Base, Telephone Directory, D 301.104/2
Hill-Burton
Hill-Burton Health Facilities Series, HE 20.6010, HE 20.6113
Hill-Burton Program, Progress Report, FS 2.95, HE 20.2509/2

Hill-Burton Project Register, FS 2.74, HE 20.2509
Hill-Burton Publications, FS 2.74/3:G-3
Hospital and Medical Facilities Series under Hill-Burton Program, FS 2.74/3
Hines
Hines Sight, VA 1.56/6
Hints
Constructive Hints, A 13.33
Hints to Settlers (on Irrigation projects), A 19.9
HIR
HIR (series), FS 3.55
Hired
Hired Farm Work Force of {year}, A 1.75, A 88.40, A 93.21, A 93.28, A 1.107
Hiring
Someone Who Cares, A Guide to Hiring an In-Home Caregiver, HE 1.1009
Hispanic
Examination Staff Procedures Manual for the Hispanic Health and Nutrition Examination Survey, HE 20.6208/2
Hispanic Focus (series), LC 24.10
Hispanic Foundation Bibliographic Series, LC 24.7
Hispanic Population in the United States, C 3.186/14-2
Hispanic Population in the United States, Advance Report, C 3.186/14
Instruction Manual: Dental Examiner's Manual for the Hispanic Health and Nutrition Survey, HE 20.6208/2-6
Instruction Manual: Dietary Interviewer's Manual for the Hispanic Health and Nutrition Examination Survey, HE 20.6208/2-2
Instruction Manual: Field Staff Operations for the Hispanic Health and Nutrition Examination Survey, HE 20.6208/2-5
Instructions for Classifying the Underlying Cause of Death: Mobile Examination Center Interviewer's Manual for the Hispanic Health and Nutrition Examination Survey, HE 20.6208/2-4
Instructions for Classifying the Underlying Cause of Death: Physician's Examination Manual for the Hispanic Health and Nutrition Examination Survey, HE 20.6208/2-3
News of the Hispanic Health and Nutrition Examination Survey, HE 20.6213/3
Progress Report to the Secretary of Education from the President's Advisory Commission on Educational Excellence for Hispanic Americans, ED 1.87
Unemployment Rate by Race and Hispanic Origin in Major Metropolitan Areas, L 2.111/6
Hispanoamericana
Airpower Journal (Hispanoamericana), D 201.26/24-3
Hispanos
Noticias De La Semana, a News Summary for Hispanos, L 1.20/7
Historian
Army Historian, D 114.2
Court Historian, Ju 13.15
Historic
Advisory List of National Register of Historic Places, I 29.76/2
Catalog of National Historic Landmarks, I 29.120
Damaged and Threatened National Historic Landmarks, I 29.117/2
Facing the Light, Historic American Portrait Daguerreotypes, SI 11.2:L 62
Historic American Buildings Survey, I 29.74
Historic American Engineering Record Catalog, I 29.84/2:C 28/976
Historic American Engineering Records Publications, I 70.9, I 29.84/2
Historic Furnishing Study (series), I 29.88/2
Historic Furnishings Report, HFC, I 29.88/2-2
Historic Resource Studies, I 29.58/3
Historic Structure and Grounds Report (series), I 29.88/4
Historic Structure Reports, I 29.88, I 70.10
National Historic Preservation Act of 1966, as Amended, Y 3.H 62:5
Preservation Tech Notes Historic Interior Spaces (series), I 29.84/3-2
Report on America's National Scenic, National Historic, and National Recreation Trails (fiscal year), I 29.130
U.S. Constitution, a National Historic Landmark Theme Study, I 29.117

Historical
Air Staff Historical Study (series), D 301.82/6
American Yesterdays, Historical Radio Scripts, I 16.57
Annotation, the Newsletter of the National Historical Publications and Records Commission, GS 4.14/2
Annual Historical Report, AMEDD Activities for the Calendar Year, D 104.30
Annual Historical Review, Armament, Munitions and Chemical Command, (AMCCOM)- (series), D 101.1/5
Annual Historical Review, Rock Island Arsenal, D 101.109
Annual Historical Review, United States Army Soldier Support Center, D 101.1/3
Annual Historical Summary; Defense Construction Supply Center, D 7.1/9
Annual Historical Summary; Defense Contract Administration Services {by region}, D 7.1/4
Annual Historical Summary; Defense Depots, D 7.1/7
Annual Historical Summary; Defense Documentation Center, D 7.1/10
Annual Historical Summary; Defense Fuel Supply Center, D 7.1/6
Annual Historical Summary; Defense General Supply Center, D 7.1/8
Annual Historical Summary; Defense Industrial Plant Equipment Center, D 7.1/3
Answer Me This: Historical Series, I 16.58/5
Archeological and Historical Data Recovery Program, I 29.59/4
Army Historical Program Fiscal Year, D 114.10/2
Army Historical Series, D 114.19
Command Historical Report, D 206.1/3
Daily Synoptic Series, Historical Weather Maps, C 30.27, C 30.38, C 30.39, C 30.40, C 30.41, C 30.42
Description of U.S. Postal Stamp, Historical and Commemorative Issues (Junior Edition), P 4.11
Engineer Historical Studies, D 103.43/2
FAA Historical Fact Book, a Chronology, 1926-1971, TD 4.2:H 62/926-71
Federal Funds for Research and Development, Detailed Historical Tables, Fiscal Years, NS 1.18/2
Fortitudine, Newsletter of Marine Corps Historical Program, D 214.20
Historical Analysis Series, D 114.19/2
Historical Base Maps (series), I 29.79/4
Historical Bibliography (series), D 110.12
Historical Chart Books, FR 1.30/2
Historical Climatology Series 6-1: Statewide Average Climatic History, C 55.287/61
Historical Climatology Series, Atlases, C 55.287/58
Historical Comparison of Budget Receipts and Expenditures by Function, Special Analysis G, PrEx 2.8/a10
Historical Compilations, C 56.222/2-2
Historical Handbook Series, I 29.58
Historical Index, C 55.287/57
Historical Monograph Series, D 208.210
Historical Monographs of Office of U.S. High Commissioner for Germany, S 1.95
Historical Notes, A 57.74
Historical Plant Cost and Annual Production Expenses for Selected Electric Plants, E 3.17/4-2
Historical Records Survey, Y 3.W 89/2:43, FW 4.14
Historical Register, U.S. Revenue Cutter Service Officers, TD 5.19/4
Historical Reports of War Administration, MC 1.30, Pr 32.4838, Pr 32.4839, Pr 32.4840, Pr 33.308, Pr 33.310, Pr 33.311
Historical Review, U.S. Army Belvoir Research and Development Center, D 101.98
Historical Review, U.S. Army Mobility Equipment Research and Development Command, D 101.98
Historical Series, TD 5.30/2
Historical Series, Independent Radio Stations (programs), I 29.16
Historical Site {brochures}, I 27.73
Historical Statistics (series), I 49.8/5

Historical Statistics of the United States, Colonial
Times to 1970, C 3.134/2:H 62
Historical Statistics on Banking, Y 3.F 31/8:26
Historical Studies, L 2.15
Historical Studies (numbered), GS 6.8
Historical Studies (series), D 114.19/3
Historical Supplement, HH 1.14/2
Historical Tables, PrEx 2.8/8
Historical Vignettes, I 1.102
Historical Weather Map, Northern Hemisphere, W
108.30
Humanities Projects in Museums and **Historical**
Organizations, NF 3.8/2-5
IRS **Historical** Studies, T 22.66
Mandrid, Columbian **Historical** Exposition, S 6.7
Marine Corps **Historical** Bibliographies, D 214.15
Marine Corps **Historical** Reference Pamphlets, D
214.14/2
Marine Corps **Historical** Reference Series, D
214.14
National **Historical** Publications Commission, GS
4.14
Navaho **Historical** Series, I 20.40
Papers of American **Historical** Association, SI 4.5
Publications **Historical** Division, D 101.42/2
Publications National **Historical** Publications
Commission, GS 4.14
QMC **Historical** Studies, D 106.8
QMC **Historical** Studies, Series II, D 106.8/2
Seventy-Fifth USA Maneuver Area Command,
Annual Report and **Historical**
Supplement, D 101.1/8
TC in the Current National Emergency, **Historical**
Report No., D 117.9, D 117.9/2
TRADOC **Historical** Monograph Series, D
101.108
TRADOC **Historical** Study Series, D 101.108/2
U.S. Army Materiel Command, Annual **Historical**
Review, D 101.1/4-2
U.S. Coast Guard **Historical** Monograph Program,
TD 5.29
United States Senate, a **Historical** Bibliography, Y
1.3:Se 5/11
USAF **Historical** Aircraft Photopaks, D 301.76/2
Historically
Faculty Graduate Study Program for **Historically**
Black Colleges and Universities, NF 3.8/
2-7
Groups with **Historically** High Incidences of
Unemployment, L 36.12
Historically Black Colleges and Universities,
Faculty Projects, Summer College
Humanities Programs for High School
Juniors, NF 3.8/2-8
White House Initiative on **Historically** Black
Colleges and Universities, Newsletter,
ED 1.89
Histories
Popular Study Series; **Histories**, I 29.45
Regimental and Squadron **Histories**, D 214.12
United States Air Force General **Histories** (series),
D 301.82/3
History
Agricultural **History** Series, A 36.133
American Military **History**, D 114.2:M 59
Army **History** D 114.20
Bibliography of the **History** of Medicine, HE
20.3615
Brief **History** of the American Labor Movement, L
2.3:1000
Calendar of United States House of Representatives
and **History** of Legislation, Y 1.2/2
Case **History** Reports for Industries, Pr 32.5223
Census of Population and Housing: **History**, C
3.223/22:90-R2
Center for Air Force **History** Publications, D
301.82/7
Civil Aeronautics Board Legislative **History** of
Regulations, C 31.206/2:L 52
Contributions from the Museum of **History** and
Technology, Papers, SI 3.3
Contributions of American Educational **History**, I
16.15
Contributions to Naval **History** (series), D 207.10/
4
Current Salary Schedules of Federal Officers and
Employees Together with a **History** of
Salary and Retirement Annuity
Adjustments, Y 4.P 84/10-15
CWIHP (Cold War International **History** Project)
Bulletin, SI 1.3/2
Earthquake **History** of the United States, C
55.202:Ea 7

Energy **History** Report, E 1.61
Energy **History** Series, E 1.78
Environmental **History** Series, D 103.43/2-2
Equine Infectious Anemia, Progress Report and
History in the United States, A 77.244
Forest Service **History** Line, A 13.98/3
GC Legislative **History** Files, GA 1.23
Harmon Memorial Lectures in Military **History**, D
305.10
History Annual Supplement, D 101.1/6
History in the House, Y 1.2/9
History of Africa, Australia, New Zealand, Etc., LC
26.9:DT-DX
History of American Naval Fighting Ships, D
207.10
History of George Washington Bicentennial
Celebration, Y 3.W 27/2:14
History of Indian Policy, I 20.2:P 75/6
History of Medical Department of Navy in World
War II, D 206.12
History of Medical Department of United States
Navy, D 206.12/2
History of the Chaplain Corps, U.S. Navy, D 201.33
History of the Economic Censuses, C 3.253/3
History of the Tariff Schedules of the United States
Annotated, ITC 1.10/2
History of Wages in the United States from
Colonial Times to 1928, L 2.3:604
Index of EPA Legal Authority Statutes and
Legislative **History**, Executive Orders,
Regulations, EP 1.5/4
Information Respecting the **History**, Conditions,
and Prospects of the Indian Tribes of the
United States, Philadelphia, Lippincott,
Grambo & Co, I 20.2:In 2
Invasion Intervention, "Intervasion": A Concise
History of the U.S. Army in Operation
Uphold Democracy, D 110.13
Legislative **History** of Titles I-XX of the Social
Security Act, HE 3.5/3
Marines in the Revolution: a **History** of
Continental Marines in the American
Revolution, D 214.13:R 32/775-83
Medical and Surgical **History** of War of Rebellion,
1861-65, W 44.10
Military **History** Section: Japanese Operational
Monograph Series, D 1.24/2
Museum of Natural **History**, Annual Report, SI 3.1/
2
National Park Service **History** Series, I 29.58/2
Natural **History** Handbook Series, I 29.62
Natural **History** Theme Studies, I 29.62/2
Naval **History** Bibliographies (series), D 221.17
Privacy and Security of Criminal **History**
Information (series), J 29.10
Proceedings Military **History** Symposium, D
301.78
Public Use Data Tape Documentation Medical
History, Ages 12-74 Years, HE 20.6226/
5
Publications Office, Chief of Military **History**, D
114.10
Report and Studies in the **History** of Art, SI 8.9
Senate **History** (series), Y 1.3/8
Smithsonian Journal of **History**, SI 1.23
Smithsonian Opportunities for Research and Study
in **History**, Art, Science, SI 1.44
Smithsonian Studies in **History** and Technology, SI
1.28
Soviet Union, Foreign Military **History** Journal,
PrEx 7.21/4-3
Special **History** Studies (series), I 29.88/5
Studies in Plains Anthropology and **History**, I
20.50
United States Air Force **History** Program, Summary
of Activities, D 301.1/2
United States Air Force **History**, a Guide to
Documentary Sources, D 301.6/5:H 62
United States Merchant Marine, Brief **History**, C
39.202:M 53/2
World War II **History** of Department of Commerce, C
1.27
Hit Kit
Army **Hit Kit** of Popular Songs, D 102.10
Army Navy **Hit Kit** of Popular Songs, M 117.7
HIV
CDC, **HIV**/AIDS Prevention, HE 20.7038/3
Facility-Based **HIV**/AIDS Education Demonstra-
tion Project FY, VA 1.97
HIV/AIDS Evaluation Monograph Series, HE
20.9515
HIV/AIDS Prevention Newsletter, HE 20.7038/2,
HE 20.7320/2
HIV/AIDS Surveillance, HE 20.7011/38

HIV/AIDS Surveillance Report, HE 20.7320
HIV Impact, HE 20.40/2
HIV/STD/TB Prevention News Update, HE
20.7318
HM
Reports, **HM**- (series), I 27.39/3
HMDA
HMDA Aggregate Reports, FR 1.63/54
HMDA Disclosure Reports, FR 1.63/55
HMO
National **HMO** Census of Prepaid Plans, HE 20.27
HMTC
HMTC Abstract Bulletin, D 7.32/2-2
Hog
Circular Letters; Corn-**Hog** Work, A 55.34, A
55.34/2, A 55.34/3
Commodity Information Series; Corn-**Hog** Leaflets,
A 55.25/7
Cooperative State-Federal **Hog** Cholera Eradication
Program Progress Report, A 77.241
Corn **Hog** Charts, A 55.14
Corn-**Hog** Circular Letters, A 55.34/3
Hog Situation, A 36.85
Publications Corn-**Hog** Board of Review, A 55.30
World **Hog** and Pork Prospects, A 36.43
Hogs
Hogs and Pigs, A 105.23/5
Hogs: Weekly Average Price per 100 Pounds, A
36.204
Holders
Schedules of Payments to **Holders** of Cotton
Options and Participation Trust
Certificates by Congressional District of
States, A 55.57
Holding
Companies **Holding** Certificates of Authority from
Secretary of Treasury As Acceptable
Securities on Federal Bonds, T 1.24, T
63.116
Holding
Releases, **Holding** Company Act of 1935, SE 1.25/2
Holdings
Cold Storage **Holdings** by States, A 36.197
Cold Storage **Holdings** of Fishery Products, I 49.8/
4
Courts-Martial Reports, **Holdings** and Decisions of
Judge Advocates General, Boards of
Review, and United States Court of
Military Appeals, D 1.29
GR 68 Quarterly Reports on **Holdings** of
Retirement Systems, C 3.242
Holdings of Selected Public Employee Retirement
Systems, GR (series), C 56.224, C 3.242
Journal **Holdings** Report, EP 1.31
Official Summary of Security Transactions and
Holdings, SE 1.9
Quarterly Reports on **Holdings** of Retirement
Systems, C 3.242
Regional Cold Storage **Holdings**, A 105.33/2
Serial **Holdings**, HE 20.7019:Se 6
Summary of Regional Cold Storage **Holdings**, A
88.20/2
Survey of Mortgage-Related Security **Holdings** of
Major Institutions, HH 1.99/4-2
Hole
Woods **Hole** Laboratory, I 49.62
Holiday
Official Opening and Closing Hours of Board of
Governors and Federal Reserve Banks,
also **Holiday** During Month, FR 1.50
Posters Federal **Holiday** Commission, Y 3.H 71:12
Holidays
Official Hours and **Holidays** to Be Observed by
Federal Reserve Offices During Year
(date), FR 1.50
World **Holidays** Listed, Guide to Business Travel,
C 42.8/a:H 717/2
Holloman
Economic Resource Impact Statement **Holloman**
AFB, New Mexico, D 301.105/6
hollow
Structural Clay Products (common brick, face brick,
vitrified paving brick, **hollow** building
tile), C 3.109
Holmes
Holmes Safety Association Bulletin, L 38.12
Holocaust
Posters United States **Holocaust** Memorial
Council, Y 3.H 74:9
President's Commission on **Holocaust**, Pr 39.8:H
74

HOM
HOM (series), D 7.8/9
Home
Analysis of HUD-Acquired **Home** Mortgage Properties, HH 1.101
Annotated Manual of Statutes and Regulations of the Federal **Home** Loan Bank Board, FHL 1.6/2:St 2
Business Situation at **Home** and Abroad, C 18.54/2
Combined Financial Statements of Members of the Federal **Home** Loan Bank System, FHL 1.12
Conventional **Home** Mortgage Rates in Early (month), FHL 1.25/3
Correction and Additions to Publications of Officers at **Home** and Abroad, N 6.6
Cost of Food at **Home** Estimated for Food Plans at Four Cost Levels, A 98.19/2
Cost of Food at **Home** Estimated for Food Plans at Three Cost Levels, Southern Region, A 106.39/5
Directory of Providers of Services of **Home** Health Services, HE 3.51
Electric **Home** and Farm Authority Publications, Y 3.T 25:9 CT
Estimated **Home** Mortgage Debt and Financing Activity, FHL 1.16
Farm-Mortgage Lending Experience of 19 Life Insurance Companies, Federal Land Banks, and Farmers **Home** Administration, A 93.9/5
Farmers **Home** Administration Features, A 84.9
Federal **Home** Loan Bank Board Digest, FHL 1.14
Federal **Home** Loan Bank Review, Y 3.F 31/3:9, FL 3.7, NHA 3.8
FHA **Home** Mortgage Insurance Operations, State, County and MSA/PMSA, HH 2.24/8
FHA Monthly Report of Operations: **Home** Mortgage Programs, HH 2.27/2
FHA Trends, Characteristics of **Home** Mortgages Insured by FHA, HH 2.24
FHLB System S & L's Combined Financial Statements: Savings and **Home** Financing Source Book, FHL 1.12/2
Food and **Home** Notes, A 21.33, A 107.9
Garden and **Home** Food Preservation Facts, A 43.29
Guidelines for {Various Health Professionals and Sub-professional} in **Home** Health Services, FS 2.6/8
Home and Abroad with Bureau of Foreign and Domestic Commerce, C 18.191
Home and Garden Bulletins, A 1.77
Home Cards, Y 3.F 73:27
Home Demonstration Review, A 43.5/14
Home Economics Circulars, I 16.25
Home Economics Letters, I 16.51
Home Economics Research Reports, A 1.87
Home Education Circulars, I 16.13
Home Education Letters, I 16.47
Home Front, HH 1.113
Home Health Agencies, FS 3.51
Home Health Agency Manual, HE 22.8/5
Home Improvement Pamphlets, I 20.32
Home Mortgage Disclosure Act Data (State), FR 1.63
Home Mortgage Interest Rates and Terms, FHL 1.25
Home Mortgage Interest Rates Continue to Decline in Early (Month), FHL 1.25/2
Home Owner's Loan Acts and Housing Acts {July 22, 1932}, Y 1.2:H 75/3
Home Owners' Loan Corporation Publications, FL 3.9, Y 3.F 31/3:8
Hymns from **Home**, W 109.13
Inspection of Several Branches of National **Home** for Disabled Volunteer Soldiers, W 9.5
Journal of the Federal **Home** Loan Bank Board, FHL 1.27
Low Income **Home** Energy Assistance Program, Report to Congress, HE 3.76, HE 25.17
Medicare **Home** Health Agency Manual, HE 22.8/5
Members of the Federal **Home** Loan Bank System, FHL 1.31
Model Town **Home** Selector, Y 3.F 31/11:33
Posters Farmers **Home** Administration, A 84.15
Press Releases Federal **Home** Loan Bank Board, FHL 1.7
Publications Bureau of **Home** Economics, A 42.5
Publications **Home** Owners' Loan Corporation, FL 3.9
Rates & Terms on Conventional **Home** Mortgages Annual Summary, FHF 1.15

Record of Changes in Memberships of National **Home** for Disabled Volunteer Soldiers, NH 1.6
Report of the Federal **Home** Loan Bank Board, FHL 1.1
Savings and **Home** Financing Chart Book, FHL 1.11/2
Savings and **Home** Financing, Source Book, FHL 1.11, T 71.17
School **Home**-Garden Circulars, I 16.16
Secondary Market Prices and Yields and Interest Rates for **Home** Loans, HH 1.99/3
Special Reports Publications Relating to **Home** Economics and Human Relations, A 77.711
Home Demonstration
Here and There with **Home Demonstration** Workers, A 43.5/13
Home Economics
Cooperative Extension Work in Agriculture and **Home Economics**, A 10.24
Home Economics in Institutions Granting Bachelor's or Higher Degrees, FS 5.283:83008, HE 5.283:83008
Notes on Graduate Studies and Research in Home Economics and **Home Economics** Education, A 1.53
Occupational **Home Economics** Education Series, HE 19.134
Home Mortgage
Annual Report, Voluntary **Home Mortgage** Credit Program, HH 1.25
Home Study
HS {**Home Study**} (series), D 14.11, D 119.15, FEM 1.13
Homebuilt
Briefs of Accidents Involving Amateur Built (**homebuilt**) Aircraft U.S. General Aviation, TD 1.109/6
Homeland
Office of **Homeland** Security (General Publication), PR 43.14
Homeless
Runaways and Otherwise **Homeless** Youth Fiscal Year, Annual Report on the Runaway Youth Act, HE 23.1309/2
Homemaker
Homemaker News, A 21.22
Popular Publications for Farmer, Suburbanite, **Homemaker**, Consumer, A 21.9/8:5, A 107.12:5
Homeowner's
Report to Congress on the Emergency **Homeowner's** Relief Act, HH 1.64
Homeownership
Housing Vacancies and **Homeownership** Survey, C 3.294
Homes
All Electric **Homes** in the United States, Annual Bills, January 1, (year), FP 1.10
All Electric **Homes**, Annual Bills, E 3.16
Construction Reports; New One-family **Homes** Sold and for Sale, C 25 (series), C 56.211/2
Energy Star **Homes** Update, EP 4.29
FHA **Homes**, Data for States, on Characteristics of FHA Operations Under Sec. 203, HH 2.24/4
FHA Low Cost Housing Trends of One-family **Homes** Insured by FHA, HH 2.26
Inspection of State Soldiers and Sailor's **Homes**, NH 1.5
Quarterly Tracking System, Energy Using and Conservation Equipment in **Homes**, E 3.23
Sales of New One-Family **Homes**, C 3.215/9
Homestead
General Land Office, Automated Records Project, Pre-1908 **Homestead** & Cash Entry Patents, I 53.57
Maps of States Showing Lands Designated by Secretary of Interior As Subject to Entry Under Enlarged **Homestead** Act of February 19, 1909, I 1.50
Homesteading
Evaluation of the Urban **Homesteading** Demonstration Program, HH 1.73
Homestudy
Homestudy Course; Communicable Disease Control, HE 20.7710
Homestudy Course; Community Health Analysis (series), HE 20.7021/8
Homestudy Course; Community Health Analysis-I Manuals, HE 20.7021/8-2

Homestudy Course; Community Health Analysis-II, HE 20.7021/8-3
Homestudy Course; Environmental Protection, HE 20.7021/10
Homestudy Course; Vectorborne Disease Control (series), HE 20.7021/7-2
Homestudy Course; Water Fluoridation, HE 20.7021/9-2
Homestudy Course; Water Fluoridation Test Exercise, HE 20.7021/9-3
Homestudy Courses; Basic Mathematics, HE 20.7021/5
Homestudy Courses; Communicable Disease Control, HE 20.7021/2
Homestudy Courses; Community Hygiene, HE 20.7021
Homestudy Courses; Foodborne Disease Control, HE 20.7021/6
Homestudy Courses; Manuals, HE 20.7021/3-2
Homestudy Courses; Principles of Epidemiology, HE 20.7021/3
Homestudy Courses; Water Fluoridation, HE 20.7021/9
Homestudy Courses; Waterborne Disease Control, HE 20.7021/4
Homicide
Homicide Surveillance, HE 20.7611/2
Hominy
Corn (**Hominy**) Grits for Domestic Distribution, A 82.3/4
Homoptera
General Catalogue of **Homoptera**, A 77.20
Honduran
Honduran-Guatemalan Boundary Commission, 1918, S 3.25
Ships Registered Under Liberian, Panamanian, and **Honduran** Flags Deemed by the Navy Department to Be Under Effective U.S. Control, C 39.228
Honey
Honey, A 92.28/2
Honey Market News, A 88.19
Honey Production, Annual Summary, A 9.28/2
Honey Report, A 88.19/2
Honey Report, Louisiana Crop Reporting Service, A 88.19/2-2
Honey Reports, A 82.12
Honey, Annual Summary, A 88.19/3, A 9.28/2
National **Honey** Market News, A 88.19
Semi-Monthly **Honey** Reports, A 36.105, A 88.19
Hong Kong
American Consulate General, **Hong Kong**, Index of Chinese Mainland Press, S 1.112
Honolulu
Honolulu District: Technical Reports, D 103.51
Pan-Pacific Educational Conference, 1st **Honolulu**, August 1921, S 5.21/2, S 5.22
Pan-Pacific Scientific Conference, 1st **Honolulu**, 1920, S 5.21/1
Honor
Medal of **Honor** Recipients, Y 4.V 64/4:M 46/3
PHA **Honor** Awards for Design Excellence, HH 3.10
Roll of **Honor**, Supplemental Statement of Disposition of Bodies of Deceased Union Soldiers and Prisoners of War Removed to National Cemeteries in Southern and Western United States, W 39.8
Roll of **Honor**, W 39.7
URA **Honor** Awards Program in Urban Renewal Design, HH 7.16
World War II **Honor** List of Dead and Missing (by States), W 107.13
Honor Awards
FHA **Honor Awards** for Presidential Design, HH 2.25
Hop
Hop Stocks, A 105.36
Hops
Stocks of **Hops**, A 88.44, A 92.30
Wheat, Rice, Feed Grains, Dry Peas, Dry Beans, Seeds, **Hops**, A 67.30:W 56
Horizon
Johnny **Horizon** Environmental Program: Action Booklets, I 1.101
Horizons
Educational **Horizons**, NAS 1.49/2
Horizons, Indian Mineral Resource, I 20.67
FAR {Far Area Research} **Horizons**, S 1.125
Horizons, S 18.58
Toward New **Horizons**, Pr 32.5023

Housing Census Separate Reports and Bulletins, C 3.950-8/4
Housing Digest, Y 3.F 31/4:14
Housing/FHA News, HH 2.29
Housing Finance Review, FHL 1.32
Housing in the Economy, HH 1.24
Housing Index-Digest, Y 3.C 33/3:7
Housing Legal Digest, Decisions, Opinions, Legislations Relating to **Housing** Construction and Finance, Y 3.C 33/3:10
Housing Monograph Series, Y 3.N 21/12:14
Housing News, Y 3.F 31/4:16
Housing Planning Information Series, HH 8.10
Housing Promotion Pointers, Y 3.F 31/11:18
Housing References, HH 1.23/2
Housing Research, HH 1.9/2
Housing Research Division Publications, HH 1.16
Housing Starts in (Month), C 3.215/2
Housing Supplement to 1st Series: **Housing** Bulletins (by States), C 3.940-31
Housing Vacancies and Homeownership Survey, C 3.294
Housing Vacancy Survey, C 224./13-2
Housing, 1st Series (by States), C 3.940-30
Housing, 2d Series (by States), C 3.940-32
Housing, 3d Series (by States), C 3.940-33
Housing, 4th Series (by States), C 3.940-34
HUD **Housing** Today, HH 1.128
Indian and Alaska Native **Housing** and Community Development Programs, Annual Report to Congress, HH 1.80
Major Programs of the U.S. Department of **Housing** and Urban Development, Fact Sheets, HH 1.43/2
Monthly Report on **Housing**, HH 1.13
National **Housing** Bulletins, NHA 1.3
National **Housing** Inventory, C 3.221
National **Housing** Production Report, HH 1.79/2
New **Housing** Units Authorized by Local Building Permits and New Dwelling Units Authorized in Local Building Permits, C 3.215/4
1950 Census of Population and **Housing** Announcements, C 3.950-4/3
1990 Census of **Housing**, Residential Finance, CH-4-1, C 3.224/13:1990 CH-4-1
1990 Census of Population and **Housing** Special Tabulation on Aging, C 3.281/2
1990 Census of Population and **Housing**, Special Tabulation on Aging, Federal Region 1, Connecticut-Maine-Massachusetts-New Hampshire-Rhode Island-Vermont, Cd 90-AOA1, C 3.218/2:CD 90-AOA
1990 **Housing** Highlights, C 3.224/3-8
Nonfarm **Housing** Characteristics, 1950 **Housing** Census Report H-B (series), C 3.950/3
Nonfarm **Housing** Starts, C 56.211/3
PHA Low-Rent **Housing** Bulletins, HH 3.3/4
PHPC (Public **Housing** Primary Care Program) Bulletin, HE 20.9121
Planning for **Housing** Security (series), HH 1.6/11
Population and **Housing** (by States), C 3.940-38
Posters **Housing** and Urban Development Department, HH 1.98
Public and Indian **Housing** FY . . . Program Fungins Plan, HH 1.80/2
Public **Housing** Management Improvement Program: Technical Memorandums, HH 1.63
Public **Housing**, FW 3.7, NHA 4.8
Report, Office of **Housing** Expediter, Y 3.H 81/2:7
Residential Energy Consumption Survey: **Housing** Characteristics, E 3.43/3
Review of Some Recent Magazine Articles Relating to **Housing**, I 40.9
Rural **Housing** (New Jersey), A 84.17
Safety Posters Federal Public **Housing** Authority, NHA 4.9
Savings, Mortgage Financing and **Housing** Data, FHL 1.10
Selected References on **Housing**, Y 3.C 33/3:8
Special Reports Central **Housing** Committee, Y 3.C 33/3:9
Status of Slum-Clearance and Low-Rent **Housing** Projects, I 40.7
Summary of Activities Senate Banking, **Housing**, and Urban Affairs Committee, Y 4.B 22/3:Ac 8
Tabulation of Project Note Sales for Low- income **Housing**, HH 1.71/2
Task Force on Low-Income **Housing**, Pr 37.8:H 81

Technical Information on Building Materials for Use in Design of Low-cost **Housing**, C 13.27
Telephone Directory **Housing** and Urban Development Department, HH 1.92
Trends Toward Open Occupancy in **Housing** Programs of Public **Housing** Administration, HH 3.8
U.S. Census of **Housing** City Blocks, Series HC (3), C 3.224/6
U.S. Census of **Housing** Components of Inventory Change, Final Report HC (4) series, C 3.224/6
U.S. Census of **Housing** Special Reports for Local **Housing** Authorities, series HC (S 1), C 3.224/8
U.S. Census of **Housing** State and Small Areas, Final Report HC (1) (series), C 3.224/3
U.S. **Housing** Market Conditions, HH 1.120
United States Censuses of Population and **Housing**: Geographic Identification Code Scheme, Phc (2) (series), C 3.223/13
Update Department of **Housing** and Urban Development, HH 1.68
Veterans Emergency **Housing** Program: Community Action Report to Mayor's Emergency **Housing** Committee, NHA 1.12, Y 3.H 81/2:8
Veterans' Emergency **Housing** Program: Community Action Bulletin, NHA 1.14
War **Housing** Technical Bulletins, NHA 4.10
Housing Characteristics
American Housing Survey: **Housing** Characteristics for Selected Metropolitan Areas ,Milwaukee, Wisconsin, Primary Metropolitan Statistical Area, C 3.215/17-29
How
How Federal Agencies Develop Management Talent, Management Staff Development Series Reports, CS 1.56
How They Do It, Illustrations of Practice in Administration of AFDC (series), HE 17.408/2
How to Find U.S. Statutes and U.S. Code Citations, GS 4.102:St 2
How to Inspect Charts, HTIC LS (series), L 16./3
How to Use Injury Statistics to Prevent Occupational Accidents, L 16.42
How to Use the Microfiche, GP 3.22/3
Howard University
Howard University, Annual Reports, I 1.18
Publications **Howard** University, FS 5.41
Hoy
Hoy, Y 3.Sp 2/7:9
HPC
HPC (High Performance Computing) Modernization Plan, D 1.106
HPMC
HPMC Performance Indicators, HH 1.57
HRA
HRA, HSA, CDS, ADAMHA Public Advisory Committees, HE 20.6013
HRCD
HRCD, Human Resources Compact Disk, PM 1.59/2
HRSA
HRSA, Care Action, HE 20.9516
HRSA, State Health Workforce Profiles, HE 20.9317
HRSA, State Health Workforce Profiles (database), HE 20.9317/2
HS
HS {Home Study} (series), D 14.11, D 119.15, FEM 1.13
HSA
HRA, **HSA**, CDS, ADAMHA Public Advisory Committees, HE 20.6013
HSMHA
HSMHA Health Reports, HE 20.2010/2
HSRA
HSRA Directory, HE 20.9015
HSS
Special Study Report, NTSB-**HSS**- (series), TD 1.120
Special Study, NTSB-**HSS** (series), TD 1.126
HTIC
How to Inspect Charts, **HTIC** LS (series), L 16./3
HTIS
HTIS Bulletin, D 7.32/3

HUD
Annual Report of **HUD** Activities Under the Uniform Relocation Assistance Policies Act of 1970, HH 1.49
Biennial **HUD** Awards for Design Excellence, HH 1.41
Executive Summary of **HUD** Research Project Report (series), HH 1.53
HUD Building Technology Reports, HH 1.72
HUD Challenge, HH 1.36
HUD Challenge Reprints, HH 1.36/a
HUD Clearinghouse Service, HCS (series), HH 1.35
HUD Guides (numbered), HH 1.6/7
HUD Handbooks (numbered), HH 1.6/6
HUD Housing Today, HH 1.128
HUD International Briefs, HH 1.40/2
HUD International Information Series, HH 1.40
HUD International Information Sources Series, HH 1.40/4
HUD International Special Reports, HE 1.40/5
HUD International Special Supplements, HH 1.40/3-2
HUD International Supplements, HH 1.40/3
HUD Library Recent Acquisitions, HH 1.23/5
HUD Minimum Property Standards, HH 1.6/9
HUD Newsletter, HH 1.15/4
HUD Program Guides, HH 1.6/5
HUD Research, HH 1.56
HUD Research Thesaurus, HH 1.56/2
HUD Sales Connection, HH 1.115
HUD Scorecard, Quality Assurance Program, HH 1.83
HUD Selling List, HH 1.6/3-2
HUD Solar Status, HH 1.69
HUD Survey Reveals Large Increase in Pension Fund Investment in Mortgage Instruments, HH 1.99/7
HUD Training Handbooks, HH 1.6/6-2
HUD User Bibliography Series, HH 1.23/7
Minority Business Enterprise in **HUD** Programs, Annual Report, HH 1.60
Programs of **HUD**, HH 1.100
Water and Sewer Facilities Grant Program, **HUD** Information Series, HH 1.17
HUD-Acquired
Analysis of **HUD-Acquired** Home Mortgage Properties, HH 1.101
HUD-IP
HUD-IP (series), HH 1.27
HUD-MP
HUD-MP (series), HH 1.28
HUD-PG
HUD-PG (series), HH 1.29
HUD-TS
HUD-TS (series), HH 1.31
Hudson's Bay
Joint Commission on **Hudson's Bay** and Puget's Sound, S 3.9
Human
Air Force **Human** Resources Laboratory: Annual Report, D 301.45/27-5
Air University, **Human** Resources Research Institute, Research Memorandum, D 301.26/7
Biblio-Profile on **Human** Communication and Its Disorders a Capsule State-of-the-art Report and Bibliography, HE 20.3513/2
Committee on the Assessment of **Human** Health Effects of Great Lakes Water Quality: Annual Report, Y 3.In 8/28:15
Country Reports on **Human** Rights Practices, Y 4.F 76/1-15, Y 4.In 8/16:15
HRCD, **Human** Resources Compact Disk, PM 1.59/2
Human Development News, HE 23.10
Human Embryology and Development Study Section, HE 20.3001/2:Em 1
Human Engineering Report, D 210.14/3
Human Genetics Informational and Educational Materials, HE 20.5117
Human Genome News, E 1.99/3
Human Genome Project Progress Report, Fiscal Years, HE 20.3063
Human Needs, HE 17.26
Human Resources, PrEx 7.21/9
Human Services, Bibliography Series, HE 1.18/4
Human Services, Monograph Series, HE 1.54
Human Systems Division, Annual Report, D 301.45/38-2
Journal of **Human** Services Abstracts, HE 1.50

National Advisory Child Health and **Human** Development Council, HE 20.3001/2:C 43

National Institute of Child Health and **Human** Development Intramural Research Program: Annual Report of the Scientific Director, HE 20.3365

Office of **Human** Development Services Budget Request, HE 23.13

Protecting **Human** Subjects, E 1.144

Publications **Human** Research Unit, D 101.46

Report on USDA **Human** Nutrition Research and Education Activities, A Report to Congress, A 1.1/5

Report of the Senate Committee on Labor and **Human** Resources Presenting its View and Estimates Pursuant to the Congressional Budget Act, Y 4.L 11/4:C 76

Report to the Advisory Child Health and **Human** Development Council, HE 20.3362/7

Report of the FCCSET Committee on Education and **Human** Resources, PrEx 8.111

Research Bulletins Air Training Command, **Human** Resources Research Center, D 301.36/3

Research Memorandum Air University, **Human** Resources Report Institute, D 301.26/7

Research Reports Air Training Command, **Human** Resources Research Center, D 301.36/6

Research Review, Air Training Command, **Human** Resources Research Center, D 301.36/4

Special Reports Publications Relating to Home Economics and **Human** Relations, A 77.711

Technical Appendixes to the Report and Recommendations to the Secretary, U.S. Department of Health and **Human** Services, Y 3.P 29:1-2

World List of Future International Meeting: Pt. 2, Social, Cultural, Commercial, **Humanistic**, LC 2.9/2

Humanities
Exploring Careers in the **Humanities**, HE 19.108:Ex 7/8

Historically Black Colleges and Universities, Faculty Projects, Summer College **Humanities** Programs for High School Juniors, NF 3.8/2-8

Humanities, NF 3.10

Humanities (2d series), NF 3.11

Humanities in America: A Report to the President, the Congress, and the American People, NF 3.21

Humanities Projects in Libraries and Archives, Guidelines and Applications Instructions, NF 3.8/2-10

Humanities Projects in Libraries, Guidelines Application Instructions, NF 3.8/2-2

Humanities Projects in Media, NF 3.16

Humanities Projects in Media, Guidelines and Application Instructions, NF 3.16

Humanities Projects in Museums and Historical Organizations, NF 3.8/2-5

Public **Humanities** Projects, Guidelines and Application Instructions, NF 3.8/2-9

Human Rights
Annual Report on International Religious Freedom (Bureau for Democracy, **Human Rights** and Labor), S 1.151

Humid
Vegetables for the Hot, **Humid** Tropics (series), A 106.26

Hungary
Tripartite Claims Commission (U.S., Austria, and **Hungary**), S 3.37

Hunger
Presidential Commissional on World **Hunger**, Pr 39.8:W 89/3

War on **Hunger**, Monthly New Report, S 18.34

World **Hunger** Working Group, Pr 39.8:W 89

Hunter
Preliminary Estimates of Waterfowl Harvest and **Hunter** Activity in the United States During the Hunting Season, I 49.106

Sandhill Crane Harvest and **Hunter** Activity in the Central Flyway During the Hunting Season, I 49.106/4

Hunting
Analysis of the 1985 National Survey of Fishing, **Hunting** and Wildlife-Associated Recreation Reports, I 49.98/3

National Survey of Fishing, **Hunting**, and Wildlife-Associated Recreation, I 49.98, I 49.98/ 2-nos., I 49.98/4

Preliminary Estimates of Age and Sex Composi- tions of Ducks and Geese Harvested in the **Hunting** Season in Comparison with Prior Years, I 49.106/3

Preliminary Estimates of Waterfowl Harvest and Hunter Activity in the United States During the **Hunting** Season, I 49.106

Summary of Federal **Hunting** Regulations for (year), I 49.24/2

Huntington's Disease
NINCDS **Huntington's** Disease Research Program, HE 20.3502:H 92/2

Hurricane
Diagnostics Report of the National **Hurricane** Center, C 55.131

Hurricane Research Progress Reports, C 55.609

National **Hurricane** Research Laboratory, Fiscal Year Programs, Fiscal Year Projections, C 55.601/3

National **Hurricane** Research Project Reports, C 30.70

Hurricanes
Forecast Tracks and Probabilities for **Hurricanes** (by name), C 55.126

Husbandman
Extension Animal **Husbandman**, A 77.214

Extension Poultry **Husbandman**, A 43.5/12

Husbandry
Animal **Husbandry** Division, A 77.209

Animal **Husbandry** Division Mimeographs, A 4.26

Hybrid
Electric and **Hybrid** Vehicle Program, Annual Report to Congress, E 1.45/2

Electric and **Hybrid** Vehicle Program, EHV/ quarterly Report, E 1.45

Hybrid Corn, A 88.12/13

Hydraulic
Bonneville **Hydraulic** Laboratory Reports, D 103.27/2

Hydraulic and Engineering Construction, C 41.47

Hydraulic and Excavation Tables, I 27.16

Hydraulic Design Series, TD 2.33

Hydraulic Engineering and Soil Improvement, C 41.47/3

Hydraulic Engineering Circulars, TD 2.27

Hydraulic Laboratory Bulletin, C 13.26/2

Hydraulic Laboratory Report, I 27.32

Hydraulic Laboratory: Technical Reports, D 103.44

Index of Straight-time Average Hourly Earnings for **Hydraulic** Turbine Operations, L 2.78/2

Indexes of Prices for Selected Materials, **Hydraulic** Turbine Industry, L 2.78

Report on Current **Hydraulic** Laboratory Research in U.S., C 13.26

Hydraulics
Experiment Station **Hydraulics** Bulletin, W 31.10

Reports of Committee on Tidal **Hydraulics**, D 103.28

Technical Bulletin of Committee on Tidal **Hydraulics**, D 103.28/2

Hydro
Division of Fossil and **Hydro** Power, Monthly Report, Y 3.T 25:48

Fossil and **Hydro** Power Monthly Report, Y 3.T 25:62

Hydro Electric Plant Construction Cost and Annual Production Expenses, E 3.17/3

Hydro Energy, E 1.99

Hydro-Electric
Federal Power Commission Laws and **Hydro- Electric** Power Development Laws (June 10, 1920), Y 1.2:F 31/7

Hydrodynamics
International Conference on Numerical Ship **Hydrodynamics**: Proceedings, D 211.9/ 5

Proceedings International Conference on Numerical Ship **Hydrodynamics**, D 211.9/5

Symposium on Naval **Hydrodynamics**, D 210.19

Hydroelectric
Evaluation Report, Water Resources Appraisal for **Hydroelectric** Licensing, FP 1.31

Hydroelectric Power Resources of the United States, Developed and Undeveloped, FP 1.123

Hydrogen
Hydrogen, E 1.99

Hydrographic
Hydrographic Bulletins, D 203.3

Hydrographic Notices, N 6.14

Hydrographic Office Publications, M 202.23, N 6.8

Ice Supplement to **Hydrographic** Bulletins, N 6.3/2

Quarterly Bulletin for Part 2, **Hydrographic** Products, D 5.351/2-2

Reprint of **Hydrographic** Information, N 6.19

Hydrographic Products
Catalog of Maps, Charts, and Related Products, Part 2, **Hydrographic Products**, D 5.351/2

Hydrography
Hydrography Division Circulars, I 19.6

Hydrologic
Compilation of **Hydrologic** Data (by area), I 19.58

Hydrologic Bulletin, Hourly and Daily Precipitation; Lower Mississippi-West Gulf District, C 30.35

Hydrologic Bulletin, Hourly and Daily Precipitation; Missouri River District, C 30.34

Hydrologic Bulletin, Hourly and Daily Precipitation; North Atlantic District, C 30.30

Hydrologic Bulletin, Hourly and Daily Precipitation; Ohio River District, C 30.32

Hydrologic Bulletin, Hourly and Daily Precipitation; Pacific District, C 30.36

Hydrologic Bulletin, Hourly and Daily Precipitation; South Pacific District, C 30.31

Hydrologic Bulletin, Hourly and Daily Precipitation; Upper Mississippi District, C 30.33

Hydrologic Bulletins, A 1.55

Hydrologic Engineering Center: General Publications, D 103.55/2

Hydrologic Engineering Center: Research Notes, D 103.55/4

Hydrologic Investigation Atlases (maps), I 19.89

Hydrologic Pamphlets, W 7.27

Hydrologic Unit Map, I 19.89/2

Notes on **Hydrologic** Activities, Bulletins, Y 3.F 31/13:3, Y 3.In 8/8:7

Selected Papers in the **Hydrologic** Sciences, I 19.13/2

Hydrology
Bibliography of **Hydrology** and Sedimentation of the United States and Canada, I 19.13

Joint **Hydrology**-Sedimentation Bulletins, Y 3.In 8/ 8:9, Y 3.W 29:9

Meterology and **Hydrology** (abstracts), C 41.78

Military **Hydrology** Bulletins, D 103.32

Plan of Work for Cooperative **Hydrology** Investigations, I 53.47

Hydrometeorological
Hydrometeorological Reports, C 55.28

Hydropac
Hydropac Message Summary, N 6.34, M 202.24

Hygiene
Child **Hygiene** (letters), T 27.41

Homestudy Courses; Community **Hygiene**, HE 20.7021

Industrial **Hygiene** News Letters, FS 2.45

Occupational Safety and Health Industrial **Hygiene** Field Operations Manual, L 35.6/3-6

Social **Hygiene** Monthly, T 27.21

Hygienic
Hygienic Laboratory Bulletins, National Institute of Health Bulletin, T 27.3

Hymns
Hymns from Home, W 109.13

Hypertension
Renal Disease and **Hypertension**, Proceedings, Annual Conference, HE 20.5412

Hypoglycemia
Hypoglycemia, National Diabetes Information Clearinghouse, HE 20.3323/2

Hysterectomy
Surgical Sterilization Surveillance, **Hysterectomy** (series), HE 20.7011/30-2

I

I & N Reporter, J 21.10/2

I Hear American Singing (radio scripts), FS 1.9

I.L.S.
Instrument Approach Charts, **I.L.S.**, C 4.9/14

IACC
IACC (Series), D 1.92

IADS
Agricultural Development, **IADS** News Digest, A 95.10/2

IADS-C
IADS-C (Consultant) (series), A 95.10/2

IADS-S
IADS-S (Survey) (series), A 95.10

Ibero

Seville, Spain, **Ibero**-American Exposition, October 12, 1928, S 6.21

Ic

Table of Cases in Both ICC Reports and **Ic** Reports, IC 1.6/5

ICA

Counterpart Funds and **ICA** Foreign Currency Accounts, J 17.11/3

ICA Bulletins (numbered), S 17.3

ICA Contracts Notice, S 7.26/2

ICA Financed Awards, S 17.26

ICA Health Summary, S 17.34

ICA Newsletter, GS 1.37

ICA Small Business Circulars, S 17.13

Small Business Memo, **ICA**/SBM Series, S 17.14

ICARUS

ICARUS: The Cadet Creative Writing Magazine, D 305.22

ICAS

ICAS Reports, Y 3.F 31/16:12

ICC

ICC Cases in Federal Courts, IC 1.6/9

ICC Register, IC 1.35

ICC Reports, Cases Cited, IC 1.6/6

Table of Cases in Both **ICC** Reports and Ic Reports, IC 1.6/5

Table of Cases on Formal Docket of **ICC** Not Disposed of in Printed Reports, IC 1.6/8

ICD 9

Instruction Manual: **ICD 9** Acme Decision Tables for Classifying Underlying Causes of Death, HE 20.6208/4-2

ICD.9.CM

ICD.9.CM International Classification of Diseases, HE 22.41/2

ICDA

Instruction Manual: **ICDA** Eighth Revision of Decision Tables for Classifying Underlying Causes of Death, HE 20.6208/4-5

Ice

Ice Supplement to Hydrographic Bulletins, N 6.3/2

Ice Supplement to North Atlantic Pilot Chart, N 6.15/2

Snow and **Ice** Bulletin, A 29.16

World Data Center A Glaciology (Snow and **Ice**), Glaciological Data Report, GD- (nos), C 55.220/6

World Data Center A Glaciology (Snow and **Ice**): New Accessions List, C 55.220/8

Iceland

Nautical Charts and Publications, Region 3, Western Europe, **Iceland**, Greenland, and the Arctic, C 55.440/3

NIMA Nautical Charts, Public Sale Region 3, Western Europe, **Iceland**, Greenland, and the Arctic, TD 4.82/3

ICF

Inertial Confinement Fusion, **ICF** Annual Report, E 1.99/7-2

ICO

ICO Information Reports, Y 3.F 31/16:9-2

ICO Pamphlets, Y 3.F 31/16:9

ICR

ICR (series), J 1.36/2

ICRDB

ICRDB Cancergram, HE 20.3173/2

ICRL-RR

Injury Control Research Laboratory: Research Report, **ICRL-RR** (series), HE 20.1116

Idaho

Activities of the U.S. Geological Survey, Water Resources Division, Status of **Idaho** Projects, I 19.55/3

Cattle on Feed, Illinois, Iowa, Nebraska, **Idaho**, and California, A 88.16/7

Idaho, Governor, Annual Reports, 1878 90, I 1.19

Reintroduction and Management of Wolves in Yellowstone National Park and the Central **Idaho** Wilderness Area, Y 3.W 83

Water Resources Development in **Idaho**, D 103.35/12

Ideas

Adult Education **Ideas**, FS 5.42

Field Works, **Ideas** for Housing and Community Development, HH 1.75/3

Ideas, 4 H and Youth Development, A 43.36

Ideas that Work, L 37.26

NASA Bits {brief **ideas**, thoughts, suggestions}, NAS 1.36

New Product **Ideas**, Process Improvements, and Cost-Saving Techniques, Relating to {various subjects}, NASA/SBA FA (series), NAS 1.56

Recruiting **Ideas**, FS 2.51

Identical

Identical Bidding in Public Procurement Report of Attorney General Under Executive Order 10936, J 1.31

Report of Federal Trade Commission on Rates of Return (after taxes) for **Identical** Companies in Selected Manufacturing Industries, FT 1.21

Identification

Census of Population and Housing: Geographic **Identification** Code Scheme, C 3.223/22:90-R5

Consolidated Address and Territorial Bulletin, VA Station Addresses, **Identification** Numbers, and Territorial Jurisdictions, VA 1.69

Federal Item **Identification** Guides for Supply Cataloging, Description Patterns, D 7.6/2:6-2

Federal Item **Identification** Guides for Supply Cataloging, Indexes, Supplements, D 7.6/2:6-1, D 7.8:1

Federal Item **Identification** Guides for Supply Cataloging, Reference Drawings, D 7.6/2:6-3

Federal Procurement Data System, Contractor **Identification** File, Alphabetical Listing, PrEx 2.24/14

Geographic **Identification** Code Scheme {by regions}, C 3.223/13-2

(HCFA) Medicare Unique Physician **Identification** Number (Directory), HE 22.414/2

HIA {Hazard **Identification** and Analysis} Special Reports, Y 3.C 76/3:17-2

Identification Lists, D 7.25

Identification Orders, J 1.14/9

Pollutant **Identification** Research Highlights, EP 1.37/3

Stock Catalog **Identification** List, GS 2.10/6:pt 2

United States Censuses of Population and Housing: Geographic **Identification** Code Scheme, Phc (2) (series), C 3.223/13

Identifications

Federal Item **Identifications** Guides for Supply Cataloging, Part 2, Description Patterns, D 7.6/2:6-2

H 6-2 Federal Item **Identifications** Guides for Supply Cataloging, Part 2, Description Patterns, D 7.6/2:6-2

Identified

Energy Information in the Federal Government, a Directory of Energy Sources **Identified** by the Interagency Task Force on Energy Information, FE 1.24

Identifier

MILSTRIP Routing and **Identifier** and Distribution Codes, D 1.87/2

MILSTRIP Routing **Identifier** Codes, D 7.6/16

Ideology

Economics, Politics, **Ideology**, PrEx 7.21/14

IER

Solar-Geophysical Data, **IER**-FB- (series), C 52.18, C 55.215

IERC

IERC Bulletin, I 20.59

IFR

Air Traffic Patterns for **IFR** and VFR Aviation, Calendar Year, TD 4.19/2

Enroute **IFR** Air Traffic Survey, C 31.165, FAA 3.11

Enroute **IFR** Air Traffic Survey, Peak Day, TD 4.19/3

Enroute **IFR** Peak Day Charts, Fiscal Year, FAA 3.11/3

Enroute **IFR**-Supplement, United States, D 5.318/7

IFR Altitude Usage Peak Day, FAA 3.11/2

IFR and VFR Pilot Exam-O-Grams, TD 4.54

IFR Area Charts (U.S.), TD 4.79/16-2

IFR Enroute High Altitude Charts (Alaska), TD 4.49/17-2

IFR Enroute High Altitude (U.S.), TD 4.79/17

IFR Enroute Low Altitude (Alaska), TD 4.79/16

IFR Enroute Low Altitude (U.S.), C 55.416/14

IFR Enroute Low Altitude (U.S.), TD 4.79/15

IFR/VFR Low Altitude Planning Chart, TD 4.79/16-3

IFR/VFR Low Altitude Planning Chart, C 55.416/15-3

IFR Wall Planning Chart: East, Low Altitude, U.S., C 55.461/7

IFR Wall Planning Chart: West, Low Altitude, U.S., C 55.416/7-1

Minimum Enroute **IFR** Altitudes Over Particular Routes and Intersections, TD 4.316

VFR/**IFR** Planning Chart, C 55.416/7

IFYGL

IFYGL Atlases, C 55.21/5

International Field Year for the Great Lakes: Proceedings, **IFYGL** Symposium, Annual Meetings of the American Geophysical Union, C 55.21/3

IG

IG Pamphlets, D 101.22/2

IGY

Daily Aerological Cross-Section Pole to Pole along Meridian 75 Degrees W for **IGY** Period, July 1957-December 1958, C 30.76

IHS

IHS Primary Care Provider, HE 20.9423, HE 20.320

IITF

IITF Activity Reports, PrEx 23.11

Illinois

Cattle on Feed, **Illinois**, Iowa, Nebraska, Idaho, and California, A 88.16/7

Medicare Hospital Mortality Information: Vol. 2, Colorado - **Illinois**, HE 22.34

Trade World **Illinois**, C 61.39/3

Water Resources Activities in **Illinois**, I 19.55/5

Water Resources Development in **Illinois**, D 103.35/13

Illness

Transactions of Research Conferences on Cooperative Chemotherapy Studies in Psychiatry and Research Approaches to Mental **Illness**, VA 1.41

Illnesses

News, BLS Reports on Survey of Occupational Injuries and **Illnesses** in ..., L 2.120/2-11

Occupational Injuries and **Illnesses** in (year), L 1.79/2-4, L 2.120/2-11

Occupational Injuries and **Illnesses** in the United States by Industry, L 2.3/11

Recordkeeping Requirements for Firms Selected to Participate in the Annual Survey of Occupational Injuries and **Illnesses**, L 2.129

Illuminating

Illuminating Glassware Manufactures, Sales and Credits, C 3.146

Illustrated

America **Illustrated**, IA 1.14, ICA 1.10

American **Illustrated** (Polish language), IA 1.14/2

American **Illustrated** {Russian Edition}, ICA 1.10

Illustrated Instructor's Reference, W 1.45

Illustrations

How They Do It, **Illustrations** of Practice in Administration of AFDC (series), HE 17.408/2

Illustrations from State Public Assistance Agencies, Current Practices in Staff Training, FS 3.20

Series of Educational **Illustrations** (Charts), A 43.5/10, A 43.22

Series of Educational **Illustrations** for Schools (posters), A 45.5

IM

Handbook **IM** (series), P 1.31/15

IM&S-M

IM&S-M Series, VA 1.48/4

IMA

IMA Update Issues, D 301.127

Image

Color **Image** Map, I 19.81/3

Imagery

Key to Meteorological Records, Environmental Satellite **Imagery** (series), C 55.219/4

Images

USAMark: Fascimile **Images** of Registered United States Trademarks, C 21.31/11

USAPAT, Facsimile **Images** of United States Patents, C 21.31

IMM

IMM (International Mail Manual), P 1.10/5

Immediate

Immediate Water Pollution Control Needs, I 67.13/5

U.S. Exports and **Imports**, Working-Day and Seasonal Adjustment Factors and Months for Cyclical Dominance (MCD), C 3.235

U.S. General **Imports** and **Imports** for Consumption, Schedule A Commodity and Country, C 3.164:135

U.S. General **Imports** Commodity, Country and Method of Transporation, C 3.164:350

U.S. General **Imports** Geographic Area, Country, Schedule A Commodity Groupings, and Method of Transporation, C 3.164:155

U.S. General **Imports** Schedule A Commodity Groupings by World Area, C 56.210:FT 150

U.S. General **Imports** Schedule A Commodity Groupings, Geographic Area, Country, and Method of Transportation, C 3.164:150

U.S. General **Imports** Various Products, C 56.210/4

U.S. General **Imports** World Area and Country of Origin by Schedule A Commodity Groupings, C 3.164:155

U.S. **Imports** and Exports of Natural Gas, E 3.25/3

U.S. **Imports** for Consumption & General Imports, Tariff Schedules Annotated by Country, C 3.150/6

U.S. **Imports** for Consumption, Harmonized TSUSA Commodity by Country of Origin, FT 247, C 3.164:247

U.S. **Imports** for Consumption and General Imports, SIC-Based Products and Area, C 3.164:210

U.S. **Imports** for Consumption and General **Imports**, SIC-Based Products and Area, C 3.164:210

U.S. **Imports** for Consumption and General Imports, Tariff Schedules Annotated by Country, C 3.150/6

U.S. **Imports** for Consumption and General Imports-TSUSA Commodity by Country: (year), C 3.164:246

U.S. **Imports** of Fruits and Vegetables under Plant Quarantine Regulations, A 93.44/3

U.S. **Imports** of Merchandise, C 3.278/2

U.S. **Imports** of Merchandise for Consumption, C 3.164:125

U.S. **Imports** of Textile and Apparel Products, C 61.52

U.S. **Imports** of Textiles and Apparel under the Multifiber Arrangement, Statistical Report, ITC 1.30

U.S. **Imports**, General and Consumption, Schedule a Commodity and Country, C 3.164:135

U.S. Merchandise Trade: Exports and General **Imports** by County, C 3.164:927

U.S. Merchandise Trade: Exports, General Imports, and **Imports** for Consumption, C 3.164:925

U.S. Lumber **Imports**, C 57.24/2

U.S. Production, **Imports** and Import/Production Ratios for Cotton, Wool and Man-made Textiles and Apparel, C 61.26

U.S. Waterborne Exports and General **Imports**, C 3.164:985

United States Airborne General **Imports** of Merchandise, Country of Origin by Commodity, C 3.164:390

United States Exports and **Imports** of Gold and Silver, Total United States Trade in Gold and Silver and United States Trade in Gold and Silver with Latin American Republics and Canada, C 3.164:859

United States General **Imports** and **Imports** for Consumption from Canada and Mexico, Exluding Strategic, Military and Critical Materials, Country by Commodity Totals, C 3.164:121

United States General **Imports** from Canada, Excluding Strategic and Critical Materials and Military Equipment, C 3.157/5

United States General **Imports** from Latin American Republics, C 3.157/3

United States General **Imports** of Cotton Manufacturers, C 3.164/2-2

United States General **Imports** of Cotton Manufacturers: Country of Origin by Geneva Agreement Category, C 56.210:130, C 3.164:130

United States General **Imports** of Cotton Manufacturers; TQ-2190, C 3.164/2-8

United States General **Imports** of Merchandise, Commodity by Country of Origin, C 3.164:10

United States General **Imports** of Textile Manufactures, Except Cotton and Wool, Grouping by Country of Origin and Schedule a Commodity by Country of Origin, TQ-2501, C 3.164/2-7

United States General **Imports** of Wool Manufacture Except Floor Coverings, Quantity Totals in Terms of Equivalent Square Yards in Country of Origin by Commodity Grouping Arrangement, TQ-2203, C 3.164/2-6

United States General **Imports** of Wool Manufacture Except for Floor Coverings, Country of Origin by Wool Grouping, TQ- 2202, C 3.164/2-5

United States General **Imports** for Immediate Consumption, Entries into Bonded Manufacturing Warehouse for Manufacture and Exports, Entries into Bonded Storage Warehouse and Withdrawals from Bonded Storage Warehouse for Consumption of Petroleum and Its Products, C 3.164:576

United States **Imports** of Aluminum, C 57.10/2

United States **Imports** of Merchandise for Consumption: Commodity by Country of Origin, C 3.164:110

United States **Imports** of Merchandise for Consumption; Country of Origin by Subgroup, C 3.164:120

United States Lumber **Imports**, C 41.101/2

United States, Airborne General **Imports** of Merchandise, Commodity by Country of Origin, C 3.164:380

Weekly Statement of Gold and Silver Exports and **Imports**, United States, C 3.195

Imposed

United States District Courts Sentences **Imposed** Chart, Ju 10.18

Imprints

U.S. **Imprints** on Sub-Saharan Africa, LC 41.12/2

Improve

Report of Cooperative Research to **Improve** the Nation's Schools, FS 5.82, HE 5.82

Research to **Improve** Health Services for Mothers and Children, HE 20.5114/2

Improved

Current IPA Projects for **Improved** State and Local Management, CS 1.94

Improved Lunar Ephemeris, D 213.8/2

Improved Manpower Management in Federal Government, Y 4.P 84/10:M 31/5

Towards **Improved** Health and Safety for America's Coal Miners, Annual Report of the Secretary of the Interior, I 1.96

Improvement

Alfalfa **Improvement** Conferences, Reports, A 19.30

Annual Report of Accomplishments Under the Airport **Improvement** Program, TD 4.61

Annual Report of Justice System **Improvement** Act Agencies, J 1.87

Annual Report on Urban Area Traffic Operations **Improvement**, TD 2.29

Annual Report to Congress on the Federal Trade Commission **Improvement** Act for the Calendar Year, FR 1.57

Breeding Research and **Improvement** Activities of Department of Agriculture Reports, A 1.91

Federal Management **Improvement** Conference, Proceedings, PrEx 2.19

Fund for the **Improvement** of Postsecondary Education: Publications (series), HE 19.9

Hatcheries and Dealers Participating in the National Poultry **Improvement** Plan, A 77.15:44-6

Home **Improvement** Pamphlets, I 20.32

Hot Springs Reservation **Improvement** Office, Annual Reports, I 1.16

Hydraulic Engineering and Soil **Improvement**, C 41.47/3

Indian Health Care **Improvement** Act, Annual Report, HE 20.5301

Industrial Energy Efficiency **Improvement** Program, Annual Report, E 1.47

Joint Financial Management **Improvement** Program, Annual Report Fiscal Year (date), GA 1.12

Management Improvement, A 1.74

Management Improvement Program, Plowback, **Improvement**s Reports, D 101.63

Management **Improvement** Series, T 1.42

National Poultry **Improvement** Plan Reports, A 106.22

Northeast Corridor **Improvement** Project Annaul Report, TD 3.13/3

President's Advisory Council on Management **Improvement**, Pr 37.8:M 31

Proceedings Southern Pasture and Forage Crop **Improvement** Conference, A 106.29

Productivity **Improvement** Program, HH 1.107

Progress in Management **Improvement**, T 1.43

Public Housing Management **Improvement** Program: Technical Memorandums, HH 1.63

Range **Improvement** Notes, A 13.65/11

Report of Alfalfa **Improvement** Conference, A 77.531

Science Course **Improvement** Projects, NS 1.24

Status Report: Workable Program for Community **Improvement**, HH 1.47

Tables on Hatchery and Flock Participation in the National Poultry **Improvement** Plan, A 77.15:44-3

Tables on Hatchery and Flock Participation in the National Turkey **Improvement** Plan, A 77.15:44-4

Technical Specification **Improvement** Program Highlights, Y 3.N 88:31/0110

Treatment **Improvement** Protocol, HE 20.8029

Work and Management **Improvement**, A 57.41

Workable Program for Community **Improvement**, Program Guides, HH 1.6/4

Improvements

Current Construction Reports, Special Studies, Expenditures for Nonresidential **Improvements** and Repairs, C 3.215/8-2

Management Improvement Program, Plowback, **Improvements** Reports, D 101.63

New Product Ideas, Process **Improvements**, and Cost-Saving Techniques, Relating to {various subjects}, NASA/SBA FA (series), NAS 1.56

Improving

Status of Open Recommendations **Improving** Operations of Federal Departments and Agencies, GA 1.13/18

Task Force on **Improving** and Prospects of Small Business, Pr 37.8:Sm 1

IMS

IMS Access, NF 4.15

IMS List Sanitation compliance and Enforcement Ratings of Interstate Milk Shippers, HE 20.4014/2

Inactive

Inactive or Discontinued Items from the 1950 Revision of the Classified List, GP 3.24, GP 3.24/2

Incentive

Assessments Completed and Referrals to Manpower Agencies by Welfare Agencies Under Work **Incentive** Program for AFDC Recipients, HE 17.619

Building for Clean Water Progress Report on Federal **Incentive** Grants for Municipal Waste Treatment Fiscal Year, FS 2.64/6

Building for Clean Water Report on Federal **Incentive** Grants for Municiapl Waste Treatment, FS 16.9

Child Care Arrangements of AFDC Recipients Under the Work **Incentive** Program, HE 17.609

Incentive Awards Bulletins, L 22.25

Incentive Awards Notes, CS 1.83, PM 1.27/2

Report to Congress, Title V **Incentive** Grants for Local Delinquency Prevention Programs, J 32.10/3

Work **Incentive** Program, HE 17.619/2

Work **Incentive** Program: Annual Report to Congress, L 1.71

Incentives

Experimental Technology **Incentives** Program, Program Area Description, C 13.57

Forestry **Incentives** Program, from Inception of Program through (date), A 82.92

Grants Contract Reports, Experimental Technology **Incentives** Program, GCR-ETIP (series), C 13.57/2

Inception

Water Bank Program, from **Inception** of Program through (date), A 82.94

Incidence
Incidence of Bluetongue Reported in Sheep During Calendar Year, A 77.231
Report on Incidence of Anthrax in Animals in United States, A 77.225
Reported Incidence of Infectious Equine Encephalomyelitis and Related Encephalitides in the United States, Calendar Year (date), A 77.230
Reported Incidence of Rabies in United States, A 77.232

Incidences
Groups with Historically High Incidences of Unemployment, L 36.12

Incident
Charges for Ginning Cotton, Costs of Selected Services Incident to Marketing, and Related Information, Season, A 88.11/12
Highway Accident/Incident Summary Reports, TD 1.117/3
Railroad Accident/Incident Summary Reports, TD 1.112/7

Incidents
Explosives Incidents, Annual Report, T 70.11
Polluting Incidents in and Around U.S. Waters, TD 5.51
Rail-Highway-Grade Crossing Accident/Incidents Bulletin, TD 3.109
Rules Pertaining to Aircraft Accidents, Incidents, Overdue Aircraft, and Safety Investigations, TD 1.106/2
Significant Incidents of Political Violence Against Americans, S 1.138/2

Income
Advance Summary of Revenues, Expenses, and Net Railway Operating Income, Class 1 Steam Railways, IC 1 ste.19/2
AFDC and Related Income Maintenance Studies, HE 3.67
After-Tax Money Income Estimates of Households, Current Population Reports, C 3.186/5
Annual Report of Indian Land and Income from Surface, I 20.61/2
Chickens and Eggs, Farm Production, Disposition, Cash Receipts and Gross Income, Chickens on Farms, Commercial Broilers, by States, A 88.15/18
Chickens and Eggs, Farm Production, Disposition, Cash Receipts and Gross Income, A 9.9/3
Classification of Income and Profit and Loss Accounts, IC 1 wat.8
Classification of Income, Profit & Loss, and General Balance Sheet Accounts, IC 1 ste.15
Consumer Income, C 3.186:P-60
Consumers' Price Index for Moderate-Income Families (adjusted series), L 2.38/2
East North Central, Population and Per Capita Income Estimates for Counties and Incorporated Places, C 3.186/27-4
Employee Retirement Income Security Act, Report to Congress, L 1.76, L 40.15
Farm Income Situation, A 88.9/2, A 93.9
Farm Production and Income from Meat Animals, A 66.34
Farm Production, Disposition, Cash Receipts and Gross Income, Turkeys, A 88.15/16, A 105.35/2
Farm Value, Gross Income, and Cash Income from Farm Production, A 36.125
Farmer's Tax Guide, Income and Self Employment Taxes, T 22.19/2:F 22
Form of Income and Profit and Loss Statement, IC 1 ste.14
Income and Expense under Rent Control, Pr 32.4225
Income and Poverty, Current Population Survey, C 3.224/12-2
Income in (year) of Persons in the United States, C 3.186:P-60
Income Limits and Section 8 Fair Market Rents (FMRs), HH 1.126
Income Maintenance Training Program, HE 3.37
Income of the Population 55 and Over, HE 3.75
Income of the Population 55 or Older, SSA 1.30
Income, Education and Unemployment in Neighborhoods (by city), L 2.88
Meat Animals, Farm Production, Disposition, and Income by States, A 88.17/3
Meat Animals, Production, Disposition, and Income, A 105.23/6
Member Bank Income, FR 1.11/3

Methodology Papers: U.S. National Income and Product Accounts, BEA-MP- (series), C 59.19
Milk Production, Disposition, and Income, A 92.10/2, A 105.17/5
Milk, Farm Production, Disposition, and Income, A 88.14/8
Mohair Production and Income, A 36.200
Money Income and Poverty Status of Families and Persons in the United States, C 3.186/11
Money Income of Households, Families, and Persons in the United States, C 3.186/2
National Income and Product Accounts of the United States, C 49.11/4:In 2, C 59.11/5, C 59.11/5-2, C 59.11/5-3
Northeast, Population and Per Capita Income Estimates for Counties and Incorporated Places, C 3.186/27
Poultry Production, Disposition and Income, A 105.12/6
Poultry Production, Disposition and Income, Final Estimates, A 1.34/5
Preliminary Reports of Income Accounting of Railways in United States, IC 1 ste.6
Preliminary Statement of Capitalization and Income, Class I Steam Railways in United States, IC 1 ste.28
Program and Demographic Characteristics of Supplemental Security Income Beneficiaries, HE 3.71/2
Program Facts on Federally Aided Public Assistance Income Maintenance Programs, HE 17.614
Proposed Multi-Year Operating Plan, Statistics of Income Division, T 22.2/3, T 22.2/10
Revenues and Income of Privately Owned Class A & B Electric Utilities in the U.S., FP 1.11/5
Revenues, Expenses, Other Income, and Statistics of Class 1 Motor Carriers of Passengers, IC 1 mot.12
Revenues, Expenses, Other Income, and Statistics of Large Motor Carriers of Property, IC 1 mot.13
Sales, Revenue, and Income for Electric Utilities, E 3.11/2-6, E 3.11/2-8
Selected Income and Balance-Sheet Items of Class I Railroads in the United States, IC 1 ste.34
Selected Revenues, Expenses, Other Income, and Statistics of Class II Carriers of Property, IC 1 mot.13/2
South, Population and Per Capita Income Estimates for Counties and Incorporated Places, C 3.186/27-5

Income
SPI State Personal Income, C 59.25
SSA Program Circulars Supplemental Security Income, HE 3.4/6
Statistics of Income, Corporation Income Tax Returns, T 22.35/5
Statistics of Income, Final Volumes, T 22.35/2
Statistics of Income, Partnership Returns, T 22.35/6
Statistics of Income, Preliminary Reports, T 22.35/3
Statistics of Income, T 22.35
Studies in Income Distribution (series), HE 3.67/2
Summary Statement of Income and Expenditures of Voluntary Relief Agencies Registered with Advisory Committee on Voluntary Foreign Aid, S 1.99/3
Supplemental Security Income Program for the Aged, Blind, and Disabled, HE 3.77
Supplemental Security Income, State and County Data, HE 3.71
West North Central, Population and Per Capita Income Estimates for Counties and Incorporated Places, C 3.186/27-3
West, Population and Per Capita Income Estimates for Counties and Incorporated Places, C 3.186/27-2

Income Tax
Bulletins, Income Tax (lettered), T 22.22
Business Income Tax Returns, T 22.35/2:B 96, T 22/35/3:B 96
Corporation Income Tax Returns, T 22.35/3:C 81, T 22.35/2:C 81
Corporation Income Tax Returns, Source Book (year), T 22.35/5-2
Digest of Income Tax Rulings, T 22.24, T 22.25/2
Effect of Income Tax Law Revision on Electric Taxes and Income, FP 1.23

Farmer's Cooperative Income Tax Returns, T 22.35/2:F 22
Federal Income Tax Guide for Older Americans, Y 4.Ag 4/2-11
Federal Income Tax Information, D 205.9
Federal Income Tax Information (for Persons in Naval Service), N 20.22
Fiduciary Income Tax Returns, T 22.35/2:F 44/2
Foreign Income Tax Returns, T 22.35/2
Foreign Tax Credit Claimed on Corporation Income Tax Returns, T 22.35/2:F 76
High Income Tax Returns, T 1.52
Income Tax Brevities for Use by Radio Broadcasting Stations, T 22.38
Income Tax Returns: Number of Individual by States, Counties, Cities, and Towns, T 22.40
Individual Income Tax Returns, T 22.35/3:In 2
Sales of Capital Assets Reported on Individual Income Tax Returns, T 22.35/2:C 17
Statistics of Income, Corporation Income Tax Returns Documentation Guides, T 22.35/7
Statistics of Income, Corporation Income Tax Returns, T 22.35/5
Your Federal Income Tax, T 22.44

Incoming
Industry Survey: Manufacturers' Inventories, Shipments, Incoming Business (and) Unfilled Orders, C 18.224

Incorporated
South, Population and Per Capita Income Estimates for Counties and Incorporated Places, C 3.186/27-5
West North Central, Population and Per Capita Income Estimates for Counties and Incorporated Places, C 3.186/27-3
West, Population and Per Capita Income Estimates for Counties and Incorporated Places, C 3.186/27-2

Incorporating
Interim List of Persons or Firms Currently Debarred for Violation of Various Public Contracts Acts Incorporating Labor Standards Provisions, GA 1.17/2

Increase
Increase & Diffusion, SI 1.46

Increases
Continued Increases in Industry Productivity in (year) Reported by BLS, L 1.79/2-3

Incubator
Incubator Times, SBA 1.39

Incurred
Total Obligations Incurred for Emergency Relief from All Public Funds by State and Local Relief Administration in Continental United States, Y 3.F 31/5:35

IND
Questions and Answers, QA-IND- (series), L 22.30

Indebtedness
Funded Indebtedness of District of Columbia, T 40.5

Indemnity
Statement of Indemnity Claims and Averages in Cooperative Bang's Disease Work, A 4.29
Statement of Indemnity Claims and Averages in Cooperative Tuberculosis Eradication, A 4.30
Summary of Bovine Tuberculosis Eradication in Cooperation with Various States, Statement of Indemnity and Averages in Cooperative Bovine Brucellosis Work, A 77.216/2
Tuberculosis Eradication: Statement of Indemnity Claims and Averages in Cooperative, A 77.214

Indemnity Claims
Bang's Disease Work; Statement of Indemnity Claims and Averages in Cooperative, A 77.211

Indenture
Releases, Trust Indenture Act of 1939, SE 1.25/7

Independence
Project Independence, FE 1.18
Rio de Janeiro, International Exposition of Centenary of Independence of Brazil, 1922-23, S 6.20

Independent
DANTES Independent Study Catalog, D 1.33/7-2
FEC Index of Independent Expenditures, Y 3.El 2/3:15-2

Index of U.S. Voluntary Engineering Standards, C 13.10:329

Index of United States Army, Joint Army-Navy, and Federal Specifications and Standards, M 101.23

Index Quartermaster Corps Specifications, D 106.11

Index to Bureau of Mines Publications, C 22.7/2

Index to Catalog of Investment Information and Opportunities, S 18.35

Index to Civil Service Commission Information, CS 1.61/4

Index to Classification, C 21.12/2

Index to Commission Decisions, SE 1.11/2

Index to Daily Consular Reports, C 14.7

Index to Decisions, Y 3.Oc 1:10-3

Index to Design, Grist, Trends, I 70.22/4

Index to Federal Civil Defense Administration Publications, FCD 1.21/2

Index to Foreign Market Reports, C 57.110, C 61.16

Index to Foreign Production and Commercial Reports, Cumulative **Index**es, C 42.15/3-3

Index to General Orders, Special Orders, Special and General Court-Martial Orders and Memoranda, W 12.16

Index to Geologic Mapping in United States (by State) Maps, I 19.37

Index to Geologic Mapping of the United States, I 19.86

Index to Geologic Names of North America, I 19.3:1056

Index to H.O. Charts on Issue, N 6.5/9

Index to Information, PM 1.44

Index to Intermediate Scale Mapping, I 19.96

Index to International Business Publications, C 57.115:In 2

Index to Land Use and Land Cover Maps and Digital Data, I 19.97/3

Index to Legislation of States to U.S. Enacted, LC 21.9

Index to Management Issuances, NAS 1.18/2

Index to Monthly Consular Reports, C 14.9

Index to Navy Procurement Information, D 201.6/11

Index to Orthophotoquad Mapping, I 19.97

Index to Publications of the Manpower Administration, L 1.34:M 31/4

Index to Reappraisement Circulars, Ju 9.4/2

Index to Reappraisements Made by Board of General Appraisers, T 20.4/2

Index to Reports and Supplements, GB 1.6

Index to Reports on Private and Public Bills and Resolutions Favorably Reported by the Committee, Y 4.J 89/1:In 2/9, Y 4.J 89/1-14

Index to Research Reports and Research and Statistics Notes, FS 3.49/2

Index to River and Harbor Act Approved, W 7.12

Index to River Surveys Made by the Geological Survey and Other Agencies, I 19.13:995

Index to Selected Outdoor Recreation Literature, I 66.15:L 71

Index to Tests of Metals at Watertown Arsenal, W 34.14/2

Index to the Published Decisions of the Accounting Officers of the United States, GA 1.5

Index to the U.S. Patent Classification, C 21.12/3

Index to Topographic and Other Map Coverage (series), I 19.41/6-3

Index to Treasury Decisions Under Customs and Other Laws, T 1.11/1a

Index to U.S. Army Specifications, W 3.48/2

Index to USGS/DMA 1:50,000-Scale, 15 Minute Quadrangle Mapping, I 19.97/2

Index to Veterans Administration Publications, VA 1.20

Index to World Trade Information Service Reports, C 42.14

Index, Coordinated Purchase Descriptions, D 106.14

Index, Research Grant Publications and Reports, I 67.13/2

Index/Journals of the Continental Congress, GS 4.2:C 76/2

Information Sharing **Index**, HE 24.12

Journals of the Continental Congress, **Index**, GS 4.2:C 76/2

Keywords **Index** to U.S. Government Technical Reports, C 41.21/5

Kidney Disease and Nephrology **Index**, HE 20.3318

Military Publications: **Index** of AMC Publications and Blank Forms, D 101.22/3:310.1

National Criminal Justice Reference Service: Document Retrieval **Index**, J 26.26

National Criminal Justice: Document Retrieval **Index**, J 1.42

News, Consumer Price **Index**, L 2.38/3-2

NINCDS **Index** to Research Grants and Awards, HE 20.3516

Numerical and Functional **Index** of Command Forms, D 301.45/14-2:0-9

Numerical **Index** for Station Catalogs, N 6.5/8

Numerical **Index** of Standard and Recurring Air Force Publications, D 301.6:0-2

Numerical **Index** of Technical Publications, M 301.13, D 301.17

Numerical **Index** Supplement to Bibliography of Technical Reports, C 35.7/3

Numerical Tables and Schedule of Volumes (for Document **Index**), GP 3.15

OAR Quarterly **Index** of Current Research Results, D 301.69/8

Ordnance Publications for Supply **Index**, W 34.23/3

Pacific Summary/**Index**, I 72.9/7

Pakistan, **Index** {cumulations}, LC 1.30/2-3

Patentee/Assignee **Index**, C 21.27

Population Sciences, **Index** of Biomedical Research, HE 20.3362/5

President's Papers **Index** Series, LC 4.7

Public Use Data Tape Documentation Medical Coding Manual and Short **Index**, HE 20.6226/9

Publications School of Aviation Medicine, **Index**, Fiscal Year, D 301.26/13-3

Quarterly **Index** of Technical Documentary Reports, D 301.45/15

Quarterly **Index** to Periodical Literature, Eastern and Southern Africa, LC 1.30/8-4

Region **Index** of Publications, Forms and Form Letters, D 7.16/2

Registry of Toxic Effects of Chemical Substances, Permuted Molecular Formula, **Index**, HE 20.7112/4

Regulatory and Technical Reports (Abstract **Index** Journal), Y 3.N 88:21-3

Research and Technology Program Digest, Flash **Index**, NAS 1.41

Research Awards **Index**, HE 20.3013/2

Research Grants **Index**, Fiscal Year, FS 2.22/7-2

Research Grants **Index**, HE 20.3013/2

Reserve Training Publications **Index**, TD 5.21

Retail Food Price **Index**, L 2.39

Retail Food Price **Index**, Washington, D.C., Area, L 2.39/3

River Mile **Index**, Y 3.P 11/4:10

Space Photography **Index**, NAS 1.43/4

State Law **Index**, LC 14.5

Subject **Index** of Current Research Grants and Contracts Administered by the National Heart, Lung, and Blood Institute, HE 20.3212

Subject Matter **Index** with Cross-Reference Table, Y 3.F 31/21:11

Subject-Matter **Index** and Table of Cases, Y 3.F 31/21-2:9

Summary Data from the Producer Price **Index** News Release, L 2.61/10-2

Supplement to **Index** to Commission Decisions, SE 1.11/2

Supplemental Digest and **Index** of Published Decisions of the Assistant Secretary of Labor for Labor-Management Relations Pursuant to Executive Order 11491, Y 3.F 31/21-3:10

T.I.S.C.A. {Technical Information System for Carrier Aviation} Technical Information Indexes: Naval Carrier Aviation Abstract Bulletin with Cross Reference **Index**, D 202.22

Technical Information Indexes: Naval Carrier Aviation Abstract Bulletin with Cross Reference **Index**, D 202.22

Technical Report **Index**, Maritime Administration Research and Development, C 39.227:T 22

Title Page and **Index** to Opinions, Ju 8.6

Tuberculosis Beds in Hospitals and Sanatoria, **Index** of Beds Available, FS 2.69

U.S. Army Equipment **Index** of Modification Work Orders, D 101.22:750-10

United States Army in World War II: Master **Index**, Reader's Guide, D 114.7/2

Unpublished Comptroller General Decisions, With **Index**, D 301.100

Weekly Health **Index**, C 3.41

Weekly Periodical **Index**, D 103.108

Wholesale (Preliminary Market) Price **Index**, L 2.61/5

Wholesale Price **Index** (1947-49=100), Indexes for Groups, Subgroups, and Project Classes of Commodities, L 2.61/2

Wholesale Price **Index** (1947-49=100), Prices and Price Relatives for Individual Commodities, 1951-53, L 2.61/6, L 2.61/6-2

Wholesale Price **Index** Series 1947-48 100: Economic Sector Indexes, L 2.61/8

Wholesale Price **Index**, Major Specification Changes 1947-53, L 2.61/7

Wholesale Price **Index**, Preliminary Estimate, L 2.61/9

World **Index** of Plastic Standards, C 13.10:352

World Port **Index**, D 203.22:150

Index-Catalogue

Index-Catalogue of Library of Surgeon General's Office, 4th Series, D 104.8

Index-Catalogue of Medical and Veterinary Zoology, A 77.219

Index-Catalogue of Medical and Veterinary Zoology {by Subject}, A 77.219/2

Index-Catalogue of Medical and Veterinary Zoology, Special Publications, (numbered), A 77.219/4

Index-Digest

Cumulative **Index-Digest**, C 31.211/3

Cumulative **Index-Digest** of Unpublished Decisions, I 1.69/2-3

Index-Digest of Decisions of the Department of the Interior in Cases Relating to Public Lands, I 1.69/3

Index-Digest of Decisions Under Federal Safety Appliance Acts, IC 1 saf.9

Index-Digest of the Published Decisions of the Comptroller General of the United States, GA 1.5/3

Index-Digest, Published and Important Unpublished Decisions, I 1.69/2

Index/Papers

Index/Papers of the Continental Congress, GS 4.2:C 76/3

Indexed

Serial Publications **Indexed** to Bibliography of Agriculture, A 17.17:75

Indexes

Abstracts of and **Indexes** For Reports and Testimony, Fiscal Year, GA 1.16/3-4

Aerospace Medicine and Biology, A Continuing Bibliography with **Indexes**, NAS 1.21:7011

Business **Indexes**, FR 1.19

Clearinghouse on Health **Indexes**, HE 20.6216/2-2

Clearinghouse on Health **Indexes**: Cumulated Annotations, HE 20.6216/2

Commanders Digest **Indexes**, D 2.15/2-2

Costs and **Indexes** for Domestic Oil and Gas Field Equipment and Production Operations, E 3.44/2

Cumulative **Indexes**, NAS 1.9/5

Daily **Indexes** and Spot Market Prices, L 2.60/2

Daily Spot Market Price **Indexes** and Prices, Weekly Summary, L 2.60

Department Store Inventory Price **Indexes**, L 2.79

Digests and **Indexes** of Treasury Decisions, T 1.12

Earth Resources, A Continuing Bibliography with **Indexes**, NAS 1.21:7041

Energy, Continuing Bibliography with **Indexes**, NAS 1.21:7043

Farmers' Bulletins (**Indexes**), A 21.9/5

Federal Item Identification Guides for Supply Cataloging, **Indexes**, Supplements, D 7.6/2:6-1, D 7.8:1

General **Indexes** to Monthly Consular Reports, S 4.8

Guide to Subject **Indexes** for Scientific and Technical Aerospace Reports, NAS 1.9/6

Indexes and Estimates of Domestic Well Drilling Costs, E 3.44

Indexes for Compilations of Records, Briefs, etc., J 1.19/1

Indexes of Average Freight Rates on Railroad Carload Traffic, IC 1.27

Indexes of Change in Straight-Time Average Hourly Earnings for Selected Shipyards, by Type of Construction and Region, L 2.81/2

Indexes of Output Per Man-Hour for the Private Economy, L 2.89/2

Indexes of Output Per Man-Hour, Hourly Compensation, and Unit Labor Costs in the Private Sector of the Economy and the Nonfarm Sector, L 2.2:Ou 8/8

Indexes of Output Per Man-Hour, Selected Industries, L 2.89

Indexes of Prices for Selected Materials, Hydraulic Turbine Industry, L 2.78

Indexes of Production Worker Employment in Manufacturing Industries by Metropolitan Area, L 2.24

Indexes of Rents by Type of Dwelling, L 2.11

Indexes of Retail Prices on Meats in Large Cities, L 2.39/2

Indexes to Advance Sheets of Consular Reports, S 4.6

Indexes to Bureau of Mines Publications, I 28.5/4

Indexes to Papers of President Franklin Delano Roosevelt, PI 1.8

Indexes to Patents (special), I 23.5

Indexes to Specifications, W 77.8/3

Indexes to Yearbooks of Department of Agriculture, A 21.12

News, Producer Price **Indexes**, L 2.61/10

NODC Quarterly Accessions, Computer Produced **Indexes**, American Meteorological Society Meteorological and Geoastrophysical Abstracts, D 203.24/6

NPA Production Series, Quarterly **Indexes** of Shipments for Products of Metalworking Industries, C 40.15

Papers in Re, **Indexes**, J 1.13/3s

Procedures **Indexes**, Y 3.R 31:26

Producer Price **Indexes**, L 2.61

Producers Prices and Price **Indexes**, L 2.61

Productivity **Indexes** for Selected Industries, L 2.3

Registration Record, Securities Act of 1933, **Indexes**, SE 1.13/2

Relative Importance of Components in the Consumer Price **Indexes**, L 2.3/9

Retail Prices and **Indexes** of Fuels and Electricity, L 2.40

Retail Prices and **Indexes** of Fuels and Utilities, L 2.40

Subject Matter **Indexes** to Decisions of the Federal Labor Relations Authority, Y 3.F 31/21-3:10-3

Supplement to Producer Prices and Price **Indexes** Data for (year), L 2.61/11

T.I.S.C.A. (Technical Information System for Carrier Aviation) Technical Information **Indexes**: Naval Carrier Aviation Abstract Bulletin with Cross Reference Index, D 202.22

Technical Information **Indexes**: Naval Carrier Aviation Abstract Bulletin with Cross Reference Index, D 202.22

Technical Publications Announcements with **Indexes**, NAS 1.9/3

Technology for Large Space Systems, a Bibliography with **Indexes**, NAS 1.21:7046

Topical **Indexes** to Decisions and Opinions of the Department of the Interior, I 1.69/2-2

Tuesday Spot Market Price **Indexes** and Prices, L 2.60

U.S. Department of State **Indexes** of Living Costs Abroad and Living Quarters Allowances, L 2.101

U.S. Department of State **Indexes** of Living Costs Abroad and Quarters Allowances, April, L 2.101/2

U.S. Department of State **Indexes** of Living Costs Abroad, S 1.76/4

U.S. Import and Export Price **Indexes**, L 2.60/3

U.S. Supreme Court, Government Briefs in Cases Argued by Solicitor General, **Indexes**, J 1.19/3

U.S. Supreme Court, Government Briefs in Cases Argued, **Indexes**, J 1.19/4

Unreported Opinions, **Indexes**, IC 1.7/4

Unreported Opinions, Reparation (**indexes**), IC 1.7/2

Wholesale Price **Index** (1947-49=100), **Indexes** for Groups, Subgroups, and Project Classes of Commodities, L 2.61/2

Wholesale Price **Index** Series 1947-48 100: Economic Sector **Indexes**, L 2.61/8

Wholesale Price **Indexes**, Advance Summary, L 2.61/10

Wholesale Prices and Price **Indexes**, L 2.61

India
India, LC 1.30
India, Accessions List, Annual Supplement, Cumulative List of Serials, LC 1.30/1-2
Accession List: **India**, LC 1.30/1
Indian
American **Indian** Calendar, I 20.2:C 1/2
Annual Report of **Indian** Land, I 20.61
Annual Report of **Indian** Land and Income from Surface, I 20.61/2
Application for Basic Grants under Library Services for **Indian** Tribes and Hawaiian Program, ED 1.53/2
Application for Grants under Adult **Indian** Education Programs, ED 1.52
Application for Grants under **Indian** Education Program, ED 1.51
Art and **Indian** Children of the Dakotas (series), I 20.63
Biographical Sketches and Ancedotes of 95 of 120 Principal Chiefs from **Indian** Tribes of North America, I 20.2:In 2/27
Carlisle **Indian** School, I 20.16
Circular Letters, Relate to **Indian** Emergency Conservation Work, I 20.23
Decisions on **Indian** Appeals, I 1.69/6
Directory of **Indian** Service Units, I 20.38
Fact Sheets: Sources of **Indian** and Eskimo Arts and Crafts, I 1.84/3
History of **Indian** Policy, I 20.2:P 75/6
Horizons, **Indian** Mineral Resource, I 20.67
Indian Affairs, (year), Progress Report from the Commissioner of **Indian** Affairs, I 20.1
Indian Affairs, (year), Progress Report from the Commissioner of **Indian** Affairs, I 20.1
Indian Affairs, Laws and Treaties, I 1.107
Indian and Alaska Native Housing and Community Development Programs, Annual Report to Congress, HH 1.80
Indian Appeals, I 1.69/6
Indian Arts and Crafts Board Publications, I 1.84
Indian Health Service Scholarship Program: Applicant Information Instruction Booklet, HE 20.9418
Census of Housing: Detailed Housing Characteristics for American **Indian** and Alaska Native Areas, C 3.224/3-5
Census of Housing: General Housing Characteristics for American **Indian** and Alaska Native Areas, C 3.224/3-2
Census of Population: General Population Characteristics for American **Indian** and Alaska Native Areas, C 3.223/6-2
Census of Population: Social and Economic Characteristics for American **Indian** and Alaska Native Areas, C 3.223/7-2
Indian Children's Own Writings, I 20.36
Indian Commissioners Board, Annual Reports, I 20.5
Indian Craftsman, I 20.16/5
Indian Education, I 20.26
Indian Forest Management, I 20.61/3
Indian Handicraft Pamphlets, I 20.31
Indian Health Care Improvement Act, Annual Report, HE 20.5301
Indian Health Highlights, HE 20.2:In 25/9
Indian Health Service Directory, HE 20.9412/2
Indian Health Service Regional Differences in **Indian** Health, HE 20.9422
Indian Health Service Scholarship Program Student Handbook, HE 20.9418/2
Indian Health Service Scholarship Program: Applicant Information Instruction Booklet, HE 20.9418
Indian Health Trends and Services, HE 20.5310
Indian Inspector for **Indian** Territory, Annual Reports, I 1.20/2
Indian Leader, I 20.39
Indian Life Readers, I 20.33
Indian Reading Series, ED 1.319
Indian Records, I 20.55
Indian School Journal, I 20.41
Indian Schools Superintendent, Annual Report, I 20.7
Indian Schools, (misc. publications), I 20.8
Indian Vital Statistics, FS 2.86/5, HE 20.2660
Information Respecting the History, Conditions, and Prospects of the **Indian** Tribes of the United States, Philadelphia, Lippincott, Grambo & Co, I 20.2:In 2
Jails in **Indian** Country, J 29.11/5-3
Kappler's Compilation of **Indian** Laws and Treaties, Y 4.In 2/2:L 44

Library Programs, Library Services for **Indian** Tribes and Hawaiian Natives Program, ED 1.18/3
Library Programs, Library Services for **Indian** Tribes and Hawaiian Natives Program, Review of Program Activities, ED 1.18/3-2
Mine Inspector for **Indian** Territory, Annual Reports, I 1.20
Mineral Frontiers on **Indian** Lands, I 20.61/4
Mineral Revenues, the Report on Receipts from Federal and **Indian** Leases, I 72.13
National **Indian** Institute Publications, I 20.29
Navajo Area **Indian** Health Service, Office of Environmental Health and Engineering: Annual Report, HE 20.5301/2
Northwest **Indian** Fisheries Commission, I 20.1/3
Opening **Indian** Reservations, I 21.14
Opinions of the Solicitor of the Department of the Interior Relating to **Indian** Affairs, I 1.69/9
Orders Bureau of **Indian** Affairs, I 20.20
Papers in Re **Indian** Claims Commission, J 1.85
Personnel Bulletins **Indian** Affairs Bureau, I 20.28
Proposals (and specifications for supplies) for **Indian** Service, I 20.14
Proposals for **Indian** Service, I 20.14
Proposals Received and Contracts Awarded for Supplies for **Indian** Service, I 20.11
Public and **Indian** Housing FY . . . Program Fungins Plan, HH 1.80/2
Regional Differences in **Indian** Health, HE 20.319
Regulations of **Indian** Office (general), I 20.13/1
Report on **Indian** Health, FS 2.86/2
Roster of Officers of **Indian** Service, I 20.10
Routes to **Indian** Agencies and Schools, I 20.19
Southwestern **Indian** Polytechnic Institute, Catalog, I 20.66
States and Their **Indian** Citizens, I 20.2:St 2/3
Statistics Concerning **Indian** Education, Fiscal Year, I 20.46
To the First Americans, Annual Report of the **Indian** Health Program, FS 2.867/4, HE 20.2014/2, HE 20.5312
Transmittal Letters (for **Indian** Service Manual), I 20.35
Trends in **Indian** Health, HE 20.316, HE 20.9421
Trends in Utilization of **Indian** Health Service and Contract Hospitals, HE 20.9417
Indian Ocean
Meterological Chart of the **Indian Ocean**, A 29.27
Nautical Charts and Publications, Region 6, **Indian Ocean**, C 55.440:6
NIMA Nautical Charts, Public Sale Region 6, **Indian Ocean**, TD 4.82:6
Oceanographic Atlas of the International **Indian Ocean** Expedition, NS 1.2:In 2/4
Pilot Chart of **Indian Ocean**, D 203.16, N 6.17, M 202.16, D 203.16
Tide Tables Central and Western Pacific Ocean and **Indian Ocean**, C 4.15/6
Tide Tables Pacific Ocean and **Indian Ocean**, C 4.15/2
Tide Tables, High and Low Water Predictions Central and Western Pacific Ocean and **Indian Ocean**, C 55.421/4
Indiana
Indiana (various subjects), I 20.51/2
Medicare Hospital Mortality Information: Vol. 3, **Indiana** - Maryland, HE 22.34
Water Resources Development in **Indiana**, D 103.35/14
Indians
Famous **Indians**, a Collection of Short Biographies, I 20.2:In 2/26
Handbook of North American **Indians**, SI 1.20/2
Indians at Work, I 20.22
Indians of (States or Areas), I 20.51
Indians on Federal Reservations in United States (by areas), FS 2.86
Indians: (various subjects), I 20.51/2
Reports of Agents and Superintendents in Charge of **Indians**, I 20.15
Status Report of the Operation and Maintenance of Sanitation Facilities Serving American **Indians** and Alaska Natives, HE 20.9416
Indicated
Cranberries, **Indicated** Production, A 92.11/6
Indicator
Indicator of the Month (series), ED 1.341

Indicators
 Annual **Indicators** of Immigration into the United
  States of Aliens in Professional and
  Related Occupations, J 21.15
 Annual Report of Energy Conservation **Indicators**
  for (year), E 3.47
 Consumer Buying **Indicators**, C 3.186:P 65
 Defense **Indicators**, C 56.110, C 59.10, C 3.241
 Description of Output **Indicators** by Function for
  the Federal Government, L 2.133
 Economic and Energy **Indicators**, C 3.14/2
 Economic **Indicators**, Y 4.Ec 7:Ec 7
 Economic **Indicators** of the Farm Sector, A 93.45
 Economic **Indicators** of the Farm Sector, Cost of
  Production: Livestock and Dairy, A
  93.45/2-2
 Economic **Indicators** Weekly Review, ER-EI
  (series), PrEx 3.13
 Education **Indicators**, ED 1.109/2
 Energy Conservation **Indicators**, Annual Report, E
  3.47
 Health, Education and Welfare **Indicators**, FS 1.20
 HPMC Performance **Indicators**, HH 1.57
 Indicators of School Crime and Safety, ED 1.347
 Indicators of Welfare Dependence, HE 1.1/4
 Metal Industry **Indicators**, I 28.173
 Monthly Energy **Indicators**, FE 1.14
 Rum: Annual Report on Selected Economic
  Indicators, ITC 1.31
 Science **Indicators**, NS 1.28/2
 Selected Economic **Indicators**, D 1.43
 Small Business Economic **Indicators**, SBA 1.1/2-2
 U.S. Automobile Industry: Monthly Report on
  Selected Economic **Indicators**, ITC 1.16/
  3
 Youth **Indicators**, Trends in the Well-Being of
  American Youth, ED 1.327
Indices
 Indices of Agricultural Production in {various}
  Countries, A 67.36, A 93.32
 Railroad Construction **Indices**, IC 1 acco.8
 Rehabilitation Service Administration, Quarterly
  Indices, HE 17.120
 Schedule of Annual and Period **Indices** for Carriers
  by Pipeline, IC 1 acco.10
 World **Indices** of Agricultural and Food
  Production, A 1.34/3
Individual
 Consumer Price Index {by **individual** cities and
  commodities}, L 2.38/5
 Foreign Agricultural Trade of the United States,
  Trade in Agricultural Products with
  Individual Countries by Calendar Year,
  A 67.19/6
 Income Tax Returns: Number of **Individual** by
  States, Counties, Cities, and Towns, T
  22.40
 Individual Income Tax Returns, T 22.35/3:In 2
 NCHSR Program Solicitation, **Individual** and
  Institutional, HE 20.6512/8
 Reports on Investigations of **Individual** Accidents,
  IC 1 acci.5
 Requirement for **Individual** Water-Supply and
  Sewage-Disposal Systems (by States),
  NHA 2.17, HH 2.11
 Sales of Capital Assets Reported on **Individual**
  Income Tax Returns, T 22.35/2:C 17
 Specifications and Code Numbers for **Individual**
  Commodities, L 2.61/3
 Territories and Possessions Reports (**Individual**
  Reports), C 3.940-17
 United States **Individual** Retirement Bonds, Tables
  of Redemption Values for All Denomina-
  tion Bonds, T 63.209/8
 Wholesale Price Index (1947-49=100), Prices and
  Price Relatives for **Individual**
  Commodities, 1951-53, L 2.61/6, L 2.61/
  6-2
Individualized
 Modular **Individualized** Learning for Electronics
  Training, D 207.109
Individuals
 Catalog of HEW Assistance Providing Financial
  Support and Service to States,
  Communities, Organizations,
  Individuals, HE 1.6/6
 Continuing Survey of Food Intake by **Individuals**,
  A 111.9/3
 Enrollment Information Guide and Plan
  Comparison Chart **Individuals**
  Receiving Compensation from the Office
  of Workers Compensation Programs, PM
  1.8/13

 Library Programs, Library Services for **Individuals**
  with Limited English Proficiency, ED
  1.18/8
 Theater, Support to **Individuals**, NF 2.8/2-30
 Volume and Composition of **Individuals'** Savings
  Federal Reserve System Board of
  Governors, FR 1.53
 Volume and Composition of **Individuals'** Savings
  Securities and Exchange Commission, SE
  1.25/6
Indochina
 Air War in **Indochina** (series), D 301.93
 Indochina Monographs (series), D 114.18
Indonesia
 Indonesia, LC 1.30/5
 Indonesia, Cumulative List of Serials, LC 1.30/5-2
 Nautical Charts and Publications, Region 7,
  Australia, **Indonesia,** and New Zealand,
  C 55.440:7
 NIMA Nautical Charts, Public Sale Region 7,
  Australia, **Indonesia,** and New Zealand,
  TD 4.82:7
Induced
 Instruction Manual: Classification and Coding
  Instructions for **Induced** Termination of
  Pregnancy Records, HE 20.6208/8
Induced
 Laser **Induced** Damage in Optical Materials, C
  13.10/4
Industrial
 Annual Historical Summary; Defense **Industrial**
  Plant Equipment Center, D 7.1/3
 Annual Report to Congress on National **Industrial**
  Reserve Under Public Law 883, 80th
  Congress, D 7.21
 Apparent Consumption of **Industrial** Explosives
  and Blasting Agents in the United
  States, I 28.112
 Area and **Industrial** Development Aids, C 41.8/2
 Area Development Aid: **Industrial** Location
  Series, C 45.8/3
 Background to **Industrial** Mobilization Manual for
  Executive Reservists, C 41.6/7
 Bibliography of Scientific and **Industrial** Reports,
  C 35.7
 Changes in Commercial and **Industrial** Loans by
  Industry, FR 1.39
 Circular of Inquiry Concerning Gold and Silver
  Coinage and Currency of Foreign
  Countries, Including Production, Import
  and Export, and **Industrial** Consumption
  of Gold and Silver, T 28.8
 Commercial and **Industrial** Loans Outstanding by
  Industry, FR 1.39/2
 Commercial and **Industrial** Loans to U.S.
  Addressess Excluding Bankers
  Acceptances and Commercial Paper, by
  Industry, FR 1.39/2
 Consumer Installment Credits of **Industrial** Loan
  Companies, FR 1.36/4
 Current **Industrial** Reports, C 3.158, C 56.216
 Current **Industrial** Reports (Multigraphed), C 3.58
 Current **Industrial** Reports, Manufacturing
  Profiles, C 3.158/4
 Current **Industrial** Reports: Manufacturing
  Technology, C 3.158/3
 Economic and **Industrial** Affairs, PrEx 7.17
 Electric Locomotives (mining and **industrial**), C
  3.81
 Electrical **Industrial** Trucks and Tractors, C 3.80
 Executive Reservist, Bulletin from **Industrial**
  Mobilization, for Members of National
  Defense Executive Reserve, C 41.113
 FIR {Fishery **Industrial** Research} Reprints, I
  49.26/2a
 Fishery **Industrial** Research, C 55.311
 Foreign Economic Collection and **Industrial**
  Espionage, Y 3.C 83/2:1-2
 For Your Information; **Industrial** Survival, FCD
  1.13/9
 Handbooks, Manuals, Guides Relating to
  Industrial Mobilization and Security, D
  3.6/3
 Industrial Activities Bulletin, S 18.10
 Industrial and Mechanical Engineering, C 51.9/16
 Industrial Area Statistical Summaries, L 2.18
 Industrial Area Studies, L 2.16
 Industrial Banking, Companies, Installment Loans
  to Consumers, C 18.219
 Industrial Civil Defense Handbooks, C 41.6/12
 Industrial Civil Defense Newsletter, C 41.110
 Industrial Classification Code, FS 3.112/2

 Industrial Classification Code, State Operations
  Bulletins, FS 3.112
 Industrial College of the Armed Forces Catalog, D
  5.11
 Industrial College of the Armed Forces:
  Perspectives in Defense Management, D
  5.16
 Industrial College of the Armed Forces:
  Publications, D 5.13
 Industrial Corporation Reports (by industries), FT
  1.17
 Industrial Development in the TVA Area, Y 3.T
  25:30-2
 Industrial Development in TVA Area During
  (date), Y 3.T 25:30 In 27
 Industrial Diamonds in (year), I 28.162
 Industrial Economics Review, C 62.19
 Industrial Education Circulars, I 16.33
 Industrial Effluent Standards, EP 1.8/4-4
 Industrial Employment Information Bulletin, L 7.8
 Industrial Energy Conservation, Fact Sheets, FE
  1.27
 Industrial Energy Efficiency Improvement
  Program, Annual Report, E 1.47
 Industrial Environmental Research Laboratory:
  (year) Research Review, EP 1.46/5-2
 Industrial Environmental Research Laboratory:
  Annual Report, EP 1.46/5
 Industrial Fact Sheets, C 45.8, C 41.90/3
 Industrial Fishery Products, (year) Annual
  Summary, C 55.309/2
 Industrial Fishery Products, Situation and
  Outlook CEA I (series), C 55.309/3, I
  49.8/9
 Industrial Health and Safety Series, L 16.9
 Industrial Hygiene News Letters, FS 2.45
 Industrial Location Series, C 41.90/2
 Industrial Machine Letters, C 18.98
 Industrial Marketing Guides, C 41.6/10
 Industrial Materials Series: Report M (series), TC
  1.27
 Industrial Mobilization, W 3.50/16
 Industrial News, C 46.7/2
 Industrial Notes, D 211.10
 Industrial Nutrition Service, A 82.66
 Industrial Outlook and Economy at Midyear, C
  41.42/4
 Industrial Personnel Security Review Program,
  Annual Reports, D 3.12
 Industrial Power Engineering {abstracts}, C
  41.60/4
 Industrial Production, FR 1.19/3
 Industrial Projects Bulletin, FO 1.18, S 17.18
 Industrial Property Bulletin, C 18.99
 Industrial Reference Service, C 18.220, C 34.10
 Industrial Reference Service, Business Service, C
  18.221
 Industrial Reports and Publications, S 18.20
 Industrial Safety Subjects, L 16.18
 Industrial Safety Summaries, L 16.20
 Industrial Security Cartoons, D 3.11/3
 Industrial Security Poster PIN (series), D 3.11
 Industrial Security Statements, D 3.11/2
 Industrial Series: Bureau of Foreign and Domestic
  Commerce, C 18.225
 Industrial Series: Children's Bureau, L 5.9
 Industrial Series: Office of Domestic Commerce, C
  36.7
 Industrial Standards, C 18.24
 Industrial Survival, for Your Information
  {Releases}, FCD 1.13/9
 Industrial Uses of Agricultural Materials,
  Situation and Outlook Report, A 93.56
 Industrial Waste Guide Series, FS 2.71
 Industrial Waste Guides, I 67.8/2
 Industry Wage Survey: **Industrial** Chemicals, L
  2.3/31
 Main Line Natural Gas Sales to **Industrial** Users, E
  3.11/14
 Motion Pictures Educational {and} **Industrial**, C
  18.116
 National **Industrial** Recovery Act, C 18.3/2
 National Resources Conference Conducted by
  Industrial College of Armed Forces, D
  5.9
 New Publications in Wages and **Industrial**
  Relations, L 2.74/2
 Newsmap, **Industrial** Edition, W 109.209
 Occupational Safety and Health **Industrial**
  Hygiene Field Operations Manual, L
  35.6/3-6
 Office of **Industrial** Technology Reports, E 1.138

OIT (Office of **Industrial** Technologies) Times, The, E 1.140/2

Patterns of **Industrial** Growth (series), C 41.90/5

President's Conference on **Industrial** Safety News Letter, L 16.30

Reports of Project on Research in Agricultural and **Industrial** Development in Tennessee Valley Region, Y 3.T 25:26

Selected **Industrial** Films SIF (series), C 41.23/3

Seminar on **Industrial** Issues (various topics), C 62.18

Special **Industrial** Relations Reports, L 2.58

Special Notice Concerning Basic Agreements Teleprocessing Services Program (TSP) **Industrial** Group 737, **Industrial** Class 7374, GS 12.13

Standard **Industrial** Classification Manual, PrEx 2.6/2:In 27

Statement of Postal Receipts at 50 **Industrial** Offices, P 4.8

Summary of War Supply and Facility Contracts by State and **Industrial** Area, Pr 32.4828

T.I.D.C. Projects on German **Industrial** Economic Disarmament, Pr 32.5813

Technical Memoranda for Municipal, **Industrial** and Domestic Water Supplies, Pollution Abatement, Public Health, FS 2.301

Typical Commercial and **Industrial** Electric Bills, FP 1.16/4

Typical Electric Bills, Typical Net Monthly Bills of January (year), for Residential Commercial and **Industrial** Services, FP 1.10

U.S. **Industrial** Outlook for 200 Industries with Projections for (year), C 62.17

U.S. **Industrial** Outlook, (year), with Projections to (year), C 57.309

U.S. **Industrial** Outlook, C 57.18, C 61.34

Voluntary **Industrial** Energy Conservation, C 57.25, E 1.22

Industrial Arts

Art and Industry Education in **Industrial Arts** and Fine Arts in United States, I 16.7

Industries

Agricultural, Pastoral, and Forest **Industries** in American Republics, TC 1.19

Analysis of Production, Wages and Employment in Manufacturing **Industries**, Y 3.C 78:7

Annual Report on the Impact of the Caribbean Basin Economic Recovery Act on U.S. **Industries** and Consumers, ITC 1.32

Bulletins (by Principal **Industries**), C 3.24/4

Bulletins, Manufacturers (by **Industries**), C 3.28/15

Case History Reports for **Industries**, Pr 32.5223

Census of Construction **Industries**: Final Reports, C 3.245/3

Census of Construction **Industries**: Final Reports, Bound Volumes, C 3.245/6

Census of Construction **Industries**: Final Reports, Special Reports, C 3.245/5

Census of Construction **Industries**; Advance Industry Reports, C 3.245

Census of Construction **Industries**; Announce- ments and Order Forms, C 3.245/2

Census of Construction **Industries**; Area Statistics, C 56.254/4

Census of Construction **Industries**; Bound Volumes, C 56.254/6

Census of Construction **Industries**; Final Reports, C 56.254/3

Census of Construction **Industries**; General Publications, C 56.254

Census of Construction **Industries**; Preliminary Reports, C 56.254/2

Census of Construction **Industries**; Special Reports, C 56.254/5

Census of Electrical **Industries**, C 3.38

Census of Financial, Insurance, and Real Estate **Industries**, C 3.291

Census of Mineral **Industries**; Area Series, C 56.236/4

Census of Mineral **Industries**; Preliminary Reports, C 56.236/2

Census of Mineral **Industries**; Subject Series, C 56.236/5

Census of Mineral **Industries**; Subject, Industry, and Area Statistics, C 56.236/6

Census of Mineral **Industries**; {Industry} Bulletins MI (series), C 56.236/3

Census of Mineral **Industries**; {Publications}, C 56.236

Census of Population and Housing: Alphabetical Index of **Industries** and Occupations, C 3.223/22:90-R3

Census of Population and Housing: Classified Index of **Industries** and Occupations, C 3.223/22:90-R4

Census of Selected Service **Industries**; Area Statistics Series, C 56.253/3

Census of Selected Service **Industries**; Final Volumes, C 56.253/5

Census of Selected Service **Industries**; General Publications, C 56.253

Census of Selected Service **Industries**; Preliminary Area Series, C 56.253/2

Census of Selected Service **Industries**; Subject Reports, C 56.253/4

Census of Service **Industries** Industry Series, C 3.257/3-4

Census of Service **Industries** Nonemployer Statistics Series, C 3.257/5

Census of Service **Industries**; Final Reports, C 3.257/4

Census of Service **Industries**; General Publica- tions, C 3.257

Census of Service **Industries**; Geographic Area Series, C 3.257/2

Census of Service **Industries**; Geographic Area Series, Advance Reports, C 3.257/2-2

Census of Service **Industries**; Preliminary Report Industry Series, C 3.257/3-3

Census of Service **Industries**; Subject Series, C 3.257/3

Company Statistics Bulletins, Census of Business, Manufactures and Mineral **Industries**, C 3.222

Employers' Estimates of Labor Needs in Selected Defense **Industries**, FS 3.121

Field Letter, National Committee for Conservation of Manpower in War **Industries**, L 1.29

Fisheries and Fishing **Industries**, FC 1.6

Indexes of Output Per Man-Hour, Selected **Industries**, L 2.89

Indexes of Production Worker Employment in Manufacturing **Industries** by Metropolitan Area, L 2.24

Industries and Reciprocal Trade Agreements, Reports on, by **Industries**, TC 1.15

Manufacturers, Minerals **Industries**, EC (series), C 3.202/16

Mineral **Industries**, C 3.940-12

Mining and Manufacturing **Industries** in the American Republics, TC 1.21

Minutes of {Meetings of Committees of Various **Industries**}, C 40.16

NPA Production Series, Quarterly Indexes of Shipments for Products of Metalworking **Industries**, C 40.15

Price Lists Federal Prison **Industries**, Inc., FPI 1.7

Production, Prices Employment, and Trade in Northwest Forest **Industries**, A 13.66/13

Productivity Indexes for Selected **Industries**, L 2.3

Productivity Measures for Selected **Industries**, L 2.3/20

Report of Federal Trade Commission on Rates of Return (after taxes) for Identical Companies in Selected Manufacturing **Industries**, FT 1.21

Reports of **Industries**, L 20.12

Safety in Mineral **Industries**, I 28.113

Small Industry Series, Cottage **Industries** Bulletins, S 17.37

Statistics for Industry Groups and **Industries**, C 3.24/9-7

Survey of American Listed Corporations, Reported Information on Selected Defense **Industries**, SE 1.18/2

Technologic and Related Trends in the Mineral **Industries**, I 28.27

U.S. Industrial Outlook for 200 **Industries** with Projections for (year), C 62.17

Walsh-Healey Public Contracts Act Minimum Wage Determination (for various **industries**), L 22.19

What Social Security Means to **Industries**, SS 1.18

Industry

Air Carrier **Industry** Scheduled Service Traffic Statistics, CAB 1.39

Airline **Industry** Economic Report, CAB 1.18, C 31.260

Area Development Aid: **Industry** Trend Series, C 45.8/2

Art and **Industry** Education in Industrial Arts and Fine Arts in United States, I 16.7

Automobile **Industry**, C 41.44

BDSA **Industry** Growth Studies, C 41.90/4

Catalog of Training Products for the Mining **Industry**, L 38.11/3

Census of Construction Industries; Advance **Industry** Reports, C 3.245

Census of Distribution **Industry** Statistics, C 3.245/6

Census of Distribution; Construction **Industry**, State Series, C 3.37/21

Census of Manufactures; **Industry** Series MC (nos.), C 56.244/6

Census of Mineral Industries; Subject, **Industry**, and Area Statistics, C 56.236/6

Census of Mineral Industries; {**Industry**} Bulletins MI (series), C 56.236/3

Census of Retail Trade; **Industry** Series, C 3.225/3-3

Census of Retail Trade; Preliminary Report **Industry** Series, C 3.255/3-2

Census of Service Industries **Industry** Series, C 3.257/3-4

Census of Service Industries; Preliminary Report **Industry** Series, C 3.257/3-3

Census of Wholesale Trade; **Industry** Series, C 3.256/6

Census of Wholesale Trade; Preliminary Report **Industry** Series, C 3.256/3-2

Changes in Commercial and Industrial Loans by **Industry**, FR 1.39

Chemical **Industry** {abstracts}, C 41.53/7

Chemical Science and **Industry** {abstracts}, C 41.53/10

Coal Rationing **Industry** Letters, Pr 32.4236

Commercial and Industrial Loans Outstanding by **Industry**, FR 1.39/2

Commercial and Industrial Loans to U.S. Addressees Excluding Bankers Acceptances and Commercial Paper, by **Industry**, FR 1.39/2

Construction and Building Materials, Monthly **Industry** Report, C 40.10

Construction and Related **Industry**, PrEx 7.22/3-2

Construction **Industry** Series, HE 19.108/2

Construction **Industry** Stabilization Commission Regulations, ES 2.6/4

Continued Increases in **Industry** Productivity in (year) Reported by BLS, L 1.79/2-3

Copper **Industry**, I 28.59/2

Copper **Industry**, Annual, I 28.59/3

Department of the Army Prime Contracts ($1 million and over) Placed with **Industry**, Non-Profit Organizations, Colleges, and Universities, D 101.22:715-4

Employment and Wages of Workers Covered by State Unemployment Insurance Laws and Unemployment Compensation for Federal Employees, by **Industry** and State, L 7.20/3, L 1.61

Facts for **Industry** Series 6-2 and 6-10, Organic Chemicals and Plastic Materials, TC 1.25/2

Fair Facts, Information for American **Industry**, C 44.8

Fashion **Industry** Series, HE 5.288

Fishery **Industry** Research, I 49.26/2

Footwear **Industry** Revitalization Program, Annual Progress Report, C 1.72

Forest Products **Industry** Notes, Y 3.T 25:28-2

Fuel Oil **Industry** Letters, Pr 32.4228

General **Industry** Standards, L 35.6/3

General Summary of Inventory Status and Movement of Capital and Producers Goods, Plants, Aircraft, and **Industry** Agent Items, Pr 33.210

General Survey of Conditions in Coal **Industry**, C 22.21

Herald of Electrical **Industry** {abstracts}, C 41.66/2

Hours and Earnings **Industry** Reports, L 2.41

Household and Commercial Pottery **Industry** in {various countries}, C 41.100

Indexes of Prices for Selected Materials, Hydraulic Turbine **Industry**, L 2.78

Industry and Product Reports, C 3.24/8-2

Industry and Trade Summary, Itc 1.33

Industry Circulars, T 70.10

Industry Information, Pr 32.4230

Industry Manpower Surveys, L 7.49, L 34.10

Industry News Letters, Pr 32.4230/2

Industry Pamphlets, L 22.29

Industry Productivity in (year) Reported by BLS, L 2.120/2-9

Industry Profiles, Accession Notices, S 18.36

Industry Releases, C 3.209/2

Industry Report, Canned Fruits and Vegetables, Production and Wholesale Distribution, C 18.234

Industry Report, Chemicals and Allied Products, C 18.235

Industry Report, Coffee, Tea and Spices, C 18.240

Industry Report, Construction and Building Materials, C 41.30

Industry Report, Construction and Construction Materials, C 18.233

Industry Report, Crude Drugs, Gums, Balsams, and Essential Oils, C 18.236

Industry Report, Drugs and Pharmaceuticals, C 18.237

Industry Report, Fats and Oils, C 18.238

Industry Report, International Iron and Steel, C 41.36

Industry Report, Leather, C 18.239

Industry Report, Rubber, C 18.241

Industry Reports, C 41.31

Industry Reports Sugar, Molasses and Confectionary, C 18.231

Industry Reports, Domestic Transportation, C 18.232

Industry Reports, Lumber, C 18.230

Industry Survey, C 3.231

Industry Survey, Manufacturers' Sales, Inventories, New and Unfilled Orders, C 43.9

Industry Survey: Manufacturers' Inventories, Shipments, Incoming Business {and} Unfilled Orders, C 18.224

Industry Trade and Technology Review, ITC 1.33/2

Industry Trend Series, C 41.90

Industry Wage Studies Memo, L 2.47/2

Industry Wage Studies, Series 3, Wage Movements, L 2.47

Industry Wage Survey Reports, L 2.106

Industry Wage Survey Summaries, L 2.3/3-2

Industry Wage Survey: Banking, L 2.3/22

Industry Wage Survey: Cigarette Manufacturing, L 2.3/26

Industry Wage Survey: Contract Cleaning Services, L 2.3/33

Industry Wage Survey: Department Stores, L 2.3/37

Industry Wage Survey: Hospitals, L 2.3/24

Industry Wage Survey: Industrial Chemicals, L 2.3/31

Industry Wage Survey: Iron and Steel Foundries, L 2.3/32

Industry Wage Survey: Meat Products (year), L 2.3/15

Industry Wage Survey: Men's and Boy's Shirts and Nightwear, L 2.3/35

Industry Wage Survey: Millwork, L 2.3/14

Industry Wage Survey: Nursing and Personal Care Facilities, L 2.3/25

Industry Wage Survey: Petroleum Refining, L 2.3/19

Industry Wage Survey: Pressed or Blown Glassware, L 2.3/29

Industry Wage Survey: Shipbuilding and Repairing, L 2.3/34

Industry Wage Survey: Structural Clay Products, L 2.3/30

Industry Wage Survey: Synthetic Fibers, L 2.3/21

Industry Wage Survey: Temporary Help Survey, L 2.3/38

Industry Wage Survey: Textile Mills, L 2.3/23

Industry Wage Survey: Wood Household Furniture, L 2.3/27

Inter-American Conference on Agriculture, Forestry, and Animal Industry, Washington, Sept. 8-20, 1930, S 5.32

Japanese Trade Studies, Special Industry Analyses, TC 1.23/3

Joint Military-Industry Packaging and Materials Handling Symposium, D 101.51

Major Collective Bargaining Settlements in Private Industry, L 2.45/2

Manpower Utilization-Job Security in Longshore Industry {by port}, L 1.50

Manufactures, Industry Series, C 3.37/26

Manufacturing Industry, Technical Document, EP 4.20

Maritime Safety Data for Shipyard Industry, L 16.47/4

Maritime Safety Data for the Stevedoring Industry, L 16.47/6

Metal Industry Indicators, I 19.129, I 28.173

Mineral Industry Health Programs, Technical Progress Reports, I 28.26/2

Mineral Industry Surveys, I 19.160, I 19.161

Mineral Industry Surveys, Directory of Principal Construction Sand and Gravel Producers in the . . ., Annual Advanced Summary Supplement, I 19.138/3

Mineral Industry Surveys, Mineral Industry of (Country) Minerals, I 19.163

Mineral Industry Surveys, Mineral Industry of [State] Minerals, I 19.162

Monthly Report on Selected Steel Industry Data, ITC 1.27

NASA-Industry Program Plans Conference, NAS 1.17

National Employment, Hours, and Earning Industry Summaries {employees in nonagricultural establishments, by industry division}, L 2.41/5

New Research and Development Reports Available to Industry, C 42.21/4

News, Average Annual Pay by State and Industry, L 2.120/2-3

Nuclear Industry, Y 3.At 7:56

Nuclear Notes for Industry, Y 3.At 7:31

Occupational Injuries and Illnesses in the United States by Industry, L 2.3/11

Occupational Safety and Health General Industry Standard and Interpretations, L 35.6/3-1

Office of Construction Industry Services: Annual Report, L 1.1/2

Office of Industry and Commerce Releases OIC (series), C 18.281/2

Preliminary Report on Production on Specified Synthetic Organic Chemicals in United States; Facts for Industry Series, TC 1.25

Publications Relating to Dairy Industry, A 44.11

Pulp and Paper Industry Reports, C 18.229

Pulp, Paper and Board Industry Report, C 40.11

Registered Group-Joint Apprenticeship Programs in Construction Industry (by trades), L 23.9

Report of the Attorney General on Competition in the Synthetic Rubber Industry, J 1.26

Research and Development in Industry, NS 1.22:In 2

Safety in Industry, L 16.3

SBIC Industry Reports, SBA 1.29

Secretary's Task Force on Competition in the U.S. Domestic Airline Industry, TD 1.57

Service and Regulatory Announcements Bureau of Animal Industry, A 4.13, A 77.208

Service and Regulatory Announcements Bureau of Dairy Industry, A 44.5

Service and Regulatory Announcements Bureau of Plant Industry, A 19.13

Small Industry Series, Cottage Industries Bulletins, S 17.37

Statistical Bulletins Philippine Islands, Commerce and Industry Bureau, W 49.52/5

Statistics for Industry Groups and Industries, C 3.24/9-7

Statistics of the Communications Industry in the United States, CC 1.35

Stories of American Industry, C 1.20

Stove Rationing Industry Letters, Pr 32.4237

Summary of Bang's Disease Control Program Conducted by Bureau of Animal Industry in Cooperation with Various States, A 4.23

Summary of Brucellosis (Bang's Disease) Control Program Conducted by Bureau of Animal Industry in Cooperation with Various States, A 77.213

Technical Terms of the Meat Industry, A 88.17/6:6

Trade and Industry Publications, L 23.16

Training within Industry Abstracts, British Engineering Bulletins, Pr 32.4822, Pr 32.5215

Training within Industry Bulletin Series, Pr 32.5208/2

Training within Industry, Bulletins, Pr 32.4011

Training within Industry, Examples, Pr 32.4012, Pr 32.4808

Training within the Industry; Bulletin, Pr 32.4816, Pr 32.5208

U.S. Auto Industry, ITC 1.16/4

U.S. Automobile Industry, C 1.84

U.S. Automobile Industry: Monthly Report on Selected Economic Indicators, ITC 1.16/3

U.S. Census of Wholesale Trade Industry Series, C 3.256/3-2

U.S. Energy Industry Financial Developments, E 3.56

U.S. Industry and Trade Outlook, C 61.48

Unemployment Insurance Tax Rates by Industry, L 7.70, L 33.11

Uranium Industry, E 3.46/5

War Changes in Industry Series, Reports, TC 1.18

Zinc Industry in (year), I 28.69/2

Zinc Industry, I 28.69

Ineligible

Consolidated List of Debarred, Suspended, and Ineligible Contractors, GS 1.28

Inertial

Inertial Confinement Fusion Quarterly Report, E 1.99/7, E 1.99/7-2

INF

INF Bulletins, CC 1.3/3

Infant

Birth Cohort Linked Birth/Infant Death Data Set, HE 20.6209/4-7

Birth Still-Birth and Infant Mortality Statistics Annual Report, C 3.26

Infant Mortality Series, L 5.5

National Advisory Council on Maternal, Infant and Fetal Nutrition: Biennial Report, A 98.14/2

Infantry

Infantry, D 102.83

Infantry School Quarterly, D 101.53

Infants

WI Communique, Issues of the Special Supplemental Food Program for Women, Infants, and Children, A 98.14

Infected

Map of District Infected with Splenetic Fever, A 4.6

Infections

National Nosocomial Infections Study, Reports, HE 20.7011/10

Infectious

Emerging Infectious Diseases, HE 20.7009/7, HE 20.7817

Equine Infectious Anemia, Progress Report and History in the United States, A 77.244

Highlights of Research Progress in Allergy and Infectious Diseases, FS 2.22/17

Infectious Disease Committee, HE 20.3001/2:In 3

Infectious Disease Research Series, HE 20.3262/2

Intramural Research, Annual Report: National Institute of Allergy and Infectious Diseases, HE 20.3211/3

Microbiology and Infectious Diseases Program, Annual Report, HE 20.3263

MMWR Surveillance Summaries from the Center for Infectious Diseases, HE 20.7009/2-3

Reported Incidence of Infectious Equine Encephalomyelitis and Related Encephalitides in the United States, Calendar Year (date), A 77.230

United States Army Medical Research Institute of Infectious Disease: Annual Progress Report, D 104.27

Inflationary

Inflationary Impact Statements, L 35.20

In-flight

Special Notices, Supplement to Radio Facility Charts and In-flight Data, Europe, D 301.9/3

United States Air Force, Navy, Royal Canadian Air Force and Royal Canadian Navy, Navy Radio Facility Charts and In-Flight Data, Alaska, Canada and North Atlantic, D 301.13/3

Influenza

Influenza Immunizations Paid for by Medicare, HE 22.21/4

Influenza-Respiratory Disease Surveillance, Reports, HE 20.2309/10

Info

Info Memo Bulletin, HE 20.3214/2

Sti-Recon Bulletin and Tech Info News, NAS 1.76

Infobase

Infobase, USIA Directives, IA 1.32

USIA INFO BASE (Quick Reference Guide), IA 1.32

InfoDisc

Energy InfoDisc, E 3.60

InfoLine

InfoLine, HE 20.3214/3

Informal
  Digest and Index of Opinions of Counsel, **Informal** Rulings of Federal Reserve Board and Matter Relating Thereto, from Federal Reserve Bulletin, FR 1.10
  Exparte Presentations in **Informal** Rulemakings, CC 1.42/3
  Informal Communications, Pr 32.413/7
  Informal Reports, D 203.26/2
Information
  Animal Welfare **Information** Center Newsletter, A 17.27/2
  Annual Forum, Federal **Information** Policies, LC 1.47
  Annual Letter of **Information**, A 35.10
  Biweekly Review, News and **Information** of Interest to Field Offices, C 41.13
  Case **Information** Sheets, Y 3.F 31/21-3:14-11
  Catalogue of **Information**, D 208.109
  Center for **Information** Management and Automation: Calendar for Fiscal Year, PM 1.51
  CERCLIS (Comprehensive Environmental Response Compensation, and Liability **Information** System), EP 1.104/5
  CERL Abstracts, **Information** Exchange Bulletin, D 103.73
  CERL Reports, **Information** Exchange Bulletin, D 103.74
  Chemical **Information** Fact Sheets, EP 5.20
  Chemical-Biological **Information**-Handling Review Committee, HE 20.3001/2:C 42
  CIO **Information** in the News, VA 1.101
  Command **Information** Package, D 101.118/5
  Computers, Control, and **Information** Theory, C 51.9/8
  Consumer **Information** Catalog, GS 11.9
  Contract Reports National Telecommunications and **Information** Administration, C 60.12
  Criminal Justice **Information** Exchange Directory, J 28.20/2
  Criminal Justice **Information** Policy (series), J 29.9/8
  Cultural Resources **Information** Series, I 53.22/11
  Current **Information** Resource Requirements of the Federal Government, PM 1.56
  Current **Information** Technology Resources Requirements of the Federal Government, PrEx 2.12/5
  Defense **Information** School: Catalog, D 1.59
  Defense Logistics **Information** System (DLIS) Procedures Manual, D 7.6/19
  Detailed Mock-Up **Information**, W 108.20
  Diabetes Dateline, the National Diabetes **Information** Clearinghouse Bulletin, HE 20.3310/3
  Digest, Disarmament **Information** Summary, Pr 34.11/2
  Directorate of Mathematical and **Information** Sciences, Air Force Office of Scientific Research, Research Summaries, D 301.45/19-10
  DISA (Defense **Information** Systems Agency), D 5.112
  DOE **Information** Bridge, E 1.137
  Electronic **Information** Products Available by Special Order, GP 3.22/5
  Electronics Engineering **Information** Bulletin, TD 5.3/3
  Enrollment **Information** Guide and Plan Comparison Chart, PM 1.8/4, PM 1.8/10, PM 1.8/11
  Enrollment **Information** Guide and Plan Comparison Chart Federal Civilian Employees in Positions Outside the Continental U.S., PM 1.8/8
  Enrollment **Information** Guide and Plan Comparison Chart Former Spouses Enrolled in the Federal Employees Health Benefits Program, PM 1.8/7
  Enrollment **Information** Guide and Plan Comparison Chart Individuals Receiving Compensation from the Office of Workers Compensation Programs, PM 1.8/13
  Enrollment **Information** Guide and Plan Comparison Chart Open Season, PM 1.8/12
  Enrollment **Information** Guide and Plan Comparison Chart Retirement Systems Participating in the Federal Employees Health Benefits Program, PM 1.8/4

  Enrollment **Information** Guide and Plan Comparison Chart U.S. Postal Service Employees, PM 1.8/5
  ERIC (Educational Resources **Information** Center) Annual Report, ED 1.301/2
  External **Information** and Cultural Relations Programs: {various countries}, IA 1.23
  Federal **Information** Locator System, PrEx 2.14/2
  Federal **Information** Processing Standards Publications, C 13.52
  FIPSE, Drug Prevention Programs in Higher Education, **Information** and Application Procedures, ED 1.23/7, ED 1.23/8
  Five Year **Information** Resource Management Plan, TD 5.64
  FOIA Annual Report (Freedom of **Information** Act), J 1.1/11
  Foreign Trade **Information** on Instrumentation, C 41.92
  Freedom of **Information** Act Annual Report, FMC 1.1/2
  Freedom of **Information** Case List, J 1.56
  Global Volcanism Program, Digital **Information** Series, SI 1.49
  Hazardous Material Control and Management/Hazardous Materials **Information** System, D 212.16
  Hazardous Materials **Information** System, D 7.32
  HCFA Forms **Information** Catalog, HE 22.32/2
  Headquarters, First United States Army, Deputy Chief of Staff, **Information** Management, Organization, Mission, and Functions, D 101.1/9
  Health Care Financing Administration **Information** Systems Development Guide, HE 22.508/2
  Highway **Information** Quarterly, TD 2.23/4
  Highway **Information** Update, TD 2.23/5
  Housing Planning **Information** Series, HH 8.10
  Hypoglycemia, National Diabetes **Information** Clearinghouse, HE 20.3323/2
  Important **Information** about You and Your Medication, VA 1.79
  Information and Technology Report, I 73.11, I 19.210
  Information (series), A 89.15
  Information Bulletins: Adjutant General's Department, W 3.82
  Information Bulletins: Bureau of Air Commerce, C 23.8
  Information Bulletins: Bureau of Land Management, I 53.9
  Information Bulletins: Coast Guard, TD 5.3/6
  Information Bulletins: Defense Civil Prepardness Agency, D 14.13/2
  Information Bulletins: Department of Energy, E 1.100
  Information Bulletins: Division of Maternal and Child Health, HE 20.9111
  Information Bulletins: Environmental **Information** Division, D 301.38/8
  Information Bulletins: Federal Civil Defense Administration, FCD 1.13/11
  Information Bulletins: Field Artillery Office, W 96.5
  Information Bulletins: General Land Office, I 21.17
  Information Bulletins: Human Resources Research Center, D 301.36/5
  Information Bulletins: Library of Congress, LC 1.18
  Information Bulletins: Metallurgical Advisory Committee on Titanium, D 105.13/2-4
  Information Bulletins: National Inventors Council, C 32.7
  Information Bulletins: National Scientific Register, Office of Education, FS 5.47/2
  Information Bulletins: Office of Civil Defense, D 13.3/2
  Information Bulletins: Office of Defense and Civilian Mobilization, Pr 34.753/2
  Information Bulletins: Office of Emergency Preparedness, PrEx 4.3/3
  Information Bulletins: Office of U.S. High Commissioner for Germany, S 1.85
  Information Bulletins: Veteran's Administration, VA 1.22/2
  Information Bulletins: Youth 2000 (series), HE 20.9203/2
  Information Circulars: Air Service, W 87.10
  Information Circulars: Bureau of Mines, C 22.11, I 28.27

  Information Circulars: Engineer Department, W 7.15
  Information Circulars: Federal National Mortgage Association, FL 5.16
  Information Circulars: Field Division, Y 3.C 83:85
  Information Circulars: Hydrographic Office, N 6.23
  Information Circulars: Inspector General's Department, W 9.8
  Information Circulars: National Institute for Occupational Safety and Health, HE 20.7130
  Information Circulars: National Youth Administration, Y 3.N 21/14:8
  Information Circulars: State Councils Section, Y 3.C 83:75
  Information Circulars: War Department Claims Board, W 93.6
  Information Collection and Exchange (series), PE 1.10
  Information Digest, Pr 32.214, Pr 32.5010
  Information Directory, C 21.28/2
  Information Guide (series), T 22.19/4
  Information Letters, W 108.21
  Information Letters {unrestricted}, W 42.41
  Information Memorandum (series), HE 23.1114
  Information Memorandums, HE 1.1013
  Information Memorandums, HE 23.3013
  Information Memorandums {issued by various departments}, HE 1.47
  Information Memorandums, OCSE-IM-(series), HE 24.15
  Information News Letter, L 1.54/3
  Information News Service, C 46.13
  Information Notes, S 1.84
  Information Pamphlets, I 20.34
  Information, Quarterly Newsletter of the National Institute of Education, HE 19.209
  Information Releases, A 82.83
  Information Reports, L 38.10
  Information Resources Directory, EP 1.12/3
  Information Resources Management Handbook (series), GS 12.17
  Information Resources Management Newsletter, GS 12.17/3
  Information Series: Bureau of Agricultural Chemistry and Engineering, A 70.11
  Information Series: Bureau of Agricultural Engineering, A 53.10
  Information Series: Bureau of Public Roads, A 22.14
  Information Series: Federal Board of Surveys and Maps, Y 3.Su 7:9
  Information Series: Federal Crop Insurance Corporation, A 76.108, A 80.907, A 82.207, A 62.9
  Information Series: National Institute of Education, HE 18.11/2
  Information Series: Office of Education, HE 19.143
  Information Service, P 1.36
  Information Service Circulars, HE 3.4
  Information Service Letters, Y 3.W 89/2:39, FW 4.15
  Information Services Fact Sheets, D 301.54
  Information Sheet, S 1.66
  Information Sheets (series), D 101.107/8
  Information Systems Security Products and Services Catalogue, D 1.69/2
  Information Systems Strategic Plan, VA 1.86
  Information Technology Newsletter, GS 1.37/2
  Inside NIDCD **Information** Clearinghouse, HE 20.3666
  Instruction and **Information** for Applicants and for Boards of Examiners, CS 1.6
  International **Information** and Cultural Affairs Office Publications, S 1.56
  International **Information** and Cultural Series, S 1.67
  International Marketing Events **Information** Series, C 57.117/2
  ISOO (**Information** Security Oversight Office) Annual Report, AE 1.101/3
  Judges **Information** Series, Ju 10.24
  Labor **Information** Bulletin, L 2.10
  Labor **Information** Circulars, SS 1.14
  Mechanized **Information** Services Catalog, C 13.46:814
  Memorandum for **Information**, S 1.62
  Minerals and Materials **Information**, I 19.120/4
  Monthly **Information** Bulletins, N 13.10
  NASA **Information** Summaries, NAS 1.90

National Air Toxics **Information** Clearinghouse: Newsletter, EP 4.23

National Clearinghouse on Child Abuse and Neglect **Information** Catalog, HE 23.1216/2

National Physical Demands **Information** Series, L 7.26

NDPO-**Information** Bulletins, J 1.14/25-3

New **Information** from the Office of Educational Research and Improvement, ED 1.303/3

Nonconventional Technical **Information** Systems in Current Use, NS 2.8

NRC **Information** Notice, Y 3.N 88:56-2

Office of Administrator, for Your **Information**, AD (series), FCD 1.13/3

Office of Solid Wastes **Information** Series, SW-(series), FS 2.305

Official Bulletin Committee on Public **Information**, Y 3.P 93/3:3

OPA **Information** Leaflets for Schools and Colleges, Pr 32.4240

Operating Experience, Bulletin **Information** Report, Y 3.N 88:13

Outer Continental Shelf Oil and Gas **Information** Program, Summary Reports (various regions), I 72.9

Pavements and Soil Trafficability **Information** Analysis Center, PSTIAC Reports, D 103.24/12

Policy **Information** Notice (series), HE 20.9118

Price **Information** for Drug Products, Invoice Level Prices, HE 22.113, HE 22.309

Privacy and Security of Criminal History **Information** (series), J 29.10

Procurement **Information** Bulletins, FO 1.3

Program **Information** Guide Series, ED 1.8/4

PROMIS {Prosecutor's Management **Information** System} Research Project Publications, J 1.52

Proposals, Advertisements, General **Information**, etc., N 1.17

Public **Information** (series), P 1.36/2

Public **Information** Communicator (series), FS 14.16

Public **Information** Series, S 1.71/5

Public **Information** {releases}, TC 1.29

Public Sector Labor Relations **Information** Exchange {publications}, L 1.66

Public Sector Labor Relations **Information** Exchange: Calendar of Events, L 1.66/2

Publications National Earthquake **Information** Center, C 55.691

Quarterly Check List, USAF/USN Flight **Information** Publications, Planning, D 301.52/2

Quarterly Circular **Information** Bulletin, D 103.42/11

Quartermaster Letters of **Information**, W 99.13/12

Rabies **Information** Exchange, HE 20.7036/2

Radio and Radar **Information** Letters, Pr 32.4836

Radio Facility Charts and Supplementary **Information**, United States, LF/MF Edition, D 301.43

Recent Releases, Selected **Information** Materials, S 1.30/2

Reference **Information** Paper, AE 1.124

Reference **Information** Series, HE 20.3614/7

Regional **Information** Series Leaflets, A 55.43/6, A 55.45/5

Regional **Information** Series, A 55.42/5, A 55.44/5, A 55.46/5

Regulations, Rules and Instructions Office of **Information** Resources Management, GS 12.15

Regulatory **Information** Service Center: General Publications, GS 1.6.11

Reprint of Hydrographic **Information**, N 6.19

Research **Information** Abstracts, A 106.37/2

Research **Information** Digest, Recent Publications of Southeastern Forest Experiment Station, A 13.63/13

Research **Information** Letter, A 106.37

Research Reports Office of **Information** for the Armed Forces, D 2.12

Resource Management Quarterly **Information** Summary, C 55.9/3

Review of Current **Information** in Treasury Library, T 23.7

Review of Operations **Information** Agency, IA 1.1/2

Route **Information** Series, W 87.21/2

Rural **Information** Center Publication Series, A 17.29

Safety Management **Information**, EP 1.7/3

Safety News Letter, Current **Information** in the Federal Safety Field, L 30.8

Satellite Applications **Information** Notes, C 55.37

Scholarship Program, Applicant **Information** Bulletin, HE 20.6023

Scholarships and Fellowship **Information**, FS 5.63

Sci-Tech **Information**, C 13.74

Science **Information** News, NS 1.17

Scientific **Information** Activities of Federal Agencies, NS 1.16

Scientific **Information** Report, Pr 34.609

Selected Technical Reports, **Information** Retrieval Bulletin, TD 4.17/2

Selective Notification of **Information** SNI, J 26.19, J 28.14

Selective Service College Qualification Test, Bulletin of **Information**, Y 3.Se 4:22

Service Reports Energy **Information** Administration, E 3.26/5

Signal Corps Technical **Information** Letters, W 42.40

Small Business Weekly Summary, Trade Opportunities and **Information** for American Suppliers, FO 1.17

Smithsonian Institution **Information** Systems Innovations, SI 1.32

Social Security **Information** Items, HE 3.82

Social Security **Information**, HE 3.52

Soil Quality **Information** Sheets, A 57.77

Solid Waste Management, Available **Information** Materials, EP 1.17:58.25

Sources for **Information** on American Firms for International Buyers, C 42.2:Am 3

Sources of **Information** on Urban Transportation Planning Methods, TD 1.51

Sources of **Information** Regarding Labor {various countries}, L 2.72/2

Sources of Travel **Information** Series, I 29.56

Soviet Bloc International Geophysical Year **Information**, C 41.40

Special Foreign Currency Science **Information** Program, List of Translations in Process for Fiscal Year, Coordinated and Administered by the National Science Foundation, C 51.12

Special **Information** Bulletins, FS 2.73

SSA Program Circulars Public **Information**, HE 3.4/3

Staff **Information** Circulars, GS 4.12

Staff **Information** Papers, GS 4.12

State Traffic Safety **Information**, TD 8.62

Stockpile **Information**, GS 10.7/2

Student **Information** Sheets (series), D 101.112/2

Sugar **Information** Series, Publications, A 63.9

Summaries of Tariff **Information**, TC 1.26

Summaries of Trade and Tariff **Information**, TC 1.26/2

Summary **Information** Report, Y 3.N 88:41

Summary of Air **Information**, W 95.11

Summary of Health **Information** for International Travel, HE 20.7315/2

Summary of Trade and Tariff **Information** (series), ITC 1.11

Supplementary Flight **Information** Document, Caribbean and South America, D 301.51

Supplements to Veneral Disease **Information** Bulletin, FS 2.10

Survey of American Listed Corporations, Reported **Information** on Selected Defense Industries, SE 1.18/2

Survival Series, For Your **Information** {releases}, FCD 1.13/10

Systems **Information** Newsletter, HE 3.68/4

Systems Technology **Information** Update, HE 3.80T.B. Folders, FS 2.42

T.I.S.C.A. {Technical **Information** System for Carrier Aviation} Technical **Information** Indexes: Naval Carrier Aviation Abstract Bulletin with Cross Reference Index, D 202.22

Tariff **Information** Series, TC 1.5

Tariff **Information** Surveys, TC 1.6

Tax **Information**, IRS Publications (numbered), T 22.44/2

Teaching Opportunities, Directory of Placement **Information**, FS 5.226:2600, HE 5.226:2600

Technical Advisory Services, Health Office, For Your **Information**, TAS (series), FCD 1.13/2

Technical **Information** Bulletins, FS 2.2/3, FS 3.52/2, HE 3.52/2

Technical **Information** Center: Bulletins, TD 1.3/2

Technical **Information** Circulars, Y 3.N 21/14:11, FS 6.14

Technical **Information** Handbooks, FTC-TIH-, D 301.45/31-4

Technical **Information** Indexes: Naval Carrier Aviation Abstract Bulletin with Cross Reference Index, D 202.22

Technical **Information** Memorandum (series), D 1.83

Technical **Information** Notes, I 40.11, FW 3.11

Technical **Information** on Building Materials for Use in Design of Low-cost Housing, C 13.27

Technical **Information** Pamphlets, D 103.53/6

Technical **Information** Release, T 22.42/2

Technical Memorandum Energy **Information** Administration, E 3.26,

Technical Memorandum National Telecommunications and **Information** Administration, C 60.11

Technical Reports Energy **Information** Administration, E 3.26/3

Thomas: Legislative **Information** on the Internet, LC 1.54/2

TIB {Technical **Information** Bulletin} (series), HE 3.52/2

Timely Extension **Information**, A 43.5/6, A 43.6

Toxics Integration **Information** Series, EP 1.79/2, EP 5.18

Trade **Information** Bulletins, C 18.25

Trademarks Pending, Bibliographic **Information** from Pending US Trademarks, C 21.31/8

Trademarks Registered, Bibliographic **Information** from Registered US Trademarks, C 21.31/7

Traffic **Information** Letters, T 58.12

Training Analysis and Development, **Information** Bulletin, D 301.38/2

Transportation Safety **Information** Report, TD 1.48

Treaty **Information** Bulletin, S 9.7

U.S. Coast Pilots Wartime **Information** to Mariners, C 4.7/6

U.S.D.A. Administrative **Information**, A 1.57

United States Advisory Commission on **Information**, Semiannual Report to Congress, S 1.93

United States Air Force and Navy Supplementary Flight **Information** Document, Pacific and Far East, D 301.50

United States Air Force and Navy Supplementary Flight **Information**, Europe, Africa, and Middle East, D 301.49

United States Air Force, Commands and Agencies Basic **Information**, D 301.26/23

United States Air Force, Navy, Royal Canadian Air Force and Royal Canadian Supplementary Flight **Information**, North American Area (excluding Mexico and Caribbean area), D 301.48

United States Air Force, Navy, Royal Canadian Air Force, and Royal Canadian Navy Supplementary Flight **Information**, North American Area (excluding Mexico and Caribbean area), D 301.48

United States Coast Guard Academy, New London, Connecticut: Bulletin of **Information**, TD 5.16/2

United States Government Flight **Information** Publication: Pacific Chart Supplement, C 55.427

United States Immigration Laws, General **Information**, J 21.5/2

United States LPPSD Technical **Information** Exchange Documents, EP 1.50

United States LPPSD {Low Pollution Power Systems Development} Technical **Information** Exchange Documents, ER 1.16

United States-United Nations **Information** Series, S 1.50

Urban Consortium **Information** Bulletins, HH 1.3/3

USAFI **Information** Letter, D 1.10/2

Useful **Information** for Newly Commissioned Officers, D 207.215

USIA Strategic **Information** Resources Management (IRM) Plan, IA 1.33
V-line, Bulletin of **Information**, PrEx 10.13/4
Value Engineering **Information** Letters, C 39.220
Veneral Disease **Information**, T 27.26, FS 2.9
Veterans Assistance **Information**, Printed and Processed, Y 3.Se 4:18
Victory Speaker; An Arsenal of **Information** for Speakers, Pr 32.5017
Viet-Nam **Information** Notes, S 1.38
Vocational Education **Information** (series), HE 19.121
Vocational Summary, Circulars of **Information**, VE 1.5
Voice of Z39, News About Library, **Information** Science, and Publishing Standards, C 13.163
Voting **Information** Bulletins, D 2.3/2
Voting **Information** News, D 1.96
War **Information** Series, Y 3.P 96/3:7
War Notes, **Information** from Abroad, N 13.7
War Series, **Information** from Abroad, N 13.8
Wartime **Information** to Mariners Supplementing U.S. Coast Pilots, C 4.7/6
Water and Sewer Facilities Grant Program, HUD **Information** Series, HH 1.17
Water **Information** Series Reports, I 19.53/4
Water Resources Scientific **Information** Center, WRSIC- (series), I 1.97
Weekly **Information** Report, Y 3.N 88:37, Y 3.N 88:50, Y 3.N 88:55
Weekly Summary of Health **Information** for International Travel, HE 20.7023
World Trade **Information** Series, C 41.13, C 49.8
Informational
 Informational Bulletins, W 108.23
 Informational Letters, FS 3.34
 Informational Memorandums, FW 2.16
 Package X, **Informational** Copies of Federal Tax Forms, T 22.2/12
Informations
 Informations, Region 6, I 49.7/2
Informative
 Informative Technical Bulletins, Pr 32.4821
InForum
 InForum, E 1.134
Infractions
 Report on Administrative Adjudication of Traffic **Infractions**, TD 8.12/4
Infrastructure
 Highlights (National **Infrastructure** Protection Center), J 1.14/23-3
Ingot
 Aluminum Alloy **Ingot**, Monthly Reports, I 28.71
 Aluminum Scrap and Secondary **Ingot**, I 28.71/2
 Aluminum Scrap and Secondary **Ingot**, Secondary Aluminum Monthly Report, I 28.71/3
Ingredients
 Project Label, Alphabetical Listings by Controlled Generic Drug **Ingredients**, J 24.24/2
Inhabitants
 U.S. Census of Population: Number of **Inhabitants**, C 3.223/5
In-Home
 Someone Who Cares, A Guide to Hiring an **In-Home** Caregiver, HE 1.1009
In-House
 In-House List of Publications, Aeronautical Research Laboratory, D 301.69/4
Initial
 C.A.B. **Initial** and Recommended Decisions of Administrative Law Judges, CAB 1.38
 Initial Analysis and Forecast Charts, C 55.281/2-6
 Initial Reports of the Deep Sea Drilling Project, NS 1.38
 Initial Sequestration Report for Fiscal Year (date), Y 4.D 36/2
 Memorandum, Opinions and Orders, **Initial** Decisions, Etc., CC 1.12/a 8
 Proceedings Ocean Drilling Program, **Initial** Reports, NS 1.38/2
 Substitute Chemical Program, **Initial** Scientific and Minieconomic Review of {various chemicals}, EP 5.13
Initiation Grants
 Applied Social and Behavioral Sciences Research **Initiation Grants**, NS 1.10/8
Initiative
 Initiative for Interdisciplinary Artists Inter-Arts, NF 2.8/2-22
 NBLIC (National Black Leadership **Initiative** on Cancer) News, HE 20.3195

Report to the Congress on the Strategic Defense **Initiative**, D 1.1/6
White House **Initiative** on Historically Black Colleges and Universities, Newsletter, ED 1.89
Initiatives
 America's Commitment: Federal Programs Benefiting Women and New **Initiatives** as Follow-up to the U.N. Fourth World Conference on Women, Pr 42.8:W 84
 ED **Initiatives**, ED 1.90
 Grants to Presenting Organizations, Special Touring **Initiatives** Application Guidelines, NF 2.8/2-29
Injuries
 Casualities and **Injuries** among Shipyard and Dock Workers, L 16.37
 Coal Mine **Injuries** and Worktime, I 28.89
 Estimated Work **Injuries**, L 2.77/5
 Federal Work **Injuries** Sustained During Calendar Year, L 26.8
 Federal Work Injury Facts, Occupational Distribution, Duration and Direct Cost Factors of Work **Injuries** to Civilian Federal Employees During Calendar Year, L 26.8/2-2
 Medical Statistics, Navy, Statistical Report of the Surgeon General, Navy, Occurrence of Diseases and **Injuries** in the Navy for Fiscal Year (date), D 206.11
 MESA Safety Reviews: Coal-Mine **Injuries** and Worktime, I 69.10/2
 MESA Safety Reviews: **Injuries** at Sand and Gravel Plants, I 69.10/3
 Mine **Injuries** and Worktime, L 38.16
 News, BLS Reports on Survey of Occupational **Injuries** and Illnesses in ..., L 2.120/2-11
 Occupational **Injuries** and Illnesses in (year), L 1.79/2-4, L 2.120/2-11
 Occupational **Injuries** and Illnesses in the United States by Industry, L 2.3/11
 Recordkeeping Requirements for Firms Selected to Participate in the Annual Survey of Occupational **Injuries** and Illnesses, L 2.129
 Report on Traffic Accidents and **Injuries** for (year), TD 8.32
 Statistics of Diseases and **Injuries** in Navy, N 10.15, M 203.10
 Work **Injuries** in Atomic Energy, L 2.71
 Work **Injuries** Reported by Longshoremen and Harbor Workers, L 26.9
 Work **Injuries**, Contract Construction, L 2.77/3
 Work **Injuries**, Trade, L 2.77/4
Injury
 Determination of **Injury** (series), TC 1.31/2
 Determination of No **Injury** or Likelihood Thereof, TC 1.31
 Fatal and **Injury** Accidents Rates on Federal-aid and Other Highway Systems, TD 2.20
 Federal Work **Injury** Facts, L 26.2:In 5/4
 Federal Work **Injury** Facts, Occupational Distribution, Duration and Direct Cost Factors of Work Injuries to Civilian Federal Employees During Calendar Year, L 26.8/2-2
 How to Use **Injury** Statistics to Prevent Occupational Accidents, L 16.42
 Injury Control Research Laboratory: Research Report, ICRL-RR (series), HE 20.1116
 Injury Control Update, HE 20.7956
 Injury Epidemiology and Control Reprints, HE 20.7009/3
 Injury Experience and Related Employment Data for Sand and Gravel Industry, I 28.108/2
 Injury Experience in Coal Mining, I 28.27, L 38.10/4, I 69.9
 Injury Experience in Metallic Mineral Industries, I 28.27, I 69.9
 Injury Experience in Nonmetallic Mining Industries, I 28.27, L 38.10/5, I 69.9
 Injury Experience in Oil and Gas Industry of United States, I 28.108
 Injury Experience in Quarrying, I 28.27, I 69.9
 Injury Experience in Stone Mining, L 38.10/3
 Injury Rates by Industry, L 2.77/2
 Injury-frequency Rates for Selected Manufacturing Industries, L 2.77
 Morbidity Weekly Report, **Injury** Prevention Reprints, HE 20.7009/4
 NASA Mishap and **Injury** Data, NAS 1.57

NEISS {National Electronic **Injury** Surveillance System} News, Product Safety, HE 20.4026, Y 3.C 76/3:7-2
NINCDS Spinal Cord **Injury** Research Program, HE 20.3502:Sp 4/2
Proceedings Annual Clinical Spinal Cord **Injury** Conference, VA 1.42
Research Reports **Injury** Control Report Laboratory, FS 2.316
Studies in Workmen's Compensation and Radiation **Injury**, Y 3.At 7:2 R 11/28
Inland
 Foreign **Inland** Waterway News, Intercoastal Waterways, Rivers, Lakes, Canals, Equipment, C 18.208
 Pilot Rules for Certain **Inland** Waters of Atlantic and Pacific Coasts of Gulf of Mexico, C 25.9
 Uniform System of Accounts for Carriers by **Inland** and Coastal Waterways, IC 1 wat.14
Inlets
 GITI {General Investigation of Tidal **Inlets**} Reports, D 103.42/7
Inmates
 Drugs and Jail **Inmates**, J 29.13/3
 Jail **Inmates**, J 29.11/5
 Prison and Jail **Inmates** at Midyear, J 29.11/5-2
 Profile of Jail **Inmates**, J 29.13/2
 Survey of State Prison **Inmates**, J 29.25
Innovation
 Abstracts of Phase I Awards, Small Business **Innovation** Research, NS 1.46
 Aerospace Technology **Innovation**, NAS 1.95
 Omnibus Solicitation of the Public Health Service for Small Business **Innovation** Research (SBIR) Grant Applications, HE 20.3047/2
 Pacesetters in **Innovation**, FS 5.220:20103, HE 5.220:20103
 Pre-Solicitation Announcements, Small Business **Innovation** Programs, SBA 1.37
 Program Solicitation, Small Business **Innovation** Research Program, A 94.16
 Results under the Small Business **Innovation** Development Act of 1982, SBA 1.1/4
 Small Business **Innovation** Research for Fiscal Year, C 1.82
 Small Business **Innovation** Research Program Solicitation, TD 10.13
 Small Business **Innovation** Research (SBIR) Program, D 1.48/3
 Solicitation of the Public Health Service and the Health Care Financing Administration for Small Business **Innovation** Research Contract Proposals, HE 22.31
Innovations
 Innovations in Election Administration, Y 3.El 2/3:18
 Innovations in the Courts: Series on Court Administration, Ju 13.12
 Innovations, Mental Health Services, Progress Reports, HE 20.2425
 Smithsonian Institution Information Systems **Innovations**, SI 1.32
 Youth Program Models and **Innovations**, L 37.19
Innovative
 Innovative and Alternative Technology Projects, a Progress Report, EP 2.30
 Innovative Finance, TD 2.75/2
 Innovative Finance Quarterly, TD 2.75
 Omnibus Solicitation for the Small Business **Innovative** Research, HE 20.28
 SITE (Superfund **Innovative** Technology Evaluation) Demonstration Bulletin, EP 1.89/4-2
 SITE (Superfund **Innovative** Technology Evaluation), EP 1.89/4
Innovators
 Information for **Innovators**, and Interdisciplinary Information Service, C 51.9/31
Inorganic
 Journal of **Inorganic** Chemistry, C 41.53/4
Inpatient
 Inpatient Utilization of Short-Stay Hospitals by Diagnosis, United States, HE 20.6209/8
Inputs
 Inputs Outlook and Situation, A 93.47
Inquiries
 Reports on Investigations and **Inquiries**, TC 1.39

Instruction Manual: Classification and Coding Instructions for Marriage Records, HE 20.6208/7

Instruction Manual: Data Preparation of the Current Sample, HE 20.6208/9

Instruction Manual: Demographic Classification and Coding Instructions for Death Records, HE 20.6208/5

Instruction Manual: Dental Examiner's Manual for the Hispanic Health and Nutrition Survey, HE 20.6208/2-6

Instruction Manual: Dietary Interviewer's Manual for the Hispanic Health and Nutrition Examination Survey, HE 20.6208/2-2

Instruction Manual: Field Staff Operations for the Hispanic Health and Nutrition Examination Survey, HE 20.6208/2-5

Instruction Manual: ICD 9 Acme Decision Tables for Classifying Underlying Causes of Death, HE 20.6208/4-2

Instruction Manual: ICDA Eighth Revision of Decision Tables for Classifying Underlying Causes of Death, HE 20.6208/4-5

Instruction Manual, Part 1, Source Records and Control Specifications, HE 20.6209/11

Instruction Manual Part 2d, NCHS Procedures for Mortality Medical Data System File Preparation and Maintenance, HE 20.6208/4-6

Instruction Manual Part 2g, Data Entry Instructions for the Mortality Medical Indexing, Classification, and Retrieval System (MICAR), HE 20.6208/4-7

Instruction Manual Part 2h, Dictionary of Valid Terms for the Mortality Medical Indexing, Classification, and Retrieval System (MICAR), HE 20.6208/4-8

Instruction Manual Part 11, Computer Edits for Mortality Data, HE 20.6208/14

Instruction Manual Part 12, Computer Edits for Natality Data, HE 20.6208/15

Instruction Manuals: Engineer Department, W 7.20

Instruction Manuals: War Plans Division, Education and Special Training Committee, W 26.17/5

Instruction Memorandum, D 212.6/2, D 212.11

Instruction Reports, D 103.24/7

Instruction Sheets, W 28.8

Instruction, Special, FR 1.8

Letters of **Instruction**, W 87.18

Military Notes on Training and **Instruction**, W 26.16/5

MSHA **Instruction** Guide Series, L 38.17/3

NDATUS **Instruction** Manual, HE 20.8021

Operating **Instruction** for Merchant Marine Examination Questions Books, Navigation General Book 3, TD 5.57/2

Planning Division, **Instruction** and Procedure, GP 1.23/3

Programmed **Instruction** (series), D 101.107/10

Programmed **Instruction** Workbooks (series), L 38.18

Publications for **Instruction**, etc. of Naval Militia, N 1.27/7

Regulations and Programme of **Instruction**, W 29.6

School of **Instruction**, T 33.11

Secretary's **Instruction**, L 1.22

Technical **Instruction** Book Manuscript, TD 4.32/13

U.S. Navy Travel Instructions, **Instruction** Memoranda, N 20.13/3

Instructional

Instructional Cassette Recordings, LC 19.11/3

Instructional Disc Recordings, LC 19.11/3-2

Instructional Faculty Salaries for Academic Year, ED 1.131

Instructional Materials . . . for U.S. Army Reserve Schools, D 103.6/8

Instructional Program Notes, VA 1.76

National Defense Language Development Program: Completed Research, Studies and **Instructional** Materials, Lists, FS 5.212:12016, HE 5.212:12016

Programs, (year), Guide to Programmed **Instructional** Materials Available to Educators by (date), FS 5.234:34015, HE 5.234:34015

Title II, Elementary and Secondary Education Act of 1965, School Library Resources, Textbooks and Other **Instructional** Materials, Annual Report, HE 5.79/2

Vocational **Instructional** Materials Available from Federal Agencies, ED 1.17/3

Vocational **Instructional** Materials for Marketing and Distributive Education, ED 1.17/3

Instructions

General **Instructions** and Regulations in Relation to Transaction of Business at Mints and Assay Offices with Coinage Laws, T 28.9

General **Instructions** for Surveys in Philippine Islands, C 4.18/4

Head Start, Child Development Program, Manual of Policies and **Instructions**, PrEx 10.8:H 34/2

Instructions and Application for Grants under the Special Needs Program, ED 1.61

Instructions and Application for Grants under the Strengthening Program, ED 1.61/2

Instructions and Data Specifications for Reporting DHHS Obligations to Institutions of Higher Education and Other Nonprofit Organizations, HE 20.3050

Instructions for Classifying Multiple Causes of Death, HE 20.6208/4-3

Instructions for Classifying the Underlying Cause of Death, HE 20.6208/4-4

Instructions for Classifying the Underlying Cause of Death: Mobile Examination Center Interviewer's Manual for the Hispanic Health and Nutrition Examination Survey, HE 20.6208/2-4

Instructions for Classifying the Underlying Cause of Death: Nonindexed Terms, Standard Abbreviations, and State Geographic Codes Used in Mortality Data Classification, HE 20.6208/4

Instructions for Classifying the Underlying Cause of Death: Physician's Examination Manual for the Hispanic Health and Nutrition Examination Survey, HE 20.6208/2-3

Instructions for Classifying the Underlying Cause of Death: Source Records and Control Specifications, HE 20.6208/11

Instructions for Classifying the Underlying Cause of Death: Vital Records Geographic Classification, HE 20.6208/3

Instructions: Bureau of Medicine and Surgery, N 10.5

Instructions: Federal Board for Vocational Education, VE 1.9

Instructions to Candidates, D 305.8/4

Instructions: Weather Bureau, A 29.12

Interpretations, Rulings and Explanations Regarding Laws, Rulings, and **Instructions**, IC 1 loc.6

Interpretations, Rulings, and **Instructions** for Inspection and Testing of Locomotives and Tenders and their Appurtenances, IC 1 loc.5

Modification **Instructions**, D 217.16/6

National Emergency Standby Regulations and **Instructions** Personnel and Manpower, CS 1.41/4:990-3

Naval Reserve Circular Letters and **Instructions**, N 25.5

O & NAV **Instructions**, D 207.8

Operations **Instructions** (series), J 21.6/2-2

Operations, **Instructions**, Regulations, and Interpretations, J 21.6/2

Ordnance **Instructions** for Navy, N 18.5

Pay and Supply **Instructions**, Circulars, N 24.26, T 47.8/2

Personnel **Instructions**, L 1.25

Photogrammetric **Instructions**, C 4.48

Preservation Programs Guidelines and Application **Instructions**, NF 3.8/2-3

Program **Instructions**, HE 1.47/2

Public Humanities Projects, Guidelines and Application **Instructions**, NF 3.8/2-9

Regulations, Rules and **Instructions** Census Bureau, C 3.6

Regulations, Rules and **Instructions** Center for Professional Development and Training, HE 20.7709

Regulations, Rules, and **Instructions**: Comptroller of the Currency, T 12.25

Regulations, Rules and **Instructions** Court of Customs Appeals, Ju 7.8/2

Regulations, Rules and **Instructions** Customs Division, T 17.5

Regulations, Rules and **Instructions** Department of Education, ED 1.47

Regulations, Rules and **Instructions** Department of Transportation, TD 1.6

Regulations, Rules and **Instructions** Federal Emergency Management Agency, FEM 1.6

Regulations, Rules and **Instructions** Food and Nutrition Service, A 98.18

Regulations, Rules, and **Instructions**: Grain Inspection, Packers and Stockyards Administration, A 113.12

Regulations, Rules and **Instructions** International Trade Commission, ITC 1.6

Regulations, Rules and **Instructions** National Center for Devices and Radiological Health, HE 20.4606

Regulations, Rules and **Instructions** National Defense University, D 5.406

Regulations, Rules and **Instructions** Naval Research Office, D 210.6

Regulations, Rules and **Instructions** Office of Information Resources Management, GS 12.15

Regulations, Rules and **Instructions** Office of Water Programs, EP 2.6

Regulations, Rules and **Instructions** Research and Special Programs Administration, TD 10.6

Regulations, Rules and **Instructions** United States Parole Commission, J 27.6

Rules, Rulings and **Instructions**, A 55.69

Staff **Instructions**, A 68.21

Systems Maintenance Division **Instructions**, FAA 1.6/7

Topographic **Instructions**, I 19.15/4

U.S. Navy Travel **Instructions**, Instruction Memoranda, N 20.13/3

Veterans Administration **Instructions**, VA 1.15

Instructor

Instructor Set (series), D 12.13

Instructor Training Bulletins, N 17.34

Instructor's

Illustrated **Instructor's** Reference, W 1.45

Instructor's Guide for Classes, First Aid Training Courses, N 10.16

Instructor's Guides, IG (series), D 14.8/4, D 119.8/7

Instructor's Training Aids Guide, D 208.9

Instructor's Work Kit, L 7.46

Instructors' Journal, D 301.38/7

Instruction

Course Management Plan and Program of **Instruction** (series), D 101.107/4

Course of **Instruction** at Merchant Marine Academy, C 39.225

epartment of Defense **Instruction** (series), D 1.6/13

Instructions

Compliance Boards **Instructions**, Y 3.N 21/8:11

Instructors

Certification; Pilots and Flight **Instructors**, TD 4.6:part 61

Instrument

Aircraft **Instrument** Approaches, Fiscal Year, FAA 1.40

Aircraft **Instrument** Bulletin, Flowmeter Series, Flowmeter Bulletins, N 28.19

Aircraft **Instrument** Bulletins, N 28.10, M 208.9

Dates of Latest Prints, **Instrument** Flight Charts, C 4.9/18

Eastern United States, Dates of Latest Prints, **Instrument** Approach Procedure Charts and Airport Obstruction Plans (OP), C 4.9/19

High Altitude **Instrument** Approach Procedures, D 5.318/2

Index of Standard **Instrument** Approach Procedures, TD 4.312

Instrument Approach and Landing Charts, C 4.9/10

Instrument Approach Chart, Radio Beacon, C 4.9/16

Instrument Approach Charts, I.L.S., C 4.9/14

Instrument Approach Procedure Charts, C 55.411, C 55.411/2

Instrument Fact Sheet, C 55.71, D 203.32/2

Instrument Flying, D 301.7:51-37

Instrument Manufacture {abstracts}, C 41.77/2

Instrument Room {or division} Circulars, A 29.11

Military Fields, United States, **Instrument** Approach Procedure Charts, C 55.418/4

Radiation **Instrument** Catalog, Y 3.At 7:20

Self-Evaluation **Instrument** (series), HE 20.7116

Standard **Instrument** Approach Procedures, FAA 5.13, TD 4.60

Standard **Instrument** Departure (SID) Charts, Eastern U.S., C 55.416/5

Standard **Instrument** Departure (SID) Charts, Western United States, C 55.416/6

Standards Laboratory **Instrument** Calibration Procedure, Department of Navy, BUWEPS-BUSHIPS Calibration Program, D 217.16/2

Standards Laboratory **Instrument** Calibration Technique, D 217.16/7

Western United States, Dates of Latest Prints, **Instrument** Approach Procedure Charts and Airport Obstruction Plans, C 4.9/20

Instrument Approach

DoD Flight Information Publication (Terminal) High Altitude **Instrument Approach** Procedures, D 5.318/2

Flight Information Publication: Low Altitude **Instrument Approach** Procedures, D 5.318

Instrumentation

Airborne **Instrumentation** Research Project Summary Catalog, NAS 1.68

Biomedical Engineering and **Instrumentation** Branch, Division of Research Branch: Annual Report, HE 20.3036/3

Engineering and **Instrumentation**, C 13.22

Foreign Trade Information on **Instrumentation**, C 41.92

Instrumentation, E 1.99

Instrumentation Papers, D 301.45/10

National Oceanographic **Instrumentation** Center Publications, C 55.72

Radio Chemical Analysis, Nuclear **Instrumenta-tion**, Radiation Techniques, **Nuclear** Chemistry, Radioisotope Techniques, C 13.46

Testing and **Instrumentation**, C 51.17/10

Instruments

HUD Survey Reveals Large Increase in Pension Fund Investment in Mortgage **Instruments**, HH 1.99/7

Scientific Reports of Higher Schools Machine Construction and **Instruments** Manufacture, C 41.65/8

Survey of Pension Fund Investment in Mortgage **Instruments**, HH 1.99/4

Insular

Annual Conference with Directors of National Reclamation Association, Memorandum of Chairman to Members of Committee on Interior and **Insular** Affairs, Y 4.In 8/13:R 24/2

News Releases and Miscellaneous Publications; Committee on Interior and **Insular** Affairs, (House), Y 4.In 8/14-2

Report to the Committee on the Budget; Views and Estimates of the Committee on Interior and **Insular** Affairs (House), Y 4.In 8/14-11

Rules for the Committee on Interior and **Insular** Affairs, Y 4.In 8/14-13

Insurance

Annual Report of **Insurance** Business Transacted in Canal Zone, CZ 1.9

Annual Report of the Board of Trustees of the Federal Old-Age and Survivors Insurance and Disability **Insurance** Trust Funds, SSA 1.1/4

Annual Report of the Health **Insurance** Benefits Advisory Council, HE 20.17

Annual Statements, Government Life **Insurance** Fund, VA 1.13

Automobile **Insurance** and Compensation Studies, TD 1.17

Benefit Series Service Unemployment **Insurance** Report, L 37.209

Business Establishment, Employment and Taxable Pay Rolls under Old-Age and Survivors **Insurance** Program, C 18.270

Census of Financial, **Insurance**, and Real Estate Industries, C 3.291

Characteristics of Social Security Disability **Insurance** Beneficiaries, HE 3.91

Comparison of State Unemployment **Insurance** Laws, L 37.212

Composite List of Eligible Institutions, National Vocation Student Loan **Insurance** Act of 1965, FS 5.83/2, HE 5.83/2

Concurrent Receipt of Public Assistance Money Payments and Old-Age, Survivors, and Disability **Insurance** Cash Benefits by Persons Aged 65 or Over, FS 17.636, HE 17.636

Crop **Insurance** Manager's Bulletins, A 112.20

Crop **Insurance** Research and Development Bulletins, A 112.17, A 62.17

Crop **Insurance** Update, A 62.13

Digest of Health and **Insurance** Plans, L 2.99/2

Digest of Rulings (Old-Age and Survivors **Insurance**), FS 3.24

Digest of Selected Health and **Insurance** Plans, L 2.99/2

Directory of Multifamily Project Mortgage **Insurance** Programs by Project Status, HH 1.50

Employment and Wages of Workers Covered by State Unemployment **Insurance** Laws and Unemployment Compensation for Federal Employees, by Industry and State, L 7.20/3, L 1.61

Employment and Wages, a Quarterly Summary of Workers Covered by State Unemploy-ment **Insurance** Laws and Unemploy-ment Compensation for Federal Employees, L 2.104

Farm-Mortgage Lending Experience of 19 Life **Insurance** Companies, Federal Land Banks, and Farmers Home Administra-tion, A 93.9/5

Federal Crop **Insurance** Corporation, A 82.201

Federal Savings and Loan **Insurance** Corporation, Financial Statements, FHL 1.2:F 31/2

FHA Home Mortgage **Insurance** Operations, State, County and MSA/PMSA, HH 2.24/8

FHA Monthly Report of Operations: Project Mortgage **Insurance** Programs, HH 2.27

Flood **Insurance** Rate Maps, HH 10.9/2

Flood **Insurance** Studies, FEM 1.209

Flood **Insurance** Studies (by State), HH 10.9

Flood **Insurance** Studies (various areas), FEM 1.209

Government Life **Insurance** Programs for Veterans and Servicemen, VA 1.46

Guide to Crop **Insurance** Protection, A 62.16

Handbook of Old-Age and Survivors **Insurance** Statistics, FS 3.40

Health **Insurance** for the Aged, HE 3.6/4, HE 3.57

Health **Insurance** Statistics, HE 3.28/5

Health **Insurance** Statistics, CMS (series), FS 3.28/4, HE 3.28/4

Health **Insurance** Statistics: Current Medicare Survey Report, HE 3.28/4

Health **Insurance** Studies: Contract Research Series, HE 22.11

Insurance and Disability Insurance Trust Funds, SSA 1.1/4

Insurance and Labor Law Series, C 18.99/2

Insurance Bulletins, T 49.9

Insurance Program Quality, HE 3.28/6-4

Monthly Benefit Statistics; Old-age, Survivors, Disability, and Health **Insurance**, Summary Benefit Data, HE 3.28/6

Monthly Benefit Statistics; Railroad Retirement and Unemployment **Insurance** Programs, RR 1.13

National Credit Union Share **Insurance** Fund: Annual Report, NCU 1.18

National Flood **Insurance** Program Community Status Book, District of Columbia, FEM 1.210/10

National Survey of Old-Age and Survivors **Insurance** Beneficiaries: Highlight Reports, FS 3.48

Old-Age and Survivors **Insurance**, Regulations, FS 3.6/2

Old-Age and Survivors **Insurance** Operating Statistics Review, SS 1.33

Operating Bank Offices Insured by the Federal Deposit **Insurance** Corporation, as of {date}, Y 3.F 31/8:18

Papers in Re World War Risk **Insurance**, J 1.13/2

Pension **Insurance** Data Book: PBGC Single-Employer Program, Y 3.P 38/2:12

Preliminary Data on Unemployment **Insurance**, L 7.43

Railroad Retirement and Unemployment **Insurance** Act, As Amended {August 29, 1935}, Y 1.2:R 13

Regulations No. 4, Old-Age and Survivors **Insurance**, FS 3.6/2

Report, Civil Service Requirement, Federal Employees' Group Life **Insurance**, Federal Employees Health Benefits, Retired Federal Employees Health Benefits, Fiscal Year (date), CS 1.29/3

Retirement and Survivors **Insurance** Semiannual Analysis, HE 3.57/2

Selected Multifamily Status Reports, Mortgage **Insurance** Programs by Name and Location of Each Project, HH 1.50

Servicemen's Group Life **Insurance** Program, Annual Report, VA 1.46/2

Significant Provisions of State Unemployment **Insurance** Laws, L 37.210

Social Security Rulings on Federal Old-age, Survivors, Disability, and Health **Insurance**, HE 3.44

SSA Program Circulars Retirement and Survivors **Insurance**, HE 3.4/5

Summary of Mortgage **Insurance** Operations and Contract Authority, HH 2.24/5

Unemployment **Insurance** Claims Weekly Report, L 37.12/2-2

Unemployment **Insurance** Claims, L 1.62, L 37.12/2

Unemployment **Insurance** Occasional Paper, L 37.213/2

Unemployment **Insurance** Occasional Papers, L 37.20

Unemployment **Insurance** Program Letters, L 7.50

Unemployment **Insurance** Quality Appraisal Results, L 37.213

Unemployment **Insurance** Quality Control, Annual Report, L 37.20/3

Unemployment **Insurance** Review, L 7.18/3

Unemployment **Insurance** Statistics, L 1.62/2, L 37.12

Unemployment **Insurance** Tax Rates by Industry, L 7.70, L 33.11

Unemployment **Insurance** Weekly Claims Reports, L 37.12/2, L 37.12/2-2

Unemployment **Insurance** Weekly Claims Reports, L 37.21/2-2

Unemployment **Insurance**, Technical Staff Papers, L 37.20/2

Insurance Companies

Nonfarm Mortgage Investments of Life **Insurance** Companies, FHL 1.18

Insured

Characteristics of the **Insured** Unemployed, Monthly Report, L 1.32

FHA Low Cost Housing Trends of One-family Homes **Insured** by FHA, HH 2.26

FHA Trends, Characteristics of Home Mortgages **Insured** by FHA, HH 2.24

FSLIC **Insured** Savings and Loan Associations, Savings and Mortgage Activity, Selected Balance Sheet Items, FHL 1.20/2

Manual of Laws Affecting Federally **Insured** State Credit Unions, NCU 1.8:St 2/2

Mortgage Interest Rates on Conventional Loans, Largest **Insured** Savings and Loan Associations, FHL 1.24

Number of Foreclosures {and rate of foreclosure} by FSLIC **Insured** Savings and Loan Associations, FHL 1.26

Report to **Insured** Banks, Y 3.F 31/8:17

Savings and Mortgage Lending Activity, Selected Balance Sheet Items, F.S.L.I.C. **Insured** Savings and Loan Associations, FHL 1.20/2

Summary of Savings Accounts by Geographic Area, FSLIC-**Insured** Savings and Loan Associations, FHL 1.29

Insurgent

Philippine **Insurgent** Records, W 6.10

Integrated

World **Integrated** Nuclear Evaluation System, E 3.51/2

IPEDS **Integrated** Postsecondary Education Data System, Institutional Characteristics, ED 1.23/6

Integration

Toxics **Integration** Information Series, EP 1.79/2, EP 5.18

Toxics **Integration** Policy Series, EP 1.79/3

Integrity

Data **Integrity** and Run to Run Balancing, T 22.58

Federal Managers' Financial **Integrity** Act, Secretary's Annual Statement and Report to the President and the Congress, I 1.96/6

HCFA Regional Office Manual; Program **Integrity**, HE 22.8/8-2

Office of Research **Integrity**, Annual Report, HE 20.1/3

President's Council on **Integrity** and Efficiency: Reports, Pr 41.8/3

Program **Integrity** Bulletin, HH 1.3/5

Steam Generator Tube **Integrity** Program, Y 3.N 88:17

Intellectual
Committee on International **Intellectual** Property, S
1.130/2:In 8
Intelligence
Air Technical **Intelligence** Technical Data Digest,
M 301.9
Army **Intelligence** Center and School: SupR
(series), D 101.112
Center for the Study of **Intelligence** Monographs,
PrEx 3.18
Current **Intelligence** Bulletin, HE 20.7115
Current **Intelligence** Bulletins, Summaries, HE
20.7115/2
Defense **Intelligence** Agency Regulations (series),
D 5.206/2
Defense **Intelligence** School: Academic Catalog, D
5.210
Directorate of **Intelligence** Publications
(numbered), PrEx 3.10/7
Engineer **Intelligence** Notes, D 103.29
Information **Intelligence** Summary, W 108.32
Military **Intelligence**, D 101.93
National Basic **Intelligence** Factbook, PrEx 3.10:N
21
National Drug **Intelligence** Center (NDIC):
General Publications, J 1.112
Posters Defense **Intelligence** Agency, D 5.213
Press **Intelligence** Bulletins, Y 3.N 21/8:13, Pr
32.209, Pr 32.5012
Quarterly Bulletin, **Intelligence** Continuing
Education Program, D 5.212
Quarterly **Intelligence** Trends, J 24.18/4
Rules of Procedure for the Permanent Select
Committee on **Intelligence**, Y 4.In 8/18-
10
Special Releases {of Foreign Broadcast **Intelligence**
Service}, W 100.9
Special Series Military **Intelligence** Division, W
100.7
Studies in **Intelligence**, PrEX 3.19
Summary of **Intelligence**, W 95.12
Intentions
Planting **Intentions**, A 36.38
Turkey Breeder Hens Hatching Season **Intentions**,
A 92.9/9
Interaction
Interaction, AA 1.13
Interactive
Interactive Courseware, D 301.118/2
Interagency
Calendar of **Interagency** Courses, GS 1.26
Cooperative Area Manpower Planning System,
Interagency Cooperative Issuances, L
1.64
Federal **Inter-Agency** River Basin Committee
Publications, I 1.81
GSA **Interagency** Training Center Newsletter, GS
1.26/3
Interagency Advisory Committee on Water Data:
Summary of Meetings, I 19.74
Interagency Advisory Group: Annual Report, CS
1.87
Interagency Auditor Training Center Bulletin, C
1.61
Interagency Committee on Women's Business
Enterprise, Annual Report to Congress,
Pr 40.8:W 84, SBA 1.23
Interagency Directory, Key Contacts for Planning,
Scientific and Technical Exchange
Programs, Educational Travel, Students,
Teachers, Lecturers, Research Scholars,
Specialists, S 1.67/3
Interagency Reports, I 19.63
Interagency Steering Committee on Radiation
Standards, Y 3.N 88:10-6
Interagency Technical Committee on Heart, Blood
Vessel, Lung, and Blood Diseases; and
Blood Resources, HE 20.3001/2:H 35
Interagency Training Catalog of Courses, PM 1.19
Interagency Training Courses, Calendar, CS 1.65/4
Interagency Training Program (various subjects)
(series), GS 1.26/2
Interagency Training Programs, CS 1.65
National Institute of Standards and Technology
Interagency Reports, NISTIR (series), C
13.58
National **Interagency** Training Curriculum, CS
1.65/6
Report of **Interagency** Substances Data Commis-
sion, EP 1.79/4
Simplifying Federal Aid to States and Communities,
Annual Report to the President of an
Interagency Program, PrEx 2.18

Studies from **Interagency** Data Linkages (series),
HE 3.62
Toward **Interagency** Coordination, Federal
Research and Development on
Adolescence, HE 23.1013
Toward **Interagency** Coordination: Federal
Research and Development on Early
Childhood, HE 23.1013/2
Yellowstone Grizzly Bear Investigations, Annual
Report of the **Interagency** Study Team, I
29.94
Inter-American
Conferences on **Inter-American** Relations, S 15.5
Cooperative **Inter-American** Plantation Rubber
Development, A 77.519
Examination of the **Inter-American** Foundation's
Financial Statements, GA 1.13/2
Grassroots Development: Journal of the **Inter-
American** Foundation, Y 3.In 8/25:15
Institute of **Inter-American** Affairs Publications, S
1.64
Inter-American Affairs Institute, Building a Better
Hemisphere Series, Point 4 in Action, S
1.64/3
Inter-American Conference for Maintenance of
Peace, 1936, S 5.38
Inter-American Conference on Agriculture,
Forestry, and Animal Industry,
Washington, Sept. 8-20, 1930, S 5.32
Inter-American Defense Board, S 5.45
Inter-American Development Commission, S 5.43
Inter-American Education Demonstration Centers,
FS 5.31
Inter-American Foundation, Y 3.In 8/25
Inter-American Series, S 1.26
Inter-American Technical Aviation Conference, S
5.40
Newsletter, Health and Sanitation Division,
Institute of **Inter-American** Affairs, S
1.51
Publications **Inter-American** Education
Demonstration Centers, FS 5.31
Inter-Arts
Initiative for Interdisciplinary Artists **Inter-Arts**,
NF 2.8/2-22
Inter-Arts, Artists' Projects: New Forms, NF 2.8/
2-26
Inter-Arts, Presenting Organizations Artist
Communities Services to the Arts,
Application Guidelines, NF 2.8/2-23
Interbank
Bank Debits to Demand Deposit Accounts (Except
Interbank and U.S. Government
Accounts), FR 1.17/2
Interbureau
Interbureau Forage Committee Publications I.F.C.,
A 1.49
Intercepted
Service and Regulatory Announcements List of
Intercepted Plant Pests, A 77.308/2
Interception
Report on Applications for Orders Authorizing or
Approving the **Interception** of Wire or
Oral Communications, Ju 10.19
Interceptor
Interceptor, D 301.70
Interchange
ETA **Interchange**, L 37.9
Information **Interchange** Service, Y 3.Ad 9/8:14
Interchange, L 1.69
President's Commission on Personnel **Inter-
change**, Pr 37.8:P 43
RRB-SSA Financial **Interchange**: Calculations for
Fiscal Year with Respect to OASI, DI,
and HI Trust Funds, RR 1.15
Interchangeability
DOD **Interchangeability** and Substitutability
(I&S), Parts I & II, D 7.36
Intercoastal
Foreign Inland Waterway News, **Intercoastal**
Waterways, Rivers, Lakes, Canals,
Equipment, C 18.208
U.S. Water Borne **Intercoastal** Traffic by Ports of
Origin and Destination and Principal
Commodities, SB 7.5/317, C 27.9/9, MC
1.9
Water Borne Commerce of United States Including
Foreign **Intercoastal** and Coastwise
Traffic and Commerce of U.S. Noncon-
tiguous Territory, SB 7.5/295
Intercom
FAA **Intercom**, TD 4.5/2
Great Lakes **Intercom**, TD 4.26/2
Headquarters **Intercom**, TD 4.5/2

Intercom: Air Force Department, D 301.101
Intercom: Forest Service, A 13.56
Interdepartment
Report of the **Interdepartment** Radio Advisory
Committee, C 60.15
Interdepartmental
Proceedings **Interdepartmental** Board on
Simplified Office Procedure, Executive
Committee Meeting, T 51.11/5
United States Government **Interdepartmental**
Standards, T 51.11/7
Interdisciplinary
Children, **Interdisciplinary** Journal for Professions
Serving Children, FS 14.109
Children, **Interdisciplinary** Journal for Professions
Serving Children, FS 14.109
Information for Innovators, and **Interdisciplinary**
Information Service, C 51.9/31
Initiative for **Interdisciplinary** Artists Inter-Arts,
NF 2.8/2-22
Quarterly Report, Government Sponsored and
Government Supported Research, Social
Sciences and **Interdisciplinary** Areas,
NS 1.9
Interest
Court Decisions of **Interest** to Labor, L 2.6/a 8
Economic Plans of **Interest** to the Americas, A
67.17
Farmers' Bulletins of **Interest** to Persons Residing
in Cities or Towns, A 21.9/2
Food Facts of **Interest** to the Trade, Pr 32.4260
Grouped **Interest** Guides, HE 20.8311/3
Home Mortgage **Interest** Rates and Terms, FHL 1.25
Home Mortgage **Interest** Rates Continue to Decline
in Early (Month), FHL 1.25/2
Interest Bearing Debt Outstanding, T 62.8
Items of **Interest**, D 201.27, D 208.3/3
Mortgage **Interest** Rates on Conventional Loans,
Largest Insured Savings and Loan
Associations, FHL 1.24
National Clearinghouse for Alcohol Information:
Grouped **Interest** Guides, HE 20.8311/3
NICHD Research Highlights and Topics of
Interest, HE 20.3364
Publications and Reports of Cryogenic **Interest**
Noted List, C 13.51
Seabee Items of **Interest**, N 21.13
Secondary Market Prices and Yields and **Interest**
Rates for Home Loans, HH 1.99/3
Selected **Interest** and Exchange Rates for Major
Countries and the U.S., FR 1.32/3
Selected **Interest** Rates and Bond Prices, FR 1.32/6,
FR 1.32/7
Selected List of Articles in Current Periodicals of
Interest to Ordnance Department, W
34.21/2
Semiannual **Interest** Rate Bulletins, T 66.3/2
Interested
Exact Location of All Ships in which Shipping
Board is **Interested**, SB 2.10
Interferences
Papers in Re in Patent Office (**Interferences**), J 1.81
Intergovernmental
Intergovernmental Personnel Notes, CS 1.86, PM
1.27
Intergovernmental Perspective, Y 3.Ad 9/8:11
Intergovernmental Solutions Newsletter, GS 1.38
Interim
Interim Decisions, J 1.102/5
Interim Decisions of the Department of Justice, J
21.11/2
Interim Directives, Pr 34.706/2, PrEx 4.612
Interim Federal Specifications, GS 2.8/5
Interim Guide for Environment Assessment, HH
1.6/3:En 8
Interim Issues, VA 1.39
Interim List of Persons or Firms Currently
Debarred for Violation of Various Public
Contracts Acts Incorporating Labor
Standards Provisions, GA 1.17/2
Interim Lists of Periodicals in Collection of
Atmospheric Sciences Library and
Marine and Earth Sciences Library, C
55.224
Interim Report of the Activities, Y 4.G 74/7-12
Interim Reports, D 103.53/5
Progress Report, **Interim** Statistical Report, Pr
34.751
Quarterly **Interim** Financial Report, Certificated
Route Air Carriers and Supplemental Air
Carriers, C 31.240/3, CAB 1.14
Quarterly Listing of **Interim** Issuances, D 7.6/
7:5025.1:pt. 2

Public Use Data Tape Documentation **Interviewer's** Manual National Interview Survey, HE 20.6226/8

Interviewing
Interviewing Aid, L 7.52
Interviewing Guides for Specific Disabilities, L 1.7/7, L 37.8/4

Interviews
Interviews, S 1.25/5
Interviews with the Past, I 16.61

Intestinal
Intestinal Parasite Surveillance, HE 20.7011/28

Intolerance
Hate Crime: The Violence of **Intolerance**, CRS Bulletin, J 23.3
Series on Religion Nationalism and **Intolerance**, Y 3.P 31:18

Intra-Alaska
Certificated Air Carrier Financial Data; Territorial **Intra-Alaska** and Other Alaska {quarterly comparisons}, C 31.243
Certificated Air Carrier Financial Data; Territorial **Intra-Alaska** and Other Than Alaska {12-month comparisons}, C 31.243/2

Intramural
Annual Report of **Intramural** Activities, HE 20.3267
Annual Report, Mental Health **Intramural** Research Program, HE 20.8136
Division of **Intramural** Research Programs, Annual Report, HE 20.8136
Intramural Annual Report, National Institute of Aging, HE 20.3866
Intramural Research, Annual Report: National Institute of Allergy and Infectious Diseases, HE 20.3211/3
Intramural Research, Annual Report: National Institute of Neurological and Communicative Disorders and Stroke, HE 20.3516/4
Intramural Research Highlights, National Medical Expenditure Survey, HE 20.6517/4
National Institute of Child Health and Human Development **Intramural** Research Program: Annual Report of the Scientific Director, HE 20.3365
National Institute of Dental Research Programs, Grants, Awards, Contracts, and **Intramural** Projects, HE 20.3402:D 43/5

In-transit
Schedule L. Statistical Classification of Foreign Merchandise Reports in **In-transit** Trade of United States, C 3.150:L
Shipping Weight and Dollar Value of Merchandise Laden on and Unladen from Vessels at United States Ports During the **In-transit** Movement of the Merchandise from One Foreign Country to Another, C 3.164:981
Statistical Classification of Foreign Merchandise Reports in **In-Transit** Trade of United States, C 3.150:L

Introduction
Catalog of Seed and Vegetable Stock Available from the Southern Regional Plant **Introduction** Station for various plants, A 106.19
Seed and Plant **Introduction** and Distribution, A 19.6

Introductions
New Plant **Introductions** (annual lists), A 19.15

Introductory
New Item **Introductory** Schedule, GS 2.22

Invasion
Invasion Intervention, "Intervasion": A Concise History of the U.S. Army in Operation Uphold Democracy, D 110.13

Inventions
Bulletin of **Inventions**, C 41.82
Catalog of Government **Inventions** Available for Licensing, C 51.16/2
Government **Inventions** for Licensing, C 51.9/23
Inventions Available for Licensing, A 77.35
Significant NASA **Inventions** Available for Licensing in Foreign Countries, NAS 1.21:7038
Status Report of the Energy-Related **Inventions** Program, C 13.72

Inventories
Annual Survey of Manufacturers, Value of Manufacturers' **Inventories**, C 3.24/9-11

Census of Manufactures; Manufacturers' **Inventories**, C 56.244/8
Coffee **Inventories** and Roastings, C 3.169
Current Business Reports; Green Coffee, **Inventories**, Imports, Roastings, BG (series), C 56.219/2
Current Business Reports; Monthly Wholesale Trade, Sales and **Inventories**, BW (series), C 56.219
Environmental **Inventories**, C 55.232
Green Coffee **Inventories** and Roastings, C 3.236
Industry Survey, Manufacturers' Sales, **Inventories**, New and Unfilled Orders, C 43.9
Industry Survey: Manufacturers' **Inventories**, Shipments, Incoming Business {and} Unfilled Orders, C 18.224
Inventories, A 6.6
Inventories and Analysis of Federal Population Research, HE 20.3362/2
Inventories of Steel Producing Mills, C 3.158:M 33 J
Manufacturers' Shipments, **Inventories** and Orders, C 56.245, C 3.231
Monthly Wholesale Trade Report: Sales and **Inventories**, C 3.133
Petroleum Products, Secondary **Inventories** and Storage Capacity, C 3.213
Preliminary **Inventories**, GS 4.10
Revised Monthly Retail Sales in **Inventories**, C 3.138/3-3
Soil and Water Conservation District Resources **Inventories** (series), A 57.38/2
Wetlands **Inventories**, I 49.64

Inventors
Patent Attorneys and Agents Available to Represent **Inventors** Before the United States Patent Office, C 21.9/2

Inventory
Acquisitions and Disposal of CCC Price-Support **Inventory**, A 82.78
Air Chief (Clearinghouse for **Inventory** and Emission Factors), EP 1.109
Annual **Inventory** of Available USDA Popular Publications for Use of State and County Extension Offices in Ordering USDA Publications, A 43.34
Annual **Inventory** of Available USDA Publications for State and County Extension Offices in Ordering USDA Publications, A 106.16/2
Automatic Data Processing Equipment **Inventory** in the United States Government As of the End of the Fiscal Year, GS 12.10
Cattle **Inventory**, A 105.23
Cattle **Inventory**, Special Report on Number of Cattle and Calves on Farms by Sex and Weight, United States, A 92.18/6-2
Cattle, Sheep and Goat **Inventory**, A 93.18/8
Coast Ecological **Inventory**, I 49.6/5
Commercial Activities **Inventory** Report and Five Year Review Schedule, D 1.64
Department Store **Inventory** Price Indexes, L 2.79
Desalting Plants **Inventory** Reports, I 1.87/4
EMRIA {Energy Mineral Rehabilitation **Inventory** and Analysis} Reports, I 1.104
Federal Program in Population Research, **Inventory** of Population Research Supported by Federal Agencies During Fiscal Year (date), HE 20.3362/2
Federal Real Property and Personal Property **Inventory** Report of the United States Government Covering its Properties Located in the U.S., in the Territories, and Overseas, as of June 30 (year), Y 4.G 74/7:P 94
Fish **Inventory** Data, Y 3.T 25:40
Florida Coastal Ecological **Inventory** Characterization, I 49.6/6
General Real and Personal Property **Inventory** Report (Civilian and Military) of the U.S. Located in the United States, in the Territories, and Overseas, As of June 30 {year}, Y 4.G 74/7:P 94
General Summary of **Inventory** Status and Movement of Capital and Producers Goods, Plants, Aircraft, and Industry Agent Items, Pr 33.210
Health Data **Inventory**, HE 1.59
Inventory and Analysis of NIH Maternal and Child Health Research, HE 20.3363
Inventory Municipal Waste Facilities, EP 2.17

Inventory of Agricultural Research, A 94.14
Inventory of American Intermodal Equipment, C 39.237, TD 11.31
Inventory of Automated Data Processing Equipment in the United States Government for Fiscal Year (date), GS 12.10
Inventory of Automatic Data Processing (ADP) Equipment in Federal Government, PrEx 2.12
Inventory of Automatic Data Processing Equipment in the United States Government, GS 2.15
Inventory of Federal Tourism Programs, Federal Agencies Commissions, Programs Reviewed for Their Participation in the Development of Recreation, Travel, and Tourism in the United States, C 47.2:T 64/3
Inventory of Knowledge Series, LC 1.41
Inventory of Nonpurchased Foreign Currencies, T 1.50
Inventory of Nonutility Electric Power Plants in the United States, E 3.29/2
Inventory of Physical Facilities in Institutions of Higher Education, HE 5.92/3, HE 19.310
Inventory of Population Research Supported by Federal Agencies, HE 20.3362/2
Inventory of Soil, Water, and Related Resources, A 57.22
Inventory of U.S. Greenhouse Gas Emissions and Sinks, EP 1.115
National Archives **Inventory** Series, GS 4.10/2
National Housing **Inventory**, C 3.221
National Water Quality **Inventory**, Report to Congress, EP 2.17/2
National Wetlands **Inventory**, I 49.6/7
Plant **Inventory**, A 77.515, A 106.11
Population Sciences, **Inventory** of Private Agency Population Research, HE 20.3362/2-2
Program Results **Inventory**, J 1.51
Project Skywater Data **Inventory** SCPP Season, I 27.57/2
Project Skywater, CRADP DAT **Inventory**, I 27.57/3
Real Estate Asset **Inventory**, Y 3.R 31/2:15
Real Property **Inventory**, C 18.42
Research Relating to Children, **Inventory** of Studies in Progress, FS 3.220
Resource **Inventory** Notes, I 53.24
Scientific **Inventory** Management Series, GS 2.6/4
Semiannual Report on Strategic Special Nuclear Material **Inventory** Differences, E 1.15/2
Toxic Chemical Release **Inventory**, EP 5.22
Toxics-Release **Inventory**: A National Prospective, EP 5.18/2
Toxics-Release **Inventory**: Executive Summary, EP 5.18/2-2
Truck **Inventory** and Use Survey (TIUS), C 3.233/6
U.S. Census of Housing Components of **Inventory** Change, Final Report HC (4) series, C 3.224/6
Vessel **Inventory** Report, C 39.221, TD 11.11
Vessel **Inventory** Report, United States Flag Dry Cargo and Tanker Fleets, 1,000 Gross Tons and Over, C 39.217

Investigated
Railroad Employee Fatalities **Investigated** by the Federal Railroad Administration in (year), TD 3.110/5
Summary of Accidents **Investigated** by the Federal Railroad Administration in Fiscal Year, TD 3.110/2, TD 3.111

Investigation
Annual Report to Secretary of Transportation on Accident **Investigation** and Reporting Activities of Federal Highway Administration, TD 2.16
Annual Report to the Secretary of Transportation on the Accident **Investigation** and Reporting Activities of the Federal Highway Administration in (year), TD 2.16
Annual Report to the Secretary on Accident **Investigation** and Reporting Activities, TD 8.17
Cancer Clinical **Investigation** Review Committee, HE 20.3001/2:C 16
Forestry **Investigation** Notes, Y 3.T 25:34
GITI {General **Investigation** of Tidal Inlets} Reports, D 103.42/7
Hydrologic **Investigation** Atlases (maps), I 19.89

Motor Carrier Accident **Investigation** Reports, TD 2.309

Motor Carrier **Investigation** Reports, IC 1 mot.18

Oil and Gas **Investigation** Charts, I 19.25/5, I 19.92

Posters Federal Bureau of **Investigation**, J 1.14/21

Railroad Accident **Investigation** Reports, TD 3.10, TD 3.110

Railroad Accident **Investigation** Reports: Compilations, TD 3.110/4

Railroad Employee Accident **Investigation** Reports, TD 3.110/3

Safety **Investigation** Regulations, SIR (series), C 31.206/4

Soil Survey **Investigation** Reports, A 57.52

Special **Investigation** Reports, TD 1.112/2

Summary of Accident **Investigation** Reports, IC 1 accu.7

Tri-level Accident **Investigation** Summaries, TD 8.19

Investigational

Investigational Reports, C 6.12, I 45.19

NCI **Investigational** Drugs, Chemical Information, HE 20.3180/2

NCI **Investigational** Drugs, Pharmaceutical Data, HE 20.3180

Investigations

Accidents Involving Civil Aircraft; Reports of **Investigations** of, C 31.213

Air Force Office of Special **Investigations**, AFOSIP (series), D 301.88

Analysis and Summary of Accident **Investigations**, TD 2.312/3

Annual Summary of **Investigations** in Support of Civil Works Program for Calendar Year, D 103.24/8

CDC Technology Branch, Summary of **Investigations**, FS 2.60/5

Coal **Investigations** Maps, I 19.25/3, I 19.85

Columbia Basin Joint **Investigations** {Reports on Problems}, I 27.23

Cooperative **Investigations** Reports (series), I 19.83

Financial Reports, a Newsletter from the Financial **Investigations** Division, T 1.61

Fish Monitoring **Investigations**, Browns Ferry Nuclear Plant, Wheeler Reservoir, Alabama, Y 3.T 25:37

Fish Monitoring **Investigations**: Sequoyah Nuclear Plant, Chickamauga Reservoir, Tennessee, Y 3.T 25:37-3

Geophysical **Investigations** Maps, I 19.25/2, I 19.87

Grain **Investigations** {publications}, A 36.93

Horticulrural **Investigations**, A 19.7

Investigations and News, Y 3.C 42/2:16

Investigations (series), ITC 1.12

Investigations in Fish Control, I 49.70

Mineral **Investigations** Resource Maps, I 19.90

Mineral **Investigations** Series, I 28.13

Mineral **Investigations**, Field Studies Maps, I 19.39

Miscellaneous Geologic **Investigations** Maps, I 19.91

Missouri River Basin **Investigations** Project Reports, I 20.52

Multidisciplinary Accident **Investigations**, TD 8.11, TD 8.11/2

Oil and Gas **Investigations** Maps, I 19.25/4, I 19.93

Papers in Re {proceedings of inquiry, general investigations, etc.}, IC 1.13/2

Plan of Work for Cooperative Hydrology **Investigations**, I 53.47

Publications Patents of Division of Insecticide **Investigations**, List of, A 77.318

Report of **Investigations**, HE 20.7131

Reports and Statistical Tables on Fur-Seal **Investigations** in Alaska, T 35.7

Reports of **Investigations** of Accidents Involving Civil Aircraft, C 31.213

Reports of **Investigations**, I 28.23

Reports on **Investigations** and Inquiries, TC 1.39

Reports on **Investigations** of Individual Accidents, IC 1 acci.5

Rules of Practice and Rules Relating to **Investigations** and Code of Behavior Governing Exparte Communications Between Persons Outside the Commission and Decisional Employees, SE 1.6:R 86/4

Rules Pertaining to Aircraft Accidents, Incidents, Overdue Aircraft, and Safety **Investigations**, TD 1.106/2

Subcommittee on Oversight and **Investigations** of the Committee on Energy and Commerce, Y 4.En 2/3-12

Surveillance and Analysis Division, Region 8: Technical **Investigations** Branch, SA/TIB-(series), EP 1.51/4

Technicap Training Courses, Technical Techniques of Water-Resources **Investigations**, I 19.15/4, I 19.15/5

Water Resources **Investigations** (numbered), I 19.42/4

Water Resources **Investigations** Folders, I 19.94

Water Resources **Investigations**, I 19.42/4-2

Waterfowl Monitoring **Investigations**, Y 3.T 25:27-2

Weekly Station Reports of Office of Dry Land Agriculture **Investigations**, A 19.24

Yellowstone Grizzly Bear **Investigations**, Annual Report of the Interagency Study Team, I 29.94

Investigative

DIS (Defense **Investigative** Service) Achievements, D 1.1/8

Investigative Hearings

Committee Rules and Rules for **Investigative** **Hearings** Conducted by Subcommittees of the Committee on Armed Services, Y 4.Ar 5/2-15

Investigator

Extramural Grant and Contract Awards by Principal **Investigator**/Contractor, HE 20.3176/3

NCI Grants Awarded, by Principal **Investigator**, HE 20.3176/2

Investigator's

Environmental Assessment of the Alaskan Continental Shelf, Principal **Investigator's** Reports, C 55.622

Outer Continental Shelf Environmental Assessment Program Final Reports of Principal **Investigators**, C 55.433

Investment

Annual Report and Strategic **Investment** Plan, D 1.97/2

Catalog of **Investment** Information and Opportunities, IP, Supplements, S 18.35/2

Catalog of **Investment** Opportunities Index, Supplements, S 18.35/3

Classification of **Investment** in Road Equipment, IC 1 ste.16

Commission on International Trade and **Investment** Policy, Pr 37.8:In 8/2

Cumulative Report of All Specific Risk **Investment** Guaranties Issued Since the Beginning of the Program through, S 18.26/3

Foreign Direct **Investment** in the United States, C 61.25/2

Foreign Direct **Investment** in the United States, Establishment Data For Manufacturing, C 59.20/3

General Rules and Regulations Under the **Investment** Company Act of 1940, as in Effect (date), SE 1.6:R 86/9

Index to Catalog of **Investment** Information and Opportunities, S 18.35

Investment Opportunities Abroad, Bulletins, C 42.3/2

Investment Opportunity Information, C 42.25

Investment, Operating and Other Budget Expenditures, Special Analysis D, PrEx 2.8/a8

Investment Properties, Y 3.F 31/8:30

Market Prices and **Investment** Values of Outstanding Bonds and Notes, T 50.5

Monthly Report on Foreign Direct **Investment** Activity in the United States, C 61.25/3

NCUA **Investment** Report, NCU 1.22

OPEC Direct **Investment** in the United States, C 61.25

Profiles of Foreign Direct **Investment** in U.S. Energy, E 3.52

Quarterly Report of All **Investment** Guaranties Issued, S 18.26

Releases, **Investment** Company Act of 1940, SE 1.25/3

Return on **Investment** Case Study, D 103.53/8

Small Business Administration and **Investment** Act, with Amendments {1953}, Y 1.2:Sm 1

Small Business Administration and **Investment** Act, Y 1.3:Sm 1

Small Business **Investment** Companies Licensed by Small Business Administration, SBA 1.23

Small Business **Investment** Companies Licensed by the Small Business Administration As of (date), SBA 1.2:In 8

Summary of Prescribed Unit Costs and Hourly Rate for Return on **Investment** and Tax Allowance, C 31.272, CAB 1.10

Survey of Pension Fund **Investment** in Mortgage Instruments, HH 1.99/4

Table of **Investment** Yields for United States Savings Bonds of Series E. Official Use, T 66.23

U.S. Direct **Investment** Abroad, Operations of U.S. Parent Companies and Their Foreign Affiliates, Preliminary Estimates, C 59.20/2

Investments

Nonfarm Mortgage **Investments** of Life Insurance Companies, FHL 1.18

Investor-Owned

Financial Statistics of Major **Investor-Owned** Electric Utilities, E 3.18/4-2

Financial Statistics of Selected **Investor-Owned** Electric Utilities, E 3.18/4-2

Invitation

Sealed Bid/**Invitation** for Bids, D 7.34

Invitations

Food Purchase Reports & **Invitations** to Bid, A 88.67

Invoice

Price Information for Drug Products, **Invoice** Level Prices, HE 22.113, HE 22.309

Invoices

Depository **Invoices**, GP 3.16

Facts for Business, Yellow Pages **Invoices** Scams, FT 1.32/2

Involved

Fully **Involved**, FEM 1.111

Fully **Involved** {special issues}, FEM 1.111/2

Getting **Involved** (various subjects) (series), HE 23.1112

Inyokern

U.S. Naval Ordnance Test Station, **Inyokern**, Technical Memorandums, D 215.11

Iodine

Iodine in (year), I 28.129

Ionospheric

Central Radio Propagation Laboratory **Iono-spheric** Predictions, C 13.31/3

Ionospheric Data, C 55.218

Iowa

Cattle on Feed, Illinois, **Iowa**, Nebraska, Idaho, and California, A 88.16/7

Water Resources Development in **Iowa**, D 103.35/15

IP

Intern Program, **IP** (series), PM 1.36

IPA

Current **IPA** Projects for Improved State and Local Management, CS 1.94

Report of **IPA** Grant Activity, GS 1.94

IPA's

Case Studies of **IPA's** in various cities, HE 20.24

IPEDS

IPEDS Integrated Postsecondary Education Data System, Institutional Characteristics, ED 1.23/6

IR

IR (series), C 41.26/2

IRAC

TELE-**IRAC** (series), C 1.60/6

Iranian

Directory of **Iranian** Officials, PrEx 3.10/7-22

IRC

IRC Bulletin, EP 2.3/3

IRG

IRG Bulletin, HE 20.8103/2

IRIG

IRIG Documents, D 105.23

IRIS

IRIS, Earth Orientation Bulletin, C 55.437

IRM

Federal **IRM** Directory, GS 12.19

IRM Forum, GS 12.17/2

USIA Strategic Information Resources Management **IRM** Plan, IA 1.33

IRMS

IRMS Directory of Assistance, GS 12.12/3

Iron

Bolts Nuts and Large Screws of **Iron** or Steel, ITC 1.17 ITC 1.17/2

Industry Report, International **Iron** and Steel, C 41.36

Industry Wage Survey: **Iron** and Steel Foundries, L 2.3/32

Iron and Steel Slag, I 28.53/5
Iron Ore, I 28.66
Iron Ore in (year), I 28.66/2
Iron Ore Monthly Reports, I 28.66
Iron Oxide Pigments in (year), I 28.163
Malleable **Iron** Castings, C 3.89
Mineral Industry Surveys, **Iron** and Steel Scrap, I 19.141
Mineral Industry Surveys, **Iron** Ore, I 19.142
Slag-**Iron** and Steel in (year), I 28.53/5

Irradiation
  Alloy Development for **Irradiation** Performance, E 1.64

Irrigation
  Bulletins, **Irrigation** (by States), C 3.14/8, C 3.28/12
  Decisions on Tort and **Irrigation** Claims, I 1.69/8
  Hints to Settlers (on **Irrigation** projects), A 19.9
  Irrigation Energy Efficiency (series), E 5.13
  Irrigation Guides {for areas}, A 57.6/3
  Irrigation of Agricultural Lands (by States), C 3.940-9
  Irrigation Operational and Maintenance Bulletin, I 27.41
  Irrigation Photographs, I 27.24
  Irrigation, Agricultural Lands, C 3.37/24
  Public Notices {concerning **irrigation** projects}, I 27.40, I 1.49
  Report of Quality of Surface Waters for **Irrigation**, Western United States, I 19.13
  Weekly Reports of Office of Western **Irrigation** Agriculture, A 19.25

IRS
  IRS Clip-sheet, T 22.49
  IRS Historical Studies, T 22.66
  IRS International Telephone Directory, T 22.48
  IRS News, T 22.55/2
  IRS Phone Book, National Office, T 22.48
  IRS Service, T 22.55/2-2
  Tax Information, **IRS** Publications (numbered), T 22.44/2
  Update, **IRS** International, T 22.2/15:7177

IS
  IS (series), I 53.26
  VA Fact Sheets, **IS**- (series), VA 1.34
  VA-DMA-**IS** (series), VA 1.53

ISC
  ISC Fact Sheets, S 17.24
  VR-**ISC** (series), FS 13.204

Island
  Island Lantern, J 16.20
  Island of Palmas Arbitration, S 3.18/6
  Rubber Laboratory, Mare **Island** Naval Shipyard, Vallejo, California, Reports, D 211.16

Islands
  High Commissioner of Trust Territory of Pacific **Islands**, I 35.16
  Pacific Coast and Pacific **Islands**, TD 5.9:3
  Quarterly Summary of Commerce of Philippine **Islands**, W 6.8

ISO
  Army Institute for Professional Development: Subcourse **ISO** (series), D 101.103

ISOO
  ISOO (Information Security Oversight Office) Annual Report, AE 1.101/3

Isotope
  Isotope Developments, Y 3.At 7:27

Isotopes
  Catalog and Price List of Stable **Isotopes** Including Related Materials and Services, Y 3.At 7:35
  Isotopes and Radiation Technology, Y 3.At 7:52
  Isotopes Branch Circulars, Y 3.At 7:12

ISP
  Series **ISP**, CENTS {Census Tabulation System}, C 56.226

Israel
  Accession List: **Israel**, LC 1.30/4
  Israel, LC 1.30/4

Issuance
  Crop Reporting Board, (year) **Issuance** Dates and Contents, A 92.35:C 88

Issuances
  Compilation of Meat and Poultry Inspection **Issuances**, A 110.9
  Cooperative Area Manpower Planning System, Interagency Cooperative **Issuances**, L 1.64
  Energy Information Administration **Issuances**, E 3.27/2
  Index to Management **Issuances**, NAS 1.18/2

Meat and Poultry Inspection Manual and Compilation of Meat and Poultry Inspection **Issuances**, A 101.8:M 46/2
Meat and Poultry Inspection Program, Program **Issuances**, A 88.17/8
Privacy Act **Issuances** Compilation, AE 2.106/4
Privacy Act **Issuances**, GS 4.107/a:P 939/2
Quarterly Listing of Interim **Issuances**, D 7.6/7:5025.1:pt. 2
Unclassified DOD **Issuances** on CD-ROM, D 1.95/3

Issue
  Current **Issue** Outline (series), C 55.235
  DNFSB Staff **Issue** Reports, Y 3.D 36/3:12
  Global **Issues**, IA 1.39
  Ground Water **Issue**, EP 1.43/2
  IMA Update **Issues**, D 301.127
  Index to H.O. Charts on **Issue**, N 6.5/9
  Issue Alert (series), SBA 1.41
  Issue Brief (series), A 107.16
  Issue Briefing Papers (series), A 107.16
  Issue Bulletin, A 1.141
  Military Standard Requisitioning and **Issue** Procedure, D 7.6/4:M 59
  Special **Issue**, Consular Reports, S 4.13

Issued
  Cumulative Report of All Specific Risk Investment Guaranties **Issued** Since the Beginning of the Program through, S 18.26/3
  Fee Licenses **Issued** for the Month, I 64.12
  Publications **Issued** Since 1897, LC 1.12
  Publications **Issued**, A 77.16/2
  Quarterly Report of All Investment Guaranties **Issued**, S 18.26
  United States Savings Bonds **Issued** and Redeemed Through (date), T 63.7

Issues
  Air Force **Issues** Book, D 301.1/3
  Concepts and **Issues**, D 214.27
  Health Care Financing: **Issues** (series), HE 22.19/8
  Immigration **Issues** (series), J 21.22
  Interim **Issues**, VA 1.39
  Issues in International Crime, J 28.23/2
  Issues in Labor Statistics, L 2.132
  Issues of Democracy, S 20.21
  Issues of Democracy, IA 1.36, S 20.21
  Mineral **Issues**, I 28.156/2
  Mineral **Issues**, an Analytical Series, I 28.156
  Research **Issues**, HE 20.8214
  Seminar on Industrial **Issues** (various topics), C 62.18
  State Legislative Summary, Children and Youth **Issues**, HE 24.16
  Tuberculosis Control **Issues**, FS 2.7/a 2
  Unresolved Safety **Issues** Summary, Aqua Book, Y 3.N 88:30
  WI Communique, **Issues** of the Special Supplemental Food Program for Women, Infants, and Children, A 98.14

Isthmian
  Manual of Information: **Isthmian** Canal Commission, W 73.11
  Proceedings Medical Association of **Isthmian** Canal Zone, W 79.12/6

Item
  Federal **Item** Identification Guides for Supply Cataloging, Description Patterns, D 7.6/2:6-2
  Federal **Item** Identification Guides for Supply Cataloging, Indexes, Supplements, D 7.6/2:6-1, D 7.8:1
  Federal **Item** Identification Guides for Supply Cataloging, Reference Drawings, D 7.6/2:6-3
  Federal **Item** Identifications Guides for Supply Cataloging, Part 2, Description Patterns, D 7.6/2:6-2
  Federal **Item** Logistics Data Records, D 7.26
  Federal **Item** Name Directory for Supply Cataloging, Handbook, D 7.6/2
  GPO Depository Union List of **Item** Selections, GP 3.32/2
  H 6-2 Federal **Item** Identifications Guides for Supply Cataloging, Part 2, Description Patterns, D 7.6/2:6-2
  Hazardous **Item** Listing, D 7.32
  Hazardous Materials Information System, Hazardous **Item** Listing, D 7.6/17
  New **Item** Introductory Schedule, GS 2.22
  State Exchange Service **Item** Series, FS 13.213
  Tariff **Item**, C 18.205

Items
  Consumer Price Index, Price Indexes for Selected **Items** and Groups, L 2.38/4

Federal Stock Number Reference Catalog, Numerical Listing of **Items** Available from General Services Administration, GS 2.10/5
FSLIC Insured Savings and Loan Associations, Savings and Mortgage Activity, Selected Balance Sheet **Items**, FHL 1.20/2
General Summary of Inventory Status and Movement of Capital and Producers Goods, Plants, Aircraft, and Industry Agent **Items**, Pr 33.210
Items of Interest, D 201.27, D 208.3/3
Morale **Items**, W 2.11
Savings and Mortgage Lending Activity, Selected Balance Sheet **Items**, F.S.L.I.C. Insured Savings and Loan Associations, FHL 1.20/2
Seabee **Items** of Interest, N 21.13
Selected Income and Balance-Sheet **Items** of Class I Railroads in the United States, IC 1 ste.34
Social Security Information **Items**, HE 3.82
Southern Region Miscellaneous Series, **Items**, A 55.45/6
Tentative Agenda **Items**, NC 2.12
Weekly Averages of Member Bank Reserves, Reserve Bank Credit and Related **Items** and Statement of Condition of the Federal Reserve Bank, FR 1.15

Itinerary
  Program and **Itinerary**, S 18.13

ITS
  ITS News, Y 3.N 88:51
  ITS Update, TD 1.60

IWR
  IWR Contract Reports, D 103.57
  IWR Proceedings (series), D 103.57/10
  IWR User's Manual, D 103.57/11

J

Jackson
  Jackson, C 55.287/20-4

JACS
  JACS {Journal Article Copy Service} Directory, C 51.11/6

JAG
  Air Force **JAG** Law Review, D 302.9
  JAG Journal, D 205.7

Jag
  United States Air Force **Jag** Law Review, D 302.9

Jail
  Drugs and **Jail** Inmates, J 29.13/3
  Jail Inmates, J 29.11/5
  Prison and **Jail** Inmates at Midyear, J 29.11/5-2
  Profile of **Jail** Inmates, J 29.13/2

Jails
  Census of Local **Jails**, J 29.21
  Jails in Indian Country, J 29.11/5-3

JANP
  JANP (series), D 5.8

January
  Typical Electric Bills, Typical Net Monthly Bills of **January** (year), for Residential Commercial and Industrial Services, FP 1.10

Japan
  Film Resources on **Japan**, HE 5.2:J 27
  Japan Productivity Center, United States Operations Mission to **Japan**, Publications, S 17.44/2
  Japan Report, PrEx 7.16
  Japan Report, Science and Technology, PrEx 7.16/6
  Japan Road Maps, Series L302, D 5.340
  Monthly Trade Report, **Japan**, C 18.155
  Report of **Japan**'s Export Shipments and Import Receipts Stated by Areas and Countries of Destination and Origin, with Value Expressed in United States Dollars, D 102.11/3
  Science and Technology in **Japan**, Reports, M 105.24, D 102.15
  Summation of Non-Military Activities in **Japan**, W 1.75, M 105.11
  Weekly Report on **Japan**, D 102.13

Japanese
  Civilian Personnel Liberated from **Japanese** Custody, W 107.12
  Directory of **Japanese** Technical Reports, C 51.19/3
  Japanese Economic Statistics Bulletin, D 102.14

Journal of Applied Chemistry {abstracts}, C 41.53/11

Journal of Executive Proceedings of Senate, Y 1.3/4

Journal of Experimental and Theoretical Physics {abstracts}, C 41.52/2

Journal of General Chemistry {abstracts}, C 41.53

Journal of Highway Research, Public Roads, C 37.8

Journal of Human Services Abstracts, HE 1.50

Journal of Inorganic Chemistry, C 41.53/4

Journal of Legal Studies, D 305.21/2

Journal of Mycology, A 28.5

Journal of Navy Civilian Manpower Management, D 204.9

Journal of Physical Chemistry {abstracts}, C 41.34/5

Journal of Public Inquiry, PR 42.8/4

Journal of Rehabilitation, Research and Development, VA 1.23/3

Journal of Research of the U.S. Geological Survey, I 19.61

Journal of Research, Bound Volumes, C 13.22/2

Journal of Scientific and Applied Photography and Cinematography {abstracts}, C 41.69

Journal of Technical Physics {abstracts}, C 42.52/6

Journal of the Federal Home Loan Bank Board, FHL 1.27

Journal of the House of Representatives, XJH

Journal of the National Cancer Institute, HE 20.3161

Journal of the Senate, XJS

Journal of Transportation and Statistics, TD 12.18

Journal of United States Artillery, W 29.5

MARATech R and D Technology Transfer **Journal**, C 39.227/2, TD 11.26

Medical Technicians Bulletin, Supplement to U.S. Armed Forces Medical **Journal**, D 1.11/2

National Institute of Justice **Journal**, J 28.14/2-2

NavSea **Journal**, D 211.24

Navy Lifeline, Naval Safety **Journal**, D 207.15

NCO **Journal**, D 101.127

Official **Journal** of the Plant Variety Protection Office, A 88.52

OHA Law **Journal**, HE 3.66/3

Parameters, **Journal** of the U.S. Army War College, D 101.72

Peace Corps Program and Training **Journal** Manual Series, AA 4.8/2

Peace Corps Programs and Training **Journal**, AA 4.10/2

Pesticides Monitoring **Journal**, Pr 37.8:En 8/P 43, PrEx 14.9, Y 3.F 31/21-9

Philippine **Journal** of Agriculture, W 49.55/5

Philippine **Journal** of Science, W 49.31/5

Program and Training **Journal** Manual Series, AA 4.8/2

Program and Training **Journal** Reprint Series, AA 4.10

Prologue, **Journal** of the National Archives, GS 4.23

Public Roads, **Journal** of Highway Research, TD 2.19

Quarterly **Journal** of Current Acquisitions, LC 2.17

Quarterly **Journal** of Library of Congress, LC 1.17

Quarterly **Journal**, Comptroller of the Currency, T 12.18

Recognitition **Journal**, W 1.69

Recruiter **Journal**, D 118.9, D 101.106/3

Recruiting and Career Counseling **Journal**, D 118.9

Recruiting **Journal**, D 102.76

Regulatory and Technical Reports (Abstract Index **Journal**), Y 3.N 88:21-3

Research Papers, Separates from the **Journal** of Research, C 13.22

Smithsonian **Journal** of History, SI 1.23

Soldier Support **Journal**, D 101.12/2

Soviet Union, Foreign Military History **Journal**, PrEx 7.21/4-3

Staff, the Congressional Staff **Journal**, Y 4.R 86/2:3

To Farm **Journal** Editors, A 55.22

U.S. Army Recruiting and Reenlisting **Journal**, D 118.9

Ukranian Mathematics **Journal** {abstracts}, C 41.61/7

United States Air Force Academy **Journal** of Professional Military Ethics, D 305.21

United States Armed Forces Medical **Journal**, D 1.11

Volpe Transportation **Journal**, TD 8.27/2

War Trade Board **Journal**, S 13.5

Journals

Energy Library, **Journals** Available, E 1.13/2

Feature Sections of **Journals** in NWC Library, D 1.26

Index/**Journals** of the Continental Congress, GS 4.2:C 76/2

Journals Available in the ERDA Library, ER 1.19

Journals of Continental Congress, Miscellaneous, LC 4.6

Journals of the Continental Congress, LC 4.5

Journals of the Continental Congress, Index, GS 4.2:C 76/2

List of **Journals** Indexed in AGRICOLA, A 17.18/5

JPL

JPL Facts (various topics), NAS 1.12/9

JPL SP

JPL-SP (series), NAS 1.12/6

JPRS

JPRS (DC) L (series), Y 3.J 66:10

JPRS (NY) L (series), Y 3.J 66:11

JPRS (NY) Reports, Y 3.J 66:8

JPRS (series), Y 3.J 66:13

JPRS (series) Science & Technology, China: Energy, PrEx 7.15/6-2

JPRS (series) Soviet Union, the Working Class & the Contemporary World, PrEx 7.21/9-2

JPRS (series) USSR Reports, Machine Tools and Metal Working Equipment, PrEx 7.21/3-3

JPRS R (series), Y 3.J 66:12

JPRS Report: East Asia, Korea, PrEx 7.16/2-2

JPRS Report: Science and Technology, Europe, PrEx 7.17/6

JPRS Report: Science and Technology, USSR, Life Sciences, PrEx 7.21/14-2

JPRS Report: Soviet Union, World Economy and International Relations, PrEx 7.21/15

JPRS {Joint Publications Research Service}, PrEx 7.13

JPRS/DC

JPRS/DC Reports, Y 3.J 66:9

JS&HQ

JS&HQ, L 35.9/3

Judge

Administrative Law **Judge** and Commission Decisions, Y 3.Oc 1:10-2

Administrative Law **Judge** Decisions, Y 3.F 31/21-3:9-3

Bulletin of **Judge** Advocate General of Army, D 108.3

Civil Law Opinions of the **Judge** Advocate General, Air Force, D 302.12

Consolidated Index of Opinions and Digests of Opinions of **Judge** Advocate General, W 10.10

Courts-Martial Reports, Holdings and Decisions of **Judge** Advocates General, Boards of Review, and United States Court of Military Appeals, D 1.29

Judge Advocate General's Department, W 3.65

Judge Advocate Legal Service, D 101.22:27

Special Text of **Judge** Advocate General's School, D 108.9

Memorandum Opinions of **Judge** Advocate General of the Army, D 108.8

Opinions of **Judge** Advocate General, Army, W 10.9

Judge-Advocate-General

Digest of Opinions, **Judge-Advocate-General** of Armed Forces, D 1.18, D 1.18/2

Digest of Opinions of **Judge-Advocate-General**, Army, W 10.8

Judgement

Notices of Insecticide Act **Judgement**, A 1.18

Notices of **Judgement** Summarizing Judicial Review of Orders under Sec. 701 (F) of Federal Food, Drug and Cosmetic Act, FS 7.17, FS 13.116

Notices of **Judgement** under Caustic Poison Act, FS 7.9, FS 13.112

Notices of **Judgement** under Federal Food, Drug, and Cosmetic Act: Cosmetics, A 46.21, FS 7.13, FS 13.113

Notices of **Judgement** under Federal Food, Drug, and Cosmetic Act: Drugs and Devices, A 46.22, FS 7.12

Notices of **Judgement** under Federal Food, Drug, and Cosmetic Act: Foods, A 46.20, FS 7.10

Notices of **Judgement** under Federal Hazardous Substances Labeling Act, FS 13.112/2

Notices of **Judgement** Under Federal Insecticide, Fungicide, and Rodenticide Act, A 77.325, A 82.56

Notices of **Judgement** Under Insecticide Act, A 82.34

Notices of **Judgement** Under the Federal Insecticide, Fungicide, and Rodenticide Act, EP 1.70

Notices of **Judgement**, Food and Drug Act, A 32.6, A 1.16

Judgements

Judgements Rendered by Court of Claims, Ju 3.6

Judges

C.A.B. Initial and Recommended Decisions of Administrative Law **Judges**, CAB 1.38

Judgment

Notice of **Judgment** under Caustic Poison Act, A 46.9

Notice of **Judgment** under Food and Drug Act, A 46.6

Notice of **Judgment** under Insecticide Act, A 46.7

Notice of **Judgment** under Regulations of Naval Stores, A 46.8

Notices of **Judgment** under: Caustic Poison Act, FS 7.9, FS 13.112

Judges

Judges Information Series, Ju 10.24

Judicial

Annual Report of the Proceedings of the **Judicial** Conference of the United States {and} Semiannual Report of the Director of the Administrative Office of the United States Courts, Ju 10.1

Federal **Judicial** Caseload Statistics JU 10.21

Federal **Judicial** Workload Statistics, Ju 10.2:W 89, Ju 10.21

Federal-State Election Law Survey: an Analysis of State Legislation, Federal Legislation and **Judicial** Decisions, Y 3.El 2/3:2 St 2

International **Judicial** Observer, Ju 13.13/2-3

Judicial Business of the United States Courts, Ju 10.1/4

Judicial Decisions, SE 1.19

Notices of Judgement Summarizing **Judicial** Review of Orders under Sec. 701 (F) of Federal Food, Drug and Cosmetic Act, FS 7.17, FS 13.116

Report of Proceedings of Regular Annual Meeting of **Judicial** Conference of the United States, Ju 10.10

Report of Proceedings of Special Session of **Judicial** Conference of the United States, Ju 10.10/2

Reports of the Proceedings of the **Judicial** Conference of the United States {and} Annual Report of the Director of the Administrative Office of the U.S. Courts, Ju 10.1/2

State - Federal **Judicial** Observer, Ju 13.13/2

Judiciary

Committee on the **Judiciary** Program, Y 4.J 89/2:P 94/22

Rules of Procedure, Committee on the **Judiciary**, Y 4.J 89/2-10

Statistical Tables for the Federal **Judiciary**, Ju 10.21/2

Juice

Commitments of Traders in Commodity Futures, Cotton, Frozen Concentrated Orange **Juice**, Potatoes, A 85.9

Futures Trading and Open Contracts in Frozen Concentrated Orange **Juice**, A 85.11/8

Juices

Consumer Buying Practices for Selected Fresh Fruits, Canned and Frozen **Juices**, and Dried Fruits, Related to Family Characteristics, Region and City Size, A 36.173

Consumer Purchases of Citrus and Other **Juices**, CPFJ (series), A 93.12

Consumer Purchases of Fruits and **Juices**, A 88.12/4

er Purchases of Fruits and **Juices** by Regions and Retail Outlets, A 36.171/2

Consumer Purchases of Selected Fresh Fruits, Canned and Frozen **Juices**, and Dried Fruits, A 36.171

Regional Distribution and Types of Stores where Consumers Buy Selected Fresh Fruits, Canned and Frozen **Juices**, and Dried Fruits, A 36.172

Jumping
Parachute **Jumping**, TD 4.6:part 105
Junior
Junior Division News-Letter, L 7.9
Junior-Year
Junior-Year Science, Mathematics, and Foreign
Language Students, First-Term, FS
5.254:54001, HE 5.254:54001
Jurisdiction
Background Material and Data on Programs within
the **Jurisdiction**, Y 4.W 36:10-4
Commission on Extraterritorial **Jurisdiction** in
China, S 3.36
Docket of Cases Pending in Court of Claims,
General **Jurisdiction**, Ju 3.12
Federal and State Commission **Jurisdiction** and
Regulations, Electric, Gas, and
Telephone Utilities, FP 1.21
Instructions to Clerks of Courts Exercising
Naturalization **Jurisdiction**, L 6.10
Weekly Report of Vessels under **Jurisdiction** of
Shipping Board, SB 2.12
Jurisdictional
Notices of Determinations by **Jurisdictional**
Agencies Under the Natural Gas Policy
Act of 1978, E 2.22
Jurisdictions
Consolidated Address and Territorial Bulletin, VA
Station Addresses, Identification
Numbers, and Territorial **Jurisdictions**,
VA 1.69
Juror
Grand and Petit **Juror** Service in U.S. District
Courts, Ju 10.13
Juror Utilization in United States District Courts,
Ju 10.13
Justice
Annual Report of **Justice** System Improvement Act
Agencies, J 1.87
Attorney General's Annual Report Federal Law
Enforcement and Criminal **Justice**
Assistance Activities, J 1.32/2
Briefs in Court of Claims Cases Prepared or Argued
by Tax Division Department of **Justice**, J
1.19/8
Building Knowledge About Crime and **Justice** J
28.36
Bureau of **Justice** Assistance Bulletin, J 26.32
Bureau of **Justice** Assistance Publications List, J
26.9/2
Bureau of **Justice** Statistics Fiscal Year: At a
Glance, J 29.1/2
Compendium of Federal **Justice** Statistics, J 29.20
Congressional Budget Request, U.S. Department of
Justice, E 1.34/3
Criminal **Justice** Agencies, J 1.39
Criminal **Justice** Information Exchange Directory, J
28.20/2
Criminal **Justice** Information Policy (series), J 29.9/
8
Criminal **Justice** Monograph Series, J 1.37/3
Criminal **Justice** Perspectives (series), J 26.14
Criminal **Justice** Research, J 28.17
Criminal **Justice** Research Series, J 1.37/4
Criminal **Justice** Research Solicitations, J 1.37/5, J
26.18
Criminal **Justice** Research Utilization Program
(series), J 28.13
Directory of Criminal **Justice** Information Sources, J
26.2:In 3, J 28.20
Directory of Law Enforcement and Criminal **Justice**
Associations and Research Centers, C
13.10:480-20
Federal **Justice** statistics Program, J 29.30

Federal Law Enforcement and Criminal **Justice**
Assistance Activities, Annual Report, J
1.32/2
Justice, J 1.101
Justice Assistance News, J 1.59
Justice Expenditure and Employment, J 29.11/2
Justice Expenditure and Employment Extracts, J
29.11/2-2
Justice Expenditure and Employment in the U.S, J
29.11/2-3
Justice Library Review, J 4.7
Juvenile **Justice** and Delinquency Prevention, Y
3.C 86:2 J 98
Juvenile **Justice** Bulletins, J 32.10
Juvenile **Justice** Conditions of Confinement, J
32.19
Juvenile **Justice**, Deinstitutionalizing Status
Offenders: A Record of Progress, J 32.20/
4

National Advisory Committee for Juvenile **Justice**
and Delinquency Prevention: Annual
Report, J 1.48/2, J 26.1/4
National Criminal **Justice** Information and
Statistics Service, J 1.37
National Criminal **Justice** Information and
Statistics Service, Statistics Center
Report, J 1.37/2
National Criminal **Justice** Information and
Statistics Service: {reports}, J 26.10
National Criminal **Justice** Reference Service
Document Data Base, J 28.31/2
National Criminal **Justice** Reference Service:
Document Retrieval Index, J 26.26
National Criminal **Justice** Reference Service:
Miscellaneous Publications Series, J
1.42/3
National Criminal **Justice**: Document Retrieval
Index, J 1.42
National Institute for Juvenile **Justice** and
Delinquency Prevention: Annual
Report, J 26.1/2
National Institute of **Justice**, Research Report, J
28.15/2
National Institute of **Justice** Catalog, J 28.14/2
National Institute of **Justice** Journal, J 28.14/2-2
National Institute of **Justice** Reports, J 28.14
National Institute of Law Enforcement and Criminal
Justice; Annual Report, J 1.1/3, J 26.1/3
National Institute of Law Enforcement and Criminal
Justice; Evaluation Series, J 26.21/2
National Institute of Law Enforcement and Criminal
Justice; Exemplary Project Reports, J
1.10
Network of Knowledge, Directory of Criminal
Justice Information Sources, J 28.20
NIJ Reports, A Bimonthly Journal of the National
Institute of **Justice**, J 28.14
Office of Juvenile **Justice** and Delinquency
Prevention: Annual Report, J 1.47
Permanent Court of International **Justice**, S 1.29
Perspectives on Crime and **Justice**, Lecture Series, J
28.24/3-2
Posters Department of **Justice**, J 1.99
Rape and Its Victims: a Report for Citizens, Health
Facilities, and Criminal **Justice**
Agencies, J 1.8/3:R 18
Register, Department of **Justice** and the Courts of
the United States, J 1.7
Report of the U.S. Department of **Justice** Pursuant
to Section 8 of the Federal Coal Leasing
Amendments Act of 1975, J 1.27/3
Reports of the Advisory Committee to the
Administrator on Standards for the
Administration of Juvenile **Justice**, J
1.48
Reports of the National Juvenile **Justice**
Assessment Centers (series), J 26.27
Research Reports National Institue of **Justice**, J
28.24/3
Sourcebook of Criminal **Justice** Statistics, J 1.42/3,
J 29.9/6, J 29.9/6-2
Special Reports **Justice** Statistics Bureau, J 29.13
Telephone Directory **Justice** Department, J 1.89
Truth in Criminal **Justice** Series, J 1.95
Justification
Budget Program **Justification** of Programs and
Estimates for Fiscal Year (date)
Submitted to Congress, Y 3.T 25:43
Congressional **Justification** for Estimates, HH
1.105
Justification of Budget and Legislative Program
for Office of Management and Budget, HE
22.30/2
Justifications
Justifications of Appropriation Estimates for
Committees on Appropriations, Fiscal
Year, HE 1.1/3, ED 1.46
Justifications of Appropriation Estimates for
Committees on Appropriations:
Department of Education, ED 1.46, ED
1.46/2
Justifications of Appropriation Estimates for
Committees on Appropriations:
Department of Health and Human
Services, HE 1.1/3
Justifications of Appropriation Estimates for
Committees on Appropriations: Health
Care Financing Administration, HE
22.33
Jute
Sisal, Hemp, **Jute** and Miscellaneous Fibers, C
18.126

Juvenile
Analysis and Evaluation, Federal **Juvenile**
Delinquency Programs, J 26.25
Annual Report on **Juvenile** Arrestees/Detainees, J
28.24/6
Grants, **Juvenile** Delinquency Prevention and
Control Act, HE 17.21
Juvenile Court Statistics, FS 17.213, HE 17.23, J
1.53
Juvenile Delinquency Prevention and Control Act
of 1968, Grants, HE 17.811
Juvenile Delinquency Reporter, HE 17.22
Juvenile Delinquency: Facts and Facets, FS 3.222,
FS 14.115
Juvenile Justice, Deinstitutionalizing Status
Offenders: A Record of Progress, J 32.20/
4
Juvenile Justice and Delinquency Prevention, Y
3.C 86:2 J 98
Juvenile Justice Bulletins, J 32.10
Juvenile Justice Conditions of Confinement, J 32.19
National Advisory Committee for **Juvenile** Justice
and Delinquency Prevention: Annual
Report, J 1.48/2, J 26.1/4
National Conference of Prevention and Control of
Juvenile Delinquency, J 1.24
National Institute for **Juvenile** Justice and
Delinquency Prevention: Annual
Report, J 26.1/2
News Notes on **Juvenile** Delinquency, FS 3.219
Office of **Juvenile** Justice and Delinquency
Prevention: Annual Report, J 1.47
Reports of the Advisory Committee to the
Administrator on Standards for the
Administration of **Juvenile** Justice, J 1.48
Reports of the National **Juvenile** Justice
Assessment Centers (series), J 26.27
Juveniles
Juveniles Taken into Custody, J 32.18

K

Kansas
BLM in New Mexico, Oklahoma, Texas and **Kansas**,
I 53.43/5
Kansas Leaflets, A 62.10
Kansas City
Average Semi-Monthly Retail Meat Prices at New
York Chicago and **Kansas City**, A
36.179
Kappler's
Kappler's Compilation of Indian Laws and
Treaties, Y 4.In 2/2:L 44
Kazakh
Herald of Academy of Sciences of **Kazakh** SSR
{abstracts}, C 41.50/9
Keep
Keep Well Series, T 27.22
Kelly
Economic Resource Impact Statement **Kelly** Air
Force Base, D 301.105/3
Kennedy
Concorde Monitoring; John F. **Kennedy**
International Airport, TD 4.49/2
Kennedy Round, Special Reports, C 42.29
Research and Activities Under Saltonstall-
Kennedy Act, Annual Report of Secretary
of Interior, I 1.1/2
Telephone Directory **Kennedy** Space Center, NAS
1.24/3
Kennewick
Area Wage Survey Summary Yakima-Richland-
Kennewick-Pasco-Walla Walla-
Pendleton, Washington-Oregon, L
2.122/47
Kentucky
Commercial Tobacco-Livestock Farms, Bluegrass
Area, **Kentucky** and Penny-Royal Grass
Area, Kentucky-Tennessee, A 93.9/11

Water Resources Development in **Kentucky**, D
103.35/17
Kerosene
Deliveries of Fuel Oil and **Kerosene** in (date), E
3.40
Fuel Oil and **Kerosene** Sales, E 3.11/11-4
Sales of Fuel Oil and **Kerosene** in (year), I 28.45/5

World Retail Prices and Taxes on Gasoline, **Kerosene**, and Motor Lubricating Oils, I 28.44

Kerr

Records and Briefs in Cases Arising Under Agricultural Adjustment Act, Bankhead Act, and **Kerr**-Smith Tobacco Act, J 1.19/7

Key

Interagency Directory, **Key** Contacts for Planning, Scientific and Technical Exchange Programs, Educational Travel, Students, Teachers, Lecturers, Research Scholars, Specialists, S 1.67/3

Key Audiovisual Personnel in Public Schools and Library Systems in State and Large Cities and In Large Public Colleges and Universities, FS 5.60/2

Key Dates, NAS 1.79

Key Facts, Employment Security Operations, L 7.60

Key Officers of Foreign Service Posts, S 1.40/5

Key Officers of Foreign Service Posts, Guide for Businessmen, S 1.40/2:Of 2

Key to Geophysical Records Documentation, C 55.219/2

Key to Meteorological Records Documentation, C 55.219

Key to Meteorological Records, Environmental Satellite Imagery (series), C 55.219/4

Key to Oceanic and Atmospheric Information Sources, C 55.219/5

Key to Oceanographic Records Documentation, C 55.219/3

Organizational Directory of **Key** Officials, PM 1.31/2

Weekly Business Survey of **Key** Cities, C 1.19

KeyNotes

KeyNotes, HH 1.121

Keyport

Naval Torpedo Station, **Keyport**, Washington: Publications, D 211.23

Keyword

Keyword Directory, T 17.6/3-3

Keyword Worksheet, T 17.6/3-2

Key West

Atlantic Coast; Cape Henry to **Key West**, C 55.422:4

Keywords

Keywords Index to U.S. Government Technical Reports, C 41.21/5

Kidnapping

Crime, **Kidnapping**, and Prison Laws {June 21, 1902}, Y 1.2:C 86

Kidney

Annual Contractors' Conference on Artificial **Kidney** Program, Proceedings, HE 20.3314

Artificial **Kidney** Bibliography, HE 20.3311

Artificial **Kidney**-Chronic Uremia Advisory Committee, HE 20.3001/2:K 54

Interstitial Cyctisis, National **Kidney** and Urologic Disease Information Clearinghouse, HE 20.3323/3

Kidney Disease and Nephrology Index, HE 20.3318

Kidney, Urology and Hematology, HE 20.3320/2-5

KU (**Kidney**/Urologic) Notes (series), HE 20.3324

National **Kidney** and Urologic Diseases Information Clearinghouse Factsheet HE 20.3323/3

National Listing of Medicare Providers Furnishing **Kidney** Dialysis and Transplant Services, HE 22.510, HE 22.216

National Listing of Providers Furnishing **Kidney** Dialysis and Transplant Services, HE 22.25

National Listing of Renal Providers Furnishing **Kidney** Dialysis and Transplant Services, HE 22.510/2

Research Updates in **Kidney** and Urologic Health, HE 20.3324/2

Kids

Caring About **Kids** (series), HE 20.8130

Killed

FBI Uniform Crime Reports: Law Enforcement Officers **Killed**, J 1.14/7-5

Killers

Hidden **Killers**, S 1.148

Kills

Fish **Kills** Caused by Pollution in (year), EP 2.24

Pollution-Caused Fish **Kills**, FS 2.94, I 67.9

Kindergarten

Energy Education Resources, **Kindergarten** Through 12th Grade, E 3.27/6

Kindergarten Extension Series, I 16.18/5

The Fund for the Improvement of Postsecondary Education (FIPSE), Special Focus Competition: College-School Partnerships to Improve Learning of Essential Academic Subjects, **Kindergarten** through College, ED 1.23/9

King

Catalogue and Index of the Publications of the Hayden, **King**, Powell, and Wheeler Survyes, I 19.3:222

Kitchen

Test **Kitchen** Series, C 55.321, I 49.39

Kit

BJS Program Application **Kit**, Fiscal Year, J 29.22

Tax Practitioner Reproducible **Kit**, T 22.51/2

Kits

Study **Kits**, C 30.78

Klamath

Klamath River Fisheries Assessment Program (series), I 49.107

Klamath Falls

Area Wage Survey Summary Eugene-Springfield-Medford-Roseburg-**Klamath Falls**-Grants Pass, Oregon, L 2.122/37

Knit

Foreign **Knit** Goods Letter; Special Bulletins, C 18.78

International **Knit** Goods, News, C 18.101

Knit Fabric Gloves, C 3.129

Knit Wool Gloves and Mittens, C 3.63

Know

Facts You Should **Know**, Statements, Pr 32.4242

Know Your Communist Enemy Series, D 2.13

U.S.A. Citizenship, **Know** It, Cherish It, Live It, J 1.25

What You Have to **Know** about SSI, HE 3.90

Knowledge

Inventory of **Knowledge** Series, LC 1.41

Knowledge for Survival, You Can Survive! Newsletter to State Extension Program Leaders, Rural Defense, A 43.35/2

Network of **Knowledge**, Directory of Criminal Justice Information Sources, J 28.20

Smithsonian Contributions to **Knowledge**, SI 1.6

Kommunist

Translation from **Kommunist**, PrEx 7.21/11

Korea

Directory of Officials of the Democratic People's Republic of **Korea**, PrEx 3.10/7-6

East Asia, **Korea**: Kulloja, PrEx 7.16/2

JPRS Report: East Asia, **Korea**, PrEx 7.16/2-2

Korea Road Maps, Series L351, D 5.341

South **Korea** Interim Government Activities, M 105.13

Summation of United States Army Military Government Activities in **Korea**, W 1.76

Korean

Korean Affairs Report, PrEx 7.16/2

KU

KU (Kidney/Urologic) Notes (series), HE 20.3324

Kulloja

East Asia, Korea: **Kulloja**, PrEx 7.16/2

KW

U.S. Nuclear Plants Cost Per **KW** Report, Office of Nuclear Power, Y 3.T 25:68

Kyanite

Kyanite and Related Minerals in (year), I 28.131

L

L

L, ED 1.76/2-4

L.S.

L.S. Series, C 30.69

La Crosse

Quarterly Report of Progress at Fish Control Laboratory, **La Crosse**, Wisconsin, Southeastern Fish Control Laboratory, Warm Springs, Georgia, and Hammond Bay Biological Station, Millersburg, Michigan, I 49.75

Lab

CDC **Lab** Manual, HE 20.7008/2

Labcert

Labcert Bulletin, EP 2.3/4

LABCOM-P

Laboratory Command: Pamphlets, **LABCOM-P**-(series), D 101.22/24

Label

Project **Label**, Alphabetical Listings by Controlled Generic Drug Ingredients, J 24.24/2

Project **Label**, Alphabetical Listings by Drug Labeler of Discontinued Products, J 24.24/3

Project **Label**, Alphabetical Listings by Drug Labeler, J 24.24

Project **Label**, Alphabetical Listings by Drug Product, J 24.24/4

Labeler

Project Label, Alphabetical Listings by Drug **Labeler** of Discontinued Products, J 24.24/3

Project Label, Alphabetical Listings by Drug **Labeler**, J 24.24

Labeling

Notices of Judgement under Federal Hazardous Substances **Labeling** Act, FS 13.112/2

Standards and **Labeling** Policy Book, A 110.18

Labels

U.S. Statutes Concerning the Registration of Prints and **Labels**, C 21.7/3

Labor

Adequacy of **Labor** Supply in Important **Labor** Market Areas, Pr 32.5217

Agricultural **Labor** Situation, A 1.56

Annual Digest of State and Federal **Labor** Legislation, L 16.3

Annual Report of Secretary, Department of Commerce and **Labor**, C 1.1

Annual Report of the Federal **Labor** Relations Authority, Y 4.P 84/10-11

Annual Report on International Religious Freedom (Bureau for Democracy, Human Rights and **Labor**), S 1.151

Bimonthly Summary of **Labor** Market Developments in Major Areas, L 7.51

Brief History of the American **Labor** Movement, L 2.3:1000

Bureau of **Labor** Statistics Catalog of Publications, Bulletins, Reports, Releases, and Periodicals, L 2.34

Bureau of **Labor** Statistics Surveys, L 2.136

Catalog of Seminars, Training Programs and Technical Assistance in **Labor** Statistics, L 2.114

Child **Labor** Bulletins, L 36.203/2

Child **Labor** Regulations, L 22.6/3

Child **Labor** Regulations, Orders, L 5.39

Child **Labor** Series, L 16.27

Child-**Labor** Bulletins, L 22.14

Classification of Important **Labor** Market Areas, L 7.19

Classification of **Labor** Market Areas According to Relative Adequacy of **Labor** Supply, L 7.19/2

Classified Index of Decisions of Regional Directors of National **Labor** Relations Board in Representation Proceedings, LR 1.8/6-2

Classified Index of Dispositions of ULP {Unfair **Labor** Practices} Charges by the General Counsel of the Federal **Labor** Relations Authority, Y 3.F 31/21-3:11

Classified Index of Dispositions of ULP {Unfair **Labor** Practices} Charges by the General Counsel of the National **Labor** Relations Board, LR 1.8/8

Classified Index of the National **Labor** Relations Board Decisions and Related Court Decisions, LR 1.8/6

Collective Bargaining Agreements Received by Bureau of **Labor** Statistics, L 2.45

Compilation . . .Between Employers and Employees, Laws {on} Disputes Between Carriers and. . ., Eight-hour Laws, Employers' Liability Laws, **Labor** and Child **Labor** Laws, Y 1.2:Em 7/6

Naval Research **Laboratory** Review (Separates), D 210.17/2 a

Oak Ridge National **Laboratory** Review, E 1.28/17

Operational Applications **Laboratory**, Air Force Cambridge Research Center, OAL- TM, D 301.45/37

Pacific Marine Environmental **Laboratory**: Annual Report, C 55.601/2

Pacific Northwest Environmental Research **Laboratory**: Quarterly Progress Report, EP 1.19

Pacific Northwest Water **Laboratory**: Quarterly Progress Report, EP 2.22

Plant **Laboratory** {abstracts}, C 41.58

Proceedings Standards **Laboratory** Conferences, C 13.10

Program and Services, Report of Educational Materials **Laboratory**, Division of International Studies and Services, FS 5.214:14031, HE 5.214:14031

Publications Navy Electronics **Laboratory**, D 211.11/2

Quarterly Progress Reports, Wildlife Research **Laboratory**, Denver, Colorado, I 49.47

Quarterly Report of Central Propagation **Laboratory**, C 13.33/2

Quarterly Report of Progress at Fish Control **Laboratory**, La Crosse, Wisconsin, Southeastern Fish Control **Laboratory**, Warm Springs, Georgia, and Hammond Bay Biological Station, Millersburg, Michigan, I 49.75

Questionnaire Design in the Cognitive Research **Laboratory**, HE 20.6209:6

Report on Current Hydraulic **Laboratory** Research in U.S., C 13.26

Research Reports Cold Regions Research and Engineering **Laboratory**, D 103.33/3

Research Reports Forest Products **Laboratory**, A 13.27/14

Research Reports Injury Control Report **Laboratory**, FS 2.316

Research Reports Naval Research **Laboratory**, D 210.22

Rodman Process **Laboratory**, Watertown Arsenal, Reports, D 105.13

Rubber **Laboratory**, Mare Island Naval Shipyard, Vallejo, California, Reports, D 211.16

Soil Survey **Laboratory** Memorandums, A 57.43, A 77.525

Southeast Environmental Research **Laboratory**: Quarterly Summary, EP 1.60

Southwestern Radiological Health **Laboratory**: Monthly Activities Report, EP 1.13

Special Reports Cold Regions Research and Engineering **Laboratory**, D 103.33/2

Special Reports Construction Engineering Research **Laboratory**, D 103.53/4

Standards **Laboratory** Cross-Check Procedure, Department of Navy, BUWEPS-BUSHIPS Calibration Program, D 217.16

Standards **Laboratory** Instrument Calibration Procedure, Department of Navy, BUWEPS-BUSHIPS Calibration Program, D 217.16/2

Standards **Laboratory** Instrument Calibration Technique, D 217.16/7

Standards **Laboratory** Measurements System Operation Procedure, Department of Navy, BUWEPS-BUSHIPS Calibration Program, D 217.16/3

State Clinical and Environmental **Laboratory** Legislation, HE 20.7028

Structural Research **Laboratory** Report, I 27.29

Technical Notes Department of the Air Force Alaskan Air Command, Arctic Aeromedical **Laboratory**, D 301.66

Technical Notes Department of the Air Force Atmospheric Analysis **Laboratory**, D 301.45/30 3

Technical Notes Department of the Air Force Meteorological Development **Laboratory**, D 301.45/17-2

Technical Notes Forest Service Forest Products **Laboratory**, A 13.27/9

Technical Plan for the Great Lakes Environmental Research **Laboratory**, C 55.620/2

Telephone Directory Jet Propulsion **Laboratory**, NASA, NAS 1.12/7-2

Textile Engineering **Laboratory** Reports, D 106.9/2-2

U.S. Army Mobility R & D **Laboratory**: USAAMRDL CR- (series), D 117.8/6

U.S. Naval Radiological Defense **Laboratory**, Research and Development Report USNRDL (series), D 211.13

Walter Reed Army Medical Center, Army Prosthetics Research **Laboratory**, Technical Reports, D 104.15/2

Watertown Arsenal **Laboratory**, Report WAL (series), D 105.13/2

Watertown Arsenal **Laboratory**: Technical Report (series), D 105.13/2-2

Western Environmental Research **Laboratory**: Annual Report, EP 1.14/2

Western Environmental Research **Laboratory**: Monthly Activities Report, EP 1.14

White Oak **Laboratory**: Technical Reports, NSWC/ WOL/TR- (series), D 201.21/3

Wildlife Research **Laboratory**: Technical Notes, I 49.47/3

Woods Hole **Laboratory**, I 49.62

Working Papers Environmental Protection Agency, Pacific Northwest Environmental Research **Laboratory**, EP 1.37/2

Labor-Management

Decisions and Reports on Rulings of the Assistant Secretary of Labor for **Labor-Management** Relations Pursuant to Executive Order 11491, L 1.51/4, Y 3.F 31/21-3:10-2

Digest and Index of Published Decisions of the Assistant Secretary of Labor for **Labor-Management** Relations Pursuant to Executive Order 11491, As Amended, L 1.51/3

Labor-Management Cooperation Brief, L 1.85

LA/C

LA/C Business Bulletin, C 61.35/2

Lacquer

Paint, Varnish, **Lacquer**, and Fillers, C 3.94

Lacquers

Sales of **Lacquers**, C 3.88

Laden

United States Foreign Trade Bunker Oil and Coal **Laden** in the United States on Vessels, C 3.164:810

Lading

Shipment Under the United States Foreign Aid Programs Made on Army- or Navy-Operated Vessels (American flag) by Port of **Lading** by Country of Destination, C 3.164:976

Lake

Catalog of Charts of the Great **Lakes** and Connecting Waters, Also **Lake** Champlain, New York Canals, Minnesota-Ontario Border Lakes, D 103.208

Lake Series, D 103.18

Publications **Lake** States Forest Experiment Station {list}, A 13.61/12

Regulations for Sale of **Lake** Survey Charts, W 33.5

Research Reports **Lake** Survey Office, D 103.209

Saint Marys Falls Canal, Michigan, Statistical Report of **Lake** Commerce Passing through Canals at Sault Ste. Marie, Michigan and Ontario, W 7.26, M 110.16, D 103.17

Technical Notes Forest Service **Lake** States Forest Experiment Station, A 13.61/10

Lake Champlain

Catalog of Charts of the Great Lakes and Connecting Waters, Also **Lake Champlain**, New York Canals, Minnesota-Ontario Border Lakes, D 103.208

Lakes

Average Monthly Discharge for 15-year Base Period at Selected Gaging Stations and Change of Storage in Certain **Lakes** and Reservoirs in Pacific Northwest, I 19.45/3-2

Catalog of Charts of the Great Lakes and Connecting Waters, Also Lake Champlain, New York Canals, Minnesota-Ontario Border **Lakes**, D 103.208

Charts of Great **Lakes**, W 33.7/2

Coast Charts of Great **Lakes**, W 33.7/3

Focus on Great **Lakes** Water Quality, Y 3.In 8/28:17

Foreign Inland Waterway News, Intercoastal Waterways, Rivers, **Lakes**, Canals, Equipment, C 18.208

General Chart of Northern and Northwestern **Lakes** {and rivers}, W 33.7/1

Great **Lakes**, TD 5.9:4, C 55.422:6

Great **Lakes** Environmental Research Laboratory: Annual Report, C 55.620

Great **Lakes** Fisheries, C 55.309/2

Great **Lakes** Intercom, TD 4.26/2

Great **Lakes** Pilot; Lake Survey Office, D 103.203

Great **Lakes** Pilot; National Ocean Survey, C 55.420

Great **Lakes** Pilotage Administration, C 1.47

Great **Lakes** Pilotage Regulations and Rules and Orders, C 1.47:R 26

Great **Lakes** Region Air Traffic Activity, TD 4.19/5

Great **Lakes** Region Aviation Systems, Ten Year Plan, TD 4.33/4

Great **Lakes** Research Advisory Board: Annual Report, Y 3.In 8/28:10

Great **Lakes** Science Advisory Board: Annual Report, Y 3.In 8/28:12, Y 3.In 8/28:16

Great **Lakes** Water Levels, C 55.420/2

Great **Lakes** Water Quality Annual Report, Y 3.In 8/28:9

Great **Lakes**-Saint Lawrence Seaway Winter Navigation Board: Annual Report, D 103.1/3

International Field Year for the Great **Lakes**: Proceedings, IFYGL Symposium, Annual Meetings of the American Geophysical Union, C 55.21/3

Land Between the **Lakes** {field guides}, Y 3.T 25:6-3

Merchant Fleet in Service on Great **Lakes**, C 27.9/5

Meterological Chart of the Great **Lakes**, A 29.13, A 29.13/2

Monthly Bulletin of Lake Levels for the Great **Lakes**, D 103.116

Monthly Mean Discharge at Selected Gaging Stations and Change of Storage in Certain **Lakes** and Reservoirs in Columbia River Basin, I 19.47

Lakeshores

Compilation of Administrative Policies for National Recreation Areas, National Seashores, National **Lakeshores**, National Parkways, National Scenic Riverways (Recreational Area Category), I 29.9/4:R 24

National **Lakeshores** {Information Circulars}, I 29.6/3

Lamb

Sheep and **Lamb** on Feed, A 88.16/13, A 105.47

Sheep and **Lamb** Situation, A 36.91

Lambs

Sheep and **Lambs**: Weekly Average Price per 100 Pounds, A 36.183

Land

Agricultural Census Analyses: Changes in **Land** in Farms by Size of Farm, A 36.137/1

Agricultural **Land** Values and Markets, Outlook and Situation Report, A 93.29/2-4

Annual Report of Indian **Land**, I 20.61

Annual Report of Indian **Land** and Income from Surface, I 20.61/2

Bureau of **Land** Management 1:100,000-Scale Maps, I 53.11/4

Bureau of **Land** Management Maps, Surface and Minerals Management Status, Scale 1:100,000, I 53.11/4-2

Certification and Operations; **Land** Airports Serving CAB-Certificated Scheduled Air Carriers Operating Large Aircraft, TD 4.6:part 139

Circular Showing Manner of Proceeding to Obtain Title to **Land**, I 21.12

Conventional Loans Made to Finance Acquisition and Development of **Land**, Federal Savings and Loan Associations, FHL 1.22

Dry **Land** Agriculture Division, Weekly Station Reports, A 77.508

Dry-**Land** Agriculture, A 19.35

Erosion and Related **Land** Use Conditions (by Projects), A 57.24

Farm-Mortgage Lending Experience of 19 Life Insurance Companies, Federal **Land** Banks, and Farmers Home Administration, A 93.9/5

Farms of Nonwhite Farm Operators, Number of Farms, **Land** in Farm, Cropland Harvested, and Value of **Land** and Buildings, by Tenure, Censuses of 1945 and 1940 (by States), C 3.193

Federal Reclamation Projects, Water and **Land** Resource Accomplishments, I 27.55

Legacy
Jefferson's **Legacy**, LC 1.56
Legal
Annual Digest of **Legal** Interpretations, Y 3.Eq 2:10-2
Annual Report of **Legal** Services Program of Office of Economic Opportunity to the American Bar Association, PrEx 10.18
Audit **Legal** Letter Guidance, PrEx 2.34
Collection of **Legal** Opinions, EP 1.63
Current **Legal** Literature, TD 4.17/4
Digest of **Legal** Interpretations Issued or Adopted by the Commission, Compilation, Y 3.Eq 2:10
Doorway to **Legal** News, Y 3.At 7:46
FLITE {Federal **Legal** Information Through Electronics} Newsletter, D 302.10
Focus on Special Education **Legal** Practices, ED 1.212
General **Legal** Bulletin, Foreign Laws Affecting American Business, C 18.95
Guide to Selected **Legal** Sources of Mainland China, LC 1.6/4:C 44
Housing **Legal** Digest, Decisions, Opinions, Legislations Relating to Housing Construction and Finance, Y 3.C 33/3:10
Index of EPA **Legal** Authority Statutes and Legislative History, Executive Orders, Regulations, EP 1.5/4
Journal of **Legal** Studies, D 305.21/2
Judge Advocate **Legal** Service, D 101.22:27
Legal Activities, J 1.109
Legal Medicine Open File, D 101.117/7
Legal Precedent Retrieval System, T 17.6/3-7
Legal Series: Children's Bureau, L 5.13
Legal Series: Welfare Administration, FS 14.17/2
Monthly Accession List of Library, **Legal** Reference Section, SS 1.22
Opinions of the Office of **Legal** Counsel, J 1.5/4
OVC's **Legal** Series Bulletin, Y 1.2/2
Procurement **Legal** Service Circulars, D 101.33/3
Revised Guide to the Law and **Legal** Literature of Mexico, L 1.36:38
Summary of Cooperative Cases, **Legal** Series, A 89.9/2
Legal Opinions
Digests of **Legal Opinions**, VB 1.13
Legislation
AEC Authorizing **Legislation**, Fiscal Year {date}, Y 4.At 7/2:L 52
Agricultural **Legislation** in the Congress, Y 4.Ag 8/1:L 52
Annual Digest of State and Federal Labor **Legislation**, L 16.3
Annual Report of Department of Treasury on Operation and Effect of Domestic International Sales Corporation **Legislation** for Calendar Year, Y 4.W 36:D 71/2
Calendar of United States House of Representatives and History of **Legislation**, Y 1.2/2
Digest of State **Legislation** of Special Interest to Women Workers, L 13.14/2
Federal-State Election Law Survey: an Analysis of State **Legislation**, Federal **Legislation** and Judicial Decisions, Y 3.El 2/3:2 St 2
Federal/State Radiation Control **Legislation**, HE 20.4115
Highlights of Current **Legislation** and Activities in Mid-Europe, LC 1.27
Highlights of **Legislation** on Aging, FS 1.13/4, FS 14.912
Index to **Legislation** of States to U.S. Enacted, LC 21.9
Information Report on State **Legislation**, Y 3.N 88:42
Legislation Relating to District of Columbia, Summary Report, Y 4.D 63/1:L 52
Major **Legislation** of the Congress, LC 14.18
Nuclear Regulatory **Legislation**, Y 4.In 8/14:N 88/5
Operation and Effect of the Domestic International Sales Corporation **Legislation**, T 1.54
State Clinical and Environmental Laboratory **Legislation**, HE 20.7028
State Labor **Legislation** in (year), L 2.6/1:L 524
State **Legislation** of 1941: Summaries of Laws Currently Received in Library of Congress, LC 14.10
State **Legislation** on Smoking and Health, HE 20.7210, HE 20.25/3
State Radiation Control **Legislation**, HE 20.1112

Survey of State **Legislation** Relating to Higher Education, FS 5.250:50008, HE 5.250:50008
Weekly Summary of Federal **Legislation** Relating to National Resources Committee, Activities Bulletins, Y 3.N 21/12:15
Legislations
Atomic Energy **Legislations** through {Congress Session}, Y 4.At 7/2:L 52/2
Housing Legal Digest, Decisions, Opinions, **Legislations** Relating to Housing Construction and Finance, Y 3.C 33/3:10
Legislative
Civil Aeronautics Board **Legislative** History of Regulations, C 31.206/2:L 52
Consumer **Legislative** Monthly Report, HE 1.510
Division of **Legislative** Analysis Highlights, HE 20.3051
Field Letter, Information, **Legislative**, Court Decisions, Opinions, L 25.8
GC **Legislative** History Files, GA 1.23
Index of EPA Legal Authority Statutes and **Legislative** History, Executive Orders, Regulations, EP 1.5/4
Justification of Budget and **Legislative** Program for Office of Management and Budget, HE 22.30/2
Legislative Calendar [Banking, Finance and Urban Affairs Committee (House)], Y 4.B 22/1-10
Legislative Calendar [District of Columbia Committee (House)], Y 4.D 63/1-10
Legislative Calendar [Education and Labor Committee (House)], Y 4.Ed 8/1-10
Legislative Calendar [Government Operations Committee (House)], Y 4.G 74/7-11
Legislative Calendar [House Administration Committee (House)], Y 4.H 81/3
Legislative Calendar [National Security Committee (House)], Y 4.Se 2/1-17
Legislative History of Titles I-XX of the Social Security Act, HE 3.5/3
Legislative Record, Y 4.W 36:10-6
Legislative Reports, FS 3.125, L 16.12
Legislative Series, L 36.115
Legislative Status Report, VA 1.58
Recent Educational Policy and **Legislative** Developments Abroad (series), HE 5.94
Research and Statistics **Legislative** Notes, FS 3.28/3

State **Legislative** Fact Sheet, TD 8.65
State **Legislative** Summary, Children and Youth Issues, HE 24.16
Summary of **Legislative** Activities, Y 4.P 96/10:L 52
Thomas: **Legislative** Information on the Internet, LC 1.54/2
Legislators
Policy Briefs, Action Guides for **Legislators** and Government Executives, J 28.8/2
Legislature
Acts and Resolutions of **Legislature**, I 35.12/5, W 75.12
Legitimate
Registered Bona Fide and **Legitimate** Farmers' Cooperative Organizations under Bituminous Coal Act of 1937, I 46.15
Leisure
Community Organization for **Leisure**, Serials, Y 3.W 89/2:28
Lend-lease
Report to Congress on **Lend-lease** Operations, S 1.43
Reports to Congress on **Lend-Lease** Operations, Pr 32.402:L 54, Pr 32.5507
United States Exports of Domestic and Foreign Merchandise To Canada (Including **Lend-Lease** Exports), C 3.157/4
United States Exports of Domestic and Foreign Merchandise Under **Lend-Lease** Program, Calendar Year, C 3.164:405
United States Exports of Domestic and Foreign Merchandise Under **Lend-Lease** Program, Commodity by Country of Destination, C 3.164:415
United States Exports of Domestic and Foreign Merchandise Under **Lend-Lease** Program, Country of Destination by Commodity, C 3.164:421, C 3.164:425
United States Exports of Domestic Merchandise (Including **Lend-Lease** Exports), C 3.164:400

Lenders
Alphabetic List of **Lenders**, ED 1.66
Numeric List of **Lenders**, ED 1.67
Lending
Estimated Mortgage **Lending** Activity of Savings and Loan Associations, HH 4.8/3
Farm-Mortgage **Lending** Experience of 19 Life Insurance Companies, Federal Land Banks, and Farmers Home Administration, A 93.9/5
Mortgage **Lending** Activity of Savings and Loan Associations, FHL 1.7/3
Savings and Mortgage **Lending** Activity, Selected Balance Sheet Items, F.S.L.I.C. Insured Savings and Loan Associations, FHL 1.20/2
Small Business **Lending** in the United States, SBA 1.52
Survey of Mortgage **Lending** Activity State Estimates, HH 1.99/2-2
Survey of Mortgage **Lending** Activity, HH 1.99, HH 1.99/2, HH 1.99/2-3
Length
Coach Traffic, Revenue, Yield and Average On-flight Trip **Length** by Fare Category for the 48-state Operations of the Domestic Trunks, C 31.269
Estimated Grade and Staple **Length** of Upland Cotton Ginned (by States), A 82.69
Estimated Grade and Staple **Length** of Upland Cotton Ginned in United States, A 88.11/7
Profiles of Scheduled Air Carrier Operations by Stage **Length**, TD 4.44/3
Trunk Carriers, Coach Class, Traffic, Revenue, Yield, Enplanements and Average On-flight Trip **Length** by Fare Category, CAB 1.24
Leningrad University
Herald of **Leningrad University**, Mathematics, Mechanics, and Astronomy Series {abstracts}, C 41.51/5
Herald of **Leningrad University**, Physics and Chemistry Series {abstracts}, C 41.52/5
Lentils
Official United States Standards for Peas & **Lentils**, A 113.10/4
Lesson
Extension Course of Medical Field Service School; **Lesson** Assignment Sheets, W 3.71
Interior Guard Duty, **Lesson** Assignment Sheets, W 3.50/7
Master **Lesson** Plans, Prepared for Use at Engineer School Only, D 103.110
Military Law; **Lesson** Assignment Sheets, W 3.50/3
Programmed **Lesson** (series), D 101.47/7
Lessons
Center for Army **Lessons** Learned (series), D 101.22/25
Correspondence Course, Elements of Surface Weather Observations, **Lessons**, C 30.26
Lessons (series), D 103.6/7
Lessons Learned in Contracting RPMA, D 103.121
TEC **Lessons** (series), D 101.6/7
Lessors
Selected Elements of Value of Property Used in Common Carrier Service, Before and After Recorded Depreciation and Amortization, Class I Line Haul Railways, Including Their **Lessors** and Proprietary Companies, IC 1 val.10
Letort
Letort Papers, D 101.146/3
Letter
Annual **Letter** of Information, A 35.10
Audit Legal **Letter** Guidance, PrEx 2.34
Chit Chat, an Administrative **Letter** for Division Employees, A 103.17
Generic **Letter** (series), Y 3.N 88:56
Information News **Letter**, L 1.54/3
Letter Circulars, C 13.16
NCUA **Letter** to Credit Unions, NCU 1.19
Patent Office News **Letter**, C 21.13
Pathologist; News **Letter** for Extension Workers Interested in Plant Disease Control, A 43.20
President's Conference on Industrial Safety News **Letter**, L 16.30
Regional and Field **Letter**, FS 1.16
Research Information **Letter**, A 106.37
Rubber News **Letter**, C 18.140/2
Safety News **Letter**, Current Information in the Federal Safety Field, L 30.8

Supplement **Litigation**, Actions and Proceedings Bulletin Index, SE 1.20/3

Little

Light List: Vol. 2, Atlantic Coast, Toms River, New Jersey to **Little** River, South Carolina, TD 5.9:v 2

Live

Commercial Livestock Slaughter, Number and **Live** Weight, by States, Meat and Lard Production, United States, by Months, A 88.16/17

Instruction Manual: Classification and Coding Instructions for **Live** Birth Records, HE 20.6208/6

U.S.A. Citizenship, Know It, Cherish It, **Live** It, J 1.25

Livestock

Commercial **Livestock** Slaughter and Meat Production, A 92.18/3

Commercial **Livestock** Slaughter, Number and Live Weight, by States, Meat and Lard Production, United States, by Months, A 88.16/17

Commercial Tobacco-**Livestock** Farms, Bluegrass Area, Kentucky and Penny-Royal Grass Area, Kentucky-Tennessee, A 93.9/11

Dairy, **Livestock**, and Poultry: U.S. Trade and Prospects, A 67.18:FDLP

Driven-In Receipts of **Livestock**, A 66.28

Economic Indicators of the Farm Sector, Cost of Production: **Livestock** and Dairy, A 93.45/2-2

Foreign Crop and **Livestock** Reports, A 27.11

Livestock and Meat, A 67.30:L 75

Livestock and Meat Situation, A 88.16/8, A 93.15, A 105.23/2

Livestock and Poultry, A 93.46

Livestock and Poultry Inventory, A 88.16/14

Livestock and Poultry Inventory, January 1, Number, Value and Classes, A 92.18/8

Livestock and Poultry: World Markets and Trade Circular Series, A 67.18:FL&P

Livestock & Seed Division, A 88.61

Livestock and Veterinary Sciences, Annual Report of the National Research Programs, A 106.33

Livestock and Wool Situation, A 36.141

Livestock, Dairy and Poultry Situation and Outlook, A 93.46/3

Livestock Health Series (Posters), A 77.222

Livestock Movement at Twelve Markets, A 36.202

Livestock Reports, A 36.33, A 66.42

Livestock Short Course, A 21.13

Livestock Situation, A 36.116

Livestock Slaughter, A 105.23/4

Livestock Slaughter and Meat Production, A 88.16/9

Livestock Slaughter by States, A 88.16/2

Livestock Slaughter, Annual Summary, A 105.23/4-2

Livestock Slaughter, Louisiana Crop Reporting Service, A 88.16/2-2

Livestock, Meat, Wool, Market News, Weekly Summary and Statistics, A 88.16/4

Livestock, Meats, and Wool, Market Statistics and Related Data, A 66.36

Livestock, Meats, and Wool; Market Review and Statistics, A 66.13, A 75.10, A 78.11, A 80.111, A 80.811, A 81.11, A 82.7

Market News, **Livestock** Division, Market Reviews and Statistics, A 88.16/4

Market Reviews and Statistical Summaries of **Livestock**, Meats and Wool, A 36.98

Markets and Crop Estimates Bureau, Foreign Crop and **Livestock** Reports, A 36.19

Meats, **Livestock**, Fats and Oils, CE 18.72/5

Radio Service **Livestock** Short Course, A 21.13/1

Receipts and Disposition of **Livestock** at 66 Public Markets, A 82.41

Receipts and Disposition of **Livestock** at Public Markets, A 88.16

Receipts and Disposition of **Livestock** at Public Stockyards, A 36.203

Salable (and total) Receipts of **Livestock** at Public Markets, in Order of Volume, A 88.16/15

Statistical Tables Showing Progress of Eradication of Brucellosis and Tuberculosis in **Livestock** in United States and Territories for Fiscal Year, A 77.212/3

Total **Livestock** Slaughter, Meat and Lard Production, A 88.16/16

Virginia Crops and **Livestock**, A 88.31

Western Range and **Livestock** Report, A 92.18/10

Working Reference of **Livestock** Regulatory Establishments, A 77.221/2

Working Reference of **Livestock** Regulatory Establishments, Circuits and Officials, A 88.16/20

Living

Ameri ca's Families and **Living** Arrangements, C 186.17-2

Changes in Cost of **Living**, L 2.6/a 5

Cost of **Living** Council News, PrEx 17.7

Living with Radiation, Y 3.At 7:43

Marital Status and **Living** Arrangements, C 3.186/6

Minimum Property Requirements for Properties of One or Two **Living** Units Located in the (various States), HH 2.17

Minimum Property Standards for 1 and 2 **Living** Units, HH 2.17/4

U.S. Department of State Indexes of **Living** Costs Abroad and Living Quarters Allowances, L 2.101

U.S. Department of State Indexes of **Living** Costs Abroad and Quarters Allowances, April, L 2.101/2

U.S. Department of State Indexes of **Living** Costs Abroad, S 1.76/4

Living Arrangements

Households, Families, Marital Status, and **Living Arrangements**, Advance Report, C 3.186/9

LMNOD-SP

Public Notice, LMNOD-SP- (series), D 103.117

Load

Electric Energy and Peak **Load** Data, E 3.11/17-9

Energy and Peak **Load** Data, E 3.11/17-3

Load Forecast and Power Supply Summary Prepared for Fiscal Year (date), Y 3.T 25:58

Local Service Air Carrier, Selected Flight **Load** Data by City Pair, by Frequency Grouping, by Aircraft Type, C 31.253/2

Monthly Comparisons of Peak Demands and Energy **Load**, E 3.11/17-5

Reports on Airline Service, Fares Traffic, **Load** Factors and Market Shares, CAB 1.27

Rotorcraft External-**Load** Operations, TD 4.6:part 133

Loaded

Statistics of Bituminous Coal **Loaded** for Shipment on Railroads and Waterways As Reported by Operators, I 28.34

Loads

Study of Methods Used in Measurement and Analysis of Sediment **Loads** in Streams, Reports, Y 3.F 31/13:9, Y 3.In 8/8:10

Loan

All Operating Savings and **Loan** Associations, Selected Balance Sheet Data, FHL 1.20

Annotated Manual of Statutes and Regulations of the Federal Home **Loan** Bank Board, FHL 1.6/2:St 2

Annual Report to Congress on the Section 312 Rehabilitation **Loan** Program, HH 1.87

Asset and Liability Trends All Operating Savings and **Loan** Associations, FHL 1.30

Class A **Loan** Bulletins, Y 3.F 31/11:26

Combined Financial Statements of Members of the Federal Home **Loan** Bank System, FHL 1.12

Composite List of Eligible Institutions, National Vocation Student **Loan** Insurance Act of 1965, FS 5.83/2, HE 5.83/2

Consumer Installment Credits of Industrial **Loan** Companies, FR 1.36/4

Consumer Loans Made Under Effective State Small **Loan** Laws, FR 1.36/3

Conventional Loans Made in Excess of 80 Percent of Property Appraisal by Federal Savings and **Loan** Associations, FHL 1.19

Conventional Loans Made to Finance Acquisition and Development of Land, Federal Savings and **Loan** Associations, FHL 1.22

Estimated Flow of Savings in Savings and **Loan** Associations, HH 4.8/2

Estimated Mortgage Lending Activity of Savings and **Loan** Associations, HH 4.8/3

Evaluation Document **Loan** Lists, J 1.20/5

Federal Farm **Loan** Act with Amendments and Farm Mortgage and Farm Credit Acts, Y 1.2:F 31

Federal Home **Loan** Bank Board Digest, FHL 1.14

Federal Home **Loan** Bank Review, Y 3.F 31/3:9, FL 3.7, NHA 3.8

Federal **Loan** Agency News, FL 1.8

Federal Savings and **Loan** Insurance Corporation, Financial Statements, FHL 1.2:F 31/2

Flow of Savings in Savings and **Loan** Associations, FHL 1.7/2

Forest Service Films Available on **Loan** for Educational Purposes to Schools, Civic Groups, Churches, Television, A 13.55

FSLIC Insured Savings and **Loan** Associations, Savings and Mortgage Activity, Selected Balance Sheet Items, FHL 1.20/2

Health Facilities Construction Program **Loan**, Loan Guarantee and Mortgage Quarterly Status Report, HE 20.9013

Home Owner's **Loan** Acts and Housing Acts (July 22, 1932), Y 1.2:H 75/3

Home Owners' **Loan** Corporation Publications, FL 3.9, Y 3.F 31/3:8

Journal of the Federal Home **Loan** Bank Board, FHL 1.27

Liberty **Loan** Acts (April 24, 1917), Y 1.2:L 61

Loan Commitments at Selected Large Commercial Banks, FR 1.39/3

Members of the Federal Home **Loan** Bank System, FHL 1.31

Monthly **Loan** Data Report, Y 3.T 25:13-3

Mortgage Interest Rates on Conventional Loans, Largest Insured Savings and **Loan** Associations, FHL 1.24

Mortgage Lending Activity of Savings and **Loan** Associations, FHL 1.7/3

National Defense and Direct Student **Loan** Program, Directory of Designated Low-Income Schools for Teacher Cancellation Benefits, ED 1.40/2

National Defense Student **Loan** Program, Including Participating Institutions, FS 5.255:55001, HE 5.255:55001

National Direct Student **Loan** Status of Default as of (date), ED 1.40

National Health Service Corps Information Bulletin, Private Practice **Loan** Program for Former Corps Members, HE 20.9110/8

National Health Service Corps Information Bulletin, Private Practice Startup **Loan** Program, HE 20.9110/7

National Woman's Liberty **Loan** Committee, T 1.27/11-19

NCJRS Document **Loan** Program, Document Lists, J 1.20/4

Number of Foreclosures (and rate of foreclosure) by FSLIC Insured Savings and **Loan** Associations, FHL 1.26

Participation **Loan** Transactions, FHL 1.17

Press Releases Federal Home **Loan** Bank Board, FHL 1.7

Publications Home Owners' **Loan** Corporation, FL 3.9

Publicity Bureau, Liberty **Loan** of 1917, T 1.25

Quarterly Review, 503 and 504 Economic Development **Loan** Programs, SBA 1.27/2

Report of the Federal Home **Loan** Bank Board, FHL 1.1

Report to the National Farm **Loan** Associations, FCA 1.23

Rules and Regulations for Federal Savings and **Loan** System, with Amendments to (date), FHL 1.6:Sa 9

Savings and **Loan** Activity in (Month), FHL 1.15/2

Savings and Mortgage Lending Activity, Selected Balance Sheet Items, F.S.L.I.C. Insured Savings and **Loan** Associations, FHL 1.20/2

Status of Perkins **Loan** Default, ED 1.40/4

Summary of **Loan** Activity and Operating Results through (date) Issued by CCC, A 82.83/2

Summary of Savings Accounts by Geographic Area, FSLIC-Insured Savings and **Loan** Associations, FHL 1.29

Trends in the Savings and **Loan** Field, FHL 1.15

War **Loan** Organization, T 1.27

Woman's Liberty **Loan** Committee (miscellaneous publications), T 1.25/5

Loan Guarantee

Health Facilities Construction Program Loan, **Loan Guarantee** and Mortgage Quarterly Status Report, HE 20.9013

Loans

Agricultural **Loans** by States, A 36.132

Automobile **Loans** by Major Finance Companies, FR 1.34/6

Bank Rates on Short-Term Business **Loans**, FR 1.32/5

CCC **Loans** on Cotton, A 82.309

Changes in Commercial and Industrial **Loans** by Industry, FR 1.39

Commercial and Industrial **Loans** Outstanding by Industry, FR 1.39/2

Commercial and Industrial **Loans** to U.S. Addresses Excluding Bankers Acceptances and Commercial Paper, by Industry, FR 1.39/2

Composite List of Eligible Institutions for Guaranteed **Loans** for College Students, Higher Education Act of 1965, FS 5.83, HE 5.83

Consumer Finance Companies, **Loans** Outstanding and Volume of **Loans** Made, FR 1.36/6

Consumer Installment **Loans** of Principal Types of Financial Institutions, FR 1.34

Consumer **Loans** Made Under Effective State Small Loan Laws, FR 1.36/3

Conventional **Loans** Made in Excess of 80 Percent of Property Appraisal by Federal Savings and Loan Associations, FHL 1.19

Conventional **Loans** Made to Finance Acquisition and Development of Land, Federal Savings and Loan Associations, FHL 1.22

Credit Unions, Installment **Loans** to Consumers, C 18.226

Current Statement of **Loans** by Years and Commodities, Y 3.C 73:12

Direct **Loans** Bulletin, ED 1.40/6

Direct **Loans** Newsletter, ED 1.40/5

Directory of Grants, Awards, and **Loans**, HE 20.6111, HE 20.6612

Handbook for Participation **Loans** with the Small Business Administration, SBA 1.19:L 78

Industrial Banking, Companies, Installment **Loans** to Consumers, C 18.219

Laws relating to **Loans** and Currency, T 26.6/1

Loans and Discounts of Farm Credit Banks and Associations, Annual Report, FCA 1.12/2

Loans and Discounts of Lending Institutions Supervised by Farm Credit Administration, FCA 1.12/2

Loans Made, United States and Territories, by Crop Years, from Date of Organization (1933) through June 30 (year), A 82.311

Member Bank **Loans**, FR 1.11/2

Monthly Report on **Loans** and Discounts, FCA 1.12

Mortgage Interest Rates on Conventional **Loans**, Largest Insured Savings and Loan Associations, FHL 1.24

Personal Finance Companies, Installment **Loans** to Consumers, C 18.222

Quarterly Report on **Loans** and Discounts, A 71.12

Secondary Market Prices and Yields and Interest Rates for Home **Loans**, HH 1.99/3

Statement of Active **Loans** and Financial Guarantees, Y 3.Ex 7/3, Y 3.Ex 7/3:12

Statement of **Loans** and Commodities Owned, A 71.7, A 82.307

Statements of **Loans** and Commodities Owned, A 80.407

Vessels Receiving Benefits of Construction **Loans** under Merchant Marine Act of 1928, SB 7.8

Local

Alaska Railroad, **Local** Passenger Tariffs, I 35.10/7

Catalog of Federal Grant-In-Aid Programs to State and **Local** Governments, Y 3.Ad 9/8:20

Census of **Local** Jails, J 29.21

Certificated Air Carrier Financial Data; Domestic **Local** Service 12-month Comparisons, C 31.235/2

Certificated Air Carrier Financial Data; Domestic **Local** Service {quarterly comparisons}, C 31.235

Construction Expenditure of State and **Local** Governments, BC (series), C 56.223, C 3.215/10

Construction Expenditure of State and **Local** Tax Revenue, C 3.215/10

Current IPA Projects for Improved State and **Local** Management, CS 1.94

Current **Local** Announcements Covering Washington, D.C. Metropolitan Area, CS 1.28:2602-WA

Current Population Reports, **Local** Population Estimates, County Population Estimates, C 3.186/20-2

Employee Benefits in State and **Local** Governments, L 2.3/10-2

Estimates of **Local** Public School System Finances, ED 1.112/3

European Program, **Local** Currency Counterpart Funds, Pr 33.911, Pr 33.911/2, FO 1.11, FO 1.11/2

Final State and **Local** Data Elements, T 1.64/2

Job Patterns For Minorities and Women in State and **Local** Government, Y 3.Eq 2:12-4

Labor Management Relations Issues in State and **Local** Governments, CS 1.80/2

List of **Local** Boards of the Selective Service System, Y 3.Se 4:24

List of State and **Local** Trade Associations (by States), C 18.200

Local Area Personal Income, C 59.18

Local Arts Agencies Program, Application Guidelines, NF 2.8/2-31

Local Authorities Participating in HAA Low-Rent Programs, HH 3.9

Local Authorities Participating in Low-Rent Housing Programs, HH 1.51

Local Board Memoranda, Y 3.Se 4:13-2

Local Board Memoranda (Compilations), Y 3.Se 4:13

Local Board Releases, Y 3.Se 4:11

Local Chairman of Better Housing Program Committee, Y 3.F 31/11:11

Local Climatological Data, C 55.217

Local Climatological Data, Annual Summaries, C 55.287

Local Climatological Data, Dulles International Airport, C 55.287/3

Local Climatological Data, National Airport, C 55.287/2

Local Climatological Data, Washington, D.C., Dulles International Airport, C 55.217/2

Local Climatological Data, (various states), C 55.286/6-54

Local Climatological Summary with Comparative Data, C 30.10/3

Local Currency Counterpart Funds, Y 4.Ec 74/3:12

Local Government Employment in Major County Areas, C 3.140/2-6

Local Government Finanaces in Selected Metropolitan Areas in (year), C 56.209, C 3.191/2

Local Government Finances in Major County Areas, C 3.191/2-9

Local Light List, C 9.42-C 9.49

Local List of Lights and Other Marine Aids, Pacific, T 47.25/2

Local Preservation, I 29.104/3

Local Programs, Application Guidelines, NF 2.8/2-21

Local Public Agency Letters, HH 7.9/2

Local School Administration Briefs, FS 5.68

Local Service Air Carrier, Selected Flight Load Data by City Pair, by Frequency Grouping, by Aircraft Type, C 31.253/2

Local Service Air Carriers' Unit Costs, C 31.253

Local Service Carrier Passenger Enplanements, C 31.266

Local Shortages in Selected Scientific and Engineering Occupations, L 7.63

Local Telephone System, N 1.23/2

Minorities and Women in State and **Local** Government, Y 3.Eq 2:12-4

New Dwelling Units Authorized by **Local** Building Permits, L 2.51/5

New Housing Units Authorized by Local Building Permits and New Dwelling Units Authorized in **Local** Building Permits, C 3.215/4

Organization and Staffing for Full Time **Local** Health Services, FS 2.80

Personnel Management Reform, Progress in State and **Local** Governments, PM 1.11/3

Precision and Accuracy Assessments for State and **Local** Air Monitoring Networks, EP 1.23/5-3

Problem-solving Technology for State and **Local** Governments, C 51.9/30

Productivity and Cost of Employment: **Local** Service Carriers, Calendar Year, C 31.263

Public Assistance, Costs of State and **Local** Administration, Services, and Training, FS 17.633, HE 17.633

Public Health Personnel in **Local** Health Units, FS 2.80

Public Use Data Tape Documentation Mortality **Local** Area Summary, HE 20.6226/7

Public Use Data Tape Documentation Natality **Local** Area Summary, HE 20.6226/3

Quarterly Summary of Federal, State, and **Local** Tax Revenue, C 3.145/6

Quarterly Summary of State and **Local** Tax Revenue, C 3.145/6, C 56.231/2

Recurrent Report of Mileage and Traffic Data Domestic **Local** Service Carriers, C 31.229

References on **Local** School Administration, FS 5.10/4

Report of Conference of **Local** Appraisers Held at New York, T 20.5

Report of State and **Local** Radiological Health Programs, HE 20.4121

Report on Plan Preparation on State and **Local** Public Works, FW 7.7

Report on Washington Conference of Mayors and Other **Local** Government Executives on National Security, FCD 1.18

Seasonally Adjusted Capacity and Traffic Scheduled Operations **Local** Service Carriers, C 31.262/4

Seasonally Adjusted Capacity and Traffic Scheduled Operations: System, Domestic, and International Trunks Plus **Local** Service Carrier, CAB 1.20

Special Analysis of Federal Aid to State and **Local** Governments in Budget, PrEx 2.8/a3

State and **Local** Government Collective Bargaining Settlements, L 2.45/4

State and **Local** Government Employment and Payrolls, L 2.41/4

State and **Local** Government Functional Profile Series, Y 3.Eq 2:14

State and **Local** Government Quarterly Employment Survey, C 3.140

State and **Local** Government Special Studies, C 3.145, C 56.231

State and **Local** Grant Awards, EP 1.35/2

State and **Local** Personnel Systems, Annual Statistical Report, CS 1.95

State and **Local** Programs on Smoking and Health, HE 20.25/4

State-**Local** Businessmen's Organizations, C 18.200/2

Statistics of **Local** Public School Systems Fall (year), HE 5.93/8

Statistics of **Local** Public School Systems Pupils and Staff, HE 19.318/4

Statistics of **Local** Public School Systems, Finance, (year), HE 19.318/2

Status of the Nation's **Local** Public Transportation, Conditions and Performance, Report to Congress, TD 7.18

To Mayor of Each City with **Local** Airline Service, C 31.256

Total Obligations Incurred for Emergency Relief from All Public Funds by State and **Local** Relief Administration in Continental United States, Y 3.F 31/5:35

Transmittal Memo {for} **Local** Board Memorandums, Y 3.Se 4:13

U.S. Census of Housing Special Reports for **Local** Housing Authorities, series HC (S 1), C 3.224/8

Unemployment in States and **Local** Areas, L 2.41/9

Unemployment Rates for States and **Local** Governments, BLS/PWEDA/QR-(series), L 2.111/3

Urban Renewal Manual, Policies and Requirements for **Local** Public Agencies, HH 7.9

Wind Erosion Conditions, Great Plains, Summary of **Local** Estimates, A 57.47

Localities

Current Housing Market Situation, Report {various **localities**}, HH 2.28/2

Harbor Charts and Charts of Special **Localities**, W 33.8

Located

List of Available Surplus Property **Located** in District of Columbia, T 58.23

Location

Airborne Anomaly **Location** Maps, Y 3.At 7:31

Annual Report on **Location** of New Federal Offices and Other Facilities, A 1.111

Area Development Aid: Industrial **Location** Series, C 45.8/3

Changes in Status of Banks and Branches During Month, Name and **Location** of Banks and Branches, FR 1.33/2

Exact **Location** of All Ships in which Shipping Board is Interested, SB 2.10

Food and Drug Administration **Location** Directory, HE 20.4037

Industrial **Location** Series, C 41.90/2

Location Directory, HE 20.4037

Location Identifiers, TD 4.310

Location of Irrigated Land, Maps (by States), C 3.950-9/4

Location of Manufacturing Plants by Industry, County, and Employment Size, C 3.24/14

Location Sheets of Maps and Charts, W 31.7/2

National Park **Location** Maps, I 29.53

Number of New Permanent Nonfarm Dwelling Units Started by Urban or Rural **Location**, Public or Private Ownership, and Type of Structure, L 2.51/4

Selected Multifamily Status Reports, Mortgage Insurance Programs by Name and **Location** of Each Project, HH 1.50

Worldwide Geographic **Location** Codes, GS 1.34

Locations

List of Illinois River Terminals, Docks, Mooring **Locations**, and Warehouses, D 103.58

List of Mississippi River Terminals, Docks, Mooring **Locations**, and Warehouses, D 103.58/2

National Union Catalog: Register of Addition **Locations**, LC 30.8/7

Locator

Federal Information **Locator** System, PrEx 2.14/2

GPO **Locator**, GP 3.37

Transmittals (NOAA Washington Area Personnel **Locator**), C 55.47

LOCATORplus

NLM **LOCATORplus**, HE 20.3626

Lock

Performance Monitoring System: Summary of **Lock** Statistics, D 103.57/12

Lockers

Steel Office Furniture, Shelving, and **Lockers**, and Fireproof Safes, C 3.108

Lockheed Aircraft Corporation

Audit of Payments from Special Bank Account to **Lockheed Aircraft Corporation** for C-5a Aircraft Program . . ., GA 1.13:L 81/2

Locomotion

Land **Locomotion** Laboratory Reports, D 105.18/2

Locomotive

Annual Report of the Director of **Locomotive** Inspection, IC 1 loc.1

Decisions Under **Locomotive** Inspection Act {individual cases}, IC 1 loc.7

Locomotive-Miles

Classification of Train-Miles, **Locomotive-Miles** and Car-Miles, IC 1 ste.11

Locomotives

Electric **Locomotives** (mining and industrial), C 3.81

Fuel and Power for **Locomotives** and Rail Motor Cars of Class I Steam Railways in United States, IC 1 ste.30

Interpretations, Rulings, and Instructions for Inspection and Testing of **Locomotives** and Tenders and Their Appurtenances, IC 1 loc.5

Laws, Rules, and Instructions for Inspection and Testing of **Locomotives** Other Than Steam, IC 1 loc.8

Laws, Rulings, and Instructions for Inspection and Testing of **Locomotives** and Tenders and Their Appurtenances, IC 1 loc.5

Railroad **Locomotives**, C 3.105

Log

Commerce **Log**, C 1.38

EPA **Log**, Weekly Log of Significant Events, EP 1.24

Log of the Laboratory, Items of Current Research, A 13.27/10

Mariners Weather **Log**, C 55.210

Loggers

War Reports for **Loggers** and Mill Men, W 107.9

Logistician

Army **Logistician**, D 101.69

Logistics

Air Force Journal and **Logistics**, D 301.91

Air Force **Logistics** Command, Hill Air Force Base, Telephone Directory, D 301.104/2

Air Force Medical **Logistics** Letter, D 304.9

Annual Department of Defense Bibliography of **Logistics** Studies and Related Documents, D 1.33/3-2

Catalog of **Logistics** Models, D 1.33/6

Defense **Logistics** Information System (DLIS) Procedures Manual, D 7.6/19

Department of Defense Bibliography of **Logistics** Studies and Related Documents, D 1.33/3

Federal Item **Logistics** Data Records, D 7.26

Logistics Leadership Series, D 208.211

Logistics Systems, D 101.119

Naval Research **Logistics** Quarterly, D 201.12

USAF Medical **Logistics** Directory, D 304.9/2

Logos

Logos, E 1.86/3

London

London, International Fisheries Exhibition, S 6.6

Records of Virginia Company of **London**, LC 1.11

Technical Reports, Naval Research Office **London**, D 210.16

Long

Comparative Statement of Foreign Commerce of United States Ports Handling Cargo Tonnage of 100,000 **Long** Tons and Over, SB 7.5/296

Long Range Acquisition Estimates, D 201.35

Long Range Plans, T 63.214

Long Record of Weather Observations, C 55.287/56

Long Staple Cotton Review, A 88.11/20

Long-Range

Long-Range Planning Series, Ju 13.16

Log Lines

Log Lines, DLA News Customers Can Use, D 7.43

Longitudinal Surveys

National **Longitudinal Surveys**, Discussion Paper, L 2.71/5-2

NLS News, National **Longitudinal Surveys**, L 2.135

Longshore

Longshore and Harbor Workers' Compensation Act, L 36.18

Manpower Utilization-Job Security in **Longshore** Industry {by port}, L 1.50

Maritime Manpower Report: Sea Faring, **Longshore**, and Shipyard Employment as of (date), C 39.202:Se 1/2, C 39.235

Longshoremen

Suggested Safe Practices for **Longshoremen**, L 16.51/3-2

Work Injuries Reported by **Longshoremen** and Harbor Workers, L 26.9

Longshoring

Longshoring, L 16.47

Maritime Safety Data; **Longshoring**, L 16.47/5

Long-Term

AHCPR **Long-Term** Care Studies (series), HE 20.6519

Division of **Long-Term** Care: Annual Report, HE 20.6001/4

Long-Term Care Information Series, HE 22.209

Long-Term Embrittlement of Cast Duplex Stainless Steels in LWR Systems, Y 3.N 88:25-5

Longview

Area Wage Survey, **Longview**-Marshall, Texas, Metropolitan Area, L 2.121/43-6

Look

Closer **Look**, HE 19.119

Report from Closer **Look**, a Project of the Parents' Campaign for Handicapped Children and Youth, ED 1.22

Loop

University of Maryland College Park 2x4 **Loop** Test Facility, Y 3.N 88:25-7

Loose Leaf

Loose Leaf Circulars, FS 5.4/2

Loran

Hydrographic/Topographic Center Publications: **Loran** Tables, D 5.317/4

Loran A

Loran A (19) Plotting Charts Series 7300, D 5.348

Loran C

Loran C Plotting Charts Series 7800, D 5.348/2

Loran Tables

Loran Tables, D 5.317

Los Alamos

Los Alamos Laboratory: Research Highlights, E 1.96/2

Los Alamos Science, E 1.96

Los Angeles

Los Angeles Air Force Station, Telephone Directory, D 301.104/3

U.S. Army Engineer District, **Los Angeles**: Reports (numbered), D 103.59

VFR Helicopter Chart of **Los Angeles**, C 55.416/12-2

Loss

Air Freight **Loss** and Damage Claims, C 31.265

Air Freight **Loss** and Damage Claims for the Six Months Ended (date), C 31.265/2

Air Freight **Loss** and Damage Claims, Annual Summaries, C 31.265/3

Classification of Income and Profit and **Loss** Accounts, IC 1 wat.8

Classification of Income, Profit & **Loss**, and General Balance Sheet Accounts, IC 1 ste.15

Fire **Loss** to Government Property, GS 1.14/2

Form of Income and Profit and **Loss** Statement, IC 1 ste.14

Quarterly Freight **Loss** and Damage Claims Reported by Common and Contract Motor Carriers of Property, IC 1 acco.11

Quarterly Freight **Loss** and Damage Claims, Class 1, Line-Haul Railroads, IC 1 acco.12

Lost

Oceangoing Merchant Ships of 1,000 Gross Tons and Over Scrapped and **Lost** During the Calendar Year (date), C 39.229

Lottery

Foreign Fraud, Unlawful, and **Lottery** Mail Orders, P 1.12

Louisiana

Agricultural Prices, **Louisiana** Crop Reporting Service, A 88.9/4

Annual Rice Summary, **Louisiana** Crop Reporting Service, A 88.18/23

General Crop Report, **Louisiana** Crop Reporting Service, A 88.24/7

Hatchery Production, **Louisiana** Crop Reporting Service, A 88.15/22

Honey Report, **Louisiana** Crop Reporting Service, A 88.19/2-2

Lamb Crop and Wool Production, **Louisiana** Crop Reporting Service, A 88.16/19

Leaflets for Distribution from Survey's Exhibition at **Louisiana** Purchase Exposition, C 4.10

Livestock Slaughter, **Louisiana** Crop Reporting Service, A 88.16/2-2

Louisiana Annual Crop Summary, **Louisiana** Crop Reporting Service, A 88.24/6

Louisiana Annual Vegetable Summary, **Louisiana** Crop Reporting Service, A 88.12/23

Louisiana Soybeans for Beans, Acreage, Yield and Production, A 88.18/25

Louisiana Weekly Weather and Crop Bulletin, A 88.49/2

Pecan Report, **Louisiana** Crop Reporting Service, A 88.10/5

Pig Crop Report, **Louisiana** Crop Reporting Service, A 88.16/3-2

Prospective Strawberry Acreage, **Louisiana** Crop Reporting Service, A 88.12/27

Rice Production, **Louisiana** Crop Reporting Service, A 88.18/26

River Summary and Forecast, New Orleans, **Louisiana**, C 55.110/2-2

Saint Louis, **Louisiana** Purchase Exposition, S 6.18

Sweetpotato Report, **Louisiana** Crop Reporting Service, A 88.12/4-2

Turkeys Raised, **Louisiana** Crop Reporting Service, A 88.15/11-2

Vegetable Report, **Louisiana** Crop Reporting Service, A 88.12/26

Winter Wheat Report, **Louisiana** Crop Reporting Service, A 88.18/24

Louisiana Purchase

Notes for **Louisiana Purchase** Exposition, Saint Louis, Missouri, LC 1.8

Low

Enroute High and **Low** Altitude, U.S., D 5.318/4

IFR Enroute **Low** Altitude (Alaska), TD 4.79/16

IFR Enroute **Low** Altitude (U.S.), TD 4.79/15

IFR/VFR **Low** Altitude Planning Chart, C 55.416/15-3

IFR/VFR **Low** Altitude Planning Chart, TD 4.79/16-3

Low Altitude Approach Procedures, United States Military Aviation Notice, D 5.318/3

Low Altitude Instrument Approach Procedures, D 5.318

Terminal **Low** Altitude, Africa and Southwest Asia, D 301.13/6

Tide Tables High and **Low** Water Prediction, C 55.421

Tide Tables, High and **Low** Water Predictions Central and Western Pacific Ocean and Indian Ocean, C 55.421/4

Magnesium and **Magnesium** Compounds in (year), I 28.101/2, I 28.101/2-2
Mineral Industry Surveys, **Magnesium**, I 19.145
Primary **Magnesium**, I 28.101
Magnetic
    Magnetic Declinations, C 4.24
    Magnetic Hourly Values HV (series), C 4.40
    Magnetic Observations, C 4.26
    Results of Observations made at C. & G. Survey **Magnetic** Observatories, C 4.16
Magnetized
    Transportation of Dangerous Articles and **Magnetized** Materials, TD 4.6:part 103
Magnetograms
    Daily **Magnetograms** for ... from the AFGL Network, D 301.45/4-4
    Magnetograms, C 4.38
    Magnetograms and Hourly Values, C 4.40/2
Mail
    Advertisements Inviting Proposals for Covered Regulation Wagon Mail-Messenger, Transfer, and **Mail** Station Service, P 1.6
    Air **Mail** Schedules, P 20.8
    Directory of International **Mail**, P 1.10/5
    Domestic **Mail** Manual, P 1.12/11
    Estimated Volume of **Mail** and Special Services and Postal Revenues, P 1.37
    Foreign Air **Mail** Service, P 8.6
    Foreign Fraud, Unlawful, and Lottery **Mail** Orders, P 1.12
    Foreign, Overseas and Territorial Air **Mail** Carriers, C 31.231
    Mail Room Companion, P 1.47/2
    Postal Laws and Regulations Applicable to Railway **Mail** Service, P 10.13
    Public **Mail** Series, PMS- (series), NAS 1.74
    Recurrent Report of Financial Data: Domestic Air **Mail** Trunk Carriers, Quarters {comparisons}, C 31.234
    Recurrent Report of Mileage and Traffic Data Domestic Air **Mail** Carriers, C 31.230
    Recurrent Report of Mileage and Traffic Data Foreign, Overseas and Territorial Air **Mail** Carriers, C 31.231
    Schedule of **Mail** Routes, P 10.12/16
    Schedule of **Mail** Trains, P 10.12
    Schemes for Separation of **Mail** by States, P 1.21
    Schemes of States (for use of publishers in distribution 2d class **mail**), P 10.10
Mail-Messenger
    Advertisements Inviting Proposals for Covered Regulation Wagon **Mail-Messenger**, Transfer, and Mail Station Service, P 1.6
Mailability
    Fraud and **Mailability**, Enforcement Action, P 1.29/2
Mailers
    Instructions for **Mailers**, P 1.12/5a
    Memo to **Mailers**, P 1.47
Mailing
    Mailing List, W 30.8
    Mailing List of Consular Service of United States, S 1.19
Mails
    Advertisements Inviting Proposals for Carrying **Mails** (miscellaneous), P 1.8
    Advertisements Inviting Proposals for Carrying **Mails** by Airplane or Seaplane, P 1.24
    Advertisements Inviting Proposals for Carrying **Mails** by Regulation Screen Wagons, P 1.7
    Advertisements Inviting Proposals for Carrying **Mails** by Star Routes (by States), P 1.22
    Advertisements Inviting Proposals for Carrying **Mails** By States, P 1.5
    Advertisements Inviting Proposals for Carrying **Mails** by Steamboat Routes (by States), P 1.23
    Schedule of Steamers Appointed to Convey **Mails** to Foreign Countries, P 8.5
Main
    Missouri River **Main** Stream Reservoir Regulation Studies, D 103.41/3
    National Household Survey on Drug Abuse: **Main** Findings, HE 20.417/3
Main Line
    Main Line Natural Gas Sales to Industrial Users, E 3.11/14
Maine
    Commercial Broiler Farms, **Maine**, Delmarva, and Georgia, A 93.9/11
Mainframes
    Directory of U.S. Government Datafiles for **Mainframes** & Microcomputers, C 51.19/4, C 51.19/5

Mainland
    Guide to Selected Legal Sources of **Mainland** China, LC 1.6/4:C 44
    Mainland Cane Sugar Orders, A 55.67
Mainstream
    Musical **Mainstream**, LC 19.12
Mainstreaming
    Mainstreaming Preschoolers (series), HE 23.1110
Maintenance
    Aerospace **Maintenance** Safety, D 306.8
    AFDC and Related Income **Maintenance** Studies, HE 3.67
    Aircraft Accident and **Maintenance** Review, D 301.58
    Conditions of Major Water System Structures and Facilities, Review of **Maintenance**, Report of Examination, {various regions and projects}, I 27.69
    Construction Reports; Residential Alterations and Repairs, Expenditures on Residential Additions, Alterations, **Maintenance** and Repairs, and Replacements, C 56.211/7
    Engineered Performance Standards for Real Property **Maintenance** Activities, D 1.6/7
    Equipment **Maintenance** Series, Bulletins, CS 1.42
    Expenditures for Additions, Alterations, **Maintenance** and Repairs, and Replacements on One-Housing-Unit Owner-Occupied Properties, C 3.215/8:Pt-2
    Expenditures on Residential Additions, Alterations, **Maintenance** and Repairs, and Replacements, C 3.215/8:Pt 1
    Focus on Health **Maintenance** Organizations, HE 20.20/2
    General **Maintenance** Alert Bulletins, C 31.163/2, FAA 1.31/2
    General **Maintenance** Inspection Aids, C 31.162
    General **Maintenance** Inspection Aids Summary and Supplements, FAA 1.31
    Health **Maintenance** Organizations, HE 20.20
    Income **Maintenance** Training Program, HE 3.37
    Inter-American Conference for **Maintenance** of Peace, 1936, S 5.38
    Irrigation Operational and **Maintenance** Bulletin, I 27.41
    Maintenance, D 301.84
    Maintenance Handbook, MS (series), P 1.31/6
    Maintenance Operations Division Instructions, C 31.106/4, FAA 1.6/3
    Maintenance, Preventive **Maintenance**, Rebuilding and Alterations, TD 4.6:part 43
    Office of Federal Airways **Maintenance** Engineering Division Newsletter, C 31.149
    Power O. and M. Report, Field Review of **Maintenance**, I 27.45/2
    Power O. and M. Reports, Field Review of Operation and **Maintenance**, I 27.45/3
    Program Facts on Federally Aided Public Assistance Income **Maintenance** Programs, HE 17.614
    Program Memorandum Health **Maintenance** Organization/Competitive Medical Plan, HE 22.28/2
    PS, the Preventive **Maintenance** Monthly, D 101.87
    REMR Bulletin: News from the Repair, Evaluation, **Maintenance** and Rehabilitation Research Program, D 103.72
    Status Report of the Operation and **Maintenance** of Sanitation Facilities Serving American Indians and Alaska Natives, HE 20.9416
    Supply and **Maintenance** Command Regulations, D 101.9/3
    Supply and **Maintenance** Command, SMC Pamphlets, D 101.22/5
    Systems **Maintenance** Division Instructions, FAA 1.6/7
    Textile **Maintenance** Notes, C 18.148
    Water Operation and **Maintenance** Bulletin, I 27.41
Major
    Alphabetical Listing of **Major** War Supply Contracts, Pr 32.4842
    Annual Report **Major** Natural Gas Companies, E 3.25/4
    Census of Retail Trade; **Major** Retail Centers in Standard Metropolitan Statistical Areas, RC (series), C 56.251/5
    Census of Retail Trade; **Major** Retail Centers Statistics, C 3.255/5

Chronologies of **Major** Developments in Selected Areas of International Relations, Y 4.F 76/1:In 8/57, Y 4.In 8/16:In 8/5
Conditions of **Major** Water System Structures and Facilities, Review of Maintenance, Report of Examination, {various regions and projects}, I 27.69
Department Store Sales and Stocks, by **Major** Departments, FR 1.24/4
Facilities Expansions Authorized Listed by **Major** Types of Products, Pr 32.4843
Farm Population, Annual Estimates by States, **Major** Geographical Division, and Regions, A 88.21
Financial Statistics of **Major** Investor-Owned Electric Utilities, E 3.18/4-2
Financial Statistics of **Major** U.S. Publicly Owned Electric Utilities, E 3.18/4-3
Listing of **Major** War Supply Contracts by State and County, Pr 32.4841
Major Activities in Programs of National Aeronautics and Space Administration, NAS 1.1/2
Major Activities in the Atomic Energy Programs, Y 3.At 7:2 P 94/2
Major BLS Programs, L 2.87
Major Collective Bargaining Settlements in Private Industry, L 2.45/2
Major Data Processing and Telecommunication Acquisition Plans of Federal Executive Agencies, PrEx 2.12/3
Major Information Technology Systems, Acquisition Plans of Federal Executive Agencies, PrEx 2.27
Major Legislation of the Congress, LC 14.18
Major Matters Before the Commission, CC 1.2:M 43
Major Matters Before the Federal Communications Commission, CC 1.50
Major Metropolitan Market Areas, C 47.15/3
Major News Releases and Speeches, A 107.18
Major Nondeposit Funds of Commercial Banks, FR 1.39/4
Major Policy Initiatives, PrEx 2.8/10
Major Programs of the U.S. Department of Housing and Urban Development, Fact Sheets, HH 1.43/2
Major Programs, Bureau of Labor Statistics, L 2.125
Major Shippers Report, C 61.53
Major Work Stoppages, L 2.45/3
Map Book of **Major** Military Installations, D 1.58
Maps of **Major** Concentrations of Poverty in Standard Metropolitan Statistical Areas of 250,000 or More Population, PrEx 10.2:P 86/9
Performance Profiles of **Major** Energy Producers, E 3.37, E 3.37/2
Quarterly Bibliography of **Major** Tropical Diseases, HE 20.3614/4
Reserve Positions of **Major** Reserve City Banks, FR 1.15/2
Residential Electric Bills in **Major** Cities, E 3.11/17-2
Selected Interest and Exchange Rates for **Major** Countries and the U.S., FR 1.32/3
Staff Papers, Background Papers and **Major** Testimony, Y 3.Ec 7/3
State Workmen's Compensation Laws, Comparison of **Major** Provisions with Recommended Standards, L 16.3:212
Storage in **Major** Power Reservoirs in the Columbia River Basin, I 19.47/2
Summary of **Major** Provisions of Convention and of Law Relating to Factory Inspection (by States), L 16.32
Survey of Mortgage-Related Security Holdings of **Major** Institutions, HH 1.99/4-2
Unemployment in **Major** Areas, L 7.64
Unemployment Rate by Race and Hispanic Origin in **Major** Metropolitan Areas, L 2.111/6
United States Army Installations and **Major** Activities in Continental U.S., D 101.22:210-1
Wholesale Price Index, **Major** Specification Changes 1947-53, L 2.61/7
Make
    Listing of Aircraft Accidents/incidents by **Make** and Model, U.S. Civil Aviation, TD 1.109/15
Maketings
    Cash Income from Farm **Maketings**, A 36.68
Making
    Making of American Scenery, I 29.10

Procedure for **Making** Soil Conservation Surveys, Outlines, A 57.17

Maktaba
Maktaba Afrikana Series, LC 2.12, LC 41.11

Malaria
Malaria Folders, FS 2.41
Malaria Surveillance, Annual Report, HE 20.2309/13
Malaria Surveillance, Annual Summary, HE 20.7011/8

Malaysia
Cumulative List of **Malaysia**, Singapore and Brunei Serials, LC 1.30/10-2

Malformations
Congenital **Malformations** Surveillance, Reports, HE 20.7011/2

Malleable
Malleable Iron Castings, C 3.89

Malmstrom
Malmstrom Air Force Base Pamphlet (series), D 301.35/7

Malta
Conferences at **Malta** and Yalta, 1945, S 1.1/3:M 29

Maltreatment
Child **Maltreatment**: Reports from the States to the National Child Abuse and Neglect Data System, HE 23.1018

Mammal
Administration of the Marine **Mammal** Protection Act of 1972, C 55.327
Administration of the Marine **Mammal** Protection Act of 1972, Report of the Secretary of the Interior, I 49.84
Rodenticides and **Mammal**, Bird and Fish Toxicants, EP 5.11/4
Survey of Federally-Funded Marine **Mammal** Research and Studies, Y 3.M 33/3:9-2

Mammalian
Mammalian Mutant Cell Lines Committee, HE 20.3001/2:M 31

Mammography
Mammography Matters, HE 20.4619

Man
Conservation **Man** (radio scripts), I 29.49
Minute **Man**, T 66.7

Managed
Medicaid **Managed** Care Enrollment Report, HE 22.13/2

Managed Care
National Summary of State Medicaid **Managed** Care Programs, HE 22.116
National Summary of State Medicaid **Managed** Care Programs, Program Descriptions, HE 22.12/3

Management
ABM (Acquisition & Business **Management**) Online, D 201.44
Administration and **Management**, TD 1.15/6
Administration and **Management**, Current Literature, C 37.15
Administration and **Management**, Current Literature Compiled by Library Staff, TD 1.15/6
Administrative **Management** Course Program Topics, SBA 1.24
Advisor, Navy Civilian Manpower **Management**, D 204.9
Airport **Management** Series, C 31.137
All Points Bulletin, the Army Financial **Management** Newsletter, D 101.96
Annual **Management** Report of the Defense Supply Agency, D 7.1/13
Annual Report on In-House Energy **Management**, E 1.50/2
Annual Report on the **Management** Efficiency Pilot Program, VA 1.1/3
Annual Report, Federal Emergency **Management** Agency (by Region), FEM 1.1/2
Annual Report, Fishery Conservation and **Management** Act, C 55.330
Army **Management** Course (series), D 101.94
Army **Management** Engineering Training Activity: Course Catalog, D 101.94/3
BEM {Bureau of Executive **Management**} Pamphlets, CS 1.48/2
BNDD Personnel **Management** Series, J 24.16
Branch of Fishery **Management** Annual Report, I 49.53
Budget and **Management** Circulars, L 1.23
Bureau of Land **Management** 1:100,000-Scale Maps, I 53.11/4
Bureau of Land **Management** Maps, Surface and Minerals Management Status, Scale 1:100,000, I 53.11/4-2

Case **Management** Information Series, PM 1.41/2
Catalog **Management** Data, D 7.29
Center for Information **Management** and Automation: Calendar for Fiscal Year, PM 1.51
Civilian Manpower **Management**, Journal of Navy and Civilian Personnel **Management**, D 201.18
Coastal Zone **Management** Technical Assistance Documents, C 55.32/2
Community Environmental **Management** Series, HE 20.1117, HE 20.1810
Comprehensive Studies of Solid Waste **Management**, Annual Report, EP 1.11
Consolidated **Management** Data List, D 7.29/6
Course **Management** Plan and Program of Instruction (series), D 101.107/4
Cultural Resource **Management** Series, I 70.11/2
Cultural Resource **Management** Studies, I 29.86, I 70.11
Cultural Resources **Management** Bulletin, I 29.86/2
Current IPA Projects for Improved State and Local **Management**, CS 1.94
Current News Defense **Management** Edition, D 2.19/5, D 301.89/8, D 301.89/11
DEA Personnel **Management** Series, J 24.16
Decisions and Reports on Rulings of the Assistant Secretary of Labor for Labor-**Management** Relations Pursuant to Executive Order 11491, L 1.51/4, Y 3.F 31/21-3:10-2
Defense Acquisition **Management** Data System Code Translations, D 1.57/10
Defense **Management** Joint Course (series), D 101.94/2
Defense **Management** Journal, D 1.38/2
Defense Systems **Management** Review, D 1.53
Department of Transportation Budget Program: Analysis of Fiscal Year DOT Program by Policy and RD&D **Management** Objectives, DOT-OST (series), TD 1.34/2
Development and **Management** of Ambulatory Care Programs, HE 20.9109/2
Digest and Index of Published Decisions of the Assistant Secretary of Labor for Labor-**Management** Relations Pursuant to Executive Order 11491, As Amended, L 1.51/3
Directory of Telecommunications **Management**, Annual Report, PrEx 4.17
Emergency **Management**, FEM 1.16
Emergency **Management** Institute, Resident Training Programs, FEM 1.17/2
Emergency **Management** Institute, Schedule of Courses, FEM 1.17/2
Emergency **Management** of National Economy, D 1.27
Energy **Management** and Control Quarterly, VA 1.82
Energy **Management** in the Federal Government, E 1.50
Equal Employment Opportunity **Management** Directives/Bulletins, Y 3.Eq 2:18-5
Executive **Management** Bulletin (series), PrEx 2.3/3
Executive Manpower **Management** Technical Assistance Papers, EMMTAP, CS 1.85
Executive/**Management** Training Handbook, HE 22.8/20
Farm **Management** Reports, A 36.118
Farm-**Management** Office-Circulars, A 1.21
Federal Coal **Management** Report, I 1.96/4
Federal Energy **Management** Program Annual Reports, FE 1.16
Federal Financial **Management** Directory, GA 1.12/2
Federal Labor-**Management** Consultant, PM 1.13, CS 1.80
Federal **Management** Circulars (numbered), GS 1.4/3
Federal **Management** Improvement Conference, Proceedings, PrEx 2.19
Federal Property **Management** Regulations Amendments, GS 1.6/8-3
Federal Supply Catalog for Civil Agencies, Descriptive and **Management** Data List, D 7.9/2
Financial **Management** Capacity Sharing Program, HH 1.82
Financial **Management** Manual, P 1.12/9
Financial **Management** Profile: Department of Health and Human Services, GA 1.26

Financial **Management** Status Report and 5-year Plan, ED 1.1/5
Financial **Management** Systems Series, C 3.243
Fire **Management** Notes, A 13.32
Fishery Conservation and **Management** Act, Annual Report, C 55.330
Flood Plain **Management** Study, A 57.64/4
Forest Insect and Disease **Management** (series), A 13.93/3, A 13.106
Forest Insect and Disease **Management**/Evaluation Reports, A 13.93
Forest Insect and Disease **Management**/Survey Reports, A 13.93/2
Forest Inspection and Disease **Management** (series), A 13.93/3
Forest **Management** Notes, A 13.42/11
Forest **Management** Papers, A 13.42/12
Forest **Management** Program Annual Report (National Summary), A 13.152
Forest Pest **Management** Methods Applications Group: Reports (series), A 13.52/10-3
General **Management** Training Center, Calendar of Training Courses, Fiscal Year, CS 1.65/5
Habitat **Management** for {various Animals}, A 57.56
Hazardous Material Control and **Management**/Hazardous Materials Information System, D 212.16
Herd **Management** Area Plan (various locations), I 53.23/2
Higher Education Planning and **Management** Data, FS 5.253:53004, HE 5.253:53004
Highlights of Natural Resources **Management**, I 29.119
How Federal Agencies Develop Management Talent, **Management** Staff Development Series Reports, CS 1.56
Improved Manpower **Management** in Federal Government, Y 4.P 84/10:M 31/5
Index to **Management** Issuances, NAS 1.18/2
Indian Forest **Management**, I 20.61/3
Industrial College of the Armed Forces: Perspectives in Defense **Management**, D 5.16
Information Resources **Management** Handbook (series), GS 12.17
Information Resources **Management** Newsletter, GS 12.17/3
Information Resources **Management** Plan (series), TD 4.33/6
Institute for Medicaid **Management**: Publications, HE 22.112
Joint Financial **Management** Improvement Program, Annual Report Fiscal Year (date), GA 1.12
Journal for Medicaid **Management**, HE 22.109
Journal of Navy Civilian Manpower **Management**, D 204.9
Labor **Management** Case Finder, CS 1.41/4:711-2
Labor **Management** News, Pr 32.4820
Labor **Management** Relations, CS 1.41/4:711-1
Labor **Management** Relations Issues in State and Local Governments, CS 1.80/2
Labor-**Management** Cooperation Brief, L 1.85
Labor-**Management** Manpower Policy Committee, Publications, Pr 34.209
Labor-**Management** Reporting and Disclosures Act, As Amended, Regulations and Interpretative Bulletins, L 1.51/2
Lake Erie Wastewater **Management** Study Public Information Fact Sheet, D 103.63/2
Management, PM 1.11/2
Management Aids, SBA 1.32
Management Aids for Small Manufacturers, SBA 1.10
Management Analysis Series, CS 1.65/7, PM 1.49
Management and Productivity Improvement Report, VA 1.89
Management Bulletins: Bureau of the Budget, Pr 32.108, Pr 33.108, Pr 34.108, PrEx 2.3/2
Management Bulletins: Department of Agriculture, A 1.3/2
Management Data List: Air Force, D 7.29/2
Management Data List: Army, D 7.29/3
Management Data List: Marine Corps, D 7.29/5
Management Data List: Navy, D 7.29/4
Management Data Series, P 1.46
Management Design and Development Technical Bulletins, HH 1.96
Management Experience Notes, FW 3.10
Management Highlights Releases, I 1.92
Management Improvement, A 1.74
Management Improvement Program, Plowback, Improvements Reports, D 101.63

Management Improvement Series, T 1.42
Management Information on ERL's Scientific and Technical Publications, C 52.21/5
Management Notes, Pr 33.114
Management of the United States Government, Fiscal Year (date), PrEx 2.8/9
Management Plan & Environmental Assessment, I 53.59/2
Management Plans (series), C 55.32/6
Management Procedure Notices, L 22.24
Management Reports, GS 1.23
Management Research Summary (series), SBA 1.12/2
Management Sciences Institute, Philadelphia Region: Bulletins, CS 1.3/2
Management Series, I 70.11/3, I 29.106
Management Service Notices, FAA 1.19
Management Statistics for United States Courts, Ju 10.14
Manual of Regulations and Procedures for Radio Frequency Management, PrEx 18.8:R 11
Maritime Labor, Management Affiliations Guide, TD 11.8/2
Medicaid Management Reports, HE 22.109/2, HE 22.410, HE 22.410/2
Midwest Region: Research/Resources Management Reports, I 29.105/2
Military Traffic Management Bulletins, D 101.3/2
Military Traffic Management Command Publications, D 101.129/3
Minerals Management Quad (maps), I 53.11/6
Model Cities Management Series, Bulletins, HH 1.42
Monthly Management Report, TD 4.53
National Emergency Readiness of Federal Personnel Management, CS 1.41/4:910-1
National Security Management, D 5.9/3, D 5.410
Navy Management Review, D 201.14
NCHSR Research Management (series), HE 20.6512/4
Office of Management and Systems Annual Performace Report, HE 20.4001/3
Outer Continental Shelf Research Management Advisory Board: Annual Report, I 1.99
Pamphlets Personnel Management Office, PM 1.10
Park Science, Resource Management Bulletin, I 29.3/4
Parts Specification Management for Reliability, D 4.9
Personnel Management Publications, I 1.73/2
Personnel Management Reform, Progress in State and Local Governments, PM 1.11/3
Personnel Management Series, CS 1.54, PM 1.28
Personnel Management Training Center: Course Catalog, CS 1.65/10
Personnel Management Training Division I, PM 1.28/2
Personnel Management Training Units, L 1.38
Perspectives in Defense Management, D 5.16
Perspectives on Medicaid and Medicare Management, HE 22.411
Posters Federal Emergency Management Agency, FEM 1.21
Posters Financial Management Service, T 63.122
Posters Minerals Management Service, I 72.16
Posters Office of Attorney Personnel Management, J 33.9
Posters Office of Management and Budget, PrEx 2.32
Posters Office of Personnel Management, PM 1.35
Presenters and Festivals Jazz Management, Jazz Special Projects, Music, Application Guidelines, NF 2.8/2-9
President's Advisory Council on Management Improvement, Pr 37.8:M 31
Procurement and Contracts Management, DOE/ PR- (series), E 1.49
Program Management Series, CS 1.65/8
Progress in Management Improvement, T 1.43
Project Management Series, PM 1.41
PROMIS (Prosecutor's Management Information System) Research Project Publications, J 1.52
Public Housing Management Improvement Program: Technical Memorandums, HH 1.63
Public Management Sources, PrEx 2.9
Public Support for Coastal Zone Management Programs Implementation of the Coastal Zone Management Act of 1972, C 55.32/ 5

Public Support for Coastal Zone Management Programs Implementation of the Coastal Zone Management Act of 1972, C 55.32/ 5
Quarterly Debt Management Report, HE 20.9311
Records Management Handbooks, GS 4.6/2
Regulations, Rules and Instructions Federal Emergency Management Agency, FEM 1.6
Regulations, Rules and Instructions Office of Information Resources Management, GS 12.15
Reintroduction and Management of Wolves in Yellowstone National Park and the Central Idaho Wilderness Area, Y 3.W 83
Report on the Significant Actions of the Office of Personnel Management, MS 1.16
Report to the Congress on Coastal Zone Management, C 55.32
Research Projects Federal Emergency Management Agency, FEM 1.22
Research/Resources Management Reports, I 29.105
Resource Management Monographs, D 1.44
Resource Management Quarterly Information Summary, C 55.9/3
Resource Management, D 101.89
Resources Management Plan Annual Update, I 53.50
Rulings on Requests for Review of the Assistant Secretary of Labor for Labor-Management Relations Pursuant to Executive Order 11491, As Amended, L 1.51/6
Safety Management Information, EP 1.7/3
Safety Management Series, L 35.19
Safety, Fire Prevention, and Occupational Health Management, by Objectives Review, D 301.99
Scientific Inventory Management Series, GS 2.6/4
Seafaring Guide, and Directory of Labor-Management Affiliations, C 39.206/3:Se 1
Secretary's Semiannual Management Report, U.S. Department of Labor, L 1.1/3
Secretary's Semiannual Management Report to the Congress, S 1.1/9
Selected Bibliography of Range Management Literature, A 13.30/9
Significant Cases, Federal Employee and Labor-Management Relations, PM 1.63
Small Business Administration Publications, Classification of Management Publications, SBA 1.18/3
Small Business Management Series, SBA 1.12
Solid Waste Management Monthly Abstracts Bulletin, EP 1.17/3
Solid Waste Management Series, EP 1.17
Solid Waste Management Training Bulletin of Courses, EP 3.12
Solid Waste Management, Available Information Materials, EP 1.17:58.25
SSA Management Newsletter for Supervisors and Management Personnel, HE 3.68/2
Standardization and Data Management Newsletter, D 1.88
State Coastal Zone Management Activities, C 55.32/3
Statewide Transportation Planning and Management Series, TD 2.57
Studies in Cultural Resource Management, A 13.101/2
Studies on Administrative Management in Government of U.S., Y 3.P 92/3:7
Summary of Operations, Labor-Management Reporting and Disclosure Act, L 1.51
Summary of Safety Management Audits, TD 2.66
Supervision and Management Series, FS 1.12
Supplemental Digest and Index of Published Decisions of the Assistant Secretary of Labor for Labor-Management Relations Pursuant to Executive Order 11491, Y 3.F 31/21-3:10
Supply and Mess Management, W 3.50/15
Surface Management Quadrangles (maps), I 53.11/ 5
Telephone Directory Office of Personnel Management, PM 1.31
USIA Strategic Information Resources Management (IRM) Plan, IA 1.33
Wastewater Management Reports, D 103.60
Water Management and Conservation Program, I 27.78

Water Quality Management Accomplishments, Compendiums, EP 1.75
Water Quality Management Bulletin, EP 1.71
Water Quality Management Five Year Strategy FY-Baseline, EP 1.91
Water Quality Management Guidance, EP 1.8/8
Wildlife Management Series Leaflets, I 49.13/2
Wildlife Research and Management Leaflets, A 5.11
Woodland Management Plan, Agreements and Farm Codes, A 57.37
Work and Management Improvement, A 57.41
Manager
    Forest-Gram South, Dispatch of Current Technical Information for Direct Use by Practicing Forest Resource Manager in the South, A 13.89
    Program Manager, D 1.60
    Quarterly Report of the General Sales Manager, A 1.117, A 67.43
Managers
    Crop Insurance Manager's Bulletins, A 112.20
    Federal Managers' Financial Integrity Act, Secretary's Annual Statement and Report to the President and the Congress, I 1.96/6
    Manager's Calendar, HE 3.81
    Proceedings Board of Managers, NH 1.6
Managing
    Managing Clinical Costs, VA 1.84
    Managing Federal Information Resources, PrEx 2.25
    Managing the Nation's Public Lands, I 53.12/2
    Managing Your Woodland, How to Do It Guides, A 13.36/3
    Starting and Managing Series, SBA 1.15
Manchurian
    Manchurian Soy Bean Trade, C 18.197
Mandrid
    Mandrid, Columbian Historical Exposition, S 6.7
Maneuver
    Maneuver Memorandum, W 99.17/19
    Seventy-Fifth USA Maneuver Area Command, Annual Report and Historical Supplement, D 101.1/8
Manganese
    Manganese, I 28.54
    Manganese in (year), I 28.54/2
    Mineral Industry Surveys, Manganese, I 19.158
Manhattan
    Annual Report Manhattan Plant Materials Center, A 57.54/3
Man-Hour
    Indexes of Output Per Man-Hour for the Private Economy, L 2.89/2
    Indexes of Output Per Man-Hour, Hourly Compensation, and Unit Labor Costs in the Private Sector of the Economy and the Nonfarm Sector, L 2.2:Ou 8/8
    Indexes of Output Per Man-Hour, Selected Industries, L 2.89
Manila
    Manila Custom-House General Orders, W 49.10/7
Man-Induced
    Report to Congress on Ocean Dumping and Other Man-Induced Changes to Ocean Ecosystems, C 55.31
Man-made
    U.S. Production, Imports and Import/Production Ratios for Cotton, Wool and Man-made Textiles and Apparel, C 61.26
Manned
    Manned Space Flight Resources Summary, Budget Estimates, NAS 1.54
    Manned Undersea Science and Technology Fiscal Year Reports, C 55.29
Manner
    Circular Showing Manner of Proceeding to Obtain Title to Land, I 21.12
Manpower
    Advisor, Navy Civilian Manpower Management, D 204.9
    American Science Manpower, NS 1.14/2
    Area Redevelopment Manpower Reports, L 7.66/2
    Assessments Completed and Referrals to Manpower Agencies by Welfare Agencies Under Work Incentive Program for AFDC Recipients, HE 17.619
    Civilian Manpower Management, Journal of Navy and Civilian Personnel Management, D 201.18
    Civilian Manpower Statistics, D 1.61/2
    Cooperative Area Manpower Planning System, Interagency Cooperative Issuances, L 1.64

Defense **Manpower** Commission Staff Studies and Supporting Papers, Y 3.D 36:9

Defense **Manpower** Policy (series), Pr 34.208

Defense **Manpower** Policy Statement, Pr 33.1010

Demonstration Notes, Experimental and Demonstration **Manpower** Programs, L 1.45/2

Education and Training, Annual Report of Secretary of Health, Education and Welfare to Congress on Training Activities Under **Manpower** Development and Training Act, FS 1.26, HE 1.26

Executive **Manpower** Management Technical Assistance Papers, EMMTAP, CS 1.85

Field Letter, National Committee for Conservation of **Manpower** in War Industries, L 1.29

Health **Manpower** Clearinghouse Series, HE 20.3114/3

Health **Manpower** Data Series, HE 20.3114/2

Health **Manpower** Source Book, FS 2.2:M 31, HE 20.2:M 31, HE 20.3109

Health **Manpower** Statistics, D 1.62/2

Impact on Public Assistance Caseloads of (a) Training Programs under **Manpower** Development and Training Act and Read Redevelopment Act, and (b) Public Assist. Work and Training Programs, FS 14.219, FS 17.409, FS 17.635

Improved **Manpower** Management in Federal Government, Y 4.P 84/10:M 31/5

Index to Publications of the **Manpower** Administration, L 1.34:M 31/4

Industry **Manpower** Surveys, L 7.49, L 34.10

Journal of Navy Civilian **Manpower** Management, D 204.9

Labor-Management **Manpower** Policy Committee, Publications, Pr 34.209

Listing of Eligible Labor Surplus Areas Under Defense **Manpower** Policy No. 4a and Executive Order 10582, L 37.17

Manpower, L 1.39/9

Manpower Administration Notice, L 1.22/4

Manpower Administration Orders, L 1.22/3

Manpower and Automation Research, L 1.39/5

Manpower Daily Reporter, L 1.39/7

Manpower Development and Training, Projects Approved, FS 5.76

Manpower Development Program Highlights, L 7.66

Manpower Development Research Program, Report, D 1.50

Manpower Evaluation Reports, L 1.39/2

Manpower Program Evaluation, L 1.45

Manpower Report of the President and Report on **Manpower** Requirements, Resources, Utilization, and Training by the U.S. Department of Labor, L 1.42/2

Manpower Report of the President and Report on **Manpower** Requirements, Resources, Utilization, and Training by the U.S. Department of Labor, L 1.42/2

Manpower Reports: Bureau of Labor Statistics, L 2.57

Manpower Reports: **Manpower** Administration, L 1.39

Manpower Requirements Report, D 1.52

Manpower Research Bulletins, L 1.3/4

Manpower Research Projects, Sponsored by the **Manpower** Administration through (date), L 1.39/6

Manpower Research Report, D 1.50/2

Manpower Review, Pr 32.5209

Manpower Technical Exchange, L 1.39/10

Manpower Training Facts, L 1.40/2

Manpower Utilization-Job Security in Longshore Industry {by port}, L 1.50

Manpower/Automation Research Monographs, L 1.39/3

Manpower/Automation Research Notices, L 1.39/4

Manual of Navy Enlisted **Manpower** and Personnel Classifications and Occupational Standards Section II Navy Enlisted Classifications, D 208.6/3-4

Maritime **Manpower** Report: Sea Faring, Longshore, and Shipyard Employment as of (date), C 39.202:Se 1/2, C 39.235

Mental Health **Manpower**, Current Statistical and Activities Reports, FS 2.54/3

Military **Manpower** Statistics, D 1.61

Monthly Release {of} Federal Civilian **Manpower** Statistics, CS 1.55/2

National Emergency Standby Regulations and Instructions Personnel and **Manpower**, CS 1.41/4:990-3

OMAT-O-GRAM, for Staff Members of Office of **Manpower**, Automation, and Training, L 1.41

Register of Projects Approved Under **Manpower** Development and Training Act, L 1.53

Reserve **Manpower** Statistics, D 1.61/7

Rural **Manpower** Developments, L 1.63

Scientific **Manpower** Bulletins, NS 1.3/2

Scientific **Manpower** Series, FS 5.47

Scientific **Manpower**, Significant Developments, Views and Statistics, NS 1.14

Selected **Manpower** Statistics, D 1.61/4

Seminar of **Manpower** Policy and Program, L 1.39/8

Statistics on **Manpower**, Supplement to **Manpower** Report of the President, L 1.42/2-2

Training and **Manpower** Development Activities Supported by the Administration on Aging Under Title IV-A of the Older Americans Act of 1965, As Amended, Descriptions of Funded Projects, HE 23.3002:T 68/2

Volunteer **Manpower** Booklet, VM (series), FCD 1.10

Worldwide **Manpower** Distribution by Geographical Area, D 1.61/3

Manprint

Manprint, D 101.3/6-2

Manprint Bulletin, D 101.3/6

Manual

Digest of Procedure **Manual** Materials, Y 3.R 31:15

Inspection Operations **Manual** Transmittal Notices, HE 20.4008/2

Instruction **Manual**, Part 1, Source Records and Control Specifications, HE 20.6209/11

Instruction **Manual** Part 2d, NCHS Procedures for Mortality Medical Data System File Preparation and Maintenance, HE 20.6208/4-6

Instruction **Manual** Part 2h, Dictionary of Valid Terms for the Mortality Medical Indexing, Classification, and Retrieval System (MICAR), HE 20.6208/4-8

Instruction **Manual** Part 12, Computer Edits for Natality Data, HE 20.6208/15

Internal Revenue **Manual**, T 22.2/15-3

Manual of Information: Philippine Islands Civil Service Bureau, W 49.5/6

Manual of Instructions, J 1.14/6

Manual Series, D 203.24:M

NIH Administrative **Manual**, HE 20.3008/3

OHD, Grants Administration **Manual**, TN-(series), HE 1.709

OPA **Manual** News Letters, Pr 32.4248

Ordnance **Manual**, W 34.7/1

Ordnance Supply **Manual**, W 34.7/2

Organization and Policy **Manual** Letters, CS 1.7/3

Outdoor Recreation Grants-In-Aid **Manual**, I 66.8

Peace Corps Program and Training Journal **Manual** Series, AA 4.8/2

PHA Grants Administration **Manual**, HE 20.8/2

Post Entitlement **Manual**, HE 3.6/6

Postal Contracting **Manual**, P 1.12/6

Postal **Manual** {issues}, P 1.12/4

Postal **Manual** {simplified Edition}, P 1.12/3

Postal **Manual**, P 1.12/2

Postal Operations **Manual**, P 1.12/8

Postal Service **Manual**, P 1.12/5

Process Design **Manual** for {various subjects} (series), EP 7.8/2

Program and Training Journal **Manual** Series, AA 4.8/2

Program Operations **Manual** System, HE 3.6/5

Programmer's **Manual** (series), D 101.107/7

Public Use Data Tape Documentation Interviewer's **Manual** National Interview Survey, HE 20.6226/8

Public Use Data Tape Documentation Medical Coding **Manual** and Short Index, HE 20.6226/9

Quality Evaluation Program **Manual**, D 7.6/4-3

Quartermaster Corps **Manual**, D 106.6/2

Registrants Processing **Manual**, Y 3.Se 4:10-2 R 26

Selective Service **Manual**, Pr 32./5280

Standard Industrial Classification **Manual**, PrEx 2.6/2:In 27

State Buy-in **Manual**, HE 22.8/11

State Medicaid **Manual**, HE 22.26, HE 22.8/10

Steamboat Inspector's **Manual**, T 38.6, C 15.6

Student **Manual**, SM- (series), D 14.8/2

Subject Cataloging **Manual**, Shelf Listing, LC 26.8/5

Subject Cataloging **Manual**: Subject Headings, LC 26.8/4

Telecommunications Engineering and Construction **Manual**, A 68.6/4

Telephone Engineering and Construction **Manual**, A 68.6/4

Telephone Operators' **Manual**, A 68.6/3

Terminal Forecasting Reference **Manual** (by Terminals), C 30.52

Training **Manual** Agency for International Development, S 18.8/2

Training **Manual** Department of Health, Education, and Welfare, FS 1.10, HE 1.10

Training **Manual** Department of War, W 1.23

Training **Manual** Federal Security Agency, FS 1.10

Training **Manual** International Cooperation Administration, S 17.6/4

Training **Manual** United States Army, W 3.39/3

Transmittal Letters {for Indian Service **Manual**}, I 20.35

Transmittal Letters, **Manual** of Regulations and Procedure, FW 1.14

U.S. Alcohol Epidemiologic Data Reference **Manual**, HE 20.8308/3

U.S. Government Printing Office Style **Manual**, GP 1.23/4:St 9

Union Wage Studies **Manual** of Procedures, L 2.55

United States Government **Manual**, GS 4.109, AE 2.108/2

United States Government Organization **Manual**, GS 4.109

United States Standard Facilities Flight Check **Manual**, FAA 5.9

United States Standard Flight Inspection **Manual**, C 31.163/3

Urban Renewal **Manual**, Policies and Requirements for Local Public Agencies, HH 7.9

User **Manual** Series, HE 23.1210/4

Wage Operations **Manual** of Procedures, L 2.54

Manuals

HCFA's Laws, Regulations, **Manuals**, HE 22.8/22

Homestudy Courses; **Manuals**, HE 20.7021/3-2

Manuals and Handbooks (miscellaneous), I 53.7/2

Manuals, AFM-(series), D 301.7

Manuals, AFSCM-(series), D 301.45/14

Manuals, DIAM-(series), D 5.208/3

Manuals, EM-(series), D 103.6/3

Manuals: Air Force Systems Command, D 301.45/14

Manuals: Air National Guard, D 301.23

Manuals: Air Weather Service, D 301.27

Manuals: Armed Forces Institute, D 1.10

Manuals: Bureau of Naval Personnel, D 208.6/2

Manuals: Bureau of Ships, D 211.7

Manuals: Civil Aeronautics Administration, C 31.107

Manuals: Civil Aeronautics Authority, CA 1.10

Manuals: Civil Air Patrol, D 301.7/4

Manuals: Defense Contract Audit Agency, D 1.46/2

Manuals: Defense Logistics Service Center, D 7.6/10

Manuals: Defense Supply Agency, D 7.6/3, D 7.6/8

Manuals: Department of Health, Education, and Welfare, FS 1.6/2

Manuals: Department of the Air Force, D 301.7

Manuals: Federal Civil Defense Administration, FCD 1.6/6

Manuals: Federal Security Agency, FS 1.6/2

Manuals: Fleet Marine Force, D 214.9/4

Manuals: General Reference and Bibliography Division, LC 2.8

Manuals: Marine Corps, D 214.9

Manuals: Military Air Transportation Service, D 301.7/6

Manuals: National Guard Bureau, D 112.7

Manuals: Ordnance Corps, D 105.6/2

Manuals: Quartermaster Corps, D 106.6/2

Manuals: Quartermaster's Department, W 39.9/2

Manuals: ROTC, D 101.48

Manuals: Volunteer Probation Programs, FS 17.8/2, HE 17.8/2

OEO **Manuals**, PrEx 10.8/5

Ordnance Corps **Manuals**, D 105.6/2

P.D.C. **Manuals**, CS 1.40

Pocket **Manuals** PM (series), FCD 1.6/8, Pr 34.761/5, PrEx 4.12/6, D 13.8/2

Procedure **Manuals**, Table of Contents by Subject, Y 3.R 31:27

Professional **Manuals**, D 119
Rate Training **Manuals**, D 207.208/2
ROTC **Manuals**, D 101.48
Safety **Manuals**, I 69.8/2, L 38.8/2
Self-Study Course 3014-G, Waterborne Disease
    Control **Manuals**, HE 20.7021/4-2
Services Research Monograph Series, National
    Polydrug Collaborative Project,
    Treatment **Manuals**, HE 20.8216/2
Ship Construction **Manuals**, N 24.37, T 47.37
State and Private Forestry: Handbooks, **Manuals**,
    Guides, A 13.110/8
Status of CAA Releases, **Manuals**, and Regula-
    tions, C 31.151
Status of Civil Air Regulations and Civil
    Aeronautics **Manuals**, FAA 1.18
Technical Handbook for Facilities Engineering and
    Construction **Manuals**, HE 1.108/2
Technical **Manuals**, D 214.9/3
Therapy **Manuals** for Drug Addiction, HE
    20.3958/2
Training **Manuals**, HE 1.10, S 18.8/2
U.S. Army Educational **Manuals**, W 3.47
U.S. Army Training **Manuals** Numbered, W 3.39/1
U.S. Army Training **Manuals**, W 3.39
VISTA **Manuals**, PrEx 10.8/2
Manufacture
    Instrument **Manufacture** {abstracts}, C 41.77/2
    Manufacture and Sale of Farm Equipment, C 3.55
    Manufacture of Tin and Terne Plates in United
        States (year), T 35.5
    Quarterly Report of **Manufacture** and Sales of
        Snuff, Smoking, and Chewing Tobacco, A
        88.34/11
    Scientific Reports of Higher Schools Machine
        Construction and Instruments
        Manufacture, C 41.65/8
    United States General Imports of Wool **Manufac-
        ture** Except Floor Coverings, Quantity
        Totals in Terms of Equivalent Square
        Yards in Country of Origin by
        Commodity Grouping Arrangement, TQ-
        2203, C 3.164/2-6
    United States General Imports of Wool **Manufac-
        ture** Except for Floor Coverings, Country
        of Origin by Wool Grouping, TQ- 2202,
        C 3.164/2-5
    United States Imports for Immediate Consumption,
        Entries into Bonded Manufacturing
        Warehouse for **Manufacture** and
        Exports, Entries into Bonded Storage
        Warehouse and Withdrawals from
        Bonded **Storage** Warehouse for
        Consumption of Petroleum and Its
        Products
Manufactured
    Annual Survey of Manufacturers, Origin of
        Manufactured Products, C 3.24/9-10
    Bulletins, **Manufactured** (by States), C 3.14/3
    Cottonseed Products **Manufactured** and on Hand
        at Oil Mills by States, C 3.125
    Manufactured Abrasives, I 28.171
    Mineral Industry Surveys, **Manufactured**
        Abrasives, I 19.146
    Production of **Manufactured** Dairy Products, A
        88.14/10
    U.S. Export and Import Trade in Leaf and
        Manufactured Tobacco, C 18.152/2
Manufacturer
    Parts **Manufacturer** Approvals, TD 4.2/11
Manufacturers
    Alphabetical Listing, Register or Planned
        Mobilization Producers, **Manufacturers**
        of War Material Registered Under
        Production Allocation Program, D 7.11
    Announcements, Census of **Manufacturers**, C 3.24/
        10
    Annual Survey of **Manufacturers**, Origin of
        Manufactured Products, C 3.24/9-10
    Annual Survey of **Manufacturers**, Value of
        Manufacturers' Inventories, C 3.24/9-11
    Automobile **Manufacturers** Measurements, FMC
        1.12
    Biennial Census of **Manufacturers**, C 3.24
    Bulletins, **Manufacturers** (by Industries), C 3.28/
        15
    Bulletins, **Manufacturers** (by States), C 3.28/14
    Census of Manufactures; **Manufacturers'**
        Inventories, C 56.244/8
    Confectionery **Manufacturers'** Sales and
        Distribution, C 41.19, C 57.13
    Federal Supply Code for **Manufacturers**, D 7.6/2:4
    H 7 **Manufacturers** Part and Drawing Numbering
        Systems, D 7.6/2:7

Industry Survey, **Manufacturers'** Sales,
    Inventories, New and Unfilled Orders, C
    43.9
Industry Survey: **Manufacturers'** Inventories,
    Shipments, Incoming Business {and}
    Unfilled Orders, C 18.224
Leather **Manufacturers** Advertising Circulars, C
    18.111
Leather **Manufacturers** Rest in Foreign Markets, C
    18.112
List of **Manufacturers** and Jobbers of Fruit and
    Vegetable Containers, A 36.60
Management Aids for Small **Manufacturers**, SBA
    1.10
Manufacturers (by Industries), C 3.940-18
Manufacturers (Miscellaneous), C 3.37/27
Manufacturers Division, Special Bulletins, C 3.7
Manufacturers Part and Drawing Numbering
    Systems, D 7.6/2:7
Manufacturers Sales and Collections on Accounts
    Receivable, C 18.195
Manufacturers' Shipments, Inventories and
    Orders, C 56.245, C 3.231
Manufacturers, Minerals Industries, EC (series), C
    3.202/16
Motor Vehicle Safety Defect Recall Campaigns
    Reported to the Department of
    Transportation by Domestic and Foreign
    Vehicle **Manufacturers**, TD 2.209
NATO Supply Code for **Manufacturers**, D 7.6/2-
    2:4-3/date
Publication Announcement and Order Form,
    Annual Survey of **Manufacturers**, C
    3.24/9-5
Special Bulletins **Manufacturers** Division, C 3.7
Stocks of Leaf Tobacco Owned by Dealers and
    Manufacturers, A 80.124
Sulphuric Acid, Production, Stocks, etc. Reported
    by Fertilizer **Manufacturers**, C 3.110
Superphosphates, Production, etc., Reported by
    Fertilizer **Manufacturers**, C 3.111
Technical Aids for Small **Manufacturers**, SBA 1.11
United States General Imports of Cotton
    Manufacturers, C 3.164/2-2
United States General Imports of Cotton
    Manufacturers: Country of Origin by
    Geneva Agreement Category, C
    56.210:130, C 3.164:130
United States General Imports of Cotton
    Manufacturers; TQ-2190, C 3.164/2-8
Annual Survey of Manufacturers, Value of
    Manufacturers' Inventories, C 3.24/9-
    11
Annual Survey of **Manufactures** , C 3.24/9, C 3.24/
    9-2, C 3.24/9-3
Annual Survey of **Manufactures** Miscellaneous
    Publications, C 3.24/9-4
Annual Survey of **Manufactures**: Annual Volumes,
    C 56.221/2
Census of **Manufactures**, C 3.24/11-/15
Census of **Manufactures**; Area Series, C 56.244/7
Census of **Manufactures**; Final Volumes, C 56.244
Census of **Manufactures**; General Publications, C
    56.244/2
Census of **Manufactures**; Industry Series MC
    (nos.), C 56.244/6
Census of **Manufactures**; Maps, C 3.24/7
Census of **Manufactures**; Preliminary Reports, C
    3.24/8
Census of **Manufactures**; **Special Reports** Bulletin
    MC (series), C 3.24/13
Census of **Manufactures**; Subject Bulletin Mc
    (Series), C 3.24/12
Census of **Manufactures**; Supplementary Reports,
    C 56.244/3
Company Statistics Bulletins, Census of Business,
    Manufactures and Mineral Industries, C
    3.222
Illuminating Glassware **Manufactures**, Sales and
    Credits, C 3.146
Manufactures and Miscellaneous and Forwarder
    Traffic, IC 1.23/14:SS-6
Manufactures, 1939: State Series, C 3.940-19
Manufactures, Industry Series, C 3.37/26
Manufactures, State Series, C 3.37/28
United States General Imports of Textile
    Manufactures, Except Cotton and Wool,
    Grouping by Country of Origin and
    Schedule a Commodity by Country of
    Origin, TQ-2501, C 3.164/2-7
Wool **Manufactures**, C 3.52/4
Manufacturing
    Analysis of Production, Wages and Employment in
        Manufacturing Industries, Y 3.C 78:7

Capacity Utilization in **Manufacturing**, Quarterly
    Averages, Seasonally Adjusted, FR 1.55
Capacity Utilization: **Manufacturing** and
    Materials, FR 1.55/2
Current Industrial Reports, **Manufacturing**
    Profiles, C 3.158/4
Current Industrial Reports: **Manufacturing**
    Technology, C 3.158/3
Foreign Direct Investment in the United States,
    Establishment Data For **Manufacturing**,
    C 59.20/3
Indexes of Production Worker Employment in
    Manufacturing Industries by
    Metropolitan Area, L 2.24
Industry Wage Survey: Cigarette **Manufacturing**,
    L 2.3/26
Injury-frequency Rates for Selected **Manufacturing**
    Industries, L 2.77
International Comparisons of Hourly Compensa-
    tion Costs for Production Workers in
    Manufacturing, L 2.130
International Comparisons of **Manufacturing**
    Productivity and Labor Costs Trends, L
    2.120/2-6
Labor Turnover in **Manufacturing**, L 2.42/3
Location of **Manufacturing** Plants by Industry,
    County, and Employment Size, C 3.24/14
Lumber **Manufacturing**, Wood Using and Allied
    Associations, A 13.77
Manufacturing, C 51.17/7
Manufacturing: Analytical Report Series, C 3.24/
    9-12
Manufacturing Energy Consumption Survey:
    Changes in Energy Efficiency, E 3.54/2
Manufacturing Energy Consumption Survey:
    Consumption of Energy, E 3.54
Manufacturing Energy Consumption Survey: Fuel
    Switching, E 3.54/3
Manufacturing Industry, Technical Document, EP
    4.20
Manufacturing Technology, C 51.9/33
Mining and **Manufacturing** Industries in the
    American Republics, TC 1.21
Occupational Employment in **Manufacturing**
    Industries, L 2.3/16
Prices Received by Farmers for **Manufacturing**
    Grade Milk in Minnesota and
    Wisconsin, A 92.16/3
Quarterly Financial Report for **Manufacturing**,
    Mining, and Trade Corporations, FT
    1.18, C 3.267
Quarterly Financial Report, United States
    Manufacturing Corporations, FT 1.18
Report of Federal Trade Commission on Rates of
    Return (after taxes) for Identical
    Companies in Selected **Manufacturing**
    Industries, FT 1.21
Reports Control Symbol Darcom **Manufacturing**
    Technology, RCS DRCMT-(series), D
    101.110
Solar Collector **Manufacturing** Activity and
    Applications in the Residential Sector, E
    3.19
Solar Collector **Manufacturing** Activity, E 3.19/2
Summary of **Manufacturing** Earnings Series, L 2.90
United States Imports for Immediate Consumption,
    Entries into Bonded **Manufacturing**
    Warehouse for Manufacture and Exports,
    Entries into Bonded Storage Warehouse
    and Withdrawals from Bonded Storage
    Warehouse for Consumption of
    Petroleum and Its Products, C 3.164:576
Update (Electronics **Manufacturing** Productivity
    Facility), D 201.36
Wage Developments in **Manufacturing**, Summary
    Release, L 2.44/2
Manuscript
    Manuscript Reports, I 49.57
    Manuscript Reports Issued by Biological
        Laboratory, Auke Bay, Alaska, I 49.57
    Museum **Manuscript** Register Series, D 214.17
    National Union Catalog of **Manuscript**
        Collections, LC 9.8
    News from the Center {for the Coordination of
        Foreign **Manuscript** Copying}, LC 1.33
    Registers of Papers in the **Manuscript** Division of
        the Library of Congress, LC 4.10
    Technical Instruction Book **Manuscript**, TD 4.32/
        13
Manuscripts
    Manuscripts Approved by Divisions for
        Publication, A 77.21
    Technical **Manuscripts**, D 103.53/2

Map
  Army **Map** Sevice Bulletins, W 7.33/4
  Circum-Pacific (CP) **Map** Series, I 19.91/2
  Color Image **Map**, I 19.81/3
  County **Map** Series, I 19.108
  GE-70 **Map** Series, C 3.62/8
  Geologic **Map** Index of (various States), I 19.41/8
  Historical Weather **Map**, Northern Hemisphere, W 108.30
  Index **Map** of Quadrangles, W 31.9/2
  Index to Topographic and Other **Map** Coverage (series), I 19.41/6-3
  Map and Chart Series, FS 2.72
  Map Book of Major Military Installations, D 1.58
  Map of Alluvial Valley of Mississippi River, Quadrangles, W 31.9
  Map of District Infected with Splenetic Fever, A 4.6
  Map Series, S 1.33
  Maps and **Map** Folders, I 53.11
  OCS **Map** Series, I 72.12/4
  Publications Army **Map** Service, D 103.20
  SE Asia Briefing **Map**, Series 5213, D 5.335
  State **Map** Series Planimetric, I 19.102
  State **Map** Series Shaded Relief, I 19.104
  State **Map** Series Topographic, I 19.103
  Topographic **Map** of the United States, I 19.12
MAPAD
  MAPAD System, D 1.7/2
Mapping
  Defense **Mapping** Agency Public Sale Nautical Charts and Publications, C 55.440
  Index to Geologic **Mapping** in United States (by State) Maps, I 19.37
  Index to Geologic **Mapping** of the United States, I 19.86
  Index to Intermediate Scale **Mapping**, I 19.96
  Index to Orthophotoquad **Mapping**, I 19.97
  Index to USGS/DMA 1:50,000-Scale, 15 Minute Quadrangle **Mapping**, I 19.97/2
  LandView II, **Mapping** of Selected EPA-Regulated Sites, TIGER/Line and Census of Population and Housing, EP 1.104/4
  National **Mapping** Program (series), I 19.80
  Topographic **Mapping**, Status and Progress of Operations, I 19.95
Mapping Products
  Bathymetric **Mapping Products** (Catalog) 5, United States Bathymetric and Fishing Maps, C 55.418:5
Maps
  Air Navigation **Maps**, W 87.22/2
  Airborne Anomaly Location **Maps**, Y 3.At 7:31
  Airway **Maps**, C 23.10
  Antarctic Research Program **Maps**, I 19.25/8
  Area Outline **Maps** Series 1105, D 5.325-D 5.325/2
  ASCS Aerial Photography Status **Maps**, A 82.84:Ae 8
  Base **Maps** by States, I 19.27
  Boaters **Maps** (series), D 103.49/2
  Bureau of Land Management 1:100,000-Scale **Maps**, I 53.11/4
  Bureau of Land Management **Maps**, Surface and Minerals Management Status, Scale 1:100,000, I 53.11/4-2
  Catalog of **Maps**, Charts, and Related Products, Part 2, Hydrographic Products, D 5.351/2
  Catalog of Published State **Maps**, I 19.14/6
  Catalog of Topographic and Other Published **Maps** (by State), I 19.41/6-2
  Census of Manufactures; **Maps**, C 3.24/7
  Climatic **Maps** of United States, C 52.11
  Cooperative State-Federal Brucellosis Eradication Program; Charts and **Maps**, A 77.212/6-2
  County Block **Maps**, C 3.62/9
  County Subdivision **Maps**, C 3.62/6
  Daily Synoptic Series, Historical Weather **Maps**, C 30.27, C 30.38, C 30.39, C 30.40, C 30.41, C 30.42
  Daily Weather **Maps**, C 55.195
  Daily Weather **Maps**, Weekly Series, C 55.213
  Defense Mapping Agency Catalog of **Maps**, Charts, and Related Products, D 5.351
  Defense Mapping Agency Catalog of **Maps**, Charts, and Related Products, Semi-Annual Bulletin Digest, Part 2, Hydrographic Products, D 5.351/2-3
  Educational Series Federal Board of Surveys and **Maps**, Y 3.Su 7:8
  Foreign Agricultural Situation, **Maps** and Charts, A 67.24
  GE-50 United States **Maps**, C 3.62/4

Geophysical Investigations **Maps**, I 19.25/2, I 19.87
Historical Base **Maps** (series), I 29.79/4
Index **Maps**, Tidal Bench Marks, C 4.32/2
Index of Topographic Quadrangle **Maps** of Alluvial Valley of Lower Mississippi River, D 103.308/2
Index to Land Use and Land Cover **Maps** and Digital Data, I 19.97/3
Japan Road **Maps**, Series L302, D 5.340
Korea Road **Maps**, Series L351, D 5.341
Land Use and Land Cover and Associated **Maps**, I 19.112
List of Books, Pamphlets, and **Maps** Received, New Series, S 8.7
List of Geological Survey Geologic and Water-Supply Reports and **Maps** for (various States), I 19.41/7
List of Rural Delivery County **Maps**, P 11.7
Lists of **Maps**, Townsite, and Farm Unit Plots, I 27.7/2
Location of Irrigated Land, **Maps** (by States), C 3.950-9/4
Location Sheets of **Maps** and Charts, W 31.7/2
Maps, C 55.22/a, I 28.157
Maps (by States), A 57.7
Maps (by Subjects), A 57.7/2
Maps (Minor Civil Divisions), C 3.61
Maps (miscellaneous) Includes U.S. Outline **Maps**, C 3.62/2
Maps (outline), C 3.62
Maps and Atlases: Agricultural Stabilization and Conservation Service, A 82.91
Maps and Atlases: Central Intelligence Agency, PrEx 3.10/4
Maps and Atlases: Department of State, S 1.33/2
Maps and Atlases: Environmental Data Service, C 55.231
Maps and Atlases: Environmental Protection Agency, EP 1.99
Maps and Atlases: Library of Congress, Processing Department, LC 30.8/5
Maps and Atlases: National Science Foundation, NS 1.41
Maps and Atlases: Veterans Administration, VA 1.70
Maps and Charts: Bureau of Federal Credit Unions, FS 3.308
Maps and Charts: Civil Rights Commission, CR 1.13
Maps and Charts: Coast and Geodetic Survey, C 4.9, C 4.9/2
Maps and Charts: Coastal and Engineering Research Center, D 103.42/8
Maps and Charts: Economic Development Administration, C 46.17
Maps and Charts: Federal Aviation Agency, FAA 1.16
Maps and Charts: National Highway Traffic Safety Commission, TD 8.31
Maps and Charts: National Weather Service, C 55.122
Maps and Charts: Naval Oceanographic Office, D 203.21
Maps and Charts: Public Health Service, FS 2.72
Maps and Charts: Weather Bureau, C 30.22, C 30.22/2
Maps and Charts: Western Area Power Administration, E 6.10
Maps and Map Folders, I 53.11
Maps and Posters: Coast Guard, TD 5.47
Maps and Posters: Corps of Engineers, D 103.49/3
Maps and Posters: Geological Survey, I 19.79
Maps and Posters: Soil Conservation Service, A 57.68
Maps and Posters: Territories Office, L 35.23
Maps, Charts, and Atlases, D 5.353
Maps for America, I 19.2:M 32/12
Maps, Indian Health Service, HE 20.311
Maps of Major Concentrations of Poverty in Standard Metropolitan Statistical Areas of 250,000 or More Population, PrEx 10.2:P 86/9
Maps of States, A 27.10
Maps of States Showing Lands Designated by Secretary of Interior As Subject to Entry Under Enlarged Homestead Act of February 19, 1909, I 1.50
Maps {Concerning Animal Industry}, A 77.238
Maps, Reclamation Service, I 19.17/5
Maps, Townsite, and Farm Unit Plots, Lists of, I 27.7/2
Mineral Investigations Resource **Maps**, I 19.90

Mineral Investigations, Field Studies **Maps**, I 19.39
Minerals Management Quad (**maps**), I 53.11/6
Miscellaneous Field Studies **Maps**, I 19.113
Miscellaneous Geologic Investigations **Maps**, I 19.91
Noteworthy **Maps**, LC 5.5
Official Postal **Maps**, P 11.8
Official Road **Maps** for Allied Forces Europe, Series M305, D 5.342
List of Books, Pamphlets, and **Maps** Received, New Oil and Gas Investigations **Maps**, I 19.25/4, I 19.93
Outline **Maps**, A 36.37
Post Route **Maps**, P 11.5
Posters and **Maps**, A 1.32, HH 2.15
Posters, Federal, **Maps**, CC 1.8
Price List of Post Route **Maps**, P 11.6
Progress **Maps**, FW 2.12
Public Sale Catalog: Topographic **Maps** and Publications, D 5.319/3, D 5.351/3
Radio Beacon System (**maps**), T 47.22
Radiobeacon System (**maps**), N 24.14
Research Division **Maps**, C 27.9/13
Rocky Mountain Research Station: **Maps**, A 13.151/3
Separate Sheets of Selected Thematic and General Reference **Maps** from the National Atlas of the United States of America, I 19.111a
Shawnee Sportsman's **Maps** (series), A 13.28/3
Slope **Maps**, I 19.109
Soil Interpretive **Maps** (for various subjects), A 57.69/2
Species Range **Maps** (series), A 13.107
State **Maps**, I 19.21/3
State Postal **Maps**, P 1.39/2
Surface Management Quadrangles (**maps**), I 53.11/5
Topographic **Maps** Circulars, I 19.11
Topographic **Maps**, I 19.40
Topographic Quadrangle **Maps** of Alluvial Valley of Lower Mississippi River, D 103.308
Topographical **Maps**, 7.5 Minute Series, I 19.81
Topographical Quadrangle **Maps**, 15' Series, I 19.81/2
Topographical Quadrangle **Maps**, I 19.81
Transportation **Maps**, A 22.9/2, FW 2.13, C 37.11
U.S. **Maps**, C 56.242/2
United States **Maps**, C 56.242, C 3.62/10
United States 1:1,000,000-Scale **Maps**, I 19.107
United States 1:1,000,000-Scale Series, Intermediate Scale **Maps**, I 19.110
United States Series of Topographic **Maps**, I 19.98
United States Topographic/Bathymetric **Maps**, I 19.101
Weather **Maps** Signal Office, W 42.23
Weather **Maps** Weather Bureau, C 30.12
MarAd
  Highlights of **MarAd** Port Activities, C 39.223/2
MARAD
  MARAD Press Clips, C 39.234/2
  MARAD Publications, TD 11.9/2
  MARAD Safety Review, C 39.219
MARATech
  MARATech R and D Technology Transfer Journal, C 39.227/2, TD 11.26
MARC
  MARC Distribution Services, LC 30.28
  MARC Serials Editing Guide, Bimonthly Updates, LC 1.6/4:M 18
March
  March of Education, FS 5.19
  March of Education, News Letter for School Officers, I 16.26/3
MARD
  MARD Safety Review, C 39.219
Mare
  Rubber Laboratory, **Mare** Island Naval Shipyard, Vallejo, California, Reports, D 211.16
Margarine
  Household Purchases of Butter, Cheese, Nonfat Dry Milk Solids and **Margarine**, A 88.14/6
  Margarine Production, A 82.26
Margin
  List of OTC **Margin** Stocks, FR 1.46/4
  Margin Notes, Y 3.T 25:21
Margins
  Heating Oil Prices and **Margins** (advance release), E 3.11/11-2
  Marketing **Margins** for Florida Oranges in Ten Major Cities, A 36.175
  Mill **Margins** Report, A 88.11/10-3

Materiel
Navy Medical and Dental **Materiel** Bulletin, D 206.3/2
U.S. Army **Materiel** Command, Annual Historical Review, D 101.1/4-2

Maternal
Inventory and Analysis of NIH **Maternal** and Child Health Research, HE 20.3363
Maternal and Child Health Information, HE 20.2761
Maternal and Child Health Services, FS 17.213
Maternal and Child Welfare Bulletins, L 5.34
National Advisory Council on **Maternal**, Infant and Fetal Nutrition: Biennial Report, A 98.14/2

Maternal Health
Bierman Jessie M. Annual Lectures in **Maternal Health** and Child Health, FS 14.110/2

Mates
List of Masters, **Mates**, {etc} of Merchant Steam, Motor, and Sail Vessels, Licensed during Calendar Year, T 38.7

Mathematical
Directorate of **Mathematical** and Information Sciences, Air Force Office of Scientific Research, Research Summaries, D 301.45/19-10
Handbook of **Mathematical** Functions, C 13.32:55
Herald of Moscow University, Physio-**Mathematical** and Natural Sciences Series {abstracts}, C 41.50/6
Mathematical Analysis Groups Reports, I 27.39
Mathematical Sciences, C 13.22
Mathematical Sciences Postdoctoral Research Fellowships, NS 1.45
Mathematical Tables, C 13.30
News of Academy of Sciences of Armenian SSR, Physyco-**Mathematical**, Natural and Technical Sciences Series, C 41.50/7
Progress of **Mathematical** Sciences {abstracts}, C 41.61/4

Mathematical Models
Computer Codes and **Mathematical Models**, Y 3.N 88:31/0083

Mathematics
Academic Year Institutes for Secondary School Teachers and Supervisors of Science and **Mathematics**, NS 1.12
Analysis of Research in the Teaching of **Mathematics**, FS 5.229:29007, HE 5.229:29007
Application for Grants under the Secretary's Discretionary Program for **Mathematics**, Science, Computer Learning and Critical Foreign Languages, ED 1.64
Applied **Mathematics** and Mechanics {abstracts}, C 41.61
Applied **Mathematics** Series, C 13.32
Herald of Leningrad University, **Mathematics**, Mechanics, and Astronomy Series {abstracts}, C 41.50/8
Homestudy Courses; Basic **Mathematics**, HE 20.7021/5
Journal of Abstracts, **Mathematics**, C 41.61/3
Junior-Year Science, **Mathematics**, and Foreign Language Students, First-Term, FS 5.254:54001, HE 5.254:54001
Mathematics Symposium {abstracts}, C 41.61/6
National Applied **Mathematics** Laboratories, Projects and Publications, Quarterly Report, C 13.43
News of Academy of Sciences of USSR; **Mathematics** Series, C 41.61/5
News of Institutes of Higher Learning; Ministry of Higher Education, USSR, **Mathematics**, C 41.61/2
Physics and **Mathematics**, PrEx 7.22/11
Programs for College Teachers of Science, **Mathematics**, and Engineering, NS 1.12
Publications National Applied **Mathematics** Laboratories, C 13.43
Research in Progress, Calendar Year Physics, Electronics, **Mathematics**, Geosciences, D 101.52/5-4
Research Participation for Teachers of Science and **Mathematics**, NS 1.12/3
Technical Memorandum National Bureau of Standards, Applied **Mathematics** Division, C 13.39
Ukranian **Mathematics** Journal {abstracts}, C 41.61/7

MATS
MATS Flyer, D 301.56
MATS Manuals, D 301.7/6

MATS Regulations, D 301.6/3

Matter
Digest and Index of Opinions of Counsel, Informal Rulings of Federal Reserve Board and **Matter** Relating Thereto, from Federal Reserve Bulletin, FR 1.10
Soil Organic **Matter** Levels in the Central Great Plains, A 77.15/3
Subject **Matter** Index with Cross-Reference Table, Y 3.F 31/21:11
Subject **Matter** Indexes to Decisions of the Federal Labor Relations Authority, Y 3.F 31/21-3:10-3

Matters
Conference in **Matters** of Pollution of Navigable Waters, Proceedings, EP 1.16/2
Digest of Unpublished Decisions of the Comptroller General of the United States on General Government **Matters**, Appropriations and Miscellaneous, GA 1.5/12
Federal Design **Matters**, NF 2.9
Major **Matters** Before the Commission, CC 1.2:M 43
Major **Matters** Before the Federal Communications Commission, CC 1.50
Mammography **Matters**, HE 20.4619
Mental Health **Matters**, HE 20.8124
Proceedings Conference in **Matters** of Pollution and Navigable Waters, EP 1.16/2
Report on U.S. Government Research and Studies in the Field of Arms Control and Disarmament **Matters**, AC 1.14
Reports on Bankruptcy **Matters**, J 1.9

Maturity
Maturity Distribution of Euro-Dollar Deposits in Foreign Branches of U.S. Banks, FR 1.54
Maturity Distribution of Outstanding Negotiable Time Certificates of Deposit, FR 1.54/2

Maumee River Basin
Maumee River Basin, Y 3.G 79/3:10

Maury
Nautical Monographs (**Maury**), N 14.11

Maximum
Annual **Maximum**, Minimum, and Mean Discharges of Mississippi River and Its Outlets and Tributaries, D 103.309/2
General **Maximum** Price Regulations, Bulletins, Pr 32.4211
Maximum Price Regulations, Pr 32.4210
Maximum Rent Regulations, Pr 32.4214
Maximum Travel Per Diem Allowances for Foreign Areas, S 1.76/3-2
Minimum Wage and **Maximum** Hours Under the Fair Labor Standards Act, L 36.9

Maximums
State **Maximums** and Other Methods of Limiting Money Payments to Recipients of Special Types of Public Assistance, HE 17.626

Mayonnaise
Salad Dressing, **Mayonnaise** and Related Products, C 57.316, C 57.514

Mayor
To **Mayor** of Each City with Local Airline Service, C 31.256

Mayor's
Veterans Emergency Housing Program: Community Action Report to **Mayor's** Emergency Housing Committee, NHA 1.12, Y 3.H 81/2:8
Report on Washington Conference of **Mayors** and Other Local Government Executives on National Security, FCD 1.18

MB
Survey of Minority-Owned Business Enterprises, **MB** (series), C 56.250, C 3.258, C 56.260

MC
MC Reports, D 201.20

McCoy
Headquarters Fort **McCoy** Regulations, D 101.9/4

MCD
MCD Series, EP 2.28
U.S. Exports and Imports, Working-Day and Seasonal Adjustment Factors and Months for Cyclical Dominance (**MCD**), C 3.235

MCH
MCH Research Series, HE 20.5114
MCH Statistical Series, HE 20.5113

MCHS
MCHS Statistics Series, HE 20.2760

MCI

MCI- (series), D 214.25

McIntire-Stennis
Forestry Research Progress in (year) **McIntire-Stennis** Cooperative Forestry Research Program, A 94.2 F 76/

McNair
McNair Papers (series), D 5.416

MCP
MCP- (series), D 304.10

MCRP
MCRP (Marine Corp Reference Publication) Series, D 214.9/8

MDSC
Milk Distributors, Sales and Costs **MDSC** (series), A 88.14/9

MDTA
MDTA Experimental and Demonstration Findings, L 1.56

Mead
Lake **Mead** Water Supply Outlook, I 27.43

Meade
Headquarters Fort George C. **Meade** Pamphlets (series), D 101.22/10

Meal
Alfalfa **Meal** Production, A 82.59/2, A 88.18/5
Commitments of Traders in Wheat, Corn, Oats, Rye, Soybeans, Soybean Oil, Soybean **Meal**, Shell Eggs, A 85.9/2
Corn **Meal**, A 82.3/8
Corn **Meal** for Domestic Distribution, A 82.3/3
Corn **Meal** for Export Distribution, A 82.3/7
Export Corn **Meal** Bulletin, A 82.3/2
Fish **Meal** and Oil, C 55.309/2
Fish **Meal** and Oil Market Review, Current Economic Analysis I, C 55.309/3
Food Selection and **Meal** Planning Charts, A 10.21/2
Futures Trading and Open Contracts in Soybean **Meal** and Cottonseed **Meal**, A 85.11/6
Meat **Meal** and Tankage Production, Semiannual Report, A 92.17/2

Mean
Accuracy of Monthly **Mean** Flow in Current Releases, I 19.45/2
Annual Maximum, Minimum, and **Mean** Discharges of Mississippi River and Its Outlets and Tributaries, D 103.309/2
Monthly **Mean** Discharge at Selected Gaging Stations and Change of Storage in Certain Lakes and Reservoirs in Columbia River Basin, I 19.47

Means
Manual of Rules of the Committee on Ways and **Means**, Y 4.W 36:WMCP 96-1
Semimonthly **Means** of Sea Surface Temperature, C 55.193
What Social Security **Means** to Industries, SS 1.18

Measels
Measels Surveillance, Reports, HE 20.2309/4, HE 20.7011

Measurement
Area **Measurement** Reports, C 3.208/2
Federal Productivity **Measurement**, PM 1.45
GE-20 Area **Measurement** Reports, C 3.208/2
Handbook of Hearing Aid **Measurement**, VA 1.22/3
Hearing Aid Performance **Measurement** Data and Hearing Aid Selection Procedures, Contract Year (date), VA 1.22
Measurement of Vessels, T 17.9/2
Measurement Systems Operation Procedure, D 217.16/4-2
Measurement Techniques {abstracts}, C 41.75
Measurement Users Bulletin, C 13.10/2
National **Measurement** Laboratory, News Features, C 13.70/2
Overlap, **Measurement** Agreement through Process Evaluation, C 13.56
Personnel **Measurement** Research and Development Center, CS 1.71
Standardization of Work **Measurement**, D 7.6/4-2
Study of Methods Used in **Measurement** and Analysis of Sediment Loads in Streams, Reports, Y 3.F 31/13:9, Y 3.In 8/8:10

Measurements
Automobile Manufacturers **Measurements**, FMC 1.12
Snow Survey and Soil Moisture **Measurements**, Basic Data Summary for Western United States, Including Columbia River Drainage in Canada, A 57.46/17

Newsletter of the U.S. Army **Medical** Department, D 104.24

North Central Regional **Medical** Education Center: Newsletter, VA 1.56/2

Notes for **Medical** Catalogers, HE 20.3611

Number of Recipients and Amounts of Payments Under Medicaid and Other **Medical** Programs Financed from Public Assistance Funds, HE 17.617/3

Pan-American **Medical** Congress, Washington, 1893, S 5.16

Permuted **Medical** Subject Headings, HE 20.3612/3-3

Posters Army **Medical** Department, D 104.34

Posters National Institute of General **Medical** Sciences, HE 20.3467

Proceedings **Medical** Association of Isthmian Canal Zone, W 79.12/6

Program Memorandum Health Maintenance Organization/Competitive **Medical** Plan, HE 22.28/2

Progress Report President's **Medical** Programs for Heart Disease, Cancer, and Stroke, and Related Diseases, FS 2.313

Public Assistance: Vendor Payments for **Medical** Care by Type of Service, Fiscal Year Ended (date), HE 17.617

Public Use Data Tape Documentation **Medical** Coding Manual and Short Index, HE 20.6226/9

Public Use Data Tape Documentation **Medical** History, Ages 12-74 Years, HE 20.6226/5

Recipients and Amounts of **Medical** Vendor Payments Under Public Assistance Programs, HE 17.617/2

Resources for **Medical** Research and Education, Reports, HE 20.3014

Resources for **Medical** Research, Reports, FS 2.22/33

Reviewing and Acting on **Medical** Certificates, CS 1.41/4:339-31

Selected Bibliography of Regional **Medical** Programs, HE 20.2612

Selected **Medical** Care Statistics, D 1.62

Special Reports Naval Submarine **Medical** Center, D 206.10/3

Station-List of Officers of **Medical** Department, W 44.13

Studies in **Medical** Care Administration, FS 2.311

Summary of Reports Received by Committee on **Medical** Research, Pr 32.413/10

Supply Table of **Medical** Department, Navy, with Allowance for Ships, N 10.8

U.S. Army **Medical** Doctrine, Publications, D 104.36

United States Air Force **Medical** Service Digest, D 304.8

United States Armed Forces **Medical** Journal, D 1.11

United States Army **Medical** Research Institute of Infectious Disease: Annual Progress Report, D 104.27

United States Naval **Medical** Bulletin, N 10.11

USAF **Medical** Logistics Directory, D 304.9/2

VA **Medical** Center, Allen Park, Michigan: Newsletter, VA 1.56/5

VA **Medical** Center, Phoenix, Arizona: Newsletter, VA 1.56/3

VA **Medical** Research Conference Abstracts, VA 1.43/2

VA **Medical** Research Service, Annual Report, VA 1.1/4

Vendor Payments for **Medical** Care Under Public Assistance, by Program and Type of Service, Fiscal Year (date), HE 17.617/4

Veterans Administration **Medical** Center, Tucson, Arizona, Formulary, VA 1.73/5

Veterans Administration Summary of **Medical** Programs, VA 1.43/5

Walter Reed Army **Medical** Center, Army Prosthetics Research Laboratory, Technical Reports, D 104.15/2

West Side VA **Medical** Center Formulary, VA 1.78

Medicare

Annual **Medicare** Program Statistics, HE 22.21/3

Directory of **Medicare** Providers and Suppliers of Services, HE 3.51/5

Guide to Health Insurance for People with **Medicare**, HE 22.8/17

(HCFA) **Medicare** Unique Physician Identification Number (Directory), HE 22.414/2

HCFA Regional Office Manual; **Medicare**, HE 22.8/8

Health Care Financing Administration Rulings on **Medicare**, Medicaid, Professional Standards Review and Related Matters, HE 22.15

Health Insurance Statistics: Current **Medicare** Survey Report, HE 3.28/4

Impact of the **Medicare** Hospital Prospective Payment System, Report to Congress, HE 22.21/3

Medicaid **Medicare** Exchange, HE 22.409

Medicare and Medicaid Program Manual, Transmittals and Program Memos, HE 22.8/23

Medicare Annual Report, HE 22.21

Medicare Carrier Quality Assurance Handbook, HE 22.8/7-5

Medicare Carriers Manual; Claims Process, HE 22.8/7

Medicare Carriers Manual; Fiscal Administration, HE 22.8/7-2

Medicare Carriers Manual; Program Administration, HE 22.8/7-3

Medicare Christian Science Sanatorium Hospital Manual Supplement, HE 22.8/2-2

Medicare Coverage Issues Manual, HE 22.8/14

Medicare Directory of Prevailing Charges, HE 22.29

Medicare Home Health Agency Manual, HE 22.8/5

Medicare Hospice Benefits, HE 22.21/5

Medicare Hospital Manual, HE 22.8/2

Medicare Hospital Mortality Information: Vol. 1, Alabama - California, HE 22.34

Medicare Hospital Mortality Information: Vol. 2, Colorado - Illinois, HE 22.34

Medicare Hospital Mortality Information: Vol. 3, Indiana - Maryland, HE 22.34

Medicare Hospital Mortality Information; Vol. 5, New Hampshire - Ohio, HE 22.34

Medicare Hospital Mortality Information; Vol. 6, Oklahoma - Tennessee, HE 22.34

Medicare Hospital Mortality Information; Vol. 7, Texas - Guam, HE 22.34

Medicare Intermediary Letters, HE 22.8/6-5

Medicare Intermediary Manual, Part 2, Audits-Reimbursement Program Administration, HE 22.8/6-2

Medicare Intermediary Manual, Part 3, Claims Process, HE 22.8/6

Medicare Newsletter, FS 3.53

Medicare Outpatient Physical Therapy Provider Manual, HE 22.8/9

Medicare Part A Intermediary Manual, Part 1, Fiscal Administration, HE 22.8/6-3

Medicare Part A Intermediary Manual, Part 4, Audit Procedures, HE 22.8/6-4

Medicare Peer Review Organizational Manual, HE 22.8/15

Medicare Program Statistics, HE 22.21/2

Medicare Program Statistics, Medicare Utilization, HE 22.21/2-2

Medicare Prospective Payment and the American Health Care System, Y 3.P 29:3

Medicare Provider Reimbursement Manual, HE 22.8/4

Medicare Renal Dialysis Facility Manual, HE 22.8/13

Medicare Rural Health Clinic Manual, HE 22.8/19

Medicare Skilled Nursing Facility Manual, HE 22.8/3

Medicare Unique Physician Identification Number Directory, HE 22.414

Medicare, Medicaid, State Operations Manual, Provider Certification, HE 22.8/12

Medicare/Medicaid Directory of Medical Facilities, HE 22.213

Medicare/Medicaid Nursing Home Information (State), HE 22.35

Medicare/Medicaid Sanction, Reinstatement Report, HE 22.36

Medicare Hospital Mortality Information; Vol. 4, Massachusetts - Nevada, HE 22.34

National Listing of **Medicare** Providers Furnishing Kidney Dialysis & Transplant Services, HE 22.216

Perspectives on Medicaid and **Medicare** Management, HE 22.411

Your **Medicare** Handbook, HE 22.8/16

Medication

Important Information about You and Your **Medication**, VA 1.79

Medicinal

Bimonthly Review of **Medicinal** Preparation Exports, C 18.50

Medicinal Chemistry A Study Section, HE 20.3001/2:M 46/5

Medicinal Chemistry B Study Section, HE 20.3001/2:M 46/6

Medicine

Aerospace **Medicine** and Biology, A Continuing Bibliography with Indexes, NAS 1.21:7011

Air University, School of Aviation **Medicine**: {publications}, D 301.26/13-2

Aviation **Medicine** Anotated Bibliography, LC 36.9

Bibliography of Soviet Sources on **Medicine** and Public Health in the U.S.S.R., HE 20.3711:So 8/2

Bibliography of the History of **Medicine**, HE 20.3615

Biology and Aerospace **Medicine**, PrEx 7.22/12

Bulletin of the School of **Medicine**, Uniformed Services University of the Health Sciences, D 1.67

Bureau of Veterinary **Medicine** Memo, BVMM (series), HE 20.4028

Case Studies in Environmental **Medicine**, HE 20.7917

Current Bibliographies in **Medicine** (series), HE 20.3615/2

Film Reference Guide for **Medicine** and Allied Sciences, HE 20.3608/2

Fogarty International Center Series on Preventive **Medicine**, HE 20.3713

Fogarty International Center Series on the Teaching of Preventative **Medicine**, HE 20.3714

General **Medicine** A Study Section, HE 20.3001/2:M 46/2

General **Medicine** B Study Section, HE 20.3001/2:M 46/3

International Congress of Military **Medicine** and Pharmacy, S 5.39

Joint NCDRH and State Quality Assurance Surveys in Nuclear **Medicine**, HE 20.4611

Legal **Medicine** Open File, D 101.117/7

Medicine and Biology, C 51.9/24

Medicine for the Layman (series), HE 20.3031

National Health Service Corps Scholarship Program Information Bulletin for Students of Allopathic Medicine, Osteopathic **Medicine**, and Dentistry, HE 20.5011

National Library of **Medicine** Audiovisuals Catalog, HE 20.3609/4

National Library of **Medicine** Catalog, LC 30.13

National Library of **Medicine** Current Catalog (Monthly Listings), FS 2.216, HE 20.3609

National Library of **Medicine** Current Catalog, Cumulative Listing, HE 20.3609/2

National Library of **Medicine** Current Catalog: Annual Cumulation, HE 20.3609/3

National Library of **Medicine** Fact Sheets, HE 20.3621

National Library of **Medicine** News, HE 20.3619

National Library of **Medicine** News: NLM Publications, HE 20.3619/2

National Library of **Medicine** Newsline HE 20.3619

National Library of **Medicine** Staff Directory, HE 20.3619/3

Office of Aviation **Medicine** Encyclopedia of Medical Program Data, TD 4.213

Oral Biology and **Medicine** Study Section, HE 20.3001/2:Or 1

Physical Fitness/Sports **Medicine** Bibliography, HE 20.111

Posters Bureau of **Medicine** and Surgery, D 206.23

Posters National Library of **Medicine**, HE 20.3622

Preventive **Medicine** Division, Bulletins, N 10.12

Publications Air University, School of Aviation **Medicine**, D 301.26/3-2

Publications School of Aviation **Medicine**, Index, Fiscal Year, D 301.26/13-3

Research Reports Naval School of Aviation **Medicine**, D 206.16

Review of War Surgery and **Medicine**, W 44.16

School of Aerospace **Medicine**: Technical Documentary Report SAM-TDR (series), D 301.26/13-6

School of Aviation **Medicine**: General Publications, D 301.26/13-5
Spawning the **Medicine** River, I 20.64
Statistics of Navy **Medicine**, D 206.15
Textbook of Military **Medicine** (series), D 104.35
Tropical **Medicine** and Parasitology Study Section, HE 20.3001/2:M 46/7
U.S. Navy **Medicine**, D 206.7

Medicines
World Trade in Prepared **Medicines**, C 18.174

Medico
Medico-Military Review for Medical Department, Army, W 44.22

Medicus
Abridged Index **Medicus**, HE 20.3612/2
Cumulated Index **Medicus**, HE 20.3612/3
Index **Medicus**, Including Bibliography of Medical Reviews, HE 20.3612
List of Journals Indexed in Index **Medicus**, HE 20.3612/4

Mediterranean
Nautical Charts and Publications, Region 5, Western Africa and the **Mediterranean**, C 55.440:5
NIMA Nautical Charts, Public Sale Region 5, Western Africa and the **Mediterranean**, TD 4.82:5

Mediterranean Sea
Tide Tables, High and Low Water Predictions Europe and West Coast of Africa, Including the **Mediterranean Sea**, C 55.421/3

Medium
Employee Benefits in **Medium** and Large Firms, L 2.3/10

MedPAC
MedPAC Report to Congress, Y 3.M 46/3:1

MEDTEP
MEDTEP Update, HE 20.6517/5

Meeting
Commission **Meeting** Agenda, CC 1.52
Literacy: **Meeting** the Challenge (series), ED 1.27
Meeting Leaders Guide, W 3.84/2, M 108.79/2
Meeting of the Canada-United States Interparliamentary Group, Y 4.F 76/1-11, Y 4.In 8/16:11
Proceedings Interdepartmental Board on Simplified Office Procedure, Executive Committee **Meeting**, T 51.11/5
Proceedings Joint **Meeting** with its Advisory Council, Y 3.Ou 8:9
Public Health Conference on Records and Statistics, National **Meeting** Announcement, HE 20.6214/2
Report of Coordinated **Meeting** of Federal Agencies (by States), Y 3.N 21/9:11
Report of Proceedings of Regular Annual **Meeting** of Judicial Conference of the United States, Ju 10.10
Summary Minutes of **Meeting**, S 5.48/12
Summary of **Meeting** Depository Library Council to the Printer, GP 3.30/2
Transcripts of Proceedings, **Meeting** of Depository Council to the Public Printer, GP 3.30
Voluntary Service National Advisory Committee: Report of Annual **Meeting**, VA 1.52
World List of Future International **Meeting**: Pt. 2, Social, Cultural, Commercial, Humanistic, LC 2.9/2

Meetings
Calendar of National **Meetings**, FS 2.315
Canada-United States Interparliamentary Group Report on **Meetings** by Senate Delegation, Y 4.F 76/2:C 16/2
Central Executive Council, Reports of **Meetings**, T 1.23/6
Cotton Educational **Meetings**, A 55.39
List of Official International Conferences and **Meetings**, S 5.49
Proceedings National Data Buoy Systems Scientific Advisory **Meetings**, TD 5.23
Proceedings Special **Meetings**, T 38.11
Quarterly Calendar of Environmental **Meetings**, EP 1.39
Transcript CONTU **Meetings** (numbered), Y 3.C 79:9
United States Section, Reports of **Meetings**, T 1.23/7
World List of Future International **Meetings** 19591969, LC 2.9

Megamarketplace
Directory of Women Business Owners, **Megamarketplace** East/West, C 1.37/3

Megamarketplace East, Directory of Women Business Owners, C 1.37/2

Melbourne
Melbourne International Exhibition, 1880, S 6.8/1, S 6.8/2

Mellitus
Diabetes **Mellitus**, HE 20.3320/2-4
Diabetes **Mellitus** Coordinating Committee, Annual Report to the Director, National Institutes of Health, Fiscal Year (date), HE 20.3028

Melons
Spring Vegetables and **Melons**, A 88.26/4
Spring Vegetables, Spring **Melons**, Spring Potatoes, A 88.26/4
Summer and Fall Vegetables for Fresh Market, Summer **Melons**, Sweetpotatoes, A 88.26/4
Summer and Fall Vegetables, **Melons**, Sweetpotatoes, A 88.26/4
Total Commercial Production of All Vegetables and **Melons** for Fresh Market and Processing, A 92.11/10-3

Member
Changes in State **Member** Banks, FR 1.33
Condition of Weekly Reporting **Member** Banks in Central Reserve Cities, FR 1.16/2
Condition of Weekly Reporting **Member** Banks in Leading Cities, FR 1.16
Condition of Weekly Reporting **Member** Banks in New York and Chicago, FR 1.16/2
List of **Member** Banks by Districts, RB 1.5
Member Bank Call Report, FR 1.11
Member Bank Earnings, FR 1.11/3
Member Bank Income, FR 1.11/3
Member Bank Loans, FR 1.11/2
State **Member** Banks of the Federal Reserve System, FR 1.11/5
Summary of Equity Security Transactions and Ownership of Directors, Officers, and Principal Stockholders of **Member** State Banks As Reported Pursuant to
Summary Report, Assets and Liabilities of **Member** Banks, FR 1.11
Weekly Averages of **Member** Bank Reserves, Reserve Bank Credit and Related Items and Statement of Condition of the Federal Reserve Bank, FR 1.15

Member Bank
Aggregate Reserves and **Member Bank** Deposits, FR 1.15/3, HE 1.210

Member Banks
Assets and Liabilities of All **Member Banks** by Districts, FR 1.28/3
Duties and Liabilities of Directors of National and **Member Banks** of Federal Reserve System, T 12.12

Members
Chiefs of State and Cabinet **Members** of Foreign Governments, CR CS- (series), PrEx 3.11/2
Combined Financial Statements of **Members** of the Federal Home Loan Bank System, FHL 1.12
Congressional Lists; List of Publications Available for Distribution by **Members** of Congress, A 21.9/3
Executive Reservist, Bulletin from Industrial Mobilization, for **Members** of National Defense Executive Reserve, C 41.113
Health Planning Newsletter for Governing Body **Members**, HE 20.6022
List of **Members** of Bureau of Mines, I 28.12
List of Publications Available for Distribution by **Members** of Congress, A 21.9/8:1
Members of Advisory Councils, Study Sections, and Committees of National Institutes of Health, FS 2.22/22
Members of the Federal Home Loan Bank System, FHL 1.31
Monthly Digest to **Members** of Congress, L 2.66
Public Advisory Committees: Authority, Structure, Functions, **Members**, HE 20.1000
Roster of **Members** of PHS Public Advisory Groups, Councils, Committees, Boards, Panels, Study Sections, HE 20.2:Ad 9/3

Membership
Annual Report to **Membership**, PrEx 1.10
Challenge Network **Membership** Directory, ED 1.30/3
Changes in State Bank **Membership**, Announcements, FR 1.33
Constitution and **Membership**, NA 1.7

North Central Regional **Membership** Relations Conference, A 89.17/2
President's Committee on Employment of the Handicapped, Annual Report to **Membership**, .PrEx 1.10/13
Union **Membership** in, L 2.120/2-12

Memberships
Record of Changes in **Memberships** of National Home for Disabled Volunteer Soldiers, NH 1.6

MEMCPM
MEMCPM Regulations, D 1.65/2

Memo
Memo, HE 20.3915
Memo AG (series), D 101.32/2
SMA **Memo**, HE 20.4614
Small Business **Memo** FOA/SMB (series), FO 1.14
Small Business **Memo**, ICA/SBM Series, S 17.14
Staff **Memo** from U.S. Secretary of Labor, L 1.33
Transmittal **Memo** {for} Local Board Memorandums, Y 3.Se 4:13

Memoirs
Bibliographical **Memoirs**, NA 1.6
Memoirs, NA 1.5
Professional **Memoirs**, W 7.16/6

Memoranda
All Participants **Memoranda**, HH 1.23/8, HH 1.37/4
Memoranda, W 87.16
Office **Memoranda**, N 16.5
Ordnance **Memoranda**, W 34.10
Scientific Inquiry **Memoranda**, C 6.15
Tax Court **Memoranda**, Ju 11.7/2
Technical **Memoranda** for Municipal, Industrial and Domestic Water Supplies, Pollution Abatement, Public Health, FS 2.301
U.S. Navy Travel Instructions, Instruction **Memoranda**, N 20.13/3

Memorandum
Conservation Planning **Memorandum**, A 57.53
Employment Security **Memorandum**, FS 3.110
Foreign Service Regulations, **Memorandum** Transmitting Mimeographed Inserts for, S 1.5/2
Memorandum for Information, S 1.62
Memorandum on Women's Alcohol, Drug Abuse, and Mental Health Issues, HE 20.8019
Memorandum Reports, D 206.10/2, TD 8.23/2
Memorandum Series, HE 20.7026
Memorandum to All Nurses in the Public Health Service, HE 20.36
Memorandum Transmitting Mimeographed Inserts for Foreign Service Regulations, S 1.5/2
NRL **Memorandum** Report (series), D 210.8/2
Operating Procedure **Memorandum**, Y 3.W 89/2:30, FW 4.8
Organized Reserves **Memorandum**, W 99.18/8
Personnel Research and Development Center: Technical **Memorandum**, CS 1.71/4
PHS Grants Policy **Memorandum**, HE 1.6/7-3, HE 20.8/3
Physicians **Memorandum**, HE 20.36/2
Planning Survey **Memorandum**, A 22.12, FW 2.9
Plant Quarantine **Memorandum**, A 77.314/2
Program **Memorandum** Health Maintenance Organization/Competitive Medical Plan, HE 22.28/2
Program **Memorandum** Medicaid State Agencies, HE 22.28
Program **Memorandum** Quality Assurance, HE 22.28/3
Program **Memorandum** State Survey Agencies, HE 22.28/4
R.O.T.C. **Memorandum**, W 99.13/10
Recreation **Memorandum**, W 99.13/9, W 99.17/9
Rehabilitation Standards **Memorandum**, FS 13.209
Research **Memorandum** Air University, Human Resources Report Institute, D 301.26/7
Research **Memorandum** National Labor Relations Board, LR 1.10
Research **Memorandum** Social Security Administration, SS 1.28, FS 1.28
Signal Corps **Memorandum**, W 42.26
Soils **Memorandum**, A 57.48
Special **Memorandum** Series, I 49.43
State Office **Memorandum**, A 55.46/10
Technical Information **Memorandum** (series), D 1.83
Technical **Memorandum** Beach Erosion Board, D 103.19
Technical **Memorandum** Defense Civil Preparedness Agency, D 119.8/5

Technical **Memorandum** Defense Communications
Agency, D 5.110
Technical **Memorandum** Energy Information
Administration, E 3.26,
Technical **Memorandum** National Aeronautics and
Space Administration, NAS 1.15
Technical **Memorandum** National Bureau of
Standards, Applied Mathematics
Division, C 13.39
Technical **Memorandum** National Telecommunica-
tions and Information Administration, C
60.11
Technical **Memorandum** Reclamation Bureau, I
27.31/2
Technical **Memorandum** Technology Assessment
Office, Y 3.T 22/2:11
Technical **Memorandum** To United States Study
Commission, Southeast River Basins, A
57.50
Technical Report **Memorandum** AFHRL (TT)-
TRM, D 301.45/27-2
Tennis **Memorandum**, W 99.14/11
Training **Memorandum**, W 99.11/8, W 99.13/8, W
99.14/8, W 99.15/8, W 99.16/8, W
99.18/10, W 99.19/11, W 99.20/7
Transportation **Memorandum**, N 9.14
Voucher Examination **Memorandum**, T 60.8, T
63.111
Memorandums
Information **Memorandums**, HE 1.1013
OT Technical **Memorandums**, C 1.60/8
Public Housing Management Improvement
Program: Technical **Memorandums**, HH
1.63
Scales and Weighing **Memorandums**, A 96.11
Selective Service **Memorandums** to All Navy
Contractors, N 1.30
Soil Survey Laboratory **Memorandums**, A 57.43,
A 77.525
Special Services **Memorandums**, A 82.109
Staff **Memorandums**, SS 1.29
Training **Memorandums**, W 1.34
Transmittal Memo {for} Local Board **Memoran-
dums**, Y 3.Se 4:13
Transportation Research and Development
Command: Research Technical
Memorandums, D 117.8
U.S. Naval Ordnance Test Station, Inyokern,
Technical **Memorandums**, D 215.11
USAREC Research **Memorandums** (numbered), D
101.106/2
Memorial
Additions to Columbus **Memorial** Library, AR 1.7
Posters United States Holocaust **Memorial**
Council, Y 3.H 74:9
Memory
A.I.D. **Memory** Documents, S 18.43
American **Memory** Digital Collections, LC 1.54/3
Memos
Resources Analysis **Memos**, HE 20.3014/2
U.S. National Commission for UNESCO **Memos**, S
5.48/14
Memphis
River Summary and Forecasts {**Memphis**, Tenn.
area}, C 55.110/2
Memphis District
Stages and Discharges of Mississippi River and
Tributaries in the **Memphis District**, D
103.45/2
Men
Corpsman, Published for **Men** and Women of Job
Corps, L 1.58/3, PrEx 10.10/2
Four Minute **Men** Bulletins, Y 3.P 96/3:6
Four Minute **Men** Division, School Bulletins, Y
3.P 96/3:17
Four Minute **Men** News, Y 3.P 96/3:13
Four Minute **Men**, Army Bulletins, Y 3.P 96/3:6
Free **Men** at Work, L 2.73
Merchant Mariner, Devoted to **Men** of American
Merchant Marine, SB 3.5
Surrenders and Apprehensions Reported of **Men**
Charged with Desertion from Army, W
3.38
U.S. Department of Commerce Periodicals to Aid
Business **Men**, C 1.54
War Reports for Loggers and Mill **Men**, W 107.9
Men's
Industry Wage Survey: **Men's** and Boy's Shirts and
Nightwear, L 2.3/35
Men's, Youth's, and Boy's Clothing Cut, C 3.92
Meningitis
Aseptic **Meningitis** Surveillance Annual Summary,
HE 20.7011/26

Mental
Hospital and **Mental** Facilities Construction
Program under Title 6 of Public Health
Service Act, Semiannual Analysis of
Projects Approved for Federal Aid, FS
2.74/2
Memorandum on Women's Alcohol, Drug Abuse,
and **Mental** Health Issues, HE 20.8019
Mental Defectives and Epileptics in State
Institutions, C 3.60
Mental Health Directory, HE 20.410/2
Mental Health Service System Reports and
Statistical Notes Publication Listing,
HE 20.8113/5
Mental Patients in State Hospitals, C 3.59
Mental Retardation Abstracts, FS 2.22/52, HE
17.113
Mental Retardation Activities of the Department of
Health, Education, and Welfare, FS 1.23/
5, HE 1.23/5
Mental Retardation and Development Disabilities
Abstracts, HE 1.49
Mental Retardation and the Law, a Report on Status
of Current Court Cases, HE 23.110
Mental Retardation and the Law, a Report on the
Status of Current Court Cases, HE 1.51
Mental Retardation Grants, Fiscal Year, HE 1.23/3
Mental Retardation Reports, FS 1.23/4, HE 1.23/4
Mental Retardation Research Committee, HE
20.3001/2:M 52
Mental Retardation Source Book, HE 1.23/6
Patient Movement Data, State and **Mental**
Hospitals, FS 2.22/46
Patients in Hospitals for **Mental** Disease, C 3.59/2
Patients in **Mental** Institutions, FS 2.59
President's Commission on **Mental** Health, Pr
39.8:M 52
Prevention Activities of the Alcohol, Drug Abuse,
and **Mental** Health Administration, HE
20.8018
Proceedings Annual Conference of **Mental** Health
Career Development Program, FS 2.22/45
Proceedings Annual Conference on Model
Reporting Area for **Mental** Hospital
Statistics, FS 2.22/44
Proceedings Annual Conference, Surgeon General,
Public Health Service, with State and
Territorial **Mental** Health Authorities, FS
2.83/3
Progress Report National **Mental** Health Program,
FS 2.65
Proposed **Mental** Retardation Programs, HE 1.23
Publications National Institute of **Mental** Health,
HE 20.8113/3
Research Project Summaries, National Institute of
Mental Health, FS 2.22/16-2
Research Reports National Institute of **Mental**
Health, HE 20.2420/4, HE 20.8114/2
State Salary Ranges, Selected Classes {of
positions} in Employment Security,
Public Welfare, Public Health, **Mental**
Health, Vocational Rehabilitation, Civil
Defense, Emergency Planning, CS 1.81,
FS 1.22, HE 1.22, GS 1.8
Statistical Notes National Institute of **Mental**
Health, HE 20.3812
Summary Proceedings of ADAMHA Annual
Conference of the State and Territorial
Alcohol, Drug Abuse, and **Mental**
Health Authorities, HE 20.8011
Transactions of Research Conferences on
Cooperative Chemotherapy Studies in
Psychiatry and Research Approaches to
Mental Illness, VA 1.41
Trends in **Mental** Health (series), HE 20.8126
Woman and **Mental** Health: a Bibliography, HE
20.8113:W 84
Mental Health
Administration in **Mental Health**, HE 20.8112
Alcohol, Drug Abuse, **Mental Health** Research
Grant Awards, HE 20.8016, HE 20.8118
Annual Report, **Mental Health** Intramural Research
Program, HE 20.8136
Center for **Mental Health** Services General
Publications, HE 20.427
Directory of Local Health and **Mental Health**
Units, HE 20.2015
Directory of Outpatient Psychiatric Clinics,
Psychiatric Day-Night Services and
Other **Mental Health** Resources in the
United States and Territories, FS 2.22/
38-4

Directory of State **Mental Health** Personnel and
Regional Offices of Department of Health,
Education, and Welfare, FS 2.22:M 52/40
Grants-In-Aid and Other Financial Assistance
Programs, Health Services and **Mental
Health** Administration, FS 2.317
Health Services and **Mental Health** Administration
Public Advisory Committees: Authority,
Structure, Functions, FS 2.321
Highlights of Progress in **Mental Health** Research,
FS 2.22/16
Innovations, **Mental Health** Services, Progress
Reports, HE 20.2425
Mental Health Demographic Profile System,
MHDPS Working Papers, HE 20.8133
Mental Health Digest, HE 20.8009
Mental Health Directory, HE 20.8123
Mental Health Directory of State and National
Agencies Administering Public **Mental
Health** and Related Programs, FS 2.22/
49
Mental Health Emergencies Alert, HE 20.8113/2
Mental Health in Deafness, HE 20.8127
Mental Health Manpower, Current Statistical and
Activities Reports, FS 2.54/3
Mental Health Matters, HE 20.8124
Mental Health Monographs, FS 2.22/31
Mental Health Program Reports, FS 2.22/50-4, HE
20.2419, HE 20.8117
Mental Health Research Findings (year), FS
2.22:M 52/44
Mental Health Research Grant Awards, Fiscal Year,
HE 20.2423
Mental Health Resources in the Greater
Washington Area, HE 20.8119
Mental Health Series, FS 2.53
Mental Health Service System Reports, HE
20.8110/2
Mental Health Statistics Series, HE 20.8110
Mental Health Statistics, Current Report Series, FS
2.115, FS 2.53/2
Mental Health Statistics: Current Facility Reports,
HE 17.117
Mental Health Training Grant Awards, FS 2.22/7-4
Mental Health, United States, HE 20.8137
National Clearinghouse for **Mental Health**
Information Abstracts, HE 20.2429
National Institute of **Mental Health** Support
Programs, HE 20.2412
National Institute of **Mental Health** Training Grant
Program, FS 2.22/42
National **Mental Health** Program Progress Reports,
FS 2.65
New Dimensions in **Mental Health**, HE 20.8122
New Dimensions in **Mental Health**, Report from the
Director (series), HE 20.8122/2
Newsletter for Research in **Mental Health** and
Behavioral Sciences, VA 1.22:15-5
Occupational **Mental Health** Notes, FS 2.22/50-3,
HE 20.2511
Posters Alcohol, Drug Abuse, and **Mental Health**
Administration, HE 20.8014
Mental Retardation
Fiscal Year Appropriations for **Mental Retardation**
Programs of the Department of Health,
Education, and Welfare, FS 1.23/2
Message from the Presidents's Committee on
Mental Retardation, Pr 36.8:M 52/M/
56
Mentally
Newsletter, Tips and Trends in Employment of the
Mentally Handicapped, PrEx 1.10/5
Special Report, Fresh Views of Employment of the
Mentally Handicapped, PrEx 1.10/4-2
Task Force on **Mentally** Handicapped, Pr 37.8:M 52
Mentally Disordered
Directory of Institutions for **Mentally Disordered**
Offenders, HE 20.2402:Of 2/2
Mentally Handicapped
Newsletter, Tips and Trends in Employment of the
Mentally Handicapped, PrEx 1.10/5
Mentally Ill
Directory of Halfway Houses and Community
Residences for the **Mentally Ill**, HE
20.8129
Directory of Halfway Houses for the **Mentally Ill**
and Alcoholics, HE 20.2402:H 13
Mentally Retarded
Hospital and Medical Facilities Series, Facilities
for the **Mentally Retarded**, FS 2.74/5
MEPCOM
MEPCOM (series), D 1.65
MEPCOM Regulations, D 1.6/9

MEPS

MEPS, (Medical Expenditure Panel Survey), Chartbook, HE 20.6517/7
MEPS (Medical Expenditure Panel Survey) Highlights, HE 20.6517/6
MEPS (Medical Expenditure Panel Survey), Research Findings, HE 20.6517/9

Merchandise

Census of Retail Trade; Retail Merchandise Lines Service, C 56.251/4, C 3.255/4
Circulars, Reappraisements of Merchandise by General Appraisers or Reappraisement Circulars, T 20.4/1
Export and Import Merchandise Trade, C 56.210:900, C 3.164:900
General Imports of Merchandise into United States by Air, Commodity by Country of Origin, C 3.164:231
General Imports of Merchandise into United States by Air, Country of Origin by Commodity, C 3.164:232
Imported Merchandise Entered for Consumption in United States, and Duties Collected Thereon During the Quarter Ending, C 18.17
Imported Merchandise Entered for Consumtion in United States, etc., C 14.18
Merchandise Line Sales, BC-MLS (series), C 3.202/19
Public Merchandise Warehousing, C 3.102
Recent Trends in U.S. Merchandise Trade, ITC 1.15/3
Schedule H. Statistical Classification and Code Numbers of Shipments of Merchandise to Alaska from United States, C 3.150:H
Schedule L. Statistical Classification of Foreign Merchandise Reports in In-transit Trade of United States, C 3.150:L
Schedule S. Statistical Classification of Domestic and Foreign Merchandise Exported from U.S., C 3.150:S
Schedule X. Statistical Classification of Domestic and Foreign Merchandise Exported from United States by Air Arranged in Shipping Commodity Groups, C 3.150:X
Shipping Weight and Dollar Value of Merchandise Laden on and Unladen from Vessels at United States Ports During the In-transit Movement of the Merchandise from One Foreign Country to Another, C 3.164:981
Statistical Classification and Code Numbers of Shipments of Merchandise to Alaska from United States, C 3.150:H
Statistical Classification of Domestic and Foreign Merchandise Exported from U.S., C 3.150:S
Statistical Classification of Foreign Merchandise Reports in In-Transit Trade of United States, C 3.150:L
U.S. Exports of Domestic Merchandise, SIC- based Products and Area, C 3.164:610
U.S. Exports of Merchandise, C 3.278/3
U.S. Imports of Merchandise, C 3.278/2
U.S. Imports of Merchandise for Consumption, C 3.164:125
U.S. Merchandise Trade: Exports and General Imports by County, C 3.164:927
U.S. Merchandise Trade: Exports, General Imports, and Imports for Consumption, C 3.164:925
U.S. Merchandise Trade Position at Midyear, C 61.40
U.S. Merchandise Trade; Selected Highlights, FT-920, C 3.164:920
United States Airborne Exports of Domestic and Foreign Merchandise, Commodity (Schedule X) by Country of Destination, C 3.164:780
United States Airborne Exports of Domestic and Foreign Merchandise, Country of Destination by Commodity, C 3.164:790
United States Airborne General Imports of Merchandise, Country of Origin by Commodity, C 3.164:390
United States Exports by Air of Domestic and Foreign Merchandise Commodity by Country of Destination, C 3.164:731
United States Exports by Air of Domestic and Foreign Merchandise Country of Destination by Commodity, C 3.164:732

United States Exports of Domestic and Foreign Merchandise Commodity by Country of Destination, C 3.164:410
United States Exports of Domestic and Foreign Merchandise Country of Destination by Subgroup, C 3.164:420
United States Exports of Domestic and Foreign Merchandise To Canada (Including Lend-Lease Exports), C 3.157/4
United States Exports of Domestic and Foreign Merchandise Under Lend-Lease Program, Calendar Year, C 3.164:405
United States Exports of Domestic and Foreign Merchandise Under Lend-Lease Program, Commodity by Country of Destination, C 3.164:415
United States Exports of Domestic and Foreign Merchandise Under Lend-Lease Program, Country of Destination by Commodity, C 3.164:421, C 3.164:425
United States Exports of Domestic and Foreign Merchandise Under United Nations Relief and Rehabilitation Program, Country of Destination by Commodity, C 3.164:426
United States Exports of Domestic and Foreign Merchandise Under United Nations Relief and Rehabilitation Program, Commodity by Country of Destination, C 3.164:416
United States Exports of Domestic Merchandise (Including Lend-Lease Exports), C 3.164:400
United States Exports of Domestic Merchandise to Latin American Republics, C 3.157
United States Exports of Foreign Merchandise to Latin American Republics, C 3.157/2
United States General Imports of Merchandise, Commodity by Country of Origin, C 3.164:10
United States Imports of Merchandise for Consumption: Commodity by Country of Origin, C 3.164:110
United States Imports of Merchandise for Consumption; Country of Origin by Subgroup, C 3.164:120
United States, Airborne General Imports of Merchandise, Commodity by Country of Origin, C 3.164:380

Merchandising

Census of Distribution; Merchandising Series, C 3.37/18
Department Store Merchandising Data, FR 1.24/5, FR 1.24/6

Merchant

American Documented Seagoing Merchant Vessels of 500 Gross Tons and Over, 4 Degree, C 11.8
Annual List of Merchant Vessels, C 11.5
Employment Report of United States Flag Merchant Fleet, Oceangoing Vessels 1,000 Gross Tons and Over, C 39.208
Foreign Flag Merchant Ships Owned by U.S. Parent Companies, TD 11.16
Handbook of Merchant Shipping Statistics, C 39.218
List of Masters, Mates, {etc} of Merchant Steam, Motor, and Sail Vessels, Licensed during Calendar Year, T 38.7
List of Merchant Vessels, T 37.11, T 30.5
List of Officers of Merchant Steam, Motor and Sail Vessels Licensed During (calendar year), C 15.7
Merchant Fleet in Service on Great Lakes, C 27.9/5
Merchant Fleet News, SB 2.16
Merchant Fleets of the World, C 39.212
Merchant Fleets of the World, Sea-Going Steam and Motor Ships of 1,000 Gross Tons and Over, TD 11.14
Merchant Ships Built in United States and Other Countries in Employment Report of United States Flag Merchant Seagoing Vessels 1,000 Tons and Over, C 39.211
Merchant Vessels of United States, TD 5.12/2, T 17.11/2
Monthly Supplement to Merchant Vessels of United States, T 17.11
Ocean Going Merchant Fleets of Principal Maritime Nations, SB 7.5/100, SB 7.5/1100, C 27.9/6, MC 1.16
Oceangoing Foreign Flag Merchant Type Ships of 1,000 Gross Tons and Over Owned by the United States Parent Companies, C 39.230

Oceangoing Merchant Ships of 1,000 Gross Tons and Over Scrapped and Lost During the Calendar Year (date), C 39.229
Our Merchant Fleet, MC 1.28
Quarterly Report on Employment of American Merchant Vessels, SB 7.5/300, C 27.9/7
Quarterly Report on Employment of American Steam and Motor Merchant Vessels, MC 1.8
Statistical Analysis of the World's Merchant Fleet, TD 11.12
Statistical Analysis of World's Merchant Fleets Showing Age, Size, Speed, and Draft by Frequency Groupings, As of (date), C 39.224
Supplement to Merchant Vessels of United States, TD 5.12
United States Merchant Marine, Brief History, C 39.202:M 53/2
Weather Service for Merchant Shipping, C 30.79
Wheat Ground and Wheat-Milling Products, Merchant and Other Mills, C 3.118

Merchant Marine

Course of Instruction at Merchant Marine Academy, C 39.225
Laws relating to Shipping and Merchant Marine, Y 1.2:Sh 6
Merchant Marine Bulletin, C 25.12
Merchant Marine Council, Proceedings, TD 5.13
Merchant Marine Data Sheet, C 39.238
Merchant Marine Examination Questions, TD 5.57
Merchant Marine Statistics, C 11.10, C 25.10, T 17.10
Merchant Mariner, Devoted to Men of American Merchant Marine, SB 3.5
National Conference on Merchant Marine, SB 1.14
News Releases and Miscellaneous Publications; Committee on Merchant Marine and Fisheries, (House), Y 4.M 53/2
Office of Merchant Marine Safety, TD 5.35
Operating Instruction for Merchant Marine Examination Questions Books, Navigation General Book 3, TD 5.57/2
Proceedings Merchant Marine Council, N 24.32, T 47.31
Status of Vessel Construction and Reconditioning under Merchant Marine Acts of 1920 and 1938, SB 7.5:1105, C 27.9/8
U.S. Merchant Marine Data Sheet, TD 11.10
Vessels Receiving Benefits of Construction Loans under Merchant Marine Act of 1928, SB 7.8

Merchant Mariner

Merchant Mariner, Devoted to Men of American Merchant Marine, SB 3.5

Merchantable

Merchantable Potato Stocks, with Comparisons, A 88.12/9

Merchants

Bulletins for Retail Merchants, Y 3.F 73:17
Digest of Trade Hints for Paint and Varnish Merchants, C 18.194
Dry Goods Merchants' World News Letter, C 18.66

Mercury

Mercury, D 101.128, I 28.55
Mercury in (year), I 28.55/2
Mercury Reports, I 28.55

Merger

Merger Decisions, Y 3.F 31/8:1-3

Mergers

F.T.C. Statistical Report on Mergers and Acquisitions, FT 1.2:M 54/3

Merit

Digest Merit Systems Protection Board, MS 1.11
Issues of Merit, MS 1.17
Life-Pass It On, President's Environmental Merit Awards Program, EP 1.34
Pamphlets Merit Systems Protection Board, MS 1.9
Posters Office of the Special Counsel, Merit Systems Protection Board, MS 1.12

Merit System

Merit System Methods, FS 1.25

Merit Systems

Directory of State Merit Systems, FS 1.2:M 54

Meritorious

Meritorious Suggestions Digest, C 1.29

Merits

Petitions for Certiorari and Briefs on Merits and in Opposition for U.S. in Supreme Court of U.S., J 1.19/6

MESA

MESA Information Report, I 69.9

MESA Reports, C 55.617
MESA Safety Reviews: Coal-Mine Fatalities, I 69.10
MESA Safety Reviews: Coal-Mine Injuries and Worktime, I 69.10/2
MESA Safety Reviews: Injuries at Sand and Gravel Plants, I 69.10/3
MESA, the Magazine of Mining Health and Safety, I 69.11
NOAA Data Report, **MESA** (series), C 55.36

Mesa Verde
Mesa Verde National Park, Annual Reports, I 1.48

Mess
Supply and **Mess** Management, W 3.50/15

Message
Hydropac **Message** Summary, N 6.34, M 202.24
Message from the Presidents's Committee on Mental Retardation, Pr 36.8:M 52/M/56
President Monroe's **Message**, SI 11.2:M 75

Messages
Civilian Medical Division Health **Messages**, W 1.54

Messenger
Parent Education **Messenger**, A 43.14

Metabolic
Highlights of Research Progress in Arthritis and **Metabolic** Diseases, FS 2.22/21

Metabolism
Metabolism Study Section, HE 20.3001/2:M 56/2
National Arthritis, **Metabolism**, and Digestive Diseases Advisory Council, HE 20.3001/2:Ar 7/2

Metal
Administration of Federal **Metal** and Nonmetallic Mine Safety Act, Annual Report of the Secretary of the Interior, I 1.96/2
Administration of the Federal **Metal** and Nonmetallic Mine Safety Act, I 28.5
Aluminum **Metal** Supply and Shipments of Products to Consumers, C 41.112/4
Annual Conference on Advanced Pollution Control for the **Metal** Finishing Industry, EP 1.80
Babbitt **Metal**, C 3.71
Brass Mill Scrap and **Metal** Consumption and Stocks at Brass and Wire Mills, I 28.79/2
Contractor Fatalities Coal and **Metal**/Nonmetal Mines, L 38.20/4
Fatal Accidents Involving Drowning at Coal and **Metal**/Nonmetal Mines, L 38.19/3-2
JPRS (series) USSR Reports, Machine Tools and **Metal** Working Equipment, PrEx 7.21/3-3
Machine Tools and **Metal** Working Equipment, PrEx 7.22/3-3
Metal Industry Indicators, I 19.129, I 28.173
Metal/Nonmetal, Surface and Underground Fatalities, L 38.19/4
Metal/Nonmetal-Surface Fatalities, L 38.19/3
Metal/Nonmetal-Underground Fatalities, L 38.19/2
Power Haulage Fatalities, Coal and **Metal**/Nonmetal Mines, L 38.19
Refined **Metal** and Copper Scrap Operations at Brass and Wire Mills, Brass Mill Report, I 28.79/2
Titanium **Metal** Report, I 28.82/2
World Trade in Wood, Furniture, Floor, **Metal** and Automobile Polishes, C 18.178

Metallic
Injury Experience in **Metallic** Mineral Industries, I 28.27, I 69.9

Metallization
Double-Level **Metallization**: Annual Report, C 13.58/6

Metallography
Metallography and Heat Treatment of Metals {abstracts}, C 41.54/7
Physics of Metals and **Metallography** {abstracts}, C 41.54/2

Metallurgical
Metallurgical Advisory Committee on Titanium Information Bulletins, D 105.13/2-4

Metallurgist
Metallurgist {abstracts}, C 41.54/3

Metallurgy
Bureau of Mines Research (year), Summary of Significant Results in Mining **Metallurgy** and Energy, I 28.115
Institute for Material Research, **Metallurgy** Division, Technical Highlights, Fiscal Year, C 13.1/5-2
Journal of Abstracts, **Metallurgy**, C 41.54/9

Materials Science and **Metallurgy**, PrEx 7.22/10
Research in Progress, Calendar Year **Metallurgy** and Materials Sciences, Mechanics and Aeronautics, Chemistry and Biological Sciences, D 101.52/5-5
Scientific Reports of Higher Schools **Metallurgy**, C 41.54/4

Metals
Ferrous **Metals** Supply/Demand Data, I 28.169
Foreign Markets for **Metals** and Minerals Circulars, C 18.85/2
Foreign Trade Notes, Minerals and **Metals**, C 18.91/2
Foreign Trade Notes, Minerals and **Metals** and Petroleum, C 18.91
Index to Tests of **Metals** at Watertown Arsenal, W 34.14/2
Metallography and Heat Treatment of **Metals** {abstracts}, C 41.54/7
Metals Laboratory Unit Report, I 27.35
Nonferrous **Metals**, C 41.54
Nonferrous **Metals** Supply, Demand Data, I 28.169/3
Physics of **Metals** and Metallography {abstracts}, C 41.54/2
Platinum Group **Metals** in (year), I 28.77/2
Platinum Group **Metals**, I 28.77
Platinum **Metals** Reports, I 28.77
Preservation Tech Notes **Metals**, I 29.84/3-8
Production of Precious **Metals**, Calendar Year, T 28.7
Test of **Metals** at Watertown Arsenal, W 34.14

Metalworking
NPA Production Series, Quarterly Indexes of Shipments for Products of **Metalworking** Industries, C 40.15

Meteorological
Annual **Meteorological** Summary, Washington, D.C., A 29.30/2
Army **Meteorological** Register, W 44.11
BOMEX {Barbados Oceanographic and **Meteorological** Experiment} Bulletin, C 55.18
Catalog of **Meteorological** Satellite Data: ESSA 9 and NOAA 1 Television Cloud Photography, C 55.219:5.3
Collected Reprints; Atlantic Oceanographic and **Meteorological** Laboratories, C 55.612
Current Federal **Meteorological** Research and Development Activities, C 30.75/2
Data Report, **Meteorological** Rocket Network Firings, C 52.16
Data Report: High Altitude **Meteorological** Data, C 55.280
Federal Coordinator for **Meteorological** Services and Supporting Research, FCM (series), C 55.12
Federal **Meteorological** Handbooks, C 1.8/4
Federal Plan for **Meteorological** Services and Supporting Research, Fiscal Year (date), C 55.16/2
International **Meteorological** Observations, W 42.7/1
Key to **Meteorological** Records Documentation, C 55.219
Key to **Meteorological** Records, Environmental Satellite Imagery (series), C 55.219/4
Federal Coordinator for **Meteorological** Services and Supporting Research, FCM (series), C 55.12
Manual of Marine **Meteorological** Observations, C 30.4:M
Meteorological Chart of the Indian Ocean, A 29.27
Meteorological Chart of the Great Lakes, A 29.13, A 29.13/2
Meteorological Chart of the North Atlantic Ocean, A 29.23
Meteorological Chart of the North Pacific Ocean, A 29.24
Meteorological Chart of the South Atlantic Ocean, A 29.25
Meteorological Chart of the South Pacific Ocean, A 29.26
Meteorological Record, W 42.24
Meteorological Summaries, C 30.16
Meteorological Summary, Washington, D.C., C 30.10
Monthly **Meteorological** Summary, A 29.30
National **Meteorological** Center Publications, C 55.190
NODC Quarterly Accessions, Computer Produced Indexes, American Meteorological Society **Meteorological** and Geoastrophysical Abstracts, D 203.24/6

Numerical Weather Prediction Activities, National **Meteorological** Center, C 55.115
Publications National **Meteorological** Center, C 55.190
Special **Meteorological** Summaries, C 30.10/2
Station **Meteorological** Summary, C 30.10
Summary and Review of International **Meteorological** Observations for Month of, W 42.7/2
Summary of Synoptic **Meteorological** Observations, D 220.10
Technical Notes Department of the Air Force **Meteorological** Development Laboratory, D 301.45/17-2
Tri-Daily **Meteorological** Record {for} Month of, W 42.8/3
United States **Meteorological** Yearbook, A 29.45, C 30.25

Meteorology
Electromagnetic **Meteorology**, Current Awareness Service, C 13.54
Meterology and Hydrology {abstracts}, C 41.78
Meterology Data Report, C 55.220/5
World Data Center A **Meteorology** Data Report, C 55.220/5
World Data Center A **Meteorology**: Publications (unnumbered), C 55.220/7

Meter
Gas and **Meter** Inspection, Annual Report, I 1.13

Methamphetamine
Annual Report on **Methamphetamine** Use Among Arrestees, J 28.15/2-7

Methane
Shipment of Liquefied Petroleum Gases and **Methane** in (year), I 28.98/5

Methanol
Production of **Methanol**, C 3.101

Method
Federal Test **Method** Standards, GS 2.8/7
Method of Transportation Code, Exports, C 3.140:N
Schedule N. **Method** of Transportation Code, Exports, C 3.150:N
Test **Method** (series), EP 1.89/3
U.S. Exports, Commodity, Country, and **Method** of Transportation, C 3.164:750
U.S. Exports, Geographic Area, Country, Schedule B Commodity Groupings, and **Method** of Transportation, C 3.164:455
U.S. Exports, Schedule B Commodity Groupings, Geographic Area, Country, and **Method** of Transportaion, C 3.164:450
U.S. General Imports Commodity, Country and **Method** of Transporation, C 3.164:350
U.S. General Imports Geographic Area, Country, Schedule A Commodity Groupings, and **Method** of Transporation, C 3.164:155
U.S. General Imports Schedule A Commodity Groupings, Geographic Area, Country, and **Method** of Transportation, C 3.164:150

Methodological
Census Bureau **Methodological** Research, (year), Annotated List of Papers and Reports, C 56.222/3:M 56
Methodological Report, HE 20.6517/8
National Medical Care Utilization and Expenditure Survey Series A, **Methodological** Report, HE 22.26/2

Methodology
Congressional **Methodology**, ED 1.81
Methodology Papers: U.S. National Income and Product Accounts, BEA-MP- (series), C 59.19
Methodology Report, HE 20.6517/8
National Center for Education Statistics, Technical/ **Methodology** Report, ED 1.328/10

Methods
Acceptable **Methods**, Techniques, and Practices: Aircraft Alterations, TD 4.28, TD 4.28/2
Acceptable **Methods**, Techniques, and Practices: Aircraft Inspection and Repair, FAA 5.15, TD 4.28/2
Circulars Relating to Plan and **Methods** of Publication of Official Records of Union Army and Confederate Army, W 45.4
Design and Evaluation **Methods** (series), S 18.52/5
Evaluation **Methods** Series, CS 1.58/2
Forest Pest Management **Methods** Applications Group: Reports (series), A 13.52/10-3
Health Planning **Methods** and Technology Series, HE 20.6110/3
Merit System **Methods**, FS 1.25

Methods for Determination of Radioactive Substances in Water and Fluvial Sediments, I 19.15/5
Methods for the Collection and Analysis of Aquatic Biological and Microbiological Samples, I 19.15/5
Methods Handbook, P 1.31/7
Methods of Urban Impact Analysis (series), HH 1.76
National Medical Expenditure Survey **Methods**, HE 20.6517/3
Personnel **Methods** Series, CS 1.58
Series Available and Estimating **Methods**, BLS Current Employment Statistics Program, L 2.124/2
Series Available and Estimating **Methods**, BLS National Payroll Employment Program, L 2.124
Sources of Information on Urban Transportation Planning **Methods**, TD 1.51
State Maximums and Other **Methods** of Limiting Money Payments to Recipients of Special Types of Public Assistance, HE 17.626
Study of **Methods** Used in Measurement and Analysis of Sediment Loads in Streams, Reports, Y 3.F 31/13:9, Y 3.In 8/8:10
Metropolitan
Annual Housing Survey: Housing Characteristics for Selected **Metropolitan** Areas, C 3.215:H-170
Annual Housing Survey: Housing Characteristics for Selected Standard **Metropolitan** Statistical Area, C 3.215/17-60
Census of Housing: Detailed Housing Characteristics for **Metropolitan** Statistical Areas, C 3.224/3-6
Census of Housing: General Housing Characteristics for **Metropolitan** Statistical Areas, C 3.224/3-3
Census of Population: General Population Characteristics for **Metropolitan** Statistical Areas, C 3.223/6-3
Census of Population: Social and Economic Characteristics for **Metropolitan** Statistical Areas, C 3.223/7-3
Census of Retail Trade; Major Retail Centers in Standard **Metropolitan** Statistical Areas, RC (series), C 56.251/5
Climate Review, **Metropolitan** Washington, C 55.129
Construction Reports; New Residential Construction in Selected Standard **Metropolitan** Statistical Areas (SMSA), C 3.215/15
Current Local Announcements Covering Washington, D.C. **Metropolitan** Area, CS 1.28:2602-WA
Facts for Marketers: Standard **Metropolitan** Statistical Areas in { } Regional Geographical Division, C 41.2:M 34/3
Indexes of Production Worker Employment in Manufacturing Industries by **Metropolitan** Area, L 2.24
Local Government Finances in Selected **Metropolitan** Areas in (year), C 56.209, C 3.191/2
Major **Metropolitan** Market Areas, C 47.15/3
Maps of Major Concentrations of Poverty in Standard **Metropolitan** Statistical Areas of 250,000 or More Population, PrEx 10.2:P 86/9
News, Annual Pay Levels in **Metropolitan** Areas, L 2.120/2-4
News, Average Annual Pay by State and Standard **Metropolitan** Statistical Area, L 2.120/2-2
News, **Metropolitan** Areas Employment and Unemployment L 2.111/5
Public Assistance Recipients in Standard **Metropolitan** Statistical Areas, HE 3.61/2
Selected **Metropolitan** Areas, L 2.3
Social Security Beneficiaries in **Metropolitan** Areas, HE 3.73/3
State and **Metropolitan** Area Data Book, C 3.134/5
State and **Metropolitan** Area Data Book, A Statistical Supplement, C 3.134/5-2
State and **Metropolitan** Area Employment and Unemployment, L 2.111/5
State and **Metropolitan** Area Unemployment, L 2.111/5

Summary Characteristics for Governmental Units and Standard **Metropolitan** Statistical Areas (series), C 3.223/23:
Unemployment Rate by Race and Hispanic Origin in Major **Metropolitan** Areas, L 2.111/6
Urban Atlas, Tract Data for Standard **Metropolitan** Statistical Areas, C 3.62/7, C 56.242/4
Wage Trends for Occupational Groups in **Metropolitan** Areas, Summary Release, L 2.86/2
Metropolitan Areas
Distribution of Bank Deposits by Counties and Standard **Metropolitan** Areas, FR 1.11/6
Metropolitan Housing
Census of Housing **Metropolitan Housing**, C 3.224/4
Mexican
Mexican Boundary Commission, S 3.19/2
Mexican Boundary Survey, S 3.19/1
United States and **Mexican** Claims Commission, 1869-76, S 3.12
Mexico
Marine Environmental Assessment, Gulf of **Mexico**, Annual Summary, C 55.237
Mexico-United States Interparliamentary Group Report of Senate Delegation, Y 4.F 76/2:M 57/8
Mixed Claims Commissions, United States and **Mexico**, S 3.34/1
Revised Guide to the Law and Legal Literature of **Mexico**, L 1.36:38
United States General Imports and Imports for Consumption from Canada and **Mexico**, Exluding Strategic, Military and Critical Materials, Country by Commodity Totals, C 3.164:121
Mexico City
International American Conference: **Mexico City**, S 5.9/2
Methyl
Methyl Bromide Alternatives, A 77.517
MHDPS
Mental Health Demographic Profile System, **MHDPS** Working Papers, HE 20.8133
MI
MI Magazine, D 101.84
MIA
POW/**MIA** Policy and Process, Y 4.P 93/8
Mica
Mica in (year), I 28.130
MICAR
Instruction Manual Part 2g, Data Entry Instructions for the Mortality Medical Indexing, Classification, and Retrieval System (**MICAR**), HE 20.6208/4-7
Instruction Manual Part 2h, Dictionary of Valid Terms for the Mortality Medical Indexing, Classification, and Retrieval System (**MICAR**), HE 20.6208/4-8
Mich.
Statistical Report of Commerce Passing through Canals at Sault Ste. Marie, **Mich.** and Ontario, Salt Water Ship Movements for Season of (year), D 103.17/2
Michigan
Business America, **Michigan**, C 61.18/3
Lake **Michigan** Cooling Water Studies Panel: Reports, EP 1.72
Saint Marys Falls Canal, **Michigan**, Statistical Report of Lake Commerce Passing through Canals at Sault Ste. Marie, **Michigan** and Ontario, W 7.26, M 110.16, D 103.17
Special Promotion Series from Office of Civil and Defense Mobilization, Battle Creek, **Michigan**, Bulletins, Pr 34.757/3
Trade World **Michigan**, C 61.39
VA Medical Center, Allen Park, **Michigan**: Newsletter, VA 1.56/5
Water Resources Development in **Michigan**, D 103.35/22
Microanalytical
Publications **Microanalytical** Division, A 46.17, FS 7.16
Microbial
Microbial Chemistry Study Section, HE 20.3001/2:M 58
Microbiological
Methods for the Collection and Analysis of Aquatic Biological and **Microbiological** Samples, I 19.15/5
Microbiology

Microbiology and Infectious Diseases Program, Annual Report, HE 20.3263
Microcard
Microcard Availability Lists, Y 3.At 7:30
Microcomputer
Microcomputer Training Catalog, The DOL Academy, L 1.86/2
Microcomputers
Directory of U.S. Government Datafiles for Mainframes & **Microcomputers**, C 51.19/4, C 51.19/5
Microcomputers in Transportation (various titles), TD 1.52
Microcopy
National Archives Microfilm Publications: Pamphlets Accompanying **Microcopy**, GS 4.20
Microdata
Public Use **Microdata** Files (PUMS), C 3.285
Microelectronics
Space **Microelectronics**, NAS 1.80
Microfiche
How to Use the **Microfiche**, GP 3.22/3
Public Documents Highlights, **Microfiche** Cumulation, GP 3.27/2
Publications Reference File on **Microfiche**, GP 3.22/3
Slim Selected Library in **Microfiche**, J 26.28
Microfiles
Statistics Research Analysis **Microfiles** Catalog, HE 3.38/4
Microfilm
Contents and Price List for **Microfilm** Publications, GS 4.20/2
List of National Archives **Microfilm** Publications, GS 4.17/2
Microfilm Lists, GS 4.17/4
National Archives **Microfilm** Publications: Pamphlets Accompanying Microcopy, GS 4.20
Newspapers in **Microfilm**, Foreign Countries, LC 30.20/2
Microfilmed
Guide to German Records **Microfilmed** at Alexandria, Va., GS 4.18
Guides to the **Microfilmed** Records of the German Navy, GS 4.18/2
Microform
Name Authorities, Cumulative **Microform** Edition, LC 30.21
National Register of **Microform** Masters, LC 30.8/8
Newspapers in **Microform**, LC 30.20
Microforms
Library of Congress Catalogs: Newspapers in **Microforms**, LC 30.20
Microgravity
Microgravity News, NAS 1.92
Microwave
Market for U.S. **Microwave**, Forward Scatter, and Other Radio Communications Equipment and Radar in {various countries}, C 41.105
Point to Point **Microwave** Radio Service, CC 1.36/8
Mid-Air Collisions
Briefs of Accidents Involving **Mid-Air Collisions** U.S. Civil Aviation, TD 1.109/7
Mid-continent
Mid-continent Memo, I 66.19/3
Mid-East
Mid-East Briefing Graphic, D 5.329
Mid-East Briefing Maps, D 5.330
Mid-Europe
Highlights of Current Legislation and Activities in **Mid**-Europe, LC 1.27
Mid-Session
Mid-Session Review of the Budget, PrEx 2.31
Mid-Year
Mid-Year Statistics, NCU 1.9/3
Midcentury
Midcentury White House Conference on Children and Youth, Progress Bulletins, FS 3.217
Middle
Educational Briefs for the **Middle** and Secondary Level Classroom, NAS 1.19/3
Regional Reports, **Middle** Atlantic Region, L 2.71/6
Retail Trade Report **Middle** Atlantic Region, C 3.174
Middle Atlantic
Middle Atlantic Fisheries, C 55.309/2

Middle Atlantic Regional Office Publications, L 2.92

Middle East
 Accession List: **Middle East**, LC 1.30/3
 Aeronautical Chart and Information Bulletin, Europe, Africa and **Middle East**, New Editions of Aeronautical Charts Published, D 301.49/3
 Agricultural Situation: Africa and the **Middle East**, A 93.29/2-2
 Flight Information Publication: Enroute High Altitude, Europe, Africa, **Middle East**, D 301.9/4
 Middle East {United Arab Republic}, LC 1.30/3
 Military Aviation Notices; Corrections to Supplementary Flight Information, Europe, Africa and **Middle East**, D 301.49/2
 Radio Facility Charts, Europe, Africa, **Middle East**, M 301.17
 United States Air Force and Navy Supplementary Flight Information, Europe, Africa, and **Middle East**, D 301.49
 United States Air Force Radio Facility Charts, Europe, Africa, **Middle East**, D 301.9
 World Agricultural Situation Supplements: Africa and the **Middle East**, A 93.29/2-2

Middle Eastern
 Near and **Middle Eastern** Series, S 1.86
 Near Eastern and **Middle Eastern** Series, S 1.86

Mideast
 Mideast Directions (series), LC 41.10

Midmanagers
 First Line, Newsletter for Federal Supervisors and **Midmanagers**, PM 1.17, CS 1.91

Midshipmen
 Regulations Governing Admission of Candidates into Naval Academy As **Midshipmen** and Sample Examination Questions, D 208.108

Midsouth
 Forest Research News for the **Midsouth**, A 13.40/11

Midwest
 Commercial Dairy Farms, Northeast and **Midwest**, A 93.9/11
 Environment **Midwest**, EP 1.28/7
 Environment **Midwest**, Together, EP 1.28/6
 Latest Consumer Price Index (Tables for U.S. and 6 Cities in **Midwest**), L 2.38/8-4
 Midwest Region Annual Science Report, I 29.113
 Midwest Regional Member Relations Conference Sponsored by American Institute of Cooperation and Farmer Cooperative Service, A 89.17
 Midwest Region: Research/Resources Management Reports, I 29.105/2

Midwestern
 Midwestern Cities, A 88.12/31:2

Midwestern Cities
 Fresh Fruit and Vegetable Unloads in **Midwestern** Cities, A 88.40/2:5

Midyear
 Industrial Outlook and Economy at **Midyear**, C 41.42/4
 U.S. Merchandise Trade Position at **Midyear**, C 61.40

Might
 This **Might** Be You (radio scripts), L 1.14

Migrant
 Migrant Health Projects, Summary of Project Data, HE 20.5116
 Traveler/El Viajero, Quarterly Newsletter for **Migrant** and Seasonal Farm Workers, PrEx 10.19

Migration
 Bird **Migration** Memorandum, I 49.31
 County-to-County **Migration** File, C 3.284
 Migration and Settlement on Pacific Coast, Reports, A 36.131
 Migration of Birds, I 49.4:16
 Net **Migration** of the Population, by Age, Sex and Color, A 93.35
 Radionuclide **Migration** around Uranium Ore Bodies Analogue of Radioactive Waste Repositories, Y 3.N 88:25-11

Migratory
 Migratory Labor Notes, L 16.43/2
 Migratory Sheep Ranches, A 93.9/11

MIL-STD
 Military Standard **MIL-STD** (Navy) Series, D 201.13
 Military Standard **MIL-STD** Series, D 7.10

Mile
 River **Mile** Index, Y 3.P 11/4:10

Mileage
 Carload Waybill Statistics, **Mileage** Block Distribution, Traffic and Revenue by Commodity Class, Territorial Movement, and Type of Rate, Products of Agriculture, 1 Percent Sample . . . MB-1, IC 1.23/2
 Carload Waybill Statistics, **Mileage** Block Distribution, Traffic and Revenue by Commodity Class, Territorial Movement, and Type of Rate, Animals and Products, 1 Percent Sample. . . MB-2, IC 1.23/3
 Carload Waybill Statistics, **Mileage** Block Distribution, Traffic and Revenue by Commodity Class, Territorial Movement, and Type of Rate, Products of Mines, 1 Percent Sample of. . . MB-3, IC 1.23/4
 Carload Waybill Statistics, **Mileage** Block Distribution, Traffic and Revenue by Commodity Class, Territorial Movement, and Type of Rate, Products of Forests, 1 Percent Sample of. . . MB-4, IC 1.23/5
 Carload Waybill Statistics, **Mileage** Block Distribution, Traffic and Revenue by Commodity Class, Territorial Movement, and Type of Rate, Manufacturers and Miscellaneous. . . Terminations Statement MB-5, IC 1.23/6
 Carload Waybill Statistics, Traffic and Revenue Progressions by Specified **Mileage** Blocks for Commodity Groups and Classes, 1 Percent Sample of Carload Terminations in Year Statement MB-6, IC 1.23/7
 Crude-oil and Refined-products Pipeline **Mileage** in the United States, I 28.45/2
 Mileage Block Progressions, IC 1.23/7:MB-6
 Mileage Conservation Letter, Pr 32.4266
 Mileage Distribution of Carloads for Each Commodity Class by Type of Car, IC 1.23/16:TC-1
 Recurrent Report of **Mileage** and Traffic Data All Certificated Air Cargo Carriers, C 31.232
 Recurrent Report of **Mileage** and Traffic Data Domestic Air Mail Carriers, C 31.230
 Recurrent Report of **Mileage** and Traffic Data Domestic Helicopter Service, Certificated Airmail Carriers, C 31.229/4
 Recurrent Report of **Mileage** and Traffic Data Domestic Local Service Carriers, C 31.229
 Recurrent Report of **Mileage** and Traffic Data Foreign, Overseas and Territorial Air Mail Carriers, C 31.231

Miles
 Classification of Train-Miles, Locomotive-**Miles** and Car-**Miles**, IC 1 ste.11

Milestones
 Milestones Along Recovery Highway, Y 3.N 21/8:18
 U.S. Central Station Nuclear Electric Generating Units, Significant **Milestones**, E 1.41

Militarily
 Militarily Critical Technologies, D 10.13

Military
 Abstracts of Selected Periodical Articles of **Military** Interest, W 55.8
 Air University Library Index to **Military** Periodicals, D 301.26/2
 American **Military** History, D 114.2:M 59
 Army-Navy-Air Force List of Products Qualified Under **Military** Specifications, D 101.30
 Changes in **Military** Laws of United States, W 1.8/4
 Courts-Martial, Courts of Inquiry, and **Military** Commissions, W 10.6
 Courts-Martial Reports, Holdings and Decisions of Judge Advocates General, Boards of Review, and United States Court of **Military** Appeals, D 1.29
 Department of Defense Dictionary of **Military** and Associated Terms, D 5.12/3
 Department of Defense **Military** Commission Order, D 1.6/18
 Detailed Listing of Real Property Owned by the United States and Used by the Department of Defense for **Military** Functions Throughout the World, GS 1.15/4-2
 Dictionary of Basic **Military** Terms: a Soviet View, D 301.79:9
 Dictionary of **Military** and Associated Terms, D 5.12:1

Engineering Manual for **Military** Construction, D 103.9, M 110.13
European Recovery Program; Joint Report of United States and United Kingdom **Military** Governors, M 105.18
Military Traffic Management Command Publications, D 101.129/3
Extracts from Reports by Regular and **Military** Officers on Joint Army and Militia Coast-Defense Exercises, W 2.7
Foreign **Military** Sales Customer Procedures (series), D 7.6/15
Foreign Military Sales, Foreign Military Construction Sales, and **Military** Assistance Facts, D 1.66
Foreign Versions, Variations, and Diminutives of English Names and Foreign Equivalents of U.S. **Military** and Civilian Titles, J 21.2:N 15
General Real and Personal Property Inventory Report (Civilian and **Military**) of the U.S. Government Covering Its Properties Located in the U.S., in the Territories, and Overseas, As of June 30 {year}, Y 4.G 74/7:P 94
H 8-1 Nongovernment Organization Codes for **Military** Standard Contract Administration Procedures: Name to Code, D 7.6/2:8-1/2
H 8-2 Nongovernment Organization Codes for **Military** Standard Contract Administration Procedures: Code to Name, D 7.6/2:8-2/2
Harmon Memorial Lectures in **Military** History, D 305.10
Index of Military Specifications and Standards, **Military** Index, D 3.10
Index of Special **Military** Subjects Contained in Books, Pamphlets and Periodicials Received During Quarter Ending, W 26.5
Index of Specifications and Related Publications Used by Air Force, **Military** Index, D 301.28
Index of Specifications and Standards used by Department of Army, **Military** Index, V. 2, D 101.34
Index of Specifications and Standards Used by Department of the Navy, **Military** Index, D 212.10
Index of U.S. Air Force, Air Force-Navy Aeronautical and **Military** (MS) Standards (sheet form), D 301.16/2
Information Relative to Appointment and Admission of Cadets of **Military** Academy, W 12.9
Joint **Military** Packaging Training Center Course Outlines, D 1.35
Joint **Military**-Industry Packaging and Materials Handling Symposium, D 101.51
Last Salute, Civil and **Military** Funerals, D 101.2:F 96
Legal Guide and Case Digest, Veterans' Reemployment Rights Under the Universal **Military** Training and Service Act, As Amended, and Related Acts, L 25.6/2:L 52
Letters Relative to Current Developments in Medical Science and Medical **Military** Information, FS 2.40
Low Altitude Approach Procedures, United States **Military** Aviation Notice, D 5.318/3
Manual of Policies and Procedure for **Military** Specifications, D 3.6/2
Map Book of Major **Military** Installations, D 1.58
Medico-**Military** Review for Medical Department, Army, W 44.22
Military Affairs, PrEx 7.21/4
Military Air Traffic Activity Report, TD 4.19/4
Military and Civil Aircraft and Aircraft Engine Production, Monthly Production Report, C 31.130
Military Assistance Program Address Directory, D 7.6/4:M 59/6
Military Aviation Notices, D 301.9/2
Military Aviation Notices; Corrections, D 301.48/2
Military Aviation Notices; Corrections to Enroute-Low Altitude-Alaska, D 301.13/4
Military Aviation Notices; Corrections to Supplementary Flight Information Document, Pacific and Far East, D 301.50/2

Military Aviation Notices; Corrections to Supplementary Flight Information, Europe, Africa and Middle East, D 301.49/2

Military Aviation Notices; North Atlantic and East Canada, D 301.11/2

Military Aviation Notices; Pacific, D 301.12/2

Military Aviation Notices; West Canada and Alaska, D 301.13/2

Military Careers: A Guide to Military Occupations and Selected Military Career Paths, D 1.6/15

Military Chaplains' Review, D 101.73, D 101.22:165, D 101.114

Military Child Care Project (series), D 1.63

Military Commands and Posts, etc., W 3.20

Military Compensation Background Papers, D 1.54

Military Discipline, Courtesies, and Customs of Service, W 3.50/12

Military Fields, United States, Instrument Approach Procedure Charts, C 55.418/4

Military Geology (series), D 103.40

Military Government of Ryukyu Islands: Ryukyu Statistical Bulletin, D 102.19

Military Government Regulations, W 1.72/4

Military Government Weekly Field Reports, W 1.81

Military Government Weekly Information Bulletins, W 1.72/5, M 101.16, M 105.8

Military Government, Austria, Report of United States Commissioner, W 1.74, M 105.10

Military History Section: Japanese Operational Monograph Series, D 1.24/2

Military Hydrology Bulletins, D 103.32

Military Intelligence, D 101.93

Military Law Review, D 101.22:27-100

Military Law; Courts-Martial, W 3.50/13

Military Law; Law of Military Offenses, W 3.50/14

Military Law; Lesson Assignment Sheets, W 3.50/3

Military Laws of United States (Army), D 108.5/2

Military Manpower Statistics, D 1.61

Military Media Review, D 101.92

Military Negotiation Regulations, D 1.8

Military Notes on Training and Instruction, W 26.16/5

Military Operations of Civil War, Guide-Index to Official Records of Union and Confederate Armies, GS 4.21

Military Personnel Update, D 1.104/3

Military Police Journal, D 101.84/2

Military Prime Contract Awards by State, D 1.57/6-2

Military Publications: Index of AMC Publications and Blank Forms, D 101.22/3:310.1

Military Renegotiation Regulations Under Renegotiation Act of 1948, RnB 1.6/4

Military Reservations, W 1.32

Military Review, D 110.7

Military Sanitation and First Aid, W 3.50/4

Military Sea Transportation Service Magazine, D 216.8

Military Sealift Command, D 216.8

Military Specifications, D 1.12

Military Specifications, Temporary, D 1.12/2

Military Standard (designs), D 202.11

Military Standard MIL-STD (Navy) Series, D 7.10, D 201.13

Military Standard Requisitioning and Issue Procedure, D 7.6/4:M 59

Military Standards, D 3.7

Military Standards (preliminary), D 7.10/2

Military Traffic Management Bulletins, D 101.3/2

Military Women in the Department of Defense, D 1.90

Military-Civilian Occupational Source Book, D 1.51

MILSTRIP, Military Standard Requisitioning and Issue Procedures, D 7.6/17

Monograph Series on American Military Participation in World War, W 26.15/6

Monthly List of Military Information, W 26.7

Monthly Report of the Military Governor for Germany (U.S.), M 105.7

National Military Command System Information Processing System 360 Formatted File System , D 5.109

National Military Establishment Standards, M 5.8

National Monuments and National Military Parks: Information Circulars, I 29.21

Naval Military Personnel Manual, D 208.6/2

Navy Military Personnel Statistics, D 208.25

Nongovernment Organization Codes for Military Standard Contract Administration Procedures: Code to Name, D 7.6/2:8-2/2

Nongovernment Organization Codes for Military Standard Contract Administration Procedures: Name to Code, D 7.6/2:8-1/2

Nongovernment Organization Codes for Military Standard Contract Administration Procedures, D 7.6/2:8

Personnel Law: Civilian Personnel and Military Personnel, GA 1.5/13

Political, Sociological and Military Affairs, PrEx 7.15/4, PrEx 7.17/2

Posters Military Sealift Command, D 216.10

Proceedings Military History Symposium, D 301.78

Publications Office, Chief of Military History, D 114.10

Publications United States Court of Military Appeals, D 1.19/2

Quarterly Review of Military Literature, W 28.10

Register of Military Personnel in the Washington, D.C. Area, TD 5.19/3

Regulations for Military Academy (general), W 12.6/1

Reports of Military Operations during Rebellion, 1860-65, W 45.9

School of Military Packaging Technology Booklets, SMPT-BKLT- (series), D 105.31

Sealift, Magazine of the Military Sealift Command, D 216.8

Semi-Monthly Military Government Report for U.S. Occupied Area of Germany, M 105.21

Sixth Quadrennial Review of Military Compensation, D 1.89

Soldier-Scholar, A Journal of Contemporary Military Thought, D 305.23

Soviet Military Power, D 1.74

Soviet Military Thought Series, D 301.79

Soviet Union, Foreign Military History Journal, PrEx 7.21/4-3

Soviet Union, Foreign Military Review, PrEx 7.21/2-3, PrEx 7.21/4-2

Special Series Military Intelligence Division, W 100.7

Statement of a Proper Military Policy for the United States, W 26.8

Statistical Bulletins Military Government of Ryukyu Islands, D 102.19

Studies in Military Engineering (series), D 103.43/4

Summation of United States Army Military Government Activities in Korea, W 1.76

Summation of United States Army Military Government Activities in Ryukyu Islands, W 1.78, M 105.12

Textbook of Military Medicine (series), D 104.35

Transition Assistance Program Military Civilian One Good Job Deserves Another Participant Manual, L 39.8/2

Trials of War Criminals Before Nuremberg Military Tribunals, D 102.8

U.S. Army Military Personnel Center: Pamphlets (series), D 101.22/16

United States Air Force Academy Journal of Professional Military Ethics, D 305.21

United States Court of Military Appeals and the Judge Advocates General of the Armed Forces and the General Counsel of the Department of the Treasury,

United States Court of Military Appeals, D 1.19/2

United States Court of Military Appeals, Pubs, D 1.19/2

United States Military Posture for Fy (date), D 5.19

USAF Military Aviation Notices, Amending SFID, Caribbean and South America, D 301.51/2

World Military Expenditures and Arms Transfer, S 22.116

World Military Expenditures and Related Data, AC 1.16

Worldwide U.S. Active Duty Military Personnel Casualties, D 1.61/6

Militia

Extracts from Reports by Regular and Military Officers on Joint Army and Militia Coast-Defense Exercises, W 2.7

Militia Bureau Regulations (general), W 70.7

Naval Militia Circular Letters, N 23.6

Publications for Instruction, etc. of Naval Militia, N 1.27/7

Register of Commissioned and Warrant Officers Naval Militia, N 1.27/6

Register of Naval Militia, N 23.5

Report on the Militia of U.S., W 3.35

Roster of Organizaed Militia of United States, by Divisions, Brigades, Regiments, Companies, and other Organizations, with their Stations, W 70.5

Transactions of Naval Militia Association of United States, N 1.27/5

Milk

Bulk Cooling Tanks on Farms Supplying Federal Milk Order Markets, A 82.81/2

Commodity Information Series; Milk Leaflets, A 55.25/3

Dry Milk Reports, A 36.180

Evaporated, Condensed, and Dry Milk Report, A 88.14

Federal Milk Order Market Statistics, A 88.14/11

Federal Milk Order Market Statistics, Summary, A 82.81

Fluid Milk and Cream Report, A 88.14/3

Fluid Milk and Cream Report, Da 1-3 (series), A 92.10/3

Fluid Milk Prices in City Markets, A 36.152

Household Purchases of Butter, Cheese, Nonfat Dry Milk Solids and Margarine, A 88.14/6

IMS List Sanitation Compliance and Enforcement Ratings of Interstate Milk Shippers, HE 20.4014/2

Milk Distributors, Sales and Costs, A 93.13/2

Milk Distributors, Sales and Costs MDSC (series), A 88.14/9

Milk Inspector Letters, A 44.8

Milk Plant Letters, A 4.17, A 44.7

Milk Production on Farms and Statistics of Dairy Plant Products, A 88.14/7

Milk Production, Disposition, and Income, A 92.10/2, A 105.17/5

Milk Sugar, A 36.165

Milk, Farm Production, Disposition, and Income, A 88.14/8

Outbreaks of Disease Caused by Milk and Milk Products as Reported by Health Authorities as having Occurred in U.S., T 27.42

Prices Received, Minnesota-Wisconsin Manufacturing Grade Milk, A 92.16/3

Service and Regulatory Announcements Import Milk, A 46.11, FS 13.114

Sources of Milk for Federal Order Markets, by State and County, A 88.40, A 88.14/11-3

Stocks of Evaporated and Condensed Milk Held by Wholesale Grocers, A 88.14/5

Summaries of Federal Milk Marketing Orders, A 88.2:M 59/28

Mill

Brass Mill Scrap and Metal Consumption and Stocks at Brass and Wire Mills, I 28.79/2

Mill Margins Report, A 88.11/10-3

Mill Margins Report, Cotton Cloth and Yarn Values, Cotton Prices and Mill Margins for Unfinished Carded Cotton Cloth and Yarn, Revised Estimates, A 88.11/10-2

Prices of Cotton Cloth and Raw Cotton, and Mill Margins for Certain Constructions of Unfinished Cloth, A 88.11/10

Refined Metal and Copper Scrap Operations at Brass and Wire Mills, Brass Mill Report, I 28.79/2

Unfinished Cotton Cloth Prices, Cotton Prices, and Mill Margins, A 82.51, A 88.11/6

War Reports for Loggers and Mill Men, W 107.9

Wholesale Prices of Lumber, Based on Actual Sales Made F.O.B. Mill, A 13.15

Milled

Rice Stocks, Rough and Milled, A 105.42

Rough and Milled Rice Stocks, A 88.18/17

Millers

List, Peanut Millers (shellers and crushers), A 92.14/3

Peanut Millers List, A 92.14/3

Milling

Milling Division Circulars, Y 3.F 73:15

Wheat Ground and Wheat-Milling Products, C 3.116

Wheat Ground and Wheat-Milling Products, by States, C 3.117

Wheat Ground and Wheat-Milling Products, Merchant and Other Mills, C 3.118

Mills

Cotton Linters Produced and on Hand at Oil Mills by Type of Cut, by States, Preliminary, C 3.148

Cottonseed Products Manufactured and on Hand at Oil **Mills** by States, C 3.125

Cottonseed Received, Crushed and on Hand; Cotton Linters Produced; and Linters on Hand at Oil **Mills**, Preliminary Reports, C 3.149

Industry Wage Survey: Textile **Mills**, L 2.3/23

Inventories of Steel Producing **Mills**, C 3.158:M 33 J

Refined Metal and Copper Scrap Operations at Brass and Wire **Mills**, Brass Mill Report, I 28.79/2

Rice, Stocks and Movement, Southern **Mills**, A 82.50

Rice, Stocks, and Movement, California **Mills**, A 82.49, A 88.18/10

Wheat and Wheat-Flour Stocks Held by **Mills**, C 3.115

Wheat Ground and Wheat-Milling Products, Merchant and Other **Mills**, C 3.118

Millwork

Industry Wage Survey: **Millwork**, L 2.3/14

MILSTRIP

MILSTRIP Routing and Identifier and Distribution Codes, D 1.87/2

MILSTRIP Routing Identifier Codes, D 7.6/16

MILSTRIP Military Standard Requisitioning and Issue Procedures, D 7.6/17

Mind

Mind over Matter, HE 20.3965/3

Mindflights

Mindflights, D 305.22/2

Mimeographed

Foreign Service Regulations, Memorandum Transmitting **Mimeographed** Inserts for, S 1.5/2

Memorandum Transmitting **Mimeographed** Inserts for Foreign Service Regulations, S 1.5/2

Mimeographed Circulars, A 47.9

Mimeographs

Pro-**Mimeographs**, T 22.30

Mine

Administration of Federal Metal and Nonmetallic **Mine** Safety Act, Annual Report of the Secretary of the Interior, I 1.96/2

Administration of the Federal Metal and Nonmetallic **Mine** Safety Act, I 28.5

Bituminous Coal and Lignite **Mine** Openings and Closings in Continental United States (dates), I 28.33/2-2

Bituminous Coal and Lignite Production and **Mine** Operations, E 3.11/7-3

Coal **Mine** Fatalities, I 28.10/2

Coal **Mine** Injuries and Worktime, I 28.89

Federal Coal **Mine** Health Program in (year), HE 20.7109

Federal Coal **Mine** Health Program, Annual Report of the Federal Coal **Mine** Health and Safety Act, HE 20.2020

Federal **Mine** Health Program for (year), HE 20.7109

Federal **Mine** Safety and Health Review Commission Index, Y 3.M 66:9-2

Gold Report {**Mine** Production}, I 28.61

Lead **Mine** Production, I 28.60

MESA Safety Reviews: Coal-**Mine** Fatalities, I 69.10

MESA Safety Reviews: Coal-**Mine** Injuries and Worktime, I 69.10/2

Mine Emergency Operations Telephone Book, L 38.21

Mine Injuries and Worktime, L 38.16

Mine Inspector for Indian Territory, Annual Reports, I 1.20

Mine Inspector for Territory of Alaska, Annual Reports, I 28.9

Mine Inspector for the Territory of New Mexico, Annual Reports, I 1.23

Mine Inspector for the Territory of Utah, Annual Reports, 1893 95, I 1.33

Mine Production of Copper, I 28.59

Mine Production of Gold, I 28.61

Mine Production of Lead, I 28.60

Mine Production of Silver, Monthly Reports, I 28.62

Mine Production of Zinc, Monthly Reports, I 28.57

Mine Safety and Health, L 38.9

Monthly Statement of Coal-**Mine** Fatalities in United States, I 28.10/1

National First-Aid and **Mine** Rescue Contest, I 28.26/5

Posters **Mine** Safety and Health Administration, L 38.14/2

Schedule of Lists for Permissible **Mine** Equipment, I 28.8

Silver {**Mine** Production}, I 28.62

Zinc **Mine** Production, I 28.57

Mineral

Annual Report on Alaska's **Mineral** Resources, I 19.4/4

Census of **Mineral** Industries; Area Series, C 56.236/4

Census of **Mineral** Industries; Preliminary Reports, C 56.236/2

Census of **Mineral** Industries; Subject Series, C 56.236/5

Census of **Mineral** Industries; Subject, Industry, and Area Statistics, C 56.236/6

Census of **Mineral** Industries; {Industry} Bulletins MI (series), C 56.236/3

Census of **Mineral** Industries; {Publications}, C 56.236

Company Statistics Bulletins, Census of Business, Manufactures and **Mineral** Industries, C 3.222

EMRIA {Energy **Mineral** Rehabilitation Inventory and Analysis} Reports, I 1.104

Horizons, Indian **Mineral** Resource, I 20.67

Injury Experience in Metallic **Mineral** Industries, I 28.27, I 69.9

Manual of Instructions for Survey of **Mineral** Lands in United States, I 21.11/4

Mineral Commodities Summaries, I 28.148

Mineral Commodity Profiles, I 28.37/3

Mineral Commodity Summaries, I 19.165

Mineral Deposits Reports, I 19.36

Mineral Facts and Problems, I 28.3

Mineral Frontiers on Indian Lands, I 20.61/4

Mineral In . . ., I 28.156/3

Mineral Industries, C 3.940-12

Mineral Industry Health Programs, Technical Progress Reports, I 28.26/2

Mineral Industry Surveys, I 19.160, I 19.161

Mineral Industry Surveys, **Mineral** Industry of (Country) **Minerals**, I 19.163

Mineral Industry Surveys, **Mineral** Industry of [State] **Minerals**, I 19.162

Mineral Industry Surveys, Directory of Principal Construction Sand and Gravel Producers in the . . ., Annual Advanced Summary Supplement, I 19.138/3

Mineral Investigations Resource Maps, I 19.90

Mineral Investigations Series, I 28.13

Mineral Investigations, Field Studies Maps, I 19.39

Mineral Issues, I 28.156/2

Mineral Issues, an Analytical Series, I 28.156

Mineral Market Reports, I 28.28

Mineral Market Reports, I.S.P. (series), I 28.53/2

Mineral Orders MO (series), DM 1.6/3

Mineral Perspectives, I 28.37/2

Mineral Products of the United States, I 19.7

Mineral Resources Newsletter, I 19.115/3

Mineral Resources of the United States, I 19.8

Mineral Resources West of Rocky Mountains, T 28.6

Mineral Revenues, the Report on Receipts from Federal and Indian Leases, I 72.13

Mineral Trade Notes, I 28.39

Monthly Lime Report, **Mineral** Market Report LM (series), I 28.28/2

Oil Lands Leasing Act of 1920 with Amendments and Other Laws Relating to **Mineral** Lands {March 2, 1919}, Y 1.2:Oi 5

Preprints from Bulletin 585, **Mineral** Facts and Problems, I 28.3/c

Raw Nonfuel **Mineral** Production in (year), I 28.165

Report of Secretary to President and Congress on **Mineral** Exploration Program, I 1.85

Reprints from Bulletin 556, **Mineral** Facts and Problems, I 28.3/b, I 28.3/c

Safety in **Mineral** Industries, I 28.113

State **Mineral** Profiles, I 28.37/4

Technologic and Related Trends in the **Mineral** Industries, I 28.27

United States **Mineral** Resources, I 19.16:820

USGS Research on **Mineral** Resources, Program and Abstracts, I 19.4/7

World **Mineral** Production in (year), I 28.81/2

Minerals

Annual Report of the Secretary of the Interior under the Mining and **Minerals** Policy Act of 1970, I 1.96/3

Bureau of Land Management Maps, Surface and **Minerals** Management Status, Scale 1:100,000, I 53.11/4-2

Foreign Markets for Metals and **Minerals** Circulars, C 18.85/2

Foreign **Minerals** Quarterly, I 28.51

Foreign **Minerals** Survey, I 28.81

Foreign Trade Notes, **Minerals** and Metals, C 18.91/2

Foreign Trade Notes, **Minerals** and Metals and Petroleum, C 18.91

Kyanite and Related **Minerals** in (year), I 28.131

Manufacturers, **Minerals** Industries, EC (series), C 3.202/16

Mineral Industry Surveys, Mineral Industry of (Country) **Minerals**, I 19.163

Mineral Industry Surveys, Mineral Industry of [State] **Minerals**, I 19.162

Minerals and Materials, a Monthly Survey, I 28.149

Minerals and Materials Information, I 28.37/7, I 19.120/4

Minerals in the U.S. Economy, I 28.2:M 66/6

Minerals Management Quad (maps), I 53.11/6

Minerals Today, I 28.149/2

Minerals Yearbook, C 22.8/2, I 28.37

Posters **Minerals** Management Service, I 72.16

War **Minerals** Reports, I 28.99

Miners

Miners Circulars, I 28.6

Towards Improved Health and Safety for America's Coal **Miners**, Annual Report of the Secretary of the Interior, I 1.96

Mines

Bulletins, **Mines** (by States), C 3.14/4

Bulletins, **Mines** and Quarries (by Industries), C 3.28/18

Bulletins, **Mines** and Quarries (by States), C 3.28/17

Bureau of **Mines** Handbooks (series), I 28.16/3

Bureau of **Mines** Research (year), Summary of Significant Results in Mining Metallurgy and Energy, I 28.115

Bureau of **Mines** Research in (year), I 28.5

Carload Waybill Statistics, Mileage Block Distribution, Traffic and Revenue by Commodity Class, Territorial Movement, and Type of Rate, Products of **Mines**, 1 Percent . . . MB-3, IC 1.23/4

Census of **Mines** and Quarries, C 3.37/32

Census of **Mines** and Quarries (by States), C 3.37/33

Contractor Fatalities Coal and Metal/Nonmetal **Mines**, L 38.20/4

Fatal Accidents Involving Drowning at Coal and Metal/Nonmetal **Mines**, L 38.19/3-2

Fatalities in Small Underground Coal **Mines**, L 38.20

Index to Bureau of **Mines** Publications, C 22.7/2

Indexes to Bureau of **Mines** Publications, I 28.5/4

List of Bureau of **Mines** Publications and Articles, I 28.5

List of Members of Bureau of **Mines**, I 28.12

Product of **Mines**, IC 1.23/12:SS-4

Publications Bureau of **Mines**, C 22.7/1, I 28.5/8

Review of Bureau of **Mines** Coal Program, I 28.17, I 28.27

Review of Bureau of **Mines** Energy Program, I 28.27

Technology News from the Bureau of **Mines**, I 28.152

Mini

Mini Conference Report (series), Y 3.W 58/4:10

NTIS Published Search **Mini** Catalog, C 51.13/2-2

Miniature

Miniature Portraits, Wildlife at National Parks, I 29.51

Minieconomic

Substitute Chemical Program, Initial Scientific and **Minieconomic** Review of {various chemicals}, EP 5.13

Minimum

Annual Maximum, **Minimum**, and Mean Discharges of Mississippi River and Its Outlets and Tributaries, D 103.309/2

HUD **Minimum** Property Standards, HH 1.6/9

Minimum Construction Requirements for New Dwellings, FL 2.11

Minimum Enroute IFR Altitudes Over Particular Routes and Intersections, TD 4.316

Minimum Property Requirements for Properties of One or Two Living Units Located in the {various States}, HH 2.17

Minimum Property Standards, HH 2.17/3

Minimum Property Standards for 1 and 2 Living Units, HH 2.17/4

Minimum Wage and Maximum Hours Under the Fair Labor Standards Act, L 36.9

Walsh-Healey Public Contracts Act **Minimum** Wage Determination (for various industries), L 22.19

Mining

Annual Report of the Secretary of Interior Under the Surface **Mining** Control and Reclamation Act of 1977, I 1.96/5

Annual Report of the Secretary of the Interior under the **Mining** and Minerals Policy Act of 1970, I 1.96/3

Bureau of Mines Research (year), Summary of Significant Results in **Mining** Metallurgy and Energy, I 28.115

Catalog of Training Products for the **Mining** Industry, L 38.11/3

Domestic Uranium **Mining** and Milling Industry, (year) Viability Assessment, E 3.46/3

Electric Locomotives (**mining** and industrial), C 3.81

Environmental Overview and Analysis of **Mining** Effects, I 29.101

Excellence in Surface Coal **Mining** and Reclamation Awards, I 71.16

Injury Experience in Coal **Mining**, I 28.27, L 38.10/ 4, I 69.9

Injury Experience in Nonmetallic **Mining** (except Stone and Coal), L 38.10/5

Injury Experience in Nonmetallic **Mining** Industries, I 28.27, I 69.9

Injury Experience in Stone **Mining**, L 38.10/3

MESA, the Magazine of **Mining** Health and Safety, I 69.11

Mining and Manufacturing Industries in the American Republics, TC 1.21

Mining Journal {abstracts}, C 41.54/4

Mining Research Contract Review, I 28.154

Mining Research Review, I 28.153

Quarterly Financial Report for Manufacturing, **Mining**, and Trade Corporations, FT 1.18, C 3.267

Summary of **Mining** and Petroleum Laws of the World, I 28.27

Technical Highlights **Mining** Research, I 28.151/2

Ministry

Directory of USSR **Ministry** of Foreign Affairs Officials, PrEx 3.10/7-17

News of Institutes of Higher Learning; **Ministry** of Higher Education USSR, Geodesy and Aerial Photography, C 41.69/2

News of Institutes of Higher Learning; **Ministry** of Higher Education, Physics, C 41.52/4

News of Institutes of Higher Learning; **Ministry** of Higher Education, USSR, Mathematics, C 41.61/2

Mink

Mink, A 105.48

Mink Production, Pelts Produced in (year), A 92.18/11

Minn.

Statistic Report of Marine Commerce of Duluth-Superior Harbor, **Minn.** and Wis., D 103.13

Minneapolis

Express Mail Next Day Service, Directory for **Minneapolis** 554, P 1.52/2

Minnesota

Catalog of Charts of the Great Lakes and Connecting Waters, Also Lake Champlain, New York Canals, **Minnesota**-Ontario Border Lakes, D 103.208

Prices Received by Farmers for Manufacturing Grade Milk in **Minnesota** and Wisconsin, A 92.16/3

Water Resources Development in **Minnesota**, D 103.35/23

Minor

Minor Nonmetals in (year), Annual Advance Summary, I 28.121

Minor Civil Divisions

Maps (**Minor Civil Divisions**), C 3.61

Minorities

Annual Accomplishments Report, Affirmative Action Program for **Minorities** and Women, C 13.68

Annual Report on the Employment of **Minorities**, Women and Handicapped Individuals in the Federal Government, Y 3.Eq 2:12-5

Higher Education Opportunities for **Minorities** and Women, ED 1.42

Job Patterns for **Minorities** and Women and Private Industry, Y 3.Eq 2:12-7

Job Patterns for **Minorities** and Women in Apprenticeship Programs and Referral Unions, Y 3.Eq 2:12-2

Job Patterns For **Minorities** and Women in State and Local Government, Y 3.Eq 2:12-4

Minorities and Women in Public Elementary and Secondary Schools, Y 3.Eq 2:12-3

Minorities and Women in State and Local Government, Y 3.Eq 2:12-4

Minorities and Women in Undergraduate Education, Geographic Distributions for Academic Year, HE 20.9314

Selected List of Postsecondary Education Opportunities for **Minorities** and Women, ED 1.42

Women and **Minorities** in Science and Engineering, NS 1.49

Minority

Commerce, Journal of **Minority** Business, C 1.78

Directory for Reaching **Minority** Groups, L 23.2:M 66

Directory of Private Programs for **Minority** Business Enterprise, C 1.56

Employment in Perspective: **Minority** Workers, L 2.41/11-2

Minority and Female Motor Carrier Listings, IC 1.38

Minority Biomedical Research Support Program, HE 20.3037/7

Minority Business Enterprise in HUD Programs, Annual Report, HH 1.60

Minority Business Today, C 1.79

Minority Programs of the National Heart, Lung, and Blood Institute, HE 20.3224

National Roster of **Minority** Professional Consulting Services, C 1.57/3

MIGMS **Minority** Program Update, HE 20.3469

OMBE Outlook, News from the Office of **Minority** Business Enterprise, C 1.57/2

Presidential Advisory Committee on Small and **Minority** Business Ownership, Annual Report, PrEx 1.16

Press Releases **Minority** Business Enterprise Office, C 1.57

Views and Estimates of Committees of the House (together with Supplemental and **Minority** Views) on the Congressional Budget for Fiscal Year (date), Y 4.B 85/3-11

Minority-Owned

Survey of **Minority-Owned** Business Enterprises, MB (series), C 56.250, C 3.258, C 56.260

Minors

State Laws and Regulations Prohibiting Employment of **Minors** in Hazardous Occupations, L 22.6/2

Mint

Posters United States **Mint**, T 28.13

Mint Set

Mint Set of Commemorative Stamps, P 1.26/4, P 1.54

Mint Set of Definitive Stamps, P 1.54/2

Mints

General Instructions and Regulations in Relation to Transaction of Business at **Mints** and Assay Offices with Coinage Laws, T 28.9

Minute

Topographical Maps, 7.5 **Minute** Series, I 19.81

Minute Man

Minute Man, T 66.7

Four **Minute Men** Bulletins, Y 3.P 96/3:6

Four **Minute Men** Division, School Bulletins, Y 3.P 96/3:17

Four **Minute Men** News, Y 3.P 96/3:13

Four **Minute Men**, Army Bulletins, Y 3.P 96/3:6

Minutes

Minutes of Annual Meeting, GS 1.14/3

Minutes of Meeting; Arkansas-White-Red Basins Inter-Agency Committee, Y 3.F 31/13-2:2 M 66

Minutes of Meeting; National Institute of Neurological and Communicative Disorders and Stroke, HE 20.3519

Minutes of the Annual Meeting of the Treasury Safety Council, T 1.41/2

Minutes of {Meetings of Committees of Various Industries}, C 40.16

Minutes, Annual Meeting, PrEx 1.10:M 66

Summary **Minutes** of Meeting, S 5.48/12

MIP

MIP {Meat Inspection Program} Guidelines, A 88.17/6

Misbranding

Misbranding Regulations, Y 3.F 31/10:10

Misbranding Rulings, Y 3.F 31/10:11

Miscellaneous

Carload Waybill Statistics, Mileage Block Distribution, Traffic and Revenue by Commodity Class, Territorial Movement, and Type of Rate, Manufacturers and **Miscellaneous** Forwarder Traffic,... MB-5, IC 1.23/6

General and **Miscellaneous**, E 1.99

Manufactrers (**Miscellaneous**), C 3.37/27

Manufactures and **Miscellaneous** and Forwarder Traffic, IC 1.23/14:SS-6

Miscellaneous, A 1.5/2

Miscellaneous Circulars, A 1.5/1

Miscellaneous Correspondence of Navy Department Concerning Schley's Court of Inquiry, N 1.21/2

Miscellaneous Extension Publications, A 43.5/18

Miscellaneous Field Studies Maps, I 19.113

Miscellaneous Geologic Investigations Maps, I 19.91

Miscellaneous Papers, A 13.62/9, D 103.15/2, D 103.24/4, D 103.31/2, D 103.38/2, D 103.42/2, D 103.57/6, D 103.210

Miscellaneous Processed Documents, AE 1.13

Miscellaneous Publications of Congress, Y 1

Miscellaneous Series, D 103.11, EP 1.23/6

Miscellaneous Special Reports, A 1.7

Miscellaneous Unclassified Publications of Both House and Senate, Y 1.1

National Criminal Justice Reference Service: **Miscellaneous** Publications Series, J 1.42/3

News Releases and **Miscellaneous** Publications; Committee on Agriculture, (House), Y 4.Ag 8/1-2

News Releases and **Miscellaneous** Publications; Committee on Agriculture, Nutrition, and Forestry, (Senate), Y 4.Ag 8/3-2

News Releases and **Miscellaneous** Publications; Committee on Armed Services, (House), Y 4.Ar 5/2-2

News Releases and **Miscellaneous** Publications; Committee on Finance, (Senate), Y 4.F 49/2

News Releases and **Miscellaneous** Publications; Committee on Interior and Insular Affairs, (House), Y 4.In 8/14-2

News Releases and **Miscellaneous** Publications; Committee on Merchant Marine and Fisheries, (House), Y 4.M 53/2

News Releases and **Miscellaneous** Publications; Committee on Post Office and Civil Service, (House), Y 4.P 84/10-2

News Releases and **Miscellaneous** Publications; Committee on the Environment and Public Works, (Senate), Y 4.P 96/10-2

Pacific Northwest Research Station: **Miscellaneous** Publications, A 13.129

Rules and Regulations (**miscellaneous**), FP 1.7

Sisal, Hemp, Jute and **Miscellaneous** Fibers, C 18.126

Smithsonian **Miscellaneous** Collection, SI 1.7

Southern Region **Miscellaneous** Series, Items, A 55.45/6

tate and Private Forestry: **Miscellaneous** Reports, A 13.110/11

Woman's Liberty Loan Committee (**miscellaneous** publications), T 1.25/5

Mishap

NASA **Mishap** and Injury Data, NAS 1.57

Missile

AFMTCP-Air Force **Missile** Test Center, D 301.45/ 23-1

Air Force Ballistic **Missile** Division, Publications, D 301.68

Air Force **Missile** Test Center: Technical Reports, AFMTC TR (series), D 301.45/23

Analysis of Work Stoppages on U.S. **Missile** Sites, Pr 35.8:M 69/W 89

Army Ballistic **Missile** Agency DC-TR (series), D 105.15

Army **Missile** Command Redstone Scientific Information Center Redstone Arsenal Alabama RSIC (series), D 105.22/3

Budget Estimates; Aircraft and **Missile** Procurement, D 301.83/2

Encyclopedia of U.S. Air Force Aircraft and **Missile** Systems, D 301.90

Missile Purchase Description, D 105.21

Publications Air Force Ballistic **Missile** Division, D 301.68

Publications Air Force **Missile** Test Center, D 301.45/23-1

Report to Congress on the Ballistic **Missile** Defense Organization, D 1.1/6

Research Reports Army Ballistic **Missile** Agency, D 105.15

Special Bibliography, Artillery and Guided **Missile** School Library, D 101.49

U.S. Army Ballistic **Missile** Agency, DG- TR- (series), D 105.15/2

Western Space and **Missile** Center: Regulations, WSMCR- (series), D 301.6/7

Missing

Briefs of Accidents Involving **Missing** Aircraft U.S. General Aviation, TD 1.109/8

OJJDP Annual Report on **Missing** Children, J 32.17

World War II Honor List of Dead and **Missing** (by States), W 107.13

Mission

Headquarters, First United States Army, Deputy Chief of Staff, Information Management, Organization, **Mission**, and Functions, D 101.1/9

Japan Productivity Center, United States Operations **Mission** to Japan, Publications, S 17.44/2

Mission, Y 3.Eq 2:15

Mission Reports, NAS 1.45

Mission Status Bulletins, NAS 1.12/8

Publications Mutual Security **Mission** to China, FO 1.27

United States Chiefs of **Mission**, S 1.69:147

United States **Mission** to the United Nations Press Releases, S 5.55

United States Operations **Mission** to the Philippines, Publications, S 18.31

United States Operations **Mission** to Vietnam, Publications, S 18.31/2

Missions

Employees of Diplomatic **Missions**, S 1.8/2

Reports of United States Trade **Missions**, C 42.19, C 48.9

Mississippi

Annual Maximum, Minimum, and Mean Discharges of **Mississippi** River and Its Outlets and Tributaries, D 103.309/2

Daily **Mississippi** River Stage and Forecast Bulletin, C 30.54

Daily Missouri-**Mississippi** River Bulletin, C 30.54

Hydrologic Bulletin, Hourly and Daily Precipitation; Lower **Mississippi**-West Gulf District, C 30.35

Hydrologic Bulletin, Hourly and Daily Precipitation; Upper **Mississippi** District, C 30.33

Light List, Lights, Buoys, and Day Marks, **Mississippi** and Ohio Rivers, C 9.29/2

Light List, **Mississippi** and Ohio Rivers and Tributaries, N 24.18, T 47.27

Mississippi Flyway, I 49.24/6

Mississippi Weekly Weather-Crops Bulletins, A 88.49

Publications Upper **Mississippi** Valley Region, A 57.18

River Summary and Forecast, {Lower **Mississippi** Region}, C 55.110/7

Upper **Mississippi** Valley Region, Publications, A 57.18

Mississippi River

Explorations and Surveys for Railroad from **Mississippi River** to Pacific Ocean, W 7.14

Index of Topographic Quadrangle Maps of Alluvial Valley of Lower **Mississippi River**, D 103.308/2

List of **Mississippi River** Terminals, Docks, Mooring Locations, and Warehouses, D 103.58/2

Map of Alluvial Valley of **Mississippi** River, Quadrangles, W 31.9

Mississippi River, D 103.66/6

Mississippi River Fisheries, C 55.309/2

Mississippi River System of the United States, TD 5.9:5

Missouri-**Mississippi River** Summary and Forecasts, C 55.110/3

Stages and Discharges of **Mississippi River** and Tributaries and Other Watersheds in the New Orleans District, D 103.45/4

Stages and Discharges of **Mississippi River** and Tributaries in the Memphis District, D 103.45/2

Stages and Discharges of **Mississippi River** and Tributaries in the St. Louis District, D 103.45/3

Stages and Discharges of **Mississippi River** and Tributaries in the Vicksburg District, D 103.45

Stages and Discharges, **Mississippi River** and its Outlets and Tributaries, W 31.5, M 110.207, D 103.309

Topographic Quadrangle Maps of Alluvial Valley of Lower **Mississippi River**, D 103.308

Missouri

Daily **Missouri**-Mississippi River Bulletin, C 30.54

Missouri-Mississippi River Summary and Forecasts, C 55.110/3

Navigation Charts; **Missouri** River, D 103.66

Notes for Louisiana Purchase Exposition, Saint Louis, **Missouri**, LC 1.8

Water Resources Development in **Missouri**, D 103.35/25

Missouri Basin

Missouri Basin Inter-Agency Committee Publications, I 1.78

Missouri Basin Survey Commission, Reports and Publications, Pr 33.22

Missouri River

Comprehensive Framework Study, **Missouri River** Basin, Y 3.M 69:9

Department of Interior in **Missouri River** Basin Progress Report, I 1.79

Hydrologic Bulletin, Hourly and Daily Precipitation; **Missouri River** District, C 30.34

Missouri River, D 103.66

Missouri River Division: M.R.D. Sediment Series, D 103.41

Missouri River Main Stream Reservoir Regulation Studies, D 103.41/3

Progress, **Missouri River** Basin, I 1.80

Stages of the **Missouri River**, W 32.6

Missouri River Basin

Missouri River Basin Investigations Project Reports, I 20.52

MISTRIP

MISTRIP, Defense Program for Redistribution of Assets (DEPRA) Procedures, D 1.87/3

Mittens

Knit Wool Gloves and **Mittens**, C 3.63

Leather Gloves and **Mittens**, C 3.42

Mixed

Mixed Claims Commission, United States and Germany, S 3.31

Mixed Claims Commissions, United States and Mexico, S 3.34/1

Payload Flight Assignments NASA **Mixed** Fleet, NAS 1.81

Venezuelan **Mixed** Claims Commissions, Caracas 1902 and 1903, S 3.17

Washington Arbitration (American-British **Mixed** Claims Commission), S 3.13/2

ML

Technical Documentary Report **ML**-TDR, D 301.45/47

MMPA

MMPA Bulletin, C 55.313/2

MMS

MMS Today, I 72.17

MMWR

MMWR CDC Surveillance Summaries, HE 20.7009/2

MMWR, Morbidity and Morality Weekly Report, HE 20.7039/3

MMWR Recommendations and Reports, HE 20.7009/2-2

MMWR Reports on AIDS, HE 20.7009/5

MMWR Surveillance Summaries from the Center for Infectious Diseases, HE 20.7009/2-3

Mobile

Armor the Magazine of **Mobile** Warfare, D 101.78/2

Common Carrier Public **Mobile** Services Information, CC 1.36/6

New Domestic Public Land **Mobile** Radio Service Applications Accepted for Filing During Past Week, CC 1.36

Mobility

Army Air **Mobility** Research and Development Laboratory Fort Eustis Virginia: USAAMRDL Technical Reports, D 117.8/2 D 117.8/4

Geographic **Mobility**, C 3.186

Geographical **Mobility**, C 3.186/18

Historical Review, U.S. Army **Mobility** Equipment Research and Development Command, D 101.98

Mobility of the Population of the United States, C 3.186:P-20

Pupil **Mobility** in Public Elementary and Secondary Schools During the (date) School Year, HE 5.93/6

The **Mobility** Forum, D 301.56/7

U.S. Army **Mobility** R & D Laboratory: USAAMRDL CR- (series), D 117.8/6

Mobilization

Alphabetical Listing, Register or Planned **Mobilization** Producers, Manufacturers of War Material Registered Under Production Allocation Program, D 7.11

Annual Report of the Activities of the Joint Committee on Defense Production with Material on **Mobilization** from Departments and Agencies, Y 4.D 36:R 29

Background to Industrial **Mobilization** Manual for Executive Reservists, C 41.6/7

Civil and Defense **Mobilization** Directory, Pr 34.708/2, PrEx 4.8/2

Defense **Mobilization** Orders, Pr 33.1006/2, Pr 34.206/2, Pr 34.706/4, PrEx 4.6/3

Executive Reservist, Bulletin from Industrial **Mobilization**, for Members of National Defense Executive Reserve, C 41.113

Farm **Mobilization** Fact Sheets, A 21.21

Handbooks, Manuals, Guides Relating to Industrial **Mobilization** and Security, D 3.6/3

Health **Mobilization** Series, FS 2.302

Industrial **Mobilization**, W 3.50/16

Mobilization Regulations, W 1.29

Mobilization Training Program, W 1.37

National Plan for Civil Defense and Defense **Mobilization**, PrEx 4.6/7

Problems of **Mobilization** and Reconversion, Reports to the President, Senate, and House of Representatives by Director of War **Mobilization** and Reconversion, Y 3.W 19/7:8

Report to the President by Director of Defense **Mobilization**, Pr 33.1008

Report to the President by Director of Office of Defense **Mobilization**, Pr 34.201

Special Promotion Series from Office of Civil and Defense **Mobilization**, Battle Creek, Michigan, Bulletins, Pr 34.757/3

Mock-Up

Detailed **Mock-Up** Information, W 108.20

Mode

Pleasure and Business Visitors to U.S. by Port of Entry and **Mode** of Travel, C 47.15/2

Model

Annual Conference of **Model** Reporting Area for Blindness Statistics, Proceedings, FS 2.22/37

Conference of **Model** Reporting Area for Blindness, Proceedings, HE 20.3759/2

Directory of Energy Information Administration **Model** Abstracts, E 3.48

Listing of Aircraft Accidents/incidents by Make and **Model**, U.S. Civil Aviation, TD 1.109/15

Model Cities Management Series, Bulletins, HH 1.42

Model Documentation Reports, E 3.26/6

Model Programs, Title III, Elementary and Secondary Education Act, HE 18.12

Model State Regulations {on various subjects} As Adopted by the National Conference on Weights and Measures, C 13.55/3

Model Town Home Selector, Y 3.F 31/11:33

Model Weights and Measures Ordinance (year), Provisions As Adopted by the National Conference on Weights and Measures, C 13.55

Oak Ridge Uranium Market **Model**, E 3.46/3-2

Oil Market Simulation **Model**, E 3.55

Proceedings Annual Conference of **Model** Reporting Area for Blindness Statistics, FS 2.22/37

Proceedings Annual Conference on **Model** Reporting Area for Mental Hospital Statistics, FS 2.22/44

Report on Quality Changes for (year) **Model** Passenger Cars, L 1.79/2, L 2.120/2-7

Statistical Report, Annual Tabulations of **Model** Reporting Area for Blindness Statistics, FS 2.22/37-2

Statistics for (year) on Blindness in the **Model** Reporting Area, HE 20.3759

Supplement to State Court **Model** Statistical Dictionary, J 29.9/3

Task Force on **Model** Cities, Pr 37.8:M 72

Taylor **Model** Basin Report, D 211.9/2

Models

Catalog of Logistics **Models**, D 1.33/6

CETA Program **Models** (series), L 37.8/6

Computer Codes and Mathematical **Models**, Y 3.N 88:31/0083

Habitat Suitability Index **Models** (series), I 49.97

Market Penetration **Models**, E 3.1/5-2

Program **Models**, J 1.54, J 26.16, J 28.9

Youth Program **Models** and Innovations, L 37.19

Moderate-Income

Consumers' Price Index for **Moderate-Income** Families (adjusted series), L 2.38/2

Modern

Applications of **Modern** Technologies to International Development, AID-OST (series), S 18.42

Deschler's Procedure, a Summary of the **Modern** Precedents and Practices of the U.S. House of Representatives, Y 1.2:D 45

Modern Foreign Language Fellowship Program, National Defense Education Act, Title 6 and NDEA Related Awards under Fullbright-Hays Act, FS 5.255:55034, HE 5.255:55034

Modern World at Work, FS 6.11

The U.S. Navy in the **Modern** World Series, D 221.16

Modernization

HPC (High Permormance Computing) **Modernization** Plan, D 1.106

Modernization Credit Plan, Bulletins, Y 3.F 31/11:12

National Implementation Plan For **Modernization** of the National Weather Service, C 55.133

Modernize

Title 1 Fall Program, **Modernize** for Winter, Special Field Bulletins, Y 3.F 31/11:34

Modification

Electronic Equipment **Modification**, C 31.161

Field Service **Modification** Work Orders, W 34.33

Modification Instructions, D 217.16/6

Modification Work Orders: Civil Aeronautics Administration, C 31.116/3

Modification Work Orders: Department of the Army, W 1.56, D 101.29

Summary Report, Weather **Modification**, C 55.27

U.S. Army Equipment Index of **Modification** Work Orders, D 101.22:750-10

Weather **Modification** Activity Reports, C 55.27/2

Weather **Modification** Reporting Program, C 55.27/3

Weather **Modification**, Annual Report, NS 1.21

Weather **Modification**, Summary Report, C 55.27

Modified

Names of Counties Declared to be **Modified** Accredited Bang's Disease-Free Areas, A 4.33

Request for New or **Modified** Broadcast Call Signs, CC 1.44

Modular

Modular Individualized Learning for Electronics Training, D 207.109

Module

Module (series): Centers for Disease Control, HE 20.7030

Module (series): Department of the Air Force, D 301.26/7-4, D 301.26/17-4

Modules

Teenage Health Teaching **Modules** (series), HE 20.7024

Mohair

Mohair Production and Income, A 36.200

Mohair Production and Value, A 92.29/4

Mohair Production and Value of Sales, A 88.35/4

Wool and **Mohair**, A 92.29/5, A 105.54

Wool and **Mohair** Prices, Marketing Year, A 88.35/5

Wool and **Mohair** Production, Price and Value, A 92.29/5

Moils

Commercial Stocks of Wool and Related Fibers, Tops, **Moils**, Waste Clips and Rags in U.S., C 3.52/3

Moisture

Snow Survey and Soil **Moisture** Measurements, Basic Data Summary for Western United States, Including Columbia River Drainage in Canada, A 57.46/17

Molasses

Industry Reports Sugar, **Molasses** and Confectionary, C 18.231

Molasses Market News, A 88.23

Molasses Market News Annual Summary, A 88.40/2:2

Molasses Market News, Market Summary, A 88.23/2, A 88.51

Weekly **Molasses** Market Reports, A 82.62

Molecular

Molecular Biology Study Section, HE 20.3001/2:M 73/2

Molecular Control Working Group, HE 20.3001/2:M 73

Registry of Toxic Effects of Chemical Substances, Permuted **Molecular** Formula, Index, HE 20.7112/4

Molluscicides

Insecticides, Acaricides, **Molluscicides**, and Antifouling Compounds, EP 5.11/3

Molybdenum

Molybdenum, I 28.58/3

Molybdenum Reports, I 28.58

Molybdenum Reports {new series}, I 28.58/2

Mineral Industry Surveys, **Molybdenum**, I 19.159

Monday

Monday Morning Highlights, J 16.29

Monetary

Monetary Conferences, S 5.13

World **Monetary** Conditions in Relation to Agricultural Trade, A 93.34/2

Money

After-Tax **Money** Income Estimates of Households, Current Population Reports, C 3.186/5

Circulation Statement of United States **Money**, T 63.308

Concurrent Receipt of Public Assistance **Money** Payments and Old-Age, Survivors, and Disability Insurance Cash Benefits by Persons Aged 65 or Over, FS 17.636, HE 17.636

Facts about United States **Money**, T 1.40

Money Income and Poverty Status of Families and Persons in the United States, C 3.186/11

Money Income of Households, Families, and Persons in the United States, C 3.186/2

Money Payments to Recipients of Special Types of Public Assistance, FS 17.627, HE 17.627

Money Stock Measures and Components of **Money** Stock Measures and Related Items, FR 1.47

National **Money** Laundering Strategy, T 1.67/2

Open-Market **Money** Rates and Bond Prices, FR 1.44

Reasons for Discontinuing **Money** Payments to Public Assistance Cases, HE 17.613/2

Recipients of Public Assistance **Money** Payments and Amounts of Such Payments, by Program, State, and County, HE 17.627/2

State Maximums and Other Methods of Limiting **Money** Payments to Recipients of Special Types of Public Assistance, HE 17.626

Trends in **Money** Laundering, T 1.67

Money Order

International List, **Money Order** Offices in Foreign Countries, P 9.6

Register of **Money Order** Post Offices in United States, P 9.5

Stolen **Money-Order** Forms, P 4.7

Moneys

(Public **Moneys** Depositaries) Circulars, W 3.25

Tables to Convert {Foreign **Moneys**, Weights and Measures into U.S. Standards}, C 1.11

Mongolia

Mongolia Report, PrEx 7.16/3

Monitor

CMC (Cooperative Monitoring Center) **Monitor** Newsletter, E 1.139

Earth System **Monitor**, C 55.52

102 **Monitor**, Environmental Impact Statements, PrEx 14.10, EP 1.76

Monitor, E 2.19

Monitoring

Action in the United States of America Related to Stratospheric **Monitoring**, S 1.132

Concorde **Monitoring**; Dulles International Airport, TD 4.49

Concorde **Monitoring**; John F. Kennedy International Airport, TD 4.49/2

CRS Media Relations, Newspapers, Magazines, Radio, Television, Informational **Monitoring** Service, J 23.7

Directory of Air Quality **Monitoring** Sites Active in (year), EP 1.2:Ai 7/5

Ecological **Monitoring** Program at the Waste Isolation Pilot Plant, Annual Report, E 1.28/16

Environmental **Monitoring**, 600/4 (series), EP 1.23/5

Federal Plan for Ocean Pollution Research, Developing, and **Monitoring**, PrEx 8.109

Federal Radiological Fallout **Monitoring** Station Directory, D 119.8/3:E 5.11

Fish **Monitoring** Investigations, Browns Ferry Nuclear Plant, Wheeler Reservoir, Alabama, Y 3.T 25:37

Fish **Monitoring** Investigations: Sequoyah Nuclear Plant, Chickamauga Reservoir, Tennessee, Y 3.T 25:37-3

Geophysical **Monitoring** for Climatic Change, C 55.618

Global Atmospheric Background **Monitoring** for Selected Environmental Parameters, C 55.284

Long Term Resource **Monitoring** Program, Program Report (series), I 49.109

Long Term Resource **Monitoring** Program, Technical Report (series), I 49.109/4

Monitoring and Air Quality Trends Report, EP 1.59

National Air **Monitoring** Program: Air Quality and Emission Trends, Annual Report, EP 1.47

National Survey Results on Drug Use from the **Monitoring** the Future Study, HE 20.3968

NDE of Stainless Steel and On-Line Leak **Monitoring** of LWRS, Annual Report, Y 3.N 88:25-5, Y 3.N 88:25-9

NRC-TLD Direct Radiation **Monitoring** Network, Y 3.N 88:43

Performance **Monitoring** System: Summary of Lock Statistics, D 103.57/12

Pesticides and Toxic Substances **Monitoring** Report, EP 5.16

Pesticides **Monitoring** Journal, Pr 37.8:En 8/P 43, PrEx 14.9, Y 3.F 31/18:9

Precision and Accuracy Assessments for State and Local Air **Monitoring** Networks, EP 1.23/5-3

Report to Congress on Ocean Pollution, **Monitoring** and Research, C 55.31/3, C 55.439

Waterfowl **Monitoring** Investigations, Y 3.T 25:27-2

Monmouth

Area Wage Survey, **Monmouth**-Ocean, New Jersey, Metropolitan Area, L 2.121/30-4

Monograph

Cancer Research Safety **Monograph** Series, HE 20.3162/2

CPR **Monograph** Series, HE 20.3362/6

Criminal Justice **Monograph** Series, J 1.37/3

Effective Programs **Monograph**, J 26.30/2

Historical **Monograph** Series, D 208.210

HIV/AIDS Evaluation **Monograph** Series, HE 20.9515

Housing **Monograph** Series, Y 3.N 21/12:14

Monograph (series): Bureau of Mines, C 22.24

Monograph (series): Childrens Bureau, C 19.5

Monograph (series): Environmental Science Services Administration, C 52.13

Monograph (series): Industrial College of the Armed Forces, D 5.10

Monograph (series): International Labor Affairs Bureau, L 29.13

Monograph (series): Joint Chiefs of Staff, D 5.9/4

Monograph (series): Law Enforcement Assistance Administration, J 26.15/2

Monograph (series): National Bureau of Standards, C 13.44

Instruction Manual Part 2h, Dictionary of Valid Terms for the **Mortality** Medical Indexing, Classification, and Retrieval System (MICAR), HE 20.6208/4-8

Instruction Manual Part 11, Computer Edits for **Mortality** Data, HE 20.6208/14

Instructions for Classifying the Underlying Cause of Death: Nonindexed Terms, Standard Abbreviations, and State Geographic Codes Used in **Mortality** Data Classification, HE 20.6208/4

Medicare Hospital **Mortality** Information: Vol. 1, Alabama - California, HE 22.34

Medicare Hospital **Mortality** Information: Vol. 2, Colorado - Illinois, HE 22.34

Medicare Hospital **Mortality** Information: Vol. 3, Indiana - Maryland, HE 22.34

Medicare Hospital **Mortality** Information: Vol. 4, Massachusetts - Nevada, HE 22.34

Medicare Hospital **Mortality** Information: Vol. 5, New Hampshire - Ohio, HE 22.34

Medicare Hospital **Mortality** Information: Vol. 6, Oklahoma - Tennessee, HE 22.34

Medicare Hospital **Mortality** Information: Vol. 7, Texas - Guam, HE 22.34

MMWR, Morbidity and **Mortality** Weekly Report, HE 20.7039/3

Morbidity and **Mortality** Weekly Report, HE 20.7009

Mortality Index, FS 2.107

Mortality Statistics, C 3.3, C 3.40

Public Use Data Tape Documentation **Mortality** Cause-of-Death Summary Data, HE 20.6226/6

Public Use Data Tape Documentation **Mortality** Local Area Summary, HE 20.6226/7

Summary of **Mortality** from Automobile Accidents, C 3.39

Mortgage

Analysis of HUD-Acquired Home **Mortgage** Properties, HH 1.101

Annual Report, Voluntary Home **Mortgage** Credit Program, HH 1.25

Conventional Home **Mortgage** Rates in Early (month), FHL 1.25/3

Directory of Multifamily Project **Mortgage** Insurance Programs by Project Status, HH 1.50

Estimated Home **Mortgage** Debt and Financing Activity, FHL 1.16

Estimated **Mortgage** Lending Activity of Savings and Loan Associations, HH 4.8/3

Farm **Mortgage** Debt, A 93.9/12

Farm-**Mortgage** Lending Experience of 19 Life Insurance Companies, Federal Land Banks, and Farmers Home Administration, A 93.9/5

Farm-**Mortgage** Recordings (by States), A 36.109

Federal Farm Loan Act with Amendments and Farm **Mortgage** and Farm Credit Acts, Y 1.2:F 31

Federal National **Mortgage** Association News, HH 6.8/2

FHA and VA **Mortgages** Owned and Available for Sale by Reconstruction Finance Corporation and Federal National **Mortgage** Association, Y 3.R 24:14

FHA Home **Mortgage** Insurance Operations, State, County and MSA/PMSA, HH 2.24/8

FHA Monthly Report of Operations: Home **Mortgage** Programs, HH 2.27/2

FHA Monthly Report of Operations: Project **Mortgage** Insurance Programs, HH 2.27

FSLIC Insured Savings and Loan Associations, Savings and **Mortgage** Activity, Selected Balance Sheet Items, FHL 1.20/2

Government National **Mortgage** Association, GNMA, Annual Report, HH 1.1/7

Home **Mortgage** Disclosure Act Data (State), FR 1.63

Home **Mortgage** Interest Rates and Terms, FHL 1.25

Home **Mortgage** Interest Rates Continue to Decline in Early (Month), FHL 1.25/2

HUD Survey Reveals Large Increase in Pension Fund Investment in **Mortgage** Instruments, HH 1.99/7

Mortgage Interest Rates on Conventional Loans, Largest Insured Savings and Loan Associations, FHL 1.24

Mortgage Lending Activity of Savings and Loan Associations, FHL 1.7/3

Mortgage Recording Letter, FHL 1.9, HH 4.9

Nonfarm **Mortgage** Investments of Life Insurance Companies, FHL 1.18

Publications Federal National **Mortgage** Association, FL 5.17

RFC **Mortgage** Company, Circulars, Y 3.R 24:9

Savings and **Mortgage** Financing Data, HH 4.10

Savings and **Mortgage** Lending Activity, Selected Balance Sheet Items, F.S.L.I.C. Insured Savings and Loan Associations, FHL 1.20/2

Savings, **Mortgage** Financing and Housing Data, FHL 1.10

Selected Multifamily Status Reports, **Mortgage** Insurance Programs by Name and Location of Each Project, HH 1.50

Summary of **Mortgage** Insurance Operations and Contract Authority, HH 2.24/5

Survey of **Mortgage** Lending Activity State Estimates, HH 1.99/2-2

Survey of **Mortgage** Lending Activity, HH 1.99, HH 1.99/2, HH 1.99/2-3

Survey of Pension Fund Investment in **Mortgage** Instruments, HH 1.99/4

Urban **Mortgage** Finance Reading Lists, NHA 2.16

Mortgage-Related

Survey of **Mortgage-Related** Security Holdings of Major Institutions, HH 1.99/4-2

Mortgages

All Approved **Mortgages**, Letters to Administrators, HH 2.6/4

Characteristics of FHA Single-Family **Mortgages**, HH 2.24/7

Estimated Amount of Nonfarm **Mortgages** of $20,000 or Less Recorded, HH 4.8/4

FHA Trends, Characteristics of Home **Mortgages** Insured by FHA, HH 2.24

Rates & Terms on Conventional Home **Mortgages** Annual Summary, FHF 1.15

MOSAIC

MOSAIC, NS 1.29

Mosaics

Lunar Charts and **Mosaics** Series, D 301.49/4

Magellan Full-Resolution Radar **Mosaics**, NAS 1.86/2

Moscow

Bulletin of **Moscow** Society of Naturalists, Geological Division, C 41.46/2

Moscow University

Herald of **Moscow University**, Physio-Mathematical and Natural Sciences Series {abstracts}, C 41.50/6

Motel

Federal Hotel/**Motel** Discount Directory, GS 8.10/2, GS 2.21/2

Motels

Eating and Drinking Places and **Motels** Wage Survey Summaries by Cities, L 2.113/4

Mothers

Center for Research for **Mothers** and Children, Progress Report, HE 20.3351/2

News Exchange, Extended School Services for Children of Working **Mothers**, Letters, FS 5.36

Research to Improve Health Services for **Mothers** and Children, HE 20.5114/2

Motion

World Wide **Motion** Picture Developments, C 18.180

Motion Picture

Motion Picture Films, I 28.35

Motion Picture Guides, FS 2.211/2

Motion Picture Theaters Throughout the World, C 18.116/2

Motion Pictures

Bibliography of **Motion Pictures** and Film Strips FS (series), C 35.11/2 C 41.23

Bimonthly List of Publications and **Motion Pictures**, A 21.6/5

Motion Pictures Abroad, C 18.115, C 41.16

Motion Pictures and Filmstrips, LC 30.8/4

Motion Pictures Distributed by Photographic Section, I 43.9

Motion Pictures Educational {and} Industrial, C 18.116

Motion Pictures of Department of Agriculture, A 43.24

Motion-Picture

Motion-Picture Films, C 22.26/1

Motions

Actions on **Motions**, Reports, CC 1.32

In Supreme Court of U.S., Briefs, Petitions, and **Motions** of Wm. Marshall Bullett, Solicitor General, J 1.19/2

Motive

Motive Power and Car Equipment of Class I Railroads in the United States, IC 1 ste.36

Motor

Accidents of Class 1 **Motor** Carriers of Passengers, TD 2.310/2

Accidents of Large **Motor** Carriers of Property, TD 2.310

Analysis of Defective Vehicle Accidents of **Motor** Carriers, IC 1 mot.20

Analysis of **Motor** Carrier Accidents Involving Vehicle Defects of Mechanical Failure, TD 2.312

Annual **Motor** Vehicle Report for Fiscal Year, GS 2.14

Annual Report to the Interstate Commerce Commission, Class I and Class II **Motor** Carriers of Household Goods, IC 1.39/3

Annual Report to the Interstate Commerce Commission, Class I and Class II **Motor** Carriers of Property, IC 1.39

Cost of Transporting Freight by Class I and Class II **Motor** Common Carriers of General Commodities, IC 1 acco.2.F 88, IC 1 acco.13

Cost of Transporting Freight, Class 1 and Class 2 **Motor** Common Carriers of General Freight, IC 1 acco.13

Federal Motor Carrier Safety Administration, Register, TD 2.314.6/4

Federal **Motor** Vehicle Fleet Reports, GS 2.18

Federal **Motor** Vehicle Safety Standards, TD 8.6/4

Federal **Motor** Vehicle Safety Standards and Regulations, TD 8.6/2

Fuel and Power for Locomotives and Rail **Motor** Cars of Class I Steam Railways in United States, IC 1 ste.30

List of Masters, Mates, {etc} of Merchant Steam, **Motor**, and Sail Vessels, Licensed during Calendar Year, T 38.7

List of Officers of Merchant Steam, **Motor** and Sail Vessels Licensed During (calendar year), C 15.7

Merchant Fleets of the World, Sea-Going Steam and **Motor** Ships of 1,000 Gross Tons and Over, TD 11.14

Minority and Female **Motor** Carrier Listings, IC 1.38

Monthly **Motor** Fuel Reported by States, TD 2.46/2

Monthly **Motor** Gasoline Reported by States, TD 2.46

Monthly **Motor** Truck Production Report, C 41.39

Motor and Vehicles Fixed Price Lists, W 77.23/9

Motor and Vehicles Lists, W 77.23/10

Motor Carrier, IC 1 mot.8/a:M

Motor Carrier Accident Investigation Reports, TD 2.309

Motor Carrier Cases, IC 1 mot.8

Motor Carrier Freight Commodity Statistics Class 1 Common and Contract Carriers of Property, IC 1 mot.22

Motor Carrier Investigation Reports, IC 1 mot.18

Motor Carrier, Finance, IC 1 mot.8/a 2

Motor Carriers of Passengers, Class 1 Accident Data, IC 1 mot.21/2

Motor Carriers of Property, Accident Data, IC 1 mot.21

Motor Carriers, Special Circulars, IC 1 mot.15

Motor Freight Transportation and Warehousing Survey, C 3.138/3-5

Motor Gasoline Watch, E 3.13/6

Motor Transport, Technical Service Bulletins, W 77.31

Motor Vehicle Report, Pr 33.112

Motor Vehicle Safety Defect Recall Campaigns, TD 8.9

Motor Vehicle Safety Defect Recall Campaigns Reported to the Department of Transportation by Domestic and Foreign Vehicle Manufacturers, TD 2.209

National **Motor** Vehicle Safety Advisory Council Summary Report, TD 1.13

On Guard, Bureau of **Motor** Carrier Safety Bulletin, TD 2.303

Quarterly Freight Loss and Damage Claims Reported by Common and Contract **Motor** Carriers of Property, IC 1 acco.11

Quarterly Report on Employment of American Steam and **Motor** Merchant Vessels, MC 1.8

Report on Activities Under the National Traffic and **Motor** Vehicle Safety Act, TD 8.12

Revenues, Expenses, and Statistics of Class 1 **Motor** Carriers of Passengers, IC 1 mot.11

Revenues, Expenses, and Statistics of Class 1 **Motor** Carriers of States, IC 1 ste.24

Revenues, Expenses, Other Income, and Statistics of Class 1 **Motor** Carriers of Passengers, IC 1 mot.12

Revenues, Expenses, Other Income, and Statistics of Large **Motor** Carriers of Property, IC 1 mot.13

Safety Related Recall Campaigns for **Motor** Vehicles and **Motor** Vehicle Equipment, Including Tires, TD 8.9/2

Selected Safety Road Checks **Motor** Carriers of Property, TD 2.311

Selected Statistics for Class 3 **Motor** Carriers of Property, IC 1 mot.14/2

Statistics of Class 1 **Motor** Carriers, IC 1 mot.14

Summary of **Motor** Carrier Accidents, IC 1 mot.21/3

Summary of **Motor** Vehicle Accident Fatalities, C 3.128/3

Territorial Studies of **Motor** Carrier Costs, Traffic and Rate Structure, IC 1 mot.16

U.S. Automotive Trade Statistics, Series A: **Motor** Vehicles, ITC 1.16

World **Motor** Vehicle and Trailer Production and Registration, C 57.21

World **Motor** Vehicle Production and Registration, C 41.17

World Retail Prices and Taxes on Gasoline, Kerosene, and **Motor** Lubricating Oils, I 28.44

Motor-Fuel

Forecast of **Motor-Fuel** Demand and Required Crude-Oil Production by States, Monthly Forecast, I 28.41

Motorboat

Motorboat Safety, T 47.49

Motorcycles

Heavyweight **Motorcycles**: Annual Report on Selected Economic Indicators, ITC 1.26/2

Heavyweight **Motorcycles**: Selected Economic Indicators, ITC 1.26

Motorists

Motorists Guides, I 29.24

Mount Rainier

Mount Rainier National Park, Annual Reports, I 1.43

Naturalist Program, **Mount Rainier** National Park, I 29.60/3

Self-Guiding Nature Trail Leaflets, **Mount Rainier** National Park, I 29.61/2

Mountain

10th **Mountain** Division (LI) and Fort Drum: Pamphlets (series), D 101.22/23

Bulletin of **Mountain** Weather Observatory, A 29.21

Employment and Earnings in the **Mountain** Plains Region, L 2.41/8

Employment in the **Mountain** States, L 2.41/6

Mountain Views, A 13.120

Number of New Dwelling Units and Permit Valuation of Building Construction Authorized by Class of Construction in **Mountain** and Pacific Division by Civil Division and State, L 2.51, L 2.51/2, L 2.51/3

Retail Trade Report **Mountain** Region, C 3.180

Rocky **Mountain** Regional Aviation System Plan, TD 4.33/5

Mountain Region

Consumer Price Index, **Mountain Region** and Plain Region, L 2.38/6

Mountains

Mineral Resources West of Rocky **Mountains**, T 28.6

Naturalist Program, Great Smokey **Mountains** National Park, I 29.60/2

Santa Monica **Mountains** and Seashore, I 29.6/7

Mourning Dove

Mourning Dove, Breeding Population Status, I 49.106/5

Mourning Dove Newsletter, I 49.50

Mourning Dove Status Report, I 49.15/3

Movement

Brief History of the American Labor **Movement**, L 2.3:1000

California Rice Stocks and **Movement** Reports, A 36.186

Carload Waybill Statistics, Mileage Block Distribution, Traffic and Revenue by Commodity Class, Territorial **Movement**, and Type of Rate, Products of Agriculture, 1 Percent Sample of. . . MB-1, IC 1.23/2

Carload Waybill Statistics, Mileage Block Distribution, Traffic and Revenue by Commodity Class, Territorial **Movement**, and Type of Rate, Animals and Products, 1 Percent Sample of. . .MB-2, IC 1.23/3

Carload Waybill Statistics, Mileage Block Distribution, Traffic and Revenue by Commodity Class, Territorial **Movement**, and Type of Rate, Products of Mines, 1 Percent Sample of. . .MB-3, IC 1.23/4

Carload Waybill Statistics, Mileage Block Distribution, Traffic and Revenue by Commodity Class, Territorial **Movement**, and Type of Rate, Products of Forests, 1 Percent Sample. . .MB-4, IC1.23/5

Carload Waybill Statistics, Mileage Block Distribution, Traffic and Revenue by Commodity Class, Territorial **Movement**, and Type of Rate, Manufacturers and Miscellaneous Forwarder Traffic,...MB-5, IC 1.23/6

Commercial Egg **Movement** Report, A 88.15/20

Estimated Refrigerator Car **Movement** of Domestic Fresh Fruits and Vegetables by Regions, A 82.42

General Summary of Inventory Status and **Movement** of Capital and Producers Goods, Plants, Aircraft, and Industry Agent Items, Pr 33.210

Livestock **Movement** at Twelve Markets, A 36.202

Patient **Movement** Data, State and Mental Hospitals, FS 2.22/46

Rice, Stocks and **Movement**, Southern Mills, A 82.50

Rice, Stocks, and **Movement**, California Mills, A 82.49, A 88.18/10

Shipping Weight and Dollar Value of Merchandise Laden on and Unladen from Vessels at United States Ports During the In-transit **Movement** of the Merchandise from One Foreign Country to Another, C 3.164:981

Southern Rice Stocks and **Movement** Reports, A 36.185

Movements

Gold and Silver **Movements**: United States, C 3.196

Industry Wage Studies, Series 3, Wage **Movements**, L 2.47

Movements of Vessels, N 17.8

Movements of Vessels {fiscal year}, N 1.28

Statistical Report of Commerce Passing through Canals at Sault Ste. Marie, Mich. and Ontario, Salt Water Ship **Movements** for Season of (year), D 103.17/2

Statistics of Capital **Movements** Between U.S. and Foreign Countries, T 62.9

United States Gold and Silver **Movements** in (Month), C 56.210:2402, C 3.164:2402

Moves

Marketing **Moves**, the Marketing Bulletin from the U.S. Government Printing Office, GP 1.38

Moving

Moving and Storage Wage Survey Summaries by Cities, L 2.113/5

Moving and Storage Wage Surveys, Summaries by State, L 2.113/5-2

MPI

MPI {Meat and Poultry Inspection} Guidelines (series), A 103.8/2

MPR

MPR Revisions, HH 2.17/2

MRBC

MRBC Basic Bulletin, Y 3.M 69/2:3

MSA

Abstracts of Earthquake Reports for the United States, **MSA** (series), C 55.223, C 55.417, I 19.69

MSA, C 4.42

MSA Country Series, Pr 33.919

Small Business Circular **MSA**/CBC (series), Pr 33.913

Trans-Atlantic, from Office of Labor Advisors, **MSA** Labor News Letter, Pr 33.915

MSA/SBM

Memo for Small Business **MSA/SBM** (series), Pr 33.914

MSHA

MSHA Instruction Guide Series, L 38.17/3

MSHA Policy Memorandum (series), L 38.17

MSHA Program Information Bulletin (series), L 38.17/2

MSHA Program Policy Letter (Series), L 38.17/2-2

MSP

Quarterly Seismology Bulletin **MSP** (series), C 4.25/4

MSPB

Study of **MSPB** Appeals Decisions for FY (year), MS 1.15

MSS

MSS, C 4.43

MTMC

MTMC Expediter, D 101.66/3

MTMC Pamphlets, D 101.22/6

Multi-Year

Proposed **Multi-Year** Operating Plan, Statistics of Income Division, T 22.2/3, T 22.2/10

Multidisciplinary

Multidisciplinary Accident Investigations, TD 8.11, TD 8.11/2

Multifactor

Multifactor Productivity Measures, L 2.120/2-10

News, **Multifactor** Productivity Measures, L 2.120/2-10

Multifamily

Directory of **Multifamily** Project Mortgage Insurance Programs by Project Status, HH 1.50

Selected **Multifamily** Status Reports, Mortgage Insurance Programs by Name and Location of Each Project, HH 1.50

Multifiber

U.S. Imports of Textiles and Apparel under the **Multifiber** Arrangement, Statistical Report, ITC 1.30

Multiphasic

Automated **Multiphasic** Health Testing Bibliography, HE 20.2710

Multiple

Instructions for Classifying **Multiple** Causes of Death, HE 20.6208/4-3

Multiple Award Federal Supply Schedule, GS 2.7/6

Multiple Risk Intervention Trial, Public Annual Report, HE 20.3213

Report on Status of **Multiple** Use and Joint Development, TD 2.121

Multiple Sclerosis

NINCDS **Multiple Sclerosis** Research Program, HE 20.3502:M 91

Multiple Use

Development of **Multiple Use** Facilities on Highway Right of Way, TD 2.121/2

Highway Joint Development and **Multiple Use**, TD 2.56

Multiplier

Multiplier, S 17.33, S 18.32

Multipurpose

Multipurpose Arthritis Centers Personnel Directory, HE 20.3322

Mumps

Mumps Surveillance, HE 20.7011/34

Municipal

Building for Clean Water Report on Federal Incentive Grants for **Municiapl** Waste Treatment, FS 16.9

Building for Clean Water Progress Report on Federal Incentive Grants for **Municipal** Waste Treatment Fiscal Year, FS 2.64/6

Inventory **Municipal** Waste Facilities, EP 2.17

List of Acquisitions of **Municipal** Reference Service, C 3.198

Municipal and Cooperative Distributors of TVA Power, (date) Operations, Y 3.T 25:1-3

Municipal Environmental Research Laboratory: Quarterly Report, EP 1.46/7

Municipal Environmental Research Laboratory: Report of Progress, EP 1.46/7-2

Municipal Government Wage Surveys, L 2.105

Municipal Water Facilities, FS 2.84/3

Policies and Trends in **Municipal** Waste Treatment (series), EP 1.26

State **Municipal** Project Priority Lists, Grants Assistance Programs, EP 1.56/3

State, County and **Municipal** Survey, L 2.13

Statistical Summary of **Municipal** Water Facilities, FS 2.84

Technical Memoranda for **Municipal**, Industrial and Domestic Water Supplies, Pollution Abatement, Public Health, FS 2.301

Municipals

Sales of Firm Electric Power for Resale, by Private Electric Utilities, by Federal Projects, by **Municipals**, FP 1.21

Munitions

Annual Historical Review, Armament, **Munitions** and Chemical Command, (AMCCOM)- (series), D 101.1/5

Munitions Board Manuals, D 3.8

Museum
  Army **Museum** Newsletter, D 114.16
  Contributions from the **Museum** of History and Technology, Papers, SI 3.3
  Interior **Museum** News, I 1.90
  Medical **Museum** of Armed Forces Institute of Pathology Publications, D 1.16/2
  Museum Assessment Program, Grant Application and Information, NF 4.11
  Museum Manuscript Register Series, D 214.17
  Museum of Natural History, Annual Report, SI 3.1/2
  Preservation Tech Notes **Museum** Collection Storage (series), I 29.84/3-3
  Publications in **Museum** Behavior, SI 1.39
  Publications **Museum** Behavior, SI 1.39
  Southwestern Monuments, **Museum** and Education Series, Letters, I 29.15/3

Museums
  Humanities Projects in **Museums** and Historical Organizations, NF 3.8/2-5
  NEH Travel to Collections, Small Grants for Research Travel to Libraries, Archives, **Museums**, and Other Repositories, NF 3.19

Mushrooms
  Mushrooms, A 92.11/10-5, A 105.24/6
  Processed **Mushrooms**, ITC 1.20

Music
  American Folk **Music** and Folklore Recordings, a Selected List, LC 39.12
  Braille Scores Catalog-Organ, **Music** and Musicians, LC 19.22
  Exploring **Music** Careers, HE 19.108:Ex 7/10
  Folk **Music** of United States, LC 12.7
  Music and **Musicians** (series), LC 19.19
  Music and Phonorecords, LC 30.8/6
  Music Circulars, LC 19.14
  Music Ensembles Chamber Music/New Music/Jazz Ensembles/Choruses/Orchestras/Composer in Residence/Consortium Commissioning, NF 2.8/2-14
  Music Fellowships: Composers, Jazz, Solo Recitalists, Applications Guidelines, NF 2.8/2-8
  Music Presenters and Festivals Jazz Management and Special Projects, NF 2.8/2-9
  Music Professional Training Career Development Organizations, Music Recording Services to Composers, Centers for New Music Resources Special Projects, Music, Application Guidelines, NF 2.8/2-5
  National 4 H **Music** Hour , A 43.25
  Presenters and Festivals Jazz Management, Jazz Special Projects, **Music**, Application Guidelines, NF 2.8/2-9
  The Library of Congress Presents a Season of Chamber **Music**, LC 12.9
  Voice of America Forum Lectures **Music** Series, IA 1.19/3

Musical
  Musical Mainstream, LC 19.12
  Opera-**Musical** Theater, Application Guidelines, NF 2.8/2-12

Musical Compositions
  Catalogue of Copyright Entries, Pt. 3, Musical **Compositions**, LC 3.6/3

Musician
  New Braille **Musician**, LC 19.12/2

Musicians
  Braille Scores Catalog-Organ, Music and **Musicians**, LC 19.22
  Music and **Musicians** (series), LC 19.19

Musketeers
  Safety **Musketeers**, I 16.63

Musketry
  Musketry Bulletins, W 95.3/2

Muskingum River
  Daily Totals of Precipitation in **Muskingum River** Basin, A 80.2010
  Precipitation in **Muskingum River** Basin, A 57.21/2

Mussles
  Certified Shippers of Fresh and Frozen Oyster, Clams, and **Mussles**, FS 2.16

Mutant Cell
  Mammalian **Mutant Cell** Lines Committee, HE 20.3001/2:M 31

Mutual

Assets Liabilities and Capital Accounts Commercial Banks and **Mutual** Savings Banks, Y 3.F 31/8:9

Background for **Mutual** Security, S 17.35/2

Mutual Security Program, Summary Presentation, S 17.35

Publications **Mutual** Security Mission to China, FO 1.27

Report of Calls, Assets, Liabilities, Capital, Accounts, Commercial and **Mutual** Savings Banks (unnumbered), Y 3.F 31/8:9-2

Review of **Mutual** Cooperation in Public Administration, S 17.46

Semiannual Report on Operations Under **Mutual** Defense Assistance Control Act of 1951, FO 1.1/2

Semiannual Reports on Operations under **Mutual** Defense Assistance Act, S 17.1/2

Semiannual Reports under **Mutual** Defense Assistance Control Act, Pr 33.901/2

Summary of Accounts and Deposits in All Commercial and **Mutual** Savings Banks, Y 3.F 31/8:22

Summary of Accounts and Deposits in All **Mutual** Savings Banks, Y 3.F 31/8:21

Mycology
  Bacteriology and **Mycology** Study Section, HE 20.3001/2:B 13
  Journal of **Mycology**, A 28.5
  Performance Evaluation Summary Analysis **Mycology**, HE 20.7037

Mycoses
  Mycoses Surveillance, Reports, HE 20.7011/3

Myogenic
  Androgenic and **Myogenic** Endocrine Bioassay Data, FS 2.22/48

N

N.I.M.H.
  Workshop Series of Pharmacology Section, **N.I.M.H.**, FS 2.310

N.L.R.B.
  N.L.R.B. Election Reports, LR 1.16
  N.L.R.B. Statistical Summary Covering the Three Month Period, LR 1.15/3
  Weekly Summary of **N.L.R.B.** Cases, LR 1.15/2

N.O.I.
  N.O.I. Publications, N 13.9

N.Y.
  Regional Research Bulletins, **N.Y.** and New England, Y 3.W 89/2:60

NACA
  Index of **NACA** Technical Publications, Y 3.N 21/5:17

NADC-CS
  Reports, **NADC-CS**- (series), D 201.22

NAEP
  NAEP Newsletter, HE 19.209/2, ED 1.316
  NAEPFacts, ED 1.335
  NAEP Trends in Academic Progress, ED 1.335/4

NA-FB/M
  NA-FB/M (series), A 13.106/3

NA-FB/P
  NA-FB/P (series), A 13.106

NAFTA
  NAFTA Review, PrEx 9.12
  NAFTA Situation and Outlook Series A 93.29/2-20

NA-GR
  NA-GR (series), A 13.106/3-2

NAMC-AEL
  NAMC-AEL (series), D 217.21

Name
  Changes in Status of Banks and Branches During Month, **Name** and Location of Banks and Branches, FR 1.33/2
  Federal Item **Name** Directory for Supply Cataloging, Handbook, D 7.6/2
  Library of Congress **Name** Headings with References, LC 30.19
  Name and Address of Air Service Officers, W 87.9
  Name Authorities, Cumulative Edition, LC 30.21
  Name Authorities, Cumulative Microform Edition, LC 30.21
  NLM **Name** and Series Authorities, HE 20.3609/5
  Nongovernment Organization Codes for Military Standard Contract Administration Procedures: Code to **Name**, D 7.6/2:8-2/2

Nongovernment Organization Codes for Military Standard Contract Administration Procedures: **Name** to Code, D 7.6/2:8-1/2

Selected Multifamily Status Reports, Mortgage Insurance Programs by **Name** and Location of Each Project, HH 1.50

Named
  First Class Post Offices with **Named** Stations and Branches, P 24.8

Names
  Color Universal Language and Dictionary of **Names**, C 13.10:440
  Decisions Geographic **Names** Board, I 33.5, I 33.6
  Directory of Awardee **Names**, E 1.35/2-7
  Foreign Versions, Variations, and Diminutives of English **Names** and Foreign Equivalents of U.S. Military and Civilian Titles, J 21.2:N 15
  Geographic **Names** in Coastal Areas (by States), C 4.37
  Geologic **Names** of North America Introduced in 1936-1955, I 19.3:1056
  GEOnet **Names** Server, D 5.319/2
  Index of Generic **Names** of Fossil Plants, I 19.3:1013
  Index to Geologic **Names** of North America, I 19.3:1056
  Lexicon of Geologic **Names** of the United States, I 19.3:1200, I 19.3:1350
  Lexicon of Geologic **Names** of the United States, Including Alaska, I 19.3:896
  List of Corporate **Names** of Common Carriers, IC 1.15
  Names of Counties Declared to be Modified Accredited Bang's Disease-Free Areas, A 4.33
  State Agricultural Departments and Marketing Agencies, with **Names** of Officials, A 66.45

NAPAP
  NAPAP Newsletter, Y 3.In 8/31:15

NAPCA
  NAPCA Abstracts-Bulletins, EP 4.11

NARA
  NARA Bulletin (series), AE 1.103

Narcotic
  Directory of **Narcotic** Addiction Treatment Agencies in the United States, HE 20.2402:N 16/3
  Narcotic and Dangerous Drug Section Monographs (series), J 1.90
  Opium and **Narcotic** Laws {February 9, 1909}, Y 1.2:Op 3

Narcotics
  International **Narcotics** Control Strategy Report, S 1.146
  Rules of the Select Committee on **Narcotics** Abuse and Control, Y 4.N 16/10

NARIC
  NARIC Quarterly, ED 1.79/2
  NARIC, Disability Research Resources, ED 1.79

Narratives
  Narratives, C 3.940-8

NASA
  AEC-**NASA** Tech Briefs, NAS 1.29/2
  Annual **NASA**-University Conference on Manual Control, NAS 1.21
  Conference Publications, **NASA** CP (series), NAS 1.55
  NASA Activities, NAS 1.46
  NASA Aeronautics Research and Technology, Annual Report, NAS 1.19/2
  NASA Annual Procurement Report, NAS 1.30
  NASA Bits {brief ideas, thoughts, suggestions}, NAS 1.36
  NASA Budget Estimates, NAS 1.85
  NASA Earth Resources Survey Program, C 51.9/11
  NASA Educational Briefs for the Classroom (series), NAS 1.69
  NASA Excellence Award for Quality and Productivity, NAS 1.78
  NASA Facts, NAS 1.20
  NASA Information Summaries, NAS 1.90
  NASA Historical Reports, NAS 1.31
  NASA History: News and Notes, NAS 1.96
  NASA Magazine, NAS 1.87
  NASA Mishap and Injury Data, NAS 1.57
  NASA Patent Abstracts Bibliography, NAS 1.21:7039
  NASA Patents, NAS 1.71
  NASA PED (series), NAS 1.84
  NASA Picture Sets, NAS 1.43/2
  NASA Posters, NAS 1.43
  NASA Procurement Regulation, NAS 1.6/2

NASA Procurement Regulation Directive, NAS 1.6/3
NASA Reference Publications, RP (series), NAS 1.61
NASA Report to Educators, NAS 1.49
NASA Republications, NAS 1.13
NASA Scientific and Technical Publications, NAS 1.21:7063
NASA SP (series), NAS 1.21
NASA STD (Series), NAS 1.82
NASA STI Directory, NAS 1.24/4
NASA Tech Briefs, NAS 1.29, NAS 1.29/3
NASA Technical Reports (bound volumes), NAS 1.12/2
NASA-Industry Program Plans Conference, NAS 1.17
Payload Flight Assignments **NASA** Mixed Fleet, NAS 1.81
Report to the Administrator by the **NASA** Aerospace Safety Advisory Panel, NAS 1.58
Significant **NASA** Inventions Available for Licensing in Foreign Countries, NAS 1.21:7038
Telephone Directory Jet Propulsion Laboratory, **NASA**, NAS 1.12/7-2
Telephone Directory **NASA**, Headquarters, Washington, D.C., NAS 1.24
Weekly Abstracts: **NASA** Earth Resources Survey Program, C 51.9/11

NASA'S
Callback from **NASA's** Aviation Safety Reporting System, NAS 1.89
NASA'S University Program, Quarterly Report of Active Grants and Research Contracts, NAS 1.42

NASA/SBA FA
New Product Ideas, Process Improvements, and Cost-Saving Techniques, Relating to {various subjects}, **NASA/SBA FA** (series), NAS 1.56

Nashville, Tennessee
Nashville, Tennessee, Centennial Exposition, 1897, S 6.15

Natality
Instruction Manual Part 12, Computer Edits for **Natality** Data, HE 20.6208/15
Public Use Data Tape Documentation Detail **Natality**, HE 20.6226/2
Public Use Data Tape Documentation **Natality** Local Area Summary, HE 20.6226/3
Public Use Data Tape Documentation **Natality** State Summary, HE 20.6226

Natick
Natick Laboratories, **Natick**, Massachusetts, Technical Reports, D 106.21
U.S. Army **Natick** Laboratories, Food Division, **Natick**, Mass. Technical Report FD-, D 106.20
Natick Laboratories, **Natick,** Massachusetts, Technical Reports, D 106.21

Nation
Factfinder for the **Nation**, CFF, C 3.252
Nation to **Nation**, J 1.105
Navajo **Nation** & Regional Areas Resource Directory, HE 20.310/3

National
Abstract of Reports of Condition of **National** Banks, T 12.5
AHCPR **National** Medical Expenditure Survey Data Summary, HE 20.6517/2
Air War College Studies in **National** Security, D 301.26/25
Americorps Leaders Program, A Service Leadership Development Program of the Corporation for **National** Service, Y 3.N 21/29:16-17
Analysis of the 1985 **National** Survey of Fishing, Hunting and Wildlife-Associated Recreation Reports, I 49.98/3
Annual Report of the **National** Digestive Diseases Advisory Board, HE 20.3027/4
Argonne **National** Laboratory: Research and Highlights, E 1.86/4
Archeological Programs of **National** Park Service, I 29.2:Ar 2/3
Biennial Report of the **National** Institutes of Health, HE 20.3001/3
CD Blind, **National** Library Service for the Blind and Physically Handicapped, LC 19.24
Check List of Birds of **National** Parks, I 29.27
Committee on **National Security**: Papers (numbered), Y 4.Se 2/1 a

Compendium of **National** Urban Mass Transportation Statistics from the 1989 Section 15 Report, TD 7.11/2-2
Department of Transportation **National** Plan for Navigation, TD 1.19
Descriptive Booklets and Folders on the Individual **National** Parks, Monuments, etc, I 29.6
Digest of Decisions Relating to **National** Banks, T 12.7/2
Education and **National** Defense Series Pamphlets, FS 5.22
Experience the Willamette **National** Forest, A 13.119
FBI **National** Academy Associates Newsletter, J 1.14/20
Government **National** Mortgage Association, GNMA, Annual Report, HH 1.1/7
Highlights of the **National** Youth Gang Survey, J 32.21/3
Highlights (**National** Infrastructure Protection Center), J 1.14/23-3
Hypoglycemia, **National** Diabetes Information Clearinghouse, HE 20.3323/2
Inspection **National** News, T 22.2/15:7371
Institute for **National** Strategic Studies: General Publications, D 5.417/2
Interstitial Cyctisis, **National** Kidney and Urologic Diseases Information Clearinghouse, HE 20.3323/3
Land Areas of the **National** Forest System, A 13.10
Lessons in Community and **National** Life, I 16.21/2
List of Record Groups in **National** Archives and Federal Records Centers, GS 4.19
Local Climatological Data, **National** Airport, C 55.287/2
Medical Devices and Diagnostic Products Standards Survey; **National** Edition, HE 20.4035/2
National Acid Precipitation Assessment Program, Report to Congress, C 55.703
National Action Plan on Breast Cancer Fact Sheets (series), HE 20.38/2
National Archives and Records Administration Telephone Directory, AE 1.122
National Archives, Calendar of Events, AE 1.129
National Atlas, I 19.111
National Center for Chronic Disease Prevention and Health Promotion (NCCDPHP), HE 20.7039, HE 20.7616
National Clearinghouse on Child Abuse and Neglect Information Catalog, HE 23.1216/2
National Climatic Data Center Periodical Publications, C 55.287/63
National Compensation Survey Bulletins, Summaries, and Supplemental Tables for National, L 2.121/57
National Compensation Survey Divisions, L 2.121/56
National Corrections Reporting Program, J 29.11/13
National Diabetes Information Clearinghouse HE 20.3323/2
National Directory of Drug Abuse and Alcoholism Treatment and Prevention Programs, HE 20.410/3
National Directory of Farmers Markets, A 88.69/2
National Disability Policy: A Progress Report, Y 3.D 63/3:1-2
National Domestic Preparedness Office - General Publications, J 1.14/25-2
National Drug Control Policy, PrEx 26.1/2
National Drug Intelligence Center (NDIC): General Publications, J 1.112
National Economic Social & Environmental Data Bank (NESEDB), C 1.88/2
National Education Goals Report, ED 1.1/3
National Export Strategy C 1.2:EX, C 1.1/6
National Forest Annual Reports (various regions), A 13.114/2, A 13.114/4
National Forests, America's Great Outdoors, A 13.122
National Health and Nutrition Examination Survey, HE 20.6209/4-8
National Hospital Discharge Survey: Annual Summary, HE 20.6209/7
National Household Survey on Drug Abuse: Main Findings, HE 20.417/3
National Household Survey on Drug Abuse: Preliminary Results..., HE 20.417/4

National Household Survey on Drug Abuse: Summary of Findings, HE 20.417/5
National Income and Product Accounts of the United States, C 59.11/5, C 59.11/5-2, C 59.11/5-3
National Institute for Literacy, Pr 41.8:L 71
National Institute of Child Health and Human Development Intramural Research Program: Annual Report of the Scientific Director, HE 20.3365
National Institute of Corrections, Annual Program Plan, Fiscal Year, J 16.110
National Institute of Justice Catalog, J 28.14/2
National Institute of Justice Journal, J 28.14/2-2
National Institute of Justice Reports, J 28.14
National Institute of Justice Research Report, J 28.15/2
National Kidney and Urologic Diseases Information Clearinghouse Factsheet HE 20.3323/3
National Land Cover Dataset, I 19.168
National Leadership Grants, Grant Application & Guidelines, NF 4.11/2
National Library of Medicine Newsline HE 20.3619
National Listing of Medicare Providers Furnishing Kidney Dialysis & Transplant Services, HE 22.216
National Medical Expenditure Survey Methods, HE 20.6517/3
National Money Laundering Strategy, T 1.67/2
National Postsecondary Student Aid Study (NPSAS), ED 1.333
National Priorities List Sites, EP 1.107
National Pseudorabies Reports, A 101.33
National Research Initiative Competitive Grants Program, A 94.24
National Science and Technology Council: General Publications, PrEx 23.14
National Security Essay Series, D 5.413
National Security Management Programs Instructor's Guide (Series), D 5.410/2
National Security Seminar: Presentation, D 5.9
National Service News, Y 3.N 21/29:16-15
National Shellfish Register of Classified Growing Waters, C 55.441
National Summary of State Medicaid Managed Care Programs, HE 22.116
National Survey of Fishing, Hunting and Wildlife-Associated Recreation, I 49.98/4
National Survey Results on Drug Use from the Monitoring the Future Study, HE 20.3968
National Toxicology Program, Annual Plan, Fiscal Year, HE 20.3551/2
National Toxicology Program, Technical Report series, HE 20.3564
National Toxicology Program, Toxicity Report series, HE 20.3564/2
National Transportation Statistics, Annual Report, TD 12.1/2
National Undersea Research Program Technical Report, C 55.29/3
National Update, J 29.24
National Water Conditions, I 19.42
NCSS (**National** Cooperative Soil Survey) Newsletter, A 57.78
NBLIC (**National** Black Leadership Initiative on Cancer) News, HE 20.3195
News from the **National** 5 A Day Program, HE 20.3161/3
NHLBI **National** Research Service Award Programs Summary Descriptions, HE 20.3211/4
NLS News, **National** Longitudinal Surveys, L 2.135
NPDP (**National** Practitioner Data Bank) News, HE 20.9316
NPS Strategic Planning, **National** Park Scan, I 29.132
NSSB (**National** Skill Standards Board) Annual Report, L 1.1/5
NWHC Technical Report (**National** Wildlife Health Center), I 19.211
Official Bulletins, **National** Trophy Matches, D 101.61
On Scene, **National** Maritime SAR {Search and Rescue} Review, TD 5.24
Open Window, the Newsletter of the **National** Library of Education, ED 1.345
Operations of **National** Weather Service, C 55.111
OSHA **National** Training Institute Catalog of Courses, L 35.25/2

Ottawa **National** Forest, A 13.28/a

Papers on the **National** Health Guidelines, HE 20.6020

Participation of Principal **National** Flags in United States Oceanborne Foreign Trade, C 39.221

Periodic Report from the **National** Digital Library Program, L 37.215

Periodicals and Serials Received in the Library of the **National** Bureau of Standards, C 13.10

Photographs of Scenes in **National** Parks (by name of park), I 29.32

Photographs of Scenes of **National** Parks, etc., I 29.29

Platt **National** Park, Annual Reports, I 1.54

Posters **National** Archives and Records Service, GS 4.26

Posters **National** Eye Institute, HE 20.3715

Posters **National** Gallery of Art, SI 8.10

Posters **National** Institute of General Medical Sciences, HE 20.3467

Posters **National** Institute on Aging, HE 20.3867

Posters **National** Library for the Blind and Physically Handicapped, LC 19.18

Posters **National** Library of Medicine, HE 20.3622

Posters **National** Ocean Service, C 55.418/6-2

Posters **National** Weather Service, C 55.130

President Research Associateships, Post- Doctoral, Tenable at **National** Bureau of Standards, C 13.47

President's Commission on **National** Agenda for the Eighties, Pr 39.8:Ag 3

President's **National** Policy Report, HH 1.75

President's **National** Urban Policy Report, HH 1.75

Press Notices **National** Bureau of Standards, C 13.18

Price Schedules **National** Bituminous Coal Commission, I 34.19

Proceedings Annual Alcoholism Conference of the **National** Institute on Alcohol Abuse and Alcoholism, HE 20.2430/2

Proceedings **National** Brucellosis Committee and Progress Report of the Cooperative State-Federal Brucellosis Eradication Program, A 77.202:B 83/16

Proceedings **National** Data Buoy Systems Scientific Advisory Meetings, TD 5.23

Proceedings **National** Security Affairs Conference, D 5.412

Proceedings **National** Shellfish Sanitation Workshop, FS 2.16/2

Professional Papers **National** Oceanic and Atmospheric Administration, C 55.25

Profile: Smithsonian **National** Portrait Gallery News, SI 11.16

Program Plan of the **National** Institute for Occupational Safety and Health, HE 20.7127

Progress Against Cancer, Report by **National** Advisory Cancer Council, HE 20.3024, HE 20.3163

Progress Report **National** Institute of Health, FS 2.22/10

Progress Report **National** Mental Health Program, FS 2.65

Projects Initiated under Title VII, **National** Defense Education Act, FS 5.234:34013, FS 5.234:34021, HE 5.234:34013, HE 5.234:34021

Prologue, Journal of the **National** Archives, GS 4.23

Public Health Conference on Records and Statistics, **National** Meeting Announcement, HE 20.6214/2

Public Use Data Tape Documentation Interviewer's Manual **National** Interview Survey, HE 20.6226/8

Public Use Data Tape Documentation **National** Health Interview Survey, HE 20.6226/10

Public Use of **National** Parks, Statistical Report, I 29.63

Public Use, Tabulation of Visitors to Areas Administrated by **National** Park Service, I 29.63

Publications Federal **National** Mortgage Association, FL 5.17

Publications **National** Air Pollution Control Administration, FS 2.93/3

Publications **National** Applied Mathematics Laboratories, C 13.43

Publications **National** Archives and Records Service, GS 4.17

Publications **National** Bureau of Standards, C 13.10:305

Publications **National** Center for Education Statistics, HE 19.317:P 96

Publications **National** Climatic Center, C 55.281

Publications **National** Committee on Wood Utilization, C 1.14

Publications **National** Conference on Air Pollution, FS 2.98

Publications **National** Conference on Water Pollution, FS 2.64/3

Publications **National** Conferences on Street and Highway Safety, C 1.21

Publications **National** Earthquake Information Center, C 55.691

Publications **National** Export Expansion Council, C 1.42/3

Publications **National** Geodetic Survey, C 55.413/3

Publications **National** Historical Publications Commission, GS 4.14

Publications **National** Institute of Mental Health, HE 20.8113/3

Publications **National** Meteorological Center, C 55.190

Publications **National** Ocean Survey, C 55.419

Publications **National** Oceanographic Data Center, D 203.24, D 203.24/2, C 55.292

Publications **National** Security Agency, D 1.25

Publications **National** Wage Stabilization Board, L 1.17

Publications of the **National** Science Foundation, NS 1.13/5

Quarterly Compilation of Periodical Literature Reflecting the Use of Records in the **National** Archives, AE 1.128

Record of Changes in Memberships of **National** Home for Disabled Volunteer Soldiers, NH 1.6

Recreation Guide to Grand Mesa, Uncompahgre and Gunnison **National** Forests, A 13.36/2-7

Regulations, Rules and Instructions **National** Center for Devices and Radiological Health, HE 20.4606

Regulations, Rules and Instructions **National** Defense University, D 5.406

Reintroduction and Management of Wolves in Yellowstone **National** Park and the Central Idaho Wilderness Area, Y 3.W 83

Report of **National** Advisory Council on Economic Opprotunity, PrEx 10.22

Report of the **National** Conference on Weights and Measures, C 13.10, C 13.10/3

Report of the **National** Defense Education Act, FS 5.210:10004

Report of the Panel on Pain to the **National** Advisory Neurological and Communicative Disorders and Stroke Council, HE 20.3517

Report on Activities Under the **National** Traffic and Motor Vehicle Safety Act, TD 8.12

Report on **National** Growth and Development, PrEx 15.9

Report on **National** Growth, PrEx 15.9

Report on the **National** Defense Education Act, HE 5.210:10004

Report on Washington Conference of Mayors and Other Local Government Executives on **National** Security, FCD 1.18

Report on Washington Conference on **National** Women's Advisory Committee on FCDA, FCD 1.18/2

Report to Congress on the Administration of the **National** Traffic Vehicle Safety Act of 1966, TD 1.10/2

Report to the **National** Farm Loan Associations, FCA 1.23

Reports of the **National** Juvenile Justice Assessment Centers (series), J 26.27

Research Division Reports **National** Endowment for the Arts, NF 2.12

Research Highlights, **National** Institutes of Health, FS 2.22/28

Research Memorandum **National** Labor Relations Board, LR 1.10

Research Notes **National** Center for Health Services Research, HE 20.6514

Research Project Summaries, **National** Institute of Mental Health, FS 2.22/16-2

Research Reports **National** Cancer Institute, FS 2.22/32

Research Reports **National** Environmental Research Center, EP 1.21/9

Research Reports **National** Institue of Justice, J 28.24/3

Research Reports **National** Institute of Mental Health, HE 20.2420/4, HE 20.8114/2

Research Reports, **National** Environmental Research Center, Las Vegas {list}, EP 1.21/9

Resident Research Associateships, Postdoctoral, Tenable and **National** Bureau of Standards, C 13.47

Resource Decisions in the **National** Forests of the Eastern Region, A 13.90

River Forecasts Provided by the **National** Weather Service, C 55.117/2, C 55.285

Rocky Mountain **National** Park, Annual Reports, I 1.57

Roll of Honor, Supplemental Statement of Disposition of Bodies of Deceased Union Soldiers and Prisoners of War Removed to **National** Cemeteries in Southern and Western United States, W 39.8

Rules and Regulations of **National** Parks, I 1.47/2

Safety Bulletins **National** Shipping Authority, C 39.209

Safety Bulletins **National** Youth Administration, FS 6.16

Safety Competition, **National** Crushed Stone Association, I 28.26/4

Safety Competition, **National** Lime Association, I 28.26/3

Safety Competition, **National** Sand and Gravel, I 28.26/3

Safety Competitions, **National** Limestone Institute, I 28.26/7

SCS **National** Engineering Handbook, A 57.6/2:En 3

Self-Guiding Nature Trail Leaflets, Glacier **National** Park, I 29.61

Self-Guiding Nature Trail Leaflets, Mount Rainier **National** Park, I 29.61/2

Separate Sheets of Selected Thematic and General Reference Maps from the **National** Atlas of the United States of America, I 19.111a

Sequoia and General Grant **National** Parks, Annual Reports, I 1.29

Serials Currently Received by the **National** Agricultural Library, A 17.18/2:Se 6

Series Available and Estimating Methods, BLS **National** Payroll Employment Program, L 2.124

Services Research Monograph Series, **National** Polydrug Collaborative Project, Treatment Manuals, HE 20.8216/2

Shawnee Quarterly, the Shawnee **National** Forest Schedule of Projects, A 13.138

Sheets of **National** Atlas of United States Agricultural Research Service, A 77.19

Sheets of **National** Atlas of United States Bureau of the Census, C 3.62/3

Sheets of **National** Atlas of United States Census of Agriculture, C 3.31/10

Sheets of **National** Atlas of United States Coast and Geodetic Survey, C 4.9/21

Sheets of **National** Atlas of United States Forest Service, A 13.28/2

Sheets of **National** Atlas of United States Geological Survey, I 19.5/3

Sheets of **National** Atlas of United States Interstate Commerce Commission, IC 1.30

Sheets of **National** Atlas of United States Tennessee Valley Authority, Y 3.T 25:7-2

Sheets of **National** Atlas of United States Weather Bureau, C 30.22/4

Shenandoah **National** Park Chips, I 29.67

Ship Operations Report, **National** Ocean Survey, C 55.423

Smoking and Health, a **National** Status Report, HE 20.7613

Special Foreign Currency Science Information Program, List of Translations in Process for Fiscal Year, Coordinated and Administered by the **National** Science Foundation, C 51.12

Special Reports **National** Archives, AE 1.18

State and **National** Reports, Y 3.N 21/9:10

Statement Showing Amount of **National** Bank Notes Outstanding {ect}, T 12.9

Statistical Notes **National** Clearinghouse on Aging, HE 23.3112

Statistical Notes **National** Institute of Mental Health, HE 20.3812

Statistical Series **National** Institute on Drug Abuse, HE 20.8212, HE 20.8212/2, HE 20.8212/3, HE 20.8212/5, HE 20.8212/6

Stumpage Prices for Sawtimber Sold from **National** Forests, by Selected Species and Region, A 13.58/2

Subject Index of Current Research Grants and Contracts Administered by the **National** Heart, Lung, and Blood Institute, HE 20.3212

Summary of Grants and Contracts Administered by the **National** Center for Health Services Research and Development, HE 20.2116

Summary Technical Report of **National** Defense Research Committee, Pr 32.413/12

Summer Research Fellowship Program at the **National** Institutes of Health, HE 20.3015/2

Supplemental Reports to the Second **National** Water Assessment, Y 3.W 29:13

Tables on Hatchery and Flock Participation in the **National** Poultry Improvement Plan, A 77.15:44-3

Tables on Hatchery and Flock Participation in the **National** Turkey Improvement Plan, A 77.15:44-4

Take Pride in America, **National** Awards Ceremony, I 1.110/2

TC in the Current **National** Emergency, Historical Report No., D 117.9, D 117.9/2

Technical Highlights of the **National** Bureau of Standards, C 13.1

Technical Memorandum **National** Aeronautics and Space Administration, NAS 1.15

Technical Memorandum **National** Bureau of Standards, Applied Mathematics Division, C 13.39

Technical Memorandum **National** Telecommunications and Information Administration, C 60.11

Technical News from Department of Commerce, **National** Bureau of Standards, C 13.36/6

Technical Notes **National** Aeronautics and Space Administration, NAS 1.14

Technical Notes **National** Bureau of Standards, C 13.46

Technical Problems Affecting **National** Defense, C 32.8

Technical Reports **National** Park Service, J 29.15, I 29.109

Teenage Victims, A **National** Crime Survey Report, J 29.23

Telephone Directory **National** Transportation Safety Board, TD 1.124

The **National** Banking Review, T 12.16

Third **National** Cancer Survey Utilization Advisory Committee, HE 20.3001/2:C 16/7

Timucuan Today and Tomorrow, A Newsletter from the **National** Park Service, I 29.128

Toxics-Release Inventory: A **National** Prospective, EP 5.18/2

Trainees and Fellows Supported by the **National** Institute of Dental Research and Trained During Fiscal Year, HE 20.3402:T 68, HE 20.3410

Translations for **National** Institutes of Health, FS 2.22/19-3

Type A Topics, **National** School Lunch Program, A 98.10

U.S. Constitution, a **National** Historic Landmark Theme Study, I 29.117

U.S. **National** Arboretum: Annual Report, A 77.26

U.S. **National** Arboretum Elite Plant, A 77.38/2

U.S. **National** Commission for UNESCO Memos, S 5.48/14

U.S. **National** Commission for UNESCO Newsletter, S 5.48/5

U.S. **National** Commission for UNESCO, S 5.48/7

U.S. **National** Committee of the CCIR {Comite Consultatif International des Radiocommunication}: Publications, S 5.56

Union Conventions, (year), **National** and International Unions, State Organizations, L 1.85

Union Conventions, **National** and International Unions, State Organizations, L 2.85

United States and United **National** Report Series, S 1.49

United States **National** Arboretum, A 1.68:309

Universities and Their Relationships with the **National** Oceanic and Atmospheric Administration, C 55.40

Update **National** Cancer Institute, HE 20.3182/2

Update **National** Commission on the Observance of Update from State, S 1.118/2

USSR Report: **National** Economy, PrEx 7.21/2-2

Visitor Accommodations Furnished by Concessioners in Areas Administered by **National** Park Service, I 29.70

Voluntary Service **National** Advisory Committee: Report of Annual Meeting, VA 1.52

Volunteers in the **National** Forests (series), A 13.112/2

Weekly Statement of Bonds Held in Trust for **National** Banks, T 40.9

Weekly Summary of Federal Legislation Relating to **National** Resources Committee, Activities Bulletins, Y 3.N 21/12:15

Weekly Weather and Crop Bulletin, **National** Summary, C 30.11, C 55.209

Wind Cave **National** Park, Annual Reports, I 1.56

Working Papers **National** Transportation Policy Study Commission, Y 3.T 68/2:10

WPA Week in **National** Defense, FW 4.37

Yellowstone **National** Park, Annual Reports, 1898-90, I 1.37

Yosemite **National** Park, Annual Reports, I 1.38

Your Changing Forest, News on the Black Hills **National** Forest Plan Revision, A 13.128

National Guard

Air **National Guard** Manuals, D 301.23

Air **National Guard** Register, D 12.9/2

Army **National Guard** Lineage Series, D 12.20

District of Columbia **National Guard**: Annual Report, D 12.1/2

Education Service Plan, Wisconsin **National Guard**, D 12.16

National Guard Bulletins, W 99.17/15

National Guard Bureau Manual, W 70.8, D 112.7

National Guard on Guard, D 12.14/2

National Guard Regulations, M 114.6, D 112.6

National Guard Update (Air), D 12.17

National Guard Update (Army), D 12.17/2

Official Army **National Guard** Register, D 12.9

Official **National Guard** Register, D 112.8

Official Register **National Guard** Bureau, D 112.8

Pamphlets **National Guard** Bureau, D 12.8

Posters **National Guard** Bureau, D 12.14

Questions for **National Guard** Officers, W 70.9

Training Circulars **National Guard** Bureau, W 70.11

Nationalism

Series on Religion **Nationalism** and Intolerance, Y 3.P 31:18

Nationality

Administrative Decisions Under Immigration and **Nationality** Laws, J 21.11

Interim Administrative Decisions under Immigration and **Nationality** Laws, J 21.11/2

Laws Applicable to Immigration and **Nationality**, J 21.5

Nation's

Compilation of Federal Laws Relating to Conservation and Development of Our **Nation's** Fish and Wildlife Resources, Environmental Quality, and Oceanography, Y 4.M 53:L 44/2

Managing the **Nation's** Public Lands, I 53.12/2

Our **Nation's** Children, FS 3.212, L 5.49

President's Committee on Employment of the Handicapped: People with Disabilities in Our **Nation's** Job Training Partnership Act Programs, PrEx 1.10/15

Report of Cooperative Research to Improve the **Nation's** Schools, FS 5.82, HE 5.82

Reports to Aid **Nation's** Defense Effort, A 13.27/13

Safeguard Our **Nation's** Youth on the Job, L 15.51/5

Status of the **Nation's** Local Public Transportation, Conditions and Performance, Report to Congress, TD 7.18

Your Navy, from the Viewpoint of the **Nation's** Finest Artists, D 201.9

Nationwide

Nationwide Food Consumption Survey (year), Preliminary Reports, A 111.9/2

Nationwide Food Consumption Survey (year), Reports, A 111.9

Nationwide Outdoor Recreation Plan, I 70.20

Nationwide Personal Transportation Study: Reports, TD 2.31

Quarterly Progress Report, **Nationwide** Urban Runoff Program, EP 1.92

Native

Alaska **Native** Medical Center: Annual Report, HE 20.5311

Indian and Alaska **Native** Housing and Community Development Programs, Annual Report to Congress, HH 1.80

Native American, HE 1.710

Native American Arts (series), I 1.84/4

Native American Monograph, HE 20.3162/4

Census of Housing: Detailed Housing Characteristics for American Indian and Alaska **Native** Areas, C 3.224/3-5

Census of Housing: General Housing Characteristics for American Indian and Alaska **Native** Areas, C 3.224/3-2

Census of Population: General Population Characteristics for American Indian and Alaska **Native** Areas, C 3.223/6-2

Census of Population: Social and Economic Characteristics for American Indian and Alaska **Native** Areas, C 3.223/7-2

Native Sulfur, I 28.63

Natives

Library Programs, Library Services for Indian Tribes and Hawaiian **Natives** Program, ED 1.18/3

Library Programs, Library Services for Indian Tribes and Hawaiian **Natives** Program, Review of Program Activities, ED 1.18/3-2

Status Report of the Operation and Maintenance of Sanitation Facilities Serving American Indians and Alaska **Natives**, HE 20.9416

NATO

NATO Parliamentarians' Conference, Report of Senate Delegation, Y 4.F 76/2:Na 81a/5

NATO Review, S 1.135

NATO Supply Code for Manufacturers, D 7.6/2-2:4-3/date

NA-TP

Pest Alert **NA-TP** series, A 13.52/10-4

Natural

Compilation of Administrative Policies for National Parks and National Monuments of Scientific Significance (**Natural** Area Category), I 29.9/4:N 21

Damaged and Threatened National **Natural** Landmarks, I 29.117/4

Directory of Research **Natural** Areas on Federal Lands of United States of America, Y 3.F 31/19:9

Exploration and Conservation of **Natural** Resources, C 41.45

Federal Research **Natural** Areas in, A 13.36/12

Herald of Moscow University, Physio-Mathematical and **Natural** Sciences Series {abstracts}, C 41.50/6

Highlights of **Natural** Resources Management, I 29.119

Land and **Natural** Resources Division Journal, J 30.9

Museum of **Natural** History, Annual Report, SI 3.1/2

Natural Charts and Other Publications Recently Issued, C 4.5/2

Natural Disaster Survey Reports, C 55.20

Natural Gas. . . Issues and Trends, E 3.11/2-11

Natural Gas Star Partner Update, EP 6.15

Natural Gasoline, I 28.47

Natural Graphite in (year), I 28.128

Natural History Handbook Series, I 29.62

Natural History Theme Studies, I 29.62/2

Natural Inquirer, A Research and Science Journal, The A 13.155

Natural Resource Development Program Annual Report, SBA 1.48

Natural Resource Year in Review, I 29.1/4

Natural Resources, C 51.9/25

Natural Resources of {state}, I 1.91

Natural Resources Reports, I 29.89

Natural Resources Section Preliminary Studies, W 1.80/2

Natural Resources Section Reports, W 1.80

Natural Resources Section Weekly Summary, D 102.12

Natural Resources, A Selection of Bibliographies, D 103.50:3

News of Academy of Sciences of Armenian SSR, Phsyco-Mathematical, **Natural** and Technical Sciences Series, C 41.50/7

Other Synthetic and **Natural** Fuels, E 1.99

Publications List Senate Committee on Energy and **Natural** Resources, Y 4.En 2:P 96

Radio (Independents) **Natural** Science Series Talks, I 29.18

Report to the Committee on the Budget Views and Estimates of the Committee on **Natural** Resources, Y 4.R 31/3-11

Supreme Commander for Allied Powers: **Natural** Resources Section Reports, D 102.20

Natural Gas

Annual Report of Major **Natural Gas** Companies, E 3.25/4

Annual Report of Secretary of Transportation of Administration of **Natural Gas** Pipelines Safety Act of 1968, TD 1.10/4

Annual Report of the Administration of the **Natural Gas** Pipeline Safety Act, TD 9.11

Financial Statistics of Electric Utilities and Interstate **Natural Gas** Pipeline Companies, E 3.11/2-8

Gas Supplies of Interstate **Natural Gas** Pipeline Companies, E 3.25/2

Liquefied **Natural Gas**, Literature Survey, C 13.37/6

Main Line **Natural Gas** Sales to Industrial Users, E 3.11/14

Natural Gas, I 28.98, E 3.11, E 1.99

Natural Gas Annual, E 3.11/2-2, E 3.11/2-10

Natural Gas Deliveries and Curtailments to End-use Customers and Potential Needs for Additional Alternate Fuels, E 3.11/2-5

Natural Gas in (year), I 28.98/4

Natural Gas Liquids, I 28.47, E 3.11/2

Natural Gas Processing Plants in United States, I 28.98/3

Natural Gas Production and Consumption, I 28.98/6

Natural Gas Weekly Market Update, E 1.133

Notices of Determinations by Jurisdictional Agencies Under the **Natural Gas** Policy Act of 1978, E 2.22

Preliminary Report of Domestic **Natural Gas** Reserves and Production Dedicated to Interstate Pipeline Companies, E 3.25/2-2

Quarterly **Natural Gas** Reports, I 28.98

Regulations Under the **Natural Gas** Act, August 1, 1967, FP 1.7:G 21/3

Sales by Producers of **Natural Gas** to Interstate Pipe-Line Companies, FP 1.21

Statistics of Interstate **Natural Gas** Pipeline Companies, E 3.25

Summary of **Natural** Hazard Deaths in the United States, C 55.134

U.S. Crude Oil and **Natural Gas** Reserves, (year) Annual Report, E 3.34

U.S. Crude Oil, **Natural Gas**, and Natural Gas Liquids Reserves (Diskettes), E 3.34

U.S. Imports and Exports of **Natural Gas**, E 3.25/3

Underground **Natural Gas** Storage in the United States, (date) Heating Year, E 3.11/2-9

Underground Storage of **Natural Gas** by Interstate Pipeline Companies, E 3.11/2-4

Uniform System of Accounts Prescribed for **Natural Gas** Companies, FP 1.7/2

World **Natural Gas** in (year), I 28.98/7

World **Natural Gas**, E 3.11/2-3

Natural Gases

Analysis of **Natural Gases** of the United States, I 28.27

Natural-Gas

Natural-Gas Production and Consumption, E 3.38

Naturalist

Naturalist Program, Arcadia National Park, I 29.60

Naturalist Program, Great Smokey Mountains National Park, I 29.60/2

Naturalist Program, Mount Rainier National Park, I 29.60/3

Naturalist Program, Shenandoah National Park, I 29.60/4

Naturalists

Bulletin of Moscow Society of **Naturalists**, Geological Division, C 41.46/2

Naturality

Naturality Laws {August 31, 1935}, Y 1.2:N 39

Naturalization

Essential Procedure and Requirements for **Naturalization** Under General Law (Form C-59), J 21.8

Instructions to Clerks of Courts Exercising **Naturalization** Jurisdiction, L 6.10

Naturalization Laws and Regulations, C 7.10/5, L 6.5

Naturalization Laws {May 9, 1918}, Y 1.2:N 21/3

Statistical Yearbook of the Immigration and **Naturalization** Service, J 21.2:St 2, J 21.2/2, J 21.2/10

Nature

Nature Notes, Clip Sheets, I 29.22

Nature to Be Commanded, I 19.16:950

Self-Guiding **Nature** Trail Leaflets, Glacier National Park, I 29.61

Self-Guiding **Nature** Trail Leaflets, Mount Rainier National Park, I 29.61/2

Nautical

Aeronautical Supplement to American **Nautical** Almanac, N 11.6/2

American Ephemeris and **Nautical** Almanac for the Year {date}, N 11.5, M 212.8, D 213.8

American **Nautical** Almanac, N 11.6, M 212.9

Astronomical Papers Prepared for Use of American Ephemeris and **Nautical** Almanac, D 213.9

Atlantic Coasters' **Nautical** Almanac, N 11.10

Defense Mapping Agency Public Sale **Nautical** Charts and Publications, C 55.440

General (38) **Nautical** Charts, D 5.343

General **Nautical** and International **Nautical** Charts, D 5.356

Guide to NOAA **Nautical** Products & Services, C 55.418:6

Monthly Corrections Affecting Portfolio Chart List and Index-Catalog of **Nautical** Charts and Publications, D 203.22/2

Nautical Almanac for the Year {date}, D 213.11

Nautical Chart Catalogs, C 55.418

Nautical Charts and Publications, C 55.440

Nautical Charts and Publications, Region 1, United States and Canada, C 55.440:1

Nautical Monographs, N 6.10

Nautical Monographs (Maury), N 14.11

NIMA **Nautical** Charts, Public Sale Region 1, United States and Canada, TD 4.82:1

NIMA **Nautical** Charts, Public Sale Region 2, Central and South America and Antarctica, TD 4.82:2

NIMA **Nautical** Charts, Public Sale Region 3, Western Europe, Iceland, Greenland, and the Arctic, TD 4.82:3

NIMA **Nautical** Charts, Public Sale Region 4, Scandinavia, Baltic and Russia, TD 4.82:4

NIMA **Nautical** Charts, Public Sale Region 5, Western Africa and the Mediterranean, TD 4.82:5

NIMA **Nautical** Charts, Public Sale Region 6, Indian Ocean, TD 4.82:6

NIMA **Nautical** Charts, Public Sale Region 7, Australia, Indonesia, and New Zealand, TD 4.82:7

NIMA **Nautical** Charts, Public Sale Region 8, Oceania, TD 4.82:8

NIMA **Nautical** Charts, Public Sale Region 9, East Asia, TD 4.82:9

Pacific Coaster's **Nautical** Almanac, N 11.8

Tables Computed for the American Ephemeris and **Nautical** Almanac, N 11.9

NAV

O & **NAV** Instructions, D 207.8

NAVAER

BUAER Instruction **NAVAER**, D 202.6/4

BUAER Notice **NAVAER**, D 202.6/6

NAVAER Publications Index, N 28.17

Navaho

Adahooniligii, **Navaho** Language Monthly, I 20.37

Navaho Historical Series, I 20.40

Navair

Navair (series), D 222.9

Navajo

Navajo Area Indian Health Service, Office of Environmental Health and Engineering: Annual Report, HE 20.5301/2

Navajo Historical Series, I 20.40

Navajo Nation & Regional Areas Resource Directory, HE 20.310/3

Navajo Yearbook of Planning in Action, I 20.44

Naval

All Hands, Bureau of **Naval** Personnel Career Publications, D 208.3

All Hands, Bureau of **Naval** Personnel Information Bulletin, D 207.17

Approach, **Naval** Aviation Safety Review, D 202.13

Bureau of **Naval** Personnel Manual, D 208.6/2

Bureau of **Naval** Weapons Directory, Organizational Listing and Correspondence Designations, D 217.25

Chief of **Naval** Air Training, CNAT- (series), D 201.31/3

Civilian Personnel of **Naval** Shore Establishment, M 204.8

Combat Connected **Naval** Casualties, World War II, by States, N 1.34/2

Contributions to **Naval** History (series), D 207.10/4, D 221.19

Dictionary of American-**Naval** Fight Ships, D 207.10

Excerpts from Slide Presentations by the Office of Chief of **Naval** Operations, D 207.14

Federal Income Tax Information {for Persons in **Naval** Service}, N 20.22

History of American **Naval** Fighting Ships, D 207.10

List and Stations of **Naval** Inspectors of Engineering Material, N 19.6

Naval Aerospace Medical Institute, D 206.18

Naval Air Development Center Reports NADA (series), D 202.23

Naval Air Development Center, Johnsville, Pennsylvania, Aeronautical Electronic and Electrical Laboratory, Report NADC-EL (series), D 202.14

Naval Aviation News, N 27.16, M 207.7/2, D 202.9, D 202.9/2, D 207.7, D 207.7/2

Naval Aviation System Plan, TD 4.33

Naval Aviation Training Schools, N 28.11

Naval Documents of the American Revolution, D 207.12

Naval Engineering Experiment Station, Annapolis, Maryland, D 211.15

Naval Engineering Memorandum, T 47.46

Naval Expenditures, D 212.8

Naval Firepower, N 18.12

Naval History Bibliographies (series), D 221.17

Naval Law Review, D 205.7

Naval Material Inspection Districts under Inspectors of **Naval** Material, N 19.6/2

Naval Medical Bulletin, D 206.3

Naval Medical Research Institute Reports, D 206.9

Naval Medical Research Institute: Lecture and Review Series, D 206.14

Naval Military Personnel Manual, D 208.6/2

Naval Militia Circular Letters, N 23.6

Naval Oceanographic Newsletter, D 203.28

Naval Ordnance Bulletins, N 18.11

Naval Ordnance Laboratory, Corona, California: Reports, D 215.13

Naval Ordnance Papers, N 18.8

Naval Petroleum and Oil Shale Reserves, Annual Report of Operations, E 1.84/2

Naval Professional Papers, N 17.5

Naval Research Laboratory Quarterly on Nuclear Science and Technology, Progress Reports, D 210.21

Naval Research Laboratory Reports, N 32.7, M 216.7

Naval Research Laboratory Review (Separates), D 210.17/2 a

Naval Research Laboratory, Annual Report, D 210.17/2

Naval Research Laboratory, Fact Book, D 210.17/3

Naval Research Laboratory, Review, D 210.17/2

Naval Research Logistics Quarterly, D 201.12

Naval Research Reviews, D 210.11

Naval Research Task Summary, D 210.20

Naval Reserve Circular Letters, N 17.28

Naval Reserve Circular Letters and Instructions, N 25.5

Naval Reserve Regulations, N 25.7/2

Naval Reservist News, D 207.309

Naval Reservist, News of Interest to the **Naval** Reservist, D 208.10

Naval Ship Research and Development Center Reports, D 211.9

Naval Ship Systems Command Technical News, D 211.8

Naval Stores, A 105.49

Naval Stores Report, A 88.29, A 88.29/2

Naval Support Force Antarctica, D 201.15/3

Naval Support Force, Antarctica, Publications, D 201.15/2

Naval Surface Warfare Center Dahlgren Division, Technical Digest, D 201.21/8

Naval Surface Weapons Center, NSWC-AP (series), D 201.21/6

Naval Surface Weapons Center, Technical Reports, D 201.21/5

Naval Torpedo Station, Keyport, Washington: Publications, D 211.23

Naval Training Bulletin, D 208.7

Naval War College Review, D 208.209

Index of United States Army, Joint Army-**Navy**, and Federal Specifications and Standards, M 101.23

Index to **Navy** Procurement Information, D 201.6/11

Joint Air Forces & **Navy** Radio Facility Charts, M 301.16

Joint Army & **Navy** Radio Facility Charts, W 108.29

Joint Army-**Navy** Publications, W 1.79

Joint Army-**Navy** Specifications, N 20.23, M 213.8

Joint Army-**Navy** Standards, N 20.28, M 5.7

Journal of **Navy** Civilian Manpower Management, D 204.9

Laws Governing Granting of Army and **Navy** Pensions, VA 2.5/2

Laws Governing Granting of Army and **Navy** Pensions and Bounty Land, I 24.14

Laws Relating Chiefly to Navy, **Navy** Department, and Marine Corps, M 201.10

Laws Relating to **Navy**, N 7.7, M 214.8

List of Addresses of **Navy** Recruiting Stations, N 17.13, N 17.21

List of Books Available for Ship and Station Libraries, **Navy**, N 17.26

Manual for Medical Department, **Navy** (separates), N 10.5/1a

Manual of Medical Department, **Navy**, D 206.8, D 206.8/2

Manual of **Navy** Enlisted Manpower and Personnel Classifications and Occupational Standards Section II **Navy** Enlisted Classifications, D 208.6/3-4

Medical Statistics, Navy, Statistical Report of the Surgeon General, Navy, Occurrence of Diseases and Injuries in the **Navy** for Fiscal Year (date), D 206.11

Military Standard MIL-STD (**Navy**) Series, D 201.13

Miscellaneous Correspondence of **Navy** Department Concerning Schley's Court of Inquiry, N 1.21/2

NavNews, a **Navy** News Service, D 201.24

Navy, D 7.29/4

Navy and Marine Corps List and Directory, N 1.24

Navy Chaplain, D 207.19/2

Navy Chaplains Bulletin, D 208.3/2, D 207.19

Navy Chaplains Newsletter, D 208.3/2

Navy Civil Engineer, D 209.13

Navy Comptroller Manual, D 201.6/2

Navy Comptroller Manual, Advance Changes, D 201.6/3

Navy Current Procurement Directives, NCPD (series), D 201.6/13

Navy Department Specifications, D 212.9

Navy Department Specifications and Federal Specifications, Monthly Bulletin, N 20.20

Navy Editor Service, D 201.26

Navy Electronics Laboratory Reports, D 211.11

Navy Electronics Laboratory, San Diego, California, Publications (misc.), D 211.11/2

Navy Expenditures, N 20.21

Navy Family Lifeline, D 201.25

Navy Guide for Retired Personnel and Their Families, D 208.26

Navy Life, Reading and Writing for Success in the **Navy**, D 208.11/3

Navy Lifeline, Naval Safety Journal, D 207.15

Navy Management Review, D 201.14

Navy Medical and Dental Materiel Bulletin, D 206.3/2

Navy Military Personnel Statistics, D 208.25

Navy Procurement Directives, D 201.6/10

Navy Property Redistribution and Disposal Regulations, D 201.6/9

Navy Recruiter, D 208.16

Navy Register, N 1.10

Navy Regulations, N 1.11/1, D 201.11

Navy Regulations, Proposed Changes, N 1.11/3

Navy Scientific and Technical Information Program, Newsletter, D 210.26

Navy Shipping Guide, N 20.17

Navy Shipping Guide, Changes, N 20.17/2

Navy Supply Corps Newsletter, D 212.14

Navy Surplus by Auction Catalogs, N 20.14/2

Navy Surplus Supplies; Catalog, N 20.14/3

Navy Training Courses, N 17.25, D 208.11

Navy Training Text Materials, D 208.11/2, D 207.208/4

Navy Transportation Schedules, N 17.10

Navy V-12 Bulletins, N 17.36

Navy War Maps, N 17.35

Navy Wifeline, D 201.25

(**Navy** Yard) Examination Orders, N 1.25

Navy Yard Orders, N 1.15

Numerical List Covering Army Air Forces and Army-**Navy** Aeronautical Standard Parts, W 108.15

Numerical List of U.S. Air Force and Air Force-**Navy** Aeronautical Standard Drawings, D 301.16

Numerical List, U.S. Air Force and Army-**Navy** Aeronautical Standard Drawings, M 301.12

Officers of **Navy** and Marine Corps in District of Columbia, N 1.20

Ordnance Instructions for **Navy**, N 18.5

Pamphlets Oceanographer of the **Navy**, D 218.9

Posters **Navy** Department, D 201.19

Publications **Navy** Electronics Laboratory, D 211.11/2

Register of Civil Engineer Corps Commissioned and Warrant Officers of United States **Navy** and Naval Reserve on Active Duty, D 209.9

Register of Commissioned and Warrant Officers **Navy** and Marine Corps and Reserve Officers on Active Duty, D 208.12

Register of Commissioned and Warrant Officers United States **Navy** and Marine Corps, M 206.10

Register of Retired Commissioned and Warrant Officers, Regular and Reserve, of the United States **Navy** and Marine Corps, D 208.12/3

Safety Posters Department of the **Navy**, N 1.31/2

Selective Service Memorandums to All **Navy** Contractors, N 1.30

Selling to **Navy** Prime Contractors, D 201.2:Se 4/2

Shift Colors, the Newsletter for **Navy** Retirees, D 208.12/3-2

Shipment Under the United States Foreign Aid Programs Made on Army- or **Navy**-Operated Vessels (American flag) by Port of Lading by Country of Destination, C 3.164:976

Ships Registered Under Liberian, Panamanian, and Honduran Flags Deemed by the **Navy** Department to Be Under Effective U.S. Control, C 39.228

Standards Laboratory Cross-Check Procedure, Department of **Navy**, BUWEPS-BUSHIPS Calibration Program, D 217.16

Standards Laboratory Instrument Calibration Procedure, Department of **Navy**, BUWEPS-BUSHIPS Calibration Program, D 217.16/2

Standards Laboratory Measurements System Operation Procedure, Department of **Navy**, BUWEPS-BUSHIPS Calibration Program, D 217.16/3

Statistics of Diseases and Injuries in **Navy**, N 10.15, M 203.10

Statistics of **Navy** Medicine, D 206.15

Supply Table of Medical Department, **Navy**, with Allowance for Ships, N 10.8

U.S. Air Force and U.S. **Navy** Flight Planning Document, D 301.52

U.S. Army and **Navy** Directory of Airfields, C 31.125

U.S. **Navy** Civil Engineer Corps Bulletin, N 21.14, M 205.7, D 209.7

U.S. **Navy** Marine Climatic Atlas of the World, D 202.2:At 6

U.S. **Navy** Medicine, D 206.7

U.S. **Navy** Regulations, D 201.11

U.S. **Navy** Travel Instructions, Instruction Memoranda, N 20.13/3

United States Air Force and **Navy** Supplementary Flight Information Document, Pacific and Far East, D 301.50

United States Air Force and **Navy** Supplementary Flight Information, Europe, Africa, and Middle East, D 301.49

United States Air Force and United States **Navy** Radio Facility Charts, Central Pacific-Far East, D 301.12

United States Air Force, **Navy**, Royal Canadian Air Force and Royal Canadian **Navy**, **Navy** Radio Facility Charts and In-Flight Data, Alaska, Canada and North Atlantic, D 301.13/3

United States Air Force, **Navy**, Royal Canadian Air Force and Royal Canadian Supplementary Flight Information, North American Area (excluding Mexico and Caribbean area), D 301.48

United States Air Force, United States **Navy** and Royal Canadian Air Force Radio Facility Charts, West Canada and Alaska, D 301.13

United States Air Force, United States **Navy** Radio Facility Charts, North Atlantic Area, D 301.11

United States **Navy** and the Vietnam Conflict (series), D 207.10/3

Your **Navy**, from the Viewpoint of the Nation's Finest Artists, D 201.9

Nazi

Nazi-Soviet Relations, 1939-41, Documents from the German Foreign Office, S 1.2:N 23

NBECS

Nonresidential Buildings Energy Consumption Survey (**NBECS**) (Diskettes), E 3.43/2-3

NBL

NBL Certified Reference Materials Catalog, E 1.98:

NBLIC

NBLIC (National Black Leadership Initiative on Cancer) News, HE 20.3195

NBS

Activities of the **NBS** Spectrochemical Analysis Section, C 13.46

NBS Consumer Information Series, C 13.53

NBS Handbook, Specifications, Tolerances, and Other Technical Requirements for Weighing and Measuring Devices, C 13.11/2

NBS Publications Newsletter, C 13.36/5

NBS Reactor: Summary of Activities, C 13.46/2

NBS Serial Holdings, C 13.58/5

NBS Standard, C 13.42

NBS Standard Reference Materials Price List, C 13.48/4-2

NBS Standard Reference Materials {announcements}, C 13.48/2

NBS Time and Frequency Broadcast Services, C 13.60

NBS Update, C 13.36/7

New Publications from **NBS**, C 13.36/2

News for Users of **NBS** Standard Reference Materials, C 13.50

NC

NC News, A 13.82/9-2

NCADI

NCADI Publications Catalog, HE 20.419, HE 20.8012/2

NCBE

NCBE Forum, ED 1.71/3

NCBI

NCBI Newsletter, HE 20.3624/2

NCCDPHP

National Center for Chronic Disease Prevention and Health Promotion (**NCCDPHP**), HE 20.7039, HE 20.7616

NCDRH

Joint **NCDRH** and State Quality Assurance Surveys in Nuclear Medicine, HE 20.4611

NCEL

NCEL Contract Report, D 209.12/4

NCEL Techdata, D 201.27

NCES

NCES Announcements, ED 1.128

NCES Bulletins, ED 1.126

NCG

NCG {Nuclear Catering Group} Technical Reports, D 103.54

NCH

NCH Statistics Series, HE 20.5113

NCHCT

NCHCT Fact Sheet, HE 20.28

NCHCT Monograph Series, HE 20.26

NCHS

Advance Data from the Vital and Health Statistics of **NCHS**, HE 20.6209/3

NCHS Atlas CD-ROM, HE 20.6209/12

NCHS Catalog of University Presentations, HE 20.6225

NCHS CD-ROM Series (23), HE 20.6209/10

NCHS Health Interview Statistics, Publications from the National Health <KEY>Instruction Manual Part 2d, **NCHS** Procedures for Mortality Medical Data System File Preparation and Maintenance, HE 20.6208/4-6

Interview Survey, Advance Data Reports, HE 20.6216/5
NCHS Publications on {various subjects}, HE 20.6220

NCHSR

NCHSR Health Care for the Aging, HE 20.6514/2
NCHSR Program Solicitation (series), HE 20.6512/9
NCHSR Program Solicitation, Grants for Health Services Dissertation Research, HE 20.6512/8-2
NCHSR Program Solicitation, Individual and Institutional, HE 20.6512/8
NCHSR Research Activities, HE 20.6512/5
NCHSR Research Digest Series, HE 20.6511
NCHSR Research Management (series), HE 20.6512/4
NCHSR Research Proceedings Series, HE 20.6512/3
NCHSR Research Report Series, HE 20.6512
NCHSR Research Summary Series, HE 20.6512/2

NCI

NCI Fact Book, HE 20.3174
NCI Grant Supported Literature Index, HE 20.3179
NCI Grants Awarded, by Principal Investigator, HE 20.3176/2
NCI Grants Awarded, Fiscal Year (date), HE 20.3176
NCI Investigational Drugs, Chemical Information, HE 20.3180/2
NCI Investigational Drugs, Pharmaceutical Data, HE 20.3180
NCI Monographs, HE 20.3162

NCIC

NCIC 2000 Newsletter, J 1.107

NCI-CG-TR

Carcinogenesis Technical Report Series, **NCI-CG-TR** (series), HE 20.3159/2

NCIC

NCIC Newsletter, J 1.14/19

NCJRS

NCJRS Abstracts Database, J 28.31/2-2
NCJRS Document Loan Program, Document Lists, J 1.20/4

NCO

NCO Call, D 101.118/3
NCO Journal, D 101.127

NCSC-TG

NCSC-TG (series), D 1.79/4

NCPTT

NCPTT Notes, I 29.136

NCSS

NCSS (National Cooperative Soil Survey) Newsletter, A 57.78
NCSS Report, H , HE 17.640
Progress Report on Staff Development for Fiscal Year, **NCSS** Report E-3, FS 17.630, HE 17.630

NCUA

NCUA Digest, NCU 1.13
NCUA Investment Report, NCU 1.22
NCUA Letter to Credit Unions, NCU 1.19
NCUA News, NCU 1.20
NCUA Quarterly, NCU 1.3/2
NCUA Report, NCU 1.12
NCUA Review, NCU 1.15

NCWM

NCWM Publications, C 13.10/3-3

NDATUS

NDATUS Instruction Manual, HE 20.8021

NDC

NDC Research Abstracts, D 5.411/2

NDE

NDE of Stainless Steel and On-Line Leak Monitoring of LWRS, Annual Report, Y 3.N 88:25-5, Y 3.N 88:25-9

NDEA

Modern Foreign Language Fellowship Program, National Defense Education Act, Title 6 and **NDEA** Related Awards under Fullbright-Hays Act, FS 5.255:55034, HE 5.255:55034
NDEA Counseling and Guidance Institutes, FS 5.255:25015, HE 5.255:25015

NDIC

National Drug Intelligence Center (**NDIC**): General Publications, J 1.112

NDPO

Beacon (**NDPO**-Monthly Newsletter), The J 1.14/25-5
NDPO Fact Sheet, J 1.14/25-4
NDPO Information Bulletins, J 1.14/25-3

NDU-DODCI

DoD Computer Institute: **NDU-DODCI** Course Catalog, D 5.414/2

NE

NE Regional Reports, L 2.71/3
NE Regional Staff Letter, A 77.29, A 106.38

Nealon

Nealon Report, The, HE 20.3152/15

Near

Near and Middle Eastern Series, S 1.86

Near East

Near East and Africa Reports, PrEx 7.20
Near East and South Asia Report, PrEx 7.20
Near East and South Asian Series, S 1.86/2

Near Eastern

Near Eastern and Middle Eastern Series, S 1.86
Near Eastern Series, S 1.31

Nebraska

Cattle on Feed, Illinois, Iowa, **Nebraska**, Idaho, and California, A 88.16/7
Nebraska Weekly Weather and Crop Report, A 36.208

NECTP

NECTP {Northeast Corridor Transportation Project} , TD 3.13

Needs

ADFC Standards for Basic **Needs**, HE 3.64
Employers' Estimates of Labor **Needs** in Selected Defense Industries, FS 3.121
Five Year Medical Facility Construction **Needs** Assessment, VA 1.68
Human **Needs**, HE 17.26
Immediate Water Pollution Control **Needs**, I 67.13/5
Instructions and Application for Grants under the Special **Needs** Program, ED 1.61
Natural Gas Deliveries and Curtailments to End-use Customers and Potential **Needs** for Additional Alternate Fuels, E 3.11/2-5
Needs and Offers List, GP 3.31
OAA and AFDC, Cost Standards for Basic **Needs** and Percent of Such Standards Met for Specified Types of Cases, FS 17.625, HE 17.625
Personnel **Needs** and Training for Biomedical and Behavioral Research, HE 20.3036/2
Soil and Water Conservation Research **Needs** Executive Summary, A 57.73
Special **Needs** Offenders, Bulletin, Ju 13.17
World Food **Needs** and Availabilities, A 93.48

Neglect

Annual Review of Child Abuse and **Neglect** Research, HE 23.1210/3
Child Abuse and **Neglect** (series), HE 1.480, HE 23.1210
Child Abuse and **Neglect** Programs, HE 1.480/4, HE 23.1211
Child Abuse and **Neglect** Reports, HE 1.480/2, HE 23.1212
Child Abuse and **Neglect** Research: Projects and Publications, HE 1.480/3, HE 23.1210/2
National Clearinghouse on Child Abuse and **Neglect** Information Catalog, HE 23.1216/2
National Conference on Child Abuse and **Neglect**: Proceedings, HE 1.480/5

Neglected

Cultivation of **Neglected** Tropical Fruits with Promise (series), A 106.26/2
Neglected or Delinquent Children Living in State Operated or Supported Institutions, HE 19.335

Negotiable

Maturity Distribution of Outstanding **Negotiable** Time Certificates of Deposit, FR 1.54/2

Negotiation

Military **Negotiation** Regulations, D 1.8

Negro

National **Negro** Health News, T 27.30, FS 2.19
Negro Economics Division, L 1.8
Negro Extension News, A 43.7/2
Negro Notes, S 1.83
Negro Population: March (year), C 3.186:P-20
Negro Statistics Bulletin, C 3.131
Survey of **Negro** World War II Veterans and Vacancy and Occupancy of Dwelling Units Available to Negroes {in city areas}, L 2.31

Negroes

Banking Institutions Owned and Operated by **Negroes** Annual Reports, C 1.23
Negroes in the United States, C 3.3

Survey of Negro World War II Veterans and Vacancy and Occupancy of Dwelling Units Available to **Negroes** {in city areas}, L 2.31

NEH

NEH Exhibitions Today, NF 3.24
NEH Fellowships University Teachers, College Teachers, and Independent Scholars Anniversary and Commemorative Initiatives, NF 3.13/4
NEH News, NF 3.7
NEH Teacher-Scholar Program for Elementary and Secondary School Teachers, Guidelines and Application Instructions, NF 3.18
NEH Travel to Collections, Small Grants for Research Travel to Libraries, Archives, Museums, and Other Repositories, NF 3.19

Neighborhood

Neighborhood Health Centers, Summary of Project Data, HE 20.5115
Neighborhood Networks Fact Sheet, HH 13.16/5
Neighborhood Networks News, HH 13.16
Neighborhood Networks News Brief, HH 1.127
Neighborhood Networks Newsline, HH 1.127/2
Neighborhood Youth Corps Publications, L 1.49

Neighborhoods

Income, Education and Unemployment in **Neighborhoods** {by city}, L 2.88

NE-INF

NE-INF (series), A 13.42/25

NEISS

NEISS Data Highlights, Y 3.C 76/3:7-3
NEISS {National Electronic Injury Surveillance System} News, Product Safety, HE 20.4026, Y 3.C 76/3:7-2

Nematicides

Annotated Index of Registered Fungicides and **Nematicides**, Their Uses in the United States, A 77.302:F 96
Fungicides and **Nematicides**, EP 5.11/2

NE/NA-INF

NE/NA-INF, A 13.110/15

Neoplasms

Conversion of **Neoplasms** by Topography and Morphology, HE 20.3197

NEPA/BRAC

NEPA/BRAC, D 103.128

Nepal

Accession List: **Nepal**, LC 1.30/6
Nepal, LC 1.30/6

NEPH

NEPH Newsletters, L 16.44

Nephrology

Kidney Disease and **Nephrology** Index, HE 20.3318

NESEDB

National Economic Social & Environmental Data Bank (**NESEDB**), C 1.88/2

NESDIS

NESDIS (series), C 55.13:**NESDIS**
NOAA Atlas **NESDIS**, C 55.242

NESS

NESS (series), C 55.13:NESS, C 55.13/2:**NESS**

Net

Net Migration of the Population, by Age, Sex and Color, A 93.35
Net (New Electronic Titles), GP 3.40
Net Spendable Earnings, L 2.75, LC 30.24
Prime Contract Awards by Statutory Authority, Number of Actions, and **Net** Value by Department, D 1.57/3-2
Typical Electric Bills, Typical **Net** Monthly Bills of January (year), for Residential Commercial and Industrial Services, FP 1.10

Network

Challenge **Network** Membership Directory, ED 1.30/3
Daily Magnetograms for ... from the AFGL **Network**, D 301.45/4-4
Defense Communications System Global, Automatic Voice **Network** Telephone Directory, D 5.111
Disability **Network** News, PrEx 1.10/20, PrEx 1.10/20-2
Drug Abuse Warning **Network** Series, HE 20.416/3
LECC **Network** News, J 31.11
Network of Knowledge, Directory of Criminal Justice Information Sources, J 28.20
Network News, HE 20.9117
Network Planning Papers (series), LC 1.37
Network, SBA 1.38, T 22.2/15:7375

Undersecretary's Report to the Field, **Newsletter** for Department of Labor Field Representatives, L 1.37

UNESCO Conference **Newsletter**, S 5.48/4

VA Medical Center, Allen Park, Michigan: **Newsletter**, VA 1.56/5

VA Medical Center, Phoenix, Arizona: **Newsletter**, VA 1.56/3

Veterans Education **Newsletter**, VA 1.49

VHA Employee **Newsletter**, VA 1.100

Western Regional **Newsletter**, J 21.17

Wildlife **Newsletter**, J 30.9/2

Women's **Newsletter**, PrEx 1.20

Youth Advisory Board **Newsletter**, EP 1.27

Newsletters

Southeastern Forest Insect and Disease **Newsletters**, A 13.63/14

State Technical Services **Newsletters**, C 1.53

Newsline

FCA **Newsline**, FCA 1.26

GSO **Newsline**, S 1.144

LC Cataloging **Newsline**, LC 1.55

Neighborhood Networks **Newsline**, HH 1.127/2

Newsline, E 1.53/3

Newslink

Health Workforce **Newslink**, HE 20.9315

Newsmakers

Sea **Newsmakers**, A 106.41

Newsmap

Newsmap for Armed Forces, W 109.207, W 109.207/2

Newsmap, Industrial Edition, W 109.209

Newsmap, Overseas Edition, W 109.208

Newsnet

Newsnet, LC 3.4/3

Newsnotes

Newsnotes on Education Around the World, FS 5.57, FS 5.214:14035, HE 5.214:14035

UMTA **Newsnotes**, TD 7.14

Newspaper

Foreign **Newspaper** and Gazette Report, LC 29.10

General **Newspaper** Releases, Y 3.W 19/2:5

Weekly **Newspaper** Service, L 1.77

Newspapers

CRS Media Relations, **Newspapers**, Magazines, Radio, Television, C 50.7/2

CRS Media Relations, **Newspapers**, Magazines, Radio, Television, Informational Monitoring Service, J 23.7

Library of Congress Catalogs: **Newspapers** in Microforms, LC 30.20

List of **Newspapers** Designated to Publish Advertisements of War Department, W 1.9

Newspapers Currently Received, LC 6.7

Newspapers in Microfilm, Foreign Countries, LC 30.20/2

Newspapers in Microform, LC 30.20

Newspictures

CD **Newspictures**, D 1.34/2, D 119.10

Newspictures, FCD 1.16/2, Pr 34.760, PrEx 4.7/3

Next

Next General Weather Radar (series), C 1.80

Treasurers **Next** Door, I 16.65/3

Next Day

Express Mail **Next Day** Service, Directory for Minneapolis 554, P 1.52/2

NFS

NFS, NS 1.3

NFS Reports, A 77.516

NFS Reports (series), A 77.516

NGB

NGB Circulars, M 114.4, D 112.4

NGB Manuals (numbered), D 12.10/2

NGB Publications Bulletin, D 12.3/2

NGF

Technical Report **NGF** (series), D 215.10

NHIS

National Health Interview Survey, (**NHIS**), HE 20.6209/4-3

NHLBI

NHLBI National Research Service Award Programs Summary Descriptions, HE 20.3211/4

NHPRC

NHPRC (year) Annual Report, GS 4.14/3

NHSC

NHSC Fact Sheets, HE 20.9110/5

NHSC in Touch, Free On-Line Service Open to Primary Care Providers, HE 20.9110/9

NHSC Notes, HE 20.9110/4

NHSQIC

NHSQIC Annual Bibliography, HE 22.212

NHTSA

NHTSA News, TD 8.25

NHTSA Technical Notes, TD 8.23

NHTSA Technical Reports, TD 8.22

NIA

NIA Report to Council on Program, HE 20.3860

Summer Jobs at **NIA**, Catalog, HE 20.3015/3

NIAA

NIAA Information and Feature Service, HE 20.8312

NIAAA

NIAAA Treatment Handbook Series, HE 20.8308/2

NIAID

NIAID Awards, HE 20.3266

NIAMDD

NIAMDD Research Advances (on various diseases), HE 20.3320

Nicaragua

Costa Rica-**Nicaragua** Boundary Arbitration, S 3.15

Directory of the Republic of **Nicaragua**, PrEx 3.10/7-19

Maritime Canal Company of **Nicaragua**, Annual Reports, I 1.21

NICHD

NICHD News Notes, HE 20.3364/3

NICHD Research Highlights and Topics of Interest, HE 20.3364

Research Report from the **NICHD**, HE 20.3364/2

Nickel

Mineral Industry Surveys, Nickel, I 19.148

Nickel, I 28.92

Nickel in (year), I 28.92/2

Nicotine

Tar, **Nicotine**, and Carbon Dioxide of the Smoke of...Varieties of Domestic Cigarettes for the Year, FT 1.36

NIDA

NIDA Capsules (Series), HE 20.8234, HE 20.3967/2

NIDA Notes, HE 20.8217/4, HE 20.3967

NIDA Research Report Series, HE 20.8217/6, HE 20.3965/2

NIDCD

Inside **NIDCD** Information Clearinghouse, HE 20.3666

NIDRR

NIDRR Program Directory, ED 1.30/5, ED 1.215

NIDR

NIDR Research Digest, HE 20.3413

NIDRR

NIDRR Consensus Statement, ED 1.86

NIE

Funding Opportunities at **NIE**, FY (year), ED 1.321

Funding Opportunities at **NIE**, Grants Competitions and Requests for Proposals in Fiscal Year, HE 19.216/2

Grants Competitions and RFPS: Planned **NIE** Activities During the Fiscal Year, HE 19.216

NIE Information, ED 1.318

NIE Papers in Education and Work, HE 19.212

NIE-R

Request for Proposal, **NIE-R-** (series), ED 1.324

Night

Directory of Outpatient Psychiatric Clinics, Psychiatric Day-**Night** Services and Other Mental Health Resources in the United States and Territories, FS 2.22/38-4

Nightwear

Industry Wage Survey: Men's and Boy's Shirts and **Nightwear**, L 2.3/35

NIGMS

NIGMS Minority Program Update, HE 20.3469

NIGMS Research Grants, HE 20.3465, HE 20.3465/2

NIGMS Training Grants, HE 20.3468

NIH

Current and Non-current Periodicals in the **NIH** Library, HE 20.3009/3

Inventory and Analysis of **NIH** Maternal and Child Health Research, HE 20.3363

News and Features from **NIH**, Portfolio Series, HE 20.3007/2

NIH Administrative Manual, HE 20.3008/3

NIH Almanac, HE 20.3061

NIH Almanac Update, HE 20.3182/5

NIH Catalyst, HE 20.3061

NIH Curriculum Supplement Series HE 20.3065

NIH Data Book, Basic Data Relating to the National Institutes of Health, HE 20.3041

NIH Extramural Data and Trends, HE 20.3055/2

NIH Extramural Programs, Funding for Research and Research Training, HE 20.3053/2

NIH Guide for Grants and Contracts, HE 20.3008/2, HE 20.3008/2-2

NIH Library Translations Index, FS 2.22:T 68/2

NIH Peer Review Notes, HE 20.3045

NIH Program Evaluation Reports, HE 20.3039

NIH Public Advisory Groups: Authority, Structure, Functions, HE 20.3018

NIH Publications List, HE 20.3009

NIH Quarterly Publications List, FS 2.22/13-9

NIH Record, FS 2.22/2, HE 20.3007/3

NIH Statistical Reference Book of International Activities, HE 20.3760

NIH Training Center Catalog and Calendar, HE 20.3060

Periodicals Currently Received in **NIH** Library, FS 2.22/13-3

Reprints of Articles Published Concerning **NIH** Consensus Development Conferences, HE 20.3030/2

Schedule of **NIH** Conferences, HE 20.3040

NIJ

NIJ Guide, J 28.8/3

NIJ Reports, A Bimonthly Journal of the National Institute of Justice, J 28.14

NIJ Reports/SNI (reprints), J 28.14/a

NIJ Research Forum, J 28.35

NIJ Research Review, The, J 28.24/10

Technology Assessment Program, **NIJ** Standard, J 28.15

Nikishka

Supplemental Tidal Predictions, Anchorage, **Nikishka**, Seldovia, and Valdez, Alaska, C 55.432

NILECJ

NILECJ Evaluation Series, J 1.46/2

NILECJ-guides, J 1.41/3

NILECJ-STD

Law Enforcement Standards Program, **NILECJ-STD** (series), J 1.41/2, J 26.20

NIMA

NIMA Aeronautical Charts and Publications, TD 4.84

NIMA Nautical Charts, Public Sale Region 1, United States and Canada, TD 4.82:1

NIMA Nautical Charts, Public Sale Region 2, Central and South America and Antarctica, TD 4.82:2

NIMA Nautical Charts, Public Sale Region 3, Western Europe, Iceland, Greenland, and the Arctic, TD 4.82:3

NIMA Nautical Charts, Public Sale Region 4, Scandinavia, Baltic and Russia, TD 4.82:4

NIMA Nautical Charts, Public Sale Region 5, Western Africa and the Mediterranean, TD 4.82:5

NIMA Nautical Charts, Public Sale Region 6, Indian Ocean, TD 4.82:6

NIMA Nautical Charts, Public Sale Region 7, Australia, Indonesia, and New Zealand, TD 4.82:7

NIMA Nautical Charts, Public Sale Region 8, Oceania, TD 4.82:8

NIMA Nautical Charts, Public Sale Region 9, East Asia, TD 4.82:9

NIMH

NIMH Analyses Series, FS 2.22/27

NIMH Library Acquisition List, HE 20.8113/4

NIMH Report to Physicians (series), HE 20.8111

NINBD

NINBD Monographs, FS 2.22/55

NINCDS

NINCDS Amyotrophic Lateral Sclerosis Research Program, HE 20.3502:Am 9/2

NINCDS Cerebral Palsy Research Program, HE 20.3502:C 33/3

NINCDS Epilepsy Research Program, HE 20.3502:Ep 4/2

NINCDS Hearing, Speech, and Language Research Program, HE 20.3502:H 35/3

NINCDS Huntington's Disease Research Program, HE 20.3502:H 92/2

NINCDS Index to Research Grants and Awards, HE 20.3516

NINCDS Multiple Sclerosis Research Program, HE 20.3502:M 91

NINCDS Neuromuscular Disorders Research Program, HE 20.3502:N 39/3

NINCDS Parkinson's Disease Research Program, HE 20.3502:P 22
NINCDS Research Program, Stroke, HE 20.3512/2
NINCDS Spinal Cord Injury Research Program, HE 20.3502:Sp 4/2
NINCDS Stroke Research Progrm HE 20.3502:St 8

NINDS
NINDS Bibliography Series, HE 20.3513/3
NINDS Index to Research Grants and Contracts, HE 20.3516
NINDS Monographs, HE 20.3510
NINDS Research Profiles, HE 20.3512

1997
1997 Economic Censuses, C 3.277/2

Nineteen Ninety Six
Nineteen Ninety Six Buy-Recycled Series, EP 1.17/8

NIOSH
NIOSH Alert, HE 20.7123
NIOSH Certified Equipment List, HE 20.7124
NIOSH Health and Safety Guides for {various businesses}, HE 20.7108/2
NIOSH Health Hazard Evaluation Report, HE 20.7125/2
NIOSH Projects for (Fiscal Year), HE 20.7127
NIOSH Publications Catalog, HE 20.7114/2
NIOSH Research Reports, HE 20.7111
NIOSH Schedule of Courses, HE 20.7128
NIOSH Surveillance Reports, HE 20.7111/3
NIOSH Technical Reports, HE 20.7111/2
NIOSH Worker Bulletin (series), HE 20.7117/2
Subfiles of the NIOSH Toxic Substances List, HE 20.7112/2

NIST
NIST Conference Calendar, C 13.10/3-2
NIST Handbook, Specifications, Tolerances, and Other Technical Requirements for Weighing and Measuring Devices, C 13.11/2
NIST Serial Holdings, C 13.58/5
NIST Update, C 13.36/7

NIST-GCR
NIST-GCR Grantee/Contractor Report, C 13.57/2

NISTIR
National Institute of Standards and Technology Interagency Reports, NISTIR (series), C 13.58

Nitro-Cellulose
Cellulose Plastic Products (Nitro-Cellulose and Cellulose Acetate Sheets, Rods and Tubes), C 3.73

Nitrogen
Nitrogen in (year), I 28.132

NLM
Index of NLM Serial Titles, HE 20.3618
NLM Catalog Supplement, HE 20.3609/3-3
NLM LOCATORplus, HE 20.3626
NLM Name and Series Authorities, HE 20.3609/5

NLRB
Classification Outline for Decisions of the NLRB and Related Court Decisions, LR 1.8/7
Digest & Index of Decisions of NLRB, LR 1.8/2
Weekly Summary of NLRB Cases, LR 1.5/2

NLS
NLS News, National Longitudinal Surveys, L 2.135

NMFS
NMFS (series), C 55.13:NMFS, C 55.13/2:NMFS
NMFS Northwest Region, Organization and Activities, Fiscal Year, C 55.301/2

NMRC
NMRC (series), C 39.244, TD 11.17

NMSS
NMSS Licensee Newsletter, Y 3.N 88:57

NOAA
Catalog of Meteorological Satellite Data: ESSA 9 and NOAA 1 Television Cloud Photography, C 55.219:5.3
NOAA, C 55.14
NOAA Atlases, C 55.22
NOAA Circular (series), C 55.4
NOAA Coastal Ocean Program, Decisions Analysis Series, C 55.49/3
NOAA Coastal Ocean Program, Project News Update, C 55.49/4
NOAA Coastal Ocean Program, Regional Synthesis Series, C 55.49/2
NOAA Computer Programs and Problems, C 55.13/3
NOAA Data Report, MESA (series), C 55.36
NOAA Data Reports, C55.36
NOAA Data Reports, OMPA (series), C 55.36
NOAA Dumpsite Evaluation Reports, C 55.35
NOAA Environmental Buoy Data, C 55.297

NOAA Estuary-of-the-Month, Seminar Series, C 55.49
NOAA Handbooks, C 55.8/2
NOAA Manuals (numbered), C 55.8/3
NOAA National Status and Trends Program and Quality Assurance Program for Marine Environmental Measurements, C 55.434
NOAA Organization Directory (series), C 55.48/2
NOAA Paleoclimate Publications Series Report (series), C 55.241
NOAA Photoessays, C 55.19
NOAA Professional Papers, C 55.25
NOAA Program Plans, C 55.15
NOAA Publications Announcements, C 55.17
NOAA Report, C 55.53
NOAA Scientific and Technical Publications Announcements, C 55.228/2
NOAA Special Reports, NOS OMA- (series), C 55.13/6
NOAA Technical Memorandums, C 55.13/2
NOAA Technical Reports, C 55.13
NOAA Western Region Computer Programs and Problems (series), C 55.13/3
Satellite Activities of NOAA, C 55.510
This Week in NOAA, C 55.9/2, C 55.46
Transmittals (NOAA Washington Area Personnel Locator), C 55.47

NOAA'S
Symposia Series for Undersea Research, NOAA'S Undersea Research Program, C 55.29/2

Nobel Prize
Nobel Prize Laureates, HE 20.3463

NODC
NODC Environmental Information Summaries, C 55.299
NODC Quarterly Accessions, Computer Produced Indexes, American Meteorological Society Meteorological and Geoastrophysical Abstracts, D 203.24/6

Noise
Background Document for {various products} Noise Emission Regulations, EP 1.6/2
Federal Aircraft Noise Abatement Plan, Fiscal Year, TD 1.16
Federal Noise Program Reports, EP 1.73
Federal Noise Research in (various subjects), EP 1.73/3
Foreign Noise Research (series), EP 1.73/2
Highway Traffic Noise in the United States: Problem and Response, TD 2.23/7
Noise Diagnostics for Safety Assessment, Standards, and Regulation, E 1.28/10
Noise Emission Standards for Construction Equipment, Background Document for {various items}, EP 1.6/3
Noise Facts Digest, EP 1.30
Noise Standards, Aircraft Type and Airworthiness Certification, TD 4.6:part 36

Noise Abatement
Office of Noise Abatement: Report FAA-NO (series), TD 4.32/2

Nomenclature
Standard Nomenclature Lists, Obsolete General Supplies, W 32.23/4
Standard Nomenclature Lists, W 34.22

Nominate
Nominate a Small Business Person or Advocate of the Year, SBA 1.43

Nomination
Election Law Guidebook, 1974, Summary of Federal and State Laws Regulating Nomination and Election of United States Senators, Revised to January 1, 1974, Y 1.93-2:S.doc. 84

Nonagricultural
Employment in Nonagricultural Establishments, FR 1.42
National Employment, Hours, and Earning Industry Summaries {employees in nonagricultural establishments, by industry division}, L 2.41/5

Non-Appropriated
Non-Appropriated Employees, CS 1.41/4:532-2

Non-Budget
Cost of Pipeline and Compressor Station Construction Under Non-Budget Type or Certificate Authorizations As Reported by Pipeline Companies, FP 1.30

Noncitrus
Fruits, Noncitrus, by State, Production, Use, Value, A 88.12/20

Noncitrus Fruits and Nuts, Annual Summary, A 105.11

Noncollegiate
Enrollments and Programs in Noncollegiate Postsecondary Schools, HE 19.337/2
Occupational Education Enrollments and Programs in Noncollegiate Postsecondary Schools, HE 19.337/2

Non-Compulsory
Non-Compulsory Radio Fixes, TD 4.311

Noncontiguous
Acts of Congress, Treaties, and Proclamations Relating to Noncontiguous Territory, W 6.12
Water Borne Commerce of United States Including Foreign Intercoastal and Coastwise Traffic and Commerce of U.S. Noncontiguous Territory, SB 7.5/295
Water-Borne Foreign and Noncontiguous Commerce and Passenger Traffic of United States, MC 1.23

Nonconventional
Nonconventional Technical Information Systems in Current Use, NS 2.8

Non-current
Current and Non-current Periodicals in the NIH Library, HE 20.3009/3

Nondeposit
Major Nondeposit Funds of Commercial Banks, FR 1.39/4

Nonemployer
Census of Retail Trade Nonemployer Statistics Series, C 3.255/7
Census of Service Industries Nonemployer Statistics Series, C 3.257/5

Nonfarm
Estimated Amount of Nonfarm Mortgages of $20,000 or Less Recorded, HH 4.8/4
Indexes of Output Per Man-Hour, Hourly Compensation, and Unit Labor Costs in the Private Sector of the Economy and the Nonfarm Sector, L 2.2:Ou 8/8
Nonfarm Housing Characteristics, 1950 Housing Census Report H-B (series), C 3.950/3
Nonfarm Housing Starts, C 56.211/3
Nonfarm Mortgage Investments of Life Insurance Companies, FHL 1.18
Nonfarm Real Estate Foreclosure Report, FHL 1.8
Non-farm Real Estate Foreclosures, Y 3.F 31/3:10, FL 3.8, NHA 3.9
Number of New Permanent Nonfarm Dwelling Units Started by Urban or Rural Location, Public or Private Ownership, and Type of Structure, L 2.51/4

Nonfat Dry Milk
Household Purchases of Butter, Cheese, Nonfat Dry Milk Solids and Margarine, A 88.14/6

Non-Federal
Federal and Non-Federal Projects Approved, Y 3.F 31/4:7

Nonferrous
Nonferrous Metals, C 41.54
Nonferrous Metals Supply, Demand Data, I 28.169/3
Nonferrous Scrap Dealers Reports, I 28.65

Nonfood
List of Proprietary Substance and Nonfood Compounds, A 110.9/2
List of Proprietary Substances and Nonfood Compounds Authorized for Use under USDA Inspection and Grading Programs, A 110.15

Nonfuel
Raw Nonfuel Mineral Production in (year), I 28.165

Nongovernment
H 8-1 Nongovernment Organization Codes for Military Standard Contract Administration Procedures: Name to Code, D 7.6/2:8-1/2
H 8-2 Nongovernment Organization Codes for Military Standard Contract Administration Procedures: Code to Name, D 7.6/2:8-2/2
Nongovernment Organization Codes for Military Standard Contract Administration Procedures: Code to Name, D 7.6/2:8-1/2, D 7.6/2:8-2/2

Nonimmigrant
Quarterly Nonimmigrant Statistics, J 21.2/10-2

Nonindexed
Instructions for Classifying the Underlying Cause of Death: **Nonindexed** Terms, Standard Abbreviations, and State Geographic Codes Used in Mortality Data Classification, HE 20.6208/4

Nonionization
Life Sciences: Effects of **Nonionization** Electromagnetic Radiation, PrEx 7.22/2

Nonmanufacturing
Occupational Employment in Selected **Nonmanufacturing** Industries, L 2.3/16-2

Nonmarket
Quarterly Report on Trade Between the United States and **Nonmarket** Economy Countries, Pursuant to Section 411 (c) of the Trade Act of 1974, Y 4.W 36:3

Quarterly Report to Congress and the East-West Foreign Trade Board on Trade Between the United States and the **Nonmarket** Economy Countries, Y 4.W 36:2

Report to Congress and East-West Foreign Trade Board on Trade Between United States and **Nonmarket** Economy Countries, TC 1.38

Report to the Congress and the Trade Policy Committee on Trade Between the U.S. and the **Nonmarket** Economy Countries, ITC 1.13

Nonmetal
Contractor Fatalities Coal and Metal/**Nonmetal** Mines, L 38.20/4

Fatal Accidents Involving Drowning at Coal and Metal/**Nonmetal** Mines, L 38.19/3-2

Metal/**Nonmetal**, Surface and Underground Fatalities, L 38.19/4

Metal/**Nonmetal**-Surface Fatalities, L 38.19/3

Metal/**Nonmetal**-Underground Fatalities, L 38.19/2

Nonmetallic
Administration of Federal Metal and **Nonmetallic** Mine Safety Act, Annual Report of the Secretary of the Interior, I 1.96/2

Administration of the Federal Metal and **Nonmetallic** Mine Safety Act, I 28.5

Injury Experience in **Nonmetallic** Mining (except Stone and Coal), L 38.10/5

Injury Experience in **Nonmetallic** Mining Industries, I 28.27, I 69.9

Nonmetals
Minor **Nonmetals** in (year), Annual Advance Summary, I 28.121

Nonmetropolitan
Financial and Technical Assistance Provided by the Department of Agriculture and the Department of Housing and Urban Development for **Nonmetropolitan** Planning District, Annual Report to Congress, A 1.113

Non-Military
Summation of **Non-Military** Activities in Japan, W 1.75, M 105.11

Nonpartisan
Nonpartisan Review, NC 3.11

Nonprocurement
List of Parties Excluded from Federal Procurement or **Nonprocurement** Programs, GS 1.28

Nonprofit
Department of the Army Prime Contracts ($1 million and over) Placed with Industry, **Non-Profit** Organizations, Colleges, and Universities, D 101.22:715-4

Educational and **Nonprofit** Institutions Receiving Prime Contract Awards for Research, Development, Test and Evaluation, D 1.57/8

Federal Support of Research and Development at Universities and Colleges and Selected **Nonprofit** Institutions, Fiscal Year, Report to the President and Congress, NS 1.30

Federal Support to Universities, Colleges, and Selected **Nonprofit** Institutions, Fiscal Year (date), Report to the President and Congress, NS 1.30

Instructions and Data Specifications for Reporting DHHS Obligations to Institutions of Higher Education and Other **Nonprofit** Organizations, HE 20.3050

Status Report, Voluntary and **Non-Profit** Agency Technical Crop Ration Contracts with International Cooperation Administration, S 17.41/2

Nonpublic
Directory of Secondary Schools with Occupational Curriculums, Public and **Nonpublic**, HE 5.96

Nonpublic Schools in Large Cities, HE 5.93/11

Statistics of **Nonpublic** Elementary and Secondary Schools, (year), HE 5.93/9

Statistics of **Nonpublic** Elementary Schools, FS 5.220:20064

Subject Offerings and Enrollments, Grades 912, **Nonpublic** Secondary Schools, FS 5.224:24012, HE 5.224:24012

Nonpurchased
Inventory of **Nonpurchased** Foreign Currencies, T 1.50

Nonresidential
Current Construction Reports, Special Studies, Expenditures for **Nonresidential** Improvements and Repairs, C 3.215/8-2

Nonresidential Buildings Energy Consumption Survey (NBECS) (Diskettes), E 3.43/2-3

Nonrubber
Nonrubber Footwear, ITC 1.21, ITC 1.21/2

Nonsurgical
Surgical and **Nonsurgical** Procedures in Shortstay Hospitals, United States, HE 20.6209/5

Non-Theatrical
Current Releases of **Non-Theatrical** Film, C 18.63

Non-U.S.
Statistical Summary and Analysis of Foreign Visitor Arrivals, U.S. Citizen and **Non-U.S.** Citizen Departures, C 47.15

Nonutility
Inventory of **Nonutility** Electric Power Plants in the United States, E 3.29/2

Nonwhite
Farms of **Nonwhite** Farm Operators, Number of Farms, Land in Farm, Cropland Harvested, and Value of Land and Buildings, by Tenure, Censuses of 1945 and 1940 (by States), C 3.193

NORDA
NORDA Reports, D 210.109

Norfolk
Area Wage Survey Summary **Norfolk**-Virginia Beach-Newport News, Virginia, L 2.122/46-2

Tide Calendar **Norfolk** and Newport News, Virginia, N 6.22

Normal
Airworthiness Standards, **Normal**, Utility, and Acrobatic Category Airplanes, TD 4.6:part 23

Hampton **Normal** and Agricultural Institute, I 20.17

Normals
Climatography of the United States; Monthly **Normals** of Temperature, Precipitation, and Heating and Cooling Degree Days, C 55.286

Decennial Census of United States, Climate: Monthly **Normals** of Temperature, Precipitation, and Heating Degree Days, C 30.71/4

Monthly **Normals** of Temperature, Precipitation, and Heating and Cooling Degree Days, C 55.286

U.S. Divisional and Station Climatic Data and **Normals**, C 55.281/2-3

North
Army Air Forces Radio and Facility Charts **North** Pacific Area, W 108.27

Cattle and Sheep, Shipments of Stocker and Feeder Cattle and Sheep into Selected **North** Central States, A 88.16/18-2

East **North** Central, Population and Per Capita Income Estimates for Counties and Incorporated Places, C 3.186/27-4

Forest Pest Conditions in the **North** East, A 13.52/9

Hydrologic Bulletin, Hourly and Daily Precipitation; **North** Atlantic District, C 30.30

Ice Supplement to **North** Atlantic Pilot Chart, N 6.15/2

Meteorological Chart of the **North** Atlantic Ocean, A 29.23

Meteorological Chart of the **North** Pacific Ocean, A 29.24

Military Aviation Notices; **North** Atlantic and East Canada, D 301.11/2

New from **North** Central, A 13.82/9

North Atlantic Coast Fisheries Arbitration, S 3.18/3

North Atlantic Route Chart, C 55.416/8

North Atlantic Route Chart, TD 4.79/9

North Central Region, A 106.39/3

North Central Regional Medical Education Center: Newsletter, VA 1.56/2

North Central Regional Membership Relations Conference, A 89.17/2

North Central Regional Office Publications, L 2.94

North Central States Regional Poultry Breeding Project, Annual Report, A 77.236

North Central Volume, HE 20.6202:N 93 NC

North Eastern Regional Office Publications, L 2.93

North Pacific Oceanic Route Chart, C 55.416/9, C 55.416/9-2

North Pacific Route Chart Northeast Area, TD 4.70/10-1

Pilot Chart of **North** Atlantic Ocean, N 6.15, M 202.17, D 203.17

Pilot Chart of **North** Pacific Ocean, D 203.19, N 6.16, M 202.19

Pilot Chart of Upper Air, **North** Atlantic Ocean, N 6.28

Pilot Chart of Upper Air, **North** Pacific Ocean, N 6.29

Publications Agricultural Adjustment Agency **North** Central Region, A 76.451, A 79.451, A 80.2151

Retail Trade Report East **North** Central, C 3.176

Retail Trade Report West **North** Central, C 3.178

Tide Tables East Coast of **North** and South America, C 4.15/4, C 4.15/5

Tide Tables, High and Low Water Predictions East Coast of **North** and South America Including Greenland, C 55.421/2

Tide Tables, High and Low Water Predictions West Coast of **North** and South America Including Hawaiian Islands, C 55.421

Tropical Cyclones of the **North** Atlantic Ocean, C 55.202:C 99/871-977

U.S. Air Force Radio Facility Charts, **North** Pacific Area, M 301.14

United States Air Force, Navy, Royal Canadian Air Force and Royal Canadian Navy, Navy Radio Facility Charts and In-Flight Data, Alaska, Canada and **North** Atlantic, D 301.13/3

United States Air Force, United States Navy Radio Facility Charts, **North** Atlantic Area, D 301.11

West Coast of **North** and South America (including the Hawaiian Islands), C 4.15/5

West **North** Central, Population and Per Capita Income Estimates for Counties and Incorporated Places, C 3.186/27-3

North America
Acid Precipitation in **North America**: Annual Data Summary from Acid Deposition System Data Base, EP 1.23/5-4

Area Planning **North America** and South America, D 5.318/5-2

Area Planning Special Use Airspace **North America** and South America, D 5.318/5-3

Biographical Sketches and Ancedotes of 95 of 120 Principal Chiefs from Indian Tribes of **North America**, I 20.2:In 2/27

East Coast of **North America** and South America (including Greenland), C 4.15/4

Geologic Names of **North America** Introduced in 1936-1955, I 19.3:1056

Index to Geologic Names of **North America**, I 19.3:1056

North America and Oceania Outlook and Situation Report, A 93.29/2-16

Tide Current Tables, Atlantic Coast of **North America**, C 55.425

North American
Abstracts of **North American** Geology, I 19.54

Bibliography of **North American** Geology, I 19.3

Handbook of **North American** Indians, SI 1.20/2

North American Fauna (series), I 49.30

Notice to Mariners, **North American**-Caribbean Edition, N 6.11/5, M 202.10, D 203.10

United States Air Force, Navy, Royal Canadian Air Force and Royal Canadian Supplementary Flight Information, **North American** Area (excluding Mexico and Caribbean area), D 301.48

North Carolina
  Commercial Tobacco Farms, Coastal Plain, **North Carolina**, A 93.9/11
  National Environmental Research Center, Research Triangle Park, **North Carolina**: Annual Report, EP 1.46
  Water Resources Development in **North Carolina**, D 103.35/33
North Dakota
  North Dakota Leaflets, A 62.12
  Water Resources Development in **North Dakota**, D 103.35/34
North-Central
  Pulpwood Production in the **North-Central** Region by County, A 13.80/5
Northeast
  Commercial Dairy Farms, **Northeast** and Midwest, A 93.9/11
  Employer Costs for Employee Compensation, **Northeast** Region, L 2.120/2-16
  Facts for **Northeast** Committeemen, A 55.14/13
  Flight Information Publication: Enroute-High Altitude, United States, **Northeast** {and Southeast}, D 301.43/3, D 301.43/3-2
  NECTP {**Northeast** Corridor Transportation Project}, TD 3.13
  Northeast Corridor Improvement Project Annaul Report, TD 3.13/3
  Northeast Corridor Transportation Project, C 1.52
  Northeast Employment Cost Index, L 2.117/2
  Northeast Region, A 106.39/2
  Northeast Region Outdoor Memo, I 66.21
  Northeast Volume, HE 20.6202:N 93 NE
  Northeast, Population and Per Capita Income Estimates for Counties and Incorporated Places, C 3.186/27
  Publications Agricultural Adjustment Agency **Northeast** Region, A 76.461, A 79.461, A 80.2161
  Pulpwood Production in the **Northeast**, A 13.80/3
  Regional Data on Compensation Show Wages, Salaries and Benefits Costs in the **Northeast**, L 2.71/6-6
Northeastern
  Genetic Bases for Resistance to Avian Diseases, **Northeastern** States Regional Project, A 94.15
  Northeastern Area State and Private Forestry {publications}, A 13.52/8
  Northeastern Area, NA-FR (series), A 13.102
  Northeastern Boundary Arbitration, S 3.10/1
  Northeastern Forest Pest Reporter, A 13.52/3
  Northeastern General Technical Reports, A 13.42/28
  Northeastern Information Series, NE-INF, A 13.106/4
  Northeastern Pest Reporter, A 13.42/22
  Northeastern Radiological Health Laboratory, BRH/NERHL (series), HE 20.4109
  Northeastern Research Notes, A 13.42/20
  Northeastern Resource Bulletins, A 13.42/26
  Northeastern States Regional Poultry Breeding Project, Annual Report, A 77.234
  Occasional Papers Forest Service **Northeastern** Forest Experiment Station, A 13.42/8, A 13.42/8-2
  Technical Notes Forest Service **Northeastern** Forest Experiment Station, A 13.67/9, A 13.42/7
  Water Supply Outlook for **Northeastern** United States, C 55.113/2
Northern
  Contributions from the Center for **Northern** Studies, I 29.99
  General Chart of **Northern** and Northwestern Lakes {and rivers}, W 33.7/1
  Light and Fog Signals of United States and Canada on **Northern** Lakes and Rivers, C 9.30
  Lights and Fog Signals, **Northern** Lakes and Rivers and Canada, T 25.17, C 9.18
  Progress Report **Northern** Rocky Mountain Forest and Range Experiment Station, A 13.30/6
  Technical Notes Forest Service **Northern** Forest Experiment Station, A 13.73/9
Northern Hemisphere
  Historical Weather Map, **Northern Hemisphere**, W 108.30
Northern Region
  Forest Insect and Disease Conditions in the **Northern** Region, A 13.52/7
  Forest Insect Conditions in the **Northern Region**, A 13.52/7

Northwest
  Annual Peak Discharge at Selected Gaging Stations in Pacific **Northwest**, I 19.45/3
  Commercial Wheat Farms, Plains and Pacific **Northwest**, A 93.9/11
  Current Discharge at Selected Stations in the Pacific **Northwest**, I 19.45, I 19.47/2
  Environmental Quality Profile, Pacific **Northwest** Region, EP 1.87/2
  Forest Insect and Disease Conditions in the Pacific **Northwest**, A 13.52/6
  Forest Insect Conditions in Pacific **Northwest** During (year), A 13.52/6
  New Reports by Geological Survey About Water in the Pacific **Northwest**, I 19.14/5
  NMFS **Northwest** Region, Organization and Activities, Fiscal Year, C 55.301/2
  Northwest Fisheries Center: Publications, C 55.326
  Northwest Indian Fisheries Commission, I 20.1/3
  Northwest Shellfish Sanitation Research Planning Conference, Proceedings, EP 2.15
  Pacific **Northwest** and Alaska Bioenergy Program Yearbook, E 5.12
  Pacific **Northwest** Environmental Research Laboratory: Quarterly Progress Report, EP 1.19
  Pacific **Northwest** Monthly Precipitation and Temperature, C 55.114
  Pacific **Northwest** Monthly Streamflow Summary, I 19.46/4
  Pacific **Northwest** Research Station: Miscellaneous Publications, A 13.129
  Pacific **Northwest** Water Laboratory: Quarterly Progress Report, EP 2.22
  Pacific **Northwest** Water Resources Summary, I 19.46
  Proceedings **Northwest** Shellfish Sanitation Research Planning Conference, EP 2.15
  Production, Prices Employment, and Trade in **Northwest** Forest Industries, A 13.66/13
  Publications Pacific **Northwest** Forest and Range Experiment Station, A 13.66/15
  Recent Publications of the Pacific **Northwest** Forest and Range Experiment Station, A 13.66/14
  Review of Power Planning in Pacific **Northwest**, Calendar Year, Y 3.P 11/4:9
  River Temperature at Selected Stations in the Pacific **Northwest**, I 19.46/2-2, I 19.46/2-3
  Weekly Runoff Report, Pacific **Northwest** Water Resources, I 19.46/2
  Working Papers Environmental Protection Agency, Pacific **Northwest** Environmental Research Laboratory, EP 1.37/2
Northwestern
  Berlin Arbitration (**Northwestern** Boundary), S 3.13/3
  General Chart of Northern and **Northwestern** Lakes {and rivers}, W 33.7/1
  Northwestern Boundary Commission, 1957 61, S 3.10/2
NOS
  NOS Oceanographic Circulatory Survey Reports, C 55.429
  NOS Publications (numbered), C 55.419
  NOS Technical Manuals, C 55.408/2
  Press Releases, **NOS** (series), C 55.415
NOS OMA
  NOAA Special Reports, **NOS OMA**- (series), C 55.13/6
Nosocomial
  National **Nosocomial** Infections Study, Reports, HE 20.7011/10
Not
  Not for Women Only, D 7.30
Notams
  International **Notams**, C 31.133, FAA 1.26, TD 4.11
Note
  Publication **Note** Series, HE 20.6216/3
  Tabulation of Project **Note** Sales for Low- income Housing, HH 1.71/2
  Technical **Note**, L 1.79/3
Notebook
  Environmental Assessment **Notebook** Series, TD 1.8/2
  Sector **Notebook** Project, EP 1.113
Notes
  Budget Explanatory **Notes** for Committee on Appropriations, A 13.130
  Chronic Disease **Notes** & Reports, HE 20.7617
  Doctrine **Notes**, D 207.416

Healthy People 2000, Statistical **Notes**, HE 20.6230
Historical **Notes**, A 57.74
Information **Notes**, S 1.84
Market Prices and Investment Values of Outstanding Bonds and **Notes**, T 50.5
Market Prices and Yields of Outstanding Bonds, **Notes**, and Bills of U.S., T 62.7
NASA History: News and **Notes**, NAS 1.96
NIDA **Notes**, HE 20.3967
Notes, D 214.30
Occupational Mental Health **Notes**, FS 2.22/50-3, HE 20.2511
Ordnance **Notes**, W 34.11
Ordnance Technical **Notes**, W 34.27
PHS Dental **Notes**, HE 20.8/4
Plasted **Notes**, D 4.11/2
Power Plant **Notes**, N 28.9
Preservation Tech **Notes** Exterior Woodwork, I 29.84/3-6
Preservation Tech **Notes** Historic Interior Spaces (series), I 29.84/3-2
Preservation Tech **Notes** Masonry, I 29.84/3-7
Preservation Tech **Notes** Mechanical Systems, I 29.84/3-9
Preservation Tech **Notes** Metals, I 29.84/3-8
Preservation Tech **Notes** Museum Collection Storage (series), I 29.84/3-3
Preservation Tech **Notes** Site, I 29.84/3-11
Preservation Tech **Notes** Temporary Protection (series), I 29.84/3-5
Preservation Tech **Notes** Windows (series), I 29.84/3-4
Preservation Tech **Notes**, I 29.84/3
Production **Notes**, SDP 1.13
Program **Notes**, A 88.55, HE 20.6512/6
Progress **Notes**, D 104.15/5
Puget Sound **Notes**, EP 1.97
Quality Control **Notes**, Pr 32.4835
R & D **Notes**, D 103.33/11
Random Forestry **Notes** for Extension Foresters, A 43.28
Range Improvement **Notes**, A 13.65/11
Research and Statistics Legislative **Notes**, FS 3.28/3
Research and Statistics **Notes**, HE 3.28/2, HE 22.17
Research **Notes** Forest Service, A 13.79
Research **Notes** National Center for Health Services Research, HE 20.6514
Resource Inventory **Notes**, I 53.24
RIIES Research **Notes**, SI 1.40/3
Rug and Floor Covering Material **Notes**, C 18.122
Russian Economic **Notes**, C 18.123
Satellite Applications Information **Notes**, C 55.37
Services Research Branch **Notes**, HE 20.8216/4
Signal Service **Notes**, W 42.14
Small Area Data **Notes**, C 56.217, C 3.238
Southern Forestry **Notes**, A 13.40/7
Statement Showing Amount of National Bank **Notes** Outstanding {ect}, T 12.9
Station and Program **Notes**, W 100.8
Station **Notes**, A 13.42/15, A 13.68/10
Statistical **Notes** for Health Planners, HE 20.6218
Statistical **Notes** National Clearinghouse on Aging, HE 23.3112
Statistical **Notes** National Institute of Mental Health, HE 20.3812
Statistical **Notes** Rehabilitation Services Administration, HE 17.114
Stratigraphic **Notes**, I 19.3/6
Survey and Reports Section Statistical **Notes**, HE 20.2424
Tables of Redemption Values for United States Savings **Notes**, T 63.210
TB **Notes**, HE 20.7013/2
Tech **Notes**, C 51.17, C 51.17/12
Tech **Notes**: Energy, C 51.17/3
Technical Development **Notes**, C 31.12, C 31.125
Technical Information **Notes**, I 40.11, FW 3.11
Technical **Notes** Ballistics Research Laboratories, D 105.10/3
Technical **Notes** Bureau of the Census, C 56.215, C 3.212/2
Technical **Notes** Coast Artillery Target Practice, W 3.37
Technical **Notes** Department of the Air Force Aeronautical Systems Division, D 301.45/26
Technical **Notes** Department of the Air Force Air Proving Ground Center, D 301.45/50
Technical **Notes** Department of the Air Force Alaskan Air Command, Arctic Aeromedical Laboratory, D 301.66

Technical **Notes** Department of the Air Force
Arnold Engineering Development
Center, D 301.45/33-3

Technical **Notes** Department of the Air Force
Atmospheric Analysis Laboratory, D
301.45/30 3

Technical **Notes** Department of the Air Force
Cambridge Research Center, D 301.45/4-
2

Technical **Notes** Department of the Air Force
Command and Control Development
Division, D 301.45/24

Technical **Notes** Department of the Air Force
Electronics Research Directorate, D
301.45/12-2

Technical **Notes** Department of the Air Force
Geophysics Research Directorate, D
301.45/16-2

Technical **Notes** Department of the Air Force
Meteorological Development
Laboratory, D 301.45/17-2

Technical **Notes** Department of the Air Force Office
of Scientific Research, D 301.45/18

Technical **Notes** Department of the Air Force Rome
Air Development Center, D 301.57/2

Technical **Notes** Department of the Air Force
Special Weapons Center, D 301.45/20-2

Technical **Notes** Department of the Air Force
Wright Air Development Center, D
301.45/13

Technical **Notes** Environmental Protection Agency,
EP 1.7/5

Technical **Notes** Forest Service Forest Products
Laboratory, A 13.27/9

Technical **Notes** Forest Service Lake States Forest
Experiment Station, A 13.61/10

Technical **Notes** Forest Service Northeastern Forest
Experiment Station, A 13.67/9, A 13.42/
7

Technical **Notes** Forest Service Northern Forest
Experiment Station, A 13.73/9

Technical **Notes** Forest Service Southeastern Forest
Experiment Station, A 13.63/8

Technical **Notes** Forest Service WSDG-TN- (nos),
A 13.27/9, A 13.87/4

Technical **Notes** National Aeronautics and Space
Administration, NAS 1.14

Technical **Notes** National Bureau of Standards, C
13.46

Technical **Notes** Naval Air Systems Command, N
28.6, M 208.10, D 202.7

Technical **Notes** Picatinny Arsenal, D 105.12/2, D
105.12/4

Technical **Notes** Weather Bureau, C 30.82

Textile Maintenance **Notes**, C 18.148

Treatment Research **Notes**, HE 20.8217/4

Tree Planters' **Notes**, A 13.51

Tropical Forest **Notes**, A 13.64/8

Urban Renewal **Notes**, HH 7.12

USAPRO Technical Research **Notes**, D 101.60

USAREC Research **Notes** (series), D 101.106

USARTL-TN, Technical **Notes**, D 117.8/4

Viet-Nam Information **Notes**, S 1.38

WADC Technical **Notes**, D 301.45/13

War **Notes**, Information from Abroad, N 13.7

Wildlife Conservation and Restoration **Notes**, A
43.5/20

Wildlife Research Laboratory: Technical **Notes**, I
49.47/3

World Economic **Notes**, C 18.282

World Trade **Notes** on Chemicals and Allied
Products, C 18.179

Noteworthy

Noteworthy Maps, LC 5.5

What's **Noteworthy** on ... (series), ED 1.9/2

Notice

Enroute Change **Notice**, DoD Flip Enroute VFR
Supplement United States, D 5.318/8-2

Notice, D 301.32

Notice and Posting System, PM 1.14/4

Notice to Mariners Relating to Great Lakes and
Tributary Waters West of Montreal, D
203.9, TD 5.10

Notice to Mariners, Great Lakes, C 9.41, T 47.20, N
24.13, T 6.12

Notice to Mariners, Restricted, N 6.11/2, M 202.8/
2, D 203.8/2

Policy Information **Notice** (series), HE 20.9118

Poster **Notice** to Mariners, C 9.38

Public **Notice**, LMNOD-SP- (series), D 103.117

Publication **Notice**; PN- (series), C 4.49

Secretary's **Notice**, L 1.22/5

Special **Notice** (series), C 55.416/18

Special **Notice** Concerning Basic Agreements
Teleprocessing Services Program (TSP)
Industrial Group 737, Industrial Class
7374, GS 12.13

Special **Notice** to Mariners, D 203.8/3, TD 5.56

SSA Administrative Directives System Transmittal
Notice, HE 3.68

USAFI Supply **Notice**, D 1.10/3

Notices

Applications, **Notices**, Orders [Department of the
Treasury], T 1.6/2

Inspection Operations Manual Transmittal **Notices**,
HE 20.4008/2

International **Notices** to Airmen, TD 4.11

Orders, **Notices**, Rulings and Decisions Issued by
Hearing Examiners and by the
Commission in Formal Docketed
Proceedings before the Federal Maritime

Patent and Trademark Office **Notices**, C 21.5/4a, C
21.5/4-2

Press **Notices** Bureau of Foreign and Domestic
Commerce, C 18.31

Press **Notices** Department of Agriculture, A 1.31

Press **Notices** Grain Corporation, Y 3.W 56:15

Press **Notices** National Bureau of Standards, C
13.18

Press **Notices** Office of Communication, A 21.7

Procurement **Notices** (series), NAS 1.6/2-2

Public **Notices** (concerning irrigation projects of
reclamation service), I 1.49

Public **Notices** {concerning irrigation projects}, I
27.40

Public **Notices**, CC 1.37, TC 1.28

Public **Notices**: Petitions for Rule Making Field,
CC 1.38

Public **Notices**: Safety and Special Radio Services,
Report, CC 1.39

Purchase and Storage **Notices**, W 77.19, W 89.8

Relief **Notices**, Y 3.F 31/5:23

Safety and Special Actions, Reports, Public
Notices, CC 1.39/2

Space Science **Notices**, NAS 1.53/2

Special **Notices** to Airmen, CA 1.7/2, C 31.10, C
31.110

Special **Notices**, C 55.416/8

Special **Notices**, Supplement to Radio Facility
Charts and In-flight Data, Europe, D
301.9/3

Supplementary **Notices** to Mariners, Correction
Sheets for Coast Pilots, N 6.11/3

Supplementary **Notices** to Mariners, Correction
Sheets for H.O. Publications, N 6.11/4

Type Approval Actions, Reports, Public **Notices**,
CC 1.48

USAF Military Aviation **Notices**, Amending SFID,
Caribbean and South America, D 301.51/
2

Veterinary Biologics Division **Notices**, A 77.226/3

Veterinary Biologics **Notices**, A 101.14

Weekly **Notices** to Airmen, C 23.15, CA 1.7, C 31.9,
C 31.109

Notification

AM Broadcast Applications Accepted for Filing
and **Notification** of Cut-off Date, CC
1.26/4

FM and TV Translator Applications Ready and
Available for Processing and
Notification of Cut-off Date, CC 1.26/6

FM Broadcast Applications Accepted for Filing
and **Notification** of Cut-off Date, CC
1.26/3

Selective **Notification** of Information SNI, J 26.19, J
28.14

TV Broadcast Applications Accepted for Filing and
Notification of Cut-off Date, CC 1.26/5

Notifications

Notifications, HCRS Information Exchange
(series), I 70.25

November

Voting and Registration in the Election of
November (date), C 3.186/3

Now

HEW **Now**, HE 1.27/2

NPA

NPA Delegations, C 40.6/3

NPA Notices, C 40.9

NPA Orders, C 40.6/4

NPA Organization Statements, C 40.6/7

NPA Production Series, Quarterly Indexes of
Shipments for Products of Metalworking
Industries, C 40.15

NPA Regulations, C 40.6/2

NPA Regulatory Material and Forms, Digest, C
40.6/8

NPC

Reliability Publications, **NPC** 250 (series), NAS
1.22/2

NPDP

NPDP (National Practitioner Data Bank) News, HE
20.9316

NPIP

Breed Distribution of **NPIP** Participating Flocks
by States and Divisions, A 77.15:44-2

NPRDC-TR

NPRDC-TR- (series), D 201.34

NPS

NPS Strategic Planning, National Park Scan, I
29.132

NPSAS

National Postsecondary Student Aid Study
(**NPSAS**), ED 1.333

NRA

NRA News, Y 3.N 21/8:9

NRAC

NRAC Technical Reports, PrEx 4.18

NRC

NRC Committee on Aviation Psychology
Publications, NA 2.9

NRC Information Notice, Y 3.N 88:56-2

NRC Public Document Room Collection, Y 3.N
88:62

NRC Regulatory Agenda, Y 3.N 88:45

NRC Switchboard, SL (series), LC 33.11

U.S. **NRC** Facilities License Application Record,
Y 3.N 88

NRC-TLD

NRC-TLD Direct Radiation Monitoring Network,
Y 3.N 88:43

NRI

NRI Annual Report, A 94.18/2

NRL

NRL Memorandum Report (series), D 210.8/2

NRL Reports, D 210.8

NRL Reprints, D 210.9

NRL {Naval Research Laboratory} Bibliographies,
D 210.13

Report of **NRL** progress, D 210.17

NRP

ARS National Research Program **NRP** (series), A
77.28

NRVSS

NRVSS Monthly Report, HE 20.7011/39

NS

System Package Program, **NS**-SPP- (series), TD
4.30

NSA

NSA Orders (National Shipping Authority), C
39.206/2

NSF

ASA/**NSF**/Census Bureau Research Fellow
Program, C 3.293

Energy Research and Technology: Abstracts of **NSF**
Research Results, NS 1.13/3

Exploratory Research and Problem Assessment:
Abstracts of **NSF** Research Results, NS
1.13/2

Listing of Peer Reviewers Used by **NSF** Divisions,
NS 1.36

National Science Foundation, Directory of **NSF**-
Supported Teacher Enhancement
Projects, NS 1.44/2

NSF Bulletin, NS 1.3

NSF Directions, NS 1.54

NSF Engineering News, NS 1.22/10

NSF Visiting Professorships for Women, NS 1.48

NSF/RANN

Abstracts of **NSF/RANN** Research Reports: Private
Sector Productivity, NS 1.13/4

Energy Research and Technology: Abstracts of
NSF/RANN Research Reports, NS 1.13/
3-2

NSHCIC

NSHCIC Bulletins, HH 1.77

NSSB

NSSB, Skills Today L 1.94

NSSB (National Skill Standards Board) Annual
Report, L 1.1/5

NSSDC

National Space Science Data Center, **NSSDC**-
(series), NAS 1.37

NSWC

NSWC MP (series), D 201.21/7

Technical Reports, **NSWC/WOL/TR**- (series), D
201.21/3

White Oak Laboratory: Technical Reports, **NSWC/ WOL/TR-** (series), D 201.21/3

NTSB
NTSB Safety Recommendation (series), TD 1.129

NTIA
NTIA Reports, C 60.10
Special Publications, **NTIA-SP-** (series), C 60.9

NTIP
Turkeys in **NTIP** Flocks and Their Distribution by States and Varieties, A 77.15:44-11

NTIS
Federal Technology Catalog, Summaries of Practical Technology, **NTIS** Tech Notes Annual Index, C 51.17/11
NTIS Digest, C 51.11/7
NTIS Information Services, C 51.11:In 3
NTIS Information Services, General Catalogs, C 51.11/4
NTIS Monthly Marketing, C 51.7/6
NTIS Products and Services Catalog, C 51.11/8
NTIS Published Search Mini Catalog, C 51.13/2-2
NTIS Searchers, C 51.13

NTP
NTP Technical Bulletin, HE 20.23/3

NTPSC
NTPSC Special Reports, Y 3.T 68/2:9

NTSB
Safety Effectiveness Evaluation, **NTSB-SEE-** (series), TD 1.125
Safety Reports, **NTSB-SR** (series), TD 1.106/4
Safety Studies, **NTSB/SS** (series), TD 1.27
Special Study Report, **NTSB-HSS-** (series), TD 1.120
Special Study, **NTSB-HSS** (series), TD 1.126

NTSB-AAR
Aircraft Accident Reports **NTSB-AAR** (series), TD 1.112

NTSB-AAS
NTSB-AAS {National Transportation Safety Board, Aspects of Aviation Safety} (series), TD 1.121

NTSB-AMM
Briefs of Aircraft Accidents Involving Turbine Powered Aircraft U.S. General Aviation Calendar Year **NTSB-AMM** (series), TD 1.109/14
Report **NTSB-AMM** (series), TD 1.109/16

NTSB-BA
Aircraft Accident Reports, Brief Format, U.S. Civil Aviation, **NTSB-BA** (series), TD 1.109/13

NTSB-PAM
NTSB-PAM (series), TD 1.123

NTSB/HZM
Hazardous Materials Accident Report, **NTSB/ HZM-** (series), TD 1.28

NTSB/RP
NTSB/RP, TD 1.130

NU
NU Reports (series), J 28.15/2

NUC
NUC Books, LC 30.26

Nuclear
Activation Analysis: Cockcroft-Walton Generator **Nuclear** Reactor, LINAC, C 13.46
Annual Radiological Environmental Operating Report, Sequoyah **Nuclear** Plant, Y 3.T 25:57
Budget Estimates **Nuclear** Regulatory Commission, Y 3.N 88:10-2
Cockcroft-Walton Generator **Nuclear** Reactor, C 13.46
Commercial **Nuclear** Power, Prospects for the United States and the World, E 3.51
Construction Status Report, **Nuclear** Power Plants, Data for Decisions, Y 3.N 88:16
Employment in **Nuclear** Energy Activities, a Highlights Report, E 1.33:0049
Environmental Radioactivity Levels Belefonte **Nuclear** Plant, Y 3.T 25:52
Environmental Radioactivity Levels Browns Ferry **Nuclear** Plant, Y 3.T 25:55
Environmental Radioactivity Levels, Sequoyah **Nuclear** Plant, Y 3.T 25:56
Environmental Radioactivity Levels Watts Bar **Nuclear** Plant, Y 3.T 25:51
Fish Monitoring Investigations, Browns Ferry **Nuclear** Plant, Wheeler Reservoir, Alabama, Y 3.T 25:37
Fish Monitoring Investigations: Sequoyah **Nuclear** Plant, Chickamauga Reservoir, Tennessee, Y 3.T 25:37-3
Fundamental **Nuclear** Energy Research, Y 3.At 7:48

Index of U.S. **Nuclear** Standards, C 13.10:483
Joint NCDRH and State Quality Assurance Surveys in **Nuclear** Medicine, HE 20.4611
NCG {**Nuclear** Catering Group} Technical Reports, D 103.54
New **Nuclear** Data, Annual Cumulations, Y 3.At 7:16-3
Nuclear Data Tables, Y 3.At 7:16-4
Nuclear Development &Proliferation PrEx 7.14/4
Nuclear Energy, E 1.68
Nuclear Fuels, E 1.99
Nuclear Industry, Y 3.At 7:56
Nuclear Notes for Industry, Y 3.At 7:31
Nuclear Reactor Technology, E 1.99
Nuclear Regulatory Commission Issuances, Y 3.N 88:11-2
Nuclear Regulatory Commission Issuances: Opinions and Decisions of the **Nuclear** Regulatory Commission with Selected Orders, Y 3.N 88:11
Nuclear Regulatory Legislation, Y 4.In 8/14:N 88/5
Nuclear Safety, Y 3.N 88:9, E 1.93
Nuclear Safety Index, Y 3.N 88:9-2
Nuclear Science Abstracts, ER 1.10
Nuclear Theory Reference Book, Y 3.At 7:53
Nuclear Waste, Quarterly Report on DOE'S Nuclear Waste Program, GA 1.13/9
Occupational Radiation Exposure at Commercial **Nuclear** Power Reactors and Other Facilities, Y 3.N 88:10-5
Radio Chemical Analysis, **Nuclear** Instrumentation, Radiation Techniques, Nuclear Chemistry, Radioisotope Techniques, C 13.46
Radioactive Materials Released from **Nuclear** Power Plants, Y 3.N 88:25-12
Radiological Impact Assessment, Browns Ferry **Nuclear** Plant, Y 3.T 25:53
Report to the U.S. Congress and the U.S. Secretary of Energy from the **Nuclear** Waste Technical Review Board, Y 3.N 88/2:1
Safety Research Programs Sponsored by Office of **Nuclear** Regulatory Research, Y 3.N 88:48
Semiannual Report on Strategic Special **Nuclear** Material Inventory Differences, E 1.15/2
Status of the Department of Energy's Implementation of **Nuclear** Waste Policy Act, GA 1.13/10
Summaries of FY (date) Research in **Nuclear** Physics, E 1.19/3
Survey of **Nuclear** Power Plant Construction Costs, E 3.17/5
Telephone Directory **Nuclear** Regulatory Commission, Y 3.N 88
U.S. Atmospheric **Nuclear** Weapons Tests, **Nuclear** Test Personnel Review, D 15.10
U.S. Central Station **Nuclear** Electric Generating Units, Significant Milestones, E 1.41
U.S. **Nuclear** Plants Cost Per KW Report, Office of Nuclear Power, Y 3.T 25:68
U.S. **Nuclear** Regulatory Commission Regulations {List}, Y 3.N 88:21
World Integrated **Nuclear** Evaluation System, E 3.51/2
World **Nuclear** Fuel Cycle Requirements, E 3.46/4

Nuclear Power
Division of **Nuclear** Power: Monthly Report, T 3.T 25:48-2

Nuclear Power Plants
Nuclear Power Plants, E 1.99

Nuclear Regulatory Commission
Contract Reports **Nuclear Regulatory Commission**, Y 3.N 88:25-2

Nuclear Science
Naval Research Laboratory Quarterly on **Nuclear Science** and Technology, Progress Reports, D 210.21

Nuclides
Trilinear Chart of **Nuclides**, Y 3.At 7:42

Number
Agricultural Census Analyses: Changes in **Number** of Farms by Size of Farm, A 36.137/2
Cattle Inventory, Special Report on **Number** of Cattle and Calves on Farms by Sex and Weight, United States, A 92.18/6-2
Chickens, **Number** Raised, Preliminary Estimates, A 92.9/7

Commercial Livestock Slaughter, **Number** and Live Weight, by States, Meat and Lard Production, United States, by Months, A 88.16/17
Farms of Nonwhite Farm Operators, **Number** of Farms, Land in Farm, Cropland Harvested, and Value of Land and Buildings, by Tenure, Censuses of 1945 and 1940 (by States), C 3.193
(HCFA) Medicare Unique Physician Identification **Number** (Directory), HE 22.414/2
Income Tax Returns: **Number** of Individual by States, Counties, Cities, and Towns, T 22.40
Livestock and Poultry Inventory, January 1, **Number**, Value and Classes, A 92.18/8
Number and Percentage of Farms Electrified with Central Station Service, A 68.20
Number of Employees at Middle of Month, IC 1 ste.25/2
Number of Farms by States, A 88.21/2
Number of Females Employed by Class 1 Steam Railways, IC 1 ste.43
Number of Foreclosures {and rate of foreclosure} by FSLIC Insured Savings and Loan Associations, FHL 1.26
Number of New Dwelling Units and Permit Valuation of Building Construction Authorized by Class of Construction in Mountain and Pacific Division by Civil Division and State, L 2.51, L 2.51/2, L 2.51/3
Number of New Permanent Nonfarm Dwelling Units Started by Urban or Rural Location, Public or Private Ownership, and Type of Structure, L 2.51/4
Number of Recipients and Amounts of Payments Under Medicaid and Other Medical Programs Financed from Public Assistance Funds, HE 17.617/3
Permit Valuation and **Number** of New Dwelling Units Provided in Housekeeping and Dwellings Authorized in Metropolitan Area of Washington, D.C. by Type of Dwelling and Source of Funds, L 2.51/7
Prime Contract Awards by Statutory Authority, **Number** of Actions, and Net Value by Department, D 1.57/3-2
Projections of the **Number** of Households and Families, C 3.186/15
Projections, **Number** of Returns to be Filed, T 22.2/13
Standard **Number** Series, N 4.7
U.S. Census of Population: **Number** of Inhabitants, C 3.223/5

Numbered
Navigation Charts; **Numbered** Rivers, D 103.66/3
Numbered River, D 103.66/3
U.S. Army Training Manuals **Numbered**, W 3.39/1

Numbered Circulars
Digest of War Department Directives and Index of General Orders, Bulletins, and **Numbered Circulars**, W 1.41
H 7 Manufacturers Part and Drawing **Numbering** Systems, D 7.6/2:7
Manufacturers Part and Drawing **Numbering** Systems, D 7.6/2:7
Recreational Boating in United States, Report of Accidents, **Numbering** and Related Activies, T 47.54

Numbers
Comparison Deck **Numbers**, FS 2.119
Estimated **Numbers** of Apple Trees by Varieties and Ages in Commercial and Farm Orchards, A 36.52
Farm **Numbers**, A 92.24/5
Index **Numbers** of Wholesale Prices, FR 1.38
Index **Numbers** of Wholesale Prices by Groups and Subgroups of Commodities, L 2.49/3
Numbers of Farms Participating in 1934 AAA Voluntary Control Programs (by States), A 55.55
Patents Snap, Concordance of U.S. Patent Application Serial **Numbers** to U.S. Patent **Numbers**, C 21.31/6
Schedule H. Statistical Classification and Code **Numbers** of Shipments of Merchandise to Alaska from United States, C 3.150:H
Specifications and Code **Numbers** for Individual Commodities, L 2.61/3
Statistical Classification and Code **Numbers** of Shipments of Merchandise to Alaska from United States, C 3.150:H

Numeric
  Numeric List of Educational Institutions, ED 1.65
  Numeric List of Lenders, ED 1.67
  Numeric List of Product Class Codes, Commodity
    Transportation Survey, C 3.163/4-2
Numerical
  Federal Stock Number Reference Catalog,
    Numerical Listing of Items Available
    from General Services Administration,
    GS 2.10/5
Numerical
  Numerical and Functional Index of Command
    Forms, D 301.45/14-2:0-9
  Numerical Index for Station Catalogs, N 6.5/8
  Numerical Index of AFSC Publications, D 301.45/
    14-2:0-2
  Numerical Index of Departmental Forms, D
    301.6:0-9
  Numerical Index of Specialty Training Standards,
    D 301.6:0-8
  Numerical Index of Standard and Recurring Air
    Force Publications, D 301.6:0-2
  Numerical Index of Technical Publications, M
    301.13, D 301.17
  Numerical Index Supplement to Bibliography of
    Technical Reports, C 35.7/3
  Numerical List Covering Army Air Forces and
    Army-Navy Aeronautical Standard Parts,
    W 108.15
  Numerical List of Treaty Series, Executive
    Agreement Series and Treaties and other
    International Acts Series, S 9.11/3
  Numerical List of U.S. Air Force and Air Force-
    Navy Aeronautical Standard Drawings,
    D 301.16
  Numerical List, U.S. Air Force and Army-Navy
    Aeronautical Standard Drawings, M
    301.12
  Numerical Lists and Schedule of Volumes of
    Reports and Documents of Congress, GP
    3.7/2
  Numerical Tables and Schedule of Volumes (for
    Document Index), GP 3.15
  Numerical Weather Prediction Activities,
    National Meteorological Center, C
    55.115
  Proceedings International Conference on
    Numerical Ship Hydrodynamics, D
    211.9/5
  United States Congressional Serial Set Catalog:
    Numerical Lists and Schedule of
    Volumes, GP 3.34
NUREG
  NUREG (series), Y 3.N 88:10
NUREG/CP
  NUREG/CP (series), Y 3.N 88:27
Nuremberg
  Trials of War Criminals Before **Nuremberg** Military
    Tribunals, D 102.8
Nurse
  Army **Nurse**, W 44.29
  Nurse Planning Information Series, HE 20.6613
  Nurse Training Act of 1975, Report to Congress,
    HE 20.6615
Nurseries
  Forest Tree **Nurseries** in the United States, A 13.74
Nursery
  Nursery Products, Production and Sales, A 88.48
Nurses
  Basic Preparatory Programs for Practical **Nurses** by
    States and Changes in Number of
    Programs, FS 5.133
  Census of **Nurses** Employed for Public Health
    Work in United States, in Territories of
    Alaska and Hawaii, and in Puerto Rico
    and Virgin Islands, FS 2.81
  Directory of Programs Preparing Registered **Nurses**
    for Expanded Roles, HE 20.6610
  Employment Data on Title 38 Physicians, Dentists,
    and **Nurses**, VA 1.75
  Memorandum to All **Nurses** in the Public Health
    Service, HE 20.36
  Nurses in Public Health, HE 20.3110
  Visitors Report to **Nurses'** Station Before Entering
    Room, HE 20.7029
Nursing
  Industry Wage Survey: **Nursing** and Personal Care
    Facilities, L 2.3/25
  Medicare Skilled **Nursing** Facility Manual, HE
    22.8/3
  Medicare/Medicaid **Nursing** Home Information
    (State), HE 22.35

Nursing Clinical Conferences Presented by the
    Nursing Department of Clinical Center,
    HE 20.3021
  {**Nursing** Education} Leaflets, FS 2.46
Nursing Home
  Directory of **Nursing Home** Facilities, HE
    20.6202:N 93
  Medicare/Medicaid **Nursing Home** Information,
    HE 22.35
Nursing Homes
  Environmental Health Factors, **Nursing Homes**, FS
    2.300/2
Nut
  Fruit and **Nut** Crop Prospects, A 66.39
Nutmeg
  Nutmeg Guidon, J 16.15
Nutrients
  Consumption of Commercial Fertilizers and Primary
    Plant **Nutrients** in United States, A
    92.37
Nutrition
  A.N.D. Animal **Nutrition** Division (series), A
    77.210
  Bibliography of U.S. Army Medical Research and
    Nutrition Laboratory Reports and
    Reprints for (year), D 104.17
  Center for Food Safety and Applied **Nutrition**
    Technical Plan, HE 20.4515
  Examination Staff Procedures Manual for the
    Hispanic Health and **Nutrition**
    Examination Survey, HE 20.6208/2
  Family Economics and **Nutrition** Review, A 98.20
  Food and **Nutrition**, A 98.11
  Food and **Nutrition** Information and Educational
    Materials Center Catalog, A 17.18/3
  Food and **Nutrition** Newsletter of the Food and
    Nutrition Service, A 98.11/2
  Food and **Nutrition** Research Briefs, A 17.30
  Food and **Nutrition** Research Briefs, A 77.518
  Food Assistance and **Nutrition** Research Program,
    A 93.61
  Food Assistance and **Nutrition** Research Report, A
    93.60
  Industrial **Nutrition** Service, A 82.66
  Instruction Manual: Dental Examiner's Manual for
    the Hispanic Health and **Nutrition**
    Survey, HE 20.6208/2-6
  Instruction Manual: Dietary Interviewer's Manual
    for the Hispanic Health and **Nutrition**
    Examination Survey, HE 20.6208/2-2
  Instruction Manual: Field Staff Operations for the
    Hispanic Health and **Nutrition**
    Examination Survey, HE 20.6208/2-5
  Instructions for Classifying the Underlying Cause
    of Death: Mobile Examination Center
    Interviewer's Manual for the Hispanic
    Health and **Nutrition** Examination
    Survey, HE 20.6208/2-4
  Instructions for Classifying the Underlying Cause
    of Death: Physician's Examination
    Manual for the Hispanic Health and
    Nutrition Examination Survey, HE
    20.6208/2-3
  National Advisory Council on Maternal, Infant and
    Fetal **Nutrition**: Biennial Report, A
    98.14/2
  National Health and **Nutrition** Examination
    Survey, HE 20.6209/4-8
  News of the Hispanic Health and **Nutrition**
    Examination Survey, HE 20.6213/3
  News Releases and Miscellaneous Publications;
    Committee on Agriculture, **Nutrition**,
    and Forestry, (Senate), Y 4.Ag 8/3-2
  Nutrition and Food Conservation Series, A 1.65
  Nutrition Charts, A 42.7
  Nutrition Education Series Pamphlets, FS 5.34
  Nutrition News Letters, A 82.48
  Nutrition Program News, A 77.710, A 106.20, A
    106.111
  Nutrition Study Section, HE 20.3001/2:N 95
  Nutrition Surveillance, Annual Summary, HE
    20.7011/24
  Nutrition Surveys {by country}, FS 2.22/57
  Posters Food and **Nutrition** Service, A 98.16
  Program in Biomedical and Behavioral **Nutrition**
    Research and Training, Fiscal Year, HE
    20.3036
  Publications **Nutrition** and Food Conservation
    Branch, A 80.123
  Regulations, Rules and Instructions Food and
    Nutrition Service, A 98.18
  Survey of Food and **Nutrition** Research in United
    States, NA 2.8

Nuts
  Bolts **Nuts** and Large Screws of Iron or Steel, ITC
    1.17 ITC 1.17/2
  Evaluation of Foreign Fruits and **Nuts**, A 77.532
  Fruit and Tree **Nuts**, A 93.12/3
  Fruits, Vegetables, Tree **Nuts**, A 67.30:F 94
  Noncitrus Fruits and **Nuts**, Annual Summary, A
    105.11
  Production, Farm Disposition, and Value of
    Principal Fruits and Tree **Nuts**, A 88.12/
    16
  Series 1, Evaluation of Foreign Fruits and **Nuts**, A
    77.533
  Sugar Confectionery, **Nuts**, C 18.72/6
NVLAP
  Directory of **NVLAP** Accredited Laboratories, C
    13.58/7
NWC
  Feature Sections of Journals in **NWC** Library, D
    1.26
  List of Periodicals in **NWC** Library, D 1.26/2
  NWC Administrative Publications (series), D
    201.21/6-2
  NWC Technical Publications, D 201.23
NWCG
  NWCG Handbooks, A 13.99
NWHC
  NWHC Technical Report (National Wildlife Health
    Center), I 19.211
NWL
  NWL Administrative Reports, D 201.21/2
  NWL Reports, D 217.17
  NWL Technical Report, D 201.21, D 215.14
NWRC
  NWRC Research Update, A 101.29
NWS-TDL-CP
  NWS-TDL-CP- (series), C 55.13/4
NYA
  Employment Hours and Earnings on Student Aid
    Projects of **NYA**, Y 3.W 89/2:27
NYLS
  News, **NYLS**- (series), L 2.71/6-2

O

O
  O & NAV Instructions, D 207.8
O. and M.
  Power **O. and M.** Bulletins, I 27.45
  Power **O. and M.** Report, Field Review of
    Maintenance, I 27.45/2
  Power **O. and M.** Reports, Field Review of
    Operation and Maintenance, I 27.45/3
O.P.O.
  O.P.O. Publications, A 60.8
O.W.I.
  O.W.I. Reports, Pr 32.5020
OA
  OA Manual, HH 1.6/2
OAA
  OAA and AFDC, Cost Standards for Basic Needs
    and Percent of Such Standards Met for
    Specified Types of Cases, FS 17.625, HE
    17.625
OAAS
  What's New, Tips for Supervisors from **OAAS**, L
    1.43
Oak Ridge
  Oak Ridge National Laboratory Review, E 1.28/17
  Oak Ridge Uranium Market Model, E 3.46/3-2
OAM
  OAM Publications, A 91.8
OAO
  OAO (series), C 55.13/2:OAO-nos.
OAQPS
  OAQPS Guideline Series, EP 1.8/6
OAR
  List of **OAR** Research Efforts, D 301.69/7
  OAR (series) (numbered), D 301.69/3
  OAR (series), C 55.13/2:OAR-nos.
  OAR News, D 301.69
  OAR Progress (year), D 301.69/3
  OAR Quarterly Index of Current Research Results,
    D 301.69/8
OASDI
  OASDI Beneficiaries by State and County, SSA
    1.17/4
OASI
  Digest of Rulings (**OASI**) Transmittal Sheets, FS
    3.24/2
  OASI- (series), FS 3.35

RRB-SSA Financial Interchange: Calculations for Fiscal Year with Respect to **OASI**, DI, and HI Trust Funds, RR 1.15

Oasis

Oasis, FS 3.36

Oats

Commitments of Traders in Wheat, Corn, **Oats**, Rye, Soybeans, Soybean Oil, Soybean Meal, Shell Eggs, A 85.9/2

Futures Trading and Open Contracts in Wheat, Corn, **Oats**, Rye, Soybeans and Products, A 85.11/7

Futures Trading and Open Contracts in {Wheat, Corn, **Oats**, etc.} on Chicago Board of Trade, A 88.11/18

OBE

Business News Reports **OBE** {release}, C 18.281, C 43.7

OBERS

OBERS, BEA Regional Projections, C 59.17

Objectives

Department of Transportation Budget Program: Analysis of Fiscal Year DOT Program by Policy and RD&D Management **Objectives**, DOT-OST (series), TD 1.34/2

Legislative **Objectives** of Veterans' Organizations, Y 4.V 64/3:L 52/8

Research **Objectives**, D 301.69/3

Safety, Fire Prevention, and Occupational Health Management, by **Objectives** Review, D 301.99

Obligations

DHEW **Obligations** to {various institutions}, HE 1.41

Federal Funds for Research and Development, Federal **Obligations** for Research by Agency and Detailed Field of Science, Fiscal Years, NS 1.18/3

HEW **Obligations** to Institutions of Higher Education, Fiscal Year, FS 1.2:Ed 8/3

Instructions and Data Specifications for Reporting DHHS **Obligations** to Institutions of Higher Education and Other Nonprofit Organizations, HE 20.3050

Total **Obligations** Incurred for Emergency Relief from All Public Funds by State and Local Relief Administration in Continental United States, Y 3.F 31/5:35

Obligors

Significant Arrearages Due the United States Government and Unpaid 90 Days or More by Official Foreign **Obligors**, T 1.45/5

Obscenity

Enforcement Report of Postal Inspection Service, Fraud, **Obscenity**, Extortion, P 1.29/2

Obscenity Enforcement Reporter, J 1.94

Obscenity Reporter, J 1.94

Observance

President's Commission for **Observance** of 25th Anniversary of the United Nations, Pr 37.8:Un 3

Update National Commission on the **Observance** of Update from State, S 1.118/2

Observation

Water Levels in **Observation** Wells in Santa Barbara County, California, I 19.49

Observational

Observational Study of Agricultural Aspects of Arkansas River Multiple-purpose Project, Annual Report, A 57.60

Observations

Correspondence Course, Elements of Surface Weather **Observations**, Lessons, C 30.26

International Meteorological **Observations**, W 42.7/1

Long Record of Weather **Observations**, C 55.287/56

Magnetic **Observations**, C 4.26

Manual of Surface **Observations**, C 30.4

Manual of Winds-Aloft **Observations**, C 30.4O

Radio **Observations**, C 3.18/4

Radiosonde **Observations**, C 1.8/4:3

Results of **Observations** made at C. & G. Survey Magnetic Observatories, C 4.16

Summary and Review of International Meteorological **Observations** for Month of, W 42.7/2

Summary of Hourly **Observations**, W 95.10

Summary of Synoptic Meteorological **Observations**, D 220.10

Observatories

Results of Observations made at C. & G. Survey Magnetic **Observatories**, C 4.16

Observatory

Annals of Astrophysical **Observatory**, SI 1.12

Astrophysical **Observatory** Reports, SI 1.1/a2

Bulletin of Mountain Weather **Observatory**, A 29.21

Hawaiian Volcano **Observatory** Summary, I 19.29/2

Monthly Bulletin of Hawaiian Volcano **Observatory**, I 19.28

News from the Naval **Observatory**, Stargazing Notes, D 213.15

Publications Naval **Observatory**, D 213.10

USGS/NGIC Geomagnetic **Observatory** Data, I 19.120/2

Observer

Aircraft **Observer**, D 301.38/4

Cooperative **Observer**, C 55.118

Forest Pest **Observer**, A 13.68/11

International Judicial **Observer**, Ju 13.13/2-3

National Cooperative **Observer** Newsletter, C 55.118/6

State - Federal Judicial **Observer**, Ju 13.13/2

Observers

Instructions for Climatological **Observers**, C 30.4:B

Observers Quarterly, C 30.86

Observing

Program for Regional **Observing** and Forecasting Services, C 55.626/2

Weather Bureau **Observing** Handbooks, C 30.6/6

Weather Service **Observing** Handbooks, C 55.108/2

Obsolete

Standard Nomenclature Lists, **Obsolete** General Supplies, W 32.23/4

Obstetrics

Department of **Obstetrics** and Gynecology, D 1.67/4

Obstruction

Airport **Obstruction** Charts, C 55.411/3

Airport **Obstruction** Plans, C 4.9/11

Eastern United States, Dates of Latest Prints, Instrument Approach Procedure Charts and Airport **Obstruction** Plans (OP), C 4.9/19

Latest Editions, Airport **Obstruction** Charts, C 55.411/3-2

Western United States, Dates of Latest Prints, Instrument Approach Procedure Charts and Airport **Obstruction** Plans, C 4.9/20

Obtained

Cotton Seed Crushed and Linters **Obtained**, C 3.22

OC

World Data Center A Oceanography, Catalogue of Data, WDCA-**OC**- (series), C 55.220/2-3

OCAHO

Office of the Chief Administrative Hearing Officer (**OCAHO**) Cases, J 1.102, J 21.23

Office of the Chief Administrative Hearing Officer **OCAHO** Files, J 1.102/2

Office of the Chief Administrative Hearing Officer (**OCAHO**) Subpoenas, J 1.102/4

OCC

OCC Advisory Letters, T 12.23

OCC Alerts, T 12.21

OCC Bulletins, T 12.20

OCC/SB

OCC/SB (series), HE 20.3165/2

Occasional

Center for International Systems Research: **Occasional** Papers, S 1.124

Development Studies Program **Occasional** Papers, S 18.59

Focus **Occasional Papers** in Bilingual Education, ED 1.49/2-2

INSS **Occasional** Paper, Regional Series, D 305.24

Occasional Forestry Papers, I 29.41

Occasional Paper, L 29.15/2

Occasional Papers Council of Scholars (series), LC 1.42

Occasional Papers Engineer Department, Engineer School, W 7.16/2

Occasional Papers Forest Service Institute of Tropical Forestry, A 13.64/10

Occasional Papers Forest Service Northeastern Forest Experiment Station, A 13.42/8, A 13.42/8-2

Occasional Papers Forest Service Southern Forest Experiment Station, A 13.40/6

Occasional Papers Marine Corps, D 214.14/3

Occasional Papers Series, S 18.57

Occasional Papers, C 3.265

Occasional Reports, I 29.14/2

Preservation and New Technology **Occasional** Papers, LC 1.43

RIIES **Occasional** Papers, SI 1.40/2

Unemployment Insurance **Occasional** Papers, L 37.20, L 37.213/2

Occupancy

Survey of Negro World War II Veterans and Vacancy and **Occupancy** of Dwelling Units Available to Negroes {in city areas}, L 2.31

Survey of World War II Veterans and Dwelling Unit Vacancy and **Occupancy** {in city areas}, L 2.30

Survey of World War II Veterans and Dwelling Unit Vacancy and **Occupancy** (in Specified Areas), C 3.194

Trends Toward Open **Occupancy** in Housing Programs of Public Housing Administration, HH 3.8

Occupant

Occupant Emergency Plan Handbook for the Frances Perkins Building, L 1.1/2-2:2-8

Occupation

Department of Commerce List of Currently Essential Activities, Department of Labor List of Currently Critical **Occupation**, L 7.65

Occupation Wage Relationships, Series 1, L 2.25

So You Want to Be a {**Occupation**}, PrEx 10.20

Occupational

Annual Training Course in **Occupational** Therapy, W 44.23/8

Citator to Decisions of the **Occupational** Safety and Health Review Commission, Y 3.Oc 1:10-4

Criteria for a Recommended Standard, **Occupational** Exposure to {various subjects}, HE 20.7110

Current Information on **Occupational** Outlook, VA 1.31

Departmental Circulars, **Occupational** Deferment Series, CS 1.38

Directory of Postsecondary Schools with **Occupational** Programs, HE 19.337

Directory of Secondary Schools with **Occupational** Curriculums, Public and Nonpublic, HE 5.96

Federal **Occupational** Health Memo Series, HE 20.9116

Federal Work Injury Facts, **Occupational** Distribution, Duration and Direct Cost Factors of Work Injuries to Civilian Federal Employees During Calendar Year, L 26.8/2-2

Guide to Organized **Occupational** Curriculums in Higher Education, FS 5.254:54012, HE 5.254:54012

Handbook of **Occupational** Groups and Series of Classes, PM 1.8/2, SE 1.13/3

How to Use Injury Statistics to Prevent **Occupational** Accidents, L 16.42

Navy Civilian **Occupational** Source Book, D 1.51

News from the President's Conference on **Occupational** Safety, L 16.35/2

News, BLS Reports on Survey of **Occupational** Injuries and Illnesses in ..., L 2.120/2-11

Occupational and Career Information (series), L 37.16

Occupational Briefs, W 1.63, M 101.28

Occupational Bulletins, Y 3.Se 4:12

Occupational Compensation Survey: Pay and Benefits, L 2.121, L 2.122

Occupational Composition Patterns, L 7.27

Occupational Earnings and Wage Trends in Metropolitan Areas, Summary, L 2.86

Occupational Earnings in All Metropolitan Areas, L 2.86/5

Occupational Earnings in Banking, Selected Metropolitan Areas Summary, L 2.86/4

Occupational Earnings in Major Labor Market Summary Release, L 2.86

Occupational Earnings in Selected Areas, Summary, L 2.86/3

Occupational Education Enrollments and Programs in Noncollegiate Postsecondary Schools, HE 19.337/2

Occupational Employment in Manufacturing Industries, L 2.3/16

Occupational Employment in Selected Nonmanufacturing Industries, L 2.3/16-2

Occupational Guide Series: Job Descriptions, L 7.32, FS 3.133

Occupational Guide Series: Labor Market Information, L 7.32/2, FS 3.133/2

Occupational Guides, L 1.7/5

Occupational Hazards to Young Workers Reports, L 16.40

Occupational Hazards to Young Workers, L 16.3

Occupational Health Reporter, CS 1.90

Occupational Health Services for Civilian Employees, CS 1.41/4:792-1

Occupational Home Economics Education Series, HE 19.134

Occupational Injuries and Illnesses in (year), L 1.79/2-4, L 2.120/2-11

Occupational Injuries and Illnesses in the United States by Industry, L 2.3/11

Occupational Mental Health Notes, FS 2.22/50-3, HE 20.2511

Occupational Outlook Briefs {Excerpts from Occupational Outlook Handbook}, L 2.3/a 2

Occupational Outlook for College Graduates, L 2.3

Occupational Outlook Handbook, L 2.3, L 2.3/4, L 2.3/4-4

Occupational Outlook Publications, L 2.70

Occupational Outlook Quarterly, L 2.70/4

Occupational Outlook Report Series, L 2.3

Occupational Outlook Review, VA 1.37

Occupational Outlook Summary, L 2.70/2

Occupational Projections and Training Data, L 2.3/4-2

Occupational Radiation Exposure at Commercial Nuclear Power Reactors and Other Facilities, Y 3.N 88:10-5

Occupational Safety Aid, Department of Labor Safety Training Programs, OSA-OSHA-(series), L 35.10

Occupational Safety and Health Construction Standards and Interpretations, L 35.6/3-3

Occupational Safety and Health Field Operations Manual, L 35.6/3-5

Occupational Safety and Health General Industry Standard and Interpretations, L 35.6/3-1

Occupational Safety and Health Hazards (series), HE 20.7117

Occupational Safety and Health Industrial Hygiene Field Operations Manual, L 35.6/3-6

Occupational Safety and Health Maritime Standards and Interpretations, L 35.6/3-2

Occupational Safety and Health Other Regulations and Procedures, L 35.6/3-4

Occupational Safety and Health Regulations, L 35.6/2

Occupational Safety and Health Statistics of the Federal Government, L 35.13

Occupational Safety Charts, L 16.8/2:Oc 1

Occupational Statistics, C 3.37/31

Occupational Wage Relationships, L 2.25

OSAHRE Reports: Decisions of the **Occupational** Safety and Health Review Commission, Y 3.Oc 1:10

President's Report on **Occupational** Safety and Health, Pr 38.2:Oc 1

Program Plan of the National Institute for **Occupational** Safety and Health, HE 20.7127

Recordkeeping Requirements for Firms Selected to Participate in the Annual Survey of **Occupational** Injuries and Illnesses, L 2.129

Reprints from the **Occupational** Outlook Handbook, Bulletins, L 2.3/4 a

Resource Guide for Health Science Students: **Occupational** and Environmental Health, HE 20.7108:H 34/2

Safety, Fire Prevention, and **Occupational** Health Management, by Objectives Review, D 301.99

Safety, **Occupational** Health and Fire Protection Bulletin, VA 1.22:13-1

Special **Occupational** Hazard Review with Control Recommendations, HE 20.7113

Standard **Occupational** Classification Manual, PrEX 2.6/3

United States Army **Occupational** Handbook, D 101.40

Vocational Education; Schools for Careers, an Analysis of **Occupational** Courses Offered by Secondary and Postsecondary Schools, HE 19.321

Wage Trends for **Occupational** Groups in Metropolitan Areas, Summary Release, L 2.86/2

Occupations

Annual Indicators of Immigration into the United States of Aliens in Professional and Related **Occupations**, J 21.15

Census of Population and Housing: Alphabetical Index of Industries and **Occupations**, C 3.223/22:90-R3

Census of Population and Housing: Classified Index of Industries and **Occupations**, C 3.223/22:90-R4

Descriptions of **Occupations**, L 2.7

Federal Civilian Work Force Statistics, **Occupations** of Federal Blue-Collar Workers, PM 1.10:Sm 59-11

Federal Civilian Work Force Statistics, **Occupations** of Federal White-Collar Workers, PM 1.10:Sm 56-13

Hazardous **Occupations** Orders, L 22.26

Job Grading System for Trades and Labor **Occupations**, CS 1.41/4:512-1, CS 1.42/2

Labor Supply and Demand in Selected Defense **Occupations**, as Reported by Public Employment Offices, J 21.15

Labor Supply Available at Public Employment Offices in Selected Defense **Occupations**, FS 3.117

Local Shortages in Selected Scientific and Engineering **Occupations**, L 7.63

Military Careers: A Guide to Military **Occupations** and Selected Military Career Paths, D 1.6/15

Occupations in Demand at Job Service Offices, Extra Edition for Students and Recent Graduates, L 37.310/2

Occupations in Demand at Job Service Offices, L 37.310

Occupations of Federal White-Collar and Blue-Collar Workers, PM 1.10/2-2

State Laws and Regulations Prohibiting Employment of Minors in Hazardous **Occupations**, L 22.6/2

Occupied

Expenditures for Additions, Alterations, Maintenance and Repairs, and Replacements on One-Housing-Unit Owner-**Occupied** Properities, C 3.215/8:Pt-2

Semi-Monthly Military Government Report for U.S. **Occupied** Area of Germany, M 105.21

Occurrence

Medical Statistics, Navy, Statistical Report of the Surgeon General, Navy, **Occurrence** of Diseases and Injuries in the Navy for Fiscal Year (date), D 206.11

Occurrences

Report to Congress on Abnormal **Occurrences**, Y 3.N 88:20

OCD

OCD News Letters, Official Bulletins, Pr 32.4408

OCDM

OCDM Regulations, PrEx 4.6/4

OCDM Telephone Directory, PrEx 4.8

OCE

REC-**OCE** Reclamation Bureau-Office of Chief Engineer (series), I 27.60

Staff Report, FPC/**OCE** (series), FP 1.7/4

Ocean

Area Wage Survey, Monmouth-**Ocean**, New Jersey, Metropolitan Area, L 2.121/30-4

Collected Reprints National **Ocean** Survey, C 55.428

Federal **Ocean** Program, Annual Report to Congress, Pr 37.11, Pr 38.11, Pr 39.12

Federal Plan for **Ocean** Pollution Research, Developing, and Monitoring, PrEx 8.109

Global **Ocean** Floor Analysis and Research Data Series, D 203.31

National **Ocean** Survey Abstracts, C 55.413/2

National **Ocean** Survey Catalog of Aeronautical Charts and Related Publications, C 55.418/2

NOAA Coastal **Ocean** Program, Decisions Analysis Series, C 55.49/3

NOAA Coastal **Ocean** Program, Project News Update, C 55.49/4

NOAA Coastal **Ocean** Program, Regional Synthesis Series, C 55.49/2

Ocean Affairs Advisory Committee, S 1.130/2:Oc 2

Ocean Dumping in the United States, EP 1.69

Ocean Dumping Report for Calendar Year (date) Dredged Material, D 103.68/2

Ocean Freight Rate Bulletin, A 88.70

Ocean Going Merchant Fleets of Principal Maritime Nations, SB 7.5/100, SB 7.5/1100, C 27.9/6, MC 1.16

Ocean Series, SI 12.9

Ocean Technology and Engineering, C 51.9/26

Ocean Thermal Energy Conversion, Report to Congress, Fiscal Year, C 55.42

Pilot Chart of Indian **Ocean**, D 203.16, N 6.17, M 202.16

Pilot Chart of North Atlantic **Ocean**, N 6.15, M 202.17, D 203.17

Pilot Chart of North Pacific **Ocean**, N 6.16, M 202.19, D 203.19

Pilot Chart of South Atlantic **Ocean**, N 6.20, M 202.18, D 203.18

Pilot Chart of South Pacific **Ocean**, N 6.12, M 202.20, D 203.20

Pilot Chart of Upper Air, North Atlantic **Ocean**, N 6.28

Pilot Chart of Upper Air, North Pacific **Ocean**, N 6.29

Posters National **Ocean** Service, C 55.418/6-2

Proceedings **Ocean** Drilling Program, Initial Reports, NS 1.38/2

Publications National **Ocean** Survey, C 55.419

Report to Congress on Administration of **Ocean** Dumping Activities, D 103.68

Report to Congress on **Ocean** Dumping and Other Man-Induced Changes to **Ocean** Ecosystems, C 55.31

Report to Congress on **Ocean** Pollution, Monitoring and Research, C 55.31/3, C 55.439

Report to Congress on **Ocean** Pollution, Overfishing, and Offshore Development, C 55.31/2

Ship Operations Report, National **Ocean** Survey, C 55.423

Tide Tables Atlantic **Ocean**, C 4.15/3

Tide Tables Central and Western Pacific **Ocean** and Indian **Ocean**, C 4.15/6

Tide Tables Pacific **Ocean** and Indian **Ocean**, C 4.15/2

Tide Tables, High and Low Water Predictions Central and Western Pacific **Ocean** and Indian **Ocean**, C 55.421/4

World **Ocean** Atlas, C 55.297

Oceanborne

Domestic **Oceanborne** and Great Lakes Commerce of the United States, C 39.222

Foreign **Oceanborne** Trade of United States Containerized Cargo Summary, Selected Trade Routes, C 39.233

Participation of Principal National Flags in United States **Oceanborne** Foreign Trade, C 39.221

Review of United States **Oceanborne** Foreign Trade, C 39.202:Oc 2

U.S. **Oceanborne** Foreign Trade Forecast, TD 11.13/2

U.S. **Oceanborne** Foreign Trade Routes, TD 11.13

United States **Oceanborne** Foreign Trade Routes, C 39.240

Oceangoing

Containerships Under Construction and on Order (including conversions) in United States and Foreign Shipyards **Oceangoing** Ships of 1,000 Gross Tons and Over, C 39.231

Employment Report of United States Flag Merchant Fleet, **Oceangoing** Vessels 1,000 Gross Tons and Over, C 39.208

New Ship Construction, **Oceangoing** Ships of 1,000 Gross Tons and Over in United States and Foreign Shipyards, C 39.212/3

Oceangoing Foreign Flag Merchant Type Ships of 1,000 Gross Tons and Over Owned by the United States Parent Companies, C 39.230

Oceangoing Merchant Ships of 1,000 Gross Tons and Over Scrapped and Lost During the Calendar Year (date), C 39.229

Oceania

Nautical Charts and Publications, Region 8, **Oceania**, C 55.440:8

NIMA Nautical Charts, Public Sale Region 8, **Oceania**, TD 4.82:8

North America and **Oceania** Outlook and Situation Report, A 93.29/2-16

Oceanic
Key to **Oceanic** and Atmospheric Information
Sources, C 55.219/5
Oceanic Biology Program Abstract Book, D
210:28
Professional Papers National **Oceanic** and
Atmospheric Administration, C 55.25
Universities and Their Relationships with the
National **Oceanic** and Atmospheric
Administration, C 55.40
Oceanographer
Pamphlets **Oceanographer** of the Navy, D 218.9
Oceanographic
BOMEX {Barbados **Oceanographic** and
Meteorological Experiment} Bulletin, C
55.18
Collected Reprints; Atlantic **Oceanographic** and
Meteorological Laboratories, C 55.612
Highlights National **Oceanographic** Data Center,
C 55.291
Key to **Oceanographic** Records Documentation, C
55.219/3
National **Oceanographic** Data Center Publica-
tions, D 203.24, D 203.24/3
National Oceanographic Data Center, List of Fully
Processed **Oceanographic** Cruise, D
203.24/5
National **Oceanographic** Fleet Operating
Schedules, D 218.11
National **Oceanographic** Instrumentation Center
Publications, C 55.72
Naval **Oceanographic** Newsletter, D 203.28
NOS **Oceanographic** Circulatory Survey Reports,
C 55.429
Oceanographic Atlas of the International Indian
Ocean Expedition, NS 1.2:In 2/4
Oceanographic Data Exchange, NS 1.32
Oceanographic Monthly Summary, C 55.123/2
Oceanographic Reports, TD 5.18
Oceanographic Unit Technical Reports, TD 5.18/2
Oceanography Semiannual Report of **Oceano-
graphic** Data Exchange, C 55.220/3
Publications National **Oceanographic** Data
Center, D 203.24, D 203.24/2, C 55.292
Publications Naval **Oceanographic** Office, D
203.22
Received or Planned Current Fisheries, **Oceano-
graphic**, and Atmospheric Translations,
A- (series), C 55.325/2
Sailing Directions Naval **Oceanographic** Office, D
203.22
Survey of Foreign Fisheries, **Oceanographic**, and
Atmospheric Literature, C- (series), C
55.325/3
Translated Tables of Contents of Current Foreign
Fisheries, **Oceanographic**, and
Atmospheric Publications, C 55.325
U.S. Naval **Oceanographic** Office Chart Correction
List, D 203.21/2
Oceanography
Collected Reprints ESSA Institute for **Oceanogra-
phy**, C 52.23
Compilation of Federal Laws Relating to
Conservation and Development of Our
Nation's Fish and Wildlife Resources,
Environmental Quality, and **Oceanogra-
phy**, Y 4.M 53:L 44/2
Fishery and **Oceanography** Translations, I 49.18/5
List of Fully Processed **Oceanography** Cruise, D
203.24/5
National **Oceanography** Data Center: Annual
Report, C 55.291/2
Oceanography Catalogue of Accessioned Soviet
Publications, C 55.220/2
Oceanography Semiannual Report of Oceano-
graphic Data Exchange, C 55.220/3
Task Force on **Oceanography**, Pr 37.8:Oc 2
World Data Center A **Oceanography**, Catalog of
Accessioned Publications, C 55.220/2-2
World Data Center A, **Oceanography**, Catalogue of
Data, C 55.220/3
World Data Center A **Oceanography**, Catalogue of
Data, WDCA-OC- (series), C 55.220/2-3
World Data Center A **Oceanography**, Data of
Accessioned Soviet Publications, C
55.220/2
World Data Center A **Oceanography**, Semiannual
Report of **Oceanography** Data Exchange,
C 55.220/3
Oceans
Questions about the **Oceans**, D 203.24:G-13
OCO
OCO Pamphlets (series), D 105.9/2

OCRWM
OCRWM Backgrounder, E 1.68/2-3
OCRWM Bulletin, E 1.68/2-2
OCRWM Publications Catalog, E 1.68/2-4
OCS
OCS Activities Report, I 72.12/12
OCS EIS/EA (Series), I 72.12/11
OCS Information Report, I 72.12/10
OCS Map Series, I 72.12/4
OCS Monographs (series), I 72.12
OCS Reports, I 72.12/3
OCS Statistical Series, I 72.12/9
OCS Studies (series), I 72.12/2
Pacific Outer Continental Shelf Studies Program
(**OCS**) Statistical Reports, I 72.12/3-4
Radiation Exposure Overview, **OCS** (series), HE
20.1111
Regional Studies Plan, Fiscal Year, Atlantic **OCS**
Region, I 72.12/15
OCSE-AT-
Action Transmittals, **OCSE-AT-** (series), HE 24.14
OCSE-IM-
Information Memorandums, **OCSE-IM-**(series), HE
24.15
October
United States Reports, Cases Adjudged in Supreme
Court at **October** Term, Ju 6.8
OCZM
OCZM Guideline Papers, C 55.32/4
ODPHP
ODPHP Healthfinder, HE 20.34/2
ODPHP Monograph Series, HE 20.34
ODPHP Publications List, HE 20.11/3
OE
OE Communique, D 101.91
OEDP
Monthly **OEDP** Status Report, C 46.21
OEG
OEG Report; Operations Evaluation Group, N
27.19
OEH
OEH Guidelines, HE 20.2658/2
OEO
OEO Handbooks, PrEx 10.8/3
OEO Manuals, PrEx 10.8/5
OEO News Summary, PrEx 10.7/3
OEO Pamphlets, PrEx 10.23
OEO Training Manuals, PrEx 10.8/4
OEP
OEP Economic Stabilization Circulars, PrEx 4.4/3
OERI
OERI Announcements (series), ED 1.75
OERI Bulletin ED 1.303/2
OERI Directory of Computer Tapes, ED 1.24/2
OES
OES Circular Letters, A 77.410
Off the Job
Off the Job Safety, OJS-LS- (series), L 16.51/9
Offenders
Directory of Institutions for Mentally Disordered
Offenders, HE 20.2402:Of 2/2
Federal **Offenders** in the United States Courts, Ju
10.11
Special Needs **Offenders**, Bulletin, Ju 13.17
Tracking **Offenders**, J 29.11/9
Offenses
Military Law; Law of Military **Offenses**, W 3.50/
14
Offered
Corporate Securities **Offered** for Cash, SE 1.25/6
Vocational Education; Schools for Careers, an
Analysis of Occupational Courses
Offered by Secondary and
Postsecondary Schools, HE 19.321
Offering
Course **Offering**, Enrollments, and Curriculum,
Practices in Public Secondary Schools,
HE 19.334/2
Offerings
Housing Authority Project Note **Offerings** on
(date), HH 1.71
Offerings and Sales of Office of Personal Property
Disposal, Y 3.W 19/8:12
Schedule of Sales **Offerings**, Pr 33.213
Subject **Offerings** and Enrollments, Grades 912,
Nonpublic Secondary Schools, FS
5.224:24012, HE 5.224:24012
Summary of **Offerings** and Enrollments in Public
and Secondary Schools, HE 19.334
Surplus Government Property Special **Offerings**,
Y 3.W 19/8:9
Offers
Needs and **Offers** List, GP 3.31

Office
Central **Office** Bulletin, HE 3.3/6
Compendium of Copyright **Office** Practices, LC
3.11
Consolidated Annual Report for the **Office** of
Community Planning and Development,
HE 23.1017
Employment **Office** Manual Series (lettered), L
7.15
Field **Office** Memorandum, T 60.7
Hydrographic **Office** Publications, N 6.8
Hydrographic **Office** Publications (numbered), M
202.23
Office and Project Directory, I 27.28
Office Equipment Guide, D 201.6/7
Office Equipment Handbook, D 201.6/6
Office Equipment News, D 201.6/8
Office Memoranda, N 16.5
Office of Administration and Resources
Management, Research Triangle Park,
N.C.: Telephone Directory, EP 1.12/2
Office of Administrative Procedure, Annual
Report, J 1.29
Office of Administrator, for Your Information, AD
(series), FCD 1.13/3
Office of Aviation Policy and Plans: Report FAA-
AV- (series), TD 4.32/4
Office of Construction Industry Services: Annual
Report, L 1.1/2
Office of Drug Evaluation Annual Report, HE
20.4618/2
Office of Energy Resources Yearbook, E 5.16
Office of Engineering Design and Construction:
Annual Report, Y 3.T 25:1-15
Office of Federal Airways Maintenance
Engineering Division Newsletter, C
31.149
Office of Health and Environmental Science:
Annual Report, Y 3.T 25:1-10
Office of Hearings and Appeals Handbook, HE
3.6/7
Office of Homeland Security (General Publica-
tion), PR 43.14
Office of Human Development Services Budget
Request, HE 23.13
Office of Industrial Technology Reports, E 1.138
Office of Industry and Commerce Releases OIC
(series), C 18.281/2
Office of Inspector General, Agricultural Research
Service: Annual Report, A 1.1/3
Office of Inspector General: Annual Report, HE
1.1/2
Office of Inspector General, Audit and Inspection
Plan, C 1.1/2-2
Office of Inspector General, DOE/IG- (series), E
1.48
Office of Inspector General FY, Annual Plan, A
1.1/6
Office of Inspector General Public Reports, E
1.136
Office of Inspector General: Report to the
Congress, HH 1.1/2
Office of Inspector General, Semiannual Report to
the Congress, Y 3.L 52:1
Office of Inspector General, Semiannual Report to
Congress Department of Education, ED
1.26
Office of Inspector General, Semiannual Report to
Congress Department of Transportation,
TD 1.1/3
Office of Inspector General, Semiannual Report to
Congress General Services Administra-
tion, GS 1.1/3
Office of Inspector General, Semiannual Report to
the Congress, IA 1.1/3
Office of Inspector General, Semiannual Report, I
1.1/7
Office of International Trade Releases OIT (series),
C 18.281/3
Office of Juvenile Justice and Delinquency
Prevention: Annual Report, J 1.47
Office of Management and Systems Annual
Performace Report, HE 20.4001/3
Office of Marine Pollution Assessment, Technical
Plan for Fiscal Year, C 55.43/2
Office of Marine Pollution Assessment: Annual
Report, C 55.43
Office of Merchant Marine Safety, TD 5.35
Office of Noise Abatement: Report FAA-NO
(series), TD 4.32/2
Office of Operations and Enforcement: Annual
Report, TD 10.11
Office of Pesticide Programs Annual Report, EP
5.1

Office of Procurement and Supply Letter, VA 1.80
Office of Research and Demonstrations
    Publications Catalog, HE 22.22/2
Office of Research and Development, Region 1:
    Annual Report, EP 1.1/3
Office of Research and Development: Reports CG-
    D- (series), TD 5.25/2
Office of Research and Statistics: Staff Papers, HE
    3.56
Office of Research {reports}, IA 1.24/3
Office of Revenue Sharing: Annual Report, T 1.1/2
Office of Saline Water, I 1.82/3
Office of Science Monograph Series, HE 20.8232
Office of Selective Service Records Regulations, Y
    3.Se 4:19
Office of Solid Wastes Information Series, SW-
    (series), FS 2.305
Office of Technical Services Reports Suitable for
    Commercial Publications, Bulletins, C
    35.10
Office of Technology and Forecast: Publications, C
    21.24
Office of Technology Assessment and Forecast:
    Publications, C 1.62
Office of Women's Jea;tj - Gemera; {ib;ocatopm. JE
    20.41/2
Office of the Chief Administrative Hearing Officer
    (OCAHO) Cases, J 1.102, J 21.23
Office of the Chief Administrative Hearing Officer
    (OCAHO) Files, J 1.102/2
Office of the Chief Administrative Hearing Officer
    (OCAHO) Subpoenas, J 1.102/4
Office of the Chief Scientist: Annual Report, I
    29.1/2
Office of the Inspector General: Annual Report, E
    1.1/2
Office of the Inspector General: Semiannual Report
    to the Congress, CSA 1.1/2
Office of the Inspector General: Semiannual
    Report, EP 1.1/5
Office of the Secretary Petitions for Reconsidera-
    tion of Actions in Rule Making
    Proceedings Filed, Public Notices, CC
    1.38/2
Office of the Secretary, DOE/S- (series), E 1.60
Office of U.S. High Commissioner for German
    Publications, S 1.91
Office of United States Economic Coordinator for
    Cento Affairs, Non-Government Central
    Treaty Organization, S 5.54
Office of United States High Commissioner for
    Austria, General Publications, S 1.89/4
Office of Water Operating Guidance and
    Accountability System, EP 2.29
Office of Water Research and Technology: Annual
    Report, I 1.1/5
Office of Women's Health - Geeral Publications,
    HE 2041/2
Office Orders, W 34.31
Office Review, Y 3.W 19/1:17
Official Gazette Adjutant General's **Office**, D
    102.16
Official Gazette of U.S. Patent **Office**, Trademarks,
    C 21.5/4
Official Gazette Patent and Trademark **Office**, C
    21.5
Official Gazette Patent **Office**, I 23.8
Official Journal of the Plant Variety Protection
    Office, A 88.52
OILA Memorandum Monthly Service of **Office** of
    International Labor Affairs, L 1.21
OIT (**Office** of Industrial Technologies) Times, The,
    E 1.140/2
OMAT-O-GRAM, for Staff Members of **Office** of
    Manpower, Automation, and Training, L
    1.41
OMBE Outlook, News from the **Office** of Minority
    Business Enterprise, C 1.57/2
ONR {**Office** of Naval Research} Reports, D
    210.15
Operations and Enforcement **Office**: Annual
    Report, TD 9.14
Operations of **Office** of Private Resources, S 18.1/2
Opinions of the **Office** of Legal Counsel, J 1.5/4
Pamphlets Federal Employees' Compensation
    Office, L 36.309
Pamphlets Personnel Management **Office**, PM 1.10
Pamphlets Worker's Compensation Programs
    Office, L 36.409
Papers in Re in Patent **Office** (Interferences), J 1.81
Passport **Office** {newsletter}, S 1.27/3
Patent and Trademark **Office** Notices, C 21.5/4a, C
    21.5/4-2

Patent Attorneys and Agents Available to
    Represent Inventors Before the United
    States Patent **Office**, C 21.9/2
Patent **Office** News Letter, C 21.13
Personnel Bulletins Government Printing **Office**,
    GP 1.20
Personnel Bulletins Personnel **Office**, Department
    of Agriculture, A 49.3/2
Plans **Office** Technical Reports, NAS 1.39
Posters **Office** of Attorney Personnel Management,
    J 33.9
Posters **Office** of Management and Budget, PrEx
    2.32
Posters **Office** of Personnel Management, PM 1.35
Posters **Office** of Pesticides and Toxic Substances,
    EP 5.21
Posters **Office** of the Special Counsel, Merit
    Systems Protection Board, MS 1.12
Power **Office**, Publications, Y 3.T 25:30
Press Notices **Office** of Communication, A 21.7
Press Releases Minority Business Enterprise
    Office, C 1.57
Price Lists Patent **Office**, I 23.16
Price Schedules **Office** of Price Administration, Pr
    32.4207
Proceedings Interdepartmental Board on Simplified
    Office Procedure, Executive Committee
    Meeting, T 51.11/5
Public Service **Office**, Series S-, S 1.106/2
Publications Air Force **Office** of Scientific
    Research, D 301.45/19-2
Publications Air Pollution Control **Office**, EP 4.9
Publications Naval Oceanographic **Office**, D
    203.22
Publications **Office** of Aerospace Research, D
    301.69/5
Publications **Office** of Air Programs, EP 4.9
Publications **Office** of Education, FS 5.9, FS 5.10,
    FS 5.211:11000, HE 5.211:11000
Publications **Office** of Technology and Forecast, C
    21.24
Publications **Office** of Technology Assessment and
    Forecast, C 1.62
Publications **Office**, Chief of Military History, D
    114.10
Publications Plant and Operations **Office**, A 60.8
Publications Scientific Research and Development
    Office, Pr 32.413
Purchasing **Office** Circulars, I 1.66
Quarterly Report on Germany, **Office** of U.S. High
    Commissioner for Germany, S 1.90
REC-OCE Reclamation Bureau-**Office** of Chief
    Engineer (series), I 27.60
Recent Research Accomplishments of the Air Force
    Office of Scientific Research, D 301.45/
    19-7
Regional **Office** Directory, Professional and
    Administrative Personnel, FS 1.17/2
Register of **Office** of Attorney General, J 1.12
Regulations of Indian **Office** (general), I 20.13/1
Regulations of the **Office** of the Secretary, TD 1.6/2
Regulations, Rules and Instructions Naval
    Research **Office**, D 210.6
Regulations, Rules and Instructions **Office** of
    Information Resources Management, GS
    12.15
Regulations, Rules and Instructions **Office** of
    Water Programs, EP 2.6
Report of Austria, **Office** of U.S. High Commis-
    sioner for Austria, S 1.89/3
Report on the Significant Actions of the **Office** of
    Personnel Management, MS 1.16
Report R-(series), **Office** of Chief Engineer, CC
    1.46
Report to Congress, **Office** of Federal Procurement
    Policy, PrEx 2.21
Report to the President by Director of **Office** of
    Defense Mobilization, Pr 34.201
Report, **Office** of Housing Expediter, Y 3.H 81/2:7
Reports of the Proceedings of the Judicial
    Conference of the United States {and}
    Annual Report of the Director of the
    Administrative **Office** of the U.S. Courts,
    Ju 10.1/2
Reports on Case Handling Developments of the
    Office of the General Counsel, Y 3.F 31/
    21-3:12
Research Papers Thrift Supervisor **Office**, T 71.16
Research Reports Lake Survey **Office**, D 103.209
Research Reports **Office** of Information for the
    Armed Forces, D 2.12

Research Reports Supported by **Office** of Water
    Resources Research Under the Water
    Resources Research Act of 1964
    Received During the Period (date), I
    1.97/2
Research Review, **Office** of Aerospace Research, D
    301.69/6
Revenues, and **Office** of Revenue Sharing
    Newsletter, T 1.49
Roster of Attorneys and Agents Registered to
    Practice before the U.S. Patent **Office**, C
    21.9
Rules of Practice General Land **Office**, I 21.9
Rules of Practice Patent and Trademark **Office**, C
    21.8
Rules of Practice Patent **Office**, I 23.12
Safety Bulletins Government Printing **Office**, GP
    1.24
Safety Research Programs Sponsored by **Office** of
    Nuclear Regulatory Research, Y 3.N
    88:48
Sailing Directions Naval Oceanographic **Office**, D
    203.22
Semi-annual List of Reports Prepared for or by the
    Office of Toxic Substances, EP 1.65
Semiannual Report, **Office** of Inspector General, A
    1.1/3
Service and Regulatory Announcements, **Office** of
    Distribution, A 80.118
Southeastern Regional **Office**: Regional Reports, L
    2.71/8
Southern Regional **Office** Publications, L 2.95
Special Action **Office** Monographs, PrEx 20.9
Special Promotion Series from **Office** of Civil and
    Defense Mobilization, Battle Creek,
    Michigan, Bulletins, Pr 34.757/3
Special Reports Executive **Office** of the President,
    PrEx 1.10/14
Special Reports Soil Conservation Service, **Office**
    of Research, Sedimentation Section, A
    76.215, A 80.2013
Special Series **Office** of Education, FS 5.41
State **Office** Memorandum, A 55.46/10
Statistical Bulletins **Office** of Civil Defense, Pr
    32.4425
Steel **Office** Furniture, Shelving, and Lockers, and
    Fireproof Safes, C 3.108
Summary of Operations, **Office** of General Counsel,
    LR 1.1/2
Summary of Passport **Office** Accomplishments, S
    1.1/5
Technical Activities, **Office** of Standard Reference
    Data, C 13.58/3
Technical Advisory Services, Health **Office**, For
    Your Information, TAS (series), FCD
    1.13/2
Technical Analysis Papers Congressional Budget
    Office, Y 10.11
Technical Memorandum Technology Assessment
    Office, Y 3.T 22/2:11
Technical Notes Department of the Air Force **Office**
    of Scientific Research, D 301.45/18
Technical Reports, Naval Research **Office** London,
    D 210.16
Technical Services **Office** General Publications, C
    41.22
Telecommunications **Office**: Press Releases, C
    1.32/7
Telephone Directory Central **Office** and Regions,
    GS 12.12
Telephone Directory General Accounting **Office**,
    GA 1.27
Telephone Directory Government Printing **Office**,
    GP 1.39
Telephone Directory **Office** of Personnel
    Management, PM 1.31
Telephone Directory United States Courts
    Administrative **Office**, Ju 10.20
Trademark Rules of Practice of the Patent **Office**,
    with Forms and Statutes, C 21.14:T 67/2
Trans-Atlantic, from **Office** of Labor Advisors, ESC
    Labor News Letter, Y 3.Ec 74/3:31
Trans-Atlantic, from **Office** of Labor Advisors,
    MSA Labor News Letter, Pr 33.915
Treasury Department-General Accounting **Office**
    Joint Regulations, T 1.38
U.S. Government Printing **Office** Style Manual,
    GP 1.23/4:St 9
U.S. Naval Oceanographic **Office** Chart Correction
    List, D 203.21/2
U.S. Nuclear Plants Cost Per KW Report, **Office** of
    Nuclear Power, Y 3.T 25:63
Victory; **Office** Weekly Bulletins, Pr 32.5008
Washington **Office** Telephone Directory, I 53.45
Weather Maps Signal **Office**, W 42.23

Weekly Reports of **Office** of Western Irrigation Agriculture, A 19.25

Weekly Station Reports of **Office** of Dry Land Agriculture Investigations, A 19.24

Working Papers **Office** on Water Programs, EP 2.23

Office Workers

Office Workers, Salaries, Hours of Work, Supplementary Benefits (by cities), L 2.43

Office-Holders

Political Activity and Political Assessments of Federal **Office-Holders** and Employees, CS 1.34

Officer

Air Force Reserve **Officer** Training Corps {textbooks}, D 301.63

Biennial **Officer** Billet Summary (Junior Officer Edition), D 208.24

Biennial **Officer Billet** Summary (Senior Officer Edition), D 208.24/2

General/Flag **Officer** Worldwide Roster, D 1.61/8

Health **Officer**, FS 2.15

Office of the Chief Administrative Hearing **Officer** (OCAHO) Files, J 1.102/2

Officer Correspondence Courses (series), D 207.208/5

Officer Directory, D 103.71

Officer Personnel Newsletter, D 208.21

Officer Specialty (series), D 101.88

Officer Text (series), D 207.208/6

Publications U.S. Antarctic Projects **Officer**, D 1.32

U.S. Antarctic Projects **Officer**, Bulletin, D 1.32/2

U.S. Antarctic Projects **Officer**, Publications, D 1.32

Officer's

Division **Officer's** Planning Guide, D 208.6/3-2

Joint Staff **Officer's** Guide, D 5.408/2

Officers

Address List of State Institutions and **Officers** in Charge of Agricultural Extension Work under Smith-Lever Act, A 10.25

Analysis of Assaults on Federal **Officers**, J 1.14/7-3

Announcements {of examinations for appointment of **officers** in Public Health Service}, FS 2.91

Assaults on Federal **Officers**, J 1.14/7-3

Catalogue of Book and Blanks Furnished by Department of Commerce to Customs **Officers**, C 1.16

Catalogue of Books and Blanks Used by **Officers** of Customs at Port of New York, T 36.5/2

Chronological List of Official Orders to Commissioned and Other **Officers**, FS 2.28

Combined Lineal List of **Officers** on Active Duty in the Marine Corps, D 214.11

Compensation of **Officers**, Directors, Etc., Class 1 Railroads, Line-Haul and Switching and Terminal Companies, IC 1.26

Conference of State and Territorial Health **Officers** with United States Public Health Service, Transactions, T 27.32, FS 2.34

Conference of State Planning and Development **Officers** with Federal Officials, Summaries, C 45.11

Correction and Additions to Publications of **Officers** at Home and Abroad, N 6.6

Directory of **Officers** and Organizations Concerned with Protection of Birds and Game, A 5.8

Directory of United States Probation **Officers**, Ju 10.15

Emergency **Officers**, Army List and Directory, W 3.10/2

Extracts from Reports by Regular and Military **Officers** on Joint Army and Militia Coast-Defense Exercises, W 2.7

FAS Letter to Agricultural Attaches and **Officers**, A 67.31/2

FBI Uniform Crime Reports: Law Enforcement **Officers** Killed, J 1.14/7-5

Historical Register, U.S. Revenue Cutter Service **Officers**, TD 5.19/4

Key **Officers** of Foreign Service Posts, S 1.40/5

Key **Officers** of Foreign Service Posts, Guide for Businessmen, S 1.40/2:Of 2

Law Enforcement **Officers** Killed and Assaulted, Uniform Crime Report, J 1.14/7-6

Laws and Executive Orders Relating to Compensation, Pension, Emergency **Officers'** Retirement, etc., VA 1.14

Leaves of Absence Granted **Officers**, N 17.14

Lineal List of Commissioned and Warrant **Officers** of the Marine Corps Reserves, D 214.11/2

List and Station of Commission **Officers**, T 33.10

List of **Officers** of Merchant Steam, Motor and Sail Vessels Licensed During (calendar year), C 15.7

March of Education, News Letter for School **Officers**, I 16.26/3

Memoranda for Information of **Officers** Pay Corps, etc., N 20.7/1

Memorandum to State Procurement **Officers**, T 58.17

Monthly List of **Officers** Absent on Leave in Excess of Time, W 3.15

Monthly Station List of **Officers**, W 36.8

Name and Address of Air Service **Officers**, W 87.9

Officers in the Marine Corps Reserve, D 214.11/3

Officers of Army in or Near District of Columbia, W 3.81

Officers of Navy and Marine Corps in District of Columbia, N 1.20

Officers on Active Duty in the Marine Corps, D 214.11

Official List of Commissioned and Other **Officers** of U.S. Public Health and Marine Hospital Service, T 27.5

Official List of **Officers** of Reserve Corps, Army, W 3.44

Official Register of **Officers** and Cadets, W 12.5, M 109.11, D 109.7

Official Roster of **Officers** and Employees, W 49.5/5

Orders to **Officers**, U.S.N., N 17.9

Pay Tables for Use of Pay **Officers**, N 20.5

Proceedings Annual Conference of the Surgeon General, Public Health Service, and Chief, Children's Bureau, with State and Territorial Health **Officers**, FS 2.83

Questions for National Guard **Officers**, W 70.9

Register of Civil Engineer Corps Commissioned and Warrant **Officers** of United States Navy and Naval Reserve on Active Duty, D 209.9

Register of Commissioned and Warrant **Officers** Coast Guard Reserve, T 47.10/2

Register of Commissioned and Warrant **Officers** Marine Corps Reserve, N 9.20

Register of Commissioned and Warrant **Officers** Naval Militia, N 1.27/6

Register of Commissioned and Warrant **Officers** Naval Reserve Force, N 25.6

Register of Commissioned and Warrant **Officers** Naval Reserve, N 17.38

Register of Commissioned and Warrant **Officers** Navy and Marine Corps and Reserve Officers on Active Duty, D 208.12

Register of Commissioned and Warrant Officers Navy and Marine Corps and Reserve **Officers** on Active Duty, D 208.12

Register of Commissioned and Warrant **Officers** United States Naval Reserve, D 208.12/2

Register of Commissioned and Warrant **Officers** United States Navy and Marine Corps, M 206.10

Register of **Officers** and Cadets, TD 5.19

Register of **Officers** and Graduates (triennial), W 12.12

Register of **Officers** and Vessels, T 33.6

Register of Reserve **Officers**, TD 5.19/2

Register of Retired Commissioned and Warrant **Officers**, Regular and Reserve, of the United States Navy and Marine Corps, D 208.12/3

Regulations Governing Uniform and Equipment of **Officers** and Enlisted Men, N 9.8

Reserve **Officers** Training Corps Bulletin, W 99.17/18

Roster and Station of **Officers** of Signal Corps, W 42.9

Roster of Commissioned **Officers** and Employees, A 29.28

Roster of Field **Officers**, I 21.15

Roster of General **Officers** of General Staff, Volunteers, W 3.7

Roster of **Officers** and Troops, W 12.8

Roster of **Officers** of Indian Service, I 20.10

Roster of **Officers**, Adjutant-General's Department, W 3.34

Roster Showing Stations and Duties of **Officers**, W 39.12, W 77.6

State Agricultural and Marketing **Officers**, A 36.55

State **Officers** Analyzer Sheets, C 46.12

Statement Showing Rank Duties and Address of **Officers** of Corps of Engineers, W 7.7

Station-List of **Officers** of Medical Department, W 44.13

Summary of Equity Security Transactions and Ownership of Directors, **Officers**, and Principal Stockholders of Member State Banks As Reported Pursuant to

Useful Information for Newly Commissioned **Officers**, D 207.215

Officers' Call, M 101.33, D 101.17, D 101.118

Offices

Annual Report on Location of New Federal **Offices** and Other Facilities, A 1.111

Offices of Processed Products Standardization and Inspection Branch, A 88.43

Official Army and Air Force Register, M 101.19, M 108.8

Official List of Rural Free Delivery **Offices**, P 13.6

Ordnance Materials Research **Offices**, Watertown Arsenal, Omro Publications, D 105.13/3

Publications Ordnance Materials Research **Offices**, D 105.13/3

Selected Agricultural Activities of Public Employment **Offices**, L 7.59

Statement of Postal Receipts at 50 Industrial **Offices**, P 4.8

Statement of Postal Receipts at 50 Selected **Offices**, P 4.9

Vocational Training Activities of Public Employment **Offices**, FS 3.119

Worldwide Public Affairs **Offices** Directory, D 101.120/2

Official

Abridged United States **Official** Postal Guide, P 1.10/2

Chronological List of Official Orders to Commissioned and Other **Officers**, FS 2.28

Circulars Relating to Plan and Methods of Publication of **Official** Records of Union Army and Confederate Army, W 45.4

Fly-By, **Official** Employee Publication of Federal Aviation Agency, FAA 1.11

French-Speaking Central Africa, a Guide to **Official** Publications in American Libraries, LC 2.8:Af 8/3

List of **Official** International Conferences and Meetings, S 5.49

List of **Official** Publications of Government Distributed for Library of Congress through Smithsonian Institution, SI 1.5

Marines, **Official** Magazine of the U.S. Marine Corps, D 214.24

Military Operations of Civil War, Guide-Index to **Official** Records of Union and Confederate Armies, GS 4.21

Official Army National Guard Register, D 12.9

Official Army Register of Volunteer Force of U.S. Army, 1861-65, W 3.12

Official Bulletin Committee on Public Information, Y 3.P 93/3:3

Official Bulletin Federal Radio Commission, RC 1.5

Official Bulletins, I 29.37/5

Official Bulletins, National Trophy Matches, D 101.61

Official Circulars, I 16.9

Official Circulars, V.D., T 27.23

Official Classification of . . . Watering Points, FS 2.75

Official Gazette Adjutant General's Office, D 102.16

Official Gazette Allied High Commission for Germany, S 1.88

Official Gazette Control Council for Germany, W 1.73, M 105.9

Official Gazette of Allied High Commission for Germany, S 1.88

Official Gazette of U.S. Patent Office, Trademarks, C 21.5/4

Official Gazette Patent and Trademark Office, C 21.5

Official Gazette Patent Office, I 23.8

Official Gazette Philippine Islands, W 49.16

Official Gazette {Japanese} English Edition, D 102.16

Official Grain Standards of the United States, A 88.6/2:G 761

Official Hours and Holidays to Be Observed by Federal Reserve Offices During Year (date), FR 1.50

Official Journal of the Plant Variety Protection Office, A 88.52

Official List of Commissioned and Other Officers of U.S. Public Health and Marine Hospital Service, T 27.5

Official List of Officers of Officers Reserve Corps, Army, W 3.44

Official List of Rural Free Delivery Offices, P 13.6

Official List of Section 13(f) Securities, SE 1.34

Official National Guard Register, D 112.8

Official Opening and Closing Hours of Board of Governors and Federal Reserve Banks, also Holiday During Month, FR 1.50

Official Opinions, P 6.5

Official Opinions of Attorney-General, W 49.23/5

Official Opinions of the Attorneys General of the United States, J 1.5

Official Parcel Post Zone Keys Hawaii, P 1.25/4

Official Parcel Post Zone Keys Puerto Rico, P 1.25/3

Official Parcel Post Zone Keys United States, P 1.25/1

Official Parcel Post Zone Keys Virgin Islands, P 1.25/2

Official Postal Maps, P 11.8

Official Record, Department of Agriculture, A 1.33

Official Records of Union and Confederal Navies in War of Rebellion, N 16.6

Official Register (or Blue Book) Biennial, I 1.25

Official Register Life-Saving Service, T 24.5

Official Register National Guard Bureau, D 112.8

Official Register of Officers and Cadets, W 12.5, M 109.11, D 109.7

Official Register of Officers Volunteers in Service of United States, W 3.21

Official Register of the United States, C 3.10, CS 1.31

Official Reports of the Supreme Court, Preliminary Prints, Ju 6.8/a

Official Road Maps for Allied Forces Europe, Series M305, D 5.342

Official Roster of Officers and Employees, W 49.5/5

Official Statement of United States Food Administration, Y 3.F 73:19

Official Statement of Wheat Director, Y 3.W 56:5

Official Summary of Security Transactions and Holdings, SE 1.9

Official Table of Distances, W 36.9

Official United States Standards for Grain, A 104.6/2, A 113.10

Official United States Standards for Beans, A 113.10/3

Official United States Standards for Peas & Lentils, A 113.10/4

Official United States Standards for Rice, A 113.10/2

Receipts for State Administered Highways, **Official** Distribution, C 37.19

Significant Arrearages Due the United States Government and Unpaid 90 Days or More by **Official** Foreign Obligors, T 1.45/5

Soil Conservation; **Official** Organ, A 76.208, A 79.207

Table of Investment Yields for United States Savings Bonds of Series E. **Official** Use, T 66.23

Turkeys Tested by **Official** State Agencies, A 88.15/4

U.S. **Official** Postal Guide, P 1.10

War of Rebellion, Compilation of **Official** Records of Union and Confederate Armies {or Rebellion Records}, W 45.5

Officials

Association of Food and Drug **Officials** Quarterly Bulletin, HE 20.4003/5

Compilation of Laws Relating to Mediation, Conciliation, and Arbitration Between Employers and Employees, Laws {on} Disputes Between Carriers and Employers and Subordinate **Officials**. . . , Y 1.2:Em 7/6

Conference of State Planning and Development Officers with Federal **Officials**, Summaries, C 45.11

Directory of **Officials** of the Democratic People's Republic of Korea, PrEx 3.10/7-6

Directory of **Officials** of the Republic of Cuba, PrEx 3.10/7-18

Directory of **Officials** of Vietnam, A Reference Aid, PrEx 3.10/7-25

Directory of Soviet **Officials**, National Organizations, PrEx 3.10/7-4

Directory of State **Officials**, HE 20.4037/2

Directory, State **Officials** Charged with Enforcement of Food, Drug, Cosmetic, and Feed Laws, FS 13.102:St 2

List of State Designated Agencies, **Officials** and Working Contracts, C 1.53/3

Officials of Department of Agriculture, A 1.89/2

Organizational Directory of Key **Officials**, PM 1.31/2

State Agricultural Departments and Marketing Agencies, with Names of **Officials**, A 66.45

Working Reference of Livestock Regulatory Establishments, Circuits and **Officials**, A 88.16/20

Offline

GLOBE **Offline**, C 55.56

Offshore

Federal **Offshore** Statistics, Leasing, Exploration, Production, Revenue, I 72.10

Offshore Scientific and Technical Publications, I 72.14, I 72.14/2

Offshore Stats, I 72.18

Report to Congress on Ocean Pollution, Overfishing, and **Offshore** Development, C 55.31/2

OFPP

OFPP Pamphlets, PrEx 2.22

OGC

OGC Adviser, GA 1.24

OH

OH (series), HE 20.2810

OHA

OHA Law Journal, HE 3.66/3, SSA 1.5/3

OHA Law Reporter, HE 3.66

OHA Newsletter, HE 3.66/2

OHA Telephone Directory, HE 3.51/6

OHD

OHD, Grants Administration Manual, TN-(series), HE 1.709

Ohio

Center for Vocational and Technical Education, **Ohio** State University: Research and Development Series, HE 18.11

Daily **Ohio** River Bulletin, C 30.54/17, C 55.110

Hourly Precipitation on Upper **Ohio** and Susquehanna Drainage Basins, A 57.31

Index of Current Water Resources Activities in **Ohio**, I 19.55/6

Light List, Lights, Buoys, and Day Marks, Mississippi and **Ohio** Rivers, C 9.29/2

Light List, Mississippi and **Ohio** Rivers and Tributaries, N 24.18, T 47.27

Medicare Hospital Mortality Information; Vol. 5, New Hampshire - **Ohio**, HE 22.34

Navigation Charts; **Ohio** River, D 103.66/2

Sun and Moon Tables for Cleveland, **Ohio**, D 203.14/2

Systems Engineering Group, Research and Technology Division, Air Force Systems Command, Wright-Patterson Air Force Base, **Ohio**, Technical Documentary Report No. SEG TDR, D 301.45/48

Trade World, **Ohio** C 61.39/6

Water Resources Development in **Ohio**, D 103.35/35

Ohio River

Hydrologic Bulletin, Hourly and Daily Precipitation; **Ohio River** District, C 30.32

Ohio River Charts, W 7.13/3

Ohio River Flood Plain Charts, W 7.13/4

Ohio River Summary and Forecasts, C 55.110

Ohio River, D 103.66/2

OHM

OHM Newsletter, TD 9.12

OHRO

OHRO Digest, HE 20.6019

OIC

Office of Industry and Commerce Releases **OIC** (series), C 18.281/2

OIG

OIG Communique, HH 1.109

OIG Highlights, I 1.1/7-2

OIG News, A 1.80/3

Oil

Analysis Report, Estimate of the (year) Cost of **Oil** Imports into the United States, E 3.26/4

Annual Outlook for **Oil** and Gas, E 3.11/7-10

Cabinet Task Force on **Oil** Import Control, Pr 37.8:Oi 5

Commitments of Traders in Wheat, Corn, Oats, Rye, Soybeans, Soybean **Oil**, Soybean Meal, Shell Eggs, A 85.9/2

Competitive **Oil** and Gas Lease Sale Results, Date of Sale, I 53.53

Conference of **Oil** Pollution of Navigable Waters, S 5.24

Costs and Indexes for Domestic **Oil** and Gas Field Equipment and Production Operations, E 3.44/2

Cotton Linters Produced and on Hand at **Oil** Mills by Type of Cut, by States, Preliminary, C 3.148

Cottonseed Products Manufactured and on Hand at **Oil** Mills by States, C 3.125

Cottonseed Received, Crushed and on Hand; Cotton Linters Produced; and Linters on Hand at **Oil** Mills, Preliminary Reports, C 3.149

Crude-**oil** and Product Pipelines, E 3.11/12

Crude-**oil** and Refined-products Pipeline Mileage in the United States, I 28.45/2

Distillate **Oil** Burners, C 3.76

Environmental Development Plan, **Oil** Shale, ER 1.33

Essential **Oil** Production and Trade, C 18.69

Estimated **Oil** and Gas Reserves, I 72.12/7

Federal **Oil** Conservation Board, I 1.67

Fish Meal and **Oil**, C 55.309/2

Fish Meal and **Oil** Market Review, Current Economic Analysis I, C 55.309/3

Forecast of Motor-Fuel Demand and Required Crude-**Oil** Production by States, Monthly Forecast, I 28.41

Fuel **Oil** and Kerosene Sales, E 3.11/11-4

Fuel **Oil** Industry Letters, Pr 32.4228

Fuel **Oil** Sales, E 3.11/11

Futures Trading and Open Contracts in Cotton and Cottonseed **Oil**, A 85.11/5

Government Vehicle Operators Guide to Service Stations for Gasoline, **Oil** and Lubrication, D 7.6/7-2

Heating **Oil** Prices and Margins (advance release), E 3.11/11-2

Injury Experience in **Oil** and Gas Industry of United States, I 28.108

International **Oil** and Gas Exploration and Development, E 3.11/20-6

International **Oil** and Gas Exploration and Development Activities, E 3.11/20-4

Measuring and Dispensing Pumps, Gasoline, **Oil**, etc. Shipments of, C 3.90

Naval Petroleum and **Oil** Shale Reserves, Annual Report of Operations, E 1.84/2

Oil and Gas Field Code Master List, E 3.34/2

Oil and Gas Investigation Charts, I 19.25/5, I 19.92

Oil and Gas Investigations Maps, I 19.25/4, I 19.93

Oil and Hazardous Material Program Series, EP 2.11

Oil Burners, C 3.93

Oil Contract Bulletin, D 11.3

Oil Crops Outlook and Situation Report, A 93.23/2

Oil Crops, Situation and Outlook Yearbook, A 93.23/2-2

Oil Import Totals, I 64.11

Oil Lands Leasing Act of 1920 with Amendments and Other Laws Relating to Mineral Lands {March 2, 1919}, Y 1.2:Oi 5

Oil Market Simulation Model, E 3.55

Oil Pollution Abstracts, EP 1.25/2

Oil Pollution Research Newsletter, EP 1.25

Oil Shales and Tar Sands, E 1.99

Outer Continental Shelf **Oil** and Gas Information Program, Summary Reports (various regions), I 72.9

Outer Continental Shelf **Oil** and Gas Leasing and Production Program Annual Report, I 72.12/3-2

Production of Linseed **Oil**, Preliminary Report, C 3.122

Report of the Attorney General Pursuant to Section 2 of the Joint Resolution of July 28, 1955, Consenting to an Interstate Compact to Conserve **Oil** and Gas, J 1.27

Sales of Fuel **Oil** and Kerosene in (year), I 28.45/5

Shipments of Measuring and Dispensing Pumps, Gasoline, **Oil**, etc., C 3.90

Transportation Revenue and Traffic of Large **Oil** Pipe Line Companies, IC 1 pip.7

Tung **Oil** Monthly, Production in America, Foreign Trade, etc., C 18.209

U.S. Crude **Oil** and Natural Gas Reserves, (year) Annual Report, E 3.34

U.S. Crude **Oil**, Natural Gas, and Natural Gas Liquids Reserves (Diskettes), E 3.34

United States Foreign Trade Bunker **Oil** and Coal Laden in the United States on Vessels, C 3.164:810

Weekly Crude **Oil** Stock Reports, I 28.46

Weekly **Oil** Update, E 3.32/2

World Crude **Oil** Production Annual (year), I 28.18/5

Oila
OILA Memorandum Monthly Service of Office of International Labor Affairs, L 1.21

Oils
Animal and Vegetable Fats and **Oils**, C 3.56

Availability of Heavy Fuel **Oils** by Sulfur Level, E 3.11/8 E 3.11/8-2

Chemistry and Technology of Fuels and **Oils** {abstracts}, C 41.55

Factory Consumption of Animal and Vegetable Fats and **Oils** by Classes of Products, C 3.154

Fats and **Oils** Subjected to Supphonation, C 3.124

Fuel **Oils** by Sulfur Content, I 28.45/4

Industry Report, Crude Drugs, Gums, Balsams, and Essential **Oils**, C 18.236

Industry Report, Fats and **Oils**, C 18.238

Meats, Livestock, Fats and **Oils**, C 18.72/5

Production, Consumption, and Stocks of Fats and **Oils**, C 3.123

Supply, Demand, and Stocks of All **Oils** by P.A.D. Districts, I 28.18/7

World Retail Prices and Taxes on Gasoline, Kerosene, and Motor Lubricating **Oils**, I 28.44

Oilseeds
Oilseeds and **Oilseed** Products, A 67.30:Oi 5

OIMA
Research Series (**OIMA**), C 1.93

OIR
OIR Reports, S 1.57

OIT
Energy Matters (**OIT** Newsletter), E 1.140/3

Office of International Trade Releases **OIT** (series), C 18.281/3

OIT (Office of Industrial Technologies) Times, The, E 1.140/2

OIT Technical Reports, E 1.140

OJJDP
OJJDP Annual Report on Missing Children, J 32.17

OJJDP Discretionary Program Announcement, J 32.22

OJJDP Fact Sheet (series), J 32.21

OJJDP Fiscal Year, Program Plan, J 32.10/2

OJJDP News @ a Glance, J 32.25

OJJDP Report & Research Report, J 32.20/3

OJJDP Summary & Program Summary, J 32.20/2

OJJDP Summary & Research Summary, J 32.20

OJJDP Youth in Action Fact Sheet, J 32.21/2

OKARNG
OKARNG- (series), D 12.12/2

Oklahoma
BLM in New Mexico, **Oklahoma**, Texas and Kansas, I 53.43/5

Contributions from Thermodynamics Laboratory, Petroleum Experiment Station, Bartlesville, **Oklahoma**, I 28.105

Cotton Grade and Staple Reports, Texas and **Oklahoma**, A 36.27/2

Medicare Hospital Mortality Information; Vol. 6, **Oklahoma** - Tennessee, HE 22.34

Oklahoma, Governor, Annual Reports, 1891-1907, I 1.26

Oklahoma City
Area Wage Survey Summary **Oklahoma City**, Oklahoma, L 2.122/36-2

Old-Age
Annual Report of the Board of Trustees of the Federal **Old-Age** and Survivors Insurance and Disability Insurance Trust Funds, SSA 1.1/4

Public Assistance Bureau, Applications: **Old-Age** Assistance, Aid to Dependent Children, Aid to the Blind {and} General Assistance, FS 3.17

Business Establishment, Employment and Taxable Pay Rolls under **Old-Age** and Survivors Insurance Program, C 18.270

Concurrent Receipt of Public Assistance Money Payments and **Old-Age**, Survivors, and Disability Insurance Cash Benefits by Persons Aged 65 or Over, FS 17.636, HE 17.636

Digest of Rulings (**Old-Age** and Survivors Insurance), FS 3.24

Handbook of **Old-Age** and Survivors Insurance Statistics, FS 3.40

Monthly Benefit Statistics; **Old-age**, Survivors, Disability, and Health Insurance, Summary Benefit Data, HE 3.28/6

National Survey of **Old-Age** and Survivors Insurance Beneficiaries: Highlight Reports, FS 3.48

Old-Age and Survivors Insurance, Regulations, FS 3.6/2

Old-Age Insurance Operating Statistics Review, SS 1.33

Regulations No. 4, **Old-Age** and Survivors Insurance, FS 3.6/2

Selected List of References on **Old-Age** Security, Y 3.F 31/5:20

Social Security Rulings on Federal **Old-age**, Survivors, Disability, and Health Insurance, HE 3.44

Older
Designs for Action for **Older** Americans (series), FS 17.310, HE 17.310

Facts and Figures on **Older** Americans, HE 1.209

Federal Income Tax Guide for **Older** Americans, Y 4.Ag 4/2-11

Older Americans in Action, AA 2.9

Statistical Reports on **Older** Americans, HE 23.3112/2

Training and Manpower Development Activities Supported by the Administration on Aging Under Title IV-A of the **Older** Americans Act of 1965, As Amended, Descriptions of Funded Projects, HE 23.3002:T 68/2

Olives
Table **Olives**, A 67.18:FOL

Olympic
President's Commission on **Olympic** Sports, Pr 38.8:Ol 9

Omaha
Omaha, Trans-Mississippi and International Exposition, 1898, S 6.16

OMAT-O-GRAM
OMAT-O-GRAM, for Staff Members of Office of Manpower, Automation, and Training, L 1.41

OMB
OMB Submission, VA 1.83

OMBE
OMBE Outlook, News from the Office of Minority Business Enterprise, C 1.57/2

Omega
Hydrographic/Topographic Center Publications: **Omega** Tables, D 5.317/5

Omega Plotting (31) Charts Series 7500, D 5.347

Omega Plotting (112) Charts Series 7600, D 5.347/2

Omega Plotting Charts, D 5.356

Omega Tables, D 5.317

Omnibus
Omnibus Solicitation for the Small Business Innovative Research, HE 20.28

Omnibus Solicitation of the Public Health Service for Small Business Innovation Research (SBIR) Grant Applications, HE 20.3047/2

OMPA
NOAA Data Reports, **OMPA** (series), C 55.36

OMRO
Ordnance Materials Research Offices, Watertown Arsenal, **OMRO** Publications, D 105.13/3

On
On the Beat: Community Oriented Policing Services J 1.107

On the Job Training Program, JP Series, D 301.38/5

On the Record, AE 1.116

On Call
On Call Positions in Spot Cotton Based on New York Cotton Futures Reported by Merchants in Special Account Status, Y 3.C 73/5:11

On Guard
On Guard Series, Y 3.F 73:11

On Guard, Bureau of Motor Carrier Safety Bulletin, TD 2.303

ONC
ONC - Operational Navigation Charts, D 5.322

Oncology
Oncology Overview, NCI/ICRDB, HE 20.3173/3

ONDCP
ONDCP Brief, PrEx 1.3/3

ONDCP Bulletin, PrEx 1.3/2

O-NET
O-NET (Online Database), L 1.96

One-family
Construction Reports; New **One-family** Homes Sold and for Sale, C 25 (series), C 56.211/2

Construction Reports; Price Index of New **One-family** Houses Sold, C 27 (series), C 3.215/9-2, C 56.211/2-2

Current Construction Reports, New **One-Family** Houses Sold and for Sale, C 3.215/9

FHA Low Cost Housing Trends of **One-family** Homes Insured by FHA, HH 2.26

One-Housing-Unit
Expenditures for Additions, Alterations, Maintenance and Repairs, and Replacements on **One-Housing-Unit** Owner-Occupied Properities, C 3.215/8:Pt-2

On-flight
Coach Traffic, Revenue, Yield and Average **On-flight** Trip Length by Fare Category for the 48-state Operations of the Domestic Trunks, C 31.269

Trunk Carriers, Coach Class, Traffic, Revenue, Yield, Enplanements and Average **On-flight** Trip Length by Fare Category, CAB 1.24

On-going
Directory of **On-going** Research in Smoking and Health, HE 20.25, HE 20.7015

On-Highway
On-Highway Diesel Prices, E 3.13/8

Onion
Onion Stocks, A 88.12/25

Online
ABM (Acquisition & Business Management) **Online**, D 201.44

GAO **Online** Service, GA 1.34

List of Serials Indexed for **Online** Users, HE 20.3618/2

NDE of Stainless Steel and **On-Line** Leak Monitoring of LWRS, Annual Report, Y 3.N 88:25-5, Y 3.N 88:25-9

NHSC in Touch, Free **On-Line** Service Open to Primary Care Providers, HE 20.91110/9

Online Literature Searching and Databases, EP 1.21/10

ONR
ONR Report ARC (series), D 210.15

ONR Reports, DR- (series), D 210.15

ONR Symposium Reports, D 210.5

ONR Technical Report RLT (series), D 210.8/3-2

ONR {Office of Naval Research} Reports, D 210.15

Ontario
Catalog of Charts of the Great Lakes and Connecting Waters, Also Lake Champlain, New York Canals, Minnesota-**Ontario** Border Lakes, D 103.208

Saint Marys Falls Canal, Michigan, Statistical Report of Lake Commerce Passing through Canals at Sault Ste. Marie, Michigan and **Ontario**, W 7.26, M 110.16, D 103.17

Statistical Report of Commerce Passing through Canals at Sault Ste. Marie, Mich. and **Ontario**, Salt Water Ship Movements for Season of (year), D 103.17/2

OOE
OOE (series), C 55.13

OP
Ordnance Pamphlets, **OP**- (series), D 215.9

OPA
OPA Bulletins for Schools and Colleges, Pr 32.4224

OPA Chart Book Releases, Pr 32.4250

OPA Economic Data Series, Pr 33.307

OPA Food Guide for Retailers, Pr 32.4241

OPA Information Leaflets for Schools and Colleges, Pr 32.4240

OPA Manual News Letters, Pr 32.4248

OPA Trade Bulletins, Pr 32.4244

OPE
OPE Reports, HE 20.4034

Certification and **Operations**; Air Carriers and Commercial Operators of Large Aircraft, TD 4.6:part 121

Certification and **Operations**; Air Travel and Clubs Using Large Airplanes, TD 4.6:part 123

Certification and **Operations**; Land Airports Serving CAB-Certificated Scheduled Air Carriers Operating Large Aircraft, TD 4.6:part 139

Certification and **Operations**; Scheduled Air Carriers with Helicopters, TD 4.6:part 127

Classification of Revenues and Expenses by Outside **Operations**, IC 1 ste.10

Classification of Revenues and Expenses of Sleeping Car **Operations**, of Auxiliary **Operations** and of Other Properties for Sleeping Car Companies, IC 1 sle.5

Coach Traffic, Revenue, Yield and Average On-flight Trip Length by Fare Category for the 48-state **Operations** of the Domestic Trunks, C 31.269

Commuter Air Carrier **Operations** As of (date), TD 4.35

Comparative Statistics of General Assistance **Operations** of Public Agencies in Selected Large Cities, FS 3.16

Costs and Indexes for Domestic Oil and Gas Field Equipment and Production **Operations**, E 3.44/2

Current Social Security Program **Operations**, FS 3.43

Daily **Operations** Highlights, TD 5.31

Emergency **Operations** Orders, Pr 34.706/6, PrEx 4.6/6

Emergency Relief Appropriation Acts, Reports of President to Congress Showing Status of Funds and **Operations** Under, T 63.114

Excerpts from Slide Presentations by the Office of Chief of Naval **Operations**, D 207.14

Federal Airways Manual of **Operations**, C 31.116/2

Federal Credit Unions, Quarterly Report on **Operations**, FCA 1.16

FHA Homes, Data for States, on Characteristics of FHA **Operations** Under Sec. 203, HH 2.24/4

FHA Monthly Report of **Operations**: Home Mortgage Programs, HH 2.27/2

FHA Monthly Report of **Operations**: Project Mortgage Insurance Programs, HH 2.27

Field **Operations** Handbook, L 22.18

Field **Operations** of Bureau of Soils, A 26.5

For Your Information; **Operations** Control Services, FCD 1.13/4

Fuel Consumption and Cost, Certificated Route and Supplemental Air Carriers, Domestic and International **Operations**, C 31.267

Fuel Cost and Consumption, Certified Route and Supplemental Air Carriers, Domestic and International **Operations**, Twelve Months Ended (date), C 31.267/2

General Relief **Operations** of Large City Public Welfare Agencies, SS 1.26

Index of Straight-time Average Hourly Earnings for Hydraulic Turbine **Operations**, L 2.78/2

Industrial Classification Code, State **Operations** Bulletins, FS 3.112

Inspection **Operations** Manual Transmittal Notices, HE 20.4008/2

Japan Productivity Center, United States **Operations** Mission to Japan, Publications, S 17.44/2

Key Facts, Employment Security **Operations**, L 7.60

Maintenance **Operations** Division Instructions, C 31.106/4, FAA 1.6/3

Manual of **Operations**, C 23.6/5, CA 1.14, C 31.116

Medicare, Medicaid, State **Operations** Manual, Provider Certification, HE 22.8/12

Military **Operations** of Civil War, Guide-Index to Official Records of Union and Confederate Armies, GS 4.21

Monthly Reports of Organizations and **Operations** of Federal Credit Unions, A 72.14

Monthly Summary of Statistics of **Operations**, L 22.21

Municipal and Cooperative Distributors of TVA Power, (date) **Operations**, Y 3.T 25:1-3

Notes on Recent **Operations**, W 95.13

OEG Report; **Operations** Evaluation Group, N 27.19

Office of **Operations** and Enforcement: Annual Report, TD 10.11

Operating Units Status Report, Licensed **Operations** Reactors Data for Decisions, Y 3.N 88:15

Operations and Enforcement Office: Annual Report, TD 9.14

Operations Instructions (series), J 21.6/2-2

Operations Letters, Pr 32.4418

Operations of National Weather Service, C 55.111

Operations of Office of Private Resources, S 18.1/2

Operations of the Bureau of Commercial Fisheries Under the Saltonstall-Kennedy Act, I 49.48

Operations of the Employment Security Program, FS 3.3/a3

Operations of the Trade Agreements Program, TC 1.14/3, ITC 1.24

Operations of the Weather Bureau, C 30.83

Operations Report, S 18.16

Operations, Instructions, Regulations, and Interpretations, J 21.6/2

Orientation Material, Tribal **Operations**, Administrative, I 20.49

Plant and **Operations** Circulars, A 60.4/3

Postal **Operations** Manual, P 1.12/8

Production Credit Associations, Annual Summary of **Operations**, FCA 1.22

Production Credit Associations, Summary of **Operations**, A 72.25

Profiles of Scheduled Air Carrier Airport **Operations** by Equipment Type, Top 100 U.S. Airports, TD 4.44/4

Profiles of Scheduled Air Carrier Airport **Operations**, Top 100 U.S. Airports, TD 4.44

Profiles of Scheduled Air Carrier **Operations** by Stage Length, TD 4.44/3

Program **Operations** Manual System, HE 3.6/5

Publications Plant and **Operations** Office, A 60.8

Quarterly Report of Budgetary **Operations**, C 1.30

Quarterly Summary of Statistics of **Operations**, L 22.20

Refined Metal and Copper Scrap **Operations** at Brass and Wire Mills, Brass Mill Report, I 28.79/2

Report of Financial Conditions and **Operations**, As of {date}, A 82.308

Report of **Operations**, D 1.46/5

Report of Urban Renewal **Operations**, HH 7.10, HH 9.9

Report to Congress on Lend-lease **Operations**, S 1.43

Report to Congress on **Operations** of UNRRA Under Act of March 28, 1944, S 1.44

Reports of Military **Operations** during Rebellion, 1860-65, W 45.9

Reports of President to Congress Showing Status of Funds and **Operations** under Emergency Relief Appropriation Acts, T 63.114

Reports to Congress on Lend-Lease **Operations**, Pr 32.402:L 54, Pr 32.5507

Reports to Congress on United States Participation in **Operations** of UNRRA under Act of March 28, 1944, Pr 32.5812

Review of **Operations** Information Agency, IA 1.1/2

Review of **Operations** Social Security Administration, FS 3.15

Rotorcraft External-Load **Operations**, TD 4.6:part 133

Rules of the Committee on Government **Operations**, Y 4.G 74/7-10

Scheduled International **Operations**, International Trunks, C 31.262

Seasonally Adjusted Capacity and Traffic Scheduled Domestic **Operations**, Domestic Trunks, C 31.262/3

Seasonally Adjusted Capacity and Traffic Scheduled International **Operations**, International Trunks, C 31.262

Seasonally Adjusted Capacity and Traffic Scheduled **Operations** Local Service Carriers, C 31.262/4

Seasonally Adjusted Capacity and Traffic Scheduled **Operations** System Trunks and Regional Carriers, C 31.262/5

Seasonally Adjusted Capacity and Traffic Scheduled **Operations**, System Trunks, C 31.262/2

Seasonally Adjusted Capacity and Traffic Scheduled **Operations**: System, Domestic, and International Trunks Plus Local Service Carrier, CAB 1.20

Semiannual Report on **Operations** Under Mutual Defense Assistance Control Act of 1951, FO 1.1/2

Semiannual Reports on **Operations** under Mutual Defense Assistance Act, S 17.1/2

Ship **Operations** Report, National Ocean Survey, C 55.423

State Education Agency **Operations**, Revenues, Expenditures, and Employees, ED 1.108/3

Statement of **Operations**, Y 3.F 31/8:1

Statistical Summary, Railroad Retirement Board **Operations**, RR 1.11

Status of Open Recommendations Improving **Operations** of Federal Departments and Agencies, GA 1.13/18

Summary of Mortgage Insurance **Operations** and Contract Authority, HH 2.24/5

Summary of **Operations** of Production Credit Associations, A 72.25

Summary of **Operations**, Labor-Management Reporting and Disclosure Act, L 1.51

Summary of **Operations**, Office of General Counsel, LR 1.1/2

Summary Report of Bureau's Financial Condition and **Operations** for Fiscal Year, I 27.1/3

Topographic Mapping, Status and Progress of **Operations**, I 19.95

U.S. Direct Investment Abroad, **Operations** of U.S. Parent Companies and Their Foreign Affiliates, Preliminary Estimates, C 59.20/2

United States **Operations** Mission to the Philippines, Publications, S 18.31

United States **Operations** Mission to Vietnam, Publications, S 18.31/2

United States Special **Operations** Forces, Posture Statement, D 1.98

Wage **Operations** Manual of Procedures, L 2.54

Water **Operations** Technical Support: WOTS, D 103.24/15

Operators

Air Taxi **Operators** and Commerical Operators of Small Aircraft, TD 4.6:part 135

Certification and Operations; Air Carriers and Commercial **Operators** of Large Aircraft, TD 4.6:part 121

Farm Returns, Summary of Reports of Farm **Operators**, A 36.124

Farms of Nonwhite Farm Operators, Number of Farms, Land in Farm, Cropland Harvested, and Value of Land and Buildings, by Tenure, Censuses of 1945 and 1940 (by States), C 3.193

Government Vehicle **Operators** Guide to Service Stations for Gasoline, Oil and Lubrication, D 7.6/7-2

Operators Letters, HH 2.21

Statistics of Bituminous Coal Loaded for Shipment on Railroads and Waterways As Reported by **Operators**, I 28.34

Telephone **Operators'** Manual, A 68.6/3

Opiate

Annual Report on **Opiate** Use Among Arrestees, J 28.15/2-4

OPIC

OPICNews, OP 1.10

Opinion

Advisory **Opinion** Digests, FT 1.12/2

Opinion Digest, SBA 1.47

Opinion Papers, LC 1.50

Opinions

Atomic Energy Commission Reports **Opinions** of the Atomic Energy Commssion with Selected Orders, Y 3.At 7:49

C.A.B. Economic Orders and **Opinions**, CAB 1.31

Civil Law **Opinions** of the Judge Advocate General, Air Force, D 302.12

Collection of Legal **Opinions**, EP 1.63

Consolidated Index of **Opinions** and Digests of **Opinions** of Judge Advocate General, W 10.10

Digest and Index of Opinions of Counsel, Informal Rulings of Federal Reserve Board and Matter Relating Thereto, from Federal Reserve Bulletin, FR 1.10

Digest of **Opinions**, J 5.5

Digest of **Opinions** of Judge-Advocate-General, Army, W 10.8

Digest of **Opinions**, Judge-Advocate-General of Armed Forces, D 1.18, D 1.18/2

Directive Orders and **Opinions**, Pr 32.5107

Federal Power Commission Reports, **Opinions**, and Orders, FP 1.20

Radionuclide Migration around Uranium **Ore** Bodies Analogue of Radioactive Waste Repositories, Y 3.N 88:25-11

Oregon
BLM Facts, **Oregon** and Washington, I 53.43/2
Conservation Vistas, Regional Conservation Education Newsletter Serving **Oregon** and Washington, A 13.72/2
Cultural Resources Series **Oregon**, I 53.22/10
Federal-State-Private Cooperative Snow Surveys: **Oregon**, A 57.46/5-2
Oregon and Washington Planned Land Sales, I 53.32
Oregon Annual Data Summary, Water Year, A 57.46/5-3
Pacific Coast, California, **Oregon**, Washington, and Hawaii, C 55.422:7
Tall Fescue, **Oregon**, A 92.19/13
U.S. Coast Pilots Pacific Coast, California, **Oregon**, Washington, and Hawaii, C 4.7/1

Organ
Organ Site Carcinogenesis Skin, HE 20.3173/2
Soil Conservation; Official **Organ**, A 76.208, A 79.207

Organic
Facts for Industry Series 6-2 and 6-10, **Organic** Chemicals and Plastic Materials, TC 1.25/2
Organic Chemistry: Air Pollution Studies Characterization of Chemical Structures; Synthesis of Research Materials, C 13.46
Preliminary Report on Production on Specified Synthetic **Organic** Chemicals in United States; Facts for Industry Series, TC 1.25
Preliminary Report on U.S. Production of Selected Synthetic **Organic** Chemicals, ITC 1.14/2
S.O.C. {Synthetic **Organic** Chemicals}, TC 1.25/3, TC 1.25/4
Soil **Organic** Matter Levels in the Central Great Plains, A 77.15/3
Synthetic **Organic** Chemicals, United States Production and Sales, Preliminaries, TC 1.33/2
Synthetic **Organic** Chemicals, United States Production and Sales, TC 1.33, ITC 1.14

Organisms
Radiation and **Organisms** Division, Reports, SI 1.1/a5

Organized
Roster of **Organizaed** Militia of United States, by Divisions, Brigades, Regiments, Companies, and other Organizations, with their Stations, W 70.5

Organization
Brief of the **Organization** and Functions Secretary of Defense Deputy Secretary of Defense etc., D 1.36
Change Sheets Applying to **Organization** Directory, W 3.42/2
Community **Organization** for Leisure, Serials, Y 3.W 89/2:28
Environmental Health Service Series on Community **Organization** Techniques, HE 20.1811
Field **Organization** News Letters, T 1.110
Functions and **Organization** of Bureau of Supplies and Accounts, Control Record, N 20.25
Government **Organization** Handbooks, GS 4.109/2
Government **Organization** Manuals, a Bibliography, LC 1.12/2:G 74
Headquarters, First United States Army, Deputy Chief of Staff, Information Management, **Organization**, Mission, and Functions, D 101.1/9
Instructions and Suggestions Relative to **Organization**, etc., of National Banks, T 12.8
Intermountain Region **Organization** Directory, A 13.36/2-3
International **Organization** and Conference Series, S 1.70
National Commission for United Nations Educational, Scientific and Cultural **Organization** Publications, S 5.48, S 5.48/9, S 5.48/10
National Institutes of Health **Organization** Handbook, FS 2.22/36
New Federal Credit Union Charters, Quarterly Report of **Organization**, FS 3.307
NMFS Northwest Region, **Organization** and Activities, Fiscal Year, C 55.301/2

Nongovernment **Organization** Codes for Military Standard Contract Administration Procedures, D 7.6/2:8
Nongovernment **Organization** Codes for Military Standard Contract Administration Procedures: Code to Name, D 7.6/2:8-1/2, D 7.6/2:8-2/2
Nongovernment **Organization** Codes for Military Standard Contract Administration Procedures: Name to Code, D 7.6/2:8-1/2
NPA **Organization** Statements, C 40.6/7
Organization and Fact Book, HE 20.3319
Organization and Policy Manual Letters, CS 1.7/3
Organization and Staffing for Full Time Local Health Services, FS 2.80
Organization Charts, Y 3.R 31:20
Organization Directory Adjutant General's Department, W 3.42
Organization Directory Civilian Production Administration, Pr 32.4830
Organization Directory, U.S. Department of Agriculture, A 60.10
Organization of Army, W 3.50/17
Organization of Federal Executive Departments and Agencies, Y 4.G 74/9-10
Organization Orders, VA 1.17
Organization Regulations, C 31.206/6
President's Advisory Council on Executive **Organization**, Pr 37.8:Ex 3
President's **Organization** of Unemployment Relief, C 1.15
Professional Standards Review **Organization**, Annual Report, HE 22.210
Program Memorandum Health Maintenance **Organization**/Competitive Medical Plan, HE 22.28/2
Publications President's **Organization** of Unemployment Relief, C 1.15
Report of United States Government to the Food and Agricultural **Organization** of the United Nations, A 67.35
Responsibilities and **Organization**, Y 10.20
Soil and Water Conservation Districts, Status of **Organization**, by States, Approximate Acreage, and Farms in Organized Districts, A 57.32
Spotlight on **Organization** and Supervision in Large High Schools, FS 5.50
Support to **Organizations** Theater, NF 2.8/2-33
Tables of **Organization** and Equipment, Department of the Air Force, M 301.7
Tables of **Organization** and Equipment, W 1.44, M 101.21, D 101.19
Tables of **Organization**, W 1.25, W 70.12
UNESCO World Review Weekly Radio News from United Nations Educational, Scientific, and Cultural **Organization**, Paris, France, S 5.48/6
United Nations Conference on International **Organization**, S 5.44
United Nations Educational, Scientific and Cultural **Organization** News {releases}, S 5.48/13
United States Government **Organization** Manual, GS 4.109
War Loan **Organization**, T 1.27

Organizational
APHIS **Organizational** Directory, A 101.21
Army **Organizational** Effectiveness Journal, D 101.91
Bureau of Naval Weapons Directory, **Organizational** Listing and Correspondence Designations, D 217.25
Forest Service **Organizational** Directory, A 13.36/2-2
Medicare Peer Review **Organizational** Manual, HE 22.8/15
Organizational Directory of Key Officials, PM 1.31/2

Organizations
Catalog of HEW Assistance Providing Financial Support and Service to States, Communities, **Organizations**, Individuals, HE 1.6/6
Cumulative List, **Organizations** Described in Section 170 (c) of the International Revenue Code of 1954, T 22.2:Or 3
Department of the Army Prime Contracts ($1 million and over) Placed with Industry, Non-Profit **Organizations**, Colleges, and Universities, D 101.22:715-4

Directory of American Agricultural **Organizations**, A 37.6
Directory of International Trade Union **Organizations**, L 29.9/2
Directory of Labor **Organizations** in {various countries}, L 2.72/4
Directory of Officers and **Organizations** Concerned with Protection of Birds and Game, A 5.8
Directory of Veterans **Organizations** and State Departments of Veterans Affairs, VA 1.62
Directory, Local Law Enforcement **Organizations** Participating in Aviation Security, TD 4.809
Exempt **Organizations** Current Developments, T 22.50
Focus on Health Maintenance **Organizations**, HE 20.20/2
Foreign Credits by United States Government, Status of Active Foreign Credits of United States Government and of International **Organizations**, T 1.45
Government **Organizations**, C 3.171
Grants to Presenting **Organizations**, Special Touring Initiatives Application Guidelines, NF 2.8/2-29
Health Maintenance **Organizations**, HE 20.20
Instructions and Data Specifications for Reporting DHHS Obligations to Institutions of Higher Education and Other Nonprofit **Organizations**, HE 20.3050
Inter-Arts, Presenting **Organizations** Artist Communities Services to the Arts, Application Guidelines, NF 2.8/2-23
International Application Guidelines, International Program: International Projects Initiative For **Organizations** Partnerships, NF 2.8/2-35
Legislative Objectives of Veterans' **Organizations**, Y 4.V 64/3:L 52/8
Monthly Reports of **Organizations** and Operations of Federal Credit Unions, A 72.14
Organizations Designated Under E.O. 10450, Consolidated List (SCS Form 385), CS 1.63
Organizations Visual Arts, Application Guidelines, NF 2.8/2-15
Register of Reporting Labor **Organizations**, L 1.84
Registered Bona Fide and Legitimate Farmers' Cooperative **Organizations** under Bituminous Coal Act of 1937, I 46.15
Roster of Organizaed Militia of United States, by Divisions, Brigades, Regiments, Companies, and other **Organizations**, with their Stations, W 70.5
State-Local Businessmen's **Organizations**, C 18.200/2
Union Conventions, (year), National and International Unions, State **Organizations**, L 1.85
Union Conventions, National and International Unions, State **Organizations**, L 2.85
United States Contributions to International **Organizations**, S 1.70, S 1.70/9
Visual Arts Grants to **Organizations**, NF 2.8/2-15
World Strength of the Communist Party **Organizations**, Annual Report, S 1.111

Organized
Guide to **Organized** Occupational Curriculums in Higher Education, FS 5.254:54012, HE 5.254:54012
Organized Reserves Bulletin, W 99.17/17
Organized Reserves Circular, W 99.16/12
Organized Reserves Memorandum, W 99.18/8

Oriental
Oriental Studies, SI 7.7

Orientation
Directory, Executive **Orientation** Courses in Automatic Data Processing, PrEx 2.12/2
IRIS, Earth **Orientation** Bulletin, C 55.437
Orientation Material, Tribal Operations, Administrative, I 20.49

Oriented
COBOL {Common Business **Oriented** Language}, D 1.31

Origin
Export **Origin** Studies {by State}, C 1.46
Foreign Agricultural Trade of the United States; Imports of Fruits and Vegetables under Quarantine by Countries of **Origin** and Ports of Entry, A 67.19/7, A 93.17/5
General Imports of Merchandise into United States by Air, Commodity by Country of **Origin**, C 3.164:231

General Imports of Merchandise into United States by Air, Country of **Origin** by Commodity, C 3.164:232

Persons of Spanish **Origin** in the United States, Advance Report, C 3.186/14

Report of Japan's Export Shipments and Import Receipts Stated by Areas and Countries of Destination and **Origin**, with Value Expressed in United States Dollars, D 102.11/3

Report on Volume of Water Borne Foreign Commerce of U.S. by Ports of **Origin** and Destination (fiscal year), C 27.9/10, MC 1.17

Science Education **Origin**, D 210.18

State Export-**Origin** Series: Exports from {State}, C 42.28

U.S. Exports of Petroleum and Petroleum Products of Domestic **Origin**, Commodity by Customs District, C 3.164:527

U.S. General Imports World Area and Country of **Origin** by Schedule A Commodity Groupings, C 3.164:155

U.S. Import for Consumption, USUSA Commodity by Country of **Origin**, C 56.210:146

U.S. Water Borne Intercoastal Traffic by Ports of **Origin** and Destination and Principal Commodities, SB 7.5/317, C 27.9/9, MC 1.9

Unemployment Rate by Race and Hispanic **Origin** in Major Metropolitan Areas, L 2.111/6

United States Airborne General Imports of Merchandise, Country of **Origin** by Commodity, C 3.164:390

United States Exports of Petroleum and Petroleum Products of Domestic **Origin**, Commodity by Country of Destination, C 3.164:526

United States General Imports of Cotton Manufacturers: Country of **Origin** by Geneva Agreement Category, C 56.210:130, C 3.164:130

United States General Imports of Merchandise, Commodity by Country of **Origin**, C 3.164:10

United States General Imports of Textile Manufactures, Except Cotton and Wool, Grouping by Country of **Origin** and Schedule a Commodity by Country of **Origin**, TQ-2501, C 3.164/2-7

United States General Imports of Wool Manufacture Except Floor Coverings, Quantity Totals in Terms of Equivalent Square Yards in Country of **Origin** by Commodity Grouping Arrangement, TQ-2203, C 3.164/2-6

United States General Imports of Wool Manufacture Except for Floor Coverings, Country of **Origin** by Wool Grouping, TQ- 2202, C 3.164/2-5

United States Imports of Merchandise for Consumption: Commodity by Country of **Origin**, C 3.164:110

United States Imports of Merchandise for Consumption; Country of **Origin** by Subgroup, C 3.164:120

United States, Airborne General Imports of Merchandise, Commodity by Country of **Origin**, C 3.164:380

Unloads of Tomatoes in 66 Cities by States of **Origin**, A 36.187

Original

Index of **Original** Surface Weather Records for Stations in {various States}, C 55.288

Originated

Tons of Revenue Freight **Originated** and Tons Terminated by States and by Commodity Class, IC 1.23/15:SS-7

Tons of Revenue Freight **Originated** and Tons Terminated in Carloads by Classes of Commodities and by Geographic Areas, Class 1 Steam Railways, IC 1 ste.42

ORO-

ORO- (series), HE 20.4113

ORP

ORP Contract Reports, EP 6.10/9

ORP/CSD

ORP/CSD (series), EP 6.10/3

ORP/SID

ORP/SID (series), EP 6.10/2

ORRC

ORRC Study Reports, Y 3.Ou 8:10

Orthophotoquad

Digital **Orthophotoquads** DOQ For, I 19.124

Index to **Orthophotoquad** Mapping, I 19.97

OSAHRE

OSAHRE Reports: Decisions of the Occupational Safety and Health Review Commission, Y 3.Oc 1:10

OSAP

OSAP Cultural Competence Series, HE 20.8018/5

OSAP Prevention Monograph (series), HE 20.8018/2

OSAP Put on the Brakes Bulletin, HE 20.8018/4

OSAP Technical Report (Series), HE 20.8018/3

OSC

OSC Update, J 21.5/3

OSERS

OSERS News in Print, ED 1.213, ED 1.85/3

OSFA

OSFA Program Book, ED 1.29/2

OSHA

Fiscal Year ... **OSHA** Training Institute Schedule of Courses and Registration Requirements, L 35.25

OSHA Documents and Files, L 35.26

OSHA National Training Institute Catalog of Courses, L 35.25/2

OSHA Safety and Health Standards Digests, L 35.6/4

OSHA Standards and Regulations, L 35.6/3

Safe Work Guide, **OSHA**, L 35.11

KEY>OSM

Technical Services and Research, **OSM**/TM-(series), I 71.3/2

Technical Services Research, **OSM**-TR-(series), I 71.3

OSPAM-

OSPAM- (series), D 105.27

OSRD

Catalog of **OSRD** Reports, LC 29.8

OSRD {reports}, Pr 32.413/3

OST

TA/**OST**- (series), S 18.42/2

OST-NDER

OST-NDER Bulletin, TD 1.43

OST/TST

OST/TST Reports, TD 1.20/3

Osteopathic

National Health Service Corps Scholarship Program Information Bulletin for Students of Allopathic Medicine, **Osteopathic** Medicine, and Dentistry, HE 20.5011

OSWER

OSWER Training Course Catalog, EP 1.103

OT

OT Contractor Reports, C 1.60/7

OT Series, L 38.20/6

OT Special Publication (series), C 1.60/2

OT Technical Memorandums, C 1.60/8

OT- (series), A 108.11

OTB

Bulletins, **OTB** (series), C 1.60/4

OTC

List of **OTC** Margin Stocks, FR 1.46/4

OTES

OTES (series), C 55.13

Other

Other Carriers {12-month comparisons}, C 31.247/2

Other Carriers {quarterly comparisons}, C 31.247

Other Regulations and Procedures, C 35.6/3

Other Synthetic and Natural Fuels, E 1.99

OTR

Reports, **OTR**- (series), C 1.60/3

Review of Selected U.S. Government Research and Development Reports, **OTR**-(series), C 13.49

OTS

OTS Briefs, C 41.102

OTS Technology Guide Circulars, C 35.12

Special Announcements Concerning Research Reports from Department of Commerce **OTS**, C 41.28/2

OTT

OTT Times, E 1.128

Ottawa

Ottawa National Forest, A 13.28/a

Our

Our Library Presents, ITC 1.9/2

Our Merchant Fleet, MC 1.28

Our Nation's Highways: Selected Facts and Figures, TD 2.23/6

Our Nation's Children, FS 3.212, L 5.49

Our Own Spanish-American Citizens and the Southwest Which They Colonized, I 29.40

Our Public Lands, I 53.12

Our Rivers, I 27.25

Our War, W 3.80

Our Wonder World, I 16.56/3

Out

Starting **Out** Series, SBA 1.35

Outbreaks

Foodborne and Waterborne Disease **Outbreaks**, Annual Summary, HE 20.7011/13

National Communicable Disease Center Foodborne **Outbreaks**, Annual Summary, FS 2.60/18

Outbreaks of Disease Caused by Milk and Milk Products as Reported by Health Authorities as having Occurred in U.S., T 27.42

Psoroptic Sheep Scabies **Outbreaks** in (State), A 77.240

Water-Related Disease **Outbreaks** Surveillance, HE 20.7011/33

Outdoor

Appraisal of Potentials for **Outdoor** Recreational Development {by Area}, A 57.57

Catalog of Guides to **Outdoor** Recreation Areas and Facilities, I 66.15:G 94

Index to Selected **Outdoor** Recreation Literature, I 66.15:L 71

Nationwide **Outdoor** Recreation Plan, I 70.20

Northeast Region **Outdoor** Memo, I 66.21

Outdoor Recreation Action, I 66.17

Outdoor Recreation Grants-In-Aid Manual, I 66.8

Outdoor Recreation Research, I 66.18

Outdoors

National Forests, America's Great **Outdoors**, A 13.122

Outdoors in the Santa Monica Mountains National Recreation Area, I 29.6/7, I 29.135

Outer

Outer Continental Shelf Environmental Assessment Program Final Reports of Principal Investigators, C 55.433

Outer Continental Shelf Environmental Studies Advisory Committee: Publications, I 1.99/2

Outer Continental Shelf Oil and Gas Information Program, Summary Reports (various regions), I 72.9

Outer Continental Shelf Oil and Gas Leasing and Production Program Annual Report, I 72.12/3-2

Outer Continental Shelf Research Management Advisory Board: Annual Report, I 1.99

Outer Continental Shelf Standard, GSS-OCS (series), I 19.73

Outer Continental Shelf Statistical Summary, I 72.12/3-3

Pacific **Outer** Continental Shelf Studies Program (OCS) Statistical Reports, I 72.12/3-4

Outlays

Federal **Outlays**, PrEx 10.24

Monthly Statement of Receipts and **Outlays** of the United States Government, T 1.5/2

Outlets

Annual Maximum, Minimum, and Mean Discharges of Mississippi River and Its **Outlets** and Tributaries, D 103.309/2

Consumer Purchases of Fruits and Juices by Regions and Retail **Outlets**, A 36.171/2

Stages and Discharges, Mississippi River and its **Outlets** and Tributaries, W 31.5, M 110.207, D 103.309

Outline

Administrative Review **Outline**, L 7.45

Area **Outline** Maps Series 1105, D 5.325-D 5.325/2

Classification **Outline** for Decisions of the NLRB and Related Court Decisions, LR 1.8/7

Classification **Outline** Scheme of Classes, LC 9.5

Consumer Study **Outline**, A 55.53

Current Issue **Outline** (series), C 55.235

Maps (miscellaneous) Includes U.S. **Outline** Maps, C 3.62/2

Outline Maps, A 36.37

Outline of Agricultural Conservation Program, A 55.44/12

Suggested Co-op Electrification Adviser Training **Outline**, A 68.16

Outlines

Cost System **Outlines**, S 17.40

Foreign Policy **Outlines**, S 1.25/3

Joint Military Packaging Training Center Course **Outlines**, D 1.35

Outlook

National Security Seminar Presentation **Outlines** and Reading List, D 5.9/2
Outlines, LR 1.11
Procedure for Making Soil Conservation Surveys, **Outlines**, A 57.17

Outlook
Agricultural and Credit **Outlook**, FCA 1.24
Agricultural Land Values and Markets, **Outlook** and Situation Report, A 93.29/2-4
Agricultural **Outlook**, A 92.10/2
Agricultural **Outlook** Chartbook, A 1.98
Agricultural **Outlook** Charts, A 88.8/3, A 88.8/2
Agricultural **Outlook** Digest, A 93.10, A 88.9/3
Agriculture **Outlook**, A 105.27
Annual Energy **Outlook**, with Projections to (year), E 3.1/4
Annual **Outlook** for Oil and Gas, E 3.11/7-10
Annual **Outlook** for U.S. Coal, E 3.11/7-8
Annual **Outlook** for U.S. Electric Power, E 3.50
Asia and Pacific Rim, Situation and **Outlook** Series, A 93.29/2-19
Basin **Outlook** Reports (Washington), A 57.46/7
Cropland Use and Supply, **Outlook** and Situation Report, A 93.29/2-14
Current Information on Occupational **Outlook**, VA 1.31
Dairy, Situation and **Outlook** Yearbook, A 93.13/2-2
Eastern Europe, Situation and **Outlook** Report, A 93.29/2-10
Employment **Outlook** for {various occupations}, L 13.2
Environmental **Outlook**, EP 1.93
Federal Employment **Outlook**, CS 1.72/3
Federal Workforce **Outlook**, CS 1.72/2
Feed **Outlook** and Situation Report, A 93.11/2
Feed, **Outlook** and Situation Yearbook, A 93.11/2-2
Five-year **Outlook** on Science and Technology, NS 1.40/2
Food Fish Situation and **Outlook**, Annual Review Issue, I 49.8/7
Food Fish, Market Review and **Outlook**, C 55.309/5
Fruit **Outlook** and Situation Report, A 93.12/3
Gateway **Outlook**, I 29.96/3
Industrial Fishery Products, Situation and **Outlook** CEA I (series), C 55.309/3, I 49.8/9
Industrial **Outlook** and Economy at Midyear, C 41.42/4
Inputs **Outlook** and Situation, A 93.47
Lake Mead Water Supply **Outlook**, I 27.43
Occupational **Outlook** Briefs {Excerpts from Occupational Outlook Handbook}, L 2.3/a 2
Occupational **Outlook** for College Graduates, L 2.3
Occupational **Outlook** Handbook, L 2.3, L 2.3/4, L 2.3/4-4
Occupational **Outlook** Publications, L 2.70
Occupational **Outlook** Quarterly, L 2.70/4
Occupational **Outlook** Report Series, L 2.3
Occupational **Outlook** Review, VA 1.37
Occupational **Outlook** Summary, L 2.70/2
Oil Crops **Outlook** and Situation Report, A 93.23/2
Oil Crops, Situation and **Outlook** Yearbook, A 93.23/2-2
OMBE **Outlook**, News from the Office of Minority Business Enterprise, C 1.57/2
Outlook, HE 20.3766
Outlook and Situation Reports (various areas), A 93.29/2
Outlook and Situation, Summary, A 93.29/2-17
Outlook and Year-End Economic Review, C 1.41
Outlook Charts, A 36.50
Outlook for Agricultural Exports, A 1.80/2
Outlook for Timber in the United States, A 13.50:20/2
Outlook for U.S. Agricultural Exports, A 93.43
Outlook, ED 1.409, J 16.14
Overseas **Outlook**, LC 19.13/3
Pacific Rim Agriculture and Trade Reports: Situation and **Outlook** Series, A 92.29/2-19
Personal Computer-Annual Energy **Outlook**, E 3.1/5
Poultry and Egg **Outlook**, A 36.72
Reprints from the Occupational **Outlook** Handbook, Bulletins, L 2.3/4 a
Rice, Situation and **Outlook** Report, A 93.11/3
Secretary's Annual Report to Congress, Posture Statement, **Outlook** and Program Review, E 1.60:0010

Shellfish Situation and **Outlook**, CEA-S (series), C 55.309/4, I 49.8/8
Short-term Energy **Outlook**, E 3.31
Snow Surveys and Water Supply **Outlook** for Alaska, A 57.46/13
South Asia **Outlook** and Situation Report, A 93.29/2-15
Sub-Saharan Africa, Situation and **Outlook** Report, A 93.29/2-13
Sugar and Sweetener, **Outlook** and Situation, A 105.53/2, A 93.31/3
Sugar and Sweetener, Situation and **Outlook** Report, A 93.31/3
Sugar and Sweetener, Situation and **Outlook** Yearbook, A 93.31/3-2
Synopsis of the Annual Energy Review and **Outlook**, E 3.1/3
Tobacco, Situation and **Outlook** Report, A 93.25
Tobacco, Situation and **Outlook** Yearbook, A 93.25/2
U.S. Industrial **Outlook** for 200 Industries with Projections for (year), C 62.17
U.S. Industrial **Outlook**, (year), with Projections to (year), C 57.309
U.S. Industrial **Outlook**, C 57.18, C 61.34
U.S. Industry and Trade **Outlook**, C 61.48
U.S. Trade Performance in (year) and **Outlook**, C 61.28
USSR Grain Situation and **Outlook**, A 67.18:SG
USSR, Situation and **Outlook** Report, A 93.29/2-8
Utah Water Supply **Outlook**, A 57.46/6
Vegetable Situation and **Outlook** Yearbook, A 93.12/2-3
Vegetable, Situation and **Outlook**, A 93.12/2
Water Supply **Outlook** for Northeastern United States, C 55.113/2
Water Supply **Outlook** for Western United States, Water Year, C 55.113
Water Supply **Outlook** Reports, A 57.46
Water Supply **Outlook**, Federal-State-Private Cooperative Snow Surveys {Colorado}, A 57.46/15
Weather **Outlook**, A 29.38, C 30.13
Western Europe, Situation and **Outlook** Report, A 93.29/2-9
Western Hemisphere, **Outlook** and Situation Report, A 93.29/2-18
Wheat **Outlook** and Situation Report, A 93.11
Wheat, **Outlook** and Situation Yearbook, A 93.11/2-3
World Agricultural **Outlook** and Situation, A 93.29/2
World Grain Situation and **Outlook**, A 67.18:FG

Outlooks
Agricultural **Outlooks** (individual), A 36.83
Food Fish, Situation and **Outlooks**, I 49.8/6

Outlying
Population, **Outlying** Possessions, C 3.940-39

Outlying Areas
Economic Censuses of **Outlying Areas**, C 56.259
Economic Censuses of **Outlying Areas**, OAC (Series), C 3.253/2

Outpatient
Directory of **Outpatient** Psychiatric Clinics, Psychiatric Day-Night Services and Other Mental Health Resources in the United States and Territories, FS 2.22/38-4
Medicare **Outpatient** Physical Therapy Provider Manual, HE 22.8/9
Outpatient Psychiatric Clinics, Community Service Activities, FS 2.22/38-3
Outpatient Psychiatric Clinics, Special Statistical Series Reports, FS 2.22/40

Output
Description of **Output** Indicators by Function for the Federal Government, L 2.133
ES 2 U.S. Commodity Exports and Imports Related to **Output**, C 3.229
Indexes of **Output** Per Man-Hour for the Private Economy, L 2.89/2
Indexes of **Output** Per Man-Hour, Hourly Compensation, and Unit Labor Costs in the Private Sector of the Economy and the Nonfarm Sector, L 2.2:Ou 8/8
Indexes of **Output** Per Man-Hour, Selected Industries, L 2.89
Output of Refineries in United States, I 28.19
U.S. Commodity Exports and Imports As Related to **Output**, C 56.232
Weekly Electric **Output**, United States, FP 1.11/7

Outreach
Outreach, D 214.31, SBA 1.46

Outside

Classification of Revenues and Expenses by **Outside** Operations, IC 1 ste.10
Monthly List of **Outside** Publications and Addresses, I 49.18/4
Where to Write for Birth and Death Records of U.S. Citizens Who Were Born or Died **Outside** of the United States and Birth Certifications for Alien Children Adopted by U.S. Citizens, FS 2.102:B 53/7

Outstanding
Commercial and Industrial Loans **Outstanding** by Industry, FR 1.39/2
Consumer Finance Companies, Loans **Outstanding** and Volume of Loans Made, FR 1.36/6
Interest Bearing Debt **Outstanding**, T 62.8
Market Prices and Investment Values of **Outstanding** Bonds and Notes, T 50.5
Market Prices and Yields of **Outstanding** Bonds, Notes, and Bills of U.S., T 62.7
Maturity Distribution of **Outstanding** Negotiable Time Certificates of Deposit, FR 1.54/2
Monthly Statement of Paper Currency of Each Denomination **Outstanding**, T 40.8
Paper Currency of Each Denomination **Outstanding**, Monthly Statements, T 63.307

OVC
OVC Fact Sheets, J 34.4
OVC's Legal Series Bulletin, J 34.3/3

Over
Over Change Claim Circulars, Y 3.R 13/2:35

Over-the-Counter
Over-the-Counter Brokers and Dealers Registered with Securities & Exchange Commission, SE 1.15

Overdue
Rules Pertaining to Aircraft Accidents, Incidents, **Overdue** Aircraft, and Safety Investigations, TD 1.106/2

Overfishing
Report to Congress on Ocean Pollution, **Overfishing**, and Offshore Development, C 55.31/2

Overlap
Overlap, Measurement Agreement through Process Evaluation, C 13.56

Overriding
General **Overriding** Regulations, ES 3.6/9

Overseas
Certificated Air Carrier Financial Data; Foreign or **Overseas** {12-month comparisons}, C 31.236/2
Certificated Air Carrier Financial Data; Foreign or **Overseas** {quarterly comparisons}, C 31.236
Federal Real Property and Personal Property Inventory Report of the United States Government Covering its Properties Located in the U.S., in the Territories, and **Overseas**, as of June 30 (year), Y 4.G 74/7:P 94
Foreign, **Overseas** and Territorial Air Mail Carriers, C 31.231
General Real and Personal Property Inventory Report (Civilian and Military) of the U.S. Government Covering Its Properties Located in the U.S., in the Territories, and **Overseas**, As of June 30 {year}, Y 4.G 74/7:P 94
Newsmap, **Overseas** Edition, W 109.208
Overseas Business Reports, C 1.50, C 57.11, C 61.12
Overseas Common Carrier Section 214 Applications for Filing, CC 1.36/4
Overseas Employment Opportunities for Educators, D 1.68
Overseas Export Promotion Calendar, C 57.117, C 61.19
Overseas Outlook, LC 19.13/3
Overseas Television Developments, IA 1.16
Overseas Trade Promotion Calendar, C 57.12
Recurrent Report of Mileage and Traffic Data Foreign, **Overseas** and Territorial Air Mail Carriers, C 31.231
U.S. Great Lakes Ports, Statistics for **Overseas** and Canadian Waterborne Commerce, TD 6.10

Oversight
Subcommittee on **Oversight** and Investigations of the Committee on Energy and Commerce, Y 4.En 2/3-12

Overview
Budget of the U.S. Government: Director's Introduction and **Overview** Tables, PrEx 2.8/11

Cultural Resources **Overview** (series), A 13.101

Environmental **Overview** and Analysis of Mining Effects, I 29.101

Oncology **Overview**, NCI/ICRDB, HE 20.3173/3

Overview of Endowment Programs, NF 3.15

Profiles in School Support, Decennial **Overview**, FS 5.222:22022, HE 5.222:22022

R & D Technology Transfer, an **Overview**, E 1.109

Radiation Exposure **Overview**, OCS (series), HE 20.1111

State Energy **Overview**, E 3.42/2

Wind Energy Program **Overview**, E 1.38/5

Overviews

Preservation Planning Series, State Program **Overviews**, I 29.102

Owl's

Woodsy **Owl's** Campaign Catalog, A 13.111

Owned

Detailed Listing of Real Property **Owned** by the United States and Used by Civil Agencies Throughout the World, GS 1.15/4

Detailed Listing of Real Property **Owned** by the United States and Used by the Department of Defense for Military Functions Throughout the World, GS 1.15/4-2

Dry Cargo Service and Area Report, United States Dry Cargo Shipping Companies by Ships **Owned** and/or Chartered Type of Service and Area Operated, A 82.307

FHA and VA Mortgages **Owned** and Available for Sale by Reconstruction Finance Corporation and Federal National Mortgage Association, Y 3.R 24:14

List of American and Foreign Ships **Owned** under Requisition of Chartered to Shipping Board, SB 2.11

Revenues and Income of Privately **Owned** Class A & B Electric Utilities in the U.S., FP 1.11/5

Statement of Loans and Commodities **Owned**, A 71.7, A 82.307

Statement of Taxes, Dividends, Salaries and Wages, Class a and Class B Privately **Owned** Electric Utilities in U.S., FP 1.22

Statements of Loans and Commodities **Owned**, A 80.407

Statistics of Electric Utilities in the United States, Classes A and B Publicly **Owned** Companies, FP 1.21

Statistics of Privately **Owned** Electric Utilities in the United States, E 3.18/2

Statistics of Publicly **Owned** Electric Utilities in the United States, E 3.18/3

Stocks of Leaf Tobacco **Owned** by Dealers and Manufacturers, A 80.124

Women **Owned** Businesses, C 3.250

Owner-Occupied

Expenditures for Additions, Alterations, Maintenance and Repairs, and Replacements on One-Housing-Unit **Owner-Occupied** Properties, C 3.215/8:Pt-2

Owners

Geographic Distribution of Radio Sets and Characteristics of Radio **Owners** in Countries of the World, IA 1.12/2

Home **Owners'** Loan Corporation Publications, FL 3.9, Y 3.F 31/3:8

Publications Home **Owners'** Loan Corporation, FL 3.9

Ownership

Number of New Permanent Nonfarm Dwelling Units Started by Urban or Rural Location, Public or Private **Ownership**, and Type of Structure, L 2.51/4

Presidential Advisory Committee on Small and Minority Business **Ownership**, Annual Report, PrEx 1.16

Summary of Equity Security Transactions and **Ownership** of Directors, Officers, and Principal Stockholders of Member State Banks As Reported Pursuant to

Owning

Cost of **Owning** and Operating Automobiles and Vans, TD 2.60

OWRT

Technology, **OWRT**-TT, I 1.97/5

Water Reuse, **OWRT**/RU- , I 1.97/3

Oxide

Iron **Oxide** Pigments in (year), I 28.163

Zinc **Oxide**, I 28.90

Oxides

Sulfur **Oxides** Control Technology Series, EP 7.12

Oxygen

Oxygen {abstracts}, C 41.50

Oyster

Certified Shippers of Fresh and Frozen **Oyster**, Clams, and Mussels, FS 2.16

P

P&SA

P&SA (series), A 96.10

P-1

Personnel Handbook, Series **P-1**, Position Description and Salary Schedules, Transmittal Letters, P 1.31

P-90

International Population Statistics Reports, P 90-(series), C 59.13/2:90

P-90 International Population Statistics Reports, C 3.205

P. and S.

P. and S. Docket, Monthly Report of Action Stockyards Act, A 88.16/5

P. and S. Docket, Monthly Report of Action Taken on Cases Arising Under Packers and Stockyards Act, A 82.14

P.A.D.

P.A.D. Districts Supply/Demand, E 3.11/6-2, E 3.11/6-3, E 3.11/6-4, I 28.18/6, I 28.18/7,

Supply, Demand, and Stocks of All Oils by **P.A.D.** Districts, I 28.18/7

P.B.A.

P.B.A. Circulars, A 49.4

P.C.

P.C. Producer-Consumer Series, A 55.65

P.D.C.

P.D.C. Manuals, CS 1.40

P.P.C.

P.P.C. (series), A 77.308/4

P.S.

P.S. Payroll Savings Bulletin, T 66.16

PA

Public Affairs **PA** (series), FCD 1.13

PA-B

{Public Affairs} Booklet **PA-B** (series), FCD 1.17/2

PA-F

Public Affairs Flyer **PA-F** (series), FCD 1.17

PACAF

PACAF {Pacific Air Forces} Basic Bibliographies, D 301.62

Pacesetter

Pacesetter, C 1.94

Pacesetters

Pacesetters in Innovation, FS 5.220:20103, HE 5.220:20103

Pacific

Airman's Guide and Flight Information Manual; **Pacific** Supplement, FAA 1.25

Airman's Guide; **Pacific** Supplement, FAA 1.25/3

Anglers' Guide to the United States **Pacific** Coast, C 55.308:An 4/2

Annual Fish Passage Report, North **Pacific** Divisions, D 103.27

Annual Peak Discharge at Selected Gaging Stations in **Pacific** Northwest, I 19.45/4

Annual Summary of Water Quality Data for Selected Sites in the **Pacific** Northwest, I 19.46/3

Army Air Forces Radio and Facility Charts North **Pacific** Area, W 108.27

Asia and **Pacific** Rim, Situation and Outlook Series, A 93.29/2-19

Average Monthly Discharge for 15-year Base Period at Selected Gaging Stations and Change of Storage in Certain Lakes and Reservoirs in **Pacific** Northwest, I 19.45/3-2

Central **Pacific**, Western **Pacific**, and South **Pacific** Fisheries Development Program Report for Calendar Year, C 55.329

Chart Supplement **Pacific**, TD 4.79/3

Climatological Data; **Pacific**, C 30.19/2

Commercial Wheat Farms, Plains and **Pacific** Northwest, A 93.9/11

Current Discharge at Selected Stations in the **Pacific** Northwest, I 19.45, I 19.47/2

East Asian and **Pacific** Series, S 1.38

Environmental Quality Profile, **Pacific** Northwest Region, EP 1.87/2

Flight Information Manual, **Pacific** Supplement, FAA 1.25/4

Flight Information Publication: Terminal High Altitude, **Pacific** and Southeast Asia, D 301.12/4

Flight Information Publication: Terminal Low Altitude, **Pacific** and Southeast Asia, D 301.12/3

Forest Insect and Disease Conditions in the **Pacific** Northwest, A 13.52/6

Forest Insect Conditions in **Pacific** Northwest During (year), A 13.52/6

High Commissioner of Trust Territory of **Pacific** Islands, I 35.16

Hydrologic Bulletin, Hourly and Daily Precipitation; **Pacific** District, C 30.36

Hydrologic Bulletin, Hourly and Daily Precipitation; South **Pacific** District, C 30.31

Important Facts About the **Pacific** Northwest Region, A 13.117

Instrument Approach Procedure Charts {Alaska, Hawaii, U.S. **Pacific** Islands}, C 55.411/2

Light List, **Pacific** Coast of United States, N 24.19, T 47.25

Lights and Fog Signals, **Pacific** Coast and British Columbia, T 25.18

Local List of Lights and Other Marine Aids, **Pacific**, T 47.25/2

Lumber Shipments from **Pacific** Coast to Atlantic Coast, SB 7.5/162

Marine Calendar, **Pacific**, A 29.42

Marine Recreational Fishery Statistics Survey, **Pacific** Coast, C 55.309/2-5

Migration and Settlement on **Pacific** Coast, Reports, A 36.131

Military Aviation Notices; Corrections to Supplementary Flight Information Document, **Pacific** and Far East, D 301.50/2

Military Aviation Notices; **Pacific**, D 301.12/2

New Reports by Geological Survey About Water in the **Pacific** Northwest, I 19.14/5

Number of New Dwelling Units and Permit Valuation of Building Construction Authorized by Class of Construction in Mountain and **Pacific** Division by Civil Division and State, L 2.51, L 2.51/2, L 2.51/3

PACAF {**Pacific** Air Forces} Basic Bibliographies, D 301.62

Pacific Airman's Guide and Chart Supplement, TD 4.16

Pacific and Arctic Coasts, Alaska, Cape Spencer to Beaufort Sea, C 55.422:9

Pacific Basin Consortium for Hazardous Waste Research Newsletter, E 1.110

Pacific Coast and **Pacific** Islands, TD 5.9:3

Pacific Coast Salmon Park, C 6.11

Pacific Coast States Fisheries, C 55.309/2

Pacific Coast, Alaska, Dixon Entrance to Cape Spencer, C 55.422:8

Pacific Coast, California, Oregon, Washington, and Hawaii, C 55.422:7

Pacific Coaster's Nautical Almanac, N 11.8

Pacific Flyway, I 49.24/5

Pacific Halibut Fishery Regulations, S 5.35:5

Pacific Marine Environmental Laboratory: Annual Report, C 55.601/2

Pacific Northwest and Alaska Bioenergy Program Yearbook, E 5.12

Pacific Northwest Environmental Research Laboratory: Quarterly Progress Report, EP 1.19

Pacific Northwest Monthly Precipitation and Temperature, C 55.114

Pacific Northwest Monthly Streamflow Summary, I 19.46/4

Pacific Northwest Research Station: Miscellaneous Publications, A 13.129

Pacific Northwest Water Laboratory: Quarterly Progress Report, EP 2.22

Pacific Northwest Water Resources Summary, I 19.46

Pacific Outer Continental Shelf Studies Program (OCS) Statistical Reports, I 72.12/3-4

Pacific Region, C 55.118/5, C 55.119

Pacific Rim Agriculture and Trade Reports: Situation and Outlook Series, A 92.29/2-19

Pacific Salmon Pack, I 49.23

Pacific Summary/Index, I 72.9/7

Pacific Waterfowl Flyway Report, I 49.55/2

Pilot Rules for Certain Inland Waters of Atlantic and Pacific Coasts of Gulf of Mexico, C 25.9

Publications Pacific Northwest Forest and Range Experiment Station, A 13.66/15

Recent Publications of the Pacific Northwest Forest and Range Experiment Station, A 13.66/14

Report of Trust Territory of Pacific Islands Transmitted to United Nations, I 35.16/8

Retail Trade Report Pacific Region, C 3.181

Review of Power Planning in Pacific Northwest, Calendar Year, Y 3.P 11/4:9

River Temperature at Selected Stations in the Pacific Northwest, I 19.46/2-2, I 19.46/2-3

Seafaring Wage Rates, Atlantic, Gulf and Pacific Districts, C 39.202:W 12

Terminal High Altitude, Pacific and Southeast Asia, D 301.12/4

Tide Tables Pacific Coast, T 11.14, C 14.14

Trust Territory of the Pacific Islands, S 1.70/7

Trust Territory of the Pacific Islands, Annual Report on Administration of the Territory of the Pacific Islands, S 1.70

U.S. Air Force Radio Facility Charts, North Pacific Area, M 301.14

U.S. Coast Pilots Pacific Coast, California, Oregon, Washington, and Hawaii, C 4.7/1

U.S. Trust Territory of the Pacific, Series 9203, D 5.339

Union Pacific Railway, Government Directors, Annual Reports, 1864-1898, I 1.30

United States Air Force and Navy Supplementary Flight Information Document, Pacific and Far East, D 301.50

United States Air Force and United States Navy Radio Facility Charts, Central Pacific-Far East, D 301.12

United States Government Flight Information Publication: Pacific Chart Supplement, C 55.427

Weekly Runoff Report, Pacific Northwest Water Resources, I 19.46/2

Working Papers Environmental Protection Agency, Pacific Northwest Environmental Research Laboratory, EP 1.37/2

Pacific Ocean

Explorations and Surveys for Railroad from Mississippi River to Pacific Ocean, W 7.14

Meteorological Chart of the North Pacific Ocean, A 29.24

Meteorological Chart of the South Pacific Ocean, A 29.26

Pilot Chart of North Pacific Ocean, N 6.16, M 202.19, D 203.19

Pilot Chart of South Pacific Ocean, N 6.12, M 202.20, D 203.20

Pilot Chart of Upper Air, North Pacific Ocean, N 6.29

Tide Tables Central and Western Pacific Ocean and Indian Ocean, C 4.15/6

Tide Tables Pacific Ocean and Indian Ocean, C 4.15/2

Tide Tables, High and Low Water Predictions Central and Western Pacific Ocean and Indian Ocean, C 55.421/4

Pack

Current Business Reports; Canned Food, Stock, Pack, Shipments, B-1 (series), C 56.219/8

Pacific Salmon Pack, I 49.23

Package

Command Information Package, D 101.118/5

Implementation Package (series), TD 2.36

Package X, Informational Copies of Federal Tax Forms, T 22.2/12

Prescriptive Package Series, J 1.8/3, J 26.13

Review of Waste Package Verification Test, Y 3.N 88:25-3

Student Package (series), D 101.47/8

System Package Program, NS-SPP- (series), TD 4.30

Packaged

Packaged Fishery Products, C 55.309/2

Packaged Literature Searches (series), C 55.229/3

Packaged-Fuel

Fuel-Briquets and Packaged-Fuel Producers, Annual, I 28.109

Packages

Consumer Information TV Program Packages, Suggested Scripts, A 21.27

Sending Gift Packages to Various Countries, C 49.9

Packaging

Army-Navy Joint Packaging Instructions, N 20.27

Containers and Packaging, C 18.242, C 40.12, C 41.33, C 57.314, C 57.513

Joint Military Packaging Training Center Course Outlines, D 1.35

Joint Military-Industry Packaging and Materials Handling Symposium, D 101.51

Packaging Requirements Code, D 7.20:726C

School of Military Packaging Technology Booklets, SMPT-BKLT- (series), D 105.31

Packed

Imported Dates Packed and Shipped, C 3.130

Packers

P. and S. Docket, Monthly Report of Action Taken on Cases Arising Under Packers and Stockyards Act, A 82.14

Packers and Stockyards Resume, A 88.16/5-2, A 96.9

Packers and Stockyards Statistical Report, A 113.15

Packet

Radio-TV Packet, FS 13.124

Page

Age Page (series), HE 20.3861

CD News Feature Page, D 1.34

Title Page and Index to Opinions, Ju 8.6

Woman's Page Feature, Y 3.F 31/11:25

Women's Page Clip Sheets, Y 3.F 31/11:15

Pageants

Plays and Pageants, Y 3.W 27/2:12

Pages

Contents, Format and Concepts of Federal Budget, Reprint of Selected Pages from Budget of United States Government, PrEx 2.8

Special Picture Pages, T 1.112

Paid

Allotments, Authorizations, and Paid Shipments, Data, FO 1.9/2

National Survey of Compensation Paid Scientists and Engineers Engaged in Research and Development Activities, E 1.34

Paid Shipments (by country), Special Statements, Y 3.Ec 74/3:13-2

Paid Shipments, European and Far East Program, FO 1.9

Paid Shipments, Y 3.Ec 74/3:13, Pr 33.909

Prices Paid by Farmers, A 36.75

Pain

Report of the Panel on Pain to the National Advisory Neurological and Communicative Disorders and Stroke Council, HE 20.3517

Paint

Digest of Trade Hints for Paint and Varnish Merchants, C 18.194

Paint, Varnish, Lacquer, and Fillers, C 3.94

Painting

National Painting and Decorating Apprenticeship and Training Standards Adopted by the National Joint Painting and Decorating Apprenticeship and Training Committee, L 23.2:P 16

Paints

Plastic Paints, Cold Water Paints, and Calcimines, C 3.96

World Trade in Paints and Varnishes, C 18.171

World Trade in Plastic Paints, C 18.172

Pakistan

Accession List: Pakistan, LC 1.30/2

Pakistan, Index {cumulations}, LC 1.30/2-3

Pakistan, LC 1.30/2

Palate

Cleft Palate Team Directory, HE 20.3402:C 58/2

Paleobiology

Smithsonian Contributions to Paleobiology, SI 1.30

Paleoclimate

NOAA Paleoclimate Publications Series Report (series), C 55.241

Paleoclimate Data Record, C 55.240

Palmas

Island of Palmas Arbitration, S 3.18/6

Palsy

NINCDS Cerebral Palsy Research Program, HE 20.3502:C 33/3

PAM

Pamphlets PAM- (series), NAS 1.75

U.S. Army Recruiting Command Pamphlets, USAREC PAM- (series), D 101.22/7

USAADASCH PAM (series), D 101.22/14

USAAVNC PAM- (series), D 101.22/11

Pamphlet

ARPC Pamphlet (series), , D 301.35/9

FB Pamphlet (series), D 103.109/3

Pamphlet EP (series), D 103.43

Session Laws of Pamphlet Laws (State Department edition), S 7.6:C & S

Session Laws, or Pamphlet Laws (Little, Brown and Company edition), S 7.13:C & S

Student Pamphlet (series), D 103.120/3

TRADOC Pamphlet (series), D 101.22/22

USAEHA Pamphlet, D 105.33

USAFAC Pamphlet (series), D 101.22/21

Pamphlets

AHS Pamphlets, D 101.22/19

CCPM Pamphlets {Commissioned Corps Personnel Manual}, HE 20.13

Changes in Marine Corps Pamphlets, N 9.12

DARCOM Pamphlets, D 101.22/3

Education and National Defense Series Pamphlets, FS 5.22

Library List of Pamphlets, Books, Etc., A 68.10

List of Books, Pamphlets, and Maps Received, New Series, S 8.7

OFPP Pamphlets, PrEx 2.22

1A Pamphlets (series), D 101.22/9-2

Ordnance Corps Pamphlets, D 105.9

Ordnance Pamphlets, OP- (series), D 215.9

Pamphlets Civil Service Commission, CS 1.48

Pamphlets Community Services Administration, CSA 1.9

Pamphlets Department of the Air Force, D 301.35/3

Pamphlets Federal Employees' Compensation Office, L 36.309

Pamphlets Merit Systems Protection Board, MS 1.9

Pamphlets National Guard Bureau, D 12.8

Pamphlets Naval Supply Systems Command, D 211.12

Pamphlets Oceanographer of the Navy, D 218.9

Pamphlets PAM- (series), NAS 1.75

Pamphlets Personnel Management Office, PM 1.10

Pamphlets Veterans Administration, VA 1.19

Pamphlets Women's Bureau, L 36.112

Pamphlets Worker's Compensation Programs Office, L 36.409

QMC Pamphlets, D 106.13

Radio Communication Pamphlets, W 42.29

Reports, Consolidated Pamphlets, Ju 11.7/a2

Safety Pamphlets, GP 1.18

Second Army Pamphlets (series), D 101.22/9

Security Pamphlets, Y 3.At 7:18

Sherman Pamphlets, I 20.30

Signal School Pamphlets, W 42.34/6

Supply and Maintenance Command, SMC Pamphlets, D 101.22/5

Technical Information Pamphlets, D 103.53/6

Technical Personnel Pamphlets, D 12.8/2

10th Mountain Division (LI) and Fort Drum: Pamphlets (series), D 101.22/23

Text Pamphlets (series), D 104.31/2

Training Pamphlets, W 42.31

Transportation Corps Pamphlets, W 109.307

U.S. Army Military Personnel Center: Pamphlets (series), D 101.22/16

U.S. Army Recruiting Command Pamphlets, USAREC PAM- (series), D 101.22/7

USAAPGISA Pamphlets (series), D 105.9/3

USAARMC Pamphlets (series), D 101.22/20

Victory Crops Series Pamphlets, FS 5.29

VISTA Pamphlets, PrEx 10.13/3

War Trade Board Pamphlets, WT 1.6

Wire Communications Pamphlets, W 42.30

Pan American

Pan American Child Congress, 6th Lima, S 5.34

Pan American Club News, FS 5.35, FS 5.26/a 2

Pan American Financial Conference, 2d, Washington, 1920, T 1.22/2

Pan American Financial Conference, Washington, D.C., May 24, 1915, T 1.22

Pan American Scientific Congress, 3d Lima, Peru, 1924-25, S 5.14/3

Leaflets Accompanying Exhibit of Coast and Geodetic Survey at Pan-American Exposition, T 11.18

Pan-American Congress of Highways, 1st, Buenos Aires, S 5.23

Pan-American Congress on Highways, 2d, Rio de Janerio, S 5.23/2

Pan-American Medical Congress, Washington, 1893, S 5.16

Pan-American Scientific Congress, 2d, Washington, D.C., S 5.14/2

Pan-American Scientific Congress, Santiago, Chile, S 5.14

Pan-Pacific

Pan-Pacific Educational Conference, 1st Honolulu, August 1921, S 5.21/2, S 5.22

Pan-Pacific Scientific Conference, 1st Honolulu, 1920, S 5.21/1

Panama

Land Joint Commission, United States and **Panama**, S 3.30

Publications **Panama** Railroad Company, D 113.9

Tide, Moon and Sunrise Tables, **Panama**, and Cristobal, Colon, W 79.8

Panama Canal

Examination of the **Panama Canal** Commission's Financial Statements for the Years Ended ..., GA 1.13/11

Executive Orders Relating to **Panama Canal**, W 79.11/8

Panama Canal Company, Annual Report, CZ 1.1

Panama Canal Review, CZ 1.8, Y 3.P 19/2:10

Panama Canal Spillway, CZ 1.11, Y 3.P 19/2:9

Retirement Reports, Fiscal Yr., C.S. Retirement Act, **Panama Canal** Annuity Act, CS 1.29/2

Panamanian

Ships Registered Under Liberian, **Panamanian**, and Honduran Flags Deemed by the Navy Department to Be Under Effective U.S. Control, C 39.228

Panel

Federal Service Impasses **Panel** Releases, Y 3.F 31/ 21-3:14-3

MEPS, (Medical Expenditure **Panel** Survey), Chartbook, HE 20.6517/7

MEPS (Medical Expenditure **Panel** Survey) Highlights, HE 20.6517/6

Panel of International Law, S 1.130/2:L 41

President's Advisory **Panel** on Timber and the Environment, Pr 37.8:T 48

President's **Panel** on Federal Compensation, Pr 38.8:C 73

Publications Army Scientific Advisory **Panel**, D 101.81

Report of the **Panel** on Pain to the National Advisory Neurological and Communicative Disorders and Stroke Council, HE 20.3517

Report to the Administrator by the NASA Aerospace Safety Advisory **Panel**, NAS 1.58

Panels

Roster of Members of PHS Public Advisory Groups, Councils, Committees, Boards, **Panels**, Study Sections, HE 20.2:Ad 9/3

Panorama

Personal **Panorama**, C 4.46

Paper

BJS Discussion **Paper**, J 29.26

ECOL Tech **Paper**, A 13.66/18

Farm **Paper** Letter, A 107.13, A 107.13/3

Government **Paper** Specification Standards, Y 4.P 93/1:7, Y 4.P 93/1:7/2

INSS Occasional **Paper**, Regional Series, D 305.24

Monthly Statement of **Paper** Currency of Each Denomination Outstanding, T 40.8

News Bulletin of **Paper** Section, C 13.28

Occasional **Paper**, L 29.15/2

Paper Currency of Each Denomination Outstanding, Monthly Statements, T 63.307

POCS Technical **Paper**, I 1.98/3, I 53.29/2

Population Division Working **Paper** Series, C 3.223/26

Population **Paper** Listings (PPL series), C 3.223/ 25

Pulp and **Paper** Industry Reports, C 18.229

Pulp, **Paper** and Board Industry Report, C 40.11

Pulp, **Paper** and Board, C 57.313, C 57.511

Reference Information **Paper**, AE 1.124

Side Runs of **Paper** Trade, C 18.124

Special Series Bureau of Foreign and Domestic Commerce, **Paper** Division, C 18.146

Staff Discussion **Paper** (series), E 2.23

U.S. Foreign Trade in Pulp and **Paper**, C 18.198

Unemployment Insurance Occasional **Paper**, L 37.213/2

Paperboard

Paperboard, C 3.95

Papers

Development Studies Program Occasional **Papers**, S 18.59

Economic **Papers**, I 28.38

McNair **Papers** (series), D 5.416

Occasional Forestry **Papers**, I 29.41

Occasional **Papers** Council of Scholars (series), LC 1.42

Occasional **Papers** Engineer Department, Engineer School, W 7.16/2

Occasional **Papers** Forest Service Institute of Tropical Forestry, A 13.64/10

Occasional **Papers** Forest Service Northeastern Forest Experiment Station, A 13.42/8, A 13.42/8-2

Occasional **Papers** Forest Service Southern Forest Experiment Station, A 13.40/6

Occasional **Papers** Marine Corps, D 214.14/3

Occasional **Papers** Series, S 18.57

Occasional **Papers**, C 3.265

Operation **Papers**, CS 1.71/8

Papers Approved for Publication or Presentation, FS 2.22/9

Papers in Education Finance, HE 19.144

Papers in Re (miscellaneous), J 1.84

Papers in Re in Circuit Courts, J 1.76

Papers in Re in Court of Appeals, J 1.77

Papers in Re in Court of Claims, J 1.80

Papers in Re in Court of Customs and Patent Appeals, J 1.79

Papers in Re in District Courts, J 1.75

Papers in Re in Patent Office (Interferences), J 1.81

Papers in Re in State Courts of Appeal, J 1.83

Papers in Re in State Supreme Courts, J 1.82

Papers in Re in Supreme Court, J 1.78

Papers in Re Indian Claims Commission, J 1.85

Papers in Re World War Risk Insurance, J 1.13/2

Papers in Re {proceedings of inquiry, general investigations, etc.}, IC 1.13/2

Papers in Re, C 31.212, J 1.13

Papers in Re, Indexes, J 1.13/3s

Papers of American Historical Association, SI 4.5

Papers on the National Health Guidelines, HE 20.6020

Papers Relating to Foreign Relations of the United States, S 1.1

Papers, {number} Congress, Y 4.Ar 5/2:a

Physical Sciences Research **Papers**, D 301.45/40

PNERL Working **Papers**, EP 1.37/2

POCS Reference **Papers** (series), I 1.98/2, I 53.29

Preservation and New Technology Occasional **Papers**, LC 1.43

President's **Papers** Index Series, LC 4.7

Professional **Papers** Engineer Department, W 7.10

Professional **Papers** Environmental Science Services Administration, C 52.20

Professional **Papers** Geological Survey, I 19.16

Professional **Papers** National Oceanic and Atmospheric Administration, C 55.25

Professional **Papers** Signal Corps, W 42.11/2

Professional **Papers** Signal Service, W 42.11/1

Public **Papers** of the Presidents of the United States, AE 2.114, GS 4.113

Reference **Papers** (series), I 71.11

Registers of **Papers** in the Manuscript Division of the Library of Congress, LC 4.10

Research Institute for the Behavioral and Social Sciences: Technical **Papers**, D 101.60

Research **Papers** Forest Service, A 13.78

Research **Papers** Thrift Supervisor Office, T 71.16

Research **Papers**, Separates from the Journal of Research, C 13.22

Research Working **Papers** (series), FHL 1.35

RIIES Occasional **Papers**, SI 1.40/2

Resource **Papers** in Administrative Law, Y 3.Ad 6:11

Selected **Papers** from Bureau of Radiological Health Seminar Program (numbered), HE 20.1109

Selected **Papers** in School Finance, ED 1.310/5

Selected **Papers** in the Hydrologic Sciences, I 19.13/2

Small-Area Statistics **Papers**, C 3.238/2

Solar Events Calendar and Call for **Papers**, E 1.91

Southwest Cultural Resources Center: Professional **Papers**, I 29.116

Special Studies **Papers**, FR 1.58

Staff Information **Papers**, GS 4.12

Staff **Papers**, Background **Papers** and Major Testimony, Y 3.Ec 7/3

Staff **Papers**, BIE-SP-(series), C 62.15

Staff **Papers**, C 45.10

Staff **Papers**, FJC-SP- (series), Ju 13.10/2

Station **Papers**, A 13.30/8, A 13.42/16, A 13.61/8, A 13.63/9, A 13.67/8, A 13.69/7, A 13.73/8

Statistical Policy Working **Papers**, C 1.70, PrEx 2.28

Surveillance and Analysis Division, Region 10: Working **Papers**, EP 1.51/6

Technical Analysis **Papers** Congressional Budget Office, Y 10.11

Technical Analysis **Papers** Department of Health, Education, and Welfare, HE 1.52

Technical **Papers**, AFHRL-TP- (series), D 301.45/ 27-4

Technical **Papers**, C 1.73, I 53.30

Technologic **Papers**, C 13.8

Territorial **Papers** of United States, GS 4.13, S 1.36

Training **Papers**, C 55.121

Treasury **Papers**, T 1.48

Unemployment Insurance Occasional **Papers**, L 37.20

Unemployment Insurance, Technical Staff **Papers**, L 37.20/2

Water Supply **Papers**, I 19.13

Weather Bureau Training **Papers**, C 30.48

Working **Papers** Bureau of the Census, C 56.229, C 3.214

Working **Papers** Corps of Engineers, D 103.57/9

Working **Papers** Department of Education, ED 1.80

Working **Papers** Environmental Protection Agency, Pacific Northwest Environmental Research Laboratory, EP 1.37/2

Working **Papers** National Transportation Policy Study Commission, Y 3.T 68/2:10

Working **Papers** Office on Water Programs, EP 2.23

Working **Papers** Social and Rehabilitation Service, HE 17.24

Working **Papers**, Publication Order Forms, C 56.229/2

WSDG Technical **Papers**, WSDG-TP- (series), A 13.87/2

Par

Federal Reserve **Par** List, October (year), FR 1.9

Program Administration Review, **PAR** (nos.), FS 13.219

Parachute

Parachute Jumping, TD 4.6:part 105

Paraguay

Commission of Inquiry and Conciliation, Bolivia and **Paraguay**, Report of Chairman, S 3.40

Parameters

Global Atmospheric Background Monitoring for Selected Environmental **Parameters**, C 55.284

Parameters, Journal of the U.S. Army War College, D 101.72

Parasite

Intestinal **Parasite** Surveillance, HE 20.7011/28

Parasitology

Performance Evaluation Summary Analysis **Parasitology**, HE 20.7037/3

Proficiency Testing Summary Analysis, **Parasitology**, HE 20.7022/3-4

Tropical Medicine and **Parasitology** Study Section, HE 20.3001/2:M 46/7

Parcel

Official **Parcel** Post Zone Keys Hawaii, P 1.25/4

Official **Parcel** Post Zone Keys Puerto Rico, P 1.25/3

Official **Parcel** Post Zone Keys United States, P 1.25/1

Official **Parcel** Post Zone Keys Virgin Islands, P 1.25/2

Parent

Emergency **Parent** Education Bulletins, Y 3.F 31/ 5:16

Foreign Flag Merchant Ships Owned by U.S. **Parent** Companies, TD 11.16

Parent Education Letters, I 16.48

Parent Education Messenger, A 43.14

U.S. Direct Investment Abroad, Operations of U.S. **Parent** Companies and Their Foreign Affiliates, Preliminary Estimates, C 59.20/2

Unemployed-**Parent** Segment of Aid to Families with Dependent Children, FS 14.210, FS 17.11, FS 17.611

Parents

Child Guidance Leaflets, Series on Eating, for **Parents**, FS 3.211

Healthy That's Me, **Parents**' Handbooks, HE 21.208/2

Parents and Beginning Readers (series), HE 5.91

Report from Closer Look, a Project of the **Parents'** Campaign for Handicapped Children and Youth, ED 1.22

Statistical Summary of Aid to Dependent Children of Unemployed **Parents**, FS 3.39/3

Paris

Fur Seal Arbitration, **Paris**, S 3.7/1, S 3.7/1a

Paris Air Show News Fillers, C 42.27/2

Paris Air Show Newsletter, C 42.27

Paris, Universal Exposition 1867, S 6.9

Paris, Universal Exposition 1878, S 6.10

Paris, Universal Exposition 1889, S 6.11

Paris, Universal Exposition 1900, S 6.12

Peace Conference, **Paris**, 1919, S 3.28

UNESCO World Review Weekly Radio News from United Nations Educational, Scientific, and Cultural Organization, **Paris**, France, S 5.48/6

Park

Annual Report of the Chief Scientist of the National **Park** Service, I 29.1/2

Areas Administered by the National **Park** Service, I 29.66

Calendar of Events in Areas Administered by National **Park** Service, I 29.66/2

Camping Facilities in Areas Administered by National **Park** Service, I 29.71

Courier, the National **Park** Service Newsletter, I 29.96

Crater Lake National **Park**, Annual Reports, I 1.42

Glacier National **Park**, Reports, I 1.52

Glen Echo **Park**, I 29.98

Laws relating to National **Park** Service, T 29.46:L 44

Mesa Verde National **Park**, Annual Reports, I 1.48

Mount Rainier National **Park**, Annual Reports, I 1.43

National Historic **Park** (series), I 29.88/6

National **Park** Conferences, I 29.5

National **Park** Location Maps, I 29.53

National **Park** Series, I 19.106

National **Park** Service Annual Science Report, I 29.1/3

National **Park** Service Bulletin, I 29.3/2

National **Park** Service Governor's Books {by State}, I 29.75

National **Park** Service Guide to the Historic Places of the American Revolution, I 29.9/2:Am 3

National **Park** Service Handbooks (numbered), I 29.9/5

National **Park** Service History Series, I 29.58/2

National **Park** System and Related Areas, Index, I 29.103

National Zoological **Park**, Reports, SI 1.1/a4

National Zoological **Park**: Annual Report, SI 1.1/2

Naturalist Program, Arcadia National **Park**, I 29.60

Naturalist Program, Great Smokey Mountains National **Park**, I 29.60/2

Naturalist Program, Mount Rainier National **Park**, I 29.60/3

Naturalist Program, Shenandoah National **Park**, I 29.60/4

NPS Strategic Planning, National **Park** Scan, I 29.132

Pacific Coast Salmon **Park**, C 6.11

Park Areas and Employment Opportunities for Summer, I 29.110

Park Practice Grist, I 29.72

Park Science, Resource Management Bulletin, I 29.3/4

Park Service Bulletins, I 29.3

Patrols with **Park** Rangers, I 29.42

Platt National **Park**, Annual Reports, I 1.54

Public Use, Tabulation of Visitors to Areas Administered by National **Park** Service, I 29.63

Reintroduction and Management of Wolves in Yellowstone National **Park** and the Central Idaho Wilderness Area, Y 3.W 83

Rocky Mountain National **Park**, Annual Reports, I 1.57

Schedules of Basic Rates (by name of **park** or monument), I 29.33

Self-Guiding Nature Trail Leaflets, Glacier National **Park**, I 29.61

Self-Guiding Nature Trail Leaflets, Mount Rainier National **Park**, I 29.61/2

Shenandoah National **Park** Chips, I 29.67

State **Park** Statistics, I 29.68

Technical Reports National **Park** Service, J 29.15, I 29.109

Timucuan Today and Tomorrow, A Newsletter from the National **Park** Service, I 29.128

Visitor Accommodations Furnished by Concessioners in Areas Administered by National **Park** Service, I 29.70

Wind Cave National **Park**, Annual Reports, I 1.56

Yearbook, **Park** and Recreation Progress, I 29.44

Yellowstone National **Park**, Annual Reports, 1898-90, I 1.37

Yosemite National **Park**, Annual Reports, I 1.38

Parkinson's

Parkinson's Disease and Related Disorders, Citations from the Literature, HE 20.3511

Parkinson's Disease and Related Disorders, International Directory of Scientists, HE 20.3511/2

Parkinson's Disease and Related Disorders: Cumulative Bibliography, HE 20.3511/3

NINCDS **Parkinson's** Disease Research Program, HE 20.3502:P 22

Parklawn

Parklawn Computer Center Technical News, HE 20.31

Parklawn Computer Center: Annual Report, HE 20.4036

Parklawn Computer Center: Computer Training Courses, HE 20.4036/2

Parklawn Training Center, Quarterly Calendar, HE 20.32/2

Parklawn Training Center: Training Catalog, HE 20.32

Parks

Art and Artists in National **Parks**, I 29.25

Celebrated Conservationists in Our National **Parks**, I 29.31

Check List of Birds of National **Parks**, I 29.27

Compilation of Administrative Policies for National **Parks** and National Monuments of Scientific Significance (Natural Area Category), I 29.9/4:N 21

Federal Surplus Real Property Public Benefit Discount Program, **Parks** and Recreation, Report to Congress, I 29.118

General Superintendent and Landscape Engineer of National **Parks**, Annual Reports, I 1.58

Laws and Regulations Relating to National **Parks**, Reservations, etc., I 1.47

Miniature Portraits, Wildlife at National **Parks**, I 29.51

National Monuments and National Military **Parks**: Information Circulars, I 29.21

National **Parks** Program {Radio Broadcasts}, I 29.17

National **Parks**, USA {poster series}, I 29.20/2

National **Parks**: Camping Guide, I 29.71

Parks, I 29.85

Photographs of Scenes in National **Parks** (by name of park), I 29.32

Photographs of Scenes of National **Parks**, etc., I 29.29

Public Use of National **Parks**, Statistical Report, I 29.63

Rules and Regulations of National **Parks**, I 1.47/2

Sequoia and General Grant National **Parks**, Annual Reports, I 1.29

Parkways

Compilation of Administrative Policies for National Recreation Areas, National Seashores, National Lakeshores, National **Parkways**, National Scenic Riverways (Recreational Area Category), I 29.9/4:R 24

Parliamentarians

NATO **Parliamentarians'** Conference, Report of Senate Delegation, Y 4.F 76/2:Na 81a/5

Parlor

Passenger Traffic Statements (other than commutation) of Class 1 Steam Railways in United States Separated Between Coach Traffic and **Parlor** and Sleeping Car Traffic, IC 1 ste.40

Passenger Traffic Statistics (other than commutation) of Class I Steam Railways in the United States Separated Between Coach Traffic and **Parlor** and Sleeping Car Traffic, IC 1 ste.39

Federal **Parole** Decision-Making: Selected Reprints, J 27.9

Parole in the United States, J 29.12/2

Parole Series, HE 17.16

Probation and **Parole**, J 29.11/6

Regulations, Rules and Instructions United States **Parole** Commission, J 27.6

Uniform **Parole** Reports, J 29.12

Paroling

Rules and Regulations Governing **Paroling** of Prisoners from Penitentiaries, State Institutions, J 1.15/5

Rules and Regulations Governing **Paroling** of Prisoners from U.S. Penitentiaries {etc.} (special), J 1.15/6

Part

H 7 Manufacturers **Part** and Drawing Numbering Systems, D 7.6/2:7

Manufacturers **Part** and Drawing Numbering Systems, D 7.6/2:7

Part 2

Quarterly Bulletin for **Part 2**, Hydrographic Products, D 5.351/2-2

Partial

United States Flag Containerships and United States Flag Ships with **Partial** Capacities for Containers And/or Vehicles, C 39.232

Participant

Study of WIC **Participant** and Program Characteristics, A 98.17

Participants

All **Participants** Memoranda, HH 1.23/8), HH 1.37/4

Summer Seminars for College Teachers Guidelines and Application Form for **Participants**, NF 3.13/2-2

Summer Seminars for Secondary School Teachers Guidelines and Applications Form for **Participants**, NF 3.13/3-2

Participating

Annual Report Colorado River Storage Project and **Participating** Projects for Fiscal Year (date), I 27.71/2

Directory, Local Law Enforcement Organizations **Participating** in Aviation Security, TD 4.809

List of **Participating** Institutions, Fiscal Year (date), J 1.43

National Defense Student Loan Program, Including **Participating** Institutions, FS 5.255:55001, HE 5.255:55001

Numbers of Farms **Participating** in 1934 AAA Voluntary Control Programs (by States), A 55.55

Recovery Guides, **Participating** Counties, Y 3.Ec 74/3:16

Participation

Announcement of Opportunities for **Participation**, NAS 1.53

Handbook for **Participation** Loans with the Small Business Administration, SBA 1.19:L 78

Inventory of Federal Tourism Programs, Federal Agencies Commissions, Programs Reviewed for Their **Participation** in the Development of Recreation, Travel, and Tourism in the United States, C 47.2:T 64/3

Monograph Series on American Military **Participation** in World War, W 26.15/6

Participation in Adult Education, ED 1.123

Participation Loan Transactions, FHL 1.17

Participation of American and Foreign-Flag Vessels in Shipments under United States Foreign Relief Programs, C 3.164:976

Participation of Principal National Flags in United States Oceanborne Foreign Trade, C 39.221

Reports to Congress on United States **Participation** in Operations of UNRRA under Act of March 28, 1944, Pr 32.5812

Research and Development: Public Awareness/**participation** Support Plan, Fiscal Year (date), EP 1.90

Research **Participation** for Teachers of Science and Mathematics, NS 1.12/3

Schedules of Payments to Holders of Cotton Options and **Participation** Trust Certificates by Congressional District of States, A 55.57

Source Catalog on Youth **Participation** (series), HE 1.312

Tables on Hatchery and Flock **Participation** in the National Poultry Improvement Plan, A 77.15:44-3

Peaches
  Marketing of South Carolina **Peaches**, Summary of
    Season, A 88.12/29
Peak
  Annual **Peak** Discharge at Selected Gaging
    Stations in Pacific Northwest, I 19.45/3
  Electric Energy and **Peak** Load Data, E 3.11/17-9
  Energy and **Peak** Load Data, E 3.11/17-3
  Enroute IFR Air Traffic Survey, **Peak** Day, TD 4.19/
    3
  Enroute IFR **Peak** Day Charts, Fiscal Year, FAA
    3.11/3
  Monthly Comparisons of **Peak** Demands and
    Energy Load, E 3.11/17-5
Peak Day
  IFR Altitude Usage **Peak Day**, FAA 3.11/2
Peanut
  List, **Peanut** Millers (shellers and crushers), A
    92.14/3
  List, **Peanut** Processors, A 92.14/4
  List, **Peanut** Processors (users of raw **peanuts**), A
    88.10/6
  List, **Peanut** Shellers and Crushers, A 88.10/3
  Peanut Letters, A 55.38
  Peanut Market News, A 88.10
  Peanut Millers List, A 92.14/3
  Peanut Processors List, A 88.10/6, A 92.14/4
  Peanut Reports, A 82.10
  Peanut Shellers and Crushers List, A 88.10/3
  Weekly **Peanut** Reports, A 36.106, A 88.10
Peanuts
  List, Peanut Processors (users of raw **peanuts**), A
    88.10/6
  Peanuts, Stocks and Processing, A 88.10/2, A
    88.10/2-2, A 105.29
Peas
  Official United States Standards for **Peas** & Lentils,
    A 113.10/4
  Wheat, Rice, Feed Grains, Dry **Peas**, Dry Beans,
    Seeds, Hops, A 67.30:W 56
Peat
  Advance Data on **Peat** in (year), I 28.107/2
  Peat, I 28.107/2
  Peat Producers in United States, I 28.107
Pecan
  Annual **Pecan** Summary, Louisiana Crop Reporting
    Service, A 88.10/5-2
  Pecan Report, Louisiana Crop Reporting Service, A
    88.10/5
PED
  NASA **PED** (series), NAS 1.84
Pedestrian
  Pedestrian Laws in the United States, October
    1974, TD 8.5/2:3/3
Peer
  Listing of **Peer** Reviewers Used by NSF Divisions,
    NS 1.36
  Medicare **Peer** Review Organizational Manual, HE
    22.8/15
  NIH **Peer** Review Notes, HE 20.3045
Pell
  Pell Grant Formula, ED 1.45/2
  Pell Grant Payment Schedule, ED 1.45/3-2
Pelts
  Mink Production, **Pelts** Produced in (year), A
    92.18/11
Pending
  Trademarks **Pending**, Bibliographic Information
    from **Pending** US Trademarks, C 21.31/8
Penetration
  Market **Penetration** Models, E 3.1/5-2
Penitentiaries
  Rules and Regulations for Government and
    Discipline of United States **Penitentia-
    ries**, J 1.16
  Rules and Regulations Governing Paroling of
    Prisoners from **Penitentiaries**, State
    Institutions, J 1.15/5
  Rules and Regulations Governing Paroling of
    Prisoners from U.S. **Penitentiaries** {etc.}
    (special), J 1.15/6
Pennsylvania
  Naval Air Development Center, Johnsville,
    Pennsylvania, Aeronautical Electronic
    and Electrical Laboratory, Report
    NADC-EL (series), D 202.14
  USA Trade World, **Pennsylvania** & Delaware, C
    61.39/4
Pennsylvania Anthracite
  Coal, **Pennsylvania Anthracite**, E 3.11/3-2
  Coal, **Pennsylvania Anthracite** in (year), I 28.50/4
  Distribution of **Pennsylvania Anthracite** for Coal
    Year (date), I 28.50/3
  Pennsylvania Anthracite Distribution, E 3.11/3-3

Pennsylvania Anthracite Weekly, E 3.11/3
Pennsylvania Anthracite, I 28.49/2
  Preliminary Estimates of Production of **Pennsylva-
    nia Anthracite** and Beehive Coke, I
    28.50
Penny-Royal Grass
  Commercial Tobacco-Livestock Farms, Bluegrass
    Area, Kentucky and **Penny-Royal Grass**
    Area, Kentucky-Tennessee, A 93.9/11
Penology
  Recent Publications of Criminology and **Penology**,
    J 16.9
Pension
  Administration on Welfare and **Pension** Plans
    Disclosure Act, L 1.55
  Annual Reports on Construction of **Pension**
    Building, I 1.27
  Corporate **Pension** Funds, SE 1.25/6
  Employee Benefits Survey Defined Benefit **Pension**
    Coding Manual, L 2.46/7
  Fact Sheets (**Pension** Benefit Guaranty Corpora-
    tion), Y 3.P 38/2:14
  Laws and Executive Orders Relating to
    Compensation, **Pension**, Emergency
    Officers' Retirement, etc., VA 1.14
  PBGC {**Pension** Benefit Guaranty Corporation}
    Fact Sheets, L 1.51/5
  Private **Pension** Plan Bulletin, L 40.16
  Pension Building, Annual Reports on Construc-
    tion of, 1883-87, I 1.27
  Pension Cases, Decisions, I 1.55
  Pension Decisions, I 24.8
  Pension Insurance Data Book: PBGC Single-
    Employer Program, Y 3.P 38/2:12
  Pension Laws {June 25, 1918}, Y 1.2:P 38/2
  President's Commission on **Pension** Policy, Pr
    39.8:P 38
  Private **Pension** Plan Bulletin, L 40.16
  Selected Compensation and **Pension** Data by State
    of Residence, VA 1.88
  Survey of **Pension** Fund Investment in Mortgage
    Instruments, HH 1.99/4
Pension Fund
  HUD Survey Reveals Large Increase in **Pension
    Fund** Investment in Mortgage
    Instruments, HH 1.99/7
Pension Plans
  Digest of Selected **Pension Plans** under Collective
    Bargaining, L 2.3
Pensioners
  List of **Pensioners**, I 24.6
Pensions
  Laws Governing Granting of Army and Navy
    Pensions, VA 2.5/2
  Laws Governing Granting of Army and Navy
    Pensions and Bounty Land, I 24.14
People
  Facts of Life and Death, Selected Statistics on
    Nation's Health and **People**, FS 2.102:H
    34
  Freedom's **People**, FS 5.27
  Health United States and Healthy **People** 2000
    Review, HE 20.7042
  Healthy **People** 2000 Review, HE 20.6223/3
  Healthy **People** 2000, Statistical Notes, HE
    20.6230
  Healthy **People** 2000 Statistics and Surveillance,
    HE 20.7040
  Peace Corps Opportunity Newsletter of Special
    Interest to Professional and Technical
    People, S 19.13
  People Land and Water, I 1.116
  President's Committee on Employment of the
    Handicapped: **People** with Disabilities
    in Our Nation's Job Training
    Partnership Act Programs, PrEx 1.10/15
  Reaching **People**, A 98.12
  Soviet Union, **People** of Asia and Africa, PrEx 7.21/
    7-3
  "We the **People**" Calendar, Y 3.H 62/2:9
Per Capita
  East North Central, Population and **Per Capita**
    Income Estimates for Counties and
    Incorporated Places, C 3.186/27-4
  Northeast, Population and **Per Capita** Income
    Estimates for Counties and Incorporated
    Places, C 3.186/27
  South, Population and **Per Capita** Income
    Estimates for Counties and Incorporated
    Places, C 3.186/27-5
  West North Central, Population and **Per Capita**
    Income Estimates for Counties and
    Incorporated Places, C 3.186/27-3

  West, Population and **Per Capita** Income Estimates
    for Counties and Incorporated Places, C
    3.186/27-2Percent
  Percent Changes in Gross Average Hourly
    Earnings Over Selected Periods, L 2.63/
    2, L 2.63/3
  Percent Changes in Gross Hourly and Weekly
    Earnings over Selected Periods, L 2.63
Per Diem
  U.S. **Per Diem** Rates (CONUS), GS 1.36
Percentage
  Number and **Percentage** of Farms Electrified with
    Central Station Service, A 68.20
Performance
  Air Navigation and Air Traffic Control Facility
    Performance and Availability Report,
    Calendar Year, TD 4.710
  Aircraft Operating Cost and **Performance** Report,
    CAB 1.22, CAB 1.22/2, C 31.259
  Alloy Development for Irradiation **Performance**, E
    1.64
  Annual **Performance** Plan, A 13.1/4
  Annual R.O.P. and **Performance** Test Summary, A
    77.15:44-7
  Background Information for Standards of
    Performance, EP 1.8/5
  Customs **Performance** Reports, T 17.25
  Development Document for Effluent Limitations
    Guidelines and New Source **Perfor-
    mance** Standards for {various
    industries}, EP 1.8/3
  Engineered **Performance** Standards for Real
    Property Maintenance Activities, D 1.6/
    7
  Engineering **Performance** Standards, D 209.14
  Facility **Performance** Report, Calendar Year, TD
    4.710/2
  Financial **Performance** Indicators, FCA 1.28
  Freight Train **Performance** of Class I Railroads in
    the United States, IC 1 ste.35
  Fuel **Performance** Annual Report, Y 3.N 88:25-4
  Hearing Aid **Performance** Measurement Data and
    Hearing Aid Selection Procedures,
    Contract Year (date), VA 1.22
  High **Performance** Computing and Communica-
    tions Implementation Plan, PrEx 23.13
  HPMC **Performance** Indicators, HH 1.57
  Insights, High **Performance** Computer and
    Communications, NAS 1.94
  Lesson **Performance** Test Grading Sheets (series),
    D 101.107/2
  National **Performance** Audit Program, Ambient
    Air Audits of Analytical Proficiency, EP
    1.23/5-2
  Office of Management and Systems Annual
    Performace Report, HE 20.4001/3
  Passenger Train **Performance** of Class I Railroads
    in the United States, IC 1 ste.37
  Performance, PM 1.32
  Performance Evaluation Summary Analysis
    Bacteriology, HE 20.7037/2
  Performance Evaluation Summary Analysis
    Mycology, HE 20.7037
  Performance Evaluation Summary Analysis
    Parasitology, HE 20.7037/3
  Performance Guides (series) Army Department, D
    101.107/3-2
  Performance Guides (series) Forest Service, A
    13.65/12-2
  Performance Monitoring System: Summary of
    Lock Statistics, D 103.57/12
  Performance Plan, Fiscal Year... and Revised Final
    Fiscal Year...Performance Plan, SSA
    1.2:P41
  Performance Profiles of Major Energy Producers,
    E 3.37/2
  Performance Profiles of Major Energy Producers,
    E 3.37
  Performance, Story of the Handicapped, PrEx
    1.10/3
  Report on the Financial Condition and **Perfor-
    mance** of the Farm Credit System, FCA
    1.1/2
  Report to Congress on Conrail **Performance**, Y 3.R
    13/4:9
  Review of Standards of **Performance** for New
    Stationary Sources, EP 4.19
  Schedule Arrival **Performance** in the Top 200
    Markets by Carrier, C 31.261, CAB 1.19
  Small Business **Performance**, by Claimant
    Program, D 1.48/2
  Status of the Nation's Local Public Transportation,
    Conditions and **Performance**, Report to
    Congress, TD 7.18

Student **Performance** Guides (series), D 101.107/3

U.S. Trade **Performance** in (year) and Outlook, C 61.28

Yard Service **Performance** of Class I Railroads in the United States, IC 1ste.38

Performances

Analysis and Summary of Conditions and **Performances** of the Farm Credit Banks and Associations, FCA 1.23/2

Performing

Performing Arts, LC 1.46

Period

Schedule of Annual and **Period** Indices for Carriers by Pipeline, IC 1 acco.10

Periodic

Bench Comment, a Periodic Guide to Recent Appellate Treatment of Practical Procedural Issues, Ju 13.8/2

Periodic Inspection Reports, D 103.310

Periodic Report from the National Digital Library Program, L 37.215

Periodic Reports of Agricultural Economics, Economic Research Service, Statistical Reporting Service, A 1.99

Periodic Supplement, Selected United States Government Publications, GP 3.17/3

Periodical

Abstracts of Selected **Periodical** Articles of Military Interest, W 55.8

Dated **Periodical** Schedules, GP 1.22

From the ACIR Library: **Periodical** Index, Y 3.Ad 9/8:12-2

Guide to Russian Scientific **Periodical** Literature, Y 3.At 7:23

Lists of Selected **Periodical** Literature, D 102.28/5

Monthly Catalog of United States Government Publications, **Periodical** Supplement, GP 3.8/8-8

National Climatic Data Center **Periodical** Publications, C 55.287/63

Quarterly Compilation of **Periodical** Literature Reflecting the Use of Records in the National Archives, AE 1.128

Quarterly Index to **Periodical** Literature, Eastern and Southern Africa, LC 1.30/8-4

Selected **Periodical** Literature, Lists, D 102.28/5

Weekly **Periodical** Index, D 103.108

Periodicals

Air University Library Index to Military **Periodicals**, D 301.26/2

Air University Library Master List of **Periodicals** 301.26/2-2

Catalogs and Lists of American and Foreign Annuals and **Periodicals**, N 16.7

Catalogue of Copyright Entries, Pt. 2, **Periodicals**, LC 3.6/2

Classification of **Periodicals**, Army Medical Library, W 44.24

Current and Non-current **Periodicals** in the NIH Library, HE 20.3009/3

EEOC Reports, Clearinghouse Service for Business Newsletters and **Periodicals**, Y 3.Eq 2:7-2

Interim Lists of **Periodicals** in Collection of Atmospheric Sciences Library and Marine and Earth Sciences Library, C 55.224

List of **Periodicals** in NWC Library, D 1.26/2

Periodicals and Serials Received in the Library of the National Bureau of Standards, C 13.10

Periodicals Currently Received in NIH Library, FS 2.22/13-3

Periodicals Supplement, GP 3.8/5

Review of Current **Periodicals**, New Series, SE 1.23

Selected List of American Agricultural Books in Print and Current Agricultural **Periodicals**, A 17.17:1

Selected List of Articles in Current **Periodicals** of Interest to Ordnance Department, W 34.21/2

U.S. Department of Commerce **Periodicals** to Aid Business Men, C 1.54

Weekly Review of **Periodicals**, FR 1.22

Periods

Present Changes in Gross Hourly and Weekly Earnings Over Selected **Periods**, L 2.63

Periscope

Periscope, J 16.16

Perishable

Digest of Decisions Secretary of Agriculture under **Perishable** Agricultural Commodities Act, A 82.55

Perkins

Occupant Emergency Plan Handbook for the Frances **Perkins** Building, L 1.1/2-2:2-8

Status of **Perkins** Loan Default, ED 1.40/4

Perlite

Perlite in (year), I 28.133

Permanent

National Portrait Gallery **Permanent** Collection Illustrated Checklist, SI 11.2:P 42

Number of New **Permanent** Nonfarm Dwelling Units Started by Urban or Rural Location, Public or Private Ownership, and Type of Structure, L 2.51/4

Permanent Court of International Justice, S 1.29

Permanent International Association of Road Congress, S 5.31

Permanent Mass Layoffs and Plant Closings, L 2.3/36

Rules of Procedure for the **Permanent** Select Committee on Intelligence, Y 4.In 8/18-10

Permissible

Schedule of Lists for **Permissible** Mine Equipment, I 28.8

Permission

Special Tariff **Permission** Under Section 224.1 of Economic Regulations, C 31.210

Special Tariff **Permission**, CA 1.16

Permit

Building **Permit** Survey, L 2.12

Construction Reports; Housing Units Authorized for Demolition in **Permit**-issuing Places, (year), C 45 (series), C 56.211/8

Number of New Dwelling Units and **Permit** Valuation of Building Construction Authorized by Class of Construction in Mountain and Pacific Division by Civil Division and State, L 2.51, L 2.51/2, L 2.51/3

Permit Valuation and Number of New Dwelling Units Provided in Housekeeping and Dwellings Authorized in Metropolitan Area of Washington, D.C. by Type of Dwelling and Source of Funds, L 2.51/7

Permits

Applications for **Permits**, CC 1.34

Building **Permits** in Principal Cities of U.S., L 2.6/a 4

Construction Reports; Building **Permits**, C 40 (series), C 3.215/7

Construction Reports; Building **Permits**: C 42 (series), C 3.215/6

Construction Reports; Housing Authorized by Building **Permits** and Public Contracts, C 56.211/4, C 3.215/11

Construction Reports; **Permits** Issued for Demolition of Residential Structures in Selected Cities, C 45 (series), C 3.215/12

Current Construction Reports, Housing Units Authorized by Building **Permits**, C 3.215/4:C 40

Housing Authorized by Building **Permits** and Public Contracts, C 3.215/4

New Dwelling Units Authorized by Local Building **Permits**, L 2.51/5

New Housing Units Authorized by Local Building **Permits** and New Dwelling Units Authorized in Local Building **Permits**, C 3.215/4

Reports of Construction **Permits** Retired to Closed Files, etc., CC 1.29

Permittees

Veterinary Biological Products, Licensees and **Permittees**, A 101.2/10

Permuted

Permuted Medical Subject Headings, HE 20.3612/3-3

Registry of Toxic Effects of Chemical Substances, **Permuted** Molecular Formula, Index, HE 20.7112/4

Personal

EIA **Personal** Computer Products, International Coal Statistics Database, E 3.11/7-11

Excess **Personal** Property Available for Transfer, Circulars, GS 2.4/3

Federal **Personal** Data Systems Subject to the Privacy Act of 1974, Annual Report of the President, Pr 38.12, Pr 39.11

Local Area **Personal** Income, C 59.18

Nationwide **Personal** Transportation Study: Reports, TD 2.31

Personal Computer-Annual Energy Outlook, E 3.1/5

Personal Finance Companies, Installment Loans to Consumers, C 18.222

Personal Panorama, C 4.46

Personal Weather Estimated from Estate Tax Returns Filed during Calendar Year, T 22.35/2:W 37

Real and **Personal** Property of the Department of Defense, As of June 30, D 1.2:P 94/8

Real and **Personal** Property, D 1.58/2

Personal Care

Industry Wage Survey: Nursing and **Personal Care** Facilities, L 2.3/25

Personal Property

Declared Excess **Personal Property** Listing, D 7.34/2

Department of Defense Exchange Sale of **Personal Property** Available for Transfer to Federal Agencies, Admin, GS 2.11

Department of Defense List of Excess **Personal Property** Available for Transfer to Federal Civil Agencies, GS 2.4/3-2

Federal Real Property and **Personal Property** Inventory Report of the U.S. Government Covering its Properties Located in the United States, in the Territories, and Overseas, as of June 30 (year), Y 4.G 74/7:P 94

General Real and **Personal** Property Inventory Report (Civilian and Military) of the U.S. Government Covering Its Properties Located in the U.S., in the Territories, and Overseas, As of June 30 {year}, Y 4.G 74/7:P 94

Offerings and Sales of Office of **Personal Property** Disposal, Y 3.W 19/8:12

Personnel

Abstracts of **Personnel** Research Reports, D 301.45/27

All Hands, Bureau of Naval **Personnel** Career Publications, D 208.3

All Hands, Bureau of Naval **Personnel** Information Bulletin, D 207.17

Army **Personnel** Bulletin, D 101.39/4

Army **Personnel** Letter, D 101.39/3

Bibliographies Guidance and Student **Personnel** Section, FS 5.16/2

BNDD **Personnel** Management Series, J 24.16

Bureau of Naval **Personnel** Manual, D 208.6/2

Bureau of **Personnel** Manual, C 4.12/2

CCPM Pamphlets {Commissioned Corps **Personnel** Manual}, HE 20.13

Civilian Manpower Management, Journal of Navy and Civilian **Personnel** Management, D 201.18

Civilian **Personnel**, D 1.6/5

Civilian **Personnel** and Payroll Letters, D 101.13

Civilian **Personnel** Bulletins (CPBs), D 101.138

Civilian **Personnel** Circulars, M 101.20, D 101.26

Civilian **Personnel** Liberated from Japanese Custody, W 107.12

Civilian **Personnel** News Letter, D 101.39

Civilian **Personnel** of Naval Shore Establishment, M 204.8

Civilian **Personnel** Phamphlets, W 1.57, M 101.35, D 101.37

Civilian **Personnel** Procedures Manual, D 101.6/3

Civilian **Personnel** Regulations, W 1.42, D 101.6/2

Commissioned Corps **Personnel** Manual, HE 20.13/3

CSRS and FERS Handbook for **Personnel** and Payroll, PM 1.14/3-3

DEA **Personnel** Management Series, J 24.16

Directory of **Personnel** Responsible for Radiological Health Programs, HE 20.4122

Directory of State Mental Health **Personnel** and Regional Offices of Department of Health, Education, and Welfare, FS 2.22:M 52/40

Directory of U.S. Government Audiovisual **Personnel**, GS 4.24

Directory, State Department of Education **Personnel** for Guidance, Counseling, and Testing, FS 5.255:25037:A, HE 5.255:25037:A

Dissertations and Theses Relating to **Personnel** Administration, CS 1.61/2

Distribution of **Personnel** by State and by Selected Locations, D 1.61/5

Education of **Exceptional** Children and Youth: Special Education Personnel in State Education Departments, FS 5.235:35003, HE 5.235:35003

Elementary School **Personnel**, FS 5.84:El 2, HE 5.84:El 2

EPDA Higher Education **Personnel** Training Programs, HE 5.258:58025

Federal **Personnel** Administration Career Programs, PM 1.41/4:931-1

Federal **Personnel** Manual: Bulletins, Installments and Letters, PM 1.14/2

Federal **Personnel** Manual: Supplements, PM 1.14/3

Federal **Personnel** Manual: Transmittal Sheets, PM 1.14

Federal Tax Information for Armed Forces **Personnel**, D 205.9

Guide Lines, Guidance and Pupil **Personnel** Service, FS 5.54

Guide to Processing **Personnel** Actions, PM 1.14/3-4

Hi-Line, Newsletters for Enlisted **Personnel**, TD 5.40

Higher Education **Personnel** Training Programs (year), Fellowship Programs, HE 5.92

Industrial **Personnel** Security Review Program, Annual Reports, D 3.12

Intergovernmental **Personnel** Notes, CS 1.86, PM 1.27

Key Audiovisual **Personnel** in Public Schools and Library Systems in State and Large Cities and In Large Public Colleges and Universities, FS 5.60/2

Link, Enlisted **Personnel** Distribution Bulletin, D 208.19

Memorandum Regarding **Personnel** and Policy Changes, I 29.3/2

Military **Personnel** Update, D 1.104/3

Monthly Report on Federal **Personnel** and Pay, Y 4.R 24/4

Multipurpose Arthritis Centers **Personnel** Directory, HE 20.3322

National Emergency Readiness of Federal **Personnel** Management, CS 1.41/4:910-1

National Emergency Standby Regulations and Instructions **Personnel** and Manpower, CS 1.41/4:990-3

Naval Military **Personnel** Manual, D 208.6/2

Navy Guide for Retired **Personnel** and Their Families, D 208.26

Navy Military **Personnel** Statistics, D 208.25

Officer **Personnel** Newsletter, D 208.21

Pamphlets **Personnel** Management Office, PM 1.10

Personnel Advisory Series, CS 1.82

Personnel and **Personnel** Practices in Public Institutions for Delinquent Children, FS 2.13

Personnel Appeals Board, Annual Report, GA 1.1/2

Personnel Bibliography Series, CS 1.61/3, PM 1.22/2

Personnel Bulletins Government Printing Office, GP 1.20

Personnel Bulletins Indian Affairs Bureau, I 20.28

Personnel Bulletins Interior Department, I 1.73

Personnel Bulletins Labor Department, L 1.3/2

Personnel Bulletins **Personnel** Office, Department of Agriculture, A 49.3/2

Personnel Circular Letters, VA 1.4/2

Personnel Circulars, A 1.44, A 49.4/2

Personnel Development for Vocational Education, HE 19.124

Personnel Handbook, Series P-1, Position Description and Salary Schedules, Transmittal Letters, P 1.31

Personnel Handbooks, P 1.31/5

Personnel Instructions, L 1.25

Personnel Law: Civilian **Personnel** and Military **Personnel**, GA 1.5/13

Personnel Literature, CS 1.62, PM 1.16

Personnel Management Publications, I 1.73/2

Personnel Management Reform, Progress in State and Local Governments, PM 1.11/3

Personnel Management Series, CS 1.54, PM 1.28

Personnel Management Training Center: Course Catalog, CS 1.65/10

Personnel Management Training Division I, PM 1.28/2

Personnel Management Training Units, L 1.38

Personnel Measurement Research and Development Center, CS 1.71

Personnel Methods Series, CS 1.58

Personnel Needs and Training for Biomedical and Behavioral Research, HE 20.3036/2

Personnel of Naval Shores Establishment, D 204.8

Personnel Records and Files, CS 1.41/4:293-31

Personnel Research and Development Center: Technical Memorandum, CS 1.71/4

Personnel Research Highlights, PM 1.57

Personnel Research Reports, CS 1.71/7, PM 1.43

Personnel Research Series, A 49.9

Personnel Section Bulletins, T 47.15

Personnel Statistics Reports, CS 1.33

Personnel, W 3.43

Political Activity of Government **Personnel** Commission, Y 3.P 75

Posters Office of Attorney **Personnel** Management, J 33.9

Posters Office of **Personnel** Management, PM 1.35

President's Commission on **Personnel** Interchange, Pr 37.8:P 43

Processing **Personnel** Actions, CS 1.41/4:296-31

Public Health **Personnel** in Local Health Units, FS 2.80

Public Welfare **Personnel**, Annual Statistical Data, HE 17.629

Regional Office Directory, Professional and Administrative **Personnel**, FS 1.17/2

Register of Military **Personnel** in the Washington, D.C. Area, TD 5.19/3

Releases Pertaining to **Personnel**, C 13.36/3

Report on the Significant Actions of the Office of **Personnel** Management, MS 1.16

Report to the President and Congress on the Status of Health **Personnel** in the United States, HE 20.9310

Report to the President and Congress on the Status of Health Professions **Personnel** in the United States, HE 20.6619

Scientific and Technical **Personnel** in the Federal Government, NS 1.22:G 74

Scientific **Personnel** Bulletin, D 210.7

Secondary School **Personnel**, FS 5.84:Se 2, HE 5.84:Se 2

Special Education **Personnel** in State Education Departments, FS 5.235:35051

SPI State **Personal** Income, C 59.25

SSA Management Newsletter for Supervisors and Management **Personnel**, HE 3.68/2

State and Local **Personnel** Systems, Annual Statistical Report, CS 1.95

Supervisor and **Personnel** Administration, C 21.14/3

Technical **Personnel** Pamphlets, D 12.8/2

Technical Research Reports Published by Air Force **Personnel** and Training Center Air Research and Development Command, D 301.26/10

Telephone Directory Office of **Personnel** Management, PM 1.31

Tips, Army **Personnel** Magazine, D 102.80

Trainers of Teachers, Other Education **Personnel** and Undergraduates, FS 5.84:T 22, HE 5.84:T 22

Transmittals (NOAA Washington Area **Personnel** Locator), C 55.47

Trends in Hospital **Personnel**, HE 20.9313

U.S. Army Military **Personnel** Center: Pamphlets (series), D 101.22/16

U.S. Atmospheric Nuclear Weapons Tests, Nuclear Test **Personnel** Review, D 15.10

What's Happening in the **Personnel** Field, D 217.13

Work Years and **Personnel** Costs, PM 1.10/4

Worldwide U.S. Active Duty Military **Personnel** Casualties, D 1.61/6

Persons

Consolidated List of **Persons** or Firms Currently Debarred for Violations of Various Public Contracts Acts Incorporating Labor Standard Provisions, GA 1.17

Income in (year) of **Persons** in the United States, C 3.186:P-60

Interim List of **Persons** or Firms Currently Debarred for Violation of Various Public Contracts Acts Incorporating Labor Standards Provisions, GA 1.17/2

Money Income and Poverty Status of Families and **Persons** in the United States, C 3.186/11

Money Income of Households, Families, and **Persons** in the United States, C 3.186/2

Persons Furnishing Cars to or on Behalf of Carriers by Railroad or Express Companies, Summary of Quarterly Reports, IC 1.18

Persons of Spanish Origin in the United States, Advance Report, C 3.186/14

Perspective

Employment in **Perspective**: Minority Workers, L 2.41/11-2

Employment in **Perspective**: Women in the Labor Force, L 2.41/11

Perspective, D 208.22

Tennessee Valley **Perspective**, Y 3.T 25:39

Perspectives

Criminal Justice **Perspectives** (series), J 26.14

Economic **Perspectives**, IA 1.37

Environmental Health **Perspectives**, Experimental Issues, HE 20.3559

Industrial College of the Armed Forces: **Perspectives** in Defense Management, D 5.16

Mineral **Perspectives**, I 28.37/2

New **Perspectives**, CR 1.12

Perspectives in Defense Management, D 5.16

Perspectives in Reading Research, ED 1.317/3

Perspectives on Crime and Justice, Lecture Series, J 28.24/3-2

Perspectives on Education Policy Research, ED 1.336/2

Perspectives on Medicaid and Medicare Management, HE 22.411

Perspectives on Policing (series), J 28.27

Perspectives, CR 1.12, D 104.28

Public Administration Practices and **Perspectives**, Digest of Current Materials, S 18.24

Rural Development **Perspectives**, A 93.41/2, A 105.40/2

Pertaining

Releases **Pertaining** to Personnel, C 13.36/3

Rules **Pertaining** to Aircraft Accidents, Incidents, Overdue Aircraft, and Safety Investigations, TD 1.106/2

Pertinent

United States Policy Toward USSR and International Communism, Monthly Digest of **Pertinent** Data Appearing in Department of State Publications, S 1.97

Peru

Arbitration Between Republic of Chile and Republic of **Peru** with Respect to Unfulfilled Provisions of Treaty of Peace of Oct. 20 1883, S 3.35

Pan American Scientific Congress, 3d Lima, **Peru**, 1924-25, S 5.14/3

Pest

Cooperative **Pest** Control Programs, A 77.327

Cooperative Plant **Pest** Report, A 101.9/2

Forest **Pest** Conditions in the North East, A 13.52/9

Forest **Pest** Leaflets, A 13.52

Forest **Pest** Management Methods Applications Group: Reports (series), A 13.52/10-3

Forest **Pest** Observer, A 13.68/11

Insect **Pest** Survey Bulletins, A 77.310

Insect **Pest** Survey, Special Supplements, A 77.310/3

Northeastern Forest **Pest** Reporter, A 13.52/3

Northeastern **Pest** Reporter, A 13.42/22

Pest Alert (NA-TP series), A 13.52/10-4

Plant **Pest** Control Cooperative Programs, Western Region, Fiscal Year (date), A 77.327/2

Plant **Pest** News, A 101.23

Review of U.S. Patents Relating to **Pest** Control, A 47.7

Review of United States Patents Related to **Pest** Control, A 77.311

Southern Forest **Pest** Reporter, A 13.52/4

Pest Control

Armed Forces **Pest Control** Board Annual Reports, D 104.18/2

Pesticide

Administration of the **Pesticide** Programs, EP 5.19

Digest of State **Pesticide** Use and Application Laws, Guide for Analyzing Pesticide Legislation, EP 5.8:P 43

Office of **Pesticide** Programs Annual Report, EP 5.1

Pesticide Data Program, A 88.60

Pesticide Registration Eligibility Decisions (REDs), EP 5.27

Pesticide Registration Standards, EP 5.17

Pesticide Review (year), A 82.76

Pesticide Station for (year), A 82.76

U.S.D.A. Summary of Registered Agricultural **Pesticide** Chemical Uses, A 77.302:P 43/4

Pesticides

Apply **Pesticides** Correctly, a Guide for Commercial Applicators (series), EP 5.8/2

EPA Compendium of Registered **Pesticides**, EP 5.11/1-5

Health Aspects of **Pesticides**, Abstracts Bulletin, HE 20.4011

Pesticides Abstracts, EP 5.9

Pesticides and Toxic Substances Monitoring Report, EP 5.16

Pesticides Documentation Bulletin, A 17.20

Pesticides Monitoring Journal, Pr 37.8:En 8/P 43, PrEx 14.9, Y 3.F 31/18:9

Pesticides Study Series, EP 2.25

Posters Office of **Pesticides** and Toxic Substances, EP 5.21

Progress Report on **Pesticides** and Related Activities, A 1.2:P 43/3

Pests

Biology and Control of Insect and Related **Pests** of {various animals}, EP 1.94

List of Intercepted Plant **Pests**, A 77.308/2, A 101.10/2:82-5

Service and Regulatory Announcements List of Intercepted Plant **Pests**, A 77.308/2

PETC

PETC Review, E 1.112

Petit

Grand and **Petit** Juror Service in U.S. District Courts, Ju 10.13

Petitions

In Supreme Court of U.S., Briefs, **Petitions**, and Motions of Wm. Marshall Bullett, Solicitor General, J 1.19/2

Petitions for Certiorari and Briefs on Merits and in Opposition for U.S. in Supreme Court of U.S., J 1.19/6

Petitions for Patent Waiver, NAS 1.18/3

Petitions, Y 3.Sp 2:5

Public Notices: **Petitions** for Rule Making Field, CC 1.38

Petroleum

Contributions from Thermodynamics Laboratory, **Petroleum** Experiment Station, Bartlesville, Oklahoma, I 28.105

Crude **Petroleum** and **Petroleum** Products, I 28.18/4

Crude **Petroleum** Reports by Refineries, I 32.9, I 28.45

Distribution of **Petroleum** Products by Petroleum Administration Districts, IC 1.24

Distribution of Petroleum Products by **Petroleum** Administration Districts, IC 1.24

District V **Petroleum** Statement, E 3.11/6, I 28.45/3

DOE **Petroleum** Demand Watch, E 1.7/3

Foreign **Petroleum** Statistics, C 18.86, C 18.86/2

Foreign Trade Notes, Minerals and Metals and **Petroleum**, C 18.91

Foreign Trade Notes, **Petroleum**, C 18.91/3

Industry Wage Survey: **Petroleum** Refining, L 2.3/19

International **Petroleum** Annual, I 28.43/3, E 3.11/5-3

International **Petroleum** Quarterly, I 28.43/2

Liquefied **Petroleum** Gas Sales, E 3.11/13

Monthly **Petroleum** Product Price Report, E 3.24, FE 1.9/5

Monthly **Petroleum** Statistics Report, E 3.12, FE 1.9/4

National **Petroleum** Reserve in Alaska Task Force Study Reports, I 1.106

Naval **Petroleum** and Oil Shale Reserves, Annual Report of Operations, E 1.84/2

News of Institutes of Higher Learning; **Petroleum** and Gas, C 41.55/4

Petroleum Economy {abstracts}, C 41.55/3

Petroleum Forecast, I 28.41

Petroleum Imports Reporting System, Weekly Situation Report, FE 1.9/2

Petroleum Market Shares, FE 1.12

Petroleum Market Shares, Report on Sales of Refined **Petroleum** Products, E 3.13

Petroleum Market Shares, Report on Sales of Retail Gasoline, E 3.13/2

Petroleum Market Shares, {reports on various subjects}, FE 1.12/2, E 3.13/3

Petroleum Marketing Monthly, E 3.13/4

Petroleum Marketing, E 3.13/4-2

Petroleum Products Survey, PPS- (series), I 28.18/3

Petroleum Products, Secondary Inventories and Storage Capacity, C 3.213

Petroleum Refineries in the United States and Puerto Rico, I 28.17/2, E 3.11/5-4

Petroleum Situation Report, FE 1.9

Petroleum Statement, I 28.18/2, I 28.18/4, E 3.11/5, E 3.11/5-2

Petroleum Statistics, I 22.9, I 22.9/2

Petroleum Supply Annual, E 3.11/5-5

Petroleum Worker {abstracts}, C 41.55/2

Petroleum, E 1.99

Recent Articles on **Petroleum** and Allied Substances, I 28.22

Shipment of Liquefied **Petroleum** Gases and Methane in (year), I 28.98/5

Standardization of **Petroleum** Specifications Committee, Bulletins, I 28.15

Status of Strategic **Petroleum** Reserve Activities as of (date), GA 1.13/3

Strategic **Petroleum** Reserve Quarterly Report, E 1.90/2

Strategic **Petroleum** Reserve, E 1.30

Summary of Mining and **Petroleum** Laws of the World, I 28.27

U.S. Exports of **Petroleum** and **Petroleum** Products of Domestic Origin, Commodity by Customs District, C 3.164:527

United States Exports of **Petroleum** and **Petroleum** Products of Domestic Origin, Commodity by Country of Destination, C 3.164:526

United States Imports for Immediate Consumption, Entries into Bonded Manufacturing Warehouse for Manufacture and Exports, Entries into Bonded Storage Warehouse and Withdrawals from Bonded Storage Warehouse for Consumption of **Petroleum** and Its Products

Weekly **Petroleum** Statistics Reports, FE 1.9/3

Weekly **Petroleum** Status Report, E 1.63, E 3.32

World **Petroleum** Statistics, I 28.91

Petroleum Industry

Bibliography of Fire Hazards and Prevention and Safety in **Petroleum Industry**, C 22.27

Petroleum Refinery

Petroleum Refinery Statistics, I 28.17, I 28.18

PG

Professional Guide-**PG** (series), D 13.8/6

PHA

PHA Grants Administration Manual, HE 20.8/2

PHA Honor Awards for Design Excellence, HH 3.10

PHA Low-Rent Housing Bulletins, HH 3.3/4

Phamphlets

Civilian Personnel **Phamphlets**, W 1.57, M 101.35, D 101.37

Pharmaceutical

NCI Investigational Drugs, **Pharmaceutical** Data, HE 20.3180

Pharmaceuticals

Industry Report, Drugs and **Pharmaceuticals**, C 18.237

Pharmacists

Data on Licensed **Pharmacists** (place), HE 20.6221

Pharmacology

Pharmacology and Biorelated Chemistry Program: Biennial Report, HE 20.3461/3

Pharmacology Research Associate Program, HE 20.3461/2

Pharmacology Study Section, HE 20.3001/2:P 49

Pharmacology-Toxicology Program Committee, HE 20.3001/2:P 49/2

Pharmacology-Toxicology Program, HE 20.3461

Workshop Series of **Pharmacology** Section, N.I.M.H., FS 2.310

Pharmacy

International Congress of Military Medicine and **Pharmacy**, S 5.39

Pharmacy Newsletter, HE 20.3054

Pharmacy Residences in Public Health Service Hospitals, FS 2.89/3

Phase

Snow Survey **Phase** of Project Skywater, Colorado, Annual Report, A 57.56/16

Phase I

Abstracts of **Phase I** Awards, Small Business Innovation Research, NS 1.46

Phc

United States Censuses of Population and Housing: Geographic Identification Code Scheme, **Phc** (2) (series), C 3.223/13

Phenomena

Astronomical **Phenomena** for the Year {date}, D 213.8/3

Center for Short-Lived **Phenomena**: Annual Report, SI 1.1/3

Philadelphia

Information Respecting the History, Conditions, and Prospects of the Indian Tribes of the United States, **Philadelphia**, Lippincott, Grambo & Co, I 20.2:In 2

Management Sciences Institute, **Philadelphia** Region: Bulletins, CS 1.3/2

Philadelphia, International Exhibition, S 6.13

Philadelphia, Sesquicentennial International Exposition, S 6.22

Philatelic

Philatelic Dedicatory Lecture Series, SI 3.12

Philatelic Releases, P 1.29/3

Philippine

Official Gazette **Philippine** Islands, W 49.16

Philippine Agricultural Review, W 49.21/7

Philippine Copra Market, C 18.199

Philippine Craftsman, W 49.6/5

Philippine Farmer, W 49.21/10

Philippine Health Service, Monthly Bulletin, W 49.15/6

Philippine Insurgent Records, W 6.10

Philippine Islands Census, 1903; Bulletins, C 3.8/2

Philippine Islands Census, 1903; Reports, C 3.8/1

Philippine Journal of Agriculture, W 49.55/5

Philippine Journal of Science, W 49.31/5

Philippine Tariffs, W 6.11

Quarterly Summary of Commerce of **Philippine** Islands, W 6.8

Philippine Islands

General Instructions for Surveys in **Philippine** Islands, C 4.18/4

Statistical Bulletins **Philippine Islands**, Commerce and Industry Bureau, W 49.52/5

U.S. Coast Pilots **Philippine Islands**, C 4.18/5

Philippines

United States Operations Mission to the **Philippines**, Publications, S 18.31

Philosophical

Bulletin of the **Philosophical** Society of Washington, SI 1.10

Phoenix

Area Wage Survey, **Phoenix**, Arizona, Metropolitan Area, L 2.121/3

Project **Phoenix** Reports, C 55.623

VA Medical Center, **Phoenix**, Arizona: Newsletter, VA 1.56/3

Phone

IRS **Phone** Book, National Office, T 22.48

Phonorecords

Music and **Phonorecords**, LC 30.8/6

Phosphate

Marketable **Phosphate** Rock, I 28.119/3

Mineral Industry Surveys, Marketable **Phosphate Rock**, I 19.147

Phosphate Crop Year, I 28.119/2

Phosphate Rock in (year), I 28.119

Phosphate Rock, I 28.119/3

Photo

Photo Series, A 1.100/2

USDA **Photo** Feature (series), A 1.137/2

Photoelastic

Photoelastic Group Reports, I 27.33

Photoessays

NOAA **Photoessays**, C 55.19

Photogrammetric

Photogrammetric Instructions, C 4.48

Photograph

Catalogue of Copyright Entries, Pt. 1, Engraving, Cuts and Prints, Chromos and Lithographs, **Photographs**, Fine Arts, LC 3.6/4

Photographic

Financial Audit, Senate Recording and **Photographic** Studios Revolving Fund, GA 1.13/5

Motion Pictures Distributed by **Photographic** Section, I 43.9

United States Foreign Trade in **Photographic** Goods, C 41.108

Photographs

Catalogue of **Photographs** and Stereoptican Slides, Y 3.P 96/3:11

Irrigation **Photographs**, I 27.24

Photographs of A-Bomb Test, Operation Doorstep, Yucca Flat, Nevada, March 17, 1953, FCD 1.11/2

Photographs of Scenes in National Parks (by name of park), I 29.32

Photographs of Scenes of National Parks, etc., I 29.29

Selected Audiovisual Records, **Photographs** of (various subjects), GS 4.17/7

Photography

Aerial **Photography** Summary Record System, APSRS (series), I 19.77

ASCS Aerial **Photography** Status Maps, A 82.84:Ae 8

Catalog of Meteorological Satellite Data: ESSA 9 and NOAA 1 Television Cloud **Photography**, C 55.219:5.3

Extent of Aerial **Photography** by Agriculture Department, Completed, in Progress and Approved, A 1.51

Journal of Scientific and Applied **Photography** and Cinematography {abstracts}, C 41.69

News of Institutes of Higher Learning; Ministry of Higher Education USSR, Geodesy and Aerial **Photography**, C 41.69/2

Space **Photography** Index, NAS 1.43/4

Photomap

Antarctic **Photomap** (series), I 19.100/6

Photometry

Titrimetry, Gravimetry, Flame **Photometry**, Spectro Photometry, and Gas Evolution, C 13.46

Photopaks

USAF Historical Aircraft **Photopaks**, D 301.76/2

Photovoltaics

National **Photovoltaics** Program Review, E 1.108

PHPC

PHPC (Public Housing Primary Care Program) Bulletin, HE 20.9121

Phrase Cards

Foreign Language **Phrase Cards**, D 208.6/5

PHS

PHS Dental Notes, HE 20.8/4

PHS Grants Administration Manual, HE 20.8/2

PHS Grants Policy Memorandum, HE 1.6/7-3, HE 20.8/3

PHS Public Advisory Groups, Authority, Structures, Functions, HE 20.2:Ad 9/2

PHS Rehabilitation Guide Series, FS 2.6/2, FS 2.6/6

Referral Guidelines for Funding Components of **PHS**, HE 20.3008/4

Roster of Members of **PHS** Public Advisory Groups, Councils, Committees, Boards, Panels, Study Sections, HE 20.2:Ad 9/3

PHS-Supported

Biomedical Index to **PHS-Supported** Research, HE 20.3013/2

Phsyco

News of Academy of Sciences of Armenian SSR, **Phsyco**-Mathematical, Natural and Technical Sciences Series, C 41.50/7

Physical

Inventory of **Physical** Facilities in Institutions of Higher Education, HE 5.92/3, HE 19.310

Journal of **Physical** Chemistry {abstracts}, C 41.34/5

Medicare Outpatient **Physical** Therapy Provider Manual, HE 22.8/9

National **Physical** Demands Information Series, L 7.26

Physical Education Series, I 16.40

Physical Fitness Research Digest, HE 20.110, Pr 37.8:P 56/2 R 31/2

Physical Fitness/Sports Medicine Bibliography, HE 20.111

Physical Land Surveys, A 76.212, A 80.2012, A 80.510

Physical Sciences Research Papers, D 301.45/40

Physical Sciences, C 51.17/9

Posters President's Council on **Physical** Fitness and Sports, HE 20.113

President's Council on **Physical** Fitness and Sports, Pr 37.8:P 56/2

President's Council on **Physical** Fitness and Sports: Research Digests, HE 20.114

Progress of **Physical** Sciences {abstracts}, C 41.52

Smithsonian **Physical** Tables, SI 1.7:120

Statistical Summary of the **Physical** Research Program as of June 30 (year), Y 3.At 7:2 P 56/2

Summary Statistics, Finances and **Physical** Features, I 27.1/4-3

Physical Sciences

Atomic Energy Research in Life Sciences and **Physical Sciences**, Y 3.At 7:48

Federal Grants and Contracts for Unclassified Research in **Physical Sciences**, NS 1.10/2

Foreign-Language and English Dictionaries in the **Physical** Sciences and Engineering, Selected Bibliography, 1952-1963, C 13.10:258

Physically Handicapped

Address List, Regional and Subregional Libraries for the Blind and **Physically Handicapped**, LC 19.17

Books for Blind and **Physically Handicapped** Individuals, LC 19.15/2

CD Blind, National Library Service for the Blind and **Physically Handicapped**, LC 19.24

Library Resources for the Blind and **Physically Handicapped**, LC 19.16

Posters National Library for the Blind and **Physically Handicapped**, LC 19.18

Task Force on **Physically Handicapped**, Pr 37.8:P 56

Physician

(HCFA) Medicare Unique **Physician** Identification Number (Directory), HE 22.414/2

Medicare Unique **Physician** Identification Number Directory, HE 22.414

Physician Requirements for {various subjects} (series), HE 20.6024

Physician's

Instructions for Classifying the Underlying Cause of Death: **Physician's** Examination Manual for the Hispanic Health and Nutrition Examination Survey, HE 20.6208/2-3

Physician's Pocket Reference to International List of Causes of Death, C 3.54

Physicians

Characteristics of **Physicians**: (by State), HE 20.6617

Employment Data on Title 38 **Physicians**, Dentists, and Nurses, VA 1.75

Handbook for Staff **Physicians**, HE 20.3044

NIMH Report to **Physicians** (series), HE 20.8111

Physicians Memorandum, HE 20.36/2

Physics

Bibliography on the High Temperature Chemistry and **Physics** of Gases and Gas-condensed Phase Reactions, C 13.37/3

Bibliography on the High Temperature Chemistry and **Physics** of Materials in the Condensed State, C 13.37/2

Collected Reprints; Atmospheric **Physics** and Chemistry Laboratory, C 55.612/3

Herald of Leningrad University, **Physics** and Chemistry Series {abstracts}, C 41.52/5

International Solar-Terrestrial **Physics** Program, NAS 1.86/3

Journal of Experimental and Theoretical **Physics** {abstracts}, C 41.52/2

Journal of Technical **Physics** {abstracts}, C 42.52/6

News of Academy of Sciences of USSR; **Physics** Series, C 41.52/3

News of Institutes of Higher Learning; Ministry of Higher Education, **Physics**, C 41.52/4

Physics and Mathematics, PrEx 7.22/11

Physics of Metals and Metallography {abstracts}, C 41.54/2

Physics Research, E 1.99

Physics, C 51.9/27

Research in Progress, Calendar Year **Physics**, Electronics, Mathematics, Geosciences, D 101.52/5-4

Summaries of FY (date) Research in Nuclear **Physics**, E 1.19/3

Technical Activities, Center for Chemical **Physics**, C 13.58/9

Physio-Mathematical

Herald of Moscow University, **Physio-Mathematical** and Natural Sciences Series {abstracts}, C 41.50/6

Physiological

Physiological Chemistry, Study Section, HE 20.3001/2:P 56/3

Physiology

Applied **Physiology** and Bioengineering Study Section, HE 20.3001/2:P 56

Physiology Study Section, HE 20.3001/2:P 56/2

Physiomathematical

News of Academy of Sciences of Estonia SSR, Technical and **Physiomathematical** Sciences, C 41.50/5

Physiotherapy

Annual Training Course in **Physiotherapy**, W 44.23/7

PI-H

PI-H (series), ES 3.11

PIC

PIC Highlights, HE 1.62

Picatinny

Technical Notes **Picatinny** Arsenal, D 105.12/2, D 105.12/4

Pictorial

United States Courts, **Pictorial** Summary, Ju 10.12

Viewpoints, a Selection from the **Pictorial** Collections of the Library of Congress, LC 25.2:V 67

Picture

Motion **Picture** Films, I 28.35

Motion **Picture** Guides, FS 2.211/2

Motion **Picture** Theaters Throughout the World, C 18.116/2

Motion-**Picture** Films, C 22.26/1

NASA **Picture** Sets, NAS 1.43/2

Picture of Subsidized Households, HH 1.124

Picture Sheets, A 56.20, A 77.320

Picture Story (series), A 21.26

Picture Story, A 1.100

Special **Picture** Pages, T 1.112

Viking **Picture** Sets, NAS 1.43/5

World Wide Motion **Picture** Developments, C 18.180

Picture Pages

Feature **Picture Pages**, T 66.13

Pictures

Bibliography of Motion **Pictures** and Film Strips FS (series), C 35.11/2 C 41.23

Motion **Pictures** Abroad, C 18.115, C 41.16

Motion **Pictures** and Filmstrips, C 18.116/3

Motion **Pictures** Distributed by Photographic Section, I 43.9

Motion **Pictures** Educational {and} Industrial, C 18.116

Motion **Pictures** of Department of Agriculture, A 43.24

Pig

Pig Crop Report, A 88.16/3

Pig Crop Report, Louisiana Crop Reporting Service, A 88.16/3-2

Pigments

Iron Oxide **Pigments** in (year), I 28.163

Pigs

Hogs and **Pigs**, A 105.23/5

Pilot

Aeronautical Communications and **Pilot** Services Handbook 7300.7, Changes, FAA 3.9/2

Great Lakes **Pilot**; Lake Survey Office, D 103.203

Great Lakes **Pilot**; National Ocean Survey, C 55.420

IFR and VFR **Pilot** Exam-O-Grams, TD 4.54

Inside Route **Pilot** (Atlantic and Gulf Coasts), C 4.6/3

Montana **Pilot** Bulletin, TD 4.66

Pilot Chart of Central American Waters, N 6.24, M 202.15, D 203.15

Pilot Chart of Greenland and Barnets Seas, N 6.15/4

Pilot Chart of Indian Ocean, N 6.17, M 202.16, D 203.16

Pilot Chart of North Atlantic Ocean, N 6.15, M 202.17, D 203.17

Pilot Chart of North Pacific Ocean, N 6.16, M 202.19, D 203.19

Pilot Chart of South Atlantic Ocean, N 6.20, M 202.18, D 203.18

Pilot Chart of South Pacific Ocean, N 6.12, M 202.20, D 203.20

Pilot Chart of Upper Air, North Atlantic Ocean, N 6.28

Pilot Chart of Upper Air, North Pacific Ocean, N 6.29

Pilot Charts of Central American Waters, D 203.15

Pilot Cities Program, J 1.46/2

Pilot Rules for Certain Inland Waters of Atlantic and Pacific Coasts of Gulf of Mexico, C 25.9

Pilot Rules for Rivers whose Waters Flow into Gulf of Mexico and Their Tributaries and Red River of the North, C 25.8

Pilot Rules, T 38.8, C 15.8

Supplement to **Pilot** Charts, N 6.26

U.S. Coast Pilots Inside Route **Pilot**, C 4.6/3

United States Coast **Pilot**, Atlantic Coast, T 11.6

United States Coast **Pilot**, Pacific Coast, Alaska, pt. 1, Dixon Entrance to Yakutat Bay, T 11.7/2

Pilot Chart

Ice Supplement to North Atlantic **Pilot Chart**, N 6.15/2

Pilot Plant

Ecological Monitoring Program at the Waste Isolation **Pilot Plant**, Annual Report, E 1.28/16

Pilot Program

Annual Report on the Management Efficiency **Pilot Program**, VA 1.1/3

Pilotage

Great Lakes **Pilotage** Administration, C 1.47

Great Lakes **Pilotage** Regulations and Rules and Orders, C 1.47:R 26

Publications Great Lakes **Pilotage** Administration, C 1.47

Statistical Report, Great Lakes **Pilotage**, C 1.47:St 2

Tactical **Pilotage** Charts, D 5.354
Pilots
Catalogs of Charts, Coast **Pilots** and Tide Tables, C
4.5, T 11.5
Certification; Flight Crewmembers other than
Pilots, TD 4.6:part 63
Certification; **Pilots** and Flight Instructors, TD
4.6:part 61
Coast **Pilots**, C 4.6/1
Supplementary Notices to Mariners, Correction
Sheets for Coast **Pilots**, N 6.11/3
U.S. Coast **Pilots** Alaska, C 4.7/2, C 4.7/3, C 4.7/7
U.S. Coast **Pilots** Atlantic Coast, C 4.6/1
U.S. Coast **Pilots** Gulf Coast, Puerto Rico, and
Virgin Islands, C 4.6, C 4.6/4
U.S. Coast **Pilots** Hawaiian Islands, C 4.7/4, C 4.7/
5
U.S. Coast **Pilots** Inside Route Pilot, C 4.6/3
U.S. Coast **Pilots** Pacific Coast, California, Oregon,
Washington, and Hawaii, C 4.7/1
U.S. Coast **Pilots** Philippine Islands, C 4.18/5
U.S. Coast **Pilots** Wartime Information to Mariners,
C 4.7/6
U.S. Coast **Pilots** West Indies, C 4.6/2
United States Coast **Pilots**, C 55.422
Wartime Information to Mariners Supplementing
U.S. Coast **Pilots**, C 4.7/6
Pipe
Uniform System of Accounts for **Pipe** Lines, IC 1
pip.5, IC 1 pip.6
Pipe-Line
Sales by Producers of Natural Gas to Interstate
Pipe-Line Companies, FP 1.21
Transportation Revenue and Traffic of Large Oil
Pipe Line Companies, IC 1 pip.7
Pipe Lines
Depreciation Rates for Property of Carriers by **Pipe
Lines**, IC 1 pip.8
Pipeline
Annual Report of the Administration of the Natural
Gas **Pipeline** Safety Act, TD 9.11
Annual Report on **Pipeline** Safety, TD 10.12
Annual Report on the Administration of the
Natural Gas Pipeline Safety Act, TD 9.11
Cost of **Pipeline** and Compressor Station
Construction Under Non-Budget Type or
Certificate Authorizations As Reported
by **Pipeline** Companies, FP 1.30
Crude-oil and Refined-products **Pipeline** Mileage
in the United States, I 28.45/2
Financial Statistics of Electric Utilities and
Interstate Natural Gas **Pipeline**
Companies, E 3.11/2-8
Gas Supplies of Interstate Natural Gas **Pipeline**
Companies, E 3.25/2
Preliminary Report of Domestic Natural Gas
Reserves and Production Dedicated to
Interstate **Pipeline** Companies, E 3.25/2-
2
Prevention **Pipeline**, HE 20.428, HE 20.8012/3
Statistics of Interstate Natural Gas **Pipeline**
Companies, E 3.25
Underground Storage of Natural Gas by Interstate
Pipeline Companies, E 3.11/2-4
Pipelines
Annual Report of Secretary of Transportation of
Administration of Natural Gas **Pipelines**
Safety Act of 1968, TD 1.10/4
Crude-oil and Product **Pipelines**, E 3.11/12
Piroplasmosis
Equine **Piroplasmosis** Progress Report, A 77.242
PK-M
PK-M (series), ES 3.6/12
PLA
Environmental Action **PLA** Reports (numbered),
TD 2.44
Place
Construction Reports; Value of New Construction
Put in **Place**, C 30 (series), C 56.211/5
Placecards
Bulletin Board **Placecards**, Pr 32.4812/2
Placement
Coordinator's Scoreboard, Review of What's New
in **Placement** of the Handicapped, CS
1.75
Evaluation of Employees for Promotion and
Internal **Placement**, CS 1.41/4:335-1
Placement Activities, Pr 32.5218
Teaching Opportunities, Directory of **Placement**
Information, FS 5.226:2600, HE
5.226:2600

Places
Eating and Drinking **Places** and Motels Wage
Survey Summaries by Cities, L 2.113/4
National Register of Historic **Places**, I 29.76, I
70.2:H 62/2, I 70.17
National Register of Historic **Places** Bulletins, I
29.76/3
Places where Civil Service Examinations are Held,
CS 1.28:2300
South, Population and Per Capita Income Estimates
for Counties and Incorporated **Places**, C
3.186/27-5
West North Central, Population and Per Capita
Income Estimates for Counties and
Incorporated **Places**, C 3.186/27-3
Places
West, Population and Per Capita Income Estimates
for Counties and Incorporated **Places**, C
3.186/27-2
Plain
Commercial Tobacco Farms, Coastal **Plain**, North
Carolina, A 93.9/11
Flood **Plain** Information (series), D 103.47
Flood **Plain** Management Study, A 57.64/4
Flood **Plain** Report {various locations}, A 57.64
Plain Talk About {various subjects}, HE 20.8128
Plain Region
Consumer Price Index, Mountain Region and **Plain
Region**, L 2.38/6
Plains
Commercial Wheat Farms, **Plains** and Pacific
Northwest, A 93.9/11
Employment and Earnings in the Mountain **Plains**
Region, L 2.41/8
Employment in the **Plains** States, L 2.41/7
Studies in **Plains** Anthropology and History, I
20.50
Plan
Air Force Energy Conservation **Plan**, D 301.89/6-2
Annual Program **Plan**, J 16.26
Annual Program **Plan** and Academy Training
Schedule, J 16.26
Aviation Capacity Enhancement **Plan**, TD 4.77
BJA Program **Plan**, J 26.1/5
Circulars Relating to **Plan** and Methods of
Publication of Official Records of Union
Army and Confederate Army, W 45.4
Comprehensive **Plan** for the National Capital, NC
2.2:P 69/2
Course Management **Plan** and Program of
Instruction (series), D 101.107/4
Current Report on Marshall **Plan**, Y 3.Ec 74/3:15
Enrollment Information Guide and **Plan**
Comparison Chart, PM 1.8/11
FAA **Plan** for Air Navigation and Air Traffic
Control Systems, FAA 1.37
Federal Aviation Administration **Plan** for Research,
Engineering, and Development, TD 4.64
Federal **Plan** for Marine Environmental Prediction,
Fiscal Year, C 55.16
Federal **Plan** for Meteorological Services and
Supporting Research, Fiscal Year (date),
C 55.16/2
Federal **Plan** for Ocean Pollution Research,
Developing, and Monitoring, PrEx
8.109
Federal **Plan** for Water-Data Acquisition, I 19.74/3
Federal Radionavigation **Plan**, D 1.84
Forward **Plan** for Health, HE 20.18
High Performance Computing and Communications
Implementation **Plan**, PrEx 23.13
Implementation **Plan** Review for {Various States}
As Required by the Energy Supply and
Environmental Coordination Act, EP
1.58
Information Systems Strategic **Plan**, VA 1.86
Inspector General: Master **Plan**, Y 3.T 25:67
Management **Plan** & Environmental Assessment, I
53.59/2
National Action **Plan** on Breast Cancer Fact Sheets
(series), HE 20.38/2
Office of Inspector General, Audit and Inspection
Plan, C 1.1/2-2
Office of Inspector General FY, Annual **Plan**, A 1.1/
6
Plan of Work for Cooperative Hydrology
Investigations, I 53.47
Program and Financial **Plan**, Basic Assumptions
and Guidelines, HE 1.610/2
Program and Project **Plan** for Fiscal Year (date), J
1.38

Program Memorandum Health Maintenance
Organization/Competitive Medical **Plan**,
HE 22.28/2
Program **Plan** by Program Areas for Fiscal Year, HE
20.7121
Program **Plan** of the National Institute for
Occupational Safety and Health, HE
20.7127
Program **Plan**, Fiscal Year (date), J 26.24
Proposed Multi-Year Operating **Plan**, Statistics of
Income Division, T 22.2/3, T 22.2/10
Questions and Answers on Controlled Materials
Plan, Q & A (series), C 40.13
Receipts and Disbursements of Government
Consolidated into Bureau of Accounts,
Fiscal Service in Treasury Department by
President's Reorganization **Plan** no. 3, T
9.11
Regional Studies **Plan**, Fiscal Year, Atlantic OCS
Region, I 72.12/15
Report on **Plan** Preparation on State and Local
Public Works, FW 7.7
Research and Development: Public Awareness/
participation Support **Plan**, Fiscal Year
(date), EP 1.90
Research and Evaluation **Plan**, J 28.25/5
Research Program **Plan**, J 28.25/3
Resource Conservation Development **Plan**, A 57.65
Resources Management **Plan** Annual Update, I
53.50
Rocky Mountain Regional Aviation System **Plan**,
TD 4.33/5
State Air Pollution Implementation **Plan** Progress
Report, EP 1.52
State Vocational Rehabilitation Agency Program
and Financial **Plan**, HE 23.4110
Tables on Hatchery and Flock Participation in the
National Poultry Improvement **Plan**, A
77.15:44-3
Tables on Hatchery and Flock Participation in the
National Turkey Improvement **Plan**, A
77.15:44-4
Tactical **Plan**, T 63.125
Technical **Plan** for the Great Lakes Environmental
Research Laboratory, C 55.620/2
Telecommunications **Plan**, TD 5.52
Tower University: Education Service **Plan**, D
101.93/2
U.S. Air Force **Plan** for Defense Research Sciences,
D 301.45/19-5
United States Arctic Research **Plan**, NS 1.51
United States Retirement **Plan** Bonds, Tables of
Redemption Values for All Denomination
Bonds, T 63.209/8-2
USC/FAR Consolidated **Plan** for Foreign Affairs
Research, PrEx 3.12
USIA Strategic Information Resources Management
(IRM) **Plan**, IA 1.33
VA ADP and Telecommunications **Plan**, VA 1.77
Watershed Work **Plan** {by Area}, A 57.59
Western U.S. Water **Plan**, (year) Progress Report, I
27.61
Woodland Management **Plan**, Agreements and Farm
Codes, A 57.37
Your Changing Forest, News on the Black Hills
National Forest **Plan** Revision, A 13.128
Plane
AVFUEL & AVOIL into **Plane** Contract Listing, D
7.24/2
Planet
ERTS-1, a New Window on Our **Planet**, I
19.16:929
Planetary
Lunar and **Planetary** Institute: Technical Reports,
NAS 1.67
Planimetric
State Map Series **Planimetric**, I 19.102, I 19.105
State Map Series: **Planimetric**, Topographic and
Shaded Relief, I 19.102
Planned
Alphabetical Listing, Register or **Planned**
Mobilization Producers, Manufacturers
of War Material Registered Under
Production Allocation Program, D 7.11
Grants Competitions and RFPS: **Planned** NIE
Activities During the Fiscal Year, HE
19.216
Oregon and Washington **Planned** Land Sales, I
53.32
Received or **Planned** Current Fisheries, Oceano-
graphic, and Atmospheric Translations,
A- (series), C 55.325/2
Register **Planned** Emergency Producers, D 7.11/2

Toxics Integration **Policy** Series, EP 1.79/3

Trade **Policy** Agenda and Annual Report of the President of the Agreements Program, PrEx 9.11

U.S. Air Force **Policy** Letter Digest, D 301.120

U.S. Foreign **Policy** Agenda, IA 1.38

United States Foreign **Policy**, S 1.71

United States **Policy** Toward USSR and International Communism, Monthly Digest of Pertinent Data Appearing in Department of State Publications, S 1.97

Working Papers National Transportation **Policy** Study Commission, Y 3.T 68/2:10

Poliomyelitis

National Communicable Disease Center Neurotropic Viral Diseases Surveillance, Annual **Poliomyelitis** Summary, FS 2.60/14:P 75

Poliomyelitis Surveillance Summary, HE 20.7011/31

Polish

American Illustrated (**Polish** language), IA 1.14/2

Translated **Polish** Patents, C 41.85/2

Polishes

World Trade in Wood, Furniture, Floor, Metal and Automobile **Polishes**, C 18.178

Politic

Akten Zur Deutschen Auswartigen **Politic**, S 1.82/2

Political

Annual Report of **Political** Committees Supporting Candidates for House of Representatives, Y 1.2/4

Laws relating to Federal Corrupt Practices and Political Activities, Federal Corrupt Practices Act, Hatch **Political** Activities Act, Miscellaneous Related Acts and Regulations, Y 1.2:F 31/8

Monthly **Political** Report, S 1.20

Monthly **Political** Reports, Confidential, Changes in Foreign Service, S 1.14

Political Activity and Political Assessments of Federal Office-Holders and Employees, CS 1.34

Political Activity of Government Personnel Commission, Y 3.P 75

Political and Sociological Affairs, PrEx 7.21/5

Political, Sociological and Military Affairs, PrEx 7.15/4, PrEx 7.17/2

Significant Incidents of **Political** Violence Against Americans, S 1.138/2

Soviet Union, **Political** Affairs, PrEx 7.21/5-2

Political Committees

Annual Reports of **Political Committees** Supporting Candidates for Senate, Y 1.3/5

Manual of Regulations and Instructions . . . Federal Campaign Funds for Candidates for the Office of President or Vice President of the United States and **Political Committees** Supporting Such Candidates, GA 1.14:C 15

Politics

Economics, **Politics**, Ideology, PrEx 7.21/14

International **Politics**, Selective Monthly Bibliography, S 1.92/4

Pollutant

National Air **Pollutant** Emission Estimates, EP 4.24

Pollutant Identification Research Highlights, EP 1.37/3

Polluting

Polluting Incidents in and Around U.S. Waters, TD 5.51

Pollution

Air **Pollution** Abstracts, EP 4.11

Air **Pollution** Aspects of Emission Sources: {various subjects}, a Bibliography with Abstracts, EP 1.21/5

Air **Pollution** Control Office Publications APTD (series), EP 4.9/2

Air **Pollution** Control Office Publications, AP (series), EP 4.9

Air **Pollution** Report, Federal Facilities, Air Quality Control Regions, EP 4.10

Air **Pollution** Technical Publications of the U.S. Environmental Protection Agency, Quarterly Bulletin, EP 1.21/8

Air Pollution Training Courses, (year) and University Training Programs, Extramural Programs, Institute for Air **Pollution** Training Planning and Special Projects, EP 4.13

Air Pollution, Sulfur Oxides **Pollution** Control, Federal Research and Development, Planning and Programming, FS 2.93/4

Annual Conference on Advanced **Pollution** Control for the Metal Finishing Industry, EP 1.80

Bulletin of Courses Water **Pollution** Control Technical Training Program, I 67.17

Chronological Schedule, Institute of Air **Pollution** Training Courses, EP 4.14/2

Coastal **Pollution** Research Highlights, EP 1.37

Compendium of State Air **Pollution** Control Agencies, 1972, EP 1.2:St 2/972

Conference in Matters of **Pollution** of Navigable Waters, Proceedings, EP 1.16/2

Conference of Oil **Pollution** of Navigable Waters, S 5.24

Economic Impact Analysis of Alternative **Pollution** Control Technologies (series), EP 1.8/10

Environmental **Pollution** and Control, C 51.9/5

EPA Annual Report to **Pollution** Engineers, EP 1.85

Estuarine **Pollution** Study Series, EP 2.19

Federal Plan for Ocean **Pollution** Research, Developing, and Monitoring, PrEx 8.109

Fish Kills Caused by **Pollution** in (year), EP 2.24

Immediate Water **Pollution** Control Needs, I 67.13/5

International Reference Group on Great Lakes **Pollution** from Land Use Activities: Annual Progress Report, Y 3.In 8/28:14

National Marine **Pollution** Program, PrEx 8.109

Office of Marine **Pollution** Assessment, Technical Plan for Fiscal Year, C 55.43/2

Office of Marine **Pollution** Assessment: Annual Report, C 55.43

Oil **Pollution** Abstracts, EP 1.25/2

Oil **Pollution** Research Newsletter, EP 1.25

Organic Chemistry: Air **Pollution** Studies Characterization of Chemical Structures; Synthesis of Research Materials, C 13.46

Pollution Prevention Handbook, I 1.77/3

Pollution Prevention News, EP 5.26

Proceedings Conference in Matters of **Pollution** and Navigable Waters, EP 1.16/2

Progress in the Prevention and Control of Air **Pollution** in (year), Report to Congress, EP 4.16

Project Register, Projects Approved Under Sec. 8 of Federal Water **Pollution** Control Act (Pub. Law 660, 84th Cong.), As Amended and Sec. 3, of Public Works

Public Health Service Water **Pollution** Surveillance System, FS 2.84/2

Publications Air **Pollution** Control Office, EP 4.9

Publications National Air **Pollution** Control Administration, FS 2.93/3

Publications National Conference on Air **Pollution**, FS 2.98

Publications National Conference on Water **Pollution**, FS 2.64/3

Report to Congress on Ocean **Pollution**, Monitoring and Research, C 55.31/3, C 55.439

Report to Congress on Ocean **Pollution**, Overfishing, and Offshore Development, C 55.31/2

State Air **Pollution** Implementation Plan Progress Report, EP 1.52

Task Force on Air **Pollution**, Pr 37.8:Ai 7

Technical Memoranda for Municipal, Industrial and Domestic Water Supplies, **Pollution** Abatement, Public Health, FS 2.301

United States LPPSD {Low **Pollution** Power Systems Development} Technical Information Exchange Documents, ER 1.16

Water **Pollution** Control Research and Training Grants, FS 2.64/7, I 67.13

Water **Pollution** Control Research Series, EP 1.16, EP 2.10

Water **Pollution** Control, Federal Costs, Report to Congress, I 67.1/2

Water **Pollution** Publications, FS 2.64

Water Supply and **Pollution** Control, FS 2.64/2

Pollution-Caused

Pollution-Caused Fish Kills, FS 2.94, I 67.9

Polydrug

Services Research Monograph Series, National **Polydrug** Collaborative Project, Treatment Manuals, HE 20.8216/2

Polymer

Polymer Science and Standards Division, Annual Report, C 13.1/7

Polytechnic

Southwestern Indian **Polytechnic** Institute, Catalog, I 20.66

POMS

POMS Program Operations Manual System, SSA 1.8/2

Popcorn

Popcorn Acreage for Harvest, A 92.11/7

Popcorn Production, A 88.12/14

Poplar River

Annual Reports to the Governments of Canada, U.S, Saskatchewan and Montana by the **Poplar River** Bilateral Monitoring Committee, S 1.147

Poppies

Poppies and Porticos, a HCRS Heritage Newsletter, I 70.21

Popular

Army Hit Kit of **Popular** Songs, D 102.10

Popular Bulletins, W 49.21/8

Popular Publications for Farmer, Suburbanite, Homemaker, Consumer, A 21.9/8:5, A 107.12:5

Popular Study Series; Histories, I 29.45

Population

After-Tax Money Income Estimates of Households, Current **Population** Reports, C 3.186/5

American Woodcock, Harvest and Breeding **Population** Status, I 49.106/6

Analysis of Federal **Population** Research, HE 20.3025

Annual Summary Progress Reports of **Population** Research Centers and Program Projects, HE 20.3362/4

Bulletins, **Population** (by States), C 3.14/1, C 3.28/8

Bulletins, **Population** (Misc.) {Including Occupations}, C 3.28/9

Census of **Population**, C 3.223/12

Census of **Population**; Advance Estimates of Social Economic, and Housing Characteristics, Supplementary Reports, PHC A2 (series), C 3.223/21-2

Census of **Population**; Advance Reports, C 3.223/4

Census of **Population** and Housing, Advance Reports, PHC, C 3.223/19

Census of **Population** and Housing: Alphabetical Index of Industries and Occupations, C 3.223/22:90-R3

Census of **Population** and Housing Block Statistics, C 3.282/3

Census of **Population** and Housing: Classified Index of Industries and Occupations, C 3.223/22:90-R4

Census of **Population** and Housing: Finders Guide to Census Tract Reports, C 3.223/11-2

Census of **Population** and Housing: Geographic Identification Code Scheme, C 3.223/22:90-R5

Census of **Population** and Housing Guide Part B, Glossary, C 3.223/22:90-R1

Census of **Population** and Housing: History, C 3.223/22:90-R2

Census of **Population** and Housing, Preliminary Reports, C 3.223/18

Census of **Population** and Housing, Public Law 94-171 DATA, C 3.281

Census of **Population** and Housing: Reference Reports, C 3.223/22:90-R

Census of **Population** and Housing Tabulation and Publication Program for Puerto Rico, C 3.223/24

Census of **Population** and Housing: Users Guide, C 3.223/22-2

Census of **Population**; Characteristics of the **Population**, C 3.223/9

Census of **Population**; Congressional Districts, C 3.223/20

Census of **Population**; Detailed Characteristics, C 3.223/8

Census of **Population**; Final Volumes (other than by States), C 3.223/10

Census of **Population**; General **Population** Characteristics, C 3.223/6

Census of **Population**: General **Population** Characteristics for American Indian and Alaska Native Areas, C 3.223/6-2

Census of Population: General **Population** Characteristics for American Indian and Alaska Native Areas, C 3.223/6-2

Census of **Population**: General **Population** Characteristics for Metropolitan Statistical Areas, C 3.223/6-3

Census of **Population**: General **Population** Characteristics for Urbanized Areas, C 3.223/6-4

Census of **Population**; General Publications, C 3.223

Census of **Population**; General Social and Economic Characteristics, C 3.223/7

Census of **Population**; Housing: Announcements, C 3.223/3

Census of **Population**; Housing: Evaluation and Research Program, C 56.223/16

Census of **Population**; Preliminary Reports, C 3.223/2

Census of **Population**; Reference Reports, C 3.223/22

Census of **Population**: Social and Economic Characteristics for American Indian and Alaska Native Areas, C 3.223/7-2

Census of **Population**: Social and Economic Characteristics for Metropolitan Statistical Areas, C 3.223/7-3

Census of **Population**: Social and Economic Characteristics for Urbanized Areas, C 3.223/7-4

Census of **Population**; Subject Reports, C 56.223/10

Census of **Population**; Supplementary Reports, C 3.223/21

Census of **Population**; Supplementary Reports PC (S1) (series), C 56.223/12

Census of The Americas, **Population** Census, Urban Area Data, C 3.211

Censuses of **Population** and Housing: Census County Division Boundary Description, Phc (3) series, C 3.223/15

Censuses of **Population** and Housing: Census Tract Reports, C 3.223/11

Center for **Population** Research, Progress Report, HE 20.3351/3

CPR **Population** Research, HE 20.3362/3

Current **Population** Reports, C 3.186, C 56.218

Current **Population** Reports, Household Economic Studies, C 3.186:P-70/2

Current **Population** Reports, Local **Population** Estimates, County **Population** Estimates, C 3.186/20-2

Current Population Reports, Local **Population** Estimates, County Population Estimates, C 3.186/20-2

Current **Population** Research Reports, FS 2.22/61

Current **Population** Survey, C 3.224/12

East North Central, **Population** and Per Capita Income Estimates for Counties and Incorporated Places, C 3.186/27-4

Employment and **Population** Changes, Special Economic Reports, C 56.240

Estimates of the **Population** of Puerto Rico and the Outlying Areas, C 3.186/19

Estimates of the **Population** of the United States, C 3.186:P-25

Farm **Population**, C 3.201

Farm **Population** and Rural Life Activities, A 36.23

Farm **Population** of the United States, C 3.186:P-27

Farm **Population**, Annual Estimates by States, Major Geographical Division, and Regions, A 88.21

Federal **Population** and Mortality Schedules (years), in the National Archives and the States, AE 1.115

Federal Program in **Population** Research, Inventory of **Population** Research Supported by Federal Agencies During Fiscal Year (date), HE 20.3362/2

Federal-State Cooperative Program for **Population** Estimates, C 3.186:P-26

Fertility of **Population**, C 3.186:P-20

Financial Statistics of Cities Having a **Population** of Over 30,000, C 3.47

Financial Statistics of Cities Having a **Population** of Over 100,000, C 3.47/2

Hispanic **Population** in the United States, C 3.186/14-2

Hispanic **Population** in the United States, Advance Report, C 3.186/14

Income and Poverty, Current **Population** Survey, C 3.224/12-2

Income of the **Population** 55 and Over, HE 3.75

Income of the **Population** 55 or Older, SSA 1.30

International **Population** Reports, C 3.186:P-95

International **Population** Reports Series, C 56.112/2

International **Population** Reports, P-91 (series), C 59.13

International **Population** Statistics Reports, C 56.112

International **Population** Statistics Reports, P 90 (series), C 59.13/2:90

Inventory and Analysis of Federal **Population** Research, HE 20.3362/2

Inventory of Federal **Population** Research, Fiscal Year, HE 20.3025

Inventory of **Population** Research Supported by Federal Agencies, HE 20.3362/2

Inventory of **Population** Research Supported by Federal Agencies, HE 20.3362/2

Mobility of the **Population** of the United States, C 3.186:P-20

Monthly State, Regional and National Cooling Degree Days Weighted by **Population**, C 55.287/60-3

Monthly State, Regional and National Heating Degree Days Weighted by **Population**, C 55.287/60-2

Mourning Dove, Breeding **Population** Status, I 49.106/5

National Health Survey: **Population** Series, Bulletins, Preliminary Reports, T 27.37

Negro **Population**: March (year), C 3.186:P-20

Net Migration of the **Population**, by Age, Sex and Color, A 93.35

1950 Census of **Population** and Housing Announcements, C 3.950-4/3

1990 Census of **Population** and Housing Special Tabulation on Aging, C 3.281/2

1990 Census of **Population** and Housing, Special Tabulation on Aging, Federal Region 1, Connecticut-Maine-Massachusetts-New Hampshire-Rhode Island-Vermont, Cd 90-AOA1, C 3.218/2:CD 90-AOA

Northeast, **Population** and Per Capita Income Estimates for Counties and Incorporated Places, C 3.186/27

P-90 International **Population** Statistics Reports, C 3.205

Population, 2d Series, C 3.940-13/2

Population, 3d Series (by States), C 3.940-37

Population, 4th Series (by States), C 3.940-37/2**Population** and Housing (by States), C 3.940-38

Population and Reproduction Research Abstracts, HE 20.3360

Population Bulletins, Families, C 3.37/10

Population Bulletins, 1st Series (by States), C 3.37/8

Population Bulletins, 2d Series (by States), C 3.37/9

Population Characteristics, C 3.186:P-20

Population {Congested Areas}, C 3.160

Population Division Working Paper Series, C 3.223/26

Population Estimates and Projection, C 3.186:P-25, C 3.223/27

Population, Outlying Possessions, C 3.940-39**Population** Paper Listings (PPL series), C 3.223/25

Population Profile of the United States, Current **Population** Reports, C 3.186/8

Population Research Committee, HE 20.3001/2:P 81

Population Research Reports, HE 20.3362

Population Research Study Section, HE 20.3001/2:P 81/2

Population Sciences, Index of Biomedical Research, HE 20.3362/5

Population Sciences, Inventory of Private Agency **Population** Research, HE 20.3362/2-2

Population, Special Reports, C 3.161**Population** Trends, C 3.288

Population Trends and Environmental Policy, I 22.10

Population-Weighted Data, C 55.287/60

Projections of the **Population** of Voting Age, for States, C 3.186/26

Provisional Estimates of the **Population** of Counties, C 3.186/20

Reports on Reproduction and **Population** Research (series), FS 2.22/13-7

South, **Population** and Per Capita Income Estimates for Counties and Incorporated Places, C 3.186/27-5

Special Studies, Current **Population** Reports, C 3.186:P-23

State **Population** and Household Estimates with Age, Sex, and Components of Change, C 3.186/21

U.S. Census of **Population**: Number of Inhabitants, C 3.223/5

United States Censuses of **Population** and Housing: Geographic Identification Code Scheme, Phc (2) (series), C 3.223/13

Weekly **Population** Report, J 16.32

West North Central, **Population** and Per Capita Income Estimates for Counties and Incorporated Places, C 3.186/27-3

West, **Population** and Per Capita Income Estimates for Counties and Incorporated Places, C 3.186/27-2

World **Population**: Recent Demographic Estimates for the Countries and Regions of the World, C 3.205/3

Populations

Correctional **Populations** in the United States, J 29.17

International **Populations** Reports, C 3.186:P-95, C 56.112/2

News, Work Experience of the **Populations**, L 2.120/2-18

Populations, 1st Series (by States), C 3.940-13

Statistics of Public Library Systems Serving **Populations** of 100,000 or more, FS 5.215:15033, HE 5.215:15033

Statistics of Public Library Systems Serving **Populations** of 50,000-99,999, FS 5.215:15034, HE 5.215:15034

Statistics of Public Library Systems Serving **Populations** of 35,00049,999, FS 5.215:15035, HE 5.215:15035

Trends in Duck Breeding **Populations**, I 49.106/2

Porcelain

Porcelain Enameled Flat Ware, C 3.98

Porcelain Plumbing Fixtures (all clay), C 3.99

Pork

World Hog and **Pork** Prospects, A 36.43

Port

Activities Relating to the **Port** and Tanker Safety Act, TD 5.34/2

Catalogue of Books and Blanks Used by Officers of Customs at **Port** of New York, T 36.5/2

Foreign **Port** Series, C 18.34

Highlights of MarAd **Port** Activities, C 39.223/2

Pleasure and Business Visitors to U.S. by **Port** of Entry and Mode of Travel, C 47.15/2

Port Allocations of {various commodities}, A 82.86

Port and Terminal Facilities, W 7.34

Port Guides, D 208.6/4

Port Safety Bulletin, TD 5.3/4

Port Security, TD 1.61

Port Series, C 39.223, D 103.8

Port Series, Maritime Administration, C 39.223

Shipment Under the United States Foreign Aid Programs Made on Army- or Navy-Operated Vessels (American flag) by **Port** of Lading by Country of Destination, C 3.164:976

World **Port** Index, D 203.22:150

Portfolio

Insured Mortgage **Portfolio**, HH 2.10

Monthly Corrections Affecting **Portfolio** Chart List and Index-Catalog of Nautical Charts and Publications, D 203.22/2

News and Features from NIH, **Portfolio** Series, HE 20.3007/2

Portfolios

Catalog of Charts and Plans Issued to Vessels of Navy, **Portfolios**, N 6.5/7

Graphic **Portfolios**, Charts, and Posters, W 1.52

Porticos

Poppies and **Porticos**, a HCRS Heritage Newsletter, I 70.21

Portions

Fish Sticks, Fish **Portions**, and Breaded Shrimp (CFS series), C 55.309/2

Portland

Area Wage Survey, **Portland**, Oregon- Washington, Metropolitan Area, L 2.121/37

Porto Rico

Climatological Data; **Porto Rico** Section, A 29.35

Monthly Summary of Commerce of **Porto Rico**, W 6.7

Special Reports **Porto Rico**, Labor Bureau, W 75.14/4

Portrait

ALA **Portrait** Index, LC 1.10

Facing the Light, Historic American **Portrait** Daguerreotypes, SI 11.2:L 62

National **Portrait** Gallery Calendar of Events, SI 11.15

Profile: Smithsonian National **Portrait** Gallery News, SI 11.16

Powers

Publications Supreme Commander for Allied **Powers**, D 102.11

Supreme Commander for Allied **Powers**, Publications, D 102.11

Supreme Commander for Allied **Powers**: Japanese Economic Statistics Bulletin, D 102.18

Supreme Commander for Allied **Powers**: Natural Resources Section Reports, D 102.20

POW/MIA

POW/MIA Policy and Process, Y 4.P 93/8

PPL

Population Paper Listings (**PPL** series), C 3.223/25

PPL Digest, E 1.103

PPS

Petroleum Products Survey, **PPS**- (series), I 28.18/3

PQ

PQ {Plant Quarantine} (series), A 77.308/3

PR

PR, HH 1.33

PR- (series), J 1.36

Practical

American **Practical** Navigator, D 5.317:9, D 203.22:9

Federal Technology Catalog, Summaries of **Practical** Technology, NTIS Tech Notes Annual Index, C 51.17/11

Practical Check Lists, W 9.8/2

Practical Exercises (series), D 101.107

Practical Guide Series, HE 20.3108/2

Tables from American **Practical** Navigator (Bowditch), D 203.22:9

Practical Nurses

Basic Preparatory Programs for **Practical Nurses** by States and Changes in Number of Programs, FS 5.133

Practice

Annual Report of Small Arms Target **Practice**, N 17.15

Bureau of Ships, Shop **Practice** Suggestions, C 41.95

Bureau **Practice**, FAA 5.10

Clinical **Practice** Guideline, HE 20.6520, HE 20.6520/3

Committeeman's **Practice** Handbooks (by States), A 82.107

Fair Employment **Practice** Committee {publications}, Pr 32.412

Federal Power Commission Rules of **Practice** and Procedure, FP 1.6

Foundry **Practice** {abstracts}, C 41.54/10

How They Do It, Illustrations of **Practice** in Administration of AFDC (series), HE 17.408/2

Labor Law and **Practice** in (country), L 2.71

Park **Practice** Grist, I 29.72

Practice and Procedure, RC 1.8

Proposed Trade **Practice** Rules, FT 1.16/2

Roster of Attorneys and Agents Registered to **Practice** before the U.S. Patent Office, C 21.9

Rules of **Practice** and Procedure, FP 1.6, TC 1.8

Rules of **Practice** and Rules Relating to Investigations and Code of Behavior Governing Exparte Communications Between Persons Outside the Commission and Decisional Employees, SE 1.6:R 86/4

Rules of **Practice** Board of Tax Appeals, Y 3.T 19:7

Rules of **Practice** Bureau of Domestic Commerce, C 41.6/11

Rules of **Practice** Federal Power Commission, FP 1.8

Rules of **Practice** Federal Trade Commission, FT 1.7

Rules of **Practice** General Land Office, I 21.9

Rules of **Practice** in Patent Cases, C 21.14:P 27

Rules of **Practice** Patent and Trademark Office, C 21.8

Rules of **Practice** Patent Office, I 23.12

Rules of **Practice** Shipping Board, SB 1.7

Rules of **Practice** under Title 4, Regulations and Orders, CA 1.14

Senate Procedure, Precedents and **Practice**, Y 1.93-1:S.doc. 21

Staff **Practice** and Procedure Digest, Y 3.N 88:23

Technical Notes Coast Artillery Target **Practice**, W 3.37

Trade **Practice** Rules, FT 1.16

Trademark Rules of **Practice** of the Patent Office, with Forms and Statutes, C 21.14:T 67/2

Welding **Practice** {abstracts}, C 41.54/8

Practices

Acceptable Methods, Techniques, and **Practices**: Aircraft Alterations, TD 4.28, TD 4.28/2

Acceptable Methods, Techniques, and **Practices**: Aircraft Inspection and Repair, FAA 5.15, TD 4.28/2

Agricultural Conservation **Practices** (by States), A 80.608

Case Book, Education Beyond High School **Practices** Underway to Meet the Problems of the Day, FS 5.65

Civil Defense Education Project, Classroom **Practices**, FS 5.45/3

Classified Index of Dispositions of ULP {Unfair Labor **Practices**} Charges by the General Counsel of the Federal Labor Relations Authority, Y 3.F 31/21-3:11

Classified Index of Dispositions of ULP {Unfair Labor **Practices**} Charges by the General Counsel of the National Labor Relations Board, LR 1.8/8

Compendium of Copyright Office **Practices**, LC 3.11

Consumer Buying **Practices** for Selected Fresh Fruits, Canned and Frozen Juices, and Dried Fruits, Related to Family Characteristics, Region and City Size, A 36.173

Country Reports on Human Rights **Practices**, Y 4.In 8/16:15

Course Offering, Enrollments, and Curriculum, **Practices** in Public Secondary Schools, HE 19.334/2

Deschler's Procedure, a Summary of the Modern Precedents and **Practices** of the U.S. House of Representatives, Y 1.2:D 45

Examining **Practices**, CS 1.41/4:330-1

Exemplary **Practices** in Federal Productivity, PM 1.37

Handbook of Conservation **Practices** (by States), A 82.111

Illustrations from State Public Assistance Agencies, Current **Practices** in Staff Training, FS 3.20

Issues and **Practices**, J 28.23

Laws relating to Federal Corrupt Practices and Political Activities, Federal Corrupt **Practices** Act, Hatch Political Activities Act, Miscellaneous Related Acts and Regulations, Y 1.2:F 31/8

Manual of Acceptable **Practices**, HH 1.6/9

National Survey of Community Solid Waste **Practices**, HE 20.1409

Personnel and Personnel **Practices** in Public Institutions for Delinquent Children, FS 2.13

Production **Practices**, 1943 Farm Program, A 79.458

Public Administration **Practices** and Perspectives, Digest of Current Materials, S 18.24

Recommended **Practices**, GS 1.14/7

Report to Congress on Voting **Practices** in the United Nations, S 1.1/8

Safe Work **Practices** Series, L 35.11/2

Soil-Binding **Practices** Applicable in State, A 55.44/10

Suggested Safe **Practices** for Longshoremen, L 16.51/3-2

Suggested Safety **Practices** for Shipyard Workers, L 16.51/3

Practicing

Forest-Gram South, Dispatch of Current Technical Information for Direct Use by **Practicing** Forest Resource Manager in the South, A 13.89

Practitioner

NPDP (National **Practitioner** Data Bank) News, HE 20.9316

Tax **Practitioner** Reproducible Kit, T 22.51/2

Tax **Practitioner** Update, T 22.51/3

PRB

PRB Reports, D 102.27/3

PRB Technical Research Notes, D 102.27

PRB Technical Research Reports, D 102.27/2

Preamble

Preamble Compilation, Radiological Health, HE 20.4006/2

Preambles

FERC Statutes and Regulations, Regulations **Preambles**, E 2.18/2

Precedents

Deschler's Procedure, a Summary of the Modern **Precedents** and Practices of the U.S. House of Representatives, Y 1.2:D 45

Senate Procedure, **Precedents** and Practice, Y 1.93-1:S.doc. 21

State Department, International Law (texts, **precedents** and discussions published by the State Department), S 7.14

Precious

Mineral Industry Surveys, **Precious Metals**, I 19.149

Production of **Precious** Metals, Calendar Year, T 28.7

Precipitation

Acid **Precipitation** in North America: Annual Data Summary from Acid Deposition System Data Base, EP 1.23/5-4

Atmospheric Turbidity and **Precipitation** Chemistry Data for the World, C 55.283

Climatography of the United States; Monthly Averages of Temperature and **Precipitation** for State Climatic Division, C 55.286/2

Climatography of the United States; Monthly Normals of Temperature, **Precipitation**, and Heating and Cooling Degree Days, C 55.286

Daily Temperature, Degree Day and **Precipitation** Normals, C 30.62

Daily Totals of **Precipitation** in Muskingum River Basin, A 80.2010

Decennial Census of United States, Climate: Monthly Normals of Temperature, **Precipitation**, and Heating Degree Days, C 30.71/4

Hourly **Precipitation** Data, C 30.59, C 55.216-C 55.216/43

Hourly **Precipitation** on Upper Ohio and Susquehanna Drainage Basins, A 57.31

Hydrologic Bulletin, Hourly and Daily **Precipitation**; Lower Mississippi-West Gulf District, C 30.35

Hydrologic Bulletin, Hourly and Daily **Precipitation**; Missouri River District, C 30.34

Hydrologic Bulletin, Hourly and Daily **Precipitation**; North Atlantic District, C 30.30

Hydrologic Bulletin, Hourly and Daily **Precipitation**; Ohio River District, C 30.32

Hydrologic Bulletin, Hourly and Daily **Precipitation**; Pacific District, C 30.36

Hydrologic Bulletin, Hourly and Daily **Precipitation**; South Pacific District, C 30.31

Hydrologic Bulletin, Hourly and Daily **Precipitation**; Upper Mississippi District, C 30.33

Monthly Averages of Temperature and **Precipitation** for State Climatic Divisions, C 55.286/2

Monthly Normals of Temperature, **Precipitation**, and Heating and Cooling Degree Days, C 55.286

National Acid **Precipitation** Assessment Program, Report to Congress, Y 3.In 8/31:1-2, C 55.703

Pacific Northwest Monthly **Precipitation** and Temperature, C 55.114

Precipitation Data from Storage-Gage Stations, C 30.59/44

Precipitation in Muskingum River Basin, A 57.21/2

Precipitation in Tennessee River Basin, Y 3.T 25:14

Storage-Gage **Precipitation** Data for Western United States, C 55.225

Tropical Strip/**Precipitation** and Observed Weather Charts, C 55.281/2-7

Precision

Precision and Accuracy Assessments for State and Local Air Monitoring Networks, EP 1.23/5-3

Precursors

Precursors to Potential Severe Core Damage Accidents, Y 3.N 88:25-6

Predator

Annual Report of the Southwestern District Branch of **Predator** & Rodent Control, I 49.61

Prediction

Climate **Prediction** Center Atlas, C 55.136

Federal Plan for Marine Environmental **Prediction**, Fiscal Year, C 55.16

Numerical Weather **Prediction** Activities, National Meteorological Center, C 55.115

Tide Tables High and Low Water **Prediction**, C 55.421

Predictions
Central Radio Propagation Laboratory Ionospheric
Predictions, C 13.31/3
Ionospheric **Predictions**, C 1.59
Supplemental Tidal **Predictions**, Anchorage,
Nikishka, Seldovia, and Valdez, Alaska,
C 55.432
Tide Tables, High and Low Water **Predictions**
Central and Western Pacific Ocean and
Indian Ocean, C 55.421/4
Tide Tables, High and Low Water **Predictions** East
Coast of North and South America
Including Greenland, C 55.421/2
Tide Tables, High and Low Water **Predictions**
Europe and West Coast of Africa,
Including the Mediterranean Sea, C
55.421/3
Tide Tables, High and Low Water **Predictions** West
Coast of North and South America
Including Hawaiian Islands, C 55.421
Preference
Veteran **Preference**, CS 1.30
Preferred
U.S. Government's **Preferred** Products List, D
1.69
Pregnancy
Instruction Manual: Classification and Coding
Instructions for Induced Termination of
Pregnancy Records, HE 20.6208/8
Prehearing
C.A.B. Notices of **Prehearing** Conference Hearings,
and Oral Arguments, CAB 1.36
C.A.B. **Prehearing** Conference Reports, CAB 1.35
C.A.B. Weekly Calendar of **Prehearing** Conferences,
Hearings and Arguments, CAB 1.33
Calendar of **Prehearing** Conferences Hearings, and
Arguments Conferences, C 31.227
Pre-Induction
Pre-Induction Training Course, W 1.40
Preliminaries
Synthetic Organic Chemicals, United States
Production and Sales, **Preliminaries**, TC
1.33/2
Preliminary
Preliminary Abstract of Statistics of Railway
Statistics, IC 1.14
Preliminary Analysis of Aircraft Accident Data,
U.S. Civil Aviation, TD 1.113/6
Preliminary Checklists, AE 1.15
Preliminary Data on Unemployment Insurance, L
7.43
Preliminary Data Summary, D 103.42/13
Preliminary Determination of Epicenters, C
55.412, I 19.66/2
Preliminary Determination of Epicenters, Monthly
Listing, C 55.690, I 19.66
Preliminary Dockets, C 31.211/2
Preliminary Estimates of Age and Sex Composi-
tions of Ducks and Geese Harvested in
the Hunting Season in Comparison with
Prior Years, I 49.106/3
Preliminary Estimates of Production of
Bituminous Coal, I 34.15, I 46.11
Preliminary Estimates of Production of Coal and
Beehive Coke, I 28.31
Preliminary Estimates of Production of
Pennsylvania Anthracite and Beehive
Coke, I 28.50
Preliminary Estimates on Production of
Bituminous Coal and Lignite, I 28.64
Preliminary Estimates of Waterfowl Harvest and
Hunter Activity in the United States
During the Hunting Season, I 49.106
Preliminary General Statistics, C 3.24/8-3
Preliminary Inventories, GS 4.10
Preliminary Monthly Statistical Report on EMIC
Program, L 5.50, FS 3.208
Preliminary Power Production, Fuel Consumption
and Installed Capacity Data, E 3.11/17-
4, E 3.11/17-6
Preliminary Prints, Ju 6.8/1
Preliminary Report and Forecast of Solar
Geophysical Data, C 55.627
Preliminary Report of Commissioner of Internal
Revenue, T 22.7
Preliminary Report of Domestic Natural Gas
Reserves and Production Dedicated to
Interstate Pipeline Companies, E 3.25/2-
2
Preliminary Report of Findings, (year) AFDC
Study, HE 17.639
Preliminary Report of Railroad Employment, Class
1 Line-haul Railroads, IC 1 ste.25/3

Preliminary Report on Harness Leather and
Skivers, C 3.44
Preliminary Report on Production on Specified
Synthetic Organic Chemicals in United
States; Facts for Industry Series, TC 1.25
Preliminary Report on U.S. Production of Selected
Synthetic Organic Chemicals, ITC 1.14/2
Preliminary Reports of Income Accounting of
Railways in United States, IC 1 ste.6
Preliminary Reports, D 103.53/3
Preliminary Statement of Capitalization and
Income, Class I Steam Railways in
United States, IC 1 ste.28
Preliminary Statistics of State School Systems, FS
5.220:20006, HE 5.220:20006, HE
5.93/4
Preliminary Study of Certain Financial Laws and
Institutions (by country), T 1.37
Production of Linseed Oil, **Preliminary** Report, C
3.122
Proposed Federal Specifications, **Preliminary**, GS
2.8/6
Soybean Crush Products, **Preliminary** Report, C
3.121
Statistics of Income, **Preliminary** Reports, T 22.35/
3
Studies of Family Clothing Supplies, **Preliminary**
Reports, A 77.712
U.S. Direct Investment Abroad, Operations of U.S.
Parent Companies and Their Foreign
Affiliates, **Preliminary** Estimates, C
59.20/2
Vegetables, **Preliminary** Acreage, Yield,
Production and Value, A 92.11/10-6
Wholesale (**Preliminary** Market) Price Index, L
2.61/5
Wholesale Price Index, **Preliminary** Estimate, L
2.61/9
Premiums
Average **Premiums** and Discounts for CCC
Settlement Purposes for Offers Received,
A 88.11/21
PREP
PREP Reports, HE 5.89, HE 18.9
Prepaid
Digest of **Prepaid** Dental Care Plans, HE 20.2:D
54/7
National HMO Census of **Prepaid** Plans, HE 20.27
Roster of **Prepaid** Dental Care Plans, FS 2.2:D 54/7
Preparation
Bimonthly Review of Medicinal **Preparation**
Exports, C 18.50
Flight Information Publication: Flight **Preparation**
Training Series, N 27.9
Guide for **Preparation** of Proposals and Project
Operation, NS 1.20/2
Instruction Manual: Data **Preparation** of the
Current Sample, HE 20.6208/9
Report on Plan **Preparation** on State and Local
Public Works, FW 7.7
Preparations
Bimonthly Review of Toilet **Preparations** Exports,
C 18.51
World Trade in Dental **Preparations** (WTDP-nos.),
C 18.168
World Trade in Toilet **Preparations**, C 18.176
World Trade in Veterinary **Preparations**, C 18.177
Preparatory
Basic **Preparatory** Programs for Practical Nurses
by States and Changes in Number of
Programs, FS 5.133
Prepared
Prepared Roofing, C 3.100
World Trade in **Prepared** Medicines, C 18.174
Preparedness
Disaster **Preparedness** Report, C 55.127
Foresight, Civil **Preparedness** Today, D 14.14
National Domestic **Prepardness** Office - General
Publications, J 1.14/25-2
National Plan for Emergency **Preparedness**, PrEx
4.6/8
Research Studies Defense Civil **Preparedness**
Agency, D 14.17
Technical Memorandum Defense Civil **Prepared-
ness** Agency, D 119.8/5
Preparing
Instructions for **Preparing** Reports, C 3.38/2
Preprimary
Preprimary Enrollment, ED 1.112/5
Preprimary Enrollment, October (year), HE 19.327
Preprints
Preprints from Bulletin 585, Mineral Facts and
Problems, I 28.3/c

Pre-School
Lesson Material on Care of **Pre-School** Child, L
5.26
Preschoolers
Mainstreaming **Preschoolers** (series), HE 23.1110
Prescribed
Summary of **Prescribed** Unit Costs and Hourly Rate
for Return on Investment and Tax
Allowance, C 31.272, CAB 1.10
Uniform System of Accounts **Prescribed** for Natural
Gas Companies, FP 1.7/2
Uniform System of Accounts **Prescribed** for Public
Utilities and Licenses, FP 1.7/3
Prescription
Approved **Prescription** Drug Products with
Therapeutic Equivalence Evaluations,
HE 20.4210
Publications Task Force on **Prescription** Drugs, FS
1.32, HE 1.32
Task Force on **Prescription** Drugs, HE 1.32
Prescriptive
Prescriptive Package Series, J 1.8/3, J 26.13
Present
Present Changes in Gross Hourly and Weekly
Earnings Over Selected Periods, L 2.63
Presentation
Congressional **Presentation** for Security
Assistance Programs, Fiscal Year (date),
D 1.85
Consolidated of Schedule B Commodity
Classifications for Use in **Presentation** of
U.S. Export Statistics, C 3.150:G
Cultural **Presentation** Programs of the Department
of State, S 1.67
Mutual Security Program, Summary **Presentation**, S
17.35
National Security Seminar **Presentation** Outlines
and Reading List, D 5.9/2
Papers Approved for Publication or **Presentation**,
FS 2.22/9
Proposed Foreign Aid Program Fiscal Year,
Summary **Presentation** to Congress, S
18.28/a
Proposed Foreign Aid Program, Summary
Presentation to Congress, S 18.28
Schedule G. Consolidation of Schedule B
Commodity Classifications for Use in
Presentation of U.S. Export Statistics, C
3.150:G
Trend Report: Graphic **Presentation** of Public
Assistance and Related Data, HE 17.612
Presentations
Cultural **Presentations** USA, (year), Report to
Congress and the Public, S 1.67
Excerpts from Slide **Presentations** by the Office of
Chief of Naval Operations, D 207.14
Exparte **Presentations** in Informal Rulemakings, CC
1.42/3
Presenters
Presenters and Festivals Jazz Management, Jazz
Special Projects, Music, Application
Guidelines, NF 2.8/2-9
Presenting
Grants to **Presenting** Organizations, Special
Touring Initiatives Application
Guidelines, NF 2.8/2-29
Presents
Our Library **Presents**, ITC 1.9/2
Preservation
Garden and Home Food **Preservation** Facts, A
43.29
Local **Preservation**, I 29.104/3
National **Preservation** Report, LC 1.36
Preservation and New Technology Occasional
Papers, LC 1.43
Preservation Briefs, I 29.84, I 70.12
Preservation Case Studies, I 29.104, I 70.12/2
Preservation Leaflets, LC 1.35
Preservation Planning Series, I 70.12/3, I 29.104/2
Preservation Planning Series, State Program
Overviews, I 29.102
Preservation Programs Guidelines and Applica-
tion Instructions, NF 3.8/2-3
Preservation Tech Notes, Doors, I 29.84/3-10
Preservation Tech Notes Exterior Woodwork, I
29.84/3-6
Preservation Tech Notes Historic Interior Spaces
(series), I 29.84/3-2
Preservation Tech Notes Masonry, I 29.84/3-7
Preservation Tech Notes Mechanical Systems, I
29.84/3-9

Preservation Tech Notes Metals, I 29.84/3-8
Preservation Tech Notes Museum Collection
Storage (series), I 29.84/3-3
Preservation Tech Notes Site, I 29.84/3-11
Preservation Tech Notes Temporary Protection
(series), I 29.84/3-5
Preservation Tech Notes Windows (series), I
29.84/3-4
Preservation Tech Notes, I 29.84/3
Technical Preservation Services Reading Lists, I
70.15/2
Tree Preservation Bulletins, I 29.26
Preserves
National Preserves (series), I 29.97
Presidency
If Elected. . . Unsuccessful Candidates for the
Presidency, SI 11.2:P 92/2
President
Annual Report of the President on Trade
Agreements Program, Pr 42.11
Biennial Report to the President of the United
States, I 49.1/8
Committees and Commissions of the President, Pr
37.8, Pr 38.8, Pr 39.8, Pr 40.8
Economic Report of the President, Pr 37.9, Pr 38.9,
Pr 39.9, Pr 40.9, Pr 41.9, Pr 42.9
Emergency Relief Appropriation Acts, Reports of
President to Congress Showing Status of
Funds and Operations Under, T 63.114
Employment and Training Report of the President,
L 1.42/2
Federal Advisory Committees, Annual Report of the
President, Pr 37.12, Pr 38.10, Pr 39.10,
Pr 40.10, Pr 41.10, Pr 42.10
Federal Managers' Financial Integrity Act,
Secretary's Annual Statement and Report
to the President and the Congress, I
1.96/6
Federal Personal Data Systems Subject to the
Privacy Act of 1974, Annual Report of
the President, Pr 38.12, Pr 39.11
Federal Support of Research and Development at
Universities and Colleges and Selected
Nonprofit Institutions, Fiscal Year,
Report to the President and Congress,
NS 1.30
Federal Support to Universities, Colleges, and
Selected Nonprofit Institutions, Fiscal
Year (date), Report to the President and
Congress, NS 1.30
Financial Conditions of {various railroads},
Annual Report to the President and the
Congress, TD 1.10/6-2
Indexes to Papers of President Franklin Delano
Roosevelt, PI 1.8
International Economic Report of the President, Pr
37.8:In 8/3/R 29/2
Manpower Report of the President and Report on
Manpower Requirements, Resources,
Utilization, and Training by the U.S.
Department of Labor, L 1.42/2
Manual of Regulations and Instructions Relating to
the Disclosure of Federal Campaign
Funds for Candidates for the Office of
President or Vice President of the United
States and . . . Candidates, GA 1.14:C 15
President Monroe's Message, SI 11.2:M 75
President Research Associateships, Post- Doctoral,
Tenable at National Bureau of Standards,
C 13.47
Problems of Mobilization and Reconversion,
Reports to the President, Senate, and
House of Representatives by Director of
War Mobilization and Reconversion, Y
3.W 19/7:8
Public Law 480, Agricultural Export Activities,
Annual Report of the President, Pr 37.13
Raising a President, L 5.42
Report of Secretary to President and Congress on
Mineral Exploration Program, I 1.85
Report of the President of the Commodity Credit
Corporation, A 82.301
Report on U.S. Export Controls to the President
and the Congress, C 57.30
Report to the President and Congress on the Drug
Abuse, Prevention, and Treatment
Functions, HE 1.58
Report to the President and Congress on the Status
of Health Personnel in the United States,
HE 20.9310
Report to the President and Congress on the Status
of Health Professions Personnel in the
United States, HE 20.6619

Report to the President and the Congress on the
Effectiveness of the Rail Passenger
Services Act, IC 1.34
Report to the President by Director of Defense
Mobilization, Pr 33.1008
Report to the President by Director of Office of
Defense Mobilization, Pr 34.201
Reports of President to Congress Showing Status
of Funds and Operations under
Emergency Relief Appropriation Acts, T
63.114
Resources for Freedom, Research to the President
by President's Materials Policy
Commission, Pr 33.15
Simplifying Federal Aid to States and Communities,
Annual Report to the President of an
Interagency Program, PrEx 2.18
Special Reports Executive Office of the President,
PrEx 1.10/14
State of Small Business, a Report to the President,
SBA 1.1/2
Statistics on Manpower, Supplement to Manpower
Report of the President, L 1.42/2-2
Supplement to Title 3, the President, GS 4.108/2
Supplements to the Employment and Training
Report of the President, L 1.42/2-3
Trade Policy Agenda and Annual Report of the
President of the Agreements Program,
PrEx 9.11
U.S. Participation in the United Nations, Report by
the President to Congress, S 1.70
President's
Life-Pass It On, President's Environmental Merit
Awards Program, EP 1.34
Posters President's Council on Physical Fitness
and Sports, HE 20.113
President's Advisory Board for Cuba Broadcasting,
Pr 41.8:Br 78
President's Advisory Council on Executive
Organization, Pr 37.8:Ex 3
President's Advisory Council on Management
Improvement, Pr 37.8:M 31
President's Advisory Panel on Timber and the
Environment, Pr 37.8:T 48
President's Awards for Distinguished Federal
Civilian Service, CS 1.64
President's Commission for Observance of 25th
Anniversary of the United Nations, Pr
37.8:Un 3
President's Commission on All-volunteer Armed
Forces, Pr 37.8:Ar 5
President's Commission on Campus Unrest, Pr
37.8:C 15
President's Commission on Coal, Pr 39.8:C 63
President's Commission on Federal Statistics, Pr
37.8:St 2
President's Commission on Holocaust, Pr 39.8:H
74
President's Commission on Mental Health, Pr
39.8:M 52
President's Commission on National Agenda for
the Eighties, Pr 39.8:Ag 3
President's Commission on Olympic Sports, Pr
38.8:Ol 9
President's Commission on Pension Policy, Pr
39.8:P 38
President's Commission on Personnel Interchange,
Pr 37.8:P 43
President's Commission on School Finance, Pr
37.8:Sch 6
President's Committee on Employment of the
Handicapped, Annual Report to
Membership, .PrEx 1.10/13
President's Committee on Employment of the
Handicapped: People with Disabilities
in Our Nation's Job Training
Partnership Act Programs, PrEx 1.10/15
President's Committee on Employment of the
Handicapped: Press Releases, PrEx 1.10/
4
President's Committee on Health Education, Pr
37.8:H 34
President's Comprehensive Triennial Report on
Immigration, J 21.21
President's Conference on Industrial Safety News
Letter, L 16.30
President's Council on Competitiveness, Pr 41.8:R
26
President's Council on Integrity and Efficiency:
Reports, Pr 41.8/3
President's Council on Physical Fitness and
Sports, Pr 37.8:P 56/2
President's Council on Physical Fitness and
Sports: Research Digests, HE 20.114

President's Council on Youth Opportunity, Pr
37.8:Y 8
President's Export Council: Publications, Pr
37.8:Ex 7
President's National Policy Report, HH 1.75
President's National Urban Policy Report, HH
1.75
President's Organization of Unemployment Relief,
C 1.15
President's Panel on Federal Compensation, Pr
38.8:C 73
President's Papers Index Series, LC 4.7
President's Reorganization Project: Publications,
PrEx 1.11
President's Report on Occupational Safety and
Health, Pr 38.2:Oc 1
Program Guide President's Committee on
Employment of the Handicapped, PrEx
1.10/7
Progress Report President's Medical Programs for
Heart Disease, Cancer, and Stroke, and
Related Diseases, FS 2.313
Progress Report to the Secretary of Education from
the President's Advisory Commission
on Educational Excellence for Hispanic
Americans, ED 1.87
Publications President's Conference on Fire
Prevention, FW 6.9
Publications President's Highway Safety
Conference, FW 2.18
Publications President's Organization of
Unemployment Relief, C 1.15
Receipts and Disbursements of Government
Consolidated into Bureau of Accounts,
Fiscal Service in Treasury Department by
President's Reorganization Plan no. 3, T
9.11
Report of President's Airport Commission, Pr
33.16
Resources for Freedom, Research to the President
by President's Materials Policy
Commission, Pr 33.15
The President's Comprehensive Triennial Report
on Immigration, L 29.17
Presidential
Ad Hoc Advisory Group on Presidential Vote for
Puerto Rico, Pr 37.8:P 96
Alphabetical Listing of (year) Presidential
Campaign Receipts, GA 1.20
Codification of Presidential Proclamations and
Executive Orders, GS 4.113/3
FHA Honor Awards for Presidential Design, HH
2.25
Presidential Advisory Committee on Small and
Minority Business Ownership, Annual
Report, PrEx 1.16
Presidential Clemency Board: Publications, Pr
38.8:C 59
Presidential Commissional on World Hunger, Pr
39.8:W 89/3
Presidential Vetoes, Y 1.3:V 64/2:798-976
Weekly Compilation of Presidential Documents,
GS 4.114, AE 2.109
Presidents
Circular Letters to Presidents or Cashiers of
National Banks Asking for Report of
Conditions of Banks, T 12.11/1
Public Papers of the Presidents of the United
States, AE 2.114, GS 4.113
Statements by Presidents of the United States on
International Cooperation in Space, Y
1.92-1:S.doc. 40
Pre-Solicitation
Pre-Solicitation Announcements, Small Business
Innovation Programs, SBA 1.37
Press
AF Press Clips, S 1.134
American Consulate General, Hong Kong, Index of
Chinese Mainland Press, S 1.112
Business Press Service, L 1.78/2
Current Review of Soviet Technical Press, C 41.94
Daily Press Digest, FS 3.26
General Press Releases, ES 3.7/1
Labor Press Service, L 1.78
President's Committee on Employment of the
Handicapped: Press Releases, PrEx 1.10/
4
Press Bulletins, A 13.6
Press Digest, Y 3.F 31/11:20, Y 3.F 31/11:38, FL
2.9, NHA 2.9
Press Feature, S 1.77
Press Intelligence Bulletins, Y 3.N 21/8:13, Pr
32.209, Pr 32.5012

Armed Services **Procurement** Manual ASPM (series), D 1.13/4

Armed Services **Procurement** Regulation, M 1.8 D 1.13

Armed Services **Procurement** Regulation Revision, D 1.13/2

Armed Services **Procurement** Regulation Supplement ASPA (series), D 1.13/2-2

Army **Procurement** Circulars, D 101.33/2

Army **Procurement** Procedures, D 101.6/4

Army **Procurement** Regulations, M 101.11

Budget Estimates; Aircraft and Missile **Procurement**, D 301.83/2

Defense **Procurement** Circulars, D 1.13/3

Defense Supply **Procurement** Regulations, D 7.6/5

Directory of Academic **Procurement** and Related Programs and Courses, GS 1.30

Federal **Procurement** Data System, PrEx 2.24

Federal **Procurement** Data System, Annual Analysis (series), PrEx 2.24/2

Federal **Procurement** Data System, Combined Special Analyses, PrEx 2.24/12

Federal **Procurement** Data System, Contractor Identification File, Alphabetical Listing, PrEx 2.24/14

Federal **Procurement** Data System, Special Analysis 3, PrEx 2.24/3

Federal **Procurement** Data System, Special Analysis 8, PrEx 2.24/8

Federal **Procurement** Data System, Special Analysis 10, PrEx 2.24/10

Federal **Procurement** Data System, Standard Report, PrEx 2.24/13

Federal **Procurement** Regulations, GS 1.6/5

Federal **Procurement** Regulations, FPR Notices, GS 1.6/5-2

GSA Bulletin FPR, Federal **Procurement**, Gs 1.6/5-3

Identical Bidding in Public **Procurement** Report of Attorney General Under Executive Order 10936, J 1.31

Index of Specifications and Bulletins Approved for U.S. Air Force **Procurement**, D 301.18

Index of Specifications Approved for AAF **Procurement**, W 108.13/3

Index to Navy **Procurement** Information, D 201.6/11

Joint Army and Air Force **Procurement** Circulars, D 101.33

Life Cycle Costing **Procurement** Cases, GS 2.19

List of Parties Excluded from Federal **Procurement** or Nonprocurement Programs, GS 1.28

Marketing and **Procurement** Briefs, C 1.57/5

Memorandum to State **Procurement** Officers, T 58.17

NASA Annual **Procurement** Report, NAS 1.30

NASA **Procurement** Regulation, NAS 1.6/2

NASA **Procurement** Regulation Directive, NAS 1.6/3

Navy Current **Procurement** Directives, NCPD (series), D 201.6/13

Navy **Procurement** Directives, D 201.6/10

Office of **Procurement** and Supply Letter, VA 1.80

Procurement and Contracts Management, DOE/PR- (series), E 1.49

Procurement Authorization and Allotments, European and Far East Programs, FO 1.8

Procurement Authorization and Allotments, Pr 33.908

Procurement Circulars Printed and Processed, W 1.31

Procurement Circulars, W 1.24/5

Procurement Division Bulletins, T 58.15

Procurement Equipment Directory D (series), D 7.13/2

Procurement from Small and Other Business Firms, D 1.48

Procurement Information Bulletins, FO 1.3

Procurement Legal Service Circulars, D 101.33/3

Procurement List, Y 3.P 97:10

Procurement Newsletter, D 301.6/4-2

Procurement Notices (series), NAS 1.6/2-2

Procurement Regulations Agency for International Development, S 18.6/2

Procurement Regulations Services of Supply, W 109.7, W 109.8, W 109.8-2

Procurement Regulatory Activity Report, PrEx 2.24/15

Property, Emergency **Procurement** and Funds, W 3.50/6

Report to Congress, Office of Federal **Procurement** Policy, PrEx 2.21

Semiannual **Procurement** Report, NAS 1.30

Survey of **Procurement** Statistics, D 201.6/14

Synopsis of U.S. Government Proposed **Procurement** and Contract Awards, C 18.284

Telephone Directory General Services Administration and Defense Materials **Procurement** Agency, GS 1.11

Produce

Volunteers Who **Produce** Books, Braille, Tape, Large Type, LC 19.21

Produced

Cotton Linters **Produced** and on Hand at Oil Mills by Type of Cut, by States, Preliminary, C 3.148

Cottonseed Received, Crushed and on Hand; Cotton Linters **Produced**; and Linters on Hand at Oil Mills, Preliminary Reports, C 3.149

List of Audiovisual Materials **Produced** by the United States Government (series), GS 4.17/5-2

Mink Production, Pelts **Produced** in (year), A 92.18/11

Reference List of Audiovisual Materials **Produced** by the United States Government, GS 4.2:Au 2

Producer

Federal Energy Regulatory Commission **Producer** Manual, E 2.12:0030

News, **Producer** Price Indexes, L 2.61/10

P.C. **Producer**-Consumer Series, A 55.65

Producer Price Indexes, L 2.61

Producer Price Indexes Data For . . ., L 2.61/11

Summary Data from the **Producer** Price Index News Release, L 2.61/10-2

Supplement to **Producer** Prices and Price Indexes Data for (year), L 2.61/11

Producers

Alphabetical Listing, Register or Planned Mobilization **Producers**, Manufacturers of War Material Registered Under Production Allocation Program, D 7.11

Broom Corn Brooms: **Producers'** Shipments Imports for Consumption Exports and Apparent Consumption, ITC 1.23

Coke **Producers**, E 3.11/16-2

Coke **Producers** in the United States in (year), I 28.30/2

Directory of Principal U.S. Gemstone **Producers** (Annual Advance Summary), I 28.117

Fuel-Briquets and Packaged-Fuel **Producers**, Annual, I 28.109

General Summary of Inventory Status and Movement of Capital and **Producers** Goods, Plants, Aircraft, and Industry Agent Items, Pr 33.210

List of Bituminous Coal **Producers** who have Accepted Bituminous Coal Code Promulgated June 21, 1972, I 34.17, I 46.9

List of Code Number **Producers** of Bituminous Coal, I 34.22

Mineral Industry Surveys, Directory of Principal Construction Sand and Gravel **Producers** in the . . ., Annual Advanced Summary Supplement, I 19.138/3

Peat **Producers** in United States, I 28.107

Performance Profiles of Major Energy **Producers**, E 3.37, E 3.37/2

Producers Prices and Price Indexes, L 2.61

Register Planned Emergency **Producers**, D 7.11/2

Sales by **Producers** of Natural Gas to Interstate Pipe-Line Companies, FP 1.21

Producing

Cotton Varieties Planted in Early **Producing** Section of Texas, (year), A 88.11/11

Product

Consumer **Product** Information, GS 11.9

Consumer **Product** Safety Review, Y 3.C 76/3:28

Crude-oil and **Product** Pipelines, E 3.11/12

Forest **Product** Notes, A 13.42/18

Forest **Product** Utilization Technical Reports, A 13.96

Focus (Joint Center for Integrated **Product** Data Environment), D 215.15

Industry and **Product** Reports, C 3.24/8-2

Interagency Task Force on **Product** Liability, C 1.66, C 1.66/2

List of Chemical Compounds Authorized for Use Under USDA Poultry, Meat, Rabbit and Egg **Products** Inspection Programs, A 88.6:C 42, A 101.6:C 42

Methodology Papers: U.S. National Income and **Product** Accounts, BEA-MP- (series), C 59.19

Monthly Petroleum **Product** Price Report, E 3.24, FE 1.9/5

Monthly **Product** Announcement, C 3.163/7

National Income and **Product** Accounts of the United States, C 49.11/4:In 2, C 59.11/5, C 59.11/5-2, C 59.11/5-3

NEISS {National Electronic Injury Surveillance System} News, **Product** Safety, HE 20.4026, Y 3.C 76/3:7-2

New **Product** Ideas, Process Improvements, and Cost-Saving Techniques, Relating to {various subjects}, NASA/SBA FA (series), NAS 1.56

Numeric List of **Product** Class Codes, Commodity Transportation Survey, C 3.163/4-2

Orders Consumer **Product** Safety Commission, Y 3.C 76/3:6-2

Product Analysis Service, Pr 33.920

Product of Mines, IC 1.23/12:SS-4

Product Primers, C 3.163/8

Product Profile, C 3.287

Product Safety Education Unit (series), Y 3.C 76/3:19

Product Standards, C 13.20/2

Product/Activity Status Bulletin, C 3.238/6

Project Label, Alphabetical Listings by Drug **Product**, J 24.24/4

Quarterly Progress Report on Fission **Product** Behavior in LWRs, E 1.28/2

Research **Product** (series), D 101.60/5

Value of **Product** Shipments, C 3.24/9-6

Production

Alfalfa Meal **Production**, A 82.59/2, A 88.18/5

Analysis of **Production**, Wages and Employment in Manufacturing Industries, Y 3.C 78:7

Annual Report of the Activities of the Joint Committee on Defense **Production** with Material on Mobilization from Departments and Agencies, Y 4.D 36:R 29

Annual Report of the National Research Programs, Crop **Production**, A 106.25, A 106.25/2

Apples, **Production** by Varieties, with Comparisons, A 88.12/15

Bituminous Coal and Lignite **Production** and Mine Operations, E 3.11/7-3

Brewers' Dried Grain **Production**, A 88.18/6, A 82.59/3

Brewers' Dried Grains United States **Production** and Stocks in Hands of Producers, A 88.18/6-2

Bush Berries, Indicated Yield and **Production**, A 92.11/13

Business Information Service: Defense **Production** Aids, C 40.7

Canned Fruits and Vegetables, **Production** and Wholesale Distribution, C 3.168

Catfish **Production**, A 92.44/2-2

Cherry **Production**, A 92.11/3

Chickens and Eggs, Farm **Production**, Disposition, Cash Receipts and Gross Income, A 9.9/3

Chickens and Eggs, Farm **Production**, Disposition, Cash Receipts and Gross Income, Chickens on Farms, Commercial Broilers, by States, A 88.15/18

Chickens and Eggs, Layers and Egg **Production**, A 88.15/14, A 92.9/13

Circular of Inquiry Concerning Gold and Silver Coinage and Currency of Foreign Countries, Including **Production**, Import and Export, and Industrial Consumption of Gold and Silver, T 28.8

Citrus Fruits by States, **Production**, Use, Value, A 88.12/21

Combined **Production** and Resources Board, United States, Great Britain, and Canada, Y 3.C 73/3

Commercial Apples, **Production** by Varieties, with Comparisons, A 92.11/9

Commercial Broiler **Production**, A 88.15/13

Commercial Broilers **Production** in 22 States, A 92.9/10

Commercial Livestock Slaughter and Meat **Production**, A 92.18/3

Commercial Livestock Slaughter, Number and Live Weight, by States, Meat and Lard **Production**, United States, by Months, A 88.16/17

Consumption of Fuel for **Production** of Electric Energy, FP 1.11/3

Copper **Production**, I 28.59/5

Corn, Estimated Planted Acreage, Yield, and **Production** by States, A 66.47

Costs and Indexes for Domestic Oil and Gas Field Equipment and **Production** Operations, E 3.44/2

Cotton Estimated Acreage, Yield, and **Production**, A 36.114, A 66.41

Cotton **Production**, A 88.11/5

Cotton **Production** Adjustments, A 55.23

Cotton **Production** and Distribution, Year Ending July 31, C 3.3

Cotton **Production** in the United States, Crop of {year}, C 3.32

Cotton **Production**, CN 1 (series), A 92.20

Cotton **Production**: Cotton and Cottonseed **Production**, A 88.11/16

Cranberries, Indicated **Production**, A 92.11/6

Creamery Butter and American Cheese **Production** Estimates, A 36.196

Crop **Production**, A 88.24, A 105.9

Crop **Production** Research, A 77.33

Crop **Production**, Acreage, A 92.24/4-2

Crop **Production**, Annual Summary, A 92.24/4, A 105.9/2

Crop **Production**, Prospective Plantings, A 88.24/4, A 88.30/2

Crop **Production**, Winter Wheat and Rye, A 88.18/11

Crop **Production**: Quarterly Grain Stocks in Farms, Revised Estimates, A 88.18/22

Crop Values, Season Average Prices Received by Farmers and Value of **Production**, A 92.24/3

Cumulative Index to Foreign **Production** and Commercial Reports, C 42.15/3-2

Cut Flowers, **Production** and Sales, A 88.47

Cutbacks Reported to **Production** Readjustment Committee, Pr 32.4834

Dairy **Production**, A 88.14/2

Defense **Production** Act, Progress Reports, Y 4.D 36:P 94

Defense **Production** Notes, DP 1.10

Defense **Production** Record, DP 1.8

Distillers' Dried Grain **Production**, A 88.18/7, A 82.59/4

Distillers' Dried Grains, United States, **Production** by Kinds by Months, A 88.18/7-2

Dry Casein, Estimated **Production** and Stocks, United States, A 36.166

Economic Indicators of the Farm Sector, Cost of **Production**: Livestock and Dairy, A 93.45/2-2

Egg Products, Liquid, Frozen, Solids **Production**, A 92.9/4

Essential Oil **Production** and Trade, C 18.69

Farm **Production** and Income from Meat Animals, A 66.34

Farm **Production** Expenditures for (year), A 92.40

Farm **Production**, Disposition, Cash Receipts and Gross Income, Turkeys, A 88.15/16, A 105.35/2

Farm Value, Gross Income, and Cash Income from Farm **Production**, A 36.125

Federal Offshore Statistics, Leasing, Exploration, **Production**, Revenue, I 72.10

Fertilizer Trends, **Production**, Consumption, and Trade, Y 3.T 25:66

Field and Seed Crops, Farm **Production**, Farm Disposition, Value, by States, A 88.30/4

Field and Seed Crops, **Production**, Farm Use, Sales, Value by States, A 92.19

Field Crops, **Production**, Disposition, Value, A 105.9/4

Floriculture Crops, **Production** Area and Sales, A 92.32

Flowers and Foliage Plants, **Production** and Sales, A 92.32

Food **Production** Memorandum, A 79.7, A 80.208

Forecast of Motor-Fuel Demand and Required Crude-Oil **Production** by States, Monthly Forecast, I 28.41

Foreign Agriculture, Review of Foreign Farm Policy, **Production** and Trade, A 36.88, A 64.7, A 67.7

Foreign **Production** and Commercial Reports, C 42.15/3

Fruits, Noncitrus, by State, **Production**, Use, Value, A 88.12/20

Gas Turbine Electric Plant Construction Cost and Annual **Production** Expenses, E 3.17/2

Gold Report {Mine **Production**}, I 28.61

Hatchery **Production**, A 88.15/5, A 105.12/3-2

Hatchery **Production**, Louisiana Crop Reporting Service, A 88.15/22

Historical Plant Cost and Annual **Production** Expenses for Selected Electric Plants, E 3.17/4-2

Honey **Production**, Annual Summary, A 9.28/2

Hydro Electric Plant Construction Cost and Annual **Production** Expenses, E 3.17/3

Index to Foreign **Production** and Commercial Reports, Cumulative Indexes, C 42.15/3-3

Indexes of **Production** Worker Employment in Manufacturing Industries by Metropolitan Area, L 2.24

Indices of Agricultural **Production** in {various} Countries, A 67.36, A 93.32

Industrial **Production**, FR 1.19/3

Industry Report, Canned Fruits and Vegetables, **Production** and Wholesale Distribution, C 18.234

Lamb Crop and Wool **Production**, Louisiana Crop Reporting Service, A 88.16/19

Layers and Egg **Production**, A 105.12/7

Lead Mine **Production**, I 28.60

Lead **Production**, I 28.87, I 28.87/3

Liquid, Frozen, and Dried Egg **Production**, A 88.15

Livestock Slaughter and Meat **Production**, A 88.16/9

Louisiana Soybeans for Beans, Acreage, Yield and **Production**, A 88.18/25

Margarine **Production**, A 82.26

Meat Animals, Farm **Production**, Disposition, and Income by States, A 88.17/3

Meat Animals, **Production**, Disposition, and Income, A 105.23/6

Meat Meal and Tankage **Production**, Semiannual Report, A 92.17/2

Meat Scraps and Tankage **Production**, A 88.17/2

Military and Civil Aircraft and Aircraft Engine Production, Monthly **Production** Report, C 31.130

Milk **Production**, A 105.17

Milk **Production** and Dairy Products, Annual Statistical Summary, A 92.10/6

Milk **Production** on Farms and Statistics of Dairy Plant Products, A 88.14/7

Milk **Production**, Disposition, and Income, A 92.10/2, A 105.17/5

Milk, Farm **Production**, Disposition, and Income, A 88.14/8

Mine **Production** of Copper, I 28.59

Mine **Production** of Gold, I 28.61

Mine **Production** of Lead, I 28.60

Mine **Production** of Silver, Monthly Reports, I 28.62

Mine **Production** of Zinc, Monthly Reports, I 28.57

Mink **Production**, Pelts Produced in (year), A 92.18/11

Mohair **Production** and Income, A 36.200

Mohair **Production** and Value, A 92.29/4

Mohair **Production** and Value of Sales, A 88.35/4

Monthly Motor Truck **Production** Report, C 41.39

National Housing **Production** Report, HH 1.79/2

Natural Gas **Production** and Consumption, E 3.38, I 28.98/6

NPA **Production** Series, Quarterly Indexes of Shipments for Products of Metalworking Industries, C 40.15

Nursery Products, **Production** and Sales, A 88.48

Organization Directory Civilian **Production** Administration, Pr 32.4830

Outer Continental Shelf Oil and Gas Leasing and **Production** Program Annual Report, I 72.12/3-2

Popcorn **Production**, A 88.12/14

Poultry and Egg **Production** Reports, A 36.102

Poultry and Egg **Production**, A 66.43

Poultry **Production** and Value, A 92.9/15

Poultry **Production**, Disposition and Income, A 105.12/6

Poultry **Production**, Disposition and Income, Final Estimates, A 1.34/5

Power **Production**, Generating Capacity, E 3.11/17-7

Preliminary Estimates of **Production** of Bituminous Coal, I 34.15, I 46.11

Preliminary Estimates of **Production** of Coal and Beehive Coke, I 28.31

Preliminary Estimates of **Production** of Pennsylvania Anthracite and Beehive Coke, I 28.50

Preliminary Estimates on **Production** of Bituminous Coal and Lignite, I 28.64

Preliminary Power **Production**, Fuel Consumption and Installed Capacity Data, E 3.11/17-6

Preliminary Power **Production**, Fuel Consumption, and Installed Capacity Data for (year), E 3.11/17-4

Preliminary Report of Domestic Natural Gas Reserves and **Production** Dedicated to Interstate Pipeline Companies, E 3.25/2-2

Preliminary Report on **Production** on Specified Synthetic Organic Chemicals in United States; Facts for Industry Series, TC 1.25

Preliminary Report on U.S. **Production** of Selected Synthetic Organic Chemicals, ITC 1.14/2

Production and Availability of Construction Materials, Pr 32.4827

Production and Carry Over of Fruit and Vegetable Containers, A 36.61

Production and Inspection Reports, A 82.59

Production and Utilization of Electric Energy in United States, FP 1.11/2

Production Credit Associations, Annual Summary of Operations, FCA 1.22

Production Credit Associations, Summary of Operations, A 72.25

Production Economics Research Branch Publications, A 77.16

Production Equipment Directory D (series), D 7.13/3

Production Notes, SDP 1.13

Production of Boots and Shoes, C 3.43

Production of Coal in United States from 1814 to Close of Calendar Year, I 19.19

Production of Electric Energy and Capacity of Generating Plants, FP 1.21

Production of Electricity for Public Use in the U.S., FP 1.11, I 19.32, I 19.33

Production of Lead in United States, Calendar Year, I 19.24

Production of Linseed Oil, Preliminary Report, C 3.122

Production of Manufactured Dairy Products, A 88.14/10

Production of Methanol, C 3.101

Production of Precious Metals, Calendar Year, T 28.7

Production of Smelter in United States (mid year statements and annual statements, calendar years), I 19.22

Production Practices, 1943 Farm Program, A 79.458

Production Research Reports, A 1.84

Production, Consumption, and Stocks of Fats and Oils, C 3.123

Production, Farm Disposition, and Value of Principal Fruits and Tree Nuts, A 88.12/16

Production, Prices Employment, and Trade in Northwest Forest Industries, A 13.66/13

Production-Conservation Program, Committeemen's Handbooks, A 80.2158

Publications **Production** Economics Research Branch, A 77.16

Pulpwood **Production** in the North-Central Region by County, A 13.80/5

Pulpwood **Production** in the Northeast, A 13.80/3

Raw Nonfuel Mineral **Production** in (year), I 28.165

Report of Egg **Production** Tests, United States and Canada, A 77.15:44-78

Rice **Production**, Louisiana Crop Reporting Service, A 88.18/26

Shorn Wool **Production**, A 88.35/2

Silver {Mine **Production**}, I 28.62

Soda Ash and Sodium Sulfate: U.S. **Production**, Trade and Consumption, I 28.135/2

Southern Pulpwood **Production**, A 13.80/4

Soybeans Harvested for Beans by Countries, Acreage, Yield, **Production**, A 88.18/19

Steam-Electric Plant Construction Cost and Annual **Production** Expenses, E 3.17

Studies in the Economics of **Production**, C 1.81

Sulphuric Acid, **Production**, Stocks, etc. Reported by Fertilizer Manufacturers, C 3.110

Summary of Operations of **Production** Credit Associations, A 72.25

Summary of Technological Developments Affecting War **Production**, L 2.17

Superphosphates, **Production**, etc., Reported by Fertilizer Manufacturers, C 3.111

Synthetic Organic Chemicals, United States **Production** and Sales, Preliminaries, TC 1.33/2

Synthetic Organic Chemicals, United States **Production** and Sales, TC 1.33, ITC 1.14

Thermal-Electric Plant Construction Cost and Annual **Production** Expenses, E 3.17/4

Total Commercial **Production** of All Vegetables and Melons for Fresh Market and Processing, A 92.11/10-3

Total Livestock Slaughter, Meat and Lard **Production**, A 88.16/16

Tung Oil Monthly, **Production** in America, Foreign Trade, etc., C 18.209

U.S. Government Campaign to Promote **Production**, Sharing, and Proper Use of Food, Pr 32.5019, Pr 32.5019/2

U.S. **Production** of Fish Fillets and Steaks, Annual Summary, C 55.309/2-6

U.S. **Production**, Imports and Import/**Production** Ratios for Cotton, Wool and Man-made Textiles and Apparel, C 61.26

U.S. Timber **Production**, Trade, Consumption, and Price Statistics, A 13.113

USDA Meat **Production** Reports, A 82.54, A 88.17

Vegetables, Fresh Market, Annual Summary, Acreage, **Production**, etc., A 92.11/10-2

Vegetables, Preliminary Acreage, Yield, **Production** and Value, A 92.11/10-6

War **Production** Drive, Progress Report, Pr 32.4815

Weekly Report on **Production** of Bituminous Coal, Etc, I 19.30

Weekly Roundup of World **Production** and Trade, WR (series), A 67.42

Wheat **Production** Adjustment, A 43.5/16

Wool and Mohair **Production**, Price and Value, A 92.29/5

Wool **Production** and Value of Sales, A 88.35/3

Wool **Production** and Value, A 92.29/3

World Agricultural **Production** and Trade, Statistical Report, A 67.8/3

World Agricultural **Production**, A 67.18:WAP

World Crop **Production**, A 67.18:WCP

World Crude Oil **Production** Annual (year), I 28.18/5

World Indices of Agricultural and Food **Production**, A 1.34/3

World Mineral **Production** in (year), I 28.81/2

World Motor Vehicle and Trailer **Production** and Registration, C 57.21

World Motor Vehicle **Production** and Registration, C 41.17

Your Guide to Federal Waterfowl **Production** Areas, I 49.6/3

Zinc Mine **Production**, I 28.57

Productions

Advance Statements of **Productions** of Copper in United States (calendar year), I 19.23

Vegetables, Processing, Annual Summary, Acreage **Productions**, etc., A 92.11/10

Productivity

Abstracts of NSF/RANN Research Reports: Private Sector **Productivity**, NS 1.13/4

Chartbook on Prices, Wages, and **Productivity**, L 2.102/2

Continued Increases in Industry **Productivity** in (year) Reported by BLS, L 1.79/2-3

Developments in Labor **Productivity**, L 2.73

Exemplary Practices in Federal **Productivity**, PM 1.37

Federal **Productivity** Measurement, PM 1.45

Industry **Productivity** in (year) Reported by BLS, L 2.120/2-9

International Comparisons of Manufacturing **Productivity** and Labor Costs Trends, L 2.120/2-6

Japan **Productivity** Center, United States Operations Mission to Japan, Publications, S 17.44/2

Management and **Productivity** Improvement Report, VA 1.89

Multifactor **Productivity** Measures, L 2.120/2-10

NASA Excellence Award for Quality and **Productivity**, NAS 1.78

National Commission on **Productivity** and Work Quality: Publications, Pr 37.8:P 94

News, Multifactor **Productivity** Measures, L 2.120/2-10

Productivity and Cost of Employment: Local Service Carriers, Calendar Year, C 31.263

Productivity and Cost of Employment: System Trunks, Calendar Year, C 31.263/2

Productivity and Costs, L 2.119

Productivity and Job Security, Y 3.P 94:9

Productivity and Technological Development Division Publications, L 2.19

Productivity Improvement Program, HH 1.107

Productivity Indexes for Selected Industries, L 2.3

Productivity Measures for Selected Industries, L 2.3/20

Productivity Research Program for Fiscal Year (date), PM 1.38

Productivity Statistics for Federal Government Functions, Fiscal Year, L 2.119/2

Productivity, Annual Report, Pr 94/R 29

Quarterly Review of **Productivity**, Wages, and Prices, L 2.102

Update (Electronics Manufacturing **Productivity** Facility), D 201.36

Products

Aluminum Metal Supply and Shipments of **Products** to Consumers, C 41.112/4

Animals and **Products**, IC 1.23/11:SS-3

Army-Navy-Air Force List of **Products** Qualified Under Military Specifications, D 101.30

Audiovisual **Products**, CC 1.56

Banned **Products** {list}, Y 3.C 76/3:9

Biological **Products** Memo, A 77.226/2

Biological **Products** Notices, A 77.226

Bulletins, Forest **Products**, C 3.28/16

Canned Fishery **Products**, C 55.309/2

Carload Waybill Statistics, Mileage Block Distribution, Traffic and Revenue by Commodity Class, Territorial Movement, and Type of Rate, **Products** of Agriculture, 1 Percent Sample of... MB-1, IC 1.23/2

Carload Waybill Statistics, Mileage Block Distribution, Traffic and Revenue by Commodity Class, Territorial Movement, and Type of Rate, Animals and **Products**, 1 Percent Sample... MB-2, IC 1.23/3

Carload Waybill Statistics, Mileage Block Distribution, Traffic and Revenue by Commodity Class, Territorial Movement, and Type of Rate, **Products** of Mines, 1 Percent Sample... MB-3, IC 1.23/4

Carload Waybill Statistics, Mileage Block Distribution, Traffic and Revenue by Commodity Class, Territorial Movement, and Type of Rate, **Products** of Forests, 1 Percent Sample... MB-4, IC 1.23/5

Cellulose Plastic **Products** (Nitro-Cellulose and Cellulose Acetate Sheets, Rods and Tubes), C 3.73

Certification Procedures for **Products** and Parts, TD 4.6:part 21

Check List of Standards for Farm **Products**, A 36.59, A 66.26

Chemicals and Allied **Products** Entered for Consumption, C 18.55

Clay **Products** of United States, I 19.18

Coal and Coal **Products**, E 1.99

Cold Storage Holdings of Fishery **Products**, I 49.8/4

Commercial News USA, New **Products** Annual Directory, C 61.10/2

Commodities Included in (various) **Products** Group for Revised Wholesale Price Index, L 2.61/3

Competitive Position of United States Farm **Products** Abroad, A 67.28

Contracts for U.S. Food **Products**, A 67.40/3

Cottonseed **Products** Manufactured and on Hand at Oil Mills by States, C 3.125

Crude Petroleum and Petroleum **Products**, I 28.18/4

Crude-oil and Refined-**products** Pipeline Mileage in the United States, I 28.45/2

Current Fishery **Products**, Annual Summary, C 55.309/2-4

Distribution of Petroleum **Products** by Petroleum Administration Districts, IC 1.24

Egg **Products**, A 105.12/2

Egg **Products**, Liquid, Frozen, Solids Production, A 92.9/4

Electronic Information **Products** Available by Special Order, GP 3.22/5

Electronic **Products** [Agriculture Department], A 1.142

Electronic **Products** [Air Force Department], D 301.118

Electronic **Products** [Animal and Plant Health Inspection Service], A 101.32

Electronic **Products** [Appalachian Regional Commission], Y 3.Ap 4/2:16

Electronic **Products** [Army Department], D 101.121/2

Electronic **Products** [Bonneville Power Administration], E 5.24

Electronic **Products** [Census Bureau], C 3.275

Electronic **Products** [Coast Guard], TD 5.67

Electronic **Products** [Commerce Department], C 1.89

Electronic **Products** [Congress], Y 1.5

Electronic **Products** [Cooperative State Research Service], A 94.22

Electronic **Products** [Defense Department], D 1.95

Electronic **Products** [Defense Logistics Agency], D 7.45

Electronic **Products** [Descriptive Cataloging Division], LC 9.17

Electronic **Products** [Education Department], ED 1.83

Electronic **Products** [Energy Department], E 1.111

Electronic **Products** [Environmental Protection Agency], EP 1.104

Electronic **Products** [Executive Office of the President], PrEx 1.21

Electronic **Products** [Farmer Cooperative Service], A 88.64

Electronic **Products** [Federal Deposit Insurance Corporation], Y 3.F 31/8:32

Electronic **Products** [Federal Highway Administration], TD 2.73

Electronic **Products** [Federal Register Office], AE 2.115

Electronic **Products** [Federal Trade Commission], FT 1.33

Electronic **Products** [Fish and Wildlife Service], I 49.113

Electronic **Products** [Food Safety and Inspection Service], A 110.20

Electronic **Products** [Forest Service], A 13.140

Electronic **Products** [General Services Administration], GS 1.35

Electronic **Products** [Geological Survey], I 19.120

Electronic **Products** [Health and Human Services Department], HE 1.60

Electronic **Products** [Housing and Urban Development Department], HH 1.114

Electronic **Products** [Interior Department], I 1.114

Electronic **Products** [International Trade Administration], C 61.47

Electronic **Products** [Justice Department], J 1.100

Electronic **Products** [Library of Congress], LC 1.54

Electronic **Products** [Medicine and Surgery Bureau], D 206.24

Electronic **Products** [Military Sealift Command], D 216.11

Electronic **Products** [National Aeronautics and Space Administration], NAS 1.86

Electronic **Products** [National Agricultural Library], A 17.31

Electronic **Products** [National Agricultural Statistics Service], A 92.51

Electronic **Products** [National Archives and Records Administration], AE 1.127

Electronic **Products** [National Cancer Institute], HE 20.3193

Electronic **Products** [National Institute of Standards and Technology], C 13.79

Electronic **Products** [National Library of Medicine], HE 20.3624/3

Electronic **Products** [National Science Foundation], NS 1.60

Electronic **Products** [Nuclear Regulatory Commission], Y 3.N 88:61

Electronic **Products** [Prisons Bureau], J 16.33

Electronic **Products** [Processing Department], LC 30.33

Electronic **Products** [Public Documents Division], GP 3.38

Electronic **Products** [Science and Technology Policy Office], PrEx 23.12

Electronic **Products** [Smithsonian Institution], SI 1.47

Electronic **Products** [State Department], S 1.142

Electronic **Products** [Transportation Department], TD 1.56

Electronic **Products** [Treasury Department], T 1.66

Electronic **Products** [United States Postal Service], P 1.59

Electronic **Products** [Veterans Affairs Department], VA 1.95

Electronic **Products** [Vice President Office], PrVp 42.17

ERIC **Products**, Bibliography of Information
Analysis Publications of ERIC
Clearinghouses, HE 5.77/2
Establishments and **Products** Licensed Under
Section 351 of the Public Health Service
Act, HE 20.4042
Facilities Expansions Authorized Listed by Major
Types of **Products**, Pr 32.4843
Factory Consumption of Animal and Vegetable Fats
and Oils by Classes of **Products**, C 3.154
Farm **Products** Prices, A 36.184
FDA Drug and Device **Products** Approvals, FDA/
BD, HE 20.4209
Fishery **Products** Report, I 49.65
Food **Products**, A 19.5
Foreign Agricultural Trade of the United States,
Trade in Agricultural **Products** with
Individual Countries by Calendar Year,
A 67.19/6
Forest **Products**, C 3.12, C 3.12/7
Forest **Products** Division Circulars, C 13.92/2
Forest **Products** Division Paper Circulars, C 18.92/
3
Forest **Products** Industry Notes, Y 3.T 25:28-2
Forest **Products** Laboratory, Madison, Wisconsin,
A 13.27
Forest **Products** Papers, A 13.67/10
Forest **Products** Review, C 62.11
Forest **Products**, (year), C 3.12/1, C 3.12/2, C 3.12/
3, C 3.12/4, C 3.12/5, C 3.12/6
Fresh **Products** Standardization and Inspection
Branch, Annual Progress Report, A
88.12/28
Frozen Fishery **Products**, C 55.309/2
Futures Trading and Open Contracts in Wheat,
Corn, Oats, Rye, Soybeans and **Products**,
A 85.11/7
Grain and Grain **Products**, C 18.72/4
Harvard Studies in Marketing Farm **Products**, A
36.169
Imports and Exports of Fishery **Products**, (year)
Annual Summary, C 55.309/2
Imports of Benzenoid Chemicals and **Products**, TC
1.36, ITC 1.19
Imports of Coal-Tar **Products**, TC 1.32
Industrial Fishery **Products**, (year) Annual
Summary, C 55.309/2
Industrial Fishery **Products**, Situation and Outlook
CEA I (series), C 55.309/3, I 49.8/9
Industry Report, Chemicals and Allied **Products**, C
18.235
Industry Wage Survey: Meat **Products** (year), L 2.3/
15
List of Plants Operating Under USDA and Egg
Grading and Egg **Products** Inspection
Programs, A 103.10
Lumber and Timber Basic **Products** Industry,
Wooden Container Industry, Employer
Report of Employment and Required
Labor Force by Standard Lumber Type
Region, Pr 32.5224
Market for U.S. **Products** {by country}, C 42.20/2
Medical Devices and Diagnostic **Products**
Standards Survey; International Edition,
HE 20.4035
Medical Devices and Diagnostic **Products**
Standards Survey; National Edition, HE
20.4035/2
Milk Production and Dairy **Products**, Annual
Statistical Summary, A 92.10/6
Milk Production on Farms and Statistics of Dairy
Plant **Products**, A 88.14/7
Mineral **Products** of the United States, I 19.7
Monthly Comparative Sales of Confectionery and
Competitive Chocolate **Products**, C
3.135
Monthly Receipts from Sale of Principal Farm
Products by States, A 36.81/2
New **Products** Annual Directory, C 61.10/2
New **Products** from the U.S. Government, GP 3.17/
6
NPA Production Series, Quarterly Indexes of
Shipments for **Products** of Metalworking
Industries, C 40.15
NTIS **Products** and Services Catalog, C 51.11/8
Nursery **Products**, Production and Sales, A 88.48
Oilseeds and Oilseed **Products**, A 67.30:Oi 5
Packaged Fishery **Products**, C 55.309/2
Petroleum Market Shares, Report on Sales of
Refined Petroleum **Products**, E 3.13
Petroleum **Products** Survey, PPS- (series), I 28.18/3
Petroleum **Products**, Secondary Inventories and
Storage Capacity, C 3.213

Price Information for Drug **Products**, Invoice Level
Prices, HE 22.113, HE 22.309
Production of Manufactured Dairy **Products**, A
88.14/10
Products and Services Catalog, C 21.30
Products and Services Catalog, C 21.39
Products List Circulars, SBA 1.4/2
Products of Agriculture, IC 1.23/10:SS-2
Products of Forest, IC 1.23/13:SS-5
Project Label, Alphabetical Listings by Drug
Labeler of Discontinued **Products**, J
24.24/3
Qualified **Products** Lists Department of Defense, D
1.17
Qualified **Products** Lists Department of the Air
Force, D 301.22
Quarterly Bulletin for Part 2, Hydrographic
Products, D 5.351/2-2
Quarterly Update of Courses and **Products**, L
38.11/4-2
Receipts from Sale of Principal Farm **Products** by
States, A 36.81/1
Recent **Products** of Applied Analysis, E 3.27/3
Reports on Foreign Markets for Agricultural
Products, A 36.8
Research in Forest **Products**, A 13.27/11
Research Reports Forest **Products** Laboratory, A
13.27/14
Rubber **Products** Trade News, C 18.201
Salad Dressing, Mayonnaise and Related **Products**,
C 57.316, C 57.514
Schedule of Blind-made **Products**, Y 3.B 61:8
Soybean Crush **Products**, Preliminary Report, C
3.121
Structural Clay **Products** (common brick, face brick,
vitrified paving brick, hollow building
tile), C 3.109
Technical Notes Forest Service Forest **Products**
Laboratory, A 13.27/9
Textiles and Allied **Products**, C 18.150
Tropical **Products**, C 18.72/7
Tropical Products: World Markets and Trade, A
67.18:FTROP
U.S. Exports of Domestic Merchandise, SIC- based
Products and Area, C 3.164:610
U.S. Exports of Petroleum and Petroleum **Products**
of Domestic Origin, Commodity by
Customs District, C 3.164:527
U.S. General Imports Various **Products**, C 56.210/4
U.S. Government's Preferred **Products** List, D 1.69
U.S. Imports for Consumption and General Imports,
SIC-Based **Products** and Area, C
3.164:210
U.S. Imports of Textile and Apparel **Products**, C
61.52
Underware and Allied **Products**, C 3.113
United States Exports of Petroleum and Petroleum
Products of Domestic Origin,
Commodity by Country of Destination, C
3.164:526
Veterinary Biological **Products**, Licensees and
Permittees, A 101.2/10
Wheat Ground and Wheat-Milling **Products**, by
States, C 3.117
Wheat Ground and Wheat-Milling **Products**, C
3.116
Wheat Ground and Wheat-Milling **Products**,
Merchant and Other Mills, C 3.118
Wood **Products**: International Trade and Foreign
Markets, A 67.18:WP
World Trade Notes on Chemicals and Allied
Products, C 18.179
Profession
Education **Profession** Series, HE 5.92/9
Professional
Annual Indicators of Immigration into the United
States of Aliens in **Professional** and
Related Occupations, J 21.15
Army Institute for **Professional** Development:
Subcourse ISO (series), D 101.103
Biannual **Professional** Development Program, ED
1.33/2
Conventions, (year): National and International
Unions, State Labor Federations,
Professional Associations, State
Employee Association {list}, L 2.103
ESSA **Professional** Papers, C 52.20
Faculty and Other **Professional** Staff in
Institutions of Higher Education, FS
5.253:53000, HE 5.253:53000
Financial Assistance for College Students,
Undergraduate and First-**Professional**,
FS 5.255:55027, HE 5.255:55027

Health Care Financing Administration Rulings on
Medicare, Medicaid, **Professional**
Standards Review and Related Matters,
HE 22.15
Music **Professional** Training Career Development
Organizations, Music Recording
Services to Composers, Centers for New
Music Resources Special Projects,
Music, Application Guidelines, NF 2.8/
2-5
National **Professional** Standards Review Council:
Annual Report, HE 1.46, HE 20.5010
National Roster of Minority **Professional**
Consulting Services, C 1.57/3
National Survey of **Professional**, Administrative,
Technical, and Clerical Pay, L 2.3
Naval **Professional** Papers, N 17.5
NOAA **Professional** Papers, C 55.25
Peace Corps Opportunity Newsletter of Special
Interest to **Professional** and Technical
People, S 19.13
Professional Guide-PG (series), D 13.8/6
Professional Manuals, D 119
Professional Memoirs, W 7.16/6
Professional Opportunities for Women in Research
and Education, NS 1.61
Professional Papers Engineer Department, W 7.10
Professional Papers Environmental Science
Services Administration, C 52.20
Professional Papers Geological Survey, I 19.16
Professional Papers National Oceanic and
Atmospheric Administration, C 55.25
Professional Papers Signal Corps, W 42.11/2
Professional Papers Signal Service, W 42.11/1
Professional Series, CS 1.71/2
Professional Standards Review Organization,
Annual Report, HE 22.210
Quartermaster **Professional** Bulletin, D 106.3/4
Regional Office Directory, **Professional** and
Administrative Personnel, FS 1.17/2
Regulations, Rules and Instructions Center for
Professional Development and Training,
HE 20.7709
Southwest Cultural Resources Center: **Profes-**
sional Papers (series), I 29.116
Summary Report, Faculty and Other **Professional**
Staff in Institutions of Higher Education,
FS 5.253:53014, HE 5.253:53014
Undergraduate Engineering Curricular Accredited
by Engineer's Council for **Professional**
Development, FS 5.61
United States Air Force Academy Journal of
Professional Military Ethics, D 305.21
VA Health **Professional** Scholarship Program:
Publications, VA 1.63
Professionals
Guidelines for {Various Health **Professionals** and
Sub-professional} in Home Health
Services, FS 2.6/8
Impaired **Professionals'** Resource Guide, HE
20.9113
Publications List for Health **Professionals**, HE
20.3183/2
Training Health **Professionals**, HE 20.6618
Professions
Children, Interdisciplinary Journal for **Professions**
Serving Children, FS 14.109
Commissioner's Report on the Education
Professions, HE 19.124
Education **Professions**, HE 5.258:58032
Health **Professions** Education Assistance Program,
Report to the President and the
Congress, HE 1.40
Hospital and Medical Facilities Series, Health
Professions Education, FS 2.74/4
Report to the President and Congress on the Status
of Health **Professions** Personnel in the
United States, HE 20.6619
Professorships
NSF Visiting **Professorships** for Women, NS 1.48
Proficiency
Blood Lead **Proficiency** Testing, HE 20.7412/2
English Language **Proficiency** Study (series), ED
1.43
Erythrocyte Protoporphyrin, **Proficiency** Testing,
HE 20.7412/4
Fluoridated Drinking Water, **Proficiency** Testing,
HE 20.7412/3
Library Programs, Library Services for Individuals
with Limited English **Proficiency**, ED
1.18/8
National Performance Audit Program, Ambient Air
Audits of Analytical **Proficiency**, EP
1.23/5-2

Proficiency Testing Summary Analysis, Parasitology, HE 20.7022/3-4
Proficiency Testing Summary Analysis, Public Health Immunology, HE 20.7022/3-3
Proficiency Testing Summary Analysis, General Immunology, HE 20.7022/3, HE 20.7412

Profile
Cadet **Profile**, United States Coast Guard Academy, TD 5.15
Education **Profile**, I 20.60
Environmental Quality **Profile**, Pacific Northwest Region, EP 1.87/2
Geographic **Profile** of Employment and Unemployment, L 2.3/12
Mental Health Demographic **Profile** System, MHDPS Working Papers, HE 20.8133
1990 Census **Profile**, C 3.223/7-5
Population **Profile** of the United States, Current Population Reports, C 3.186/8
Product **Profile**, C 3.287
Profile, D 1.41, HE 20.9016
Profile of Jail Inmates, J 29.13/2
Profile of Labor Conditions (various countries), L 29.14
Profile on Fire in the United States, FEM 1.117/2
Profile: Smithsonian National Portrait Gallery News, SI 11.16
Reading is Fundamental, Inc., Book Supplier **Profile**, SI 1.36/2
State and Local Government Functional **Profile** Series, Y 3.Eq 2:14
State Health **Profile**, HE 20.7043/1—51
Statistical **Profile** Series SP, C 3.228
Statistical **Profile**, Redevelopment Area Series, C 1.45
Toxicological **Profile** (TP), HE 20.7918
Urban Business **Profile**, C 46.27
Workforce **Profile**, T 17.24

Profiles
Community **Profiles**, PrEx 10.9/5
Country Demographic **Profiles** for Foreign Country Series, ISP 30 (series), C 56.218/2
Country **Profiles**, S 18.53
Current Industrial Reports, Manufacturing **Profiles**, C 3.158/4
Demographic **Profiles** of the Airway Facilities Work Force, TD 4.65
Employment **Profiles** for Selected Low-Income Areas, PHC (3) (series), C 3.223/17
Environmental Quality **Profiles** (various States), EP 1.87
Industry **Profiles**, Accession Notices, S 18.36
Mineral Commodity **Profiles**, I 28.37/3
NINDS Research **Profiles**, HE 20.3512
Patent **Profiles**, C 21.25
Performance **Profiles** of Major Energy Producers, E 3.37, E 3.37/2
Profiles in School Support, Decennial Overview, FS 5.222:22022, HE 5.222:22022
Profiles of Foreign Direct Investment in U.S. Energy, E 3.52
Profiles of Scheduled Air Carrier Airport Operations by Equipment Type, Top 100 U.S. Airports, TD 4.44/4
Profiles of Scheduled Air Carrier Airport Operations, Top 100 U.S. Airports, TD 4.44
Profiles of Scheduled Air Carrier Operations by Stage Length, TD 4.44/3
Profiles of Scheduled Air Carrier Passenger Traffic, Top 100 U.S. Airports, TD 4.44/2
Regional **Profiles**, S 18.54
Research **Profiles**, FS 2.22/43
Small Business **Profiles**, SBA 1.50
State Data **Profiles**, Calendar Year (date), Selected Ascs Program Activity and Other Agricultural Data, A 82.90
State Higher Education **Profiles**, ED 1.116/3
State Mineral **Profiles**, I 28.37/4
State Workers' Compensation: Administration **Profiles**, L 36.16
Statistical **Profiles**, Rural Redevelopment Areas, SP (Series), C 1.45/2
{**Profiles**} P Series, C 31.146/2

Profit
Classification of Income and **Profit** and Loss Accounts, IC 1 wat.8
Classification of Income, **Profit** & Loss, and General Balance Sheet Accounts, IC 1 ste.15
Form of Income and **Profit** and Loss Statement, IC 1 ste.14

Profits
Sales, **Profits**, and Dividends of Large Corporations, FR 1.40
War **Profits** Studies, Pr 32.4227, Pr 33.312

Progeny
DHIA Cow Performance Index List, Registered **Progeny** of DHIA Sires, A 77.15:44

Program
ACCP (Atlantic Climate Change **Program**) Newsletter, C 55.55
ACTION **Program** Highlights, AA 1.9/4
Ad Hoc Committee for Review of the Special Virus Cancer **Program**, HE 20.3001/2:V 81/5
Advanced Education **Program** in General Dentistry, D 304.11
Americorps Leaders **Program**, A Service Leadership Development **Program** of the Corporation for National Service, Y 3.N 21/29:16-17
Animal Damage Control **Program**, A 101.28
Annual **Program** Plan, J 16.26
Annual **Program** Plan and Academy Training Schedule, J 16.26
Annual Report of the President on Trade Agreements **Program**, Pr 42.11
Application for Grants under Handicapped Children's Early Education **Program** Demonstration and Auxiliary Activities, ED 1.50/3
Arts III Computer **Program** Functional Specifications (CPFS), TD 4.46
ASA/NSF/Census Bureau Research Fellow **Program**, C 3.293
BJA **Program** Plan, J 26.1/5
BJS **Program** Application Kit, Fiscal Year, J 29.22
Census of Population and Housing Tabulation and Publication **Program** for Puerto Rico, C 3.223/24
Challenge Cost-Share **Program** Report, A 13.124/2
Challenge Grants **Program** Guidelines and Application Materials, NF 3.8/2-4
CHR **Program** Update, HE 20.318
Community Action **Program** for Traffic Safety, Guides (numbered), TD 8.8/2
Compliance **Program** Guide Manual, HE 20.4008/7
Computer **Program** Abstracts, NAS 1.44
Conservation Reserve **Program** of Soil Bank, Statistical Summaries, A 82.79/2
Consolidated Supply **Program**, HH 1.90
Consumer Information TV **Program** Packages, Suggested Scripts, A 21.27
Course Management Plan and **Program** of Instruction (series), D 101.107/4
Department of Labor **Program** Reports, L 1.57
Development Studies **Program** Occasional Papers, S 18.59
Diabetes Control **Program** Update, HE 20.7314
Electronic Computer **Program** Library Memorandum, C 37.20
Employee Counseling Service **Program** Memo, HE 20.9113/2
Energy **Program** Technical Reports, Y 3.N 42/2:9
Expenditures for Public Assistance Payments and for Administrative Costs, by **Program** and Source of Funds, HE 17.632
Federal Women's **Program** Newsletter, I 28.170
Foreign Buyer **Program** Export Interest Directory (series), C 61.19/2
Forest Management **Program** Annual Report (National Summary), A 13.152
General Research Support **Program** Advisory Committee, HE 20.3001/2:R 31/2
GEO-Drug Enforcement **Program** Six-month Statistics, J 24.18
Global Volcanism **Program**, Digital Information Series, SI 1.49
Guide to Computer **Program** Directories, C 13.10:500-42
HCFA Regional Office Manual; **Program** Integrity, HE 22.8/8-2
Head Start **Program** Data, HE 23.1115
Instructional **Program** Notes, VA 1.76
Instructions and Application for Grants under the Special Needs **Program**, ED 1.61
Instructions and Application for Grants under the Strengthening **Program**, ED 1.61/2
Insurance **Program** Quality, HE 3.28/6-4
Intern **Program**, IP (series), PM 1.36
International Solar-Terrestrial Physics **Program**, NAS 1.86/3
Literacy Leader Fellowship **Program** Reports, Y 3.L 71:16

Local Arts Agencies **Program**, Application Guidelines, NF 2.8/2-31
Medicaid Statistics, **Program** and Financial Statistics, HE 22.115
Medicare Carriers Manual; **Program** Administration, HE 22.8/7-3
Medicare **Program** Statistics, HE 22.21/2
Medicare **Program** Statistics, Medicare Utilization, HE 22.21/2-2
Monthly Summary of Export Credit Guarantee **Program** Activity, A 67.47
Monthly Summary of Export Credit Guarantee **Program** Activity, Commodity Credit Corporation, A 67.18:ECG
National Acid Precipitation Assessment **Program**, Report to Congress, C 55.703
National Toxicology **Program**, Technical Report series, HE 20.3564
National Toxicology **Program**, Toxicity Report series, HE 20.3564/2
Natural Resource Development **Program** Annual Report, SBA 1.48
NCHSR **Program** Solicitation (series), HE 20.6512/9
NCHSR **Program** Solicitation, Grants for Health Services Dissertation Research, HE 20.6512/8-2
NCHSR **Program** Solicitation, Individual and Institutional, HE 20.6512/8
NIDRR **Program** Directory, ED 1.30/5
NOAA Coastal Ocean **Program**, Project News Update, C 55.49/4
Oceanic Biology **Program** Abstract Book, D 210:28
Oil and Hazardous Material **Program** Series, EP 2.11
OJJDP Discretionary **Program** Announcement, J 32.22
OJJDP Fiscal Year, **Program** Plan, J 32.10/2
On the Job Training **Program**, JP Series, D 301.38/5
Operations of the Employment Security **Program**, FS 3.3/a3
Operations of the Trade Agreements **Program**, TC 1.14/3, ITC 1.24
OSFA **Program** Book, ED 1.29/2
Outer Continental Shelf Environmental Assessment **Program** Final Reports of Principal Investigators, C 55.433
Outer Continental Shelf Oil and Gas Information **Program**, Summary Reports (various regions), I 72.9
Outer Continental Shelf Oil and Gas Leasing and Production **Program** Annual Report, I 72.12/3-2
Outline of Agricultural Conservation **Program**, A 55.44/12
Pacific Northwest and Alaska Bioenergy **Program** Yearbook, E 5.12
Paid Shipments, European and Far East **Program**, FO 1.9
Peace Corps **Program** and Training Journal Manual Series, AA 4.8/2
Peace Corps **Program** Directory, S 19.16
Pension Insurance Data Book: PBGC Single-Employer **Program**, Y 3.P 38/2:12
Periodic Report from the National Digital Library **Program**, L 37.215
Pesticide Data **Program**, A 88.60
Pharmacology Research Associate **Program**, HE 20.3461/2
Pharmacology-Toxicology **Program** Committee, HE 20.3001/2:P 49/2
Pharmacology-Toxicology **Program**, HE 20.3461
PHPC (Public Housing Primary Care **Program**) Bulletin, HE 20.9121
Pilot Cities **Program**, J 1.46/2
Power **Program** Summary, Y 3.T 25:1-16
Preliminary Monthly Statistical Report on EMIC **Program**, L 5.50, FS 3.208
Preservation Planning Series, State **Program** Overviews, I 29.102
Price Support **Program**, Charts and Tables, Selected Activities, A 82.310/2
Proceedings Annual Conference of Mental Health Career Development **Program**, FS 2.22/45
Proceedings National Brucellosis Committee and Progress Report of the Cooperative State-Federal Brucellosis Eradication **Program**, A 77.202:B 83/16
Proceedings Ocean Drilling **Program**, Initial Reports, NS 1.38/2

Production Practices, 1943 Farm **Program**, A 79.458

Production-Conservation **Program**, Committeemen's Handbooks, A 80.2158

Productivity Improvement **Program**, HH 1.107

Productivity Research **Program** for Fiscal Year (date), PM 1.38

Program Activity Reports, Public Law 85-864, FS 5.71

Program Administration Review, PAR (nos.), FS 13.219

Program Aids Defense Savings Staff, T 1.109

Program Aids Department of Agriculture, A 1.68

Program Alert, Y 3.H 75:16

Program Analysis (series), FS 1.29, HE 1.29

Program and Demographic Characteristics of Supplemental Security Income Beneficiaries, HE 3.71/2

Program and Financial Plan, Basic Assumptions and Guidelines, HE 1.610/2

Program and Itinerary, S 18.13

Program and Progress Report, FAA 2.1

Program and Project Plan for Fiscal Year (date), J 1.38

Program and Resource Digest, J 1.86

Program and Services, Report of Educational Materials Laboratory, Division of International Studies and Services, FS 5.214:14031, HE 5.214:14031

Program and Training Journal Manual Series, AA 4.8/2

Program and Training Journal Reprint Series, AA 4.10

Program Announcement, Graduate Research Fellowship **Program**, J 28.25

Program Announcement, Visiting Fellowship **Program**, J 28.25/2

Program Application Reports, HE 17.25/2

Program Approval Documents, Executive Summaries, ER 1.22

Program Brief, J 26.31, J 28.24/9

Program Data, HE 1.610/3

Program Development Handbooks for State and Area Agencies on {various subjects}, HE 23.3009

Program Facts on Federally Aided Public Assistance Income Maintenance Programs, HE 17.614

Program Focus, J 28.30

Program for Regional Observing and Forecasting Services, C 55.626/2

Program Guide Environmental Protection Agency, EP 1.8/9

Program Guide Federal Civil Defense Administration, FCD 1.6/7

Program Guide President's Committee on Employment of the Handicapped, PrEx 1.10/7

Program Guide Veterans Administration, VA 1.10/3

Program Highlights, HE 20.3033

Program in Biomedical and Behavioral Nutrition Research and Training, Fiscal Year, HE 20.3036

Program Information Guide Series, ED 1.8/4

Program Instructions, HE 1.47/2

Program Integrity Bulletin, HH 1.3/5

Program Management Series, CS 1.65/8

Program Manager, D 1.60

Program Memorandum Health Maintenance Organization/Competitive Medical Plan, HE 22.28/2

Program Memorandum Medicaid State Agencies, HE 22.28

Program Memorandum Quality Assurance, HE 22.28/3

Program Memorandum State Survey Agencies, HE 22.28/4

Program Models, J 1.54, J 26.16, J 28.9

Program Notes, A 88.55, HE 20.6512/6

Program of University Research Report Reprinted, TD 1.20/6-2

Program of Water Resources Division, Texas District, and Summary of District Activities, Fiscal Year, I 19.55/2

Program Operations Manual System, HE 3.6/5

Program Plan by Program Areas for Fiscal Year, HE 20.7121

Program Plan of the National Institute for Occupational Safety and Health, HE 20.7127

Program Plan, Fiscal Year (date), J 26.24

Program Regulation Guides {issued by various departments}, HE 1.47/3

Program Report of the United States Travel Service, C 47.1

Program Reports {various subjects}, NS 1.37

Program Research and Development Announcements, ER 1.30

Program Results Inventory, J 1.51

Program Solicitation (series), NS 1.33

Program Solicitation, Small Business Innovation Research Program, A 94.16

Program Summary Report, Y 3.N 88:26

Program Year, I 1.105/3

Progress in Rural Development **Program**, Annual Reports, A 1.85

Progress Report Hill-Burton **Program**, FS 2.96

Progress Report National Mental Health **Program**, FS 2.65

Proposed Foreign Aid **Program** Fiscal Year, Summary Presentation to Congress, S 18.28/a

Proposed Foreign Aid **Program**, Summary Presentation to Congress, S 18.28

Proposed Streamflow Data **Program** for {State}, I 19.59

Public Employment **Program**, Annual Report to Congress, L 1.68

Public Housing Management Improvement **Program**: Technical Memorandums, HH 1.63

Publications Federal-Aid Airport **Program**, FAA 8.10

Publications Russian Scientific Translation **Program**, FS 2.22/19

Publications Scientific Translation **Program**, FS 2.214

Quality Evaluation **Program** Manual, D 7.6/4-3

Quarterly Bulletin, Intelligence Continuing Education **Program**, D 5.212

Quarterly Progress Report, Nationwide Urban Runoff **Program**, EP 1.92

Quarterly Report on **Program** Cost and Schedule, E 1.68/2-6

Quarterly Report, Demonstration Projects **Program**, TD 2.40/2

Quarterly Statistical Bulletin, Electric **Program**, A 68.13/2

Quarterly Statistical Bulletin, Telephone **Program**, A 68.13/3

Questions from Answer Me This, Radio **Program**, I 16.58/2

Reading **Program**, S 1.64/2

Reagents Evaluation **Program**, HE 20.7809, HE 20.7810/2

Recap, Reclamation's Current Awareness **Program**, I 27.52

Recipients of Public Assistance Money Payments and Amounts of Such Payments, by **Program**, State, and County, HE 17.627/2

Refugee Relief **Program**, S 1.110

Refugee Resettlement **Program**, Report to Congress, HE 3.72, HE 25.16

Regulatory Licensing, Status Summary Report, Systematic Evaluation **Program**, Y 3.N 88:29

Regulatory **Program** of the United States Government, PrEx 2.30

REMR Bulletin: News from the Repair, Evaluation, Maintenance and Rehabilitation Research **Program**, D 103.72

Renewable Resources Remote Sensing Research **Program** Report, NAS 1.70

Report of Classified **Program** of Exports and Value by American Agencies Voluntarily Registered with Advisory Committee on Voluntary Foreign Aid, S 1.99/2

Report of Secretary to President and Congress on Mineral Exploration **Program**, I 1.85

Report of Urban Planning Assistance **Program**, HH 7.11

Report of Virgin Islands Agricultural Research and Extension **Program**, A 77.491

Report on Progress of Works **Program**, Y 3.W 89/2:32

Report to Congress on Foreign Assistance **Program**, S 18.1

Report to Congress on United States Foreign Relief **Program**, S 1.63

Research and Technology **Program** Digest, Flash Index, NAS 1.41

Research and Technology **Program**, Fiscal Year (date), HH 1.88

Research and Technology **Program**, HH 1.88

Research **Program** Plan, J 28.25/3

Residential Solar **Program** Reports, HH 1.74

Residential **Program** Highlights, FEM 1.17

Review of Bureau of Mines Coal **Program**, I 28.17, I 28.27

Review of Bureau of Mines Energy **Program**, I 28.27

Review of the Air Force Materials Research and Development **Program**, D 301.45

Rural Development **Program** News, A 21.25

Russian Scientific Translation **Program** Publications, FS 2.22/19

Saline Water Conservation **Program**, Reports and Publications, I 1.83

Scholarship **Program**, Applicant Information Bulletin, HE 20.6023

Science and Technology Fellowship **Program**, C 1.86

Scientific Translation **Program** Publications, FS 2.214

Secretary's Annual Report to Congress, Posture Statement, Outlook and **Program** Review, E 1.60:0010

Security **Program**, TD 1.33

Selected Papers from Bureau of Radiological Health Seminar **Program** (numbered), HE 20.1109

Semiannual Report to Congress on the Effectiveness of the Civil Aviation Security **Program**, TD 4.810

Seminar of Manpower Policy and **Program**, L 1.39/8

Series Available and Estimating Methods, BLS Current Employment Statistics **Program**, L 2.124/2

Series Available and Estimating Methods, BLS National Payroll Employment **Program**, L 2.124

Servicemen's Group Life Insurance **Program**, Annual Report, VA 1.46/2

Shipbuilding and Conversion **Program**, D 207.13

Simplifying Federal Aid to States and Communities, Annual Report to the President of an Interagency **Program**, PrEx 2.18

Small Business Performance, by Claimant **Program**, D 1.48/2

Small-scale Appropriate Energy Technology Grants **Program**, E 1.76

Smaller War Plants Corporation **Program** and Progress Reports, Pr 32.4825

Solar Thermal Power Systems: **Program** Summary, E 1.38/2-2

Space Science and Applications **Program**, NAS 1.33

Special Foreign Currency Science Information **Program**, List of Translations in Process for Fiscal Year, Coordinated and Administered by the National Science Foundation, C 51.12

Special Notice Concerning Basic Agreements Teleprocessing Services **Program** (TSP) Industrial Group 737, Industrial Class 7374, GS 12.13

SSA **Program** Circulars Disability, HE 3.4/4

SSA **Program** Circulars General Series, HE 3.4/2

SSA **Program** Circulars Public Information, HE 3.4/3

SSA **Program** Circulars Retirement and Survivors Insurance, HE 3.4/5

SSA **Program** Circulars Supplemental Security Income, HE 3.4/6

Standards Laboratory Cross-Check Procedure, Department of Navy, BUWEPS-BUSHIPS Calibration **Program**, D 217.16

Standards Laboratory Instrument Calibration Procedure, Department of Navy, BUWEPS-BUSHIPS Calibration **Program**, D 217.16/2

Standards Laboratory Measurements System Operation Procedure, Department of Navy, BUWEPS-BUSHIPS Calibration **Program**, D 217.16/3

State Data Profiles, Calendar Year (date), Selected Ascs **Program** Activity and Other Agricultural Data, A 82.90

State Safety **Program** Work Sheets, L 16.39

State Vocational Rehabilitation Agency **Program** and Financial Plan, HE 23.4110

State Vocational Rehabilitation Agency: **Program** Data, HE 23.4110/2

Station and **Program** Notes, W 100.8

Program Facts on Federally Aided Public Assistance Income Maintenance **Programs**, HE 17.614

Programs (numbered), Y 3.W 27/2:9

Programs and Plans, Environmental Research Laboratories, C 55.615/2

Programs and Schedules, Services of Supply Staff Course, W 28.11/3

Programs by States, A 55.42/9

Programs for College Teachers of Science, Mathematics, and Engineering, NS 1.12

Programs for the Handicapped, HE 1.23/4

Programs of HUD, HH 1.100

Programs, (year), Guide to Programmed Instructional Materials Available to Educators by (date), FS 5.234:34015, HE 5.234:34015

Progress Report President's Medical **Programs** for Heart Disease, Cancer, and Stroke, and Related Diseases, FS 2.313

Proposed Mental Retardation **Programs**, HE 1.23

Public Health Service Support of Cardiovascular Research, Training and Community **Programs**, FS 2.22/11-2

Public **Programs**, NF 3.26

Public School Finance **Programs**, HE 19.126

Public Support for Coastal Zone Management **Programs** Implementation of the Coastal Zone Management Act of 1972, C 55.32/5

Publications Office of Air **Programs**, EP 4.9

Quarterly Awards Listing Grants Assistance **Programs**, EP 1.35

Quarterly Review, 503 and 504 Economic Development Loan **Programs**, SBA 1.27/2

Recipients and Amounts of Medical Vendor Payments Under Public Assistance **Programs**, HE 17.617/2

Registered Group-Joint Apprenticeship **Programs** in Construction Industry (by trades), L 23.9

Regulations, Rules and Instructions Office of Water **Programs**, EP 2.6

Regulations, Rules and Instructions Research and Special **Programs** Administration, TD 10.6

Report of Secretary of Defense to the Congress on the Budget, Authorization Request, and Defense **Programs**, D 1.1

Report of State and Local Radiological Health **Programs**, HE 20.4121

Reports on Apprentice Selection **Programs**, L 23.11

Research and Training Opportunities Abroad (year), Educational **Programs** in Foreign Language and Area Studies, HE 5.99

Research **Programs** in Aging, FS 2.22/25-2

Revenue **Programs** for the Public Schools in the United States, FS 5.222:22013, HE 5.222:22013

Safety Research **Programs** Sponsored by Office of Nuclear Regulatory Research, Y 3.N 88:48

Sanitation Handbook of Consumer Protection **Programs**, A 88.6/4:Sa 5

Selected Bibliography of Regional Medical **Programs**, HE 20.2612

Selected Multifamily Status Reports, Mortgage Insurance **Programs** by Name and Location of Each Project, HH 1.50

Shipment Under the United States Foreign Aid **Programs** Made on Army- or Navy-Operated Vessels (American flag) by Port of Lading by Country of Destination, C 3.164:976

Social Security **Programs** in the United States, SSA 1.24/2

Social Security **Programs** Throughout the World, HE 3.49:31, HE 3.49/3

Solar Educational **Programs** and Courses, E 1.85

Special Analysis of Federal Credit **Programs** in Budget, PrEx 2.8/a5

Special Analysis of Federal Research and Development **Programs** in Budget, PrEx 2.8/a4

Special Analysis of Principal Federal Statistical **Programs** in Budget, PrEx 2.8/a6

Sponsored Research **Programs**, J 28.24/2

Spotlight on Affirmative Employment **Programs**, PM 1.18/4

Staff Training in Extramural **Programs**, HE 20.3053

State Air **Programs**, Digest, Fiscal Year (date), EP 1.33

State and Local **Programs** on Smoking and Health, HE 20.25/4

State Expenditures for Public Assistance **Programs**, HE 17.2:St 2/2

State Municipal Project Priority Lists, Grants Assistance **Programs**, EP 1.56/3

State **Programs** for Public School Support, FS 5.222:22023, HE 5.222:22023

State **Programs**, NF 1.8/2-17

States and Small Business: **Programs** and Activities, SBA 1.34

Statistical **Programs** of the United States Government, PrEx 2.10/3

Statistical Summaries {various commodity **programs**}, A 82.37/3

Status of Handicapped Children in Head Start **Programs**, HE 23.1012

Status Report on Water and Power Resources Service **Programs** Within (various States), I 27.74

Student Guide, Five Federal Financial Aid **Programs**, ED 1.8/2

Student Work Sheets, Department of Labor Safety Training **Programs**, SWS-LS-(series), L 16.51

Summary of SBA **Programs**, Y 4.Sm 1/12

Trends Toward Open Occupancy in Housing **Programs** of Public Housing Administration, HH 3.8

United States Antarctic **Programs**, Annual Report, D 201.15

Upper Atmospheric **Programs** Bulletin, NAS 1.63

Veterans Administration Summary of Medical **Programs**, VA 1.43/5

Voluntary Foreign Relief **Programs**, Activities of Registered American Voluntary Agencies, S 18.19

Wastewater Treatment Construction Grants Data Base, Public Law 92-500 Project Records, Grants Assistance **Programs**, New Projects Funded During (Month), EP 1.56

Working Papers Office on Water **Programs**, EP 2.23

Progress

Annual Report of **Progress** on Engineering Research, I 27.54

Annual Report of Safety **Progress** for (year), T 1.41/3

Bureau of Reclamation **Progress**, I 27.56

Coastal America **Progress** Report, PrEx 1.18

EM **Progress**, E 1.90/6

Equipment Development and Test Program, **Progress**, Plans, Fiscal Year, A 13.49/5

Extent of Aerial Photography by Agriculture Department, Completed, in **Progress** and Approved, A 1.51

Forestry Research **Progress** in (year) McIntire-Stennis Cooperative Forestry Research Program, A 94.2 F 76/

General Letters to State Works **Progress** Administrators, Y 3.W 89/2:23

General **Progress** Bulletins, New Alotments, Y 3.R 88:12

Government-Supported Research, International Affairs, Research Completed and in **Progress**, S 1.101/9

Highlights of **Progress** in Mental Health Research, FS 2.22/16

Highlights of **Progress** in Research in Cancer, FS 2.22/14

Highlights of **Progress** in Research on Neurologic Disorders, FS 2.22/12

Highlights of **Progress** in Research on Oral Diseases, FS 2.22/23

Highlights of Research **Progress** in Allergy and Infectious Diseases, FS 2.22/17

Highlights of Research **Progress** in Arthritis and Metabolic Diseases, FS 2.22/21

Highlights of Research **Progress** in General Medical Sciences, FS 2.22/20

Highway **Progress**, TD 2.21

Highway **Progress** (year) Annual Report of the Bureau of Public Roads, C 37.1

Highway Research and Development News, Plant Ecology and Esthetics, **Progress** and Implementation, TD 2.113/2

Information from Plans for **Progress**, L 1.54/2

Joint Stock Land Banks, **Progress** in Liquidation Including Statements of Condition, A 72.16

{Letters} to State Works **Progress** Administrators, Y 3.W 89/2:21

Municipal Environmental Research Laboratory: Report of **Progress**, EP 1.46/7-2

National Assessment of Education **Progress**: Reports, HE 19.312

National Assessment of Educational **Progress** {reports} (unnumbered), HE 19.312/2

OAR **Progress** (year), D 301.69/3

Patterns for **Progress** in Aging Case Studies, FS 1.13/3, FS 14.9/5

Patterns for **Progress** in Aging, HE 1.211

Personnel Management Reform, **Progress** in State and Local Governments, PM 1.11/3

Plans for **Progress** Publications, L 1.54

Progress, Y 3.T 25:65

Progress Against Cancer (series), HE 20.3169

Progress Against Cancer, Report by National Advisory Cancer Council, HE 20.3024, HE 20.3163

Progress American Women, Y 3.In 8/21:7-2

Progress Analysis, Pr 33.214

Progress Bulletins, General, A 68.8

Progress Check Book (series), D 101.107/15

Progress During. . .Strong-Motion Earthquake in California and Elsewhere, C 4.25/3

Progress in Aging, Y 4.Ag 4/2:Ag 4/5

Progress in American Education, HE 5.210:10064

Progress in Candy Research, Reports, A 77.109

Progress in Fishery Research, I 49.96

Progress in Management Improvement, T 1.43

Progress in Radiation Protection, HE 20.4117

Progress in Rural Development Program, Annual Reports, A 1.85

Progress in Soil and Water Conservation Research, Quarterly Reports, A 77.528

Progress in the Prevention and Control of Air Pollution in (year), Report to Congress, EP 4.16

Progress Maps, FW 2.12

Progress Notes, D 104.15/5

Progress of Chemistry {abstracts}, C 41.53/3

Progress of Education in the U.S. of America, HE 19.133, ED 1.41

Progress of Mathematical Sciences {abstracts}, C 41.61/4

Progress of Physical Sciences {abstracts}, C 41.52

Progress of Public Education in the United States of America, FS 5.210:10005, HE 5.210:10005

Progress of Public Education in United States of America, FS 5.62

Progress, Missouri River Basin, I 1.80

Progress, U.S. Army, D 101.50

Projects in **Progress**, ED 1.33/2-2

Quarterly Report of **Progress** at Fish Control Laboratory, La Crosse, Wisconsin, Southeastern Fish Control Laboratory, Warm Springs, Georgia, and Hammond Bay Biological Station, Millersburg, Michigan, I 49.75

Report of NRL **Progress**, D 210.17

Report of **Progress** in (year) on the Status of Women, Y 3.In 8/21:1

Report on **Progress** in (year) of the Status of Women, Y 3.In 8/21:1

Report on **Progress** of Works Program, Y 3.W 89/2:32

Research and Development **Progress**, C 39.202:R 31

Research Bulletins Works **Progress** Administration, Y 3.W 89/2:13

Research for **Progress** in Education, Annual Report, HE 5.212:12051

Research in **Progress**, Calendar Year Metallurgy and Materials Sciences, Mechanics and Aeronautics, Chemistry and Biological Sciences, D 101.52/5-5

Research in **Progress**, Calendar Year Physics, Electronics, Mathematics, Geosciences, D 101.52/5-4

Research in **Progress**, Calendar Year, D 101.52/5

Research **Progress** (year), A 13.66/1

Research **Progress** and Plans of the Weather Bureau, C 30.75

Research **Progress** in (year), a Report of the Agricultural Research Service, A 77.1

Research Relating to Children, Inventory of Studies in **Progress**, FS 3.220

Safety Bulletins Works **Progress** Administration, Y 3.W 89/2:11

State Solid Waste Planning Grants, Agencies, and **Progress**, Report of Activities, EP 3.10

Statistical Bulletins Works **Progress** Administration, Y 3.W 89/2:58

Statistical Tables Showing **Progress** of Eradication of Brucellosis and Tuberculosis in Livestock in United States and Territories for Fiscal Year, A 77.212/3

Summary of **Progress**, SS 1.16

Technical **Progress** Bulletin, C 13.58/11

Tests in **Progress** Sheet, D 203.32, C 55.70

Topographic Mapping, Status and **Progress** of Operations, I 19.95

TOX-TIPS, Toxicology Testing in **Progress**, HE 20.3620

Works **Progress** Administration Orders, Y 3.R 31:21

Year of **Progress**, Annual Summary, A 95.1

Yearbook, Park and Recreation **Progress**, I 29.44

Progress Report

Annual **Progress Report**, D 104.15/3

Building for Clean Water **Progress Report** on Federal Incentive Grants for Municipal Waste Treatment Fiscal Year, FS 2.64/6

CIP Cataloging in Publication, **Progress Report**, LC 30.16

Conservation Highlights, Digest of the **Progress Report** of the Soil Conservation Service, A 57.1/2

Cooperative State-Federal Brucellosis Eradication Program; **Progress Report**, A 77.15:91-57

Cooperative State-Federal Hog Cholera Eradication Program **Progress Report**, A 77.241

Cooperative State-Federal Sheep and Cattle Scabies Eradication, **Progress Report**, A 77.233

Cooperative State-Federal Tuberculosis Eradication, **Progress Report**, A 77.15:91-44

Equine Piroplasmosis **Progress Report**, A 77.242

Experimental Safety Vehicle Program and Vehicle Safety Research, **Progress Report**, TD 8.16/2

Family **Progress Report**, Releases, A 80.709

Federal Scientific and Technical Communication, **Progress Report**, NS 2.12

Fresh Products Standardization and Inspection Branch, Annual **Progress Report**, A 88.12/28

Innovative and Alternative Technology Projects, a **Progress Report**, EP 2.30

Institute for Telecommunication Sciences: Annual Technical **Progress Report**, C 60.14

International Reference Group on Great Lakes Pollution from Land Use Activities: Annual **Progress Report**, Y 3.In 8/28:14

Medical Research and Development Board, Research **Progress Report**, D 104.12, D 104.12/2

Monthly **Progress Report**, C 51.10

Pacific Northwest Environmental Research Laboratory: Quarterly **Progress Report**, EP 1.19

Pacific Northwest Water Laboratory: Quarterly **Progress Report**, EP 2.22

Proceedings National Brucellosis Committee and **Progress Report** of the Cooperative State-Federal Brucellosis Eradication Program, A 77.202:B 83/16

Program and **Progress Report**, FAA 2.1

Progress Report Air Service, Engineering Division, W 87.14

Progress Report Department of Commerce, C 1.32

Progress Report Federal Civil Defense Administration, FCD 1.1/2

Progress Report Forest Taxation Inquiry, A 13.21

Progress Report Hill-Burton Program, FS 2.96

Progress Report National Institute of Health, FS 2.22/10

Progress Report National Mental Health Program, FS 2.65

Progress Report Northern Rocky Mountain Forest and Range Experiment Station, A 13.30/6

Progress Report on Pesticides and Related Activities, A 1.2:P 43/3

Progress Report on Staff Development for Fiscal Year, NCSS Report E-3, FS 17.630, HE 17.630

Progress Report on Staff Development, FS 14.220

Progress Report President's Medical Programs for Heart Disease, Cancer, and Stroke, and Related Diseases, FS 2.313

Progress Report School Facilities Survey, FS 5.46

Progress Report to Congress by War Assets Administration, Pr 33.211, Y 3.W 19/8:11

Progress Report to the Secretary of Education from the President's Advisory Commission on Educational Excellence for Hispanic Americans, ED 1.87

Progress Report War Assets Administration, Pr 33.215

Progress Report, Annual Varietal and Environmental Study of Fiber and Spinning Properties of Cottons, A 77.530

Progress Report, Interim Statistical Report, Pr 34.751

Quarterly **Progress Report** on Fission Product Behavior in LWRs, E 1.28/2

Quarterly **Progress Report** on Veterans Administration-Armed Forces Study on Chemotherapy of Tuberculosis, VA 1.40

Quarterly **Progress Report**, D 103.33/10

Quarterly **Progress Report**, Nationwide Urban Runoff Program, EP 1.92

Research and Special Studies **Progress Report**, D 301.26/15

Research Divison, Quarterly **Progress Report**, D 103.33/9

Saval Ranch Research and Evaluation Project, **Progress Report**, I 53.40

Shipbuilding **Progress Report** for Month Ending, C 39.216

Solar Thermal Power Systems, Annual Technical **Progress Report**, E 1.38/2

State Air Pollution Implementation Plan **Progress Report**, EP 1.52

Statistical Summary, Rural Areas Development and Area Redevelopment, Quarterly **Progress Report**, A 43.38

Summary **Progress Report**, Tropical Deterioriation Committee, Pr 32.413/11

Surgical Research Unit, Brooke Army Medical Center, Fort Sam Houston, Texas: Annual Research **Progress Report**, D 104.22

United States Army Medical Research Institute of Infectious Disease: Annual **Progress Report**, D 104.27

War Production Drive, **Progress Report**, Pr 32.4815

Western U.S. Water Plan, (year) **Progress Report**, I 27.61

Progress Reports

California Region, **Progress Reports**, Progress in (year), A 13.1/2

Continental Divide Trail Study **Progress Reports**, I 66.19/2

Hurricane Research **Progress Reports**, C 55.609

Innovations, Mental Health Services, **Progress Reports**, HE 20.2425

International Decade of Ocean Exploration, **Progress Reports**, C 55.227

Investigations of Floods in Hawaii, **Progress Reports**, I 19.57

Mineral Industry Health Programs, Technical **Progress Reports**, I 28.26/2

Plant Materials Annual **Progress Reports**, A 57.55

Quarterly **Progress Reports** by Surplus Property Board to Congress, Y 3.W 19/7:207

Quarterly **Progress Reports**, Wildlife Research Laboratory, Denver, Colorado, I 49.47

Rehabilitation R and D **Progress Reports**, VA 1.23/3-2

Research and Development **Progress Reports**, I 1.88

Research on Bird Repellents, **Progress Reports**, I 49.47/2

Saline Water Research and Development **Progress Reports**, I 1.88

Smaller War Plants Corporation Program and **Progress Reports**, Pr 32.4825

Soil Survey Interpretations for Woodlands, **Progress Reports**, A 57.58

State Planning Activities **Progress Reports**, Y 3.N 21/12:9

Status and **Progress Reports**, Releases, A 61.19

Technical **Progress Reports**, I 28.26/6

Voluntary Business Energy Conservation Program, **Progress Reports**, E 1.39

Progressions

Carload Waybill Statistics, Traffic and Revenue **Progressions** by Specified Mileage Blocks for Commodity Groups and Classes, 1 Percent Sample of Carload Terminations in Year Statement MB-6, IC 1.23/7

Mileage Block **Progressions**, IC 1.23/7:MB-6

Progressive

Progressive Fish Culturist, I 49.35

Prohibiting

State Laws and Regulations **Prohibiting** Employment of Minors in Hazardous Occupations, L 22.6/2

Prohibition

Digest of Supreme Court Decisions Interpreting National **Prohibition** Act, T 54.6

Project

Annual Report Colorado River Storage **Project** and Participating Projects for Fiscal Year (date), I 27.71/2

Census Library **Project** Series, LC 29.7

Central Valley Project Studies {Reports on Problems}, I 27.26

Central Valley **Project**, Annual Report, I 27.26/2

Civil Defense Education **Project**, Classroom Practices, FS 5.45/3

Civil Defense Education **Project**, Information Sheets, FS 5.45/2

College Curriculum Support **Project**, Updates, C 3.163/9

Colorado River Basin **Project**, Annual Report, I 27.71/3

Community Education **Project** Description for Fiscal Year, HE 19.132

Comprehensive Health Services **Projects**, Summary of **Project** Data, CHSP Reports, HE 20.5115

Conservation **Project** Support Grant Application and Information, NF 4.10

Critical **Project** Status Report, E 2.14

Current Research **Project** Grants, HE 20.3111

Cutter Radar **Project** Newsletter, TD 5.38

FHA Monthly Report of Operations: **Project** Mortgage Insurance Programs, HH 2.27

Forest Research **Project** Reports, A 13.41

Guide for Preparation of Proposals and **Project** Operation, NS 1.20/2

Heart and Lung Program **Project** Committee, HE 20.3001/2:H 35/2

Listing of Land in Urban Renewal **Project** Areas Available for Private Redevelopment, HH 7.15

NOAA Coastal Ocean Program, **Project** News Update, C 55.49/4

Office and **Project** Directory, I 27.28

Planners and **Project** Managers Annual Report, D 1.1/11

Planners and **Project** Managers Program, D 103.132

President's Reorganization **Project**: Publications, PrEx 1.11

Program and **Project** Plan for Fiscal Year (date), J 1.38

Project Analysis Series, Pr 32.5411, I 52.10

Project Connection: Best Strategy (series), HE 20.8221/2

Project DAWN {Drug Abuse Warning Network}, Annual Report, J 24.19/2

Project Facts Sheets, E 1.90/8

Project Head Start (series), PrEx 10.12, HE 21.212, HE 1.469

Project Head Start, HE 1.36

Project Independence, FE 1.18

Project Label, Alphabetical Listings by Controlled Generic Drug Ingredients, J 24.24/2

Project Label, Alphabetical Listings by Drug Labeler of Discontinued Products, J 24.24/3

Project Label, Alphabetical Listings by Drug Labeler, J 24.24

Project Label, Alphabetical Listings by Drug Product, J 24.24/4

Project Management Series, PM 1.41

Project Match Monograph, HE 20.8323

Project on the Status and Education of Women, Field Evaluation Draft, ED 1.42/2

Project Phoenix Reports, C 55.623

Project Planning Reports, I 27.44

Project Register, I 67.16

Project Register, Projects Approved Under Sec. 8 of Federal Water Pollution Control Act (Pub. Law 660, 84th Cong.), As Amended and Sec. 3, of Public Works

Project Register, Waste Water Treatment Construction Grants, EP 1.9/2, EP 1.56/2

Project Reports, N 10.21

Project Skywater Data Inventory SCPP Season, I 27.57/2

Project Skywater, Annual Report, I 27.57

Project Skywater, CRADP DAT Inventory, I 27.57/3

Project Stormfury, Annual Report, D 220.9

Annual Report on Cooperative State-Federal **Psoroptic** Sheep and Cattle Scabies Eradication Activities, Fiscal Year (date), A 77.233

Psoroptic Sheep Scabies Outbreaks in (State), A 77.240

PSTIAC

Pavements and Soil Trafficability Information Analysis Center, **PSTIAC** Reports, D 103.24/12

Psychiatric

Directory of Outpatient **Psychiatric** Clinics, **Psychiatric** Day-Night Services and Other Mental Health Resources in the United States and Territories, FS 2.22/38-4

Outpatient **Psychiatric** Clinics, Community Service Activities, FS 2.22/38-3

Outpatient **Psychiatric** Clinics, Special Statistical Series Reports, FS 2.22/40

Psychiatry

Transactions of Research Conferences on Cooperative Chemotherapy Studies in **Psychiatry** and Research Approaches to Mental Illness, VA 1.41

Psychological

Psychological Warfare School Special Texts, D 101.44

Psychology

Aviation **Psychology** Program Research Reports, W 108.25

Experimental **Psychology** Study Section, HE 20.3001/2:P 95

NRC Committee on Aviation **Psychology** Publications, NA 2.9

Psychopharmacology

Psychopharmacology Abstracts, HE 20.8109/2

Psychopharmacology Bulletin, HE 20.8109

Pseudorabies

National **Pseudorabies** Reports, A 101.33

PT

Programmed Text, USAAVNA **PT**- (series), D 101.47/5

PTO

PTO Pulse, C 21.33

PTSD

PTSD Research Quarterly, VA 1.94

PTSD (Post-Traumatic Stress Disorder) Clinical Quarterly, VA 1.94/2

Pubic School

Current Expenditures Per Pupil in **Pubic School** Systems, FS 5.222:22000, HE 5.222:22000

Public

Accelerated **Public** Works Program, Directory of Approved Projects, C 46.19

Acts and **Public** Resolutions, W 49.7/3

Administration of **Public** Laws 81-874 and 81-815, Annual Report of the Commissioner of Education, ED 1.1/2, HE 19.101/2

Administrative Decisions, Walsh-Healey **Public** Contracts Act, Index-Digest, L 21.2:In 2

Advance Release of Statistics on **Public** Assistance, FS 3.14/2, FS 14.209, FS 17.10, FS 17.610

Advance Sheets of 3d Edition of Checklist of United States **Public** Documents, GP 3.14

Advertisements for Bids, Specifications, etc., for Equipment of **Public** Buildings, T 39.9

Air Force **Public** Information Letter, D 301.46

Amendments to Regulations, **Public** Health Service, T 27.8/2

Analysis of Constitutional Provisions Affecting **Public** Welfare in States, Y 3.W 89/2:36

Annual Report on **Public** Information and Education Countermeasure of Alcohol Safety Action Projects, TD 8.20

Applications and Case Dispositions for **Public** Assistance, HE 3.60/3, HE 17.613/3

Applications, Cases Approved, and Cases Discontinued for **Public** Assistance, HE 17.641

Areas Eligible for Financial Assistance Designated Under the **Public** Works and Economic Development Act of 1965 Reports, C 46.25/2

Bibliography of Publications for **Public** Education and Membership Training, T 47.50/2

Bibliography of Soviet Sources on Medicine and **Public** Health in the U.S.S.R., HE 20.3711:So 8/2

Bibliography of United States **Public** Documents Department Lists, GP 3.10

Bond Sales for **Public** School Purposes, HE 19.323

Business and **Public** Administration Notes, FS 5.72

Case Records in **Public** Assistance, FS 3.23

CDC Veterinary **Public** Health Notes, HE 20.7010

Census of Nurses Employed for **Public** Health Work in United States, in Territories of Alaska and Hawaii, and in Puerto Rico and Virgin Islands, FS 2.81

Changes in Different Types of **Public** and Private Relief in Urban Areas, L 5.33

Changing **Public** Attitudes on Governments and Taxes, Y 3.Ad 9/8:17

Children Saved by **Public** Welfare Agencies and Voluntary Child Welfare Agencies and Institutions, HE 17.645

Commissioner of **Public** Buildings, Annual Reports, I 1.51

Community Facilities Administration News about New Accelerated **Public** Works Program, HH 5.7/2

Comparative Statistics of General Assistance Operations of **Public** Agencies in Selected Large Cities, FS 3.16

Compilation of **Public** Health Service Regulations, FS 2.52

Concurrent Receipt of **Public** Assistance Money Payments and Old-Age, Survivors, and Disability Insurance Cash Benefits by Persons Aged 65 or Over, FS 17.636, HE 17.636

Condition of **Public** School Plants, FS 5.221:21033, HE 5.221:21033

Consolidated Annual Report on State and Territorial **Public** Health Laboratories, HE 20.7001/2

Consolidated List of Persons or Firms Currently Debarred for Violations of Various **Public** Contracts Acts Incorporating Labor Standard Provisions, GA 1.17

Construction Committees {various cities}, **Public** Sector Bid Calendars by Agencies, L 1.75

Construction Reports; Housing Authorized by Building Permits and **Public** Contracts, C 3.215/11

Construction Reports; Housing Authorized by Building Permits and **Public** Contracts, C 40 (series), C 56.211/4

Course Offering, Enrollments, and Curriculum, Practices in **Public** Secondary Schools, HE 19.334/2

CPSC **Public** Calendar, Y 3.C 76/3:26

Cultural Presentations USA, (year), Report to Congress and the **Public**, S 1.67

Defense Housing Financed by **Public** Funds, Summaries, Pr 32.4307

Depository Library Council Report to the **Public** Printer, GP 1.35

Depository Library Council to the **Public** Printer: Addresses, GP 1.36

Designated Redevelopment Areas Under the **Public** Works and Economic Development Act of 1965, C 46.25/3

Direction, the Navy **Public** Affairs Magazine, D 201.17

Directory of **Public** and Secondary Schools in Selected District, Enrollment and Staff by Racial/Ethnic Group, HE 1.38

Directory of **Public** Training Schools Serving Delinquent Children, FS 14.102:T 68

Directory of Secondary Schools with Occupational Curriculums, **Public** and Nonpublic, HE 5.96

Disposition of **Public** Assistance Cases Involving Question of Fraud, HE 3.63

Education Directory: **Public** School Systems, HE 19.324/2

Establishments and Products Licensed Under Section 351 of the **Public** Health Service Act, HE 20.4042

Estimates of Local **Public** School System Finances, ED 1.112/3

Expenditures and Revenues for **Public** Elementary and Secondary Education, HE 19.313

Expenditures for **Public** Assistance Payments and for Administrative Costs, by Program and Source of Funds, HE 17.632

Expenditures for **Public** Assistance Programs, HE 3.69

Experimental Actions, Reports, **Public** Notices, CC 1.37/3

Fact Sheets of **Public**-Private Partnerships for Child Care, HE 20.1402

Fair Hearings in **Public** Assistance, HE 17.644

Fall (year) Statistics of **Public** Schools, Advance Report, HE 5.93/5, HE 5.220:20119

Fall {year} Enrollment, Teachers, and School-Housing in Full-Time **Public** Elementary and Secondary Day Schools, FS 5.220:20007, HE 5.220:20007

Farm Labor Contractor Registration Act, **Public** Registry, National Listing of Contractors and Employees Registered, L 36.14

FCDA **Public** Affairs Newsletter, FCD 1.15

Federal Communications Commission Reports, Decisions, Reports, **Public** Notices, and Other Documents of the Federal Communications Commission (2d series), CC 1.12/2a

Federal Surplus Real Property **Public** Benefit Discount Program, Parks and Recreation, Report to Congress, I 29.118

Federal Work Programs and **Public** Assistance, FW 4.32

Finances of **Public** School Systems, C 3.191/2-6

Financial Statistics for **Public** Assistance, Calendar Year, FS 3.14/3

Fixed **Public** Service Applications Received for Filing During Past Week, **Public** Notices, CC 1.40

Food News Notes for **Public** Libraries, Y 3.F 73:9

Forum for Applied Research and **Public** Policy, Y 3.T 25:61

GAO, Office of **Public** Information, Reports, GA 1.16/3

General Relief Operations of Large City **Public** Welfare Agencies, SS 1.26

Hazardous Substances and **Public** Health, HE 20.516, HE 20.7915

Health Consequences of Smoking, A **Public** Health Service Review, FS 2.309

Hearings in **Public** Assistance, HE 17.644

Highway Progress (year) Annual Report of the Bureau of **Public** Roads, C 37.1

Holdings of Selected **Public** Employee Retirement Systems, GR (series), C 56.224, C 3.242

Hospital and Mental Facilities Construction Program under Title 6 of **Public** Health Service Act, Semiannual Analysis of Projects Approved for Federal Aid, FS 2.74/2

Housing Authorized by Building Permits and **Public** Contracts, C 3.215/4

HRA, HSA, CDS, ADAMHA **Public** Advisory Committees, HE 20.6013

Identical Bidding in **Public** Procurement Report of Attorney General Under Executive Order 10936, J 1.31

Illustrations from State **Public** Assistance Agencies, Current Practices in Staff Training, FS 3.20

Impact on **Public** Assistance Caseloads of (a) Training Programs under Manpower Development and Training Act and Read Redevelopment Act, and (b) **Public** Assistance Work and Training Programs, FS 14.219, FS 17.409, FS 17.635

Index to Reports on Private and **Public** Bills and Resolutions Favorably Reported by the Committee, Y 4.J 89/1:In 2/9, Y 4.J 89/1-14

Index-Digest of Decisions of the Department of the Interior in Cases Relating to **Public** Lands, I 1.69/3

Interim List of Persons or Firms Currently Debarred for Violation of Various **Public** Contracts Acts Incorporating Labor Standards Provisions, GA 1.17/2

Journal of Highway Research, **Public** Roads, C 37.8

Journal of **Public** Inquiry, PR 42.8/4

Key Audiovisual Personnel in **Public** Schools and Library Systems in State and Large Cities and In Large **Public** Colleges and Universities, FS 5.60/2

Labor Supply and Demand in Selected Defense Occupations, as Reported by **Public** Employment Offices, FS 3.116

Labor Supply Available at **Public** Employment Offices in Selected Defense Occupations, FS 3.117

Lake Erie Wastewater Management Study **Public** Information Fact Sheet, D 103.63/2

Latin American **Public** Utilities Survey, Y 3.Ec 74/2:7

Library Programs, **Public** Library Construction: An Overview and Analysis, ED 1.18/7

List of Electric Power Suppliers with Annual
Operating Revenues of $2,500,000 or
More Classified As Public Utilities
Under Federal Power Act, FP 1.28
List of Health Information Leaflets and Pamphlets
of the Public Health Service, FS 2.24:In 3
Local Public Agency Letters, HH 7.9/2
Managing the Nation's Public Lands, I 53.12/2
Manual of Instructions for Survey of Public Lands
of United States, I 53.7
Medicaid and Other Medical Care Financed from
Public Assistance Funds, HE 17.620,
HE 17.621
Medical Assistance Financed under Public
Assistance Titles of Social Security Act,
FS 17.2:M 46/2, HE 17.2:M 46/2
Medical Care in Public Assistance, Guides and
Recommended Standards, FS 14.208/2
Medical Internship in U.S. Public Health Service
Hospitals, FS 2.89
Mental Health Directory of State and National
Agencies Administering Public Mental
Health and Related Programs, FS 2.22/49
Minorities and Women in Public Elementary and
Secondary Schools, Y 3.Eq 2:12-3
Money Payments to Recipients of Special Types of
Public Assistance, FS 17.627, HE
17.627
Monthly Statement of Public Debt of the United
States, T 1.5/3
Multiple Risk Intervention Trial, Public Annual
Report, HE 20.3213
National Conference on Public Health Training,
Report to the Surgeon General, FS 2.2:T
68/6, HE 20.2:T 68/6
New Domestic Public Land Mobile Radio Service
Applications Accepted for Filing During
Past Week, CC 1.36
News in Public Roads, C 37.16
News Releases and Miscellaneous Publications;
Committee on the Environment and
Public Works, (Senate), Y 4.P 96/10-2
NIMA Nautical Charts, Public Sale Region 1,
United States and Canada, TD 4.82:1
NIMA Nautical Charts, Public Sale Region 2,
Central and South America and
Antarctica, TD 4.82:2
NIMA Nautical Charts, Public Sale Region 3,
Western Europe, Iceland, Greenland, and
the Arctic, TD 4.82:3
NIMA Nautical Charts, Public Sale Region 4,
Scandinavia, Baltic and Russia, TD
4.82:4
NIMA Nautical Charts, Public Sale Region 5,
Western Africa and the Mediterranean,
TD 4.82:5
NIMA Nautical Charts, Public Sale Region 6,
Indian Ocean, TD 4.82:6
NIMA Nautical Charts, Public Sale Region 7,
Australia, Indonesia, and New Zealand,
TD 4.82:7
NIMA Nautical Charts, Public Sale Region 8,
Oceania, TD 4.82:8
NIMA Nautical Charts, Public Sale Region 9, East
Asia, TD 4.82:9
NRC Public Document Room Collection, Y 3.N
88:62
Number of New Permanent Nonfarm Dwelling
Units Started by Urban or Rural
Location, Public or Private Ownership,
and Type of Structure, L 2.51/4
Number of Recipients and Amounts of Payments
Under Medicaid and Other Medical
Programs Financed from Public
Assistance Funds, HE 17.617/3
Office of Inspector General Public Reports, E 1.136
Office of the Secretary Petitions for Reconsideration
of Actions in Rule Making Proceedings
Filed, Public Notices, CC 1.38/2
Official Bulletin Committee on Public Information,
Y 3.P 93/3:3
Official List of Commissioned and Other Officers of
U.S. Public Health and Marine Hospital
Service, T 27.5
Omnibus Solicitation of the Public Health Service
for Small Business Innovation Research
(SBIR) Grant Applications, HE 20.3047/
2
Our Public Lands, I 53.12
Personnel and Personnel Practices in Public
Institutions for Delinquent Children, FS
2.13
Pharmacy Residences in Public Health Service
Hospitals, FS 2.89/3

PHPC (Public Housing Primary Care Program)
Bulletin, HE 20.9121
PHS Public Advisory Groups, Authority,
Structures, Functions, HE 20.2:Ad 9/2
Plans of Public Buildings, T 39.6/2
Position Classification and Pay in State and
Territorial Public Health Laboratories,
HE 20.7413
Price Lists Division of Public Documents, GP 3.9
Prices and Yields of Public Marketable Securities
Issued by United States Government and
by Federal Agencies, T 68.7
Proceedings Annual Conference of the Surgeon
General, Public Health Service, and
Chief, Children's Bureau, with State and
Territorial Health Officers, FS 2.83
Proceedings Annual Conference, Surgeon General,
Public Health Service, with State and
Territorial Mental Health Authorities, FS
2.83/3
Proceedings Biennial Conference of State and
Territorial Dental Directors with Public
Health Service and Children's Bureau,
FS 2.83/2
Proceedings Public Health Conference on Records
and Statistics, FS 2.122, HE 20.2214,
HE 20.6214
Production of Electricity for Public Use in the U.S.,
I 19.32, I 19.33
Production of Electricity for Public Use in U.S., FP
1.11
Proficiency Testing Summary Analysis, Public
Health Immunology, HE 20.7022/3-3
Program Activity Reports, Public Law 85-864, FS
5.71
Program Facts on Federally Aided Public
Assistance Income Maintenance
Programs, HE 17.614
Progress of Public Education in the United States
of America, FS 5.62, FS 5.210:10005, HE
5.210:10005
Proposals for Construction of Public Buildings;
Specifications and Proposals for Repairs,
etc. at Public Buildings, T 39.7
Public Acts and Resolutions Relating to Post
Office Department and Postal Service, P
1.20
Public Administration Bulletin {for Vietnam}, S
18.38
Public Administration Practices and Perspectives,
Digest of Current Materials, S 18.24
Public Advisories, IC 1.31
Public Advisory Board, Reports, Y 3.Ec 74/3:7
Public Advisory Committees: Authority, Structure,
Functions, HE 20.4022
Public Advisory Committees: Authority, Structure,
Functions, Members, HE 20.1000
Public Affairs Abstracts (new series), LC 14.14
{Public Affairs} Booklet PA-B (series), FCD 1.17/2
Public Affairs Bulletin, LC 14.9
Public Affairs Flyer PA-F (series), FCD 1.17
Public Affairs PA (series), FCD 1.13
Public and Indian Housing FY . . . Program
Fungins Plan, HH 1.80/2
Public Assistance Bureau, Applications: Old- Age
Assistance, Aid to Dependent Children,
Aid to the Blind {and} General
Assistance, FS 3.17
Public Assistance Recipients and Cash Payments,
HE 3.61
Public Assistance Recipients in Standard
Metropolitan Statistical Areas, HE 3.61/
2
Public Assistance Reports, HE 17.19
Public Assistance Statistics, HE 3.60, HE 17.610
Public Assistance, Annual Statistical Data, FS
14.212, FS 17.13, FS 17.615, HE 17.615
Public Assistance, Costs of State and Local
Administration, Services, and Training,
FS 17.633, HE 17.633
Public Assistance, FS 3.3/a2, FS 2.13/3
Public Assistance, Quarterly Review of Statistics
for U.S., SS 1.13
Public Assistance, Statistics for U.S., SS 1.25/a 1
Public Assistance: Vendor Payments for Medical
Care by Type of Service, Fiscal Year
Ended (date), HE 17.617
Public Booklet PB (series), Pr 34.764, D 13.11
Public Buildings Act of 1926, with Amendments,
Condemnation Laws with Amendments,
Public Works and Construction Laws
{May 7, 1926}, Y 1.2:P 96/3
Public Circulars, T 1.33
Public Construction, GS 1.7

Public Debt and Cash in Treasury, T 9.9
Public Documents Highlights, GP 3.27
Public Documents Highlights, Microfiche
Cumulation, GP 3.27/2
Public Elementary and Secondary Education in the
United States, ED 1.112/2
Public Elementary and Secondary Education
Statistics: School Year, ED 1.328/12
Public Employment in (year), C 3.140/2, C 3.140/2-
4
Public Employment Program, Annual Report to
Congress, L 1.68
Public Health Bibliography Series, FS 2.21
Public Health Broadcasts, T 27.35
Public Health Bulletins, T 27.12, FS 2.3
Public Health Conference on Records and
Statistics, National Meeting Announce-
ment, HE 20.6214/2
Public Health Conference on Records and
Statistics, Proceedings, FS 2.122
Public Health Engineering Abstracts, T 27.28, FS
2.13
Public Health Monograph Series, HE 20.2018
Public Health Monographs, FS 2.62
Public Health Personnel in Local Health Units, FS
2.80
Public Health Reports, HE 20.30, HE 20.6011
Public Health Service Bibliography Series, HE
20.11
Public Health Service Film Catalog, FS 2.36/2
Public Health Service Grants and Awards, HE
20.3013
Public Health Service International Postdoctorate
Research Fellowships Awards for Study
in the United States, HE 20.3709
Public Health Service Posters, FS 2.26/2
Public Health Service Prospective Payment
Activity, HE 20.6516
Public Health Service Support of Cardiovascular
Research, Training and Community
Programs, FS 2.22/11-2
Public Health Service Water Pollution Surveillance
System, FS 2.84/2
Public Health Technical Monographs, FS 2.62
Public Hearings, Y 3.Se 5:14
Public Hearings (various cities), Y 3.Al 1:9
Public Housing Management Improvement
Program: Technical Memorandums, HH
1.63
Public Housing, FW 3.7, NHA 4.8
Public Humanities Projects, Guidelines and
Application Instructions, NF 3.8/2-9
Public Information (series), P 1.36/2
Public Information Communicator (series), FS 14.16
Public Information Series, S 1.71/5
Public Information {releases}, TC 1.29
Public Land Statistics, I 53.1/2
Public Law 85-742, Safety and Health Administra-
tion, Annual Report, L 16.48
Public Law 480, Agricultural Export Activities,
Annual Report of the President, Pr 37.13
Public Laws and Resolutions, W 49.7/1
Public Laws with Amendments, W 49.7/2
Public Laws, S 7.5/3
Public Library Data, ED 1.334/3
Public Libraries in the United States, ED 1.134
Public Mail Series, PMS- (series), NAS 1.74
Public Management Sources, PrEx 2.9
Public Merchandise Warehousing, C 3.102
(Public Moneys Depositaries) Circulars, W 3.25
Public Notice, LMNOD-SP- (series), D 103.117
Public Notices (concerning irrigation projects of
reclamation service), I 1.49
Public Notices {concerning irrigation projects}, I
27.40
Public Notices, CC 1.37, TC 1.28
Public Notices: Petitions for Rule Making Field,
CC 1.38
Public Notices: Safety and Special Radio Services,
Report, CC 1.39
Public Papers of the Presidents of the United
States, AE 2.114, GS 4.113
Public Programs, NF 3.26
Public Relations, HH 1.12
Public Report of the Vice President's Task Force on
Combatting Terrorism, PrVp 40.2:T 27
Public Resolutions, GS 4.110/2, S 7.5/2
Public Roads Round-Up, C 37.29
Public Roads, Journal of Highway Research, TD
2.19
Public Safety Newsletter, Y 3.At 7:58
Public Sale Catalog: Aeronautical Charts and
Publications, D 5.351/3-2

Public Sale Catalog: Topographical Maps and Publications, D 5.351/3, D 5.319/3

Public School Finance Programs, HE 19.126

Public Sector Labor Relations Information Exchange {publications}, L 1.66

Public Sector Labor Relations Information Exchange: Calendar of Events, L 1.66/2

Public Service Office, Series S-, S 1.106/2

Public Sewage Treatment Plant Construction, FS 2.56/2

Public Support for Coastal Zone Management Programs Implementation of the Coastal Zone Management Act of 1972, C 55.32/5

Public Use Data Tape Documentation Chest X-Ray, Pulmonary Diffusion, and Tuberculin Test Results Ages 25-74, HE 20.6226/5-2

Public Use Data Tape Documentation Detail Natality, HE 20.6226/2

Public Use Data Tape Documentation Divorce Data, Detail, HE 20.6226/4

Public Use Data Tape Documentation Fetal Deaths Detail Records, HE 20.6226/11

Public Use Data Tape Documentation Interviewer's Manual National Interview Survey, HE 20.6226/8

Public Use Data Tape Documentation Medical Coding Manual and Short Index, HE 20.6226/9

Public Use Data Tape Documentation Medical History, Ages 12-74 Years, HE 20.6226/5

Public Use Data Tape Documentation Mortality Cause-of-Death Summary Data, HE 20.6226/6

Public Use Data Tape Documentation Mortality Local Area Summary, HE 20.6226/7

Public Use Data Tape Documentation Natality Local Area Summary, HE 20.6226/3

Public Use Data Tape Documentation Natality State Summary, HE 20.6226

Public Use Data Tape Documentation National Health Interview Survey, HE 20.6226/10

Public Use Files Catalog HE 22.616

Public Use Microdata Files (PUMS), C 3.285

Public Use of National Parks, Statistical Report, I 29.63

Public Use, Tabulation of Visitors to Areas Administered by National Park Service, I 29.63

Public Welfare Personnel, Annual Statistical Data, HE 17.629

Public Works Administration of Federal Works Agency, Reports Showing Status of Funds and Analyses of Expenditures, T 63.108

Public Works Digest, D 103.122/3

Public Works of Art Project, T 1.30

Publications Bureau of **Public** Roads, A 22.5

Publications List for the **Public** and Patients, HE 20.3183

Publications **Public** Health and Marine-Hospital Service, T 27.16

Pupil Mobility in **Public** Elementary and Secondary Schools During the (date) School Year, HE 5.93/6

Qualified Areas Under **Public** Works and Economic Development Act of 1965, **Public** Law 89-136, Reports, C 46.25

Quarterly **Public** Assistance Statistics, HE 3.60/4, HE 25.15

Reasons for Discontinuing Money Payments to **Public** Assistance Cases, HE 17.613/2

Reasons for Opening and Closing **Public** Assistance Cases, FS 3.45, FS 14.214, FS 17.411, FS 17.613

Reasons for Opening **Public** Assistance Cases, HE 17.613

Receipts and Disposition of Livestock at 66 **Public** Markets, A 82.41

Receipts and Disposition of Livestock at **Public** Markets, A 88.16

Receipts and Disposition of Livestock at **Public** Stockyards, A 36.203

Receipts from and Payments to the **Public**, Pr 33.113

Recipients and Amounts of Medical Vendor Payments Under **Public** Assistance Programs, HE 17.617/2

Recipients of **Public** Assistance Money Payments and Amounts of Such Payments, by Program, State, and County, HE 17.627/2

Region V **Public** Report, EP 1.28/5

Regulations for Government of **Public** Health and Marine Hospital Service, T 27.8

Report on Disposition of **Public** Assistance Cases Involving Questions of Fraud, Fiscal Year, HE 17.642

Report on Plan Preparation on State and Local **Public** Works, FW 7.7

Report to Congress on Implementation of **Public** Law 94-142, HE 19.117/2, ED 1.32

Report to Congress on the Economic Impact of Energy Actions As Required by **Public** Law 93-275, Section 18 (d), E 1.59, FE 1.15/2

Report to the Congress on the Status of the **Public** Ports of the United States, TD 11.30

Report to the **Public**, T 34.1/2

Report to the Senate and House Committees on the Budget As Required by **Public** Law 93-344, Y 10.13

Reports Showing Status of Funds and Analyses of Expenditures, **Public** Works Administration Federal Works Agency, T 60.14

Reprints from **Public** Health Reports, T 27.6/a

Request for Hearings in **Public** Assistance, Fiscal Year (date), HE 3.60/2

Research and Development: **Public** Awareness/participation Support Plan, Fiscal Year (date), EP 1.90

Research and Training Grants and Awards of **Public** Health Service, FS 2.22/8

Revenue Programs for the **Public** Schools in the United States, FS 5.222:22013, HE 5.222:22013

Revenues and Expenditures for **Public** and Elementary and Secondary Education, ED 1.119

Review of Mutual Cooperation in **Public** Administration, S 17.46

Roster of Members of PHS **Public** Advisory Groups, Councils, Committees, Boards, Panels, Study Sections, HE 20.2:Ad 9/3

Safety and Special Actions, Reports, **Public** Notices, CC 1.39/2

Safety Posters Federal **Public** Housing Authority, NHA 4.9

Salable {and total} Receipts of Livestock at **Public** Markets, in Order of Volume, A 88.16/15

Salaries of State **Public** Health Workers, FS 2.82

Selected Agricultural Activities of **Public** Employment Offices, L 7.59

Slip Laws: **Public** Laws, S 7.5:C.S.

Solicitation of the **Public** Health Service and the Health Care Financing Administration for Small Business Innovation Research Contract Proposals, HE 22.31

Solicitation of the **Public** Health Service for Small Business Research (SBIR) Contract Proposals, HE 20.28/2

Some Recent Books on **Public** Affairs Available for Circulation in the Book Forms, LC 1.25

Source of Funds Expended for **Public** Assistance Payments and for Cost of Administration, Services, and Training, HE 17.634

Source of Funds Expended for **Public** Assistance Payments, FS 14.215, FS 17.631, HE 17.631, HE 17.19/2

Special Analysis of Federal Activities in **Public** Works and Other Construction in Budget, PrEx 2.8/a2

Specifications for **Public** Buildings, T 39.6

SSA Program Circulars **Public** Information, HE 3.4/3

State Distribution of **Public** Employment in (year), C 3.140/2

State Expenditures for **Public** Assistance Programs, HE 17.2:St 2/2

State Maximums and Other Methods of Limiting Money Payments to Recipients of Special Types of **Public** Assistance, HE 17.626

State of the **Public** Range in Wyoming, I 53.56

State Programs for **Public** School Support, FS 5.222:22023, HE 5.222:22023

State Salary Ranges, Selected Classes {of positions} in Employment Security, **Public** Welfare, **Public** Health, Mental Health, Vocational Rehabilitation, Civil Defense, Emergency Planning, CS 1.81, FS 1.22, HE 1.22, GS 1.8

Statement of **Public** Debt of United States, T 63.112

Statistics of Local **Public** School Systems Fall (year), HE 5.93/8

Statistics of Local **Public** School Systems Pupils and Staff, HE 19.318/4

Statistics of Local **Public** School Systems, Finance, (year), HE 19.318/2

Statistics of **Public** Elementary and Secondary Day Schools, HE 19.326

Statistics of **Public** Libraries, ED 1.122/2

Statistics of **Public** Library Systems Serving Populations of 100,000 or more, FS 5.215:15033, HE 5.215:15033

Statistics of **Public** Library Systems Serving Populations of 50,000-99,999, FS 5.215:15034, HE 5.215:15034

Statistics of **Public** Library Systems Serving Populations of 35,000-49,999, FS 5.215:15035, HE 5.215:15035

Statistics of **Public** School Libraries, FS 5.215:51049, HE 5.215:15049

Statistics of **Public** School Systems in Twenty Largest U.S. Cities, ED 1.112/4

Statistics of **Public** Schools, Advance Report, Fall, HE 19.318

Status of Compliance, **Public** School districts, 17 Southern and Border States, Reports, FS 5.80, HE 5.80

Status of the Nation's Local **Public** Transportation, Conditions and Performance, Report to Congress, TD 7.18

Summary of Offerings and Enrollments in **Public** and Secondary Schools, HE 19.334

Surplus Property Disposed of to **Public** Health and Educational Institutions, FS 1.15

Tables and Formulas for Use of Surveyors and Engineers on **Public** Land Surveys, I 21.11/3

Technical Memoranda for Municipal, Industrial and Domestic Water Supplies, Pollution Abatement, **Public** Health, FS 2.301

Total Obligations Incurred for Emergency Relief from All **Public** Funds by State and Local Relief Administration in Continental United States, Y 3.F 31/5:35

Transcripts of Proceedings, Meeting of Depository Council to the **Public** Printer, GP 3.30

Trend Report: Graphic Presentation of **Public** Assistance and Related Data, HE 17.612

Trends Toward Open Occupancy in Housing Programs of **Public** Housing Administration, HH 3.8

Type Approval Actions, Reports, **Public** Notices, CC 1.48

U.S. Air Force **Public** Affairs Staff Directory, D 301.104/4

U.S. Government Films for **Public** Educational Use, FS 5.234:34006, HE 5.234:34006

Uniform System of Accounts Prescribed for **Public** Utilities and Licenses, FP 1.7/3

United States Import Duties Annotated, **Public** Bulletins, C 3.150/5

Urban Renewal Manual, Policies and Requirements for Local **Public** Agencies, HH 7.9

Vendor Payments for Medical Care Under **Public** Assistance, by Program and Type of Service, Fiscal Year (date), HE 17.617/4

Vocational Training Activities of **Public** Employment Offices, FS 3.119

Walsh-Healey **Public** Contracts Act Minimum Wage Determination (for various industries), L 22.19

Walsh-Healey **Public** Contracts Act, Decisions, L 22.23

Wastewater Treatment Construction Grants Data Base, **Public** Law 92-500 Project Records, Grants Assistance Programs, New Projects Funded During (Month), EP 1.56

Worldwide **Public** Affairs Offices Directory, D 101.120/2

Public Domain

CRS Studies in the **Public Domain** (series), LC 14.20

Publication

Census of Population and Housing Tabulation and **Publication** Program for Puerto Rico, C 3.223/24

Consolidated **Publication** of Component Lists, D 101.16/3

Cultural Landscape **Publication**, I 29.86/4

Customs **Publication** (series), T 17.26

Papers Approved for **Publication** or Presentation, FS 2.22/9

Publication Announcement and Order Form, Annual Survey of Manufacturers, C 3.24/9-5

Publication Announcements, NAS 1.9

Publication Catalogue and Order Form, HE 20.3183/3

Publication Note Series, HE 20.6216/3

Publication Notice; PN- (series), C 4.49

Rural Information Center **Publication** Series, A 17.29

Publications

Bibliographies and Lists of **Publications** [Aging Administration], HE 1.1011

Bibliographies and Lists of **Publications** [Children's Bureau], HE 23.1216

Bibliographies and Lists of **Publications** [Drug Evaluation Research Center], HE 20.4709

Bibliographies and Lists of **Publications** [Juvenile Justice and Delinquency Prevention Office], J 32.11

Bibliographies and Lists of **Publications** [National Institute of Corrections], J 16.111

Bibliographies and Lists of **Publications** [National Institute on Drug Abuse], HE 20.3959

Bibliographies and Lists of **Publications** [United States Holocaust Memorial Council], Y 3.H 74:13

Bureau of Justice Assistance **Publications** List, J 26.9/2

Catalog of **Publications**, Audiovisuals, and Software, HE 20.3619/2

Catalog of U.S. Government **Publications** (online), GP 3.8/8-9

Center for Air Force History **Publications**, D 301.82/7

Civil Defense **Publications** Available from Superintendent of Documents, FCD 1.21

Committee **Publications** and Policies Governing their Distribution, Y 4.Ec 7-10

DLAPS **Publications**, D 7.41

FBIS **Publications** Reports, PrEx 7.10/3

Federal Information Processing Standards **Publications**, C 13.52

Index, Research Grant **Publications** and Reports, I 67.13/2

List of Available USDA **Publications** for Sale from GPO, A 43.51

Monthly Catalog of United States Government **Publications**, Periodical Supplement, GP 3.8/8-8

National Climatic Data Center Periodical **Publications**, C 55.287/63

Nautical Charts and **Publications**, C 55.440

New **Publications** Rocky Mountain Research Station, A 13.151/2-2

NIMA Aeronautical Charts and **Publications**, TD 4.84

NIOSH **Publications** Catalog, HE 20.7114/2

ODPHP **Publications** List, HE 20.11/3

Office of Research and Demonstrations **Publications** Catalog, HE 22.22/2

Office of Technical Services Reports Suitable for Commercial **Publications**, Bulletins, C 35.10

Offshore Scientific and Technical **Publications**, I 72.14, I 72.14/2

Orders **Publications** Relating to the Care of Animals and Poultry, A 77.218

Ordnance **Publications** for Supply Index, W 34.23/3

Pacific Northwest Research Station: Miscellaneous **Publications**, A 13.129

Periodic Supplement, Selected United States Government **Publications**, GP 3.17/3

Popular **Publications** for Farmer, Suburbanite, Homemaker, Consumer, A 21.9/8:5, A 107.12:5

Posters **Publications** Relating to Ordnanace, D 105.32

Public Sale Catalog - Topographical Maps and **Publications**, D 5.319/3

Publications (unnumbered), C 55.220/4

Publications {year}, A 13.69/10-2

Publications, A Quarterly Guide, EP 1.21/7-3

Publications Announcements, GP 3.21

Publications Available for Free Distribution, I 27.10

Publications Available for Purchase, U.S. Army Engineer Waterways Experiment Station and Other Corps of Engineers Agencies, D 103.39

Publications Available for Sale, I 27.10/2

Publications Bulletin, D 101.139

Publications Bureau of Community Health Services, HE 20.5110:P 96

Publications Catalog of the U.S. Department of Commerce, C 1.54/2-2

Publications Catalog, U.S. Department of Health and Human Services, HE 3.38/5

Publications for Sale, I 27.10/2

Publications from the National Center for Health Statistics, HE 20.7042/7

Publications in Print, LC 1.12/2-3

Publications Issued Since 1897, LC 1.12

Publications Issued, A 77.16/2

Publications List, Y 4.Ag 4:P 96, Y 4.En 2:P 96

Publications List: National Institute on Deafness and Other Communication Disorders, HE 20.3659/2

Publications National Historical **Publications** Commission, GS 4.14

Publications Newly Available, A 13.62/11-3

Publications Received, A 93.18

Publications Reference File on Microfiche, GP 3.22/3

Publications Sale, L 2.34/3

Publications Series, S 18.62

Recent **Publications** of the Department of Education, ED 1.317/2

Reports and **Publications**, Y 3.B 49, Y 4.Se 2

Reserve Training **Publications** Index, TD 5.21

Rocky Mountain Research Station: Bibliographies and Lists of **Publications**, A 13.151/2

Selected List of **Publications** Added to the Library, W 34.21/4

Selected **Publications** of the United States International Trade Commission, ITC 1.9/3

Small Business Administration **Publications**, Classification of Management Publications, SBA 1.18/3

Social Security Administration **Publications** Catalog, HE 3.38/3

Soldier Training **Publications**, D 101.20/4

Southern Research Station: Bibliographies and Lists of **Publications**, A 13.150/2

Southern Regional Office **Publications**, L 2.95

State **Publications** Issued in Cooperation with Agricultural Marketing Service, A 88.42/2

State **Publications** Issued in Cooperation with Federal Extension Service, A 43.37

Supplementary Notices to Mariners, Correction Sheets for H.O. **Publications**, N 6.11/4

Tax Information, IRS **Publications** (numbered), T 22.44/2

Technical **Publications**, A 57.15, TD 5.43

U.S. Army Medical Doctrine, **Publications**, D 104.36

Vocational Education Study **Publications**, HE 19.219

Publicity

Publications Recruiting **Publicity** Bureau, D 102.75

Publicity Bureau, Liberty Loan of 1917, T 1.25

Publicity Bureau, T 1.27/21-29

Recruiting **Publicity** Bureau Posters, D 102.78

Recruiting **Publicity** Bureau Publications, D 102.75

Thunderbird **Publicity** Book, D 301.98

Publicly

Financial Statistics of Major U.S. **Publicly** Owned Electric Utilities, E 3.18/4-3

Financial Statistics of Selected **Publicly** Owned Electric Utilities, E 3.18/4-3

Statistics of Electric Utilities in the United States, Classes A and B **Publicly** Owned Companies, FP 1.21

Statistics of **Publicly** Owned Electric Utilities in the United States, E 3.18/3

Title List of Documents Made **Publicly** Available, Y 3.N 88:21-2

Publish

List of Newspapers Designated to **Publish** Advertisements of War Department, W 1.9

Published

Abstracts of Recent **Published** Material on Soil and Water Conservation, A 1.68, A 57.36, A 77.15:41

Digest and Index of **Published** Decisions of the Assistant Secretary of Labor for Labor-Management Relations Pursuant to Executive Order 11491, As Amended, L 1.51/3

Guide to **Published** Research on Atomic Energy, Y 3.At 7:7

Index to the **Published** Decisions of the Accounting Officers of the United States, GA 1.5

Index-Digest of the **Published** Decisions of the Comptroller General of the United States, GA 1.5/3

Index-Digest, **Published** and Important Unpublished Decisions, I 1.69/2

NTIS **Published** Search Mini Catalog, C 51.13/2-2

Published Ordinances, Firearms, T 70.5:F 51

Published Search Bibliographies, C 51.13/2

Reprints of Articles **Published** Concerning NIH Consensus Development Conferences, HE 20.3030/2

State Laws and **Published** Ordinances, T 70.14

Supplemental Digest and Index of **Published** Decisions of the Assistant Secretary of Labor for Labor-Management Relations Pursuant to Executive Order 11491, Y 3.F 31/21-3:10

Technical Reports **Published** in (year), D 117.8/2-2

Technical Research Reports **Published** by Air Force Personnel and Training Center Air Research and Development Command, D 301.26/10

Publishers

Eastern Africa, Annual **Publishers** Directory, LC 1.30/8-3

Schemes of States (for use of **publishers** in distribution 2d class mail), P 10.10

Publishing

Air Education and Training Command Electronic **Publishing** Library, AETCEPL, 301.116/3

Air Force Electronic **Publishing** Library of Departmental Publications and Forms, D 301.116

Printing and **Publishing**, C 62.9, C 57.311, C 57.510

Voice of Z39, News About Library, Information Science, and **Publishing** Standards, C 13.163

PubMed

PubMed, He 20.3627

PubScience

PubScience, E. 1.137/2

Puerto Rico

Ad Hoc Advisory Group on Presidential Vote for **Puerto Rico**, Pr 37.8:P 96

Annual Report of Vegetable Breeding in Southeastern United States, Hawaii, and **Puerto Rico**, A 77.532

Atlantic Coast; Gulf of Mexico **Puerto Rico** and Virgin Islands, C 55.422:5

Census of Nurses Employed for Public Health Work in United States, in Territories of Alaska and Hawaii, and in **Puerto Rico** and Virgin Islands, FS 2.81

Census of Population and Housing Tabulation and Publication Program for **Puerto Rico**, C 3.223/24

Climatological Summary, San Juan, **Puerto Rico**, C 30.45

Commodity Classification for Reporting Shipments from **Puerto Rico** to U.S., C 3.150:P

Cuba and **Puerto Rico** Special Commissioner, T 1.16

Estimates of the Population of **Puerto Rico** and the Outlying Areas, C 3.186/19

Official Parcel Post Zone Keys **Puerto Rico**, P 1.25/3

Petroleum Refineries in the United States and **Puerto Rico**, I 28.17/2, E 3.11/5-4

Puerto Rico Administrative Rulings, A 55.18/3

Puerto Rico Censuses, Announcements, C 3.219

Puerto Rico Orders, A 63.8

Puerto Rico Special Commissioner (Carroll), T 1.17

Puerto Rico Sugar Orders, A 55.18

Puerto Rico Tax Fund Orders, A 55.18/2

Puerto Rico, Education Department Annual Reports, I 1.39

Puerto Rico, Interior Department Annual Reports, I 1.40

Schedule P. Commodity Classification for Reporting Shipments from **Puerto Rico** to U.S., C 3.150:P

U.S. Coast Pilots Gulf Coast, **Puerto Rico**, and Virgin Islands, C 4.6, C 4.6/4

United States Trade with **Puerto Rico** and with United States Possessions, C 56.210:800, C 3.164:800, C 3.164:895

Puget Sound
  Puget Sound Notes, EP 1.97
  Joint Commission on Hudson's Bay and **Puget's Sound**, S 3.9

Pullet
  Pullet Chick Replacements for Broiler Hatchery Supply Flocks, A 88.15/19
  Pullet Chicks for Broiler Hatchery Supply Flocks, Pou 2-7 (series), A 92.90

Pulmonary
  Analysis of Current **Pulmonary** Research Programs Supported by the National Heart, Lung, and Blood Institute, HE 20.3202:P 96/2
  Cardiovascular and **Pulmonary** Study Section, HE 20.3001/2:C 17/6
  Public Use Data Tape Documentation Chest X-Ray, **Pulmonary** Diffusion, and Tuberculin Test Results Ages 25-74, HE 20.6226/5-2
  Transactions of Research Conferences in **Pulmonary** Diseases, VA 1.40/2

Pulp
  Pulp and Paper Industry Reports, C 18.229
  Pulp, Paper and Board Industry Report, C 40.11
  Pulp, Paper and Board, C 57.313, C 57.511
  U.S. Foreign Trade in **Pulp** and Paper, C 18.198

Pulpwood
  Pulpwood Prices in the Southeast, A 13.79/2
  Pulpwood Production in the Lake States, A 13.80/5-2
  Pulpwood Production in the North-Central Region by County, A 13.80/5
  Pulpwood Production in the Northeast, A 13.80/3
  Southern **Pulpwood** Production, A 13.80/4

Pulse
  PTO **Pulse**, C 21.33
  Pulse, VA 1.51
  Pulse Check, PrEx 26.10

Pulverized
  New Orders for Pulverizers, for **Pulverized** Fuel Installations, C 3.103
  Pulverizers, for **Pulverized** Fuel Installations, New Order for, C 3.103

Pulverizers
  New Orders for **Pulverizers**, for Pulverized Fuel Installations, C 3.103
  Pulverizers, for Pulverized Fuel Installations, New Order for, C 3.103

Pumice
  Pumice and Pumicite in (year), I 28.122
  Pumice and Volcanic Cinder in (year), I 28.122

Pumicite
  Pumice and **Pumicite** in (year), I 28.122

Pumps
  Domestic **Pumps**, Water Systems, and Windmills, Shipments of, C 3.77
  Measuring and Dispensing **Pumps**, Gasoline, Oil, etc. Shipments of, C 3.90
  Shipments of Domestic **Pumps**, Water Systems, and Windmills, C 3.77
  Shipments of Measuring and Dispensing **Pumps**, Gasoline, Oil, etc., C 3.90
  Public Use Microdata Files (**PUMS**), C 3.285

Pupil
  Current Expenditures Per **Pupil** in Pubic School Systems, FS 5.222:22000, HE 5.222:22000
  Guide Lines, Guidance and **Pupil** Personnel Service, FS 5.54
  Pupil Mobility in Public Elementary and Secondary Schools During the (date) School Year, HE 5.93/6
  State Supervisors of **Pupil** Transportation, Directory, FS 5.2:T 68/2
  Statistics on **Pupil** Transportation, FS 5.220:20022, HE 5.220;20022

Pupils
  Statistics of Local Public School Systems **Pupils** and Staff, HE 19.318/4

Purchase
  Chemical Corps **Purchase** Description, D 116.10
  Food **Purchase** Reports & Invitations to Bid, A 88.67

FSQS Food **Purchase**, Annual Summary, A 103.11/2

Index, Coordinated **Purchase** Descriptions, D 106.14

Institutional Meat **Purchase** Specifications, A 88.17/4, A 103.15

Leaflets for Distribution from Survey's Exhibition at Louisiana **Purchase** Exposition, C 4.10

Missile **Purchase** Description, D 105.21

Notes for Louisiana **Purchase** Exposition, Saint Louis, Missouri, LC 1.8

Publications Available for **Purchase**, U.S. Army Engineer Waterways Experiment Station and Other Corps of Engineers Agencies, D 103.39

Purchase and Sales Reports, A 82.61/2
Purchase and Storage Notices, W 77.19, W 89.8
Purchase Circulars, GP 1.21
Purchase Descriptions, P 1.33
Purchase Report, A 82.44, A 82.60
Reports of Special Agent for **Purchase** and Distribution of Seeds, A 24.5
Saint Louis, Louisiana **Purchase** Exposition, S 6.18

Purchased
  Annual Report of Energy **Purchased** by REA Borrowers, A 68.1/4, A 68.3
  Finance Rate and Other Terms on New Car and Used Car Installment Credit Contracts **Purchased** from Dealers of Major Auto Finance Companies, FR 1.34/5

Purchases
  AMS Food **Purchases**, A 88.57
  Commodity **Purchases** for Domestic Distribution, A 82.87
  Commodity **Purchases** for Export Distribution, A 82.87/2
  Consumer **Purchases** of Citrus and Other Juices, CPFJ (series), A 93.12
  Consumer **Purchases** of Fruits and Juices, A 88.12/4
  Consumer **Purchases** of Fruits and Juices by Regions and Retail Outlets, A 36.171/2
  Consumer **Purchases** of Selected Fresh Fruits, Canned and Frozen Juices, and Dried Fruits, A 36.171
  FSQS Food **Purchases**, A 103.11/4
  Household **Purchases** of Butter, Cheese, Nonfat Dry Milk Solids and Margarine, A 88.14/6
  Notice of **Purchases** (of miscellaneous materials, etc.), N 20.9
  Notice of **Purchases** (of miscellaneous materials, etc., for western States), N 20.10
  Recent **Purchases** of Cars, Houses and Other Durables and Expectations to Buy During the Month Ahead: Survey Data Through, C 3.186:P-65
  Study of Consumer **Purchases**, A 42.8
  Uranium **Purchases** Report, E 3.46/5-2

Purchasing
  EPP (Environmentally Preferable **Purchasing**) Update, EP 5.28
  Purchasing Office Circulars, I 1.66
  U.S. Government **Purchasing** and Sales Directory Guide for Selling or Buying in the Government Market, SBA 1.13/3
  U.S. Government **Purchasing** Directory, SBA 1.13

Pursuant
  Quarterly Report on Trade Between the United States and Nonmarket Economy Countries, **Pursuant** to Section 411 (c) of the Trade Act of 1974, Y 4.W 36:3

PWA
  PWA Bulletins, Y 3.F 31/4:24
  PWA Circulars, Y 3.F 31/4:23

PWEDA
  Unemployment Rates for States and Local Governments, BLS/**PWEDA**/QR- (series), L 2.111/3

Pyrophyllite
  Talc, Soapstone and **Pyrophyllite** in (year), I 28.136

Pyroxylin-Coated
  Pyroxylin-Coated Textiles, C 3.104

Q

Q & A
  Q & A (series), C 46.16

Questions and Answers on Controlled Materials Plan, **Q & A** (series), C 40.13

QA
  Quality Assurance, **QA** Reporter, D 7.23
  Questions and Answers, **QA**-IND- (series), L 22.30

QMC
  QMC Historical Studies, D 106.8
  QMC Historical Studies, Series II, D 106.8/2
  QMC Pamphlets, D 106.13

QMFCIAF
  QMFCIAF Reports, D 106.16

QMG
  QMG Circulars, M 112.4
  QMS- (series), D 101.6/9

QR
  Unemployment Rates for States and Local Governments, BLS/PWEDA/**QR**- (series), L 2.111/3

Quad
  Minerals Management **Quad** (maps), I 53.11/6

Quadrangle
  Geologic **Quadrangle** Maps, I 19.38
  Geological **Quadrangle** Maps, I 19.88
  Index of Topographic **Quadrangle** Maps of Alluvial Valley of Lower Mississippi River, D 103.308/2
  Index to USGS/DMA 1:50,000-Scale, 15 Minute **Quadrangle** Mapping, I 19.97/2
  Topographic **Quadrangle** Maps of Alluvial Valley of Lower Mississippi River, D 103.308
  Topographical **Quadrangle** Maps, 15' Series, I 19.81/2
  Topographical **Quadrangle** Maps, I 19.81

Quadrangles
  Index Map of **Quadrangles**, W 31.9/2
  Surface Management **Quadrangles** (maps), I 53.11/5

Quadrennial
  Sixth **Quadrennial** Review of Military Compensation, D 1.89

Quads
  Quads, Report on Energy Activities, A 13.98/2

Qualification
  Development of **Qualification** Standards, CS 1.41/4:271-1
  Selective Service College **Qualification** Test, Bulletin of Information, Y 3.Se 4:22

Qualifications
  Marksmanship **Qualifications**, M 209.7, N 9.10

Qualified
  Qualified Areas Under Public Works and Economic Development Act of 1965, Public Law 89-136, Reports, C 46.25
  Qualified Products Lists Department of Defense, D 1.17
  Qualified Products Lists Department of the Air Force, D 301.22

Qualifying
  Qualifying Facilities Report, E 2.12/3

Quality
  Air Pollution Report, Federal Facilities, Air **Quality** Control Regions, EP 4.10
  Air **Quality** Criteria (series), EP 1.53/2
  Air **Quality** Data from National Air Surveillance Networks and Contributing State and Local Networks, FS 2.307
  Air **Quality** Data, (date) Quarter Statistics, EP 1.53
  Ambient Water **Quality** Criteria for {various chemicals}, EP 1.29/3
  Annual Report of Secretary of Health, Education, and Welfare to Congress in Compliance with Public Law 90-148, Air **Quality** Act of 1967, FS 1.35
  Annual Report of the Activities of the Effluent Standards and Water **Quality** Information Advisory Committee, EP 1.1/2
  Annual Summary of Cost and **Quality** of Steam-Electric Plant Fuels, FP 1.2:F 95
  Annual Summary of Water **Quality** Data for Selected Sites in the Pacific Northwest, I 19.46/3
  Annual Water **Quality** Analyses Report for Nevada, I 53.44
  Annual Water **Quality** Data Report, E 1.28/15
  Biennial Report Under the Great Lakes Water **Quality** Agreement of 1978, Y 3.In 8/28:11
  Carrier **Quality** Assurance Report, HE 22.415
  Citizens Advisory Committee on Environmental **Quality**, Pr 37.8:En 8
  Citizens' Advisory Committee on Environmental **Quality**: Annual Report, PrEx 14.1/2
  Committee on the Assessment of Human Health Effects of Great Lakes Water **Quality**: Annual Report, Y 3.In 8/28:15

Compilation of Federal Laws Relating to Conservation and Development of Our Nation's Fish and Wildlife Resources, Environmental **Quality**, and Oceanography, Y 4.M 53:L 44/2

Cost and **Quality** of Fuels, E 3.11/15

Cost and **Quality** of Fuels for Electric Utility Plants, E 3.11/15-2

Cotton **Quality** Crop of (year), A 88.11

Cotton **Quality** Report for Ginnings, Western Upland Cotton, A 82.68

Cotton **Quality** Reports for Ginnings, A 82.70

Cotton **Quality** Statistics, A 1.34

Cottonseed **Quality**, Crop of (year), A 88.11/15

Environmental and Water **Quality** Operational Studies, D 103.24/15

Environmental **Quality**, PrEx 7.14

Environmental **Quality** Profile, Pacific Northwest Region, EP 1.87/2

Environmental **Quality** Profiles (various States), EP 1.87

EPA Newsletter, **Quality** Assurance, EP 1.98

Federal **Quality** News, PM 1.58

Focus on Great Lakes Water **Quality**, Y 3.In 8/28:17

Grain Crop **Quality**, (year) Crops, A 88.40/2:44

Great Lakes Water **Quality** Annual Report, Y 3.In 8/28:9

HUD Scorecard, **Quality** Assurance Program, HH 1.83

Insurance Program **Quality**, HE 3.28/6-4

Joint NCDRH and State **Quality** Assurance Surveys in Nuclear Medicine, HE 20.4611

Lake Erie Water **Quality** Newsletter, D 103.63

Monitoring and Air **Quality** Trends Report, EP 1.59

NASA Excellence Award for **Quality** and Productivity, NAS 1.78

National Air Monitoring Program: Air **Quality** and Emission Trends, Annual Report, EP 1.47

National Commission on Productivity and Work **Quality**: Publications, Pr 37.8:P 94

National Reference List of Water **Quality** Stations, Water Year (date), I 19.53/3

National Status and Trends Program, Water **Quality** Cruise Data Reports (series), C 55.436, C 55.436/4

National Water **Quality** Inventory, Report to Congress, EP 2.17/2

Program Memorandum **Quality** Assurance, HE 22.28/3

Quality and Prices of Cotton Linters Produced in United States, A 66.37

Quality and Reliability Assurance Handbooks, D 7.6/11

Quality Assurance, QA Reporter, D 7.23

Quality Control and Reliability Technical Reports, D 7.15

Quality Control Digests, C 31.166, FAA 5.11

Quality Control Notes, Pr 32.4835

Quality Control Reports, Pr 32.4833

Quality Evaluation Program Manual, D 7.6/4-3

Quality of Cotton Classed Under Smith-Doxey Act, United States, A 88.11/23

Quality of Cotton in Carry-Over, A 88.11/14

Quality of Grain Crops Based on Inspected Receipts at Representative Markets, A 36.206

Quality of Surface Waters of the United States, I 19.13

Quality Publications, NPC 200 (series), NAS 1.22

Radiological Health **Quality** Assurance Series, HE 20.4108/2

Radiological **Quality** of the Environment, EP 6.11

Reliability and **Quality** Assurance Publications, NAS 1.22/3

Report of **Quality** of Surface Waters for Irrigation, Western United States, I 19.13

Report on **Quality** Changes for (year) Model Passenger Cars, L 1.79/2, L 2.120/2-7

Reports for Consultation on Air **Quality** Control Regions, FS 2.93/5

RSI **Quality** Appraisal Awards and Disallowances Monthly Statistical Summary, HE 3.28/9

RSI **Quality** Appraisal Postadjudicative Monthly Statistical Summary, HE 3.28/8

Selected References on Environmental **Quality** As It Relates to Health, HE 20.3616

Soil **Quality** Information Sheets, A 57.77

Staff Report of Monthly Report Cost and **Quality** of Fuels for Electric Utility Plants, E 2.13

Staff Report on Monthly Report of Cost and **Quality** of Fuels for Steam-Electric Plant, FP 1.32

U.S. Cotton **Quality** Report for Ginnings, A 80.134, A 80.824

U.S. Export Corn **Quality**, A 104.12

U.S. Export Soybean **Quality**, A 104.12/2

U.S. Export Wheat **Quality**, A 104.12/2-2

U.S. Grain Export **Quality** Report, Wheat, Corn, Soybeans, A 104.12/2-3

U.S. Wheat **Quality**, A 104.12/2-5

Unemployment Insurance **Quality** Appraisal Results, L 37.213

Unemployment Insurance **Quality** Control, Annual Report, L 37.20/3

United States Cotton **Quality** Report for Ginnings, A 82.28

Water **Quality** Management Accomplishments, Compendiums, EP 1.75

Water **Quality** Management Bulletin, EP 1.71

Water **Quality** Management Five Year Strategy FY-Baseline, EP 1.91

Water **Quality** Management Guidance, EP 1.8/8

Water **Quality** Records of {States}, I 19.53/2

Water **Quality** Standards Criteria Digest, Compilation of Federal/State Criteria on {various subjects}, EP 1.29/2

Water **Quality** Standards Summary {for various States} (series), EP 1.29

Water Resources, Water **Quality**, Y 3.T 25:59-2

Quantity

United States General Imports of Wool Manufacture Except Floor Coverings, **Quantity** Totals in Terms of Equivalent Square Yards in Country of Origin by Commodity Grouping Arrangement, TQ-2203, C 3.164/2-6

Quarantine

Administrative Instructions {under sections of the Plant **Quarantine** Act}, A 77.306/2

Entomology and Plant **Quarantine** Bureau, Notices of **Quarantine**, A 77.317

Foreign Agricultural Trade of the United States; Imports of Fruits and Vegetables under **Quarantine** by Countries of Origin and Ports of Entry, A 67.19/7, A 93.17/5

Handbooks, Manuals, Guides {relating to Entomology and Plant **Quarantine**}, A 77.306/3

Notice of **Quarantine**, A 48.5

Notices of **Quarantine**, A 77.317

Plant **Quarantine** Decisions, A 35.6

Plant **Quarantine** Import Requirements of (country), A 77.339

Plant **Quarantine** Memorandum, A 77.314/2

Plant **Quarantine**, A 77.217/2

PQ {Plant **Quarantine**} (series), A 77.308/3

Quarantine Laws and Regulations, T 27.9

Service and Regulatory Announcements Bureau of Entomology and Plant **Quarantine**, A 56.14

Service and Regulatory Announcements Bureau of Plant **Quarantine**, A 48.7

Service and Regulatory Announcements Publications Relating to Entomology and Plant **Quarantine**, A 77.308

U.S. Imports of Fruits and Vegetables under Plant **Quarantine** Regulations, A 93.44/3

Quarantines

Foreign Plant **Quarantines** in Service Training Series, A 56.25

Quarries

Bulletins, Mines and **Quarries** (by Industries), C 3.28/18

Bulletins, Mines and **Quarries** (by States), C 3.28/17

Census of Mines and **Quarries**, C 3.37/32

Census of Mines and **Quarries** (by States), C 3.37/33

Quarrying

Injury Experience in **Quarrying**, I 28.27, I 69.9

Quarterly

ASC MSRC, **Quarterly** Journal, D 301.121

Highway Information **Quarterly**, TD 2.23/4

Joint Force **Quarterly**, D 5.20

OAR **Quarterly** Index of Current Research Results, D 301.69/8

Observers **Quarterly**, C 30.86

Occupational Outlook **Quarterly**, L 2.70/4

Other Carriers {**quarterly** comparisons}, C 31.247

Pacific Northwest Environmental Research Laboratory: **Quarterly** Progress Report, EP 1.19

Pacific Northwest Water Laboratory: **Quarterly** Progress Report, EP 2.22

Parklawn Training Center, **Quarterly** Calendar, HE 20.32/2

Peace Corps Volunteer, **Quarterly** Statistical Summary, S 19.11

Persons Furnishing Cars to or on Behalf of Carriers by Railroad or Express Companies, Summary of **Quarterly** Reports, IC 1.18

PTSD Research **Quarterly**, VA 1.94

Quarterly Awards Listing Grants Assistance Programs, EP 1.35

Quarterly Benefit Statistics Report, RR 1.16

Quarterly Bibliography of Major Tropical Diseases, HE 20.3614/4

Quarterly Bulletin for Part 2, Hydrographic Products, D 5.351/2-2

Quarterly Bulletin, Intelligence Continuing Education Program, D 5.212

Quarterly Calendar of Environmental Meetings, EP 1.39

Quarterly Canned Foods Stocks Reports, C 3.136

Quarterly Cargo Review, C 31.264

Quarterly Check List, USAF/USN Flight Information Publications, Planning, D 301.52/2

Quarterly Circular Information Bulletin, D 103.42/11

Quarterly Coke Report, E 3.11/9

Quarterly Compilation of Periodical Literature Reflecting the Use of Records in the National Archives, AE 1.128

Quarterly Cumulative Report of Technical Assistance, C 46.23

Quarterly Debt Management Report, HE 20.9311

Quarterly Digest of Unpublished Decisions of the Comptroller General of the United States: Personnel Law, Civilian Personnel, GA 1.5/5, GA 1.5/10, GA 1.5/11

Quarterly Economic and Financial Review: Federal Republic of Germany and Western Sectors of Berlin, S 1.91/2

Quarterly Financial Report for Manufacturing, Mining, and Trade Corporations, FT 1.18, C 3.267

Quarterly Financial Report, United States Manufacturing Corporations, FT 1.18

Quarterly Financial Report, United States Retail and Wholesale Corporations, FT 1.20

Quarterly Flax Market Review, A 36.115

Quarterly Freight Loss and Damage Claims Reported by Common and Contract Motor Carriers of Property, IC 1 acco.11

Quarterly Freight Loss and Damage Claims, Class 1, Line-Haul Railroads, IC 1 acco.12

Quarterly Graduate Bulletin, D 5.210/2

Quarterly Gypsum Reports, C 22.33, I 28.32

Quarterly Index of Technical Documentary Reports, D 301.45/15

Quarterly Index to Periodical Literature, Eastern and Southern Africa, LC 1.30/8-4

Quarterly Intelligence Trends, J 24.18/4

Quarterly Interim Financial Report, Certificated Route Air Carriers and Supplemental Air Carriers, CAB 1.14

Quarterly Interim Financial Report, Certified Route Air Carriers and Supplemental Air Carriers, C 31.240/3

Quarterly Journal of Current Acquisitions, LC 2.17

Quarterly Journal, Comptroller of the Currency, T 12.18

Quarterly Listing of Interim Issuances, D 7.6/7:5025.1:pt. 2

Quarterly Natural Gas Reports, I 28.98

Quarterly Nonimmigrant Statistics, J 21.2/10-2

Quarterly Operating Data of 70 Telephone Carriers, CC 1.14

Quarterly Operating Data of Telegraph Carriers, CC 1.13

Quarterly Progress Report on Fission Product Behavior in LWRs, E 1.28/2

Quarterly Progress Report on Veterans Administration-Armed Forces Study on Chemotherapy of Tuberculosis, VA 1.40

Quarterly Progress Report, D 103.33/10

Quarterly Progress Report, Nationwide Urban Runoff Program, EP 1.92

Quarterly Progress Reports by Surplus Property Board to Congress, Y 3.W 19/7:207

Quarterly Progress Reports, Wildlife Research Laboratory, Denver, Colorado, I 49.47

Quarterly Public Assistance Statistics, HE 3.60/4, HE 25.15

Quarterly R & D Summary, D 301.45/27-6

Quarterly Report Disciplinary and Related Actions, T 22.2/15:5528

Quarterly Report of Air Carrier Operating Factors, C 31.240

Quarterly Report of All Investment Guaranties Issued, S 18.26

Quarterly Report of Applications in Process, S 18.26/2

Quarterly Report of Budgetary Operations, C 1.30

Quarterly Report of Central Propagation Laboratory, C 13.33/2

Quarterly Report of Manufacture and Sales of Snuff, Smoking, and Chewing Tobacco, A 88.34/11

Quarterly Report of Progress at Fish Control Laboratory, La Crosse, Wisconsin, Southeastern Fish Control Laboratory, Warm Springs, Georgia, and Hammond Bay Biological Station, Millersburg, Michigan, I 49.75

Quarterly Report of the General Sales Manager, A 1.117, A 67.43

Quarterly Report on Case Developments, LR 1.15/4

Quarterly Report on Employment of American Merchant Vessels, SB 7.5/300, C 27.9/7

Quarterly Report on Employment of American Steam and Motor Merchant Vessels, MC 1.8

Quarterly Report on Germany, Office of U.S. High Commissioner for Germany, S 1.90

Quarterly Report on Loans and Discounts, A 71.12

Quarterly Report on Private Grievances and Redresses, E 1.73, FE 1.26

Quarterly Report on Program Cost and Schedule, E 1.68/2-6

Quarterly Report on Trade Between the United States and Nonmarket Economy Countries, Pursuant to Section 411 (c) of the Trade Act of 1974, Y 4.W 36:3

Quarterly Report to Congress and the East-West Foreign Trade Board on Trade Between the United States and the Nonmarket Economy Countries, Y 4.W 36:2

Quarterly Report, Demonstration Projects Program, TD 2.40/2

Quarterly Report, E 5.1/2, PrEx 22.9

Quarterly Report, Government Sponsored and Government Supported Research, Social Sciences and Interdisciplinary Areas, NS 1.9

Quarterly Reports on Holdings of Retirement Systems, C 3.242

Quarterly Reports Showing Imports and Exports, T 37.6

Quarterly Review of Commission Proceedings, NC 2.11

Quarterly Review of Military Literature, W 28.10

Quarterly Review of Productivity, Wages, and Prices, L 2.102

Quarterly Review, 503 and 504 Economic Development Loan Programs, SBA 1.27/2

Quarterly Review, VA 1.25

Quarterly Seismology Bulletin MSP (series), C 4.25/4

Quarterly Soybean Market Review, A 80.129

Quarterly Statistical Brochure, HE 20.8212/4

Quarterly Statistical Bulletin, Electric Program, A 68.13/2

Quarterly Statistical Bulletin, Telephone Program, A 68.13/3

Quarterly Statistical Report, J 24.18/3

Quarterly Status of Department of Energy Projects, E 1.35/3

Quarterly Summary of Commerce of Philippine Islands, W 6.8

Quarterly Summary of Federal, State, and Local Tax Revenue, C 3.145/6

Quarterly Summary of Foreign Commerce of the United States, C 3.147

Quarterly Summary of Future Construction Abroad, C 57.113

Quarterly Summary of State and Local Tax Revenue, C 3.145/6, C 56.231/2

Quarterly Summary of Statistics of Operations, L 22.20

Quarterly Survey on Certain Stainless Steel and Alloy Tool Steel, ITC 1.25

Quarterly Tracking System, Energy Using and Conservation Equipment in Homes, E 3.23

Quarterly Trade Report, Southeastern Asia, C 18.156

Quarterly Update, J 1.102/3

Quarterly Update, a Comprehensive Listing of New Audiovisual Materials and Services Offered by the Audiovisual Center, GS 4.17/5-3, AE 1.109

Quarterly Update, Index of Administrative Law Judge and Chief Administrative Hearing Officer Decisions, J 21.23/2

Quarterly Update of Courses and Products, L 38.34/11/4-2

Rehabilitation Service Administration, **Quarterly** Indicies, HE 17.120

Research Divison, **Quarterly** Progress Report, D 103.33/9

Resource Management **Quarterly** Information Summary, C 55.9/3

Revenue Sharing **Quarterly** Payment, T 1.53/3

RRB **Quarterly** Review, RR 1.7/3

Shawnee **Quarterly**, the Shawnee National Forest Schedule of Projects, A 13.138

Southern Asia, Publications in Western Languages, **Quarterly** Accessions List, LC 17.7

State and Local Government **Quarterly** Employment Survey, C 3.140

State **Quarterly** Economic Developments, C 59.16/1, C 59.16/52

Supplement to LC Subject Headings, **Quarterly** Cumulative Supplement, LC 26.7

Traveler/El Viajero, **Quarterly** Newsletter for Migrant and Seasonal Farm Workers, PrEx 10.19

TVA Power, **Quarterly** Report, Y 3.T 25:33

United States **Quarterly** Book List, LC 1.20

World Tobacco Analysis (**Quarterly**), A 67.25

Quartermaster

Army **Quartermaster** School Correspondence Subcourse QM (series), D 106.22

Quartermaster Corps Manual, D 106.6/2

Quartermaster Food and Container Institute for Armed Forces: Library Bulletin, D 106.3/2

Quartermaster Letters of Information, W 99.13/12

Quartermaster Professional Bulletin, D 106.3/4

Statistical Yearbook of the **Quartermaster** Corps, D 106.12

Quartermaster Corps

Index **Quartermaster Corps** Specifications, D 106.11

Manual for **Quartermaster Corps**, W 7.16/1

Quartermaster's

Regulations for **Quartermaster's** Department (general), W 39.9/1

Quarters

U.S. Department of State Indexes of Living Costs Abroad and Living **Quarters** Allowances, L 2.101, L 2.101/2

Quartz

Quartz Crystals in (year), I 28.164

Quebec

Conference at **Quebec**, 1944, S 1.1/3:Q 3

Conferences at Washington and **Quebec**, S 1.1/3:W 27/2

Query

Instruction Manual Part 18, Guidelines For Implementing Field and **Query** Programs For Registration of Births and Deaths, HE 20.6208/16

Question

Disposition of Public Assistance Cases Involving **Question** of Fraud, HE 3.63

Question and Answer Handbooks, I 28.48, I 28.48/2

Questionnaire

Questionnaire Design in the Cognitive Research Laboratory, HE 20.6209:6

Questionnaires, FP 1.9

Questions

Merchant Marine Examination **Questions**, TD 5.57

Operating Instruction for Merchant Marine Examination **Questions** Books, Navigation General Book 3, TD 5.57/2

Questions and Answers About..., HE 20.3917

Questions & Answer Service, C 35.14

Questions about the Oceans, D 203.24:G-13

Questions and Answers on Controlled Materials Plan, Q & A (series), C 40.13

Questions and Answers on Rent Control, ES 5.7/2

Questions and Answers, QA-IND- (series), L 22.30

Questions and Answers, S 1.107

Questions for National Guard Officers, W 70.9

Questions from Answer Me This, Radio Program, I 16.58/2

Regulations Governing Admission of Candidates into Naval Academy As Midshipmen and Sample Examination **Questions**, D 208.108

Report on Disposition of Public Assistance Cases Involving **Questions** of Fraud, Fiscal Year, HE 17.642

Quick

Catalog and **Quick** Index to Taxpayer Information Publications, T 22.44/3

Quick Bibliographic Series, A 17.18/4

Quick Reference Guide for Clinicians, HE 20.6520/2

Quick Draw, HE 1.65

Quick-quiz (series), A 1.118

USIA INFO BASE (**Quick** Reference Guide), IA 1.32

Quicklist

Quicklist (series), HE 3.74

Quiz

Quick-**quiz** (series), A 1.118

Quotas

Cotton Marketing **Quotas** Letters, A 55.43/10

FAS Report, Status of U.S. Sugar Import **Quotas**, A 67.42/2

S.R. {Sugar Requirements and **Quotas**} (series), A 82.6/2

Quotations

Daily Spot Cotton **Quotations**, A 88.11/4

Farmers Weekly Cotton Price **Quotations**, A 82.67

Spot Cotton **Quotations**, Designated Markets, A 82.73, A 88.11/4

Quotes

News and **Quotes**, T 66.20

R

R & D

Federal **R & D** Funding by Budget Function, NS 1.18/4

MARATech **R and D** Technology Transfer Journal, C 39.227/2, TD 11.26

Quarterly **R & D** Summary, D 301.45/27-6

R & D Highway & Safety Transportation System Studies, TD 2.24

R & D Monographs, L 37.14

R & D Notes, D 103.33/11

R & D Systems Studies: Technical Reports, HE 19.215

R & D Technology Transfer, an Overview, E 1.109

Recreation Boating Safety **R & D**, Annual Report, TD 5.28/4

Rehabilitation **R and D** Progress Reports, VA 1.23/3-2

U.S. Army Mobility **R & D** Laboratory: USAAMRDL CR- (series), D 117.8/6

R.O.P.

Annual **R.O.P.** and Performance Test Summary, A 77.15:44-7

R.O.T.C.

R.O.T.C. Memorandum, W 99.13/10

RA

RA-DET, Y 3.At 7:19

Rabbit

List of Chemical Compounds Authorized for Use Under USDA Meat, Poultry, **Rabbit** and Egg Inspection Programs, A 103.13

List of Chemical Compounds Authorized for Use Under USDA Poultry, Meat, **Rabbit** and Egg Products Inspection Programs, A 88.6:C 42, A 101.6:C 42

Rabies

Rabies Information Exchange, HE 20.7036/2

Rabies, Zoonosis Surveillance, Summary, HE 20.7011/11

Reported Incidence of **Rabies** in United States, A 77.232

Race

Unemployment Rate by **Race** and Hispanic Origin in Major Metropolitan Areas, L 2.111/6

Race/ethnicity
    National Household Survey on Drug Abuse: **Race/ ethnicity**, . . ., HE 20.417
Racial
    Directory of Public and Secondary Schools in Selected District, Enrollment and Staff by **Racial**/Ethnic Group, HE 1.38
Radar
    Cutter **Radar** Project Newsletter, TD 5.38
    Market for U.S. Microwave, Forward Scatter, and Other Radio Communications Equipment and **Radar** in {various countries}, C 41.105
    Magellan Full-Resolution **Radar** Mosaics, NAS 1.86/2
    Next General Weather **Radar** (series), C 1.80
    Radar Bulletins, N 27.15
    Radio and **Radar** Information Letters, Pr 32.4836
RADC
    Technical Documentary Report **RADC**-TDR- (series), D 301.57/3
Radiation
    Annual Report of **Radiation** Exposures for DOE and DOE Contractor Employees, E 1.42
    Biological Effects of Electromagnetic **Radiation**, D 101.52/8
    Center for **Radiation** Research, Technical Highlights, Fiscal Year, C 13.1/2
    Chemical, Environmental, and **Radiation** Carcinogenesis, HE 20.3173/2
    Environmental **Radiation** Data Reports, EP 6.12
    EPA Review of **Radiation** Protection Activities, EP 6.1/2
    Federal/State **Radiation** Control Legislation, HE 20.4115
    Interagency Steering Committee on **Radiation** Standards, Y 3.N 88:10-6
    Interagency Working Group on Medical **Radiation**: Federal Guidance Reports, EP 1.68
    Isotope and **Radiation** Source Technology, E 1.99
    Isotopes and **Radiation** Technology, Y 3.At 7:52
    Life Sciences: Effects of Nonionization Electromagnetic **Radiation**, PrEx 7.22/2
    Living with **Radiation**, Y 3.At 7:43
    Monthly Summary Solar **Radiation** Data, C 55.289
    National Conference on **Radiation** Control, HE 20.4118
    National Conference on **Radiation** Control Proceedings, HE 20.4118
    NRC-TLD Direct **Radiation** Monitoring Network, Y 3.N 88:43
    Occupational **Radiation** Exposure at Commercial Nuclear Power Reactors and Other Facilities, Y 3.N 88:10-5
    Progress in **Radiation** Protection, HE 20.4117
    Radiation and Organisms Division, Reports, SI 1.1/a5
    Radiation Data and Reports, EP 6.9
    Radiation Exposure Overview, OCS (series), HE 20.1111
    Radiation Instrument Catalog, Y 3.At 7:20
    Radiation Recommendations (series), HE 20.4123, HE 20.4615
    Radiation Study Section, HE 20.3001/2:R 11
    Radio Chemical Analysis, Nuclear Instrumentation, **Radiation** Techniques, Nuclear Chemistry, Radioisotope Techniques, C 13.46
    State **Radiation** Control Legislation, HE 20.1112
    Studies in Workmen's Compensation and **Radiation** Injury, Y 3.At 7:2 R 11/28
    Ultraviolet **Radiation** and Skin Cancer Working Group, HE 20.3001/2:R 11/2
Radiators
    Convection-type **Radiators**, C 3.75
Radio
    America's Hour of Destiny, **Radio** Series, I 29.30, I 29.30/2
    Applications Accepted for Filing by Private **Radio** Bureau, CC 1.36/9
    Applications Accepted for Filing by Safety and Special **Radio** Services Bureau, CC 1.39/4
    Applications Pending in Commission for Exemption from **Radio** Provisions of International Convention for Safety of Life at Sea Convention, London, 1929, Title 3, . . ., Reports, CC 1.19
    Army Air Forces **Radio** and Facility Charts Atlantic and Caribbean Areas, W 108.26
    Army Air Forces **Radio** and Facility Charts North Pacific Area, W 108.27

Basic **Radio** Propagation Predictions, C 13.31
Central **Radio** Propagation Laboratory Ionospheric Predictions, C 13.31/3
Central **Radio** Propagation Laboratory Reports, C 13.33
Clean Water, Announcements {for **radio** and television}, FS 2.64/5
Conservation Man (**radio** scripts), I 29.49
Correction to USAFE **Radio** Facility Chart, Weekly Notices to Airmen, M 301.17/2
Crop and Market News **Radio** Broadcast Schedules, A 36.26
CRS Media Relations, Newspapers, Magazines, **Radio**, Television, C 50.7/2
CRS Media Relations, Newspapers, Magazines, **Radio**, Television, Informational Monitoring Service, J 23.7
Educational AM and FM **Radio** and Education Television Stations, FS 5.234:34016, HE 5.234:34016
Electrical and **Radio** World Trade News, C 18.67
Epoch Discoveries of the Past, Scientific **Radio** Scripts, I 16.66
Foreign **Radio** Broadcasting Services, C 18.87
Fruit Flashes, Foreign News on Fruits by Cable and **Radio**: Citrus {fruits}, A 67.9
Fruit Flashes, Foreign News on Fruits by Cable and **Radio**: Deciduous {fruits}, A 67.10
Geographic Distribution of Radio Sets and Characteristics of **Radio** Owners in Countries of the World, IA 1.12/2
Income Tax Brevities for Use by **Radio** Broadcasting Stations, T 22.38
Instrument Approach Chart, **Radio** Beacon, C 4.9/16
IRAC {Interdepartment **Radio** Advisory Committee} Gazetteer, C 1.60/5
Joint Air Forces & Navy **Radio** Facility Charts, M 301.16
Joint Army & Navy **Radio** Facility Charts, W 108.29
List of **Radio** Broadcast Stations, CC 1.10
List of **Radio** Broadcast Stations by Frequency, CC 1.22
List of **Radio** Broadcast Stations by State and City, CC 1.23
List of **Radio** Broadcast Stations, Alphabetically by Call Letters, CC 1.21
List of **Radio** Broadcast Stations, by Zone and State, CC 2.12
List of **Radio** Stations of United States, C 11.7/6
Manual of Regulations and Procedures for **Radio** Frequency Management, PrEx 18.8:R 11
Market for U.S. Microwave, Forward Scatter, and Other **Radio** Communications Equipment and Radar in {various countries}, C 41.105
Media Arts: Film/**Radio**/Television, NF 2.8/2-10
New Domestic Public Land Mobile **Radio** Service Applications Accepted for Filing During Past Week, CC 1.36
Non-Compulsory **Radio** Fixes, TD 4.311
Official Bulletin Federal **Radio** Commission, RC 1.5
Point to Point Microwave **Radio** Service, CC 1.36/8
Private **Radio** Bureau, CC 1.36/10
Public Notices: Safety and Special **Radio** Services, Report, CC 1.39
Questions from Answer Me This, **Radio** Program, I 16.58/2
Radio (Independents) Natural Science Series Talks, I 29.18
Radio Aids to Navigation, Great Lakes, United States and Canada, T 47.26/2
Radio and Radar Information Letters, Pr 32.4836
Radio Beacon System (maps), T 47.22
Radio Broadcast Stations in United States, Containing Alterations and Corrections, CC 1.24
Radio Charts, C 4.9/3
Radio Chemical Analysis, Nuclear Instrumentation, Radiation Techniques, Nuclear Chemistry, Radioisotope Techniques, C 13.46
Radio Circulars, C 30.23
Radio Communication Charts, N 22.5
Radio Communication Laws and Regulations, C 11.7/5
Radio Communication Pamphlets, W 42.29
Radio Compass Bulletin, N 19.10
Radio Engineering and Electronics {abstracts}, C 41.49/2

Radio Engineering {abstracts}, C 41.49
Radio Facility Charts and Supplementary Information, United States, LF/MF Edition, D 301.43
Radio Facility Charts United States, VOR edition, D 301.43/2
Radio Facility Charts, C 4.9/12
Radio Facility Charts, Caribbean and South American Area, M 301.19
Radio Facility Charts, Europe, Africa, Middle East, M 301.17
Radio Laws of the United States {June 24, 1910}, Y 1.2:R 11
Radio Markets Checklist of Circulars, C 18.120/3
Radio Observations, C 3.18/4
Radio Propagation Forecasts, C 13.31/2
Radio Propagation, C 13.22
Radio Records, A 21.13/5
Radio Science, C 13.22, C 52.9
Radio Service Agriculture in Defense, A 21.13/9
Radio Service Bulletins, CC 1.3/2, CC 1.25
Radio Service Consumer Facts, A 21.13/6
Radio Service Dairy Short Course, A 21.13/2
Radio Service Farm Flashes, A 21.13/7
Radio Service Housekeepers' Charts, A 21.13/8
Radio Service Livestock Short Course, A 21.13/1
Radio Service Poultry Short Course, A 21.13/3
Radio Stations of United States, C 11.7/6, C 24.5
Radio Talks Bureau of Agricultural Economics, A 13.144
Radio Talks Bureau of Foreign and Domestic Commerce, C 18.40
Radio War Guide, Pr 32.5009
Radio, Telephone, Telegraph, C 18.220/2
Radio-Television News, C 52.7/2
Radio-TV Defense Dialog, D 2.19/2
Radio-TV Packet, FS 13.124
Report of the Interdepartment **Radio** Advisory Committee, C 60.15
Reports of Applications Received in **Radio** Broadcast Stations, CC 1.26
Safety and Special **Radio** Services Bulletins, CC 1.39/3
Special Notices, Supplement to **Radio** Facility Charts and In-flight Data, Europe, D 301.9/3
Tabulation of Air Navigation **Radio** Aids, C 23.18, CA 1.9, C 31.8, C 31.108
This Might Be You (**radio** scripts), L 1.14
Treasure Trails, **Radio** Scripts, I 29.34
Two on a Trip; **Radio** Series, Scripts, I 29.43
U.S. Air Force **Radio** Facility Charts, Atlantic and Caribbean Area, M 301.15
U.S. Air Force **Radio** Facility Charts, North Pacific Area, M 301.14
UNESCO World Review Weekly **Radio** News from United Nations Educational, Scientific, and Cultural Organization, Paris, France, S 5.48/6
United States Air Force and United States Navy **Radio** Facility Charts, Central Pacific-Far East, D 301.12
United States Air Force **Radio** Facility Charts, Caribbean and South American Area, D 301.10
United States Air Force **Radio** Facility Charts, Europe, Africa, Middle East, D 301.9
United States Air Force, Navy, Royal Canadian Air Force and Royal Canadian Navy, Navy **Radio** Facility Charts and In-Flight Data, Alaska, Canada and North Atlantic, D 301.13/3
United States Air Force, United States Navy and Royal Canadian Air Force **Radio** Facility Charts, West Canada and Alaska, D 301.13
United States Air Force, United States Navy **Radio** Facility Charts, North Atlantic Area, D 301.11
What We Defend (**Radio** Scripts), I 29.48
World is Yours (**Radio** Scripts), I 16.56/2, FS 5.14/1
World **Radio** Market Series, C 18.120/2
World **Radio** Markets, C 18.120
Worldwide Distribution of **Radio** Receiver Sets, IA 1.12
Radio Scripts
    American Yesterdays, Historical **Radio Scripts**, I 16.57
    Broadcasting **Radio Stations** of the United States, RC 1.9
    Historical Series, Independent **Radio** Stations (programs), I 29.16

Surveys of Wage and Wage **Rates** in Agriculture, Reports, A 36.156
Treasury Reporting **Rates** of Exchange As of (date), T 63.102:Ex 2
Treasury Reporting **Rates** of Exchange, T 63.121
Unemployment Insurance Tax **Rates** by Industry, L 7.70, L 33.11
Unemployment **Rates** for States and Local Governments, BLS/PWEDA/QR-(series), L 2.111/3
Wage **Rates** in Selected Farm Activities, L 7.55/2-2

Ration
Status Report, Voluntary and Non-Profit Agency Technical Crop **Ration** Contracts with International Cooperation Administration, S 17.41/2

Rationing
Coal **Rationing** Industry Letters, Pr 32.4236
New Passenger Automobile **Rationing** Regulations, Orders, Pr 32.4208
Stove **Rationing** Industry Letters, Pr 32.4237
Tire **Rationing** Guides, Pr 32.4220

Ratios
Commitments of Traders in Commodity Futures with Market Concentration **Ratios**, Y 3.C 73/5:9
U.S. Production, Imports and Import/Production **Ratios** for Cotton, Wool and Man-made Textiles and Apparel, C 61.26

Raw
Foreign Markets Bulletins for **Raw** Materials, C 18.109/2
Leather **Raw** Materials Bulletin, C 18.186
List, Peanut Processors (users of **raw** peanuts), A 88.10/6
Prices of Cotton Cloth and **Raw** Cotton, and Mill Margins for Certain Constructions of Unfinished Cloth, A 88.11/10
Raw and Vulcanized Rubber, C 41.70
Raw Nonfuel Mineral Production in (year), I 28.165
Textile **Raw** Materials, C 18.149
Weekly Bulletin on **Raw** Materials, Y 3.W 19/2:35

Rayon
Rayon and Other Synthetic Textile Fiber Imports, C 18.121
Silk and **Rayon** and Other Synthetic Textile Fibers, C 18.125

Rays
Sensory Biology of Sharks, Skates, and **Rays**, D 210.2

RB
Reference Books, **RB**- (series), D 110.10

RCS
Reports Control Symbol Darcom Manufacturing Technology, **RCS** DRCMT-(series), D 101.110

R & D
Federal **R&D** Project Summaries, E 1.142 429-X-24

RD
Technical Reports, MA-**RD**- (series), C 39.246, TD 11.23

RD&A
Army **RD&A** Bulletin, D 101.52/3

RDA
Research and Development Abstracts of USAEC, **RDA** (series), Y 3.At 7:51

RDT&E
Five-hundred Contractors Receiving the Largest Dollar Volume of Prime Contracts for **RDT&E**, D 1.57/2

Re
Papers in **Re** (miscellaneous), J 1.84
Papers in **Re** in Circuit Courts, J 1.76
Papers in **Re** in Court of Appeals, J 1.77
Papers in **Re** in Court of Claims, J 1.80
Papers in **Re** in Court of Customs and Patent Appeals, J 1.79
Papers in **Re** in District Courts, J 1.75
Papers in **Re** in Patent Office (Interferences), J 1.81
Papers in **Re** in State Courts of Appeal, J 1.83
Papers in **Re** in State Supreme Courts, J 1.82
Papers in **Re** in Supreme Court, J 1.78
Papers in **Re** Indian Claims Commission, J 1.85
Papers in **Re** World War Risk Insurance, J 1.13/2
Papers in **Re** {proceedings of inquiry, general investigations, etc.}, IC 1.13/2
Papers in **Re**, C 31.212, J 1.13
Papers in **Re**, Indexes, J 1.13/3s

RE-TR
Reports, **RE-TR**- (series), D 105.22

REA
Annual Report of Energy Purchased by **REA** Borrowers, A 68.1/4, A 68.3
Current **REA** Publications, A 68.3
Daily Index of **REA** News, Y 3.R 88:15
List of Material Acceptable for Use on Systems of **REA** Electrification Borrowers and List of Materials Accepted on a Trial Basis, A 68.6/2
List of Materials Acceptable for Use on Telephone Systems of **REA** Borrowers, A 68.6/5
REA Bulletins, A 68.3

Reaching
Reaching People, A 98.12

Reactions
Bibliography on the High Temperature Chemistry and Physics of Gases and Gas-condensed Phase **Reactions**, C 13.37/3
Monthly Report on Adverse **Reactions** to Drugs and Therapeutic Devices, FS 13.123
Surface **Reactions** in the Space Environment, D 301.45/19-11

Reactor
Activation Analysis: Cockcroft-Walton Generator Nuclear **Reactor**, LINAC, C 13.46
Cockcroft-Walton Generator Nuclear **Reactor**, C 13.46
High-Temperature Gas-Cooled **Reactor** Safety Studies, E 1.28/7
High-Temperature Gas-Cooled Reactor Safety Studies for the Division of **Reactor** Safety Research Quarterly Progress Report, E 1.28/7
NBS **Reactor**: Summary of Activities, C 13.46/2
Nuclear **Reactor** Technology, E 1.99
Power **Reactor** Events, Y 3.N 88:12-2
Reactor and Fuel Processing Technology, Y 3.At 7:36
Reactor Fuel Processing, Y 3.At 7:37
Reactor Materials, Y 3.At 7:38
Reactor Plant Fiscal Year End Review, E 1.105
Water **Reactor** Safety Research, Buff Book I, Y 3.N 88:18

Reactor Safety
High-Temperature Gas-cooled **Reactor Safety** Studies for the Division of Reactor Safety Research Quarterly Progress Report, E 1.28/7

Reactors
Current Events: Power **Reactors**, Y 3.N 88:12
Licensed Operating **Reactors**, Status Summary Report, Y 3.N 88:15
Occupational Radiation Exposure at Commercial Nuclear Power **Reactors** and Other Facilities, Y 3.N 88:10-5
Operating **Reactors** Licensing Actions Summary, Y 3.N 88:35
Operating Units Status Report, Licensed Operations **Reactors** Data for Decisions, Y 3.N 88:15

Read
Impact on Public Assistance Caseloads of (a) Training Programs under Manpower Development and Training Act and **Read** Redevelopment Act, and (b) Public Assistance Work and Training Programs, FS 14.219, FS 17.409, FS 17.635
Right to **Read**, ED 1.12, HE 19.125

Readable
Machine **Readable** Cataloging, LC 30.27/2-2

Reader's
United States Army in World War II: Master Index, **Reader's** Guide, D 114.7/2

Readers
Foreign Service Institute, **Readers**, S 1.114/2-2
Indian Life **Readers**, I 20.33
Parents and Beginning **Readers** (series), HE 5.91

Readiness
BPR Emergency **Readiness** Newsletter, C 37.31
CJCS Guide to the Chairman's **Readiness** System, D 5.8/2
CTC Trends, Joint **Readiness** Training Center, D 101.22/28
Environmental **Readiness** Documents, DOE/ERD (series), E 1.16/2
National Emergency **Readiness** of Federal Personnel Management, CS 1.41/4:910-1

Reading
Foster Family Services Selected **Reading** List, HE 1.452:F 81/4
Indian **Reading** Series, ED 1.319
National Security Seminar Presentation Outlines and **Reading** List, D 5.9/2

Navy Life, **Reading** and Writing for Success in the Navy, D 208.11/3
Perspectives in **Reading** Research, ED 1.317/3
Reading Books (series), D 101.107/5
Reading Courses, I 16.12
Reading Guide to Cancer-Virology Literature, FS 2.22/56
Reading is Fundamental, Inc., Book Supplier Profile, SI 1.36/2
Reading Program, S 1.64/2
RIF {**Reading** Is Fundamental} Newsletter, SI 1.36
Technical Preservation Services **Reading** Lists, I 70.15/2
Urban Mortgage Finance **Reading** Lists, NHA 2.16

Readings
Elective Course **Readings** (series), D 5.415/9
Selected **Readings** and Documents on Postwar American Defense Policy, D 305.12/2:D 36

Readjustment
Civil **Readjustment** Bulletins, N 24.38, T 47.33
Cutbacks Reported to Production **Readjustment** Committee, Pr 32.4834
Readjustment Allowance Activities, VA 1.24
Readjustment Regulations, W 1.62

Ready
FM and TV Translator Applications **Ready** and Available for Processing and Notification of Cut-off Date, CC 1.26/6
Standard Broadcast Applications **Ready** and Available for Processing Pursuant to Sec. 1.354 (c) of Commission's Rules, Lists, CC 1.26/2

Reagents
Monthly Report of **Reagents** Evaluation, HE 20.7032, HE 20.7810
Reagents Evaluation Program, HE 20.7809, HE 20.7810/2

Real
Real and Personal Property of the Department of Defense, As of June 30, D 1.2:P 94/8
Real and Personal Property, D 1.58/2
Real Earnings, L 2.115

Real Estate
Census of Financial, Insurance, and **Real Estate** Industries, C 3.291
Current Developments in Farm **Real Estate** Market, A 77.13
Farm **Real Estate** Debt, RED (series), A 93.9/9
Farm **Real Estate** Market Developments, A 93.9/4, A 105.19/2
Farm **Real Estate** Taxes, A 36.63
Farm **Real Estate** Taxes, Recent Trends and Developments, A 93.9/6
Non-farm **Real Estate** Foreclosures, Y 3.F 31/3:10, FL 3.8, NHA 3.9
Nonfarm **Real Estate** Foreclosure Report, FHL 1.8
Real Estate Asset Inventory, Y 3.F 31/8:31, Y 3.R 31/2:15
Real Estate Foreclosure Report, FHL 1.8/2
Survey of **Real Estate** Trends, Y 3.F 31/8:28
Tax Delinquency of Rural **Real Estate**, A 36.78
Trends in Selected Economic and **Real Estate** Factors in United States, NHA 2.15
U. S. Agricultural **Real Estate** Trends, FCA 1.24/2

Real Property
Classification of Expenditures for Real **Property** and Equipment, IC 1 wat.7
Classification of Expenditures for **Real Property** and Equipment of Express Companies, IC 1 exp.5
Detailed Listing of **Real Property** Owned by the United States and Used by Civil Agencies Throughout the World, GS 1.15/4
Detailed Listing of **Real Property** Owned by the United States and Used by the Department of Defense for Military Functions Throughout the World, GS 1.15/4-2
Engineered Performance Standards for **Real Property** Maintenance Activities, D 1.6/7
Federal **Real Property** and Personal Property Inventory Report of the U.S. Government Covering its Properties Located in the United States, in the Territories, and Overseas, as of June 30 (year), Y 4.G 74/7:P 94
Federal Surplus **Real Property** Public Benefit Discount Program, Parks and Recreation, Report to Congress, I 29.118

Recent Research Accomplishments of the Air Force Office of Scientific Research, D 301.45/19-7

Recent Research Results, HH 1.84

Recent Reviews, Cancer Diagnosis and Therapy, Supplement to the Cancergrams, HE 20.3173/2-3

Recent Reviews, Cancer Virology and Biology, Supplement to the Cancergrams, HE 20.3173/2-4

Recent Reviews, Carcinogenesis, HE 20.3173/2-2

Recent Translation, Selected List, HE 20.3009/2

Recent Trends in U.S. Merchandise Trade, ITC 1.15/3

Research Information Digest, **Recent** Publications of Southeastern Forest Experiment Station, A 13.63/13

Research Library, **Recent** Acquisitions, FR 1.29, FR 1.29/2

Review of Some **Recent** Magazine Articles Relating to Housing, I 40.9

Selected List of **Recent** Additions to the Library, L 1.19

Some **Recent** Books on Public Affairs Available for Circulation in the Book Forms, LC 1.25

Weekly Review of **Recent** Developments, L 2.56

World Population: **Recent** Demographic Estimates for the Countries and Regions of the World, C 3.205/3

Recessions
Training Publications, **Recessions**, W 1.21/3

Recipes
Tested **Recipes** (numbered), Y 3.F 73:22

Recipient
Assessments Completed and Referrals to Manpower Agencies by Welfare Agencies Under Work Incentive Program for AFDC **Recipients**, HE 17.619

Recipients
Child Care Arrangements of AFDC **Recipients** Under the Work Incentive Program, HE 17.609

Medal of Honor **Recipients**, Y 4.V 64/4:M 46/3

Money Payments to **Recipients** of Special Types of Public Assistance, FS 17.627, HE 17.627

Number of **Recipients** and Amounts of Payments Under Medicaid and Other Medical Programs Financed from Public Assistance Funds, HE 17.617/3

Public Assistance **Recipients** and Cash Payments, HE 3.61

Public Assistance **Recipients** in Standard Metropolitan Statistical Areas, HE 3.61/2

Recipients and Amounts of Medical Vendor Payments Under Public Assistance Programs, HE 17.617/2

Recipients of Public Assistance Money Payments and Amounts of Such Payments, by Program, State, and County, HE 17.627/2

SSI **Recipients** by State and County, HE 3.71, SSA 1.17

State Maximums and Other Methods of Limiting Money Payments to **Recipients** of Special Types of Public Assistance, HE 17.626

State Assistance Programs for SSI **Recipients**, SSA 1.17/2

State Tables Fiscal Year (date), Medicaid: **Recipients**, Payments and Services, HE 22.12

Reciprocal
Emergency Tariff Laws of 1921 and **Reciprocal** Trade Agreement Act of 1934, with all Amendments {May, 1934}, Y 1.2:T 17/2

Imports Under **Reciprocal** Trade Agreements, by Countries, TC 1.13

Industries and **Reciprocal** Trade Agreements, Reports on, by Industries, TC 1.15

Reclamation
Annual Conference with Directors of National **Reclamation** Association, Memorandum of Chairman to Members of Committee on Interior and Insular Affairs, Y 4.In 8/13:R 24/2

Annual Report of the Secretary of Interior Under the Surface Mining Control and **Reclamation** Act of 1977, I 1.96/5

Bureau of **Reclamation** Progress, I 27.56

Bureau of **Reclamation** Projects (by States), I 27.55/2

Excellence in Surface Coal Mining and **Reclamation** Awards, I 71.16

Federal **Reclamation** Laws, I 27.27:L 44

Federal **Reclamation** Projects, Water and Land Resource Accomplishments, I 27.55

Library Accessions of the Bureau of **Reclamation**, I 27.10/4

Manual of the Bureau of **Reclamation**, I 27.20

Maps, **Reclamation** Service, I 19.17/5

Public Notices (concerning irrigation projects of **reclamation** service), I 1.49

REC-OCE **Reclamation** Bureau-Office of Chief Engineer (series), I 27.60

Reclamation Era, I 27.5

Reclamation Safety News, I 27.18

Reclamation Service, I 19.17

Resource and Potential **Reclamation** Evaluation Reports, I 53.31

Settlement Opportunities on **Reclamation** Projects, I 27.49

Specifications **Reclamation** Bureau, I 27.8

Summary Report of the Commissioner, Bureau of **Reclamation** {and} Statistical Appendix, I 27.1/2

Technical Memorandum **Reclamation** Bureau, I 27.31/2

Telephone Directory **Reclamation** Bureau, I 27.77

The **Reclamation** Reform Act of 1982, Annual Report to the Congress, I 27.27/2

Trees for **Reclamation** (series), A 13.42/24

Work of **Reclamation** Project Experiment Farm, A 19.14

Reclamation's
Recap, **Reclamation's** Current Awareness Program, I 27.52

Reclassification
CADO **Reclassification** Bulletin, D 301.37

Reclassification Orders (series), C 21.3/3

Recognition
Recognition Journal, W 1.69

Survival Plant **Recognition** Cards, D 210.14/5

Union **Recognition** in the Federal Government, Statistical Summary, PM 1.47

Recombinant
Recombinant DNA Advisory Committee, Minutes of Meeting, HE 20.3043/2

Recombinant DNA Research (series), HE 20.3043

Recombinant DNA Technical Bulletin, HE 20.3460, HE 20.3264

Recommendations
Findings of Fact and **Recommendations** of Reference, L 21.14

Limitation of Variety **Recommendations**, C 13.12/2

Literature **Recommendations**, S 17.42

MMWR **Recommendations** and Reports, HE 20.7009/2-2

Radiation **Recommendations** (series), HE 20.4123, HE 20.4615

Recommendations and Reports of the Administrative Conference of the United States, Y 3.Ad 6:9

Recommendations of the DNFSB, Y 3.D 36/3:10

Report and **Recommendations** of Fact-Finding Boards, L 1.16

Safety **Recommendations**, TD 1.106/3

Simplified Practice **Recommendations**, C 13.12

Special Occupational Hazard Review with Control **Recommendations**, HE 20.7113

Status of Open **Recommendations** Improving Operations of Federal Departments and Agencies, GA 1.13/18

Technical Appendixes to the Report and **Recommendations** to the Secretary, U.S. Department of Health and Human Services, Y 3.P 29:1-2

Wilderness **Recommendations** for {various areas}, I 29.79

Recommended
Criteria for a **Recommended** Standard, Occupational Exposure to {various subjects}, HE 20.7110

Medical Care in Public Assistance, Guides and **Recommended** Standards, FS 14.208/2

Recommended Lists, I 33.5/3

Recommended Practices, GS 1.14/7

Recommended Standards, HE 20.7110/2

Reports and Orders **Recommended** by Joint Boards, IC 1 mot.19

State Workmen's Compensation Laws, Comparison of Major Provisions with **Recommended** Standards, L 16.3:212

Reconciliation
Check Payment and **Reconciliation** Memoranda, CP & R (series), T 63.8

Reconditioned
Reconditioned Steel Barrels and Drums Report, C 3.218

Reconditioning
Status of Vessel Construction and **Reconditioning** under Merchant Marine Acts of 1920 and 1938, SB 7.5:1105, C 27.9/8

Reconnaissance
Alaska **Reconnaissance** Topographic Series, I 19.41

Reconnection
Reconnection, AA 1.16

Reconstruction
Daily Digest of **Reconstruction** News, Y 3.C 83:95

FHA and VA Mortgages Owned and Available for Sale by **Reconstruction** Finance Corporation and Federal National Mortgage Association, Y 3.R 24:14

International Bank for **Reconstruction** and Development, S 5.51

International Monetary Fund and International Bank for **Reconstruction** and Development, S 5.46

Reconstruction Finance Corporation Act with Amendments and Small Business Administration Act with Amendments Including Related Acts on Small Business, Y 1.2:R 24/2

Reconversion
Problems of Mobilization and **Reconversion**, Reports to the President, Senate, and House of Representatives by Director of War Mobilization and **Reconversion**, Y 3.W 19/7:8

Record
Canal **Record**, W 73.8

Congressional **Record**, X 1.1

Congressional **Record** Digest, CS 1.77

Congressional **Record** Review, S 18.46

Congressional **Record**, Proceedings and Debates, X/a

Experiment Station **Record**, A 10.6, A 77.408

Federal Election Commission **Record**, Y 3.El 2/3:11

Federal Election Commission **Record**, Index, Y 3.El 2/3:11-2

4-H **Record**, National 4-H Club Camp, Washington, D.C., A 43.15/2

Functions and Organization of Bureau of Supplies and Accounts, Control **Record**, N 20.25

General Index to Experiment Station **Record**, A 10.6/2

Guide to **Record** Retention Requirements, GS 4.107/a:R 245

Historic American Engineering **Record** Catalog, I 29.84/2:C 28/976

List of Record Groups in National Archives and Federal **Records** Centers, GS 4.19

Monthly **Record**, Administration of Packers and Stockyards Act, A 39.5, A 4.28

Official **Record**, Department of Agriculture, A 1.33

On the **Record**, AE 1.116

Paleoclimate Data **Record**, C 55.240

Record [Health Care Financing Administration], HE 22.3

Record [State Department], S 1.42

Record Book of Business Statistics, C 3.33/2

Record, News from the National Archives and Records Administration, AE 1.117/2

Record of Changes in Memberships of National Home for Disabled Volunteer Soldiers, NH 1.6

Registration **Record**, Securities Act of 1933, Indexes, SE 1.13/2

Registration **Record**, Securities Act of 1933, SE 1.13/1

Rehabilitation **Record**, FS 13.216, FS 17.109, HE 17.109

Signal Corps Library **Record**, W 42.39

Social and Rehabilitation **Record**, HE 17.27

Transportation Research **Record** (series), NA 1.10

U.S. NRC Facilities License Application **Record**, Y 3.N 88

Where to Write for Marriage **Record**, FS 2.102:M 34

Recorded
Estimated Amount of Nonfarm Mortgages of $20,000 or Less **Recorded**, HH 4.8/4

Patents Assign, U.S. Patents Assignments **Recorded** at the USPTO, C 21.31/4

Trademarks Assign, U.S. Trademarks Assignments **Recorded** at the USPTO, C 21.31/9

Recordfacts
Recordfacts Update, AE 1.121

Recording
Financial Audit, House **Recording** Studio Revolving Fund, GA 1.13/5-2
Financial Audit, Senate **Recording** and Photographic Studios Revolving Fund, GA 1.13/5
Mortgage **Recording** Letter, FHL 1.9, HH 4.9
Music Professional Training Career Development Organizations, Music **Recording** Services to Composers, Centers for New Music Resources Special Projects, Music, Application Guidelines, NF 2.8/2-5

Recordings
American Folk Music and Folklore **Recordings**, a Selected List, LC 39.12
Farm-Mortgage **Recordings** (by States), A 36.109
Folk **Recordings**, Selected from the Archive of Folk Song, LC 40.2:F 71
Instructional Cassette **Recordings**, LC 19.11/3
Instructional Disc **Recordings**, LC 19.11/3-2
Sound **Recordings**, LC 3.6/5:part 14

Recordkeeping
Recordkeeping Requirements for Firms Selected to Participate in the Annual Survey of Occupational Injuries and Illnesses, L 2.129

Records
Annotation, the Newsletter of the National Historical Publications and **Records** Commission, GS 4.14/2
Case **Records** in Public Assistance, FS 3.23
Circulars Relating to Plan and Methods of Publication of Official **Records** of Union Army and Confederate Army, W 45.4
Compilation of **Records** of Surface Waters of the United States, I 19.13
Guide to German **Records** Microfilmed at Alexandria, Va., GS 4.18
Guides to the Microfilmed **Records** of the German Navy, GS 4.18/2
Historic American Engineering **Records** Publications, I 70.9, I 29.84/2
Historical **Records** Survey, Y 3.W 89/2:43, FW 4.14
Index of Original Surface Weather **Records** for Stations in {various States}, C 55.288
Index of Surface-water **Records** to (date), I 19.4/2
Indexes for Compilations of **Records**, Briefs, etc., J 1.19/1
Indian **Records**, I 20.55
Instruction Manual: Classification and Coding Instructions for Marriage **Records**, HE 20.6208/7
Instructions for Classifying the Underlying Cause of Death: Source **Records** and Control Specifications, HE 20.6208/11
Interagency **Records** Administration Conference, Reports of Meetings, GS 4.16
Key to Geophysical **Records** Documentation, C 55.219/2
Key to Meteorological **Records** Documentation, C 55.219
Key to Meteorological **Records**, Environmental Satellite Imagery (series), C 55.219/4
Key to Oceanographic **Records** Documentation, C 55.219/3
List of Forms, **Records**, Laws, and Regulations Pertaining to Internal Revenue Service, T 22.39
List of Record Groups in National Archives and Federal **Records** Centers, GS 4.19
Medical Subject Headings; Supplementary Chemical **Records**, HE 20.3612/3-7
Military Operations of Civil War, Guide-Index to Official **Records** of Union and Confederate Armies, GS 4.21
National Archives and **Records** Administration Telephone Directory, AE 1.122
Office of Selective Service **Records** Regulations, Y 3.Se 4:19
Official **Records** of Union and Confederal Navies in War of Rebellion, N 16.6
Personnel **Records** and Files, CS 1.41/4:293-31
Philippine Insurgent **Records**, W 6.10
Posters National Archives and **Records** Service, GS 4.26
Procedure Material Insert **Records**, Y 3.R 31:28

Proceedings Public Health Conference on **Records** and Statistics, FS 2.122, HE 20.2214, HE 20.6214
Public Health Conference on **Records** and Statistics, National Meeting Announcement, HE 20.6214/2
Public Health Conference on **Records** and Statistics, Proceedings, FS 2.122
Public Use Data Tape Documentation Fetal Deaths Detail **Records**, HE 20.6226/11
Publications National Archives and **Records** Service, GS 4.17
Quarterly Compilation of Periodical Literature Reflecting the Use of **Records** in the National Archives, AE 1.128
Radio **Records**, A 21.13/5
Records Administration Studies, AE 1.14
Records Administration Training, AE 2.112
Records and Briefs in Cases Arising Under Agricultural Adjustment Act, Bankhead Act, and Kerr-Smith Tobacco Act, J 1.19/7
Records and Briefs in Circuit Courts of Appeals and Court of Appeals, District of Columbia, J 1.19/5
Records and Briefs in U.S. Cases Decided by Supreme Court of United States, J 1.19
Records Management Handbooks, GS 4.6/2
Records of Virginia Company of London, LC 1.11
Selected Audiovisual **Records**, Photographs of (various subjects), GS 4.17/7
State Educational **Records** and Reports Series, HE 19.308/2
The More Important Insect **Records**, A 77.310/2
War of Rebellion, Compilation of Official **Records** of Union and Confederate Armies {or Rebellion **Records**}, W 45.5
War **Records** Project, Reports, A 36.150
War **Records**, Monographs, A 1.69
Wastewater Treatment Construction Grants Data Base, Public Law 92-500 Project **Records**, Grants Assistance Programs, New Projects Funded During (Month), EP 1.56
Water Quality **Records** of {States}, I 19.53/2
Where to Write for Birth and Death **Records** of U.S. Citizens Who Were Born or Died Outside of the United States and Birth Certifications for Alien Children Adopted by U.S. Citizens, W 45.5, FS 2.102:B 53/7
Where to Write for Birth and Death **Records**, FS 2.102:B 53/3
Where to Write for Divorce **Records**, FS 2.102:D 64
Where to Write for Vital **Records**, HE 20.6210/2
World Weather **Records**, SI 1.7

Recovery
Archeological and Historical Data **Recovery** Program, I 29.59/4
Current Developments Report on European **Recovery**, S 1.72
Disaster Response and **Recovery**, FEM 1.211
European **Recovery** Program, Commodity Study, Y 3.Ec 74/3:11
European **Recovery** Program; Joint Report of United States and United Kingdom Military Governors, M 105.18
Interim Report on European **Recovery** Programme, Y 3.Ec 74/3:18
Milestones Along **Recovery** Highway, Y 3.N 21/8:18
National Industrial **Recovery** Act, C 18.3/2
Recovery Guides, Participating Counties, Y 3.Ec 74/3:16
Recovery Plans, I 49.77/5
Recovery Times, FEM 1.26
Report to Congress, Endangered and Threatened Species **Recovery** Program, I 49.77/3

Recreation
Analysis of the 1985 National Survey of Fishing, Hunting and Wildlife-Associated **Recreation** Reports, I 49.98/3
Army Morale Welfare and **Recreation** Fiscal Year Annual Report, D 102.82/2
Catalog of Guides to Outdoor **Recreation** Areas and Facilities, I 66.15:G 94
Compilation of Administrative Policies for National **Recreation** Areas, National Seashores, National Lakeshores, National Parkways, National Scenic Riverways (Recreational Area Category), I 29.9/4:R 24

Federal **Recreation** Fee Program (year), Including Federal **Recreation** Visitation Data, a Report to the Congress, I 70.18
Federal **Recreation** Fee Report, I 29.108
Federal **Recreation** Fees, I 66.23
Federal Surplus Real Property Public Benefit Discount Program, Parks and **Recreation**, Report to Congress, I 29.118
Index to Selected Outdoor **Recreation** Literature, I 66.15:L 71
Inventory of Federal Tourism Programs, Federal Agencies Commissions, Programs Reviewed for Their Participation in the Development of **Recreation**, Travel, and Tourism in the United States, C 47.2:T 64/3
National **Recreation** Areas I 29.39
National Survey of Fishing, Hunting, and Wildlife-Associated **Recreation**, I 49.98, I 49.98/2, I 49.98/4
National Urban **Recreation** Study (series), I 66.24
Nationwide Outdoor **Recreation** Plan, I 70.20
Operation Golden Eagle, Directory of Federal **Recreation** Areas Changing Entrance, Admission and User Fees, I 66.16
Outdoor **Recreation** Action, I 66.17
Outdoor **Recreation** Grants-In-Aid Manual, I 66.8
Outdoors in the Santa Monica Mountains National **Recreation** Area, I 29.6/7
Recovery Program for the Endangered Fishes of the Upper Colorado, I 49.77/4
Recreation and Welfare News, GP 1.17
Recreation Boating Safety R & D, Annual Report, TD 5.28/4
Recreation Bulletins, FS 8.8, Pr 32.4509, FS 9.7
Recreation Futures for Colorado, I 53.48
Recreation Guide, A 13.36/2-6
Recreation Guide to Grand Mesa, Uncompahgre and Gunnison National Forests, A 13.36/2-7
Recreation Information Series, I 53.52
Recreation Memorandum, W 99.13/9
Report on America's National Scenic, National Historic, and National **Recreation** Trails (fiscal year), I 29.130
Tourist and **Recreation** Potential {by areas}, I 66.13
Travel and **Recreation** News Letters, I 29.37/7
Yearbook, Park and **Recreation** Progress, I 29.44

Recreational
Appraisal of Potentials for Outdoor **Recreational** Development {by Area}, A 57.57
Compilation of Administrative Policies for National **Recreation** Areas, National Seashores, National Lakeshores, National Parkways, National Scenic Riverways (**Recreational Area** Category), I 29.9/4:R 24
Marine **Recreational** Fisheries, C 55.339
Marine **Recreational** Fishery Statistics Survey, Atlantic and Gulf Coasts, C 55.309/2-3
Marine **Recreational** Fishery Statistics Survey, Pacific Coast, C 55.309/2-5
Recreational Boating Guide, TD 5.8:B 63
Recreational Boating in United States, Report of Accidents, Numbering and Related Activies, T 47.54
Recreational Charts (series), C 55.418/5
Recreational Demonstration Area (by area), I 29.39

Recruiter
Civil Service **Recruiter**, CS 1.68
Navy **Recruiter**, D 208.16
Recruiter Journal, D 118.9, D 101.106/3
The **Recruiter**: A Newsletter For the Health Professional Recruiter, HE 20.9017

Recruiting
Army Life and United States **Recruiting** News, M 108.77
Focus, **Recruiting**, TD 5.39
List of Addresses of Navy **Recruiting** Stations, N 17.13, N 17.21
Ordnance **Recruiting** Bulletins, W 34.22
Ordnance **Recruiting** Posters, W 34.29/2
Publications **Recruiting** Publicity Bureau, D 102.75
Recruiting and Career Counseling Journal, D 118.9
Recruiting Authority Circulars, CS 1.53
Recruiting Bulletins Agricultural Marketing Service, A 88.3/2
Recruiting Bulletins Army and Corps Areas and Departments, Seventh Corps Area, W 99.17/10

NBS Standard **Reference** Materials Price List, C 13.48/4-2

NBS Standard **Reference** Materials {announcements}, C 13.48/2

News for Users of NBS Standard **Reference** Materials, C 13.50

NIH Statistical **Reference** Book of International Activities, HE 20.3760

Nuclear Theory **Reference** Book, Y 3.At 7:53

Physician's Pocket **Reference** to International List of Causes of Death, C 3.54

POCS **Reference** Papers (series), I 1.98/2, I 53.29

Price List of Standard **Reference** Materials, C 13.10

Publications International **Reference** Service, C 34.11

Publications **Reference** File on Microfiche, GP 3.22/3

Quick Reference Guide for Clinicians, HE 20.6520/2

Reference Aids, PrEx 3.11

Reference Book (series), D 110.10, D 101.111

Reference Circulars, LC 6.4/3, LC 19.4/2

Reference Data Report, C 13.48/3

Reference Guides (Series), FS 2.22/4, LC 1.6/5

Reference Information Paper, AE 1.124

Reference Information Series, HE 20.3614/7

Reference List of Audiovisual Materials Produced by the United States Government, GS 4.2:Au 2

Reference Lists, Pr 32.216

Reference Papers (series), I 71.11, I 72.11

Reference Publications, D 218.10, NAS 1.61

Research-**Reference** Accessions, Y 3.R 31:29, A 61.15, A 36.110

Selected **Reference** Series, HE 20.8215/2

Separate Sheets of Selected Thematic and General **Reference** Maps from the National Atlas of the United States of America, I 19.111a

Special **Reference** Briefs, A 17.24

Standard **Reference** Materials, C 13.10:260, C 13.48/4

Statistical **Reference** Book of International Activities, HE 20.3712

Standard **Reference** Materials Price List, C 13.48/4-3

Student **Reference** Book (series), D 101.47/6

Student **Reference** Sheets, SR- (series), FS 13.122

Technical Activities, Office of Standard **Reference** Data, C 13.58/3

Technical **Reference** (series), I 53.35

Terminal Forecasting **Reference** Manual (by Terminals), C 30.52

U.S. Alcohol Epidemiologic Data **Reference** Manual, HE 20.8308/3

United States Air Force **Reference** Series, D 301.82/5

USIA INFO BASE (Quick **Reference** Guide), IA 1.32

Working **Reference** of Livestock Regulatory Establishments, A 77.221/2

Working **Reference** of Livestock Regulatory Establishments, Circuits and Officials, A 88.16/20

References

Adult Education **References**, FS 5.49

Atomic Energy: Significant **References** Covering Various Aspects of Subject Arranged Topically, LC 14.13

Commodity Exchange Administration Literature, Selected **References** Catalogued in the Library, A 59.8

Cotton Literature, Selected **References**, A 1.50

Housing and Planning **References**, New Series, HH 1.23/3

Housing **References**, HH 1.23/2

Library of Congress Name Headings with **References**, LC 30.19

Plant Science Literature, Selected **References**, A 19.22/2, A 17.11

References on Local School Administration, FS 5.10/4

Selected List of **References** on Old-Age Security, Y 3.F 31/5:20

Selected **References** for Labor Attaches, List of Readily Available Materials, L 1.34/2

Selected **References** on Aging, FS 1.18/2, FS 14.9/4, FS 15.12/2

Selected **References** on Environmental Quality As It Relates to Health, HE 20.3616

Selected **References** on Housing, Y 3.C 33/3:8

Selected **References** on {various subjects}, LC 33.9/2

Selected **References**, FS 5.43, FS 5.220:20002A, HE 5.220:20002A

Soil Conservation Literature, Selected Current **References**, A 57.20, A 17.15

Technical **References**, TR-LS- (series), L 16.51/6

Referral

Clinical Center, Current Clinical Studies and Patient **Referral** Procedures, HE 20.3010

Energy Information **Referral** Directory, E 3.33

Information and **Referral** Services (series), HE 1.208/2

Job Patterns for Minorities and Women in Apprenticeship Programs and **Referral** Unions, Y 3.Eq 2:12-2

National Environmental Data **Referral** Service Publication, C 55.238

National **Referral** Center for Science and Technology Publications, LC 1.31

Referral Guidelines for Funding Components of PHS, HE 20.3008/4

Referrals

Assessments Completed and **Referrals** to Manpower Agencies by Welfare Agencies Under Work Incentive Program for AFDC Recipients, HE 17.619

Refined

Petroleum Market Shares, Report on Sales of **Refined** Petroleum Products, E 3.13

Refined Metal and Copper Scrap Operations at Brass and Wire Mills, Brass Mill Report, I 28.79/2

Refined-products

Crude-oil and **Refined-products** Pipeline Mileage in the United States, I 28.45/2

Refineries

Crude Petroleum Reports by **Refineries**, I 32.9, I 28.45

Output of **Refineries** in United States, I 28.19

Petroleum **Refineries** in the United States and Puerto Rico, I 28.17/2, E 3.11/5-4

Stocks on Hand at **Refineries**, I 28.20, I 28.21

Refiners

Cobalt {**refiners**}, I 28.76/2

Refining

Industry Wage Survey: Petroleum **Refining**, L 2.3/19

Proceedings Technical Session on Cane Sugar **Refining** Research, A 106.27/2

Reflections

Reflections, T 22.2/15:7583

Reform

Personnel Management **Reform**, Progress in State and Local Governments, PM 1.11/3

Reforms

FIPSE, Disseminating Proven **Reforms**, ED 1.23/11

Refractories

Refractories, C 41.76

Refrigerated

Capacity of **Refrigerated** Warehouses, A 105.33/3

Capacity of **Refrigerated** Warehouses in United States, A 88.20/3, A 92.21/3

Directory of **Refrigerated** Warehouses in the United States, A 92.34:1

Survey of Capacity of **Refrigerated** Storage Warehouses in United States, A 82.58

Refrigeration

Household **Refrigeration** Charts, A 42.7/2

Refrigerator

Estimated **Refrigerator** Car Movement of Domestic Fresh Fruits and Vegetables by Regions, A 82.42

Refrigerator Engineering, C 41.83

Refueling

Economic Resource Impact Statement 305th Air **Refueling** Wing, Grissom Air Force Base, Indiana, D 301.105/8

Refuge

Refuges 2003: A Plan for the Future of the National Wildlife **Refuge** System, I 49.44/4

Refuge Leaflets, I 49.44

Refugee

HEW **Refugee** Task Force, Report to the Congress, HE 1.55

Refugee Relief Program, S 1.110

Refugee Resettlement Program, Report to Congress, HE 3.72, HE 25.16

Refugees

Interagency Task Force for Indochina **Refugees**, Pr 38.8:R 25

Refuges

Refuges 2003: A Plan for the Future of the National Wildlife Refuge System, I 49.44/4

National Wildlife **Refuges**, I 49.44/2

National Wildlife **Refuges** Planning Update, I 49.44/3

Refuse

Refuse Hauling Wage Survey Summaries by Cities, L 2.113/3

Regarding

Memorandum **Regarding** Personnel and Policy Changes, I 29.3/2

Sources of Information **Regarding** Labor {various countries}, L 2.72/2

Regents

Board of **Regents**, HE 20.3001/2:R 26

Report of the Secretary and Financial Report of the Executive Committee of the Board of **Regents**, SI 1.1/a

Regimental

Extracts from General Orders and Bulletins, War Department Relating to **Regimental** and Company Administration, W 3.40

Regimental and Squadron Histories, D 214.12

Regiments

Roster of Organizaed Militia of United States, by Divisions, Brigades, **Regiments**, Companies, and other Organizations, with their Stations, W 70.5

Region

Alaska **Region** Leaflets, A 13.103/2

Alaska **Region** Reports, A 13.103

Alaska **Region**-Ten Year Plan, TD 4.56

California **Region**, Progress Reports, Progress in (year), A 13.1/2

Central **Region**, C 55.118/3

Consumer Buying Practices for Selected Fresh Fruits, Canned and Frozen Juices, and Dried Fruits, Related to Family Characteristics, **Region** and City Size, A 36.173

Corn and Wheat **Region** Bulletins, C 30.7

Cotton **Region** Bulletin, C 30.9

Cotton **Region** Weather Crop Bulletin, A 29.20

Eastern **Region**, C 55.118/4

Employer Costs for Employee Compensation, Northeast **Region**, L 2.120/2-16

Intermountain **Region** Organization Directory, A 13.36/2-3

Intermountain **Region** Yearbooks, A 13.57

Midwest **Region** Annual Science Report, I 29.113

Midwest **Region**: Research/Resources Management Reports, I 29.105/2

NMFS Northwest **Region**, Organization and Activities, Fiscal Year, C 55.301/2

NOAA Western **Region** Computer Programs and Problems (series), C 55.13/3

North Central **Region**, A 106.39/3

Northeast **Region**, A 106.39/2

Northeast **Region** Outdoor Memo, I 66.21

Office of Research and Development, **Region** 1: Annual Report, EP 1.1/3

Pacific **Region**, C 55.118/5, C 55.119

Plant Pest Control Cooperative Programs, Western **Region**, Fiscal Year (date), A 77.327/2

Prime Contract Awards by **Region** and State, D 1.57/5

Publications Agricultural Adjustment Agency East Central **Region**, A 76.441, A 79.441, A 80.2141

Publications Agricultural Adjustment Agency North Central **Region**, A 76.451, A 79.451, A 80.2151

Publications Agricultural Adjustment Agency Northeast **Region**, A 76.461, A 79.461, A 80.2161

Publications Agricultural Adjustment Agency Southern **Region**, A 76.471, A 79.471, A 80.2171

Publications Agricultural Adjustment Agency Western **Region**, A 76.481, A 79.481, A 80.2181

Publications Upper Mississippi Valley **Region**, A 57.18

Pulpwood Production in the North-Central **Region** by County, A 13.80/5

Recruiting Circulars, 4th Civil Service **Region**, CS 1.35/2

Region 2 Report, EP 1.7/8

Region 4: Annual Report, I 49.1/4

Region 6: Regional Report Series, L 2.71/9

Region Index of Publications, Forms and Form Letters, D 7.16/2

Region V Public Report, EP 1.28/5

Regional Reports, Middle Atlantic Region, L 2.71/6

Regional Review, Region 1, I 29.36

Regional Studies Plan, Fiscal Year, Atlantic OCS Region, I 72.12/15

Reports of Project on Research in Agricultural and Industrial Development in Tennessee Valley Region, Y 3.T 25:26

Resource Decisions in the National Forests of the Eastern Region, A 13.90

Retail Trade Report Middle Atlantic Region, C 3.174

Retail Trade Report Mountain Region, C 3.180

Retail Trade Report Pacific Region, C 3.181

Retail Trade Report South Atlantic Region, C 3.175

River Summary and Forecast, {Lower Mississippi Region}, C 55.110/7

Seafood Dealers of the Southwest Region, C 55.337/2

Southern Region Agricultural Conservation, A 55.45/8

Southern Region Miscellaneous Series, Items, A 55.45/6

Southern Region Report, A 13.56

Southern Region, C 55.118/2

State of the Rocky Mountain Region, I 29.125

Stumpage Prices for Sawtimber Sold from National Forests, by Selected Species and Region, A 13.58/2

Surveillance and Analysis Division, Region 8, Denver Colo., Technical Support Branch: SA/TSB-1- (series), EP 1.51/3

Surveillance and Analysis Division, Region 8: Technical Investigations Branch, SA/TIB-(series), EP 1.51/4

Surveillance and Analysis Division, Region 9, San Francisco, California: Technical Reports, EP 1.51

Surveillance and Analysis Division, Region 10: Working Papers, EP 1.51/6

Telephone Directory Automated Data and Telecommunications Service, Region 1, GS 12.12/2:1

Telephone Directory Geological Survey, Central Region, I 19.84/2

Upper Mississippi Valley Region, Publications, A 57.18

Wage Developments in the New England Region, L 2.49/5

Weekly Corn and Wheat Region Bulletin, A 29.43

Weekly Cotton Region Bulletins, A 29.39

Western Region, C 55.118

Regional

Address List, Regional and Subregional Libraries for the Blind and Physically Handi-capped, LC 19.17

Catalog of Seed and Vegetable Stock Available from the Southern Regional Plant Introduction Station for various plants, A 106.19

Classified Index of Decisions of Regional Directors of National Labor Relations Board in Representation Proceedings, LR 1.8/6-2

Conservation Vistas, Regional Conservation Education Newsletter Serving Oregon and Washington, A 13.72/2

Crops Research: Results of Regional Cotton Variety Tests by Cooperating Agricultural Experiment Stations, A 77.15:34

Directory of Federal Regional Structure, GS 4.119

Directory of State Mental Health Personnel and Regional Offices of Department of Health, Education, and Welfare, FS 2.22:M 52/40

East Central Regional Office Publications, L 2.91

Federal Regional Council, Pr 37.8:R 26

INSS Occasional Paper, Regional Series, D 305.24

International Organization and Conference Series II, Regional, S 1.70/2

Market News Service (Regional) Publications, I 49.52/2

Navajo Nation & Regional Areas Resource Directory, HE 20.310/3

NE Regional Reports, L 2.71/3

NE Regional Staff Letter, A 77.29, A 106.38

News Regional and State Employment and Unemployment, L 2.111/7

North Central Regional Medical Education Center: Newsletter, VA 1.56/2

North Central Regional Membership Relations Conference, A 89.17/2

North Central Regional Office Publications, L 2.94

North Central States Regional Poultry Breeding Project, Annual Report, A 77.236

North Eastern Regional Office Publications, L 2.93

Northeastern States Regional Poultry Breeding Project, Annual Report, A 77.234

OBERS, BEA Regional Projections, C 59.17

Program for Regional Observing and Forecasting Services, C 55.626/2

Region 6: Regional Report Series, L 2.71/9

Regional Aeronautical Charts, C 23.10/4, C 4.9/5

Regional Air Cargo Workshop, C 31.258

Regional and Field Letter, FS 1.16

Regional Brief, S 1.71/6

Regional Bulletins, A 57.16

Regional Cold Storage Holdings, A 105.33/2

Regional Contract Charts, A 55.7/2, A 55.7/3, A 55.7/4

Regional Cotton Variety Tests, A 106.28

Regional Data on Compensation Show Wages, Salaries and Benefits Costs in the Northeast, L 2.71/6-6

Regional Differences in Indian Health, HE 20.319

Regional Distribution and Types of Stores where Consumers Buy Selected Fresh Fruits, Canned and Frozen Juices, and Dried Fruits, A 36.172

Regional Economic Information System (REIS), C 59.24

Regional Handbooks, A 57.22

Regional Information Series Leaflets, A 55.43/6, A 55.45/5

Regional Information Series, A 55.42/5, A 55.44/5, A 55.46/5

Regional Labor Statistics Bulletin, L 2.71/7

Regional Office Directory, Professional and Administrative Personnel, FS 1.17/2

Regional Profiles, S 18.54

Regional Reports (numbered), L 2.71/3

Regional Reports (series), L 2.71/4

Regional Reports, L 2.71/2

Regional Reports, Middle Atlantic Region, L 2.71/6

Regional Research Bulletins, N.Y. and New England, Y 3.W 89/2:60

Regional Review, Region 1, I 29.36

Regional Studies Plan, Fiscal Year, Atlantic OCS Region, I 72.12/15

Regional Tide and Tidal Current Tables, C 55.425/3

Results of Regional Cotton Variety Tests by Cooperating Agricultural Experiment Stations, A 77.15:34

Rocky Mountain Regional Aviation System Plan, TD 4.33/5

Seasonally Adjusted Capacity and Traffic Scheduled Operations System Trunks and Regional Carriers, C 31.262/5

Selected Bibliography of Regional Medical Programs, HE 20.2612

Southeastern Regional Office: Regional Reports, L 2.71/8

Southern Regional Office Publications, L 2.95

State and Regional Unemployment, L 2.120/2

Summary of Regional Cold Storage Holdings, A 88.20/2

Western Regional Newsletter, J 21.17

Western States Regional Turkey Breeding Project, Annual Report, A 77.235

Regions

Cold Regions Research and Engineering Laboratory R & D Notes, D 103.33/11

Cold Regions Science and Engineering, D 103.33/7

Cold Regions Technical Digest (series), D 103.33/14

Conditions of Major Water System Structures and Facilities, Review of Maintenance, Report of Examination, {various regions and projects}, I 27.69

Reports for Consultation on Air Quality Control Regions, FS 2.93/5

Research Reports Cold Regions Research and Engineering Laboratory, D 103.33/3

Special Reports Cold Regions Research and Engineering Laboratory, D 103.33/2

Telephone Directory Central Office and Regions, GS 12.12

World Population: Recent Demographic Estimates for the Countries and Regions of the World, C 3.205/3

Registar

Registar, C 3.126, FS 2.111

The Registar, C 3.126

Register

Advisory List of National Register of Historic Places, I 29.76/2

Air Force Register, D 303.7

Air National Guard Register, D 12.9/2

Alphabetical Listing, Register or Planned Mobilization Producers, Manufacturers of War Material Registered Under Production Allocation Program, D 7.11

Annual Register, N 12.5

Annual Register of the United States Naval Academy, D 208.107

Annual Report of the Register of Copyrights, LC 3.1

Army Meteorological Register, W 44.11

Army Register, D 102.9

Biographic Register, S 1.69

Equal Employment Opportunity Federal Register, Y 3.Eq 2:18-6

FDA Federal Register Documents, Chronological Document Listing, 1936-1976, HE 20.4016:C 46

Federal Motor Carrier Safety Administration, Register, TD 2.314.6/4

Federal Register, GS 4.107, AE 2.106

Federal Register Proposed Amendments, Y 3.F 31/21-3:9-5

Federal Register Update, GS 4.107/2

Federal Register, What It Is and How to Use It, GS 4.6/2:F 31

Hill-Burton Project Register, FS 2.74, HE 20.2509

Historical Register, U.S. Revenue Cutter Service Officers, TD 5.19/4

ICC Register, IC 1.35

International Shipborne Barge Register, C 39.241, TD 11.24

Museum Manuscript Register Series, D 214.17

National Register of Historic Places, I 29.76, I 70.2:H 62/2, I 70.17

National Register of Historic Places Bulletins, I 29.76/3

National Register of Microform Masters, LC 30.8/8

National Shellfish Register of Classified Growing Waters, C 55.441

National Union Catalog: Register of Addition Locations, LC 30.8/7

Navy Register, N 1.10

Official Army and Air Force Register, M 101.19, M 108.8

Official Army National Guard Register, D 12.9

Official Army Register of Volunteer Force of U.S. Army, 1861-65, W 3.12

Official National Guard Register, D 112.8

Official Register (or Blue Book) Biennial, I 1.25

Official Register Life-Saving Service, T 24.5

Official Register National Guard Bureau, D 112.8

Official Register of Officers and Cadets, W 12.5, M 109.11, D 109.7

Project Register, I 67.16

Project Register, Projects Approved Under Sec. 8 of Federal Water Pollution Control Act (Pub. Law 660, 84th Cong.), As Amended and Sec. 3, of Public Works

Project Register, Waste Water Treatment Construction Grants, EP 1.9/2, EP 1.56/2

Register of Civil Engineer Corps Commissioned and Warrant Officers of United States Navy and Naval Reserve on Active Duty, D 209.9

Register of Commissioned and Warrant Officers Coast Guard Reserve, T 47.10/2

Register of Commissioned and Warrant Officers Marine Corps Reserve, N 9.20

Register of Commissioned and Warrant Officers Naval Militia, N 1.27/6

Register of Commissioned and Warrant Officers Naval Reserve Force, N 25.6

Register of Commissioned and Warrant Officers Naval Reserve, N 17.38

Register of Commissioned and Warrant Officers Navy and Marine Corps and Reserve Officers on Active Duty, D 208.12

Register of Commissioned and Warrant Officers United States Naval Reserve, D 208.12/2

Register of Commissioned and Warrant Officers United States Navy and Marine Corps, M 206.10

Register of Debates, X 43 X 71

Register of Employees, P 1.14

Register of Military Personnel in the Washington, D.C. Area, TD 5.19/3

Register of Money Order Post Offices in United States, P 9.5

Register of Naval Militia, N 23.5

Register of Office of Attorney General, J 1.12

Register of Officers and Cadets, TD 5.19

Register of Officers and Graduates (triennial), W 12.12

Register of Officers and Vessels, T 33.6

Register of Projects Approved Under Manpower Development and Training Act, L 1.53

Register of Reporting Employers, L 1.81

Register of Reporting Labor Organizations, L 1.84

Register of Reporting Surety Companies, L 1.82

Register of Reserve Officers, TD 5.19/2

Register of Retired Commissioned and Warrant Officers, Regular and Reserve, of the United States Navy and Marine Corps, D 208.12/3

Register of the Department of the Interior, I 1.28

Register of U.S. Commissioners, J 1.18

Register of Visitors, S 1.52

Register of Voluntary Agencies, S 18.12

Register of War Department, W 1.10

Register Planned Emergency Producers, D 7.11/2

Register, Department of Justice and the Courts of the United States, J 1.7

Register, Department of State, S 1.6

Register, Y 3.Se 4:27

Reports, **Register** of Approved Recurring Reports, D 101.22/3:335-1

Technical Standards **Register**, C 31.143/2

Treasury **Register**, T 1.13

United States Civil Aircraft **Register**, TD 4.18/2

Registered

Annotated Index of **Registered** Fungicides and Nematicides, Their Uses in the United States, A 77.302:F 96

Caveat List of United States **Registered** Bonds, T 26.7

DHIA Cow Performance Index List, **Registered** Progeny of DHIA Sires, A 77.15:44

EPA Compendium of **Registered** Pesticides, EP 5.11/1-5

Farm Labor Contractor Registration Act, Public Registry, National Listing of Contractors and Employees **Registered**, L 36.14

List of Stocks **Registered** on National Securities Exchange and of Redeemable Securities of Certain Investment Companies, FR 1.46

Registered Bona Fide and Legitimate Farmers' Cooperative Organizations under Bituminous Coal Act of 1937, I 46.15

Registered Distributors under Bituminous Coal Act of 1973 {lists}, I 46.14

Registered Group-Joint Apprenticeship Programs in Construction Industry (by trades), L 23.9

Report of Classified Program of Exports and Value by American Agencies Voluntarily **Registered** with Advisory Committee on Voluntary Foreign Aid, S 1.99/1

Schedule of Sailings of Steam Vessels **Registered** Under Laws of United States and Intended to Load General Cargo at Ports in United States for Foreign Destinations, IC 1 rat.8

Ships **Registered** Under Liberian, Panamanian, and Honduran Flags Deemed by the Navy Department to Be Under Effective U.S. Control, C 39.228

Summary Statement of Income and Expenditures of Voluntary Relief Agencies **Registered** with Advisory Committee on Voluntary Foreign Aid, S 1.99/3

Trademarks **Registered**, Bibliographic Information from **Registered** US Trademarks, C 21.31/7

U.S.D.A. Summary of **Registered** Agricultural Pesticide Chemical Uses, A 77.302:P 43/4

USAMark: Fascimile Images of **Registered** United States Trademarks, C 21.31/11

Voluntary Foreign Relief Programs, Activities of **Registered** American Voluntary Agencies, S 18.19

Registered Nurses

Directory of Programs Preparing **Registered Nurses** for Expanded Roles, HE 20.6610

Registers

Registers of Papers in the Manuscript Division of the Library of Congress, LC 4.10

Registrant

Registrant Facts, J 24.17

Registrants

Registrants Processing Manual, Y 3.Se 4:10-2 R 26

Registration

Aircraft **Registration**, TD 4.6:part 47

Automobile **Registration** Characteristics, FW 2.17

Farm Labor Contractor **Registration** Act, Public Registry, National Listing of Contractors and Employees Registered, L 36.14

Foreign Service Written Examination **Registration** and Application Form, S 1.137

Graves **Registration** Service Bulletins, W 95.16

Pesticide **Registration** Eligibility Decisions (REDs), EP 5.27

Pesticide **Registration** Standards, EP 5.17

Registration Record, Securities Act of 1933, Indexes, SE 1.13/2

Registration Record, Securities Act of 1933, SE 1.13/1

Registration, Employment and Unemployment, U.S. Zone, Statistical Report, W 1.72/3

Report of the Attorney General to the Congress of the United States on the Administration of the Foreign Agents **Registration** Act of 1938, As Amended, J 1.30

U.S. Statutes Concerning the **Registration** of Prints and Labels, C 21.7/3

U.S. Statutes Concerning the **Registration** of Trademarks, C 21.7/2

Voting and **Registration** in the Election of (name), C 3.186/3-2

Voting and **Registration** in the Election of November (date), C 3.186/3

World Motor Vehicle and Trailer Production and **Registration**, C 57.21

World Motor Vehicle Production and **Registration**, C 41.17

Registry

Agency for Toxic Substances and Disease **Registry** Annual Report, HE 20.501/2

Farm Labor Contractor Registration Act, Public **Registry**, National Listing of Contractors and Employees Registered, L 36.14

Registry of Toxic Effects of Chemical Substances (cumulative) Supplement, HE 20.7112/5

Registry of Toxic Effects of Chemical Substances, HE 20.7112/3

Registry of Toxic Effects of Chemical Substances, Permuted Molecular Formula, Index, HE 20.7112/4

Subfile of the **Registry** of Toxic Effects of Chemical Substances, HE 20.7112/2

Regular

Corps of **Regular** Army, W 44.27

Extracts from Reports by **Regular** and Military Officers on Joint Army and Militia Coast-Defense Exercises, W 2.7

Register of Retired Commissioned and Warrant Officers, **Regular** and Reserve, of the United States Navy and Marine Corps, D 208.12/3

Regulate

Prosecutions Under Act to **Regulate** Commerce, IC 1 act.6

Regulated

Monthly Commodity Futures Statistics on Futures Trading in Commodities **Regulated** under the Commodity Exchange Act, A 85.15/2

Regulating

Election Law Guidebook, 1974, Summary of Federal and State Laws **Regulating** Nomination and Election of United States Senators, Revised to January 1, 1974, Y 1.93-2:S.doc. 84

Regulation

Acquisition **Regulation** Staff Manual, HE 1.6/8

Advertisements Inviting Proposals for Carrying Mails by **Regulation** Screen Wagons, P 1.7

Advertisements Inviting Proposals for Covered **Regulation** Wagon Mail-Messenger, Transfer, and Mail Station Service, P 1.6

Armed Services Procurement **Regulation**, M 1.8, D 1.13

Armed Services Procurement **Regulation** Revision, D 1.13/2

Armed Services Procurement **Regulation** Supplement ASPA (series), D 1.13/2-2

Federal Acquisition **Regulation**, GP 3.38/2

Missouri River Main Stream Reservoir **Regulation** Studies, D 103.41/3

NASA Procurement **Regulation**, NAS 1.6/2

NASA Procurement **Regulation** Directive, NAS 1.6/3

Noise Diagnostics for Safety Assessment, Standards, and **Regulation**, E 1.28/10

Program **Regulation** Guides {issued by various departments}, HE 1.47/3

Regulations

Abstracts of Defense **Regulations**, GS 4.112

Administrative Rules and **Regulations** Under Sections of National Housing Act, HH 2.6/2

Advance Copy Proposed Rules and **Regulations**, NCU 1.6/a

Adverse Action, Law and **Regulations**, Annotated, CS 1.41/4:752-1

AF **Regulations**, M 301.6

Amendment to Rules and **Regulations** Under Sections of National Housing Act, HH 2.6/3

Amendments to **Regulations**, Public Health Service, T 27.8/2

Annotated Manual of Statutes and **Regulations** of the Federal Home Loan Bank Board, FHL 1.6/2:St 2

Annual Review, Airworthiness Civil Air **Regulations** Meeting, C 31.245

Army Material Command **Regulations**, D 101.9/2

Army Procurement **Regulations**, M 101.11

Army **Regulations** AR (series), W 1.6 D 101.9

Atomic Energy Commission Rules and **Regulations**, Y 3.At 7:6-2

Background Document for {various products} Noise Emission **Regulations**, EP 1.6/2

BDSA **Regulations**, C 41.6/2

Brewers' Code **Regulations**, Y 3.F 31/10:7

Budget-Treasury **Regulations**, Pr 33.106/2

C.A.B. Notices of Proposed Rulemaking and Amendments to All **Regulations**, CAB 1.37

Calendar of Federal **Regulations**, Y 3.R 26:9

Ceiling Price **Regulations**, ES 3.6/5

Changes in Army **Regulations**, W 1.6/2

Changes in Drill **Regulations**, W 42.13/2

Changes in Engineer **Regulations**, W 7.11/4

Changes in Navy **Regulations**, N 1.11/2

Changes in **Regulations**, N 17.16/2

Changes in **Regulations** (compilations), W 70.7/3

Changes in **Regulations** (general), W 70.7/2

Changes in **Regulations** and Instructions (numbered), W 2.6/2, W 26.9/2

Changes in Training **Regulations**, W 1.21/2

Changes in Uniform **Regulations**, N 1.18/2

Changes to Rules, **Regulations** and Instructions, W 77.10/2

Child Labor **Regulations**, L 22.6/3

Child Labor **Regulations**, Orders, L 5.39

Chinese Exclusion Treaties, Laws and **Regulations**, C 7.5

Civil Aeronautics Board Legislative History of **Regulations**, C 31.206/2:L 52

Civil Air **Regulations**, C 31.209

Civil Air **Regulations** (compilations), C 23.6/2, C 23.6/3

Civil Air **Regulations** Draft Release, C 31.209/2

Civilian Personnel **Regulations**, W 1.42, D 101.6/2

Code of Federal **Regulations** (Hardcopy), AE 2.106/3

Code of Federal **Regulations** of United States, AE 2.9

Code of **Regulations** of U.S. of America, AE 2.8

Commercial **Regulations** of Foreign Countries, S 1.9

Commodity Exchange Act, As Amended, **Regulations** of the Secretary of Agriculture Thereunder, Orders of the Commodity Exchange Commission Pursuant to Sec. 4a and 5a(4), A 85.6:C 73

Compendium of General Orders Amending Army **Regulations**, W 3.13

Compilation of Public Health Service **Regulations**, FS 2.52

Compilations and Digest of Orders, Circulars, **Regulations**, and Decisions, W 7.11/3

Comptroller General's Special **Regulations**, GA 1.7

Construction Industry Stabilization Commission **Regulations**, ES 2.6/4
Consular **Regulations**, S 1.5
Coordination Service, Digest of Interpretations of Specific Price Schedules and **Regulations**, Pr 32.4249
Customs **Regulations**, T 1.9/1
Customs **Regulations** of the United States, T 17.9
Customs Tariff and **Regulations**, W 1.7
Digests of Decisions and **Regulations**, T 22.8/2
Distribution **Regulations**, ES 3.6/8
DPS **Regulations** (numbered), C 41.6/2-2
Drill **Regulations**, W 3.16
Drill **Regulations**, Manuals, and Instructions for Army, W 3.16/1
Economic **Regulations** (compilation), C 31.220/2
Enforcement and Procedure **Regulations**, ES 3.6/6
Equal Employment Opportunity, Code of Federal **Regulations** Title 29, Y 3.Eq 2:18-4
Export Administration **Regulations**, C 57.409, C 61.23, C 63.28
Export Control **Regulations**, C 42.11/3, C 57.409
F.D.C. **Regulations**, FS 13.106/2
Federal Acquisition **Regulations**, D 1.6/11
Federal and State Commission Jurisdiction and **Regulations**, Electric, Gas, and Telephone Utilities, FP 1.21
Federal Aviation **Regulations**, TD 4.6
Federal Energy Guidelines: Statutes and **Regulations**, E 2.18
Federal Food, Drug, and Cosmetic Act, as Amended, and General **Regulations** for its Enforcement, FS 13.105:F 73
Federal Motor Vehicle Safety Standards and **Regulations**, TD 8.6/2
Federal Procurement **Regulations**, GS 1.6/5
Federal Procurement **Regulations**, FPR Notices, GS 1.6/5-2
Federal Property Management **Regulations** Amendments, GS 1.6/8-3
Federal Rules and **Regulations**, Correction Sheets, CC 1.7/3
Federal Travel **Regulations**, GS 1.6/8-2
FERC Statutes and Regulations, Proposed **Regulations**, E 2.18/3
FERC Statutes and **Regulations**, **Regulations** Preambles, E 2.18/2
FHA **Regulations**, HH 2.6
Field Manual and Field **Regulations**, W 1.33
First Army, 1a **Regulations**, D 101.9/6
Foreign Service **Regulations** (by chapters), S 1.5/3
Foreign Service **Regulations**, Memorandum Transmitting Mimeographed InsertsRegulations for, S 1.5/2
Foreign Trade **Regulations** of (country), C 1.50, C 57.11
General Ceiling Price **Regulations**, ES 3.6/4
General Instructions and **Regulations** in Relation to Transaction of Business at Mints and Assay Offices with Coinage Laws, T 28.9
General Maximum Price **Regulations**, Bulletins, Pr 32.4211
General Overriding **Regulations**, ES 3.6/9
General **Regulations** for the Enforcement of the Federal Food, Drug, and Cosmetic Act, FS 13.106/2:1/2
General Rules and **Regulations** Prescribed by Board of Supervising Inspectors of Steamboats, T 38.9
General Rules and **Regulations** Under the Investment Company Act of 1940, as in Effect (date), SE 1.6:R 86/9
General Rules and **Regulations** Under the Securities Act of 1933, as in Effect (date), SE 1.6:R 86/2
General Rules and **Regulations** Under the Securities Exchange Act of 1934, as in Effect (date), SE 1.6:R 86/3
General Salary Stabilization **Regulations** GSSR (series), ES 4.6/2
General Wage **Regulations**, ES 2.6/3
Government Printing and Binding **Regulations**, Y 4.P 93/1:6
Great Lakes Pilotage **Regulations** and Rules and Orders, C 1.47:R 26
GSA FIRMR/FAR **Regulations**, GS 12.15/2
HCFA's Laws, **Regulations,** Manuals, HE 22.8/22
Headquarters Fort McCoy **Regulations**, D 101.9/4
Immigration Laws and **Regulations**, W 6.5
Import **Regulations**, A 1.11/2
Imports and Exports of Commodities by U.S. Coastal Districts and Foreign Trade **Regulations**, SB 7.5/275, C 27.9/4, MC 1.11

Index of Current **Regulations** of Federal Maritime Board, Maritime Administration, National Shipping Authority, C 39.106/2, C 39.206/4, TD 11.22
Index of EPA Legal Authority Statutes and Legislative History, Executive Orders, **Regulations**, EP 1.5/4
Inserts to Postal Laws and **Regulations**, P 1.11/2
Instructions and **Regulations**, N 25.7
Internal Revenue **Regulations** and Instructions, T 22.29
Investment Advisers Act of 1940 and General Rules and **Regulations** Thereunder As in Effect (date), SE 1.5:In 8/2
Joint Army and Air Force **Regulations**, M 101.15
Joint Travel **Regulations**, D 1.6/4
Labor-Management Reporting and Disclosures Act, As Amended, **Regulations** and Interpretative Bulletins, L 1.51/2
Laws and **Regulations**, HE 3.5/2
Laws and **Regulations** Enforced or Administered by the United States Customs Service, T 17.6/2
Laws and **Regulations** for Protection of Commercial Fisheries of Alaska, I 45.11
Laws and **Regulations** Relating to Lighthouse Establishment, C 9.16
Laws and **Regulations** Relating to National Parks, Reservations, etc., I 1.47
Laws relating to Federal Corrupt Practices and Political Activities, Federal Corrupt Practices Act, Hatch Political Activities Act, Miscellaneous Related Acts and **Regulations**, Y 1.2:F 31/8
Laws, Executive Orders, Rules and **Regulations**, CS 1.41/4:990-1
Laws, Rules and **Regulations**, CS 1.7
Laws, Rules and **Regulations** (special), CS 1.7/2
Legal Compilation, Statutes and Legislative History, Executive Orders, **Regulations**, Guidelines and Reports, EP 1.5/3
License **Regulations** (numbered), Y 3.F 73:18
List of Forms, Records, Laws, and **Regulations** Pertaining to Internal Revenue Service, T 22.39
Manual of **Regulations**, I 28.11
Manual of **Regulations** and Instructions Relating to the Disclosure of Federal Campaign Funds for Candidates for the Office of President or Vice President of the United States and . . . Candidates, GA 1.14:C 15
Manual of **Regulations** and Procedures for Radio Frequency Management, PrEx 18.8:R 11
Manual of Rules **Regulations**, Transmittal Letters, FW 4.30
Maximum Price **Regulations**, Pr 32.4210
Maximum Rent **Regulations**, Pr 32.4214
Meat and Poultry Inspection **Regulations**, A 110.6/2, A 103.6/4
Meat Inspection Division **Regulations**, A 77.206:M 46
MEMCPM **Regulations**, D 1.65/2
Memorandum Transmitting Mimeographed Inserts for Foreign Service **Regulations**, S 1.5/2
MEPCOM **Regulations**, D 1.6/9
Military Government **Regulations**, W 1.72/4
Military Negotiation **Regulations**, D 1.8
Military Renegotiation **Regulations** Under Renegotiation Act of 1948, RnB 1.6/4
Militia Bureau **Regulations** (general), W 70.7
Misbranding **Regulations**, Y 3.F 31/10:10
Mobilization **Regulations**, W 1.29
Model State **Regulations** {on various subjects} As Adopted by the National Conference on Weights and Measures, C 13.55/3
National Credit Union Administration Rules and **Regulations**, NCU 1.6:R 86
National Emergency Standby **Regulations** and Instructions Personnel and Manpower, CS 1.41/4:990-3
National Guard **Regulations**, M 114.6, D 112.6
Naturalization Laws and **Regulations**, C 7.10/5, L 6.5
Naval Reserve **Regulations**, N 25.7/2
Navy Property Redistribution and Disposal **Regulations**, D 201.6/9
Navy **Regulations**, N 1.11/1, D 201.11
Navy **Regulations**, Proposed Changes, N 1.11/3
New Passenger Automobile Rationing **Regulations**, Orders, Pr 32.4208
Notice of Judgment under **Regulations** of Naval Stores, A 46.8
NPA **Regulations**, C 40.6/2

Occupational Safety and Health Other **Regulations** and Procedures, L 35.6/3-4
Occupational Safety and Health **Regulations**, L 35.6/2
OCDM **Regulations**, PrEx 4.6/4
Office of Selective Service Records **Regulations**, Y 3.Se 4:19
Old-Age and Survivors Insurance, **Regulations**, FS 3.6/2
Operations, Instructions, **Regulations**, and Interpretations, J 21.6/2
Orders and **Regulations**, D 103.6/2
Organization **Regulations**, C 31.206/6
OSHA Standards and **Regulations**, L 35.6/3
Other **Regulations** and Procedures, C 35.6/3
Pacific Halibut Fishery **Regulations**, S 5.35:5
Postal Laws and **Regulations** (General), P 1.11
Postal Laws and **Regulations** Applicable to Railway Mail Service, P 10.13
Postal Laws and **Regulations** {special}, P 1.12
Priorities **Regulations**, Pr 32.4010, Pr 32.4807
Procedural **Regulations**, Pr 32.4209
Procurement **Regulations** Agency for International Development, S 18.6/2
Procurement **Regulations** Services of Supply, W 109.7, W 109.8, W 109.8-2
Property **Regulations** (numbered), VB 1.14
Quarantine Laws and **Regulations**, T 27.9
Radio Communication Laws and **Regulations**, C 11.7/5
Readjustment **Regulations**, W 1.62
Regulations [Export Administration Bureau], C 63.23
Regulations, AFSCR (series), D 301.45/14-2
Regulations, Alcohol Tax Unit, T 22.17/2
Regulations and Interpretations, L 22.9
Regulations and Interpretive Bulletins, L 1.7/4
Regulations and Policy Statements, C 31.224/2
Regulations and Procedure, VB 1.10/3, VB 1.10/4
Regulations and Programme of Instruction, W 29.6
Regulations, ER- (series), D 103.6/4
Regulations for Clerks of Courts Who Take Passport Applications, S 1.18
Regulations for Government of Ordnance Department (general), W 34.12/1
Regulations for Government of Public Health and Marine Hospital Service, T 27.8
Regulations for Government of United States Army General Hospital, W 44.15
Regulations for Military Academy (general), W 12.6/1
Regulations for Quartermaster's Department (general), W 39.9/1
Regulations for Revenue-Cutter Service (general), T 33.7
Regulations for Sale of Lake Survey Charts, W 33.5
Regulations for Subsistence Department, W 5.7
Regulations for the Administration and Enforcement of the Radiation Control for Health and Safety Act of 1968, HE 20.4606/2
Regulations for United States Corps of Cadets Prescribed by Commandant of Cadets, M 109.6/2
Regulations Governing Admission of Candidates into Naval Academy As Midshipmen and Sample Examination Questions, D 208.108
Regulations Governing Meat Inspection of the U.S. Department of Agriculture, A 88.6/3:188
Regulations Governing Uniform and Equipment of Officers and Enlisted Men, N 9.8
Regulations Governing Uniforms, N 1.18/1, T 27.7
Regulations No. 4, Old-Age and Survivors Insurance, FS 3.6/2
Regulations (numbered), Pr 32.4406
Regulations of Administrator, C 31.140, FAA 1.6/4
Regulations of Department of Agriculture, A 1.19
Regulations of General Services Administration, GS 1.6/4
Regulations of Indian Office (general), I 20.13/1
Regulations of the Civil Aeronautics Board, C 31.206/7, CAB 1.16
Regulations of the Office of the Secretary, TD 1.6/2
Regulations (pt. nos. of Title 26 of the Code of Federal **Regulations**), T 70.6/2
Regulations (pt. nos. of Title 27 Code of Federal **Regulations**), T 22.17/4, T 70.6/3
Regulations, Plant, A 35.8
Regulations, Rules, Instructions, J 36.6

Regulations, Rules and Instructions [Census Bureau], C 3.6

Regulations, Rules and Instructions [Center for Professional Development and Training], HE 20.7709

Regulations, Rules, and Instructions [Comptroller of the Currency], T 12.25

Regulations, Rules and Instructions [Court of Customs Appeals], Ju 7.8/2

Regulations, Rules and Instructions [Customs Division], T 17.5

Regulations, Rules and Instructions [Department of Education], ED 1.47

Regulations, Rules and Instructions [Department of Transportation], TD 1.6

Regulations, Rules and Instructions [Federal Emergency Management Agency], FEM 1.6

Regulations, Rules and Instructions [Food and Nutrition Service], A 98.18

Regulations, Rules, and Instructions [Grain Inspection, Packers and Stockyards Administration], A 113.12

Regulations, Rules and Instructions [International Trade Commission], ITC 1.6

Regulations, Rules and Instructions [National Center for Devices and Radiological Health, HE 20.4606

Regulations, Rules and Instructions [National Defense University], D 5.406

Regulations, Rules and Instructions [Naval Research Office], D 210.6

Regulations, Rules and Instructions [Office of Information Resources Management], GS 12.15

Regulations, Rules and Instructions [Office of Water Programs], EP 2.6

Regulations, Rules and Instructions [Research and Special Programs Administration], TD 10.6

Regulations, Rules and Instructions [United States Parole Commission], J 27.6

Regulations (special), T 17.5

Regulations S-X Under the Securities Act of 1933, SE 1.6:F 49

Regulations Series 5, T 22.15

Regulations, Title 29, Code of Federal Regulations], L 36.206/2

Regulations Under Fair Labor Standards Act, L 22.22

Regulations Under Federal Power Act, FP 1.7:P 87/2

Regulations Under the Natural Gas Act, August 1, 1967, FP 1.7:G 21/3

Regulations Under the Perishable Agricultural Commodoties Act 1930, and Perishable Agricultural Commodities Act, A 88.6:P 41

Renegotiation Board **Regulations**, RnB 1.6/2

Revised Customs **Regulations**, T 1.9/2

Rules and **Regulations** (miscellaneous), FP 1.7

Rules and **Regulations** and Statements of Procedure, LR 1.6:R 86

Rules and **Regulations** for Federal Savings and Loan System, with Amendments to {date}, FHL 1.6:Sa 9

Rules and **Regulations** for Foreign Vessels Operating in the Navigable Waters of the United States, TD 5.6:V 63/7

Rules and **Regulations** for Government and Discipline of United States Penitentiaries, J 1.16

Rules and **Regulations** Governing Paroling of Prisoners from Penitentiaries, State Institutions, J 1.15/5

Rules and **Regulations** Governing Paroling of Prisoners from U.S. Penitentiaries {etc.} (special), J 1.15/6

Rules and **Regulations** of Bureau of Imports, WT 4.5

Rules and **Regulations** of National Parks, I 1.47/2

Rules and **Regulations** of Service, IC 1.12/1

Rules and **Regulations**, Title 10, Code of Federal **Regulations**, Chapter 1, Y 3.N 88:6

Rules of Practice under Title 4, **Regulations** and Orders, CA 1.14

Safety Investigation **Regulations**, SIR (series), C 31.206/4

Salary Procedural **Regulations**, ES 4.6/5

Selective Service **Regulations**, Y 3.Se 4:6, Y 3.Se 4:7

Special Civil Air **Regulations**, C 31.206/3

Special **Regulations**, W 1.18

Special Tariff Permission Under Section 224.1 of Economic **Regulations**, C 31.210

Standardized Government Civilian Allowance **Regulations**, Allowance Circulars, S 1.76

Standardized Government Post Differential **Regulations**, Differential Circulars, S 1.76/2

Standardized **Regulations** (Government Civilians, Foreign Areas), S 1.76/3

State Laws and **Regulations** Prohibiting Employment of Minors in Hazardous Occupations, L 22.6/2

Status of CAA Releases, Manuals, and **Regulations**, C 31.151

Status of Civil Air **Regulations** and Civil Aeronautics Manuals, FAA 1.18

Status of Federal Aviation **Regulations**, New, TD 4.13

Summary of Federal Hunting **Regulations** for (year), I 49.24/2

Summary of U.S. Export Control **Regulations**, C 42.6:Ex 7/2

Supplement to General Rules and **Regulations**, C 15.9/2

Supply and Maintenance Command **Regulations**, D 101.9/3

Surplus War Property Administration **Regulations**, Pr 32.5908

Temporary Joint **Regulations**, Y 3.F 31/10:14

Temporary **Regulations**, Y 3.F 31/10:13

Training **Regulations**, W 1.21

Transmittal Letters, Manual of **Regulations** and Procedure, FW 1.14

Treasury Department-General Accounting Office Joint **Regulations**, T 1.38

U.S. Imports of Fruits and Vegetables under Plant Quarantine **Regulations**, A 93.44/3

U.S. Navy **Regulations**, D 201.11

U.S. Nuclear Regulatory Commission **Regulations** {List}, Y 3.N 88:21

USAREC **Regulations**, D 101.9/5

Weekly Summary of Orders and **Regulations**, C 31.208

Western Space and Missile Center: **Regulations**, WSMCR- (series), D 301.6/7

Wholesale Code **Regulations**, Y 3.F 31/10:15

Regulators

Herbicides and Plant **Regulators**, EP 5.11

Regulatory

Buyer-Seller Codes Authorized for Reporting to the Federal Energy **Regulatory** Commission, E 3.35

Congressional Budget Request, Federal Energy **Regulatory** Commission, E 1.34/4

Databases and Browseable Lists of the **Regulatory** Plan and the Unified Agenda of Federal Regulatory and Deregulatory Actions, GS 1.6/11-2

Draft **Regulatory** Guide, DG-, Y 3.N 88:6-3

Federal Energy **Regulatory** Commission Producer Manual, E 2.12:0030

Final **Regulatory** Analysis, I 70.14

Final **Regulatory** Analysis, OSM-RA- (series), I 1.77/4

NPA **Regulatory** Material and Forms, Digest, C 40.6/8

NRC **Regulatory** Agenda, Y 3.N 88:45

Nuclear **Regulatory** Commission Issuances, Y 3.N 88:11-2

Nuclear Regulatory Commission Issuances: Opinions and Decisions of the Nuclear **Regulatory** Commission with Selected Orders, Y 3.N 88:11

Nuclear **Regulatory** Legislation, Y 4.In 8/14:N 88/5

Orders Federal Energy **Regulatory** Commission, E 2.10

Plant **Regulatory** Announcements, A 77.308/5

Procurement **Regulatory** Activity Report, PrEx 2.24/15

Regulatory and Technical Reports (Abstract Index Journal), Y 3.N 88:21-3

Regulatory Alert, NCU 1.6/2

Regulatory Announcements, I 49.24

Regulatory Calendar, E 2.16

Regulatory DataBases and Browseable Lists of the Regulatory Plan and the Unified Agenda of Federal Regulatory and Deregulatory Actions, GS 1.6/11-2

Regulatory Guide List, Y 3.N 88:6-4

Regulatory Guides, Y 3.N 88:6-2

Regulatory Impact Analysis (series), EP 6.14/2

Regulatory Information Service Center: General Publications, GS 1.6.11

Regulatory Licensing Status Summary Reports, Y 3.N 88:44

Regulatory Licensing, Status Summary Report, Systematic Evaluation Program, Y 3.N 88:29

Regulatory Procedures Manual, HE 20.4008/6

Regulatory Program of the United States Government, PrEx 2.30

Regulatory Reporter, Y 3.R 26/2:9

Safety Research Programs Sponsored by Office of Nuclear **Regulatory** Research, Y 3.N 88:48

Service and **Regulatory** Announcements Agricultural Marketing Administration, A 75.16

Service and **Regulatory** Announcements Agricultural Marketing Service, A 66.27, A 88.6/3

Service and **Regulatory** Announcements Agricultural Research Service, A 77.6/2

Service and **Regulatory** Announcements Agricultural Stabilization and Conservation Service, A 82.23

Service and **Regulatory** Announcements Alaska Game Commission, A 5.10/5

Service and **Regulatory** Announcements Bureau of Agricultural Economics, A 36.5

Service and **Regulatory** Announcements Bureau of Animal Industry, A 4.13, A 77.208

Service and **Regulatory** Announcements Bureau of Biological Survey, A 5.6

Service and **Regulatory** Announcements Bureau of Chemistry, A 7.6

Service and **Regulatory** Announcements Bureau of Dairy Industry, A 44.5

Service and **Regulatory** Announcements Bureau of Entomology and Plant Quarantine, A 56.14

Service and **Regulatory** Announcements Bureau of Plant Industry, A 19.13

Service and **Regulatory** Announcements Bureau of Plant Quarantine, A 48.7

Service and **Regulatory** Announcements Bureau of Soils, A 26.7

Service and **Regulatory** Announcements Caustic Poison, A 46.13, FS 13.110

Service and **Regulatory** Announcements Civil Service Commission, CS 1.5

Service and **Regulatory** Announcements Federal Horticulture Board, A 35.9

Service and **Regulatory** Announcements Food and Drug, A 46.12

Service and **Regulatory** Announcements Food, Drug, and Cosmetic, A 46.19, FS 7.8, FS 13.115

Service and **Regulatory** Announcements Import Milk, A 46.11, FS 13.114

Service and **Regulatory** Announcements Insecticide and Fungicide Board, A 34.6

Service and **Regulatory** Announcements Insecticide and Fungicide, A 46.15

Service and **Regulatory** Announcements List of Intercepted Plant Pests, A 77.308/2

Service and **Regulatory** Announcements Naval Stores, A 46.18

Service and **Regulatory** Announcements Publications Relating to Entomology and Plant Quarantine, A 77.308

Service and **Regulatory** Announcements Publications Relating to the Care of Animals and Poultry, A 77.208

Service and **Regulatory** Announcements SRA-C&MS- (series), A 88.6/3

Service and **Regulatory** Announcements Tea, A 46.14, FS 7.14

Service and **Regulatory** Announcements, Office of Distribution, A 80.118

State **Regulatory** Commissions and Fuel Tax Divisions, IC 1.3/2-2

Telephone Directory Federal Energy **Regulatory** Commission, E 2.12/2

Telephone Directory Nuclear **Regulatory** Commission, Y 3.N 88

Transportation Safety **Regulatory** Bulletin, E 1.135

U.S. Nuclear **Regulatory** Commission Regulations {List}, Y 3.N 88:21

Working Reference of Livestock **Regulatory** Establishments, A 77.221/2

Working Reference of Livestock **Regulatory** Establishments, Circuits and Officials, A 88.16/20

Relative
    Classification of Labor Market Areas According to **Relative** Adequacy of Labor Supply, L 7.19/2
    Procedure **Relative** to Claims, A 55.45/10
    Relative Cost of Shipbuilding, TD 11.15/2
    Relative Cost of Shipbuilding in Various Coastal Districts of the United States, Report to Congress, C 39.216/2
    Relative Importance of Components in the Consumer Price Indexes, L 2.3/9
Relatives
    Wholesale Price Index (1947-49=100), Prices and Price **Relatives** for Individual Commodities, 1951-53, L 2.61/6, L 2.61/6-2
Relay
    Cable Television **Relay** Service, Applications, Reports, Public Notices, CC 1.47/2
    Relay Broadcast Stations, CC 1.31
Release
    Pretrial **Release** of Felony Defendants, J 29.11/14
    Release (of action taken) Prior to January 22, 1936, Reports, CC 4.8
    Release for Publication (series), FP 1.25/2
    Summary Data from the Employment Situation News **Release**, L 2.53/2-2
    Summary Data from the Producer Price Index News **Release**, L 2.61/10-2
    Technical Information **Release**, T 22.42/2
    Toxic Chemical **Release** Inventory, EP 5.22
    Toxics-**Release** Inventory: A National Prospective, EP 5.18/2
    Toxics-**Release** Inventory: Executive Summary, EP 5.18/2-2
    Wage Developments in Manufacturing, Summary **Release**, L 2.44/2
    Wage Trends for Occupational Groups in Metropolitan Areas, Summary **Release**, L 2.86/2
    Wartime Report **Release** Lists, Y 3.N 21/5:12
Released
    Radioactive Materials **Released** from Nuclear Power Plants, Y 3.N 88:25-12
Releases
    Census Bureau News **Releases**, C 3.295
    Current **Releases** of Non-Theatrical Film, C 18.63
    Energy Efficiency and **Renewable** Energy, Clearinghouse, E 1.99/13
    News **Releases** and Other News Material, A 1.143
    Office of Industry and Commerce **Releases** OIC (series), C 18.281/2
    Office of International Trade **Releases** OIT (series), C 18.281/3
    OPA Chart Book **Releases**, Pr 32.4250
    Philatelic **Releases**, P 1.29/3
    President's Committee on Employment of the Handicapped: Press **Releases**, PrEx 1.10/4
    Press **Releases** Alaska Railroad, I 1.82/2
    Press **Releases** Department of Education, ED 1.25
    Press **Releases** Federal Home Loan Bank Board, FHL 1.7
    Press **Releases** Minority Business Enterprise Office, C 1.57
    Press **Releases** Securities and Exchange Commission, SE 1.25/8
    Press **Releases**, NOS (series), C 55.415
    Recent **Releases**, Selected Information Materials, S 1.30/2
    Releases CGS (series), C 3.209
    Releases Pertaining to Personnel, C 13.36/3
    Releases Relating to Orders, ES 3.7/3
    Releases, Air Research and Development Command, D 301.45/3
    Releases, Corporate Reorganization, SE 1.25/1
    Releases, Holding Company Act of 1935, SE 1.25/2
    Releases, Investment Company Act of 1940, SE 1.25/3
    Releases, ITC 1.7
    Releases, Securities Act of 1933, SE 1.25/4
    Releases, Securities Exchange Act of 1934, SE 1.25/5
    Releases, Trust Indenture Act of 1939, SE 1.25/7
    Research News (press **releases**), HE 20.3407
    Selected Speeches and News **Releases**, A 1.134, A 21.24/2
    Special Market Study **Releases**, SE 1.28
    Special **Releases** {of Foreign Broadcast Intelligence Service}, W 100.9
    State Prisoners: Admissions and **Releases**, J 16.23/2

Status and Progress Reports, **Releases**, A 61.19
Status of CAA **Releases**, Manuals, and Regulations, C 31.151
Summary of CPI News **Releases**, L 2.38/10
Survival Series, For Your Information {**releases**}, FCD 1.13/10
Telecommunications Office: Press **Releases**, C 1.32/7
United Nations Educational, Scientific and Cultural Organization News {**releases**}, S 5.48/13
United States Mission to the United Nations Press **Releases**, S 5.55
Wage Stabilization Committee **Releases**, WSC (series), ES 2.7/2
Weekly Summary: AAA Press **Releases**, A 55.64
Reliability
    Aircraft Utilization and Propulsion **Reliability** Report, TD 4.59
    Parts Specification Management for **Reliability**, D 4.9
    Quality and **Reliability** Assurance Handbooks, D 7.6/11
    Quality Control and **Reliability** Technical Reports, D 7.15
    Reliability Abstracts and Technical Reviews, NAS 1.35
    Reliability and Quality Assurance Publications, NAS 1.22/3
    Reliability Publications, NPC 250 (series), NAS 1.22/2
Relics
    Firearms, and Ammunition Curios and **Relics** List, T 70.15
Relief
    Administration of **Relief** Committees, Y 3.P 92:6
    Beyond **Relief**, Y 3.Af 8:10
    Changes in Different Types of Public and Private **Relief** in Urban Areas, L 5.33
    Current Statistics of **Relief** in Rural and Town Areas, Y 3.W 89/2:25, SS 1.23
    Emergency **Relief** Appropriation Acts, Reports of President to Congress Showing Status of Funds and Operations Under, T 63.114
    Emergency **Relief** Appropriation Acts, Reports Showing Status of Funds, T 63.107
    Emergency **Relief** Appropriation Acts, Reports Showing Status of Funds and Analyses to Expenditures, T 63.109
    Emergency **Relief** Bulletins, Y 3.R 24:8
    Employment and Pay Rolls, Emergency Work **Relief** Program, Y 3.F 31/5:31
    Farm **Relief** and Agricultural Adjustment Acts {June 15, 1929}, Y 1.2:F 22
    Federal Emergency **Relief** Administration Grants, Y 3.F 31/5:32
    Federal Emergency **Relief** Administration Grants Distributed According to Programs and Periods for which Grants were Made, Y 3.F 31/5:33
    General **Relief** Operations of Large City Public Welfare Agencies, SS 1.26
    Intensity of **Relief** Maps, Y 3.F 31/5:36
    Monthly Expenditures for Family **Relief**, L 5.28
    Monthly **Relief** Bulletin, L 5.29
    Participation of American and Foreign-Flag Vessels in Shipments under United States Foreign **Relief** Programs, C 3.164:976
    President's Organization of Unemployment **Relief**, C 1.15
    Publications President's Organization of Unemployment **Relief**, C 1.15
    Refugee **Relief** Program, S 1.110
    Relief in Rural and Town Areas, SS 1.25/a 2
    Relief in Urban Areas, SS 1.10, SS 1.25/a 3
    Relief Notices, Y 3.F 31/5:23
    Report to Congress on the Emergency Homeowner's **Relief** Act, HH 1.64
    Report to Congress on United States Foreign **Relief** Program, S 1.63
    Reports of President to Congress Showing Status of Funds and Operations under Emergency **Relief** Appropriation Acts, T 63.114
    Reports Showing Financial Status of Funds Provided in Emergency **Relief** Appropriation Acts, T 60.11
    Reports Showing Status of Funds Provided in Emergency **Relief** Appropriation Acts, T 60.12
    Research Bulletins Federal Emergency **Relief** Administration, Y 3.F 31/5:28

Safety Bulletins Federal Emergency **Relief** Administration, Y 3.F 31/5:24
Soldiers' and Sailors' Civil **Relief** Act of 1940 and Amendments, Y 1.2:So 4/7, Y 1.2:So 4/2
State Map Series Shaded **Relief**, I 19.104
Summary of Emergency **Relief** Statistics, Y 3.F 31/5:34
Summary Statement of Income and Expenditures of Voluntary **Relief** Agencies Registered with Advisory Committee on Voluntary Foreign Aid, S 1.99/3
Total Obligations Incurred for Emergency **Relief** from All Public Funds by State and Local **Relief** Administration in Continental United States, Y 3.F 31/5:35
Trend of **Relief** in Continental United States, Y 3.F 31/5:37
Trend of Urban **Relief**, Y 3.F 31/5:25, SS 1.15
United States Exports of Domestic and Foreign Merchandise Under United Nations **Relief** and Rehabilitation Program, Country of Destination by Commodity, C 3.164:426
United States Exports of Domestic and Foreign Merchandise Under United Nations **Relief** and Rehabilitation Program, Commodity by Country of Destination, C 3.164:416
United States Exports Under United Nations **Relief** and Rehabilitation Program, C 3.164:960
Voluntary Foreign **Relief** Programs, Activities of Registered American Voluntary Agencies, S 18.19
Religion
    Series on **Religion** Nationalism and Intolerance, Y 3.P 31:18
Religious
    Annual Report on International **Religious** Freedom (Bureau for Democracy, Human Rights and Labor), S 1.151
    Census of **Religious** Bodies, C 3.35
    Religious Press Bulletin, Y 3.F 73:13
Relocation
    Annual Report of HUD Activities Under the Uniform **Relocation** Assistance Policies Act of 1970, HH 1.49
    Federal-Aid Highway **Relocation** Assistance and Payment Statistics, TD 2.28
    Relocation from Urban Renewal Project Areas, HH 7.14
Reminders
    Technical Assistance **Reminders**, L 31.8/2
Remote
    Renewable Resources **Remote** Sensing Research Program Report, NAS 1.70
Removal
    General Drawings of Snow **Removal** Equipment, W 7.31/2
Removals
    Information Concerning **Removals**, Reductions, Suspensions and Furloughs, CS 1.24
    Superfund Emergency Response Actions, A Summary of Federally-Funded **Removals**, Annual Report, EP 1.89/5
REMR
    REMR Bulletin: News from the Repair, Evaluation, Maintenance and Rehabilitation Research Program, D 103.72
Renal
    Cardiovascular and **Renal** Study Section, HE 20.3001/2:C 17/5
    End-Stage **Renal** Disease Medical Information System Facility Reports, HE 22.9
    End-Stage **Renal** Disease Program Medical Information System, Facility Survey Tables (year), HE 22.9/3
    End-Stage **Renal** Disease Program, Annual Report to Congress, HE 22.9/2
    Medicare **Renal** Dialysis Facility Manual, HE 22.8/13
    National Listing of **Renal** Providers Furnishing Kidney Dialysis and Transplant Services, HE 22.510/2
    Renal Disease and Hypertension, Proceedings, Annual Conference, HE 20.5412
    United States **Renal** Data System, Annual Data Report, HE 20.3325
Renegotiation
    Military **Renegotiation** Regulations Under **Renegotiation** Act of 1948, RnB 1.6/4
    Renegotiation Board Regulations, RnB 1.6/2

Directory, Directors of State Agencies for Surplus
  Property and Regional **Representatives**,
  Division of Surplus Property
  Utilization, FS 1.2:Su 7/2
DNFSB Site **Representatives** Weekly Activities
  Reports, Y 3.D 36/3:11
Handbook for Veterans Administration Contract
  Representatives, VA 1.10/5:232-68-1/2
International Civil Aviation Organization Report
  of **Representatives** of United States, S
  5.52
Journal of the House of **Representatives**, XJH
National Conference Veterans' Employment
  Representatives, FS 3.123
Rules Adopted by the Committees of the House of
  Representatives, Y 4.R 86/1-12
Telephone Directory House of **Representatives**, Y
  1.2/7
U.S. House of **Representatives**, Detailed Statement
  of Disbursements, Y 4.H 81/3:D 63
Undersecretary's Report to the Field, Newsletter
  for Department of Labor Field
  Representatives, L 1.37
Represented
  Subject Catalog, Cumulative List of Works
    Represented by Library of Congress
    Printed Cards, LC 30.11
Reprint
  Contents, Format and Concepts of Federal Budget,
    Reprint of Selected Pages from Budget of
    United States Government, PrEx 2.8
  EPA Journal **Reprint**, EP 1.67/a
  Information Collection and Exchange, **Reprint**
    Series, AA 4.12
  Program and Training Journal **Reprint** Series, AA
    4.10
  Reprint and Circular Series, NA 2.5
  Reprint of Hydrographic Information, N 6.19
  Reprint Series, Y 3.Se 5:15
  Technology Sharing **Reprint** Series, TD 1.49
Reprints
  Collected **Reprints**, C 52.23, C 55.334, C 55.428
  Collected **Reprints**; Atlantic Oceanographic and
    Meteorological Laboratories, C 55.612
  Collected **Reprints**; Atmospheric Physics and
    Chemistry Laboratory, C 55.612/3
  Collected **Reprints**; Wave Propagation Laboratory,
    C 55.612/2
  Injury Epidemiology and Control **Reprints**, HE
    20.7009/3
  Reprints from Bulletin 556, Mineral Facts and
    Problems, I 28.3/b, I 28.3/c
  Reprints from Marketing Activities, A 82.17/1
  Reprints from Public Health Reports, T 27.6/a
  Reprints from the Occupational Outlook
    Handbook, Bulletins, L 2.3/4 a
  Reprints of Articles Published Concerning NIH
    Consensus Development Conferences,
    HE 20.3030/2
  Reprints, R- (series), D 103.42/4
  Technical **Reprints**, NAS 1.27
Reproducible
  Fixed **Reproducible** Tangible Wealth of the United
    States, C 59.27
  Reproducible Federal Tax Forms for Use in
    Libraries, T 22.57
  Tax Practitioner **Reproducible** Kit, T 22.51/2
Reproduction
  Population and **Reproduction** Research Abstracts,
    HE 20.3360
  Reports on **Reproduction** and Population Research
    (series), FS 2.22/13-7
Republic
  Quarterly Economic and Financial Review: Federal
    Republic of Germany and Western
    Sectors of Berlin, S 1.91/2
  Telephone Directory **Republic** 7500, Executive
    6300, District 0525, GS 6.7
Republic of Liberia
  International Commission of Inquiry into Existence
    of Slavery and Forced Labor in **Republic
    of Liberia**, S 5.33
Republican
  Platforms of the Democratic Party and the
    Republican Party, Y 1.2:P 69
Republications
  NASA **Republications**, NAS 1.13
Republics
  Economic Control and Commercial Policy in
    American **Republics**, TC 1.20
  Mining and Manufacturing Industries in the
    American **Republics**, TC 1.21
  Recent Developments in Foreign Trade of American
    Republics, TC 1.22

United States Exports and Imports of Gold and
  Silver, Total United States Trade in Gold
  and Silver and United States Trade in
  Gold and Silver with Latin American
  Republics and Canada, C 3.164:859
United States Exports of Domestic Merchandise to
  Latin American **Republics**, C 3.157
United States Exports of Foreign Merchandise to
  Latin American **Republics**, C 3.157/2
United States General Imports from Latin American
  Republics, C 3.157/3
Request
  Congressional Budget **Request**, E 1.34
  Congressional Budget **Request**, Federal Energy
    Regulatory Commission, E 1.34/4
  Congressional Budget **Request**, U.S. Department of
    Justice, E 1.34/3
  Congressional Budget **Request**, U.S. Department of
    the Interior, E 1.34/2
  Report of Secretary of Defense to the Congress on
    the Budget, Authorization **Request**, and
    Defense Programs, D 1.1
  Request for Grant Applications (series), HE
    20.3220
  Request for Hearings in Public Assistance, Fiscal
    Year (date), HE 3.60/2
  Request for New or Modified Broadcast Call Signs,
    CC 1.44
  Request for Proposal (series), ED 1.72
  Request for Proposal, NIE-R- (series), ED 1.324
  Request for Proposals, J 16.28
  Request for Research Grant Applications (series),
    HE 20.3864
Requests
  CATV **Requests** Filed Pursuant to Sec. 74.1107(a)
    of the Rules, Public Notice, CC 1.45
  Funding Opportunities at NIE, Grants Competi-
    tions and **Requests** for Proposals in
    Fiscal Year, HE 19.216/2
  Manual on Uniform Traffic Control Devices for
    Streets and Highways: Official Rulings
    on **Requests** for Interpretations,
    Changes, and Experimentations, TD 2.8/
    2
  Rulings on **Requests** for Review of the Assistant
    Secretary of Labor for Labor- Manage-
    ment Relations Pursuant to Executive
    Order 11491, As Amended, L 1.51/6
Required
  Forecast of Motor-Fuel Demand and **Required**
    Crude-Oil Production by States,
    Monthly Forecast, I 28.41
  Lumber and Timber Basic Products Industry,
    Wooden Container Industry, Employer
    Report of Employment and **Required**
    Labor Force by Standard Lumber Type
    Region, Pr 32.5224
Requirement
  Report, Civil Service **Requirement**, Federal
    Employees' Group Life Insurance,
    Federal Employees Health Benefits,
    Retired Federal Employees Health
    Benefits, Fiscal Year (date), CS 1.29/3
  Requirement for Individual Water-Supply and
    Sewage-Disposal Systems (by States),
    NHA 2.17, HH 2.11
  Requirement Forms, T 45.7
Requirements
  Current Information Resource **Requirements** of the
    Federal Government, PM 1.56
  Current Information Technology Resources
    Requirements of the Federal Govern-
    ment, PrEx 2.12/5
  Driver License Administration **Requirements** and
    Fees, TD 2.61
  Essential Procedure and **Requirements** for
    Naturalization Under General Law (Form
    C-59), J 21.8
  Guide to Record Retention **Requirements**, GS
    4.107/a:R 245
  Guidelines for Implementation of Sanitary
    Requirements in Poultry Establish-
    ments, A 88.6/4:P 86/2
  Manpower Report of the President and Report on
    Manpower **Requirements**, Resources,
    Utilization, and Training by the U.S.
    Department of Labor, L 1.42/2
  Manpower **Requirements** Report, D 1.52
  Minimum Construction **Requirements** for New
    Dwellings, FL 2.11
  Minimum Property **Requirements** for Properties of
    One or Two Living Units Located in the
    {various States}, HH 2.17

NBS Handbook, Specifications, Tolerances, and
  Other Technical **Requirements** for
  Weighing and Measuring Devices, C
  13.11/2
NIST Handbook, Specifications, Tolerances, and
  Other Technical **Requirements** for
  Weighing and Measuring Devices, C
  13.11/2
Packaging **Requirements** Code, D 7.20:726C
Physician **Requirements** for {various subjects}
  (series), HE 20.6024
Plant Quarantine Import **Requirements** of {various
  countries}, A 101.11
Plant **Requirements** Reports (series), FO 1.28, S
  17.28
Plant **Requirements**, S 18.22
Recordkeeping **Requirements** for Firms Selected to
  Participate in the Annual Survey of
  Occupational Injuries and Illnesses, L
  2.129
S.R. {Sugar **Requirements** and Quotas} (series), A
  82.6/2
Urban Renewal Manual, Policies and **Require-
  ments** for Local Public Agencies, HH
  7.9
Visa **Requirements** of Foreign Governments, S
  1.2:V 82/2
World Nuclear Fuel Cycle **Requirements**, E 3.46/4
Requirments
  Safety and Health **Requirments**, L 16.23
Requisition
  List of American and Foreign Ships Owned under
    Requisition of Chartered to Shipping
    Board, SB 2.11
Requisitioned
  Contract and **Requisitioned** Steamships, SB 2.13
Requisitioning
  Military Standard **Requisitioning** and Issue
    Procedure, D 7.6/4:M 59
  MILSTRIP, Military Standard **Requisitioning** and
    Issue Procedures, D 7.6/17
Resale
  Sales of Firm Electric Power for **Resale**, by Private
    Electric Utilities, by Federal Projects, by
    Municipals, FP 1.21
Rescue
  Air Sea **Rescue** Bulletin, N 24.35, T 47.32
  National First-Aid and Mine **Rescue** Contest, I
    28.26/5
  On Scene, National Maritime SAR {Search and
    Rescue} Review, TD 5.24
Research
  A.I.D. **Research** Abstracts, TN-AAA (series), S
    18.47
  Abstracts of Completed **Research**, D 206.21/2
  Abstracts of NSF/RANN **Research** Reports:
    Private Sector Productivity, NS 1.13/4
  Abstracts of Personnel **Research** Reports, D
    301.45/27
  Abstracts of USAPRO **Research** Publications, D
    101.60
  ACR **Research** Reports, D 210.15
  ACS **Research** Report (series), A 109.10
  Active Foreign Agricultural **Research**, A 106.42/2
  Advances in Education **Research**, ED 1.317/4
  Adult Development and Aging **Research**
    Committee, HE 20.3001/2:Ad 9
  Advanced Waste Treatment **Research**, I 67.13/
    3:AWTR
  AEC **Research** and Development Reports, Y 3.At
    7:22
  Aeromedical **Research** Unit, Fort Rucker, Ala.;
    USAARU Reports, D 104.21
  Aeronautical **Research** Laboratory, ARL (series), D
    301.69/2
  Agricultural Economics **Research**, A 36.167, A
    88.27, A 93.26, A 105.21
  Agricultural Economics **Research**, A 105.21
  Agricultural **Research**, A 106.9
  Agricultural **Research** and Marketing Act
    Publications, A 1.72
  Agricultural **Research** Results, A 106.13
  Agricultural **Research** Results, ARR (series), A
    106.12, A 77.32
  AHCPR **Research** Activities HE 20.6512/5
  AHRQ **Research** Activities HE 20.6512/5
  Air Force Cambridge **Research** Center: AFCRC
    Technical Reports, D 301.45/4
  Air Force **Research** Resumes, D 301.69/3
  Air Force **Research** Review, D 301.69/6-2
  Air Force Scientific **Research** Bibliography, D
    301.45/19-2:700

Air Force Weapons Laboratory, **Research** and Technology Division, AFWL-TDR, D 301.45/35

Air Pollution, Sulfur Oxides Pollution Control, Federal **Research** and Development, Planning and Programming, FS 2.93/4

Air **Research** and Development Command: Technical Reports, ARDC-TR , D 301.45/21

Air University Compendium of **Research** Topics, D 301.26/3-2

Air University Documentary **Research** Study, Publications, D 301.26/3

Air University, Human Resources **Research** Institute, **Research** Memorandum, D 301.26/7

Airborne Instrumentation **Research** Project Summary Catalog, NAS 1.68

Alaska Forest **Research** Center, A 13.73

Alcohol Health and **Research** World, HE 20.2430, HE 20.3813, HE 20.8309

Alcohol **Research** and Health HE 20.8309

Alcohol, Drug Abuse, Mental Health **Research** Grant Awards, HE 20.8016, HE 20.8118

Allergic Diseases **Research** (series), HE 20.3262

Analysis of Current Pulmonary **Research** Programs Supported by the National Heart, Lung, and Blood Institute, HE 20.3202:P 96/2

Analysis of Federal Population **Research**, HE 20.3025

Analysis of **Research** in the Teaching of Mathematics, FS 5.229:29007, HE 5.229:29007

Analysis of **Research** in the Teaching of Science, FS 5.229:29000, HE 5.229:29000

Animal Health Science **Research** Advisory Board, A 106.40

Annual Conference Report on Cotton-Insect **Research** and Control, A 106.28/2

Annual International Aviation **Research** and Development Symposium, Report of Proceedings, FAA 2.9

Annual Report of Progress on Engineering **Research**, I 27.54

Annual Report of **Research**, A 13.27/1

Annual Report of the National **Research** Programs, Crop Production, A 106.25, A 106.25/2

Annual Report to Congress on Administration of the Marine Protection **Research** and Sanctuaries Act of 1972, EP 1.69

Annual Report, Mental Health Intramural **Research** Program, HE 20.8136

Annual **Research** Symposium, EP 1.83

Annual Review of Child Abuse and Neglect **Research**, HE 23.1210/3

Annual Summary Progress Reports of Population **Research** Centers and Program Projects, HE 20.3362/4

Antarctic **Research** Program Maps, I 19.25/8

Arbovirus Surveillance, Reference, and **Research**, HE 20.7811

Archaeological **Research** Series, I 29.59

Arctic **Research** of the United States, NS 1.51/2

Argonne National Laboratory: **Research** and Highlights, E 1.86/4

Armed Forces Radiobiology **Research** Institute: Annual **Research** Report, D 15.1/2

Armed Forces Radiobiology **Research** Institute: Scientific Reports, D 15.12

Armed Forces Radiobiology **Research** Institute: Technical Reports, D 15.12/2

Army Air Mobility **Research** and Development Laboratory Fort Eustis Virginia: USAAMRDL Technical Reports, D 117.8/2 D 117.8/4

Army Electronics Command Fort Monmouth N.J.: **Research** and Development Technical Reports ECOM (series), D 111.9/4

Army Medical **Research** Laboratory Reports, D 104.14

Army Prosthetics **Research** Laboratory Technical Reports, D 104.15/2

Army **Research** and Development, D 101.52/3

Army **Research** Institute for Behavioral and Social Sciences: **Research** Reports, D 101.60/2

Army **Research** Institute for Behavioral and Social Sciences: **Research** Reports, D 101.60/2

Army **Research** Laboratory Strategic Plan for Fiscal Year, D 101.1/11-2

Army **Research** Task Summaries, D 101.52/2

Army Transportation **Research** Command: Interim Reports, D 117.8/3

ARS National **Research** Program NRP (series), A 77.28

ASA/NSF/Census Bureau **Research** Fellow Program, C 3.293

Atoll **Research** Bulletin, SI 1.25

Atomic Energy Commission **Research** Reports for Sale by Office of Technical Services, C 41.29

Atomic Energy **Research** in Life Sciences and Physical Sciences, Y 3.At 7:48

Aviation Psychology Program **Research** Reports, W 108.25

Behavioral Sciences **Research** Contract Review Committee, HE 20.3001/2:B 39

Belvior **Research**, Development, and Engineering Center: Handbooks, (series), D 101.6/10

Belvoir **Research** and Development Center: Container System Hardware Status Report, D 101.115

BIA Education **Research** Bulletin, I 20.57

Bibliography of U.S. Army Medical **Research** and Nutrition Laboratory Reports and Reprints for (year), D 104.17

Biomedical Engineering and Instrumentation Branch, Division of **Research** Branch: Annual Report, HE 20.3036/3

Biomedical Index to PHS-Supported **Research**, HE 20.3013/2

BLMR **Research** Studies, L 31.11

Breeding **Research** and Improvement Activities of Department of Agriculture Reports, A 1.91

Building **Research** Summary Reports, C 13.40

Bulletin of Prosthetics **Research**, VA 1.23/3

Bureau of International Economic Policy and **Research**: Reports, Studies, Data, C 57.26

Bureau of Mines **Research** (year), Summary of Significant Results in Mining Metallurgy and Energy, I 28.115

Bureau of Mines **Research** in (year), I 28.5

Bureau of Radiological Health **Research** Grants Program, Fiscal Year, (date), HE 20.4116

Cancer **Research** Center Review Committee, HE 20.3001/2:C 16/10

Cancer **Research** Safety Monograph Series, HE 20.3162/2

Catalog of Current Joint Publications **Research** Publications, Y 3.J 66:15

Catalog of **Research** Projects, I 1.88/2

Census Bureau Methodological **Research**, (year), Annotated List of Papers and Reports, C 56.222/3:M 56

Census of Population; Housing: Evaluation and **Research** Program, C 56.223/16

Center for International Systems **Research**: Occasional Papers, S 1.124

Center for Population **Research**, Progress Report, HE 20.3351/3

Center for Radiation **Research**, Technical Highlights, Fiscal Year, C 13.1/2

Center for **Research** for Mothers and Children, Progress Report, HE 20.3351/2

Center for Vocational and Technical Education, Ohio State University: **Research** and Development Series, HE 18.11

CERC Bulletin and Summary Report of **Research**, Fiscal Year (date), D 103.42/3

Checklist of Reports Issued by Economic **Research** Service and Statistical Reporting Service, A 1.97

Child Abuse and Neglect Research: Projects and Publications, HE 1.480/3, HE 23.1210/2

Cityscape - A Journal of Policy Development and **Research**, HH 1.75/2

Coastal Pollution **Research** Highlights, EP 1.37

Cold Regions **Research** and Engineering Laboratory R & D Notes, D 103.33/11

Compass: Recent Publications of the Southern **Research** Station, A 13.150/5

Computer **Research** and Technology Divisions: Technical Reports, HE 20.3011

Conference Report on Cotton Insect **Research** and Control, A 77.328

Congressional **Research** Service Review, LC 14.19

Conservation **Research** Reports, A 1.114, A 77.23

Consumer Goods **Research**, C 57.118

Contraceptive Evaluation **Research** Contract Review Committee, HE 20.3001/2:C 76/2

Contract **Research** Reports, TD 8.15/2

Contractor **Research** and Development Reports, E 1.28

Cooperative **Research** and Service Division, Quarterly Reports, A 72.22

Cooperative **Research** Program: Projects under Contract, FS 5.69

Cooperative **Research** Reports, A 105.38

Cooperative Water Resources, **Research** and Training, I 1.1/4

CPR Population **Research**, HE 20.3362/3

CR {Crop **Research**} (series), A 77.534

Crashworthiness **Research** News, TD 8.61

Criminal Justice **Research**, J 28.17

Criminal Justice **Research** Series, J 1.37/4

Criminal Justice **Research** Solicitations, J 1.37/5, J 26.18

Criminal Justice **Research** Utilization Program (series), J 28.13

Crop Insurance **Research** and Development Bulletins, A 112.17, A 62.17

Crop Production **Research**, A 77.33

Crops **Research**: Results of Regional Cotton Variety Tests by Cooperating Agricultural Experiment Stations, A 77.15:34

CSRS **Research** Information Letter, A 94.13

Current Federal Aid **Research** Report, Wildlife, I 49.94/2

Current Federal Meteorological **Research** and Development Activities, C 30.75/2

Current Federal **Research** Reports, Fish, I 49.94

Current Population **Research** Reports, FS 2.22/61

Current Projects on Economic and Social Implications of Scientific **Research** and Development, NS 1.23

Current **Research** and Developments in Scientific Documentation, NS 1.15, NS 2.10

Current **Research** Project Grants, HE 20.3111

Dental **Research** in the United States, Canada and Great Britain, Fiscal Year (Date), HE 20.3402:D 43

Department of Defense Program for **Research** and Development, D 1.81

Directorate of Mathematical and Information Sciences, Air Force Office of Scientific **Research**, **Research** Summaries, D 301.45/19-10

Directorate of **Research** Analysis, AFOSR/DRA (series), D 301.45/19-4

Directory of Labor **Research** Advisory Council to the Bureau of Labor Statistics, L 2.83/2

Directory of Law Enforcement and Criminal Justice Associations and **Research** Centers, C 13.10:480-20

Directory of On-going **Research** in Smoking and Health, HE 20.25, HE 20.7015

Directory of **Research** Natural Areas on Federal Lands of United States of America, Y 3.F 31/19:9

Directory of **Research**, Development and Demonstration Projects, TD 7.9

Directory of the Labor **Research** Advisory Council to the Bureau of Labor Statistics, L 2.109

Directory, Business **Research** Advisory Council of the Bureau of Labor Statistics, L 2.83

Dissemination of **Research** Results {on Poultry and Egg Marketing Subjects}, A 82.75, A 88.15/8

Division of Cancer Epidemiology and Genetics, Annual **Research** Directory, HE 20.3188/2

Division of Cancer **Research** Resources and Centers: Annual Report, HE 20.3151/2

Division of Clinical Sciences, Annual **Research** Directory, HE 20.3151/9

Division of **Research** Service: Annual Report, HE 20.3035

DRG {Division of **Research** Grants} Newsletter, HE 20.3022

Drug Abuse **Research** and Development, Federally Supported Drug Abuse and Tobacco **Research** and Development, Fiscal Year (date), HE 20.8220

Drug Abuse Services **Research** Series, HE 20.8235

DWRC **Research** Update, A 101.29

EARI Development **Research** Series, Reports, D 103.50

Ecological **Research** Series, EP 2.32

Ecological **Research**, 600/3 (series), EP 1.23

Economic Development **Research** Reports, C 46.29

Economic Redevelopment **Research**, C 46.24

Economic **Research** Reports, C 3.259

EDRO **Research** Programs, Progress Reports, HE 20.4031

EDRO SARAP **Research** Technical Reports, HE 20.4031/2
Education **Research** Bulletin, ED 1.303/2
Education **Research** Consumer Guide, ED 1.308/2
Education **Research** Report, ED 1.322/3
Educational and Nonprofit Institutions Receiving Prime Contract Awards for **Research**, Development, Test and Evaluation, D 1.57/8
Electronic **Research** Directorate Technical Memorandum ERD-CRRK-TM (series), D 301.45/12
Employment Security **Research** and Reporting Exchange Series, L 7.56/2
Employment Security **Research** Exchange, L 7.56/3
Energy Efficiency **Research**, ER 1.29
Energy **Research** Abstracts, E 1.17
Energy **Research** and Technology: Abstracts of NSF **Research** Results, NS 1.13/3
Energy **Research** and Technology: Abstracts of NSF/RANN **Research** Reports, NS 1.13/3-2
Energy **Research**, DOE/ER (series), E 1.19
Engineer **Research** and Development Laboratories Reports, D 103.25
Engineering Laboratory **Research**, Y 3.T 25:35
Engineering Postdoctoral **Research** Associateship Program, C 13.65/2
Environmental Health Effects **Research**, 600/1 (series), EP 1.23/4
Environmental **Research** Brief (series), EP 1.96
Environmental **Research** in (year), EP 1.46/2
Environmental **Research** Laboratory, Duluth: Quarterly Report, EP 1.46/6
Environmental **Research** Papers, D 301.45/39
ERDA Energy **Research** Abstracts, ER 1.15
ESCS **Research** Abstracts, A 105.25/2
ESSA **Research** Laboratories Technical Manuals, C 52.8/2
Evaluation and **Research** Reports ER (series), C 3.223/16
Executive Summary of HUD **Research** Project Report (series), HH 1.53
Experimental Safety Vehicle Program and Vehicle Safety **Research**, Progress Report, TD 8.16/2
Exploratory **Research** and Problem Assessment: Abstracts of NSF **Research** Results, NS 1.13/2
External **Research** Papers, S 1.101/3
External **Research** Report, Memorandums, S 1.101/4
External **Research** Report **Research** Lists, S 1.101
External **Research** Reports, Policy **Research** Brief PRB (series), S 1.101/5
External **Research** Studies, S 1.101/11
FAA Aviation Medical **Research** Reports, FAA 7.10
FAR {Far Area **Research**} Horizons, S 1.125
Farm Resources and Facilities **Research** Advisory Committee Report, A 1.103
FCA **Research** Journal, FCA 1.25
FCS **Research** Reports, A 89.19
Federal Aviation Administration Plan for **Research**, Engineering, and Development, TD 4.64
Federal Coordinator for Meterological Services and Supporting **Research**, FCM (series), C 55.12
Federal Funds for **Research** and Development, Detailed Historical Tables, Fiscal Years, NS 1.18/2
Federal Funds for **Research** and Development, Federal Obligations for **Research** by Agency and Detailed Field of Science, Fiscal Years, NS 1.18/3
Federal Funds for **Research**, Development, and Other Scientific Activities, NS 1.18
Federal Grants and Contracts for Unclassified **Research** in Life Sciences, NS 1.10
Federal Grants and Contracts for Unclassified **Research** in Physical Sciences, NS 1.10/2
Federal Noise **Research** in (various subjects), EP 1.73/3
Federal Plan for Meteorological Services and Supporting **Research**, Fiscal Year (date), C 55.16/2
Federal Plan for Ocean Pollution **Research**, Developing, and Monitoring, PrEx 8.109

Federal Program in Population **Research**, Inventory of Population **Research** Supported by Federal Agencies During Fiscal Year (date), HE 20.3362/2
Federal **Research** Natural Areas in, A 13.36/12
Federal Support of **Research** and Development at Universities and Colleges and Selected Nonprofit Institutions, Fiscal Year, Report to the President and Congress, NS 1.30
Federal Water Resources **Research** Program for Fiscal Year, PrEx 8.9
Federally Coordinated Program of Highway **Research** and Development, TD 2.42
Fermilab **Research** Program Workbook, E 1.92
FHA **Research** and Statistics Release, HH 2.18/3
FHWA **Research** and Development Implementation Catalog, TD 2.36/3
FIR {Fishery Industrial **Research**} Reprints, I 49.26/2a
Fire **Research** Publications, C 13.58/4
Fiscal Year Priorities and Fiscal Year Accomplishments For **Research**, Extension, and Higher Education, A Report to the Secretary of Agriculture, A 1.2/13
Fish and Wildlife **Research** (series), I 49.99
Fish-Passage **Research** Program Progress Reports, I 49.63
Fisheries and Wildlife **Research**, I 49.92
Fishery Industrial **Research**, C 55.311
Fishery Industry **Research**, I 49.26/2
Food and Agriculture Competitively Awarded **Research** and Education Grants, A 106.42
Food Assistance and Nutrition **Research** Program, A 93.61
Food Assistance and Nutrition **Research** Report, A 93.60
Food & Nutrition **Research** Briefs, A 17.30
Foreign Affairs **Research** Papers Available, S 1.126
Foreign Affairs **Research** Special Papers Available, S 1.126/2
Foreign Affairs **Research**, a Directory of Government Resources, S 1.2:F 76a/4
Foreign Area **Research** Documentation Center: Papers Available, S 1.126
Foreign Noise **Research** (series), EP 1.73/2
Forest **Research** News for the Midsouth, A 13.40/11
Forest **Research** News for the South, A 13.40/11
Forest **Research** Notes, A 13.62/7, A 13.66/7
Forest **Research** Project Reports, A 13.41
Forestry **Research** Progress in (year) McIntire-Stennis Cooperative Forestry **Research** Program, A 94.2 F 76/
Forestry **Research** West, A 13.95/2
Forestry **Research**: What's New in the West, A 13.95
Fundamental Nuclear Energy **Research**, Y 3.At 7:48
Funds for **Research** at State Agricultural Experimental Stations, A 94.10
General Clinical **Research** Centers Committee, HE 20.3001/2:C 61/2
General Publications Relating to Dairy **Research**, A 77.602
General **Research** Support Program Advisory Committee, HE 20.3001/2:R 31/2
General **Research**, GR- (series), I 27.72
Geological Survey **Research**, I 19.16
Geophysical **Research** Papers, D 301.45/2
Geothermal Energy **Research**, Development and Demonstration Program, Annual Report, ER 1.31
Geriatric **Research**, Education, and Clinical Centers, VA 1.92
Global Ocean Floor Analysis and **Research** Data Series, D 203.31
Government-Supported **Research** on Foreign Affairs, Current Project Information, S 1.101/10
Government-Supported Research, International Affairs, **Research** Completed and in Progress, S 1.101/9
GP-PIA Joint **Research** Bulletins, GP 1.25
GRD **Research** Notes, Geophysics **Research** Directorate, D 301.45/16
Great Lakes Environmental **Research** Laboratory: Annual Report, C 55.620
Great Lakes **Research** Advisory Board: Annual Report, Y 3.In 8/28:10
Guide to Published **Research** on Atomic Energy, Y 3.At 7:7

Handbooks, Manuals, Guides Relating to **Research** and Development, D 4.10
Health Care Financing **Research** and Demonstration Series, HE 22.16
Health Care Financing, **Research** Reports, HE 22.19/2
Health Care Financing: Grants for **Research** and Demonstrations, Fiscal Year, HE 22.19/3
Health Insurance Studies: Contract **Research** Series, HE 22.11
Heart **Research** News, FS 2.22/34
High-Temperature Gas-Cooled Reactor Safety Studies for the Division of Reactor Safety **Research** Quarterly Progress Report, E 1.28/7
Higher Education Act Title 2-b, Library **Research** and Demonstration Program, Abstracts, Fiscal Year (date), HE 19.135
Highlights of Progress in Mental Health **Research**, FS 2.22/16
Highlights of Progress in **Research** in Cancer, FS 2.22/14
Highlights of Progress in **Research** on Neurologic Disorders, FS 2.22/12
Highlights of Progress in **Research** on Oral Diseases, FS 2.22/23
Highlights of **Research** Progress in Allergy and Infectious Diseases, FS 2.22/17
Highlights of **Research** Progress in Arthritis and Metabolic Diseases, FS 2.22/21
Highlights of **Research** Progress in General Medical Sciences, FS 2.22/20
Highlights of VA Medical **Research**, VA 1.43/3
Highway **Research** and Development News, Plant Ecology and Esthetics, Progress and Implementation, TD 2.113/2
Highway **Research** and Development Studies using Federal-Aid **Research** and Planning Funds, TD 2.113
Highway **Research** Newsletter, C 37.24
Historical Review, U.S. Army Belvoir **Research** and Development Center, D 101.98
Historical Review, U.S. Army Mobility Equipment **Research** and Development Command, D 101.98
Home Economics **Research** Reports, A 1.87
Hospital Cost and Utilization Project **Research** Notes, HE 20.6514
Housing **Research**, HH 1.9/2
Housing **Research** Division Publications, HH 1.16
HUD **Research**, HH 1.56
HUD **Research** Thesaurus, HH 1.56/2
Hurricane **Research** Progress Reports, C 55.609
Hydrologic Engineering Center: **Research** Notes, D 103.55/4
In-House List of Publications, Aeronautical **Research** Laboratory, D 301.69/4
Index to **Research** Reports and **Research** and Statistics Notes, FS 3.49/2
Index, **Research** Grant Publications and Reports, I 67.13/2
Industrial Environmental **Research** Laboratory: (year) **Research** Review, EP 1.46/5-2
Industrial Environmental **Research** Laboratory: Annual Report, EP 1.46/5
Infectious Disease **Research** Series, HE 20.3262/2
Injury Control **Research** Laboratory: **Research** Report, ICRL-RR (series), HE 20.1116
Institute for Material **Research**, Metallurgy Division, Technical Highlights, Fiscal Year, C 13.1/5-2
Institute for Materials **Research**, Technical Highlights, Fiscal Year, C 13.1/5
Institute for Water Resources: **Research** Reports, D 103.57/5
Interagency Directory, Key Contacts for Planning, Scientific and Technical Exchange Programs, Educational Travel, Students, Teachers, Lecturers, **Research** Scholars, Specialists, S 1.67/3
Interagency Energy-Environment **Research** and Development Program Reports, EP 1.23/8
International Cancer **Research** Data Bank Program, HE 20.3170
International Cancer **Research** Data Bank: Special Listing (series), HE 20.3173
International Marketing Events, Market **Research** Summary, C 61.21
International **Research** Documents, C 3.205/6, C 56.226/2
Intramural **Research**, Annual Report, HE 20.3211/3

ONR {Office of Naval **Research**} Reports, D 210.15

Operational Applications Laboratory, Air Force Cambridge **Research** Center, OAL- TM, D 301.45/37

Ordnance Materials **Research** Offices, Watertown Arsenal, Omro Publications, D 105.13/3

Organic Chemistry: Air Pollution Studies Characterization of Chemical Structures; Synthesis of **Research** Materials, C 13.46

Outer Continental Shelf **Research** Management Advisory Board: Annual Report, I 1.99

Pacific Basin Consortium for Hazardous Waste **Research** Newsletter, E 1.110

Pacific Northwest Environmental **Research** Laboratory: Quarterly Progress Report, EP 1.19

Pacific Northwest **Research** Station: Miscellaneous Publications, A 13.129

Periodic Reports of Agricultural Economics, Economic **Research** Service, Statistical Reporting Service, A 1.99

Personnel Measurement **Research** and Development Center, CS 1.71

Personnel Needs and Training for Biomedical and Behavioral **Research**, HE 20.3036/2

Personnel **Research** and Development Center: Technical Memorandum, CS 1.71/4

Personnel **Research** Highlights, PM 1.57

Personnel **Research** Reports, CS 1.71/7, PM 1.43

Personnel **Research** Series, A 49.9

Perspectives in Reading **Research**, ED 1.317/3

Perspectives on Education Policy **Research**, ED 1.336/2

Pharmacology **Research** Associate Program, HE 20.3461/2

Physical Fitness **Research** Digest, HE 20.110, Pr 37.8:P 56/2 R 31/2

Physical Sciences **Research** Papers, D 301.45/40

Physics **Research**, E 1.99

Policy **Research** Studies, S 1.101/8

Pollutant Identification **Research** Highlights, EP 1.37/3

Population and Reproduction **Research** Abstracts, HE 20.3360

Population **Research** Committee, HE 20.3001/2:P 81

Population **Research** Reports, HE 20.3362

Population **Research** Study Section, HE 20.3001/2:P 81/2

Population Sciences, Index of Biomedical **Research**, HE 20.3362/5

Population Sciences, Inventory of Private Agency Population **Research**, HE 20.3362/2-2

Post Harvest Science and Technology **Research**, A 77.34

Postdoctoral **Research** Associateships, C 13.65

PRB Technical **Research** Notes, D 102.27

PRB Technical **Research** Reports, D 102.27/2

President **Research** Associateships, Post-Doctoral, Tenable at National Bureau of Standards, C 13.47

Prevention **Research** Reports, HE 20.8217/5

Price List, Selective Bibliography of Government **Research** Reports and Translations, C 41.21/3

Primate **Research** Centers Advisory Committee, HE 20.3001/2:P 93

Priorities for **Research**, Extension and Higher Education, A 1.2/10

Proceedings Northwest Shellfish Sanitation **Research** Planning Conferences, EP 2.15

Proceedings Technical Session on Cane Sugar Refining **Research**, A 106.27/2

Production Economics **Research** Branch Publications, A 77.16

Production **Research** Reports, A 1.84

Productivity **Research** Program for Fiscal Year (date), PM 1.38

Professional Opportunities for Women in **Research** and Education, NS 1.61

Program Announcement, Graduate **Research** Fellowship Program, J 28.25

Program in Biomedical and Behavioral Nutrition **Research** and Training, Fiscal Year, HE 20.3036

Program of University **Research** Report Reprinted, TD 1.20/6-2

Program **Research** and Development Announcements, ER 1.30

Program Solicitation, Small Business Innovation **Research** Program, A 94.16

Programs and Plans, Environmental **Research** Laboratories, C 55.615/2

Progress in Candy **Research**, Reports, A 77.109

Progress in Fishery **Research**, I 49.96

Progress in Soil and Water Conservation **Research**, Quarterly Reports, A 77.528

PROMIS {Prosecutor's Management Information System} **Research** Project Publications, J 1.52

PTSD **Research** Quarterly, VA 1.94

Public Health Service International Postdoctorate **Research** Fellowships Awards for Study in the United States, HE 20.3709

Public Health Service Support of Cardiovascular **Research**, Training and Community Programs, FS 2.22/11-2

Public Roads, Journal of Highway **Research**, TD 2.19

Publications Air Force Cambridge **Research** Laboratories, D 301.45/23-3

Publications Air Force Office of Scientific **Research**, D 301.45/19-2

Publications Air University, Documentary **Research** Study, D 301.26/3

Publications Human **Research** Unit, D 101.46

Publications Office of Aerospace **Research**, D 301.69/5

Publications Ordnance Materials **Research** Offices, D 105.13/3

Publications Production Economics **Research** Branch, A 77.16

Publications **Research** and Analysis Branch, Y 3.C 78/3:7, W 2.13

Publications Scientific **Research** and Development Office, Pr 32.413

Publications Weather **Research** Center, W 108.16

Quarterly Progress Reports, Wildlife **Research** Laboratory, Denver, Colorado, I 49.47

Quarterly Report, Government Sponsored and Government Supported **Research**, Social Sciences and Interdisciplinary Areas, NS 1.9

Questionnaire Design in the Cognitive **Research** Laboratory, HE 20.6209:6

Range **Research** Hi-lites, A 13.30/10

Range **Research** Reports, A 13.66/9

RBS **Research** Report, A 109.10

Recent Publications of Range **Research**, Arid South Area, A 77.17/6

Recent **Research** Accomplishments of the Air Force Office of Scientific Research, D 301.45/19-7

Recent **Research** Results, HH 1.84

Recombinant DNA **Research** (series), HE 20.3043

Regional **Research** Bulletins, N.Y. and New England, Y 3.W 89/2:60

Regulations, Rules and Instructions Naval **Research** Office, D 210.6

Regulations, Rules and Instructions **Research** and Special Programs Administration, TD 10.6

Releases, Air **Research** and Development Command, D 301.45/3

REMR Bulletin: News from the Repair, Evaluation, Maintenance and Rehabilitation **Research** Program, D 103.72

Renewable Resources Remote Sensing **Research** Program Report, NAS 1.70

Report of Activities under **Research** and Marketing Act, A 77.8

Report of Agricultural Aviation **Research** Conferences, A 77.2:Av 5

Report of Cooperative **Research** to Improve the Nation's Schools, FS 5.82

Report of Dry Bean **Research** Conference, A 77.15:74

Report of Secretary of Labor to Congress on **Research** and Training Activities, L 1.42

Report of Virgin Islands Agricultural **Research** and Extension Program, A 77.491

Report of Water Resources **Research**, I 19.75

Report on Cooperative **Research** to Improve the Nation's Schools, HE 5.82

Report on Current Hydraulic Laboratory **Research** in U.S., C 13.26

Report on Dry Bean **Research** Conference, A 77.15:74

Report on Scientific **Research** Projects Conducted During Fiscal Year, Y 3.T 25:32

Report on U.S. Government **Research** and Studies in the Field of Arms Control and Disarmament Matters, AC 1.14

Report on USDA Human Nutrition **Research** and Education Activities, A Report to Congress, A 1.1/5

Report to Congress on Ocean Pollution, Monitoring and **Research**, C 55.31/3, C 55.439

Reports from USDA's Economic **Research** Service, A 93.18/3

Reports of Division of **Research** , C 31.131

Reports of Project on **Research** in Agricultural and Industrial Development in Tennessee Valley Region, Y 3.T 25:26

Reports on Reproduction and Population **Research** (series), FS 2.22/13-7

Request for **Research** Grant Applications (series), HE 20.3864

Research (year), Annotated List of **Research** and Demonstration Grants, HE 17.15

Research Abstracts, A 93.39, J 28.24/4, Y 3.N 21/5:14

Research Accomplished, A 13.40/8-4

Research Achievement Sheet, A 77.7

Research and Activities Under Saltonstall-Kennedy Act, Annual Report of Secretary of Interior, I 1.1/2

Research and Demonstrations Brief {Bring **Research** into Effective Focus}, HE 17.18

Research and Demonstrations in Health Care Financing, HE 22.16/2

Research and Development Abstracts of USAEC, RDA (series), Y 3.At 7:51

Research and Development Contracts, Fiscal Year Funds, HE 20.3013/4

Research and Development Division Reports, D 212.12

Research and Development Findings, L 1.56

Research and Development in Industry, NS 1.22:In 2

Research and Development Progress Reports, I 1.88

Research and Development Progress, C 39.202:R 31

Research and Development Projects, C 13.2:R 31/4

Research and Development Report, E 5.10/2, ED 1.328/6

Research and Development Reports, C 21.18, ER 1.11

Research and Development Series, HE 19.218

Research and Development Technical Reports, D 211.13/2

Research and Development Yearbook, E 5.10

Research and Development: Public Awareness/participation Support Plan, Fiscal Year (date), EP 1.90

Research and Discovery, Advances in Behavioral and Social Science Research, HE 20.3036/4

Research and Evaluation Plan, J 28.25/5

Research and Evaluation Report Series, L 37.22/2

Research and Special Studies Progress Report, D 301.26/15

Research and Statistics Legislative Notes, FS 3.28/3

Research and Statistics Letters, FS 3.28

Research and Statistics Notes, HE 3.28/2, HE 22.17

Research and Technology Fiscal Year (date) Annual Report of the Goddard Space Flight Center, NAS 1.65/2

Research and Technology Program Digest, Flash Index, NAS 1.41

Research and Technology Program, Fiscal Year (date), HH 1.88

Research and Technology Program, HH 1.88

Research and Technology Transporter, TD 2.70

Research and Technology Work on Explosives, Explosions, and Flames, T 28.27

Research and Technology, Annual Report of the Langley **Research** Center, NAS 1.65/3

Research and Technology, Annual Report, NAS 1.65

Research and Training Grants and Awards of Public Health Service, FS 2.22/8

Research and Training Opportunities Abroad (year), Educational Programs in Foreign Language and Area Studies, HE 5.99

Research Announcement, NAS 1.53/3

Research Areas, E 1.106

Research at Southeastern Forest Experiment Station, A 13.63/3

Research Attainment Report, Fiscal Year, A 13.82/11

Research Awards Index, HE 20.3013/2

Research Briefs, FS 17.18

Research Bulletins Air Training Command, Human Resources **Research** Center, D 301.36/3

Research Bulletins Federal Emergency Relief Administration, Y 3.F 31/5:28

Research Bulletins Works Progress Administration, Y 3.W 89/2:13

Research Bulletins, J 28.19

Research Demonstration and Evaluation Studies, HE 23.1010

Research Division Maps, C 27.9/13

Research Division Reports Bureau of Apprenticeship and Training, L 23.19

Research Division Reports National Endowment for the Arts, NF 2.12

Research Divison, Quarterly Progress Report, D 103.33/9

Research Documentation List, C 3.232

Research Documents, C 56.248

Research Facilities Center: Annual Report, C 55.601/4

Research for Progress in Education, Annual Report, HE 5.212:12051

Research Grants Index, Fiscal Year, FS 2.22/7-2

Research Grants Index, HE 20.3013/2

Research Grants, Data Book, HE 20.3516/2

Research Grants, Environmental Engineering and Food Protection, FS 2.300/3

Research Grants, Training Awards, Summary Tables, HE 20.3516/3

Research Highlights in Aging, FS 2.22/25

Research Highlights, EP 1.81

Research Highlights, National Institutes of Health, FS 2.22/28

Research Highlights of the NMC Development Division, C 55.197

Research in Action (series), J 28.15/2-2, J 28.24/3-2

Research in Brief, ED 1.322, J 28.24

Research in Education, FS 5.77, HE 5.77, HE 18.10

Research in Forest Products, A 13.27/11

Research in Progress, Calendar Year Metallurgy and Materials Sciences, Mechanics and Aeronautics, Chemistry and Biological Sciences, D 101.52/5-5

Research in Progress, Calendar Year Physics, Electronics, Mathematics, Geosciences, D 101.52/5-4

Research in Progress, Calendar Year, D 101.52/5

Research in the Teaching of Science, FS 5.229:29000, HE 5.229:29000

Research Information Abstracts, A 106.37/2

Research Information Digest, Recent Publications of Southeastern Forest Experiment Station, A 13.63/13

Research Information Letter, A 106.37

Research Institute for the Behavioral and Social Sciences: Technical Papers, D 101.60

Research Issues, HE 20.8214

Research Library Abstracts; Domestic, Y 3.W 89/2:20

Research Library, Recent Acquisitions, FR 1.29, FR 1.29/2

Research Memorandum Air University, Human Resources Report Institute, D 301.26/7

Research Memorandum National Labor Relations Board, LR 1.10

Research Memorandum Social Security Administration, SS 1.28, FS 1.28

Research Monograph Series, HE 20.8216

Research Monographs, Y 3.W 89/2:17, FW 4.35

Research News (press releases), HE 20.3407

Research News, Y 3.N 88:54

Research Notes Forest Service, A 13.79

Research Notes National Center for Health Services **Research**, HE 20.6514

Research Objectives, D 301.69/3

Research on Bird Repellents, Progress Reports, I 49.47/2

Research on U.S. International Trade, C 42.32

Research Opportunities at the Census Bureau, C 3.293

Research Opportunities for Women Scientists and Engineers, NS 1.48/2

Research Papers Forest Service, A 13.78

Research Papers Thrift Supervisor Office, T 71.16

Research Papers, Separates from the Journal of **Research**, C 13.22

Research Participation for Teachers of Science and Mathematics, NS 1.12/3

Research Plan, J 28.25/3

Research Preview, J 28.24/7

Research Product (series), D 101.60/5

Research Profiles, FS 2.22/43

Research Program Plan, J 28.25/3

Research Programs in Aging, FS 2.22/25-2

Research Progress (year), A 13.66/1

Research Progress and Plans of the Weather Bureau, C 30.75

Research Progress in (year), a Report of the Agricultural **Research** Service, A 77.1

Research Project Summaries, National Institute of Mental Health, FS 2.22/16-2

Research Projects Department of State, S 1.96

Research Projects Federal Emergency Management Agency, FEM 1.22

Research Publications of the National Biological Service, I 73.9

Research Relating to Children, Bulletins, HE 19.120

Research Relating to Children, FS 17.211

Research Relating to Children, Inventory of Studies in Progress, FS 3.220

Research Relating to Special Groups of Children, FS 3.220/2, FS 14.114/2

Research Report AFPTRC-TN (series), D 301.36/6

Research Report from the NICHD, HE 20.3364/2

Research Report, A 13.43/8

Research Reports, Y 3.Em 7/3:10/nos

Research Reports Air Force Academy, D 305.14

Research Reports Air Training Command, Human Resources **Research** Center, D 301.36/6

Research Reports Air University, D 301.26/13

Research Reports Arms Control and Disarmament Agency, AC 1.15

Research Reports Army Ballistic Missile Agency, D 105.15

Research Reports Bureau of Federal Credit Unions, FS 3.309

Research Reports Children's Bureau, FS 17.214

Research Reports Cold Regions **Research** and Engineering Laboratory, D 103.33/3

Research Reports Department of the Air Force, D 301.26/7-2

Research Reports Economics, Statistics, and Cooperatives Service, A 105.31

Research Reports Farm Security Administration, A 61.15

Research Reports Forest Products Laboratory, A 13.27/14

Research Reports Injury Control Report Laboratory, FS 2.316

Research Reports Lake Survey Office, D 103.209

Research Reports National Cancer Institute, FS 2.22/32

Research Reports National Environmental **Research** Center, EP 1.21/9

Research Reports National Institue of Justice, J 28.24/3

Research Reports National Institute of Mental Health, HE 20.2420/4, HE 20.8114/2

Research Reports Naval **Research** Laboratory, D 210.22

Research Reports Naval School of Aviation Medicine, D 206.16

Research Reports Office of Information for the Armed Forces, D 2.12

Research Reports Publications Relating to Horticulture, A 77.522

Research Reports Smithsonian Institution, SI 1.37

Research Reports Social Security Administration, FS 3.49, HE 3.49

Research Reports Southwestern Forest and Range Experiment Station, A 13.43/8

Research Reports Supported by Office of Water Resources **Research** Under the Water Resources **Research** Act of 1964 Received During the Period (date), I 1.97/2

Research Reports Walter Reed Army Institute of **Research**, D 104.15

Research Reports Waterways Experiment Station, D 103.24/5

Research Reports, A 96.10

Research Reports, National Environmental **Research** Center, Las Vegas {list}, EP 1.21/9

Research Resources Reporter, HE 20.3013/6

Research Results Utilization, **Research** Project Control System, Status Summary Report, Y 3.N 88:36

Research Review, Air Training Command, Human Resources **Research** Center, D 301.36/4

Research Review, Department of the Air Force, D 301.69/6-2

Research Review, Economic Development Administration, C 46.26

Research Review, Office of Aerospace **Research**, D 301.69/6

Research Series, J 1.44

Research Series (OIMA), C 1.93

Research Studies Defense Civil Preparedness Agency, D 14.17

Research Studies Department of State, S 1.101/12

Research Study (series), NCU 1.21

Research Summary (series), E 1.107, EP 1.89, SBA 1.20/3

Research Surveys, D 110.11

Research Technical Library Biweekly Accession List, PrEx 4.15

Research to Improve Health Services for Mothers and Children, HE 20.5114/2

Research Update, C 13.78, HE 20.3222

Research Updates in Kidney and Urologic Health, HE 20.3324/2

Research Utilization Series, FS 2.22/41

Research Working Papers (series), FHL 1.35

Research, Demonstration, and Evaluation Studies, HE 1.402:R 31

Research, Evaluation, and Demonstration Projects, L 37.22

Research-Reference Accessions, Y 3.R 31:29, A 61.15, A 36.110

Research/Resources Management Reports, I 29.105

Resident **Research** Associateships, Postdoctoral, Tenable and National Bureau of Standards, C 13.47

Resources for Biomedical **Research** and Education, Reports, HE 20.3014

Resources for Freedom, **Research** to the President by President's Materials Policy Commission, Pr 33.15

Resources for Medical **Research** and Education, Reports, HE 20.3014

Resources for Medical **Research**, Reports, FS 2.22/33

Review of Current DHHS, DOE, and EPA **Research** Related to Toxicology, HE 20.3563

Review of Selected U.S. Government **Research** and Development Reports, OTR-(series), C 13.49

Review of the Air Force Materials **Research** and Development Program, D 301.45

Reviews of Data on **Research** and Development, NS 1.11

RIIES **Research** Notes, SI 1.40/3

Rocky Mountain **Research** Station: Bibliographies and Lists of Publications, A 13.151/2

Rocky Mountain **Research** Station Directory, A 13.151/4-2

Rocky Mountain **Research** Station: General Publications, A 13.151

Rocky Mountain **Research** Station: Handbooks, Manuals, Guides, A 13.151/4

Rocky Mountain **Research** Station: Maps, A 13.151/3

Rolla **Research** Center Annual Progress Report FY, I 28.154/2

Rural Development **Research** Reports, A 93.41, A 105.40

Safety **Research** Programs Sponsored by Office of Nuclear Regulatory **Research**, Y 3.N 88:48

Sagamore Army Materials **Research** Conference Proceedings (series), D 101.122

Saline Water **Research** and Development Progress Reports, I 1.88

Saval Ranch **Research** and Evaluation Project, Progress Report, I 53.40

Scientific and Engineering **Research** Facilities at Universities and Colleges, NS 1.53

Scientific and Technical Publications of ESSA **Research** Laboratories, C 52.21/4, C 52.21/4-2

Scientific **Research** Institutes of the USSR, LC 38.10

Sea Water Conversion, Solar **Research** Station (series), I 1.87

Search, Administrative **Research** Bulletins, ARB-(series), VA 1.47

Selected Abstracts of Completed **Research** Studies, Fiscal Year (date), SBA 1.18/4

Selected List of Additions to **Research** Library, FR 1.22/2

Selected Summaries of Water **Research**, I 67.12

Service and Regulatory Announcements Agricultural **Research** Service, A 77.6/2

Services **Research** Branch Notes, HE 20.8216/4

Services **Research** Monograph Series, HE 20.8216/2-2

Services **Research** Monograph Series, National Polydrug Collaborative Project, Treatment Manuals, HE 20.8216/2

Services **Research** Reports, HE 20.8216/3

Sex Roles: a **Research** Bibliography, HE 20.8113:Se 9

Sheets of National Atlas of United States Agricultural **Research** Service, A 77.19

Small Business Innovation **Research** for Fiscal Year, C 1.82

Small Business **Research** Series, SBA 1.20

Smithsonian Opportunities for **Research** and Study in History, Art, Science, SI 1.44

Snake River Birds of Prey **Research** Project, Annual Report, I 53.39

Social and Rehabilitation Service **Research** and Demonstration Projects, FS 17.15

Social **Research** Reports, A 61.10

Soil and Water Conservation **Research** Needs Executive Summary, A 57.73

Soil, Water, Air Sciences **Research** Annual Report, A 106.14

Solar Energy **Research** and Development Report, E 1.38, ER 1.32

Solicitation of the Public Health Service and the Health Care Financing Administration for Small Business Innovation **Research** Contract Proposals, HE 22.31

Solicitation of the Public Health Service for Small Business **Research** (SBIR) Contract Proposals, HE 20.28/2

Southeast Environmental **Research** Laboratory: Quarterly Summary, EP 1.60

Southern Forest **Research**, A 13.40/10

Southern **Research** Station Annual Report, A 13.150/1

Southern **Research** Station: Bibliographies and Lists of Publications, A 13.150/2

Southern **Research** Station Directory of **Research** Scientists, A 13.150/4

Southern **Research** Station: General Publications, A 13.150

Southern **Research** Station: Handbooks, Manuals, Guides, A 13.150/3

Southwest Fisheries Center: **Research** Highlights, Monthly Report, C 55.331

Soviet-Bloc **Research** in Geophysics, Astronomy and Space, Y 3.J 66:14

Special Analysis of Federal **Research** and Development Programs in Budget, PrEx 2.8/a4

Special Announcements Concerning **Research** Reports from Department of Commerce OTS, C 41.28/2

Special Reports Coastal Engineering **Research** Center, D 103.42/6

Special Reports Cold Regions **Research** and Engineering Laboratory, D 103.33/2

Special Reports Construction Engineering **Research** Laboratory, D 103.53/4

Special Reports Soil Conservation Service, Office of **Research**, Sedimentation Section, A 76.215, A 80.2013

Special Resources for **Research** (series), LC 30.31

Special Series Reports of Division of **Research**, C 31.131/2

Sponsored **Research** Programs, J 28.24/2

Sport Fishery and Wildlife **Research**, I 49.1/6

Staff **Research** Studies, TC 1.37

Staff **Research** Study (series), ITC 1.22

Statistical Summary of the Physical **Research** Program as of June 30 (year), Y 3.At 7:2 P 56/2

Statistics **Research** Analysis Microfiles Catalog, HE 3.38/4

Structural **Research** Laboratory Report, I 27.29

Subject Index of Current **Research** Grants and Contracts Administered by the National Heart, Lung, and Blood Institute, HE 20.3212

Summaries of FY (date) **Research** in Nuclear Physics, E 1.19/3

Summaries of **Research** Reported on During Calendar Year (date), D 206.17

Summary of Grants and Contracts Administered by the National Center for Health Services **Research** and Development, HE 20.2116

Summary of Reports Received by Committee on Medical **Research**, Pr 32.413/10

Summaries of **Research**, Naval Dental **Research** Institute, D 206.1/2

Summary of **Research** Projects Monthly Reports, A 57.34

Summary Report of Utilization **Research** and Development, Fiscal Year (date), A 77.2:Ut 3

Summary Technical Report of National Defense **Research** Committee, Pr 32.413/12

Summer **Research** Fellowship Program at the National Institutes of Health, HE 20.3015/2

Surgical **Research** Unit, Brooke Army Medical Center, Fort Sam Houston, Texas: Annual **Research** Progress Report, D 104.22

Surgical **Research** Unit, Brooke Army Medical Center, Fort Sam Houston, Texas: Annual **Research** Progress Report, D 104.22

Survey of Federally-Funded Marine Mammal **Research** and Studies, Y 3.M 33/3:9-2

Survey of Food and Nutrition **Research** in United States, NA 2.8

Symposia Series for Undersea **Research**, NOAA'S Undersea **Research** Program, C 55.29/2

Systems Engineering Group, **Research** and Technology Division, Air Force Systems Command, Wright-Patterson Air Force Base, Ohio, Technical Documentary Report No. SEG TDR, D 301.45/48

Tax Policy **Research** Studies, T 1.44

Technical Highlights Mining **Research**, I 28.151/2

Technical Literature **Research** Series, N 29.17

Technical Notes Ballistics **Research** Laboratories, D 105.10/3

Technical Notes Department of the Air Force Cambridge **Research** Center, D 301.45/4-2

Technical Notes Department of the Air Force Electronics **Research** Directorate, D 301.45/12-2

Technical Notes Department of the Air Force Geophysics **Research** Directorate, D 301.45/16-2

Technical Notes Department of the Air Force Office of Scientific **Research**, D 301.45/18

Technical Plan for the Great Lakes Environmental **Research** Laboratory, C 55.620/2

Technical Report Index, Maritime Administration **Research** and Development, C 39.227:T 22

Technical Reports, Naval **Research** Office London, D 210.16

Technical **Research** Reports Published by Air Force Personnel and Training Center Air **Research** and Development Command, D 301.26/10

Technical Services and **Research**, OSM/TM-(series), I 71.3/2

Technical Services **Research**, OSM-TR-(series), I 71.3

Telecommunication Policy, **Research** and Development, PrEx 7.14/5

Telecommunications **Research** and Engineering Reports, C 1.60

Toward Interagency Coordination, Federal **Research** and Development on Adolescence, HE 23.1013

Toward Interagency Coordination: Federal **Research** and Development on Early Childhood, HE 23.1013/2

Toxicology **Research** Projects Directory, HE 1.48

Traffic Safety Evaluation **Research** Review, TD 8.18/2

Trainees and Fellows Supported by the National Institute of Dental **Research** and Trained During Fiscal Year, HE 20.3402:T 68, HE 20.3410

Transactions of **Research** Conferences in Pulmonary Diseases, VA 1.40/2

Transactions of **Research** Conferences on Cooperative Chemotherapy Studies in Psychiatry and **Research** Approaches to Mental Illness, VA 1.41

Transportation **Research** and Development Command: **Research** Technical Memorandums, D 117.8

Transportation **Research** Record (series), NA 1.10

Treatment **Research** Monograph (series), HE 20.8217/2

Treatment **Research** Notes, HE 20.8217/4

Treatment **Research** Reports, HE 20.8217/3

U.S. Air Force Plan for Defense **Research** Sciences, D 301.45/19-5

U.S. Army **Research** and Development Program Guide, D 101.52/4

U.S. Dairy Forage **Research** Center, A 77.37

U.S. Government **Research**, C 41.21, C 51.9/3

U.S. Naval Radiological Defense Laboratory, **Research** and Development Report USNRDL (series), D 211.13

Union Catalog, Selected List of Unlocated **Research** Books, LC 18.7

United States Arctic **Research** Plan, NS 1.51

United States Army Medical **Research** Institute of Infectious Disease: Annual Progress Report, D 104.27

United States Army **Research** and Development Series, D 101.52

United States Employment Service Test **Research** Reports, L 7.69

University Centers of Foreign Affairs **Research**, Selective Directory, S 1.2:Un 3

University **Research**: Summary of Awards, Program of University **Research**, TD 1.45

USAPRO Technical **Research** Notes, D 101.60

USAPRO Technical **Research** Reports, D 101.60/2

USAREC **Research** Memorandums (numbered), D 101.106/2

USAREC **Research** Notes (series), D 101.106

USC/FAR Consolidated Plan for Foreign Affairs **Research**, PrEx 3.12

Uses of **Research** Sponsored by the Administration on Aging, Case Studies, HE 23.3012

Uses Test **Research** Reports (series), L 37.312

USGS **Research** on Energy Resources, Program and Abstracts, I 19.4/5, I 19.4/7

USRL **Research** Reports, D 210.22

Utilization **Research** Reports, A 1.88

VA Health Services **Research** & Development Service Progress Reports, VA 1.1/7

VA Medical **Research** Conference Abstracts, VA 1.43/2

VA Medical **Research** Service, Annual Report, VA 1.1/4

Vision **Research** Program Committee, HE 20.3001/2:V 82/3

Vocational Rehabilitation Administration **Research** and Demonstration Projects, FS 13.202:R 31/2

Walter Reed Army Institute of **Research**, **Research** Reports WRAIR (series), D 104.15

Walter Reed Army Medical Center, Army Prosthetics **Research** Laboratory, Technical Reports, D 104.15/2

Water Pollution Control **Research** and Training Grants, FS 2.64/7, I 67.13

Water Pollution Control **Research** Series, EP 1.16, EP 2.10

Water Reactor Safety **Research**, Buff Book I, Y 3.N 88:18

Water **Research** Capsule Report (series), I 1.103

Water Resources **Research** Catalog, I 1.94

Water Resources **Research** Program of the U.S. Geological Survey, I 19.42/4-3

Welfare **Research** Researchs, FS 14.14

Western Environmental **Research** Laboratory: Annual Report, EP 1.14/2

Western Environmental **Research** Laboratory: Monthly Activities Report, EP 1.14

What's New in **Research**, A 13.62/13

Wildlife **Research** and Management Leaflets, A 5.11

Wildlife **Research** Bulletins, I 49.19

Wildlife **Research** Center, Denver, Colorado: Annual Report, I 49.47/5

Wildlife **Research** Laboratory: Technical Notes, I 49.47/3

Wildlife **Research** Reports, I 49.47/4

Working Papers Environmental Protection Agency, Pacific Northwest Environmental **Research** Laboratory, EP 1.37/2

Researchers

Archives II **Researcher** Bulletin, AE 1.123

Graduate Student **Researchers** Program, NAS 1.42/2

United States Fisheries Systems and Social Sciences: a Bibliography of Work and Directory of **Researchers**, C 55.332:So 1

Reservation

Hot Springs **Reservation** Commission, Annual Reports, I 1.15

Hot Springs **Reservation** Improvement Office, Annual Reports, I 1.16

Cultural **Resource** Management Series, I 70.11/2
Cultural **Resource** Management Studies, I 29.86, I 70.11
Cultural **Resource** Series (Utah), I 53.22/2
Cultural **Resources** Information Series, I 53.22/11
Current Information **Resource** Requirements of the Federal Government, PM 1.56
Current Information Technology **Resources** Requirements of the Federal Government, PrEx 2.12/5
Diplomatic Security Training **Resources**, etc. Fiscal Year, S 1.139/2
Economic **Resource** Impact Statement 305th Air Refueling Wing, Grissom Air Force Base, Indiana, D 301.105/8
Economic **Resource** Impact Statement Andrews Air Force Base, D 301.105/7
Economic **Resource** Impact Statement George Air Force Base, California, D 301.105/4
Economic **Resource** Impact Statement Grand Forks Air Force Base, D 301.105/2
Economic **Resource** Impact Statement Holloman AFB, New Mexico, D 301.105/6
Economic **Resource** Impact Statement Kelly Air Force Base, D 301.105/3
Economic **Resource** Impact Statement K. I. Sawyer AFB, D 301.105
Economic **Resource** Impact Statement Luke Air Force Base, New Mexico, D 301.105/5
EMS {Emergency Medical Services} **Resource** Exchange Bulletin, FEM 1.110/3
Environmental/**Resource** Assessment and Information, C 55.233
Environmental/**Resource** Assessment and Information, U.S. Energy/Climate Section, C 55.233/2
Federal Reclamation Projects, Water and Land **Resource** Accomplishments, I 27.55
Forest **Resource** Reports, A 13.50
Forest-Gram South, Dispatch of Current Technical Information for Direct Use by Practicing Forest **Resource** Manager in the South, A 13.89
Higher Education and the Handicapped, **Resource** Directory, ED 1.32/2
Historic **Resource** Studies, I 29.58/3
Horizons, Indian Mineral **Resource**, I 20.67
Impaired Professionals' **Resource** Guide, HE 20.9113
Information from Health **Resource** Center, ED 1.22
Long Term **Resource** Monitoring Program, Program Report (series), I 49.109
Long Term **Resource** Monitoring Program, Technical Report (series), I 49.109/4
Midwest Region: Research/**Resources** Management Reports, I 29.105/2
Mineral Investigations **Resource** Maps, I 19.90
National Blood **Resource** Program Advisory Committee, HE 20.3001/2:B 62/2
Natural **Resource** Development Program Annual Report, SBA 1.48
National Trends in Electric Energy **Resource** Use, E 3.11/17
National Uranium **Resource** Evaluation: Annual Activity Report, E 1.51
Navajo Nation & Regional Areas **Resource** Directory, HE 20.310/3
Northeastern **Resource** Bulletins, A 13.42/26
Park Science, **Resource** Management Bulletin, I 29.3/4
Program and **Resource** Digest, J 1.86
Report of the FCCSET Committee on Education and Human **Resources**, PrEx 8.111
Research **Resources** Reports (separates), HE 20.3013/6 a
Resource and Potential Reclamation Evaluation Reports, I 53.31
Resource Applications, E 1.30
Resource Bulletins, A 13.80
Resource Conservation and Development Plans, A 57.62
Resource Conservation Development Plan, A 57.65
Resource Decisions in the National Forests of the Eastern Region, A 13.90
Resource Directory, HE 20.3660/2
Resource Exchange Bulletin, FEM 1.110
Resource Guide for Health Science Students: Occupational and Environmental Health, HE 20.7108:H 34/2
Resource Inventory Notes, I 53.24
Resource Management Monographs, D 1.44

Resource Management Quarterly Information Summary, C 55.9/3
Resource Management, D 101.89
Resource Papers in Administrative Law, Y 3.Ad 6:11
Resource Publications, I 49.66
Resource Reports, A 13.80/2, C 55.317
Resource Status Reports, I 49.67
Rural **Resource** Leaflets, A 21.25/2
Social Service **Resource** Directories, J 16.7
Studies in Cultural **Resource** Management, A 13.101/2

Resources
Activities of Water **Resources** Division, California District, I 19.55
Agricultural **Resources**, Cropland, Water, and Conservation, A 93.47/2
Air Force Human **Resources** Laboratory: Annual Report, D 301.45/27-5
Air **Resources** Atmospheric Turbulence and Diffusion Laboratory: Annual Report, C 55.621
Air University, Human **Resources** Research Institute, Research Memorandum, D 301.26/7
Alaska **Resources** Development Studies, I 68.9
Animal **Resources** Advisory Committee, HE 20.3001/2:An 5
Announcement of Water-**Resources** Reports Released for Public Inspection, I 19.48
Annual Earth **Resources** Program Review, NAS 1.47
Annual Report on Alaska's Mineral **Resources**, I 19.4/4
Annual Report on Sharing Medical **Resources**, Y 4.V 64/4:M 46/5
Annual Report, Title 2, Elementary and Secondary Education Act of 1965, School Library **Resources**, Textbooks, and Other Instructional Materials, FS 5.220:20108, HE 5.220:20108
Application for Grants under Strengthening Research Library **Resources** Program, ED 1.53
Biotechnology **Resources**, HE 20.3002:B 52/4
Blood Diseases and **Resources** Advisory Committee, HE 20.3001/2:B 62
Coal **Resources** of the United States, I 19.3:1412
Combined Production and **Resources** Board, United States, Great Britain, and Canada, Y 3.C 73/3
Compilation of Federal Laws Relating to Conservation and Development of Our Nation's Fish and Wildlife **Resources**, Environmental Quality, and Oceanography, Y 4.M 53:L 44/2
Cooperative Water **Resources**, Research and Training, I 1.1/4
Cultural **Resources** Management Bulletin, I 29.86/2
Cultural **Resources** Overview (series), A 13.101
Cultural **Resources** Publications (series), I 53.22/4
Cultural **Resources** Reports, I 29.86/3
Cultural **Resources** Series, I 53.22
Cultural **Resources** Series (Nevada), I 53.22/3
Cultural **Resources** Series Arizona, I 53.22/8
Cultural **Resources** Series Montana, I 53.22/5
Cultural **Resources** Series New Mexico, I 53.22/9
Cultural **Resources** Series Oregon, I 53.22/10
Cultural **Resources** Series Utah, I 53.22/2
Cultural **Resources** Series Wyoming, I 53.22/7
Directory of Information **Resources** in Agriculture and Biology, A 17.2:D 62
Directory of Information **Resources** in the United States, LC 1.31
Directory of Outpatient Psychiatric Clinics, Psychiatric Day-Night Services and Other Mental Health **Resources** in the United States and Territories, FS 2.22/38-4
Directory of **Resources** for Cultural and Educational Exchanges and International Communication, ICA 1.12
Earth **Resources** Satellite Data Applications Series, NAS 1.64
Earth **Resources** Technology Satellite: Standard Catalog, NAS 1.488
Earth **Resources**, A Continuing Bibliography with Indexes, NAS 1.21:7041
Economic **Resources** Impact Statements, D 103.105
ERIC (Educational **Resources** Information Center) Annual Report, ED 1.301/2

Evaluation Report, Water **Resources** Appraisal for Hydroelectric Licensing, FP 1.31
Exploration and Conservation of Natural **Resources**, C 41.45
Farm **Resources** and Facilities Research Advisory Committee Report, A 1.103
Federal Water **Resources** Research Program for Fiscal Year, PrEx 8.9
Film **Resources** on Japan, HE 5.2:J 27
Fishery **Resources**, Fiscal Year (date), I 49.87
Foreign Affairs Research, a Directory of Government **Resources**, S 1.2:F 76a/4
Health **Resources** News, HE 20.6014
Health **Resources** Opportunity Office: Annual Report, HE 20.6001/3
Health **Resources** Statistics, HE 20.6212
Health **Resources** Studies, HE 20.6012
Higher Education Act, Title II-C, FY Abstracts Strengthening Library **Resources** Program, ED 1.18
Highlights of Natural **Resources** Management, I 29.119
HRCD, Human **Resources** Compact Disk, PM 1.59/2
Human **Resources**, PrEx 7.21/9
Hydroelectric Power **Resources** of the United States, Developed and Undeveloped, FP 1.123
Information **Resources** Directory, EP 1.12/3
Information **Resources** Management Handbook (series), GS 12.17
Information **Resources** Management Newsletter, GS 12.17/3
Information **Resources** Management Plan (series), TD 4.33/6
Institute for Water **Resources**: Research Reports, D 103.57/5
Integrated **Resources** and Services for {various subjects}, C 1.77
Interagency Technical Committee on Heart, Blood Vessel, Lung, and Blood Diseases; and Blood **Resources**, HE 20.3001/2:H 35
Inventory of Water **Resources**, Y 3.N 21/12:10
Land and Natural **Resources** Division Journal, J 30.9
Library **Resources** for the Blind and Physically Handicapped, LC 19.16
Life Sciences: Agrotechnology and Food **Resources**, PrEx 7.22/3
Manned Space Flight **Resources** Summary, Budget Estimates, NAS 1.54
Manpower Report of the President and Report on Manpower Requirements, **Resources**, Utilization, and Training by the U.S. Department of Labor, L 1.42/2
Mental Health **Resources** in the Greater Washington Area, HE 20.8119
Mineral **Resources** Newsletter, I 19.115/3
Mineral **Resources** of the United States, I 19.8
Mineral **Resources** West of Rocky Mountains, T 28.6
Monographs and Data for Health **Resources** Planning Series, HE 20.6110
NASA Earth **Resources** Survey Program, C 51.9/11
National Health **Resources** Advisory Committee: Reports of Meetings, GS 13.9
National Patterns of Science and Technology **Resources**, NS 1.22/2
National **Resources** Conference Conducted by Industrial College of Armed Forces, D 5.9
Natural **Resources**, C 51.9/25
Natural **Resources** of {state}, I 1.91
Natural **Resources** Reports, I 29.89
Natural **Resources** Section Preliminary Studies, W 1.80/2
Natural **Resources** Section Reports, W 1.80
Natural **Resources** Section Weekly Summary, D 102.12
Natural **Resources**, A Selection of Bibliographies, D 103.50:3
Office of Administration and **Resources** Management, Research Triangle Park, N.C.: Telephone Directory, EP 1.12/2
Office of Energy **Resources** Yearbook, E 5.16
Operations of Office of Private **Resources**, S 18.1/2
Pacific Northwest Water **Resources** Summary, I 19.46
Posters Health **Resources** and Services Administration, HE 20.9012
Prevention **Resources** Series, HE 20.8224
Program of Water **Resources** Division, Texas District, and Summary of District Activities, Fiscal Year, I 19.55/2

Radiological Health Training **Resources** Catalog, HE 20.4610

Regulations, Rules and Instructions Office of Information **Resources** Management, GS 12.15

Renewable **Resources** Remote Sensing Research Program Report, NAS 1.70

Report of the Senate Committee on Labor and Human **Resources** Presenting its View and Estimates Pursuant to the Congressional Budget Act, Y 4.L 11/4:C 76

Report of Water **Resources** Research, I 19.75

Report to the Committee on the Budget Views and Estimates of the Committee on Natural **Resources**, Y 4.R 31/3-11

Research Bulletins Air Training Command, Human **Resources** Research Center, D 301.36/3

Research Memorandum Air University, Human **Resources** Report Institute, D 301.26/7

Research Reports Air Training Command, Human **Resources** Research Center, D 301.36/6

Research Reports Supported by Office of Water **Resources** Research Under the Water **Resources** Research Act of 1964 Received During the Period (date), I 1.97/2

Research **Resources** Reporter, HE 20.3013/6

Research Review, Air Training Command, Human **Resources** Research Center, D 301.36/4

Research/**Resources** Management Reports, I 29.105

Resources (series), HE 20.8218

Resources Analysis Memos, HE 20.3014/2

Resources and Staffing, HE 20.4102:R 31

Resources Atlas Project: Thailand, Atlas, D 103.49

Resources Evaluation Newsletter, A 13.69/14

Resources for Biomedical Research and Education, Reports, HE 20.3014

Resources for Change, a Guide to Projects, HE 19.9:R 31

Resources for Freedom, Research to the President by President's Materials Policy Commission, Pr 33.15

Resources for Medical Research and Education, Reports, HE 20.3014

Resources for Medical Research, Reports, FS 2.22/33

Resources in Education, ED 1.11, HE 19.210

Resources in Women's Educational Equality, ED 1.17/2, HE 19.128:W 84/2

Resources Management Plan Annual Update, I 53.50

Reviews of Data on Science **Resources**, NS 1.11/2

Science **Resources** Studies Highlights, NS 1.31

Selected Water **Resources** Abstracts, I 1.94/2

Soil and Water Conservation District **Resources** Inventories (series), A 57.38/2

Southwest Cultural **Resources** Center: Professional Papers, I 29.116

Special **Resources** for Research (series), LC 30.31

State **Resources** and Services for Alcohol and Drug Abuse Problems, HE 20.8319

Status Report on Water and Power **Resources** Service Programs Within (various States), I 27.74

Supreme Commander for Allied Powers: Natural **Resources** Section Reports, D 102.20

Surveys of Science **Resources** Series, NS 1.22

Title II, Elementary and Secondary Education Act of 1965, School Library **Resources**, Textbooks and Other Instructional Materials, Annual Report, HE 5.79/2

Topical Briefs: Fish and Wildlife **Resources** and Electric Power Generation, I 49.78

United States Mineral **Resources**, I 19.16:820

USGS Research on Energy **Resources**, Program and Abstracts, I 19.4/5

USGS Research on Mineral **Resources**, Program and Abstracts, I 19.4/7

USIA Strategic Information **Resources** Management (IRM) Plan, IA 1.33

Water and Related Land **Resources** {by area}, A 1.105

Water **Resources** Activities in Illinois, I 19.55/5

Water **Resources** Bulletins, I 19.3/3

Water **Resources** Data for {State}, I 19.53/2

Water **Resources** Data, I 19.15/6

Water **Resources** Development by Army Corps of Engineers in {State}, D 103.35

Water **Resources** Development by Corps of Engineers by Area, D 103.35

Water **Resources** Development in Delaware in (year), D 103.35/8

Water **Resources** Development in District of Columbia, D 103.35/51

Water **Resources** Development in Idaho, D 103.35/12

Water **Resources** Development in Illinois, D 103.35/13

Water **Resources** Development in Indiana, D 103.35/14

Water **Resources** Development in Iowa, D 103.35/15

Water **Resources** Development in Kentucky, D 103.35/17

Water **Resources** Development in Maryland, D 103.35/20

Water **Resources** Development in Massachusetts, D 103.35/21

Water **Resources** Development in Michigan, D 103.35/22

Water **Resources** Development in Minnesota, D 103.35/23

Water **Resources** Development in Missouri, D 103.35/25

Water **Resources** Development in Nevada, D 103.35/28

Water **Resources** Development in New Jersey (year), D 103.35/30

Water **Resources** Development in New Mexico, D 103.35/31

Water **Resources** Development in New York, D 103.35/32

Water **Resources** Development in North Carolina, D 103.35/33

Water **Resources** Development in North Dakota, D 103.35/34

Water **Resources** Development in Ohio, D 103.35/35

Water **Resources** Development in South Carolina, D 103.35/40

Water **Resources** Development in Virginia, D 103.35/46

Water **Resources** Development in West Virginia, D 103.35/48

Water **Resources** Development in Wisconsin, D 103.35/49

Water **Resources** Development in {State}, D 103.35, D 103.35/53

Water **Resources** Divisions Bulletin of Training, I 19.3/4

Water **Resources** Investigations (numbered), I 19.42/4

Water **Resources** Investigations Folders, I 19.94

Water **Resources** Investigations, I 19.42/4-2

Water **Resources** Reports, WR- (series), Y 3.T 25:59

Water **Resources** Research Catalog, I 1.94

Water **Resources** Research Program of the U.S. Geological Survey, I 19.42/4-3

Water **Resources** Review, Annual Summary, Water Year, I 19.42/2

Water **Resources** Review, I 19.42

Water **Resources** Scientific Information Center, WRSIC- (series), I 1.97

Water **Resources** Teaching Guide (series), I 27.76

Water **Resources**/Water Quality, Y 3.T 25:59-2

Water-**Resources** Bulletins, I 19.3/3

Weekly Abstracts: NASA Earth **Resources** Survey Program, C 51.9/11

Weekly Runoff Report, Pacific Northwest Water **Resources**, I 19.46/2

Weekly Summary of Federal Legislation Relating to National **Resources** Committee, Activities Bulletins, Y 3.N 21/12:15

Respiratory

Influenza-**Respiratory** Disease Surveillance, Reports, HE 20.2309/10

Response

CERCLIS (Comprehensive Environmental **Response** Compensation, and Liability Information System), EP 1.104/5

Challenge-**Response** {papers}, HH 1.62

Disaster **Response** and Recovery, FEM 1.211

Response, Report on Actions for a Better Environment, A 21.30

Superfund Emergency **Response** Actions, A Summary of Federally-Funded Removals, Annual Report, EP 1.89/5

Responsibilities

Responsibilities and Organization, Y 10.20

Task Force on Women's Rights and **Responsibilities**, Pr 37.8:W 84

Your Social Security Rights & **Responsibilities**, Retirement & Survivors Benefits, HE 3.88/2, HE 3.93

Your Social Security Rights and **Responsibilities**, Disability Benefits, HE 3.88

Rest

Leather Manufacturers **Rest** in Foreign Markets, C 18.112

Restaurant

Financial Audit, House **Restaurant** Revolving Fund's Financial Statements, GA 1.13/8

Restaurants

Financial Audit, Senate **Restaurants** Revolving Fund for Fiscal Years, GA 1.13/8-2

Restoration

Defense Environmental **Restoration** Program: Annual Report to Congress, D 1.97

Federal Aid in Fish and Wildlife **Restoration**, I 49.29/3

Statistical Summary for Fish and Wildlife **Restoration**, I 49.29/4

Wildlife Conservation and **Restoration** Notes, A 43.5/20

Restored

Involvement for Community Organizations with Employment of the Mentally **Restored**, PrEx 1.10/4-3

Restraint

Statement of Voluntary Credit **Restraint** Committee, FR 1.35

Results

Agricultural Research **Results**, A 106.13

Agricultural Research **Results**, ARR (series), A 106.12, A 77.32

Bureau of Mines Research (year), Summary of Significant **Results** in Mining Metallurgy and Energy, I 28.115

Consumer Expenditure Survey **Results**, L 2.120/2-5

Cotton Fiber and Processing Test **Results**, A 88.11/17

Search: **Results** of Regional Cotton Variety Tests by Cooperating Agricultural Experiment Stations, A 77.15:34

Dissemination of Research **Results** {on Poultry and Egg Marketing Subjects}, A 82.75, A 88.15/8

Energy Research and Technology: Abstracts of NSF Research **Results**, NS 1.13/3

Exploratory Research and Problem Assessment: Abstracts of NSF Research **Results**, NS 1.13/2

National Survey **Results** on Drug Use from the Monitoring the Future Study, HE 20.3968

Program **Results** Inventory, J 1.51

Public Use Data Tape Documentation Chest X-Ray, Pulmonary Diffusion, and Tuberculin Test **Results** Ages 25-74, HE 20.6226/5-2

Recent Research **Results**, HH 1.84

Research **Results** Utilization, Research Project Control System, Status Summary Report, Y 3.N 88:36

Results of Observations made at C. & G. Survey Magnetic Observatories, C 4.16

Results of Regional Cotton Variety Tests by Cooperating Agricultural Experiment Stations, A 77.15:34

Results of Services Conference, C 61.56

Results under the Small Business Innovation Development Act of 1982, SBA 1.1/4

Summary of Cotton Fiber and Processing Test **Results**, Crop of (year), A 88.11/17-2

Summary of Loan Activity and Operating **Results** through (date) Issued by CCC, A 82.83/2

Tabulated **Results** of Discharge Measurements, W 31.6

Unemployment Insurance Quality Appraisal **Results**, L 37.213

Resume

Packers and Stockyards **Resume**, A 88.16/5-2, A 96.9

Resume of U.S. Civil Air Carrier and General Aviation Aircraft Accidents, Calendar Year, C 31.244

Retail

Advance Monthly **Retail** Sales Report, C 3.138/4

Annual Benchmark Report for **Retail** Trade, C 138/3-8

Annual **Retail** Trade Report, C 3.138/3-2

Average Semi-Monthly **Retail** Meat Prices at New York Chicago and Kansas City, A 36.179

Bulletins for **Retail** Merchants, Y 3.F 73:17

Census of Business; 1939, **Retail** Trade (by States), C 3.940-23

Census of Business; 1939, **Retail** Trade (Miscellaneous), C 3.940-22

Census of Business; 1939, **Retail** Trade, Commodity Sales (by Commodities), C 3.940-24

Census of Business; **Retail** Trade Bulletins (by States), C 3.202/2

Census of Distribution; **Retail** Distribution (by States), C 3.37/22

Census of Distribution; **Retail** Distribution Trade Series, C 3.37/39

Census of **Retail** Trade; Area Statistics (series), C 56.251/2

Census of **Retail** Trade; Final Volumes, C 56.251/6, C 3.255/6

Census of **Retail** Trade; General Publications, C 3.255, C 56.251

Census of **Retail** Trade; Geographic Area Series, C 225/8-2

Census of **Retail** Trade; Geographic Area Statistics, C 3.255/2

Census of **Retail** Trade; Geographic Area Statistics, Advance Reports, C 3.255/2-2

Census of **Retail** Trade; Geographic Area - Summary, C 225/8

Census of **Retail** Trade; Industry Series, C 3.225/3-3

Census of **Retail** Trade; Major **Retail** Centers in Standard Metropolitan Statistical Areas, RC (series), C 56.251/5

Census of **Retail** Trade; Major **Retail** Centers in Standard Metropolitan Statistical Areas, RC (series), C 56.251/5

Census of **Retail** Trade; Major **Retail** Centers Statistics, C 3.255/5

Census of **Retail** Trade Nonemployer Statistics Series, C 3.255/7

Census of **Retail** Trade; Preliminary Area Reports, C 56.251/7

Census of **Retail** Trade; Preliminary Report Industry Series, C 3.255/3-2

Census of **Retail** Trade; **Retail** Merchandise Lines Service, C 56.251/4, C 3.255/4

Census of **Retail** Trade; Subject Reports, C 56.251/3, C 3.255/3

Combined Annual and Revised Monthly **Retail** Trade, C 3.138/3-7

Consumer Purchases of Fruits and Juices by Regions and **Retail** Outlets, A 36.171/2

Current Business Reports; Advance Monthly **Retail** Sales, CB (series), C 56.219/6

Current Business Reports; Monthly **Retail** Trade, Sales and Accounts Receivable, BR (series), C 56.219/4

Current Business Reports; **Retail** Trade, C 56.219/4-2

Current Business Reports; Weekly **Retail** Sales, CB (series), C 56.219/7

Current **Retail** Trade Reports, C 3.138

Estimated **Retail** Food Prices by Cities, L 2.37

Farm-**Retail** Price Spreads, A 36.138

Indexes of **Retail** Prices on Meats in Large Cities, L 2.39/2

Monthly **Retail** Sales, C 3.138/3-3

Monthly **Retail** Trade Report, C 3.138/3

Petroleum Market Shares, Report on Sales of **Retail** Gasoline, E 3.13/2

Quarterly Financial Report, United States **Retail** and Wholesale Corporations, FT 1.20

Retail Bulletins, Y 3.N 21/8:12

Retail Food Price Index, L 2.39

Retail Food Price Index, Washington, D.C., Area, L 2.39/3

Retail Furniture Report, FR 1.41

Retail Gasoline Prices, E 3.13/9

Retail Installment Credit and Furniture and Household Appliance Stores, FR 1.34/2

Retail Prices and Indexes of Fuels and Electricity, L 2.40

Retail Prices and Indexes of Fuels and Utilities, L 2.40

Retail Prices on Food, L 2.3

Retail Prices, L 2.6/a 2

Retail Sales, Independent Stores, Summary for States, C 3.138

Retail Stores Section Flyers, Y 3.F 73:16

Retail Trade (by States), C 3.940-10

Retail Trade Bulletins, C 3.202/2

Retail Trade Report East North Central, C 3.176

Retail Trade Report East South Central, C 3.177

Retail Trade Report Middle Atlantic Region, C 3.174

Retail Trade Report Mountain Region, C 3.180

Retail Trade Report New England, C 3.173

Retail Trade Report Pacific Region, C 3.181

Retail Trade Report South Atlantic Region, C 3.175

Retail Trade Report United States Summary, C 3.138/2

Retail Trade Report West North Central, C 3.178

Retail Trade Report West South Central, C 3.179

Retail, Wholesale, Service Trades, Subject Bulletin, RWS (series), C 3.202/9

Revised Monthly **Retail** Sales in Inventories, C 3.138/3-3

Specifications for **Retail** Prices, L 2.65

Supplies of Important Foods in **Retail** Stores, L 2.67

Weekly **Retail** Sales Report, C 3.138/5

World **Retail** Prices and Taxes on Gasoline, Kerosene, and Motor Lubricating Oils, I 28.44

Retailers

Digests for **Retailers**, Pr 32.4218

OPA Food Guide for **Retailers**, Pr 32.4241

Retailers' Bulletins, Pr 32.4221

Retailing

Information for Business Executives {and} Firms with **Retailing** and Wholesale Interests, Y 3.P 93/4:9

Retardation

Fiscal Year Appropriations for Mental **Retardation** Programs of the Department of Health, Education, and Welfare, FS 1.23/2

Mental **Retardation** Abstracts, FS 2.22/52, HE 17.113

Mental **Retardation** Activities of the Department of Health, Education, and Welfare, FS 1.23/5, HE 1.23/5

Mental **Retardation** and Development Disabilities Abstracts, HE 1.49

Mental **Retardation** and the Law, a Report on Status of Current Court Cases, HE 23.110

Mental **Retardation** and the Law, a Report on the Status of Current Court Cases, HE 1.51

Mental **Retardation** Grants, Fiscal Year, HE 1.23/3

Mental **Retardation** Reports, FS 1.23/4, HE 1.23/4

Mental **Retardation** Research Committee, HE 20.3001/2:M 52

Mental **Retardation** Source Book, HE 1.23/6

Message from the Presidents's Committee on Mental **Retardation**, Pr 36.8:M 52/M/56

Proposed Mental **Retardation** Programs, HE 1.23

Retarded

Hospital and Medical Facilities Series, Facilities for the Mentally **Retarded**, FS 2.74/5

Retention

Guide to Record **Retention** Requirements, GS 4.107/a:R 245

Retired

Navy Guide for **Retired** Personnel and Their Families, D 208.26

Listing of Awardee Names, **Retired Awards**, E 1.35/2-6

Register of **Retired** Commissioned and Warrant Officers, Regular and Reserve, of the United States Navy and Marine Corps, D 208.12/3

Reports of Construction Permits **Retired** to Closed Files, etc., CC 1.29

Retiree

Retiree Newsletter, TD 5.45

Retirees

Shift Colors, the Newsletter for Navy **Retirees**, D 208.12/3-2

Retirement

Board of Actuaries of the Civil Service **Retirement** System Annual Report, Y 4.P 84/10:R 31/30

Current Salary Schedules of Federal Officers and Employees Together with a History of Salary and **Retirement** Annuity Adjustments, Y 4.P 84/10-15

Dates of **Retirement** of Officers of Corps of Engineers, W 7.17

Digest of Selected Federal **Retirement** Systems, CS 1.29/4

Employee **Retirement** Income Security Act, Report to Congress, L 1.76, L 40.15

Enrollment Information Guide and Plan Comparison Chart **Retirement** Systems Participating in the Federal Employees Health Benefits Program, PM 1.8/4

Finances of Employee-**Retirement** Systems of State and Local Governments in (year), C 56.209, C 3.191/2

GR 68 Quarterly Reports on Holdings of **Retirement** Systems, C 3.242

Holdings of Selected Public Employee **Retirement** Systems, GR (series), C 56.224, C 3.242

Laws and Executive Orders Relating to Compensation, Pension, Emergency Officers' **Retirement**, etc., VA 1.14

Laws relating to Civil Service **Retirement**, Y 1.2:R 31/2

Legal Opinions, Rulings in Administration of Railroad **Retirement** Act and Railroad Unemployment Insurance Act, RR 1.12

Monthly Benefit Statistics; Railroad **Retirement** and Unemployment Insurance Programs, RR 1.13

Quarterly Reports on Holdings of **Retirement** Systems, C 3.242

Railroad **Retirement** and Unemployment Insurance Act, As Amended {August 29, 1935}, Y 1.2:R 13

Retirement and Survivors Insurance Semiannual Analysis, HE 3.57/2

Retirement Circulars, CS 1.29

Retirement Reports, Fiscal Yr., C.S. **Retirement** Act, Panama Canal Annuity Act, CS 1.29/2

Retirement, CS 1.41/4:831-1

SSA Program Circulars **Retirement** and Survivors Insurance, HE 3.4/5

Statistical Summary, Railroad **Retirement** Board Operations, RR 1.11

TVA **Retirement** System: Annual Report, Y 3.T 25:1-14

United States Individual **Retirement** Bonds, Tables of Redemption Values for All Denomination Bonds, T 63.209/8

United States **Retirement** Plan Bonds, Tables of Redemption Values for All Denomination Bonds, T 63.209/8-2

When You Get Social Security **Retirement** or Survivors Benefits, What You Need to Know, SSA 1.20

Your Social Security Rights & Responsibilities, **Retirement** & Survivors Benefits, HE 3.88/2, HE 3.93

Retirements

Expenditures for Plant and Equipment, Book Value of Fixed Assets, Rental Payments for Buildings and Equipment, Depreciation and **Retirements**, C 3.24/9-8

Retreat

National Sea Grant Program Annual **Retreat** Report, C 55.38/2

Retrieval

Bibliographies of Technical Reports Information **Retrieval** Lists, FAA 1.10/2

Documents **Retrieval** Index, J 28.22

ENTREZ: Document **Retrieval** System, HE 20.3624

Legal Precedent **Retrieval** System, T 17.6/3-7

National Criminal Justice Reference Service: Document **Retrieval** Index, J 26.26

National Criminal Justice: Document **Retrieval** Index, J 1.42

Selected Technical Reports, Information **Retrieval** Bulletin, TD 4.17/2

Return

Report of Federal Trade Commission on Rates of **Return** (after taxes) for Identical Companies in Selected Manufacturing Industries, FT 1.21

Return on Investment Case Study, D 103.53/8

Summary of Prescribed Unit Costs and Hourly Rate for **Return** on Investment and Tax Allowance, C 31.272, CAB 1.10

Returning

Best Bets for **Returning** Veterans in Washington D.C. Area, CS 1.43/2

Returns

Corporation Income Tax **Returns**, T 22.35/3:C 81, T 22.35/2:C 81

Corporation Income Tax **Returns**, Source Book (year), T 22.35/5-2

Cost and **Returns**, A 93.9/11

Costs and **Returns**, A 93.9/11

Farm **Returns**, Summary of Reports of Farm Operators, A 36.124

Farmer's Cooperative Income Tax **Returns**, T 22.35/2:F 22

Fiduciary Income Tax **Returns**, T 22.35/2:F 44/2

Foreign Income Tax **Returns**, T 22.35/2

Comparative Law Series, Monthly World **Review**, C 18.79

Conditions of Major Water System Structures and Facilities, **Review** of Maintenance, Report of Examination, {various regions and projects}, I 27.69

Congressional Record **Review**, S 18.46

Congressional Research Service **Review**, LC 14.19

Consolidated **Review** of Current Information, T 23.7/2

Contraceptive Development Contract **Review** Committee, HE 20.3001/2:C 76

Contraceptive Evaluation Research Contract **Review** Committee, HE 20.3001/2:C 76/2

Cottonseed **Review**, South Central Area, A 82.65

Courts-Martial Reports, Holdings and Decisions of Judge Advocates General, Boards of **Review**, and United States Court of Military Appeals, D 1.29

Current **Review** of Soviet Technical Press, C 41.94

Domestic Council **Review** Group on Regulatory Reform, Pr 38.8:R 26

ERIC **Review**, ED 1.331

Friday **Review** of Defense Literature, D 1.33/2

FSIS Food Safety **Review**, A 110.17

Gulf War **Review**, VA 1.104

Health Care Financing **Review**, HE 22.512

Health Care Financing **Review** Annual Supplement, HE 22.18/2

Manual for **Review** and Comment, HE 20.2588/2

Mid-Session **Review** of the Budget, PrEx 2.31

Military Law **Review**, D 101.22:27-100

Monthly **Review**, J 21.10, RR 1.7/2

Oak Ridge National Laboratory **Review**, E 1.28/17

Occupational Outlook **Review**, VA 1.37

Office **Review**, Y 3.W 19/1:17

Old-Age Insurance Operating Statistics **Review**, SS 1.33

OPM, the Year in **Review**, PM 1.1

Oral Argument {before a panel of the **Review** Board}, CC 1.42/4

OSAHRE Reports: Decisions of the Occupational Safety and Health **Review** Commission, Y 3.Oc 1:10

Outlook and Year-End Economic **Review**, C 1.41

Panama Canal **Review**, CZ 1.8, Y 3.P 19/2:10

Pesticide **Review** (year), A 82.76

Philippine Agricultural **Review**, W 49.21/7

Power O. and M. Report, Field **Review** of Maintenance, I 27.45/2

Power O. and M. Reports, Field **Review** of Operation and Maintenance, I 27.45/3

Press **Review**, W 95.9

Price Trends and Controls in Latin America, Fortnightly **Review**, Pr 32.4246

Professional Standards **Review** Organization, Annual Report, HE 22.210

Program Administration **Review**, PAR (nos.), FS 13.219

Public Assistance, Quarterly **Review** of Statistics for U.S., SS 1.13

Publications Corn-Hog Board of **Review**, A 55.30

Quarterly Cargo **Review**, C 31.264

Quarterly Economic and Financial **Review**: Federal Republic of Germany and Western Sectors of Berlin, S 1.91/2

Quarterly Flax Market **Review**, A 36.115

Quarterly **Review** of Commission Proceedings, NC 2.11

Quarterly **Review** of Military Literature, W 28.10

Quarterly **Review** of Productivity, Wages, and Prices, L 2.102

Quarterly **Review**, 503 and 504 Economic Development Loan Programs, SBA 1.27/2

Quarterly **Review**, VA 1.25

Quarterly Soybean Market **Review**, A 80.129

Reactor Plant Fiscal Year End **Review**, E 1.105

Reappraisement Decisions, for **Review** by U.S. Customs Court As Published in Weekly Treasury Decisions, T 1.11/2a

Regional **Review**, Region 1, I 29.36

Report to the U.S. Congress and the U.S. Secretary of Energy from the Nuclear Waste Technical **Review** Board, Y 3.N 88/2:1

Research **Review**, Air Training Command, Human Resources Research Center, D 301.36/4

Research **Review**, Department of the Air Force, D 301.69/6-2

Research **Review**, Economic Development Administration, C 46.26

Research **Review**, Office of Aerospace Research, D 301.69/6

Reserve Fleet Safety **Review**, C 39.219

Review of Alcohol as a Cause Factor, TD 1.129

Review of Arms Control and Disarmament Activities, Y 4.Ar 5/2-16

Review of Budget, Pr 34.107/3

Review of Bureau of Mines Coal Program, I 28.17, I 28.27

Review of Bureau of Mines Energy Program, I 28.27

Review of Current DHHS, DOE, and EPA Research Related to Toxicology, HE 20.3563

Review of Current Information in Treasury Library, T 23.7

Review of Current Periodicals, New Series, SE 1.23

Review of Foreign Developments, Prepared for Internal Circulation, FR 1.49

Review of Month, L 2.59

Review of Mutual Cooperation in Public Administration, S 17.46

Review of Operations Information Agency, IA 1.1/2

Review of Operations Social Security Administration, FS 3.15

Review of Power Planning in Pacific Northwest, Calendar Year, Y 3.P 11/4:9

Review of Selected U.S. Government Research and Development Reports, OTR-(series), C 13.49

Review of Some Recent Magazine Articles Relating to Housing, I 40.9

Review of Soviet Ground Forces, D 5.209

Review of Standards of Performance for New Stationary Sources, EP 4.19

Review of the Air Force Materials Research and Development Program, D 301.45

Review of the Economy, Y 4.Ec 7:Ec 7/40

Review of the Month, Pr 33.212

Review of the World's Commerce, S 4.12, C 14.15

Review of U.S. Patents Relating to Insecticides and Fungicides, A 7.9

Review of U.S. Patents Relating to Pest Control, A 47.7

Review of United States Oceanborne Foreign Trade, C 39.202:Oc 2

Review of United States Patents Related to Pest Control, A 77.311

Review of USTTA International Markets, and Summary of Cooperative Advertising Opportunities, C 47.20

Review of War Surgery and Medicine, W 44.16

Review of Waste Package Verification Test, Y 3.N 88:25-3

Review of World's Commerce, C 10.9

Review, Statistical **Review** of Ordnance Accident Experiment, W 34.42

Rice Market **Review**, A 82.33

RRB Quarterly **Review**, RR 1.7/3

RTC **Review**, T 71.20, Y 3.R 31/2:17

Rulings on Requests for **Review** of the Assistant Secretary of Labor for Labor-Management Relations Pursuant to Executive Order 11491, As Amended, L 1.51/6

Safety **Review**, D 204.7

Safety, Fire Prevention, and Occupational Health Management, by Objectives **Review**, D 301.99

SBA Economic **Review**, SBA 1.27

Science and Technology **Review**, E 1.53

SEC Monthly Statistical **Review**, SE 1.20

Secretary's Annual Report to Congress, Posture Statement, Outlook and Program **Review**, E 1.60:0010

Shellfish Market **Review**, Current Economic Analysis S, C 55.309/4

Sixth Quadrennial **Review** of Military Compensation, D 1.89

Soviet Union, Foreign Military **Review**, PrEx 7.21/2-3, PrEx 7.21/4-2

Special Hazard **Review**, HE 20.7113

Special Occupational Hazard **Review** with Control Recommendations, HE 20.7113

SSA Training Data **Review** Technician, Basic Training Course, HE 3.69/3

Statistical Supplement of Monthly Domestic Dairy Markets **Review**, A 88.13/2

Statistical Supplement to Monthly Egg and Poultry Market **Review**, A 88.13/4

Substitute Chemical Program, Initial Scientific and Minieconomic **Review** of {various chemicals}, EP 5.13

Summary and **Review** of International Meteorological Observations for Month of, W 42.7/2

Synopsis of the Annual Energy **Review** and Outlook, E 3.1/3

The National Banking **Review**, T 12.16

Tobacco Market **Review**, A 88.34/5-8

Topical Report **Review** Status, Y 3.N 88:34

Trade **Review** of Canada, C 18.157

Traffic Safety Evaluation Research **Review**, TD 8.18/2

U.S. Army Materiel Command, Annual Historical **Review**, D 101.1/4-2

U.S. Atmospheric Nuclear Weapons Tests, Nuclear Test Personnel **Review**, D 15.10

Unemployment Insurance **Review**, L 7.18/3

UNESCO World **Review** Weekly Radio News from United Nations Educational, Scientific, and Cultural Organization, Paris, France, S 5.48/6

United States Air Force Jag Law **Review**, D 302.9

United States Waterborne Foreign Commerce, a **Review** of {year}, C 3.211/2

USAF Fighter Weapons **Review**, D 301.102

Vessel Safety **Review**, TD 5.12/3

Virus Cancer Program Scientific **Review** Committee A, HE 20.3001/2:V 81/2

Virus Cancer Program Scientific **Review** Committee B, HE 20.3001/2:V 81/3

Volume **Review** Exercise (series), D 301.26/17-5

Water Resources **Review**, Annual Summary, Water Year, I 19.42/2

Water Resources **Review**, I 19.42

Weekly Cotton Linters **Review**, A 88.11/3

Weekly Cotton Market **Review**, A 88.11/2

Weekly Feed **Review**, A 88.18/4

Weekly **Review** of Periodicals, FR 1.22

Weekly **Review** of Recent Developments, L 2.56

Weekly **Review**, RR 1.7, Y 3.W 19/2:6

Weekly Rice Market **Review**, A 88.18/9

Welfare in **Review**, HE 17.9

Wildlife **Review**, I 49.17

Year in **Review** at Goddard Space Flight Center, NAS 1.1/3

Reviewers

Listing of Peer **Reviewers** Used by NSF Divisions, NS 1.36

Reviewing

Reviewing and Acting on Medical Certificates, CS 1.41/4:339-31

Reviews

Current **Reviews** of Economic and Social Problems in United Nations, S 1.81

News, **Reviews**, and Comment, Y 3.N 88:49

Recent **Reviews**, Cancer Diagnosis and Therapy, Supplement to the Cancergrams, HE 20.3173/2-3

Recent **Reviews**, Cancer Virology and Biology, Supplement to the Cancergrams, HE 20.3173/2-4

Recent **Reviews**, Carcinogenesis, HE 20.3173/2-2

Reliability Abstracts and Technical **Reviews**, NAS 1.35

Reports to Congress on Audits, **Reviews**, and Examinations, GA 1.13

Reviews and Lectures, D 211.13/3

Reviews of Data on Research and Development, NS 1.11

Reviews of Data on Science Resources, NS 1.11/2

Reviews of New Reports, HE 20.6229

Reviews of New Reports from the Centers for Disease Control and Prevention/National Center for Health Statistics, HE 20.6216/6

Tobacco Market **Reviews**, A 36.189

Revise

Commission to **Revise** the Laws of the United States: Publications, J 1.10

Revised

Combined Annual and **Revised** Monthly Wholesale Trade, C 3.133/4

Commercial Grain Stocks {**Revised** Figures for Calendar Year}, A 88.18/2-2, A 82.31/2

Commodities Included in (various) Products Group for **Revised** Wholesale Price Index, L 2.61/3

Revised Customs Regulations, T 1.9/2

Revised Guide to the Law and Legal Literature of Mexico, L 1.36:38

Revised Monthly Retail Sales in Inventories, C 3.138/3-3

Revised Statutes, S 7.10

Revision

Effect of Income Tax Law **Revision** on Electric Taxes and Income, FP 1.23

International Conference for **Revision** of Convention of 1914 for Safety of Life at Sea, S 5.29

Revision of Rules (all classes), C 15.9/3

Your Changing Forest, News on the Black Hills National Forest Plan **Revision**, A 13.128

Revisions
Budget **Revisions**, PrEx 2.8/7
MPR **Revisions**, HH 2.17/2

Revitalization
Footwear Industry **Revitalization** Program, Annual Progress Report, C 1.72

Revolution
Marines in the Revolution: a History of Continental Marines in the American **Revolution**, D 214.13:R 32/775-83
National Park Service Guide to the Historic Places of the American **Revolution**, I 29.9/2:Am 3
Naval Documents of the American **Revolution**, D 207.12
War of the American **Revolution**, D 114.2:Am 3

Revolving
Financial Audit, House Recording Studio **Revolving** Fund, GA 1.13/5-2
Financial Audit, House Restaurant **Revolving** Fund's Financial Statements, GA 1.13/8
Financial Audit, House Stationery **Revolving** Fund Statements, GA 1.13/19
Financial Audit, Senate Recording and Photographic Studios **Revolving** Fund, GA 1.13/5
Financial Audit, Senate Restaurants **Revolving** Fund for Fiscal Years, GA 1.13/8-2

RFC
RFC Mortgage Company, Circulars, Y 3.R 24:9
RFC Small Business Activities, FL 5.15
RFC Surplus Property News, FL 5.12

RFPS
Grants Competitions and **RFPS**: Planned NIE Activities During the Fiscal Year, HE 19.216

RG-TR
Reports, **RG-TR**- (series), D 105.22/2-2

Rh
Rh Hemolytic Disease Surveillance, HE 20.7011/19

Rhenium
Rhenium in (year), I 28.145

Rheumatic
Arthritis and **Rheumatic** Diseases Abstracts, HE 20.3312

Rheumatic Diseases
Arthritis, **Rheumatic Diseases**, and Related Disorders, HE 20.3320/2

Rheumatoid Arthritis
Rheumatoid Arthritis, Handout on Health, HE 20.3916

Rice
Annual **Rice** Summary, Louisiana Crop Reporting Service, A 88.18/23
California **Rice** Stocks and Movement Reports, A 36.186
Futures Trading and Open Contracts in Potatoes and **Rice**, A 85.11
Official United States Standards for **Rice**, A 113.10/2
Rice Administration Orders, A 55.20
Rice Annual Market Summary, A 88.40/2:18
Rice Market News Supplement, Rough **Rice** Receipts, A 88.18/20
Rice Market News, A 88.18/9
Rice Market Review, A 82.33
Rice Production, Louisiana Crop Reporting Service, A 88.18/26
Rice Situation, A 88.18/18, A 93.11/3, A 105.20/4
Rice Stocks, A 92.43
Rice Stocks, Rough and Milled, A 105.42
Rice, Situation and Outlook Report, A 93.11/3
Rice, Stocks and Movement, Southern Mills, A 82.50
Rice, Stocks, and Movement, California Mills, A 82.49, A 88.18/10
Rice Yearbook, A 93.11/4
Rough and Milled **Rice** Stocks, A 88.18/17
Southern **Rice** Inspected for Export, A 88.18/28
Southern **Rice** Stocks and Movement Reports, A 36.185
U.S. **Rice** Distribution Patterns, A 93.51
Weekly **Rice** Market Review, A 88.18/9
Wheat, **Rice**, Feed Grains, Dry Peas, Dry Beans, Seeds, Hops, A 67.30:W 56
World News on **Rice**, C 18.72/9

Richland
Area Wage Survey Summary Yakima-**Richland**-Kennewick-Pasco-Walla Walla-Pendleton, Washington-Oregon, L 2.122/47

Rickettsial
Rickettsial Disease Surveillance, HE 20.7011/27

RIF
RIF {Reading Is Fundamental} Newsletter, SI 1.36

Right
Development of Multiple Use Facilities on Highway **Right** of Way, TD 2.121/2
Right to Read, ED 1.12, HE 19.125

Rights
Civil **Rights** Forum, J 1.104
Country Reports on Human **Rights** Practices, Y 4.F 76/1-15
Layman's Guide to Individual **Rights** Under the United States Constitution, Y 4.J 89/2:R 44
Legal Guide and Case Digest, Veterans' Reemployment **Rights** Under the Universal Military Training and Service Act, As Amended, and Related Acts, L 25.6/2:L 52
Task Force on Women's **Rights** and Responsibilities, Pr 37.8:W 84
Telephone Directory Civil **Rights** Commission, CR 1.16
Veterans' Reemployment **Rights** Handbooks, L 25.6/2:V 64
Your Social Security **Rights** & Responsibilities, Retirement & Survivors Benefits, HE 3.88/2, HE 3.93
Your Social Security **Rights** and Responsibilities, Disability Benefits, HE 3.88

RIIES
RIIES Bibliographic Studies, SI 1.40
RIIES Occasional Papers, SI 1.40/2
RIIES Research Notes, SI 1.40/3

Rim
Pacific **Rim** Agriculture and Trade Reports: Situation and Outlook Series, A 92.29/2-19

Ring
Council **Ring**, I 29.38
Let Freedom **Ring** (Radio Scripts), I 16.62/1

Rings
Rings of Saturn, NAS 1.22:343

Rio de Janeiro
International American Conference; **Rio de Janeiro**, S 5.9/3
Rio de Janeiro, International Exposition of Centenary of Independence of Brazil, 1922-23, S 6.20
Pan-American Congress on Highways, 2d, **Rio de Janerio**, S 5.23/2

Rio Grande
Federal-State-Private Cooperative Snow Surveys: Colorado, **Rio Grande**, Platte, and Arkansas Drainage Basins, A 57.46/9-2
International Commission for Equitable Distribution of Water of **Rio Grande**, S 3.19/4
Light List, Atlantic Coast of U.S. Intercoastal Waterway, Hampton Roads to **Rio Grande** Including Inside Waters, N 24.17, T 47.28

Risk
Behavioral **Risk** Factor Surveillance System, HE 20.7611/3
All-**Risk** Update, A 62.13
Cumulative Report of All Specific **Risk** Investment Guaranties Issued Since the Beginning of the Program through, S 18.26/3
Multiple **Risk** Intervention Trial, Public Annual Report, HE 20.3213
Papers in Re World War **Risk** Insurance, J 1.13/2
Risk Analysis of Farm Credit System Operations and Economic Outlook, FCA 1.23/2-2

River
Annual Maximum, Minimum, and Mean Discharges of Mississippi **River** and Its Outlets and Tributaries, D 103.309/2
Colorado **River** Basin Project, Annual Report, I 27.71/3
Comprehensive Framework Study, Missouri **River** Basin, Y 3.M 69:9
Daily **River** Bulletin, C 30.54/7, C 30.55, C 55.110/2
Daily **River** Stages, A 29.10, C 30.24, C 55.117
Daily Weather and **River** Bulletin {New Orleans, La. Area}, C 55.110/5
Daily Weather and **River** Bulletin {Shreveport, La. Area}, C 55.110/6
Eel **River** Charts, W 7.13/2
Fall Water Supply Summary for **River** Basins, A 57.46/8

Federal Inter-Agency **River** Basin Committee Publications, I 1.81
Index to **River** and Harbor Act Approved, W 7.12
Index to **River** Surveys Made by the Geological Survey and Other Agencies, I 19.13:995
List of Illinois **River** Terminals, Docks, Mooring Locations, and Warehouses, D 103.58
List of Mississippi **River** Terminals, Docks, Mooring Locations, and Warehouses, D 103.58/2
Maumee **River** Basin, Y 3.G 79/3:10
Numbered **River**, D 103.66/3
Potomac **River** Naval Command Publications, D 201.12
River Basins of the United States, I 19.56
River Currents, TD 5.27
River Forecasts Provided by the National Weather Service, C 55.117/2, C 55.285
River Mile Index, Y 3.P 11/4:10
River Summary and Forecast, New Orleans, Louisiana, C 55.110/2-2
River Summary and Forecast, {Lower Mississippi Region}, C 55.110/7
River Summary and Forecasts {Memphis, Tenn. area}, C 55.110/2
River Temperature at Selected Stations in the Pacific Northwest, I 19.46/2-2, I 19.46/2-3
Spawning the Medicine **River**, I 20.64
Special **River** Bulletins, A 29.19
Technical Memorandum To United States Study Commission, Southeast **River** Basins, A 57.50
Wabash **River** Charts, W 7.13/5

Rivers
Alleghaney and Monongahela **Rivers**, D 103.66/4
Annual Report of the **Rivers** and Trails Conservation Programs, I 29.124
Board of Engineers for **Rivers** and Harbors Report of Hearings, D 103.23
Flood Hazard Studies {various **rivers**, creeks, and areas}, A 57.64/3
Foreign Inland Waterway News, Intercoastal Waterways, **Rivers**, Lakes, Canals, Equipment, C 18.208
General Chart of Northern and Northwestern Lakes {and rivers}, W 33.7/1
Light and Fog Signals of United States and Canada on Northern Lakes and **Rivers**, C 9.30
Light List, Lights, Buoys, and Day Marks, Mississippi and Ohio **Rivers**, C 9.29/2
Light List, Mississippi and Ohio **Rivers** and Tributaries, N 24.18, T 47.27
Lights and Fog Signals, Northern Lakes and **Rivers** and Canada, T 25.17, C 9.18
Lights on Western **Rivers**, C 9.21
National **Rivers** {information circulars}, I 29.6/4
Our **Rivers**, I 27.25
Pilot Rules for **Rivers** whose Waters Flow into Gulf of Mexico and Their Tributaries and Red River of the North, C 25.8
Post Lights on Western **Rivers**, T 25.20

Riverways
Compilation of Administrative Policies for National Recreation Areas, National Seashores, National Lakeshores, National Parkways, National Scenic **Riverways** (Recreational Area Category), I 29.9/4:R 24

RMRScience
RMRScience, A 13.151/6

RM-TT
RM-TT- (series), A 13.69/15

RMP
RMP Bulletin, I 72.3/2

RO/EERL
RO/EERL Series, EP 6.10

Road
Alaska **Road** Commission, I 35.10/21
Classification of Expenditures for **Road** and Equipment, IC 1 ste.8
Classification of Investment in **Road** Equipment, IC 1 ste.16
Japan **Road** Maps, Series L302, D 5.340
Korea **Road** Maps, Series L351, D 5.341
Official **Road** Maps for Allied Forces Europe, Series M305, D 5.342
Permanent International Association of **Road** Congress, S 5.31
Road & Rec, D 301.72/2
Road to the United States Census 2000, C 3.296
Selected Safety **Road** Checks Motor Carriers of Property, TD 2.311

Roads
Bureau of Steam **Roads**, IC 1 ste.1
Classification of Expenditures for **Roads** and
Equipment of Electric Railways, IC 1
eler.6
Highway Progress (year) Annual Report of the
Bureau of Public **Roads**, C 37.1
Journal of Highway Research, Public **Roads**, C
37.8
Laws relating to Federal Aid and Construction of
Roads, Y 1.2:R 53
News in Public **Roads**, C 37.16
Operating Revenues and Operating Expenses of
Large Steam **Roads** with Annual
Operating Revenues Above
$25,000,000, IC 1 ste.20
Operating Statistics of Class 1 Steam **Roads**,
Freight and Passenger Service, IC 1
ste.21
Public **Roads** Round-Up, C 37.29
Public **Roads**, Journal of Highway Research, TD
2.19
Publications Bureau of Public **Roads**, A 22.5
Roads Circular, I 20.24
Unit Costs (selected expense accounts) of Class 1
Steam **Roads**, IC 1 ste.23
Roadside
BMCS National **Roadside** Inspection, TD 2.313/2
Roastings
Coffee Inventories and **Roastings**, C 3.169
Current Business Reports; Green Coffee,
Inventories, Imports, **Roastings**, BG
(series), C 56.219/2
Green Coffee Inventories and **Roastings**, C 3.236
Roadsides
Green **Roadsides**, TD 2.30/16-2
Rock
Marketable Phosphate **Rock**, I 28.119/3
Phosphate **Rock** in (year), I 28.119
Phosphate **Rock**, I 28.119/3
Rock Island Arsenal
Annual Historical Review, **Rock Island Arsenal**,
D 101.109
Rocket
Data Catalog, Satellite and **Rocket** Experiments,
NSSDA (nos), NAS 1.37
Data Report, Meteorological **Rocket** Network
Firings, C 52.16
Rockwell
Rockwell International, Rocky Flats Plant, E 1.12/
4
Telephone Directory **Rockwell** International,
Rocky Flats Plant, E 1.12/4
Rocky
Rockwell International, **Rocky** Flats Plant, E 1.12/
4
Telephone Directory Rockwell International,
Rocky Flats Plant, E 1.12/4
Rocky Mountain
Forest Insect and Disease Conditions in the **Rocky
Mountain** Region, A 13.52/13
Mineral Resources West of **Rocky Mountains**, T
28.6
Progress Report Northern **Rocky Mountain** Forest
and Range Experiment Station, A 13.30/
6
Publications **Rocky Mountain** Forest and Range
Experiment Station, A 13.69/10-2
Rocky Mountain National Park, Annual Reports, I
1.57
Rocky Mountain Regional Aviation System Plan,
TD 4.33/5
Rocky Mountain Research Station: Bibliographies
and Lists of Publications, A 13.151/2
Rocky Mountain Research Station Directory, A
13.151/4-2
Rocky Mountain Research Station: General
Publications, A 13.151
Rocky Mountain Research Station: Handbooks,
Manuals, Guides, A 13.151/4
Rocky Mountain Research Station: Maps, A
13.151/3
State of the **Rocky Mountain** Region, I 29.125
ROD
ROD Annual Report FY, EP 1.1/7
Rodent
Annual Report of the Southwestern District Branch
of Predator & **Rodent** Control, I 49.61
Rodenticide
Notices of Judgement Under Federal Insecticide,
Fungicide, and **Rodenticide** Act, A
77.325, A 82.56

Notices of Judgement Under the Federal Insecticide,
Fungicide, and **Rodenticide** Act, EP
1.70
Rodenticides
Rodenticides and Mammal, Bird and Fish Toxicants,
EP 5.11/4
Rodman
Rodman Process Laboratory, Watertown Arsenal,
Reports, D 105.13
Rods
Cellulose Plastic Products (Nitro-Cellulose and
Cellulose Acetate Sheets, **Rods** and
Tubes), C 3.73
Role
International Direct Investment, Global Trends and
the U.S. **Role**, C 61.29
Roles
Directory of Programs Preparing Registered Nurses
for Expanded **Roles**, HE 20.6610
Sex **Roles**: a Research Bibliography, HE
20.8113:Se 9
Roll
Roll of Honor, Supplemental Statement of
Disposition of Bodies of Deceased
Union Soldiers and Prisoners of War
Removed to National Cemeteries in
Southern and Western United States, W
39.8
Roll of Honor, W 39.7
Rolla
Rolla Research Center Annual Progress Report FY,
I 28.154/2
Romanian
Directory of **Romanian** Officials, A Reference Aid,
PrEx 3.10/7-24
Rome
American Embassy, **Rome**: Quarterly Statistical
Bulletin, S 1.115
Technical Notes Department of the Air Force **Rome**
Air Development Center, D 301.57/2
Roofing
Prepared **Roofing**, C 3.100
Room
Visitors Report to Nurses' Station Before Entering
Room, HE 20.7029
Instrument **Room** {or division} Circulars, A 29.11
Roosevelt
Franklin D. **Roosevelt** Library, Annual Report of
Archivist of United States, GS 4.9
Indexes to Papers of President Franklin Delano
Roosevelt, PI 1.8
Roosevelt Library, Annual Report of Archivest of
United States, GS 4.9
Roots
Table of All Primitive **Roots** for Primes Less Than
5000, D 210.8:7070
Roseburg
Area Wage Survey Summary Eugene-Springfield-
Medford-**Roseburg**-Klamath Falls-
Grants Pass, Oregon, L 2.122/37
Rosenwal
Rosenwal (Lessing J.) Collection Catalog, LC
1.2:R 72/3
Rosin
Gum Turpentine and Gum **Rosin** Circular Letters, Y
3.C 73:11
Roster
General/Flag Officer Worldwide **Roster**, D 1.61/8
Library Vacancy **Roster**, LC 1.32/3
National **Roster** of Minority Professional
Consulting Services, C 1.57/3
Official **Roster** of Officers and Employees, W 49.5/5
Roster and Directory of Troops in Hawaiian
Department, W 81.5
Roster and Station of Officers of Signal Corps, W
42.9
Roster of Attorneys and Agents Registered to
Practice before the U.S. Patent Office, C
21.9
Roster of Commissioned Officers and Employees, A
29.28
Roster of Disqualified Attorneys, I 24.12
Roster of Examining Surgeons, I 24.10
Roster of Field Officers, I 21.15
Roster of General Officers of General Staff,
Volunteers, W 3.27
Roster of Members of PHS Public Advisory
Groups, Councils, Committees, Boards,
Panels, Study Sections, HE 20.2:Ad 9/3
Roster of Officers and Troops, W 12.8
Roster of Officers of Indian Service, I 20.10
Roster of Officers, Adjutant-General's Department,
W 3.34

Roster of Organizaed Militia of United States, by
Divisions, Brigades, Regiments,
Companies, and other Organizations,
with their Stations, W 70.5
Roster of Prepaid Dental Care Plans, FS 2.2:D 54/7
Roster of Subsistence Department, W 5.8
Roster Showing Stations and Duties of Officers, W
39.12, W 77.6
Rotated
Thesaurus of ERIC Descriptors **Rotated** Display,
ED 1.310/3-4
ROTC
Air Force **ROTC** Four Year College Scholarship
Program Application Booklet for High
School Students Entering College in the
(year) Fall Term, D 301.95
Army **ROTC** (pamphlets), D 101.22/31
ROTC Manuals, D 101.48
Rotocraft
Briefs of Accidents Involving **Rotocraft** U.S.
General Aviation, TD 1.109/5
Rotoprint
Distribution of Sales (**Rotoprint**), C 3.57
Rotorcraft
Rotorcraft External-Load Operations, TD 4.6:part
133
Type Certificate Data Sheets and Specifications,
Rotorcraft, Gliders, and Balloons, TD
4.15/6
Rough
Rice Market News Supplement, **Rough** Rice
Receipts, A 88.18/20
Rice Stocks, **Rough** and Milled, A 105.42
Rough and Milled Rice Stocks, A 88.18/17
Rough List of More Important Additions, W 11.7
Round
Kennedy **Round**, Special Reports, C 42.29
Round-Up
Food Fights for Freedom **Round-Up**, A 21.19
Public Roads **Round-Up**, C 37.29
Rounds
Rounds of the Teaching Staff, VA 1.61
Roundup
ARA News **Roundup**, S 1.134/2
Weekly **Roundup** of World Production and Trade,
WR (series), A 67.42
Roundups
Weekly **Roundups**, Economic Letter, S 1.80
Route
Atlanta Helicopter **Route** Chart, C 55.416/12-8
Boston Helicopter **Route** Chart, C 55.416/12-7
Chicago Helicopter **Route** Chart, C 55.416/12-5
Fuel Consumption and Cost, Certificated **Route** and
Supplemental Air Carriers, Domestic and
International Operations, C 31.267
Fuel Cost and Consumption, Certified **Route** and
Supplemental Air Carriers, Domestic and
International Operations, Twelve
Months Ended (date), C 31.267/2
Houston Helicopter **Route** Chart, C 55.416/12-9
Inside **Route** Pilot (Atlantic and Gulf Coasts), C
4.6/3
New York Helicopter **Route** Chart, C 55.416/12-3
Post **Route** Maps, P 11.5
Price List of Post **Route** Maps, P 11.6
Quarterly Interim Financial Report, Certificated
Route Air Carriers and Supplemental Air
Carriers, CAB 1.14
Quarterly Interim Financial Report, Certified **Route**
Air Carriers and Supplemental Air
Carriers, C 31.240/3
Route Charts, C 4.9/9, C 4.9/17
Route Information Series, W 87.21/2
U.S. Coast Pilots Inside **Route** Pilot, C 4.6/3
Uniform System of Accounts and Reports for
Certificated **Route** Air Carriers in
Accordance with Sec. 407 of the Federal
Aviation Act, C 31.206/5
Washington Helicopter **Route** Chart, C 55.416/12-
4
Routes
Cooperative Creamery **Routes**, A 72.20
Essential United States Foreign Trade **Routes**, C
39.202:F 76
Foreign Oceanborne Trade of United States
Containerized Cargo Summary, Selected
Trade **Routes**, C 39.233
Minimum Enroute IFR Altitudes Over Particular
Routes and Intersections, TD 4.316
Routes to Indian Agencies and Schools, I 20.19
Schedule of Mail **Routes**, P 10.12/16
U.S. Oceanborne Foreign Trade **Routes**, TD 11.13
United States Oceanborne Foreign Trade **Routes**, C
39.240

Routing
　　MILSTRIP **Routing** and Identifier and Distribution
　　　　Codes, D 1.87/2
　　MILSTRIP **Routing** Identifier Codes, D 7.6/16
Royal
　　United States Air Force, Navy, **Royal** Canadian Air
　　　　Force and **Royal** Canadian Navy, Navy
　　　　Radio Facility Charts and In- Flight
　　　　Data, Alaska, Canada and North
　　　　Atlantic, D 301.13/3
　　United States Air Force, Navy, **Royal** Canadian Air
　　　　Force and **Royal** Canadian Supplemen-
　　　　tary Flight Information, North American
　　　　Area (excluding Mexico and Caribbean
　　　　area), D 301.48
　　United States Air Force, United States Navy and
　　　　Royal Canadian Air Force Radio Facility
　　　　Charts, West Canada and Alaska, D
　　　　301.13
Royal Grass
　　Commercial Tobacco-Livestock Farms, Bluegrass
　　　　Area, Kentucky and Penny-**Royal Grass**
　　　　Area, Kentucky-Tennessee, A 93.9/11
RPI
　　RPI (series), D 101.43/2
RPMA
　　Lessons Learned in Contracting **RPMA**, D 103.121
RRB
　　RRB Actuarial Studies, RR 1.14
　　RRB Quarterly Review, RR 1.7/3
　　RRB-SSA Financial Interchange: Calculations for
　　　　Fiscal Year with Respect to OASI, DI,
　　　　and HI Trust Funds, RR 1.15
RSC
　　RSC (series), D 101.104
RSI
　　RSI Quality Appraisal Awards and Disallowances
　　　　Monthly Statistical Summary, HE 3.28/9
　　RSI Quality Appraisal Postadjudicative Monthly
　　　　Statistical Summary, HE 3.28/8
RSIC
　　Army Missile Command Redstone Scientific
　　　　Information Center Redstone Arsenal
　　　　Alabama **RSIC** (series), D 105.22/3
RSIM
　　RSIM (series), A 77.529
RSVP
　　RSVP Exchange, AA 1.9/11-2
RT
　　Technical Reports, **RT-** (series), D 105.14
RT-TR
　　Reports, **RT-TR-** (series), D 105.22/2
RTC
　　RTC Review, T 71.20, Y 3.R 31/2:17
RTD
　　RTD Technology Briefs, D 301.45/34
　　Technical Documentary Report **RTD**-TDR- (series),
　　　　D 301.45/34-2
RTP
　　RTP-TR- (series), J 24.14
RU
　　Water Reuse, OWRT/**RU**- , I 1.97/3
Rubber
　　Chemical and **Rubber**, C 41.35
　　Cooperative Inter-American Plantation **Rubber**
　　　　Development, A 77.519
　　Industry Report, **Rubber**, C 18.241
　　Raw and Vulcanized **Rubber**, C 41.70
　　Report of the Attorney General on Competition in
　　　　the Synthetic **Rubber** Industry, J 1.26
　　Rubber Laboratory, Mare Island Naval Shipyard,
　　　　Vallejo, California, Reports, D 211.16
　　Rubber News Letter, C 18.140/2
　　Rubber Products Trade News, C 18.201
　　Rubber Series, L 16.19
　　Rubber, Annual Report, C 1.28
　　United States Consumption of **Rubber**, C 40.14, C
　　　　41.31
Rubella
　　National Communicable Disease Center **Rubella**
　　　　Surveillance {Reports}, FS 2.60/16
　　Rubella Surveillance, {reports}, HE 20.7011/12
Rubidium
　　Cesium and **Rubidium** in (year), I 28.139
Rug
　　Rug and Floor Covering Material Notes, C 18.122
Rule Making
　　Office of the Secretary Petitions for Reconsideration
　　　　of Actions in **Rule Making** Proceedings
　　　　Filed, Public Notices, CC 1.38/2
　　Public Notices: Petitions for **Rule Making** Field,
　　　　CC 1.38

Rulemaking
　　C.A.B. Notices of Proposed **Rulemaking** and
　　　　Amendments to All Regulations, CAB
　　　　1.37
Rulemakings
　　Exparte Presentations in Informal **Rulemakings**,
　　　　CC 1.42/3
Rules
　　Administrative **Rules** and Regulations Under
　　　　Sections of National Housing Act, HH
　　　　2.6/2
　　Advance Copy Proposed **Rules** and Regulations,
　　　　NCU 1.6/a
　　Amendment to **Rules** and Regulations Under
　　　　Sections of National Housing Act, HH
　　　　2.6/3
　　Atomic Energy Commission **Rules** and Regula-
　　　　tions, Y 3.At 7:6-2
　　CATV Requests Filed Pursuant to Sec. 74.1107(a)
　　　　of the **Rules**, Public Notice, CC 1.45
　　Changes to **Rules**, Regulations and Instructions, W
　　　　77.10/2
　　Committee Rules and **Rules** for Investigative
　　　　Hearings Conducted by Subcommittees
　　　　of the Committee on Armed Services, Y
　　　　4.Ar 5/2-15
　　Federal **Rules** and Regulations, Correction Sheets,
　　　　CC 1.7/3
　　Federal **Rules** of Appellate Procedure with Forms,
　　　　Y 4.J 89/1-10
　　Federal **Rules** of Evidence, Y 4.J 89/1-13
　　General Operating and Flight **Rules**, TD 4.6:part
　　　　91
　　General **Rules** and Regulations Prescribed by
　　　　Board of Supervising Inspectors of
　　　　Steamboats, T 38.9
　　General **Rules** and Regulations Under the
　　　　Investment Company Act of 1940, as in
　　　　Effect (date), SE 1.6:R 86/9
　　General **Rules** and Regulations Under the
　　　　Securities Act of 1933, as in Effect (date),
　　　　SE 1.6:R 86/2
　　General **Rules** and Regulations Under the
　　　　Securities Exchange Act of 1934, as in
　　　　Effect (date), SE 1.6:R 86/3
　　Great Lakes Pilotage Regulations and **Rules** and
　　　　Orders, C 1.47:R 26
　　House **Rules** of Procedure, Y 4.B 85/3-10
　　Investment Advisers Act of 1940 and General
　　　　Rules and Regulations Thereunder As in
　　　　Effect (date), SE 1.5:In 8/2
　　Laws, Executive Orders, **Rules** and Regulations,
　　　　CS 1.41/4:990-1
　　Manual of **Rules** of the Committee on Ways and
　　　　Means, Y 4.W 36:WMCP 96-1
　　Manual of **Rules** Regulations, Transmittal Letters,
　　　　FW 4.30
　　National Credit Union Administration **Rules** and
　　　　Regulations, NCU 1.6:R 86
　　Pilot **Rules** for Certain Inland Waters of Atlantic
　　　　and Pacific Coasts of Gulf of Mexico, C
　　　　25.9
　　Pilot **Rules** for Rivers whose Waters Flow into
　　　　Gulf of Mexico and Their Tributaries and
　　　　Red River of the North, C 25.8
　　Pilot **Rules**, T 38.8, C 15.8
　　Proposed Trade Practice **Rules**, FT 1.16/2
　　Regulations, **Rules** and Instructions Census
　　　　Bureau, C 3.6
　　Regulations, **Rules** and Instructions Center for
　　　　Professional Development and Training,
　　　　HE 20.7709
　　Regulations, **Rules**, Instructions: Comptroller of
　　　　the Currency, T 12.25
　　Regulations, **Rules** and Instructions Court of
　　　　Customs Appeals, Ju 7.8/2
　　Regulations, **Rules** and Instructions Customs
　　　　Division, T 17.5
　　Regulations, **Rules** and Instructions Department of
　　　　Education, ED 1.47
　　Regulations, **Rules** and Instructions Department of
　　　　Transportation, TD 1.6
　　Regulations, **Rules** and Instructions Federal
　　　　Emergency Management Agency, FEM
　　　　1.6
　　Regulations, **Rules** and Instructions Food and
　　　　Nutrition Service, A 98.18
　　Regulations, **Rules**, Instructions: Grain Inspection,
　　　　Packers and Stockyards Administration,
　　　　A 113.12
　　Regulations, **Rules** and Instructions International
　　　　Trade Commission, ITC 1.6

Regulations, **Rules** and Instructions National
　　Center for Devices and Radiological
　　Health, HE 20.4606
Regulations, **Rules** and Instructions National
　　Defense University, D 5.406
Regulations, **Rules** and Instructions Naval
　　Research Office, D 210.6
Regulations, **Rules** and Instructions Office of
　　Information Resources Management, GS
　　12.15
Regulations, **Rules** and Instructions Office of Water
　　Programs, EP 2.6
Regulations, **Rules** and Instructions Research and
　　Special Programs Administration, TD
　　10.6
Regulations, **Rules** and Instructions United States
　　Parole Commission, J 27.6
Regulations, **Rules**, Instructions, J 36.6
Revision of **Rules** (all classes), C 15.9/3
Rules Adopted by the Committees of the House of
　　Representatives, Y 4.R 86/1-12
Rules and Regulations (miscellaneous), FP 1.7
Rules and Regulations and Statements of
　　Procedure, LR 1.6:R 86
Rules and Regulations for Federal Savings and
　　Loan System, with Amendments to
　　{date}, FHL 1.6:Sa 9
Rules and Regulations for Foreign Vessels
　　Operating in the Navigable Waters of the
　　United States, TD 5.6:V 63/7
Rules and Regulations for Government and
　　Discipline of United States Penitentia-
　　ries, J 1.16
Rules and Regulations Governing Paroling of
　　Prisoners from Penitentiaries, State
　　Institutions, J 1.15/5
Rules and Regulations Governing Paroling of
　　Prisoners from U.S. Penitentiaries {etc.}
　　(special), J 1.15/6
Rules and Regulations of Bureau of Imports, WT
　　4.5
Rules and Regulations of National Parks, I 1.47/2
Rules and Regulations of Service, IC 1.12/1
Rules and Regulations, Title 10, Code of Federal
　　Regulations, Chapter 1, Y 3.N 88:6
Rules for Inspection of Safety Appliances, IC 1 saf.6
Rules for the Committee on Interior and Insular
　　Affairs, Y 4.In 8/14-13
Rules Governing Monthly Reports of Railway
　　Accidents, IC 1 acci.6
Rules of Civil Procedure for District Courts in U.S.,
　　Ju 6.9/3
Rules of Civil Procedure for the United States
　　District Courts, Y 4.J 89/1-11
Rules of Courts (by States), Ju 10.7
Rules of Criminal Procedure for the United States
　　District Courts, Y 4.J 89/1-12
Rules of Flight, FAA 1.6/9
Rules of Practice and Procedure, FP 1.6, TC 1.8
Rules of Practice and **Rules** Relating to
　　Investigations and Code of Behavior
　　Governing Exparte Communications
　　Between Persons Outside the
　　Commission and Decisional Employees,
　　SE 1.6:R 86/4
Rules of Practice Board of Tax Appeals, Y 3.T 19:7
Rules of Practice Bureau of Domestic Commerce, C
　　41.6/11
Rules of Practice Federal Power Commission, FP
　　1.8
Rules of Practice Federal Trade Commission, FT 1.7
Rules of Practice General Land Office, I 21.9
Rules of Practice in Patent Cases, C 21.14:P 27
Rules of Practice Patent and Trademark Office, C
　　21.8
Rules of Practice Patent Office, I 23.12
Rules of Practice Shipping Board, SB 1.7
Rules of Practice under Title 4, Regulations and
　　Orders, CA 1.14
Rules of Procedure, Committee on the Judiciary, Y
　　4.J 89/2-10
Rules of Procedure for the Permanent Select
　　Committee on Intelligence, Y 4.In 8/18-
　　10
Rules of Procedure of the Committee on House
　　Administration, Y 4.H 81/3-10
Rules of Procedure, Y 4.Ag 4/2, Y 4.Ag 4/2-12, Y
　　4.St 2/3-11
Rules of the Committee on Government Operations,
　　Y 4.G 74/7-10
Rules of the Committee on International Relations,
　　Y 4.In 8/16:18
Rules of the Committee on Small Business, Y 4.Sm
　　1-10

Rules of the Select Committee on Narcotics Abuse and Control, Y 4.N 16/10
Rules of United States Court of Customs and Patent Appeals, Ju 7.8
Rules Pertaining to Aircraft Accidents, Incidents, Overdue Aircraft, and Safety Investigations, TD 1.106/2
Rules, Ju 3.10
Rules, Rulings and Instructions, A 55.69
Special Air Traffic Rules and Airport Traffic Patterns, TD 4.6:part 93
Special Rules, WT 2.6
Standard Broadcast Applications Ready and Available for Processing Pursuant to Sec. 1.354 (c) of Commission's Rules, Lists, CC 1.26/2
Supplement to General Rules and Regulations, C 15.9/2
Trade Practice Rules, FT 1.16
Trademark Rules of Practice of the Patent Office, with Forms and Statutes, C 21.14:T 67/2
Treaty, Laws and Rules Governing Admission of Chinese, L 3.7, L 15.12

Rulings
Administrative Rulings {under House of Service Act}, IC 1 hou.6
Classification Rulings and Decisions: Index Harmonized Tariff Schedules of the United States of America, T 17.6/3-6
Compiled Rulings of Provost Marshal General, W 37.7
Comptroller General's Rulings, Y 3.R 31:14
Conference Rulings Bulletins, IC 1.8, FT 1.6
Decisions and Reports on Rulings of the Assistant Secretary of Labor for Labor-Management Relations Pursuant to Executive Order 11491, L 1.51/4, Y 3.F 31/21-3:10-2
Decisions/Rulings, T 17.6/3
Digest and Index of Opinions of Counsel, Informal Rulings of Federal Reserve Board and Matter Relating Thereto, from Federal Reserve Bulletin, FR 1.10
Digest of Rulings, FR 1.12
Digest of Rulings (OASI) Transmittal Sheets, FS 3.24/2
Digest of Rulings (Old-Age and Survivors Insurance), FS 3.24
Digest Rulings, FR 1.12
HCFA Rulings, HE 22.38
Health Care Financing Administration Rulings on Medicare, Medicaid, Professional Standards Review and Related Matters, HE 22.15
Interpretations, Rulings and Explanations Regarding Laws, Rulings, and Instructions, IC 1 loc.6
Interpretations, Rulings, and Instructions for Inspection and Testing of Locomotives and Tenders and Their Appurtenances, IC 1 loc.5
Legal Opinions, Rulings in Administration of Railroad Retirement Act and Railroad Unemployment Insurance Act, RR 1.12
Manual on Uniform Traffic Control Devices for Streets and Highways: Official Rulings on Requests for Interpretations, Changes, and Experimentations, TD 2.8/2
Meat Inspection Rulings, A 4.12
Misbranding Rulings, Y 3.F 31/10:11
Orders, Notices, Rulings and Decisions Issued by Hearing Examiners and by the Commission in Formal Docketed Proceedings before the Federal Maritime
Puerto Rico Administrative Rulings, A 55.18/3
Renegotiation Board Rulings, RnB 1.6/5
Rules, Rulings and Instructions, A 55.69
Rulings and Interpretations, L 22.11
Rulings on Requests for Review of the Assistant Secretary of Labor for Labor- Management Relations Pursuant to Executive Order 11491, As Amended, L 1.51/6
Sales Tax Rulings, Cumulative Bulletin, T 22.27
Sales Tax Rulings, T 22.26
Social Security Rulings on Federal Old-age, Survivors, Disability, and Health Insurance, HE 3.44
Social Security Rulings, Cumulative Bulletins, HE 3.44/2

Rum
Rum War at Sea, T 47.2:R 86
Rum: Annual Report on Selected Economic Indicators, ITC 1.31

Run
Data Integrity and Run to Run Balancing, T 22.58

Runaway

Annual Report on Activities Conducted to Implement the Runaway Youth Act, HE 23.1309
Runaways and Otherwise Homeless Youth Fiscal Year, Annual Report on the Runaway Youth Act, HE 23.1309/2

Runoff
Quarterly Progress Report, Nationwide Urban Runoff Program, EP 1.92
Selected Urban Storm Water Runoff Abstracts, EP 2.10:11024
Weekly Runoff Report, Pacific Northwest Water Resources, I 19.46/2

Runs
Side Runs of Paper Trade, C 18.124

Rural
Annual Report on the HEW/USDA Rural Health Facilities Agreement, A 84.12
Annual Statistical Report, Rural Electrification Borrowers, A 68.1/2
Annual Statistical Report, Rural Telecommunications Borrowers, A 68.1/3
Catalyst for Rural Development, A 21.31
Census of Distribution; Small City and Rural Trade Series, C 3.37/38
Current Statistics of Relief in Rural and Town Areas, Y 3.W 89/2:25, SS 1.23
Directory of Teachers Giving Courses in Rural Sociology and Rural Life, A 36.57
Extension Service Update, Community and Rural Development (CRD), A 43.49/3
Farm Population and Rural Life Activities, A 36.23
Knowledge for Survival, You Can Survive! Newsletter to State Extension Program Leaders, Rural Defense, A 43.35/2
List of Rural Delivery County Maps, P 11.7
Medicare Rural Health Clinic Manual, HE 22.8/19
News Letter for State Supervisors of Rural Research, Y 3.F 31/5:26, Y 3.W 89/2:16
Number of New Permanent Nonfarm Dwelling Units Started by Urban or Rural Location, Public or Private Ownership, and Type of Structure, L 2.51/4
Official List of Rural Free Delivery Offices, P 13.6
Progress in Rural Development Program, Annual Reports, A 1.85
Relief in Rural and Town Areas, SS 1.25/a 2
Report of the Administrator of the Rural Electrification Administration, A 68.1
Residents of Farms & Rural Areas, C 3.186/25
Rural Areas Development Newsletter, A 21.25/3
Rural Child Welfare Series, L 5.11
Rural Conditions and Trends, A 93.41/3
Rural Development Goals, Annual Report of the Secretary of Agriculture to the Congress, A 1.85/2
Rural Development Goals, Pr 37.14
Rural Development Perspectives, A 93.41/2, A 105.40/2
Rural Development Program News, A 21.25
Rural Development Research Reports, A 93.41, A 105.40
Rural Electrification News, A 68.9
Rural Housing (New Jersey), A 84.17
Rural Information Center Publication Series, A 17.29
Rural Life Studies, A 36.136
Rural Lines, A 68.18
Rural Manpower Developments, L 1.63
Rural Opportunities, PrEx 10.14
Rural Rehabilitation, Y 3.F 31/5:11
Rural Resource Leaflets, A 21.25/2
Rural School Circulars, I 16.42
Rural School Leaflets, I 16.35
Rural Telephone Bank Annual Report, A 1.116
Rural Telephone Bank Publications, A 1.116
Statistical Bulletins Rural Electrification Administration, A 68.13
Statistical Profiles, Rural Redevelopment Areas, SP (Series), C 1.45/2
Statistical Summary, Rural Areas Development and Area Redevelopment, Quarterly Progress Report, A 43.38
Task Force on Rural Development, Pr 37.8:R 88
Tax Delinquency of Rural Real Estate, A 36.78
You Can Survive, Rural Defense Fact Sheets, A 43.35
Working Together for Rural America, A 13.125

Russia
NIMA Nautical Charts, Public Sale Region 4, Scandinavia, Baltic and Russia, TD, 4.82:4

Russian
Amepnka, This Is a Russian Edition of America, S 1.55
American Illustrated {Russian Edition}, ICA 1.10
Astronomical Papers Translated from the Russian, SI 1.12/4
Bibliography of Translations from Russian Scientific and Technical Literature, LC 1.26
Bulletin of Translations from Russian Medical Sciences, FS 2.22/19-2
Guide to Russian Scientific Periodical Literature, Y 3.At 7:23
Monthly Index of Russian Accessions, LC 30.10
Publications Russian Scientific Translation Program, FS 2.22/19
Russian Economic Notes, C 18.123
Russian Scientific Translation Program Publications, FS 2.22/19
Russian Series, S 1.17

RWS
Retail, Wholesale, Service Trades, Subject Bulletin, RWS (series), C 3.202/9

Rye
Commitments of Traders in Wheat, Corn, Oats, Rye, Soybeans, Soybean Oil, Soybean Meal, Shell Eggs, A 85.9/2
Commodity Information Series; Rye Leaflets, A 55.25/8
Crop Production, Winter Wheat and Rye, A 88.18/ 11
Futures Trading and Open Contracts in Wheat, Corn, Oats, Rye, Soybeans and Products, A 85.11/7
Small Grains, Annual Summary and Crop Winter Wheat and Rye Seedings, A 105.20/6, A 92.42
Stocks of Wheat and Rye, A 36.174/2
United States Winter Wheat and Rye Reports, A 36.74
Wheat and Rye Summary, Crop Year, A 88.18/16
Winter Wheat and Rye Reports, A 66.48

Ryukyu
Military Government of Ryukyu Islands: Ryukyu Statistical Bulletin, D 102.19

Ryukyu Islands
Civil Affairs Activities in Ryukyu Islands, D 102.19/3
Military Government of Ryukyu Islands: Ryukyu Statistical Bulletin, D 102.19
Special Bulletins United States Administration of Ryukyu Islands, D 102.19/2
Statistical Bulletins Military Government of Ryukyu Islands, D 102.19
Summation of United States Army Military Government Activities in Ryukyu Islands, W 1.78, M 105.12
United States Civil Administration of Ryukyu Islands; Special Bulletins, D 102.19/2

S

S & L's
FHLB System S & L's Combined Financial Statements: Savings and Home Financing Source Book, FHL 1.12/2

S-X
Regulations S-X Under the Securities Act of 1933, SE 1.6:F 49

S.O.C.
S.O.C. {Synthetic Organic Chemicals}, TC 1.25/3, TC 1.25/4

S.R.
S.R. {Sugar Requirements and Quotas} (series), A 82.6/2
Sugar Requirements and Quotas S.R. (series), A 82.6/2

SA
SA-FR (series), A 13.102/2
Surveillance and Analysis Division, Region 8, Denver Colo., Technical Support Branch: SA/TSB-1- (series), EP 1.51/3
Surveillance and Analysis Division, Region 8: Technical Investigations Branch, SA/ TIB-(series), EP 1.51/4
Technical Publications, SA-TP (series), A 13.40/12

Sabotage
Laws relating to Espionage, Sabotage, etc., Y 1.2:Es 6

Safe
Safe Work Guide, OSHA, L 35.11
Safe Work Guides, SWG LS-(series), L 16.51/2
Safe Work Practices Series, L 35.11/2

Suggested **Safe** Practices for Longshoremen, L 16.51/3-2

Safeguard

Safeguard Our Nation's Youth on the Job, L 15.51/5

Safes

Steel Office Furniture, Shelving, and Lockers, and Fireproof **Safes**, C 3.108

Safety

Activities Relating to the Port and Tanker **Safety** Act, TD 5.34/2

Activities Relating to Title II, Ports and Waterways **Safety** Act of 1972, Report to Congress, TD 5.34

Administration of Federal Metal and Nonmetallic Mine **Safety** Act, Annual Report of the Secretary of the Interior, I 1.96/2

Administration of the Federal Metal and Nonmetallic Mine **Safety** Act, I 28.5

Aerospace Maintenance **Safety**, D 306.8

Aerospace **Safety**, D 301.44

Aerospace **Safety** Advisory Panel, Annual Report, NAS 1.1/7

Annual Report by the President to the Congress on the Administration of the Federal Railroad **Safety** Act of 1970, TD 1.10/7

Annual Report Director of the Bureau of **Safety**, IC 1 saf.1

Annual Report of **Safety** Progress for (year), T 1.41/3

Annual Report of Secretary of Transportation of Administration of Natural Gas Pipelines **Safety** Act of 1968, TD 1.10/4

Annual Report of the Administration of the Natural Gas Pipeline **Safety** Act, TD 9.11

Annual Report on Pipeline **Safety**, TD 10.12

Annual Report on Public Information and Education Countermeasure of Alcohol **Safety** Action Projects, TD 8.20

Annual Report on School **Safety**, E 1.1/7

Annual Report on the Administration of the Natural Gas Pipeline **Safety** Act, TD 9.11

Applications Accepted for Filing by **Safety** and Special Radio Services Bureau, CC 1.39/4

Applications Pending in Commission for Exemption from Radio Provisions of International Convention for **Safety** of Life at Sea Convention, London, 1929, Title 3,. . ., Reports, CC 1.19

Approach, Naval Aviation **Safety** Review, D 202.13

Auto and Traffic **Safety**, TD 8.36

Bibliography of Fire Hazards and Prevention and **Safety** in Petroleum Industry, C 22.27

Boating **Safety** Circulars, TD 5.4/3

Boating **Safety** Newsletter, TD 5.28

Bureau of Aviation **Safety** Report, BASR (series), TD 1.114

Bureau of **Safety** and Service Laws, IC 1 saf.5/2

Bureau of **Safety** Pamphlet BOSP (series), C 31.252

Bureau of **Safety** Reports, C 31.252/2

Callback from NASA's Aviation **Safety** Reporting System, NAS 1.89

Cancer Research **Safety** Monograph Series, HE 20.3162/2

Chemical **Safety** Data Sheets, EDS-LS- (series), L 16.51/7

Citator to Decisions of the Occupational **Safety** and Health Review Commission, Y 3.Oc 1:10-4

Community Action Program for Traffic **Safety**, Guides (numbered), TD 8.8/2

Comparisons of State **Safety** Codes with A S A, L 16.7/2

Consumer Product **Safety** Review, Y 3.C 76/3:28

Executive Summaries, National Highway **Safety** Bureau Contractors Report, TD 2.212

Experimental **Safety** Vehicle Program and Vehicle **Safety** Research, Progress Report, TD 8.16/2

Explosives **Safety**, D 211.26

Fathom, Surface Ship and Submarine **Safety** Review, D 202.20, D 201.32

FAA Aviation **Safety** Journal, TD 4.68

FDA **Safety** Alerts (on various subjects), HE 20.4616

Federal Coal Mine Health Program, Annual Report of the Federal Coal Mine Health and **Safety** Act, HE 20.2020

Federal Mine **Safety** and Health Review Commission Index, Y 3.M 66:9-2

Federal Motor Carrier **Safety** Administration, Register, TD 2.314.6/4

Federal Motor Vehicle **Safety** Standards, TD 8.6/4

Federal Motor Vehicle **Safety** Standards and Regulations, TD 8.6/2

Federal **Safety** News, FIS 1.8

Fire **Safety** Activities, GS 1.14/8

Fire **Safety** Activities {list} Administrative, GS 1.14/8

Fire **Safety** Focus Sheets, Y 3.C 76/3:24

Flight **Safety** Bulletins, TD 5.3/7, D 202.10

Food **Safety** Educator, A 110.19

FSIS Food **Safety** Review, A 110.17

Health and **Safety**, E 1.99

Health and **Safety** Laboratory: Environmental Quarterly, ER 1.27

Health and **Safety** Statistics, I 28.26

High-Temperature Gas-Cooled Reactor **Safety** Studies, E 1.28/7

High-Temperature Gas-Cooled Reactor **Safety** Studies for the Division of Reactor **Safety** Research Quarterly Progress Report, E 1.28/7

Highlights (year) **Safety** Standards Activity, L 16.52

Highway and Traffic **Safety**, TD 8.12/3

Highway **Safety** Literature Annual Cumulations, TD 8.10/3

Highway **Safety** Literature, Supplements, TD 8.10/4

Highway **Safety** Program Manual, TD 8.8/3

Highway **Safety** Program Standards, TD 2.38, TD 8.8/4

Highway **Safety** Stewardship Report, TD 2.58

Holmes **Safety** Association Bulletin, L 38.12

Index-Digest of Decisions Under Federal **Safety** Appliance Acts, IC 1 saf.9

Indicators of School Crime and **Safety**, ED 1.347

Industrial Health and **Safety** Series, L 16.9

Industrial **Safety** Subjects, L 16.18

Industrial **Safety** Summaries, L 16.20

International Conference for Revision of Convention of 1914 for **Safety** of Life at Sea, S 5.29

International Conference on **Safety** at Sea, Reports, C 1.10

International Conference on **Safety** of Life at Sea, London, 1929, Reports, C 1.10/2

International Congress on Automotive **Safety**: Proceedings, TD 8.21

Job **Safety** and Health, L 35.9/2

MARAD **Safety** Review, C 39.219

Marine **Safety** Newsletter, TD 5.3/11

Maritime **Safety** Data for Shipyard Industry, L 16.47/4

Maritime **Safety** Data for the Stevedoring Industry, L 16.47/6

Maritime **Safety** Data; Longshoring, L 16.47/5

Maritime **Safety** Digest, L 16.47

Maritime **Safety** Digest: Shipyards, L 35.12

MESA **Safety** Reviews: Coal-Mine Fatalities, I 69.10

MESA **Safety** Reviews: Coal-Mine Injuries and Worktime, I 69.10/2

MESA **Safety** Reviews: Injuries at Sand and Gravel Plants, I 69.10/3

MESA, the Magazine of Mining Health and **Safety**, I 69.11

Mine **Safety** and Health, L 38.9

Minutes of the Annual Meeting of the Treasury **Safety** Council, T 1.41/2

Monthly **Safety** Bulletin, Y 3.Em 3:10, Y 3.C 49:7

Motor Vehicle **Safety** Defect Recall Campaigns, TD 8.9

Motor Vehicle **Safety** Defect Recall Campaigns Reported to the Department of Transportation by Domestic and Foreign Vehicle Manufacturers, TD 2.209

Motorboat **Safety**, T 47.49

National Conferences on Street and Highway **Safety**, C 1.21

National Farm **Safety** Week, A 1.96

National Farm **Safety** Week: Annual Report, Y 3.T 25:1-8

National Farm **Safety** Week: Bulletins, Y 3.T 25:3-2

National Farm **Safety** Week: Circulars, Y 3.T 25:4-2

National Highway **Safety** Advisory Committee: Annual Report, TD 1.13/2

National Highway **Safety** Bureau Contracts, TD 8.15

National Motor Vehicle **Safety** Advisory Council Summary Report, TD 1.13

National Shipping Authority: **Safety** Bulletin, C 39.209

National Traffic **Safety** Newsletter, TD 8.18

National Transportation **Safety** Board Decisions, TD 1.122

Navy Lifeline, Naval **Safety** Journal, D 207.15

NEISS {National Electronic Injury Surveillance System} News, Product **Safety**, HE 20.4026, Y 3.C 76/3:7-2

News from the President's Conference on Occupational **Safety**, L 16.35/2

NIOSH Health and **Safety** Guides for {various businesses}, HE 20.7108/2

Noise Diagnostics for **Safety** Assessment, Standards, and Regulation, E 1.28/10

NTSB **Safety** Recommendation (series), TD 1.129

NTSB-AAS {National Transportation **Safety** Board, Aspects of Aviation **Safety**} (series), TD 1.121

Nuclear **Safety**, Y 3.N 88:9, E 1.93

Nuclear **Safety** Index, Y 3.N 88:9-2

Occupational **Safety** Aid, Department of Labor **Safety** Training Programs, OSA-OSHA- (series), L 35.10

Occupational **Safety** and Health Construction Standards and Interpretations, L 35.6/3-3

Occupational **Safety** and Health Field Operations Manual, L 35.6/3-5

Occupational **Safety** and Health General Industry Standard and Interpretations, L 35.6/3-1

Occupational **Safety** and Health Hazards (series), HE 20.7117

Occupational **Safety** and Health Industrial Hygiene Field Operations Manual, L 35.6/3-6

Occupational **Safety** and Health Maritime Standards and Interpretations, L 35.6/3-2

Occupational **Safety** and Health Other Regulations and Procedures, L 35.6/3-4

Occupational **Safety** and Health Regulations, L 35.6/2

Occupational **Safety** and Health Statistics of the Federal Government, L 35.13

Occupational **Safety** Charts, L 16.8/2:Oc 1

Off the Job **Safety**, OJS-LS- (series), L 16.51/9

Office of Merchant Marine **Safety**, TD 5.35

On Guard, Bureau of Motor Carrier **Safety** Bulletin, TD 2.303

Orders Consumer Product **Safety** Commission, Y 3.C 76/3:6-2

Ordnance Department **Safety** Bulletin, D 105.7

OSAHRE Reports: Decisions of the Occupational **Safety** and Health Review Commission, Y 3.Oc 1:10

OSHA **Safety** and Health Standards Digests, L 35.6/4

Plant **Safety** Branch Handbooks, FS 2.22/24

Port **Safety** Bulletin, TD 5.3/4

Posters Food **Safety** and Inspection Service, A 103.18

Posters Mine **Safety** and Health Administration, L 38.14/2

President's Conference on Industrial **Safety** News Letter, L 16.30

President's Report on Occupational **Safety** and Health, Pr 38.2:Oc 1

Product **Safety** Education Unit (series), Y 3.C 76/3:19

Program Plan of the National Institute for Occupational **Safety** and Health, HE 20.7127

Public Law 85-742, **Safety** and Health Administration, Annual Report, L 16.48

Public Notices: **Safety** and Special Radio Services, Report, CC 1.39

Public **Safety** Newsletter, Y 3.At 7:58

Publications National Conferences on Street and Highway **Safety**, C 1.21

Publications President's Highway **Safety** Conference, FW 2.18

R & D Highway & **Safety** Transportation System Studies, TD 2.24

Reclamation **Safety** News, I 27.18

Recreation Boating **Safety** R & D, Annual Report, TD 5.28/4

Regulations for the Administration and Enforcement of the Radiation Control for Health and **Safety** Act of 1968, HE 20.4606/2

Report on Activities Under Highway **Safety** Act, TD 8.12/2

Report on Activities Under the National Traffic and Motor Vehicle **Safety** Act, TD 8.12

Report on the International Technical Conference on Experimental **Safety** Vehicles, TD 8.16

Report to Congress on the Administration of the Highway **Safety** Act of 1966, TD 1.10/3

Report to Congress on the Administration of the National Traffic Vehicle **Safety** Act of 1966, TD 1.10/2

Report to the Administrator by the NASA Aerospace **Safety** Advisory Panel, NAS 1.58

Reserve Fleet **Safety** Review, C 39.219

Rules for Inspection of **Safety** Appliances, IC 1 saf.6

Rules Pertaining to Aircraft Accidents, Incidents, Overdue Aircraft, and **Safety** Investigations, TD 1.106/2

Safety and Fire Protection Bulletins, Y 3.At 7:3

Safety and Health Requirments, L 16.23

Safety and Special Actions, Reports, Public Notices, CC 1.39/2

Safety and Special Radio Services Bulletins, CC 1.39/3

Safety Appliances Act {text}, IC 1 saf.5

Safety Bulletins Bureau of Employees' Compensation, FS 13.307, L 26.7

Safety Bulletins Civil Aeronautics Board, C 31.214

Safety Bulletins Civil Conservation Corps, FS 4.8

Safety Bulletins Employees Compensation Commission, EC 1.9

Safety Bulletins Federal Emergency Relief Administration, Y 3.F 31/5:24

Safety Bulletins Government Printing Office, GP 1.24

Safety Bulletins National Shipping Authority, C 39.209

Safety Bulletins National Youth Administration, FS 6.16

Safety Bulletins Works Progress Administration, FW 4.20, Y 3.W 89/2:11

Safety Bus Checks, TD 2.302:B 96

Safety Competition, National Crushed Stone Association, I 28.26/4

Safety Competition, National Lime Association, I 28.26/3

Safety Competition, National Sand and Gravel, I 28.26/3

Safety Competitions, National Limestone Institute, I 28.26/7

Safety Conference Guides, I 1.77/3

Safety Department Bulletins, Y 3.F 31/7:10

Safety Digest, W 34.37, D 101.22/3:385

Safety Division Bulletins, Y 3.Em 3:8

Safety Effectiveness Evaluation, NTSB-SEE-(series), TD 1.125

Safety Evaluation Series, TD 2.62

Safety in Industry, L 16.3

Safety in Mineral Industries, I 28.113

Safety Investigation Regulations, SIR (series), C 31.206/4

Safety Management Information, EP 1.7/3

Safety Management Series, L 35.19

Safety Manuals, I 69.8/2, L 38.8/2

Safety Musketeers, I 16.63

Safety News, Y 3.C 76/3:11-4

Safety News Letter, Y 3.F 31/5:17

Safety News Letter, Current Information in the Federal Safety Field, L 30.8Safety Pamphlets, GP 1.18

Safety Post Cards, I 29.54

Safety Posters Department of the Navy, N 1.31/2

Safety Posters Federal Public Housing Authority, NHA 4.9

Safety Recommendations, TD 1.106/3

Safety Related Recall Campaigns for Motor Vehicles and Motor Vehicle Equipment, Including Tires, TD 8.9/2

Safety Reports, NTSB-SR (series), TD 1.106/4

Safety Research Programs Sponsored by Office of Nuclear Regulatory Research, Y 3.N 88:48

Safety Review, D 204.7

Safety Section Circulars, Y 3.R 13/2:26

Safety Series, Bulletins, IC 1 mot.10

Safety Standards, L 35.9

Safety Studies, C 31.223

Safety Studies, NTSB/SS (series), TD 1.27

Safety, Fire Prevention, and Occupational Health Management, by Objectives Review, D 301.99

Safety, Occupational Health and Fire Protection Bulletin, VA 1.22:13-1

Schools and **Safety** Staffing Survey, ED 1.332

Selected **Safety** Road Checks Motor Carriers of Property, TD 2.311

Spot the Danger, User's Guide to {various products} **Safety** Series, Y 3.C 76/3:8-3

State **Safety** Digest, L 16.29

State **Safety** Program Work Sheets, L 16.39

State Traffic **Safety** Information, TD 8.62

Student Work Sheets, Department of Labor **Safety** Training Programs, SWS-LS-(series), L 16.51

Subject Bibliographies from Highway **Safety** Literature, SB- (series), TD 8.13/3

Suggested **Safety** Practices for Shipyard Workers, L 16.51/3

Summary of **Safety** Management Audits, TD 2.66

Survey with **Safety**, C 4.51

Task Force on Highway **Safety**, Pr 37.8:H 53

Telephone Directory National Transportation **Safety** Board, TD 1.124

Towards Improved Health and **Safety** for America's Coal Miners, Annual Report of the Secretary of the Interior, I 1.96

Traffic **Safety** Data ASCII and SAS Versions, TD 1.56/3

Traffic **Safety** Digest, TD 8.40

Traffic **Safety** Evaluation Research Review, TD 8.18/2

Traffic **Safety** Newsletter, TD 8.18

Transportation **Safety** Information Report, TD 1.48

Transportation **Safety** Regulatory Bulletin, E 1.135

Treasury **Safety** Council Safety Bulletin, Administrative, T 1.41

Unresolved **Safety** Issues Summary, Aqua Book, Y 3.N 88:30

Vessel **Safety** Review, TD 5.12/3

Water Reactor **Safety** Research, Buff Book I, Y 3.N 88:18

Water **Safety** Program Catalog, D 103.124

Safety Studies

Safetyline
    Safetyline, D 207.15/2

Sagamore
    Sagamore Army Materials Research Conference Proceedings (series), D 101.122

Sail
    List of Masters, Mates, {etc} of Merchant Steam, Motor, and **Sail** Vessels, Licensed during Calendar Year, T 38.7

    List of Officers of Merchant Steam, Motor and **Sail** Vessels Licensed During (calendar year), C 15.7

Sailing
    Catalog of Charts, **Sailing** Directions and Tide Tables, C 4.18/1

    Explanations and **Sailing** Directions to Accompany Wind and Current Charts, N 14.9

    Great Circle (8) **Sailing** and Polar Charts, D 5.345

    Hydrographic/Topographic Center Publications: Sailing Directions, D 5.317/3

    Sailing Dates of Steamships from the Principal Ports of the United States to Ports in Foreign Countries, C 15.19, C 18.10

    Sailing Directions Coast and Geodetic Survey, C 4.18/3

    Sailing Directions Naval Oceanographic Office, D 203.22

    Sailing Directions, D 5.317

Sailings
    Schedule of **Sailings** of Steam Vessels Registered Under Laws of United States and Intended to Load General Cargo at Ports in United States for Foreign Destinations, IC 1 rat.8

Sailor
    Soldier, **Sailor**, Airman, Marine (SAM), D 1.55

Sailor's
    Inspection of State Soldiers and **Sailor's** Homes, NH 1.5

Sailors
    Soldiers' and **Sailors'** Civil Relief Act of 1940 and Amendments, Y 1.2:So 4/7, Y 1.2:So 4/2

Saint Elizabeth's
    Saint Elizabeth's Hospital, Sun Dial, I 1.14/5

Saint Lawrence
    Great Lakes-**Saint Lawrence** Seaway Winter Navigation Board: Annual Report, D 103.1/3

    Saint Lawrence Survey {reports}, C 1.22

Saint Louis
    Notes for Louisiana Purchase Exposition, **Saint Louis**, Missouri, LC 1.8

    Saint Louis, Louisiana Purchase Exposition, S 6.18

Saint Marys
    Saint Marys Falls Canal, Michigan, Statistical Report of Lake Commerce Passing through Canals at Sault Ste. Marie, Michigan and Ontario, W 7.26, M 110.16, D 103.17

Salable
    Salable {and total} Receipts of Livestock at Public Markets, in Order of Volume, A 88.16/15

Salad
    Salad Dressing, Mayonnaise and Related Products, C 57.316, C 57.514

Salaries
    Faculty **Salaries** in Land-Grant Colleges and State Universities, FS 5.253:53023, HE 5.253:53023

    Higher Education **Salaries**, FS 5.253:53015, HE 5.253:53015

    Instructional Faculty **Salaries** for Academic Year, ED 1.131

    Office Workers, **Salaries**, Hours of Work, Supplementary Benefits (by cities), L 2.43

    Receipts and Classes of Post Offices, with Basic **Salaries** of Postmasters, P 24.7, P 25.8

    Regional Data on Compensation Show Wages, **Salaries** and Benefits Costs in the Northeast, L 2.71/6-6

    Salaries and Fringe Benefits, HE 19.332

    Salaries of State Public Health Workers, FS 2.82

    Statement of Taxes, Dividends, **Salaries** and Wages, Class a and Class B Privately Owned Electric Utilities in U.S., FP 1.22

    White-Collar **Salaries**, L 2.43/2

Salary
    Current **Salary** Schedules of Federal Officers and Employees Together with a History of Salary and Retirement Annuity Adjustments, Y 4.P 84/10-15

    Earnings and Employment Data for Wage and **Salary** Workers Covered under Social Security by State and County, HE 3.95, SSA 1.17/3

    General Accounting Office **Salary** Tables, GA 1.10, GA 1.6/10

    General **Salary** Orders, ES 4.6/3

    General **Salary** Stabilization Regulations GSSR (series), ES 4.6/2

    Government **Salary** Tables, T 13.6

    Laws relating to Civil Service **Salary** Classification, Civil Service Preference, Etc., Y 1.2:Sa 3/2

    Personnel Handbook, Series P-1, Position Description and **Salary** Schedules, Transmittal Letters, P 1.31

    Salary Procedural Regulations, ES 4.6/5

    Salary Tables, Executive Branch of the Government, CS 1.73, PM 1.9

    State **Salary** Ranges, Selected Classes {of positions} in Employment Security, Public Welfare, Public Health, Mental Health, Vocational Rehabilitation, Civil Defense, Emergency Planning, CS 1.81, FS 1.22, HE 1.22, GS 1.8

    U.S. Government **Salary** Tables, Post-Office Dept, P 1.15

    Usual Weekly Earnings of Wage and **Salary** Workers, L 2.126

    Weekly Earnings of Wage and **Salary** Workers, L 2.126

Sale
    Catalogs and Advertisements of Surplus Equipment for **Sale**, N 20.14

Sale
    Competitive Oil and Gas Lease **Sale** Results, Date of Sale, I 53.53

    Construction Reports; New One-family Homes Sold and for **Sale**, C 25 (series), C 56.211/2

    Current Construction Reports, New One-Family Houses Sold and for **Sale**, C 3.215/9

    FHA and VA Mortgages Owned and Available for **Sale** by Reconstruction Finance Corporation and Federal National Mortgage Association, Y 3.R 24:14

    Land **Sale**, I 53.32/2

    List of Atomic Energy Commission Documents Available for **Sale**, Y 3.At 7:15

    Manufacture and **Sale** of Farm Equipment, C 3.55

Monthly Receipts from **Sale** of Principal Farm
Products by States, A 36.81/2

National Forest Timber **Sale** Accomplishments for
Fiscal Year, A 13.58

Price List of Publications of Department of
Agriculture for **Sale** by Superintendent
of Documents, A 21.8

Public **Sale** Catalog: Aeronautical Charts and
Publications, D 5.351/3-2

Public **Sale** Catalog: Topographic Maps and
Publications, D 5.351/3

Publications Available for **Sale**, I 27.10/2

Publications for **Sale**, I 27.10/2

Publications **Sale**, L 2.34/3

Receipts from **Sale** of Principal Farm Products by
States, A 36.81/1

Regulations for **Sale** of Lake Survey Charts, W 33.5

Sales

Advance Monthly Retail **Sales** Report, C 3.138/4

American Listed Corporations, Survey of:
Quarterly **Sales** Data, SE 1.22

Annual Report of Department of Treasury on
Operation and Effect of Domestic
International **Sales** Corporation
Legislation for Calendar Year, Y 4.W
36:D 71/2

Asphalt **Sales**, E 3.11/18

Asphalt **Sales** in (year), I 28.110/2

Bond **Sales** for Higher Education, FS 5.252:52004
HE 5.252:52004

Bond **Sales** for Public School Purposes, HE 19.323

Cattle, Calves, and Vealers: Top Prices and Bulk of
Sales, Chicago, A 36.207

CCC Monthly **Sales** List, A 1.101

Census of Business; 1939, Retail Trade, Commodity
Sales (by Commodities), C 3.940-24

Census of Wholesale Trade; Wholesale Commodity
Line **Sales**, C 3.256/5

Confectionery Manufacturers' **Sales** and
Distribution, C 41.19, C 57.13

Current Business Reports; Advance Monthly
Retail **Sales**, CB (series), C 56.219/6

Current Business Reports; Monthly Retail Trade,
Sales and Accounts Receivable, BR
(series), C 56.219/4

Current Business Reports; Monthly Wholesale
Trade, **Sales** and Inventories, BW
(series), C 56.219

Current Business Reports; Weekly Retail **Sales**, CB
(series), C 56.219/7

Cut Flowers, Production and **Sales**, A 88.47

Department Store **Sales**, FR 1.24

Department Store **Sales** and Stocks, by Major
Departments, FR 1.24/4

Department Store **Sales**, by Cities, FR 1.24/2

Department Store **Sales**, Preliminary Reports, FR
1.20

Department Store Trade, United States Departmental **Sales** Indexes, without Seasonal
Adjustment, FR 1.24/9, FR 1.24/10

Department Store Trade, United States Distribution
of **Sales** by Months, FR 1.24/7, FR 1.24/
8

Distribution of **Sales** (Rotoprint), C 3.57

Electric **Sales** and Revenue, E 3.22

Electricity **Sales** Statistics, Y 3.T 25:13

Electricity **Sales** Statistics, Distribution of
Electricity at TVA Wholesale and Retail
Rates, Y 3.T 25:13-2

Electricity **Sales** Statistics: Rate of Initial Service
at TVA Rates and Wholesale Purchases
from TVA, Y 3.T 25:13-2

Exhausted GPO **Sales** Publications Reference File,
GP 3.22/3-3

Export **Sales** Promotions Announcements, C 42.23/
2

Field and Seed Crops, Production, Farm Use, **Sales**,
Value by States, A 92.19

Floriculture Crops, Production Area and **Sales**, A
92.32

Flowers and Foliage Plants, Production and **Sales**,
A 92.32

Foreign Military **Sales** Customer Procedures
(series), D 7.6/15

Foreign Military Sales, Foreign Military
Construction **Sales**, and Military
Assistance Facts, D 1.66

Fuel Oil and Kerosene **Sales**, E 3.11/11-4

Fuel Oil **Sales**, E 3.11/11

Generation and **Sales** Statistics, I 44.8

GPO **Sales** Publications Reference File, GP 3.22/3

GPO **Sales** Publications Reference File, Update,
GP 3.22/3-2

HUD **Sales** Connection, HH 1.115

Illuminating Glassware Manufactures, **Sales** and
Credits, C 3.146

Industry Survey, Manufacturers' **Sales**, Inventories,
New and Unfilled Orders, C 43.9

Inventories and **Sales** of Fuel Oil and Motor
Gasoline, Wholesale Distributions, C
3.263/3

Main Line Natural Gas **Sales** to Industrial Users, E
3.11/14

Manufacturers **Sales** and Collections on Accounts
Receivable, C 18.195

Merchandise Line **Sales**, BC-MLS (series), C 3.202/
19

Milk Distributors, **Sales** and Costs, A 88.14/9, A
93.13/2

Mohair Production and Value of **Sales**, A 88.35/4

Monthly Comparative **Sales** of Confectionery, C
18.72/11

Monthly Comparative **Sales** of Confectionery and
Competitive Chocolate Products, C
3.135

Monthly Department Store **Sales** in Selected Areas,
C 3.211/5

Monthly Electric Utility **Sales** and Revenue Report
with State Distributions, E 3.11/17-14

Monthly Retail **Sales**, C 3.138/3-3

Monthly Wholesale Trade Report: **Sales** and
Inventories, C 3.133

Newsletter to **Sales** Agents, GP 3.25

Nursery Products, Production and **Sales**, A 88.48

Offerings and **Sales** of Office of Personal Property
Disposal, Y 3.W 19/8:12

Operation and Effect of the Domestic International
Sales Corporation Legislation, T 1.54

Oregon and Washington Planned Land **Sales**, I
53.32

Petroleum Market Shares, Report on **Sales** of
Refined Petroleum Products, E 3.13

Petroleum Market Shares, Report on **Sales** of Retail
Gasoline, E 3.13/2

Purchase and **Sales** Reports, A 82.61/2

Quarterly Report of Manufacture and **Sales** of Snuff,
Smoking, and Chewing Tobacco, A
88.34/11

Quarterly Report of the General **Sales** Manager, A
1.117, A 67.43

Reports on Hatchery **Sales** in California, A 36.194

Retail **Sales**, Independent Stores, Summary for
States, C 3.138

Revised Monthly Retail **Sales** in Inventories, C
3.138/3-3

Sales by Producers of Natural Gas to Interstate
Pipe-Line Companies, FP 1.21

Sales Finance Companies Bureau of the Census, C
3.151

Sales Finance Companies Federal Reserve System
Board of Governors, FR 1.26

Sales of Capital Assets Reported on Individual
Income Tax Returns, T 22.35/2:C 17

Sales of Condemned Ordnance and Stores, W 34.15

Sales of Electric Energy to Ultimate Consumers, FP
1.11/6

Sales of Firm Electric Power for Resale, by Private
Electric Utilities, by Federal Projects, by
Municipals, FP 1.21

Sales of Fuel Oil and Kerosene in (year), I 28.45/5

Sales of Lacquers, C 3.88

Sales of New One-Family Homes, C 3.215/9

Sales Reports, A 82.61

Sales Tax Rulings, Cumulative Bulletin, T 22.27

Sales Tax Rulings, T 22.26

Sales Product Catalog (online), GP 3.22/7

Sales, Profits, and Dividends of Large Corporations, FR 1.40

Sales, Revenue, and Income for Electric Utilities, E
3.11/2-6

Sales, Revenue, and Income of Electric Utilities, E
3.11/2-8

Schedule of **Sales** Offerings, Pr 33.213

Schedule of **Sales**, Y 3.W 19/8:8

Special Current Business Reports: Monthly
Department Store **Sales** in Selected
Areas, BD- (series), C 56.219/3

Summary of Financial Statements and **Sales**
Statistics, Distributors of TVA Power, Y
3.T 25:1-16

Survey of American Listed Corporations: Quarterly
Sales Data, SE 1.22

Synthetic Organic Chemicals, United States
Production and **Sales**, Preliminaries, TC
1.33/2

Synthetic Organic Chemicals, United States
Production and **Sales**, TC 1.33, ITC 1.14

Tabulation of Project Note **Sales** for Low- income
Housing, HH 1.71/2

U.S. Export **Sales**, A 67.40

U.S. Export **Sales**, Outstanding Export Sales
(unshipped balances) On, A 67.48

U.S. Government Purchasing and **Sales** Directory
Guide for Selling or Buying in the
Government Market, SBA 1.13/3

U.S. Real Property **Sales** List, GS 1.15/5

Water and Sewer Bond **Sales** in United States, FS
2.56/4, I 67.10

Weekly Retail **Sales** Report, C 3.138/5

Wholesale Prices of Lumber, Based on Actual **Sales**
Made F.O.B. Each Market, A 13.17

Wholesale Prices of Lumber, Based on Actual **Sales**
Made F.O.B. Mill, A 13.15

Wool Production and Value of **Sales**, A 88.35/3

Salesmen

News Letter to **Salesmen**, Y 3.N 21/8:21

Saline

Office of **Saline** Water, I 1.82/3

Saline Water Conservation Program, Reports and
Publications, I 1.83

Saline Water Conversion Demonstration Plant, I
1.87/2

Saline Water Conversion Report for (year), I 1.1/3

Saline Water Research and Development Progress
Reports, I 1.88

Salmon

Annual Report Dall Porpoise-**Salmon** Research, C
55.343

Annual Reports on **Salmon** Fisheries, C 2.1

Pacific Coast **Salmon** Park, C 6.11

Pacific **Salmon** Pack, I 49.23

Report on **Salmon** Fisheries of Alaska, T 35.6

Salmonella

National Communicable Disease Center
Salmonella Surveillance, Annual
Summary, FS 2.60/12-2

National Communicable Disease Center
Salmonella Surveillance, Reports, FS
2.60/12

Salmonella Surveillance, Annual Summary, HE
20.7011/15

Salmonella Surveillance, Reports, HE 20.2309

Salt

Directory of Companies Producing **Salt** in the
United States, I 28.134/2

Salt in (year), I 28.134

Statistical Report of Commerce Passing through
Canals at Sault Ste. Marie, Mich. and
Ontario, **Salt** Water Ship Movements for
Season of (year), D 103.17/2

Salt Lake City

Telephone Directory Internal Revenue Service, **Salt
Lake City** District, T 22.48/3

Telephone Directory **Salt Lake City** District, T
22.48/3

Saltonstall

Operations of the Bureau of Commercial Fisheries
Under the **Saltonstall**-Kennedy Act, I
49.48

Research and Activities Under **Saltonstall**-
Kennedy Act, Annual Report of
Secretary of Interior, I 1.1/2

Salute

Last **Salute**, Civil and Military Funerals, D 101.2:F
96

Salvador

U.S. v. **Salvador** Arbitration Tribunal, S 3.14

Salvage

Publications in **Salvage** Archeology, SI 1.22

Salvage News Letters, Pr 32.4823

SAM

School of Aerospace Medicine: Technical
Documentary Report **SAM**-TDR (series),
D 301.26/13-6

Soldier, Sailor, Airman, Marine (**SAM**), D 1.55

Technical Documentary Report **SAM**-TDR- (series),
D 301.26/13-6:1056

Technical Reports, **SAM**-TR- (series), D 301.26/13-
6:1057

Uncle **Sam** Says, T 66.19

SAMHSA

SAMHSA News, HE 20.425

SAMHSA News, HE 20.8026

Sample

1953 **Sample** Census of Agriculture, C 3.31/6

Carload Waybill Statistics, Traffic and Revenue
Progressions by Specified Mileage
Blocks for Commodity Groups and
Classes, 1 Percent **Sample** of Carload
Terminations in Year Statement MB-6, IC
1.23/7

Carload Waybill Statistics,..., Traffic and Revenue by Commodity Class, Territorial Movement, and Type of Rate, Products of Agriculture, 1 Percent **Sample** of Terminations in Statement MB-1, IC 1.23/2

Carload Waybill Statistics,..., Traffic and Revenue by Commodity Class, Territorial Movement, and Type of Rate, Animals and Products, 1 Percent **Sample** of Terminations in Statement MB-2, IC 1.23/3

Carload Waybill Statistics,..., Traffic and Revenue by Commodity Class, Territorial Movement, and Type of Rate, Products of Mines, 1 Percent **Sample** of Terminations in Statement MB-3, IC 1.23/4

Carload Waybill Statistics,..., Traffic and Revenue by Commodity Class, Territorial Movement, and Type of Rate, Products of Forests, 1 Percent **Sample** of Terminations in Statement MB-4, IC 1.23/5

Instruction Manual: Data Preparation of the Current **Sample**, HE 20.6208/9

Regulations Governing Admission of Candidates into Naval Academy As Midshipmen and **Sample** Examination Questions, D 208.108

Samples

Catalog of Cell Cultures and DNA **Samples**, HE 20.3464

Certificate of Analyses of Standard **Samples**, C 13.17

Methods for the Collection and Analysis of Aquatic Biological and Microbiological **Samples**, I 19.15/5

San Angelo

Area Wage Survey, **San Angelo**, Texas, Metropolitan Area, L 2.121/43-5

San Diego, California

Navy Electronics Laboratory, **San Diego, California**, Publications (misc.), D 211.11/2

Neuropsychiatric Research Unit, **San Diego, California**, Abstracts of Completed Research, D 206.21/2

San Francisco

Surveillance and Analysis Division, Region 9, **San Francisco**, California: Technical Reports, EP 1.51

San Juan, Puerto Rico

Climatological Summary, **San Juan, Puerto Rico**, C 30.45

Sanatoria

Tuberculosis Beds in Hospitals and **Sanatoria**, Index of Beds Available, FS 2.69

Sanatorium

Medicare Christian Science **Sanatorium** Hospital Manual Supplement, HE 22.8/2-2

Sanctions

Administrative Decisions Under Employer **Sanctions** and Unfair Immigration-Related Employment Practices Law of the United States, J 1.103

Sanctuaries

Annual Report to Congress on Administration of the Marine Protection Research and **Sanctuaries** Act of 1972, EP 1.69

Sand

Crushed Stone and **Sand** and Gravel in the Quarter of, I 28.118/4

Injury Experience and Related Employment Data for **Sand** and Gravel Industry, I 28.108/2

MESA Safety Reviews: Injuries at **Sand** and Gravel Plants, I 69.10/3

Mineral Industry Surveys, Crushed Stone and **Sand**, I 19.138

Mineral Industry Surveys, Directory of Principal Construction **Sand** and Gravel Producers in the . . ., Annual Advanced Summary Supplement, I 19.138/3

Safety Competition, National **Sand** and Gravel, I 28.26/3

Sand and Gravel (Construction) in . . ., I 28.146/2

Sand and Gravel in (year), I 28.146

Sandhill

Sandhill Crane Harvest and Hunter Activity in the Central Flyway During the Hunting Season, I 49.106/4

Sandia

Sandia Technology, E 1.20/5

Sands

Oil Shales and Tar **Sands**, E 1.99

Singing **Sands** Almanac, I 29.6/3-2

Sandy Hook

Atlantic Coast; Cape Cod to **Sandy Hook**, C 55.422:2

Atlantic Coast; **Sandy Hook** to Cape Henry, C 55.422:3

Sanitary

Approved List **Sanitary** Inspected Fish Establishments, C 55.338

Conference of State **Sanitary** Engineers, Report of Proceedings, HE 20.14

Guidelines for Implementation of **Sanitary** Requirements in Poultry Establishments, A 88.6/4:P 86/2

International **Sanitary** Conference, Washington, 1881, S 5.11

Proceedings Conference of State **Sanitary** Engineers, FS 2.83/4

Sanitary Climatology Circulars, A 29.15

Sanitation

FES Aid: **Sanitation** Series, A 43.40

Health and **Sanitation** Division Newsletters, Pr 32.4610

IMS List **Sanitation** Compliance and Enforcement Ratins of Interstate Milk Shippers, HE 20.4014/2

Military **Sanitation** and First Aid, W 3.50/4

National Shellfish **Sanitation** Workshop, Proceedings, HE 20.4032

Newsletter, Health and **Sanitation** Division, Institute of Inter-American Affairs, S 1.51

Northwest Shellfish **Sanitation** Research Planning Conference, Proceedings, EP 2.15

Proceedings National Shellfish **Sanitation** Workshop, FS 2.16/2

Proceedings Northwest Shellfish **Sanitation** Research Planning Conference, EP 2.15

Sanitation Handbook of Consumer Protection Programs, A 88.6/4:Sa 5

Sanitation Series, A 43.40

School **Sanitation** Leaflets, I 16.24

Status Report of the Operation and Maintenance of **Sanitation** Facilities Serving American Indians and Alaska Natives, HE 20.9416

Summary of **Sanitation** Inspection of International Cruise Ships, HE 20.7511

Santa Barbara

Water Levels in Observation Wells in **Santa Barbara** County, California, I 19.49

Santa Monica

Outdoors in the **Santa Monica** Mountains National Recreation Area, I 29.6/7

Santa Monica Mountains and Seashore, I 29.6/7

Santa Monica Mountains

Outdoors in the **Santa Monica Mountains** National Recreation Area, I 29.135

Santiago

International American Conference; **Santiago**, Chile, S 5.9/5

Pan-American Scientific Congress, **Santiago**, Chile, S 5.14

Santiago, Chile, International Exhibition, 1875, S 6.5

Santitation

List of Acceptable Interstate Carrier Equipment Having **Santitation** Significances, FS 2.78

SAR

National Maritime **SAR** Review, TD 5.24

On Scene, National Maritime **SAR** {Search and Rescue} Review, TD 5.24

SAR Statistics, TD 5.50

SARAP

EDRO **SARAP** Research Technical Reports, HE 20.4031/2

SARE/ACE

National **SARE/ACE** Report to Congress, A 94.19

SAS

Traffic Safety Data ASCII and **SAS** Versions, TD 1.56/3

Saskatchewan

Annual Reports to the Governments of Canada, U.S. **Saskatchewan** and Montana by the Poplar River Bilateral Monitoring Committee, S 1.147

Satcom

Satcom Quarterly, NAS 1.12/7:410-33

Satellite

Annual Report on Activities and Accomplishments Under the Communications **Satellite** Act of 1962, PrEx 18.9

Appalachian Education **Satellite** Project Technical Reports, Y 3.Ap 4/2:12

Bibliography of National Environmental **Satellite** Service, C 55.509

Catalog of Meteorological **Satellite** Data: ESSA 9 and NOAA 1 Television Cloud Photography, C 55.219:5.3

Data Catalog, **Satellite** and Rocket Experiments, NSSDA (nos), NAS 1.37

Domestic Fixed **Satellite** Services, CC 1.47/4

Earth Resources **Satellite** Data Applications Series, NAS 1.64

Earth Resources Technology **Satellite**: Standard Catalog, NAS 1.488

International **Satellite** and Space Probe Summary {and charts}, NAS 1.16

Key to Meteorological Records, Environmental **Satellite** Imagery (series), C 55.219/4

Satellite Activities of NOAA, C 55.510

Satellite Applications Information Notes, C 55.37

Satellite Situation Report, NAS 1.40

Saturn

Rings of **Saturn**, NAS 1.22:343

Sault Ste. Marie

Saint Marys Falls Canal, Michigan, Statistical Report of Lake Commerce Passing through Canals at **Sault Ste. Marie**, Michigan and Ontario, W 7.26, M 110.16, D 103.17

Statistical Report of Commerce Passing through Canals at **Sault Ste. Marie**, Mich. and Ontario, Salt Water Ship Movements for Season of (year), D 103.17/2

Saval

Saval Ranch Research and Evaluation Project, Progress Report, I 53.40

Savannah

Tide Calendar **Savannah**, Georgia, N 6.22/3, M 202.14, D 203.14

Saver

War **Saver**, T 1.26/7

Saving

New Way of **Saving** (series), GS 12.11

Savings

All Operating **Savings** and Loan Associations, Selected Balance Sheet Data, FHL 1.20

Asset and Liability Trends All Operating **Savings** and Loan Associations, FHL 1.30

Assets Liabilities and Capital Accounts Commercial Banks and Mutual **Savings** Banks, Y 3.F 31/8:9

BondPro, U.S. **Savings** Bond Pricing System, T 63.217

Bond Tips from Your U.S. **Savings** Bond Reporter, T 66.24

Conventional Loans Made in Excess of 80 Percent of Property Appraisal by Federal **Savings** and Loan Associations, FHL 1.19

Conventional Loans Made to Finance Acquisition and Development of Land, Federal **Savings** and Loan Associations, FHL 1.22

Cooperative **Savings** with Federal Credit Unions, FCA 1.14, FCA 1.14/2

Defense **Savings** Staff News, T 1.108

Estimated Flow of **Savings** in **Savings** and Loan Associations, HH 4.8/2

Estimated Mortgage Lending Activity of **Savings** and Loan Associations, HH 4.8/3

Federal **Savings** and Loan Insurance Corporation, Financial Statements, FHL 1.2:F 31/2

FHLB System S & L's Combined Financial Statements: **Savings** and Home Financing Source Book, FHL 1.12/2

Flow of **Savings** in **Savings** and Loan Associations, FHL 1.7/2

FSLIC Insured **Savings** and Loan Associations, **Savings** and Mortgage Activity, Selected Balance Sheet Items, FHL 1.20/2

Information about Postal **Savings** System, P 19.7/2

Insured **Savings** and Loan Associations, Average Annual Dividend Rates Paid, FHL 1.21

Investment of Individuals in **Savings** Accounts, U.S. **Savings** Bonds and Life Insurance Reserves, FHL 1.13

Mortgage Interest Rates on Conventional Loans, Largest Insured **Savings** and Loan Associations, FHL 1.24

Mortgage Lending Activity of **Savings** and Loan Associations, FHL 1.7/3

National War **Savings** Committee, T 1.26

Number of Foreclosures {and rate of foreclosure} by FSLIC Insured **Savings** and Loan Associations, FHL 1.26

P.S. Payroll **Savings** Bulletin, T 66.16

Program Aids Defense **Savings** Staff, T 1.109

Schedule of Sailings of Steam Vessels Registered Under Laws of United States and Intended to Load General Cargo at Ports in United States for Foreign Destinations, IC 1 rat.8

Schedule of Sales Offerings, Pr 33.213

Schedule of Sales, Y 3.W 19/8:8

Schedule of Steamers Appointed to Convey Mails to Foreign Countries, P 8.5

Schedule of Training and Services for Fiscal Year, J 16.109

Schedule of Volumes (for document index), GP 3.11

Schedule P. Commodity Classification for Reporting Shipments from Puerto Rico to U.S., C 3.150:P

Schedule Q. Commodity Classification for Compiling Statistics on Shipments from U.S., C 3.150:Q

Schedule R. Code Classification and Definitions of Foreign Trade Areas, C 3.150:R

Schedule S. Statistical Classification of Domestic and Foreign Merchandise Exported from U.S., C 3.150:S

Schedule T. Statistical Classification of Imports into U.S. Arranged in Shipping Commodity GROUPS., C 3.150:T

Schedule W. Statistical Classification of U.S. Waterborne Exports and Imports, C 3.150:W

Schedule X. Statistical Classification of Domestic and Foreign Merchandise Exported from United States by Air Arranged in Shipping Commodity Groups, C 3.150:X

Schedule Y. Statistical Classification of Imports into United States Arranged in Shipping Commodity Groups, C 3.150:Y

Shawnee Quarterly, the Shawnee National Forest **Schedule** of Projects, A 13.138

Single Award Federal Supply **Schedule**, GS 2.7/7

U.S. Export, **Schedule** B, Commodity by Country, C 3.164:446

U.S. Exports, Geographic Area, Country, **Schedule** B Commodity Groupings, and Method of Transportation, C 3.164:455

U.S. Exports, Harmonized **Schedule** B Commodity by Country, FT-447, C 3.164:447

U.S. Exports, **Schedule** B Commodity Groupings, Geographic Area, Country, and Method of Transportaion, C 3.164:450

U.S. Exports, World Area by **Schedule** E Commodity Groupings, C 3.164:455

U.S. General Imports and Imports for Consumption, **Schedule** A Commodity and Country, C 3.164:135

U.S. General Imports Geographic Area, Country, **Schedule** A Commodity Groupings, and Method of Transporation, C 3.164:155

U.S. General Imports **Schedule** A Commodity Groupings by World Area, C 56.210:FT 150

U.S. General Imports **Schedule** A Commodity Groupings, Geographic Area, Country, and Method of Transportation, C 3.164:150

U.S. General Imports **Schedule** World Area and Country of Origin by **Schedule** A Commodity Groupings, C 3.164:155

U.S. Imports, General and Consumption, **Schedule** A Commodity and Country, C 3.164:135

United States Airborne Exports of Domestic and Foreign Merchandise, Commodity (**Schedule** X) by Country of Destination, C 3.164:780

United States Congressional Serial Set Catalog: Numerical Lists and **Schedule** of Volumes, GP 3.34

United States General Imports of Textile Manufactures, Except Cotton and Wool, Grouping by Country of Origin and **Schedule** a Commodity by Country of Origin, TQ-2501, C 3.164/2-7

Western Training Center, Catalogs and **Schedule** of Courses, D 13.16

Scheduled

Air Carrier Industry **Scheduled** Service Traffic Statistics, CAB 1.39

Air Carrier Industry **Scheduled** Series: Traffic Statistics Quarterly, TD 12.15

Certification and Operations; Land Airports Serving CAB-Certificated **Scheduled** Air Carriers Operating Large Aircraft, TD 4.6:part 139

Certification and Operations; **Scheduled** Air Carriers with Helicopters, TD 4.6:part 127

Congressional Hearings **Scheduled**, I 20.45/2

Profiles of **Scheduled** Air Carrier Airport Operations by Equipment Type, Top 100 U.S. Airports, TD 4.44/4

Profiles of **Scheduled** Air Carrier Airport Operations, Top 100 U.S. Airports, TD 4.44

Profiles of **Scheduled** Air Carrier Operations by Stage Length, TD 4.44/3

Profiles of **Scheduled** Air Carrier Passenger Traffic, Top 100 U.S. Airports, TD 4.44/2

Scheduled International Operations, International Trunks, C 31.262

Seasonally Adjusted Capacity and Traffic **Scheduled** Domestic Operations, Domestic Trunks, C 31.262/3

Seasonally Adjusted Capacity and Traffic **Scheduled** International Operations, International Trunks, C 31.262

Seasonally Adjusted Capacity and Traffic **Scheduled** Operations Local Service Carriers, C 31.262/4

Seasonally Adjusted Capacity and Traffic **Scheduled** Operations System Trunks and Regional Carriers, C 31.262/5

Seasonally Adjusted Capacity and Traffic **Scheduled** Operations, System Trunks, C 31.262/2

Seasonally Adjusted Capacity and Traffic **Scheduled** Operations: System, Domestic, and International Trunks Plus Local Service Carrier, CAB 1.20

Trends in **Scheduled** All-Cargo Service, C 31.264/2

Schedules

Air Mail **Schedules**, P 20.8

Amortization **Schedules**, Y 3.F 31/11:36, FL 2.13

Classification Rulings and Decisions: Index Harmonized Tariff **Schedules** of the United States of America, T 17.6/3-6

Classification **Schedules**, C 14.17, C 18.18

Comprehensive Export Control **Schedules**, Y 3.Ec 74/2:108

Comprehensive Export **Schedules**, Pr 32.5808, C 34.8, C 18.267, C 42.11/a, C 49.208

Coordination Service, Digest of Interpretations of Specific Price **Schedules** and Regulations, Pr 32.4249

Crop and Market News Radio Broadcast **Schedules**, A 36.26

Current Salary **Schedules** of Federal Officers and Employees Together with a History of Salary and Retirement Annuity Adjustments, Y 4.P 84/10-15

Export Control **Schedules** (numbered), Y 3.Ec 74/2:107

History of the Tariff **Schedules** of the United States Annotated, ITC 1.10/2

Irrigation and Investigation **Schedules**, A 10.8

Library of Congress Classification **Schedules**, LC 26.9

National Oceanographic Fleet Operating **Schedules**, D 218.11

Navy Transportation **Schedules**, N 17.10

Personnel Handbook, Series P-1, Position Description and Salary **Schedules**, Transmittal Letters, P 1.31

Price **Schedules** National Bituminous Coal Commission, I 34.19

Price **Schedules** Office of Price Administration, Pr 32.4207

Programs and **Schedules**, Services of Supply Staff Course, W 28.11/3

Proposals and Specifications for Supplies, **Schedules**, P 1.13/2

Schedules of Basic Rates (by name of park or monument), I 29.33

Schedules of Payments to Holders of Cotton Options and Participation Trust Certificates by Congressional District of States, A 55.57

Schedules of Railway Post Offices, P 10.5

Schedules, SE 1.10

Tariff **Schedules** of the United States, Annotated, TC 1.35/2, ITC 1.10

Tariff **Schedules** of the United States, TC 1.35/3

U.S. Foreign Trade: **Schedules**, C 56.210/3

U.S. Imports for Consumption & General Imports, Tariff **Schedules** Annotated by Country, C 3.150/6

Scheley

Scheley Court of Inquiry Proceedings, N 1.21/1

Scheme

Classification Outline **Scheme** of Classes, LC 9.5

Scheme of City Distribution, P 1.18

United States Censuses of Population and Housing: Geographic Identification Code **Scheme**, Phc (2) (series), C 3.223/13

Schemes

Schemes for Separation of Mail by States, P 1.21

Schemes of City Distribution, P 10.9

Schemes of States (for use of publishers in distribution 2d class mail), P 10.10

Schemes of States (from certain standpoints), P 10.8

Schemes of States (general), P 10.6

Schizophrenia

Schizophrenia Bulletin, HE 20.2414, HE 20.8115

Schley's

Miscellaneous Correspondence of Navy Department Concerning **Schley's** Court of Inquiry, N 1.21/2

Scholar

NEH Teacher-**Scholar** Program for Elementary and Secondary School Teachers, Guidelines and Application Instructions, NF 3.18

Scholars

Interagency Directory, Key Contacts for Planning, Scientific and Technical Exchange Programs, Educational Travel, Students, Teachers, Lecturers, Research **Scholars**, Specialists, S 1.67/3

NEH Fellowships University Teachers, College Teachers, and Independent **Scholars** Anniversary and Commemorative Initiatives, NF 3.13/4

Occasional Papers Council of **Scholars** (series), LC 1.42

Trident **Scholars**, D 208.111

Younger **Scholars**, NF 3.8/2-6

Scholarship

Air Force ROTC Four Year College **Scholarship** Program Application Booklet for High School Students Entering College in the (year) Fall Term, D 301.95

Indian Health Service **Scholarship** Program Student Handbook, HE 20.9418/2

Indian Health Service **Scholarship** Program: Applicant Information Instruction Booklet, HE 20.9418

National Health Service Corps **Scholarship** Program Information Bulletin for Students of Allopathic Medicine, Osteopathic Medicine, and Dentistry, HE 20.5011

National Health Service Corps **Scholarship** Program, Report by Secretary of Health, Education, and Welfare to Congress, HE 20.6616

Scholarship Program, Applicant Information Bulletin, HE 20.6023

Scholarship Program, Applicant Information Instruction Booklet, HE 20.317

VA Health Professional **Scholarship** Program: Publications, VA 1.63

Scholorships

Scholorships and Fellowship Information, FS 5.63

School

Academic Year Institutes for Secondary **School** Teachers and Supervisors of Science and Mathematics, NS 1.12

Adjutant General's **School**, Fort Benjamin Harrison, Indiana, Reports and Publications, D 102.25

Agriculture Department Graduate **School** Publications, A 1.42

Annual Report on **School** Safety, E 1.1/7

Annual Report, Title 2, Elementary and Secondary Education Act of 1965, **School** Library Resources, Textbooks, and Other Instructional Materials, FS 5.220:20108, HE 5.220:20108

Annual **School** Calendar, I 20.16/6

Army Ordnance Center and **School** Aberdeen Proving Ground Maryland: Special Texts, D 105.25

Bond Sales for Public **School** Purposes, HE 19.323

Bulletin of the **School** of Medicine, Uniformed Services University of the Health Sciences, D 1.67

Carlisle Indian **School**, I 20.16

Case Book, Education Beyond High **School** Practices Underway to Meet the Problems of the Day, FS 5.65

City **School** Circulars, I 16.69

City **School** Leaflets, I 16.36

Condition of Public **School** Plants, FS 5.221:21033, HE 5.221:21033

Courses, Engineer **School**, Fort Belvoir, Virginia, D 103.111

Current Expenditures Per Pupil in Pubic **School** Systems, FS 5.222:22000, HE 5.222:22000

Defense Information **School**: Catalog, D 1.59

Drug Abuse Among American **School** Students, HE 20.8222

Drug Use Among American High **School** Students, HE 20.8219

Education Directory: Public **School** Systems, HE 19.324/2

Elementary **School** Personnel, FS 5.84:El 2, HE 5.84:El 2

Engineer **School** Library Bulletin, D 103.107

Engineer **School** Special Text, ST (series), D 103.109

Estimates of Local Public **School** System Finances, ED 1.112/3

Extension Course of Medical Field Service **School**; Lesson Assignment Sheets, W 3.71

Extension **School** Bulletin, W 99.17/14

Extension **School** Memorandum, W 99.13/14

Fall {year} Enrollment, Teachers, and School-Housing in Full-Time Public Elementary and Secondary Day Schools, FS 5.220:20007, HE 5.220:20007

Federal **School** Code (Database), ED 1.92/2

Federal **School** Code List, ED 1.92

Finance **School** Texts, W 97.8/7

Finances of Public **School** Systems, C 3.191/2-6

Four Minute Men Division, **School** Bulletins, Y 3.P 96/3:17

Graduate **School** Announcement of Courses, C 13.41

High School News Service Report, Basic Fact Edition, **School** Year, D 1.41/2

Indian **School** Journal, I 20.41

Indicators of **School** Crime and Safety, ED 1.347

Infantry **School** Quarterly, D 101.53

Local **School** Administration Briefs, FS 5.68

March of Education, News Letter for **School** Officers, I 16.26/3

Master Lesson Plans, Prepared for Use at Engineer **School** Only, D 103.110

National Stay-in-**School** Campaign, L 1.36

NEH Teacher-Scholar Program for Elementary and Secondary **School** Teachers, Guidelines and Application Instructions, NF 3.18

News Exchange, Extended **School** Services for Children of Working Mothers, Letters, FS 5.36

Occasional Papers Engineer Department, Engineer **School**, W 7.16/2

Preliminary Statistics of State **School** Systems, FS 5.220:20006, HE 5.220:20006, HE 5.93/4

President's Commission on **School** Finance, Pr 37.8:Sch 6

Profiles in **School** Support, Decennial Overview, FS 5.222:22022, HE 5.222:22022

Progress Report **School** Facilities Survey, FS 5.46

Psychological Warfare **School** Special Texts, D 101.44

Public **School** Finance Programs, HE 19.126

Publications Adjutant General's **School**, D 102.25

Publications Air University, **School** of Aviation Medicine, D 301.26/3-2

Publications Army Language **School**, D 101.64

Publications **School** of Aviation Medicine, Index, Fiscal Year, D 301.26/13-3

References on Local **School** Administration, FS 5.10/4

Research Reports Naval **School** of Aviation Medicine, D 206.16

Rural **School** Circulars, I 16.42

Rural **School** Leaflets, I 16.35

School Children and the War Series, Leaflets, FS 5.32

School Desegregation in {various localities}, CR 1.14

School District Data Book, ED 1.334/6

School Enrollment, Social and Economic Characteristics of Students, C 3.186/12

School Enrollment: October (year), C 3.186:P-20

School Facilities Service (lists & references), FS 5.10/2

School Garden Army Leaflets (general), I 16.28/6

School Health Studies, I 16.38

School Home-Garden Circulars, I 16.16

School Life, I 16.26, FS 5.7

School Lunch Series, A 73.13, A 75.18

School of Aerospace Medicine: Technical Documentary Report SAM-TDR (series), D 301.26/13-6

School of Advanced Airpower Studies, D 301.26/6-9

School of Aviation Medicine: General Publications, D 301.26/13-5

School of Instruction, T 33.11

School of Military Packaging Technology Booklets, SMPT-BKLT- (series), D 105.31

School Sanitation Leaflets, I 16.24

Selected Papers in **School** Finance, ED 1.310/5

Summer Seminars For Directors, For College Teachers, For **School** Teachers, Guidelines and Application Form for Participants, NF 3.13/3-5

Secondary **School** Circulars, I 16.22

Secondary **School** Personnel, FS 5.84:Se 2, HE 5.84:Se 2

Signal **School** Pamphlets, W 42.34/6

Summer Seminars Participants, for College Teachers and **School** Teachers, NF 3.13/3-6

Social and Economic Characteristics of U.S. **School** Districts, HE 19.336

Special Bibliography, Artillery and Guided Missile **School** Library, D 101.49

Special Text of Judge Advocate General's **School**, D 108.9

Standard **School** Lectures, Civilian Protection, Pr 32.4411

State Programs for Public **School** Support, FS 5.222:22023, HE 5.222:22023

Statistics of Local Public **School** Systems Fall (year), HE 5.93/8

Statistics of Local Public **School** Systems Pupils and Staff, HE 19.318/4

Statistics of Local Public **School** Systems, Finance, (year), HE 19.318/2

Statistics of Public **School** Libraries, FS 5.215:51049, HE 5.215:15049

Statistics of Public **School** Systems in Twenty Largest U.S. Cities, ED 1.112/4

Statistics of State **School** Systems, HE 19.318/3

Status of Compliance, Public **School** districts, 17 Southern and Border States, Reports, FS 5.80, HE 5.80

Summer Seminars for Secondary **School** Teachers Guidelines and Application Form for Directors, NF 3.13/3-3

Summer Seminars for Secondary **School** Teachers Guidelines and Applications Form for Participants, NF 3.13/3-2

Summer Seminars for Secondary **School** Teachers, NF 3.13/3

Summer Seminars for Secondary **School** Teachers, Seminar Descriptions, NF 3.13/3-4

Title II, Elementary and Secondary Education Act of 1965, **School** Library Resources, Textbooks and Other Instructional Materials, Annual Report, HE 5.79/2

Training Bulletin, **School** Series, FCD 1.9/3

Treasury of Stamps Album, **School** Year (date), P 1.49

Type A Topics, National **School** Lunch Program, A 98.10

U.S.A. Armor **School** Subcourses, D 101.78

Schools

Annual Test Report, Department of Defense Dependents **Schools**, D 1.1/10

Course Offering, Enrollments, and Curriculum, Practices in Public Secondary **Schools**, HE 19.334/2

Dependents **Schools** Manuals, D 1.6/2-2

Directory of Postsecondary **Schools** with Occupational Programs, HE 19.337

Directory of Public and Secondary **Schools** in Selected District, Enrollment and Staff by Racial/Ethnic Group, HE 1.38

Directory of Public Training **Schools** Serving Delinquent Children, FS 14.102:T 68

Directory of Secondary **Schools** with Occupational Curriculums, Public and Nonpublic, HE 5.96

Drug Abuse Prevention Materials for **Schools**, PrEx 13.2:D 84

Enrollments and Programs in Noncollegiate Postsecondary **Schools**, HE 19.337/2

Fall (year) Statistics of Public **Schools**, Advance Report, HE 5.93/5, HE 5.220:20119

Fall {year} Enrollment, Teachers, and School-Housing in Full-Time Public Elementary and Secondary Day **Schools**, FS 5.220:20007, HE 5.220:20007

Forest Service Films Available on Loan for Educational Purposes to **Schools**, Civic Groups, Churches, Television, A 13.55

Indian **Schools** Superintendent, Annual Report, I 20.7

Indian **Schools**, (misc. publications), I 20.8

Instructional Materials . . . for U.S. Army Reserve **Schools**, D 103.6/8

Key Audiovisual Personnel in Public **Schools** and Library Systems in State and Large Cities and In Large Public Colleges and Universities, FS 5.60/2

Minorities and Women in Public Elementary and Secondary **Schools**, Y 3.Eq 2:12-3

National Defense and Direct Student Loan Program, Directory of Designated Low-Income **Schools** for Teacher Cancellation Benefits, ED 1.40/2

Nonpublic **Schools** in Large Cities, HE 5.93/11

Occupational Education Enrollments and Programs in Noncollegiate Postsecondary **Schools**, HE 19.337/2

OPA Bulletins for **Schools** and Colleges, Pr 32.4224

OPA Information Leaflets for **Schools** and Colleges, Pr 32.4240

Pupil Mobility in Public Elementary and Secondary **Schools** During the (date) School Year, HE 5.93/6

Report on Cooperative Research to Improve the Nation's **Schools**, HE 5.82

Revenue Programs for the Public **Schools** in the United States, FS 5.222:22013, HE 5.222:22013

Routes to Indian Agencies and **Schools**, I 20.19

Schools at War, War Savings News Bulletins for Teachers, T 66.9

Scientific Reports of Higher **Schools** Chemistry and Chemical Technology, C 41.53/9

Scientific Reports of Higher **Schools** Electro-Mechanics and Automation, C 41.65/7

Scientific Reports of Higher **Schools** Machine Construction and Instruments Manufacture, C 41.65/8

Scientific Reports of Higher **Schools** Metallurgy, C 41.54/4

Schools and Safety Staffing Survey, ED 1.332

Semi-Annual Report of **Schools** for Freedmen, W 41.5

Series of Educational Illustrations for **Schools** (posters), A 45.5

Service Bulletins of Defense Training in Vocational **Schools**, FS 5.24

Spotlight on Organization and Supervision in Large High **Schools**, FS 5.50

Statistics of Nonpublic Elementary and Secondary **Schools**, (year), HE 5.93/9

Statistics of Nonpublic Elementary **Schools**, FS 5.220:20064

Statistics of Public Elementary and Secondary Day **Schools**, HE 19.326

Statistics of Public **Schools**, Advance Report, Fall, HE 19.318

Subject Offerings and Enrollments, Grades 912, Nonpublic Secondary **Schools**, FS 5.224:24012, HE 5.224:24012

Summary of Offerings and Enrollments in Public and Secondary **Schools**, HE 19.334

USAF Formal **Schools**, D 301.6:50-5

Vocational Education; **Schools** for Careers, an Analysis of Occupational Courses Offered by Secondary and Postsecondary Schools, HE 19.321

SCID

SCID-TR- (series), J 24.14

Science

Academic Year Institutes for Secondary School Teachers and Supervisors of **Science** and Mathematics, NS 1.12

Activities of the Federal Council for **Science** and Technology and the Federal Coordinating Council for **Science**, Engineering and Technology, Report, PrEx 23.9

Agricultural **Science** Review, A 94.11

Agronomy, Weed **Science**, Soil Conservation, Agricultural Programs, A 106.36

American **Science** Manpower, NS 1.14/2

Analysis of Research in the Teaching of **Science**, FS 5.229:29000, HE 5.229:29000

Animal Health **Science** Research Advisory Board, A 106.40

Materials **Sciences**, C 51.9/7

Mathematical **Sciences**, C 13.22

Mathematical **Sciences** Postdoctoral Research Fellowships, NS 1.45

Medical and Health Related **Sciences** Thesaurus, HE 20.3023

National Advisory Environmental Health **Sciences** Council, HE 20.3001/2:En 8

National Advisory General Medical **Sciences** Council, HE 20.3001/2:M 46

National Atmospheric **Sciences** Program, PrEx 8.110

National Institute of Environmental Health **Sciences** Research Programs, HE 20.3561

News of Academy of **Sciences** of Armenian SSR, Phsyco-Mathematical, Natural and Technical **Sciences** Series, C 41.50/7

News of Academy of **Sciences** of Estonia SSR, Technical and Physiomathematical **Sciences**, C 41.50/5

News of Academy of **Sciences** of USSR; Department of Chemical Science, C 41.53/2

News of Academy of **Sciences** of USSR; Department of Technical Services, C 41.50/3

News of Academy of **Sciences** of USSR; Geography Series, C 41.46/4

News of Academy of **Sciences** of USSR; Geology Series, C 41.52/7

News of Academy of **Sciences** of USSR; Mathematics Series, C 41.61/5

News of Academy of **Sciences** of USSR; Physics Series, C 41.52/3

Newsletter for Research in Mental Health and Behavioral **Sciences**, VA 1.22:15-5

Physical **Sciences** Research Papers, D 301.45/40

Physical **Sciences**, C 51.17/9

Population **Sciences**, Index of Biomedical Research, HE 20.3362/5

Population **Sciences**, Inventory of Private Agency Population Research, HE 20.3362/2-2

Posters National Institute of General Medical **Sciences**, HE 20.3467

Progress of Mathematical **Sciences** {abstracts}, C 41.61/4

Progress of Physical **Sciences** {abstracts}, C 41.52

Quarterly Report, Government Sponsored and Government Supported Research, Social **Sciences** and Interdisciplinary Areas, NS 1.9

Reports of Academy of **Sciences** of USSR, C 41.50

Research in Progress, Calendar Year Metallurgy and Materials Sciences, Mechanics and Aeronautics, Chemistry and Biological **Sciences**, D 101.52/5-5

Research Institute for the Behavioral and Social **Sciences**: Technical Papers, D 101.60

Selected Papers in the Hydrologic **Sciences**, I 19.13/2

Self-Study Course 3010-G, Environmental Health **Sciences** (series), HE 20.7021/11

Smithsonian Contributions to Earth **Sciences**, SI 1.26

Smithsonian Contributions to the Marine **Sciences**, SI 1.41

Soil, Water, Air **Sciences** Directory, A 106.14/2

Soil, Water, Air **Sciences** Research Annual Report, A 106.14

Special Reports Earth **Sciences** Division, D 106.17/2

U.S. Air Force Plan for Defense Research **Sciences**, D 301.45/19-5

United States Fisheries Systems and Social **Sciences**: a Bibliography of Work and Directory of Researchers, C 55.332:So 1

Visual **Sciences** A Study Section, HE 20.3001/2:V 82

Visual **Sciences** B Study Section, HE 20.3001/2:V 82/2

Scientific

Advanced Abstracts of **Scientific** and Technical Papers Submitted for Publication and Presentation, D 104.23/2

Air Force **Scientific** Research Bibliography, D 301.45/19-2:700

Armed Forces Radiobiology Research Institute: **Scientific** Reports, D 15.12

Army Missile Command Redstone **Scientific** Information Center Redstone Arsenal Alabama RSIC (series), D 105.22/3

Bibliography of **Scientific** and Industrial Reports, C 35.7

Bibliography of Translations from Russian **Scientific** and Technical Literature, LC 1.26

Board of **Scientific** Counselors, HE 20.3001/2:Sci 2

Board of **Scientific** Counselors Division of Cancer Biology and Diagnosis, HE 20.3001/2:Sci 2/4

Board of **Scientific** Counselors Division of Cancer Treatment, HE 20.3001/2:Sci 2/3

Board of **Scientific** Counselors National Eye Institute, HE 20.3001/2:Sci 2/2

Board of **Scientific** Counselors National Institute of Allergy and Infectious Diseases, HE 20.3001/2:Sci 2/7

Board of **Scientific** Counselors National Institute of Arthritis, Metabolism, and Digestive Diseases, HE 20.3001/2:Sci 2/5

Board of **Scientific** Counselors National Institute of Child Health and Human Development, HE 20.3001/2:Sci 2/6

Board of **Scientific** Counselors National Institute of Dental Research, HE 20.3001/2:Sci 2/8

Board of **Scientific** Counselors National Institute of Environmental Health Sciences, HE 20.3001/2:Sci 2/10

Board of **Scientific** Counselors National Institute on Drug Abuse, HE 20.3001/2:Sci 2/9

Carcinogenesis Program **Scientific** Review Committee A, HE 20.3001/2:C 17/2

Carcinogenesis Program **Scientific** Review Committee B, HE 20.3001/2:C 17/3

Carcinogenesis Program **Scientific** Review Committee C, HE 20.3001/2:C 17/4

Compilation of Administrative Policies for National Parks and National Monuments of **Scientific** Significance (Natural Area Category), I 29.9/4:N 21

Current Projects on Economic and Social Implications of **Scientific** Research and Development, NS 1.23

Current Research and Developments in **Scientific** Documentation, NS 1.15, NS 2.10

Directorate of Mathematical and Information Sciences, Air Force Office of **Scientific** Research, Research Summaries, D 301.45/19-10

Directory of Contacts for International Educational, Cultural and **Scientific** Exchange Programs, S 1.67/4

Epoch Discoveries of the Past, **Scientific** Radio Scripts, I 16.66

Federal Funds for Research, Development, and Other **Scientific** Activities, NS 1.18

Federal **Scientific** and Technical Communication, Progress Report, NS 2.12

Federal **Scientific** and Technical Workers: Numbers and Characteristics, NS 1.14/3

Guide to Russian **Scientific** Periodical Literature, Y 3.At 7:23

Guide to Subject Indexes for **Scientific** and Technical Aerospace Reports, NAS 1.9/6

Helium: Bibliography of Technical and **Scientific** Literature, (year), Including Papers on Alpha-Particles, I 28.27

Independent **Scientific** Advisory Board (ISAB) Documents, Y 3.N 81/8:16

Independent **Scientific** Review Panel (ISRP) Documents, Y 3.N 81/8:17

Interagency Directory, Key Contacts for Planning, **Scientific** and Technical Exchange Programs, Educational Travel, Students, Teachers, Lecturers, Research Scholars, Specialists, S 1.67/3

Journal of **Scientific** and Applied Photography and Cinematography {abstracts}, C 41.69

List of International and Foreign **Scientific** and Technical Meetings, NS 1.8

List of Recent Accessions and Foreign Patent Translations of the **Scientific** Library, C 21.17/2

Local Shortages in Selected **Scientific** and Engineering Occupations, L 7.63

Management Information on ERL's **Scientific** and Technical Publications, C 52.21/5

NASA **Scientific** and Technical Publications, NAS 1.21:7063

National Commission for United Nations Educational, **Scientific** and Cultural Organization Publications, S 5.48, S 5.48/9, S 5.48/10

National Institute of Child Health and Human Development Intramural Research Program: Annual Report of the **Scientific** Director, HE 20.3365

National Institutes of Health **Scientific** Directory, (year), and Annual Bibliography, FS 2.21

Navy **Scientific** and Technical Information Program, Newsletter, D 210.26

NOAA **Scientific** and Technical Publications Announcements, C 55.228/2

Offshore **Scientific** and Technical Publications, I 72.14, I 72.14/2

Pan American **Scientific** Congress, 3d Lima, Peru, 1924-25, S 5.14/3

Pan-American **Scientific** Congress, 2d, Washington, D.C., S 5.14/2

Pan-American **Scientific** Congress, Santiago, Chile, S 5.14

Pan-Pacific **Scientific** Conference, 1st Honolulu, 1920, S 5.21/1

Proceedings National Data Buoy Systems **Scientific** Advisory Meetings, TD 5.23

Publications Air Force Office of **Scientific** Research, D 301.45/19-2

Publications Army **Scientific** Advisory Panel, D 101.81

Publications Russian **Scientific** Translation Program, FS 2.22/19

Publications **Scientific** Research and Development Office, Pr 32.413

Publications **Scientific** Translation Program, FS 2.214

Recent Research Accomplishments of the Air Force Office of **Scientific** Research, D 301.45/19-7

Report on **Scientific** Research Projects Conducted During Fiscal Year, Y 3.T 25:32

Russian **Scientific** Translation Program Publications, FS 2.22/19

Scientific Activities in Universities and Colleges, NS 1.22:C 83/3

Scientific Affairs, PrEx 7.17/3

Scientific Aids to Learning Committee, Publications, NA 2.6

Scientific and Engineering Research Facilities at Universities and Colleges, NS 1.53

Scientific and Technical Aerospace Reports, NAS 1.9/4

Scientific and Technical Assessments Reports, EP 1.23/7

Scientific and Technical Personnel in the Federal Government, NS 1.22:G 74

Scientific and Technical Publications of ESSA Research Laboratories, C 52.21/4, C 52.21/4-2

Scientific Bulletin, D 210.3/3

Scientific Directory and Annual Bibliography, HE 20.3017

Scientific Information Activities of Federal Agencies, NS 1.16

Scientific Information Report, Pr 34.609

Scientific Inquiry Memoranda, C 6.15

Scientific Inventory Management Series, GS 2.6/4

Scientific Manpower Bulletins, NS 1.3/2

Scientific Manpower Series, FS 5.47

Scientific Manpower, Significant Developments, Views and Statistics, NS 1.14

Scientific Monograph Series, I 29.80

Scientific Monographs, D 201.16/3

Scientific Personnel Bulletin, D 210.7

Scientific Reports of Higher Schools Chemistry and Chemical Technology, C 41.53/9

Scientific Reports of Higher Schools Electro-Mechanics and Automation, C 41.65/7

Scientific Reports of Higher Schools Machine Construction and Instruments Manufacture, C 41.65/8

Scientific Reports of Higher Schools Metallurgy, C 41.54/4

Scientific Research Institutes of the USSR, LC 38.10

Scientific Translation Program Publications, FS 2.214

Special **Scientific** Report: Fisheries, C 55.312

STAR, **Scientific** and Technical Aerospace Reports, NAS 1.9/4

Substitute Chemical Program, Initial **Scientific** and Minieconomic Review of {various chemicals}, EP 5.13

Technical Notes Department of the Air Force Office of **Scientific** Research, D 301.45/18

UNESCO World Review Weekly Radio News from
United Nations Educational, **Scientific**,
and Cultural Organization, Paris, France,
S 5.48/6

United Nations Educational, **Scientific** and
Cultural Organization News {releases},
S 5.48/13

USSR and Eastern European **Scientific** Abstracts,
Geophysics, Astronomy, and Space, Y 3.J
66:14

USSR Reports (**Scientific** and Technical), PrEx 7.22

Virus Cancer Program **Scientific** Review Committee
A, HE 20.3001/2:V 81/2

Virus Cancer Program **Scientific** Review Committee
B, HE 20.3001/2:V 81/3

Water Resources **Scientific** Information Center,
WRSIC- (series), I 1.97

Scientist

Annual Report of the Chief **Scientist** of the National
Park Service, I 29.1/2

Office of the Chief **Scientist**: Annual Report, I 29.1/
2

Scientists

Current Employment Market for Engineers,
Scientists, and Technicians, L 7.63/2

Directory of Environmental Life **Scientists**, 1974, D
103.43:1105-2-3

Energy-Related Doctoral **Scientists** and Engineers
in the United States, E 1.21

Federal **Scientists** and Engineers, NS 1.22/9

Immigrant **Scientists** and Engineers, NS 1.22/5

National Survey of Compensation Paid **Scientists**
and Engineers Engaged in Research and
Development Activities, E 1.34

Parkinson's Disease and Related Disorders,
International Directory of **Scientists**, HE
20.3511/2

Research Opportunities for Women **Scientists** and
Engineers, NS 1.48/2

Southern Research Station Directory of Research
Scientists, A 13.150/4

U.S. **Scientists** and Engineers, NS 1.22/7

Sci-Tech

Sci-Tech Information, C 13.74

SCLD

SCLD (State Cancer Legislative Database) Update,
HE 20.3182/9

Sclerosis

NINCDS Amyotrophic Lateral **Sclerosis** Research
Program, HE 20.3502:Am 9/2

NINCDS Multiple **Sclerosis** Research Program, HE
20.3502:M 91

Scoreboard

Coordinator's **Scoreboard**, Review of What's New
in Placement of the Handicapped, CS
1.75

Scorecard

HUD **Scorecard**, Quality Assurance Program, HH
1.83

Scorekeeping

Budget **Scorekeeping** Report, Y 4.R 24/4:B 85/2

Congressional Budget **Scorekeeping** Reports, Y
10.10

Senate Budget **Scorekeeping** Report, Y 1.3/7

Scores

Braille **Scores** Catalog-Organ, Music and
Musicians, LC 19.22

Large-Print **Scores** and Books, LC 19.11/3-3

SCP

SCP Exchange, Y 3.N 21/29:15

SCPP

Project Skywater Data Inventory **SCPP** Season, I
27.57/2

Scrap

Aluminum **Scrap** and Secondary Ingot, I 28.71/2

Aluminum **Scrap** and Secondary Ingot, Secondary
Aluminum Monthly Report, I 28.71/3

Brass Mill **Scrap** and Metal Consumption and
Stocks at Brass and Wire Mills, I 28.79/2

Copper **Scrap** Consumers, I 28.79

Iron and Steel **Scrap** in (year), I 28.53/2-2

Iron and Steel **Scrap** Stock Reports, I 28.53

Lead **Scrap** Consumers Reports, I 28.67

Nonferrous **Scrap** Dealers Reports, I 28.65

Refined Metal and Copper **Scrap** Operations at
Brass and Wire Mills, Brass Mill Report,
I 28.79/2

Zinc **Scrap** Consumers Reports, I 28.68

Zinc **Scrap**, I 28.68

Scrapped

Oceangoing Merchant Ships of 1,000 Gross Tons
and Over **Scrapped** and Lost During the
Calendar Year (date), C 39.229

Scraps

Meat **Scraps** and Tankage Production, A 88.17/2

Screening

Advance Training for Workers in the Early and
Periodic **Screening**, Diagnosis and
Treatment Program: Publications, HE
22.111

Screw Thread

National **Screw Thread** Commission, C 13.23

Screws

Bolts Nuts and Large **Screws** of Iron or Steel, ITC
1.17, ITC 1.17/2

Scripts

Conservation Man (radio **scripts**), I 29.49

Consumer Information TV Program Packages,
Suggested **Scripts**, A 21.27

Epoch Discoveries of the Past, Scientific Radio
Scripts, I 16.66

This Might Be You (radio **scripts**), L 1.14

Treasure Trails, Radio **Scripts**, I 29.34

Two on a Trip; Radio Series, **Scripts**, I 29.43

What We Defend (Radio **Scripts**), I 29.48

World is Yours (Radio **Scripts**), I 16.56/2, FS 5.14/
1

SCS

SCS Aids, A 57.40

SCS Flood Reports, A 57.40/3

SCS National Engineering Handbook, A 57.6/
2:En 3

SCS-CI- {Conservation Aids} (series), A 57.45

SD

SD Developments, S 18.67

SD-TR (series), D 301.45/21-2

SE

Report, **SE**- (series), C 55.220/5

SE Asia Briefing Map, Series 5213, D 5.335

Sea

Air **Sea** Rescue Bulletin, N 24.35, T 47.32

Applications Pending in Commission for
Exemption from Radio Provisions of
International Convention for Safety of
Life at **Sea** Convention, London, 1929,
Title 3, Pt. 2 of Communications Act of
1934, etc., Reports, CC 1.19

Bering **Sea** Claims Commission, S 3.7/2

Density of **Sea** Water (D.W.), C 4.33

Initial Reports of the Deep **Sea** Drilling Project, NS
1.38

International Conference for Revision of
Convention of 1914 for Safety of Life at
Sea, S 5.29

International Conference on Safety at **Sea**, Reports,
C 1.10

International Conference on Safety of Life at **Sea**,
London, 1929, Reports, C 1.10/2

Law of the **Sea**, PrEx 7.14/3

Mariners Worldwide Climatic Guide to Tropical
Storms at **Sea**, D 220.8:St 7

Maritime Manpower Report: **Sea** Faring,
Longshore, and Shipyard Employment as
of (date), C 39.202:Se 1/2, C 39.235

Military **Sea** Transportation Service Magazine, D
216.8

National **Sea** Grant Program Annual Retreat
Report, C 55.38/2

Rum War at **Sea**, T 47.2:R 86

Sea Clipper, D 208.8

Sea Grant Annual Report, C 55.38

Sea Newsmakers, A 106.41

Sea Water Conversion, Solar Research Station
(series), I 1.87

Semimonthly Means of **Sea** Surface Temperature, C
55.193

Sea-Going

Merchant Fleets of the World, **Sea-Going** Steam and
Motor Ships of 1,000 Gross Tons and
Over, TD 11.14

Seabee

Seabee Items of Interest, N 21.13

Seafaring

Seafaring Guide, and Directory of Labor-
Management Affiliations, C 39.206/3:Se
1

Seafaring Wage Rates, Atlantic, Gulf and Pacific
Districts, C 39.202:W 12

Seafood

Seafood Dealers of the Southwest Region, C
55.337/2

Seagoing

American Documented **Seagoing** Merchant Vessels
of 500 Gross Tons and Over, 4 Degree, C
11.8

Merchant Ships Built in United States and Other
Countries in Employment Report of
United States Flag Merchant **Seagoing**
Vessels 1,000 Tons and Over, C 39.211

Seal

Fur **Seal** Arbitration, Paris, S 3.7/1, S 3.7/1a

Reports and Statistical Tables on Fur-**Seal**
Investigations in Alaska, T 35.7

Sealed

Sealed Bid/Invitation for Bids, D 7.34

Sealed Bids (series), D 7.34

Sealed Source and Device Newsletter (SS&D), Y
3.N 21/29:18-1

Sealift

Military **Sealift** Command, D 216.8

Posters Military **Sealift** Command, D 216.10

Sealift, Magazine of the Military Sealift Command,
D 216.8

Seamen

Seamen's Act As Amended and Other Laws
Relating to **Seamen** {March 4, 1915}, Y
1.2:Se 1/2

SEAN

SEAN Bulletin, SI 3.13

Seaplane

Advertisements Inviting Proposals for Carrying
Mails by Airplane or **Seaplane**, P 1.24

Seaplane Bases

Directory of Airports and **Seaplane Bases**,
Airman's Guide Supplement, FAA 1.23/
2

Search

BISNIS **Search** of Partners, C 61.42/2

Continuation Application for Grants under Talent
Search Program, ED 1.55

On Scene, National Maritime SAR {**Search** and
Rescue} Review, TD 5.24

Patents Assist, Full Text of Patent **Search** Tools, C
21.31/5

Published **Search** Bibliographies, C 51.13/2

Search for Health (series), HE 20.3038

Search Tips Series, A 17.25

Search, Administrative Research Bulletins, ARB-
(series), VA 1.47

Searchers

Literature **Searchers** (numbered), HE 20.3614/2

NTIS **Searchers**, C 51.13

Searches

Packaged Literature **Searches** (series), C 55.229/3

Searching

Online Literature **Searching** and Databases, EP
1.21/10

Seas

Limits in the **Seas** (series), S 1.119/5

Pilot Chart of Greenland and Barnets **Seas**, N 6.15/
4

Seashore

National **Seashore**, I 29.6/2

Santa Monica Mountains and **Seashore**, I 29.6/7

Seashores

Compilation of Administrative Policies for
National Recreation Areas, National
Seashores, National Lakeshores,
National Parkways, National Scenic
Riverways (Recreational Area Category),
I 29.9/4:R 24

Season

Charges for Ginning Cotton, Costs of Selected
Services Incident to Marketing, and
Related Information, **Season**, A 88.11/12

Crop Values, **Season** Average Prices Received by
Farmers and Value of Production, A
92.24/3

Marketing of South Carolina Peaches, Summary of
Season, A 88.12/29

Open **Season** for Game, A 5.9

Project Skywater Data Inventory SCPP **Season**, I
27.57/2

Season Tobacco Market News Reports Type 12, A
36.188

Sugarcane Variety Tests in Florida, Harvest **Season**,
A 106.27

The Library of Congress Presents a **Season** of
Chamber Music, LC 12.9

Turkey Breeder Hens Hatching **Season** Intentions,
A 92.9/9

Seasonal

Department Store Trade, United States Departmental Sales Indexes, without **Seasonal**
Adjustment, FR 1.24/9, FR 1.24/10

Monthly and **Seasonal** Weather Outlook, C 55.109

Potatoes and Sweetpotatoes, Estimates by States
and **Seasonal** Groups, A 88.12/19

Traveler/El Viajero, Quarterly Newsletter for Migrant and **Seasonal** Farm Workers, PrEx 10.19

U.S. Exports and Imports, Working-Day and **Seasonal** Adjustment Factors and Months for Cyclical Dominance (MCD), C 3.235

Seasonally

Capacity Utilization in Manufacturing, Quarterly Averages, **Seasonally** Adjusted, FR 1.55

Flow of Funds, **Seasonally** Adjusted and Unadjusted, FR 1.56

Seasonally Adjusted Capacity and Traffic Scheduled Domestic Operations, Domestic Trunks, C 31.262/3

Seasonally Adjusted Capacity and Traffic Scheduled International Operations, International Trunks, C 31.262

Seasonally Adjusted Capacity and Traffic Scheduled Operations Local Service Carriers, C 31.262/4

Seasonally Adjusted Capacity and Traffic Scheduled Operations System Trunks and Regional Carriers, C 31.262/5

Seasonally Adjusted Capacity and Traffic Scheduled Operations, System Trunks, C 31.262/2

Seasonally Adjusted Capacity and Traffic Scheduled Operations: System, Domestic, and International Trunks Plus Local Service Carrier, CAB 1.20

Seaway

Great Lakes-Saint Lawrence **Seaway** Winter Navigation Board: Annual Report, D 103.1/3

Traffic Report of the St. Lawrence **Seaway**, TD 6.9

Seaword

Seaword, Developments in American Flag Shipping, C 39.236

SE

Statistical Series Securities and Exchange Commission, **SE** Statistical Series, Annual Data, Data from the Drug Abuse Warning Network (DAWN), Series I, HE 20.8212/11

Season

Statistical Report of Commerce Passing through Canals at Sault Ste. Marie, Mich. and Ontario, Salt Water Ship Movements for **Season** of (year), D 103.17/2

SEC

Final Report of the **SEC** Government-Business Forum on Small Business Capital Formation, SE 1.35/2

SEC Docket, SE 1.29

SEC Monthly Statistical Review, SE 1.20

SEC Special Studies, SE 1.38

Standard Broadcast Applications Ready and Available for Processing Pursuant to **Sec.** 1.354 (c) of Commission's Rules, Lists, CC 1.26/2

Sec. 8

Project Register, Projects Approved Under **Sec. 8** of Federal Water Pollution Control Act (Pub. Law 660, 84th Cong.), As Amended and Sec. 3, of Public Works

Second

Publications, **Second** Series, M 212.10

Second Army Pamphlets (series), D 101.22/9

Second Army, 2A Circulars (series), D 101.4/3

Second Supplement on Aging, HE 20.6232

Supplemental Reports to the **Second** National Water Assessment, Y 3.W 29:13

Training Circulars Army and Corps Areas and Departments, **Second** Corps Area, W 99.12/8

Tumors of the Adrenal, **Second** Series, D 101.117/3

Second-Order

Second-Order Leveling, List of Standard Elevations, C 4.39

Secondary

Academic Year Institutes for **Secondary** School Teachers and Supervisors of Science and Mathematics, NS 1.12

Adult Basic and **Secondary** Level Program Statistics, Students and Staff Data, HE 19.319

Aluminum Scrap and **Secondary** Ingot, I 28.71/2

Aluminum Scrap and **Secondary** Ingot, Secondary Aluminum Monthly Report, I 28.71/3

Annual Report of Compensatory Education Programs under Title I, Elementary and **Secondary** Education Act of 1965, FS 5.79

Annual Report, Title 2, Elementary and **Secondary** Education Act of 1965, School Library Resources, Textbooks, and Other Instructional Materials, FS 5.220:20108, HE 5.220:20108

Course Offering, Enrollments, and Curriculum, Practices in Public **Secondary** Schools, HE 19.334/2

Directory of Public and **Secondary** Schools in Selected District, Enrollment and Staff by Racial/Ethnic Group, HE 1.38

Directory of **Secondary** Schools with Occupational Curriculums, Public and Nonpublic, HE 5.96

Educational Briefs for the Middle and **Secondary** Level Classroom, NAS 1.19/3

Expenditures and Revenues for Public Elementary and **Secondary** Education, HE 19.313

Fall {year} Enrollment, Teachers, and School-Housing in Full-Time Public Elementary and **Secondary** Day Schools, FS 5.220:20007, HE 5.220;20007

Implementing Title IX and Attaining Sex Equity; A Workshop for Elementary-**Secondary** Educators, HE 19.141/2

Minorities and Women in Public Elementary and **Secondary** Schools, Y 3.Eq 2:12-3

Model Programs, Title III, Elementary and **Secondary** Education Act, HE 18.12

NEH Teacher-Scholar Program for Elementary and **Secondary** School Teachers, Guidelines and Application Instructions, NF 3.18

Petroleum Products, **Secondary** Inventories and Storage Capacity, C 3.213

Public Elementary and **Secondary** Education in the United States, ED 1.112/2

Public Elementary and **Secondary** Education Statistics: School Year, ED 1.328/12

Pupil Mobility in Public Elementary and **Secondary** Schools During the (date) School Year, HE 5.93/6

Revenues and Expenditures for Public and Elementary and **Secondary** Education, ED 1.119

Secondary Aluminum, I 28.71/3

Secondary Education, FS 5.53

Secondary Market Prices and Yields and Interest Rates for Home Loans, HH 1.99/3

Secondary School Circulars, I 16.22

Secondary School Personnel, FS 5.84:Se 2, HE 5.84:Se 2

Space Benefits: **Secondary** Application of Aerospace Technology in Other Sectors of the Economy, NAS 1.66

Statistics of Nonpublic Elementary and **Secondary** Schools, (year), HE 5.93/9

Statistics of Public Elementary and **Secondary** Day Schools, HE 19.326

Subject Offerings and Enrollements, Grades 912, Nonpublic **Secondary** Schools, FS 5.224:24012, HE 5.224:24012

Summary of Offerings and Enrollments in Public and **Secondary** Schools, HE 19.334

Summer Seminars for **Secondary** School Teachers Guidelines and Application Form for Directors, NF 3.13/3-3

Summer Seminars for **Secondary** School Teachers Guidelines and Applications Form for Participants, NF 3.13/3-2

Summer Seminars for **Secondary** School Teachers, NF 3.13/3

Summer Seminars for **Secondary** School Teachers, Seminar Descriptions, NF 3.13/3-4

Title 1, Elementary and **Secondary** Education Act of 1965, States Report, FS 5.79, HE 5.79

Title 1 of Elementary and **Secondary** Education Act of 1965; Annual Report, FS 5.237:37013, HE 5.237:37013

Title II, Elementary and **Secondary** Education Act of 1965, School Library Resources, Textbooks and Other Instructional Materials, Annual Report, HE 5.79/2

Vocational Education; Schools for Careers, an Analysis of Occupational Courses Offered by **Secondary** and Postsecondary Schools, HE 19.321

Secretaries

Secretaries of State, Portraits and Biographical Sketches, S 1.69:162

Secretary

Commerce in {year}, Annual Report of the **Secretary** of Commerce, C 1.1

Commodity Exchange Act, As Amended, Regulations of the **Secretary** of Agriculture Thereunder, Orders of the Commodity Exchange Commission Pursuant to Sec. 4a and 5a(4), A 85.6:C 73

Companies Holding Certificates of Authority from **Secretary** of Treasury As Acceptable Securities on Federal Bonds, T 1.24, T 63.116

Office of the **Secretary** Petitions for Reconsideration of Actions in Rule Making Proceedings Filed, Public Notices, CC 1.38/2

Office of the **Secretary**, DOE/S- (series), E 1.60

Progress Report to the **Secretary** of Education from the President's Advisory Commission on Educational Excellence for Hispanic Americans, ED 1.87

Regulations of the Office of the **Secretary**, TD 1.6/2

Report of **Secretary** of Defense to the Congress on the Budget, Authorization Request, and Defense Programs, D 1.1

Report of **Secretary** of Labor to Congress on Research and Training Activities, L 1.42

Report of **Secretary** to President and Congress on Mineral Exploration Program, I 1.85

Report of the **Secretary** and Financial Report of the Executive Committee of the Board of Regents, SI 1.1/a

Report of the **Secretary** of Agriculture, A 1.1

Report to Congress by the **Secretary** of the Interior and the **Secretary** of Agriculture on Administration of the Wild Free-roaming Horses and Burro Act, I 1.100

Report to the U.S. Congress and the U.S. **Secretary** of Energy from the Nuclear Waste Technical Review Board, Y 3.N 88/2:1

Research and Activities Under Saltonstall-Kennedy Act, Annual Report of **Secretary** of Interior, I 1.1/2

Rulings on Requests for Review of the Assistant **Secretary** of Labor for Labor-Management Relations Pursuant to Executive Order 11491, As Amended, L 1.51/6

Rural Development Goals, Annual Report of the **Secretary** of Agriculture to the Congress, A 1.85/2

Secretary of State Press Conferences, S 1.25/4

Secretary of State's Advisory Committee on Private International Law: Publications, S 1.130

Semi-Annual Report of the **Secretary** of Commerce on the United States Travel Service, C 47.1

Smithsonian Year (date), Statement by the **Secretary**, SI 1.1/4

Staff Memo from U.S. **Secretary** of Labor, L 1.33

Supplemental Digest and Index of Published Decisions of the Assistant **Secretary** of Labor for Labor-Management Relations Pursuant to Executive Order 11491, Y 3.F 31/21-3:10

Technical Appendixes to the Report and Recommendations to the **Secretary**, U.S. Department of Health and Human Services, Y 3.P 29:1-2

Towards Improved Health and Safety for America's Coal Miners, Annual Report of the **Secretary** of the Interior, I 1.96

Training and Employment Report of the **Secretary** of Labor, L 37.23

Secretary's

Federal Managers' Financial Integrity Act, **Secretary's** Annual Statement and Report to the President and the Congress, I 1.96/6

Secretary's Annual Report to Congress, Posture Statement, Outlook and Program Review, E 1.60:0010

Secretary's Community Health Promotion Awards, HE 20.7612

Secretary's Instruction, L 1.22

Secretary's Letter, FS 1.30

Secretary's Notice, L 1.22/5

Secretary's Orders, L 1.22/2

Secretary's Semiannual Management Report to the Congress, S 1.1/9

Secretary's Semiannual Management Report, U.S. Department of Labor, L 1.1/3

Secretary's Semiannual Report to the Congress, HH 1.1/6, TD 1.1/4

Secretary's Task Force on Competition in the U.S. Domestic Airline Industry, TD 1.57

Section

Compendium of National Urban Mass Transportation Statistics from the 1989 **Section** 15 Report, TD 7.11/2-2

Depreciation **Section** Series Circulars, IC 1 acco.5

Education **Section** News Letter, T 66.21

Hospital **Section** Orders, VB 1.11

Official List of **Section** 13(f) Securities, SE 1.34

Overseas Common Carrier **Section** 214 Applications for Filing, CC 1.36/4

Patent Abstract **Section**, C 21.5/a 8

Pathology A Study **Section**, HE 20.3001/2:P 27

Pathology B Study **Section**, HE 20.3001/2:P 27/2

Personnel **Section** Bulletins, T 47.15

Pharmacology Study **Section**, HE 20.3001/2:P 49

Physiological Chemistry, Study **Section**, HE 20.3001/2:P 56/3

Physiology Study **Section**, HE 20.3001/2:P 56/2

Population Research Study **Section**, HE 20.3001/2:P 81/2

Publications Land Economics Division, Water Utilization **Section**, A 36.149

Quarterly Report on Trade Between the United States and Nonmarket Economy Countries, Pursuant to **Section** 411 (c) of the Trade Act of 1974, Y 4.W 36:3

Radiation Study **Section**, HE 20.3001/2:R 11

Report of the Attorney General Pursuant to **Section** 2 of the Joint Resolution of July 28, 1955, Consenting to an Interstate Compact to Conserve Oil and Gas, J 1.27

Report of the Attorney General, Pursuant to **Section** 252(i) of the Energy Policy and Conservation Act, J 1.27/2

Report of the U.S. Department of Justice Pursuant to **Section** 8 of the Federal Coal Leasing Amendments Act of 1975, J 1.27/3

Report to Congress on the Economic Impact of Energy Actions As Required by Public Law 93-275, **Section** 18 (d), E 1.59, FE 1.15/2

Reports of Applications Received in Telegraph **Section**, CC 1.27, CC 1.28

Retail Stores **Section** Flyers, Y 3.F 73:16

Safety **Section** Circulars, Y 3.R 13/2:26

Section 16(a) of the Securities Exchange Act of 1934, FR 1.31/2

Section 106 Update, Y 3.H 62:9

Special Reports Soil Conservation Service, Office of Research, Sedimentation **Section**, A 76.215, A 80.2013

Special Tariff Permission Under **Section** 224.1 of Economic Regulations, C 31.210

Supreme Commander for Allied Powers: Natural Resources **Section** Reports, D 102.20

Surgery A Study **Section**, HE 20.3001/2:Su 7

Surgery B Study **Section**, HE 20.3001/2:Su 7/2

Survey and Reports **Section** Statistical Notes, HE 20.2424

Tariff Circulars Rate **Section**, Interstate Commerce Commission, IC 1 rat.4

Technical **Section** Bulletins, W 95.21/7

Toxicology Study **Section**, HE 20.3001/2:T 66

Tropical Medicine and Parasitology Study **Section**, HE 20.3001/2:M 46/7

United States **Section**, Reports of Meetings, T 1.23/7

Virology Study **Section**, HE 20.3001/2:V 81

Visual Sciences A Study **Section**, HE 20.3001/2:V 82

Visual Sciences B Study **Section**, HE 20.3001/2:V 82/2

Workshop Series of Pharmacology **Section**, N.I.M.H., FS 2.310

World Dairy and Poultry News **Section**, C 18.72/8

Sectional

Sectional Aeronautical Charts, C 55.416/10

Sectional Aeronautical Charts, TD 4.79/11

Sections

Interstate Commerce Act, Including Text or Related **Sections** of Other Acts, IC 1 act.5

Roster of Members of PHS Public Advisory Groups, Councils, Committees, Boards, Panels, Study **Sections**, HE 20.2:Ad 9/3

Use Book **Sections**, A 13.14/2

Sector

Economic Indicators of the Farm **Sector**, A 93.45

Economic Indicators of the Farm **Sector**, Cost of Production: Livestock and Dairy, A 93.45/2-2

Indexes of Output Per Man-Hour, Hourly Compensation, and Unit Labor Costs in the Private Sector of the Economy and the Nonfarm **Sector**, L 2.2:Ou 8/8

Public **Sector** Labor Relations Information Exchange {publications}, L 1.66

Public **Sector** Labor Relations Information Exchange: Calendar of Events, L 1.66/2

Sector Notebook Project, EP 1.113

Solar Collector Manufacturing Activity and Applications in the Residential **Sector**, E 3.19

USIA Private **Sector** Committees Annual Report, IA 1.28

Wholesale Price Index Series 1947-48 100: Economic **Sector** Indexes, L 2.61/8

Sectoral

Country Market **Sectoral** Surveys, C 57.119

Sectors

Space Benefits: Secondary Application of Aerospace Technology in Other **Sectors** of the Economy, NAS 1.66

Securities

Companies Holding Certificates of Authority from Secretary of Treasury As Acceptable **Securities** on Federal Bonds, T 1.24, T 63.116

Computer **Security** Guide, C 1310:800-18

Corporate **Securities** Offered for Cash, SE 1.25/6

Directory of Companies Filing Annual Reports with the **Securities** and Exchange Commission, SE 1.27

General Rules and Regulations Under the **Securities** Act of 1933, as in Effect (date), SE 1.6:R 86/2

General Rules and Regulations Under the **Securities** Exchange Act of 1934, as in Effect (date), SE 1.6:R 86/3

Laws Relating to **Securities** Commission, Exchanges and Holding Companies, Y 1.2:Se 2

List of Stocks Registered on National Securities Exchange and of Redeemable **Securities** of Certain Investment Companies, FR 1.46

Official List of Section 13(f) **Securities**, SE 1.34

Over-the-Counter Brokers and Dealers Registered with **Securities** & Exchange Commission, SE 1.15

Press Releases **Securities** and Exchange Commission, SE 1.25/8

Prices and Yields of Public Marketable **Securities** Issued by United States Government and by Federal Agencies, T 68.7

Registration Record, **Securities** Act of 1933, Indexes, SE 1.13/2

Registration Record, **Securities** Act of 1933, SE 1.13/1

Regulations S-X Under the **Securities** Act of 1933, SE 1.6:F 49

Releases, **Securities** Act of 1933, SE 1.25/4

Releases, **Securities** Exchange Act of 1934, SE 1.25/5

Report Coordinating Group Annual Report to the **Securities** and Exchange Commission, SE 1.32

Section 16(a) of the **Securities** Exchange Act of 1934, FR 1.31/2

Securities Act of 1933, As Amended to (date), SE 1.5:Se 2/3

Securities Exchange Act of 1934, As Amended to (date), SE 1.5:Se 2

Securities Traded on Exchanges Under the **Securities** Exchange Act, SE 1.16

Statistical Bulletins **Securities** and Exchange Commission, SE 1.20

Statistical Series **Securities** and Exchange Commission, SE Statistical Series, Annual Data, Data from the Drug Abuse Warning Network (DAWN), Series I, HE 20.8212/11

U.S. Government **Securities** Yields and Prices, FR 1.46/2

Volume and Composition of Individuals' Savings **Securities** and Exchange Commission, SE 1.25/6

Security

Background for Mutual **Security**, S 17.35/2

Computer **Security** Center, CSC-EPL- (series), D 1.79

Congressional Presentation for **Security** Assistance Programs, Fiscal Year (date), D 1.85

Digest **Security** and Cooperation in Europe Commission, Y 4.Se 2/11:13/3

Diplomatic **Security** Training Resources, etc. Fiscal Year, S 1.139/2

Directory of Local Employment **Security** Offices, L 37.18, L 1.59

Directory, Local Law Enforcement Organizations Participating in Aviation **Security**, TD 4.809

Employee Retirement Income **Security** Act, Report to Congress, L 1.76, L 40.15

Employment **Security** Activities, L 7.40

Employment **Security** Exchange Series, L 7.56

Employment **Security** Memorandum, FS 3.110

Employment **Security** Research and Reporting Exchange Series, L 7.56/2

Employment **Security** Research Exchange, L 7.56/3

Facility **Security** Program Bulletins, Pr 32.4420

Family **Security** Circulars, Pr 32.4511

Family **Security** Confidential Bulletins, FS 8.9

Handbooks, Manuals, Guides Relating to Industrial Mobilization and **Security**, D 3.6/3

Industrial Personnel **Security** Review Program, Annual Reports, D 3.12

Industrial **Security** Cartoons, D 3.11/3

Industrial **Security** Poster PIN (series), D 3.11

Industrial **Security** Statements, D 3.11/2

Information Systems **Security** Products and Services Catalogue, D 1.69/2

ISOO (Information **Security** Oversight Office) Annual Report, AE 1.101/3

Key Facts, Employment **Security** Operations, L 7.60

Manpower Utilization-Job **Security** in Longshore Industry {by port}, L 1.50

National **Security** Affairs Issue Papers, D 5.409/2

National **Security** Affairs Monographs, D 5.409

National **Security** Agency Publications, D 1.25

National **Security** Management, D 5.9/3, D 5.410

National **Security** Seminar Presentation Outlines and Reading List, D 5.9/2

Office of Homeland **Security** (General Publications), PR 43.14

Official Summary of **Security** Transactions and Holdings, SE 1.9

Operations of the Employment **Security** Program, FS 3.3/a3

Planning for Housing **Security** (series), HH 1.6/11

Port **Security**, TD 1.61

Privacy and **Security** of Criminal History Information (series), J 29.10

Proceedings National **Security** Affairs Conference, D 5.412

Productivity and Job **Security**, Y 3.P 94:9

Program and Demographic Characteristics of Supplemental **Security** Income Beneficiaries, HE 3.71/2

Publications Mutual **Security** Mission to China, FO 1.27

Publications National **Security** Agency, D 1.25

Report on Washington Conference of Mayors and Other Local Government Executives on National **Security**, FCD 1.18

Report to Congress on Title 20 of the Social **Security** Act, HE 23.2009

Research Reports Farm **Security** Administration, A 61.15

Security Awareness Bulletin, D 1.3/3

Security Pamphlets, Y 3.At 7:18

Security Procedures, GP 1.23/2

Security Program, TD 1.33

Selected List of References on Old-Age **Security**, Y 3.F 31/5:20

Semiannual Report to Congress on the Effectiveness of the Civil Aviation **Security** Program, TD 4.810

Social **Security** Administration Baltimore Directory, HE 3.58/2

SSA Program Circulars Supplemental **Security** Income, HE 3.4/6

State Salary Ranges, Selected Classes {of positions} in Employment **Security**, Public Welfare, Public Health, Mental Health, Vocational Rehabilitation, Civil Defense, Emergency Planning, CS 1.81, FS 1.22, HE 1.22, GS 1.8

Summary of Equity **Security** Transactions and Ownership of Directors, Officers, and Principal Stockholders of Member State Banks As Reported Pursuant to

Supplemental **Security** Income Program for the Aged, Blind, and Disabled, HE 3.77

Supplemental **Security** Income, State and County Data, HE 3.71

Selected Technical Reports, Information Retrieval Bulletin, TD 4.17/2
Selected Topic Digests, J 1.42/2
Selected United States Government Publications, GP 3.17, GP 3.17/2
Selected United States Marketing Terms and Definitions, English {foreign Language}, C 41.93
Selected Urban Storm Water Runoff Abstracts, EP 2.10:11024
Selected Water Resources Abstracts, I 1.94/2
Selected Worldwide Weather Broadcasts, C 55.119
Selected-Current Acquisitions, TC 1.34/2
Separate Sheets of **Selected** Thematic and General Reference Maps from the National Atlas of the United States of America, I 19.111a
Slim **Selected** Library in Microfiche, J 26.28
Soil Conservation Literature, **Selected** Current References, A 57.20, A 17.15
Special Current Business Reports: Monthly Department Store Sales in **Selected** Areas, BD- (series), C 56.219/3
State Data Profiles, Calendar Year (date), **Selected** Ascs Program Activity and Other Agricultural Data, A 82.90
State Salary Ranges, **Selected** Classes {of positions} in Employment Security, Public Welfare, Public Health, Mental Health, Vocational Rehabilitation, Civil Defense, Emergency Planning, CS 1.81, FS 1.22, HE 1.22, GS 1.8
State, County and **Selected** City Employment and Unemployment, BLS/PWEDA/MR- (series), L 2.111/2
State, County and **Selected** City Employment and Unemployment, BLS/PWEDA/SP- (series), L 2.111/4
State, County and **Selected** City Employment and Unemployment, L 2.111
Statement of Postal Receipts at 50 **Selected** Offices, P 4.9
Stumpage Prices for Sawtimber Sold from National Forests, by **Selected** Species and Region, A 13.58/2
Survey of American Listed Corporations, Reported Information on **Selected** Defense Industries, SE 1.18/2
Telephone Companies, **Selected** Financial and Operating Data from Annual Reports, IC 1 telp.7
Trends in **Selected** Economic and Real Estate Factors in United States, NHA 2.15
Trends in **Selected** Economic Factors, United States, HH 2.16
U.S. Automobile Industry: Monthly Report on **Selected** Economic Indicators, ITC 1.16/3
U.S. Trade Shifts in **Selected** Commodity Areas, ITC 1.15
Union Catalog, **Selected** List of Unlocated Research Books, LC 18.7
Wage Rates in **Selected** Farm Activities, L 7.55/2-2
Weekly List of **Selected** U.S. Government Publications, GP 3.17

Selection
Clothing **Selection** Charts, A 42.7/5
Food **Selection** and Meal Planning Charts, A 10.21/2
Hearing Aid Performance Measurement Data and Hearing Aid **Selection** Procedures, Contract Year (date), VA 1.22
List of Items for **Selection** by Depository Libraries, GP 3.32
Programme of Competition for **Selection** of Architect for Building for Department, T 39.10
Reports on Apprentice **Selection** Programs, L 23.11
Selection of Patients for X-Ray Examinations (series), HE 20.4617
Viewpoints, a **Selection** from the Pictorial Collections of the Library of Congress, LC 25.2:V 67

Selections
GPO Depository Union List of Item **Selections**, GP 3.32/2

Selective
List of Local Boards of the **Selective** Service System, Y 3.Se 4:24
Medical Circulars of **Selective** Service Bureau, Pr 32.5281
Office of **Selective** Service Records Regulations, Y 3.Se 4:19
Price List, **Selective** Bibliography of Government Research Reports and Translations, C 41.21/3

Selective Notification of Information SNI, J 26.19
Selective Notification of Information, J 28.14
Selective Service Act As Amended {May 18, 1917}, Y 1.2:Se 4
Selective Service College Qualification Test, Bulletin of Information, Y 3.Se 4:22
Selective Service Manual, Pr 32./5280
Selective Service Memorandums to All Navy Contractors, N 1.30
Selective Service News, Y 3.Se 4:20
Selective Service Regulations, Y 3.Se 4:6, Y 3.Se 4:7
Selective Service, Y 3.Se 4:9, Pr 32.5279, Y 3.Se 4:20
Telephone Directory **Selective** Service System, Y 3.Se 4:26
University Centers of Foreign Affairs Research, **Selective** Directory, S 1.2:Un 3

Selenium
Selenium and Tellurium in (year), I 28.104/2
Selenium Report, I 28.104
Selenium, I 28.104

Self
Farmer's Tax Guide, Income and **Self** Employment Taxes, T 22.19/2:F 22

Self-Employment
Self-Employment Claims and Payment by Agencies, VA 1.35

Self-Evaluation
Self-Evaluation Instrument (series), HE 20.7116

Self-Guiding
Self-Guiding Nature Trail Leaflets, Glacier National Park, I 29.61
Self-Guiding Nature Trail Leaflets, Mount Rainier National Park, I 29.61/2

Self-Help
Cooperative **Self-Help**, Y 3.F 31/5:22

Self-Instructional
Self-Instructional Texts (series), D 101.107/6

Self-Study
Self-Study Course 3010-G, Environmental Health Sciences (series), HE 20.7021/11
Self-Study Course 3014-G, Waterborne Disease Control Manuals, HE 20.7021/4-2

Sell
News to Use, Wartime Facts about Goods You **Sell**, Pr 32.4819

Seller
Buyer-**Seller** Codes Authorized for Reporting to the Federal Energy Regulatory Commission, E 3.35
Marine Surplus **Seller**, MC 1.26, Pr 33.216

Selling
HUD **Selling** List, HH 1.6/3-2
Selling in (country), C 1.50, C 57.11
Selling in Army and Air Force Careers, W 3.84, M 108.79
Selling to Navy Prime Contractors, D 201.2:Se 4/2
U.S. Government Purchasing and Sales Directory Guide for **Selling** or Buying in the Government Market, SBA 1.13/3

Selma
Area Wage Survey (summary): **Selma**, Alabama, L 2.122/1-6

Semana
Noticias De La **Semana**, a News Summary for Hispanos, L 1.20/7

Semi-Annual
Semi-Annual Checklist of the EEOC Orders, Y 3.Eq 2:19
Semi-annual List of Reports Prepared for or by the Office of Toxic Substances, EP 1.65
Semi-Annual Report of Schools for Freedmen, W 41.5
Semi-annual Report of the Inspector General, U.S. Small Business Administration, SBA 1.1/3
Semi-Annual Report of the Secretary of Commerce on the United States Travel Service, C 47.1

Semiannual
Oceanography **Semiannual** Report of Oceanographic Data Exchange, C 55.220/3
Office of Inspector General, **Semiannual** Report to Congress Department of Education, ED 1.26
Office of Inspector General, **Semiannual** Report to Congress Department of Transportation, TD 1.1/3
Office of Inspector General, **Semiannual** Report to Congress General Services Administration, GS 1.1/3
Office of Inspector General, **Semiannual** Report, I 1.1/7

Office of the Inspector General: **Semiannual** Report to the Congress, CSA 1.1/2
Office of the Inspector General: **Semiannual** Report, EP 1.1/5
Retirement and Survivors Insurance **Semiannual** Analysis, HE 3.57/2
Secretary's **Semiannual** Management Report to the Congress, S 1.1/9
Secretary's **Semiannual** Management Report, U.S. Department of Labor, L 1.1/3
Semiannual Checklist, Bureau of International Commerce International Business Publications, C 42.15:C 41
Semiannual Consolidated Report of Balances of Foreign Currencies Acquired Without Payment of Dollars As of December 31 (year), T 63.117
Semiannual Interest Rate Bulletins, T 66.3/2
Semiannual Procurement Report, NAS 1.30
Semiannual Report of the Inspector General to Congress, C 1.1/2
Semiannual Report of the Inspector General, L 1.74, VA 1.55
Semiannual Report on Operations Under Mutual Defense Assistance Control Act of 1951, FO 1.1/2
Semiannual Report on Strategic Special Nuclear Material Inventory Differences, E 1.15/2
Semiannual Report to Congress on the Effectiveness of the Civil Aviation Security Program, TD 4.810
Semiannual Report, Implementation of Helsinki Accord, S 1.129
Semiannual Report, Office of Inspector General, A 1.1/3
Semiannual Report, Y 3.Se 4:1
Semiannual Reports on Operations under Mutual Defense Assistance Act, S 17.1/2
Semiannual Reports under Mutual Defense Assistance Control Act, Pr 33.901/2
Semiannual Reports, NAS 1.1
United States Advisory Commission on Information, **Semiannual** Report to Congress, S 1.93
World Data Center A Oceanography, **Semiannual** Report of Oceanography Data Exchange, C 55.220/3

Semimonthly
Semi-Monthly Honey Reports, A 36.105, A 88.19
Semimonthly Means of Sea Surface Temperature, C 55.193
Semi-Monthly Military Government Report for U.S. Occupied Area of Germany, M 105.21
Semi-Monthly News Letter, Federal Theatre Project, Y 3.W 89/2:33
Semi-monthly Report on Employment Situation, L 2.53

Seminar
Executive **Seminar** Centers {programs}, CS 1.65/3
Publications Technology Transfer **Seminar**, EP 7.10
Science Writer **Seminar** Series, HE 20.3859
Selected Papers from Bureau of Radiological Health **Seminar** Program (numbered), HE 20.1109
Seminar of Manpower Policy and Program, L 1.39/8
Seminar on Industrial Issues (various topics), C 62.18
Social **Seminar** Discussion Guides, HE 20.2408/2
Summer Seminars for College Teachers, **Seminar** Descriptions, NF 3.13
Summer Seminars for Secondary School Teachers, **Seminar** Descriptions, NF 3.13/3-4
Technology Transfer **Seminar** Publications, EP 7.10

Seminars
Application for **Seminars** Abroad Program, ED 1.59/2
Catalog of **Seminars**, Training Programs and Technical Assistance in Labor Statistics, L 2.114
Summer **Seminars** for College Teachers Guidelines and Application Form for Participants, NF 3.13/2-2
Summer **Seminars** for College Teachers, Guidelines and Application Forms for Directors, NF 3.13/2
Summer **Seminars** for College Teachers, NF 3.13/2-3
Summer **Seminars** for College Teachers, Seminar Descriptions, NF 3.13

Summer **Seminars** For Directors, For College Teachers, For School Teachers, Guidelines and Application Form for Participants, NF 3.13/3-5

Summer **Seminars** for Secondary School Teachers Guidelines and Application Form for Directors, NF 3.13/3-3

Summer **Seminars** for Secondary School Teachers Guidelines and Applications Form for Participants, NF 3.13/3-2

Summer **Seminars** for Secondary School Teachers, NF 3.13/3

Summer **Seminars** for Secondary School Teachers, Seminar Descriptions, NF 3.13/3-4

Summer **Seminars** Participants, for College Teachers and School Teachers, NF 3.13/3-6

Teacher Exchange Opportunities Abroad, Teaching, Summer **Seminars** under International Educational Exchange Program of Department of States {announcements}, FS 5.64/2

Semper Fidelis
Semper Fidelis, D 214.35

Senate
Annual Reports of Political Committees Supporting Candidates for **Senate**, Y 1.3/5

Canada-United States Interparliamentary Group Report on Meetings by **Senate** Delegation, Y 4.F 76/2:C 16/2

Federal Elections . . ., Election Results for the U.S. **Senate** and U.S. House of Representatives, Y 3.El 2/3:16

Final Cumulative Finding Aid, House and **Senate** Bills, GP 3.28

Financial Audit, **Senate** Recording and Photographic Studios Revolving Fund, GA 1.13/5

Financial Audit, **Senate** Restaurants Revolving Fund for Fiscal Years, GA 1.13/8-2

Journal of Executive Proceedings of **Senate**, Y 1.3/4
Journal of the **Senate**, XJS

List of Committee Hearings, Committee Prints and Publications of the United States **Senate**, Y 1.3/10

Problems of Mobilization and Reconversion, Reports to the President, **Senate**, and House of Representatives by Director of War Mobilization and Reconversion, Y 3.W 19/7:8

Procedures and Guidelines for Impeachment Trials in the U.S. **Senate**, Y 1.93-2:S.doc 102

Publications List **Senate** Committee on Energy and Natural Resources, Y 4.En 2:P 96

Publications List **Senate** Special Committee on Aging, Y 4.Ag 4:P 96

Report of the **Senate** Committee on Labor and Human Resources Presenting its View and Estimates Pursuant to the Congressional Budget Act, Y 4.L 11/4:C 76

Report of the **Senate** Impeachment Trial Committee, Y 4.Im 7/2

Report to the **Senate** and House Committees on the Budget As Required by Public Law 93-344, Y 10.13

Senate Budget Scorekeeping Report, Y 1.3/7
Senate Concurrent Resolutions, Y 1.1/4
Senate Executive Reports and Documents, Y 1.Cong.
Senate History (series), Y 1.3/8
Senate Procedure, Precedents and Practice, Y 1.93-1:S.doc. 21
Senate Treaty Documents, Y 1.1/4
Summary of Activities **Senate** Banking, Housing, and Urban Affairs Committee, Y 4.B 22/3:Ac 8
U.S. **Senate** Telephone Directory, Y 1.3/10
United States **Senate**, a Historical Bibliography, Y 1.3:Se 5/11
Views of the Committee on Appropriations, United States **Senate**, on the First Concurrent Resolution on the Budget, Y 4.Ap 6/2:B 85/5

Senators
Election Law Guidebook, 1974, Summary of Federal and State Laws Regulating Nomination and Election of United States **Senators**, Revised to January 1, 1974, Y 1.93-2:S.doc. 84

Sending
Sending Gift Packages to Various Countries, C 49.9

Senior
Senior Executive Service Newsletter, PM 1.64
Senior Executive Service, Forum Series, L 1.95

Sensing
Renewable Resources Remote **Sensing** Research Program Report, NAS 1.70

Sensory
Sensory Biology of Sharks, Skates, and Rays, D 210.2

Sentenced
Felons **Sentenced** to Probation in State Courts, J 29.11/12

Sentences
Felony **Sentences** in State Courts, J 29.11/11
Felony **Sentences** in the United States, J 29.11/11-2
United States District Courts **Sentences** Imposed Chart, Ju 10.18

Sentencing
Guideline **Sentencing** Update, Ju 13.8/3
State **Sentencing** of Convicted Felons, J 29.11/11-3

Sentencing Commission
Minutes of U.S. **Sentencing Commission** Meetings, Y 3.Se 5:16

Sentinel
Border **Sentinel**, J 16.17
Border **Sentinel** Comment, J 16.17/2
Community and Family **Sentinel**, D 102.81

Separate
Housing Census **Separate** Reports and Bulletins, C 3.950-8/4
Separate Sheets of Selected Thematic and General Reference Maps from the National Atlas of the United States of America, I 19.111a

Separates
Research Papers, **Separates** from the Journal of Research, C 13.22
United States Census of Agriculture, 1950: V. 2 General Report (**separates**), C 3.950-9/5

Separation
Schemes for **Separation** of Mail by States, P 1.21

Sepulveda
Formulary, VA Medical Center **Sepulveda, Georgia**, VA 1.73/6

Sequences
Entrez: **Sequences**, HE 20.3624

Sequestration
Initial **Sequestration** Report for Fiscal Year (date), Y 4.D 36/2
Sequestration Report for Fiscal Year (date): A Summary, Y 10.18

Sequoia
Sequoia and General Grant National Parks, Annual Reports, I 1.29

Sequoyah
Annual Radiological Environmental Operating Report, **Sequoyah** Nuclear Plant, Y 3.T 25:57
Environmental Radioactivity Levels, **Sequoyah** Nuclear Plan, Y 3.T 25:56
Fish Monitoring Investigations: **Sequoyah** Nuclear Plant, Chickamauga Reservoir, Tennessee, Y 3.T 25:37-3

Sequoyah Nuclear Plant
Aquatic Environmental Conditions in Chickamauga Reservoir During Operation of **Sequoyah Nuclear Plant**, Y 3.T 25:54

Sergeants
Sergeants' Business, D 101.118/3

Serial
Eastern Africa, Annual **Serial** Supplement, LC 1.30/8-2
Index of NLM **Serial** Titles, HE 20.3618
NBS **Serial** Holdings, C 13.58/5
New **Serial** Titles, LC 1.23/3
Patents Snap, Concordance of U.S. Patent Application **Serial** Numbers to U.S. Patent Numbers, C 21.31/6
Serial Holdings, HE 20.7019:Se 6
Serial Publications Indexed to Bibliography of Agriculture, A 17.17:75
Serial Titles Newly Received, LC 1.23
United States Congressional **Serial** Set Catalog: Numerical Lists and Schedule of Volumes, GP 3.34
United States Congressional **Serial** Set Supplement, GP 3.8/6
Wright Aeronautical **Serial** Reports, D 301.45/22

Serials
Annual List of **Serials**, American Libraries Book Procurement Centers, Karachi, Dacca, LC 1.30/2-2
Cumulative List of Malaysia, Singapore and Brunei **Serials**, LC 1.30/10-2

India, Accessions List, Annual Supplement, Cumulative List of **Serials**, LC 1.30/1-2
Indonesia, Cumulative List of **Serials**, LC 1.30/5-2
List of **Serials** Indexed for Online Users, HE 20.3618/2
MARC **Serials** Editing Guide, Bimonthly Updates, LC 1.6/4:M 18
Periodicals and **Serials** Received in the Library of the National Bureau of Standards, C 13.10
Serials Currently Received by the National Agricultural Library, A 17.18/2:Se 6

Series
Daily **Series**, Synoptic Weather Maps, C 55.213/2
Diskette **Series**, HE 20.6209/4-4
Drug Abuse Warning Network **Series**, HE 20.416/3
Galveston Bay Fact Sheet **Series**, I 49.110
Global Volcanism Program, Digital Information **Series**, SI 1.49
HIV/AIDS Evaluation Monograph **Series**, HE 20.9515
Judges Information **Series**, Ju 10.24
Methodological **Series**, HE 20.422
Monograph **Series**, Y 3.Em 7/3:11
Monthly **Series** on Mass Layoffs, L 1.94
On Guard **Series**, Y 3.F 73:11
Order **Series**, A 55.36
Population Division Working Paper **Series**, C 3.223/26
Philatelic Dedicatory Lecture **Series**, SI 3.12
Publications, Second **Series**, M 212.10
Radio (Independents) Natural Science **Series** Talks, I 29.18
Recruiting **Series** Posters, W 3.46/2
Reprint and Circular **Series**, NA 2.5
Reprint **Series**, Y 3.Se 5:15
Route Information **Series**, W 87.21/2
Rubber **Series**, L 16.19
Rural Child Welfare **Series**, L 5.11
Safety Evaluation **Series**, TD 2.62
Safety Management **Series**, L 35.19
Series 1, Evaluation of Foreign Fruits and Nuts, A 77.533
Series Available and Estimating Methods, BLS Current Employment Statistics Program, L 2.124/2
Series Available and Estimating Methods, BLS National Payroll Employment Program, L 2.124
Series Data Handbook, HH 2.24/6
Series H/HH Savings Bonds, T 63.209/8-4
Series HC Reports, C 3.950-4/2
Series ISP, CENTS {Census Tabulation System}, C 56.226
Series of Educational Illustrations (Charts), A 43.5/10, A 43.22
Series of Educational Illustrations for Schools (posters), A 45.5
Series PC Reports, C 3.950-4
Series W-(numbered), VA 1.57
Spectrum **Series**, HE 20.3417
Table of Investment Yields for United States Savings Bonds of **Series** E. Official Use, T 66.23
Table of Redemption Values for United States Savings Bonds, **Series** A to E, Inclusive, T 63.209/2
Tables of Redemption Values for $50 **Series** EE and $25 **Series** E Savings Bond, T 63.209/5-2
Tables of Redemption Values for United States Savings Bonds **Series** A-E, T 63.209
Tables of Redemption Values for United States Savings Bonds **Series** EE, T 63.209/7
Tables of Redemption Values for United States Savings Bonds **Series** J, T 63.209/3
Tables of Redemption Values for United States **Series E** Savings Bonds and Savings Notes, T 63.210/2
Tables of Redemption Values of $25 **Series** E Savings Bonds **Series**, T 63.209/5
Test Kitchen **Series**, C 55.321, I 49.39
Textile **Series** Reports, D 106.9/2
Toxics Integration Information **Series**, EP 1.79/2, EP 5.18
Toxics Integration Policy **Series**, EP 1.79/3
Transition **Series**, GA 1.33
Two on a Trip; Radio **Series**, Scripts, I 29.43
U.S. Air Force Fine Arts **Series**, D 301.76/4
U.S. Army in Action **Series**, D 114.7/4
U.S. Automotive Trade Statistics, **Series** A: Motor Vehicles, ITC 1.16

U.S. Automotive Trade Statistics, **Series B,** Passenger Automobiles, ITC 1.16/2
U.S. Census of Housing City Blocks, **Series HC (3),** C 3.224/6
Understanding the Atom **Series,** Y 3.At 7:54
Unemployment Compensation Interpretation Service, Benefit **Series,** SS 1.32, FS 3.108
Unemployment Compensation Interpretation Service, Federal Service, Federal **Series,** SS 1.20
Unemployment Compensation Interpretation Service, State **Series,** SS 1.21, FS 3.109
Union **Series,** L 13.13
United States 1:1,000,000-Scale **Series,** Intermediate Scale Maps, I 19.110
United States and United National Report **Series,** S 1.49
United States Army Research and Development **Series,** D 101.52
United States **Series** of Topographic Maps, I 19.98
United States, **Series** 8205 and 8206, D 5.337
United States-United Nations Information **Series,** S 1.50
USAF Southeast Asia Monograph **Series,** D 301.86
User Manual **Series,** HE 23.1210/4
USSR-Administrative Areas, **Series** 5103, D 5.332
Utilities Demonstration **Series,** HH 1.66
Veneer and Plywood **Series,** C 18.159
Victory Crops **Series** Pamphlets, FS 5.29
Visiting Expert **Series,** S 1.87
Visitor Services Training **Series,** I 29.9/3-2
Vocational Rehabilitation **Series** Bulletins, FS 5.28, FS 10.7
Vocational Rehabilitation **Series,** Opportunity Monographs, VE 1.6
Voice of America Forum Lectures Mass Communication **Series,** IA 1.19
Voice of America Forum Lectures Music **Series,** IA 1.19/3
Voice of America Forum Lectures Space Science **Series,** IA 1.19/2
Voice of America Forum Lectures University **Series,** IA 1.19/4
Wage Chronology **Series** 4, L 2.64
Wage Chronology **Series,** L 2.6/a 10
Wage **Series** Reports, RL 1.8
Wage Structure, **Series** 2, L 2.27
War Changes in Industry **Series,** Reports, TC 1.18
War Information **Series,** Y 3.P 96/3:7
War **Series,** Information from Abroad, N 13.8
Water and Sewer Facilities Grant Program, HUD Information **Series,** HH 1.17
Water Information **Series** Reports, I 19.53/4
Water Pollution Control Research **Series,** EP 1.16, EP 2.10
Water Supply and Waste Disposal **Series,** TD 2.32
Weekly Anthracite Report, WAR **Series,** I 28.49/2
Weekly News **Series,** A 43.27
Western European **Series,** S 1.28
Wholesale Price Index **Series** 1947-48 100: Economic Sector Indexes, L 2.61/8
Wildlife Management **Series** Leaflets, I 49.13/2
Wildlife Portrait **Series,** I 49.71
Wildlife Unit Technical **Series,** A 13.32/2-2
Wind and Current Charts, **Series** A, Tract Charts, N 14.10/1
Wings at War **Series,** W 108.24
Women's Studies, Monograph **Series,** HE 19.220
Workers' Health **Series,** FS 2.33
Workshop **Series** of Pharmacology Section, N.I.M.H., FS 2.310
World of the Atom **Series** Booklets, Y 3.At 7:54-2
World Plotting **Series, Series** 1147, D 5.327
World Radio Market **Series,** C 18.150/2
World Trade Information **Series,** C 41.13, C 49.8
World Trade **Series,** C 42.9/2
Wounded Americans **Series,** T 66.10
You and Your USA **series,** D 2.11
Serologic
   Serologic Tests for Syphilis, FS 2.60/7:Sy 7/2, HE 20.2308:Sy 7/2
SERVE
   SERVE General Publications, ED 1.348/3
   SERVE Special Report, A, ED 1.348/2
   Vision (Newsletter of **SERVE),** The, ED 1.348
Service
   ACS **Service** Report, A 109.9
   Administrative Reference **Service** Reports, N 1.32
   Administrative Rulings {under House of **Service** Act}, IC 1 hou.6
   Administrative **Service** Series, FS 13.212
   Airports **Service,** Standards Division Index of Advisory Circulars, TD 4.110

Americorps Leaders Program, A **Service** Leadership Development Program of the Corporation for National **Service,** Y 3.N 21/29:16-17
Bureau of Safety and **Service** Laws, IC 1 saf.5/2
Cable Television Relay **Service,** Applications, Reports, Public Notices, CC 1.47/2
Cable Television **Service** Applications, Reports, Public Notices, CC 1.47
Career **Service** Board for Science Reports, FS 1.33
Catalog of HEW Assistance Providing Financial Support and **Service** to States, Communities, Organizations, Individuals, HE 1.6/6
Cataloging **Service** Bulletin, LC 30.7, LC 30.7/2
CD Blind, National Library **Service** for the Blind and Physically Handicapped, LC 19.24
Census of Business; **Service** Trades Bulletins (by States), C 3.202/4
Census of Selected **Service** Industries; Area Statistics Series, C 56.253/3
Census of Selected **Service** Industries; Final Volumes, C 56.253/5
Census of Selected **Service** Industries; General Publications, C 56.253
Census of Selected **Service** Industries; Preliminary Area Series, C 56.253/2
Census of Selected **Service** Industries; Subject Reports, C 56.253/4
Census of **Service** Industries: Geographic Area Series, C 257/6-2
Census of **Service** Industries: Geographic Area Summary, C 257/6
Census of **Service** Industries Industry Series, C 3.257/3-4
Census of **Service** Industries Nonemployer Statistics Series, C 3.257/5
Census of **Service** Industries; Final Reports, C 3.257/4
Census of **Service** Industries; General Publications, C 3.257
Census of **Service** Industries; Geographic Area Series, C 3.257/2
Census of **Service** Industries; Geographic Area Series, Advance Reports, C 3.257/2-2
Census of **Service** Industries; Preliminary Report Industry Series, C 3.257/3-3
Census of **Service** Industries; Subject Series, C 3.257/3
Certificated Air Carrier Financial Data; Domestic Helicopter **Service** {12-month comparisons}, C 31.242/2
Certificated Air Carrier Financial Data; Domestic Helicopter **Service** {quarterly comparisons}, C 31.242
Certificated Air Carrier Financial Data; Domestic Local **Service** 12-month Comparisons, C 31.235/2
Certificated Air Carrier Financial Data; Domestic Local **Service** {quarterly comparisons}, C 31.235
Changes in Air **Service** Information Circular, W 87.11/3
Checklist of Reports Issued by Economic Research **Service** and Statistical Reporting Service, A 1.97
Chemical Warfare Field **Service** Bulletins, W 91.7
Chemical Warfare **Service** Bulletin, W 99.17/12
Community **Service** and Continuing Education, Title 1, Higher Education Act of 1965, FS 5.78
Compilation of Public Health **Service** Regulations, FS 2.52
Congressional Research **Service** Review, LC 14.19
Contract Advisory **Service** Summaries, IC 1.36
Cooperative Research and **Service** Division, Quarterly Reports, A 72.22
Coordination **Service,** Digest of Interpretations of Specific Price Schedules and Regulations, Pr 32.4249
Current Business Reports **Service** Annual Survey, C 3.138/3-4
Current Business Reports; Monthly Selected **Service** Receipts, BS (series), C 56.219/5
Decisions Under Hours of **Service** Act {compilations}, IC 1 hou.8
Decisions Under Hours of **Service** Act {individual cases}, IC 1 hou.7
Dialog for the **Service** Education Officer, D 1.10/5
Directory of Air **Service** Stations, W 87.9/2
Directory of Indian **Service** Units, I 20.38
Dry Cargo **Service** and Area Report, United States Dry Cargo Shipping Companies by Ships Owned and/or Chartered Type of **Service** and Area Operated, C 39.213

Education **Service** Plan, Wisconsin National Guard, D 12.16
EEOC Reports, Clearinghouse **Service** for Business Newsletters and Periodicals, Y 3.Eq 2:7-2
Employees' Health **Service** Folders, FS 2.49
Employment **Service** Manual, Pr 32.5221
Employment **Service** News, L 7.14, FS 3.107
Employment **Service** Review, L 7.18, FS 3.130
Employment **Service** Statistics, L 7.18/2-2, L 1.60
Employment **Service** Technical Reports, L 1.70
Extension **Service** Circulars, A 43.4
Extension **Service** Review, A 43.7
Federal Contract Air **Service** and Travel Directory, GS 8.10
Federal **Service** Impasses Panel Releases, Y 3.F 31/21-3:14-3
Fixed Public **Service** Applications Received for Filing During Past Week, Public Notices, CC 1.40
Food **Service** Equipment Catalog, D 7.38
Food **Service** Information Bulletin, D 214.22
Foreign Plant Quarantines in **Service** Training Series, A 56.25
Foreign **Service** Classification List, S 1.7/2
Foreign **Service** Institute Bulletin, S 1.114/4
Foreign **Service** Institute Courses, S 1.114/2
Foreign **Service** Institute, General Publications, S 1.114/3
Foreign **Service** Institute, Quarterly Projection of Courses, S 1.114
Foreign **Service** Institute, Readers, S 1.114/2-2
Foreign **Service** List, S 1.7
Foreign **Service** Manual, Transmittal Letters, S 1.5/4
Foreign **Service** News Letter, S 1.109
Foreign **Service** on Vegetables, A 64.13, A 67.14
Foreign **Service** Regulations (by chapters), S 1.5/3
Foreign **Service** Regulations, Memorandum Transmitting Mimeographed Inserts for, S 1.5/2
Foreign **Service** Reports, A 36.39, A 67.11
Forest **Service** Comments on Resolutions Relating to the National Forest System As Adopted, A 13.86
Forest **Service** Films Available on Loan for Educational Purposes to Schools, Civic Groups, Churches, Television, A 13.55
Forest **Service** History Line, A 13.98/3
Forest **Service** Translations, A 13.81
Government Vehicle Operators Guide to **Service** Stations for Gasoline, Oil and Lubrication, D 7.6/7-2
Grand and Petit Juror **Service** in U.S. District Courts, Ju 10.13
Handbook for **Service** Attaches Accredited to the Department of the Air Force, D 301.6/5-2
Hours of **Service** Act Text of Act, IC 1 hou.5
HUD Clearinghouse **Service,** HCS (series), HH 1.35
Indian Health **Service** Directory, HE 20.9412/2
Information News **Service,** C 46.13
Land **Service** Bulletin, I 21.16
Legal Guide and Case Digest, Veterans' Reemployment Rights Under the Universal Military Training and **Service** Act, As Amended, and Related Acts, L 25.6/2:L 52
Local **Service** Air Carrier, Selected Flight Load Data by City Pair, by Frequency Grouping, by Aircraft Type, C 31.253/2
Local **Service** Air Carriers' Unit Costs, C 31.253
Local **Service** Carrier Passenger Enplanements, C 31.266
Memorandum Transmitting Mimeographed Inserts for Foreign **Service** Regulations, S 1.5/2
National **Service** News, Y 3.N 21/29:16-15
NHLBI National Research **Service** Award Programs Summary Descriptions, HE 20.3211/4
Number and Percentage of Farms Electrified with Central Station **Service,** A 68.20
Occasional Papers Forest **Service** Southern Forest Experiment Station, A 13.40/6
Operating Statistics of Class 1 Steam Roads, Freight and Passenger **Service,** IC 1 ste.21
Orders United States Postal **Service,** P 1.19
Ordnance Field **Service** Bulletins, W 34.26, W 34.32
Ordnance Field **Service** Technical Bulletins, W 34.36
Outpatient Psychiatric Clinics, Community **Service** Activities, FS 2.22/38-3
Park **Service** Bulletins, I 29.3

Pay Structure on the Federal Civil Service, CS 1.48:33

Pecan Report, Louisiana Crop Reporting Service, A 88.10/5

Performance Guides (series) Forest Service, A 13.65/12-2

Periodic Reports of Agricultural Economics, Economic Research Service, Statistical Reporting Service, A 1.99

Pharmacy Residences in Public Health Service Hospitals, FS 2.89/3

Philippine Health Service, Monthly Bulletin, W 49.15/6

Pig Crop Report, Louisiana Crop Reporting Service, A 88.16/3-2

Places where Civil Service Examinations are Held, CS 1.28:2300

Point to Point Microwave Radio Service, CC 1.36/8

Postal Inspection Service Bulletin, P 1.3/2

Postal Laws and Regulations Applicable to Railway Mail Service, P 10.13

Postal Service Institute Bulletin, P 1.44

Postal Service Manual, P 1.12/5

Postal Service News, P 1.30

Postal Service Orders, P 1.12/5-2

Posters Civil Service Commission, CS 1.89

Posters Customs Service, T 17.21

Posters Financial Management Service, T 63.122

Posters Food and Nutrition Service, A 98.16

Posters Food Safety and Inspection Service, A 103.18

Posters General Service Administration, GS 1.32

Posters Minerals Management Service, I 72.16

Posters National Archives and Records Service, GS 4.26

Posters National Ocean Service, C 55.418/6-2

Posters National Weather Service, C 55.130

Posters Soil Conservation Service, A 57.71

Posters United States Marshals Service, J 25.12

President's Awards for Distinguished Federal Civilian Service, CS 1.64

Prime Contract Awards by Service Category and Federal Supply Classification, D 1.57/4

Proceedings Annual Conference of the Surgeon General, Public Health Service, and Chief, Children's Bureau, with State and Territorial Health Officers, FS 2.83

Proceedings Annual Conference, Surgeon General, Public Health Service, with State and Territorial Mental Health Authorities, FS 2.83/3

Proceedings Biennial Conference of State and Territorial Dental Directors with Public Health Service and Children's Bureau, FS 2.83/2

Procurement Legal Service Circulars, D 101.33/3

Product Analysis Service, Pr 33.920

Productivity and Cost of Employment: Local Service Carriers, Calendar Year, C 31.263

Program Report of the United States Travel Service, C 47.1

Progress Report Air Service, Engineering Division, W 87.14

Proposals (and specifications for supplies) for Indian Service, I 20.14

Proposals for Indian Service, I 20.14

Proposals Received and Contracts Awarded for Supplies for Indian Service, I 20.11

Prospective Strawberry Acreage, Louisiana Crop Reporting Service, A 88.12/27

Public Acts and Resolutions Relating to Post Office Department and Postal Service, P 1.20

Public Assistance: Vendor Payments for Medical Care by Type of Service, Fiscal Year Ended (date), HE 17.617

Public Health Service Bibliography Series, HE 20.11

Public Health Service Film Catalog, FS 2.36/2

Public Health Service Grants and Awards, HE 20.3013

Public Health Service International Postdoctorate Research Fellowships Awards for Study in the United States, HE 20.3709

Public Health Service Posters, FS 2.26/2

Public Health Service Prospective Payment Activity, HE 20.6516

Public Health Service Support of Cardiovascular Research, Training and Community Programs, FS 2.22/11-2

Public Health Service Water Pollution Surveillance System, FS 2.84/2

Public Notices (concerning irrigation projects of reclamation service), I 1.49

Public Service Office, Series S-, S 1.106/2

Public Use, Tabulation of Visitors to Areas Administrated by National Park Service, I 29.63

Publications Army Map Service, D 103.20

Publications Environmental Data Service, C 55.228

Publications International Reference Service, C 34.11

Publications National Archives and Records Service, GS 4.17

Publications Public Health and Marine-Hospital Service, T 27.16

Publications United States Postal Service, P 1.57

Qualification Standards for Postal Field Service, CS 1.45

Questions & Answer Service, C 35.14

Radio Service Agriculture in Defense, A 21.13/9

Radio Service Bulletins, CC 1.3/2, CC 1.25

Radio Service Consumer Facts, A 21.13/6

Radio Service Dairy Short Course, A 21.13/2

Radio Service Farm Flashes, A 21.13/7

Radio Service Housekeepers' Charts, A 21.13/8

Radio Service Livestock Short Course, A 21.13/1

Radio Service Poultry Short Course, A 21.13/3

Rail Passenger Service Act, Report to Congress, TD 1.10/5

Reclamation Service, I 19.17

Recruiting Bulletins Agricultural Marketing Service, A 88.3/2

Recurrent Report of Mileage and Traffic Data Domestic Helicopter Service, Certificated Airmail Carriers, C 31.229/4

Recurrent Report of Mileage and Traffic Data Domestic Local Service Carriers, C 31.229

Regulations for Government of Public Health and Marine Hospital Service, T 27.8

Regulations for Revenue-Cutter Service (general), T 33.7

Regulations, Rules and Instructions Food and Nutrition Service, A 98.18

Rehabilitation Service Administration, Quarterly Indicies, HE 17.120

Rehabilitation Service Series, FS 13.207, FS 17.110/3, HE 17.110/3

Report of Career Service Board for Science, HE 1.33

Report of Forest Service Training Activities, Civilian Conservation Corps, A 13.71

Report of the Chief of the Forest Service, A 13.1

Report of the Forest Service, Fiscal Year (date), A 13.1/3

Report on Internal Audit Activities of the Internal Revenue Service, T 22.53

Report, Civil Service Requirement, Federal Employees' Group Life Insurance, Federal Employees Health Benefits, Retired Federal Employees Health Benefits, Fiscal Year (date), CS 1.29/3

Reports from USDA's Economic Research Service, A 93.18/3

Reports Issued by Agricultural Marketing Service, A 66.19

Reports on Airline Service, Fares Traffic, Load Factors and Market Shares, CAB 1.27

Reports Prepared for Foreign Service of United States, Listings, C 42.22

Research and Training Grants and Awards of Public Health Service, FS 2.22/8

Research Notes Forest Service, A 13.79

Research Papers Forest Service, A 13.78

Research Progress in (year), a Report of the Agricultural Research Service, A 77.1

Research Reports Economics, Statistics, and Cooperatives Service, A 105.31

Retail, Wholesale, Service Trades, Subject Bulletin, RWS (series), C 3.202/9

Rice Production, Louisiana Crop Reporting Service, A 88.18/26

River Forecasts Provided by the National Weather Service, C 55.117/2, C 55.285

Roster of Officers of Indian Service, I 20.10

Rules and Regulations of Service, IC 1.12/1

School Facilities Service (lists & references), FS 5.10/2

Seasonally Adjusted Capacity and Traffic Scheduled Operations Local Service Carriers, C 31.262/4

Seasonally Adjusted Capacity and Traffic Scheduled Operations: System, Domestic, and International Trunks Plus Local Service Carrier, CAB 1.20

Selected Decision of Comptroller General Applicable to Naval Service, N 20.7/4

Selected Elements of Value of Property Used in Common Carrier Service, Before and After Recorded Depreciation and Amortization, Class I Line Haul Railways, Including Their Lessors and Proprietary Companies, IC 1 val.10

Selective Service Act As Amended {May 18, 1917}, Y 1.2:Se 4

Selective Service College Qualification Test, Bulletin of Information, Y 3.Se 4:22

Selective Service Manual, Pr 32./5280

Selective Service Memorandums to All Navy Contractors, N 1.30

Selective Service News, Y 3.Se 4:20

Selective Service Regulations, Y 3.Se 4:6, Y 3.Se 4:7

Selective Service, Y 3.Se 4:9, Pr 32.5279, Y 3.Se 4:20

Semi-Annual Report of the Secretary of Commerce on the United States Travel Service, C 47.1

Service and Regulatory Announcements Agricultural Marketing Administration, A 75.16

Service and Regulatory Announcements Agricultural Marketing Service, A 66.27, A 88.6/3

Service and Regulatory Announcements Agricultural Research Service, A 77.6/2

Service and Regulatory Announcements Agricultural Stabilization and Conservation Service, A 82.23

Service and Regulatory Announcements Alaska Game Commission, A 5.10/5

Service and Regulatory Announcements Bureau of Agricultural Economics, A 36.5

Service and Regulatory Announcements Bureau of Animal Industry, A 4.13, A 77.208

Service and Regulatory Announcements Bureau of Biological Survey, A 5.6

ice and Regulatory Announcements Bureau of Chemistry, A 7.6

Service and Regulatory Announcements Bureau of Dairy Industry, A 44.5

Service and Regulatory Announcements Bureau of Entomology and Plant Quarantine, A 56.14

Service and Regulatory Announcements Bureau of Plant Industry, A 19.13

Service and Regulatory Announcements Bureau of Plant Quarantine, A 48.7

Service and Regulatory Announcements Bureau of Soils, A 26.7

Service and Regulatory Announcements Caustic Poison, A 46.13, FS 13.110

Service and Regulatory Announcements Civil Service Commission, CS 1.5

Service and Regulatory Announcements Federal Horticulture Board, A 35.9

Service and Regulatory Announcements Food and Drug, A 46.12

Service and Regulatory Announcements Food, Drug, and Cosmetic, A 46.19, FS 7.8, FS 13.115

Service and Regulatory Announcements Import Milk, A 46.11, FS 13.114

Service and Regulatory Announcements Insecticide and Fungicide Board, A 34.6, A 46.15

Service and Regulatory Announcements List of Intercepted Plant Pests, A 77.308/2

Service and Regulatory Announcements Naval Stores, A 46.18

Service and Regulatory Announcements Publications Relating to Entomology and Plant Quarantine, A 77.308

Service and Regulatory Announcements Publications Relating to the Care of Animals and Poultry, A 77.208

Service and Regulatory Announcements SRA-C&MS- (series), A 88.6/3

Service and Regulatory Announcements Tea, A 46.14, FS 7.14

Service and Regulatory Announcements, Office of Distribution, A 80.118

Service Bulletin, I 19.26

Service Bulletins of Defense Training in Vocational Schools, FS 5.24

Service Coordinators Chronicle, HH 1.125

Service Directory, A 13.8/2

Service Establishments (by States), C 3.940-11

Service Letters, VA 1.32

Service Reports Energy Information Administration, E 3.26/5

Service Reports Farmer Cooperative Service, A 89.12

Service Series Posters, W 3.46/3

Service Series Special Posters, W 3.46/4

Service Survey, I 49.22

Service Trade Bulletins, Pr 32.4222

Service Trade Reports, C 3.185

Service, USDA's Report to Consumers, A 21.29, A 107.11

Sheets of National Atlas of United States Agricultural Research Service, A 77.19

Sheets of National Atlas of United States Forest Service, A 13.28/2

Signal Service Notes, W 42.14

Smithsonian International Exchange Service Annual Report, SI 1.1/a3

Social and Rehabilitation Service Reports Bulletins, HE 17.29

Social and Rehabilitation Service Research and Demonstration Projects, FS 17.15

Social Service Resource Directories, J 16.7

Soil Conservation Service, A 57.1/3

Solicitation of the Public Health Service and the Health Care Financing Administration for Small Business Innovation Research Contract Proposals, HE 22.31

Solicitation of the Public Health Service for Small Business Research (SBIR) Contract Proposals, HE 20.28/2

Speakers Guide for Service Spokesmen, D 6.8

Speakers' Guide for Service Spokesmen, Power for Peace, Armed Forces Day, D 1.6/3

Special Bulletins Civil Service Commission, CS 1.47

Special Features Service, Y 3.P 96/3:8

Special Releases {of Foreign Broadcast Intelligence Service}, W 100.9

Special Reports Farmer Cooperative Service, A 89.20

Special Reports Soil Conservation Service, A 57.72

Special Reports Soil Conservation Service, Office of Research, Sedimentation Section, A 76.215, A 80.2013

Special Service Digest, W 109.108

Specifications United States Postal Service, P 1.16, P 1.32

Stars in Service, T 66.14

State Exchange Service Item Series, FS 13.213

State Publications Issued in Cooperation with Agricultural Marketing Service, A 88.42/2

State Publications Issued in Cooperation with Federal Extension Service, A 43.37

State Reports Issued in Cooperation with Statistical Reporting Service, A 92.36

Statistical Analysis of Carrier's Monthly Hours of Service Reports, IC 1 hou.9

Statistical Series Social and Rehabilitation Service, HE 17.23

Statistical Yearbook of the Immigration and Naturalization Service, J 21.2:St 2, J 21.2/2, J 21.2/10

Status Report on Water and Power Resources Service Programs Within (various States), I 27.74

Steamboat-Inspection Service Bulletin, C 15.10

Summary of Activities Animal and Plant Health Inspection Service, A 101.27

Sweetpotato Report, Louisiana Crop Reporting Service, A 88.12/4-2

Technical Digest Service, C 41.24

Technical Inquiry Service, S 18.23

Technical Notes Forest Service Forest Products Laboratory, A 13.27/9

Technical Notes Forest Service Lake States Forest Experiment Station, A 13.61/10

Technical Notes Forest Service Northeastern Forest Experiment Station, A 13.67/9, A 13.42/7

Technical Notes Forest Service Northern Forest Experiment Station, A 13.73/9

Technical Notes Forest Service Southeastern Forest Experiment Station, A 13.63/8

Technical Notes Forest Service WSDG-TN-(nos), A 13.27/9, A 13.87/4

Technical Reports National Park Service, J 29.15, I 29.109

Telephone and Service Directory, HE 20.3037

Telephone Directory Automated Data and Telecommunications Service, Region 1, GS 12.12/2:1

Telephone Directory Customs Service, T 17.15

Telephone Directory Internal Revenue Service, Salt Lake City District, T 22.48/3

Telephone Directory Selective Service System, Y 3.Se 4:26

Timucuan Today and Tomorrow, A Newsletter from the National Park Service, I 29.128

To Mayor of Each City with Local Airline Service, C 31.256

Tower University: Education Service Plan, D 101.93/2

Traffic Service Letters, GS 2.9

Train and Yard Service of Class I Railroads in the United States, IC 1 ste.38/2

Transmittal Letters {for Indian Service Manual}, I 20.35

Trends in Scheduled All-Cargo Service, C 31.264/2

Trends in Utilization of Indian Health Service and Contract Hospitals, HE 20.9417

Turkeys Raised, Louisiana Crop Reporting Service, A 88.15/11-2

U.S. Air Service in World War I, D 301.82/2

U.S. Army and Air Force Recruiting Service Letter, M 208.76

U.S. Book Exchange Service, S 18.27

Unemployment Compensation Interpretation Service, Benefit Series, SS 1.32, FS 3.108

Unemployment Compensation Interpretation Service, Federal Service, Federal Series, SS 1.20

Unemployment Compensation Interpretation Service, State Series, SS 1.21, FS 3.109

United States Air Force Medical Service Digest, D 304.8

United States Employment Service Test Research Reports, L 7.69

Urban Renewal Service Bulletins, HH 7.7/3

VA Medical Research Service, Annual Report, VA 1.1/4

Vegetable Report, Louisiana Crop Reporting Service, A 88.12/26

Vendor Payments for Medical Care Under Public Assistance, by Program and Type of Service, Fiscal Year (date), HE 17.617/4

Veterans Employment Service Handbooks, L 7.30

Visitor Accommodations Furnished by Concessioners in Areas Administered by National Park Service, I 29.70

Voluntary Service National Advisory Committee: Report of Annual Meeting, VA 1.52

Weather Service Bulletin, W 108.35

Weather Service for Merchant Shipping, C 30.79

Weather Service Observing Handbooks, C 55.108/2

Weekly Cotton Service Bulletins, C 18.162

Weekly Newspaper Service, L 1.77

Wildlife Service Leaflets, I 49.13/3

Winter Wheat Report, Louisiana Crop Reporting Service, A 88.18/24

Working Papers Social and Rehabilitation Service, HE 17.24

Yard Service Performance of Class I Railroads in the United States, IC 1ste.38

Servicemen

Government Life Insurance Programs for Veterans and Servicemen, VA 1.46

Servicemen's Group Life Insurance Program, Annual Report, VA 1.46/2

Services

Administrative Services, DOE/OAS (series), E 1.46

Aeronautical Communications and Pilot Services Handbook 7300.7, Changes, FAA 3.9/2

Air Force Engineering and Services Quarterly, D 301.65

Annual Report of Legal Services Program of Office of Economic Opportunity to the American Bar Association, PrEx 10.18

Calibration and Test Services of the National Bureau of Standards, C 13.10:250

Catalog and Price List of Stable Isotopes Including Related Materials and Services, Y 3.At 7:35

Charges for Ginning Cotton, Costs of Selected Services Incident to Marketing, and Related Information, Season, A 88.11/12

Commodities and Services Manual, L 2.46/2

Common Carrier Public Mobile Services Information, CC 1.36/6

Comprehensive Health Services Projects, Summary of Project Data, CHSP Reports, HE 20.5115

Computer Services Newsletter, T 22.2/15-2

Current Business Reports: Annual Survey of Communication Services, C 3.138/3-6

Directory of Commodities and Services, ES 3.10

Directory of Commodities and Services Exempted or Suspended from Price Control, ES 3.10/2

Directory of Facilities Obligated to Provide Uncompensated Services by State and City, HE 20.9209

Directory of Medicare Providers and Suppliers of Services, HE 3.51/5

Directory of Outpatient Psychiatric Clinics, Psychiatric Day-Night Services and Other Mental Health Resources in the United States and Territories, FS 2.22/38-4

Directory of Providers of Services of Extended Care Facilities, HE 3.51/3

Directory of Providers of Services of Home Health Services, HE 3.51

Directory of Providers of Services of Hospitals, HE 3.51/2

Directory of Providers of Services of Independent Laboratories, HE 3.51/4

Directory of Services, ED 1.30/4

Directory of Suppliers of Services: Independent Laboratories, FS 3.51/4

Directory of United States Poison Control Centers and Services, HE 20.4003/2-2

Disease Control Services Activities, A 77.212/9

Drug Abuse Services Research Series, HE 20.8235

Educational Services Brochure and Schedule of Courses, D 101.93

Employment Services for Veterans, Annual Report, L 7.30/2

EMS {Emergency Medical Services} Resource Exchange Bulletin, FEM 1.110/3

EMSC (Emergency Medical Services for Children) News, HE 20.9212

Estimated Volume of Mail and Special Services and Postal Revenues, P 1.37

Facts and Services from the U.S. Department of Labor, L 1.31

Family Planning Services, HE 20.7011/21

Federal Coordinator for Meterological Services and Supporting Research, FCM (series), C 55.12

Federal Plan for Meteorological Services and Supporting Research, Fiscal Year (date), C 55.16/2

Federal-State Market News Reports, Directory of Services Available, A 88.40/2:21

Flight Services Handbook, TD 4.308:F 64

For Your Information; Education Services, FCD 1.13/5

Foreign Radio Broadcasting Services, C 18.87

Foster Family Services Selected Reading List, HE 1.452:F 81/4

Graduate Education Bulletin, Uniformed Services University of the Health Sciences, D 1.67/2

Group Services Bulletins, Pr 32.4232

Human Services, Bibliography Series, HE 1.18/4

Integrated Resources and Services for {various subjects}, C 1.77

Inter-Arts, Presenting Organizations Artist Communities Services to the Arts, Application Guidelines, NF 2.8/2-23

National Listing of Providers Furnishing Kidney Dialysis and Transplant Services, HE 22.25

NTIS Products and Services Catalog, C 51.11/8

Office of Construction Industry Services: Annual Report, L 1.1/2

Office of Human Development Services Budget Request, HE 23.13

Organization and Staffing for Full Time Local Health Services, FS 2.80

Pamphlets Community Services Administration, CSA 1.9

Posters Health Resources and Services Administration, HE 20.9012

Procurement Regulations Services of Supply, W 109.7, W 109.8, W 109.8-2

Products and Services Catalog, C 21.30

Products and Services Catalog, C 21.39

Professional Papers Environmental Science Services Administration, C 52.20

Program and Services, Report of Educational Materials Laboratory, Division of International Studies and Services, FS 5.214:14031, HE 5.214:14031

Program for Regional Observing and Forecasting Services, C 55.626/2

Programs and Schedules, Services of Supply Staff Course, W 28.11/3

Protection Services Division {Reports}, Pr 32.4427

Shawnee
Shawnee Quarterly, the **Shawnee** National Forest
Schedule of Projects, A 13.138
Shawnee Sportsman's Maps (series), A 13.28/3
Sheep
Annual Report of Cooperative State-Federal **Sheep**
Scabies Eradication Activities, Fiscal
Year (date), A 77.233/2
Annual Report on Cooperative State-Federal
Psoroptic **Sheep** and Cattle Scabies
Eradication Activities, Fiscal Year
(date), A 77.233
Cattle and **Sheep**, Shipments of Stocker and Feeder
Cattle and **Sheep** into Selected North
Central States, A 88.16/18-2
Cattle, **Sheep** and Goat Inventory, A 93.18/8
Cooperative State-Federal **Sheep** and Cattle Scabies
Eradication, Progress Report, A 77.233
Cooperative State-Federal **Sheep** and Cattle
Scabies, Epidemiology and Related
Activities, A 77.233/4
Incidence of Bluetongue Reported in **Sheep** During
Calendar Year, A 77.231
International Trade in **Sheep** Skins, C 18.186/3
Psoroptic **Sheep** Scabies Outbreaks in (State), A
77.240
Sheep, A 92.18/9
Sheep and Goats, A 105.23/8
Sheep and Lamb on Feed, A 88.16/13, A 105.47
Sheep and Lamb Situation, A 36.91
Sheep and Lambs: Weekly Average Price per 100
Pounds, A 36.183
Shipments of Stocker and Feeder Cattle and **Sheep**,
A 88.16/18
Sheet
Classification of Income, Profit & Loss, and General
Balance **Sheet** Accounts, IC 1 ste.15
Consumer Fact **Sheet**, TD 5.60
HCFA Fact **Sheet** (series), HE 22.40
OJJDP Fact **Sheet** (series), J 32.21
Research Achievement **Sheet**, A 77.7
Savings and Mortgage Lending Activity, Selected
Balance **Sheet** Items, F.S.L.I.C. Insured
Savings and Loan Associations, FHL
1.20/2
State Vocational Rehabilitation Agency: Fact **Sheet**
Booklets, HE 17.119/2, HE 1.610
Tech Data **Sheet** (series), D 201.27
Tests in Progress **Sheet**, D 203.32, C 55.70
U.S. Agricultural Imports, Fact **Sheet**, A 67.32/2, A
93.30, A 93.30/2
U.S. Department of Labor Program Highlights, Fact
Sheet (Series), L 1.88
U.S. Merchant Marine Data **Sheet**, TD 11.10
VD Fact **Sheet**, HE 20.7018
Sheets
Case Information **Sheets**, Y 3.F 31/21-3:14-11
Cellulose Plastic Products (Nitro-Cellulose and
Cellulose Acetate **Sheets**, Rods and
Tubes), C 3.73
Change **Sheets** Applying to Organization
Directory, W 3.42/2
Clip **Sheets**, A 21.15
Extension Course of Medical Field Service School;
Lesson Assignment **Sheets**, W 3.71
Fact **Sheets** [Animal and Plant Health Inspection
Service], A 101.31
Job **Sheets**, A 57.40/2
Lesson Performance Test Grading **Sheets** (series), D
101.107/2
Location **Sheets** of Maps and Charts, W 31.7/2
PBGC {Pension Benefit Guaranty Corporation}
Fact **Sheets**, L 1.51/5
Picture **Sheets**, A 56.20, A 77.320
Price Control Fact **Sheets**, Pr 32.4268
Separate **Sheets** of Selected Thematic and General
Reference Maps from the National Atlas
of the United States of America, I 19.111a
Sheets of National Atlas of United States
Agricultural Research Service, A 77.19
Sheets of National Atlas of United States Bureau of
the Census, C 3.62/3
Sheets of National Atlas of United States Census of
Agriculture, C 3.31/10
Sheets of National Atlas of United States Coast and
Geodetic Survey, C 4.9/21
Sheets of National Atlas of United States Forest
Service, A 13.28/2
Sheets of National Atlas of United States
Geological Survey, I 19.5/3
Sheets of National Atlas of United States Interstate
Commerce Commission, IC 1.30
Sheets of National Atlas of United States Tennessee
Valley Authority, Y 3.T 25:7-2

Sheets of National Atlas of United States Weather
Bureau, C 30.22/4
State Officers Analyzer **Sheets**, C 46.12
State Safety Program Work **Sheets**, L 16.39
Student Information **Sheets** (series), D 101.112/2
Student Reference **Sheets**, SR- (series), FS 13.122
Student Work **Sheets**, Department of Labor Safety
Training Programs, SWS-LS-(series), L
16.51
Supplementary Notices to Mariners, Correction
Sheets for Coast Pilots, N 6.11/3
Supplementary Notices to Mariners, Correction
Sheets for H.O. Publications, N 6.11/4
Technical Fact **Sheets**, Y 3.C 76/3:11-2
Type Certificate Data **Sheets** and Specifications,
Rotorcraft, Gliders, and Balloons, TD
4.15/6
United States Treaty Developments, Transmittal
Sheets, S 9.11/2
VA Fact **Sheets**, IS- (series), VA 1.34
Water Fact **Sheets** (series), I 19.114
Women's Page Clip **Sheets**, Y 3.F 31/11:15
You Can Survive, Rural Defense Fact **Sheets**, A
43.35
Your New Social Security, Fact **Sheets**, FS 3.25
Shelf
Outer Continental **Shelf** Environmental
Assessment Program Final Reports of
Principal Investigators, C 55.433
Outer Continental **Shelf** Environmental Studies
Advisory Committee: Publications, I
1.99/2
Outer Continental **Shelf** Oil and Gas Information
Program, Summary Reports (various
regions), I 72.9
Outer Continental **Shelf** Oil and Gas Leasing and
Production Program Annual Report, I
72.12/3-2
Outer Continental **Shelf** Research Management
Advisory Board: Annual Report, I 1.99
Outer Continental **Shelf** Standard, GSS-OCS
(series), I 19.73
Outer Continental **Shelf** Statistical Summary, I
72.12/3-3
Subject Cataloging Manual, **Shelf** Listing, LC
26.8/5
Shell
Commitments of Traders in Wheat, Corn, Oats, Rye,
Soybeans, Soybean Oil, Soybean Meal,
Shell Eggs, A 85.9/2
Shellers
List, Peanut Millers (**shellers** and crushers), A
92.14/3
List, Peanut **Shellers** and Crushers, A 88.10/3
Peanut **Shellers** and Crushers List, A 88.10/3
Shellfish
Interstate Certified **Shellfish** Shippers List, HE
20.4014
Interstate **Shellfish** Shippers List, HE 20.4014
National **Shellfish** Register of Classified Growing
Waters, C 55.441
National **Shellfish** Sanitation Workshop,
Proceedings, HE 20.4032
Northwest **Shellfish** Sanitation Research Planning
Conference, Proceedings, EP 2.15
Proceedings National **Shellfish** Sanitation
Workshop, FS 2.16/2
Proceedings Northwest **Shellfish** Sanitation
Research Planning Conference, EP 2.15
Shellfish Market Review, Current Economic
Analysis S, C 55.309/4
Shellfish Situation and Outlook, CEA-S (series), C
55.309/4, I 49.8/8
Shelter
Protective Structures, **Shelter** Design Series, D
13.15
Sheltered
News and Clues for **Sheltered** Workshop, PrEx
1.10/4-4
Shelving
Steel Office Furniture, **Shelving**, and Lockers, and
Fireproof Safes, C 3.108
Shenandoah
Naturalist Program, **Shenandoah** National Park, I
29.60/4
Shenandoah National Park Chips, I 29.67
Sherman
Sherman Pamphlets, I 20.30
Shield
Eagle and the **Shield**, S 1.69:161
Shift
Shift Colors, the Newsletter for Navy Retirees, D
208.12/3-2

Shifts
U.S. Trade **Shifts** in Selected Commodity Areas, ITC
1.15
Shigella
National Communicable Disease Center **Shigella**
Surveillance, Reports, FS 2.60/16
Shigella Surveillance, Reports, HE 20.7011/18
Shingles
Red Cedar **Shingles**, C 3.119
Ship
Fathom, Surface **Ship** and Submarine Safety Review,
D 202.20, D 201.32
International Conference on Numerical **Ship**
Hydrodynamics: Proceedings, D 211.9/5
List of Books Available for **Ship** and Station
Libraries, Navy, N 17.26
Naval **Ship** Research and Development Center
Reports, D 211.9
Naval **Ship** Systems Command Technical News, D
211.8
New **Ship** Construction, TD 11.15
New **Ship** Construction, Oceangoing Ships of
1,000 Gross Tons and Over in United
States and Foreign **Ship**yards, C 39.212/
3
New **Ship** Deliveries, Calendar Year, C 39.212/2
New **Ship** Techniques and Development of Research
Services Division, Annual Report, D
301.45/11
Proceedings International Conference on Numerical
Ship Hydrodynamics, D 211.9/5
SCC {**Ship** Structure Committee}, Y 3.Sh 6:6/SSC
Ship Construction Manuals, N 24.37, T 47.37
Ship Operations Report, National Ocean Survey, C
55.423
Ship Structure Committee, TD 5.63
Statistical Report of Commerce Passing through
Canals at Sault Ste. Marie, Mich. and
Ontario, Salt Water **Ship** Movements for
Season of (year), D 103.17/2
Steam Railways in Hands of Receivers and Trustees,
and Changes in List of Companies
Affected by Receiver **Ship** of Trusteeship,
IC 1 ste.45
Shipborne
International **Shipborne** Barge Register, C 39.241,
TD 11.24
Shipbuilders
Shipbuilders Bulletin, SB 2.9
Shipbuilding
Industry Wage Survey: **Shipbuilding** and
Repairing, L 2.3/34
National **Shipbuilding** Research Program (various
subjects) (series), C 39.245
Relative Cost of **Shipbuilding**, TD 11.15/2
Relative Cost of **Shipbuilding** in Various Coastal
Districts of the United States, Report to
Congress, C 39.216/2
Report on Survey of U.S. **Shipbuilding** and Repair
Facilities, TD 11.25
Shipbuilding and Conversion Program, D 207.13
Shipbuilding Progress Report for Month Ending, C
39.216
Shipment
Ordnance Storage and **Shipment** Charts, W 34.38
Shipment of Liquefied Petroleum Gases and
Methane in (year), I 28.98/5
Shipment Under the United States Foreign Aid
Programs Made on Army- or Navy-
Operated Vessels (American flag) by Port
of Lading by Country of Destination, C
3.164:976
Statistics of Bituminous Coal Loaded for **Shipment**
on Railroads and Waterways As
Reported by Operators, I 28.34
Shipments
Allotments, Authorizations, and Paid **Shipments**,
Data, FO 1.9/2
Aluminum Metal Supply and **Shipments** of
Products to Consumers, C 41.112/4
Asphalt **Shipments** in (year), I 28.110
Broom Corn Brooms: Producers' **Shipments**
Imports for Consumption Exports and
Apparent Consumption, ITC 1.23
Car-Lot **Shipments** of Fruits and Vegetables, by
Commodities, States, and Months, A
1.34, A 66.24
Carlot **Shipments** of, from Stations in U.S., A 66.24/
2
Cattle and Sheep, **Shipments** of Stocker and Feeder
Cattle and Sheep into Selected North
Central States, A 88.16/18-2
Commodity Classification for Compiling Statistics
on **Shipments** from U.S., C 3.140:Q

Commodity Classification for Reporting **Shipments** from Puerto Rico to U.S., C 3.150:P

Current Business Reports; Canned Food, Stock, Pack, **Shipments**, B-1 (series), C 56.219/8

Distribution of Coal **Shipments**, I 28.24

Fire Extinguishing Equipment, Report of **Shipments**, C 3.84

Fresh Fruit and Vegetable **Shipments** by States, Commodities, Counties, Stations, Calendar Year (date), A 88.12/31:6, A 88.40/2:12

Fresh Fruit and Vegetable **Shipments**, by Commodities, States, Months, Calendar Year (date), A 88.12/31:7, A 88.40/2:14

Industry Survey: Manufacturers' Inventories, **Shipments**, Incoming Business {and} Unfilled Orders, C 18.224

Lumber **Shipments** from Pacific Coast to Atlantic Coast, SB 7.5/162

Manufacturers' **Shipments**, Inventories and Orders, C 56.245, C 3.231

NPA Production Series, Quarterly Indexes of **Shipments** for Products of Metalworking Industries, C 40.15

Paid **Shipments** (by country), Special Statements, Y 3.Ec 74/3:13-2

Paid **Shipments**, European and Far East Program, FO 1.9

Paid **Shipments**, Y 3.Ec 74/3:13, Pr 33.909

Participation of American and Foreign-Flag Vessels in **Shipments** under United States Foreign Relief Programs, C 3.164:976

Report of Japan's Export **Shipments** and Import Receipts Stated by Areas and Countries of Destination and Origin, with Value Expressed in United States Dollars, D 102.11/3

Schedule H. Statistical Classification and Code Numbers of **Shipments** of Merchandise to Alaska from United States, C 3.150:H

Schedule P. Commodity Classification for Reporting **Shipments** from Puerto Rico to U.S., C 3.150:P

Schedule Q. Commodity Classification for Compiling Statistics on **Shipments** from U.S., C 3.150:Q

Shipments of Asphalt, I 28.110

Shipments of Domestic Pumps, Water Systems, and Windmills, C 3.77

Shipments of Domestic Water Softening Apparatus, C 3.78

Shipments of Measuring and Dispensing Pumps, Gasoline, Oil, etc., C 3.90

Shipments of Stocker and Feeder Cattle and Sheep, A 88.16/18

State Carlot **Shipments** of Fruits and Vegetables, by Commodities, Counties, and Billing Stations, A 88.12/10

Statistical Classification and Code Numbers of **Shipments** of Merchandise to Alaska from United States, C 3.150:H

Steel Import Data, **Shipments** from Exporting Countries in Calendar Year, C 57.209

Summary of Carlot **Shipments**, A 82.45

Value of Product **Shipments**, C 3.24/9-6

Weekly Summary of Fruit and Vegetable Carlot **Shipments**, A 88.12

Shipped
   Imported Dates Packed and **Shipped**, C 3.130

Shippers
   Certified **Shippers** of Fresh and Frozen Oyster, Clams, and Mussles, FS 2.16
   IMS List **Sanitation** Compliance and Enforcement Ratings of Interstate Milk Shippers, HE 20.4014/2
   Interstate Certified Shellfish **Shippers** List, HE 20.4014
   Interstate Shellfish **Shippers** List, HE 20.4014
   Major **Shippers** Report, C 61.53

Shipping
   Current **Shipping** Data, C 25.7
   Daily Depository **Shipping** List, GP 3.16/3
   Daily **Shipping** Bulletins, N 22.6, SB 1.12
   Dry Cargo Service and Area Report, United States Dry Cargo **Shipping** Companies by Ships Owned and/or Chartered Type of Service and Area Operated, C 39.213
   Exact Location of All Ships in which **Shipping** Board is Interested, SB 2.10
   Foreign **Shipping** News, C 18.89
   Handbook of Merchant **Shipping** Statistics, C 39.218

Index of Current Regulations of Federal Maritime Board, Maritime Administration, National **Shipping** Authority, C 39.106/2, C 39.206/4, TD 11.22

Laws relating to **Shipping** and Merchant Marine, Y 1.2:Sh 6

List of American and Foreign Ships Owned under Requisition of Chartered to **Shipping** Board, SB 2.11

National **Shipping** Authority: Safety Bulletin, C 39.209

Navy **Shipping** Guide, N 20.17

Navy **Shipping** Guide, Changes, N 20.17/2

NSA Orders (National **Shipping** Authority), C 39.206/2

Rules of Practice **Shipping** Board, SB 1.7

Safety Bulletins National **Shipping** Authority, C 39.209

Schedule T. Statistical Classification of Imports into U.S. Arranged in **Shipping** Commodity GROUPS., C 3.150:T

Schedule X. Statistical Classification of Domestic and Foreign Merchandise Exported from United States by Air Arranged in **Shipping** Commodity Groups, C 3.150:X

Schedule Y. Statistical Classification of Imports into United States Arranged in **Shipping** Commodity Groups, C 3.150:Y

Seaword, Developments in American Flag **Shipping**, C 39.236

Shipping Coordinating Committee, S 1.130/2:Sh 6

Shipping Point Inspection Circulars, A 36.201

Shipping Weight and Dollar Value of Merchandise Laden on and Unladen from Vessels at United States Ports During the In-transit Movement of the Merchandise from One Foreign Country to Another, C 3.164:981

Statistical Classification of Imports into U.S. Arranged in **Shipping** Commodity Groups, C 3.150:T

Statistical Classification of Imports into United States Arranged in **Shipping** Commodity Groups, C 3.150:Y

Tariff Circulars **Shipping** Board, SB 1.8

U.S. Airborne Exports and General Imports, **Shipping** Weight and Value, C 3.164:986

U.S. Naval Control of **Shipping** Report, D 201.30

Weather Service for Merchant **Shipping**, C 30.79

Weekly Report of Vessels under Jurisdiction of **Shipping** Board, SB 2.12

Weekly Summary of F.O.B. Prices of Fresh Fruits and Vegetables in Representative **Shipping** Districts, A 88.12/2, A 82.53

Ships
   Bureau of **Ships** Technical Manual, D 211.7/3
   Bureau of **Ships** Translations, D 211.14
   Bureau of **Ships**, Shop Practice Suggestions, C 41.95
   Catalogs of **Ships** and Crew's Libraries of the U.S., N 5.6, N 17.19
   Containerships Under Construction and on Order (including conversions) in United States and Foreign Shipyards Oceangoing **Ships** of 1,000 Gross Tons and Over, C 39.231
   Dry Cargo Service and Area Report, United States Dry Cargo Shipping Companies by **Ships** Owned and/or Chartered Type of Service and Area Operated, C 39.213
   Exact Location of All **Ships** in which Shipping Board is Interested, SB 2.10
   Foreign Flag Merchant **Ships** Owned by U.S. Parent Companies, TD 11.16
   History of American Naval Fighting **Ships**, D 207.10
   List of American and Foreign **Ships** Owned under Requisition of Chartered to Shipping Board, SB 2.11
   Manual of Bureau of **Ships** (by chapters), N 29.13
   Merchant **Ships** Built in United States and Other Countries in Employment Report of United States Flag Merchant Seagoing Vessels 1,000 Tons and Over, C 39.211
   New Ship Construction, Oceangoing **Ships** of 1,000 Gross Tons and Over in United States and Foreign Shipyards, C 39.212/3
   Oceangoing Foreign Flag Merchant Type **Ships** of 1,000 Gross Tons and Over Owned by the United States Parent Companies, C 39.230

Oceangoing Merchant **Ships** of 1,000 Gross Tons and Over Scrapped and Lost During the Calendar Year (date), C 39.229

Ships Registered Under Liberian, Panamanian, and Honduran Flags Deemed by the Navy Department to Be Under Effective U.S. Control, C 39.228

Supply Table of Medical Department, Navy, with Allowance for **Ships**, N 10.8

Summary of Sanitation Inspection of International Cruise **Ships**, HE 20.7511

United States Flag Containerships and United States Flag **Ships** with Partial Capacities for Containers And/or Vehicles, C 39.232

Shipyard
   Casualities and Injuries among **Shipyard** and Dock Workers, L 16.37
   Maritime Manpower Report: Sea Faring, Longshore, and **Shipyard** Employment as of (date), C 39.202:Se 1/2, C 39.235
   Maritime Safety Data for **Shipyard** Industry, L 16.47/4
   Rubber Laboratory, Mare Island Naval **Shipyard**, Vallejo, California, Reports, D 211.16
   Shipyard Bulletin, SB 2.8
   Suggested Safety Practices for **Shipyard** Workers, L 16.51/3

Shipyards
   Containerships Under Construction and on Order (including conversions) in United States and Foreign **Shipyards** Oceangoing Ships of 1,000 Gross Tons and Over, C 39.231
   Employees in Private and Government **Shipyards** by Region, L 2.81
   Indexes of Change in Straight-Time Average Hourly Earnings for Selected **Shipyards**, by Type of Construction and Region, L 2.81/2
   Maritime Safety Digest: **Shipyards**, L 35.12
   New Ship Construction, Oceangoing Ships of 1,000 Gross Tons and Over in United States and Foreign **Shipyards**, C 39.212/3

Shipyards, L 16.47/3

Shirts
   Industry Wage Survey: Men's and Boy's **Shirts** and Nightwear, L 2.3/35

Shock
   Shock and Vibration Bulletin, D 210.27/2
   Shock and Vibration Digest, D 4.12/2, D 210.27
   Shock and Vibration Monographs, D 1.42, D 210.27/3

Shoes
   Market for U.S. Leather and **Shoes** in {various foreign countries}, C 41.98
   Production of Boots and **Shoes**, C 3.43

Shooting
   Shooting News, W 82.5

Shop
   Bureau of Ships, **Shop** Practice Suggestions, C 41.95
   Rates of Pay of **Shop** Crafts, RL 1.10

Shore
   Civilian Personnel of Naval **Shore** Establishment, M 204.8

Shores
   Personnel of Naval **Shores** Establishment, D 204.8

Shorn
   Shorn Wool Production, A 88.35/2

Short
   Advance United States **Short** Wave Broadcast Programs, S 9.13
   Livestock **Short** Course, A 21.13
   Poultry **Short** Course, A 21.13/3
   Radio Service Dairy **Short** Course, A 21.13/2
   Radio Service Livestock **Short** Course, A 21.13/1
   Radio Service Poultry **Short** Course, A 21.13/3

Shortages
   Local **Shortages** in Selected Scientific and Engineering Occupations, L 7.63

Short-Lived
   Center for **Short-Lived** Phenomena: Annual Report, SI 1.1/3

Short-Stay
   Detailed Diagnoses and Procedures for Patients Discharged from **Short-Stay** Hospitals, United States, HE 20.6209/9
   Detailed Diagnoses and Surgical Procedures for Patients Discharged from **Short-Stay** Hospitals, HE 20.6222
   Inpatient Utilization of **Short-Stay** Hospitals by Diagnosis, United States, HE 20.6209/8

Surgical and Nonsurgical Procedures in **Shortstay**
Hospitals, United States, HE 20.6209/5
Utilization of **Short-Stay** Hospitals United States,
Annual Summary, HE 20.6209/7

Short-Term
Bank Rates on **Short-Term** Business Loans, FR
1.32/5
Short-term Energy Outlook, E 3.31

Show
Paris Air **Show** News Fillers, C 42.27/2
Paris Air **Show** Newsletter, C 42.27
Regional Data on Compensation **Show** Wages,
Salaries and Benefits Costs in the
Northeast, L 2.71/6-6

Showing
Quarterly Reports **Showing** Imports and Exports, T
37.6
Statement **Showing** Amount of National Bank
Notes Outstanding {ect}, T 12.9
Statistical Tables **Showing** Progress of Eradication
of Brucellosis and Tuberculosis in
Livestock in United States and
Territories for Fiscal Year, A 77.212/3

Shows
Soldier **Shows**, Blueprint Specials, W 109.114
Soldier **Shows**, Folios, W 109.116

Shreveport
Daily Weather and River Bulletin {**Shreveport**, La.
Area}, C 55.110/6

Shrimp
Fish Sticks, Fish Portions, and Breaded **Shrimp**
(CFS series), C 55.309/2
Gulf Coast **Shrimp** Data, I 49.60
Shrimp Landings, C 55.309/2

SI
Laboratory Report **SI** Series, I 27.45

SIC
U.S. Exports of Domestic Merchandise, **SIC**- based
Products and Area, C 3.164:610
U.S. Imports for Consumption and General Imports,
SIC-Based Products and Area, C
3.164:210

Sickle Cell
Sickle Cell Disease Advisory Committee, HE
20.3001/2:Si 1

Sickness
Employee Benefits Survey **Sickness** and Accident
Coding Manual, L 2.46/6
National Health Survey: **Sickness** and Medical
Care Series, Bulletins, Preliminary
Reports, T 27.38

SID
Standard Instrument Departure (**SID**) Charts,
Eastern U.S., C 55.416/5
Standard Instrument Departure (**SID**) Charts,
Western United States, C 55.416/6

Side
Side Runs of Paper Trade, C 18.124
West **Side** VA Medical Center Formulary, VA 1.78

SIF
Selected Industrial Films **SIF** (series), C 41.23/3

SIG
U.S. Army Electronic Proving Ground, USAEPG-
SIG (series), D 111.12

SIGCAT
SIGCAT CD-ROM Compendium, GP 3.22/6

Sight
Hines **Sight**, VA 1.56/6

Signal
Changes in **Signal** Corps Manuals (numbered), W
42.22/3
Drill Books, **Signal** Books and Code Lists, N
17.12/1
Index of **Signal** Corps Specifications and Standards,
D 111.8
List of Unclassified Reports Received from
Department of Army, **Signal** Corps, C
13.33/4
Professional Papers **Signal** Corps, W 42.11/2
Professional Papers **Signal** Service, W 42.11/1
Roster and Station of Officers of **Signal** Corps, W
42.9
Signal Communication for All Arms and Services,
W 3.50/8
Signal Corps Bulletin, W 42.3
Signal Corps Library Record, W 42.39
Signal Corps Memorandum, W 42.26
Signal Corps Technical Information Letters, W
42.40
Signal School Pamphlets, W 42.34/6
Signal Service Notes, W 42.14
Weather Maps **Signal** Office, W 42.23

Signals
International Code of **Signals**, United States
Edition, D 203.22:102
Light and Fog **Signals** of United States and Canada
on Northern Lakes and Rivers, C 9.30
Lights and Fog **Signals**, Atlantic and Gulf Coasts,
T 25.16
Lights and Fog **Signals**, Northern Lakes and
Rivers and Canada, T 25.17, C 9.18
Lights and Fog **Signals**, Pacific Coast and British
Columbia, T 25.18
List of Lights and Fog **Signals**, D 203.22
Tabulation of Statistics Pertaining to Block
Signals and Telegraph and Telephone for
Transmission of Train Orders, IC 1 blo.5
Tabulations of Statistics Pertaining to **Signals**,
Interlocking, Automatic, Train Control,
Telegraph and Telephone for Transmis-
sion of Train Orders, and Spring
Switches As Used on Railroads of
United States, IC 1 saf.10

Significance
Compilation of Administrative Policies for
National Parks and National Monuments
of Scientific **Significance** (Natural Area
Category), I 29.9/4:N 21

Significances
List of Acceptable Interstate Carrier Equipment
Having Sanitation **Significances**, FS
2.78

Significant
Atomic Energy: **Significant** References Covering
Various Aspects of Subject Arranged
Topically, LC 14.13
Enforcement Actions, **Significant** Actions
Resolved, Y 3.N 88:47
EPA Log, Weekly Log of **Significant** Events, EP
1.24
Food and Drug Administration, Summary of
Significant Accomplishment and
Activities, HE 20.4046
Report on the **Significant** Actions of the Office of
Personnel Management, MS 1.16
Scientific Manpower, **Significant** Developments,
Views and Statistics, NS 1.14
Significant Arrearages Due the United States
Government and Unpaid 90 Days or
More by Official Foreign Obligors, T
1.45/5
Significant Cases, Federal Employee and Labor-
Management Relations, PM 1.63
Significant Features of Fiscal Federalism, Y 3.Ad
9/8:18
Significant NASA Inventions Available for
Licensing in Foreign Countries, NAS
1.21:7038
Significant Provisions of State Unemployment
Compensation Laws, SS 1.19, L 33.10
Significant Provisions of State Unemployment
Insurance Laws, L 37.210
U.S. Central Station Nuclear Electric Generating
Units, **Significant** Milestones, E 1.41

Signs
Request for New or Modified Broadcast Call **Signs**,
CC 1.44

Silicon
Mineral Industry Surveys, **Silicon**, I 19.150
Silicon, I 28.75
Silicon in (year), I 28.75/2
Silicon Report, I 28.106

Silk
Silk and Rayon and Other Synthetic Textile Fibers,
C 18.125

Silver
Circular of Inquiry Concerning Gold and **Silver**
Coinage and Currency of Foreign
Countries, Including Production, Import
and Export, and Industrial Consumption
of Gold and **Silver**, T 28.8
Gold and **Silver**, I 28.61/2
Gold and **Silver** Exports and Imports: Weekly
Statement of, United States, C 3.195
Gold and **Silver** in (year), I 28.61/3
Gold and **Silver** Movements: United States, C
3.196
Silver {Mine Production}, I 28.62
Silver Lining, Y 3.R 31/2:16
Summary of U.S. Exports and Imports of Gold and
Silver, Calendar Year, C 3.196/3
Summary of U.S. Exports and Imports of Gold and
Silver, Fiscal Year, C 3.196/2
The **Silver** Lining, T 71.22

United States Exports and Imports of Gold and
Silver, Total United States Trade in Gold
and Silver and United States Trade in
Gold and Silver with Latin American
Republics and Canada, C 3.164:859
United States Gold and **Silver** Movements in
(Month), C 56.210:2402, C 3.164:2402
Weekly Statement of Gold and **Silver** Exports and
Imports, United States, C 3.195

Silvical
Forest Planting, Seeding, and **Silvical** Treatments
in the United States, A 13.51/2
Silvical Leaflets, A 13.12
Silvical Series, A 13.66/11

Simplified
Proceedings Interdepartmental Board on
Simplified Office Procedure, Executive
Committee Meeting, T 51.11/5
Simplified Practice Recommendations, C 13.12

Simplifying
Simplifying Federal Aid to States and Communities, Annual Report to the President of
an Interagency Program, PrEx 2.18

Simulation
Oil Market **Simulation** Model, E 3.55

Singapore
Cumulative List of Malaysia, **Singapore** and Brunei
Serials, LC 1.30/10-2

Singing
I Hear American **Singing** (radio scripts), FS 1.9
Singing Sands Almanac, I 29.6/3-2

Single
Single Award Federal Supply Schedule, GS 2.7/7

Single-Employer
Pension Insurance Data Book: PBGC **Single-
Employer** Program, Y 3.P 38/2:12

Single-Family
Characteristics of FHA **Single-Family** Mortgages,
HH 2.24/7

Sinking
Annual Report of **Sinking** Fund and Funded Debt
of District of Columbia, for Fiscal Year, T
40.6

Sinks
Inventory of U.S. Greenhouse Gas Emissions and
Sinks, EP 1.115

SIPP
SIPP Data News, C 3.274

SIPRE
SIPRE Reports, D 103.26

SIR
Safety Investigation Regulations, **SIR** (series), C
31.206/4

Sire
DHIA **Sire** Summary List, A 77.15:44

Sisal
Sisal, Hemp, Jute, and Miscellaneous Fibers, C
18.126

Site
DNFSB **Site** Representatives Weekly Activities
Reports, Y 3.D 36/3:11
Historical **Site** {brochures}, I 27.73
Operation Breakthrough, **Site** Planner's Report
(series), HH 1.48
Organ **Site** Carcinogenesis Skin, HE 20.3173/2
Preservation Rech Notes **Site**, I 29.84/3-11
SITE (Superfund Innovative Technology
Evaluation), EP 1.89/4
SITE (Superfund Innovative Technology
Evaluation) Demonstration Bulletin, EP
1.89/4-2
SITE Technology Demonstration Summary, EP
1.89/4-3

Sites
Analysis of Work Stoppages on U.S. Missile **Sites**,
Pr 35.8:M 69/W 89
Directory of Air Quality Monitoring **Sites** Active
in (year), EP 1.2:Ai 7/5
National Historic **Sites** Information Circulars, I
29.6/6

Situation
Agricultural **Situation**, A 36.15, A 88.8, A 92.23,
A 105.10
Agricultural **Situation** in Relation to Banking, A
36.129
Agricultural **Situation** Supplements (various
areas), A 93.29/2-2
Agricultural **Situation**, Special Edition for Crop
and Price Reports, A 36.15/2
Agricultural **Situation**: Africa and the Middle East,
A 93.29/2-2
Asia and Pacific Rim, **Situation** and Outlook
Series, A 93.29/2-19
Business **Situation** at Home and Abroad, C 18.54/2

Snakes
Poisonous **Snakes** of the World, D 206.6/3:Sn 1
Snap
Patents BIB and Patents **SNAP**, C 21.31/16
Patents **Snap**, Concordance of U.S. Patent
Application Serial Numbers to U.S.
Patent Numbers, C 21.31/6
SNI
Selective Notification of Information **SNI**, J 26.19
Snow
Alaska **Snow** Survey, Annual Data Summary, A
57.46/13-3
Alaska **Snow** Surveys and Federal-State Private
Cooperative Surveys, A 57.46/13
Colorado Water Supply Outlook and Federal-State-
Private Cooperative **Snow** Survey, A
57.46/19
Federal State Cooperative **Snow** Surveys and Water
Supply Forecasts, A 57.46/9-2
Federal-State-Private Cooperative **Snow** Surveys:
Colorado, Rio Grande, Platte, and
Arkansas Drainage Basins, A 57.46/9-2
Federal-State-Private Cooperative **Snow** Surveys:
Montana, A 57.46/3-2
Federal-State-Private Cooperative **Snow** Surveys:
Oregon, A 57.46/5-2
Federal-State-Private Cooperative **Snow** Surveys:
Utah, A 57.46/6-1
General Drawings of **Snow** Removal Equipment, W
7.31/2
Snow and Ice Bulletin, A 29.16
Snow Survey and Soil Moisture Measurements,
Basic Data Summary for Western United
States, Including Columbia River
Drainage in Canada, A 57.46/17
Snow Survey Phase of Project Skywater, Colorado,
Annual Report, A 57.56/16
Snow Surveys and Water Supply Outlook for
Alaska, A 57.46/13
Snow Surveys for Alaska, A 57.46/13
Water Supply Outlook, Federal-State-Private
Cooperative **Snow** Surveys {Colorado},
A 57.46/15
World Data Center A Glaciology (**Snow** and Ice),
Glaciological Data Report, GD-(nos), C
55.220/6
World Data Center A Glaciology (**Snow** and Ice):
New Accessions List, C 55.220/8
Snuff
Quarterly Report of Manufacture and Sales of **Snuff**,
Smoking, and Chewing Tobacco, A
88.34/11
Soapstone
Talc, **Soapstone** and Pyrophyllite in (year), I
28.136
Sobre
Datos **Sobre** el Cancer (Cancer Facts), HE 20.3182/
6-2
Datos **Sobre** Tipos de Cancer (series), HE 20.3182/
6
Social
Applied **Social** and Behavioral Sciences Research
Initiation Grants, NS 1.10/8
Army Research Institute for Behavioral and **Social**
Sciences: Research Reports, D 101.60/2
Army Research Institute for the Behavioral and
Social Sciences: Special Reports (series),
D 101.60/6
Basic Research in Behavioral and **Social** Sciences:
U.S. Army Research Institute Annual
Report, D 101.1/7-2
Census of Population; Advance Estimates of **Social**
Economic, and Housing Characteristics,
Supplementary Reports, PHC A2
(series), C 3.223/21-2
Census of Population; General **Social** and
Economic Characteristics, C 3.223/7
Census of Population: **Social** and Economic
Characteristics for American Indian and
Alaska Native Areas, C 3.223/7-2
Census of Population: **Social** and Economic
Characteristics for Metropolitan
Statistical Areas, C 3.223/7-3
Census of Population: **Social** and Economic
Characteristics for Urbanized Areas, C
3.223/7-4
Current Projects on Economic and **Social**
Implications of Scientific Research and
Development, NS 1.23
Current Reviews of Economic and **Social** Problems
in United Nations, S 1.81
Division of **Social** Sciences Quarterly Grant List,
NS 1.10/5

Economic and **Social** Analysis Workshop:
Proceedings, D 103.57/10
Environmental-**Social** Aspects of Energy
Technologies, E 1.99
ERIC Clearinghouse for **Social** Studies, **Social**
Science Education: Interpretive Studies,
HE 18.13
Foreign **Social** Science Bibliographies, C 3.163/5
Institute of **Social** Anthropology Publications, SI
1.16
National Economic **Social** & Environmental Data
Bank (NESEDB), C 1.88/2
News Bulletin of **Social** Statistics in Child Welfare
and Related Fields, L 5.31
Quarterly Report, Government Sponsored and
Government Supported Research, **Social**
Sciences and Interdisciplinary Areas, NS
1.9
Research and Discovery, Advances in Behavioral
and **Social** Science Research, HE
20.3036/4
Research Institute for the Behavioral and **Social**
Sciences: Technical Papers, D 101.60
School Enrollment, **Social** and Economic
Characteristics of Students, C 3.186/12
Social and Economic Characteristics of U.S. School
Districts, HE 19.336
Social and Rehabilitation Record, HE 17.27
Social and Rehabilitation Service Reports
Bulletins, HE 17.29
Social and Rehabilitation Service Research and
Demonstration Projects, FS 17.15
Social Hygiene Monthly, T 27.21
Social Problems, Y 3.W 89/2:57, FW 4.19
Social Research Reports, A 61.10
Social Seminar Discussion Guides, HE 20.2408/2
Social Service Resource Directories, J 16.7
Social Services for Families and Children, HE
17.618
Social Services U.S.A., HE 17.647, HE 23.2010
Social Statistics in Child Welfare and Related
Fields, L 5.27
Social Statistics, L 5.36
Statistical Report on **Social** Services, Form FS-
2069, Quarter Ended (date), FS 17.12, FS
17.628
Statistical Series **Social** and Rehabilitation Service,
HE 17.23
Status, a Monthly Chartbook of **Social** and
Economic Trends, C 3.251
Studies in **Social** Change, HE 20.8132
United States Fisheries Systems and **Social**
Sciences: a Bibliography of Work and
Directory of Researchers, C 55.332:So 1
Working Papers **Social** and Rehabilitation Service,
HE 17.24
World List of Future International Meeting: Pt. 2,
Social, Cultural, Commercial,
Humanistic, LC 2.9/2
Social Security
Amendments to Social **Security** Laws, SSI, HE
3.25/2
Annual Statistical Supplement to the **Social**
Security Bulletin, SSA 1.22/2
Annual Statistics on Workers Under **Social**
Security, HE 3.40
Author Index Title Index and Subject Index to the
Social Security Bulletin, HE 3.3/5
Characteristics of **Social Security** Disability
Insurance Beneficiaries, HE 3.91
Characteristics of State Plans for Aid to Families
with Dependent Children Under the
Social Security Act Title IV-A, HE 3.65/
2
Current **Social Security** Program Operations, FS
3.43
Earnings and Employment Data for Wage and
Salary Workers Covered under **Social**
Security by State and County, HE 3.95
Fast Facts & Figures About **Social Security**, HE
3.94
From **Social Security** Survey of Institutionalized
Adults, Reports, HE 3.54/3
From the **Social Security** Survey of the Disabled,
Reports, HE 3.54/2
Laws Relating to **Social Security** and Unemploy-
ment Compensation, Y 1.2:So 1
Legislative History of Titles I-XX of the **Social**
Security Act, HE 3.5/3
Medical Assistance (Medicaid) Financed Under
Title XIX of **Social Security** Act, HE
17.616
Medical Assistance Financed under Assistance
Titles of **Social Security** Act, FS 17.616

Medical Assistance Financed under Public
Assistance Titles of **Social Security** Act,
FS 17.2:M 46/2, HE 17.2:M 46/2
Report of Advisory Council on **Social Security**
Financing, HE 3.41
Report to Congress on Title 20 of the **Social**
Security Act, HE 23.2009
Research Memorandum **Social Security** Administra-
tion, SS 1.28, FS 1.28
Research Reports **Social Security** Administration,
FS 3.49, HE 3.49
Review of Operations **Social Security** Administra-
tion, FS 3.15
Social Security Administration Baltimore
Directory, HE 3.58/2
Social Security Administration Publications
Catalog, HE 3.38/3
Social Security Agreements (various countries SSA
1.29
Social Security Beneficiaries by State and County,
HE 3.73/2
Social Security Beneficiaries by Zip Code Area, HE
3.73
Social Security Beneficiaries in Metropolitan
Areas, HE 3.73/3
Social Security Bulletin, HE 3.3
Social Security Bulletin, Statistical Supplement,
HE 3.3/3
Social Security Handbooks, HE 3.6/3:So 1/3, HE
3.6/8
Social Security Information Items, HE 3.82
Social Security Information, HE 3.52
Social Security Programs in the United States, SSA
1.24/2
Social Security Programs Throughout the World,
HE 3.49:31, HE 3.49/3
Social Security Rulings on Federal Old-age,
Survivors, Disability, and Health
Insurance, HE 3.44
Social Security Rulings, Cumulative Bulletins, HE
3.44/2
Social Security Student Gazette, HE 3.59
Social Security Today, SSA 1.28
Social Security Yearbook, FS 3.3/2
What **Social Security** Means to Industries, SS 1.18
Your New **Social Security**, Fact Sheets, FS 3.25
Your **Social Security** Rights & Responsibilities,
Retirement & Survivors Benefits, HE
3.88/2, HE 3.93
Your **Social Security** Rights and Responsibilities,
Disability Benefits, HE 3.88
Your **Social Security**, HE 3.89
Social Work
Interdisciplinary Glossary on Child Abuse and
Neglect: Legal, Medical, **Social Work**
Terms, HE 23.1210:G 51
Society
Behavior and **Society**, C 51.9/12
Congress of International **Society** of Soil Science
Publications, A 57.49
Publications Congress of International **Society** of
Soil Science, A 57.49
U.S. **Society** & Values, IA 1.35, S 20.19
Socioeconomic
Socioeconomic Environmental Studies, EP 1.23/3
Sociological
Political and **Sociological** Affairs, PrEx 7.21/5
Political, **Sociological** and Military Affairs, PrEx
7.15/4, PrEx 7.17/2
Sociological Studies, PrEx 7.21/13
Sociology
Directory of Teachers Giving Courses in Rural
Sociology and Rural Life, A 36.57
Soda
Mineral Industry Surveys, **Soda Ash** and Sodium
Sulfate, I 19.151
Soda Ash and Sodium Sulfate: U.S. Production,
Trade and Consumption, I 28.135/2
Sodium
Mineral Industry Surveys, Soda Ash and **Sodium**
Sulfate, I 19.151
Soda Ash and **Sodium** Sulfate: U.S. Production,
Trade and Consumption, I 28.135/2
Sodium Carbonate in (year), I 28.135, I 28.135/3
Sodium Compounds, I 28.135/2
Sodium Sulfate in (year), I 28.135/4
Softening
Shipments of Domestic Water **Softening** Apparatus,
C 3.78
Software
Catalog of Publications, Audiovisuals, and
Software, HE 20.3619/2
Directory of Computer **Softwear** Applications, C
51.11/5

Directory of Computerized Data Files and Related **Software** Available from Federal Agencies, C 51.11/2

Directory of Computerized **Software**, C 51.11/2

Directory of U.S. Government **Software** for Mainframes & Microcomputers, C 51.19/5

Enhanced UTCS **Software** Operator's Manual, Implementation Package (series), TD 2.36

Federal **Software** Exchange Catalog, GS 12.14

Federal **Software** Exchange Catalog Supplement, GS 12.14/2-2

U.S. Government Environmental Datafiles & **Software**, C 51.20

Softwood

End-Matched **Softwood** Lumber Series, C 18.68

SOI

SOI Bulletin, T 22.35/4

Soil

Abstracts of Recent Published Material on **Soil** and Water SodiumConservation, A 1.68, A 57.36, A 77.15:41

AgronSodiumomy, Weed Science, **Soil** Conservation, Agricultural Programs, A 106.36

Congress of International Society of **Soil** Science Publications, A 57.49

Conservation Highlights, Digest of the Progress Report of the **Soil** Conservation Service, A 57.1/2

Conservation Reserve Program of **Soil** Bank, Statistical Summaries, A 82.79/2

Hydraulic Engineering and **Soil** Improvement, C 41.47/3

Inventory of **Soil**, Water, and Related Resources, A 57.22

Land Use and **Soil** Conservation, Informational Materials Available to Public, Leaflets (by Regions), A 57.26

List of Laboratories Approved to Receive **Soil**, A 101.34

Lists of Published **Soil** Surveys, A 57.38

Mechanical Analyses of Data for **Soil** Types {by County}, A 57.39

NCSS (National Cooperative **Soil** Survey) Newsletter, A 57.78

Pavements and **Soil** Trafficability Information Analysis Center, PSTIAC Reports, D 103.24/12

Posters **Soil** Conservation Service, A 57.71

Procedure for Making **Soil** Conservation Surveys, Outlines, A 57.17

Progress in **Soil** and Water Conservation Research, Quarterly Reports, A 77.528

Publications Congress of International Society of **Soil** Science, A 57.49

Snow Survey and **Soil** Moisture Measurements, Basic Data Summary for Western United States, Including Columbia River Drainage in Canada, A 57.46/17

Soil and Water Conservation District Resources Inventories (series), A 57.38/2

Soil and Water Conservation Districts, Status of Organization, by States, Approximate Acreage, and Farms in Organized Districts, A 57.32

Soil and Water Conservation Research Needs Executive Summary, A 57.73

Soil and Water Conservation News, A 57.9/2

Soil Bank Handbooks, A 82.6/3

Soil Bank Summaries, A 82.79

Soil Conservation Bibliographies, A 57.27/2

Soil Conservation Districts, A 76.214, A 80.2009, A 80.508

Soil Conservation Literature, Selected Current References, A 57.20, A 17.15

Soil Conservation Service, A 57.1/3

Soil Conservation, A 80.2007, A 80.507, A 57.9

Soil Conservation; Official Organ, A 76.208, A 79.207

Soil Interpretive Maps (for various subjects), A 57.69/2

Soil Organic Matter Levels in the Central Great Plains, A 77.15/3

Soil Quality Information Sheets, A 57.77

Soil Survey (of States), A 47.5/2

Soil Survey Field Letter, A 57.42, A 77.524

Soil Survey Interpretations for Woodlands, Progress Reports, A 57.58

Soil Survey Investigation Reports, A 57.52

Soil Survey Laboratory Memorandums, A 57.43, A 77.525

Soil Survey Reports, A 47.5, A 19.31, A 19.32, A 77.514

Soil Surveys, A 57.38

Soil, Water, Air Sciences Directory, A 106.14/2

Soil, Water, Air Sciences Research Annual Report, A 106.14

Soil-Binding Practices Applicable in State, A 55.44/10

Special Reports **Soil** Conservation Service, A 57.72

Special Reports **Soil** Conservation Service, Office of Research, Sedimentation Section, A 76.215, A 80.2013

State Law for **Soil** Conservation, A 13.60

Soil-Binding

Soil-Binding Practices Applicable in State, A 55.44/10

Soils

Classification and Correlation of **Soils** {by areas}, A 57.61

Field Operations of Bureau of **Soils**, A 26.5

Service and Regulatory Announcements Bureau of **Soils**, A 26.7

Soils Memorandum, A 57.48

Solar

Active **Solar** Installations Survey, E 3.19/3

Conservation and **Solar** Applications, DOE/CS (series), E 1.36

Discovery, the Newsletter of the **Solar** System Exploration Division, NAS 1.91

HUD **Solar** Status, HH 1.69

Intermediate Minimum Property Standards for **Solar** Heating and Domestic Hot Water Systems, HH 1.6/9:So 4

International **Solar**-Terrestrial Physics Program, NAS 1.86/3

Preliminary Report and Forecast of **Solar** Geophysical Data, C 55.627

Residental **Solar** Program Reports, HH 1.74

Sea Water Conversion, **Solar** Research Station (series), I 1.87

Solar Bibliography (series), HH 1.23/6

Solar Bulletin, E 1.58

Solar Collector Manufacturing Activity and Applications in the Residential Sector, E 3.19

Solar Collector Manufacturing Activity, E 3.19/2

Solar Detox Update, E 1.99/5-2

Solar Educational Programs and Courses, E 1.85

Solar Energy Research and Development Report, E 1.38, ER 1.32

Solar Energy, E 1.99

Solar Events Calendar and Call for Papers, E 1.91

Solar Law Reporter, E 1.38/4

Solar Thermal Power Systems, Annual Technical Progress Report, E 1.38/2

Solar Thermal Power Systems: Program Summary, E 1.38/2-2

Solar Thermal Report, E 1.83

Solar-Geophysical Data, IER-FB-(series), C 52.18, C 55.215

Sold

Catalogue of Articles to be **Sold** at Auction, P 7.5

Cattle and Calves on Feed, Cattle **Sold** for Slaughter, Selected Markets, A 92.18/6

Construction Report: Price Index of New One-Family Houses **Sold**, C 27 (series), C 56.211/2-2

Construction Reports; New One-family Homes **Sold** and for Sale, C 25 (series), C 56.211/2

Current Construction Reports, New One-Family Houses **Sold** and for Sale, C 3.215/9

Stumpage Prices for Sawtimber **Sold** from National Forests, by Selected Species and Region, A 13.58/2

Soldier

Annual Historical Review, United States Army **Soldier** Support Center, D 101.1/3

Life of **Soldier** and Airman, D 102.77

Post-War Plans for **Soldier** Series, Reports, W 109.214

Soldier, Sailor, Airman, Marine (SAM), D 1.55

Soldier Shows, Blueprint Specials, W 109.114

Soldier Shows, Folios, W 109.116

Soldier Support Journal, D 101.12/2

Soldier Training Publications, D 101.20/4

What the **Soldier** Thinks, Monthly Digest of War Department Studies on Attitudes of American Troops, W 1.65

Soldiers

Inspection of Several Branches of National Home for Disabled Volunteer **Soldiers**, W 9.5

Inspection of State **Soldiers** and Sailor's Homes, NH 1.5

Record of Changes in Memberships of National Home for Disabled Volunteer **Soldiers**, NH 1.6

Roll of Honor, Supplemental Statement of Disposition of Bodies of Deceased Union **Soldiers** and Prisoners of War Removed to National Cemeteries in Southern and Western United States, W 39.8

Soldiers' and Sailors' Civil Relief Act of 1940 and Amendments, Y 1.2:So 4/7, Y 1.2:So 4/2

Soldiers' Handbook, W 3.29

Soldiers' Scene, D 101.118/4

Soldiers, D 101.12

Soldier-Scholar

Soldier-Scholar, A Journal of Contemporary Military Thought, D 305.23

Sole

Source Book, **Sole** Proprietorship Returns, T 22.35/5-3

Solicitation

BLM Contract **Solicitation**, I 53.38

NCHSR Program **Solicitation** (series), HE 20.6512/9

NCHSR Program **Solicitation**, Grants for Health Services Dissertation Research, HE 20.6512/8-2

NCHSR Program **Solicitation**, Individual and Institutional, HE 20.6512/8

Omnibus **Solicitation** for the Small Business Innovative Research, HE 20.28

Omnibus **Solicitation** of the Public Health Service for Small Business Innovation Research (SBIR) Grant Applications, HE 20.3047/2

Program **Solicitation** (series), NS 1.33

Program **Solicitation**, Small Business Innovation Research Program, A 94.16

Small Business Innovation Research Program **Solicitation**, TD 10.13

Solicitation (series), J 28.33

Solicitation of the Public Health Service and the Health Care Financing Administration for Small Business Innovation Research Contract Proposals, HE 22.31

Solicitation of the Public Health Service for Small Business Research (SBIR) Contract Proposals, HE 20.28/2

Solicitations

Criminal Justice Research **Solicitations**, J 1.37/5, J 26.18

Solicitor

In Supreme Court of U.S., Briefs, Petitions, and Motions of Wm. Marshall Bullett, **Solicitor** General, J 1.19/2

Opinions of the **Solicitor** of the Department of the Interior Relating to Indian Affairs, I 1.69/9

U.S. Supreme Court, Government Briefs in Cases Argued by **Solicitor** General, Indexes, J 1.19/3

Solicitor's

Decisions, **Solicitor's** Opinions, I 1.69/4

Interior Department Decisions, **Solicitor's** Opinions, I 1.69/4

Solid

Accession Bulletin, **Solid** Waste Information Retrieval System, EP 1.18, EP 3.3/2

National Survey of Community **Solid** Waste Practices, HE 20.1409

Solid Waste Management, Available Information Materials, EP 1.17:58.25

Solid Waste News Brief, EP 1.17/4

State **Solid** Waste Planning Grants, Agencies, and Progress, Report of Activities, EP 3.10

World Data Center A for **Solid** Earth Geophysics Report, SE Series, C 55.220/5

Solids

Egg Products, Liquid, Frozen, **Solids** Production, A 92.9/4

Solo

Music Fellowships: Composers, Jazz, **Solo** Recitalists, Applications Guidelines, NF 2.8/2-8

Solutions

Intergovernmental **Solutions** Newsletter, GS 1.38

Someone

Someone Who Cares, A Guide to Hiring an In-Home Caregiver, HE 1.1009

Something

Something About (series), I 49.51

Song

Answer Me This: **Song** Series, I 16.58/4

Armed Forces **Song** Folio, D 1.14

Folk Recordings, Selected from the Archive of Folk **Song**, LC 40.2:F 71

Songs

Army Hit Kit of Popular **Songs**, D 102.10

Army Navy Hit Kit of Popular **Songs**, M 117.7

Sound

Sound Recordings, LC 3.6/5:part 14

Sour

Sour Cherry Report, A 88.12/11, A 92.11/3

Source

Corporation Income Tax Returns, **Source** Book (year), T 22.35/5-2

Development Document for Effluent Limitations Guidelines and New **Source** Performance Standards for {various industries}, EP 1.8/3

Expenditures for Public Assistance Payments and for Administrative Costs, by Program and **Source** of Funds, HE 17.632

FHLB System S & L's Combined Financial Statements: Savings and Home Financing **Source** Book, FHL 1.12/2

Health Manpower **Source** Book, FS 2.2:M 31, HE 20.2:M 31, HE 20.3109

Instruction Manual, Part 1, **Source** Records and Control Specifications, HE 20.6209/11

Instructions for Classifying the Underlying Cause of Death: **Source** Records and Control Specifications, HE 20.6208/11

Isotope and Radiation **Source** Technology, E 1.99

Reducing Waste at Its **Source** (series), EP 1.17/2

Savings and Home Financing, **Source** Book, FHL 1.11, T 71.17

Sealed **Source** and Device Newsletter (SS&D), Y 3.N 21/29:18-1

Source Book, HE 20.8229

Source Book, Partnership Returns, T 22.35/6-2

Source Book Series, I 29.50

Source Book, Sole Proprietorship Returns, T 22.35/5-3

Source Catalog on Youth Participation (series), HE 1.312

Source Category Survey (series), EP 4.17

Source of Funds Expended for Public Assistance Payments and for Cost of Administration, Services, and Training, HE 17.634

Source of Funds Expended for Public Assistance Payments, FS 14.215, FS 17.631, HE 17.631, HE 17.19/2

Stationary **Source** Enforcement Series, EP 1.8/7

Vista **Source**, Y 3.N 21/29:16-16

Sourcebook

Congressional **Sourcebook** Series, GA 1.22

Sourcebook of Criminal Justice Statistics, J 1.42/3, J 29.9/6, J 29.9/6-2

Sources

Energy Information in the Federal Government, a Directory of Energy **Sources** Identified by the Interagency Task Force on Energy Information, FE 1.24

Guide to Selected Legal **Sources** of Mainland China, LC 1.6/4:C 44

HUD International Information **Sources** Series, HH 1.40/4

Information **Sources** on International Travel, C 47.8

Key to Oceanic and Atmospheric Information **Sources**, C 55.219/5

Public Management **Sources**, PrEx 2.9

Review of Standards of Performance for New Stationary **Sources**, EP 4.19

Sources for Information on American Firms for International Buyers, C 42.2:Am 3

Sources of Information on Urban Transportation Planning Methods, TD 1.51

Sources of Information Regarding Labor {various countries}, L 2.72/2

Sources of Milk for Federal Order Markets, by State and County, A 88.40, A 88.14/11-3

Sources of Morbidity Data, FS 2.76

Sources of Travel Information Series, I 29.56

United States Air Force History, a Guide to Documentary **Sources**, D 301.6/5:H 62

South

Forest Research News for the **South**, A 13.40/11

Forest-Gram South, Dispatch of Current Technical Information for Direct Use by Practicing Forest Resource Manager in the **South**, A 13.89

Near East and **South** Asia Report, PrEx 7.20

Near East and **South** Asian Series, S 1.86/2

Pilot Chart of **South** Atlantic Ocean, D 203.18, N 6.20, M 202.18, D 203.18

Pilot Chart of **South** Pacific Ocean, D 203.20, N 6.12, M 202.20, D 203.20

Recent Publications of Range Research, Arid **South** Area, A 77.17/6

Retail Trade Report East **South** Central, C 3.177

Retail Trade Report **South** Atlantic Region, C 3.175

Retail Trade Report West **South** Central, C 3.179

South and East Asia Report, PrEx 7.16/4

South Asia Outlook and Situation Report, A 93.29/2-15

South Asia, LC 1.30/10-3

South Atlantic Fisheries, C 55.309/2

South Cherry Report, A 88.12/11

South Korea Interim Government Activities, M 105.13

South Volume, HE 20.6202:N 93 S

South, Population and Per Capita Income Estimates for Counties and Incorporated Places, C 3.186/27-5

South Africa

South Africa, Serials Supplement, LC 1.30/10-4

South America

Area Planning North America and **South America**, D 5.318/5-2

Area Planning Special Use Airspace North America and **South America**, D 5.318/5-3

Central Pacific, Western Pacific, and **South** Pacific Fisheries Development Program Report for Calendar Year, C 55.329

Central, Western, and **South** Pacific Fisheries Development Program Report for Calendar Year, C 55.329

Cottonseed Review, **South** Central Area, A 82.65

East Coast of North America and **South America** (including Greenland), C 4.15/4

Hydrologic Bulletin, Hourly and Daily Precipitation; **South** Pacific District, C 30.31

Nautical Charts and Publications, Region 2, Central and **South America** and Antarctica, C 55.440:2

NIMA Nautical Charts, Public Sale Region 2, Central and **South America** and Antarctica, TD 4.82:2

Supplementary Flight Information Document, Caribbean and **South America**, D 301.51

Tide Tables, High and Low Water Predictions East Coast of North and **South America** Including Greenland, C 55.421/2

Tide Tables, High and Low Water Predictions West Coast of North and **South America** Including Hawaiian Islands, C 55.421

Tide Tables East Coast of North and **South** America, C 4.15/4

Tide Tables West Coast of North and **South** America, C 4.15/5

USAF Military Aviation Notices, Amending SFID, Caribbean and **South America**, D 301.51/2

West Coast of North and **South America** (including the Hawaiian Islands), C 4.15/5

South American

Radio Facility Charts, Caribbean and **South American** Area, M 301.19

United States Air Force Radio Facility Charts, Caribbean and **South American** Area, D 301.10

South Carolina

Light List: Vol. 2, Atlantic Coast, Toms River, New Jersey to Little River, **South Carolina**, TD 5.9:v 2

Marketing of **South** Carolina Peaches, Summary of Season, A 88.12/29

Water Resources Development in **South Carolina**, D 103.35/40

South Dakota

Area Wage Survey, **South Dakota**, L 2.122/41

Southeast

Accession List: **Southeast** Asia, LC 1.30/10

Flight Information Publication: Enroute-High Altitude, United States, Northeast {and **Southeast**}, D 301.43/3, D 301.43/3-2

Flight Information Publication: Terminal High Altitude, Pacific and **Southeast** Asia, D 301.12/4

Flight Information Publication: Terminal Low Altitude, Pacific and **Southeast** Asia, D 301.12/3

Pulpwood Prices in the **Southeast**, A 13.79/2

Southeast Asia Report, PrEx 7.16/4

Southeast Asia, Burma, Thailand, and Laos, LC 1.30/10-5

Southeast Asia, LC 1.30/10

Southeast Environmental Research Laboratory: Quarterly Summary, EP 1.60

Technical Memorandum To United States Study Commission, **Southeast** River Basins, A 57.50

Terminal High Altitude, Pacific and **Southeast** Asia, D 301.12/4

United States Air Force in **Southeast** Asia (series), D 301.86/2

USAF **Southeast** Asia Monograph Series, D 301.86

Southeastern

Annual Report of Vegetable Breeding in **Southeastern** United States, Hawaii, and Puerto Rico, A 77.532

Quarterly Report of Progress at Fish Control Laboratory, La Crosse, Wisconsin, **Southeastern** Fish Control Laboratory, Warm Springs, Georgia, and Hammond Bay Biological Station, Millersburg, Michigan, I 49.75

Quarterly Trade Report, **Southeastern** Asia, C 18.156

Research at **Southeastern** Forest Experiment Station, A 13.63/3

Research Information Digest, Recent Publications of **Southeastern** Forest Experiment Station, A 13.63/13

Southeastern Forest Insect and Disease Newsletters, A 13.63/14

Southeastern Power Administration: Annual Report, E 1.95

Southeastern Regional Office: Regional Reports, L 2.71/8

Technical Notes Forest Service **Southeastern** Forest Experiment Station, A 13.63/8

Southeastern Massachusetts

Area Wage Survey Summary **Southeastern Massachusetts**, L 2.122/21-2

Southern

Catalog of Seed and Vegetable Stock Available from the **Southern** Regional Plant Introduction Station **for various plants**, A 106.19

Compass: Recent Publications of the **Southern** Research Station, A 13.150/5

Cost of Food at Home Estimated for Food Plans at Three Cost Levels, **Southern** Region, A 106.39/5

Fresh Fruit and Vegetable Unloads in **Southern** Cities, A 88.40/2:6

Light List, Atlantic Coast of United States, **Southern** Part, N 24.16, T 47.24

Occasional Papers Forest Service **Southern** Forest Experiment Station, A 13.40/6

Proceedings **Southern** Pasture and Forage Crop Improvement Conference, A 106.29

Publications Agricultural Adjustment Agency **Southern** Region, A 76.471, A 79.471, A 80.2171

Publications **Southern** Forest Experiment Station, A 13.40/8-3

Quarterly Index to Periodical Literature, Eastern and **Southern** Africa, LC 1.30/8-4

Rice, Stocks and Movement, **Southern** Mills, A 82.50

Roll of Honor, Supplemental Statement of Disposition of Bodies of Deceased Union Soldiers and Prisoners of War Removed to National Cemeteries in **Southern** and Western United States, W 39.8

Southern Asia, Publications in Western Languages, Quarterly Accessions List, LC 17.7

Southern Cities, A 88.12/31:3

Southern Economic Extension, A 43.5/15

Southern Forest Insect Reporter, A 13.40/9

Southern Forest Pest Reporter, A 13.52/4

Southern Forest Research, A 13.40/10

Southern Forestry Notes, A 13.40/7

Southern Pulpwood Production, A 13.80/4

Southern Region Agricultural Conservation, A 55.45/8

Southern Region Annual Monitoring and Evaluation Reports, A 13.157

Southern Region Miscellaneous Series, Items, A 55.45/6

Southern Region Report, A 13.56

Southern Region, C 55.118/2

Southern Regional Office Publications, L 2.95

Southern Research Station Annual Report, A 13.150/1

Southern Research Station: Bibliographies and Lists of Publications, A 13.150/2

Southern Research Station Directory of Research Scientists, A 13.150/4

Spectrum
   AMEDD **Spectrum**, D 104.26
   Specturm, D 103.48
   Spectrum Series, HE 20.3417
Speech
   NINCDS Hearing, **Speech**, and Language Research
      Program, HE 20.3502:H 35/3
Speeches
   Federal Maritime Commission **Speeches**, FMC 1.9
   GAO Documents, Catalog of Reports, Decisions
      and Opinions, Testimonies and **Speeches**,
      GA 1.16/4
   Major News Releases and **Speeches**, A 107.18
   Selected **Speeches** and News Releases, A 1.134, A
      21.24/2
Speed
   Report on High **Speed** Ground Transportation Act
      of 1965, TD 1.10
   Statistical Analysis of World's Merchant Fleets
      Showing Age, Size, **Speed**, and Draft by
      Frequency Groupings, As of (date), C
      39.224
   Traffic **Speed** Trends, TD 2.115
SPEEDE/ExPRESS
   SPEEDE/ExPRESS Newsletter, ED 1.133
Speedy
   Report on the Implementation to Title 1 and Title 2
      of the **Speedy** Trial Act of 1974, Ju 10.16
Spendable
   Net **Spendable** Earnings, L 2.75, LC 30.24
SPI
   SPI State Personal Income, C 59.25
Spices
   Industry Report, Coffee, Tea and **Spices**, C 18.240
Spillway
   Panama Canal **Spillway**, CZ 1.11, Y 3.P 19/2:9
Spinal Cord
   NINCDS **Spinal Cord** Injury Research Program,
      HE 20.3502:Sp 4/2
   Proceedings Annual Clinical **Spinal Cord** Injury
      Conference, VA 1.42
Spindles
   Report of Cotton Consumed, on Hand, Imported and
      Exported and Active **Spindles**, C 3.21
Spinning
   Activity in Cotton **Spinning** Industry, C 3.53
   Progress Report, Annual Varietal and Environmen-
      tal Study of Fiber and **Spinning**
      Properties of Cottons, A 77.530
Spinoff
   Spinoff, Annual Report, NAS 1.1/4
Spirits
   Alcohol and Tobacco Summary Statistics, Distilled
      Spirits, Wine, Beer, Tobacco,
      Enforcement Taxes, Fiscal Year, T 70.9
   Distilled **Spirits**, T 70.9/3
   Trends in Wholesale Winers and **Spirits** Trade, C
      3.200
Splenetic Fever
   Map of District Infected with **Splenetic Fever**, A 4.6
Spoilation
   Commission Appointed to Examine French
      Spoilation Claims Presented Under
      Treaty with France of July 4, 1831, S 3.5
Spokefish
   Spokefish Monthly, C 55.50
Spokesmen
   Speakers Guide for Service **Spokesmen**, D 6.8
   Speakers' Guide for Service **Spokesmen**, Power for
      Peace, Armed Forces Day, D 1.6/3
Sponsored
   Quarterly Report, Government **Sponsored** and
      Government Supported Research, Social
      Sciences and Interdisciplinary Areas, NS
      1.9
   Sponsored Reports Series, HE 19.311
   Sponsored Research Programs, J 28.24/2
   Uses of Research **Sponsored** by the Administration
      on Aging, Case Studies, HE 23.3012
Sport
   Bureau of **Sport** and Fisheries and Wildlife's In-
      sight, I 49.50/2
   Publications Bureau of **Sport** Fisheries and
      Wildlife, I 49.18/6
   Sport Fishery Abstracts, I 49.40/2
   Sport Fishery and Wildlife Research, I 49.1/6
Sports
   Physical Fitness/**Sports** Medicine Bibliography,
      HE 20.111
   Posters President's Council on Physical Fitness
      and **Sports**, HE 20.113
   President's Commission on Olympic **Sports**, Pr
      38.8:Ol 9

President's Council on Physical Fitness and
   Sports, Pr 37.8:P 56/2
President's Council on Physical Fitness and
   Sports: Research Digests, HE 20.114
Sportsman's
   Shawnee **Sportsman's** Maps (series), A 13.28/3
Spot
   Daily Indexes and **Spot** Market Prices, L 2.60/2
   Daily **Spot** Cotton Quotations, A 88.11/4
   Daily **Spot** Market Price Indexes and Prices,
      Weekly Summary, L 2.60
   On Call Positions in **Spot** Cotton Based on New
      York Cotton Futures Reported by
      Merchants in Special Account Status, Y
      3.C 73/5:11
   Spot Announcements, L 22.28
   Spot Cotton Quotations, Designated Markets, A
      82.73, A 88.11/4
   Spot News from Field, Y 3.F 31/11:22
   Spot the Danger, User's Guide to {various
      products} Safety Series, Y 3.C 76/3:8-3
   Tuesday **Spot** Market Price Indexes and Prices, L
      2.60
Spotlight
   EEO **Spotlight**, CS 1.76
   Spotlight on Affirmative Employment Programs,
      PM 1.18/4
   Spotlight on Organization and Supervision in
      Large High Schools, FS 5.50
   Spotlight, PM 1.18
SPP
   System Package Program, NS-**SPP**- (series), TD 4.30
Spreads
   Farm-Retail Price **Spreads**, A 36.138
Spring
   Spring and Early-Summer Potatoes, A 88.26/4
   Spring Potatoes, A 88.26/4
   Spring Vegetables and Melons, A 88.26/4
   Spring Vegetables, **Spring** Melons, Spring
      Potatoes, A 88.26/4
   Tabulations of Statistics Pertaining to Signals,
      Interlocking, Automatic, Train Control,
      Telegraph and Telephone for Transmis-
      sion of Train Orders, and **Spring**
      Switches As Used on Railroads of
      United States, IC 1 saf.10
Springfield
   Area Wage Survey Summary Eugene-**Springfield**-
      Medford-Roseburg-Klamath Falls-Grants
      Pass, Oregon, L 2.122/37
Squadron
   Aeronautical Chart and Information **Squadron**
      Bulletin, D 301.59/3
   Regimental and **Squadron** Histories, D 214.12
   Squadron Bulletin, D 301.59/3
Square
   United States General Imports of Wool Manufacture
      Except Floor Coverings, Quantity Totals
      in Terms of Equivalent **Square** Yards in
      Country of Origin by Commodity
      Grouping Arrangement, TQ-2203, C
      3.164/2-6
SR
   Safety Reports, NTSB-**SR** (series), TD 1.106/4
   Student Reference Sheets, **SR**- (series), FS 13.122
SRA
   Service and Regulatory Announcements **SRA**-
      C&MS- (series), A 88.6/3
SRE
   SRE Special Publication, FO 1.23
SRF
   Clean Water **SRF** Program Information for the State
      of..., EP 2.33
SRS
   SRS Data Brief, NS 1.11/3
   SRS (series), A 92.34
SS
   Safety Studies, NTSB/**SS** (series), TD 1.27
SSA
   RRB-**SSA** Financial Interchange: Calculations for
      Fiscal Year with Respect to OASI, DI,
      and HI Trust Funds, RR 1.15
   SSA Administrative Directives System Transmittal
      Notice, HE 3.68
   SSA Baltimore Telephone Directory, SSA 1.9/2
   SSA Management Newsletter for Supervisors and
      Management Personnel, HE 3.68/2
   SSA Program Circulars Disability, HE 3.4/4
   SSA Program Circulars General Series, HE 3.4/2
   SSA Program Circulars Public Information, HE 3.4/
      3
   SSA Program Circulars Retirement and Survivors
      Insurance, HE 3.4/5

SSA Program Circulars Supplemental Security
   Income, HE 3.4/6
SSA Training (series): Technical CORE Curriculum,
   HE 3.69/2
SSA Training Data Review Technician, Basic
   Training Course, HE 3.69/3
SSA Workload Analysis Report, HE 3.79
SSA's
   SSA's Accountability Report for FY..., SSA 1.1/2
   SSA's Accountability Report for FY...Summary, SSA
      1.1/3
SS&D
   Sealed Source and Device Newsletter (**SS&D**), Y
      3.N 21/29:18-1
SSC
   SSC, Y 3.Sh 6:SSC
SSI
   SSI Recipients by State and County, HE 3.71, SSA
      1.17
   State Assistance Programs for **SSI** Recipients, SSA
      1.17/2
   What You Have to Know about **SSI**, HE 3.90
SSIG
   SSIG and SG, ED 1.76/2-3
ST
   Student Texts, **ST**- (series), D 5.352/2
St. Lawrence
   Traffic Report of the **St. Lawrence** Seaway, TD 6.9
St. Louis District
   Stages and Discharges of Mississippi River and
      Tributaries in the **St. Louis District**, D
      103.45/3
St. Petersburg
   Area Wage Survey, Tampa-**St. Petersburg**-
      Clearwater, Florida, Metropolitan Area,
      L 2.121/9-6
Stability
   Prices, Escalation, and Economic **Stability**, L 2.100
Stabilization
   Committee on Channel **Stabilization**: Technical
      Reports, D 103.64
   Community **Stabilization** Case Studies, HH 1.67
   Construction Industry **Stabilization** Commission
      Regulations, ES 2.6/4
   Economic **Stabilization** Program Quarterly Report,
      PrEx 17.9
   Economic **Stabilization** Program, Bi-weekly
      Summary, PrEx 17.9/2
   Feed Grain and Wheat **Stabilization** Program, A
      82.37/3:F 32/2
   General Salary **Stabilization** Regulations GSSR
      (series), ES 4.6/2
   OEP Economic **Stabilization** Circulars, PrEx 4.4/3
   Publications National Wage **Stabilization** Board, L
      1.17
   Service and Regulatory Announcements
      Agricultural **Stabilization** and
      Conservation Service, A 82.23
   Wage **Stabilization** Bulletin, L 22.17
   Wage **Stabilization** Committee Releases, WSC
      (series), ES 2.7/2
   Wage **Stabilization**, General Orders and
      Interpretations, Pr 32.5112
Stable
   Care of Animals and **Stable** Management, W 3.50/9
   Catalog and Price List of Stable Isotopes Including
      Related Materials and Services, Y 3.At
      7:35
Staff
   Clinical Center: Medical **Staff** Directory, HE
      20.3002:M 46/4
   Congressional **Staff** Journal, Y 4.H 81/3:2, Y 4.R
      86/2:3
   DNFSB **Staff** Issue Reports, Y 3.D 36/3:12
   Economic **Staff** Papers, SE 1.30
   Energy Action **Staff**: Annual Report, HE 20.6001/
      2
   ERS **Staff** Reports, A 93.44
   Faculty and Other Professional **Staff** in
      Institutions of Higher Education, FS
      5.253:53000, HE 5.253:53000
   Handbook for **Staff** Physicians, HE 20.3044
   How Federal Agencies Develop Management
      Talent, Management **Staff** Development
      Series Reports, CS 1.56
   Investment Guaranties **Staff** Circular Letters, S
      17.43
   Joint **Staff** Officer's Guide, D 5.408/2
   Office of Research and Statistics: **Staff** Papers, HE
      3.56
   OMAT-O-GRAM, for **Staff** Members of Office of
      Manpower, Automation, and Training, L
      1.41

Program Aids Defense Savings **Staff**, T 1.109

Programs and Schedules, Services of Supply **Staff** Course, W 28.11/3

Progress Report on **Staff** Development for Fiscal Year, NCSS Report E-3, FS 17.630, HE 17.630

Progress Report on **Staff** Development, FS 14.220

Publications by **Staff** and Cooperators, Intermountain Forest and Range Experiment Station, A 13.65/14

Publications **Staff** and Cooperators, Intermountain Forest and Range Experiment Station, A 13.65/14

Renegotiation **Staff** Bulletins, RnB 1.6/3

Report of the Chief of **Staff** of the United States Army, D 101.1/2

Report to Field **Staff**, L 23.14

Roster of General Officers of General **Staff**, Volunteers, W 3.27

Rounds of the Teaching **Staff**, VA 1.61

Staff Accounting Bulletins, SE 1.31

Staff Development Series, FS 14.208/4

Staff Discussion Paper (series), E 2.23

Staff Economic Studies, FR 1.51

Staff Information Circulars, GS 4.12

Staff Information Papers, GS 4.12

Staff Instructions, A 68.21

Staff Manual Guide, HE 20.4008/4

Staff Memo from U.S. Secretary of Labor, L 1.33

Staff Memorandums, SS 1.29

Staff Papers, Background Papers and Major Testimony, Y 3.Ec 7/3

Staff Papers, BIE-SP- (series), C 62.15

Staff Papers, C 45.10

Staff Papers, FJC-SP- (series), Ju 13.10/2

Staff Practice and Procedure Digest, Y 3.N 88:23

Staff Publications, A 13.62/11

Staff Report of Monthly Report Cost and Quality of Fuels for Electric Utility Plants, E 2.13

Staff Report on Monthly Report of Cost and Quality of Fuels for Steam-Electric Plant, FP 1.32

Staff Report, FPC/OCE (series), FP 1.7/4

Staff Reports, C 1.48

Staff Research Studies, TC 1.37

Staff Research Study (series), ITC 1.22

Staff Training in Extramural Programs, HE 20.3053

Staff, the Congressional **Staff** Journal, Y 4.R 86/2:3

Statistics of Local Public School Systems Pupils and **Staff**, HE 19.318/4

Summary Report, Faculty and Other Professional **Staff** in Institutions of Higher Education, FS 5.253:53014, HE 5.253:53014

Transportation, Current Literature Compiled by Library **Staff**, TD 1.15/4

U.S. Air Force Public Affairs **Staff** Directory, D 301.104/4

Unemployment Insurance, Technical **Staff** Papers, L 37.20/2

Urban Transportation and Planning, Current Literature Compiled by Library **Staff**, TD 1.15/5

Staffing

Organization and **Staffing** for Full Time Local Health Services, FS 2.80

Resources and **Staffing**, HE 20.4102:R 31

Schools and Safety **Staffing** Survey, ED 1.332

Staffing Analysis Report, T 22.56

Stage

Daily Mississippi River **Stage** and Forecast Bulletin, C 30.54

Portraits of the American **Stage**, SI 1.2:St 1, SI 11.2:St 1/771-971

Profiles of Scheduled Air Carrier Operations by **Stage** Length, TD 4.44/3

Stages

Daily River **Stages**, A 29.10, C 30.24, C 55.117

Stages and Discharges of Mississippi River and Tributaries and Other Watersheds in the New Orleans District, D 103.45/4

Stages and Discharges of Mississippi River and Tributaries in the Memphis District, D 103.45/2

Stages and Discharges of Mississippi River and Tributaries in the St. Louis District, D 103.45/3

Stages and Discharges of Mississippi River and Tributaries in the Vicksburg District, D 103.45

Stages and Discharges, Mississippi River and its Outlets and Tributaries, W 31.5, M 110.207, D 103.309

Stages of the Missouri River, W 32.6

Stainless

Quarterly Survey on Certain **Stainless** Steel and Alloy Tool Steel, ITC 1.25

Annual Survey on Certain **Stainless Steel** and Alloy Tool Steel, ITC 1.25/2

NDE of **Stainless Steel** and On-Line Leak Monitoring of LWRS, Annual Report, Y 3.N 88:25-5, Y 3.N 88:25-9

Long-Term Embrittlement of Cast Duplex **Stainless Steels** in LWR Systems, Y 3.N 88:25-5

Stalking

Domestic Violence and **Stalking**, J 35.21

Stamp

Benjamin Franklin **Stamp** Club, P 1.50

Commemorative **Stamp** Posters, P 1.26/2

Duck **Stamp** Data, I 49.93

Food **Stamp** Series, A 73.11

U.S. Treasury Savings **Stamp** News, T 66.22

USPS **Stamp** Posters, P 1.26/3

Stamps

Mint Set of Commemorative **Stamps**, P 1.26/4, P 1.54

Mint Set of Definitive **Stamps**, P 1.54/2

Postage **Stamps** of the United States, P 4.10

Treasury of **Stamps** Album, School Year (date), P 1.49

Standard

Alphabetical List Covering Army Air Forces and Army-Navy Aeronautical **Standard** Parts, W 108.15/2, M 301.11

Alphabetical List, U.S. Air Force and Air Force-Navy Aeronautical **Standard** Drawings, D 301.15

Catalog of **Standard** Reference Materials, C 13.10

Certificate of Analyses of **Standard** Samples, C 13.17

Commercial **Standard** CS (series), C 41.25

Consolidated List of Persons or Firms Currently Debarred for Violations of Various Public Contracts Acts Incorporating Labor **Standard** Provisions, GA 1.17

Criteria for a Recommended **Standard**, Occupational Exposure to {various subjects}, HE 20.7110

Distribution of Bank Deposits by Counties and **Standard** Metropolitan Areas, FR 1.11/6

Earth Resources Technology Satellite: **Standard** Catalog, NAS 1.488

Facts for Marketers: **Standard** Metropolitan Statistical Areas in { } Regional Geographical Division, C 41.2:M 34/3

Federal **Standard** Stock Catalog: Sec. 4, Pt. 5, Emergency Federal Specifications, GS 2.8/4

Index of **Standard** Forms, A 13.23

Index of **Standard** Instrument Approach Procedures, TD 4.312

Lumber and Timber Basic Products Industry, Wooden Container Industry, Employer Report of Employment and Required Labor Force by **Standard** Lumber Type Region, Pr 32.5224

National **Standard** Reference Data Series, C 13.48

NBS **Standard**, C 13.42

NBS **Standard** Reference Materials Price List, C 13.48/4-2

NBS **Standard** Reference Materials {announcements}, C 13.48/2

News for Users of NBS **Standard** Reference Materials, C 13.50

Nongovernment Organization Codes for Military **Standard** Contract Administration Procedures, D 7.6/2:8

Nongovernment Organization Codes for Military **Standard** Contract Administration Procedures: Code to Name, D 7.6/2:8-2/2

Nongovernment Organization Codes for Military **Standard** Contract Administration Procedures: Name to Code, D 7.6/2:8-1/2

Numerical Index of **Standard** and Recurring Air Force Publications, D 301.6:0-2

Numerical List Covering Army Air Forces and Army-Navy Aeronautical **Standard** Parts, W 108.15

Numerical List of U.S. Air Force and Air Force-Navy Aeronautical **Standard** Drawings, D 301.16

Numerical List, U.S. Air Force and Army-Navy Aeronautical **Standard** Drawings, M 301.12

Occupational Safety and Health General Industry **Standard** and Interpretations, L 35.6/3-1

Outer Continental Shelf **Standard**, GSS-OCS (series), I 19.73

Price List of **Standard** Reference Materials, C 13.10

Public Assistance Recipients in **Standard** Metropolitan Statistical Areas, HE 3.61/2

Second-Order Leveling, List of **Standard** Elevations, C 4.39

Standard and Optional Forms Facsimile Handbook, GS 4.6/3, GS 12.18

Standard Broadcast Applications Ready and Available for Processing Pursuant to Sec. 1.354 (c) of Commission's Rules, Lists, CC 1.26/2

Standard Designs, I 27.6

Standard Distribution List, TD 5.61

Standard Field Tables, I 53.10

Standard Forms Catalog, GS 2.10/4

Standard Industrial Classification Manual, PrEx 2.6/2:In 27

Standard Instrument Approach Procedures, FAA 5.13, TD 4.60

Standard Instrument Departure (SID) Charts, Eastern U.S., C 55.416/5

Standard Instrument Departure (SID) Charts, Western United States, C 55.416/6

Standard Nomenclature Lists, Obsolete General Supplies, W 32.23/4

Standard Nomenclature Lists, W 34.22

Standard Number Series, N 4.7

Standard Occupational Classification Manual, PrEX 2.6/3

Standard Posters, A 13.20/2

Standard Reference Materials, C 13.10:260, C 13.48/4

Standard School Lectures, Civilian Protection, Pr 32.4411

Standard Specification, I 27.11

Standard Specifications Bureau of Yards and Docks, N 21.10

Standard Specifications Engineer Department, W 7.18

Standard Specifications for Construction of Airports, TD 4.24

Standard Terminal Arrival (STAR) Charts, C 55.416/3

Summary Characteristics for Governmental Units and **Standard** Metropolitan Statistical Areas (series), C 3.223/23:

Technical Activities, Office of **Standard** Reference Data, C 13.58/3

Technical **Standard** Order Authorizations, TD 4.6:part 37

Technology Assessment Program, NIJ **Standard**, J 28.15

United States **Standard** Facilities Flight Check Manual, FAA 5.9

United States **Standard** Flight Inspection Manual, C 31.163/3

Urban Atlas, Tract Data for **Standard** Metropolitan Statistical Areas, C 3.62/7, C 56.242/4

Standardization

Active **Standardization** Projects, Standards, Specifications, Studies and Handbooks, D 7.12

Defense Cataloging and **Standardization** Act of 1952, Y 4.Ar 5/2-14

Defense **Standardization** and Specification Program Policies, Procedures and Instructions, D 7.6/3:4120.3-M

Defense **Standardization** Program, Directory of Points of Interest, D 7.13/2

Directory of United States **Standardization** Activities, C 13.10:288, C 13.10:417

Egg **Standardization** Leaflets, A 36.24

Federal Supply Classification Listing of DoD **Standardization** Documents, D 7.14/2

Fresh Products **Standardization** and Inspection Branch, Annual Progress Report, A 88.12/28

Grain **Standardization**, A 19.11

Standardization and Data Management Newsletter, D 1.88

Standardization Directories, D 7.13

Standardization of Petroleum Specifications Committee, Bulletins, I 28.15

Standardization of Work Measurement, D 7.6/4-2

Standardization {abstracts}, C 41.72

Standardized
  Standardized Government Civilian Allowance
    Regulations, Allowance Circulars, S
    1.76
  Standardized Government Post Differential
    Regulations, Differential Circulars, S
    1.76/2
  Standardized Regulations (Government Civilians,
    Foreign Areas), S 1.76/3
Standards
  Active Standardization Projects, **Standards**,
    Specifications, Studies and Handbooks,
    D 7.12
  ADFC **Standards** for Basic Needs, HE 3.64
  Administrative **Standards** Bulletins, FS 3.111
  AFDC **Standards** for Basic Needs, HE 3.64
  Air Force-Navy Aeronautical Design **Standards**, D
    301.29
  Air Force-Navy Aeronautical **Standards**, D 301.30
  Airport Design **Standards**, TD 4.8/4, TD 4.111
  Airports Service, **Standards** Division Index of
    Advisory Circulars, TD 4.110
  Airworthiness **Standards**, Aircraft Engines, TD
    4.6:part 33
  Airworthiness **Standards**, Normal, Utility, and
    Acrobatic Category Airplanes, TD
    4.6:part 23
  Airworthiness **Standards**, Transport Category
    Airplanes, TD 4.6:part 25
  American Marine **Standards** Committee, C 13.19
  Annual Report of the Activities of the Effluent
    Standards and Water Quality
    Information Advisory Committee, EP
    1.1/2
  Apprenticeship **Standards**, L 16.14
  Armed Services Electro **Standards** Agency Lists, D
    101.38
  Army-Navy Aeronautical **Standards** Index, Y 3.Ae
    8:7
  Background Information for **Standards** of
    Performance, EP 1.8/5
  Bureau of Medical Devices **Standards** Survey,
    International Edition, HE 20.4309
  Bureau of Medical Devices **Standards** Survey,
    National Edition, HE 20.4309/2
  Calibration and Test Services of the National
    Bureau of **Standards**, C 13.10:250
  Check List of **Standards** for Farm Products, A
    36.59, A 66.26
  Commercial **Standards**, C 13.20, C 13.21
  Construction **Standards**, L 35.6/3
  Cost Analysis of Correctional **Standards**, {various
    subjects}, J 1.49
  Development Document for Effluent Limitations
    Guidelines and New Source Performance
    Standards for {various industries}, EP
    1.8/3
  Directory of **Standards** Laboratories in the United
    States, C 13.2:St 2/2
  Economic Analysis of Pretreatment **Standards**
    Series, EP 1.8/4-2
  Electrical **Standards**, C 18.30
  Engineered Performance **Standards** for Real
    Property Maintenance Activities, D 1.6/
    7
  Engineering Performance **Standards**, D 209.14
  FDA Medical Device **Standards** Publication,
    Technical Reports, FDA-T, HE 20.4310/2
  FDA Medical Device **Standards** Publications,
    MDS (series), HE 20.4310
  Federal Information Processing **Standards**
    Publications, C 13.52
  Federal Motor Vehicle Safety **Standards**, TD 8.6/4
  Federal Motor Vehicle Safety **Standards** and
    Regulations, TD 8.6/2
  Federal **Standards**, GS 2.8/3
  Federal Test Method **Standards**, GS 2.8/7
  Flight **Standards** Information Manual, TD 4.8/3
  Folders, Grain **Standards**, A 36.53
  General Industry **Standards**, L 35.6/3
  Government Paper Specification **Standards**, Y 4.P
    93/1:7, Y 4.P 93/1:7/2
  HCFA Regional Office Manual; **Standards** and
    Certification Guidelines, HE 22.8/8-3
  Highlights (year) Safety **Standards** Activity, L
    16.52
  Highway Safety Program **Standards**, TD 2.38, TD
    8.8/4
  HUD Minimum Property **Standards**, HH 1.6/9
  Index of Federal Specifications, **Standards**, and
    Handbooks, GS 2.8/2
  Index of International **Standards**, C 13.10:390
  Index of Military Specifications and **Standards**,
    Military Index, D 3.10

  Index of Signal Corps Specifications and
    Standards, D 111.8
  Index of Specifications and **Standards**, D 1.76
  Index of Specifications and **Standards** used by
    Department of Army, Military Index, V. 2,
    D 101.34
  Index of Specifications and **Standards** Used by
    Department of the Navy, Military Index,
    D 212.10
  Index of Specifications and **Standards** Used by
    Department of the Navy, Specifications
    Cancelled or Superseded, D 212.10/2
  Index of State Specifications and **Standards**, C
    13.10:375
  Index of U.S. Air Force, Air Force-Navy
    Aeronautical and Military (MS)
    Standards (sheet form), D 301.16/2
  Index of U.S. Nuclear **Standards**, C 13.10:483
  Index of U.S. Voluntary Engineering **Standards**, C
    13.10:329
  Index of United States Army, Joint Army-Navy, and
    Federal Specifications and **Standards**, M
    101.23
  Industrial Effluent **Standards**, EP 1.8/4-4
  Industrial **Standards**, C 18.24
  Inspection **Standards**, Memeographed, W 9.6
  Institute for Basic **Standards**, Technical
    Highlights, Fiscal Year, C 13.1/4
  Interim List of Persons or Firms Currently Debarred
    for Violation of Various Public Contracts
    Acts Incorporating Labor **Standards**
    Provisions, GA 1.17/2
  Intermediate Minimum Property **Standards** for
    Solar Heating and Domestic Hot Water
    Systems, HH 1.6/9:So 4
  Joint Army-Navy **Standards**, N 20.28, M 5.7
  Labor **Standards**, L 16.11/1
  Labor **Standards** Clearinghouse, L 16.46
  Law Enforcement **Standards** Program, LESP-RPT
    (series), J 1.41
  Law Enforcement **Standards** Program, NILECJ-
    STD (series), J 1.41/2, J 26.20
  List of Inspection Points Under the Grain
    Standards Act, A 88.2:G 76/6
  Maritime **Standards**, L 35.6/3
  Medical Care in Public Assistance, Guides and
    Recommended **Standards**, FS 14.208/2
  Medical Devices and Diagnostic Products
    Standards Survey; International
    Edition, HE 20.4035
  Medical Devices and Diagnostic Products
    Standards Survey; National Edition,
    HE 20.4035/2
  National Apprenticeship and Training **Standards**
    for {various occupations}, L 37.106/2
  National Bureau of **Standards** Certificate of
    Calibration, C 13.45
  National Bureau of **Standards** Interagency Reports,
    C 13.58
  National Carpentry Apprenticeship and Training
    Standards, L 23.2:C 22
  National Institute of **Standards** and Technology
    Interagency Reports, NISTIR (series), C
    13.58
  National Painting and Decorating Apprenticeship
    and Training **Standards** Adopted by the
    National Joint Painting and Decorating
    Apprenticeship and Training Committee,
    L 23.2:P 16
  National Professional **Standards** Review Council:
    Annual Report, HE 1.46, HE 20.5010
  Noise Diagnostics for Safety Assessment,
    Standards, and Regulation, E 1.28/10
  Noise Emission **Standards** for Construction
    Equipment, Background Document for
    {various items}, EP 1.6/3
  Noise **Standards**, Aircraft Type and Airworthiness
    Certification, TD 4.6:part 36
  Occupational Safety and Health Construction
    Standards and Interpretations, L 35.6/3-
    3
  Occupational Safety and Health Maritime
    Standards and Interpretations, L 35.6/3-
    2
  Official Grain **Standards** of the United States, A
    88.6/2:G 761
  Official United States **Standards** for Grain, A
    104.6/2, A 113.10
  OSHA Safety and Health **Standards** Digests, L
    35.6/4
  OSHA **Standards** and Regulations, L 35.6/3
  Periodicals and Serials Received in the Library of
    the National Bureau of **Standards**, C
    13.10

  Pesticide Registration **Standards**, EP 5.17
  Polymer Science and **Standards** Division, Annual
    Report, C 13.1/7
  Position Classification **Standards** for Positions
    Subject to the Classification Act of 1949,
    CS 1.39, PM 1.30
  President Research Associateships, Post- Doctoral,
    Tenable at National Bureau of **Standards**,
    C 13.47
  Press Notices National Bureau of **Standards**, C
    13.18
  Proceedings **Standards** Laboratory Conferences, C
    13.10
  Product **Standards**, C 13.20/2
  Professional **Standards** Review Organization,
    Annual Report, HE 22.210
  Publications National Bureau of **Standards**, C
    13.10:305
  Qualification **Standards** for Wage Board Positions,
    CS 1.45
  Qualification **Standards** for White Collar
    Positions Under the General Schedule,
    CS 1.45:X-118, PM 1.8/3:X-118
  Recommended **Standards**, HE 20.7110/2
  Regulations Under Fair Labor **Standards** Act, L
    22.22
  Rehabilitation **Standards** Memorandum, FS 13.209
  Reports of the Advisory Committee to the
    Administrator on **Standards** for the
    Administration of Juvenile Justice, J 1.48
  Resident Research Associateships, Postdoctoral,
    Tenable and National Bureau of
    Standards, C 13.47
  Review of **Standards** of Performance for New
    Stationary Sources, EP 4.19
  Safety **Standards**, L 35.9
  Specifications, International Aircraft **Standards**, C
    13.9
  Standards and Labeling Policy Book, A 110.18
  Standards Development Status Summary Report, Y
    3.N 88:32
  Standards for Fruits and Vegetables, A 104.6/3
  Standards for Specifying Construction of Airports,
    TD 4.24
  Standards Laboratory Cross-Check Procedure,
    Department of Navy, BUWEPS-
    BUSHIPS Calibration Program, D
    217.16
  Standards Laboratory Instrument Calibration
    Procedure, Department of Navy,
    BUWEPS-BUSHIPS Calibration
    Program, D 217.16/2
  Standards Laboratory Instrument Calibration
    Technique, D 217.16/7
  Standards Laboratory Measurements System
    Operation Procedure, Department of
    Navy, BUWEPS-BUSHIPS Calibration
    Program, D 217.16/3
  Standards Support and Environmental Impact
    Statements, EP 1.57/5
  Standards Yearbooks, C 13.10
  Standards, FAA-STD (series), TD 4.24/2
  State Child-Labor **Standards** (by States), L 16.21
  State Workmen's Compensation Laws, Comparison
    of Major Provisions with Recommended
    Standards, L 16.3:212
  Tables to Convert {Foreign Moneys, Weights and
    Measures into U.S. **Standards**}, C 1.11
  Technical Highlights of the National Bureau of
    Standards, C 13.1
  Technical Memorandum National Bureau of
    Standards, Applied Mathematics
    Division, C 13.39
  Technical News from Department of Commerce,
    National Bureau of **Standards**, C 13.36/6
  Technical Notes National Bureau of **Standards**, C
    13.46
  Technical **Standards** Orders, C 31.143, FAA 1.38
  Technical **Standards** Register, C 31.143/2
  Technical **Standards** Training Guides, HH 2.6/7
  Tentative Airworthiness **Standards**, TD 4.411
  U.S. Air Force **Standards**, D 301.31
  U.S. **Standards** for Fruits and Vegetables, A 66.16
  United States Government Interdepartmental
    Standards, T 51.11/7
  United States **Standards** for Fruits and Vegetables,
    A 36.35, A 75.19, A 80.121, A 80.822
  United States **Standards** for Grades of {commod-
    ity}, A 88.6/2
  United States **Standards** for Grades of {fruits,
    vegetables, etc.}, A 82.20
  United States **Standards** for {various foods}, A
    103.6/2
  United States **Standards**, A 36.35/2

Voice of Z39, News About Library, Information Science, and Publishing **Standards**, C 13.163

Water Quality **Standards** Criteria Digest, Compilation of Federal/State Criteria on {various subjects}, EP 1.29/2

Water Quality **Standards** Summary {for various States} (series), EP 1.29

World Index of Plastic **Standards**, C 13.10:352

Standby

National Emergency **Standby** Regulations and Instructions Personnel and Manpower, CS 1.41/4:990-3

Staple

Cotton Grade and **Staple** Reports, Georgia, A 36.27/1

Cotton Grade and **Staple** Reports, Texas and Oklahoma, A 36.27/2

Estimated Grade and **Staple** Length of Upland Cotton Ginned (by States), A 82.69

Estimated Grade and **Staple** Length of Upland Cotton Ginned in United States, A 88.11/7

Long **Staple** Cotton Review, A 88.11/20

Star

Advertisements Inviting Proposals for Carrying Mails by **Star** Routes (by States), P 1.22

Energy Star Homes Update, EP 4.29

Science and Technology Agriculture Reporter (**STAR**), S 18.64

Standard Terminal Arrival (**STAR**) Charts, C 55.416/3

STAR, Scientific and Technical Aerospace Reports, NAS 1.9/4

Stargazing

News from the Naval Observatory, **Stargazing** Notes, D 213.15

Stars

Ephemeris of Sun, Polaris, and Other Selected **Stars**, D 213.12

Ephemeris of the Sun, Polaris and Other Selected **Stars** with Companion Data and Tables for the year {date}, I 53.8

Stars in Service, T 66.14

Started

Number of New Permanent Nonfarm Dwelling Units **Started** by Urban or Rural Location, Public or Private Ownership, and Type of Structure, L 2.51/4

Starting

Starting and Managing Series, SBA 1.15

Starting Out Series, SBA 1.35

Starts

Construction Reports; Housing **Starts**, C 20 (Series), C 56.211/3

Housing **Starts** in (Month), C 3.215/2

Nonfarm Housing **Starts**, C 56.211/3

Startup

National Health Service Corps Information Bulletin, Private Practice **Startup** Loan Program, HE 20.9110/7

STAT-USA

STAT-USA, C 1.91

State

Atlas/**State** Data Abstract for the United States, D 1.58/4

Catalog of Federal Grant-In-Aid Programs to **State** and Local Governments, Y 3.Ad 9/8:20

Chiefs of **State** and Cabinet Members of Foreign Governments, CR CS- (series), PrEx 3.11/2

Consolidated Annual Report on **State** and Territorial Public Health Laboratories, HE 20.7001/2

Cultural Presentation Programs of the Department of **State**, S 1.67

Current Employment Statistics **State** Operating Manual, L 2.46/4

Digest of **State** Laws Relating to Taxation and Revenue, C 3.50

Digest of **State** Program Plans, EP 2.21

Documents and **State** Papers, S 1.73

EM **State** Fact Sheets, E 1.90/7

Employee Benefits in **State** and Local Governments, L 2.3/10-2

Extramural Grant and Contract Awards by **State**, City Institution and Number, HE 20.3176/4

Fed **State** Bulletin, T 22.2/15:7208

Federal and **State** Endangered Species Expenditures, I 49.77/6

Felons Sentenced to Probation in **State** Courts, J 29.11/12

Final **State** and Local Data Elements, T 1.64/2

HRSA **State** Health Workforce Profiles, HE 20.9317

HRSA **State** Health Workforce Profiles (database), HE 20.9317/2

Monthly Electric Utility Sales and Revenue Report with **State** Distributions, E 3.11/17-14

Monthly List of **State** Publications, LC 7.6

National Summary of **State** Medicaid Managed Care Programs, HE 22.116

National Summary of **State Medicaid** Managed Care Programs, Program Descriptions, HE 22.12/3

News Regional and **State** Employment and Unemployment, L 2.111/7

Papers in Re in **State** Courts of Appeal, J 1.83

Papers in Re in **State** Supreme Courts, J 1.82

Patient Movement Data, **State** and Mental Hospitals, FS 2.22/46

Personnel Management Reform, Progress in **State** and Local Governments, PM 1.11/3

Position Classification and Pay in **State** and Territorial Public Health Laboratories, HE 20.7413

Precision and Accuracy Assessments for **State** and Local Air Monitoring Networks, EP 1.23/5-3

Preliminary Statistics of **State** School Systems, FS 5.220:20006, HE 5.220:20006, HE 5.93/4

Preservation Planning Series, **State** Program Overviews, I 29.102

Prime Contract Awards by Region and **State**, D 1.57/5

Prime Contract Awards by **State**, D 1.57/6

Prisoners in **State** and Federal Institutions on (date), J 29.9/7

Prisoners in **State** and Federal Institutions, J 16.23

Problem-solving Technology for **State** and Local Governments, C 51.9/30

Proceedings Annual Conference of the Surgeon General, Public Health Service, and Chief, Children's Bureau, with **State** and Territorial Health Officers, FS 2.83

Proceedings Annual Conference, Surgeon General, Public Health Service, with **State** and Territorial Mental Health Authorities, FS 2.83/3

Proceedings Assembly of **State** Librarians, LC 30.14

Proceedings Biennial Conference of **State** and Territorial Dental Directors with Public Health Service and Children's Bureau, FS 2.83/2

Proceedings Conference of **State** Sanitary Engineers, FS 2.83/4

Proceedings National Brucellosis Committee and Progress Report of the Cooperative **State**-Federal Brucellosis Eradication Program, A 77.202:B 83/16

Program Development Handbooks for **State** and Area Agencies on {various subjects}, HE 23.3009

Program Memorandum Medicaid **State** Agencies, HE 22.28

Program Memorandum **State** Survey Agencies, HE 22.28/4

Prosecutors in **State** Courts, J 29.11/15

Public Assistance, Costs of **State** and Local Administration, Services, and Training, FS 17.633, HE 17.633

Public Use Data Tape Documentation Natality **State** Summary, HE 20.6226

Publications Department of **State**, Quarterly List, S 1.30

Quarterly Summary of Federal, **State**, and Local Tax Revenue, C 3.145/6

Quarterly Summary of **State** and Local Tax Revenue, C 3.145/6, C 56.231/2

Rate Series 2, **State** Reports, FP 1.10/2

Receipts for **State** Administered Highways, Official Distribution, C 37.19

Recipients of Public Assistance Money Payments and Amounts of Such Payments, by Program, **State**, and County, HE 17.627/2

Register, Department of **State**, S 1.6

Report of **State** and Local Radiological Health Programs, HE 20.4121

Report on Plan Preparation on **State** and Local Public Works, FW 7.7

Research Projects Department of **State**, S 1.96

Research Studies Department of **State**, S 1.101/12

Rules and Regulations Governing Paroling of Prisoners from Penitentiaries, **State** Institutions, J 1.15/5

Salaries of **State** Public Health Workers, FS 2.82

Secretaries of **State**, Portraits and Biographical Sketches, S 1.69:162

Secretary of **State** Press Conferences, S 1.25/4

Selected Compensation and Pension Data by **State** of Residence, VA 1.88

Selected **State** Department Publications, S 1.30/3-2

Session Laws of Pamphlet Laws (**State** Department edition), S 7.6:C & S

Significant Provisions of **State** Unemployment Compensation Laws, SS 1.19, L 33.10

Significant Provisions of **State** Unemployment Insurance Laws, L 37.210

Social Security Beneficiaries by **State** and County, HE 3.73/2

Soil-Binding Practices Applicable in **State**, A 55.44/10

Sources of Milk for Federal Order Markets, by **State** and County, A 88.40, A 88.14/11-3

Special Analysis of Federal Aid to **State** and Local Governments in Budget, PrEx 2.8/a3

Special Education Personnel in **State** Education Departments, FS 5.235:35051

Specifications **State** Department, S 1.32

SPI **State** Personal Income, C 59.25

State Administered Federal Engineer Funds, HE 19.122

State Agricultural and Marketing Officers, A 36.55

State Agricultural Departments and Marketing Agencies, with Names of Officials, A 66.45

State Air Pollution Implementation Plan Progress Report, EP 1.52

State Air Programs, Digest, Fiscal Year (date), EP 1.33

State and Federal Marketing Activities and Other Economic Work, A 36.21

State and Local Government Collective Bargaining Settlements, L 2.45/4

State and Local Government Employment and Payrolls, L 2.41/4

State and Local Government Functional Profile Series, Y 3.Eq 2:14

State and Local Government Quarterly Employment Survey, C 3.140

State and Local Government Special Studies, C 3.145, C 56.231

State and Local Grant Awards, EP 1.35/2

State and Local Personnel Systems, Annual Statistical Report, CS 1.95

State and Local Programs on Smoking and Health, HE 20.25/4

State and Metropolitan Area Data Book, C 3.134/5

State and Metropolitan Area Data Book, A Statistical Supplement, C 3.134/5-2

State and Metropolitan Area Employment and Unemployment, L 2.111/5

State and Metropolitan Area Unemployment, L 2.111/5

State and National Reports, Y 3.N 21/9:10

State and Private Forestry: Forestry Bulletins, A 13.110/10

State and Private Forestry: Forestry Reports, A 13.110/9

State and Private Forestry: General Publications, A 13.110/2

State and Private Forestry: General Reports, A 13.110/12

State and Private Forestry: Handbooks, Manuals, Guides, A 13.110/8

State and Private Forestry: Miscellaneous Reports, A 13.110/11

State and Private Forestry: Technical Publications, A 13.110/13

State and Private Forestry: Technical Reports, A 13.110/14

State and Regional Unemployment, L 2.120/2

State Bulletins, 2d Series (Statistics by counties), C 3.31/3

State Bulletins, C 3.31/2

State Buy-in Manual, HE 22.8/11

State Carlot Shipments of Fruits and Vegetables, by Commodities, Counties, and Billing Stations, A 88.12/10

State Chartered Credit Unions, Annual Report, NCU 1.1/2

State Child-Labor Standards (by States), L 16.21

State Climatologist, C 55.281/3

State Clinical and Environmental Laboratory Legislation, HE 20.7028

Official **Statement** of United States Food Administration, Y 3.F 73:19

Official **Statement** of Wheat Director, Y 3.W 56:5

Petroleum **Statement**, I 28.18/2, I 28.18/4, E 3.11/5, E 3.11/5-2

Preliminary **Statement** of Capitalization and Income, Class I Steam Railways in United States, IC 1 ste.28

Roll of Honor, Supplemental **Statement** of Disposition of Bodies of Deceased Union Soldiers and Prisoners of War Removed to National Cemeteries in Southern and Western United States, W 39.8

Secretary's Annual Report to Congress, Posture **Statement**, Outlook and Program Review, E 1.60:0010

Smithsonian Year (date), **Statement** by the Secretary, SI 1.1/4

Statement (various topics), HE 20.3182/8

Statement of a Proper Military Policy for the United States, W 26.8

Statement of Active Loans and Financial Guarantees, Y 3.Ex 7/3, Y 3.Ex 7/3:12

Statement of Balances, Appropriations, and Disbursements, T 9.7

Statement of Condition of Federal Land Banks, Joint Stock Land Banks, etc., FCA 1.7

Statement of Expenditures, A 76.409

Statement of Federal Financial Accounting Concepts, PrEX 2.35

Statement of Federal Financial Accounting Standards, PrEX 2.35/2

Statement of Financial Condition, HH 2.22

Statement of Foreign Commerce and Immigration, T 37.5

Statement of Foreign Currencies Purchased with Dollars, T 63.118/3

Statement of Indemnity Claims and Averages in Cooperative Bang's Disease Work, A 4.29

Statement of Indemnity Claims and Averages in Cooperative Tuberculosis Eradication, A 4.30

Statement of Loans and Commodities Owned, A 71.7, A 82.307

Statement of Operations, Y 3.F 31/8:1

Statement of Postal Receipts at 50 Industrial Offices, P 4.8

Statement of Postal Receipts at 50 Selected Offices, P 4.9

Statement of Public Debt of United States, T 63.112

Statement of Recruiting for Line of Army at General Recruiting Stations and Their Auxiliaries, W 3.17/2

Statement of Taxes, Dividends, Salaries and Wages, Class a and Class B Privately Owned Electric Utilities in U.S., FP 1.22

Statement of Treasury, Daily, T 9.8

Statement of United States Currency and Coin, T 63.188, T 63.308

Statement of Voluntary Credit Restraint Committee, FR 1.35

Statement Showing Amount of National Bank Notes Outstanding {ect}, T 12.9

Statement Showing Rank Duties and Address of Officers of Corps of Engineers, W 7.7

Summary of Bovine Tuberculosis Eradication in Cooperation with Various States, **Statement** of Indemnity and Averages in Cooperative Bovine Brucellosis Work, A 77.216/2

Summary **Statement** of Income and Expenditures of Voluntary Relief Agencies Registered with Advisory Committee on Voluntary Foreign Aid, S 1.99/3

Superintendent's **Statement** to Board of Visitors, D 208.110

Tuberculosis Eradication: **Statement** of Indemnity Claims and Averages in Cooperative, A 77.214

U.S. House of Representatives, Detailed **Statement** of Disbursements, Y 4.H 81/3:D 63

United States Naval Academy, Superintendent's **Statement** to Board of Visitors, D 208.110

United States Special Operations Forces, Posture **Statement**, D 1.98

Weekly Averages of Member Bank Reserves, Reserve Bank Credit and Related Items and **Statement** of Condition of the Federal Reserve Bank, FR 1.15

Weekly **Statement** of Bonds Held in Trust for National Banks, T 40.9

Weekly **Statement** of Gold and Silver Exports and Imports, United States, C 3.195

Statements

102 Monitor, Environmental Impact **Statements**, PrEx 14.10, EP 1.76

Combined Financial **Statements** of Members of the Federal Home Loan Bank System, FHL 1.12

Condensed Consolidated Statistical **Statements**, Class 1 Railways Having Annual Railway Operating Revenues of $10,000,000 or More, IC 1 ste.46

Consolidated Financial **Statements** of the United States Government, Fiscal Year, T 63.113/3

Current Information **Statements**, A 55.33

Environmental Impact **Statements**, E 2.11/3

Industrial Security **Statements**, D 3.11/2

Joint Stock Land Banks, Progress in Liquidation Including **Statements** of Condition, A 72.16

Paid Shipments (by country), Special **Statements**, Y 3.Ec 74/3:13-2

Paper Currency of Each Denomination Outstanding, Monthly **Statements**, T 63.307

Passenger Traffic **Statements** (other than commutation) of Class 1 Steam Railways in United States Separated Between Coach Traffic and Parlor and Sleeping Car Traffic, IC 1 ste.40

Regulations and Policy **Statements**, C 31.224/2

Rules and Regulations and **Statements** of Procedure, LR 1.6:R 86

Standards Support and Environmental Impact **Statements**, EP 1.57/5

Statements by Presidents of the United States on International Cooperation in Space, Y 1.92-1:S.doc. 40

Statements of Condition of Joint Stock Land Banks, FCA 1.7/2

Statements of Conditions of Federal Land Banks, etc., T 48.6

Statements of Expenditures, A 55.62

Statements of Facts, and Briefs, J 10.5/1

Statements of Loans and Commodities Owned, A 80.407

Statements, S 1.25/6

Trend of Employment in U.S. (Monthly summary **statements**), L 2.9/2

Staten Island

Dietetic Internship, Public Health Service Hospital, **Staten Island**, N.Y., FS 2.89/4

States

North Central **States** Regional Poultry Breeding Project, Annual Report, A 77.236

Pacific Coast **States** Fisheries, C 55.309/2

Potatoes and Sweetpotatoes, Estimates by **States** and Seasonal Groups, A 88.12/19

Procedure (by **States**), A 55.46/12

Programs by **States**, A 55.42/9

Projections of the Population of Voting Age, for **States**, C 3.186/26

Projects Operated by Work Projects Administration, Accomplishments on (by **States**), FW 4.31

Publications Central **States** Forest Experiment Station, A 13.68/12-2

Publications Lake **States** Forest Experiment Station {list}, A 13.61/12

Rate Series B (by **States**), FP 1.16

Receipts from Sale of Principal Farm Products by **States**, A 36.81/1

Report on Cotton Ginnings by **States** (Preliminary), C 3.20

Requirement for Individual Water-Supply and Sewage-Disposal Systems (by **States**), NHA 2.17, HH 2.11

Retail Sales, Independent Stores, Summary for **States**, C 3.138

Retail Trade (by **States**), C 3.940-10

Revenues, Expenses, and Statistics of Class 1 Motor Carriers of **States**, IC 1 ste.24

Rules of Courts (by **States**), Ju 10.7

Schedule of Examinations for 4th-class Postmasters (by **States**), CS 1.27

Schedules of Payments to Holders of Cotton Options and Participation Trust Certificates by Congressional District of **States**, A 55.57

Schemes for Separation of Mail by **States**, P 1.21

Schemes of **States** (for use of publishers in distribution 2d class mail), P 10.10

Schemes of **States** (from certain standpoints), P 10.8

Schemes of **States** (general), P 10.6

Service Establishments (by **States**), C 3.940-11

Simplifying Federal Aid to **States** and Communities, Annual Report to the President of an Interagency Program, PrEx 2.18

Soil and Water Conservation Districts, Status of Organization, by **States**, Approximate Acreage, and Farms in Organized Districts, A 57.32

Soil Survey (of **States**), A 47.5/2

State Child-Labor Standards (by **States**), L 16.21

States, EP 1.1/9

States Activities Report, C 55.438

States and Small Business: Programs and Activities, SBA 1.34

States and Their Indian Citizens, I 20.2:St 2/3

States and Urban Strategies (various **States**) (series), HH 1.89

Status of Compliance, Public School districts, 17 Southern and Border **States**, Reports, FS 5.80, HE 5.80

Status Report on Water and Power Resources Service Programs Within (various **States**), I 27.74

Summary of Bang's Disease Control Program Conducted by Bureau of Animal Industry in Cooperation with Various **States**, A 4.23

Summary of Bang's Disease Work in Cooperation with Various **States**, A 4.21

Summary of Bovine Brucellosis Eradication Activities in Cooperation with **States**, A 77.212/2

Summary of Bovine Tuberculosis Eradication in Cooperation with Various **States**, Statement of Indemnity and Averages in Cooperative Bovine Brucellosis Work, A 77.216/2

Summary of Brucellosis (Bang's Disease) Control Program Conducted by Bureau of Animal Industry in Cooperation with Various **States**, A 77.213

Summary of Brucellosis Eradication Activities in Cooperation with Various **States** Under Cull and Dry Cow Testing Program, A 77.212/7

Summary of Bucellosis Eradication Activities in Cooperation with the Various **States** Under the Market Cattle Testing Program, A 77.212/8

Summary of Tuberculosis Eradication in Cooperation with Various **States**, A 77.216

Tall Fescue, Southern **States**, A 92.19/12

Tax Capacity of the **States**, Y 3.Ad 9/8:19

Teacher Exchange Opportunities Abroad, Teaching, Summer Seminars under International Educational Exchange Program of Department of **States** {announcements}, FS 5.64/2

Technical Notes Forest Service Lake **States** Forest Experiment Station, A 13.61/10

Title 1, Elementary and Secondary Education Act of 1965, **States** Report, FS 5.79, HE 5.79

Tons of Revenue Freight Originated and Tons Terminated by **States** and by Commodity Class, IC 1.23/15:SS-7

Truck Crop Farms, Adjustments on (by **States**), A 36.135

Tuberculosis Statistics, (year), **States** and Cities (date), HE 20.7013

Turkeys in NTIP Flocks and Their Distribution by **States** and Varieties, A 77.15:44-11

Unemployment Bulletins (by **States**), C 3.37/16

Unemployment in **States**, L 2.111/5-2

Unemployment in **States** and Local Areas, L 2.41/9

Unemployment Rates for **States** and Local Governments, BLS/PWEDA/QR-(series), L 2.111/3

Unloads of Tomatoes in 66 Cities by **States** of Origin, A 36.187

Water Facilities Area Plans (by **States**), A 36.148

Water Quality Records of {**States**}, I 19.53/2

Water Quality Standards Summary {for various **States**} (series), EP 1.29

Western **States** Regional Turkey Breeding Project, Annual Report, A 77.235

Wheat Ground and Wheat-Milling Products, by **States**, C 3.117

Workmen's Compensation (by **States**), L 16.22

World War II Honor List of Dead and Missing (by **States**), W 107.13

ZIP Code Directories {by **States**}, P 1.10/7

Statewide

Statewide Highway Planning Surveys; News Bulletins, FW 2.10

Statewide Transportation Planning and Management Series, TD 2.57

Station

Central States Forest Experiment **Station**, A 13.68

Contributions from Thermodynamics Laboratory, Petroleum Experiment **Station**, Bartlesville, Oklahoma, I 28.105

Dry Land Agriculture Division, Weekly **Station** Reports, A 77.508

Experiment **Station** Hydraulics Bulletin, W 31.10

Experiment **Station** Letters, A 94.12

Experiment **Station** Office, A 77.400

Experiment **Station** Record, A 10.6, A 77.408

Experiment **Station** Reports, A 57.19

Experiment **Station** Work, A 1.9, A 10.11

Federal Radiological Fallout Monitoring **Station** Directory, D 119.8/3:E 5.11

General Index to Experiment **Station** Record, A 10.6/2

Introduction to **Station** Catalogs, N 6.5/10

List and **Station** of Commission Officers, T 33.10

List of Books Available for Ship and **Station** Libraries, Navy, N 17.26

List of Station Publications Received by Office of Experiment **Stations**, A 10.17

Number and Percentage of Farms Electrified with Central **Station** Service, A 68.20

Numerical Index for **Station** Catalogs, N 6.5/8

Occasional Papers Forest Service Northeastern Forest Experiment **Station**, A 13.42/8, A 13.42/8-2

Occasional Papers Forest Service Southern Forest Experiment **Station**, A 13.40/6

Pacific Northwest Research **Station**: Miscellaneous Publications, A 13.129

Pesticide **Station** for (year), A 82.76

Progress Report Northern Rocky Mountain Forest and Range Experiment **Station**, A 13.30/6

Publications Available for Purchase, U.S. Army Engineer Waterways Experiment **Station** and Other Corps of Engineers Agencies, D 103.39

Publications by Staff and Cooperators, Intermountain Forest and Range Experiment **Station**, A 13.65/14

Publications Central States Forest Experiment **Station**, A 13.68/12-2

Publications Lake States Forest Experiment **Station** {list}, A 13.61/12

Publications Naval Torpedo **Station**, D 211.23

Publications Pacific Northwest Forest and Range Experiment **Station**, A 13.66/15

Publications Rocky Mountain Forest and Range Experiment **Station**, A 13.69/10-2

Publications Southern Forest Experiment **Station**, A 13.40/8-3

Publications Staff and Cooperators, Intermountain Forest and Range Experiment **Station**, A 13.65/14

Recent Publications of the Pacific Northwest Forest and Range Experiment **Station**, A 13.66/14

Research at Southeastern Forest Experiment **Station**, A 13.63/3

Research Information Digest, Recent Publications of Southeastern Forest Experiment **Station**, A 13.63/13

Research Reports Southwestern Forest and Range Experiment **Station**, A 13.43/8

Research Reports Waterways Experiment **Station**, D 103.24/5

Rocky Mountain Research **Station**: Bibliographies and Lists of Publications, A 13.151/2

Rocky Mountain Research **Station** Directory, A 13.151/4-2

Rocky Mountain Research **Station**: General Publications, A 13.151

Rocky Mountain Research **Station**: Handbooks, Manuals, Guides, A 13.151/4

Rocky Mountain Research **Station**: Maps, A 13.151/3

Roster and **Station** of Officers of Signal Corps, W 42.9

Sea Water Conversion, Solar Research **Station** (series), I 1.87

Southern Research **Station**: Bibliographies and Lists of Publications, A 13.150/2

Southern Research **Station** Directory of Research Scientists, A 13.150/4

Southern Research **Station**: General Publications, A 13.150

Southern Research **Station**: Handbooks, Manuals, Guides, A 13.150/3

Station and Program Notes, W 100.8

Station Directory, N 12.9

Station List, W 24.8

Station Meterological Summary, C 30.10

Station Notes, A 13.42/15, A 13.68/10

Station Papers, A 13.30/8, A 13.42/16, A 13.61/8, A 13.63/9, A 13.67/8, A 13.69/7, A 13.73/8

Station-List of Officers of Medical Department, W 44.13

Technical Notes Forest Service Lake States Forest Experiment **Station**, A 13.61/10

Technical Notes Forest Service Northeastern Forest Experiment **Station**, A 13.67/9, A 13.42/7

Technical Notes Forest Service Northern Forest Experiment **Station**, A 13.73/9

Technical Notes Forest Service Southeastern Forest Experiment **Station**, A 13.63/8

U.S. Central **Station** Nuclear Electric Generating Units, Significant Milestones, E 1.41

U.S. Divisional and **Station** Climatic Data and Normals, C 55.281/2-3

U.S. Naval Ordnance Test **Station**, Inyokern, Technical Memorandums, D 215.11

Visitors Report to Nurses' **Station** Before Entering Room, HE 20.7029

Waterways Experiment **Station** Capabilities, D 103.24/10

Weekly **Station** Reports of Office of Dry Land Agriculture Investigations, A 19.24

Stationary

Review of Standards of Performance for New **Stationary** Sources, EP 4.19

Stationary Source Enforcement Series, EP 1.8/7

Financial Audit, House **Stationery** Revolving Fund Statements, GA 1.13/19

Stations

Address List of Agricultural Experiment **Stations**, A 10.19

Annual Peak Discharge at Selected Gaging **Stations** in Pacific Northwest, I 19.45/3

Broadcasting Radio **Stations** of the United States, RC 1.9

Broadcasting **Stations** of the World, PrEx 7.9

Carlot Shipments of, from **Stations** in U.S., A 66.24/2

Catalog of Information on Water Data: Index to **Stations** in Coastal Areas, I 19.42/6

Climatological Data; Antarctic **Stations**, C 30.21/3

Climatological Data; Artic **Stations**, C 30.21/2

Crops Research: Results of Regional Cotton Variety Tests by Cooperating Agricultural Experiment **Stations**, A 77.15:34

Current Discharge at Selected **Stations** in the Pacific Northwest, I 19.45, I 19.47/2

Directory of Air Service **Stations**, W 87.9/2

Directory of World Seismograph **Stations**, C 55.220/5:25

Educational AM and FM Radio and Education Television **Stations**, FS 5.234:34016, HE 5.234:34016

First Class Post Offices with Named **Stations** and Branches, P 24.8

Fresh Fruit and Vegetable Shipments by States, Commodities, Counties, **Stations**, Calendar Year (date), A 88.12/31:6, A 88.40/2:12

Funds for Research at State Agricultural Experimental **Stations**, A 94.10

Historical Series, Independent Radio **Stations** (programs), I 29.16

Income Tax Brevities for Use by Radio Broadcasting **Stations**, T 22.38

Index of Original Surface Weather Records for **Stations** in {various States}, C 55.288

List and **Stations** of Naval Inspectors of Engineering Material, N 19.6

List of Addresses of Navy Recruiting **Stations**, N 17.13, N 17.21

List of Changes of **Stations**, Etc., T 27.13

List of Extension Publications of State Agricultural Colleges Received by Office of Experiment **Stations** Library, A 43.5/9

List of Radio Broadcast **Stations**, CC 1.10

List of Radio Broadcast **Stations** by Frequency, CC 1.22

List of Radio Broadcast **Stations** by State and City, CC 1.23

List of Radio Broadcast **Stations**, Alphabetically by Call Letters, CC 1.21

List of Radio Broadcast **Stations**, by Zone and State, CC 2.12

List of Radio **Stations** of United States, C 11.7/6

List of Station Publications Received by Office of Experiment **Stations**, A 10.17

List of Wireless Telegraph **Stations** of the World, N 19.7

Monthly Mean Discharge at Selected Gaging **Stations** and Change of Storage in Certain Lakes and Reservoirs in Columbia River Basin, I 19.47

Precipitation Data from Storage-Gage **Stations**, C 30.59/44

Radio Broadcast **Stations** in United States, Containing Alterations and Corrections, CC 1.24

Radio **Stations** of United States, C 11.7/6, C 24.5

Relay Broadcast **Stations**, CC 1.31

Report on Agricultural Experiment **Stations**, A 10.1/2

Reports of Applications Received in Radio Broadcast **Stations**, CC 1.26

Results of Regional Cotton Variety Tests by Cooperating Agricultural Experiment **Stations**, A 77.15:34

River Temperature at Selected **Stations** in the Pacific Northwest, I 19.46/2-2, I 19.46/2-3

Roster of Organizaed Militia of United States, by Divisions, Brigades, Regiments, Companies, and other Organizations, with their **Stations**, W 70.5

Roster Showing **Stations** and Duties of Officers, W 39.12, W 77.6

State Carlot Shipments of Fruits and Vegetables, by Commodities, Counties, and Billing **Stations**, A 88.12/10

Statement of Recruiting for Line of Army at General Recruiting **Stations** and Their Auxiliaries, W 3.17/2

Stations of Army, W 3.30, W 40.5

Water Temperatures, Coast and Geodetic Survey Tide **Stations**, C 4.34

Statistic

Statistic Report of Marine Commerce of Duluth-Superior Harbor, Minn. and Wis., D 103.13

Statistical

Agricultural Conservation Program, **Statistical** Summary, A 90.10

Annual Grazing **Statistical** Report, A 13.83

Annual Housing Survey: Housing Characteristics for Selected Standard Metropolitan **Statistical** Area, C 3.215/17-60

Annual **Statistical** Digest, FR 1.59

Annual **Statistical** Report, Fiscal Year (date), D 14.1/2, D 119.1/2

Annual **Statistical** Report, Rural Electrification Borrowers, A 68.1/2

Annual **Statistical** Report, Rural Telephone Borrowers, A 68.1/3

Annual **Statistical** Review, Hospital and Medical Services, FS 2.86/6

Annual **Statistical** Summary, T 34.9

Annual **Statistical** Summary, Fiscal Year, HE 20.5409

Annual **Statistical** Supplement, FS 3.3/3

Astronauts and Cosmonauts Biographical and **Statistical** Data, Y 4.Sci 2:95

Aviation Accident **Statistical** Summary Calendar Year, TD 4.413

Bi-annual **Statistical** Summary, AA 1.12

Census Bureau **Statistical** Daily, C 3.237

Census of Housing: Detailed Housing Characteristics for Metropolitan **Statistical** Areas, C 3.224/3-6

Census of Housing: General Housing Characteristics for Metropolitan **Statistical** Areas, C 3.224/3-3

Census of Population: General Population Characteristics for Metropolitan **Statistical** Areas, C 3.223/6-3

Census of Population: Social and Economic Characteristics for Metropolitan **Statistical** Areas, C 3.223/7-3

Census of Retail Trade; Major Retail Centers in Standard Metropolitan **Statistical** Areas, RC (series), C 56.251/5

Checklist of Reports Issued by Economic Research Service and **Statistical** Reporting Service, A 1.97

Condensed Consolidated **Statistical** Statements, Class 1 Railways Having Annual Railway Operating Revenues of $10,000,000 or More, IC 1 ste.46

Conservation Reserve Program of Soil Bank, **Statistical** Summaries, A 82.79/2

Construction and Building Materials, **Statistical** Supplements, C 41.30/2

Construction Reports; New Residential Construction in Selected Standard Metropolitan **Statistical** Areas (SMSA), C 3.215/15

Cooperative State-Federal Bovine Tuberculosis Eradication Program, **Statistical** Tables, A 101.18

Cooperative State-Federal Brucellosis Eradication Program; **Statistical** Tables, A 101.18/2

Cooperative State-Federal Brucellosis Eradication Program; **Statistical** Tables, Fiscal Year (date), A 77.212/4

Cooperative State-Federal Tuberculosis Eradication Program, **Statistical** Tables, Fiscal Year (date), A 77.212/5

Copper, (year) Annual **Statistical** Supplement, C 57.512/2

Directory of Federal **Statistical** Data Files, C 51.15

Emergency Conservation Program, Fiscal Year **Statistical** Summary, A 112.1/2

F.T.C. **Statistical** Report on Mergers and Acquisitions, FT 1.2:M 54/3

FAA **Statistical** Handbook of Civil Aviation, TD 4.20

Facts for Marketers: Standard Metropolitan **Statistical** Areas in { } Regional Geographical Division, C 41.2:M 34/3

Federal Bureau of Prisons **Statistical** Tables, J 16.23/4

Federal Meat and Poultry Inspection, **Statistical** Summary for (year), A 101.6/3

Federal Meat Inspection, **Statistical** Summary for (year), A 88.40/2:54

Federal **Statistical** Directory, PrEx 2.10, C 1.75

Foreign Agricultural Trade of the United States, **Statistical** Report, A 93.17

Foreign Agricultural Trade **Statistical** Report, A 105.14/2

Foreign **Statistical** Publications, Accessions List, C 56.238

General Aviation Accidents (non-air carrier), **Statistical** Analysis, C 31.160/2, FAA 1.15

Grain Market News and **Statistical** Report, A 82.71, A 88.18

Healthy People 2000, **Statistical** Notes, HE 20.6230

Industrial Area **Statistical** Summaries, L 2.18

International Economic and Energy **Statistical** Review, ER-IEESR (series), PrEx 3.14/2

International Energy Biweekly **Statistical** Review, ER-IEBSR (series), PrEx 3.14

International Energy **Statistical** Review, ER-IESR (series), PrEx 3.14/2

International **Statistical** Congress, S 5.5

ISP {International **Statistical** Program} Supplemental Course Series, C 3.205/4

ISPO {International **Statistical** Program Office}, C 3.205/3

Maps of Major Concentrations of Poverty in Standard Metropolitan **Statistical** Areas of 250,000 or More Population, PrEx 10.2:P 86/9

Market Reviews and **Statistical** Summaries of Livestock, Meats and Wool, A 36.98

MCH **Statistical** Series, HE 20.5113

Medical Statistics, Navy, **Statistical** Report of the Surgeon General, Navy, Occurrence of Diseases and Injuries in the Navy for Fiscal Year (date), D 206.11

Mental Health Manpower, Current **Statistical** and Activities Reports, FS 2.54/3

Mental Health Service System Reports and **Statistical** Notes Publication Listing, HE 20.8113/5

Midyear Financial & **Statistical** Report, NCU 1.9/3-2

Monthly **Statistical** Release: Wines, T 70.9/5

New Drug Evaluation **Statistical** Report, HE 20.4211

News, Average Annual Pay by State and Standard Metropolitan **Statistical** Area, L 2.120/2-2

NIH **Statistical** Reference Book of International Activities, HE 20.3760

NLRB **Statistical** Summary Covering the Three Month Period, LR 1.15/3

OCS **Statistical** Series, I 72.12/9

Outer Continental Shelf **Statistical** Summary, I 72.12/3-3

Outpatient Psychiatric Clinics, Special **Statistical** Series Reports, FS 2.22/40

Packers and Stockyards **Statistical** Report, A 113.15

Peace Corps Volunteer, Quarterly **Statistical** Summary, S 19.11

Periodic Reports of Agricultural Economics, Economic Research Service, **Statistical** Reporting Service, A 1.99

Preliminary Monthly **Statistical** Report on EMIC Program, L 5.50, FS 3.208

Proceedings Annual **Statistical** Engineering Symposium, D 116.12

Progress Report, Interim **Statistical** Report, Pr 34.751

Public Assistance Recipients in Standard Metropolitan **Statistical** Areas, HE 3.61/2

Public Assistance, Annual **Statistical** Data, FS 14.212, FS 17.13, FS 17.615, HE 17.615

Public Use of National Parks, **Statistical** Report, I 29.63

Public Welfare Personnel, Annual **Statistical** Data, HE 17.629

Quarterly **Statistical** Brochure, HE 20.8212/4

Quarterly **Statistical** Bulletin, Electric Program, A 68.13/2

Quarterly **Statistical** Bulletin, Telephone Program, A 68.13/3

Quarterly **Statistical** Report, J 24.18/3

Registration, Employment and Unemployment, U.S. Zone, **Statistical** Report, W 1.72/3

Report of United States High Commissioner, **Statistical** Annex, U.S. Element, Allied Commission for Austria, S 1.89/2

Reports and **Statistical** Tables on Fur-Seal Investigations in Alaska, T 35.7

Review, **Statistical** Review of Ordnance Accident Experiment, W 34.42

RSI Quality Appraisal Awards and Disallowances Monthly **Statistical** Summary, HE 3.28/9

RSI Quality Appraisal Postadjudicative Monthly **Statistical** Summary, HE 3.28/8

Saint Marys Falls Canal, Michigan, **Statistical** Report of Lake Commerce Passing through Canals at Sault Ste. Marie, Michigan and Ontario, W 7.26, M 110.16, D 103.17

Schedule H. **Statistical** Classification and Code Numbers of Shipments of Merchandise to Alaska from United States, C 3.150:H

Schedule L. **Statistical** Classification of Foreign Merchandise Reports in In-transit Trade of United States, C 3.150:L

Schedule S. **Statistical** Classification of Domestic and Foreign Merchandise Exported from U.S., C 3.150:S

Schedule T. **Statistical** Classification of Imports into U.S. Arranged in Shipping Commodity GROUPS., C 3.150:T

Schedule W. **Statistical** Classification of U.S. Waterborne Exports and Imports, C 3.150:W

Schedule X. **Statistical** Classification of Domestic and Foreign Merchandise Exported from United States by Air Arranged in Shipping Commodity Groups, C 3.150:X

Schedule Y. **Statistical** Classification of Imports into United States Arranged in Shipping Commodity Groups, C 3.150:Y

SEC Monthly **Statistical** Review, SE 1.20

Selected **Statistical** Data by Sex, S 18.56

SL {**Statistical** Lists} (series), I 49.42

Social Security Bulletin, **Statistical** Supplement, HE 3.3/3

Special Analysis of Principal Federal **Statistical** Programs in Budget, PrEx 2.8/a6

Special **Statistical** Reports on United States Waterborne Commerce, C 3.203

State and Local Personnel Systems, Annual **Statistical** Report, CS 1.95

State and Metropolitan Area Data Book, A **Statistical** Supplement, C 3.134/5-2

State Reports Issued in Cooperation with **Statistical** Reporting Service, A 92.36

State **Statistical** and Economic Abstract Series, C 1.87

Statistical Schedule A. **Statistical** Classification on Commodities Imported into the United States with Rates of Duty and Tariff Paragraphs, C 3.150:A

Statistical Schedule B. **Statistical** Classification of Domestic and Foreign Commodities Exported from the United States, C 3.150:B

Statistical Abstract of the United States, C 3.134, C 3.134/7, C 56.243

Statistical Analysis of Carrier's Monthly Hours of Service Reports, IC 1 hou.9

Statistical Analysis of the World's Merchant Fleet, TD 11.12

Statistical Analysis of World's Merchant Fleets Showing Age, Size, Speed, and Draft by Frequency Groupings, As of (date), C 39.224

Statistical Analysis Report, ED 1.120/2, ED 1.328/5

Statistical Brief from the Bureau of the Census (series), C 3.205/8

Statistical Briefs (series), VA 1.74

Statistical Briefs from Around the World, C 3.205/2

Statistical Bulletins Bureau of Fisheries, C 6.5, I 45.8, I 49.8

Statistical Bulletins Department of Agriculture, A 1.34

Statistical Bulletins Farm Credit Administration, FCA 1.3/2

Statistical Bulletins Fish Commission, FC 1.5

Statistical Bulletins Military Government of Ryukyu Islands, D 102.19

Statistical Bulletins Office of Civil Defense, Pr 32.4425

Statistical Bulletins Philippine Islands, Commerce and Industry Bureau, W 49.52/5

Statistical Bulletins Rural Electrification Administration, A 68.13

Statistical Bulletins Securities and Exchange Commission, SE 1.20

Statistical Bulletins Work Projects Administration, FW 4.13

Statistical Bulletins Works Progress Administration, Y 3.W 89/2:58

Statistical Cards, L 5.25

Statistical Circulars, I 16.39, FS 5.39

Statistical Classification and Code Numbers of Shipments of Merchandise to Alaska from United States, C 3.150:H

Statistical Classification of Domestic and Foreign Commodities Exported from the United States, C 3.150:B

Statistical Classification of Domestic and Foreign Merchandise Exported from U.S., C 3.150:S

Statistical Classification of Foreign Merchandise Reports in In-Transit Trade of United States, C 3.150:L

Statistical Classification of Imports into U.S. Arranged in Shipping Commodity Groups, C 3.150:T

Statistical Classification of Imports into United States Arranged in Shipping Commodity Groups, C 3.150:Y

Statistical Classification of U.S. Waterborne Exports and Imports, C 3.150:W

Statistical Classification on Commodities Imported into the United States with Rates of Duty and Tariff Paragraphs, C 3.150:A

Statistical Compendium, I 28.37/6

Statistical Compendium on Alcohol and Health, HE 20.8317

Statistical Digests, C 55.316, I 49.32

Statistical Evaluation Reports, PrEx 2.13

Statistical Handbook of Civil Aviation, C 31.144

Statistical Letter, FS 2.11/3

Statistical Materials, Y 3.N 21/8:24

Statistical Notes for Health Planners, HE 20.6218

Statistical Notes National Clearinghouse on Aging, HE 23.3112

Statistical Notes National Institute of Mental Health, HE 20.3812

Statistical Notes Rehabilitation Services Administration, HE 17.114

Statistical Policy Working Papers, C 1.70, PrEx 2.28

Statistical Profile Series SP, C 3.228

Statistical Profile, Redevelopment Area Series, C 1.45

Statistical Profiles, Rural Redevelopment Areas, SP (Series), C 1.45/2

Statistical Programs of the United States Government, PrEx 2.10/3

Statistical Publications, A 55.60

Statistical Reference Book of International Activities, HE 20.3712

Statistical Report of Commerce Passing through Canals at Sault Ste. Marie, Mich. and Ontario, Salt Water Ship Movements for Season of (year), D 103.17/2

Statistical Report of Marine Commerce of Duluth-Superior Harbor, Minn. and Wis., D 103.13

Statistical Report on Social Services, Form FS-2069, Quarter Ended (date), FS 17.12, FS 17.628

Statistical Report, Annual Tabulations of Model Reporting Area for Blindness Statistics, FS 2.22/37-2

Statistical Report, Fiscal Year (date), J 16.2:P 93/3

Statistical Report, Great Lakes Pilotage, C 1.47:St 2

Statistical Report, J 1.55, J 16.23/5, J 31.10

Statistical Reporter, C 1.69, PrEx 2.11

Statistical Reports on Older Americans, HE 23.3112/2

Statistical Reports, FT 1.28

Statistical Series Annual Data, Data from the Drug Abuse Warning Network (DAWN) Series I, HE 20.8212/11

Statistical Series Children's Bureau, FS 3.214, FS 14.113, FS 17.213

Statistical Series Circulars, IC 1.4/3

Statistical Series Federal Power Commission, FP 1.21

Statistical Series National Institute on Drug Abuse, HE 20.8212, HE 20.8212/2, HE 20.8212/3, HE 20.8212/5, HE 20.8212/6

Statistical Series, Quarterly Report, HE 20.8212

Statistical Series Securities and Exchange Commission, SE Statistical Series, Annual Data, Data from the Drug Abuse Warning Network (DAWN), Series I, HE 20.8212/11

Statistical Series Social and Rehabilitation Service, HE 17.23

Statistical Series, Quarterly Report, Series D, HE 20.8212/2

Statistical Series, Reports, I 66.12

Statistical Series, Series A, HE 20.8212/5

Statistical Series, Series B, HE 20.8212/8

Statistical Series, Series C, HE 20.8212/9

Statistical Series, Series E, HE 20.8212/3

Statistical Series, Series F, HE 20.8212/6

Statistical Series, Series G, HE 20.8212/7

Statistical Series, Series H, HE 20.8212/10

Statistical Study of U.S. Civil Aircraft, C 31.160, FAA 1.32/2

Statistical Summaries {various commodity programs}, A 82.37/3

Statistical Summary and Analysis of Foreign Visitor Arrivals, U.S. Citizen and Non-U.S. Citizen Departures, C 47.15

Statistical Summary for Fish and Wildlife Restoration, I 49.29/4

Statistical Summary of Aid to Dependent Children of Unemployed Parents, FS 3.39/3

Statistical Summary of Municipal Water Facilities, FS 2.84

Statistical Summary of the Physical Research Program as of June 30 (year), Y 3.At 7:2 P 56/2

Statistical Summary, A 88.28

Statistical Summary, Railroad Retirement Board Operations, RR 1.11

Statistical Summary, Rural Areas Development and Area Redevelopment, Quarterly Progress Report, A 43.38

Statistical Supplement of Monthly Domestic Dairy Markets Review, A 88.13/2

Statistical Supplement to Monthly Egg and Poultry Market Review, A 88.13/4

Statistical Tables for the Federal Judiciary, Ju 10.21/2

Statistical Tables Showing Progress of Eradication of Brucellosis and Tuberculosis in Livestock in United States and Territories for Fiscal Year, A 77.212/3

Statistical Yearbook of the Immigration and Naturalization Service, J 21.2:St 2, J 21.2/2, J 21.2/10

Statistical Yearbook of the Quartermaster Corps, D 106.12

Statistical Yearbook, HH 1.38

Summary Characteristics for Governmental Units and Standard Metropolitan Statistical Areas (series), C 3.223/23:

Summary Report of the Commissioner, Bureau of Reclamation {and} Statistical Appendix, I 27.1/2

Supplement to State Court Model Statistical Dictionary, J 29.9/3

Supplements to Statistical Abstract of United States, C 3.134/2

Supplements to the Statistical Abstract of the United States, C 56.243/2

Survey and Reports Section Statistical Notes, HE 20.2424

Tables (Statistical), A 13.45

The USAF Statistical Digest, D 301.83/3

U.S. Foreign Agricultural Trade Statistical Report, A 93.17/3

U.S. Imports of Textiles and Apparel under the Multifiber Arrangement, Statistical Report, ITC 1.30

Union Recognition in the Federal Government, Statistical Summary, PM 1.47

United States Air Force Statistical Digest, D 301.112

United States Foreign Trade Statistical Publications, C 3.166

Urban Atlas, Tract Data for Standard Metropolitan Statistical Areas, C 3.62/7, C 56.242/4

USA Counties, a Statistical Abstract Supplement, C 3.134/6

VA Statistical Summary, VA 1.27

VD Statistical Letter, HE 20.7018/2, HE 20.7309

Weekly Statistical News, Y 3.W 19/2:36

Weekly Statistical Reports, Y 3.F 31/11:24

World Agricultural Production and Trade, Statistical Report, A 67.8/3

Statistics

Adult Basic and Secondary Level Program Statistics, Students and Staff Data, HE 19.319

Adult Basic Education Program Statistics (series), HE 5.97

Advance Data from the Vital and Health Statistics of NCHS, HE 20.6209/3

Advance Release of Statistics on Public Assistance, FS 3.14/2, FS 14.209, FS 17.10, FS 17.610

Advance Report Immigration Statistics: Fiscal Year, J 21.20

Agricultural Finance Statistics, AFS (series), A 93.9/10-2

Agricultural Statistics Board Catalog, A 92.35/2

Agriculture Statistics, A 1.47

Air Carrier Analytical Charts and Summaries, Including Supplemental Air Carrier Statistics, C 31.241/2

Air Carrier Financial Statistics, CAB 1.17, C 31.240

Air Carrier Industry Scheduled Service Traffic Statistics, CAB 1.39

Air Carrier Traffic Statistics, C 31.241, CAB 1.13

Airport Activity Statistics on Certificated Route Air Carriers, C 31.251, TD 4.14

Alaska Agriculture Statistics, A 92.48

Annual Cancer Statistics Review, HE 20.3186

Annual Conference of Model Reporting Area for Blindness Statistics, Proceedings, FS 2.22/37

Annual Medicare Program Statistics, HE 22.21/3

Annual Report of the United States National Committee on Vital and Health Statistics, HE 20.6211

Annual Reports on Statistics of Express Companies in the United States, IC 1 exp.1

Annual Reports on Statistics of Railways in United States, IC 1 ste.11

Annual Statistics, NCU 1.9/2

Annual Statistics on Workers Under Social Security, HE 3.40

Arrivals and Departures by Selected Ports Statistics of Foreign Visitor Arrivals and U.S. Citizen Departures Analyzed by U.S. Ports of Entry and Departure, C 47.15/4

Birth Still-Birth and Infant Mortality Statistics Annual Report, C 3.26

Boating Statistics, TD 5.11

Bulletin of Hardwood Market Statistics, A 13.79/3

Bureau of Justice Statistics Fiscal Year: At a Glance, J 29.1/2

Bureau of Labor Statistics Catalog of Publications, Bulletins, Reports, Releases, and Periodicals, L 2.34

Bureau of Labor Statistics Surveys, L 2.136

Business Statistics, C 59.11/3

Business Statistics, Biennial Supplement to Survey of Current Business, C 56.109/3

Business Statistics, Weekly Supplement, C 59.11/2

Business Statistics, Weekly Supplement to Survey of Current Business, C 56.109/2

Carload Waybill Statistics, Distribution of Freight Traffic and Revenue Averages by Commodity Classes, IC 1.23/8

Carload Waybill Statistics, Mileage Block Distribution, Traffic and Revenue by Commodity Class, Territorial Movement, and Type of Rate, Products of Agriculture, 1 Percent Sample of... MB-1, IC1.23/2

Carload Waybill Statistics, Quarterly Comparisons, Traffic and Revenue by Commodity Classes, IC 1.23

Carload Waybill Statistics, Statement TD-1, TD 1.22

Carload Waybill Statistics, Territorial Distribution Traffic and Revenue by Commodity Classes, TD 3.14

Carload Waybill Statistics, Traffic and Revenue Progressions by Specified Mileage Blocks for Commodity Groups and Classes, 1 Percent Sample of Carload Terminations in Year Statement MB-6, IC 1.23/7

Carload Waybill Statistics,..., Traffic and Revenue by Commodity Class, Territorial Movement, and Type of Rate, Animals and Products, 1 Percent Sample of Terminations in Statement MB-2, IC 1.23/3

Carload Waybill Statistics,..., Traffic and Revenue by Commodity Class, Territorial Movement, and Type of Rate, Products of Mines, 1 Percent Sample of Terminations in Statement MB-3, IC 1.23/4

Carload Waybill Statistics,..., Traffic and Revenue by Commodity Class, Territorial Movement, and Type of Rate, Products of Forests, 1 Percent Sample of Terminations in Statement MB-4, IC 1.23/5

Carload Waybill Statistics,..., Traffic and Revenue by Commodity Class, Territorial Movement, and Type of Rate, Manufacturers and Miscellaneous Forwarder Traffic, One Percent Sampling... MB-5, IC 1.23/6

Catalog of Publications of the National Center for Health Statistics, HE 20.6216/4

Catalog of Seminars, Training Programs and Technical Assistance in Labor Statistics, L 2.114

Catalogue of Publications of the National Center for Health Statistics, HE 20.6216:C 29

Census of Construction Industries; Area Statistics, C 56.254/4

Census of Distribution Industry Statistics, C 3.245/6

Census of Housing; Block Statistics, C 3.224/5

Census of Population and Housing Block Statistics, C 3.282/3

Census of Retail Trade Nonemployer Statistics Series, C 3.255/7

Census of Retail Trade; Area Statistics (series), C 56.251/2

Census of Retail Trade; Geographic Area Statistics, C 3.255/2

Census of Retail Trade; Geographic Area Statistics, Advance Reports, C 3.255/2-2

Census of Retail Trade; Major Retail Centers Statistics, C 3.255/5

Census of Selected Service Industries; Area Statistics Series, C 56.253/3

Census of Service Industries Nonemployer Statistics Series, C 3.257/5

Central Business District Statistics Bulletin CBD (series), C 3.202/13

CHAMPUS Chartbook of Statistics, D 1.82

Child Welfare Statistics, HE 17.638

Civilian Manpower Statistics, D 1.61/2

Collective Bargaining Agreements Received by Bureau of Labor Statistics, L 2.45

Commodity Classification for Compiling Statistics on Shipments from U.S., C 3.140:Q

Commodity Statistics, A 1.73

Commuter Air Carrier Traffic Statistics, C 31.241/3, CAB 1.11

Company Statistics Bulletins, Census of Business, Manufactures and Mineral Industries, C 3.222

Company **Statistics** Series (Economic Census), C 3.277/3

Comparative **Statistics** of General Assistance Operations of Public Agencies in Selected Large Cities, FS 3.16

Consolidated of Schedule B Commodity Classifications for Use in Presentation of U.S. Export **Statistics**, C 3.150:G

Containerzied Cargo **Statistics**, C 39.233, TD 11.21

Continerized Cargo **Statistics**, C 39.233

Cotton Price **Statistics**, A 88.11/9, A 82.13

Cotton Price **Statistics**, Monthly Averages, A 80.128

Cotton Quality **Statistics**, A 1.34

Credit Union **Statistics**, NCU 1.9

Cuba, Handbook of Trade **Statistics**, PrEx 3.20

Current Employment **Statistics** State Operating Manual, L 2.46/4

Current Fisheries **Statistics** CFS (series), C 55.309/ 2

Current Fishery **Statistics**, I 49.8/2

Current Listing and Topical Index to the Vital and Health **Statistics** Series, HE 20.2202:V 83

Current **Statistics** of Relief in Rural and Town Areas, Y 3.W 89/2:25, SS 1.23

Dairy and Poultry Market **Statistics** Annual Summaries, A 1.34, A 36.54, A 66.35

DEA Drug Enforcement **Statistics** Report, J 24.18/2

Digest of Educational **Statistics**, ED 1.326, HE 19.315

Disability **Statistics** Abstract, ED 1.215/4

Disability **Statistics** Report (series), ED 1.84

Educational **Statistics**, ED 1.328/13

EIA Personal Computer Products, International Coal **Statistics** Database, E 3.11/7-11

Election **Statistics**, Y 1.2/10

Electric Power **Statistics**, FP 1.24, FP 1.27, E 3.18

Electricity Sales **Statistics**, Y 3.T 25:13

Electricity Sales **Statistics**, Distribution of Electricity at TVA Wholesale and Retail Rates, Y 3.T 25:13-2

Electricity Sales **Statistics**: Rate of Initial Service at TVA Rates and Wholesale Purchases from TVA, Y 3.T 25:13-2

Employment and Earnings **Statistics** for the United States, L 2.3

Employment Service **Statistics**, L 7.18/2-2, L 1.60

Enterprise **Statistics**, C 3.226, C 56.228

Enterprise **Statistics**, Preliminary Reports, C 3.230/ 2

ES 3 Enterprise **Statistics**, C 3.230

Facts of Life and Death, Selected **Statistics** on Nation's Health and People, FS 2.102:H 34

Fall (year) **Statistics** of Public Schools, Advance Report, HE 5.93/5, HE 5.220:20119

Farmer Cooperative **Statistics**, A 109.11/2

FDIC **Statistics** on Banking, Y 3.F 31/8:1-2

Federal Civilian Work Force **Statistics** , PM 1.10/2, PM 1.15, CS 1.55/2

Federal Civilian Work Force **Statistics**, Occupations of Federal Blue-Collar Workers, PM 1.10:Sm 59-11

Federal Civilian Work Force **Statistics**, Occupations of Federal White-Collar Workers, PM 1.10:Sm 56-13

Federal Employment **Statistics** Bulletin, CS 1.55

Federal Judicial Caseload **Statistics** JU 10.21

Federal Judicial Workload **Statistics**, Ju 10.2:W 89, Ju 10.21

Federal Justice **Statistics** Program, J 29.30

Federal Milk Order Market **Statistics**, A 88.14/11

Federal Milk Order Market **Statistics**, Summary, A 82.81

Federal Offshore **Statistics**, Leasing, Exploration, Production, Revenue, I 72.10

Federal Reserve Chart Book on Financial and Business **Statistics**, FR 1.30

Federal **Statistics**, PrEx 2.10/2

Federal-Aid Highway Relocation Assistance and Payment **Statistics**, TD 2.28

Feed Market News, Weekly Summary and **Statistics**, A 88.18/4

FHA Research and **Statistics** Release, HH 2.18/3

Field Studies and **Statistics** Program, HE 20.3178

Financial and Operating **Statistics**, Class I Railroads, IC 1 ste.19/4

Financial **Statistics** for Public Assistance, Calendar Year, FS 3.14/3

Financial **Statistics** of Cities, C 3.142

Financial **Statistics** of Cities Having a Population of Over 30,000, C 3.47

Financial **Statistics** of Cities Having a Population of Over 100,000, C 3.47/2

Financial **Statistics** of Electric Utilities and Interstate Natural Gas Pipeline Companies, E 3.11/2-8

Financial **Statistics** of Institutions of Higher Education, HE 19.316/2-2, ED 1.116

Financial **Statistics** of Institutions of Higher Education, Current Funds, Revenues, and Expenditures, HE 19.316/2

Financial **Statistics** of Institutions of Higher Education: Property, HE 19.316

Financial **Statistics** of Major Investor-Owned Electric Utilities, E 3.18/4-2

Financial **Statistics** of Major U.S. Publicly Owned Electric Utilities, E 3.18/4-3

Financial **Statistics** of Selected Electric Utilities, E 3.18/4

Financial **Statistics** of Selected Investor-Owned Electric Utilities, E 3.18/4-2

Financial **Statistics** of Selected Publicly Owned Electric Utilities, E 3.18/4-3

Financial **Statistics** of State and Local Government, C 3.49, C 3.49/2

Financial **Statistics** of State Governments, C 3.29

Financial **Statistics** of States, C 3.48, C 3.141

Fishery **Statistics** of the United States, C 55.316

Foreign Petroleum **Statistics**, C 18.86, C 18.86/2

Foreign **Statistics** on Apples and Other Deciduous Fruits, A 67.12

Foreign Trade **Statistics** Notes, C 3.167

Forest Fire **Statistics**, A 13.32/2

Forest **Statistics** Series (by States), A 13.42/21

Freight Commodity **Statistics** of Class I Railroads in the United States, IC 1 ste.26

Freight Commodity **Statistics**, Class I Railroads in the United States for Year Ended December 31 (date), IC 1 ste.29

Generation and Sales **Statistics**, I 44.8

GEO-Drug Enforcement Program Six-month **Statistics**, J 24.18

Geographic Area **Statistics**, C 3.24/9-9

Grain Market News, Quarterly Summary and **Statistics**, A 88.18/21

Guide to Foreign Trade **Statistics**, (year), C 56.210/ 2

Handbook of Airline **Statistics**, C 31.249

Handbook of Economic **Statistics**, S 1.91/3

Handbook of Labor **Statistics**, L 2.3

Handbook of Merchant Shipping **Statistics**, C 39.218

Handbook of Old-Age and Survivors Insurance **Statistics**, FS 3.40

Health and Safety **Statistics**, I 28.26

Health Care Financing Program **Statistics**, HE 22.19/4-2

Health Insurance **Statistics**, HE 3.28/5

Health Insurance **Statistics**, CMS (series), FS 3.28/ 4, HE 3.28/4

Health Insurance **Statistics**: Current Medicare Survey Report, HE 3.28/4

Health Manpower **Statistics**, D 1.62/2

Health Resources **Statistics**, HE 20.6212

Health **Statistics** from the U.S. National Health Survey, FS 2.85

Health **Statistics** Plan, HE 20.16

Health **Statistics** Report, Fiscal Year (date), HE 20.16/2

Healthy People 2000 **Statistics** and Surveillance, HE 20.7040

Highway **Statistics**, TD 2.23

Highway **Statistics** Summary, TD 2.23/2

Historical **Statistics** (series), I 49.8/5

Historical **Statistics** of the United States, Colonial Times to 1970, C 3.134/2:H 62

Historical **Statistics** on Banking, Y 3.F 31/8:26

How to Use Injury **Statistics** to Prevent Occupational Accidents, L 16.42

Index to Research Reports and Research and **Statistics** Notes, FS 3.49/2

Indian Vital **Statistics**, FS 2.86/5, HE 20.2660

International Population **Statistics** Reports, C 56.112

International Population **Statistics** Reports, P 90-(series), C 59.13/2:90

International Trade **Statistics** Series, C 42.9/3

International Training Programs in Labor **Statistics**, L 2.128

Issues in Labor **Statistics**, L 2.132

Japanese Economic **Statistics** Bulletin, D 102.14

Journal of Transportation and **Statistics**, TD 12.18

Juvenile Court **Statistics**, FS 17.213, HE 17.23, J 1.53

Labor **Statistics** Series, L 2.72

Library **Statistics** of Colleges and Universities, HE 19.338, ED 1.122, ED 1.222/3

Library **Statistics** of Colleges and Universities; Analytic Report, FS 5.215:15031, HE 5.215:15031

Library **Statistics** of Colleges and Universities; Fall (year) Summary Data, HE 19.338

Library **Statistics** of Colleges and Universities; Fall (year), Part C, Analytic Report, HE 5.92/7

Library **Statistics** of Colleges and Universities; Institutional Data, FS 5.215:15023, HE 5.215:15023

List of Reports and Publications Relating to Vital **Statistics**, C 3.137

Livestock, Meat, Wool, Market News, Weekly Summary and **Statistics**, A 88.16/4

Livestock, Meats, and Wool, Market **Statistics** and Related Data, A 66.36

Livestock, Meats, and Wool; Market Review and **Statistics**, A 66.13, A 75.10, A 78.11, A 80.111, A 80.811, A 81.11, A 82.7

Management **Statistics** for United States Courts, Ju 10.14

Manual of Finance and **Statistics** Memorandum, FS 6.17

Manual of Finance and **Statistics** Memorandum of National Youth Administration, Pr 32.5258

Marine Recreational Fishery **Statistics** Survey, Atlantic and Gulf Coasts, C 55.309/2-3

Marine Recreational Fishery **Statistics** Survey, Pacific Coast, C 55.309/2-5

Market News, Livestock Division, Market Reviews and **Statistics**, A 88.16/4

Market News, Livestock Division, Market Reviews and **Statistics**, A 88.16/4

MCHS **Statistics** Series, HE 20.2760

Medicaid **Statistics**, HE 22.13

Medicaid **Statistics**, Program and Financial **Statistics**, HE 22.115

Medical **Statistics** Bulletins, Y 3.Se 4:15

Medical **Statistics**, Navy, Statistical Report of the Surgeon General, Navy, Occurrence of Diseases and Injuries in the Navy for Fiscal Year (date), D 206.11

Medicare Program **Statistics**, HE 22.21/2

Medicare Program **Statistics**, Medicare Utilization, HE 22.21/2-2

Merchant Marine **Statistics**, C 11.10, C 25.10, T 17.10

Mid-Year **Statistics**, NCU 1.9/3

Monthly Commodity Futures **Statistics** on Futures Trading in Commodities Regulated under the Commodity Exchange Act, A 85.15/2

Monthly Vital **Statistics** Bulletins, C 3.127

Monthly Vital **Statistics** Report, HE 20.6009, HE 20.6217

National Criminal Justice Information and **Statistics** Service, J 1.37

National Criminal Justice Information and Statistics Service, **Statistics** Center Report, J 1.37/ 2

National Criminal Justice Information and **Statistics** Service: {reports}, J 26.10

National Prisoner **Statistics**, J 16.23

National Prisoner **Statistics** Bulletin, J 1.33/5

National Transportation **Statistics**, Annual Report, TD 10.9, TD 12.1/2

National Urban Mass Transportation **Statistics**, TD 7.11/2

Navy Military Personnel **Statistics**, D 208.25

NCH **Statistics** Series, HE 20.5113

NCHS Health Interview **Statistics**, Publications from the National Health Interview Survey, Advance Data Reports, HE 20.6216/5

Negro **Statistics** Bulletin, C 3.131

News Bulletin of Social **Statistics** in Child Welfare and Related Fields, L 5.31

News of the Cooperative Health **Statistics** System, HE 20.6213

Occupational Safety and Health **Statistics** of the Federal Government, L 35.13

Occupational **Statistics**, C 3.37/31

Office of Research and **Statistics**: Staff Papers, HE 3.56

Old-Age Insurance Operating **Statistics** Review, SS 1.33

Operating **Statistics** of Class 1 Steam Roads, Freight and Passenger Service, IC 1 ste.21

Operating **Statistics** of Large Railroads, Selected Items, IC 1 ste.22

P-90 International Population **Statistics** Reports, C 3.205

Passenger Traffic **Statistics** (other than commutation) of Class I Steam Railways in the United States Separated Between Coach Traffic and Parlor and Sleeping Car Traffic, IC 1 ste.39

Performance Monitoring System: Summary of Lock **Statistics**, D 103.57/12

Personnel **Statistics** Reports, CS 1.33

Petroleum Refinery **Statistics**, I 28.17, I 28.18

Petroleum **Statistics**, I 22.9, I 22.9/2

Poison Control **Statistics**, HE 20.4019

Postal Union Transit **Statistics**, P 8.7

Preliminary Abstract of **Statistics** of Railway **Statistics**, IC 1.14

Preliminary General **Statistics**, C 3.24/8-3

Preliminary **Statistics** of State School Systems, FS 5.220:20006, HE 5.220:20006, HE 5.93/4

President's Commission on Federal **Statistics**, Pr 37.8:St 2

Proceedings Annual Conference of Model Reporting Area for Blindness **Statistics**, FS 2.22/37

Proceedings Annual Conference on Model Reporting Area for Mental Hospital **Statistics**, FS 2.22/44

Proceedings Interstate Conference on Labor **Statistics**, L 2.80

Proceedings Public Health Conference on Records and **Statistics**, FS 2.122, HE 20.2214, HE 20.6214

Processed Fishery **Statistics**, Annual Summary, C 55.309/2-9

Productivity **Statistics** for Federal Government Functions, Fiscal Year, L 2.119/2

Projections of Educational **Statistics**, HE 19.320, ED 1.120

Proposed Multi-Year Operating Plan, **Statistics** of Income Division, T 22.2/3, T 22.2/10

Public Assistance **Statistics**, HE 3.60, HE 17.610

Public Assistance, Quarterly Review of **Statistics** for U.S., SS 1.13

Public Assistance, **Statistics** for U.S., SS 1.25/a 1

Public Elementary and Secondary Education **Statistics**: School Year, ED 1.328/12

Public Health Conference on Records and **Statistics**, National Meeting Announcement, HE 20.6214/2

Public Health Conference on Records and **Statistics**, Proceedings, FS 2.122

Public Land **Statistics**, I 53.1/2

Publications Bureau of Labor **Statistics**, L 2.71

Publications National Center for Education **Statistics**, HE 19.317:P 96

Quarterly Benefit **Statistics** Report, RR 1.16

Quarterly Nonimmigrant **Statistics**, J 21.2/10-2

Quarterly Public Assistance **Statistics**, HE 3.60/4, HE 25.15

Quarterly Summary of **Statistics** of Operations, L 22.20

Record Book of Business **Statistics**, C 3.33/2

Regional Labor **Statistics** Bulletin, L 2.71/7

Research and **Statistics** Legislative Notes, FS 3.28/3

Research and **Statistics** Letters, FS 3.28

Research and **Statistics** Notes, HE 3.28/2, HE 22.17

Research Reports Economics, **Statistics**, and Cooperatives Service, A 105.31

Reserve Manpower **Statistics**, D 1.61/7

Revenue Traffic **Statistics** of Class I Railroads in the United States, IC 1 ste.24

Revenues, Expenses, and **Statistics** of Class 1 Motor Carriers of Passengers, IC 1 mot.11

Revenues, Expenses, and **Statistics** of Class 1 Motor Carriers of States, IC 1 ste.24

Revenues, Expenses, and **Statistics** of Freight Forwarders, IC 1.19

Revenues, Expenses, Other Income, and **Statistics** of Class 1 Motor Carriers of Passengers, IC 1 mot.12

Revenues, Expenses, Other Income, and **Statistics** of Large Motor Carriers of Property, IC 1 mot.13

SAR **Statistics**, TD 5.50

Schedule G. Consolidation of Schedule B Commodity Classifications for Use in Presentation of U.S. Export **Statistics**, C 3.150:G

Schedule Q. Commodity Classification for Compiling **Statistics** on Shipments from U.S., C 3.150:Q

Scientific Manpower, Significant Developments, Views and **Statistics**, NS 1.14

Selected Manpower **Statistics**, D 1.61/4

Selected Medical Care **Statistics**, D 1.62

Selected Revenues, Expenses, Other Income, and **Statistics** of Class II Carriers of Property, IC 1 mot.13/2

Selected **Statistics** for Class 3 Motor Carriers of Property, IC 1 mot.14/2

Series Available and Estimating Methods, BLS Current Employment **Statistics** Program, L 2.124/2

Sexually Transmitted Disease **Statistics**, HE 20.7309

Small-Area **Statistics** Papers, C 3.238/2

Small-Area **Statistics**, C 56.217/2

Social **Statistics** in Child Welfare and Related Fields, L 5.27

Social **Statistics**, L 5.36

Sourcebook of Criminal Justice **Statistics**, J 1.42/3, J 29.9/6, J 29.9/6-2

Special Reports Justice **Statistics** Bureau, J 29.13

State Park **Statistics**, I 29.68

Statistical Report, Annual Tabulations of Model Reporting Area for Blindness **Statistics**, FS 2.22/37-2

Statistics and Agriculture, A 36.134

Statistics Bulletins, HH 1.11

Statistics Concerning Indian Education, Fiscal Year, I 20.46

Statistics for (year) on Blindness in the Model Reporting Area, HE 20.3759

Statistics for Industry Groups and Industries, C 3.24/9-7

Statistics in Brief, ED 1.328/4

Statistics of American Listed Corporations, SE 1.17/3

Statistics of Bituminous Coal Loaded for Shipment on Railroads and Waterways As Reported by Operators, I 28.34

Statistics of Capital Movements Between U.S. and Foreign Countries, T 62.9

Statistics of Class 1 Motor Carriers, IC 1 mot.14

Statistics of Class a Telephone Carriers Reporting Annually to the Commission, As of December 31 (year) and for Year Then Ended, CC 1.14/2

Statistics of Communications Common Carriers, CC 1.35

Statistics of Diseases and Injuries in Navy, N 10.15, M 203.10

Statistics of Education in the United States, FS 5.220:20032, HE 5.220:20032

Statistics of Electric Utilities in the United States, Classes A and B Publicly Owned Companies, FP 1.21

Statistics of Farmer Cooperatives, A 89.19

Statistics of Income, Corporation Income Tax Returns Documentation Guides, T 22.35/7

Statistics of Income, Corporation Income Tax Returns, T 22.35/5

Statistics of Income, Final Volumes, T 22.35/2

Statistics of Income, Partnership Returns, T 22.35/6

Statistics of Income, Preliminary Reports, T 22.35/3

Statistics of Income, T 22.35

Statistics of Interstate Natural Gas Pipeline Companies, E 3.25

Statistics of Land-Grant Colleges and Universities, FS 5.250:50002, HE 5.250:5002

Statistics of Local Public School Systems Fall (year), HE 5.93/8

Statistics of Local Public School Systems Pupils and Staff, HE 19.318/4

Statistics of Local Public School Systems, Finance, (year), HE 19.318/2

Statistics of Navy Medicine, D 206.15

Statistics of Nonpublic Elementary and Secondary Schools, (year), HE 5.93/9

Statistics of Nonpublic Elementary Schools, FS 5.220:20064

Statistics of Principal Domestic and International Telegraph Carriers Reporting to the Commission As of December 31 (year) and for Year Then Ended, CC 1.41

Statistics of Privately Owned Electric Utilities in the United States, E 3.18/2

Statistics of Public Elementary and Secondary Day Schools, HE 19.326

Statistics of Public Libraries, ED 1.122/2

Statistics of Public Library Systems Serving Populations of 100,000 or more, FS 5.215:15033, HE 5.215:15033

Statistics of Public Library Systems Serving Populations of 50,000-99,999, FS 5.215:15034, HE 5.215:15034

Statistics of Public Library Systems Serving Populations of 35,000-49,999, FS 5.215:15035, HE 5.215:15035

Statistics of Public School Libraries, FS 5.215:51049, HE 5.215:15049

Statistics of Public School Systems in Twenty Largest U.S. Cities, ED 1.112/4

Statistics of Public Schools, Advance Report, Fall, HE 19.318

Statistics of Publicly Owned Electric Utilities in the United States, E 3.18/3

Statistics of State School Systems, HE 19.318/3

Statistics of the Communications Industry in the United States, CC 1.35

Statistics of Trends in Education, HE 19.302:St 2/2

Statistics on Banking, Y 3.F 31/8:1-2

Statistics on Manpower, Supplement to Manpower Report of the President, L 1.42/2-2

Statistics on Pupil Transportation, FS 5.220:20022, HE 5.220;20022

Statistics Research Analysis Microfiles Catalog, HE 3.38/4

Statistics Technical Reports, J 1.40

Statistics, Distributors of TVA Power Fiscal Years, Y 3.T 25:1-18

Sugar Market **Statistics**, A 92.41, A 105.53

Summary of Air Carrier **Statistics**, C 31.240/2

Summary of Emergency Relief **Statistics**, Y 3.F 31/5:34

Summary of Passport **Statistics**, S 1.27/2

Summary **Statistics** Project Data, I 27.1/4-2

Summary **Statistics**, Finances and Physical Features, I 27.1/4-3

Summary **Statistics**, Water, Land and Related Data, I 27.1/4

Supplement to Carload Waybill **Statistics**, IC 1.23/20

Supplements to the Monthly Vital **Statistics** Report, HE 20.6209:24

Supreme Commander for Allied Powers: Japanese Economic **Statistics** Bulletin, D 102.18

Survey of Procurement **Statistics**, D 201.6/14

Tables of Bankruptcy **Statistics**, Ju 10.9

Tabulation of **Statistics** Pertaining to Block Signals and Telegraph and Telephone for Transmission of Train Orders, IC 1 blo.5

Tabulations of **Statistics** Pertaining to Signals, Interlocking, Automatic, Train Control, Telegraph and Telephone for Transmission of Train Orders, and Spring Switches As Used on Railroads of United States, IC 1 saf.10

Technical Appendix from Vital **Statistics** of the United States, HE 20.6210/a

Transport **Statistics** in the United States, IC 1.25

Trend Analyses and Related **Statistics**, T 22.2:T 72

Tuberculosis **Statistics**, (year), States and Cities (date), HE 20.7013

U.S. Automotive Trade **Statistics**, Series A: Motor Vehicles, ITC 1.16

U.S. Automotive Trade **Statistics**, Series B, Passenger Automobiles, ITC 1.16/2

U.S. Great Lakes Ports, **Statistics** for Overseas and Canadian Waterborne Commerce, TD 6.10

U.S. International Air Travel **Statistics**, Calendar Year, TD 1.40/3

U.S. International Air Travel **Statistics**, Fiscal Year, TD 1.40/2

U.S. International Air Travel **Statistics**, TD 1.40

U.S. Timber Production, Trade, Consumption, and Price **Statistics**, A 13.113

Unemployment Insurance **Statistics**, L 1.62/2, L 37.12

United States Foreign Trade **Statistics** Publications, C 3.166

United States Foreign Trade **Statistics**, C 18.185

USA **Statistics** in Brief, C 3.134/2:St 2, C 3.134/2-2

U.S. Foreign Waterborne Transportation **Statistics** Quarterly, TD 11.35

Vital and Health **Statistics**, HE 20.6209

Vital and Health **Statistics**, Series 1, HE 20.6209:1

Vital **Statistics** Bulletin, FS 2.110

Vital **Statistics** of Latin America, C 18.160

Vital **Statistics** of the United States, HE 20.6210, C 3.139

Vital **Statistics**, Special Reports (abstracts), C 3.67/2

Vital **Statistics**, Special Reports, C 3.67

Wage **Statistics** of Class 1 Railroads in the United States, IC 1 ste.25

Weekly Petroleum **Statistics** Reports, FE 1.9/3

Wildfire **Statistics**, A 13.32/2

World Petroleum **Statistics**, I 28.91

Stats

Offshore **Stats**, I 72.18

Status

Designation **Status** Reports, C 46.14

ASCS Aerial Photography **Status** Maps, A 82.84:Ae 8

Budget **Status** Report, TD 1.34

Bureau of Land Management Maps, Surface and Minerals Management **Status**, Scale 1:100,000, I 53.11/4-2

Changes in **Status** of Banks and Branches During Month, Name and Location of Banks and Branches, FR 1.33/2

Construction **Status** Report, Nuclear Power Plants, Data for Decisions, Y 3.N 88:16

Critical Project **Status** Report, E 2.14

Cumulative Price and **Status** Change Report, GP 3.22/3-4

Draft Environmental **Status** Report, EP 1.57/6

Emergency Relief Appropriation Acts, Reports of President to Congress Showing **Status** of Funds and Operations Under, T 63.114

Emergency Relief Appropriation Acts, Reports Showing **Status** of Funds, T 63.107

Emergency Relief Appropriation Acts, Reports Showing **Status** of Funds and Analyses to Expenditures, T 63.109

FAS Report, **Status** of U.S. Sugar Import Quotas, A 67.42/2

Foreign Credits by United States Government, **Status** of Active Foreign Credits of United States Government and of International Organizations, T 1.45

General Summary of Inventory **Status** and Movement of Capital and Producers Goods, Plants, Aircraft, and Industry Agent Items, Pr 33.210

Hearing Process **Status** Report (White Book), E 2.14/2

HUD Solar **Status**, HH 1.69

Inventory Report of Jurisdictional **Status** of Federal Areas Within the States, As of June 30, GS 1.15/3

Legal **Status** of Homemakers in {various States}, Y 3.W 84:9

Legal **Status** of Women in the United States, L 36.103

Legislative **Status** Report, VA 1.58

Licensed Fuel Facility **Status** Report, Y 3.N 88:28

Licensee Contractor and Vendor Inspection **Status** Report, Y 3.N 88:24

Life Sciences **Status** Reports, NAS 1.62

Marital Status and Family **Status**, C 3.186:P-20

National Direct Student Loan **Status** of Default as of (date), ED 1.40

National **Status** and Trends Program for Marine Environmental Quality, C 55.436/2

National **Status** and Trends Program for Marine Environmental Quality, FY Program Description, C 55.436/3

National **Status** and Trends Program, Water Quality Cruise Data Reports (series), C 55.436, C 55.436/4

NOAA National **Status** and Trends Program and Quality Assurance Program for Marine Environmental Measurements, C 55.434

Operating Units **Status** Report, Licensed Operations Reactors Data for Decisions, Y 3.N 88:15

Planning **Status** Reports, FP 1.29

Product/Activity **Status** Bulletin, C 3.238/6

Project on the **Status** and Education of Women, Field Evaluation Draft, ED 1.42/2

Public Works Administration of Federal Works Agency, Reports Showing **Status** of Funds and Analyses of Expenditures, T 63.108

Quarterly **Status** of Department of Energy Projects, E 1.35/3

Regulatory Licensing **Status** Summary Reports, Y 3.N 88:44

Regulatory Licensing, **Status** Summary Report, Systematic Evaluation Program, Y 3.N 88:29

Report on Progress in (year) of the **Status** of Women, Y 3.In 8/21:1

Report on **Status** of Multiple Use and Joint Development, TD 2.121

Report to the Congress on the **Status** of the Public Ports of the United States, TD 11.30

Report to the President and Congress on the **Status** of Health Personnel in the United States, HE 20.9310

Report to the President and Congress on the **Status** of Health Professions Personnel in the United States, HE 20.6619

Reports of President to Congress Showing **Status** of Funds and Operations under Emergency Relief Appropriation Acts, T 63.114

Reports Showing Financial **Status** of Funds Provided in Emergency Relief Appropriation Acts, T 60.11

Reports Showing **Status** of Funds and Analyses of Expenditures, Emergency Appropriation Acts, T 60.13

Reports Showing **Status** of Funds and Analyses of Expenditures, Public Works Administration Federal Works Agency, T 60.14

Reports Showing **Status** of Funds Provided in Emergency Relief Appropriation Acts, T 60.12

Research Results Utilization, Research Project Control System, **Status** Summary Report, Y 3.N 88:36

Resource **Status** Reports, I 49.67

Selected Multifamily **Status** Reports, Mortgage Insurance Programs by Name and Location of Each Project, HH 1.50

Smoking and Health, a National **Status** Report, HE 20.7613

Soil and Water Conservation Districts, **Status** of Organization, by States, Approximate Acreage, and Farms in Organized Districts, A 57.32

Standards Development **Status** Summary Report, Y 3.N 88:32

Status and Progress Reports, Releases, A 61.19

Status of Active Foreign Credits of the United States Government: Foreign Credits by United States Government Agencies, T 1.45/2

Status of CAA Releases, Manuals, and Regulations, C 31.151

Status of Children, HE 23.1009

Status of Civil Air Regulations and Civil Aeronautics Manuals, FAA 1.18

Status of Compliance, Public School districts, 17 Southern and Border States, Reports, FS 5.80, HE 5.80

Status of Federal Aviation Regulations, New, TD 4.13

Status of Handicapped Children in Head Start Programs, HE 23.1012

Status of Open Recommendations Improving Operations of Federal Departments and Agencies, GA 1.13/18

Status of Perkins Loan Default, ED 1.40/4

Status of Slum-Clearance and Low-Rent Housing Projects, I 40.7

Status of Strategic Petroleum Reserve Activities as of (date), GA 1.13/3

Status of the Department of Energy's Implementation of Nuclear Waste Policy Act, GA 1.13/10

Status of the Nation's Local Public Transportation, Conditions and Performance, Report to Congress, TD 7.18

Status of Vessel Construction and Reconditioning under Merchant Marine Acts of 1920 and 1938, SB 7.5:1105, C 27.9/8

Status of Waterfowl & Fall Flight Forecast, I 49.100/3

Status Report of the Energy-Related Inventions Program, C 13.72

Status Report of the Operation and Maintenance of Sanitation Facilities Serving American Indians and Alaska Natives, HE 20.9416

Status Report of the U.S. Treasury-Owned Gold, T 63.131

Status Report on Water and Power Resources Service Programs Within (various States), I 27.74

Status Report, Voluntary and Non-Profit Agency Technical Crop Ration Contracts with International Cooperation Administration, S 17.41/2

Status Report, Y 3.F 31/15:10

Status Report: Workable Program for Community Improvement, HH 1.47

Status, a Monthly Chartbook of Social and Economic Trends, C 3.251

Topical Report Review **Status**, Y 3.N 88:34

Topographic Mapping, **Status** and Progress of Operations, I 19.95

TSCA **Status** Report for Existing Chemicals, EP 5.15/4

U.S. Trade **Status** with Communist Countries, C 57.28, C 57.413, C 61.22

Waterfowl **Status** Report, I 49.15/3, I 49.100/2

Weekly Petroleum **Status** Report, E 1.63, E 3.32

Woodcock **Status** Report, I 49.15/3

Stat-USA

Stat-USA: The Newsletter, C 1.91/2

Statutes

Aeronautical **Statutes** and Related Material, Federal Aviation Act of 1958 and Other Provisions Relating to Civil Aeronautics, C 31.205:Ae 8

Annotated Manual of **Statutes** and Regulations of the Federal Home Loan Bank Board, FHL 1.6/2:St 2

Current Laws, **Statutes** and Executive Orders, EP 1.5:L 44

Federal Energy Guidelines: **Statutes** and Regulations, E 2.18

FERC **Statutes** and Regulations, Proposed Regulations, E 2.18/3

FERC **Statutes** and Regulations, Regulations Preambles, E 2.18/2

Headings and Subheads for Index to Federal **Statutes**, LC 10.6

How to Find U.S. **Statutes** and U.S. Code Citations, GS 4.102:St 2

Index Analysis of Federal **Statutes**, LC 10.5

Index of EPA Legal Authority **Statutes** and Legislative History, Executive Orders, Regulations, EP 1.5/4

Interpretation of War **Statutes**, Bulletins, J 1.17

Legal Compilation, **Statutes** and Legislative History, Executive Orders, Regulations, Guidelines and Reports, EP 1.5/3

Revised **Statutes**, S 7.10

Statutes and Court Decisions, FT 1.13

Statutes and Decisions Pertaining to the Federal Trade Commission, FT 1.13/2

Statutes at Large, S 7.9

Trademark Rules of Practice of the Patent Office, with Forms and **Statutes**, C 21.14:T 67/2

U.S. **Statutes** Concerning the Registration of Prints and Labels, C 21.7/3

U.S. **Statutes** Concerning the Registration of Trademarks, C 21.7/2

United States **Statutes** at Large, GS 4.111, AE 2.111

Statutory

Prime Contract Awards by **Statutory** Authority, Number of Actions, and Net Value by Department, D 1.57/3-2

Statutory Debt Limitation As of, T 63.208

Stay-in-School

National **Stay-in-School** Campaign, L 1.36

STD

Directory of **STD** Clinics, HE 20.7316

HIV/**STD**/TB Prevention News Update, HE 20.7318

NASA **STD** (Series), NAS 1.82

Standards, FAA-**STD** (series), TD 4.24/2

Steaks

U.S. Production of Fish Fillets and **Steaks**, Annual Summary, C 55.309/2-6

Steam

Advance Summary of Revenues, Expenses, and Net Railway Operating Income, Class 1 **Steam** Railways, IC 1 ste.19/2

Bulletins of Revenues and Expenses of **Steam** Roads, IC 1 ste.3

Bureau of **Steam** Roads, IC 1 ste.1

Commission to Arbitrate Claims of Venezuela **Steam** Transportation Company of New York against Venezuela, S 3.11

Comparative Statement of Operating Averages, Class I **Steam** Railways in United States, IC 1 ste.27

Females Employed by Class 1 **Steam** Railways, Number of, IC 1 ste.43

Fuel and Power for Locomotives and Rail Motor Cars of Class I **Steam** Railways in United States, IC 1 ste.30

List of Masters, Mates, {etc} of Merchant **Steam**, Motor, and Sail Vessels, Licensed during Calendar Year, T 38.7

Publications National Conferences on **Street** and Highway Safety, C 1.21
Street Directory of Principal Cities of United States, P 7.6
TIGER/Census Tract **Street** Index, Version 2, C 3.279/2:CD-CTSI

Streets
Manual on Uniform Control Devices for **Streets** and Highways, TD 2.8:T 67
Manual on Uniform Traffic Control Devices for **Streets** and Highways: Official Rulings on Requests for Interpretations, Changes, and Experimentations, TD 2.8/2
Tiger/Census Tract **Street** Index, C 3.279/2

Strength
World **Strength** of the Communist Party Organizations, Annual Report, S 1.111

Strengthening
Awards Higher Education Act of 1965 (P.L. 89-329) as Amended Title 3 **Strengthening** Developing Institutions, HE 5.92/2 HE 19.139
Higher Education Act, Title II-C, FY Abstracts **Strengthening** Library Resources Program, ED 1.18
Instructions and Application for Grants under the **Strengthening** Program, ED 1.61/2
Strengthening Developing Institutions, Title 3 of the Higher Education Act of 1965, Annual Report, HE 19.139/2
Strengthening Research Library Resources Program, ED 1.53
Application for Grants under Strengthening **Research Library** Resources Program, ED 1.53

Stress
PTSD (Post-Traumatic **Stress** Disorder) Clinical Quarterly, VA 1.94/2

Strikes
Analysis of **Strikes**, L 2.6/a 6
Strikes in the United States, L 2.3:651
Strikes in, L 2.69

Striped
Emergency **Striped** Bass Research Study, I 49.103

Stroke
Intramural Research, Annual Report: National Institute of Neurological and Communicative Disorders and **Stroke**, HE 20.3516/4
National Advisory Neurological and Communicative Disorders and **Stroke** Council, HE 20.3001/2:N 39/5
Neurological Diseases and **Stroke** Science Information Program Advisory Committee, HE 20.3001/2:N 39/6
NINCDS Research Program, **Stroke**, HE 20.3512/2
NINCDS **Stroke** Research Program, HE 20.3502:St 8
Progress Report President's Medical Programs for Heart Disease, Cancer, and **Stroke**, and Related Diseases, FS 2.313
Report of the Panel on Pain to the National Advisory Neurological and Communicative Disorders and **Stroke** Council, HE 20.3517

Strong-Motion
Progress During. . .**Strong-Motion** Earthquake in California and Elsewhere, C 4.25/3
Strong-Motion Program Report, I 19.4/6

Strontium
Strontium in (year), I 28.166

Structural
Civil and **Structural** Engineering, C 51.9/21
Industry Wage Survey: **Structural** Clay Products, L 2.3/30
Structural Clay Products (common brick, face brick, vitrified paving brick, hollow building tile), C 3.109
Structural Engineering Bulletin, HH 1.95
Structural Engineering Series, TD 2.48
Structural Research Laboratory Report, I 27.29

Structure
Directory of Federal Regional **Structure**, GS 4.119
Health Services and Mental Health Administration Public Advisory Committees: Authority, **Structure**, Functions, FS 2.321
Historic **Structure** and Grounds Report (series), I 29.88/4
Historic **Structure** Reports, I 29.88, I 70.10
NIH Public Advisory Groups: Authority, **Structure**, Functions, HE 20.3018

Number of New Permanent Nonfarm Dwelling Units Started by Urban or Rural Location, Public or Private Ownership, and Type of **Structure**, L 2.51/4
Pay **Structure** on the Federal Civil Service, CS 1.48:33
Public Advisory Committees: Authority, **Structure**, Functions, HE 20.4022
Public Advisory Committees: Authority, **Structure**, Functions, Members, HE 20.1000
SCC {Ship **Structure** Committee}, Y 3.Sh 6:6/SSC
Territorial Studies of Motor Carrier Costs, Traffic and Rate **Structure**, IC 1 mot.16
Wage **Structure**, Series 2, L 2.27

Structures
Building Materials and **Structures** Report, C 13.29
Conditions of Major Water System **Structures** and Facilities, Review of Maintenance, Report of Examination, {various regions and projects}, I 27.69
Construction Reports; Permits Issued for Demolition of Residential **Structures** in Selected Cities, C 45 (series), C 3.215/12
Large Space **Structures** and Systems in the Space Station Era, A Bibliography with Indexes, NAS 1.21:7085
Medical Subject Headings; Tree **Structures**, HE 20.3602:H 34/2, HE 20.3612/3-5
Organic Chemistry: Air Pollution Studies Characterization of Chemical **Structures**; Synthesis of Research Materials, C 13.46
PHS Public Advisory Groups, Authority, **Structures**, Functions, HE 20.2:Ad 9/2
Protective **Structures**, Shelter Design Series, D 13.15

Student
Bibliographies Guidance and **Student** Personnel Section, FS 5.16/2
College Costs, Basic **Student** Charges 2-year and 4-year Institutions, ED 1.121/3
College Costs, Basic **Student** Charges, 2-year Institutions, ED 1.121/2
College Costs, Basic **Student** Charges, 4-year Institutions, ED 1.121
Composite List of Eligible Institutions, National Vocation **Student** Loan Insurance Act of 1965, FS 5.83/2, HE 5.83/2
Counselor's Handbook, a Federal **Student** Aid Reference, ED 1.45
Education Update: **Student** Liaison Officer's Monthly Memo to Students, ED 1.41/2
EFC Formula Book, The Expected Family Contribution for Federal **Student** Aid, ED 1.45/5
Employment Hours and Earnings on **Student** Aid Projects of NYA, Y 3.W 89/2:27
Exploring Careers, a **Student** Guidebook, HE 19.108
Faculty and **Student** Programs, E 1.86/6
Federal **Student** Financial Aid Handbook, ED 1.45/4
Federal **Student** Loan Program Bulletin, ED 1.3/3
Graduate **Student** Researchers Program, NAS 1.42/2
Higher Education Basic **Student** Charges, HE 19.328
Highlights from **Student** Drug Use in America, HE 20.8219/2
Indian Health Service Scholarship Program **Student** Handbook, HE 20.9418/2
Interdisciplinary **Student**/teacher Materials in Energy, the Environment, and the Economy, E 1.9
National Defense and Direct **Student** Loan Program, Directory of Designated Low-Income Schools for Teacher Cancellation Benefits, ED 1.40/2
National Defense **Student** Loan Program, Including Participating Institutions, FS 5.255:55001, HE 5.255:55001
National Direct **Student** Loan Status of Default as of (date), ED 1.40
National Postsecondary **Student** Aid Study (NPSAS), ED 1.333
Social Security **Student** Gazette, HE 3.59
Student Conference on United States Affairs, D 109.9
Student Guide, Five Federal Financial Aid Programs, ED 1.8/2
Student Handbook (series) Corps of Engineers, D 103.120/2
Student Handbook (series) Department of Defense, D 1.67/3

Student Handbook (series) Department of the Army, D 101.47/3, D 101.47/4
Student Information Sheets (series), D 101.112/2
Student Manual, SM- (series), D 14.8/2
Student Package (series), D 101.47/8
Student Pamphlet (series), D 103.120/3
Student Performance Guides (series), D 101.107/3
Student Reference Book (series), D 101.47/6
Student Reference Sheets, SR- (series), FS 13.122
Student Report (series), D 301.26/7-3
Student Texts, ST- (series), D 5.352/2
Student Work Sheets, Department of Labor Safety Training Programs, SWS-LS-(series), L 16.51
Student Workout (series), D 103.120
Summer **Student** Trainee Report, C 30.77

Students
Adult Basic and Secondary Level Program Statistics, **Students** and Staff Data, HE 19.319
Air Force ROTC Four Year College Scholarship Program Application Booklet for High School **Students** Entering College in the (year) Fall Term, D 301.95
Clinical Electives for Medical and Dental **Students** at the National Institutes of Health, Catalog, HE 20.3042
Composite List of Eligible Institutions for Guaranteed Loans for College **Students**, Higher Education Act of 1965, FS 5.83, HE 5.83
Continuation Application for Grants under Special Services for Disadvantage **Students** Program, ED 1.60
Drug Abuse Among American School **Students**, HE 20.8222
Drug Use Among American High School **Students**, HE 20.8219
Education Update: Student Liaison Officer's Monthly Memo to **Students**, ED 1.41/2
Federal Career Directory, Guide for College **Students**, CS 1.7/4:C 18
Financial Assistance for College **Students**, Undergraduate and First-Professional, FS 5.255:55027, HE 5.255:55027
Graduate **Students** and Postdoctorates in Science and Engineering, NS 1.22/11
Higher Education: **Students** Enrolled for Advanced Degrees, Fall (year), HE 19.330
Interagency Directory, Key Contacts for Planning, Scientific and Technical Exchange Programs, Educational Travel, **Students**, Teachers, Lecturers, Research Scholars, Specialists, S 1.67/3
Junior-Year Science, Mathematics, and Foreign Language **Students**, First-Term, FS 5.254:54001, HE 5.254:54001
National Health Service Corps Scholarship Program Information Bulletin for **Students** of Allopathic Medicine, Osteopathic Medicine, and Dentistry, HE 20.5011
Resource Guide for Health Science **Students**: Occupational and Environmental Health, HE 20.7108:H 34/2
School Enrollment, Social and Economic Characteristics of **Students**, C 3.186/12
Students Enrolled for Advanced Degrees, HE 19.330
Summary Report on Survey of **Students** Enrolled for Advanced Degrees: Fall (year), FS 5.254:54009, HE 5.254:54009
White House Report to **Students**, PrEx 1.12

Studies
Active Standardization Projects, Standards, Specifications, **Studies** and Handbooks, D 7.12
Actuarial **Studies**, HE 3.19, SS 1.34, SSA 1.25/2
Beneficiary **Studies** Notes, FS 3.46
Case **Studies** in Environmental Medicine, HE 20.7917
Clearinghouse of **Studies** on Higher Education, Reporter, FS 5.250:50004, HE 5.250:50004
Clinical Center, Current Clinical **Studies** and Patient Referral Procedures, HE 20.3010
Community Development: Case **Studies**, S 18.17/2
Comprehensive **Studies** of Solid Waste Management, Annual Report, EP 1.11
Contributions from the Center for Northern **Studies**, I 29.99
Cooperative **Studies** Reports, C 30.61
Cooperative **Studies** Technical Papers, C 30.61/2
Copyright Law **Studies**, LC 3.9

Country Law **Studies**, D 1.40
CRS **Studies** in the Public Domain (series), LC 14.20
Cultural Resource Management **Studies**, I 29.86, I 70.11
Current Construction Reports, Special **Studies**, Expenditures for Nonresidential Improvements and Repairs, C 3.215/8-2
Defense Manpower Commission Staff **Studies** and Supporting Papers, Y 3.D 36:9
Development **Studies** Program Occasional Papers, S 18.59
Disability **Studies** Notes, FS 3.54
Distribution Cost **Studies**, C 18.33
Educational Programs in Foreign Language and Area **Studies** (series), HE 5.99
Environmental and Water Quality Operational **Studies**, D 103.24/15
Environmental **Studies** Division, FY (year) Program, EP 1.44
Export Origin **Studies** {by State}, C 1.46
External Research **Studies**, S 1.101/11
Field Initiated **Studies** Program, Abstracts of Funded Projects, ED 1.337
Field **Studies** and Statistics Program, HE 20.3178
Geologic **Studies** in Alaska by the U.S. Geological Survey, I 19.4/8
Geological **Studies** in Alaska by the U.S. Geological Survey, I 19.4/3
Harvard **Studies** in Marketing Farm Products, A 36.169
Health Resources **Studies**, HE 20.6012
High-Temperature Gas-Cooled Reactor Safety **Studies**, E 1.28/7
Highway Research and Development **Studies** using Federal-Aid Research and Planning Funds, TD 2.113
Historical **Studies**, L 2.15
Historical **Studies** (numbered), GS 6.8
Industrial Area **Studies**, L 2.16
Industry Wage **Studies** Memo, L 2.47/2
Industry Wage **Studies**, Series 3, Wage Movements, L 2.47
Institute Programs for Advanced **Studies**, FS 5.84, HE 5.84
International Labor **Studies**, L 29.8
International Law **Studies**, D 208.207
Inventory of Recent Publications and Research **Studies** in the Field of International and Cultural Affairs, S 1.30/4
IRS Historical **Studies**, T 22.66
Japanese Trade **Studies**, TC 1.23
Japanese Trade **Studies**, Special Industry Analyses, TC 1.23/3
Lake Michigan Cooling Water **Studies** Panel: Reports, EP 1.72
List of Current **Studies**, BR (series), S 1.101/6
List of Technical **Studies**, HH 2.23/2
National Defense Language Development Program: Completed Research, **Studies** and Instructional Materials, Lists, FS 5.212:12016, HE 5.212:12016
National War College Strategic **Studies** (series), D 5.415
Notes on Graduate **Studies** and Research in Home Economics and Home Economics Education, A 1.53
OCS **Studies** (series), I 72.12/2
Operation **Studies**, D 106.19
Organic Chemistry: Air Pollution **Studies** Characterization of Chemical Structures; Synthesis of Research Materials, C 13.46
Oriental **Studies**, SI 7.7
Outer Continental Shelf Environmental **Studies** Advisory Committee: Publications, I 1.99/2
Patterns for Progress in Aging Case **Studies**, FS 1.13/3, FS 14.9/5
Policy Research **Studies**, S 1.101/8
Policy **Studies** (series), D 103.57/8
Postwar Economic **Studies**, FR 1.27
Preservation Case **Studies**, I 29.104, I 70.12/2
Procedural **Studies** of 1950 Censuses, C 3.950-10
Procedural **Studies** of Censuses, C 3.225
Program and Services, Report of Educational Materials Laboratory, Division of International **Studies** and Services, FS 5.214:14031, HE 5.214:14031
QMC Historical **Studies**, D 106.8
QMC Historical **Studies**, Series II, D 106.8/2
R & D Highway & Safety Transportation System **Studies**, TD 2.24
R & D Systems **Studies**: Technical Reports, HE 19.215

Records Administration **Studies**, AE 1.14
Regional **Studies** Plan, Fiscal Year, Atlantic OCS Region, I 72.12/15
Report and **Studies** in the History of Art, SI 8.9
Report on U.S. Government Research and **Studies** in the Field of Arms Control and Disarmament Matters, AC 1.14
Research and Special **Studies** Progress Report, D 301.26/15
Research and Training Opportunities Abroad (year), Educational Programs in Foreign Language and Area **Studies**, HE 5.99
Research Demonstration and Evaluation **Studies**, HE 23.1010
Research Relating to Children, Inventory of **Studies** in Progress, FS 3.220
Research **Studies** Defense Civil Preparedness Agency, D 14.17
Research **Studies** Department of State, S 1.101/12
Research, Demonstration, and Evaluation **Studies**, HE 1.402:R 31
RIIES Bibliographic **Studies**, SI 1.40
RRB Actuarial **Studies**, RR 1.14
Rural Life **Studies**, A 36.136
Safety **Studies**, C 31.223
Safety **Studies**, NTSB/SS (series), TD 1.27
School Health **Studies**, I 16.38
School of Advanced Airpower **Studies**, D 301.26/6-9
Science Resources **Studies** Highlights, NS 1.31
Sedimentation **Studies**, A 57.14
Selected Abstracts of Completed Research **Studies**, Fiscal Year (date), SBA 1.18/4
Smithsonian Folklife **Studies**, SI 1.43
Smithsonian **Studies** in Air and Space, SI 1.42
Smithsonian **Studies** in History and Technology, SI 1.28
Socioeconomic Environmental **Studies**, EP 1.23/3
Sociological **Studies**, PrEx 7.21/13
Special History **Studies** (series), I 29.88/5
Special **Studies** Papers, FR 1.58
Special **Studies** Series, D 114.17
Special **Studies**, C 3.186:P-23, D 102.29, S 18.52/3
Special **Studies**, Current Population Reports, C 3.186:P-23
Staff Economic **Studies**, FR 1.51
Staff Research **Studies**, TC 1.37
State and Local Government Special **Studies**, C 3.145, C 56.231
Studies (numbered), Y 3.Ai 7/5:10
Studies from Interagency Data Linkages (series), HE 3.62
Studies in Administrative Law and Procedure, Y 3.Ad 6:10
Studies in American Folklife, LC 39.11
Studies in Asymmetry, D 101.146/8
Studies in Communist Affairs, D 301.85
Studies in Comparative Education, Bibliography, Publications, FS 5.214, HE 5.214
Studies in Comparative Education, Education in {country}, FS 5.212, HE 5.212
Studies in Comparative Education, FS 5.59
Studies in Cultural Resource Management, A 13.101/2
Studies in Delinquency, HE 17.16/4
Studies in Income Distribution (series), HE 3.67/2
Studies in Intelligence, PrEX 3.19
Studies in Medical Care Administration, FS 2.311
Studies in Military Engineering (series), D 103.43/4
Studies in Plains Anthropology and History, I 20.50
Studies in Social Change, HE 20.8132
Studies in the Economics of Production, C 1.81
Studies in Workmen's Compensation and Radiation Injury, Y 3.At 7:2 R 11/28
Studies of Automatic Technology, L 2.76
Studies of Family Clothing Supplies, Preliminary Reports, A 77.712
Studies of Small Business Finance, Y 3.In 8/29:9
Studies on Administrative Management in Government of U.S., Y 3.P 92/3:7
Studies on Household Sewage Disposal System, FS 2.56
Summaries of **Studies** in Agricultural Education Supplements, FS 5.281:81002, HE 5.281:81002
Survey of Federally-Funded Marine Mammal Research and **Studies**, Y 3.M 33/3:9-2
Tax Policy Research **Studies**, T 1.44
Technical **Studies** Reports, EP 2.26, HH 2.23
Territorial **Studies** of Motor Carrier Costs, Traffic and Rate Structure, IC 1 mot.16

Transactions of Research Conferences on Cooperative Chemotherapy **Studies** in Psychiatry and Research Approaches to Mental Illness, VA 1.41
Union Wage Scale **Studies**, L 2.29
Union Wage **Studies** Manual of Procedures, L 2.55
United States Air Force Special **Studies**, D 301.82/4
Urban **Studies** Division Bulletins, NHA 1.7
Urban **Studies**, CR 1.11
USAF Warrior **Studies**, D 301.96
Uses of Research Sponsored by the Administration on Aging, Case **Studies**, HE 23.3012
Utilization of American Cotton **Studies**, A 36.64
Vietnam **Studies** (series), D 101.74
War Background **Studies**, SI 1.14
War Profits **Studies**, Pr 32.4227, Pr 33.312
What the Soldier Thinks, Monthly Digest of War Department **Studies** on Attitudes of American Troops, W 1.65
Women's **Studies**, Monograph Series, HE 19.220
Work and Wage Experience **Studies**, Reports, L 2.28

Study
Allergy and Immunology **Study** Section, HE 20.3001/2:Al 5
Cell Biology **Study** Section, HE 20.3001/2:C 33
Censuses Use **Study** Reports, C 3.244
Center for the **Study** of Intelligence Monographs, PrEx 3.18
Communicative Sciences **Study** Section, HE 20.3001/2:C 73/2
Comprehensive Framework **Study**, Missouri River Basin, Y 3.M 69:9
Computer and Biomathematical Sciences **Study** Section, HE 20.3001/2:C 73
Consumer **Study** Outline, A 55.53
Continental Divide Trail **Study** Progress Reports, I 66.19/2
DANTES Independent **Study** Catalog, D 1.33/7-2
Developmental Behavioral Sciences **Study** Section, HE 20.3001/2:B 39/2
Endocrinology **Study** Section, HE 20.3001/2:En 2
English Teaching **Study** Units, IA 1.17/3
Epidemiology and Disease Control **Study** Section, HE 20.3001/2:Ep 4/2
Estuarine Pollution **Study** Series, EP 2.19
Experimental Psychology **Study** Section, HE 20.3001/2:P 95
Experimental Therapeutics **Study** Section, HE 20.3001/2:T 34/2
General Medicine A **Study** Section, HE 20.3001/2:M 46/2
General Medicine B **Study** Section, HE 20.3001/2:M 46/3
Genetics **Study** Section, HE 20.3001/2:G 28
Historic Furnishing **Study** (series), I 29.88/2
HS {Home **Study**} (series), D 14.11, D 119.15, FEM 1.13
Immunobiology **Study** Section, HE 20.3001/2:Im 6/2
Immunological Sciences **Study** Section, HE 20.3001/2:Im 6
Interstate System Traveled-Way **Study** Reports, TD 2.118
Lake Erie Wastewater Management **Study** Public Information Fact Sheet, D 103.63/2
Members of Advisory Councils, **Study** Sections, and Committees of National Institutes of Health, FS 2.22/22
National Agricultural Lands **Study**: Interim Reports, A 1.30/2
National Health Survey: Hearing **Study** Series, Bulletins; Preliminary Report, T 27.39
National Independent **Study** Center: Correspondence Courses, CS 1.92
National Survey Results on Drug Use from the Monitoring the Future **Study**, HE 20.3968
Nutrition **Study** Section, HE 20.3001/2:N 95
Observational **Study** of Agricultural Aspects of Arkansas River Multiple-purpose Project, Annual Report, A 57.60
Oral Biology and Medicine **Study** Section, HE 20.3001/2:Or 1
ORRC **Study** Reports, Y 3.Ou 8:10
Pathology A **Study** Section, HE 20.3001/2:P 27
Pathology B **Study** Section, HE 20.3001/2:P 27/2
Pesticides **Study** Series, EP 2.25
Pharmacology **Study** Section, HE 20.3001/2:P 49
Physiological Chemistry, **Study** Section, HE 20.3001/2:P 56/3
Physiology **Study** Section, HE 20.3001/2:P 56/2
Popular **Study** Series; Histories, I 29.45

Summary of Major Provisions of Convention and of Law Relating to Factory Inspection (by States), L 16.32

Summary of Manufacturing Earnings Series, L 2.90

Summary of Meeting Depository Library Council to the Printer, GP 3.30/2

Summary of Mining and Petroleum Laws of the World, I 28.27

Summary of Monthly Reports of Large Telephone Companies, IC 1 telp.6

Summary of Mortality from Automobile Accidents, C 3.39

Summary of Mortgage Insurance Operations and Contract Authority, HH 2.24/5

Summary of Motor Carrier Accidents, IC 1 mot.21/3

Summary of Motor Vehicle Accident Fatalities, C 3.128/3

Summary of Offerings and Enrollments in Public and Secondary Schools, HE 19.334

Summary of Operations of Production Credit Associations, A 72.25

Summary of Operations, Labor-Management Reporting and Disclosure Act, L 1.51

Summary of Operations, Office of General Counsel, LR 1.1/2

Summary of Orders, ES 3.6/10

Summary of Passport Office Accomplishments, S 1.1/5

Summary of Passport Statistics, S 1.27/2

Summary of Policies, Reports, and Other Publications, Y 3.F 31/5:14

Summary of Prescribed Unit Costs and Hourly Rate for Return on Investment and Tax Allowance, C 31.272, CAB 1.10

Summary of Press Comments, A 55.27

Summary of Progress, SS 1.16

Summary of Regional Cold Storage Holdings, A 88.20/2

Summary of Report, A 93.50

Summary of Reports Received by Committee on Medical Research, Pr 32.413/10

Summary of Research Projects Monthly Reports, A 57.34

Summary of Safety Management Audits, TD 2.66

Summary of Savings Accounts by Geographic Area, FSLIC-Insured Savings and Loan Associations, FHL 1.29

Summary of Sanitation Inspection of International Cruise Ships, HE 20.7511

Summary of SBA Programs, Y 4.Sm 1/12

Summary of Small Business Financing by SBIC's, SBA 1.28

Summary of State Government Finances in (year), C 56.209, C 3.191/2

Summary of State Labor Laws for Women, L 13.14/2

Summary of State Unemployment Compensation Laws, SS 1.19/2

Summary of Supplemental Type Certificates and Approved Replacement Parts, FAA 1.14, FAA 5.12

Summary of Supplemental Type Certificates, TD 4.36

Summary of Surplus Property, C 33.11, FL 5.11

Summary of Synoptic Meteorological Observations, D 220.10

Summary of Technological Developments Affecting War Production, L 2.17

Summary of the Budget, EP 1.1/4

Summary of Trade and Tariff Information (series), ITC 1.11

Summary of Transportation, Pr 32.4844

Summary of Tuberculosis Eradication in Cooperation with Various States, A 77.216

Summary of U.S. Export Control Regulations, C 42.6:Ex 7/2

Summary of U.S. Exports and Imports of Gold and Silver, Calendar Year, C 3.196/3

Summary of U.S. Exports and Imports of Gold and Silver, Fiscal Year, C 3.196/2

Summary of War Supply and Facility Contracts by State and Industrial Area, Pr 32.4828

Summary of Watershed Conditions Affecting Water Supply of the Lower Colorado River, I 27.43

Summary Proceedings of ADAMHA Annual Conference of the State and Territorial Alcohol, Drug Abuse, and Mental Health Authorities, HE 20.8011

Summary Progress Report, Tropical Deteriorioration Committee, Pr 32.413/11

Summary Report of Bachelor's and Higher Degrees Conferred During (school year), FS 5.254:54010, HE 5.254:54010

Summary Report of Bureau's Financial Condition and Operations for Fiscal Year, I 27.1/3

Summary Report of the Commissioner, Bureau of Reclamation {and} Statistical Appendix, I 27.1/2

Summary Report of Utilization Research and Development, Fiscal Year (date), A 77.2:Ut 3

Summary Report on Survey of Students Enrolled for Advanced Degrees: Fall (year), FS 5.254:54009, HE 5.254:54009

Summary Report, Assets and Liabilities of Member Banks, FR 1.11

Summary Report, Faculty and Other Professional Staff in Institutions of Higher Education, FS 5.253:53014, HE 5.253:53014

Summary Report, Weather Modification, C 55.27

Summary Reports of Accidents, U.S. Civil Aviation, C 31.244/4

Summary, Special Labor Force Reports, L 2.98/2

Summary Statement of Income and Expenditures of Voluntary Relief Agencies Registered with Advisory Committee on Voluntary Foreign Aid, S 1.99/3

Summary Statistics Project Data, I 27.1/4-2

Summary Statistics, Finances and Physical Features, I 27.1/4-3

Summary Statistics, Water, Land and Related Data, I 27.1/4

Summary Tape Files - STF 4, C 3.282/2-2

Summary Technical Report of National Defense Research Committee, Pr 32.413/12

Superfund Emergency Response Actions, A **Summary** of Federally-Funded Removals, Annual Report, EP 1.89/5

Technical Committee Executive **Summary** (series), Y 3.W 58/4:11

Time Distribution **Summary**, L 7.42

Tobacco Crop **Summary**, A 88.34/9

Tobacco Market News **Summary**, A 88.34/10

Toxics-Release Inventory: Executive **Summary**, EP 5.18/2-2

Trend of Employment in U.S. (Monthly **summary** statements), L 2.9/2

Trichinosis Surveillance, Annual **Summary**, HE 20.7011/4

U.S. Department of Agriculture Budget **Summary**, A 1.138

U.S. Production of Fish Fillets and Steaks, Annual **Summary**, C 55.309/2-6

U.S. Waterborne Foreign Trade, **Summary** Report, C 3.164:985

U.S.D.A. **Summary** of Registered Agricultural Pesticide Chemical Uses, A 77.302:P 43/4

UI Data **Summary**, L 37.214

Uniform Crime Reports Bomb **Summary**, J 1.14/7-7

Union Recognition in the Federal Government, Statistical **Summary**, PM 1.47

United States Air Force History Program, **Summary** of Activities, D 301.1/2

United States Courts, Pictorial **Summary**, Ju 10.12

University Research: **Summary** of Awards, Program of University Research, TD 1.45

Unresolved Safety Issues **Summary**, Aqua Book, Y 3.N 88:30

Utah, Annual Data **Summary**, A 57.46/6-3

Utilization of Short-Stay Hospitals United States, Annual **Summary**, HE 20.6209/7

VA Statistical **Summary**, VA 1.27

Vegetables, (year) Annual **Summary**, A 105.24/2

Vegetables, Fresh Market, Annual **Summary**, Acreage, Production, etc., A 92.11/10-2

Vegetables, Processing, Annual **Summary**, Acreage Productions, etc., A 92.11/10

Veterans Administration **Summary** of Medical Programs, VA 1.43/5

Vocational **Summary**, Circulars of Information, VE 1.5

Wage Developments in Manufacturing, **Summary** Release, L 2.44/2

Wage Trends for Occupational Groups in Metropolitan Areas, **Summary** Release, L 2.86/2

Washington Annual Data **Summary** Water Year, A 57.46/7-2

Water Quality Standards **Summary** {for various States} (series), EP 1.29

Water Resources Review, Annual **Summary**, Water Year, I 19.42/2

Weather Modification, **Summary** Report, C 55.27

Weekly News **Summary**, HH 1.15/2

Weekly **Summary** (Press Division), A 107.17

Weekly **Summary** of Banking and Credit Measures, FR 1.52

Weekly **Summary** of Export Opportunities for Small Business, Pr 33.917

Weekly **Summary** of F.O.B. Prices of Fresh Fruits and Vegetables in Representative Shipping Districts, A 88.12/2, A 82.53

Weekly **Summary** of Federal Legislation Relating to National Resources Committee, Activities Bulletins, Y 3.N 21/12:15

Weekly **Summary** of Fruit and Vegetable Carlot Shipments, A 88.12

Weekly **Summary** of Health Information for International Travel, HE 20.7023

Weekly **Summary** of N.L.R.B. Cases, LR 1.15/2

Weekly **Summary** of NLRB Cases, LR 1.5/2

Weekly **Summary** of Orders and Regulations, C 31.208

Weekly **Summary** of Wholesale Prices of Fresh Fruits and Vegetables at New York City and Chicago, A 88.12/3, A 82.52

Weekly **Summary**, A 21.6/6

Weekly **Summary**: AAA Press Releases, A 55.64

Weekly Tobacco Market News **Summary**, A 88.34/7

Weekly Weather and Crop Bulletin, National **Summary**, C 30.11, C 55.209

Wheat and Rye **Summary**, Crop Year, A 88.18/16

Wholesale Price Indexes, Advance **Summary**, L 2.61/10

Wholesale Prices of Fruits and Vegetables at New York and Chicago, Weekly **Summary** of, A 82.52

Wind Erosion Conditions, Great Plains, **Summary** of Local Estimates, A 57.47

Year of Progress, Annual **Summary**, A 95.1

Summation

Summation of Non-Military Activities in Japan, W 1.75, M 105.11

Summation of United States Army Military Government Activities in Korea, W 1.76

Summation of United States Army Military Government Activities in Ryukyu Islands, W 1.78, M 105.12

Summer

Cooperative Graduate Fellowship Program for Fiscal Year, Fellowship Awards {and} Program of **Summer** Fellowships for Graduate Teaching Assistants for Fiscal Year, NS 1.19/2

Historically Black Colleges and Universities, Faculty Projects, **Summer** College Humanities Programs for High School Juniors, NF 3.8/2-8

Park Areas and Employment Opportunities for **Summer**, I 29.110

Summer and Fall Vegetables for Fresh Market, Summer Melons, Sweetpotatoes, A 88.26/4

Summer and Fall Vegetables, Melons, Sweetpotatoes, A 88.26/4

Summer Jobs at NIA, Catalog, HE 20.3015/3

Summer Research Fellowship Program at the National Institutes of Health, HE 20.3015/2

Summer Seminars for College Teachers, NF 3.13/2-3

Summer Seminars for College Teachers Guidelines and Application Form for Participants, NF 3.13/2-2

Summer Seminars for College Teachers, Guidelines and Application Forms for Directors, NF 3.13/2

Summer Seminars for College Teachers, Seminar Descriptions, NF 3.13

Summer Seminars for Secondary School Teachers Guidelines and Application Form for Directors, NF 3.13/3-3

Summer Seminars for Secondary School Teachers Guidelines and Applications Form for Participants, NF 3.13/3-2

Summer Seminars for Secondary School Teachers, NF 3.13/3

Summer Seminars for Secondary School Teachers, Seminar Descriptions, NF 3.13/3-4

Summer Stipends, NF 3.22

Summer Stipends, Guidelines and Application Forms, NF 3.8/2

Summer Student Trainee Report, C 30.77

Summer Training Camp Bulletins, W 99.19/10

Summer Youth Opportunity Campaign, TD 2.15

Summer Youth Opportunity Program Annual
Report, TD 1.12
Teacher Exchange Opportunities Abroad, Teaching,
Summer Seminars under International
Educational Exchange Program of
Department of States {announcements},
FS 5.64/2
Sun
Ephemeris of **Sun**, Polaris, and Other Selected Stars,
D 213.12
Ephemeris of the **Sun**, Polaris and Other Selected
Stars with Companion Data and Tables
for the year {date}, I 53.8
Saint Elizabeth's Hospital, **Sun** Dial, I 1.14/5
Sun and Moon Tables for Cleveland, Ohio, D
203.14/2
Tide, Moon and **Sun** Calendar, Baltimore, Md., D
203.12
Sunrise
Tide, Moon and **Sunrise** Tables, Panama, and
Cristobal, Colon, W 79.8
Superconducting
Superconducting Devices and Materials, C 13.37/5
Superconducting Devices, C 13.75/5
Superconducting Devices, Literature Survey, C
13.37/5
Superfund
SITE (**Superfund** Innovative Technology
Evaluation) Demonstration Bulletin, EP
1.89/4-2
SITE (**Superfund** Innovative Technology
Evaluation), EP 1.89/4
Superfund Accomplishments in . . ., EP 1.112
Superfund Emergency Response Actions, A
Summary of Federally-Funded Removals,
Annual Report, EP 1.89/5
Superfund Innovative Technology Evaluation
Program, Annual Report to Congress, EP
1.89/4-4
Superintendent
Chief Clerk and **Superintendent** of Buildings,
Annual Report, I 1.60
Five Civilized Tribes, **Superintendent**, Annual
Reports, I 20.21
General **Superintendent** and Landscape Engineer of
National Parks, Annual Reports, I 1.58
Indian Schools **Superintendent**, Annual Report, I
20.7
Posters **Superintendent** of Documents, GP 3.21/2
Price List of Publications of Department of
Agriculture for Sale by **Superintendent**
of Documents, A 21.8
Superintendent of Documents
Civil Defense Publications Available from
Superintendent of Documents, FCD
1.21
Superintendent's
Superintendent's Statement to Board of Visitors, D
208.110
United States Naval Academy, **Superintendent's**
Statement to Board of Visitors, D
208.110
Reports of Agents and **Superintendents** in Charge
of Indians, I 20.15
Superior Harbor
Statistic Report of Marine Commerce of Duluth-
Superior Harbor, Minn. and Wis., D
103.13
Statistical Report of Marine Commerce of Duluth-
Superior Harbor, Minn. and Wis., D
103.13
Superphosphates
Superphosphates, Production, etc., Reported by
Fertilizer Manufacturers, C 3.111
Superseded
Index of Specifications and Standards Used by
Department of the Navy, Specifications
Cancelled or **Superseded**, D 212.10/2
Supervised
Loans and Discounts of Lending Institutions
Supervised by Farm Credit Administra-
tion, FCA 1.12/2
Notices, Activities of Licensed Establishments
Supervised by Virus-Serum Control
Division, A 4.31, A 77.217
Supervising
General Rules and Regulations Prescribed by
Board of **Supervising** Inspectors of
Steamboats, T 38.9
Proceedings Board of **Supervising** Inspectors, T
38.10
Supervision
Basic **Supervision**, C 31.155

Spotlight on Organization and **Supervision** in
Large High Schools, FS 5.50
Supervision and Management Series, FS 1.12
Supervision Series, C 1.35
Supervisor
Census **Supervisor**, C 3.206
Research Papers Thrift **Supervisor** Office, T 71.16
Supervisor and Personnel Administration, C
21.14/3
Supervisor's
Supervisor's Bulletins (occasional), L 1.24
Supervisor's Guide Series, L 1.24/2
Supervisors
Academic Year Institutes for Secondary School
Teachers and **Supervisors** of Science and
Mathematics, NS 1.12
Alert, Administrative News Highlights for
Supervisors, A 1.129/2
Conference for **Supervisors** of Elementary
Education in Large Cities, FS 5.58/2
First Line, Newsletter for Federal **Supervisors** and
Midmanagers, PM 1.17, CS 1.91
News Letter for State **Supervisors** of Rural
Research, Y 3.F 31/5:26, Y 3.W 89/2:16
SSA Management Newsletter for **Supervisors** and
Management Personnel, HE 3.68/2
State **Supervisors** of Pupil Transportation,
Directory, FS 5.2:T 68/2
What's New, Tips for **Supervisors** from Oaas, L
1.43
Supphonation
Fats and Oils Subjected to **Supphonation**, C 3.124
Supplement
Mineral Industry Surveys, Directory of Principal
Construction Sand and Gravel Producers
in the . . ., Annual Advanced Summary
Supplement, I 19.138/3
Monthly Catalog of United States Government
Publications, Periodical **Supplement**,
GP 3.8/8-8
NLM Catalog **Supplement**, HE 20.3609/3-3
Pacific Airman's Guide and Chart **Supplement**, TD
4.16
Periodic **Supplement**, Selected United States
Government Publications, GP 3.17/3
Periodicals **Supplement**, GP 3.8/5
Recent Reviews, Cancer Diagnosis and Therapy,
Supplement to the Cancergrams, HE
20.3173/2-3
Recent Reviews, Cancer Virology and Biology,
Supplement to the Cancergrams, HE
20.3173/2-4
Registry of Toxic Effects of Chemical Substances
(cumulative) **Supplement**, HE 20.7112/5
Second **Supplement** on Aging, HE 20.6232
Seventy-Fifth USA Maneuver Area Command,
Annual Report and Historical
Supplement, D 101.1/8
Social Security Bulletin, Statistical **Supplement**,
HE 3.3/3
South Africa, Serials **Supplement**, LC 1.30/10-4
Special Notices, **Supplement** to Radio Facility
Charts and In-flight Data, Europe, D
301.9/3
Statistical **Supplement** of Monthly Domestic Dairy
Markets Review, A 88.13/2
Statistical **Supplement** to Monthly Egg and
Poultry Market Review, A 88.13/4
Statistics on Manpower, **Supplement** to Manpower
Report of the President, L 1.42/2-2
Supplement Alaska, TD 4.79/2
Supplement Litigation, Actions and Proceedings
Bulletin Index, SE 1.20/3
Supplement to Carload Waybill Statistics, IC 1.23/
20
Supplement to Employment and Earnings, L 2.41/
2-2
Supplement to General Rules and Regulations, C
15.9/2
Supplement to Index to Commission Decisions, SE
1.11/2
Supplement to LC Subject Headings, Quarterly
Cumulative Supplement, LC 26.7
Supplement to Merchant Vessels of United States,
TD 5.12
Supplement to Pilot Charts, N 6.26
Supplement to Producer Prices and Price Indexes
Data for (year), L 2.61/11
Supplement to State Court Model Statistical
Dictionary, J 29.9/3
Supplement to Table of Cases Decided, LR 1.8/9
Supplement to Title 3, the President, GS 4.108/2
Theater, **Support** to Individuals, NF 2.8/2-30
Trademark **Supplement**, C 21.5/a 3

United States Congressional Serial Set **Supple-
ment**, GP 3.8/6
United States Government Flight Information
Publication: Pacific Chart **Supplement**,
C 55.427
VFR-Supplement, United States, D 5.318/8
Supplemental
Fuel Consumption and Cost, Certificated Route and
Supplemental Air Carriers, Domestic
and International Operations, C 31.267
Fuel Cost and Consumption, Certified Route and
Supplemental Air Carriers, Domestic
and International Operations, Twelve
Months Ended (date), C 31.267/2
Program and Demographic Characteristics of
Supplemental Security Income
Beneficiaries, HE 3.71/2
Quarterly Interim Financial Report, Certificated
Route Air Carriers and **Supplemental**
Air Carriers, CAB 1.14, C 31.240/3
Roll of Honor, **Supplemental** Statement of
Disposition of Bodies of Deceased
Union Soldiers and Prisoners of War
Removed to National Cemeteries in
Southern and Western United States, W
39.8
SSA Program Circulars **Supplemental** Security
Income, HE 3.4/6
Summary of **Supplemental** Type Certificates and
Approved Replacement Parts, FAA 1.14,
FAA 5.12
Summary of **Supplemental** Type Certificates, TD
4.36
Supplemental Digest and Index of Published
Decisions of the Assistant Secretary of
Labor for Labor-Management Relations
Pursuant to Executive Order 11491, Y
3.F 31/21-3:10
Supplemental Reports to the Second National
Water Assessment, Y 3.W 29:13
Supplemental Security Income Program for the
Aged, Blind, and Disabled, HE 3.77
Supplemental Security Income, State and County
Data, HE 3.71
Supplemental Tidal Predictions, Anchorage,
Nikishka, Seldovia, and Valdez, Alaska,
C 55.432
Supplemental Training Material (series), D 105.28
Views and Estimates of Committees of the House
(together with **Supplemental** and
Minority Views) on the Congressional
Budget for Fiscal Year (date), Y 4.B.85/3-
11
WI Communique, Issues of the Special **Supplemen-
tal** Food Program for Women, Infants, and
Children, A 98.14
Supplementary
Office Workers, Salaries, Hours of Work,
Supplementary Benefits (by cities), L
2.43
Radio Facility Charts and **Supplementary**
Information, United States, LF/MF
Edition, D 301.43
Supplementary Cotton Program Series, A 73.12
Supplementary Flight Information Document,
Caribbean and South America, D 301.51
Supplementary Notices to Mariners, Correction
Sheets for Coast Pilots, N 6.11/3
Supplementary Notices to Mariners, Correction
Sheets for H.O. Publications, N 6.11/4
United States Air Force and Navy **Supplementary**
Flight Information Document, Pacific and
Far East, D 301.50
United States Air Force and Navy **Supplementary**
Flight Information, Europe, Africa, and
Middle East, D 301.49
United States Air Force, Navy, Royal Canadian Air
Force and Royal Canadian **Supplemen-
tary** Flight Information, North American
Area (excluding Mexico and Caribbean
area), D 301.48
United States Air Force, Navy, Royal Canadian Air
Force, and Royal Canadian Navy
Supplementary Flight Information,
North American Area (excluding Mexico
and Caribbean area), D 301.48
Supplementing
Wartime Information to Mariners **Supplementing**
U.S. Coast Pilots, C 4.7/6
Supplements
General Maintenance Inspection Aids Summary and
Supplements, FAA 1.31
Index to Reports and **Supplements**, GB 1.6
Plant Disease Reporter **Supplements**, A 77.512

Federal **Support** to Universities, Colleges, and Selected Nonprofit Institutions, Fiscal Year (date), Report to the President and Congress, NS 1.30

General Operating **Support** Grant Application and Information, NF 4.9

General Research **Support** Program Advisory Committee, HE 20.3001/2:R 31/2

Inventory of Federal Programs that **Support** Health Manpower Training, HE 20.3114/3

National Institute of Mental Health **Support** Programs, HE 20.2412

Naval **Support** Force Antarctica, D 201.15/3

Naval **Support** Force, Antarctica, Publications, D 201.15/2

Price **Support** Program, Charts and Tables, Selected Activities, A 82.310/2

Profiles in School **Support**, Decennial Overview, FS 5.222:22022, HE 5.222:22022

Public Health Service **Support** of Cardiovascular Research, Training and Community Programs, FS 2.22/11-2

Public **Support** for Coastal Zone Management Programs Implementation of the Coastal Zone Management Act of 1972, C 55.32/5

Publications Naval **Support** Force, Antarctica, D 201.15/2

Research and Development: Public Awareness/participation **Support** Plan, Fiscal Year (date), EP 1.90

Soldier **Support** Journal, D 101.12/2

Standards **Support** and Environmental Impact Statements, EP 1.57/5

State Programs for Public School **Support**, FS 5.222:22023, HE 5.222:22023

Support to Organizations Theater, NF 2.8/2-33

Surveillance and Analysis Division, Region 8, Denver Colo., Technical **Support** Branch: SA/TSB-1- (series), EP 1.57/3

Training **Support** Developments, D 210.14/4

Supported

Drug Abuse Research and Development, Federally **Supported** Drug Abuse and Tobacco Research and Development, Fiscal Year (date), HE 20.8220

Trainees and Fellows **Supported** by the National Institute of Dental Research and Trained During Fiscal Year, HE 20.3402:T 68, HE 20.3410

Training and Manpower Development Activities **Supported** by the Administration on Aging Under Title IV-A of the Older Americans Act of 1965, As Amended, Descriptions of Funded Projects, HE 23.3002:T 68/2

Supporting

Annual Report of Political Committees **Supporting** Candidates for House of Representatives, Y 1.2/4

Federal Coordinator for Meterological Services and **Supporting** Research, FCM (series), C 55.12

Federal Plan for Meteorological Services and **Supporting** Research, Fiscal Year (date), C 55.16/2

Supporting Papers

Defense Manpower Commission Staff Studies and **Supporting Papers**, Y 3.D 36:9

SupR

Army Intelligence Center and School: **SupR** (series), D 101.112

Supreme

Publications **Supreme** Allied Commander in Europe, D 9.8

Publications **Supreme** Commander for Allied Powers, D 102.11

Supreme Commander for Allied Powers, Publications, D 102.11

Supreme Commander for Allied Powers: Japanese Economic Statistics Bulletin, D 102.18

Supreme Commander for Allied Powers: Natural Resources Section Reports, D 102.20

Supreme Court

Cases Argued and Decided in **Supreme Court** of United States, Ju 6.8/4

Condensed Reports of Cases in **Supreme Court** of United States, Ju 6.8/3

Docket of **Supreme Court**, Ju 6.10

In **Supreme Court** of U.S., Briefs, Petitions, and Motions of Wm. Marshall Bullett, Solicitor General, J 1.19/2

In the **Supreme Court** of the United States (series), Ju 6.13

Official Reports of the **Supreme Court**, Preliminary Prints, Ju 6.8/a

Opinions of **Supreme Court**, Ju 6.8/1b

Papers in Re in State **Supreme** Courts, J 1.82

Papers in Re in **Supreme Court**, J 1.78

Petitions for Certiorari and Briefs on Merits and in Opposition for U.S. in **Supreme Court** of U.S., J 1.19/6

Records and Briefs in U.S. Cases Decided by **Supreme Court** of United States, J 1.19

Tax Cases Decided with Opinions by the **Supreme Court**, Y 4.In 8/11:T 19/3

U.S. **Supreme Court**, Government Briefs in Cases Argued by Solicitor General, Indexes, J 1.19/3

U.S. **Supreme Court**, Government Briefs in Cases Argued, Indexes, J 1.19/4

United States Reports, Cases Adjudged in **Supreme Court** at October Term, Ju 6.8

Sureties

Companies Authorized under Act of August 13, 1894 to be Accepted as **Sureties** on Federal Bonds, T 2.5

Surety

Register of Reporting **Surety** Companies, L 1.82

Surf

Surf 'n' Turf, D 5.320

Surface

A Report of the Secretary of Transportation Pursuant to the Intermodal **Surface** Transportation Efficiency Act of 1991, TD 1.1/5

Annual Report of Indian Land and Income from **Surface**, I 20.61/2

Annual Report of the Secretary of Interior Under the **Surface** Mining Control and Reclamation Act of 1977, I 1.96/5

Bureau of Land Management Maps, **Surface** and Minerals Management Status, Scale 1:100,000, I 53.11/4-2

Coal, **Surface** and Underground Fatalities, L 38.20/5

Compilation of Records of **Surface** Waters of the United States, I 19.13

Correspondence Course, Elements of **Surface** Weather Observations, Lessons, C 30.26

Excellence in **Surface** Coal Mining and Reclamation Awards, J 71.16

Fathom, **Surface** Ship and Submarine Safety Review, D 202.20, D 201.32

Index of Original **Surface** Weather Records for Stations in {various States}, C 55.288

Manual of **Surface** Observations, C 30.4

Metal/Nonmetal, **Surface** and Underground Fatalities, L 38.19/4

Metal/Nonmetal-**Surface** Fatalities, L 38.19/3

Naval **Surface** Warfare Center Dahlgren Division, Technical Digest, D 201.21/8

Naval **Surface** Weapons Center, NSWC-AP (series), D 201.21/6

Naval **Surface** Weapons Center, Technical Reports, D 201.21/5

Quality of **Surface** Waters of the United States, I 19.13

Report of Quality of **Surface** Waters for Irrigation, Western United States, I 19.13

Semimonthly Means of Sea **Surface** Temperature, C 55.193

Surface and Upper Air Weather Charts, C 55.281/2-5

Surface Management Quadrangles (maps), I 53.11/5

Surface Reactions in the Space Environment, D 301.45/19-11

Surface Transportation Board Reports TD 13.6/2

Surface Warfare, D 207.18

Surface Water Records of {states}, I 19.53

Surface Water Supply of the United States, I 19.13

Technical Activities, **Surface** Science Division, C 13.71

Surface-water

Index of **Surface-water** Records to (date), I 19.4/2

Surgeon

Flight **Surgeon** Topics, W 44.25

Surgeon General

Annual Report, **Surgeon General**, United States Army, D 104.1

Health Consequences of Smoking, Report to the **Surgeon General**, HE 20.2019

Medical Statistics, Navy, Statistical Report of the **Surgeon General**, Navy, Occurrence of Diseases and Injuries in the Navy for Fiscal Year (date), D 206.11

National Conference on Public Health Training, Report to the **Surgeon General**, FS 2.2:T 68/6, HE 20.2:T 68/6

Proceedings Annual Conference of the **Surgeon General**, Public Health Service, and Chief, Children's Bureau, with State and Territorial Health Officers, FS 2.83

Proceedings Annual Conference, **Surgeon General**, Public Health Service, with State and Territorial Mental Health Authorities, FS 2.83/3

Reports of the **Surgeon General**, HE 20.7615

Surgeon General's

Index-Catalogue of Library of **Surgeon General's** Office, 4th Series, D 104.8

Surgeons

Federal Air **Surgeons** Medical Bulletin, TD 4.215

Instructions to Examining **Surgeons**, I 24.13

Roster of Examining **Surgeons**, I 24.10

Surgery

Posters Bureau of Medicine and **Surgery**, D 206.23

Review of War **Surgery** and Medicine, W 44.16

Surgery A Study Section, HE 20.3001/2:Su 7

Surgery B Study Section, HE 20.3001/2:Su 7/2

Surgical

Annual Report of the **Surgical** Service, VA 1.1/2

Detailed Diagnoses and **Surgical** Procedures for Patients Discharged from Short-Stay Hospitals, HE 20.6222

Medical and **Surgical** History of War of Rebellion, 1861-65, W 44.10

Surgical and Nonsurgical Procedures in Shortstay Hospitals, United States, HE 20.6209/5

Surgical Research Unit, Brooke Army Medical Center, Fort Sam Houston, Texas: Annual Research Progress Report, D 104.22

Surgical Sterilization Surveillance, Hysterectomy (series), HE 20.7011/30-2

Surgical Sterilization Surveillance, Tubal Sterilization, HE 20.7011/30

Surplus

BuShips **Surplus** Material List Series, N 29.16

Catalogs and Advertisements of **Surplus** Equipment for Sale, N 20.14

Directory, Directors of State Agencies for Surplus Property and Regional Representatives, Division of **Surplus** Property Utilization, FS 1.2:Su 7/2

Facts on **Surplus** Foods, A 69.8

Federal **Surplus** Real Property Public Benefit Discount Program, Parks and Recreation, Report to Congress, I 29.118

Field **Surplus** Lists, T 58.14

List of Available **Surplus** Property Located in District of Columbia, T 58.23

Listing of Eligible Labor **Surplus** Areas Under Defense Manpower Policy No. 4a and Executive Order 10582, L 37.17

Marine **Surplus** Seller, MC 1.26, Pr 33.216

Navy **Surplus** by Auction Catalogs, N 20.14/2

Navy **Surplus** Supplies; Catalog, N 20.14/3

Prime Contract Awards in Labor **Surplus** Area, D 1.57/7

Quarterly Progress Reports by **Surplus** Property Board to Congress, Y 3.W 19/7:207

Report to Congress on Foreign **Surplus** Disposal, S 1.47

RFC **Surplus** Property News, FL 5.12

Summary of **Surplus** Property, C 33.11, FL 5.11

Surplus Government Property Special Listings, FL 5.13, Pr 33.209

Surplus Government Property Special Offerings, Y 3.W 19/8:9

Surplus Leather and Harness Lists, W 77.23/5

Surplus Lists, T 58.13

Surplus Materials Bulletins, M 1.27

Surplus Property Act of 1944, and Amendments, Y 1.2:Su 7

Surplus Property Bulletins, PrEx 4.3/5

Surplus Property Disposed of to Public Health and Educational Institutions, FS 1.15

Surplus Property Lists, T 45.9

Surplus Property News, Pr 33.207

Surplus Reporter, FL 5.14, Pr 33.208

Surplus Subsistence Lists, W 77.23/11

Surplus War Property Administration Regulations, Pr 32.5908

Value of Prime Contracts Awarded by Federal Agencies in Areas of Substantial Labor **Surplus**, C 46.10

Surpluses

What We Are Doing About Agricultural **Surpluses**, A 82.80

Surrenders
  Surrenders and Apprehensions Reported of Men Charged with Desertion from Army, W 3.38
Surveillance
  Abortion Surveillance, Annual Summary, HE 20.7011/20
  Adverse Events Following Immunization Surveillance, HE 20.7011/36
  Arbovirus Surveillance, Reference, and Research, HE 20.7811
  Aseptic Meningitis Surveillance Annual Summary, HE 20.7011/26
  Behavioral Risk Factor Surveillance System, HE 20.7611/3
  Biologics Surveillance, HE 20.7011/37
  Congenital Malformations Surveillance, Reports, HE 20.7011/2
  Encephalitis Surveillance, Annual Summary, HE 20.7011/25
  Enterovirus Surveillance, HE 20.7011/35
  Guillain Barre Syndrome Surveillance, HE 20.7011/32
  Healthy People 2000 Statistics and Surveillance, HE 20.7040
  Hepatitis Surveillance, Reports, HE 20.7011/6
  HIV/AIDS Surveillance, HE 20.7011/38
  HIV/AIDS Surveillance Report, HE 20.7320
  Homicide Surveillance, HE 20.7611/2
  Influenza-Respiratory Disease Surveillance, Reports, HE 20.2309/10
  Intestinal Parasite Surveillance, HE 20.7011/28
  Leptospirosis Surveillance, Annual Summary, HE 20.7011/17
  Malaria Surveillance, Annual Report, HE 20.2309/13
  Malaria Surveillance, Annual Summary, HE 20.7011/8
  Measels Surveillance, Reports, HE 20.2309/4, HE 20.7011
  Measles Surveillance, Reports, HE 20.7011
  MMWR CDC Surveillance Summaries, HE 20.7009/2
  MMWR Surveillance Summaries from the Center for Infectious Diseases, HE 20.7009/2-3
  National Communicable Disease Center Hepatitis Surveillance, Reports, FS 2.60/13
  National Communicable Disease Center Neurotropic Viral Diseases Surveillance {reports}, FS 2.60/14
  National Communicable Disease Center Neurotropic Viral Diseases Surveillance, Annual Poliomyelitis Summary, FS 2.60/14:P 75
  National Communicable Disease Center Rubella Surveillance {Reports}, FS 2.60/16
  National Communicable Disease Center Salmonella Surveillance, Annual Summary, FS 2.60/12-2
  National Communicable Disease Center Salmonella Surveillance, Reports, FS 2.60/12
  National Communicable Disease Center Shigella Surveillance, Reports, FS 2.60/16
  National Communicable Disease Center Zoonoses Surveillance {reports}, FS 2.60/15
  National Communicable Disease Center Zoonoses Surveillance, Annual Summary, Psittacosis, FS 2.60/15:P 95
  National Communicable Disease Center, Neurotropic Viral Diseases Surveillance: Annual Encephalitis Summary, FS 2.60/14:En 1
  National Tick Surveillance Program, A 77.237/2
  NEISS {National Electronic Injury Surveillance System} News, Product Safety, HE 20.4026, Y 3.C 76/3:7-2
  Neurotropic Viral Diseases Surveillance, HE 20.7011/5
  NIOSH Surveillance Reports, HE 20.7111/3
  Nutrition Surveillance, Annual Summary, HE 20.7011/24
  Poliomyelitis Surveillance Summary, HE 20.7011/31
  Primate Zoonoses Surveillance, Reports, Annual Summary, HE 20.7011/9
  Public Health Service Water Pollution Surveillance System, FS 2.84/2
  Rabies, Zoonosis Surveillance, Summary, HE 20.7011/11
  Rh Hemolytic Disease Surveillance, HE 20.7011/19
  Rickettsial Disease Surveillance, HE 20.7011/27
  Rubella Surveillance, {reports}, HE 20.7011/12

  Salmonella Surveillance, Annual Summary, HE 20.7011/15
  Salmonella Surveillance, Reports, HE 20.2309
  Sexually Transmitted Disease Surveillance, HE 20.7309/2
  Shigella Surveillance, Reports, HE 20.7011/18
  Suicide Surveillance Summary, HE 20.7611
  Surgical Sterilization Surveillance, Hysterectomy (series), HE 20.7011/30-2
  Surgical Sterilization Surveillance, Tubal Sterilization, HE 20.7011/30
  Surveillance and Analysis Division, Region 8, Denver Colo., Technical Support Branch: SA/TSB-1- (series), EP 1.51/3
  Surveillance and Analysis Division, Region 8: Technical Investigations Branch, SA/TIB-(series), EP 1.51/4
  Surveillance and Analysis Division, Region 9, San Francisco, California: Technical Reports, EP 1.51
  Surveillance and Analysis Division, Region 10: Working Papers, EP 1.51/6
  Surveillance Reports, HE 20.8324
  Surveillance Summaries, HE 20.7009/2
  Trichinosis Surveillance, Annual Summary, HE 20.7011/4
  Water-Related Disease Outbreaks Surveillance, HE 20.7011/33
Survey
  AHCPR National Medical Expenditure Survey Data Summary, HE 20.6517/2
  Air Transportation Wage Survey, L 2.113/7
  American Community Survey, C 3.297
  American Housing Brief (AHB) from the American Housing Survey, C 3.215/20
  American Housing Survey, C 3.215/19
  Annual Survey of Manufacturers, Origin of Manufactured Products, C 3.24/9-10
  Annual Survey of Manufacturers, Value of Manufacturers' Inventories, C 3.24/9-11
  Annual Survey on Certain Stainless Steel and Alloy Tool Steel, ITC 1.25/2
  Collected Reprints National Ocean Survey, C 55.428
  Commercial Buildings Energy Consumption Survey, E 3.43/2-4
  Consumer Survey Handbooks, FT 1.8/3
  Continuing Survey of Food Intake by Individuals, A 111.9/3
  Current Population Survey, C 3.224/12
  Eating and Drinking Places and Motels Wage Survey Summaries by Cities, L 2.113/4
  End-Stage Renal Disease Program Medical Information System, Facility Survey Tables (year), HE 22.9/3
  Enroute IFR Air Traffic Survey, C 31.165, FAA 3.11
  Industry Wage Survey Reports, L 2.106
  Liquefied Natural Gas, Literature Survey, C 13.37/6
  Materials Survey, I 28.97
  Materials Survey Reports, C 40.17
  MEPS, (Medical Expenditure Panel Survey), Chartbook, HE 20.6517/7
  MEPS (Medical Expenditure Panel Survey) Highlights, HE 20.6517/6
  National Health and Nutrition Examination Survey, HE 20.6209/4-8
  National Household Survey on Drug Abuse: Main Findings, HE 20.417/3
  National Medical Expenditure Survey Methods, HE 20.6517/3
  National Survey of Fishing, Hunting and Wildlife-Associated Recreation, I 49.98/4
  National Survey Results on Drug Use from the Monitoring the Future Study, HE 20.3968
  Occupational Compensation Survey: Pay and Benefits, L 2.121, L 2.122
  Petroleum Products Survey, PPS- (series), I 28.18/3
  Planning Survey Memorandum, A 22.12, FW 2.9
  Plant Disease Survey Special Publications, A 77.520
  Price and Availability List of U.S. Geological Survey Publications, I 19.41/9
  Professional Papers Geological Survey, I 19.16
  Program Memorandum State Survey Agencies, HE 22.28/4
  Progress Report School Facilities Survey, FS 5.46
  Public Use Data Tape Documentation Interviewer's Manual National Interview Survey, HE 20.6226/8
  Public Use Data Tape Documentation National Health Interview Survey, HE 20.6226/10

  Publication Announcement and Order Form, Annual Survey of Manufacturers, C 3.24/9-5
  Publications Coast and Geodetic Survey, C 4.19/2
  Publications National Geodetic Survey, C 55.413/3
  Publications National Ocean Survey, C 55.419
  Quarterly Survey on Certain Stainless Steel and Alloy Tool Steel, ITC 1.25
  Recent Purchases of Cars, Houses and Other Durables and Expectations to Buy During the Month Ahead: Survey Data Through, C 3.186:P-65
  Recordkeeping Requirements for Firms Selected to Participate in the Annual Survey of Occupational Injuries and Illnesses, L 2.129
  Refuse Hauling Wage Survey Summaries by Cities, L 2.113/3
  Regulations for Sale of Lake Survey Charts, W 33.5
  Report on Survey of U.S. Shipbuilding and Repair Facilities, TD 11.25
  Research Reports Lake Survey Office, D 103.209
  Residential Energy Consumption Survey, E 3.43, E 3.43/4
  Residential Energy Consumption Survey: Housing Characteristics, E 3.43/3
  Results of Observations made at C. & G. Survey Magnetic Observatories, C 4.16
  Sailing Directions Coast and Geodetic Survey, C 4.18/3
  Saint Lawrence Survey {reports}, C 1.22
  Service and Regulatory Announcements Bureau of Biological Survey, A 5.6
  Service Survey, I 49.22
  Sheets of National Atlas of United States Coast and Geodetic Survey, C 4.9/21
  Sheets of National Atlas of United States Geological Survey, I 19.5/3
  Ship Operations Report, National Ocean Survey, C 55.423
  Snow Survey and Soil Moisture Measurements, Basic Data Summary for Western United States, Including Columbia River Drainage in Canada, A 57.46/17
  Snow Survey Phase of Project Skywater, Colorado, Annual Report, A 57.56/16
  Soil Survey (of States), A 47.5/2
  Soil Survey Field Letter, A 57.42, A 77.524
  Soil Survey Interpretations for Woodlands, Progress Reports, A 57.58
  Soil Survey Investigation Reports, A 57.52
  Soil Survey Laboratory Memorandums, A 57.43, A 77.525
  Soil Survey Reports, A 47.5, A 19.31, A 19.32, A 77.514
  Source Category Survey (series), EP 4.17
  Special Supplements to Survey of Current Business, C 56.109/4
  Special Supplements to the Survey of Current Business, C 59.11/4
  Specifications Geological Survey, I 19.17/6
  State and Local Government Quarterly Employment Survey, C 3.140
  State, County and Municipal Survey, L 2.13
  Strategic Bombing Survey Publications, W 1.71
  Summary Report on Survey of Students Enrolled for Advanced Degrees: Fall (year), FS 5.254:54009, HE 5.254:54009
  Superconducting Devices, Literature Survey, C 13.37/5
  Survey and Reports Section Statistical Notes, HE 20.2424
  Survey of Activities of the Committee on Foreign Affairs, Y 4.F 76/1:Ac 8
  Survey of American Listed Corporations, General Publications, SE 1.17/2
  Survey of American Listed Corporations, Reported Information on Selected Defense Industries, SE 1.18/2
  Survey of American Listed Corporations, Reports, SE 1.18/3
  Survey of American Listed Corporations, SE 1.18
  Survey of American Listed Corporations: Quarterly Sales Data, SE 1.22
  Survey of Capacity of Refrigerated Storage Warehouses in United States, A 82.58
  Survey of College Graduates, ED 1.127
  Survey of Compounds which have Been Tested for Carcinogenic Activity, HE 20.3187
  Survey of Current Business, C 3.33/1, C 56.109, C 59.11, C 59.11/1
  Survey of Current Business, Weekly Supplements, C 3.34
  Survey of Federal Libraries, HE 19.311:L 61

Task Force on Environmental Cancer and Heart and Lung Diseases: Annual Report to Congress, EP 1.82
Task Force on Higher Education, Pr 37.8:Ed 8
Task Force on Highway Safety, Pr 37.8:H 53
Task Force on Improving and Prospects of Small Business, Pr 37.8:Sm 1
Task Force on Low-Income Housing, Pr 37.8:H 81
Task Force on Mentally Handicapped, Pr 37.8:M 52
Task Force on Model Cities, Pr 37.8:M 72
Task Force on Oceanography, Pr 37.8:Oc 2
Task Force on Physically Handicapped, Pr 37.8:P 56
Task Force on Prescription Drugs, HE 1.32
Task Force on Problems of Aging, Pr 37.8:Ag 4/Ct
Task Force on Rural Development, Pr 37.8:R 88
Task Force on Science Policy, Pr 37.8:Sci 2
Task Force on Urban Renewal, Pr 37.8:Ur 1
Task Force on Women's Rights and Responsibilities, Pr 37.8:W 84

Tax
Briefs in Court of Claims Cases Prepared or Argued by Tax Division Department of Justice, J 1.19/8
Bulletins, Income Tax (lettered), T 22.22
Business Income Tax Returns, T 22.35/2:B 96, T 22/35/3:B 96
Construction Expenditure of State and Local Tax Revenue, C 3.215/10
Corporation Income Tax Returns, T 22.35/3:C 81, T 22.35/2:C 81
Digest of Income Tax Rulings, T 22.24, T 22.25/2
Effect of Income Tax Law Revision on Electric Taxes and Income, FP 1.23
Employment Tax, T 22.19/3:3
Estate and Gift Tax, T 22.19/3:2
Estimates of Federal Tax Expenditures for Fiscal Year, Y 4.T 19/4-10
Farmer's Cooperative Income Tax Returns, T 22.35/2:F 22
Farmer's Tax Guide, Income and Self Employment Taxes, T 22.19/2:F 22
Federal Income Tax Information, D 205.9
Federal Income Tax Information {for Persons in Naval Service}, N 20.22
Federal Tax Collections, Calendar Year, T 22.7/2
Federal Tax Forms, Includes Non-calendar Year Products, T 22.51/4
Federal Tax Information for Armed Forces Personnel, D 205.9
Federal Tax Products, GP 3.38/3
Fiduciary Income Tax Returns, T 22.35/2:F 44/2
Foreign Income Tax Returns, T 22.35/2
Foreign Tax Credit Claimed on Corporation Income Tax Returns, T 22.35/2:F 76
Hawaii Tax Fund Orders, A 55.28
High Income Tax Returns, T 1.52
Income Tax Brevities for Use by Radio Broadcasting Stations, T 22.38
Income Tax Returns: Number of Individual by States, Counties, Cities, and Towns, T 22.40
Individual Income Tax Returns, T 22.35/3:In 2
Internal Revenue Bulletin Index-Digest Quarterly System, Service 1, Tax Matters Other Than Alcohol, Tobacco, and Firearms, T 22.25/3
Opinions United States Tax Court Reports, Ju 11.7/a
Package X, Informational Copies of Federal Tax Forms, T 22.2/12
Personal Weather Estimated from Estate Tax Returns Filed during Calendar Year, T 22.35/2:W 37
Puerto Rico Tax Fund Orders, A 55.18/2
Quarterly Summary of Federal, State, and Local Tax Revenue, C 3.145/6
Quarterly Summary of State and Local Tax Revenue, C 3.145/6, C 56.231/2
Regulations, Alcohol Tax Unit, T 22.17/2
Reports of the Tax Court, Ju 11.7
Reproducible Federal Tax Forms for Use in Libraries, T 22.57
Rules of Practice Board of Tax Appeals, Y 3.T 19:7
Sales of Capital Assets Reported on Individual Income Tax Returns, T 22.35/2:C 17
Sales Tax Rulings, Cumulative Bulletin, T 22.27
Sales Tax Rulings, T 22.26
State Forest Tax Law Digest, A 13.21/2
State Government Tax Collections, C 3.191/2-8
State Regulatory Commissions and Fuel Tax Divisions, IC 1.3/2-2
State Tax Collections in (year), C 56.209, C 3.191/2

Statistics of Income, Corporation Income Tax Returns Documentation Guides, T 22.35/7
Summary of Prescribed Unit Costs and Hourly Rate for Return on Investment and Tax Allowance, C 31.272, CAB 1.10
Tax Capacity of the States, Y 3.Ad 9/8:19
Tax Cases Decided with Opinions by the Supreme Court, Y 4.In 8/11:T 19/3
Tax Court Memoranda, Ju 11.7/2
Tax Delinquency of Rural Real Estate, A 36.78
Tax Guide for Small Business, T 22.19/2:Sm 1, T 22.19/2-3
Tax Guide for U.S. Citizens Abroad, T 22.19/2:C 49
Tax Information, IRS Publications (numbered), T 22.44/2
Tax Policy and Administration ... Annual Report on GAO'S Tax-Related Work, GA 1.13/6
Tax Policy Research Studies, T 1.44
Tax Practitioner Reproducible Kit, T 22.51/2
Tax Practitioner Update, T 22.51/3
Tobacco Tax Guide, T 22.19/5
Treasury Inspector General for Tax Administration, T 1.1/6
Unemployment Insurance Tax Rates by Industry, L 7.70, L 33.11
Your Federal Income Tax, T 22.44

Tax Returns

Tax-Related
Tax Policy and Administration ... Annual Report on GAO'S Tax-Related Work, GA 1.13/6

Taxable
Business Establishment, Employment and Taxable Pay Rolls under Old-Age and Survivors Insurance Program, C 18.270

Taxation
Digest of State Laws Relating to Taxation and Revenue, C 3.50
Guide to Federal Estate and Gift Taxation, T 22.19/2:Es 8
Operation and Effect of the Possessions Corporation System of Taxation, T 1.55
Progress Report Forest Taxation Inquiry, A 13.21
Task Force on Business Taxation, Pr 37.8:B 96

Taxes
Alcohol and Tobacco Summary Statistics, Distilled Spirits, Wine, Beer, Tobacco, Enforcement Taxes, Fiscal Year, T 70.9
Changing Public Attitudes on Governments and Taxes, Y 3.Ad 9/8:17
Effect of Income Tax Law Revision on Electric Taxes and Income, FP 1.23
Excise Taxes, T 22.19/3:4
Farm Real Estate Taxes, A 36.63
Farm Real Estate Taxes, Recent Trends and Developments, A 93.9/6
Farmer's Tax Guide, Income and Self Employment Taxes, T 22.19/2:F 22
Highway Taxes and Fees: How They are Collected and Distributed, TD 2.64
Internal Revenue Bulletin Index-Digest Quarterly System, Service 2, Alcohol, Tobacco, and Firearms Taxes, T 22.25/4
Statement of Taxes, Dividends, Salaries and Wages, Class a and Class B Privately Owned Electric Utilities in U.S., FP 1.22
Understanding Taxes, Teacher's Guide, T 22.19/2-2
World Retail Prices and Taxes on Gasoline, Kerosene, and Motor Lubricating Oils, I 28.44

Taxfax
Taxfax, T 22.64

Taxpayer
Catalog and Quick Index to Taxpayer Information Publications, T 22.44/3

Taylor
Taylor Model Basin Report, D 211.9/2

TB
TB Notes, HE 20.7013/2
HIV/STD/TB Prevention News Update, HE 20.7318

TBT
TBT News, C 13.70

TC
TC in the Current National Emergency, Historical Report No., D 117.9, D 117.9/2
Term Contract, TC- (series), GS 2.12

TD
USGS-TD- (series), I 19.64
{Truck Crops} TD-Series, A 88.16/6-2

TDA
TDA Update, TDA 1.15
USGS-TD

TDC
TDA Update, TDA 1.15

TDL
TDL-CP- (series), C 55.13/5

TDR
School of Aerospace Medicine: Technical Documentary Report SAM-TDR (series), D 301.26/13-6
Space Systems Division: Technical Documentary Report TDR (series), D 301.71
Technical Documentary Report AAL-TDR- (series), D 301.45/30-2
Technical Documentary Report AEDC-TDR- (series), D 301.45/33-2
Technical Documentary Report AFSWC-TDR- (series), D 301.45/20-3
Technical Documentary Report AL-TDR- (series), D 301.45/45
Technical Documentary Report AMRL-TDR- (series), D 301.45/32
Technical Documentary Report APL-TDR, D 301.45/51
Technical Documentary Report ASD-TDR- (series), D 301.45/26-3
Technical Documentary Report ESD-TDR- (series), D 301.45/28-2
Technical Documentary Report FDL-TDR, D 301.45/46
Technical Documentary Report ML-TDR, D 301.45/47
Technical Documentary Report RADC-TDR- (series), D 301.57/3
Technical Documentary Report RTD-TDR- (series), D 301.45/34-2
Technical Documentary Report SAM-TDR- (series), D 301.26/13-6:1056
Technical Documentary Report SEG-TDR, D 301.45/48
Technical Documentary Report WADC-TDR- (series), D 301.45/5

Tea
Industry Report, Coffee, Tea and Spices, C 18.240
Service and Regulatory Announcements Tea, A 46.14, FS 7.14

Teacher
Elementary Teacher Education Program, Feasibility Studies, HE 5.87
Interdisciplinary Student/teacher Materials in Energy, the Environment, and the Economy, E 1.9
International Teacher Development Program, Annual Report to Bureau of Educational and Cultural Affairs, Department of State, FS 5.214:14003
National Defense and Direct Student Loan Program, Directory of Designated Low-Income Schools for Teacher Cancellation Benefits, ED 1.40/2
National Science Foundation, Directory of NSF-Supported Teacher Enhancement Projects, NS 1.44/2
NEH Teacher-Scholar Program for Elementary and Secondary School Teachers, Guidelines and Application Instructions, NF 3.18
NEH Teacher-Scholar Program for Elementary and Secondary School Teachers, Guidelines and Application Instructions, NF 3.18
Teacher Exchange Opportunities Abroad, Teaching, Summer Seminars under International Educational Exchange Program of Department of States {announcements}, FS 5.64/2
Teacher Exchange Opporunities under International Educational Exchange Program, FS 5.64, FS 5.214:14047, HE 5.214:14047

Teacher's
Understanding Taxes, Teacher's Guide, T 22.19/2-2

Teachers
Academic Year Institutes for Secondary School Teachers and Supervisors of Science and Mathematics, NS 1.12
Announcements of Summary Conferences for College Teachers, NS 1.12/2
Directory of Teachers Giving Courses in Rural Sociology and Rural Life, A 36.57
Fall {year} Enrollment, Teachers, and School-Housing in Full-Time Public Elementary and Secondary Day Schools, FS 5.220:20007, HE 5.220:20007

Interagency Directory, Key Contacts for Planning, Scientific and Technical Exchange Programs, Educational Travel, Students, **Teachers**, Lecturers, Research Scholars, Specialists, S 1.67/3

NEH Fellowships University **Teachers**, College Teachers, and Independent Scholars Anniversary and Commemorative Initiatives, NF 3.13/4

Opportunities Abroad for **Teachers** (series), HE 5.99/2, ED 1.19

Opportunities for **Teachers** Abroad, HE 19.112

Opportunities for **Teachers** of French Language and Literature, FS 5.64/3

Opportunities for **Teachers** of Spanish and Portuguese, FS 5.64/4

Programs for College **Teachers** of Science, Mathematics, and Engineering, NS 1.12

Research Participation for **Teachers** of Science and Mathematics, NS 1.12/3

Schools at War, War Savings News Bulletins for **Teachers**, T 66.9

Summer Seminars for College **Teachers**, NF 3.13/2-3

Summer Seminars for College **Teachers** Guidelines and Application Form for Participants, NF 3.13/2-2

Summer Seminars for College **Teachers**, Guidelines and Application Forms for Directors, NF 3.13/2

Summer Seminars for College **Teachers**, Seminar Descriptions, NF 3.13

Summer Seminars for Secondary School **Teachers** Guidelines and Application Form for Directors, NF 3.13/3-3

Summer Seminars for Secondary School **Teachers** Guidelines and Applications Form for Participants, NF 3.13/3-2

Summer Seminars for Secondary School **Teachers**, NF 3.13/3

Summer Seminars for Secondary School **Teachers**, Seminar Descriptions, NF 3.13/3-4

Today's Health Problems, Series for **Teachers**, FS 2.97

Trainers of **Teachers**, Other Education Personnel and Undergraduates, FS 5.84:T 22, HE 5.84:T 22

Teachers'
Teachers' Leaflets, I 16.20

Teaching
Analysis of Research in the **Teaching** of Mathematics, FS 5.229:29007, HE 5.229:29007

Analysis of Research in the **Teaching** of Science, FS 5.229:29000, HE 5.229:29000

Conservation **Teaching** Aids, A 13.72

Cooperative Graduate Fellowship Program for Fiscal Year, Fellowship Awards {and} Program of Summer Fellowships for Graduate **Teaching** Assistants for Fiscal Year, NS 1.19/2

English **Teaching** Forum, IA 1.17, ICA 1.11, S 21.15

English **Teaching** Study Units, IA 1.17/3

Fogarty International Center Series on the **Teaching** of Preventative Medicine, HE 20.3714

National Research and **Teaching** Conference in Agricultural Cooperation, A 89.18

Research in the **Teaching** of Science, FS 5.229:29000, HE 5.229:29000

Rounds of the **Teaching** Staff, VA 1.61

Selected English **Teaching** Materials Catalogue, IA 1.17/2

Teacher Exchange Opportunities Abroad, **Teaching**, Summer Seminars under International Educational Exchange Program of Department of States {announcements}, FS 5.64/2

Teaching Aids for Developing International Understanding, FS 5.52

Teaching Opportunities, Directory of Placement Information, FS 5.226:2600, HE 5.226:2600

Teenage Health **Teaching** Modules (series), HE 20.7024

Water Resources **Teaching** Guide (series), I 27.76

Team
Cleft Palate **Team** Directory, HE 20.3402:C 58/2

Engineer Center **Team** Minutes, D 103.112/4

Yellowstone Grizzly Bear Investigations, Annual Report of the Interagency Study **Team**, I 29.94

Teamwork
Teamwork, Y 3.T 25:22

TEB
Training and Education Bulletin **TEB** (series), FCD 1.9

TEC
TEC Lessons (series), D 101.6/7

Tech
AEC-NASA **Tech** Briefs, NAS 1.29/2

Bio **Tech** Brief, E 6.11

ECOL **Tech** Paper, A 13.66/18

NASA **Tech** Briefs, NAS 1.29, NAS 1.29/3

NTIS **Tech** Express, C 51.21

Preservation **Tech** Notes, Doors, I 29.84/3-10

Preservation **Tech** Notes Exterior Woodwork, I 29.84/3-6

Preservation **Tech** Notes Historic Interior Spaces (series), I 29.84/3-2

Preservation **Tech** Notes Masonry, I 29.84/3-7

Preservation **Tech** Notes Mechanical Systems, I 29.84/3-9

Preservation **Tech** Notes Metals, I 29.84/3-8

Preservation **Tech** Notes Museum Collection Storage (series), I 29.84/3-3

Preservation **Tech** Notes Site, I 29.84/3-11

Preservation **Tech** Notes Temporary Protection (series), I 29.84/3-5

Preservation **Tech** Notes Windows (series), I 29.84/3-4

Preservation **Tech** Notes, I 29.84/3

Sti-Recon Bulletin and **Tech** Info News, NAS 1.76

Tech Data Sheet (series), D 201.27

Tech Notes, C 51.17, C 51.17/12

Tech Notes: Energy, C 51.17/3

Tech Transfer Highlights, E 1.86/10

Tech Trends, EP 1.106

TechBeat
TechBeat, J 28.37

Tech-Tran
Tech-Tran, D 103.125

Techdata
NCEL **Techdata**, D 201.27

Technical
Abstracts from Annual and **Technical** Reports Submitted by USAMRDC Contractors/Grantees, D 104.23

Access: A **Technical** Circular for the End-User Computing Community, HE 3.4/7

ACER **Technical** Memorandum (series), I 27.75

ACIC **Technical** Reports, D 301.59/2

Advanced Abstracts of Scientific and **Technical** Papers Submitted for Publication and Presentation, D 104.23/2

AF **Technical** Reports, Wright Air Development Center, D 301.45/6

AFCRC **Technical** Notes TN (series), D 301.45/4-2

AFCRC **Technical** Reports, D 301.45/4

Agriculture Technology for Developing Countries, **Technical** Series Papers, S 18.45

Agronomy **Technical** Notes, A 57.67

Air Corps **Technical** Reports, W 87.26

Air Force Avionics Laboratory **Technical** Reports, AFAL-TR-(series), D 301.45/45-2

Air Force Cambridge Research Center: AFCRC **Technical** Reports, D 301.45/4

Air Force Command and Control Development Division: **Technical** Notes AFCCDD-TN (nos.), D 301.45/24

Air Force Missile Test Center: **Technical** Reports, AFMTC TR (series), D 301.45/23

Air Material Command: **Technical** Reports, D 301.67

Air Pollution **Technical** Publications of the U.S. Environmental Protection Agency, Quarterly Bulletin, EP 1.21/8

Air Research and Development Command: **Technical** Reports, ARDC-TR, D 301.45/21

Air Technical Intelligence **Technical** Data Digest, M 301.9

Air Weather Service, **Technical** Reports, D 301.40

Alaska Technical Report, I 53.28

Alaskan Air Command, Arctic Aeromedical Laboratory: **Technical** Notes, D 301.66

Alcohol Fuels Programs **Technical** Review, E 1.80/2

AMC Laboratories and Research, Development and Engineering Centers, **Technical** Accomplishments, D 101.1/4

AMS **Technical** Manuals, D 103.20/2

Annapolis Field Office, Middle Atlantic Region 3, Philadelphia, Pa.: **Technical** Reports, EP 1.51/2

Annotated Bibliography of **Technical** Films {by subject}, S 17.29/2

Annual Report on the **Technical** Assistance Training Program in Education, FS 5.214:14046, HE 5.214:14046

Annual **Technical** Report of the Cape May Plant Materials Center, HE 3.67/2

Appalachian Education Satellite Project **Technical** Reports, Y 3.Ap 4/2:12

Aquatic Plant Control Program **Technical** Reports, D 103.24/13

ARDC **Technical** Program Planning Document AF ARPD, D 301.45/49

Area Redevelopment **Technical** Leaflets, I 1.93

ARL **Technical** Reports, D 301.45/25

Armed Forces Radiobiology Research Institute: **Technical** Reports, D 15.12/2

Army Air Mobility Research and Development Laboratory Fort Eustis Virginia: USAAMRDL **Technical** Reports, D 117.8/2 D 117.8/4

Army Electronics Command Fort Monmouth N.J.: Research and Development **Technical** Reports ECOM (series), D 111.9/4

Army Prosthetics Research Laboratory **Technical** Reports, D 104.15/2

ASD **Technical** Note TN (series), D 301.45/26

Atmospheric Sciences Laboratory: **Technical** Reports ASL-TR (series), D 111.9/5

Ballistic Systems Division **Technical** Documentary Report BSD-TDR, D 301.45/36

BCD **Technical** Papers, C 3.226/2

Bibliographies of **Technical** Reports Information Retrieval Lists, FAA 1.10/2

Bibliography of Translations from Russian Scientific and **Technical** Literature, LC 1.26

BRH **Technical** Information Accession Bulletin, HE 20.4103/2

Bulletin of Courses Water Pollution Control **Technical** Training Program, I 67.17

Bureau of Ships **Technical** Manual, D 211.7/3

C & G S **Technical** Manuals, C 4.12/5

CADO **Technical** Data Digest, D 301.14

CAORF **Technical** Reports (series), TD 11.18

Carcinogenesis **Technical** Report Series, NCI-CG-TR (series), HE 20.3159/2

Catalog of Seminars, Training Programs and **Technical** Assistance in Labor Statistics, L 2.114

Catalog of **Technical** Reports CTR (series), C 41.21/3

Center for Food Safety and Applied Nutrition **Technical** Plan, HE 20.4515

Center for Radiation Research, **Technical** Highlights, Fiscal Year, C 13.1/2

Center for Vocational and **Technical** Education, Ohio State University: Research and Development Series, HE 18.11

CETA **Technical** Assistance Documents, L 37.8/2

CETA **Technical** Documents (series), L 37.8/3

Chanute **Technical** Training Center Economic Resource Impact Statement, D 301.105/9

Chemical and Plastics Division, **Technical** Report CP (series), D 106.9/5

Civil Defense **Technical** Bulletins, Pr 34.753, PrEx 4.3/2

Climatic Impact Assessment Program; **Technical** Abstract Report, TD 1.38

Coal Conversion Systems **Technical** Data Book, E 1.56

Coal **Technical** Reports, ER 1.28/5

Coastal Engineering **Technical** Aids (numbered), D 103.42/12

Coastal Zone Management **Technical** Assistance Documents, C 55.32/2

Cold Regions **Technical** Digest (series), D 103.33/14

Commandant's International **Technical** Series, TD 5.48

Committee on Channel Stabilization: **Technical** Reports, D 103.64

Computer Research and Technology Divisions: **Technical** Reports, HE 20.3011

Conservation Agronomy **Technical** Notes, A 57.63

Consolidated Abstracts of **Technical** Reports, FAA 2.11

Consolidated Abstracts of **Technical** Reports: General Distribution, FAA 2.11/2

Cooperative Studies **Technical** Papers, C 30.61/2

CSAP **Technical** Report, HE 20.415/3

Current Review of Soviet **Technical** Press, C 41.94

Customer Care **Technical** Brief, E 6.1/2

Directory of Computerized Data Files and Related **Technical** Reports, C 1.11/2-2

Directory of Japanese **Technical** Reports, C 51.19/3

Earth Sciences Division: **Technical** Report ES (series), D 106.17
EDRO SARAP Research **Technical** Reports, HE 20.4031/2
Electronic Research Directorate Technical Memorandum ERD-CRRK-TM (series), D 301.45/12
Employment Service **Technical** Reports, L 1.70
Energy Materials Coordinating Committee: Annual **Technical** Report, E 1.52
Energy Program **Technical** Reports, Y 3.N 42/2:9
Engineering **Technical** Information System: EM (series), A 13.84/2
Engineering **Technical** Information System: **Technical** Reports, A 13.84
English Abstracts of Selected Articles from Soviet Bloc and Mainland China **Technical** Journals, C 41.84
Entomology **Technical** Series, A 56.11
Environmental Protection Division, **Technical** Report EP (series), D 106.9/4
EPA **Technical** Notes, EP 1.7/5
ESSA Research Laboratories **Technical** Manuals, C 52.8/2
ESSA **Technical** Memorandums, C 52.15/2
ESSA **Technical** Reports, C 52.15
ET {Entomological Technical} (series), A 77.313
Executive Manpower Management **Technical** Assistance Papers, EMMTAP, CS 1.85
FDA Medical Device Standards Publication, **Technical** Reports, FDA-T, HE 20.4310/2
FDA **Technical** Bulletins, HE 20.4040
Federal Scientific and **Technical** Communication, Progress Report, NS 2.12
Federal Scientific and **Technical** Workers: Numbers and Characteristics, NS 1.14/3
FEDLINK **Technical** Notes, LC 1.32/5
Financial and **Technical** Assistance Provided by the Department of Agriculture and the Department of Housing and Urban Development for Nonmetropolitan Planning District, Annual Report to Congress, A 1.113
Fiscal Year ... Air Force **Technical** Objective Document, D 301.45/27-10
Fish and Wildlife **Technical** Reports (series), I 49.100
Food and Drug **Technical** Bulletins, FS 13.103/2
For Your Information; **Technical** Advisory Services, Health Office, FCD 1.13/2
Forest Product Utilization **Technical** Reports, A 13.96
Forest-Gram South, Dispatch of Current **Technical** Information for Direct Use by Practicing Forest Resource Manager in the South, A 13.89
Frankford Arsenal: **Technical** Memorandums, D 105.17/3
Frankford Arsenal: **Technical** Reports, D 105.17/4
General **Technical** Reports, A 13.88
Goddard Space Flight Center, **Technical** Abstracts, NAS 1.28
Grants, Preventive Services, Training, **Technical** Assistance and Information Services, HE 1.310
GRD **Technical** Report, D 301.45/16-3
Guide to Subject Indexes for Scientific and **Technical** Aerospace Reports, NAS 1.9/6
Helium: Bibliography of **Technical** and Scientific Literature, (year), Including Papers on Alpha-Particles, I 28.27
Highway Planning **Technical** Reports, TD 2.25
Honolulu District: **Technical** Reports, D 103.51
Hydraulic Laboratory: **Technical** Reports, D 103.44
Index of NACA **Technical** Publications, Y 3.N 21/5:17
Information and **Technical** Assistance Delivered by the Department of Agriculture in Fiscal Year, A 1.1/2
Informative **Technical** Bulletins, Pr 32.4821
Institute for Applied Technology, **Technical** Highlights, Fiscal Year, C 13.1/3
Institute for Basic Standards, **Technical** Highlights, Fiscal Year, C 13.1/4
Institute for Material Research, Metallurgy Division, **Technical** Highlights, Fiscal Year, C 13.1/5-2
Institute for Materials Research, **Technical** Highlights, Fiscal Year, C 13.1/5
Institute for Telecommunication Sciences: Annual **Technical** Progress Report, C 60.14

Inter-American **Technical** Aviation Conference, S 5.40
Interagency Directory, Key Contacts for Planning, Scientific and **Technical** Exchange Programs, Educational Travel, Students, Teachers, Lecturers, Research Scholars, Specialists, S 1.67/3
Interagency **Technical** Committee on Heart, Blood Vessel, Lung, and Blood Diseases; and Blood Resources, HE 20.3001/2:H 35
Interim **Technical** Reports, A 13.53
International Field Year for the Great Lakes: **Technical** Manual Series, C 55.21/4
International **Technical** Cooperation Series, HE 3.33
Japanese **Technical** Literature Bulletin, C 1.90
Jet Propulsion Laboratory: **Technical** Reports, NAS 1.12/3
Journal of **Technical** Physics {abstracts}, C 42.52/6
Keywords Index to U.S. Government **Technical** Reports, C 41.21/5
List of International and Foreign Scientific and **Technical** Meetings, NS 1.8
List of **Technical** Studies, HH 2.23/2
Lunar and Planetary Institute: **Technical** Reports, NAS 1.67
Management Design and Development **Technical** Bulletins, HH 1.96
Management Information on ERL's Scientific and **Technical** Publications, C 52.21/5
Manpower **Technical** Exchange, L 1.39/10
Manufacturing Industry, **Technical** Document, EP 4.20
NASA Scientific and **Technical** Publications, NAS 1.21:7063
NASA **Technical** Reports (bound volumes), NAS 1.12/2
Natick Laboratories, Natick, Massachusetts, **Technical** Reports, D 106.21
National Plant Materials Centers: Annual **Technical** Reports, A 57.54
National Survey of Professional, Administrative, **Technical**, and Clerical Pay, L 2.3
National Toxicology Program, **Technical** Report series, HE 20.3564
National Undersea Research Program **Technical** Report, C 55.29/3
Naval Ship Systems Command **Technical** News, D 211.8
Naval Surface Weapons Center, **Technical** Reports, D 201.21/5
NavFac **Technical** Training Center: NTTC Courses, D 209.16
Navy Scientific and **Technical** Information Program, Newsletter, D 210.26
NCG {Nuclear Catering Group} **Technical** Reports, D 103.54
News of Academy of Sciences of Armenian SSR, Phsyco-Mathematical, Natural and **Technical** Sciences Series, C 41.50/7
News of Academy of Sciences of Estonia SSR, **Technical** and Physiomathematical Sciences, C 41.50/5
News of Academy of Sciences of USSR; Department of **Technical** Services, C 41.50/3
Newsletter of Community Development in **Technical** Cooperation, FO 1.31, S 17.31
NHTSA **Technical** Notes, TD 8.23
NHTSA **Technical** Reports, TD 8.22
NIOSH **Technical** Reports, HE 20.7111/2
NIST Handbook, Specifications, Tolerances, and Other **Technical** Requirements for Weighing and Measuring Devices, C 13.11/2
NOAA Scientific and **Technical** Publications Announcements, C 55.228/2
NOAA **Technical** Memorandums, C 55.13/2
NOAA **Technical** Reports, C 55.13
Nonconventional **Technical** Information Systems in Current Use, NS 2.8
Northeastern General **Technical** Reports, A 13.42/28
NOS **Technical** Manuals, C 55.408/2
NRAC **Technical** Reports, PrEx 4.18
NTP **Technical** Bulletin, HE 20.23/3
Numerical Index of **Technical** Publications, M 301.13, D 301.17
Numerical Index Supplement to Bibliography of **Technical** Reports, C 35.7/3
NWC **Technical** Publications, D 201.23
NWHC **Technical** Report (National Wildlife Health Center), I 19.211
NWL **Technical** Report, D 201.21, D 215.14
Oceanographic Unit **Technical** Reports, TD 5.18/2

Office of Marine Pollution Assessment, **Technical** Plan for Fiscal Year, C 55.43/2
Office of **Technical** Services Reports Suitable for Commercial Publications, Bulletins, C 35.10
Offshore Scientific and **Technical** Publications, I 72.14, I 72.14/2
ONR **Technical** Report RLT (series), D 210.8/3-2
Ordnance Field Service **Technical** Bulletins, W 34.36
Ordnance **Technical** Library Bulletins, W 34.21/3
Ordnance **Technical** Notes, W 34.27
OSAP **Technical** Report (Series), HE 20.8018/3
OT **Technical** Memorandums, C 1.60/8
Parklawn Computer Center **Technical** News, HE 20.31
Peace Corps Opportunity Newsletter of Special Interest to Professional and **Technical** People, S 19.13
Personnel Research and Development Center: **Technical** Memorandum, CS 1.71/4
Plans Office **Technical** Reports, NAS 1.39
Plastics **Technical** Evaluation Center: Plastic Reports, D 4.11, D 4.11/2
POCS **Technical** Paper, I 1.98/3, I 53.29/2
PRB **Technical** Research Notes, D 102.27
PRB **Technical** Research Reports, D 102.27/2
Proceedings **Technical** Session on Cane Sugar Refining Research, A 106.27/2
Public Health **Technical** Monographs, FS 2.62
Public Housing Management Improvement Program: **Technical** Memorandums, HH 1.63
Quality Control and Reliability **Technical** Reports, D 7.15
Quarterly Cumulative Report of **Technical** Assistance, C 46.23
Quarterly Index of **Technical** Documentary Reports, D 301.45/15
R & D Systems Studies: **Technical** Reports, HE 19.215
Recombinant DNA **Technical** Bulletin, HE 20.3460, HE 20.3264
Regulatory and **Technical** Reports (Abstract Index Journal), Y 3.N 88:21-3
Reliability Abstracts and **Technical** Reviews, NAS 1.35
Report on the International **Technical** Conference on Experimental Safety Vehicles, TD 8.16
Report to the U.S. Congress and the U.S. Secretary of Energy from the Nuclear Waste **Technical** Review Board, Y 3.N 88/2:1
Reports of **Technical** Study Groups on Soviet Agriculture, A 1.94
Research and Development **Technical** Reports, D 211.13/2
Research Institute for the Behavioral and Social Sciences: **Technical** Papers, D 101.60
Research **Technical** Library Biweekly Accession List, PrEx 4.15
School of Aerospace Medicine: **Technical** Documentary Report SAM-TDR (series), D 301.26/13-6
Scientific and **Technical** Aerospace Reports, NAS 1.9/4
Scientific and **Technical** Assessments Reports, EP 1.23/7
Scientific and **Technical** Personnel in the Federal Government, NS 1.22:G 74
Scientific and **Technical** Publications of ESSA Research Laboratories, C 52.21/4, C 52.21/4-2
Selected List of **Technical** Reports in Dentistry, HE 20.3412
Selected **Technical** Publications, HE 20.4023
Selected **Technical** Reports, Information Retrieval Bulletin, TD 4.17/2
Signal Corps **Technical** Information Letters, W 42.40
Solar Thermal Power Systems, Annual **Technical** Progress Report, E 1.38/2
Space Systems Division: **Technical** Documentary Report TDR (series), D 301.71
SSA Training (series): **Technical** CORE Curriculum, HE 3.69/2
STAR, Scientific and **Technical** Aerospace Reports, NAS 1.9/4
State and Private Forestry: **Technical** Publications, A 13.110/13
State and Private Forestry: **Technical** Reports, A 13.110/14
State **Technical** Services Newsletters, C 1.53
Statistics **Technical** Reports, J 1.40

Status Report, Voluntary and Non-Profit Agency **Technical** Crop Ration Contracts with International Cooperation Administration, S 17.41/2

Summary **Technical** Report of National Defense Research Committee, Pr 32.413/12

Surveillance and Analysis Division, Region 8, Denver Colo., **Technical** Support Branch: SA/TSB-1- (series), EP 1.51/3

Surveillance and Analysis Division, Region 8: **Technical** Investigations Branch, SA/TIB-(series), EP 1.51/4

Surveillance and Analysis Division, Region 9, San Francisco, California: **Technical** Reports, EP 1.51

Systems Engineering Group, Research and Technology Division, Air Force Systems Command, Wright-Patterson Air Force Base, Ohio, **Technical** Documentary Report No. SEG TDR, D 301.45/48

T.I.S.C.A. (**Technical** Information System for Carrier Aviation) **Technical** Information Indexes: Naval Carrier Aviation Abstract Bulletin with Cross Reference Index, D 202.22

Technical Activities, Center for Analytical Chemistry, C 13.58/2

Technical Activities, Center for Chemical Physics, C 13.58/9

Technical Activities, Office of Standard Reference Data, C 13.58/3

Technical Activities, Surface Science Division, C 13.71

Technical Advisory Services, Health Office, For Your Information, TAS (series), FCD 1.13/2

Technical Aids for Small Business, Annuals, SBA 1.11/2

Technical Aids for Small Manufacturers, SBA 1.11

Technical Aids, L 1.49/2

Technical Alfalfa Conference, Proceedings, A 77.15:74

Technical Analysis Papers Congressional Budget Office, Y 10.11

Technical Analysis Papers Department of Health, Education, and Welfare, HE 1.52

Technical Analysis Report DASA (series), D 5.14

Technical Appendix from Vital Statistics of the United States, HE 20.6210/a

Technical Appendixes to the Report and Recommendations to the Secretary, U.S. Department of Health and Human Services, Y 3.P 29:1-2

Technical Assistance Aids, L 1.48, L 31.8

Technical Assistance Bulletins [Outdoor Recreation Bureau], I 66.22

Technical Assistance Bulletins [Substance Abuse and Mental Health Services Administration], HE 20.415/2

Technical Assistance Guides, L 37.308/2

Technical Assistance Guide (series), J 1.8/4

Technical Assistance Publication Series, HE 20.415, HE 20.8025

Technical Assistance Reminders, L 31.8/2

Technical Bulletin of Committee on Tidal Hydraulics, D 103.28/2

Technical Bulletin, D 203.32/3

Technical Circulars, HH 2.12

Technical Committee Executive Summary (series), Y 3.W 58/4:11

Technical Committee Reports, Y 3.W 58/4:12

Technical Data Digest, W 108.18

Technical Development Notes, C 31.12, C 31.125

Technical Development Reports, CA 1.20, C 31.11, C 31.119, FAA 2.8

Technical Digest Bureau of Yards and Docks, M 205.8

Technical Digest Feature, S 18.18

Technical Digest International Cooperation Administration, S 17.45

Technical Digest Naval Facilities Engineering Command, D 209.8

Technical Digest Service, C 41.24

Technical Disclosure Bulletin, D 210.3/2

Technical Division Report, TAS (series), C 41.26

Technical Division Reports, C 35.13

Technical Documentary Report AAL-TDR- (series), D 301.45/30-2

Technical Documentary Report AEDC-TDR- (series), D 301.45/33-2

Technical Documentary Report AFSWC-TDR- (series), D 301.45/20-3

Technical Documentary Report AL-TDR- (series), D 301.45/45

Technical Documentary Report AMRL-TDR- (series), D 301.45/32

Technical Documentary Report APL-TDR, D 301.45/51

Technical Documentary Report ASD-TDR- (series), D 301.45/26-3

Technical Documentary Report ESD-TDR- (series), D 301.45/28-2

Technical Documentary Report FDL-TDR, D 301.45/46

Technical Documentary Report ML-TDR, D 301.45/47

Technical Documentary Report RADC-TDR- (series), D 301.57/3

Technical Documentary Report RTD-TDR- (series), D 301.45/34-2

Technical Documentary Report SAM-TDR- (series), D 301.26/13-6:1056

Technical Documentary Report SEG-TDR, D 301.45/48

Technical Documentary Report WADC-TDR- (series), D 301.45/5

Technical Equipment Reports, A 13.49/3

Technical Fact Sheets, Y 3.C 76/3:11-2

Technical Handbook for Facilities Engineering and Construction Manuals, HE 1.108/2

Technical Highlights Mining Research, I 28.151/2

Technical Highlights of the National Bureau of Standards, C 13.1

Technical Information Bulletins, FS 2.2/3, FS 3.52/2, HE 3.52/2

Technical Information Center: Bulletins, TD 1.3/2

Technical Information Circulars, Y 3.N 21/14:11, FS 6.14

Technical Information Handbooks, FTC-TIH-, D 301.45/31-4

Technical Information Indexes: Naval Carrier Aviation Abstract Bulletin with Cross Reference Index, D 202.22

Technical Information Memorandum (series), D 1.83

Technical Information Notes, I 40.11, FW 3.11

Technical Information on Building Materials for Use in Design of Low-cost Housing, C 13.27

Technical Information Pamphlets, D 103.53/6

Technical Information Release, T 22.42/2

Technical Inquiry Service, S 18.23

Technical Instruction Book Manuscript, TD 4.32/13

Technical Letter, A 57.35

Technical Library Bibliographic Series, D 106.10

Technical Literature Research Series, N 29.17

Technical Manuals, D 214.9/3

Technical Manuscripts, D 103.53/2

Technical Memoranda for Municipal, Industrial and Domestic Water Supplies, Pollution Abatement, Public Health, FS 2.301

Technical Memorandum Beach Erosion Board, D 103.19

Technical Memorandum Defense Civil Preparedness Agency, D 119.8/5

Technical Memorandum Defense Communications Agency, D 5.110

Technical Memorandum Energy Information Administration, E 3.26,

Technical Memorandum National Aeronautics and Space Administration, NAS 1.15

Technical Memorandum National Bureau of Standards, Applied Mathematics Division, C 13.39

Technical Memorandum National Telecommunications and Information Administration, C 60.11

Technical Memorandum Reclamation Bureau, I 27.31/2

Technical Memorandum Technology Assessment Office, Y 3.T 22/2:11

Technical Memorandum To United States Study Commission, Southeast River Basins, A 57.50

Technical Monographs, Y 3.T 25:16

Technical News Bulletin, C 13.13

Technical News from Department of Commerce, National Bureau of Standards, C 13.36/6

Technical Note, L 1.79/3

Technical Notes Ballistics Research Laboratories, D 105.10/3

Technical Notes Bureau of the Census, C 56.215, C 3.212/2

Technical Notes Coast Artillery Target Practice, W 3.37

Technical Notes Department of the Air Force Aeronautical Systems Division, D 301.45/26

Technical Notes Department of the Air Force Air Proving Ground Center, D 301.45/50

Technical Notes Department of the Air Force Alaskan Air Command, Arctic Aeromedical Laboratory, D 301.66

Technical Notes Department of the Air Force Arnold Engineering Development Center, D 301.45/33-3

Technical Notes Department of the Air Force Atmospheric Analysis Laboratory, D 301.45/30 3

Technical Notes Department of the Air Force Cambridge Research Center, D 301.45/4-2

Technical Notes Department of the Air Force Command and Control Development Division, D 301.45/24

Technical Notes Department of the Air Force Electronics Research Directorate, D 301.45/12-2

Technical Notes Department of the Air Force Geophysics Research Directorate, D 301.45/16-2

Technical Notes Department of the Air Force Meteorological Development Laboratory, D 301.45/17-2

Technical Notes Department of the Air Force Office of Scientific Research, D 301.45/18

Technical Notes Department of the Air Force Rome Air Development Center, D 301.57/2

Technical Notes Department of the Air Force Special Weapons Center, D 301.45/20-2

Technical Notes Department of the Air Force Wright Air Development Center, D 301.45/13

Technical Notes Environmental Protection Agency, EP 1.7/5

Technical Notes Forest Service Forest Products Laboratory, A 13.27/9

Technical Notes Forest Service Lake States Forest Experiment Station, A 13.61/10

Technical Notes Forest Service Northeastern Forest Experiment Station, A 13.67/9, A 13.42/7

Technical Notes Forest Service Northern Forest Experiment Station, A 13.73/9

Technical Notes Forest Service Southeastern Forest Experiment Station, A 13.63/8

Technical Notes Forest Service WSDG-TN- (nos), A 13.27/9, A 13.87/4

Technical Notes National Aeronautics and Space Administration, NAS 1.14

Technical Notes National Bureau of Standards, C 13.46

Technical Notes Naval Air Systems Command, N 28.6, M 208.10, D 202.7

Technical Notes Picatinny Arsenal, D 105.12/2, D 105.12/4

Technical Notes Weather Bureau, C 30.82

Technical Orders, D 202.8

Technical Papers, AFHRL-TP- (series), D 301.45/27-4

Technical Papers, C 1.73, I 53.30

Technical Personnel Pamphlets, D 12.8/2

Technical Plan for the Great Lakes Environmental Research Laboratory, C 55.620/2

Technical Preservation Services Reading Lists, I 70.15/2

Technical Problems Affecting National Defense, C 32.8

Technical Procedures Bulletins, C 55.128

Technical Progress Bulletin, C 13.58/11

Technical Progress Reports, I 28.26/6

Technical Publication Announcements, C 13.58/10

Technical Publications (series), I 19.14/7

Technical Publications Announcements with Indexes, NAS 1.9/3

Technical Publications for Air Force Technical Libraries, Book Lists, D 301.20

Technical Publications NAVDOCKS TP, D 209.10

Technical Publications, A 57.15, TD 5.43

Technical Publications, SA-TP (series), A 13.40/12

Technical Reference (series), I 53.35

Technical References, TR-LS- (series), L 16.51/6

Technical Report, [Education Department], ED 1.328/7

Technical Report, [Veteran's Affairs Department], VA 1.45

Technical Report (numbered), L 37.309

Technical Report (series), E 3.26/3

Technical Report, AFAPL-TR, D 301.45/51-2
Technical Report AFML-TR, D 301.45/47-2
Technical Report Analysis Condensation Evaluation (Trace), D 301.45/27-3
Technical Report, APGC-TR, D 301.45/50-2
Technical Report, BRL TR (series), D 105.10/3-2
Technical Report Index, Maritime Administration Research and Development, C 39.227:T 22
Technical Report Memorandum AFHRL (TT)-TRM, D 301.45/27-2
Technical Report NGF (series), D 215.10
Technical Report Summaries, D 301.45/19-6
Technical Report Series: Federal Emergency Management Administration, FEM 1.115
Technical Report Series: Research Customer Service Group, C 55.287/62
Technical Reports [Animal and Plant Health Inspection Service], A 101.30
Technical Reports [Energy Information Administration], E 3.26/3
Technical Reports [Environmental Protection Agency], EP 1.78
Technical Reports [Federal Energy Administration], FE 1.20
Technical Reports [National Park Service], J 29.15, I 29.109
Technical Reports, AEDC-TR, D 301.45/33
Technical Reports, AFFDL-TR, D 301.45/46-2
Technical Reports, AFHRL-TR- (series), D 301.45/27
Technical Reports, AFMDC-TRN(series), D 301.45/17
Technical Reports, AFOSR-TR-, D 301.45/19
Technical Reports, AFSWC-TR, D 301.45/20
Technical Reports, AFWAL-TR- (series), D 301.45/57
Technical Reports, AMD-TR- (series), D 301.45/52
Technical Reports, AMRA CR- (series), D 105.26
Technical Reports, ASD-TR- (series), D 301.45/26-2
Technical Reports, DNA-TR- (series), D 15.13
Technical Reports, DTIC-TR- (series), D 7.15/2
Technical Reports, ESD-TR- (series), D 301.45/28
Technical Reports, FRL-TR- (series), D 105.12/3
Technical Reports from the Study of the Sustaining Effects of Compensatory Education on Basic Skills, HE 19.137
Technical Reports, FTC-TR- (series), D 301.45/31
Technical Reports, MA-RD- (series), C 39.246, TD 11.23
Technical Reports, Naval Research Office London, D 210.16
Technical Reports, NAVTRADEVCEN-(series), D 210.14
Technical Reports News Letters, C 41.21/2
Technical Reports, NSWC/WOL/TR- (series), D 201.21/3
Technical Reports Published in (year), D 117.8/2-2
Technical Reports, R- (series), NAS 1.12
Technical Reports, RT- (series), D 105.14
Technical Reports, SAM-TR- (series), D 301.26/13-6:1057
Technical Reports, TR- (series), D 103.25/2
Technical Reprints, NAS 1.27
Technical Research Reports Published by Air Force Personnel and Training Center Air Research and Development Command, D 301.26/10
Technical Section Bulletins, W 95.21/7
Technical Series, A 9.8
Technical Series Bulletins, S 18.50
Technical Series Reports, C 55.33
Technical Services and Research, OSM/TM-(series), I 71.3/2
Technical Services Office General Publications, C 41.22
Technical Services Research, OSM-TR-(series), I 71.3
Technical Services, C 35.8
Technical Specification Improvement Program Highlights, Y 3.N 88:31/0110
Technical Standard Order Authorizations, TD 4.6:part 37
Technical Standards Orders, C 31.143, FAA 1.38
Technical Standards Register, C 31.143/2
Technical Standards Training Guides, HH 2.6/7
Technical Studies Reports, EP 2.26, HH 2.23
Technical Tables, A 57.21
Technical Terms of the Meat Industry, A 88.17/6:6
Technical Translations, NAS 1.13/2, NAS 1.77
Technical Working Paper Series, C 3.223/27
Technicap Training Courses, **Technical** Techniques of Water-Resources Investigations, I 19.15/4, I 19.15/5

TIB {**Technical** Information Bulletin} (series), HE 3.52/2
Transportation Research and Development Command: Research **Technical** Memorandums, D 117.8
U.S. Army Natick Laboratories, Food Division, Natick, Mass. **Technical** Report FD-, D 106.20
U.S. Naval Ordnance Test Station, Inyokern, **Technical** Memorandums, D 215.11
Unemployment Insurance, **Technical** Staff Papers, L 37.20/2
United States LPPSD **Technical** Information Exchange Documents, EP 1.50
United States LPPSD {Low Pollution Power Systems Development} **Technical** Information Exchange Documents, ER 1.16
USAPRO **Technical** Research Notes, D 101.60
USAPRO **Technical** Research Reports, D 101.60/2
USARTL-TN, **Technical** Notes, D 117.8/4
USSR Reports (Scientific and **Technical**), PrEx 7.22
Vocational and **Technical** Education Abstracts, C 41.62
WADC **Technical** Notes, D 301.45/13
Walter Reed Army Medical Center, Army Prosthetics Research Laboratory, **Technical** Reports, D 104.15/2
War Housing **Technical** Bulletins, NHA 4.10
Watertown Arsenal Laboratory: **Technical** Report (series), D 105.13/2-2
Watertown Arsenal: **Technical** Report Ward, TR (series), D 105.13/2-3
White Oak Laboratory: **Technical** Reports, NSWC/WOL/TR- (series), D 201.21/3
Wildlife Research Laboratory: **Technical** Notes, I 49.47/3
Wildlife Unit **Technical** Series, A 13.32/2-2
WSDG **Technical** Papers, WSDG-TP- (series), A 13.87/2
Wyoming BLM Wildlife **Technical** Bulletins, I 53.34
Technicap
  Technicap Training Courses, Technical Techniques of Water-Resources Investigations, I 19.15/4, I 19.15/5
Technician
  SSA Training Data Review **Technician**, Basic Training Course, HE 3.69/3
Technicians
  Current Employment Market for Engineers, Scientists, and **Technicians**, L 7.63/2
  Medical **Technicians** Bulletin, Supplement to U.S. Armed Forces Medical Journal, D 1.11/2
Technique
  Standards Laboratory Instrument Calibration **Technique**, D 217.16/7
Techniques
  Acceptable Methods, Techniques, and Practices: Aircraft Alterations, TD 4.28, TD 4.28/2
  Acceptable Methods, **Techniques**, and Practices: Aircraft Inspection and Repair, FAA 5.15, TD 4.28/2
  Environmental Health Service Series on Community Organization **Techniques**, HE 20.1811
  Instruments and Experiment **Techniques** {abstracts}, C 41.77
  Measurement **Techniques** {abstracts}, C 41.75
  New Product Ideas, Process Improvements, and Cost-Saving **Techniques**, Relating to {various subjects}, NASA/SBA FA (series), NAS 1.56
  New Ship **Techniques** and Development of Research Services Division, Annual Report, D 301.45/11
  Radio Chemical Analysis, Nuclear Instrumentation, Radiation **Techniques**, Nuclear Chemistry, Radioisotope **Techniques**, C 13.46
  Technicap Training Courses, Technical **Techniques** of Water-Resources Investigations, I 19.15/4, I 19.15/5
Technologic
  Technologic and Related Trends in the Mineral Industries, I 28.27
  Technologic Papers, C 13.8
Technological
  Productivity and **Technological** Development Division Publications, L 2.19
  Summary of **Technological** Developments Affecting War Production, L 2.17

Technologies
  Applications of Modern **Technologies** to International Development, AID-OST (series), S 18.42
  Appropriate **Technologies** for Development (series), PE 1.10
  Department of Defense Critical **Technologies** Plan for the Committees on Armed Service, United States Congress, D 1.91
  Economic Impact Analysis of Alternative Pollution Control **Technologies** (series), EP 1.8/10
  Environmental-Social Aspects of Energy **Technologies**, E 1.99
Technology
  Activities of the Federal Council for Science and **Technology** and the Federal Coordinating Council for Science, Engineering and **Technology**, Report, PrEx 23.9
  Advanced **Technology** Program Performance of Completed Projects (Special Publication 950-1), C 13.10:950-1
  Advances in Agricultural **Technology**, AAT (series), A 106.24, A 77.31
  Aerospace **Technology** Innovation, NAS 1.95
  Agricultural **Technology** Circulars, A 19.20
  Agriculture **Technology** for Developing Countries, Technical Series Papers, S 18.45
  Air Force Institute of **Technology**: New Books in Library, D 301.45/44
  Air Force Weapons Laboratory, Research and **Technology** Division, AFWL-TDR, D 301.45/35
  Applied **Technology** Laboratory, U.S. Army Research and Technology Laboratories, D 117.8/2
  Army **Technology**, D 101.1/16
  Biomedical **Technology** and Engineering, C 51.9/13
  Building **Technology**, C 51.9/10
  CDC **Technology** Branch, Summary of Investigations, FS 2.60/5
  Center for Building **Technology**, Project Summaries, C 13.59
  Chemistry and **Technology** of Fuels and Oils {abstracts}, C 41.55
  Clearinghouse Announcements in Science and **Technology**, C 51.7/5
  Commercial Fisheries **Technology** Leaflets, I 49.46
  Computer Research and **Technology** Divisions: Technical Reports, HE 20.3011
  Contributions from the Museum of History and **Technology**, Papers, SI 3.3
  Current Awareness Buildings Energy **Technology**, DOE/BET, E 1.119
  Current Industrial Reports: Manufacturing **Technology**, C 3.158/3
  Current Information **Technology** Resources Requirements of the Federal Government, PrEx 2.12/5
  Cybernetics, Computers, and Automation **Technology**, PrEx 7.22/5
  Devices and **Technology** Branch Contractors Meeting, Summary and Abstracts, HE 20.3219
  Directory of Federal Laboratory and **Technology** Resources, a Guide to Services, Facilities, and Expertise, C 51.19/2-2
  Directory of Federal **Technology** Transfer, PrEx 23.10
  Division of Computer Research and **Technology**: Annual Report, HE 20.3011/2
  Earth Resources **Technology** Satellite: Standard Catalog, NAS 1.488
  Emerging **Technology** Bulletin, EP 1.3/4
  Energy and **Technology** Review, E 1.53
  Energy Research and **Technology**: Abstracts of NSF Research Results, NS 1.13/3
  Energy Research and **Technology**: Abstracts of NSF/RANN Research Reports, NS 1.13/3-2
  Energy **Technology**, DOE/ET (series), E 1.18
  Environmental Protection **Technology**, EP 1.23/2
  Environmental **Technology** Partnerships, EP 1.23/10
  EPA **Technology** Transfer Capsule Reports, EP 7.11
  Experimental **Technology** Incentives Program, Program Area Description, C 13.57
  Evidence Report/**Technology** Assessment, HE 20.6524
  Federal Technology Catalog, Summaries of Practical **Technology**, NTIS Tech Notes Annual Index, C 51.17/11
  Fire **Technology** Abstracts, C 58.11, FEM 1.109

Five-year Outlook on Science and **Technology**, NS 1.40/2

Foreign **Technology**, C 51.9/32

Foreign **Technology** Alert: Bibliography (series), C 51.13/3

Geoscience and **Technology** Bulletin, LC 38.12

Grants Contract Reports, Experimental **Technology** Incentives Program, GCR-ETIP (series), C 13.57/2

Health Planning Methods and **Technology** Series, HE 20.6110/3

Health **Technology** Assessment Reports (series), HE 20.6512/7

Health **Technology** Review, HE 20.6522

HUD Building **Technology** Reports, HH 1.72

Industry Trade and **Technology** Review, ITC 1.33/2

Information and **Technology** Report, I 73.11, I 19.210

Information **Technology** Newsletter, GS 1.37/2

Innovative and Alternative **Technology** Projects, a Progress Report, EP 2.30

Institute for Applied **Technology**, Technical Highlights, Fiscal Year, C 13.1/3

International Science and **Technology** Data Update, NS 1.52

Isotope and Radiation Source **Technology**, E 1.99

Isotopes and Radiation **Technology**, Y 3.At 7:52

Japan Report, Science and **Technology**, PrEx 7.16/6

JPRS (series) Science & **Technology**, China: Energy, PrEx 7.15/6-2

JPRS Report: Science and **Technology**, Europe, PrEx 7.17/6

JPRS Report: Science and **Technology**, USSR, Life Sciences, PrEx 7.21/14-2

Laramie Energy **Technology** Center: Annual Report, E 1.1/3

Liquid Fossil Fuel **Technology**, DOE/BETC/QPR (series), E 1.97

Major Information **Technology** Systems, Acquisition Plans of Federal Executive Agencies, PrEx 2.27

Manned Undersea Science and **Technology** Fiscal Year Reports, C 55.29

Manufacturing **Technology**, C 51.9/33

MARATech R and D **Technology** Transfer Journal, C 39.227/2, TD 11.26

NASA Aeronautics Research and **Technology**, Annual Report, NAS 1.19/2

National Institute of Standards and **Technology** Interagency Reports, NISTIR (series), C 13.58

National Patterns of Science and **Technology** Resources, NS 1.22/2

National Referral Center for Science and **Technology** Publications, LC 1.31

National Science and **Technology** Council: General Publications, PrEx 23.14

Naval Research Laboratory Quarterly on Nuclear Science and **Technology**, Progress Reports, D 210.21

Nevada Today, Developments in Business, **Technology** and International Trade, C 1.65

News of Institutes of Higher Learning; Chemistry, and Chemistry **Technology**, C 41.53/8

Nuclear Reactor **Technology**, E 1.99

Ocean **Technology** and Engineering, C 51.9/26

Office of Industrial **Technology** Reports, E 1.138

Office of **Technology** and Forecast: Publications, C 21.24

Office of **Technology** Assessment and Forecast: Publications, C 1.62

Office of Water Research and **Technology**: Annual Report, I 1.1/5

OIT (Office of Industrial **Technology**) Times, The, E 1.140/2

OTS **Technology** Guide Circulars, C 35.12

Post Harvest Science and **Technology** Research, A 77.34

Preservation and New **Technology** Occasional Papers, LC 1.43

Problem-solving **Technology** for State and Local Governments, C 51.9/30

Project Summaries FY (year), Center for Building **Technology**, C 13.59

Publications Office of **Technology** and Forecast, C 21.24

Publications Office of **Technology** Assessment and Forecast, C 1.62

Publications **Technology** Transfer Seminar, EP 7.10

Publications U.S. Army Foreign Science and **Technology** Center, D 101.79

R & D **Technology** Transfer, an Overview, E 1.109

Reactor and Fuel Processing **Technology**, Y 3.At 7:36

Reports Control Symbol Darcom Manufacturing **Technology**, RCS DRCMT-(series), D 101.110

Research and **Technology** Fiscal Year (date) Annual Report of the Goddard Space Flight Center, NAS 1.65/2

Research and **Technology** Program Digest, Flash Index, NAS 1.41

Research and **Technology** Program, Fiscal Year (date), HH 1.88

Research and **Technology** Program, HH 1.88

Research and **Technology** Work on Explosives, Explosions, and Flames, T 28.27

Research and **Technology**, Annual Report of the Langley Research Center, NAS 1.65/3

Research and **Technology**, Annual Report, NAS 1.65

Research and **Technology** Transporter, TD 2.70

RTD **Technology** Briefs, D 301.45/34

School of Military Packaging **Technology** Booklets, SMPT-BKLT- (series), D 105.31

Science and **Technology**, PrEx 7.15/6, PrEx 7.18/2

Science and **Technology** Agriculture Reporter (STAR), S 18.64

Science and **Technology**, Annual Report to Congress, NS 1.40

Science and **Technology** Fellowship Program, C 1.86

Science and **Technology** in Japan, Reports, M 105.24, D 102.15

Science & **Technology** in Review, E 1.28/18

Science and **Technology** News Features, C 1.32/2

Science and **Technology** Policy, PrEx 7.22/14

Science and **Technology** Review, E 1.53

Science, **Technology**, and American Diplomacy, Y 4.F 76/1-12, Y 4.In 8/16:12

Scientific Reports of Higher Schools Chemistry and Chemical **Technology**, C 41.53/9

SITE (Superfund Innovative **Technology** Evaluation), EP 1.89/4

SITE (Superfund Innovative **Technology** Evaluation) Demonstration Bulletin, EP 1.89/4-2

SITE **Technology** Demonstration Summary, EP 1.89/4-3

Small-scale Appropriate Energy **Technology** Grants Program, E 1.76

Smithsonian Studies in History and **Technology**, SI 1.28

Space Benefits: Secondary Application of Aerospace **Technology** in Other Sectors of the Economy, NAS 1.66

Space Science and **Technology** Today (series), NAS 1.51

Studies of Automatic **Technology**, L 2.76

Sulfur Oxides Control **Technology** Series, EP 7.12

Summary of Activities House Science and **Technology** Committee, Y 4.Sci 2-10

Superfund Innovative **Technology** Evaluation Program, Annual Report to Congress, EP 1.89/4-4

Systems Engineering Group, Research and **Technology** Division, Air Force Systems Command, Wright-Patterson Air Force Base, Ohio, Technical Documentary Report No. SEG TDR, D 301.45/48

Systems **Technology** Information Update, HE 3.80T.B. Folders, FS 2.42

Technical Memorandum **Technology** Assessment Office, Y 3.T 22/2:11

Technology and Development Program, A 13.137

Technology Applications (series), E 1.72

Technology Applications Report, D 1.91/2

Technology Assessment and Forecast, Report, C 21.24:T 22

Technology Assessment Program, NIJ Standard, J 28.15

Technology at a Glance, C 13.75

Technology Fact Sheet, E 1.90/10

Technology for Large Space Systems, a Bibliography with Indexes, NAS 1.21:7046

Technology News from the Bureau of Mines, I 28.152

Technology, OWRT-TT, I 1.97/5

Technology Sharing Reprint Series, TD 1.49

Technology Transfer, EP 7.9

Technology Transfer Opportunities, A 13.27:15

Technology Transfer Seminar Publications, EP 7.10

Technology Transfer Today, Gaining the Competitive Edge, D 201.42

Technology Transfer Update, I 28.151/3

Urban **Technology**, C 51.9/14

TEDS

Treatment Episode Data Set (**TEDS**), HE 20.423/2

Teenage

Teenage Health Teaching Modules (series), HE 20.7024

Teenage Victims, A National Crime Survey Report, J 29.23

Tehran

Conferences at Cairo and **Tehran**, 1943, 1961, S 1.1/3:C 12

TELE

TELE-IRAC (series), C 1.60/6

Telecommunication

Institute for **Telecommunication** Sciences: Annual Technical Progress Report, C 60.14

International **Telecommunication** Union, S 5.50

Major Data Processing and **Telecommunication** Acquisition Plans of Federal Executive Agencies, PrEx 2.12/3

Telecommunication Policy, Research and Development, PrEx 7.14/5

Telecommunications

ADA and **Telecommunications** Standards Index, GS 12.10/2

Annual Statistical Report, Rural **Telecommunications** Borrowers A 68.1/3

Contract Reports National **Telecommunications** and Information Administration, C 60.12

Current FAA **Telecommunications**, Fiscal Year . . ., TD 4.73

Directory of **Telecommunications** Management, Annual Report, PrEx 4.17

FAA Future **Telecommunications** Plan "Fuchsia Book", TD 4.83

Federal **Telecommunications** System Telephone Directory, Y 3.At 7:55-2

Market for U.S. **Telecommunications** Equipment in {various countries}, C 41.104

Technical Memorandum National **Telecommunications** and Information Administration, C 60.11

Telecommunications Bulletin, TD 5.3/8

Telecommunications Engineering and Construction Manual, A 68.6/4

Telecommunications Office: Press Releases, C 1.32/7

Telecommunications Plan, TD 5.52

Telecommunications Research and Engineering Reports, C 1.60

Telecommunications Update, IA 1.16/2

Telephone Directory Automated Data and **Telecommunications** Service, Region 1, GS 12.12/2:1

VA ADP and **Telecommunications** Plan, VA 1.77

Telegrams

Division of **Telegrams** and Reports for Benefit of Commerce and Agriculture, Circular, W 42.21

Telegraph

Actions of Commission, Reports (Telephone and **Telegraph**), CC 1.20/3

International **Telegraph** Conference, Brussels, 1928, S 5.27/2

International **Telegraph** Conference, Paris, 1925, S 5.27

List of Wireless **Telegraph** Stations of the World, N 19.7

Operating Data from Monthly Reports of Large **Telegraph** Cable, and Radiotelegraph Carriers, CC 1.13

Quarterly Operating Data of **Telegraph** Carriers, CC 1.13

Radio, Telephone, **Telegraph**, C 18.220/2

Reports of Applications Received in **Telegraph** Section, CC 1.27, CC 1.28

Statistics of Principal Domestic and International **Telegraph** Carriers Reporting to the Commission As of December 31 (year) and for Year Then Ended, CC 1.41

Tabulation of Statistics Pertaining to Block Signals and **Telegraph** and Telephone for Transmission of Train Orders, IC 1 blo.5

Telegraph Accounting Circulars, CC 1.17

Uniform System of Accounts for **Telegraph** and Cable Companies, IC 1 telg.5

Telemechanics

Automatics and **Telemechanics** Abstracts, C 41.43/2

Telephone

Actions of Commission, Reports (**Telephone** and Telegraph), CC 1.20/3

Annual Statistical Report, Rural **Telephone** Borrowers, A 68.1/3

Newly Reported Tuberculosis Cases and Tuberculosis Deaths, United States and **Territories**, FS 2.42/2

Rail Carload Cost Scales by **Territories** for Year (date), IC 1 acco.7

Statistical Tables Showing Progress of Eradication of Brucellosis and Tuberculosis in Livestock in United States and **Territories** for Fiscal Year, A 77.212/3

Territories and Possessions Reports (Individual Reports), C 3.940-17

United States Trade with the **Territories** and Possessions, C 3.164:980

Territory

Acts of Congress, Treaties, and Proclamations Relating to Noncontiguous **Territory**, W 6.12

High Commissioner of Trust **Territory** of Pacific Islands, I 35.16

Indian Inspector for Indian **Territory**, Annual Reports, I 1.20/2

Report of Trust **Territory** of Pacific Islands Transmitted to United Nations, I 35.16/8

Trust **Territory** of the Pacific Islands, Annual Report on Administration of the Territory of the Pacific Islands, S 1.70

Trust Territory of the Pacific Islands, Annual Report on Administration of the **Territory** of the Pacific Islands, S 1.70

Trust **Territory** of the Pacific Islands, S 1.70/7

U.S. Trust **Territory** of the Pacific, Series 9203, D 5.339

Water Borne Commerce of United States Including Foreign Intercoastal and Coastwise Traffic and Commerce of U.S. Noncontiguous **Territory**, SB 7.5/295

Terrorism

Patterns of Global **Terrorism**, S 1.138

Public Report of the Vice President's Task Force on Combatting **Terrorism**, PrVp 40.2:T 27

Terrorism in the United States, J 1.14/22

Terrorism, PrEx 7.14/6

TES

Fisheries, Wildlife, and **TES** Species Challenge Cost-Share Program Report for the Intermountain Region, A 13.124

Report **TES** (series), TD 1.35

Test

AFMTCP-Air Force Missile **Test** Center, D 301.45/23-1

Air Force Missile **Test** Center: Technical Reports, AFMTC TR (series), D 301.45/23

Annual R.O.P. and Performance **Test** Summary, A 77.15:44-7

Calibration and **Test** Services of the National Bureau of Standards, C 13.10:250

Cotton Fiber and Processing **Test** Results, A 88.11/17

Educational and Nonprofit Institutions Receiving Prime Contract Awards for Research, Development, **Test** and Evaluation, D 1.57/8

Equipment Development and **Test** Program, Progress, Plans, Fiscal Year, A 13.49/5

Equipment Development and **Test** Reports, EDT (Series), A 13.49/4

Federal **Test** Method Standards, GS 2.8/7

Homestudy Course; Water Fluoridation **Test** Exercise, HE 20.7021/9-3

Lesson Performance **Test** Grading Sheets (series), D 101.107/2

Photographs of A-Bomb **Test**, Operation Doorstep, Yucca Flat, Nevada, March 17, 1953, FCD 1.11/2

Public Use Data Tape Documentation Chest X-Ray, Pulmonary Diffusion, and Tuberculin **Test** Results Ages 25-74, HE 20.6226/5-2

Publications Air Force Missile **Test** Center, D 301.45/23-1

Review of Waste Package Verification **Test**, Y 3.N 88:25-3

Selective Service College Qualification **Test**, Bulletin of Information, Y 3.Se 4:22

Summary of Cotton Fiber and Processing **Test** Results, Crop of (year), A 88.11/17-2

Test and Evaluation Reports, D 210.25

Test Design (series), J 28.12

Test Highlights, D 301.45/33-4

Test Kitchen Series, C 55.321, I 49.39

Test Method (series), EP 1.89/3

Test of Metals at Watertown Arsenal, W 34.14

U.S. Atmospheric Nuclear Weapons Tests, Nuclear **Test** Personnel Review, D 15.10

U.S. Naval Ordnance **Test** Station, Inyokern, Technical Memorandums, D 215.11

United States Employment Service **Test** Research Reports, L 7.69

University of Maryland College Park 2x4 Loop **Test** Facility, Y 3.N 88:25-7

Uses **Test** Research Reports (series), L 37.312

Tested

Survey of Compounds which have Been **Tested** for Carcinogenic Activity, HE 20.3187

Tested Recipes (numbered), Y 3.F 73:22

Title Survey of Compounds which Have Been **Tested** for Carcinogenic Activity, HE 20.3187

Turkeys and Chickens **Tested**, A 92.9/2

Turkeys **Tested** by Official State Agencies, A 88.15/4

Testimonies

GAO Documents, Catalog of Reports, Decisions and Opinions, **Testimonies** and Speeches, GA 1.16/4

Testimony

Abstracts of and Indexes For Reports and **Testimony**, Fiscal Year, GA 1.16/3-4

Abstracts of Reports and **Testimony**, GA 1.16/3-3

Reports and **Testimony**, GA 1.16/3

Staff Papers, Background Papers and Major **Testimony**, Y 3.Ec 7/3

Testing

Automated Multiphasic Health **Testing** Bibliography, HE 20.2710

Blood Lead Proficiency **Testing**, HE 20.7412/2

Compliance **Testing** Reports (series), TD 8.34

Cow **Testing** Association Letter, A 44.6

Directory, State Department of Education Personnel for Guidance, Counseling, and **Testing**, FS 5.255:25037:A, HE 5.255:25037:A

Erythrocyte Protoporphyrin, Proficiency **Testing**, HE 20.7412/4

Fluoridated Drinking Water, Proficiency **Testing**, HE 20.7412/3

Interpretations, Rulings, and Instructions for Inspection and **Testing** of Locomotives and Tenders and their Appurtenances, IC 1 loc.5

Interpretations, Rulings, and Instructions for Inspection and **Testing** of Locomotives and Tenders and Their Appurtenances, IC 1 loc.5

Laws, Rules, and Instructions for Inspection and **Testing** of Locomotives Other Than Steam, IC 1 loc.8

Laws, Rulings, and Instructions for Inspection and **Testing** of Locomotives and Tenders and Their Appurtenances, IC 1 loc.5

Proficiency **Testing** Summary Analysis, Parasitology, HE 20.7022/3-4

Proficiency **Testing** Summary Analysis, Public Health Immunology, HE 20.7022/3-3

Proficiency **Testing** Summary Analysis: General Immunology, HE 20.7022/3, HE 20.7412

Summary of Brucellosis Eradication Activities in Cooperation with Various States Under Cull and Dry Cow **Testing** Program, A 77.212/7

Summary of Bucellosis Eradication Activities in Cooperation with the Various States Under the Market Cattle **Testing** Program, A 77.212/8

Testing and Instrumentation, C 51.17/10

TOX-TIPS, Toxicology **Testing** in Progress, HE 20.3620

Tests

Crops Research: Results of Regional Cotton Variety **Tests** by Cooperating Agricultural Experiment Stations, A 77.15:34

Index to **Tests** of Metals at Watertown Arsenal, W 34.14/2

Regional Cotton Variety **Tests**, A 106.28

Report of Egg Production **Tests**, United States and Canada, A 77.15:44-78

Results of Regional Cotton Variety **Tests** by Cooperating Agricultural Experiment Stations, A 77.15:34

Serologic **Tests** for Syphilis, FS 2.60/7:Sy 7/2, HE 20.2308:Sy 7/2

Sugarcane Variety **Tests** in Florida, Harvest Season, A 106.27

Tests and Other Applicant Appraisal Procedures, CS 1.41/4:271-2

Tests in Progress Sheet, 2003.32, C 55.70

U.S. Atmospheric Nuclear Weapons **Tests**, Nuclear Test Personnel Review, D 15.10

Texas

BLM in New Mexico, Oklahoma, **Texas** and Kansas, I 53.43/5

Cotton Grade and Staple Reports, **Texas** and Oklahoma, A 36.27/2

Cotton Varieties Planted in Early Producing Section of **Texas**, (year), A 88.11/11

Medicare Hospital Mortality Information; Vol. 7, **Texas** - Guam, HE 22.34

Program of Water Resources Division, **Texas** District, and Summary of District Activities, Fiscal Year, I 19.55/2

Report of the Office of the United States Attorney General for the Southern District of **Texas**, Year in Review, J 1.1/12

Surgical Research Unit, Brooke Army Medical Center, Fort Sam Houston, **Texas**: Annual Research Progress Report, D 104.22

Texas, Year in Review, J 1.1/12

Text

AFROTC **Text** Books, D 201.26/12

Engineer School Special **Text**, ST (series), D 103.109

Hours of Service Act **Text** of Act, IC 1 hou.5

Interstate Commerce Act, Including **Text** or Related Sections of Other Acts, IC 1 act.5

Navy Training **Text** Materials, D 208.11/2, D 207.208/4

Officer **Text** (series), D 207.208/6

Patents Assist, Full **Text** of Patent Search Tools, C 21.31/5

Programmed **Text**, USAAVNA PT- (series), D 101.47/5

Special **Text** (series), D 101.107/14, D 101.111/2

Special **Text** of Judge Advocate General's School, D 108.9

Special **Text**, M 114.8

Text Pamphlets (series), D 104.31/2

Training **Text** (series), A 13.36/4

Textbook

Federal **Textbook** on Citizenship, J 21.9

Textbook of Military Medicine (series), D 104.35

Textbook/Coursebook (series), D 305.19

Textbooks

Annual Report, Title 2, Elementary and Secondary Education Act of 1965, School Library Resources, **Textbooks**, and Other Instructional Materials, FS 5.220:20108, HE 5.220:20108

Title II, Elementary and Secondary Education Act of 1965, School Library Resources, **Textbooks** and Other Instructional Materials, Annual Report, HE 5.79/2

Textile

Industry Wage Survey: **Textile** Mills, L 2.3/23

Rayon and Other Synthetic **Textile** Fiber Imports, C 18.121

Silk and Rayon and Other Synthetic **Textile** Fibers, C 18.125

Special Bulletins Bureau of Foreign and Domestic Commerce, **Textile** Division, C 18.127

Textile and Apparel Trade Balance Report, C 61.51

Textile Engineering Laboratory Reports, D 106.9/2-2

Textile Lists, W 77.23/12

Textile Maintenance Notes, C 18.148

Textile Raw Materials, C 18.149

Textile Series Reports, D 106.9/2

U.S. Imports of **Textile** and Apparel Products, C 61.52

U.S. **Textile** and Apparel Category System, C 61.54

United States General Imports of **Textile** Manufactures, Except Cotton and Wool, Grouping by Country of Origin and Schedule a Commodity by Country of Origin, TQ-2501, C 3.164/2-7

Textiles

Pyroxylin-Coated **Textiles**, C 3.104

Textiles and Allied Products, C 18.150

U.S. Exports of **Textiles** and Apparel Products, C 61.50

U.S. Imports of **Textiles** and Apparel under the Multifiber Arrangement, Statistical Report, ITC 1.30

U.S. Production, Imports and Import/Production Ratios for Cotton, Wool and Man-made **Textiles** and Apparel, C 61.26

Texts

Finance School **Texts**, W 97.8/7

Programmed **Texts**, D 103.109/2

Psychological Warfare School Special **Texts**, D 101.44

Self-Instructional **Texts** (series), D 101.107/6
Special **Texts**, D 105.25
State Department, International Law (**texts**, precedents and discussions published by the State Department), S 7.14
Student **Texts**, ST- (series), D 5.352/2
Training **Texts**, A 13.85
Thailand
Resources Atlas Project: **Thailand**, Atlas, D 103.49
Southeast Asia, Burma, **Thailand**, and Laos, LC 1.30/10-5
Theater
Exploring **Theater** and Media Careers, HE 19.108:Ex 7/6
Mary Pickford **Theater** in the Library of Congress, LC 40.10
Opera-Musical **Theater**, Application Guidelines, NF 2.8/2-12
Theater Application Guidelines, NF 2.8/2-6
Theater, Support to Individuals, NF 2.8/2-30
Semi-Monthly News Letter, Federal **Theatre** Project, Y 3.W 89/2:33
Support to Organizations **Theater**, NF 2.8/2-33
Thematic
Separate Sheets of Selected **Thematic** and General Reference Maps from the National Atlas of the United States of America, I 19.111a
Theme
Natural History **Theme** Studies, I 29.62/2
U.S. Constitution, a National Historic Landmark **Theme** Study, I 29.117
Theoretical
Journal of Experimental and **Theoretical** Physics {abstracts}, C 41.52/2
Theory
Computers, Control, and Information **Theory**, C 51.9/8
Nuclear **Theory** Reference Book, Y 3.At 7:53
Theory of Probability and Its Applications, C 41.61/8
Therapeutic
Approved Drug Products with **Therapeutic** Equivalence Evaluations, HE 20.4210, HE 20.4715
Approved Prescription Drug Products with **Therapeutic** Equivalence Evaluations, HE 20.4210
Therapeutic Evaluations Committee, HE 20.3001/2:T 34
Therapeutics
Experimental **Therapeutics** Study Section, HE 20.3001/2:T 34/2
Therapy
Annual Training Course in Occupational **Therapy**, W 44.23/8
Diagnosis and **Therapy**, HE 20.3173/2
Medicare Outpatient Physical **Therapy** Provider Manual, HE 22.8/9
Recent Reviews, Cancer Diagnosis and **Therapy**, Supplement to the Cancergrams, HE 20.3173/2-3
Therapy Manuals for Drug Addiction, HE 20.3958/2
Thermal
Ocean **Thermal** Energy Conversion, Report to Congress, Fiscal Year, C 55.42
Solar **Thermal** Power Systems, Annual Technical Progress Report, E 1.38/2
Solar **Thermal** Power Systems: Program Summary, E 1.38/2-2
Solar **Thermal** Report, E 1.83
Thermal Properties of Gases {tables}, C 13.34
Thermal-Electric Plant Construction Cost and Annual Production Expenses, E 3.17/4
Thermodynamics
Contributions from **Thermodynamics** Laboratory, Petroleum Experiment Station, Bartlesville, Oklahoma, I 28.105
Thermoelectricty
Thermoelectricty Abstracts, D 210.23
Thesaurus
HUD Research **Thesaurus**, HH 1.56/2
Medical and Health Related Sciences **Thesaurus**, HE 20.3023
Thesaurus of ERIC Descriptors Alphabetical Display, ED 1.310/3-2
Thesaurus of ERIC Descriptors Rotated Display, ED 1.310/3-4
Thesaurus of ERIC Descriptors, ED 1.310/3
Theses
Dissertations and **Theses** Relating to Personnel Administration, CS 1.61/2

Third
Third Branch, a Bulletin of the Federal Courts, Ju 10.3/2
Third National Cancer Survey Utilization Advisory Committee, HE 20.3001/2:C 16/7
Thomas
Thomas: Legislative Information on the Internet, LC 1.54/2
Thorium
Rare Elements and **Thorium** in (year), I 28.144
Thought
Soviet Military **Thought** Series, D 301.79
Thoughts
NASA Bits {brief ideas, **thoughts**, suggestions}, NAS 1.36
Thread
National Screw **Thread** Commission, C 13.23
Threatened
Damaged and **Threatened** National Historic Landmarks, I 29.117/2
Damaged and **Threatened** National Natural Landmarks, I 29.117/4
Report to Congress, Endangered and **Threatened** Species Recovery Program, I 49.77/3
Three Rivers
Three Rivers Review, I 29.133
Thrift
Food **Thrift** Series, A 1.24
Monthly **Thrift** Data, T 71.21
Research Papers **Thrift** Supervisor Office, T 71.16
Thrift Institution Activity in (month), FHL 1.33
Thrombolysis
Fibrinolysis, **Thrombolysis**, and Blood Clotting, Bibliography, FS 2.22/13-6, HE 20.3209
Thrombosis
Hemostasis and **Thrombosis**, Bibliography, HE 20.3209/2
Thunderbird
Thunderbird Publicity Book, D 301.98
TIB
Surveillance and Analysis Division, Region 8: Technical Investigations Branch, SA/**TIB**-(series), EP 1.51/4
TIB {Technical Information Bulletin} (series), HE 3.52/2
TIBER
TIBER/Line Files; 1990 Census Version, C 3.279
Tick
National **Tick** Surveillance Program, A 77.237/2
Report of Cooperative Cattle Fever **Tick** Eradication Activities, Fiscal Year (date), A 77.237
Tidal
GITI {General Investigation of **Tidal** Inlets} Reports, D 103.42/7
Index Maps, **Tidal** Bench Marks, C 4.32/2
Regional Tide and **Tidal** Current Tables, C 55.425/3
Reports of Committee on **Tidal** Hydraulics, D 103.28
Supplemental **Tidal** Predictions, Anchorage, Nikishka, Seldovia, and Valdez, Alaska, C 55.432
Technical Bulletin of Committee on **Tidal** Hydraulics, D 103.28/2
Tidal Bench Marks, C 4.32
Tidal Current Charts, C 55.424
Tidal Current Tables, C 4.22, C 4.23, C 55.425
Tidal Harmonic Constants, C 4.35
Tidal Power, E 1.99
Tide & **Tidal Current** Tables, C 55.421/5
Tide
Catalog of Charts, Sailing Directions and **Tide** Tables, C 4.18/1
Catalogs of Charts, Coast Pilots and **Tide** Tables, C 4.5, T 11.5
Regional **Tide** and Tidal Current Tables, C 55.425/3
Tide & Tidal Current Tables, C 55.421/5
Tide Calendar Baltimore and Cape Henry, N 6.22/2
Tide Calendar Hampton Roads (Sewalls Point), Virginia, M 202.13, D 203.13
Tide Calendar Norfolk and Newport News, Virginia, N 6.22
Tide Calendar Savannah, Georgia, N 6.22/3, M 202.14, D 203.14
Tide Current Tables, Atlantic Coast of North America, C 55.425
Tide Tables Atlantic Coast of (Calendar Year), T 11.13, C 4.13
Tide Tables Atlantic Ocean, C 4.15/3
Tide Tables Balboa and Cristobal, Canal Zone, M 115.7, D 113.7

Tide Tables Central and Western Pacific Ocean and Indian Ocean, C 4.15/6
Tide Tables East Coast of North and South America, C 4.15/4
Tide Tables Europe and East Coast of Africa, C 4.15/7
Tide Tables High and Low Water Prediction, C 55.421
Tide Tables Pacific Coast, T 11.14, C 14.14
Tide Tables Pacific Ocean and Indian Ocean, C 4.15/2
Tide Tables West Coast of North and South America, C 4.15/5
Tide Tables, High and Low Water Predictions Central and Western Pacific Ocean and Indian Ocean, C 55.421/4
Tide Tables, High and Low Water Predictions East Coast of North and South America Including Greenland, C 55.421/2
Tide Tables, High and Low Water Predictions Europe and West Coast of Africa, Including the Mediterranean Sea, C 55.421/3
Tide Tables, High and Low Water Predictions West Coast of North and South America Including Hawaiian Islands, C 55.421
Tide Tables, T 11.15, C 4.15, C 4.27, C 55.421
Tide, Moon and Sun Calendar, Baltimore, Md., D 203.12
Tide, Moon and Sunrise Tables, Panama, and Cristobal, Colon, W 79.8
Water Temperatures, Coast and Geodetic Survey **Tide** Stations, C 4.34
Tidings
Export Expansion **Tidings**, C 1.42
Tie
Tie Series, C 18.151
Ties
World Trade in Coal Tar **Ties**, C 18.167
TIG
TIG Brief, D 301.119
Tiger/Census Tract
Tiger/Census Tract Street Index, C 3.279/2
TIGER/Census Tract Street Index, Version 2, C 3.279/2:CD-CTSI
TIGER/Line
TIGER/Line, TD 1.56/5:CD
TIGER/Line Redistricting - Census, C 3.279/3
Tile
Floor and Wall **Tile** (except quarry tile), C 3.85
Structural Clay Products (common brick, face brick, vitrified paving brick, hollow building **tile**), C 3.109
Timber
Lumber and **Timber** Basic Products Industry, Wooden Container Industry, Employer Report of Employment and Required Labor Force by Standard Lumber Type Region, Pr 32.5224
National Forest **Timber** Sale Accomplishments for Fiscal Year, A 13.58
National **Timber** Bridge Initiative Fiscal Year, A 13.113/2
Outlook for **Timber** in the United States, A 13.50:20/2
President's Advisory Panel on **Timber** and the Environment, Pr 37.8:T 48
U.S. **Timber** Production, Trade, Consumption, and Price Statistics, A 13.113
Time
Maturity Distribution of Outstanding Negotiable **Time** Certificates of Deposit, FR 1.54/2
NBS **Time** and Frequency Broadcast Services, C 13.60
Time and Frequency Bulletin, C 13.3/4
Time Distribution Summary, L 7.42
Time Deposit
Deposits of County Banks: Index Numbers of Total, Demand and **Time Deposits** Selected Groups of States, Specified Periods, A 77.14/3, A 93.9/7
Timely
Timely Extension Information, A 43.5/6, A 43.6
Times
Bicentennial **Times**, Y 3.Am 3/6:10
Incubator **Times**, SBA 1.39
OTT **Times**, E 1.128
Peace Corps **Times**, AA 4.10/2, PE 1.9
Prime **Times**, AA 2.10
Recovery **Times**, FEM 1.26
Timothy
Timothy Seed, A 105.18/4
Timothy, A 92.19/11

Domestic and International Business News to Use for **Trade** Association Periodicals, C 1.32/6

Domestic **Trade** Digest, C 18.283

Domestic Waterborne **Trade** of the United States, C 39.222, TD 11.19

East-West Foreign **Trade** Board Report, Y 3.T 67:1

East-West **Trade** Policy Staff Papers, Y 61.17

Electric **Trade** in the United States, E 3.11/17-12

Electrical and Radio World **Trade** News, C 18.67

Emergency Tariff Laws of 1921 and Reciprocal **Trade** Agreement Act of 1934, with all Amendments {May, 1934}, Y 1.2:T 17/2

Essential Oil Production and **Trade**, C 18.69

Essential United States Foreign **Trade** Routes, C 39.202:F 76

Europe Update, Agriculture and **Trade** Report, A 93.29/2-21

Export and Import Merchandise **Trade**, C 56.210:900, C 3.164:900

Global **Trade** Talk, T 17.28

Facts for Apparel **Trade**, Pr 32.4262

Facts for Consumer Durables **Trade**, Pr 32.4267

Federal **Trade** Commission Decisions, FT 1.11/2

Fertilizer Trends, Production, Consumption, and **Trade**, Y 3.T 25:66

Fishery **Trade**, Landings, Receipts, Processing, and Storage, Monthly Summary of, I 49.34

Food Facts of Interest to the **Trade**, Pr 32.4260

Food **Trade** Letters, A 71.9, A 80.125, A 80.410

Foreign Agricultural **Trade**, A 67.19

Foreign Agricultural **Trade** Digest of United States, A 67.19/8

Foreign Agricultural **Trade** of the United States, A 93.17/7, A 105.14

Foreign Agricultural **Trade** of the United States Digest, A 93.17/2

Foreign Agricultural **Trade** of the United States, Fiscal Year, A 93.17/6

Foreign Agricultural **Trade** of the United States, Statistical Report, A 93.17

Foreign Agricultural **Trade** of the United States, **Trade** by Commodities, A 93.17/8

Foreign Agricultural **Trade** of the United States, **Trade** by Countries, A 93.17/4

Foreign Agricultural **Trade** of the United States, **Trade** in Agricultural Products with Individual Countries by Calendar Year, A 67.19/6

Foreign Agricultural **Trade** of the United States; Imports of Fruits and Vegetables under Quarantine by Countries of Origin and Ports of Entry, A 67.19/7, A 93.17/5

Foreign Agricultural **Trade** Statistical Report, A 105.14/2

Foreign Agriculture, A Review of Foreign Farm Policy, Production, and **Trade**, A 67.7

Foreign Agriculture, Review of Foreign Farm Policy, Production and **Trade**, A 36.88, A 64.7, A 67.7

Foreign Oceanborne **Trade** of United States Containerized Cargo Summary, Selected **Trade** Routes, C 39.233

Foreign **Trade** in Farm Machinery and Supplies, A 67.21

Foreign **Trade** Information on Instrumentation, C 41.92

Foreign **Trade** Mark Application Service, C 18.90

Foreign **Trade** Notes, Minerals and Metals, C 18.91/2

Foreign **Trade** Notes, Minerals and Metals and Petroleum, C 18.91

Foreign **Trade** Notes, Petroleum, C 18.91/3

Foreign **Trade** Regulations of (country), C 1.50, C 57.11

Foreign **Trade** Reports, C 3.164

Foreign **Trade** Series, FT 1.9

Foreign **Trade** Statistics Notes, C 3.167

Foreign **Trade** {reports by States}, S 1.54

Foreign Year **Trade** Notes, C 18.92

Fur **Trade** Developments, C 18.94

Futures Trading and Open Contracts in {Wheat, Corn, Oats, etc.} on Chicago Board of **Trade**, A 88.11/18

General Description of Foreign-**trade** Zones, FTZ 1.8

Grain, World Markets and **Trade**, A 67.18:FG

Guide to Foreign **Trade** Statistics, (year), C 56.210/2

Hardware **Trade** Bulletin, C 18.76

Highlights of U.S. Exports and Import **Trade**, C 3.164:990

Imports and Exports of Commodities by U.S. Coastal Districts and Foreign **Trade** Regulations, SB 7.5/275, C 27.9/4, MC 1.11

Imports Under Reciprocal **Trade** Agreements, by Countries, TC 1.13

Index of **Trade** Opportunities, C 61.13/2

Index to World **Trade** Information Service Reports, C 42.14

Industries and Reciprocal **Trade** Agreements, Reports on, by Industries, TC 1.15

Industry and **Trade** Summary, Itc 1.33

Industry **Trade** and Technology Review, ITC 1.33/2

Interdepartmental **Trade** Agreements Organization, Publications, TC 1.14/2

International Coal **Trade**, I 28.42

International Petroleum **Trade**, I 28.43

International **Trade** in Goatskins, C 18.186/2

International **Trade** in Sheep Skins, C 18.186/3

International **Trade** Series, C 18.273

International **Trade** Statistics Series, C 42.9/3

Japanese **Trade** Studies, TC 1.23

Japanese **Trade** Studies, Special Industry Analyses, TC 1.23/3

List of State and Local **Trade** Associations (by States), C 18.200

Livestock and Poultry: World Markets and **Trade** Circular Series, A 67.18:FL&P

Manchurian Soy Bean **Trade**, C 18.197

Monthly Summary of Fishery **Trade**, Landings, Receipts, Processing, and Storage, I 49.34

Monthly **Trade** Update, C 61.46

National **Trade** Data Bank, C 1.88

National **Trade** Estimate, Report on Foreign **Trade** Barriers, PrEx 1.14, PrEx 9.10

Nevada Today, Developments in Business, Technology and International **Trade**, C 1.65

Notice to **Trade** {various commodities}, C 57.315

Office of International **Trade** Releases OIT (series), C 18.281/3

OPA **Trade** Bulletins, Pr 32.4244

Operations of the **Trade** Agreements Program, TC 1.14/3, ITC 1.24

OPS **Trade** Aid TA (series), ES 3.6/15

OPS **Trade** Bulletins, ES 3.9

OPS **Trade** Guide TP (series), ES 3.6/13

Overseas **Trade** Promotion Calendar, C 57.12

Pacific Rim Agriculture and **Trade** Reports: Situation and Outlook Series, A 92.29/2-19

Participation of Principal National Flags in United States Oceanborne Foreign **Trade**, C 39.221

Posters Federal **Trade** Commission, FT 1.31

Production, Prices Employment, and **Trade** in Northwest Forest Industries, A 13.66/13

Proposed **Trade** Practice Rules, FT 1.16/2

Prospects for Foreign **Trade** in {various commodities}, A 67.30

Quarterly Financial Report for Manufacturing, Mining, and **Trade** Corporations, FT 1.18, C 3.267

Quarterly Report on **Trade** Between the United States and Nonmarket Economy Countries, Pursuant to Section 411 (c) of the **Trade** Act of 1974, Y 4.W 36:3

Quarterly Report to Congress and the East-West Foreign **Trade** Board on **Trade** Between the United States and the Nonmarket Economy Countries, Y 4.W 36:2

Quarterly **Trade** Report, Southeastern Asia, C 18.156

Recent Developments in Foreign **Trade** of American Republics, TC 1.22

Recent Trends in U.S. Merchandise **Trade**, ITC 1.15/3

Regulations, Rules and Instructions International **Trade** Commission, ITC 1.6

Report of Federal **Trade** Commission on Rates of Return (after taxes) for Identical Companies in Selected Manufacturing Industries, FT 1.21

Report on **Trade** Conditions, C 10.11

Report to Congress and East-West Foreign **Trade** Board on **Trade** Between United States and Nonmarket Economy Countries, TC 1.38

Report to the Congress and the **Trade** Policy Committee on **Trade** Between the U.S. and the Nonmarket Economy Countries, ITC 1.13

Reports of **Trade** Conditions, C 1.7

Reports of United States **Trade** Missions, C 42.19, C 48.9

Reports on **Trade** Conditions, C 1.7

Research on U.S. International **Trade**, C 42.32

Retail **Trade** (by States), C 3.940-10

Retail **Trade** Bulletins, C 3.202/2

Retail **Trade** Report East North Central, C 3.176

Retail **Trade** Report East South Central, C 3.177

Retail **Trade** Report Middle Atlantic Region, C 3.174

Retail **Trade** Report Mountain Region, C 3.180

Retail **Trade** Report New England, C 3.173

Retail **Trade** Report Pacific Region, C 3.181

Retail **Trade** Report South Atlantic Region, C 3.175

Retail **Trade** Report United States Summary, C 3.138/2

Retail **Trade** Report West North Central, C 3.178

Retail **Trade** Report West South Central, C 3.179

Review of United States Oceanborne Foreign **Trade**, C 39.202:Oc 2

Rubber Products **Trade** News, C 18.201

Rules of Practice Federal **Trade** Commission, FT 1.7

Schedule K. Code Classification of Foreign Ports by Geographic **Trade** Area and Country, C 3.150:K

Schedule L. Statistical Classification of Foreign Merchandise Reports in In-transit **Trade** of United States, C 3.150:L

Schedule R. Code Classification and Definitions of Foreign **Trade** Areas, C 3.150:R

Selected Publications of the United States International **Trade** Commission, ITC 1.9/3

Service **Trade** Bulletins, Pr 32.4222

Service **Trade** Reports, C 3.185

Side Runs of Paper **Trade**, C 18.124

Small Business Weekly Summary, **Trade** Opportunities and Information for American Suppliers, FO 1.17

Soda Ash and Sodium Sulfate: U.S. Production, **Trade** and Consumption, I 28.135/2

Special Foreign **Trade** Reports, C 3.164/2

Special Reports to Congress and East-West Foreign **Trade** Board, TC 1.38/2

Statistical Classification of Foreign Merchandise Reports in In-Transit **Trade** of United States, C 3.150:L

Statutes and Decisions Pertaining to the Federal **Trade** Commission, FT 1.13/2

Stocks of Grain in Deliverable Positions for Chicago Board of **Trade**, Futures Contracts in Exchange-Approved and Federally Licensed Warehouses, as Reported by Those Warehouses, A 85.14, Y 3.C 73/5:10

Summaries of **Trade** and Tariff Information, TC 1.26/2

Summary of **Trade** and Tariff Information (series), ITC 1.11

Textile and Apparel **Trade** Balance Report, C 61.51

Trade Agreement Digest, TC 1.24

Trade Agreements (by countries), TC 1.14

Trade and Employment, C 3.269

Trade and Industry Publications, L 23.16

Trade Center Announcements, C 1.51

Trade Data (series), C 57.17

Trade in Cotton Futures, A 82.30

Trade in Grain Futures, A 82.29

Trade in Wool Top Futures, A 59.12, A 75.210

Trade Information Bulletins, C 18.25

Trade Leads, A 67.40/2

Trade List Catalog, C 42.10/2

Trade Lists, C 57.22

Trade of the United States with, C 18.204

Trade Opportunity Program, TOP Bulletin, C 57.27

Trade Policies and Market Opportunities for U.S. Farm Exports, Annual Report, A 67.40/5

Trade Policy Agenda and Annual Report of the President of the Agreements Program, PrEx 9.11

Trade Practice Rules, FT 1.16

Trade Promotion Series, C 18.27

Trade Relations Bulletin, C 34.9

Trade Review of Canada, C 18.157

Trade World Illinois, C 61.39/3

Trade World Michigan, C 61.39

Trade World, New York, C 61.39/5

Trade World, OHIO, C 61.39/6

Trend of U.S. Foreign **Trade**, C 18.190

Trends in Drug **Trade**, C 3.182

Trends in Dry Goods **Trade**, C 3.197

Trends in Electrical Goods **Trade**, C 3.172

Trends in Grocery **Trade**, C 3.183
Trends in Jewelry **Trade**, C 3.190
Trends in Tobacco **Trade**, C 3.184
Trends in U.S. Foreign **Trade**, C 57.23
Trends in Wholesale Winers and Spirits **Trade**, C 3.200
Tropical Products: World Markets and **Trade**, A 67.18:FTROP
Tung Oil Monthly, Production in America, Foreign **Trade**, etc., C 18.209
Two Centuries of Tariffs, the Background and Emergence of the U.S. International **Trade** Commission, TC 1.2:T 17/20
U.S. Agricultural **Trade** Update, A 93.17/7-5
U.S. Automotive **Trade** Statistics, Series A: Motor Vehicles, ITC 1.16
U.S. Automotive **Trade** Statistics, Series B, Passenger Automobiles, ITC 1.16/2
U.S. Census of Wholesale **Trade** Industry Series, C 3.256/3-2
U.S. Export and Import **Trade** in Leaf and Manufactured Tobacco, C 18.152/2
U.S. Foreign Agricultural **Trade** Statistical Report, A 93.17/3
U.S. Foreign **Trade** (by Commodities), C 18.211
U.S. Foreign **Trade** Highlights, C 61.28/2
U.S. Foreign **Trade** in Pulp and Paper, C 18.198
U.S. Foreign **Trade** {reports}, C 56.210
U.S. Foreign **Trade**: Schedules, C 56.210/3
U.S. Global **Trade** Outlook, C 61.34/2
U.S. Global **Trade** Outlook 1995-2000 Toward the 21st Century, C 61.34/3
U.S. Industry and **Trade** Outlook, C 61.48
U.S. Merchandise **Trade**: Exports and General Imports by County, C 3.164:927
U.S. Merchandise **Trade**: Exports, General Imports, and Imports for Consumption, C 3.164:925
U.S. Merchandise **Trade** Position at Midyear, C 61.40
U.S. Merchandise **Trade**: Selected Highlights, FT-920, C 3.164:920
U.S. Oceanborne Foreign **Trade** Forecast, TD 11.13/2
U.S. Oceanborne Foreign **Trade** Routes, TD 11.13
U.S. Planting Seed **Trade**, A 67.18/3
U.S. Timber Production, **Trade**, Consumption, and Price Statistics, A 13.113
U.S. **Trade** Performance in (year) and Outlook, C 61.28
U.S. **Trade** Shifts in Selected Commodity Areas, ITC 1.15
U.S. **Trade** Status with Communist Countries, C 57.28, C 57.413, C 61.22
U.S. **Trade** with Puerto Rico and U.S. Possessions, FT-895, C 3.164:895
U.S. Waterborne Foreign **Trade**, Summary Report, C 3.164:985
U.S. Waterborne Foreign **Trade**, **Trade** Area by U.S. Coastal District, C 3.164:600
United States Airborne Foreign **Trade**, Customs District by Continent, C 3.164:986
United States Court of International **Trade** Reports, Ju 9.5/2
United States Exports and Imports of Gold and Silver, Total United States **Trade** in Gold and Silver and United States **Trade** in Gold and Silver with Latin American Republics and Canada, C 3.164:859
United States Foreign **Trade** Bunker Oil and Coal Laden in the United States on Vessels, C 3.164:810
United States Foreign **Trade** in Photographic Goods, C 41.108
United States Foreign **Trade** Statistical Publications, C 3.166
United States Foreign **Trade** Statistics, C 18.185
United States Foreign **Trade**, C 3.164:930, C 3.164:950
United States Foreign **Trade**, **Trade** by Air, C 3.164:971
United States Foreign **Trade**, **Trade** by Customs District, C 3.164:970
United States Foreign **Trade**, **Trade** with E.C.A. Countries, C 3.164:951
United States Foreign **Trade**, **Trade** with U.S.S.R. and Other Eastern Europe, C 3.164:954
United States Foreign **Trade**, Waterborne **Trade** by **Trade** Area, C 3.164:973
United States Foreign **Trade**, Waterborne **Trade** by United States Ports, C 3.164:972
United States Oceanborne Foreign **Trade** Routes, C 39.240

United States **Trade** with Puerto Rico and with United States Possessions, C 56.210:800, C 3.164:800
United States **Trade** with the Territories and Possessions, C 3.164:980
USA **Trade** World Nevada, C 61.39/2
USA **Trade** World, Ohio, C 61.39/6
USA **Trade** World, Pennsylvania & Delaware, C 61.39/4
War **Trade** Board Journal, S 13.5
War **Trade** Board Pamphlets, WT 1.6
Weekly Consular and **Trade** Reports, C 10.14
Weekly Roundup of World Production and **Trade**, WR (series), A 67.42
Wholesale **Trade** in U.S., FR 1.21
Wholesale **Trade**, C 18.196
Wood Products: International **Trade** and Foreign Markets, A 67.18:WP
Work Injuries, **Trade**, L 2.77/4
World Agricultural Production and **Trade**, Statistical Report, A 67.8/3
World Economic Conditions in Relation to Agricultural **Trade**, A 93.34/2, A 105.22/2
World **Trade** Directory Reports, C 18.280
World **Trade** in Coal Tar Ties, C 18.167
World **Trade** in Dental Preparations (WTDP-nos.), C 18.168
World **Trade** in Explosives, C 18.169
World **Trade** in Insecticides, C 18.170
World **Trade** in Paints and Varnishes, C 18.171
World **Trade** in Plastic Paints, C 18.172
World **Trade** in Plastics, C 18.173
World **Trade** in Prepared Medicines, C 18.174
World **Trade** in Synthetic Aromatics, C 18.175
World **Trade** in Toilet Preparations, C 18.176
World **Trade** in Veterinary Preparations, C 18.177
World **Trade** in Wood, Furniture, Floor, Metal and Automobile Polishes, C 18.178
World **Trade** Information Series, C 41.13, C 49.8
World **Trade** Notes on Chemicals and Allied Products, C 18.179
World **Trade** Series, C 42.9/2

Traded
Securities **Traded** on Exchanges Under the Securities Exchange Act, SE 1.16

Trademark
Consolidated Listing of Official Gazette Notices Re Patent and **Trademark** Office Practices and Procedures, Patent Notices, C 21.5/5
Decisions of the Commissioner of Patents and of United States Courts in Patent and **Trademark** Cases, C 21.6
Official Gazette Patent and **Trademark** Office, C 21.5
Patent and **Trademark** Office Notices, C 21.5/4a, C 21.5/4-2
Rules of Practice Patent and **Trademark** Office, C 21.8
Trademark Examining Procedure Directives, C 21.15/2
Trademark Laws, C 21.7/4
Trademark Public Advisory Committee Annual Report, C 21.1/3
Trademark Rules of Practice of the Patent Office, with Forms and Statutes, C 21.14:T 67/2
Trademark Supplement, C 21.5/a 3

Trademarks
General Information Concerning **Trademarks**, C 21.2:T 67, C 21.26
Index of **Trademarks** Issued from the Patent Office, C 21.5/3
Official Gazette of U.S. Patent Office, **Trademarks**, C 21.5/4
Patents and **Trademarks**, ASSIGN, C 21.31/13
Trademarks Assign, U.S. **Trademarks** Assignments Recorded at the USPTO, C 21.31/9
Trademarks Assist, C 21.31/10
Trademarks BIB, C 21.31/18
Trademarks Pending, Bibliographic Information from Pending US **Trademarks**, C 21.31/8
Trademarks Registered, C 21.31/14
Trademarks Registered, Bibliographic Information from Registered US **Trademarks**, C 21.31/7
U.S. Statutes Concerning the Registration of **Trademarks**, C 21.7/2
USAMark: Fascimile Images of Registered United States **Trademarks**, C 21.31/11

Traders
Commitments of Large **Traders** in Cotton Futures, A 85.9

Commitments of **Traders** in Commodity Futures, Y 3.C 73/5:9/2
Commitments of **Traders** in Commodity Futures with Market Concentration Ratios, Y 3.C 73/5:9
Commitments of **Traders** in Commodity Futures, Cotton, Frozen Concentrated Orange Juice, Potatoes, A 85.9
Commitments of **Traders** in Commodity Futures, Cotton, Wool, Potatoes, A 85.9
Commitments of **Traders** in Wheat, Corn, Oats, Rye, Soybeans, Soybean Oil, Soybean Meal, Shell Eggs, A 85.9/2
Commitments of **Traders** in Wool and Wool Top Futures, New York Cotton Exchange, A 85.9/3

Trades
Census of Business; Service **Trades** Bulletins (by States), C 3.202/4
Current Distribution Developments in Hardware and Allied **Trades**, C 18.215
Job Grading System for **Trades** and Labor Occupations, CS 1.41/4:512-1, CS 1.42/2
Retail, Wholesale, Service **Trades**, Subject Bulletin, RWS (series), C 3.202/9

Tradewinds
Tradewinds, C 61.27, C 61.36

Trading
Control and Employment of Vessels **Trading** with United States, SB 5.6
Enemy **Trading** List, WT 1.7
Futures **Trading** and Open Contracts in Butter, Eggs and Potatoes, A 85.11/4
Futures **Trading** and Open Contracts in Cotton and Cottonseed Oil, A 85.11/5
Futures **Trading** and Open Contracts in Frozen Concentrated Orange Juice, A 85.11/8
Futures **Trading** and Open Contracts in Potatoes, A 85.11/3
Futures **Trading** and Open Contracts in Potatoes and Rice, A 85.11
Futures **Trading** and Open Contracts in Soybean Meal and Cottonseed Meal, A 85.11/6
Futures **Trading** and Open Contracts in Wheat, Corn, Oats, Rye, Soybeans and Products, A 85.11/7
Futures **Trading** and Open Contracts in {Wheat, Corn, Oats, etc.} on Chicago Board of Trade, A 88.11/18
Futures **Trading** in Cotton, Wool and Wool Tops, A 85.11/2
Microcomputer **Training** Catalog, The DOL Academy, L 1.86/2
Monthly Commodity Futures Statistics on Futures **Trading** in Commodities Regulated under the Commodity Exchange Act, A 85.15/2
Report on Vessels **Trading** with United States, SB 5.5
Telephone Directory, Bureau of Apprenticeship and **Training**, L 37.109
Weekly **Trading** Data on New York Exchanges, SE 1.25/6

Traditional Arts
Folk and **Traditional Arts**, Application Guidelines For Fiscal Years, NF 2.8/2-36

TraDiv
TraDiv Letters, N 17.33

TRADOC
TRADOC Historical Monograph Series, D 101.108
TRADOC Historical Study Series, D 101.108/2
TRADOC Pamphlet (series), D 101.22/22

Traffic
Activities at Air **Traffic** Control Facilities, Fiscal Year, FAA 1.27/2
Air Carrier Industry Scheduled Series: **Traffic** Statistics Quarterly, TD 12.15
Air Carrier Industry Scheduled Service **Traffic** Statistics, CAB 1.39
Air Carrier **Traffic** Statistics, C 31.241, CAB 1.13
Air Carrier **Traffic** Statistics Monthly, TD 10.9/3, TD 12.15/2
Air Commerce **Traffic** Patterns, C 3.153, FAA 4.11
Air Commerce **Traffic** Patterns (scheduled carriers), Fiscal Year, FAA 8.9
Air **Traffic** Control Handbook, TD 4.308:Ai 7/3
Air **Traffic** Control Procedures, FAA 3.9
Air **Traffic** Patterns for IFR and VFR Aviation, Calendar Year, TD 4.19/2
Air **Traffic** Publications Library, TD 4.78
Air **Traffic** Survey {maps}, C 31.218
Airline **Traffic** Survey, C 31.225

ANC Procedures for Control of Air **Traffic**, C 31.106/2

Annual Report on Urban Area **Traffic** Operations Improvement, TD 2.29

Auto and **Traffic** Safety, TD 8.36

Carload Waybill Analyses, Distribution of Freight **Traffic** and Revenue Averages by Commodity Groups and Rate Territories, IC 1.20

Carload Waybill Analyses, Territorial Distribution, **Traffic** and Revenue by Commodity Groups, IC 1.22

Carload Waybill Statistics, . . ., **Traffic** and Revenue by Commodity Class, Territorial Movement, and Type of Rate, Products of Agriculture, 1 Percent Sample of Terminations in Statement MB-1, IC 1.23/2

Carload Waybill Statistics, . . ., **Traffic** and Revenue by Commodity Class, Territorial Movement, and Type of Rate, Animals and Products, 1 Percent Sample of Terminations in Statement MB-2, IC 1.23/3

Carload Waybill Statistics, . . ., **Traffic** and Revenue by Commodity Class, Territorial Movement, and Type of Rate, Products of Mines, 1 Percent Sample of Terminations in Statement MB-3, IC 1.23/4

Carload Waybill Statistics, . . ., **Traffic** and Revenue by Commodity Class, Territorial Movement, and Type of Rate, Products of Forests, 1 Percent Sample of Terminations in Statement MB-4, IC 1.23/5

Carload Waybill Statistics, . . ., **Traffic** and Revenue by Commodity Class, Territorial Movement, and Type of Rate, Manufacturers and Miscellaneous Forwarder Traffic, One Percent Sampling. . . MB-5, IC 1.23/6

Carload Waybill Statistics, . . ., **Traffic** and Revenue by Commodity Class, Territorial Movement, and Type of Rate, Manufacturers and Miscellaneous Forwarder Traffic, One Percent Sampling. . . MB-5, IC 1.23/6

Carload Waybill Statistics, Distribution of Freight **Traffic** and Revenue Averages by Commodity Classes, IC 1.23/8

Carload Waybill Statistics, Quarterly Comparisons, **Traffic** and Revenue by Commodity Classes, IC 1.23

Carload Waybill Statistics, Territorial Distribution **Traffic** and Revenue by Commodity Classes, TD 3.14

Carload Waybill Statistics, **Traffic** and Revenue Progressions by Specified Mileage Blocks for Commodity Groups and Classes, 1 Percent Sample of Carload Terminations in Year Statement MB-6, IC 1.23/7

Coach **Traffic**, Revenue, Yield and Average On-flight Trip Length by Fare Category for the 48-state Operations of the Domestic Trunks, C 31.269

Community Action Program for **Traffic** Safety, Guides (numbered), TD 8.8/2

Commuter Air Carrier **Traffic** Statistics, C 31.241/3, CAB 1.11

Distribution of Freight **Traffic** and Revenue Averages by Commodity Classes, IC 1.23/8:MS-1

En Route Air **Traffic** Control, TD 4.308:En 1

Enroute IFR Air **Traffic** Survey, C 31.165, FAA 3.11

Enroute IFR Air **Traffic** Survey, Peak Day, TD 4.19/3

FAA Air **Traffic** Activity, TD 4.19

FAA Plan for Air Navigation and Air **Traffic** Control Systems, FAA 1.37

Federal Airways Air **Traffic** Activity, C 31.158

Federal **Traffic** Board, T 51.10

Great Lakes Region Air **Traffic** Activity, TD 4.19/5

Highway and **Traffic** Safety, TD 8.12/3

Highway **Traffic** Noise in the United States: Problem and Response, TD 2.23/7

Indexes of Average Freight Rates on Railroad Carload **Traffic**, IC 1.27

Intercoastal **Traffic**, SB 7.5/158

International Air Commerce **Traffic** Pattern, U.S. Flag Carriers, Calendar Year, C 31.153/2

Manual on Uniform **Traffic** Control Devices for Streets and Highways: Official Rulings on Requests for Interpretations, Changes, and Experimentations, TD 2.8/2

Manufactures and Miscellaneous and Forwarder **Traffic**, IC 1.23/14:SS-6

Marine Air **Traffic** Control Detachment Handbook, PCN nos, D 214.9/7

Military **Traffic** Management Command Publications, D 101.129/3

Monthly **Traffic** Fatality Report, TD 8.38

National **Traffic** Safety Newsletter, TD 8.18

Passenger **Traffic** Statements (other than commutation) of Class 1 Steam Railways in United States Separated Between Coach Traffic and Parlor and Sleeping Car **Traffic**, IC 1 ste.40

Passenger Traffic Statements (other than commutation) of Class 1 Steam Railways in United States Separated Between Coach **Traffic** and Parlor and Sleeping Car Traffic, IC 1 ste.40

Passenger **Traffic** Statistics (other than commutation) of Class I Steam Railways in the United States Separated Between Coach Traffic and Parlor and Sleeping Car **Traffic**, IC 1 ste.39

Profiles of Scheduled Air Carrier Passenger **Traffic**, Top 100 U.S. Airports, TD 4.44/2

Railways Freight and Passenger **Traffic** Handled on Highways, Class 1 Steam Railways, IC 1 ste.41

Recurrent Report of Mileage and **Traffic** Data All Certificated Air Cargo Carriers, C 31.232

Recurrent Report of Mileage and **Traffic** Data Domestic Air Mail Carriers, C 31.230

Recurrent Report of Mileage and **Traffic** Data Domestic Helicopter Service, Certificated Airmail Carriers, C 31.229/4

Recurrent Report of Mileage and **Traffic** Data Domestic Local Service Carriers, C 31.229

Recurrent Report of Mileage and **Traffic** Data Foreign, Overseas and Territorial Air Mail Carriers, C 31.231

Report on Activities Under the National **Traffic** and Motor Vehicle Safety Act, TD 8.12

Report on Administrative Adjudication of **Traffic** Infractions, TD 8.12/4

Report on **Traffic** Accidents and Injuries for (year), TD 8.32

Report to Congress on the Administration of the National **Traffic** Vehicle Safety Act of 1966, TD 1.10/2

Reports on Airline Service, Fares **Traffic**, Load Factors and Market Shares, CAB 1.27

Revenue and **Traffic** Carriers by Water, IC 1 wat.11

Revenue and **Traffic** of Class A and B Water Carriers, IC 1 wat.11

Revenue **Traffic** Statistics of Class I Railroads in the United States, IC 1 ste.24

Seasonally Adjusted Capacity and **Traffic** Scheduled Domestic Operations, Domestic Trunks, C 31.262/3

Seasonally Adjusted Capacity and **Traffic** Scheduled International Operations, International Trunks, C 31.262

Seasonally Adjusted Capacity and **Traffic** Scheduled Operations Local Service Carriers, C 31.262/4

Seasonally Adjusted Capacity and **Traffic** Scheduled Operations System Trunks and Regional Carriers, C 31.262/5

Seasonally Adjusted Capacity and **Traffic** Scheduled Operations, System Trunks, C 31.262/2

Seasonally Adjusted Capacity and **Traffic** Scheduled Operations: System, Domestic, and International Trunks Plus Local Service Carrier, CAB 1.20

Special Air **Traffic** Rules and Airport Traffic Patterns, TD 4.6:part 93

State **Traffic** Safety Information, TD 8.62

Study of Air **Traffic** Control, Reports, C 31.123

Terminal Air **Traffic** Control, TD 4.308:T 27

Territorial Distribution, **Traffic** and Revenue by Commodity Classes, IC 1.23/18:TD-1

Territorial Studies of Motor Carrier Costs, **Traffic** and Rate Structure, IC 1 mot.16

Traffic and Revenue by Commodity Classes, IC 1.23:QC-1

Traffic Circulars, MC 1.21

Traffic, Decisions, IC 1.6/a

Traffic in Opium and Other Dangerous Drugs, J 24.9

Traffic Information Letters, T 58.12

Traffic Laws Commentary, TD 8.5/2

Traffic Report of the St. Lawrence Seaway, TD 6.9

Traffic Safety Data ASCII and SAS Versions, TD 1.56/3

Traffic Safety Digest, TD 8.40

Traffic Safety Evaluation Research Review, TD 8.18/2

Traffic Safety Newsletter, TD 8.18

Traffic Service Letters, GS 2.9

Traffic Speed Trends, TD 2.115

Traffic Techs, TD 8.63

Traffic Volume Trends, FW 2.11, FW 2.14, GS 3.7, C 37.9, TD 2.50

Transportation Revenue and **Traffic** of Large Oil Pipe Line Companies, IC 1 pip.7

Trunk Carriers, Coach Class, **Traffic**, Revenue, Yield, Enplanements and Average On-flight Trip Length by Fare Category, CAB 1.24

U.S. International Air Freight **Traffic**, C 31.265/4

U.S. Water Borne Intercoastal **Traffic** by Ports of Origin and Destination and Principal Commodities, SB 7.5/317, C 27.9/9, MC 1.9

Water Borne Commerce of United States Including Foreign Intercoastal and Coastwise **Traffic** and Commerce of U.S. Noncontiguous Territory, SB 7.5/295

Water Borne Passenger **Traffic** of U.S., SB 7.5/157, C 27.9/12

Water-Borne Foreign and Noncontiguous Commerce and Passenger **Traffic** of United States, MC 1.23

Waterborne Passenger **Traffic** of U.S., MC 1.15

Trafficability

Pavements and Soil **Trafficability** Information Analysis Center, PSTIAC Reports, D 103.24/12

Trafficking

Drug **Trafficking** in the United States, J 24.29

Victims of **Trafficking** and Violence Protection Act: 2000, Trafficking in Persons Report, S 1.152

Trail

Continental Divide **Trail** Study Progress Reports, I 66.19/2

Self-Guiding Nature **Trail** Leaflets, Glacier National Park, I 29.61

Self-Guiding Nature **Trail** Leaflets, Mount Rainier National Park, I 29.61/2

Trailer

World Motor Vehicle and **Trailer** Production and Registration, C 57.21

Trails

Annual Report of the Rivers and **Trails** Conservation Programs, I 29.124

National Historic **Trails** (series), I 29.88/3

National Scenic **Trails** Information Circulars, I 29.6/5

National **Trails** Directory Series, I 29.123

Report on America's National Scenic, National Historic, and National Recreation **Trails** (fiscal year), I 29.130

Treasure **Trails**, Radio Scripts, I 29.34

Train

Freight **Train** Performance of Class I Railroads in the United States, IC 1 ste.35

Passenger **Train** Performance of Class I Railroads in the United States, IC 1 ste.37

Tabulation of Statistics Pertaining to Block Signals and Telegraph and Telephone for Transmission of **Train** Orders, IC 1 blo.5

Tabulations of Statistics Pertaining to Signals, Interlocking, Automatic, **Train** Control, Telegraph and Telephone for Transmission of **Train** Orders, and Spring Switches As Used on Railroads of United States, IC 1 saf.10

Train and Yard Service of Class I Railroads in the United States, IC 1 ste.38/2

Train of Thought, TD 3.18

Train-Miles

Classification of **Train-Miles**, Locomotive-Miles and Car-Miles, IC 1 ste.11

Trained

Trainees and Fellows Supported by the National Institute of Dental Research and **Trained** During Fiscal Year, HE 20.3402:T 68, HE 20.3410

Trainee

Summer Student **Trainee** Report, C 30.77

Recent **Translation**, Selected List, HE 20.3009/2
Russian Scientific **Translation** Program
 Publications, FS 2.22/19
Scientific **Translation** Program Publications, FS
 2.214
Translation from Kommunist, PrEx 7.21/11
Translation Lists, Y 3.At 7:44-2
Translation Series, DOE-TR-, E 1.43
Translation Series, Y 3.N 88:39
USERDA **Translation** Lists, ER 1.18
Translations
 Bibliography of Medical **Translations**, FS 2.209/3
 Bibliography of **Translations** from Russian
  Scientific and Technical Literature, LC
  1.26
 Bulletin of **Translations** from Russian Medical
  Sciences, FS 2.22/19-2
 Bureau of Ships **Translations**, D 211.14
 Current Awareness of **Translations**, EP 1.21/3
 Fishery and Oceanography **Translations**, I 49.18/5
 Forest Service **Translations**, A 13.81
 List of Recent Accessions and Foreign Patent
  Translations of the Scientific Library, C
  21.17/2
 NIH Library **Translations** Index, FS 2.22:T 68/2
 Price List, Selective Bibliography of Government
  Research Reports and **Translations**, C
  41.21/3
 Received or Planned Current Fisheries, Oceano-
  graphic, and Atmospheric **Translations**,
  A- (series), C 55.325/2
 Special Foreign Currency Science Information
  Program, List of **Translations** in Process
  for Fiscal Year, Coordinated and
  Administered by the National Science
  Foundation, C 51.12
 Survey of Foreign Fisheries, Translated Tables of
  Contents, and New **Translations**, C
  55.325/4
 Technical **Translations**, NAS 1.13/2, NAS 1.77
 Translations for National Institutes of Health, FS
  2.22/19-3
 Translations of {Foreign} Patents, C 21.22
 Translations, D 103.24/3, D 103.31/3, D 203.25,
  D 301.64, D 103.33/4
Translator
 FM and TV **Translator** Applications Ready and
  Available for Processing and
  Notification of Cut-off Date, CC 1.26/6
Translog
 Translog, D 101.66/2
 Translog, Defense Transportation System Bulletin,
  D 101.66/2-2
Transmission
 Tabulation of Statistics Pertaining to Block Signals
  and Telegraph and Telephone for
  Transmission of Train Orders, IC 1 blo.5
Trans-Mississippi
 Omaha, **Trans-Mississippi** and International
  Exposition, 1898, S 6.16
Transmittal
 Administrative Handbook, **Transmittal** Sheets, L
  1.26
 Digest of Rulings (OASI) **Transmittal** Sheets, FS
  3.24/2
 Federal Personnel Manual: **Transmittal** Sheets,
  PM 1.14
 Foreign Service Manual, **Transmittal** Letters, S
  1.5/4
 Import/Export Manual, **Transmittal** Letters, I 49.6/
  8
 Inspection Operations Manual **Transmittal**
  Notices, HE 20.4008/2
 Manual **Transmittal** Letter, L 7.44
 Medical **Transmittal** Memorandums, Y 3.Se 4:16
 Personnel Handbook, Series P-1, Position
  Description and Salary Schedules,
  Transmittal Letters, P 1.31
 SSA Administrative Directives System **Transmit-
  tal** Notice, HE 3.68
 Transmittal Letters {for Indian Service Manual}, I
  20.35
 Transmittal Letters, Manual of Regulations and
  Procedure, FW 1.14
 Transmittal Memo {for} Local Board Memoran-
  dums, Y 3.Se 4:13
 United States Treaty Developments, **Transmittal**
  Sheets, S 9.11/2
Transmittals
 Action **Transmittals**, OCSE-AT- (series), HE 24.14
 Federal Energy Guidelines, **Transmittals**, FE 1.8/5
 Medicaid Action **Transmittals**, HE 22.28
 Transmittals (NOAA Washington Area Personnel
  Locator), C 55.47

Transmitted
 Sexually **Transmitted** Disease Statistics, HE
  20.7309
 Sexually **Transmitted** Disease Surveillance, HE
  20.7309/2
 Sexually **Transmitted** Diseases, Abstracts and
  Bibliographies, HE 20.7311
Transmitting
 Circular Letter **Transmitting** Blank Reports, T
  12.11/2
 Memorandum **Transmitting** Mimeographed Inserts
  for Foreign Service Regulations, S 1.5/2
Transplant
 National Listing of Medicare Providers Furnishing
  Kidney Dialysis and **Transplant**
  Services, HE 22.510
 National Listing of Providers Furnishing Kidney
  Dialysis and **Transplant** Services, HE
  22.25
 National Listing of Medicare Providers Furnishing
  Kidney Dialysis & **Transplant** Services,
  HE 22.216
 National Listing of Renal Providers Furnishing
  Kidney Dialysis and **Transplant**
  Services, HE 22.510/2
Transplantation
 Transplantation and Immunology Committee, HE
  20.3001/2:T 68
Transpo
 Transpo Topics, TD 1.25/2
Transport
 Air **Transport** Economics in Jet Age, Staff Research
  Reports, C 31.250
 Airworthiness Standards, **Transport** Category
  Airplanes, TD 4.6:part 25
 Highways **Transport** Committee Circulars, Y 3.C
  83:24
 Transport Economics, IC 1.17
 Transport Statistics in the United States, IC 1.25
Transportation
 Abstract of Reports of Free and Reduced-Fare
  Transportation Rendered by Air-mail
  Carriers, IC 1 air.7
 Air **Transportation** Wage Survey, L 2.113/7
 Annual Report of the Secretary of **Transportation**
  of Administration of Natural Gas
  Pipelines Safety Act of 1968, TD 1.10/4
 Annual Report of the Secretary of **Transportation**
  on Hazardous Materials Control, TD
  1.24
 Annual Report of the Secretary of **Transportation**
  on Hazardous Materials Transportation,
  TD 9.15
 Annual Report to Secretary of **Transportation** on
  Accident Investigation and Reporting
  Activities of Federal Highway
  Administration, TD 2.16
 Annual Report to the President and the Congress
  Submitted by the Secretary of
  Transportation Under the Emergency
  Rail Service Act of 1970, TD 1.10/6
 Annual Report to the Secretary of **Transportation**
  on the Accident Investigation and
  Reporting Activities of the Federal
  Highway Administration in (year), TD
  2.16
 Army **Transportation** Engineering Agency:
  USATEA Reports, D 117.11
 Army **Transportation** Research Command: Interim
  Reports, D 117.8/3
 Census of **Transportation**, Communications, and
  Utilities, C 3.292
 Census of **Transportation**; Final Reports, C 3.233/
  5, C 56.246/2
 Census of **Transportation**; General Publications, C
  56.246
 Census of **Transportation**; Publication Program, C
  3.233/4-2
 Census of **Transportation**; {Volumes}, C 56.246/3
 Commission to Arbitrate Claims of Venezuela Steam
  Transportation Company of New York
  against Venezuela, S 3.11
 Compendium of National Urban Mass **Transporta-
  tion** Statistics from the 1989 Section 15
  Report, TD 7.11/2-2
 Department of **Transportation** Budget Program:
  Analysis of Fiscal Year DOT Program by
  Policy and RD&D Management
  Objectives, DOT-OST (series), TD 1.34/
  2
 Design, Art, and Architecture in **Transportation**,
  TD 1.47
 European **Transportation** Survey, Pr 32.5810

Grain **Transportation** Prospect, A 88.68/2
Grain **Transportation** Report, A 88.68
Grain **Transportation** Situation, A 108.12
Hazardous Materials **Transportation** Training
 Modules TD 10.16
Highway and Urban Mass **Transportation**, TD
 2.18
Transportation, TD 2.18
Highway **Transportation** Surveys, A 22.8
Implementing **Transportation** Policy, TD 1.28
Industry Reports, Domestic **Transportation**, C
 18.232
Invitation for Bids for **Transportation** of Enlisted
 Men of Navy and Marine Corps, N 17.11
Journal of **Transportation** and Statistics, TD 12.18
Latin American **Transportation** Survey, Y 3.Ec 74/
 2:8
Laws relating to Interstate Commerce and
 Transportation, Y 1.2:In 8/3
Marketing and **Transportation** Situation, A 88.26/
 2, A 93.14
Motor Freight **Transportation** and Warehousing
 Survey, C 3.138/3-5
National **Transportation** Report, TD 1.26
National **Transportation** Safety Board Decisions,
 TD 1.122
National **Transportation** Statistics, Annual
 Report, TD 10.9, TD 12.1/2
National Urban Mass **Transportation** Statistics,
 TD 7.11/2
Nationwide Personal **Transportation** Study:
 Reports, TD 2.31
Navy **Transportation** Schedules, N 17.10
NECTP {Northeast Corridor **Transportation**
 Project}, TD 3.13
1990 Census **Transportation** Planning Package,
 TD 1.56/2
Northeast Corridor **Transportation** Project, C 1.52
NTSB-AAS {National **Transportation** Safety
 Board, Aspects of Aviation Safety}
 (series), TD 1.121
Numeric List of Product Class Codes, Commodity
 Transportation Survey, C 3.163/4-2
R & D Highway & Safety **Transportation** System
 Studies, TD 2.24
Regulations, Rules and Instructions Department of
 Transportation, TD 1.6
Report on High Speed Ground **Transportation** Act
 of 1965, TD 1.10
Report to Congress Concerning the Demonstration
 of Fare-Free Mass **Transportation**, TD
 7.13
Schedule N. Method of **Transportation** Code,
 Exports, C 3.150:N
Selected Library Acquisitions Department of
 Transportation, TD 1.15/3
Sources of Information on Urban **Transportation**
 Planning Methods, TD 1.51
State Supervisors of Pupil **Transportation**,
 Directory, FS 5.2:T 68/2
Statewide **Transportation** Planning and
 Management Series, TD 2.57
Statistics on Pupil **Transportation**, FS
 5.220:20022, HE 5.220;20022
Status of the Nation's Local Public **Transporta-
 tion**, Conditions and Performance,
 Report to Congress, TD 7.18
Summary of **Transportation**, Pr 32.4844
Surface **Transportation** Board Reports TD 13.6/2
Telephone Directory National **Transportation**
 Safety Board, TD 1.124
Translog, Defense **Transportation** System Bulletin,
 D 101.66/2-2
Transportation Acquisition Circular, Summary of
 Items, TD 1.6/3
Transportation Bulletins, Pr 32.4416
Transportation Committee Bulletins, Pr 32.4235
Transportation Committee News, Pr 32.4261
Transportation Corps Pamphlets, W 109.307
Transportation Corps, D 101.66/4
Transportation Forecast, TD 1.14
Transportation Link, TD 1.25/4
Transportation Maps, A 22.9/2, FW 2.13, C 37.11
Transportation Memorandum, N 9.14
Transportation of Dangerous Articles and
 Magnetized Materials, TD 4.6:part 103
Transportation Proceedings, D 101.66
Transportation Research and Development
 Command: Research Technical
 Memorandums, D 117.8
Transportation Research Record (series), NA 1.10
Transportation Revenue and Traffic of Large Oil
 Pipe Line Companies, IC 1 pip.7
Transportation Safety Information Report, TD 1.48

Transportation Safety Regulatory Bulletin, E 1.135

Transportation Series Bureau of Foreign and Domestic Commerce, C 18.274

Transportation Series Corps of Engineers, D 103.10

Transportation Series Engineer Department, W 7.23, M 110.17

Transportation Statistics Annual Report, TD 12.1

Transportation Statistics in Brief, TD 12.16

Transportation Topics for Consumers, TD 1.25

Transportation Update, A 108.9

Transportation USA, TD 1.27

Transportation, C 51.9/8, C 51.9/9, PrEx 7.21/10, TD 1.15/4

Transportation, Current Literature Compiled by Library Staff, TD 1.15/4

U.S. Department of **Transportation** FY...Procurement Forecast, TD 1.62

U.S. Exports, Commodity, Country, and Method of **Transportation**, C 3.164:750

U.S. Exports, Geographic Area, Country, Schedule B Commodity Groupings, and Method of **Transportation**, C 3.164:455

U.S. Exports, Schedule B Commodity Groupings, Geographic Area, Country, and Method of **Transportation**, C 3.164:450

U.S. Foreign Waterborne **Transporation** Statistics Quarterly, TD 11.35

U.S. General Imports Commodity, Country and Method of **Transportation**, C 3.164:350

U.S. General Imports Geographic Area, Country, Schedule A Commodity Groupings, and Method of **Transportation**, C 3.164:155

U.S. General Imports Schedule A Commodity Groupings, Geographic Area, Country, and Method of **Transportation**, C 3.164:150

University **Transportation** Center Project Abstracts, TD 10.14

Urban Mass **Transportation** Abstracts, TD 7.10/3

Urban **Transportation** and Planning, Current Literature Compiled by Library Staff, TD 1.15/5

Urban **Transportation** and Planning, TD 1.15/5

User-Oriented Materials for UTPS {Urban **Transportation** Planning System}, TD 2.54

Volpe **Transportation** Journal, TD 8.27/2

Working Papers National **Transportation** Policy Study Commission, Y 3.T 68/2:10

Transported
Freight Revenue and Wholesale Value at Destination of Commodities **Transported** by by Class I Line-haul Railroads, IC 1.29

Transporter
Research and Technology **Transporter**, TD 2.70

Transporting
Cost of **Transporting** Freight by Class I and Class II Motor Common Carriers of General Commodities, IC 1 acco 2.F 88, IC 1 acco.13

Transshipped
U.S. Exports and Imports **Transshipped** Via Canadian Ports, TD 11.28

TranStats
TranStats, TD 12.19

Travel
Air **Travel** Consumer Report, TD 1.54

Certification and Operations; Air **Travel** and Clubs Using Large Airplanes, TD 4.6:part 123

Eastern **Travel** Today, I 29.37/9

Federal Contract Air Service and **Travel** Directory, GS 8.10

Federal **Travel** Directory, GS 2.21, GS 1.29

Federal **Travel** Regulations, GS 1.6/8-2

Health Information for International **Travel**, HE 20.7009, HE 20.7818

Health Information for **Travel** in {area}, HE 20.2:T 69

Information Sources on International **Travel**, C 47.8

Interagency Directory, Key Contacts for Planning, Scientific and Technical Exchange Programs, Educational **Travel**, Students, Teachers, Lecturers, Research Scholars, Specialists, S 1.67/3

Inventory of Federal Tourism Programs, Federal Agencies Commissions, Programs Reviewed for Their Participation in the Development of Recreation, **Travel**, and Tourism in the United States, C 47.2:T 64/3

Joint Federal **Travel** Regulations, Vol. 1, D 1.6/4-2

Joint **Travel** Regulations, D 1.6/4, D 1.6/4-5

Marine Corps **Travel** Instructions Manual, D 214.29

Maximum **Travel** Per Diem Allowances for Foreign Areas, S 1.76/3-2

NEH **Travel** to Collections, Small Grants for Research Travel to Libraries, Archives, Museums, and Other Repositories, NF 3.19

Passenger **Travel** between United States and Foreign Countries {annual summary reports}, J 21.13

Patterns of Foreign **Travel** in the U.S., C 47.18

Pleasure and Business Visitors to U.S. by Port of Entry and Mode of **Travel**, C 47.15/2

Program Report of the United States **Travel** Service, C 47.1

Report of Passenger **Travel** between the United States and Foreign Countires, J 21.13/2

Semi-Annual Report of the Secretary of Commerce on the United States **Travel** Service, C 47.1

Sources of **Travel** Information Series, I 29.56

Study of the International **Travel** Market {various countries}, C 47.19

Summary and Analysis of International **Travel** to the U.S., C 47.15

Summary of Health Information for International **Travel**, HE 20.7818/2

Summary of Health Information for International **Travel**, HE 20.7315/2, HE 20. 7818/2

Travel and Recreation News Letters, I 29.37/7

Travel Folders, USTS (series), C 47.16

Travel USA Bulletin, I 29.55

U.S. International Air **Travel** Statistics, Calendar Year, TD 1.40/3

U.S. International Air **Travel** Statistics, Fiscal Year, TD 1.40/2

U.S. International Air **Travel** Statistics, TD 1.40

U.S. Navy **Travel** Instructions, Instruction Memoranda, N 20.13/3

U.S. **Travel** Bureau, I 29.37

Weekly Summary of Health Information for International **Travel**, HE 20.7023

World Holidays Listed, Guide to Business **Travel**, C 42.8/a:H 717/2

Traveled
Interstate System **Traveled**-Way Study Reports, TD 2.118

Traveler
Traveler/El Viajero, Quarterly Newsletter for Migrant and Seasonal Farm Workers, PrEx 10.19

Traveler's
Traveler's Guides to Special Attractions, C 47.12/2

Travelers
International **Travelers** to the U.S., Annual Summary, C 47.15/5

Traveling
New Mexico, **Traveling** Auditor and Bank Examiner, Annual Reports, I 1.24/2

Traveling Exhibitions, Administrative, SI 1.18

Travers
Antarctic **Travers** (series), C 4.56

Treasure
Treasure Trails, Radio Scripts, I 29.34

Treasurers
Treasurers Next Door, I 16.65/3

Treasury
Annual Report of the Department of **Treasury** on Operation and Effect of Domestic International Sales Corporation Legislation for Calendar Year, Y 4.W 36:D 71/2

Annual Report of the Secretary of the **Treasury** on the State of the Finances, T 1.1

Budget-**Treasury** Regulations, Pr 33.106/2

Companies Holding Certificates of Authority from Secretary of **Treasury** As Acceptable Securities on Federal Bonds, T 1.24, T 63.116

Contents of Vaults {of} **Treasury** Department, T 40.10

Daily Statement of the **Treasury**, T 1.5

Daily **Treasury** Statement, T 63.113/2-2

Index to **Treasury** Decisions Under Customs and Other Laws, T 1.11/1a

Public Debt and Cash in **Treasury**, T 9.9

Reappraisement Decisions, for Review by U.S. Customs Court As Published in Weekly **Treasury** Decisions, T 1.11/2a

Receipts and Disbursements of Government Consolidated into Bureau of Accounts, Fiscal Service in **Treasury** Department by President's Reorganization Plan no. 3, T 9.11

Review of Current Information in **Treasury** Library, T 23.7

Statement of **Treasury**, Daily, T 9.8

Status Report of the U.S. **Treasury**-Owned Gold, T 63.131

Treasury Bulletin, T 1.3, T 63.103/2

Treasury Cattle Commission, Reports, T 1.20

Treasury Decisions Under Internal Revenue Laws, T 22.8

Treasury Decisions, T 1.11/1, T 1.11/2

Treasury Department-General Accounting Office Joint Regulations, T 1.38

Treasury Inspector General for Tax Administration, T 1.1/6

Treasury News, SSA 1.25

Treasury of Stamps Album, School Year (date), P 1.49

Treasury Papers, T 1.48

Treasury Register, T 1.13

Treasury Reporting Rates of Exchange As of (date), T 63.102:Ex 2

Treasury Reporting Rates of Exchange, T 63.121

Treasury Safety Council Safety Bulletin, Administrative, T 1.41

United States Court of Military Appeals and the Judge Advocates General of the Armed Forces and the General Counsel of the Department of the **Treasury**,

U.S. **Treasury** Savings Stamp News, T 66.22

Treaties
Acts of Congress, **Treaties**, and Proclamations Relating to Noncontiguous Territory, W 6.12

Chinese Exclusion **Treaties**, Laws and Regulations, C 7.5

Foreign **Treaties** and Conventions (United States not a Signatory), S 9.6

Indian Affairs, Laws and **Treaties**, I 1.107

Kappler's Compilation of Indian Laws and **Treaties**, Y 4.In 2/2:L 44

Lists of Commercial **Treaties** and Conventions, and Agreements Affected by Exchange of Notes or Declarations in Force Between United States and Other Countries, S 9.9

Numerical List of Treaty Series, Executive Agreement Series and **Treaties** and other International Acts Series, S 9.11/3

Postal **Treaties** and Conventions, P 1.9, S 9.5/3

Treaties and Agreements, I 20.18

Treaties and Other International Acts of U.S., S 9.5/1

Treaties and Other International Acts Series, S 9.10

Treaties and Other International Agreements of United States, S 9.12/2

Treaties in Force, S 9.14

United States **Treaties** and Other International Agreements, S 9.12

Treating
Clinical Handbook on Economic Poisons, Emergency Information for **Treating** Poisoning, EP 5.8:P 75

Treatment
Advance Training for Workers in the Early and Periodic Screening, Diagnosis and **Treatment** Program: Publications, HE 22.111

Advanced Training for Workers in the Early and Periodic Screening, Diagnosis and **Treatment** Program: Publications, HE 22.111

Bench Comment, a Periodic Guide to Recent Appellate **Treatment** of Practical Procedural Issues, Ju 13.8/2

Breast Cancer **Treatment** Committee, HE 20.3001/2:B 74/3

Building for Clean Water Progress Report on Federal Incentive Grants for Municipal Waste **Treatment** Fiscal Year, FS 2.64/6

Building for Clean Water Report on Federal Incentive Grants for Municiapl Waste **Treatment**, FS 16.9

Cancer Control **Treatment** and Rehabilitation Review Committee, HE 20.3001/2:C 16/15

Cancer **Treatment** Advisory Committee, HE 20.3001/2:C 16/11

Cancer **Treatment** Symposia, HE 20.3172/2

Action in the **United States** of America Related to Stratospheric Monitoring, S 1.132

Activities of the **U.S.** Geological Survey Water Resources Division, Hawaii, I 19.55/7

Activities of the **U.S.** Geological Survey, Water Resources Division, Status of Idaho Projects, I 19.55/3

Adjudications of Attorney General of **United States**, J 1.28

Advance Sheets from Monthly Summary of the Foreign Commerce of the **United States**, C 18.8

Advance Sheets of 3d Edition of Checklist of **United States** Public Documents, GP 3.14

Advance Statements of Productions of Copper in **United States** (calendar year), I 19.23

Advance **United States** Short Wave Broadcast Programs, S 9.13

Air Force Driver, the Automotive Magazine of the **U.S.** Air Force, D 301.72

Air Pollution Technical Publications of the **U.S.** Environmental Protection Agency, Quarterly Bulletin, EP 1.21/8

Aircraft Accident Reports, Brief Format, **U.S.** Civil Aviation, NTSB-BA- (series), TD 1.109/13

All Banks in the **United States** and Other Areas, Principal Assets and Liabilities by States, FR 1.28/2

All-Electric Homes in the **United States**, Annual Bills, January 1, (year), FP 1.10

Alphabetical List, **U.S.** Air Force and Air Force-navy Aeronautical Standard Drawings, D 301.15

American Flag Services in Foreign Trade and with **U.S.** Possessions, MC 1.12

American Flag Services in Foreign Trade with **U.S.**, C 27.9/1

Analysis of Accidents Involving Air Taxi Operations, **U.S.** General Aviation, TD 1.113/4

Analysis of Aircraft Accident Data, **U.S.** Air Carrier Operations, TD 1.113/5

Analysis of Aircraft Accident Data, **U.S.** General Aviation, TD 1.113/3

Analysis of Economic Groups of Domestic Exports from and Imports into **U.S.**, C 18.6/3

Analysis of Natural Gases of the **United States**, I 28.27

Analysis of Work Stoppages on **U.S.** Missile Sites, Pr 35.8:M 69/W 89

Analysis Report, Estimate of the (year) Cost of Oil Imports into the **United States**, E 3.26/4

Anglers' Guide to the **United States** Atlantic Coast, C 55.308:An 4

Anglers' Guide to the **United States** Pacific Coast, C 55.308:An 4/2

Annapolis, the **United States** Naval Academy Catalog, D 208.109

Annotated Index of Registered Fungicides and Nematicides, Their Uses in the **United States**, A 77.302:F 96

Annual Evaluation Report on Programs Administered by the **U.S.** Office of Education, HE 19.101/3

Annual Historical Review, **United States** Army Soldier Support Center, D 101.1/3

Annual Indicators of In-migration into the **United States** of Aliens in Professional and Related Occupations, J 21.15

Annual Outlook for **U.S.** Coal, E 3.11/7-8

Annual Outlook for **U.S.** Electric Power, E 3.50

Annual Register of the **United States** Naval Academy, D 208.107

Annual Report, Authorized by 38 **U.S.C.** 5057, Administrator, Veterans' Affairs, on Sharing Medical Facilities, Fiscal Year (date), Y 4.V 64/4:M 46

Annual Report of Lands under Control of the **U.S.** Fish and Wildlife Service, I 49.102

Annual Report of the Attorney General of the **United States**, J 1.1

Annual Report of the Comptroller General of the **United States**, GA 1.1

Annual Report of the President of the **United States** on Trade Agreements Program, Pr 37.10, Pr 40.11

Annual Report of the Proceedings of the Judicial Conference of the **United States** [and] Semiannual Report of the Director of the Administrative Office of the **United States** Courts, Ju 10.1

Annual Report of the **United States** National Committee on Vital and Health Statistics, HE 20.6211

Annual Report of Vegetable Breeding in Southeastern **United States**, Hawaii, and Puerto Rico, A 77.532

Annual Report on the Impact of the Caribbean Basin Economic Recovery Act on **U.S.** Industries and Consumers, ITC 1.32

Annual Report, Surgeon General, **United States** Army, D 104.1

Annual Reports on Statistics of Express Companies in the **United States**, IC 1 exp.1

Annual Reports on Statistics of Railways in **United States**, IC 1 ste.11

Annual Review of Aircraft Accident Data, **U.S.** Air Carrier Operations, TD 1.113/5

Annual Review of Aircraft Accident Data, **U.S.** General Aviation, TD 1.113

Annual Review of **U.S.** Air Carrier Accidents Occurring in Calendar Year (date), TD 1.113/2

Annual Review of **U.S.** General Aviation Accidents Occurring in Calendar Year, TD 1.113

Antarctic Journal of the **United States**, NS 1.26

Apparent Consumption of Industrial Explosives and Blasting Agents in the **United States**, I 28.112

Appeals Pending Before **United States** Courts in Customs Cases, T 17.8

Appendix, Budget of the **United States** Government, Department of Commerce Chapter, C 1.86

Applied Technology Laboratory, **U.S.** Army Research and Technology Laboratories, D 117.8/2

Approved Conference, Rate and Interconference Agreements of Steamship Lines in the Foreign Commerce of the **United States**, FMC 1.11

Arctic Research of the **United States**, NS 1.51/2

Area Charts, **U.S.**, D 5.318/6

Army Life and **United States** Recruiting News, M 108.77

Arrearage Tables of Amounts Due and Unpaid, 90 Days or More on Foreign Credits of the **United States** Government, T 1.45/4

Arrivals and Departures by Selected Ports, Statistics of Foreign Visitor Arrivals and **U.S.** Citizen Departures Analyzed by **U.S.** Ports of Entry and Departure, C 47.15/4

Art and Industry, Education in Industrial and Fine Arts in **United States**, I 16.7

Art in the **United States** Capitol, Y 1.91-2:H.doc 368

Assets and Liabilities of All Banks in the **United States**, FR 1.28

Assets and Liabilities of All Commercial Banks in **United States**, FR 1.28/4

Atlantic and Gulf Coast of the **United States**, TD 5.9:2

Atlas/State Data Abstract for the **United States**, D 1.58/4

Attorney General's Advisory Committee of **United States** Attorneys Annual Report, J 1.1/8

Automatic Data Processing Equipment Inventory in the **United States** Government As of the End of the Fiscal Year, GS 12.10

Background Facts on Women Workers in the **United States**, L 36.114/2

Band News from the **United States** Air Force Band, Washington, D.C., D 301.108

Bank Debits to Demand Deposit Accounts (Except Interbank and **U.S.** Government Accounts), FR 1.17/2

Bankruptcy Laws of the **United States**, Y 1.2:B 22/2

Basic Research in Behavioral and Social Sciences: **U.S.** Army Research Institute Annual Report, D 101.1/7-2

Bathymetric Mapping Products (Catalog) 5, **United States** Bathymetric and Fishing Maps, C 55.418:5

Ben's Guide to U.S. Government for Kids, GP 3.39

Bibliographies; **United States** Institute of Peace, Y 3.P 31:17

Bibliography of Hydrology and Sedimentation of the **United States** and Canada, I 19.13

Bibliography of **U.S.** Army Medical Research and Nutrition Laboratory Reports and Reprints for (year), D 104.17

Bibliography of **United States** Public Documents, Department Lists, GP 3.10

Bicycling Laws in the **United States**, TD 8.5/2:3/2

Biennial Report of Depository Libraries, **U.S.** Summary, GP 3.33

Biennial Survey of Education in **United States**, FS 5.23

Bituminous Coal and Lignite Mine Openings and Closings in Continental **United States**, (dates), I 28.33/2-2

Bond Tips from You **U.S.** Savings Bond Reporter, T 66.24

Boundaries of the **United States** and the Several States, I 19.3:1212

Brewers' Dried Grains, **United States**, Production and Stocks in Hands of Producers, A 88.18/6-2

Bridges Over Navigable Waters of the **U.S.**, D 103.2:B 76

Briefs of Accidents Involving -

Briefs of Accidents Involving Aerial Applications Operations, **U.S.** General Aviation, TD 1.109/4

Briefs of Accidents Involving Air Taxi Operations, **U.S.** General Aviation, TD 1.109/3

Briefs of Accidents Involving Alcohol As a Cause/Factor, **U.S.** General Aviation, TD 1.109/9

Briefs of Accidents Involving Amateur Built (homebuilt) Aircraft, **U.S.** General Aviation, TD 1.109/6

Briefs of Accidents Involving Corporate/Executive Aircraft, **U.S.** General Aviation, TD 1.109/10

Briefs of Accidents Involving Mid-Air Collisions, **U.S.** Civil Aviation, TD 1.109/7

Briefs of Accidents Involving Missing Aircraft, **U.S.** General Aviation, TD 1.109/8

Briefs of Accidents Involving Rotocraft, **U.S.** General Aviation, TD 1.109/5

Briefs of Accidents, **U.S.** Civil Aviation, TD 1.109, C 31.244/6

Briefs of Accidents, **U.S.** General Aviation , C 31.244/5

Briefs of Aircraft Accidents Involving Turbine Powered Aircraft, **U.S.** General Aviation, Calendar Year, NTSB-AMM- (series), TD 1.109/14

Briefs of Fatal Accidents Involving Weather As a Cause/Factor, **U.S.** General Aviation, TD 1.109/12

Broadcasting Radio Stations of the **United States**, RC 1.9

Budget Estimates, Excerpts from the **United States** Government Budget, HH 1.1/4

Budget Estimates, **United States** Department of Agriculture, A 1.93

Budget of the **U.S.** Government: Director's Introduction and Overview Tables, PrEx 2.8/11

Budget of the **United States** Government, PrEx 2.8

Budget of **United States** Government, District of Columbia, PrEx 2.8/4

Budget of **United States** Government, Pr 32.107, Pr 33.107, Pr 34.107

Building Construction in Urban Areas in **United States**, L 2.36

Building Permits in Principal Cities of **U.S.**, L 2.6/a 4

Cadet Profile, **United States** Coast Guard Academy, TD 5.15

Calendar of **United States** House of Representatives and History of Legislation, Y 1.2/2

Canada-**United States** Interparliamentary Group Report on Meetings by Senate Delegation, Y 4.F 76/2:C 16/2

Cancer Services, Facilities and Programs in **United States**, HE 20.2:C 16/5

Capacity of Refrigerated Warehouses in **United States**, A 88.20/3, A 92.21/3

Careers in the **United States** Department of the Interior, I 1.73/2:3

Carlot Shipments of, from Stations in **U.S.**, A 66.24/2

Cases Argued and Decided in Supreme Court of **United States**, Ju 6.8/4

Cases Decided in the Court of Claims of the **United States**, Ju 3.9

Cases Decided in **United States** Court of Appeals for the Federal Circuit, Ju 7.5

Cases Decided in **United States** Court of Appeals for the Federal Circuit: Customs Cases Adjudged in the Court of Appeals for the Federal Circuit, Ju 7.5/2

Catalog and Index, **U.S.** Department of Commerce Publications, C 1.54/2

Directory of Information Resources in the **United States**, LC 1.31

Directory of Narcotic Addiction Treatment Agencies in the **United States**, HE 20.2402:N 16/3

Directory of National and International Labor Unions in the **United States**, L 2.3

Directory of Outpatient Psychiatric Clinics, Psychiatric Day-Night Services and Other Mental Health Resources in the **United States** and Territories, FS 2.22/38-4

Directory of Principal Crushed Stone Producers in the **United States** in (year), I 28.118/2

Directory of Principal Dimension Stone Producers in the **United States**, I 28.118/3

Directory of Principal **U.S.** Gemstone Producers (Annual Advance Summary), I 28.117

Directory of Refrigerated Warehouses in the **United States**, A 92.34:1

Directory of Research Natural Areas on Federal Lands of **United States** of America, Y 3.F 31/19:9

Directory of Standards Laboratories in the **United States**, C 13.2:St 2/2

Directory of **U.S.** Government Audiovisual Personnel, GS 4.24

Directory of **U.S.** Government Datafiles for Mainframes & Microcomputers, C 51.19/4

Directory of **U.S.** Institutions of Higher Education, Fall (year), FS 5.250:50052, HE 5.250:50052

Directory of **United States** Poison Control Centers and Services, HE 20.4003/2-2

Directory of **United States** Probation and Pretrial Services Officers, Ju 10.15

Directory of **United States** Probation Officers, Ju 10.15

Directory of **United States** Standardization Activities, C 13.10:288, C 13.10:417

Directory, **United States**, Territories, and Canada, HE 20.6213/2

Disability Days, **United States**, HE 20.6209/5

Distillers' Dried Grains, **United States**, Production by Kinds by Months, A 88.18/7-2

DoD Document Identifiers, Low Altitude Approach Procedures, **United States** Military Aviation Notice, D 5.318/3

Domestic Oceanborne and Great Lakes Commerce of the **United States**, C 39.222

Domestic Waterborne Trade of the **United States**, C 39.222

Domestic Waterborne Trade of the **United States**, TD 11.19

Dropout Rates in the **United States**, ED 1.329

Dry Cargo Service and Area Report, **United States** Dry Cargo Shipping Companies by Ships Owned And/or Chartered Type of Service and Area Operated, C 39.213

Dry Casein, Estimated Production and Stocks, **United States**, A 36.166

Drug Trafficking in the **United States**, J 24.29

Earthquake History of the **United States**, C 55.202:Ea 7

Earthquakes in the **United States**, I 19.4/2

Eastern **United States**, Dates of Latest Prints, Instrument Approach Procedure Charts and Airport Obstruction Plans (OP), C 4.9/19

Economic Characteristics of Households in the **United States**, C 3.186:P-70/2

Economic Development U.S.A., C 46.9/3

Economic Forces in **United States** in Facts and Figures, FO 1.30, S 17.8

Economic Trends and Their Implications for the **United States**, C 42.30

Educational Attainment in the **United States**, C 3.186/23

Election Law Guidebook, 1974, Summary of Federal and State Laws Regulating Nomination and Election of **United States** Senators, Revised to January 1, 1974, Y 1.93-2:S.doc. 84

Electric Trade in the **United States**, E 3.11/17-12

Employment and Earnings Statistics for the **United States**, L 2.3

Employment Bulletin, Current Openings, G-11 and Above, at Army Material Command Activities Throughout the **United States**, D 101.3/5

Employment Report of **United States** Flag Merchant Fleet, Oceangoing Vessels 1,000 Gross Tons and Over, C 39.208

Encyclopedia of **U.S.** Air Force Aircraft and Missile Systems, D 301.90

Energy-Related Doctoral Scientists and Engineers in the **United States**, E 1.21

Enrollment Information Guide and Plan Comparison Chart: Federal Civilian Employees in Positions Outside the Continental **U.S.**, PM 1.8/8

Enrollment Information Guide and Plan Comparison Chart: **U.S.** Postal Service Employees, PM 1.8/5

Enroute Area Charts (**U.S.**) Low Altitude, C 55.416/14, C 55.416/15-2

Enroute Change Notice, DoD Flip Enroute VFR Supplement **United States**, D 5.318/8-2

Enroute High Altitude Planning Charts (**U.S.**), C 55.416/17

Enroute High and Low Altitude, **U.S.**, C 55.416/16, D 5.318/4

Enroute IFR-Supplement, **United States**, D 5.318/7

Environmental/Resource Assessment and Information, **U.S.** Energy/Climate Section, C 55.233/2

Equine Infectious Anemia, Progress Report and History in the **United States**, A 77.244

Essential **United States** Foreign Trade Routes, C 39.202:F 76

Estimated Grade and Staple Length of Upland Cotton Ginned in **United States**, A 88.11/7

Estimated Use of Water in the **United States**, I 19.4/9

Estimates of the Population of the **United States** and Components of Change, C 3.186/7-3

Estimates of the Population of the **United States**, by Age, Sex, and Race, C 3.186/7-2

Estimates of the Population of the **United States**, C 3.186:P-25, C 3.186/7

European Community/**United States** of America Joint Consortia for Cooperation in Higher Education, ED 1.23/10

European Recovery Program; Joint Report of **United States** and United Kingdom Military Governors, M 105.18

Export Markets of **U.S.** Grain and Products, A 67.18:EMG

Exporting to the **United States**, T 17.5/2:Ex 7

Exports Declared for **United States**, S 4.11

Facts about **U.S.** Agriculture, A 1.38/2

Facts about **United States** Money, T 1.40

Facts and Services from the **U.S.** Department of Labor, L 1.31

Farm Population of the **United States**, C 3.186:P-27, C 3.186/25

FAS Report, Status of **U.S.** Sugar Import Quotas, A 67.42/2

Federal Elections . . ., Election Results for the **U.S.** Senate and **U.S.** House Film Strips of **U.S.D.A.**, Price Lists, A 43.23

Federal Offenders in the **United States** Courts, Ju 10.11

Federal Real and Personal Property Inventory Report (Civilian and Military) of the **United States** Government Covering its Properties Located in the **United States**, in the Territories, and Overseas, as of June 30 (year), Y 4.G 74/7:P 94

Federal Specifications Board, **United States** Government Master Specifications, C 13.24

Film Strips of **U.S.D.A.**, Price Lists, A 43.23

Final Bulletins (**U.S.** Territorial Possessions), C 3.37/30

Financial Characteristics of **U.S.** Farms, A 1.75/2

Financial Statistics of Major **U.S.** Publicly Owned Electric Utilities, E 3.18/4-3

FIPSE EFinancial Statistics of Major **U.S.** Publicly Owned Electric Utilities, E 3.18/4-3

Fire in the **United States**, C 58.13, FEM 1.117

Fisheries of the **United States** and Alaska, a Preliminary Review, I 49.28

Fisheries of the **United States**, C 55.309/2

Fishery Statistics of the **United States**, C 55.316

Fixed Reproducible Tangible Wealth of the **United States**, C 59.27

Flight Information Publication: Area Charts, **U.S.**, D 5.318/6

Flight Information Publication: Enroute High and Low Altitude, **U.S.**, D 5.318/4

Flight Information Publication; Enroute Intermediate Altitude, **United States**, D 301.13/5

Flight Information Publication; Enroute-High Altitude, **United States**, Northeast [and Southeast], D 301.43/3, D 301.43/3-2

Folk Music of **United States**, LC 12.7

Foreign Agricultural Trade Digest of **United States**, A 67.19/8

Foreign Agricultural Trade of the **United States**, A 93.17/7, A 105.14

Foreign Aid by the **U.S.** Government, C 18.279

Foreign Claims Settlement Commission of the **United States**: Annual Report, J 1.1/6

Foreign Commerce and Navigation of **United States**, C 3.159

Foreign Consular Offices in the **U.S.**, S 1.34, S 1.69, S 1.69/2

Foreign Countries and Plants Certified to Export Meat and Poultry to the **United States**, A 110.14/2

Foreign Credits by **United States** Government, C 43.11/2

Foreign Credits by **United States** Government, Status of Active Foreign Credits of **United States** Government and of International Organizations, T 1.45

Foreign Direct Investment in the **U.S.**, Operations of **U.S.** Affiliates of Foreign Companies, C 59.20

Foreign Direct Investment in the **United States**, C 61.25/2, C 59.20

Foreign Economic Trends and Their Implications for the **United States**, C 57.111, C 61.11

Foreign Flag Merchant Ships Owned by **U.S.** Parent Companies, TD 11.16

Foreign Grants and Credits by the **United States** Government, C 43.11

Foreign Oceanborne Trade of **United States** Containerized Cargo Summary, Selected Trade Routes, C 39.233

Foreign Plants Certified to Export Meat to the **United States**, A 110.14

Foreign Relations of the **United States**, S 1.1

Foreign Relations of **United States**, Diplomatic Papers: Conferences, S 1.1/3

Foreign Transactions of **U.S.** Government, C 18.278

Foreign Treaties and Conventions (**United States** not a Signatory), S 9.6

Foreign Versions, Variations, and Diminutives of English Names and Foreign Equivalents of **U.S.** Military and Civilian Titles, J 21.2:N 15

Foreign-Owned **U.S.** Firms, FOF (series), C 3.254

Forest and Windbarrier Planting and Seeding in the **United States**, Report, A 13.51/2

Forest Insect Conditions in the **United States**, A 13.52/2

Forest Planting, Seeding, and Silvical Treatments in the **United States**, A 13.51/2

Forest Tree Nurseries in the **United States**, A 13.74

Forms; **United States** Institute of Peace, Y 3.P 31:13

Franklin D. Roosevelt Library, Annual Report of Archivist of **United States**, GS 4.9

Freight Commodity Statistics of Class I Railroads in the **United States**, IC 1 ste.26

Freight Commodity Statistics, Class I Railroads in the **United States** for Year Ended December 31 (date), IC 1 ste.29

Freight Train Performance of Class I Railroads in the **United States**, IC 1 ste.35

Fuel and Power for Locomotives and Rail Motor Cars of Class I Steam Railways in **United States**, IC 1 ste.30

GE-50 **United States** Maps, C 3.62/4

General Imports of Merchandise into **United States** by Air, Commodity by Country of Origin, C 3.164:231

General Imports of Merchandise into **United States** by Air, Country of Origin by Commodity, C 3.164:232

General Real and Personal Property Inventory Report (Civilian and Military) of the **United States** Government Covering Its Properties Located in the **United States**, in the Territories, and Overseas, As of June 30 [year], Y 4.G 74/7:P 94

Geologic Atlas of the **United States**, I 19.5/1

Geologic Studies in Alaska by the **U.S.** Geological Survey, I 19.4/8

Geological Studies in Alaska by the **U.S.** Geological Survey, I 19.4/3

Gold and Silver Exports and Imports: Weekly Statement of, **United States**, C 3.195

Gold and Silver Movements: **United States**, C 3.196

Governmental Finances in **United States**, C 3.191

Grand and Petit Juror Service in **U.S.** District Courts, Ju 10.13

Great Britain and **United States** Claims Commission, S 3.8

Ground-Water Levels in the **United States**, I 19.13

Guide of the **U.S.** Development of Energy, Board of Contract Appeals and Contract Adjustment Board, E 1.8/4

Guide to the National Archives of the **United States**, GS 4.6/2:N 21

Guide to the **U.S.** Department of Energy, Board of Contract Appeals and Contract Adjustment Board, E 1.8/4

Handbook of the Hospital Corps, **United States** Navy, D 206.6/3:H 79

Harmonized Tariff Schedule of the **U.S.** Annotated for Statistical Reporting Purposes, ITC 1.10

Harmonized Tariff Schedule of the **United States**, ITC 1.10/4

Headquarters, First **United States** Army, Deputy Chief of Staff, Information Management, Organization, Mission, and Functions, D 101.1/9

Health Statistics from the **U.S.** National Health Survey, FS 2.85

Health, **United States**, HE 20.21, HE 20.6018, HE 20.6223

Helium Resources of the **United States**, I 28.167

Highlights of **U.S.** Exports and Import Trade, C 3.164:990

Highway Traffic Noise in the **United States**: Problem and Response, TD 2.23/7

Hispanic Population in the **United States**, Advance Report, C 3.186/14

Hispanic Population in the **United States**, C 3.186/14-2

Historical Monographs of Office of **U.S.** High Commissioner for Germany, S 1.95

Historical Register, **U.S.** Revenue Cutter Service Officers, TD 5.19/4

Historical Review, **U.S.** Army Belvoir Research and Development Center, D 101.98

Historical Review, **U.S.** Army Mobility Equipment Research and Development Command, D 101.98

Historical Statistics of the **United States**, Colonial Times to 1970, C 3.134/2:H 62

History of Medical Department of **United States** Navy, D 206.12/2

History of the Chaplain Corps, **U.S.** Navy, D 201.33

History of the Tariff Schedules of the **United States** Annotated, ITC 1.10/2

History of Wages in the **United States** from Colonial Times to 1928, L 2.3:604

Household Economic Studies, Economic Characteristics of Households in the **United States**, C 3.186:P-70

How to Find **U.S.** Statutes and **U.S.** Code Citations, GS 4.102:St 2

Hydroelectric Power Resources of the **United States**, Developed and Undeveloped, FP 1.123

IFR Wall Planning Chart: East, Low Altitude, **U.S.**, C 55.461/7

IFR Wall Planning Chart: West, Low Altitude, **U.S.**, C 55.416/7-1

Imported Merchandise Entered for Consumtion in **United States**, and Duties Collected Thereon During the Quarter Ending, C 18.17

Imported Merchandise Entered for Consumtion in **United States**, etc., C 14.18

Importing into the **United States**, T 17.17

Imports and Exports of Commodities by **U.S.** Coastal Districts and Foreign Trade Regulations, SB 7.5/275, C 27.9/4, MC 1.11

Imports under Items 806.30 and 807.00 of the Tariff Schedules of the **United States**, ITC 1.10/3

In Supreme Court of **U.S.**, Briefs, Petitions, and Motions of Wm. Marshall Bullett, Solicitor General, J 1.19/2

In the Supreme Court of the **United States** (series), Ju 6.13

Income in (year) of Persons in the **United States**, C 3.186:P-60

Index of Specifications and Bulletins Approved for **U.S.** Air Force Procurement, D 301.18

Index of **U.S.** Air Force, Air Force-Navy Aeronautical and Military (MS) Standards (sheet form), D 301.16/2

Index of **U.S.** Nuclear Standards, C 13.10:483

Index of **U.S.** Voluntary Engineering Standards, C 13.10:329

Index of **United States** Army, Joint Army-Navy, and Federal Specifications and Standards, M 101.23

Index to Geologic Mapping in **United States** (by State) Maps, I 19.37

Index to Geologic Mapping of the **United States**, I 19.86

Index to Legislation of States to **U.S.** Enacted, LC 21.9

Index to the Published Decisions of the Accounting Officers of the **United States**, GA 1.5

Index to the **U.S.** Patent Classification, C 21.12/3

Index to **U.S.** Army Specifications, W 3.48/2

Index-Digest of the Published Decisions of the Comptroller General of the **United States**, GA 1.5/3

Indians on Federal Reservations in **United States** [by areas], FS 2.86

Information Bulletins; Office of **U.S.** High Commissioner for Germany, S 1.85

Information Collection Budget of the **United States**, PrEx 2.29

Information for **United States** Businessmen [by country], C 49.11

Information Respecting the History, Conditions, and Prospects of the Indian Tribes of the **United States**, Philadelphia, Lippincott, Grambo & Co., I 20.2:In 2

Injury Experience in Oil and Gas Industry of **United States**, I 28.108

Inpatient Utilization of Short-Stay Hospitals by Diagnosis, **United States**, HE 20.6209/8

Institutions in **United States** Giving Instruction in Agriculture, A 10.18

Instructional Materials . . . for **U.S.** Army Reserve Schools, D 103.6/8

Instrument Approach Procedure Charts [Alaska, Hawaii, **U.S.** Pacific Islands], C 55.411/2

International Air Commerce Traffic Pattern, **U.S.** Flag Carriers, Calendar Year, C 31.153/2

International Boundary Commission, **U.S.**-Mexico, Chamizal Arbitration, S 3.19/3

International Civil Aviation Organization Report of Representatives of **United States**, S 5.52

International Code of Signals, **United States** Edition, D 203.22:102

International Direct Investment, Global Trends and the **U.S.** Role, C 61.29

International Joint Commission on Boundary Waters Between **United States** and Canada, 1909, S 3.23

International Travelers to the **U.S.**, Annual Summary, C 47.15/5

Interstate Commerce Commission Reports, Decisions of the Interstate Commerce Commission of the **United States**, IC 1.6

Inventory of Automatic Data Processing Equipment in the **United States** Government, GS 2.15

Inventory of Automated Data Processing Equipment in the **United States** Government for Fiscal Year (date), GS 12.10

Inventory of Federal Tourism Programs, Federal Agencies, Commissions, Programs Reviewed for Their Participation in the Development of Recreation, Travel, and Tourism in the **United States**, C 47.2:T 64/3

Inventory of Nonutility Electric Power Plants in the **United States**, E 3.29/2

Inventory of Power Plants in the **United States**, E 3.29

Inventory Report on Real Property Leased to the **United States** throughout the World, GS 1.15/2

Inventory Report on Real Property Owned by the **United States** throughout the World, GS 1.15

Investment of Individuals in Savings Accounts, **U.S.** Savings Bonds and Life Insurance Reserves, FHL 1.13

Japan Productivity Center, **United States** Operations Mission to Japan, Publications, S 17.44/2

Journal of Research of the **U.S.** Geological Survey, I 19.61

Journal of **United States** Artillery, W 29.5

Journal; **U.S.** Army Intelligence and Security Command, D 101.85

Journal; **United States** Institute of Peace, Y 3.P 31:15

Judicial Business of the **United States** Courts, Ju 10.1/4

Juror Utilization in **United States** District Courts, Ju 10.13

Keywords Index to **U.S.** Government Technical Reports, C 41.21/5

Labor Offices in the **United States** and Canada, L 16.3

Labor Offices in **U.S.** and Foreign Countries, L 2.6/a 3

Land Joint Commission, **United States** and Panama, S 3.30

Landsat: Non-**U.S.** Standard Catalog, NAS 1.48/2

Landsat: **U.S.** Standard Catalog, NAS 1.48

Latest Consumer Price Index (Tables for **U.S.** and 6 Cities in Midwest), L 2.38/8-4

Latest Editions of **U.S.** Air Force Aeronautical Charts, C 55.418/3

Laws and Regulations Enforced or Administered by the **United States** Customs Service, T 17.6/2

Layman's Guide to Individual Rights Under the **United States** Constitution, Y 4.J 89/2:R 44

Legal Status of Women in the **United States**, L 36.103

Lexicon of Geologic Names of the **United States**, 1936-1960, I 19.3:1200

Lexicon of Geologic Names of the **United States**, 1961-1967, I 19.3:1350

Lexicon of Geologic Names of the **United States**, Including Alaska, I 19.3:896

Light and Fog Signals of **United States** and Canada on Northern Lakes and Rivers, C 9.30

Light List: Atlantic and Gulf Coasts of **United States**, N 24.30, T 47.35

Light List: Atlantic Coast of **United States**, Southern Part, N 24.16, T 47.24

Light List: Great Lakes, **United States** and Canada, N 24.20, T 47.26

Light List: Pacific Coast of **United States**, N 24.19, T 47.25

Light List;Atlantic Coast of **U.S.** Intercoastal Waterway, Hampton Roads to Rio Grande Including Inside Waters, N 24.17, T 47.28

Lime Plants in the **United States**, I 28.28/4

List of Audiovisual Materials Produced by the **United States** Government (series), GS 4.17/5-2, AE 1.110/2

List of Available Publications of the **United States** Department of Agriculture, A 21.9/8:11

List of Classes in 1950 Revision of Classified List of **United States** Government Publications by Departments and Bureaus, GP 3.24

List of Committee Hearings, Committee Prints and Publications of the **United States** Senate, Y 1.3/10

List of Fishery Cooperatives in the **United States**, C 55.338/2

List of Foreign Consular Officers in **United States**, S 1.12

List of Radio Stations of **United States**, C 11.7/6

List of **U.S.** Air Carriers, CAB 1.26

List of **U.S.** Carriers, C 31.254

List of **U.S.** Judges, Attorneys and Marshals, J 1.11

Listing of Aircraft Accidents/incidents by Make and Model, **U.S.** Civil Aviation, TD 1.109/15

Lists of Commercial Treaties and Conventions, and Agreements Affected by Exchange of Notes or Declarations in Force Between **United States** and Other Countries, S 9.9

Lists of **U.S.** Judges, Attorneys and Marshals, J 1.11

Loans Made, **United States** and Territories, by Crop Years, from Date of Organization (1933) through June 30 (year), A 82.311

Low Altitude Approach Procedures, **United States** Military Aviation Notice, D 5.318/3

Mailing List of Consular Service of **United States**, S 1.19

Major Programs of the **U.S.** Department of Housing and Urban Development, Fact Sheets, HH 1.43/2

Management of the **United States** Government, Fiscal Year (date), PrEx 2.8/9

Management Statistics for **United States** Courts, Ju 10.14

Manpower Report of the President and Report on Manpower Requirements, Resources, Utilization, and Training by the **U.S.** Department of Labor, L 1.42/2

Manual for Courts-Martial: **United States**, D 1.15

Manual of Instructions for Survey of Mineral Lands in **United States**, I 21.11/4

Manual of Instructions for Survey of Public Lands of **United States**, I 53.7

Manual of Regulations and Instructions Relating to the Disclosure of Federal Campaign Funds for Candidates for the Office of President or Vice President of the **United States** and Political Committees Supporting Such Candidates, GA 1.14:C 15

Manufacture of Tin and Terne Plates in **United States** (year), T 35.5

Maps (listed in) Bathymetric Mapping Products Catalog 5, **United States** Bathymetric and Fishing Maps, C 55.418/7

Maps (miscellaneous) Includes **U.S.** Outline Maps, C 3.62/2

Marines, Official Magazine of the **U.S.** Marine Corps, D 214.24

Market for Selected **U.S.** Electric Housewares in [various countries], C 41.103

Market for Selected **U.S.** Household and Commercial Gas Appliances in [various countries], C 41.106

Market for **U.S.** Leather and Shoes in [various foreign countries], C 41.98

Market for **U.S.** Microwave, Forward Scatter, and Other Radio Communications Equipment and Radar in [various countries], C 41.105

Market for **U.S.** Products [by country], C 42.20/2

Market for **U.S.** Telecommunications Equipment in [various countries], C 41.104

Market Prices and Yields of Outstanding Bonds, Notes, and Bills of **U.S.**, T 62.7

Marketing Moves, the Marketing Bulletin from the **U.S.** Government Printing Office, GP 1.38

Marketing **U.S.** Tourism Abroad, C 47.20

Materials in the **U.S.** Economy, I 28.2:M 66/6

Maturity Distribution of Euro-Dollar Deposits in Foreign Branches of **U.S.** Banks, FR 1.54

Medical Catalog of Audiovisual Materials Produced by the **United States** Government, GS 4.17/6

Medical Department, **United States** Army in Vietnam, D 104.11/2

Medical Internship in **U.S.** Public Health Service Hospitals, FS 2.89

Medical Technicians Bulletin, Supplement to **U.S.** Armed Forces Medical Journal, D 1.11/2

Meeting of the Canada-**United States** Interparliamentary Group, Y 4.F 76/1-11, Y 4.In 8/16:11

Mental Health, **United States**, HE 20.8137

Merchant Ships Built in **United States** and Other Countries in Employment Report of **United States** Flag Merchant Seagoing Vessels 1,000 Tons and Over, C 39.211

Merchant Vessels of **United States**, TD 5.12/2, T 17.11/2

Merchant Vessels of **United States**: Monthly Supplement to, T 17.11

Methodology Papers: **U.S.** National Income and Product Accounts, BEA-MP- (series), C 59.19

Mexico-**United States** Interparliamentary Group Report of Senate Delegation, Y 4.F 76/2:M 57/8

Military Fields, **United States**, Instrument Approach Procedure Charts, C 55.418/4

Military Government, Austria, Report of **United States** Commissioner, W 1.74, M 105.10

Military Laws of **United States** (Army), D 108.5/2

Mineral Products of the **United States**, I 19.7

Mineral Resources of the **United States**, I 19.8

Minerals in the **U.S.** Economy, I 28.2:M 66/6

Mississippi River System of the **United States**, TD 5.9:5

Mixed Claims Commission, **United States** and Germany, S 3.31

Mixed Claims Commissions, **United States** and Mexico, S 3.34/1

Mobility of the Population of the **United States**, C 3.186:P-20

Money Income and Poverty Status of Families and Persons in the **United States**, C 3.186/11

Money Income of Households, Families, and Persons in the **United States**, C 3.186/2

Monthly Catalog of **United States** Government Publications, GP 3.8

Monthly Catalog of **United States** Government Publications, Periodical Supplement, GP 3.8/8-8

Monthly Report of Condition for **U.S.** Agencies, Branches and Domestic Banking Subsidiaries of Foreign Banks, FR 1.16/3

Monthly Report of the Military Governor for German **(U.S.)**, M 105.7

Monthly Report on Foreign Direct Investment Activity in the **United States**, C 61.25/3

Monthly Statement of Coal-Mine Fatalities in **United States**, I 28.10/1

Monthly Statement of Public Debt of the **United States**, T 1.5/3

Monthly Statement of Receipts and Outlays of the **United States** Government, T 1.5/2

Monthly Statement of the Public Department of the **United States**, T 63.215

Monthly Summary of Foreign Commerce of **United States**, C 18.7

Monthly Supplement to Merchant Vessels of **United States**, T 17.11

Monthly Treasury Statement of Receipts and Outlays of the **United States** Government, T 63.113/2

Motive Power and Car Equipment of Class I Railroads in the **United States**, IC 1 ste.36

National Atlas of the **United States**, I 19.2:N 21 a, I 19.111

National Gazatteer of the **United States**, I 19.16

National Income and Product Accounts of the **United States**, C 49.11/4:In 2, C 59.11/5, C 59.11/5-2, C 59.11/3

Natural Gas Processing Plants in **United States**, I 28.98/3

Navigation Laws of **U.S.**, C 25.5/2

Negroes in the **United States**, C 3.3

New Ship Construction, Oceangoing Ships of 1,000 Gross Tons and Over in **United States** and Foreign Shipyards, C 39.212/3

Newly Reported Tuberculosis Cases and Tuberculosis Deaths, **United States** and Territories, FS 2.42/2

News, Employment and Wages in Foreign-Owned Businesses in the **United States**, L 2.41/12

Newsletter of the **U.S.** Army Medical Department, D 104.24

Newsletter: Commission of the Bicentennial of the **United States** Consitution, Y 3.B 47/2:15

Newsletter: **United States** Holocaust Memorial Council, Y 3.H 74:10

Newsletter: **United States** Travel Service, C 47.14

Notes on Forest Trees Suitable for Planting in the **U.S.**, A 13.7

Numerical List of **U.S.** Air Force and Air Force-navy Aeronautical Standard Drawings, D 301.16

Numerical List, **U.S.** Air Force and Army- Navy Aeronautical Standard Drawings, M 301.12

Occupational Injuries and Illnesses in the **United States** by Industry, L 2.3/11

Ocean Dumping in the **United States**, EP 1.69

Oceangoing Foreign Flag Merchant Type Ships of 1,000 Gross Tons and Over Owned by the **United States** Parent Companies, C 39.230

Office of Inspector General, Semiannual Report to Congress, **United States** Information Agency, IA 1.1/3

Office of **U.S.** High Commissioner for German Publications, S 1.91

Office of **United States** Economic Coordinator for Cento Affairs, Non-Government Central Treaty Organization, S 5.54

Office of **United States** High Commissioner for Austria, General Publications, S 1.89/4

Official Army Register of Volunteer Force of **U.S.** Army, 1861-65, W 3.12

Official Gazette of **U.S.** Patent Office, Trademarks, C 21.5/4

Official Grain Standards of the **United States**, A 88.6/2:G 761

Official List of Commissioned and Other Officers of **U.S.** Public Health and Marine Hospital Service, T 27.5

Official Opinions of the Attorneys General of the **United States**, J 1.5

Official Parcel Post Zone Keys, **United States**, P 1.25/1

Official Register of Officers Volunteers in Service of **United States**, W 3.21

Official Register of the **United States**, C 3.10, CS 1.31

Official Statement of **United States** Food Administration, Y 3.F 73:19

Official **United States** Standards for Beans, A 113.10/3

Official **United States** Standards for Grain, A 104.6/2, A 113.10

Official **United States** Standards for Peas & Lentils, A 113.10/4

Official **United States** Standards for Rice, A 113.10/2

OPEC Direct Investment in the **United States**, C 61.25

Operating Revenues and Operating Expenses by Class of Service, Class 1 Steam Railways in **United States**, IC 1 ste.32

Operating Revenues and Operating Expenses Class 1 Steam Railway in **United States**, IC 1 ste.19

Operating Revenues and Operating Expenses of Class I Railroads in the **United States**, IC 1 ste.19/3

Opinions **United States** Tax Court Reports, Ju 11.7/a

Order of Battle of **United States** Land Forces, D 114.10

Orders to Officers, **U.S.N.**, N 17.9

Orders: **United States** Postal Service, P 1.19

Organization Directory, **U.S.** Department of Agriculture, A 60.10

Outbreaks of Disease Caused by Milk and Milk Products as Reported by Health Authorities as having Occurred in **U.S.**, T 27.42

Outlook for Timber in the **United States**, A 13.50:20/2

Outlook for **U.S.** Agricultural Exports, A 93.43

Output of Refineries in **United States**, I 28.19

Papers Relating to Foreign Relations of the **United States**, S 1.1

Parameters, Journal of the **U.S.** Army War College, D 101.72

Parole in the **United States**, J 29.12/2

Participation of American and Foreign-Flag Vessels in Shipments under **United States** Foreign Relief Programs, C 3.164:976

Participation of Principal National Flags in **United States** Oceanborne Foreign Trade, C 39.221

Passenger Traffic Statements (other than commutation) of Class 1 Steam Railways in **United States** Separated Between Coach Traffic and Parlor and Sleeping Car Traffic, IC 1 ste.40

Passenger Traffic Statistics (other than commutation) of Class I Steam Railways in the **United States** Separated Between Coach Traffic and Parlor and Sleeping Car Traffic, IC 1 ste.39

Passenger Train Performance of Class I Railroads in the **United States**, IC 1 ste.37

Passenger Travel between **United States** and Foreign Countries [annual summary reports], J 21.13

Patent Attorneys and Agents Available to Represent Inventors Before the **United States** Patent Office, C 21.9/2

Patents Assign, **U.S.** Patents Assignments Recorded at the USPTO, C 21.31/4

Patents Class, Current Classifications of **U.S.** Patents, C 21.31/3

Patents Snap, Concordance of **U.S.** Patent Application Serial Numbers to **U.S.** Patent Numbers, C 21.31/6

Patterns of Foreign Travel in the **U.S.**, C 47.18

Peace and War, **United States** Foreign Policy, S 1.2:P 31/8

Peat Producers in **United States**, I 28.107

Pedestrian Laws in the **United States**, October 1974, TD 8.5/2:3/3

Periodic Supplement, Selected **United States** Government Publications, GP 3.17/3

Persons of Spanish Origin in the **United States**, Advance Report, C 3.186/14

Petitions for Certiorari and Briefs on Merits and in Opposition for **U.S.** in Supreme Court of **U.S.**, J 1.19/6

Petroleum Refineries in the **United States** and Puerto Rico, I 28.17/2, E 3.11/5-4

Plant and Equipment Expenditures of **U.S.** Business, SE 1.25/6

Plant Tours for International Visitors to the **United States**, C 47.2:P 69

Pleasure and Business Visitors to **U.S.** by Port of Entry and Mode of Travel, C 47.15/2

Polluting Incidents in and Around **U.S.** Waters, TD 5.51

Population Profile of the **United States**, Current Population Reports, C 3.186/8

Postage Stamps of the **United States**, P 4.10

Postal Decisions of **United States** and Other Courts Affecting Post Office Department and Postal Service, P 14.5

Posters: Bicentennial of the **United States** Constitution Commission, Y 3.B 47/2:12

Posters: **United States** Holocaust Memorial Council, Y 3.H 74:9

Posters: **United States** Information Agency, IA 1.31

Posters: **United States** Marshals Service, J 25.12

Posters: **United States** Mint, T 28.13

Poverty in the **United States**, C 3.186/22

Preliminary Analysis of Aircraft Accident Data, **U.S.** Civil Aviation, TD 1.113/6

Preliminary Estimates of Waterfowl Harvest and Hunter Activity in the **United States** During the Hunting Season, I 49.106

Preliminary Report on Production on Specified Synthetic Organic Chemicals in **United States**; Facts for Industry Series, TC 1.25

Preliminary Report on **U.S.** Production of Selected Synthetic Organic Chemicals, ITC 1.14/2

Preliminary Reports of Income Accounting of Railways in **United States**, IC 1 ste.6

Preliminary Statement of Capitalization and Income, Class I Steam Railways in **United States**, IC 1 ste.28

Price and Availability List of **U.S.** Geological Survey Publications, I 19.41/9

Prices and Yields of Public Marketable Securities Issued by **United States** Government and by Federal Agencies, T 68.7

Procedures and Guidelines for Impeachment Trials in the **U.S.** Senate, Y 1.93-2:S.doc 102

Production and Utilization of Electric Energy in **United States**, FP 1.11/2

Production of Coal in **United States** from 1814 to Close of Calendar Year, I 19.19

Production of Electricity for Public Use in the **U.S.**, I 19.32, I 19.33

Production of Electricity for Public Use in **U.S.**, FP 1.11

Production of Lead in **United States**, Calendar Year, I 19.24

Production of Smelter in **United States** (mid year statements and annual statements, calendar years), I 19.22

Profile on Fire in the **United States**, FEM 1.117/2

Profiles of Foreign Direct Investment in **U.S.** Energy, E 3.52

Profiles of Scheduled Air Carrier Airport Operations by Equipment Type, Top 100 **U.S.** Airports, TD 4.44/4

Profiles of Scheduled Air Carrier Airport Operations, Top 100 **U.S.** Airports, TD 4.44

Profiles of Scheduled Air Carrier Passenger Traffic, Top 100 **U.S.** Airports, TD 4.44/2

Program Report of the **United States** Travel Service, C 47.1

Progress of Education in the **U.S.** of America, HE 19.133, ED 1.41

Progress of Public Education in the **United States** of America, FS 5.210:10005, HE 5.210:10005

Progress of Public Education in **United States** of America, FS 5.62

Progress, **U.S.** Army, D 101.50

Public Assistance, Quarterly Review of Statistics for **U.S.**, SS 1.13

Public Assistance, Statistics for **U.S.**, SS 1.25/a 1

Public Elementary and Secondary Education in the **United States**, ED 1.112/2

Public Health Service International Postdoctorate Research Fellowships Awards for Study in the **United States**, HE 20.3709

Public Libraries in the **United States**, ED 1.134

Public Papers of the Presidents of the **United States**, AE 2.114, GS 4.113

Publications Catalog of the **U.S.** Department of Commerce, C 1.54/2-2

Publications Catalog, **U.S.** Department of Health and Human Services, HE 3.38/5

Publications: Available for Purchase, **U.S.** Army Engineer Waterways Experiment Station and Other Corps of Engineers Agencies, D 103.39

Publications: **U.S.** Antarctic Projects Officer, D 1.32

Publications: **U.S.** Army Foreign Science and Technology Center, D 101.79

Publications: **U.S.** Army Headquarters in Europe, D 101.42

Publications: **United States** Court of Military Appeals, D 1.19/2

Publications: **United States** Postal Service, P 1.57

Quality and Prices of Cotton Linters Produced in **United States**, A 66.37

Quality of Cotton Classed Under Smith- Doxey Act, **United States**, A 88.11/23

Quality of Surface Waters of the **United States**, I 19.13

Quarterly Digest of Unpublished Decisions of the Comptroller General of the **United States**: Personnel Law, Civilian Personnel, GA 1.5/5, GA 1.5/10, GA 1.5/11

Quarterly Financial Report, **United States** Manufacturing Corporations, FT 1.18

Quarterly Financial Report, **United States** Retail and Wholesale Corporations, FT 1.20

Quarterly Report on Germany, Office of **U.S.** High Commissioner for Germany, S 1.90

Quarterly Report on Trade Between the **United States** and Nonmarket Economy Countries, Pursuant to Section 411 (c) of the Trade Act of 1974, Y 4.W 36:3

Quarterly Report to Congress and the East- West Foreign Trade Board on Trade Between the **United States** and the Nonmarket Economy Countries, Y 4.W 36:2

Quarterly Summary of Foreign Commerce of the **United States**, C 3.147

Radio Aids to Navigation, Great Lakes, **United States** and Canada, T 47.26/2

Radio Broadcast Stations in **United States**, Containing Alterations and Corrections, CC 1.24

Radio Facility Charts and Supplementary Information, **United States**, LF/MF Edition, D 301.43

Radio Facility Charts **United States**, VOR edition, D 301.43/2

Radio Laws of the **United States** [June 24, 1910], Y 1.2:R 11

Radio Stations of **United States**, C 11.7/6, C 24.5

Reappraisal Decisions, for Review by **U.S.** Customs Court As Published in Weekly Treasury Decisions, T 1.11/2a

Recommendations and Reports of the Administrative Conference of the **United States**, Y 3.Ad 6:9

Records and Briefs in **U.S.** Cases Decided by Supreme Court of **United States**, J 1.19

Records and Briefs in **U.S.** Cases Decided by Supreme Court of **United States**, J 1.19

Recreational Boating in **United States**, Report of Accidents, Numbering and Related Activies, T 47.54

Reference List of Audiovisual Materials Produced by the **United States** Government, GS 4.2:Au 2

Register of Civil Engineer Corps Commissioned and Warrant Officers of **United States** Navy and Naval Reserve on Active Duty, D 209.9

Register of Commissioned and Warrant Officers; **United States** Naval Reserve, D 208.12/2

Register of Commissioned and Warrant Officers; **United States** Navy and Marine Corps, M 206.10

Register of Money Order Post Offices in **United States**, P 9.5

Register of Retired Commissioned and Warrant Officers, Regular and Reserve, of the **United States** Navy and Marine Corps, D 208.12/3

Register of **U.S.** Commissioners, J 1.18

Register, Department of Justice and the Courts of the **United States**, J 1.7

Registration, Employment and Unemployment, **U.S.** Zone, Statistical Report, W 1.72/3

Regulations for Government of **United States** Army General Hospital, W 44.15

Regulations for **United States** Corps of Cadets Prescribed by Commandant of Cadets, M 109.6/2

Regulations Governing Meat Inspection of the **U.S.** Department of Agriculture, A 88.6/3:188

Regulations, Rules and Instructions: **United States** Parole Commission, J 27.6

Regulatory Program of the **United States** Government, PrEx 2.30

Relative Cost of Shipbuilding in Various Coastal Districts of the **United States**, Report to Congress, C 39.216/2

Report of Austria, Office of **U.S.** High Commissioner for Austria, S 1.89/3

Report of Egg Production Tests, **United States** and Canada, A 77.15:44-78

Report of Forest and Windbarrier Planting in the **United States**, A 13.75

Report of Japan's Export Shipments and Import Receipts Stated by Areas and Countries of Destination and Origin, with Value Expressed in **United States** Dollars, D 102.11/3

Report of Passenger Travel between the **United States** and Foreign Countires, J 21.13/2

Report of Proceedings of Regular Annual Meeting of Judicial Conference of the **United States**, Ju 10.10

Report of Proceedings of Special Session of Judicial Conference of the **United States**, Ju 10.10/2

Report of Quality of Surface Waters for Irrigation, Western **United States**, I 19.13

Report of the Attorney General to the Congress of the **United States** on the Administration of the Foreign Agents Registration Act of 1938, As Amended, J 1.30

Report of the Chief of Staff of the **United States** Army, D 101.1/2

Report of the **U.S.** Attorney General for the District of (area) to the Attorney General, J 31.9

Report of the **U.S.** Department of Justice Pursuant to Section 8 of the Federal Coal Leasing Amendments Act of 1975, J 1.27/3

Report of the **United States** Attorney for the District of Columbia, J 1.1/4

Report of the **United States** Delegation to the World Health Assembly, HE 20.19

Report of **United States** Government to the Food and Agricultural Organization of the United Nations, A 67.35

Report of **United States** High Commissioner, Statistical Annex, **U.S.** Element, Allied Commission for Austria, S 1.89/2

Report of **United States** High Commissioner, Statistical Annex, **U.S.** Element, Allied Commission for Austria, S 1.89/2

Report of **United States** High Commissioner, **U.S.** Element, Allied Commission for Austria, S 1.89

Report of **United States** High Commissioner, **U.S.** Element, Allied Commission for Austria, S 1.89

Report on Austria, Office of **U.S.** High Commissioner for Austria, S 1.89/3

Report on Current Hydraulic Laboratory Research in **U.S.**, C 13.26

Report on Foreign Currencies Held by the **U.S.** Government Fiscal Year and Transition Quarter, T 63.118/2

Report on Incidence of Anthrax in Animals in **United States**, A 77.225

Report on Survey of **U.S.** Shipbuilding and Repair Facilities, TD 11.25

Report on the Militia of **U.S.**, W 3.35

Report on **U.S.** Export Controls to the President and the Congress, C 57.30

Report on **U.S.** Government Research and Studies in the Field of Arms Control and Disarmament Matters, AC 1.14

Report on Vessels Trading with **United States**, SB 5.5

Report on Volume of Water Borne Foreign
Commerce of **U.S.** by Ports of Origin and
Destination (fiscal year), C 27.9/10, MC
1.17

Report to Congress and East-West Foreign Trade
Board on Trade Between **United States**
and Nonmarket Economy Countries, TC
1.38

Report to Congress on **United States** Foreign Relief
Program, S 1.63

Report to the Congress and the Trade Policy
Committee on Trade Between the **U.S.**
and the Nonmarket Economy Countries,
ITC 1.13

Report to the Congress on the Status of the Public
Ports of the **United States**, TD 11.30

Report to the President and Congress on the Status
of Health Personnel in the **United States**,
HE 20.9310

Report to the President and Congress on the Status
of Health Professions Personnel in the
United States, HE 20.6619

Report to the **United States**Congress and the **U.S.**
Secretary of Energy from the Nuclear
Waste Technical Review Board, Y 3.N
88/2:1

Report to the **United States** Congress on Federal
Activities on Alcohol Abuse and
Alcoholism, HE 20.8316

Reported Incidence of Infectious Equine
Encephalomyelitis and Related
Encephalitides in the **United States**,
Calendar Year (date), A 77.230

Reported Incidence of Rabies in **United States**, A
77.232

Reports of the Proceedings of the Judicial
Conference of the **United States** [and]
Annual Report of the Director of the
Administrative Office of the **U.S.** Courts,
Ju 10.1/2

Reports of the Proceedings of the Judicial
Conference of the **United States** [and]
Annual Report of the Director of the
Administrative Office of the **U.S.** Courts,
Ju 10.1/2

Reports of **United States** Trade Missions, C 42.19,
C 48.9

Reports on Condition of Banks in U.S., T 1.6

Reports Prepared for Foreign Service of **United**
States, Listings, C 42.22

Reports to Congress on **United States** Participation in Operations of UNRRA under Act
of March 28, 1944, Pr 32.5812

Research on **U.S.** International Trade, C 42.32

Resume of **U.S.** Civil Air Carrier and General
Aviation Aircraft Accidents, Calendar
Year, C 31.244

Retail Trade Report: **United States** Summary, C
3.138/2

Revenue Programs for the Public Schools in the
United States, FS 5.222:22013, HE
5.222:22013

Revenue Traffic Statistics of Class I Railroads in the
United States, IC 1 ste.24

Revenues and Income of Privately Owned Class a &
B Electric Utilities in the U.S., FP 1.11/5

Review of Selected **U.S.** Government Research and
Development Reports, OTR-(series), C
13.49

Review of **U.S.** Patents Relating to Insecticides and
Fungicides, A 7.9

Review of **U.S.** Patents Relating to Pest Control, A
47.7

Review of **United States** Oceanborne Foreign
Trade, C 39.202:Oc 2

Review of **United States** Patents Related to Pest
Control, A 77.311

River Basins of the **United States**, I 19.56

Road to the **United States** Census 2000, C 3.296

Roll of Honor, Supplemental Statement of
Disposition of Bodies of Deceased
Union Soldiers and Prisoners of War
Removed to National Cemeteries in
Southern and Western **United States**, W
39.8

Roosevelt Library, Annual Report of Archivest of
United States, GS 4.9

Roster of Attorneys and Agents Registered to
Practice before the **U.S.** Patent Office, C
21.9

Roster of Organizaed Militia of **United States**, by
Divisions, Brigades, Regiments,
Companies, and other Organizations,
with their Stations, W 70.5

Rules and Regulations for Foreign Vessels
Operating in the Navigable Waters of the
United States, TD 5.6:V 63/7

Rules and Regulations for Government and
Discipline of **United States** Penitentiaries, J 1.16

Rules and Regulations Governing Paroling of
Prisoners from **U.S.** Penitentiaries [etc.]
(special), J 1.15/6

Rules of Civil Procedure for District Courts in U.S.,
Ju 6.9/3

Rules of Civil Procedure for the **United States**
District Courts, Y 4.J 89/1-11

Rules of Criminal Procedure for the **United States**
District Courts, Y 4.J 89/1-12

Rules of **United States** Court of Customs and Patent
Appeals, Ju 7.8

Sailing Dates of Steamships from the Principal
Ports of the **United States** to Ports in
Foreign Countries, C 15.19, C 18.10

Schedule A. Statistical Classification on
Commodities Imported into the **United**
States with Rates of Duty and Tariff
Paragraphs, C 3.150:A

Schedule B. Statistical Classification of Domestic
and Foreign Commodities Exported from
the **United States**, C 3.150:B

Schedule D. Code Classification of **U.S.** Customs
Districts and Ports, C 3.150:D

Schedule G. Consolidation of Schedule B
Commodity Classifications for Use in
Presentation of **U.S.** Export Statistics, C
3.150:G

Schedule H. Statistical Classification and Code
Numbers of Shipments of Merchandise to
Alaska from **United States**, C 3.150:H

Schedule L. Statistical Classification of Foreign
Merchandise Reports in In-transit Trade
of **United States**, C 3.150:L

Schedule of Sailings of Steam Vessels Registered
Under Laws of **United States** and
Intended to Load General Cargo at Ports
in **United States** for Foreign Destinations, IC 1 rat.8

Schedule P. Commodity Classification for
Reporting Shipments from Puerto Rico to
U.S., C 3.150:P

Schedule Q. Commodity Classification for
Compiling Statistics on Shipments from
U.S., C 3.150:Q

Schedule S. Statistical Classification of Domestic
and Foreign Merchandise Exported from
U.S., C 3.150:S

Schedule T. Statistical Classification of Imports into
U.S. Arranged in Shipping Commodity
GROUPS., C 3.150:T

Schedule W. Statistical Classification of **U.S.**
Waterborne Exports and Imports, C
3.150:W

Schedule X. Statistical Classification of Domestic
and Foreign Merchandise Exported from
United States by Air Arranged in
Shipping Commodity Groups, C 3.150:X

Schedule Y. Statistical Classification of Imports
into **United States** Arranged in Shipping
Commodity Groups, C 3.150:Y

Secretary's Semiannual Management Report, **U.S.**
Department of Labor, L 1.1/3

Secretary's Task Force on Competition in the **U.S.**
Domestic Airline Industry, TD 1.57

Selected Income and Balance-Sheet Items of Class I
Railroads in the **United States**, IC 1
ste.34

Selected Interest and Exchange Rates for Major
Countries and the **U.S.**, FR 1.32/3

Selected Publications of the **United States**
International Trade Commission, ITC 1.9/
3

Selected **United States** Government Publications,
GP 3.17, GP 3.17/2

Selected **United States** Marketing Terms and
Definitions, English [foreign Language],
C 41.93

Semi-annual Report of the Inspector General, **U.S.**
Small Business Administration, SBA
1.1/3

Semi-Annual Report of the Secretary of Commerce
on the **United States** Travel Service, C
47.1

Semi-Monthly Military Government Report for **U.S.**
Occupied Area of Germany, M 105.21

Separate Sheets of Selected Thematic and General
Reference Maps from the National Atlas
of the **United States** of America, I
19.111a

Sheets of National Atlas of **United States**:
Agricultural Research Service, A 77.19

Sheets of National Atlas of **United States**: Bureau
of the Census, C 3.62/3

Sheets of National Atlas of **United States**: Census
of Agriculture, C 3.31/10

Sheets of National Atlas of **United States**: Coast
and Geodetic Survey, C 4.9/21

Sheets of National Atlas of **United States**: Forest
Service, A 13.28/2

Sheets of National Atlas of **United States**:
Geological Survey, I 19.5/3

Sheets of National Atlas of **United States**:
Interstate Commerce Commission, IC 1.30

Sheets of National Atlas of **United States**:
Tennessee Valley Authority, Y 3.T 25:7-2

Sheets of National Atlas of **United States**: Weather
Bureau, C 30.22/4

Shipment Under the **United States** Foreign Aid
Programs Made on Army- or Navy-
Operated Vessels (American flag) by Port
of Lading by Country of Destination, C
3.164:976

Shipping Weight and Dollar Value of Merchandise
Laden on and Unladen from Vessels at
United States Ports During the In-
transit Movement of the Merchandise
from One Foreign Country to Another, C
3.164:981

Ships Registered Under Liberian, Panamanian, and
Honduran Flags Deemed by the Navy
Department to Be Under Effective **U.S.**
Control, C 39.228

Significant Arrearages Due the **United States**
Government and Unpaid 90 Days or
More by Official Foreign Obligors, T
1.45/5

Small Business Lending in the **United States**, SBA
1.52

Snow Survey and Soil Moisture Measurements,
Basic Data Summary for Western **United**
States, Including Columbia River
Drainage in Canada, A 57.46/17

Social and Economic Characteristics of **U.S.** School
Districts, HE 19.336

Social Security Programs in the **United States**, SSA
1.24/2

Social Services U.S.A., HE 17.647, HE 23.2010

Soda Ash and Sodium Sulfate: **U.S.** Production,
Trade and Consumption, I 28.135/2

Special Analyses, Budget of **United States** Fiscal
Year, PrEx 2.8/5

Special Analysis, **United States** Budget, Fiscal
Year, PrEx 2.8/5

Special Report to the **U.S.** Congress on Alcohol
and Health, HE 20.8313

Specifications: **United States** Administration of
Ryukyu Islands, D 102.19/2

Staff Memo from **U.S.** Secretary of Labor, L 1.33

Standard Instrument Departure (SID) Charts,
Eastern **U.S.**, C 55.416/5

Standard Instrument Departure (SID) Charts,
Western **United States**, C 55.416/6

Statement of a Proper Military Policy for the **United**
States, W 26.8

Statement of Public Debt of **United States**, T 63.112

Statement of Taxes, Dividends, Salaries and Wages,
Class a and Class B Privately Owned
Electric Utilities in U.S., FP 1.22

Statement of **United States** Currency and Coin, T
63.188, T 63.308

Statements by Presidents of the **United States** on
International Cooperation in Space, Y
1.92-1:S.doc. 40

Statistical Abstract of the **United States**, C 3.134, C
56.243

Statistical Classification and Code Numbers of
Shipments of Merchandise to Alaska from
United States, C 3.150:H

Statistical Classification of Domestic and Foreign
Commodities Exported from the **United**
States, C 3.150:B

Statistical Classification of Domestic and Foreign
Merchandise Exported from U.S., C
3.150:S

Statistical Classification of Foreign Merchandise
Reports in In-Transit Trade of **United**
States, C 3.150:L

Statistical Classification of Imports into **U.S.** Arranged in Shipping Commodity Groups, C 3.150:T

Statistical Classification of Imports into **United States** Arranged in Shipping Commodity Groups, C 3.150:Y

Statistical Classification of **U.S.** Waterborne Exports and Imports, C 3.150:W

Statistical Classification on Commodities Imported into the **United States** with Rates of Duty and Tariff Paragraphs, C 3.150:A

Statistical Programs of the **United States** Government, PrEx 2.10/3

Statistical Study of **U.S.** Civil Aircraft, C 31.160, FAA 1.32/2

Statistical Summary and Analysis of Foreign Visitor Arrivals, **U.S.** Citizen and Non-**U.S.** Citizen Departures, C 47.15

Statistical Tables Showing Progress of Eradication of Brucellosis and Tuberculosis in Livestock in **United States** and Territories for Fiscal Year, A 77.212/3

Statistics of Capital Movements Between **U.S.** and Foreign Countries, T 62.9

Statistics of Education in the **United States**, FS 5.220:20032, HE 5.220:20032

Statistics of Electric Utilities in the **United States**, Calasses A and B Publicly Owned Companies, FP 1.21

Statistics of Privately Owned Electric Utilities in the **United States**, E 3.18/2

Statistics of Public School Systems in Twenty Largest **U.S.** Cities, ED 1.112/4

Statistics of Publicly Owned Electric Utilities in the **United States**, E 3.18/3

Statistics of the Communications Industry in the **United States**, CC 1.35

Status of Active Foreign Credits of the **United States** Government: Foreign Credits by **United States** Government Agencies, T 1.45/2

Storage-Gage Precipitation Data for Western **United States**, C 55.225

Street Directory of Principal Cities of **United States**, P 7.6

Strikes in the **United States**, L 2.3:651

Student Conference on **United States** Affairs, D 109.9

Studies on Administrative Management in Government of U.S., Y 3.P 92/3:7

Subsidy for **United States** Certificated Air Carriers, C 31.257

Summary and Analysis of International Travel to the **U.S.**, C 47.15

Summary of Foods in the **United States**, I 19.13

Summary of **U.S.** Export Control Regulations, C 42.6:Ex 7/2

Summary of **U.S.** Exports and Imports of Gold and Silver, Calendar Year, C 3.196/3

Summary of **U.S.** Exports and Imports of Gold and Silver, Fiscal Year, C 3.196/2

Summary Reports of Accidents, **U.S.** Civil Aviation, C 31.244/4

Summation of **United States** Army Military Government Activities in Korea, W 1.76

Summation of **United States** Army Military Government Activities in Ryukyu Islands, W 1.78, M 105.12

Supplement to Merchant Vessels of **United States**, TD 5.12

Supplements to Statistical Abstract of **United States**, C 3.134/2

Supplements to the Statistical Abstract of the **United States**, C 56.243/2

Supply and Distribution of Cotton in **United States**, C 3.36

Surface Water Supply of the **United States**, I 19.13

Surgical and Nonsurgical Procedures in Shortstay Hospitals, **United States**, HE 20.6209/5

Survey of Capacity of Refrigerated Storage Warehouses in **United States**, A 82.58

Survey of Food and Nutrition Research in **United States**, NA 2.8

Survey of **U.S.** Uranium Exploration Activity, E 3.46

Survey of **United States** Uranium Marketing Activity, E 3.46/2

Synopsis of **U.S.** Government Proposed Procurement and Contract Awards, C 18.284

Synthetic Organic Chemicals, **United States** Production and Sales, Preliminaries, TC 1.33/2

Synthetic Organic Chemicals, **United States** Production and Sales, TC 1.33, ITC 1.14

Table of Investment Yields for **United States** Savings Bonds of Series E. Official Use, T 66.23

Table of Redemption Values for **United States** Savings Bonds, Series A to E, Inclusive, T 63.209/2

Tables of Redemption Values for **United States** Savings Bonds, T 63.209

Tables of Redemption Values for **United States** Savings Notes, T 63.210

Tables of Redemption Values for **United States** Series E Savings Bonds and Savings Notes, T 63.210/2

Tables to Convert [Foreign Moneys, Weights and Measures into **U.S.** Standards], C 1.11

Tabulations of Statistics Pertaining to Signals, Interlocking, Automatic, Train Control, Telegraph and Telephone for Transmission of Train Orders, and Spring Switches As Used on Railroads of **United States**, IC 1 saf.10

Tariff Schedules of the **United States**, Annotated, TC 1.35/2, ITC 1.10

Tariff Schedules of the **United States**, TC 1.35/3

Tax Guide for **U.S.** Citizens Abroad, T 22.19/2:C 49

Technical Appendix from Vital Statistics of the **United States**, HE 20.6210/a

Technical Appendixes to the Report and Recommendations to the Secretary, **U.S.** Department of Health and Human Services, Y 3.P 29:1-2

Technical Memorandum-To **United States** Study Commission, Southeast River Basins, A 57.50

Telephone Directory: **United States** Courts Administrative Office, Ju 10.20

Territorial Papers of **United States**, GS 4.13, S 1.36

Terrorism in the **United States**, J 1.14/22

Topographic Atlas of the **United States**, I 19.10

Topographic Map of the **United States**, I 19.12

Total Obligations Incurred for Emergency Relief from All Public Funds by State and Local Relief Administration in Continental **United States**, Y 3.F 31/5:35

Trade of the **United States** with, C 18.204

Trade Policies and Market Opportunities for **U.S.** Farm Exports, Annual Report, A 67.40/5

Trademarks Assign, **U.S.** Trademarks Assignments Recorded at the USPTO, C 21.31/9

Trademarks Pending, Bibliographic Information from Pending **U.S.** Trademarks, C 21.31/8

Trademarks Registered, Bibliographic Information from Registered **U.S.** Trademarks, C 21.31/7

Train and Yard Service of Class I Railroads in the **United States**, IC 1 ste.38/2

Training Manual: **United States** Army, W 3.39/3

Transactions of Naval Militia Association of **United States**, N 1.27/5

Transport Statistics in the **United States**, IC 1.25

Treaties and Other International Acts of **U.S.**, S 9.5/1

Treaties and Other International Agreements of **United States**, S 9.12/2

Trend of Employment in **U.S.** (Monthly summary statements), L 2.9/2

Trend of Relief in Continental **United States**, Y 3.F 31/5:37

Trend of **U.S.** Foreign Trade, C 18.190

Trends in Selected Economic and Real Estate Factors in **United States**, NHA 2.15

Trends in Selected Economic Factors, **United States**, HH 2.16

Trends in **U.S.** Foreign Trade, C 57.23

Tripartite Claims Commission (**U.S.**, Austria, and Hungary), S 3.37

Tuberculosis in the **United States**, HE 20.7310

Two Centuries of Tariffs, the Background and Emergence of the **U.S.** International Trade Commission, TC 1.2:T 17/20

U.S. Agricultural Exports, A 67.32

U.S. Agricultural Imports, Fact Sheet, A 67.32/2, A 93.30, A 93.30/2

U.S. Agricultural Real EstateTrends, FCA 1.24/2

U.S. Agricultural Trade Update, A 93.17/7-5

U.S. Air Force Academy Bulletin, D 305.8/2

U.S. Air Force and **U.S.** Navy Flight Planning Document, D 301.52

U.S. Air Force Fine Arts Series, D 301.76/4

U.S. Air Force Plan for Defense Research Sciences, D 301.45/19-5

U.S. Air Force Policy Letter Digest, D 301.120

U.S. Air Force Public Affairs Staff Directory, D 301.104/4

U.S. Air Force Radio Facility Charts, Atlantic and Caribbean Area, M 301.15

U.S. Air Force Radio Facility Charts, North Pacific Area, M 301.14

U.S. Air Force Standards, D 301.31

U.S. Air Service in World War I, D 301.82/2

U.S. Airborne Exports and General Imports, Shipping Weight and Value, C 3.164:986

U.S. Alcohol Epidemiologic Data Reference Manual, HE 20.8308/3

U.S. Antarctic Projects Officer, Bulletin, D 1.32/2

U.S. Antarctic Projects Officer, Publications, D 1.32

U.S. Area Handbook for (country), D 101.22:550

U.S. Arms Control and Disarmament Agency, Annual Report, Y 4.F 76/1-16

U.S. Army and Air Force Recruiting Service Letter, M 208.76

U.S. Army and Navy Directory of Airfields, C 31.125

U.S. Army Audit Agency Bulletins, D 101.3/3

U.S. Army Ballistic Missile Agency, DG- TR- (series), D 105.15/2

U.S. Army Campaigns of World War II, D 114.7/5

U.S. Army Educational Manuals, W 3.47

U.S. Army Electronic Proving Ground, USAEPG-SIG (series), D 111.12

U.S. Army Engineer District, Los Angeles: Reports (numbered), D 103.59

U.S. Army Equipment Index of Modification Work Orders, D 101.22:750-10

U.S. Army in Action Series, D 114.7/4

U.S. Army Materiel Command, Annual Historical Review, D 101.1/4-2

U.S. Army Medical Doctrine, Publications, D 104.36

U.S. Army Military Personnel Center: Pamphlets (series), D 101.22/16

U.S. Army Mobility R & D Laboratory: USAAMRDL CR- (series), D 117.8/6

U.S. Army Natick Laboratories, Food Division, Natick, Mass. Technical Report FD-, D 106.20

U.S. Army Pocket Recruiting Guide, D 101.6/11

U.S. Army Recruiting and Reenlisting Journal, D 118.9

U.S. Army Recruiting Command Pamphlets, USAREC PAM- (series), D 101.22/7

U.S. Army Research and Development Program Guide, D 101.52/4

U.S. Army Specifications, W 3.48/1, W 1.49, M 101.26, D 101.28

U.S. Army Training Manuals Numbered, W 3.39/1

U.S. Army Training Manuals, W 3.39

U.S. Atmospheric Nuclear Weapons Tests, Nuclear Test Personnel Review, D 15.10

U.S. Auto Industry, ITC 1.16/4

U.S. Automobile Industry, C 1.84

U.S. Automobile Industry: Monthly Report on Selected Economic Indicators, ITC 1.16/3

U.S. Automotive Trade Statistics, Series A: Motor Vehicles, ITC 1.16

U.S. Automotive Trade Statistics, Series B, Passenger Automobiles, ITC 1.16/2

U.S. Average, A 106.39

U.S. Book Exchange Service, S 18.27

U.S. Census of Housing: City Blocks, Series HC (3), C 3.224/6

U.S. Census of Housing: Components of Inventory Change, Final Report HC (4) series, C 3.224/6

U.S. Census of Housing: Special Reports for Local Housing Authorities, series HC (S 1), C 3.224/8

U.S. Census of Housing: State and Small Areas, Final Report HC (1) (series), C 3.224/3

U.S. Census of Population: Number of Inhabitants, C 3.223/5

U.S. Census of Wholesale Trade Industry Series, C 3.256/3-2

U.S. Central Station Nuclear Electric Generating Units, Significant Milestones, E 1.41

U.S. Civil Aviation Briefs of Accidents, C 31.244/6

U.S. Coast Guard Historical Monograph Program, TD 5.29

U.S. Coast Pilots: Alaska, C 4.7/2, C 4.7/3, C 4.7/7

U.S. Coast Pilots: Atlantic Coast, C 4.6/1

U.S. Coast Pilots: Gulf Coast, Puerto Rico, and Virgin Islands, C 4.6, C 4.6/4

U.S. Production, Imports and Import/Production Ratios for Cotton, Wool and Man-made Textiles and Apparel, C 61.26

U.S. Real Property Sales List, GS 1.15/5

U.S. Rice Distribution Patterns, A 93.51

U.S. Savings Bond Comprehensive Savings Bond Value Tables (Series EE, I Bond, Series E and Savings Notes), T 63.210/3

U.S. Scientists and Engineers, NS 1.22/7

U.S. Seed Exports, A 67.18:FFVS

U.S. Senate Telephone Directory, Y 1.3/10

U.S. Society & Values, IA 1.35, S 20.19

U.S. Standards for Fruits and Vegetables, A 66.16

U.S. Statutes Concerning the Registration of Prints and Labels, C 21.7/3

U.S. Statutes Concerning the Registration of Trademarks, C 21.7/2

U.S. Supreme Court, Government Briefs in Cases Argued by Solicitor General, Indexes, J 1.19/3

U.S. Supreme Court, Government Briefs in Cases Argued, Indexes, J 1.19/4

U.S. Terminal Procedures, C 55.411

U.S. Textile and Apparel Category System, C 61.54

U.S. Timber Production, Trade, Consumption, and Price Statistics, A 13.113

U.S. Trade Performance in (year) and Outlook, C 61.28

U.S. Trade Shifts in Selected Commodity Areas, ITC 1.15

U.S. Trade Status with Communist Countries, C 57.28, C 57.413, C 61.22

U.S. Trade with Puerto Rico and U.S. Possessions, FT-895, C 3.164:895

U.S. Travel Bureau, I 29.37

U.S. Treasury Savings Stamp News, T 66.22

U.S. Trust Territory of the Pacific, Series 9203, D 5.339

U.S. v. Salvador Arbitration Tribunal, S 3.14

U.S. Warehouse Act Licensed Warehouses, A 112.22

U.S. Water Borne Intercoastal Traffic by Ports of Origin and Destination and Principal Commodities, SB 7.5/317, C 27.9/9, MC 1.9

U.S. Waterborne Exports and General Imports, C 3.164:985

U.S. Waterborne Foreign Trade, Summary Report, C 3.164:985

U.S. Waterborne Foreign Trade, Trade Area by U.S. Coastal District, C 3.164:600

U.S. Wheat Quality, A 104.12/2-5

U.S. Working Women: a Databook, L 2.3:1977

U.S.A. Armor School Subcourses, D 101.78

U.S.A. Citizenship-Know It, Cherish It, Live It, J 1.25

U.S.A. Life, S 1.59/4

U.S.A., Pr 32.5025

U.S.D.A, A 1.57

U.S.D.A. Administrative Information, A 1.57

U.S.D.A. Summary of Registered Agricultural Pesticide Chemical Uses, A 77.302:P 43/4

USPTO

USPTO Today, C 21.33/2, C 21.33/2-2

U.S.T.S. [poster series], C 47.10/2

IFR Enroute High Altitude United States, TD 4.79/17

IFR Enroute low Altitude United States, TD 4.79/15

NIMA Nautical Charts, Public Sale Region 1, United States and Canada, TD 4.82:1

Underground Natural Gas Storage in the United States, (date) Heating Year, E 3.11/2-9

Uniform Crime Reports for the United States, J 1.14/7

United States 1:1,000,000-Scale Maps, I 19.107

United States 1:1,000,000-Scale Series, Intermediate Scale Maps, I 19.110

United States Active Civil Aircraft by State and County, C 31.132/2, FAA 1.35

United States Advisory Commission on Information, Semiannual Report to Congress, S 1.93

United States Air Force Academy Assembly, Proceedings, D 305.11

United States Air Force Academy Journal of Professional Military Ethics, D 305.21

United States Air Force and Navy Supplementary Flight Information Document, Pacific and Far East, D 301.50

United States Air Force and Navy Supplementary Flight Information, Europe, Africa, and Middle East, D 301.49

United States Air Force and United States Navy Radio Facility Charts, Central Pacific-Far East, D 301.12

United States Air Force Fact Sheets, D 301.128

United States Air Force General Histories (series), D 301.82/3

United States Air Force History Program, Summary of Activities, D 301.1/2

United States Air Force History, a Guide to Documentary Sources, D 301.6/5:H 62

United States Air Force in Southeast Asia (series), D 301.86/2

United States Air Force Jag Law Review, D 302.9

United States Air Force Medical Service Digest, D 304.8

United States Air Force Radio Facility Charts, Caribbean and South American Area, D 301.10

United States Air Force Radio Facility Charts, Europe, Africa, Middle East, D 301.9

United States Air Force Reference Series, D 301.82/5

United States Air Force Special Studies, D 301.82/4

United States Air Force, Commands and Agencies Basic Information, D 301.26/23

United States Air Force, Navy, Royal Canadian Air Force and Royal Canadian Navy, Navy Radio Facility Charts and In-Flight Data, Alaska, Canada and North Atlantic, D 301.13/3

United States Air Force, Navy, Royal Canadian Air Force and Royal Canadian Supplementary Flight Information, North American Area (excluding Mexico and Caribbean area), D 301.48

United States Air Force, Navy, Royal Canadian Air Force, and Royal Canadian Navy Supplementary Flight Information, North American Area (excluding Mexico and Caribbean area), D 301.48

United States Air Force, United States Navy and Royal Canadian Air Force Radio Facility Charts, West Canada and Alaska, D 301.13

United States Air Force, United States Navy Radio Facility Charts, North Atlantic Area, D 301.11

United States Airborne Exports of Domestic and Foreign Merchandise, Commodity (Schedule X) by Country of Destination, C 3.164:780

United States Airborne Exports of Domestic and Foreign Merchandise, Country of Destination by Commodity, C 3.164:790

United States Airborne Foreign Trade, Customs District by Continent, C 3.164:986

United States Airborne General Imports of Merchandise, Country of Origin by Commodity, C 3.164:390

United States and Canada Cattle, A 92.18/6-3

United States and Canadian Great Lakes Fleets, C 39.214

United States and Chilean Claims Commission, 1892-94, S 3.21/2

United States and Chilean Claims Commission, 1900-01, S 3.21/3

United States and Mexican Claims Commission, 1869-76, S 3.12

United States and United National Report Series, S 1.49

United States Antarctic Programs, Annual Report, D 201.15

United States Arctic Research Plan, NS 1.51

United States Armed Forces Medical Journal, D 1.11

United States Army in Vietnam (series), D 114.7/3

United States Army in World War II, D 114.7

United States Army in World War II: Master Index, Reader's Guide, D 114.7/2

United States Army in World War, M 103.9

United States Army Installations and Major Activities in Continental U.S., D 101.22:210-1

United States Army Medical Research Institute of Infectious Disease: Annual Progress Report, D 104.27

United States Army Occupational Handbook, D 101.40

United States Army Research and Development Series, D 101.52

United States Army Training Publications, W 3.39/2

United States Attorney's Bulletins, J 31.12

United States Census of Agriculture, 1950: Announcements, C 3.950-9/6

United States Census of Agriculture, 1950: V. 2 General Report (separates), C 3.950-9/5

United States Censuses of Population and Housing: Geographic Identification Code Scheme, Phc (2) (series), C 3.223/13

United States Chiefs of Mission, S 1.69:147

United States Civil Administration of Ryukyu Islands; Special Bulletins, D 102.19/2

United States Civil Aircraft Register, TD 4.18/2

United States Coast Guard Academy, New London, Connecticut: Bulletin of Information, TD 5.16/2

United States Coast Guard Annotated Bibliography, TD 5.21/3

United States Coast Pilot, Atlantic Coast, T 11.6

United States Coast Pilot, Pacific Coast, Alaska, pt. 1, Dixon Entrance to Yakutat Bay, T 11.7/2

United States Coast Pilots, C 55.422

United States Code, Y 1.2/5, Y 1.2/5-2, Y 4.J 89/1:Un 3/3

United States Congressional Serial Set Catalog: Numerical Lists and Schedule of Volumes, GP 3.34

United States Congressional Serial Set Supplement, GP 3.8/6

United States Consumption of Rubber, C 40.14, C 41.31

United States Contributions to International Organizations, S 1.70, S 1.70/9

United States Cotton Quality Report for Ginnings, A 82.28

United States Court Directory, Ju 10.17

United States Court of International Trade Reports, Ju 9.5/2

United States Court of Military Appeals and the Judge Advocates General of the Armed Forces and the General Counsel of the Department of the Treasury,

United States Court of Military Appeals, D 1.19/2

United States Court of Military Appeals, Pubs, D 1.19/2

United States Courts, Pictorial Summary, Ju 10.12

United States Customs Court Reports, Ju 9.5

United States Department of Commerce News, C 1.32/8

United States District Courts Sentences Imposed Chart, Ju 10.18

United States Earthquakes, C 55.417/2, I 19.65/2

United States Employment Service Test Research Reports, L 7.69

United States Exports and Imports of Gold and Silver, Total United States Trade in Gold and Silver and United States Trade in Gold and Silver with Latin American Republics and Canada, C 3.164:859

United States Exports by Air of Domestic and Foreign Merchandise Commodity by Country of Destination, C 3.164:731

United States Exports by Air of Domestic and Foreign Merchandise Country of Destination by Commodity, C 3.164:732

United States Exports of Aluminum, C 41.112/2, C 57.10

United States Exports of Domestic and Foreign Merchandise: Commodity by Country of Destination, C 3.164:410

United States Exports of Domestic and Foreign Merchandise: Country of Destination by Subgroup, C 3.164:420

United States Exports of Domestic and Foreign Merchandise: To Canada (Including Lend-Lease Exports), C 3.157/4

United States Exports of Domestic and Foreign Merchandise: Under Lend-Lease Program, Calendar Year, C 3.164:405

United States Exports of Domestic and Foreign Merchandise: Under Lend-Lease Program, Commodity by Country of Destination, C 3.164:415

United States Exports of Domestic and Foreign Merchandise: Under Lend-Lease Program, Country of Destination by Commodity, C 3.164:421, C 3.164:425

Water-Borne Foreign and Noncontiguous
Commerce and Passenger Traffic of
United States, MC 1.23
Waterborne Commerce of the **United States**, D
103.1/2
Waterborne Passenger Traffic of **U.S.**, MC 1.15
Week in the **United States**, S 1.79
Weekly Census Report of **U.S.** Marine and Contract
Hospitals, T 26.36
Weekly Electric Output, **United States**, FP 1.11/7
Weekly List of Selected **U.S.** Government
Publications, GP 3.17
Weekly Statement of Gold and Silver Exports and
Imports, **United States**, C 3.195
Western **U.S.** Water Plan, (year) Progress Report, I
27.61
Western **United States**, Dates of Latest Prints,
Instrument Approach Procedure Charts
and Airport Obstruction Plans, C 4.9/20
Where to Write for Birth and Death Records of **U.S.**
Citizens Who Were Born or Died
Outside of the **United States** and Birth
Certifications for Alien Children
Adopted by **U.S.** Citizens, FS 2.102:B
53/7
Where to Write for Birth and Death Records of **U.S.**
Citizens Who Were Born or Died
Outside of the **United States** and Birth
Certifications for Alien Children
Adopted by **U.S.** Citizens, FS 2.102:B
53/7
Wholesale Trade in **U.S.**, FR 1.21
Wildlife Imported into the **United States**, I 49.13
Working Capital of **U.S.** Corporations, SE 1.25/6
Worldwide **U.S.** Active Duty Military Personnel
Casualties, D 1.61/6
Yard Service Performance of Class I Railroads in the
United States, IC 1ste.38

Units
Construction Reports; Housing **Units** Authorized
for Demolition in Permit-issuing Places,
(year), C 45 (series), C 56.211/8
Number of New Dwelling **Units** and Permit
Valuation of Building Construction
Authorized by Class of Construction in
Mountain and Pacific Division by Civil
Division and State, L 2.51, L 2.51/2, L
2.51/3
Number of New Permanent Nonfarm Dwelling
Units Started by Urban or Rural
Location, Public or Private Ownership,
and Type of Structure, L 2.51/4
Operating **Units** Status Report, Licensed
Operations Reactors Data for Decisions,
Y 3.N 88:15
Permit Valuation and Number of New Dwelling
Units Provided in Housekeeping and
Dwellings Authorized in Metropolitan
Area of Washington, D.C. by Type of
Dwelling and Source of Funds, L 2.51/7
Personnel Management Training **Units**, L 1.38
Public Health Personnel in Local Health **Units**, FS
2.80
Summary Characteristics for Governmental **Units**
and Standard Metropolitan Statistical
Areas (series), C 3.223/23:
Survey of Negro World War II Veterans and Vacancy
and Occupancy of Dwelling **Units**
Available to Negroes {in city areas}, L
2.31
U.S. Central Station Nuclear Electric Generating
Units, Significant Milestones, E 1.41

Universal
Color **Universal** Language and Dictionary of
Names, C 13.10:440
Legal Guide and Case Digest, Veterans'
Reemployment Rights Under the
Universal Military Training and Service
Act, As Amended, and Related Acts, L
25.6/2:L 52
Paris, **Universal** Exposition 1867, S 6.9
Paris, **Universal** Exposition 1878, S 6.10
Paris, **Universal** Exposition 1889, S 6.11
Paris, **Universal** Exposition 1900, S 6.12

Universities
Correspondence Courses Offered by Participating
Colleges and **Universities** through the
United States Armed Forces Institute, D
1.10/6
Department of the Army Prime Contracts ($1
million and over) Placed with Industry,
Non-Profit Organizations, Colleges, and
Universities, D 101.22:715-4

Education Directory: Colleges and **Universities**,
HE 19.324
Faculty Graduate Study Program for Historically
Black Colleges and **Universities**, NF 3.8/
2-7
Faculty Salaries in Land-Grant Colleges and State
Universities, FS 5.253:53023, HE
5.253:53023
Fall Enrollment Colleges and **Universities**, ED
1.124
Federal Support of Research and Development at
Universities and Colleges and Selected
Nonprofit Institutions, Fiscal Year,
Report to the President and Congress,
NS 1.30
Federal Support to **Universities**, Colleges, and
Selected Nonprofit Institutions, Fiscal
Year (date), Report to the President and
Congress, NS 1.30
Historically Black Colleges and **Universities**,
Faculty Projects, Summer College
Humanities Programs for High School
Juniors, NF 3.8/2-8
Key Audiovisual Personnel in Public Schools and
Library Systems in State and Large
Cities and In Large Public Colleges and
Universities, FS 5.60/2
Land-Grant Colleges and **Universities**, Preliminary
Report for Year Ended June 30, FS
5.250:50025, HE 5.250:50025
Library Statistics of Colleges and **Universities**, HE
19.338, ED 1.122, ED 1.222/3
Library Statistics of Colleges and **Universities**;
Analytic Report, FS 5.215:15031, HE
5.215:15031
Library Statistics of Colleges and **Universities**;
Fall (year) Summary Data, HE 19.338
Library Statistics of Colleges and **Universities**;
Fall (year), Part C, Analytic Report, HE
5.92/7
Library Statistics of Colleges and **Universities**;
Institutional Data, FS 5.215:15023, HE
5.215:15023
National Advisory Committee on Black Higher
Education and Black Colleges and
Universities: Annual Report, HE
19.140, ED 1.21
Scientific Activities in **Universities** and Colleges,
NS 1.22:C 83/3
Scientific and Engineering Research Facilities at
Universities and Colleges, NS 1.53
Selected Data on Federal Support to **Universities**
and Colleges, Fiscal Year, NS 1.30/2-2
Statistics of Land-Grant Colleges and **Universities**,
FS 5.250:50002, HE 5.250:5002
Universities and Their Relationships with the
National Oceanic and Atmospheric
Administration, C 55.40
White House Initiative on Historically Black
Colleges and **Universities**, Newsletter,
ED 1.89

University
Air Pollution Training Courses, (year) and
University Training Programs,
Extramural Programs, Institute for Air
Pollution Training Planning and Special
Projects, EP 4.13
Air **University** Catalog, D 301.26/16
Air **University** Compendium of Research Topics, D
301.26/3-2
Air **University** Documentary Research Study,
Publications, D 301.26/3
Air **University** Library Index to Military
Periodicals, D 301.26/2
Air **University** Library Master List of Periodicals,
D 301.26/2-2
Air **University** Publications, D 301.26/6
Air **University** Review, D 301.26
Air **University**, AFROTC {text books}, D 301.26/
12
Air **University**, Human Resources Research
Institute, Research Memorandum, D
301.26/7
Air **University**, School of Aviation Medicine:
{publications}, D 301.26/13-2
Annual NASA-**University** Conference on Manual
Control, NAS 1.21
Bulletin of the School of Medicine, Uniformed
Services University of the Health
Sciences, D 1.67
Center for Vocational and Technical Education,
Ohio State **University**: Research and
Development Series, HE 18.11

CSU-PHS {Colorado State **University**-Public
Health Service} Collaborative
Radiological Health Laboratory: Annual
Report, HE 20.4119, HE 20.4613
Extension Course Institute, Air **University**: Career
Development Course, D 301.26/17-2
Graduate Education Bulletin, Uniformed Services
University of the Health Sciences, D
1.67/2
Herald of Leningrad **University**, Mathematics,
Mechanics, and Astronomy Series
{abstracts}, C 41.50/8
Herald of Leningrad **University**, Physics and
Chemistry Series {abstracts}, C 41.52/5
Herald of Moscow **University**, Physio-Mathemati-
cal and Natural Sciences Series
{abstracts}, C 41.50/6
Institutes for College and **University** Faculty, NF
3.14
Maritime Administration **University** Research
Program, TD 11.33
NASA'S **University** Program, Quarterly Report of
Active Grants and Research Contracts,
NAS 1.42
National Defense **University** Catalogue, D 5.414
NCHS Catalog of **University** Presentations, HE
20.6225
NEH Fellowships **University** Teachers, College
Teachers, and Independent Scholars
Anniversary and Commemorative
Initiatives, NF 3.13/4
Program of **University** Research Report Reprinted,
TD 1.20/6-2
Publications Air **University**, D 301.26/6
Publications Air **University**, Documentary
Research Study, D 301.26/3
Publications Air **University**, School of Aviation
Medicine, D 301.26/3-2
Publications Howard **University**, FS 5.41
Regulations, Rules and Instructions National
Defense **University**, D 5.406
Research Memorandum Air **University**, Human
Resources Report Institute, D 301.26/7
Research Reports Air **University**, D 301.26/13
Tower **University**: Education Service Plan, D
101.93/2
University Centers of Foreign Affairs Research,
Selective Directory, S 1.2:Un 3
University of Maryland College Park 2x4 Loop Test
Facility, Y 3.N 88:25-7
University Research: Summary of Awards, Program
of **University** Research, TD 1.45
University-Federal Agency Conference on Career
Development, Conference Reports, CS
1.70
University Transportation Center Project
Abstracts, TD 10.14
Voice of America Forum Lectures **University** Series,
IA 1.19/4

Unlawful
Foreign Fraud, **Unlawful**, and Lottery Mail Orders,
P 1.12

Unload
Fresh Fruit and Vegetable **Unload** Totals for 41
Cities, Calendar Year (date), A 88.40/2:7

Unloads
Car-Lot **Unloads** of Certain Fruits and Vegetables,
A 66.40
Carlot **Unloads** of Fruits and Vegetables at
Washington, D.C., A 82.46
Carlot **Unloads** of Fruits and Vegetables by
Commodities, A 88.12/5
Fresh Fruit and Vegetable **Unloads** in Eastern
Cities, A 88.40/2:3
Fresh Fruit and Vegetable **Unloads** in Midwestern
Cities, A 88.40/2:5
Fresh Fruit and Vegetable **Unloads** in Southern
Cities, A 88.40/2:6
Fresh Fruit and Vegetable **Unloads** in Western
Cities, A 88.40/2:4
Fresh Fruit and Vegetable **Unloads**, FVUS (series),
A 88.12/31
Unloads of Tomatoes in 66 Cities by States of
Origin, A 36.187
Washington, D.C. **Unloads** of Fresh Fruits and
Vegetables, A 88.12/17

Unlocated
Union Catalog, Selected List of **Unlocated**
Research Books, LC 18.7

Unpublished
Cumulative Index-Digest of **Unpublished**
Decisions, I 1.69/2-3

Mill Margins Report, Cotton Cloth and Yarn **Values**, Cotton Prices and Mill Margins for Unfinished Carded Cotton Cloth and Yarn, Revised Estimates, A 88.11/10-2

Table of Redemption **Values** for United States Savings Bonds, Series A to E, Inclusive, T 63.209/2

Tables of Redemption **Values** for $50 Series EE and $25 Series E Savings Bond, T 63.209/5-2

Tables of Redemption **Values** for United States Savings Bonds Series A-E, T 63.209

Tables of Redemption **Values** for United States Savings Bonds Series E, T 63.209/6

Tables of Redemption **Values** for United States Savings Bonds Series EE, T 63.209/7

Tables of Redemption **Values** for United States Savings Bonds Series J, T 63.209/3

Tables of Redemption **Values** for United States Savings Notes, T 63.210

Tables of Redemption **Values** for United States Series E Savings Bonds and Savings Notes, T 63.210/2

Tables of Redemption **Values** of $25 Series E Savings Bonds Series, T 63.209/5

Total **Values** of Imports and Exports, T 37.7, C 14.12, C 18.6

U.S. Society & **Values**, IA 1.35

United States Individual Retirement Bonds, Tables of Redemption **Values** for All Denomination Bonds, T 63.209/8

United States Retirement Plan Bonds, Tables of Redemption **Values** for All Denomination Bonds, T 63.209/8-2

U.S. Society and **Values**, S 20.19

Values of German Exports of Electrical Apparatus and Equipment, C 18.158

Vanadium
Mineral Industry Surveys, **Vanadium**, I 19.156
Vanadium in (year), I 28.78/2
Vanadium, I 28.78

Vandenberg
Strategic Air Command, **Vandenberg** Air Force Base Telephone Directory, D 301.104/7

Vandium
Vandium Reports, I 28.78

Vanguard
Vanguard, VA 1.93

Vans
Cost of Owning and Operating Automobiles and **Vans**, TD 2.60

Variations
Climate **Variations** Bulletin, C 55.287/61
Foreign Versions, **Variations**, and Diminutives of English Names and Foreign Equivalents of U.S. Military and Civilian Titles, J 21.2:N 15

Varietal
Progress Report, Annual **Varietal** and Environmental Study of Fiber and Spinning Properties of Cottons, A 77.530

Varieties
Apples, Production by **Varieties**, with Comparisons, A 88.12/15
Commercial Apples, Production by **Varieties**, with Comparisons, A 92.11/9
Cotton **Varieties** Planted, A 88.11/13
Cotton **Varieties** Planted in Early Producing Section of Texas, (year), A 88.11/11
New Crop **Varieties**, A 43.33/2
Trends in Forage Crops **Varieties**, A 43.33
Turkeys in NTIP Flocks and Their Distribution by States and **Varieties**, A 77.15:44-11

Variety
Crops Research: Results of Regional Cotton **Variety** Tests by Cooperating Agricultural Experiment Stations, A 77.15:34
Limitation of **Variety** Recommendations, C 13.12/2
Official Journal of the Plant **Variety** Protection Office, A 88.52
Regional Cotton **Variety** Tests, A 106.28
Results of Regional Cotton **Variety** Tests by Cooperating Agricultural Experiment Stations, A 77.15:34
Sugarcane **Variety** Tests in Florida, Harvest Season, A 106.27

Various
Crop Report as of . . . **Various** Crops, A 88.24/2
Relative Cost of Shipbuilding in **Various** Coastal Districts of the United States, Report to Congress, C 39.216/2
Sending Gift Packages to **Various** Countries, C 49.9

U.S. General Imports **Various** Products, C 56.210/4

Varnish
Digest of Trade Hints for Paint and **Varnish** Merchants, C 18.194
Paint, **Varnish**, Lacquer, and Fillers, C 3.94

Varnishes
World Trade in Paints and **Varnishes**, C 18.171

Varying
Farm Labor Reports **Varying** Title, A 66.10

Vascular
Rare and Endangered **Vascular** Plant Species in (various States), I 49.95

Vaults
Contents of **Vaults** {of} Treasury Department, T 40.10

VCR
VCR and Film Catalog, IA 1.27/2

VD
NavMed **VD** {leaflets}, N 10.19
Special **VD** Education Circulars, FS 2.38
VD Education Circulars, FS 2.39
VD Fact Sheet, HE 20.7018
VD Folderes, FS 2.32
VD Statistical Letter, HE 20.7018/2, HE 20.7309

Vealers
Cattle, Calves, and **Vealers**: Top Prices and Bulk of Sales, Chicago, A 36.207

Vectorborne
Homestudy Course; **Vectorborne** Disease Control (series), HE 20.7021/7, HE 20.7021/7-2

Vegetable
Animal and **Vegetable** Fats and Oils, C 3.56
Annual Report of **Vegetable** Breeding in Southeastern United States, Hawaii, and Puerto Rico, A 77.532
Catalog of Seed and **Vegetable** Stock Available from the Southern Regional Plant Introduction Station for various plants, A 106.19
Factory Consumption of Animal and **Vegetable** Fats and Oils by Classes of Products, C 3.154
Fresh Fruit and **Vegetable** Arrival Totals, A 88.12/31-4
Fresh Fruit and **Vegetable** Market News, Weekly Summary, A 88.12/22
Fresh Fruit and **Vegetable** Shipments by States, Commodities, Counties, Stations, Calendar Year (date), A 88.12/31:6, A 88.40/2:12
Fresh Fruit and **Vegetable** Shipments, by Commodities, States, Months, Calendar Year (date), A 88.12/31:7, A 88.40/2:14
Fresh Fruit and **Vegetable** Unload Totals for 41 Cities, Calendar Year (date), A 88.40/2:7
Fresh Fruit and **Vegetable** Unloads in Eastern Cities, A 88.40/2:3
Fresh Fruit and **Vegetable** Unloads in Midwestern Cities, A 88.40/2:5
Fresh Fruit and **Vegetable** Unloads in Southern Cities, A 88.40/2:6
Fresh Fruit and **Vegetable** Unloads in Western Cities, A 88.40/2:4
Fresh Fruit and **Vegetable** Unloads, FVUS (series), A 88.12/31
Fresh Fruit and **Vegetable** Wholesale Market Prices, A 88.12/22-2
Fruit and **Vegetable** Crops and Diseases Division, Semi-monthly News Letters, A 77.510
Fruit and **Vegetable** Inspection Service, Inspector's Guides, A 36.193
Fruit and **Vegetable** Market News, Weekly Arrival Summary, A 88.12/18
Fruit and **Vegetable** Situation, A 36.95
Fruit and **Vegetable** Truck Cost Report, A 108.10
Fruit and **Vegetable** Truck Rate Report, A 88.12/32
List of Manufacturers and Jobbers of Fruit and **Vegetable** Containers, A 36.60
Louisiana Annual **Vegetable** Summary, Louisiana Crop Reporting Service, A 88.12/23
Production and Carry Over of Fruit and **Vegetable** Containers, A 36.61
Seed Crops, **Vegetable** Seed Report, A 92.19/7
Vegetable Report, Louisiana Crop Reporting Service, A 88.12/26
Vegetable Seed Stocks, A 92.19/6
Vegetable Seeds, A 92.19/17
Vegetable Situation and Outlook Yearbook, A 93.12/2-3
Vegetable Situation, A 88.12/8, A 93.12/1, A 105.24
Vegetable, Situation and Outlook, A 93.12/2
Vegetable-Seed Stocks, A 88.30/5
Weekly Summary of Fruit and **Vegetable** Carlot Shipments, A 88.12

Vegetables
Agricultural Chemical Usage, **Vegetables**, Summary, A 92.50
Canned Fruits and **Vegetables**, Production and Wholesale Distribution, C 3.168
Car-Lot Shipments of Fruits and **Vegetables**, by Commodities, States, and Months, A 1.34, A 66.24
Car-Lot Unloads of Certain Fruits and **Vegetables**, A 66.40
Carlot Unloads of Fruits and **Vegetables** at Washington, D.C., A 82.46
Carlot Unloads of Fruits and **Vegetables** by Commodities, A 88.12/5
Cold Storage Stocks of Frozen Fruits and **Vegetables** by Container Size, A 82.36
Commercial **Vegetables** TC (series), A 88.12/6
Estimated Refrigerator Car Movement of Domestic Fresh Fruits and **Vegetables** by Regions, A 82.42
Foreign Agricultural Trade of the United States; Imports of Fruits and **Vegetables** under Quarantine by Countries of Origin and Ports of Entry, A 67.19/7, A 93.17/5
Foreign News on **Vegetables**, A 36.46
Foreign Service on **Vegetables**, A 64.13, A 67.14
Fresh Fruits and **Vegetables**, C 18.72/3
Fruits, **Vegetables**, Tree Nuts, A 67.30:F 94
Market News Service of Fruits and **Vegetables**, A 88.12/30
Marketing Order Actions, a Summary of Actions Under Marketing Orders for Fruit, **Vegetables**, and Speciality Crops, A 88.12/33
Memorandum to Editors {wholesale prices selected fruits and **vegetables**}, L 1.20/5
Plants Under USDA Continuous Inspection, Processed Fruits and **Vegetables** and Related Products, A 88.43/2
Spring **Vegetables** and Melons, A 88.26/4
Spring **Vegetables**, Spring Melons, Spring Potatoes, A 88.26/4
Standards for Fruits and **Vegetables**, A 104.6/3
State Carlot Shipments of Fruits and **Vegetables**, by Commodities, Counties, and Billing Stations, A 88.12/10
Summer and Fall **Vegetables** for Fresh Market, Summer Melons, Sweetpotatoes, A 88.26/4
Summer and Fall **Vegetables**, Melons, Sweetpotatoes, A 88.26/4
Total Commercial Production of All **Vegetables** and Melons for Fresh Market and Processing, A 92.11/10-3
Truck Receipts of Fresh and Fruits and **Vegetables**, A 66.20
U.S. Imports of Fruits and **Vegetables** under Plant Quarantine Regulations, A 93.44/3
U.S. Standards for Fruits and **Vegetables**, A 66.16
United States Standards for Fruits and **Vegetables**, A 36.35, A 75.19, A 80.121, A 80.822
United States Standards for Grades of {fruits, **vegetables**, etc.}, A 82.20
Vegetables for the Hot, Humid Tropics (series), A 106.26
Vegetables, (year) Annual Summary, A 105.24/2
Vegetables, A 105.24/2-2
Vegetables, Fresh Market {and} Processing, A 92.11
Vegetables, Fresh Market, Annual Summary, Acreage, Production, etc., A 92.11/10-2
Vegetables, Preliminary Acreage, Yield, Production and Value, A 92.11/10-6
Vegetables, Processing, A 92.11/14
Vegetables, Processing, Annual Summary, Acreage Productions, etc., A 92.11/10
Washington, D.C. Unloads of Fresh Fruits and **Vegetables**, A 88.12/17
Weekly Summary of F.O.B. Prices of Fresh Fruits and **Vegetables** in Representative Shipping Districts, A 88.12/2, A 82.53
Weekly Summary of Wholesale Prices of Fresh Fruits and **Vegetables** at New York City and Chicago, A 88.12/3, A 82.52

Vehicle
Analysis of Defective **Vehicle** Accidents of Motor Carriers, IC 1 mot.20
Analysis of Motor Carrier Accidents Involving **Vehicle** Defects of Mechanical Failure, TD 2.312
Annual Motor **Vehicle** Report for Fiscal Year, GS 2.14
Electric and Hybrid **Vehicle** Program, Annual Report to Congress, E 1.45/2

Electric and Hybrid **Vehicle** Program, EHV/
quarterly Report, E 1.45
Experimental Safety **Vehicle** Program and **Vehicle**
Safety Research, Progress Report, TD
8.16/2
Farm **Vehicle** Activity Memorandums, Pr 32.4910
Federal Motor **Vehicle** Fleet Reports, GS 2.18
Federal Motor **Vehicle** Safety Standards, TD 8.6/4
Federal Motor **Vehicle** Safety Standards and
Regulations, TD 8.6/2
Government **Vehicle** Operators Guide to Service
Stations for Gasoline, Oil and
Lubrication, D 7.6/7-2
Motor Vehicle Safety Defect Recall Campaigns
Reported to the Department of
Transportation by Domestic and Foreign
Vehicle Manufacturers, TD 2.209
National Motor **Vehicle** Safety Advisory Council
Summary Report, TD 1.13
Report on Activities Under the National Traffic and
Motor **Vehicle** Safety Act, TD 8.12
Report to Congress on the Administration of the
National Traffic **Vehicle** Safety Act of
1966, TD 1.10/2
Safety Related Recall Campaigns for Motor Vehicles
and Motor **Vehicle** Equipment, Including
Tires, TD 8.9/2
Summary of Motor **Vehicle** Accident Fatalities, C
3.128/3
World Motor **Vehicle** and Trailer Production and
Registration, C 57.21
World Motor **Vehicle** Production and Registration,
C 41.17
Vehicles
Report on the International Technical Conference
on Experimental Safety **Vehicles**, TD 8.16
Safety Related Recall Campaigns for Motor **Vehicles**
and Motor Vehicle Equipment, Including
Tires, TD 8.9/2
U.S. Automotive Trade Statistics, Series A: Motor
Vehicles, ITC 1.16
United States Flag Containerships and United
States Flag Ships with Partial Capacities
for Containers And/or **Vehicles**, C 39.232
Vendor
Licensee Contractor and **Vendor** Inspection Status
Report, Y 3.N 88:24
Public Assistance: **Vendor** Payments for Medical
Care by Type of Service, Fiscal Year
Ended (date), HE 17.617
Recipients and Amounts of Medical **Vendor**
Payments Under Public Assistance
Programs, HE 17.617/2
Vendor Payments for Medical Care Under Public
Assistance, by Program and Type of
Service, Fiscal Year (date), HE 17.617/4
Veneer
Veneer and Plywood Series, C 18.159
Venereal
Supplements to **Veneral** Disease Information
Bulletin, FS 2.10
Veneral Disease Bulletins, T 27.20, FS 2.11
Veneral Disease Information, T 27.26, FS 2.9
Venereal
Abstracts of Current Literature on **Venereal**
Disease, FS 2.11/2
CLVD (Current Literature on **Venereal** Disease)
Abstracts and Bibliography, HE 20.7311
Current Literature on **Venereal** Disease, FS 2.11/2,
HE 20.2311
Venezuela
Commission to Arbitrate Claims of **Venezuela** Steam
Transportation Company of New York
against **Venezuela**, S 3.11
Venezuelan
Venezuelan Mixed Claims Commissions, Caracas
1902 and 1903, S 3.17
Verific
Verific Vessel Entrances and Clearances: Calendar
Year (date), C 56.210:975, C 3.174:975
Verification
Review of Waste Package **Verification** Test, Y 3.N
88:25-3
Version
TIBER/Line Files; 1990 Census **Version**, C 3.279
Versions
Foreign **Versions**, Variations, and Diminutives of
English Names and Foreign Equivalents
of U.S. Military and Civilian Titles, J
21.2:N 15
Vesicular
Report of Developments on Eradication of
Vesicular Exanthema, A 77.224

Vessel
Code Classification of Flag of **Vessel**, C 3.150:J
Estimated **Vessel** Operating Expenses, C 39.242
National Heart, Blood **Vessel**, Lung, and Blood
Program: Annual Report of the Director
of the National Heart and Lung Institute,
HE 20.3211, HE 20.3211/2
Navigation and **Vessel** Inspection Circulars, N
24.27, T 47.34, TD 5.4/2
Schedule J. Code Classification of Flag of **Vessel**, C
3.150:J
Status of **Vessel** Construction and Reconditioning
under Merchant Marine Acts of 1920 and
1938, SB 7.5:1105, C 27.9/8
Verific **Vessel** Entrances and Clearances: Calendar
Year (date), C 56.210:975, C 3.174:975
Vessel Inventory Report, C 39.221, TD 11.11
Vessel Inventory Report, United States Flag Dry
Cargo and Tanker Fleets, 1,000 Gross
Tons and Over, C 39.217
Vessel Safety Review, TD 5.12/3
Vessels
Allowance of Articles under Cognizance of Bureau
of Construction and Repair for **Vessels** of
the Navy, N 4.5
Allowances for **Vessels** of the Navy, N 5.5
American Documented Seagoing Merchant **Vessels**
of 500 Gross Tons and Over, 4 Degree, C
11.8
Annual List of Merchant **Vessels**, C 11.5
Catalog of Charts and Plans Issued to **Vessels** of
Navy, Portfolios, N 6.5/7
Charter Report, Government-Owned Dry-Cargo
Vessels, Operated by Bareboat Charters
and/or Agents of Maritime Administra-
tion, C 39.215
Control and Employment of **Vessels** Trading with
United States, SB 5.6
Employment Report of United States Flag Merchant
Fleet, Oceangoing **Vessels** 1,000 Gross
Tons and Over, C 39.208
General Specifications for Building **Vessels** of
Navy, N 29.7, M 210.7
List of Masters, Mates, {etc} of Merchant Steam,
Motor, and Sail **Vessels**, Licensed during
Calendar Year, T 38.7
List of Merchant **Vessels**, T 37.11, T 30.5
List of Officers of Merchant Steam, Motor and Sail
Vessels Licensed During (calendar year),
C 15.7
Measurement of **Vessels**, T 17.9/2
Merchant Ships Built in United States and Other
Countries in Employment Report of
United States Flag Merchant Seagoing
Vessels 1,000 Tons and Over, C 39.211
Participation of American and Foreign-Flag **Vessels**
in Shipments under United States
Foreign Relief Programs, C 3.164:976
Quarterly Report on Employment of American
Merchant **Vessels**, SB 7.5/300, C 27.9/7
Quarterly Report on Employment of American
Steam and Motor Merchant **Vessels**, MC
1.8
Register of Officers and **Vessels**, T 33.6
Report on **Vessels** Trading with United States, SB
5.5
Rules and Regulations for Foreign **Vessels**
Operating in the Navigable Waters of the
United States, TD 5.6:V 63/7
Schedule of Sailings of Steam **Vessels** Registered
Under Laws of United States and
Intended to Load General Cargo at Ports
in United States for Foreign Destina-
tions, IC 1 rat.8
Shipment Under the United States Foreign Aid
Programs Made on Army- or Navy-
Operated **Vessels** (American flag) by Port
of Lading by Country of Destination, C
3.164:976
Shipping Weight and Dollar Value of Merchandise
Laden on and Unladen from **Vessels** at
United States Ports During the In-transit
Movement of the Merchandise from One
Foreign Country to Another, C
3.164:981
Supplement to Merchant **Vessels** of United States,
TD 5.12
United States Foreign Trade Bunker Oil and Coal
Laden in the United States on **Vessels**, C
3.164:810
Vessels Receiving Benefits of Construction Loans
under Merchant Marine Act of 1928, SB
7.8

Weekly Report of **Vessels** under Jurisdiction of
Shipping Board, SB 2.12
Vesting
Vesting Orders, Pr 33.507
Veteran
Veteran Preference , CS 1.30
Veterans
Annual Report, Authorized by 38 U.S.C. 5057,
Administrator, **Veterans**' Affairs, on
Sharing Medical Facilities, Fiscal Year
(date), Y 4.V 64/4:M 46
Best Bets for Returning **Veterans** in Washington
D.C. Area, CS 1.43/2
Board of **Veterans**' Appeals Decisions, VA 1.95/2
Data on Female **Veterans**, VA 1.2/12
Data on Vietnam Era **Veterans**, VA 1.2/2, VA 1.2/10
Department of **Veterans** Affairs, FY Budget in Brief
and Budget Submission, VA 1.83/2
Directory of **Veterans** Administration Facilities, VA
1.62/2-2
Directory of **Veterans** Organizations and State
Departments of Veterans Affairs, VA 1.62
Disabled **Veterans**, Affirmative Action Plan, P 1.56
Employment of Disabled and Vietnam Era **Veterans**
in Federal Government, CS 1.93
Employment Services for **Veterans**, Annual Report,
L 7.30/2
Federal Benefits for **Veterans** and Dependents, VA
1.34:1
Government Life Insurance Programs for **Veterans**
and Servicemen, VA 1.46
Handbook for **Veterans** Administration Contract
Representatives, VA 1.10/5:232-68-1/2
Laws relating to **Veterans**, Y 1.2:V 64
Legal Guide and Case Digest, **Veterans**'
Reemployment Rights Under the
Universal Military Training and Service
Act, As Amended, and Related Acts, L
25.6/2:L 52
Legislative Objectives of **Veterans**' Organizations,
Y 4.V 64/3:L 52/8
Medical Research in **Veterans** Administration,
Annual Report, VA 1.43
National Conference **Veterans**' Employment
Representatives, FS 3.123
Pamphlets **Veterans** Administration, VA 1.19
Program Guide **Veterans** Administration, VA 1.10/
3
Quarterly Progress Report on **Veterans** Administra-
tion-Armed Forces Study on Chemo-
therapy of Tuberculosis, VA 1.40
Report to the Committee on the Budget from the
Committee on **Veterans**' Affairs, Y 4.V
64/3-10
Survey of Negro World War II **Veterans** and
Vacancy and Occupancy of Dwelling
Units Available to Negroes {in city
areas}, L 2.31
Survey of World War II **Veterans** and Dwelling
Unit Vacancy and Occupancy {in city
areas}, L 2.30
Survey of World War II **Veterans** and Dwelling
Unit Vacancy and Occupancy (in
Specified Areas), C 3.194
Telephone Directory **Veterans** Administration, VA
1.60
Veterans Administration Activities, Submitted by
the Veterans Administration, Y 4.V 64/
4:V 64
Veterans Administration Instructions, VA 1.15
Veterans Administration Medical Center, Tucson,
Arizona, Formulary, VA 1.73/5
Veterans Administration Medical Research Service,
Annual Report, VA 1.1/4
Veterans Administration Summary of Medical
Programs, VA 1.43/5
Veterans Assistance Information, Printed and
Processed, Y 3.Se 4:18
Veterans Education Newsletter, VA 1.49
Veterans Emergency Housing Program: Community
Action Report to Mayor's Emergency
Housing Committee, NHA 1.12, Y 3.H
81/2:8
Veterans Employment News, L 7.29
Veterans Employment Service Handbooks, L 7.30
Veterans'
Selected Reports of Cases before **Veterans**'
Education Appeals Board, Y 3.V 64:7
Veterans' Emergency Housing Program:
Community Action Bulletin, NHA 1.14
Veterans' Reemployment Rights Handbooks, L
25.6/2:V 64
Veterinarian
FDA **Veterinarian**, HE 20.4410

Veterinary
Bureau of **Veterinary** Medicine Memo, BVMM (series), HE 20.4028
CDC **Veterinary** Public Health Notes, HE 20.7010
International **Veterinary** Congress Proceedings, A 4.19
Livestock and **Veterinary** Sciences, Annual Report of the National Research Programs, A 106.33
Veterinary Biological Products, Licensees and Permittees, A 101.2/10
Veterinary Biologics Division Notices, A 77.226/3
Veterinary Biologics Notices, A 101.14
Veterinary Bulletins, W 44.21/9
World Trade in **Veterinary** Preparations, C 18.177

Vetoes
Presidential **Vetoes**, Y 1.3:V 64/2:798-976

VFR
Air Traffic Patterns for IFR and **VFR** Aviation, Calendar Year, TD 4.19/2
Enroute Change Notice, DoD Flip Enroute **VFR** Supplement United States, D 5.318/8-2
Grand Canyon **VFR** Aeronautical Chart, (general aviation), C 55.416/12-6
Grand Canyon **VFR** Aeronautical Chart, TD 4.79/13-6
IFR/**VFR** Low Altitude Planning Chart, TD 4.79/16-3
Terminal Area Charts (**VFR**), C 55.416/11
U.S. Gulf Coast **VFR** Aeronautical Chart, C 55.416/12
U.S. Gulf Coast **VFR** Aeronautical Chart, TD 4.79/13
VFR Helicopter Chart of Los Angeles, C 55.416/12-2
VFR/IFR Planning Chart, C 55.416/7
VFR Low Altitude Planning Chart, C 55.416/15-3
VFR-Supplement, United States, D 5.318/8

VHA
VHA Employee Newsletter, VA 1.100

Vibration
Shock and **Vibration** Bulletin, D 210.27/2
Shock and **Vibration** Digest, D 4.12/2, D 210.27
Shock and **Vibration** Monographs, D 1.42, D 210.27/3

Vice President's
Public Report of the **Vice President's** Task Force on Combatting Terrorism, PrVp 40.2:T 27

Vicksburg District
Stages and Discharges of Mississippi River and Tributaries in the **Vicksburg District**, D 103.45

Victimization
Bureau of Justice Statistics Bulletin, Criminal **Victimization**, J 29.11/10
Criminal **Victimization** in the United States, J 1.42/3
Criminal **Victimization** in the United States: Trends, J 29.9/2-2
Victimization, Fear of Crime and Altered Behavior (series), HH 1.70

Victims
Rape and Its **Victims**: a Report for Citizens, Health Facilities, and Criminal Justice Agencies, J 1.8/3:R 18
Teenage **Victims**, A National Crime Survey Report, J 29.23
Victims of Trafficking and Violence Protection Act: 2000, Trafficking in Persons Report, S 1.152

Victory
Education for **Victory**, FS 5.26
Special Bulletin Addressed to **Victory** Speakers, Pr 32.5017/2
Victory Crops Series Pamphlets, FS 5.29
Victory Fleet, MC 1.24
Victory Speaker; An Arsenal of Information for Speakers, Pr 32.5017
Victory, Pr 32.5021
Victory; Office Weekly Bulletins, Pr 32.5008

Video
USIA **Video** Library Catalog, IA 1.30

Videos
Catalog of Captioned Feature and Special Interest Films and **Videos** for the Hearing Impaired, ED 1.209/2-3
Catalog of Educational Captioned Films/**Videos** for the Deaf, ED 1.209/2-2

Vienna
Vienna, International Exhibition, 1873, S 6.14

Viet-Nam
Viet-Nam Information Notes, S 1.38

Vietnam
Data on **Vietnam** Era Veterans, VA 1.2/2, VA 1.2/10
Directory of Officials of **Vietnam**, A Reference Aid, PrEx 3.10/7-25
East Asia, **Vietnam**: TAP CHI CONG SAN, PrEx 7.16/4-2
Employment of Disabled and **Vietnam** Era Veterans in Federal Government, CS 1.93
Medical Department, United States Army in **Vietnam**, D 104.11/2
Public Administration Bulletin {for **Vietnam**}, S 18.38
United States Army in **Vietnam** (series), D 114.7/3
United States Navy and the **Vietnam** Conflict (series), D 207.10/3
United States Operations Mission to **Vietnam**, Publications, S 18.31/2
Vietnam Report, PrEx 7.16/5
Vietnam Studies (series), D 101.74

Viewpoint
Center for the Book **Viewpoint** Series, LC 1.38
Your Navy, from the **Viewpoint** of the Nation's Finest Artists, D 201.9

Viewpoints
Viewpoints, a Selection from the Pictorial Collections of the Library of Congress, LC 25.2:V 67

Views
News and **Views**, Ju 10.23
Mountain **Views**, A 13.120
Report to the Committee on the Budget; **Views** and Estimates of the Committee on Interior and Insular Affairs (House), Y 4.In 8/14-11
Report to the Committee on the Budget **Views** and Estimates of the Committee on Natural Resources, Y 4.R 31/3-11
Scientific Manpower, Significant Developments, **Views** and Statistics, NS 1.14
Special Report, Fresh **Views** of Employment of the Mentally Handicapped, PrEx 1.10/4-2
Views and Estimates of Committees of the House (together with Supplemental and Minority Views) on the Congressional Budget for Fiscal Year (date), Y 4.B 85/3-11
Views and Estimates of the Committee on Education, Y 4.Ed 8/1-11
Views and Estimates of the Committee on Foreign Affairs on the Budget, Y 4.F 76/1:B 85
Views and Estimates on the Budget Proposed for Fiscal Year (date), Y 4.Ap 6/1-10
Views of the Committee on Appropriations, United States Senate, on the First Concurrent Resolution on the Budget, Y 4.Ap 6/2:B 85/5

Vigileer
Aviano **Vigileer**, D 301.123

Vignettes
Historical **Vignettes**, I 1.102

Viking
Viking Picture Sets, NAS 1.43/5

Violations
Consolidated List of Persons or Firms Currently Debarred for **Violations** of Various Public Contracts Acts Incorporating Labor Standard Provisions, GA 1.17

Violence
Closing the Gap, Waging War on **Violence**, HE 20.40
CSAP, Substance Abuse Resource Code, **Violence**, HE 20.409/2
Domestic **Violence** and Stalking, J 35.21
Domestic **Violence** Information Series, HE 23.1015
Domestic **Violence** Monograph Series, HE 23.1015/2
Hate Crime: The **Violence** of Intolerance, CRS Bulletin, J 23.3
Significant Incidents of Political **Violence** Against Americans, S 1.138/2
Victims of Trafficking and **Violence** Protection Act: 2000, Trafficking in Persons Report, S 1.152
Violence Against Women Act News, J 35.20
Violence Surveillance Summary Series, HE 20.7957

Viral
National Communicable Disease Center Neurotropic **Viral** Diseases Surveillance {reports}, FS 2.60/14
National Communicable Disease Center Neurotropic **Viral** Diseases Surveil-lance, Annual Poliomyelitis Summary, FS 2.60/14:P 75

National Communicable Disease Center, Neurotropic **Viral** Diseases Surveil-lance: Annual Encephalitis Summary, FS 2.60/14:En 1
Viral Tumorigenesis Report, HE 20.3167

Viral Diseases
Neurotropic **Viral Diseases** Surveillance, HE 20.7011/5

Virgin Islands
Atlantic Coast; Gulf of Mexico Puerto Rico and **Virgin Islands**, C 55.422:5
Census of Nurses Employed for Public Health Work in United States, in Territories of Alaska and Hawaii, and in Puerto Rico and **Virgin Islands**, FS 2.81
Laws Administered by Governor of **Virgin Islands**, I 35.13/5
Official Parcel Post Zone Keys **Virgin Islands**, P 1.25/2
Report of **Virgin Islands** Agricultural Research and Extension Program, A 77.491
Special Census, 1923, High Point, N.C.; **Virgin Islands** 1917, C 3.23
U.S. Coast Pilots Gulf Coast, Puerto Rico, and **Virgin Islands**, C 4.6, C 4.6/4

Virginia
Guides to German Records Microfilmed at Alexandria, **Virginia**, GS 4.18
Records of **Virginia** Company of London, LC 1.11
Tide Calendar Hampton Roads (Sewalls Point), **Virginia**, M 202.13, D 203.13
Tide Calendar Norfolk and Newport News, **Virginia**, N 6.22
Virginia Crops and Livestock, A 88.31
Water Resources Development in **Virginia**, D 103.35/46

Virginia Beach
Area Wage Survey Summary Norfolk-**Virginia Beach**-Newport News, Virginia, L 2.122/46-2

Virology
Reading Guide to Cancer-**Virology** Literature, FS 2.22/56
Recent Reviews, Cancer **Virology** and Biology, Supplement to the Cancergrams, HE 20.3173/2-4
Virology Study Section, HE 20.3001/2:V 81

Virus
Ad Hoc Committee for Review of the Special **Virus** Cancer Program, HE 20.3001/2:V 81/5
Arthropod-Borne **Virus** Information Exchange, HE 20.7036
Solid Tumor **Virus** Working Group, HE 20.3001/2:T 83/2
Tumor **Virus** Detection Working Group, HE 20.3001/2:T 83
Virus Cancer Program Advisory Committee, HE 20.3001/2:V 81/4
Virus Cancer Program Scientific Review Committee A, HE 20.3001/2:V 81/2
Virus Cancer Program Scientific Review Committee B, HE 20.3001/2:V 81/3

Virus-Serum
Notices, Activities of Licensed Establishments Supervised by **Virus-Serum** Control Division, A 4.31, A 77.217

VISA
Annual Report of the **VISA** Office, S 1.1/4
Visa Bulletin, S 1.3/4
Visa Requirements of Foreign Governments, S 1.2:V 82/2

Vision
National Advisory Eye Council: Annual Report on **Vision** Research Projects, HE 20.3752:R 31/4
Vision (Newsletter of SERVE), The, ED 1.348
Vision Research Program Committee, HE 20.3001/2:V 82/3

Visitation
Federal Recreation Fee Program (year), Including Federal Recreation **Visitation** Data, a Report to the Congress, I 70.18

Visiting
Program Announcement, **Visiting** Fellowship Program, J 28.25/2
Visiting Expert Series, S 1.87
Visiting Fellowship Program Reports, J 26.11

Visitor
Arrivals and Departures by Selected Ports Statistics of Foreign **Visitor** Arrivals and U.S. Citizen Departures Analyzed by U.S. Ports of Entry and Departure, C 47.15/4

Statistical Series Securities and Exchange Commission, SE Statistical Series, Annual Data, Data from the Drug Abuse **Warning** Network (DAWN), Series I, HE 20.8212/11

Warrant

Lineal List of Commissioned and **Warrant** Officers of the Marine Corps Reserves, D 214.11/2

Register of Civil Engineer Corps Commissioned and **Warrant** Officers of United States Navy and Naval Reserve on Active Duty, D 209.9

Register of Commissioned and **Warrant** Officers Coast Guard Reserve, T 47.10/2

Register of Commissioned and **Warrant** Officers Marine Corps Reserve, N 9.20

Register of Commissioned and **Warrant** Officers Naval Militia, N 1.27/6

Register of Commissioned and **Warrant** Officers Naval Reserve Force, N 25.6

Register of Commissioned and **Warrant** Officers Naval Reserve, N 17.38

Register of Commissioned and **Warrant** Officers Navy and Marine Corps and Reserve Officers on Active Duty, D 208.12

Register of Commissioned and **Warrant** Officers United States Naval Reserve, D 208.12/2

Register of Commissioned and **Warrant** Officers United States Navy and Marine Corps, M 206.10

Register of Retired Commissioned and **Warrant** Officers, Regular and Reserve, of the United States Navy and Marine Corps, D 208.12/3

Warren

F.E. **Warren** AFB, FEWP- (series), D 301.35/6

Warren Grant Magnuson

Warren Grant Magnuson Clinical Center: Annual Brochure, HE 20.3052/2

Warrior

USAF **Warrior** Studies, D 301.96

Wartime

Adjustment of College Curriculum to **Wartime** Conditions and Needs, Reports, FS 5.33

News to Use, **Wartime** Facts about Goods You Sell, Pr 32.4819

U.S. Coast Pilots **Wartime** Information to Mariners, C 4.7/6

Wartime Information to Mariners Supplementing U.S. Coast Pilots, C 4.7/6

Wartime Report Release Lists, Y 3.N 21/5:12

Wartime Reports, Y 3.N 21/5:11

Washington

Arbitrations Under Treaty of **Washington**, S 3.13

Basin Outlook Reports **Washington**, A 57.46/7

BLM Facts, Oregon and **Washington**, I 53.43/2

Bulletin of the Philosophical Society of **Washington**, SI 1.10

Circular DC-Nos. **Washington** Store, GS 2.4/2

Climate Review, Metropolitan **Washington**, C 55.129

Conference on Limitation of Armament, **Washington**, 1921n22, S 3.29

Conferences at **Washington** and Quebec, S 1.1/3:W 27/2

Conferences at **Washington**, 1941-1942, and Casablanca, S 1.1/3:W 27

Conservation Vistas, Regional Conservation Education Newsletter Serving Oregon and **Washington**, A 13.72/2

History of George **Washington** Bicentennial Celebration, Y 3.W 27/2:14

Naval Torpedo Station, Keyport, **Washington**: Publications, D 211.23

Oregon and **Washington** Planned Land Sales, I 53.32

Pacific Coast, California, Oregon, **Washington**, and Hawaii, C 55.422:7

Pan American Financial Conference, 2d, **Washington**, 1920, T 1.22/2

Pan-American Medical Congress, **Washington**, 1893, S 5.16

Price List of Subsistence Stores in **Washington** Barracks, D.C., W 77.9

Report on **Washington** Conference of Mayors and Other Local Government Executives on National Security, FCD 1.18

Report on **Washington** Conference on National Women's Advisory Committee on FCDA, FCD 1.18/2

Telephone Listing, **Washington** Area, T 63.202/10

Transmittals (NOAA **Washington** Area Personnel Locator), C 55.47

U.S. Coast Pilots Pacific Coast, California, Oregon, **Washington**, and Hawaii, C 4.7/1

Washington Annual Data Summary Water Year, A 57.46/7-2

Washington Aqueduct, Annual Reports, I 1.45

Washington Arbitration (American-British Mixed Claims Commission), S 3.13/2

Washington Helicopter Route Chart, C 55.416/12-4

Washington Hospital for Foundlings, Annual Reports, I 1.34

Washington Office Telephone Directory, I 53.45

Washington, Governor, Annual Reports, 1878-90, I 1.35

Writings of George **Washington**, Y 3.W 27/2:13

Washington D.C.

Authorized Construction—**Washington D.C.** Area, C 3.215/5

Best Bets for Returning Veterans in **Washington D.C.** Area, CS 1.43/2

Carlot Unloads of Fruits and Vegetables at **Washington, D.C.**, A 82.46

Construction Reports; Authorized Construction, **Washington, D.C.** Area, C 56.211/6

Consumer Price Index, **Washington, D.C.** Area, L 2.38/8

Current Local Announcements Covering **Washington, D.C.** Metropolitan Area, CS 1.28:2602-WA

Local Climatological Data, **Washington, D.C.**, Dulles International Airport, C 55.217/2

Pan American Financial Conference, **Washington, D.C.**, May 24, 1915, T 1.22

Pan-American Scientific Congress, 2d, **Washington, D.C.**, S 5.14/2

Permit Valuation and Number of New Dwelling Units Provided in Housekeeping and Dwellings Authorized in Metropolitan Area of **Washington, D.C.** by Type of Dwelling and Source of Funds, L 2.51/7

Register of Military Personnel in the **Washington, D.C.** Area, TD 5.19/3

Report to Employees FY, **Washington, D.C.** Post Office, P 1.1/2

Retail Food Price Index, **Washington, D.C.**, Area, L 2.39/3

Telephone Directory NASA, Headquarters, **Washington, D.C.**, NAS 1.24

Washington, D.C. Unloads of Fresh Fruits and Vegetables, A 88.12/17

Waste

Accession Bulletin, Solid **Waste** Information Retrieval System, EP 1.18, EP 3.3/2

Advanced **Waste** Treatment Research, I 67.13/3:AWTR

Building for Clean Water Progress Report on Federal Incentive Grants for Municipal **Waste** Treatment Fiscal Year, FS 2.64/6

Building for Clean Water Report on Federal Incentive Grants for Municiapl **Waste** Treatment, FS 16.9

Commercial Stocks of Wool and Related Fibers, Tops, Moils, **Waste** Clips and Rags in U.S., C 3.52/3

Comprehensive Studies of Solid **Waste** Management, Annual Report, EP 1.11

Ecological Monitoring Program at the **Waste** Isolation Pilot Plant, Annual Report, E 1.28/16

Elimination of **Waste** Series, C 1.13

Inventory Municipal **Waste** Facilities, EP 2.17

National Survey of Community Solid **Waste** Practices, HE 20.1409

Nuclear **Waste**, Quarterly Report on DOE'S Nuclear Waste Program, GA 1.13/9

Pacific Basin Consortium for Hazardous **Waste** Research Newsletter, E 1.110

Policies and Trends in Municipal **Waste** Treatment (series), EP 1.26

Project Register, **Waste** Water Treatment Construction Grants, EP 1.9/2, EP 1.56/2

Radionuclide Migration around Uranium Ore Bodies Analogue of Radioactive **Waste** Repositories, Y 3.N 88:25-11

Reducing **Waste** at Its Source (series), EP 1.17/2

Report to the U.S. Congress and the U.S. Secretary of Energy from the Nuclear **Waste** Technical Review Board, Y 3.N 88/2:1

Review of **Waste** Package Verification Test, Y 3.N 88:25-3

Solid **Waste** Management Monthly Abstracts Bulletin, EP 1.17/3

Solid **Waste** Management Series, EP 1.17

Solid **Waste** Management Training Bulletin of Courses, EP 3.12

Solid **Waste** Management, Available Information Materials, EP 1.17:58.25

Solid **Waste** News Brief, EP 1.17/4

State Solid **Waste** Planning Grants, Agencies, and Progress, Report of Activities, EP 3.10

Status of the Department of Energy's Implementation of Nuclear **Waste** Policy Act, GA 1.13/10

Water Supply and **Waste** Disposal Series, TD 2.32

Wastes

Office of Solid **Wastes** Information Series, SW-(series), FS 2.305

Wastewater

Lake Erie **Wastewater** Management Study Public Information Fact Sheet, D 103.63/2

Wastewater

State Priority Lists for Construction Grants for **Wastewater** Treatment Works, Fiscal Year (date), EP 1.56/4

Wastewater Management Reports, D 103.60

Wastewater Treatment Construction Grants Data Base, Public Law 92-500 Project Records, Grants Assistance Programs, New Projects Funded During (Month), EP 1.56

Watch

Congressional **Watch**, Y 3.Ad 9/8:13

Distillate **Watch**, E 3.13/5

DOE Petroleum Demand **Watch**, E 1.7/3

HCFA Health **Watch**, HE 22.43

Motor Gasoline **Watch**, E 3.13/6

Peace **Watch**, Y 3.P 31:15-2

Proliferation **Watch**, Y 4.G 74/9-11

Propane **Watch**, E 3.13/7

Water

Abstracts of Recent Published Material on Soil and **Water** Conservation, A 1.68, A 57.36, A 77.15:41

Activities of the U.S. Geological Survey **Water** Resources Division, Hawaii, I 19.55/7

Activities of the U.S. Geological Survey, **Water** Resources Division, Status of Idaho Projects, I 19.55/3

Activities of **Water** Resources Division, California District, I 19.55

Agricultural Resources, Cropland, **Water**, and Conservation, A 93.47/2

Aircraft Emergency Procedures Over **Water**, T 47.32/2

Alaska **Water** Laboratory Quarterly Research Reports, EP 1.22/2

Alaska **Water** Laboratory, College, Alaska: Reports, EP 1.22

Ambient **Water** Quality Criteria for {various chemicals}, EP 1.29/3

Announcement of **Water**-Resources Reports Released for Public Inspection, I 19.48

Annual Report of the Activities of the Effluent Standards and **Water** Quality Information Advisory Committee, EP 1.1/2

Annual Summary of **Water** Quality Data for Selected Sites in the Pacific Northwest, I 19.46/3

Annual **Water** Quality Analyses Report for Nevada, I 53.44

Annual **Water** Quality Data Report, E 1.28/15

Arkansas River **Water** Basin News, D 103.30/2

Basic Data Series Ground-**Water** Releases (series), I 19.82

Biennial Report Under the Great Lakes **Water** Quality Agreement of 1978, Y 3.In 8/28:11

Building for Clean **Water** Progress Report on Federal Incentive Grants for Municipal Waste Treatment Fiscal Year, FS 2.64/6

Building for Clean **Water** Report on Federal Incentive Grants for Municiapl Waste Treatment, FS 16.9

Building for Clear **Water**, I 67.15

Bulletin of Courses **Water** Pollution Control Technical Training Program, I 67.17

Carriers by **Water**, Selected Financial and Operating Data Form Annual Reports, IC 1 wat.10

Catalog of Information on **Water** Data, I 19.42/5

Catalog of Information on **Water** Data: Index to Stations in Coastal Areas, I 19.42/6

Clean **Water**, Announcements {for radio and television}, FS 2.64/5

Clean **Water**, Report to Congress (year), EP 1.43
Clean **Water** SRF Program Information for the State
of..., EP 2.33
Colorado **Water** Supply Outlook and Federal-
State-Private Cooperative Snow Survey,
A 57.46/19
Committee on the Assessment of Human Health
Effects of Great Lakes **Water** Quality:
Annual Report, Y 3.In 8/28:15
Comparative Summary of **Water** Borne Foreign
Commerce, SB 7.5/399, C 27.9/3, MC
1.19
Conditions of Major **Water** System Structures and
Facilities, Review of Maintenance,
Report of Examination, {various regions
and projects}, I 27.69
Cooperative **Water** Resources, Research and
Training, I 1.1/4
Cost of Clean **Water** , EP 2.14
Density of Sea **Water** (D.W.), C 4.33
Division of **Water** Control Planning: Annual
Report, Y 3.T 25:1-12
Division of **Water** Control Planning: Reports, Y
3.T 25:38
Domestic Pumps, **Water** Systems, and Windmills,
Shipments of, C 3.77
Domestic **Water** Softening Apparatus, Shipments
of, C 3.78
Environmental and **Water** Quality Operational
Studies, D 103.24/15
Evaluation of {various States} **Water** Supply
Program, EP 1.61
Evaluation Report, **Water** Resources Appraisal for
Hydroelectric Licensing, FP 1.31
Fall **Water** Supply Summary for Nevada, A 57.46/
14
Fall **Water** Supply Summary for River Basins, A
57.46/8
Fall **Water** Supply Summary for Utah, A 57.46/6-1
Federal Reclamation Projects, **Water** and Land
Resource Accomplishments, I 27.55
Federal State Cooperative Snow Surveys and
Water Supply Forecasts, A 57.46/9-2
Federal **Water** Resources Research Program for
Fiscal Year, PrEx 8.9
Fluoridated Drinking **Water**, HE 20.7022/4
Fluoridated Drinking **Water**, Proficiency Testing,
HE 20.7412/3
Focus on Great Lakes **Water** Quality, Y 3.In 8/
28:17
Galvanized Range Broilers and Tanks for Hot
Water Heaters, C 3.86
Great Lakes **Water** Levels, C 55.420/2
Great Lakes **Water** Quality Annual Report, Y 3.In
8/28:9
Ground **Water** Issue, EP 1.43/2
Ground-**Water** Levels in the United States, I 19.13
Homestudy Course; **Water** Fluoridation, HE
20.7021/9-2
Homestudy Course; **Water** Fluoridation Test
Exercise, HE 20.7021/9-3
Homestudy Courses; **Water** Fluoridation, HE
20.7021/9
Index of Current **Water** Resources Activities in
Ohio, I 19.55/6
Interagency Advisory Committee on **Water** Data:
Summary of Meetings, I 19.74
Intermediate Minimum Property Standards for Solar
Heating and Domestic Hot **Water**
Systems, HH 1.6/9:So 4
International Commission for Equitable
Distribution of **Water** of Rio Grande, S
3.19/4
Inventory of Interstate Carrier **Water** Supply
Systems, EP 1.41
Inventory of Soil, **Water**, and Related Resources, A
57.22
Inventory of **Water** Resources, Y 3.N 21/12:10
Lake Erie **Water** Quality Newsletter, D 103.63
Lake Mead **Water** Supply Outlook, I 27.43
Lake Michigan Cooling **Water** Studies Panel:
Reports, EP 1.72
Land and **Water** Conservation Fund Grants
Manual, I 29.107
Land and **Water** Conservation Fund, Grants-in-
Aid Program, Annual Report, I 29.107/2
National Reference List of **Water** Quality Stations,
Water Year (date), I 19.53/3
National Status and Trends Program, **Water**
Quality Cruise Data Reports (series), C
55.436, C 55.436/4
National **Water** Conditions, I 19.42
National **Water** Quality Inventory, Report to
Congress, EP 2.17/2

National **Water** Summary, I 19.13/3
Nevada Annual Data Summary **Water** Year, A
57.46/4-2
New Reports by Geological Survey About **Water**
in the Pacific Northwest, I 19.14/5
Office of Saline **Water**, I 1.82/3
Office of **Water** Environmental and Program
Information Systems Compendium, EP
2.29/2
Office of **Water** Operating Guidance and
Accountability System, EP 2.29
Office of **Water** Research and Technology: Annual
Report, I 1.1/5
Oregon Annual Data Summary, **Water** Year, A
57.46/5-3
Pacific Northwest **Water** Laboratory: Quarterly
Progress Report, EP 2.22
Pacific Northwest **Water** Resources Summary, I
19.46
People Land and **Water**, I 1.116:v.nos.nos
Plastic Paints, Cold **Water** Paints, and Calcimines,
C 3.96
Program of **Water** Resources Division, Texas
District, and Summary of District
Activities, Fiscal Year, I 19.55/2
Progress in Soil and **Water** Conservation Research,
Quarterly Reports, A 77.528
Project Register, Projects Approved Under Sec. 8
of Federal **Water** Pollution Control Act
(Pub. Law 660, 84th Cong.), As
Amended and Sec. 3, of Public Works
Project Register, Waste **Water** Treatment
Construction Grants, EP 1.9/2, EP 1.56/
2
Public Health Service **Water** Pollution
Surveillance System, FS 2.84/2
Publications Land Economics Division, **Water**
Utilization Section, A 36.149
Publications National Conference on **Water**
Pollution, FS 2.64/3
Regulations, Rules and Instructions Office of
Water Programs, EP 2.6
Report of **Water** Resources Research, I 19.75
Report on Volume of **Water** Borne Foreign
Commerce of U.S. by Ports of Origin and
Destination (fiscal year), C 27.9/10, MC
1.17
Research Reports Supported by Office of **Water**
Resources Research Under the **Water**
Resources Research Act of 1964
Received During the Period (date), I
1.97/2
Revenue and Traffic Carriers by **Water**, IC 1 wat.11
Revenue and Traffic of Class A and B **Water**
Carriers, IC 1 wat.11
Saline **Water** Conservation Program, Reports and
Publications, I 1.83
Saline **Water** Conversion Demonstration Plant, I
1.87/2
Saline **Water** Conversion Report for (year), I 1.1/3
Saline **Water** Research and Development Progress
Reports, I 1.88
Sea **Water** Conversion, Solar Research Station
(series), I 1.87
Selected Summaries of **Water** Research, I 67.12
Selected Urban Storm **Water** Runoff Abstracts, EP
2.10:11024
Selected **Water** Resources Abstracts, I 1.94/2
Sewage and **Water** Works Construction, I 67.11
Shipments of Domestic Pumps, **Water** Systems, and
Windmills, C 3.77
Shipments of Domestic **Water** Softening Apparatus,
C 3.78
Snow Surveys and **Water** Supply Outlook for
Alaska, A 57.46/13
Soil and **Water** Conservation District Resources
Inventories (series), A 57.38/2
Soil and **Water** Conservation Districts, Status of
Organization, by States, Approximate
Acreage, and Farms in Organized
Districts, A 57.32
Soil and **Water** Conservation News, A 57.9/2
Soil and **Water** Conservation Research Needs
Executive Summary, A 57.73
Soil, **Water**, Air Sciences Directory, A 106.14/2
Soil, **Water**, Air Sciences Research Annual Report,
A 106.14
Statistical Report of Commerce Passing through
Canals at Sault Ste. Marie, Mich. and
Ontario, Salt **Water** Ship Movements for
Season of (year), D 103.17/2
Statistical Summary of Municipal **Water** Facilities,
FS 2.84

Status Report on **Water** and Power Resources
Service Programs Within (various
States), I 27.74
Summary of Watershed Conditions Affecting **Water**
Supply of the Lower Colorado River, I
27.43
Summary Statistics, **Water**, Land and Related Data,
I 27.1/4
Supplemental Reports to the Second National
Water Assessment, Y 3.W 29:13
Surface **Water** Records of {states}, I 19.53
Surface **Water** Supply of the United States, I 19.13
Technical Memoranda for Municipal, Industrial and
Domestic **Water** Supplies, Pollution
Abatement, Public Health, FS 2.301
Tide Tables High and Low **Water** Prediction, C
55.421
Tide Tables, High and Low **Water** Predictions
Central and Western Pacific Ocean and
Indian Ocean, C 55.421/4
Tide Tables, High and Low **Water** Predictions East
Coast of North and South America
Including Greenland, C 55.421/2
Tide Tables, High and Low **Water** Predictions
Europe and West Coast of Africa,
Including the Mediterranean Sea, C
55.421/3
Tide Tables, High and Low **Water** Predictions
West Coast of North and South America
Including Hawaiian Islands, C 55.421
U.S. **Water** Borne Intercoastal Traffic by Ports of
Origin and Destination and Principal
Commodities, SB 7.5/317, C 27.9/9, MC
1.9
Utah **Water** Supply Outlook, A 57.46/6
Washington Annual Data Summary **Water** Year, A
57.46/7-2
Water and Related Land Resources {by area}, A
1.105
Water and Sewer Bond Sales in United States, FS
2.56/4, I 67.10
Water and Sewer Facilities Grant Program, HUD
Information Series, HH 1.17
Water Bank Program, from Inception of Program
through (date), A 82.94
Water Borne Commerce of United States Including
Foreign Intercoastal and Coastwise
Traffic and Commerce of U.S. Noncon-
tiguous Territory, SB 7.5/295
Water Borne Foreign and Domestic Commerce of
U.S., C 27.9/11, MC 1.20
Water Borne Foreign Commerce of United States,
SB 7.5/216, SB 7.7
Water Borne Passenger Traffic of U.S., SB 7.5/157,
C 27.9/12
Water Conservation Report WC (series), I 27.53
Water Data Coordination Directory, I 19.118
Water Facilities Area Plans (by States), A 36.148
Water Fact Sheets (series), I 19.114
Water Information Series Reports, I 19.53/4
Water Levels in Observation Wells in Santa
Barbara County, California, I 19.49
Water Management and Conservation Program, I
27.78
Water Operation and Maintenance Bulletin, I
27.41
Water Operations Technical Support: WOTS, D
103.24/15
Water Pollution Control Research and Training
Grants, FS 2.64/7, I 67.13
Water Pollution Control Research Series, EP 1.16,
EP 2.10
Water Pollution Control, Federal Costs, Report to
Congress, I 67.1/2
Water Pollution Publications, FS 2.64
Water Quality in Galveston Bay, I 49.110
Water Quality Management Accomplishments,
Compendiums, EP 1.75
Water Quality Management Bulletin, EP 1.71
Water Quality Management Five Year Strategy FY-
Baseline, EP 1.91
Water Quality Management Guidance, EP 1.8/8
Water Quality Records of {States}, I 19.53/2
Water Quality Standards Criteria Digest,
Compilation of Federal/State Criteria on
{various subjects}, EP 1.29/2
Water Quality Standards Summary {for various
States} (series), EP 1.29
Water Reactor Safety Research, Buff Book I, Y 3.N
88:18
Water Research Capsule Report (series), I 1.103
Water Resources Activities in Illinois, I 19.55/5
Water Resources Bulletins, I 19.3/3
Water Resources Data for {State}, I 19.53/2

Water Resources Data, I 19.15/6

Water Resources Development by Army Corps of Engineers in {State}, D 103.35

Water Resources Development by Corps of Engineers by Area, D 103.35

Water Resources Development in Delaware in (year), D 103.35/8

Water Resources Development in District of Columbia, D 103.35/11

Water Resources Development in Idaho, D 103.35/12

Water Resources Development in Illinois, D 103.35/13

Water Resources Development in Indiana, D 103.35/14

Water Resources Development in Iowa, D 103.35/15

Water Resources Development in Kentucky, D 103.35/17

Water Resources Development in Maryland, D 103.35/20

Water Resources Development in Massachusetts, D 103.35/21

Water Resources Development in Michigan, D 103.35/22

Water Resources Development in Minnesota, D 103.35/23

Water Resources Development in Missouri, D 103.35/25

Water Resources Development in Nevada, D 103.35/28

Water Resources Development in New Jersey (year), D 103.35/30

Water Resources Development in New Mexico, D 103.35/31

Water Resources Development in New York, D 103.35/32

Water Resources Development in North Carolina, D 103.35/33

Water Resources Development in North Dakota, D 103.35/34

Water Resources Development in Ohio, D 103.35/35

Water Resources Development in South Carolina, D 103.35/40

Water Resources Development in Virginia, D 103.35/46

Water Resources Development in West Virginia, D 103.35/48

Water Resources Development in Wisconsin, D 103.35/49

Water Resources Development in {State}, D 103.35D 103.35/53

Water Resources Divisions Bulletin of Training, I 19.3/4

Water Resources Investigations (numbered), I 19.42/4

Water Resources Investigations Folders, I 19.94

Water Resources Investigations, I 19.42/4-2

Water Resources Research Catalog, I 1.94

Water Resources Research Program of the U.S. Geological Survey, I 19.42/4-3

Water Resources Review, Annual Summary, Water Year, I 19.42/2

Water Resources Review, I 19.42

Water Resources Scientific Information Center, WRSIC- (series), I 1.97

Water Resources Teaching Guide (series), I 27.76

Water Resources/Water Quality, Y 3.T 25:59-2

Water Reuse, OWRT/RU- , I 1.97/3

Water Resources Research Catalog, I 1.94

Water Safety Program Catalog, D 103.124

Water Spectrum, D 103.48

Water Supply and Pollution Control, FS 2.64/2

Water Supply and Waste Disposal Series, TD 2.32

Water Supply Bulletins, I 19.3/5

Water Supply Forecasts, C 30.58

Water Supply Outlook for Northeastern United States, C 55.113/2

Water Supply Outlook for Western United States, Water Year, C 55.113

Water Supply Outlook Reports, A 57.46

Water Supply Outlook, Federal-State-Private Cooperative Snow Surveys {Colorado}, A 57.46/15

Water Supply Papers, I 19.13

Water Temperatures, Coast and Geodetic Survey Tide Stations, C 4.34

Water-Related Disease Outbreaks Surveillance, HE 20.7011/33

Water-Resources Bulletins, I 19.3/3

Weekly Runoff Report, Pacific Northwest Water Resources, I 19.46/2

Western U.S. Water Plan, (year) Progress Report, I 27.61

Working for Clean Water, EP 1.8/12

Working Papers Office on Water Programs, EP 2.23

Waterborne

Domestic Waterborne Trade of the United States, C 39.222, TD 11.19

Foodborne and Waterborne Disease Outbreaks, Annual Summary, HE 20.7011/13

Homestudy Courses; Waterborne Disease Control, HE 20.7021/4

Schedule W. Statistical Classification of U.S. Waterborne Exports and Imports, C 3.150:W

Self-Study Course 3014-G, Waterborne Disease Control Manuals, HE 20.7021/4-2

Special Statistical Reports on United States Water-borne Commerce, C 3.203

Statistical Classification of U.S. Waterborne Exports and Imports, C 3.150:W

U.S. Foreign Waterborne Transportation Statistics Quarterly, TD 11.35

U.S. Great Lakes Ports, Statistics for Overseas and Canadian Waterborne Commerce, TD 6.10

U.S. Waterborne Exports and General Imports, C 3.164:985

U.S. Waterborne Foreign Trade, Summary Report, C 3.164:985

U.S. Waterborne Foreign Trade, Trade Area by U.S. Coastal District, C 3.164:600

United States Foreign Trade, Waterborne Trade by Trade Area, C 3.164:973

United States Foreign Trade, Waterborne Trade by United States Ports, C 3.164:972

United States Waterborne Foreign Commerce, a Review of {year}, C 3.211/2

United States Waterborne Foreign Commerce, Great Lakes Area {year}, C 3.211/2

Waterborne Commerce of the United States, D 103.1/2

Water-Borne Foreign and Noncontiguous Commerce and Passenger Traffic of United States, MC 1.23

Waterborne Passenger Traffic of U.S., MC 1.15

Water-Data

Federal Plan for Water-Data Acquisition, I 19.74/3

Waterfowl

Annual Waterfowl Report Alaska, I 49.55

Pacific Waterfowl Flyway Report, I 49.55/2

Preliminary Estimates of Waterfowl Harvest and Hunter Activity in the United States During the Hunting Season, I 49.106

Status of Waterfowl & Fall Flight Forecast, I 49.100/3

Waterfowl Monitoring Investigations, Y 3.T 25:27-2

Waterfowl Status Report, I 49.15/3, I 49.100/2

Waterfowl 2000, I 49.100/4

Your Guide to Federal Waterfowl Production Areas, I 49.6/3

Watering

Official Classification of . . . Watering Points, FS 2.75

Watermark

Watermark, FEM 1.23

Water-Related

Water-Related Disease Outbreaks Surveillance, HE 20.7011/33

Water-Resources

Technicap Training Courses, Technical Techniques of Water-Resources Investigations, I 19.15/4, I 19.15/5

Waters

Bridges Over Navigable Waters of the U.S., D 103.2:B 76

Catalog of Charts of the Great Lakes and Connecting Waters, Also Lake Champlain, New York Canals, Minnesota-Ontario Border Lakes, D 103.208

Compilation of Records of Surface Waters of the United States, I 19.13

Conference in Matters of Pollution of Navigable Waters, Proceedings, EP 1.16/2

Conference of Oil Pollution of Navigable Waters, S 5.24

Environmental Factors on Coastal and Estaurine Waters, Bibliographic Series, I 67.14/2

International Joint Commission on Boundary Waters Between United States and Canada, 1909, S 3.23

Laws Relating to Construction of Bridges over Navigable Waters, W 7.6/2

Light List, Atlantic Coast of U.S. Intercoastal Waterway, Hampton Roads to Rio Grande Including Inside Waters, N 24.17, T 47.28

National Shellfish Register of Classified Growing Waters, C 55.441

Notice to Mariners Relating to Great Lakes and Tributary Waters West of Montreal, D 203.9, TD 5.10

Pilot Chart of Central American Waters, N 6.24, M 202.15, D 203.15

Pilot Charts of Central American Waters, D 203.15

Pilot Rules for Certain Inland Waters of Atlantic and Pacific Coasts of Gulf of Mexico, C 25.9

Pilot Rules for Rivers whose Waters Flow into Gulf of Mexico and Their Tributaries and Red River of the North, C 25.8

Polluting Incidents in and Around U.S. Waters, TD 5.51

Proceedings Conference in Matters of Pollution and Navigable Waters, EP 1.16/2

Quality of Surface Waters of the United States, I 19.13

Report of Quality of Surface Waters for Irrigation, Western United States, I 19.13

Rules and Regulations for Foreign Vessels Operating in the Navigable Waters of the United States, TD 5.6:V 63/7

Watershed

Summary of Watershed Conditions Affecting Water Supply of the Lower Colorado River, I 27.43

Watershed Work Plan {by Area}, A 57.59

Watersheds

Stages and Discharges of Mississippi River and Tributaries and Other Watersheds in the New Orleans District, D 103.45/4

Water-Supply

List of Geological Survey Geologic and Water-Supply Reports and Maps for (various States), I 19.41/7

Requirement for Individual Water-Supply and Sewage-Disposal Systems (by States), NHA 2.17, HH 2.11

Watertown

Ordnance Materials Research Offices, Watertown Arsenal, Omro Publications, D 105.13/3

Rodman Process Laboratory, Watertown Arsenal, Reports, D 105.13

Test of Metals at Watertown Arsenal, W 34.14

Watertown Arsenal Laboratory, Report WAL (series), D 105.13/2

Watertown Arsenal Laboratory: Technical Report (series), D 105.13/2-2

Watertown Arsenal: Technical Report Ward, TR (series), D 105.13/2-3

Waterway

Foreign Inland Waterway News, Intercoastal Waterways, Rivers, Lakes, Canals, Equipment, C 18.208

Light List, Atlantic Coast of U.S. Intercoastal Waterway, Hampton Roads to Rio Grande Including Inside Waters, N 24.17, T 47.28

Waterways

Activities Relating to Title II, Ports and Waterways Safety Act of 1972, Report to Congress, TD 5.34

Foreign Inland Waterway News, Intercoastal Waterways, Rivers, Lakes, Canals, Equipment, C 18.208

Publications Available for Purchase, U.S. Army Engineer Waterways Experiment Station and Other Corps of Engineers Agencies, D 103.39

Research Reports Waterways Experiment Station, D 103.24/5

Statistics of Bituminous Coal Loaded for Shipment on Railroads and Waterways As Reported by Operators, I 28.34

Uniform System of Accounts for Carriers by Inland and Coastal Waterways, IC 1 wat.14

Waterways Experiment Station Capabilities, D 103.24/10

Watts Bar

Environmental Radioactivity Levels Watts Bar Nuclear Plant, Y 3.T 25:51

Wave

Cold Wave Bulletin, A 29.9

Collected Reprints; Wave Propagation Laboratory, C 55.612/2

Wave Propagation Group Reports, Pr 32.413/6

Waves
    Air **Waves**, Y 3.Ai 7/5:9
    Coastal **Waves** Program Field Wave Data, C 55.435
Way
    New **Way** of Saving (series), GS 12.11
Way Study
    Interstate System Traveled-**Way Study** Reports, TD
        2.118
Waybill
    Carload **Waybill** Analyses, Distribution of Freight
        Traffic and Revenue Averages by
        Commodity Groups and Rate Territories,
        IC 1.20
    Carload **Waybill** Analyses, State by State
        Distribution of Tonnage by Commodity
        Groups, IC 1.21
    Carload **Waybill** Analyses, Territorial Distribution,
        Traffic and Revenue by Commodity
        Groups, IC 1.22
    Carload **Waybill** Statistics, . . ., Traffic and Revenue
        by Commodity Class, Territorial
        Movement, and Type of Rate, Products of
        Agriculture, 1 Percent Sample of
        Terminations in Statement MB-1, IC 1.23/
        2
    Carload **Waybill** Statistics, . . ., Traffic and Revenue
        by Commodity Class, Territorial
        Movement, and Type of Rate, Animals
        and Products, 1 Percent Sample of
        Terminations in Statement MB-2, IC 1.23/
        3
    Carload **Waybill** Statistics, . . ., Traffic and Revenue
        by Commodity Class, Territorial
        Movement, and Type of Rate, Products of
        Mines, 1 Percent Sample of Terminations
        in Statement MB-3, IC 1.23/4
    Carload **Waybill** Statistics, . . ., Traffic and Revenue
        by Commodity Class, Territorial
        Movement, and Type of Rate, Products of
        Forests, 1 Percent Sample of Terminations
        in Statement MB-4, IC 1.23/5
    Carload **Waybill** Statistics, . . ., Traffic and Revenue
        by Commodity Class, Territorial
        Movement, and Type of Rate, Manufactur-
        ers and Miscellaneous Forwarder Traffic,
        One Percent Sampling. . . MB-5, IC 1.23/
        6
    Carload **Waybill** Statistics, Distribution of Freight
        Traffic and Revenue Averages by
        Commodity Classes, IC 1.23/8
    Carload **Waybill** Statistics, Quarterly Comparisons,
        Traffic and Revenue by Commodity
        Classes, IC 1.23
    Carload **Waybill** Statistics, Statement TD-1, TD
        1.22
    Carload **Waybill** Statistics, Territorial Distribution
        Traffic and Revenue by Commodity
        Classes, TD 3.14
    Carload **Waybill** Statistics, Traffic and Revenue
        Progressions by Specified Mileage
        Blocks for Commodity Groups and
        Classes, 1 Percent Sample of Carload
        Terminations in Year Statement MB-6, IC
        1.23/7
    Rail **Waybill** Data, TD 1.56/4
    Supplement to Carload **Waybill** Statistics, IC 1.23/
        20
Ways
    Manual of Rules of the Committee on **Ways** and
        Means, Y 4.W 36:WMCP 96-1
WB/BC
    Bibliography on the Climate of {Country} **WB/BC**
        (series), C 52.21
WC
    Water Conservation Report **WC** (series), I 27.53
WDCA
    World Data Center A Oceanography, Catalogue of
        Data, **WDCA**-OC- (series), C 55.220/2-3
We
    "**We** the People" Calendar, Y 3.H 62/2:9
    We the Americans (series), C 56.234
    What **We** Defend (Radio Scripts), I 29.48
Wealth
    Fixed Reproducible Tangible **Wealth** of the United
        States, C 59.27
Weapon
    Weapon Systems, D 101.95
Weapons
    Air Force **Weapons** Laboratory, Research and
        Technology Division, AFWL-TDR, D
        301.45/35
    Bureau of Naval **Weapons** Directory, Organiza-
        tional Listing and Correspondence
        Designations, D 217.25

Naval Surface **Weapons** Center, NSWC-AP
    (series), D 201.21/6
Naval Surface **Weapons** Center, Technical Reports,
    D 201.21/5
Technical Notes Department of the Air Force
    Special **Weapons** Center, D 301.45/20-2
U.S. Atmospheric Nuclear **Weapons** Tests, Nuclear
    Test Personnel Review, D 15.10
USAF Fighter **Weapons** Review, D 301.102
Wearing
    Wearing Apparel in World Markets, C 18.161
Weather
    Air **Weather** Service: Bibliography, D 301.42
    Air **Weather** Service Manual, D 301.27
    Air **Weather** Service, Technical Reports, D 301.40
    Air **Weather** Service: Training Guides, D 301.39
    Average Monthly **Weather** Outlook, C 55.109
    Aviation **Weather** System Plan, TD 4.62
    Briefs of Fatal Accidents Involving **Weather** As a
        Cause-Factor U.S. General Aviation, TD
        1.109/12
    Bulletin of Mountain **Weather** Observatory, A
        29.21
    Correspondence Course, Elements of Surface
        Weather Observations, Lessons, C
        30.26
    Cotton Region **Weather** Crop Bulletin, A 29.20
    Daily Bulletin of Simultaneous **Weather** Reports
        with Synopses Indications, and Facts for
        Month of, W 42.8/1
    Daily Series, Synoptic **Weather** Maps, C 55.213/2
    Daily **Weather** and River Bulletin {New Orleans,
        La. Area}, C 55.110/5
    Daily **Weather** and River Bulletin {Shreveport, La.
        Area}, C 55.110/6
    Daily **Weather** Bulletin, C 30.43
    Daily **Weather** Maps, C 55.195
    Daily **Weather** Maps, Weekly Series, C 55.213
    Directory of **Weather** Broadcasts, C 30.73
    Historical **Weather** Map, Northern Hemisphere, W
        108.30
    International Geophysical Year World **Weather**
        Maps, C 30.22/5
    Long Record of **Weather** Observations, C 55.287/
        56
    Louisiana Weekly **Weather** and Crop Bulletin, A
        88.49/2
    Marine **Weather** Services Charts, C 55.112
    Mariners **Weather** Log, C 55.135, C 55.210
    Monthly **Weather** Review, C 55.11
    Monthly **Weather** Review, Signal Office, W 42.20
    National Implementation Plan For Modernization
        of the National **Weather** Service, C
        55.133
    National **Weather** Bulletin, A 29.7
    Nebraska Weekly **Weather** and Crop Report, A
        36.208
    New England Highway **Weather** Bulletin, A 29.32
    Next General **Weather** Radar (series), C 1.80
    Numerical **Weather** Prediction Activities, National
        Meteorological Center, C 55.115
    Operations of National **Weather** Service, C 55.111
    Operations of the **Weather** Bureau, C 30.83
    Personal **Weather** Estimated from Estate Tax
        Returns Filed during Calendar Year, T
        22.35/2:W 37
    Posters National **Weather** Service, C 55.130
    Publications Directorate of **Weather**; Special
        Series, W 108.17
    Publications **Weather** Bureau Available for
        Distribution, A 29.31
    Publications **Weather** Bureau, C 30.17/2
    Publications **Weather** Research Center, W 108.16
    Research Progress and Plans of the **Weather**
        Bureau, C 30.75
    River Forecasts Provided by the National **Weather**
        Service, C 55.117/2, C 55.285
    Selected Worldwide **Weather** Broadcasts, C 55.119
    Sheets of National Atlas of United States **Weather**
        Bureau, C 30.22/4
    Summary Report, **Weather** Modification, C 55.27
    Surface and Upper Air **Weather** Charts, C 55.281/2-
        5
    Technical Notes **Weather** Bureau, C 30.82
    Tropical Strip/Precipitation and Observed
        Weather Charts, C 55.281/2-7
    Weather Bureau Engineering Handbooks EHB-
        (series), C 30.6/5
    Weather Bureau Forecasters Handbooks, C 30.6/4
    Weather Bureau Marine Services Charts, C 30.22/6
    Weather Bureau Observing Handbooks, C 30.6/6
    Weather Bureau Training Papers, C 30.48
    Weather, Crops, and Markets, A 36.11

Weather Maps Signal Office, W 42.23
Weather Maps Weather Bureau, C 30.12
Weather Modification Activity Reports, C 55.27/2
Weather Modification Reporting Program, C
    55.27/3
Weather Modification, Annual Report, NS 1.21
Weather Modification, Summary Report, C 55.27
Weather Outlook, A 29.38, C 30.13
Weather Service Bulletin, W 108.35
Weather Service for Merchant Shipping, C 30.79
Weather Service Observing Handbooks, C 55.108/
    2
Weather-Crop Bulletin, W 42.27
Weekly **Weather** and Crop Bulletin, C 55.209
Weekly **Weather** and Crop Bulletin, National
    Summary, C 30.11, C 55.209
Weekly **Weather** Chronicle, W 42.18
World **Weather** Records, SI 1.7
Worldwide Marine **Weather** Broadcasts, C 55.119
Web
    Smithsonian (**Web** Magazine), S 1.10
WEEA
    WEEA Equity Resource Center EDC Catalog, ED
        1.411
Weed
    Agronomy, **Weed** Science, Soil Conservation,
        Agricultural Programs, A 106.36
    Bibliography of **Weed** Investigations, A 77.521
    Weed & Seed In-Sites, J 1.110
Week
    Prices for **Week**, L 2.49/2
    Primary Sugar Distribution for **Week**, A 82.72
    This **Week** in Defense, Pr 32.215
    This **Week** in NOAA, C 55.9/2, C 55.46
    Week in the United States, S 1.79
    Week of the War, Pr 32.5014
    WPA **Week** in National Defense, FW 4.37
Weekly
    Daily Weather Maps, **Weekly** Series, C 55.213
    DNFSB Site Representatives **Weekly** Activities
        Reports, Y 3.D 36/3:11
    Farmers **Weekly** Cotton Price Quotations, A 82.67
    Natural Gas **Weekly** Market Update, E 1.133
    MMWR, Morbidity and Morality **Weekly** Report,
        HE 20.7039/3
    Pennsylvania Anthracite **Weekly**, E 3.11/3
    Percent Changes in Gross Hourly and **Weekly**
        Earnings over Selected Periods, L 2.63
    Petroleum Imports Reporting System, **Weekly**
        Situation Report, FE 1.9/2
    Present Changes in Gross Hourly and **Weekly**
        Earnings Over Selected Periods, L 2.63
    Sheep and Lambs: **Weekly** Average Price per 100
        Pounds, A 36.183
    Small Business **Weekly** Summary, Trade Opportuni-
        ties and Information for American
        Suppliers, FO 1.17
    Survey of Current Business, **Weekly** Supplements,
        C 3.34
    Unemployment Insurance Claims **Weekly** Report, L
        37.12/2-2
    Unemployment Insurance **Weekly** Claims Reports,
        L 37.12/2, L 37.12/2-2
    UNESCO World Review **Weekly** Radio News from
        United Nations Educational, Scientific,
        and Cultural Organization, Paris, France,
        S 5.48/6
    Usual **Weekly** Earnings of Wage and Salary
        Workers, L 2.126
    Victory; Office **Weekly** Bulletins, Pr 32.5008
    Weekly Abstracts: NASA Earth Resources Survey
        Program, C 51.9/11
    Weekly Accession List (of) Library, SS 1.17, FS 3.8
    Weekly Accident Bulletins, C 3.128
    Weekly Advertising Digest, Y 3.F 31/11:30
    Weekly Anthracite and Beehive Coke Reports, I
        28.49
    Weekly Anthracite Report, WAR Series, I 28.49/2
    Weekly Averages of Member Bank Reserves,
        Reserve Bank Credit and Related Items
        and Statement of Condition of the Federal
        Reserve Bank, FR 1.15
    Weekly Bulletin on Raw Materials, Y 3.W 19/2:35
    Weekly Bulletins, Y 3.F 73:5
    Weekly Business Survey of 33 Cities, C 3.66
    Weekly Business Survey of Key Cities, C 1.19
    Weekly Census Report of U.S. Marine and Contract
        Hospitals, T 26.36
    Weekly Climate Bulletin, C 55.129/2
    Weekly Coal Report, I 28.33, E 3.11/4
    Weekly Compilation of Presidential Documents,
        GS 4.114, AE 2.109

Weekly Condition Report of Large Commercial Banks in New York and Chicago, FR 1.16

Weekly Consular and Trade Reports, C 10.14

Weekly Corn and Wheat Region Bulletin, A 29.43

Weekly Cotton Linters Review, A 88.11/3

Weekly Cotton Market Review, A 88.11/2

Weekly Cotton Region Bulletins, A 29.39

Weekly Cotton Service Bulletins, C 18.162

Weekly Crude Oil Stock Reports, I 28.46

Weekly Earnings of Wage and Salary Workers, L 2.126

Weekly Electric Output, United States, FP 1.11/7

Weekly European Citrus Fruit Market Cable, A 36.67

Weekly Feed Review, A 88.18/4

Weekly Fruit Exports, C 18.72/13

Weekly Government Abstracts, WGA-(series), C 51.9/5C 51.9/30

Weekly Health Index, C 3.41

Weekly Information Report, Y 3.N 88:37, Y 3.N 88:50, Y 3.N 88:55

Weekly Labor News Digest, L 1.28, L 2.50

Weekly List of Selected U.S. Government Publications, GP 3.17

Weekly Molasses Market Reports, A 82.62

Weekly News Letter {to Crop Correspondents}, A 1.22

Weekly News Series, A 43.27

Weekly News Summary, HH 1.15/2

Weekly Newspaper Service, L 1.77

Weekly Notices to Airmen, C 23.15, CA 1.7, C 31.9, C 31.109

Weekly Oil Update, E 3.32/2

Weekly Peanut Reports, A 36.106, A 88.10

Weekly Periodical Index, D 103.108

Weekly Petroleum Statistics Reports, FE 1.9/3

Weekly Petroleum Status Report, E 1.63, E 3.32

Weekly Population Report, J 16.32

Weekly Poultry Slaughter Report, A 88.15/7

Weekly Report of Certificated Stock in Licensed Warehouses, A 88.11/24

Weekly Report of Vessels under Jurisdiction of Shipping Board, SB 2.12

Weekly Report on Japan, D 102.13

Weekly Report on Production of Bituminous Coal, Etc, I 19.30

Weekly Report {Cotton}, A 85.12

Weekly Reports of Office of Western Irrigation Agriculture, A 19.25

Weekly Retail Sales Report, C 3.138/5

Weekly Review of Periodicals, FR 1.22

Weekly Review of Recent Developments, L 2.56

Weekly Review, RR 1.7, Y 3.W 19/2:6

Weekly Rice Market Review, A 88.18/9

Weekly Roundup of World Production and Trade, WR (series), A 67.42

Weekly Roundups, Economic Letter, S 1.80

Weekly Runoff Report, Pacific Northwest Water Resources, I 19.46/2

Weekly Statement of Bonds Held in Trust for National Banks, T 40.9

Weekly Statement of Gold and Silver Exports and Imports, United States, C 3.195

Weekly Station Reports of Office of Dry Land Agriculture Investigations, A 19.24

Weekly Statistical News, Y 3.W 19/2:36

Weekly Statistical Reports, Y 3.F 31/11:24

Weekly Summary (Press Division), A 107.17

Weekly Summary of Banking and Credit Measures, FR 1.52

Weekly Summary of Export Opportunities for Small Business, Pr 33.917

Weekly Summary of F.O.B. Prices of Fresh Fruits and Vegetables in Representative Shipping Districts, A 88.12/2, A 82.53

Weekly Summary of Federal Legislation Relating to National Resources Committee, Activities Bulletins, Y 3.N 21/12:15

Weekly Summary of Fruit and Vegetable Carlot Shipments, A 88.12

Weekly Summary of Health Information for International Travel, HE 20.7023

Weekly Summary of N.L.R.B. Cases, LR 1.15/2

Weekly Summary of NLRB Cases, LR 1.5/2

Weekly Summary of Orders and Regulations, C 31.208

Weekly Summary of Wholesale Prices of Fresh Fruits and Vegetables at New York City and Chicago, A 82.52, A 88.12/3

Weekly Summary, A 21.6/6

Weekly Summary: AAA Press Releases, A 55.64

Weekly Tobacco Market News Summary, A 88.34/7

Weekly Trading Data on New York Exchanges, SE 1.25/6

Weekly Weather and Crop Bulletin, C 55.209

Weekly Weather and Crop Bulletin, National Summary, C 30.11, C 55.209

Weekly Weather Chronicle, W 42.18

Wholesale Prices of Fruits and Vegetables at New York and Chicago, **Weekly** Summary of, A 82.52

Weighing

Foreign Markets for Scales and Other **Weighing** Devices, C 18.85

NBS Handbook, Specifications, Tolerances, and Other Technical Requirements for **Weighing** and Measuring Devices, C 13.11/2

NIST Handbook, Specifications, Tolerances, and Other Technical Requirements for **Weighing** and Measuring Devices, C 13.11/2

Scales and **Weighing** Memorandums, A 96.11

Weight

Average **Weight** of Measured Cup of Various Foods, A 1.87:41

Cattle Inventory, Special Report on Number of Cattle and Calves on Farms by Sex and **Weight**, United States, A 92.18/6-2

Commercial Livestock Slaughter, Number and Live **Weight**, by States, Meat and Lard Production, United States, by Months, A 88.16/17

Shipping **Weight** and Dollar Value of Merchandise Laden on and Unladen from Vessels at United States Ports During the In-transit Movement of the Merchandise from One Foreign Country to Another, C 3.164:981

U.S. Airborne Exports and General Imports, Shipping **Weight** and Value, C 3.164:986

Weight Distribution of Carloads for Each Commodity Class by Type of Car, IC 1.23/16:TC-2

Weights

Conference on **Weights** and Measures, C 13.7

Directory of Associate Members, National Conference on **Weights** and Measures, C 13.66/3

Model Weights and Measures Ordinance (year), Provisions As Adopted by the National Conference on **Weights** and Measures, C 13.55

National **Weights** and Measures Law, (year), C 13.55/2

Report of the National Conference on **Weights** and Measures, C 13.10, C 13.10/3

Tables to Convert {Foreign Moneys, **Weights** and Measures into U.S. Standards}, C 1.11

Weights and Measures Directory, C 13.66

Weights and Measures Today, C 13.66/2

Welcoming

Welcoming America's Newest Commonwealth: Reports, Y 3.N 81/6:9

Welding

Automatic **Welding** {abstracts}, C 41.54/6

Welding Practice {abstracts}, C 41.54/8

Welfare

Administration on **Welfare** and Pension Plans Disclosure Act, L 1.55

Analysis of Constitutional Provisions Affecting Public **Welfare** in States, Y 3.W 89/2:36

Animal **Welfare** Enforcement Fiscal Year, A 101.22/2

Animal **Welfare** Information Center Newsletter, A 17.27/2

Animal **Welfare** Legislation: Bills and Public Laws, A 17.26

Animal **Welfare**: List of Licensed Dealers, A 101.26

Annual Report of **Welfare** Programs, HE 17.28

Army Morale **Welfare** and Recreation Fiscal Year Annual Report, D 102.82/2

Assessments Completed and Referrals to Manpower Agencies by **Welfare** Agencies Under Work Incentive Program for AFDC Recipients, HE 17.619

Catalog, Department of Health, Education, and **Welfare**, Publications, HE 1.18/3

Child **Welfare** News Summary, L 5.23

Child **Welfare** Reports, FS 3.215, L 5.52

Child **Welfare** Statistics, HE 17.638

Child **Welfare** Training (series), HE 23.1213

Community Child-**Welfare** Series, L 5.18

Digest of Public **Welfare** Provisions under Laws of States, Y 3.W 89/2:35

General Relief Operations of Large City Public **Welfare** Agencies, SS 1.26

Handbooks on Programs of Department of Health, Education and **Welfare**, FS 1.6/5, HE 1.6/5

Health, Education and **Welfare** Indicators, FS 1.20

Health, Education and **Welfare** Trends, FS 1.19, HE 1.19

Indicators of **Welfare** Dependence, HE 1.1/4

Manual on Fund-raising Within the Federal Services for Voluntary Health and **Welfare** Agencies, CS 1.7/5

Maternal and Child **Welfare** Bulletins, L 5.34

News Bulletin of Social Statistics in Child **Welfare** and Related Fields, L 5.31

Public **Welfare** Personnel, Annual Statistical Data, HE 17.629

Recreation and **Welfare** News, GP 1.17

Rural Child **Welfare** Series, L 5.11

Social Statistics in Child **Welfare** and Related Fields, L 5.27

State Salary Ranges, Selected Classes {of positions} in Employment Security, Public **Welfare**, Public Health, Mental Health, Vocational Rehabilitation, Civil Defense, Emergency Planning, CS 1.81, FS 1.22, HE 1.22, GS 1.8

Technical Analysis Papers Department of Health, Education, and **Welfare**, HE 1.52

Training Manual Department of Health, Education, and **Welfare**, FS 1.10, HE 1.10

Welfare in Review, HE 17.9

Welfare Research Researchs, FS 14.14

Welfare Work Series, Y 3.C 83:35

Well

Keep **Well** Series, T 27.22

Well-Being

Trends in the **Well-Being** of America's Children and Youth, HE 1.63

Youth Indicators, Trends in the **Well-Being** of American Youth, ED 1.327

Wellness

HUD **Wellness** Newsletter, HH 1.120/2

Wells

Water Levels in Observation **Wells** in Santa Barbara County, California, I 19.49

West

East-**West** Foreign Trade Board Report, Y 3.T 67:1

East-**West** Trade Policy Staff Papers, C 61.17

Forestry Research **West**, A 13.95/2

Forestry Research: What's New in the **West**, A 13.95

Formulary, **West** Side Medical Center, Chicago, Illinois, VA 1.73/4

Quarterly Report to Congress and the East- **West** Foreign Trade Board on Trade Between the United States and the Nonmarket Economy Countries, Y 4.W 36:2

Retail Trade Report **West** North Central, C 3.178

Retail Trade Report **West** South Central, C 3.179

Special Reports to Congress and East-**West** Foreign Trade Board, TC 1.38/2

Tide Tables **West** Coast of North and South America, C 4.15/5

Tide Tables, High and Low Water Predictions Europe and **West** Coast of Africa, Including the Mediterranean Sea, C 55.421/3

Tide Tables, High and Low Water Predictions **West** Coast of North and South America Including Hawaiian Islands, C 55.421

United States Air Force, United States Navy and Royal Canadian Air Force Radio Facility Charts, **West** Canada and Alaska, D 301.13

West Coast of North and South America (including the Hawaiian Islands), C 4.15/5

West Europe Report, PrEx 7.18

West North Central, Population and Per Capita Income Estimates for Counties and Incorporated Places, C 3.186/27-3

West Side VA Medical Center Formulary, VA 1.78

West, Population and Per Capita Income Estimates for Counties and Incorporated Places, C 3.186/27-2

West Indies

Climatological Data; **West Indies** and Caribbean Service, A 29.36, C 30.20

U.S. Coast Pilots **West Indies**, C 4.6/2

West Virginia

Area Wage Survey Summary **West Virginia**, L 2.122/48

Water Resources Development in **West Virginia**, D 103.35/48

Western

Annual Report on the Archeological Programs of the **Western** Region, I 29.59/3

BLM **Westfornet** Monthly Alert, I 53.17/2

Central Pacific, **Western** Pacific, and South Pacific Fisheries Development Program Report for Calendar Year, C 55.329

Central, **Western**, and South Pacific Fisheries Development Program Report for Calendar Year, C 55.329

Cotton Quality Report for Ginnings, **Western** Upland Cotton, A 82.68

Fresh Fruit and Vegetable Unloads in **Western** Cities, A 88.40/2:4

Lights on **Western** Rivers, C 9.21

Nautical Charts and Publications, Region 3, **Western** Europe, Iceland, Greenland, and the Arctic, C 55.440:3

Nautical Charts and Publications, Region 5, **Western** Africa and the Mediterranean, C 55.440:5

NIMA, Nautical Charts, Public Sale Region 3, **Western** Europe, Iceland, Greenland, and the Arctic, TD 4.82:3

NIMA, Nautical Charts, Public Sale Region 5, **Western** Africa and the Mediterranean, TD 4.82:5

NOAA **Western** Region Computer Programs and Problems (series), C 55.13/3

Plant Pest Control Cooperative Programs, **Western** Region, Fiscal Year (date), A 77.327/2

Post Lights on **Western** Rivers, T 25.20

Proceedings Annual **Western** International Forest Disease Work Conference, A 13.69/13

Publications Agricultural Adjustment Agency **Western** Region, A 76.481, A 79.481, A 80.2181

Quarterly Economic and Financial Review: Federal Republic of Germany and **Western** Sectors of Berlin, S 1.91/2

Report of Quality of Surface Waters for Irrigation, **Western** United States, I 19.13

Roll of Honor, Supplemental Statement of Disposition of Bodies of Deceased Union Soldiers and Prisoners of War Removed to National Cemeteries in Southern and **Western** United States, W 39.8

Snow Survey and Soil Moisture Measurements, Basic Data Summary for **Western** United States, Including Columbia River Drainage in Canada, A 57.46/17

Southern Asia, Publications in **Western** Languages, Quarterly Accessions List, LC 17.7

Standard Instrument Departure (SID) Charts, **Western** United States, C 55.416/6

Storage-Gage Precipitation Data for **Western** United States, C 55.225

Tide Tables Central and **Western** Pacific Ocean and Indian Ocean, C 4.15/6

Tide Tables, High and Low Water Predictions Central and **Western** Pacific Ocean and Indian Ocean, C 55.421/4

Water Supply Outlook for **Western** United States, Water Year, C 55.113

Weekly Reports of Office of **Western** Irrigation Agriculture, A 19.25

Western Cities, A 88.12/31:4

Western Environmental Research Laboratory: Annual Report, EP 1.14/2

Western Environmental Research Laboratory: Monthly Activities Report, EP 1.14

Western Europe Reports, PrEx 7.18

Western Europe, Situation and Outlook Report, A 93.29/2-9

Western European Series, S 1.28

Western Hemisphere, Outlook and Situation Report, A 93.29/2-18

Western Range and Livestock Report, A 92.18/10

Western Range, A 13.29

Western Region, C 55.118

Western Regional Newsletter, J 21.17

Western Space and Missile Center: Regulations, WSMCR- (series), D 301.6/7

Western States Regional Turkey Breeding Project, Annual Report, A 77.235

Western Training Center, Catalogs and Schedule of Courses, D 13.16

Western U.S. Water Plan, (year) Progress Report, I 27.61

Western United States, Dates of Latest Prints, Instrument Approach Procedure Charts and Airport Obstruction Plans, C 4.9/20

Western Volume, HE 20.6202:N 93 W

Westfornet

Westfornet Monthly Alert, A 13.108

Wetlands

National **Wetlands** Inventory, I 49.6/7

National Wetlands Inventory (maps) by States, I 49.6/7-nos.

Wetlands Inventories, I 49.64

WGA

Weekly Government Abstracts, **WGA**-(series), C 51.9/5C 51.9/30

What

What Price America, I 43.8

What Social Security Means to Industries, SS 1.18

What the Soldier Thinks, Monthly Digest of War Department Studies on Attitudes of American Troops, W 1.65

What We Are Doing About Agricultural Surpluses, A 82.80

What We Defend (Radio Scripts), I 29.48

What You Have to Know about SSI, HE 3.90

What's

What's Doing in Your Town, Y 3.F 31/11:23

What's Happening in the Personnel Field, D 217.13

What's New in Research, A 13.62/13

What's New, Tips for Supervisors from Oaas, L 1.43

What's Noteworthy on ... (series), ED 1.9/2

Wheat

Circular Letters; **Wheat** Work, A 55.35

Commercial **Wheat** Farms, Plains and Pacific Northwest, A 93.9/11

Commitments of Traders in **Wheat**, Corn, Oats, Rye, Soybeans, Soybean Oil, Soybean Meal, Shell Eggs, A 85.9/2

Commodity Information Series; **Wheat** Circulars, A 55.25/4

Commodity Information Series; **Wheat** Leaflets, A 55.25/5

Corn and **Wheat** Region Bulletins, C 30.7

Crop Production, Winter **Wheat** and Rye, A 88.18/11

Export **Wheat** Flour Bulletin, A 82.3/5

Feed Grain and **Wheat** Stabilization Program, A 82.37/3:F 32/2

Futures Trading and Open Contracts in **Wheat**, Corn, Oats, Rye, Soybeans and Products, A 85.11/7

Futures Trading and Open Contracts in {**Wheat**, Corn, Oats, etc.} on Chicago Board of Trade, A 88.11/18

National Conference on **Wheat** Utilization Research, Proceedings, A 77.15:74

Official Statement of **Wheat** Director, Y 3.W 56:5

Small Grains, Annual Summary and Crop Winter **Wheat** and Rye Seedings, A 105.20/6, A 92.42

Smutty **Wheat** Reports, A 36.56, A 66.30

Stocks of **Wheat** and Rye, A 36.174/2

U.S. Export **Wheat** Quality, A 104.12/2-2

U.S. Grain Export Quality Report, **Wheat**, Corn, Soybeans, A 104.12/2-3

United States **Wheat** Quality, A 104.12/2-5

United States Winter **Wheat** and Rye Reports, A 36.74

Weekly Corn and **Wheat** Region Bulletin, A 29.43

Wheat and Rye Summary, Crop Year, A 88.18/16

Wheat and **Wheat**-Flour Stocks Held by Mills, C 3.115

Wheat Flour for Domestic Distribution, A 82.3/6

Wheat Flour for Export Distribution, A 82.3/9

Wheat Flour, A 82.3/10

Wheat Ground and **Wheat**-Milling Products, by States, C 3.117

Wheat Ground and **Wheat**-Milling Products, C 3.116

Wheat Ground and **Wheat**-Milling Products, Merchant and Other Mills, C 3.118

Wheat Outlook and Situation Report, A 93.11

Wheat Pasture Report, A 92.33

Wheat Production Adjustment, A 43.5/16

Wheat Situation and Outlook Yearbook, A 93.11/2-3

Wheat Situation, A 88.18/8, A 93.11, A 105.20/3

Wheat, Outlook and Situation Yearbook, A 93.11/2-3

Wheat, Rice, Feed Grains, Dry Peas, Dry Beans, Seeds, Hops, A 67.30:W 56

Winter **Wheat** and Rye Reports, A 66.48

Winter **Wheat** Report, Louisiana Crop Reporting Service, A 88.18/24

World **Wheat** Prospects, A 36.44

Wheeler

Catalogue and Index of the Publications of the Hayden, King, Powell, and **Wheeler** Survyes, I 19.3:222

Where

Where to Write for Birth and Death Records of U.S. Citizens Who Were Born or Died Outside of the United States and Birth Certifications for Alien Children Adopted by U.S. Citizens, FS 2.102:B 53/7

Where to Write for Birth and Death Records, FS 2.102:B 53/3

Where to Write for Divorce Records, FS 2.102:D 64

Where to Write for Marriage Record, FS 2.102:M 34

Where to Write for Vital Records, HE 20.6210/2

White

Red, **White**, and Blue Series, Y 3.P 96/3:6

White Book

Hearing Process Status Report (**White Book**), E 2.14/2

White Collar

Qualification Standards for **White Collar** Positions Under the General Schedule, CS 1.45:X-118, PM 1.8/3:X-118

White House

Inside the **White House**, PrEx 1.12/2

Report from the **White House** Conference on Families, Y 3.W 58/22:9

Reports and Guidelines from **White House** Conference on Aging (series), FS 1.13/2

White House Conference Happenings, Y 3.W 58:6

White House Fellowships, Pr 40.12, Pr 41.12, Pr 42.12

White House Report to Students, PrEx 1.12

White Oak

White Oak Laboratory: Technical Reports, NSWC/WOL/TR- (series), D 201.21/3

White Pine

White Pine Blister Control, Annual Report, A 13.59

White River

White River Charts, W 7.13/6

White-Collar

Federal Civilian Work Force Statistics, Occupations of Federal **White-Collar** Workers, PM 1.10:Sm 56-13

National Survey of **White-Collar** Pay, L 2.43/3

Occupations of Federal **White-Collar** and Blue-Collar Workers, PM 1.10/2-2

White-Collar Salaries, L 2.43/2

Whiteman

Digest of International Laws, **Whiteman** Series, S 7.12/2

Wholesale

Annual Benchmark Report for **Wholesale** Trade, C 3.133/5

Average **Wholesale** Prices and Index Numbers of Individual Commodities, L 2.33

Canned Fruits and Vegetables, Production and **Wholesale** Distribution, C 3.168

Census of Business; 1939, **Wholesale** Trade (by States), C 3.940-25

Census of Business; 1939, **Wholesale** Trade (Miscellaneous), C 3.940-26

Census of Distribution; **Wholesale** Distribution, Special Series, C 3.37/37

Census of Distribution; **Wholesale** Distribution, Trade Series, C 3.37/35

Census of Distribution; **Wholesale** Trade Bulletins, State Series, C 3.37/23

Census of **Wholesale** Trade; Area Statistics (series), C 56.252/3

Census of **Wholesale** Trade; Final Reports, C 3.256/4

Census of **Wholesale** Trade; Final Volumes, C 56.252/5

Census of **Wholesale** Trade; General Publications, C 56.252, C 3.256

Census of **Wholesale** Trade; Geographic Area Series, Advance Reports, C 3.256/2-2

Census of **Wholesale** Trade; Geographic Area Series, C 256/7-2, C 3.256/2

Census of **Wholesale** Trade: Geographic Area - Summary, C 256/7

Census of **Wholesale** Trade; Industry Series, C 3.256/6

Census of **Wholesale** Trade; Preliminary Area Series, C 56.252/2

Census of **Wholesale** Trade; Preliminary Report Industry Series, C 3.256/3-2

Assessments Completed and Referrals to Manpower Agencies by Welfare Agencies Under **Work** Incentive Program for AFDC Recipients, HE 17.619

Census of Nurses Employed for Public Health **Work** in United States, in Territories of Alaska and Hawaii, and in Puerto Rico and Virgin Islands, FS 2.81

Child Care Arrangements of AFDC Recipients Under the **Work** Incentive Program, HE 17.609

Circular Letters, Relate to Indian Emergency Conservation **Work**, I 20.23

Circular Letters; Corn-Hog **Work**, A 55.34, A 55.34/2, A 55.34/3

Circular Letters; Wheat **Work**, A 55.35

Continuing Education is **Work**, Y 3.Ed 8/8:1

Cooperative Extension **Work** Office, A 43.5

Demographic Profiles of the Airway Facilities **Work** Force, TD 4.65

Directory of Representative **Work** Education Programs, HE 5.2:W 89/2

Emergency Conservation **Work** Bulletins, L 1.11

Emergency Conservation **Work**, Project Training Publications, I 29.28

yment and Pay Rolls, Emergency **Work** Relief Program, Y 3.F 31/5:31

Estimated **Work** Injuries, L 2.77/5

Experiment Station **Work**, A 1.9, A 10.11

Extension **Work** Circulars, W 49.21/9

Federal Civilian **Work** Force Statistics , PM 1.10/2, PM 1.15, CS 1.55/2

Federal Civilian **Work** Force Statistics, Occupations of Federal Blue-Collar Workers, PM 1.10:Sm 59-11

Federal Civilian **Work** Force Statistics, Occupations of Federal White-Collar Workers, PM 1.10:Sm 56-13

Federal **Work** and Construction Projects, FW 4.33, Y 3.W 89/2:61

Federal **Work** Injuries Sustained During Calendar Year, L 26.8

Federal **Work** Injury Facts, L 26.2:In 5/4

Federal **Work** Injury Facts, Occupational Distribution, Duration and Direct Cost Factors of **Work** Injuries to Civilian Federal Employees During Calendar Year, L 26.8/2-2

Federal **Work** Programs and Public Assistance, FW 4.32

Field Service Modification **Work** Orders, W 34.33

Field **Work** Series, L 7.10

Free Men at **Work**, L 2.73

Hired Farm **Work** Force of {year}, A 1.75, A 88.40, A 93.21, A 93.28, A 1.107

Ideas that **Work**, L 37.26

List of Small Companies for Research and Development **Work**, SBA 1.16

Major **Work** Stoppages, L 2.45/3

Mechanization of Labor and Heavy **Work**, C 41.65/5

Monthly Summary of **Work**, FT 1.15

National Commission on Productivity and **Work** Quality: Publications, Pr 37.8:P 94

News, **Work** Experience of the Populations, L 2.120/2-18

NIE Papers in Education and **Work**, HE 19.212

Office Workers, Salaries, Hours of **Work**, Supplementary Benefits (by cities), L 2.43

Plan of **Work** for Cooperative Hydrology Investigations, I 53.47

Proceedings Annual Western International Forest Disease **Work** Conference, A 13.69/13

Projects Operated by **Work** Projects Administration, Accomplishments on (by States), FW 4.31

Research and Technology **Work** on Explosives, Explosions, and Flames, T 28.27

Safe **Work** Guide, OSHA, L 35.11

Safe **Work** Guides, SWG LS- (series), L 16.51/2

Safe **Work** Practices Series, L 35.11/2

Standardization of **Work** Measurement, D 7.6/4-2

State and Federal Marketing Activities and Other Economic **Work**, A 36.21

State Safety Program **Work** Sheets, L 16.39

Statement of Indemnity Claims and Averages in Cooperative Bang's Disease **Work**, A 4.29

Statistical Bulletins **Work** Projects Administration, FW 4.13

Student **Work** Sheets, Department of Labor Safety Training Programs, SWS-LS-(series), L 16.51

Summary of Bang's Disease **Work** in Cooperation with Various States, A 4.21

Summary of Bovine Tuberculosis Eradication in Cooperation with Various States, Statement of Indemnity and Averages in Cooperative Bovine Brucellosis **Work**, A 77.216/2

Tax Policy and Administration ... Annual Report on GAO'S Tax-Related **Work**, GA 1.13/6

Tomorrow's **Work**, FS 6.10

U.S. Army Equipment Index of Modification **Work** Orders, D 101.22:750-10

United States Fisheries Systems and Social Sciences: a Bibliography of **Work** and Directory of Researchers, C 55.332:So 1

Watershed **Work** Plan {by Area}, A 57.59

Welfare **Work** Series, Y 3.C 83:35

Women and **Work**, L 1.20/8

Work and Management Improvement, A 57.41

Work and Wage Experience Studies, Reports, L 2.28

Work Clothing (garments cut), C 3.64

Work Incentive Program, HE 17.619/2

Work Incentive Program: Annual Report to Congress, L 1.71

Work Injuries in Atomic Energy, L 2.71

Work Injuries Reported by Longshoremen and Harbor Workers, L 26.9

Work Injuries, Contract Construction, L 2.77/3

Work Injuries, Trade, L 2.77/4

Work Life, PrEx 1.10/3-3

Work Materials, Y 3.N 21/8:25

Work of Reclamation Project Experiment Farm, A 19.14

Work Stoppages, L 2.62, L 2.62/2, L 2.62/3

Work with Children Coming before the Courts, FS 3.223, FS 14.116

Work Years and Personnel Costs, PM 1.10/4

Work-Study Reports (series), ED 1.74

Workable

Status Report: **Workable** Program for Community Improvement, HH 1.47

Workable Program for Community Improvement, Program Guides, HH 1.6/4

Workbook

Fermilab Research Program **Workbook**, E 1.92

Workbook (series), D 101.105

Workbooks

Camp Life Arithmetic **Workbooks**, FS 4.10

Programmed Instruction **Workbooks** (series), L 38.18

Worker

Employment and Wages, a Quarterly Summary of **Workers** Covered by State Unemployment Insurance Laws and Unemployment Compensation for Federal Employees, L 2.104

Forest **Worker**, A 13.19

NIOSH **Worker** Bulletin (series), HE 20.7117/2

Petroleum **Worker** {abstracts}, C 41.55/2

Women **Worker**, L 13.8

Worker's

Pamphlets **Worker's** Compensation Programs Office, L 36.409

Workers

Advance Training for **Workers** in the Early and Periodic Screening, Diagnosis and Treatment Program: Publications, HE 22.111

Annual Statistics on **Workers** Under Social Security, HE 3.40

Background Facts on Women **Workers** in the United States, L 36.114/2

Casualities and Injuries among Shipyard and Dock **Workers**, L 16.37

Concerning **Workers'** Education, Y 3.F 31/4:12

Digest of State Legislation of Special Interest to Women **Workers**, L 13.14/3

Earnings and Employment Data for Wage and Salary **Workers** Covered under Social Security by State and County, HE 3.95, SSA 1.17/3

Earnings of **Workers** and Their Families, L 2.118

Employment and Wages of **Workers** Covered by State Unemployment Compensation Laws: Estimated, FS 3.122

Employment and Wages of **Workers** Covered by State Unemployment Insurance Laws and Unemployment Compensation for Federal Employees, by Industry and State, L 7.20/3, L 1.61

Employment in Perspective: Minority **Workers**, L 2.41/11-2

Extension Pathologist; News Letter for Extension **Workers** Interested in Plant Disease Control, A 43.20

Facts on Women **Workers**, L 13.15

Federal Civilian Employment and Wages of **Workers** Covered by Unemployment Compensation for Federal Employees, L 7.20/4

Federal Civilian Work Force Statistics, Occupations of Federal Blue-Collar **Workers**, PM 1.10:Sm 59-11

Federal Civilian Work Force Statistics, Occupations of Federal White-Collar **Workers**, PM 1.10:Sm 56-13

Federal Scientific and Technical **Workers**: Numbers and Characteristics, NS 1.14/3

Forage Crop Gazette, News Letter for Staff **Workers**, Division of Forage Crops and Diseases, A 77.509

Handbook on Women **Workers**, L 36.103

Here and There with Home Demonstration **Workers**, A 43.5/13

Job Guide for Young **Workers**, L 1.7/6

List of **Workers** in Subjects Pertaining to Agriculture, A 10.23

Occupational Hazards to Young **Workers** Reports, L 16.40

Occupational Hazards to Young **Workers**, L 16.3

Occupations of Federal White-Collar and Blue-Collar **Workers**, PM 1.10/2-2

Pathologist; News Letter for Extension **Workers** Interested in Plant Disease Control, A 43.20

Salaries of State Public Health **Workers**, FS 2.82

State **Workers'** Compensation: Administration Profiles, L 36.16

Suggested Safety Practices for Shipyard **Workers**, L 16.51/3

Traveler/El Viajero, Quarterly Newsletter for Migrant and Seasonal Farm **Workers**, PrEx 10.19

Usual Weekly Earnings of Wage and Salary **Workers**, L 2.126

Weekly Earnings of Wage and Salary **Workers**, L 2.126

Which Jobs for Young **Workers**, L 5.45

Women **Workers** in {State} (year), L 36.114

Work Injuries Reported by Longshoremen and Harbor **Workers**, L 26.9

Workers Health Posters, FS 2.25

Workers'

Workers' Health Series, FS 2.33

Workforce

Current Federal **Workforce** Data, CS 1.72

Federal **Workforce** Outlook, CS 1.72/2

Health **Workforce** Newslink, HE 20.9315

HRSA State Health **Workforce** Profiles, HE 20.9317

HRSA State Health **Workforce** Profiles (database), HE 20.9317/2

Report on the American **Workforce**, L 1.90/2

U.S. Coast Guard Civilian **Workforce** Report, Fiscal Year, TD 5.65

Workforce Profile, T 17.24

Working

Compensation and **Working** Conditions, L 2.44, L 2.44/4

Economic **Working** Papers, T 12.22

Facts on **Working** Women, L 36.114/3

JPRS (series) Soviet Union, the **Working** Class & the Contemporary World, PrEx 7.21/9-2

List of State Designated Agencies, Officials and **Working** Contracts, L 1.53/3

Machine Tools and Metal **Working** Equipment, PrEx 7.22/3-3

News Exchange, Extended School Services for Children of **Working** Mothers, Letters, FS 5.36

PNERL **Working** Papers, EP 1.37/2

Population Division **Working** Paper Series, C 3.223/26

Research **Working** Papers (series), FHL 1.35

Solid Tumor Virus **Working** Group, HE 20.3001/2:T 83/2

Statistical Policy **Working** Papers, C 1.70, PrEx 2.28

Surveillance and Analysis Division, Region 10: **Working** Papers, EP 1.51/6

Technical **Working** Paper Series, C 3.223/27

Tumor Virus Detection **Working** Group, HE 20.3001/2:T 83

U.S. **Working** Women: a Databook, L 2.3:1977

Ultraviolet Radiation and Skin Cancer **Working** Group, HE 20.3001/2:R 11/2

U.S. Government Security **Yields** and Prices
(**Yields** in per cent per annum), FR 1.46/3
Yosemite
Yosemite National Park, Annual Reports, I 1.38
You
Census and **You**, C 3.238
Facts **You** Should Know, Statements, Pr 32.4242
So **You** Want to Be a {Occupation}, PrEx 10.20
This Might Be **You** (radio scripts), L 1.14
What **You** Have to Know about SSI, HE 3.90
You and Your USA series, D 2.11
You Can Survive, Rural Defense Fact Sheets, A 43.35
You-in (series), HE 20.3116
Young
Job Guide for **Young** Workers, L 1.7/6
Occupational Hazards to **Young** Workers Reports, L 16.40
Occupational Hazards to **Young** Workers, L 16.3
Which Jobs for **Young** Workers, L 5.45
Younger
Younger Scholars, NF 3.8/2-6
Your
For **Your** Information; Education Services, FCD 1.13/5
For **Your** Information; Industrial Survival, FCD 1.13/9
For **Your** Information; Office of Administrator, FCD 1.13/3
For **Your** Information; Office of Executive Assistant Administrator, FCD 1.13/6
For **Your** Information; Office of General Counsel, FCD 1.13/7
For **Your** Information; Operations Control Services, FCD 1.13/4
For **Your** Information; Planning Staff, FCD 1.13/8
For **Your** Information; Technical Advisory Services, Health Office, FCD 1.13/2
Survival Series, For **Your** Information {releases}, FCD 1.13/10
Technical Advisory Services, Health Office, For **Your** Information, TAS (series), FCD 1.13/2
What's Doing in **Your** Town, Y 3.F 31/11:23
Working with **Your** Schools, CR 1.6/3
You and **Your** USA series, D 2.11
Your Changing Forest, News on the Black Hills National Forest Plan Revision, A 13.128
Your Defense Budget, D 1.1/4
Your Federal Budget, Pr 34.107/4
Your Federal Income Tax, T 22.44
Your Guide to Federal Waterfowl Production Areas, I 49.6/3
Your Medicare Handbook, HE 22.8/16
Your Navy, from the Viewpoint of the Nation's Finest Artists, D 201.9
Your New Social Security, Fact Sheets, FS 3.25
Your Social Security Rights & Responsibilities, Retirement & Survivors Benefits, HE 3.88/2, HE 3.93
Your Social Security Rights and Responsibilities, Disability Benefits, HE 3.88
Your Social Security, HE 3.89
Yours
Greatfully **Yours**, HE 20.3625
World is **Yours** (Radio Scripts), I 16.56/2, FS 5.14/1
Youth
Annual Report on Activities Conducted to Implement the Runaway **Youth** Act, HE 23.1309
Education of Exceptional Children and **Youth**: Special Education Personnel in State Education Departments, FS 5.235:35003, HE 5.235:35003
Engineering for **Youth** {abstracts}, C 41.57
Highlights of the National **Youth** Gang Survey, J 32.21/3
Letters to State **Youth** Directors, Y 3.N 21/14:7
Manual of Finance and Statistics Memorandum of National **Youth** Administration, Pr 32.5258
OJJDP **Youth** in Action Fact Sheet, J 32.21/2

President's Council on **Youth** Opportunity, Pr 37.8:Y 8
Report from Closer Look, a Project of the Parents' Campaign for Handicapped Children and **Youth**, ED 1.22
Runaways and Otherwise Homeless **Youth** Fiscal Year, Annual Report on the Runaway **Youth** Act, HE 23.1309/2
Safeguard Our Nation's **Youth** on the Job, L 15.51/5
Safety Bulletins National **Youth** Administration, FS 6.16
Source Catalog on **Youth** Participation (series), HE 1.312
State Legislative Summary, Children and **Youth** Issues, HE 24.16
Summer **Youth** Opportunity Campaign, TD 2.15
Summer **Youth** Opportunity Program Annual Report, TD 1.12
Trends in the Well-Being of America's Children and **Youth**, HE 1.63
Youth Advisory Board Newsletter, EP 1.27
Youth Employment Tables TS (series), L 16.41
Youth Fatal Crash and Alcohol Facts, TD 8.39
Youth in Action Bulletin, J 32.21/2-2
Youth Indicators, Trends in the Well-Being of American Youth, ED 1.327
Youth Program Models and Innovations, L 37.19
Youth Reporter, HE 1.311
Youth Reports, HE 21.109
Youth Corps
Neighborhood **Youth Corps** Publications, L 1.49
Youth's
Men's, **Youth's**, and Boy's Clothing Cut, C 3.92
Yucca Flat
Photographs of A-Bomb Test, Operation Doorstep, **Yucca Flat**, Nevada, March 17, 1953, FCD 1.11/2
Yugoslav
Directory of **Yugoslav** Officials, PrEx 3.10/7-8

Z

Z39
Voice of **Z39**, News About Library, Information Science, and Publishing Standards, C 13.163
Zinc
Mineral Industry Surveys, **Zinc**, I 19.157
Monthly Slab **Zinc** Reports, I 28.56
Slab **Zinc** Reports, I 28.56
Zinc Industry in (year), I 28.69/2
Zinc Industry, I 28.69
Zinc Mine Production, I 28.57
Zinc Oxide, I 28.90
Zinc Reports, I 28.69
Zinc Scrap Consumers Reports, I 28.68
Zinc Scrap, I 28.68
Zinc, I 28.69/2
ZIP
Labor Surplus Area **Zip** Code Reference, GS 1.33
National Five-Digit **ZIP** Code & Post Office Directory, P 1.10/8
National **Zip** Code and Post Office Directory, P 1.10/8
National **Zip** Code Directory, P 1.10/8
Social Security Beneficiaries by **Zip** Code Area, HE 3.73
ZIP Code Business Patterns, C 3.294
ZIP Code Business Patterns C 3.298
ZIP Code Directories {by States}, P 1.10/7
ZIP + 4, State Directories, P 1.10/9
Zirconium
Zirconium and Hafnium in (year), I 28.83/2
Zirconium Reports, I 28.83
Zone
Coastal **Zone** and Estuarine Studies (series), C 55.335
Coastal **Zone** Management Technical Assistance Documents, C 55.32/2
List of Radio Broadcast Stations, by **Zone** and State, CC 2.12
Official Parcel Post **Zone** Keys Hawaii, P 1.25/4
Official Parcel Post **Zone** Keys Puerto Rico, P 1.25/3
Official Parcel Post **Zone** Keys United States, P 1.25/1

Official Parcel Post **Zone** Keys Virgin Islands, P 1.25/2
Postal **Zone** Directories, P 1.35
Registration, Employment and Unemployment, U.S. **Zone**, Statistical Report, W 1.72/3
Report to the Congress on Coastal **Zone** Management, C 55.32
State Coastal **Zone** Management Activities, C 55.32/3
Store Stock Catalog, General Services Administration, **Zone** Price Lists, **Zone** 1, GS 2.10
Zones
General Description of Foreign-trade **Zones**, FTZ 1.8
Zoological Park
National **Zoological Park**, Reports, SI 1.1/a4
National **Zoological Park**: Annual Report, SI 1.1/2
Zoology
Smithsonian Contributions to **Zoology**, SI 1.27
Zoonoses
National Communicable Disease Center **Zoonoses** Surveillance {reports}, FS 2.60/15
National Communicable Disease Center **Zoonoses** Surveillance, Annual Summary, Psittacosis, FS 2.60/15:P 95
Primate **Zoonoses** Surveillance, Reports, Annual Summary, HE 20.7011/9

Preface

In the 1950s, the size of the United States government started growing rapidly, and with this growth, so did the volume of publications produced by the various government agencies. Libraries became repositories for vast amounts of information. The size and scope of federal documents collections were beginning to generate difficulty for the librarian in both the cataloging and retrieval of documents. Thus John Andriot, a librarian, sought to fill the need for publications which would aid in the bibliographic control of government publications. In 1959, Mr. Andriot published the *Guide to U.S. Government Serials and Periodicals,* which later became the *Guide to U.S. Government Publications.*

In 1999, Gale purchased Documents Index, Inc., along with **Guide to U.S. Government Publications**, and is continuing the tradition of providing a comprehensive, yet concise annotated guide to the important series, periodicals, and reference tools published by U.S. Government agencies.

A guide to the Sudocs classification system precedes the actual entries contained in this edition. Entries, listed by Sudocs class number, contain such information as title, starting dates, frequency, earlier and later references, item number, Dewey number, L.C. classification number, L.C. card number and annotations.

A popular and valuable feature of this *Guide* is the agency class chronology which gives the complete history of current Class number assignments and traces them back historically to previous number assignments, allowing the user to track the many changes of older serials.

Over the years, the index section of the *Guide to U.S. Government Publications* has expanded to more than 36,000 entries. Agencies are indexed first, then titles, followed by a keyword in title index which allows quick and easy referencing without knowing the intricacies of the Sudocs system.

Forty years since its inception, the *Guide to U.S. Government Publications,* formerly known as *Andriot,* has become a standard reference source in Federal documents collections. We at Gale strive to continue this service. We welcome your comments and suggestions so that we may continue to answer your needs.

Guide to U.S. Government Publications
Gale Group
27500 Drake Rd.
Farmington Hills, MI 48331
Toll-Free: (800) 347-GALE
Telephone: (248) 699-4253
Fax: (248) 699-8069
Email: BusinessProducts@gale.com

A Practical Guide
To the Superintendent of Documents
Classification System

Foreword

The Superintendent of Documents Classification System was formed in the library of the Government Printing Office sometime between 1895 and 1903. The first explanation of it was given in October 1903 by William Leander Post, then in charge of the Library, in the preface to *List of Publications of the Agriculture Department 1862-1902, Department list No. 1,* issued by the Superintendent of Documents in 1904.

Mr. Post gives credit for the basis of the system (classification by governmental author) to Miss Adelaide R. Hasse, who used this basis in assigning classification numbers to a *List of Publications of the U.S. Department of Agriculture from 1841 to June 30, 1895, inclusive.* Miss Hasse prepared the 1895 list while assistant librarian in the Los Angeles Public Library but it was published by the Department of Agriculture in 1895 as its library Bulletin No. 9.

Like other classification systems in use for many years, this one has expanded as the Federal Government has grown, and has changed in some details and methods of use, though still retaining the principles upon which it is based.

It has one fundamental weakness-the position in the scheme, of the publications of any Government author (i.e. department, bureau, office, etc.) is determined by the current organizational status of the author. Thus it is at the mercy of any Government reorganization which may be directed by the President, by Congress or by the head of a department or agency, with the result that the publications of some authors may be located in as many as three different places in the scheme.

Despite this functional weakness, it has stood the test of time as a workable arrangement for publications of the United States Goverment, having been used for over 50 years by the library of the Documents Area for the collection of public documents which has accumulated as a by-product of the Department's cataloging and publishing functions, and as a catalog system for the stocks of Government publications sold by the Superintendent of Documents.

Introduction

The United States Government issues a large number of publications each year. The Superintendent of Documents classification system, which has been developed and expanded over the years, has proved to be a most efficient method of classifying these publications. The adequacy of the system has been confirmed by the number of libraries changing from Library of Congress, Dewey Decimal, and original systems to the Superintendent of Documents classification scheme to classify their Government publications.

The basis of the Superintendent of Documents Classification System is the grouping together of publications of any Government author, the various departments, bureaus, and agencies being considered the authors. In the grouping, the organizational structure of the United States Government is followed: that is, subordinate bureaus and divisions are grouped with the parent organization. Because the class numbers reflect the organization of the Government, they should be changed as necessary to keep abreast of changes in Government organization.

A Superintendent of Documents classification number consists of a capital letter or letters representing a Government department or agency.

> Example: TD for Transportation Department

The letters are followed by a number representing the agency as a whole, or a subordinate office. This figure is followed by a period.

> Example: TD 4. for Federal Aviation
> Administration.

After the period, there is a number designating the series or category grouping of publications, followed by a colon.

> Example: TD 4.10/4: FAA airworthiness
> directive biweekly listing.

The numbers after the colon represent individual publications in the series.

> Example: TD 4.10/4:83-7 for issue 83-7.

Thus, from the class alone it can be determined that the publication in the example is issued by the Transportation Department, Federal Aviation Administration, and that it has a number **83-7** printed on it. If the user also knows individual series class numbers, he will know at a glance exactly what publication this number represents. Each publication must have its own unique number.

Each separate piece, such as a map in a pocket of a publication, should have its own separate class number written on it, so that it may be identified when separated from the basic publication. The class is added to each bit and piece solely for identification of stray pieces, and not for cataloging purposes. No documentation is needed in any files for these separate pieces.

One of the most important things to remember when assigning numbers in the system is to check all classification possibilities before making a final decision.

Chapter 1

Author Symbols

(before the period)

Section I,
Departments and Independent Agencies

The first letter or letters in the classification number represent the department or independent agency issuing the publication. Each department or independent agency has a unique letter or combination of letters assigned to it. In early years, when the classification system was first established, the departments were assigned a single letter (Example: A for Agriculture Department), and independent agencies were assigned two letters (Example: **GP** for Government Printing Office). However, this is no longer the practice. As more departments were established, there were conflicts, and changes were required. For example **T** was assigned to Treasury Department; therefore, **T** could not be used alone for the Transportation Department when it was established later. The **TD** designation was assigned to the Transportation Department.

Practical Application

Capital letters are used for the department and agency designations. On occasions, a lower case letter with a capital may be used as in the case of the President (**Pr**) to separate it from Post Office (**P**).

Capital letters should be used if the initials of the agency are used.

> Examples: **A** (Agriculture), **C** (Commerce), **T** (Treasury). **CR** (Civil Rights).

Lower case letters should be used if the second or other letters of the names of the agencies are used in the classes.

> Examples: **Pr, PrEx** (Executive Office Of the President), **RnB** (Renegotiation Board).

Use capital initials of agencies if possible. Use the lower case letters only when necessary to avoid conflict.

In general, the author symbols are easy to determine by looking at the publications being classified, when the issuing office is represented by one or more initials.

> Examples: **A** for Agriculture, **C** for Commerce, **D** for Defense, **E** for Energy.

Exceptions to this are the classes for publications of the United States Congress which are classified in **X** and **Y** classes. The boards, commissions, and committees established by act of Congress or under authority of act of Congress, not specifically designated in the Executive Branch of the Government are grouped under: **Y 3.**, one of the symbols assigned to Congressional publications. Series designations are handled differently in the **X** and **Y** classes and are covered in Chapter IV of this manual.

New agency classes

When a new agency or department is established, it is important to find the authority for setting up the organization so that it can be assigned to its correct place in the classification scheme. These authorities may be public laws, Executive Orders of the President or departmental directives. It may be necessary to call the new agency to locate this infomation.

Problems

Occasionally a publication will appear without an issuing office name printed on it and classification difficulties result. Usually, somewhere inside the publication is a letter of transmittal, preface, or foreword which gives information or at least an agency contact, where more information may be obtained to help identify the publication. The Government Printing Office jacket number identification is another source for determining the issuing agency.

Joint publications

A publication may be issued by two or more agencies. If this is the case, all of the agency names will be listed on the publication with more or less equal treatment. Classify the publication under the first agency listed.

If the publication is a serial and the order of the agencies changes with later issues, retain the original class if the first agency is still listed as a publisher.

The publication may or may not carry one or more series designations. Do not come to the conclusion immediately that the series class is where the publication belongs. First, decide the issuing agency to be used in the class. After the proper issuing agency has been determined, classify in the series appropriate to that agency. It may be the first or second series listed, but it must agree with the issuing office.

For example, the National Bureau of Standards, Commerce Department and the National Institute for Occupational Safety and Health, Health and Human Services Department, issued a booklet designated *NBS/NIOSH publication*. The publication carried a **NIOSH** number as well as the designation **NBSIR 83-2693**. The National Bureau of Standards was the first agency listed, so the publication was classified **C 13.58**

If a double series is issued routinely by two agencies, and the publications are not consistent in assigning the agency and series designations in uniform order, classify the publications in one class consistently.

A joint publication may carry only one series designation. If the agency listed first is not the agency associated with the series, then the publication should be classified in a general class under the agency selected as the issuing agency.

A revised edition of a joint publication should be classified with the original if both agencies are issuing the revision, regardless of the order in which the agencies are listed on the publication. However, if only one of the agencies issued the revision, it should be classified under the revising agency regardless of where it was classified originally.

Publications prepared by one agency for another pose a somewhat different problem. First, determine which agency is the actual publisher of the book in question, and classify under that agency. In most cases, the agency for which the publication was prepared is the issuing agency; however, on occasion the preparing agency will publish it. Usually this can be determined by the title page or cover format.

For example, if the book was prepared by Geological Survey for the Commerce Department, and a U.S. Gelogical Survey open-file report number appears on the publication, and a Commerce Department series does not, do not let the Geological Survey series number be the deciding factor in determining the issuing office. If the Commerce Department issued the publication, that is where it should be classified. If the Geological Survey is determined to be the issuing office, use the series printed on the publication as the class.

Section 2

Suboordinate offices

To set off the subordinate bureaus, administrations, and offices, numbers are added to the author letter and followed by a period. The figure 1 is always used for the office of the secretary of a department or the administrator of an independent agency. The **1** class also should be used for any publication carrying only the department or agency name with no subordinate bureau listed.

As a general rule, the classification number is not broken down below the level of the first subordinate office.

When the classification system was established, the subordinate offices were arranged alphabetically with numbers assigned sequentially. It is rarely possible to obtain enough Information on new departments and their plans for organization to continue following this practice. Also, new departments and agencies frequently reorganize and change the names of the subordinate offices. A chronological arrangement determined by receipt of publications is followed rather than an alphabetical arrangement at the present time.

Examples:

A 1.	Agriculture Department as whole, and/or the Secretary's Office
A 13.	Forest Service
A 68.	Rural Electrification Administration
A 88.	Agricultural Marketing Service

On occasion, second level offices are broken down to a smaller level for a finer organization of the office's publications. This is done by using 100 or 1000 numbers after the parent agency's assigned number, depending upon how small a breakdown is necessary for clarity.

Examples:

C 1.	Commerce Department (level 1)
C 55.	National Oceanographic and Atmospheric Administration (level 2)
C 55.100's	National Weather Service(level 3)
.200's	Environmental Data & Information Service (level 3)
.300's	National Marine Fisheries Service (level 3)
.400's	National Ocean Survey (level 3)
HE 1.	Health and Human Services Department (level 1)
HE 20.	Public Health Services (level 2)
HE 20.3000's	National Institutes of Health (level 3)
.3150's	National Cancer Institute (level 4)
.3200 to .3249	National Heart, Lung, and Blood Institute (level 4)
.3250's	National Instutute of Allergy & Infectious Diseases Level 4)
HE 20.3600's	National Library of Medicine (level 4)
HE 20.4000's	Food and Drug Administration (level 4)
.4100's	Radiological Health Bureau (level 4)
HE 20.5000's	Health Services Administration (level 3) with subordinate agencies broken down by 100's.

In the case of the Public Health Service, National Institutes of Health, there are so many separate institutes that the **3000** numbers are broken by **50's** to have a number for each of the institutes. Currently, the Health and Human Services Department classes are the only ones using **1000** numbers.

The publications of third and fourth level offices not expected to issue a great many publications may be treated as series rather than as publications with subordinate office classes. This means that distinguishing numbers assigned to publications of the office appear after the period instead of before it.

Example:

A 13.	Forest Service
A 13.40/1:	Southern Forest Experiment Station: Annual report
A 13.40/2:	Same: General publications
A 13.40/5:	Same: Occasional papers (numbered)
A 13.40/8-3:	Same: Publications of Southern Forest Experiment Station (list)

A 13.40/ has been reserved for publications of the Southern Forest Experiment Station. Each of the Forest Service experiment stations has a number reserved for it. As new classes are established, new slash numbers are used as necessary.

Practical application

A publication should be classified under the subordinate office printed on the title page. the verso of the title page, pages 1, 2, 3 and 4 of the cover, or the spine. Under ordinary circumtances. use whichever of the above sources that provides the most complete information. However, in cases of conflict, prefer the information found on the title page.

Pages 1-4 of cover are both sides of the front and back cover. In general, thesubordinate office should not be taken from a letter of transmittal, preface, or foreword and used as the issuing office. Also, the bureau or office listed with the personal author, in most cases, should not be used as a determining factor.

When a joint publication, not in a numbered series, carries twoequally subordinate bureaus under the same department, classify the publication under the bureau which is listed first on the document to be classified. If it carries three or more equally subordinate offices, ignore the bureaus and classify the publication in a class under the parent agency. The *U.S. Government Manual* and the *Federal Executive Directory* should be consulted when making the above determination. If these sources don't have the needed information, then a cataloger should be contacted who will search the authority files and the MUMS data base.

Example 1.

Information as shown on the title page:

Annual report on the administration of Government

waste.

Issued by: Bureau of Efficiency

Office X

Office Y

Hierarchy of the Bureau of Efficiency in one of the reference tools:

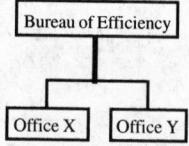

The publication would be classified under Office X.

Example 2.

Information as shown on the title page:

Annual report on the distribution of electronic data bases.

Issued by: Bureau of Efficiency

Office X

Office Y

Hierarchy of the Bureau of Efficiency in one of the reference tools:

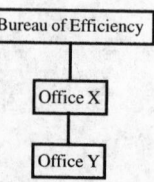

The publication would be classified under Office Y.